Income
Tax
Regulations

Including
Proposed
Regulations

As of November 2, 2018

Volume 5

§ 31.3101-1–End

Wolters Kluwer Editorial Staff Publication

This publication is designed to provide accurate and authoritative information in regard to the subject matter covered. It is sold with the understanding that the publisher is not engaged in rendering legal, accounting, or other professional service. If legal advice or other expert assistance is required, the services of a competent professional person should be sought.

ISBN 978-0-8080-4780-3 (Set)
ISBN 978-0-8080-5104-6 (Volume 1)
ISBN 978-0-8080-5055-1 (Volume 2)
ISBN 978-0-8080-5056-8 (Volume 3)
ISBN 978-0-8080-5057-5 (Volume 4)
ISBN 978-0-8080-5058-2 (Volume 5)
ISBN 978-0-8080-5059-9 (Volume 6)

2700 Lake Cook Road
Riverwoods, IL 60015
800 344 3734
CCHCPELink.com

Printed in the United States of America

SUSTAINABLE FORESTRY INITIATIVE   Certified Sourcing
www.sfiprogram.org
SFI-01681

EMPLOYMENT TAXES

Federal Insurance Contributions Act

INTRODUCTION

See p. 20,601 for regulations not amended to reflect law changes

[Reg. §31.0-1]

§31.0-1. Introduction.—(a) *In general.*—The regulations in this part relate to the employment taxes imposed by subtitle C (chapters 21 to 25, inclusive) of the Internal Revenue Code of 1954, as amended. References in the regulations to the "Internal Revenue Code" or the "Code" are references to the Internal Revenue Code of 1954, as amended, unless otherwise indicated. References to the Federal Insurance Contributions Act, the Railroad Retirement Tax Act, and the Federal Unemployment Tax Act are references to chapters 21, 22, and 23, respectively, of the Code. References to sections of law are references to sections of the Internal Revenue Code unless otherwise indicated. The regulations in this part also provide rules relating to the deposit of other taxes by electronic funds transfer.

(b) *Division of regulations.*—The regulations in this part are divided into 7 subparts. Subpart A contains provisions relating to general definitions and use of terms, the division and scope of the regulations in this part, and the extent to which the regulations in this part supersede prior regulations relating to employment taxes. Subpart B relates to the taxes under the Federal Insurance Contributions Act. Subpart C relates to the taxes under the Railroad Retirement Tax Act. Subpart D relates to the tax under the Federal Unemployment Tax Act. Subpart E relates to the collection of income tax at source on wages under chapter 24 of the Code. Subpart F relates to the provisions of chapter 25 of the Code which are applicable in respect of the taxes imposed by chapters 21 to 24, inclusive, of the Code. Subpart G relates to selected provisions of subtitle F of the Code, relating to procedure and administration, which have special application in respect of the taxes imposed by subtitle C of the Code. Inasmuch as these regulations constitute Part 31 of Title 26 of the Code of Federal Regulations, each section of the regulations is preceded by a section symbol and 31 followed by a decimal point (§31.). Sections of law or references thereto are preceded by "Sec." or the word "section". [Reg. §31.0-1.]

☐ [T.D. 6516, 12-20-60. *Amended by T.D. 8723,* 7-11-97.]

[Reg. §31.0-2]

§31.0-2. **General definitions and use of terms.**—(a) *In general.*—As used in the regulations in this part, unless otherwise expressly indicated—

(1) The terms defined in the provisions of law contained in the regulations in this part shall have the meanings so assigned to them.

(2) The Internal Revenue Code of 1954 means the Act approved August 16, 1954 (26 U.S.C.), entitled "An act to revise the internal revenue laws of the United States", as amended.

(3) The Internal Revenue Code of 1939 means the Act approved February 10, 1939 (53 Stat., Part 1), as amended.

(4) The Social Security Act means the Act approved August 14, 1935 (42 U.S.C. c.7), as amended.

(5)(i) The Social Security Amendments of 1954 means the act approved September 1, 1954 (68 Stat. 1052), as amended.

(ii) The Social Security Amendments of 1956 means the act approved August 1, 1956 (70 Stat. 807), as amended.

(iii) The Social Security Amendments of 1958 means the act approved August 28, 1958 (72 Stat. 1013), as amended.

(iv) The Social Security Amendments of 1960 means the act approved September 13, 1960 (74 Stat. 924).

(v) The Social Security Amendments of 1961 means the act approved June 30, 1961 (75 Stat. 131).

(vi) The Social Security Amendments of 1965 means the act approved July 30, 1965 (79 Stat. 286).

(vii) The Social Security Amendments of 1967 means the act approved January 2, 1968 (81 Stat. 821).

(viii) The Social Security Amendments of 1972 means the act approved October 30, 1972 (86 Stat. 1329).

(6) The Social Security Administration means the Social Security Administration of the Department of Health, Education, and Welfare. (See the Statement of Organization and Delegations of Authority of the Department of Health, Education, and Welfare (20 F.R. 1996).)

(7) District director means district director of internal revenue. The term also includes the Director of International Operations in all cases where the authority to perform the functions which may be performed by a district director has been delegated to the Director of International Operations.

(8) Person includes an individual, a corporation, a partnership, a trust or estate, a joint-stock company, an association, or a syndicate, group, pool, joint venture or other unincorporated organization or group, through or by means of which any business, financial operation, or venture is carried on. It includes a guardian, committee, trustee, executor, administrator, trustee in bankruptcy, receiver, assignee for the benefit of creditors, conservator, or any person acting in a fiduciary capacity.

(9) Calendar quarter means a period of 3 calendar months ending on March 31, June 30, September 30, or December 31.

(10) Account number means the identifying number of an employee assigned, as the case may be, under the Internal Revenue Code of 1954, under subchapter A of chapter 9 of the Internal Revenue Code of 1939, or under title VIII of the Social Security Act. See also § 301.7701-11 of this chapter (Regulations on Procedure and Administration).

(11) Identification number means the identifying number of an employer assigned, as the case may be, under the Internal Revenue Code of 1954, under subchapter A or D of chapter 9 of the Internal Revenue Code of 1939, or under title VIII of the Social Security Act. See also § 301.7701-12 of this chapter (Regulations on Procedure and Administration).

(12) Regulations 90 means the regulations approved February 17, 1936 (26 CFR (1939) Part 400), as amended, relating to the excise tax on employers under title IX of the Social Security Act, and such regulations as made applicable to subchapter C of chapter 9 and other provisions of the Internal Revenue Code of 1939 by Treasury Decision 4885, approved February 11, 1939 (26 CFR (1939) 1943 Cum. Supp., p. 5876), together with any amendments to such regulations as so made applicable to the Internal Revenue Code of 1939.

(13) Regulations 91 means the regulations approved November 9, 1936 (26 CFR (1939) Part 401), as amended, relating to the employees' tax and the employers' tax under title VIII of the Social Security Act, and such regulations as made applicable to subchapter A of chapter 9 and other provisions of the Internal Revenue Code of 1939 by Treasury Decision 4885, approved February 11, 1939 (26 CFR (1939) 1943 Cum. Supp., p. 5876), together with any amendments to such regulations as so made applicable to the Internal Revenue Code of 1939.

(14) Regulations 106 means the regulations approved February 24, 1940 (26 CFR (1939) Part 402), as amended, relating to the employees' tax and the employers' tax under the Federal Insurance Contributions Act (subchapter A of chapter 9 of the Internal Revenue Code of 1939) with respect to the period after 1939 and before 1951.

(15) Regulations 107 means the regulations approved September 12, 1940 (26 CFR (1939) Part 403), as amended, relating to the excise tax on employers under the Federal Unemployment Tax Act (subchapter C of chapter 9 of the Internal Revenue Code of 1939) with respect to the period after 1939 and before 1955.

(16) Regulations 114 means the regulations approved December 30, 1948 (26 CFR (1939) Part 411), as amended, relating to the employers' tax, employees' tax, and employee representatives' tax under the Railroad Retirement Tax Act (subchapter B of chapter 9 of the Internal Revenue Code of 1939) with respect to compensation paid after 1948 for services rendered after 1946 and before 1955.

(17) Regulations 120 means the regulations approved December 22, 1953 (26 CFR (1939) Part 406), as amended, relating to collection of income tax at source on wages under subchapter D of chapter 9 of the Internal Revenue Code of 1939 with respect to the period after 1953 and before 1955.

(18) Regulations 128 means the regulations approved December 6, 1951 (26 CFR (1939) Part 408), as amended, relating to the employee tax and the employer tax under the Federal Insurance Contributions Act (subchapter A of chapter 9 of the Internal Revenue Code of 1939) with respect to the period after 1950 and before 1955.

(19) The cross references in the regulations in this part to other portions of the regulations, when the word "see" is used, are made only for convenience and shall be given no legal effect.

(b) *Subpart B.*—As used in subpart B of this part, unless otherwise expressly indicated—

(1) Act means the Federal Insurance Contributions Act.

(2) Taxes means the employee tax and the employer tax, as respectively defined in this paragraph.

(3) Employee tax means the tax (with respect to wages received by an employee after December 31, 1965, the taxes) imposed by section 3101 of the Code.

(4) Employer tax means the tax (with respect to wages paid by an employer after December 31, 1965, the taxes) imposed by section 3111 of the Code.

(c) *Subpart C.*—As used in subpart C of this part, unless otherwise expressly indicated—

(1) Act means the Railroad Retirement Tax Act.

(2) Railway Labor Act means the Act approved May 20, 1926 (45 U.S.C. c.8), as amended.

(3) Railroad Retirement Act of 1937 means the Act approved June 24, 1937 (45 U.S.C. 228a and following), as amended.

(4) Railroad Retirement Board means the board established pursuant to section 10 of the Railroad Retirement Act of 1937 (45 U.S.C. 228j).

(5) Tax means the employee tax, the employee representative tax, or the employer tax, as respectively defined in this paragraph.

(6) Employee tax means the tax imposed by section 3201 of the Code.

(7) Employee representative tax means the tax imposed by section 3211 of the Code.

(8) Employer tax means the tax imposed by section 3221 of the Code.

(d) *Subpart D.*—As used in subpart D of this part, unless otherwise expressly indicated—

(1) Act means the Federal Unemployment Tax Act.

(2) Railroad Unemployment Insurance Act means the Act approved June 25, 1938 (45 U.S.C. c. 11), as amended.

(3) Tax means the tax imposed by section 3301 of the Code.

(e) *Subpart E.*—As used in subpart E of this part, unless otherwise expressly indicated, tax means the tax required to be deducted and withheld from wages under section 3402 of the Code. [Reg. § 31.0-2.]

☐ [*T.D.* 6516,12-20-60. *Amended by* T.D.6606, 8-25-62; *T.D.* 6658, 6-27-63; *T.D.* 6983, 12-4-68 *and* T.D. 7280, 7-10-73.]

[Reg. § 31.0-3]

§ 31.0-3. Scope of regulations.—(a) *Subpart B.*—The regulations in his part relate to the imposition of the employee tax and the employer tax under the Federal Insurance Contributions Act with respect to wages paid and received after 1954 for employment performed after 1936. In addition to employment in the case of remuneration therefor paid and received after 1954, the regulations in Subpart B of this part relate also to employment performed after 1954 in the case of remuneration therefor paid and received before 1955. The regulations in Subpart B of this part include provisions relating to the definition of terms applicable in the determination of the taxes under the Federal Insurance Contributions Act, such as "employee", "wages", and "employment". The provisions of Subpart B of this part relating to "employment" are applicable also, (1) to the extent provided in § 31.3121(b)-2, to services performed before 1955 the remuneration for which is paid after 1954, and (2) to the extent provided in § 31.3121(k)-3, to services performed before 1955 the remuneration for which was paid before 1955. (For prior regulations on similar subject matter, see 26 CFR (1939) Part 408 (Regulations 128).)

(b) *Subpart C.*—The regulations in subpart C of this part relate to the imposition of the employee tax, the employee representative tax, and the employer tax under the Railroad Retirement Tax Act with respect to compensation paid after 1954, for services rendered after such date. The regulations in subpart C of this part include provisions relating to the definition of terms applicable in the determination of the taxes under the Railroad Retirement Tax Act, such as "employee", "employee representative", "employer", and "compensation". (For prior regulations on similar subject matter, see 26 CFR (1939) Part 411 (Regulations 114).)

(c) *Subpart D.*—The regulations in subpart D of this part relate to the imposition on employers of the excise tax under the Federal Unemployment Tax Act for the calendar year 1955 and subsequent calendar years with respect to wages paid after 1954 for employment performed after 1938. In addition to employment in the case of remuneration therefor paid after 1954, the regulations in subpart D of this part relate also to employment performed after 1954 in the case of remuneration therefor paid before 1955. The regulations in subpart D of this part include provisions relating to the definition of terms applicable in the determination of the tax under the Federal Unemployment Tax Act, such as

"employee", "employer", "employment", and "wages". The regulations in subpart D of this part also include provisions relating to the credits against the Federal tax for State contributions. (For prior regulations on similar subject matter, see 26 CFR (1939) Part 403 (Regulations 107).)

(d) *Subpart E.*—The regulations in subpart E of this part relate to the withholding under chapter 24 of the Code of income tax at source on wages paid after 1954, regardless of when such wages were earned. The regulations in subpart E of this part include provisions relating to the definition of terms applicable in the determination of the tax under chapter 24 of the Code, such as "employee", "employer", and "wages". (For prior regulations on similar subject matter, see 26 CFR (1939) Part 406 (Regulations 120).)

(e) *Subpart F.*—The regulations in subpart F of this part deal with the general provisions contained in chapter 25 of the Code, which relate to the employment taxes imposed by chapters 21 to 24, inclusive, of the Code. (For prior regulations on the subject matter of section 3503, see 26 CFR (1939) 411.802 and 408.803 (Regulations 114 and 128, respectively). (For prior regulations on the subject matter of section 3504, see 26 CFR (1939) 406.807 and 408.906 (Regulations 120 and 128, respectively).)

(f) *Subpart G.*—The regulations in subpart G of this part, which are prescribed under selected provisions of subtitle F of the Code, relate to the procedural and administrative requirements in respect of records, returns, deposits, payments, and related matters applicable to the employment taxes imposed by subtitle C (chapters 21 to 25, inclusive) of the Code. In addition, the provisions of subpart G of this part relate to adjustments and to claims for refund, credit, or abatement, made after 1954, in connection with the employment taxes imposed by subtitle C of the Internal Revenue Code of 1954, by chapter 9 of the Internal Revenue Code of 1939, or by the corresponding provisions of prior law, but not to any adjustment reported, or credit taken, in whole or in part on any return or supplemental return filed on or before July 31, 1960. The provisions of subpart G of this part also relate to deposits of taxes imposed by subchapter B of chapter 9 of the 1939 Code or by corresponding provisions of prior law with respect to compensation paid after 1954 for services rendered before 1955. For other administrative provisions which have application to the employment taxes imposed by subtitle C of the Code, see Part 301 of this chapter (Regulations on Procedure and Administration). (The administrative and procedural regulations applicable with respect to a particular employment tax for a prior period were combined with the substantive regulations relating to such tax for such period. For the regulations applicable to the respective taxes for prior periods, see paragraphs (a), (b), (c), and (d) of this section.) Subpart G of this part also provides rules relating to the deposit of other taxes by electronic funds transfer. [Reg. § 31.0-3.]

☐ *[T.D. 6516, 12-20-60. Amended by T.D. 6744, 7-2-64 and T.D. 8723, 7-11-97.]*

[Reg. §31.0-4]

§31.0-4. Extent to which the regulations in this part supersede prior regulations.—The regulations in this part, with respect to the subject matter within the scope thereof, supersede 25 CFR (1939) Parts 403, 406, 408, and 411 (Regulations 107, 120, 128, and 114, respectively). The Regulations on Monthly Returns and Payment of Employment Taxes (23 F.R. 5006) are also superseded. [Reg. §31.0-4.]

☐ *[T.D. 6516, 12-20-60.]*

TAX ON EMPLOYEES

[Reg. §31.3101-1]

§31.3101-1. Measure of employee tax.—The employee tax is measured by the amount of wages received after 1954 with respect to employment after 1936. See §31.3121(a)-1, relating to wages; and §§31.3121(b)-1 to 31.3121(b)-4, inclusive, relating to employment. For provisions relating to the time of receipt of wages, see §31.3121(a)-2.[Reg. §31.3101-1.]

☐ *[T.D. 6190, 7-14-56. Republished in T.D. 6516, 12-20-60. Amended by T.D. 6744, 7-2-64.]*

⋙→ *Caution: This regulation has not been amended to reflect the changes enacted by P.L. 95-216.*

[Reg. §31.3101-2]

§31.3101-2. Rates and computation of employee tax.—(a) *Old-Age, Survivors, and Disability Insurance.*—The rates of employee tax for Old-Age, Survivors, and Disability Insurance (OASDI) with respect to wages received in calendar years after 1983 are as follows (these regulations do not reflect off-Code revisions to the following rates):

Calendar year	Percent
1984, 1985, 1986, or 1987	5.7
1988 or 1989	6.06
1990 and subsequent years	6.2

(b)(1) *Hospital Insurance.*—The rates of employee tax for Hospital Insurance (HI) with respect to wages received in calendar years after 1973 are as follows:

Calendar year	Percent
1974, 1975, 1976, or 1977	0.90
1978	1.00
1979 or 1980	1.05
1981, 1982, 1983, or 1984	1.30
1985	1.35
1986 and subsequent years	1.45

(2) *Additional Medicare Tax.*—(i) The rate of Additional Medicare Tax with respect to wages received in taxable years beginning after December 31, 2012, is as follows:

Taxable year	Percent
Beginning after December 31, 2012	0.9

(ii) Individuals are liable for Additional Medicare Tax with respect to wages received in taxable years beginning after December 31, 2012, which are in excess of:

Filling Status	Threshold
Married individual filing a joint return	$250,000
Married individual filing a separate return	$125,000
Any other case	$200,000

(c) *Computation of employee tax.*—The employee tax is computed by applying to the wages received by the employee the rates in effect at the time such wages are received.

Example. In 1989, A performed services for X which constituted employment (see §31.3121(b)-2). In 1990 A receives from X $1,000 as remuneration for such services. The tax is payable at the 6.2 percent OASDI rate and the 1.45 percent HI rate in effect for the calendar year 1990 (the year in which the wages are received) and not at the 6.06 percent OASDI rate and the 1.45 percent HI rate which were in effect for the calendar year 1989 (the year in which the services were performed).

(d) *Effective/applicability date.*—Paragraphs (a), (b), and (c) of this section apply to quarters beginning on or after November 29, 2013. [Reg. §31.3101-2.]

☐ *[T.D. 6190, 7-14-56. Republished in T.D. 6516, 12-20-60. Amended by T.D. 6744, 7-2-64; T.D. 6983, 12-4-68; T.D. 7374, 7-24-75 and T.D. 9645, 11-26-2013 (corrected 1-28-2014).]*

[Reg. §31.3101-3]

§31.3101-3. When employee tax attaches.— The employee tax attaches at the time that the wages are received by the employee. For provisions relating to the time of such receipt see §31.3121(a)-2. [Reg. §31.3101-3.]

☐ [T.D. 6190, 7-14-56. *Republished in T.D. 6516, 12-20-60.*]

[Reg. §31.3102-1]

§31.3102-1. Collection of, and liability for, employee tax; in general.—(a) The employer shall collect from each of his employees the employee tax with respect to wages for employment performed for the employer by the employee. The employer shall make the collection by deducting or causing to be deducted the amount of the employee tax from such wages as and when paid. (For provisions relating to the time of such payment, see §31.3121(a)-2.) The employer is required to collect the tax, notwithstanding the wages are paid in something other than money, and to pay over the tax in money. (As to the exclusion from wages of remuneration paid in any medium other than cash for certain types of services, see §31.3121(a)(7)-1, relating to such remuneration paid for service not in the course of the employer's trade or business or for domestic service in a private home of the employer; and §31.3121(a)(8)-1, relating to such remuneration paid for agricultural labor.) For provisions relating to the collection of, and liability for, employee tax in respect of tips, see §31.3102-3. For special rules relating to Additional Medicare Tax imposed under section 3101(b)(2), see §31.3102-4.

(b) The employer is permitted, but not required, to deduct amounts equivalent to employee tax from payments to an employee of cash remuneration to which the sections referred to in this paragraph (b) are applicable prior to the time that the sum of such payments equals—

(1) $100 in the calendar year, for service not in the course of the employer's trade or business, to which §31.3121(a)(7)-1 is applicable;

(2) The applicable dollar threshold (as defined in section 3121(x)) in the calendar year, for domestic service in a private home of the employer, to which §31.3121(a)(7)-1 is applicable;

(3) $150 in the calendar year, for agricultural labor, to which §31.3121(a)(8)-1(c)(1)(i) is applicable; or

(4) $100 in the calendar year, for service performed as a home worker, to which §31.3121(a)(10)-1 is applicable.

(c) At such time as the sum of the cash payments in the calendar year for a type of service referred to in paragraph (b)(1), (b)(2), (b)(3) or (b)(4) of this section equals or exceeds the amount specified, the employer is required to collect from the employee any amount of employee tax not previously deducted. If an employer pays cash remuneration to an employee for two or more of the types of service referred to in paragraph (b)(1), (b)(2), (b)(3) or (b)(4) of this section, the provisions of paragraph (b) of this section and this paragraph (c) are to be applied separately to the amount of remuneration attributable to each type of service. For provisions relating to the repayment to an employee, or other disposition, of amounts deducted from an employee's remuneration in excess of the correct amount of employee tax, see §31.6413(a)-1.

(d) In collecting employee tax, the employer shall disregard any fractional part of a cent of such tax unless it amounts to one-half cent or more, in which case it shall be increased to 1 cent. The employer is liable for the employee tax with respect to all wages paid by him to each of his employees whether or not it is collected from the employee. If, for example, the employer deducts less than the correct amount of tax, or if he fails to deduct any part of the tax, he is nevertheless liable for the correct amount of the tax. Until collected from him the employee also is liable for the employee tax with respect to all the wages received by him. Any employee tax collected by or on behalf of an employer is a special fund in trust for the United States. See section 7501. The employer is indemnified against the claims and demands of any person for the amount of any payment of such tax made by the employer to the district director.

(e)(1) The provisions of paragraphs (a) and (d) of this section apply to any payment made on or after January 1, 1955.

(2) The provisions of paragraphs (b) and (c) of this section that apply to any payment made for service not in the course of the employer's trade or business or for service performed as a home worker within the meaning of section 3121(d)(3)(C) apply to any such payment made on or after January 1, 1978. The provisions of paragraphs (b) and (c) of this section that apply to any payment made for domestic service in a private home of the employer apply to any such payment made on or after January 1, 1994. The provisions of paragraphs (b) and (c) of this section that apply to any payment made for agricultural labor apply to any such payment made on or after January 1, 1988. For rules applicable to any payment for these services made prior to the dates set forth in this paragraph (e)(2), see §31.3102-1 in effect at such time (see 26 CFR part 31 contained in the edition of 26 CFR Parts 30 to 39, revised as of April 1, 2006).

(f) *Effective/applicability date.*—Paragraph (a) of this section applies to quarters beginning on or after November 29, 2013. [Reg. §31.3102-1.]

☐ [T.D. 6190, 7-14-56. *Republished in T.D. 6516, 12-20-60. Amended by T.D. 6744, 7-2-64; T.D. 7001, 1-23-69; T.D. 9266, 6-16-2006 and T.D. 9645, 11-26-2013.*]

[Reg. §31.3102-2]

§31.3102-2. Manner and time of payment of employee tax.—The employee tax is payable to the district director in the manner and at the time prescribed in Subpart G of the regulations in this part. For provisions relating to the payment by an employee of employee tax in respect of tips, see paragraph (d) of §31.3102-3. [Reg. §31.3102-2.]

☐ [T.D. 6190, 7-14-56. *Republished in T.D. 6516, 12-20-60; T.D. 7001, 1-23-69.*]

Reg. §31.3102-2

[Reg. § 31.3102-3]

§ 31.3102-3. Collection of, and liability for, employee tax on tips.—(a) *Collection of tax from employee.*—(1) *In general.*—Subject to the limitations set forth in subparagraph (2) of this paragraph, the employer shall collect from each of his employees the employee tax on those tips received by the employee which constitute wages for purposes of the tax imposed by section 3101. (For provisions relating to the treatment of tips as wages, see §§ 31.3121(a)(12) and 31.3121(q).) The employer shall make the collection by deducting or causing to be deducted the amount of the employee tax from wages (exclusive of tips) which are under the control of the employer or other funds turned over by the employee to the employer (see subparagraph (3) of this paragraph). For purposes of this section the term "wages (exclusive of tips) which are under the control of the employer" means, with respect to a payment of wages, an amount equal to wages as defined in section 3121(a) except that tips and noncash remuneration which are wages are not included, less the sum of—

(i) The tax under section 3101 required to be collected by the employer in respect of wages as defined in section 3121(a) (exclusive of tips);

(ii) The tax under section 3402 required to be collected by the employer in respect of wages as defined in section 3401(a) (exclusive of tips); and

(iii) The amount of taxes imposed on the remuneration of an employee withheld by the employer pursuant to State and local law (including amounts withheld under an agreement between the employer and the employee pursuant to such law) except that the amount of taxes taken into account in this subdivision shall not include any amount attributable to tips.

(2) *Limitations.*—An employer is required to collect employee tax on tips which constitute wages only in respect of those tips which are reported by the employee to the employer in a written statement furnished to the employer pursuant to section 6053(a). The employer is responsible for the collection of employee tax on tips reported to him only to the extent that the employer can—

(i) During the period beginning at the time the written statement is submitted to him and ending at the close of the 10th day of the month following the month in which the statement was submitted, or

(ii) In the case of an employer who elects to deduct the tax on an estimated basis (see paragraph (c) of this section), during the period beginning at the time the written statement is submitted to him and ending at the close of the 30th day following the quarter in which the statement was submitted,

collect the employee tax by deducting it or causing it to be deducted as provided in subparagraph (1).

(3) *Furnishing of funds to employer.*—If the amount of employee tax in respect of tips reported by the employee to the employer in a written statement (or statements) furnished pursuant to section 6053(a) exceeds the wages (exclusive of tips) which are under the control of the employer, the employee may furnish to the employer, within the period specified in subparagraph (2)(i) or (ii) of this paragraph (whichever is applicable), an amount of money equal to the amount of such excess.

(b) *Less than $20 of tips.*—Notwithstanding the provisions of paragraph (a) of this section, if an employee furnishes to his employer a written statement—

(1) Covering a period of less than one month, and

(2) The statement is furnished to the employer prior to the close of the 10th day of the month following the month in which the tips were actually received by the employee, and

(3) The aggregate amount of tips reported in the statement and in all other statements previously furnished by the employee covering periods within the same month is less than $20, and the statements, collectively, do not cover the entire month,

the employer may deduct amounts equivalent to employee tax on such tips from wages (exclusive of tips) which are under the control of the employer or other funds turned over by the employee to the employer. For provisions relating to the repayment to an employee, or other disposition, of amounts deducted from an employee's remuneration in excess of the correct amount of employee tax, see § 31.6413(a)-1. (As to the exclusions from wages of tips of less than $20, see § 31.3121(a)(12)-1.)

(c) *Collection of employee tax on estimated basis.*—(1) *In general.*—Subject to certain limitations and conditions, an employer may, at his discretion, make collection of the employee tax in respect of tips reported by an employee to the employer on an estimated basis. An employer who elects to make collection of the employee tax on an estimated basis shall:

(i) In respect of each employee, make an estimate of the amount of tips that will be reported, pursuant to section 6053(a), by the employee to the employer in a calendar quarter.

(ii) Determine the amount which must be deducted upon each payment of wages (exclusive of tips) which are under the control of the employer to be made during the quarter by the employer to the employee in order to collect from the employee during the quarter an amount equal to the amount obtained by multiplying the estimated quarterly tips by the sum of the rates of tax under subsections (a) and (b) of section 3101.

(iii) Deduct from any payment of such employee's wages (exclusive of tips) which are under the control of the employer, or from funds referred to in paragraph (a)(3) of this section, such amount as may be necessary to adjust the amount of tax withheld on the estimated basis to conform to the amount of employee tax imposed upon, and required to be deducted in respect of, tips reported by the employee to the employer during the calendar quarter in written statements furnished to the employer pursuant to section 6053(a). If an adjustment is required, the additional employee tax required to be collected may be deducted upon any payment of the employee's wages (exclusive of tips) which are under the control of the employer during the quarter and within the first 30 days following the quarter or from funds turned over by the employee to the employer for such purposes within such period. For provisions relating to the repayment to an employee, or other disposition, of amounts deducted from an employee's remuneration in excess of the correct amount of employee tax, see § 31.6413(a)-1.

(2) *Estimating tips employee will report.*— (i) *Initial estimate.*—The initial estimate of the amount of tips that will be reported by a particular employee in a calendar quarter shall be made on the basis of the facts and circumstances surrounding the employment of that employee. However, if a number of employees are employed under substantially the same circumstances and working conditions, the initial estimate established for one such employee may be used as the initial estimate for other employees in that group.

(ii) *Adjusting estimate.*—If the quarterly estimate of tips in respect of a particular employee continues to differ substantially from the amount of tips reported by the employee and there are no unusual factors involved (for example, an extended absence from work due to illness) the employer shall make an appropriate adjustment of his estimate of the amount of tips that will be reported by the employee.

(iii) *Reasonableness of estimate.*—The employer must be prepared, upon request of the district director, to disclose the factors upon which he relied in making the estimate, and his reasons for believing that the estimate is reasonable.

(d) *Employee tax not collected by employer.*—If—

(1) The amount of the employee tax imposed by section 3101 in respect of those tips received by an employee which constitute wages exceeds

(2) The amount of employee tax imposed by section 3101 (in respect of tips reported by the employee to the employer) which can be collected by the employer from such employee's wages (exclusive of tips) which are under the control of the employer or from funds referred to in paragraph (a)(3) of this section,

the employee shall be liable for the payment of tax in an amount equal to such excess. For provisions relating to the manner and time of payment of employee tax by an employee, see

paragraph (d) of § 31.6011(a)-1 and paragraph (a)(4) of § 31.6071(a)-1. For provisions relating to statements required to be furnished by employers to employees in respect of uncollected employee tax on tips reported to the employer, see § 31.6053-2. [Reg. § 31.3102-3.]

☐ [*T.D.* 7001, 1-23-69, *as corrected* 1-31-69.]

[Reg. § 31.3102-4]

§ 31.3102-4. Special rules regarding Additional Medicare Tax.—(a) *Collection of tax from employee.*—An employer is required to collect from each of its employees the tax imposed by section 3101(b)(2) (Additional Medicare Tax) with respect to wages for employment performed for the employer by the employee only to the extent the employer pays wages to the employee in excess of $200,000 in a calendar year. This rule applies regardless of the employee's filing status or other income. Thus, the employer disregards any amount of wages or Railroad Retirement Tax Act (RRTA) compensation paid to the employee's spouse. The employer also disregards any RRTA compensation paid by the employer to the employee or any wages or RRTA compensation paid to the employee by another employer.

Example. H, who is married and files a joint return, receives $100,000 in wages from his employer for the calendar year. I, H's spouse, receives $300,000 in wages from her employer for the same calendar year. H's wages are not in excess of $200,000, so H's employer does not withhold Additional Medicare Tax. I's employer is required to collect Additional Medicare Tax only with respect to wages it pays which are in excess of the $200,000 threshold (that is, $100,000) for the calendar year.

(b) *Collection of amounts not withheld.*—To the extent the employer does not collect Additional Medicare Tax imposed on the employee by section 3101(b)(2), the employee is liable to pay the tax.

Example. J, who is married and files a joint return, receives $190,000 in wages from his employer for the calendar year. K, J's spouse, receives $150,000 in wages from her employer for the same calendar year. Neither J's nor K's wages are in excess of $200,000, so neither J's nor K's employers are required to withhold Additional Medicare Tax. J and K are liable to pay Additional Medicare Tax on $90,000 ($340,000 minus the $250,000 threshold for a joint return).

(c) *Employer's liability for tax.*—If the employer deducts less than the correct amount of Additional Medicare Tax, or if it fails to deduct any part of Additional Medicare Tax, it is nevertheless liable for the correct amount of tax that it was required to withhold, unless and until the employee pays the tax. If an employee subsequently pays the tax that the employer failed to deduct, the tax will not be collected from the employer. The employer will not be relieved of its liability for payment of the tax required to be withheld unless it can show that the tax under section 3101(b)(2) has been paid. The employer, however, will remain subject to any applicable penalties or additions to tax resulting from the failure to withhold as required.

(d) *Effective/applicability date.*—This section applies to quarters beginning on or after November 29, 2013. [Reg. § 31.3102-4.]

☐ [T.D. 9645, 11-26-2013.]

TAX ON EMPLOYERS

[Reg. § 31.3111-1]

§ 31.3111-1. Measure of employer tax.—The employer tax is measured by the amount of wages paid after 1954 with respect to employment after 1936. See § 31.3121(a)-1, relating to wages, and §§ 31.3121(b)-1 to 31.3121(b)-4, inclusive, relating to employment. For provisions relating to time of payment of wages, see § 31.3121(a)-2. [Reg. § 31.3111-1.]

☐ [T.D. 6190, 7-14-56. *Republished in T.D.* 6516, 12-20-60. *Amended by T.D.* 6744, 7-2-64.]

»»→ *Caution: This regulation has not been amended to reflect the changes enacted by P.L. 95-216.*

[Reg. § 31.3111-2]

§ 31.3111-2. Rates and computation of employer tax.—(a) *Old-age, survivors, and disability insurance.*—The rates of employer tax for old-age survivors, and disability insurance with respect to wages paid in calendar years after 1954 are as follows:

Calendar years	Percent
1955 and 1956	2
1957 and 1958	2.25
1959	2.5
1960 and 1961	3
1962	3.125
1963 to 1965, both inclusive	3.625
1966	3.85
1967	3.9
1968	3.8
1969 and 1970	4.2
1971 and 1972	4.6
1973	4.85
1974 to 2010, both inclusive	4.95
2011 and subsequent calendar years	5.95

(b) *Hospital insurance.*—The rates of employer tax for hospital insurance with respect to wages paid in calendar years after 1965 are as follows:

Calendar years	Percent
1966	0.35
1967	0.50
1968 to 1972, both inclusive	0.60
1973	1.0
1974 to 1977, both inclusive	0.90
1978 to 1980, both inclusive	1.10
1981 to 1985, both inclusive	1.35
1986 and subsequent calendar years	1.50

(c) *Computation of employer tax.*—The employer tax is computed by applying to the wages paid by the employer the rate in effect at the time such wages are paid. [Reg. § 31.3111-2.]

☐ [T.D. 6190, 7-14-56. *Republished in T.D.* 6516, 12-20-60. *Amended by T.D.* 6744, 7-2-64, T.D. 6983, 12-4-68 *and T.D.* 7374, 7-24-75.]

[Reg. § 31.3111-3]

§ 31.3111-3. When employer tax attaches.—The employer tax attaches at the time that the wages are paid by the employer. For provisions relating to the time of such payment, see § 31.3121(a)-2. [Reg. § 31.3111-3.]

☐ [T.D. 6190, 7-14-56. *Republished in T.D.* 6516, 12-20-60.]

[Reg. § 31.3111-4]

§ 31.3111-4. Liability for employer tax.—The employer is liable for the employer tax with respect to the wages paid to his employees for employment performed for him. [Reg. § 31.3111-4.]

☐ [T.D. 6190, 7-14-56. *Republished in T.D.* 6516, 12-20-60.]

[Reg. § 31.3111-5]

§ 31.3111-5. Manner and time of payment of employer tax.—The employer tax is payable to the district director in the manner and at the time prescribed in subpart G of the regulations in this part. [Reg. § 31.3111-5.]

☐ [T.D. 6190, 7-14-56. *Republished in T.D.* 6516, 12-20-60.]

[Reg. § 31.3112-1]

§ 31.3112-1. Instrumentalities of the United States specifically exempted from the employer tax.—Section 3112 makes ineffectual as to the employer tax imposed by section 3111 those provisions of law which grant to an instrumentality of the United States an exemption from taxation from taxation, unless such provisions grant a specific exemption from the tax imposed by section 3111 by an express reference to such section or the corresponding section of prior law (section 1410 of the Internal Revenue Code 1939). Thus, the general exemptions from Federal taxation granted by various statutes to certain instrumentalities of the United States without specific reference to the tax imposed by section 3111 or by section 1410 of the 1939 Code are rendered inoperative insofar as such exemptions relate to the tax imposed by section 3111. For provisions relating to the exception from employment of services performed in the employ of an instrumentality of the United States specifically exempted from the employer tax, see § 31,3121(b)(5)-1. For provisions relating to services performed for an instrumentality exempt on December 31, 1950, from the employer tax, see paragraph (c) of § 31,3121(b)(6)-1. [Reg. § 31.3112-1.]

☐ [T.D. 6190, 7-14-56. *Republished in T.D.* 6516, 12-20-60.]

GENERAL PROVISIONS

[Reg. §31.3121(a)-1]

§31.3121(a)-1. **Wages.**—(a) Whether remuneration paid after 1954 for employment performed after 1936 constitutes wages is determined under section 3121 (a). This section and §§31.3121(a)(1)-1 to 31.3121(a)(15)-1, inclusive (relating to the statutory exclusions from wages), apply with respect only to remuneration paid after 1954 for employment performed after 1936. Whether remuneration paid after 1936 and before 1940 for employment performed after 1936 constitutes wages shall be determined in accordance with the applicable provisions of law and of 26 CFR (1939) Part 401 (Regulations 91). Whether remuneration paid after 1939 and before 1951 for employment performed after 1936 constitutes wages shall be determined in accordance with the applicable provisions of law and of 26 CFR (1939) Part 402 (Regulations 106). Whether remuneration paid after 1950 and before 1955 for employment performed after 1936 constitutes wages shall be determined in accordance with the applicable provisions of law and of 26 CFR (1939) Part 408 (Regulations 128).

(b) The term "wages" means all remuneration for employment unless specifically excepted under section 3121(a) (see §§31.3121(a)(1)-1 to 31.3121(a)(15)-1, inclusive) or paragraph (j) of this section.

(c) The name by which the remuneration for employment is designated is immaterial. Thus, salaries, fees, bonuses, and commissions on sales or on insurance premiums, are wages if paid as compensation for employment.

(d) Generally the basis upon which the remuneration is paid is immaterial in determining whether the remuneration constitutes wages. Thus, it may be paid on the basis of piecework, or a percentage of profits; and it may be paid hourly, daily, weekly, monthly, or annually. See, however, §31.3121(a)(8)-1 which relates to the treatment of cash remuneration computed on a time basis for agricultural labor.

(e) Generally the medium in which the remuneration is paid is also immaterial. It may be paid in cash or in something other than cash, as for example, goods, lodging, food, or clothing. Remuneration paid in items other than cash shall be computed on the basis of the fair value of such items at the time of payment. See, however, §§31.3121(a)(7)-1, 31.3121(a)(8)-1, 31.3121-(a)(10)-1, and 31.3121(a)(12)-1, relating to the treatment of remuneration paid in any medium other than cash for services not in the course of the employer's trade or business and for domestic service in a private home of the employer, for agricultural labor, for services performed by certain home workers, and as tips, respectively.

(f) Ordinarily, facilities or privileges (such as entertainment, medical services, or so-called "courtesy" discounts on purchases), furnished or offered by an employer to his employees generally, are not considered as remuneration for employment if such facilities or privileges are of relatively small value and are offered or furnished by the employer merely as a means of promoting the health, good will, contentment, or efficiency of his employees. The term "facilities or privileges," however, does not ordinarily include the value of meals or lodging furnished, for example, to restaurant or hotel employees, or to seamen or other employees aboard vessels, since generally these items constitute an appreciable part of the total remuneration of such employees.

(g) Amounts of so-called "vacation allowances" paid to an employee constitute wages. Thus, the salary of an employee on vacation, paid notwithstanding his absence from work, constitutes wages.

(h) Amounts paid specifically—either as advances or reimbursements—for traveling or other bona fide ordinary and necessary expenses incurred or reasonably expected to be incurred in the business of the employer are not wages. For amounts that are received by an employee on or after July 1, 1990, with respect to expenses paid or incurred on or after July 1, 1990, see §31.3121(a)-3.

(i) Remuneration for employment, unless such remuneration is specifically excepted under section 3121(a) or paragraph (j) of this section, constitutes wages even though at the time paid the relationship of employer and employee no longer exists between the person in whose employ the services were performed and the individual who performed them.

Example. A is employed by B during the month of January 1955 in employment and is entitled to receive remuneration of $100 for the services performed for B, the employer, during the month. A leaves the employ of B at the close of business on January 31, 1955. On February 15, 1955 (when A is no longer an employee of B), B pays A the remuneration of $100 which was earned for the services performed in January. The $100 is wages and the taxes are payable with respect thereto.

(j) In addition to the exclusions specified in §§31.3121(a)(1)-1 to 31.3121(a)(15)-1, inclusive, the following types of payments are excluded from wages:

(1) Remuneration for services which do not constitute employment under section 3121(b) and which are not deemed to be employment under section 3121(c) (see §31.3121(c)-1).

(2) Remuneration for services which are deemed not to be employment under section 3121(c) (see §31.3121(c)-1).

(3) Tips or gratuities paid, prior to January 1, 1966, directly to an employee by a customer of

an employer, and not accounted for by the employee to the employer. For provisions relating to the treatment of tips received by an employee after December 31, 1965, as wages, see §§ 31.3121(a)(12) and 31.3121(q).

(k) *Split-dollar life insurance arrangements.*—Except as otherwise provided under section 3121(v), see §§ 1.61-22 and 1.7872-15 of this chapter for rules relating to the treatment of split-dollar life insurance arrangements. [Reg. § 31.3121(a)-1.]

☐ [*T.D.* 6190, 7-14-56. *Republished in T.D.* 6516, 12-20-60. *Amended by T.D.* 6744, 7-2-64; *T.D.* 7374, 7-24-75; *T.D.* 8324, 12-17-90 *and T.D.* 9092, 9-11-2003.]

[Reg. § 31.3121(a)-1T]

§ 31.3121(a)-1T. Question and answer relating to the definition of wages in section 3121(a) (Temporary).—The following question and answer relates to the definition of wages in section 3121(a) of the Internal Revenue Code of 1954, as amended by section 531(d)(1)(A) of the Tax Reform Act of 1984 (98 Stat. 885):

Q-1: Are fringe benefits included in the definition of "wages" under section 3121(a)?

A-1: Yes, unless specifically excluded from the definition of "wages" pursuant to section 3121(a)(1) through (20). For example, a fringe benefit provided to or on behalf of an employee is excluded from the definition of "wages" if at the time such benefit is provided it is reasonable to believe that the employee will be able to exclude such benefit from income under section 117 or 132. [Temporary Reg. § 31.3121(a)-1T.]

☐ [*T.D.* 8004, 1-2-85.]

[Reg. § 31.3121(a)-2]

§ 31.3121(a)-2. Wages; when paid and received.—(a) In general, wages are received by an employee at the time that they are paid by the employer to the employee. Wages are paid by an employer at the time that they are actually or constructively paid unless under paragraph (c) of this section they are deemed to be subsequently paid. For provisions relating to the time when tips received by an employee are deemed paid to the employee, see § 31.3121(q)-1.

(b) Wages are constructively paid when they are credited to the account of or set apart for an employee so that they may be drawn upon by him at any time although not then actually reduced to possession. To constitute payment in such a case the wages must be credited to or set apart for the employee without any substantial limitation or restriction as to the time or manner of payment or condition upon which payment is to be made, and must be made available to him so that they may be drawn upon at any time, and their payment brought within his own control and disposition. For provisions relating to the treatment of deductions from remuneration as payments of remuneration, see § 31.3123-1.

(c)(1) The first $100 of cash remuneration paid, either actually or constructively, by an employer in any calendar year to an employee for—

(i) Service not in the course of the employer's trade or business, to which § 31.3121(a)(7)-1 is applicable, shall be deemed to be paid by the employer to the employee at the first moment of time in such calendar year that the sum of such cash payments made within such year is at least $100; or

(ii) Service performed as a home worker within the meaning of section 3121(d)(3)(C), to which § 31.3121(a)(10)-1 is applicable, shall be deemed to be paid by the employer to the employee at the first moment of time in such calendar year that the sum of such cash payments made within such year is at least $100.

(2) Cash remuneration paid, either actually or constructively, by an employer in any calendar year to an employee for domestic service in a private home of the employer to which § 31.3121(a)(7)-1 is applicable, and before the sum of the payments of such cash remuneration equals or exceeds the applicable dollar threshold (as defined in section 3121(x)) for such year, shall be deemed to be paid by the employer to the employee at the first moment of time in such calendar year that the sum of such cash payments made within such year equals or exceeds the applicable dollar threshold (as defined in section 3121(x)) for such year.

(3) Cash remuneration paid, either actually or constructively, by an employer in any calendar year to an employee for agricultural labor to which § 31.3121(a)(8)-1 is applicable, and before either of the events described in paragraphs (c)(3)(i) and (c)(3)(ii) of this section has occurred, shall be deemed to be paid by the employer to the employee at the first moment of time in such calendar year that—

(i) The sum of the payments of such remuneration is $150 or more; or

(ii) The employer's expenditures for agricultural labor in such calendar year equals or exceeds $2,500, except that this paragraph (c)(3)(ii) shall not apply in determining when such remuneration is deemed to be paid under this paragraph if such employee—

(A) Is employed as a hand-harvest laborer and is paid on a piece rate basis in an operation which has been, and is customarily and generally recognized as having been, paid on a piece rate basis in the region of employment;

(B) Commutes daily from his permanent residence to the farm on which he is so employed; and

(C) Has been employed in agriculture less than 13 weeks during the preceding calendar year.

(4) If an employer pays cash remuneration to an employee for two or more of the types of service referred to in this paragraph, the provisions of this paragraph are to be applied separately to the amount of remuneration attributable to each type of service.

(d)(1) The provisions of paragraphs (a) and (b) of this section apply to any payment of wages made on or after January 1, 1955.

(2) The provisions of paragraph (c) of this section that apply to any payment of wages made for service not in the course of the employer's trade or business or for service performed as a home worker within the meaning of section 3121(d)(3)(C) apply to any such payment made on or after January 1, 1978. The provisions of paragraph (c) of this section that apply to any payment of wages made for domestic service in a private home of the employer apply to any such payment made on or after January 1, 1994. The provisions of paragraph (c) of this section that apply to any payment of wages made for agricultural labor apply to any such payment made on or after January 1, 1988. For rules applicable to any payment of wages for these services made prior to the dates set forth in this paragraph (d)(2), see §31.3121(a)-2 in effect at such time (see 26 CFR part 31 contained in the edition of 26 CFR Parts 30 to 39, revised as of April 1, 2006). [Reg. §31.3121(a)-2.]

☐ [T.D. 6190, 12-14-56. *Republished in T.D.* 6516, 12-20-60. *Amended by T.D.* 6744, 7-2-64; *T.D.* 7001, 1-23-69 *and T.D.* 9266, 6-16-2006.]

[Reg. §31.3121(a)-3]

§31.3121(a)-3. Reimbursement and other expense allowance amounts.—(a) *When excluded from wages.*—If a reimbursement or other expense allowance arrangement meets the requirements of section 62(c) of the Code and §1.62-2 and the expenses are substantiated within a reasonable period of time, payments made under the arrangement that do not exceed the substantiated expenses are treated as paid under an accountable plan and are not wages. In addition, if both wages and the reimbursement or other expense allowance are combined in a single payment, the reimbursement or other expense allowance must be identified either by making a separate payment or by specifically identifying the amount of the reimbursement or other expense allowance.

(b) *When included in wages.*—(1) *Accountable plans.*—(i) *General rule.*—Except as provided in paragraph (b)(1)(ii) of this section, if a reimbursement or other expense allowance arrangement satisfies the requirements of section 62(c) and §1.62-2, but the expenses are not substantiated within a reasonable period of time or amounts in excess of the substantiated expenses are not returned within a reasonable period of

time, the amount paid under the arrangement in excess of the substantiated expenses is treated as paid under a nonaccountable plan, is included in wages, and is subject to withholding and payment of employment taxes no later than the first payroll period following the end of the reasonable period.

(ii) *Per diem or mileage allowances.*—If a reimbursement or other expense allowance arrangement providing a per diem or mileage allowance satisfies the requirements of section 62(c) and §1.62-2, but the allowance is paid at a rate for each day or mile of travel that exceeds the amount of the employee's expenses deemed substantiated for a day or mile of travel, the excess portion is treated as paid under a nonaccountable plan and is included in wages. In the case of a per diem or mileage allowance paid as a reimbursement, the excess portion is subject to withholding and payment of employment taxes when paid. In the case of a per diem or mileage allowance paid as an advance, the excess portion is subject to withholding and payment of employment taxes no later than the first payroll period following the payroll period in which the expenses with respect to which the advance was paid (i.e., the days or miles of travel) are substantiated. The Commissioner may, in his discretion, prescribe special rules in pronouncements of general applicability regarding the timing of withholding and payment of employment taxes on per diem and mileage allowances.

(2) *Nonaccountable plans.*—If a reimbursement or other expense allowance arrangement does not satisfy the requirements of section 62(c) and §1.62-2 (e.g., the arrangement does not require expenses to be substantiated or require amounts in excess of the substantiated expenses to be returned), all amounts paid under the arrangement are treated as paid under a nonaccountable plan, are included in wages, and are subject to withholding and payment of employment taxes when paid.

(c) *Effective dates.*—This section generally applies to payments made under reimbursement or other expense allowance arrangements received by an employee on or after July 1, 1990, with respect to expenses paid or incurred on or after July 1, 1990. Paragraph (b)(1)(ii) of this section applies to payments made under reimbursement or other expense allowance arrangements received by an employee on or after January 1, 1991, with respect to expenses paid or incurred on or after January 1, 1991. [Reg. §31.3121(a)-3.]

☐ [T.D. 8324, 12-17-90.]

⧸⧸⧸→ *Caution: Reg. §31.3121(a)(1)-1 does not reflect P.L. 95-216 or P.L. 101-508.*

[Reg. §31.3121(a)(1)-1]

§31.3121(a)(1)-1. Annual wage limitation.—(a) *In general.*—(1) The term "wages" does not include that part of the remuneration paid by an employer to an employee within any calendar year—

(i) After 1954 and before 1959 which exceeds the first $4,200 of remuneration,

(ii) After 1958 and before 1966 which exceeds the first $4,800 of remuneration,

(iii) After 1965 and before 1968 which exceeds the first $6,600 of remuneration,

(iv) After 1967 and before 1972 which exceeds the first $7,800 of remuneration,

(v) After 1971 and before 1973 which exceeds the first $9,000 of remuneration,

(vi) After 1972 and before 1974 which exceeds the first $10,800 of remuneration,

(vii) After 1973 and before 1975 which exceeds the first $13,200 of remuneration, or

(viii) After 1974 which exceeds the amount equal to the contribution and benefit base (as determined under section 230 of the Social Security Act) which is effective for such calendar year

(exclusive of remuneration excepted from wages in accordance with paragraph (j) of §31.3121(a)-1 or §§31.3121(a)(2)-1 to 31.3121(a)(15)-1, inclusive) paid within the calendar year by an employer to the employee for employment performed for him at any time after 1936. For provisions relating to the treatment of tips for purposes of the annual wage limitation see §31.3121(q)-1.

(2) The annual wage limitation applies only if the remuneration received during any one calendar year by an employee from the same employer for employment performed after 1936 exceeds the amount of such limitation. The limitation in such case relates to the amount of remuneration received during any one calendar year for employment after 1936 and not to the amount of remuneration for employment performed in any one calendar year.

Example. Employee A, in 1967 receives $7,000 from employer B in part payment of $8,000 due him from employment performed in 1967. In 1968 A receives from employer B the balance of $1,000 due him for employment performed in 1967, and thereafter in 1968 also receives $7,000 for employment performed in 1968 for employer B. The first $6,600 of the $7,000 received during 1967 is subject to the taxes in 1967. The remaining $400 received in 1967 is not included as wages and is not subject to the taxes. The balance of $1,000 received in 1968 for employment during 1967 is subject to the taxes during 1968 as is also the first $6,800 of the $7,000 thereafter received in 1968 ($1,000 plus $6,800 totaling $7,800, which is the annual wage limitation applicable to remuneration received in 1968 by an employee from any one employer). The remaining $200 received in 1968 is not included as wages and is not subject to the taxes.

(3) If during a calendar year the employee receives remuneration from more than one employer, the annual wage limitation does not apply to the aggregate remuneration received from all of such employers, but instead applies to the remuneration received during such calendar year from each employer with respect to employment after 1936. In such case the first remuneration received in any calendar year after 1974 up to the amount equal to the contribution and benefit base (as determined under section 230 of the Social Security Act) (the first $13,200 received in 1974, the first $10,800 received in 1973, the first $9,000 received in 1972, the first $7,800 received in any calendar year after 1967 and before 1972, the first $6,600 received in any calendar year after 1965 and before 1968, the first $4,800 received in any calendar year after 1958 and before 1966, or the first $4,200 received in any calendar year after 1954 and before 1959) from each employer constitutes wages and is subject to the taxes, even though, under section 6413(c), the employee may be entitled to a special credit or refund of a portion of the employee tax deducted from his wages received during the calendar year. In this connection and in connection with the two examples immediately following, see §31.6413(c)-1, relating to special credits or refunds of employee tax. In connection with the annual wage limitation in the case of remuneration paid for services performed in the employ of the United States or a wholly owned instrumentality thereof, see §31.3122. In connection with the annual wage limitation in the case of remuneration paid for services performed in the employ of the Government of Guam, the Government of American Samoa, the District of Columbia, a political subdivision of the Government of Guam, or the Government of American Samoa, or any instrumentality of any of the foregoing which is wholly owned thereby, see §31.3125. In connection with the application of the annual wage limitation, see also paragraph (b) of this section, relating to the circumstances under which wages paid by a predecessor employer are deemed to be paid by his successor. In connection with the annual wage limitation in the case of remuneration paid after December 31, 1978, from two or more related corporations that compensate an employee through a common paymaster, see §31.3121(s)-1.

Example (1). During 1968 employee C receives from employer D a salary of $1,300 a month for employment performed for D during the first 7 months of 1968, or total remuneration of $9,100. At the end of the sixth month C has received $7,800 from employer D, and only that part of his total remuneration from D constitutes wages subject to the taxes. The $1,300 received by employee C from employer D in the seventh month is not included as wages and is not subject to the taxes. At the end of the seventh month C leaves the employ of D and enters the employ of E. C receives remuneration of $1,560 a month from employer E in each of the remaining 5 months of 1968, or total remuneration of $7,800 from employer E. The entire $7,800 received by C from employer E constitutes wages and is subject to the taxes. Thus, the first $7,800 received from employer D and the entire $7,800 received from employer E constitute wages.

Example (2). During the calendar year 1968 F is simultaneously an officer (an employee) of the X Corporation, the Y Corporation, and the Z Corporation and during such year receives a salary of $7,800 from each corporation. Each $7,800 received by F from each of the Corporations X, Y, and Z (whether or not such corporations are related) constitutes wages and is subject to the taxes.

(b) *Wages paid by predecessor attributed to successor.*—(1) If an employer (hereinafter referred to as a successor) during any calendar year acquires substantially all the property used in a trade or business of another employer (hereinafter referred to as a predecessor), or used in a separate unit of a trade or business of a predecessor, and if immediately after the acquisition the successor employs in his trade or business an individual who immediately prior to the acquisition was employed in the trade or business of such predecessor, then, for purposes of the application of the annual wage limitation set forth in paragraph (a) of this section, any remuneration (exclusive of remuneration excepted from wages in accordance with paragraph (j) of § 31.3121(a)-1 or § § 31.3121(a)(2)-1 to 31.3121(a)(15)-1, inclusive) with respect to employment paid (or considered under this paragraph as having been paid) to such individual by the predecessor during such calendar year and prior to the acquisition shall be considered as having been paid by the successor.

(2) The wages paid, or considered as having been paid, by a predecessor to an employee shall, for purposes of the annual wage limitation, be treated as having been paid to such employee by a successor, if:

(i) the successor during a calendar year acquired substantially all the property used in a trade or business, or used in a separate unit of a trade or business, of the predecessor;

(ii) such employee was employed in the trade or business of the predecessor immediately prior to the acquisition and is employed by the successor in his trade or business immediately after the acquisition; and

(iii) such wages were paid during the calendar year in which the acquisition occurred and prior to such acquisition.

(3) The method of acquisition by an employer of the property of another employer is immaterial. The acquisition may occur as a consequence of the incorporation of a business by a sole proprietor or a partnership, the continuance without interruption of the business of a previously existing partnership by a new partnership or by a sole proprietor, or a purchase or any other transaction whereby substantially all the property used in a trade or business, or used in a separate unit of a trade or business, of one employer is acquired by another employer.

(4) Substantially all the property used in a separate unit of a trade or business may consist of substantially all the property used in the performance of an essential operation of the trade or business, or it may consist of substantially all the property used in a relatively self-sustaining entity which forms a part of the trade or business.

Example (1). The M Corporation which is engaged in the manufacture of automobiles, including the manufacture of automobile engines, discontinues the manufacture of the engines and transfers all the property used in such manufacturing operation to the N Company. The N Company is considered to have acquired a separate unit of the trade or business of the M Corporation, namely, its engine manufacturing unit.

Example (2). The R Corporation which is engaged in the operation of a chain of grocery stores transfers one of such stores to the S Company. The S Company is considered to have acquired a separate unit of the trade or business of the R Corporation.

(5) A successor may receive credit for wages paid to an employee by a predecessor only if immediately prior to the acquisition the employee was employed by the predecessor in his trade or business which was acquired by the successor and if immediately after the acquisition such employee is employed by the successor in his trade or business (whether or not in the same trade or business in which the acquired property is used). If the acquisition involves only a separate unit of a trade or business of the predecessor, the employee need not have been employed by the predecessor in that unit provided he was employed in the trade or business of which the acquired unit was a part.

Example. The Y Corporation in 1968 acquires by purchase all the property of the X Company and immediately after the acquisition employs in its trade or business employee A, who, immediately prior to the acquisition, was employed by the X Company. The X Company has in 1968 (the calendar year in which the acquisition occurs) and prior to the acquisition paid $5,000 of wages to A. The Y Corporation in 1968 pays to A remuneration of $5,000 with respect to employment. Only $2,800 of the remuneration paid by the Y Corporation is considered to be wages. For purposes of the $7,800 limitation, the Y Corporation is credited with the $5,000 paid to A by the X Company. If, in the same calendar year, the Z Company acquires the property by purchase from the Y Corporation and A immediately after the acquisition is employed by the Z Company in its trade or business, no part of the remuneration paid to A by the Z Company in the year of the acquisition will be considered to be wages. The Z Company will be credited with the remuneration paid to A by the Y Corporation and also with the wages paid to A by the X Company (considered for purposes of the application of the $7,800 limitation as having also been paid by the Y Corporation).

(6) Where a corporation described in section 501(c)(3) which is exempt from income tax under section 501(a) has in effect a certificate filed pursuant to section 3121(k), or pursuant to section 1426(l) of the Internal Revenue Code of 1939, waiving its exemption from the taxes imposed by the Act, the activity in which such corporation is engaged is considered to be its trade or business for the purpose of determining whether the transferred property was used in the trade or business of the predecessor and for the purpose of determining whether the employment by the predecessor and the successor of an individual whose services were retained by the successor constitute employment in a trade or business. Thus, if a charitable or religious organization, subject to the taxes by virtue of its certificate, acquires all the property of another such organization likewise subject to the taxes and retains the services of employees of the predecessor, wages paid to such employees by the prede-

cessor in the year of the acquisition (and prior to such acquisition) will be attributed to the successor for purposes of the annual wage limitation. [Reg. § 31.3121(a)(1)-1.]

>>>→ *Caution: Regulation §31.3121(a)(2)-1 does not reflect changes made by P.L. 100-203.*

[Reg. § 31.3121(a)(2)-1]

§ 31.3121(a)(2)-1. Payments on account of sickness or accident disability, medical or hospitalization expenses, or death.—(a) The term "wages" does not include the amount of any payment (including any amount paid by an employer for insurance or annuities, or into a fund, to provide for any such payment) made to, or on behalf of, an employee or any of his dependents under a plan or system established by an employer which makes provision for his employees generally (or for his employees generally and their dependents) or for a class or classes of his employees (or for a class or classes of his employees and their dependents), on account of—

(1) Sickness or accident disability of an employee or any of his dependents, only if payment is received under a workers' compensation law,

(2) Medical or hospitalization expenses in connection with sickness or accident disability of an employee or any of his dependents, or

(3) Death of an employee or any of his dependents.

(b) The plan or system established by an employer need not provide for payments on account of all of the specified items, but such plan or system may provide for any one or more of such items. Payments for any one or more of such items under a plan or system established by an employer solely for the dependents of his employees are not within this exclusion from wages.

(c) Dependents of an employee include the employee's husband or wife, children, and any other members of the employee's immediate family.

(d) *Workers' compensation law.*—(1) For purposes of paragraph (a)(1) of this section, a payment made under a workers' compensation law includes a payment made pursuant to a statute in the nature of a workers' compensation act.

(2) For purposes of paragraph (a)(1) of this section, a payment made under a workers' compensation law does not include a payment made pursuant to a State temporary disability insurance law.

(3) If an employee receives a payment on account of sickness or accident disability that is not made under a workers' compensation law or a statute in the nature of a workers' compensation act, the payment is not excluded from wages as defined by section 3121(a)(2)(A) even if the payment must be repaid if the employee receives a workers' compensation award or an award under a statute in the nature of a workers' compensation act with respect to the same period of absence from work.

(4) If an employee receives a payment on account of non-occupational injury sickness or accident disability such payment is not excluded from wages, as defined by section 3121(a)(2)(A).

(e) *Examples.*—The following examples illustrate the principles of paragraph (d) of this section:

Example 1. A local government employee is injured while performing work-related activities. The employee is not covered by the State workers' compensation law, but is covered by a local government ordinance that requires the local government to pay the employee's full salary when the employee is out of work as a result of an injury incurred while performing services for the local government. The ordinance does not limit or otherwise affect the local government's liability to the employee for the work-related injury. The local ordinance is not a workers' compensation law, but it is in the nature of a workers' compensation act. Therefore, the salary the employee receives while out of work as a result of the work-related injury is excluded from wages under section 3121(a)(2)(A).

Example 2. The facts are the same as in *Example 1* except that the local ordinance requires the employer to continue to pay the employee's full salary while the employee is unable to work due to an injury whether or not the injury is work-related. Thus, the local ordinance does not limit benefits to instances of work-related disability. A benefit paid under an ordinance that does not limit benefits to instances of work-related injuries is not a statute in the nature of a workers' compensation act. Therefore, the salary the injured employee receives from the employer while out of work is wages subject to FICA even though the employee's injury is work-related.

Example 3. The facts are the same as in *Example 1* except that the local ordinance includes a rebuttable presumption that certain injuries, including any heart attack incurred by a firefighter or other law enforcement personnel is work-related. The presumption in the ordinance does not eliminate the requirement that the injury be work-related in order to entitle the injured worker to full salary. Therefore, the ordinance is a statute in the nature of a workers' compensation act, and the salary the injured employee receives pursuant to the ordinance is excluded from wages under section 3121(a)(2)(A).

(f) It is immaterial for purposes of this exclusion whether the amount or possibility of such benefit payments is taken into consideration in fixing the amount of an employee's remuneration or whether such payments are required, expressly or impliedly, by the contract of service. [Reg. § 31.3121(a)(2)-1.]

□ [*T.D.* 6190, 12-14-56. *Republished in T.D.* 6516, 12-20-60. *Amended by T.D.* 6744, 7-2-64; *T.D.* 6983, 12-4-68; *T.D.* 7374, 7-24-75 *and T.D.* 7660, 12-19-79.]

□ [*T.D.* 6190, 7-14-56. *Republished in T.D.* 6516, 12-20-60. *Amended by T.D.* 9233, 12-14-2005.]

»»→ *Caution: Temporary Regulation §32.1, below, is applicable to payments made on account of sickness or accident disability on or after January 1, 1982.*

[Reg. §32.1]

§32.1. Social security taxes with respect to payments on account of sickness or accident disability.—(a) *General rule.*—The amount of any payment on or after January 1, 1982, made to, or on behalf of, an employee or any of his dependents on account of sickness or accident disability is not excluded from the term wages as defined in section 3121(a)(2)(A) unless such payment is—

(1) Received under a workmen's compensation law (as defined in 31.3121(a)(2)-1(d)(3) for payments made on or after December 15, 2005, or

(2) Made by a third party pursuant to a contractual agreement between the employer and third party entered into prior to December 14, 1981, but then only if—

(i) The third party's coverage for that employee's group ceases prior to March 1, 1982,

(ii) No third party payment is made to such employee under that contract after February 28, 1982, and

(iii) The cessation of the third party's coverage for that employee's group indefinitely terminates the contractual relationship between the third party and the employer as to sickness and accident disability benefits for that employee's group.

See section 3121(a)(4) and §31.3121(a)(4)-1 for the exclusion from the term "wages" of any payment on account of sickness or accident disability made after the expiration of 6 calendar months following the last calendar month in which the employee worked.

(b) *Examples.*—The application of the provisions of subparagraph (2) of paragraph (a) may be illustrated by the following examples:

Example (1). Company Q enters into a contract on August 31, 1981, with Insurance Company R to provide sickness and accident disability payments to Q's employees. The contract expires on February 28, 1982. On March 1, 1982, Q enters into a new contract with R to provide sickness and accident disability payments to Q's employees. Payments made by R pursuant to the contract expiring February 28, 1982, are included in "wages" as defined in section 3121(a)(2)(B).

Example (2). Company S enters into a contract on November 15, 1981, with Insurance Company T to provide sickness and accident disability payments to S's employees. The contract expires on February 15, 1982, and is not renewed. A, one of S's employees, has been receiving sickness payments from T since December 1, 1981. T makes its final payment to A on February 22, 1982. The payments made by T to A pursuant to its contract with S are not included in "wages" as defined in section 3121(a)(2)(B).

(c) *Workmen's compensation laws.*—(1) For purposes of paragraph (a)(1) of this section, a payment made under a workmen's compensation law does not include a payment made pursuant to a State temporary disability insurance law.

(2) If an employee receives a payment on account of sickness or accident disability which is not made under a workmen's compensation law and which must be repaid if the employee receives a workmen's compensation award with respect to the same period of absence from work, such payment is not excluded from the term "wages" as defined in section 3121(a)(2)(B).

(d) *Sickness or accident disability.*—For purposes of paragraph (a) of this section, a payment made on account of sickness or accident disability includes any payment for personal injuries or sickness includible in gross income under section 105(a) and the regulations thereunder and thus does not include—

(1) Any amount which is expended for medical care as described in section 105(b) and §1.105-2,

(2) Any payment which is unrelated to absence from work as described in section 105(c) and §1.105-3, or

(3) Any payment or a portion thereof which is attributable to a contribution by the employee as determined in paragraphs (d) and (e) of §1.105-1.

A payment made on account of sickness or accident disability does not include any payment which is excludable from gross income under section 104(a)(2), (4), or (5). An employee who elects to reduce his compensation or to forgo an increase in his compensation under a salary reduction agreement with an employer will not be deemed to have made employee contributions to the sickness or accident disability plan or system if the employee is not subject to income or social security taxes on the reduction in compensation. A tax which is paid by an employee to fund a State temporary disability insurance program is considered a contribution by the employee for purposes of paragraph (d)(3) of this section.

(e) *Payments by third parties.*—(1) Any third party making a payment on account of sickness or accident disability which payment is not excluded from the term "wages" under paragraph (a) of this section shall be treated as the employer with respect to such wages, except as provided in subparagraphs (2) and (3) of this paragraph. Accordingly, such third party must withhold from such payment the tax imposed on the employee by section 3101, pay the tax imposed on employers by section 3111, deposit such taxes pursuant to section 6302 and §31.6302(c)-1(a), and provide the receipts required by section 6051 and §§31.6051-1 and 31.6051-2.

(2) If any third party who is treated as the employer solely by reason of the applicability of subparagraph (1) of this paragraph promptly—

(i) Withholds the tax imposed on the employee by section 3101,

Reg. §32.1(e)(2)(i)

(ii) Deposits such tax pursuant to section 6302 and §31.6302(c)-1(a), and

(iii) Notifies the employer for whom services are normally rendered of the amount of wages paid on which tax was withheld and deposited, then the employer (and not the third party) shall be required to pay the tax imposed by section 3111 and to comply with the requirements of section 6051 and §§31.6051-1 and 31.6051-2 with respect to the wages. For purposes of subdivision (ii) of this subparagraph, the taxes described in subdivision (i) shall be treated by the third party as if included in the term "taxes" as defined in §31.6302(c)-1(a)(1)(iii). For purposes of subdivision (iii) of this subparagraph, the notice must be provided by the third party within the time required for the deposit of the tax under subdivision (ii) of this subparagraph. For the purpose of providing the notice, the rules of section 7502(a), relating to timely mailing being treated as timely filing, shall apply. The employer, if notified pursuant to subdivision (iii) of this subparagraph by a third party who has complied with the requirements of subdivisions (i) and (ii) of this subparagraph, must deposit the tax imposed by section 3111 in accordance with §31.6302(c)-1(a). For purposes of §31.6302(c)-1(a)(1)(iii)(b), with respect to the employer for whom services are normally rendered the term "taxes" shall not include any tax imposed on employers by section 3111 that is required to be paid by a third party under subparagraph (1) of this paragraph until the employer receives notification from the third party under subdivision (iii) of this subparagraph (2).

(3) A third party making a payment on account of sickness or accident disability to an employee as agent for the employer or making such a payment directly to the employer shall not be treated as the employer under subparagraph (1) with respect to such payment unless the agency agreement so provides. The determining factor as to whether a third party is an agent of the employer is whether the third party bears any insurance risk. If the third party bears no insurance risk and is reimbursed on a cost plus fee basis, the third party is an agent of the employer even if the third party is responsible for making determinations of the eligibility of individual employees of the employer for payments on account of sickness or accident disability. If the third party is paid an insurance premium and not reimbursed on a cost plus fee basis, the third party is not an agent of the employer, but the third party is treated as the employer as provided in subparagraph (1) of this paragraph (e).

(4) In order to avoid overpayment of taxes which would result from paying taxes—

(i) On remuneration which exceeds the annual contribution and benefit base (as described in section 3121(a)(1)),

(ii) With respect to a period of time which exceeds the 6-calendar-month period described in section 3121(a)(4), or

(iii) On a payment or a portion thereof which is attributable to a contribution by the employee,

the third party may request information from the employer as the total wages earned by the employee for the calendar year in which the third party is making payments, as to the last date on which the employee worked for the employer during such year, and as to the amount of any contribution by the employee. Except if the third party has reason not to believe any information supplied by the employer as the result of a request made pursuant to the preceding sentence, the third party may rely on such information in complying with the requirements of subparagraphs (1) and (2) of this paragraph (e). The third party may not rely on representations of the employee as to the information which may be requested of the employer in complying with the requirements of subparagraphs (1) and (2) of this paragraph (e).

(5) The application of the provisions of this paragraph may be illustrated by the following examples:

Example (1). Pursuant to an agreement with Company U, Insurance Company V makes payments on account of sickness or accident disability to U's employees. Such payments are not made under a workmen's compensation law. U reimburses V for all such payments and pays V a fee for its expenses of administering the payments. V is not treated as the employer with respect to such payments.

Example (2). Pursuant to an agreement with Company W, Insurance Company X indemnifies W for the amount of any payments which W must make to an employee on account of sickness or accident disability. Such payments are not made under a workmen's compensation law. X makes its indemnity payments directly to W. W makes the payments to its employees. X is not treated as the employer with respect to such payments.

Example (3). Pursuant to an agreement with company Y (which is not an agency agreement described in subparagraph (3) of this §32.1(e)). Insurance Company Z makes payments on account of sickness or accident disability to Y's employees. Such payments are not made under a workmen's compensation law. Z does not notify Y of the amount of such payments. Z is treated as the employer with respect to such payments.

(f) *Penalties and interest on payments made from January 1, 1982, to June 30, 1982.*—[Note: An *IRS Release* of 7-2-82 extended the grace period to September 30, 1982—CCH.] No penalty under section 6656(a) or interest under section 6601 will be assessed for the failure to make timely payments of the tax imposed by section 3101 or section 3111 on payments made on account of sickness or accident disability, which payments of tax are made after December 31, 1981, and before July 1, 1982, to the extent that the failure is due to reasonable cause and not willful neglect.

Reg. §32.1(e)(2)(ii)

(g) *Special rules.*—(1) For purposes of subdivision (iii) of paragraph (e)(2), the last employer for whom the employee worked prior to becoming sick or disabled or for whom the employee was working at the time he became sick or disabled shall be deemed to be the employer for whom services are normally rendered, provided that such employer made contributions on behalf of such employee to the plan or system under which the employee is being paid.

(2) The application of the provisions of subparagraph (1) of this paragraph (g) may be illustrated by the following examples:

Example (1). B is employed by Company M. B becomes sick and is absent from work for 3 months. While B is absent from work, he receives sick pay from Insurance Company N pursuant to a plan established by M and to which M has made contributions on behalf of B. M is the employer for whom services are normally rendered by B.

Example (2). C is employed by Company O and is also employed on a part-time basis by Company Q. C becomes sick while at work at Q's place of business. C is absent from work for 3 months. While C is absent from work, he receives sick pay from Insurance Company P pursuant to a plan established by O and to which O has made contributions on behalf of C. O is the employer for whom services are normally rendered by C.

Example (3). D is a member of a labor union whose members receive health and welfare benefit payments from a trust fund which is supported by the contributions of the various employers who employ the labor union's members. D has been employed by Company R for 4 days when he becomes sick and is absent from work for 3 months. While D is absent from work he receives sick pay from his union's trust fund to which R has made contributions on D's half. R is the employer for whom services are normally rendered by D.

(3) For purposes of paragraph (e) of this section, in the case of payments on account of sickness or accident disability made to employees by a third party insurer pursuant to a contract of insurance with a multiemployer plan which is obligated to make payments on account of sickness or accident disability to such employees pursuant to a collectively bargained agreement, if the third party insurer making the payments complies with the requirements of subdivisions (i) and (ii) of subparagraph (2) of paragraph (e) and notifies the plan of the amount of wages paid on which tax was withheld and deposited within the time required for notification of the employer under subparagraph (2) of paragraph (e), then the plan (and not the third party insurer) shall be required to pay the tax imposed by section 3111 and to comply with the requirements of section 6051 and §§31.6051-1 and 31.6051-2 with respect to such payments unless, within 6 business days of the receipt of such notification, the plan notifies the employer for whom services are normally rendered of the amount of the wages on which tax was withheld and deposited. If the plan provides such notice to the employer, the employer (and not the plan) shall be required to pay the tax imposed by section 3111 and to comply with the requirements of section 6051 and §§31.6051-1 and 31.6051-2 with respect to the wages. [Reg. §32.1.]

☐ [*T.D.* 7823, 7-6-82. *Amended by T.D.* 7867, 1-7-83 *and T.D.* 9233, 12-14-2005.]

[Reg. §32.2]

§32.2. Railroad retirement taxes with respect to payments on account of sickness or accident disability.—[Not reproduced—CCH.]

⋙➔ *Caution: Reg. §31.3121(a)(3)-1 does not reflect changes made by P.L. 98-21.*

[Reg. §31.3121(a)(3)-1]

§31.3121(a)(3)-1. Retirement payments.—The term "wages" does not include any payment made by an employer to an employee (including any amount paid by an employer for insurance or annuities, or into a fund, to provide for any such payment) on account of the employee's retirement. Thus, payments made to an employee on account of his retirement are excluded from wages under this exception even though not made under a plan or system. [Reg. §31.3121(a)(3)-1.]

☐ [*T.D.* 6190, 7-14-56. *Republished in T.D.* 6516, 12-20-60.]

[Reg. §31.3121(a)(4)-1]

§31.3121(a)(4)-1. Payments on account of sickness or accident disability, or medical or hospitalization expenses.—The term "wages" does not include any payment made by an employer to, or on behalf of, an employee on account of the employee's sickness or accident disability or the medical or hospitalization expenses in connection with the employee's sickness or accident disability, if such payment is made after the expiration of six calendar months following the last calendar month in which such employee worked for such employer. Such payments are excluded from wages under this exception even though not made under a plan or system. If the employee does not actually perform services for the employer during the requisite period, the existence of the employer-employee relationship during that period is immaterial. [Reg. §31.3121(a)(4)-1.]

☐ [*T.D.* 6190, 7-14-56. *Republished in T.D.* 6516, 12-20-60.]

»»→ *Caution: Reg. §31.3121(a)(5)-1 has not been amended to reflect the change made by P.L. 96-222 and P.L. 96-499.*

[Reg. §31.3121(a)(5)-1]

§31.3121(a)(5)-1. Payments from or to certain tax-exempt trusts, or under or to certain annuity plans or bond purchase plans.—(a) *Payments from or to certain tax-exempt trusts.*—The term "wages" does not include any payment made—

(1) By an employer, on behalf of an employee or his beneficiary, into a trust, or

(2) To, or on behalf of; an employee or his beneficiary from a trust, if at the time of such payment the trust is exempt from tax under section 501(a) as an organization described in section 401(a). A payment made to an employee of such a trust for services rendered as an employee of the trust and not as a beneficiary thereof is not within this exclusion from wages.

(b) *Payments under or to certain annuity plans.*—(1) The term "wages" does not include any payment made after December 31, 1962—

(i) By an employer, on behalf of an employee or his beneficiary, into an annuity plan, or

(ii) To, or on behalf of, an employee or his beneficiary under an annuity plan, if at the time of such payment the annuity plan is a plan described in section 403(a).

(2) The term "wages" does not include any payment made before January 1, 1963—

(i) By an employer, on behalf of an employee or his beneficiary, into an annuity plan, or

(ii) To, or on behalf of, an employee or his beneficiary under an annuity plan, if at the time of such payment the annuity plan meets the requirements of section 401(a)(3), (4), (5) and (6).

(c) *Payments under or to certain bond purchase plans.*—The term "wages" does not include any payment made after December 31, 1962—

(1) By an employer, on behalf of an employee or his beneficiary, into a bond purchase plan, or

(2) To, or on behalf of, an employee or his beneficiary under a bond purchase plan, if at the time of such payment the plan is a qualified bond purchase plan described in section 405(a). [Reg. §31.3121(a)(5)-1.]

☐ [*T.D. 6190, 7-14-56. Republished in T.D. 6516, 12-20-60. Amended by T.D. 6876, 2-10-66.*]

[Reg. §31.3121(a)(5)-2]

§31.3121(a)(5)-2. Payments under or to an annuity contract described in section 403(b)..—(a) *Salary reduction agreement defined.*—For purposes of section 3121(a)(5)(D), the term *salary reduction agreement* means a plan or arrangement (whether evidenced by a written instrument or otherwise) whereby payment will be made by an employer, on behalf of an employee or his or her beneficiary, under or to an annuity contract described in section 403(b)—

(1) If the employee elects to reduce his or her compensation pursuant to a cash or deferred election as defined at §1.401(k)-1(a)(3) of this chapter;

(2) If the employee elects to reduce his or her compensation pursuant to a one-time irrevocable election made at or before the time of initial eligibility to participate in such plan or arrangement (or pursuant to a similar arrangement involving a one-time irrevocable election); or

(3) If the employee agrees as a condition of employment (whether such condition is set by statute, contract, or otherwise) to make a contribution that reduces his or her compensation.

(b) *Effective/applicability date.*—This section is applicable on November 15, 2007. [Reg. §31.3121(a)(5)-2.]

☐ [*T.D. 9367, 11-14-2007.*]

»»→ *Caution: This regulation has not been amended to reflect the change made by P.L. 96-499.*

[Reg. §31.3121(a)(6)-1]

§31.3121(a)(6)-1. Payment by an employer of employee tax under section 3101 or employee contributions under a State law.—The term "wages" does not include any payment by an employer (without deduction from the remuneration of, or other reimbursement from, the employee) of either (a) the employee tax imposed by section 3101 or the corresponding section of prior law, or (b) any payment required from an employee under a State unemployment compensation law. [Reg. §31.3121(a)(6)-1.]

☐ [*T.D. 6190, 7-14-56. Republished in T.D. 6516, 12-20-60.*]

[Reg. §31.3121(a)(7)-1]

§31.3121(a)(7)-1. Payments for services not in the course of employer's trade or business or for domestic service.—(a) *Meaning of terms.*—

(1) *Services not in the course of employer's trade or business.*—The term "services not in the course of the employer's trade or business" includes services that do not promote or advance the trade or business of the employer. Such term does not include services performed for a corporation. As used in this section, the term does not include service not in the course of the employer's trade or business performed on a farm operated for profit or domestic service in a private home of the employer. See paragraph (f) of §31.3121(g)-1 for provisions relating to services not in the course of the employer's trade or business performed on a farm operated for profit.

(2) *Domestic service in a private home of the employer.*—Services of a household nature performed by an employee in or about a private home of the person by whom he is employed constitute domestic service in a private home of the employer. A private home is a fixed place of

abode of an individual or family. A separate and distinct dwelling unit maintained by an individual in an apartment house, hotel, or other similar establishment may constitute a private home. If a dwelling house is used primarily as a boarding or lodging house for the purpose of supplying board or lodging to the public as a business enterprise, it is not a private home. In general, services of a household nature in or about a private home include services performed by cooks, waiters, butlers, housekeepers, governesses, maids, valets, baby sitters, janitors, laundresses, furnacemen, caretakers, handymen, gardeners, footmen, grooms, and chauffeurs of automobiles for family use. The term "domestic service in a private home of the employer" does not include the services enumerated above unless such services are performed in or about a private home of the employer. Services not of a household nature, such as services performed as a private secretary, tutor, or librarian, even though performed in the employer's home, are not included within the term "domestic service in a private home of the employer." As used in this section, the term does not include domestic service in a private home of the employer performed on a farm operated for profit or service not in the course of the employer's trade or business. See paragraph (f) of §31.3121(g)-1 for provisions relating to domestic service in a private home of the employer performed on a farm operated for profit.

(b) *Payments other than in cash.*—The term "wages" does not include remuneration paid in any medium other than cash (1) for service not in the course of the employer's trade or business, or (2) for domestic service in a private home of the employer. Cash remuneration includes checks and other monetary media of exchange. Remuneration paid in any medium other than cash, such as lodging, food, clothing, car tokens, transportation passes or tickets, or other goods or commodities, for service not in the course of the employer's trade or business or for domestic service in a private home of the employer does not constitute wages.

(c) *Cash payments.*—(1) The term wages does not include cash remuneration paid by an employer in any calendar year to an employee for—

(i) Domestic service in a private home of the employer, unless the cash remuneration paid in such year by the employer to the employee for such service equals or exceeds the applicable dollar threshold (as defined in section 3121(x)) for such year; or

(ii) Service not in the course of the employer's trade or business, unless the cash remuneration paid in such year by the employer to the employee for such service equals or exceeds $100.

(2) The tests relating to cash remuneration are based on the remuneration paid in a calendar year rather than on the remuneration earned during a calendar year. The following example illustrates this provision:

Example. On March 31, 2004, employer X pays employee A cash remuneration of $100 for service not in the course of X's trade or business. Such remuneration constitutes wages subject to the taxes even though $10 thereof represents payment for such service performed by A for X in December 2003.

(3) In determining whether wages have been paid either for domestic service in a private home of the employer or for service not in the course of the employer's trade or business, only cash remuneration for such service shall be taken into account. Cash remuneration includes checks and other monetary media of exchange. Remuneration paid in any other medium, such as lodging, food, clothing, car tokens, transportation passes or tickets, or other goods or commodities, is disregarded in determining whether the cash-remuneration test is met. If an employee receives cash remuneration from an employer in a calendar year for both types of services the pertinent cash-remuneration test is to be applied separately to each type of service. If an employee receives cash remuneration from more than one employer in a calendar year for domestic service in a private home of the employer or for service not in the course of the employer's trade or business, the pertinent cash-remuneration test is to be applied separately to the remuneration received from each employer.

(d) *Cross references.*—(1) For provisions relating to deduction of employee tax or amounts equivalent to the tax from cash payments for the services described in this section, see §31.3102-1;

(2) For provisions relating to time of payment of wages for such services, see §31.3121(a)-2;

(3) For provisions relating to computations to the nearest dollar of any payment of cash remuneration for domestic service in a private home of the employer, see §31.3121(i)-1.

(e) *Effective dates.*—(1) The provisions of this section apply to any cash payment for service not in the course of the employer's trade or business made on or after January 1, 1978 and for domestic service in a private home of the employer made on or after January 1, 1994.

(2) For rules applicable to any cash payment made prior to the dates set forth in paragraph (e)(1), see §31.3121(a)(7)-1 in effect at such time (see 26 CFR part 31 contained in the edition of 26 CFR Parts 30 to 39, revised as of April 1, 2006). [Reg. §31.3121(a)(7)-1.]

☐ [*T.D.* 6190, 7-14-56. *Republished in T.D.* 6516, 12-20-60. *Amended by T.D.* 9266, 6-16-2006.]

[Reg. §31.3121(a)(8)-1]

§31.3121(a)(8)-1. Payments for agricultural labor.—(a) *Scope of this section.*—For purposes of the regulations in this section, the term "agricultural labor" means only such agricultural labor (see §31.3121(g)-1) as constitutes employment or is deemed to constitute employment by reason of the rules relating to included and excluded services contained in section 3121(c) (see §31.3121(c)-1) or the corresponding section of prior law.

(b) *Payments other than in cash.*—The term "wages" does not include remuneration paid in any medium other than cash for agricultural labor. For meaning of the term "cash remuneration", see paragraph (f) of the regulations in this section.

(c) *Cash payments.*—(1) The term wages does not include cash remuneration paid by an employer in any calendar year to an employee for agricultural labor unless—

(i) The cash remuneration paid in such year by the employer to the employee for such labor is $150 or more; or

(ii) The employer's expenditures for agricultural labor in such year equal or exceed $2,500, except that this paragraph (c)(1)(ii) shall not apply in determining whether remuneration paid to an employee constitutes wages for agricultural labor if such employee—

(A) Is employed as a hand-harvest laborer and is paid on a piece rate basis in an operation which has been, and is customarily and generally recognized as having been, paid on a piece rate basis in the region of employment;

(B) Commutes daily from his permanent residence to the farm on which he is so employed; and

(C) Has been employed in agriculture less than 13 weeks during the preceding calendar year.

(2) The application of the provisions of paragraph (c)(1) of this section may be illustrated by the following example:

Example. Employer X pays A $140 in cash for agricultural labor in calendar year 2004. X makes no other payments to A during the year and makes no other payment for agricultural labor to any other employee. Employee A is not employed as a hand-harvest laborer. Neither the $150-cash-remuneration test nor the $2,500-employer's-expenditures-for-agricultural-labor test is met. Accordingly, the remuneration paid by X to A is not subject to the taxes. If in 2004 X had paid A $140 in cash for agricultural labor and had made expenditures of $2,360 or more to other employees for agricultural labor, the $140 paid by X to A would have been subject to tax because the $2,500-employer's-expenditures-for-agricultural-labor test would have been met. Or, if X had paid A $150 in cash in 2004 and made no other payments to any other employee for agricultural labor, the $150 paid by X to A would have been subject to tax because the $150-cash-remuneration test would have been met.

(d) *Application of cash-remuneration test.*—(1) If an employee receives cash remuneration from an employer both for services which constitute agricultural labor and for services which do not constitute agricultural labor, only the amount of such remuneration which is attributable to agricultural labor shall be included in determining whether cash remuneration of $150 or more has been paid in the calendar year by the employer to the employee for agricultural labor. The following example illustrates this paragraph (d)(1):

Example. Employer X operates a store and also is engaged in farming operations. Employee A, who regularly performs services for X in connection with the operation of the store, works on X's farm when additional help is required for the farm activities. In the calendar year 2004, X pays A $140 in cash for services performed in agricultural labor, and $4,000 for services performed in connection with the operation of the store. X has no additional expenditures for agricultural labor in 2004. Since the cash remuneration paid by X to A in the calendar year 2004 for agricultural labor is less than $150, the $150-cash-remuneration test is not met. The $140 paid by X to A in 2004 for agricultural labor does not constitute wages and is not subject to the taxes.

(2) The test relating to cash remuneration of $150 or more is based on the cash remuneration paid in a calendar year rather than on the remuneration earned during a calendar year. It is immaterial if such cash remuneration is paid in a calendar year other than the year in which the agricultural labor is performed. The following example illustrates this paragraph (d)(2):

Example. Employer X pays cash remuneration of $150 in the calendar year 2004 to employee A for agricultural labor. Such remuneration constitutes wages even though $10 of such amount represents payment for agricultural labor performed by A for X in December 2003.

(3) In determining whether $150 or more has been paid to an employee for agricultural labor, only cash remuneration for such labor shall be taken into account. If an employee receives cash remuneration in any one calendar year from more than one employer for agricultural labor, the cash-remuneration test is to be applied with respect to the remuneration received by the employee from each employer in such calendar year for such labor.

(e) *Application of employer's-expenditures-for-agricultural-labor test.*—(1) If an employer has expenditures in a calendar year for agricultural labor and for non-agricultural labor, only the amount of such expenditures for agricultural labor shall be included in determining whether the employer's expenditures for agricultural labor in such year equal or exceed $2,500. The following example illustrates this paragraph (e)(1):

Example. Employer X operates a store and also is engaged in farming operations. Employee A, who regularly performs services for X in connection with the operation of the store, works on X's farm when additional help is required for the farm activities. In calendar year 2004, X pays A $140 in cash for services performed in agricultural labor, and $4,000 for services performed in connection with the operation of the store. X has no additional expenditures for agricultural labor in 2004. Since X's expenditures for agricultural labor in 2004 are less than $2,500, the employer's-expenditures-for-agricultural-labor test is not met. The $140 paid by X to A in 2004 for agricultural labor does not constitute wages and is not subject to the taxes.

(2) The test relating to an employer's expenditures of $2,500 or more for agricultural labor is based on the expenditures paid by the employer in a calendar year rather than on the expenses incurred by the employer during a calendar year. It is immaterial if the expenditures are paid in a calendar year other than the year in which the agricultural labor is performed. The following example illustrates this paragraph (e)(2):

Example. Employer X employs A to construct fences on a farm owned by X. The work constitutes agricultural labor and is performed over the course of November and December 2003. A is not employed by X at any other time, however X does have other employees to whom X pays remuneration of $2,000 for agricultural labor in 2003. X pays A $140 in cash in November 2003 and $140 in cash in January 2004, in full payment for the work. The $140 payment to A made in November is not wages for calendar year 2003 because the $150-cash-remuneration test is not met and X's total expenditures for agricultural labor for such year are not equal to or in excess of $2,500. The $140 payment to A made in January is not wages for 2004 because the $150 cash-remuneration test is not met. However, if X pays additional remuneration to employees for agricultural labor in 2004 that equals or exceeds $2,360, the employer's-expenditures-for-agricultural-labor test will be met and the $140 paid by X to A in 2004 will be considered wages. It is immaterial that the work was performed in 2003.

(f) *Meaning of "cash remuneration."*—Cash remuneration includes checks and other monetary media of exchange. Cash remuneration does not include payments made in any other medium, such as lodging, food, clothing, car tokens, transportation passes or tickets, farm products, or other goods or commodities.

(g) *Cross references.*—(1) For provisions relating to deduction of employee tax or amounts equivalent to the tax from cash payments for agricultural labor, see § 31.3102-1.

(2) For provisions relating to the time of payment of wages for agricultural labor, see § 31.3121(a)-2.

(3) For provisions relating to records to be kept with respect to agricultural labor, see paragraph (b) of § 31.6001-2.

(h) *Effective dates.*—The provisions of this section apply to any payment for agricultural labor made on or after January 1, 1988. For rules applicable to any payment for agricultural labor made prior to January 1, 1988, see § 31.3121(a)(8)-1 in effect at such time (see 26 CFR part 31 contained in the edition of 26 CFR Parts 30 to 39, revised as of April 1, 2006). [Reg. § 31.3121(a)(8)-1.]

☐ [T.D. 6190, 7-14-56. *Republished in T.D.* 6516, 12-20-60. *Amended by T.D.* 6744, 7-2-64 and T.D. 9266, 6-16-2006.]

⟫⟫→ *Caution: This regulation has not been amended to reflect P.L. 98-21.*

[Reg. § 31.3121(a)(9)-1]

§ 31.3121(a)(9)-1. Payments to employees for nonwork periods.—(a) The term "wages" does not include any payment (other than vacation or sick pay) made by an employer to an employee for a period throughout which the employment relationship exists between the employer and the employee, but in which the employee does not work (other than being subject to call for the performance of work) for the employer, if such payment is made after the calendar month in which—

(1) The employee attains age 65, if the employee is a man to whom the payment is made before January 1975, or if the employee is a woman to whom the payment is made before November 1956, or

(2) The employee attains age 62, if the employee is a man to whom the payment is made after December 1974, or if [the employee is a woman to whom the] payment is made after October 1956.

(b) Vacation or sick pay is not within this exclusion from wages. If the employee does any work for the employer in the period for which the payment is made, no remuneration paid by such employer to such employee with respect to such period is within this exclusion from wages.

Example. Mrs. A, an employee of X, attained the age of 62 on September 15, 1956, and discontinued the performance of regular work for X on September 30, 1956. Their employment relationship continued for several years until Mrs. A's death, and X paid Mrs. A $50 per month as consideration for Mrs. A's agreement to work when asked by X. The payment for each month was made on the first day of each succeeding month. After September 30, 1956, the only work performed by Mrs. A for X was performed on one day in October 1956. The payment made by X to Mrs. A on November 1 (for October 1956) is not excluded from wages under this exception, but the payments made thereafter are excluded from wages. The payment on November 1 was not excluded because Mrs. A worked for X on one day in October 1956. (Inasmuch as Mrs. A had attained age 62 in September 1956, the November 1 payment would have been excluded if Mrs. A had not performed any work for X in October 1956.) [Reg. § 31.3121(a)(9)-1.]

☐ [T.D. 6190, 7-14-56. *Republished in T.D.* 6516, 12-20-60. *Amended by T.D.* 6744, 7-2-64, *and T.D.* 7373, 7-24-75.]

[Reg. § 31.3121(a)(10)-1]

§ 31.3121(a)(10)-1. Payments to certain home workers.—(a) The term wages does not include remuneration paid by an employer in any calendar year to an employee for service performed as a home worker who is an employee by reason of the provisions of section 3121(d)(3)(C) (see

§ 31.3121(d)-1(d)), unless the cash remuneration paid in such calendar year by the employer to the employee for such services is $100 or more. The test relating to cash remuneration of $100 or more is based on remuneration paid in a calendar year rather than on remuneration earned during a calendar year. If cash remuneration of $100 or more is paid in a particular calendar year, it is immaterial whether such remuneration is in payment for services performed during the year of payment or during any other year.

(b) The application of paragraph (a) of this section may be illustrated by the following example:

Example. A, a home worker, performs services for X, a manufacturer, in 2003 and 2004. In the performance of the home work A is an employee by reason of section 3121(d)(3)(C). In March 2004, A returns to X articles made by A at home from materials received by A from X in 2003. X pays A cash remuneration of $100 for such work when the finished articles are delivered. The $100 includes $10 which represents remuneration for home work performed by A in 2003. The entire $100 is subject to the taxes. Any additional cash remuneration paid by X to A in 2004 for such services is also subject to the taxes.

(c) In the event an employee receives remuneration in any one calendar year from more than one employer for services performed as a home worker of the character described in paragraph (a) of this section, the regulations in this section are to be applied with respect to the remuneration received by the employee from each employer in such calendar year for such services. This exclusion from wages has no application to remuneration paid for services performed as a home worker who is an employee under section 3121(d)(2) (see § 31.3121(d)-1(c)) relating to common law employees.

(d) Cash remuneration includes checks and other monetary media of exchange. Remuneration paid in any other medium, such as clothing, car tokens, transportation passes or tickets, or other goods or commodities, is disregarded in determining whether the $100 cash-remuneration test is met. If the cash remuneration paid in any calendar year by an employer to an employee for services performed as a home worker of the character described in paragraph (a) of this section is $100 or more, then no remuneration, whether in cash or in any medium other than cash, paid by the employer to the employee in such calendar year for such services is excluded from wages under this exception.

(e)(1) For provisions relating to deductions of employee tax or amounts equivalent to the tax from cash payments for services performed as a home worker within the meaning of section 3121(d)(3)(C), see § 31.3102-1.

(2) For provisions relating to the time of payment of wages for services performed as a home worker within the meaning of section 3121(d)(3)(C), see § 31.3121(a)-2.

(3) For provisions relating to records to be kept with respect to payment of wages for services performed as a home worker within the meaning of section 3121(d)(3)(C), see § 31.6001-2.

(f) The provisions of this section apply to any payment for services performed as a home worker within the meaning of section 3121(d)(3)(C) made on or after January 1, 1978. For rules applicable to any payment for services performed as a home worker within the meaning of section 3121(d)(3)(C) made prior to January 1, 1978, see § 31.3121(a)(10)-1 in effect at such time (see 26 CFR part 31 contained in the edition of 26 CFR Parts 30 to 39, revised as of April 1, 2006). [Reg. § 31.3121(a)(10)-1.]

□ [*T.D.* 6190, 7-14-56. *Republished in T.D.* 6516, 12-20-60. *Amended by T.D.* 9266, 6-16-2006.]

[Reg. § 31.3121(a)(11)-1]

§ 31.3121(a)(11)-1. Moving   expenses.— (a) The term "wages" does not include remuneration paid on or after November 1, 1964, to or on behalf of an employee, either as an advance or a reimbursement, specifically for moving expenses incurred or expected to be incurred, if (and to the extent that) at the time of payment it is reasonable to believe that a corresponding deduction is or will be allowable to the employee under section 217. The reasonable belief contemplated by the statute may be based upon any evidence reasonably sufficient to induce such belief, even though such evidence may be insufficient upon closer examination by the district director or the courts finally to establish that a deduction is allowable under section 217. The reasonable belief shall be based upon the application of section 217 and the regulations thereunder in Part 1 of this chapter (Income Tax Regulations). When used in this section, the term "moving expenses" has the same meaning as when used in section 217 and the regulations thereunder.

(b) Except as otherwise provided in paragraph (a) of this section, or in a numbered paragraph of section 3121(a), amounts paid to or on behalf of an employee for moving expenses are wages for purposes of section 3121(a). [Reg. § 31.3121(a)(11)-1.]

□ [*T.D.* 7375, 7-12-75.]

[Reg. § 31.3121(a)(12)-1]

§ 31.3121(a)(12)-1. Tips.—The term "wages" does not include remuneration received by an employee after December 1965 in the form of tips if—

(a) The tips are paid in any medium other than cash, or

(b) The cash tips received by an employee in any calendar month in the course of his employment by an employer are less than $20.

If the cash tips received by an employee in a calendar month after December 1965 in the course of his employment by an employer amount to $20 or more, none of the cash tips received by the employee in such calendar month are excluded from the term "wages" under this section. The cash tips to which this section applies include checks and other monetary media of exchange. Tips received by an employee in any medium other than cash, such as passes, tickets, or other goods or commodities do not constitute wages. If an employee in any calendar month performs services for two or more employers and receives tips in the course of his employment by each employer, the $20 test is to be applied separately with respect to the cash tips received by the employee in respect of his services for each employer and not to the total cash tips received by the employee during the month. As to the time tips are deemed paid, see § 31.3121(q)-1. For provisions relating to the treatment of tips received by an employee prior to 1966, see paragraph (j)(3) of § 31.3121(a)-1. [Reg. § 31.3121(a)(12)-1.]

☐ [T.D. 7001, 1-23-69.]

>>>→ *Caution: This regulation has not been amended to reflect the changes made by the Social Security Amendments of 1983 (P.L. 98-21).*

[Reg. § 31.3121(a)(13)-1]

§ 31.3121(a)(13)-1. Payments under certain employers' plans after retirement, disability, or death.—(a) *In general.*—The term "wages" does not include the amount of any payment or series of payments made after January 2, 1968, by an employer to, or on behalf of, an employee or any of his dependents under a plan established by the employer which makes provisions for his employees generally (or for his employees generally and their dependents) or for a class or classes of his employees (or for a class or classes of his employees and their dependents), which is paid or commences to be paid upon or within a reasonable time after the termination of an employee's employment relationship because of the employee's—

(1) Death,

(2) Retirement for disability, or

(3) Retirement after attaining an age specified in the plan established by the employer or in a pension plan of the employer at the age at which a person in the employee's circumstances is eligible for retirement.

A payment or series of payments made under the circumstances described in the preceding sentence is excluded from "wages" even if made pursuant to an incentive compensation plan which also provides for the making of other types of payments. However, any payment or series of payments which would have been paid if the employee's relationship had not been terminated is not excluded from "wages" under this section and section 3121(a)(13). For example, lump-sum payments for unused vacation time or a final pay-check received after retirement are payments which the employee would have received whether or not he retired and therefore are not excluded from "wages" under this section. Further, if any payment is made upon or after termination of employment for any reason other than those set out in subparagraphs (1), (2), and (3) of this paragraph such payment is not excludable from "wages" by this section. For example, if a pension plan provides for retirement upon disability, completion of 30 years of service, or attainment of age 65, and if an employee who is not disabled retires at age 61 after 30 years of service, none of the retirement payments made to the employee under the pension plan (including any made after he is 65) is excludable from "wages" under this section. However, if the pension plan had conditioned retirement after 30 years of service upon attainment of age 60, all of the retirement payments would have been excludable.

(b) *Plan.*—The plan or system established by an employer need not provide for payments because of termination of employment for all the reasons set out in subparagraphs (1), (2), and (3) of paragraph (a), but such plan or system may provide for payments because of termination for any one or more of such reasons. Payments because of termination of employment for any one or more of such reasons under a plan or system established by an employer solely for the dependents of his employees are not within this exclusion from wages.

(c) *Dependents.*—Dependents of an employee include the employee's husband or wife, children, and any other members of the employee's immediate family.

(d) *Benefit payment.*—It is immaterial for purposes of this exclusion whether the amount or possibility of benefit payments is paid on account of services rendered or taken into consideration in fixing the amount of an employee's remuneration or whether such payments are required, expressly or impliedly, by the contract of service.

(e) *Example.*—The application of this section may be illustrated by the following example:

Example. A, an employee, receives a salary of $1,500 a month, payable on the 5th day of the month following the month for which the salary is earned. A's employer has established an incentive compensation plan for a class of his employees, including A, providing for the payment of deferred compensation on termination of employment, including termination upon an employee's death, retirement at age 65 (the retirement age specified in the plan), or retirement for disability. On March 1, 1973, A attains the age of 65 and retires. On March 5, 1973, A receives $5,500 from his employer of which $1,500 represents A's salary for services he performed in February 1973, and $4,000 represents incentive compensation paid under the employer's plan. The amount of $4,000 is excluded from "wages" under this section. The amount of $1,500 is not excluded from "wages" under this section. [Reg. § 31.3121(a)(13)-1.]

☐ [T.D. 7374, 7-24-75.]

[Reg. § 31.3121(a)(14)-1]

§ 31.3121(a)(14)-1. Payments by employer to survivor or estate of former employee.—The term "wages" does not include any payment by an employer to a survivor or the estate of a former employee made after 1972 and after the calendar year in which such employee died. [Reg. § 31.3121(a)(14)-1.]

☐ [T.D. 7373, 7-24-75.]

[Reg. § 31.3121(a)(15)-1]

§ 31.3121(a)(15)-1. Payments by employer to disabled former employee.—The term "wages" does not include any payment made after 1972 by an employer to an employee, if at the time such payment is made such employee is entitled to disability insurance benefits under section 223(a) of the Social Security Act and such entitlement commenced prior to the calendar year in which such payment is made, and if such employee did not perform any service for such employer during the period for which such payment is made. [Reg. § 31.3121(a)(15)-1.]

☐ [T.D. 7373, 7-24-75.]

[Reg. § 31.3121(a)(18)-1]

§ 31.3121(a)(18)-1. Payments or benefits under a qualified educational assistance program.—The term "wages" does not include any payment made, or benefit furnished, to or for the benefit of an employee in a taxable year beginning after December 31, 1978, if at the time of such payment or furnishing it is reasonable to believe that the employee will be able to exclude such payment or benefit from income under section 127. [Reg. § 31.3121(a)(18)-1.]

☐ T.D. 7898, 7-6-83.

[Reg. § 31.3121(b)-1]

§ 31.3121(b)-1. Employment; services to which the regulations in this subpart apply.—(a) The provisions of the regulations in this subpart relating to the term "employment" apply with respect to services performed after 1954. Certain provisions also apply with respect to services performed before 1955 for which the remuneration is paid after 1954 (see paragraph (b) of § 31.3121(b)-2). For provisions relating generally to services performed before 1955, see paragraph (a) of § 31.3121(b)-2. For provisions relating to the circumstances under which services which do not constitute employment are nevertheless deemed to be employment, and relating to the circumstances under which services which constitute employment are nevertheless deemed not to be employment, see § 31.3121(c)-1. For provisions relating to who are employees and who are employers, see § § 31.3121(d)-1 and 31.3121(d)-2, respectively.

(b) The taxes apply with respect to remuneration paid after 1954 for services performed before 1955, as well as for services performed after 1954, to the extent that the remuneration and services constitute wages and employment. See § § 31.3121(a)-1 to 31.3121(a)(13)-1 relating to wages. [Reg. § 31.3121(b)-1.]

☐ T.D. 6190, 7-14-56. Republished in T.D. 6516, 12-20-60. Amended by T.D. 6983, 12-4-68.

[Reg. § 31.3121(b)-2]

§ 31.3121(b)-2. Employment; services performed before 1955.—(a) General rule.—(1) Subject to the provisions of paragraph (b) of this section:

(i) Services performed after 1936 and before 1955 which were employment under the applicable law in effect before 1955 constitute employment under section 3121(b).

(ii) Services performed after 1936 and before 1955 which were not employment under the applicable law in effect before 1955 do not constitute employment under section 3121(b).

(2) Except as provided in paragraph (b) of this section, determination of whether services performed before 1955 constitute employment shall be made in accordance with the applicable provisions of law in effect before 1955 and of the regulations thereunder. The regulations applicable in determining whether services performed after 1936 and before 1955 constitute employment are as follows:

(i) Services performed after 1936 and before 1940—26 CFR (1939) Part 401 (Regulations 91).

(ii) Services performed after 1939 and before 1951—26 CFR (1939) Part 402 (Regulations 106).

(iii) Services performed after 1950 and before 1955—26 CFR (1939) Part 408 (Regulations 128).

(b) Certain services performed before 1955 the remuneration for which is paid after 1954.—(1) Services of the following character performed before 1955, for which remuneration is paid after 1954, constitute employment under section 3121(b):

(i) Agricultural labor, as defined in section 3121(g) (see § 31.3121(g)-1), other than services of the character described in section 3121(b)(1) (relating to services performed in connection with the production or harvesting of certain oleoresinous products and services performed by certain foreign agricultural workers), which, at the time performed, constituted employment under section 1426(b) of the 1939 Code, or would have constituted employment except for the provisions of section 1426(b)(1) of such Code, as in effect at the time the services were performed.

(ii) Services not in the course of the employer's trade or business (see paragraph (a)(1) of § 31.3121(a)(7)-1 which, at the time performed, constituted employment under section 1426(b) of the 1939 Code, or would have constituted employment except for the provisions of section 1426(b)(3) of such Code, as in effect at the time the services were performed.

(2) Services of the character described in paragraphs (a) and (b) of § 31.3121(b)(1)-1, which were performed by certain foreign agricultural workers before 1955 and the remuneration for which is paid after 1954, do not constitute employment under section 3121(b), irrespective of whether they constituted employment under

section 1426(b) of the 1939 Code, as in effect at the time the services were performed.

(3) This paragraph has no application to services performed before 1955 and the remuneration for which was paid before 1955. [Reg. § 31.3121(b)-2.]

☐ *T.D. 6190, 7-14-56. Republished in T.D. 6516, 12-20-60. Amended by T.D. 6744, 7-2-64.*

[Reg. § 31.3121(b)-3]

§ 31.3121(b)-3. Employment; services performed after 1954.—(a) *In general.*—Whether services performed after 1954 constitute employment is determined in accordance with the provisions of section 3121(b).

(b) *Services performed within the United States.*—Services performed after 1954 within the United States (see § 31.3121(e)-1) by an employee for his employer, unless specifically excepted by section 3121(b), constitute employment. With respect to services performed within the United States, the place where the contract of service is entered into is immaterial. The citizenship or residence of the employee or of the employer also is immaterial except to the extent provided in any specific exception from employment. Thus, the employee and the employer may be citizens and residents of a foreign country and the contract of service may be entered into in a foreign country, and yet, if the employee under such contract performs services within the United States, there may be to that extent employment.

(c) *Services performed outside the United States.*—(1) *In general.*—Except as provided in subparagraphs (2) and (3) of this paragraph, services performed outside the United States (see § 31.3121(e)-1) do not constitute employment.

(2) *On or in connection with an American vessel or American aircraft.*—(i) Services performed after 1954 by an employee for an employer "on or in connection with" an American vessel or American aircraft outside the United States (see § 31.3121(e)-1) constitute employment if:

    (*a*) The employee is also employed "on and in connection with" such vessel or aircraft when outside the United States; and

    (*b*) The services are performed under a contract of service, between the employee and the employer, which is entered into within the United States, or during the performance of the contract under which the services are performed and while the employee is employed on the vessel or aircraft it touches at a port within the United States; and

    (*c*) The services are not excepted under section 3121(b).

(ii) An employee performs services on and in connection with the vessel or aircraft if he performs services on such vessel or aircraft which are also in connection with the vessel or aircraft. Services performed on the vessel by employees as officers or members of the crew, or as employees of concessionaires, of the vessel, for example, are performed under such circumstances, since such services are also connected

with the vessel. Similarly, services performed *on* the aircraft by employees as officers or members of the crew of the aircraft are performed on and in connection with such aircraft. Services may be performed on the vessel or aircraft, however, which have no connection with it, as in the case of services performed by an employee while on the vessel or aircraft merely as a passenger in the general sense. For example, the services of a buyer in the employ of a department store while he is a passenger on a vessel are not in connection with the vessel.

(iii) If services are performed by an employee "on and in connection with" an American vessel or American aircraft when outside the United States and conditions listed in subdivision (i)(b) and (c) of this subparagraph are met, then the services of that employee performed on or in connection with the vessel or aircraft constitute employment. The expression "on or in connection with" refers not only to services performed on the vessel or aircraft but also to services connected with the vessel or aircraft which are not actually performed on it (for example, shore services performed as officers or members of the crew, or as employees of concessionaires, of the vessel).

(iv) Services performed by a member of the crew or other employee whose contract of service is not entered into within the United States, and during the performance of which and while the employee is employed on the vessel or aircraft it does not touch at a port within the United States, do not constitute employment under this subparagraph, notwithstanding services performed by other members of the crew or other employees on or in connection with the vessel or aircraft may constitute employment.

(v) A vessel includes every description of watercraft, or other contrivance, used as a means of transportation on water. An aircraft includes every description of craft, or other contrivance, used as a means of transportation through the air. In the case of an aircraft, the term "port" means an airport. An airport means an area on land or water used regularly by aircraft for receiving or discharging passengers or cargo. For definitions of "American vessel" and "American aircraft," see § 31.3121(f)-1.

(vi) With respect to services performed outside the United States on or in connection with an American vessel or American aircraft, the citizenship or residence of the employee is immaterial, and the citizenship or residence of the employer is material only in case it has a bearing in determining whether a vessel is an American vessel.

(3) *By a citizen of the United States as an employee for an American employer.*—Services performed after 1954 outside the United States by a citizen of the United States as an employee for an American employer constitute employment provided the services are not specifically excepted under section 3121(b). For definitions of "citizen of the United States" and "American employer", see § § 31.3121(e)-1 and 31.3121(h)-1, respectively.

(4) *By a citizen of the United States as an employee for a foreign subsidiary corporation.*—For provisions relating to the extension of the Federal old-age and survivors insurance system established by title II of the Social Security Act to certain services not constituting employment which are performed outside the United States by citizens of the United States in the employ of a foreign subsidiary of a domestic corporation, see section 3121(l) and Part 36 of this chapter (Regulations Relating to Contract Coverage of Employees of Foreign Subsidiaries). [Reg. § 31.3121(b)-3.]

☐ *T.D.* 6190, 7-14-56. *Republished in T.D.* 6516, 12-20-60. *Amended by T.D.* 6744, 7-2-64.

[Reg. § 31.3121(b)-4]

§ 31.3121(b)-4. Employment; excepted services in general.—(a) Services performed by an employee for an employer do not constitute employment for purposes of the taxes if they are specifically excepted from employment under any of the numbered paragraphs of section 3121(b). Services so excepted do not constitute employment for purposes of the taxes even though they are performed within the United States, or are performed outside the United States on or in connection with an American vessel or American aircraft, or are performed outside the United States by a citizen of the United States for an American employer. If not otherwise provided in the regulations relating to the numbered paragraphs of section 3121(b), such regulations apply to services performed after 1954.

(b) The exception attaches to the services performed by the employee and not to the employee as an individual; that is, the exception applies only to the services in an excepted class rendered by the employee.

Example. A is an individual who is employed part time by B to perform services which are specifically excepted from employment under one of the numbered paragraphs of section 3121(b). A is also employed by C part time to perform services which constitute employment. While no tax liability is incurred with respect to A's remuneration for services performed in the employ of B (the services being excepted from employment), the exception does not embrace the services performed by A in the employ of C (which constitute employment) and the taxes attach with respect to the wages (see § 31.3121(a)-1) for such services.

(c) For provisions relating to the circumstances under which services which are excepted are nevertheless deemed to be employment, and relating to the circumstances under which services which are not excepted are nevertheless deemed not to be employment, see § 31.3121(c)-1. [Reg. § 31.3121(b)-4.]

☐ *T.D.* 6190, 7-14-56. *Republished in T.D.* 6516, 12-20-60. *Amended by T.D.* 6744, 7-2-64.

[Reg. § 31.3121(b)(1)-1]

§ 31.3121(b)(1)-1. Certain services performed by foreign agricultural workers, or performed before 1959 in connection with oleoresinous products.—(a) *Services of workers from Mexico.*—Services performed before 1965 by foreign agricultural workers from the Republic of Mexico under contracts entered into in accordance with title V of the Agricultural Act of 1949, as amended, are excepted from employment. Contracts entered into pursuant to the provisions of such title V may provide for the performance only of services which constitute "agricultural employment". The term "agricultural employment" includes certain services which do not constitute "agricultural labor" as that term is defined in section 3121(g) (see § 31.3121(g)-1). For purposes of title V of the Agricultural Act of 1949, as amended, the term "agricultural employment" includes services or activities included within the provisions of section 3(f) of the Fair Labor Standards Act of 1938, as amended, or section 3121(g) of the Internal Revenue Code. Under section 507 of the Agricultural Act of 1949, as amended, and as in effect before October 3, 1961, the term "agricultural employment" included also horticultural employment, cotton ginning, compressing and storing, crushing of oil seeds, and the packing, canning, freezing, drying, or other processing of perishable or seasonable agricultural products.

(b) *Services of workers from British West Indies.*—Services performed by a foreign agricultural worker lawfully admitted to the United States from the Bahamas, Jamaica, or the other British West Indies, on a temporary basis to perform agricultural labor are excepted from employment.

(c) *Services performed after 1956 by foreign workers.*—Services performed after 1956 by a foreign agricultural worker lawfully admitted to the United States from any foreign country or possession thereof, including the Republic of Mexico, on a temporary basis to perform agricultural labor are excepted from employment.

(d) *Services performed before 1959 in connection with the production or harvesting of certain oleoresinous products.*—Services performed before 1959 in connection with the production or harvesting of crude gum (oleoresin) from a living tree or the processing of such crude gum into gum spirits of turpentine and gum rosin, provided the processing is carried on by the original producer of the crude gum, are excepted from employment. However, the services to which this paragraph relates constitute agricultural labor as defined in section 3121(g) (see paragraph (d) of § 31.3121(g)-1). Thus, any cash remuneration paid for such services, to the extent that the services are deemed to constitute employment by reason of the rules relating to included and excluded services contained in section 3121(c) (see § 31.3121(c)-1), is taken into account in applying the test prescribed in section 3121(a)(8)(B) for determining whether cash remuneration paid for agricultural labor constitutes wages (see paragraph (c) of § 31.3121(a)(8)-1).

(e) *Cross-reference.*—See paragraph (b) of § 31.3121(b)-2 for provisions relating to the status of services of the character to which paragraphs (a) and (b) of this section apply which were performed before 1955 and the remuneration for which is paid after 1954. [Reg. § 31.3121(b)(1)-1.]

☐ T.D.6190, 7-14-56. *Republished in T.D.* 6516, 12-20-60. *Amended by T.D.* 6744, 7-2-64.

[Reg. § 31.3121(b)(2)-1]

§ 31.3121(b)(2)-1. Domestic service performed by students for certain college organizations.—(a) Services of a household nature performed in or about the club rooms or house of a local college club, or in or about the club rooms or house of a local chapter of a college fraternity or sorority, by a student who is enrolled and regularly attending classes at a school, college, or university are excepted from employment. For the purposes of this exemption, the statutory tests are the type of services performed by the employee, the character of the place where the services are performed, and the status of the employee as a student enrolled and regularly attending classes at a school, college, or university.

(b) In general, services of a household nature in or about the club rooms or house of a local college club or local chapter of a college fraternity or sorority include services rendered by cooks, waiters, butlers, maids, janitors, laundresses, furnacemen, handymen, gardeners, housekeepers, and housemothers.

(c) A local college club or local chapter of a college fraternity or sorority does not include an alumni club or chapter. If the club rooms or house of a local college club or local chapter of a college fraternity or sorority is used primarily for the purpose of supplying board or lodging to students or the public as a business enterprise, the services performed therein are not within the exception.

(d) An organization is a *school, college, or university* within the meaning of section 3121(b)(2) if its primary function is the presentation of formal instruction, it normally maintains a regular faculty and curriculum, and it normally has a regularly enrolled body of students in attendance at the place where its educational activities are regularly carried on. See section 170(b)(1)(A)(ii) and the regulations thereunder.

(e) Services of a household nature are not within the exception if performed in or about rooming or lodging houses, boarding houses, clubs (except local college clubs), hotels, hospitals, eleemosynary institutions, or commercial offices or establishments.

(f) For provisions relating to domestic service in a private home of the employer, see § 31.3121(a)(7)-1. [Reg. § 31.3121(b)(2)-1.]

☐ *T.D.* 6190, 7-14-56. *Republished in T.D.* 6516, 12-20-60. *Amended by T.D.* 9167, 12-20-2004.

⟫⟫→ *Caution: This regulation has not been amended to reflect changes enacted by the Omnibus Budget Reconciliation Act of 1987 (P.L. 100-203).*

[Reg. § 31.3121(b)(3)-1]

§ 31.3121(b)(3)-1. Family employment.—(a) Certain services are excepted from employment because of the existence of a family relationship between the employee and the individual employing him. The exceptions are as follows:

(1) Services performed by an individual in the employ of his or her spouse;

(2)(i) Services performed before 1961 by a father or mother in the employ of his or her son or daughter;

(ii) Services not in the course of the employer's trade or business, or domestic service in a private home of the employer, performed after 1960 but prior to 1968 by a father or mother in the employ of his or her son or daughter;

(iii) Services not in the course of the employer's trade or business, or domestic service in a private home of the employer, performed after 1967 by a father or mother in the employ of his or her son or daughter unless (*a*) the employer has a child (including an adopted child or stepchild) living in his or her home who is under age 18 or who has a mental or physical condition which requires the personal care and supervision of an adult for at least 4 continuous weeks in the calendar quarter in which the services are rendered; and (*b*) the employer is during the calendar quarter in which the services are rendered:

(1) A widow or widower;

(2) A divorced person who has not remarried; or

(3) A married person who has a spouse living in the home who has a mental or physical condition which results in such spouse's being incapable of caring for such child for at least 4 continuous weeks in the calendar quarter in which the services are rendered; and

(3) Services performed by a son or daughter under the age of 21 in the employ of his or her father or mother.

(b) Under paragraph (a)(1) and (2)(i) of this section, the exception is conditioned solely upon the family relationship between the employee and the individual employing him. Under paragraph (a)(2)(ii) and (iii) of this section, in addition to the family relationship, there is a further requirement that the services performed after 1960 and before 1968 for purposes of paragraph (a)(2)(ii) and after 1967 for purposes of paragraph (a)(2)(iii) shall be services not in the course of the employer's trade or business or shall be domestic service in a private home of the employer. The terms "services not in the course of the employer's trade or business" and "domestic service in a private home of the employer" have the same meaning as when used in § 31.3121(a)(7)-1, except that it is immaterial under paragraphs (a)(2)(ii) and (iii) of this section whether or not such services are performed on a farm operated for profit. The mere fact that a mental or physical disability, whether temporary or permanent, renders a child or spouse incapable of self-support does not necessarily mean that the child requires the personal care and supervision of an adult or that the spouse is incapable of caring for a child within the meaning of paragraph (a)(2)(iii) of this section. A written statement by a doctor of the existence of the mental or physical condition of the child or spouse which states that the child requires the personal care and supervision of an adult or that the spouse is incapable of caring for a child and which sets forth the period of time during which the condition has existed and is likely to exist will usually be sufficient evidence to establish the existence and duration of the condition at the time of the statement. Under paragraph (a)(3) of this section, in addition to the family relationship, there is a further requirement that the son or daughter shall be under the age of 21, and the exception continues only during the time that the son or daughter is under the age of 21.

(c) Services performed in the employ of a partnership are within the exception described in paragraph (a) of this section only if the requisite family relationship exists between the employee and each of the partners comprising the partnership.

(d) Services performed in the employ of a corporation are not within the exception described in paragraph (a) of this section, except that services performed in the employ of an entity that is treated as a corporation under § 301.7701-2(c)(2)(iv)(B) of this chapter may qualify for the exception if the requirements of the exception are otherwise met. An entity that is treated as a corporation under § 301.7701-2(c)(2)(iv)(B) of this chapter is not treated as the employer for purposes of applying section 3121(b)(3) and this section. For purposes of applying section 3121(b)(3) and this section, the owner of an entity that is treated as a corporation under § 301.7701-2(c)(2)(iv)(B) of this chapter is treated as the employer.

(e) Paragraphs (c) and (d) of this section apply to wages paid on or after November 1, 2011. However, taxpayers may apply paragraphs (c) and (d) of this section to wages paid on or after January 1, 2009. [Reg. § 31.3121(b)(3)-1.]

☐ [T.D. 6190, 7-14-56. Republished in T.D. 6516, 12-20-60. Amended by T.D. 6744, 7-2-64; T.D. 7374, 7-24-75, T.D. 9554, 10-31-2011 and T.D. 9670, 6-25-2014.]

[Reg. § 31.3121(b)(4)-1]

§ 31.3121(b)(4)-1. Services performed on or in connection with a non-American vessel or aircraft.—(a) Services performed within the United States by an employee for an employer "on or in connection with" a vessel not an American vessel, or "on or in connection with" an aircraft not an American aircraft, are excepted from employment if—

(1) The employee is employed by such employer "on and in connection with" such vessel or aircraft when outside the United States, and

(2)(i) The employee is not a citizen of the United States, or (ii) the employer is not an American employer.

(b) An employee performs services on and in connection with the vessel or aircraft if he performs services on the vessel or aircraft when outside the United States which are also in connection with the vessel or aircraft. Services performed on the vessel outside the United States by employees as officers or members of the crew, or by employees of concessionaires, of the vessel, for example, are performed under such circumstances, since such services are also connected with the vessel. Similarly, services performed on the aircraft outside the United States by employees as officers or members of the crew of the aircraft are performed on and in connection with such aircraft. Services may be performed on the vessel or aircraft, however, which have no connection with it, as in the case of services performed by an employee while on the vessel or aircraft merely as a passenger in the general sense. For example, the services of a buyer in the employ of a department store while he is a passenger on a vessel are not in connection with the vessel.

(c) The expression "on or in connection with" refers not only to services performed on the vessel or aircraft but also to services connected with the vessel or aircraft which are not actually performed on it (for example, shore services performed as officers or members of the crew, or as employees of concessionaires, of the vessel).

(d) Services performed within the United States on or in connection with a non-American vessel or aircraft for an employer by an employee who is not a citizen of the United States are excepted from employment, irrespective of whether the employer is or is not an American employer, provided the employee also is employed by such employer on and in connection with the vessel or aircraft when outside the United States. Services performed within the United States on or in connection with a non-American vessel or aircraft by an employee for an employer who is not an American employer also are excepted from employment, irrespective of whether the employee is or is not a citizen of the United States, provided the employee also is employed by such employer on and in connection with the vessel or aircraft when outside the United States. Services performed within the United States on or in connection with a non-American vessel or aircraft for an American employer by an employee who is a citizen of the United States are not excepted from employment under section 3121(b)(4), irrespective of whether the employee is employed by such employer on and in connection with the vessel or aircraft when outside the United States. Further, section 3121(b)(4) does not except from employment services performed within the United States for an employer, whether or not an American employer, on or in connection with a non-American vessel or aircraft by an employee, whether or not a citizen of the United States, who is not also employed by such employer on and in connection with the vessel or aircraft when outside the United States.

(e) Services performed outside the United States on or in connection with a vessel not an American vessel, or on or in connection with an aircraft not an American aircraft, by a citizen of the United States as an employee for an American employer are not excepted from employment under section 3121(b)(4), irrespective of whether the employee is employed on and in connection with such vessel or aircraft when outside the United States. Services performed outside the United States on or in connection with a vessel not an American vessel or on or in connection with an aircraft not an American aircraft, either by an employee who is not a citizen of the United States or for an employer who is not an American employer, do not, in any event, constitute employment. See paragraph (c) of §31.3121(b)-3, relating to services performed outside the United States which constitute employment.

(f) See paragraph (c)(2)(v) of §31.3121(b)-3 for definitions of "vessel" and "aircraft," §31.3121(f)-1, for definitions of "American vessel" and "American aircraft," §31.3121(e)-1, for definition of "citizen of the United States," and §31.3121(h)-1, for definition of "American employer." [Reg. §31.3121(b)(4)-1.]

☐ *T.D. 6190, 7-14-56. Republished in T.D. 6516,* 12-20-60.

[Reg. §31.3121(b)(5)-1]

§31.3121(b)(5)-1. Services in employ of an instrumentality of the United States specifically exempted from the employer.—Services performed in the employ of an instrumentality of the United States are excepted from employment if such instrumentality is exempt from the employer tax imposed by section 3111 by virtue of any other provision of law which specifically refers to such section 3111 or the corresponding section of prior law (section 1410 of the Internal Revenue Code of 1939) in granting exemption from the employer tax. This exception does not operate to exclude from employment services performed in the employ of an instrumentality of the United States unless the Congress has granted to such instrumentality a specific exemption from the tax imposed by section 3111 or the corresponding section of prior law. For provisions which make general exemptions from Federal taxation ineffectual as to the employer tax imposed by section 3111, see §31.3112-1. For other exceptions from employment applicable with respect to services performed in the employ of an instrumentality of the United States, see §31.3121(b)(6)-1.

The IRS has revoked, effective July 1, 1992, previously issued but unidentified letter rulings under which an exempt organization did not have to pay the employer's portion of the FICA tax imposed by Code Sec. 3111. The IRS applied this revocation prospectively after finding that: (1) there was no misstatement or omission of material facts by the organization; (2) any differences between the facts now and the facts on which the rulings were based were not material; (3) while there has been a change in applicable law, that change did not impact upon the tax at issue here; (4) that ruling was issued in connection with an ongoing transaction; and (5) the organization reasonably relied on the rulings, and retroactive revocation would be to the taxpayer's detriment. [Reg. §31.3121(b)(5)-1.]

☐ *T.D. 6190, 7-14-56. Republished in T.D. 6516,* 12-20-60.

>>>→ *Caution: This regulation has not been amended to reflect changes enacted by the Social Security Amendments of 1983 (P.L. 98-21).*

[Reg. §31.3121(b)(6)-1]

§31.3121(b)(6)-1. Services in employ of United States or instrumentality thereof.— (a) *In general.*—This section relates to services performed in the employ of the United States Government or in the employ of an instrumentality of the United States. Particular services which are not excepted from employment under one rule set forth in this section may nevertheless be excepted under another rule set forth in this section or under §31.3121(b)(5)-1, relating to services in the employ of an instrumentality of the United States specifically exempted from the employer tax. Moreover, services performed in the employ of the United States or of any instrumentality thereof which are not excepted from employment under paragraph (5) or (6) of section 3121(b) may nevertheless be excepted under some other paragraph of such section. For provisions relating generally to the application of the taxes in the case of services performed in the employ of the United States or a wholly owned instrumentality thereof, see §31.3122. For provisions relating to the computation of remuneration for service performed by an individual as a member of a uniformed service or for service performed by an individual as a volunteer or volunteer leader within the meaning of the Peace Corps Act, see §31.3121(i)-2 and §31.3121(i)-3, respectively.

(b) *Services covered under a retirement system established by a law of the United States.*—Services performed in the employ of the United States or in the employ of any instrumentality thereof are excepted from employment under section 3121(b)(6)(A) if such services are covered under a law enacted by the Congress of the United States which specifically provides for the establishment of a retirement system for employees of the United States or of such instrumentality. Determinations as to whether services are covered by a retirement system of the requisite character are to be made as of the time such services are performed. Services of an employee who has an option to have his services covered under a retirement system are not covered under such retirement system unless and until he exercises such option. The test is whether particular services performed by an employee are covered by a retirement system of the requisite character rather than whether the position in which such services are performed is covered by such retirement system.

(c) *Services performed for an instrumentality not subject to employer tax on December 31, 1950, and covered under a retirement system established by such instrumentality.*—(1) Subject to the provisions of subparagraph (4) of this paragraph, services performed in the employ of an instrumentality of the United States are excepted from employment under section 3121(b)(6)(B) if—

(i) The particular instrumentality was not subject on December 31, 1950, to the employer tax imposed by section 1410 of the Internal Revenue Code of 1939, and

(ii) The services are covered by a retirement system established by such instrumentality.

(2) If the particular instrumentality was not in existence on December 31, 1950, but is created thereafter under a law which was in effect on December 31, 1950, services performed in the employ of such instrumentality are excepted from employment (unless otherwise provided in subparagraph (c)(4) of this paragraph) if—

(i) The instrumentality had it been in existence on December 31, 1950, would not have been subject on that date to the employer tax imposed by section 1410 of the Internal Revenue Code of 1939, and

(ii) The services are covered by a retirement system established by such instrumentality..—It is immaterial, for purposes of this exception, whether the exemption from the employer tax on December 31, 1950, resulted, or would have resulted, from a tax exemption as such in effect on December 31, 1950, or from the provisions of section 1426(b)(6) of the Internal Revenue Code of 1939 in effect on that date, relating to the exception from employment of services performed in the employ of certain instrumentalities of the United States.

(3) Determinations as to whether services performed in the employ of an instrumentality referred to in subparagraph (1) or (2) of this paragraph are covered by a retirement system established by such instrumentality are to be made as of the time such services are performed. Services of an employee who has an option to have his services covered under a retirement system established by the instrumentality are not covered under such retirement system unless and until he exercises such option. The test is whether particular services performed by an employee are covered by a retirement system established by the instrumentality rather than whether the position in which such services are performed is covered by such retirement system.

(4) The exception from employment provided in section 3121(b)(6)(B) has no application

with respect to any of the following classes of services:

(i) Services performed in the employ of a corporation which is wholly owned by the United States;

(ii) Services performed in the employ of a production credit association, a Federal Reserve Bank, or a Federal Credit Union; services performed before December 31, 1959, in the employ of a national farm loan association; services performed after December 30, 1959, in the employ of a Federal land bank association; and services performed after December 31, 1959, in the employ of a Federal land bank, a Federal intermediate credit bank, or a bank for cooperatives; services performed after December 31, 1972, in the employ of a Federal home loan bank; and services performed after December 31, 1966, and before January 1, 1973, in the employ of a Federal home loan bank, in the case of individuals who are in such employ on the latter date, provided that an amount equal to the taxes imposed by sections 3101 and 3111 with respect to all such services performed by all such individuals are paid under the provisions of section 3122 by July 1, 1973;

(iii) Services performed in the employ of a State, county, or community committee under the Commodity Stabilization Service;

(iv) Services performed by a civilian employee, not compensated from funds appropriated by the Congress, in the Army and Air Force Exchange Service, Army and Air Force Motion Picture Service, Navy Exchanges, Marine Corps Exchanges, or other activities, conducted by an instrumentality of the United States subject to the jurisdiction of the Secretary of Defense, at installations of the Department of Defense for the comfort, pleasure, contentment, and mental and physical improvement of personnel of such Department, or

(v) Services performed by a civilian employee, not compensated from funds appropriated by the Congress, in the Coast Guard Exchanges or other activities, conducted by an instrumentality of the United States subject to the jurisdiction of the Secretary of the Treasury, at installations of the Coast Guard for the comfort, pleasure, contentment, and mental and physical improvement of personnel of the Coast Guard.

(d) *Special classes of services.*—The following classes of services performed either in the employ of the United States or in the employ of any instrumentality thereof are excepted from employment under section 3121(b)(6)(C):

(1) Services performed as the President or Vice President of the United States or as a Member, Delegate, or Resident Commissioner, of or to the Congress of the United States;

(2) Services performed in the legislative branch of the United States Government;

(3) Services performed in a penal institution of the United States by an inmate thereof;

(4)(i) Except as provided in subdivision (ii) of this subparagraph, services performed by student nurses, medical or dental interns, residents in training, student dietitians, student physical therapists, or student occupational therapists, assigned or attached to a hospital, clinic, or medical or dental laboratory operated by any department, agency, or instrumentality of the United States Government, or by certain other student employees described in section 5351(2) of title 5, United States Code.

(ii) The provisions of subdivision (i) of this subparagraph have no application to services performed after 1965 by medical or dental interns or by medical or dental residents in training.

(5) Services performed by an individual as an employee serving on a temporary basis in case of fire, storm, earthquake, flood, or other similar emergency; and

(6)(i) Except as provided in subdivision (ii) of this subparagraph, services performed by an individual to whom subchapter III of chapter 83 of title 5, United States Code (civil service retirement) does not apply because he is, with respect to such services, subject to another retirement system, established either by a law of the United States or by the agency or instrumentality of the United States for which such services are performed.

(ii) The provisions of subdivision (i) of this subparagraph have no application to service performed by an individual to whom subchapter III of chapter 83 of title 5, United States Code (civil service retirement) does not apply because such individual is subject to the retirement system of the Tennessee Valley Authority, if such service is subject to the plan approved by the Secretary of Health, Education, and Welfare on December 28, 1956, pursuant to section 104(i)(2) of the Social Security Amendments of 1956 (70 Stat. 827). See section 201(m)(4) of such Amendments for provisions relating to the timeliness of payment of tax with respect to remuneration paid before 1957 for such services, and barring the imposition of interest on the amount of any such tax due for any period before December 28, 1956. [Reg. § 31.3121(b)(6)-1.]

☐ *T.D.* 6190, 7-14-56. *Republished in T.D.* 6516, 12-20-60. *Amended by T.D.* 6744, 7-2-64, *T.D.* 6983, 12-4-68, *and T.D.* 7373, 7-24-75.

[Reg. § 31.3121(b)(7)-1]

§ 31.3121(b)(7)-1. Services in employ of States or their political subdivisions or instrumentalities.—(a) *In general.*—Except as provided in other paragraphs of this section, services performed in the employ of any State, any political subdivision of a State, or any instrumentality of one or more States or political subdivisions thereof which is wholly owned by one or more States or political subdivisions are excepted from employment. For the definition of the term "State," as used in this section, see § 31.3121(e)-1.

(b) *Covered transportation service.*—The exception from employment under section 3121(b)(7) does not apply to covered transportation service

as defined in section 3121(j). See §§ 31.3121(j) and 31.3121(j)-1.

(c) *Government of American Samoa.*—The exception from employment under section 3121(b)(7) does not apply to services performed after 1960 in the employ of the Government of American Samoa, any political subdivision thereof, or any instrumentality of such Government or political subdivision, or combination thereof, which is wholly owned thereby, performed by an officer or employee thereof (including a member of the legislature of such Government or political subdivision).

(d) *District of Columbia.*—The exception from employment under section 3121(b)(7) does not apply to services performed after September 30, 1965, in the employ of the District of Columbia or any instrumentality which is wholly owned thereby, if such service is not covered by a retirement system established by a law of the United States. Notwithstanding the preceding sentence the following classes of services performed either in the employ of the District of Columbia or in the employ of any instrumentality which is wholly owned thereby are excepted from employment:

(1) Services performed in a hospital or penal institution by a patient or inmate thereof.

(2) Services performed by student nurses, student dietitians, student physical therapists, or student occupational therapists assigned or attached to a hospital, clinic, or medical or dental laboratory operated by the District of Columbia or by any wholly owned instrumentality thereof, or by certain other student employees described in section 5351(2) of title 5, United States Code. This subparagraph does not apply to services performed by medical or dental interns or by medical or dental residents in training described in such section 5351(2).

(3) Services performed by an individual as an employee serving on a temporary basis in case of fire, storm, snow, earthquake, flood, or other similar emergency.

(4) Services performed by a member of a board, committee, or council of the District of Columbia, paid on a per diem, meeting, or other fee basis.

(e) *Government of Guam.*—The exception from employment under section 3121(b)(7) does not apply to services performed after 1972 in the employ of the Government of Guam or any instrumentality which is wholly owned thereby, by an employee properly classified as a temporary or intermittent employee, if such service is not covered by a retirement system established by a law of Guam. The preceding sentence shall not apply to the services performed by an elected official or a member of the legislature or in a hospital or penal institution by a patient or inmate thereof. For purposes of this paragraph—

(1) Any person whose services as an officer or employee of such Government or instrumentality are not covered by a retirement system established by a law of the United States shall

not, with respect to such service, be regarded as an employee of the United States or any agency or instrumentality thereof, and

(2) The remuneration for services described in subparagraph (1) (including fees paid to a public official) shall be deemed to have been paid by such Government or instrumentality. [Reg. § 31.3121(b)(7)-1.]

☐ *T.D. 6190, 7-14-56. Republished in T.D. 6516, 12-20-60. Amended by T.D. 6744, 7-2-64, T.D. 6983, 12-4-68, and T.D. 7373, 7-24-75.*

[Reg. § 31.3121(b)(7)-2]

§ 31.3121(b)(7)-2. Service by employees who are not members of a public retirement system.—(a) *Table of contents.*—This paragraph contains a listing of the major headings of this section 31.3121(b)(7)-2.

§ 31.3121(b)(7)-2 Service by employees who are not members of a public retirement system.

    (a) Table of contents.

    (b) Introduction.

    (c) General rule.

        (1) Inclusion in employment of service by employees who are not members of a retirement system.

        (2) Treatment of individuals employed in more than one position.

    (d) Definition of qualified participant.

        (1) General rule.

        (2) Special rule for part-time, seasonal and temporary employees.

        (3) Alternative lookback rule.

        (4) Treatment of former participants.

    (e) Definition of retirement system.

        (1) Requirement that system provide retirement-type benefits.

        (2) Requirement that system provide minimum level of benefits.

    (f) Transition rules.

        (1) Application of qualified participant rules during 1991.

        (2) Additional transition rules for plans in existence on November 5, 1990.

(b) *Introduction.*—Under section 3121(b)(7)(F), wages of an employee of a State or local government are generally subject to tax under FICA after July 1, 1991, unless the employee is a member of a retirement system maintained by the State or local government entity. This section 31.3121(b)(7)-2 provides rules for determining whether an employee is a "member of a retirement system". These rules generally treat an employee as a member of a retirement system if he or she participates in a system that provides retirement benefits, and has an accrued benefit or receives an allocation under the system that is comparable to the benefits he or she would have or receive under Social Security. In the case of part-time, seasonal and temporary employees, this minimum retirement benefit is required to be nonforfeitable.

(c) *General rule.*—(1) *Inclusion in employment of service by employees who are not members of a retire-*ment system.—Except in the case of service described in section 3121(b)(7)(F)(i) through (v), the exception from employment under section 3121(b)(7) does not apply to service in the employ of a State or any political subdivision thereof, or of any instrumentality of one or more of the foregoing that is wholly owned thereby, after July 1, 1991, unless the employee is a member of a retirement system of such State, political subdivision or instrumentality at the time the service is performed. An employee is not a member of a retirement system at the time service is performed unless at that time he or she is a qualified participant (as defined in paragraph (d) of this section) in a retirement system that meets the requirements of paragraph (e) of this section with respect to that employee.

(2) *Treatment of individuals employed in more than one position.*—Under section 3121(b)(7)(F), whether an employee is a member of a retirement system is determined on an entity-by-entity rather than a position-by-position basis. Thus, if an employee is a member of a retirement system with respect to service he or she performs in one position in the employ of a State, political subdivision or instrumentality thereof, the employee is generally treated as a member of a retirement system with respect to all service performed for the same State, political subdivision or instrumentality in any other positions. A State is a separate entity from its political subdivisions, and an instrumentality is a separate entity from the State or political subdivision by which it is owned for purposes of this rule. See paragraph (e)(2) of this section, however, for rules relating to service and compensation required to be taken into account in determining whether an employee is a member of a retirement system for purposes of this section. This rule is illustrated by the following examples:

Example (1). An individual is employed full-time by a county and is a qualified participant (as defined in paragraph (d) of this section) in its retirement plan with regard to such employment. In addition to this full-time employment, the individual is employed part-time in another position with the same county. The part-time position is not covered by the county retirement plan, however, and neither the service nor the compensation in the part-time position is considered in determining the employee's retirement benefit under the county retirement plan. Nevertheless, if the retirement plan meets the requirements of paragraph (e) of this section with respect to the individual, the exclusion from employment under section 3121(b)(7) applies to both the employee's full-time and part-time service with the county.

Example (2). An individual is employed full-time by a State and is a member of its retirement plan. The individual is also employed part-time by a city located in the State, but does not participate in the city's retirement plan. The services of the individual for the city are not excluded from employment under section 3121(b)(7), because the determination of whether services constitute employment for such purposes is made separately with respect to each political subdivision for which services are performed.

(d) *Definition of qualified participant.*—(1) *General rule.*—(i) *Defined benefit retirement systems.*— Whether an employee is a qualified participant in a defined benefit retirement system is determined as services are performed. An employee is a qualified participant in a defined benefit retirement system (within the meaning of paragraph (e)(1) of this section) with respect to services performed on a given day if, on that day, he or she is or ever has been an actual participant in the retirement system and, on that day, he or she actually has a total accrued benefit under the retirement system that meets the minimum retirement benefit requirement of paragraph (e)(2) of this section. An employee may not be treated as an actual participant or as actually having an accrued benefit for this purpose to the extent that such participation or benefit is subject to any conditions (other than vesting), such as a requirement that the employee attain a minimum age, perform a minimum period of service, make an election in order to participate, or be present at the end of the plan year in order to be credited with an accrual, that have not been satisfied. The rules of this paragraph (d)(1)(i) are illustrated by the following examples:

Example (1). A State maintains a defined benefit plan that is a retirement system within the meaning of paragraph (e)(1) of this section. Under the terms of the plan, employees in positions covered by the plan must complete 6 months of service before becoming participants. The exception from employment in section 3121(b)(7) does not apply to services of an employee during the employee's 6 months of service prior to his or her initial entry into the plan. The same result occurs even if, upon the satisfaction of this service requirement, the employee is given credit under the plan for all service with the employer (i.e., if service is credited for the 6-month waiting period). This is true even if the employee makes a required contribution in order to gain the retroactive credit. The same result also occurs if the employee can elect to participate in the plan before the end of the 6-month waiting period, but does not elect to do so.

Example (2). A political subdivision maintains a defined benefit plan that is a retirement system within the meaning of paragraph (e)(1) of this section. Under the terms of the plan, service during a plan year is not credited for accrual purposes unless a participant has at least 1,000 hours of service during the year. Benefits that accrue only upon satisfaction of this 1,000-hour requirement may not be taken into account in determining whether an employee is a qualified participant in the plan before the 1,000-hour requirement is satisfied.

(ii) *Defined contribution retirement systems.*—Whether an employee is a qualified participant in a defined contribution retirement system is determined as services are performed. An employee is a qualified participant in a de-

fined contribution or other individual account retirement system (within the meaning of paragraph (e)(1) of this section) with respect to services performed on a given day if, on that day, he or she has satisfied all conditions (other than vesting) for receiving an allocation to his or her account (exclusive of earnings) that meets the minimum retirement benefit requirement of paragraph (e)(2) of this section with respect to compensation during any period ending on that day and beginning on or after the beginning of the plan year of the retirement system. This is the case regardless of whether the allocations were made or accrued before the effective date of section 3121(b)(7)(F). This rule is illustrated by the following examples:

Example (1). A State-owned hospital maintains a nonelective defined contribution plan that is a retirement system within the meaning of paragraph (e)(1) of this section. Under the terms of the plan, employees must be employed on the last day of a plan year in order to receive any allocation for the year. Employees may not be treated as qualified participants in the plan before the last day of the year.

Example (2). Assume the same facts as in *Example (1)* except that, under the terms of the plan, an employee who terminates service before the end of a plan year receives a pro rata portion of the allocation he or she would have received at the end of the year, e.g., based on compensation earned since the beginning of the plan year. If the pro rata allocation available on a given day would meet the minimum retirement benefit requirement of paragraph (e)(2) of this section with respect to compensation from the beginning of the plan year through that day (or some later day), employees are treated as qualified participants in the plan on that day.

Example (3). A political subdivision maintains an elective defined contribution plan that is a retirement system within the meaning of paragraph (e)(1) of this section. The plan has a calendar year plan year and two open seasons—in December and June—when employees can change their contribution elections. In December, an employee elects not to contribute to the plan. In June, the employee elects (beginning July 1) to contribute a uniform percentage of compensation for each pay period to the plan for the remainder of the plan year. The employee is not a qualified participant in the plan during the period January-June, because no allocations are made to the employee's account with respect to compensation during that time, and it is not certain at that time that any allocations will be made. If the level of contributions during the period July-December meets the minimum retirement benefit requirement of paragraph (e)(2) of this section with respect to compensation during that period, however, the employee is treated as a qualified participant during that period.

Example (4). Assume the same facts as in *Example (3)*, except that the plan allows participants to cancel their elections in cases of economic hardship. In October, the employee suffers an economic hardship and cancels the election (effective November 1). If the contributions during the period July-October are high enough to meet the minimum retirement benefit requirement of paragraph (e)(2) of this section with respect to compensation during that period, the employee is treated as a qualified participant during that period. In addition, if the contributions during the period July-October are high enough to meet the requirements for the entire period July-December, the employee is treated as a qualified participant in the plan throughout the period July-December, even though no allocations are made to the employee's account in the last two months of the year. There is no requirement that the period used to determine whether an employee is a qualified participant on a given day remain the same from day to day, as long as the period begins on or after the beginning of the plan year and ends on the date the determination is being made.

(2) *Special rule for part-time, seasonal and temporary employees.*—(i) *In general.*—A part-time, seasonal or temporary employee is generally not a qualified participant on a given day unless any benefit relied upon to meet the requirements of paragraph (d)(1) of this section is 100-percent nonforfeitable on that day. This requirement may be applied solely to the portion of an employee's benefit under the retirement system attributable to compensation and service while an employee is a part-time, seasonal or temporary employee, provided that such service is taken into account with respect to the remaining portion of the benefit for vesting purposes. Rules similar to the rules in section 411(a)(11) are applicable in determining whether a benefit is nonforfeitable. Thus, a benefit does not fail to be nonforfeitable solely because it can be immediately distributed upon separation of service without the consent of the employee, provided that the present value of the benefit does not exceed the cash-out limit in effect under § 1.411(a)-11(c)(3)(ii) of this chapter.

(ii) *Treatment of employees entitled to certain distributions upon death or separation from service.*—A part-time, seasonal or temporary employee's benefit under a retirement system is considered nonforfeitable within the meaning of paragraph (d)(2)(i) of this section on a given day if on that day the employee is unconditionally entitled under the retirement system to a single-sum distribution on account of death or separation from service of an amount that is at least equal to 7.5 percent of the participant's compensation (within the meaning of paragraph (e)(2)(iii)(B) of this section) for all periods of credited service taken into account in determining whether the employee's benefit under the retirement system meets the minimum retirement benefit requirement of paragraph (e)(2) of this section. An employee will be considered to be unconditionally entitled to a single-sum distribution notwithstanding the fact that the distribution may be forfeitable (in whole or in part) upon a finding of such employee's criminal mis-

conduct. The participant must be entitled to interest on the distributable amount through the date of distribution, at a rate meeting the requirements of paragraph (e)(2)(iii)(C) of this section, as part of the single sum. See paragraph (f)(2)(i)(C) for a transition rule relating to this nonforfeitable benefit safe harbor. The rule of this paragraph (d)(2)(ii) is illustrated by the following example:

Example. An employee is required to contribute 7.5 percent of his or her compensation to a State's defined benefit plan each year. The contribution is "picked up" by the employer in accordance with section 414(h). Under the plan, these amounts plus interest accrued since the date each amount was contributed are refundable to the employee in all cases upon the employee's death or separation from service with the employer. If the interest rate meets the requirements of paragraph (e)(2)(iii)(C) of this section, then the employee's benefits under the plan are considered nonforfeitable and thus meet the requirement of paragraph (d)(2)(i) of this section. Of course, the benefit under the plan must still meet the minimum retirement benefit requirement for defined benefit plans of paragraph (e)(2)(ii) of this section.

(iii) *Definitions of part-time, seasonal and temporary employee.*—(A) *Definition of part-time employee.*—For purposes of this section, a part-time employee is any employee who normally works 20 hours or less per week. A teacher employed by a post-secondary educational institution (e.g., a community or junior college, post-secondary vocational school, college, university or graduate school) is not considered a part-time employee for purposes of this section if he or she normally has classroom hours of one-half or more of the number of classroom hours designated by the educational institution as constituting full-time employment, provided that such designation is reasonable under all the facts and circumstances. In addition, elected officials and election workers (otherwise described in section 3121(b)(7)(F)(iv) but paid in excess of $100 annually) are not considered part-time, seasonal or temporary employees for purposes of this section. The rules of this paragraph (d)(2)(iii) are illustrated by the following example:

Example. A community college treats a teacher as a full-time employee if the teacher is assigned to work 15 classroom hours per week. A new teacher is assigned to work 8 classroom hours per week. Because the assigned classroom hours of the teacher are at least one-half of the school's definition of full-time teacher, the teacher is not a part-time employee.

(B) *Definition of seasonal employee.*—For purposes of this section, a seasonal employee is any employee who normally works on a full-time basis less than 5 months in a year. Thus, for example, individuals who are hired by a political subdivision during the tax return season in order to process incoming returns and work full-time over a 3-month period are seasonal employees.

(C) *Definition of temporary employee.*—
For purposes of this section, a temporary employee is any employee performing services under a contractual arrangement with the employer of 2 years or less duration. Possible contract extensions may be considered in determining the duration of a contractual arrangement, but only if, under the facts and circumstances, there is a significant likelihood that the employee's contract will be extended. Future contract extensions are considered significantly likely to occur for purposes of this rule if on average 80 percent of similarly situated employees (i.e., those in the same or a similar job classification with expiring employment contracts) have had bona fide offers to renew their contracts in the immediately preceding 2 academic or calendar years. In addition, future contract extensions are considered significantly likely to occur if the employee with respect to whom the determination is being made has a history of contract extensions with respect to his or her current position. An employee is not considered a temporary employee for purposes of this rule solely because he or she is included in a unit of employees covered by a collective bargaining agreement of 2 years or less duration.

(D) *Treatment of employees participating in certain systems.*—Whether an employee is a part-time, seasonal or temporary employee with respect to allocations or benefits under a retirement system is generally determined based on service in the position in which the allocations or benefits were earned, and does not take into account service in other positions with the same or different States, political subdivisions or instrumentalities thereof. All of an employee's service in other positions with the same or different States, political subdivisions or instrumentalities thereof may be taken into account for purposes of determining whether an employee is a part-time, seasonal or temporary employee with respect to benefits under the retirement system, however, provided that: the employee's service in the other positions is or was covered by the retirement system; all service aggregated for purposes of determining whether an employee is a part-time, seasonal or temporary employee (and related compensation) is aggregated under the system for all purposes in determining benefits (including vesting); and the employee is treated at least as favorably as a full-time employee under the retirement system for benefit accrual purposes. The rule of this paragraph (d)(2)(iii)(D) is illustrated by the following example:

Example. Assume that an employee works 15 hours per week for a county and 10 hours per week for a municipality, and that both of these political subdivisions contribute to the same state-wide public employee retirement system. Assume further that the employee's service in both positions is aggregated under the system for all purposes in determining benefits (including vesting). If the employee is covered under the retirement system with respect to both posi-

tions and is treated for benefit accrual purposes at least as favorably as full-time employees under the retirement system, then the employee is not considered a part-time employee of either the county or the municipality for purposes of the nonforfeitable benefit requirement of paragraph (d)(2)(i) of this section.

(3) *Alternative lookback rule.*—(i) *In general.*—An employee may be treated as a qualified participant in a retirement system throughout a calendar year if he or she was a qualified participant in such system (within the meaning of paragraphs (d)(1) and (2) of this section) at the end of the plan year of the system ending in the previous calendar year. This rule is illustrated by the following examples:

Example 1. A political subdivision maintains a plan that is a retirement system within the meaning of paragraph (e)(1) of this section. An employee is a qualified participant within the meaning of paragraph (d)(1) of this section in the plan on the last day of the plan year ending on May 31, 1995. If the alternative lookback rule is used to determine FICA liability, no such liability exists with respect to the employee or employer for calendar year 1996 by reason of section 3121(b)(7)(F). The same result would apply if the determination is being made with respect to calendar year 1992 and the lookback year was the plan year ending May 31, 1991, even though that plan year ended before the effective date of section 3121(b)(7)(F).

Example 2. A political subdivision maintains an elective defined contribution plan described in section 457(b) of the Code. An employee is eligible to participate in the plan but does not elect to contribute for a plan year. Under the general rule of paragraph (d)(1) of this section, the employee is not a qualified participant in the plan during the plan year because contributions sufficient to meet the minimum retirement benefit requirement of paragraph (e)(2) of this section are not being made. However, if an employee's status as a qualified participant is being determined under the alternative lookback rule, then the employee is a qualified participant for the calendar year in which the determination is being made if he or she was a qualified participant as of the end of the plan year that ended in the previous calendar year.

(ii) *Application in first year of participation.*—If the alternative lookback rule is used, an employee who participates in the retirement system may be treated as a qualified participant on any given day during his or her first plan year of participation in a retirement system (within the meaning of paragraph (e)(1) of this section) if and only if it is reasonable on such day to believe that the employee will be a qualified participant (within the meaning of paragraphs (d)(1) and (2) of this section) on the last day of such plan year. In the case of a defined contribution retirement system, the determination of whether the employee is actually (or is expected to be) a qualified participant at the end of the plan year must

Reg. §31.3121(b)(7)-2(d)(3)(ii)

take into account all compensation since the commencement of participation. See paragraph (d)(3)(iv) of this section. If this reasonable belief is correct, and the employee is a qualified participant on the last day of his or her first year of participation, then the exception from employment in section 3121(b)(7) will apply without regard to section 3121(b)(7)(F) to services of the employee for the balance of the calendar year in which the plan year ends. For purposes of this paragraph (d)(3)(ii), it is not reasonable to assume the establishment of a new plan until such establishment actually occurs. In addition, the rule in this paragraph (d)(3)(ii) may not be used to treat an employee as a qualified participant until the employee actually becomes a participant in the retirement system. In the case of a retirement system that does not permit a new employee to participate until the first day of the first month beginning after the employee's commencement of service, or some earlier date, a new employee who is not a part-time, seasonal or temporary employee may be treated as a qualified participant until such date. This 1-month rule of administrative convenience applies without regard to whether the employer has a reasonable belief that the employee will be a qualified participant. The rules of this paragraph (d)(3)(ii) are illustrated by the following examples:

Example 1. A political subdivision maintains a plan that is a retirement system within the meaning of paragraph (e)(1) of this section and uses the alternative lookback rule of this paragraph (d)(3). Under the terms of the plan, service during a plan year is not credited for accrual purposes unless a participant has at least 1,000 hours of service during the year. Assume that an employee becomes a participant. If it is reasonable to believe that the employee will be credited with 1,000 hours of service by the last day of his or her first year of participation and thereby become a qualified participant by reason of accruing a benefit that meets the minimum retirement benefit requirement of paragraph (e)(2) of this section, the services of the employee are not subject to FICA tax from the date of initial participation until the end of that plan year. If the employee is a qualified participant on the last day of his or her first plan year of participation, then the exception from employment for purposes of FICA will apply to services of the employee for the balance of the calendar year in which the plan year ended.

Example 2. Assume the same facts as *Example 1,* except that the employee is a newly hired employee and the plan provides that an employee may not participate until the first day of his or her first full month of employment. Under the 1-month rule of convenience, the employee may be treated as a qualified participant until the first date on which he or she could participate in the plan.

(iii) *Application in last year of participation.*—If the alternative lookback rule is used, an employee may be treated as a qualified partici-

pant on any given day during his or her last year of participation in a retirement system (within the meaning of paragraph (e)(1) of this section) if and only if it is reasonable to believe on such day that the employee will be a qualified participant (within the meaning of paragraphs (d)(1) and (2) of this section) on his or her last day of participation. For purposes of this paragraph (d)(3)(iii), an employee's last year of participation means the plan year that the employer reasonably ascertains is the final year of such employee's participation (e.g., where the employee has a scheduled retirement date or where the employer intends to terminate the plan).

(iv) *Special rule for defined contribution retirement systems.*—An employee may not be treated as a qualified participant in a defined contribution retirement system under this paragraph (d)(3) if compensation for less than a full plan year or other 12-month period is regularly taken into account in determining allocations to the employee's account for the plan year unless, under all of the facts and circumstances, such arrangement is not a device to avoid the imposition of FICA taxes. For example, an arrangement under which compensation taken into account is limited to the contribution base described in section 3121(x)(1) is not considered a device to avoid FICA taxes by reason of such limitation. See paragraph (e)(2)(iii)(B) of this section for a rule permitting the use of such limitation. This rule is illustrated by the following example:

Example. A political subdivision maintains a defined contribution plan that covers all of its full-time employees and is a retirement system within the meaning of paragraph (e)(1) of this section. Under the plan, a portion of each participant's compensation in the final month of every plan year is allocated to the participant's account. Employees covered under the plan generally may not be treated as qualified participants under the alternative lookback rule for any portion of the calendar year following the year in which such allocation is made.

(v) *Consistency requirement.*—Beginning with calendar year 1992, if the alternative lookback rule is used to determine whether an employee is a qualified participant, it must be used consistently from year to year and with respect to all employees of the State, political subdivision or instrumentality thereof making the determination. If a retirement system is sponsored by more than one State, political subdivision or instrumentality, this consistency requirement applies separately to each plan sponsor.

(4) *Treatment of former participants.*—(i) *In general.*—In general, the rules of this paragraph (d) apply equally to former participants who continue to perform service for the same State, political subdivision or instrumentality thereof or who return after a break in service. Thus, for example, a former employee of a political subdivision with a deferred benefit under a defined benefit retirement system maintained by the political subdivision who is reemployed by the po-

litical subdivision but does not resume participation in the retirement system, may continue to be a qualified participant in the system after becoming reemployed if his or her total accrued benefit under the system meets the minimum retirement benefit requirement of paragraph (e)(2) of this section (taking into account all periods of service (including current service) required to be taken into account under that paragraph). See also paragraph (e)(2)(v) of this section for situations in which benefits under a retirement system may be taken into account even though they relate to service for another employer.

(ii) *Treatment of re-hired annuitants.*—An employee who is a former participant in a retirement system maintained by a State, political subdivision or instrumentality thereof, who has previously retired from service with the State, political subdivision or instrumentality, and who is either in pay status (i.e., is currently receiving retirement benefits) under the retirement system or has reached normal retirement age under the retirement system, is deemed to be a qualified participant in the retirement system without regard to whether he or she continues to accrue a benefit or whether the distribution of benefits under the retirement system has been suspended pending cessation of services. This rule also applies in the case of an employee who has retired from service with another State, political subdivision or instrumentality thereof that maintains the same retirement system as the current employer, provided the employee is a former participant in the system by reason of the employee's former employment. Thus, for example, if a teacher retires from service with a school district that participates in a state-wide teachers' retirement system, begins to receive benefits from the system, and later becomes a substitute teacher in another school district that participates in the same state-wide system, the employee is treated as a re-hired annuitant under this paragraph (d)(4)(ii).

(e) *Definition of retirement system.*—(1) *Requirement that system provide retirement-type benefits.* For purposes of section 3121(b)(7)(F), a retirement system includes any pension, annuity, retirement or similar fund or system within the meaning of section 218 of the Social Security Act that is maintained by a State, political subdivision or instrumentality thereof to provide retirement benefits to its employees who are participants. Whether a plan is maintained to provide retirement benefits with respect to an employee is determined under the facts and circumstances of each case. For example, a plan providing only retiree health insurance or other deferred welfare benefits is not considered a retirement system for this purpose. The legal form of the system is generally not relevant. Thus, for example, a retirement system may include a plan described in section 401(a), an annuity plan or contract under section 403 or a plan described in section 457(b) or (f) of the Internal Revenue Code. In addition, the Social Security system is

not a retirement system for purposes of section 3121(b)(7)(F) and this section. These rules are illustrated by the following examples:

Example 1. Under an employment arrangement, a portion of an employee's compensation is regularly deferred for 5 years. Because a plan that defers the receipt of compensation for a short span of time rather than until retirement is not a plan that provides retirement benefits, this arrangement is not a retirement system for purposes of section 3121(b)(7)(F).

Example 2. An individual holds two positions with the same political subdivision. The wages earned in one position are subject to FICA tax pursuant to an agreement (under section 218 of the Social Security Act) between the Secretary of Health and Human Services and the State in which the political subdivision is located. Because the Social Security system is not a retirement system for purposes of section 3121(b)(7)(F), the exception from employment in section 3121(b)(7) does not apply to service in the other position unless the employee is otherwise a member of a retirement system of such political subdivision.

(2) *Requirement that system provide minimum level of benefits.*—(i) *In general.*—A pension, annuity, retirement or similar fund or system is not a retirement system with respect to an employee unless it provides a retirement benefit to the employee that is comparable to the benefit provided under the Old-Age portion of the Old-Age, Survivor and Disability Insurance program of Social Security. Whether a retirement system meets this requirement is generally determined on an individual-by-individual basis. Thus, for example, a pension plan that is not a retirement system with respect to an employee may nevertheless be a retirement system with respect to other employees covered by the system.

(ii) *Defined benefit retirement systems.*—A defined benefit retirement system maintained by a State, political subdivision or instrumentality thereof meets the requirements of this paragraph (e)(2) with respect to an employee on a given day if and only if, on that day, the employee has an accrued benefit under the system that entitles the employee to an annual benefit commencing on or before his or her Social Security retirement age that is at least equal to the annual Primary Insurance Amount the employee would have under Social Security. For this purpose, the Primary Insurance Amount an individual would have under Social Security is determined as it would be under the Social Security Act if the employee had been covered under Social Security for all periods of service with the State, political subdivision or instrumentality, had never performed service for any other employer, and had been fully insured within the meaning of section 214(a) of the Social Security Act, except that all periods of service with the State, political subdivision or instrumentality must be taken into account (i.e., without reduction for low-earning years).

Reg. §31.3121(b)(7)-2(e)(2)(ii)

(iii) *Defined contribution retirement systems.*—(A) *In general.*—A defined contribution retirement system maintained by a state, political subdivision or instrumentality thereof meets the requirements of paragraph (e)(2)(i) of this section with respect to an employee if and only if allocations to the employee's account (not including earnings) for a period are at least 7.5 percent of the employee's compensation for service for the State, political subdivision or instrumentality during the period. Matching contributions by the employer may be taken into account for this purpose.

(B) *Definition of compensation.*—The definition of compensation used in determining whether a defined contribution retirement system meets the minimum retirement benefit requirement must generally be no less inclusive than the definition of the employee's base pay as designated by the employer or the retirement system, provided such designation is reasonable under all the facts and circumstances. Thus, for example, a defined contribution retirement system will not fail to meet this requirement merely because it disregards for all purposes one or more of the following: overtime pay, bonuses, or single-sum amounts received on account of death or separation from service under a bona fide vacation, compensatory time or sick pay plan, or under severance pay plans. Furthermore, any compensation remaining after such amounts are disregarded that is in excess of the contribution base described in section 3121(x)(1) at the beginning of the plan year may also be disregarded. The rules of this paragraph are illustrated by the following example:

Example. A political subdivision maintains an elective defined contribution plan that is a retirement system within the meaning of paragraph (e)(1) of this section. The plan has a calendar year plan year. In 1995, an employee contributes to the plan at a rate of 7.5 percent of base pay. Assume that the employee will reach the maximum contribution base described in section 3121(x)(1) in October of 1995. The employee is a qualified participant in the plan for all of the 1995 plan year without regard to whether the employee ceases to participate at any time after reaching the maximum contribution base.

(C) *Reasonable interest rate requirement.*—A defined contribution retirement system does not satisfy this paragraph (e)(2) with respect to an employee unless the employee's account is credited with earnings at a rate that is reasonable under all the facts and circumstances, or employees' accounts are held in a separate trust that is subject to general fiduciary standards and are credited with actual earnings on the trust fund. Whether the interest rate with which an employee's account is credited is reasonable is determined after reducing the rate to adjust for the payment of any administrative expenses. The rule of this paragraph (e)(2)(iii)(C) is illustrated by the following example:

Example. A political subdivision maintains a defined contribution plan described in section 457(b). Under the plan, the accounts of participants are credited annually on the basis of a variable interest rate formula determined as of the beginning of the plan year. The formula requires an interest rate (after adjustment for administrative expense payments) equal to 100 percent of the Applicable Federal Rate for long-term debt instruments. This interest rate constitutes a reasonable rate of interest.

(iv) *Treatment of employees employed in more than one position with the same entity.*—All service and compensation of an employee with respect to his or her employment with a State, political subdivision or instrumentality thereof must generally be considered in determining whether a benefit meets the requirement of this paragraph (e)(2). However, for individuals employed simultaneously in multiple positions with the same entity, this determination may (but is not required to) be made solely by reference to the service and compensation related to a single position of the employee with the State, political subdivision or instrumentality thereof making the determination, provided that the position is not a part-time, seasonal or temporary position.

(v) *Treatment of employees participating in certain systems.*—In general, only compensation from and service for the State, political subdivision or instrumentality thereof that employs the employee (and the allocations or benefits related to such compensation or service) on a given day are considered in determining whether the employee's benefit under the retirement system on that day meets the requirements of this paragraph (e)(2), even if the employee has other allocations or benefits under the same retirement system from service with another State, political subdivision or instrumentality thereof. However, an employee's total allocations or benefits under a retirement system maintained by multiple States, political subdivisions or instrumentalities thereof (including the current employer) may be taken into account if:

(A) The compensation and service on which the additional allocations or benefits are based are also taken into account in determining whether the employee's allocations or benefits satisfy the minimum retirement benefit requirement;

(B) The retirement system takes all service and compensation of the employee in all positions covered by the system into account for all benefit determination purposes; and

(C) If the employee is a part-time, seasonal or temporary employee, he or she is treated under the plan for benefit accrual purposes in as favorable a manner as a full-time employee participating in the system.

(vi) *Additional testing methods.*—Additional testing methods may be designated by the Commissioner in revenue procedures, revenue rulings, notices or other documents of general applicability.

(f) *Transition rules.*—(1) *Application of qualified participant rules during 1991.*—(i) *In general.*—An employee may be treated as a qualified participant in a retirement system (within the meaning of paragraph (e)(1) of this section) on a given day during the period July 1 through December 31, 1991, if it is reasonable on that day to believe that he or she will be a qualified participant under the general rule in paragraphs (d)(1) and (2) of this section by January 1, 1992 (taking into account only service and compensation on or after such date). For purposes of this paragraph (f)(1)(i), given the facts and circumstances of a particular case, it may be reasonable to assume that the terms of a plan will be changed or that a new retirement system will be established by the end of calendar year 1991, as long as affirmative steps have been taken to accomplish this result.

(ii) *Extension of reliance period if legislative action required.*—If a plan amendment or other action is necessary in order to treat an employee as a member of a retirement system for purposes of this section, such amendment or other action may only be taken by a legislative body that does not convene during the period July 1, 1991, through December 31, 1991, and the other requirements of paragraph (f)(1)(i) of this section are met, the end of the reasonable reliance period (including the rule that service and compensation prior to that date may be disregarded) provided under paragraph (f)(1)(i) of this section is extended from December 31, 1991, to the date that is the last day of the first legislative session commencing after December 31, 1991. These rules are illustrated by the following examples:

Example 1. A State maintains a defined benefit plan that meets the requirements of paragraph (e) of this section. The plan does not cover a particular class of full-time employees as of July 1, 1991. However, in light of the enactment of section 3121(b)(7)(F), state officials administering the plan for the State intend to request that the legislature amend the State statute to include that class of employees in the existing plan and otherwise to modify the terms of the plan to meet the requirements of section 3121(b)(7)(F) and this section. The State legislature meets from January through March each year, and legislative action is required to expand coverage under the plan. State officials administering the plan have publicized the proposed amendment providing for the addition of these employees to the plan. Under the transition rule for 1991, if it is reasonable to believe that the legislature will pass this bill in the 1992 session, service by the employees who will be covered under the plan by reason of the amendment is not treated as employment by reason of section 3121(b)(7)(F) during the period prior to April 1, 1992. This is true regardless of whether the plan provides retroactive coverage for the period July 1, 1991 through March 31, 1992.

Example 2. Assume the same facts as in *Example 1*, except that legislative action is not required in order to expand coverage under the plan, and that publication of the proposed change to the plan occurs in 1991. Assume further that coverage is expanded under the plan to include the new class of full-time employees as of April 1, 1992. Despite this action, in this situation the service by those employees during the period January 1, 1992 through March 31, 1992 is not excluded from "employment" under section 3121(b)(7)(F), and wages for that period are generally subject to FICA taxes even if the plan provides retroactive coverage for any portion of the period July 1, 1991 to March 31, 1992.

(2) *Additional transition rules for plans in existence on November 5, 1990.*—(i) *Application of minimum retirement benefit requirement to defined benefit retirement systems in plan years beginning before 1993.*—(A) *In general.*—A defined benefit retirement system maintained by a State, political subdivision or instrumentality thereof on November 5, 1990, is not subject to the minimum retirement benefit requirement of paragraph (e)(2) of this section for any plan year beginning before January 1, 1993, with respect to individuals who were actually covered under the system on November 5, 1990. Such a retirement system is also not subject to the minimum retirement benefit requirement of paragraph (e)(2) of this section with respect to an employee who becomes a participant after November 5, 1990, if he or she is employed in a position that was covered under the retirement system on November 5, 1990, without regard to whether such coverage was mandatory or elective. A retirement system is not described in this paragraph (f)(2)(i)(A) if there has been a material decrease in the level of retirement benefits under the retirement system pursuant to an amendment adopted subsequent to November 5, 1990. Whether such a material decrease in benefits has occurred is determined under the facts and circumstances of each case. A decrease in benefits is not material to the extent that it does not decrease the benefit payable at normal retirement age. These rules are illustrated by the following examples:

Example 1. The retirement formula under a retirement plan that was in existence on November 5, 1990, is amended to use career average compensation instead of a high 3-year average, without any increase in the benefit formula. This amendment constitutes a material decrease in the level of benefit under the retirement plan. Therefore, the retirement plan is subject to the minimum retirement benefit requirement for the plan year for which the amendment is effective and for all succeeding plan years.

Example 2. A defined benefit retirement plan that was in existence on November 5, 1990, is subsequently amended to include part-time employees. Previously, this class of employees was not covered under the plan either on a mandatory or on an elective basis. The plan is subject to the minimum retirement benefit requirement with respect to the part-time employees because this class of employees was previously excluded from coverage under the retirement plan. Of course, the nonforfeitable benefit rule applies to the benefit relied upon to meet the minimum retirement benefit requirement with respect to any part-time, seasonal or temporary employee covered during this period.

(B) *Treatment in plan years beginning after 1992 of benefits accrued during previous plan years.*—The general rule that a defined benefit retirement system meets the minimum retirement benefit requirement on the basis of total benefits and service accrued to date is modified for plans in existence on November 5, 1990. If a defined benefit retirement system in existence on November 5, 1990, does not meet the minimum retirement benefit requirement solely because the benefits accrued for an employee (with respect to whom the system is entitled to relief under paragraph (f)(2)(i)(A) of this section) as of the last day of the last plan year beginning before January 1, 1993, do not meet the minimum retirement benefit requirement of paragraph (e)(2) of this section with respect to service and compensation before that time, then the retirement system will be deemed to comply with the requirements of paragraph (e)(2) of this section if the future service accruals would comply with the requirement of paragraph (e)(2) of this section. If retirement benefits under a retirement system in existence on November 5, 1990, are materially decreased within the meaning of paragraph (f)(2)(i)(A) of this section, then the date the decrease is effective is substituted for January 1, 1993, for purposes of this paragraph. The rule of this paragraph (f)(2)(i)(B) is illustrated by the following example:

Example. A defined benefit plan maintained by a State was in existence on November 5, 1990. It provides a retirement benefit on the last day of the 1992 plan year that is insufficient to meet the requirements of paragraph (e)(2) of this section based on employees' total service and compensation with the State at that time. The plan will nevertheless meet the requirements of paragraph (e)(2) of this section if it is amended to provide benefits sufficient to meet the requirements of paragraph (e)(2) of this section based on employees' service and compensation in plan years beginning after December 31, 1992.

(C) *Treatment of part-time, seasonal or temporary employees.*—A defined benefit retirement system is not exempt from the minimum retirement benefit requirement with respect to a part-time, seasonal or temporary employee during the transition period provided in paragraph (f)(2)(i)(A) of this section unless any retirement benefit provided to the employee is 100-percent nonforfeitable within the meaning of paragraph (d)(2) of this section. In determining whether the benefit is nonforfeitable, the special rule in paragraph (d)(2)(ii) of this section is modified in two respects during the transition period: first, the percentage of compensation required to be available for distribution is reduced from 7.5 percent to 6 percent; and second, the period of service with respect to which compensation must be determined is modified to include all periods of participation by the employee in the system since July 1, 1991.

(ii) *Application of minimum retirement benefit requirement to defined contribution retirement systems in plan years beginning before 1993.*—A defined contribution retirement system maintained by a State, political subdivision or instrumentality thereof on November 5, 1990, meets the minimum retirement benefit requirement of paragraph (e)(2) of this section with respect to an employee for any plan year beginning before January 1, 1993, if mandatory allocations to the employee's account (not including earnings) for a period are at least 6 percent (rather than 7.5 percent) of the employee's compensation for service to the State, political subdivision or instrumentality during the period, and the plan otherwise meets the requirements of paragraph (e)(2)(iii) of this section. This transition rule is only available with respect to an employee who is actually covered under the system on November 5, 1990, and to an employee who becomes a participant after November 5, 1990, if he or she is employed in a position that was covered under the retirement system on November 5, 1990, without regard to whether such coverage was mandatory or elective. In addition, this transition rule is not available with respect to a part-time, seasonal or temporary employee unless the mandatory allocation required under this paragraph (f)(2)(ii) is 100-percent nonforfeitable within the meaning of paragraph (d)(2) of this section. A retirement system is not described in this paragraph (f)(2)(ii) if there has been a material decrease in the level of retirement benefits under the retirement system pursuant to an amendment adopted subsequent to November 5, 1990. Whether such a material decrease in benefits has occurred is determined under all the facts and circumstances.

(iii) *Application of qualified participant rules.*—A participant with respect to whom relief is granted under paragraph (f)(2)(i)(A) of this section may be treated as a qualified participant in the defined benefit retirement system on a given day if, on that day, he or she is actually a participant in the retirement system, and, on that day, it is reasonable to believe that the participant will actually accrue a benefit before the end of the plan year of such retirement system in which the determination is made. A participant is not treated as accruing a benefit for purposes of this rule if his or her accrued benefits increase solely as a result of an increase in compensation. However, an employee is treated as a qualified participant for a plan year if the employee meets all of the applicable conditions for accruing the maximum current benefit for such year but fails to accrue a benefit solely because of a uniformly applicable benefit limit under the plan. In addition, an employee may be treated as a qualified participant in the system on a given day if the employee is a re-hired annuitant within the meaning of paragraph (d)(4)(ii) of this section. This rule is illustrated by the following example:

Example. A political subdivision maintains a defined benefit plan that is a retirement system within the meaning of paragraph (e)(1) of this section but does not meet the requirements of paragraph (e)(2) of this section. If the plan is not subject to the minimum retirement benefit requirement, an employee who is a participant in the retirement plan as of the end of a plan year beginning before January 1, 1993, and may reasonably be expected to accrue a benefit under the plan by the end of such plan year may be treated as a qualified participant in the plan throughout the plan year regardless of the actual amount of the accrual. [Reg. § 31.3121(b)(7)-2.]

☐ *[T.D. 8354, 6-28-91. Amended by T.D. 8794, 12-18-98 and T.D. 8891, 7-18-2000.]*

≫→ *Caution: The following regulation has not been revised to reflect the automatic extension of self-employment coverage to ministers, Christian Science practitioners, and members of religious orders who have not applied for an exemption from coverage.*

[Reg. § 31.3121(b)(8)-1]

§ 31.3121(b)(8)-1. Services performed by a minister of a church or a member of a religious order.—(a) *In general.*—Services performed by a duly ordained, commissioned, or licensed minister of a church in the exercise of his ministry, or by a member of a religious order in the exercise of duties required by such order, are excluded from employment, except that services performed by a member of such an order in the exercise of such duties (whether performed for the order or for another employer) are included in employment if an election of coverage under section 3121(r) and § 31.3121(r)-1 is in effect with respect to such order or with respect to the autonomous subdivision thereof to which such member belongs. For provisions relating to the election available to certain ministers and members of religious orders with respect to the extension of the Federal old-age, survivors, and disability insurance system established by Title II of the Social Security Act to certain services performed by them, see Part 1 of this chapter (Income Tax Regulations).

(b) *Service by a minister in the exercise of his ministry.*—Except as provided in paragraph (c)(3) of this section, service performed by a minister in the exercise of his ministry includes the ministration of sacerdotal functions and the conduct of religious worship, and the control, conduct, and maintenance of religious organizations (including the religious boards, societies, and other integral agencies of such organizations), under the authority of a religious body constituting a church or church denomination. The following rules are applicable in determining whether services performed by a minister are performed in the exercise of his ministry:

(1) Whether service performed by a minister constitutes the conduct of religious worship or the ministration of sacerdotal functions depends on the tenets and practices of the particular religious body constituting his church or church denomination.

(2) Service performed by a minister in the control, conduct, and maintenance of a religious organization relates to directing, managing, or promoting the activities of such organization. Any religious organization is deemed to be under the authority of a religious body constituting a church or church denomination if it is organized and dedicated to carrying out the tenets and principles of a faith in accordance with either the requirements or sanctions governing the creation of institutions of the faith. The term "religious organization" has the same meaning and application as is given to the term for income tax purposes.

(3)(i) If a minister is performing service in the conduct of religious worship or the ministration of sacerdotal functions, such service is in the exercise of his ministry whether or not it is performed for a religious organization.

(ii) The rule in subdivision (i) of this subparagraph may be illustrated by the following example:

Example. M, a duly ordained minister, is engaged to perform service as chaplain at N university. M devotes his entire time to performing his duties as chaplain which include the conduct of religious worship, offering spiritual counsel to the university students, and teaching class in religion. M is performing service in the exercise of his ministry.

(4)(i) If a minister is performing service for an organization which is operated as an integral agency of a religious organization under the authority of a religious body constituting a church or church denomination, all service performed by the minister in the conduct of religious worship, in the ministration of sacerdotal functions, or in the control, conduct, and maintenance of such organization (see subparagraph (2) of this paragraph) is in the exercise of his ministry.

(ii) The rule in subdivision (i) of this subparagraph may be illustrated by the following example:

Example. M, a duly ordained minister, is engaged by the N Religious Board to serve as director of one of its departments. He performs no other service. The N Religious Board is an integral agency of O, a religious organization operating under the authority of a religious body constituting a church denomination. M is performing service in the exercise of his ministry.

(5)(i) If a minister, pursuant to an assignment or designation by a religious body constituting his church, performs service for an organization which is neither a religious organization nor operated as an integral agency of a religious organization, all service performed by him, even though such service may not involve the conduct of religious worship or the ministration of sacerdotal functions, is in the exercise of his ministry.

(ii) The rule in subdivision (i) of this subparagraph may be illustrated by the following example:

Example. M, a duly ordained minister, is assigned by X, the religious body constituting his church, to perform advisory service to Y Company in connection with the publication of a book dealing with the history of M's church denomination. Y is neither a religious organization nor operated as an integral agency of a religious organization. M performs no other service for X or Y. M is performing service in the exercise of his ministry.

(c) *Service by a minister not in the exercise of his ministry.*—(1) Section 3121(b)(8)(A) does not except from employment service performed by a duly ordained, commissioned, or licensed minister of a church which is not in the exercise of his ministry.

(2)(i) If a minister is performing service for an organization which is neither a religious organization nor operated as an integral agency of a religious organization and the service is not performed pursuant to an assignment or designation by his ecclesiastical superiors, then only the service performed by him in the conduct of religious worship or the ministration of sacerdotal functions is in the exercise of his ministry. See, however, subparagraph (3) of this paragraph.

(ii) The rule in subdivision (i) of this subparagraph may be illustrated by the following example:

Example. M, a duly ordained minister, is engaged by N University to teach history and mathematics. He performs no other service for N although from time to time he performs marriages and conducts funerals for relatives and friends. N University is neither a religious organization nor operated as an integral agency of a religious organization. M is not performing the service for N pursuant to an assignment or des-

ignation by his ecclesiastical superiors. The service performed by M for N University is not in the exercise of his ministry. However, service performed by M in performing marriages and conducting funerals is in the exercise of his ministry.

(3) Service performed by a duly ordained, commissioned, or licensed minister of a church as an employee of the United States, or a State, Territory, or possession of the United States, or the District of Columbia, or a foreign government, or a political subdivision of any of the foregoing, is not considered to be in the exercise of his ministry for purposes of the taxes, even though such service may involve the ministration of sacerdotal functions or the conduct of religious worship. Thus, for example, service performed by an individual as a chaplain in the Armed Forces of the United States is considered to be performed by a commissioned officer in his capacity as such, and not by a minister in the exercise of his ministry. Similarly, service performed by an employee of a State as a chaplain in a State prison is considered to be performed by a civil servant of the State and not by a minister in the exercise of his ministry.

(d) *Service in the exercise of duties required by a religious order.*—Service performed by a member of a religious order in the exercise of duties required by such order includes all duties required of the member by the order. The nature or extent of such service is immaterial so long as it is a service which he is directed or required to perform by his ecclesiastical superiors. [Reg. § 31.3121(b)(8)-1.]

☐ [*T.D.* 6190, 7-14-56. *Republished in T.D.* 6516, 12-20-60. *Amended by T.D.* 7280, 7-10-73.]

>>>→ *Caution: This regulation has not been amended to reflect the changes in nonprofit organization status under P.L. 98-21.*

[Reg. § 31.3121(b)(8)-2]

§ 31.3121(b)(8)-2. Services in employ of religious, charitable, educational, or certain other organizations exempt from income.—(a) Services performed by an employee in the employ of a religious, charitable, educational, or other organization described in section 501(c)(3) which is exempt from income tax under section 501(a) are excepted from employment. However, this exception does not apply to services with respect to which a certificate, filed pursuant to section 3121(k) or (r), section 1426(l) of the Internal Revenue Code of 1939, is in effect. For provisions relating to the services with respect to which such a certificate is in effect, see § 31.3121(k)-1 and 31.3121(r)-1.

(b) For provisions relating to exemption from income tax of an organization described in section 501(c)(3), see Part 1 of this chapter (Income Tax Regulations). For provisions relating to waiver by an organization of its exemption from the taxes imposed by sections 3101 and 3111, see § 31.3121(k)-1. See also § 31.3121(b)(8)-1, relating to services performed by a minister of a church in the exercise of his ministry or by a member of

a religious order in the exercise of duties required by such order; § 31.3121(b)(10)-1, relating to services for remuneration of less than $50 for calendar quarter in the employ of certain organizations exempt from income tax; § 31.3121(b)(10)-2, relating to services performed in the employ of a school, college, or university by certain students; and § 31.3121(b)(13)-1, relating to services performed by certain student nurses and hospital interns. [Reg. § 31.3121(b)(8)-2.]

☐ [*T.D.* 6190, 7-14-56. *Republished in T.D.* 6516, 12-20-60. *Amended by T.D.* 7280, 7-10-73.]

[Reg. § 31.3121(b)(9)-1]

§ 31.3121(b)(9)-1. Railroad industry; services performed by an employee or an employee representative as defined in section 3231.—Services performed by an individual as an "employee" or as an "employee representative," as those terms are defined in section 3231, are excepted from employment. For definitions of employee and employee representative, see §§ 31.3231(b)-1 and 31.3231(c)-1. [Reg. § 31.312(b)(9)-1.]

☐ [*T.D.* 6190, 7-14-56.]

»»→ *Caution: This regulation has not been amended to reflect the new test for low-paid employees of exempt organizations.*

[Reg. §31.3121(b)(10)-1]

§31.3121(b)(10)-1. **Services for remuneration of less than $50 for calendar quarter in the employ of certain organizations exempt from income tax.**—(a) Services performed by an employee in a calendar quarter in the employ of an organization exempt from income tax under section 501(a) (other than an organization described in section 401(a)) or under section 521 are excepted from employment, if the remuneration for the services is less than $50. The test relating to remuneration of $50 is based on the remuneration earned during a calendar quarter rather than on the remuneration paid in a calendar quarter. The exception applies separately with respect to each organization for which the employee renders services in a calendar quarter. The type of services performed by the employee and the place where the services are performed are immaterial; the statutory tests are the character of the organization in the employ of which the services are performed and the amount of the remuneration for services performed by the employee in the calendar quarter. For provisions relating to exemption from income tax under section 501(a) or 521, see Part 1 of this chapter (Income Tax Regulations).

Example (1). X is a local lodge of a fraternal organization and is exempt from income tax under section 501(a) as an organization of the character described in section 501(c)(8). X has two paid employees, A, who serves exclusively as recording secretary for the lodge, and B, who performs services for the lodge as janitor of its clubhouse. For services performed during the first calendar quarter of 1955 (that is, January 1, 1955, through March 31, 1955, both dates inclusive) A earns a total of $30. For services performed during the same calendar quarter B earns $180. Since the remuneration for the services performed by A during such quarter is less than $50, all of such services are excepted, and the taxes do not attach with respect to any of the remuneration for such services. Since the remuneration for the services performed by B during such quarter, however, is not less than $50, none of such services are excepted, and the taxes attach with respect to all of the remuneration for such services (that is, $180) as and when paid.

Example (2). The facts are the same as in example (1), above, except that on April 1, 1955, A's salary is increased and, for services performed during the calendar quarter beginning on that date (that is, April 1, 1955, through June 30, 1955, both dates inclusive), A earns a total of $60. Although all of the services performed by A during the first quarter were excepted, none of A's services performed during the second quarter are excepted since the remuneration for such services is not less than $50. The taxes attach with respect to all of the remuneration for services performed during the second quarter (that is, $60) as and when paid.

Example (3). The facts are the same as in example (1), above, except that A earns $120 for services performed during the year 1955, and such amount is paid to him in a lump sum at the end of the year. The services performed by A in any calendar quarter during the year are excepted if the portion of the $120 attributable to services performed in that quarter is less than $50. If, however, the portion of the $120 attributable to services performed in any calendar quarter during the year is not less than $50, the services during that quarter are not excepted, and the taxes attach with respect to that portion of the remuneration attributable to his services in that quarter.

(b) See §31.3121(b)(8)-2, relating to services performed in the employ of religious, charitable, educational, and certain other organizations exempt from income tax; §31.3121(b)(8)-1, relating to services performed by a minister of a church in the exercise of his ministry or by a member of a religious order in the exercise of duties required by such order; §31.3121(b)(10)-2, relating to services performed by certain students in the employ of a school, college, or university or of a nonprofit organization auxiliary to a school, college, or university; and §31.3121(b)(13)-1, relating to services performed by certain student nurses and hospital interns. [Reg. §31.3121(b)(10)-1.]

☐ [T.D. 6190, 7-14-56. *Republished in T.D.* 6516, 12-20-60. *Amended by T.D.* 7373, 7-24-75.]

[Reg. §31.3121(b)(10)-2]

§31.3121(b)(10)-2. **Services performed by certain students in the employ of a school, college, or university, or of a nonprofit organization auxiliary to a school, college, or university.**—(a) *General rule.*—(1) Services performed in the employ of a school, college, or university within the meaning of paragraph (c) of this section (whether or not the organization is exempt from income tax) are excepted from employment, if the services are performed by a student within the meaning of paragraph (d) of this section who is enrolled and is regularly attending classes at the school, college, or university.

(2) Services performed in the employ of an organization which is—

(i) Described in section 509(a)(3) and §1.509(a)-4;

(ii) Organized, and at all times thereafter operated, exclusively for the benefit of, to perform the functions of, or to carry out the purposes of a school, college, or university within the meaning of paragraph (c) of this section; and

(iii) Operated, supervised, or controlled by or in connection with the school, college, or university; are excepted from employment, if the services are performed by a student who is enrolled and regularly attending classes within the meaning of paragraph (d) of this section at the school, college, or university. The preceding sentence shall not apply to services performed in the employ of a school, college, or university of a State or a political subdivision thereof by a student referred to in section 218(c)(5) of the Social Security Act (42 U.S.C. 418(c)(5)) if such services are covered under the agreement between the Commissioner of Social Security and such State entered into pursuant to section 218 of such Act. For the definitions of "operated, supervised, or controlled by", "supervised or controlled in connection with", and "operated in connection with", see paragraphs (g), (h), and (i), respectively, of § 1.509(a)-4.

(b) *Statutory tests.*—For purposes of this section, if an employee has the status of a student within the meaning of paragraph (d) of this section, the amount of remuneration for services performed by the employee, the type of services performed by the employee, and the place where the services are performed are not material. The statutory tests are:

(1) The character of the organization in the employ of which the services are performed as a school, college, or university within the meaning of paragraph (c) of this section, or as an organization described in paragraph (a)(2) of this section, and

(2) The status of the employee as a student enrolled and regularly attending classes within the meaning of paragraph (d) of this section at the school, college, or university within the meaning of paragraph (c) of this section by which the employee is employed or with which the employee's employer is affiliated within the meaning of paragraph (a)(2) of this section.

(c) *School, college, or university.*—An organization is a *school, college, or university* within the meaning of section 3121(b)(10) if its primary function is the presentation of formal instruction, it normally maintains a regular faculty and curriculum, and it normally has a regularly enrolled body of students in attendance at the place where its educational activities are regularly carried on. See section 170(b)(1)(A)(ii) and the regulations thereunder.

(d) *Student status—general rule.*—Whether an employee has the status of a student performing the services shall be determined based on the relationship of the employee with the organization employing the employee. In order to have the status of a student, the employee must perform services in the employ of a school, college, or university within the meaning of paragraph (c) of this section at which the employee is enrolled and regularly attending classes in pursuit of a course of study within the meaning of paragraphs (d)(1) and (2) of this section. In addition, the employee's services must be incident to and for the purpose of pursuing a course of study within the meaning of paragraph (d)(3) of this section at such school, college, or university. An employee who performs services in the employ of an affiliated organization within the meaning of paragraph (a)(2) of this section must be enrolled and regularly attending classes at the affiliated school, college, or university within the

meaning of paragraph (c) of this section in pursuit of a course of study within the meaning of paragraphs (d)(1) and (2) of this section. In addition, the employee's services must be incident to and for the purpose of pursuing a course of study within the meaning of paragraph (d)(3) of this section at such school, college, or university.

(1) *Enrolled and regularly attending classes.*—An employee must be enrolled and regularly attending classes at a school, college, or university within the meaning of paragraph (c) of this section at which the employee is employed to have the status of a student within the meaning of section 3121(b)(10). An employee is enrolled within the meaning of section 3121(b)(10) if the employee is registered for a course or courses creditable toward an educational credential described in paragraph (d)(2) of this section. In addition, the employee must be regularly attending classes to have the status of a student. For purposes of this paragraph (d)(1), a class is an instructional activity led by a faculty member or other qualified individual hired by the school, college, or university within the meaning of paragraph (c) of this section for identified students following an established curriculum. Traditional classroom activities are not the sole means of satisfying this requirement. For example, research activities under the supervision of a faculty advisor necessary to complete the requirements for a Ph.D. degree may constitute classes within the meaning of section 3121(b)(10). The frequency of these and similar activities determines whether an employee may be considered to be regularly attending classes.

(2) *Course of study.*—An employee must be pursuing a course of study in order to have the status of a student. A course of study is one or more courses the completion of which fulfills the requirements necessary to receive an educational credential granted by a school, college, or university within the meaning of paragraph (c) of this section. For purposes of this paragraph, an educational credential is a degree, certificate, or other recognized educational credential granted by an organization described in paragraph (c) of this section. A course of study also includes one or more courses at a school, college or university within the meaning of paragraph (c) of this section the completion of which fulfills the requirements necessary for the employee to sit for an examination required to receive certification by a recognized organization in a field.

(3) *Incident to and for the purpose of pursuing a course of study.*—(i) *General rule.*—An employee's services must be incident to and for the purpose of pursuing a course of study in order for the employee to have the status of a student. Whether an employee's services are incident to and for the purpose of pursuing a course of study shall be determined on the basis of the relationship of the employee with the organization for which such services are performed as an employee. The educational aspect of the relationship between the employer and the employee, as

compared to the service aspect of the relationship, must be predominant in order for the employee's services to be incident to and for the purpose of pursuing a course of study. The educational aspect of the relationship is evaluated based on all the relevant facts and circumstances related to the educational aspect of the relationship. The service aspect of the relationship is evaluated based on all the relevant facts and circumstances related to the employee's employment. The evaluation of the service aspect of the relationship is not affected by the fact that the services performed by the employee may have an educational, instructional, or training aspect. Except as provided in paragraph (d)(3)(iii) of this section, whether the educational aspect or the service aspect of an employee's relationship with the employer is predominant is determined by considering all the relevant facts and circumstances. Relevant factors in evaluating the educational and service aspects of an employee's relationship with the employer are described in paragraphs (d)(3)(iv) and (v) of this section respectively. There may be facts and circumstances that are relevant in evaluating the educational and service aspects of the relationship in addition to those described in paragraphs (d)(3)(iv) and (v) of this section.

(ii) *Student status determined with respect to each academic term.*—Whether an employee's services are incident to and for the purpose of pursuing a course of study is determined separately with respect to each academic term. If the relevant facts and circumstances with respect to an employee's relationship with the employer change significantly during an academic term, whether the employee's services are incident to and for the purpose of pursuing a course of study is reevaluated with respect to services performed during the remainder of the academic term.

(iii) *Full-time employee.*—The services of a full-time employee are not incident to and for the purpose of pursuing a course of study. The determination of whether an employee is a full-time employee is based on the employer's standards and practices, except regardless of the employer's classification of the employee, an employee whose normal work schedule is 40 hours or more per week is considered a full-time employee. An employee's normal work schedule is not affected by increases in hours worked caused by work demands unforeseen at the start of an academic term. However, whether an employee is a full-time employee is reevaluated for the remainder of the academic term if the employee changes employment positions with the employer. An employee's work schedule during academic breaks is not considered in determining whether the employee's normal work schedule is 40 hours or more per week. The determination of an employee's normal work schedule is not affected by the fact that the services performed by the employee may have an educational, instructional, or training aspect.

(iv) *Evaluating educational aspect.*—The educational aspect of an employee's relationship with the employer is evaluated based on all the relevant facts and circumstances related to the educational aspect of the relationship. The educational aspect of an employee's relationship with the employer is generally evaluated based on the employee's course workload. Whether an employee's course workload is sufficient in order for the employee's employment to be incident to and for the purpose of pursuing a course of study depends on the particular facts and circumstances. A relevant factor in evaluating an employee's course workload is the employee's course workload relative to a full-time course workload at the school, college or university within the meaning of paragraph (c) of this section at which the employee is enrolled and regularly attending classes.

(v) *Evaluating service aspect.*—The service aspect of an employee's relationship with the employer is evaluated based on the facts and circumstances related to the employee's employment. Services of an employee with the status of a full-time employee within the meaning of paragraph (d)(3)(iii) of this section are not incident to and for the purpose of pursuing a course of study. Relevant factors in evaluating the service aspect of an employee's relationship with the employer are described in paragraphs (d)(3)(v)(A), (B), and (C) of this section.

(A) *Normal work schedule and hours worked.*—If an employee is not a full-time employee within the meaning of paragraph (d)(3)(iii) of this section, then the employee's normal work schedule and number of hours worked per week are relevant factors in evaluating the service aspect of the employee's relationship with the employer. As an employee's normal work schedule or actual number of hours worked approaches 40 hours per week, it is more likely that the service aspect of the employee's relationship with the employer is predominant. The determination of an employee's normal work schedule and actual number of hours worked is not affected by the fact that some of the services performed by the employee may have an educational, instructional, or training aspect.

(B) *Professional employee.*—(1) If an employee has the status of a professional employee, then that suggests. the service aspect of the employee's relationship with the employer is predominant. A professional employee is an employee—

(i) Whose primary duty consists of the performance of work requiring knowledge of an advanced type in a field of science or learning customarily acquired by a prolonged course of specialized intellectual instruction and study, as distinguished from a general academic education, from an apprenticeship, and from training in the performance of routine mental, manual, or physical processes;

(ii) Whose work requires the consistent exercise of discretion and judgment in its performance; and

(iii) Whose work is predominantly intellectual and varied in character (as opposed to routine mental, manual, mechanical, or physical work) and is of such character that the output produced or the result accomplished cannot be standardized in relation to a given period of time.

(2) Licensed, professional employee.—If an employee is a licensed, professional employee, then that further suggests the service aspect of the employee's relationship with the employer is predominant. An employee is a licensed, professional employee if the employee is required to be licensed under state or local law to work in the field in which the employee performs services and the employee is a professional employee within the meaning of paragraph (d)(3)(v)(B)(1) of this section.

(C) Employment benefits.—Whether an employee is eligible to receive one or more employment benefits is a relevant factor in evaluating the service aspect of an employee's relationship with the employer. For example, eligibility to receive vacation, paid holiday, and paid sick leave benefits; eligibility to participate in a retirement plan or arrangement described in sections 401(a), 403(b), or 457(a); or eligibility to receive employment benefits such as reduced tuition (other than qualified tuition reduction under section 117(d)(5) provided to a teaching or research assistant who is a graduate student), or benefits under sections 79 (life insurance), 127 (qualified educational assistance), 129 (dependent care assistance programs), or 137 (adoption assistance) suggest that the service aspect of an employee's relationship with the employer is predominant. Eligibility to receive health insurance employment benefits is not considered in determining whether the service aspect of an employee's relationship with the employer is predominant. The weight to be given the fact that an employee is eligible for a particular employment benefit may vary depending on the type of benefit. For example, eligibility to participate in a retirement plan is generally more significant than eligibility to receive a dependent care employment benefit. Additional weight is given to the fact that an employee is eligible to receive an employment benefit if the benefit is generally provided by the employer to employees in positions generally held by non-students. Less weight is given to the fact that an employee is eligible to receive an employment benefit if eligibility for the benefit is mandated by state or local law.

(e) *Examples.*—The following examples illustrate the principles of paragraphs (a) through (d) of this section:

Example 1. (i) Employee C is employed by State University T to provide services as a clerk in T's administrative offices, and is enrolled and regularly attending classes at T in pursuit of a

B.S. degree in biology. C has a course workload during the academic term which constitutes a full-time course workload at T. C is considered a part-time employee by T during the academic term, and C's normal work schedule is 20 hours per week, but occasionally due to work demands unforeseen at the start of the academic term C works 40 hours or more during a week. C is compensated by hourly wages, and receives no other compensation or employment benefits.

(ii) In this *example,* C is employed by T, a school, college, or university within the meaning of paragraph (c) of this section. C is enrolled and regularly attending classes at T in pursuit of a course of study. C is not a full-time employee based on T's standards, and C's normal work schedule does not cause C to have the status of a full-time employee, even though C may occasionally work 40 hours or more during a week due to unforeseen work demands. C's part-time employment relative to C's full-time course workload indicates that the educational aspect of C's relationship with T is predominant. Additional facts supporting this conclusion are that C is not a professional employee, and C does not receive any employment benefits. Thus, C's services are incident to and for the purpose of pursuing a course of study. Accordingly, C's services are excepted from employment under section 3121(b)(10).

Example 2. (i) Employee D is employed in the accounting department of University U, and is enrolled and regularly attending classes at U in pursuit of an M.B.A. degree. D has a course workload which constitutes a half-time course workload at U. D is considered a full-time employee by U under U's standards and practices.

(ii) In this *example,* D is employed by U, a school, college, or university within the meaning of paragraph (c) of this section. In addition, D is enrolled and regularly attending classes at U in pursuit of a course of study. However, because D is considered a full-time employee by U under its standards and practices, D's services are not incident to and for the purpose of pursuing a course of study. Accordingly, D's services are not excepted from employment under section 3121(b)(10).

Example 3. (i) The facts are the same as in Example 2, except that D is not considered a full-time employee by U, and D's normal work schedule is 32 hours per week. In addition, D's work is repetitive in nature and does not require the consistent exercise of discretion and judgment, and is not predominantly intellectual and varied in character. However, D receives vacation, sick leave, and paid holiday employment benefits, and D is eligible to participate in a retirement plan maintained by U described in section 401(a).

(ii) In this *example,* D's half-time course workload relative to D's hours worked and eligibility for employment benefits indicates that the service aspect of D's relationship with U is predominant, and thus D's services are not incident to and for the purpose of pursuing a course of study. Accordingly, D's services are not excepted from employment under section 3121(b)(10).

Example 4. (i) Employee E is employed by University V to provide patient care services at a teaching hospital that is an unincorporated division of V. These services are performed as part of a medical residency program in a medical specialty sponsored by V. The residency program in which E participates is accredited by the Accreditation Counsel for Graduate Medical Education. Upon completion of the program, E will receive a certificate of completion, and be eligible to sit for an examination required to be certified by a recognized organization in the medical specialty. E's normal work schedule, which includes services having an educational, instructional, or training aspect, is 40 hours or more per week.

(ii) In this *example*, E is employed by V, a school, college, or university within the meaning of paragraph (c) of this section. However, E's normal work schedule calls for E to perform services 40 or more hours per week. E is therefore a full-time employee, and the fact that some of E's services have an educational, instructional, or training aspect does not affect that conclusion. Thus, E's services are not incident to and for the purpose of pursuing a course of study. Accordingly, E's services are not excepted from employment under section 3121(b)(10) and there is no need to consider other relevant factors, such as whether E is a professional employee or whether E is eligible for employment benefits.

Example 5. (i) Employee F is employed in the facilities management department of University W. F has a B.S. degree in engineering, and is completing the work experience required to sit for an examination to become a professional engineer eligible for licensure under state or local law. F is not attending classes at W.

(ii) In this *example*, F is employed by W, a school, college, or university within the meaning of paragraph (c) of this section. However, F is not enrolled and regularly attending classes at W in pursuit of a course of study. F's work experience required to sit for the examination is not a course of study for purposes of paragraph (d)(2) of this section. Accordingly, F's services are not excepted from employment under section 3121(b)(10).

Example 6. (i) Employee G is employed by Employer X as an apprentice in a skilled trade. X is a subcontractor providing services in the field in which G wishes to specialize. G is pursuing a certificate in the skilled trade from Community College C. G is performing services for X pursuant to an internship program sponsored by C under which its students gain experience, and receive credit toward a certificate in the trade.

(ii) In this *example*, G is employed by X. X is not a school, college or university within the meaning of paragraph (c) of this section. Thus, the exception from employment under section 3121(b)(10) is not available with respect to G's services for X.

Example 7. (i) Employee H is employed by a cosmetology school Y at which H is enrolled and

regularly attending classes in pursuit of a certificate of completion. Y's primary function is to carry on educational activities to prepare its students to work in the field of cosmetology. Prior to issuing a certificate, Y requires that its students gain experience in cosmetology services by performing services for the general public on Y's premises. H is scheduled to work and in fact works significantly less than 30 hours per week. H's work does not require knowledge of an advanced type in a field of science or learning, nor is it predominantly intellectual and varied in character. H receives remuneration in the form of hourly compensation from Y for providing cosmetology services to clients of Y, and does not receive any other compensation and is not eligible for employment benefits provided by Y.

(ii) In this *example*, H is employed by Y, a school, college or university within the meaning of paragraph (c) of this section, and is enrolled and regularly attending classes at Y in pursuit of a course of study. Factors indicating the educational aspect of H's relationship with Y is predominant are that H's hours worked are significantly less than 30 per week, H is not a professional employee, and H is not eligible for employment benefits. Based on the relevant facts and circumstances, the educational aspect of H's relationship with Y is predominant. Thus, H's services are incident to and for the purpose of pursuing a course of study. Accordingly, H's services are excepted from employment under section 3121(b)(10).

Example 8. (i) Employee J is a graduate teaching assistant at University Z. J is enrolled and regularly attending classes at Z in pursuit of a graduate degree. J has a course workload which constitutes a full-time course workload at Z. J's normal work schedule is 20 hours per week, but occasionally due to work demands unforeseen at the start of the academic term J works more than 40 hours during a week. J's duties include grading quizzes and exams pursuant to guidelines set forth by the professor, providing class and laboratory instruction pursuant to a lesson plan developed by the professor, and preparing laboratory equipment for demonstrations. J receives a cash stipend and employment benefits in the form of eligibility to make elective employee contributions to an arrangement described in section 403(b). In addition, J receives qualified tuition reduction benefits within the meaning of section 117(d)(5) with respect to the tuition charged for the credits earned for being a graduate teaching assistant.

(ii) In this *example*, J is employed by Z, a school, college, or university within the meaning of paragraph (c) of this section, and is enrolled and regularly attending classes at Z in pursuit of a course of study. J's full-time course workload relative to J's normal work schedule of 20 hours per week indicates that the educational aspect of J's relationship with Z is predominant. In addition, J is not a professional employee because J's work does not require the consistent exercise of discretion and judgment in its performance. On the other hand, the fact that J receives employment benefits in the form of eligibility to make elective employee contributions to an arrangement described in section 403(b) indicates that the employment aspect of J's relationship with Z is predominant. Balancing the relevant facts and circumstances, the educational aspect of J's relationship with Z is predominant. Thus, J's services are incident to and for the purpose of pursuing a course of study. Accordingly, J services are excepted from employment under section 3121(b)(10).

(f) *Effective date.*—Paragraphs (a), (b), (c), (d) and (e) of this section apply to services performed on or after April 1, 2005.

(g) For provisions relating to domestic service performed by a student in a local college club, or local chapter of a college fraternity or sorority, see § 31.3121(b)(2)-1. [Reg. § 31.3121(b)(10)-2.]

☐ [*T.D. 6190,* 7-14-56. *Republished in T.D. 6516,* 12-20-60. *Amended by T.D. 7373, 7-24-75 and T.D. 9167, 12-20-2004.*]

[Reg. § 31.3121(b)(11)-1]

§ 31.3121(b)(11)-1. Services in the employ of foreign government.—(a) Services performed by an employee in the employ of a foreign government are excepted from employment. The exception includes not only services performed by ambassadors, ministers, and other diplomatic officers and employees but also services performed as a consular or other officer or employee of a foreign government, or as a non-diplomatic representative thereof.

(b) For purposes of this exception, the citizenship or residence of the employee is immaterial. It is also immaterial whether the foreign government grants an equivalent exemption with respect to similar services performed in the foreign country by citizens of the United States. [Reg. § 31.2121(b)(11)-1.]

☐ [*T.D. 6190,* 7-14-56. *Republished in T.D. 6516,* 12-20-60.]

[Reg. § 31.3121(b)(12)-1]

§ 31.3121(b)(12)-1. Services in employ of wholly owned instrumentality of foreign government.—(a) Services performed by an employee in the employ of certain instrumentalities of a foreign government are excepted from employment. The exception includes all services performed in the employ of an instrumentality of the government of a foreign country, if—

(1) The instrumentality is wholly owned by the foreign government;

(2) The services are of a character similar to those performed in foreign countries by employees of the United States Government or of an instrumentality thereof; and

(3) The Secretary of State certifies to the Secretary of the Treasury that the foreign government, with respect to whose instrumentality and employees thereof exemption is claimed, grants an equivalent exemption with respect to services performed in the foreign country by employees

of the United States Government and of instrumentalities thereof.

(b) For purposes of this exception, the citizenship or residence of the employee is immaterial. [Reg. § 31.31212(b)(12)-1.]

☐ [*T.D. 6190,* 7-14-56. *Republished in T.D. 6516,* 12-20-60.]

[Reg. § 31.3121(b)(13)-1]

§ 31.3121(b)(13)-1. Services of student nurse or hospital intern.—(a) Services performed as a student nurse in the employ of a hospital or a nurses' training school are excepted from employment, if the student nurse is enrolled and regularly attending classes in a nurses' training school and such nurses' training school is chartered or approved pursuant to State law.

(b) Services performed before 1966 as an intern (as distinguished from a resident doctor), in the employ of a hospital are excepted from employment, if the intern has completed a 4 years' course in a medical school chartered or approved pursuant to State law. [Reg. § 31.3121(b)(13)-1.]

☐ [*T.D. 6190,* 7-14-56. *Republished in T.D. 6516,* 12-20-60. *Amended by T.D. 6983, 12-4-68.*]

[Reg. § 31.3121(b)(14)-1]

§ 31.3121(b)(14)-1. Services in delivery or distribution of newspapers, shopping news, or magazines.—(a) *Services of individuals under age 18.*—Services performed by an employee under the age of 18 in the delivery or distribution of newspapers or shopping news, not including delivery or distribution (as, for example, by a regional distributor) to any point for subsequent delivery or distribution, are excepted from employment. Thus, the services performed by an employee under the age of 18 in making house-to-house delivery or sale of newspapers or shopping news, including handbills and other similar types of advertising material, are excepted from employment. The services are excepted irrespective of the form or method of compensation. Incidental services by the employee who makes the house-to-house delivery, such as services in assembling newspapers, are considered to be within the exception. The exception continues only during the time that the employee is under the age of 18.

(b) *Services of individuals of any age.*—Services performed by an employee in, and at the time of, the sale of newspapers or magazines to ultimate consumers under an arrangement under which the newspapers or magazines are to be sold by him at a fixed price, his compensation being based on the retention of the excess of such price over the amount at which the newspapers or magazines are charged to him, are excepted from employment. The services are excepted whether or not the employee is guaranteed a minimum amount of compensation for such services, or is entitled to be credited with the unsold newspapers or magazines turned back. Moreover, the services are excepted without regard to the age of the employee. Services performed other than at the time of sale to the ultimate consumer are not within the exception. Thus, the services of a regional distributor which are antecedent to but not immediately part of the sale to the ultimate consumer are not within the exception. However, incidental services by the employee who makes the sale to the ultimate consumer, such as services in assembling newspapers or in taking newspapers or magazines to the place of sale, are considered to be within the exception. [Reg. §31.3121(b)(14)-1.]

□ [T.D. 6190, 7-14-56. *Republished in T.D.* 6516, 12-20-60.]

[Reg. §31.3121(b)(15)-1]

§31.3121(b)(15)-1. Services in employ of international organization.—(a) Subject to the provisions of section 1 of the International Organizations Immunities Act (22 U.S.C. 288), services performed in the employ of an international organization as defined in section 7701(a)(18) are excepted from employment.

(b)(1) Section 7701(a)(18) provides as follows:

Sec. 7701. *Definitions.* (a) When used in this title, where not otherwise distinctly expressed or manifestly incompatible with the intent thereof—

* * *

(18) *International organization.* The term "international organization" means a public international organization entitled to enjoy privileges, exemptions, and immunities as an international organization under the International Organizations Immunities Act (22 U.S.C. 288-288f).

(2) Section 1 of the International Organizations Immunities Act provides as follows:

Sec. 1. [*International Organizations Immunities Act.*]For the purposes of this title [International Organizations Immunities Act], the term "international organization" means a public international organization in which the United States participates pursuant to any treaty or under the authority of any Act of Congress authorizing such participation or making an appropriation for such participation, and which shall have been designated by the President through appropriate Executive order as being entitled to enjoy the privileges, exemptions, and immunities herein provided. The President shall be authorized, in the light of the functions performed by any such international organization, by appropriate Executive order to withhold or withdraw from any such organization or its officers or employees any of the privileges, exemptions, and immunities provided for in this title (including the amendments made by this title) or to condition or limit the enjoyment by any such organization or its officers or employees of any such privilege, exemption, or immunity. The President shall be authorized, if in his judgment such action should be justified by reason of the abuse by an international organization or its officers and employees of the privileges, exemptions, and immunities herein provided or for any other reason, at any time to revoke the designa-

tion of any international organization under this section, whereupon the international organization in question shall cease to be classed as an international organization for the purposes of this title. [Reg. §31.3121(b)(15)-1.]

□ [T.D. 6190, 7-14-56. *Republished in T.D.* 6516, 12-20-60.]

[Reg. §31.3121(b)(16)-1]

§31.3121(b)(16)-1. Services performed under share-farming arrangement.—(a) The term "employment" does not include services performed by an individual under an arrangement with the owner or tenant of land pursuant to which—

(1) Such individual undertakes to produce agricultural or horticultural commodities (including livestock, bees, poultry, and fur-bearing animals and wildlife) on such land,

(2) The agricultural or horticultural commodities produced by such individual, or the proceeds therefrom, are to be divided between such individual and such owner or tenant, and

(3) The amount of such individual's share depends on the amount of the agricultural or horticultural commodities produced.

For purposes of this exception, the arrangement pursuant to which the individual's services are performed must meet the specified statutory conditions.

(b) If the arrangement between the parties provides that the individual who undertakes to produce a crop or livestock is to be compensated at a specified rate of pay or is to receive a fixed sum of money or a stipulated quantity of the commodities to be produced, without regard to the amount actually produced, as distinguished from a proportionate share of the crop or livestock, or the proceeds therefrom, the services performed by such individual in the production of such crop or livestock is not within the exception.

(c) For provisions relating to the status, under the Self-Employment Contributions Act of 1954, of the services which are excepted from "employment" under this section, see the regulations under section 1402(a) in Part 1 of this chapter (Income Tax Regulations). [Reg. §31.3121(16)-1.]

□ [T.D. 6744, 7-2-64.]

[Reg. §31.3121(b)(17)-1]

§31.3121(b)(17)-1. Services in employ of Communist organization.—The term "employment" does not include services performed in the employ of any organization in any calendar quarter beginning after June 30, 1956, and during any part of which such organization is registered, or there is in effect a final order of the Subversive Activities Control Board requiring such organization to register, under the Internal Security Act of 1950 (50 U.S.C. 781 *et seq.*), as amended, as a Communist-action organization, a Communist-front organization, or a Communist-infiltrated organization. [Reg. §31.3121(b)(17)-1.]

□ [T.D. 6744, 7-2-64.]

[Reg. §31.3121(b)(18)-1]

§31.3121(b)(18)-1. Services performed by a resident of the Republic of the Philippines while temporarily in Guam.—(a) Services performed after 1960 by a resident of the Republic of the Philippines while in Guam on a temporary basis as a nonimmigrant alien admitted to Guam pursuant to section 101(a)(15)(H)(ii) of the Immigration and Nationality Act (8 U.S.C. 1101) are excepted from employment.

(b) Section 101(a)(15)(H) of the Immigration and Nationality Act provides as follows:

* * *

Sec. 101. *Definitions.* [Immigration and Nationality Act (66 Stat. 166)]

(a) As used in this chapter—

* * *

≫→ *Caution: This regulation has not been amended to reflect changes enacted by the Social Security Independence and Program Improvements Act of 1994 (P.L. 103-296).*

[Reg. §31.3121(b)(19)-1]

§31.3121(b)(19)-1. Services of certain nonresident aliens.—(a)(1) Services performed after 1961 by a nonresident alien individual who is temporarily present in the United States as a nonimmigrant under subparagraph (F) or (J) of section 101(a)(15) of the Immigration and Nationality Act (8 U.S.C. 1101), as amended, are excepted from employment if the services are performed to carry out a purpose for which the individual was admitted. For purposes of this section an alien individual who is temporarily present in the United States as a nonimmigrant under such subparagraph (F) or (J) is deemed to be a nonresident alien individual. The preceding sentence does not apply to the extent it is inconsistent with section 7701(b) and the regulations under that section. A nonresident alien individual who is temporarily present in the United States as a nonimmigrant under subparagraph (J) includes an alien individual admitted to the United States as an "exchange visitor" under section 201 of the United States Information and Educational Exchange Act of 1948 (22 U.S.C. 1446).

(2) If services are performed by a nonresident alien individual's alien spouse or minor child, who is temporarily present in the United States as a nonimmigrant under subparagraph (F) or (J) of section 101(a)(15) of the Immigration and Nationality Act, as amended, the services are not deemed for purposes of this section to be performed to carry out a purpose for which such individual was admitted. The services of such spouse or child are excepted from employment under this section only if the spouse or child was admitted for a purpose specified in such subparagraph (F) or (J) and if the services are performed to carry out such purpose.

(b) Section 101 of the Immigration and Nationality Act (8 U.S.C. 1101), as amended, provides in part as follows:

(15) The term "immigrant" means every alien except an alien who is within one of the following classes of nonimmigrant aliens—

* * *

(H) An alien having a residence in a foreign country which he has no intention of abandoning (i) who is of distinguished merit and ability and who is coming temporarily to the United States to perform temporary services of an exceptional nature requiring merit and ability; or (ii) who is coming temporarily to the United States to perform other temporary services or labor, if unemployed persons capable of performing such service or labor cannot be found in this country; or (iii) who is coming temporarily to the United States as an industrial trainee;

* * *

[Reg. §31.3121(b)(18)-1.]

☐ [T.D. 6744, 7-2-64.]

Sec. 101. *Definitions.* [Immigration and Nationality Act (66 Stat. 166)]

(a) As used in this chapter—

* * *

(15) The term "immigrant" means every alien except an alien who is within one of the following classes of nonimmigrant aliens—

* * *

(F)(i) An alien having a residence in a foreign country which he has no intention of abandoning, who is a bona fide student qualified to pursue a full course of study and who seeks to enter the United States temporarily and solely for the purpose of pursuing such a course of study at an established institution of learning or other recognized place of study in the United States, particularly designated by him and approved by the Attorney General after consultation with the Office of Education of the United States, which institution or place of study shall have agreed to report to the Attorney General the termination of attendance of each nonimmigrant student, and if any such institution of learning or place of study fails to make reports promptly the approval shall be withdrawn, and (ii) the alien spouse and minor children of any such alien if accompanying him or following to join him;

* * *

(J) An alien having a residence in a foreign country which he has no intention of abandoning who is a bona fide student, scholar, trainee, teacher, professor, research assistant, specialist, or leader in a field of specialized knowledge or skill, or other person of similar description who is coming temporarily to the United States as a participant in a program designated by the Secretary of State, for the purpose of teaching, instructing or lecturing, studying, observing, conducting research, consulting, demonstrating special skills, or receiving training and who, if he is coming to the United States to participate in a program under which he will receive graduate medical education or training, also meets the requirements of section 1182(j) of this title, and of the alien spouse and minor children of any such alien if accompanying him or following to join him.

* * *

[Sec. 101, Immigration and Nationality Act, as amended by sec. 101, Act of June 27, 1952, 66 Stat. 166; sec.109, Act of Sept. 21,1961. 75 Stat. 534]

[Reg. § 31.3121(b)(19)-1.]

☐ [*T.D.* 6744, 7-2-64. *As amended by T.D.* 8411, 4-27-92. Note that Sec. 101(a)(15) of the Immigration and Nationality Act as reproduced above does not reflect current law.—CCH.]

[Reg. § 31.3121(b)(20)-1]

§ 31.3121(b)(20)-1. Service performed on a boat engaged in catching fish.—(a) *In general.*— (1) *Service performed on or after December 31, 1954, by an individual on a boat engaged in catching fish or other forms of aquatic animal life (hereinafter "fish") are excepted from employment if*—

(i) The individual receives a share of the boat's (or boats' for a fishing operation involving more than one boat) catch of fish or a share of the proceeds from the sale of the catch.

(ii) The amount of the individual's share depends solely on the amount of the boat's (or boats' for a fishing operation involving more than one boat) catch of fish.

(iii) The individual does not receive and is not entitled to receive, any cash remuneration, other than remuneration that is described in subdivision (1) of this subparagraph, and

(iv) The crew of the boat (or of each boat from which the individual receives a share of the catch) normally is made up of fewer than 10 individuals.

(2) The requirement of subdivision (ii) of subparagraph (1) is not satisfied if there exists an agreement with the boat's (or boats') owner or operator by which the individual's remuneration is determined partially or fully by a factor not dependent on the size of the catch. For example, if a boat is operated under a remuneration arrangement, *e.g.,* a collective agreement which specifies that crew members, in addition to receiving a share of the catch, are entitled to an hourly wage for repairing nets, regardless of whether this wage is actually paid, then all the crew members covered by the arrangement are entitled to receive cash remuneration other than a share of the catch and their services are not excepted from employment by section 3121(b)(20).

(3) The operating crew of a boat includes all persons on the boat (including the captain) who receive any form of remuneration in exchange for services rendered while on a boat engaged in catching fish. See § 1.6050A-1 for reporting requirements for the operator of a boat engaged in catching fish with respect to individuals performing services described in this section.

(4) During the same return period, service performed by a crew member may be excepted from employment by section 3121(b)(20) and this section for one voyage and not so excepted on a subsequent voyage on the same or on a different boat.

(5) During the same voyage, service performed by one crew member may be excepted from employment by section 3121(b)(20) and this section but service performed by another crew member may not be so excepted.

(b) *Special rule.*—Services performed after December 31, 1954, and before October 4, 1976, on a boat by an individual engaged in catching fish are not excepted from employment for any voyage (for purposes of section 3121(b) and the corresponding regulations), even though the individual satisfies the requirements of subdivision (i) through (iv) of paragraph (a)(1) of this section, if the owner or operator of the boat engaged in catching fish treated the individual as an employee. For purposes of this subparagraph, the individual was treated as an employee if—

(1) Form 941 was voluntarily filed by the boat operator or owner, regardless of whether the tax imposed by chapter 21 was withheld. For purposes of this subdivision, the filing of Form 941 is not voluntary if the filing was the result of action taken by the Service pursuant to section 6651(a) (relating to addition to the tax for failure to file tax return or to pay tax);

(2) The boat owner or operator withheld from the individual's share the tax imposed by chapter 21, regardless of whether the tax was paid over to the Service; or

(3) The boat owner or operator made full or partial payment of the tax imposed by chapter 21, unless the payment was made pursuant to section 7422(a) (relating to no civil actions for refund prior to filing claim for refund). However, for purposes of this paragraph crew members whose services, but for subdivisions (i) through (iii), would have been excepted from employment by section 3121(b)(20) are not required to pay self-employment tax on income earned in performing those services. See § 1.1402(c)-3(g). Moreover, in such cases the employer is not entitled to a refund of the employer's share of any tax imposed by chapter 21 that was paid. [Reg. § 31.3121(b)(20)-1.]

☐ [*T.D.* 7716, 8-27-80.]

[Reg. § 31.3121(c)-1]

§ 31.3121(c)-1. Included and excluded services.—(a) If a portion of the services performed by an employee for an employer during a pay period constitutes employment, and the remainder does not constitute employment, all the services performed by the employee for the employer during the period shall for purposes of the taxes be treated alike, that is, either all as included or all as excluded. The time during which the employee performs services which under section 3121(b) constitute employment, and the time during which he performs services which under such section do not constitute employment, within the pay period, determine whether all the services during the pay period shall be deemed to be included or excluded.

(b) If one-half or more of the employee's time in the employ of a particular person in a pay period is spent in performing services which constitute employment, then all the services of that employee for that person in that pay period shall be deemed to be employment.

(c) If less than one-half of the employee's time in the employ of a particular person in a pay period is spent in performing services which constitute employment, then none of the services of that employee for that person in that pay period shall be deemed to be employment.

(d) The application of the provisions of paragraphs (a), (b), and (c) of this section may be illustrated by the following example:

Example. The AB Club, which is a local college club within the meaning of section 3121(b)(2), employs D, a student who is enrolled and is regularly attending classes at a university, to perform domestic service for the club and to keep the club's books. The domestic services performed by D for the AB Club do not constitute employment, and his services as the club's bookkeeper constitute employment. D receives a payment at the end of each month for all services which he performs for the club. During a particular month D spends 60 hours in performing domestic service for the club and 40 hours as the club's bookkeeper. None of D's services during the month are deemed to be employment, since less than one-half of his services during the month constitutes employment. During another month D spends 35 hours in the performance of domestic services and 60 hours in keeping the club's books. All of D's services during the month are deemed to be employment, since one-half or more of his services during the month constitutes employment.

(e) For purposes of this section, a "pay period" is the period (of not more than 31 consecutive calendar days) for which a payment of remuneration is ordinarily made to the employee by the employer. Thus, if the periods for which payments of remuneration are made to the employee by the employer are of uniform duration, each such period constitutes a "pay period." If,

however, the periods occasionally vary in duration, the "pay period" is the period for which a payment of remuneration is ordinarily made to the employee by the employer, even though that period does not coincide with the actual period for which a particular payment of remuneration is made. For example, if an employer ordinarily pays a particular employee for each calendar week at the end of the week, but the employee receives a payment in the middle of the week for the portion of the week already elapsed and receives the remainder at the end of the week, the "pay period" is still the calendar week; or if, instead, that employee is sent on a trip by such employer and receives at the end of the third week a single remuneration payment for three weeks' services, the "pay period" is still the calendar week.

(f) If there is only one period (and such period does not exceed 31 consecutive calendar days) for which a payment of remuneration is made to the employee by the employer, such period is deemed to be a "pay period" for purposes of this section.

(g) The rules set forth in this section do not apply (1) with respect to any services performed by the employee for the employer if the periods for which such employer makes payments of remuneration to the employee vary to the extent that there is no period "for which a payment or remuneration is ordinarily made to the employee," or (2) with respect to any services performed by the employee for the employer if the period for which a payment of remuneration is ordinarily made to the employee by such employer exceeds 31 consecutive calendar days, or (3) with respect to any service performed by the employee for the employer during a pay period if any of such service is excepted by section 3121(b)(9) (see §31.3121(b)(9)-1).

(h) If during any period for which a person makes a payment of remuneration to an employee only a portion of the employee's services constitutes employment, but the rules prescribed in this section are not applicable, the taxes attach with respect to such services as constitute employment as defined in section 3121(b). [Reg. §31.3121(c)-1.]

☐ [T.D. 6190, 7-14-56. *Republished in T.D. 6516,* 12-20-60, *Amended by T.D. 7-2-64.*]

≫≫→ *Caution: Reg. §31.3121(d)-1 has not been amended to reflect §530 of P.L. 95-600 or P.L. 104-188.*

[Reg. §31.3121(d)-1]

§31.3121(d)-1. Who are employees.—(a) *In general.*—(1) Whether an individual is an employee with respect to services performed after 1954 is determined in accordance with section 3121(d) and (o) and section 3506. This section of the regulations applies with respect only to services performed after 1954. Whether an individual is an employee with respect to services performed after 1936 and before 1940 shall be determined in accordance with the applicable provisions of law and of 26 CFR (1939) Part 401 (Regulations 91). Whether an individual is an employee with respect to services performed af-

ter 1939 and before 1951 shall be determined in accordance with the applicable provisions of law and of 26 CFR (1939) Part 402 (Regulations 106). Whether an individual is an employee with respect to services performed after 1950 and before 1955 shall be determined in accordance with the applicable provisions of law and of 26 CFR (1939) Part 408. (Regulations 128).

(2) Section 3121(d) contains three separate and independent tests for determining who are employees. Paragraphs (b), (c), and (d) of this section relate to the respective tests. Paragraph (b) relates to the test for determining whether an officer of a corporation is an employee of the

corporation. Paragraph (c) relates to the test for determining whether an individual is an employee under the usual common law rules. Paragraph (d) relates to the test for determining which individuals in certain occupational groups who are not employees under the usual common law rules are included as employees. If an individual is an employee under any one of the tests, he is to be considered an employee for purposes of the regulations in this subpart whether or not he is an employee under any of the other tests.

(3) If the relationship of employer and employee exists, the designation or description of the relationship by the parties as anything other than that of employer and employee is immaterial. Thus, if such relationship exists, it is of no consequence that the employee is designated as a partner, co-adventurer, agent, independent contractor, or the like.

(4) All classes or grades of employees are included within the relationship of employer and employee. Thus, superintendents, managers, and other supervisory personnel are employees.

(5) Although an individual may be an employee under this section, his services may be of such a nature, or performed under such circumstances, as not to constitute employment (see § 31.3121(b)-3).

(b) *Corporate officers.*—Generally, an officer of a corporation is an employee of the corporation. However, an officer of a corporation who as such does not perform any services or performs only minor services and who neither receives nor is entitled to receive, directly or indirectly, any remuneration is considered not to be an employee of the corporation. A director of a corporation in his capacity as such is not an employee of the corporation.

(c) *Common law employees.*—(1) Every individual is an employee if under the usual common law rules the relationship between him and the person for whom he performs services is the legal relationship of employer and employee.

(2) Generally such relationship exists when the person for whom services are performed has the right to control and direct the individual who performs the services, not only as to the result to be accomplished by the work but also as to the details and means by which that result is accomplished. That is, an employee is subject to the will and control of the employer not only as to what shall be done but how it shall be done. In this connection, it is not necessary that the employer actually direct or control the manner in which the services are performed; it is sufficient if he has the right to do so. The right to discharge is also an important factor indicating that the person possessing that right is an employer. Other factors characteristic of an employer, but not necessarily present in every case, are the furnishing of tools and the furnishing of a place to work, to the individual who performs the services. In general, if an individual is subject to the control or direction of another merely as to the result to be accomplished by the work and

not as to the means and methods for accomplishing the result, he is an independent contractor. An individual performing services as an independent contractor is not as to such services an employee under the usual common law rules. Individuals such as physicians, lawyers, dentists, veterinarians, construction contractors, public stenographers, and auctioneers, engaged in the pursuit of an independent trade, business, or profession, in which they offer their services to the public, are independent contractors and not employees.

(3) Whether the relationship of employer and employee exists under the usual common law rules will in doubtful cases be determined upon an examination of the particular facts of each case.

(d) *Special classes of employees.*—(1) In addition to individuals who are employees under paragraph (b) or (c) of this section, other individuals are employees if they perform services for remuneration under certain prescribed circumstances in the following occupational groups:

(i) as an agent-driver or commission-driver engaged in distributing meat products, vegetable products, fruit products, bakery products, beverages (other than milk), or laundry or dry-cleaning services for his principal;

(ii) as a full-time life insurance salesman;

(iii) as a homeworker performing work, according to specifications furnished by the person for whom the services are performed, on materials or goods furnished by such person which are required to be returned to such person or a person designated by him; or

(iv) as a traveling or city salesman, other than as an agent-driver or commission-driver, engaged upon a full-time basis in the solicitation on behalf of, and the transmission to, his principal (except for side-line sales activities on behalf of some other person) of orders from wholesalers, retailers, contractors, or operators of hotels, restaurants, or other similar establishments for merchandise for resale or supplies for use in their business operations.

(2) In order for an individual to be an employee under this paragraph, the individual must perform services in an occupation falling within one of the enumerated groups. If the individual does not perform services in one of the designated occupational groups, he is not an employee under this paragraph. An individual who is not an employee under this paragraph may nevertheless be an employee under paragraph (b) or (c) of this section. The language used to designate the respective occupational groups relates to fields of endeavor in which particular designations are not necessarily in universal use with respect to the same service. The designations are addressed to the actual services without regard to any technical or colloquial labels which may be attached to such services. Thus, a determination whether services fall within one of the designated occupational groups depends upon the facts of the particular situation.

Reg. §31.3121(d)-1(d)(2)

(3) The factual situations set forth below are illustrative of some of the individuals falling within each of the above enumerated occupational groups. The illustrative factual situations are as follows:

(i) *Agent-driver or commission-driver.*—This occupational group includes agent-drivers or commission-drivers who are engaged in distributing meat or meat products, vegetables or vegetable products, fruit or fruit products, bakery products, beverages (other than milk), or laundry or dry-cleaning services for their principals. An agent-driver or commission-driver includes an individual who operates his own truck or the truck of the person for whom he performs services, serves customers designated by such person as well as those solicited on his own, and whose compensation is a commission on his sales or the difference between the price he charges his customers and the price he pays to such person for the product or service.

(ii) *Full-time life insurance salesman.*—An individual whose entire or principal business activity is devoted to the solicitation of life insurance or annuity contracts, or both, primarily for one life insurance company is a full-time life insurance salesman. Such a salesman ordinarily uses the office space provided by the company or its general agent, and stenographic assistance, telephone facilities, forms, rate books, and advertising materials are usually made available to him without cost. An individual who is engaged in the general insurance business under a contract or contracts of service which do not contemplate that the individual's principal business activity will be the solicitation of life insurance or annuity contracts, or both, for one company, or any individual who devotes only part time to the solicitation of life insurance contracts, including annuity contracts, and is principally engaged in other endeavors, is not a full-time life insurance salesman.

(iii) *Home workers.*—This occupational group includes a worker who performs services off the premises of the person for whom the services are performed, according to specifications furnished by such person, on materials or goods furnished by such person which are required to be returned to such person or a person designated by him. For provisions relating to the determination of wages in the case of a home worker to whom this subdivision is applicable, see § 31.3121(a)(10)-1.

(iv) *Traveling or city salesman.*—(a) This occupational group includes a city or traveling salesman who is engaged upon a full-time basis in the solicitation on behalf of, and the transmission to, his principal (except for side-line sales activities on behalf of some other person or persons) of orders from wholesalers, retailers, contractors, or operators of hotels, restaurants, or other similar establishments for merchandise for resale or supplies for use in their business operations. An agent-driver or commission-driver is not within this occupational group. City or traveling salesmen who sell to retailers or to the others specified, operate off the premises of their principals, and are generally compensated on a commission basis, are within this occupational group. Such salesmen are generally not controlled as to the details of their services or the means by which they cover their territories, but in the ordinary case they are expected to call on regular customers with a fair degree of regularity.

(b) In order for a city or traveling salesman to be included within this occupational group, his entire or principal business activity must be devoted to the solicitation of orders for one principal. Thus, the multiple-line salesman generally is not within this occupational group. However, if the salesman solicits orders primarily for one principal, he is not excluded from this occupational group solely because of side-line sales activities on behalf of one or more other persons. In such a case, the salesman is within this occupational group only with respect to the services performed for the person for whom he primarily solicits orders and not with respect to the services performed for such other persons. The following examples illustrate the application of the foregoing provisions:

Example (1). Salesman A's principal business activity is the solicitation of orders from retail pharmacies on behalf of the X Wholesale Drug Company. A also occasionally solicits orders for drugs on behalf of the Y and Z companies. A is within this occupational group with respect to his services for the X Company but not with respect to his services for either the Y Company or the Z Company.

Example (2). Salesman B's principal business activity is the solicitation of orders from retail hardware stores on behalf of the R Tool Company and the S Cooking Utensil Company. B regularly solicits orders on behalf of both companies. B is not within this occupational group with respect to the services performed for either the R Company or the S Company.

Example (3). Salesman C's principal business activity is the house-to-house solicitation of orders on behalf of the T brush company. C occasionally solicits such orders from retail stores and restaurants. C is not within this occupational group.

(4)(i) The fact that an individual falls within one of the enumerated occupational groups, however, does not make such individual an employee under this paragraph unless (*a*) the contract of service contemplates that substantially all the services to which the contract relates in the particular designated occupation are to be performed personally by such individual, (*b*) such individual has no substantial investment in the facilities used in connection with the performance of such services (other than in facilities for transportation), and (*c*) such services are part of a continuing relationship with the person for whom the services are performed and are not in the nature of a single transaction.

(ii) The term "contract of service," as used in this paragraph, means an arrangement, formal or informal, under which the particular services are performed. The requirement that the contract of service shall contemplate that substantially all the services to which the contract relates in the particular designated occupation are to be performed personally by the individual means that it is not contemplated that any material part of the services to which the contract relates in such occupation will be delegated to any other person by the individual who undertakes under the contract to perform such services.

(iii) The facilities to which reference is made in this paragraph include equipment and premises available for the work or enterprise as distinguished from education, training, and experience, but do not include such tools, instruments, equipment, or clothing, as are commonly or frequently provided by employees. An investment in an automobile by an individual which is used primarily for his own transportation in connection with the performance of services for another person has no significance under this paragraph, since such investment is comparable to outlays for transportation by an individual performing similar services who does not own an automobile. Moreover, the investment in facilities for the transportation of the goods or commodities to which the services relate is to be excluded in determining the investment in a particular case. If an individual has a substantial investment in facilities of the requisite character, he is not an employee within the meaning of this paragraph, since a substantial investment of the requisite character standing alone is sufficient to exclude the individual from the employee concept under this paragraph.

(iv) If the services are not performed as part of a continuing relationship with the person for whom the services are performed, but are in the nature of a single transaction, the individual performing such services is not an employee of such person within the meaning of this paragraph. The fact that the services are not performed on consecutive workdays does not indicate that the services are not performed as part of a continuing relationship. [Reg. §31.3121(d)-1.]

☐ [T.D. 6190, 7-14-56. *Republished in T.D. 6516,* 12-20-60. *Amended by T.D. 6744, 7-2-64 and T.D. 7691, 4-9-80.*]

[Reg. §31.3121(d)-2]

§31.3121(d)-2. Who are employers.— (a) Every person is an employer if he employs one or more employees. Neither the number of employees employed nor the period during which any such employee is employed is material for the purpose of determining whether the person for whom the services are performed is an employer.

(b) An employer may be an individual, a corporation, a partnership, a trust, an estate, a joint-stock company, an association, or a syndicate, group, pool, joint venture, or other unincorporated organization, group, or entity. A trust or estate, rather than the fiduciary acting for or on behalf of the trust or estate, is generally the employer.

(c) Although a person may be an employer under this section, services performed in his employ may be of such a nature, or performed under such circumstances, as not to constitute employment (see §31.3121(b)-3). [Reg. §31.3121(d)-2.]

☐ [T.D. 6190, 7-14-56. *Republished in T.D. 6516,* 12-20-60.]

[Reg. §31.3121(e)-1]

§31.3121(e)-1. State, United States, and citizen.— (a) When used in the regulations in this subpart, the term "State" includes the District of Columbia, the Commonwealth of Puerto Rico, the Virgin Islands, the Territories of Alaska and Hawaii before their admission as States, and (when used with respect to services performed after 1960) Guam and American Samoa.

(b) When used in the regulations in this subpart, the term "United States", when used in a geographical sense, means the several states (including the Territories of Alaska and Hawaii before their admission as States), the District of Columbia, the Commonwealth of Puerto Rico, and the Virgin Islands. When used in the regulations in this subpart with respect to services performed after 1960, the term "United States" also includes Guam and American Samoa when the term is used in a geographical sense. The term "citizen of the United States" includes a citizen of the Commonwealth of Puerto Rico or the Virgin Islands, and, effective January 1, 1961, a citizen of Guam or American Samoa. [Reg. §31.3121(e)-1.]

☐ [T.D. 6190, 7-14-56. *Republished in T.D. 6516,* 12-20-60. *Amended by T.D. 6744, 7-2-64.*]

[Reg. §31.3121(f)-1]

§31.3121(f)-1. American vessel and aircraft.— (a) The term "American vessel" means any vessel which is documented (that is, registered, enrolled, or licensed) or numbered in conformity with the laws of the United States. It also includes any vessel which is neither documented nor numbered under the laws of the United States, nor documented under the laws of any foreign country, if the crew of such vessel is employed solely by one or more citizens or residents of the United States or corporations organized under the laws of the United States or of any State. (For provisions relating to the terms "State" and "citizens", see §31.3121(e)-1.)

(b) The term "American aircraft" means any aircraft registered under the laws of the United States.

(c) For provisions relating to services performed outside the United States on or in connection with an American vessel or American aircraft, see paragraph (c)(2) of §31.3121(b)-3. [Reg. §31.3121(f)-1.]

□ [T.D. 6190, 7-14-56. *Republished in T.D.* 6516, 12-20-60. *Amended by T.D.* 6744, 7-2-64.]

[Reg. § 31.3121(g)-1]

§ 31.3121(g)-1. Agricultural labor.—(a) *In general.*—(1) The term "agricultural labor" as defined in section 3121(g) includes services of the character described in paragraphs (b), (c), (d), (e) and (f) of this section. In general, however, the term does not include services performed in connection with forestry, lumbering, or landscaping.

(2) The term "farm" as used in the regulations in this subpart includes stock, dairy, poultry, fruit, fur-bearing animal, and truck farms, plantations, ranches, nurseries, ranges, orchards, and such greenhouses and other similar structures as are used primarily for the raising of agricultural or horticultural commodities. Greenhouses and other similar structures used primarily for other purposes (for example, display, storage, and fabrication of wreaths, corsages, and bouquets) do not constitute "farms".

(3) For provisions relating to the exception from employment provided with respect to services performed by certain foreign agricultural workers and to services performed before 1959 in connection with the production or harvesting of certain oleo-resinous products, see § 31.3121(b)(1)-1. For provisions relating to the exclusion from wages of remuneration paid in any medium other than cash for agricultural labor and to the test for determining whether cash remuneration paid for agricultural labor constitutes wages, see § 31.3121(a)(8)-1.

(b) *Services described in section 3121(g)(1).*—(1) Services performed on a farm by an employee of any person in connection with any of the following activities constitute agricultural labor:

(i) The cultivation of the soil;

(ii) The raising, shearing, feeding, caring for, training, or management of livestock, bees, poultry, fur-bearing animals, or wildlife; or

(iii) The raising or harvesting of any other agricultural or horticultural commodity.

(2) Services performed in connection with the production or harvesting of maple sap, or in connection with the raising or harvesting of mushrooms, or in connection with the hatching of poultry constitute agricultural labor only if such services are performed on a farm. Thus, services performed in connection with the operation of a hatchery, if not operated as part of a poultry or other farm, do not constitute agricultural labor.

(c) *Services described in section 3121(g)(2).*—(1) The following services performed by an employee in the employ of the owner or tenant or other operator of one or more farms constitute agricultural labor, provided the major part of such services is performed on a farm:

(i) Services performed in connection with the operation, management, conservation, improvement, or maintenance of any of such farms or its tools or equipment; or

(ii) Services performed in salvaging timber, or clearing land of brush and other debris, left by a hurricane.

(2) The services described in subparagraph (1)(i) of this paragraph may include, for example, services performed by carpenters, painters, mechanics, farm supervisors, irrigation engineers, bookkeepers, and other skilled or semi-skilled workers, which contribute in any way to the conduct of the farm or farms, as such, operated by the person employing them, as distinguished from any other enterprise in which such person may be engaged.

(3) Since the services described in this paragraph must be performed in the employ of the owner or other operator of the farm, the term "agricultural labor" does not include services performed by employees of a commercial painting concern, for example, which contracts with a farmer to renovate his farm properties.

(d) *Services described in section 3121(g)(3).*—Services performed by an employee in the employ of any person in connection with any of the following operations constitute agricultural labor without regard to the place where such services are performed:

(1) The ginning of cotton;

(2) The operation or maintenance of ditches, canals, reservoirs, or waterways, not owned or operated for profit, used exclusively for supplying or storing water for farming purposes; or

(3) The production or harvesting of crude gum (oleoresin) from a living tree or the processing of such crude gum into gum spirits of turpentine and gum rosin, provided such processing is carried on by the original producer of such crude gum.

(e) *Services described in section 3121(g)(4).*—(1) Services performed by an employee in the handling, planting, drying, packing, packaging, processing, freezing, grading, storing, or delivering to storage or to market or to a carrier for transportation to market, of any agricultural or horticultural commodity constitute agricultural labor if:

(i) Such services are performed by the employee in the employ of an operator of a farm or in the employ of a group of operators of farms (other than a cooperative organization);

(ii) Such services are performed with respect to the commodity in its unmanufactured state; and

(iii) Such operator produced more than one-half of the commodity with respect to which such services are performed during the pay period, or such group of operators produced all of the commodity with respect to which such services are performed during the pay period.

(2) The term "operator of a farm" as used in this paragraph means an owner, tenant, or other person, in possession of a farm and engaged in the operation of such farm.

(3) The services described in this paragraph do not constitute agricultural labor if performed

in the employ of a cooperative organization. The term "organization" includes corporations, joint-stock companies, and associations which are treated as corporations pursuant to section 7701(a)(3) of the Internal Revenue Code. For purposes of this paragraph, any unincorporated group of operators shall be deemed a cooperative organization if the number of operators comprising such group is more than 20 at any time during the calendar quarter in which the services involved are performed.

(4) Processing services which change the commodity from its raw or natural state do not constitute agricultural labor. For example, the extraction of juices from fruits or vegetables is a processing operation which changes the character of the fruits or vegetables from their raw or natural state and, therefore, does not constitute agricultural labor. Likewise, services performed in the processing of maple sap into maple sirup or maple sugar do not constitute agricultural labor. On the other hand, services rendered in the cutting and drying of fruits or vegetables are processing operations which do not change the character of the fruits or vegetables and, therefore, constitute agricultural labor, if the other requisite conditions are met. Services performed with respect to a commodity after its character has been changed from its raw or natural state by a processing operation do not constitute agricultural labor.

(5) The term "commodity" refers to a single agricultural or horticultural product, for example, all apples are to be treated as a single commodity, while apples and peaches are to be treated as two separate commodities. The services with respect to each such commodity are to be considered separately in determining whether the condition set forth in subparagraph (1)(iii) of this paragraph has been satisfied. The portion of the commodity produced by an operator or group of operators with respect to which the services described in this paragraph are performed by a particular employee shall be determined on the basis of the pay period in which such services were performed by such employee.

(6) The services described in this paragraph do not include services performed in connection with commercial canning or commercial freezing or in connection with any commodity after its delivery to a terminal market for distribution for consumption. Moreover, since the services described in this paragraph must be rendered in the actual handling, planting, drying, packing, packaging, processing, freezing, grading, storing, or delivering to storage or to market or to a carrier for transportation to market, of the commodity, such services do not, for example, include services performed as stenographers, bookkeepers, clerks, and other office employees, even though such services may be in connection with such activities. However, to the extent that the services of such individuals are performed in the employ of the owner or tenant or other operator of a farm and are rendered in major part on a farm, they may be within the provisions of paragraph (c) of this section.

(f) *Services described in section 3121(g)(5).*—(1) Service not in the course of the employer's trade or business (see paragraph (a)(1) of §31.3121(a)(7)-1) or domestic service in a private home of the employer (see paragraph (a)(2) of §31.3121(a)(7)-1) constitutes agricultural labor if such service is performed on a farm operated for profit. The determination whether remuneration for any such service performed on a farm operated for profit constitutes wages is to be made under §31.3121(a)(8)-1 rather than under §31.3121(a)(7)-1. For provisions relating to the exception from employment provided with respect to any such service performed after 1960 by a father or mother in the employ of his or her son or daughter, see §31.3121(b)(3)-1.

(2) Generally, a farm is not operated for profit if it is occupied by the employer primarily for residential purposes, or is used primarily for the pleasure of the employer or his family such as for the entertainment of guests or as a hobby of the employer or his family. [Reg. §31.3121(g)-1.]

□ [T.D. 6190, 7-14-56. *Republished in T.D. 6516,* 12-20-60. *Amended by T.D. 6744, 7-2-64.*]

[Reg. §31.3121(h)-1]

§31.3121(h)-1. **American employer.**—(a) The term "American employer" means an employer which is (1) the United States or any instrumentality thereof, (2) an individual who is a resident of the United States, (3) a partnership, if two-thirds or more of the partners are residents of the United States, (4) a trust, if all of the trustees are residents of the United States, or (5) a corporation organized under the laws of the United States or of any State. For provisions relating to the terms "State" and "United States," see §31.3121(e)-1.

(b) For provisions relating to services performed outside the United States by a citizen of the United States as an employee for an American employer, see paragraph (c)(3) of §31.3121(b)-3 and paragraph (e) of §31.3121(b)(4)-1. [Reg. §31.3121(h)-1.]

□ [T.D. 6190, 7-14-56. *Republished in T.D. 6516,* 12-20-60. *Amended by T.D. 6744, 7-2-64.*]

[Reg. §31.3121(i)-1]

§31.3121(i)-1. **Computation to nearest dollar of cash remuneration for domestic service.**—(a) An employer may, for purposes of the Act, elect to compute to the nearest dollar any payment of cash remuneration for domestic service described in section 3121(a)(7)(B) (see §31.3121(a)(7)-1) which is more or less than a whole-dollar amount. For the purpose of the computation to the nearest dollar, the payment of a fractional part of a dollar shall be disregarded unless it amounts to one-half dollar or more, in which case it shall be increased to one dollar. For example, any amount actually paid between $4.50 and $5.49, inclusive, may be treated as $5 for purposes of the taxes imposed by the Act. If an employer elects this method of computation with respect to any payment of cash remuneration made in a calendar year for domestic service in his private home, he must use the same method in computing each payment of cash remuneration of more or less than a whole-dollar amount made to each of his employees in such calendar year for domestic service in his private home. Moreover, if an employer elects this method of computation with respect to payments of the prescribed character made in any calendar year, the amount of each payment of cash remuneration so computed to the nearest dollar shall, in lieu of the amount actually paid, be deemed to constitute the amount of cash remuneration for purposes of the Act. Thus, the amount of cash payments so computed to the nearest dollar shall be used for purposes of determining whether such payments constitute wages, for purposes of apply-ing the employee and employer tax rates to the wage payments, for purposes of any required record keeping, and for purposes of reporting and paying the employee tax and employer tax with respect to such wage payments.

(b) The provisions of this section apply to any cash payment for domestic service in a private home of the employer made on or after January 1, 1994. For rules applicable to any cash payment for domestic service in a private home of the employer made prior to January 1, 1994, see § 31.3121(i)-1 in effect at such time (see 26 CFR part 31 contained in the edition of 26 CFR Parts 30 to 39, revised as of April 1, 2006). [Reg. § 31.3121(i)-1.]

☐ [*T.D.* 6190, 7-14-56. *Republished in T.D.* 6516, 12-20-60. *Amended by T.D.* 9266, 6-16-2006.]

⫸→ *Caution: This regulation has not been amended to reflect changes enacted by the Omnibus Budget Reconciliation Act of 1987 (P.L. 100-203).*

[Reg. § 31.3121(i)-2]

§ 31.3121(i)-2. Computation of remuneration for service performed by an individual as a member of a uniformed service.—In the case of an individual performing service after December 31, 1956, as a member of a uniformed service (see § 31.3121(n)), to which the provisions of section 3121(m)(1) (see § 31.3121(m)) are applicable, the term "wages" shall, subject to the provisions of section 3121(a)(1) (see § 31.3121(a)-1), include as the individual's remuneration for such service only his basic pay as described in section 102(10) of the Servicemen's and Veterans' Survivor Benefits Act (38 U.S.C., 401(1), 403; 72 Stat. 1126). [Reg. § 31.3121(i)-2.]

☐ [*T.D.* 6744, 7-2-64.]

⫸→ *Caution: This regulation has not been amended to reflect changes enacted by the Omnibus Budget Reconciliation Act of 1987 (P.L. 100-203).*

[Reg. § 31.3121(i)-3]

§ 31.3121(i)-3. Computation of remuneration for service performed by an individual as a volunteer or volunteer leader within the meaning of the Peace Corps Act.—In the case of an individual performing service in his capacity as a volunteer or volunteer leader within the meaning of the Peace Corps Act (see § 31.3121(p)), the term "wages" shall, subject to the provisions of section 3121(a)(1) (see § 31.3121(a)-1), include as such individual's remuneration for such service only amounts paid pursuant to section 5(c) or section 6(1) of the Peace Corps Act (22 U.S.C. 2501; 75 Stat. 612). [Reg. § 31.3121(i)-3.]

☐ [*T.D.* 6744, 7-2-64.]

[Reg. § 31.3121(i)-4]

§ 31.3121(i)-4. Computation of remuneration for service performed by certain members or religious orders.—In any case where an individual is a member of a religious order (as defined in section 3121(r)(2) and paragraph (b) of § 31.3121(r)-1) performing service in the exercise of duties required by such order, and an election of coverage under section 3121(r) and § 31.3121(r)-1 is in effect with respect to such order or its autonomous subdivision to which such member belongs, the term "wages" shall, subject to the provisions of section 3121(a)(1) (relating to definition of wages), include as such individual's remuneration for such service the fair market value of any board, lodging, clothing, and other perquisites furnished to such member by such order or subdivision or by any other person or organization pursuant to an agreement (whether written or oral) with such order or subdivision. Such other perquisites shall include any cash either paid by such order or subdivision or paid by another employer and not required by such order or subdivision to be remitted to it. For purposes of this section, perquisites shall be considered to be furnished over the period during which the member receives the benefit of them. (See example (4) of this section.) In no case shall the amount included as such individual's remuneration under this paragraph be less than $100 a month. All relevant facts and elements of value shall be considered in every case. Where the fair market value of any board, lodging, clothing, and other perquisites furnished to all members of an electing religious order or autonomous subdivision (or to all in a group of members) does not vary significantly, such order or subdivision may treat all of its members (or all in such group of members) as having a uniform wage. The provisions of this section may be illustrated by the following examples of the treatment of particular perquisites:

Example (1). M is a religious order which requires its members to take a vow of poverty and which has made an election under section 3121(r). Under section 3121(i)(4), M must include in the wages of its members the fair market value of the clothing it provides for its members. M and several other religious orders using essentially the same type of religious habit purchase clothing for their members from either of two suppliers in arms-length transactions. The fair market value of such clothing (*i.e.,* the price at which such items would change hands between a willing buyer and a willing seller, neither being under any compulsion to buy or to sell) is determined by reference to the actual sales price of these suppliers to the religious orders.

Example (2). N is a religious order which requires its members to take a vow of poverty and which has made an election under section 3121(r). N operates a seminary adjacent to a university. Students at the university obtain lodging and board on campus from the university for its fair market value of $2,000 for the school year. Such lodging and board is essentially the same as that provided by N at its seminary to N's members subject to a vow of poverty. Accordingly, the amount to be included in the "wages" of such members with respect to lodging and board for the same period of time is $2,000.

Example (3). O is a religious order which requires its members to take a vow of poverty and to observe silence, and which has made an election under section 3121(r). O operates a monastery in a remote rural area. Under section 3121(i)(4), O must include in the wages of its members assigned to this monastery the fair market value of the board and lodging furnished to them. In making a determination of the fair market value of such board and lodging, the remoteness of the monastery, as well as the smallness of the rooms and the simplicity of their furnishings, affect this determination. However, the facts that the facility is used by a religious order as a monastery and that the order's members maintain silence do not affect the fair market value of such items.

Example (4). P is a religious order which requires its members to take a vow of poverty and which has made an election under section 3121(r). Several of P's members are attending a university on a full-time basis. The fair market value of the board and lodging of each of such members at the university is $1,000 per semester. P pays the university $1,000 at the beginning of each semester for the board and lodging of each of such members. In addition, P gives each such member a $400 cash advance to cover his miscellaneous expenses during the semester. Under section 3121(i)(4), P must prorate the fair market value of such members' board and lodging, as well as the miscellaneous items, over the semester and include such value in the determination of "wages."

Example (5). Q is a religious order which is a corporation organized under the laws of Wisconsin, which requires its members to take a vow of poverty, and which has made an election under section 3121(r). Q has convents in rural South America and in suburbs and central city areas of the United States. Characteristically, in the United States its suburban convents provide somewhat larger and newer rooms for its members than do its convents in city areas. Moreover, its suburban convents have more extensive grounds and somewhat more elaborate facilities than do its older convents in city areas. However, both types of convents limit resident members to a single, plainly furnished room and provide them meals which are comparable. Q's members in South America live in extremely primitive dwellings and otherwise have extremely modest perquisites. Under section 3121(i)(4), Q may report a uniform wage for its members who live in suburban convents and city convents in the United States, as the board, lodging, and perquisites furnished these members do not vary significantly from one convent to the other. Q may report another uniform wage (but not less than $100 per month apiece) for its members who are citizens of the United States and who reside in South America based on the fair market value of the perquisites furnished these individuals, as the fair market value of the perquisites furnished these individuals varies significantly from that of those furnished its members who live in its domestic convents but does not vary significantly among members in South America whose wages are subject to tax. [Reg. § 31.3121(i)-4.]

□ [T.D. 7280, 7-10-73.]

[Reg. § 31.3121(j)-1]

§ 31.3121(j)-1. Covered transportation service.—(a) *Transportation systems acquired in whole or in part after 1936 and before 1951.*—(1) *In general.*—Except as provided in subparagraph (2) of this paragraph, all service performed in the employ of a State or political subdivision thereof in connection with its operation of a public transportation system constitutes covered transportation service if any part of the transportation system was acquired from private ownership after 1936 and before 1951. For purposes of this subparagraph, it is immaterial whether any part of the transportation system was acquired before 1937 or after 1950, whether the employee was hired before, during, or after 1950, or whether the employee had been employed by the employer from whom the State or political subdivision acquired its transportation system or any part thereof.

(2) *General retirement system protected by State constitution.*—Except as provided in subparagraph (3) of this paragraph, service performed in the employ of a State or political subdivision in connection with its operation of a public transportation system acquired in whole or in part from private ownership after 1936 and before 1951 does not constitute covered transportation service, if substantially all service in connection with the operation of the transportation system was, on December 31, 1950, covered under a general retirement system providing benefits which are protected from diminution or impairment under the State constitution by reason of an express provision, dealing specifically with retirement systems established by the State or political subdivisions of the State, which forbids such diminution or impairment.

(3) *Additions to certain transportation systems by acquisition after 1950.*—This subparagraph is applicable only in case of an acquisition after 1950 from private ownership of an addition to an

existing public transportation system which was acquired in whole or in part by a State or political subdivision thereof from private ownership after 1936 and before 1951 and then only in case service for such existing transportation system did not constitute covered transportation service by reason of the provisions of subparagraph (2) of this paragraph. Service in connection with the operation of such transportation system (including any additions acquired after 1950) constitutes covered transportation service commencing with the first day of the third calendar quarter following the calendar quarter in which the addition to the existing transportation system was acquired, if such service is performed by an employee who became an employee of the State or political subdivision in connection with and at the time of its acquisition from private ownership of such addition and who before the acquisition of such addition rendered service in employment in connection with the operation of the addition so acquired by such State or political subdivision. However, service performed by such employee in connection with the operation of the transportation system does not constitute covered transportation service if, on the first day of the third calendar quarter following the calendar quarter in which the addition was acquired, such service is covered by a general retirement system which does not, with respect to such employee, contain special provisions applicable only to employees who became employees of the State or political subdivision in connection with and at the time of its acquisition of such addition.

(b) *Transportation systems in operation on December 31, 1950, no part of which was acquired after 1936 and before 1951.*—(1) *In general.*—Except as provided in subparagraph (2) of this paragraph, no service performed in the employ of a State or a political subdivision thereof in connection with its operation of a public transportation system constitutes covered transportation service if no part of such transportation system operated by the State or political subdivision on December 31, 1950, was acquired from private ownership after 1936 and before 1951.

(2) *Additions acquired after 1950.*—This subparagraph is applicable only in case of an acquisition after 1950 from private ownership of an addition to an existing public transportation system which was operated by a State or political subdivision on December 31, 1950, but no part of which was acquired from private ownership after 1936 and before 1951. Service in connection with the operation of such transportation system (including any additions acquired after 1950) constitutes covered transportation service commencing with the first day of the third calendar quarter following the calendar quarter in which the addition to the existing transportation system was acquired, if such service is performed by an employee who became an employee of the State or political subdivision in connection with and at the time of its acquisition from private ownership of such addition and who before the

acquisition of such addition rendered service in employment in connection with the operation of the addition so acquired by such State or political subdivision. However, service performed by such employee in connection with the operation of the transportation system does not constitute covered transportation service if, on the first day of the third calendar quarter following the calendar quarter in which the addition was acquired, such service is covered by a general retirement system which does not, with respect to such employee, contain special provisions applicable only to employees who became employees of the State or political subdivision in connection with and at the time of its acquisition of such addition.

(c) *Transportation systems acquired after 1950.*—All service performed in the employ of a State or political subdivision thereof in connection with its operation of a public transportation system constitutes covered transportation service if the transportation system was not operated by the State or political subdivision before 1951 and, at the time of its first acquisition after 1950 from private ownership of any part of its transportation system, the State or political subdivision did not have a general retirement system covering substantially all service performed in connection with the operation of the transportation system.

(d) *Definitions.*—For purposes of this section:

(1) The term "general retirement system" means any pension, annuity, retirement, or similar fund or system established by a State or by a political subdivision thereof for employees of the State, political subdivision, or both; but such term does not include such a fund or system which covers only service performed in positions connected with the operation of its public transportation system.

(2) A transportation system or a part thereof is considered to have been acquired by a State or political subdivision from private ownership if prior to the acquisition service performed by employees in connection with the operation of the system or an acquired part thereof constituted employment under the Act or under subchapter A of chapter 9 of the Internal Revenue Code of 1939 or was covered by an agreement entered into pursuant to section 218 of the Social Security Act, and some of such employees became employees of the State or political subdivision in connection with and at the time of such acquisition.

(3) The term "political subdivision" includes an instrumentality of a State, of one or more political subdivisions of a State, or of a State and one or more of its political subdivisions.

(4) The term "employment" includes service covered by an agreement entered into pursuant to section 218 of the Social Security Act. [Reg. § 31.3121(j)-1.]

☐ [*T.D. 6190, 7-14-56. Republished in T.D. 6516,* 12-20-60.]

Reg. § 31.3121(j)-1(b)

[Reg. §31.3121(k)-1]

§31.3121(k)-1. Waiver of exemption from taxes.—(a) *Who may file a waiver certificate.*—(1) *In general.*—If services performed in the employ of an organization are excepted from employment under section 3121(b)(8)(B), the organization may file a waiver certificate on Form SS-15, together with a list on Form SS-15a, certifying that it desires to have the Federal old-age, survivors, and disability insurance system established by title II of the Social Security Act extended to services performed by its employees. (For provisions relating to the exception under section 3121(b)(8)(B), see §§31.3121(b)(8) and 31.3121(b)(8)-2.) A certificate in effect under section 1426(1) of the Internal Revenue Code of 1939 on December 31, 1954, remains in effect under, and is subject to the provisions of, section 3121(k). If the period covered by a certificate filed under section 3121(k), or under section 1426(l) of the Internal Revenue Code of 1939, is terminated by an organization, a certificate may not thereafter be filed by the organization under section 3121(k). For regulations relating to certificates filed under section 1426(1) of the Internal Revenue Code of 1939, see 26 CFR (1939) 408.216 (Regulations 128).

(2) *Organizations having two separate groups of employees.*—If an organization is eligible to file a certificate under section 3121(k), and the organization employs both individuals who are in positions covered by a pension, annuity, retirement, or similar fund or system established by a State or by a political subdivision thereof and individuals who are not in such positions, the organization shall divide its employees into two separate groups for purposes of any certificate filed after August 28, 1958. One group shall consist of all employees who are in positions covered by such a fund or system and (i) are members of such fund or system, or (ii) are not members of such fund or system but are eligible to become members thereof. The other group shall consist of all remaining employees. An organization which has so divided its employees into two groups may file a certificate after August 28, 1958, with respect to the employees in either group, or may file a separate certificate after such date with respect to employees in each group.

(3) *Certificates filed before September 14, 1960.*—A certificate filed before September 14, 1960, is void unless at least two-thirds of the employees, determined on the basis of the facts which existed as of the date the certificate was filed, concurred in the filing of the certificate, and the organization certified to such concurrence in the certificate. All individuals who were employees of the organization within the meaning of section 3121(d) (see §31.3121(d)-1) shall be included in determining whether two-thirds of the employees of the organization concurred in the filing of the certificate; except that there shall not be included (i) those employees who at the time of the filing of the certificate were perform-ing for the organization services only of the character specified in paragraphs (8)(A), (10)(B), and (13) of section 3121(b) (see §§31.3121(b)(8)-1, 31.3121(b)(10)-2, and 31.3121(b)(13)-1, respectively), (ii) those alien employees who at the time of the filing of the certificate were performing services for such organization under an arrangement which provided for the performance only of services outside the United States not on or in connection with an American vessel or American aircraft, and (iii) in connection with certificates filed after August 28, 1958, those employees who at the time of the filing of the certificate were in a group to which such certificate was not applicable because of the provisions of section 3121(k)(1)(E). (See subparagraph (2) of this paragraph.) As used in this subparagraph, the term "alien employee" does not include an employee who was a citizen of the Commonwealth of Puerto Rico or a citizen of the Virgin Islands, and the term "United States" includes Puerto Rico and the Virgin Islands.

(b) *Execution and amendment of certificate.*—(1) *Use of prescribed forms.*—An organization filing a certificate pursuant to section 3121(k) shall use Form SS-15, in accordance with the regulations and instructions applicable thereto. The certificate may be filed only if it is accompanied by a list on Form SS-15a, containing the signature, address, and social security account number, if any, of each employee, if any, who concurs in the filing of the certificate. (For provisions relating to account numbers, see §31.6011(b)-2.) If no employee concurs in a certificate filed after September 13, 1960, that fact should be stated on the Form SS-15a. (For provisions relating to the concurrence of employees in certificates filed before September 14, 1960, see paragraph (a)(3) of this section.)

(2) *Amendment of list on Form SS-15a.*—(i) *Certificate filed after August 28, 1958.*—The list on Form SS-15a accompanying a certificate filed after August 28, 1958, under section 3121(k), may be amended at any time before the expiration of the twenty-fourth month following the calendar quarter in which the certificate is filed, by filing a supplemental list or lists on Form SS-15a Supplement, containing the signature, address, and social security account number, if any, of each additional employee who concurs in the filing of the certificate.

(ii) *Certificate filed before August 29, 1958.*—The list on Form SS-15a which accompanied a certificate filed before August 29, 1958, under section 3121(k) or under section 1426(1) of the Internal Revenue Code of 1939, may be amended by filing a supplemental list or lists on Form SS-15a Supplement at any time after August 31, 1954, and before the expiration of the twenty-fourth month following the first calendar quarter for which the certificate was in effect, or before January 1, 1959, whichever is the later.

(3) *Where to file certificate or amendment.*—The certificate on Form SS-15 and accompanying list on Form SS-15a of an organization which is

required to make a return on Form 941 pursuant to §31.6011(a)-1 or §31.6011(a)-4 shall be filed with the internal revenue officer designated in the instructions applicable to Form SS-15 and Form SS-15a. The Form SS-15 and Form SS-15a of any other organization shall be filed in accordance with the provisions of §31.6091-1 which are otherwise applicable to returns. Each Form SS-15a Supplement shall be filed with the internal revenue officer with whom the related Forms SS-15 and SS-15a were filed.

(c) *Effect of waiver.*—(1) *In general.*—The exception from employment under section 3121(b)(8)(B) does not apply to services with respect to which a certificate, filed pursuant to section 3121(k), or section 1426(1) of the Internal Revenue Code of 1939, is in effect. (See §§31.3121(b)(8) and 31.3121(b)(8)-2.) If an organization has divided its employees into two groups, as set forth in paragraph (a)(2) of this section, a certificate filed with respect to either group shall have no effect with respect to services performed by an employee as a member of the other group; and the provisions of this subsection shall apply as if each group were separately employed by a different organization. A certificate is not terminated if the organization loses its exemption under section 501(a) as an organization of the character described in section 501(c)(3), but continues effective with respect to any subsequent periods during which the organization is so exempt. The certificate of an organization may be in effect without being applicable to services performed by every employee of the organization. Subparagraph (2) of this paragraph relates to the beginning of the period for which a certificate is in effect. Subparagraph (3) of this paragraph relates to the services with respect to which a certificate is in effect. Even though a certificate is in effect with respect to the services of an employee, such services may be excepted from employment under some provision of section 3121(b) other than paragraph (8)(B) thereof. For example, service performed in any calendar quarter in the employ of an organization described in section 501(c)(3) and exempt from income tax under section 501(a) is excepted from employment under section 3121(b)(10)(A) if the remuneration for such service is less than $50, regardless of whether the organization files a certificate.

(2) *Beginning of effective period of waiver.*—(i) *Certificate filed after July 30, 1965.*—A certificate filed after July 30, 1965, by an organization pursuant to section 3121(k) shall be in effect for the period beginning with one of the following dates, which shall be designated by the organization on the certificate:

(a) The first day of the calendar quarter in which the certificate is filed,

(b) The first day of the calendar quarter immediately following the quarter in which the certificate is filed, or

(c) The first day of any calendar quarter preceding the calendar quarter in which the certificate is filed, except that such date may not

be earlier than the first day of the twentieth calendar quarter preceding the quarter in which such certificate is filed. Thus, a certificate filed in December 1965 may be made effective, pursuant to this subdivision (c), for the period beginning with the first day of the calendar quarter beginning October 1, 1960, or the first day of any other calendar quarter beginning after October 1, 1960, and before October 1, 1965.

(ii) *Certificate filed after August 28, 1958, and before July 31, 1965.*—A certificate filed after August 28, 1958, and before July 31, 1965, by an organization pursuant to section 3121(k) shall be in effect for the period beginning with one of the following dates, which shall be designated by the organization on the certificate:

(a) The first day of the calendar quarter in which the certificate is filed,

(b) The first day of the calendar quarter immediately following the quarter in which the certificate is filed, or

(c) The first day of any calendar quarter preceding the calendar quarter in which the certificate is filed, except that, in the case of a certificate filed before 1960, such date may not be earlier than January 1, 1956, and in the case of a certificate filed after 1959 (but before July 31, 1965), such date may not be earlier than the first day of the fourth calendar quarter preceding the quarter in which the certificate is filed. Thus, a certificate filed in December 1959 may be made effective for the calendar quarter beginning January 1, 1956; but a certificate filed in January 1960 may not be made effective for a calendar quarter beginning before January 1, 1959.

(iii) *Certificate filed after 1956 and before August 29, 1958.*—A certificate filed by an organization after 1956 and before August 29, 1958, pursuant to section 3121(k), became effective for the period beginning with one of the following dates, as designated by the organization on the certificate:

(a) The first day of the calendar quarter in which the certificate was filed, or

(b) The first day of the calendar quarter immediately following the quarter in which the certificate was filed.

(iv) *Certificate filed before 1957.*—A certificate filed before 1957 pursuant to section 3121(k) became effective for the period beginning with the first day following the close of the calendar quarter in which the certificate was filed. In no case, however, shall a certificate filed under the provisions of section 3121(k) be in effect with respect to services performed before January 1, 1955. (For regulations relating to waiver certificates filed under section 1426(l) of the Internal Revenue Code of 1939, see 26 CFR (1939) 408.216 (Regulations 128).)

(3) *Services to which certificate applies.*—(i) *In general.*—If an organization's certificate is in effect (see subparagraph (2) of this paragraph), the certificate becomes effective with respect to services performed in its employ by each individual

(a) who enters the employ of the organization after the calendar quarter in which the certificate is filed, as set forth in subdivision (ii) of this subparagraph, or (b) whose signature appears on the list on Form SS-15a, as set forth in subdivision (iii) of this subparagraph, or (c) whose signature appears on a Form SS-15a Supplement, as set forth in subdivision (iv) or (v) of this subparagraph. The first date on which such a certificate becomes effective with respect to an employee's services shall be the earliest date applicable under this subparagraph. An organization's certificate is not effective with respect to the services of an employee who is in its employ in the calendar quarter in which the certificate is filed and who does not sign Form SS-15a or Form SS-15a Supplement, so long as his employment relationship with the organization, at the close of the calendar quarter in which the certificate is filed and thereafter, continues without interruption.

(ii) *Employee hired after quarter in which certificate is filed.*—If an individual enters the employ of an organization on or after the first day following the close of the calendar quarter in which the organization files a certificate pursuant to section 3121(k), the certificate shall be in effect with respect to services performed by the individual in the employ of the organization on and after the day he enters the employ of the organization. A former employee of the organization who is rehired on or after the first day following the close of the calendar quarter in which such a certificate is filed shall be considered to have entered the employ of the organization after such calendar quarter, regardless of whether such individual concurred in the filing of the certificate.

(iii) *Employee who signs Form SS-15a.*—A certificate on Form SS-15 filed by an organization pursuant to section 3121(k) shall be in effect with respect to services performed by an individual in the employ of the organization on and after the first day for which the certificate is in effect, if such individual's signature appears on the list on Form SS-15a which accompanies such certificate.

(iv) *Employee who signs Form SS-15a Supplement to concur in certificate filed after August 28, 1958.*—If the list on Form SS-15a accompanying a certificate filed after August 28, 1958, by an organization pursuant to section 3121(k) is amended in accordance with paragraph (b)(2)(i) of this section by the filing of a supplemental list on Form SS-15a Supplement, the certificate shall be in effect with respect to the services of each individual whose signature appears on the supplemental list, performed in the employ of the organization—

(a) On and after the first day for which the certificate is in effect, if the supplemental list is filed on or before the last day of the month following the calendar quarter in which the certificate is filed, or

(b) On and after the first day of the calendar quarter in which the supplemental list is filed, if such list is filed after the close of the first month following the calendar quarter in which the certificate is filed.

(v) *Employer who signed Form SS-15a Supplement to concur in certificate filed before August 29, 1958.*—If the list on Form SS-15a which accompanied a certificate filed before August 29, 1958, by an organization pursuant to section 3121(k), or pursuant to section 1426(l) of the Internal Revenue Code of 1939, was amended in accordance with paragraph (b)(2)(ii) of this section by the filing of a supplemental list on Form SS-15a Supplement, the certificate shall be in effect with respect to the services of each individual whose signature appears on the supplemental list, performed in the employ of the organization—

(a) On and after the first day for which the certificate is in effect, if the supplemental list was filed on or before the last day of the month following the first calendar quarter for which the certificate was in effect, or

(b) On and after the first day following the close of the calendar quarter in which the supplemental list was filed, but not before January 1, 1955, if such list was filed after the close of the first month following the first calendar quarter for which the certificate is in effect.

(4) *Administrative provisions applicable when certificate has retroactive effect.*—For purposes of computing interest and for purposes of section 6651 (relating to addition to tax for failure to file tax return), in any case in which a certificate filed pursuant to section 3121(k)(l) is effective pursuant to section 3121(k)(1)(B)(iii) (as originally enacted and as amended by section 316(a) of the Social Security Amendments of 1965) for one or more calendar quarters prior to the quarter in which the certificate is filed, the due date for the return and payment of the tax for such prior calendar quarters resulting from the filing of such certificate shall be the last day of the calendar month following the calendar quarter in which the certificate is filed. The statutory period for the assessment of the tax for such prior calendar quarters shall not expire before the expiration of 3 years from such due date. A waiver certificate (as described in section 3121(k)(1) and this section) furnished to the Internal Revenue Service after February 12, 1976, shall not be considered filed with the Internal Revenue Service unless interest paid to the organization (or credited to its account) in connection with a claim for credit or refund of taxes, which claim was based upon the exemption from taxes the organization is waiving by such certificate, is repaid. The interest so paid must be repaid only to the extent such interest relates to any taxes for which the organization or its employees would be liable by reason of the waiver certificate. Furthermore, when a waiver certificate has been filed prior to the payment of a refund of taxes based upon the exemption from taxes the organization is waiving, no credit or refund in respect of the taxes for which the exemption has been waived shall be allowed. If repayment of the

interest is made as required by this subparagraph, on or before the last day of the calendar month following the calendar quarter in which the certificate is furnished to the Internal Revenue Service, such certificate shall be considered to have been filed on the date it was originally furnished. If repayment occurs after that day, such certificate shall be considered to have been filed on the date of the repayment. References in this subparagraph to a waiver certificate refer also to any supplement to such a certificate.

(d) *Termination of waiver by organization.*— (1) The period for which a certificate filed pursuant to section 3121(k), or pursuant to section 1426(1) of the Internal Revenue Code of 1939, is in effect may be terminated by the organization upon giving to the district director with whom the organization is filing returns 2 years' advance notice in writing of its desire to terminate the effect of the certificate at the end of a specified calendar quarter, but only if, at the time of the receipt of such notice by the district director, the certificate has been in effect for a period of not less than 8 years. The notice of termination shall be signed by the president or other principal officer of the organization. Such notice shall be dated and shall show (i) the title of the officer signing the notice, (ii) the name, address, and identification number of the organization, (iii) the district director with whom the certificate was filed, (iv) the date on which the certificate became effective, and (v) the date on which the certificate is to be terminated. No particular form is prescribed for the notice of termination.

(2) In computing the effective period which must precede the date of receipt of the notice of termination, there shall be disregarded any period or periods as to which the organization was not exempt from income tax under section 501(a) as an organization of the character described in section 501(c)(3) or under section 101(6) of the Internal Revenue Code of 1939.

(3) The notice of termination may be revoked by the organization by giving, prior to the close of the calendar quarter specified in the notice of termination, a written notice of such revocation. The notice of revocation shall be filed with the district director with whom the notice of termination was filed. The notice of revocation shall be signed by the president or other principal officer of the organization. Such notice shall be dated and shall show (i) the title of the officer signing the notice, (ii) the name, address, and identification number of the organization, and (iii) the date of the notice of termination to be revoked. No particular form is prescribed for the notice of revocation.

(e) *Termination of waiver by Commissioner.*— (1) The period for which a certificate filed pursuant to section 3121(k), or pursuant to section 1426(l) of the Internal Revenue Code of 1939, is in effect may be terminated by the Commissioner, with the prior concurrence of the Secretary of Health, Education, and Welfare, upon a finding by the Commissioner that the organization has failed to comply substantially with the requirements applicable with respect to the taxes imposed by the Act (or the corresponding provisions of prior law) or is no longer able to comply therewith. The Commissioner shall give the organization not less than 60 days' advance notice in writing that the period covered by the certificate will terminate at the end of the calendar quarter specified in the notice of termination.

(2) The notice of termination may be revoked by the Commissioner, with the prior concurrence of the Secretary of Health, Education, and Welfare, by giving written notice of revocation to the organization before the close of the calendar quarter specified in the notice of termination. [Reg. § 31.3121(k)-1.]

☐ [*T.D.* 6190, 7-14-56. *Republished in T.D.* 6516, 12-20-60. *Amended by T.D.* 6744, 7-2-64; *T.D.* 6983, 12-4-68, *T.D.* 7012, 5-15-69, and *T.D.* 7476, 4-4-77.]

≫≫→ *Caution: This regulation has not been amended to reflect the repeal of §3121(k) by P.L. 98-21.*

[Reg. §31.3121(k)-2]

§31.3121(k)-2. Waivers of exemption; original effective date changed retroactively.— (a) *Certificates filed after 1955 and before August 29, 1958.*—(1) An organization which filed a certificate under section 3121(k) after 1955 and before August 29, 1958, may file a request on Form SS-15b at any time before 1960 to have such certificate made effective, with respect to the services of individuals who concurred in the filing of such certificate (initially, or by signing a supplemental list on Form SS-15a Supplement which was filed before August 29, 1958) and whose signatures also appeared on such request on Form SS-15b, for the period beginning with the first day of any calendar quarter after 1955 which preceded the first calendar quarter for which the certificate originally was effective.

(2) For purposes of computing interest and for purposes of section 6651 (relating to addition to tax for failure to file tax return), the due date

for the return and payment of the tax for any calendar quarter resulting from the filing of a request referred to in subparagraph (1) of this paragraph shall be the last day of the calendar month following the calendar quarter in which the request is filed. The statutory period for the assessment of such tax shall not expire before the expiration of 3 years from such due date.

(b) *Certificate filed before 1966.*—(1) An organization which filed a certificate on Form SS-15 under section 3121(k)(1)(A) before January 1, 1966, may amend such certificate during 1965 or 1966 to make the certificate effective beginning with the first day of a calendar quarter preceding the date designated by the organization on the certificate (see paragraph (c)(2) of § 31.3121(k)-1). The amendment of the certificate shall be made by filing a Certificate For Retroactive Coverage on Form SS-15b. A certificate on Form SS-15 may be amended to be effective for the period beginning with the first day of any calendar quarter which precedes the calendar quarter for which the certificate was originally effective, except that such a certificate may not be made effective, through an amendment, for any calendar quarter which begins earlier than the twentieth calendar quarter preceding the calendar quarter in which the organization files a Certificate For Retroactive Coverage on Form SS-15b. Thus, if a Certificate For Retroactive Coverage is filed in May 1966 in respect of a certificate on Form SS-15 filed in 1965, the certificate on Form SS-15 may not be made effective for a calendar quarter preceding the quarter beginning April 1, 1961. A certificate on Form SS-15 which is amended by a Certificate For Retroactive Coverage on Form SS-15b will be effective for the period preceding the first calendar quarter for which the certificate originally was effective only with respect to the services of individuals who concurred in the filing of the certificate (initially, or by signing a supplemental list on Form SS-15a Supplement

which was filed prior to the date on which the Certificate For Retroactive Coverage was filed) and whose signatures also appear on the Certificate For Retroactive Coverage on Form SS-15b. A Certificate For Retroactive Coverage shall be filed with the district director with whom the related Form SS-15 was filed.

(2) For purposes of computing interest and for purposes of section 6651 (relating to addition to tax for failure to file tax return), the due date for the return and payment of the tax for any calendar quarter resulting from the filing of an amendment referred to in subparagraph (1) of this paragraph shall be the last day of the calendar month following the calendar quarter in which the amendment is filed. The statutory period for the assessment of such tax shall not expire before the expiration of 3 years from such due date. [Reg. § 31.3121(k)-2.]

☐ [*T.D. 6744, 7-2-64. Amended by T.D. 6983,* 12-4-68.]

>>>→ *Caution: Reg. §31.3121(k)-3 does not reflect P.L. 98–21.*

[Reg. §31.3121(k)-3]

§31.3121(k)-3. **Request for coverage of individual employed by exempt organization before August 1, 1956.**—(a) *Application of this section.*—This section is applicable to requests made after July 31, 1956, and before September 14, 1960, under section 403 of the Social Security Amendments of 1954, as amended, except that nothing in this section shall render invalid any act performed pursuant to, and in accordance with, Revenue Ruling 57-11, Cumulative Bulletin 1957-1, page 344, or Revenue Ruling 58-514, Cumulative Bulletin 1958-2, page 733. (For regulations relating to requests made before August 1, 1956, under section 403 of the Social Security Amendments of 1954, see 26 CFR (1939) 408.216(c) and (d) (Regulations 128).)

(b) *Organization which did not have waiver certificate in effect.*—(1) *Coverage requested by employee before August 27, 1958.*—Pursuant to section 403(a) of the Social Security Amendments of 1954, as amended by section 401 of the Social Security Amendments of 1956, any individual who, as an employee, performed services after December 31, 1950, and before August 1, 1956, for an organization described in section 501(c)(3) which was exempt from income tax under section 501(a), or which was exempt from income tax under section 101(6) of the Internal Revenue Code of 1939, but which failed to file, before August 1, 1956, a valid waiver certificate under section 3121(k), or under section 1426(l) of the Internal Revenue Code of 1939, may request after July 31, 1956, and before August 27, 1958, that such part of the remuneration received by him for services performed in the employ of the organization after 1950 and before 1957 with respect to which employee and employer taxes were paid be deemed to constitute remuneration for employment, if:

(i) Any of the services performed by the individual after December 31, 1950, and before January 1, 1957, would have constituted employ-

ment if such a certificate on Form SS-15 filed by the organization had been in effect for the period during which the services were performed and the individual's signature had appeared on the accompanying list on Form SS-15a;

(ii) The employee and employer taxes were paid with respect to any part of the remuneration received by the individual from the organization for such services;

(iii) A part of such taxes was paid before August 1, 1956;

(iv) Such taxes as were paid before August 1, 1956, were paid by the organization in good faith and upon the assumption that it had filed a valid certificate under section 3121(k), or under section 1426(l) of the Internal Revenue Code of 1939; and

(v) No refund (or credit) of such taxes had been obtained by either the employee or the employer, exclusive of any refund (or credit) which would have been allowable if the services performed by the individual had constituted employment.

(2) *Coverage requested by employee after August 26, 1958, and before September 14, 1960.*—Requests may be made after August 26, 1958, and before September 14, 1960, pursuant to section 403(a) of the Social Security Amendments of 1954, as amended by section 401 of the Social Security Amendments of 1956, by the Act of August 27, 1958 (Public Law 85-785, 72 Stat. 938), and by section 105(b)(6) of the Social Security Amendments of 1960. Any individual who, as an employee, performed services after December 31, 1950, and before August 1, 1956, for an organization described in section 501(c)(3) which was exempt from income tax under section 501(a), or which was exempt from income tax under section 101(6) of the Internal Revenue Code of 1939, but which did not have in effect during the entire period in which the individual was so employed a valid waiver certificate under section 3121(k), or under section 1426(l) of the Inter-

nal Revenue Code of 1939, may request after August 26, 1958, and before September 14, 1960, that such part of the remuneration received by him for services performed in the employ of the organization after 1950 and before 1957 with respect to which employee and employer taxes were paid be deemed to constitute remuneration for employment, if:

(i) Any of the services performed by the individual after December 31, 1950, and before January 1, 1957, would have constituted employment if such a certificate on Form SS-15 filed by the organization had been in effect for the period during which the services were performed and the individual's signature had appeared on the accompanying list on Form SS-15a;

(ii) The employee and employer taxes were paid with respect to any part of the remuneration received by the individual from the organization for such services performed during the period in which the organization did not have a valid waiver certificate in effect;

(iii) A part of such taxes was paid before August 1, 1956;

(iv) Such taxes as were paid before August 1, 1956, were paid by the organization in good faith, and either without knowledge that a waiver certificate was necessary or upon the assumption that it had filed a valid certificate under section 3121(k), or under section 1426(l) of the Internal Revenue Code of 1939; and

(v) No refund (or credit) of such taxes has been obtained by either the employee or the employer, exclusive of any refund (or credit) which would be allowable if the services performed by the individual had constituted employment.

(3) *Execution and filing of request.*—(i) Except where the alternative procedure set forth in subdivision (ii) of this subparagraph is followed, the request of an individual under section 403(a) of the Social Security Amendments of 1954, as amended, is required to be made and filed as provided in this subdivision. The request shall be made in writing, be signed and dated by the individual, and include:

(a) The name and address of the organization for which the services were performed;

(b) The name, address, and social security account number of the individual;

(c) A statement that the individual has not obtained refund or credit (other than a refund or credit which would have been allowable if the services had constituted employment) from the district director of any part of the employee tax paid with respect to remuneration received by him from the organization for services performed after 1950 and before 1957; and

(d) A request that all remuneration received by him from the organization for such services with respect to which employee and employer taxes had been paid shall be deemed to constitute remuneration for employment to the extent authorized by section 403(a) of the Social Security Amendments of 1954, as amended.

The request of an individual shall be accompanied by a statement of the organization incorporating the substance of each of the five conditions listed in subparagraph (1) or (2), whichever is appropriate, of this paragraph. The statement of the organization shall show also that the individual performed services for the organization after December 31, 1950, and before August 1, 1956; that the organization was an organization described in section 501(c)(3) which was exempt from income tax under section 501(a) or was exempt from income tax under section 101(6) of the Internal Revenue Code of 1939, and the district director with whom returns on Form 941 were filed. The organization's statement shall be signed by the president or other principal officer of the organization who shall certify that the statement is correct to the best of his knowledge and belief. If the statement of the organization is not submitted with the individual's request, the individual shall include in his request an explanation of his inability to submit the statement. Other information may be required, but should be submitted only upon receipt of a specific request therefor. No particular form is prescribed for the request of the individual or the statement of the organization required to be submitted with the request. The individual's request should be filed with the district director with whom the organization files returns on Form 941. If the individual is deceased or mentally incompetent and the request is made by the legal representative of the individual or other person authorized to act on his behalf, the request shall be accompanied by evidence showing such person's authority to make the request.

(ii) An organization which has or had in its employ individuals with respect to whom section 403(a) of the Social Security Amendments of 1954, as amended, is applicable may, if it so desires, prepare a form or forms for use by any such individual or individuals in making requests under such section. Any such form shall provide space for the signature of the individual or individuals and contain such information as required to be included in a request (see subdivision (i) of this subparagraph). Any such form used by more than one individual, and any such form used by one individual which is signed and returned to the organization, shall be submitted by the organization, together with its statement (as required in subdivision (i) of this subparagraph), to the district director with whom the organization files its returns on Form 941. An individual is not required to use a form prepared by the organization but may, at his election, file his request in accordance with the provisions of subdivision (i) of this subparagraph.

(4) *Optional tax payments by organization.*— An organization which prior to August 1, 1956, reported and paid employee and employer taxes with respect to any portion of the remuneration paid to an individual, who is eligible to file a request under section 403(a) of the Social Security Amendments of 1954, as amended, for services performed by him after 1950 and before

Reg. §31.3121(k)-3(b)(2)(i)

1957, may report and pay such taxes before September 14, 1960, with respect to any remaining portion of such remuneration which would have constituted wages if a certificate had been in effect with respect to such services. Such taxes may be reported as an adjustment without interest in the manner prescribed in subpart G of the regulations in this part.

(5) *Effect of request.*—If a request is made and filed under the conditions stated in this paragraph with respect to one or more individuals, remuneration for services performed by each such individual after 1950 and before 1957, with respect to which the employee and employer taxes are paid on or before the date on which the request was filed with the district director, will be deemed to constitute remuneration for employment to the extent that such services would have constituted employment as defined in section 3121(b), or in section 1426(b) of the Internal Revenue Code of 1939, if a certificate had been in effect with respect to such services. However, the provisions of section 3121(a) and §§31.3121(a)-1 to 31.3121(a)(10)-1, inclusive, of the regulations in this part or the provisions of section 1426(a) of the Internal Revenue Code of 1939 and the regulations in 26 CFR (1939) 408.226 and 408.227 (Regulations 128), as the case may be, are applicable in determining the extent to which such remuneration for employment constitutes wages for purposes of the employee and employer taxes.

(c) *Individual who failed to sign list of concurring employees.*—(1) *In general.*—Pursuant to section 403(b) of the Social Security Amendments of 1954, as amended, any individual who, as an employee, performed services after December 31, 1950, and before August 1, 1956, for an organization which filed a valid certificate under section 3121(k), or under section 1426(l) of the Internal Revenue Code of 1939, but who failed to sign the list of employees concurring in the filing of such certificate, may request on or before January 1, 1959, that the remuneration received by him for such services be deemed to constitute remuneration for employment, if:

(i) Any of the services performed by the individual after December 31, 1950, and before August 1, 1956, would have constituted employment if the signature of such individual had appeared on the list of employees who concurred in the filing of the certificate;

(ii) The employee and employer taxes were paid before August 1, 1956, with respect to any part of the remuneration received by the individual from the organization for such services; and

(iii) No refund (or credit) of such taxes has been obtained either by the employee or the employer, exclusive of any refund (or credit) which would be allowable if the services performed by the individual had constituted employment.

(2) *Execution and filing of request.*—(i) Except where the alternative procedure set forth in sub-

division (ii) of this subparagraph is followed, the request of an individual under section 403(b) of the Social Security Amendments of 1954, as amended, shall be made and filed as provided in this subdivision. The request shall be filed on or before January 1, 1959, be made in writing, be signed and dated by the individual, and include:

(a) The name and address of the organization for which the services were performed;

(b) The name, address, and social security account number of the individual;

(c) A statement that the individual has not obtained a refund or credit (other than a refund or credit which would be allowable if the services had constituted employment) from the district director of any part of the employee tax paid before August 1, 1956, with respect to remuneration received by him from the organization;

(d) A request that all remuneration received by the individual from the organization for services performed after 1950 and before August 1, 1956, with respect to which employee and employer taxes were paid before August 1, 1956, shall be deemed to constitute remuneration for employment to the extent authorized by section 403(b) of the Social Security Amendments of 1954, as amended; and

(e) A statement that the individual understands that, upon the filing of such request with the district director, (1) he will be deemed to have concurred in the certificate which was previously filed by the organization, and (2) the employee and employer taxes will be applicable to all wages received, and to be received, by him for services performed for the organization on or after the effective date of such certificate to the extent that such taxes would have been applicable if he had signed the list on Form SS-15a submitted with the certificate.

The request of an individual shall be accompanied by a statement of the organization incorporating the substance of each of the three conditions listed in subparagraph (1) of this paragraph. The statement of the organization should also show that the individual performed services for the organization after December 31, 1950, and before August 1, 1956; that the organization filed a valid certificate under section 3121(k), or under section 1426(l) of the Internal Revenue Code of 1939; and the district director with whom returns on Form 941 are filed. Such statement shall be signed by the president or other principal officer of the organization who shall certify that the statement is correct to the best of his knowledge and belief. If the statement of the organization is not submitted with the individual's request, the individual shall include in his request an explanation of his inability to submit such statement. Other information may be required, but should be submitted only upon receipt of a specific request therefor. No particular form is prescribed for the request of the individual or the statement of the organization required to be submitted with the request. The individual's request should be filed with the district director with whom the organization files returns on Form 941. If the individual is deceased or mentally incompetent and the request is made by the legal representative of the individual or other person authorized to act on his behalf, the request shall be accompanied by evidence showing such person's authority to make the request.

(ii) An organization which has or had in its employ individuals with respect to whom section 403(b) of the Social Security Amendments of 1954, as amended, is applicable, may, if it so desires, prepare a form or forms for use by any such individual or individuals in making requests under such section. Any such form shall provide space for the signature of the individual or individuals and contain such information as is required by subdivision (i) of this subparagraph to be included in a request. Any such form used by more than one individual, and any such form used by one individual which is signed and returned to the organization, shall be submitted by the organization, together with its statement (as required in subdivision (i) of this subparagraph), to the district director with whom the organization files returns on Form 941. An individual is not required to use a form prepared by the organization but may, at his election, file his

request in accordance with the provisions of subdivision (i) of this subparagraph.

(3) *Effect of request.*—An individual who makes and files a request under the conditions stated in this paragraph with respect to services performed as an employee of an organization described in section 501(c)(3) which was exempt from income tax under section 501(a), or which was exempt from income tax under section 101(6) of the Internal Revenue Code of 1939, will be deemed to have signed the list accompanying the certificate filed by the organization under section 3121(k), or under section 1426(l) of the Internal Revenue Code of 1939. Accordingly, all services performed by the individual for the organization on and after the effective date of the certificate will constitute employment to the same extent as if he had, in fact, signed the list. The employee tax and employer tax are applicable with respect to any remuneration paid to the employee by the organization which constitutes wages. If less than the correct amount of such taxes has been paid, the additional amount due should be reported as an adjustment without interest within the time specified in subpart G of the regulations in this part.[Reg. § 31.3121(k)-3.]

□ [T.D. 6744, 7-2-64.]

⋙→ *Caution: Reg. §31.3121(k)-4 does not reflect P.L. 98–21.*

[Reg. § 31.3121(k)-4]

§ 31.3121(k)-4. Constructive filing of waivers of exemption from social security taxes by certain tax-exempt organizations.—(a) *Constructive filing of waiver certificate where no refund or credit has been allowed.*—(1) This paragraph applies (except as provided in subparagraph (3) of this paragraph) to an organization if all of the following four conditions are met.

(i) The organization is one described in section 501(c)(3) of the Internal Revenue Code of 1954, which is exempt from income tax under section 501(a) of the Code.

(ii) The organization did not file a valid waiver certificate under section 3121(k)(1) of the Internal Revenue Code of 1954 (or the corresponding provision of prior law) as of the later of October 19, 1976, or the earliest date on which it satisfies subdivision (iii) of this subparagraph.

(iii) The taxes imposed by sections 3101 and 3111 of the Code were paid with respect to remuneration paid by the organization to its employees, as though such certificate had been filed, during any period that includes all or part of at least three consecutive calendar quarters and that did not terminate before the end of the third calendar quarter of 1973.

(iv) The Internal Revenue Service did not allow (or erroneously allowed) a refund or credit of any part of the taxes paid as described in subdivision (iii) of this subparagraph with respect to remuneration for services performed on or after April 1, 1973. For purposes of the previous sentence, a refund or credit which would have been allowed, even if a valid waiver certificate filed under section 3121(k)(1) had been in

effect, shall be disregarded. A refund or credit will be regarded as having been erroneously allowed if it was credited by the Internal Revenue Service to the taxpayer account of the organization or any of its employees on or after September 9, 1976, even though it was properly made under the law in effect when made.

(2)(i) An organization to which this paragraph applies shall be deemed to have filed a valid waiver certificate under section 3121(k)(l) (or the corresponding provision of prior law) for purposes of section 210(a)(8)(B) of the Social Security Act and section 3121(b)(8)(B). The waiver certificate shall be deemed to have been filed on the first day of the period described in subparagraph (1)(iii) of this paragraph and shall be effective on the first day of the calendar quarter in which such period began. However, such waiver is effective only with respect to remuneration for services performed after 1950.

(ii) The waiver certificate shall be deemed to have been accompanied by a list containing the signature, address, and social security number (if any) of each employee with respect to whom the taxes imposed by sections 3101 and 3111 were paid as described in subparagraph (1)(iii) of this paragraph. Each such employee shall be deemed to have concurred in the filing of the certificate for purposes of section 210(a)(8)(B) of the Social Security Act and section 3121(b)(8)(B). A statement containing the name, address, and employer identification number of the organization, and the name, last known address, and social security number (if any) of each employee described in the preceding sentence shall be filed by the organization at the request of the Internal Revenue Service.

(iii) The services of all employees entering or reentering the employ of an organization on or after the first day following the close of the calendar quarter in which the organization is deemed to have filed the waiver certificate, performed on or after the day of such entry or reentry, shall be covered by the certificate.

(3) This paragraph (a) shall not apply to an organization if—

(i) Prior to the end of the period referred to in subparagraph (1)(iii) (and, in addition, in the case of an organization organized on or before October 9, 1969, prior to October 19, 1976), the organization had applied for a ruling or determination letter acknowledging it to be exempt from income tax under section 501(c)(3);

(ii) The organization subsequently received such ruling or determination letter;

(iii) The organization did not pay any taxes under sections 3101 and 3111 with respect to any employee for any calendar quarter ending after the twelfth month following the date of mailing of the ruling or determination letter; and

(iv) The organization did not pay any taxes under sections 3101 and 3111 with respect to any calendar quarter beginning after the later of December 31, 1975, or the date on which the ruling or determination letter was issued.

(4) In the case of an organization which is deemed under this paragraph to have filed a valid waiver certificate under section 3121(k)(1), if the period with respect to which the taxes imposed by sections 3101 and 3111 were paid by the organization (as described in paragraph (a)(1)(iii) of this section) terminated prior to October 1, 1976, taxes under sections 3101 and 3111 with respect to remuneration paid by the organization after the termination of such period and prior to July 1, 1977, which remained unpaid on December 20, 1977 (or which were paid after October 19, 1976, but prior to December 20, 1977), shall not be due or payable (or, if paid, shall be refunded). Similarly, an organization that received a refund or credit of the taxes described in paragraph (a)(1)(iii) of this section after September 8, 1976, shall not be liable for the taxes imposed by sections 3101 and 3111 with respect to remuneration paid by it prior to July 1, 1977, for which the organization received the refund or credit. The waiver certificate, which an organization described in this subparagraph is deemed to have filed, shall not apply to any service with respect to the remuneration for which the taxes imposed by sections 3101 and 3111 are not due or payable (or are refunded) by reason of this subparagraph.

(5) In the case of an organization which is deemed under this paragraph to have filed a valid waiver certificate under section 3121(k)(1), if the taxes imposed by sections 3101 and 3111 were not paid during the period referred to in paragraph (a)(1)(iii) of this section (whether the period has terminated or not) with respect to remuneration paid by the organization to individuals who became its employees after the close of the calendar quarter in which such period

began, taxes under sections 3101 and 3111 with respect to remuneration paid prior to July 1, 1977, to such employees, which remain unpaid on December 20, 1977 (or which were paid after October 19, 1976, but prior to December 20, 1977), shall not be due or payable (or, if paid, shall be refunded). The waiver certificate, which an organization described in this subparagraph is deemed to have filed, shall not apply to any service with respect to remuneration for which the taxes imposed by sections 3101 and 3111 are not due or payable (or are refunded) by reason of this subparagraph.

(6) This subparagraph allows certain employees to obtain social security coverage for service not covered by a deemed-filed waiver certificate by reason of section 3121(k)(4)(C) and subparagraph (4) or (5) of this paragraph. To qualify under this subparagraph, all of the following conditions must be met.

(i) An individual performed service as an employee of an organization which is deemed under this paragraph to have filed a waiver certificate under section 3121(k)(1), on or after the first day of the period described in subparagraph (1)(iii) of this paragraph and before July 1, 1977.

(ii) The service performed by the individual does not constitute employment (as defined in section 21(a) of the Social Security Act and section 3121(b) of the Code) because the waiver certificate which the organization is deemed to have filed is inapplicable to such service by reason of section 3121(k)(4)(C), but would constitute employment (as so defined) in the absence of section 3121(k)(4)(C).

(iii) The individual files a request on or before April 15, 1980, in the manner and form, and with such official, as may be prescribed by regulations under title II of the Social Security Act.

(iv) That request is accompanied by full payment of the taxes, which would have been paid under section 3101 with respect to the remuneration for the service described in subdivision (ii) of this subparagraph but for the application of section 3121(k)(4)(C) (or by satisfactory evidence that appropriate arrangements have been made for the payment of such taxes in installments as provided in section 3121(k)(8) and paragraph (d) of this section).

If these conditions are satisfied, the remuneration paid for the service described in subdivision (i) of this subparagraph shall be deemed to constitute remuneration for employment. In any case where remuneration paid by an organization to an individual is deemed under this subparagraph to constitute remuneration for employment, such organization shall be liable (notwithstanding any other provision of the Code or regulations) for payment of the taxes it would have been required to pay under section 3111 with respect to such remuneration but for the application of section 3121(k)(4)(C). The due date for the return and payment by the organization of the taxes described in the preceding sentence shall be the last day of the calendar month fol-

Reg. §31.3121(k)-4(a)(6)(iv)

lowing the calendar quarter in which the organization is notified in writing of the employee's request. However, see paragraph (d) of this section which permits the payment of these taxes in installments.

(b) *Constructive filing of waiver certificate where refund or credit has been allowed and new certificate is not filed.*—(1) This paragraph applies to an organization which meets two conditions. First, it must be an organization to which paragraph (a) of this section would apply but for its failure to satisfy the requirement of paragraph (a)(1)(iv) of this section because a refund or credit of taxes was allowed before September 9, 1976. Second, it must not have filed an actual valid waiver certificate under section 3121(k)(1) in accordance with the requirements of paragraph (c) of this section.

(2) An organization to which this paragraph applies shall be deemed, for purposes of section 210(a)(8)(B) of the Social Security Act and section 3121(b)(8)(B), to have filed a valid waiver certificate under section 3121(k)(1) on April 1, 1978. Such certificate shall be effective for the period beginning on the first day of the first calendar quarter with respect to which the refund or credit referred to in subparagraph (1) of this paragraph was allowed (or, if later, on July 1, 1973).

(3) If an organization is deemed under this paragraph to have filed a waiver certificate on April 1, 1978, the provisions of paragraph (a)(2)(ii) and (iii) of this section (relating to employees covered by a deemed-filed waiver certificate) shall apply. Such certificate shall supersede any certificate which may have been actually filed by such organization prior to that date.

(4) Where an organization is deemed under this paragraph to have filed a waiver certificate on April 1, 1978, the due date for the return and payment of the taxes imposed by sections 3101 and 3111 for wages paid prior to April 1, 1978, with respect to services constituting employment by reason of such certificate shall be August 1, 1978. However, see paragraph (d) of this section which permits the payment of these taxes in installments. Such taxes (along with the amount of any interest paid in connection with the refund or credit described in subparagraph (1) of this paragraph) shall be a liability of such organization, payable from its own funds. No portion of such taxes (or interest) shall be deducted from the wages of (or otherwise collected from) the individuals who performed such services, and those individuals shall have no liability for the payment thereof.

(5) This subparagraph allows certain employees of organizations covered under this paragraph to obtain social security coverage for periods prior to those covered by a deemed-filed waiver certificate. To qualify under this subparagraph, all of the following conditions must be met.

(i) An individual performed service, as an employee of an organization deemed under this paragraph to have filed a waiver certificate

under section 3121(k)(1), at any time prior to the period for which such certificate is effective.

(ii) The taxes imposed by sections 3101 and 3111 were paid with respect to remuneration paid for such service, but such service (or any part thereof) does not constitute employment (as defined in section 210(a) of the Social Security Act and section 3121 (b)) because the applicable taxes so paid were refunded or credited (otherwise than through a refund credit which would have been allowed if a valid waiver certificate filed under section 3121(k)(1) had been in effect) prior to September 9, 1976.

(iii) Any portion of such service (with respect to which taxes were paid and refunded or credited as described in subdivision (ii) of this subparagraph) would constitute employment (as so defined) if the organization had actually filed under section 3121(k)(1) a valid waiver certificate effective as provided in paragraph (c)(2) of this section (with such individual's signature appearing on the accompanying list).

If this subparagraph applies, the remuneration paid for the portion of such service described in subdivision (iii) of this subparagraph shall be deemed to constitute remuneration for employment (as defined in section 210(a) of the Social Security Act and section 3121(b)), where such individual filed a request on or before April 15, 1980 (in the manner and form, and with such official, as may be prescribed by regulations under title II of the Social Security Act), accompanied by full repayment of the taxes which were paid under section 3101 with respect to such remuneration and were refunded or credited (or by satisfactory evidence that arrangements have been made for the payment of such taxes in installments as provided in section 3121(k)(8) and paragraph (d) of this section). In any case where remuneration paid by an organization to an individual is deemed under this subparagraph to constitute remuneration for employment such organization shall be liable (notwithstanding any other provision of the Code or regulations) for repayment of any taxes which it paid under section 3111 with respect to such remuneration and which were refunded or credited to it. Any interest received by the organization or its employees in connection with a refund or credit with respect to such taxes shall be remitted with the repayment of taxes pursuant to this subparagraph.

(c) *Actual filing of waiver certificate by April 1, 1978, where refund or credit has been allowed.*—(1) An organization may file an actual waiver certificate in accordance with subparagraphs (2) and (3) of this paragraph if it is an organization to which paragraph (a) of this section would apply but for its failure to meet the condition set forth in paragraph (a)(1)(iv) of this section.

(2) An organization described in subparagraph (1) of this paragraph was permitted to file an actual waiver certificate on or before April 1, 1978. This certificate must be effective for the period beginning on or before the first day of the first calendar quarter with respect to which a

refund or credit described in paragraph (b)(1) of this section was allowed (or, if later, with the first day of the earliest calendar quarter for which such certificate may be in effect under section 3121(k)(1)(B)(iii)). Such waiver certificate must have been accompanied by a list described in section 3121(k)(1)(A), containing the signature, address, and social security number of each concurring employee (if any).

(3) Such a waiver certificate shall be valid only if the organization complied with the following notification requirements and, on or before April 30, 1978, filed (with the service center of the Internal Revenue Service with which the waiver certificate was filed) a certification that it had complied with these notification requirements. However, these requirements shall be conclusively presumed to have been met with respect to any employees who concurred in the filing of the waiver certificate.

(i) Written notification of the option to obtain social security coverage for the retroactive period covered by the waiver certificate is required to have been given to all current and former employees of the organization with respect to whose remuneration taxes imposed sections 3101 and 3111 were paid for any part of the period covered by the waiver certificate. For purposes of the preceding sentence, in the case of a former employee a mailing of notification to his or her last known address shall constitute delivery to the former employee. This notification must have been given at least 30 days prior to the date by which the employee was required to inform the organization whether he or she elects the retroactive social security coverage.

(ii) The notification required by this subparagraph must have stated the earliest date for which the waiver certificate is effective and the date by which the employee must have informed the organization of a decision to elect the retroactive coverage. In addition, the notification must have advised the employee how to obtain information as to the quarters of social security coverage to be obtained and any taxes or interest for which the employee would be liable if the election was made. The organization must have provided this information to any interested employee at least 14 days prior to the last day on which such employee was to have informed the organization of any election.

(iii) If the notification resulted in any employee electing the retroactive coverage whose signature did not appear on the list of concurring employees which accompanied a previously filed waiver certificate, the certification that was supplied on or before April 30, 1978, must have been accompanied by a special amendment to that list. Any employee whose name appears on this special amended list shall be treated as if his or her name appeared on the list of concurring employees filed with the waiver certificate. The preceding sentence shall only apply with respect to amended lists of concurring employees filed to comply with the requirements of this subparagraph.

(4) Any interest received in connection with a refund or credit described in paragraph (b)(1) of this section must have been repaid on or before April 30, 1978, with respect to each employee who concurs in the filing of a waiver certificate pursuant to this paragraph. Notwithstanding the provisions of paragraph (c)(4) of §31.3121(k)-1, if such interest was repaid on or before April 30, 1978, the waiver certificate shall be considered to have been filed on the date it was originally furnished to the Internal Revenue Service.

(d) *Installment payment of taxes for retroactive coverage.*—This paragraph applies if—

(1) An organization is deemed under paragraph (a) of this section to have filed a valid waiver certificate, but the applicable period described in paragraph (a)(1)(iii) has terminated and all or part of the taxes imposed by sections 3101 and 3111, with respect to remuneration paid by such organization to its employees after the close of such period, remains payable notwithstanding section 3121(k)(4)(C) and paragraph (a)(4) of this section; or

(2) An organization described in paragraph (c) files a valid waiver certificate by March 31, 1978, or, not having filed the certificate by that date, is deemed to have filed the certificate on April 1, 1978, under paragraph (b); or

(3) An individual files a request under paragraph (a)(6) or (b)(5) to have service treated as constituting remuneration for employment (as defined in section 210 (a) of the Social Security Act and section 3121(b)).

If this paragraph applies, the taxes due under sections 3101 and 3111 (together with any additions to tax or interest other than interest described in paragraph (c)(4)) with respect to service constituting employment by reason of the waiver certificate for any period prior to the first day of the calendar quarter in which the certificate is filed or deemed filed, or with respect to service constituting employment by reason of an employee request, may be paid in installments over an appropriate period of time, as determined by the district director. In determining the appropriate period of time, the district director shall exercise forbearance and, to the extent possible, grant the organization an installment agreement that will allow it sufficient funds to carry out its basic mission. If any installment is not paid on or before the date fixed for its payment, the total unpaid amount shall become payable immediately and shall be paid upon notice and demand.

(e) *Application of certain provisions to cases of constructive filing.*—(1) Except as provided in subparagraphs (2) and (3) of this paragraph, all of the provisions of section 3121(k) (other than subparagraphs (B), (F), and (H) of section 3121(k)(1)) and the regulations thereunder (including the provisions requiring the payment of taxes under sections 3101 and 3111 with respect to the services involved), shall apply with respect to any certificate which is deemed to have

Reg. §31.3121(k)-4(e)(1)

been filed under paragraph (a) or (b) of this section, in the same way they would apply if the certificate had been actually filed on that day under section 3121(k)(1).

(2) The provisions of section 3121(k)(1)(E) shall not apply unless the taxes described in paragraph (a)(1)(iii) of this section were paid by the organization as though a separate certificate had been filed with respect to one or both of the groups to which such provisions relate.

(3) The action of the organization in obtaining the refund or credit described in paragraph (b)(1) of this section shall not be considered a termination of such organization's coverage period for purposes of section 3121(k)(3).

(4) Any organization which is deemed to have filed a waiver certificate under paragraph (a) or (b) of this section shall be considered for purposes of section 3102(b) to have been required to deduct the taxes imposed by section 3101 with respect to the services involved. [Reg. § 31.3121(k)-4.]

☐ [T.D. 7647, 10-16-79.]

[Reg. § 31.3121(l)-1]

§ 31.3121(l)-1. Agreements entered into by domestic corporations with respect to foreign subsidiaries.—For provisions relating to the extension of the Federal old-age, survivors, and disability insurance system established by title II of the Social Security Act to certain services performed outside the United States by citizens of the United States in the employ of a foreign subsidiary of a domestic corporation, see the Regulations Relating to Contract Coverage of Employees of Foreign Subsidiaries (Part 36 of this chapter). [Reg. § 31.3121(l)-1.]

☐ [T.D. 6190, 7-14-56. Republished in T.D. 6516, 12-20-60.]

[Reg. § 36.3121(l)-0]

§ 36.3121(l)-0. Introduction.—(a) The regulations in this part deal with the circumstances under which a domestic corporation may enter into an agreement with the Internal Revenue Service for the purpose of extending the insurance system established by title II of the Social Security Act to certain services performed outside the United States by citizens of the United States as employees of a foreign subsidiary of the domestic corporation, and with the obligations of a domestic corporation which enters into such an agreement. The provisions of the Internal Revenue Code of 1954, as amended, to which the regulations in this part pertain are contained in section 3121(1). The liabilities assumed under an agreement entered into pursuant to such section are based on the remuneration for services covered by the agreement. Such agreement may not be effective prior to January 1, 1955.

(b) Although the obligations incurred under an agreement entered into pursuant to section 3121(1) of the Internal Revenue Code of 1954, as amended, must be distinguished from the obligations imposed on employers with respect to the taxes under the Federal Insurance Contributions Act, the two are similar in many respects. Accordingly, the regulations in this part are prescribed as a supplement to the regulations (26 CFR (1954), Part 31, Subpart B) relating to the employee tax and the employer tax imposed by the Federal Insurance Contributions Act. The terms used in the regulations in this part have the same meaning, unless otherwise provided, as when used in the regulations relating to the taxes imposed by such act.

(c) The regulations in this part constitute Part 36 of title 26 of the Code of Federal Regulations. As used in the regulations in this part, the word "Code" means the Internal Revenue Code of 1954, as amended, and the term "Federal Insurance Contributions Act" means chapter 21 of such Code. All references to sections of law are references to the Code unless otherwise indicated. The number of each section of the regulations begins with 36 followed by a decimal point (36.). Numbers which do not begin with 36 followed by a decimal point are numbers of sections of law unless otherwise indicated. In identifying sections of regulations, the symbol "§" is used. [Reg. § 36.3121(l)-0.]

☐ [T.D. 6145, 12-31-60. Amended by T.D. 7012, 5-15-69 and T.D. 7665, 1-25-80.]

[Reg. § 36.3121(l)(1)-1]

§ 36.3121(l)(1)-1. Agreements entered into by domestic corporations with respect to foreign subsidiaries.—(a) In general.—(1) Any domestic corporation having one or more foreign subsidiaries may request the Internal Revenue Service to enter into an agreement for the purpose of extending the Federal old-age, survivors, and disability insurance system established by title II of the Social Security Act to certain services performed outside the United States by all citizens of the United States who are employees of any such foreign subsidiary. See § 36.3121(l)(8)-1, relating to the definition of foreign subsidiary. Except as provided in § 36.3121(l)(5)-1, relating to the effect of the termination of an agreement entered into pursuant to the provisions of section 3121(1), the Internal Revenue Service shall, at the request of a domestic corporation enter into such agreement on Form 2032 in any case where a Form 2032 is executed, and submitted by the domestic corporation in the manner prescribed in this section. A domestic corporation may not have in effect at the same moment of time more than one agreement on Form 2032.

(2) An agreement authorized in section 3121(l)(1) may not be made applicable to any services performed outside the United States which would not constitute employment, for purposes of the taxes imposed under the Federal Insurance Contributions Act, if the services were performed within the United States. Thus, such an agreement shall have no application with respect to any services performed outside the United States which, if performed within the United States, would be specifically excepted

from employment under any of the numbered paragraphs of section 3121(b), or which, although not so excepted, would be deemed not to be employment by application of section 3121(c), relating to included and excluded services. Further, an agreement may not be made applicable with respect to any services performed outside the United States which constitute employment, as defined in section 3121(b). Thus, an agreement may not be made applicable to services for any employer performed by any employee on or in connection with an American vessel or American aircraft when outside the United States, if (i) performed under a contract of service which is entered into within the United States or (ii) during the performance of which and while the employee is employed on the vessel or aircraft it touches at a port in the United States, because such services constitute employment as defined in section 3121(b). An agreement may not be made applicable to remuneration which would not constitute wages, as defined in section 3121(a), even if the services to which such remuneration is attributable had constituted employment.

(3) The terms "corporation", "domestic", and "foreign", as used in the regulations in this part, have the meaning assigned by paragraphs (3), (4), and (5), respectively, of section 7701(a). Section 701(a) (3), (4), and (5) provides as follows:

SEC. 7701. *Definitions.* (a) When used in this title [Internal Revenue Code of 1954], where not otherwise distinctly expressed or manifestly incompatible with the intent thereof—

* * *

(3) *Corporation.* The term "corporation" includes associations, joint-stock companies, and insurance companies.

(4) *Domestic.* The term "domestic" when applied to a corporation * * * means created or organized in the United States or under the law of the United States or of any State or Territory.

(5) *Foreign.* The term "foreign" when applied to a corporation * * * means a corporation * * which is not domestic.

(b) *Form and contents of agreement.*—Form 2032 is the form prescribed for the agreement authorized in section 3121(l)(1). The agreement shall include provisions substantially as follows:

(1) That the agreement shall apply to all services performed outside the United States by all citizens of the United States who are in the employ of the foreign subsidiary or subsidiaries to which the agreement is made applicable, but only to the extent that the remuneration paid each employee for such services would constitute wages if paid by one employer for services performed in the United States;

(2) That the agreement shall not apply to any services which constitute employment within the meaning of section 3121;

(3) That the agreement shall become effective on the first day of the calendar quarter in which the Form 2032 is signed by the district

director or director of the service center or on the first day of the next succeeding calendar quarter, whichever is specified in the agreement;

(4) That the domestic corporation will pay, as required by the regulations in this part, amounts equivalent to the sum of the taxes which would be imposed by sections 3101 and 3111, respectively, if the remuneration for the services covered by the agreement constituted wages;

(5) That the domestic corporation will pay, in accordance with written notification and demand therefor to the domestic corporation, amounts equivalent to the interest, additions to the taxes, additional amounts, and penalties which would be applicable if the remuneration for services covered by the agreement constituted wages; and

(6) That the domestic corporation will comply with all provisions of the regulations in this part.

(c) *Execution and filing of Form 2032.*—The request of any domestic corporation that the Internal Revenue Service enter into an agreement with the corporation on Form 2032 shall be signified by the corporation by executing and filing Form 2032 in triplicate. Such form shall be executed and filed in accordance with the regulations in this part and the instructions relating to the form. Each copy of the form shall be signed and dated by the officer of the corporation authorized to enter into the agreement, shall show the title of such officer, and shall have the corporate seal affixed thereto. A certified copy of the minutes of the meeting of the board of directors of the domestic corporation, or other evidence, showing the authority of such officer so to act shall accompany the form. Form 2032 executed and filed as provided in this paragraph shall be signed and dated by the district director or director of the service center and, upon such signing, the Form 2032 so executed and filed will constitute the agreement authorized in section 3121(l)(1). The Internal Revenue Service will return one copy of the agreement to the domestic corporation, will transmit one copy of the Department of Health, Education, and Welfare, and will retain one copy (together with all related papers). [Reg. §36.3121(l)(1)-1.]

☐ [T.D. 6145, 9-8-55. *Amended by T.D. 7012,* 5-15-69.]

[Reg. §36.3121(l)(1)-2]

§36.3121(l)(1)-2. Amendment of agreement.—(a) An agreement entered into by a domestic corporation as provided in §36.3121(l)(1)-1 may be amended so as to be made applicable, in the same manner and under the same conditions, with respect to any one or more of the foreign subsidiaries of the domestic corporation not previously named in the agreement. See §36.3121(l)(2)-1(b), relating to the effective period of an amendment of an agreement.

(b) Form 2032 Supplement is the form prescribed for use in amending an agreement entered into by a domestic Corporation as provided in §36.3121(l)(1)-1.

(c) A domestic corporation shall signify its desire to amend an agreement entered into by the corporation as provided in §36.3121(l)(1)-1 by executing and filing Form 2032 Supplement in triplicate.

(d) Form 2032 Supplement shall be executed and filed in the manner and in conformity with the requirements prescribed in the instructions relating to such form and in §36.3121(l)(1)-1(c) in respect of an agreement on Form 2032. Form 2032 Supplement executed and filed as provided in this paragraph shall be signed and dated by the district director or director of the service center, and, upon such signing, the Form 2032 Supplement so executed and filed will constitute an amendment of the agreement entered into on Form 2032. The Internal Revenue Service will return one copy of the amendment to the domestic corporation, will transmit one copy to the Department of Health, Education, and Welfare, and will retain one copy (together with all related papers). [Reg. §36.3121(l)(1)-2.]

☐ [T.D. 6145, 12-31-60. Amended by T.D. 7012, 5-15-69.]

[Reg. §36.3121(l)(1)-3]

§36.3121(l)(1)-3. Effect of agreement.—(a) Liability for amounts equivalent to tax.—(1) In general.—A domestic corporation which has entered into an agreement (as provided in §36.3121(l)(1)-1, or any amendment thereof (as provided in §36.3121(l)(1)-2, incurs liability under the agreement in respect of certain remuneration paid by each foreign subsidiary named in the agreement, or any amendment thereof. Liability is incurred in respect of the remuneration paid to all those employees of the foreign subsidiaries who are citizens of the United States and who perform services outside the United States (other than services which constitute employment) for the foreign subsidiaries. However, liability is incurred only with respect to that portion of such remuneration paid by the foreign subsidiary which is attributable to services performed during the period for which the agreement is in effect with respect to such subsidiary, and then only to the extent that the remuneration would constitute wages if the services to which the remuneration is attributable were performed in the United States. Liability with respect to such remuneration is incurred in an amount equivalent to the sum of the employee and employer taxes which would be imposed by sections 3101 and 3111, respectively, if such remuneration constituted wages. If an individual performs services for more than one of the foreign subsidiaries named in an agreement, including any amendment thereof, such services are regarded as being performed in the employ of a single employer for purposes of determining the amount of the remuneration for such services which would constitute wages if the services were performed in the United States. See §36.3121(l)(9)-1, relating to the treatment of a domestic corporation as a separate entity in its capacity as a party to an agreement.

(2) Examples.—The application of paragraph (a)(1) of this section may be illustrated by the following examples:

Example 1. P. a domestic corporation, has entered into an agreement as provided in §36.3121(l)(1)-1, effective with respect to services performed on and after January 1, 1955. Three foreign subsidiaries, S-1, S-2, and S-3 are named in the agreement. A, a citizen of the United States, is employed during 1955 by S-1, S-2, and S-3, for the performance outside the United States of services covered by the agreement. In 1955 A is paid remuneration of $2,500 for such services by each of the foreign subsidiaries. The circumstances are such that the entire $7,500 would constitute wages if the services has been performed in the United States. However, only $4,200 of such remuneration would constitute wages if the services had been performed in the United States for a single employer, and it is with respect to this amount only that P incurs liability under its agreement.

Example 2. On August 1, 1955, P, the domestic corporation in the preceding example, amends its agreement to include therein its foreign subsidiary S-4. The amendment is in effect with respect to S-4 for the period beginning with October 1, 1955. B, a citizen of the United States, is employed by S-4 throughout 1955 for the performance of services outside the United States. B is paid remuneration of $500 in each month of 1955 for these services. The circumstances are such that the first $4,200 of such remuneration would constitute wages if the services had been performed in the United States, and, except for the $4,200 limitation, the remainder of such remuneration would constitute wages if the services had been so performed. P incurs no liability with respect to remuneration paid B for services performed for S-4 prior to October 1, 1955. However, P incurs liability under its agreement with respect to the $1,500 paid B in October, November, and December 1955, for services performed in these months. Since the remuneration paid to B for services performed during the first nine months of 1955 is not covered by the agreement, such remuneration is not taken into account in computing the $4,200 limitation or the liability under the agreement.

Example 3. Assume the same facts as in example 2 except that B's services for S-4 during December 1955 are of a character which if performed within the United States would be excepted from employment. Accordingly, P incurs no liability under the agreement with respect to the $500.00 paid in December 1955 for such services.

(3) Determination of liability.—The amount of the liability referred to in paragraph (a)(1) of this section incurred by a domestic corporation for any period shall be determined in the same manner as liability for the employee tax and for the employer tax imposed by the Federal Insurance Contributions Act is determined, pursuant to

regulations relating to the taxes under such act as in effect for the same period, with respect to wages paid by an employer to an employee.

(b) *Liability for amounts equivalent to interest or penalties.*—A domestic corporation which has entered into an agreement as provided in § 36.3121(l)(1)-1 also incurs liability under the agreement for amounts equivalent to the amount of interest, additions to the taxes, additional amounts, and penalties which would be applicable if the remuneration for services covered by the agreement constituted wages.

(c) *Deductions from employees' remuneration.*— There is no obligation to deduct, or cause to be deducted, from the remuneration of any employee of a foreign subsidiary any part of the amount due from a domestic corporation under its agreement. Whether such deduction shall be made is a matter for settlement between the employee and the domestic corporation or such other person as may be concerned.

(d) *Cross reference.*—For other obligations of a domestic corporation under an agreement, see § 36.3121(l)(1)-1. [Reg. § 36.3121(l)(1)-3.]

☐ [*T.D.* 6145, 9-8-55. *Amended by T.D.* 6390, 6-13-59.]

[Reg. § 36.3121(l)(2)-1]

§ 36.3121(l)(2)-1. Effective period of agreement.—(a) *In general.*—An agreement entered into as provided in § 36.3121(l) (1)-1 shall be in effect for the period beginning with the first day of the calendar quarter in which the agreement is signed by the district director or director of the service center, or the first day of the calendar quarter following the calendar quarter in which the agreement is signed by the district director or director of the service center, whichever is specified in the agreement. In no case, however, shall the agreement be effective for any calendar quarter which begins prior to January 1, 1955.

(b) *Amendment of agreement.*—If an amendment on Form 2032 Supplement (filed by a domestic corporation to include in its agreement services performed for a foreign subsidiary not previously named therein) is signed by the district director or director of the service center, within the quarter for which the agreement is first effective or within the first calendar month following such quarter, the agreement shall be effective with respect to the subsidiary named in the amendment as of the date such agreement first became effective. However, if the amendment is signed by the district director or director of the service center after the last day of the fourth month for which the agreement is in effect, such agreement shall be in effect with respect to the subsidiary named in the amendment for the period beginning with the first day of the calendar quarter following the calendar quarter in which the amendment is signed by the district director or director of the service center. [Reg. § 36.3121(l)(2)-1.]

☐ [*T.D.* 7012, 5-15-69.]

[Reg. § 36.3121(l)(3)-1]

§ 36.3121(l)(3)-1. Termination of agreement by domestic corporation or by reason of change in stock ownership.—(a) *Termination by domestic corporation.*—(1) A domestic corporation which has entered into an agreement under section 3121(l)(1) with respect to one or more of its foreign subsidiaries may terminate such agreement in part or in its entirety by giving (for calendar quarters beginning before 1969, to the district director for the internal revenue district in which is located the principal place of business in the United States of the domestic corporation; and for calendar quarters beginning after 1968, except as provided in paragraph (b) of § 301.6091-1 (relating to hand-carried documents) to the director of the service center serving such internal revenue district 2 years' advance notice in writing of its desire so to terminate the agreement at the end of a specified calendar quarter: *Provided,* That, at the time of the receipt of such notice by such internal revenue officer, the agreement has been in effect with respect to the subsidiary or subsidiaries covered by the notice for at least 8 years. The notice of termination shall be signed and dated and shall show (i) the title of the officer authorized to sign the notice, (ii) the name, address, and identification number of the domestic corporation, (iii) the internal revenue officer with whom the agreement was entered into, (iv) the name and address of each foreign subsidiary with respect to which the agreement is to be terminated, (v) the date on which the agreement became effective with respect to each such foreign subsidiary, and (vi) the date on which the agreement is to be terminated with respect to each such foreign subsidiary. The notice shall be submitted in duplicate and shall be accompanied by a certified copy of the minutes of the meeting of the board of directors of the domestic corporation, or other evidence, showing authorization for the notice of termination. No particular form is prescribed for the notice of termination. The Internal Revenue Service will transmit one copy of the notice of termination to the Department of Health, Education, and Welfare.

(2) A notice of termination given by a domestic corporation in respect of any one or more of its foreign subsidiaries may be revoked by the corporation with respect to any such subsidiary or subsidiaries by giving, prior to the close of the calendar quarter specified in the notice of termination, written notice of revocation. The notice of revocation shall be filed with the internal revenue officer with whom the notice of termination was filed. Such notice of revocation shall be signed and dated and shall show (i) the title of the officer authorized to sign the notice of revocation, (ii) the name, address, and identification number of the domestic corporation, (iii) the name and address of each foreign subsidiary with respect to which the notice of termination is revoked, and (iv) the date of the notice of termination to be revoked. The notice shall be submitted in duplicate and shall be accompanied by a

certified copy of the minutes of the meeting of the board of directors of the domestic corporation, or other evidence, showing authorization for the notice of revocation. No particular form is prescribed for the notice of revocation. The Internal Revenue Service will transmit one copy of the notice of revocation to the Department of Health, Education, and Welfare.

(b) *Termination by reason of change in stock ownership.*—(1) The period for which an agreement entered into by a domestic corporation as provided in §36.3121(l)(1)-1 is in effect with respect to a foreign corporation is automatically terminated at the end of the calendar quarter in which the foreign corporation ceases, at any time in such quarter, to be a foreign subsidiary of the domestic corporation. See §36.3121(l)(8)-1, relating to definition of foreign subsidiary.

(2) A domestic corporation which has entered into an agreement as provided in §36.3121(l)(1)-1 shall furnish (for calendar quarters beginning before 1969, to the district director for the internal revenue district in which is located its principal place of business in the United States; and for calendar quarters beginning after 1968, except as provided in paragraph (b) of §301.6091-1 (relating to hand-carried documents) to the director of the service center serving such internal revenue district) written notification in the event that a foreign corporation named in the agreement, including any amendment thereof, as a foreign subsidiary of the domestic corporation ceases to be its foreign subsidiary. The written notification shall be furnished in duplicate on or before the last day of the first month following the close of the calendar quarter in which the foreign corporation ceases, at any time in such quarter, to be a foreign subsidiary of the domestic corporation. Such notification shall be signed and dated by the president or other principal officer of the domestic corporation. The written notification shall show (i) the title of the officer signing the notice, (ii) the name, address, and identification number of the domestic corporation, (iii) the internal revenue officer with whom the agreement was entered into, (iv) the date on which the agreement was entered into, (v) the name and address of the foreign corporation with respect to which the notification is furnished, and (vi) the date on which the foreign corporation ceased to be a foreign subsidiary of the domestic corporation. No particular form is prescribed for the written notification. The Internal Revenue Service will transmit one copy of the written notification to the Department of Health, Education, and Welfare. [Reg. §36.3121(l)(3)-1.]

☐ [*T.D.* 6145, 12-31-60. *Amended by T.D.* 7012, 5-15-69.]

[Reg. §36.3121(l)(4)-1]

§36.3121(l)(4)-1. **Termination of agreement by Commissioner.**—(a) *Notice of termination.*— The period for which an agreement entered into with a domestic corporation as provided in §36.3121(l)(1)-1 is in effect may be terminated by

the Commissioner, with the prior concurrence of the Secretary of Health, Education, and Welfare, upon a finding by the Commissioner that the domestic corporation has failed to comply substantially with the terms of the agreement. The Commissioner shall give the corporation not less than 60 days' advance notice in writing that the period for which the agreement is in effect will terminate at the end of the calendar quarter specified in the notice of termination.

(b) *Revocation of notice of termination.*—A notice of termination given to a domestic corporation by the Commissioner may be revoked by the Commissioner, with the prior concurrence of the Secretary of Health, Education and Welfare by giving written notice of revocation to the corporation prior to the close of the calendar quarter specified in the notice of termination. [Reg. §36.3121(l)(4)-1.]

☐ [*T.D.* 6145, 9-8-55, 12-31-60.]

[Reg. §36.3121(l)(5)-1]

§36.3121(l)(5)-1. **Effect of termination.**— (a) *Termination of entire agreement.*—(1) If the effective period of an agreement entered into by a domestic corporation as provided in §36.3121(l)(1)-1 is terminated by the domestic corporation, pursuant to §36.3121(l)(3)-1(a), with respect to all foreign subsidiaries named in the agreement, including any amendment thereof, an agreement may not again be entered into by the domestic corporation under the provisions of section 3121(l)(1).

(2) If the effective period of an agreement entered into by a domestic corporation as provided in §36.3121(l)(1)-1 is terminated by the Commissioner, pursuant to §36.3121(l)(4)-1 (a), an agreement may not again be entered into by the domestic corporation under the provisions of section 3121(l)(1).

(3) If the effective period of an agreement entered into by a domestic corporation as provided in §36.3121(l)(1)-1 is terminated automatically by reason of a change in stock ownership (see §36.3121(l)(3)-1(b)) with respect to all foreign corporations named in the agreement, including any amendment thereof, a new agreement may be entered into by the domestic corporation, as provided in §36.3121(l)(1)-1, with respect to any foreign corporation which is a foreign subsidiary of the domestic corporation.

(b) *Partial termination of agreement.*—(1) If the effective period of an agreement entered into by a domestic corporation as provided in §36.3121(l)(1)-1 is terminated by the domestic corporation, pursuant to §36.3121(l)(3)-1(a), with respect to one or more foreign subsidiaries named in the agreement, including any amendment thereof, the period for which the agreement is in effect will continue with respect to any other foreign subsidiary or subsidiaries named in the agreement (or amendment). However, the agreement may not thereafter be amended to include any foreign subsidiary with respect to which the effective period of the agreement has been terminated.

(2) If the effective period of an agreement entered into by a domestic corporation as provided in §36.3121(l)(1)-1 is terminated automatically by reason of a change in stock ownership (see §36.3121(l)(3)-1(b)) with respect to a foreign corporation which has ceased to be a foreign subsidiary of the domestic corporation, but the period for which the agreement is in effect continues with respect to one or more other foreign subsidiaries, the agreement may not thereafter be amended to include such foreign corporation even though the foreign corporation may again become a foreign subsidiary of the domestic corporation. [Reg. §36.3121(l)(5)-1.]

☐ [T.D. 6145, 9-8-55, 12-31-60.]

[Reg. §36.3121(l)(7)-1]

§36.3121(l)(7)-1. Overpayments and underpayments.—(a) *Adjustments.*—(1) *In general.*—Errors in the payment of amounts for which liability equivalent to the employee and employer taxes with respect to any payment of remuneration is incurred by a domestic corporation pursuant to its agreement are adjustable by the domestic corporation in certain cases without interest. However, not all corrections made under this section constitute adjustments within the meaning of the regulations in this part. The various situations in which such corrections constitute adjustments are set forth in paragraphs (a)(2) and (3) of this section. All corrections in respect of underpayments and all adjustments or credits in respect of overpayments made under this section must be reported on a return filed by the domestic corporation under the regulations in this part and not on a return filed with respect to the employee and employer taxes imposed by sections 3101 and 3111, respectively. Every return on which such a correction (by adjustment, credit, or otherwise) is reported pursuant to this section must have securely attached as a part thereof a statement explaining the error in respect of which the correction is made, designating the calendar quarter in which the error was ascertained, and setting forth such other information as would be required if the correction were in respect of an overpayment or underpayment of taxes under the Federal Insurance Contributions Act. An error is ascertained when the domestic corporation has sufficient knowledge of the error to be able to correct it. An underpayment may not be corrected under this section after receipt from the district director or director of the service center of written notification of the amount due and demand for payment thereof, but the amount shall be paid in accordance with such notification.

(2) *Underpayments.*—If a domestic corporation fails to report, on a return filed under the regulations in this part, all or any part of the amount for which liability equivalent to the employee and employer taxes is incurred under its agreement with respect to any payment of remuneration, the domestic corporation shall adjust the underpayment by reporting the additional

amount due as an adjustment on a return or supplemental return filed on or before the last day on which the return for the return period in which the error is ascertained is required to be filed. The amount of each underpayment adjusted in accordance with this subparagraph shall be paid, without interest, at the time fixed for reporting the adjustment. If an adjustment is reported pursuant to this subparagraph but the amount thereof is not paid when due, interest thereafter accrues.

(3) *Overpayments.*—If a domestic corporation pays more than the amount for which liability equivalent to the employee and employer taxes is incurred under its agreement with respect to any payment of remuneration, the domestic corporation may correct the error, subject to the requirements and under the conditions stated in this paragraph, by deducting the amount of the overpayment from the amount of liability reported on a return filed by the domestic corporation, except that—

(i) A correction may not be made in respect of any part of an overpayment which was collected from an individual by reason of the agreement unless the domestic corporation (a) has repaid the amount so collected to the individual, has secured the written receipt of the individual showing the date and amount of the repayment, and retains such receipt as a part of its records, or (b) has reimbursed the individual by reducing the amounts which otherwise should have been deducted from his remuneration by reason of the agreement; and

(ii) A correction may not be made in one calendar year in respect of any part of an overpayment which was collected from an individual in a prior calendar year unless the domestic corporation has secured the written statement of the individual showing that he has not claimed and will not claim refund or credit of the amount so collected, and retains such receipt as a part of its records. See §31.6413(c)-1 of this chapter, relating to claims for special credit or refund.

The correction constitutes an adjustment under this subparagraph only if it is reported on the return for the period in which the error is ascertained or on the return for the next following period, and then only if the correction is reported within the statutory period of limitation upon refund or credit of overpayments of amounts due under the agreement. See paragraph (b)(2)(iii) of this section relating to such statutory period. A claim for credit or refund may be filed in accordance with the provisions of paragraph (b)(2) of this section for any overpayment of an amount due under the agreement which is not adjusted under this subparagraph.

(b) *Errors not adjustable.*—(1) *Underpayments.*—If a domestic corporation fails to report all or any part of the amount for which liability equivalent to the employee and employer taxes is incurred under its agreement with respect to any payment of remuneration, and such underpayment is not reported as an adjustment

Reg. §36.3121(l)(7)-1(b)(1)

within the time prescribed by paragraph (a)(2) of this section, the amount of such underpayment shall be reported on the domestic corporation's next return, or shall be reported immediately on a supplemental return for the return period in which such payment of remuneration was made. The reporting of an underpayment under this subparagraph does not constitute an adjustment without interest.

(2) *Overpayments.*—(i) If more than the correct amount due from a domestic corporation pursuant to its agreement (including the amount of any interest or addition) is paid and the amount of the overpayment is not adjusted under paragraph (a) (3) of this section, the domestic corporation may file a claim for refund or credit. Except as otherwise provided in this subparagraph, such claim shall be made in the same manner and subject to the same conditions as to allowance of the claim as would be the case if the claim were in respect of an overpayment of taxes under the Federal Insurance Contributions Act. Refund or credit of an amount erroneously paid by a domestic corporation under its agreement may be allowed only to the domestic corporation.

(ii) Any claim filed under this subparagraph shall be plainly marked "Claim under section 3121(1)."

(iii) No refund or credit of an overpayment of the amount due from a domestic corporation under its agreement will be allowed after the expiration of 2 years after the date of payment of such overpayment, except upon one or more of the grounds set forth in a claim filed prior to the expiration of such 2-year period.

(c) *Deductions from employees' remuneration.*—If a domestic corporation deducts, or causes to be deducted, from the remuneration of an individual for services covered by the agreement amounts which are more or less than the employee tax which would be deductible therefrom if such remuneration constituted wages, any repayment to the individual (except to the extent otherwise provided in this section), or further collection from the individual, in respect of such deduction is a matter for settlement between the individual and the domestic corporation or such other person as may be concerned. [Reg. §36.3121(l)(7)-1.]

☐ [*T.D.* 6145, 12-31-60. *Amended by T.D.* 7012, 5-15-69.]

[Reg. §36.3121(l)(8)-1]

§36.3121(l)(8)-1. Definition of foreign subsidiary.—(a) *Prior to August 1, 1956.*—(1) For the period January 1, 1955 to July 31, 1956, inclusive, a foreign corporation is a foreign subsidiary of a domestic corporation, within the meaning of the regulations in this part, if—

(i) More than 50 percent of the voting stock of the foreign corporation is owned by the domestic corporation; or

(ii) More than 50 percent of the voting stock of the foreign corporation is owned by a second foreign corporation and more than 50 percent of the voting stock of the second foreign corporation is owned by the domestic corporation.

(2) The application of subparagraph (1) of this paragraph may be illustrated by the following examples:

Example 1. P, a domestic corporation, owns 51 percent of the voting stock of S-1, a foreign corporation. S-1 owns 51 percent of the voting stock of S-2, a foreign corporation. S-2 owns 51 percent of the voting stock of S-3, a foreign corporation. S-1 and S-2 are foreign subsidiaries of P for purposes of the regulations in this part. Since neither P nor S-1 owns more than 50 percent of the voting stock of S-3, S-3 is not a foreign subsidiary of P within the meaning of the regulations in this part.

Example 2. Assume the same facts as those stated in example 1 except that 25 percent of the voting stock of S-2 is transferred by S-1 to P. P owns no other voting stock of S-2. Accordingly, after the transfer, P and S-1 together own more than 50 percent of the voting stock of S-2, but neither P nor S-1 alone owns more than 50 percent of such stock. S-2 ceases to be a foreign subsidiary of P when such transfer is effected.

(b) *On or after August 1, 1956.*—(1) Beginning August 1, 1956, a foreign corporation is a foreign subsidiary of a domestic corporation, within the meaning of the regulations in this part, if—

(i) Not less than 20 percent of the voting stock of the foreign corporation is owned by the domestic corporation; or

(ii) More than 50 percent of the voting stock of the foreign corporation is owned by a second foreign corporation and not less than 20 percent of the voting stock of the second foreign corporation is owned by the domestic corporation.

(2) The application of subparagraph (1) of this paragraph may be illustrated by the following examples:

Example 1. P, a domestic corporation owns 20 percent of the voting stock of S-1, a foreign corporation. S-1 is, therefore, a foreign subsidiary of P. S-1 owns 51 percent and P owns 15 percent of the voting stock of S-2, a foreign corporation. S-2 is also a foreign subsidiary of P, and this would be so even if P owned none of the voting stock of S-2. S-2 owns 51 percent, S-1 owns 39 percent, and P owns 10 percent of the voting stock of S-3, a foreign corporation. Since P owns less than 20 percent of the voting stock of S-2 and less than 20 percent of the voting stock of S-3, and since S-1 owns not more than 50 percent of the voting stock of S-3, S-3 is not a foreign subsidiary of P within the meaning of the regulations in this part.

Example 2. Assume the same facts as those stated in example 1 except that 4 percent of the voting stock of S-2 is transferred by S-1 to P. After, as well as before, the transfer of 66 percent of the voting stock of S-2 is owned by P and S-1 together. After the transfer, however, P owns less than 20 percent and S-1 owns not more than

50 percent of the voting stock of S-2. When such transfer is effected S-2 ceases to be a foreign subsidiary of P for purposes of the regulations in this part.

(c) *Transfer of stock ownership.*—The transfer of the voting stock of a foreign corporation which is a foreign subsidiary of a domestic corporation within the meaning of section 3121(l)(8) will not affect the status of the foreign corporation as such a foreign subsidiary if at all times either of the percentage tests stated in section 3121(l)(8), relating to ownership of the voting stock of such foreign corporation, is met.

(d) *Meaning of "stock".*—The term "stock", as used in the regulations in this part, has the meaning assigned by paragraph (7) of section 7701(a). Section 7701(a)(7) provides as follows:

SEC. 7701. *Definitions.* (a) When used in this title [Internal Revenue Code of 1954], where not otherwise distinctly expressed or manifestly incompatible with the intent thereof—

* * *

(7) *Stock.* The term "stock" includes shares in an association, joint-stock company, or insurance company.
[Reg. § 36.3121(l)(8)-1.]

☐ [*T.D.* 6390, 6-13-59.]

[Reg. § 36.3121(l)(9)-1]

§ 36.3121(l)(9)-1. Domestic corporation as separate entity.—A domestic corporation which enters into an agreement as provided in § 36.3121(l)(1)-1 shall, for purposes of the regulations in this part and for purposes of section 6413(c)(2)(C), relating to special credits or refunds, be considered an employer in its capacity as a party to such agreement separate and apart from its identity as an employer incurring liability for the employee tax and employer tax on the wages of its own employees. Thus, if a citizen of the United States performs services in employment for the domestic corporation and at any time within the same calendar year performs services covered by the agreement as an employee of one or more foreign subsidiaries named therein, the limitation on wages provided in section 3121(a) (1) has application separately as to the wages for employment performed in the employ of the domestic corporation and as to the remuneration for services covered by the agreement performed in the employ of such foreign subsidiary or subsidiaries. All services covered by the agreement whether performed in the employ of one or more than one such foreign subsidiary are regarded for purposes of the wage limitation as having been performed in the employ of the domestic corporation in its separate capacity as a party to the agreement. Similarly, any remuneration for such services which, if the services were performed in the United States, would be excluded from wages unless a certain amount of such remuneration is paid by a single employer within a specified period (for example, remuneration for agricultural labor) is regarded, for purposes of determining whether the domestic corporation incurs liability under its agreement with respect to such remuneration, as having been paid by the domestic corporation in its separate capacity as a party to the agreement. All remuneration received by an employee for services covered by the agreement is deemed, for purposes of the special credit or refund provisions contained in section 6413(c), to have been received from the domestic corporation as an employer in its separate capacity as a party to the agreement. [Reg. § 36.3121(l)(9)-1.]

☐ [*T.D.* 6145, 9-8-55, 12-31-60.]

[Reg. § 36.3121(l)(10)-1]

§ 36.3121(l)(10)-1. Requirements in respect of liability under agreement.—To the extent not inconsistent with, or otherwise provided in, the regulations in this part, the requirements and duties (relating to identification number, account numbers, wage information statements to employees, record keeping, etc.) imposed on an employer for any period with respect to the taxes imposed by the Federal Insurance Contributions Act are hereby made applicable to a domestic corporation with respect to its obligations and liabilities, for the same period, under an agreement entered into as provided in § 36.3121(l)(1)-1. [Reg. § 36.3121(l)(10)-1.]

☐ [*T.D.* 6145, 9-8-55, 12-31-60.]

[Reg. § 36.3121(l)(10)-2]

§ 36.3121(l)(10)-2. Identification.—
(a) *Domestic corporation.*—A domestic corporation which has secured, or is required to secure, an identification number as an employer having in its employ one or more individuals in employment for wages is not required to secure an identification number under the regulations in this part.

(b) *Employees.*—Every employee performing services covered by an agreement shall have the same duties in respect of an account number as would be the case if the employee were performing services in employment for the domestic corporation. [Reg. § 36.3121(l)(10)-2.]

☐ [*T.D.* 6145, 9-8-55, 12-31-60.]

[Reg. § 36.3121(l)(10)-3]

§ 36.3121(l)(10)-3. Returns.—(a) The forms prescribed for use in making returns of the taxes imposed by the Federal Insurance Contributions Act (except any forms particularly prescribed for use by household employers or by employers filing returns in Puerto Rico) shall be used by a domestic corporation in making returns of its liability under an agreement entered into as provided in § 36.3121(l)(1)-1. Returns of such liability shall be made separate and apart from any returns required of the domestic corporation in respect of the taxes imposed by the Federal Insurance Contributions Act. The domestic corporation shall plainly mark "3121(l) Agreement" at the top of each return, each detachable schedule thereof, and each paper or document constituting a part of the return, filed by the domestic corporation pursuant to the regulations in this part. Returns required under the regulations in this part shall be made by the domestic corporation as if all services covered by the agreement, whether performed in the employ of one or more than one foreign subsidiary, were performed in the employ of the domestic corporation as an employer in its separate capacity as a party to the agreement.

(b) Each return required under the regulations in this part must be filed on or before the last day of the month following the period for which the return is made. [Reg. § 36.3121(l)(10)-3.]

☐ [T.D. 6145, 9-8-55. *Amended by T.D. 6390, 6-13-59.*]

[Reg. § 36.3121(l)(10)-4]

§ 36.3121(l)(10)-4. Payment of amounts equivalent to tax.—A domestic corporation which has entered into an agreement as provided in § 36.3121(l)(1)-1 is not required to make deposits with an authorized financial institution of any amount for which liability is incurred under its agreement. [Reg. § 36.3121(l)(10)-4.]

☐ [T.D. 6145, 9-8-55, 12-31-60. *Amended by T.D. 7953, 5-9-84 and T.D. 8952, 6-26-2001.*]

[Reg. § 31.3121(o)-1]

§ 31.3121(o)-1. Crew leader.—The term "crew leader" means an individual who furnishes indi-viduals to perform agricultural labor for another person, if such individual pays (either on his own behalf or on behalf of such person) the individuals so furnished by him for the agricultural labor performed by them and if such individual has not entered into a written agreement with such person whereby such individual has been designated as an employee of such person. For purposes of this chapter a crew leader is deemed to be the employer of the individuals furnished by him to perform agricultural labor, after 1956, for another person, and the crew leader is deemed not to be an employee of such other person with respect to the performance of services by him after 1956 in furnishing such individuals or as a member of the crew. An individual is not a crew leader within the meaning of section 3121(o) and of this section if he does not pay the agricultural workers furnished by him to perform agricultural labor for another person, or if there is an agreement between such individual and the person for whom the agricultural labor is performed whereby such individual is designated as an employee of such person. Whether or not such individual is an employee will be determined under the usual common-law rules (see paragraph (c) of § 31.3121(d)-1). [Reg. § 31.3121(o)-1].

☐ [T.D. 6744, 7-2-64.]

»»→ Caution: *This regulation has not been amended to reflect changes enacted by the Omnibus Budget Reconciliation Act of 1987 (P.L. 100-203).*

[Reg. § 31.3121(q)-1]

§ 31.3121(q)-1. Tips included for employee taxes.—(a) *In general.*—Except as otherwise provided in paragraph (b) of this section, tips received after 1965 by an employee in the course of his employment shall be considered remuneration for employment. (For definition of the term "employee" see §§ 31.3121(d) and 31.3121(d)-1.) Tips reported by an employee to his employer in a written statement furnished to the employer pursuant to section 6053(a) (see § 31.6053-1) shall be deemed to be paid to the employee at the time the written statement is furnished to the employer. Tips received by an employee which are not reported to his employer in a written statement furnished pursuant to section 6053(a) shall be deemed to be paid to the employee at the time the tips are actually received by the employee. For provisions relating to the collection of employee tax in respect of tips from the employee, see § 31.3102-3.

(b) *Tips not included for employer taxes.*—Tips received after 1965 by an employee in the course of his employment do not constitute remuneration for employment for purposes of computing wages subject to the taxes imposed by subsections (a) and (b) of section 3111.

(c) *Tips received by an employee in course of his employment.*—Tips are considered to be received by an employee in the course of his employment for an employer regardless of whether the tips are received by the employee from a person other than his employer or are paid to the employee by the employer. However, only those tips which are received by an employee on his own behalf (as distinguished from tips received on behalf of another employee) shall be considered as remuneration paid to the employee. Thus, where employees practice tip splitting (for example, where waiters pay a portion of the tips received by them to the busboys), each employee who receives a portion of a tip left by a customer of the employer is considered to have received tips in the course of his employment.

(d) *Computation of annual wage limitation.*—In connection with the application of the annual wage limitation (see § 31.3121(a)(1)-1), tips reported by an employee to his employer in a written statement furnished to the employer pursuant to section 6053(a) shall be taken into account for purposes of the tax imposed by section 3101. However, since tips received by an employee in the course of his employment do not constitute remuneration for employment for purposes of the tax imposed by section 3111, they are disregarded for purposes of the annual wage limitation in respect of such tax. Accordingly, separate computations for purposes of the annual wage limitation may be required in respect of an employee who receives tips. The provisions of this paragraph may be illustrated by the following example:

Example. During 1966, A is employed as a waiter by X restaurant and is paid wages by X restaurant at the rate of $100 a week. At the end of October 1966, A has been paid weekly wages in the amount of $4,300 and has reported tips in the amount of $2,200. On November 6, 1966, A is paid an additional week's wages in the amount of $100 and on November 9, 1966, A furnishes X restaurant a report of tips actually received by him during October. The annual wage limitation of $6,600 (weekly wages of $4,400 ($4,300 plus $100) and tips of $2,200) had been reached for purposes of the tax imposed by section 3101 prior to November 9 and, accordingly, no portion of the tips included in the report furnished on that date constitutes wages. However, since tips do not constitute remuneration for employment for purposes of the tax imposed by section 3111, the weekly wages paid to A during the remainder of 1966 will be subject to the tax imposed by section 3111. [Reg. § 31.3121(q)-1.]

☐ [*T.D.* 7001, 1-23-69.]

[Reg. §31.3121(r)-1]

§31.3121(r)-1. Election of coverage by religious orders.—(a) *In general.*—A religious order whose members are required to take a vow of poverty, or any autonomous subdivision of such an order, may elect to have the Federal old-age, survivors, and disability insurance system established by title II of the Social Security Act extended to services performed by its members in the exercise of duties required by such order or subdivision. See section 3121(i)(4) and §31.3121(i)-4 for provisions relating to the computation of the amount of remuneration of such members. For purposes of this section, a subdivision of a religious order is autonomous if it directs and governs its members, if it is responsible for its members' care and maintenance, if it is responsible for the members' support and maintenance in retirement, and if the members live under the authority of a religious superior who is elected by them or appointed by higher authority.

(b) *Definition of member.*—(1) *In general.*—For purposes of section 3121(r) and this section, a member of a religious order means any individual who is subject to a vow of poverty as a member of such order, who performs tasks usually required (and to the extent usually required) of an active member of such order, and who is not considered retired because of old age or total disability.

(2) *Retirement because of old age.*—(i) *In general.*—For purposes of section 3121(r)(2) and this paragraph, an individual is considered retired because of old age if (A) in view of all the services performed by the individual and the surrounding circumstances it is reasonable to consider him to be retired, and (B) his retirement occurred by reason of old age. Even though an individual performs some services in the exercise of duties required by the religious order, the first test (the retirement test) is met where it is reasonable to consider the individual to be retired.

(ii) *Factors to be considered.*—In determining whether it is reasonable to consider an individual to be retired, consideration is first to be given to all of the following factors:

(A) *Nature of services.*—Consideration is given to the nature of the services performed by the individual in the exercise of duties required by his religious order. The more highly skilled and valuable such services are, the more likely the individual rendering such services is not reasonably considered retired. Also, whether such services are of a type performed principally by retired members of the individual's religious order may be significant.

(B) *Amount of time.*—Consideration is also given to the amount of time the individual devotes to the performance of services in the exercise of duties required by his religious order. This time includes all the time spent by him in any activity in connection with services which might appropriately be performed in the exercise of duties required of active members by the order. Normally, an individual who, solely by reason of his advanced age, performs services of less than 45 hours per month shall be considered retired. In no event shall an individual who, solely by reason of his advanced age, performs services of less than 15 hours per month not be considered retired.

(C) *Comparison of services rendered before and after retirement.*—In addition, consideration is given to the nature and extent of the services rendered by the individual before he "retired," as compared with the services performed thereafter. A large reduction in the importance or amount of services performed by the individual in the exercise of duties required by his religious order tends to show that the individual is retired; absence of such reduction tends to show that the individual is not retired. Normally, an individual who reduces by at least 75 percent the amount of services performed shall be considered retired. Where consideration of the factors described in paragraph (b)(2)(ii) of this section does not establish whether an individual is or is not reasonably considered retired, all other factors are considered.

(iii) *Examples.*—The rules of this subparagraph may be illustrated by the following examples:

Example (1). A is a member of a religious order who is subject to a vow of poverty. A's religious order is principally engaged in providing nursing services, and A has been fully trained in the nursing profession. In accordance with the practices of her order, upon attaining the age of 65, A is relieved of her nursing duties by reason of her age, and is assigned to a mother house where she is required to perform only such duties as light housekeeping and ordinary gardening. A is reasonably considered retired since the services she is performing are simple in nature, are markedly less skilled than those professional services which she previously performed, are of a type performed principally by retired members of her order, and are performed at a location to which members frequently retire.

Example (2). Assume the same facts as in example (1) except that A is not reassigned to a mother house. Instead, she is reassigned to full-time duties in a hospital not utilizing her nursing skills. Whether A has met the retirement test requires consideration of the nature of her work. If A's new duties are almost entirely of a make-work nature primarily to occupy her body and mind, she is reasonably considered retired. However, if they are essential to the operation of the hospital, she is not reasonably considered retired.

Example (3). B is a member of a religious order who is subject to a vow of poverty. As such, he provides supportive services to his order, such as housekeeping, cooking, and gardening. By reason of having attained the age of 62, he reduces the number of hours spent per day in these services from 8 hours to 2 hours. B is reasonably considered retired in view of the large reduction in the amount of time he devotes to his duties.

Example (4). C is a member of a religious order who is subject to a vow of poverty. In his capacity as a member of the order, he performs duties as president of a university. Upon attaining the age of 65, C is relieved of his duties as president of the university and instead becomes a member of its faculty, teaching two courses whereas full time members of the faculty normally teach four comparable courses. Although C's duties are no longer as demanding as those he previously performed, and although the amount of his time required for them is less than full time, he is nonetheless performing duties requiring a high degree of skill for a substantial amount of time. Accordingly, C is not reasonably considered retired.

Example (5). Assume the same facts as in example (4), except that C teaches only one course upon being relieved of his position as president by reason of age. C is reasonably considered retired.

Example (6). D is a member of a contemplative order who is subject to a vow of poverty. In accordance with the practices of his order, upon attaining the age of 70, D reduces by 50 percent the amount of time spent performing the normal duties of active members of his order. D is not reasonably considered retired.

Example (7). Assume the same facts as in example (6), except that because of his age D no longer participates in the more rigorous liturgical services of the order and that the amount of time which he spends in all duties which might appropriately be performed by active members of his order is reduced by 75 percent. D is reasonably considered retired in view of the large reduction in his participation in the usual devotional routine of his order.

(3) *Retirement because of total disability.*—For purposes of section 3121(r)(2) and this paragraph, an individual is considered retired because of total disability (i) if he is unable, by

reason of a medically determinable physical or mental impairment, to perform the tasks usually required of an active member of his order to the extent necessary to maintain his status as an active member, and (ii) if such impairment is reasonably expected to prevent his resumption of the performance of such tasks to such extent. A physical or mental impairment is an impairment that results from anatomical, physiological, or psychological abnormalities which are demonstrable by medically acceptable clinical and laboratory diagnostic techniques. Statements of the individual, including his own description of his impairment (symptoms), are, alone, insufficient to establish the presence of a physical or mental impairment.

(4) *Evidentiary requirements with respect to retirement.*—There shall be attached to the return of taxes paid pursuant to an election under section 3121(r) a summary of the facts upon which any determination has been made by the religious order or autonomous subdivision that one or more of its members retired during the period covered by such return. Each summary shall contain the name and social security number of each such retired member as well as the date of retirement. Such order or subdivision shall maintain records of the details relating to each such "retirement" sufficient to show whether or not such member or members has in fact retired.

(c) *Certificates of election.*—(1) *In general.*—A religious order or an autonomous subdivision of such an order desiring to make an election of coverage pursuant to section 3121(r) and this section SS-16 shall file a certificate of election on Form SS-16 in accordance with the instructions thereto. However, in the case of an election made before [30th day after the date of publication of this section in final regulations] a document other than Form SS-16 shall constitute a certificate of election if it purports to be a binding election of coverage and if it is filed with an appropriate official of the Internal Revenue Service. Such a document shall be given the effect it would have if it were a certificate of election containing the provisions required by subparagraph (2) of this paragraph. However, it should subsequently be supplemented by a Form SS-16.

(2) *Provisions of certificates.*—Each certificate of election shall provide that—

(i) Such election of coverage by such order or subdivision shall be irrevocable,

(ii) Such election shall apply to all current and future members of such order, or in the case of a subdivision thereof to all current and future members of such order who belong to such subdivision,

(iii) All services performed by a member of such order or subdivision in the exercise of duties required by such order or subdivision shall be deemed to have been performed by such member as an employee of such order or subdivision, and

(iv) The wages of each member, upon which such order or subdivision shall pay the taxes imposed on employees and employers by sections 3101 and 3111, will be determined as provided in section 3121(i)(4).

(d) *Effective date of election.*—(1) *In general.*—Except as provided in paragraph (e) of this section, a certificate of election of coverage filed by a religious order or its subdivision pursuant to section 3121(r) and this section shall be in effect, for purposes of section 3121(b)(8)(A) and for purposes of section 210(a)(8)(A) of the Social Security Act, for the period beginning with whichever of the following may be designated by the electing religious order or subdivision:

(i) The first day of the calendar quarter in which the certificate is filed,

(ii) The first day of the calendar quarter immediately following the quarter in which the certificate is filed, or

(iii) The first day of any calendar quarter preceding the calendar quarter in which the certificate is filed, except that such date may not be earlier than the first day of the 20th calendar quarter preceding the quarter in which such certificate is filed.

(2) *Retroactive elections.*—Whenever a date is designated as provided in paragraph (d)(1)(iii) of this section, the election shall apply to services performed before the quarter in which the certificate is filed only if the member performing such services was a member at the time such services were performed and is living on the first day of the quarter in which such certificate is filed. Thus, the election applies to an individual who is no longer a member of a religious order on the first day of such quarter if he performed services as a member at any time on or after the date so designated and is living on the first day of the quarter in which such certificate is filed. For purposes of computing interest and for purposes of section 6651 (relating to additions to tax for failure to file tax return or to pay tax), in any case in which such a date is designated the due date for the return and payment of the tax, for calendar quarters prior to the quarter in which the certificate is filed, resulting from the filing of such certificate shall be the last day of the calendar month following the calendar quarter in which the certificate is filed. The statutory period for the assessment of the tax for such prior calendar quarters shall not expire before the expiration of 3 years from such due date.

(e) *Coordination with coverage of lay employees.*—If at the time the certificate of election of coverage is filed by a religious order or autonomous subdivision, a certificate of waiver of exemption under section 3121(k) (extending coverage to any lay employees) is not in effect, the certificate of election shall not become effective unless the order or subdivision files a Form SS-15, and a Form SS-15a to accompany the certificate on Form SS-15, as provided by section 3121(k) and §§ 31.3121(k)-1 through 31.3121(k)-3. The preceding sentence applies even though an order or subdivision has no lay employees at the time it files a certificate of election of coverage.

The effective date of the certificate of waiver of exemption must be no later than the date on which the certificate of election becomes effective, and it must be specified on the certificate of waiver of exemption that such certificate is irrevocable. The certificate of waiver of exemption required under this paragraph shall be filed notwithstanding the provisions of section 3121(k)(3) (relating to no renewal of the waiver of exemption) which otherwise would prohibit the filing of a waiver of exemption if an earlier waiver of exemption had previously been terminated. If at the time the certificate of election of coverage is filed a certificate of waiver of exemption is in effect with respect to the electing religious order or autonomous subdivision, the filing of the certificate of election shall constitute an amendment of the certificate of waiver of exemption making the latter certificate irrevocable. [Reg. § 31.3121(r)-1.]

☐ [*T.D.* 7280, 7-10-73.]

[Reg. § 31.3121(s)-1]

§ 31.3121(s)-1. Concurrent employment by related corporations with common paymaster.—(a) *In general.*—For purposes of section 3102, 3111, and 3121(a)(1), except as otherwise provided in paragraph (c) of this section, when two or more related corporations concurrently employ the same individual and compensate that individual through a common paymaster which is one of the related corporations that employs the individual, each of the corporations is considered to have paid only the remuneration it actually disburses to that individual. This rule applies whether the remuneration was paid with respect to the employment relationship of the individual with the disbursing corporation or was paid on behalf of another related corporation. Accordingly, if all of the remuneration to the individual from the related corporations is disbursed through the common paymaster, the total amount of taxes imposed with respect to the remuneration under sections 3102 and 3111 is determined as though the individual has only one employer (the common paymaster). The common paymaster is responsible for filing information and tax returns and issuing Forms W-2 with respect to wages it is considered to have paid under this section. Section 3121(s) and this section apply only to remuneration disbursed in the form of money, check, or similar instrument by one of the related corporations or its agent.

(b) *Definitions.*—The definitions contained in this paragraph are applicable only for purposes of this section and § 31.3306(p)-1.

(1) *Related corporations.*—Corporations shall be considered related corporations for an entire calendar quarter (as defined in § 31.0-2(a)(9)) if they satisfy any one of the following four tests at any time during that calendar quarter:

(i) The corporations are members of a "controlled group of corporations", as defined in section 1563 of the Code, or would be members if section 1563(a)(4) and (b) did not apply and if the phrase "more than 50 percent" were substituted for the phrase "at least 80 percent" wherever it appears in section 1563(a).

(ii) In the case of a corporation that does not issue stock, either fifty percent or more of the members of one corporation's board of directors (or other governing body) are members of the other corporation's board of directors (or other governing body), or the holders of fifty percent or more of the voting power to select such members are concurrently the holders of fifty percent or more of that power with respect to the other corporation.

(iii) Fifty percent or more of one corporation's officers are concurrently officers of the other corporation.

(iv) Thirty percent or more of one corporation's employees are concurrently employees of the other corporation.

The following examples illustrate the application of this paragraph:

Example (1). (a) X Corporation employs individuals A, B, D, E, F, G, and H. Y Corporation employs individuals A, B, and C. Z Corporation employs individuals A, C, I, J, K, L, and M. X Corporation is the paymaster for all thirteen individuals. The corporations have no officers or stockholders in common.

(b) X and Y are related corporations because at least 30 percent of Y's employees are also employees of X. Y and Z are related corporations because at least 30 percent of Y's employees are also employees of Z. X and Z are not related corporations because neither corporation has 30 percent of its employees concurrently employed by the other corporation.

(c) For purposes of determining the amount of the tax liability under sections 3102 and 3111, individual B is treated as having one employer. Individual C has two employers for these purposes, although Y and Z are related corporations, because C is not employed by X Corporation, the common paymaster. Individual A also is treated as having two employers for the purposes of these sections because X and Y Corporations are treated as one employer, and Z Corporation is treated as a second employer (since it is not related to the paymaster, X Corporation). Of course, individuals D, E, F, G, H, I, J, K, L, and M are not concurrently employed by two or more corporations, and, accordingly, section 3121(s) is inapplicable to them.

Example (2). M and N Corporations are both related to Corporation O but are not related to each other. Individual A is concurrently employed by all three corporations and paid by O, their common paymaster. Although M and N are not related, O is treated as the employer for A's employment with M, N, and O.

Example (3). Corporations X, Y, and Z meet the definition of related corporations for the first time on April 12, 1979, and cease to meet it on July 5, 1979. A is concurrently employed by X, Y, and Z throughout 1979. In each of the four calendar quarters of 1979, A's remuneration from X, Y, and Z is $2,000, $10,000, and $30,000, respectively. All of the remuneration to A from X, Y, and Z for the year is disbursed by X, the common paymaster. Under these circumstances, the amount of wages subject to sections 3102 and 3111 is as follows:

	X	Y	Z
For the first calendar quarter	$2,000	$10,000	$22,900
For the second calendar quarter	$20,900 ($22,900 – $2,000)	0	0
For the third calendar quarter	0	0	0
For the fourth calendar quarter	0	$10,000	0

Of course, if the corporations had been related throughout all of 1979, only $22,900 of X's first quarter disbursement would have constituted wages subject to sections 3102 and 3111.

(2) *Common paymaster.*—(i) *In general.*—A common paymaster of a group of related corporations is any member thereof that disburses remuneration to employees of two or more of those corporations on their behalf and that is responsible for keeping books and records for the payroll with respect to those employees. The common paymaster is not required to disburse remuneration to all the employees of those two or more related corporations, but the provisions of this section do not apply to any remuneration to an employee that is not disbursed through a common paymaster. The common paymaster may pay concurrently employed individuals under this section by one combined paycheck, drawn on a single bank account, or by separate paychecks, drawn by the common paymaster on the accounts of one or more employing corporations.

(ii) *Multiple common paymasters.*—A group of related corporations may have more than one common paymaster. Some of the related corporations may use one common paymaster and others of the related corporations use another common paymaster with respect to a certain class of employees. A corporation that uses a common paymaster to disburse remuneration to certain of its employees may use a different common paymaster to disburse remuneration to other employees.

(iii) *Examples.*—The rules of this subparagraph are illustrated by the following examples:

Example (1). S, T, U, and V are related corporations with 2,000 employees collectively. Forty of these employees are concurrently employed by two or more of the corporations, during a calendar quarter. The four corporations arrange for S to disburse remuneration to thirty of these forty employees for their services. Under these facts, S is the common paymaster of S, T, U, and V with respect to the thirty employees. S is not a common paymaster with respect to the remaining employees.

Example (2). (a) W, X, Y, and Z are related corporations. The corporations collectively have 20,000 employees. Two hundred of the employees are top-level executives and managers, sixty of whom are concurrently employed by two or more of the corporations during a calendar quarter. Six thousand of the employees are skilled artisans, all of whom are concurrently employed by two or more of the corporations during the calendar year. The four corporations arrange for Z to disburse remuneration to the sixty executives who are concurrently employed by two or more of the corporations. W and X arrange for X to disburse remuneration to the artisans who are concurrently employed by W and X.

(b) A is an executive who is concurrently employed only by W, Y, and Z during the calendar year. Under these facts, Z is a common paymaster for W, Y, and Z with respect to A. Assuming that the other requirements of this section are met, the amount of the tax liability under sections 3102 and 3111 is determined as if Z were A's only employer for the calendar quarter.

(c) B is a skilled artisan who is concurrently employed only by W and X during the calendar year. Under these facts, X is a common paymaster for S and X with respect to B. Assuming that the other requirements of this section are met, the amount of the tax liability under sections 3102 and 3111 is determined as if X were B's only employer for the calendar quarter.

(3) *Concurrent employment.*—For purposes of this section, the term "concurrent employment" means the contemporaneous existence of an employment relationship (within the meaning of section 3121 (b)) between an individual and two or more corporations. Such a relationship contemplates the performance of services by the employee for the benefit of the employing corporation (not merely for the benefit of the group of corporations), in exchange for remuneration which, if deductible for the purposes of Federal income tax, would be deductible by the employing corporation. The contemporaneous existence of an employment relationship with each corporation is the decisive factor; if it exists, the fact that a particular employee is on leave or otherwise temporarily inactive is immaterial. However, employment is not concurrent with respect to one of the related corporations if the employee's employment relationship with that corporation is completely nonexistent during periods when the employee is not performing services for that corporation. An employment relationship is completely nonexistent if all rights and obligations of the employer and employee with respect to employment have terminated, other than those that customarily exist after employment relationships terminate. Exam-

ples of rights and obligations that customarily exist after employment relationships terminate include those with respect to remuneration not yet paid, employer's property used by the employee not yet returned to the employer, severance pay, and lump-sum termination payments from a deferred compensation plan. Circumstances that suggest that an employment relationship has become completely nonexistent include unconditional termination of participation in deferred compensation plans of the employer, forfeiture of seniority claims, and forfeiture of unused fringe benefits such as vacation or sick pay. Of course, the continued existence of an employment relationship between an individual and a corporation is not necessarily established by the individual's continued participation in a deferred compensation plan, retention of seniority rights, etc., since continuation of those benefits may be attributable to employment with a second corporation related to the first corporation if the corporations have common benefit plans or if the benefits are continued as a matter of corporate reciprocity. An individual who does not perform substantial services in exchange for remuneration from a corporation is presumed not employed by that corporation. Concurrent employment need not exist for any particular length of time to meet the requirements of this section, but this section only applies to remuneration disbursed by a common paymaster to an individual who is concurrently employed by the common paymaster and at least one other related corporation at the time the individual performs the services for which the remuneration is paid. If the employment relationship is nonexistent during a quarter, that employee may not be counted towards the 30-percent test set forth in paragraph (b)(1)(iv) of this section; however, even if the employment relationship is nonexistent, section 3121(s) of the Code applies to remuneration paid to the former employee for services rendered while the employee was a common employee. The principles of this subparagraph are illustrated by the following examples:

Example (1). M, N, and O are related corporations which use N as a common paymaster with respect to officers. Their respective headquarters are located in three separate cities several hundred miles apart. A is an officer of M, N, and O who performs substantial services for each corporation. A does not work a set length of time at each corporate headquarters, and when A leaves one corporate headquarters, it is not known when A will return, although it is expected that A will return. Under these facts, A is concurrently employed by the three corporations.

Example (2). P, Q, and R are related corporations whose geographical zones of business activity do not overlap. P, Q, and R have a common pension plan and arrange for Q to be a common paymaster for managers and executives. All three corporations maintain cafeterias for the use of their employees. B is a cafeteria manager who has worked at P's headquarters for 3 years. On June 1, 1980, B is transferred from P to the position of cafeteria manager of R. There are no plans for B's return to P. B's accrued pension benefits, vacation and sick pay, do not change as a result of the transfer. The decision to transfer B was made by Q, the parent corporation. Under these facts, B is not concurrently employed by P and R, because B's employment relationship with P was completely nonexistent during B's employment with R. Furthermore, section 3121(s) is inapplicable since B also was not employed by Q, the common paymaster, because B never contracted to perform services for remuneration from Q, and Q did not have the right to control the day-to-day duties of B's work.

Example (3). C is employed by two related corporations, S and T. C was concurrently employed by these corporations between April 1, 1979, and June 30, 1979. The corporations used T as the common paymaster with respect to C's wages between May 1, 1979, and September 30, 1979. T pays C on May 15 for services performed between April 1 and April 30, on July 15 for services performed between June 1 and June 30, and on August 15 for services performed between July 1 and July 31. Section 3121(s) applies to the first two payments but does not apply to the third payment (there was no concurrent employment). However, if the third payment was made by T for services performed for T, T counts the amounts previously disbursed to C in 1979 while C was concurrently employed by S and T towards the wage base (see section 3121(a)(1)).

(c) *Allocation of employment taxes.*—(1) *Responsibility to pay tax.*—If the requirements of this section are met, the common paymaster has the primary responsibility for remitting taxes pursuant to sections 3102 and 3111 with respect to the remuneration it disburses as the common paymaster. The common paymaster computes these taxes as though it were the sole employer of the concurrently employed individuals. If the common paymaster fails to remit these taxes (in whole or in part), it remains liable for the full amount of the unpaid portion of these taxes. In addition, each of the other related corporations using the common paymaster is jointly and severally liable for its appropriate share of these

$$\frac{\text{Portion of wage payment constituting remuneration to the employee for services performed for the corporation}}{\text{Total wage payment constituting remuneration to the employee for all services performed for the related corporations using the common paymaster}}$$

If the remuneration disbursed to an employee for services performed for a corporation is inappropriate, the district director may adjust the remuneration records of the related corporations to reflect appropriate remuneration. The district director may use the principles of § 1.482-2(b) in making the adjustments.

taxes. That share is an amount equal to the lesser of:

(i) The amount of the liability of the common paymaster under section 3121(s), after taking account of any tax payments made, or

(ii) The amount of the liability under sections 3102 and 3111 which, but for section 3121(s), would have existed with respect to the remuneration from such other related corporation, reduced by an allocable portion of any taxes previously paid by the common paymaster with respect to that remuneration.

The portion of taxes previously paid by the common paymaster that is allocable to each related corporation is determined by multiplying the amount of taxes paid by a fraction, the numerator of which is the portion of the amount of employment tax liability of the common paymaster under section 3121(s) that is allocable to such related corporation under paragraph (c)(2) of this section, and the denominator of which is the total amount of the common paymaster's liability under section 3121(s), both determined without regard to any prior tax payments. These rules apply whether or not the tax on employees was withheld from the employees' wages.

(2) *Allocation of tax.*—(i) *In general.*—If the related corporations maintain a record of the remuneration disbursed to the employee for services performed for each corporation, the remuneration-based allocation rules of paragraph (c)(2)(ii) of this section apply. If the related corporations do not maintain this record of remuneration, the group-wide allocation rules of paragraph (c)(2)(iii) of this section apply. In all cases, allocations must be made with respect to each payment of wages. The allocation of employment tax liabilities pursuant to this subparagraph also determines which related corporation may be entitled to income tax deductions with respect to the payments of those taxes.

(ii) *Remuneration-based allocation rules.*—Under the remuneration-based method of allocation, each related corporation that remunerates an employee through a common paymaster has allocated to it for each pay period an amount of tax determined according to the following formula:

$$\times \quad \begin{array}{l}\text{Tax on employees under section 3102} \\ \text{and tax on employers under section} \\ \text{3111 that the common paymaster is} \\ \text{required to remit with respect to the} \\ \text{wage payment.}\end{array}$$

Example. (i) X and Y are related corporations which use Y as common paymaster for their executives. A is a concurrently employed executive who performs services during the first quarter of 1979 for X and Y. Y remunerates $4,000 gross pay every week to A, calculated as follows:

| Wage payments | Remuneration | | | Tax on employers under section 3111 | Tax on employees withheld under section 3102 | Total |
	X	Y	Total			
1	$3,000	$1,000	$4,000	$245.20	$245.20	$490.40
2—3	....	8,000	8,000	490.40	490.40	980.80
4	1,000	3,000	4,000	245.20	245.20	490.40
5	4,000	....	4,000	245.20	245.20	490.40
6	2,000	2,000	4,000	177.77	177.77	355.54
7—13	10,000	18,000	28,000	0	0	0
	$20,000	$32,000	$52,000	$1,403.77	$1,403.77	$2,807.54

The amounts of remuneration to A are determined by the district director to be appropriate. Under these facts, the tax is allocated to X and Y in the following amounts:

Wage Payments	X	Y
1	$\dfrac{\$3,000}{\$4,000} \times \$490.40 = \$367.80$	$\dfrac{\$1,000}{\$4,000} \times \$490.40 = \$122.60$
2—3	....	$\dfrac{\$8,000}{\$8,000} \times \$980.80 = \$980.80$
4	$\dfrac{\$1,000}{\$4,000} \times \$490.40 = \$122.60$	$\dfrac{\$3,000}{\$4,000} \times \$490.40 = \$367.80$
5	$\dfrac{\$4,000}{\$4,000} \times \$490.40 = \$490.40$	....
6	$\dfrac{\$2,000}{\$4,000} \times \$355.54 = \$177.77$	$\dfrac{\$2,000}{\$4,000} \times \$355.54 = \$177.77$
7—13	$\dfrac{\$10,000}{\$28,000} \times \text{—0—} = \text{—0—}$	$\dfrac{\$28,000}{\$28,000} \times \text{—0—} = \text{—0—}$
	$1,158.57	$1,648.97

Example (ii) If Y remits none of the taxes to the Internal Revenue Service, X is liable for $2,452.00 (the entire amount due pursuant to sections 3102 and 3111 with respect to the remuneration to A from X) (12.26% × $20,000). Any amount remitted by X to the Internal Revenue Service under these circumstances is also credited against the liability of the common paymaster, Y. However, only the portion of the employment taxes allocated to X under (i) above may be deducted by X as employment taxes paid by it in respect of wages paid by it to its employees.

Example (iii) If Y remits $1,000.00 of the total $2,807.54 due, Y as common paymaster remains liable for $1,807.54 ($2,807.54 minus $1,000). X's liability is the lesser of $1,807.54 (the liability of the common paymaster), or X's total liability, in the absence of section 3121(s), on wages paid through the common paymaster

$2,452.00) minus a credit for an allocable part of the amount remitted by Y. The part is $412.66

$$\dfrac{\$1,158.57 \;(\text{X's allocable share of tax})}{\$2,807.54 \;(\text{total tax})} \times \$1,000$$

(tax remitted). Since $1,807.54 is less than $2,039.34 ($2,452.00 minus $412.66), X and Y are jointly and severally liable for $1,807.54.

(iii) *Group-wide allocation rules.*—Under the group-wide method of allocation, the Commissioner may allocate the taxes imposed by sections 3102 and 3111 in an appropriate manner to a related corporation that remunerates an employee through a common paymaster if the common paymaster fails to remit the taxes to the Internal Revenue Service. Allocation in an appropriate manner varies according to the circumstances. It may be based on sales, property, corporate payroll, or any other basis that reflects the distribution of the services performed by the

Reg. §31.3121(s)-1(c)(2)(iii)

employee, or a combination of the foregoing bases. To the extent practicable, the Commissioner may use the principles of §1.482-2(b) of this chapter in making the allocations with respect to wages paid after December 31, 1978, and on or before July 31, 2009. To the extent practicable, the Commissioner may use the principles of §1.482-9 of this chapter in making the allocations with respect to wages paid after July 31, 2009.

(d) *Effective/applicability date.*—(1) *In general.*— This section is applicable with respect to wages paid after December 31, 1978. The fourth sentence of paragraph (c)(2)(iii) of this section is applicable with respect to wages paid after December 31, 1978, and on or before July 31, 2009. The fifth sentence of paragraph (c)(2)(iii) of this section is applicable with respect to wages paid after July 31, 2009.

(2) *Election to apply regulation to earlier taxable years.*—A person may elect to apply the fifth sentence of paragraph (c)(2)(iii) of this section to earlier taxable years in accordance with the rules set forth in §1.482-9(n)(2) of this chapter. [Reg. §31.3121(s)-1.]

☐ *[T.D. 7660, 12-19-79, as corrected, 3-20-80. Amended by T.D. 9278, 7-31-2006 and T.D. 9456, 7-31-2009.]*

[Reg. §31.3121(v)(2)-1]

§31.3121(v)(2)-1. Treatment of amounts deferred under certain nonqualified deferred compensation plans.—(a) *Timing of wage inclusion.*—(1) *General timing rule for wages.*—Remuneration for employment that constitutes wages within the meaning of section 3121(a) generally is taken into account for purposes of the Federal Insurance Contributions Act (FICA) taxes imposed under sections 3101 and 3111 at the time the remuneration is actually or constructively paid. See §31.3121(a)-2(a).

(2) *Special timing rule for an amount deferred under a nonqualified deferred compensation plan.*— (i) *In general.*—To the extent that remuneration deferred under a nonqualified deferred compensation plan constitutes wages within the meaning of section 3121(a), the remuneration is subject to the special timing rule described in this paragraph (a)(2). Remuneration is considered deferred under a nonqualified deferred compensation plan within the meaning of section 3121(v)(2) and this section only if it is provided pursuant to a plan described in paragraph (b) of this section. The amount deferred under a nonqualified deferred compensation plan is determined under paragraph (c) of this section.

(ii) *Special timing rule.*—Except as otherwise provided in this section, an amount deferred under a nonqualified deferred compensation plan is required to be taken into account as wages for FICA tax purposes as of the later of—

(A) The date on which the services creating the right to that amount are performed (within the meaning of paragraph (e)(2) of this section); or

(B) The date on which the right to that amount is no longer subject to a substantial risk of forfeiture (within the meaning of paragraph (e)(3) of this section).

(iii) *Inclusion in wages only once (nonduplication rule).*—Once an amount deferred under a nonqualified deferred compensation plan is taken into account (within the meaning of paragraph (d)(1) of this section), then neither the amount taken into account nor the income attributable to the amount taken into account (within the meaning of paragraph (d)(2) of this section) is treated as wages for FICA tax purposes at any time thereafter.

(iv) *Benefits that do not result from a deferral of compensation.*—If a nonqualified deferred compensation plan (within the meaning of paragraph (b)(1) of this section) provides both a benefit that results from the deferral of compensation (within the meaning of paragraph (b)(3) of this section) and a benefit that does not result from the deferral of compensation, the benefit that does not result from the deferral of compensation is not subject to the special timing rule described in this paragraph (a)(2). For example, if a nonqualified deferred compensation plan provides retirement benefits which result from the deferral of compensation and disability pay (within the meaning of paragraph (b)(4)(iv)(C) of this section) which does not result from the deferral of compensation, the retirement benefits provided under the plan are subject to the special timing rule in this paragraph (a)(2) and the disability pay is not.

(v) *Remuneration that does not constitute wages.*—If remuneration under a nonqualified deferred compensation plan does not constitute wages within the meaning of section 3121(a), then that remuneration is not taken into account as wages for FICA tax purposes under either the general timing rule described in paragraph (a)(1) of this section or the special timing rule described in this paragraph (a)(2). For example, benefits under a death benefit plan described in section 3121(a)(13) do not constitute wages for FICA tax purposes. Therefore, these benefits are not included as wages under the general timing rule described in paragraph (a)(1) of this section or the special timing rule described in this paragraph (a)(2), even if the death benefit plan would otherwise be considered a nonqualified deferred compensation plan within the meaning of paragraph (b)(1) of this section.

(b) *Nonqualified deferred compensation plan.*— (1) *In general.*—For purposes of this section, the term *nonqualified deferred compensation plan* means any plan or other arrangement, other than a plan described in section 3121(a)(5), that is established (within the meaning of paragraph (b)(2) of this section) by an employer for one or more of its employees, and that provides for the deferral of compensation (within the meaning of paragraph (b)(3) of this section). A nonqualified deferred compensation plan may be adopted unilaterally by the employer or may be negotiated among or agreed to by the employer and one or more employees or employee representatives. A plan may constitute a nonqualified deferred compensation plan under this section without regard to whether the deferrals under the plan are made pursuant to an election by the employee or whether the amounts deferred are treated as deferred compensation for income tax purposes (e.g., whether the amounts are subject to the deduction rules of section 404). In addition, a plan may constitute a nonqualified deferred compensation plan under this section whether or not it is an employee benefit plan under section 3(3) of the Employee Retirement Income Security Act of 1974 (ERISA), as amended (29 U.S.C. 1002(3)). For purposes of this section, except where the context indicates otherwise, the term *plan* includes a plan or other arrangement.

(2) *Plan establishment.*—(i) *Date plan is established.*—For purposes of this section, a plan is established on the latest of the date on which it is adopted, the date on which it is effective, and the date on which the material terms of the plan are set forth in writing. For purposes of this section, a plan will be deemed to be set forth in writing if it is set forth in any other form that is approved by the Commissioner. The material terms of the plan include the amount (or the method or formula for determining the amount) of deferred compensation to be provided under the plan and the time when it may or will be provided.

(ii) *Plan amendments.*—In the case of an amendment that increases the amount deferred under a nonqualified deferred compensation plan, the plan is not considered established with respect to the additional amount deferred until the plan, as amended, is established in accordance with paragraph (b)(2)(i) of this section.

(iii) *Transition rule for written plan requirement.*—For purposes of this section, an unwritten plan that was adopted and effective before March 25, 1996, is treated as established under this section as of the later of the date on which it was adopted or became effective, provided that the material terms of the plan are set forth in writing before January 1, 2000.

(3) *Plan must provide for the deferral of compensation.*—(i) *Deferral of compensation defined.*—A plan provides for the *deferral of compensation* with respect to an employee only if, under the terms of the plan and the relevant facts and circumstances, the employee has a legally binding right during a calendar year to compensation that has not been actually or constructively received and that, pursuant to the terms of the plan, is payable to (or on behalf of) the employee in a later year. An employee does not have a legally binding right to compensation if that compensation may be unilaterally reduced or eliminated by the employer after the services creating the right to the compensation have been performed. For this purpose, compensation is not considered subject to unilateral reduction or

elimination merely because it may be reduced or eliminated by operation of the objective terms of the plan, such as the application of an objective provision creating a substantial risk of forfeiture (within the meaning of section 83). Similarly, an employee does not fail to have a legally binding right to compensation merely because the amount of compensation is determined under a formula that provides for benefits to be offset by benefits provided under a plan that is qualified under section 401(a), or because benefits are reduced due to investment losses or, in a final average pay plan, subsequent decreases in compensation.

(ii) *Compensation payable pursuant to the employer's customary payment timing arrangement.*—There is no deferral of compensation (within the meaning of this paragraph (b)(3)) merely because compensation is paid after the last day of a calendar year pursuant to the timing arrangement under which the employer ordinarily compensates employees for services performed during a payroll period described in section 3401(b).

(iii) *Short-term deferrals.*—If, under a nonqualified deferred compensation plan, there is a deferral of compensation (within the meaning of this paragraph (b)(3)) that causes an amount to be deferred from a calendar year to a date that is not more than a brief period of time after the end of that calendar year, then, at the employer's option, that amount may be treated as if it were not subject to the special timing rule described in paragraph (a)(2) of this section. An employer may apply this option only if the employer does so for all employees covered by the plan and all substantially similar nonqualified deferred compensation plans. For purposes of this paragraph (b)(3)(iii), whether compensation is deferred to a date that is not more than a brief period of time after the end of a calendar year is determined in accordance with §1.404(b)-1T, Q&A-2, of this chapter.

(4) *Plans, arrangements, and benefits that do not provide for the deferral of compensation.*—(i) *In general.*—Notwithstanding paragraph (b)(3)(i) of this section, an amount or benefit described in any of paragraphs (b)(4)(ii) through (viii) of this section is not treated as resulting from the deferral of compensation for purposes of section 3121(v)(2) and this section and, thus, is not subject to the special timing rule of paragraph (a)(2) of this section.

(ii) *Stock options, stock appreciation rights, and other stock value rights.*—The grant of a stock option, stock appreciation right, or other stock value right does not constitute the deferral of compensation for purposes of section 3121(v)(2). In addition, amounts received as a result of the exercise of a stock option, stock appreciation right, or other stock value right do not result from the deferral of compensation for purposes of section 3121(v)(2) if such amounts are actually or constructively received in the calendar year of the exercise. For purposes of this paragraph

Reg. §31.3121(v)(2)-1(b)(4)(ii)

(b)(4)(ii), a *stock value right* is a right granted to an employee with respect to one or more shares of employer stock that, to the extent exercised, entitles the employee to a payment for each share of stock equal to the excess, or a percentage of the excess, of the value of a share of the employer's stock on the date of exercise over a specified price (greater than zero). Thus, for example, the term stock value right does not include a phantom stock or other arrangement under which an employee is awarded the right to receive a fixed payment equal to the value of a specified number of shares of employer stock.

(iii) *Restricted property.*—If an employee receives property from, or pursuant to, a plan maintained by an employer, there is no deferral of compensation (within the meaning of section 3121(v)(2)) merely because the value of the property is not includible in income (under section 83) in the year of receipt by reason of the property being nontransferable and subject to a substantial risk of forfeiture. However, a plan under which an employee obtains a legally binding right to receive property (whether or not the property is restricted property) in a future year may provide for the deferral of compensation within the meaning of paragraph (b)(3) of this section and, accordingly, may constitute a nonqualified deferred compensation plan, even though benefits under the plan are or may be paid in the form of property.

(iv) *Certain welfare benefits.*—(A) *In general.*—Vacation benefits, sick leave, compensatory time, disability pay, severance pay, and death benefits do not result from the deferral of compensation for purposes of section 3121(v)(2), even if those benefits constitute wages within the meaning of section 3121(a).

(B) *Severance pay.*—Benefits that are provided under a severance pay arrangement (within the meaning of section 3(2)(B)(i) of ERISA) that satisfies the conditions in 29 CFR 2510.3-2(b)(1)(i) through (iii) are considered severance pay for purposes of this paragraph (b)(4)(iv). If benefits are provided under a severance pay arrangement (within the meaning of section 3(2)(B)(i) of ERISA), but do not satisfy one or more of the conditions in 29 CFR 2510.3-2(b)(1)(i) through (iii), then whether those benefits are severance pay within the meaning of this paragraph (b)(4)(iv) depends upon the relevant facts and circumstances. For this purpose, relevant facts and circumstances include whether the benefits are provided over a short period of time commencing immediately after (or shortly after) termination of employment or for a substantial period of time following termination of employment and whether the benefits are provided after any termination or only after retirement (or another specified type of termination). Benefits provided under a severance pay arrangement (within the meaning of section 3(2)(B)(i) of ERISA) are in all cases severance pay within the meaning of this paragraph (b)(4)(iv) if the benefits payable under the plan upon an employee's termination of employment are payable only if that termination is involuntary.

(C) *Death benefits and disability pay.*—(1) *General definition.*—Payments made under a nonqualified deferred compensation plan in the event of death are death benefits within the meaning of this paragraph (b)(4)(iv), but only to the extent the total benefits payable under the plan exceed the lifetime benefits payable under the plan. Similarly, payments made under a nonqualified deferred compensation plan in the event of disability are disability pay within the meaning of this paragraph (b)(4)(iv), but only to the extent the disability benefits payable under the plan exceed the lifetime benefits payable under the plan. Accordingly, any benefits that a nonqualified deferred compensation plan provides in the event of death or disability that are associated with an amount deferred under this section are disregarded in applying this section to the extent the benefits payable under the plan in the event of death or in the event of disability have a value in excess of the lifetime benefits payable under the plan.

(2) *Total benefits payable defined.*—For purposes of paragraph (b)(4)(iv)(C)(1) of this section, the term *total benefits payable* under a plan means the present value of the total benefits payable to or on behalf of the employee (including benefits payable in the event of the employee's death) under the plan, disregarding any benefits that are payable only in the event of disability and determined separately with respect to each form of distribution or other election that may apply with respect to the employee.

(3) *Disability benefits payable defined.*—For purposes of paragraph (b)(4)(iv)(C)(1) of this section, the term *disability benefits payable* under a plan means the present value of the benefits payable to or on behalf of the employee under the plan, including benefits payable in the event of the employee's disability but excluding death benefits within the meaning of this paragraph (b)(4)(iv).

(4) *Lifetime benefits payable defined.*—For purposes of paragraph (b)(4)(iv)(C)(1) of this section, the term *lifetime benefits payable* under a plan means the present value of the benefits that could be payable to the employee under the plan during the employee's lifetime, determined under the plan's optional form of distribution or other election that is or was available to the employee at any time with respect to the amount deferred and that provides the largest present value to the employee during the employee's lifetime of any such form or election so available.

(5) *Rules of application.*—For purposes of determining present value under this paragraph (b)(4)(iv)(C), present value is determined as of the time immediately preceding the time the amount deferred under a nonqualified deferred compensation plan is required to be taken into account under paragraph (e) of this section,

using actuarial assumptions that are reasonable as of that date but taking into consideration only benefits that result from the deferral of compensation, as determined under this paragraph (b), and benefits payable in the event of death or disability. In addition, for purposes of paragraph (b)(4)(iv)(C)(4) of this section, present value must be determined without any discount for the probability that the employee may die before benefit payments commence and without regard to any benefits payable solely in the event of disability.

(v) *Certain benefits provided in connection with impending termination.—(A) In general.—*Benefits provided in connection with impending termination of employment under paragraph (b)(4)(v)(B) or (C) of this section do not result from the deferral of compensation within the meaning of section 3121(v)(2).

(B) *Window benefits.—(1) In general.—*For purposes of this paragraph (b)(4)(v), except as provided in paragraph (b)(4)(v)(B)(3) of this section, a window benefit is provided in connection with impending termination of employment. For this purpose, a *window benefit* is an early retirement benefit, retirement-type subsidy, social security supplement, or other form of benefit made available by an employer for a limited period of time (no greater than one year) to employees who terminate employment during that period or to employees who terminate employment during that period under specified circumstances.

(2) *Special rule for recurring window benefits.—*A benefit will not be considered a window benefit if an employer establishes a pattern of repeatedly providing for similar benefits in similar situations for substantially consecutive, limited periods of time. Whether the recurrence of these benefits constitutes a pattern of amendments is determined based on the facts and circumstances. Although no one factor is determinative, relevant factors include whether the benefits are on account of a specific business event or condition, the degree to which the benefits relate to the event or condition, and whether the event or condition is temporary or discrete or is a permanent aspect of the employer's business.

(3) *Transition rule for window benefits.—*In the case of a window benefit that is made available for a period of time that begins before January 1, 2000, an employer may choose to treat the window benefit as a benefit that results from the deferral of compensation if the sole reason the window benefit would otherwise fail to be provided pursuant to a nonqualified deferred compensation plan is the application of paragraph (b)(4)(v)(B)(1) of this section.

(C) *Termination within 12 months of establishment of a benefit or plan.—*For purposes of this paragraph (b)(4)(v), a benefit is provided in connection with impending termination of employment, without regard to whether it constitutes a window benefit, if—

(1) An employee's termination of employment occurs within 12 months of the establishment of the plan (or amendment) providing the benefit; and

(2) The facts and circumstances indicate that the plan (or amendment) is established in contemplation of the employee's impending termination of employment.

(vi) *Benefits established after termination.—*Benefits established with respect to an employee after the employee's termination of employment do not result from a deferral of compensation within the meaning of section 3121(v)(2). However, cost-of-living adjustments on benefit payments under a nonqualified deferred compensation plan (within the meaning of paragraph (b) of this section) shall not be considered benefits established after the employee's termination of employment for purposes of this paragraph (b)(4)(vi) merely because the employee does not obtain the right to the adjustment until after the employee's termination of employment. For purposes of the preceding sentence, *cost-of-living adjustments* are payments that satisfy conditions similar to those of 29 CFR 2510.3-2(g)(1)(ii) and (iii).

(vii) *Excess parachute payments.—*An excess parachute payment (as defined in section 280G(b)) under an agreement entered into or renewed after June 14, 1984, in taxable years ending after such date, does not result from the deferral of compensation within the meaning of section 3121(v)(2). For this purpose, any contract entered into before June 15, 1984, that is amended after June 14, 1984, in any relevant significant aspect, is treated as a contract entered into after June 14, 1984.

(viii) *Compensation for current services.—*A plan does not provide for the deferral of compensation within the meaning of section 3121(v)(2) if, based on the relevant facts and circumstances, the compensation is paid for current services.

(5) *Examples.—*This paragraph (b) is illustrated by the following examples:

Example 1. (i) In December of 2001, Employer L tells Employee A that, if specified goals are satisfied for 2002, Employee A will receive a bonus on July 1, 2003, equal to a specified percentage of 2002 compensation. Because Employee A meets the specified goals, Employer L pays the bonus to Employee A on July 1, 2003, consistent with its oral commitment.

(ii) This arrangement is not a nonqualified deferred compensation plan under this section because its terms were not set forth in writing and, therefore, it was not established in accordance with paragraph (b)(2) of this section.

Example 2. (i) In 2004, Employer M establishes a compensation arrangement for Employee B under which Employer M agrees to pay Employee B a specified amount based on a percentage of his salary for 2004. The amount due is to be paid out of the general assets of Employer M and is payable in 2008.

(ii) Employee B has a legally binding right during 2004 to an amount of compensation that has not been actually or constructively received and that, pursuant to the terms of the arrangement, is payable in a later year. Therefore, the arrangement provides for the deferral of compensation.

Example 3. (i) Employer N establishes a nonqualified deferred compensation plan (within the meaning of paragraph (b)(1) of this section) for Employee C in 1984. The plan is amended on January 1, 2001, to increase benefits, and the amendment provides that the increase in benefits is on account of Employee C's performance of services for Employer N from 1985 through 2000.

(ii) The additional benefits that resulted from the plan amendment cannot be taken into account as amounts deferred for 1985 through 2000, even though the plan was established before then. Pursuant to paragraphs (b)(2)(ii) and (e)(1) of this section, the additional benefits cannot be taken into account before the latest of the date on which the amendment is adopted, the date on which the amendment is effective, or the date on which the material terms of the plan, as amended, are set forth in writing.

Example 4. (i) In 2002, Employer O, a state or local government, establishes a plan for certain employees that provides for the deferral of compensation and that is subject to section 457(a).

(ii) Paragraph (b)(1) of this section provides that nonqualified deferred compensation plan means any plan that is established by an employer and that provides for the deferral of compensation, other than a plan described in section 3121(a)(5). Section 3121(a)(5) lists, among other plans, an exempt governmental deferred compensation plan as defined in section 3121(v)(3). Under section 3121(v)(3)(A), this definition does not include any plan to which section 457(a) applies. Thus, the plan established by Employer O is not an exempt governmental deferred compensation plan described in section 3121(v)(3) and, consequently, is not a plan described in section 3121(a)(5). Accordingly, the plan is a nonqualified deferred compensation plan within the meaning of section 3121(v)(2) and paragraph (b)(1) of this section.

(iii) However, the general timing rule of paragraph (a)(1) of this section and the special timing rule of paragraph (a)(2) of this section apply only to remuneration for employment that constitutes wages. Under section 3121(b)(7), certain service performed in the employ of a state, or any political subdivision of a state, is not employment. Thus, even though the plan is a nonqualified deferred compensation plan, the extent to which section 3121(v)(2) applies to a participating employee will depend on whether or not the service performed for Employer O is excluded from the definition of employment under section 3121(b)(7).

Example 5. (i) In 2000, Employer P establishes a plan that provides for bonuses to be paid to employees based on an objective formula that takes into account the employees' performance for the year. Employer P does not have the discretion to reduce the amount of any employee's bonus after the end of the year. The bonus is not actually calculated until March 1 of the following year, and is paid on March 15 of that following year.

(ii) The plan provides for the deferral of compensation because the employees have a legally binding right, as of the last day of a calendar year, to an amount of compensation that has not been actually or constructively received and, pursuant to the terms of the plan, that compensation is payable in a later year. However, because the bonuses under the plan are paid within a brief period of time after the end of the calendar year from which they are deferred, Employer P may choose, pursuant to paragraph (b)(3)(iii) of this section, to treat all the bonuses as if they are not subject to the special timing rule of paragraph (a)(2) of this section.

(iii) If the employer uses the special timing rule, the amount deferred would be taken into account as wages on December 31, 2000. If the employer chooses not to use the special timing rule, the amount of the bonus is wages on the date it is actually or constructively paid, March 15, 2000.

Example 6. (i) Employer Q establishes a plan under which bonuses based on performance in one year may be paid on February 1 of the following year at the discretion of the board of directors. The board of directors meets in January of each year to determine the amount, if any, of the bonuses to be paid based on performance in the prior year.

(ii) Because an employee does not have a legally binding right to any bonus until January of the year in which the bonus is paid, any bonus paid under the plan in that year is not deferred from the preceding calendar year, and the plan does not provide for the deferral of compensation within the meaning of paragraph (b)(3)(i) of this section.

Example 7. (i) Employer R maintains a plan for employees that provides nonqualified stock options described in § 1.83-7(a) of this chapter. Under the plan, employees are granted in 2001 the option to acquire shares of employer stock at the fair market value of the shares on the date of grant ($50 per share). The options can be exercised at any time from the date of grant through 2010. The options do not have a readily ascertainable fair market value for purposes of section 83 at the date of grant, and shares are issued upon the exercise of the options without being subject to a substantial risk of forfeiture within the meaning of section 83. In 2005, when the fair market value of a share of employer stock is $80, Employee D exercises an option to acquire 1,000 shares.

(ii) Under paragraph (b)(4)(ii) of this section, neither the grant of a stock option nor amounts received currently as a result of the exercise of a stock option result from the deferral of compensation for purposes of section 3121(v)(2). Thus, under the general timing rule of paragraph (a)(1) of this section, the $30,000 spread between the amount paid for the shares ($50,000) and the fair market value of the shares on the date of exercise ($80,000) is taken into account as wages for FICA tax purposes in the year of exercise.

(iii) If the options had been granted at $45 per share, $5 per share below the fair market value on date of grant, the $35,000 spread between the amount paid for the shares ($45,000) and the fair market value of the shares on the date of exercise ($80,000) would similarly be taken into account as wages for FICA tax purposes in the year of exercise.

Example 8. (i) Employer T establishes a phantom stock plan for certain employees. Under the plan, an employee is credited on the last day of each calendar year with a dollar amount equal to the fair market value of 1,000 shares of employer stock. Upon termination of employment for any reason, each employee is entitled to receive the value on the date of termination, in cash or employer stock, of the shares with which he or she has been credited.

(ii) Because compensation to which the employee has a legally binding right as of the last day of one year is paid in a subsequent year, the phantom stock plan provides for the deferral of compensation. The phantom stock plan does not provide stock value rights within the meaning of paragraph (b)(4)(ii) of this section because it provides for awards equal in value to the full fair market value of a specified number of shares of Employer T stock, rather than the excess of that fair market value over a specified price.

Example 9. (i) Employer U establishes a severance pay arrangement (within the meaning of section 3(2)(b)(i) of ERISA) which provides for payments solely upon an employee's death, disability, or dismissal from employment. The amount of the payments to an employee is based on the length of continuous active service with Employer U at the time of dismissal, and is paid in monthly installments over a period of three years.

(ii) Because benefits payable under the plan upon termination of employment are payable only upon an employee's involuntary termination, the plan is a severance pay plan within the meaning of paragraph (b)(4)(iv)(B) of this section. Thus, the benefits are not treated as resulting from the deferral of compensation for purposes of section 3121(v)(2).

Example 10. (i) Employer V establishes a nonqualified deferred compensation plan under which employees will receive benefit payments commencing at age 65 as a life annuity or in one of several actuarially equivalent annuity forms. If an employee dies before benefit payments commence under the plan, a benefit is payable to the employee's designated beneficiary in a single lump sum payment equal to the present value of the employee's annuity benefit. This benefit

(sometimes called a full reserve death benefit) is calculated using the applicable interest rate specified in section 417(e) and, for the period after age 65, the applicable mortality table specified in section 417(e), both of which are reasonable actuarial assumptions. During 2002, Employee E obtains a legally binding right to an annuity benefit under the plan, payable at age 65. This annuity benefit has a present value of $10,000 at the end of 2002, determined using the same assumptions as are used under the plan to calculate the full reserve death benefit.

(ii) The present value, at the end of 2002, of the total benefits payable to or on behalf of Employee E (i.e., the sum of the present value of the annuity benefit commencing at age 65, and the present value of the full reserve death benefit, with both determined using the actuarial assumptions described in paragraph (i) of this *Example 10*, except also taking into account the probability of death prior to age 65) is $10,000. This present value does not exceed the present value of the annuity benefits that could be payable to Employee E under the plan during Employee E's lifetime determined without a discount for the possibility that Employee E might die before age 65 (also $10,000). Thus, the benefit payable in the event of Employee E's death is not a death benefit for purposes of paragraph (b)(4)(iv) of this section.

(iii) The same result would apply in the case of a plan that bases benefits on an interest bearing account balance and pays the account balance at termination of employment or death (because the sum of the deferred benefits payable in the future if the employee terminates employment before death with a discount for the probability of death before that date plus the present value of the benefit payable in the event of death necessarily equals the present value of the deferred benefits payable with no discount for the probability of death).

Example 11. (i) The facts are the same as in *Example 10*, except that, in lieu of the full reserve death benefit, the plan provides a monthly life annuity benefit to an employee's spouse in the event of the employee's death before benefit payments commence equal to 100 percent of the monthly annuity that would be payable to the employee at age 65 under the life annuity form. Employee E is age 63 and has a spouse who is age 51. The sum of the present value of Employee E's annuity benefit commencing at age 65 determined with a discount for the possibility that Employee E might die before age 65 and the present value of the 100 percent annuity death benefit for Employee E's spouse exceeds $10,000.

(ii) The amount deferred for 2002 is $10,000 (because the 100 percent annuity death benefit for Employee E's spouse is disregarded to the extent that the total benefits payable to or on behalf of Employee E exceeds the present value of the annuity benefits that could be payable to Employee E under the plan during Employee E's lifetime without a discount for the probability of Employee E's death before benefit payments commence).

Reg. §31.3121(v)(2)-1(b)(5)

Example 12. (i) On January 1, 2001, Employer W establishes a plan that covers only Employee F, who owns a significant portion of the business and who has 30 years of service as of that date. The plan provides that, upon Employee F's termination of employment at any time, he will receive $200,000 per year for each of the immediately succeeding five years. Employee F terminates employment on March 1, 2001.

(ii) Because Employee F terminates employment within 12 months of the establishment of the plan and the facts and circumstances set forth above indicate that the plan was established in contemplation of impending termination of employment, the plan is considered to be established in connection with impending termination within the meaning of paragraph (b)(4)(v) of this section. Therefore, the benefits provided under the plan are not treated as resulting from the deferral of compensation for purposes of section 3121(v)(2).

Example 13. (i) Employer X establishes a plan on January 1, 2004, to supplement the qualified retirement benefits of recently hired 55-year old Employee G, who forfeited retirement benefits with her former employer in order to accept employment with Employer X. The plan provides that Employee G will receive $50,000 per year for life beginning at age 65, regardless of when she terminates employment. On April 15, 2004, Employee G unexpectedly terminates employment.

(ii) The facts and circumstances indicate that the plan was not established in contemplation of impending termination. Thus, even though Employee G terminated employment within 12 months of the establishment of the plan, the plan is not considered to be established in connection with impending termination within the meaning of paragraph (b)(4)(v) of this section. Benefits provided under the plan are treated as resulting from the deferral of compensation for purposes of section 3121(v)(2).

Example 14. (i) Employer Y establishes a plan to provide supplemental retirement benefits to a group of management employees who are at various stages of their careers. All employees covered by the plan are subject to the same benefit formula. Employee H is planning to (and actually does) retire within six months of the date on which the plan is established.

(ii) Even though Employee H terminated employment within 12 months of the establishment of the plan, the plan is not considered to have been established in connection with Employee H's impending termination within the meaning of paragraph (b)(4)(v) of this section because the facts and circumstances indicate otherwise.

Example 15. (i) Employee J owns 100 percent of Employer Z, a corporation that provides consulting services. Substantially all of Employer Z's revenue is derived as a result of the services performed by Employee J. In each of 2001, 2002, and 2003, Employer Z has gross receipts of $180,000 and expenses (other than salary) of $80,000. In each of 2001 and 2002, Employer Z pays Employee J a salary of $100,000 for services performed in each of those years. On December 31, 2002, Employer Z establishes a plan to pay Employee J $80,000 in 2003. The plan recites that the payment is in recognition of prior services. In 2003, Employer Z pays Employee J a salary of $20,000 and the $80,000 due under the plan.

(ii) The facts and circumstances described above indicate that the $80,000 paid pursuant to the plan is based on services performed by Employee J in 2003 and, thus, is paid for current services within the meaning of paragraph (b)(4)(viii) of this section. Accordingly, the plan does not provide for the deferral of compensation within the meaning of section 3121(v)(2), and the $80,000 payment is included as wages in 2003 under the general timing rule of paragraph (a)(1) of this section.

(c) *Determination of the amount deferred.*— (1) *Account balance plans.*—(i) *General rule.*—For purposes of this section, if benefits for an employee are provided under a nonqualified deferred compensation plan that is an account balance plan, the amount deferred for a period equals the principal amount credited to the employee's account for the period, increased or decreased by any income attributable to the principal amount through the date the principal amount is required to be taken into account as wages under paragraph (e) of this section.

(ii) *Definitions.*—(A) *Account balance plan.*—For purposes of this section, an *account balance plan* is a nonqualified deferred compensation plan under the terms of which a principal amount (or amounts) is credited to an individual account for an employee, the income attributable to each principal amount is credited (or debited) to the individual account, and the benefits payable to the employee are based solely on the balance credited to the individual account.

(B) *Income.*—For purposes of this section, *income* means any increase or decrease in the amount credited to an employee's account that is attributable to amounts previously credited to the employee's account, regardless of whether the plan denominates that increase or decrease as income.

(iii) *Additional rules.*—(A) *Commingled accounts.*—A plan does not fail to be an account balance plan merely because, under the terms of the plan, benefits payable to an employee are based solely on a specified percentage of an account maintained for all (or a portion of) plan participants under which principal amounts and income are credited (or debited) to such account.

(B) *Bifurcation permitted.*—An employer may treat a portion of a nonqualified deferred compensation plan as a separate account balance plan if that portion satisfies the requirements of this paragraph (c)(1) and the amount payable to employees under that portion is determined independently of the amount payable under the other portion of the plan.

(C) *Actuarial equivalents.*—A plan does not fail to be an account balance plan merely because the plan permits employees to elect to receive their benefits under the plan in a form of benefit other than payment of the account balance, provided the amount of benefit payable in that other form is actuarially equivalent to payment of the account balance using actuarial assumptions that are reasonable. Conversely, a plan is not an account balance plan if it provides an optional form of benefit that is not actuarially equivalent to the account balance using actuarial assumptions that are reasonable. For this purpose, the determination of whether forms are actuarially equivalent using actuarial assumptions that are reasonable is determined under the rules applicable to nonaccount balance plans under paragraph (c)(2)(iii) of this section.

(2) *Nonaccount balance plans.*—(i) *General rule.*—For purposes of this section, if benefits for an employee are provided under a nonqualified deferred compensation plan that is not an account balance plan (a nonaccount balance plan), the amount deferred for a period equals the present value of the additional future payment or payments to which the employee has obtained a legally binding right (as described in paragraph (b)(3)(i) of this section) under the plan during that period.

(ii) *Present value defined.*—For purposes of this section, *present value* means the value as of a specified date of an amount or series of amounts due thereafter, where each amount is multiplied by the probability that the condition or conditions on which payment of the amount is contingent will be satisfied, and is discounted according to an assumed rate of interest to reflect the time value of money. For purposes of this section, the present value must be determined as of the date the amount deferred is required to be taken into account as wages under paragraph (e) of this section using actuarial assumptions and methods that are reasonable as of that date. For this purpose, a discount for the probability that an employee will die before commencement of benefit payments is permitted, but only to the extent that benefits will be forfeited upon death. In addition, the present value cannot be discounted for the probability that payments will not be made (or will be reduced) because of the unfunded status of the plan, the risk associated with any deemed or actual investment of amounts deferred under the plan, the risk that the employer, the trustee, or another party will be unwilling or unable to pay, the possibility of future plan amendments, the possibility of a future change in the law, or similar risks or contingencies. Nor is the present value affected by the possibility that some of the payments due under the plan will be eligible for one of the exclusions from wages in section 3121(a).

(iii) *Treatment of actuarially equivalent benefits.*—(A) *In general.*—In the case of a nonaccount balance plan that permits employees to receive their benefits in more than one form or commencing at more than one date, the amount deferred is determined by assuming that payments are made in the normal form of benefit commencing at normal commencement date if the requirements of paragraph (c)(2)(iii)(B) of this section are satisfied. Accordingly, in the case of a nonaccount balance plan that permits employees to receive their benefits in more than one form or commencing at more than one date, unless the requirements of paragraph (c)(2)(iii)(B) of this section are satisfied, the amount deferred is treated as not reasonably ascertainable under the rules of paragraph (e)(4)(i)(B) of this section until a form of benefit and a time of commencement are selected.

(B) *Use of normal form commencing at normal commencement date.*—The requirements of this paragraph (c)(2)(iii)(B) are satisfied by a nonaccount balance plan if the plan has a single normal form of benefit commencing at normal commencement date for the amount deferred and each other optional form is actuarially equivalent to the normal form of benefit commencing at normal commencement date using actuarial assumptions that are reasonable. For this purpose, each form of benefit for payment of the amount deferred commencing at a date is a separate optional form. For purposes of this paragraph (c)(2)(iii)(B), each optional form is actuarially equivalent to the normal form of benefit commencing at normal commencement date only if the terms of the plan in effect when the amount is deferred provide for every optional form to be actuarially equivalent and further provide for actuarial assumptions to determine actuarial equivalency that will be reasonable at the time the optional form is selected, without regard to whether market interest rates are higher or lower at the time the optional form is selected than at the time the amount is deferred. Thus, a plan that provides for every optional form to be actuarially equivalent satisfies this paragraph (c)(2)(iii)(B) if it provides for actuarial equivalence to be determined—

(1) When an optional form is selected or when benefit payments under the optional form commence, based on assumptions that are reasonable then;

(2) Based on an index that reflects market rates of interest from time to time (for example, the plan specifies that all benefits will be actuarially equivalent using the applicable interest rate and applicable mortality table specified in section 417(e)); or

(3) Based on actuarial assumptions specified in the plan and provides for those assumptions to be revised to be reasonable assumptions if they cease to be reasonable assumptions.

(C) *Fixed mortality assumptions permitted.*—A plan does not fail to satisfy paragraph (c)(2)(iii)(B) of this section merely because the plan specifies a fixed mortality assumption that is reasonable at the time the amount is deferred, even if that assumption is not reasonable at the time the optional form is selected. (But see paragraph (c)(2)(iii)(E) of this section for additional rules that apply if the mortality assumption is not reasonable at the time the optional form is selected.)

(D) *Normal form of benefit commencing at normal commencement date defined.*—For purposes of this paragraph (c)(2)(iii), the normal form of benefit commencing at normal commencement date under the plan is the form, and date of commencement, under which the payments due to the employee under the plan are expressed, prior to adjustments for form or timing of commencement of payments.

(E) *Rule applicable if actuarial assumptions cease to be reasonable.*—If the terms of the plan in effect when an amount is deferred provide for actuarial assumptions to determine actuarial equivalency that will be reasonable at the time the optional form is selected or payments commence as provided in paragraph (c)(2)(iii)(B) of this section, but, at that time, the actuarial assumptions used under the plan are not reasonable, the employee will be treated as obtaining a legally binding right at that time (or, if earlier, at the date on which the plan is amended to provide actuarial assumptions that are not reasonable) to any additional benefits that result from the use of an unreasonable actuarial assumption. This might occur, for example, if the plan specifies that the actuarial assumptions will be reasonable assumptions to be set at the time the optional form is selected and the assumptions used are in fact not reasonable at that time.

(3) *Separate determination for each period.*— The amount deferred under this paragraph (c) is determined separately for each period for which there is an amount deferred under the plan. In addition, paragraphs (d) and (e) of this section are applied separately with respect to the amount deferred for each such period. Thus, for example, the fraction described in paragraph (d)(1)(ii)(B) of this section and the amount of the true-up at the resolution date described in paragraph (e)(4)(ii)(B) of this section are determined separately with respect to each amount deferred. See paragraph (e)(4)(ii)(D) of this section for special rules for allocating amounts deferred over more than one year.

(4) *Examples.*—This paragraph (c) is illustrated by the following examples. (The examples illustrate the rules in this paragraph (c) and include various interest rate and mortality table assumptions, including the applicable section 417(e) mortality table, the GAM 83 (male) mortality table, and UP-84 mortality table. These tables can be obtained from the Society of Actuaries at its internet site at *http://www.soa.org.*) The examples are as follows:

Example 1. (i) Employer M establishes a nonqualified deferred compensation plan for Employee A. Under the plan, 10 percent of annual compensation is credited on behalf of Employee A on December 31 of each year. In addition, a reasonable rate of interest is credited quarterly on the balance credited to Employee A as of the

last day of the preceding quarter. All amounts credited under the plan are 100 percent vested and the benefits payable to Employee A are based solely on the balance credited to Employee A's account.

(ii) The plan is an account balance plan. Thus, pursuant to paragraph (c)(1) of this section, the amount deferred for a calendar year is equal to 10 percent of annual compensation.

Example 2. (i) Employer N establishes a nonqualified deferred compensation plan for Employee B. Under the plan, 2.5 percent of annual compensation is credited quarterly on behalf of Employee B. In addition, a reasonable rate of interest is credited quarterly on the balance credited to Employee B's account as of the last day of the preceding quarter. All amounts credited under the plan are 100 percent vested, and the benefits payable to Employee B are based solely on the balance credited to Employee B's account. As permitted by paragraph (e)(5) of this section, any amount deferred under the plan for the calendar year is taken into account as wages on the last day of the year.

(ii) The plan is an account balance plan. Thus, pursuant to paragraph (c)(1) of this section, the amount deferred for a calendar year equals 10 percent of annual compensation (i.e., the sum of the principal amounts credited to Employee B's account for the year) plus the interest credited with respect to that 10 percent principal amount through the last day of the calendar year. If Employer N had not chosen to apply paragraph (e)(5) of this section and, thus, had taken into account 2.5 percent of compensation quarterly, the interest credited with respect to those quarterly amounts would not have been treated as part of the amount deferred for the year.

Example 3. (i) Employer O establishes a nonqualified deferred compensation plan for a group of five employees. Under the plan, a specified sum is credited to an account for the benefit of the group of employees on July 31 of each year. Income on the balance of the account is credited annually at a rate that is reasonable for each year. The benefit payable to an employee is equal to one-fifth of the account balance and is payable, at the employee's option, in a lump sum or in 10 annual installments that reflect income on the balance.

(ii) The plan is an account balance plan notwithstanding the fact that the employee's benefit is equal to a specified percentage of an account maintained for a group of employees.

Example 4. (i) The facts are the same as in *Example 3,* except that the plan also permits an employee to elect a life annuity that is actuarially equivalent to the account balance based on the applicable interest rate and applicable mortality table specified in section 417(e) at the time the benefit is elected by the employee.

(ii) Under paragraphs (c)(1)(iii)(C) and (c)(2)(iii) of this section, the plan does not fail to be an account balance plan merely because the plan permits employees to elect to receive their benefits under the plan in a form that is actuarially equivalent to payment of the account balance using actuarial assumptions that are reasonable at the time the form is selected.

Example 5. (i) Employer P establishes a nonqualified deferred compensation plan for a group of employees. Under the plan, each participating employee has a fully vested right to receive a life annuity, payable monthly beginning at age 65, equal to the product of 2 percent for each year of service and the employee's highest average annual compensation for any 3-year period. The plan also provides that, if an employee dies before age 65, the present value of the future payments will be paid to his or her beneficiary. As permitted under paragraph (e)(5) of this section, any amount deferred under the plan for a calendar year is taken into account as FICA wages as of the last day of the year. As of December 31, 2002, Employee C is age 60, has 25 years of service, and high 3-year average compensation of $100,000 (the average for the years 2000 through 2002). As of December 31, 2003, Employee C is age 61, has 26 years of service, and has high 3-year average compensation of $104,000. As of December 31, 2004, Employee C is age 62, has 27 years of service, and has high 3-year average compensation of $105,000. The assumptions that Employer P uses to determine the amount deferred for 2003 (a 7 percent interest rate and, for the period after commencement of benefit payments, the GAM 83 (male) mortality table) and for 2004 (a 7.5 percent interest rate and, for the period after commencement of benefit payments, the GAM 83 (male) mortality table) are assumed, solely for purposes of this example, to be reasonable actuarial assumptions.

(ii) As of December 31, 2002, Employee C has a legally binding right to receive lifetime payments of $50,000 (2 percent × 25 years × $100,000) per year. As of December 31, 2003, Employee C has a legally binding right to receive lifetime payments of $54,080 (2 percent × 26 years × $104,000) per year. Thus, during 2003, Employee C has earned a legally binding right to additional lifetime payments of $4,080 ($54,080 – $50,000) per year beginning at age 65. The amount deferred for 2003 is the present value, as

of December 31, 2003, of these additional payments, which is $28,767 ($4,080 × the present value factor for a deferred annuity payable at age 65, using the specified actuarial assumptions for 2003). Similarly, during 2004, Employee C has earned a legally binding right to additional lifetime payments of $2,620 (2 percent × 27 years × $105,000, minus $54,080) per year beginning at age 65. The amount deferred for 2004 is the present value, as of December 31, 2004, of these additional payments, which is $18,845 ($2,620 × the present value factor for a deferred annuity payable at age 65, using the specified actuarial assumptions for 2004).

Example 6. (i) Employer Q establishes a nonqualified deferred compensation plan for Employee D on January 1, 2001, when Employee D is age 63. During 2001, Employee D obtains a fully vested right to receive a life annuity under the nonqualified deferred compensation plan equal to the excess of $200,000 over the life annuity benefits payable to Employee D under a qualified defined benefit pension plan sponsored by Employer Q. The life annuity benefit payable annually under the qualified plan is the lesser of $200,000 and the section 415(b)(1)(A) limitation in effect for the year, where the section 415(b)(1)(A) limitation is automatically adjusted to reflect changes in the cost of living. Benefits under both the qualified and nonqualified plan are payable monthly beginning at age 65. For purposes of this example, the section 415(b)(1)(A) limit for 2001 is assumed to be $140,000. The nonqualified plan provides no benefits in the event Employee D dies prior to commencement of benefit payments. As permitted under paragraph (e)(5) of this section, any amount deferred under the plan for a calendar year is taken into account as FICA wages as of the last day of the year. The assumptions that Employer Q uses to determine the amount deferred for 2001 (a 7 percent interest rate, a 3 percent increase in the cost of living and the GAM 83 (male) mortality table) are assumed, solely for purposes of this example, to be reasonable actuarial assumptions. As of December 31, 2001, Employee D has a legally binding right to receive lifetime payments as set forth in the following table:

Year	Annual Gross Amount	Assumed Qualified Plan Annual Payment (based on cost of living)	Net Annual Payment under Nonqualified Plan
2003	$200,000	$145,000	$55,000
2004	$200,000	$150,000	$50,000
2005	$200,000	$155,000	$45,000
2006	$200,000	$160,000	$40,000
2007	$200,000	$165,000	$35,000
2008	$200,000	$170,000	$30,000
2009	$200,000	$175,000	$25,000
2010	$200,000	$180,000	$20,000
2011	$200,000	$185,000	$15,000
2012	$200,000	$190,000	$10,000
2013	$200,000	$195,000	$5,000
2014 and thereafter	$200,000	$205,000 or greater	$0

Reg. §31.3121(v)(2)-1(c)(4)

(ii) The amount deferred for 2001 is the present value, as of December 31, 2001, of the net lifetime payments under the nonqualified plan, or $223,753.

(d) *Amounts taken into account and income attributable thereto.*—(1) *Amounts taken into account.*—(i) *In general.*—For purposes of this section, an amount deferred under a nonqualified deferred compensation plan is taken into account as of the date it is included in computing the amount of *wages* as defined in section 3121(a), but only to the extent that any additional FICA tax that results from such inclusion (including any interest and penalties for late payment) is actually paid before the expiration of the applicable period of limitations for the period in which the amount deferred was required to be taken into account under paragraph (e) of this section. Because an amount deferred for a calendar year is combined with the employee's other wages for the year for purposes of computing FICA taxes with respect to the employee for the year, if the employee has other wages that equal or exceed the wage base limitations for the Old-Age, Survivors, and Disability Insurance (OASDI) portion (or, in the case of years before 1994, the Hospital Insurance (HI) portion) of FICA for the year, no portion of the amount deferred will actually result in additional OASDI (or HI) tax. However, because there is no wage base limitation for the HI portion of FICA for years after 1993, the entire amount deferred (in addition to all other wages) is subject to the HI tax for the year and, thus, will not be considered taken into account for purposes of this section unless the HI tax relating to the amount deferred is actually paid. In determining whether any additional FICA tax relating to the amount deferred is actually paid, any FICA tax paid in a year is treated as paid with respect to an amount deferred only after FICA tax is paid on all other wages for the year.

(ii) *Amounts not taken into account.*—(A) *Failure to take an amount deferred into account under the special timing rule.*—If an amount deferred for a period (as determined under paragraph (c) of this section) is not taken into account, then the nonduplication rule of paragraph (a)(2)(iii) of this section does not apply, and benefit payments attributable to that amount deferred are included as wages in accordance with the general timing rule of paragraph (a)(1) of this section. For example, if an amount deferred is required to be taken into account in a particular year under paragraph (e) of this section, but the employer fails to pay the additional FICA tax resulting from that amount, then the amount deferred and the income attributable to that amount must be included as wages when actually or constructively paid.

(B) *Failure to take a portion of an amount deferred into account under the special timing rule.*—If, as of the date an amount deferred is required to be taken into account, only a portion of the amount deferred (as determined under para-graph (c) of this section) has been taken into account, then a portion of each subsequent benefit payment that is attributable to that amount is excluded from wages pursuant to the nonduplication rule of paragraph (a)(2)(iii) of this section and the balance is subject to the general timing rule of paragraph (a)(1) of this section. The portion that is excluded from wages is fixed immediately before the attributable benefit payments commence (or, if later, the date the amount deferred is required to be taken into account) and is determined by multiplying each such payment by a fraction, the numerator of which is the amount that was taken into account (plus income attributable to that amount determined under paragraph (d)(2) of this section through the date the portion is fixed) and the denominator of which is the present value of the future benefit payments attributable to the amount deferred, determined as of the date the portion is fixed. For this purpose, if the requirements of paragraph (c)(2)(iii)(B) of this section are satisfied, the present value is determined by assuming that payments are made in the normal form of benefit commencing at normal commencement date. In addition, if the employer demonstrates that the amount deferred was determined using reasonable actuarial assumptions as determined by the Commissioner, the present value of the future benefit payments attributable to the amount deferred is determined using those assumptions. In any other case, see paragraph (d)(2)(iii) of this section.

(2) *Income attributable to the amount taken into account.*—(i) *Account balance plans.*—(A) *In general.*—For purposes of the nonduplication rule of paragraph (a)(2)(iii) of this section, in the case of an account balance plan, the *income attributable to the amount taken into account* means any amount credited on behalf of an employee under the terms of the plan that is income (within the meaning of paragraph (c)(1)(ii)(B) of this section) attributable to an amount previously taken into account (within the meaning of paragraph (d)(1) of this section), but only if the income reflects a rate of return that does not exceed either the rate of return on a predetermined actual investment (as determined in accordance with paragraph (d)(2)(i)(B) of this section) or, if the income does not reflect the rate of return on a predetermined actual investment (as so determined), a reasonable rate of interest (as determined in accordance with paragraph (d)(2)(i)(C) of this section).

(B) *Rules relating to actual investment.*—(1) *In general.*—For purposes of this paragraph (d)(2)(i), the rate of return on a predetermined actual investment for any period means the rate of total return (including increases or decreases in fair market value) that would apply if the account balance were, during the applicable period, actually invested in one or more investments that are identified in accordance with the plan before the beginning of the period. For this purpose, an account balance plan can determine income based on the rate of return of a predetermined actual investment regardless of whether assets associated with the plan or the employer are actually invested therein and regardless of whether that investment is generally available to the public. For example, an account balance plan could provide that income on the account balance is determined based on an employee's prospective election among various investment alternatives that are available under the employer's section 401(k) plan, even if one of those investment alternatives is not generally available to the public. In addition, an actual investment includes an investment identified by reference to any stock index with respect to which there are positions traded on a national securities exchange described in section 1256(g)(7)(A).

(2) *Certain rates of return not based on predetermined actual investment.*—A rate of return will not be treated as the rate of return on a predetermined actual investment within the meaning of this paragraph (d)(2)(i)(B) if the rate of return (to any extent or under any conditions) is based on the greater of the rate of return of two or more actual investments, is based on the greater of the rate of return on an actual investment and a rate of interest (whether or not the rate of interest would otherwise be reasonable under paragraph (d)(2)(i)(C) of this section), or is based on the rate of return on an actual investment that is not predetermined. For example, if a plan bases the rate of return on the greater of the rate of return on a predetermined actual investment (such as the value of the employer's stock), and a 0 percent interest rate (i.e., without regard to decreases in the value of that investment), the plan is using a rate of return that is not a rate of return on a predetermined actual investment within the meaning of this paragraph (d)(2)(i)(B).

(C) *Rules relating to reasonable interest rates.*—(1) *In general.*—If income for a period is credited to an account balance plan on a basis other than the rate of return on a predetermined actual investment (as determined in accordance with paragraph (d)(2)(i)(B) of this section), then, except as otherwise provided in this paragraph (d)(2)(i)(C), the determination of whether the income for the period is based on a reasonable rate of interest will be made at the time the amount deferred is required to be taken into account and annually thereafter.

(2) *Fixed rates permitted.*—If, with respect to an amount deferred for a period, an account balance plan provides for a fixed rate of interest to be credited, and the rate is to be reset under the plan at a specified future date that is not later than the end of the fifth calendar year that begins after the beginning of the period, the rate is reasonable at the beginning of the period, and the rate is not changed before the reset date, then the rate will be treated as reasonable in all future periods before the reset date.

(ii) *Nonaccount balance plans.*—For purposes of the nonduplication rule of paragraph (a)(2)(iii) of this section, in the case of a nonaccount balance plan, the *income attributable to the amount taken into account* means the increase, due solely to the passage of time, in the present value of the future payments to which the employee has obtained a legally binding right, the present value of which constituted the amount taken into account (determined as of the date such amount was taken into account), but only if the amount taken into account was determined using reasonable actuarial assumptions and methods. Thus, for each year, there will be an increase (determined using the same interest rate used to determine the amount taken into account) resulting from the shortening of the discount period before the future payments are made, plus, if applicable, an increase in the present value resulting from the employee's survivorship during the year. As a result, if the amount deferred for a period is determined using a reasonable interest rate and other reasonable actuarial assumptions and methods, and the amount is taken into account when required under paragraph (e) of this section, then, under the nonduplication rule of paragraph (a)(2)(iii) of this section, none of the future payments attributable to that amount will be subject to FICA tax when paid.

(iii) *Unreasonable rates of return.*—(A) *Account balance plans.*—This paragraph (d)(2)(iii)(A) applies to an account balance plan under which the income credited is based on neither a predetermined actual investment, within the meaning of paragraph (d)(2)(i)(B) of this section, nor a rate of interest that is reasonable, within the meaning of paragraph (d)(2)(i)(C) of this section, as determined by the Commissioner. In that event, the employer must calculate the amount that would be credited as income under a reasonable rate of interest, determine the excess (if any) of the amount credited under the plan over the income that would be credited using the reasonable rate of interest, and take that excess into account as an additional amount deferred in the year the income is credited. If the employer fails to calculate the amount that would be credited as income under a reasonable rate of interest and to take the excess into account as an additional amount deferred in the year the income is credited, or the employer otherwise fails to take the full amount deferred into account, then the excess of the income credited under the plan over the income that would be credited using AFR will be treated as an amount deferred in the year the income is credited. For purposes of this section, *AFR* means the mid-term applicable federal rate (as defined pursuant to section 1274(d)) for January 1 of the calendar year, compounded annually. In addition, pursuant to paragraph (d)(1)(ii) of this section, the excess over the income that would result from the application of AFR and any income attributable to that excess are subject to the general timing rule of paragraph (a)(1) of this section.

(B) *Nonaccount balance plans.*—If any actuarial assumption or method used to determine the amount taken into account under a nonaccount balance plan is not reasonable, as determined by the Commissioner, then the income attributable to the amount taken into account is limited to the income that would result from the application of the AFR and, if applicable, the applicable mortality table under section 417(e)(3)(A)(ii)(I) (the 417(e) mortality table), both determined as of the January 1 of the calendar year in which the amount was taken into account. In addition, paragraph (d)(1)(ii)(B) of this section applies and, in calculating the fraction described in paragraph (d)(1)(ii)(B) of this section (at the date specified in paragraph (d)(1)(ii)(B) of this section), the numerator is the amount taken into account plus income (as limited under this paragraph (d)(2)(iii)(B)), and the present value in the denominator is determined using the AFR, the 417(e) mortality table, and reasonable assumptions as to cost of living, each determined as of the time the amount deferred was required to be taken into account.

(3) *Examples.*—This paragraph (d) is illustrated by the following examples:

Example 1. (i) In 2001, Employer M establishes a nonqualified deferred compensation plan for Employee A under which all benefits are 100 percent vested. In 2002, Employee A has $200,000 of current annual compensation from Employer M that is subject to FICA tax. The amount deferred under the plan on behalf of Employee A for 2002 is $20,000. Thus, Employee A has total wages for FICA tax purposes of $220,000. Because Employee A has other wages that exceed the OASDI wage base for 2002, no additional OASDI tax is due as a result of the $20,000 amount deferred. Because there is no wage base limitation for the HI portion of FICA, additional HI tax liability results from the $20,000 amount deferred. However, Employer M fails to pay the additional HI tax.

(ii) Under paragraph (d)(1)(i) of this section, an amount deferred is considered taken into account as wages for FICA tax purposes as of the date it is included in computing FICA wages, but only if any additional FICA tax liability that results from inclusion of the amount deferred is actually paid. Because the HI tax resulting from the $20,000 amount deferred was not paid, that amount deferred was not taken into account within the meaning of paragraph (d)(1) of this section. Thus, pursuant to paragraph (d)(1)(ii) of this section, benefit payments attributable to the $20,000 amount deferred will be included as wages in accordance with the general timing rule of paragraph (a)(1) of this section and will be subject to the HI portion of FICA tax when actually or constructively paid (and the OASDI portion of FICA tax to the extent Employee A's wages do not exceed the OASDI wage base limitation).

Example 2. (i) The facts are the same as in *Example 1*, except that Employer M takes all actions necessary to correct its failure to pay the additional tax before the applicable period of limitations expires for 2002 (including payment of any applicable interest and penalties).

(ii) Because the HI tax resulting from the $20,000 amount deferred is paid, that amount

deferred is considered taken into account for 2002. Thus, in accordance with paragraph (a)(2)(iii) of this section, neither the amount deferred nor the income attributable to the amount taken into account will be treated as wages for FICA tax purposes at any time thereafter.

Example 3. (i) Employer N establishes a nonqualified deferred compensation plan under which all benefits are 100 percent vested. Under the plan, an employee's account is credited with a contribution equal to 10 percent of salary on December 31 of each year. The employee's account balance also is increased each December 31 by *interest* on the total amounts credited to the employee's account as of the preceding December 31. The interest rate specified in the plan results in income credits that are not based on the rate of return on a predetermined actual investment within the meaning of paragraph (d)(2)(i)(B) of this section, and that are greater than the income that would result from application of a reasonable rate of interest within the meaning of paragraph (d)(2)(i)(C) of this section. Employer N fails to take into account an additional amount for the excess of the income credited under the plan over a reasonable rate of interest.

(ii) Pursuant to paragraph (d)(2)(iii)(A) of this section, the income credits in excess of the income that would be credited using the AFR are considered additional amounts deferred in the year credited.

Example 4. (i) The facts are the same as in *Example 3*, except that the annual increase is based on Moody's Average Corporate Bond Yield.

(ii) Because this index reflects a reasonable rate of interest, the income credited under the plan is considered income attributable to the amount taken into account within the meaning of paragraph (d)(2)(i) of this section.

Example 5. (i) The facts are the same as in *Example 3*, except that the annual increase (or decrease) is based on the rate of total return on Employer N's publicly traded common stock.

(ii) Because the income credited under the plan does not exceed the actual rate of return on a predetermined actual investment, the income credited is considered income attributable to the amount taken into account within the meaning of paragraph (d)(2)(i) of this section.

Example 6. (i) The facts are the same as in *Example 3*, except that the annual rate of increase or decrease is equal to the greater of the rate of total return on a specified aggressive growth mutual fund or the rate of return on a specified income-oriented mutual fund. Employer N fails to take into account an additional amount for the excess of the income credited under the plan over a reasonable rate of interest.

(ii) Because the rate of increase or decrease is based on the greater of two rates of returns, the increase is not based on the return on a predetermined actual investment within the meaning of paragraph (d)(2)(i)(B) of this section. Thus, if the rate of return credited under the plan (i.e., the greater of the rates of return of the two mutual funds) exceeds the income that would be credited using the AFR, the excess is not considered income attributable to the amount taken into account within the meaning of paragraph (d)(2)(i) of this section and, pursuant to paragraph (d)(2)(iii)(A) of this section, is considered an additional amount deferred.

Example 7. (i) The facts are the same as in *Example 6*, except that the annual increase or decrease with respect to 50 percent of the employee's account is equal to the rate of total return on the specified aggressive growth mutual fund and the annual increase or decrease with respect to the other 50 percent of the employee's account is equal to the increase or decrease in the Standard & Poor's 500 Index.

(ii) Because the increase or decrease attributable to any portion of the employee's account is based on the return on a predetermined actual investment, the entire increase or decrease is considered income attributable to the amount taken into account within the meaning of paragraph (d)(2)(i) of this section.

Example 8. (i) The facts are the same as in *Example 3*, except that, pursuant to the terms of the plan, before the beginning of each year, the board of directors of Employer N designates a specific investment on which the following year's annual increase or decrease will be based. The board is authorized to switch investments more frequently on a prospective basis. Before the beginning of 2004, the board designates Company A stock as the investment for 2004. Before the beginning of 2005, the board designates Company B stock as the investment for 2005. At the end of 2005, the board determines that the return on Company B stock was lower than expected and changes its designation for 2005 to the rate of return on Company C stock, which had a higher return during 2005. Employer N fails to take into account an additional amount for the excess of the income credited under the plan over a reasonable rate of interest.

(ii) The annual increase or decrease for 2004 is based on the return of a predetermined actual investment. Although the annual increase or decrease for 2005 is based on an actual investment, the actual investment is not predetermined since it was not designated before the beginning of 2005. Pursuant to paragraph (d)(2)(iii)(A) of this section, the excess of the income credited under the plan over the income determined using AFR is an additional amount deferred for 2005.

Example 9. (i) Employer O establishes a nonqualified deferred compensation plan for Employee B. Under the plan, if Employee B survives until age 65, he has a fully vested right to receive a lump sum payment at that age, equal to the product of 10 percent per year of service and Employee B's highest average annual compensation for any 3-year period, but no benefits are payable in the event Employee B dies prior to age 65. As permitted under paragraph (e)(5) of this section, any amount deferred under the plan

for the calendar year is taken into account as wages as of the last day of the year. As of December 31, 2002, Employee B has 25 years of service and Employee B's high 3-year average compensation is $100,000 (the average for the years 2000 through 2002). As of December 31, 2002, Employee B has a legally binding right to receive a payment at age 65 of $250,000 (10 percent × 25 years × $100,000). As of December 31, 2003, Employee B is age 63, has 26 years of service, and has high 3-year average compensation of $104,000. As of December 31, 2003, Employee B has a legally binding right to receive a payment at age 65 of $270,400 (10 percent × 26 years × $104,000). Thus, during 2003, Employee B has earned a legally binding right to an additional payment at age 65 of $20,400 ($270,400 − $250,000). The assumptions that Employer O uses to determine the amount deferred for 2003 are a 7 percent interest rate and the GAM 83 (male) mortality table, which, solely for purposes of this example, are assumed to be reasonable actuarial assumptions. The amount deferred for 2003 is the present value, as of December 31, 2003, of the $20,400 payment, which is $17,353. Employer O takes this amount into account by including it in Employee B's FICA wages for 2003 and paying the additional FICA tax.

(ii) Under paragraph (d)(2)(ii) of this section, the income attributable to the amount that was taken into account is the increase in the present value of the future payment due solely to the passage of time, because the amount deferred was determined using reasonable actuarial assumptions and methods. As of the payment date at age 65, the present value of the future payment earned during 2003 is $20,400. The entire difference between the $20,400 and the $17,353 amount deferred ($3,047) is the increase in the present value of the future payment due solely to the passage of time, and thus constitutes income attributable to the amount taken into account. Because the amount deferred was taken into account, the entire payment of $20,400 represents either an amount deferred that was previously taken into account ($17,353) or income attributable to that amount ($3,047). Accordingly, pursuant to the nonduplication rule of paragraph (a)(2)(iii) of this section, none of the payment is included in wages.

Example 10. (i) The facts are the same as in *Example 9*, except that, instead of providing a lump sum equal to 10 percent of average compensation per year of service, the plan provides Employee B with a fully vested right to receive a life annuity, payable monthly beginning at age 65, equal to the product of 2 percent for each year of service and Employee B's highest average annual compensation for any 3-year period. The plan also provides that, if Employee B dies before age 65, the present value of the future payments will be paid to his or her beneficiary. As of December 31, 2002, Employee B has a legally binding right to receive lifetime payments of $50,000 (2 percent × 25 years × $100,000) per year. As of December 31, 2003, Employee B has a legally binding right to receive lifetime payments of $54,080 (2 percent × 26 years × $104,000) per year. Thus, during 2003, Employee B has earned a legally binding right to additional lifetime payments of $4,080 ($54,080 $50,000) per year beginning at age 65. The amount deferred for 2003 is $32,935, which is the present value, as of December 31, 2003, of these additional payments, determined using the same actuarial assumptions and methods used in *Example 9*, except that there is no discount for the probability of death prior to age 65. Employer O takes this amount into account by including it in Employee B's FICA wages for 2003 and paying the additional FICA tax.

(ii) Under paragraph (d)(2)(ii) of this section, the income attributable to the amount that was taken into account is the increase in the present value of the future payments due solely to the passage of time, because the amount deferred was determined using reasonable actuarial assumptions and methods. Because the amount deferred was taken into account, each annual payment of $4,080 attributable to the amount deferred in 2003 represents either an amount deferred that was previously taken into account or income attributable to that amount. Accordingly, pursuant to the nonduplication rule of paragraph (a)(2)(iii) of this section, none of the payments are included in wages.

Example 11. (i) The facts are the same as in *Example 10*, except that no amount is taken into account for 2003 because Employer O fails to pay the additional FICA tax.

(ii) Under paragraph (d)(1)(ii)(A) of this section, if an amount deferred for a period is not taken into account, then the benefit payments attributable to that amount deferred are included as wages in accordance with the general timing rule of paragraph (a)(1) of this section. In this case, assuming that the amounts deferred in other periods were taken into account, $4,080 of each year's total benefit payments will be included in wages when actually or constructively paid, in accordance with the general timing rule.

Example 12. (i) Employer P establishes an account balance plan on January 1, 2002, under which all benefits are 100 percent vested. The plan provides that amounts deferred will be credited annually with interest beginning in 2002 at a rate that is greater than a reasonable rate of interest. Employer P treats the excess over the applicable interest rate in section 417(e) as an additional amount deferred for 2002 and in each year thereafter, and takes the additional amount into account by including it in FICA wages and paying the additional FICA tax for the year.

(ii) Under the nonduplication rule in paragraph (a)(2)(iii) of this section, the benefits paid under the plan will be excluded from wages for FICA tax purposes.

Example 13. (i) The facts are the same as in *Example 9*, except that, in determining the amount deferred, Employer O uses a 15 percent interest rate, which, solely for purposes of this example, is assumed not to be a reasonable interest rate. Employer O determines that the amount

deferred for 2003 is the present value, as of December 31, 2003, of the $20,400 payment, which is $15,023. Employer O includes $15,023 in wages and pays any resulting FICA tax. Solely for purposes of this example, it is assumed that the AFR as of January 1, 2003, is 7 percent.

(ii) Under paragraph (d)(2)(iii)(B) of this section, if any actuarial assumption or method is not reasonable, then the income attributable to the amount taken into account is limited to the income that would result from application of the AFR and, if applicable, the 417(e) mortality table. Because the 15 percent interest rate is unreasonable, the income attributable to the amount taken into account is limited to the income that would result from using a 7 percent interest rate and, in this case, an increase for survivorship using the 417(e) mortality table. Under these assumptions, the income attributable to the $15,023 amount taken into account for 2003 is $1,199 in 2004 and $1,313 in 2005. Under paragraph (d)(1)(ii) of this section, the sum of these amounts ($17,535) is excluded from Employee B's wages pursuant to the nonduplication rule of paragraph (a)(2)(iii) of this section, and the balance of the payment ($2,865) is subject to the general timing rule of paragraph (a)(1) of this section and, thus, is included in Employee B's wages when actually or constructively paid.

(iii) The same result can be reached by multiplying the attributable benefit payments by a fraction, the numerator of which is the amount taken into account, and the denominator of which is the amount deferred that would have been taken into account at the same time had the amount deferred been calculated using the AFR and the 417(e) mortality table. These assumptions are determined as of January 1 of the calendar year in which the amount was taken into account. In this *Example 13*, the fraction would be $15,023 divided by $17,478, which equals .85954. The $20,400 payment is multiplied by this fraction to determine the amount of the payment that is excluded from wages pursuant to the nonduplication rule of paragraph (a)(2)(iii) of this section. Thus, $17,535 ($20,400 × .85954) is excluded from wages and the balance ($2,865) is subject to FICA tax when actually or constructively paid.

Example 14. (i) The facts are the same as *Example 10*, except that Employer O calculates the amount deferred for 2003 as $18,252 and takes that amount into account by including that amount in wages and paying any resulting FICA tax. The assumptions that Employer O uses to determine the amount deferred are a 15 percent interest rate and, for the period after commencement of benefit payments, the GAM 83 (male) mortality table. The 15 percent interest rate is assumed, solely for purposes of this example, not to be a reasonable actuarial assumption. Solely for purposes of this example, it is assumed that the AFR as of January 1, 2003, is 7 percent.

(ii) Under paragraph (d)(2)(iii)(B) of this section, if any actuarial assumption or method used is not reasonable, then the income attributable to the amount taken into account is limited to the income that would result from application of the AFR and, if applicable, the 417(e) mortality table. Because the 15 percent interest rate is not reasonable, the income attributable to the amount taken into account is equal to the income that would result from using a 7 percent interest rate and the amount taken into account is treated as if it represented a portion of the amount deferred for purposes of applying paragraph (d)(1)(ii)(B) of this section. Under these assumptions, the income attributable to the $18,252 amount taken into account for 2003 is $1,278 in 2004 and $1,367 in 2005. Under paragraph (d)(1)(ii)(B) of this section, the portion of each benefit payment attributable to the amount deferred that is excluded from wages pursuant to the nonduplication rule of paragraph (a)(2)(iii) of this section is determined at benefit commencement by multiplying each benefit payment by a fraction, the numerator of which is the amount taken into account (plus income attributable to that amount) and the denominator of which is the present value of future benefit payments attributable to the amount deferred. Because the interest rate assumption is not reasonable, not only is the income limited to the application of the AFR, but the present value in the denominator must be determined using the AFR and (if applicable) the 417(e) mortality table. In this case, the present value is $40,283 and thus the fraction is $20,897 divided by $40,283, or .51875. Thus, $2,116 (.51875 × $4,080) of each year's benefit payment is excluded from wages and the balance of each year's payment ($1,964) is subject to the general timing rule of paragraph (a)(1) of this section and is included in wages when actually or constructively paid.

(iii) The same result can be reached by multiplying the attributable benefit payments by a fraction the numerator of which is the amount taken into account, and the denominator of which is the amount deferred that would have been taken into account at the same time had the amount deferred been calculated using the AFR and the 417(e) mortality table. These assumptions are determined as of January 1 of the calendar year in which the amount was taken into account. In this *Example 14*, the fraction would be $18,252 divided by $35,185, which equals .51875. The $4,080 annual payment is multiplied by this fraction to determine the amount of the payment that is excluded from wages pursuant to the nonduplication rule of paragraph (a)(2)(iii) of this section. Thus, $2,116 ($4,080 × .51875) is excluded from wages and the balance ($1,964) is subject to FICA tax when actually or constructively paid.

(e) *Time amounts deferred are required to be taken into account.*—(1) *In general.*—Except as otherwise provided in this paragraph (e), an amount deferred under a nonqualified deferred compensation plan must be taken into account as wages for FICA tax purposes as of the later of the date on which services creating the right to the amount deferred are performed (within the

meaning of paragraph (e)(2) of this section) or the date on which the right to the amount deferred is no longer subject to a substantial risk of forfeiture (within the meaning of paragraph (e)(3) of this section). However, in no event may any amount deferred under a nonqualified deferred compensation plan be taken into account as wages for FICA tax purposes prior to the establishment of the plan providing for the amount deferred (or, if later, the plan amendment providing for the amount deferred). Therefore, if an amount is deferred pursuant to the terms of a legally binding agreement that is not put in writing until after the amount would otherwise be taken into account under this paragraph (e)(1), the amount deferred (including any attributable income) must be taken into account as wages for FICA tax purposes as of the date the material terms of the plan are put in writing.

(2) *Services creating the right to an amount deferred.*—For purposes of this section, services creating the right to an amount deferred under a nonqualified deferred compensation plan are considered to be performed as of the date on which, under the terms of the plan and all the facts and circumstances, the employee has performed all of the services necessary to obtain a legally binding right (as described in paragraph (b)(3)(i) of this section) to the amount deferred.

(3) *Substantial risk of forfeiture.*—For purposes of this section, the determination of whether a substantial risk of forfeiture exists must be made in accordance with the principles of section 83 and the regulations thereunder.

(4) *Amount deferred that is not reasonably ascertainable under a nonaccount balance plan.*—(i) *In general.*—(A) *Date required to be taken into account.*—Notwithstanding any other provision of this paragraph (e), an amount deferred under a nonaccount balance plan is not required to be taken into account as wages under the special timing rule of paragraph (a)(2) of this section until the first date on which all of the amount deferred is reasonably ascertainable (the resolution date). In this case, the amount required to be taken into account as of the resolution date is determined in accordance with paragraph (c)(2) of this section.

(B) *Definition of reasonably ascertainable.*—For purposes of this paragraph (e)(4), an amount deferred is considered reasonably ascertainable on the first date on which the amount, form, and commencement date of the benefit payments attributable to the amount deferred are known, and the only actuarial or other assumptions regarding future events or circumstances needed to determine the amount deferred are interest and mortality. For this purpose, the form and commencement date of the benefit payments attributable to the amount deferred are treated as known if the requirements of paragraph (c)(2)(iii)(B) of this section (under which payments are treated as being made in the normal form of benefit commencing at normal commencement date) are satisfied. In addition,

Reg. §31.3121(v)(2)-1(e)(4)(i)(B)

an amount deferred does not fail to be reasonably ascertainable on a date merely because the exact amount of the benefit payable cannot readily be calculated on that date or merely because the exact amount of the benefit payable depends on future changes in the cost of living. If the exact amount of the benefit payable depends on future changes in the cost of living, the amount deferred must be determined using a reasonable assumption as to the future changes in the cost of living. For example, the amount of a benefit is treated as known even if the exact amount of the benefit payable cannot be determined until future changes in the cost of living are reflected in the section 415 limitation on benefits payable under a qualified retirement plan.

(ii) *Earlier inclusion permitted.*—(A) *In general.*—With respect to an amount deferred that is not reasonably ascertainable, an employer may choose to take an amount into account at any date or dates (an early inclusion date or dates) before the resolution date (but not before the date described in paragraph (e)(1) of this section with respect to the amount deferred). Thus, for example, with respect to an amount deferred under a nonaccount balance plan that is not reasonably ascertainable because the plan permits employees to receive their benefits in more than one form or commencing at more than one date (and the requirements of paragraph (c)(2)(iii) of this section are not satisfied), an employer may choose to take an amount into account on the date otherwise described in paragraph (e)(1) of this section before the form and commencement date are selected (based on assumptions as to the form and commencement date for the benefit payments) or may choose to wait until the form and commencement date of the benefit payments are selected. An employer that chooses to take an amount into account at an early inclusion date under this paragraph (e)(4)(ii) for an employee under a plan is not required until the resolution date to identify the period to which the amount taken into account relates.

(B) *True-up at resolution date.*—If, with respect to an amount deferred for a period, an employer chooses to take an amount into account as of an early inclusion date in accordance with this paragraph (e)(4)(ii) and the benefit payments attributable to the amount deferred exceed the benefit payments that are actuarially equivalent to the amount taken into account at the early inclusion date (payable in the same form and using the same commencement date as the benefit payments attributable to the amount deferred), then the present value of the difference in the benefits, determined in accordance with paragraph (c)(2) of this section, must be taken into account as of the resolution date.

(C) *Actuarial assumptions.*—For purposes of determining the benefits that are actuarially equivalent to the amount taken into account as of an early inclusion date, the amount taken into account is converted to an actuarially

equivalent benefit payable in the same form and commencing on the same date as the actual benefit payments attributable to the amount deferred using an interest rate, and, if applicable, mortality and cost-of-living assumptions, that were reasonable as of the early inclusion date. Thus, with respect to an amount deferred for a period, the amount required to be taken into account as of the resolution date is the present value (determined using an interest rate, and, if applicable, mortality and cost-of-living assumptions, that are reasonable as of the resolution date) of the excess, if any, of the future benefit payments attributable to the amount deferred over the future benefits payable in the same form and commencing on the same date that are actuarially equivalent to the portion of the amount deferred that was taken into account as of the early inclusion date (where actuarial equivalence is determined using an interest rate, and, if applicable, mortality and cost-of-living assumptions, that were reasonable as of the early inclusion date).

(D) *Allocation rules for amounts deferred over more than one period.*—(1) *General rule.*—The rules of this paragraph (e)(4)(ii)(D) apply for purposes of determining whether an amount has been included under this paragraph (e)(4) before the earliest date permitted under paragraph (e)(1) of this section.

(2) *Future compensation increases.*—Increases in an employee's compensation after the early inclusion date must be disregarded.

(3) *Early retirement subsidies.*—An early retirement subsidy that the employee ultimately receives may be taken into account at an early inclusion date if the employee would have a legally binding right to the subsidy at the early inclusion date but for any condition that the employee continue to render services. Accordingly, an employer may take into account at an early inclusion date any early retirement subsidy that the employee ultimately receives to the extent that elimination or reduction of that subsidy would violate section 411(d)(6)(B)(i) if that section applied to the plan.

(4) *Allocation with respect to offsets.*—In any case in which a series of amounts are deferred over more than one period, the amounts deferred are not reasonably ascertainable until a single resolution date and the benefit payments attributable to the entire series are determined under a formula that provides a gross benefit that in the aggregate is subject to an objective reduction for future events under the terms of the plan, such as an offset for the aggregate benefits payable under a plan qualified under section 401(a), the attribution of benefit payments to the amount deferred in each period is determined under the rules of this paragraph (e)(4)(ii)(D)(4). In a case described in the preceding sentence, the benefit payments made as a result of the series of amounts deferred may be treated as attributable to the amount deferred as of the earliest period in which the employee

obtained a legally binding right to a benefit under the plan equal to the excess, if any, of the amount of the gross benefit attributable to that period (determined at the resolution date), over the amount of the reduction determined as of the end of that period. Thus, for example, if an employee obtains a legally binding right in each of several years to benefit payments from a non-qualified deferred compensation plan that provides for a specified gross benefit for the years to be offset by the benefits payable under a qualified plan, the amount deferred in the first year may be treated as equal to the gross benefit for the year, reduced by the offset applicable at the end of the year (even if the offset increases after the end of the year).

(E) *Treatment of benefits paid before the resolution date.*—If a benefit payment is attributable to an amount deferred that is not reasonably ascertainable at the time of payment (or is paid before the date selected under paragraph (e)(5) of this section), and the employer has previously taken an amount into account with respect to the amount deferred under the early inclusion rule of this paragraph (e)(4), then, in lieu of the pro rata rule provided in paragraph (d)(1)(ii)(B) of this section, a first-in-first-out rule applies in determining the portion of the benefit payment attributable to the amount taken into account. Under this first-in-first-out rule, the benefit payment is compared to the sum of the amount taken into account at the early inclusion date and the income attributable to that amount. If the benefit payment equals or exceeds the amount taken into account at the early inclusion date and the income attributable to that amount as of the date of the benefit payment, the benefit payment is included as wages under the general timing rule of paragraph (a)(1) of this section to the extent of any excess, and the amount taken into account at the early inclusion date (and income attributable to that amount) is disregarded thereafter with respect to the amount deferred. If the amount taken into account at the early inclusion date and the income attributable to that amount as of the date of the benefit payment exceeds the benefit payment, the benefit payment is not included as wages under the general timing rule of paragraph (a)(1) of this section and, in determining the amount that must be taken into account thereafter with respect to the amount deferred, the amount taken into account at the early inclusion date, plus attributable income as of the date of the benefit payment, is reduced by the amount of the benefit payment, and only the excess plus future income attributable to the excess (credited using assumptions that were reasonable on the early inclusion date) is taken into consideration. If amounts have been taken into account at more than one early inclusion date, this paragraph (e)(4)(ii)(E) applies on a first-in-first-out basis, beginning with the amount taken into account at the earliest early inclusion date (including income attributable thereto).

(5) *Rule of administrative convenience.*—For purposes of this section, an employer may treat an amount deferred as required to be taken into account under this paragraph (e) on any date that is later than, but within the same calendar year as, the actual date on which the amount deferred is otherwise required to be taken into account under this paragraph (e). For example, if services creating the right to an amount deferred are considered performed under paragraph (e)(2) of this section periodically throughout a year, the employer may nevertheless treat the services creating the right to that amount deferred as performed on December 31 of that year. If an employer uses the rule of administrative convenience described in this paragraph (e)(5), any determination of whether the income attributable to an amount deferred under an account balance plan is based on a reasonable rate of interest or whether the actuarial assumptions used to determine the present value of an amount deferred in a nonaccount balance plan are reasonable will be made as of the date the employer selects to take the amount into account.

(6) *Portions of an amount deferred required to be taken into account on more than one date.*—If different portions of an amount deferred are required to be taken into account under paragraph (e)(1) of this section on more than one date (e.g., on account of a graded vesting schedule), then each such portion is considered a separate amount deferred for purposes of this section.

(7) *Examples.*—This paragraph (e) is illustrated by the following examples:

Example 1. (i) Employer M establishes a nonqualified deferred compensation plan for Employee A on November 1, 2005. Under the plan, which is an account balance plan, Employee A obtains a legally binding right on the last day of each calendar year (if Employee A is employed on that date) to be credited with a principal amount equal to 5 percent of compensation for the year. In addition, a reasonable rate of interest is credited quarterly. Employee A's account balance is nonforfeitable and is payable upon Employee A's termination of employment. For 2006, the principal amount credited to Employee A under the plan (which, in this case, is also the amount deferred within the meaning of paragraph (c) of this section) is $25,000.

(ii) Under paragraph (e)(2) of this section, the services creating the right to the $25,000 amount deferred are considered performed as of December 31, 2006, the date on which Employee A has performed all of the services necessary to obtain a legally binding right to the amount deferred. Thus, in accordance with paragraph (e)(1) of this section, the $25,000 amount deferred must be taken into account as of December 31, 2006, which is the later of the date on which services creating the right to the amount deferred are performed or the date on which the right to the amount deferred is no longer subject to a substantial risk of forfeiture.

Example 2. (i) The facts are the same as in *Example 1*, except that the principal amount credited under the plan on the last day of each year (and attributable interest) is forfeited if the employee terminates employment within five years of that date.

(ii) Under paragraph (e)(3) of this section, the determination of whether the right to an amount deferred is subject to a substantial risk of forfeiture is made in accordance with the principles of section 83. Under § 1.83-3(c) of this chapter, a substantial risk of forfeiture generally exists where rights in property that are transferred are conditioned, directly or indirectly, upon the future performance of substantial services. Because Employee A's right to receive the $25,000 principal amount (and attributable interest) is conditioned on the performance of services for five years, a substantial risk of forfeiture exists with respect to that amount deferred until December 31, 2011.

(iii) December 31, 2011, is the later of the date on which services creating the right to the amount deferred are performed or the date on which the right to the amount deferred is no longer subject to a substantial risk of forfeiture. Thus, in accordance with paragraph (e)(1) of this section, the amount deferred (which, pursuant to paragraph (c)(1) of this section, is equal to the $25,000 principal amount credited to Employee A's account on December 31, 2006, plus the interest credited with respect to that principal amount through December 31, 2011) must be taken into account as of December 31, 2011.

Example 3. (i) The facts are the same as in *Example 2*, except that the principal amount credited under the plan on the last day of each year (and attributable interest) becomes nonforfeitable according to a graded vesting schedule under which 20 percent is vested as of December 31, 2007; 40 percent is vested as of December 31, 2008; 60 percent is vested as of December 31, 2009; 80 percent is vested as of December 31, 2010; and 100 percent is vested as of December 31, 2011. Because these dates are later than the date on which the services creating the right to the amount deferred are considered performed (December 31, 2006), the amount deferred is required to be taken into account as of these dates that fall in five different years.

(ii) Paragraph (e)(6) of this section provides that, if different portions of an amount deferred are required to be taken into account under paragraph (e)(1) of this section on more than one date, then each such portion is considered a separate amount deferred for purposes of this section. Thus, $5,000 of the principal amount, plus interest credited through December 31, 2007, is taken into account as an amount deferred on December 31, 2007; $5,000 of the principal amount, plus interest credited through December 31, 2008, is taken into account as a separate amount deferred on December 31, 2008; etc.

Example 4. (i) On November 21, 2001, Employer N establishes a nonqualified deferred compensation plan under which all benefits are 100 percent vested. The plan provides for Employee B (who is age 45) to receive a lump sum

benefit of $500,000 at age 65. This benefit will be forfeited if Employee B dies before age 65.

(ii) Because the amount, form, and commencement date of the benefit are known, and the only assumptions needed to determine the amount deferred are interest and mortality, the amount deferred is reasonably ascertainable within the meaning of paragraph (e)(4)(i) of this section on November 21, 2001.

Example 5 (i) The facts are the same as in *Example 4*, except that plan provides that the lump sum will be paid at the later of age 65 or termination of employment and provides that the $500,000 payable to Employee B is increased by 5 percent per year for each year that payment is deferred beyond age 65.

(ii) Because the commencement date of the benefit payment is contingent on when Employee B terminates employment, the commencement date of the benefit payment is not known. Thus, the amount deferred is not reasonably ascertainable within the meaning of paragraph (e)(4)(i) of this section, unless the plan satisfies the requirements of paragraph (c)(2)(iii)(B) of this section. Because the fixed 5 percent factor may not be reasonable at the time benefit payments commence (i.e., 5 percent might be higher or lower than a reasonable interest rate when payments commence), the plan fails to satisfy paragraph (c)(2)(iii)(B) of this section and accordingly the amount deferred is not reasonably ascertainable until termination of employment.

Example 6. (i) The facts are the same as in *Example 4*, except that the $500,000 is payable to Employee B at the later of age 55 or termination of employment.

(ii) Because the commencement date of the benefit payment is contingent on when Employee B terminates employment, the commencement date of the benefit payment is not known. Thus, the amount deferred is not reasonably ascertainable until termination of employment.

Example 7. (i) The facts are the same as in *Example 4*, except that Employee B may elect to take the benefit in the form of a life annuity of $50,000 per year (commencing at age 65).

(ii) Because the plan permits employees to elect to receive benefits in more than one form and the alternative forms may not have the same value when Employee B makes his election, the plan fails to satisfy the requirements of paragraph (c)(2)(iii)(B) of this section until a form of benefit is selected. Thus, the amount deferred is not reasonably ascertainable until then.

Example 8. (i) Employer O establishes a nonqualified deferred compensation plan. The plan is a supplemental executive retirement plan (SERP) that provides Employee C with a fully vested right to receive a pension, in the form of a life annuity payable monthly, beginning at age 65, equal to the excess of 3 percent of Employee C's final 3-year average pay for each year of participation up to 15 years, over the amount payable to Employee C from Employer O's qualified pension plan. The amount payable under the qualified pension plan is a life annuity payable monthly, beginning at age 65, equal to 1.5 percent of final 3-year average pay for each year of employment, excluding pay in excess of the section 401(a)(17) compensation limit. No benefits are payable under the SERP if Employee C dies before age 65. Employee C becomes a participant in the SERP on January 1, 2001, at age 44. The amount deferred under the SERP for any year is not reasonably ascertainable prior to termination of employment because the amount of the benefit is not known and the determination of the amount deferred requires assumptions other than interest and mortality (e.g., an assumption as to Employee C's average pay for the final three years of employment). As permitted by paragraph (e)(4)(i) of this section, Employer O chooses not to take any amount into account for any year before the resolution date. Employee C terminates employment on December 31, 2018 when he is age 62.

(ii) As of the date Employee C terminates employment, the amount of the benefit is known and the only actuarial or other assumptions needed to determine the amount deferred are an interest rate assumption and a mortality assumption. At that time, the amount deferred in each past year becomes reasonably ascertainable, and Employer O is able to determine that during 2001 Employee C earned a legally binding right to a life annuity of $4,000 per year beginning in 2021 when Employee C is age 65. Employer O determines the present value of Employee C's future benefit payments under the SERP as of this resolution date (December 31, 2018), using a 7 percent interest rate and the UP-84 mortality table, which, solely for purposes of this example, are assumed to be reasonable actuarial assumptions for December 31, 2018. The special timing rule will be satisfied if the resulting present value, $26,950, is taken into account on that date in accordance with paragraph (d)(1) of this section.

Example 9. (i) The facts are the same as in *Example 8*, except that the plan provides that Employee C may choose to receive early retirement benefits on an unreduced basis at any time after age 60 if Employee C has completed 15 years of service by that date.

(ii) As of the date Employee C terminates employment, the amount of the benefit is known and the only actuarial or other assumptions needed to determine the amount deferred are an interest rate assumption and a mortality assumption. At that time, the amount deferred in each past year becomes reasonably ascertainable, and Employer O is able to determine that during 2001 Employee C earned a legally binding right to a life annuity of $4,000 per year beginning on December 31, 2018 when Employee C is age 62. Employer O determines the present value of Employee C's future benefit payments under the SERP as of this resolution date (December 31, 2018), using a 7 percent interest rate and the UP-84 mortality table, which, solely for purposes of this example, are assumed to be reasonable

actuarial assumptions for December 31, 2018. The special timing rule will be satisfied if the resulting present value, $37,576, is taken into account on that date in accordance with paragraph (d)(1) of this section.

Example 10. (i) The facts are the same as in *Example 9*, except that, as permitted under paragraph (e)(4)(ii) of this section, Employer O chooses to take an amount into account before the amount deferred for 2001 is reasonably ascertainable. The amount that Employer O takes into account on December 31, 2001, is $13,043 (the present value of a life annuity of $4,000 per year, payable at age 62, using a 6 percent interest rate and the UP-84 mortality table). Employer O does not take any other amount into account before the resolution date.

(ii) In accordance with paragraph (e)(4)(ii)(B) of this section, Employer O must determine any additional amount required to be taken into account in 2018. If the $4,000 payable in the form of a life annuity beginning at age 62 exceeds the life annuity which is actuarially equivalent to the $13,043 previously taken into account, the present value of the excess must be taken into account. In this *Example 10*, the $13,043 previously taken into account is actuarially equivalent to a $4,000 annuity commencing at age 62 using a 6 percent interest rate and the UP-84 mortality table (which, solely for purposes of this example, are assumed to be reasonable actuarial assumptions for December 31, 2001). Accordingly, no additional amount need be taken into account in 2018, regardless of any changes in market rates of interest between 2001 and 2018.

Example 11. (i) The facts are the same as in *Example 9*, except that, as permitted under paragraph (e)(4)(ii) of this section, Employer O chooses to take an amount into account before the amount deferred for 2001 is reasonably ascertainable. The amount that Employer O takes into account on December 31, 2001, is $9,569 (the present value of a life annuity of $4,000 per year, payable at age 65, using a 6 percent interest rate and the UP-84 mortality table). Employer O does not take any other amount into account before the resolution date.

(ii) In accordance with paragraph (e)(4)(ii)(B) of this section, Employer O must determine any additional amount required to be taken into account in 2018. If the $4,000 payable in the form of a life annuity beginning in 2018 at age 62 exceeds the life annuity which is actuarially equivalent to the $9,569 previously taken into account, the present value of the excess must be taken into account. In this case, the $9,569 previously taken into account is actuarially equivalent to a $2,935 annuity commencing at age 62 using a 6 percent interest rate and the UP-84 mortality table (which, solely for purposes of this example, are assumed to be reasonable actuarial assumptions for December 31, 2001). Accordingly, an additional amount needs to be taken into account in 2018 equal to the present value of the excess of the $4,000 annual stream of benefit payments to which Employee C obtained a legally binding right during 2001 over the $2,935 annual stream of benefit payments which is actuarially equivalent to the amount previously taken into account. This present value (i.e., the present value of a life annuity equal to $4,000 minus $2,935, or $1,065 annually) is determined by Employer O to be $10,005 as of the resolution date using a 7 percent interest rate and the UP-84 mortality table (which, solely for purposes of this example, are assumed to be reasonable actuarial assumptions for December 31, 2018).

Example 12. (i) The facts are the same as in *Example 9*, except that the amount that Employer O takes into account on December 31, 2001, is $15,834 (the present value of $4,000, payable at age 60, using a 6 percent interest rate and the UP-84 mortality table). Employer O does not take any other amount into account before the resolution date.

(ii) In accordance with paragraph (e)(4)(ii)(B) of this section, Employer O must determine any additional amount required to be taken into account in 2018. If the $4,000 payable in the form of a life annuity beginning at age 62 exceeds the life annuity which is actuarially equivalent to the $15,834 previously taken into account, the present value of the excess must be taken into account. In this case, the $15,834 previously taken into account is actuarially equivalent to a $4,856 annuity commencing at age 62 using a 6 percent interest rate and the UP-84 mortality table (which, solely for purposes of this example, are assumed to be reasonable actuarial assumptions for December 31, 2001). Because the life annuity of $4,856 per year (which is equivalent to the amount taken into account at the early inclusion date) exceeds the $4,000 annuity attributable to the amount deferred in 2001, no additional amount is required to be taken into account for that amount deferred as of the resolution date. Employer O may claim a refund or credit for the overpayment of FICA tax with respect to amounts taken into account prior to the resolution date to the extent permitted by sections 6402, 6413, and 6511.

Example 13. (i) The facts are the same as in *Example 12*, except that Employee C became a participant in the SERP on January 1, 2000. In addition, Employer O determines in 2018 that during 2000 Employee C earned a legally binding right to a life annuity of $1,500 per year beginning on December 31, 2018.

(ii) Employer O may allocate the $15,834 previously taken into account among any amounts deferred on or before the early inclusion date. At the resolution date, Employer O will have to take into account the present value of an annuity equal to the excess of the life annuity attributable to the amounts deferred for 2000 and 2001 over a life annuity of $4,856 per year.

Example 14. (i) In 2003, Employer P establishes a nonqualified deferred compensation plan for Employee D. The plan provides that, in consideration of Employee D's services to be performed on Project X in 2004, Employee D will have a nonforfeitable right to receive 1 percent per year of Employer P's net profits associated with Project X for each of the immediately succeeding three years. No services beyond 2004 are required. The 1 percent of net profits payable each year will be paid on March 31 of the immediately succeeding year. One percent of net profits associated with Project X is $750,000 in 2005, $400,000 in 2006, and $90,000 in 2007. Employee D receives $750,000 on March 31, 2006, $400,000 on March 31, 2007, and $90,000 on March 31, 2008.

(ii) Because the services creating the right to all of the amount deferred are performed in 2004, the benefit payments based on the 2005, 2006, and 2007 net profits are all attributable to the amount deferred in 2004. However, because the present value of Employee D's future benefit is contingent on future profits, the determination of the amount deferred requires the use of assumptions other than interest, mortality, and cost of living. Thus, all of the amount deferred in 2004 will not be reasonably ascertainable within the meaning of paragraph (e)(4)(i) of this section until December 31, 2007 (which is the resolution date). Employer P does not choose to take any amount into account prior to the amount deferred becoming reasonably ascertainable.

(iii) However, paragraph (d)(1)(ii)(A) of this section provides that a benefit payment attributable to an amount deferred under a nonqualified deferred compensation plan must be included as wages when actually or constructively paid if the amount deferred has not been taken into account as wages under the special timing rule of paragraph (a)(2) of this section. Thus, the benefit payments in 2006 and 2007 must be included as wages when paid.

(iv) As of December 31, 2007, all of the amount deferred under the plan becomes reasonably ascertainable because the amount of the benefit payable attributable to the amount deferred is treated as known under paragraph (e)(4)(i)(B) of this section, and the only assumption needed to determine the present value of the future benefits is interest. However, since Employer P was required to treat the payments in 2006 and 2007 as wages when paid under the general timing rule of paragraph (a)(1) of this section, only the present value of the payment to be made in 2008 is required to be taken into account as of the resolution date (December 31, 2007) under the special timing rule of paragraph (a)(2) of this section. Using an interest rate of 10 percent per year (which, solely for purposes of this *Example 14*, is assumed to be reasonable), Employer P determines that on December 31, 2007, the present value of the future benefits is $87,881, and Employer P includes that additional amount in wages for 2007. (Note that Employer P can choose to use the lag method of withholding described in paragraph (f)(3) of this section, which allows the resolution date amount to be taken into account no later than March 31, 2008, provided that the amount deferred is increased by interest using the AFR for January of 2008.)

Example 15. (i) The facts are the same as in *Example 14*, except that Employer P chooses the early inclusion option permitted by paragraph (e)(4)(ii) of this section to take $1,000,000 into account on December 31, 2004, before the amount deferred for 2004 is reasonably ascertainable.

(ii) Pursuant to paragraph (e)(4)(ii)(E) of this section, in applying the nonduplication rule of paragraph (a)(2)(iii) of this section, a first-in-first-out rule applies in determining the benefit payments that are attributable to amounts previously taken into account. Using the 10 percent interest rate, Employer P determines that the $750,000 benefit payment on March 31, 2006, and the March 31, 2007, benefit payment of $400,000 are less than the $1,000,000 taken into account at the early inclusion date, plus attributable income, and, therefore, are not included in wages when paid.

(iii) Under paragraph (e)(4)(ii)(E) of this section, if an employer chooses to take an amount into account before the resolution date, the amount taken into account (plus income attributable to that amount) is disregarded to the extent the amount is attributed to benefit payments made before the resolution date. Thus, Employer P must reduce the $1,000,000 taken into account in 2004 (plus income attributable to that amount) based upon the two benefit payments ($750,000 and $400,000) that were excluded from wages. Using an interest rate of 10 percent, Employer P determines that the amount taken into account in 2004 plus interest to the resolution date and reduced based upon the two benefit payments is $15,228 and the additional amount that is required to be taken into account as of December 31, 2007, is $72,653 ($87,881 − $15,228).

Example 16. (i) Employee E obtains a fully vested, legally binding right during 2002, 2003, and 2004 to payments from a nonqualified deferred compensation plan of Employer Q under which the benefits are based on a formula that includes an actuarial offset by the account balance under a qualified defined contribution plan of Employer Q as of December 31, 2004. The payments from the nonqualified deferred compensation plan are to commence on December 31, 2005. At the resolution date for the amounts earned during 2002, 2003, and 2004, which is December 31, 2004, Employee E has a legally binding right to a net annual benefit of $100,000 payable for life to commence on December 31, 2005. On the resolution date, Employer Q determines that on December 31, 2002, Employee E had a legally binding right to receive $100,000 annually for life beginning on December 31, 2005 (as a result of the gross benefit under the nonqualified plan being $120,000 annually for life, and the offset being $20,000 annually for life, as of December 31, 2002). On December 31, 2003, Employee E had a legally binding right to receive $95,000 annually for life beginning on December 31, 2005 (as a result of the gross benefit under the nonqualified plan being $135,000 annually for life, and the offset being $40,000 annually for life, as of December 31, 2003). On December 31, 2004, Employee E had a legally binding right to receive $100,000 annually for life beginning on December 31, 2005 (as a result of the gross benefit under the nonqualified plan being $145,000 annually for life, and the offset being $45,000 annually for life, as of December 31, 2004).

(ii) In this case, pursuant to paragraph (e)(4)(ii)(D)(4) of this section, Employer Q can attribute the entire $100,000 life annuity to the amount deferred for 2002, even though Employee E's benefit under the nonqualified deferred compensation plan is reduced to $95,000 in 2003.

Example 17. (i) In 2010, Employee F performs services for which she earns a right to 10 percent of the proceeds from the sale of a motion picture. In 2011, Employee F performs services for which she earns a right to 10 percent of the proceeds from the sale of another motion picture. These proceeds are calculated by subtracting the total advertising expenses for both movies. Payment is to be made in the year following the date on which both pictures have been sold, but not later than 2018. At the end of 2010, the advertising expenses for both pictures totaled $300,000. The first motion picture is sold for $10,000,000 in 2014. The second motion picture is sold for $17,000,000 in 2017. At the end of 2017, the advertising expenses totaled $1,700,000. In 2018, Employee F is paid $2,530,000 (10 percent of the sum of $10,000,000 and $17,000,000 minus $1,700,000).

(ii) Pursuant to paragraph (e)(4)(ii)(D)(4) of this section, $970,000 (10 percent of the excess of the gross proceeds from the sale of the first motion picture at the resolution date in 2017 over the advertising expenses incurred at the end of 2010) of the payment made in 2018 can be attributed to the amount deferred in 2010 (and with the remaining payment of $1,560,000 to be attributed to the amount deferred in 2011).

(f) *Withholding.*—(1) *In general.*—Unless an employer applies an alternative method described in paragraph (f)(2) or (3) of this section, an amount deferred under a nonqualified deferred compensation plan for any employee is treated, for purposes of withholding and depositing FICA tax, as wages paid by the employer and received by the employee at the time it is taken into account in accordance with paragraph (e) of this section. However, paragraphs (f)(2) and (3) of this section provide alternative methods which may be used with respect to an amount deferred for an employee. An employer is not required to be consistent in applying the alternatives described in this paragraph (f) with respect to different employees or amounts deferred.

(2) *Estimated method.*—(i) *In general.*—Under the alternative method provided in this paragraph (f)(2), the employer may make a reasonable estimate of the amount deferred on the date on which the amount is taken into account in accordance with paragraph (e) of this section and take that estimated amount into account as

wages paid by the employer and received by the employee on that date (the estimate date), for purposes of withholding and depositing FICA tax.

    (ii) *Underestimate of the amount deferred.*— (A) *General rule.*—If the employer underestimates the amount deferred (as determined after calculating the actual amount deferred that should have been taken into account as of the date on which the amount was taken into account in accordance with paragraph (e) of this section, using an interest rate and other actuarial assumptions that are reasonable as of that date), the employer may treat the shortfall as wages paid as of the estimate date or as of any date that is no later than three months after the estimate date. In either case, the shortfall does not include the income credited to the amount deferred after the amount is taken into account in accordance with paragraph (e) of this section.

    (B) *Shortfall is treated as wages paid on a date after the estimate date.*—If the employer chooses to treat the shortfall as wages paid on a date that is no later than three months after the estimate date, the employer must take that shortfall into account as wages paid by the employer and received by the employee on that date, for purposes of withholding and depositing FICA tax.

    (C) *Shortfall is treated as wages paid on the estimate date.*—If the employer chooses to treat the shortfall as wages paid as of the estimate date, the shortfall is treated as an error for purposes of withholding and depositing FICA tax. Appropriate adjustments may be made in accordance with section 6205(a) and the regulations thereunder; however, for purposes of §31.6205-1(b), the error need not be treated as ascertained before the date that is three months after the estimate date.

    (D) *Reporting.*—The employer must report the shortfall as wages on Form 941, Employer's Quarterly Federal Tax Return (and, if applicable, Form 941c, Supporting Statement to Correct Information) and Form W-2, Wage and Tax Statement (or, if applicable, Form W-2c, Corrected Wage and Tax Statement) in accordance with its treatment of the shortfall under paragraph (f)(2)(ii)(B) or (C) of this section.

    (iii) *Overestimate of the amount deferred.*—If the employer overestimates the amount deferred (as determined after calculating the actual amount deferred that should have been taken into account as of the date on which the amount was taken into account in accordance with paragraph (e) of this section, using an interest rate and actuarial assumptions that are reasonable as of that date) and deposits more than the amount required, the employer may claim a refund or credit in accordance with sections 6402, 6413, and 6511. A Form 941c, or an equivalent statement, must accompany each claim for refund. In addition, Form W-2 or, if applicable, Form W-2c

must also reflect the actual amount deferred that should have been taken into account.

    (3) *Lag method.*—Under the alternative method provided in this paragraph (f)(3), an amount deferred, plus interest, may be treated as wages paid by the employer and received by the employee, for purposes of withholding and depositing FICA tax, on any date that is no later than three months after the date the amount is required to be taken into account in accordance with paragraph (e) of this section. For purposes of this paragraph (f)(3), the amount deferred must be increased by interest through the date on which the wages are treated as paid, at a rate that is not less than AFR. If the employer withholds and deposits FICA tax in accordance with this paragraph (f)(3), the employer will be treated as having taken into account the amount deferred plus income to the date on which the wages are treated as paid.

    (4) *Examples.*—This paragraph (f) is illustrated by the following examples:

    Example 1. (i) Employer M maintains a nonqualified deferred compensation plan that is an account balance plan. The plan provides for annual bonuses based on current year profits to be deferred until termination of employment. Employer M's profits for 2003, and thus the amount deferred, is reasonably ascertainable, but Employer M calculates the amount deferred on March 3, 2004, when the relevant data is available.

    (ii) In accordance with the alternative method described in paragraph (f)(2) of this section, Employer M makes a reasonable estimate that the amount deferred that must be taken into account as of December 31, 2003, for Employee A is $20,000, and withholds and deposits FICA tax on that amount as if it were wages paid by Employer M and received by Employee A on that date. In January of 2004, Employer M files and furnishes Form W-2 for Employee A including the $20,000 in FICA wages. On March 3, 2004, Employer M determines that the actual amount deferred that should have been taken into account on December 31, 2003, was $22,000.

    (iii) In accordance with the alternative method described in paragraph (f)(2)(ii) of this section, Employer M may treat the additional $2,000 as wages paid to and received by Employee A on December 31, 2003, the estimate date. Employer M may treat the $2,000 shortfall as an error ascertained on March 3, 2004, and withhold and deposit FICA tax on that amount. Form W-2c for Employee A for 2003 must include the $2,000 shortfall in FICA wages. Employer M must also correct the information on Form 941 for the last quarter of 2003, reporting the adjustment on Form 941 for the first quarter of 2004, accompanied by Form 941c for the last quarter of 2003.

    (iv) Instead, Employer M may treat the $2,000 shortfall as wages paid on March 31, 2004, and withhold and deposit FICA tax on that amount as if it were wages paid by Employer M and received by Employee A on that date. Form W-2 for Employee A for 2004 and Form 941 for the first quarter of 2004 must include the $2,000 shortfall in FICA wages.

Example 2. (i) The facts are the same as in *Example 1,* except that on March 3, 2004, Employer M determines that the actual amount deferred that should have been taken into account on December 31, 2003, was $19,000.

(ii) Under paragraph (f)(2)(iii) of this section, Employer M may, in accordance with sections 6402, 6413, and 6511, claim a refund or credit for the overpayment of tax resulting from the overestimate. In addition, Employer M must file and furnish a Form W-2c for Employee A and must correct the information on Form 941 for the last quarter of 2003.

Example 3. (i) The facts are the same as in *Example 1,* except that Employer M does not make a reasonable estimate of the amount deferred that must be taken into account as of December 31, 2003. Instead, Employer M withholds and deposits FICA tax on the amount deferred plus interest on that amount using AFR (for January 2004) as if it were wages paid by Employer M and received by Employee A on March 15, 2004.

(ii) Under the alternative method described in paragraph (f)(3) of this section, the amount taken into account on March 15, 2004 (including the interest), will be treated as FICA wages paid to and received by Employee A on March 15, 2004.

Example 4. (i) The facts are the same as in *Example 1,* except that an amount is also deferred for Employee B which is required to be taken into account on October 15, 2003, and Employer M chooses to use the lag method in paragraph (f)(3) of this section in order to provide time to calculate the amount deferred.

(ii) Employer M may use any date not later than January 15, 2004, to take the amount deferred into account (provided that the amount deferred includes interest, at AFR for January 1, 2003, through December 31, 2003, and at AFR for January 1, 2004, through January 15, 2004).

(g) *Effective date and transition rules.*—(1) *General effective date.*—Except for paragraphs (g)(2) through (4) of this section, this section is applicable on and after January 1, 2000. Thus, paragraphs (a) through (f) of this section apply to amounts deferred on or after January 1, 2000; to amounts deferred before January 1, 2000, which cease to be subject to a substantial risk of forfeiture on or after January 1, 2000, or for which a resolution date occurs on or after January 1, 2000; and to benefits actually or constructively paid on or after January 1, 2000.

(2) *Reasonable, good faith interpretation for amounts deferred and benefits paid before January 1, 2000.*—(i) *In general.*—For periods before January 1, 2000 (including amounts deferred before January 1, 2000, and any benefits actually or constructively paid before January 1, 2000, that are attributable to those amounts deferred), an employer may rely on a reasonable, good faith interpretation of section 3121(v)(2), taking into account pre-existing guidance. An employer will be deemed to have determined FICA tax liability and satisfied FICA withholding requirements in accordance with a reasonable, good faith interpretation of section 3121(v)(2) if the employer has complied with paragraphs (a) through (f) of this section. For purposes of paragraphs (g)(2) through (4) of this section, and subject to paragraphs (g)(2)(ii) and (iii) of this section, whether an employer that has not complied with paragraphs (a) through (f) of this section has determined FICA tax liability and satisfied FICA withholding requirements in accordance with a reasonable, good faith interpretation of section 3121(v)(2) will be determined based on the relevant facts and circumstances, including consistency of treatment by the employer and the extent to which the employer has resolved unclear issues in its favor.

(ii) *Plan must be established or adopted.*—If an amount is deferred under a plan before January 1, 2000, and benefit payments attributable to that amount are actually or constructively paid on or after January 1, 2000, then in no event will an employer's treatment of the amount deferred be considered to be in accordance with a reasonable, good faith interpretation of section 3121(v)(2) if the employer treats that amount as taken into account as wages for FICA tax purposes prior to the establishment of the plan (within the meaning of paragraph (b)(2) of this section) providing for the deferred compensation (or, if later, the establishment of the plan as amended to provide for the deferred compensation, as provided in paragraph (b)(2)(ii) of this section). If an amount is deferred under a plan before January 1, 2000, and benefit payments attributable to that amount are actually or constructively paid before January 1, 2000, then in no event will the employer's treatment of that amount deferred be considered to be in accordance with a reasonable, good faith interpretation of section 3121(v)(2) if the employer treats that amount as taken into account as wages for FICA tax purposes prior to the adoption of the plan providing for the deferred compensation (or, if later, the adoption of the plan amendment providing the deferred compensation). For example, awards, bonuses, raises, incentive payments, and other similar amounts granted under a plan as compensation for past services may not be taken into account under section 3121(v)(2) prior to the establishment (or, if applicable, the adoption) of the plan.

(iii) *Certain changes in position for stock options, stock appreciation rights, and other stock value rights not reasonable, good faith interpretation.*—In the case of a stock option, stock appreciation right, or other stock value right (as defined in paragraph (b)(4)(ii) of this section) that is exercised before January 1, 2000, an employer that treats the exercise as not subject to FICA tax as a result of the nonduplication rule of section 3121(v)(2)(B) is not acting in accordance with a reasonable, good faith interpretation of section 3121(v)(2) if the employer has not treated that grant and all earlier grants as subject to section 3121(v)(2) by reporting the current value of such options and rights as FICA wages on Form 941 filed for the quarter during which each grant was made (or, if later, for the quarter during which each grant ceased to be subject to a substantial risk of forfeiture).

(3) *Optional adjustments to conform with this section for pre-effective-date open periods.*— (i) *General rule.*—If an employer determined FICA tax liability with respect to section 3121(v)(2) in any period ending before January 1, 2000, for which the applicable period of limitations has not expired on January 1, 2000 (pre-effective-date open periods), in a manner that was not in accordance with this section, the employer may adjust its FICA tax determination for that period to conform to this section. Thus, if an amount deferred was taken into account in a pre-effective-date open period when it was not required to be taken into account (e.g., an amount taken into account before it became reasonably ascertainable), the employer may claim a refund or credit for any FICA tax paid on that amount to the extent permitted by sections 6402, 6413, and 6511.

(ii) *Consistency required.*—In the case of a plan that is not a nonqualified deferred compensation plan (within the meaning of paragraph (b)(1) of this section), if any payment was actually or constructively paid to an employee under the plan in a pre-effective-date open period and that payment was not included in FICA wages by reason of the employer's treatment of the plan as a nonqualified deferred compensation plan, then the employer may claim a refund or credit for FICA tax paid on amounts treated as amounts deferred under the plan (in accordance with the employer's treatment of the plan as a nonqualified deferred compensation plan) for that employee for pre-effective-date open periods only to the extent that the FICA tax paid on all amounts treated as amounts deferred for the employee in all pre-effective-date open periods under the plan exceeds the FICA tax that would have been due on the benefits actually or constructively paid to the employee in those periods under the plan if those benefits were included in FICA wages when paid. If any benefit payments attributable to amounts deferred after December 31, 1993, were actually or constructively paid to an employee under a nonqualified deferred compensation plan (within the meaning of paragraph (b)(1) of this section) in a pre-effective-date open period, but these payments were treated as subject to FICA tax because the employer treated the plan as not being a nonqualified deferred compensation plan, then the employer may claim a refund or credit for the FICA tax paid on those benefit payments only to the extent that the FICA tax paid on those benefit payments exceeds the FICA tax that would have been due on the amounts deferred to which those benefit payments are attributable if those

amounts deferred had been taken into account when they would have been required to have been taken into account under this section (if this section had been in effect then).

(iii) *Reporting.*—Any employer that adjusts its FICA tax determination in accordance with paragraphs (g)(3)(i) and (ii) of this section must make appropriate adjustments on Form 941 and Form 941c for the affected periods, and, in addition, must file and furnish Form W-2, or, if applicable, Form W-2c, for any affected employee so that the Social Security Administration may correctly post the amount deferred to the employee's earnings record. The adjustments may be made in accordance with section 6205(a) and the regulations thereunder; however, for purposes of § 31.6205-1(b), the error is not required to be treated as ascertained before March 31, 2000.

(4) *Application of reasonable, good faith standard.*—(i) *Plans that are not subject to section 3121(v)(2).*—If a plan is not a nonqualified deferred compensation plan within the meaning of paragraph (b)(1) of this section, but, for a period ending prior to January 1, 2000, and, pursuant to a reasonable, good faith interpretation of section 3121(v)(2), an amount under the plan was taken into account (within the meaning of paragraph (d)(1) of this section) as an amount deferred under a nonqualified deferred compensation plan, then, pursuant to paragraph (g)(2) of this section, the following rules shall apply—

(A) With respect to benefit payments actually or constructively paid before January 1, 2000, that are attributable to amounts previously taken into account under the plan, no additional FICA tax will be due;

(B) On or after January 1, 2000, benefit payments under the plan must be taken into account as wages when actually or constructively paid in accordance with paragraph (a)(1) of this section; and

(C) To the extent permitted by paragraph (g)(3) of this section, the empl6oyer may claim a refund or credit for FICA tax actually paid on amounts taken into account prior to January 1, 2000.

(ii) *Plans that are subject to section 3121(v)(2) for which the amount deferred has not been fully taken into account.*—(A) *In general.*—The rules of paragraphs (g)(4)(ii)(B) through (E) of this section apply if a plan is a nonqualified deferred compensation plan (within the meaning of paragraph (b)(1) of this section) and, with respect to an amount deferred under the plan for an employee prior to January 1, 2000, the employer, in accordance with a reasonable, good faith interpretation of section 3121(v)(2), either took into account an amount that is less than the amount that would have been required to be taken into account if paragraphs (a) through (f) of this section had been in effect for that period or took no amount into account. Thus, paragraphs (g)(4)(ii)(B) through (E) of this section apply both to an employer that treated the plan as if it were not a nonqualified deferred compensation plan within the meaning of section 3121(v)(2) (by withholding and paying FICA tax due on benefits actually or constructively paid under the plan during that period, if any) and to an employer that treated the plan as a nonqualified deferred compensation plan within the meaning of section 3121(v)(2).

(B) *No additional tax required.*—Pursuant to paragraph (g)(2) of this section, no additional FICA tax will be due for any period ending prior to January 1, 2000.

(C) *General timing rule applicable.*—In accordance with paragraph (d)(1)(ii) of this section, except as provided in paragraphs (g)(4)(ii)(D) and (E), the general timing rule described in paragraph (a)(1) of this section applies to benefits actually or constructively paid on or after January 1, 2000, attributable to an amount deferred in a period before January 1, 2000, to the extent the amount taken into account was less than the amount that would have been required to be taken into account if paragraphs (a) through (f) of this section had been in effect before January 1, 2000.

(D) *Special rule for amounts deferred before 1994.*—The difference between the amount that was taken into account in any period ending prior to January 1, 1994, and the amount that would have been required or permitted to be taken into account in that period if paragraphs (a) through (f) of this section had been in effect is treated as if it had been taken into account within the meaning of paragraph (d)(1) of this section. For example, in the case of an amount deferred before 1994 that was not reasonably ascertainable (and which was not subject to a substantial risk of forfeiture), the employer is treated as if it had anticipated the actual amount, form, and commencement date for the benefit payments attributable to the amount deferred and had taken the amount deferred into account at an early inclusion date before 1994 using a method permitted under this section. Thus, with respect to such an amount deferred, the employer is not required to take any additional amount into account when the amount deferred becomes reasonably ascertainable, and no additional FICA tax will be due when the benefit payments attributable to the amount deferred are actually or constructively paid.

(E) *Special rule for amounts required to be taken into account in 1994 or 1995.*—In the case of an amount deferred that would have been required to be taken into account in 1994 or 1995 if paragraphs (a) through (f) of this section had been in effect, an employer will be treated as taking the amount deferred into account under paragraph (d)(1) of this section to the extent the employer takes the amount into account by treating it as wages paid by the employer and received by the employee as of any date prior to April 1, 2000.

(iii) *Plans that are subject to section 3121(v)(2) for which more than the amount deferred has been taken into account.*—If a plan is a nonqualified deferred compensation plan (within the meaning of paragraph (b)(1) of this section) and an amount was taken into account under the plan for an employee before January 1, 2000, in accordance with a reasonable, good faith interpretation of section 3121(v)(2), but that amount could not have been taken into account before January 1, 2000, if paragraphs (a) through (f) of this section had been in effect then, the following rules apply—

(A) The determination of the amount deferred for any period beginning on or after January 1, 2000, must be made in accordance with paragraph (c) of this section, and the time when amounts deferred under the plan are required to be taken into account must be determined in accordance with paragraph (e) of this section, without regard to any such amount that was taken into account for any period ending before January 1, 2000; and

(B) To the extent permitted by sections 6402, 6413, and 6511, the employer may claim a refund or credit for an overpayment of tax caused by the overinclusion of wages that occurred before January 1, 2000.

(5) *Examples.*—This paragraph (g) is illustrated by the following examples:

Example 1. (i) In 1996, Employer M establishes a nonqualified deferred compensation plan that is a nonaccount balance plan for Employee A. All benefits under the plan are 100 percent vested. In order to determine the amount deferred on behalf of Employee A under the plan for 1996 and 1997, Employer M must make assumptions as to the date on which Employee A will retire and the form of benefit Employee A will elect, in addition to interest, mortality, and cost-of-living assumptions. Based on assumptions made with respect to all of these contingencies, Employer M determines that the amount deferred for 1996 is $50,000 and the amount deferred for 1997 is $55,000. In 1996 and 1997, Employee A's total wages (without regard to the amounts deferred) exceed the OASDI wage bases. Employer M withholds and deposits HI tax on the $50,000 and $55,000 amounts. Employee A does not retire before January 1, 2000. Employer M chooses under paragraph (g)(3) of this section to apply this section to 1996 and 1997 before the January 1, 2000, general effective date.

(ii) Under this section, the amounts deferred in 1996 and 1997 are not reasonably ascertainable (within the meaning of paragraph (e)(4)(i) of this section) before January 1, 2000. Thus, as long as the applicable period of limitations has not expired for the periods in 1996 and 1997, Employer M may, to the extent permitted under paragraph (g)(3) of this section, apply for a refund or credit for the HI tax paid on the amounts deferred for 1996 and 1997 and, in accordance with paragraph (e)(4) of this section, take into account the amounts deferred when they become reasonably ascertainable.

Reg. §31.3121(v)(2)-1(g)(5)

Example 2. (i) Employer N adopts a plan on January 1, 1994, that covers Employee B, who has 10 years of service as of that date. The plan provides that, in consideration of Employee B's outstanding services over the past 10 years, Employee B will be paid a $500,000 lump sum distribution upon termination of employment at any time. On January 15, 1996, Employee B terminates employment with Employer N. Employer N determines, based on a reasonable, good faith interpretation of section 3121(v)(2), that the plan is a nonqualified deferred compensation plan under that section. Employer N treats the $500,000 as having been taken into account as an amount deferred in 1993 and earlier years.

(ii) Under paragraph (g)(2)(ii) of this section, if all amounts are deferred and all benefits are paid under a plan before January 1, 2000, then in no event will an employer's treatment of amounts deferred under the plan be considered to be in accordance with a reasonable, good faith interpretation of section 3121(v)(2) if the employer treats these amounts as taken into account as wages for FICA tax purposes prior to the adoption of the plan. Accordingly, Employer N's treatment is not in accordance with a reasonable, good faith interpretation of section 3121(v)(2) because Employer N treated amounts as taken into account in years before the adoption of the plan. As a result, the payment made to Employee B in 1996 was subject to both the OASDI and HI portions of FICA tax when paid.

Example 3. (i) Employer O adopts a bonus plan on December 1, 1993, that becomes effective and legally binding on January 1, 1994. Under the plan, which is not set forth in writing, a specified bonus amount (which is 100 percent vested) is credited to Employee C's account each December 31. A reasonable rate of interest on Employee C's account balance is credited quarterly. Employee C's account balance will begin to be paid in equal annual installments over 10 years beginning on January 1, 2000. Employer O determines, based on a reasonable, good faith interpretation of section 3121(v)(2), that the bonus plan is a nonqualified deferred compensation plan under that section and, therefore, treats the amounts credited from January 1, 1994, through December 31, 1999, as amounts deferred and, in accordance with a reasonable, good faith interpretation of section 3121(v)(2), takes those amounts deferred into account as wages for FICA tax purposes as of those dates. The bonus plan is set forth in writing on May 1, 1999, and, thus, is treated as established as of January 1, 1994.

(ii) Under paragraph (g)(2)(ii) of this section, if an amount is deferred before January 1, 2000, and the attributable benefit is paid on or after January 1, 2000, then in no event will an employer's treatment of the amount deferred under a plan be considered to be in accordance with a reasonable, good faith interpretation of section 3121(v)(2) if the employer treats the amount deferred as taken into account as wages for FICA tax purposes prior to the establishment of the

plan (within the meaning of paragraph (b)(2) of this section). Because the bonus plan is treated as established on January 1, 1994 (pursuant to the transition rule for unwritten plans in paragraph (b)(2)(iii) of this section), and because Employer O, in accordance with a reasonable, good faith interpretation of section 3121(v)(2), took amounts deferred into account in 1994 through 1999, the amounts paid to Employee C attributable to those amounts deferred will not be subject to FICA tax when paid.

Example 4. (i) In 1985, Employer P establishes a compensation arrangement for Employee D that provides for a lump sum payment to be made after termination of employment but the arrangement is not a nonqualified deferred compensation plan (within the meaning of paragraph (b)(1) of this section). However, prior to January 1, 2000, and in accordance with a reasonable, good faith interpretation of section 3121(v)(2), Employer P treats the arrangement as a nonqualified deferred compensation plan under section 3121(v)(2). Employer P determines that Employee D's total wages (without regard to the amount deferred) for each year from 1985 through 1993 exceed the applicable OASDI and HI wage bases for each of those years and, consequently, there is no FICA tax liability with respect to the amounts deferred for those years. In 1994, Employee D's total wages (without regard to the amount deferred) exceed the OASDI wage base. However, because there is no limit on the HI wage base, the amount deferred for 1994 results in additional HI tax liability of $290, which is timely paid by Employer P.

(ii) Employee D terminates employment with Employer P in 1995 and receives a plan payment of $50,000. In that year, Employee D also receives wages of $60,000 from Employer P. In accordance with its treatment of the plan as a nonqualified deferred compensation plan under section 3121(v)(2), Employer P does not treat the $50,000 payment in 1995 as wages for FICA tax purposes in that year.

(iii) Because amounts under a plan were taken into account (within the meaning of paragraph (d)(1) of this section) as amounts deferred under a nonqualified deferred compensation plan pursuant to a reasonable, good faith interpretation of section 3121(v)(2)(A), but that plan is not a nonqualified deferred compensation plan within the meaning of paragraph (b)(1) of this section, the transition rules provided in paragraph (g)(4)(i) of this section apply. Thus, no additional FICA tax will be due on the benefits paid in 1995.

(iv) Because $290 of HI tax was paid on the amount deferred in 1994, Employer P is entitled to a refund or credit for that amount to the extent permitted under sections 6402, 6413, and 6511— but only to the extent that $290 exceeds the FICA tax that would have been due on the $50,000 payment in 1995 if that payment had been subject to FICA tax when paid (i.e., if paragraphs (a) through (f) of this section had been effective for those years). In 1995, Employee D had other wages of $60,000. Thus, only $1,200 (the $61,200

OASDI wage base, less the $60,000 of other wages) of the $50,000 payment would have been subject to OASDI; the full $50,000 would have been subject to HI. This would have resulted in $148.80 of OASDI tax ($1,200 × 12.4 percent) and $1,450 of HI tax ($50,000 × 2.9 percent). Employer P is not entitled to a refund or credit under the consistency rule of paragraph (g)(3)(ii) because the $290 of HI tax paid in 1994 is less than the total $1,598.80 of FICA tax liability that would have resulted if this section had applied for 1995.

(v) However, if the benefit payment is instead actually or constructively paid on or after January 1, 2000, the benefit payment must be taken into account as wages when actually or constructively paid in accordance with the general timing rule of paragraph (a)(1) of this section (and paragraph (g)(4)(i)(B) of this section).

Example 5. (i) In 1985, Employer Q establishes a compensation arrangement for Employee E that is a nonqualified deferred compensation plan within the meaning of paragraph (b)(1) of this section. However, prior to January 1, 2000, Employer Q determines, based on a reasonable, good faith interpretation of section 3121(v)(2), that the arrangement is not a nonqualified deferred compensation plan within the meaning of that section. Thus, when Employee E retires at the end of 1996 and benefit payments under the arrangement begin in 1997, Employer Q withholds and deposits FICA tax on the amounts paid to Employee E. Payments under the arrangement continue on or after January 1, 2000. Employer Q does not choose (under paragraph (g)(3) of this section) to adjust its FICA tax determination for a pre-effective-date open period by treating this section as in effect for all amounts deferred and benefits actually or constructively paid for any such period. The periods in 1994 and 1995 are not pre-effective-date open periods for Employer Q.

(ii) Under paragraph (g)(4)(ii) of this section, for purposes of determining whether benefits actually or constructively paid on or after January 1, 2000, were previously taken into account for purposes of applying the nonduplication rule of section 3121(v)(2)(B), any amount that would have been required to have been taken into account before 1994 will be treated as if it had been taken into account within the meaning of paragraph (d)(1) of this section. Under the nonduplication rule, benefit payments attributable to an amount that has been so treated as taken into account is not treated as wages for FICA tax purposes at any later time (such as upon payment).

(iii) Because Employer Q does not adjust its FICA tax determination by treating this section as in effect for all amounts deferred for periods ending after December 31, 1993, any benefit payments attributable to amounts deferred in periods ending after December 31, 1993, will be included in wages when actually or constructively paid in accordance with the general timing rule of paragraph (a)(1) of this section.

Example 6. (i) The facts are the same as in *Example 5,* except that Employer Q chooses (in accordance with paragraph (g)(3) of this section) to adjust its FICA tax determination for all pre-effective-date open periods by treating this section as in effect for all amounts deferred for those periods. In addition, Employer Q chooses (in accordance with paragraph (g)(4)(ii)(E) of this section) to take the amounts deferred for 1994 and 1995 into account by treating these amounts as FICA wages paid and received by Employee E on January 15, 2000.

(ii) In accordance with the nonduplication rule of paragraph (a)(2)(iii) of this section, because all amounts deferred for Employee E under the plan were taken into account (or treated as taken into account), any benefit payments made to Employee E under the plan will not be included as FICA wages when actually or constructively paid.

Example 7. (i) The facts are the same as in *Example 5,* except that Employer Q does not withhold and deposit the FICA tax due on benefits actually or constructively paid before January 1, 2000.

(ii) Because Employer Q did not withhold and deposit the FICA tax due on benefits actually or constructively paid before January 1, 2000, Employer Q did not determine FICA tax liability and satisfy FICA tax withholding requirements in accordance with a reasonable, good faith interpretation of section 3121(v)(2). Thus, the transition rules provided in paragraphs (g)(3) and (4) of this section do not apply. As a result, any amount that would have been required to have been taken into account under this section before 1994 is not treated as if it had been so taken into account under paragraph (g)(4)(ii)(D) of this section, and benefit payments attributable to amounts deferred before January 1, 2000, are treated as FICA wages when actually or constructively paid in accordance with the general timing rule of paragraph (a)(1) of this section.

Example 8. (i) In 1993, Employer R establishes a nonqualified deferred compensation plan for Employee F under which Employee F will have a fully vested right to receive a lump sum payment in 2000 equal to 50 percent of Employee F's highest rate of salary. On December 31, 1993, Employee F's highest salary is $1 million. In accordance with a reasonable, good faith interpretation of section 3121(v)(2), Employer R determines that, for 1993, there is an amount deferred that must be taken into account as wages for FICA tax purposes. Based on Employer R's estimate that Employee F's highest salary will be $3 million in 2000, Employer R determines that the amount deferred is equal to the present value in 1993 of $1.5 million payable in 2000. However, because Employee F has other wages in 1993 that exceed the applicable OASDI and HI wage bases for that year, no additional FICA tax is paid as a result of that amount deferred being taken into account for 1993. In addition, Employer R takes no amounts into account under the plan after 1993 for Employee F.

Under paragraphs (e)(1) and (4)(ii)(D)(2) of this section, the largest amount that could have been taken into account in 1993 is the present value of a lump sum payment of $500,000, payable in 2000, because that is the maximum amount to which Employee F has a legally binding right as of December 31, 1993. Employee F's highest salary is, in fact, $3 million in 2000 and Employee F receives $1.5 million under the plan on December 31, 2000.

(ii) In accordance with paragraphs (g)(1) and (4)(iii)(A) of this section, the determination of the amount deferred under the plan for any period beginning on or after January 1, 2000, and the time when that amount deferred is required to be taken into account must be determined in accordance with this section. In addition, these determinations must be made without regard to any amount deferred that was taken into account for any period ending before January 1, 2000, that could not be taken into account before January 1, 2000, if paragraphs (a) through (f) of this section had been in effect. Because no FICA tax was actually paid on that $1 million in 1993, no overpayment of tax was caused by the overinclusion of wages in 1993 and, thus, Employer R is not entitled to a refund or credit (even assuming that the period of limitations has been kept open for periods in 1993). In addition, because the difference between the present value of the $1.5 million payment and the present value of a $500,000 payment was not taken into account for periods beginning on or after January 1, 1994, $1 million must be included in FICA wages under the general timing rule when paid.

[Reg. § 31.3121(v)(2)-1.]

☐ [*T.D.* 8814, 1-28-99 (corrected 3-31-99).]

[Reg. § 31.3121(v)(2)-2]

§ 31.3121(v)(2)-2. Effective dates and transition rules.—(a) *General statutory effective date.*— Except as otherwise provided in paragraphs (b) through (e) of this section, section 3121(v)(2) and the amendments made to section 3121(a)(2), (a)(3), and (a)(13) by the Social Security Amendments of 1983 (Public Law 98-21, 97 Stat. 65), as amended by section 2662(f)(2) of the Deficit Reduction Act of 1984 (Public Law 98-369, 98 Stat. 494), apply to amounts deferred and benefits paid after December 31, 1983.

(b) *Definitions.*—For purposes of § 31.3121(v)(2)-1 and this section, the following definitions apply:

(1) *FICA.*—*FICA* means the Federal Insurance Contributions Act (26 U.S.C. 3101 et seq.).

(2) *457(a) plan.*—A *457(a) plan* means an eligible deferred compensation plan of a State or local government or of a tax-exempt organization to which section 457(a) applies.

(3) *Gap agreement.*—*Gap agreement* means an agreement adopted after March 24, 1983, and on or before December 31, 1983, between an individual and a nonqualified deferred compensation plan within the meaning of

§ 31.3121(v)(2)-1(b). Such an agreement does not fail to be a gap agreement merely because the terms of the plan are changed after December 31, 1983.

(4) *Individual party to a gap agreement.*—*Individual party to a gap agreement* means an individual who was eligible to participate in a gap agreement on December 31, 1983, under the terms of the agreement on that date. An individual will be treated as an individual party to a gap agreement even if the individual has not accrued any benefits under the plan by December 31, 1983, and regardless of whether the individual has taken any specific action to become a party to the agreement. However, an individual who becomes eligible to participate in a gap agreement after December 31, 1983, is not an individual party to a gap agreement.

(5) *Individual party to a March 24, 1983 agreement.*—*Individual party to a March 24, 1983 agreement* means an individual who was eligible to participate in a March 24, 1983 agreement under the terms of the agreement on March 24, 1983. An individual will be treated as an individual party to a March 24, 1983 agreement even if the individual has not accrued any benefits under the plan by March 24, 1983, and regardless of whether the individual has taken any specific action to become a party to the agreement. However, an individual who becomes eligible to participate in a March 24, 1983 agreement after March 24, 1983, is not an individual party to a March 24, 1983 agreement.

(6) *March 24, 1983 agreement.*—*March 24, 1983 agreement* means an agreement in existence on March 24, 1983, between an individual and a nonqualified deferred compensation plan within the meaning of § 31.3121(v)(2)-1(b). Such an agreement does not fail to be a March 24, 1983 agreement merely because the terms of the plan are changed after March 24, 1983. In addition, for purposes of this paragraph (b)(6) only, any plan (or agreement) that provides for payments that qualify for one of the retirement payment exclusions is treated as a nonqualified deferred compensation plan. For example, § 31.3121(v)(2)-1(b)(4)(v) provides that certain benefits established in connection with impending termination do not result from the deferral of compensation and thus are not considered deferred under a nonqualified deferred compensation plan. However, a plan that provides such benefits and that was in existence on March 24, 1983, is treated as a nonqualified deferred compensation plan for purposes of this paragraph (b) to the extent it provides benefits that would have satisfied one of the retirement payment exclusions.

(7) *Retirement payment exclusions.*—*Retirement payment exclusions* are the exclusions from wages (for FICA tax purposes) for retirement payments under section 3121(a)(2)(A), (a)(3), and (a)(13)(A)(iii), as in effect on April 19, 1983 (the day before enactment of the Social Security Amendments of 1983).

(8) *Transition benefits.*—Transition benefits are payments made after December 31, 1983, attributable to services rendered before January 1, 1984. For this purpose, transition benefits are determined without regard to any changes made in the terms of the plan after March 24, 1983, in the case of a March 24, 1983 agreement or after December 31, 1983, in the case of a gap agreement.

(c) *Transition rules.*—(1) *In general.*—Except as provided in paragraph (c)(2) or (3) of this section, the general statutory effective date described in paragraph (a) of this section applies to benefit payments after December 31, 1983. Thus, except as provided in paragraph (c)(2) or (3) of this section, section 3121(v)(2) applies, and the retirement payment exclusions do not apply, to benefit payments made after December 31, 1983, even if the benefit payments are made under a March 24, 1983 agreement or a gap agreement.

(2) *Transition benefits under a March 24, 1983 agreement.*—With respect to an individual party to a March 24, 1983 agreement, transition benefits paid under that March 24, 1983 agreement (except for those paid under a 457(a) plan) are not subject to the special timing rule of section 3121(v)(2) and are subject to section 3121(a) as in effect on April 19, 1983. Thus, transition benefits under a March 24, 1983 agreement (except for those under a 457(a) plan) to an individual party to a March 24, 1983 agreement are excluded from wages (for FICA tax purposes) only if they qualify for any of the retirement payment exclusions (or any other exclusion provided under section 3121(a) as in effect on April 19, 1983).

(3) *Transition benefits under a gap agreement.*—With respect to an individual party to a gap agreement, the payor of transition benefits under the gap agreement must choose to either—

(i) Take the transition benefits into account as wages when paid; or

(ii) Take the amount deferred (within the meaning of § 31.3121(v)(2)-1(c)) with respect to the transition benefits into account as wages under section 3121(v)(2) (as if section 3121(v)(2) had applied before its general statutory effective date).

(d) *Determining transition benefit portion.*—For purposes of determining the portion of total benefits under a nonqualified deferred compensation plan that represents transition benefits, if, under the terms of the plan, benefit payments are not attributed to specific years of service, the employer may use any reasonable method. For example, if a plan provides that the employee will receive benefits equal to 2 percent of high 3-year average compensation multiplied by years of service, and the employee retires after 25 years of service, 9 of which are before 1984, the employer may determine that 9/25 of the total benefit payments to be received beginning in 2000 are transition benefits attributable to services performed before 1984.

(e) *Order of payment.*—If an employer determines, in accordance with paragraph (d) of this section, that a portion of the total benefits under a nonqualified deferred compensation plan constitutes transition benefits, then, for purposes of determining the portion of each benefit payment that constitutes transition benefits, the employer must treat each benefit payment as consisting of transition benefits in the same proportion as the transition benefits that have not been paid (as of January 1, 2000) bear to total benefits that have not been paid (as of January 1, 2000), unless such allocation is inconsistent with the terms of the plan. However, for a benefit payment made before January 1, 2000, the employer may use any reasonable allocation method to determine the portion of a payment that consists of transition benefits, provided that the allocation method is consistent with the terms of the plan. [Reg. § 31.3121(v)(2)-2.]

☐ [*T.D.* 8814, 1-28-99.]

[Reg. § 31.3123-1]

§ 31.3123-1. Deductions by an employer from remuneration of an employee.—Any amount deducted by an employer from the remuneration of an employee is considered to be part of the employee's remuneration and is considered to be paid to the employee as remuneration at the time that the deduction is made. It is immaterial that any act of Congress or the law of any State requires or permits such deductions and the payment of the amount thereof to the United States, a State, or any political subdivision thereof. [Reg. § 31.3123-1.]

☐ [*T.D.* 6190, 7-14-56. *Republished in T.D.* 6516, 12-20-60.]

[Reg. § 31.3127-1]

§ 31.3127-1. Exemption for employers and their employees if both are members of religious faiths opposed to participation in Social Security Act programs.—(a) *Exemption.*—(1) *Employer.*—Except as provided in paragraph (b) of this section, an employer is exempt from the taxes imposed by section 3111 on wages paid to an employee if—

(i) The employer (or if the employer is a partnership, each partner therein) and its employee are members of a recognized religious sect or division described in section 1402(g)(1);

(ii) Both the employer (or if the employer is a partnership, each partner therein) and the employee adhere to the tenets and teachings of that sect; and

(iii) Both the employer and the employee have filed and had approved applications under section 3127(b) for exemption from the taxes imposed by sections 3111 and 3101.

(2) *Employee.*—If an employer is exempt from the taxes imposed by section 3111 under paragraph (a)(1) of this section, then each employee described in paragraph (a)(1) of this section is exempt from the taxes imposed by section 3101 on the wages received with respect to employment with that employer.

Reg. § 31.3127-1(a)(2)

(b) *Corporation.*—Services performed in the employ of a corporation are not within the exemption described in paragraph (a) of this section, except that services performed in the employ of an entity that is treated as a corporation under § 301.7701-2(c)(2)(iv)(B) of this chapter may qualify for the exemption if the requirements of the exemption are otherwise met. An entity that is treated as a corporation under § 301.7701-2(c)(2)(iv)(B) of this chapter is not treated as the employer for purposes of applying section 3127 and this section. For purposes of applying section 3127 and paragraph (a) of this section, the owner of an entity that is treated as a corporation under § 301.7701-2(c)(2)(iv)(B) of this chapter is treated as the employer.

(c) *Effective/applicability date.*—This section applies to wages paid on or after November 1, 2011. However, taxpayers may apply this section to wages paid on or after January 1, 2009. [Reg. § 31.3127-1.]

☐ [*T.D.* 9670, 6-25-2014.]

Railroad Retirement Tax Act

TAX ON EMPLOYEES

See p. 20,601 for regulations not amended to reflect law changes

[Reg. § 31.3201-1]

§ 31.3201-1. Measure of employee tax.—The employee tax is measured by the amount of compensation received for services rendered as an employee. For provisions relating to compensation, see § 31.3231(e)-1. For provisions relating to the circumstances under which certain compensation is to be disregarded for the purpose of determining the employee tax, see paragraphs (b)(1) and (2) of § 31.3231(e)-1. [Reg. § 31.3201-1.]

☐ [*T.D.* 8582, 12-23-94.]

[Reg. § 31.3201-2]

§ 31.3201-2. Rates and computation of employee tax.—(a) *Rates.*—(1)(i) *Tier 1 tax.*—The Tier 1 employee tax rate equals the sum of the tax rates in effect under section 3101(a) relating to old-age, survivors, and disability insurance, and section 3101(b), relating to hospital insurance. The Tier 1 employee tax rate is applied to compensation up to the contribution base described in section 3231(e)(2)(B)(i). The contribution base is determined under section 230 of the Social Security Act and is identical to the old-age, survivors, and disability insurance wage base and the hospital insurance wage base, respectively, under the Federal Insurance Contributions Act.

(ii) *Example.*—The rule in paragraph (a)(1)(i) of this section is illustrated by the following example.

Example. A received compensation of $60,000 in 1992. The section 3101(a) rate of 6.2 percent would be applied to A's compensation up to $55,500, the applicable contribution base for 1992. The section 3101(b) rate of 1.45 percent would be applied to the entire $60,000 of A's compensation because the applicable contribution base for 1992 is $130,200.

(2)(i) *Tier 2 tax.*—The Tier 2 employee tax rate equals the percentage set forth in section 3201(b) of the Code. This rate is applied to compensation up to the contribution base described in section 3231(e)(2)(B)(ii).

(ii) *Example.*—The rule in paragraph (a)(2)(i) of this section is illustrated by the following example.

Example. A received compensation of $60,000 in 1992. The section 3201(b) rate of 4.90 percent would be applied to A's compensation up to $41,400, the applicable contribution base for 1992.

(b)(1) *Computation.*—The employee tax is computed by multiplying the amount of the employee's compensation with respect to which the employee tax is imposed by the rate applicable to such compensation, as determined under paragraph (a) of this section. The applicable rate is the rate in effect when the compensation is received by the employee. For rules relating to the time of receipt, see § 31.3121(a)-2 (a) and (b).

(2) *Example.*—The rule in paragraph (b)(1) of this section is illustrated by the following example.

Example. In 1990, employee A received compensation of $1,000 as remuneration for services performed for employer R in 1989. The employee tax is payable at the rate of 12.55 percent (7.65 percent plus 4.90 percent) in effect for 1990 (the year the compensation was received), and not the 12.41 percent rate (7.51 percent plus 4.90 percent) in effect for 1989 (the year the services were performed).

[Reg. § 31.3201-2.]

☐ [*T.D.* 8582, 12-23-94.]

[Reg. § 31.3202-1]

§ 31.3202-1. Collection of, and liability for, employee tax.—(a) *Collection; general rule.*—The employer shall collect from each of his employees the employee tax imposed with respect to the compensation of the employee by deducting or causing to be deducted the amount of such tax from the compensation subject to the tax as and when such compensation is paid. As to the measure of the employee tax, see § 31.3201-1.

(b) *Collection; payments by two or more employers in excess of annual compensation limitation.*—For rules relating to payments by two or more employers in excess of the annual compensation limitation see § 31.3121(a)(1)-1.

(c) *Undercollections or overcollections.*—Any undercollection or overcollection of employee tax resulting from the employer's inability to determine, at the time compensation is paid, the correct amount of compensation with respect to which the deduction should be made shall be corrected in accordance with the provisions of Subpart G of the regulations in this part relating to adjustments, credits, refunds, and abatements.

(d) *When fractional part of cent may be disregarded.*—In collecting the employee tax, the employer shall disregard any fractional part of a cent of such tax unless it amounts to one-half cent or more, in which case it shall be increased to one cent.

(e) *Employer's liability.*—The employer is liable for the employee tax with respect to compensation paid by him, whether or not collected from the employee. If the employer deducts less than the correct amount of employee tax or fails to deduct any part of the tax, he is nevertheless liable for the correct amount of the tax. Until collected from him, the employee is also liable for the employee tax. Any employee tax collected by or on behalf of an employer is a special fund in trust for the United States. See section 7501. An employer is not liable to any person for the amount of the employee tax deducted by him and paid to the district director.

(f) *Concurrent employment.*—If two or more related corporations who are rail employers concurrently employ the same individual and compensate that individual through a common paymaster, which is one of the related corporations employing the individual, see § 31.3121(s)-1.

(g) *Special rules regarding Additional Medicare Tax.*—(1) An employer is required to collect from each of its employees the portion of the tax imposed by section 3201(a) (as calculated under section 3101(b)(2)) (Additional Medicare Tax) with respect to compensation for employment performed for the employer by the employee only to the extent the employer pays compensation to the employee in excess of $200,000 in a calendar year. This rule applies regardless of the employee's filing status or other income. Thus, the employer disregards any amount of compensation or Federal Insurance Contributions Act (FICA) wages paid to the employee's spouse.

The employer also disregards any FICA wages paid by the employer to the employee or any compensation or FICA wages paid to the employee by another employer.

Example. A, who is married and files a joint return, receives $100,000 in compensation from her employer for the calendar year. B, A's spouse, receives $300,000 in compensation from his employer for the same calendar year. A's compensation is not in excess of $200,000, so A's employer does not withhold Additional Medicare Tax. B's employer is required to collect Additional Medicare Tax only with respect to compensation it pays to B that is in excess of the $200,000 threshold (that is, $100,000) for the calendar year.

(2) To the extent the employer does not collect Additional Medicare Tax imposed on the employee by section 3201(a) (as calculated under section 3101(b)(2)), the employee is liable to pay the tax.

Example. C, who is married and files a joint return, receives $190,000 in compensation from her employer for the calendar year. D, C's spouse, receives $150,000 in compensation from his employer for the same calendar year. Neither C's nor D's compensation is in excess of $200,000, so neither C's nor D's employers are required to withhold Additional Medicare Tax. C and D are liable to pay Additional Medicare Tax on $90,000 ($340,000 minus the $250,000 threshold for a joint return).

(3) If the employer deducts less than the correct amount of Additional Medicare Tax, or if it fails to deduct any part of Additional Medicare Tax, it is nevertheless liable for the correct amount of tax that it was required to withhold, unless and until the employee pays the tax. If an employee subsequently pays the tax that the employer failed to deduct, the tax will not be collected from the employer. The employer will not be relieved of its liability for payment of the tax required to be withheld unless it can show that the tax under section 3201(a) (as calculated under section 3101(b)(2)) has been paid. The employer, however, will remain subject to any applicable penalties or additions to tax resulting from the failure to withhold as required.

(h) *Effective/applicability date.*—Paragraph (g) of this section applies to quarters beginning on or after November 29, 2013. [Reg. § 31.3202-1.]

☐ [*T.D. 6516, 12-20-60. Amended by T.D. 6541, 1-20-61; T.D. 6727, 5-5-64; T.D. 8582, 12-23-94 and T.D. 9645, 11-26-2013.*]

TAX ON EMPLOYEE REPRESENTATIVES

[Reg. § 31.3211-1]

§ 31.3211-1. Measure of employee representative tax.—The employee representative tax is measured by the amount of compensation received for services rendered as an employee representative. For provisions relating to compensation, see § 31.3231(e)-1. [Reg. § 31.3211-1.]

☐ [*T.D. 8582, 12-23-94.*]

[Reg. § 31.3211-2]

§ 31.3211-2. Rates and computation of employee representative tax.—(a) *Rates.*—(1)(i) *Tier 1 tax.*—The Tier 1 employee representative tax rate equals the sum of the tax rates in effect under sections 3101(a) and 3111(a), relating to the employee and the employer tax for old-age, survivors, and disability insurance, and sections 3101(b) and 3111(b), relating to the employee and the employer tax for hospital insurance. The Tier 1 employee representative tax rate is applied to compensation up to the contribution base described in section 3231(e)(2)(B)(i). The contribution base is determined under section 230 of the Social Security Act, and is identical to the old-age, survivors, and disability insurance wage base and the hospital insurance wage base, respectively, under the Federal Insurance Contributions Act.

    (ii) *Example.*—The rule in paragraph (a)(1)(i) of this section is illustrated by the following example.

    Example. B, an employee representative received compensation of $60,000 in 1992. The sections 3101(a) and 3111(a) rates of 12.4 percent (6.2 percent plus 6.2 percent) would be applied to B's compensation up to $55,500, the applicable contribution base for 1992. The sections 3101(b) and 3111(b) rates of 2.9 percent (1.45 percent plus 1.45 percent) would be applied to the entire $60,000 of B's compensation because the applicable contribution base for 1992 is $130,200.

    (2)(i) *Tier 2 tax.*—The Tier 2 employee representative tax rate equals the percentage set forth in section 3211(a)(2) of the Code. This rate is applied up to the contribution base described in section 3231(e)(2)(B)(ii).

    (ii) *Example.*—The rule in paragraph (a)(2)(i) of this section is illustrated by the following example.

    Example. B received compensation of $60,000 in 1992. The section 3211(a)(2) rate of 14.75 percent would be applied to B's compensation up to $41,400, the applicable contribution base for 1992.

    (3) *Supplemental annuity tax.*—The supplemental annuity tax for each work-hour for which compensation is paid to an employee representative for services rendered as an employee representative is imposed at the same rate as the excise tax imposed on every employer under section 3221(c). See also § 31.3211-3.

    (b)(1) *Computation.*—The employee representative tax is computed by multiplying the amount of the employee representative's compensation with respect to which the employee representative tax is imposed by the rate applicable to such compensation, as determined under paragraph (a) of this section. The applicable rate is the rate in effect when the compensation is received by the employee representative. For rules relating to the time of receipt, see § 31.3121(a)-2 (a) and (b).

    (2) *Example.*—The rule in paragraph (b)(1) of this section is illustrated by the following example.

    Example. In 1990, employee representative B received $1,000 as remuneration for services performed for employer R in 1989. The employee representative tax is payable at the rate of 30.05 percent (15.30 percent plus 14.75 percent) in effect for 1990 (the year the compensation was received), and not the 29.77 percent rate (15.02 percent plus 14.75 percent) in effect for 1989 (the year the services were performed).

    (c)(1) *Rule where compensation is received both as an employee representative and employee.*—The following rule applies to an individual who renders service both as an employee representative and as an employee. The employee representative tax is imposed on compensation received as an employee representative under the rules described in § 31.3211-2. The employee tax is imposed on compensation received as an employee under the rules described in § 31.3201-2. However, if the total compensation received is greater than the applicable contribution base, the employee representative tax is imposed on the amount equal to the contribution base less the amount received for services rendered as an employee.

    (2) *Example.*—The rule in paragraph (c)(1) of this section is illustrated by the following example.

    Example. C performed services both as an employee and an employee representative in 1992. *C* received compensation of $40,000 as an employee and $20,000 as an employee representative. *C's* entire compensation of $40,000 is subject to tax under the rules described in § 31.3201-2. The amount of employee representative compensation subject to the section 3101(a) and the section 3111(a) rate is $15,500 ($55,500 − $40,000). The entire $20,000 is subject to the sections 3101(b) and 3111(b) rates since the combined compensation is less than $130,200, the applicable contribution base for 1992. The amount of the employee representative compensation subject to the section 3211(a)(2) rate is $1,400 ($41,400 − $40,000).

[Reg. § 31.3211-2.]

    ☐ [*T.D.* 8582, 12-23-94.]

[Reg. § 31.3211-3]

    § 31.3211-3. Employee representative supplemental tax.—See paragraphs (a), (b), and (c) of § 31.3221-3 for rules applicable to the supplemental tax for each work-hour for which compensation is paid to an employee representative for services rendered as an employee representative. [Reg. § 31.3211-3.]

    ☐ [*T.D.* 8525, 3-1-94.]

[Reg. § 31.3212-1]

    § 31.3212-1. Determination of compensation.—See § 31.3231(e)-1 for regulations applicable to compensation. [Reg. § 31.3212-1.]

TAX ON EMPLOYERS

[Reg. §31.3221-1]

§31.3221-1. Measure of employer tax.— (a) *General rule.*—The employer tax is measured by the amount of compensation paid by an employer to its employees. For provisions relating to compensation, see §31.3231(e)-1. For provisions relating to the circumstances under which certain compensation is to be disregarded for purposes of determining the employer tax, see paragraphs (b) (1) and (2) of §31.3231(e)-1.

(b) *Payments by two or more employers in excess of annual compensation limitation.*—For rules relating to payments by two or more employers in excess of the annual compensation limitation, see §31.3121(a)(1)-1.

(c) *Underpayments or overpayments.*—Any underpayment or overpayment of employer tax resulting from the employer's inability to determine, at the time such tax is paid, the correct amount of compensation with respect to which the tax should be paid shall be corrected in accordance with the provisions of Subpart G of the regulations in this part relating to adjustments, credits, refunds, and abatements. [Reg. §31.3221-1.]

☐ [*T.D.* 6516, 12-20-60. *Amended by T.D.* 6541, 1-20-61 *and T.D.* 8582, 12-23-94.]

[Reg. §31.3221-2]

§31.3221-2. Rates and computation of employer tax.—(a) *Rates.*—(1)(i) *Tier 1 tax.*—The Tier 1 employer tax rate equals the sum of the tax rates in effect under section 3111(a), relating to old-age, survivors, and disability insurance, and section 3111(b) relating to hospital insurance. The Tier 1 employer tax rate is applied to compensation up to the contribution base described in section 3231(e)(2)(B)(i). The contribution base is determined under section 230 of the Social Security Act and is identical to the old-age, survivors, and disability insurance wage base and the hospital insurance wage base, respectively, under the Federal Insurance Contributions Act.

(ii) *Example.*—The rule in paragraph (a)(1)(i) of this section is illustrated by the following example.

Example. R's employee, A, received compensation of $60,000 in 1992. The section 3111(a) rate of 6.2 percent would be applied to A's compensation up to $55,500, the applicable contribution base for 1992. The section 3111(b) rate of 1.45 percent would be applied to the entire $60,000 of A's compensation because the applicable contribution base for 1992 is $130,200.

(2)(i) *Tier 2 tax.*—The Tier 2 employer tax rate equals the percentage set forth in section 3221(b) of the Internal Revenue Code. This rate is applied up to the contribution base described in section 3231(e)(2)(B)(ii).

(ii) *Example.*—The rule in paragraph (a)(2)(i) of this section is illustrated by the following example.

Example. R's employee, A, received compensation of $60,000 in 1992. The section 3221(b) rate of 16.10 percent would be applied to A's compensation up to $41,400, the applicable contribution base for 1992.

(3) *Supplemental annuity tax.*—The supplemental annuity tax for each work-hour for which compensation is paid by an employer for services rendered during any calendar quarter by employees is imposed at the tax rate determined each calendar quarter by the Railroad Retirement Board. See also §31.3221-3.

(b)(1) *Computation.*—The employer tax is computed by multiplying the amount of the compensation with respect to which the employer tax is imposed by the rate applicable to such compensation, as determined under paragraph (a) of this section. The applicable rate is the rate in effect at the time the compensation is paid. For rules relating to the time of payment, see §31.3121(a)-2(a) and (b).

(2) *Example.*—The rule in paragraph (b)(1) of this section is illustrated by the following example.

Example. In 1990, R's employee A received $1,000 as remuneration for services performed for R in 1989. The employer tax is payable at the rate of 23.75 percent (7.65 percent plus 16.10 percent) in effect for 1990 (the year the compensation was received) and not the 23.61 percent rate (7.51 percent plus 16.10 percent) in effect for 1989 (the year the services were performed). [Reg. §31.3221-2.]

☐ [*T.D.* 8582, 12-23-94.]

[Reg. §31.3221-3]

§31.3221-3. Supplemental tax.— (a) *Introduction.*—(1) *In general.*—Section 3221(c) imposes an excise tax on every employer, as defined in section 3231(a) and §31.3231(a)-1, with respect to individuals employed by the employer. The tax is imposed for each work-hour for which the employer pays compensation, as defined in section 3231(e) and §31.3231(e)-1, for services rendered to the employer during a calendar quarter. This §31.3221-3 provides rules for determining the number of taxable work-hours.

(2) *Overview.*—Paragraph (b) of this section defines *work-hours.* Paragraph (c) of this section demonstrates the calculation of work-hours. Paragraph (d) of this section offers a safe harbor calculation of work-hours for use by any employer in lieu of calculating the number of work-hours for each employee.

(b) *Definition of work-hours.*—(1) *In general.*—For purposes of section 3221(c) and this section, *work-hours* are hours for which the employee is compensated, whether or not the employee performs services.

(i) *Payments included in work-hours.*—Work-hours include regular time worked; overtime; time paid for vacations and holidays; time allowed for meals; away-from-home terminal time; called and not used, runaround, and deadheading time; time for attending court, participating in investigations, and attending claim and safety meetings; and guaranteed time not worked. Work-hours also include conversion hours, that is, compensation converted into work-hours. Conversion hours may be derived from payment by the mile or by the piece. Work-hours also include time for which the employee is paid for periods of absence not due to sickness or accident disability, such as for routine medical and dental examinations or for time lost.

(ii) *Payments excluded from work-hours.*—Certain kinds of payments are not subject to conversion into work-hours. These include those payments that are specifically excluded from compensation within the meaning of section 3231(e), such as certain sick pay payments (section 3231(e)(1)(i)); tips (section 3231(e)(1)(ii)); and amounts paid specifically (either as an advance, as reimbursement, or allowance) for traveling expenses (section 3231(e)(1)(iii)). Traveling expenses paid under a nonaccountable plan are excluded from work-hours even though they are includible in compensation. See §31.3231(e)-1(a)(5). Also excluded from work-hours are amounts representing bonuses, amounts received pursuant to the exercise of an employee stock option, and all separation payments or severance allowances.

(2) *Hourly compensation.*—Because the tax under section 3221(c) is calculated on the basis of work-hours, the number of hours for which an employee receives compensation is the figure used to determine work-hours. In the case of an hourly-rated employee, each hour for which the employee receives compensation is one work-hour.

(3) *Daily, weekly, monthly compensation.*—(i) If an employee is paid by the day, week, month, or other period of time, the tax is imposed on the number of hours comprehended in the rate and, if any, the number of overtime hours for which additional compensation is paid. Thus, in the case of an office worker who receives an annual salary based on an 8-hour, 5-day-a-week work schedule that includes paid holidays, vacations, and sick time, the number of work-hours for one month is 174 (2088 hours/year ÷ 12 months).

(ii) The rule in paragraph (b)(3)(i) of this section is illustrated by the following examples.

Example 1. A, an office worker, receives an annual salary that is paid monthly. The salary is based on an 8-hour, Monday through Friday work schedule. *A* is not paid for overtime hours. *A* is not expected to work on holidays, during *A*'s annual vacation, or during periods that *A* is ill. The number of work-hours for one month is 174 (2088 hours/year ÷ 12 months). This figure remains constant, even though some months have more workdays than others.

Example 2. B is paid a stated amount for each day *B* works, regardless of the number of hours worked. However, if *B* works more than 8

hours during any day, *B* is paid overtime for each additional hour worked that day. *B* is not paid for holidays, vacations, or sick time. During May, *B* worked 6 hours on 4 days, 7 hours on 6 days, 8 hours on 6 days, and 9 hours on 5 days. Because *B* is paid a daily rate for up to 8 hours, 8 hours are comprehended in the daily rate. Therefore, the number of work-hours for May is 173 (21 days × 8 hours/day + 5 overtime hours), even though *B* actually worked 159 hours.

(4) *Conversion hours.*—(i) Compensation not based on time (hour, day, month, etc.), such as compensation paid by the mile or by the piece, must be converted into the number of hours represented by the compensation paid. Thus, if an employee is paid by the mile, 1 work-hour equals the number of miles constituting a workday, divided by 8 hours. However, in the case of a collective bargaining agreement that specifies a number of hours as constituting a workday, the number of hours specified under the agreement may be used instead of 8.

(ii) The rule in paragraph (b)(4)(i) of this section is illustrated by the following example.

Example. C's normal workday consists of 2 150-mile round trips that together take 6 hours. *C* is paid by the mile. The collective bargaining agreement does not specify the number of hours in a workday. Thus, the number of work-hours for each day *C* works is 8, or 1 work-hour for each 37.5 miles (300 miles/day ÷ 8 hours/day)). If the applicable collective bargaining agreement specifies that 6 hours constitute a workday, the number of work-hours for each day *C* works would be 6.

(c) *Calculation of work-hours.*—(1) An employer may calculate the work-hours separately for each employee, as described in the examples in this paragraph. If the employer chooses to calculate work-hours separately for each employee, the employer must calculate the number of regular hours, overtime hours, and conversion hours for each employee for each month. In lieu of separate calculations, the employer may calculate the work-hours for all the employer's employees using the safe harbor formula described in paragraph (d) of this section.

(2) The rules in paragraph (c) of this section are illustrated by the following examples.

Example 1. D worked 8 hours a day, Monday through Friday, during the months of February and March 1992. *D* did not work on President's Day, but was paid for the holiday. *D*'s work-hours for February were 160 (19 days × 8 hours a day + 8 holiday hours). *D*'s work-hours for March were 176 (22 days × 8 hours a day).

Example 2. E worked 7-hour shifts every Tuesday through Saturday during the months of February and March 1992. *E* also worked 7 overtime hours during February and 21 overtime hours during March. Also, *E* was paid for 7 hours on President's Day, even though *E* did not work on that day. The number of work-hours for February was 161 (21 days × 7 hours a day + 7 overtime hours + 7 holiday hours). The number of work-hours for March was 168 (21 days × 7 hours a day + 21 overtime hours). Because *E* receives an hourly wage and was paid for the President's Day holiday, the number of hours (7) for which *E* was paid are added to the hours *E* actually worked. If *E* had worked on President's Day and had received extra pay for working on a holiday and holiday pay for 7 hours, the employer would include 14 hours in *E*'s work-hours for that day, the 7 hours *E* actually worked and the 7 holiday hours for which *E* was paid.

Example 3. Employment beginning during month. *F* began employment on March 16, a Monday, and worked 8 hours a day, Monday through Friday. The employer calculates that *F*'s hours for the month were 96, because *F* worked 12 8-hour days during the month. If March 16 were on a Friday, the employer would calculate 11 days, or 88 hours.

Example 4. Employment ending during month. *G*'s last day of employment was Friday, March 13. *G* worked 8 hours a day, Monday through Friday, except for March 3, when *G* was ill. *G* was paid for 8 hours for March 3. The employer calculates that *G*'s work-hours for March were 80, because *G* worked 9 8-hour days and was paid for an additional 8 hours.

(d) *Safe harbor.*—(1) *In general.*—In lieu of calculating work-hours separately for each employee, an employer may use the safe harbor for all employees. If the employer elects to use the safe harbor for a calendar year, the employer must use the safe harbor for all employees for the entire calendar year. If an employer uses the safe harbor for a calendar year, the employer need not elect the safe harbor for the following calendar year. An employer that elects the safe harbor for a calendar year may not subsequently elect to separately calculate employee work-hours for that calendar year.

(2) *Method of calculation.*—The safe harbor treats each employee of the employer as receiving monthly compensation for a number of hours equal to the safe harbor number. To determine the number of work-hours for a month, the employer multiplies the safe harbor number by the number that equals the total number of employees to whom the employer paid compensation during the month.

(i) *Safe harbor number defined.*—The safe harbor number is the number established in guidance of general applicability promulgated by the Commissioner.

(ii) *Employee defined.*—Solely for purposes of this paragraph, an employee is any individual who is paid compensation, within the meaning of § 31.3231(e)-1, regardless of the amount, during the month. Thus, for example, a part-time, temporary, or seasonal employee is counted as an employee. A terminated employee is counted in the month of termination (provided the terminated employee received compensation in the month of termination), but not in any subsequent month in which the employee does not perform service for the employer as an em-

ployee, even if the terminated employee is paid compensation in a subsequent month. Thus, for example, an employee who terminates employment during the month, receives compensation during the month of termination, and receives a final paycheck the following month is counted as an employee of the employer for the month of termination but not for the following month.

(3) *Method of election.*—An employer makes the safe harbor election for a calendar year on the employment tax return filed for the previous calendar year.

(4) *Additional rules.*—The Commissioner may, in revenue procedures, revenue rulings, notices, or other guidance of general applicability, revise the safe harbor number or provide additional safe harbors that satisfy section 3221(c).

(e) *Effective dates.*—This § 31.3221-3 is effective for calendar years beginning after December 31, 1992, except that paragraph (d) is effective for calendar years beginning after December 31, 1993. Taxpayers may apply the rules in paragraphs (a), (b), and (c) of this section before January 1, 1993. [Reg. § 31.3221-3.]

☐ [T.D. 8525, 3-1-94.]

[Reg. § 31.3221-4]

§ 31.3221-4. Exception from supplemental tax.—(a) *General rule.*—Section 3221(d) provides an exception from the excise tax imposed by section 3221(c). Under this exception, the excise tax imposed by section 3221(c) does not apply to an employer with respect to employees who are covered by a supplemental pension plan, as defined in paragraph (b) of this section, that is established pursuant to an agreement reached through collective bargaining between the employer and employees, within the meaning of paragraph (c) of this section.

(b) *Definition of supplemental pension plan.*—(1) *In general.*—A plan is a supplemental pension plan covered by the section 3221(d) exception described in paragraph (a) of this section only if it meets the requirements of paragraphs (b)(2) through (b)(4) of this section.

(2) *Pension benefit requirement.*—A plan is a supplemental pension plan within the meaning of this section only if the plan is a pension plan within the meaning of § 1.401-1(b)(1)(i) of this chapter. Thus, a plan is a supplemental pension plan only if the plan provides for the payment of definitely determinable benefits to employees over a period of years, usually for life, after retirement. A plan need not be funded through a qualified trust that meets the requirements of section 401(a) or an annuity contract that meets the requirements of section 403(a) in order to meet the requirements of this paragraph (b)(2). A plan that is a profit-sharing plan within the meaning of § 1.401-1(b)(1)(ii) of this chapter or a stock bonus plan within the meaning of § 1.401-1(b)(1)(iii) of this chapter is not a supplemental pension plan within the meaning of this paragraph (b).

(3) *Railroad Retirement Board determination with respect to the plan.*—A plan is a supplemental pension plan within the meaning of this paragraph (b) with respect to an employee only during any period for which the Railroad Retirement Board has made a determination under 20 CFR 216.42(d) that the plan is a private pension, the payments from which will result in a reduction in the employee's supplemental annuity payable under 45 U.S.C. 231a(b). A plan is not a supplemental pension plan for any time period before the Railroad Retirement Board has made such a determination, or after that determination is no longer in force.

(4) *Other requirements.*—[Reserved]

(c) *Collective bargaining agreement.*—A plan is established pursuant to a collective bargaining agreement with respect to an employee only if, in accordance with the rules of § 1.410(b)-6(d)(2) of this chapter, the employee is included in a unit of employees covered by an agreement that the Secretary of Labor finds to be a collective bargaining agreement between employee representatives and one or more employers, provided that there is evidence that retirement benefits were the subject of good faith bargaining between employee representatives and the employer or employers.

(d) *Substitute section 3221(d) excise tax.*—Section 3221(d) imposes an excise tax on any employer who has been excepted from the excise tax imposed under section 3221(c) by the application of section 3221(d) and paragraph (a) of this section with respect to an employee. The excise tax is equal to the amount of the supplemental annuity paid to that employee under 45 U.S.C. 231a(b), plus a percentage thereof determined by the Railroad Retirement Board to be sufficient to cover the administrative costs attributable to such payments under 45 U.S.C. 231a(b).

(e) *Effective date.*—(1) *In general.*—Except as provided in paragraph (e)(2) of this section, this section applies beginning on October 1, 1998.

(2) *Delayed effective date for collective bargaining agreement provisions.*—Paragraph (c) of this section applies beginning on January 1, 2000. [Reg. § 31.3221-4.]

☐ [*T.D.* 8832, 8-5-99.]

GENERAL PROVISIONS

[Reg. § 31.3231(a)-1]

§ 31.3231(a)-1. Who are employers.—(a) Each of the following persons is an employer within the meaning of the act:

(1) Any carrier, that is, any express carrier, sleeping car carrier, or rail carrier providing transportation subject to subchapter I of chapter 105 of title 49;

(2) Any company—

(i) Which is directly or indirectly owned or controlled by one or more employers as defined in paragraph (a)(1) of this section, or under common control therewith, and

(ii) Which operates any equipment or facility or performs any service (except trucking service, casual service, and the casual operation of equipment or facilities) in connection with—

(a) The transportation of passengers or property by railroad, or

(b) The receipt, delivery, elevation, transfer in transit, refrigeration or icing, storage, or handling of property transported by railroad;

(3) Any receiver, trustee, or other individual or body, judicial or otherwise, when in the possession of the property or operating all or any part of the business of any employer as defined in paragraph (a)(1) or (2) of this section;

(4) Any railroad association, traffic association, tariff bureau, demurrage bureau, weighing and inspection bureau, collection agency, and any other association, bureau, agency, or organization controlled and maintained wholly or principally by two or more employers as defined in paragraph (a)(1), (2) or (3) of this section and engaged in the performance of services in connection with or incidental to railroad transportation;

(5) Any railway labor organization, national in scope, which has been or may be organized in accordance with the provisions of the Railway Labor Act; and

(6) Any subordinate unit of a national railway-labor-organization employer, that is, any State or National legislative committee, general committee, insurance department, or local lodge or division, of an employer as defined in paragraph (a)(5) of this section, established pursuant to the constitution and bylaws of such employer.

(b) As used in paragraph (a)(2) of this section, the term "controlled" includes direct or indirect control, whether legally enforceable and however exercisable or exercised. The control may be by means of stock ownership, or by agreements, licenses, or any other devices which insure that the operation of the company is in the interest of one or more carriers. It is the reality of the control, however, which is decisive, not its form nor the mode of its exercise.

(c) As used in paragraph (a)(2) of this section, the term *casual* applies when the service rendered or the operation of equipment or facilities by a controlled company or person in connection with the transportation of passengers or property by railroad is so irregular or infrequent as to afford no substantial basis for an inference that such service or operation will be repeated, or whenever such service or operation is insubstantial.

(d) The term "employer" does not include any street, interurban, or suburban electric railway, unless such railway is operating as a part of a general steam-railroad system of transportation, but shall not exclude any part of the general steam-railroad system of transportation which is operated by any other motive power.

(e) The term "employer" does not include any company by reason of its being engaged in the mining of coal, the supplying of coal to an employer where delivery is not beyond the mine tipple and the operation of equipment or facilities for such mining or supplying of coal, or in any of such activities.

(f) Any company that is described in paragraph (a)(2) of this section is an employer under section 3231. In certain cases, based on all the facts and circumstances, it may be appropriate to segregate those businesses engaged in rail services and therefore subject to the Railroad Retirement Tax Act from those businesses engaged exclusively in nonrail services and therefore not subject to the Railroad Retirement Tax Act. The factors considered are set forth in guidance published by the Internal Revenue Service. [Reg. § 31.3231(a)-1.]

☐ [*T.D.* 6516, 12-20-60. *Amended by T.D.* 8582, 12-23-94.]

[Reg. §31.3231(b)-1]

§31.3231(b)-1. Who are employees.—(a) *In general.*—(1) An individual who is in the service of one or more employers for compensation is an employee within the meaning of the act. (For definitions of the terms "employer", "service", and "compensation", see subsections (a), (d), and (e), respectively, of section 3231.) An individual is in the service of an employer, with respect to services rendered for compensation, if—

(i) He is subject to the continuing authority of the employer to supervise and direct the manner in which he renders such services; or

(ii) He is rendering professional or technical services and is integrated into the staff of the employer; or

(iii) He is rendering, on the property used in the employer's operations, other personal services the rendition of which is integrated into the employer's operations.

(2) In order that an individual may be in the service of an employer within the meaning of paragraph (a)(1)(i) of this section, it is not necessary that the employer actually direct or control the manner in which the services are rendered; it is sufficient if the employer has the right to do so. The right of an employer to discharge an individual is also an important factor indicating that the individual is subject to the continuing authority of the employer to supervise and direct the manner of rendition of the services. Other factors indicating that an individual is subject to the continuing authority of the employer to supervise and direct the manner of rendition of the services are the furnishing of tools and the furnishing of a place to work by the employer to the individual who renders the services.

(3) In general, if an individual is subject to the control or direction of an employer merely as to the result to be accomplished by the work and not as to the means and methods for accomplishing the result, he is an independent contractor. On individual performing services as an independent contractor is not, as to such services, in the service of an employer within the meaning of paragraph (a)(1)(i) of this section. However, an individual performing services as an independent contractor may be, as to such services, in the service of an employer within the meaning of paragraph (a)(1) (ii) or (iii) of this section.

(4) Whether or not an individual is an employee will be determined upon an examination of the particular facts of the case.

(5) If an individual is an employee, it is of no consequence that he is designated as a partner, coadventurer, agent, independent contractor, or otherwise, or that he performs services on a part-time basis.

(6) No distinction is made between classes or grades of employees. Thus, superintendents, managers, and other supervisory personnel are employees within the meaning of the act. An officer of an employer is an employee, but a director as such is not.

(7) In determining whether an individual is an employee with respect to services rendered within the United States, the citizenship or residence of the individual, or the place where the contract of service was entered into is immaterial.

(8) If an individual performs services for an employer (other than a local lodge or division or a general committee of a railway-labor-organization employer) which does not conduct the principal part of its business within the United States, such individual shall be deemed to be in the service of such employer only to the extent that he performs services for it in the United States. Thus, with respect to services rendered for such employer outside the United States, such individual is not in the service of an employer.

(9) If an individual performs services for an employer (other than a local lodge or division or a general committee of a railway-labor-organization employer) which conducts the principal part of its business within the United States, he is in the service of such employer whether his services are rendered within or without the United States. In the case of an individual, not a citizen or resident of the United States, rendering services in a place outside the United States to an employer which is required under the laws applicable in such place to employ, in whole or in part, citizens or residents thereof, such individual shall not be deemed to be in the service of an employer with respect to services so rendered.

(10) The term "employee" does not include any individual while he is engaged in the physical operations consisting of the mining of coal, the preparation of coal, the handling (other than movement by rail with standard railroad locomotives) of coal not beyond the mine tipple, or the loading of coal at the tipple.

Reg. §31.3231(b)-1(a)(10)

(b) *Employees of local lodges or divisions of railway-labor-organization employers.*—(1) An individual is in the service of a local lodge or division of a railway-labor-organization employer (see paragraph (a)(6) of §31.3231(a)-1) only if—

(i) All, or substantially all, the individuals constituting the membership of such local lodge or division are employees of an employer conducting the principal part of its business in the United States; or

(ii) The headquarters of such local lodge or division is located in the United States.

(2)(i) An individual in the service of a local lodge or division is not an employee within the meaning of the act unless he was, on or after August 29, 1935, in the service of a carrier (see §31.3231(g) for definition of carrier) or he was, on August 29, 1935, in the "employment relation" to a carrier.

(ii) An individual shall be deemed to have been in the employment relation to a carrier on August 29, 1935, if (a) he was on that date on leave of absence from his employment expressly granted to him by the carrier by whom he was employed, or by a duly authorized representative or such carrier, and the grant of such leave of absence was established to the satisfaction of the Railroad Retirement Board before July 1947; or (b) he was in the service of a carrier after August 29, 1935, and before January 1946 in each of six calendar months whether or not consecutive; or (c) before August 29, 1935, he did not retire and was not retired or discharged from the service of the last carrier by whom he was employed or its corporate or operating successor, but (1) solely by reason of his physical or mental disability he ceased before August 29, 1935, to be in the service of such carrier and thereafter remained continuously disabled until he attained age sixty-five or until August 1945, or (2) solely for such last stated reason a carrier by whom he was employed before August 29, 1935, or a carrier who is its successor did not on or after August 29, 1935, and before August 1945 call him to return to service, or (3) if he was so called he was solely for such reason unable to render service in six calendar months as provided in (b) of this subdivision; or (d) he was on August 29, 1935, absent from the service of a carrier by reason of a discharge which, within one year after the effective date thereof, was protested, to an appropriate labor representative or to the carrier, as wrongful, and which was followed within 10 years of the effective date thereof by his reinstatement in good faith to his former service with all his seniority rights. However, an individual shall not be deemed to have been in the employment relation to a carrier on August 29, 1935, if before that date he was granted a pension or gratuity on the basis of which a pension was awarded to him pursuant to section 6 of the Railroad Retirement Act of 1937 (45 U.S.C. 228f), or if during the last payroll period before August 29, 1935, in which he rendered service to a carrier he was not, with respect to any service

in such payroll period, in the service of an employer (see paragraph (a) of this section).

(c) *Employees of general committees of railway-labor-organization employers.*—An individual is in the service of a general committee of a railway-labor-organization employer (see paragraph (a)(6) of §31.3231(a)-1) only if—

(1) He is representing a local lodge or division described in paragraph (b)(1) of this section; or

(2) All, or substantially all, the individuals represented by such general committee are employees of an employer conducting the principal part of its business in the United States; or

(3) He acts in the capacity of a general chairman or an assistant general chairman of a general committee which represents individuals rendering service in the United States to an employer. In such case, if his office or headquarters is not located in the United States and the individuals represented by such general committee are employees of an employer not conducting the principal part of its business in the United States, only a part of his remuneration for such service shall be regarded as compensation. The part of his remuneration regarded as compensation shall be in the same proportion to his total remuneration as the mileage in the United States under the jurisdiction of such general committee bears to the total mileage under its jurisdiction, unless such mileage formula is inapplicable, in which case such other formula as the Railroad Retirement Board may have prescribed pursuant to section 1(c) of the Railroad Retirement Act of 1937 (45 U.S.C. 228a) shall be applicable. However, no part of his remuneration for such service shall be regarded as compensation if the application of such mileage formula, or such other formula as the Railroad Retirement Board may have prescribed, would result in his compensation for the service being less than 10 percent of his remuneration for such service. [Reg. §31.3231(b)-1.]

[Reg. §31.3231(c)-1]

§31.3231(c)-1. Who are employee representatives.—(a) An employee representative within the meaning of the act is—

(1) Any officer or official representative of a railway labor organization which is not included as an employer under section 3231(a) who—

(i) Was in the service of an employer either before or after June 29, 1937, and

(ii) Is duly authorized and designated to represent employees in accordance with the Railway Labor Act.

For railway labor organizations which are employers under section 3231(a), see paragraph (a) (5) and (6) of §31.3231(a)-1.

(2) Any individual who is regularly assigned to or regularly employed by an employee representative, as defined in paragraph (a)(1) of this section, in connection with the duties of such employee representative's office.

(b) In determining whether an individual is an employee representative, his citizenship or residence is material only insofar as those factors may affect the determination of whether he was "in the service of an employer" (see paragraph (a) of §31.3231(b)-1). [Reg. §31.3231(c)-1.]

[Reg. §31.3231(d)-1]

§31.3231(d)-1. **Service.**—See §31.3231(b)-1 for regulations relating to the term "in the service of an employer." [Reg. §31.3231(d)-1.]

[Reg. §31.3231(e)-1]

§31.3231(e)-1. **Compensation.**—
(a) *Definition.*—(1) The term *compensation* has the same meaning as the term *wages* in section 3121(a), determined without regard to section 3121(b)(9), except as specifically limited by the Railroad Retirement Tax Act (chapter 22 of the Internal Revenue Code) or regulation. The Commissioner may provide any additional guidance that may be necessary or appropriate in applying the definitions of sections 3121(a) and 3231(e).

(2) A payment made by an employer to an individual through the employer's payroll is presumed, in the absence of evidence to the contrary, to be compensation for services rendered as an employee of the employer. Likewise, a payment made by an employee organization to an employee representative through the organization's payroll is presumed, in the absence of evidence to the contrary, to be compensation for services rendered by the employee representative as such. For rules regarding the treatment of deductions by an employer from remuneration of an employee, see §31.3123-1.

(3) The term *compensation* is not confined to amounts paid for active service, but includes amounts paid for an identifiable period during which the employee is absent from the active service of the employer and, in the case of an employee representative, amounts paid for an identifiable period during which the employee representative is absent from the active service of the employee organization.

(4) Compensation includes amounts paid to an employee for loss of earnings during an identifiable period as the result of the displacement of the employee to a less remunerative position or occupation as well as pay for time lost.

(5) For rules regarding the treatment of reimbursement and other expense allowance amounts, see §31.3121(a)-3. For rules regarding the inclusion of fringe benefits in compensation, see §31.3121(a)-1T.

(6) *Split-dollar life insurance arrangements.*— See §§1.61-22 and 1.7872-15 of this chapter for rules relating to the treatment of split-dollar life insurance arrangements.

(b) *Special rules.*—(1) If the amount of compensation earned in any calendar month by an individual as an employee in the service of a local lodge or division of a railway-labor-organization employer is less than $25, the amount is disregarded for purposes of determining the employee tax under section 3201 and the employer tax under section 3221.

(2) Compensation for service as a delegate to a national or international convention of a railway-labor-organization employer is disregarded for purposes of determining the employee tax under section 3201 and the employer tax under section 3221 if the individual rendering the service has not previously rendered service, other than as a delegate, which may be included in the individual's years of service for purposes of the Railroad Retirement Act.

(3) For special provisions relating to the compensation of certain general chairs or assistant general chairs of a general committee of a railway-labor-organization employer, see paragraph (c)(3) of §31.3231(b)-1. [Reg. §31.3231(e)-1.]

☐ *T.D.* 8582, 12-23-94. *Amended by T.D.* 9092, 9-11-2003.]

[Reg. §31.3231(e)-2]

§31.3231(e)-2. **Contribution base.**—The term *compensation* does not include any remuneration paid during any calendar year by an employer to an employee for services rendered in excess of the applicable contribution base. For rules applying this provision, see §31.3121(a)(1)-1. [Reg. §31.3231(e)-2.]

☐ [*T.D.* 8582, 12-23-94.]

Federal Unemployment Tax Act

See p. 20,601 for regulations not amended to reflect law changes

[Reg. §31.3301-1]

§31.3301-1. **Persons liable for tax.**—Every person who is an employer as defined in section 3306(a) (see §31.3306(a)-1) is liable for the tax. Even if an employer is not subject to any State unemployment compensation law, he or she is nevertheless liable for the tax. However, if the employer is subject to such a State law, he or she may be entitled to certain credits against the tax (see §§31.3302(a)-1 to 31.3302(c)-1, inclusive). For provisions relating to payment of the tax, see Subpart G of the regulations in this part. [Reg. §31.3301-1.]

☐ [*T.D.* 6199, 9-5-56. *Republished in T.D.* 6516, 12-20-60.]

[Reg. §31.3301-2]

§31.3301-2. **Measure of tax.**—The tax for any calendar year is measured by the amount of wages paid by the employer during such year with respect to employment after December 31, 1938. (See §31.3306(b)-1, relating to wages, and §§31.3306(c)-1 to 31.3306(c)-3, inclusive, relating to employment.) [Reg. §31.3301-2.]

☐ [*T.D.* 6199, 9-5-56. *Republished in T.D.* 6516, 12-20-60; *T.D.* 6658, 6-27-63.]

>>>→ *Caution: Reg. §31.3301-3 does not reflect P.L. 91-373, P.L. 92-329, P.L. 94-566, P.L. 100-203 or P.L. 105-33.*

[Reg. §31.3301-3]

§31.3301-3. Rate and computation of tax.—
(a) The rates of tax with respect to wages paid in calendar years after 1954 are as follows:

	Percent
In the calendar years 1955 to 1960, both inclusive	3
In the calendar year 1961	3.1
In the calendar year 1962	3.5
In the calendar year 1963	3.35
In the calendar year 1964 and subsequent calendar years . . .	3.1

(b) The tax is computed by applying to the wages paid in calendar year, with respect to employment after December 31, 1938, the rate in effect at the time the wages are paid. [Reg. §31.3301-3.]

☐ [*T.D.* 6199, 9-5-56. *Republished in T.D. 6516,* 12-20-60; *T.D.* 6658, 6-27-63.]

[Reg. §31.3301-4]

§31.3301-4. When wages are paid.—Wages are paid when actually or constructively paid. Wages are constructively paid when they are credited to the account of or set apart for an employee so that they may be drawn upon by him at any time although not then actually reduced to possession. To constitute payment in such a case the wages must be credited to or set apart for the employee without any substantial limitation or restriction as to the time or manner of payment or condition upon which payment is to be made, and must be made available to him so that they may be drawn upon at any time, and their payment brought within his own control and disposition. See §31.6011(a)-3, relating to the return on which wages are to be reported. [Reg. §31.3301-4.]

☐ [*T.D.* 6199, 9-5-56. *Republished in T.D. 6516,* 12-20-60.]

>>>→ *Caution: Reg. §31.3302(a)-1 does not reflect P.L. 91-373, P.L. 92-329 and P.L. 94-566.*

[Reg. §31.3302(a)-1]

§31.3302(a)-1. Credit against tax for contributions paid.—(a) *In general.*—Subject to the provisions of paragraphs (b) and (c) of this section and to the provisions of §31.3302(c)-1, the taxpayer may credit against the tax for any taxable year the total amount of contributions paid by him into an unemployment fund maintained during such year under a State law which has been found by the Secretary of Labor to contain the provisions specified in section 3304(a); *Provided, however,* That no credit may be taken for contributions under a State law if such State has not been duly certified for the calendar year to the Secretary of the Treasury by the Secretary of Labor. The contributions may be credited against the tax whether or not they are paid with respect to employment as defined in section 3306(c). For provisions relating to additional credit against the tax, see §31.3302(b)-1.

(b) *Limitation on the taxable year with respect to which contributions are allowable.*—In order to be allowable as credit against the tax for any taxable year, the contributions must have been paid with respect to such year.

Example (1). Under the unemployment compensation law of State X, employer M is required to report in his contribution return for the quarter ending December 31, 1955, all remuneration payable for services rendered in such quarter. A portion of such remuneration is not paid to his employees until February 1, 1956. On January 20, 1056, M pays to the State the total amount of contributions due with respect to all remuneration so required to be reported. Such contributions, including those with respect to the remuneration paid on February 1, 1956, may be included in computing the credit against the tax for the calendar year 1955. This is true even though the remuneration paid on February 1, 1956 (if it constitutes "wages") is required to be

reported in the Federal return for 1956 and not in the Federal return for 1955.

Example (2). Under the unemployment compensation law of State Y, employer N is required to include in his contribution return for the quarter ending December 31, 1955, certain remuneration paid on December 30, 1955, to an employee for services to be rendered after December 31. On January 20, 1956, N pays to the State the total amount of contributions due with respect to all remuneration required to be reported on the contribution return. Such contributions, including those with respect to the remuneration paid on December 30, 1955, may be included in computing the credit against the tax for the calendar year 1955.

(c) *Limitation on amount of credit allowable based on time when contributions are paid.*—(1) *In general.*—The amount of credit allowable for contributions paid into a State unemployment fund depends in part on the time of payment of such contributions. Although contributions paid at any time may be credited against the tax (subject to the limitations referred to in subparagraphs (2) and (3) of this paragraph), no refund or credit of the tax based on credit for contributions paid will be allowed unless the contributions are paid prior to the expiration of the period of limitations applicable to refund or credit of the tax. For general provisions relating to the limitation period and to refunds, credits and abatements of the tax, see respectively §§301.6511(a)-1, 301.6402-2 and 301.6404-1 of this chapter (Regulations on Procedure and Administration).

(2) *Amount of credit allowable when contributions are paid on or before last day for filing return.*—Contributions paid into a State unemployment fund on or before the last day upon which the Federal return for the taxable year is required to be filed may be credited against the tax in an amount equal to such contributions, but not,

however, to exceed the total credits determined pursuant to §31.3302(c)-1. For provisions relating to the time for filing the return, see §31.6071(a)-1 in Subpart G of this part.

(3) *Amount of credit allowable when contributions are paid after last day for filing return.*—Contributions paid into a State unemployment fund after the last day upon which the Federal return for the taxable year is required to be filed may be credited against the tax in an amount not to exceed 90 percent of the amount which would have been allowable as credit on account of such contributions had they been paid into a State unemployment fund on or before such last day. However, see subparagraph (4) of this paragraph relating to the payment of contributions to the wrong State. For general provisions relating to refunds, credits, or abatements of the tax, see §§301.6402-2 and 301.6404-1 of this chapter (Regulations on Procedure and Administration).

Example (1). The Federal return of the M Company for the calendar year 1961 discloses total wages of $400,000. The Federal tax, imposed at the rate of 3.1 percent, is $12,400. The company is liable for total State contributions of $8,000 for 1961. The due date of the Federal return is January 31, 1962, no extension of time for filing the return having been granted. The contributions are not paid until February 1, 1962. If the contributions had been paid on or before January 31, 1962, the entire amount of $8,000 could have been credited against the tax. (Credits could not exceed 2.7 percent of the wages, or $10,800. See §31.3302(c)-1.) Since the contributions were paid after January 31, 1962, the M Company is entitled to a credit of 90 percent of the amount which would have been allowable as credit had the contributions been paid on time (90 percent of $8,000, or $7,200), the net liability for Federal tax being $5,200 ($12,400 minus $7,200).

Example (2). The facts are the same as in example (1), except that the M Company is liable for and pays total State contributions of $12,000, instead of $8,000. If the contributions had been paid on or before January 31, 1962, the amount allowable as credit would have been $10,800 (2.7 percent of wages of $400,000). Since the contributions were paid after January 31, 1962, the M Company is entitled to a credit of 90 percent of $10,800, or $9,720, the net liability for Federal tax being $2,680 ($12,400 minus $9,720).

Example (3). The Federal return of the R Company for the calendar year 1961 discloses a total tax of $3,100. The company is liable for total State contributions of $2,700 for such year. The due date of the Federal return is January 31, 1962, no extension of time for filing the return having been granted. The R Company pays $1,700 of the total State contributions on or before such date, and the remaining $1,000 on February 1, 1962. If the $1,000 had been paid on or before January 31, 1962, that amount could have been credited against the tax (such amount plus the $1,700 paid on or before January 31,

1962, not exceeding the aggregate credit allowable). Since the $1,000 was paid after January 31, 1962, the R Company is entitled to a credit of 90 percent of this amount or $900, plus the credit of $1,700 allowable for the contributions paid on or before January 31, 1962. The net liability for Federal tax is thus $500 ($3,100 minus $2,600).

(4) *Amount of credit allowable when contributions are paid to wrong State.*—Contributions for the taxable year paid into a State unemployment fund which are required under the unemployment compensation law of that State, but which are paid with respect to remuneration on the basis of which the taxpayer had, prior to such payment, erroneously paid an amount as contributions under another unemployment compensation law, shall be deemed for purposes of the credit to have been paid at the time of the erroneous payment. If, by reason of such other law, the taxpayer was entitled to cease paying contributions for such taxable year with respect to services subject to such other law, the payment into the proper fund shall be deemed for purposes of credit to have been made on the date the Federal return for such year was actually filed by the taxpayer under §31.6011(a)-(3).

Example. Employer N, whose Federal return for the calendar year 1961 discloses a total tax of $3,100, employs individuals in State X and State Y during the calendar year 1961. N assumes in good faith that the services of his employees are covered by the unemployment compensation law of State Y, and pays as contributions to State Y the amount of $2,700 based upon the remuneration of the employees. All of the services were in fact covered by the unemployment compensation law of State X, and none by the law of State Y. The payment to State Y was made on January 31, 1962. When the error was discovered thereafter, N paid to State X contributions in the amount of $2,700 based upon such remuneration. Since the contributions were paid to State Y on January 31, 1962, the contributions to State X are, for purposes of the credit, deemed to have been paid on such date. N is entitled to a credit of $2,700 against the Federal tax of $3,100, the net liability for Federal tax being $400 ($3,100 minus $2,700). [Reg. §31.3302(a)-1.]

☐ [*T.D.* 6199, 9-5-56. *Republished in T.D.* 6516, 12-20-60; *T.D.* 6658, 6-27-63.]

[Reg. §31.3302(a)-2]

§31.3302(a)-2. Refund of State contributions.—If, subsequent to the filing of the return, a refund is made by a State to the taxpayer of any part of his contribution credited against the tax, the taxpayer is required to advise the district director of the date and amount of such refund and the reason therefor, and to pay the tax, if any, due as a result of such refund, together with interest from the date when the tax was due. [Reg. §31.3302(a)-2.]

☐ [*T.D.* 6199, 9-5-56. *Republished in T.D.* 6516, 12-20-60.]

[Reg. §31.3302(a)-3]

§31.3302(a)-3. Proof of credit under section 3302(a).—Credit against the tax for any calendar year for contributions paid into State unemployment funds shall not be allowed unless there is submitted to the district director:

(a) A certificate of the proper officer of each State (the laws of which required the contributions to be paid) showing, for the taxpayer:

(1) The total amount of contributions required to be paid under the State law with respect to such calendar year (exclusive of penalties and interest) which was actually paid on or before the date the Federal return is required to be filed; and

(2) The amounts and dates of such required payments (exclusive of penalties and interest) actually paid after the date the Federal return is required to be filed.

(b) A statement by the taxpayer that no part of any payment made by him into a State unemployment fund for such calendar year, which is claimed as a credit against the tax, was deducted or is to be deducted from the remuneration of individuals in his employ. Such statement shall contain or be verified by a written declaration that it is made under the penalties of perjury.

(c) Such other or additional proof as the Commissioner or the district director may deem necessary to establish the right to the credit provided for under section 3302(a). [Reg. §31.3302(a)-3.]

□ [T.D. 6199, 9-5-56. *Republished in T.D. 6516,* 12-20-60.]

[Reg. §31.3302(b)-1]

§31.3302(b)-1. Additional credit against tax.—(a) *In general.*—In addition to the credit against the tax allowable for contributions actually paid to State unemployment funds (see §31.3302(a)-1), the taxpayer may be entitled to a credit under section 3302(b). This additional credit is allowable to the taxpayer with respect to the amount of contributions which he is relieved from paying to an unemployment fund under the provisions of a State law which have been certified for the taxable year as provided in section 3303. Generally, an additional credit is available to an employer, if under the provisions of a State law which have been so certified he is permitted to pay contributions to such State for the taxable year, or portion thereof, at a rate which is both lower than the highest rate applied under such law in such year and lower than 2.7 percent. No additional credit is allowable except with respect to a State law certified by the Secretary of Labor for the taxable year as provided in section 3303 (or with respect to any provisions thereof so certified).

(b) *Method of computing amount of additional credit allowable with respect to a State law.*—(1) *Certification of a State law as a whole.*—In ascertaining the additional credit for any taxable year with respect to a particular State law which the Secretary of Labor certifies as a whole to the

Secretary of the Treasury in accordance with the provisions of section 3303, the taxpayer must first compute the following amounts:

(i) The amount of contributions (whether or not with respect to employment as defined in section 3306(c)) which the taxpayer would have been required to pay under the State law for such year if throughout the year he had been subject to the highest rate applied under such law in such year, or to a rate of 2.7 percent, whichever rate is lower.

(ii) The amount of contributions (whether or not with respect to employment as defined in section 3306(c)) he was required to pay under the State law with respect to such year, whether or not paid.

The amount computed under subdivision (ii) of this subparagraph should then be subtracted from the amount computed under subdivision (i) of this subparagraph and the result will be the additional credit for the taxable year with respect to the law of that State.

Example. A employs individuals only in State X during the calendar year 1955. The unemployment compensation law of State X has been certified in its entirety to the Secretary of the Treasury by the Secretary of Labor for such year. The highest rate applied in such year under such State law to any taxpayer is 3 percent. However, A has obtained a rate of 1 percent under the law of such State and is required to pay his entire year's contribution at that rate. The amount of remuneration of A's employees subject to contributions under such State law is $25,000. A's additional credit under section 3302(b) is $425, computed as follows:

Remuneration subject to contributions	$25,000
Contributions at 2.7 percent rate . . .	675
Less:	
Contributions required to be paid at 1 percent rate	250
Additional credit to A	$425

Since the 2.7 percent rate is less than the highest rate applied (3 percent), the 2.7 percent rate is used in computing the amount ($675) from which the amount of contributions required to be paid at the 1 percent rate ($250) is deducted in order to ascertain the additional credit ($425).

(2) *Certification with respect to particular provisions of a State law.*—If the Secretary of Labor makes a certification to the Secretary of the Treasury with respect to particular provisions of a State law for any taxable year pursuant to section 3303, the additional credit of the taxpayer for such year with respect to such law shall be computed in such manner as the Commissioner shall determine.

(c) *Amount of additional credit allowable to taxpayer with respect to more than one State law.*—If the taxpayer is entitled to additional credit with respect to more than one State law in any taxable year, the additional credit allowable with respect to each State law shall be computed separately (in accordance with paragraph (b) of this section) and the total additional credit allowable against the tax for such year shall be the aggregate of the additional credits allowable with respect to such State laws. For limitation on total credits, see § 31.3302(c)-1. [Reg. § 31.3302(b)-1.]

☐ [T.D. 6199, 9-5-56. *Republished in T.D.* 6516, 12-20-60; T.D. 6658, 6-27-63.]

[Reg. § 31.3302(b)-2]

§ 31.3302(b)-2. Proof of additional credit under section 3302(b).—Additional credit under section 3302(b) shall not be allowed against the tax for any calendar year unless there is submitted—

(a) To the Commissioner a certificate of the proper officer of each State (with respect to the law of which the additional credit is claimed) showing the highest rate of contributions applied under the State law in such calendar year to any person having individuals in his employ; and

(b) To the district director a certificate of the proper officer of each State (with respect to the law of which the additional credit is claimed) showing for the taxpayer—

(1) The total remuneration with respect to which contributions were required to be paid by the taxpayer under the State law with respect to such calendar year; and

(2) The rate of contributions applied to the taxpayer under the State law with respect to such calendar year.

If under the law of such State different rates of contributions were applied to the taxpayer during particular periods of such calendar year, the certificate shall set forth the information called for in subparagraphs (1) and (2) of this paragraph with respect to each such period.

(c) Such other or additional proof as the Commissioner or the district director may deem necessary to establish the right to the additional credit provided for under section 3302(b). [Reg. § 31.3302(b)-2.]

☐ [T.D. 6199, 9-5-56. *Republished in T.D.* 6516, 12-20-60.]

>>>→ *Caution: The following regulation has not been revised to reflect provisions of P.L. 94-45 regarding repayment of advances, or to reflect certain technical amendments in P.L. 94-455, or to reflect the cap on federal credit reductions in the Omnibus Budget Reconciliation Act of 1981 (P.L. 97-35).*

[Reg. § 31.3302(c)-1]

§ 31.3302(c)-1. Limit on total credits.—(a) *In general.*—Paragraph (b) of this section relates to the limitation on the aggregate of the credits allowable under section 3302(a) and (b). Paragraph (c) of this section relates to reductions, under certain circumstances, of the total credits allowable after applying section 3302(a), (b), and (c)(1). In paragraph (c) of this section, subparagraphs (1), (2), and (3) relate, respectively, to reductions of credits in respect of advances under title XII of the Social Security Act before September 13, 1960, advances under title XII of the Social Security Act after September 12, 1960, and payments under the Temporary Unemployment Compensation Act of 1958. A reduction of credit under subparagraph (1), (2), or (3) of paragraph (c) of this section applies separately from, and in addition to, a reduction under any other such subparagraph. See section 3302(d) and § 31.3302(d)-1 for definitions and special rules relating to section 3302(c), and for a provision that, in applying section 3302(c), the Federal tax shall be computed at the rate of 3 percent.

(b) *Limitation on aggregate credit.*—The aggregate of the credit under section 3302(a) and the additional credit under section 3302(b) shall not exceed 90 percent of the tax against which credit is taken, computed as if the tax were imposed at the rate of 3 percent. Thus, the aggregate of the credit which is allowable to an employer for any taxable year shall not exceed 2.7 percent of the wages paid by the employer during the year.

(c) *Reductions of amount of credit otherwise allowable.*—(1) *Advances before September 13, 1960, under title XII of Social Security Act.*—(i) *Credit reductions for 1961 and 1962.*—Pursuant to section 3302(c)(2), as applicable to credit allowable for any year ended before 1963, the total credits otherwise allowable under section 3302 to a taxpayer subject to the unemployment compensation law of the State of—

(a) Alaska shall be reduced for the taxable year 1961 by an amount equal to 0.15 percent of the wages paid by the taxpayer during 1961 which are attributable to Alaska, and shall be reduced for the taxable year 1962 by an amount equal to 0.3 percent of the wages paid by the taxpayer during 1962 which are attributable to Alaska; or

(b) Michigan shall be reduced for the taxable year 1962 by an amount equal to 0.15 percent of the wages paid by the taxpayer during 1962 which are attributable to Michigan.

(ii) *Credit reductions for 1963 and subsequent years.*—If any balance of an advance or advances under title XII of the Social Security Act, made before September 13, 1960, to the unemployment account of a State, remains unpaid on January 1, 1963, or on January 1 of any succeeding taxable year, the total credits otherwise allowable under section 3302 to a taxpayer subject to the unemployment compensation law of the State shall be reduced for the taxable year unless—

(a) No balance of such advance or advances exists as of the beginning of November 10 of the taxable year, or

(b) The State pays into the Federal unemployment account, before November 10 of the taxable year, the amount certified by the Secretary of Labor pursuant to section 3302(c)(2), and designates such payment as being made for purposes of the last sentence of section 3302(c)(2).

The credit reduction for a taxable year shall be a percentage of the wages paid by the taxpayer during that taxable year which are attributable to the State. The percentage for the taxable year 1963, or for any succeeding taxable year beginning before January 1, 1968, is 0.15 percent (that is, 5 percent of the Federal tax, computed as if imposed at the rate of 3 percent of the wages.) The percentage for any taxable year beginning on or after January 1, 1968, is the percentage reduction for the immediately preceding taxable year plus 0.15 percent. Thus, for 1968 the percentage is 0.3 percent, for 1969 the percentage is 0.45 percent, and for 1970 the percentage is 0.6 percent.

(2) *Advances after September 12, 1960 under the title XII of Social Security Act.*—(i) *In general.*—If any balance of an advance or advances under title XII of the Social Security Act, made after September 12, 1960, to the unemployment account of a State, remains unpaid on January 1 of two consecutive taxable years, the total credits otherwise allowable under section 3302 to a taxpayer subject to the unemployment compensation law of the State shall be reduced for the taxable year beginning with the second consecutive January 1, unless prior to November 10 of that taxable year the total amount of any such advance or advances made to the account of the State has been fully repaid. The reduction made pursuant to this subdivision in the total credits otherwise allowable for the taxable year beginning with the second consecutive January 1 shall be .3 percent of the wages paid by the taxpayer during the taxable year which are attributable to the State (that is, 10 percent of the Federal tax, computed as if imposed at the rate of 3 percent of the wages). In the case of any succeeding taxable year beginning with a consecutive January 1 on which there exists such a balance of an unreturned advance or advances made after September 12, 1960, the total credits otherwise allowable shall be further reduced unless prior to November 10 of that succeeding taxable year the total amount of any such advance or advances made to the account of the State has been fully repaid. The reduction for each such succeeding taxable year beginning with a consecutive January 1 on which such a balance exists shall be a percentage of the wages paid by the taxpayer during that succeeding taxable year which are attributable to the State. The percentage reduction for any such succeeding taxable year shall be the aggregate of (*a*) the percentage reduction (without regard to subdivision (ii) or (iii) of this subparagraph) for the immediately preceding taxable year, (*b*) .3 percent of the wages paid by the taxpayer during the taxable year which are attributable to the State, and (*c*) the percentage, if any, described in subdivision (ii) or (iii) of this subparagraph.

(ii) *Additional reduction if a balance of advances exists after third or fourth consecutive January 1.*—If the credit reduction described in subdivision (i) of this subparagraph is made for the

third or fourth consecutive taxable year, the total credits otherwise allowable under section 3302 to a taxpayer subject to the unemployment compensation law of the State shall be further reduced for the taxable year unless the average employer contribution rate (see section 3302(d)(4)) for such State for the calendar year preceding such taxable year is at least 2.7 percent. The percentage of reduction, if any, under this subdivision shall be the percentage referred to in section 3302(c)(3)(B) which is certified by the Secretary of Labor pursuant to section 3302(d)(7).

(iii) *Additional reduction if a balance of advances exists after fifth or any succeeding consecutive January 1.*—If the credit reduction described in subdivision (i) of this subparagraph is made for the fifth or any succeeding taxable year, the total credits otherwise allowable under section 3302 to a taxpayer subject to the unemployment compensation law of the State shall be further reduced for the taxable year unless the average employer contribution rate (see section 3302(d)(4)) for the State for the calendar year preceding such taxable year equals or exceeds the 5-year benefit cost rate (see section 3302(d)(5)) applicable to the State for the taxable year or 2.7 percent, whichever is higher. The percentage of reduction, if any, under this subdivision for a taxable year shall be the percentage referred to in section 3302(c)(3)(C) which is certified by the Secretary of Labor pursuant to section 3302(d)(7).

(3) *Payments under the Temporary Unemployment Compensation Act of 1958.*—If any amount of temporary unemployment compensation was paid in a State under the Temporary Unemployment Compensation Act of 1958, the total credits otherwise allowable under section 3302 to a taxpayer with respect to wages attributable to the State for the taxable year beginning January 1, 1963, and for each taxable year thereafter, shall be reduced unless prior to November 10 of the taxable year—

(i) There have been restored to the Treasury the amounts of temporary unemployment compensation paid in the State (except amounts paid to individuals who exhausted their unemployment compensation under title XV of the Social Security Act and title IV of the Veterans' Readjustment Assistance Act of 1952 prior to their making their first claims under the Temporary Unemployment Compensation Act of 1958), the amount of costs incurred in the administration of the Temporary Unemployment Compensation Act of 1958 with respect to the State, and the amount estimated by the Secretary of Labor as the State's proportionate share of other costs incurred in the administration of such Act, or

(ii) The State restores to the general fund of the Treasury the amount certified by the Secretary of Labor pursuant to section 104 of the Temporary Unemployment Compensation Act of 1958, and designates such restoration as being made for purposes of the last sentence of such section.

The credit reduction for a taxable year shall be a percentage of the wages paid by the taxpayer during that year which are attributable to the State. The percentage for the taxable year 1963 is 0.15 percent (that is, 5 percent of the Federal tax, computed as if imposed at the rate of 3 percent). The precentage for any succeeding year is 0.3 percent (that is, 10 percent of the Federal tax, computed as if imposed at the rate of 3 percent).

(4) *Example.*—The cumulative effect of the credit reductions described in this paragraph may be illustrated by the following example:

Example. Advances to the unemployment account of State X were made in 1957 and in 1961 under title XII of the Social Security Act. Payments under the Temporary Unemployment Compensation Act of 1958 were made in State X in 1958. No portion of the advances or payments is returned before November 10, 1964. As a consequence:

(a) The credit reduction applicable under subparagraph (1) of this paragraph is made for 1964 at the rate of 0.15 percent;

(b) The credit reduction described in subparagraph (2) of this paragraph has been made for 1963 (the second successive year after 1961) at the rate of 0.3 percent. The rate of credit reduction under subparagraph (2) for 1964 is 1 percent (the aggregate of 0.6 percent under section 3302(c)(3)(A) and 0.4 percent (assumed for purposes of this example to be the percentage referred to in section 3302(c)(3)(B) which is certified by the Secretary of Labor); and

(c) The credit reduction described in subparagraph (3) of this paragraph has been made for 1963 at the rate of 0.15 percent. The rate of credit reduction for 1964 is 0.3 percent.

The cumulative rate of credit reduction applicable for 1964 to wages attributable to State X is 1.45 percent, representing the aggregate of the percentage reductions applicable under subparagraphs (1), (2), and (3) of this paragraph (.0.15 percent, 1 percent, and 0.3 percent, respectively). In 1964 Employer A paid wages of $100,000, all of which are subject to the unemployment compensation law of State X. The credit which would be allowable (under section 3302(a), (b), and (c)(1)) if there were no credit reduction is $2,700. Employer A's tax is computed as follows for 1964:

Total taxable wages (attributable to State X)	$100,000
Gross Federal tax (3.1 percent of wages)	3,100
Less credit:	
Gross credit $2,700	
Credit reduction (1.45 percent of wages) 1,450	
Net credit	1,250
Amount of Federal tax due	$1,850

[Reg. §31.3302(c)-1.]

   □ [T.D. 6199, 9-5-56. *Republished in T.D.* 6516, 12-20-60; T.D. 6658, 6-27-63; T.D. 6708, 3-10-64.]

≫→ *Caution: The following regulation has not been revised to reflect technical changes in IRC §3302(c) enacted by P.L. 94-455.*

[Reg. §31.3302(d)-1]

§31.3302(d)-1. Definitions and special rules relating to limit on total credits.—(a) *Rate of tax deemed to be 3 percent.*—In applying the provisions of section 3302(c) relating to the limitation on total credits, and to reductions of credits otherwise allowable, the tax imposed by section 3301 shall be computed at the rate of 3 percent in lieu of any other rate prescribed in section 3301 (see §31.3301-3).

(b) *Wages attributable to a particular State.*—For purposes of section 3302(c)(2) or (3), wages are attributable to a particular State if they are subject to the unemployment compensation law of the State. If wages are not subject to the unemployment compensation law of any State, the determination as to whether such wages, or any portion thereof, are attributable to the particular State with respect to which the reduction in total credits is imposed shall be made in accordance with rules prescribed by the Commissioner.

(c) *Employment Security Act of 1960.*—The Employment Security Act of 1960, referred to in section 3302(c)(2), means title V of the Social Security Amendments of 1960. [Reg. §31.3302(d)-1.]

   □ [T.D. 6658, 6-27-63.]

[Reg. §31.3302(e)-1]

§31.3302(e)-1. Successor employer.—(a) *In general.*—In addition to the credits against the tax allowable under section 3302(a) and (b) for any taxable year after 1960, the taxpayer may be entitled to an amount of credit under section 3302(e). Credit under section 3302(e) is provided in the case of a taxpayer who (1) acquires substantially all of the property used in a trade or business, or in a separate unit of a trade or business, of another person (referred to in this section as a predecessor) who is not an employer (see §31.3306(a)-1) for the calendar year in which the acquisition takes place, and (2) immediately after the acquisition employs in his trade or business one or more individuals who immediately prior to the acquisition were employed in the trade or business of the predecessor.

(b) *Method of computing credit under section 3302(e).*—(1) Except as provided in subparagraph (2) of this paragraph, the amount of credit to which the taxpayer may be entitled under section 3302(e) is the amount of credit to which the predecessor would be entitled under section 3302(a), (b), and (e), without regard to the limits in section 3302(c), if the predecessor were an employer.

(2) If, during the calendar year in which the acquisition takes place, the predecessor pays re-

muneration, subject to contributions under the unemployment compensation law of a State, to any employee other than the individuals referred to in paragraph (a) of this section, the taxpayer will be entitled only to a portion of the amount of credit described in subparagraph (1) of this paragraph. The portion is determined by multiplying such amount by a fraction. The numerator of the fraction is the total amount of remuneration, subject to such contributions, paid by the predecessor during such year to the individuals referred to in paragraph (a) of this section. The denominator of the fraction is the total amount of remuneration, subject to such contributions, paid by the predecessor during such year to all employees for services performed by them in the trade or business, or unit thereof, acquired by the taxpayer.

Example. In April 1961 the X Partnership terminated after selling all of its property to the Y Corporation. During 1961, the X Partnership paid its employees and former employees a total of $1,000,000 as remuneration subject to contributions under the employment compensation law of a State. (Note that the X Partnership did not qualify as an employer for 1961 for purposes of the Federal unemployment tax, because it had employees during less than 20 weeks in 1961). When the Y Corporation acquired the property it concurrently employed all individuals who were then in the employ of the X Partnership. Assume that the X Partnership, if it had qualified as an employer for 1961, would have been entitled to a total credit against the Federal tax of $30,000 under section 3302(a) and (b), without regard to the limits in section 3302(c). Of the $1,000,000 remuneration paid by the X Partnership in 1961, one-fifth (or $200,000) was paid to individuals who were employed by the Y Corporation at the time it acquired the property of the X Partnership. Under section 3302(e), therefore, the Y Corporation is entitled to credit of $6,000, which is one-fifth of the credit ($30,000) which would have been available to the X Partnership.

(3) The aggregate amount of credit allowable to the taxpayer under section 3302(a), (b), and (e) is subject to the limits in section 3302(c).

(c) *Proof of credit under section 3302(e).*—Credit under section 3302(e) shall not be allowed against the tax for any taxable year unless there is submitted to the district director (1) such information or proof as may be called for in the return on which the credit is reported, or in the instructions relating to the return, and (2) such other or additional proof as the Commissioner or the district director may deem necessary to establish the right to the credit provided for under section 3302(e).

(d) *Cross-references.*—See paragraph (b) of § 31.3306(b)(1)-1 for examples of the acquisition of property used in a trade or business, or in a separate unit thereof. [Reg. § 31.3302(e)-1.]

☐ [T.D. 6658, 6-27-63.]

»»→ Caution: *The following regulation has not been revised to reflect the amendments affecting "employer" status made by P.L. 91-373 and P.L. 94-566.*

[Reg. § 31.3306(a)-1]

§ 31.3306(a)-1. Who are employers.—(a) *Definition.*—(1) *For calendar years 1956 through 1969, inclusive.*—Every person who employs 4 or more employees in employment (within the meaning of section 3306 (c) and (d)) on a total of 20 or more calendar days during any calendar year after 1955 and before 1970, each such day being in a different calendar week, is with respect to such year an employer subject to the tax.

(1a) *For 1970 and subsequent calendar years.*—Every person who employs 4 or more employees in employment (within the meaning of section 3306 (c) and (d)) on a total of 20 or more calendar days during a calendar year after 1969, or during the calendar year immediately preceding such a calendar year, each such day being in a different calendar week, is with respect to such year an employer subject to the tax.

(2) *For calendar year 1955.*—Every person who employs 8 or more employees in employment (within the meaning of section 3306(c) and (d)) on a total of 20 or more calendar days during the calendar year 1955, each such day being in a different calendar week, is with respect to such year an employer subject to the tax.

(3) *General agents of the Secretary of Commerce.*—For provisions relating to the circumstances under which an employee who performs services as an officer or member of the crew of an American vessel (i) which is owned by or bareboat chartered to the United States and (ii) whose business is conducted by a general agent of the Secretary of Commerce shall be deemed to be performing services for such general agent rather than for the United States, see § 31.3306(n)-1.

(b) The several weeks in each of which occurs a day on which the prescribed number of employees are employed need not be consecutive weeks. It is not necessary that the employees so employed be the same individuals; they may be different individuals on each day. Neither is it necessary that the prescribed number of employees be employed at the same moment of time or for any particular length of time or on any particular basis of compensation. It is sufficient if the total number of employees employed during the 24 hours of a calendar day is 4 or more (8 or more for the calendar year 1955).

(c) In determining whether a person employs a sufficient number of employees to be an employer subject to the tax, each employee is counted with respect to services which constitute employment as defined in section 3306(c) (see § 31.3306(c)-2). No employee is counted with respect to services which do not constitute employment as so defined. See, however, paragraph (d) of this section.

(d) The provisions of paragraph (c) of this section are subject to the provisions of section 3306(d), relating to services which do not constitute employment but which are deemed to be employment, and relating to services which constitute employment but which are deemed not to be employment (see § 31.3306(d)-1). For example, if the services of an employee during a pay period are deemed to be employment under section 3306(d), even though a portion thereof does not constitute employment under section 3306(c), the employee is counted with respect to all services during the pay period. On the other hand, if the services of an employee during a pay period are deemed not to be employment, even though a portion thereof constitutes employment, the employee is not counted with respect to any services during the pay period. [Reg. § 31.3306(a)-1.]

☐ [T.D. 6199, 9-5-56. *Republished in T.D. 6516,* 12-20-60. *Amended by T.D. 7037, 4-28-70.*]

[Reg. § 31.3306(b)-1]

§ **31.3306(b)-1. Wages.**—(a) *Applicable law and regulations.*—(1) *Remuneration paid after 1954.*— Whether remuneration paid after 1954 for employment performed after 1938 constitutes wages is determined under section 3306(b). Accordingly, only remuneration paid after 1954 for employment performed after 1938 is covered by this section of the regulations and by the sections relating to the statutory exclusions from wages (§§ 31.3306(b)(1)-1 to 31.3306(b)(10)-1).

(2) *Remuneration paid after 1939 and before 1955.*—Whether remuneration paid after 1939 and before 1955 for employment performed after 1938 constitutes wages shall be determined in accordance with the applicable provisions of law and of 26 CFR (1939) Part 403 (Regulations 107).

(3) *Remuneration paid in 1939.*—Whether remuneration paid in 1939 for employment performed after 1938 constitutes wages shall be determined in accordance with the applicable provisions of law and of 26 CFR (1939) Part 400 (Regulations 90).

(b) The term "wages" means all remuneration for employment unless specifically excepted under section 3306(b) (see §§ 31.3306(b)(1)-1 to 31.3306(b)(10)-1, inclusive) or paragraph (j) of this section.

(c) The name by which the remuneration for employment is designated is immaterial. Thus, salaries, fees, bonuses, and commissions are wages if paid as compensation for employment.

(d) The basis upon which the remuneration is paid is immaterial in determining whether the remuneration constitutes wages. Thus, it may be paid on the basis of piecework or a percentage of profits; and it may be paid hourly, daily, weekly, monthly, or annually.

(e) Except in the case of remuneration paid for services not in the course of the employer's trade or business (see § 31.3306(b)(7)-1), the medium in which the remuneration is paid is also immaterial. It may be paid in cash or in something other than cash, as for example, goods, lodging, food, or clothing. Remuneration paid in items other than cash shall be computed on the basis of the fair value of such items at the time of payment.

(f) Ordinarily, facilities or privileges (such as entertainment, medical services, or so-called "courtesy" discounts on purchases), furnished or offered by an employer to his employees generally, are not considered as remuneration for employment if such facilities or privileges are of relatively small value and are offered or furnished by the employer merely as a means of promoting the health, good will, contentment, or efficiency of his employees. The term "facilities or privileges," however, does not ordinarily include the value of meals or lodging furnished, for example, to restaurant or hotel employees, or to seamen or other employees aboard vessels, since generally these items constitute an appreciable part of the total remuneration of such employees.

(g) Amounts of so-called "vacation allowances" paid to an employee constitute wages. Thus, the salary of an employee on vacation, paid notwithstanding his absence from work, constitutes wages.

(h) Amounts paid specifically—either as advances or reimbursements—for traveling or other bona fide ordinary and necessary expenses incurred or reasonably expected to be incurred in the business of the employer are not wages. For amounts that are received by an employee on or after July 1, 1990, with respect to expenses paid or incurred on or after July 1, 1990, see § 31.3306(b)-2.

(i) Remuneration paid by an employer to an individual for employment, unless such remuneration is specifically excepted under section 3306(b), constitutes wages even though at the time paid the individual is no longer an employee.

Example. A is employed by B, an employer, during the month of June 1955 in employment and is entitled to receive remuneration of $100 for the services performed for B during the month. A leaves the employ of B at the close of business on June 30, 1955. On July 15, 1955 (when A is no longer an employee of B), B pays A the remuneration of $100 which was earned for the services performed in June. The $100 is wages, and the tax is payable with respect thereto.

(j) In addition to the exclusions specified in §§ 31.3306(b)(1)-1 to 31.3306(b)(10)-1, inclusive, the following types of payments are excluded from wages:

(1) Remuneration for services which do not constitute employment under section 3306(c).

(2) Remuneration for services which are deemed not to be employment under section 3306(d) (§ 31.3306(d)-1).

(3) Tips or gratuities paid directly to an employee by a customer of an employer, and not accounted for by the employee to the employer.

(k) For provisions relating to the treatment of deductions from remuneration as payments of remuneration, see § 31.3307-1.

(l) *Split-dollar life insurance arrangements.*—Except as otherwise provided under section 3306(r), see §§ 1.61-22 and 1.7872-15 of this chapter for rules relating to the treatment of split-dollar life insurance arrangements. [Reg. § 31.3306(b)-1.]

  ☐ [*T.D.* 6199, 9-5-56. *Republished in T.D.* 6516, 12-20-60; *T.D.* 6658, 6-27-63. *Amended by T.D.* 7375, 9-12-75; *T.D.* 8324, 12-17-90 *and T.D.* 9092, 9-11-2003.]

[Reg. § 31.3306(b)-2]

§ 31.3306(b)-2. Reimbursement and other expense allowance amounts.—(a) *When excluded from wages.*—If a reimbursement or other expense allowance arrangement meets the requirements of section 62(c) of the Code and § 1.62-2 and the expenses are substantiated within a reasonable period of time, payments made under the arrangement that do not exceed the substantiated expenses are treated as paid under an accountable plan and are not wages. In addition, if both wages and the reimbursement or other expense allowance are combined in a single payment, the reimbursement or other expense allowance must be identified either by making a separate payment or by specifically identifying the amount of the reimbursement or other expense allowance.

(b) *When included in wages.*—(1) *Accountable plans.*—(i) *General rule.*—Except as provided in paragraph (b)(1)(ii) of this section, if a reimbursement or other expense allowance arrangement satisfied the requirements of section 62(c) and § 1.62-2, but the expenses are not substantiated within a reasonable period of time or amounts in excess of the substantiated expenses are not returned within a reasonable period of time, the amount paid under the arrangement in excess of the substantiated expenses is treated as paid under a nonaccountable plan, is included in wages, and is subject to withholding and payment of employment taxes no later than the first payroll period following the end of the reasonable period.

(ii) *Per diem or mileage allowances.*—If a reimbursement or other expense allowance arrangement providing a per diem or mileage allowance satisfies the requirements of section 62(c) and § 1.62-2, but the allowance is paid at a rate for each day or mile of travel that exceeds the amount of the employee's expenses deemed substantiated for a day or mile of travel, the excess portion is treated as paid under a nonaccountable plan and is included in wages. In the case of a per diem or mileage allowance paid as a reimbursement, the excess portion is subject to withholding and payment of employment taxes when paid. In the case of a per diem or mileage allowance paid as an advance, the excess portion is subject to withholding and payment of employment taxes no later than the first payroll period following the payroll period in which the expenses with respect to which the advance was paid (i.e., the days or miles of travel) are substantiated. The Commissioner may, in his discretion, prescribe special rules in pronouncements of general applicability regarding the timing of withholding and payment of employment taxes on per diem and mileage allowances.

(2) *Nonaccountable plans.*—If a reimbursement or other expense allowance arrangement does not satisfy the requirements of section 62(c) and § 1.62-2 (e.g., the arrangement does not require expenses to be substantiated or require amounts in excess of the substantiated expenses to be returned), all amounts paid under the arrangement are treated as paid under a nonaccountable plan, are included in wages, and are subject to withholding and payment of employment taxes when paid.

(c) *Effective dates.*—This section generally applies to payments made under reimbursement or other expense allowance arrangements received by an employee on or after July 1, 1990, with respect to expenses paid or incurred on or after July 1, 1990. Paragraph (b)(1)(ii) of this section applies to payments made under reimbursement or other expense allowance arrangements received by an employee on or after January 1, 1991, with respect to expenses paid or incurred on or after January 1, 1991. [Reg. § 31.3306(b)-2.]

  ☐ [*T.D.* 8324, 12-17-90.]

⋙→ *Caution: The following regulation has not been revised to reflect the increases in the taxable wage base to $4,200 after 1971 as enacted by P.L. 91-373, to $6,000 after 1977 as enacted by P.L. 94-566, and to $7,000 after 1982 as enacted by P.L. 97-248.*

[Reg. § 31.3306(b)(1)-1]

§ 31.3306(b)(1)-1. $3,000 limitation.—(a) *In general.*—(1) The term "wages" does not include that part of the remuneration paid within any calendar year by an employer to an employee which exceeds the first $3,000 of remuneration (exclusive of remuneration excepted from wages in accordance with paragraph (j) of § 31.3306(b)-1 or §§ 31.3306(b)(2)-1 to 31.3306(b)(8)-1, inclusive), paid within such calendar year by such employer to such employee for employment performed for him at any time after 1938.

(2) The $3,000 limitation applies only if the remuneration paid during any one calendar year by an employer to the same employee for employment performed after 1938 exceeds $3,000. The limitation in such case relates to the amount of remuneration paid during any one calendar year for employment after 1938 and not to the amount of remuneration for employment performed in any one calendar year.

Example. Employer B, in 1955, pays employee A $2,500 on account of $3,000 due him for employment performed in 1955. In 1956 employer B pays employee A the balance of $500 due him for employment performed in the prior year (1955), and thereafter in 1956 also pays A $3,000 for employment performed in 1956. The $2,500 paid in 1955 is subject to tax in 1955. The balance of $500 paid in 1956 for employment during 1955 is subject to tax in 1956, as is also the first $2,500 paid of the $3,000 for employment during 1956 (this $500 for 1955 employment added to the first $2,500 paid for 1956 employment constitutes the maximum wages subject to the tax which could be paid in 1956 by B to A). The final $500 paid by B to A in 1956 is not included as wages and is not subject to the tax.

(3) If during a calendar year an employee is paid remuneration by more than one employer, the limitation of wages to the first $3,000 of remuneration paid applies, not to the aggregate remuneration paid by all employers with respect to employment performed after 1938, but instead to the remuneration paid during such calendar year by each employer with respect to employment performed after 1938. In such case the first $3,000 paid during the calendar year by each employer constitutes wages and is subject to the tax. In connection with the application of the $3,000 limitation, see also paragraph (b) of this section relating to the circumstances under which wages paid by a predecessor employer are deemed to be paid by his successor. In connection with the annual wage limitation in the case of remuneration after December 31, 1978 from two or more related corporations that compensate an employee through a common paymaster, see § 31.3306(p)-1.

Example (1). During 1955 employer D pays to employee C a salary of $600 a month for employment performed for D during the first seven months of 1955, or total remunderation of $4,200. At the end of the fifth month C has been paid $3,000 by employer D, and only that part of his total remuneration from D constitutes wages subject to the tax. The $600 paid to employee C by employer D in the sixth month, and the like amount paid in the seventh month, are not included as wages and are not subject to the tax. At the end of the seventh month C leaves the employ of D and enters the employ of E. Employer E pays to C remuneration of $600 a month in each of the remaining five months of 1955, or total remuneration of $3,000. The entire $3,000 paid by E to employee C constitutes wages and is subject to the tax. Thus, the first $3,000 paid by employer D and the entire $3,000 paid by employer E constitute wages.

Example (2). During the calendar year 1955 F is simultaneously an officer (an employee) of the X Corporation, the Y Corporation, and the Z Corporation, each such corporation being an employer for such year. During such year F is paid a salary of $3,000 by each corporation. Each $3,000 paid to F by each of the corporations, X, Y, and Z (whether or not such corporations are related), constitutes wages and is subject to the tax.

(b) *Wages paid by predecessor attributed to successor.*—(1) If an employer (hereinafter referred to as a successor) during any calendar year acquires substantially all the property used in a trade or business of another employer (hereinafter referred to as a predecessor), or used in a separate unit of a trade or business of a predecessor, and if immediately after the acquisition the successor employs in his trade or business an individual who immediately prior to the acquisition was employed in the trade or business of such predecessor, then, for purposes of the application of the $3,000 limitation set forth in paragraph (a) of this section, any remuneration (exclusive of remuneration excepted from wages in accordance with paragraph (j) of § 31.3306(b)-1 or § § 31.3306(b)(2)-1 to 31.3306(b)(8)-1, inclusive), with respect to employment paid (or considered under this provision as having been paid) to such individual by such predecessor during such calendar year and prior to such acquisition shall be considered as having been paid by such successor. Wages paid by a predecessor shall not be considered as having been paid by the successor unless both the predecessor and the successor are employers as defined in section 3306(a) for the calendar year in which the acquisition occurs (see § 31.3306(a)-1, relating to who are employers).

(2) The wages paid, or considered as having been paid, by a predecessor to an employee shall, for purposes of the $3,000 limitation, be treated as having been paid to such employee by a successor, if:

(i) The successor during a calendar year acquired substantially all the property used in a trade or business, or used in a separate unit of a trade or business, of the predecessor;

(ii) Such employee was employed in the trade or business of the predecessor immediately prior to the acquisition and is employed by the successor in his trade or business immediately after the acquisition; and

(iii) Such wages were paid during the calendar year in which the acquisition occurred and prior to such acquisition.

(3) The method of acquisition by an employer of the property of another employer is immaterial. The acquisition may occur as a consequence of the incorporation of a business by a sole proprietor or a partnership, the continuance without interruption of the business of a previously existing partnership by a new partnership or by a sole proprietor, or a purchase or any other transaction whereby substantially all the property used in a trade or business, or used in a separate unit of a trade or business, of one employer is acquired by another employer.

(4) Substantially all the property used in a separate unit of a trade or business may consist of substantially all the property used in the performance of an essential operation of the trade or business, or it may consist of substantially all the property used in a relatively self-sustaining entity which forms a part of the trade or business.

Example (1). The M Corporation which is engaged in the manufacture of automobiles, including the manufacture of automobile engines, discontinues the manufacture of the engines and transfers all the property used in such manufacturing operations to the N Company. The N Company is considered to have acquired a separate unit of the trade or business of the M Corporation, namely, its engine manufacturing unit.

Example (2). The R Corporation which is engaged in the operation of a chain of grocery stores transfers one of such stores to the S Company. The S Company is considered to have acquired a separate unit of the trade or business of the R Corporation.

(5) A successor may receive credit for wages paid to an employee by a predecessor only if immediately prior to the acquisition the employee was employed by the predecessor in his trade or business which was acquired by the successor and if immediately after the acquisition such employee is employed by the successor in his trade or business (whether or not in the same trade or business in which the acquired property is used). If the acquisition involves only a separate unit of a trade or business of the predecessor, the employee need not have been employed by the predecessor in that unit provided he was employed in the trade or business of which the acquired unit was a part.

Example. The Y Corporation in 1955 acquires all the property of the X Manufacturing Company and immediately after the acquisition employs in its trade or business employee A, who, immediately prior to the acquisition, was employed by the X Company. Both the Y Corporation and the X Company are employers, as defined in the Act, for the calendar year 1955. The X Company has in 1955 (the calendar year in which the acquisition occurs) and prior to the acquisition paid $2,000 of wages to A. The Y Corporation in 1955 pays to A remuneration with respect to employment of $2,000. Only $1,000 of such remuneration is considered to be wages. For purposes of the $3,000 limitation, the Y Corporation is credited with the $2,000 paid to A by the X Company. If, in the same calendar year, the property is acquired from the Y Corporation by the Z Company, an employer for such year, and A immediately after the acquisition is employed by the Z Company in its trade or business, no part of the remuneration paid to A by the Z Company in the year of the acquisition will be considered to be wages. The Z Company will be credited with the remuneration paid to A by the Y Corporation and also with the wages paid to A by the X Company (considered for purposes of the application of the $3,000 limitation as having also been paid by the Y Corporation). [Reg. § 31.3306(b)(1)-1.]

☐ [*T.D.* 6199, 9-5-56. *Republished in T.D.* 6516, 12-20-60; *T.D.* 6658, 6-27-63; *T.D.* 7660, 12-19-79.]

≫→ *Caution: This regulation has not been amended to reflect the fact that, effective in 1985, most sick pay is includible in taxable wages.*

[Reg. § 31.3306(b)(2)-1]

§ 31.3306(b)(2)-1. Payments under employers' plans on account of retirement, sickness or accident disability, medical or hospitalization expenses, or death.—(a) The term "wages" does not include the amount of any payment (including any amount paid by an employer for insurance or annuities, or into a fund, to provide for any such payment) made to, or on behalf of, an employee or any of his dependents under a plan or system established by an employer which makes provision for his employees generally (or for his employees generally and their dependents) or for a class or classes of his employees (or for a class or classes of his employees and their dependents), on account of:

(1) An employee's retirement,

(2) Sickness or accident disability of an employee or any of his dependents,

(3) Medical or hospitalization expenses in connection with sickness or accident disability of an employee or any of his dependents, or

(4) Death of an employee or any of his dependents.

(b) The plan or system established by an employer need not provide for payments on account of all of the specified items, but such plan or system may provide for any one or more of such items. Payments for any one or more of such items under a plan or system established by an employer solely for the dependents of his employees are not within this exclusion from wages.

(c) Dependents of an employee include the employee's husband or wife, children, and any other members of the employee's immediate family.

(d) It is immaterial for purposes of this exclusion whether the amount or possibility of such benefit payments is taken into consideration in fixing the amount of an employee's remuneration or whether such payments are required, expressly or impliedly, by the contract of service. [Reg. § 31.3306(b)(2)-1.]

☐ [*T.D.* 6199, 9-5-56. *Republished in T.D.* 6516, 12-20-60.]

≫→ *Caution: This regulation has not been amended to reflect the repeal of IRC §3306(b)(3), as made by P.L. 98-21, §324(b)(3)(B).*

[Reg. § 31.3306(b)(3)-1]

§ 31.3306(b)(3)-1. Retirement payments.—The term "wages" does not include any payment made by an employer to an employee (including any amount paid by an employer for insurance or annuities, or into a fund, to provide for any such payment) on account of the employee's retirement. Thus, payments made to an employee on account of his retirement are excluded from wages under this exception even though not made under a plan or system. [Reg. § 31.3306(b)(3)-1.]

☐ [*T.D.* 6199, 9-5-56. *Republished in T.D.* 6516, 12-20-60.]

[Reg. § 31.3306(b)(4)-1]

§ 31.3306(b)(4)-1. Payments on account of sickness or accident disability, or medical or hospitalization expenses.—The term "wages" does not include any payment made by an employer to, or on behalf of, an employee on account of the employee's sickness or accident disability or the medical or hospitalization expenses in connection with the employee's sickness or accident disability, if such payment is made after the expiration of 6 calendar months following the last calendar month in which such employee worked for such employer. Such payments are excluded from wages under this exception even though not made under a plan or system. If the employee does not actually perform services for the employer during the requisite period, the existence of the employer-employee relationship during that period is immaterial.[Reg. § 31.3306(b)(4)-1.]

☐ [*T.D.* 6199, 9-5-56. *Republished in T.D.* 6516, 12-20-60.]

»»→ *Caution: This regulation has not been amended to reflect the change made by P.L. 96-222.*

[Reg. § 31.3306(b)(5)-1]

§ 31.3306(b)(5)-1. Payments from or to certain tax-exempt trusts, or under or to certain annuity plans or bond purchase plans.—(a) *Payments from or to certain tax-exempt trusts.*—The term "wages" does not include any payment made—

(1) By an employer, on behalf of an employee or his beneficiary, into a trust, or

(2) To, or on behalf of, an employee or his beneficiary from a trust,

if at the time of such payment the trust is exempt from tax under section 501(a) as an organization described in section 401(a). A payment made to an employee of such a trust for services rendered as an employee of the trust and not as a beneficiary thereof is not within this exclusion from wages.

(b) *Payments under or to certain annuity plans.*—(1) The term "wages" does not include any payment made after December 31, 1962,—

(i) By an employer, on behalf of an employee or his beneficiary, into an annuity plan, or

(ii) To, or on behalf of, an employee or his beneficiary under an annuity plan,

if at the time of such payment the annuity plan is a plan described in section 403(a).

(2) The term "wages" does not include any payment made before January 1, 1963,—

(i) By an employer, on behalf of an employee or his beneficiary, into an annuity plan, or

(ii) To, or on behalf of, an employee or his beneficiary under an annuity plan,

if at the time of such payment the annuity plan meets the requirements of section 401(a)(3), (4), (5), and (6).

(c) *Payments under or to certain bond purchase plans.*—The term "wages" does not include any payment made after December 31, 1962,—

(1) By an employer, on behalf of an employee or his beneficiary, into a bond purchase plan, or

(2) To, or on behalf of, an employee or his beneficiary under a bond purchase plan,

if at the time of such payment the plan is a qualified bond purchase plan described in section 405(a). [Reg. § 31.3306(b)(5)-1.]

☐ [*T.D.* 6199, 9-5-56. *Republished in T.D.* 6516, 12-20-60; *T.D.* 6658, 6-27-63.]

»»→ *Caution: This regulation has not been amended to reflect the change made by P.L. 96-499.*

[Reg. § 31.3306(b)(6)-1]

§ 31.3306(b)(6)-1. Payment by an employer of employee tax under sectin 3101 or employee contributions under a State law.—The term "wages" does not include any payment by an employer (without deduction from the remuneration of, or other reimbursement from, the employee) of either (a) the employee tax imposed by section 3101 [FICA employee tax] or the corresponding section of prior law, or (b) any payment required from an employee under a State unemployment compensation law. [Reg. § 31.3306(b)(6)-1.]

☐ [*T.D.* 6199, 9-5-56. *Republished in T.D.* 6516, 12-20-60.]

[Reg. § 31.3306(b)(7)-1]

§ 31.3306(b)(7)-1. Payments other than in cash for service not in the course of employer's trade or business.—The term "wages" does not include remuneration paid in any medium other than cash for service not in the course of the employer's trade or business. Cash remuneration includes checks and other monetary media of exchange. Remuneration paid in any medium other than cash, such as lodging, food, or other goods or commodities, for service not in the course of the employer's trade or business does not constitute wages. Remuneration paid in any medium other than cash for other types of services does not come within this exclusion from wages. For provisions relating to the circumstances under which service not in the course of the employer's trade or business does not constitute employment, see § 31.3306(c)(3)-1. [Reg. § 31.3306(b)(7)-1.]

☐ [*T.D.* 6199, 9-5-56. *Republished in T.D.* 6516, 12-20-60].

[Reg. § 31.3306(b)(8)-1]

§ 31.3306(b)(8)-1. Payments to employees for non-work periods.—The term "wages" does not include any payment (other than vacation or sick pay) made by an employer to an employee after the calendar month in which the employee attains age 65, if—

(a) Such employee does no work (other than being subject to call for the performance of work) for such employer in the period for which such payment is made; and

(b) The employer-employee relationship exists between the employer and employee throughout the period for which such payment is made.

Vacation or sick pay is not within this exclusion from wages. If the employee does any work for the employer in the period for which the payment is made, no remuneration paid by such employer to such employee with respect to such period is within this exclusion from wages. For example, if employee A, who attained the age of 65 in January 1955, is employed by the X Company on a stand-by basis and is paid $200 by the X Company for being subject to call during the month of February 1955 and an additional $25 for work performed for the X Company on one day in February 1955, then none of the $225 is excluded from wages under this exception. [Reg. § 31.3306(b)(8)-1.]

☐ [T.D. 6199, 9-5-56. *Republished in T.D. 6516, 12-20-60; T.D. 6708, 3-10-64.*]

[Reg. § 31.3306(b)(9)-1]

§ 31.3306(b)(9)-1. **Moving expenses.**—(a) The term "wages" does not include remuneration paid on or after November 1, 1964, to or on behalf of an employee, either as an advance or a reimbursement, specifically for moving expenses incurred or expected to be incurred, if (and to the extent that) at the time of payment it is reasonable to believe that a corresponding deduction is or will be allowable to the employee under section 217. The reasonable belief contemplated by the statute may be based upon any evidence reasonably sufficient to induce such belief, even though such evidence may be insufficient upon closer examination by the district director or the courts finally to establish that a deduction is allowable under section 217. The reasonable belief shall be based upon the application of section 217 and the regulations thereunder in Part 1 of this chapter (Income Tax Regulations). When used in this section, the term "moving expenses" has the same meaning as when used in section 217 and the regulations thereunder.

(b) Except as otherwise provided in paragraph (a) of this section, or in a numbered paragraph of section 3306(b), amounts paid to or on behalf of an employee for moving expenses are wages for purposes of section 3306(b). [Reg. § 31.3306(b)(9)-1.]

☐ [T.D. 7375, 9-12-75.]

[Reg. § 31.3306(b)(10)-1]

§ 31.3306(b)(10)-1. **Payments under certain employers' after retirement, disability, or death.**—(a) *In general.*—The term "wages" does not include the amount of any payment or series of payments made after January 2, 1968, by an employer to, or on behalf of, an employee or any of his dependents under a plan established by the employer which makes provisions for his employees generally (or for his employees generally and their dependents) or for a class or

classes of his employees (or for a class or classes of his employees and their dependents), which is paid or commences to be paid under or within a reasonable time after the termination of an employee's employment relationship because of the employee's—

(1) Death,

(2) Retirement for disability, or

(3) Retirement after attaining an age specified in the plan established by the employer or in a pension plan of the employer at the age at which a person in the employee's circumstances is eligible for retirement.

A payment or series of payments made under the circumstances described in the preceding sentence is excluded from "wages" even if made pursuant to an incentive compensation plan which also provides for the making of other types of payments. However, any payment or series of payments which would have been paid if the employee's relationship had not been terminated is not excluded from "wages" under this section and section 3306(b)(10). For example, lump-sum payments for unused vacation time or a final paycheck received after retirement are payments which the employee would have received whether or not he retired and therefore are not excluded from "wages." Further, if any payment is made upon or after termination of employment for any reason other than those set out in subparagraphs (1), (2), and (3) of this paragraph such payment is not excludable from "wages" by this section. For example, if a pension plan provides for retirement upon disability, completion of 30 years of service, or attainment of age 65, and if an employee who is not disabled retires at age 61 after 30 years of service, none of the retirement payments made to the employee under the pension plan (including any made after he is 65) is excludable from "wages" under this section. However, if the pension plan had conditioned retirement after 30 years of service upon attainment of age 60, all of the retirement payments would have been excludable.

(b) *Plan.*—The plan or system established by an employer need not provide for payments because of termination of employment for all the reasons set out in subparagraphs (1), (2), and (3) of paragraph (a), but such plan or system may provide for payments because of termination for any one or more of such reasons. Payments because of termination of employment for any one or more of such reasons under a plan or system established by an employer solely for the dependents of his employes are not within this exclusion from wages.

(c) *Dependents.*—Dependents of an employee include the employee's husband or wife, children, and any other members of the employee's immediate family.

(d) *Benefit payments.*—It is immaterial for purposes of this exclusion whether the amount or possibility of such benefit payments is paid on account of services rendered or taken into consideration in fixing the amount of an employee's remuneration or whether such payments are required expressly or impliedly, by the contract of service.

(e) *Example.*—The application of this section may be illustrated by the following example:

Example. A, an employee, receives a salary of $1,500 a month, payable on the 5th day of the month following the month for which the salary is earned. A's employer has established an incentive compensation plan for a class of his employees, including A, providing for the payment of deferred compensation on termination of employment, including termination upon an employee's death, retirement at age 65 (the retirement age specified in the plan), or retirement for disability. On March 1, 1973, A attains the age of 65 and retires. On March 5, 1973, A receives $5,500 from his employer of which $1,500 represents A's salary for services he performed in February 1973, and $4,000 represents incentive compensation paid under the employer's plan. The amount of $4,000 is excluded from "wages" under this section. The amount of $1,500 is not excluded from "wages" under this section. [Reg. § 31.3306(b)(10)-1.]

☐ [T.D. 7374, 7-24-75.]

[Reg. § 31.3306(b)(13)-1]

§ 31.3306(b)(13)-1. Payments or benefits under a qualified educational assistance program.—The term "wages" does not include any payment made, or benefit furnished, to or for the benefit of an employee in a taxable year beginning after December 31, 1978, if at the time of such payment or furnishing it is reasonable to believe that the employee will be able to exclude such payment or benefit from income under section 127. [Reg. § 31.3306(b)(13)-1.]

☐ [T.D. 7898, 7-6-83.]

[Reg. § 31.3306(b)-1T]

§ 31.3306(b)-1T. Question and answer relating to the definition of wages in section 3306(b) (Temporary).—

The following question and answer relate to the definition of wages in section 3306(b) of the Internal Revenue Code of 1954, as amended by section 531(d)(3) of the Tax Reform Act of 1984 (98 Stat. 885):

Q-1: Are fringe benefits included in the definition of wages under section 3306(b)?

A-1: Yes, unless specifically excluded from the definition of "wages" pursuant to section 3306(b)(1) through (16). For example, a fringe benefit provided to or on behalf of an employee is excluded from the definition of "wages" if at the time such benefit is provided it is reasonable to believe that the employee will be able to ex-

clude such benefit from income under section 117 or 132. [Temporary Reg. § 31.3306(b)-1T.]

☐ [T.D. 8004, 1-7-85. *Amended by* T.D. 8009, 2-20-85.]

[Reg. § 31.3306(c)-1]

§ 31.3306(c)-1. Employment; services performed after 1955.—(a) Services performed after 1938 and before 1955 constitute employment under section 3306(c) if such services were employment under the law applicable to the period in which they were performed.

(b) The tax applies with respect to remuneration paid by an employer after 1954 for services performed after 1938 and before 1955, as well as for services performed after 1954, to the extent that the remuneration and services constitute wages and employment. See § § 31.3306(b)-1 to 31.3306(b)(8)-1, inclusive, relating to wages.

(c) Determination of whether services performed after 1938 and before 1955 constitute employment shall be made in accordance with the provisions of law applicable to the period in which they were performed and of the regulations thereunder. The regulations applicable in determining whether services performed after 1938 and before 1955 constitute employment are as follows:

(1) Services performed in 1939-26 CFR (1939) Part 400 (Regulations 90).

(2) Services performed after 1939 and before 1955-26 CFR (1939) Part 403 (Regulations 107). [Reg. § 31.3306(c)-1.]

☐ [T.D. 6199, 9-5-56. *Republished in* T.D. 6516, 12-20-60.]

[Reg. § 31.3306(c)-2]

§ 31.3306(c)-2. Employment; services performed after 1954.—(a) *In general.*—Whether services performed after 1954 constitute employment is determined under subsection (c) and (n) of section 3306.

(b) *Services performed within the United States.*—Services performed after 1954 within the United States (see § 31.3306(j)-1) by an employee for the person employing him, unless specifically excepted under section 3306(c), constitute employment. With respect to services performed within the United States, the place where the contract of service is entered into is immaterial. The citizenship or residence of the employee or of the person employing him also is immaterial except to the extent provided in any specific exception from employment. Thus, the employee and the person employing him may be citizens and residents of a foreign country and the contract of service may be entered into in a foreign country, and yet, if the employee under such contract performs services within the United States, there may be to that extent employment.

⮕ *Caution: The following provisions of the regulation have not been revised to reflect the amendments made by P.L. 91-373 and 94-566.*

(c) *Services performed outside the United States.*—(1) *In general.*—Except as provided in subparagraph (2) of this paragraph, services per-

formed outside the United States (see § 31.3306(j)-1) do not constitute employment.

(2) *On or in connection with an American vessel or American aircraft.*—(i) This subparagraph relates to services performed after 1954 "on or in connection with" an American vessel, and to services performed after 1961 "on or in connection with" an American aircraft to the extent that the remuneration for the latter services is paid after 1961. Such services performed outside the United States by an employee for the person employing him constitute employment if:

(a) The employee is also employed "on and in connection with" such vessel or aircraft when outside the United States; and

(b) The services are performed under a contract of service, between the employee and the person employing him, which is entered into within the United States, or during the performance of the contract under which the services are performed and while the employee is employed on the vessel or aircraft it touches at a port within the United States; and

(c) The services are not excepted under section 3306(c). (See particularly § 31.3306(c)(17)-1, relating to fishing.)

(ii) An employee performs services on and in connection with the vessel or aircraft if he performs services on the vessel or aircraft which are also in connection with the vessel or aircraft. Services performed on the vessel by employees as officers or members of the crew, or as employees of concessionaires, of the vessel, for example, are performed under such circumstances, since the services are also connected with the vessel. Similarly, services performed on the aircraft by employees as officers or members of the crew of the aircraft are performed on and in connection with such aircraft. Services may be performed on the vessel or aircraft, however, which have no connection with it, as in the case of services performed by an employee while on the vessel or aircraft merely as a passenger in the general sense. For example, the services of a buyer in the employ of a department store while he is a passenger on a vessel are not in connection with the vessel.

(iii) If services are performed by an employee "on and in connection with" an American vessel or American aircraft when outside the United States and the conditions in (b) and (c) of subdivision (i) of this subparagraph are met, then the services of that employee performed on or in connection with the vessel or aircraft constitute employment. The expression "on or in connection with" refers not only to services performed on the vessel or aircraft but also to services connected with the vessel or aircraft which are not actually performed on it (for example, shore services performed as officers or members of the crew, or as employees of concessionaires, of the vessel).

(iv) Services performed by a member of the crew or other employee whose contract of service is not entered into within the United States, and during the performance of which and while the employee is employed on the vessel or aircraft it does not touch at a port within the United States, do not constitute employment, notwithstanding that services performed by other members of the crew or other employees on or in connection with the vessel or aircraft may constitute employment.

(v) A vessel includes every description of watercraft, or other contrivance, used as a means of transportation on water. An aircraft includes every description of craft, or other contrivance, used as a means of transportation through the air. In the case of an aircraft, the term "port" means an airport. An airport means an area on land or water used regularly by aircraft for receiving or discharging passengers or cargo. For definitions of "American vessel" and "American aircraft", see § 31.3306(m)-1.

(vi) With respect to services performed outside the United States on or in connection with an American vessel or American aircraft, the citizenship or residence of the employee is immaterial, and the citizenship or residence of the employer is material only in case it has a bearing in determining whether a vessel is an American vessel. [Reg. § 31.3306(c)-2.]

☐ [*T.D.* 6199, 9-5-56. *Republished in T.D.* 6516, 12-20-60; *T.D.* 6658, 6-27-63.]

[Reg. § 31.3306(c)-3]

§ 31.3306(c)-3. Employment; excepted services in general.—(a) Services performed by an employee for the person employing him do not constitute employment for purposes of the tax if they are specifically excepted from employment under any of the numbered paragraphs of section 3306(c). Services so excepted do not constitute employment for purposes of the tax even though they are performed within the United States, or are performed outside the United States on or in connection with an American vessel or American aircraft. If not otherwise provided in the regulations relating to the numbered paragraphs of section 3306(c), such regulations apply with respect to services performed after 1954.

(b) The exception attaches to the services performed by the employee and not to the employee as an individual; that is, the exception applies only to the services rendered by the employee in an excepted class.

Example. A is an individual who is employed part time by B to perform services which constitute "agricultural labor" (see § 31.3306(k)-1). A is also employed by C part time to perform services as a grocery clerk in a store owned by him. While A's services which constitute "agricultural labor" are excepted, the exception does not embrace the services performed by A as a grocery clerk in the employ of C and the latter services are not excepted from employment.

(c) For provisions relating to the circumstances under which services which are excepted are nevertheless deemed to be employment, and relating to the circumstances under which services which are not excepted are nevertheless deemed not to be employment, see § 31.3306(d)-1. [Reg. § 31.3306(c)-3.]

☐ [*T.D.* 6199, 9-5-56. *Republished in T.D.* 6516, 12-20-60; *T.D.* 6658, 6-27-63.]

[Reg. §31.3306(c)(1)-1]

§31.3306(c)(1)-1. Agricultural labor.—Services performed by an employee for the person employing him which constitute "agricultural labor" as defined in section 3306(k) are excepted from employment. For provisions relating to the definition of the term "agricultural labor," see §31.3306(k)-1. [Reg. §31.3306(c)(1)-1.]

☐ [*T.D.* 6199, 9-5-56. *Republished in T.D.* 6516, 12-20-60.]

[Reg. §31.3306(c)(2)-1]

§31.3306(c)(2)-1. Domestic service.—(a) *In a private home.*—(1) Services of a household nature performed by an employee in or about a private home of the person by whom he is employed are excepted from the employment. A private home is a fixed place of abode of an individual or family. A separate and distinct dwelling unit maintained by an individual in an apartment house, hotel, or other similar establishment may constitute a private home. If a dwelling house is used primarily as a boarding or lodging house for the purpose of supplying board or lodging to the public as a business enterprise, it is not a private home and the services performed therein are not excepted.

(2) In general, services of a household nature in or about a private home include services performed by cooks, waiters, butlers, housekeepers, governesses, maids, valets, baby sitters, janitors, laundresses, furnacemen, caretakers, handymen, gardeners, footmen, grooms, and chauffeurs of automobiles for family use.

(b) *In a local college club or local chapter of a college fraternity or sorority.*—(1) Services of a household nature performed by an employee in or about the club rooms or house of a local college club or of a local chapter of a college fraternity or sorority by which he is employed are excepted from employment. A local college club or local chapter of a college fraternity or sorority does not include an alumni club or chapter. If the club room or house of a local college club or local chapter of a college fraternity or sorority is used primarily for the purpose of supplying board or lodging to students or the public as a business enterprise the services performed therein are not within the exception.

(2) In general, services of a household nature in or about the club rooms or house of a local college club or local chapter of a college fraternity or sorority include services rendered by cooks, waiters, butlers, maids, janitors, laundresses, furnacemen, handymen, gardeners, housekeepers, and housemothers.

(c) *Services not excepted.*—Services not of a household nature, such as services performed as a private secretary, tutor, or librarian, even though performed in the employer's private home or in a local college club or local chapter of a college fraternity or sorority, are not within the exception. Services of a household nature are not within the exception if performed in or about rooming or lodging houses, boarding houses, clubs (except local college clubs), hotels, hospitals, eleemosynary institutions, or commercial offices or establishments. [Reg. §31.3306(c)(2)-1.]

☐ [*T.D.* 6199, 9-5-56. *Republished in T.D.* 6516, 12-20-60.]

[Reg. §31.3306(c)(3)-1]

§31.3306(c)(3)-1. Services not in the course of employer's trade or business.—(a) Services not in the course of the employer's trade or business performed by an employee for an employer in a calendar quarter are excepted from employment unless—

(1) The cash remuneration paid for such services performed by the employee for the employer in the calendar quarter is $50 or more; and

(2) Such employee is regularly employed in the calendar quarter by such employer to perform such services.

Unless the tests set forth in both subparagraphs (1) and (2) of this paragraph are met, the services are excepted from employment.

(b) The term "services not in the course of the employer's trade or business" includes services that do not promote or advance the trade or business of the employer. Services performed for a corporation do not come within the exception.

(c) The test relating to cash remuneration of $50 or more is based on the remuneration earned during a calendar quarter rather than on the remuneration paid in a calendar quarter. However, for purposes of determining whether the test is met, it is also required that the remuneration be paid, although it is immaterial when the remuneration is paid. Furthermore, in determining whether $50 or more has been paid for services not in the course of the employer's trade or business, only cash remuneration for such services shall be taken into account. The term "cash remuneration" includes checks and other monetary media of exchange. Remuneration paid in any other medium, such as lodging, food, or other goods or commodities, is disregarded in determining whether the cash-remuneration test is met.

(d) For purposes of this exception, an individual is deemed to be regularly employed by an employer during a calendar quarter only if—

(1) Such individual performs services not in the course of the employer's trade or business for such employer for some portion of the day on at least 24 days (whether or not consecutive) during such calendar quarter; or

(2) Such individual was regularly employed (as determined under subparagraph (1) of this paragraph) by such employer in the performance of services not in the course of the employer's trade or busines during the preceding calendar quarter (including the last calendar quarter of 1954).

(e) In detemining whether an employee has performed services not in the course of the employer's trade or business on at least 24 days during a calendar quarter, there shall be counted as one day—

(1) Any day or portion thereof on which the employee actually performs such services; and

(2) Any day or portion thereof on which the employee does not perform services of the prescribed character but with respect to which cash remuneration is paid or payable to the employee for such services, such as a day on which the employee is sick or on vacation.

An employee who on a particualr day reports for work and, at the direction of his employer, holds himself in readiness to perform services not in the course of the employer's trade or business shall be considered to be engaged in the actual performance of such services on that day. For purposes of this exception, a day is a period of 24 hours commencing at midnight and ending at midnight.

(f) For provisions relating to the exclusion from wages of remuneration paid in any medium oher than cash for services not in the course of the employer's trade or business, see §31.3306(b)(7)-1. [Reg. §31.3306(c)(3)-1.]

□ [*T.D.* 6199, 9-5-56. *Republished in T.D.* 6516, 12-20-60.]

[Reg. §31.3306(c)(4)-1]

§31.3306(c)(4)-1. Services on or in connection with a non-American vessel or aircraft.—
(a) Services performed within the United States by an employee for an employer "on or in connection with" a vessel not an American vessel, or "on or in connection with" an aircraft not an American aircraft, are excepted from employment if the employee is employed by the employer "on and in connection with" the vessel or aircraft when outside the United States.

(b) An employee performs services on and in connection with the vessel or aircraft if he performs services on the vessel or aircraft when outside the United States which are also in connection with the vessel or aircraft. Services performed on the vessel outside the United States by employees as officers or members of the crew, or by employees of concessionaires, of the vessel, for example, are performed under such circumstances, since such services are also connected with the vessel. Similarly, services performed on the aircraft outside the United States by employees as officers or members of the crew of the aircraft are performed on and in connection with such aircraft. Services may be performed on the vessel or aircraft, however, which have no connection with it, as in the case of services performed by an employee while on the vessel or aircraft merely as a passenger in the general sense. For example, the services of a buyer in the employ of a department store while he is a passenger on a vessel are not in connection with the vessel.

(c) The expression "on or in connection with" refers not only to services performed on the vessel or aircraft but also to services connected with the vessel or aircraft which are not actually per-

formed on it (for example, shore services performed as officers or members of the crew, or as employees of concessionaires, of the vessel).

(d) The citizenship or residence of the employee and the place where the contract of service is entered into are immaterial for purposes of this exception, and the citizenship or residence of the person employing him is material only in case it has a bearing in determining whether the vessel is an American vessel. For definitions of the terms "vessel" and "aircraft", see paragraph (c)(2)(v) of §31.3306(c)-2. For definitions of the terms "American vessel" and "American aircraft", see §31.3306(m)-1.

(e) Since the only services performed outside the United States which constitute employment are those described in section 3306(c) and paragraph (c) of §31.3306(c)-2 (relating to services performed outside the United States on or in connection with an American vessel or American aircraft), services performed outside the United States on or in connection with a vessel not an American vessel, or an aircraft not an American aircraft, do not constitute employment in any event.

(f) The provisions of section 3306(c)(4) and of this section, insofar as they relate to services performed on or in connection with an aircraft not an American aircraft, apply only to services performed after 1961 for which remuneration is paid after 1961. [Reg. §31.3306(c)(4)-1.]

□ [*T.D.* 6199, 9-5-56. *Republished in T.D.* 6516, 12-20-60; *T.D.* 6658, 6-27-63.]

[Reg. §31.3306(c)(5)-1]

§31.3306(c)(5)-1. Family employment.—
(a) Certain services are excepted from employment because of the existence of a family relationship between the employee and the individual employing him. The exceptions are as follows:

(1) Services performed by an individual in the employ of his or her spouse;

(2) Services performed by a father or mother in the employ of his or her son or daughter; and

(3) Services performed by a son or daughter under the age of 21 in the employ of his or her father or mother.

(b) Under paragraph (a)(1) and (2) of this section, the exception is conditioned solely upon the family relationship between the employee and the individual employing him. Under paragraph (a)(3) of this section, in addition to the family relationship, there is a further requirement that the son or daughter shall be under the age of 1, and the exception continues only during the time that such son or daughter is under the age of 21.

(c) Services performed in the employ of a partnership are within the exception described in paragraph (a) of this section only if the requisite family relationship exists between the employee and each of the partners comprising the partnership.

(d) Services performed in the employ of a corporation are not within the exception described in paragraph (a) of this section, except that services performed in the employ of an entity that is treated as a corporation under § 301.7701-2(c)(2)(iv)(B) of this chapter may qualify for the exception if the requirements of the exception are otherwise met. An entity that is treated as a corporation under § 301.7701-2(c)(2)(iv)(B) of this chapter is not treated as the employer for purposes of applying section 3306(c)(5) and this section. For purposes of applying section 3306(c)(5) and this section, the owner of an entity that is treated as a corporation under § 301.7701-2(c)(2)(iv)(B) of this chapter is treated as the employer.

(e) Paragraphs (c) and (d) of this section apply to wages paid on or after November 1, 2011. However, taxpayers may apply paragraphs (c) and (d) of this section to wages paid on or after January 1, 2009. [Reg. § 31.3306(c)(5)-1.]

☐ [T.D. 6199, 9-5-56. *Republished in T.D.* 6516, 12-20-60. *Amended by T.D.* 9554, 10-31-2011 *and* T.D. 9670, 6-25-2014.]

[Reg. § 31.3306(c)(6)-1]

§ 31.3306(c)(6)-1. Services in employ of United States or instrumentality thereof.— (a) *Services in employ of United States or wholly-owned instrumentality thereof.*—Services performed in the employ of the United States Government, except as provided in section 3306(n) (see § 31.3306(n)-1), are excepted from employment. Services performed in the employ of an instrumentality of the United States which is wholly owned by the United States also are excepted from employment.

(b) *Services in employ of instrumentality not wholly owned by United States.*—(1) *Services performed after 1961.*—Services performed after 1961 in the employ of an instrumentality of the United States which is partially owned by the United States are excepted from employment, if the remuneration for such service is paid after 1961. Services performed after 1961 in the employ of an instrumentality of the United States which is neither wholly owned or partially owned by the United States are excepted from employment if (i) the instrumentality is exempt from the tax imposed by section 3301 by virtue of any provision of law which specifically refers to section 3301 or the corresponding section of prior law in granting exemption from such tax, and (ii) the remuneration for such service is paid after 1961. For provisions which make general exemptions from Federal taxation ineffectual as to the tax imposed by section 3301, see § 31.3308-1.

(2) *Services performed before 1962.*—Services performed in the employ of an instrumentality of the United States which is not wholly owned by the United States are excepted from employment if the instrumentality is exempt from the tax imposed by section 3301 by virtue of any other provision of law, and (i) the services are performed before 1962 or (ii) remuneration for the services is paid before 1962. [Reg. § 31.3306(c)(6)-1.]

☐ [T.D. 6199, 9-5-56. *Republished in T.D.* 6516, 12-20-60; *T.D.* 6658, 6-27-63.]

⠀⠀⠀⠀ Caution: *P.L. 91-373 has made state coverage of certain services performed for state, county, and municipal hospitals and institutions of higher learning a condition for approval of state laws after 1971.*

[Reg. § 31.3306(c)(7)-1]

§ 31.3306(c)(7)-1. Services in employ of States or their political subdivisions or instrumentalities.—(a) Services performed in the employ of any State, or of any political subdivision thereof, are excepted from employment. Services performed in the employ of an instrumentality of one or more States or political subdivisions thereof are excepted if the instrumentality is wholly owned by one or more of the foregoing. Services performed in the employ of an instrumentality of one or more of the several States or political subdivisions thereof which is not wholly owned by one or more of the foregoing are excepted only to the extent that the instrumentality is with respect to such services immune under the Constitution of the United States from the tax imposed by section 3301.

(b) For provisions relating to the term "State" see § 31.3306(j)-1. [Reg. § 31.3306(c)(7)-1.]

☐ [T.D. 6199, 9-5-56. *Republished in T.D.* 6516, 12-20-60; *T.D.* 6658, 6-27-63.]

⠀⠀⠀⠀ Caution: *P.L. 91-373 has made state coverage of certain services performed for nonprofit organizations a condition for approval of state laws after 1971.*

[Reg. § 31.3306(c)(8)-1]

§ 31.3306(c)(8)-1. Services in employ of religious, charitable, educational, or certain other organizations exempt from income tax.— (a) *Services performed after 1961.*—Services performed by an employee after 1961 in the employ of a religious, charitable, educational, or other organization described in section 501(c)(3) which is exempt from income tax under section 501(a) are excepted from employment, if the remuneration for such service is paid after 1961. For provisions relating to exemption from income tax of an organization described in section 501(c)(3),

see Part 1 of this chapter (Income Tax Regulations).

(b) *Services performed before 1962.*—(1) Services performed by an employee in the employ of an organization described in section 3306(c)(8) as in effect before 1962, that is, a corporation, community chest, fund, or foundation, organized and operated exclusively for religious, charitable, scientific, testing for public safety, literary, or educational purposes, or for the prevention of cruelty to children or animals, no part of the net earnings of which inures to the benefit of any private shareholder or individual, and no substantial part of the activities of which is carrying on propaganda, or otherwise attempting, to influence legislation, are excepted from employment if (i) the services are performed before 1962, or (ii) remuneration for the services is paid before 1962.

(2) Any organization which is an organization of a type described in section 501(c)(3) and which—

(i) Is exempt from income tax under section 501(a), or

(ii) Has been denied exemption from income tax under section 501(a) by reason of the provisions of section 503 or 504, relating to prohibited transactions and to accumulations out of income, respectively,

is an organization of a type described in section 3306(c)(8) as in effect before 1962. An organization which would be an organization of a type described in section 501(c)(3) except for those provisions of section 501(c)(3) which are contained in section 3306(c)(8) as in effect before 1962 (provisions relating to participation or intervention in a political campaign on behalf of a candidate for public office) is also an organization of a type described in section 3306(c)(8) as in effect before 1962. [Reg. § 31.3306(c)(8)-1.]

☐ [*T.D.* 6199, 9-5-56. *Republished in T.D.* 6516, 12-20-60; *T.D.* 6658, 6-27-63.]

[Reg. § 31.3306(c)(9)-1]

§ 31.3306(c)(9)-1. Railroad industry; services performed by an employee or an employee representative under the Railroad Unemployment Insurance Act.—(a) Services performed by an individual as an "employee" or as an "employee representative", as those terms are defined in section 1 of the Railroad Unemployment Insurance Act, as amended, are excepted from employment.

(b) Section 1 of the Railroad Unemployment Insurance Act (45 U.S.C. 351), as amended, provides, in part, as follows:

For the purposes of this Act, except when used in amending the provisions of other Acts—

(a) The term "employer" means any carrier (as defined in subsection (b) of this section), and any company which is directly or indirectly owned or controlled by one or more such carriers or under common control therewith, and which operates any equipment or facility or performs any service (except trucking service, casual service, and the casual operation of equipment or facilities) in connection with the transportation of passengers or property by railroad, or the receipt, delivery, elevation, transfer in transit, refrigeration or icing, storage, or handling of property transported by railroad, and any receiver, trustee, or other individual or body, judicial or otherwise, when in the possession of the property or operating all or any part of the business of any such employer: *Provided, however,* That the term "employer" shall not include any street, interurban, or suburban electric railway, unless such railway is operating as a part of a general steam-railroad system of transportation,

but shall not exclude any part of the general steam-railroad system of transportation now or hereafter operated by any other motive power. The Interstate Commerce Commission is hereby authorized and directed upon request of the Board, or upon complaint of any party interested, to determine after hearing whether any line operated by electric power falls within the terms of this proviso. The term "employer" shall also include railroad associations, traffic associations, tariff bureaus, demurrage bureaus, weighing and inspection bureaus, collection agencies, and other associations, bureaus, agencies, or organizations controlled and maintained wholly or principally by two or more employers as hereinbefore defined and engaged in the performance of services in connection with or incidental to railroad transportation; and railway labor organizations, national in scope, which have been or may be organized in accordance with the provisions of the Railway Labor Act, and their State and National legislative committees and their general committees pursuant to the constitution and bylaws of such organizations. The term "employer" shall not include any company by reason of its being engaged in the mining of coal, the supplying of coal to an employer where delivery is not beyond the mine tipple, and the operation of equipment or facilities therefor, or in any of such activities.

(b) The term "carrier" means an express company, sleeping-car company, or carrier by railroad, subject to part I of the interstate Commerce Act.

(c) The term "company" includes corporations, associations, and joint-stock companies.

(d) The term "employee" (except when used in phrases establishing a different meaning) means any individual who is or has been (i) in the service of one or more employers for compensation, or (ii) an employee representative. The term "employee" shall include an employee of a local lodge or division defined as an employer in section 1(a) only if he was in the service of a carrier on or after August 29, 1935. The term "employee" includes an officer of an employer.

The term "employee" shall not include any individual while such individual is engaged in the physical operations consisting of the mining of coal, the preparation of coal, the handling (other than movement by rail with standard railroad locomotives) of coal not beyond the mine tipple, or the loading of coal at the tipple.

(e) An individual is in the service of an employer whether his service is rendered within or without the United States if (i) he is subject to the continuing authority of the employer to supervise and direct the manner of rendition of his service, or he is rendering professional or technical services and is integrated into the staff of the employer, or he is rendering, on the property used in the employer's operations, other personal services the rendition of which is integrated into the employer's operations, and (ii) he renders such service for compensation: *Provided, however,* That an individual shall be deemed to be in the service of an employer, other than a local lodge or division or a general committee of a railway-labor-organization employer, not conducting the principal part of its business in the United States only when he is rendering service to it in the United States; and an individual shall be deemed to be in the service of such a local lodge or division only if (1) all, or substantially all, the individuals constituting its membership are employees of an employer conducting the principal part of its business in the United States; or (2) the headquarters of such local lodge or division is located in the United States; and an individual shall be deemed to be in the service of such a general committee only if (1) he is representing a local lodge or division described in clauses (1) or (2) immediately above; or (2) all, or substantially all, the individuals represented by it are employees of an employer conducting the principal part of its business in the United States; or (3) he acts in the capacity of a general chairman or an assistant general chairman of a general committee which represents individuals rendering service in the United States to an employer, but in such case if his office or headquarters is not located in the United States and the individuals represented by such general committee are employees of an employer not conducting the principal part of its business in the United States, only such proportion of the remuneration for such service shall be regarded as compensation as the proportion which the mileage in the United States under the jurisdiction of such general committee bears to the total mileage under its jurisdiction, unless such mileage formula is inapplicable, in which case the Board may prescribe such other formula as it finds to be equitable, and if the application of such mileage formula, or such other formula as the Board may prescribe, would result in the compensation of the individual being less than 10 per centum of his remuneration for such service no part of such remuneration shall be regarded as compensation: *Provided further,* That an individual not a citizen or resident of the United States shall not be deemed to be in the service of an employer when rendering service outside the United States to an employer who is required under the laws applicable in the place where the service is rendered to employ therein, in whole or in part, citizens or residents thereof.

(f) The term "employee representative" means any officer or official representative of a railroad labor organization other than a labor organization included in the term employer as defined in section 1(a) who before or after August 29, 1935, was in the service of an employer as defined in section 1(a) and who is duly authorized and designated to represent employees in accordance with the Railway Labor Act, and any individual who is regularly assigned to or regularly employed by such officer or official representative in connection with the duties of his office.

* * *

(i) The term "compensation" means any form of money remuneration, including pay for time lost but excluding tips, paid for services rendered as an employee to one or more employers, or as an employee representative: *Provided, however,* That in computing the compensation paid to an employee, no part of any month's compensation in excess of $300 for any month before July 1, 1954, or in excess of $350 for any month after June 30, 1954, and before the calendar month next following the month [May] in which this Act was amended in 1959, or in excess of $400 for any month after the month [May] in which this Act was so amended, shall be recognized. A payment made by an employer to an individual through the employer's pay roll shall be presumed, in the absence of evidence to the contrary, to be compensation for service rendered by such individual as an employee of the employer in the period with respect to which the payment is made. An employee shall be deemed to be paid, "for time lost" the amount he is paid by an employer with respect to an identifiable period of absence from the active service of the employer, including absence on account of personal injury, and the amount he is paid by the employer for loss of earnings resulting from his displacement to a less remunerative position or occupation. If a payment is made by an employer with respect to a personal injury and includes pay for time lost, the total payment shall be deemed to be paid for time lost unless, at the time of payment, a part of such payment is specifically apportioned to factors other than time lost, in which event only such part of the payment as is not so apportioned shall be deemed to be paid for time lost. Compensation earned in any calendar month before 1947 shall be deemed paid in such month regardless of whether or when payment will have been in fact made, and compensation earned in any calendar year after 1946 but paid after the end of such calendar year shall be deemed to be compensation paid in the calendar year in which it will have been earned if it is so reported by the employer before February 1 of the next succeeding calendar year or, if the employee establishes, subject to the provisions of section 8, the period during which such compensation will have been earned.

* * *

(r) The term "Board" means the Railroad Retirement Board.

(s) The term "United States", when used in a geographical sense, means the States, Alaska, Hawaii, and the District of Columbia.

* * *

[Sec. 1, Railroad Unemployment Insurance Act, as amended by secs. 1 and 2, Act of June 20, 1939, 53 Stat. 845; secs. 1 and 3, Act of Aug. 13, 1940, 54 Stat. 785, 786; sec. 15, Act of Apr. 8, 1942, 56 Stat. 210; secs. 1 and 2, Act of July 31, 1946, 60 Stat. 722; sec. 302, Act of Aug. 31, 1954, 68 Stat. 1040; sec. 301, Act of May 19, 1959, Pub. Law 86-28, 7 Stat. 30.] [Reg. § 31.3306(c)(9)-1.]

☐ [*T.D.* 6199, 9-5-56. *Republished in T.D.* 6516, 12-20-60; *T.D.* 6658, 6-27-63.]

Reg. §31.3306(c)(9)-1(i)

[Reg. §31.3306(c)(10)-1]

§31.3306(c)(10)-1. **Services in the employ of certain organizations exempt from income tax.**—(a) *In general.*—(1) This section deals with the exception from employment of certain services performed in the employ of any organization exempt from income tax under section 501(a) (other than an organization described in section 401(a)) or under section 521. (See the provisions of §§1.401-1, 1.501(a)-1, and 1.521-1 of this chapter (Income Tax Regulations).) If the services meet the tests set forth in paragraphs (b), (c), (d), or (e) of this section, the services are excepted.

(2) See also §31.3306(c)(8)-1 for provisions relating to the exception of services performed in the employ of religious, charitable, educational, or certain other organizations exempt from income tax; §31.3306(c)(10)-2 for provisions relating to the exception of services performed by certain students in the employ of a school, college, or university; and §31.3306(c)(10)-3 for provisions relating to the exception of services performed before 1962 in the employ of certain employees' beneficiary associations.

(b) *Remuneration less than $50 for calendar quarter.*—Services performed by an employee in a calendar quarter in the employ of an organization exempt from income tax under section 501(a) (other than an organization described in section 401(a)) or under section 521 are excepted from employment, if the remuneration for the services is less than $50. The test relating to remuneration of $50 is based on the remuneration earned during a calendar quarter rather than on the remuneration paid in a calendar quarter. The exception applies separately with respect to each organization for which the employee renders services in a calendar quarter. The type of services performed by the employee and the place where the services are performed are immaterial; the statutory tests are the character of the organization in the employ of which the services are performed and the amount of the remuneration for services performed by the employee in the calendar quarter.

Example (1). X is a local lodge of a fraternal organization and is exempt from income tax under section 501(a) as an organization of the character described in section 501(c)(8). X has a number of paid employees, among them being A who serves exclusively as recording secretary for the lodge, and B who performs services for the lodge as janitor of its clubhouse. For services performed during the first calendar quarter of 1955 (that is, January 1, 1955, through March 31, 1955, both dates inclusive) A earns a total of $30. For services performed during the same calendar quarter of 1955 (that is, January 1, 1955, through March 31, 1955, both dates inclusive) A earns a total of $30. For services performed during the same calendar quarter B earns $180. Since the remuneration for the services performed by A during such quarter is less than $50, all of such services are excepted. Thus, A is not counted as

an employee in employment on any of the days during such quarter for purposes of determining whether the X organization is an employer (see §31.3306(a)-1). Even though it is subsequently determined that X is an employer, A's remuneration of $30 for services performed during the first calendar quarter of such year is not subject to tax. B's services, however, are not excepted during such quarter since the remuneration therefor is not less than $50. Thus, B is counted as an employee in employment during all of such quarter for purposes of determining whether the X organization is an employer. If it is determined that the X organization is an employer, B's remuneration of $180 for services performed during the first calendar quarter is included in computing the tax.

Example (2). The facts are the same as in example (1), above, except that on April 1, 1955, A's salary is increased and, for services performed during the calendar quarter beginning on that date (that is, April 1, 1955, through June 30, 1955, both dates inclusive), A earns $60. Although all of the services performed by A during the first quarter were excepted, none of A's services performed during the second quarter are excepted since the remuneration for such services is not less than $50. A, therefore, is counted as an employee in employment during all of the second quarter for the purpose of determining whether the X organization is an employer. If it is determined that the X organization is an employer, A's remuneration of $60 for services performed during the second calendar quarter is included in computing the tax.

Example (3). The facts are the same as in example (1), above, except that A earns $120 for services performed during the year 1955, and such amount is paid to him in a lump sum at the end of the year. The services performed by A in any calendar quarter during the year are excepted if the portion of the $120 attributable to services performed in that quarter is less than $50. In such case, A is not counted as an employee in employment on any of the days during such quarter for purposes of determining whether the X organization is an employer. If, however, the portion of the $120 attributable to services performed in any calendar quarter during the year is not less than $50, the services during that quarter are not excepted. In the latter case, A is counted as an employee in employment during all of such quarter and, if it is determined that the X organization is an employer, that portion of the $120 attribuable to services performed in such quarter is included in computing the tax.

(c) *Collection of dues or premiums for fraternal beneficiary societies, and ritualistic services in connection with such societies, before 1962.*—The following services performed by an employee in the employ of a fraternal beneficiary society, order, or association exempt from income tax under section 501(a) are excepted from employment if the services are performed before 1962 or if remuneration for the services is paid before 1962:

(1) Services performed away from the home office of such a society, order, or association in connection with the collection of dues or premiums for such society, order, or association; and

(2) Ritualistic services (wherever performed) in connection with such a society, order, or association.

For purposes of this paragraph the amount of the remuneration for services performed by the employee in the calendar quarter is immaterial; the tests are the character of the organization in whose employ the services are performed, the type of services, and, in the case of collection of dues or premiums, the place where the services are performed.

(d) *Students employed before 1962.*—(1) Services performed in the employ of an organization exempt from income tax under section 501(a) (other than an organization described in section 401(a)) or under section 521 by a student who is enrolled and is regularly attending classes at a school, college, or university, are excepted from employment if the services are performed before 1962 or if remuneration for the services is paid before 1962. For purposes of this paragraph, the amount of remuneration for services performed by the employee in the calendar quarter, the type of services, and the place where the services are performed are immaterial; the tests are the character of the organization in whose employ the services are performed and the status of the employee as a student enrolled and regularly attending classes at a school, college, or university.

(2) The term "school, college, or university" as used in this paragraph is to be taken in its commonly or generally accepted sense. For provisions relating to services performed before 1962 by a student enrolled and regularly attending classes at a school, college, or university not exempt from income tax in the employ of such school, college, or university, see paragraph (b) of §31.3306(c)(10)-2. For provisions relating to services performed after 1961 by a student en-

rolled and regularly attending classes at a school, college, or university in the employ of such school, college, or university, see paragraph (a) of §31.3306(c)(10)-2.

(e) *Services performed before 1962 in employ of agricultural or horticultural organization exempt from income tax.*—(1) Services performed by an employee in the employ of an agricultural or horticultural organization which is described in section 501(c)(5) and the regulations thereunder and which is exempt from income tax under section 501(a) are excepted from employment if the services are performed before 1962 or if remuneration of the services is paid before 1962.

(2) For purposes of this paragraph, the type of services performed by the employee, the amount of remuneration for the services, and the place where the services are performed are immaterial; the test is the character of the organization in whose employ the services are performed. [Reg. §31.3306(c)(10)-1.]

☐ [*T.D.* 6199, 9-5-56. *Republished in T.D.* 6516, 12-20-60; *T.D.* 6658, 6-27-63.]

[Reg. §31.3306(c)(10)-2]

§31.3306(c)(10)-2. Services of student in employ of school, college, or university.—(a) *Services performed after 1961.*—Services performed after 1961 in the employ of a school, college, or university, by a student who is enrolled and is regularly attending classes at the school, college, or university, are excepted from employment (whether or not the school, college, or university is exempt from income tax), if remuneration for the services is paid after 1961.

(b) *Services performed before 1962.*—Services performed in the employ of a school, college, or university not exempt from income tax under section 501(a), by a student who is enrolled and is regularly attending classes at the school, college, or university, are excepted from employment if the services are performed before 1962 or if remuneration for the services is paid before 1962.

≫→ *Caution: Reg. §31.3306(c)(10)-2(c), below, prior to amendment by T.D. 9167, is applicable for services performed before April 1, 2005.*

(c) *Application of section.*—(1) For purposes of this section, the type of services performed by the employee, the place where the services are performed, and the amount of remuneration for services performed by the employee are immaterial; the tests are the character of the organization in the employ of which the services are performed and the status of the employee as a student enrolled and regularly attending classes at the school, college, or university in the employ of which he performs the services.

(2) The status of the employee as a student performing the services shall be determined on the basis of the relationship of such employee

with the organization for which the services are performed. An employee who performs services in the employ of a school, college, or university as an incident to and for the purpose of pursuing a course of study at such school, college, or university has the status of a student in the performance of such services.

(3) The term "school, college, or university" as used in this section is to be taken in its commonly or generally accepted sense.

(4) For provisions relating to services performed before 1962 by a student in the employ of an organization exempt from income tax, see paragraph (d) of §31.3306(c)(10)-1.

>>> *Caution: Reg. §31.3306(c)(10)-2(c), below, as amended by T.D. 9167, is applicable for services performed on or after April 1, 2005.*

(c) *General rule.*—(1) For purposes of this section, the tests are the character of the organization in the employ of which the services are performed and the status of the employee as a student enrolled and regularly attending classes at the school, college, or university described in paragraph (c)(2) of this section, in the employ of which the employee performs the services. If an employee has the status of a student within the meaning of paragraph (d) of this section, the type of services performed by the employee, the place where the services are performed, and the amount of remuneration for services performed by the employee are not material.

(2) *School, college, or university.*—An organization is a *school, college, or university* within the meaning of section 3306(c)(10)(B) if its primary function is the presentation of formal instruction, it normally maintains a regular faculty and curriculum, and it normally has a regularly enrolled body of students in attendance at the place where its educational activities are regularly carried on. See section 170(b)(1)(A)(ii) and the regulations thereunder.

(d) *Student status—general rule.*—Whether an employee has the status of a student within the meaning of section 3306(c)(10)(B) performing the services shall be determined based on the relationship of the employee with the organization for which the services are performed. In order to have the status of a student within the meaning of section 3306(c)(10)(B), the employee must perform services in the employ of a school, college, or university described in paragraph (c)(2) of this section at which the employee is enrolled and regularly attending classes in pursuit of a course of study within the meaning of paragraphs (d)(1) and (2) of this section. In addition, the employee's services must be incident to and for the purpose of pursuing a course of study at such school, college, or university within the meaning of paragraph (d)(3) of this section.

(1) *Enrolled and regularly attending classes.*—An employee must be enrolled and regularly attending classes at a school, college, or university within the meaning of paragraph (c)(2) of this section at which the employee is employed to have the status of a student within the meaning of section 3306(c)(10)(B). An employee is enrolled within the meaning of section 3306(c)(10)(B) if the employee is registered for a course or courses creditable toward an educational credential described in paragraph (d)(2) of this section. In addition, the employee must be regularly attending classes to have the status of a student. For purposes of this paragraph (d)(1), a class is an instructional activity led by a faculty member or other qualified individual hired by the school, college, or university within the meaning of paragraph (c)(2) of this section for identified students following an established curriculum. The frequency of these and similar activities determines whether an employee may be considered to be regularly attending classes.

(2) *Course of study.*—An employee must be pursuing a course of study in order to have the status of a student within the meaning of section 3306(c)(10)(B). A course of study is one or more courses the completion of which fulfills the requirements necessary to receive an educational credential granted by a school, college, or university within the meaning of paragraph (c)(2) of this section. For purposes of this paragraph, an educational credential is a degree, certificate, or other recognized educational credential granted by an organization described in paragraph (c)(2) of this section. In addition, a course of study is one or more courses at a school, college or university within the meaning of paragraph (c)(2) of this section the completion of which fulfills the requirements necessary for the employee to sit for an examination required to receive certification by a recognized organization in a field.

(3) *Incident to and for the purpose of pursuing a course of study.*—(i) *General rule.*—An employee's services must be incident to and for the purpose of pursuing a course of study in order for the employee to have the status of a student. Whether an employee's services are incident to and for the purpose of pursuing a course of study shall be determined on the basis of the relationship of the employee with the organization for which such services are performed as an employee. The educational aspect of the relationship between the employer and the employee, as compared to the service aspect of the relationship, must be predominant in order for the employee's services to be incident to and for the purpose of pursuing a course of study. The educational aspect of the relationship is evaluated based on all the relevant facts and circumstances related to the educational aspect of the relationship. The service aspect of the relationship is evaluated based on all the relevant facts and circumstances related to the employee's employment. The evaluation of the service aspect of the relationship is not affected by the fact that the services performed by the employee may have an educational, instructional, or training aspect. Except as provided in paragraph (d)(3)(iii) of this section, whether the educational aspect or the service aspect of an employee's relationship with the employer is predominant is determined by considering all the relevant facts and circumstances. Relevant factors in evaluating the educational and service aspects of an employee's relationship with the employer are described in paragraphs (d)(3)(iv) and (v) of this section respectively. There may be facts and circumstances that are relevant in evaluating the educational and service aspects of the relationship in addition to those described in paragraphs (d)(3)(iv) and (v) of this section.

(ii) *Student status determined with respect to each academic term.*—Whether an employee's services are incident to and for the purpose of pursuing a course of study is determined separately with respect to each academic term. If the relevant facts and circumstances with respect to an employee's relationship with the employer change significantly during an academic term, whether the employee's services are incident to and for the purpose of pursuing a course of study is reevaluated with respect to services performed during the remainder of the academic term.

(iii) *Full-time employee.*—The services of a full-time employee are not incident to and for the purpose of pursuing a course of study. The determination of whether an employee is a full-time employee is based on the employer's standards and practices, except regardless of the employer's classification of the employee, an employee whose normal work schedule is 40 hours or more per week is considered a full-time employee. An employee's normal work schedule is not affected by increases in hours worked caused by work demands unforeseen at the start of an academic term. However, whether an employee is a full-time employee is reevaluated for the remainder of the academic term if the employee changes employment positions with the employer. An employee's work schedule during academic breaks is not considered in determining whether the employee's normal work schedule is 40 hours or more per week. The determination of the employee's normal work schedule is not affected by the fact that the services performed by the individual may have an educational, instructional, or training aspect.

(iv) *Evaluating educational aspect.*—The educational aspect of an employee's relationship with the employer is evaluated based on all the relevant facts and circumstances related to the educational aspect of the relationship. The educational aspect of an employee's relationship with the employer is generally evaluated based on the employee's course workload. Whether an employee's course workload is sufficient in order for the employee's employment to be incident to and for the purpose of pursuing a course of study depends on the particular facts and circumstances. A relevant factor in evaluating an employee's course workload is the employee's course workload relative to a full-time course workload at the school, college or university within the meaning of paragraph (c)(2) of this section at which the employee is enrolled and regularly attending classes.

(v) *Evaluating service aspect.*—The service aspect of an employee's relationship with the employer is evaluated based on the facts and circumstances related to the employee's employment. Services of an employee with the status of a full-time employee within the meaning of paragraph (d)(3)(iii) of this section are not incident to and for the purpose of pursuing a course of study. Relevant factors in evaluating the service aspect of an employee's relationship with the

employer are described in paragraphs (d)(3)(v)(A), (B), and (C) of this section.

(A) *Normal work schedule and hours worked.*—If an employee is not a full-time employee within the meaning of paragraph (d)(3)(iii) of this section, then the employee's normal work schedule and number of hours worked per week are relevant factors in evaluating the service aspect of the employee's relationship with the employer. As an employee's normal work schedule or actual number of hours worked approaches 40 hours per week, it is more likely that the service aspect of the employee's relationship with the employer is predominant. The determination of the employee's normal work schedule and actual number of hours worked is not affected by the fact that some of the services performed by the individual may have an educational, instructional, or training aspect.

(B) *Professional employee.*—(1) If an employee has the status of a professional employee, then that suggests that the service aspect of the employee's relationship with the employer is predominant. A professional employee is an employee—

(i) Whose primary duty consists of the performance of work requiring knowledge of an advanced type in a field of science or learning customarily acquired by a prolonged course of specialized intellectual instruction and study, as distinguished from a general academic education, from an apprenticeship, and from training in the performance of routine mental, manual, or physical processes;

(ii) Whose work requires the consistent exercise of discretion and judgment in its performance; and

(iii) Whose work is predominantly intellectual and varied in character (as opposed to routine mental, manual, mechanical, or physical work) and is of such character that the output produced or the result accomplished cannot be standardized in relation to a given period of time.

(2) *Licensed, professional employee.*—If an employee is a licensed, professional employee, then that further suggests the service aspect of the employee's relationship with the employer is predominant. An employee is a licensed, professional employee if the employee is required to be licensed under state or local law to work in the field in which the employee performs services and the employee is a professional employee within the meaning of paragraph (d)(3)(v)(B)(1) of this section.

(C) *Employment benefits.*—Whether an employee is eligible to receive employment benefits is a relevant factor in evaluating the service aspect of an employee's relationship with the employer. For example, eligibility to receive vacation, paid holiday, and paid sick leave benefits; eligibility to participate in a retirement plan described in section 401(a); or eligibility to receive employment benefits such as reduced tuition, or benefits under section 79 (life insurance), 127 (qualified educational assistance), 129 (dependent care assistance programs), or 137 (adoption assistance) suggest that the service aspect of an employee's relationship with the employer is predominant. Eligibility to receive health insurance employment benefits is not considered in determining whether the service aspect of an employee's relationship with the employer is predominant. The weight to be given the fact that an employee is eligible for a particular benefit may vary depending on the type of employment benefit. For example, eligibility to participate in a retirement plan is generally more significant than eligibility to receive a dependent care employment benefit. Additional weight is given to the fact that an employee is eligible to receive an employment benefit if the benefit is generally provided by the employer to employees in positions generally held by non-students.

(e) *Effective date.*—Paragraphs (c) and (d) of this section apply to services performed on or after April 1, 2005. [Reg. § 31.3306(c)(10)-2.]

☐ [*T.D.* 6199, 9-5-56. *Republished in T.D.* 6516, 12-20-60; *T.D.* 6658, 6-27-63 *and T.D.* 9167, 12-20-2004.]

[Reg. § 31.3306(c)(10)-3]

§ 31.3306(c)(10)-3. **Services before 1962 in employ of certain employees' beneficiary associations.**—(a) *Voluntary employees' beneficiary associations.*—Services performed by an employee in the employ of a voluntary employees' beneficiary association providing for the payment of life, sick, accident, or other benefits to the members of such association or their dependents are excepted from employment if—

(1) No part of its net earnings inures (other than through such payments) to the benefit of any private shareholder or individual,

(2) 85 percent or more of the income consists of amounts collected from members for the sole purpose of making such payments and meeting expenses, and

(3) The services are performed before 1962, or remuneration for the services is paid before 1962.

(b) *Federal employees' beneficiary associations.*—Services performed by an employee in the employ of a voluntary employees' beneficiary association providing for the payment of life, sick, accident, or other benefits to the members of such association or their dependents or their designated beneficiaries are excepted from employment if—

(1) Admission to membership in the association is limited to individuals who are officers or employees of the United States Government,

(2) No part of the net earnings of the association inures (other than through such payments) to the benefit of any private shareholder or individual, and

(3) The services are performed before 1962, or remuneration for the services is paid before 1962.

(c) *Application of tests.*—For purposes of this section, the type of services performed by the employee, the amount of remuneration for the services, and the place where the services are performed are immaterial; the test is the character of the organization in whose employ the services are performed. [Reg. § 31.3306(c)(10)-3.]

☐ [*T.D.* 6199, 9-5-56. *Republished in T.D.* 6516, 12-20-60; *T.D.* 6658, 6-27-63.]

[Reg. § 31.3306(c)(11)-1]

§ 31.3306(c)(11)-1. **Services in employ of foreign government.**—(a) Services performed by an employee in the employ of a foreign government are excepted from employment. The exception includes not only services performed by ambassadors, ministers, and other diplomatic officers and employees but also services performed as a consular or other officer or employee of a foreign government, or as a nondiplomatic representative thereof.

(b) For purposes of this exception, the citizenship or residence of the employee is immaterial. It is also immaterial whether the foreign government grants an equivalent exemption with respect to similar services performed in the foreign country by citizens of the United States.[Reg. § 31.3306(c)(11)-1.]

☐ [*T.D.* 6199, 9-5-56. *Republished in T.D.* 6516, 12-20-60.]

[Reg. § 31.3306(c)(12)-1]

§ 31.3306(c)(12)-1. **Services in employ of wholly owned instrumentality of foreign government.**—(a) Services performed by an employee in the employ of certain instrumentalities of a foreign government are excepted from employment. The exception includes all services performed in the employ of an instrumentality of the government of a foreign country, if—

(1) The instrumentality is wholly owned by the foreign government;

(2) The services are of a character similar to those performed in foreign countries by employees of the United States Government or of an instrumentality thereof; and

(3) The Secretary of States certifies to the Secretary of the Treasury that the foreign government, with respect to whose instrumentality exemption is claimed, grants an equivalent exemption with respect to services performed in the foreign country by employees of the United States Government and of instrumentalities thereof.

(b) For purposes of this exception, the citizenship or residence of the employee is immaterial. [Reg. § 31.3306(c)(12)-1.]

☐ [*T.D.* 6199, 9-5-56. *Republishd in T.D.* 6516, 12-20-60.]

[Reg. § 31.3306(c)(13)-1]

§ 31.3306(c)(13)-1. **Services of student nurse or hospital intern.**—(a) Services performed as a student nurse in the employ of a hospital or a nurses' training school are excepted from employment, if the student nurse is enrolled and regularly attending classes in a nurses' training school and such nurses' training school is chartered or approved pursuant to State law.

(b) Services performed as an intern (as distinguished from a resident doctor) in the employ of a hospital are excepted from employment, if the intern has completed a 4 years' course in a medical school chartered or approved pursuant to State law. [Reg. § 31.3306(c)(13)-1.]

☐ [T.D. 6199, 9-5-56. *Republished in T.D. 6516,* 12-20-60.]

[Reg. § 31.3306(c)(14)-1]

§ 31.3306(c)(14)-1. Services of insurance agent or solicitor.—(a) Services performed for a person by an employee as an insurance agent or insurance solicitor are excepted from employment, if all such services performed for such person by such individual are performed for remuneration solely by way of commission.

(b) If all or any part of the remuneration of an employee for services performed as an insurance agent or insurance solicitor for a person is a salary, none of his services performed as an insurance agent or insurance solicitor for such person are excepted from employment, and his total remuneration (for example, salary, or salary and commissions) for such services is included for purposes of computing the tax. [Reg. § 31.3306(c)(14)-1.]

☐ [T.D. 6199, 9-5-56. *Republished in T.D. 6516,* 12-20-60.]

[Reg. § 31.3306(c)(15)-1]

§ 31.3306(c)(15)-1. Services in delivery or distribution of newspapers, shopping news or magazines.—(a) *Services of individuals under age 18.*—Services performed by an employee under the age of 18 in the delivery or distribution of newspapers or shopping news, not including delivery or distribution (as, for example, by a regional distributor) to any point for subsequent delivery or distribution, are excepted from employment. Thus, the services performed by an employee under the age of 18 in making house-to-house delivery or sale of newspapers or shopping news, including handbills and other similar types of advertising material, are excepted. The services are excepted irrespective of the form or method of compensation. Incidental services by the employee who makes the house-to-house delivery, such as services in assembling newspapers, are considered to be within the exception. The exception continues only during the time that the employee is under the age of 18.

(b) *Services of individuals of any age.*—Services performed by an employee in, and at the time of, the sale of newspapers or magazines to ultimate consumers under an arrangement under which the newspapers or magazines are to be sold by him at a fixed price, his compensation being based on the retention of the excess of such price over the amount at which the newspapers or magazines are charged to him, are excepted from employment. The services are excepted whether or not the employee is guaranteed a minimum

amount of compensation for such services, or is entitled to be credited with the unsold newspapers or magazines turned back. Moreover, the services are excepted without regard to the age of the employee. Services performed other than at the time of sale to the ultimate consumer are not within the exception. Thus, the services of a regional distributor which are antecedent to but not immediately part of the sale to the ultimate consumer are not within the exception. However, incidental services by the employee who makes the sale to the ultimate consumer, such as services in assembling newspapers or in taking newspapers or magazines to the place of sale, are considered to be within the exception. [Reg. § 31.3306(c)(15)-1.]

☐ [T.D. 6199, 9-5-56. *Republished in T.D. 6516,* 12-20-60.]

[Reg. § 31.3306(c)(16)-1]

§ 31.3306(c)(16)-1. Services in employ of international organization.—(a) Subject to the provisions of section 1 of the International Organizations Immunities Act (22 U.S.C. 288), services performed in the employ of an international organization as defined in section 7701 (a)(18) are excepted from employment.

(b)(1) Section 7701(a)(18) provides as follows:

Sec. 7701. *Definitions.* (a) When used in this title, where not otherwise distinctly expressed or manifestly incompatible with the intent thereof—

* * *

(18)*International organization.* The term "international organization" means a public international organization entitled to enjoy privileges, exemptions, and immunities as an international organization under the International Organizations Immunities Act (22 U.S.C. 288-288f).

(2) Section 1 of the International Organizations Immunities Act provides as follows:

Sec. 1. [*International Organizations Immunities Act.*]For the purposes of this title [International Organizations Immunities Act], the term "international organization" means a public international organization in which the United States participates pursuant to any treaty or under the authority of any Act of Congress authorizing such participation or making an appropriation for such participation, and which shall have been designated by the President through appropriate Executive order as being entitled to enjoy the privileges, exemptions, and immunities herein provided. The President shall be authorized, in the light of the functions performed by any such international organization, by appropriate Executive order to withhold or withdraw from any such organization or its officers or employees any of the privileges, exemptions, and immunities provided for in this title (including the amendments made by this title) or to condition or limit the enjoyment by any such organization or its officers or employees of any such privilege, exemption, or immunity. The President shall be authorized, if in his judgment such action should be justified by reason of the abuse by an international organization or its officers and employees of the privileges, exemptions, and immunities herein provided or for any other reason, at any time to revoke the designation of any international organization under this section, whereupon the international organization in question shall cease to be classed as an international organization for the purposes of this title. [Reg. § 31.3306(c)(16)-1.]

☐ [*T.D. 6199, 9-5-56. Republished in T.D. 6516,* 12-20-60.]

[Reg. § 31.3306(c)(17)-1]

§ 31.3306(c)(17)-1. Fishing services.—(a) *In general.*—Subject to the limitations prescribed in paragraphs (b) and (c) of this section, services described in this paragraph are excepted from employment. Services performed by an individual in the catching, taking, harvesting, cultivating, or farming of any kind of fish, shellfish (for example, oysters, clams, and mussels), crustacea (for example, lobsters, crabs, and shrimps), sponges, seaweeds, or other aquatic forms of animal and vegetable life are excepted. The exception extends to services performed as an officer or member of the crew of a vessel while the vessel is engaged in any such activity whether or not the officer or member of the crew is himself so engaged. In the case of an individual who is engaged in any such activity in the employ of any person, the services performed, by such individual in the employ of such person, as an ordinary incident to any such activity are also excepted. Similarly, for example, the shore services of an officer or member of the crew of a vessel engaged in any such activity are excepted if such services are an ordinary incident to any such activity. Services performed as an ordinary incident to any such activity may include, for example, services performed in such cleaning, icing, and packing of fish as are necessary for the immediate preservation of the catch.

(b) *Salmon and halibut fishing.*—Services performed in connection with the catching or taking of salmon or halibut, for commercial purposes, are not within the exception. Thus, neither the services of an officer or member of the crew of a vessel (irrespective of its tonnage) which is engaged in the catching or taking of salmon or halibut, for commercial purposes, nor the services of any other individual in connection with such activity, are within the exception.

(c) *Vessels of more than 10 net tons.*—Services described in paragraph (a) of this section performed on or in connection with a vessel of more than 10 net tons are not within the exception. For purposes of the exception, the tonnage of the vessel shall be determined in the manner provided for determining the register tonnage of merchant vessels under the laws of the United States. [Reg. § 31.3306(c)(17)-1.]

☐ [*T.D. 6199, 9-5-56. Republished in T.D. 6516,* 12-20-60.]

>>>→ *Caution: This regulation has not been amended to reflect the changes made by P.L. 100-647.*

[Reg. § 31.3306(c)(18)-1]

§ 31.3306(c)(18)-1. Services of certain nonresident aliens.—(a)(1) Services performed after 1961 by a nonresident alien individual who is temporarily present in the United States as a nonimmigrant under subparagraph (F) or (J) of section 101(a)(15) of the Immigration and Nationality Act (8 U.S.C. 1101), as amended, are excepted from employment if the services are performed to carry out a purpose for which the individual was admitted. For purposes of this section an alien individual who is temporarily present in the United States as a nonimmigrant under such subparagraph (F) or (J) is deemed to be a nonresident alien individual. The preceding sentence does not apply to the extent it is inconsistent with section 7701(b) and the regulations under that section. A nonresident alien individual who is temporarily present in the United States as a nonimmigrant under such subparagraph (J) includes an alien individual admitted to the United States as an "exchange visitor" under section 201 of the United States Information and Educational Exchange Act of 1948 (22 U.S.C. 1446).

(2) If services are performed by a nonresident alien individual's alien spouse or minor child, who is temporarily present in the United States as a nonimmigrant under subparagraph (F) or (J) of section 101(a)(15) of the Immigration and Nationality Act, as amended, the services are not deemed for purposes of this section to be performed to carry out a purpose for which such individual was admitted. The services of such spouse or child are excepted from employment under this section only if the spouse or child was admitted for a purpose specified in such subparagraph (F) or (J) and if the services are performed to carry out such purpose.

(b) Section 101 of the Immigration and Nationality Act (8 U.S.C. 1101), as amended, provides, in part, as follows:

Sec. 101. *Definitions.* [Immigration and Nationality Act (66 Stat. 166)]

(a) As used in this chapter—* * *

(15) The term *immigrant* means every alien except an alien who is within one of the following classes of nonimmigrant aliens—

* * *

(F)(i) An alien having a residence in a foreign country which he has no intention of abandoning, who is a bona fide student qualified to pursue a full course of study and who seeks to enter the United States temporarily and solely for the purpose of pursuing such a course of study at an established institution of learning or other recognized place of study in the United States, particularly designated by him and approved by the Attorney General after consultation with the Office of Education of the United States, which institution or place of study shall have agreed to report to the Attorney General the termination of attendance of each nonimmigrant student, and if any such institution of learning or place of study fails to make reports promptly the approval shall be withdrawn, and (ii) the alien spouse and minor children of any such alien if accompanying him or following to join him:

* * *

(J) An alien having a residence in a foreign country which he has no intention of abandoning who is a bona fide student, scholar, trainee, teacher, professor, research assistant, specialist, or leader in a field of specialized knowledge or skill, or other person of similar description, who is coming temporarily to the United States as a participant in a program designated by the Secretary of State, for the purpose of teaching, instructing or lecturing, studying, observing, conducting research, consulting, demonstrating special skills, or receiving training, and the alien spouse and minor children of any such alien if accompanying him or following to join him.

* * *

[Sec. 101, Immigration and Nationality Act, as amended by sec. 101, Act of June 27, 1952, 66 Stat. 166; sec. 109, Act of Sept. 21, 1961, 75 Stat. 534] [Reg. § 31.3306(c)(18)-1.]

☐ [T.D. 6658, 6-27-63. *Amended by T.D.* 8411, 4-27-92.]

[Reg. § 31.3306(d)-1]

§ 31.3306(d)-1. Included and excluded service.—(a) If a portion of the services performed by an employee for the person employing him during a pay period constitutes employment, and the remainder does not constitute employment, all the services of the employee during the period shall for purposes of the tax be treated alike, that is, either all as included or all as excluded. The time during which the employee performs services which under section 3306(c) constitute employment, and the time during which he performs services which under such section do not constitute employment, within the pay period, determine whether all the services during the pay period shall be deemed to be included or excluded.

(b) If one-half or more of the employee's time in the employ of a particular person in a pay period is spent in performing services which constitute employment, then all the services of that employee for that person in that pay period shall be deemed to be employment.

(c) If less than one-half of the employee's time in the employ of a particular person in a pay period is spent in performing services which constitute employment, then none of the services of that employee for that person in that pay period shall be deemed to be employment.

(d) The application of the provisions of paragraphs (a), (b), and (c) of this section may be illustrated by the following examples:

Example (1). Employer B, who operates a farm and a store, employs A to perform services in connection with both operations. A's services on the farm are such that they are excepted as agricultural labor and do not constitute employ-

ment, and his services in the store constitute employment. He is paid at the end of each month. During a particular month A works 120 hours on the farm and 80 hours in the store. None of A's services during the month are deemed to be employment, since less than one-half of his services during the month constitutes employment. During another month A works 75 hours on the farm and 120 hours in the store. All of A's services during the month are deemed to be employment, since one-half or more of his services during the month constitutes employment.

Example (2). Employee C is employed as a maid by D, a medical doctor, whose home and office are located in the same building. C's services in the home are excepted as domestic service and do not constitute employment, and her services in the office constitute employment. She is paid each week. During a particular week C works 20 hours in the home and 20 hours in the office. All of C's services during that week are deemed to be employment, since one-half or more of her services during the week constitutes employment. During another week C works 22 hours in the home and 15 hours in the office. None of C's services during that week are deemed to be employment, since less than one-half of her services during the week constitutes employment.

(e) For purposes of this section, a "pay period" is the period (of not more than 31 consecutive calendar days) for which a payment of remuneration is ordinarily made to the employee by the person employing him. Thus, if the periods for which payments of remuneration are made to the employee by such person are of uniform duration, each such period constitutes a "pay period." If, however, the periods occasionally vary in duration, the "pay period" is the period for which a payment of remuneration is ordinarily made to the employee by such person, even though that period does not coincide with the actual period for which a particular payment of remuneration is made. For example, if a person ordinarily pays a particular employee for each calendar week at the end of the week, but the employee receives a payment in the middle of the week for the portion of the week already elapsed and receives the remainder at the end of the week, the "pay period" is still the calendar week; or if, instead, that employee is sent on a trip by such person and receives at the end of the third week a single remuneration payment for 3 weeks' services, the "pay period" is still the calendar week.

(f) If there is only one period (and such period does not exceed 31 consecutive calendar days) for which a payment of remuneration is made to the employee by the person employing him, such period is deemed to be a "pay period" for purposes of this section.

(g) The rules set forth in this section do not apply (1) with respect to any services performed by the employee for the person employing him if the periods for which such person makes payments of remuneration to the employee vary to the extent that there is no period "for which a payment of remuneration is ordinarily made to the employee," or (2) with respect to any services performed by the employee for the person employing him if the period for which a payment of remuneration is ordinarily made to the employee by such person exceeds 31 consecutive calendar days, or (3) with respect to any service performed by the employee for the person employing him during a pay period if any of such service is excepted by section 3306(c)(9) (see § 31.3306(c)(9)-1).

(h) If during any period for which a person makes a payment of remuneration to an employee only a portion of the employee's services constitutes employment, but the rules prescribed in this section are not applicable, the tax attaches with respect to such services as constitute employment as defined in section 3306(c) (provided such person is an employer as defined in section 3306(a) and § 31.3306(a)-1). [Reg. § 31.3306(d)-1.]

☐ [T.D. 6199, 9-5-56. *Republished in T.D.* 6516, 12-20-60.]

»»→ *Caution: The following regulation has not been revised to reflect the amendments made by P.L. 91-373.*

[Reg. § 31.3306(i)-1]

§ 31.3306(i)-1. Who are employees.—
(a) Every individual is an employee if the relationship between him and the person for whom he performs services is the legal relationship of employer and employee. (The word "employer" as used in this section only, notwithstanding the provisions of § 31.3306(a)-1, includes a person who employs one or more employees.)

(b) Generally such relationship exists when the person for whom services are performed has the right to control and direct the individual who performs the services, not only as to the result to be accomplished by the work but also as to the details and means by which that result is accomplished. That is, an employee is subject to the will and control of the employer not only as to what shall be done but how it shall be done. In this connection, it is not necessary that the employer actually direct or control the manner in which the services are performed; it is sufficient if he has the right to do so. The right to discharge is also an important factor indicating that the person possessing that right is an employer. Other factors characteristic of an employer, but not necessarily present in every case, are the furnishing of tools and the furnishing of a place to work, to the individual who performs the services. In general, if an individual is subject to the control or direction of another merely as to the result to be accomplished by the work and not as to the means and methods for accomplishing the result, he is an independent contractor. An individual performing services as an independent contractor is not as to such services an employee. Individuals such as physicians, lawyers, dentists, veterinarians, construction contractors, public stenographers, and auctioneers, engaged in the pursuit of an independent trade, business, or profession, in which they offer their services to the public, are independent contractors and not employees.

(c) Whether the relationship of employer and employee exists will in doubtful cases be determined upon an examination of the particular facts of each case.

(d) If the relationship of employer and employee exists, the designation or description of the relationship by the parties as anything other than that of employer and employee is immaterial. Thus, if such relationship exists, it is of no consequence that the employee is designated as a partner, coadventurer, agent, independent contractor, or the like.

(e) All classes or grades of employees are included within the relationship of employer and employee. Thus, superintendents, managers, and other supervisory personnel are employees. Generally, an officer of a corporation is an employee of the corporation. However, an officer of a corporation who as such does not perform any services or performs only minor services and who neither receives nor is entitled to receive, directly or indirectly, any remuneration is considered not to be an employee of the corporation. A director of a corporation in his capacity as such is not an employee of the corporation.

(f) Although an individual may be an employee under this section, his services may be of such a nature, or performed under such circumstances, as not to constitute employment (see § 31.3306(c)-2). [Reg. § 31.3306(i)-1.]

☐ [T.D. 6199, 9-5-56. *Republished in T.D.* 6516, 12-20-60.]

»»→ *Caution: The following regulation has not been revised to reflect the amendments made by P.L. 94-566.*

[Reg. § 31.3306(j)-1]

§ 31.3306(j)-1. State, United States, and citizen.—(a) When used in the regulations in this subpart, the term "State" includes the District of Columbia, the Territories of Alaska and Hawaii before their admission as States, and (when used with respect to remuneration paid after 1960 for services performed after 1960) the Commonwealth of Puerto Rico.

(b) When used in the regulations in this subpart, the Term "United States", when used in a geographical sense, means the several States (including the Territories of Alaska and Hawaii before their admission as States), and the District of Columbia. When used in the regulations in this subpart with respect to remuneration paid after 1960 for services performed after 1960, the term "United States" also includes the Commonwealth of Puerto Rico when the term is used in a geographical sense, and the term "citizen of the United States" includes a citizen of the Commonwealth of Puerto Rico. [Reg. § 31.3306(j)-1.]

☐ [T. D. 6658, 6-27-63.]

»»→ *Caution: The following regulation has not been revised to reflect the amendments made by P.L. 91-373.*

[Reg. §31.3306(k)-1]

§31.3306(k)-1. Agricultural labor.—(a) *In general.*—(1) Services performed by an employee for the person employing him which constitute "agricultural labor" as defined in section 3306(k) are excepted from employment by reason of section 3306(c)(1). See §31.3306(c)(1)-1. The term "agricultural labor" as defined in section 3306(k) includes services of the character described in paragraphs (b), (c), (d), and (e) of this section. In general, however, the term does not include services performed in connection with forestry, lumbering, or landscaping.

(2) The term "farm" as used in this subpart includes stock, dairy, poultry, fruit, fur-bearing animal, and truck farms, plantations, ranches, nurseries, ranges, orchards, and such greenhouses and other similar structures as are used primarily for the raising of agricultural or horticultural commodities. Greenhouses and other similar structures used primarily for other purposes (for example, display, storage, and fabrication of wreaths, corsages, and bouquets) do not constitute "farms."

(b) *Services described in section 3306(k)(1).*—Services performed on a farm by an employee of any person in connection with any of the following activities constitute agricultural labor:

(1) The cultivation of the soil;

(2) The raising, shearing, feeding, caring for, training, or management of livestock, bees, poultry, fur-bearing animals, or wildlife; or

(3) The raising or harvesting of any other agricultural or horticultural commodity.

(c) *Services described in section 3306(k)(2).*—(1) The following services performed by an employee in the employ of the owner or tenant or other operator of one or more farms constitute agricultural labor, if the major part of such services is performed on a farm:

(i) Services performed in connection with the operation, management, conservation, improvement, or maintenance of any such farms or its tools or equipment; or

(ii) Services performed in salvaging timber, or clearing land of brush and other debris, left by a hurricane.

(2) The services described in subparagraph (1)(i) of this paragraph may include, for example, services performed by carpenters, painters, mechanics, farm supervisors, irrigation engineers, bookkeepers, and other skilled or semiskilled workers, which contribute in any way to the conduct of the farm or farms, as such, operated by the person employing them, as distinguished from any other enterprise in which such person may be engaged.

(3) Since the services described in this paragraph must be performed in the employ of the owner or tenant or other operator of the farm, services performed by employees of a commercial painting concern, for example, which contracts with a farmer to renovate his farm properties, do not constitute agricultural labor.

(d) *Services described in section 3306(k)(3).*—Services performed by an employee in the employ of any person in connection with any of the following operations constitute agricultural labor without regard to the place where such services are performed:

(1) The ginning of cotton;

(2) The hatching of poultry;

(3) The raising or harvesting of mushrooms;

(4) The operation or maintenance of ditches, canals, reservoirs, or waterways used exclusively for supplying or storing water for farming purposes;

(5) The production or harvesting of maple sap or the processing of maple sap into maple sirup or maple sugar (but not the subsequent blending or other processing of such sirup or sugar with other products); or

(6) The production or harvesting of crude gum (oleoresin) from a living tree or the processing of such crude gum into gum spirits of turpentine and gum rosin, provided such processing is carried on by the original producer of such crude gum.

(e) *Services described in section 3306(k)(4).*—(1)(i) Services performed by an employee in the employ of a farmer or a farmers' cooperative organization or group in the handling, planting, drying, packing, packaging, processing, freezing, grading, storing, or delivering to storage or to market or to a carrier for transportation to market, of any agricultural or horticultural commodity, other than fruits and vegetables (see subparagraph (2) of this paragraph), produced by such farmer or farmer-members of such organization or group of farmers constitute agricultural labor, if such services are performed as an incident to ordinary farming operations.

(ii) Generally services are performed "as an incident to ordinary farming operations" within the meaning of this paragraph if they are services of the character ordinarily performed by the employees of a farmer or of a farmers' cooperative organization or group as a prerequisite to the marketing, in its unmanufactured state, of any agricultural or horticultural commodity produced by such farmer or by the members of such farmers' organization or group. Services performed by employees of such farmer or farmers' organization or group in the handling, planting, drying, packing, packaging, processing, freezing, grading, storing, or delivering to storage or to market or to a carrier for transportation to market, of commodities produced by persons other than such farmer or members of such farmers' organization or group are not performed "as an incident to ordinary farming operations".

(2) Services performed by an employee in the employ of any person in the handling, planting, drying, packing, packaging, processing, freezing, grading, storing, or delivering to storage or to market or to a carrier for transportation

to market, of fruits and vegetables, whether or not of a perishable nature, constitute agricultural labor, if such services are performed as an incident to the preparation of such fruits and vegetables for market. For example, if services in the sorting, grading, or storing of fruits, or in the cleaning of beans, are performed as an incident to their preparation for market, such services may constitute agricultural labor, whether performed in the employ of a farmer, a farmers' cooperative, or a commercial handler of such commodities.

(3) The services described in subparagraphs (1) and (2) of this paragraph do not include services performed in connection with commercial canning or commercial freezing or in connection with any commodity after its delivery to a terminal market for distribution for consumption. Moreover, since the services described in such subparagraphs must be rendered in the actual handling, planting, drying, packing, packaging, processing, freezing, grading, storing, or delivering to storage or to market or to carrier for transportation to market, of the commodity, such services do not, for example, include services performed as stenographers, bookkeepers, clerks, and other office employees, even though such services may be in connection with such activities. However, to the extent that the services of such individuals are performed in the employ of the owner or tenant or other operator of a farm and are rendered in major part on a farm, they may be within the provisions of paragraph (c) of this section. [Reg. § 31.3306(k)-1.]

☐ [T. D. 6199, 9-5-56. *Republished in T. D.* 6516, 12-20-60.]

[Reg. § 31.3306(m)-1]

§ 31.3306(m)-1. American vessel and aircraft.—(a) The term "American vessel" means any vessel which is documented (that is, registered, enrolled, or licensed) or numbered in conformity with the laws of the United States. It also includes any vessel which is neither documented nor numbered under the laws of the United States, nor documented under the laws of any foreign country, if the crew of such vessel is employed solely by one or more citizens or residents of the United States or corporations organized under the laws of the United States or of any State. (For provisions relating to the terms "State" and citizen", see § 31.3306(j)-1.)

(b) The term "American aircraft" means any aircraft registered under the laws of the United States.

(c) For provisions relating to services performed outside the United States on or in connection with an American vessel or American aircraft, see paragraph (c) of § 31.3306(c)-2. [Reg. § 31.3306(m)-1.]

☐ [T.D. 6199, 9-5-56. *Republished in T.D.* 6516, 12-20-60; T.D. 6658, 6-27-63.]

[Reg. § 31.3306(n)-1]

§ 31.3306(n)-1. Services on American vessel whose business is conducted by general agent of Secretary of Commerce.—(a) Section 3306(n)

and this section of the regulations apply with respect only to services performed by an officer or member of the crew of an American vessel (1) which is owned by or bareboat chartered to the United States, and (2) whose business is conducted by a general agent of the Secretary of Commerce. Whether services performed by such an officer or member of a crew under the above conditions constitute employment is determined under section 3306(c) and (n), but without regard to section 3306(c)(6). See § 31.3306(c)(6)-1, relating to services performed in the employ of the United States and instrumentalities thereof. If, without regard to section 3306(c)(6), such services constitute employment, they are not excepted from employment by reason of the fact that they are performed on or in connection with an American vessel which is owned by or bareboat chartered to the United States and whose business is conducted by a general agent of the Secretary of Commerce, that is, such services are not excepted from employment by section 3306(c)(6). For provisions relating to services performed within the United States and services performed outside the United States which constitute employment, see § 31.3306(c)-2.

(b) The expression "officer or member of the crew" includes the master or officer in charge of the vessel, however, designated, and every individual, subject to his authority, serving on board and contributing in any way to the operation and welfare of the vessel. Thus, the expression includes, for example, the master, mates, pilots, pursers, surgeons, stewards, engineers, firemen, cooks, clerks, carpenters, and deck hands.

(c) An employee of the United States who performs services as an officer or member of the crew of an American vessel which is owned by or bareboat chartered to the United States and whose business is conducted by a general agent of the Secretary of Commerce shall be deemed, under section 3306(n), to be performing services for such general agent rather than for the United States. Any such general agent of the Secretary of Commerce is considered a legal entity in his capacity as such general agent, separate and distinct from his identity as a person employing individuals on his own account. Each such general agent who in his capacity as such qualifies as an employer under section 3306(a) is with respect to each calendar year for which he so qualifies subject to the tax imposed by section 3301, and to all the requirements imposed upon an employer as defined in section 3306(a) by the regulations in this part, with respect to services which constitute employment by reason of section 3306(n) and this section of the regulations. [Reg. § 31.3306(n)-1.]

☐ [T.D. 6199, 9-5-56. *Republished in T.D.* 6516, 12-20-60.]

[Reg. § 31.3306(p)-1]

§ 31.3306(p)-1. Employees or related corporations.—(a) *In general.*—For purposes of sections 3301, 3302, and 3306(b)(1), when two or more related corporations concurrently employ the same individual and compensate that individual through a common paymaster which is one of the related corporations for which the individual performs services, each of the corporations is considered to have paid only the remuneration it actually disburses to that individual (unless the disbursing corporation fails to remit the taxes due). Paragraphs (b) and (c) of §31.3121(s)-1 contains rules defining related corporations, common paymasters, and concurrent employment, and rules for determining the liability of the other related corporations for employment taxes if the common paymaster fails to remit the taxes pursuant to sections 3102 and 3111, and for allocating these taxes among the related corporations. Those rules also apply to the tax under section 3301. For purposes of applying those rules to this section, references in those rules to section 3111 are considered references to sections 3301 and 3302, and references to section 3121 are considered references to section 3306.

(b) *Allocation of credit for contributions to State unemployment funds.*—A special rule for applying the rules of §31.3121(s)-1 to this section applies if it is necessary to determine the ultimate liability of each related corporation for which services are performed in the event the common paymaster fails to remit the tax to the Internal Revenue Service. In determining the ultimate liability of a corporation, the credit for contributions to State unemployment funds that the corporation may claim under section 3302 is calculated as if each corporation were a separate employer.

(c) *Effective date.*—This section is effective with respect to wages paid after December 31, 1978. [Reg. §31.3306(p)-1.]

□ [*T.D.* 7660, 12-19-79.]

[Reg. §31.3306(r)(2)-1]

§31.3306(r)(2)-1. Treatment of amounts deferred under certain nonqualified deferred compensation plans.—(a) *In general.*—Section 3306(r)(2) provides a special timing rule for the tax imposed by section 3301 with respect to any amount deferred under a nonqualified deferred compensation plan. Section 31.3121(v)(2)-1 contains rules relating to when amounts deferred under certain nonqualified deferred compensation plans are wages for purposes of sections 3121(v)(2), 3101, and 3111. The rules in §31.3121(v)(2)-1 also apply to the special timing rule of section 3306(r)(2). For purposes of applying the rules in §31.3121(v)(2)-1 to section 3306(r)(2) and this paragraph (a), references to the Federal Insurance Contributions Act are considered references to the Federal Unemployment Tax Act (26 U.S.C. 3301 et seq.), references to FICA are considered references to FUTA, references to section 3101 or 3111 are considered references to section 3301, references to section 3121(v)(2) are considered references to section 3306(r)(2), references to section 3121(a), (a)(5),

and (a)(13) are considered references to section 3306(b), (b)(5), and (b)(10), respectively, and references to §31.3121(a)-2(a) are considered references to §31.3301-4.

(b) *Effective dates and transition rules.*—Except as otherwise provided, section 3306(r)(2) applies to remuneration paid after December 31, 1984. Section 31.3121(v)(2)-2 contains effective date rules for certain remuneration paid after December 31, 1983, for purposes of section 3121(v)(2). The rules in §31.3121(v)(2)-2 also apply to section 3306(r)(2). For purposes of applying the rules in §31.3121(v)(2)-2 to section 3306(r)(2) and this paragraph (b), references to section 3121(v)(2) are considered references to section 3306(r)(2), and references to section 3121(a)(2), (a)(3), or (a)(13) are considered references to section 3306(b)(2), (b)(3), or (b)(10), respectively. In addition, references to §31.3121(v)(2)-1 are considered references to paragraph (a) of this section. For purposes of applying the rules of §31.3121(v)(2)-2 to this paragraph (b)—

(1) References to "December 31, 1983" are considered references to "December 31, 1984";

(2) References to "before 1984" are considered references to "before 1985";

(3) References to "Federal Insurance Contributions Act" are considered references to "Federal Unemployment Tax Act"; and

(4) References to "FICA" are considered references to "FUTA". [Reg. §31.3306(r)(2)-1.]

□ [*T.D.* 8815, 1-28-99.]

[Reg. §31.3307-1]

§31.3307-1. Deductions by an employer from remuneration of an employee.—Any amount deducted by an employer from the remuneration of an employee is considered to be a part of the employee's remuneration and is considered to be paid to the employee as remuneration at the time that the deduction is made. It is immaterial that any act of Congress or the law of any State requires or permits such deductions and the payment of the amount thereof to the United States, a State, or any political subdivision thereof. [Reg. §31.3307-1.]

□ [*T.D.* 6199, 9-5-56. *Republished in T.D.* 6516, 12-20-60.]

[Reg. §31.3308-1]

§31.3308-1. Instrumentalities of the United States specifically exempted from tax imposed by section 3301.—Section 3308 makes ineffectual as to the tax imposed by section 3301 (with respect to remuneration paid after 1961 for services performed after 1961) those provisions of law which grant to an instrumentality of the United States an exemption from taxation, unless such provisions grant a specific exemption from the tax imposed by section 3301 by an express reference to such section or the corresponding section of prior law. Thus, the general exemptions from Federal taxation granted by various statutes to certain instrumentalities of the United States without specific reference to the tax imposed by section 3301 or the corresponding section of prior law are rendered inoperative insofar as such exemptions relate to the tax imposed by section 3301. For provisions relating to the exception from employment of services performed in the employ of an instrumentality of the United States specificially exempted from the tax imposed by section 3301, see § 31.3306(c)(6)-1. [Reg. § 31.3308-1.]

☐ [*T.D.* 6658, 6-27-63.]

Collection of Income Tax at Source on Wages
WITHHOLDING FROM WAGES

See p. 20,601 for regulations not amended to reflect law changes

[Reg. § 31.3401(a)-1]

§ 31.3401(a)-1. Wages.—(a) *In general.*— (1) The term "wages" means all remuneration for services performed by an employee for his employer unless specifically excepted under section 3401(a) or excepted under section 3402(e).

(2) The name by which the remuneration for services is designated is immaterial. Thus, salaries, fees, bonuses, commission on sales or on insurance premiums, pensions, and retired pay are wages within the meaning of the statute if paid as compensation for services performed by the employee for his employer.

(3) The basis upon which the remuneration is paid is immaterial in determining whether the remuneration constitutes wages. Thus, it may be paid on the basis of piecework, or a percentage of profits; and may be paid hourly, daily, weekly, monthly, or annually.

(4) Generally the medium in which remuneration is paid is also immaterial. It may be paid in cash or in something other than cash, as for example, stocks, bonds, or other forms of property. (See, however, § 31.3401(a)(11)-1, relating to the exclusion from wages of remuneration paid in any medium other than cash for services not in the course of the employer's trade or business, and § 31.3401(a)(16)-1, relating to the exclusion from wages of tips paid in any medium other than cash.) If services are paid for in a medium other than cash, the fair market value of the thing taken in payment is the amount to be included as wages. If the services were rendered at a stipulated price, in the absence of evidence to the contrary, such price will be presumed to be the fair value of the remuneration received. If a corporation transfers to its employees its own stock as remuneration for services rendered by the employee, the amount of such remuneration is the fair market value of the stock at the time of the transfer.

(5) Remuneration for services, unless such remuneration is specifically excepted by the statute, constitutes wages even though at the time paid the relationship of employer and employee no longer exists between the person in whose employ the services were performed and the individual who performed them.

Example. A is employed by R during the month of January 1955 and is entitled to receive remuneration of $100 for the services performed for R, the employer, during the month. A leaves the employ of R at the close of business on January 31, 1955. On February 15, 1955 (when A is no longer an employee of R), R pays A the remuneration of $100 which was earned for the services performed in January. The $100 is wages within the meaning of the statute.

(b) *Certain specific items.*—(1) *Pensions and retirement pay.*—(i) In general, pensions and retired pay are wages subject to withholding. However, no withholding is required with respect to amounts paid to an employee upon retirement which are taxable as annuities under the provisions of section 72 or 403. So-called pensions awarded by one to whom no services have been rendered are mere gifts or gratuities and do not constitute wages. Those payments of pensions or other benefits by the Federal Government under Title 38 of the United States Code which are excluded from gross income are not wages subject to withholding.

(ii) Amounts received as retirement pay for service in the Armed Forces of the United States, the Coast and Geodetic Survey, or the Public Health Service or as a disability annuity paid under the provisions of section 831 of the Foreign Service Act of 1946, as amended (22 U.S.C. 1081; 60 Stat. 1021), are subject to withholding unless such pay or disability annuity is excluded from gross income under section 104(a)(4), or is taxable as an annuity under the provisions of section 72. Where such retirement pay or disability annuity (not excluded from gross income under section 104(a)(4) and not taxable as an annuity under the provisions of section 72) is paid to a nonresident alien individual, withholding is required only in the case of such amounts paid to a nonresident alien individual who is a resident of Puerto Rico.

(2) *Traveling and other expenses.*—Amounts paid specifically—either as advances or reimbursements—for traveling or other bona fide ordinary and necessary expenses incurred or reasonably expected to be incurred in the business of the employer are not wages and are not subject to withholding. Traveling and other reimbursed expenses must be identified either by making a separate payment or by specifically indicating the separate amounts where both wages and expense allowances are combined in a single payment. For amounts that are received

by an employee on or after July 1, 1990, with respect to expenses paid or incurred on or after July 1, 1990, see §31.3401(a)-4.

(3) *Vacation allowances.*—Amounts of so-called "vacation allowances" paid to an employee constitute wages. Thus, the salary of an employee on vacation, paid notwithstanding his absence from work, constitutes wages.

(4) *Dismissal payments.*—Any payments made by an employer to an employee on account of dismissal, that is, involuntary separation from the service of the employer, constitute wages regardless of whether the employer is legally bound by contract, statute, or otherwise to make such payments.

(5) *Deductions by employer from remuneration of an employee.*—Any amount deducted by an employer from the remuneration of an employee is considered to be a part of the employee's remuneration and is considered to be paid to the employee as remuneration at the time that the deduction is made. It is immaterial that any act of Congress, or the law of any State or of Puerto Rico, requires or permits such deductions and the payment of the amounts thereof to the United States, a State, a Territory, Puerto Rico, or the District of Columbia, or any political subdivision of any one or more of the foregoing.

(6) *Payment by an employer of employee's tax, or employee's contributions under a State law.*—The term "wages" includes the amount paid by an employer on behalf of an employee (without deduction from the remuneration of, or other reimbursement from, the employee) an account of any payment required from an employee under a State unemployment compensation law, or on account of any tax imposed upon the employee by any taxing authority, including the taxes imposed by sections 3101 and 3201.

(7) *Remuneration for services as employee of nonresident alien individual or foreign entity.*—The term "wages" includes remuneration for services performed by a citizen or resident (including, in regard to wages paid after February 28, 1979, an individual treated as a resident under section 6013(g) or (h)) of the United States as an employee of a nonresident alien individual, foreign partnership, or foreign corporation whether or not such alien individual or foreign entity is engaged in trade or business within the United States. Any person paying wages on behalf of a nonresident alien individual, foreign partnership, or foreign corporation, not engaged in trade or business within the United States (including Puerto Rico as if a part of the United States), is subject to all the provisions of law and regulations applicable with respect to an employer. See §31.3401(d)-1, relating to the term "employer", and §31.3401(a)(8)(C)-1, relating to remuneration paid for services performed by a citizen of the United States in Puerto Rico.

(8) *Amounts paid under accident or health plans.*—(i) *Amounts paid in taxable years beginning on or after January 1, 1977.*—(a) *In general.*—With-holding is required on all payments of amounts includible in gross income under section 105(a) and §1.105-1 (relating to amounts attributable to employer contributions), made in taxable years beginning on or after January 1, 1977, to an employee under an accident or health plan for a period of absence from work on account of personal injuries or sickness. Payments on which withholding is required by this subdivision are wages as defined in section 3401(a), and the employer shall deduct and withhold in accordance with the requirements of chapter 24 of subtitle C of the Code. Third party payments of sick pay, as defined in section 3402(o) and the regulations thereunder, are not wages for purposes of this section.

(b) *Payments made by an agent of the employer.*—(1) Payments are considered made by the employer if a third party makes the payments as an agent of the employer. The determining factor as to whether a third party is an agent of the employer is whether the third party bears any insurance risk. If the third party bears no insurance risk and is reimbursed on a cost plus fee basis, the third party is an agent of the employer even if the third party is responsible for making determinations of the eligibility of individual employees of the employer for sick pay payments. If the third party is paid an insurance premium and not reimbursed on a cost plus fee basis, the third party is not an agent of the employer, but the third party is a payor of third party sick pay for purposes of voluntary withholding from sick pay under sections 3402(o) and 6051(f) and the regulations thereunder. If a third party and an employer enter into an agency agreement as provided in paragraph (c) of §31.6051-3 (relating to statements required in case of sick pay paid by third parties), that agency agreement does not make the third party an agent of the employer for purposes of this paragraph.

(2) Payments made by agents subject to this paragraph are supplemental wages as defined in §31.3402(g)-1, and are therefore subject to the rules regarding withholding tax on supplemental wages provided in §31.3402(g)-1. For purposes of those rules, unless the agent is also an agent for purposes of withholding tax from the employee's regular wages, the agent may deem tax to have been withheld from regular wages paid to the employee during the calendar year.

(3) This paragraph is only applicable to amounts paid on or after May 25, 1983, unless the agent actually withheld taxes before that date.

(c) *Exceptions to withholding.*—(1) Withholding is not required on payments that are specifically excepted under the numbered paragraphs of section 3401(a) (relating to the definition of wages), under section 3402(e) (relating to included and excluded wages), or under section 3402(n) (relating to employees incurring no income tax liability).

Reg. §31.3401(a)-1(b)(8)(i)(c)(1)

(2) Withholding is not required on disability payments to the extent that the payments are excludable from gross income under section 105(d). In determining the excludable portion of the disability payments, the employer may assume that payments that the employer makes to the employee are the employee's sole source of income. This exception applies only if the employee furnishes the employer with adequate verification of disability. A certificate from a qualified physician attesting that the employee is permanently and totally disabled (within the meaning of section 105(d)) shall be deemed to constitute adequate verification. This exception does not affect the requirement that a statement (which includes any amount paid under section 105(d)) be furnished under either section 6041 (relating to information at source) or section 6051 (relating to receipts for employees) and the regulations thereunder.

(ii) *Amounts paid after December 31, 1955 and before January 1, 1977.—(a) In general.*—The term "wage continuation payment", as used in this subdivision, means any payment to an employee which is made after December 31, 1955, and before January 1, 1977, under a wage continuation plan (as defined in paragraph (a)(2)(i) of § 1.105-4 and § 1.105-5 of Part 1 of this chapter (Income Tax Regulations)) for a period of absence from work on account of personal injuries or sickness, to the extent such payment is attributable to contributions made by the employer which were not includible in the employee's gross income or is paid by the employer. Any such payment, whether or not excluded from the gross income of the employee under section 105(d), constitutes "wages" (unless specifically excepted under any of the numbered paragraphs of section 3401(a) or under section 3402(e)) and withholding thereon is required except as provided in paragraphs (b)(8)(ii)(b), (c), and (d) of this section.

(b) *Amounts paid before January 1, 1977, by employer for whom services are performed for period of absence beginning after December 31, 1963.*—(1) Withholding is not required upon the amount of any wage continuation payment for a period of absence beginning after December 31, 1963, paid before January 1, 1977, to an employee directly by the employer for whom he performs services to the extent that such payment is excludable from the gross income of the employee under the provisions of section 105(d) in effect with respect to such payments, provided the records maintained by the employer—

(i) Separately show the amount of each such payment and the excludable portion thereof, and

(ii) Contain data substantiating the employee's entitlement to the exclusion provided in section 105(d) with respect to such amount, either by a written statement from the employee specifying whether his absence from work during the period for which the payment was made was due to a personal injury or to sickness and whether he was hospitalized for at least one day during this period; or by any other information which the employer reasonably believes establishes the employee's entitlement to the exclusion under section 105(d). Employers shall not be required to ascertain the accuracy of any written statement submitted by an employee in accordance with this subdivision (b)(1)(ii).

For purposes of this subdivision (b)(1), wage continuation payments reasonably expected by the employer to be made on behalf of the employer by another person shall be taken into account in determining whether the 75 percent test contained in section 105(d) is met and in computing the amount of any wage continuation payment made directly by the employer for whom services are performed by the employee which is within the $75 or $100 weekly rate of exclusion from the gross income of the employee provided in section 105(d). In making this latter computation, the amount excludable under section 105(d) shall be applied first against payments reasonably expected to be made on behalf of the employer by the other person and then, to the extent any part of the exclusion remains, against the payments made directly by the employer. In a case in which wage continuation payments are not paid at a constant rate for the first 30 calendar days of the period of absence, the determination of whether the 75 percent test contained in section 105(d) is met shall be based upon the length of the employee's absence as of the end of the period for which the payment by the employer is made, without regard to the effect which any further extension of such absence may have upon the excludability of the payment.

(2) The computation of the amount of any wage continuation payment with respect to which the employer may refrain from withholding may be illustrated by the following examples:

Example (1). A, an employee of B, normally works Monday through Friday and has a regular weekly rate of wages of $100. On Monday, November 5, 1974, A becomes ill, and as a result is absent from work for two weeks, returning to work on Monday, November 19, 1974. A is not hospitalized. Under B's noncontributory wage continuation plan, A receives no benefits for the first three working days of absence and is paid benefits directly by B at the rate of $85 a week thereafter ($34 for the last two days of the first week of absence and $85 for the second week of absence). No wage continuation payment is made by any other person. Since the benefits are entirely attributable to contributions to the plan by B, such benefits are wage continuation payments in their entirety. The wage continuation payments for the first seven calendar days of absence are not excludable from A's gross income because A was not hospitalized for at least one day during his period of absence, and therefore B must withhold with respect to such payments. Under section 105(d), the wage continuation payments attributable to absence after the first seven calendar days of absence are excludable to the extent that they do not exceed a rate of $75 a week. Under the principles stated in paragraph (e)(6)(iv) of § 1.105-4 of this chapter (Income Tax Regulations), the wage continuation payments in the case are at a rate not in excess of 75 percent (119/200 or 59.5 percent) of A's regular weekly rate of wages. Accordingly, B may refrain from withholding with respect to $75 of the wage continuation payment attributable to the second week of absence.

Example (2). Assume the facts in example (1) except that A is unable to return to work until Monday, February 11, 1975, and that, of the $85 a week of wage continuation payments $35 is paid directly by B and $50 is reasonably expected by B to be paid by C, an insurance company, on behalf of B. In such a case, both the $50 and the $35 payments constitute wage continuation payments and the amount of such payments which is attributable to the first 30 calendar days of absence is at a rate not in excess of 75 percent (323/440 or 73.4 percent) of A's regular weekly rate of wages. Therefore, under section 105(d), the portion of such payments which is attributable to absence after the first seven calendar days of absence is excludable to the extent that it does not exceed a rate of $75 a week for the eighth through the thirtieth calendar day of absence and does not exceed a rate of $100 a week thereafter. B may refrain from withholding with respect to $25 a week (the amount by which the $75 maximum excludable amount exceeds the $50 reasonably expected by B to be paid by C) of his direct payments for the eighth through the thirtieth calendar days of absence. Thereafter, B may refrain from withholding with respect to the entire $35 paid directly by him, since the maximum excludable amount ($100 a week) exceeds the total of payments made by B and payments which B reasonably expects will be made by C.

(c) Amounts paid by employer for whom services are performed for period of absence beginning before January 1, 1964.—Withholding is not required upon the amount of any wage continuation payment for a period of absence beginning before January 1, 1964, made to an employee directly by the employer for whom he performs services to the extent that such payment is excludable from the gross income of the employee under the provisions of section 105(d) in effect with respect to such payments, provided the records maintained by the employer—

(1) Separately show the amount of each such payment and the excludable portion thereof, and

(2) Contain data substantiating the employee's entitlement to the exclusion provided in section 105(d) with respect to such amount, either by a written statement from the employee specifying whether his absence from work during the period for which the payment was made was due to a personal injury or whether such absence was due to sickness, and, if the latter, whether he was hospitalized for at least one day during this period; or by any other information which the employer reasonably be-

lieves establishes the employee's entitlement to the exclusion under section 105(d). Employers shall not be required to ascertain the accuracy of the information contained in any written statement submitted by an employee in accordance with this paragraph (b)(8)(ii)*(c)(2).*

For purposes of this paragraph (b)(8)(ii)*(c),* the computation of the amount excludable from the gross income of the employee under section 105(d) may be made either on the basis of the wage continuation payments which are made directly by the employer for whom the employee performs services, or on the basis of such payments in conjunction with any wage continuation payments made on behalf of the employer by a person who is regarded as an employer under section 3401(d)(1).

(d) Amounts paid before January 1, 1977 by person other than the employer for whom services are performed.—No tax shall be withheld upon any wage continuation payment made to an employee by or on behalf of a person who is not the employer for whom the employee performs services but who is regarded as an employer under section 3401(d)(1). For example, no tax shall be withheld with respect to wage continuation payments made on behalf of an employer by an insurance company under an accident or health policy, by a separate trust under an accident or health plan, or by a State agency from a sickness and disability fund maintained under State law.

(e) Cross references.—See sections 6001 and 6051 and the provisions thereunder in subpart G of the regulations in this part for rules with respect to the records which must be maintained in connection with wage continuation payments and for rules with respect to the statements which must be furnished an employee in connection with wage continuation payments, respectively. See also section 105 and the provisions thereunder in the Income Tax Regulations (26 CFR Part 1).

(9) Value of meals and lodging.—The value of any meals or lodging furnished to an employee by his employer is not subject to withholding if the value of the meals or lodging is excludable from the gross income of the employee. See the Income Tax Regulations (Part 1 of this chapter) under section 119.

(10) Facilities or privileges.—Ordinarily, facilities or privileges (such as entertainment, medical services, or so-called "courtesy" discounts on purchases), furnished or offered by an employer to his employees generally, are not considered as wages subject to withholding if such facilities or privileges are of relatively small value and are offered or furnished by the employer merely as a means of promoting the health, good will, contentment, or efficiency of his employees.

(11) Tips or gratuities.—Tips or gratuities paid, prior to January 1, 1966, directly to an employee by a customer of an employer, and not accounted for by the employee to the employer are not subject to withholding. For provisions

Reg. §31.3401(a)-1(b)(11)

relating to the treatment of tips received by an employee after December 31, 1965, as wages, see §§ 31.3401(f)-1 and 31.3402(k)-1.

(12) *Remuneration for services performed by permanent resident of Virgin Islands.*— (i) *Exemption from withholding.*—No tax shall be withheld for the United States under chapter 24 from a payment of wages by an employer, including the United States or any agency thereof, to an employee if at the time of payment it is reasonable to believe that the employee will be required to satisfy his income tax obligations with respect to such wages under section 28(a) of the Revised Organic Act of the Virgin Islands. That section provides that all persons whose permanent residence is in the Virgin Islands "shall satisfy their income tax obligations under applicable taxing statutes of the United States by paying their tax on income derived from all sources both within and outside the Virgin Islands into the treasury of the Virgin Islands".

(ii) *Claiming exemption.*—If the employee furnishes to the employer a statement in duplicate that he expects to satisfy his income tax obligations under section 28(a) of the Revised Organic Act of the Virgin Islands with respect to all wages subsequently to be paid to him by the employer during the taxable year to which the statement relates, the employer may, in the absence of information to the contrary, rely on such statement as establishing reasonable belief that the employee will so satisfy his income tax obligations. The employee's statement shall identify the taxable year to which it relates, and both the original and the duplicate copy thereof shall be signed and dated by the employee.

(iii) *Disposition of statement.*—The original of the statement shall be retained by the employer. The duplicate copy of the statement shall be sent by the employer to the Director of International Operations, Washington 25, D.C., on or before the last day of the calendar year in which the employer receives the statement from the employee.

(iv) *Applicability of subparagraph.*—This subparagraph has no application with respect to any payment of remuneration which is not subject to withholding by reason of any other provision of the regulations in this subpart.

(13) *Federal employees resident in Puerto Rico.*—Except as provided in paragraph (d) of § 31.3401(a)(6)-1, the term "wages" includes remuneration for services performed by a nonresident alien individual who is a resident of Puerto Rico if such services are performed as an employee of the United States or any agency thereof. The place where the services are performed is immaterial for purposes of this subparagraph.

(14) *Supplemental unemployment compensation benefits.*—(i) Supplemental unemployment compensation benefits paid to an individual after December 31, 1970, shall be treated (for purposes of the provisions of Subparts E, F, and G of

this part which relate to withholding of income tax) as if they were wages, to the extent such benefits are includible in the gross income of such individual.

(ii) For purposes of this subparagraph, the term "supplemental unemployment compensation benefits" means amounts which are paid to an employee, pursuant to a plan to which the employer is a party, because of the employee's involuntary separation from the employment of the employer, whether or not such separation is temporary, but only when such separation is one resulting directly from a reduction in force, the discontinuance of a plant or operation, or other similar conditions.

(iii) For the meanings of the terms "involuntary separation from the employment of the employer" and "other similar conditions", see subparagraphs (3) and (4) of § 1.501(c)(17)-1(b) of this chapter (Income Tax Regulations).

(iv) As used in this subparagraph, the term "employee" means an employee within the meaning of paragraph (a) of § 31.3401(c)-1, the term "employer" means an employer within the meaning of paragraph (a) of § 31.3401(d)-1, and the term "employment" means employment as defined under the common law rules.

(v) References in this chapter to wages as defined in section 3401(a) shall be deemed to refer also to supplemental unemployment compensation benefits which are treated under this subparagraph as if they were wages.

(15) *Split-dollar life insurance arrangements.*— See § 1.61-22 of this chapter for rules relating to the treatment of split-dollar life insurance arrangements.

(c) *Geographical definitions.*—For definition of the term "United States" and for other geographical definitions relating to the continental shelf, see section 638 and § 1.638-1 of this chapter. [Reg. § 31.3401(a)-1.]

☐ [T.D. 6155, 12-29-55 *and* T.D. 6259, 10-25-57. Amended by T.D. 6654, 5-27-63; T.D. 6908, 12-30-66; T.D. 7001, 1-17-69; T.D. 7068, 11-10-70; T.D. 7277, 5-14-73; T.D. 7493, 6-29-77; T.D. 7670, 1-30-80; T.D. 7888, 4-22-83; T.D. 8276, 12-7-89; T.D. 8324, 12-14-90; T.D. 9092, 9-11-2003 *and* T.D. 9276, 7-24-2006.]

[Reg. § 31.3401(a)-1T]

§31.3401(a)-1T. Question and answer relating to the definition of wages in section 3401(a).—The following question and answer relates to the definition of wages in section 3401(a) of the Internal Revenue Code of 1954, as amended by section 531(d)(4) of the Tax Reform Act of 1984 (98 Stat. 886):

Q-1: Are fringe benefits included in the definition of "wages" under section 3401(a)?

A-1: Yes, unless specifically excluded from the definition of "wages" pursuant to section 3401(a)(1) through (20). For example, a fringe benefit provided to or on behalf of an employee is excluded from the definition of "wages" if at the time such benefit is provided it is reasonable to believe that the employee will be able to exclude such benefit from income under section 117 or 132. [Reg. § 31.3401(a)-1T.]

☐ [T.D. 8004, 1-2-85.]

[Reg. § 31.3401(a)-2]

§ 31.3401(a)-2. Exclusions from wages.—(a) *In general.*—(1) The term "wages" does not include any remuneration for services performed by an employee for his employer which is specifically excepted from wages under section 3401(a).

(2) The exception attaches to the remuneration for services performed by an employee and not to the employee as an individual; that is, the exception applies only to the remuneration in an excepted category.

Example. A is an individual who is employed part time by B to perform domestic service in his home (see § 31.3401(a)(3)-1). A is also employed by C part time to perform services as a clerk in a department store owned by him. While no withholding is required with respect to A's remuneration for services performed in the employ of B (the remuneration being excluded from wages), the exception does not embrace the remuneration for services performed by A in the employ of C and withholding is required with respect to the wages for such services.

(3) For provisions relating to the circumstances under which remuneration which is excepted is nevertheless deemed to be wages, and relating to the circumstances under which remuneration which is not excepted is nevertheless deemed not to be wages, see § 31.3402(e)-1.

(4) For provisions relating to payments with respect to which a voluntary withholding agreement is in effect, which are not defined as wages in section 3401(a) but which are nevertheless deemed to be wages, see § § 31.3401(a)-3 and 31.3402 (p)-1.

(b) *Fees paid a public official.*—(1) Authorized fees paid to public officials such as notaries public, clerks of courts, sheriffs, etc., for services rendered in the performance of their official duties are excepted from wages and hence are not subject to withholding. However, salaries paid such officials by the Government, or by a Government agency or instrumentality, are subject to withholding.

(2) Amounts paid to precinct workers for services performed at election booths in State, county, and municipal elections and fees paid to jurors and witnesses are in the nature of fees paid to public officials and therefore are not subject to withholding. [Reg. § 31.3401(a)-2.]

☐ [T.D. 6259, 10-25-59. *Amended by T.D.* 6654, 5-27-63 *and T.D.* 7096, 3-17-71.]

[Reg. § 31.3401(a)-3]

§ 31.3401(a)-3. Amounts deemed wages under voluntary withholding agreements.— (a) *In general.*—Notwithstanding the exceptions to the definition of wages specified in section 3401(a) and the regulations thereunder, the term "wages" includes the amounts described in paragraph (b)(1) of this section with respect to which there is a voluntary withholding agreement in effect under section 3402(p). References in this chapter to the definition of wages contained in section 3401(a) shall be deemed to refer also to this section (§ 31.3401(a)-3).

(b) *Remuneration for services.*—(1) Except as provided in subparagraph (2) of this paragraph, the amounts referred to in paragraph (a) of this section include any remuneration for services performed by an employee for an employer which, without regard to this section, does not constitute wages under section 3401(a). For example, remuneration for services performed by an agricultural worker or a domestic worker in a private home (amounts which are specifically excluded from the definition of wages by section 3401(a)(2) and (3), respectively) are amounts with respect to which a voluntary withholding agreement may be entered into under section 3402(p). See § § 31.3401(c)-1 and 31.3401(d)-1 for the definitions of "employee" and "employer."

(2) For purposes of this paragraph, remuneration for services shall not include amounts not subject to withholding under § 31.3401(a)-1(b)(12) (relating to remuneration for services performed by a permanent resident of the Virgin Islands), § 31.3401(a)-2(b) (relating to fees paid to a public official), section 3401(a)(5) (relating to remuneration for services for foreign government or international organization), section 3401(a)(8)(B) (relating to remuneration for services performed in a possession of the United States (other than Puerto Rico) by citizens of the United States), section 3401(a)(8)(C) (relating to remuneration for services performed in Puerto Rico by citizens of the United States), section 3401(a)(11) (relating to remuneration other than in cash for service not in the course of employer's trade or business), section 3401(a)(12) (relating to payments from or to certain tax-exempt trusts, or under or to certain annuity plans or bond purchase plans), section 3401(a)(14) (relating to group-term life insurance), section 3401(a)(15) (relating to moving expenses), or section 3401(a)(16)(A) (relating to tips paid in any medium other than cash). [Reg. § 31.3401(a)-3.]

☐ [T.D. 7096, 3-17-71.]

[Reg. § 31.3401(a)-4]

§ 31.3401(a)-4. Reimbursements and other expense allowance amounts.—(a) *When excluded from wages.*—If a reimbursement or other expense allowance arrangement meets the requirements of section 62(c) of the Code and § 1.62-2 and the expenses are substantiated within a reasonable period of time, payments made under the arrangement that do not exceed the substantiated expenses are treated as paid under an accountable plan and are not wages. In addition, if both wages and the reimbursement or other expense allowance are combined in a single payment, the reimbursement or other expense allowance must be identified either by making a separate payment or by specifically identifying the amount of the reimbursement or other expense allowance.

(b) *When included in wages.*—(1) *Accountable plans.*—(i) *General rule.*—Except as provided in paragraph (b)(1)(ii) of this section, if a reimbursement or other expense allowance arrangement satisfies the requirements of section 62(c) and §1.62-2, but the expenses are not substantiated within a reasonable period of time or amounts in excess of the substantiated expenses are not returned within a reasonable period of time, the amount paid under the arrangement in excess of the substantiated expenses is treated as paid under a nonaccountable plan, is included in wages, and is subject to withholding and payment of employment taxes no later than the first payroll period following the end of the reasonable period.

(ii) *Per diem or mileage allowances.*—If a reimbursement or other expense allowance arrangement providing a per diem or mileage allowance satisfies the requirements of section 62(c) and §1.62-2, but the allowance is paid at a rate for each day or mile of travel that exceeds the amount of the employee's expenses deemed substantiated for a day or mile of travel, the excess portion is treated as paid under a nonaccountable plan and is included in wages. In the case of a per diem or mileage allowance paid as a reimbursement, the excess portion is subject to withholding and payment of employment taxes when paid. In the case of a per diem or mileage allowance paid as an advance, the excess portion is subject to withholding and payment of employment taxes no later than the first payroll period in which the expenses with respect to which the advance was paid (i.e., the days or miles of travel) are substantiated. The Commissioner may, in his discretion, prescribe special rules in pronouncements of general applicability regarding the timing of withholding and payment of employment taxes on per diem and mileage allowances.

(2) *Nonaccountable plans.*—If a reimbursement or other expense allowance arrangement does not satisfy the requirements of section 62(c) and §1.62-2 (e.g., the arrangement does not require expenses to be substantiated or require amounts in excess of the substantiated expenses to be returned), all amounts paid under the arrangement are treated as paid under a nonaccountable plan, are included in wages, and are subject to withholding and payment of employment taxes when paid.

(c) *Withholding rate.*—Payments made under reimbursement or other expense allowance arrangements that are subject to income tax withholding are supplemental wages as defined in §31.3402(g)-1. Accordingly, withholding on such supplemental wages is calculated under the rules provided with respect to supplemental wages in §31.3402(g)-1.

(d) *Effective date.*—This section applies to payments made under reimbursement or other expense allowance arrangements received by an employee on or after July 1, 1990, with respect to expenses paid or incurred on or after July 1, 1990. Paragraph (b)(1)(ii) of this section applies to payments made under reimbursement or other expense allowance arrangements received by an employee on or after January 1, 1991, with respect to expenses paid or incurred on or after January 1, 1991. [Reg. §31.3401(a)-4.]

☐ [*T.D.* 8324, 12-14-90. *Amended by T.D.* 9276, 7-24-2006.]

[Reg. §31.3401(a)(1)-1]

§31.3401(a)(1)-1. Remuneration of members of the Armed Forces of the United States for active service in combat zone or while hospitalized as a result of such service.—Remuneration paid for active service as a member of the Armed Forces of the United States performed in a month during any part of which such member served in a combat zone (as determined under section 112) or is hospitalized at any place as a result of wounds, disease, or injury incurred while serving in such a combat zone is excepted from wages and is, therefore, not subject to withholding. The exception with respect to hospitalization is applicable, however, only if during all of such month there are combatant activities in some combat zone (as determined under section 112). See the Income Tax Regulations (Part 1 of this chapter) under section 112. [Reg. §31.3401(a)(1)-1.]

☐ [*T.D.* 6259, 10-25-57.]

[Reg. §31.3401(a)(2)-1]

§31.3401(a)(2)-1. Agricultural labor.—The term "wages" does not include remuneration for services which constitute agricultural labor as defined in section 3121(g). For regulations relating to the definition of the term "agricultural labor", see §31.3121(g)-1 in subpart B of this part. [Reg. §31.3401(a)(2)-1.]

☐ [*T.D.* 6259, 10-25-57.]

[Reg. §31.3401(a)(3)-1]

§31.3401(a)(3)-1. Remuneration for domestic service.—(a) *In a private home.*—(1) Remuneration paid for services of a household nature performed by an employee in or about a private home of the person by whom he is employed is excepted from wages and hence is not subject to withholding. A private home is a fixed place of abode of an individual or family. A separate and distinct dwelling unit maintained by an individual in an apartment house, hotel, or other similar establishment may constitute a private home. If a dwelling house is used primarily as a boarding or lodging house for the purpose of supplying board or lodging to the public as a business enterprise, it is not a private home, and the remuneration paid for services performed therein is not within the exception.

(2) In general, services of a household nature in or about a private home include services

performed by cooks, waiters, butlers, housekeepers, governesses, maids, valets, baby sitters, janitors, laundresses, furnacemen, caretakers, handymen, gardeners, footmen, grooms, and chauffeurs of automobiles for family use.

(b) *In a local college club or local chapter of a college fraternity or sorority.*—(1) Remuneration paid for services of a household nature performed by an employee in or about the club rooms or house of a local college club or of a local chapter of a college fraternity or sorority by which he is employed is excepted from wages and hence is not subject to withholding. A local college club or local chapter of a college fraternity or sorority does not include an alumni club or chapter. If the club rooms or house of a local college club or local chapter of a college fraternity or sorority is used primarily for the purpose of supplying board or lodging to students or the public as a business enterprise, the remuneration paid for services performed therein is not within the exception.

(2) In general, services of a household nature in or about the club rooms or house of a local college club or local chapter of a college fraternity or sorority include services rendered by cooks, waiters, butlers, maids, janitors, laundresses, furnacemen, handymen, gardeners, housekeepers and housemothers.

(c) *Remuneration not excepted.*—Remuneration paid for services not of a household nature, such as services performed as a private secretary, tutor, or librarian, even though performed in the employer's private home or in a local college club or local chapter of a college fraternity or sorority, is not within the exception. Remuneration paid for services of a household nature is not within the exception if performed in or about rooming or lodging houses, boarding houses, clubs (except local college clubs), hotels, hospitals, eleemosynary institutions, or commercial offices or establishments. [Reg. § 31.3401(a)(3)-1.]

□ [T.D. 6259, 10-25-57.]

[Reg. § 31.3401(a)(4)-1]

§ 31.3401(a)(4)-1. Cash remuneration for service not in the course of employer's trade or business.—(a) Cash remuneration paid for services not in the course of the employer's trade or business performed by an employee for an employer in a calendar quarter is excepted from wages and hence is not subject to withholding unless—

(1) The cash remuneration paid for such services performed by the employee for the employer in the calendar quarter is $50 or more; and

(2) Such employee is regularly employed in the calendar quarter by such employer to perform such services.
Unless the tests set forth in both subparagraphs (1) and (2) of this paragraph are met, cash remuneration for service not in the course of the employer's trade or business is excluded from wages. (For provisions relating to the exclusion from wages of remuneration paid in any medium other than cash for services not in the course of the employer's trade or business, see § 31.3401(a)(11)-1.)

(b) The term "services not in the course of the employer's trade or business" includes services that do not promote or advance the trade or business of the employer. As used in this section, the term does not include service not in the course of the employer's trade or business performed on a farm operated for profit or domestic service in a private home, local college club, or local chapter of a college fraternity or sorority. Accordingly, this exception does not apply with respect to remuneration which is excepted from wages, under section 3401(a)(2) or section 3401(a)(3) (see § § 31.3401(a)(2)-1 and 31.3401(a)(3)-1, respectively). Remuneration paid for service performed for a corporation does not come within the exception.

(c) The test relating to cash remuneration of $50 or more is based on the remuneration earned during a calendar quarter rather than on the remuneration paid in a calendar quarter. However, for purposes of determining whether the test is met, it is also required that the remuneration be paid, although it is immaterial when the remuneration is paid. Furthermore, in determining whether $50 or more has been paid for service not in the course of the employer's trade or business, only cash remuneration for such service shall be taken into account. The term "cash remuneration" includes checks and other monetary media of exchange. Remuneration paid in any other medium, such as lodging, food, or other goods or commodities, is disregarded in determining whether the cash-remuneration test is met.

(d) For purposes of this exception, an individual is deemed to be regularly employed by an employer during a calendar quarter only if—

(1) Such individual performs service not in the course of the employer's trade or business for such employer for some portion of the day on at least 24 days (whether or not consecutive) during such calendar quarter; or

(2) Such individual was regularly employed (as determined under subparagraph (1) of this paragraph) by such employer in the performance of service not in the course of the employer's trade or business during the preceding calendar quarter.

(e) In determining whether an employee has performed service not in the course of the employer's trade or business on at least 24 days during a calendar quarter, there shall be counted as one day—

(1) Any day or portion thereof on which the employee actually performs such service; and

(2) Any day or portion thereof on which the employee does not perform service of the prescribed character but with respect to which cash remuneration is paid or payable to the employee for such service, such as a day on which the employee is sick or on vacation.

An employee who on a particular day reports for work and, at the direction of his employer, holds himself in readiness to perform service not in the course of the employer's trade or business shall be considered to be engaged in the actual performance of such service on that day. For purposes of this exception, a day is a continuous period of 24 hours commencing at midnight and ending at midnight. [Reg. § 31.3401(a)(4)-1.]

☐ [T.D. 6259, 10-25-57.]

[Reg. § 31.3401(a)(5)-1]

§ 31.3401(a)(5)-1. **Remuneration for services for foreign government or international organization.**—(a) *Services for foreign government.*—(1) Remuneration paid for services performed as an employee of a foreign government is excepted from wages and hence is not subject to withholding. The exception includes not only remuneration paid for services performed by ambassadors, ministers, and other diplomatic officers and employees but also remuneration paid for services performed as a consular or other officer or employee of a foreign government or as a nondiplomatic representative of such a government. However, the exception does not include remuneration for services performed for a corporation created or organized in the United States or under the laws of the United States or any State (including the District of Columbia or the Territory of Alaska or Hawaii) or of Puerto Rico even though such corporation is wholly owned by such a government.

(2) The citizenship or residence of the employee and the place where the services are performed are immaterial for purposes of the exception.

(b) *Services for international organization.*—(1) Subject to the provisions of section 1 of the International Organizations Immunities Act, remuneration aid for services performed within or without the United States by an employee for an international organization as defined in section 7701(a)(18) is excepted from wages and hence is not subject to withholding. The term "employee" as used in the preceding sentence includes not only an employee who is a citizen or resident of the United States but also an employee who is a nonresident alien individual. The term "employee" also includes an officer. An organization designated by the President through appropriate Executive order as entitled to enjoy the privileges, exemptions, and immunities provided in the International Organizations Immunities Act may enjoy the benefits of the exclusion from wages with respect to remuneration paid for services performed for such organization prior to the date of the issuance of such Executive order, if (i) the Executive order does not provide otherwise and (ii) the organization is a public international organization in which the United States participates, pursuant to a treaty or under the authority of an Act of Congress authorizing such participation or making an appropriation for such participation, at the time such services are performed.

(2) Section 7701(a)(18) provides as follows:
"Sec. 7701. *Definitions.* (a) When used in this title, where not otherwise distinctly expressed or manifestly incompatible with the intent thereof—

* * *

"(18) *International organization.* The term 'international organization' means a public international organization entitled to enjoy privileges, exemptions, and immunities as an international organization under the International Organizations Immunities Act (22 U.S.C. 288-288f)."

(3) Section 1 of the International Organizations Immunities Act provides as follows:

"Section 1. [International Organizations Immunities Act.] For the purposes of this title [International Organizations Immunities Act], the term 'international organization' means a public international organization in which the United States participates pursuant to any treaty or under the authority of any Act of Congress authorizing such participation or making an appropriation for such participation, and which shall have been designated by the President through appropriate Executive order as being entitled to enjoy the privileges, exemptions, and immunities herein provided. The President shall be authorized, in the light of the functions performed by any such international organization, by appropriate Executive order to withhold or withdraw from any such organization or its officers or employees any of the privileges, exemptions, and immunities provided for in this title (including the amendments made by this title) or to condition or limit the enjoyment by any such organization or its officers or employees of any such privilege, exemption, or immunity. The President shall be authorized, if in his judgment such action should be justified by reason of the abuse by an international organization or its officers and employees of the privileges, exemptions, and immunities herein provided or for any other reason, at any time to revoke the designation of any international organization under this section, whereupon the international organization in question shall cease to be classed as an international organization for the purposes of this title." [Reg. § 31.3401(a)(5)-1.]

☐ [T.D. 6259, 10-25-57.]

[Reg. § 31.3401(a)(6)-1]

§ 31.3401(a)(6)-1. **Remuneration for services of nonresident alien individuals.**—(a) *In general.*—All remuneration paid after December 31, 1966, for services performed by a nonresident alien individual, if such remuneration otherwise constitutes wages within the meaning of § 31.3401(a)-1 and if such remuneration is effectively connected with the conduct of a trade or business within the United States, is subject to withholding under section 3402 unless excepted from wages under this section. In regard to wages paid under this section after February 28, 1979, the term "nonresident alien individual" does not include a nonresident alien individual treated as a resident under section 6013(g) or (h).

(b) *Remuneration for services performed outside the United States.*—Remuneration paid to a non-resident alien individual (other than a resident of Puerto Rico) for services performed outside the United States is excepted from wages and hence is not subject to withholding.

(c) *Remuneration for services of residents of Canada or Mexico who enter and leave the United States at frequent intervals.*—(1) *Transportation service.*—Remuneration paid to a nonresident alien individual who is a resident of Canada or Mexico and who, in the performance of his duties in transportation service between points in the United States and points in such foreign country, enters and leaves the United States at frequent intervals, is excepted from wages and hence is not subject to withholding. This exception applies to personnel engaged in railroad, bus, truck, ferry, steamboat, aircraft, or other transportation services and applies whether the employer is a domestic or foreign entity. Thus, the remuneration of a nonresident alien individual who is a resident of Canada and an employee of a domestic railroad, for services as a member of the crew of a train operating between points in Canada and points in the United States, is not subject to withholding under section 3402.

(2) *Service on international projects.*—Remuneration paid to a nonresident alien individual who is a resident of Canada or Mexico and who, in the performance of his duties in connection with the construction, maintenance, or operation of a waterway, viaduct, dam, or bridge traversed by, or traversing, the boundary between the United States and Canada or the boundary between the United States and Mexico, as the case may be, enters and leaves the United States at frequent intervals, is excepted from wages and hence is not subject to withholding. Thus, the remuneration of a nonresident alien individual who is a resident of Canada, for services as an employee in connection with the construction, maintenance, or operation of the Saint Lawrence Seaway and who, in the performance of such services, enters and leaves the United States at frequent intervals, is not subject to withholding under section 3402.

(3) *Limitation.*—The exceptions provided by this paragraph do not apply to the remuneration of a resident of Canada or of Mexico who is employed wholly within the United States as, for example, where such a resident is employed to perform service at a fixed point or points in the United States, such as a factory, store, office, or designated area or areas within the United States, and who commutes from his home in Canada or Mexico, in the pursuit of his employment within the United States.

(4) *Certificate required.*—In order for an exception provided by this paragraph to apply for any taxable year, the nonresident alien employee must furnish his employer a statement in duplicate for the taxable year setting forth the employee's name, address, and taxpayer identifying number,and certifying (i) that he is not a citizen or resident of the United States, (ii) that he is a resident of Canada or Mexico, as the case may be, and (iii) that he expects to meet the requirements of subparagraph (1) or (2) of this paragraph with respect to remuneraion to be paid during the taxable year in respect of which the statement is filed. The statement shall be dated, shall identify the taxable year to which it relates, shall be signed by the employee, and shall contain, or be verified by, a written declaration that is made under the penalties of perjury. No particular form is prescribed for this statement. The duplicate copy of each statement filed during any calendar year pursuant to this paragraph shall be forwarded by the employer with, and attached to, the Form 1042S required by paragraph (c) of §1.1461-2 with respect to such remuneration for such calendar year.

(d) *Remuneration for services performed by residents of Puerto Rico.*—(1) Remuneration paid for services performed in Puerto Rico by a nonresident alien individual who is a resident of Puerto Rico for an employer (other than the United States or any agency thereof) is excepted from wages and hence is not subject to withholding.

(2) Remuneration paid for services performed outside the United States but not in Puerto Rico by a nonresident alien individual who is a resident of Puerto Rico for an employer (other than the United States or any agency thereof) is excepted from wages and hence is not subject to withholding if such individual does not expect to be a resident of Puerto Rico during the entire taxable year. In order for the exception provided by this subparagraph to apply for any taxable year, the nonresident alien employee must furnish his employer a statement for the taxable year setting forth the employee's name and address and certifying (i) that he is not a citizen or resident of the United States and (ii) that he is a resident of Puerto Rico but does not expect to be a resident of Puerto Rico during the entire taxable year. The statement shall be dated, shall identify the taxable year to which it relates, shall be signed by the employee, and shall contain, or be verified by, a written declaration that it is made under the penalties of perjury. No particular form is prescribed for this statement.

(3) Remuneration paid for services performed outside the United States by a nonresident alien individual who is a resident of Puerto Rico as an employee of the United States or any agency thereof is excepted from wages and hence is not subject to withholding if such individual does not expect to be a resident of Puerto Rico during the entire taxable year. In order for the exception provided by this subparagraph to apply for any taxable year, the nonresident alien employee must furnish his employer a statement for the taxable year setting forth the employee's name and address and certifying (i) that he is not a citizen or resident of the United States and (ii) that he is a resident of Puerto Rico but does not expect to be a resident of Puerto Rico during the entire taxable year. This statement shall be

dated, shall identify the taxable year to which it relates, shall be signed by the employee, and shall contain, or be verified by, a written declaration that it is made under the penalties of perjury. No particular form is prescribed for this statement.

(e) *Exemption from income tax for remuneration paid for services performed before January 1, 2001.*— Remuneration paid for services performed within the United States by a nonresident alien individual before January 1, 2001, is excepted from wages and hence is not subject to withholding if such remuneration is, or will be, exempt from income tax imposed by chapter 1 of the Internal Revenue Code by reason of a provision of the Internal Revenue Code or an income tax convention to which the United States is a party. In order for the exception provided by this paragraph to apply for any taxable year, the nonresident alien employee must furnish his employer a statement in duplicate for the taxable year setting forth the employee's name, address, and taxpayer identifying number, and certifying (1) that he is not a citizen or resident of the United States, (2) that the remuneration to be paid to him during the taxable year is, or will be, exempt from the tax imposed by chapter 1 of the Code, and (3) the reason why such remuneration is so exempt from tax. If the remuneration is claimed to be exempt from tax by reason of a provision of an income tax convention to which the United States is a party, the statement shall also indicate the provision and tax convention under which the exemption is claimed, the country of which the employee is a resident, and sufficient facts to justify the claim to exemption. The statement shall be dated, shall identify the taxable year for which it is to apply and the remuneration to which it relates, shall be signed by the employee, and shall contain, or be verified by, a written declaration that is made under the penalties of perjury. No particular form is prescribed for this statement. The duplicate copy of each statement filed during any calendar year pursuant to this paragraph shall be forwarded by the employer with, and attached to, the Form 1042S required by paragraph (c) of § 1.1461-2 with respect to such remuneration for such calendar year.

(f) *Exemption from income tax for remuneration paid for services performed after December 31, 2000.*—Remuneration paid for services performed within the United States by a nonresident alien individual after December 31, 2000, is excepted from wages and hence is not subject to withholding if such remuneration is, or will be, exempt from the income tax imposed by chapter 1 of the Internal Revenue Code by reason of a provision of the Internal Revenue Code or an income tax convention to which the United States is a party. An employer may rely on a claim that the employee is entitled to an exemption from tax if it complies with the requirements of § 1.1441-1(e)(1)(ii) of this chapter (for a claim based on a provision of the Internal Revenue Code) or § 1.1441-4(b)(2) of this chapter (for a

claim based on an income tax convention). [Reg. § 31.3401(a)(6)-1.]

☐ [*T.D.* 6908, 12-30-66. *Amended by T.D.* 7670, 1-30-80; *T.D.* 7977, 9-19-84; *T.D.* 8734, 10-6-97; *T.D.* 8804, 12-30-98 *and T.D.* 8856, 12-29-99.]

[Reg. § 31.3401(a)(7)-1]

§ 31.3401(a)(7)-1. Remuneration paid before January 1, 1967, for services performed by nonresident alien individuals who are residents of a contiguous country and who enter and leave the United States at frequent intervals.— (a) *Transportation service.*—Remuneration paid to nonresident aliens who are residents of a contiguous country (Canada or Mexico) and who, in the performance of their duties in transportation service between points in the United States and points in a contiguous country, enter and leave the United States at frequent intervals, is expected from wages and hence is not subject to withholding. This exception applies to personnel engaged in railroad, bus, ferry, steamboat, and aircraft services and applies whether the employer is a domestic or foreign entity. This, the remuneration of a nonresident alien individual who is a resident of Canada and an employee of a domestic railroad, for services as a member of the crew of a train operating between points in Canada and points in the United States, is not subject to withholding under section 3402.

(b) *Service on international projects.*—Remuneration paid to nonresident aliens who are residents of a contiguous country (Canada or Mexico) and who, in the performance of their duties in connection with the construction, maintenance or operation of a waterway, viaduct, dam, or bridge traversed by or traversing the boundary between the United States and Canada or the boundary between the United States and Mexico, as the case may be, enter and leave the United States at frequent intervals, is expected from wages and hence is not subject to withholding. Thus, the remuneration of a nonresident alien individual who is a resident of Canada, for services as an employee in connection with the construction, maintenance, or operation of the Saint Lawrence Seaway and who, in the performance of such services, enters and leaves the United States at frequent intervals, is not subject to withholding under section 3402.

(c) *Limitation on application of section.*—The exception provided by this section has no application to the remuneration of a resident of Canada or of Mexico who is employed wholly within the United States as, for example, where such a resident is employed to performed service at a fixed point or points in the United States, such as a factory, store, office, or designated area or areas within the United States, and who commutes from his home in Canada or Mexico in the pursuit of his employment within the United States.

(d) *Certificate required.*—In order for the exception to apply, the nonresident alien employee must furnish his employer a statement setting forth the employee's name and address and certifying (1) that his is not a citizen of the United States, (2) that he is a resident of Canada or Mexico, as the case may be, and (3) the approximate period of time during which he has had such status. Such statement shall be dated, shall be signed by the employee, and shall contain, or be verified by, a written declaration that it is made under the penalties of perjury. No particular form is prescribed for this statement.

(e) *Effective date.*—This section shall not apply with respect to remuneration paid after December 31, 1966. For rules with respect to such remuneration see §31.3401(a)(6)-1. [Reg. §31.3401(a)(7)-1.]

☐ [T.D. 6259, 10-25-57. *Republished in T.D.* 6516, 12-19-60. *Amended by T.D. 6908, 12-30-66.*]

[Reg. §31.3401(a)(8)(A)-1]

§31.3401(a)(8)(A)-1. Remuneration for services performed outside the United States by citizens of the United States.—(a) *Remuneration excluded from gross income under section 911.*— (1)(i) Remuneration paid for services performed outside the United States for an employer (other than the United States or any agency thereof) by a citizen of the United States does not constitute wages and hence is not subject to withholding, if at the time of payment it is reasonable to believe that such remuneration will be excluded from gross income under the provisions of section 911. The reasonable belief contemplated by the statute may be based upon any evidence reasonably sufficient to induce such belief, even though such evidence may be insufficient upon closer examination by the district director or the courts finally to establish that the remuneration is excludable from gross income under the provisions of section 911. The reasonable belief shall be based upon the application of section 911 and the regulations thereunder in Part 1 of this chapter (Income Tax Regulations).

(ii) Remuneration paid by an employer to an employee constitutes wages, and hence is subject to withholding, only to the extent that the remuneration is expected to exceed the aggregate amount which is excludable from the employee's gross income under section 911(a). For amounts paid after December 31, 1984, the determination of the amount subject to withholding shall be made by applying the excludable amount, on a pro rata basis, to each payment of remuneration to the employee. For this purpose, an employer is not required to ascertain information with respect to amounts received by his employee from any other source; but, if the employer has such information, he shall take it into account in determining whether the earned income of the employee is in excess of the applicable limitation. For purposes of section 911(d)(5) and §1.911-2(c), relating to an employee who states to the authorities of a foreign country that he is not a resident of that country, the employer is not required to ascertain whether such a statement has been made; but if an employer knows that such a statement has been made, he shall presume that the employee is not a bona fide

resident of that country, unless the employer also knows that the authorities of the foreign country have determined, notwithstanding the statement, that the employee is a resident of that country. For purposes of section 911(d)(1) or §1.911-2(a) relating to the definition of a qualified individual, the reasonable belief contemplated by the statute may be based on a presumption as set forth in subparagraph (2) or (3) of this paragraph. For purposes of sections 911(a)(2) and 911(c)(2) and §1.911-4(b) and (d)(1), relating to the housing cost amount exclusion and the definition of housing expenses, the reasonable belief contemplated by the statute may be based on the presumption set forth in subparagraph (4) of this paragraph.

(2)(i) The employer may, in the absence of cause for a reasonable belief to the contrary, presume that an employee will maintain a tax home in a foreign country or countries and be a bona fide resident of a foreign country or countries, within the meaning of section 911(d)(1), for an uninterrupted period which includes each taxable year of the employee, or applicable portion thereof, in respect of which the employee properly executes and delivers to the employer a statement that the employee meets or will meet the requirement of §1.911-2(a) relating to maintaining a tax home and a bona fide residence in a foreign country for the taxable year. This statement must set forth the facts alleged as the basis for this determination and contain a declaration by the employee that the statement is made under the penalties of perjury. Sample forms of acceptable statements may be obtained by writing to the Foreign Operations District, Internal Revenue Service, Washington, D.C. 20225 (Form IO-673).

(ii) If the employer was entitled to presume for the two consecutive taxable years immediately preceding an employee's current taxable year that such employee was a bona fide resident of a foreign country or countries for an uninterrupted period which includes such preceding taxable years, he may, if such employee is residing in a foreign country on the first day of such current taxable year, presume, in the absence of cause for a reasonable belief to the contrary, and without obtaining from the employee the statement prescribed in subdivision (i) of this subparagraph, that the employee will be a bona fide resident of a foreign country or countries in such current taxable year.

(3) The employer may, in the absence of cause for a reasonable belief to the contrary, presume that an employee will maintain a tax home in a foreign country or countries and be present in a foreign country or countries during at least 330 full days during any period of twelve consecutive months, within the meaning of section 911(d)(1), and that such period includes each taxable year of the employee, or applicable portion thereof, in respect of which the employee properly executes and delivers to the employer a statement that the employee meets or will meet the requirements of §1.911-2(a) relating to maintaining a tax home and being physically present

in a foreign country for the taxable year. This statement must set forth the facts alleged as the basis for this determination and contain a declaration by the employee that the statement is made under the penalties of perjury. Sample forms of acceptable statements may be obtained by writing to the Foreign Operations District, Internal Revenue Service, Washington, D.C. 20225 (Form IO-673).

(4) The employer may, in the absence of cause for a reasonable belief to the contrary, presume that an employee's housing cost amount will be the amount shown on a statement properly executed and delivered to the employer. This statement must set forth the employee's estimation of the following items: housing expenses (as defined in § 1.911-4(b)), the housing cost amount exclusion (as defined in § 1.911-4(d)(1)), and the qualifying period (as defined in § 1.911-2(a)). The statement must contain a declaration by the employee that it is made under the penalties of perjury. Sample forms of acceptable statements may be obtained by writing to the Foreign Operations District, Internal Revenue Service, Washington, D.C. 20225 (IO-673). The employer may not rely on a statement from an employee if the employer, based on his or her knowledge of housing costs in the vicinity of the employee's tax home (as defined in § 1.911-2(b)), believes the employee's housing expenses are lavish or extravagant under the circumstances.

(b) *Remuneration subject to withholding of income tax under law of a foreign country or a possession of the United States.*—(1) Remuneration paid for services in a foreign country or in a possession of the United States for an employer (other than the United States or any agency thereof) by a citizen of the United States does not constitute wages and hence is not subject to withholding, if at the time of the payment of such remuneration the employer is required by the law of any foreign country or of any possession of the United States to withhold income tax upon such remuneration. This paragraph, insofar as it relates to remuneration paid for services performed in a possession of the United States, applies only with respect to remuneration paid on or after August 9, 1955.

(2) Remuneration is not exempt from withholding under this paragraph if the employer is not required by the law of a foreign country or of a possession of the United States to withhold income tax upon such remuneration. Mere agreements between the employer and the employee whereby the estimated income tax of a foreign country or of a possession of the United States is withheld from the remuneration in anticipation of actual liability under the law of such country or possession will not suffice.

(3) The exemption from withholding provided by this paragraph does not apply by reason of withholding of income tax pursuant to the law of a territory of the United States, of a political subdivision of a possession of the United

States, or of a political subdivision of a foreign state.

(4) For provisions relating to remuneration for services performed by a permanent resident of the Virgin Islands, see paragraph (b)(12) of § 31.3401(a)-1.

(c) *Limitation on application of section.*—This section has no application to the remuneration paid to a citizen of the United States for services performed outside the United States as an employee of the United States or any agency thereof. [Reg. § 31.3401(a)(8)(A)-1.]

☐ [*T.D.* 6259, 10-25-57. *Amended by T.D.* 6697, 12-16-63, *and T.D.* 8006, 1-17-85.]

[Reg. § 31.3401(a)(8)(B)-1]

§ 31.3401(a)(8)(B)-1. Remuneration for services performed in possession of the United States (other than Puerto Rico) by citizen of the United States.—(a) Remuneration paid for services for an employer (other than the United States or any agency thereof) performed by a citizen of the United States within a possession of the United States (other than Puerto Rico) does not constitute wages and hence is not subject to withholding, if it is reasonable to believe that at least 80 percent of the remuneration to be paid to the employee by such employer during the calendar year will be for such services. The reasonable belief contemplated by section 3401(a)(8)(B) may be based upon any evidence reasonably sufficient to induce such belief, even though such evidence may be insufficient upon closer examination by the district director or the courts finally to establish that at least 80 percent of the remuneration paid by the employer to the employee during the calendar year was for services performed within such a possession of the United States.

(b) This section has no application to remuneration paid to a citizen of the United States for services performed in any possession of the United States as an employee of the United States or any agency thereof.

(c) For provisions relating to remuneration for services performed by a permanent resident of the Virgin Islands, see § 31.3401(a)-1(b)(12). [Reg. § 31.3401(a)(8)(B)-1.]

☐ [*T.D.* 6259, 10-25-57.]

[Reg. § 31.3401(a)(8)(C)-1]

§ 31.3401(a)(8)(C)-1. Remuneration for services performed in Puerto Rico by citizen of the United States.—(a) Remuneration paid for services performed within Puerto Rico for an employer (other than the United States or any agency thereof) by a citizen of the United States does not constitute wages and hence is not subject to withholding, if it is reasonable to believe that during the entire calendar year the employee will be a bona fide resident of Puerto Rico. The reasonable belief contemplated by section 3401(a)(8)(C) may be based upon any evidence reasonably sufficient to induce such belief, even though such evidence may be insufficient upon closer examination by the district director or the courts finally to establish that the employee was a bona fide resident of Puerto Rico for the entire calendar year.

(b) The employer may, in the absence of cause for a reasonable belief to the contrary, presume that an employee will be a bona fide resident of Puerto Rico during the entire calendar year—

(1) Unless the employee is known by the employer to have maintained his abode at a place outside Puerto Rico at some time during the current or the preceding calendar year; or

(2) In any case where the employee files with the employer a statement (containing a declaration under the penalties of perjury that such statement is true to the best of the employees's knowledge and belief) that such employee has at all times during the current calendar year been a bona fide resident of Puerto Rico and that he intends to remain a bona fide resident of Puerto Rico during the entire remaining portion of such current calendar year.

(c) This section has no application to remuneration paid to a citizen of the United States for services performed in Puerto Rico as an employee of the United States or any agency thereof. [Reg. § 31.3401(a)(8)(C)-1.]

☐ *[T.D. 6259, 10-25-57.]*

[Reg. § 31.3401(a)(9)-1]

§ 31.3401(a)(9)-1. Remuneration for services performed by a minister of a church or a member of a religious order.—(a) *In general.*—Remuneration paid for services performed by a duly ordained, commissioned, or licensed minister of a church in the exercise of his ministry, or by a member of a religious order in the exercise of duties required by such order, is excepted from wages and hence is not subject to withholding.

(b) *Service by a minister in the exercise of his ministry.*—Except as provided in paragraph (c)(3) of this section, service performed by a minister in the exercise of his ministry includes the ministration of sacerdotal functions and the conduct of religious worship, and the control, conduct, and maintenance of religious organizations (including the religious boards, societies, and other integral agencies of such organizations), under the authority of a religious body, constituting a church or church denomination. The following rules are applicable in determining whether services performed by a minister are performed in the exercise of his ministry:

(1) Whether service performed by a minister constitutes the conduct of religious worship or the ministration of sacerdotal functions depends on the tenets and practices of the particular religious body constituting his church or church denomination.

(2) Service performed by a minister in the control, conduct, and maintenance of a religious organization relates to directing, managing, or promoting the activities of such organization. Any religious organization is deemed to be under the authority of a religious body constituting a church or church denomination if it is organized and dedicated to carrying out the tenets and principles of a faith in accordance with either the requirements or sanctions governing the creation of institutions of the faith. The term "religious organization" has the same meaning and application as is given to the term for income tax purposes.

(3)(i) If a minister is performing service in the conduct of religious worship or the ministration of sacerdotal functions, such service is in the exercise of his ministry whether or not it is performed for a religious organization.

(ii) The rule in subdivision (i) of this subparagraph may be illustrated by the following example:

Example. M, a duly ordained minister, is engaged to perform service as chaplain at N University. M devotes his entire time to performing his duties as chaplain which include the conduct of religious worship, offering spiritual counsel to the university students, and teaching a class in religion. M is performing service in the exercise of his ministry.

(4)(i) If a minister is performing service for an organization which is operated as an integral agency of a religious organization under the authority of a religious body constituting a church or church denomination, all service performed by the minister in the conduct of religious worship, in the ministration of sacerdotal functions, or in the control, conduct, and maintenance of such organization (see subparagraph (2) of this paragraph) is in the exercise of his ministry.

(ii) The rule in subdivision (i) of this subparagraph may be illustrated by the following example:

Example. M, a duly ordained minister, is engaged by the N Religious Board to serve as director of one of its departments. He performs no other service. The N Religious Board is an integral agency of O, a religious organization operating under the authority of a religious body constituting a church denomination. M is performing service in the exercise of his ministry.

(5)(i) If a minister, pursuant to an assignment or designation by a religious body constituting his church, performs service for an organization which is neither a religious organization nor operated as an integral agency of a religious organization, all service performed by him, even though such service may not involve the conduct of a religious worship or the ministration of sacerdotal functions, is in the exercise of his ministry.

(ii) The rule in subdivision (i) of this subparagraph may be illustrated by the following example:

Example. M, a duly ordained minister, is assigned by X, the religious body constituting his church, to perform advisory service to Y Company in connection with the publication of a book dealing with the history of M's church denomination. Y is neither a religious organization nor operated as an integral agency of a religious organization. M performs no other service for X or Y. M is performing service in the exercise of his ministry.

(c) *Service by a minister not in the exercise of his ministry.*—(1) Section 3401(a)(9) does not except from wages remuneration for service performed by a duly ordained, commissioned, or licensed minister of a church which is not in the exercise of his ministry.

(2)(i) If a minister is performing service for an organization which is neither a religious organization nor operated as an integral agency of a religious organization and the service is not performed pursuant to an assignment or designation by his ecclesiastical superiors, then only the service performed by him in the conduct of religious worship or the ministration of sacerdotal functions is in the exercise of his ministry. See, however, subparagraph (3) of this paragraph.

(ii) The rule in subdivision (i) of this subparagraph may be illustrated by the following example:

Example. M, a duly ordained minister, is engaged by N University to teach history and mathematics. He performs no other service for N although from time to time he performs marriages and conducts funerals for relatives and friends. N University is neither a religious organization nor operated as an integral agency of a religious organization. M is not performing the service for N pursuant to an assignment or designation by his ecclesiastical superiors. However, service performed by M in performing marriages and conducting funerals is in the exercise of his ministry.

(3) Service performed by a duly ordained, commissioned, or licensed minister of a church as an employee of the United States, or a State, Territory, or possession of the United States, or the District of Columbia, or a foreign government, or a political subdivision of any of the foregoing, is not considered to be in the exercise of his ministry for purposes of the collection of income tax at source on wages, even though such service may involve the ministration of sacerdotal functions or the conduct of religious worship. Thus, for example, service performed by an individual as a chaplain in the Armed Forces of the United States is considered to be performed by a commissioned officer in his capacity as such, and not by a minister in the exercise of his ministry. Similarly, service performed by an employee of a State as a chaplain in a State prison is considered to be performed by a civil servant of the State and not by a minister in the exercise of his ministry.

(d) *Service in the exercise of duties required by a religious order.*—Service performed by a member of a religious order in the exercise of duties required by such order includes all duties required of the member by the order. The nature or extent of such service is immaterial so long as it is a service which he is directed or required to perform by his ecclesiastical superiors. [Reg. § 31.3401(a)(9)-1.]

☐ [*T.D.* 6259, 10-25-57.]

[Reg. § 31.3401(a)(10)-1]

§ 31.3401(a)(10)-1. Remuneration for services in delivery or distribution of newspapers, shopping news, or magazines.—(a) *Services of individuals under age 18.*—Remuneration for services performed by an employee under the age of 18 in the delivery or distribution of newspapers, or shopping news, not including delivery or distribution (as, for example, by a regional distributor) to any point for subsequent delivery or distribution, is excepted from wages and hence is not subject to withholding. Thus, remuneration for services performed by an employee under the age of 18 in making house-to-house delivery or sale of newspapers or shopping news, including handbills and other similar types of advertising material, is excepted from wages. The remuneration is excepted irrespective of the form or method thereof. Remuneration for incidental services by the employee who makes the house-to-house delivery, such as services in assembling newspapers, is considered to be within the exception. The exception continues only during the time that the employee is under the age of 18.

(b) *Services of individuals of any age.*—Remuneration for services performed by an employee in, and at the time of, the sale of newspapers or magazines to ultimate consumers under an arrangement under which the newspapers or magazines are to be sold by him at at fixed price, his remuneration being based on the retention of the excess of such price over the amount at which the newspapers or magazines are charged to him, is excepted from wages and hence is not subject to withholding. The remuneration is excepted whether or not the employee is guaranteed a minimum amount of remuneration, or is entitled to be credited with the unsold newspapers or magazines turned back. Moreover, the remuneration is excepted without regard to the age of the employee. Remuneration for services performed other than at the time of sale to the ultimate consumer is not within the exception. Thus, remuneration for services of a regional distributor which are antecedent to but not immediately part of the sale to the ultimate consumer is not within the exception. However, remuneration for incidental services by the employee who makes the sale to the ultimate consumer, such as services in assembling newspapers or in taking newspapers or magazines to the place of sale, is considered to be within the exception. [Reg. § 31.3401(a)(10)-1.]

☐ [*T.D.* 6259, 10-25-57.]

[Reg. § 31.3401(a)(11)-1]

§ 31.3401(a)(11)-1. Remuneration other than in cash for service not in the course of employer's trade or business.—(a) Remuneration paid in any medium other than cash for services not in the course of the employer's trade or business is excepted from wages and hence is not subject to withholding. Cash remuneration includes checks and other monetary media of exchange. Remuneration paid in any medium other than cash, such as lodging, food, or other goods or commodities, for services not in the course of the employer's trade or business does not constitute wages. Remuneration paid in any medium other than cash for other types of services does not come within this exception from wages. For provisions relating to cash remuneration for service not in the course of employer's trade or business, see § 31.3401(a)(4)-1.

(b) As used in this section, the term "services not in the course of the employer's trade or business" has the same meaning as when used in § 31.3401(a)(4)-1. [Reg. § 31.3401(a)(11)-1.]

☐ *[T.D. 6259, 10-25-57.]*

[Reg. § 31.3401(a)(12)-1]

§ 31.3401(a)(12)-1. Payments from or to certain tax-exempt trusts, or under or to certain annuity plans or bond purchase plans.—
(a) *Payments from or to certain tax-exempt trusts.—* The term "wages" does not include any payment made—

    (1) By an employer, on behalf of an employee or his beneficiary, into a trust, or

    (2) To, or on behalf of, an employee or his beneficiary from a trust, if at the time of such payment the trust is exempt from tax under section 501(a) as an organization described in section 401(a). A payment made to an employee of such a trust for services rendered as an employee of the trust and not as a beneficiary thereof is not within this exclusion from wages. Also, since supplemental unemployment compensation benefits are treated under paragraph (b)(14) of § 31.3401(a)-1 as if they were wages for purposes of this chapter, this section does not apply to such benefits.

(b) *Payments under or to certain annuity plans.—* (1) The term "wages" does not include any payment made after December 31, 1962,—

    (i) By an employer, on behalf of an employee or his beneficiary, into an annuity plan, or

    (ii) To, or on behalf of, an employee or his beneficiary under an annuity plan,

if at the time of such payment the annuity plan is a plan described in section 403(a).

    (2) The term "wages" does not include any payment made before January 1, 1963,—

    (i) By an employer, on behalf of an employee or his beneficiary, into an annuity plan, or

    (ii) To, or on behalf of, an employee or his beneficiary under an annuity plan,

if at the time of such payment the annuity plan meets the requirements of section 401(a)(3), (4), (5), and (6).

(c) *Payments under or to certain bond purchase plans.—*The term "wages" does not include any payment made after December 31, 1962,—

    (1) By an employer, on behalf of an employee or his beneficiary, into a bond purchase plan, or

    (2) To, or on behalf of, an employee or his beneficiary under a bond purchase plan,

if at the time of such payment the plan is qualified bond purchase plan described in section 405(a).

(d) *Payment to individual retirement plans.—* (1) The term "wages" does not include any payment to an individual retirement plan described in section 7701(a)(37) by an employer after December 31, 1974, on behalf of an employee, if, at the time of such payment, it is reasonable for the employer to believe that the employee will be entitled to a deduction for such payment under section 219(a).

(2) The term "wages" does not include any payment to an individual retirement plan described in section 7701(a)(37) by an employer after December 31, 1976, on behalf of an employee, if, at the time of such payment, it is reasonable for the employer to believe that the employee on whose behalf the payment is made will be entitled to a deduction for such payment under section 220(a).

(3) The term "wages" does not include any payment to a simplified employee pension arrangement described in section 408(k) by an employer after December 31, 1978, on behalf of an employee, if, at the time of such payment, it is reasonable for the employer to believe that the employee on whose behalf the payment is made will be entitled to a deduction for such payment under section 219(a). [Reg. § 31.3401(a)(12)-1.]

☐ *[T.D. 6259, 10-25-57. Amended by T.D. 6654, 5-27-63, T.D. 7068, 11-10-70 and T.D. 7730, 10-31-80.]*

[Reg. § 31.3401(a)(13)-1]

§ 31.3401(a)(13)-1. Remuneration for services performed by Peace Corps volunteers.—
(a) Remuneration paid after September 22, 1961, for services performed as a volunteer or volunteer leader within the meaning of the Peace Corps Act (22 U.S.C. 2501) is excepted from wages, and hence is not subject to withholding, unless the remuneration is paid pursuant to section 5(c) or section 6(1) of the Peace Corps Act.

(b) Sections 5 and 6 of the Peace Corps Act (22 U.S.C. 2504, 2505) provide, in part, as follows:

Sec. 5. *Peace Corps Volunteers* [Peace Corps Act (75 Stat. 613); as amended by sec. 2(b), Act of December 13, 1963 (P.L. 88-200, 77 Stat. 359); sec 2(a), Act of August 24, 1965, (P.L. 89-134, 79 Stat. 549); sec. 3(a), Act of July 24, 1970 (P.L. 91-352, 84 Stat. 464)]

* * *

(c) *Readjustment allowances.* Volunteers shall be entitled to receive a readjustment allowance at a rate not to exceed $75 for each month of satisfactory service as determined by the President; except that, in the cases of volunteers who have one or more minor children at the time of their entering a period of pre-enrollment training, one parent shall be entitled to receive a readjustment allowance at a rate not to exceed $125 for each month of satisfactory service as determined by the President. The readjustment allowance of each volunteer shall be payable on his return to the United States: *Provided, however,* That, under such circumstances as the President may determine, the accrued readjustment allowance, or any part thereof, may be paid to the volunteer, members of his family or others, during the period of his service, or prior to his return to the United States. In the event of the volunteer's death during the period of his service, the amount of any unpaid readjustment allowance shall be paid in accordance with the provisions of section 5582(b) of Title 5. For purposes of the Internal Revenue Code of 1954, a volunteer shall be deemed to be paid and to receive each amount of a readjustment allowance to which he is entitled after December 31, 1964, when such amount is transferred from funds made available under this chapter to the fund from which such readjustment allowance is payable.

* * *

Sec. 6. *Peace Corps Volunteer Leaders; number; applicability of chapter; benefits* [Peace Corps Act (75 Stat. 615), as amended by sec. 3, Act of December 13, 1963 (P.L. 88-200, 77 Stat. 360)] The President may enroll in the Peace Corps qualified citizens or nationals of the United States whose services are required for supervisory or other special duties or responsibilities in connection with programs under this chapter (referred to in this Act as "volunteer leaders"). The ratio of the total number of volunteer leaders to the total number of volunteers in service at any one time shall not exceed one to twenty-five. Except as otherwise provided in this Act, all of the provisions of this Act applicable to volunteers shall be applicable to volunteer leaders, and the term "volunteers" shall include "volunteer leaders": *Provided, however,* That—

(1) Volunteer leaders shall be entitled to receive a readjustment allowance at a rate not to exceed $125 for each month of satisfactory service as determined by the President;

* * *

[Reg. § 31.3401(a)(13)-1.]

☐ [*T.D.* 62654, 5-27-63 *Amended by T.D.* 7943, 6-29-77.]

[Reg. § 31.3401(a)(14)-1]

§ 31.3401(a)(14)-1. Group-term life insurance.—(a) The cost of group-term life insurance on the life of an employee is excepted from wages, and hence is not subject to withholding. For provisions relating generally to such remuneration, and for reporting requirements with respect to such remuneration, see sections 79 and 6052, respectively, and the regulations thereunder in Part 1 of this chapter (Income Tax Regulations).

(b) The cost of group-term life insurance on the life of an employee's spouse or children is not subject to withholding if it is excludable from the employee's gross income because it is merely incidental. See paragraph (d)(2)(ii)(b) of § 1.161-2 in Part 1 of this chapter (Income Tax Regulations). [Reg. § 31.3401(a)(14)-1.]

☐ [*T.D.* 7493, 6-29-77.]

[Reg. § 31.3401(a)(15)-1]

§ 31.3401(a)(15)-1. Moving expenses.—(a) An amount paid to or on behalf of an employee after March 4, 1964, either as an advance or a reimbursement, specifically for moving expenses incurred or expected to be incurred is excepted from wages, and hence is not subject to withholding, if (and to the extent that) at the time of payment it is reasonable to believe that a corresponding deduction is or will be allowable to the employee under section 217. The reasonable belief contemplated by the statute may be based upon any evidence reasonably sufficient to induce such belief, even though such evidence may be insufficient upon closer examination by the district director or the courts finally to establish that a deduction is allowable under section 217. The reasonable belief shall be based upon the application of section 217 and the regulations thereunder in Part 1 of this chapter (Income Tax Regulations). When used in this section, the term "moving expenses" has the same meaning as when used in section 217. See § 1.6041-2(a) in Part 1 of this chapter (Income Tax Regulations), relating to return of information as to payments to employees, and § 31.6051-1(e), relating to the reporting of reimbursements of or payments of certain moving expenses.

(b) Except as otherwise provided in paragraph (a) of this section, or in a numbered paragraph of section 3401(a), amounts paid to or on behalf of an employee for moving expenses constitute wages subject to withholding. [Reg. § 31.3401(a)(15)-1.]

☐ [*T.D.* 7493, 6-29-77.]

[Reg. § 31.3401(a)(16)-1]

§ 31.3401(a)(16)-1. Tips.—Tips paid to an employee are excepted from wages and hence not subject to withholding if—

(a) The tips are paid in any medium other than cash, or

(b) The cash tips received by an employee in any calendar month in the course of his employment by an employer are less than $20.

However, if the cash tips received by an employee in a calendar month in the course of his employment by an employer amount to $20 or more, none of the cash tips received by the employee in such calendar month are excepted from wages under this section. The cash tips to which this section applies include checks and other monetary media of exchange. Tips received by an employee in any medium other than cash, such as passes, tickets, or other goods or commodities do not constitute wages. If an employee in any calendar month performs services for two or more employers and receives tips in the course of his employment by each employer, the $20 test is to be applied separately with respect to the cash tips received by the employee in respect of his services for each employer and not to the total cash tips received by the employee during the month. As to the time tips are deemed paid, see § 31.3401(f)-1. For provisions relating to the treatment of tips received by an employee prior to 1966, see paragraph (b)(11) of § 31.3401(a)-1. [Reg. § 31.3401(a)(16)-1.]

☐ [*T.D.* 7001, 1-17-69.]

[Reg. § 31.3401(a)(17)-1]

§ 31.3401(a)(17)-1. Remuneration for services performed on a boat engaged in catching fish.—(a) Remuneration for services performed on or after December 31, 1954, by an individual on a boat engaged in catching fish or other forms of aquatic animal life (hereinafter "fish") is excepted from wages and hence is not subject to withholding if—

(1) The individual receives a share of the boat's (or boats' for a fishing operation involving more than one boat) catch of fish or a share of the proceeds from the sale of the catch,

(2) The amount of the individual's share depends solely on the amount of the boat's (or boats' for a fishing operation involving more than one boat) catch of fish,

(3) The individual does not receive, and is not entitled to receive, any cash remuneration, other than remuneration that is described in subparagraph (1) of this paragraph, and

(4) The crew of the boat (or of each boat from which the individual receives a share of the catch) normally is made up of fewer than 10 individuals.

(b) The requirement of subparagraph (2) of paragraph (a) is not satisfied if there exists an agreement with the boat's (or boats') owner or operator by which the individual's remuneration is determined partially or fully by a factor not dependent on the size of the catch. For example, if a boat is operated under a remuneration arrangement, *e.g.*, a union contract, which specifies that crew members, in addition to receiving a share of the catch, are entitled to an hourly wage for repairing nets, regardless of whether this wage is actually paid, then all the crew members covered by the arrangement are entitled to receive cash remuneration other than as a share of the catch and are not excepted from employment by section 3121(b)(20).

(c) The operating crew of a boat includes all persons on the boat (including the captain) who receive any form of remuneration in exchange for services rendered while on a boat engaged in catching fish. See § 1.6050A-1 for reporting requirements for the operator of a boat engaged in catching fish with respect to individuals performing services described in this section.

(d) During the same return period, service performed by a crew member may be excepted from employment by section 3121(b)(20) and this section for one voyage and not so excepted on a subsequent voyage on the same or on a different boat. [Reg. § 31.3401(a)(17)-1.]

☐ [*T.D.* 7716, 8-26-80.]

[Reg. § 31.3401(a)(18)-1]

§ 31.3401(a)(18)-1. Payments or benefits under a qualified educational assistance program.—A payment made, or benefit furnished, to or for the benefit of an employee in a taxable year beginning after December 31, 1978, does not constitute wages and hence is not subject to withholding if, at the time of such payment or furnishing, it is reasonable to believe that the employee will be able to exclude such payment or benefit from income under section 127. [Reg. § 31.3401(a)(18)-1.]

☐ [*T.D.* 7898, 7-5-83.]

[Reg. § 31.3401(a)(19)-1]

§ 31.3401(a)(19)-1. Reimbursements under a self-insured medical reimbursement plan.—Amounts reimbursed to or on behalf of an employee after December 31, 1979, as a medical care reimbursement under a self-insured medical reimbursement plan (within the meaning of section 105(h)(6)) do not constitute wages and hence are not subject to withholding even though such reimbursement is includible in the gross income of an employee. For rules with respect to self-insured medical reimbursement plans, see section 105(h) and § 1.105-11 of this Chapter (Income Tax Regulations). [Reg. § 31.3401(a)(19)-1.]

☐ [*T.D.* 7754, 1-13-81.]

[Reg. § 31.3401(b)-1]

§ 31.3401(b)-1. Payroll period.—(a) The term "payroll period" means the period of service for which a payment of wages is ordinarily made to an employee by his employer. It is immaterial that the wages are not always paid at regular intervals. For example, if an employer ordinarily pays a particular employee for each calendar week at the end of the week, but if for some reason the employee in a given week receives a payment in the middle of the week for the portion of the week already elapsed and receives the remainder at the end of the week, the payroll period is still the calendar week; or if, instead, that employee is sent on a 3-week trip by his employer and receives at the end of the trip a single wage payment for three weeks' services, the payroll period is still the calendar week, and the wage payment shall be treated as though it were three separate weekly wage payments.

(b) For the purpose of section 3402, an employee can have but one payroll period with respect to wages paid by any one employer. Thus, if an employee is paid a regular wage for a weekly payroll period and in addition thereto is paid supplemental wages (for example, bonuses) determined with respect to a different period, the payroll period is the weekly payroll period. For computation of tax on supplemental wage payments, see § 31.3402(g)-1.

(c) The term "payroll period" also means the period of accrual of supplemental unemployment compensation benefits for which a payment of such benefits is ordinarily made. Thus if benefits are ordinarily accrued and paid on a monthly basis, the payroll period is deemed to be monthly.

(d) The term "miscellaneous payroll period" means a payroll period other than a daily, weekly, biweekly, semimonthly, monthly, quarterly, semiannual, or annual payroll period. [Reg. § 31.3401(b)-1.]

☐ [*T.D. 6259, 10-25-57. Amended by T.D. 7068, 11-10-70.*]

[Reg. § 31.3401(c)-1]

§ 31.3401(c)-1. **Employee.**—(a) The term "employee" includes every individual performing services if the relationship between him and the person for whom he performs such services is the legal relationship of employer and employee. The term includes officers and employees, whether elected or appointed, of the United States, a State, Territory, Puerto Rico, or any political subdivision thereof, or the District of Columbia, or any agency or instrumentality of any one or more of the foregoing.

(b) Generally the relationship of employer and employee exists when the person for whom services are performed has the right to control and direct the individual who performs the services, not only as to the result to be accomplished by the work but also as to the details and means by which that result is accomplished. That is, an employee is subject to the will and control of the employer not only as to what shall be done but how it shall be done. In this connection, it is not necessary that the employer actually direct or control the manner in which the services are performed; it is sufficient if he has the right to do so. The right to discharge is also an important factor indicating that the person possessing that right is an employer. Other factors characteristic of an employer, but not necessarily present in every case, are the furnishing of tools and the furnishing of a place to work to the individual who performs the services. In general, if an individual is subject to the control or direction of another merely as to the result to be accomplished by the work and not as to the means and methods for accomplishing the result, he is not an employee.

(c) Generally, physicians, lawyers, dentists, veterinarians, contractors, subcontractors, public stenographers, auctioneers, and others who follow an independent trade, business, or profession, in which they offer their services to the public, are not employees.

(d) Whether the relationship of employer and employee exists will in doubtful cases be determined upon an examination of the particular facts of each case.

(e) If the relationship of employer and employee exists, the designation or description of the relationship by the parties as anything other than that of employer and employee is immaterial. Thus, if such relationship exists, it is of no consequence that the employee is designated as a partner, coadventurer, independent contractor, or the like.

(f) All classes or grades of employees are included within the relationship of employer and employee. Thus, superintendents, managers, and other supervisory personnel are employees. Generally, an officer of a corporation is an employee of the corporation. However, an officer of a cor-

poration who as such does not perform any services or performs only minor services and who neither receives nor is entitled to receive, directly or indirectly, any remuneration is not considered to be an employee of the corporation. A director of a corporation in his capacity as such is not an employee of the corporation.

(g) The term "employee" includes every individual who receives a supplemental unemployment compensation benefit which is treated under paragraph (b)(14) of § 31.3401(a)-1 as if it were wages.

(h) Although an individual may be an employee under this section, his services may be of such a nature, or performed under such circumstances, that the remuneration paid for such services does not constitute wages within the meaning of section 3401(a). [Reg. § 31.3401(c)-1.]

☐ [*T.D. 6259, 10-25-57. Amended by T.D. 7068, 11-10-70.*]

[Reg. § 31.3401(d)-1]

§ 31.3401(d)-1. **Employer.**—(a) The term "employer" means any person for whom an individual performs or performed any service, of whatever nature, as the employee of such person.

(b) It is not necessary that the services be continuing at the time the wages are paid in order that the status of employer exist. Thus, for purposes of withholding, a person for whom an individual has performed past services for which he is still receiving wages from such person is an "employer."

(c) An employer may be an individual, a corporation, a partnership, a trust, an estate, a joint-stock company, an association, or a syndicate, group, pool, joint venture, or other unincorporated organization, group, or entity. A trust or estate, rather than the fiduciary acting for or on behalf of the trust or estate, is generally the employer.

(d) The term "employer" embraces not only the individuals and organizations engaged in trade or business, but organizations exempt from income tax, such as religious and charitable organizations, educational institutions, clubs, social organizations and societies, as well as the governments of the United States, the States, Territories, Puerto Rico, and the District of Columbia, including their agencies, instrumentalities, and political subdivisions.

(e) The term "employer" also means (except for the purpose of the definition of "wages") any person paying wages on behalf of a nonresident alien individual, foreign partnership, or foreign corporation, not engaged in trade or business within the United States (including Puerto Rico as if a part of the United States).

(f) If the person for whom the services are or were performed does not have legal control of the payment of the wages for such services, the term "employer" means (except for the purpose of the definition of "wages") the person having such control. For example, where wages, such as certain types of pensions or retired pay, are paid by a trust and the person for whom the services were performed has no legal control over the payment of such wages, the trust is the "employer."

(g) The term "employer" also means a person making a payment of a supplemental unemployment compensation benefit which is treated under paragraph (b)(14) of §31.3401(a)-1 as if it were wages. For example, if supplemental unemployment compensation benefits are paid from a trust which was created under the terms of a collective bargaining agreement, the trust shall generally be deemed to be the employer. However, if the person making such payment is acting solely as an agent for another person, the term "employer" shall mean such other person and not the person actually making the payment.

(h) It is a basic purpose to centralize in the employer the responsibility for withholding, returning, and paying the tax, and for furnishing the statements required under section 6051 and §31.6051-1. The special definitions of the term "employer" in paragraphs (e), (f), and (g) of this section are designed solely to meet special or unusual situations. They are not intended as a departure from the basic purpose. [Reg. §31.3401(d)-1.]

☐ [T.D. 6259, 10-25-57. Amended by T.D. 7068, 11-10-70.]

[Reg. §31.3401(e)-1]

§31.3401(e)-1. Number of withholding exemptions claimed.—(a) The term "number of withholding exemptions claimed" means the number of withholding exemptions claimed in a withholding exemption certificate in effect under section 3402(f) or in effect under section 1622(h) of the Internal Revenue Code of 1939. If no such certificate is in effect, the number of withholding exemptions claimed shall be considered to be zero. The number of withholding exemptions claimed must be taken into account in determining the amount of tax to be deducted and withheld under section 3402, whether the employer computes the tax in accordance with the provisions of subsection (a) or subsection (c) of section 3402.

(b) The employer is not required to ascertain whether or not the number of withholding exemptions claimed is greater than the number of withholding exemptions to which the employee is entitled. For rules relating to invalid withholding exemption certificates, see §31.3402(f)(2)-1(e), and for rules relating to required submission of copies of certain withholding exemption certificates to the Internal Revenue Service, see §31.3402(f)(2)-1(g).

(c) As to the number of withholding exemptions to which an employee is entitled, see §31.3402(f)(1)-1. [Reg. §31.3401(e)-1.]

☐ [T.D. 6259, 10-25-57. Amended by T.D. 7423, 6-24-76; T.D. 7682, 3-10-80; T.D. 7772, 3-17-81 and T.D. 7803, 1-21-82.]

[Reg. §31.3401(f)-1]

§31.3401(f)-1. Tips.—(a) *Tips considered wages.*—Tips received after 1965 by an employee in the course of his employment are considered to be wages, and thus subject to withholding of income tax at source. For an exception to the rule that tips constitute wages, see §§31.3401(a)(16) and 31.3401(a)(16)-1, relating to tips paid in a medium other than cash and cash tips of less than $20. For definition of the term "employee", see §§31.3401(c) and 31.3401(c)-1.

(b) *When tips deemed paid.*—Tips reported by an employee to his employer in a written statement furnished to the employer pursuant to section 6053(a) (see §31.6053-1) shall be deemed to be paid to the employee at the time the written statement is furnished to the employer. Tips received by an employee which are not reported to his employer in a written statement furnished pursuant to section 6053(a) shall be deemed to be paid to the employee at the time the tips are actually received by the employee. [Reg. §31.3401(f)-1.]

☐ [T.D. 7001, 1-17-69.]

[Reg. §31.3402(a)-1]

§31.3402(a)-1. Requirement of withholding.—(a) Section 3402 provides alternative methods, at the election of the employer, for use in computing the amount of income tax to be collected at source on wages. Under the percentage method of withholding (see §31.3402(b)-1), the employer is required to deduct and withhold a tax computed in accordance with the provisions of section 3402(a). Under the wage bracket method of withholding (see §31.3402(c)-1), the employer is required to deduct and withhold a tax determined in accordance with the provisions of section 3402(c). The employer may elect to use the percentage method, the wage bracket method, or certain other methods (see §31.3402(h)(4)-1). Different methods may be used by the employer with respect to different groups of employees.

(b) The employer is required to collect the tax by deducting and withholding the amount thereof from the employee's wages as and when paid, either actually or constructively. Wages are constructively paid when they are credited to the account of or set apart for an employee so that they may be drawn upon by him at any time although not then actually reduced to possession. To constitute payment in such a case, the wages must be credited to or set apart for the employee without any substantial limitation or restriction as to the time or manner of payment or condition upon which payment is to be made, and must be made available to him so that they may be drawn upon at any time, and their payment brought within his own control and disposition.

(c) Except as provided in sections 3402(j) and (k) (see §§31.3402(j)-1 and 31.3402(k)-1, relating to noncash remuneration paid to retail commission salesman and to tips received by an employee in the course of his employment, respectively), an employer is required to deduct and withhold the tax notwithstanding the wages are paid in something other than money (for example, wages paid in stocks or bonds; see §31.3401(a)-1) and to pay over the tax in money. If wages are paid in property other than money, the employer should make necessary arrangements to insure that the amount of the tax required to be withheld is available for payment in money.

(d) For provisions relating to the circumstances under which tax is required to be deducted and withheld from certain amounts received under accident and health plans, see paragraph (b)(8) of §31.3401(a)-1.

(e) As a matter of business administration, certain of the mechanical details of the withholding process may be handled by representatives of the employer. Thus, in the case of an employer having branch offices, the branch manager or other representative may actually, as a matter of internal administration, withhold the tax or prepare the statements required under section 6051. Nevertheless, the legal responsibility for withholding, paying, and returning the tax and furnishing such statements rests with the employer. For provisions relating to statements under section 6051, see the regulations under such section in Subpart G of this part.

(f) The amount of any tax withheld and collected by the employer is a special fund in trust for the United States. See section 7501. [Reg. §31.3402(a)-1.]

☐ [T.D. 6259, 10-25-57. Amended by T.D. 7001, 1-17-69, T.D. 7115, 5-20-71 and T.D. 7888, 4-22-83.]

[Reg. §31.3402(b)-1]

§31.3402(b)-1. Percentage method of withholding.—With respect to wages paid after April 30, 1975, the amount of tax to be deducted and withheld under the percentage method of withholding shall be determined under the applicable percentage method withholding table contained in Circular E (Employer's Tax Guide) according to the instructions contained therein. [Reg. §31.3402(b)-1.]

☐ [T.D. 7915, 9-26-83.]

[Reg. §31.3402(c)-1]

§31.3402(c)-1. Wage bracket withholding.—(a) In general.—(1) The employer may elect to use the wage bracket method provided in section 3402(c) instead of the percentage method with respect to any employee. The tax computed under the wage bracket method shall be in lieu of the tax required to be deducted and withheld under section 3402(a). With respect to wages paid after July 13, 1968, the correct amount of withholding shall be determined under the applicable wage bracket withholding table contained in the Circular E (Employer's Tax Guide) issued for use with respect to the period in which such wages are paid.

(2) For provisions relating to the treatment of wages paid under accident and health plans and wages paid other than in cash to retail commission salesmen, see §§31.3401(a)-1(b)(8) and 31.3402(j)-1, respectively.

(b) Established payroll periods, other than daily or miscellaneous, covered by wage bracket withholding tables.—The wage bracket withholding tables contained in Circular E for established periods other than daily or miscellaneous should be used in determining the tax to be withheld for any such period without reference to the time the employee is actually engaged in the performance of services during such payroll period.

Example (1). On June 30, 1971, employee A is paid wages for a semimonthly payroll period. A has in effect a withholding exemption certificate indicating that he claims two withholding exemptions and that he is married. A's wages are determined at the rate of $2 per hour. During a certain payroll period he works only 24 hours and earns $48. Although A worked only 24 hours during the semimonthly payroll period, the applicable wage bracket withholding table contained in Circular E for a semimonthly payroll period for an employee who is married should be used in determining the tax to be withheld. Under this table it will be found that no tax is required to be withheld from a wage payment of $48 when two withholding exemptions are claimed.

Example (2). On May 14, 1971, employee B is paid wages for a weekly payroll period. B has in effect a withholding exemption certificate indicating that he claims one withholding exemption and that he is single. B's wages are determined at the rate of $2 per hour. During a certain payroll period B works 18 hours and earns $36. Although B worked only 18 hours during the weekly payroll period, the applicable wage bracket withholding table for a weekly payroll period for an employee who is single should be used in determining the tax to be withheld. Under this table it will be found that $0.50 is the amount of tax to be withheld from a wage payment of $36 when one withholding exemption is claimed.

(c) Periods to which the tables for a daily or miscellaneous payroll period are applicable.—(1) In general.—The tables applicable to a daily or miscellaneous payroll period show the tax for employees who are to be withheld from as single persons and for employees who are to be withheld from as married persons on the amount of wages for one day. Where the withholding is computed under the rules applicable to a miscellaneous payroll period, the wages and the amounts shown in the applicable table must be placed on a comparable basis. This may be accomplished by reducing the wages paid for the period to a daily basis by dividing the total wages by the number of days (including Sundays and holidays) in the period. The amount of the tax shown in the applicable table as the tax required to be withheld from the wages, as so reduced to a daily basis, should then be multiplied by the number of days (including Sundays and holidays) in the period.

(2) *Period not a payroll period.*—If wages are paid for a period which is not a payroll period, the amount to be deducted and withheld under the wage bracket method shall be the amount applicable in the case of a miscellaneous payroll period containing a number of days (including Sundays and holidays) equal to the number of days (including Sundays and holidays) in the period with respect to which such wages are paid.

Example. An individual performs services for a contractor in connection with a construction project. He has in effect a withholding exemption certificate indicating that he claims two withholding exemptions and that he is married. Wages have been fixed at the rate of $36 per day, to be paid upon completion of the project. The project is completed before July 1, 1971, in 12 consecutive days, at the end of which period the individual is paid wages of $360 for 10 days' services performed during the period. Under the wage bracket method the amount to be deducted and withheld from such wages is determined by dividing the amount of the wages ($360) by the number of days in the period (12), the result being $30. The amount of tax required to be withheld is determined under the appropriate table applicable to a miscellaneous payroll period for an employee who is married. Under this table the tax required to be withheld is $47.40 (12 × $3.95).

(3) *Wages paid without regard to any period.*— If wages are paid to an employee without regard to any particular period, as, for example, commissions paid to a salesman upon consummation of a sale, the amount of tax to be deducted and withheld shall be determined in the same manner as in the case of a miscellaneous payroll period containing a number of days (including Sundays and holidays) equal to the number of days (including Sundays and holidays) which have elapsed, beginning with the latest of the following days:

(i) The first day after the last payment of wages to such employee by such employer in the calendar year, or

(ii) The date on which such individual's employment with such employer began in the calendar year, or

(iii) January 1 of such calendar year, and ending with (and including) the date on which such wages are paid.

Example. On April 2, 1971, C is employed by the X Real Estate Company to sell real estate on a commission basis, commissions to be paid only upon consummation of sales. C has in effect a withholding exemption certificate indicating that he claims one withholding exemption and that he is not married. On May 22, 1971, C receives a commission of $300, his first commission since April 2, 1971. Again, on June 19, 1971, C receives a commission of $420. Under the wage bracket method, the amount of tax to be deducted and withheld in respect of the commission paid on May 22, is $10.00, which amount is obtained by multiplying $0.20 (tax per day under the appropriate wage bracket table applicable to a daily or miscellaneous payroll period for an employee who is not married where wages are at least $6 but less than $6.25 a day) by 50 (number of days elapsed); and the amount of tax to be withheld with respect to the commission paid on June 19 is $54.60, which amount is obtained by multiplying $1.95 (tax under the appropriate wage bracket table for a daily or miscellaneous payroll period where wages are at least $15 but less than $15.50 a day) by 28 (number of days elapsed).

(d) *Period or elapsed time less than one week.*— (1) It is the general rule that if wages are paid for a payroll period or other period of less than one week, the tax to be deducted and withheld under the wage bracket method shall be the amount computed for a daily payroll period, or for a miscellaneous payroll period containing the same number of days (including Sundays and holidays) as the payroll period, or other period, for which such wages are paid. In the case of wages paid without regard to any period, if the elapsed time computed as provided in paragraph (c) of this section is less than 1 week, the same rule is applicable.

Example (1). On May 14, 1971, an employee who has a daily payroll period is paid wages of $15 per day. The employee has in effect a withholding exemption certificate indicating that he claims one withholding exemption and that he is not married. Under the applicable table for a daily payroll period for an employee who is not married, the amount of tax to be deducted and withheld from each such payment of wages is $1.95.

Example (2). An employee works for a certain employer on four consecutive days for which he is paid wages totalling $60 on July 25, 1971 The employee has in effect a withholding exemption certificate claiming two withholding exemptions and indicating that he is married. The amount of tax to be deducted and withheld under the wage bracket method is $5.60 (4 × $1.40).

(2) If the payroll period, other period, or elapsed time where wages are paid without regard to any period, is less than one week, the employer may, under certain conditions, elect to deduct and withhold the tax determined by the application of the wage table for a weekly payroll period to the aggregate of the wages paid to the employee during the calendar week. The election to use the weekly wage table in such cases is subject to the limitations and conditions prescribed in Circular E with respect to employers using the percentage method in similar cases.

(3) As used in this paragraph the term "calendar week" means a period of seven consecutive days beginning with Sunday and ending with Saturday.

Reg. §31.3402(c)-1(d)(3)

(e) *Rounding off of wage payment.*—In determining the amount to be deducted and withheld under the wage bracket method the wages may, at the election of the employer, be computed to the nearest dollar, provided such wages are in excess of the highest wage bracket of the applicable table. For the purpose of the computation to the nearest dollar, the payment of a fractional part of a dollar shall be disregarded unless it amounts to one-half dollar or more, in which case it shall be increased to $1.00. Thus, if the payroll period of an employee is weekly and the wage payment of such employee is $255.49, the employer may compute the tax on the excess over $200 as if the excess were $55 instead of $55.49. If the weekly wage payment is $255.50, the employer may, in computing the tax, consider the excess over $200 to be $56 instead of $55.50. [Reg. § 31.3402(c)-1.]

☐ [*T.D.* 6259, 10-25-57. *Amended by T.D.* 6860, 11-3-65, *T.D.* 7115, 5-20-71, *T.D.* 7888, 4-22-83 *and T.D.* 7915, 9-26-83.]

[Reg. § 31.3402(d)-1]

§ 31.3402(d)-1. Failure to withhold.—If the employer in violation of the provisions of section 3402 fails to deduct and withhold the tax, and thereafter the income tax against which the tax under section 3402 may be credited is paid, the tax under section 3402 shall not be collected from the employer. Such payment does not, however, operate to relieve the employer from liability for penalties or additions to the tax applicable in respect of such failure to deduct and withhold. The employer will not be relieved of his liability for payment of the tax required to be withheld unless he can show that the tax against which the tax under section 3402 may be credited has been paid. See § 31.3403-1, relating to liability for tax. [Reg. § 31.3402(d)-1.]

☐ [*T.D.* 6259, 10-25-57.]

[Reg. § 31.3402(e)-1]

§ 31.3402(e)-1. Included and excluded wages.—(a) If a portion of the remuneration paid by an employer to his employee for services performed during a payroll period of not more than 31 consecutive days constitutes wages, and the remainder does not constitute wages, all the remuneration paid the employee for services performed during such period shall for purposes of withholding be treated alike, that is, either all included as wages or all excluded. The time during which the employee performs services, the remuneration for which under section 3401(a) constitutes wages, and the time during which he performs services, the remuneration for which under such section does not constitute wages, determine whether all the remuneration for services performed during the payroll period shall be deemed to be included or excluded.

(b) If one-half or more of the employee's time in the employ of a particular employer in a payroll period is spent in performing services the remuneration for which constitutes wages, then all the remuneration paid the employee for services performed in that payroll period shall be deemed to be wages.

(c) If less than one-half of the employee's time in the employ of a particular employer in a payroll period is spent in performing services the remuneration for which constitutes wages, then none of the remuneration paid the employee for services performed in that payroll period shall be deemed to be wages.

(d) The application of the provisions of paragraphs (a), (b), and (c) of this section may be illustrated by the following examples:

Example (1). Employer B, who operates a store and a farm, employs A to perform services in connection with both operations. The remuneration paid A for services on the farm is excepted as remuneration for agricultural labor, and the remuneration for services performed in the store constitutes wages. Employee A is paid on a monthly basis. During the particular month, A works 120 hours on the farm and 80 hours in the store. None of the remuneration paid by B to A for services performed during the month is deemed to be wages, since the remuneration paid for less than one-half of the services performed during the month constitutes wages. During another month A works 75 hours on the farm and 120 hours in the store. All of the remuneration paid by B to A for services performed during the month is deemed to be wages since the remuneration paid for one-half or more of the services performed during the month constitutes wages.

Example (2). Employee C is employed as a maid by D, a physician, whose home and office are located in the same building. The remuneration paid C for services in the home is excepted as remuneration for domestic service, and the remuneration paid for her services in the office constitutes wages. C is paid on a weekly basis. During a particular week C works 20 hours in the home and 20 hours in the office. All of the remuneration paid [by] D to C for services performed during that week is deemed to be wages, since the remuneration paid for one-half or more of the services performed during the week constitutes wages. During another week C works 22 hours in the home and 15 hours in the office. None of the remuneration paid by D to C for services performed during that week is deemed to be wages, since the remuneration paid for less than one-half of the services performed during the week constitutes wages.

(e) The rules set forth in this section do not apply (1) with respect to any remuneration paid for services performed by an employee for his employer if the periods for which remuneration is paid by the employer vary to the extent that there is no period which constitutes a payroll period within the meaning of section 3401(b) (see § 31.3401(b)-1), or (2) with respect to any remuneration paid for services performed by an employee for his employer if the payroll period for which remuneration is paid exceeds 31 consecutive days. In any such case withholding is required with respect to that portion of such remuneration which constitutes wages. [Reg. § 31.3402(e)-1.]

☐ [*T.D.* 6259, 10-25-57.]

[Reg. §31.3402(f)(1)-1]

§31.3402(f)(1)-1. Withholding exemptions.—
(a) *In general.*—(1) Except as otherwise provided in section 3402(f)(6) (see §31.3402(f)(6)-1), an employee receiving wages shall on any day be entitled to withholding exemptions as provided in section 3402(f)(1). In order to receive the benefit of such exemptions, the employee must file with his employer a withholding exemption certificate as provided in section 3402(f)(2). See §31.3402(f)(2)-1.

(2) The number of exemptions to which an employee is entitled on any day depends upon his status as single or married, upon his status as to old age and blindness, upon the number of his dependents, upon the number of exemptions claimed by his spouse (if he is married), and upon the number of withholding allowances to which he is entitled under section 3402(m).

(b) *Withholding exemptions to which an employee is entitled in respect of himself.*—An employee is entitled to one withholding exemption for himself. An employee shall on any day be entitled to an additional withholding exemption for himself if he will have attained the age of 65 before the close of his taxable year which begins in, or with, the calendar year in which such day falls. If the employee is blind, he may claim an additional withholding exemption for blindness. For purposes of claiming a withholding exemption for blindness, an individual shall be considered blind only if his central visual acuity does not exceed 20/200 in the better eye with correcting lenses or if his visual acuity is greater than 20/200 but is accompanied by a limitation in the fields of vision such that the widest diameter of the visual field subtends an angle no greater than 20 degrees. For definition of the term "blindness," see section 151(d)(3). An employee may also be entitled under section 3402(m) to withholding exemptions with respect to withholding allowances (see §31.3402(m)-1).

(c) *Withholding exemptions to which an employee is entitled in respect of his spouse.*—(1) A married employee, whose spouse is an employee receiving wages, is entitled to claim any withholding exemption to which his spouse is entitled under paragraph (b) of this section, unless the spouse has in effect a withholding exemption certificate claiming such withholding exemption. A married employee, whose spouse is not an employee receiving wages, is entitled to claim any withholding exemption to which his spouse would be entitled under paragraph (b) of this section if the spouse were an employee receiving wages.

Example (1). Assume that both the husband and wife have attained the age of 65 and are employees receiving wages. Each spouse is entitled under paragraph (b) of this section to claim 2 withholding exemptions in respect of himself or herself. Either spouse may claim, in addition to the withholding exemptions to which he or she is entitled in respect of himself or herself,

any withholding exemption to which the other spouse is entitled under such paragraph (b) but does not claim on a withholding exemption certificate.

Example (2). Assume the same facts as in Example (1) except that only the husband is an employee receiving wages. The husband is entitled to claim 4 withholding exemptions, that is, the 2 withholding exemptions to which he is entitled in respect of himself and the 2 withholding exemptions to which his spouse would be entitled under paragraph (b) of this section if she were an employee receiving wages.

(2) In determining the number of withholding exemptions to which an employee is entitled for himself and his spouse on any day, the employee's status as a single person or a married person and, if married, whether a withholding exemption is claimed by his spouse, shall be determined as of such day. However, in the case of an employee whose spouse dies in the taxable year of the employee which begins in, or with, the calendar year in which the spouse dies, any withholding exemption which would be allowable to the employee in respect of such spouse, if living and not an employee receiving wages, may be claimed by the employee for that portion of the calendar year which occurs after his spouse's death. For provisions applicable in the case of an employee whose taxable year is not a calendar year, and whose spouse dies in that portion of the calendar year which precedes the first day of the taxable year of the employee which begins in the calendar year, see paragraph (b) of §31.3402(f)(2)-1. An employee legally separated from his spouse under a decree of divorce or of separate maintenance or an employee who is a surviving spouse (as defined in section 2 and the regulations thereunder) shall not be entitled to any withholding exemptions in respect of his spouse.

(d) *Withholding exemptions to which an employee is entitled in respect of dependents.*—Subject to the limitations stated in this paragraph, an employee shall be entitled on any day to a withholding exemption for each individual who may reasonably be expected to be his dependent for his taxable year beginning in, or with, the calendar year in which such day falls. For purposes of the withholding exemption for an individual who may reasonably be expected to be a dependent, the following rules shall apply:

(1) The determination that an individual may or may not reasonably be expected to be a dependent shall be made on the basis of facts existing at the beginning of the day for which a withholding exemption for such individual is to be claimed. The individual in respect of whom an exemption is claimed by an employee must, on the day in question, be in existence and be within one of the categories listed in section 152(a), which defines the term "dependent." However, a withholding exemption for a dependent who dies continues for the portion of the

Reg. §31.3402(f)(1)-1(d)(1)

calendar year which occurs after the dependent's death, except that, in the case of an employee whose taxable year is not a calendar year, the withholding exemption does not continue for a dependent, within the meaning of section 152(a)(9) or (10), whose death occurs before the first day of the employee's taxable year beginning in the calendar year of death.

(2) The determination that an individual may or may not reasonably be expected to be a dependent shall be made for the taxable year of the employee in respect of which amounts deducted and withheld in the calendar year in which the day in question falls are allowed as a credit. In general, amounts deducted and withheld during any calendar year are allowed as a credit against the tax imposed by chapter 1 of the Code for the taxable year which begins in, or with, such calendar year. Thus, in order for an employee to be able to claim for a calendar year a withholding exemption with respect to a particular individual as a dependent there must be a reasonable expectation that the employee will be allowed an exemption with respect to such individual under section 151(e) for his taxable year which begins in, or with, such calendar year.

(3) For the employee to be entitled on any day of the calendar year to a withholding exemption for an individual as a dependent, such individual must on such day—

(i) Be an individual referred to in one of the numbered paragraphs in section 152(a),

(ii) Reasonably be expected to receive over one-half of his support, within the meaning of section 152, from the employee in the calendar year, and

(iii) Either (a) reasonably be expected to have gross income of less than the amount determined pursuant to § 1.151-2 of this chapter (Income Tax Regulations) applicable to the calendar year in which the taxable year of the taxpayer begins, or (b) be a child (son, stepson, daughter, stepdaughter, adopted son, or adopted daughter) of the employee who (1) will not have attained the age of 19 at the close of the calendar year or (2) is a student as defined in section 151.

(4) An employee is not entitled to claim a withholding exemption for an individual otherwise reasonably expected to be a dependent of the employee if such individual is not a citizen of the United States, unless such individual (i) is at any time during the calendar year a resident of the United States (including, in regard to wages paid after February 28, 1979, an individual treated as a resident under section 6013(g) or (h)), Canada, Mexico, the Canal Zone, or the Republic of Panama, or (ii) is a child of the employee born to him, or legally adopted by him, in the Philippine Islands before January 1, 1956, and the child is a resident of the Republic of the Philippines, and the employee was a member of the Armed Forces of the United States at the time the child was born to him or legally adopted by him.

(e) *Additional withholding exemption to which an employee is entitled in respect of the standard deduc-* tion.—After November 30, 1986, an employee is entitled to one additional withholding exemption unless:

(1) The employee is married (as determined under section 143) and the employee's spouse is an employee receiving wages subject to withholding, or

(2) The employee has withholding exemption certificates in effect with respect to more than one employer.

These restrictions do not apply if the combined wages of the employee and the spouse (if any) from other than one employer is less than the amount specified in the instructions to Form W-4 or W-4A (Employee's Withholding Allowance Certificate). [Reg. § 31.3402(f)(1)-1.]

☐ [T.D. 6259, 10-25-57. *Amended by* T.D. 6654, 5-27-63, T.D. 7065, 10-22-70, T.D. 7114, 5-17-71, T.D. 7115, 5-20-71, T.D. 7670, 1-30-80, T.D. 7915, 9-26-83 *and* T.D. 8164, 11-30-87.]

[Reg. § 31.3402(f)(2)-1]

§ 31.3402(f)(2)-1. **Withholding exemption certificates.**—(a) *On commencement of employment.*— On or before the date on which an individual commences employment with an employer, the individual shall furnish the employer with a signed withholding exemption certificate relating to his marital status and the number of withholding exemptions which he claims, which number shall in no event exceed the number to which he is entitled, or, if the statements described in § 31.3402(n)-1 are true with respect to an individual, he may furnish his employer with a signed withholding exemption certificate which contains such statements in lieu of the first-mentioned certificate. For form and contents of such certificates, see § 31.3402(f)(5)-1. The employer is required to request a withholding exemption certificate from each employee, but if the employee fails to furnish such certificate, such employee shall be considered as a single person claiming no withholding exemptions.

(b) *Change in status which affects calendar year.*—(1) If, on any day during the calendar year, the number of withholding exemptions to which the employee is entitled is less than the number of withholding exemptions claimed by him on the withholding exemption certificate then in effect, the employee must within 10 days after the change occurs furnish the employer with a new withholding exemption certificate relating to the number of withholding exemptions which the employee then claims, which must in no event exceed the number to which he is entitled on such day. The number of withholding exemptions to which an employee is entitled decreases, for example, for any one of the following reasons:

(i) The employee's wife (or husband) for whom the employee has been claiming a withholding exemption (a) is divorced or legally separated from the employee, or (b) claims her (or his) own withholding exemptions on a separate certificate.

(ii) In the case of an employee whose taxable year is not a calendar year, the employee's wife (or husband) for whom the employee has been claiming a withholding exemption dies in that portion of the calendar year which precedes the first day of the taxable year of the employee which begins in the calendar year in which the spouse dies.

(iii) The employee finds that no exemption for his taxable year which begins in, or with, the current calendar year will be allowable to him under section 151(e) in respect of an individual claimed as a dependent on the employee's withholding exemption certificate.

(iv) It becomes unreasonable for the employee to believe that his wages for an estimation year will not be more, or that the determinable additional amount for each item under § 31.3402(m)-1 for an estimation year will not be less, than the corresponding figure used in connection with a claim by him under section 3402(m) of a withholding allowance to such an extent that the employee would no longer be entitled to such withholding allowance.

(v) It becomes unreasonable for an employee who has in effect a withholding exemption certificate on which he claims a withholding allowance under section 3402(m), computed on the basis of the preceding taxable year, to believe that his wages and the determinable additional amounts for each item under § 31.3402(m)-1 in such preceding taxable year or in his present taxable year will entitle him to such withholding allowance in the present taxable year.

(2) If, on any day during the calendar year, the number of withholding exemptions to which the employee is entitled is more than the number of withholding exemptions claimed by him on the withholding exemption certificate then in effect, the employee may furnish the employer with a new withholding exemption certificate on which the employee must in no event claim more than the number of withholding exemptions to which he is entitled on such day.

(3) If, on any day during the calendar year, the statements described in § 31.3402(n)-1 are true with respect to an employee, such employee may furnish his employer with a withholding exemption certificate which contains such statements.

(4) If, on any day during the calendar year, it is not reasonable for an employee, who has furnished his employer with a withholding exemption certificate which contains the statements described in § 31.3402(n)-1, to anticipate that he will incur no liability for income tax imposed under subtitle A (as defined in § 31.3402(n)-1) for his current taxable year, the employee must within 10 days after such day furnish the employer with a new withholding exemption certificate which does not contain such statements. If, on any day during the calendar year, it is not reasonable for such an employee whose liability for income tax imposed under subtitle A is determined on a basis other than the calendar year to so anticipate with respect to his taxable year following his current taxable year, the employee must furnish the employer with a new withholding exemption certificate which does not contain such statements within 10 days after such day or on or before the first day of the last month of his current taxable year, whichever is later.

(c) *Change in status which affects next calendar year.*—(1) If, on any day during the calendar year, the number of exemptions to which the employee will be, or may reasonably be expected to be, entitled under sections 151 and 3402(m) for his taxable year which begins in, or with, the next calendar year is different from the number to which the employee is entitled on such day, the following rules shall be applicable:

(i) If such number is less than the number of withholding exemptions claimed by the employee on a withholding exemption certificate in effect on such day, the employee must, on or before December 1 of the year in which the change occurs, unless such change occurs in December, furnish his employer with a new withholding exemption certificate reflecting the decrease in the number of withholding exemptions. If the change occurs in December, the new certificate must be furnished within 10 days after the change occurs. The number of exemptions to which an employee is entitled for his taxable year which begins in, or with, the next calendar year decreases, for example, for any of the following reasons:

(*a*) The spouse or a dependent of the employee dies.

(*b*) The employee finds that it is not reasonable to expect that an individual claimed as a dependent on the employee's withholding exemption certificate will qualify as a dependent of the employee for such taxable year.

(*c*) It becomes unreasonable for an employee who has in effect a withholding exemption certificate on which he claims a withholding allowance under section 3402(m) to believe that his wages and the determinable additional amounts for each item under § 31.3402(m)-1 for his taxable year which begins in, or with, the next calendar year will entitle him to such withholding allowance for such taxable year.

(ii) If such number is greater than the number of withholding exemptions claimed by the employee on a withholding exemption certificate in effect on such day, the employee may, on or before December 1 of the year in which such change occurs, unless such change occurs in December, furnish his employer with a new withholding exemption certificate reflecting the increase in the number of withholding exemptions. If the change occurs in December, the certificate may be furnished on or after the date on which the change occurs.

(2) If, on any day during the calendar year, it is not reasonable for an employee, who has furnished his employer with a withholding exemption certificate which contains the statements described in § 31.3402(n)-1 and whose liability for such tax is determined on a calendar-

Reg. § 31.3402(f)(2)-1(c)(2)

year basis, to anticipate that he will incur no liability for income tax imposed under subtitle A (as defined in § 31.3402(n)-1) for his taxable year which begins with the next calendar year, the employee must furnish his employer with a new withholding exemption certificate which does not contain such statements, on or before December 1 of the first-mentioned calendar year. If it first becomes unreasonable for the employee to so anticipate in December, the new certificate must be furnished within 10 days after the day on which it first becomes unreasonable for the employee to so anticipate.

(3) Before December 1 of each year, every employer should request each of his employees to file a new withholding exemption certificate for the ensuing calendar year, in the event of change in the employee's exemption status since the filing of his latest certificate.

(d) *Inclusion of account number on withholding exemption certificate.*—Every individual to whom an account number has been assigned shall include such number on any withholding exemption certificate filed with an employer. For provisions relating to the obtaining of an account number, see § 31.6011(b)-2.

(e) *Invalid withholding exemption certificates.*— Any alteration of or unauthorized addition to a withholding exemption certificate shall cause such certificate to be invalid; see paragraph (b) of § 31.3402(f)(5)-1 for the definitions of alteration and unauthorized addition. Any withholding exemption certificate which the employee clearly indicates to be false by an oral statement or by a written statement (other than one made on the withholding exemption certificate itself) made by him to the employer on or before the date on which the employee furnishes such certificate is also invalid. For purposes of the preceding sentence, the term "employer" includes any individual authorized by the employer either to receive withholding exemption certificates, to make withholding computations, or to make payroll distributions. If an employer receives an invalid withholding exemption certificate, he shall consider it a nullity for purposes of computing withholding; he shall inform the employee who submitted the certificate that it is invalid, and shall request another withholding exemption certificate from the employee. If the employee who submitted the invalid certificate fails to comply with the employer's request, the employer shall withhold from the employee as from a single person claiming no exemptions (see § 31.3402(f)(2)-1(a)); if, however, a prior certificate is in effect with respect to the employee, the employer shall continue to withhold in accordance with the prior certificate. This paragraph applies only with respect to withholding exemption certificates received by any employer after July 26, 1976.

(f) *Applicability of withholding exemption certificate to qualified State individual income taxes.*—The withholding exemption certificate shall be used for purposes of withholding with respect to

qualified State individual income taxes as well as Federal tax. For provisions relating to the withholding exemption certificate with respect to such State taxes, see paragraph (d)(3)(i) of § 301.6361-1 of this chapter (Regulation on Procedure and Administration).

(g) *Submission of certain withholding exemption certificates and notice of the maximum number of withholding exemptions permitted.*—(1) *Submission of certain withholding exemption certificates.*—(i) *In general.*—An employer must submit to the Internal Revenue Service (IRS) a copy of any currently effective withholding exemption certificate as directed in a written notice to the employer from the IRS or as directed in published guidance.

(A) *Notice to submit withholding exemption certificates.*—A notice to the employer to submit withholding exemption certificates may relate either to one or more named employees, to one or more reasonably segregable units of the employer, or to withholding exemption certificates under certain specified criteria. The notice will designate the IRS office where the copies of the withholding exemption certificates must be submitted. Alternatively, upon notice from the IRS, the employer must make available for inspection by an IRS employee withholding exemption certificates received from one or more named employees, from one or more reasonably segregable units of the employer, or from employees who have furnished withholding exemption certificates under certain specified criteria.

(B) *Published guidance.*—Employers may also be required to submit copies of withholding exemption certificates under certain specified criteria when directed to do so by the IRS in published guidance. For purposes of the preceding sentence, the term published guidance means a revenue procedure or notice published in the Internal Revenue Bulletin (see § 601.601(d)(2) of this chapter).

(ii) *Withholding after submission of withholding exemption certificate.*—After a copy of a withholding exemption certificate has been submitted to the IRS under this paragraph (g)(1), the employer must withhold tax on the basis of the withholding exemption certificate, if the withholding exemption certificate meets the requirements of § 31.3402(f)(5)-1. However, the employer may not withhold on the basis of the withholding exemption certificate if the certificate must be disregarded based on a notice of the maximum number of withholding exemptions permitted under the provisions of paragraph (g)(2) of this section.

(2) *Notice of the maximum number of withholding exemptions permitted.*—(i) *Notice to employer.*—The IRS may notify the employer in writing that the employee is not entitled to claim a complete exemption from withholding or more than the maximum number of withholding exemptions specified by the IRS in the written

notice. The notice will also specify the applicable marital status for purposes of calculating the required amount of withholding. The notice will specify the IRS office to be contacted for further information. The notice of maximum number of withholding exemptions permitted may be issued if—

(A) The IRS determines that a copy of a withholding exemption certificate submitted under paragraph (g)(1) of this section or otherwise provided to the IRS contains a materially incorrect statement or determines, after a request to the employee for verification of the statements on the certificate, that the IRS lacks sufficient information to determine if the certificate is correct.

(B) The IRS otherwise determines that the employee is not entitled to claim a complete exemption from withholding and is not entitled to claim more than a specified number of withholding exemptions.

(ii) *Notice to employee.*—If the IRS provides a notice to the employer under this paragraph (g)(2), the IRS will also provide the employer with a similar notice for the employee (employee notice) that identifies the maximum number of withholding exemptions permitted and specifies the marital status to be used for calculating the required amount of withholding. The employee notice will also indicate the process by which the employee can provide additional information to the IRS for purposes of determining the appropriate number of withholding exemptions and/or modifying the specified marital status. The IRS will also mail a similar notice to the employee's last known address. For further guidance regarding the definition of last known address, see § 301.6212-2 of this chapter. If the IRS is unable to determine a last known address for the employee, the IRS will use other available information as appropriate to mail the notice to the employee.

(iii) *Requirement to furnish.*—If the employee is employed by the employer as of the date of the notice, the employer must furnish the employee notice to the employee within 10 business days of receipt. The employer may follow any reasonable business practice to furnish the copy of the notice to the employee. For purposes of this paragraph (g)(2)(iii), the determination of whether an employee is employed as of the date of the notice is based on all the facts and circumstances, including whether the employer has treated the employment relationship as terminated for other purposes. An employee that is not performing services for the employer as of the date of the notice is employed by the employer as of the date of the notice for purposes of this paragraph (g)(2)(iii) if—

(A) The employer pays wages with respect to prior employment to the employee subject to income tax withholding on or after the date specified in the notice;

(B) The employer reasonably expects the employee to resume the performance of ser-

vices for the employer within twelve months of the date of the notice; or

(C) The employee is on a bona fide leave of absence if the period of such leave does not exceed twelve months or the employee retains a right to reemployment with the employer under an applicable statute or by contract.

(iv) *Requirement to notify the IRS.*—If the employer is not required to furnish the notice to the employee under paragraph (g)(2)(iii) of this section, the employer must send a written response to the IRS office designated in the notice indicating that the employee is not employed by the employer.

(v) *Requirement to withhold based on the notice.*—If the employer is required to furnish the employee notice to the employee under paragraph (g)(2)(iii) of this section, then the employer must withhold tax on the basis of the maximum number of withholding exemptions and the marital status specified in the notice for any wages paid after the date specified in the notice, except as provided in paragraphs (g)(2)(vi), (vii), (viii), (ix), and (x) of this section. The employer must withhold tax in accordance with the notice as of the date specified in the notice, which shall be no earlier than 45 calendar days after the date of the notice.

(vi) *Employment resumes after twelve months.*—If the employer is required to furnish the employee notice to the employee only pursuant to paragraph (g)(2)(iii)(B) of this section and the employee resumes the performance of services for the employer more than 12 months after the date of the notice, then the employer is not required to withhold based on the notice.

(vii) *Requirement to withhold based on an existing Form W-4.*—If a withholding exemption certificate is in effect with respect to the employee before the employer receives a notice of the maximum number of withholding exemptions permitted under this paragraph (g)(2) of this section, the employer must continue to withhold tax in accordance with the existing withholding exemption certificate, rather than on the basis of the notice, if the existing withholding exemption certificate does not claim complete exemption from withholding and claims a marital status, a number of withholding exemptions, and any additional withholding that results in more withholding than would result from applying the marital status and number of withholding exemptions specified in the notice.

(viii) *Modification notice.*—After issuing the notice specifying the maximum number of withholding exemptions permitted and the marital status, the IRS may issue a subsequent notice that modifies the original notice (modification notice). The modification notice may change the marital status and/or the number of withholding exemptions permitted. The employer must withhold based on the modification notice as of the date specified in the modification notice.

Reg. §31.3402(f)(2)-1(g)(2)(viii)

(ix) *Requirement to withhold after termination of employment.*—If the employee is employed as of the date of the notice under paragraph (g)(2)(iii) of this section, but the employer or employee terminates the employment relationship after the date of the notice, the employer must continue to withhold based on the maximum number of withholding exemptions and the marital status specified in the notice or a modification notice if any wages subject to income tax withholding are paid with respect to the prior employment after such date. Furthermore, the employer must withhold based on the notice or modification notice if the employee resumes an employment relationship with the employer within 12 months after the termination of the employment relationship. Whether the employment relationship is terminated is based on all the facts and circumstances.

(x) *Requirement to withhold based on new Form W-4.*—The employee may furnish a new withholding exemption certificate after the employer receives a notice or modification notice from the IRS of the maximum number of withholding exemptions permitted under this paragraph (g)(2).

(A) *Employee requests more withholding.*—If the employee furnishes a new withholding exemption certificate after the employer receives the notice or modification notice, the employer must withhold tax on the basis of that new certificate only if the new certificate does not claim complete exemption from withholding and claims a marital status, a number of withholding exemptions, and any additional withholding that results in more withholding than would result under the notice or modification notice.

(B) *Employee requests less withholding.*—If the employee furnishes a new withholding exemption certificate after the employer receives the notice or modification notice, the employer must disregard the new certificate and withhold on the basis of the notice or modification notice if the employee claims complete exemption from withholding or claims a marital status, a number of withholding exemptions, and any additional withholding that results in less withholding than would result under the notice or modification notice. If the employee wants to put a new certificate into effect that results in less withholding than that required under the notice or modification notice, the employee must contact the IRS. The employer must withhold on the basis of the notice or modification notice unless the IRS subsequently notifies the employer to withhold based on the new certificate.

(3) *Definition of employer.*—For purposes of this paragraph (g), the term employer includes any person authorized by the employer to receive withholding exemption certificates, to make withholding computations, or to make payroll distributions.

(4) *Examples.*—The following examples illustrate the rules of this section.

Example 1. Employer U receives a notice from the IRS that identifies the maximum number of withholding exemptions permitted and specifies the marital status for Employee A. Employee A is not currently performing any services for Employer U. However, Employer U is continuing to make certain wage payments to Employee A. Employer U must furnish the employee notice to Employee A within 10 business days of receipt and must withhold based on the notice on any wages paid to Employee A on or after the date specified in the notice.

Example 2. Employer V receives a notice in October of Year 1 from the IRS that identifies the maximum number of withholding exemptions permitted and specifies the marital status for Employee B. Employee B has not performed services for Employer V since August of Year 1. However, since Employee B has performed services for Employer V for several years on a seasonal basis, Employer V reasonably expects Employee B to resume the performance of services for Employer V in June of Year 2, a date that is within 12 months of the date of the notice. Employer V is required to furnish the notice to Employee B within 10 business of receipt. Employee B does not resume the performance of services until June of Year 3. Employer V is not required to withhold based on the notice.

Example 3. Employer W receives a notice from the IRS that identifies the maximum number of withholding exemptions permitted and specifies the marital status for Employee C. Employee C began a 4-month unpaid maternity leave of absence three weeks before Employer W received the notice. Employer W must furnish the employee notice to Employee C within 10 business days of receipt. When Employee C resumes performing services when her maternity leave ends, Employer W must withhold based on the notice.

Example 4. Employer X receives a notice from the IRS in Year 1 that identifies the maximum number of withholding exemptions permitted and specifies the marital status for Employee D. Employer X must furnish the employee notice to Employee D within 10 business days of receipt and withhold based on the notice. In Year 2, Employee D terminates the employment relationship. Employee D applies for a different position with Employer X and resumes employment 10 months after having left her previous position with Employer X. Since Employer X rehired Employee D within 12 months after the termination of employment, Employer X must withhold based on the notice.

Example 5. Employer Y receives a notice from the IRS that identifies the maximum number of withholding exemptions permitted and specifies the marital status for Employee E. Employer Y must furnish the employee notice to Employee E within 10 business days of receipt. After receipt of this notice, Employee E contacts the IRS and establishes that he is entitled to claim a higher number of withholding exemptions. Employer Y receives a modification notice from the IRS that changes the maximum number of withholding exemptions permitted for Employee E. Employer Y must withhold tax based on the modification notice as of the date specified in such notice.

Example 6. Employer Z pays remuneration to Employee F, a United States citizen, for services performed in Country M. Employer Z receives a notice from the IRS in Year 1 that identifies the maximum number of withholding exemptions permitted and specifies the marital status for Employee F. Employer Z must furnish the employee notice to Employee F within 10 business days of receipt. Employer Z reasonably believes all the remuneration paid to Employee F in Year 1 is excluded from Employee F's gross income under section 911 of the Internal Revenue Code. Since section 3401(a)(8)(B) excludes such remuneration from wages for income tax withholding purposes, Employer X does not have to withhold on such remuneration, notwithstanding the maximum number of exemptions permitted and marital status specified in the notice. In Year 2, Employee F returns to the United States to perform services. Employer Z does not reasonably believe any part of Employee F's remuneration paid in Year 2 is excluded from Employee F's gross income under section 911. Rather, Employer Z reasonably believes that remuneration paid to Employee F in Year 2 is subject to income tax withholding. Employer Z must withhold on the remuneration paid to Employee F based on the notice.

(5) *Effective/applicability date.*—Except as provided in this paragraph (g)(5), paragraph (g) applies on April 14, 2005. Paragraphs (g)(2)(iii)(A), (B), and (C) and paragraph (g)(2)(ix) apply on October 11, 2007, except taxpayers may rely on such paragraphs for notices issued prior to such date. [Reg. § 31.3402(f)(2)-1.]

☐ [*T.D.* 6259, 10-25-57. *Amended by T.D.* 6606, 8-24-62, *T.D.* 6654, 5-27-63, *T.D.* 7048, 6-23-70, *T.D.* 7065, 10-22-70, *T.D.* 7423, 6-24-76, *T.D.* 7577, 12-19-78, *T.D.* 7598, 3-12-79, *T.D.* 7682, 3-10-80, *T.D.* 7772, 3-17-81, *T.D.* 7083, 1-21-82, *T.D.* 7915, 9-26-82, *T.D.* 8164, 11-30-87 *T.D.* 9196, 4-13-2005 *and T.D.* 9337, 7-12-2007.]

[Reg. § 31.3402(f)(3)-1]

§ 31.3402(f)(3)-1. When withholding exemption certificate takes effect.—(a) A withholding exemption certificate furnished the employer in any case in which no previous withholding exemption certificate is in effect with such employer, shall take effect as of the beginning of the first payroll period ending, or the first payment of wages made without regard to a payroll period, on or after the date on which such certificate is so furnished.

(b) A withholding exemption certificate furnished the employer in any case in which a previous withholding exemption certificate is in effect with such employer shall, except as hereinafter provided, take effect with respect to the

first payment of wages made on or after the first status determination date which occurs at least 30 days after the date on which such certificate is so furnished. However, at the election of the employer, except as hereinafter provided, such certificate may be made effective with respect to any payment of wages made on or after the date on which such certificate is so furnished and before such status determination date.

(c) A withholding exemption certificate furnished the employer pursuant to section 3402(f)(2)(C) (see paragraph (c) of § 31.3402(f)(2)-1 or paragraph (b)(2)(ii) of § 31.3402(l)-1) which effects a change for the next calendar year, shall not take effect, and may not be made effective, with respect to the calendar year in which the certificate is furnished. A withholding exemption certificate furnished the employer by an employee who determines his income tax liability on a basis other than a calendar-year basis, as required by paragraph (b)(4) of § 31.3402(f)(2)-1, which effects a change for the employee's next taxable year, shall not take effect, and may not be made effective, with respect to the taxable year of the employee in which the certificate is furnished.

(d) For purposes of this section, the term "status determination date" means January 1, May 1, July 1, and October 1 of each year. [Reg. § 31.3402(f)(3)-1.]

☐ [*T.D.* 6259, 10-25-57. *Amended by T.D.* 7048, 6-23-70, *T.D.* 7065, 10-22-70, *T.D.* 7115, 5-20-71 *and T.D.* 7915, 9-26-83.]

[Reg. § 31.3402(f)(4)-1]

§ 31.3402(f)(4)-1. Period during which withholding exemption certificate remains in effect.—(a) *In general.*—Except as provided in paragraphs (b) and (c) of this section, a withholding exemption certificate which takes effect under section 3402(f) of the Internal Revenue Code of 1954, or which on December 31, 1954, was in effect under section 1622(h) of the Internal Revenue Code of 1939, shall continue in effect with respect to the employee until another withholding exemption certificate takes effect under section 3402(f). Paragraphs (b) and (c) of this section are applicable only for withholding exemption certificates furnished by the employee to the employer before January 1, 1982. See § 31.3402(f)(4)-2 for the rules applicable to withholding exemption certificates furnished by the employee to the employer after December 31, 1981.

(b) *Withholding allowances under section 3402(m) for itemized deductions.*—In no case shall the portion of a withholding exemption certificate relating to withholding allowances under section 3402(m) for itemized deductions be effective with respect to any payment of wages made to an employee—

(1) In the case of an employee whose liability for tax under subtitle A of the Code is determined on a calendar-year basis, after April 30 of the calendar year immediately following the calendar year which was his estimation year for

purposes of determining the withholding allowance or allowances claimed on such exemption certificate, or

(2) In the case of an employee to whom subparagraph (1) of this paragraph does not apply, after the last day of the fourth month immediately following his taxable year which was his estimation year for purposes of determining the withholding allowance or allowances claimed on such exemption certificate.

(c) *Statements under section 3402(n) eliminating requirement of withholding.*—The statements described in §31.3402(n)-1 made by an employee with respect to his preceding taxable year and current taxable year shall be deemed to have been made also with respect to his current taxable year and his taxable year immediately thereafter, respectively, until either a new withholding exemption certificate furnished by the employee takes effect or the existing certificate which contains such statements expires. In no case shall a withholding exemption certificate which contains such statements be effective with respect to any payment of wages made to an employee—

(1) In the case of an employee whose liability for tax under subtitle A is determined on a calendar-year basis, after April 30 of the calendar year immediately following the calendar year which was his original current taxable year for purposes of such statements, or

(2) In the case of an employee to whom subparagraph (1) of this paragraph does not apply, after the last day of the fourth month immediately following his original current taxable year for purposes of such statements. [Reg. §31.3402(f)(4)-1.]

☐ [T.D. 6259, 10-25-57. *Amended by T.D. 7048,* 6-23-70; *T.D. 7065, 10-22-70 and T.D. 7915,* 9-26-83.]

[Reg. §31.3402(f)(4)-2]

§31.3402(f)(4)-2. Effective period of withholding exemption certificate.—(a) *In general.*— Except as provided in paragraphs (b) and (c) of this section, a withholding exemption certificate that takes effect under section 3402(f) of the Internal Revenue Code of 1954, or that on December 31, 1954, was in effect under section 1622(h) of the Internal Revenue Code of 1939, shall continue in effect with respect to the employee until another withholding exemption certificate takes effect under section 3402(f). Paragraphs (b) and (c) are applicable only for withholding exemption certificates furnished by the employee to the employer after December 31, 1981. See §31.3402(f)(4)-1 for the rules applicable to withholding exemption certificates furnished by the employee to the employer before January 1, 1982.

(b) *Withholding allowances under section 3402(m).*—See paragraphs (b) and (c) of §31.3402(f)(2)-1 (relating to withholding exemption certificates) for information as to when an employee claiming withholding allowances

under section 3402(m) and the regulations thereunder must file a new withholding exemption certificate with his employer.

(c) *Statements under section 3402(n) eliminating requirement of withholding.*—The statements described in §31.3402(n)-1 made by an employee with respect to his preceding taxable year and current taxable year shall be effective until either a new withholding exemption certificate furnished by the employee takes effect or the existing certificate that contains such statements expires. In no case shall a withholding exemption certificate that contains such statements be effective with respect to any payment of wages made to an employee—

(1) In the case of an employee whose liability for tax under subtitle A is determined on a calendar year basis, after February 15 of the calendar year following the estimation year, or

(2) In the case of an employee to whom subparagraph (1) of this paragraph does not apply, after the 15th day of the 2nd calendar month following the last day of the estimation year.

(d) *Estimation year.*—The estimation year is the taxable year including the day on which the employee files the withholding exemption certificate with his employer, except that if the employee files the withholding exemption certificate with his employer and specifies on the certificate that the certificate is not to take effect until a specified future date, the estimation year shall be the taxable year including that specified future date. [Reg. §31.3402(f)(4)-2.]

☐ [T.D. 7915, 9-26-83.]

[Reg. §31.3402(f)(5)-1]

§31.3402(f)(5)-1. Form and contents of withholding exemption certificate.—(a)(1) *Form W-4.*—Form W-4, "Employee's Withholding Allowance Certificate," is the form prescribed for the withholding exemption certificate required to be furnished under section 3402(f)(2). A withholding exemption certificate must be prepared in accordance with the instructions and regulations applicable thereto, and must set forth fully and clearly the data that is called for therein. Blank copies of paper Forms W-4 will be supplied to employers upon request to the Internal Revenue Service (IRS). An employer may also download and print Form W-4 from the IRS Internet site at www.irs.gov. In lieu of the prescribed form, employers may prepare and use a form the provisions of which are identical with those of the prescribed form, but only if employers also provide employees with all the tables, instructions, and worksheets contained in the Form W-4 in effect at that time, and only if employers comply with all revenue procedures relating to substitute forms in effect at that time.

(2) Employers are prohibited from accepting a substitute form developed by an employee, and the employee submitting such form will be treated as failing to furnish a withholding exemption certificate. For further guidance regarding the employer's obligations when an em-

Collection of Income Tax at Source on Wages
See p. 20,601 for regulations not amended to reflect law changes
61,561

ployee is treated as failing to furnish a withholding exemption certificate, see § 31.3402(f)(2)-1.

(3) *Effective/applicability date.*—Paragraph (a)(1) applies on April 14, 2005. Paragraph (a)(2) applies to any substitute withholding exemption certificate furnished to an employer on or after October 11, 2007.

(b) *Invalid Form W-4.*—A Form W-4 does not meet the requirements of section 3402(f)(5) or this section and is invalid if it contains an alteration or unauthorized addition. For purposes of § 31.3402(f)(2)-1(e) and this paragraph—

(1) An alteration of a withholding exemption certificate is any deletion of the language of the jurat or other similar provision of such certificate by which the employee certifies or affirms the correctness of the completed certificate, or any material defacing of such certificate;

(2) An unauthorized addition to a withholding exemption certificate is any writing on such certificate other than the entries requested (*e.g.,* name, address, and number of exemptions claimed).

(c) *Electronic Form W-4.*—(1) *In general.*—An employer may establish a system for its employees to file withholding exemption certificates electronically.

(2) *Requirements.*—(i) *In general.*—The electronic system must ensure that the information received is the information sent, and must document all occasions of employee access that result in the filing of a Form W-4. In addition, the design and operation of the electronic system, including access procedures, must make it reasonably certain that the person accessing the system and filing the Form W-4 is the employee identified in the form.

(ii) *Same information as paper Form W-4.*—The electronic filing must provide the employer with exactly the same information as the paper Form W-4.

(iii) *Jurat and signature requirements.*—The electronic filing must be signed by the employee under penalties of perjury.

(A) *Jurat.*—The jurat (perjury statement) must contain the language that appears on the paper Form W-4. The electronic program must inform the employee that he or she must make the declaration contained in the jurat and that the declaration is made by signing the Form W-4. The instructions and the language of the jurat must immediately follow the employee's income tax withholding selections and immediately precede the employee's electronic signature.

(B) *Electronic signature.*—The electronic signature must identify the employee filing the electronic Form W-4 and authenticate and verify the filing. For this purpose, the terms "authenticate" and "verify" have the same meanings as they do when applied to a written signature on a paper Form W-4. An electronic signature can be

in any form that satisfies the foregoing requirements. The electronic signature must be the final entry in the employee's Form W-4 submission.

(iv) *Copies of electronic Forms W-4.*—Upon request by the Internal Revenue Service, the employer must supply a hardcopy of the electronic Form W-4 and a statement that, to the best of the employer's knowledge, the electronic Form W-4 was filed by the named employee. The hardcopy of the electronic Form W-4 must provide exactly the same information as, but need not be a facsimile of, the paper Form W-4.

(3) *Effective date.*—(i) *In general.*—This paragraph applies to all withholding exemption certificates filed electronically by employees on or after January 2, 1997.

(ii) *Special rule for certain Forms W-4.*—In the case of an electronic system that precludes the filing of Forms W-4 required on commencement of employment and Forms W-4 claiming more than 10 withholding exemptions or exemption from withholding, the requirements of paragraph (c)(2)(iii) of this section will be treated as satisfied if the Form W-4 is filed electronically before January 1, 1999. [Reg. § 31.3402(f)(5)-1.]

☐ [*T.D. 6259, 10-25-57. Amended by T.D. 7048, 6-23-70; T.D. 7423, 6-24-76; T.D. 7915, 9-26-83; T.D. 8706, 12-31-96; T.D. 9196, 4-13-2005 and T.D. 9337, 7-12-2007.*]

[Reg. § 31.3402(f)(6)-1]

§ 31.3402(f)(6)-1. Withholding exemptions for nonresident alien individuals.—A nonresident alien individual (other than, in regard to wages paid after February 28, 1979, a nonresident alien individual treated as a resident under section 6013(g) or (h)) subject to withholding under section 3402 on any 1 day entitled under section 3402(f)(1) and § 31.3402(f)(1)-1 to the number of withholding exemptions corresponding to the number of personal exemptions to which he is entitled on such day by reason of the application of section 873(b)(3) or section 876, whichever applies. Thus, a nonresident alien individual who is not a resident of Canada or Mexico and who is not a resident of Puerto Rico during the entire taxable year is allowed under section 3402(f)(1) only one withholding exemption. [Reg. § 31.3402(f)(6)-1.]

☐ [*T.D. 6654, 5-27-63. Amended by T.D. 6908, 12-30-66 and T.D. 7670, 1-30-80.*]

[Reg. § 31.3402(g)-1]

§ 31.3402(g)-1. Supplemental wage payments.—(a) *In general and withholding on supplemental wages in excess of $1,000,000.*—(1) *Determination of supplemental wages and regular wages.*—(i) *Supplemental wages.*—An employee's remuneration may consist of regular wages and supplemental wages. Supplemental wages are all wages paid by an employer that are not regular wages. Supplemental wages include wage payments made without regard to an employee's payroll period, but also may include payments made for a payroll period. Examples of wage payments that are included in supplemental wages include reported tips (except as provided in paragraph (a)(1)(v) of this section), overtime pay (except as provided in paragraph (a)(1)(iv) of this section), bonuses, back pay, commissions, wages paid under reimbursement or other expense allowance arrangements, nonqualified deferred compensation includible in wages, wages paid as noncash fringe benefits, sick pay paid by a third party as an agent of the employer, amounts that are includible in gross income under section 409A, income recognized on the exercise of a nonstatutory stock option, wages from imputed income for health coverage for a non-dependent, and wage income recognized on the lapse of a restriction on restricted property transferred from an employer to an employee. Amounts that are described as supplemental wages in this definition are supplemental wages regardless of whether the employer has paid the employee any regular wages during either the calendar year of the payment or any prior calendar year. Thus, for example, if the only wages that an employer has ever paid an employee are payments of noncash fringe benefits and income recognized on the exercise of a nonstatutory stock option, such payments are classified as supplemental wages.

(ii) *Regular wages.*—As distinguished from supplemental wages, regular wages are amounts that are paid at a regular hourly, daily, or similar periodic rate (and not an overtime rate) for the current payroll period or at a predetermined fixed determinable amount for the current payroll period. Thus, among other things, wages that vary from payroll period to payroll period (such as commissions, reported tips, bonuses, or overtime pay) are not regular wages, except that an employer may treat tips as regular wages under paragraph (a)(1)(v) of this section and an employer may treat overtime pay as regular wages under paragraph (a)(1)(iv) of this section.

(iii) *Amounts that are not wages subject to income tax withholding.*—If an amount of remuneration is not wages subject to income tax withholding, it is neither regular wages nor supplemental wages. Thus, for example, income from the disqualifying dispositions of shares of stock acquired pursuant to the exercise of statutory stock options, as described in section 421(b), is not included in regular wages or supplemental wages.

(iv) *Optional treatment of overtime pay as regular wages.*—Employers may treat overtime pay as regular wages rather than supplemental wages. For this purpose, overtime pay is defined as any pay required to be paid pursuant to federal (Fair Labor Standards Act), state, or local governmental laws at a rate higher than the normal wage rate of the employee because the employee has worked hours in excess of the number of hours deemed to constitute a normal work week or work day.

(v) *Optional treatment of tips as regular wages.*—Employers may treat tips as regular wages rather than supplemental wages. For this purpose, tips are defined as including all tips which are reported to the employer pursuant to section 6053.

(vi) *Amount to be withheld.*—The calculation of the amount of the income tax withholding with respect to supplemental wage payments is provided for under paragraph (a)(2) through (a)(7) of this section.

(2) *Mandatory flat rate withholding.*—If a supplemental wage payment, when added to all supplemental wage payments previously made by one employer (as defined in paragraph (a)(3) of this section) to an employee during the calendar year, exceeds $1,000,000, the rate used in determining the amount of withholding on the excess (including any excess which is a portion of a supplemental wage payment) shall be equal to the highest rate of tax applicable under section 1 for such taxable years beginning in such calendar year. This flat rate shall be applied without regard to whether income tax has been withheld from the employee's regular wages, without allowance for the number of withholding allowances claimed by the employee on Form W-4, "Employee's Withholding Allowance Certificate," without regard to whether the employee has claimed exempt status on Form W-4, without regard to whether the employee has requested additional withholding on Form W-4, and without regard to the withholding method used by the employer. Withholding under this paragraph (a)(2) is mandatory flat rate withholding.

(3) *Certain persons treated as one employer.*—(i) *Persons under common control.*—For purposes of paragraph (a)(2) of this section, all persons treated as a single employer under subsection (a) or (b) of section 52 shall be treated as one employer.

(ii) *Agents.*—For purposes of paragraph (a)(2) of this section, any payment made to an employee by a third party acting as an agent for the employer (regardless of whether such person shall have been designated as an agent pursuant to section 3504) shall be considered as made by the employer except as provided in paragraph (a)(4)(iii) of this section.

(4) *Treatment of certain items in determining applicability of mandatory flat rate withholding.*—(i) *Optional treatment of compensation not subject to income tax withholding.*—For purposes of paragraph (a)(2) of this section, employers may determine whether an employee has received $1,000,000 of supplemental wages during a calendar year by including in supplemental wages amounts includible in income but not subject to withholding that are reported as wages, tips, other compensation on Form W-2.

(ii) *Allocation of salary reduction deferrals.*—In allocating salary reduction deferral amounts excludable from wages for purposes of determining whether the employer has paid

$1,000,000 of supplemental wages under paragraph (a)(2) of this section, employers must allocate such salary reduction deferral amounts to the type of compensation (i.e., gross amounts of regular wage payments or gross amounts of supplemental wage payments) actually being deferred.

(iii) *Optional de minimis exception for certain payments by agents.*—For purposes of paragraph (a)(2) of this section, if an agent makes total wage payments (including regular wages and supplemental wages) of less than $100,000 to an individual during any calendar year, an employer or other agent may disregard such payments in determining whether the individual has received $1,000,000 of supplemental wages during the calendar year, and such agent need not consider whether the individual has received other supplemental wages in determining the amount of income tax to be withheld from the payments. An employer may not avail itself of this exception if the employer is making payments to the employee using five or more agents and a principal effect of such use of agents is to reduce the applicability of mandatory flat rate withholding to the employee. For purposes of paragraph (a)(2) of this section, if an agent makes total wage payments of $100,000 or more to an individual during any calendar year, the entire amount of supplemental wages paid by the agent during the calendar year to the employee must be taken into account (by other agents of the employer that make total wage payments to the employee of $100,000 or more, by the agent, and by the employer for which the agent is acting) in determining whether the employee has received $1,000,000 of supplemental wages.

(iv) *Treatment of supplemental wage payment exceeding $1,000,000 cumulative threshold.*— In the case of a supplemental wage payment that, when added to all supplemental wage payments previously made by the employer to the employee in the calendar year, results in the employee having received in excess of $1,000,000 supplemental wages for the calendar year, the employer is required to impose withholding under paragraph (a)(2) of this section only on the portion of the payment that is in excess of $1,000,000 (taking into account all prior supplemental wage payments during the year). However, an employer may subject the entire amount of such supplemental wage payment to the withholding imposed by paragraph (a)(2) of this section.

(5) *Withholding on supplemental wages that are not subject to mandatory flat rate withholding.*—To the extent that paragraph (a)(2) of this section does not apply to a supplemental wage payment (or a portion of a payment), the amount of the tax required to be withheld on the supplemental wages when paid shall be determined under the rules provided in paragraphs (a)(6) and (7) of this section.

(6) *Aggregate procedure for withholding on supplemental wages.*—(i) *Applicability.*—The employer is required to determine withholding upon supplemental wages under this paragraph (a)(6) if paragraph (a)(2) of this section does not apply to the payment or portion of the payment and if paragraph (a)(7) of this section may not be used with respect to the payment. In addition, employers have the option of using this paragraph (a)(6) to calculate withholding with respect to a supplemental wage payment, if paragraph (a)(2) of this section does not apply to the payment, but if paragraph (a)(7) of this section could be used with respect to the payment.

(ii) *Procedure.*—Provided this procedure applies under paragraph (a)(6)(i) of this section, the supplemental wages, if paid concurrently with wages for a payroll period, are aggregated with the wages paid for such payroll period. If not paid concurrently, the supplemental wages are aggregated with the wages paid or to be paid within the same calendar year for the last preceding payroll period or for the current payroll period, if any. The amount of tax to be withheld is determined as if the aggregate of the supplemental wages and the regular wages constituted a single wage payment for the regular payroll period. The withholding method used by the employer with respect to regular wages would then be used to calculate the withholding on this single wage payment and the employer would take into consideration the Form W-4 submitted by the employee. This procedure is the aggregate procedure for withholding on supplemental wages.

(7) *Optional flat rate withholding on supplemental wages.*—(i) *Applicability.*—The employer may determine withholding upon supplemental wages under this paragraph (a)(7) if three conditions are met—

(A) Paragraph (a)(2) of this section does not apply to the payment or the portion of the payment;

(B) The supplemental wages are either not paid concurrently with regular wages or are separately stated on the payroll records of the employer; and

(C) Income tax has been withheld from regular wages of the employee during the calendar year of the payment or the preceding calendar year.

(ii) *Procedure.*—The determination of the tax to be withheld under paragraph (a)(7)(iii) of this section is made without reference to any payment of regular wages, without allowance for the number of withholding allowances claimed by the employee on Form W-4, and without regard to whether the employee has requested additional withholding on Form W-4. Withholding under this procedure is optional flat rate withholding.

(iii) *Rate applicable for purposes of optional flat rate withholding.*—Provided the conditions of paragraph (a)(7)(i) of this section have been met, the employer may determine the tax to be withheld—

Reg. § 31.3402(g)-1(a)(7)(iii)

(A) From supplemental wages paid after April 30, 1966, and prior to January 1, 1994, by using a flat percentage rate of 20 percent;

(B) From supplemental wages paid after December 31, 1993, and on or before August 6, 2001, by using a flat percentage rate of 28 percent;

(C) From supplemental wages paid after August 6, 2001, and on or before December 31, 2001, by using a flat percentage rate of 27.5 percent;

(D) From supplemental wages paid after December 31, 2001, and on or before May 27, 2003, by using a flat percentage rate of 27 percent;

(E) From supplemental wages paid after May 27, 2003, and on or before December 31, 2004, by using a flat percentage rate of 25 percent; and

(F) From supplemental wages paid after December 31, 2004, by using a flat percentage rate of 28 percent (or the corresponding rate in effect under section 1(i)(2) for taxable years beginning in the calendar year in which the payment is made).

(8) *Examples.*—For purposes of these examples, it is assumed that the rate for purposes of mandatory flat rate withholding for 2007 is 35 percent, and the rate for purposes of optional flat rate withholding for 2007 is 25 percent. The following examples illustrate this paragraph (a):

Example 1. (i) Employee A is an employee of three entities (X, Y, and Z) that are treated as a single employer under section 52(a) or (b). In 2007, X pays regular wages to A on a monthly payroll period for services performed for X, Y, and Z. The regular wages are paid on the third business day of each month. Income tax is withheld from the regular wages of A during the year. A receives only the following supplemental wage payments during 2007 in addition to the regular wages paid by X—

(A) A bonus of $600,000 from X on March 15, 2007;

(B) A bonus of $2,300,000 from Y on November 15, 2007; and

(C) A bonus of $10,000 from Z on December 31, 2007.

(ii) In this *Example 1*, the $600,000 bonus from X is a supplemental wage payment. The withholding on the $600,000 payment from X could be determined under either paragraph (a)(6) or (7) of this section because income tax has been withheld from the regular wages of A. If X elects to use the aggregate procedure under paragraph (a)(6) of this section, the amount of withholding on the supplemental wages would be based on aggregating the supplemental wages and the regular wages paid by X either for the current or last payroll period and treating the total of the regular wages paid by X and the $600,000 supplemental wages as a single wage payment for a regular payroll period. The withholding method used by the employer with re-

spect to regular wages would then be used to calculate the withholding on this single wage payment, and the employer would take into consideration the Form W-4 furnished by the employee.

(iii) In this *Example 1*, the $2,300,000 bonus from Y is a supplemental wage payment. To calculate the withholding on the $2,300,000 supplemental wage payment from Y, the $600,000 of supplemental wages X has already paid to A in 2007 must be taken into account because X and Y are treated as the same employer under section 52(a) or (b). Thus, the withholding on the first $400,000 of the payment (i.e., the cumulative supplemental wages not in excess of $1,000,000) is computed separately from the withholding on the remaining $1,900,000 of the payment (i.e., the amount of the cumulative supplemental wages in excess of $1,000,000). With respect to the first $400,000, the withholding could be computed under either paragraph (a)(6) or (a)(7) of this section, because income tax has been withheld from the regular wages of the employee. If Y elected to withhold income tax using paragraph (a)(7) of this section, Y would withhold on the $400,000 component at 25 percent (pursuant to paragraph (a)(7)(iii)(F) of this section), which would result in $100,000 tax withheld. The remaining $1,900,000 of the bonus would be subject to mandatory flat rate withholding at the maximum rate of tax in effect under section 1 for 2007 (35%) without regard to the Form W-4 submitted by A. The amount withheld from the $1,900,000 would be $665,000. The withholding on the first component and the withholding on the second component then would be added together to determine the total income tax withholding on the supplemental wage payment from Y. Alternatively, under paragraph (a)(4)(iv) of this section, Y could treat the entire $2,300,000 bonus payment as subject to mandatory flat rate withholding at the maximum rate of tax (35%), in which case the amount to be withheld would be 35 percent of $2,300,000, or $805,000.

(iv) The $10,000 bonus paid from Z is also a supplemental wage payment. To calculate the withholding on the $10,000 bonus, the $2,900,000 in cumulative supplemental wages already paid to A in 2007 by X and Y must be taken into account because X, Y, and Z are treated as a single employer. The entire $10,000 bonus would be subject to mandatory flat rate withholding at the maximum rate of tax in effect under section 1 for 2007. The income tax required to be withheld on this payment would be 35 percent of $10,000 or $3,500.

Example 2. Employees B and C work for employer M. Each employee receives a monthly salary of $3,000 in 2007. As a result of the withholding allowances claimed by B, there has been no income tax withholding on the regular wages M pays to B during either 2007 or 2006. In contrast, M has withheld income tax from regular wages M pays to C during 2007. Together with the monthly salary check paid in December 2007 to each employee, M includes a bonus of $2,000, which is the only supplemental wage payment each employee receives from M in 2007. The bonuses are separately stated on the payroll records of M. Because M has withheld no income tax from B's regular wages during either the calendar year of the $2,000 bonus or the preceding calendar year, M cannot use optional flat rate withholding provided under paragraph (a)(7) of this section to calculate the income tax withholding on B's $2,000 bonus. Consequently, M must use the aggregate procedure set forth in paragraph (a)(6) of this section to calculate the income tax withholding due on the $2,000 bonus to B. With respect to the bonus paid to C, M has the option of using either the aggregate procedure provided under paragraph (a)(6) of this section or the optional flat rate withholding provided under paragraph (a)(7) of this section to calculate the income tax withholding due.

Example 3. (i) Employee D works as an employee of Corporation R. Corporations R and T are treated as a single employer under section 52(a) or (b). R makes regular wage payments to Employee D of $200,000 on a monthly basis in 2007, and income tax is withheld from those wages. R pays D a bonus for his services as an employee equal to $3,000,000 on June 30, 2007. Unrelated company U pays D sick pay as an agent of the employer R and such sick pay is supplemental wages pursuant to § 31.3401(a)-1(b)(8)(i)(*b*)(2). U pays D $50,000 of sick pay on October 31, 2007. Corporation T decides to award bonuses to all employees of R and T, and pays a bonus of $100,000 to D on December 31, 2007. D received no other payments from R, T, or U.

(ii) In chronological summary, D is paid the following wages other than the regular monthly wages paid by R:

(A) June 30, 2007 — $3,000,000 (bonus from R);

(B) October 31, 2007 — $50,000 (sick pay from U); and

(C) December 31, 2007 — $100,000 (bonus from T).

(iii) In this *Example 3*, each payment of wages other than the regular monthly wage payments from R is considered to be supplemental wages for purposes of withholding under § 31.3402(g)-1(a)(2). The amount of regular wages from R is irrelevant in determining when mandatory flat rate withholding on supplemental wages must be applied.

(iv) Because income tax has been withheld on D's regular wages, income tax may be withheld on $1,000,000 of the $3,000,000 bonus paid on June 30, 2007, under either paragraph (a)(6) or (7) of this section. If R elects to use optional flat rate withholding provided under paragraph (a)(7)(iii)(f) of this section, withholding would be calculated at 25 percent of the $1,000,000 portion of the payment and would be $250,000.

(v) Income tax withheld on the following supplemental wage payments (or portion of a payment) as follows is required to be calculated at the maximum rate in effect under section 1, or 35 percent in 2007—

(A) $2,000,000 of the $3,000,000 bonus paid by R on June 30, 2007; and

(B) all of the $100,000 bonus paid by T on December 31, 2007.

(vi) Pursuant to paragraph (a)(4)(iii) of this section, because the total wage payments made by U, an agent of the employer, to D are less than $100,000, U is permitted to determine the amount of income tax to be withheld without regard to other supplemental wage payments made to the employee. Income tax withholding on the $50,000 in sick pay may be determined under either paragraph (a)(6) or (7) of this section. If U elects to withhold income tax at the flat rate provided under paragraph (a)(7)(iii)(F) of this section, withholding on the $50,000 of sick pay would be calculated at 25 percent of the $50,000 payment and would be $12,500. Alternatively, U may choose to take account of the $3,000,000 in supplemental wages paid by the employer during 2007 prior to payment of the $50,000 sick pay, and withholding on the $50,000 of sick pay could be calculated applying the mandatory flat rate of 35 percent, resulting in withholding of $17,500 on the $50,000 payment.

Example 4. (i) Employer J has decided it wants to grant its employee B a $1,000,000 net bonus (after withholding) to be paid in 2007. Employer J has withheld income tax from the regular wages of the employee. Employer J has made no other supplemental wage payments to B during the year.

(ii) This *Example 4* requires grossing up the supplemental wage payment to determine the gross wages necessary to result in a net payment of $1,000,000. If the employer elected to use optional flat rate withholding, the first $1,000,000 of the wages would be subject to 25 percent withholding. However, any wages above that, including amounts representing gross-up payments, would be subject to mandatory 35 percent withholding. The withholding applicable to the first $1,000,000 (i.e., $250,000) would thus be required to be grossed-up at a 35 percent rate to determine the gross wage amount in excess of $1,000,000. Thus, the wages in excess of $1,000,000 would be equal to $250,000 divided by .65 (computed by subtracting .35 from 1) or $384,615.38. Thus the total supplemental wage payment, taking into account income tax withholding only (and not Federal Insurance Contributions Act taxes), to B would be $1,384,615.38, and the total withholding with respect to the payment if Employer J elected optional flat rate withholding with respect to the first $1,000,000, would be $384,615.38.

(9) *Certain noncash payments to retail commission salesmen.*—For provisions relating to the treatment of wages that are not subject to paragraph (a)(2) of this section and that are paid other than in cash to retail commission salesmen, see § 31.3402(j)-1.

(10) *Alternative methods.*—The Secretary may provide by publication in the Internal Revenue Bulletin (see § 601.601(d)(2)(ii)(b) of this chapter) for alternative withholding methods that will allow an employer to meet its responsibility for the mandatory flat rate withholding required by paragraph (a)(2) of this section.

(b) *Special rule where aggregate withholding exemption exceeds wages paid.*—(1) *Procedure.*—This rule does not apply to the extent that paragraph (a)(2) of this section applies to the supplemental wage payment. If supplemental wages are paid to an employee during a calendar year for a period which involves two or more consecutive payroll periods, for which other wages also are paid during such calendar year, and the aggregate of such other wages is less than the aggregate of the amounts determined under the table provided in section 3402(b)(1) as the withholding exemptions applicable for such payroll periods, the amount of the tax required to be withheld on the supplemental wages shall be computed as follows:

Step 1. Determine an average wage for each of such payroll periods by dividing the sum of the supplemental wages and the wages paid for such payroll periods by the number of such payroll periods.

Step 2. Determine a tax for each payroll period as if the amount of the average wage constituted the wages paid for such payroll period.

Step 3. From the sum of the amounts of tax determined in Step 2 subtract the total amount of tax withheld, or to be withheld, from the wages, other than the supplemental wages, for such payroll periods. The remainder, if any, shall constitute the amount of the tax to be withheld upon the supplemental wages.

Example. An employee has a weekly payroll period ending on Saturday of each week, the wages for which are paid on Friday of the succeeding week. On the 10th day of each month he is paid a bonus based upon production during the payroll periods for which wages were paid in the preceding month. The employee is paid a weekly wage of $64 on each of the five Fridays occurring in July 1966. On August 10, 1966, the employee is paid a bonus of $125 based upon production during the five payroll periods covered by the wages paid in July. On the date of payment of the bonus, the employee, who is married and has three children, has a withholding exemption certificate in effect indicating that he is married and claiming five withholding exemptions. The amount of the tax to be withheld from the bonus paid on August 10, 1966, is computed as follows:

Wages paid in July 1966 for 5 payroll periods (5 × $64)	$320.00
Bonus paid August 10, 1966	125.00
Aggregate of wages and bonus	$445.00
Average wage per payroll period ($445 ÷ 5)	$89.00
Computation of tax under percentage method: Withholding exemptions (5 × $13.50)	$67.50
Remainder subject to tax	$21.50
Tax on average wage for 1 week under percentage method of withholding (married person with weekly payroll period) (14 percent of $17.50 (excess over $4))	$2.45
Tax on average wage for 5 weeks	$12.25
Less: Tax previously withheld on weekly wage payments of $64	None
Tax to be withheld on supplemental wages	$12.25
Computation of tax under wage bracket method: Tax on $89 wage under weekly wage table for married person ($2.50 per week for 5 weeks)	$12.50
Less: Tax previously withheld on weekly wage payments of $64	None
Tax to be withheld on supplemental wages	$12.50

(2) *Applicability.*—The rules prescribed in this paragraph (b) shall, at the election of the employer, be applied in lieu of the rules prescribed in paragraph (a) of this section except that this paragraph shall not be applicable in any case in which the payroll period of the employee is less than one week or to the extent that paragraph (a)(2) of this section applies to the supplemental wage payment.

(c) *Vacation allowances.*—Amounts of so-called "vacation allowances" shall be subject to withholding as though they were regular wage payments made for the period covered by the vacation. If the vacation allowance is paid in addition to the regular wage payment for such period, the rules applicable with respect to supplemental wage payments shall apply to such vacation allowance. [Reg. § 31.3402(g)-1.]

☐ [*T.D.* 6259, 10-25-57. *Amended by T.D.* 6860, 11-3-65; *T.D.* 6882, 4-11-66 *and T.D.* 9276, 7-24-2006 (*corrected* 10-2-2006 *and* 12-26-2006).]

[Reg. § 31.3402(g)-2]

§ 31.3402(g)-2. Wages paid for payroll period of more than one year.—If wages are paid to an employee for a payroll period of more than one year, for the purpose of determining the amount of tax required to be deducted and withheld in respect of such wages—

(a) Under the percentage method, the amount of the tax shall be determined as if such payroll period constituted an annual payroll period, and

(b) Under the wage bracket method, the amount of the tax shall be determined as if such payroll period constituted a miscellaneous payroll period of 365 days. [Reg. § 31.3402(g)-2.]

☐ [*T.D.* 6259, 10-25-57.]

[Reg. §31.3402(g)-3]

§31.3402(g)-3. Wages paid through an agent, fiduciary, or other person on behalf of two or more employers.—(a) If a payment of wages is made to an employee by an employer through an agent, fiduciary, or other person who also has the control, receipt, custody, or disposal of, or pays the wages payable by another employer to such employee, the amount of the tax required to be withheld on each wage payment made through such agent, fiduciary, or person shall, whether the wages are paid separately on behalf of each employer or paid in a lump sum of all such employers, be determined upon the aggregate amount of such wage payment or payments in the same manner as if such aggregate amount had been paid by one employer. Hence, under either the percentage method or the wage bracket method the tax shall be determined upon the aggregate amount of the wage payment.

(b) In any such case, each employer shall be liable for the return and payment of a pro rata portion of the tax so determined, such portion to be determined in the ratio which the amount contributed by the particular employer bears to the aggregate of such wages.

(c) For example, three companies maintain a central management agency which carries on the administrative work of the several companies. The central agency organization consists of a staff of clerks, bookkeepers, stenographers, etc., who are the common employees of the three companies. The expenses of the central agency, including wages paid to the foregoing employees, are borne by the several companies in certain agreed proportions. Company X pays 45 percent, Company Y pays 35 percent and Company Z pays 20 percent of such expenses. The amount of the tax required to be withheld on the wages paid to persons employed in the central agency should be determined in accordance with the provisions of this section. In such event, Company X is liable as an employer for the return and payment of 45 percent of the tax required to be withheld, Company Y is liable for the return and payment of 35 percent of the tax and Company Z is liable for the return and payment of 20 percent of the tax. (See §31.3504-1, relating to acts to be performed by agents.) [Reg. §31.3402(g)-3.]

☐ [*T.D.* 6259, 10-25-57.]

[Reg. §31.3402(h)(1)-1]

§31.3402(h)(1)-1. Withholding on basis of average wages.—(a) *In general.*—An employer may determine the amount of tax to be deducted and withheld upon a payment of wages to an employee on the basis of the employee's average estimated wages, with necessary adjustments, for any quarter. This paragraph applies only where the method desired to be used includes wages other than tips (whether or not tips are also included).

(b) *Withholding on the basis of average estimated tips.*—(1) *In general.*—Subject to certain limitations and conditions, an employer may, at his discretion, withhold the tax under section 3402 in respect of tips reported by an employee to the employer on an estimated basis. An employer who elects to make withholding of the tax on an estimated basis shall:

(i) In respect of each employee, make an estimate of the amount of tips that will be reported, pursuant to section 6053, by the employee to the employer in a calendar quarter.

(ii) Determine the amount which must be deducted and withheld upon each payment of wages (exclusive of tips) which are under the control of the employer to be made during the quarter by the employer to the employee. The total amount which must be deducted and withheld shall be determined by assuming that the estimated tips for the quarter represent the amount of wages to be paid to the employee in the form of tips in the quarter and that such tips will be ratably (in terms of pay periods) paid during the quarter.

(iii) Deduct and withhold from any payment of wages (exclusive of tips) which are under the control of the employer, or from funds referred to in section 3402(k) (see §§31.3402(k) and 31.3402(k)-1), such amount as may be necessary to adjust the amount of tax withheld on the estimated basis to conform to the amount required to be withheld in respect of tips reported by the employee to the employer during the calendar quarter in written statements furnished to the employer pursuant to section 6053(a). If an adjustment is required, the additional tax required to be withheld may be deducted upon any payment of wages (exclusive of tips) which are under the control of the employer during the quarter and within the first 30 days following the quarter or from funds turned over by the employee to the employer for such purpose within such period. For provisions relating to the repayment to an employee, or other disposition, of amounts deducted from an employee's remuneration in excess of the correct amount of tax, see §31.6413(a)-1.

(2) *Estimating tips employee will report.*— (i) *Initial estimate.*—The initial estimate of the amount of tips that will reported by a particular employee in a calendar quarter shall be made on the basis of the facts and circumstances surrounding the employment of that employee. However, if a number of employees are employed under substantially the same circumstances and working conditions, the initial estimate established for one such employee may be used as the initial estimate for other employees in that group.

(ii) *Adjusting estimate.*—If the quarterly estimate of tips in respect of a particular employee continues to differ substantially from the amount of tips reported by the employee and there are no unusual factors involved (for example, an extended absence from work due to illness) the employer shall make an appropriate adjustment of his estimate of the amount of tips that will be reported by the employee.

(iii) *Reasonableness of estimate.*—The employer must be prepared, upon request of the district director, to disclose the factors upon which he relied in making the estimate, and his reasons for believing that the estimate is reasonable. [Reg. § 31.3402(h)(1)-1.]

☐ [*T.D.* 6259, 10-27-57. *Amended by T.D.* 7001, 1-17-69 *and T.D.* 7053, 7-20-70.]

[Reg. § 31.3402(h)(2)-1]

§ 31.3402(h)(2)-1. Withholding on basis of annualized wages.—An employer may determine the amount of tax to be deducted and withheld upon a payment of wages to an employee by taking the following steps:

Step 1. Multiply the amount of the employee's wages for the payroll period by the number of such periods in the calendar year.

Step 2. Determine the amount of tax which would be required to be deducted and withheld upon the amount determined in Step 1 if that amount constituted the actual wages for the calendar year and the payroll period of the employee were an annual payroll period.

Step 3. Divide the amount of tax determined in Step 2 by the number of periods by which the employee's wages were multiplied in Step 1.

Example. On July 1, 1970, A, a single person who is on a weekly payroll period and claims one exemption, receives wages of $100 from X Co., his employer. X Co. multiplies the weekly wage of $100 by 52 weeks to determine an annual wage of $5,200. It then subtracts $650 for A's withholding exemption and arrives at a balance of $4,550. The applicable table in section 3402(a) for annual payroll periods indicates that the amount of tax to be withheld thereon is $376 plus $314.50 (17 percent of excess over $2,700), or a total of $690.50. The annual tax of $690.50, when divided by 52 to arrive at the portion thereof attributable to the weekly payroll period, equals $13.28. X Co. may, if it chooses, withhold $13.28 rather than the amount specified in sec-

tion 3402(a) or (c) for a weekly payroll period. [Reg. § 31.3402(h)(2)-1.]

☐ [*T.D.* 7053, 7-20-70.]

[Reg. § 31.3402(h)(3)-1]

§ 31.3402(h)(3)-1. Withholding on basis of cumulative wages.—(a) *In general.*—In the case of an employee who has in effect a request that the amount of tax to be withheld from his wages be computed on the basis of his cumulative wages, and whose wages since the beginning of the current calendar year have been paid with respect to the same category of payroll period (e.g., weekly or semimonthly) the employer may determine the amount of tax to be deducted and withheld upon a payment of wages made to the employee after December 31, 1969, by taking the following steps:

Step 1. Add the amount of the wages to be paid the employee for the payroll period to the total amount of wages paid by the employer to the employee during the calendar year.

Step 2. Divide the aggregate amount of wages computed in Step 1 by the number of payroll periods to which that amount relates.

Step 3. Compute the total amount of tax that would have been required to be deducted and withheld under section 3402(a) if the average amount of wages (as computed in Step 2) had been paid to the employee for the number of payroll periods to which the aggregate amount of wages (computed in Step 1) relates.

Step 4. Determine the excess, if any, of the amount of tax computed in Step 3 over the total amount of tax already deducted and withheld by the employer from wages paid to the employee during the calendar year.

Example. On July 1, 1970, Y Co. employs B, a single person claiming one exemption. Y Co. pays B the following amounts of wages on the basis of a biweekly payroll period on the following pay days:

July 20	$1,000
August 3	300
August 17	300
August 31	300
September 14	300
September 28	300

On October 5, B requests that Y Co. withhold on the basis of his cumulative wages with respect to his wages to be paid on October 12 and thereafter. Y Co. adds the $300 in wages to be paid to B on October 12 to the payments of wages already made to B during the calendar year, and determines that the aggregate amount of wages is $2,800. The average amount of wages for the 7 biweekly payroll periods is $400. The total amount of tax required to be deducted and withheld for payments of $400 for each of 7 biweekly payroll periods is $485.87 under section 3402(a). Since the total amount of tax which has been deducted and withheld by Y Co. through September 28 is $484.86, Y Co. may, if it chooses, deduct and withhold $1.01 (the amount by

which $485.87 exceeds the total amount already withheld by Y Co.) from the payment of wages to B on October 12 rather than the amount specified in section 3402(a) or (c).

(b) *Employee's request and revocation of request.*—An employee's request that his employer withhold on the basis of his cumulative wages and a notice of revocation of such request shall be in writing and in such form as the employer may prescribe. An employee's request furnished to his employer pursuant to this section shall be effective, and may be acted upon by his employer, after the furnishing of such request and before a revocation thereof is effective. A revocation of such request may be made at any time by

Collection of Income Tax at Source on Wages
61,569
See p. 20,601 for regulations not amended to reflect law changes

the employee furnishing his employer with a notice of revocation. The employer may give immediate effect to a revocation, but, in any event, a revocation shall be effective with respect to payments of wages made on or after the first "status determination date" (see section 3402(f)(3)(B)) which occurs at least 30 days after the date on which such notice is furnished.

(c) *Requests due to increases or decreases in allowances.*—An employee may request pursuant to this section that his employer withhold on the basis of the employee's cumulative wages when the employee is entitled to claim an increased or decreased number of withholding allowances under §31.3402(m)-1 during the estimation year (as defined in §31.3402(m)-1(c)(1)). [Reg. §31.3402(h)(3)-1.]

☐ [*T.D. 7053, 7-20-70. Amended by T.D. 7915, 9-26-83.*]

[Reg. §31.3402(h)(4)-1]

§31.3402(h)(4)-1. Other methods.—(a) *Maximum permissible deviations.*—An employer may use any other method of withholding under which the employer will deduct and withhold upon wages paid to an employee after December 31, 1969, for a payroll period substantially the same amount as would be required to be deducted and withheld by applying section 3402(a) with respect to the payroll period. For purposes of section 3402(h)(4) and this section, an amount is substantially the same as the amount required to be deducted and withheld under section 3402(a) if its deviation from the latter amount is not greater than the maximum permissible deviation prescribed in this paragraph. The maximum permissible deviation under this paragraph is determined by annualizing wages as provided in Step 1 of §31.3402(h)(2)-1 and applying the following table to the amount of tax required to be deducted and withheld under section 3402(a) with respect to such annualized wages, as determined under Step 2 of §31.3402(h)(2)-1:

If the tax required to be withheld under the annual percentage rate schedule is—	The maximum permissible annual deviation is—
$10 to $100	$10, plus 10% of excess over $10
$100 to $1,000	$19, plus 3% of excess over $100
$1,000 or over	$46, plus 1% of excess over $1,000

In any case, an amount which is less than $10 more or less per year than the amount required to be deducted and withheld under section 3402(a) is substantially the same as the latter amount. If any method produces results which are not greater than the prescribed maximum deviations only with respect to some of his employees, the employer may use such method only with respect to such employees. An employer should thoroughly test any method which he contemplates using to ascertain whether it meets the tolerances prescribed by this paragraph. An employer may not use any method one of the principal purposes of which is to consistently produce amounts to be deducted and withheld which are less (though substantially the same) than the amount required to be deducted and withheld by applying section 3402(a).

(b) *Combined FICA and income tax withholding.*—In addition to the methods authorized by paragraph (a) of this section, an employer may determine the amount of tax to be deducted and withheld under section 3402 upon a payment of wages to an employee by using tables prescribed by the Commissioner which combine the amounts of tax to be deducted under sections 3102 and 3402. Such tables shall provide for the deduction of the sum of such amounts, computed on the basis of the midpoints of the wage brackets in the tables prescribed under section 3402(c). The portion of such sum which is to be treated as the tax deducted and withheld under section 3402 shall be the amount obtained by subtracting from such sum the amount of tax required to be deducted by section 3102. Such tables may be used only with respect to payments which are wages under both sections 3121(a) and 3401(a).

(c) *Part-year employment method of withholding.*—(1) *In general.*—In addition to the methods authorized by other paragraphs of this section, in the case of part-year employment (as defined in subparagraph (4) of this paragraph) of an employee who determines his liability for tax under subtitle A of the Code on a calendar-year basis and who has in effect a request that the amount of tax to be withheld from his wages be computed according to the part-year employment method described in this paragraph, the employer may determine the amount of tax to be deducted and withheld upon a payment of wages made to the employee on or after January 5, 1973, by taking the following steps:

Step 1. Add the amount of wages to be paid to the employee for the current payroll period to the total amount of wages paid by the employer to the employee for all preceding payroll periods included in the current term of continuous employment (as defined in subparagraph (3) of this paragraph) of the employee by the employer;

Step 2. Divide the aggregate amount of wages computed in Step 1 by the total of the number of payroll periods to which that amount relates plus the equivalent number of payroll periods (as defined in subparagraph (2) of this paragraph) in the employee's term of continuous unemployment immediately preceding the current term of continuous employment, such term of continuous unemployment to be exclusive of any days prior to the beginning of the current calendar year;

Step 3. Determine the total amount of tax that would have been required to be deducted and withheld under section 3402 if the average amount of wages (as computed in Step 2) had been paid to the employee for the number of payroll periods determined in Step 2 (including the equivalent number of payroll periods); and

Step 4. Determine the excess, if any, of the amount of tax computed in Step 3 over the total amount of tax already deducted and withheld by the employer from wages paid to the employee for all payroll periods during the current term of continuous employment.

The use of the method described in this paragraph does not preclude the employee from claiming additional withholding allowances pursuant to section 3402(m) or the standard deduction allowance pursuant to section 3402(f)(1)(G).

(2) *Equivalent number of payroll periods.*—For purposes of this paragraph, the equivalent number of payroll periods shall be determined by dividing the number of calendar days contained in the current payroll period into the number of calendar days between the later of (i) the day certified by the employee as his last day of employment prior to his current term of continuous employment during the calendar year in which such term commenced, or (ii) the last day of the calendar year immediately preceding the current calendar year, and the first day of the current term of continuous employment. For purposes of the preceding sentence, the term "calendar days" includes holidays, Saturdays, and Sundays. In determining the equivalent number of payroll periods, any fraction obtained in the division described in the first sentence of this subparagraph shall be disregarded. An employee paid for a miscellaneous payroll period shall be considered to have a daily payroll period for purposes of this subparagraph. In a case in which an employee is paid for a daily or miscellaneous payroll period and the employer elects under Circular E to compute the tax to be withheld as if the aggregate of the wages paid to the employee during the calendar week were paid for a weekly period, the employer shall determine the equivalent number of payroll periods for purposes of the computation of the tax to be withheld for the calendar week on the basis of a weekly payroll period (notwithstanding the fact that a determination of the equivalent number of payroll periods for purposes of the computation of the tax to be withheld upon wages paid for daily or miscellaneous payroll periods within such calendar week has been made on the basis of a daily or miscellaneous payroll period).

(3) *Term of continuous employment.*—For purposes of this paragraph, a term of employment is continuous if it is either a single term of employment or two or more consecutive terms of employment with the same employer. A term of continuous employment begins on the first day on which any services are performed by the employee for the employer for which compensation is paid or payable. Such term ends on the earlier of (i) the last day during the current term of continuous employment on which any services are performed by the employee for the employer, or (ii) if the employee performs no services for the employer for a period of more than 30 calendar days, the last day preceding such period on which any services are performed by the employee for the employer. For example, a professional athlete who signs a contract on December 31, 1973, to perform services from July 1 through December 31 for the calendar years 1974, 1975, and 1976 has a new term of employment beginning each July 1 and accordingly may qualify for use of the part-year withholding method in each of such years. Likewise, a term of continuous employment is not broken by a temporary layoff of no more than 30 days. On the other hand, when an employment relationship is actually terminated the term of continuous employment is ended even though a new employment relationship is established with the same employer within 30 days. A "term of continuous employment" includes all days on which an employee performs any services for an employer and includes days on which services are not performed because of illness or vacation, or because such days are holidays or are regular days off (such as Saturdays and Sundays, or days off in lieu of Saturdays and Sundays), or other days for which the employee is not scheduled to work. For example, an employee who is employed two days a week for the same employer from March 1 through December 31 has a term of continuous employment of 306 days.

(4) *Part-year employment.*—For purposes of this paragraph, "part-year employment" means one or more terms of continuous employment with all employers which term or terms will not aggregate more than 245 days within a calendar year. For example, A graduates from college in May and was not employed from January through May. A accepts a permanent position with X Co., beginning June 1. Since the total duration of A's term of continuous employment will, during the current calendar year, not exceed 245 days it does qualify as part-year employment for purposes of this section. If, however, A had also worked for Y Co. from December 15 of the previous year through February 5 of the current calendar year, the total duration of A's terms of continuous employment will, during the current calendar year, exceed 245 days (36 days (January 1 through February 5) plus 214 days (June 1 through December 31) equals 250 days). This year's employment does not therefore qualify as part-year employment for purposes of this section.

(5) *Employee's request.*—(i) An employee's request that his employer withhold according to the part-year employment method shall be in writing and in such form as the employer may

prescribe. Such request shall be made under the penalties of perjury and shall contain the following information—

(a) The last day of employment (if any) by any employer prior to the current term of continuous employment during the calendar year in which such term commenced,

(b) A statement that the employee reasonably anticipates that he will be employed for an aggregate of no more than 245 days in all terms of continuous employment during the current calendar year, and

(c) The employee uses a calendar-year accounting period.

An employee's request furnished to his employer pursuant to this section shall be effective, and may be acted upon by his employer, with respect to wages paid after the furnishing of such request, and shall cease to be effective with respect to any wages paid on or after the beginning of the payroll period during which the current calendar year will end.

(ii) If, on any day during the calendar year, any of the anticipations stated by the employee in his statement provided pursuant to subdivision (i)(b) of this subparagraph becomes unreasonable, the employee shall revoke the request described in this subparagraph before the end of the payroll period during which it becomes unreasonable. The revocation shall be effective as of the beginning of the payroll period during which it is made. [Reg. § 31.3402(h)(4)-1.]

□ [T.D. 7053, 7-20-70. Amended by T.D. 7251, 12-29-72, and T.D. 7915, 9-26-83.]

[Reg. § 31.3402(i)-1]

§ 31.3402(i)-1. Additional withholding.— (a) In addition to the tax required to be deducted and withheld in accordance with the provisions of section 3402, the employer and employee may agree that an additional amount shall be withheld from the employee's wages. The agreement shall be in writing and shall be in such form as the employer may prescribe. The agreement shall be effective for such period as the employer and employee mutually agree upon. However, unless the agreement provides for an earlier termination, either the employer, or the employee, by furnishing a written notice to the other, may terminate the agreement effective with respect to the first payment of wages made on or after the first "status determination date" (see paragraph (d) of § 31.3402(f)(3)-1) which occurs at least 30 days after the date on which such notice is furnished.

(b) The amount deducted and withheld pursuant to an agreement between the employer and employee shall be considered as tax required to be deducted and withheld under section 3402. All provisions of law and regulations applicable with respect to the tax required to be deducted and withheld under section 3402 shall be applicable with respect to any amount deducted and withheld pursuant to the agreement.

(c) This section is applicable only to agreements made before October 1, 1981. Any such agreement shall remain in effect in accordance

with paragraph (a). See § 31.3402(i)-2 for rules relating to increases in withholding after September 30, 1981. [Reg. § 31.3402(i)-1.]

□ [T.D. 6259, 10-25-57. Amended by T.D. 7065, 10-22-70, and T.D. 7915, 9-26-83.]

[Reg. § 31.3402(i)-2]

§ 31.3402(i)-2. Increases or decreases in withholding.—(a) *Increases in withholding.*—(1) *In general.*—In addition to the tax required to be deducted and withheld in accordance with the provisions of section 3402, the employee may request, after September 30, 1981, that the employer deduct and withhold an additional amount from the employee's wages. The employer must comply with the employee's request, except that the employer shall comply with the employee's request only to the extent that the amount that the employee requests to be deducted and withheld under this section does not exceed the amount that remains after the employer has deducted and withheld all amounts otherwise required to be deducted and withheld by Federal law (other than by section 3402 (i) and this section), State law, and local law (other than by State or local law that provides for voluntary withholding). The employer must comply with the employee's request in accordance with the time limitations of § 31.3402(f)(3)-1 (relating to when withholding exemption certificate takes effect). The employee must make his request on Form W-4 as provided in § 31.3402(f)(5)-1 (relating to form and contents of withholding exemption certificates), and this Form W-4 shall take effect and remain effective in accordance with section 3402(f) and the regulations thereunder.

(2) *Amount deducted considered to be tax.*— The amount deducted and withheld pursuant to subparagraph (1) shall be considered to be tax required to be deducted and withheld under section 3402. All provisions of law and regulations applicable with respect to the tax required to be deducted and withheld under section 3402 shall be applicable with respect to any amount deducted and withheld under subparagraph (1).

(b) *Decreases in withholding.*—[RESERVED] [Reg. § 31.3402(i)-2.]

□ [T.D. 7915, 9-26-83.]

[Reg. § 31.3402(j)-1]

§ 31.3402(j)-1. Remuneration other than in cash for service performed by retail commission salesman.—(a) *In general.*—(1) An employer, in computing the amount to be deducted and withheld as tax in accordance with section 3402, may, at his election, disregard any wages paid, after August 9, 1955, in a medium other than cash for services performed for him by an employee if (i) the noncash remuneration is paid for services performed by the employee as a retail commission salesman and (ii) the employer ordinarily pays the employee remuneration solely by way of cash commissions for services performed by him as a retail commission salesman.

(2) Section 3402(j) and this section are not applicable with respect to wages paid to the employee that are subject to withholding under §31.3402(g)-1(a)(2). Section 3402(j) and this section are not applicable with respect to noncash wages paid to a retail commission salesman for services performed by him in a capacity other than as such a salesman. Such sections are not applicable with respect to noncash wages paid by an employer to an employee for services performed as a retail commission salesman if the employer ordinarily pays the employee remuneration other than by way of cash commissions for such services. Thus, noncash remuneration may not be disregarded in computing the amount to be deducted and withheld in a case where the employee, for services performed as a retail commission salesman, is paid both a salary and cash commissions on sales, or is ordinarily paid in something other than cash (stocks, bonds or other forms of property) notwithstanding that the amount of remuneration paid to the employee is measured by sales.

(b) *Retail commission salesman.*—For purposes of section 3402(j) and this section, the term "retail commission salesman" includes an employee who is engaged in the solicitation of orders at retail, that is, from the ultimate consumer, for merchandise or other products offered for sale by his employer. The term does not include an employee salesman engaged in the solicitation on behalf of his employer of orders from wholesalers, retailers, or others, for merchandise for resale. However, if the salesman solicits orders for more than one principal, he is not excluded from the term solely because he solicits orders from wholesalers or retailers on behalf of one or more principals. In such case the salesman may be a retail commission salesman with respect to services performed for one or more principals and not with respect to services performed for his other principals.

(c) *Noncash remuneration.*—The term "noncash remuneration" includes remuneration paid in any medium other than cash, such as goods or commodities, stocks, bonds, or other forms of property. The term does not include checks or other monetary media of exchange.

(d) *Cross reference.*—For provisions relating to records required to be kept and statements which must be furnished an employee with respect to wage payments, see sections 6001 and 6051 and the regulations thereunder in Subpart G of this part. [Reg. §31.3402(j)-1.]

☐ [*T.D. 6259,* 10-25-57. *Amended by T.D. 9276,* 7-24-2006.]

[Reg. §31.3402(k)-1]

§31.3402(k)-1. Special rule for tips.— (a) *Withholding of income tax in respect of tips.*— (1) *In general.*—Subject to the limitations set forth in subparagraph (2) of this paragraph, an employer is required to deduct and withhold from each of his employees tax in respect of those tips received by the employee which constitute wages. (For provisions relating to the treatment of tips as wages, see §§31.3401(a)(16) and 31.3401(f).) The employer shall make the withholding by deducting or causing to be deducted the amount of the tax from wages (exclusive of tips) which are under control of the employer or other funds turned over by the employee to the employer (see subparagraph (3) of this paragraph). For purposes of this section the term "wages (exclusive of tips) which are under the control of the employer" means, with respect to a payment of wages, an amount equal to wages as defined in section 3401(a) except that tips and noncash remuneration which are wages are not included, less the sum of—

(i) The tax under section 3101 required to be collected by the employer in respect of wages as defined in section 3121(a) (exclusive of tips);

(ii) The tax under section 3402 required to be collected by the employer in respect of wages as defined in section 3401(a) (exclusive of tips); and

(iii) The amount of taxes imposed on the remuneration of an employee withheld by the employer pursuant to State and local law (including amounts withheld under an agreement between the employer and the employee pursuant to such law) except that the amount of taxes taken into account in this subdivision shall not include any amount attributable to tips.

(2) *Limitations.*—An employer is required to deduct and withhold the tax on tips which constitute wages only in respect of those tips which are reported by the employee to the employer in a written statement furnished to the employer pursuant to section 6053(a). The employer is responsible for the collection of the tax on tips reported to him only to the extent that the employer can, during the period beginning at the time the written statement is submitted to him and ending at the close of the calendar year in which the statement was submitted, collect the tax by deducting it or causing it to be deducted as provided in subparagraph (1) of this paragraph.

(3) *Furnishing of funds to employer.*—If the amount of the tax in respect of tips reported by the employee to the employer in a written statement furnished pursuant to section 6053(a) exceeds the wages (exclusive of tips) which are under the control of the employer from which the employer is required to withhold the tax in respect of such tips, the employee may furnish to the employer, within the period specified in subparagraph (2) of this paragraph, an amount of money equal to the amount of such excess.

(b) *Less than $20 of tips.*—Notwithstanding the provisions of paragraph (a) of this section, if an employee furnishes to his employer a written statement—

(1) Covering a period of less than one month, and

(2) The statement is furnished to the employer prior to the close of the 10th day of the month following the month in which the tips were actually received by the employee, and

(3) The aggregate amount of tips reported in the statement and in all other statements previously furnished by the employee covering periods within the same month is less than $20, and such statements, collectively, do not cover the entire month,

the employer may deduct amounts equivalent to the tax on such tips from wages (exclusive of tips) which are under the control of the employer or other funds turned over by the employee to the employer. For provisions relating to the repayment to an employee, or other disposition, of amounts deducted from an employee's remuneration in excess of the correct amount of tax, see §31.6413(a)-1. (As to the exclusion from wages of tips of less than $20, see §31.3401(a)(16)-1.)

(c) *Priority of tax collection.*—(1) *In general.*—In the case of a payment of wages (exclusive of tips), the employer shall deduct or cause to be deducted in the following order:

(i) The tax under section 3101 and the tax under section 3402 with respect to such payment of wages.

(ii) Any tax under section 3101 which, at the time of the payment of the wages, the employer is required to collect—

(a) In respect of tips reported by the employee to the employer in a written statement furnished to the employer pursuant to section 6053(a), or

(b) By reason of the employer's election to make collection of the tax under section 3101 in respect of tips on an estimated basis,

but which has not been collected by the employer and which cannot be deducted from funds turned over by the employee to the employer for such purpose. (See §31.3102-3, relating to collection of, and liability for, employee tax on tips.)

(iii) Any tax under section 3402 which, at the time of the payment of the wages, the employer is required to collect—

(a) In respect of tips reported by the employee to the employer in a written statement furnished to the employer pursuant to section 6053(a), or

(b) By reason of the employer's election to make collection of the tax under section 3402 in respect of tips on an estimated basis,

but which has not been collected by the employer and which cannot be deducted from funds turned over by the employee to the employer for such purpose. For provisions relating to the withholding of tax on the basis of average estimated tips, see paragraph (b) of §31.3402(h)(1)-1.

(2) *Examples.*—The application of subparagraph (1) of this paragraph may be illustrated by the following examples (The amounts used in the following examples are intended for illustrative purposes and do not necessarily reflect currently effective rates or amounts.):

Example (1). W is a waiter employed by R restaurant. W's principal remuneration for his services is in the form of tips received from patrons of R; however, he also receives a salary from R of $40 per week, which is paid to him every Friday. W is a member of a labor union which has a contract with R pursuant to which R is to collect dues for the union by withholding from the wages of its employees at the rate of $1 per week. In addition to the taxes required to be withheld under the Internal Revenue Code, W's wages are subject to withholding of a state income tax imposed upon both his regular wage and his tips received and reported to R.

On Monday of a given week W furnishes a written statement to R pursuant to section 6053(a) in which he reports the receipt of $160 in tips. The $40 wage to be paid to W on Friday of the same week is subject to the following items of withholding:

	Taxes with Respect to Regular Wage	Taxes with Respect to Tips	Total
Section 3101 (F.I.C.A.)	$1.76	$7.04	$8.80
Section 3402 (Income Tax at Source)	5.65	28.30	33.95
State Income Tax	1.20	4.80	6.00
Union Dues			1.00
Total			$49.75

W does not turn over any funds to R. R should satisfy the taxes imposed by sections 3101 and 3402 out of W's $40 wage as follows: The taxes imposed with respect to the regular wage (a total of $7.41) should be satisfied first. The taxes imposed with respect to tips are to be withheld only out of "wages (exclusive of tips) which are under the control of the employer" as that phrase is defined in §§31.3102-3(a)(1) and 31.3402(k)-1a(1). The amount of such wages under the control of employer in this example is $31.39, or $40, less the amounts applied in satisfaction of the Federal and state withholding taxes imposed with respect to the regular $40 wage ($8.61). This $31.39 is applied first in satisfaction of the tax under section 3101 with respect to tips ($7.04) and the balance of $24.35 is applied in partial satisfaction of the withholding of income tax at source under section 3402 with respect to tips. The amount of the tax with respect to tips under section 3402 which remains unsatisfied ($3.95) should be withheld from wages under the control of the employer the following week.

Example (2). During the week following the week dealt with in example (1), W furnishes a

Reg. §31.3402(k)-1(c)(2)

written statement to R pursuant to section 6053(a) in which he reports the receipt of $130 in tips. In addition, R receives a notice of garnishment of W's wages issued by the state court, pursuant to which R is required to withhold $10 per week from W's wages for a period of ten weeks. The $40 wage to be paid to W at the end of the week is subject to the following items of withholding:

	Taxes with Respect to Regular Wage	Taxes with Respect to Tips	Total
Section 3101 (F.I.C.A.)	$1.76	$5.72	$7.48
Section 3402 (Income Tax at Source):			
Current week	5.65	22.30	27.95
Carryover from prior week	..	3.95	3.95
State Income Tax	1.20	3.90	5.10
Union Dues			1.00
Garnishment			10.00
Total			$55.48

As in example (1), the amount of "wages (exclusive of tips) which are under the control of the employer" is $31.39. This amount is applied first in satisfaction of the tax under section 3101 with respect to tips ($5.72) and the balance is applied in partial satisfaction of the withholding of income tax at source under section 3402 with respect to tips (a total of $26.25), including that portion of the amount required to be withheld from the prior week's wages which remained unsatisfied. The amount of the tax with respect to tips under section 3402 which remains unsatisfied ($0.58) should be withheld from wages under the control of the employer the following week. [Reg. § 31.3402(k)-1.]

☐ [T.D. 7001, 1-17-69. Amended by T.D. 7053, 7-20-70.]

[Reg. § 31.3402(l)-1]

§ 31.3402(l)-1. Determination and disclosure of marital status.—(a) *Determination of status by employer.*—An employer in computing the tax to be deducted and withheld from an employee's wages paid after April 30, 1966, shall apply the applicable percentage method or wage bracket method withholding table (see section 3402(a), (b), and (c) and the regulations thereunder) for the pertinent payroll period which relates to employees who are single persons, unless there is in effect with respect to such payment of wages a withholding exemption certificate furnished to the employer by the employee after March 15, 1966, indicating that the employee is married in which case the employer shall apply the applicable table relating to employees who are married persons.

(b) *Disclosure of status by employee.*—(1) An employee shall be entitled to furnish the employer with a withholding exemption certificate indicating he is married only if, on the day of such furnishing, he is married (determined by application of the rules in paragraph (c) of this section). Thus, an employee who is contemplating marriage may not, prior to the actual marriage, furnish the employer with a withholding exemption certificate indicating that he is a married person.

(2)(i) If, on any day during the calendar year, the marital status (as determined by application of the rules in paragraph (c) of this section) of an employee who has in effect a withholding exemption certificate indicating that he is a married person, changes from married to single, the employee must within 10 days after the change occurs furnish the employer with a new withholding exemption certificate indicating that the employee is a single person.

(ii) If an employee who has in effect a withholding exemption certificate indicating that he is a married person, is considered married solely because of the application of subparagraph (2)(ii) of paragraph (c) of this section, and his spouse died during the taxable year which precedes by two years the current taxable year, the employee must, on or before December 1 of the current taxable year, furnish the employer with a new withholding exemption certificate indicating that he is a single person. Such certificate shall not, however, become effective until the next calendar year (see paragraph (c) of § 31.3402(f)(3)-1).

(3) If, on any day during the calendar year, the marital status (as determined by application of the rules in paragraph (c) of this section) of an employee who has in effect a withholding exemption certificate indicating that he is a single person changes from single to married, the employee may furnish the employer with a new withholding exemption certificate indicating that the employee is a married person.

(c) *Determination of marital status.*—For the purposes of section 3402(l)(2) and paragraph (b) of this section, the following rules shall be applied in determining whether an employee is a married person or a single person—

(1) An employee shall on any day be considered as a single person if—

(i) He is legally separated from his spouse under a decree of divorce or separate maintenance, or

(ii) Either he or his spouse is, or on any preceding day within the same calendar year was, a nonresident alien.

(2) An employee shall on any day be considered as a married person if—

(i) His spouse (other than a spouse referred to in subparagraph (1) of this paragraph) died within the portion of his taxable year which precedes such day, or

(ii) His spouse died during one of the two taxable years immediately preceding the current taxable year and, on the basis of facts existing at the beginning of such day, he reasonably expects, at the close of his taxable year, to be a surviving spouse as defined in section 2 and the regulations thereunder. [Reg. § 31.3402(l)-1.]

☐ [T.D. 7115, 5-20-71.]

[Reg. § 31.3402(m)-1]

§ 31.3402(m)-1. Withholding allowances.—
(a) *General rule.*—An employee may claim, with respect to wages paid after December 31, 1981, a number of withholding allowances determined in accordance with this section. In order to receive the benefit of such allowances, the employee must have in effect with his employer a withholding exemption certificate claiming such allowances.

(b) *Items that may be taken into account.*—The following items may be taken into account in determining the number of withholding allowances an employee may claim:

(1) Estimated itemized deductions allowable under chapter 1,

(2) The estimated tax credits allowable under subpart A of part IV of subchapter A of chapter 1, except:

(i) For the credit for tax withheld on wages under section 31(a) (relating to wage withholding),

(ii) For the credit for tax withheld at source on nonresident aliens and foreign corporations and on tax-free convenant bonds under section 32,

(iii) That the employee may claim the credit uses of gasoline and special fuels under section 39 only to the extent the employee has not filed for a quarterly tax refund of the credit on Form 843,

(iv) That the employee may claim the credit for earned income under section 43 only to the extent the employee has not filed for advance payments of the credit on Form W-5, and

(v) For the credit for overpayment of tax under section 45,

(3) The estimated trade and business deductions of employees described in section 62(2) and allowed by part VI of subchapter B of chapter 1,

(4) The estimated deduction for payments to pension, profit-sharing, annuity, and bond purchase plans of self-employed individuals described in section 62(7) and allowed by section 404 and section 405(c),

(5) The estimated deduction for penalties forfeited because of premature withdrawal of funds from time savings accounts or deposits described in section 62(12) and allowed by section 165,

(6) The estimated direct charitable deduction under section 170(i),

(7) The estimated deduction for net operating loss carryovers under section 172,

(8) The estimated deduction for alimony, etc., payments under section 215,

(9) The estimated deduction for moving expenses under section 217 but only to the extent that the amount of such deduction is not excluded from the definition of wages by section 3401(a)(15),

(10) The estimated deduction for certain retirement savings under section 219 but only to the extent that the amount of such deduction is not excluded from the definition of wages by section 3401(a)(12)(D),

(11) The estimated deduction for two-earner married couples under section 221,

(12) The estimated net losses from schedules C (Profit or (Loss) From Business or Profession), D (Capital Gains and Losses), E (Supplemental Income Schedule), and F (Farm Income and Expenses) of Form 1040 and from the last line of Part II of Form 4797 (Supplemental Schedule of Gains and Losses),

(13) The estimated amount of decrease of tax due attributable to income averaging under sections 1301 through 1305.

The employee must first use these items ((1) through (13) of this paragraph (b)) to eliminate any payment of estimated tax (as defined in section 6015(d)). Only amounts of these items remaining after the employee has done this may be taken into account in determining the number of withholding allowances the employee may claim.

(c) *Definitions.*—(1) *Estimated.*—The term "estimated" as used in this section to modify the terms "deduction", "deductions", "credits", "losses", and "amount of decrease" means with respect to an employee the aggregate dollar amount of a particular item that the employee reasonably expects will be allowable to him for the estimation year under the section of the Code specified for each item. In no event shall that amount exceed the sum of—

(i) The amount shown for that particular item on the income tax return that the employee has filed for the taxable year preceding the estimation year (or, if such return has not yet been filed, then the income tax return that the employee filed for the taxable year preceding such year), which amount the employee also reasonably expects to show on the income tax return for the estimation year, plus

(ii) The determinable additional amounts for each item for the estimation year.
The determinable additional amounts are amounts that are not included in paragraph (c)(1)(i) of this section and that are demonstrably attributable to identifiable events during the estimation year or the preceding year. Amounts are demonstrably attributable to identifiable events

if they relate to payments already made during the estimation year, to binding obligations to make payments (including the payment of taxes) during the year, and to other transactions or occcurrences, the implementation of which has begun and is verifiable at the time the employee files a withholding exemption certificate claiming withholding allowances relating thereto. The estimation year is the taxable year including the day on which the employee files the withholding exemption certificate with his employer, except that if the employee files the withholding exemption certificate with his employer and specifies on the certificate that the certificate is not to take effect until a specified future date, the estimation year shall be the taxable year including that specified future date. It is not reasonable for an employee to include in his or her withholding computation for the estimation year any amount that is shown for a particular item on the income tax return that the employee has filed for the taxable year preceding the estimation year (or, if such return has not yet been filed, then the income tax return that the employee filed for the taxable year preceding such year) and that has been disallowed by the Service as part of a proposed adjustment described in §601.103(b) (relating to examination and determination of tax liability) and §601.105(b) (relating to examination of returns).

(2) *Amount of decrease of tax due.*—The term "amount of decrease of tax due" as used in paragraph (b)(13) of this section means—

(i) The amount of tax that the taxpayer would owe on his taxable income without using Schedule G (Form 1040), minus

(ii) The amount of tax that the taxpayer would owe on his taxable income using Schedule G (Form 1040).

(d) *Computing allowances.*—(1) The employee shall compute the number of allowances he may claim for the items specified in paragraph (b) of this section in accordance with the tables and instructions on Form W-4.

(2) If the employee—

(i) Pays or accrues amounts demonstrably attributable to identifiable events (as defined in paragraph (c)(1) of this section) that are—

(A) Interest attributable to ownership of real property and deductible under section 163(a), or

(B) Taxes deductible under section 164(a)(1), or

(C) Interest or taxes deductible under section 216(a), and

(ii) Is obligated to pay or accrue such amounts for at least 2 years subsequent to the estimation year,

then the employee may compute the portion of estimated itemized deductions attributable to such amounts for purposes of paragraph (b)(1) of this section by multiplying the total of such amounts to be paid or accrued in the estimation year by 12 and by then dividing that result by

the number of months from the 1st month in the estimation year in which the employee pays or accrues such amounts through the last month of the estimation year. If such amounts decrease during the term of the obligation, the employee must, at the beginning of each subsequent calendar year, recompute the number of allowances being claimed as required by paragraph (c)(1) of this section. If the employee uses the computation described in this subparagraph (2), the employee may not request that his employer withhold on the basis of the employee's cumulative wages as provided in §31.3402(h)(3)-1.

(e) *Examples.*—The application of this section may be illustrated by the following examples:

Example (1). Employee A has an estimated net loss from a partnership of $2,000 which would be reported on Schedule E. Employee A is not required to make any payments of estimated tax. Employee A may take her $2,000 partnership loss into consideration in determining the number of withholding allowances to which she is entitled in accordance with the tables and instructions on Form W-4.

Example (2). Employee B has an estimated net loss from a business of $3,000 which would be reported on Schedule C. Employee B would also otherwise be required to make payments of estimated tax on income of $3,000. Employee B may not take his business loss into consideration in determining the number of withholding allowances to which he is entitled in accordance with the tables and instructions on Form W-4.

Example (3). Employee C has an estimated net loss from a farm of $5,000 which would be reported on Schedule F. Employee C would also otherwise be required to make payments of estimated tax on income of $4,000. Employee C may only take her farm loss into consideration to the extent of $1,000 ($5,000–4,000) in determining the number of withholding allowances to which she is entitled in accordance with the tables and instructions on Form W-4.

(f) *Special rules.*—(1) *Married individuals.*—(i) Except as provided in subdivision (ii) of this subparagraph, a husband and wife shall determine the number of withholding allowances to which they are entitled under section 3402(m) on the basis of their combined wages and allowable items. The withholding allowances to which a husband and wife are entitled may be claimed by the husband, by the wife, or they may be allocated between them. However, they may not both have withholding exemption certificates in effect claiming the same withholding allowance.

(ii) If a husband and wife file separate income tax returns for the taxable year preceding the estimation year and reasonably expect to file separate returns for the estimation year, the husband and wife shall determine the number of withholding exemptions to which they are entitled under section 3402(m) on the basis of their individual wages and allowable items, and they shall be considered to be single for purposes of the tables on Form W-4.

Reg. §31.3402(m)-1(c)(2)

(2) Only one certificate to be in effect.—An employee who is entitled to one or more withholding allowances under section 3402(m) and who has, at the same time, two or more employers, may claim such withholding allowance or allowances with only one of his employers. [Reg. § 31.3402(m)-1.]

☐ *[T.D. 7065, 10-22-70. Amended by T.D. 7915, 9-26-83.]*

[Reg. § 31.3402(n)-1]

§ 31.3402(n)-1. Employees incurring no income tax liability.—(a) *In general.*—Notwithstanding any other provision of this subpart (except to the extent a payment of wages is subject to withholding under § 31.3402(g)-1(a)(2)), an employer shall not deduct and withhold any tax under chapter 24 upon a payment of wages made to an employee, if there is in effect with respect to the payment a withholding exemption certificate furnished to the employer by the employee which certifies that—

(1) The employee incurred no liability for income tax imposed under subtitle A of the Internal Revenue Code for his preceding taxable year; and

(2) The employee anticipates that he will incur no liability for income tax imposed under subtitle A for his current taxable year.

(b) *Mandatory flat rate withholding.*—To the extent wages are subject to income tax withholding under § 31.3402(g)-1(a)(2), such wages are subject to such income tax withholding regardless of whether a withholding exemption certificate under section 3402(n) and the regulations thereunder has been furnished to the employer.

(c) *Rules about withholding exemption certificates.*—For rules relating to invalid withholding exemption certificates, see § 31.3402(f)(2)-1(e), and for rules relating to disregarding certain withholding exemption certificates on which an employee claims a complete exemption from withholding, see § 31.3402(f)(2)-1T(g).

(d) *Examples.*—The following examples illustrate this section:

Example 1. Employee A, an unmarried, calendar-year basis taxpayer, files his income tax return for 2005 on April 10, 2006. A has adjusted gross income of $5,000 and is not liable for any income tax. He had $180 of income tax withheld during 2005. A anticipates that his gross income for 2006 will be approximately the same amount, and that he will not incur income tax liability for that year. On April 20, 2006, A commences employment and furnishes his employer a withholding exemption certificate certifying that he incurred no liability for income tax imposed under subtitle A for 2005, and that he anticipates that he will incur no liability for income tax imposed under subtitle A for 2006. A's employer shall not deduct and withhold on payments of wages made to A on or after April 20, 2006. Under § 31.3402(f)(4)-2(c), unless A furnishes a new withholding exemption certificate certifying

the statements described in paragraph (a) of this section to his employer, his employer is required to deduct and withhold upon payments of wages to A made after February 15, 2007.

Example 2. Assume the facts are the same as in *Example 1* except that A had been employed by his employer prior to April 20, 2006, and had furnished his employer a withholding exemption certificate prior to furnishing the withholding exemption certificate certifying the statements described in paragraph (a) of this section on April 20, 2006. Under section 3402(f)(3)(B)(i), his employer would be required to give effect to the new withholding exemption certificate no later than the beginning of the first payroll period ending (or the first payment of wages made without regard to a payroll period) on or after May 20, 2006. However, under section 3402(f)(3)(B)(ii), his employer could, if it chose, make the new withholding exemption certificate effective with respect to any payment of wages made on or after April 20, 2006, and before the effective date mandated by section 3402(f)(3)(B)(i). Under § 31.3402(f)(4)-2(c), unless A furnishes a new withholding exemption certificate certifying the statements described in § 31.3402(n)-1(a) to his employer, his employer is required to deduct and withhold upon payments of wages to A made after February 15, 2007.

Example 3. Assume the facts are the same as in *Example 1* except that for 2005 A has taxable income of $8,000, income tax liability of $839, and income tax withheld of $1,195. Although A received a refund of $356 due to income tax withholding of $1,195, he may not certify on his withholding exemption certificate that he incurred no liability for income tax imposed by subtitle A for 2005. [Reg. § 31.3402(n)-1.]

☐ *[T.D. 7048, 6-23-70. Amended by T.D. 7423, 6-24-76, T.D. 7577, 12-19-78, T.D. 7598, 3-12-79, T.D. 7682, 3-10-80, T.D. 7772, 3-17-81; T.D. 7803, 1-21-82 and T.D. 9276, 7-24-2006.]*

[Reg. § 31.3402(o)-1]

§ 31.3402(o)-1. Extension of withholding to supplemental unemployment compensation benefits.—(a) *In general.*—Withholding of income tax is required under section 3402(o) with respect to payments of supplemental unemployment compensation benefits made after December 31, 1970, which are treated under paragraph (b)(14) of § 31.3401(a)-1 as if they were wages.

(b) *Withholding exemption certificates.*—For purposes of section 3402(f)(2) and (3) and the regulations thereunder (relating to withholding exemption certificates), in the case of supplemental unemployment compensation benefits an employment relationship shall be considered to commence with either the date on which such benefits begin to accrue or January 1, 1971, whichever is later, and the withholding exemption certificate furnished the employer with respect to such commencement of employment shall be considered the first certificate furnished the employer. The withholding exemption certificate furnished by the employee to his former employer (with whom his employment has been involuntarily terminated, within the meaning of paragraph (b)(14)(ii) of §31.3401(a)-1) shall be treated as meeting the requirements of section 3402(f)(2)(A) and the regulations thereunder if such former employer furnishes such certificate to the employee's current employer, as defined in paragraph (g) of §31.3401(d)-1, or if such former employer is the agent of such current employer with respect to the employee's withholding exemption certificate. However, the preceding sentence shall not be applicable if such employee furnishes a new withholding exemption certificate to such current employer (or his agent), provided that such withholding exemption certificate meets the requirements of section 3402(f)(2)(A) and the regulations thereunder. See the definitions of payroll period in paragraph (c) of §31.3401(b)-1 and of employee in paragraph (g) of §31.3401(c)-1. [Reg. §31.3402(o)-1.]

□ [T.D. 7068, 11-10-70.]

[Reg. §31.3402(o)-2]

§31.3402(o)-2. Extension of withholding to annuity payments if requested by payee.— (a) *In general.*—Under section 3402(o) of the Internal Revenue Code of 1954 and this section, the payee (as defined in paragraph (g)(2) of this section) of an annuity (as defined in paragraph (g)(1) of this section) may request the payor (as defined in paragraph (g)(3) of this section) of the annuity to withhold income tax with respect to payments of the annuity made after December 31, 1970. If such a request is made, the payor shall deduct and withhold as requested.

(b) *Manner of making request.*—A payee who wishes a payor to deduct and withhold income tax from annuity payments shall file a request with the payor to deduct and withhold a specific whole dollar amount from each annuity payment. Such specific dollar amount requested shall be at least $5 per month and shall not reduce the net amount of any annuity payment received by the payee below $10. The request shall be made on Form W-4P (annuitant's withholding exemption certificate and request) in accordance with the instructions applicable thereto, and shall set forth fully and clearly the data therein called for. In lieu of Form W-4P, payers may prepare and use a form the provisions of which are identical with those of Form W-4P. For the requirements relating to Form W-4P with respect to qualified State individual income taxes, see paragraph (d)(3)(i) of §301.6361-1 of this chapter (Regulations on Procedure and Administration).

(c) *When request takes effect.*—Upon receipt of a request under this section the payor of the annuity with respect to which such request was made shall deduct and withhold the amount specified in such request from each annuity payment commencing with the first annuity payment made on or after the date which occurs—

(1) In a case in which no previous request is in effect, three calendar months after the date on which such request is furnished to such payor, and

(2) In a case in which a previous request is in effect, the first status determination date (see section 3402(f)(3)(B) and paragraph (d) of §31.3402(f)(3)-1 of this chapter) which occurs at least 30 days after the date on which such request is so furnished.

However, the payor may, at his election, commence to deduct and withhold such specified amount with respect to an annuity payment which is made prior to the annuity payment described in the preceding sentence with respect to which the payor must commence to deduct and withhold.

(d) *Duration and termination of request.*—A request under this section shall continue in effect until terminated. The payee may terminate the request by furnishing the payor a signed written notice of termination. Such notice of termination shall, except as hereinafter provided, take effect with respect to the first payment of an amount in respect of which the request is in effect which is made on or after the first status determination date (see section 3402(f)(3)(B) and paragraph (d) of §31.3402(f)(3)-1 of this chapter) which occurs at least 30 days after the date on which such notice is so furnished. However, at the election of such payor, such notice may be made effective with respect to any payment of an amount in respect of which the request is in effect which is made on or after the date on which such notice is so furnished and before such status determination date.

(e) *Special rules.*—For purposes of chapter 24 of subtitle C of the Internal Revenue Code of 1954 (relating to collection of income tax at source on wages) and of subtitle F of such Code (relating to procedure and administration), and the regulations thereunder—

(1) An amount which is requested to be withheld pursuant to this section shall be deemed a tax required to be deducted and withheld under section 3402.

(2) An amount deducted and withheld pursuant to this section shall be deemed an amount deducted and withheld under section 3402.

(3) The term "wages" includes the gross amount of an annuity payment with respect to which there is in effect a request for withholding under this section. However, references to the definition of wages in section 3401(a) which are made in section 6014 (relating to election by the taxpayer not to compute the tax on his annual return) and section 6015(a) (relating to declaration of estimated tax by individuals) shall not be deemed to include any portion of such an annuity payment.

(4) The term "employer" includes a payor with respect to whom a request for withholding is in effect under this section.

(5) The term "employee" includes a payee with respect to whom a request for withholding is in effect under this section.

(6) The term "payroll period" includes the period of accrual with respect to which payments of an annuity which is subject to withholding under this section are ordinarily made.

(f) *Returns of income tax withheld and statements for payees.*—(1) Form W-2P is to be used in lieu of Form W-2, which is required to be furnished by an employer to an employee under §31.6051-1 of this chapter and to the Social Security Administration under paragraph (a) of §31.6051-2 of this chapter, with respect to an annuity subject to withholding under this section. If an amount is required to be deducted and withheld under this section from any or all of the payments made to a payee under an annuity contract during a calendar year, all payments with respect to that annuity contract are required to be reported on Form W-2P, in lieu of Form 1099, as prescribed in §§1.6041-1, 1.6041-2, and 1.6047-1 of this chapter; any other annuity payments made by the same payor to the same payee may, at the option of the payor, be reported on Form W-2P.

(2) Each statement on Form W-2P shall show the following:

(i) The gross amount of annuity payments made during the calendar year, whether or not income tax withholding under this section was in effect with respect to all such payments,

(ii) The total amount deducted and withheld as tax under section 3402 of this section, and

(iii) The information required to be shown by Form W-2P and the instructions applicable thereto.

For the requirements relating to Form W-2P with respect to qualified State individual income taxes, see paragraph (d)(3)(ii) of §301.6361-1 of this chapter (Regulations on Procedure and Administration).

(3) The provisions of §1.9101-1 of this chapter (relating to permission to submit information required by certain returns and statements on magnetic tape) shall be applicable to the information required to be furnished on Form W-2P.

(4) The provisions of §31.6109-1 of this chapter (relating to supplying of identifying numbers) shall be applicable to Form W-2P and to any payee of an annuity to whom a statement on Form W-2P is required to be furnished.

(g) *Definitions.*—For purposes of this section—

(1) The term "annuity" means periodic payments which are payable over a period greater than one year and which are treated under section 72 as amounts received as an annuity, whether or not such periodic payments are variable in amount. Also, periodic payments to an individual who is retired before the normal retirement age for reasons of disability, to which the provisions of section 105(d) apply, shall be deemed to be an annuity for purposes of this section. A lump-sum payment (including a total distribution under section 72(n)) is not an annuity.

(2) The term "payee" means an individual who is a citizen or resident of the United States and who receives an annuity payment.

(3) The term "payor" means a person making an annuity payment except that, if the person making the payment is acting solely as an agent for another person, the term "payor" shall mean such other person and not the person actually making the payment. For example, if a bank makes an annuity payment only as agent for an employees' trust, the trust shall be deemed to be the "payor." Notwithstanding the preceding two sentences, any person who, under section 3401(a)(5) or (8), would not be required to deduct and withhold the tax under section 3402 if the annuity payment were remuneration for services shall not be considered a "payor." [Reg. §31.3402(o)-2.]

☐ [*T.D.* 7804, 1-21-82.]

[Reg. §31.3402(o)-3]

§31.3402(o)-3. Extension of withholding to sick pay.—(a) *In general.*—Under section 3402(o) of the Internal Revenue Code of 1954 and this section, the payee (as defined in subparagraph (h)(2) of this section) of sick pay (as defined in subparagraph (h)(1) of this section) may request the payor (as defined in subparagraph (h)(3) of this section) of the sick pay to withhold income tax with respect to payments of sick pay made on or after May 1, 1981. If such a request is made, the payor must deduct and withhold as requested.

(b) *Manner of making request.*—A payee who wishes a payor to deduct and withhold income tax from sick pay shall file a written request with the payor to deduct and withhold a specific whole dollar amount (subject to the limitations of paragraph (c) of this section) from each sick pay payment. The request shall be made on Form W-4S in accordance with the instructions applicable thereto, and shall set forth fully and clearly the data therein called for. In lieu of Form W-4S, payors may prepare and use a form the provisions of which are identical to those of Form W-4S. The payee must include his social security account number in the request.

(c) *Amount requested to be withheld.*—The payee shall request that the payor withhold a specific whole dollar amount. The specific whole dollar amount shall be at least $20 per weekly payment of sick pay. If the payee is paid sick pay computed on a daily basis, the specific whole dollar amount shall be at least $4 per daily payment of sick pay. If the payee is paid sick pay on a biweekly basis, the specific whole dollar amount shall be at least $40 per 2 week payment of sick pay. If the payee is paid sick pay on a semi-monthly basis, the specific whole dollar amount shall be at least $44 per semimonthly payment of sick pay. If the payee is paid sick pay on a monthly basis, the specific whole dollar amount shall be at least $88 per monthly payment of sick pay. If the payee is paid sick pay on a basis other than weekly, daily, biweekly, semimonthly, or monthly, the specific whole dollar amount shall be the equivalent of at least $4 per day, assuming a 5 day work week of 8 hours per day (40 hours total) in each 7 day calendar week. In the case of a payment which is greater or less than a full payment, the amount withheld is to bear the same relation to the specific whole dollar amount requested to be withheld as such payment bears to a full payment. For example, assume an individual receives sick pay of $100 per week and requests that $25 per week be withheld for taxes. After 4 full weeks of absence, the individual returns to work on a Wednesday (having been absent on sick leave Monday and Tuesday). For the week the individual returns to work, the individual would be entitled to $40 of sick pay, $10 of which would be withheld for taxes. The payor may, at his option, permit the payee to request that the payor withhold a specific percentage from each payment. The specific percentage shall be at least 10 percent. If the payor so opts, the payor must also accept requests under the whole dollar method. If the amount requested to be withheld under either the whole dollar method or the optional percentage method reduces the net amount of a sick pay payment received by the payee to below $10, no income tax shall be withheld from that payment by the payor.

(d) *When request takes effect.*—The payor must deduct and withhold the amount specified in the request with respect to payments made more than 7 days after the date on which the request is received by the payor. At the election of the payor, the request may take effect before this deadline.

(e) *Duration and termination of request.*—A request under this section shall continue in effect until changed or terminated. The payee may change the request by filing a new written request that meets all of the requirements of paragraphs (b) and (c) of this section. The new request shall take effect as specified in paragraph (d) of this section and the old request shall be deemed terminated when the new request takes effect. The payee may terminate the request by furnishing the payor a signed written notice of termination containing both a request to terminate withholding and all the information contained in the request to withhold. This written notice of termination shall take effect with respect to payments made more than 7 days after the date on which the notice of termination is received by the payor. At the election of the payor, the request may take effect before this deadline.

(f) *Special rules.*—For purposes of chapter 24 of subtitle C of the Internal Revenue Code of 1954 (relating to collection of income tax at source on wages) and of subtitle F of the Code (relating to procedure and administration), and the regulations thereunder—

(1) An amount which is requested to be withheld pursuant to this section shall be deemed a tax required to be deducted and withheld under section 3402.

(2) An amount deducted and withheld pursuant to this section shall be deemed an amount deducted and withheld under section 3402.

(3) The term "wages" includes the gross amount of a sick pay payment with respect to which there is in effect a request for withholding under this section. However, references to the definition of wages in section 3401(a) which are made in section 6014 (relating to election by the taxpayer not to compute the tax on his annual return) and section 6015(a) (relating to declaration of estimated tax by individuals) shall not be deemed to include any portion of such a sick pay payment.

(4) The term "employer" includes a payor with respect to whom a request for withholding is in effect under this section.

(5) The term "employee" includes a payee with respect to whom a request for withholding is in effect under this section.

(6) The term "payroll period" includes the period of accrual with respect to which payments of sick pay which are subject to withholding under this section are ordinarily made.

(g) *Statements required to be furnished to payees.*—See section 6051(f) and the regulations thereunder for requirements relating to statements required to be furnished to payees.

(h) *Definitions.*—(1)(i) The term "sick pay" means any payment made to an individual which does not constitute wages (determined without regard to section 3402(o) and this section), which is paid to an employee pursuant to a plan to which the employer is a party, and which constitutes remuneration or a payment in lieu of remuneration for any period during which the employee is temporarily absent from work on account of personal injuries or sickness. The term "personal injuries or sickness" shall have the same meaning as ascribed thereto by section 105(a) and the regulations thereunder. The term "sick pay" does not include any amounts either excludable from gross income under section 104(a)(1), (2), (4), or (5) or section 105(b) or (c) or paid under section 3402(o)(1)(B). The term "sick pay" does not include amounts paid under a plan if all amounts paid under the plan are paid to individuals who are described in the first sentence of section 105(d)(4) (relating to the definition of permanent and total disability) and the regulations thereunder. Amounts paid under any other plan shall be deemed to be paid for a period during which the employee is temporarily absent from work. For sick pay paid in 1981 only, however, the payor may opt not to follow the rules of the two preceding sentences but to follow instead the rule that an employee is temporarily absent if his absence is not described in section 105(d)(4) (relating to the definition of permanent and total disability) and the regulations thereunder. An employer is not a party to the plan if the plan is a contract between only employees and a third party payor or the employer makes no contributions to provide sick pay benefits under the plan, even if the employer withholds amounts from the employees' salaries and pays the amounts over to the third party payor.

(ii) This subparagraph (1) may be illustrated by the following examples:

Example (1). Employee A works for P Company and Employee B works for Q Company. P Company has contracted with R Insurance Company for R to pay P's employees the equivalent of their normal wages when they are temporarily absent from work because of sickness or personal injury. Q Company has neither entered into such a contract nor will it make such payments directly from its own funds. B consequently goes to S Insurance Company and purchases directly an insurance policy which will pay him the equivalent of his normal wages when he is unable to work because of sickness or personal injury. Both A and B are subsequently temporarily absent from work on account of sickness or personal injuries. A receives payments from R and B receives payments from S. Neither the payments made by R to A nor the payments made by S to B constitute wages (determined without regard to section 3402(o) and this section). A may request that R withhold income taxes under section 3402(o) and this section from the payments he receives because the payments are sick pay as defined in section 3402(o) and this section. B may not request that S withhold income taxes under section 3402(o) and this section from the payments he receives because the payments are not paid pursuant to a plan to which Q Company is a party and thus are not sick pay as defined in section 3402(o) and this section.

Example (2). Employees C and D both work for T Company, which has contracted with U Insurance Company for U to pay T's employees for all sickness or injury claims. Employee C is sick and out from work for a month. U pays C the equivalent of C's regular pay. Employee D loses his arm in an accident and U pays D $10,000. C may request that U withhold income taxes under section 3402(o) and this section from the payments he receives because the payments constitute remuneration or a payment in lieu of remuneration for any period during which the employee is temporarily absent from work on account of sickness or personal injuries. D may not request that U withhold income taxes from the payments he receives because the payments do not constitute remuneration or a payment in lieu of remuneration for any period during which the employee is temporarily absent from work on account of sickness or personal injuries.

(2) The term "payee" means an individual who is a citizen or resident of the United States and who receives a sick pay payment.

(3)(i) The term "payor" means any person making a sick pay payment who is not the employer (as defined in section 3401 and in §31.3401(d)-1 (except paragraph (f) thereof)) of the payee. If however the person making the payment is acting solely as an agent for another person, the term "payor" shall mean the other person and not the person actually making the payment.

(ii) This subparagraph (3) may be illustrated by the following examples:

Example (1). X Company contracts with Y Insurance Company for Y to pay X's employees the equivalent of their normal wages when they are temporarily absent from work because of sickness or personal injury. Y computes the amount to be paid and determines the date payment is to be made for each of X's employees. Y then instructs Z Bank to issue a check for that amount on that date. Y reimburses Z for the amount of the check plus Z's administrative costs. Under these circumstances, Z is the agent of Y and Y is the payor under section 3402(o) and this section.

Example (2). V Company contracts with W Company for W to pay V's employees the equivalent of their normal wages when they are temporarily absent from work on account of sickness or personal injury. Under the contractual arrangement, V advises W of the wages normally paid to each of V's employees. V tells W when an employee of V is temporarily absent from work on account of sickness or personal injury, and W computes the amount to be paid the employee and makes payments of sick pay to the employee during the period of the employee's absence. V subsequently reimburses W for the amount of those payments and pays W a fee for W's services. Under these circumstances, W is acting solely as the agent of V, and a payee may not request under section 3402(o) and these regulations that W withhold income taxes from his payments. However, see section 3401 and the regulations thereunder for the obligation of V to withhold income taxes from the payments that W makes as the agent of V, which are not excluded from income under section 105 and the regulations thereunder and which are wages under section 3401 and the regulations thereunder. See also §31.3402(g)-1 (relating to supplemental wage payments) for the conditions under which a flat percentage rate of withholding may be used.

Example (3). Assume the same facts as in Example (2), except that the consideratin for W's services is a set insurance premium rather than reimbursement for costs plus a fee. Under these circumstances W is the payor and is not acting solely as the agent of V. An employee of V to whom W makes payments under the agreement may request under section 3402(o) and the regulations thereunder that W withhold income taxes from those payments.

(i) *Special rules for sick pay paid pursuant to certain collective-bargaining agreements.*—(1) Special rules (enumerated in subparagraph (2)) apply to sick pay where all of the following tests are met.

(i) The sick pay must be paid pursuant to a collective-bargaining agreement between employee representatives and one or more employers.

(ii) The agreement must contain a provision that section 3402(o)(5) is to apply to sick pay paid pursuant to the agreement.

(iii) The agreement must contain a provision for determining the amount to be deducted and withheld from each payment of sick pay.

(iv) The social security number of the payee must be furnished to the payor. The agreement may provide that the employer will furnish this or the payee may furnish his social security number directly to the payor.

(v) The payor must be furnished with information that is necessary for the payor to determine whether the payment is pursuant to the agreement and to determine the amount to be deducted and withheld. The agreement may provide that the employer will furnish this information directly to the payor.

(2) The following special rules apply to sick pay where all of the tests of subparagraph (1) are met.

(i) The requirement of section 3402(o)(1)(c) and this section that a request for withholding be in effect does not apply.

(ii) The amount to be deducted and withheld from the sick pay shall be determined according to the provisions of the agreement and not according to this section. This rule shall not however apply—

(A) To payments enumerated in section 3402(n) (relating to employees incurring no income tax liability) and the regulations thereunder, or

(B) To payments made to a payee more than 7 days after the date that the payor receives a statement from the payee that the payee expects to claim an exclusion from gross income under section 105(d). Such statement must include adequate verification of disability. A certificate from a qualified physician attesting that the employee is permanently and totally disabled (within the meaning of section 105(d)) shall be deemed to constitute adequate verification. If the payor receives such a statement, the payor shall not withhold any income tax from the payments made to the payee, regardless of the provisions of the collective bargaining agreement. This exception from withholding does not affect the requirements of § 31.6051-3. [Reg. § 31.3402(o)-3.]

☐ [*T.D. 7813, 3-15-82. Amended by T.D. 7915, 9-26-83.*]

[Reg. § 31.3402(p)-1]

§ 31.3402(p)-1. Voluntary withholding agreements.—(a) *Employer-employee agreement.*—An employee and his employer may enter into an agreement under section 3402(p)(3)(A) to provide for the withholding of income tax upon payments of amounts described in paragraph (b)(1) of § 31.3401(a)-3, made after December 31, 1970. An agreement may be entered into under this section only with respect to amounts which

are includible in the gross income of the employee under section 61, and must be applicable to all such amounts paid by the employer to the employee. The amount to be withheld pursuant to an agreement under section 3402(p)(3)(A) shall be determined under the rules contained in section 3402 and the regulations thereunder. See § 31.3405(c)-1, Q&A-3 concerning agreements to have more than 20-percent Federal income tax withheld from eligible rollover distributions within the meaning of section 402.

(b) *Form and duration of employer-employee agreement.*—(1)(i) Except as provided in subdivision (ii) of this subparagraph, an employee who desires to enter into an agreement under section 3402(p)(3)(A) shall furnish his employer with Form W-4 (withholding exemption certificate) executed in accordance with the provisions of section 3402(f) and the regulations thereunder. The furnishing of such Form W-4 shall constitute a request for withholding.

(ii) In the case of an employee who desires to enter into an agreement under section 3402(p)(3)(A) with his employer, if the employee performs services (in addition to those to be the subject of the agreement) the remuneration for which is subject to mandatory income tax withholding by such employer, or if the employee wishes to specify that the agreement terminate on a specific date, the employee shall furnish the employer with a request for withholding which shall be signed by the employee, and shall contain—

(a) The name, address, and social security number of the employee making the request,

(b) The name and address of the employer,

(c) A statement that the employee desires withholding of Federal income tax, and, if applicable, of qualified State individual income tax (see paragraph (d)(3)(i) of § 301.6361-1 of this chapter (Regulations on Procedure and Administration)), and

(d) If the employee desires that the agreement terminate on a specific date, the date of termination of the agreement.

If accepted by the employer as provided in subdivision (iii) of this subparagraph, the request shall be attached to, and constitute part of, the employee's Form W-4. An employee who furnishes his employer a request for withholding under this subdivision shall also furnish such employer with Form W-4 if such employee does not already have a Form W-4 in effect with such employer.

(iii) No request for withholding under section 3402(p)(3)(A) shall be effective as an agreement between an employer and an employee until the employer accepts the request by commencing to withhold from the amounts with respect to which the request was made.

(2) An agreement under section 3402(p)(3)(A) shall be effective for such period as the employer and employee mutually agree upon. However, either the employer or the em-

ployee may terminate the agreement prior to the end of such period by furnishing a signed written notice to the other. Unless the employer and employee agree on an earlier termination date, the notice shall be effective with respect to the first payment of an amount in respect of which the agreement is in effect which is made on or after the first "status determination date" (January 1, May 1, July 1, and October 1 of each year) that occurs at least 30 days after the date on which the notice is furnished. If the employee executes a new Form W-4, the request upon which an agreement under section 3402(p)(3)(A) is based shall be attached to, and constitute a part of, such new Form W-4.

(c) *Other payments.*—The Secretary may issue guidance by publication in the Internal Revenue Bulletin (IRB) (which will be available at www.IRS.gov) describing other payments for which withholding under a voluntary withholding agreement would be appropriate and authorizing payors to agree to withhold income tax on such payments if requested by the payee. Requirements regarding the form and duration of voluntary withholding agreements authorized by this paragraph (c) will be provided in the IRB guidance issued regarding specific types of payments.

(d) *Effective/applicability date.*—(1) This section applies on and after September 16, 2014. [Reg. §31.3402(p)-1.]

☐ [*T.D. 7096, 3-17-71. Amended by T.D. 7577, 12-19-78; T.D. 8619, 9-15-95 and T.D. 9692, 9-15-2014.*]

[Reg. §31.3402(q)-1]

§31.3402(q)-1. Extension of withholding to certain gambling winnings.—(a) *Withholding obligation.*—(1) *General rule.*—Every person, including the Government of the United States, a State, or a political subdivision thereof, or any instrumentality of any of the foregoing making any payment of "winnings subject to withholding" (defined in paragraph (b) of the section) must deduct and withhold a tax in an amount equal to the product of the third lowest rate of tax applicable under section 1(c) and the payment. The tax must be deducted and withheld upon payment of the winnings by the person making the payment ("payer"). See paragraph (c)(5)(ii) of this section for a special rule relating to the time for making deposits of withheld amounts and filing the return with respect to those amounts. Any person receiving a payment of winnings subject to withholding must furnish the payer a statement as required in paragraph (d) of this section. Payers of winnings subject to withholding must file a return with the Internal Revenue Service and furnish a statement to the payee as required in paragraph (e) of this section. With respect to reporting requirements for certain payments of gambling winnings not subject to withholding, see section 6041 and the regulations thereunder.

(2) *Exceptions.*—The tax imposed under section 3402(q)(1) and this section shall not apply (i)

with respect to a payment of winnings which is made to a nonresident alien individual or foreign corporation under the circumstances described in paragraph (c)(4) of this section or (ii) with respect to a payment of winnings from a slot machine play, or a keno or bingo game.

(b) *Winnings subject to withholding.*—(1) *In general.*—Winnings subject to withholding means any payment from—

(i) A wager placed in a State-conducted lottery (defined in paragraph (c)(2) of this section) but only if the proceeds from the wager exceed $5,000;

(ii) A wager placed in a sweepstakes, wagering pool, or lottery other than a State-conducted lottery but only if the proceeds from the wager exceed $5,000; or

(iii) Any other wagering transaction (as defined in paragraph (c)(3) of this section) but only if the proceeds from the wager:

(A) Exceed $5,000; and

(B) Are at least 300 times as large as the amount of the wager.

(2) *Total proceeds subject to withholding.*—If proceeds from the wager qualify as winnings subject to withholding, then the total proceeds from the wager, and not merely amounts in excess of $5,000, are subject to withholding.

(c) *Definitions; special rules.*—(1) *Rules for determining amount of proceeds from a wager.*—(i) *In general.*—The amount of proceeds from a wager is the amount paid with respect to the wager, less the amount of the wager.

(ii) *Amount of the wager in the case of horse races, dog races, and jai alai.*—In the case of a wagering transaction with respect to horse races, dog races, or jai alai, all wagers placed in a single parimutuel pool and represented on a single ticket are aggregated and treated as a single wager for purposes of determining the amount of the wager. A ticket in the case of horse races, dog races, or jai alai is a written or electronic record that the payee must present to collect proceeds from a wager or wagers.

(iii) *Amount paid with respect to a wager.*— (A) *Identical wagers.*—Amounts paid with respect to identical wagers are treated as paid with respect to a single wager for purposes of calculating the amount of proceeds from a wager. Two or more wagers are identical wagers if winning depends on the occurrence (or non-occurrence) of the same event or events; the wagers are placed with the same payer; and, in the case of horse races, dog races, or jai alai, the wagers are placed in the same parimutuel pool. Wagers may be identical wagers even if the amounts wagered differ as long as the wagers are otherwise treated as identical wagers under this paragraph (c)(1)(iii)(A). Tickets purchased in a lottery generally are not identical wagers, because the designation of each ticket as a winner generally would not be based on the occurrence of the same event, for example, the drawing of a particular number.

(B) *Non-monetary proceeds.*—In determining the amount paid with respect to a wager, proceeds which are not money are taken into account at the fair market value.

(C) *Periodic payments.*—Periodic payments, including installment payments or payments which are to be made periodically for the life of a person, are aggregated for purposes of determining the amount paid with respect to the wager. The aggregate amount of periodic payments to be made for a person's life is based on that person's life expectancy. See §§ 1.72–5 and 1.72–9 of this chapter for rules used in computing the expected return on annuities. For purposes of determining the amount subject to withholding, the first periodic payment must be reduced by the amount of the wager.

(2) *Wager placed in a State-conducted lottery.*—The term "wager placed in a State-conducted lottery" means a wager placed in a lottery conducted by an agency of the State acting under authority of State law provided that the wager is placed with the State agency conducting such lottery or with its authorized employees or agents. This term includes wagers placed in State- conducted lotteries in which the amount of winnings is determined by a parimutuel system.

(3) *Other wagering transaction.*—The term "other wagering transaction" means any wagering transaction other than one in a lottery, sweepstakes, or wagering pool. This term includes a wagering transaction in a parimutuel pool with respect to horse races, dog races, or jai alai.

(4) *Certain payments to nonresident aliens or foreign corporations.*—A payment of winnings that is subject to withholding tax under section 1441(a) (relating to withholding on nonresident aliens) or 1442(a) (relating to withholding on foreign corporations) is not subject to the tax imposed by section 3402(q) and this section when the payee is a foreign person, as determined under the rules of section 1441(a) and the regulations thereunder. A payment is treated as being subject to withholding tax under section 1441(a) or 1442(a) notwithstanding that the rate of such tax is reduced (even to zero) as may be provided by an applicable treaty with another country. However, a reduced or zero rate of withholding of tax must not be applied by the payer in lieu of the rate imposed by sections 1441 and 1442 unless the person receiving the winnings has provided to the payer the documentation required by §1.1441-6 of this chapter to establish entitlement to treaty benefits.

(5) *Gambling winnings treated as payments by employer to employee.*—(i) Except as provided in subdivision (ii), for purposes of sections 3403 and 3404 and the regulations thereunder and for purposes of so much of subtitle F (except section 7205) and the regulations thereunder as relate to chapter 24, payments to any person of winnings subject to withholding under this section shall be treated as if they are wages paid by an employer to an employee.

(ii) Solely for purposes of applying the deposit rules under 6302(c) and the return requirement of section 6011, the withholding from winnings shall be deemed to have been made no earlier than at the time the winner's identity is known to the payer. Thus, for example, winnings from a State-conducted lottery are subject to withholding when actually or constructively paid, whichever is earlier; however, the time for depositing the withheld taxes and filing a return with respect thereto shall be determined by reference to the date on which the winner's identity is known to the State, if such date is later than the date on which the winnings are actively or constructively paid. If a payer's obligation to pay winnings terminates other than by payment, all liabilities and requirements resulting from the requirement that the payer deduct and withhold with respect to such winnings shall also terminate.

(d) *Statement furnished by payee.*—(1) *In general.*—Each person who is making a payment subject to withholding under this section must obtain from the payee a statement described in paragraph (d)(2) of this section.

(2) *Contents of statement.*—Each person who is to receive a payment of winnings subject to withholding under this section must furnish the payer a statement on Form W–2G or 5754 (whichever is applicable) made under the penalties of perjury containing—

(i) The name, address, and taxpayer identification number of the winner accompanied by a declaration that no other person is entitled to any portion of such payment, or

(ii) The name, address, and taxpayer identification number of the payee and of every person entitled to any portion of the payment.

(3) *Multiple payments.*—If more than one payment of winnings subject to withholding is to be made with respect to a single wager, for example in the case of an annuity, the payee is required to furnish the payer a statement with respect to the first payment only, provided that the other payments are taken into account in a return required by paragraph (e) of this section.

(4) *Reliance on statement for identical wagers.*—If the payee furnishes the statement which may be required pursuant to §1.6011–3 of this chapter (regarding the requirement of a statement from payees of certain gambling winnings), indicating that the payee (and any other persons entitled to a portion of the winnings) is entitled to winnings from identical wagers, as defined in paragraph (c)(1)(iii)(A) of this section, and indicating the amount of the winnings, if any, then the payer may rely upon the statement in determining the total amount of proceeds from the wager under paragraph (c)(1) of this section.

(e) *Return of payer.*—(1) *In general.*—Every person making payment of winnings for which a statement is required under paragraph (d) of this section must file a return on Form W–2G at the Internal Revenue Service location designated in the instructions to the form on or before February 28 (March 31 if filed electronically) of the calendar year following the calendar year in which the payment of winnings is made. The return required by this paragraph (e) need not include the statement by the payee required by paragraph (d) of this section and, therefore, need not be signed by the payee, provided the statement is retained by the payer as long as its contents may become material in the administration of any internal revenue law. In addition, the return required by this paragraph (e) need not contain the information required by paragraph (e)(1)(v) of this section provided the information is obtained with respect to the payee and retained by the payer as long as its contents may become material in the administration of any internal revenue law. For payments to more than one winner, a separate Form W–2G, which in no event need be signed by the winner, must be filed with respect to each such winner. Each Form W–2G must contain the following:

(i) The name, address, and taxpayer identification number of the payer;

(ii) The name, address, and taxpayer identification number of the winner;

(iii) The date, amount of the payment, and amount withheld;

(iv) The type of wagering transaction;

(v) Except with respect to winnings from a wager placed in a State-conducted lottery, a general description of the two types of identification (as described in paragraph (e)(2) of this section), one of which must have the payee's photograph on it (except in the case of tribal member identification cards in certain circumstances as described in paragraph (e)(3) of this section), that the payer relied on to verify the payee's name, address, and taxpayer identification number;

(vi) The amount of winnings from identical wagers; and

(vii) Any other information required by the form, instructions, or other applicable guidance published in the Internal Revenue Bulletin.

(2) *Identification.*—The following items are treated as identification for purposes of paragraph (e)(1)(v) of this section—

(i) Government-issued identification (for example, a driver's license, passport, social security card, military identification card, tribal member identification card issued by a federally-recognized Indian tribe, or voter registration card) in the name of the payee; and

(ii) A Form W-9, "Request for Taxpayer Identification Number and Certification," signed by the payee that includes the payee's name, address, taxpayer identification number, and other information required by the form. A Form W-9 is not acceptable for this purpose if the payee has modified the form (other than pursuant to instructions to the form) or if the payee has deleted the jurat or other similar provisions by which the payee certifies or affirms the correctness of the statements contained on the form.

(3) *Special rule for tribal member identification cards.*—A tribal member identification card need not contain the payee's photograph to meet the identification requirement described in paragraph (e)(1)(v) of this section if—

(i) The payee is a member of a federally-recognized Indian tribe;

(ii) The payee presents the payer with a tribal member identification card issued by a federally-recognized Indian tribe stating that the payee is a member of such tribe; and

(iii) The payer is a gaming establishment (as described in § 1.6041-10(b)(2)(iv) of this chapter) owned or licensed (in accordance with 25 U.S.C. 2710) by the tribal government that issued the tribal member identification card referred to in paragraph (e)(3)(ii) of this section.

(4) *Transmittal form.*—Persons making payments of winnings subject to withholding must use Form 1096 to transmit Forms W–2G to the Internal Revenue Service.

(5) *Furnishing a statement to the payee.*—Every payer required to make a return under paragraph (e)(1) of this section must also make and furnish to each payee, with respect to each payment of winnings subject to withholding, a written statement that contains the information that is required to be included on the return under paragraph (e)(1) of this section. The payer must furnish the statement to the payee on or before January 31st of the year following the calendar year in which payment of the winnings subject to withholding is made. The statement will be considered furnished to the payee if it is provided to the payee at the time of payment or if it is mailed to the payee on or before January 31st of the year following the calendar year in which payment was made.

(f) *Examples.*—The provisions of this section may be illustrated by the following examples:

Example (1). A purchases a lottery ticket for $1 in the State W lottery from an authorized agent of State W. On February 1, 1977, the drawing is held and A wins $5,001. Since the proceeds of the wager ($5,001 – $1) are not greater than $5,000, State W is not required to withhold or deduct any amount from A's winnings.

Example (2). Assume the same facts as in example (1) except that A purchases two $1 tickets and that A wins $5,002 when one of the tickets is drawn. State W must deduct and withhold tax at a rate of 20% from $5,001 ($5,002 less the $1 wager), or $1,000.20.

Example (3). C purchases a lottery ticket for $1. On June 1, 1979, the lottery drawing is held and C wins the grand prize of $50,000, payable $500 monthly. The payer must deduct and withhold tax at the rate of 20% from each payment of winnings. Therefore, $99.80 must be withheld from the first monthly payment to B (($500 − $1) × 20% = $99.80) and $100 ($500 × 20%) must be withheld from each monthly payment thereafter.

Example (4). Assume the same facts as in example (3), except that C wins an automobile rather than the grand prize. The fair market value of the automobile on the date on which it is made available to C is $10,001. The payer must deduct and withhold a tax of $2,000 (($10,001 − $1) × 20%). This may be accomplished, for example, if C pays $2,000 to the payer. Alternatively, if the payer, as part of the prize, pays all taxes required to be deducted and withheld, the payer must deduct and withhold tax not only on the fair market value of the automobile less the wager, but also on the taxes it pays that are required to be deducted and withheld. This results in a pyramiding of taxes requiring the use of an algebraic formula. Under this formula, the payer must deduct and withhold a tax of 25 percent of the fair market value of the automobile less the wager ($2,500) and, in addition, the payer must indicate on Form W-2G the amount of such winnings as $12,501 ($10,001 + 25% ($10,001 − $1)).

Example (5). D purchases a ticket for $1 in the State Y lottery from an authorized agent of State Y. On January 1, 1976, a drawing is held and D wins $100 a month for the rest of D's life. It is actuarially determined that, on January 3, 1977, D's life expectancy is 5 years. Based on that determination, the proceeds from the wager paid to D on or after January 3, 1977, will exceed $5,000. Therefore, State Y must deduct and withhold $20 from each monthly payment made on or after January 3, 1977. (None of such payments is reduced by the amount of the wager because the amount of the wager was offset by the first payment of winnings which was made before January 3, 1977.)

Example (6). Assume the same facts as in example (5) except that State Y purchases in its own name, as owner, an annuity of $100 a month for D's life from E Corporation, in order to fund its own obligation to make the payments. Although State Y remains liable for the withholding of tax, E Corporation as paying agent for State Y, making payments directly to D, should deduct and withhold from each monthly payment in the manner described in example (5).

Example (7). E purchases a sweepstakes ticket for $1 in a sweepstakes conducted by W. E purchases the ticket on behalf of himself and on behalf of F and G, who have contributed equal amounts toward the purchase of the ticket and who have agreed to share equally in any prizes won. The ticket which E purchases wins $1,002. Since the proceeds of the wager ($1,002 − $1) are greater than $1,000 W is required to withhold and deduct 20 percent of such proceeds.

Example (8). On February 1, 1977, a drawing is held in the State X lottery in which a winning ticket is selected. The person holding the winning ticket is entitled to proceeds of $100,000 payable either as a lump sum upon demand or $10,000 a year for 10 years. Under State law, the winning ticket must be presented to an author-

ized agent of State X before February 1, 1978. Until the ticket is presented, State X does not know the identity of the winner. On December 1, 1977, H, the winner, presents the winning ticket to an authorized agent of the State X lottery. The winnings are constructively paid to H on February 1, 1977. Since H has the option of receiving the entire proceeds upon demand, State X is required to deduct and withhold $20,000 ($100,000 × 20%) from the proceeds of H's winnings on February 1, 1977; but for purposes of determining the time at which the deposit and inclusion on Form 941 of these taxes is to be made, the withholding shall be deemed to have been made on December 1, 1977.

Example (9). J purchases a subscription to N magazine, at the regular subscription price. All new subscribers are automatically eligible for a special drawing. The drawing is held and J wins $50,000. Since J has not paid any more than the regular subscription price, J has not placed a wager or entered a wagering transaction. Therefore, N is not required to deduct and withhold from J's winnings.

Example 10. (i) B places a $15 bet at the cashier window at the racetrack for horse A to win the fifth race at the racetrack that day. After placing the first bet, B gains confidence in horse A's prospects to win and places an additional $40 bet at the cashier window at the racetrack for horse A to win the fifth race, receiving a second ticket for this second bet. Horse A wins the fifth race, and B wins a total of $5,500 (100 to 1 odds) on those bets. The $15 bet and the $40 bet are identical wagers under paragraph (c)(1)(iii)(A) of this section because winning on both bets depended on the occurrence of the same event and the bets are placed in the same parimutuel pool with the same payer. This is true regardless of the fact that the amount of the wager differs in each case.

(ii) B cashes the tickets at different cashier windows. Pursuant to paragraph (d) of this section and §1.6011-3, B completes a Form W-2G indicating that the amount of winnings is from identical wagers and provides the form to each cashier. The payments by each cashier of $1,500 and $4,000 are less than the $5,000 threshold for withholding, but under paragraph (c)(1)(iii)(A) of this section, identical wagers are treated as paid with respect to a single wager for purposes of determining the proceeds from a wager. The payment is not subject to withholding or reporting because although the proceeds from the wager are $5,445 ($1,500 + $4,000 - $55), the proceeds from the wager are not at least 300 times as great as the amount wagered ($55 x 300 = $16,500).

Example 11. B makes two $1,000 bets in a single "show" pool for the same jai alai game, one bet on Player X to show and one bet on Player Y to show. A show bet is a winning bet if the player comes in first, second, or third in a single game. The bets are placed at the same time at the same cashier window, and B receives a single ticket showing both bets. Player X places second in the game, and Player Y does not place first, second, or third in the game. B wins $8,000 from his bet

Reg. §31.3402(q)-1(f)

on Player X. Because winning on both bets does not depend on the occurrence of the same event, the bets are not identical bets under paragraph (c)(1)(iii)(A) of this section. However, pursuant to the rule in paragraph (c)(1)(ii) of this section, the amount of the wager is the aggregate amount of both wagers ($2,000) because the bets were placed in a single parimutuel pool and reflected on a single ticket. The payment is not subject to withholding or reporting because although the proceeds from the wager are $6,000 ($8,000 - $2,000), the proceeds from the wager are not at least 300 times as great as the amount wagered ($2,000 x 300 = $600,000).

Example 12. B bets a total of $120 on a three-dog exacta box bet ($20 for each one of the six combinations played) at the dog racetrack and receives a single ticket reflecting the bet from the cashier. B wins $5,040 from one of the selected combinations. Pursuant to the rule in paragraph (c)(1)(ii) of this section, the amount of the wager is $120, not $20 for the single winning combination of the six combinations played. The payment is not subject to withholding under section 3402(q) because the proceeds from the wager are $4,920 ($5,040-$120), which is below the section 3402(q) withholding threshold.

Example 13. B makes two $12 Pick 6 bets at the horse racetrack at two different cashier windows and receives two different tickets each representing a single $12 Pick 6 bet. In his two Pick 6 bets, B selects the same horses to win races 1-5 but selects different horses to win race 6. All Pick 6 bets on those races at that racetrack are part of a single parimutuel pool from which Pick 6 winning bets are paid. B wins $5,020 from one of his Pick 6 bets. Pursuant to the rule in paragraph (c)(1)(ii) of this section, the bets are not aggregated for purposes of determining the amount of the wager because the bets are reflected on separate tickets. Assuming that the applicable rate is 25%, the racetrack must deduct and withhold $1,252 (($5,020-$12) x 25%) because the amount of the proceeds of $5,008 ($5,020 - $12) is greater than $5,000 and is at least 300 times as great as the amount wagered ($12 x 300 = $3,600). The racetrack also must report B's winnings on Form W-2G pursuant to paragraph (e) of this section and furnish a copy of the Form W-2G to B.

Example 14. C makes two $50 bets in two different parimutuel pools for the same jai alai game. One bet is an "exacta" in which C bets on player M to win and player N to "place." The other bet is a "trifecta" in which C bets on player M to win, player N to "place," and player O to "show." C wins both bets and is paid $2,000 with respect to the bet in the "exacta" pool and $3,100 with respect to the bet in the "trifecta" pool. Under paragraph (c)(1)(iii)(A) of this section, the bets are not identical bets. Under paragraph (c)(1)(ii) of this section, the bets are not aggregated for purposes of determining the amount of the wager for either payment because they are not wagers in the same parimutuel pool. No section 3402(q) withholding is required on either payment because neither payment separately exceeds the $5,000 withholding threshold.

Example 15. C makes two $100 bets for the same dog to win a particular race. C places one bet at the racetrack and one bet at an off-track betting establishment, but the two pools constitute a single pool. C receives separate tickets for each bet. C wins both bets and is paid $4,000 from the racetrack and $4,000 from the off-track betting establishment. Under paragraph (c)(1)(ii) of this section, the bets are not aggregated for purposes of determining the amount of the wager because the wager placed at the racetrack and the wager placed at the off-track betting establishment are reflected on separate tickets, despite being placed in the same parimutuel pool. No section 3402(q) withholding is required because neither payment separately exceeds the $5,000 withholding threshold.

Example 16. C places a $200 Pick 6 bet for a series of races at the racetrack on a particular day and receives a single ticket for the bet. No wager correctly picks all six races that day, so that portion of the pool carries over to the following day. On the following day, C places an additional $200 Pick 6 bet for that day's series of races and receives a new ticket for that bet. C wins $100,000 on the second day. Pursuant to the rule in paragraph (c)(1)(ii) of this section, the bets are on two separate tickets, so C's two Pick 6 bets are not aggregated for purposes of determining the amount of the wager. Assuming that the applicable rate is 25%, the racetrack must deduct and withhold $24,950 (($100,000 - $200) x 25%) because the amount of the proceeds of $99,800 ($100,000 - $200) is greater than $5,000, and is at least 300 times as great as the amount wagered ($200 x 300 = $60,000). The racetrack also must report C's winnings on Form W-2G pursuant to paragraph (e) of this section and furnish a copy of the Form W-2G to C.

(g) *Applicability date.*—The rules in this section apply to payments made with respect to a winning event that occurs after November 13, 2017. For rules that apply to payments made with respect to a winning event on or before that date, see § 31.3402(q)-1 as contained in 26 CFR part 31, revised April 1, 2017. [Reg. § 31.3402(q)-1.]

☐ *[T.D. 7787, 9-22-81. Amended by T.D. 7919, 10-11-83; T.D. 7943, 2-10-84; T.D. 8895, 8-17-2000 and T.D. 9824, 9-25-2017.]*

[Reg. § 31.3402(r)-1]

§ 31.3402(r)-1. Withholding on distributions of Indian gaming profits to tribal members.—(a)(1) *General rule.*—Section 3402(r)(1) requires every person, including an Indian tribe, making a payment to a member of an Indian tribe from the net revenues of any class II or class III gaming activity, as defined in 25 U.S.C. 2703, conducted or licensed by such tribe to deduct and withhold from such payment a tax in an amount equal to such payment's proportionate share of the annualized tax, as that term is defined in section 3402(r)(3).

(2) *Withholding tables.*—Except as provided in paragraph (a)(4) of this section, the amount of

a payment's proportionate share of the annualized tax shall be determined under the applicable table provided by the Commissioner.

(3) *Annualized amount of payment.*—Section 3402(r)(5) provides that payments shall be placed on an annualized basis under regulations prescribed by the Secretary. A payment may be placed on an annualized basis by multiplying the amount of the payment by the total number of payments to be made in a calendar year. For example, a monthly payment may be annualized by multiplying the amount of the payment by 12. Similarly, a quarterly payment may be annualized by multiplying the amount of the payment by 4.

(4) *Alternate withholding procedures.*—(i) *In general.*—Any procedure for determining the amount to be deducted and withheld under section 3402(r) may be used, provided that the amount of tax deducted and withheld is substantially the same as it would be using the tables provided by the Commissioner under paragraph (a)(2) of this section. At the election of an Indian tribe, the amount to be deducted and withheld under section 3402(r) shall be determined in accordance with this alternate procedure.

(ii) *Method of election.*—It is sufficient for purposes of making an election under this paragraph (a)(4) that an Indian tribe evidence the election in any reasonable way, including use of a particular method. Thus, no written election is required.

(5) *Additional withholding permitted.*—Consistent with the provisions of section 3402(p), a tribal member and a tribe may enter into an agreement to provide for the deduction and withholding of additional amounts from payments in order to satisfy the anticipated tax liability of the tribal member. The agreement may be made in a manner similar to that described in §31.3402(p)-1 (with respect to voluntary withholding agreements between employees and employers).

(b) *Effective date.*—This section applies to payments made after December 31, 1994. [Reg. §31.3402(r)-1.]

☐ *[T.D. 8634, 12-18-95.]*

[Reg. §31.3403-1]

§31.3403-1. Liability for tax.—Every employer required to deduct and withhold the tax under section 3402 from the wages of an employee is liable for the payment of such tax whether or not it is collected from the employee by the employer. If, for example, the employer deducts less than the correct amount of tax, or if he fails to deduct any part of the tax, he is nevertheless liable for the correct amount of the tax. See, however, §31.3402(d)-1. The employer is relieved of liability to any other person for the amount of any such tax withheld and paid to the district director or deposited with a duly designated depositary of the United States. [Reg. §31.3403-1.]

☐ *[T.D. 6259, 10-25-57.]*

[Reg. §31.3404-1]

§31.3404-1. Return and payment by governmental employer.—If the United States, or a State, Territory, Puerto Rico, or a political subdivision thereof, or the District of Columbia, or any agency or instrumentality of any one or more of the foregoing, is an employer required to deduct and withhold tax under chapter 24, the return of the amount deducted and withheld as such tax may be made by the officer or employee having control of the payment of the wages or other officer or employee appropriately designated for that purpose. (For provisions relating to the execution and filing of returns, see Subpart G of the regulations in this part.) [Reg. §31.3404-1.]

☐ *[T.D. 6259, 10-25-57.]*

[Reg. §31.3405(c)-1]

§31.3405(c)-1. Withholding on eligible rollover distributions; questions and answers.—The following questions and answers relate to withholding on eligible rollover distributions under section 3405(c) of the Internal Revenue Code of 1986, as added by section 522(b) of the Unemployment Compensation Amendments of 1992 (Public Law 102-318, 106 Stat. 290) (UCA). For additional UCA guidance under sections 401(a)(31), 402(c), 402(f), and 403(b)(8) and (10), see §§1.401(a)(31)-1, 1.402(c)-2, 1.402(f)-1, and 1.403(b)-2 of this chapter, respectively.

LIST OF QUESTIONS

Q-1: What are the withholding requirements under section 3405 for distributions from qualified plans and section 403(b) annuities?

Q-2: May a distributee elect under section 3405(c) not to have Federal income tax withheld from an eligible rollover distribution?

Q-3: May a distributee be permitted to elect to have more than 20-percent Federal income tax withheld from an eligible rollover distribution?

Q-4: Who has responsibility for complying with section 3405(c) relating to the 20-percent income tax withholding on eligible rollover distributions?

Q-5: May the plan administrator shift the withholding responsibility to the payor and, if so, how?

Q-6: How does the 20-percent withholding requirement under section 3405(c) apply if a distributee elects to have a portion of an eligible rollover distribution paid to an eligible retirement plan in a direct rollover and to have the remainder of that distribution paid to the distributee?

Q-7: Will the plan administrator be subject to liability for tax, interest, or penalties for failure to withhold 20 percent from an eligible rollover distribution that, because of erroneous information provided by a distributee, is not paid to an eligible retirement plan even though the distributee elected a direct rollover?

Q-8: Is an eligible rollover distribution that is paid to a qualified defined benefit plan subject to 20-percent withholding?

Q-9: If property other than cash, employer securities, or plan loans is distributed, how is the 20-percent income tax withholding required under section 3405(c) accomplished?

Q-10: What assumptions may a plan administrator make regarding whether a benefit is an eligible rollover distribution for purposes of determining the amount of a distribution that is subject to 20-percent mandatory withholding?

Q-11: Are there special rules for applying the 20-percent withholding requirement to employer securities and a plan loan offset amount distributed in an eligible rollover distribution?

Q-12: How does the mandatory withholding rule apply to net unrealized appreciation from employer securities?

Q-13: Does the 20-percent withholding requirement apply to eligible rollover distributions from a qualified plan distributed annuity contract?

Q-14: Must a payor or plan administrator withhold tax from an eligible rollover distribution for which a direct rollover election was not made if the amount of the distribution is less than $200?

Q-15: If eligible rollover distributions are made from a qualified plan, who has responsibility for making the returns and reports required under these regulations?

Q-16: What eligible rollover distributions must be reported on Form 1099-R?

Q-17: Must the plan administrator, trustee or custodian of the eligible retirement plan report amounts received in a direct rollover?

QUESTIONS AND ANSWERS

Q-1: What are the withholding requirements under section 3405 for distributions from qualified plans and section 403(b) annuities?

A-1: (a) *General rule.* Section 3405(c), added by UCA, provides that any designated distribution that is an eligible rollover distribution (as defined in section 402(f)(2)(A)) from a qualified plan or a section 403(b) annuity is subject to income tax withholding at the rate of 20 percent unless the distributee of the eligible rollover distribution elects to have the distribution paid directly to an eligible retirement plan in a direct rollover. See § 1.402(c)-2, Q&A-2 of this chapter for the definition of a qualified plan and § 1.403(b)-7(b) of this chapter for the definition of a section 403(b) annuity. For purposes of section 3405 and this section, with respect to a distribution from a qualified plan, an eligible retirement plan is a trust qualified under section 401(a), an annuity plan described in section 403(a), or an individual retirement plan (as described in § 1.402(c)-2, Q&A-2 of this chapter). For purposes of section 3405 and this section, with respect to a distribution from a section 403(b) annuity, an eligible retirement plan is an annuity contract, a custodial account, a retirement income account described in section 403(b), or an individual retirement plan. If a designated distribution is not an eligible rollover distribution, it is subject to the elective withholding provisions of section 3405(a) and (b) and § 35.3405-1 of this

chapter and is not subject to the mandatory withholding provisions of section 3405(c) and this section.

(b) *Application of other statutory provisions.* See § 1.401(a)(31)-1 of this chapter concerning the requirements and the procedures for electing a direct rollover under section 401(a)(31). See section 402(c)(2) and (4), and § 1.402(c)-2, Q&A-3 through Q&A-10 and Q&A-14 of this chapter for rules to determine what constitutes an eligible rollover distribution. See § 1.402(f)-1, Q&A-1 through Q&A-3 and § 1.403(b)-7(b) of this chapter concerning the notice that must be provided to a distributee, within a reasonable period of time before making an eligible rollover distribution. See § 1.403(b)-7(b) of this chapter for guidance concerning the rollover provisions and direct rollover requirements for distributions from annuities described in section 403(b).

(c) *Effective date*—(1) *Statutory effective date*—(i) *General rule.* Section 3405(c), as added by UCA, applies to eligible rollover distributions made on or after January 1, 1993, even if the employee's employment with the employer maintaining the plan terminated before January 1, 1993 and even if the eligible rollover distribution is part of a series of payments that began before January 1, 1993.

(ii) *Special rule for governmental section 403(b) annuities.* Section 522 of UCA provides a special effective date for governmental section 403(b) annuities. This special effective date appears in § 1.403(b)-2T of this chapter (as it appeared in the April 1, 1995 edition of 26 CFR part 1).

(2) *Regulatory effective date.* This section applies to eligible rollover distributions made on or after October 19, 1995. For eligible rollover distributions made on or after January 1, 1993 and before October 19, 1995, § 31.3405(c)-1T (as it appeared in the April 1, 1995 edition of 26 CFR part 1), applies. However, for any distribution made on or after January 1, 1993 but before October 19, 1995, a plan administrator or payor may comply with the withholding requirements of section 3405(c) by substituting any or all provisions of this section for the corresponding provisions of § 31.3405(c)-1T, if any.

Q-2: May a distributee elect under section 3405(c) not to have Federal income tax withheld from an eligible rollover distribution?

A-2: No. The 20-percent income tax withholding imposed under section 3405(c)(1) applies to an eligible rollover distribution unless the distributee elects under section 401(a)(31) to have the eligible rollover distribution paid directly to an eligible retirement plan in a direct rollover. See § 1.401(a)(31)-1 and § 1.403(b)-7(b) of this chapter for provisions concerning the requirement that a distributee of an eligible rollover distribution be permitted to elect a distribution in the form of a direct rollover.

Q-3: May a distributee be permitted to elect to have more than 20-percent Federal income tax withheld from an eligible rollover distribution?

A-3: Yes. Under section 3402(p), a distributee of an eligible rollover distribution and the plan administrator or payor are permitted to enter into an agreement to provide for withholding in excess of 20 percent from an eligible rollover distribution. Any agreement must be made in accordance with applicable forms and instructions. However, no request for withholding will be effective between the plan administrator or payor and the distributee until the plan administrator or payor accepts the request by commencing to withhold from the amounts with respect to which the request was made. An agreement under section 3402(p) shall be effective for such period as the plan administrator or payor and the distributee mutually agree upon. However, either party to the agreement may terminate the agreement prior to the end of such period by furnishing a signed written notice to the other.

Q-4: Who has responsibility for complying with section 3405(c) relating to the 20-percent income tax withholding on eligible rollover distributions?

A-4: Section 3405(d) generally requires the plan administrator of a qualified plan and the payor of a section 403(b) annuity to withhold under section 3405(c)(1) an amount equal to 20 percent of the portion of an eligible rollover distribution that the distributee does not elect to have paid in a direct rollover. When an amount is paid under a qualified plan distributed annuity contract as defined in § 1.402(c)-2, Q&A-10 of this chapter, the payor is treated as the plan administrator. See Q&A-13 of this section concerning eligible rollover distributions from a qualified plan distributed annuity contract.

Q-5: May the plan administrator shift the withholding responsibility to the payor and, if so, how?

A-5: Yes. The plan administrator may shift the withholding responsibility to the payor by following the procedures set forth in § 35.3405-1, Q&A E-2 through E-5 of this chapter (relating to elective withholding on pensions, annuities and certain other deferred income) with appropriate adjustments, including the plan administrator's identification of amounts that constitute required minimum distributions.

Q-6: How does the 20-percent withholding requirement under section 3405(c) apply if a distributee elects to have a portion of an eligible rollover distribution paid to an eligible retirement plan in a direct rollover and to have the remainder of that distribution paid to the distributee?

A-6: If a distributee elects to have a portion of an eligible rollover distribution paid to an eligible retirement plan in a direct rollover and to receive the remainder of the distribution, the 20-percent withholding requirement under section 3405(c) applies only to the portion of the eligible rollover distribution that the distributee receives and not to the portion that is paid in a direct rollover.

Q-7: Will the plan administrator be subject to liability for tax, interest, or penalties for failure to withhold 20 percent from an eligible rollover distribution that, because of erroneous informa-tion provided by a distributee, is not paid to an eligible retirement plan even though the distributee elected a direct rollover?

A-7: (a) *General rule.* If the plan administrator reasonably relied on adequate information provided by the distributee (as described in paragraph (b) of this Q&A), the plan administrator will not be subject to liability for taxes, interest, or penalties for failure to withhold income tax from an eligible rollover distribution solely because the distribution is paid to an account or plan that is not an eligible retirement plan (as defined, with respect to distributions from qualified plans, in section 402(c)(8)(B) and § 1.402(c)-2, Q&A-2 of this chapter and, with respect to distributions from section 403(b) annuities, in § 1.403(b)-7(b) of this chapter. Although the plan administrator is not required to verify independently the accuracy of information provided by the distributee, the plan administrator's reliance on the information furnished must be reasonable. For example, it is not reasonable for the plan administrator to rely on information that is clearly erroneous on its face.

(b) *Adequate information.* The plan administrator has obtained from the distributee adequate information on which to rely in making a direct rollover if the distributee furnishes to the plan administrator: the name of the eligible retirement plan; a representation that the recipient plan is an individual retirement plan, a qualified plan, or a section 403(b) annuity, as appropriate; and any other information that is necessary in order to permit the plan administrator to accomplish the direct rollover by the means it has selected. This information must include any information needed to comply with the specific requirements of § 1.401(a)(31)-1, Q&A-3 and Q&A-4 of this chapter. For example, if the direct rollover is to be made by mailing a check to the trustee of an individual retirement account, the plan administrator must obtain, in addition to the name of the individual retirement account and the representation described above, the name and address of the trustee of the individual retirement account.

Q-8: Is an eligible rollover distribution that is paid to a qualified defined benefit plan subject to 20-percent withholding?

A-8: No. If an eligible rollover distribution is paid in a direct rollover to an eligible retirement plan within the meaning of section 402(c)(8), including a qualified defined benefit plan, it is reasonable to believe that the distribution is not includible in gross income pursuant to section 402(c)(1). Accordingly, pursuant to section 3405(e)(1)(B), the distribution is not a designated distribution and is not subject to 20-percent withholding.

Q-9: If property other than cash, employer securities, or plan loans is distributed, how is the 20-percent income tax withholding required under section 3405(c) accomplished?

A-9: When all or a portion of an eligible rollover distribution subject to 20-percent income tax withholding under section 3405(c) consists of property other than cash, employer securities, or plan loan offset amounts, the plan administrator or payor must apply § 35.3405-1, Q&A F-2 of this chapter and may apply § 35.3405-1, Q&A F-3 of this chapter in determining how to satisfy the withholding requirements.

Q-10: What assumptions may a plan administrator make regarding whether a benefit is an eligible rollover distribution for purposes of determining the amount of a distribution that is subject to 20-percent mandatory withholding?

A-10: (a) *In general*. For purposes of determining the amount of a distribution that is subject to 20-percent mandatory withholding, a plan administrator may make the assumptions described in paragraphs (b), (c), and (d) of this Q&A in determining the amount of a distribution that is an eligible rollover distribution and a designated distribution. Section 1.401(a)(31)-1, Q&A-18 of this chapter provides assumptions for purposes of complying with section 401(a)(31). See § 1.402(c)-2, Q&A-15 of this chapter concerning the effect of these assumptions for purposes of section 402(c).

(b) *$5,000 death benefit*. A plan administrator may assume that a distribution that qualifies for the $5,000 death benefit exclusion under section 101(b) is the only death benefit being paid with respect to a deceased employee that qualifies for that exclusion. Thus, in such a case, the plan administrator may assume that the distribution is not an eligible rollover distribution to the extent that it would be excludible from gross income based on this assumption.

(c) *Required minimum distributions*. The plan administrator is permitted to determine the amount of the minimum distribution required to satisfy section 401(a)(9)(A) for any calendar year by assuming that there is no designated beneficiary.

(d) *Valuation of property*. In the case of a distribution that includes property, in calculating the amount of the distribution for purposes of applying section 3405(c), the value of the property may be determined in accordance with § 35.3405-1, Q&A F-1 of this chapter.

Q-11: Are there special rules for applying the 20-percent withholding requirement to employer securities and a plan loan offset amount distributed in an eligible rollover distribution?

A-11: Yes. The maximum amount to be withheld on any designated distribution (including any eligible rollover distribution) under section 3405(c) must not exceed the sum of the cash and the fair market value of property (excluding employer securities) received in the distribution. The amount of the sum is determined without regard to whether any portion of the cash or property is a designated distribution or an eligible rollover distribution. For purposes of this rule, any plan loan offset amount, as defined in § 1.402(c)-2, Q&A-9 of this chapter, is treated in the same manner as employer securities. Thus, although employer securities and plan loan offset amounts must be included in the amount that is multiplied by 20-percent, the total amount required to be withheld for an eligible rollover

distribution is limited to the sum of the cash and the fair market value of property received by the distributee, excluding any amount of the distribution that is a plan loan offset amount or that is distributed in the form of employer securities. For example, if the only portion of an eligible rollover distribution that is not paid in a direct rollover consists of employer securities or a plan loan offset amount, withholding is not required. In addition, if a distribution consists solely of employer securities and cash (not in excess of $200) in lieu of fractional shares, no amount is required to be withheld as income tax from the distribution under section 3405 (including section 3405(c) and this section). For purposes of section 3405 and this section, employer securities means securities of the employer corporation within the meaning of section 402(e)(4)(E)(ii).

Q-12: How does the mandatory withholding rule apply to net unrealized appreciation from employer securities?

A-12: An eligible rollover distribution can include net unrealized appreciation from employer securities, within the meaning of section 402(e)(4), even if the net unrealized appreciation is excluded from gross income under section 402(e)(4). However, to the extent that it is excludible from gross income pursuant to section 402(e)(4), net unrealized appreciation is not a designated distribution pursuant to section 3405(e)(1)(B) because it is reasonable to believe that it is not includible in gross income. Thus, to the extent that net unrealized appreciation is excludible from gross income pursuant to section 402(e)(4), net unrealized appreciation is not included in the amount of an eligible rollover distribution that is subject to 20-percent withholding.

Q-13: Does the 20-percent withholding requirement apply to eligible rollover distributions from a qualified plan distributed annuity contract?

A-13: The 20-percent withholding requirement applies to eligible rollover distributions from a qualified plan distributed annuity contract as defined in Q&A-10 of § 1.402(c)-2 of this chapter. In the case of an eligible rollover distribution from such an annuity contract, the payor is treated as the plan administrator for purposes of section 3405. See § 1.401(a)(31)-1, Q&A-17 of this chapter concerning the direct rollover requirements that apply to distributions from such an annuity contract and see § 1.402(c)-2, Q&A-10 of this chapter concerning the treatment of distributions from such annuity contracts as eligible rollover distributions.

Q-14: Must a payor or plan administrator withhold tax from an eligible rollover distribution for which a direct rollover election was not made if the amount of the distribution is less than $200?

A-14: No. However, all eligible rollover distributions received within one taxable year of the distributee under the same plan must be aggregated for purposes of determining whether the $200 floor is reached. If the plan administrator or

Reg. §31.3405(c)-1

payor does not know at the time of the first distribution (that is less than $200) whether there will be additional eligible rollover distributions during the year for which aggregation is required, the plan administrator need not withhold from the first distribution. If distributions are made within one taxable year under more than one plan of an employer, the plan administrator or payor may, but need not, aggregate distributions for purposes of determining whether the $200 floor is reached. However, once the $200 threshold has been reached, the sum of all payments during the year must be used to determine the applicable amount to be withheld from subsequent payments during the year.

Q-15: If eligible rollover distributions are made from a qualified plan, who has responsibility for making the returns and reports required under these regulations?

A-15: Generally, the plan administrator, as defined in section 414(g), is responsible for maintaining the records and making the required reports with respect to eligible rollover distributions from qualified plans. However, if the plan administrator fails to keep the required records and make the required reports, the employer maintaining the plan is responsible for the reports and returns.

Q-16: What eligible rollover distributions must be reported on Form 1099-R?

A-16: Each eligible rollover distribution, including each eligible rollover distribution that is paid directly to an eligible retirement plan in a direct rollover, must be reported on Form 1099-R in accordance with the instructions for Form 1099-R. For purposes of the reporting required under section 6047(e), a direct rollover is treated as a distribution that is immediately rolled over to an eligible retirement plan. Distributions that are not eligible rollover distributions are subject to the reporting requirements set forth in § 35.3405-1 of this chapter and applicable forms and instructions.

Q-17: Must the plan administrator, trustee or custodian of the eligible retirement plan report amounts received in a direct rollover?

A-17: (a) *Individual retirement plan.* If a distributee elects to have an eligible rollover distribution paid to an individual retirement plan in a direct rollover, the eligible rollover distribution is reported on Form 5498 as a rollover contribution to the individual retirement plan, in accordance with the instructions for Form 5498.

(b) *Qualified plan or section 403(b) annuity.* If a distributee elects to have an eligible rollover distribution paid to a qualified plan or section 403(b) annuity, the recipient plan or annuity is not required to report the receipt of the rollover contribution.

[Reg. § 31.3405(c)-1.]

☐ [T.D. 8619, 9-15-95. *Amended by T.D. 8880,* 4-20-2000 *and T.D. 9340, 7-23-2007.*]

[Reg. § 35.3405-1]

§ 35.3405-1. Questions and answers relating to withholding on pensions, annuities, and certain other deferred income.—The following questions and answers relate to withholding on pensions, annuities, and other deferred income under section 3405 of the Internal Revenue Code of 1986, as added by section 334 of the Tax Equity and Fiscal Responsibility Tax Act of 1982 (Public Law 97-248) (TEFRA).

a-1 through d-34 [Reserved]. For further guidance, see § 35.3405-1T.

d-35. Q. *Through what medium may a payor provide the notice required under section 3405 to a payee?*

A. A payor may provide the notice required under section 3405 (including the abbreviated notice described in d-27 of § 35.3405-1T and the annual notice described in d-31 of § 35.3405-1T) to a payee on a written paper document. However, see § 1.401(a)-21 of this chapter for rules permitting the use of electronic media to provide applicable notices to recipients with respect to retirement plans and individual retirement plans.

[Reg. § 35.3405-1.]

☐ [T.D. 8873, 2-7-2000 (*corrected* 3-30-2000) *and* T.D. 9294, 10-19-2006.]

[Reg. § 35.3405-1T]

§ 35.3405-1T. Questions and answers relating to withholding on pensions, annuities, and certain other deferred income (temporary).—The following questions and answers relate to withholding on pensions, annuities, and other deferred income under section 3405 of the Internal Revenue Code of 1954, as added by section 334 of the Tax Equity and Fiscal Responsibility Act of 1982 (P.L. 97-248) (TEFRA):

TABLE OF CONTENTS
A. In general.
B. Periodic payments.
C. Nonperiodic distributions.
D. Notice and election procedures.
E. Reporting and recordkeeping.

A. In general.
A-1. Q. How did TEFRA change the law on withholding requirements for pensions, annuities, and other deferred income?

A. TEFRA amended the Internal Revenue Code to impose withholding requirements on designated distributions paid after December 31, 1982. Further, although under prior law individuals could elect to have Federal income tax withheld from certain pension and annuity payments, TEFRA requires withholding on all designated distributions unless the payee elects not to have withholding apply.

A-2. Q. What type of payment is a designated distribution that is subject to the new withhholding rules?

A. A designated distribution is any distribution or payment from or under an employer deferred compensation plan, an individual retirement plan (as defined in section 7701(a)(37)), or a commercial annuity. However, a designated distribution does not include any portion of a distribution which it is reasonable to believe is not includible in the gross income of the payee. For rules concerning when it is reasonable to believe that all or part of a distribution is not includible in the gross income of the recipient, see questions A-24 through A-33. In addition, a payment or distribution that is treated as wages under section 3401(a) is not a designated distribution subject to the new withholding rules. For examples of these payments, see questions A-18 through A-23.

A-3. Q. What is an employer deferred compensation plan for purposes of the new withholding rules?

A. An employer deferred compensation plan is any pension, annuity, profit-sharing, stock bonus, or other plan that defers the receipt of compensation.

A-4. Q. What is a commercial annuity for purposes of the new withholding rules?

A. A commercial annuity is an annuity, endowment, or life insurance contract issued by an insurance company licensed to do business under the laws of any State. See, also, question F-21.

A-5. Q. When does the new law take effect?

A. In general, withholding is required on any designated distribution made after December 31, 1982. In the case of periodic payments beginning before January 1, 1983, the first payment after December 31, 1982 is treated as the first periodic payment for purposes of the withholding requirements. The Secretary has authority to delay (but not beyond June 30, 1983) the application of these withholding provisions to any payor if the payor can establish that it is impossible to comply with these provisions without undue hardship. Additionally, no penalty will be imposed for failure to withhold on periodic payments if the failure occurs before July 1, 1983, and if a good faith attempt is made to comply.

Procedures for requesting a delay in implementation of the withholding provisions are under consideration.

A-6. Q. What effect does the new law have on the old law provisions relating to withholding of tax from annuity payments by request?

A. If payment is part of a designated distribution, the rules of section 3402(o) (relating to voluntary withholding on certain payments) do not apply. Therefore, a payee receiving amounts that are subject to withholding under the new provisions described in this regulation may not choose to use the voluntary withholding system of section 3402(o) with respect to those amounts. Also, if a payee had a fixed amount withheld by request, a different amount will probably be withheld when the new provisions take effect unless the rule provided in question A-7 applies. However, section 3402(o) will continue to apply to annuity payments that are not designated distributions, to sick pay, and to supplemental unemployment benefits.

A-7. Q. If a recipient of a pension or annuity has previously elected voluntary withholding under section 3402(o), is the Form W-4P effective for withholding on payments after December 31, 1982?

A. Yes, if the plan administrator or payor wishes to honor it; the Form W-4P can be treated by the plan administrator or payor as an election to withhold the flat dollar amount specified on the form if the payee is notified of his right to elect out of withholding and if he is notified that his previously filed W-4P will remain effective unless he elects out of withholding or files a new withholding certificate. If these requirements are met the plan administrator or payor may treat the Form W-4P as a voluntary withholding agreement under section 3402(p). See, also, section 3402(i). These amounts withheld should be reported in the same manner as amounts withheld under section 3405.

A-8. Q. What amount of Federal income tax will be withheld from designated distributions?

A. The amount to be withheld by any payor (or, in certain cases, a plan administrator) depends upon whether the payment is a periodic payment, a nonperiodic distribution other than a qualified total distribution, or a qualified total distribution. However, the maximum amount to be withheld cannot exceed the sum of the amount of money and the fair market value of property (other than employer securities as defined in section 402(a)(3)) received in the distribution.

A-9. Q. What is a periodic payment?

A. A periodic payment is an annuity or similar periodic payment whether paid by a licensed life insurance company, a financial institution, or a plan. The term "annuity" means a series of payments payable over a period greater than one year and taxable under section 72 as amounts received as an annuity, whether or not the payments are variable in amount.

A-10. Q. How will Federal income tax be withheld from a periodic payment?

A. In the case of a periodic payment, amounts are withheld as if the payment were a payment of wages by an employer to the employee for the appropriate payroll period. If the payee has not filed a withholding certificate, the amount to be withheld is calculated by treating the payee as a married individual claiming three withholding allowances.

For additional questions and answers concerning periodic payments, see part B.

A-11. Q. How will Federal income tax be withheld from a "qualified total distribution?"

A. A "qualified total distribution" means any designated distribution which it is reasonable to believe is made within one taxable year of the payee, is made from or under a qualified plan described in section 401(a) or section 403(a), and consists of the balance to the credit of the employee under the plans. For additional questions and answers concerning qualified total distributions, see part C. The amount to be withheld on qualified total distributions will be determined

Reg. § 35.3405-1T

under tables prescribed by the Secretary that approximate the tax that would be imposed under section 402(e) if the payee elected to treat the distribution as a lump sum distribution within the meaning of section 402(e)(4)(A). See, in this respect, question C-8.

A-12. Q. What amount of Federal income tax will be withheld from a designated distribution that is not a periodic payment or a qualified total distribution?

A. If a designated distribution is not a periodic payment or a qualified total distribution, the amount to be withheld is computed by multiplying the amount of the designated distribution by 10 percent.

A-13. Q. Who must withhold?

A. Generally, the payor of a designated distribution must withhold, and is liable for payment of, the tax required to be withheld. However, in the case of a distribution from a plan described in section 401(a) (relating to pension, profit-sharing, and stock bonus plans), section 403(a) (relating to certain annuity plans), or section 301(d) of the Tax Reduction Act of 1975 (relating to certain employee stock ownership plans, sometimes called "TRASOP's"), the plan administrator must withhold, and is liable for payment of, the withheld tax unless he directs the payor to withhold the tax and furnishes the payor with any information that may be required by the Secretary in forms or regulations. This provision applies to qualified plans as well as once qualified plans that are no longer qualified. For a description of the material that the plan administrator must furnish to the payor, see question E-3.

A-14. Q. Who is a plan administrator?

A. Under section 414(g), the plan administrator is the person specifically designated as the plan administrator by the terms of the plan or trust. If the plan or trust does not specifically designate the plan administrator (as provided in section 1.414(g)-1(a) of the Income Tax Regulations), then the plan administrator is generally determined as follows:

(1) In the case of a plan maintained by a single employer, the employer is the plan administrator.

(2) In the case of a plan maintained by two or more employers or jointly by one or more employers and one or more employee organizations, the association, committee, joint board of trustees, or other similar group of representatives who maintain the plan is the plan administrator.

(3) In the case in which (1) or (2) does not apply, the person actually responsible for the control, disposition, or management of the assets is the plan administrator.

A-15. Q. If a bank trustee, regulated investment company, or insurance company makes a periodic payment to a payee solely at the direction of an employer sponsored individual retirement account (IRA), is the bank trustee, regulated investment company or insurance company a payor subject to the pension withholding provisions?

A. Yes. The term "payor" generally means the person actually paying the annuity or other payment (even if the person is acting as an agent). Because this is not a payment from a plan described in section 401(a) or 403(a), responsibility for withholding is on the bank trustee, regulated investment company, or insurance company and not on the employer who sponsors the account.

A-16. Q. If a bank trustee transfers plan funds to the employer who sponsors a plan described in section 410(a) and the employer makes the designated distributions, is the employer a payor?

A. Yes. The employer is a payor because it acts as an agent for the bank trustee. Even though the plan administrator has transferred liability to the bank trustee under section 3405(c)(2), the transfer of funds to the employer does not relieve the bank trustee of its liability for withholding because the rule on transfer of liability only applies to plan administrators. Therefore, if the employer fails to withhold on designated distributions, either the employer or the bank trustee may be liable for failure to withhold. Note, however, that the plan administrator could transfer liability for withholding to the employer as payor under section 3405(c)(2). See, in this respect, questions E-2 and E-3.

A-17. Q. Do the withholding provisions apply to annuities paid from an employer deferred compensation plan, an individual retirement plan, or a commercial annuity to the surviving spouse or other beneficiary or a deceased payee?

A. Yes.

A-18. Q. Do these withholding provisions apply to designated distributions under all nonqualified employer deferred compensation plans?

A. No. The withholding provisions relating to pensions and annuities do not apply to any amounts that are wages without regard to these provisions. Wages to which the general wage withholding rules apply mean any remuneration paid by an employer for services performed by an employee unless the amount paid falls within one of the exceptions of section 3401(a). For example, wages do not include remuneration paid to, or on behalf of, an employee or beneficiary from or to a trust qualified under section 401(a) and tax-exempt under section 501(a). There is no exception for contributions to, or benefits paid from, some nonqualified plans. In general, any contributions to, or benefits from, a nonqualified plan that are taxable under section 83 are subject to wage withholding at the time that they are includible in the recipient's gross income.

A-19. Q. Do these withholding provisions apply to designated distributions from a bond purchase plan described in section 405(a)?

A. Yes. Although, a bond purchase plan is not a qualified plan, section 3402(a) does not apply to contributions to, or distributions from, such a plan. Therefore, designated distributions from a bond purchase plan are subject to the new withholding rules of section 3405. Similarly, the new withholding rules apply to designated distributions of an individual retirement bond described in section 409 or from an annuity plan described in section 403(a). For purposes of the withholding provisions of section 3405, a designated distribution from a bond purchase plan described in section 405(a) or an individual retirement bond described in section 409 occurs when an individual redeems a bond.

A-20. Q. Do these withholding provisions apply to designated distributions from a tax-sheltered annuity described in section 403(b)?

A. Yes. Section 31.3401(a)-1(b)(1)(i) of the Employment Tax Regulations provides that there is no withholding required under the wage withholding provisions to the extent that any amounts are taxable under the rules of section 72 or 403. Because designated distributions are not subject to the general wage withholding provisions, the new provisions of section 3405 apply to these designated distributions.

A-21. Q. An employer maintains a nonqualified deferred compensation plan such as a supplemental executive retirement ("top hat") plan. Payments under the plan are made in the form of a single sum payment at retirement. Amounts paid at retirement are includible in income as compensation in the year received. Must the payor withhold on these amounts according to the rules in section 3405?

A. No. Section 3405(d)(1)(B)(i) provides that a designated distribution on which withholding is required does not include amounts that are wages without regard to the rules of section 3405. Therefore, withholding on payments that are includible in income as compensation are based on the rules for withholding on wages contained in section 3402.

A-22. Q. Do the withholding provisions of section 3405 apply to a retirement plan maintained by a State or local government on behalf of its employees?

A. Yes. A retirement plan maintained by a State or local government on behalf of its employees is a plan that defers the receipt of compensation. The fact that a plan deferring the receipt of compensation is maintained by a governmental unit does not make the withholding provisions inapplicable. Thus, annuity payments and other distributions under the Federal Civil Service Retirement System or under the plan of any State or municipality are subject to withholding.

A-23. Q. Are payments from a state or local plan of deferred compensation described in section 457 subject to the withholding requirements of section 3405?

A. No. Amounts paid from a plan described in section 457 are paid from a plan that defers the receipt of compensation. However, amounts paid from a deferred compensation plan described in section 457 are wages under section 3401(a). Therefore, the general wage withholding rules, not the special rules of section 3405, apply to these payments.

A-24. Q. An individual retires and begins receiving periodic payments under a commercial annuity contract that was distributed to him from a contributory qualified plan. The insurance company is the payor and is liable for withholding because the plan administrator has transferred liability under the rules of section 3405(c)(2). Must the payor determine whether the employee's investment in the contract is recoverable within three years?

A. Yes. Under section 72(d), if the annuity payments during the first three years equal or exceed the amount contributed by the employee to the plan, no amounts are includible in income until the employee's contributions are recovered. Because the application of section 72(d) may affect the extent to which it is reasonable to believe that amounts are not includible in income and, therefore, not subject to withholding, the payor must determine whether section 72(d) applies to the annuity payments. As a general rule, the information necessary to determine the employee's investment in the contract must be provided to the payor by the plan administrator. See, however, questions A-27 and A-33.

A-25. Q. If the payor in question A-24 determines that the employee's investment in the contract is not recoverable within 3 years, must the payor compute the exclusion ratio under section 72(b) to calculate the amount of each payment that is not includible in gross income?

A. Yes. The operation of section 72(b) affects the extent to which it is reasonable to believe that amounts are not includible in gross income. Therefore, the payor must compute the exclusion ratio to determine what portion of each payment is subject to withholding under section 3405. As a general rule, the information necessary to determine the employee's exclusion ratio must be provided to the payor by the plan administrator. See, however, questions A-27 and A-33.

A-26. Q. In questions A-24 and A-25, may the payor (*i.e.*, the insurance company) rely on the information furnished by the plan administrator to determine the amounts that are includible in gross income?

A. In the absence of information to the contrary supplied by the payee, the payor may rely on the information furnished by the plan administrator. See, with respect to the plan administrator's duty to report to the payor, questions E-2 and E-3.

A-27. Q. What is the result in questions A-24 and A-25 if the plan administrator fails to provide the payor with any information concerning the amount of employee contributions?

A. Until the earlier of December 31, 1983, or the date on which the plan administrator provides the payor with information concerning the amount of employee contributions, it is reasonable for the payor to assume that the employee's investment in the annuity contract is zero unless the payor has independent specific knowledge of the amount of employee contributions. Additionally, if the payee notifies the payor of the amount of employee contributions, the payor

Reg. §35.3405-1T

must compute the taxable portion of the payment based on the information supplied by the payee. If the plan administrator fails to provide the payor with this information on or before December 31, 1983, the plan administrator will be liable for failure to withhold and pay the tax due. See questions E-2 through E-5 for rules on the plan administrator's ability to transfer liability for withholding to the payor. See also question A-33 with respect to the plan administrator's failure to provide the necessary information prior to December 31, 1983.

A-28. Q. If a beneficiary receives the balance to the credit of an employee from an annuity described in section 403(b) on account of the employee's death, is it reasonable to believe that the $5,000 death benefit exclusion of section 101(b) is not includible in gross income?

A. Yes. Although the amount of the death benefit exclusion allowable may be limited by section 101(b)(2)(B)(iii), the payor, for withholding purposes, may use the maximum death benefit exclusion ($5,000) in computing the amount of the distribution that is subject to withholding. See also, in this respect, question C-3.

A-29. Q. What is the appropriate treatment of a distribution (whether periodic or nonperiodic) that includes employer securities?

A. Employer securities are significant in the calculation of amounts subject to withholding in two respects. First, the maximum amount to be withheld cannot exceed the sum of the amount of money plus the fair market value of property received, *except* employer securities. In other words, a payor will not be forced to dispose of employer securities in order to meet withholding tax liability. Thus, for example, if an individual receives a distribution from a stock bonus plan that includes $1,000 worth of employer stock and $5 in cash for payment of fractional shares of stock, all of the cash, but none of the stock, may be retained by the payor to satisfy the withholding obligation. Second, under certain circumstances, the net unrealized appreciation in employer securities is not includible in gross income. See, in this respect, the rules of sections 402(a)(1) and 402(e)(4)(J).

A-30. Q. Is it reasonable to believe that all net unrealized appreciation from employer securities is not includible in gross income in the case of a qualified total distribution?

A. Yes. Although a qualified total distribution may include a distribution that is not a lump sum distribution, it is reasonable to believe that all net unrealized appreciation from employer securities is not includible in gross income.

A-31. Q. Is it reasonable to believe that a distribution is not includible in gross income if the distribution consists of employee contributions from a plan described in section 401(a) and the amount distributed is not specifically designated as accumulated deductible employee contributions?

A. Yes. Employee contributions to a plan described in section 401(a) are not deductible from gross income when contributed unless they are deductible employee contributions under section 72(o)(5). Unless the payor has specific knowledge that employee contributions distributed from a plan described in section 401(a) are accumulated deductible employee contributions, it is reasonable to assume that the amounts are excludible from gross income in the year when received.

A-32. Q. In the case of disability payments paid under a noncontributory plan to a disability retiree who has not attained age 65, is it reasonable to believe that all amounts paid to the payee are includible in gross income?

A. Yes. Whether or not all or part of the disability payments paid under a noncontributory plan to a permanently disabled retiree who has not attained age 65 are includible in gross income depends on the adjusted gross income of the taxpayer and on whether the taxpayer is permanently and totally disabled. In this situation, it is reasonable for the payor to assume that all amounts paid to the payee are includible in gross income unless the payor has specific independent knowledge that all or part of the periodic payments are not includible in gross income. Additionally, if the payee notifies the payor of the amount excludible from gross income, the payor must compute the taxable portion of the payment based on information provided by the payee.

A-33. Q. In the case of a periodic payment, is it reasonable to believe that all amounts paid to the payee are includible in gross income?

A. Yes. As an alternative to the general rule that a designated distribution does not include amounts which it is reasonable to believe are not includible in gross income, the payor of any periodic payment may assume that the entire amount of the payment is includible in gross income. The wage withholding tables must be used without adjustment for the fact that Federal income tax is being withheld on the gross amount. If the payor uses this alternative method of calculating the amount of the designated distribution, he must include with the notice of the election not to have withholding apply to the following additional statements:

(1) tax will be withheld on the gross amount of the payment even though the payee may be receiving amounts that are not subject to withholding because they are excludible from gross income;

(2) this withholding procedure may result in excess withholding on the payment; and

(3) the payee may adjust the allowances claimed on the withholding certificate if he wants a lesser amount withheld from each payment or he may provide the payor with the information necessary to calculate the taxable portion of each payment.

This alternative will not apply to periodic payments made after the earlier of December 31, 1983, or the date on which the plan administrator supplies the payor with the information necessary to calculate the taxable portion of the distribution.

Reg. §35.3405-1T

See, also, questions E-3, E-4, and E-5.

A-34. Q. May the payor rely on a plan administrator's computation of the amount to be withheld?

A. Yes. Although the plan administrator is not required to compute the amount to be withheld in order to transfer liability for withholding to the payor, the plan administrator may provide such information to the payor, and the payor may rely on such computations unless the payor knows or has reason to know that the computations are incorrect.

A-35. Q. Under the plans of certain States, individuals may receive payments from more than one retirement system, such as payments from the state's teacher's retirement plan and from the state's regular retirement plan. Must these payments be aggregated for purposes of providing a single notice and election to a payee or for purposes of determining whether the floor on withholding tax (i.e., $5,400 for a married individual claiming three allowances) has been reached?

A. No. However, if it is feasible to aggregate payments under more than one retirement system, the payor is permitted to do so for these purposes.

A-36. Q. If a payment is made by one check to more than one beneficiary, such as a surviving spouse and a minor child, how is the amount to be withheld computed?

A. The payor may compute the withholding on a payment made by one check to more than one beneficiary as if the payment were made to only one beneficiary. In this case, the payor must base withholding for the total amount of the designated distribution on the withholding certificate of the payee to whom the election was sent.

Alternatively, if each payee files a withholding certificate and the payor knows the amount of the payment to which each payee is entitled, the payor may determine the amount to be withheld with respect to each payee. If the payor does not know the amount of the payment to which each payee is entitled, he may treat the payment as being made pro-rata to each payee. If only one withholding certificate is received, the payor must base withholding for the total amount of the designated distribution on the withholding certificate of one of the payees, such as the surviving spouse's certificate. Thus, if notice of the election not to have withholding apply is supplied to each payee at the times required in section 3405(c)(10) and only one payee makes the election or files a certificate, the payor must assume that the election or filing was made by the payee on behalf of the other payees.

A-37. Q. If a payor makes an error in computing the amount of a designated distribution that is subject to withholding, must the payor make a retroactive correction of the error?

A. No, provided the error was a reasonable one. Thus, if a payor either underwithholds or overwithholds because the amount of the designated distribution (i.e., the taxable portion of the

payment) was incorrectly calculated, no retroactive make-up is required if one of the following applies: (1) the payor reasonably relied on information furnished by the plan administrator (including the computation of the amount to be withheld), (2) the payor relied on a payee's representations on the withholding certificate, (3) the payor reasonably relied on the rules of this regulation, or (4) the payor made a mathematical error in computations. However, if the amount of the designated distribution is correctly computed, but the payor makes an error in applying the withholding tables, the normal rules concerning failure to withhold and pay the tax will apply.

B. Withholding on Periodic Payments.

B-1. Q. Is the payor of periodic payments required to aggregate such payments with a payee's compensation to determine the amount of tax to be withheld under section 3405(a)(1)?

A. No. Although the payor must withhold from any periodic payment the amount that has to be withheld if the payment were a payment of wages by an employer to an employee for a payroll period, the amount to be withheld under section 3405(a)(1) is calculated separately of any amounts that actually are wages to the payee for the same period.

B-2. Q. Can either the percentage method (section 3402(b)) or the wage bracket method (section 3402(c)) be used to determine the withholding liability on a periodic payment?

A. Yes. Withholding on a periodic payment is accomplished by treating the payment as if it were wages. Therefore, unless the employee has elected not to have withholding apply, any method of withholding that is an appropriate method for withholding on wages is also an appropriate method for withholding on periodic payments. Refer to the Employer's Tax Guide (Circular E) and Publication 493, Alternative Tax Withholding Methods and Tables for the general procedures on withholding, deposit, payment, and reporting of Federal income tax withheld. Note, however, that any specific procedures contained in this regulation take precedence over any contrary rules in Circular E and Publication 493.

B-3. Q. Do rules similar to those for wage withholding apply to the filing of a withholding certificate for periodic payments?

A. Yes. Unless the rules of section 3405 specifically conflict with the rules of section 3402, the rules for withholding on periodic payments will parallel the rules for wage withholding. Thus, if a withholding certificate is filed by a payee, it will generally take effect as provided in section 3402(f)(3) for certificates filed to replace existing certificates. If a withholding certificate is furnished by a payee on or before the date on which payments commence, it takes effect with respect to payments made more than 30 days after the certificate is furnished, unless the payor elects to make it effective at an earlier date. If a withholding certificate is furnished by a payee after the date on which payments commence, it takes effect with respect to payments made on or after the status determination date (January 1, May 1, July 1, or October 1) that is at least 30 days after the date the certificate is filed, unless the payor elects to make it effective at an earlier date. If no withholding certificate is filed, the amount withheld is determined as if the payee were a married person claiming three withholding allowances.

B-4. Q. If no withholding certificate has been filed and the payor is aware that the payee is single, is it still appropriate to base withholding on a married individual claiming three allowances?

A. Yes. If no withholding certificate is filed, the payor is not required or permitted to base withholding on the amount of allowances the payee actually is entitled to claim. Thus, the payor must base withholding on the rates for a married person with three withholding allowances.

B-5. Q. May a payor determine whether payments to an individual are subject to withholding based on the amount of the first periodic payment for the year?

A. No. Periodic payments can vary during a calendar year because of make-up or past due payments, variable rates of payments, or cost-of-living adjustments, so that withholding based on the first payment within a year may be an inaccurate measure of withholding on total payments for the year. Therefore, the amount to be withheld is determined each payment period in the same manner as applies to withholding on wages. See, in this respect, Circular E and the regulations under section 3402.

B-6. Q. If a payment period is specified as by the terms of a commercial annuity contract, must this period be used as the appropriate period for determining the amount to be withheld?

A. Yes. Similarly, if the payment period is designated in a plan administrator's report or on an individual retirement account payout schedule agreed to by payor and payee, this period must be used as the appropriate payment period.

B-7. Q. If the payor received no report from the plan administrator or beneficiary concerning the payment period, but knows the frequency of payments, can the known frequency be used as the appropriate payment period?

A. Yes. However, if no report is received and the payor has no knowledge of the frequency of payments, then he must treat the distribution as a nonperiodic distribution. Therefore, a distribution cannot be a periodic payment unless the frequency of payments is known. See, in this respect, questions B-8 and C-2. For rules concerning the plan administrator's failure to provide this information, see questions E-2 and E-3.

B-8. Q. If a payee receives a one-time payment that is a make-up payment resulting from an insurance company's incorrect calculation of a monthly annuity amount, is the one-time payment part of a series of periodic payments?

A. Yes. Because the one-time payment is a catch-up of prior amounts due as periodic payments, it is treated as part of a series of periodic payments. These payments are treated for with-

holding purposes in a manner similar to the treatment of supplemental wage payments in section 31.3402(g)-1 of the Employment Tax Regulations.

C. Withholding on Nonperiodic Distributions.

C-1. Q. Must an individual receive a lump-sum distribution within the meaning of section 402(e)(4) to have a qualified total distribution?

A. No. A "qualified total distribution" is any distribution that (i) is a designated distribution, (ii) is reasonable to believe is made within one taxable year of the recipient, (iii) is made under a plan described in section 401(a) or 403(a), and (iv) consists of the balance to the credit of the employee under such plan. Thus, a distribution from a plan described in section 401(a) that does not meet the requirements (such as the minimum 5-year period of participation in section 402(e)(4)(H)) for a lump sum distribution within the meaning of section 402(e)(4) may still be a qualified total distribution for purposes of withholding.

C-2. Q. If a class year plan permits annual withdrawal of participants' vested amounts, are these withdrawals considered periodic payments?

A. No. A class year plan is a plan under which amounts contributed by an employer for a year become vested a number of years (*e.g.,* five years) after the year in which the amounts are contributed. Generally, class year plans permit withdrawals each year of amounts that have vested during the year. However, these distributions are not made with respect to an established frequency of payments, so the withdrawals must be treated as nonperiodic distributions, subject to withholding at the 10 percent rate.

C-3. Q. If a beneficiary receives the balance to the credit of a payee from an annuity contract on account of the payee's death, is this final payment a nonperiodic distribution?

A. Yes. The lump sum death benefit in this situation is a one-time payment that cannot be characterized as a periodic payment. The payment may be a qualified total distribution if the requirements of section 3405(c)(4) are satisfied, but otherwise it will be treated as a nonperiodic distribution other than a qualified total distribution.

C-4. Q. Is it permissible to assume that an individual is a calendar year taxpayer for purposes of determining whether a distribution is a "qualified total distribution?"

A. Yes, unless the payor or plan administrator has reason to believe that the payee is not a calendar year taxpayer. The payor or plan administrator has reason to believe that the payee is not a calendar year taxpayer if the payee tells the payor or plan administrator that he is not a calendar year taxpayer.

C-5. Q. Is a distribution of accumulated deductible employee contributions with earnings that is paid on account of an employee's separation from service treated as a qualified total distribution?

A. Yes. As long as the other requirements for a qualified total distribution are met, a distribution of accumulated deductible employee contribu-

Reg. §35.3405-1T

Collection of Income Tax at Source on Wages
See p. 20,601 for regulations not amended to reflect law changes
61,599

tions with earnings is eligible for withholding at the rate applicable to qualified total distributions even though the distribution could never be a lump sum distribution. Because accumulated deductible employee contributions are treated separately in determining whether a distribution is a qualified total distribution, the answer would be the same even if the recipient received none (or a portion) of the vested employer contributions in his account.

C-6. Q. What is meant by the "balance to the credit" of an employee under a plan described in section 401(a) or 403(a)?

A. In general, the balance to the credit of an employee includes any amount credited to the employee under the plan on the date the distribution commences. The balance to the credit of an employee includes an amount credited after the date the distribution commences if it is attributable to services performed before that date or is attributable to earnings on an amount credited to the employee before that date. Additionally, the balance to the credit of an employee includes any amount payable as an annuity with respect to the employee under the plan. Amounts that have been placed in a separate account for the funding of medical benefits under section 401(h) or amounts that are forfeitable under the plan are not included in the balance to the credit of an employee. Finally, accumulated deductible employee contributions (within the meaning of section 72(o)(5)(B)) are not included in the balance to the credit of an employee for the purposes of determining whether a distribution is a "qualified total distribution."

C-7. Q. Can a payor rely on a plan administrator's report in determining whether a distribution consists of the balance to the credit of an employee under a plan?

A. Yes. If the plan administrator does not inform the payor that the distribution consists of the balance to the credit of the employee, the payor may not assume that the distribution is a qualified total distribution and must treat the distribution as a nonperiodic distribution that is not a qualified total distribution. However, the payor may rely on the payee's representations that a distribution does consist of the balance to the credit of the employee under the plan.

C-8. Q. What table must be used to calculate the amount to be withheld from a "qualified total distribution?"

A. The table to be used for withholding on "qualified total distributions" will be published by the Secretary in the near future.

D. Notice and Election Procedures.

D-1. Q. May a payee elect not to have Federal income tax withheld from a designated distribution?

A. Yes. Withholding is not required on any periodic payment or nonperiodic distribution if the payee elects not to have withholding apply. If the payee makes this election, it is effective until revoked. The payor is required to provide each payee with notice of the right to elect not to have withholding apply and of the right to revoke the election.

D-2. Q. In the case of a designated distribution made on account of the death of an employee, who makes the election not to have withholding apply?

A. The election may be made by the beneficiary of plan benefits specified by the decedent in accordance with plan procedures or, if there is no designated beneficiary, by the beneficiary specified under the terms of the plan. If there is not a designated beneficiary and the terms of the plan do not specify a beneficiary, then the election may be made by the executor or the personal representative of the decedent.

D-3. Q. Who is required to provide notice to the payee of the payee's right not to have withholding apply?

A. Section 3405(d)(10)(B) requires the payor to provide notice to the payee of the payee's right to elect not to have withholding apply. Thus, even if the plan administrator has failed to transfer liability for withholding to the payor, the payor must provide notice to the payees.

D-4. Q. When must notice of the right to elect not to have withholding apply be given for periodic payments?

A. In the case of periodic payments, notice of the election must be provided not earlier than six months before the first payment and not later than when making the first payment. However, even if notice is provided at a date before the first payment, notice must also be given when making the first payment. Thereafter, notice must be provided at least once each calendar year of the right to make the election and to revoke the election.

D-5. Q. Must notice of the right to elect not to have withholding apply be provided to those payees whose annual payments are less than $5,400?

A. Yes. However, under the statute, notice is only required to be provided when making the first payment. Therefore, a payor may provide notice to a payee with annual payments less than $5,400 by indicating to the payee when making the first payment that no Federal income tax will be withheld unless the payee chooses to have withholding apply by filing a withholding certificate, if the payor also provides information concerning where a withholding certificate may be obtained.

D-6. Q. Must notice of the right to elect not to have withholding apply be provided in the same manner to all payees?

A. No. If the payor provides notice to all payees when making the first payment, the payor may, in addition, provide earlier notice as provided in section 3405(d)(10)(B)(i)(I) to selected groups of payees, such as those payees whose annual payments are over $5,400.

D-7. Q. Must notice be attached to the first payment to satisfy the requirement that notice be provided "when making" the first payment?

A. No. Because many payees utilize electronic funds transfer to deposit their pension or annuity checks, notice does not have to be attached physically to the check.

D-8. Q. If a payee utilizes electronic funds transfer and notice is mailed directly to the payee at the same time the check is issued, is the notice requirement satisfied even though the payee receives the notice fifteen days after the check is deposited?

A. Yes. Although it is desirable that the notice reach the payee immediately prior to or concurrent with receipt of the check, the notice requirement is deemed to be satisfied if the payee receives the notice within 15 days before or after receipt of the first payment.

D-9. Q. When is the payor required to notify the payee of his right to elect not to have withholding apply to a nonperiodic distribution?

A. Section 3405(d)(10)(B)(ii) requires that notice must be provided to the payee at the time of a nonperiodic distribution. Since notice provided at the time of the distribution could result in delay of receipt of the benefit check if the payee elects out of withholding, notice for nonperiodic distributions should be given not earlier than six months prior to the distribution and not later than the time that will give the payee reasonable time to elect not to have withholding apply and to reply to the payor with the election information. What is reasonable time depends upon the facts and circumstances of each case.

D-10. Q. What is a "reasonable time" for notice with respect to a nonperiodic distribution from a qualified plan?

A. The "reasonable time" requirement is satisfied with respect to a nonperiodic distribution if the notice is included in the basic claim for benefits application that is provided to the participant by the plan administrator.

D-11. Q. If the payor of a periodic payment provides notice of the election not to have withholding apply within the time specified by section 3405(d)(10)(B)(i)(I), may the payor specify a time prior to distribution by which the election must be made?

A. Yes. The election not to have withholding apply is generally given effect as provided in section 3402(f)(3) for a certificate filed to replace an existing certificate. However, the payor may require that the election is made up to 30 days before the first payment to be effective for the first payment. See question B-3.

D-12. Q. If the payor of a nonperiodic distribution provides notice of the election not to have withholding apply within a reasonable time prior to the distribution, may the payor specify a time prior to distribution by which the election must be made?

A. No. The payee has the right to make or revoke an election at any time prior to the distribution. Therefore, the payor may place a deadline on the time to elect without delaying payment of the distribution, but must accept any election or revocation made up to the time of distribution.

D-13. Q. What is a "reasonable time" for notice with respect to a distribution from an individual retirement account?

A. A payor may provide notice of the election not to have withholding apply at the time the beneficiary requests a withdrawal from his individual retirement account. This rule also applies to distributions from bank sponsored prototype plans and other plans that permit withdrawals on request.

D-14. Q. If notice is provided to a payee prior to the first payment of a periodic payment, why must it also be provided at the time of the first payment or distribution?

A. Section 3405(d)(10)(B)(i)(II) of the Internal Revenue Code requires such notice. In addition, because the payee has the right to make an election or to revoke a prior election at any time prior to the beginning of the payment period, notice must be provided when making the first payment in order to offer the payee ample opportunity to make or revoke an election not to have withholding apply even if the election will not be effective until later payments.

D-15. Q. If a payee who has been receiving periodic payments is rehired by the same employer, has his benefits suspended, and then recommences receiving periodic payments, must notice again be provided to the payee?

A. Yes. Upon recommencement of benefits, the first payment thereafter is treated as the first payment for purposes of the notice requirements.

D-16. Q. Must a payor provide notice if it is reasonable to believe that the entire amount payable is excludible from the payee's gross income?

A. No. Amounts which it is reasonable to believe are not includible in gross income are not designated distributions. Therefore, no notice is required of the ability to elect not to have withholding apply.

D-17. Q. If the payor of a periodic payment under a qualified plan knows that an employee's investment in an annuity contract will be recovered within three years, must he provide notice of the right to elect out of withholding at the time the first payment is made?

A. No. The first payment is not a designated distribution, and, therefore, is not a periodic payment subject to the notice requirements of section 3405(d)(10)(B)(i). There is no withholding obligation until the employee's investment in the contract is recovered because those amounts that

Reg. § 35.3405-1T

equal the investment in the contract are not includible in gross income and, therefore, are not designated distributions. Therefore, the first payment after the employee's investment in the contract is recouped is the first payment for purposes of the notice requirements.

D-18. Q. What information concerning the election not to have withholding apply must be provided by the payor to the payee?

A. Notice to a payee must contain the following information:

(1) notice of the payee's right to elect not to have withholding apply to any payment or distribution and how to make that election,

(2) notice of the payee's right to revoke such an election at any time and a statement that the election remains effective until revoked,

(3) a statement to advise payees that penalties may be incurred under the estimated tax payment rules if the payments of estimated tax are not adequate and sufficient tax is not withheld from the payment or distribution.

In the event that the payor does not know what part of a distribution is includible in gross income and treats these payments as provided in question A-33, the following additional statements must be included with the notice:

(1) tax will be withheld on the gross amount of the payment even though the payee may be receiving amounts that are not subject to withholding because they are excludible from gross income,

(2) this withholding procedure may result in excess withholding on the payment, and

(3) the payee may adjust his allowances claimed on the withholding certificate if he wants a lesser amount withheld from each payment or he may provide the payor with the information necessary to calculate the taxable portion of each payment.

D-19. Q. Is there any information that, although not required, it is desirable to include in the notice to payees?

A. It is desirable to include a statement in the notice to payees that the election not to have withholding apply is prospective only and that any election made after a payment or distribution to the payee is not an election with respect to that payment or distribution.

D-20. Q. May the plan administrator provide the notice to payees on behalf of the payor?

A. The plan administrator may provide notice on behalf of the payor. However, the payor has sole responsibility for providing this notice whether or not the plan administrator has shifted liability for withholding to the payor, and if the plan administrator fails to provide adequate notice, the payor is responsible.

D-21. Q. Is there a sample notice that can be used to satisfy the notice requirement for periodic payments?

A. Yes. Any payor who uses the following sample notice is deemed to satisfy the notice requirement if notice is timely provided:

NOTICE OF WITHHOLDING ON PERIODIC PAYMENTS

Beginning on January 1, 1983, the [pension] OR [annuity] payments you receive from the [insert name of plan or company] will be subject to Federal income tax withholding unless you elect not to have withholding apply. Withholding will only apply to the portion of your [pension]OR [annuity] payment that is already included in your income subject to Federal income tax and will be like wage withholding. Thus, there will be no withholding on the return of your own nondeductible contributions to the [plan] OR [contract].

You may elect not to have withholding apply to your [pension]OR [annuity] payments by returning the signed and dated election [manner may be specified] to [insert name and address]. Your election will remain in effect until you revoke it. You may revoke your election at any time by returning the signed and dated revocation to [insert appropriate name or address]. Any election or revocation will be effective no later than the January 1, May 1, July 1, or October 1 after it is received, so long as it is received at least 30 days before that date. You may make and revoke elections not to have withholding apply as often as you wish. Additional elections may be obtained from [insert name and address].

If you do not return the election by [insert date], Federal income tax will be withheld from the taxable portion of your [pension]OR [annuity] payments as if you were a married individual claiming three withholding allowances. As a result, no Federal income tax will be withheld if the taxable portion of your annual [pension] OR [annuity]payments are less than $5,400.

If you elect not to have withholding apply to your [pension]OR [annuity] payments, or if you do not have enough Federal income tax withheld from your [pension] OR [annuity] payments, you may be responsible for payment of estimated tax. You may incur penalties under the estimated tax rules if your withholding and estimated tax payments are not sufficient.

D-22. Q. Is there sample language that may be used to elect not to have withholding apply or to revoke a prior election not to have withholding apply?

A. Yes. A payee may elect not to have withholding apply or revoke a prior election in any manner that clearly shows the payee's intent. The following language would suffice:

ELECTION FOR RECIPIENTS OF PERIODIC PAYMENTS

Instructions: Check Box A if you do not want any Federal income tax withheld from your [pension] OR [annuity]. Check Box B to revoke an election not to have withholding apply. Return the signed and dated election to [insert name and address].

Even if you elect not to have Federal income tax withheld, you are liable for payment of Federal income tax on the taxable portion of your [pension] OR [annuity]. You also may be subject to tax penalties under the estimated tax payment

Reg. §35.3405-1T

rules if your payments of estimated tax and withholding, if any, are not adequate.

A ☐ I do not want to have Federal income tax withheld from my [pension] OR [annuity].

B ☐ I want to have Federal income tax withheld from my [pension] OR [annuity].

Signed: . . . .
  Name   Date

Return your completed election to: [insert name and address]

D-23. Q. May the payee's election be combined with a withholding certificate?

A. Yes. The payor may provide a single statement for the payee to fill out and return that would enable the payee to elect not to have withholding apply or to revoke a previous election and, at the same time, would enable the payee to claim the number of withholding allowances and, also, the dollar amount the payee wants withheld.

D-24. Q. Will a notice mailed to the last known address of the payee fulfill notice requirement of section 3405(d)(10)(B)?

A. Yes.

D-25. Q. Is there a sample notice that can be used to satisfy the notice requirement for nonperiodic distributions?

A. Yes. Any payor who uses the following sample notice is deemed to satisfy the notice requirement if notice is timely provided:

NOTICE OF WITHHOLDING ON DISTRIBUTIONS OR WITHDRAWALS FROM ANNUITIES, IRAS, PENSION, PROFIT SHARING, STOCK BONUS, AND OTHER DEFERRED COMPENSATION PLANS

The [distributions] or [withdrawals] you receive from the [insert name of plan or company] are subject to Federal income tax withholding unless you elect not to have withholding apply. Withholding will only apply to the portion of your [distribution] OR [withdrawal] that is included in your income subject to Federal income tax. Thus, for example, there will be no withholding on the return of your own nondeductible contributions to the [plan] OR [contract].

You may elect not to have withholding apply to your [distribution]OR [withdrawal] payments by signing and dating the attached election and returning it [manner may be specified] to [insert name and address].

If you do not return the election by [insert date]receipt of your payments may be delayed. If you do not respond by the date your [distribution] OR [withdrawal] is scheduled to begin, Federal income tax will be withheld from the taxable portion of your [distribution]OR [withdrawal]. [Insert information on rates if desired].

If you elect not to have withholding apply to your [distribution]OR [withdrawal] payments, or if you do not have enough Federal income tax withheld from your [distribution] OR [withdrawal], you may be responsible for payment of estimated tax. You may incur penalties under the estimated tax rules if your withholding and estimated tax payments are not sufficient.

D-26. Q. Is there sample language that may be used for payees of nonperiodic distributions to elect not to have withholding apply?

A. Yes. A payee of a nonperiodic distribution may elect not to have withholding apply in any manner that clearly shows the payee's intent. The following language would suffice:

ELECTION FOR PAYEES OF NONPERIODIC PAYMENTS

Instructions: If you do not want any Federal income tax withheld from your [distribution] OR [withdrawal], sign and date this election and return it to [insert name and address].

Even if you elect not to have Federal income tax withheld, you are liable for payment of Federal income tax on the taxable portion of your [distribution] OR [withdrawal]. You also may be subject to tax penalties under the estimated tax payment rules if your payments of estimated tax and withholding, if any, are not adequate.

I do not want to have Federal income tax withheld from my [distribution]OR [withdrawal].

Signed: . . . .
  Name   Date

Return your completed election to: [insert name and address]

D-27. Q. If the payor provides notice prior to making the first payment, can an abbreviated notice be used to satisfy the notice requirement of section 3405(d)(10)(B)(i)(II)?

A. Yes. It is permissible to provide with the payment a statement that the payee has the right to elect out of withholding. For example, the following sample notice could be used to satisfy the notice requirement if the payor has provided notice previously:

If Federal income taxes have been withheld from the [pension]OR [annuity] payments you are receiving and if you do not wish to have taxes withheld, you should notify [insert name and address]. However, if you elect not to have withholding apply to your [pension]OR [annuity] payments, or if you do not have enough Federal income tax withheld from your [pension] OR [annuity] payment, you may be responsible for payment of estimated tax. You may incur penalties under the estimated tax rules if your withholding and estimated tax payments are not sufficient.

If Federal income taxes are not being withheld from your [pension]OR [annuity] payment because you have elected not to have withholding apply and if you wish to revoke that election and have Federal income taxes withheld from your [pension] OR [annuity] payments, you should notify [insert name and address].

D-28. Q. Must an employee who receives a distribution from a plan described in section 401(a) that includes amounts attributable to employer contributions and to accumulated deductible employee contributions make two elections not to have withholding apply?

A. No. Although accumulated deductible employee contributions are treated separately in determining whether a distribution is a qualified total distribution, an employee needs to make only one election not to have withholding apply to any distributions occurring at the same time from or under the same plan. However, the plan administrator could require the employee to make separate elections with respect to the distributions.

D-29. Q. If the administrator of a plan described in section 401(a) makes a qualified total distribution to an employee out of funds contained in two or more trusts, must the employee make a separate election not to have withholding apply with respect to the distribution from each trust?

A. No. The fact that a plan may use several trusts does not eliminate treatment of the distribution as a single qualified total distribution for which only one election is necessary.

D-30. Q. Is it permissible to provide notice to persons already in pay status on January 1, 1983, in a newsletter of the plan administrator?

A. Yes, provided that this notice is received by the payee within 15 days of the payee's receipt of the first periodic payment after December 31, 1982, and such notice provides the means to make an election and instructions for electing not to have withholding apply. It is desirable that payees be afforded the maximum opportunity to make the election provided by section 3405(a)(2). Payors are encouraged to give payees notice of their election opportunities at least 30 days before the first periodic payment after December 31, 1982.

D-31. Q. Is it permissible to provide the annual notice required by section 3405(d)(10)(B)(i)(III) on January 1, 1984, December 31, 1985, and January 1, 1986?

A. No. The annual notice required by section 3405(d)(10)(B)(i)(III) should be provided at approximately the same time each calendar year.

D-32. Q. Under what circumstances may an election made with respect to a nonperiodic distribution apply to subsequent distributions?

A. Generally, any election not to have withholding apply to a nonperiodic distribution may apply to any subsequent payment or distribution from or under the same plan or arrangement. However, the payor must still provide notice of the election and revocation procedures upon each subsequent distribution and must include the statement concerning liability for payment of estimated tax if the payee does not have withholding applied.

D-33. Q. How may a payee who intends to make a qualifying rollover (as defined in section 402(a)(5) or section 408(d)(3)) of a distribution elect not to have Federal income tax withheld from the distribution?

A. The payee may elect not to have withholding apply by making the election on the form provided by the payor. Alternatively, if the payee directs the payor to pay over the distribution to a qualified plan or an individual retirement account, the payor may treat this direction as an election not to have withholding apply.

D-34. Q. If a payee claims more than 14 withholding allowances on a withholding certificate, must the payor remit a copy of the withholding certificate to the Internal Revenue Service?

A. No. Because a payee may, at any time, elect out of withholding, the rules of section 31.3402(f)(2)-1(g) of the Employment Tax Regulations do not apply. Therefore, a payee may claim more than 14 allowances and the payor need not remit the withholding certificate to the Internal Revenue Service.

E. Reporting and Recordkeeping.

E-1. Q. If designated distributions are made from or under a plan described in section 401(a), who has responsibility for making the returns and reports required by section 6047(e)?

A. Generally, the plan administrator, as defined in section 414(g), is responsible for maintaining the records and making the reports required by section 6047(e). However, if the plan administrator fails to keep the required records and make the required reports, the employer maintaining the plan is responsible for the reports and returns.

E-2. Q. How may a plan administrator of a plan described in section 401(a) or 403(a) transfer his duty to withhold to a payor?

A. A plan administrator of a plan described in section 401(a) or 403(a) may transfer the liability for withholding by (1) directing the payor in writing to withhold the tax and (2) providing the payor with any required information. This direction is presumed to remain in effect until the plan administrator revokes it in writing.

E-3. Q. What information must the plan administrator provide to the payor in order to transfer his liability for withholding?

A. The general rule is that the plan administrator must provide the payor with all information necessary to compute correctly the withholding tax liability. To satisfy this requirement, the plan administrator must explicitly inform the payor of the information that would be reportable on the Form W-2P or 1099R or that such information is not applicable to a particular payee or to any payments under the plan. For example, if the plan administrator is silent with respect to any employee contributions, he has not satisfied his reporting obligation even if there are no employee contributions to the plan. Thus, the plan administrator is expected to provide the payor with the following minimum information:

(1) the name, address, and social security number of the payee and the payee's spouse or other beneficiary if applicable,

(2) the existence and amount of any employee contributions,

(3) the amount of accumulated deductible employee contributions, if any,

(4) the payee's cost basis in any employer securities and the current fair market value of the securities,

(5) the existence and amount of any premiums paid for the current cost of life insurance that were previously includible in income,

(6) a statement of the reason (*e.g.*, death, disability, retirement) for the payment or distribution,

(7) the date on which payments commence and the amount and frequency of payments,

(8) the age of the payee and of the payee's spouse or designated beneficiary if applicable, and

(9) any other information required by Form W-2P or 1099R.

If, prior to December 31, 1983, the plan administrator fails to provide the payor with the information required in items (2) through (5) the payor is liable for withholding. However, the payor may withhold on the payment as if all amounts are includible in gross income. See question A-33.

E-4. Q. If, after December 31, 1983, the plan administrator does not notify the payor of the amount of employee contributions with respect to one payee, has withholding liability shifted to the payor?

A. Yes. The plan administrator satisfies the requirements of question E-3 as to the information that must be supplied to the payor so long as the failure to provide the required information occurs on an infrequent basis or the plan administrator informs the payor in writing that he has made a good faith effort to supply all the required information but the amount of employee contributions as to a particular payee is unavailable.

E-5. Q. If, after December 31, 1983, the plan administrator fails to supply the payor with any information concerning the existence or amount of any employee contributions, has withholding liability shifted to the payor?

A. No. The plan administrator has not satisfied his reporting obligation as required in question E-3 as to employee contributions even if there are no employee contributions unless he affirmatively states that there are no employee contributions or states that the reporting of this item is not applicable in determining the payee's tax liability.

E-6. Q. Is it permissible to satisfy the requirements of section 6047(e) by maintaining records necessary to provide the information contained on Forms W-2P and 1099R?

A. Section 6047(e) will be satisfied if, in addition to the information necessary to complete Forms W-2P and 1099R, the following information is maintained:

(1) payee's date of birth (if known), and date of spouse's or designated beneficiary's birth (if applicable and known);

(2) plan administrator's name, address, and employer identification number (EIN);

(3) plan's name and identification number and sponsor's name, address, and EIN; and

(4) date on which payments commence and amount and frequency of payments.

E-7. Q. If the interim method of withholding on periodic payments (*i.e.*, withholding on the gross amount) is used, must the employer, plan administrator, or issuer of any contract still maintain the information required by Form W-2P?

A. Yes. Even if this interim method is used, the recipient must be provided with the information that will enable him to determine his tax liability and adjust his claimed exemptions or claim a credit or refund.

E-8. Q. What events trigger the reporting requirements of section 6047(e)?

A. Reporting is required any time there is a designated distribution to which section 3405 applies. Therefore, the old law rule that distributions of less than $600 per year do not require reporting no longer applies. Additionally, an exchange of insurance contracts under which any designated distribution (including a tax-free exchange under section 1035) may be made is a reportable event even though a designated distribution does not occur. To insure proper reporting when a designated distribution is made under the new contract, it is anticipated that the issuer of the contract to be exchanged will provide the information necessary to compute the amount to be withheld to the policyholder and to the issuer of the new contract.

E-9. Q. Will the reporting requirement be satisfied if Form W-2P or Form 1099R is filed?

A. Yes. In the absence of other forms or regulations, the reporting requirement is satisfied if Form W-2P or Form 1099R is filed with respect to each payee.

E-10. Q. How should the payor or plan administrator remit payments of amounts withheld under section 3405?

A. The payor or plan administrator must deposit the amount withheld under section 3405 with an authorized financial institution in accordance with the provisions of § 31.6302(c)-1(a)(1)(i) of the Procedure and Administration Regulations, which provides the procedures for depositing employment taxes. For purposes of applying these procedures to amounts withheld under section 3405, the term "taxes" as defined in § 31.6302(c)-1(a)(1)(iii) includes the income tax withheld under section 3405 with respect to designated distributions. A payor or plan administrator who remits these amounts in accordance with those rules must report the amounts deposited on the same Form 941 or 941E, whichever is appropriate, that he uses to report the employment taxes he had deposited under § 31.6302(c)-1(a)(1)(i).

F. Other.

F-1. Q. If a plan administrator or other payor distributes property other than cash to payees, is it permissible to use the value of the property as of the last preceding valuation date to determine the amount of Federal income tax that must be withheld from each distribution?

A. Yes. In many situations, the plan administrator or payor will not be able to determine the value of property to be distributed as of the date of distribution without delaying payment to the payee. In these cases, the plan administrator or tion date prior to the date of distribution, as long as the valuation is made at least once each year. If the most recent valuation date occurred within the 90 days immediately preceding the date of distribution, the next most recent valuation date may be used.

F-2. Q. How is withholding accomplished if a payee receives only property other than employer securities?

A. A payor or plan administrator must satisfy the obligation to withhold on distributions of property other than employer securities even if this requires selling all or part of the property and distributing the cash remaining after Federal income tax is withheld. However, the payor or plan administrator may instead permit the payee to remit to the payor or plan administrator sufficient cash to satisfy the withholding obligation. Additionally, if a distribution of property other than cash includes property that is not includible in a designated distribution, such as the distribution of U.S. Savings Bonds or an annuity contract, such property need not be sold or redeemed to meet any withholding obligation.

F-3. Q. If a designated distribution includes cash and property other than employer securities, is it permissible to satisfy the withholding obligation with respect to the entire distribution by using the cash distributed, provided the cash distributed is sufficient to satisfy the withholding obligation?

A. Yes, as long as there is sufficient cash to satisfy the withholding obligation for the entire distribution. There is no requirement that tax be withheld from each type of property in proportion to its value.

F-4. Q. If a loan from a qualified plan is treated as a distribution under section 72(p), is the amount of the loan subject to withholding under section 3405?

A. Yes. If, and to the extent that, the loan is treated as a distribution when made, withholding is accomplished by withholding tax from the amount of the loan that is treated as a distribution. Thus, for example, if a loan of $12,000 that must be repaid within 5 years is made to a common law employee with a vested account balance of $5,000, $2,000 is treated as a distribution under section 72(p), and the payor or plan administrator must withhold tax from the $2,000.

F-5. Q. Is a loan that is treated as a distribution under section 72(p) a nonperiodic distribution other than a qualified total distribution?

A. Yes.

F-6. Q. Must a payor or plan administrator withhold tax on a nonperiodic distribution (including a qualified total distribution) if the amount of the distribution is less than $200?

A. No. However, all amounts received within one taxable year of the payee from the payor or plan administrator under the same plan or arrangement must be aggregated for purposes of determining whether the $200 floor is reached. If the payor or plan administrator does not know at the time a first payment of $200 or less is made whether there will be additional payments

during the year for which aggregation is required, the payor or plan administrator need not withhold from the first payment. If distributions are made within one taxable year under more than one plan of an employer, the plan administrator or payor may, but need not, aggregate the distributions for purposes of determining whether the $200 floor is reached.

F-7. Q. If a nonperiodic distribution (including a qualified total distribution) to a payee will be less than $200, must the payor provide notice to the payee of the right to elect not to have withholding apply?

A. No.

F-8. Q. How is withholding accomplished if a qualified total distribution is paid in installments during one taxable year of the payee?

A. Withholding can be accomplished on a qualified total distribution that is paid in installments within one taxable year by either one of the following methods:

Under Option 1, the tax on the first installment is calculated under the qualified total distribution table. The tax on each subsequent installment is calculated by finding the tax under the table on the cumulative amount of the installments for the year and subtracting the amount of tax already withheld from the tax due with respect to the cumulative amount of the installments.

Under Option 2, the payor or plan administrator can withhold the tax on all installments except the final installment at a 10 percent rate. The tax on the final installment may be calculated by finding the tax under the qualified total distribution table on the cumulative amount of the installments for the year and subtracting the amount of tax already withheld from the installments. Option 2 may be used even if the amount of the tax that should be withheld from the final installment under the qualified total distribution tables exceeds the amount of the final installment. The plan administrator or payor will not be subject to penalties under section 6651 with respect to the difference between the tax that should have been withheld from the final installment under the qualified total distribution tables and the amount of the final installment.

The effect of these alternatives is illustrated by the following example:

An individual receives within one taxable year the balance to his credit under a plan described in section 401(a) or 403(a). The balance to his credit is paid in three installments of $1,000, $10,000, and $60,000. The amount of tax to be withheld from the installments may be calculated under Option 1 or Option 2.

Option 1—Withholding on each installment computed by finding tax under qualified total distribution tables on the cumulative amount of the distribution and subtracting the tax already withheld.

A. 1. Amount of installment 1 . . . . . $1,000
  2. Withholding obligation on
     installment 1   50

B. 1. Amount of installments 1 and 2 . . . . $11,000
    2. Withholding obligation on installments 1 and 2 550
    3. Withholding paid on installment 1 50
    4. Withholding obligation on installment 2 500
    (2 minus 3)
C. 1. Amount of installments 1, 2, and 3 . . . . $71,000
    2. Withholding obligation on installments 1, 2, and 3 9,580
    3. Withholding paid on installments 1 and 2 550
    4. Withholding obligation on installment 3 . . . . $9,030
    (2 minus 3)
            Total withholding obligation $9,580

Option 2—Withholding computed by withholding at 10 percent rate for all but the final installment. Withholding on the final installment computed by finding tax under qualified total distribution table for the cumulative amount of the distribution and subtracting the amount of tax already withheld:

A. 1. Amount of installment 1 . . . . . $1,000
    2. Withholding obligation on installment 1 100
B. 1. Amount of installment 2 . . . . . $10,000
    2. Withholding obligation on installment 2 1,000
C. 1. Amount of installments 1, 2, and 3 . . . . $71,000
    2. Withholding obligation on installments 1, 2, and 3 9,580
    3. Withholding paid on installments 1 and 2 1,100
    4. Withholding obligation on installment 3 8,480
    (2 minus 3)
            Total withholding obligation $9,580

F-9. Q. A plan described in section 401(a) invests in life insurance contracts for its participants. Each year the current cost of the life insurance element (PS 58 cost) is taxable to the participants under section 72. Is withholding required on this amount even though there is no amount actually distributed to the participant?

A. No. Because the PS 58 costs are not distributed or deemed to be distributed, they are not designated distributions for which withholding is required.

F-10. Q. The plan administrator or payor of a plan described in section 401(a) has been properly reporting distributions on a multiple contract basis for purposes of section 72. How should the plan administrator or payor determine the amount of each payment that is includible in gross income for withholding purposes?

A. In the absence of revenue rulings or regulations to the contrary, the plan administrator or payor of a plan that properly reports distributions on a multiple contract basis should use that method to determine the taxable portion of a payment for withholding purposes.

F-11. Q. The plan administrator or payor of a plan described in section 401(a) has been reporting distributions on a multiple contract basis for purposes of section 72 and has properly switched to the single contract method for reporting distributions. How should the plan administrator or payor determine the amount of each payment that is includible in gross income for withholding purposes?

A. If a plan has properly switched from the multiple contract basis to the single contract basis for reporting distributions, the plan administrator or payor may assume that all amounts prior to the year of switch were reported by the payees on a multiple contract basis. Therefore, for example, in the case of an individual whose annuity payments have not commenced prior to the date of the switch to a single contract basis, the payee's investment in the contract can be assumed to have been recovered on a multiple contract basis prior to the year of the switch and on a single contract basis thereafter for purposes of determining the amount of each payment that is includible in gross income for withholding purposes. This rule applies even though payees may have amended their income tax returns for prior years to report all payments on a single contract basis.

F-12. Q. If a plan that makes payments subject to the withholding and notice requirements of section 3405 makes separate payments to the same individual as a retired participant and as a surviving spouse of a retired participant, must the two payments be aggregated for withholding purposes?

A. No, unless the payor wishes to aggregate them.

F-13. Q. An insurance company makes payments under certain variable annuity contracts. The Investment Company Act of 1940 (§ 22(e)) applies to these variable annuity contracts and requires that the insurance company make a pay-out within 7 days after a payee requests a withdrawal from his contract. Under these circumstances, how may notice be provided to a payee of his right to elect out of withholding for a nonperiodic distribution?

A. In this situation, the insurance company has only seven days in which to notify a payee of his right to elect out of withholding. It is not feasible for the insurance company to secure an election in writing unless the payee supplies the written election at the time he requests a withdrawal. Therefore, the notice and election can be provided in the following manner: 1) the insurance company may mail a notice to a payee on the day the request for withdrawal is received and 2) the notice may specify that unless the payee calls the company at a toll-free telephone number supplied on the notice within seven days of the date the request was received, the company will withhold from the distribution.

Notice provided in this manner is deemed to satisfy the "reasonable time" requirement of question d-9. Insurance companies that encounter this problem are encouraged to supply an election form to a payee at the time an annuity contract is purchased. If a payee supplies an election with the request for withdrawal, notice still must be given but the insurance company may honor the election received if no other communication is received after notice is provided to the payee.

F-14. Q. If an individual receives periodic payments from two or more plans of one member of a controlled group of corporations, separate periodic payments from two members of a controlled group of corporations out of one plan, or periodic payments from separate plans of two members of a controlled group, must the periodic payments be aggregated for withholding purposes?

A. No, unless the plan administrator or payor wishes to aggregate the payments. Section 414(b) does not require that plans of a controlled group of corporations be aggregated for withholding purposes. The same rule applies to a group of trades or businesses under common control or an affiliated service group described in section 414(c) or (m).

F-15. Q. How is withholding applied to a designated distribution from an individual retirement account (IRA) described in section 408(a) that is payable upon demand even though payments are scheduled to be made over a period certain greater than one year?

A. Distributions from IRAs that are payable upon demand are not periodic payments taxable under section 72 because they do not constitute annuity contracts within the meaning of section 408(d)(2). Therefore, designated distributions from an IRA that are payable upon demand are treated as nonperiodic distributions subject to withholding at the 10% rate even if the distributions are paid over a period certain.

F-16. Q. Under the rules of section 72, a portion of certain payments that may vary because of investment experience, cost of living indices, or similar criteria is treated as not received as an annuity. For withholding purposes, must these amounts be treated as nonperiodic distributions even though part of each payment is a periodic payment?

A. No. For withholding purposes, amounts will be considered periodic payments even though a portion of each payment is treated as an amount not received as an annuity under § 1.72-2(b)(3) of the Income Tax Regulations.

F-17. Q. Is the payor of distributions under a funded nonqualified deferred compensation plan that are payable as an annuity and taxable under section 72 required to withhold under section 3405?

A. Yes. Section 31.3401(a)-1(b)(1)(i) of the Employment Tax Regulations provides that any amounts received as an annuity and taxable under section 72 are excepted from the general definition of wages. Therefore, to the extent that section 402(b) requires that distributions from nonqualified plans which are received as an annuity are taxable under the rules of section 72, section 3405 will apply. See, however, question a-18 for the rules relating to distributions from a nonqualified deferred compensation plan that are taxable under section 83. Therefore, whether the payor or plan administrator of a nonqualified plan is required to withhold under section 3402 or section 3405 depends upon what section of the Code governs the taxation of amounts contributed or distributed.

F-18. Q. Are amounts paid in connection with a partial or complete surrender or upon the maturity or endowment of a commercial annuity subject to the new withholding rules?

A. Yes. Amounts paid in connection with a partial or complete surrender or upon the maturity or endowment of a commercial annuity are subject to the new withholding rules to the extent that they are designated distributions. Thus, withholding is required on the complete or partial surrender of an annuity, life insurance or endowment contract to the extent they are designated distributions.

F-19. Q. Are amounts paid in connection with a partial surrender of a commercial annuity periodic payments?

A. Generally, no. Unless the amount paid in connection with the partial surrender is one of a series of payments payable over a period of greater than one year and taxable under section 72 as an amount received as an annuity, the amount paid is not a periodic payment.

F-20. Q. Are amounts paid in connection with a complete surrender of a commercial annuity a qualified total distribution?

A. A qualified total distribution must be made under a plan described in section 401(a) or 403(a). Unless the commercial annuity is surrendered under such a plan and meets the other requirements for a qualified total distribution, the total surrender will be treated as a nonperiodic payment that is not a qualified total distribution.

F-21. Q. Is it reasonable to believe that amounts distributed in connection with a commercial annuity that was acquired on or before August 13, 1982, or are otherwise described in section 72(e)(5), which are not treated as amounts received as an annuity under section 72, will not be includible in the gross income of the recipient?

A. Generally, yes. Under the rules of section 72(e) prior to the passage of TEFRA, amounts not received as an annuity were not taxable until the investment in the contract was recovered. Thus, for distributions that are not received as an annuity under a commercial annuity contract acquired on or before August 13, 1982, it is reasonable to believe that amounts distributed are not includible in the payee's gross income to the extent they represent unrecovered investment in the contract. The special transitional rule of question a-33, available for plan administrators, may be used until December 31, 1983, by payors of commercial annuities who lack records with regard to the payee's unrecovered investment in the contract.

F-22. Q. For commercial annuity contracts entered into after August 13, 1982, which are not described in section 72(e)(5), is it reasonable to believe that amounts distributed, which are not amounts received as an annuity under section 72, are not includible in gross income?

A. Generally, no. TEFRA amended section 72(e) to provide that amounts not received as an annuity will be includible in gross income until all earnings or other amounts that are not part of the investment in the contract have been distributed. Thus, it is not reasonable to believe that amounts distributed in connection with a comercial annuity contract entered into after August 13, 1982, are excludible from gross income until all earnings or other amounts that are not part of the investment in the contract have been distributed. This new rule does not apply to distributions from commercial annuities described in section 72(e)(5). Question f-21 provides the proper rule with respect to distributions from commercial annuities described in section 72(e)(5).

F-23. Q. Is it reasonable to believe that amounts involved solely in connection with an exchange of commercial annuities under section 1035 of the Code will not be includible in the gross income of the recipient?

A. Yes. Designated distributions include only amounts that it is reasonable to believe are includible in the gross income of the recipient. In the case of a commercial annuity exchange under section 1035 in which no cash or other property is exchanged, it is reasonable to believe that no portion is includible in the gross income of a recipient. An annuity exchange includes an exchange of annuity, endowment, or life insurance contracts issued by a life insurance company licensed to do business under the laws of any State. Thus, such exchanges are not subject to the withholding rules of section 3405. However, see question e-8 concerning recordkeeping requirements with respect to the nontaxable exchange of commercial annuity contracts under section 1035.

F-24. Q. Is it reasonable to believe that amounts distributed in connection with a surrender of a life insurance or endowment contract, or in connection with an exchange of life insurance or endowment contracts in which cash or other property is distributed, will not be includible in gross income?

A. Generally, no. Amounts distributed in connection with the surrender of a life insurance or endowment contract, or in connection with an exchange of life insurance or endowment contracts in which cash or other property is distributed are includible in income to the extent that the amount received exceeds the policyholder's investment in the contract. However, if a life insurance or endowment contract issued before August 13, 1982, is surrendered within ten years of the date of its issuance, or is exchanged within

ten years of the date of its issuance, the payor may assume that no amounts are includible in the gross income of the policyholder if the cash or other property received by the policyholder in connection with the surrender or exchange of the life insurance or endowment contract does not exceed $10,000. If a life insurance or endowment contract issued before August 13, 1982, is surrendered or exchanged ten years or more after the date of its issuance, the payor may assume that no amounts are includible in the gross income of the policyholder if the cash or other property received by the policyholder in connection with the surrender or exchange of the life insurance or endowment contract does not exceed $5,000. If the payor utilizes the special rule in the two preceding sentences, the payor must notify the policyholder, at the time described in question d-4, that all or part of the amount distributed may be includible in the policyholder's gross income. See question f-23 for additional rules concerning certain exchanges of annuity contracts.

F-25. Q. Do the requirements of section 3405(d)(10), relating to the time at which notice must be provided, also apply to the time at which an election out of withholding may be made?

A. Generally, yes. For example, an individual may not at commencement of employment execute an election out of withholding to be honored by a plan administrator or payor when the individual terminates employment and receives a distribution from a deferred compensation plan. See, however, question f-13 for a special rule applicable to certain annuity contracts.

F-26. Q. If a payor provided notice prior to January 1, 1983, but failed to include all of the information required by question d-18, may the abbreviated notice of question d-27 be supplied when making the first payment?

A. Yes, as long as the abbreviated notice contains all of the information required by question d-18 that was not supplied with the earlier notice.

F-27. Q. When must notice of the right to elect not to have withholding apply be given as to designated distributions from an individual retirement account (IRA) described in section 408(a) that is payable on demand even though payments are scheduled to be made over a period greater than one year?

A. Under question f-15, designated distributions from an IRA that are payable upon demand are treated as nonperiodic distributions subject to withholding at the 10 percent rate even if the distributions are paid over a period certain. Section 3405(d)(10)(B)(i) requires the payor of a nonperiodic distribution to transmit to the payee notice, at the time of the distribution or at such earlier time as may be provided in regulations, of the right to elect not to have withholding apply. If distributions from an IRA have begun and are scheduled to be made at quarterly or more frequent intervals, then, in lieu of providing a notice at the time of each distribution, the payor may furnish a blanket notice applicable to all such distributions that are expected to be made to the payee from the account during a calendar year. Such a blanket notice must be furnished at a reasonable time before the first payment made in the calendar year to which the notice relates, except that a blanket notice relating to distributions from the IRA during 1983 may be made by the later of October 1, 1983, or the date of the first designated distribution from the IRA.

G. Delay Procedures.

G-1. Q. When does the new law take effect?

A. In general, withholding is required on any designated distributions made after December 31, 1982.

G-2. Q. Is there a penalty for failure to withhold under section 3405 on designated distributions made after December 31, 1982?

A. Yes. In general, section 6651 governs the failure to file a return and to withhold tax under section 3405.

G-3. Q. Are there any circumstances under which the withholding and notice requirements of section 3405 may be delayed to a date later than January 1, 1983?

A. Yes. The Secretary has authority to delay, but not beyond June 30, 1983, the application of these withholding provisions to any payor or plan administrator if the payor or plan administrator can establish that he is unable to comply with these provisions without undue hardship.

G-4. Q. Under what circumstances may a payor or plan administrator who is experiencing undue hardship in complying with section 3405 delay implementation of the notice and withholding requirements?

A. For those payors and plan administrators who experience undue hardship in complying with the provisions of section 3405, the withholding and notice requirements of section 3405 may be delayed so long as undue hardship exists up to July 1, 1983.

G-5. Q. Must approval be obtained from the Internal Revenue Service to be entitled to the delay referred to in question g-4 if the delay will be no later than April 1, 1983?

A. No. If a payor or plan administrator can establish that undue hardship would result if required to comply with the provisions of this section before April 1, 1983, prior approval from the Internal Revenue Service is not required and should not be requested. For purposes of this delay up to April 1, 1983, undue hardship will be presumed to exist, in the absence of bad faith, as long as the payor or plan administrator can establish that at least one of the conditions listed in question g-6 is present.

The payor or plan administrator should prepare and retain a statement of undue hardship as described in question g-9 and should maintain any documents necessary to support the representations made in that statement.

G-6. Q. What constitutes undue hardship?

A. For purposes of these delay procedures, the term "undue hardship" generally means more than an inconvenience or increased costs to the payor or plan administrator. In the case of a payor or plan administrator who complies with the notice and withholding requirements of section 3405 on or before April 1, 1983, undue hardship will be presumed to exist if one or more of the following conditions is present:

(1) The payor or plan administrator encounters significant delay or other substantial difficulty in obtaining authorization for funds to develop forms, to mail notices, to process responses, to develop new computer programs, or to obtain and train personnel to implement withholding.

(2) The payor or plan administrator incurs substantial increases in unbudgeted costs to develop forms, to mail notices, to process responses, to develop new computer programs, or to obtain and train personnel.

(3) There is difficulty in obtaining trained personnel, including professional or semi-professional individuals, whose skills are necessary to implement withholding.

(4) Training new or present employees or hiring new employees to implement withholding would cause substantially increased costs or would disrupt the payor's or plan administrator's operations, and such disruption or increased costs would not occur if withholding were implemented at a later date.

(5) Plan benefits change due to a collective bargaining agreement concluded between October 1, 1982, and April 1, 1983.

(6) A payor who provided notice prior to January 1, 1983, receives a substantial number of inquiries from payees. These inquiries indicate the payees' lack of understanding of the new withholding provisions and the payor cannot answer all questions and receive responses by January 1, 1983.

(7) The payor or plan administrator is unable to implement withholding on account of the occurrence of an event, such as fire, flood, earthquake, explosion, or strike, beyond the control of the payor or plan administrator.

(8) The payor or plan administrator is scheduled to install a new data processing hardware package or system between December 1, 1982, and July 1, 1983, that will be used for the process of pension withholding.

An example of a circumstance not considered as resulting in undue hardship would be changes in the withholding tables effective July 1, 1983.

The following examples illustrate situations in which an undue hardship that will permit delay in implementation of the notice and withholding provisions exists:

Example (1). A is the payor and plan administrator of a deferred compensation plan that is the subject of a collective bargaining agreement. The collectively bargained plan has fewer than 100 participants receiving annuity payments. All of

Reg. § 35.3405-1T

A's available budget is scheduled to be used to pay plan benefits and administrative costs, and no funds are available to implement the new withholding requirements. A must obtain authorization to expend funds to implement withholding. Meetings at which A can obtain such authorization are held August 1 and February 1 of each year. After obtaining authorization on February 1, 1983, A will need to develop and mail withholding notices and elections, process responses and determine the amount to be withheld from each payee's annuity payment. A can implement withholding on April 1, 1983, without substantially disrupting its operations, but earlier implementation would disrupt its normal operations. Under these facts, A experiences undue hardship until at least April 1, 1983, as a result of the circumstances described in items (1) and (4) of question g-6.

Example (2). B, a bank, is a payor of pensions and annuities under plans described in section 401(a). The plan administrators of all these plans have transferred liability to B for withholding under section 3405. After T.D. 7839, relating to withholding from pensions, annuities and other deferred income, was published in the Federal Register on October 14, 1982, B determines that the withholding provisions can be implemented before April 1, 1983, on a reasonable schedule, without substantial increases in costs or disruption of daily bank operations, according to the following schedule:

(a) B's counsel analyzes regulations and reports requirements to operations personnel; operations personnel develop new forms, which are reviewed and revised by management and legal personnel; new forms are printed; personnel begin reprogramming computers	8 weeks (Dec. 9, 1982)
(b) Forms distributed to branch offices	1 week (Dec. 16, 1982)
(c) Forms mailed to payees	1 week (Dec. 23, 1982)
(d) Time allowed for response to mailing of notices, answering questions, mailing follow-up notices to payees	6 weeks (Feb. 3, 1983)
(e) Withholding calculated and entered into payment system	6 weeks (Mar. 17, 1983)
Total:	22 weeks

Implementation is scheduled to begin March 17, 1983. Implementation prior to March 17, 1983, would substantially increase costs and would disrupt B's operations.

Under these facts, B experiences undue hardship under item (4) of question g-6 up to March 17, 1983, the scheduled date of implementation.

G-7. Q. If a payor or plan administrator qualifies for the delay described in question g-5, is there a procedure for requesting an additional delay up to July 1, 1983?

A. Yes. However, any request made for this additional delay will be considered on a case-by-case basis. It is anticipated these requests will be carefully scrutinized and generally will be granted only in circumstances where the payor or plan administrator can reasonably expect that more than one of the conditions described in question g-6 will exist on or after April 1, 1983, and up to July 1, 1983.

G-8. Q. How may a payor or plan administrator request this additional delay of up to 3 months for undue hardship?

A. The payor or plan administrator may request an additional delay of up to 3 months by filing in duplicate a written statement of undue hardship signed under penalties of perjury with the director of the service center where the payor or plan administrator files Form 941 or Form 941E. This written request must state on the envelope and at the top of the letter "PENSION WITHHOLDING: Undue Hardship" and must include all the information required in a statement of undue hardship as described in question g-9.

G-9. Q. What information must the statement of undue hardship include?

A. The statement of undue hardship must include the following information:

(1) The name, address, and taxpayer identification number of the payor or plan administrator.

(2) A complete statement of the facts upon which the payor is relying to show a delay beyond April 1, 1983, is warranted. This statement must include as many of the conditions of undue hardship listed in question g-6 as pertain to the payor or plan administrator.

(3) A schedule or plan of implementation showing dates on which the payor will implement the provisions of this section, with no date later than July 1, 1983. This schedule should provide a complete timetable that includes such items as development of forms, mailing of notices, time for responses, programming computers, and calculation of withholding.

(4) An explanation of the steps taken which demonstrate the payor's or plan administrator's good faith attempt to comply with these notice and withholding requirements.

G-10. Q. When must the plan administrator or payor file this request for delay and statement of undue hardship?

A. Payors or plan administrators must file the statement of undue hardship on or before March 1, 1983. However, no request for delay may be filed with the Internal Revenue Service before January 1, 1983.

Collection of Income Tax at Source on Wages
See p. 20,601 for regulations not amended to reflect law changes
61,611

G-11. Q. Who must request the delay?

A. The delay should be requested by the payor or plan administrator who is actually liable for withholding. Therefore, generally the payor should request the delay. However, in the case of a distribution from a plan described in section 401(a), section 403(a), or section 301(d) of the Tax Reduction Act of 1975, the plan administrator is liable for withholding and should request the delay unless the plan administrator has transferred liability for withholding to the payor under section 3405(c).

G-12. Q. If a plan administrator has not yet transferred liability for withholding under section 3405(c) or has inadequately transferred liability, and the payor requests a delay, will the request for delay be treated as if the plan administrator had requested it?

A. Yes.

G-13. Q. If a plan administrator and a payor both file requests for delay and statements of undue hardship with respect to the same plan, will there be two separate three-month extensions?

A. No. A request for delay will delay the effective date only up to three months and in no case will it extend it past July 1, 1983.

G-14. Q. What are the consequences for failure to file the request for delay and statement of undue hardship in a timely manner?

A. If the request for delay and statement of undue hardship are not filed in a timely manner, the payor or plan administrator will not be entitled to any delay beyond the delay to which he may be entitled under question g-5. This rule will not apply in the case of an event such as strike, fire, flood, earthquake, or explosion that occurs after March 1, 1983, if compliance with the withholding provisions would have been possible absent the occurrence of the event.

G-15. Q. Will a payor or plan administrator receive a response from the Internal Revenue Service as to whether a delay after April 1, 1983, has been granted?

A. Yes. Since these requests for delay will be reviewed on a case-by-case basis, the payor or plan administrator will receive a response by April 1, 1983, as to whether or not a requested delay has been granted. If the request for delay is denied by the director of the service center, the payor or plan administrator is required to begin withholding by the later of April 1, 1983, or 10 days from the date of the response. No penalties will be imposed under section 6651 for failure to withhold between April 1, 1983, and the day 10 days from the date on the response.

G-16. Q. If the director of the service center grants a delay up to July 1, 1983, must the payor or plan administrator retain a copy of the response from the Internal Revenue Service?

A. Yes. In addition, the payor or plan administrator must attach a copy of the response to the first Form 941 or 941E filed after the response is received.

G-17. Q. If a plan administrator or payor begins withholding before April 1, 1983, or July 1, 1983, can the payee request a refund from the plan administrator or payor of the amounts withheld?

A. No. Because plan administrators and payors are required to comply with the withholding and notice requirements as soon as they no longer experience undue hardship, they cannot refund any amounts withheld to a payee, except as provided in the regulations under section 6413 (in the case of a mistake by the payor or plan administrator).

G-18. Q. If a payor or plan administrator properly files the statement of undue hardship and receives a delay as provided in question g-7, will withholding from payments made after the delay period be required to make up for amounts that would have been withheld if there had been no delay granted?

A. No. No catch-up withholding is required for plan administrators or payors who are entitled to a delay up to April 1, 1983, as provided in question g-5 or granted a delay up to July 1, 1983, as provided in question g-7. However, if a payor or plan administrator who is entitled to a delay up to April 1, 1983, as provided in question g-5, is not granted a delay up to July 1, 1983, but is unable to implement withholding until July 1, 1983, despite a good faith effort to comply, no penalties will be imposed under section 6651 if the payor or plan administrator withholds between July 1, 1983, and December 31, 1983, both the amounts required to be withheld during that period and the amounts that should have been withheld between April 1, 1983, and June 30, 1983.

G-19. Q. If a payor or plan administrator does not receive and is not otherwise entitled to a delay under these regulations, will withholding from future payments be required to make up for amounts that would have been withheld if there had been no delay?

A. Yes, to the extent possible. An example of a situation in which a payor or plan administrator would not be able to withhold enough from subsequent payments to satisfy pre-July 1, 1983, withholding obligations is one where the recipient of a single life annuity died on July 1, 1983, before the payor or plan administrator began to withhold income tax from the annuity. In addition, a payor or plan administrator would not be able to satisfy the pre-July 1, 1983, withholding requirements if the payee elects out of withholding before all of the make-up withholding has been accomplished.

G-20. Q. What are the consequences if the payor or plan administrator cannot establish undue hardship and does not comply on January 1, 1983?

A. In general, if the payor or plan administrator cannot establish undue hardship and fails to withhold beginning January 1, 1983, the payor or plan administrator will be liable for the tax that should have been withheld and, in addition, the penalties provided in section 6651 will apply.

Reg. §35.3405-1T

However, the payor or plan administrator will not be liable for penalties for failure to file a return and for failure to pay the tax if a good faith effort is made to comply, and if, to the extent possible, withholding from post-implementation payments is sufficient to satisfy the pre-implementation withholding obligation. Whether the payor or plan administrator has made a good faith effort to comply depends on the facts and circumstances of each case. The facts and circumstances that will be considered include, but are not limited to, those conditions listed in question g-6.

G-21. Q. If a payor or plan administrator is required to make up amounts that should have been withheld, must he withhold from the first subsequent payment the entire amount that should have been previously withheld?

A. No. A payor or plan administrator may withhold a proportional amount out of each subsequent payment made before January 1, 1984.

G-22. Q. Will the notice requirements of section 3405 apply before July 1, 1983, with respect to recipients of periodic payments that total less than $5,400 per year?

A. No.

G-23. Q. Will the notice and withholding requirements of section 3405 apply before July 1, 1983, with respect to payments to nonresident alien individuals?

A. No.

G-24. Q. Does a payor or plan administrator who requested a delay prior to the publication of these procedures in the Federal Register need to resubmit the request in light of these procedures?

A. Yes. In order to be entitled to a delay, payors and plan administrators must follow the procedures required by these temporary regulations.

G-25. Q. Will the notice and withholding requirements of section 3405 apply before January 1, 1984, with respect to the exchange or complete or partial surrender of a commercial annuity under which the recipient had not irrevocably chosen, prior to January 1, 1984, to receive payments in the form of an annuity?

A. In the case of the exchange or complete or partial surrender of a commercial annuity under which the recipient had not irrevocably chosen, prior to January 1, 1984, to receive payments in the form of an annuity, the application of the notice and withholding provisions of this section may be delayed, so long as undue hardship exists, up to January 1, 1984. Prior approval from the Internal Revenue Service is not required for such delay, and should not be requested. For purposes of this delay, undue hardship will be presumed to exist, in the absence of bad faith, so long as the payor can establish that at least one of the conditions in question g-6 is present. The payor should prepare and retain a statement of undue hardship as described in question g-9 and should maintain any documents necessary to support the representations made in that statement.

[Temporary Reg. § 35.3405-1T.]

☐ [*T.D.* 7839, 10-8-82. *Amended by T.D.* 7858, 11-26-82 *and T.D.* 7904, 8-2-83. *Redesignated by T.D.* 8873, 2-7-2000. *Amended by T.D.* 8952, 6-25-2001.]

[Reg. § 31.3406-0]

§ 31.3406-0. Outline of the backup withholding regulations.—This section lists paragraphs contained in §§ 31.3406(a)-1 through 31.3406(i)-1.

§ 31.3406(a)-1 Backup withholding requirement on reportable payments.

    (a) Overview.

    (b) Conditions that invoke the backup withholding requirement.

        (1) Conditions applicable to all reportable payments.

        (2) Conditions applicable only to reportable interest or dividend payments.

    (c) Exceptions.

    (d) Cross references.

§ 31.3406(a)-2 Definition of payors obligated to backup withhold.

    (a) In general.

    (b) Persons treated as payors.

    (c) Persons not treated as payors.

    (d) Effective date.

§ 31.3406(a)-3 Scope and extent of accounts subject to backup withholding.

§ 31.3406(a)-4 Time when payments are considered to be paid and subject to backup withholding.

    (a) Timing.

        (1) In general.

        (2) Special rules for dividends.

    (b) Amounts reportable under section 6045.

        (1) In general.

        (2) Special rule for interest accrued on bonds.

    (c) Middlemen.

        (1) In general.

        (2) Special rule for common trust funds.

        (3) Special rule for certain grantor trusts.

§ 31.3406(b)(2)-1 Reportable interest payment.

    (a) Interest subject to backup withholding.

        (1) In general.

        (2) Special rule for tax-exempt interest.

    (b) Amount subject to backup withholding.

        (1) In general.

        (2) Special rule to adjust for premature withdrawal penalty.

§ 31.3406(b)(2)-2 Original issue discount.

    (a) Original issue discount subject to backup withholding.

    (b) Amount subject to backup withholding and time when backup withholding is imposed with respect to short-term obligations.

    (c) Transferred short-term obligations.

        (1) Subsequent holder may establish purchase price.

        (2) Subsequent holder unable (or not permitted) to establish purchase price.

(3) Transferred obligation.

(d) Amount subject to backup withholding and time when backup withholding is imposed with respect to long-term obligations.

(1) No cash payments prior to maturity.

(2) Registered long-term obligations with cash payments prior to maturity.

(3) Transferred registered long-term obligations with payments prior to maturity.

(e) Bearer long-term obligations.

(1) Payments prior to maturity.

(2) Payments at maturity.

§ 31.3406(b)(2)-3 *Window transactions.*

(a) Requirement to backup withhold.

(b) Window transaction defined.

(c) Manner of furnishing taxpayer identification number in the case of a window transaction.

§ 31.3426(b)(2)-4 *Reportable dividend payment.*

(a) Dividends subject to backup withholding.

(b) Dividends not subject to backup withholding.

(c) Amount subject to backup withholding.

(1) In general.

(2) Reasonable estimate of amount of dividend subject to backup withholding.

(3) Reinvested dividends.

§ 31.3406(b)(2)-5 *Reportable patronage dividend payment.*

(a) Patronage dividends subject to backup withholding.

(b) Amount subject to backup withholding.

(1) Failure to provide taxpayer identification number or notification of incorrect taxpayer identification number.

(2) Notified payee underreporting or payee certification failure.

§ 31.3406(b)(3)-1 *Reportable payments of rents, commissions, nonemployee compensation, etc.*

(a) Section 6041 and 6041A(a) payments subject to backup withholding.

(b) Amount subject to backup withholding.

(1) In general.

(2) Net commissions.

(3) Payments aggregating $600 or more for the calendar year.

§ 31.3406(b)(3)-2 *Reportable barter exchanges and gross proceeds of sales of securities or commodities by brokers.*

(a) Transactions subject to backup withholding.

(b) Amount subject to backup withholding.

(1) In general.

(2) Forward contracts, including foreign currency contracts, and regulated futures contracts.

(3) Security sales made through a margin account.

(4) Security short sales.

(5) Fractional shares.

§ 31.3406(b)(3)-3 *Reportable payments by certain fishing boat operators.*

(a) Payments subject to backup withholding.

(b) Amount subject to backup withholding.

§ 31.3406(b)(3)-4 *Reportable payments of royalties.*

(a) Royalty payments subject to backup withholding.

(b) Amount subject to backup withholding.

§ 31.3406(b)(3)-5 *Reportable payments of payment card and third party network transactions.*

(a) Payment card and third party network transactions subject to backup withholding.

(b) Amount subject to backup withholding.

(c) Time when payments are considered to be subject to backup withholding.

(d) Backup withholding from an alternate source.

(e) Effective/applicability date.

§ 31.3406(b)(4)-1 *Exemption for certain minimal payments.*

(a) In general.

(b) Manner of making the election.

(c) How to annualize.

(1) In general.

(2) Special aggregation rule for reportable interest and dividends.

(d) Exception for window transactions and original issue discount.

§ 31.3406(c)-1 *Notified payee underreporting of reportable interest or dividend payments.*

(a) Overview.

(b) Definitions.

(1) Notified payee underreporting.

(2) Payee underreporting.

(c) Notice to payors regarding backup withholding due to notified payee underreporting.

(1) In general.

(2) Additional requirements for payors that are also brokers.

(3) Payor identification of accounts of the payee subject to backup withholding due to notified payee underreporting.

(d) Notice from payors of backup withholding due to notified payee underreporting.

(1) In general.

(2) Procedures.

(e) Period during which backup withholding is required.

(1) In general.

(2) Stop withholding.

(3) Dormant accounts.

(f) Notice to payees from the Internal Revenue Service.

(1) Notice period.

(2) Payee subject to backup withholding.

(3) Disclosure of names of payors and brokers.

(4) Backup withholding certification.

(g) Determination by the Internal Revenue Service that backup withholding should not start or should be stopped.

Reg. §31.3406-0

(1) In general.

(2) Date notice to stop backup withholding will be provided.

(3) Grounds for determination.

(4) No underreporting.

(5) Correcting any payee underreporting.

(6) Undue hardship.

(7) Bona fide dispute.

(h) Payees filing a joint return.

(1) In general.

(2) Exceptions.

(i) [Reserved.]

(j) Penalties.

§ 31.3406(d)-1 Manner required for furnishing a taxpayer identification number.

(a) Requirement to backup withhold.

(b) Reportable interest or dividend account.

(1) Manner required for furnishing a taxpayer identification number with respect to a pre-1984 account or instrument.

(2) Determination of pre-1984 account or instrument.

(3) Manner required for furnishing a taxpayer identification number with respect to an account or instrument that is not a pre-1984 account.

(4) Special rule with respect to the acquisition of a readily tradable instrument in a transaction between certain parties acting without the assistance of a broker.

(c) Brokerage account.

(1) Manner required for furnishing a taxpayer identification number with respect to a brokerage relationship that is not a post-1983 brokerage account.

(2) Manner required for furnishing a taxpayer identification number with respect to a post-1983 brokerage account.

(d) Rents, commissions, nonemployee compensation, and certain fishing boat operators, etc.—Manner required for furnishing a taxpayer identification number.

§ 31.3406(d)-2 Payee certification failure.

(a) Requirement to backup withhold.

(b) Exceptions.

§ 31.3406(d)-3 Special 30-day rules for certain reportable payments.

(a) Accounts or readily tradable instruments acquired directly from the payor (including a broker who holds an instrument in street name) by electronic transmission or by mail.

(b) Sale of an instrument for a customer by electronic transmission or by mail.

(c) Application to foreign payees.

§ 31.3406(d)-4 Special rules for readily tradable instruments acquired through a broker.

(a) Readily tradable instruments acquired through post-1983 brokerage accounts with a broker who is not a payor.

(1) In general.

(2) Additional requirements.

(3) Transactions entered into through a brokerage account that is not a post-1983 brokerage account.

(4) Payor must notify payee.

(b) Notices.

(1) Form of notice by broker to payor.

(2) Form of notice by payor to payee.

(c) Payor's reliance on information from broker.

(1) In general.

(2) Amount subject to backup withholding.

§ 31.3406(d)-5 Backup withholding when the Service or a broker notifies the payor to withhold because the payee's taxpayer identification number is incorrect.

(a) Overview.

(b) Definitions and special rules.

(1) Definition of an incorrect name/TIN combination.

(2) Definition of account.

(3) Definition of business day.

(4) Certain exceptions.

(c) Notice regarding an incorrect name/TIN combination.

(1) In general.

(2) Additional requirements for payors that are also brokers.

(3) Payor identification of the account or accounts of the payee that have the incorrect taxpayer identification number.

(4) Special rule for joint accounts.

(5) Date of receipt.

(d) Notice from payors of backup withholding due to an incorrect name/TIN combination.

(1) In general.

(2) Procedures.

(e) Period during which backup withholding is required due to notification of an incorrect name/TIN combination.

(1) In general.

(2) Grace periods.

(3) Dormant accounts.

(f) Manner required for payee to furnish certified taxpayer identification number.

(g) Receipt of two notices within a 3-year period.

(1) In general.

(2) Notice to payee who has provided two incorrect name/TIN combinations within 3 calendar years.

(3) Period during which backup withholding is required due to a second notice of an incorrect name/TIN combination within 3 calendar years.

(4) Receipt of two notices in one calendar year.

(5) Notification from the Social Security Administration (or the Internal Revenue Service) validating a name/TIN combination.

(h) Payors must use newly provided certified number.

(i) Effective date.

(j) Examples.

§ 31.3406(e)-1 *Period during which backup withholding is required.*

  (a) In general.

  (b) Failure to furnish a taxpayer identification number in the manner required.

    (1) Start withholding.

    (2) Stop withholding.

  (c) Notification of an incorrect taxpayer identification number.

  (d) Notified payee underreporting.

  (e) Payee certification failure.

    (1) Start withholding.

    (2) Stop withholding.

  (f) Rule for determining when the payor receives a taxpayer identification number or certificate from a payee.

§ 31.3406(f)-1 *Confidentiality of information.*

  (a) Confidentiality and liability for violation.

  (b) Permissible use of information.

    (1) In general.

    (2) Window transactions.

  (c) Specific restrictions on the use of information.

§ 31.3406(g)-1 *Exception for payments to certain payees and certain other payments.*

  (a) Exempt recipients.

    (1) In general.

    (2) Nonexclusive list.

  (b) Determination of whether a person is described in paragraph (a)(1) of this section.

  (c) Prepaid or advance premium life-insurance contracts.

  (d) Reportable payments made to Canadian nonresident alien individuals.

  (e) Certain reportable payments made outside the United States by foreign persons, foreign offices of United States banks and brokers, and others.

  (f) Special rule for certain payment card transactions.

§ 31.3406(g)-2 *Exception for reportable payments for which backup withholding is otherwise required.*

  (a) In general.

  (b) Payment of wages.

  (c) Distribution from a pension, annuity, or other plan of deferred compensation.

  (d) Gambling winnings.

    (1) In general.

    (2) Definition of a reportable gambling winning and determination of amount subject to backup withholding.

    (3) Special rules.

  (e) Certain real estate transactions.

  (f) Certain payments after an acquisition of accounts or instruments.

  (g) Certain gross proceeds.

  (h) Applicability date.

§ 31.3406(g)-3 *Exemption while payee is waiting for a taxpayer identification number.*

  (a) In general.

    (1) Backup withholding not required for 60 days.

    (2) Reserve method.

    (3) Alternative rule; 7-day grace period.

  (b) Special rule for readily tradable instruments.

  (c) Exceptions.

    (1) In general.

    (2) Special rule for amounts subject to reporting under section 6045 other than proceeds of redemptions of bearer obligations.

  (d) Awaiting-TIN certificate.

  (e) Form for awaiting-TIN certificate.

§ 31.3406(h)-1 *Definitions.*

  (a) In general.

  (b) Taxpayer identification number.

    (1) In general.

    (2) Obviously incorrect number.

  (c) Broker.

  (d) Readily tradable instrument.

  (e) Day.

  (f) Business day.

§ 31.3406(h)-2 *Special rules.*

  (a) Joint accounts.

    (1) Relevant name and taxpayer identification number combination.

    (2) Optional rule for accounts subject to backup withholding under section 3406(a)(1)(B) or (C) where the names are switched.

    (3) Joint foreign payees.

  (b) Backup withholding from an alternative source.

    (1) In general.

    (2) Exceptions for payments made in property.

  (c) Trusts.

  (d) Adjustment of prior withholding by middleman.

  (e) Conversion of amounts paid in foreign currency into United States dollars.

  (f) Coordination with other sections.

  (g) Tax liabilities and penalties.

  (h) To whom payor is liable for amount withheld.

§ 31.3406(h)-3 *Certificates.*

  (a) Prescribed form to furnish information under penalties of perjury.

    (1) In general.

    (2) Use of a single or multiple Forms W-9 for accounts of the same payee.

  (b) Prescribed form to furnish a noncertified taxpayer identification number.

  (c) Forms prepared by payors or brokers.

    (1) Substitute forms; in general.

    (2) Form for exempt recipient.

  (d) Special rule for brokers.

  (e) Reasonable reliance on certificate.

    (1) In general.

Reg. § 31.3406-0

(2) Circumstances establishing reasonable reliance.

(f) Who may sign certificate.

(1) In general.

(2) Notified payee underreporting.

(g) Retention of certificates.

(1) Accounts or instruments that are not pre-1984 accounts and brokerage relationships that are post-1983 brokerage accounts.

(2) Accounts or instruments that are pre-1984 accounts and brokerage relationships that are not post-1983 brokerage accounts.

(h) Cross references.

[Reg. §31.3406-0.]

☐ [*T.D.* 8409, 4-10-92. *Amended by T.D.* 8637, 12-20-95; *T.D.* 8734, 10-6-97 (*T.D.* 8804 delayed the effective date of T.D. 8734 from January 1, 1999, to January 1, 2000; T.D. 8856 further delayed the effective date of T.D. 8734 until January 1, 2001); *T.D.* 9010, 7-25-2002; *T.D.* 9496, 8-13-2010 *and T.D.* 9824, 9-25-2017.]

[Reg. §31.3406(a)-1]

§31.3406(a)-1. Backup withholding requirement on reportable payments.—(a) *Overview.*— Under section 3406, a payor must deduct and withhold 31 percent of a reportable payment if a condition for withholding exists. *Reportable payments* mean interest and dividend payments (as defined in section 3406(b)(2)) and other reportable payments (as defined in section 3406(b)(3)). The conditions described in paragraph (b)(1) of this section apply to all reportable payments, including reportable interest and dividend payments. The conditions described in paragraph (b)(2) of this section apply only to reportable interest and dividend payments.

(b) *Conditions that invoke the backup withholding requirement.*—(1) *Conditions applicable to all reportable payments.*—A payor of a reportable payment must deduct and withhold under section 3406 if—

(i) The payee of the reportable payment does not furnish the payee's taxpayer identification number to the payor, as required in section 3406(a)(1)(A) and §31.3406(d)-1; or

(ii) The Internal Revenue Service or a broker notifies the payor that the taxpayer identification number furnished by its payee for a reportable payment is incorrect, as described in section 3406(a)(1)(B) and §31.3406(d)-5.

(2) *Conditions applicable only to reportable interest or dividend payments.*—A payor of a reportable interest or dividend payment must deduct and withhold under section 3406 if—

(i) The Internal Revenue Service or a broker notifies the payor that its payee has underreported interest or dividend income, as described in section 3406(a)(1)(C) and §31.3406(c)-1; or

(ii) The payee fails to certify to the payor or broker that the payee is not subject to withholding due to notified payee underreporting, as described in section 3406(a)(1)(D) and §31.3406(d)-2.

(c) *Exceptions.*—The requirement to withhold does not apply to certain minimal payments as described in §31.3406(b)(4)-1 or to payments exempt from withholding under §§31.3406(g)-1 through 31.3406(g)-3.

(d) *Cross references.*—For the definition of *payor*, see §31.3406(a)-2. For the definition of *taxpayer identification number*, see §31.3406(h)-1(b). [Reg. §31.3406(a)-1.]

☐ [*T.D.* 8637, 12-20-95.]

[Reg. §31.3406(a)-2]

§31.3406(a)-2. Definition of payors obligated to backup withhold.—(a) *In general.*—*Payor* means the person that is required to make an information return under section 6041, 6041A(a), 6042, 6044, 6045, 6049, 6050A, 6050N, or 6050W with respect to any reportable payment (as described in section 3406(b)), or that is described in paragraph (b) of this section.

(b) *Persons treated as payors.*—The following persons are treated as payors for purposes of section 3406—

(1) A grantor trust established after December 31, 1995, all of which is owned by two or more grantors (treating for this purpose spouses filing a joint return as one grantor);

(2) A grantor trust with ten or more grantors established on or after January 1, 1984 but before January 1, 1996;

(3) A common trust fund; and

(4) A partnership or an S corporation that makes a reportable payment.

(c) *Persons not treated as payors.*—A person on the following list is not treated as a payor for purposes of section 3406 if the person does not have a reporting obligation under the section on information reporting to which the payment relates—

(1) A trust (other than a grantor trust as described in paragraph (b)(1) or (2) of this section) that files a Form 1041 containing information required to be shown on an information return, including amounts withheld under section 3406; or

(2) A partnership making a payment of a distributive share or an S corporation making a similar distribution.

(d) *Effective date.*—The provisions of this section apply to payments made after December 31, 2002. [Reg. §31.3406(a)-2.]

[*T.D.* 8637, 12-20-95. *Amended by T.D.* 9010, 7-25-2002 *and T.D.* 9496, 8-13-2010.]

[Reg. §31.3406(a)-3]

§31.3406(a)-3. Scope and extent of accounts subject to backup withholding.—A payor who is required to withhold under §31.3406(a)-1 must withhold—

(a) On the accounts subject to withholding under §31.3406(a)-1(b)(1)(i) or (b)(2)(ii); and

(b) On the accounts subject to withholding under §31.3406(a)-1(b)(1)(ii) or (b)(2)(i), as described under §31.3406(d)-5 (relating to notification of incorrect TIN) or §31.3406(c)-1 (relating to notified payee underreporting), respectively. [Reg. §31.3406(a)-3.]

☐ [*T.D.* 8637, 12-20-95.]

[Reg. §31.3406(a)-4]

§31.3406(a)-4. Time when payments are considered to be paid and subject to backup withholding.—(a) *Timing.*—(1) *In general.*—If backup withholding is required under section 3406 on a reportable payment (as defined in section 3406(b)), the payor must withhold at the time it makes the payment to the payee or to the payee's account that is subject to withholding. Amounts are considered paid when they are credited to the account of, or made available to, the payee. Amounts are not considered paid solely because they are posted (e.g., an informational notation on the payee's passbook) if they are not actually credited to the payee's account or made available to the payee. See paragraph (c) of this section for the timing of withholding by a middleman.

(2) *Special rules for dividends.*—For purposes of section 3406 and this section—

(i) *Record date earlier than payment date.*—In the case of stock for which the record date is earlier than the payment date, the dividends are considered paid on the payment date.

(ii) *Dividends paid in corporate reorganizations.*—In the case of a corporate reorganization, if a payee is required to exchange stock held in the former corporation for stock in the new corporation before the dividends that have been paid with respect to the stock in the new corporation will be provided to the payee, the dividend is considered paid on the date the payee actually exchanges the stock and receives the dividend.

(b) *Amounts reportable under section 6045.*—(1) *In general.*—Notwithstanding paragraph (a) of this section, in the case of a transaction reportable under section 6045 (except in the case of forward contracts (including foreign currency contracts), regulated futures contracts, and security short sales), the obligation to withhold under section 3406 arises on the date the sale is entered on the books of the broker or the date the exchange occurs as provided in §1.6045-1(f)(3) of this chapter. A broker (in its capacity as payor) is not required, however, to satisfy its withholding liability until payment is made. See §31.3406(b)(3)-2(b)(2) for special rules applicable to forward contracts (including foreign currency contracts), regulated futures contracts, and security short sales.

(2) *Special rule for interest accrued on bonds.*—For purposes of determining the time that interest is considered paid and subject to withholding under section 3406 when bonds are sold between interest payment dates, the portion of the sales price representing interest accrued to the date of sale is considered a portion of a reportable payment of gross proceeds under section 6045 (pro-

vided that the accrued interest is not tax-exempt as described in section 103(a), relating to certain governmental obligations), and is not considered to be a payment of interest for purposes of section 6049.

(c) *Middlemen.*—(1) *In general.*—A person that is a middleman and is a person defined in §31.3406(a)-2(b) or in the section on information reporting to which the payment relates must withhold under section 3406 at the time the reportable payment is received by or credited to the middleman. If the middleman makes or credits the reportable payment to the payee prior to the middleman's receipt of the corresponding payment, the middleman may withhold at the time the reportable payment is made or credited to the payee.

(2) *Special rule for common trust funds.*—A common trust fund (as defined in section 584) must withhold either—

(i) At the time the reportable payment is received by or credited to the common trust fund as provided in paragraph (c)(1) of this section;

(ii) On the date on which the assets of the common trust fund are valued; or

(iii) At the time the common trust fund pays or credits the reportable payment to a participant of the common trust fund.

(3) *Special rule for certain grantor trusts.*—For grantor trusts described in §31.3406(a)-2(b)(1) or (2), reportable payments made to the trust are treated as paid by the trust to each grantor, in an amount equal to the distribution made by the trust to each grantor, on the date that the reportable payment is paid to the trust (except for gross proceeds reportable under section 6045). Paragraph (b)(2) of this section applies to a grantor trust making a payment of gross proceeds under section 6045 subject to withholding under section 3406. For purposes of this paragraph (c)(3) a husband and wife filing a joint return are considered to be one grantor. [Reg. §31.3406(a)-4.]

☐ [*T.D.* 8637, 12-20-95. *Amended by T.D.* 9010, 7-25-2002.]

[Reg. §31.3406(b)(2)-1]

§31.3406(b)(2)-1. Reportable interest payment.—(a) *Interest subject to backup withholding.*—(1) *In general.*—A payment of a kind, and to a payee, that is required to be reported under section 6049 (relating to returns regarding interest and original issue discount) is a reportable payment for purposes of section 3406, subject to the special rules of §31.3406(b)(2)-2 (relating to original issue discount) and §31.3406(b)(2)-3 (relating to window transactions). See §31.6051-4 for the requirement to furnish a statement to the payee if tax is withheld under section 3406.

(2) *Special rule for tax-exempt interest.*—When an issuer is required to make an information return under §1.6049-4(d)(8) of this chapter because a payee provided a signed written statement on the envelope or shell incorrectly

claiming that the interest was exempt from taxation under section 103(a)(as described in § 1.6049-5(b)(1)(ii) of this chapter), the issuer is not required to impose withholding under section 3406.

(b) *Amount subject to backup withholding.*— (1) *In general.*—The amount of interest subject to withholding under section 3406 is the amount subject to reporting under section 6049.

(2) *Special rule to adjust for premature withdrawal penalty.*—Solely for purposes of computing the amount subject to withholding under section 3406, the payor may elect not to withhold from the portion of any interest payment that is not received by the payee because a penalty is in fact imposed for premature withdrawal of funds deposited in a time savings account, certificate of deposit, or similar class of deposit. [Reg. § 31.3406(b)(2)-1.]

☐ [*T.D.* 8637, 12-20-95.]

[Reg. § 31.3406(b)(2)-2]

§ 31.3406(b)(2)-2. Original issue discount.— (a) *Original issue discount subject to backup withholding.*—The amount of original issue discount, treated as interest, subject to withholding under section 3406 is the amount subject to reporting under section 6049, but is limited to the amount of cash paid. In addition, if an original issue discount obligation, subject to reporting under section 6045, is sold prior to maturity and with respect to the seller a condition exists for imposing withholding under section 3406 on the gross proceeds, then withholding under § 31.3406(b)(3)-2 applies to the gross proceeds of the sale reportable under section 6045, and not to the amount of any original issue discount includible in the gross income of the seller for the calendar year of the sale. See § 31.6051-4 for the requirement to furnish a statement to the payee if tax is withheld under section 3406.

(b) *Amount subject to backup withholding and time when backup withholding is imposed with respect to short-term obligations.*—In the case of an obligation with a fixed maturity date not exceeding one year from the date of issue (a short-term obligation), withholding under section 3406 applies to any payment of original issue discount on the obligation includible in the gross income of the holder to the extent of the cash amount of the payment. See § 1.1273-1 of this chapter to determine the amount of original issue discount on a short-term obligation. See § 1.446-2(e)(1) of this chapter to determine the amount of a payment treated as original issue discount.

(c) *Transferred short-term obligations.*—(1) *Subsequent holder may establish purchase price.*—(i) *In general.*—At maturity of a short-term obligation, a subsequent holder (i.e., any person who purchased or otherwise obtained the obligation after the obligation was issued to the original holder) may establish the price of the obligation. The price established by the subsequent holder must then be treated as the original issue price for

purposes of computing the amount of the original issue discount subject to withholding under section 3406. The price of a short-term obligation may be established by confirmation receipt or other record of a similar type or, if the obligation is redeemed by or through the person from whom the obligation was purchased or otherwise obtained, by the records of the person from whom or through whom the obligation was purchased or otherwise obtained. The subsequent holder is not required to certify under penalties of perjury that the price determined under this paragraph (c)(1)(i) is correct.

(ii) *Exception.*—A payor may elect to disregard the price at which the subsequent holder purchased or otherwise obtained the obligation if the payor's computer or recordkeeping system on which the details of the obligation are stored is not able to accept that price without significant manual intervention.

(2) *Subsequent holder unable (or not permitted) to establish purchase price.*—If a subsequent holder fails (or is unable, pursuant to paragraph (c)(1)(ii) of this section) to establish the purchase price of the obligation, then the person redeeming the obligation must determine the amount subject to withholding under section 3406 as though the obligation had been purchased by the holder on the date of issue. If the person redeeming the obligation is the issuer of the obligation, then the issuer must determine the amount subject to withholding from its records. If a person other than the issuer of the obligation redeems the obligation and the obligation is listed in Internal Revenue Service Publication 1212, List of Original Issue Discount Obligations, that person must determine the amount subject to withholding by using the issue price indicated in Publication 1212.

(3) *Transferred obligation.*—If a short-term obligation is transferred, no part of the purchase price is considered a reportable interest payment under section 6049. Withholding under section 3406 applies, however, to the gross proceeds of the sale of the obligation if the transfer is subject to reporting under section 6045 and a condition exists for imposing withholding. For the rules regarding withholding for amounts subject to reporting under section 6045, see § 31.3406(b)(3)-2.

(d) *Amount subject to backup withholding and time when backup withholding is imposed with respect to long-term obligations.*—(1) *No cash payments prior to maturity.*—In the case of an obligation with a fixed maturity date that is more than one year from the date of issue (a long-term obligation) and with no cash payments prior to maturity, withholding under section 3406 applies at the maturity of the obligation to the amount of original issue discount includible in the gross income of the holder for the calendar year in which the obligation matures. The amount required to be withheld must not exceed the amount of the cash payment.

(2) *Registered long-term obligations with cash payments prior to maturity.*—In the case of a long-term obligation in registered form that provides for cash payments prior to maturity, withholding under section 3406 applies at the time cash payments are made to the sum of the amounts of qualified stated interest and original issue discount includible in the gross income of the holder for the calendar year in which the cash payments are made. The amount required to be withheld at the time of any cash payment, however, must not exceed the amount of the cash payment. If more than one cash payment is made during a calendar year, the tax that is required to be withheld with respect to original issue discount must be allocated among all the expected cash payments in the ratio that each cash payment bears to the total of the expected cash payments.

(3) *Transferred registered long-term obligations with payments prior to maturity.*—In the case of a long-term obligation that is transferred after its issuance from the original holder, the amount subject to withholding under section 3406 with respect to a subsequent holder is the amount of original issue discount includible in the gross income of all holders during the calendar year (without regard to any amount paid by a subsequent holder at the time of transfer). If the person redeeming the obligation at maturity is the issuer of the obligation, the issuer must determine the amount subject to withholding through its records by treating the holder as if he were the original holder. If a person redeeming the obligation at maturity is a person other than the issuer of the obligation, and the obligation is listed in Internal Revenue Service Publication 1212, List of Original Issue Discount Obligations, the person must determine the amount subject to withholding by using the issue price indicated in Publication 1212.

(e) *Bearer long-term obligations.*—In the case of a bearer long-term obligation with cash payments prior to maturity—

(1) *Payments prior to maturity.*—Withholding under section 3406 applies prior to maturity only to the payment of qualified stated interest (and not to any amount of original issue discount) includible in the gross income of the holder for the calendar year.

(2) *Payments at maturity.*—At maturity of the obligation, withholding applies to the sum of any qualified stated interest payment made at maturity and the total amount of original issue discount includible in the gross income of the holder during the calendar year of maturity. The amount required to be withheld at the time of the cash payment, however, must not exceed the amount of the cash payment. [Reg. § 31.3406(b)(2)-2.]

☐ [*T.D.* 8637, 12-20-95.]

[Reg. § 31.3406(b)(2)-3]

§ 31.3406(b)(2)-3. Window transactions.— (a) *Requirement to backup withhold.*—Withholding

under section 3406 applies to a window transaction (as defined in paragraph (b) of this section) only if the payee does not furnish a taxpayer identification number to the payor in the manner required in paragraph (c) of this section or furnishes an obviously incorrect number as described in § 31.3406(h)-1(b)(2). Withholding does not apply to a window transaction even though the Internal Revenue Service notifies the payor of the payee's incorrect taxpayer identification number under section 3406(a)(1)(B) or of notified payee underreporting under section 3406(a)(1)(C). The payee in a window transaction is not required to certify under penalties of perjury that the payee is not subject to withholding due to notified payee underreporting (as described in § 31.3406(d)-2(b)(2)).

(b) *Window transaction defined. Window transaction.*—means payment of interest with respect to any of the following obligations:

(1) An interest coupon in bearer form that is subject to taxation (i.e., other than exempt interest described in § 1.6049-5(b)(1)(ii) of this chapter);

(2) A United States savings bond; or

(3) A discount obligation having a maturity at issue of one year or less, including commercial paper and bankers' acceptances that are in definitive form (i.e., evidenced by a paper document other than a confirmation receipt) but not including short-term government obligations (as defined in section 1271(a)(3)(B)).

(c) *Manner of furnishing taxpayer identification number in the case of a window transaction.*—A payee must furnish the payee's taxpayer identification number to the payor with respect to a window transaction either orally or in writing at the time that the window transaction occurs. See § 31.3406(g)-3(c)(1)(i), which provides that a payee may not claim the payee is awaiting receipt of a taxpayer identification number with respect to a window transaction. The payee is not required to certify, under penalties of perjury, that the taxpayer identification number provided is correct. [Reg. § 31.3406(b)(2)-3.]

☐ [*T.D.* 8637, 12-20-95.]

[Reg. § 31.3406(b)(2)-4]

§ 31.3406(b)(2)-4. Reportable dividend payment.—(a) *Dividends subject to backup withholding.*—A payment of a kind, and to a payee, that is required to be reported under section 6042 (relating to returns regarding payments of dividends and corporate earnings and profits) is a reportable payment for purposes of section 3406. See paragraph (b) of this section for certain dividends not subject to withholding under section 3406. See § 31.6051-4 for the requirement to furnish a statement to the payee if tax is withheld under section 3406.

(b) *Dividends not subject to backup withholding.*—Except as provided in § 31.3406(b)(3)-2 (relating to transactions reportable under section 6045), withholding under section 3406 does not apply to—

(1) Any amount treated as a taxable dividend by reason of section 302 (relating to redemptions of stock), section 304 (relating to redemptions through the use of related corporations), section 306 (relating to disposition of certain stock), section 356 (relating to receipt of additional consideration in connection with certain reorganizations), or section 1081(e)(2)(relating to certain distributions pursuant to an order of the Securities and Exchange Commission);

(2) Any exempt-interest dividend, as defined in section 852(b)(5)(A), paid by a regulated investment company; or

(3) Any amount paid or treated as paid during a year by a regulated investment company, provided that the payor reasonably estimates, as provided in paragraph (c)(2) of this section, that 95 percent or more of all dividends paid or treated as paid during the year are exempt-interest dividends.

(c) *Amount subject to backup withholding.*—(1) *In general.*—The amount of a dividend subject to withholding under section 3406 is the amount subject to reporting under section 6042, including any dividend that is reinvested pursuant to a plan under which a shareholder may elect to receive stock as a dividend instead of property. Except as otherwise provided in this paragraph (c), withholding applies to the entire amount of the distribution.

(2) *Reasonable estimate of amount of dividend subject to backup withholding.*—Pursuant to section 6042(b)(3) and §1.6042-3(c) of this chapter, if the payor is unable to determine the portion of a distribution that is a dividend, the entire amount of the distribution must be treated as a dividend for information reporting under section 6042. Hence, withholding applies to the entire amount of the distribution. If a payor is able reasonably to estimate under section 6042 and §1.6042-3(c) of this chapter the portion of a distribution that is not a dividend, however, the payor must not withhold on that portion (which is not considered a dividend). A payor making a payment, all or a portion of which may not be a dividend, may use previous experience to estimate the portion of a distribution that is not a dividend. The payor's estimate is considered reasonable if—

(i) The estimate does not exceed the proportion of the distributions made by the payor during the most recent calendar year for which a Form 1099 was required to be filed that was not reported by the payor as a dividend; and

(ii) The payor has no reasonable basis to expect that the proportion of the distribution that is not a dividend will be substantially different for the current year.

(3) *Reinvested dividends.*—In the case of a dividend paid pursuant to a dividend reinvestment plan, withholding under section 3406 applies, pursuant to §31.3406(a)-4(a), at the time and to the amount made available to the shareholder or credited to the shareholder's account. At the discretion of the payor, withholding

under section 3406 need not be applied to any excess of the fair market value of the shares of stock received by the shareholder or credited to the shareholder's account over the purchase price of the shares (including shares acquired by the shareholder at a discount in connection with the dividend distribution) or to any fee that is paid by the payor in the nature of a broker's fee for purchase of the stock or service charge for maintenance of the shareholder's account. The payor must, however, treat any excess amounts and fees on a consistent basis for each calendar year. [Reg. §31.3406(b)(2)-4.]

☐ [*T.D.* 8637, 12-20-95.]

[Reg. §31.3406(b)(2)-5]

§31.3406(b)(2)-5. Reportable patronage dividend payment.—(a) *Patronage dividends subject to backup withholding.*—A payment of a kind, and to a payee, that is required to be reported under section 6044 (relating to returns regarding patronage dividends) is a reportable payment for purposes of section 3406. See §31.6051-4 for the requirement to furnish a statement to the payee if tax is withheld under section 3406.

(b) *Amount subject to backup withholding.*—(1) *Failure to provide taxpayer identification number or notification of incorrect taxpayer identification number.*—For purposes of sections 3406(a)(1)(A) and (B), the amount of a payment described in paragraph (a) of this section that is subject to withholding under section 3406 is the amount subject to reporting under section 6044, but only to the extent the payment is made in money. For purposes of this paragraph (b), *money* includes cash or a qualified check (as defined in section 1388(c)(4)).

(2) *Notified payee underreporting or payee certification failure.*—For purposes of sections 3406(a)(1)(C) and (D), the amount of a payment described in paragraph (a) of this section that is subject to withholding under section 3406 is the amount subject to withholding under paragraph (b)(1) of this section, but only if 50 percent or more of that reportable amount is paid in money. Thus, a payor is required to withhold according to this paragraph (b)(2) on a payment if—

(i) There has been a notified payee underreporting described in section 3406(a)(1)(C) and §31.3406(c)-1 or there has been a payee certification failure described in section 3406(a)(1)(D) and §31.3406(d)-2;

(ii) The payor makes a reportable payment subject to reporting under section 6044 to the payee; and

(iii) Fifty percent or more of the payment is in cash or by qualified check. [Reg. §31.3406(b)(2)-5.]

☐ [*T.D.* 8637, 12-20-95.]

[Reg. §31.3406(b)(3)-1]

§31.3406(b)(3)-1. Reportable payments of rents, commissions, nonemployee compensation, etc.—(a) *Section 6041 and 6041A(a) payments* *subject to backup withholding.*—A payment of a kind, and to a payee, that is required to be reported under section 6041 (relating to information reporting of rents, commissions, nonemployee compensation, etc.) or a payment that is required to be reported under section 6041A(a)(relating to information reporting of payments to nonemployees for services) is a reportable payment for purposes of section 3406. See paragraph (b) of this section for an exception concerning payments aggregating less than $600. See §31.6051-4 for the requirement to furnish a statement to the payee if tax is withheld under section 3406.

(b) *Amount subject to backup withholding.*—(1) *In general.*—The amount of a payment described in paragraph (a) of this section subject to withholding under section 3406 is the amount subject to reporting under section 6041 or section 6041A(a).

(2) *Net commissions.*—Withholding under section 3406 does not apply to net commissions paid to unincorporated special agents with respect to insurance policies that are subject to reporting under section 6041, provided that no cash is actually paid by the payor to the special agent.

(3) *Payments aggregating $600 or more for the calendar year.*—(i) *In general.*—A payment is a reportable payment under paragraph (a) of this section only if the aggregate amount of the current payment and all previous payments to the payee during the calendar year aggregate $600 or more. The amount subject to withholding is the entire amount of the payment that causes the total amount paid to the payee to equal $600 or more and the amount of any subsequent payments made to the payee during the calendar year. This paragraph (b)(3)(i) does not apply to gambling winnings (as provided in §31.3406(g)-2(e)(1)).

(ii) *Exceptions.*—(A) *The $600 aggregation rule.*—The $600 aggregation rule of paragraph (b)(3)(i) of this section does not apply if the payor was required to make an information return under section 6041 or 6041A(a) for the preceding calendar year with respect to payments to the payee, or the payor was required to withhold under section 3406 during the preceding calendar year with respect to payments to the payee that were reportable under section 6041 or 6041A(a).

(B) *Determination of whether payments aggregate $600 or more.*—In determining whether payments to a payee aggregate $600 or more during a calendar year for purposes of withholding under section 3406, the payor must aggregate only payments of the same kind made to the same payee. For this purpose, payments are of the same kind if they are of the same type, regardless of whether they are reportable under the same section. However, a payor with different paying departments making reportable payments of the same kind is not required to

aggregate payments made by all those departments unless it is the payor's customary method to aggregate those payments. A payor may, in its discretion, aggregate—

(1) Payments not of the same kind to the same payee, reportable under either section 6041 or 6041A(a); and

(2) Payments reportable under section 6041 with payments reportable under section 6041A(a). [Reg. §31.3406(b)(3)-1.]

☐ [*T.D.* 8637, 12-20-95.]

[Reg. §31.3406(b)(3)-2]

§31.3406(b)(3)-2. **Reportable barter exchanges and gross proceeds of sales of securities or commodities by brokers.**—(a) *Transactions subject to backup withholding.*—A payment of a kind, and to a payee, that any broker (as defined in section 6045(c) and §1.6045-1(a)(1) of this chapter) or any barter exchange (as defined in section 6045(c) and §1.6045-1(a)(4) of this chapter) is required to report under section 6045 is a reportable payment for purposes of section 3406. See §31.6051-4 for the requirement to furnish a statement to the payee if tax is withheld under section 3406.

(b) *Amount subject to backup withholding.*—(1) *In general.*—The amount subject to withholding under section 3406 is the amount subject to reporting under section 6045. The amount subject to withholding with respect to broker reporting is the amount of gross proceeds (as determined under §1.6045-1(d)(5) of this chapter). The amount subject to withholding with respect to barter exchanges is the amount received by any member or client (as determined under §1.6045-1(f)(4) of this chapter).

(2) *Forward contracts, including foreign currency contracts, and regulated futures contracts.*—(i) *In general.*—If a customer is subject to withholding under section 3406 with respect to a forward contract (subject to information reporting under §1.6045-1(c)(5) of this chapter), including a foreign currency contract (as defined in section 1256(g)(2)), or a regulated futures contract (as defined in section 1256(g)(1)), or with respect to an account through which those contracts are disposed of or acquired, the broker must withhold on both of the following amounts:

(A) All cash or property withdrawn from the account by the customer during the relevant year; and

(B) The amount of cash in the account available for withdrawal by the customer at the relevant year-end (including both gross proceeds and variation margin).

(ii) *Rules concerning withdrawals.*—A withdrawal includes the use of money (including both gross proceeds and variation margin) or property in the account to purchase any property other than property acquired in connection with the closing of a contract. For this purpose, the acceptance of a warehouse receipt or other taking of delivery to close a contract is in connection with the closing of a contract only if the property acquired is disposed of by the close of the seventh trading day following the trading day that the customer takes delivery under the contract. In addition, making delivery to close a contract is in connection with the closing of a contract only if the broker is able to determine that the property used to close the contract was acquired no earlier than the seventh trading day prior to the trading day on which delivery is made. Withdrawals do not include repayments of debt incurred in connection with making or taking delivery that meets the requirements of this paragraph (b)(2). Withdrawals also do not include payments of commissions, fees, transfers of cash from the account to another futures account that is subject to this paragraph (b)(2) or cash withdrawals traceable to dispositions of property other than futures (not including profit on the contract separately reportable under § 1.6045-1(c)(5)(i)(*b*) of this chapter).

(iii) *Special rule for forward contracts, including foreign currency contracts, and regulated futures contracts.*—The determination of whether the customer is subject to withholding under section 3406 with respect to an account containing forward contracts, including foreign currency contracts, or regulated futures contracts must be made at the time of the cash or property withdrawals or the relevant year-end, whichever is applicable.

(3) *Security sales made through a margin account.*—The amount described in paragraph (a) of this section that is subject to withholding under section 3406 in the case of a security sale made through a margin account (as defined in 12 CFR part 220 (Regulation T)) is the gross proceeds (as defined in § 1.6045-1(d)(5) of this chapter) of the sale. The amount required to be withheld with respect to the sale, however, is limited to the amount of cash available for withdrawal by the customer immediately after the settlement of the sale. For this purpose, the amount available for withdrawal by the customer does not include amounts required to satisfy margin maintenance under Regulation T, rules and regulations of the National Association of Securities Dealers and national securities exchanges, and generally applicable self-imposed rules of the margin account carrier.

(4) *Security short sales.*—(i) *Amount subject to backup withholding.*—The amount subject to withholding under section 3406 with respect to a short sale of securities is the gross proceeds (as defined in § 1.6045-1(d)(5) of this chapter) of the short sale. At the option of the broker, however, the amount subject to withholding may be the gain upon the closing of the short sale (if any); consequently, the obligation to withhold under section 3406 would be deferred until the closing transaction. A broker may use this alternative method of determining the amount subject to withholding under section 3406 with respect to a short sale only if at the time the short sale is initiated, the broker expects that the amount of

gain realized upon the closing of the short sale will be determinable from the broker's records. If, due to events unforeseen at the time the short sale was initiated, the broker is unable to determine the basis of the property used to close the short sale, the property must be assumed for this purpose to have a basis of zero.

(ii) *Time of backup withholding.*—The determination of whether a short seller is subject to withholding under section 3406 must be made on the date of the initiation or closing, as the case may be, or on the date that the initiation or closing, as the case may be, is entered on the broker's books and records.

(5) *Fractional shares.*—A broker is not required to withhold under section 3406 with respect to a sale of a fractional share of stock resulting in less than $20 of gross proceeds (as described in § 1.6045-1(c)(3)(x) of this chapter). [Reg. § 31.3406(b)(3)-2.]

☐ [*T.D.* 8637, 12-20-95. Amended by *T.D.* 9010, 7-25-2002.]

[Reg. § 31.3406(b)(3)-3]

§ 31.3406(b)(3)-3. Reportable payments by certain fishing boat operators.—(a) *Payments subject to backup withholding.*—A payment of a kind, and to a payee, that is required to be reported under section 6050A (relating to information reporting by certain fishing boat operators) is a reportable payment for purposes of section 3406. See § 31.6051-4 for the requirement to furnish a statement to the payee if tax is withheld under section 3406.

(b) *Amount subject to backup withholding.*—The amount described in paragraph (a) of this section subject to withholding under section 3406 is the amount subject to reporting under section 6050A, but only to the extent the amount is paid in money and represents a share of the proceeds of the catch. [Reg. § 31.3406(b)(3)-3.]

☐ [*T.D.* 8637, 12-20-95.]

[Reg. § 31.3406(b)(3)-4]

§ 31.3406(b)(3)-4. Reportable payments of royalties.—(a) *Royalty payments subject to backup withholding.*—A payment of a kind, and to a payee, that is required to be reported under section 6050N (relating to *information* reporting of payments of royalties) is a reportable payment for purposes of section 3406. See § 31.6051-4 for the requirement to furnish a statement to the payee if tax is withheld under section 3406.

(b) *Amount subject to backup withholding.*—In general, the amount described in paragraph (a) of this section that is subject to withholding under section 3406 is the amount *subject* to reporting under section 6050N. However, if the reportable payment is for an oil or gas interest, the amount subject to withholding is the net amount the payee receives (i.e., the gross proceeds less production-related taxes such as state severance taxes). [Reg. § 31.3406(b)(3)-4.]

☐ [*T.D.* 8637, 12-20-95.]

⋙→ *Caution: Reg. §31.3406(b)(3)-5, below, applies to amounts paid after December 31, 2011.*

[Reg. §31.3406(b)(3)-5]

§31.3406(b)(3)-5. Reportable payments of payment card and third party network transactions.—(a) *Payment card and third party network transactions subject to backup withholding.*—The gross amount of a reportable transaction that is required to be reported under section 6050W (relating to information reporting for payment card and third party network transactions) is a reportable payment for purposes of section 3406. See §31.6051-4 for the requirement to furnish a statement to the payee if tax is withheld under section 3406.

(b) *Amount subject to backup withholding.*—In general, the amount described in paragraph (a) of this section that is subject to withholding under section 3406 is the amount subject to reporting under section 6050W. In the case of payments made in settlement of third party network transactions, the amount subject to withholding under section 3406 is determined without regard to the exception for de minimis payments by third party settlement organizations in section 6050W(e) and the associated regulations.

(c) *Time when payments are considered to be subject to backup withholding.*—(1) *In general.*—In the case of a payment card or third party network transaction reportable under section 6050W, the obligation to withhold arises on the date of the transaction. A payor is not required, however, to satisfy its withholding liability until the time that payment is made.

(2) *Example.*—The provisions of paragraph (c)(1) are illustrated by the following example:

Example. On Day 1, Customer A uses a payment card to purchase $100 worth of goods from Merchant B. Bank X, the merchant acquiring entity for B, is the party with the contractual obligation to make payment to B in settlement of the transaction. On Day 2, X, after deducting fees of $2, makes payment of $98 to settle the transaction for the sale of goods from B to A. Under paragraph (a)(6) of §1.6050W-1, X must report the amount of $100, the amount of the transaction on Day 1, without any reduction for fees or any other amount, as the gross amount of this reportable payment transaction on the annual information return filed under paragraph (a)(1) of §1.6050W-1. Under paragraph (c)(1) of this section, X's obligation, if any, to backup withhold arises on Day 1, the backup withholding obligation must be satisfied on Day 2, and the amount subject to backup withholding is $100 (the gross amount of the reportable payment transaction (as defined in paragraph (a)(6) of §1.6050W-1)).

(d) *Backup withholding from an alternate source.*—(1) *In general.*—A payor may not withhold under section 3406 from a source maintained by the payor other than the source with respect to which there exists a liability to withhold under section 3406 with respect to the payee. See section 3403 and §31.3403-1, which

provide that the payor is liable for the amount required to be withheld regardless of whether the payor withholds.

(2) *Exceptions for backup withholding when there are no funds available.*—(i) *Backup withholding from an alternative source.*—In the event there are no funds available in the source with respect to which there exists a liability to withhold under section 3406 with respect to the payee, the payor may withhold under section 3406 from another source maintained by the payee with the payor. The source from which the tax is withheld under section 3406 must be payable to at least one of the persons listed on the account subject to withholding. If the account or source is not payable exclusively to the same person or persons listed on the account subject to withholding under section 3406, then the payor must obtain a written statement from all other persons to whom the account or source is payable authorizing the payor to withhold under section 3406 from the alternative account or source. A payor that elects to withhold under section 3406 from an alternative source may determine the account or source from which the tax is to be withheld, or may allow the payee to designate the alternative source.

(ii) *Deferral of withholding.*—If the payor cannot locate, with reasonable care (following procedures substantially similar to those set forth in §31.3406(d)-5(c)(3)(ii)(A) and (B)), an alternative source of cash from which the payor may satisfy its withholding obligation pursuant to paragraph (d)(2)(i) of this section, the payor may defer its obligation to withhold under section 3406 until the earlier of—

(A) The date on which cash, in a sufficient amount to satisfy the obligation in full, is deposited in the account subject to withholding under section 3406; or

(B) The close of the fourth calendar year after the obligation arose.

(iii) *Termination of obligation to backup withhold.*—If, at the close of the fourth calendar year after the backup withholding arose, the payor has not located an alternate source of cash from which the payor may satisfy its withholding obligation, and sufficient cash to satisfy the obligation in full has not been deposited in the account subject to withholding under section 3406, then the obligation to backup withhold terminates at the close of the fourth calendar year.

(e) *Effective/applicability date.*—The provisions of this section apply to amounts paid after December 31, 2011. [Reg. §31.3406(b)(3)-5.]

□ [*T.D.* 9496, 8-13-2010.]

[Reg. §31.3406(b)(4)-1]

§31.3406(b)(4)-1. Exemption for certain minimal payments.—(a) *In general.*—A payor of reportable interest or dividends (as described in section 3406(b)(2)) or of royalties (as described in section 3406(b)(3)(E)) may elect not to withhold from a payment that does not exceed $10 and that on an annualized basis does not exceed $10 (see paragraph (c) of this section). A broker or barter exchange may elect not to withhold on gross proceeds of $10 or less without regard to the annualization requirement. See §31.6051-4 for the requirement to furnish a statement to the payee if tax is withheld under section 3406.

(b) *Manner of making the election.*—The election not to withhold from payments that do not exceed $10 can be made only for payments described in paragraph (a) of this section. The election may be made on a payment-by-payment basis.

(c) *How to annualize.*—(1) *In general.*—To annualize a reportable interest payment, dividend payment, or royalty payment, a payor must calculate what the amount of the payment would be if it were paid for a 1-year period (instead of the period for which it actually is paid). The annualized amount is determined by dividing the amount of the payment by the number of days in the period for which it is being paid and then multiplying that result by the number of days in the year. If the annualized amount is $10 or less, the payor may elect not to withhold on that payment regardless of whether more than $10 may be or has been paid to the payee in other reportable payments during the calendar year. Conversely, if the annualized amount is more than $10, withholding applies even if $10 or less is actually paid to the payee during the calendar year. For purposes of computing the annualized amount, the payor may assume that February always consists of 28 days and that the year always consists of 360 days. For amounts that are deposited with a payor in a new account or certificate between the dates on which the payor customarily pays or credits interest, the payor may assume that the period for which the interest is paid is the payor's customary period for paying or crediting interest.

(2) *Special aggregation rule for reportable interest and dividends.*—If a payor maintains records that reflect multiple holdings of one payee and the payor makes an aggregate payment of reportable interest or dividends (as defined in section 3406(b)(2)) with respect to those multiple holdings (such as a dividend check that reflects payment on all stock owned by the payee), the payor must annualize the aggregate payment.

(d) *Exception for window transactions and original issue discount.*—A payor is not required to annualize payments made in window transactions (as defined in §31.3406(b)(2)-3(b)) or payments of original issue discount. With respect to a window transaction, however, the payor is required to aggregate all payments made in the same transaction (e.g., payments made with respect to coupons or obligations presented for payment at the same time as described in §1.6049-4(e)(4) of this chapter). [Reg. §31.3406(b)(4)-1.]

□ [*T.D.* 8637, 12-20-95.]

[Reg. §31.3406(c)-1]

§31.3406(c)-1. Notified payee underreporting of reportable interest or dividend payments.— (a) *Overview.*—Withholding under section 3406(a)(1)(C) applies to any reportable interest or dividend payment (as defined in section 3406(b)(2)) made with respect to an account of a payee if the Internal Revenue Service or a broker notifies a payor under paragraph (c)(1) or (2) of this section that the payee is subject to withholding due to notified payee underreporting (as defined in paragraph (b)(1) of this section), and the payor is required under paragraph (c)(3) of this section to identify that account. After receiving the notice and identifying accounts, the payor must notify the payee, in accordance with paragraph (d) of this section, that withholding due to notified payee underreporting has started. Paragraph (e) of this section describes the period for which withholding due to notified payee underreporting is required. Paragraph (f) of this section provides rules concerning notices that the Internal Revenue Service will send to a payee before notifying a payor that the payee is subject to withholding due to notified payee underreporting. Paragraph (g) of this section provides rules that a payee can use to prevent withholding due to notified payee underreporting from starting or to stop it once it has started. Paragraph (h) of this section provides special rules for joint accounts of payees who have filed a joint return. See section 6682 for the penalties that may apply to a payee subject to withholding under section 3406(a)(1)(C).

(b) *Definitions.*—(1) *Notified payee underreporting.*—Notified payee underreporting means that the Internal Revenue Service has—

(i) Determined that there was a payee underreporting (as defined in paragraph (b)(2) of this section);

(ii) Mailed at least four notices under paragraph (f)(1) of this section to the payee (over a period of at least 120 days) with respect to the underreporting; and

(iii) Assessed any deficiency attributable to the underreporting in the case of any payee who has filed a return.

(2) *Payee underreporting.*—(i) *In general.*— Payee underreporting means that the Internal Revenue Service has determined, for a taxable year, that—

(A) A payee failed to include in the payee's return of tax under chapter 1 of the Internal Revenue Code for that year any portion of a reportable interest or dividend payment required to be shown on that tax return; or

(B) A payee may be required to file a return for that year and to include a reportable interest or dividend payment in the return, but failed to file the return.

(ii) *Payments included in making payee underreporting determination.*—The determination of whether there is payee underreporting is made by treating as reportable interest or dividend

Collection of Income Tax at Source on Wages
61,625
See p. 20,601 for regulations not amended to reflect law changes

payments, all payments of dividends reported under section 6042, all patronage dividends reported under section 6044, and all interest and original issue discount reported under section 6049, regardless of whether withholding due to notified payee underreporting applies to those payments.

(c) *Notice to payors regarding backup withholding due to notified payee underreporting.*—(1) *In general.*—If the Internal Revenue Service or a broker notifies a payor that a payee is subject to withholding due to notified payee underreporting, the payor must—

(i) Identify any accounts of the payee under the rules of paragraph (c)(3) of this section; and

(ii) Notify the payee and withhold under section 3406 on reportable interest or dividend payments made with respect to any identified account under the rules of paragraphs (d) and (e) of this section.

(2) *Additional requirements for payors that are also brokers.*—(i) *In general.*—A broker must notify the payor of a readily tradable instrument that the payee of the instrument is subject to withholding due to notified payee underreporting if—

(A) The broker (in its capacity as a payor) receives a notice from the Internal Revenue Service under paragraph (c)(1) of this section that a payee is subject to withholding due to notified payee underreporting and the broker is required to identify an account of the payee under paragraph (c)(3) of this section;

(B) The payee subsequently acquires the instrument from the broker through the same account; and

(C) The acquisition of the instrument occurs after the close of the 30th business day after the date that the broker receives the notice (or on any earlier date that the broker may begin applying this paragraph (c)(2) after receipt of the notice described in paragraph (c)(1) of this section).

(ii) *Transfer out of street name.*—For purposes of this paragraph (c)(2), an acquisition includes a transfer of an instrument out of street name into the name of the registered owner (i.e., the payee).

(iii) *Method of providing notice.*—A broker must provide the notice required under this paragraph (c)(2) to the payor of the instrument with the transfer instructions for the acquisition. See § 31.3406(d)-4(a)(2).

(iv) *Termination of obligation to provide information.*—The obligation of a broker to provide notice to payors under this paragraph (c)(2) terminates simultaneously with the termination of the broker's obligation to withhold (in its capacity as payor) due to notified payee underreporting on reportable interest or dividends made with respect to the account.

(3) *Payor identification of accounts of the payee subject to backup withholding due to notified payee underreporting.*—(i) *In general.*—(A) *Notice from the Internal Revenue Service.*—If a payor receives a notice from the Internal Revenue Service under paragraph (c)(1) of this section, the payor must identify, exercising reasonable care, all accounts using the same taxpayer identification number for information reporting purposes as the one provided in the notice. The notice may provide, however, that the payor need only identify the account or accounts corresponding to any account number or designation and related taxpayer identification number used for information reporting purposes as that listed on the notice.

(B) *Notice from a broker.*—If a payor receives a notice from a broker under paragraphs (c)(1) and (2) of this section, the payor is not required to identify any account other than the account identified in the notice.

(ii) *Exercise of reasonable care.*—If an account identified pursuant to paragraph (c)(3)(i)(A) of this section contains a customer identifier that can be used to retrieve systemically any other accounts that use the same taxpayer identification number for information reporting purposes, the payor must identify all accounts that can be so retrieved. Otherwise, a payor is considered to exercise reasonable care in identifying accounts subject to withholding under section 3406(a)(1)(C) if the payor searches any computer or other recordkeeping system for the region, division, or branch that serves the geographic area in which the payee's mailing address is located and that was established (or is maintained) to reflect reportable interest or dividend payments.

(iii) *Newly opened accounts.*—(A) In general, a new account is not subject to withholding under section 3406(a)(1)(C) if the payee provides to the payor a Form W-9 (or other acceptable substitute) on which the payor may reasonably rely (within the meaning of § 31.3406(h)-3(e)(2) without regard to § 31.3406(h)-3(e)(2)(v)), unless the payor has actual knowledge (within the meaning of paragraph (c)(3)(iii)(B) of this section) that the statements made on the form are not true.

(B) For purposes of paragraph (c)(3)(iii)(A) of this section, a payor is considered to have actual knowledge that a payee's statement that the payee is not subject to withholding under section 3406(a)(1)(C) is not true if—

(1) The employee or individual agent of the payor who receives the payee's certification knows that the statement is not true;

(2) In conducting the investigation, if any, required by paragraph (c)(3)(iii)(C) of this section, the payor identifies any other accounts of the payee that are already subject to withholding under section 3406(a)(1)(C); or

(3) In the course of processing the certification or in administering an account to which a certification relates, the payor discovers

Reg. § 31.3406(c)-1(c)(3)(iii)(B)(3)

61,626
Collection of Income Tax at Source on Wages
See p. 20,601 for regulations not amended to reflect law changes

that the payor was previously notified by the Internal Revenue Service that the payee is subject to withholding under section 3406(a)(1)(C) and no notice was received to stop withholding pursuant to section 3406(c)(3) prior to the time of the discovery.

(C) Except as provided in this paragraph (c)(3)(iii)(C), a payor is not required to investigate whether the statements made on the Form W-9 described in paragraph (c)(3)(iii)(A) of this section are true. If, however, in opening a new account, the payor relies on the same Form W-9 (or appropriate substitute) that it relied on previously in opening another account, the payor must investigate whether any such existing account is subject to withholding under section 3406(a)(1)(C). Similarly, if the payor utilizes a universal account system described in the first sentence of paragraph (c)(3)(ii) of this section, and in opening a new account the payor searches its records to determine whether the new account should be identified under an existing identifier (because the payee has existing accounts with the payor), the payor must investigate whether any existing accounts identified with the same identifier are subject to withholding under section 3406(a)(1)(C).

(d) *Notice from payors of backup withholding due to notified payee underreporting.*—(1) *In general.*— If a payor receives notice from the Internal Revenue Service or a broker under paragraph (c)(1) of this section and is required to identify an account under paragraph (c)(3) of this section as an account of the payee, the payor must notify the payee in accordance with paragraph (d)(2) of this section that withholding due to notified payee underreporting has started.

(2) *Procedures.*—The payor must send the notice required by paragraph (d)(1) of this section to the payee no later than 15 days after the date that the payor makes the first payment subject to withholding due to notified payee underreporting. The payor must send the notice by first-class mail to the payee at the payee's last known address. The notice to the payee required by paragraph (d)(1) of this section must state—

(i) That the Internal Revenue Service has given notice that the payee has underreported reportable interest or dividends;

(ii) That, as a result of the underreporting, the payor is required under section 3406(a)(1)(C) of the Internal Revenue Code to withhold 31 percent of reportable interest or dividend payments made to the payee;

(iii) The date that the payor started (or plans to start) withholding due to notified payee underreporting under section 3406(a)(1)(C);

(iv) The account number or numbers that are subject to withholding due to notified payee underreporting;

(v) That the payee must obtain a determination from the Internal Revenue Service in order to stop the withholding due to notified payee underreporting; and

(vi) That while the payee is subject to withholding due to notified payee underreporting, the payee may not certify to a payor making reportable interest or dividend payments (or to a broker acquiring a readily tradable instrument for the payee) that the payee is not subject to withholding due to notified underreporting.

(e) *Period during which backup withholding is required.*—(1) *In general.*—If a payor receives notice from the Internal Revenue Service or a broker under paragraph (c)(1) of this section, the payor must impose withholding under section 3406(a)(1)(C) on all reportable interest or dividend payments with respect to any account of the payee required to be identified under paragraph (c)(3) of this section made after the close of the 30th business day after the day on which the payor receives that notice and before the stop date (as described in paragraph (e)(2) of this section). A payor may choose to start withholding under this paragraph (e)(1) at any time during the 30-business-day period described in the preceding sentence.

(2) *Stop withholding.*—(i) *When no underreporting exists or undue hardship exists.*—(A) *Stop date.*—In the case of a determination under paragraph (g)(3)(i) or (iii) of this section that no underreporting exists or that an undue hardship exists, the stop date is the day that is 30 days after the earlier of—

(1) The date on which the payor receives written notification from the Internal Revenue Service under paragraph (g) of this section that withholding is to stop; or

(2) The date on which the payor receives a copy of the written certification provided to the payee by the Internal Revenue Service under paragraph (g) of this section that withholding is to stop.

(B) *Acceleration of stop date.*—A payor may choose to stop withholding at any time during the 30-day period described in paragraph (e)(2)(i)(A) of this section.

(ii) *When underreporting is corrected or bona fide dispute exists.*—In the case of a determination under paragraph (g)(3)(ii) or (iv) of this section that the underreporting has been corrected or that a bona fide dispute exists, the stop date occurs on the first day of January (immediately following a period of at least twelve months ending on October 15 of any calendar year in which the determination has been made) or if later, the stop date determined under paragraph (e)(2)(i) of this section.

(3) *Dormant accounts.*—The requirement that a payor withhold under this paragraph (e) on reportable interest or dividend payments made with respect to an account terminates no later than the close of the third calendar year ending after the later of—

(i) The date that the most recent reportable interest or dividend payment was made with respect to that account; or

Reg. §31.3406(c)-1(c)(3)(iii)(C)

(ii) The date that the payor received notice under paragraph (c)(1) of this section.

(f) *Notice to payees from the Internal Revenue Service.*—(1) *Notice period.*—After the Internal Revenue Service determines under paragraph (b)(2) of this section that payee underreporting exists, the Internal Revenue Service will mail to the payee at least four notices over a period of at least 120 days (the notice period) before payors will be notified under paragraph (c)(1) of this section that the payee is subject to withholding due to notified payee underreporting. The notices may be accompanied by, or incorporated in, other notices provided to the payee by the Internal Revenue Service.

(2) *Payee subject to backup withholding.*—After the Internal Revenue Service provides the notices described in paragraph (f)(1) of this section, the Internal Revenue Service will send notices to payors under paragraph (c)(1) of this section unless—

(i) A payee obtains a determination under paragraph (g) of this section; or

(ii) In the case of a payee who has filed a tax return, the Internal Revenue Service has not assessed the deficiency attributable to the underreporting.

(3) *Disclosure of names of payors and brokers.*—Pursuant to section 3406(c)(5) the Internal Revenue Service may require a payee subject to withholding due to notified payee underreporting to disclose the names of all the payee's payors of reportable interest or dividend payments and the names of all of the brokers with whom the payee has accounts which may involve reportable interest or dividend payments. To the extent required in the request from the Internal Revenue Service, the payee must also provide the payee's account numbers and other information necessary to identify the payee's accounts.

(4) *Backup withholding certification.*—After a payee receives a final notice from the Internal Revenue Service under paragraph (f)(1) of this section, the payee is not permitted to certify to any payor or broker, under penalties of perjury, that the payee is not subject to withholding under section 3406(a)(1)(C), until the payee receives the certification from the Internal Revenue Service under paragraph (g) of this section advising the payee that the payee is no longer subject to withholding under section 3406(a)(1)(C). A final notice will contain the information described in this paragraph (f)(4). See sections 6682 and 7205(b) for civil and criminal penalties for making a false certification.

(g) *Determination by the Internal Revenue Service that backup withholding should not start or should be stopped.*—(1) *In general.*—A payee may prevent withholding due to notified payee underreporting from starting, or stop the withholding once it has started, by requesting and receiving a determination from the Internal Revenue Service under one or more of the provisions of paragraph (g)(3) of this section. Following its review

of a request for a determination under paragraph (g)(3) of this section, the Internal Revenue Service will either make the determination or provide the payee with a written report informing the payee that the request for determination is being denied and the reasons for the denial. If a determination is made during the notice period (as defined in paragraph (f)(1) of this section), the payee is not subject to withholding due to notified payee underreporting with respect to any taxable year for which a determination was made. If a determination is made after the notice period, the Internal Revenue Service will, at the time prescribed in paragraph (g)(2) of this section, provide written certification to a payee that withholding is to stop, and will notify payors who were contacted pursuant to paragraph (c)(1) of this section to stop withholding. A broker who (in its capacity as payor) under this paragraph (g)(1) receives a notice from the Internal Revenue Service or a copy of the certification provided to a payee by the Internal Revenue Service is not required to provide a corresponding notice to any payors whom the broker has previously notified under paragraph (c)(2) of this section.

(2) *Date notice to stop backup withholding will be provided.*—(i) *Underreporting corrected or bona fide dispute.*—If the Internal Revenue Service makes a determination under paragraph (g)(3)(ii) or (iv) of this section during the 12-month period ending on October 15 of any calendar year (as described in paragraph (e)(2)(ii) of this section), the Internal Revenue Service will provide the certification and the notices described in paragraph (g)(1) of this section no later than December 1 of that calendar year.

(ii) *No underreporting or undue hardship.*—If the Internal Revenue Service makes a determination under paragraph (g)(3)(i) or (iii) of this section, the Internal Revenue Service will provide the notices described in paragraph (g)(1) of this section no later than the 45th day after the day on which the Internal Revenue Service makes its determination.

(3) *Grounds for determination.*—The Internal Revenue Service will make a determination that withholding due to notified payee underreporting should not start or should stop once it has started if the payee—

(i) Shows that there was no payee underreporting (as provided in paragraph (g)(4) of this section) for each taxable year with respect to which the Internal Revenue Service determined under paragraph (b)(2) of this section that there was payee underreporting;

(ii) Corrects any payee underreporting (as provided in paragraph (g)(5) of this section) for each taxable year with respect to which the Internal Revenue Service determined under paragraph (b)(2) of this section that there was payee underreporting;

(iii) Shows that withholding will cause or is causing an undue hardship (as defined in paragraph (g)(6) of this section) and that it is

Reg. §31.3406(c)-1(g)(3)(iii)

unlikely that the payee will underreport interest or dividend payments again; or

(iv) Shows that a bona fide dispute exists regarding whether any underreporting has occurred (as provided in paragraph (g)(7) of this section) for each taxable year with respect to which the Internal Revenue Service determined under paragraph (b)(2) of this section that there was payee underreporting.

(4) *No underreporting.*—A payee may show that no underreporting of reportable interest or dividends payments exists by presenting—

(i) Receipts or other satisfactory documentation to the Internal Revenue Service showing that all taxes relating to the payments were reported; or

(ii) Evidence showing that the payee did not have to file a return for the taxable year in question (e.g., because the payee did not make enough income) or that the underreporting determination was based upon a factual, clerical, or other error.

(5) *Correcting any payee underreporting.*— (i) *Before issuance of a statutory notice of deficiency.*—Before a statutory notice of deficiency is issued to a payee pursuant to section 6212, the payee may correct underreporting—

(A) By filing a return if one was not previously filed and including the unreported interest and dividends thereon;

(B) By filing an amended return in the event a return was filed and including the unreported interest and dividends thereon; or

(C) By consenting to the additional assessment according to applicable notices and forms sent to the payee by the Internal Revenue Service with respect to the underreporting, and paying taxes, penalties, and interest due with respect to any underreported interest or dividend payments.

(ii) *After issuance of a statutory notice of deficiency.*—After a statutory notice of deficiency is issued to a payee—

(A) The payee may correct underreporting at any time, by filing a return if one was not previously filed and paying the entire deficiency and any other taxes including penalties and interest attributable to any payee underreporting of interest or dividend payments; or

(B) The payee may correct underreporting after the mailing of the statutory notice of deficiency but before the expiration of the 90-day or 150-day period described in section 6213(a) or, if a petition is filed with the United States Tax Court, before the decision of the Tax Court is final, by making a remittance to the Internal Revenue Service of the amounts described in paragraph (g)(5)(ii)(A) of this section. The payee must specifically designate in writing that the remittance is a deposit in the nature of a cash bond.

(iii) *Special rules.*—For purposes of paragraph (g)(5)(ii) of this section, the payee will not be deemed to have corrected the payee underreporting under paragraph (g)(5)(ii)(B) of this sec-

tion after the remittance is returned to the payee in the manner described in any applicable administrative procedure. For further guidance on a deposit in the nature of a cash bond, see subparagraph 2 of section 4.01 of Rev. Proc. 84-58 (1984-2 C.B. 501). (See § 601.601(d)(2) of this chapter.) Once the remittance is returned to the payee, the rules of this section will apply. If the Internal Revenue Service previously contacted payors of the payee to start withholding with respect to the notified payee underreporting, however, the Internal Revenue Service will recontact those payors to start withholding under paragraph (c)(1) of this section with respect to the payee underreporting without regard to paragraph (f) of this section.

(6) *Undue hardship.*—(i) *In general.*—A determination of undue hardship will be based on the overall impact to the payee of having reportable interest or dividend payments withheld at a 31 percent rate under section 3406. In addition, a determination of undue hardship will be made only if the Internal Revenue Service concludes that it is unlikely that any payee underreporting will occur again.

(ii) *Factors.*—Factors that will be considered in determining whether withholding causes undue hardship include, but are not limited to, the following—

(A) Whether estimated tax payments, and other credits for current tax liabilities, or amounts withheld on employee wages or pensions, in addition to withholding under section 3406, would cause significant overwithholding;

(B) The payee's health, including the payee's ability to pay foreseeable medical expenses;

(C) The extent of the payee's reliance on interest and dividend payments to meet necessary living expenses and the existence, if any, of other sources of income;

(D) Whether other income of the payee is limited or fixed (e.g., social security, pension, and unearned income);

(E) The payee's ability to sell or liquidate stocks, bonds, bank accounts, trust accounts, or other assets, and the consequences of doing so;

(F) Whether the payee reported and timely paid the most recent year's tax liability, including interest and dividend income; and

(G) Whether the payee has filed a bankruptcy petition with the United States Bankruptcy Court.

(7) *Bona fide dispute.*—The Internal Revenue Service may make a determination under this paragraph (g)(7) if there is a dispute between the payee and the Internal Revenue Service on a question of fact or law that is material to a determination under paragraph (g)(3)(i) of this section and, based upon all the facts and circumstances, the Internal Revenue Service finds that the dispute is asserted in good faith by the payee and there is a reasonable basis for the payee's position.

Reg. §31.3406(c)-1(g)(3)(iv)

(h) *Payees filing a joint return.*—(1) *In general.*—For purposes of this section, if payee underreporting is found to exist with respect to a joint return, then the provisions of this section apply to both payees (i.e., the husband and wife). As a result, both payees are subject to withholding on accounts in their individual names as well as accounts in their joint names. Either or both payees may satisfy the criteria for a determination that no payee underreporting exists, that the underreporting has been corrected, or that a bona fide dispute exists (as provided in paragraph (g)(3)(i), (ii), or (iv) of this section). Both payees, however, must satisfy the criteria for a determination that withholding will cause or is causing undue hardship (as provided in paragraph (g)(3)(iii) of this section).

(2) *Exceptions.*—(i) *Innocent spouse.*—A spouse who files a joint return may obtain a determination that withholding should stop or not start with respect to payments made to his or her individual accounts, if the spouse shows that—

(A) He or she did not underreport income because he or she is a spouse described in section 6013(e), i.e, innocent spouse; or

(B) There is a bona fide dispute regarding whether he or she is an innocent spouse and hence did not underreport income.

(ii) *Divorced or legally separated payee.*—A payee who, at the time of the request for a determination under paragraph (g) of this section, is divorced or separated under state law may obtain a determination that undue hardship exists (or would exist) under paragraph (g)(3)(iii) of this section with respect to reportable interest or dividend payments made to his or her individual accounts if the divorced or legally separated payee satisfies the criteria for a determination under paragraph (g)(6) of this section.

(i) *Reserved.*

(j) *Penalties.*—For the application of penalties related to this section, see sections 6682 and 7205(b). [Reg. §31.3406(c)-1.]

☐ [*T.D.* 8637, 12-20-95.]

[Reg. §31.3406(d)-1]

§31.3406(d)-1. Manner required for furnishing a taxpayer identification number.—(a) *Requirement to backup withhold.*—Withholding under section 3406(a)(1)(A) applies to a reportable payment (as defined in section 3406(b)) if the payee does not furnish the payee's taxpayer identification number to the payor in the manner required by this section. The period for which withholding is required is described in §31.3406(e)-1(b). See §31.3406(d)-3(a) and (b) for special rules when an account is established directly with, or an instrument is acquired directly from, the payor by electronic transmission or by mail, or an instrument is sold through a broker by electronic transmission or by mail. See §31.3406(d)-4 for special rules applicable to read-

ily tradable instruments acquired through a broker. See §31.3406(h)-3(e) for the rules on when a payor may rely on a Form W-9. See also §31.3406(g)-3 for rules regarding a payee awaiting receipt of a taxpayer identification number. See the applicable information reporting sections and section 6109 and the regulations thereunder to determine whose taxpayer identification number should be provided.

(b) *Reportable interest or dividend account.*—(1) *Manner required for furnishing a taxpayer identification number with respect to a pre-1984 account or instrument.*—A payee must furnish the payee's taxpayer identification number to the payor with respect to any obligation, deposit, certificate, share, membership, contract, investment, account, or other relationship or instrument established or acquired on or before December 31, 1983 (a pre-1984 account) and with respect to which the payor makes a reportable interest or dividend payment (as defined in section 3406(b)(2)). The manner of determining whether an account or an instrument is a pre-1984 account is described in paragraph (b)(2) of this section. The payee of a pre-1984 account may furnish the payee's taxpayer identification number to the payor orally or in writing. The payee is not required to certify under penalties of perjury that the taxpayer identification number is correct.

(2) *Determination of pre-1984 account or instrument.*—(i) *In general.*—An account that is in existence before January 1, 1984, will be considered a pre-1984 account, regardless of whether additional deposits are made to the account on or after January 1, 1984. An account established as an expansion of a credit union prime account in existence prior to January 1, 1984, constitutes a pre-1984 account. If funds taken from one account in existence prior to January 1, 1984, are used to create a new account on or after that date, however, the new account does not constitute a pre-1984 account except as provided in the preceding sentence. An instrument acquired prior to January 1, 1984, is a pre-1984 account. Regardless of when an instrument was acquired, if it is negotiated in a window transaction as defined in §31.3406(b)(2)-3(b), it is treated as an instrument acquired after December 31, 1983. An obligation in bearer form and subject to reporting under section 6045, whenever acquired, is not a pre-1984 account. Any instrument, whenever acquired, that is held in a brokerage account is considered a pre-1984 account if the brokerage account is not a post-1983 brokerage account (as described in paragraph (c)(1)(ii) of this section). If shares of a corporation are held before January 1, 1984 (or considered held before that date by operation of this paragraph (b)(2)), and additional shares are acquired by the holder, irrespective of whether the shares are received by reason of a stock dividend, investing new cash, or otherwise, the new shares, in the discretion of the payor, may be considered a pre-1984 account. In the case of a qualified employee trust

that distributes instruments in kind, any instrument distributed from the trust is considered a pre-1984 account with respect to employees who were participants in the trust before 1984. Similarly, when a payor offers participants in a plan the opportunity to purchase stock of the payor after a specified time, using the money that the payee invested during that period of time, the stock so purchased after December 31, 1983, is considered a pre-1984 account with respect to participants in the plan who either owned shares or invested money in the plan before January 1, 1984.

(ii) *Account or instrument automatically acquired on the maturity or termination of an account.*—When an account is opened, or an instrument is acquired, automatically on the maturity or termination of an account that was in existence or an instrument that was held before January 1, 1984 (or considered to have been in existence or held before that date by operation of this paragraph (b)(2)(ii)), without the participation of the payee, the new account or instrument, in the discretion of the payor, may be considered a pre-1984 account. For purposes of the preceding sentence, a payee is not considered to have participated in the acquisition of the new account or instrument solely because the payee failed to exercise a right to withdraw funds at the maturity or termination of the old account or instrument.

(iii) *Insurance policies.*—In the case of insurance policies in effect on December 31, 1983, the election of a dividend accumulation option pursuant to which interest is paid (as defined in § 1.6049-5(a)(4) of this chapter), or the creation of an account in which proceeds of a policy are held for the policy beneficiary, may, in the payor's discretion, be treated as a pre-1984 account.

(iv) *Acquisitions of accounts and instruments.*—(A) *Pre-1984 or post-1983 status known.*—If a payor acquires accounts or instruments of another payor (including through a tax-free reorganization under section 368), the acquiring payor must treat the persons specified in this paragraph (b)(2)(iv)(A) as having the same requirement to furnish a taxpayer identification number in the manner required under this paragraph (b) to the acquiring payor for information reporting, withholding, and related tax provisions as existed with respect to the payor whose accounts or instruments were acquired. Persons specified in this paragraph (b)(2)(iv)(A) are persons who held accounts or instruments in the other payor immediately before the acquisition and who receive an account or instrument in the acquiring payor immediately after the acquisition.

(B) *Pre-1984 or post-1983 status unknown.*—If the acquiring payor, as described in paragraph (b)(2)(iv)(A) of this section, is unable to identify from the business records of the other payor whether any or all of the accounts or instruments of the persons specified in para-

graph (b)(2)(iv)(A) of this section are pre-1984 (or post-1983) accounts or instruments, then the acquiring payor may treat these unidentified accounts or instruments as pre-1984 accounts or instruments.

(C) *Cross reference.*—See § 31.3406(g)-2(g) for the limited exception from withholding under section 3406(a)(1)(A) on accounts or instruments described in paragraphs (b)(2)(iv)(A) and (B) of this section for which the payor does not have a taxpayer identification number.

(3) *Manner required for furnishing a taxpayer identification number with respect to an account or instrument that is not a pre-1984 account.*—A payee who receives reportable interest or dividend payments (as defined in section 3406(b)(2)) from a payor must certify under penalties of perjury that the taxpayer identification number the payee furnishes to the payor is the payee's correct taxpayer identification number. The payee must make the certification only with respect to an account or instrument that is not a pre-1984 account (as described in paragraph (b)(2) of this section). See § 31.3406(h)-3 for a description of the certificate on which the certification must be made. See § 31.3406(d)-2 for the requirement that the payee must certify under penalties of perjury that the payee is not subject to withholding due to notified payee underreporting. See § 31.3406(d)-3(a) with respect to an account established directly with, or an instrument acquired directly from, the payor by electronic transmission or by mail. See § 31.3406(d)-4 for the rules applicable to readily tradable instruments acquired through a broker.

(4) *Special rule with respect to the acquisition of a readily tradable instrument in a transaction between certain parties acting without the assistance of a broker.*—If a payee, at any time, acquires a readily tradable instrument without the assistance of a broker, and no party to the acquisition is a broker or an agent of the payor, the payee must furnish the payee's taxpayer identification number to the payor prior to the time reportable payments are made on the instrument. The payee is not required to certify under penalties of perjury that the number is correct. See § 31.3406(d)-2 for the rule that a payee is not subject to withholding due to notified payee underreporting with respect to a readily tradable instrument acquired in the manner described in this paragraph (b)(4). A broker is considered to provide assistance in the acquisition of an instrument if the person effecting the acquisition would be required to make an information return under section 6045 if such person were to sell the instrument. See § 31.3406(d)-4 for rules relating to an acquisition of a readily tradable instrument when a broker is involved.

(c) *Brokerage account.*—(1) *Manner required for furnishing a taxpayer identification number with respect to a brokerage relationship that is not a post-1983 brokerage account.*—(i) *In general.*—With respect to any instrument, investment, or deposit made through a brokerage account that is not a post-1983 brokerage account, a payee must furnish the payee's taxpayer identification number to the broker either orally or in writing. The payee is not required to certify under penalties of perjury that the taxpayer identification number is correct. See paragraph (b)(2)(i) of this section for the rule that any instrument, whenever acquired, that is held in a brokerage account that is not a post-1983 brokerage account, is considered held in an account that is not a post-1983 brokerage account. For example, in 1983 a payee established and acquired a readily tradable instrument from a brokerage account; no activity took place through that account until the payee purchased a readily tradable instrument in 1995. That readily tradable instrument is not held in a post-1983 brokerage account; therefore, the payee need not certify under penalties of perjury that the payee's taxpayer identification number is correct.

(ii) *Definition of a brokerage account that is not a post-1983 brokerage account.*—A brokerage account that was established by a payee before January 1, 1984, through which during 1983 the broker either bought or sold securities for the payee or held securities on behalf of the payee as a nominee (i.e., in street name), is an account that is not a post-1983 brokerage account.

(2) *Manner required for furnishing a taxpayer identification number with respect to a post-1983 brokerage account.*—(i) *In general.*—With respect to a post-1983 brokerage account, the payee must furnish the payee's taxpayer identification number to the broker and certify under penalties of perjury that the taxpayer identification number furnished is correct, except as provided in §31.3406(d)-3(b).

(ii) *Definition of a post-1983 brokerage account.*—A brokerage account established after December 31, 1983 (or before January 1, 1984, through which during 1983 the broker neither bought nor sold securities nor held securities on behalf of the payee as a nominee (i.e., in street name)), is a post-1983 brokerage account.

(d) *Rents, commissions, nonemployee compensation, certain fishing boat operators, and payment card and third party network transactions, etc.—Manner required for furnishing a taxpayer identification number.*—For accounts, contracts, or relationships subject to information reporting under section 6041 (relating to information reporting at source on rents, royalties, salaries, etc.), section 6041A(a) (relating to information reporting of payments for nonemployee services), section 6050A (relating to information reporting by certain fishing boat operators), section 6050N (relating to information reporting of payments of royalties), or section 6050W (relating to information reporting for payment card and third party network transactions), the payee must furnish the payee's taxpayer identification number to the payor either orally or in writing. Except as provided in §31.3406(d)-5, the payee is not required to certify under penalties of perjury that the

taxpayer identification number is correct regardless of when the account, contract, or relationship is established. [Reg. §31.3406(d)-1.]

☐ [*T.D.* 8637, 12-20-95. *Amended by T.D.* 9496, 8-13-2010.]

[Reg. §31.3406(d)-2]

§31.3406(d)-2. Payee certification failure.—(a) *Requirement to backup withhold.*—Withholding under section 3406(a)(1)(D) applies to a reportable interest or dividend payment (as defined in section 3406(b)(2)) if, and only if, the payee fails to certify to the payor, under penalties of perjury, that the payee is not subject to withholding due to notified payee underreporting under section 3406(a)(1)(C). The period for which withholding applies is described in §31.3406(e)1(e). See §31.3406(d)-3(a) for special rules when an account is established directly with, or an instrument is acquired directly from, the payor by electronic transmission or by mail. See §31.3406(c)-1(c)(3)(iv) for rules with respect to a payor's reliance on a payee certification for a new account following notified payee underreporting. See §31.3406(d)-4 for special rules relating to the acquisition of a readily tradable instrument through a broker. The certificate on which the certification should be made is described in §31.3406(h)-3.

(b) *Exceptions.*—Withholding under section 3406(a)(1)(D) and paragraph (a) of this section does not apply to reportable interest or dividend payments (as defined in section 3406(b)(2)) made—

(1) With respect to a pre-1984 account (as defined in §31.3406(d)-1(b)(1);

(2) In a window transaction (as defined in §31.3406(b)(2)-3(b));

(3) With respect to a readily tradable instrument described in §31.3406(d)-1(b)(2)(iv) or §31.3406(d)-4(a)(3); or

(4) During the period and with respect to an account or readily tradable instrument described in §31.3406(d)-3. [Reg. §31.3406(d)-2.]

☐ [*T.D.* 8637, 12-20-95.]

[Reg. §31.3406(d)-3]

§31.3406(d)-3. Special 30-day rules for certain reportable payments.—(a) *Accounts or readily tradable instruments acquired directly from the payor (including a broker who holds an instrument in street name) by electronic transmission or by mail.*—In the case of an account established directly with, or a readily tradable instrument acquired directly from, the payor by means of electronic transmission (i.e., telephone or wire instruction) or by mail, the payor may permit the payee to furnish the certifications required in §31.3406(d)-1(b)(3)(relating to certification that the payee's taxpayer identification number is correct) and §31.3406(d)-2 (relating to certification of notified payee underreporting) within 30 days after the establishment or acquisition without subjecting the account to withholding during the 30 days. The preceding sentence applies only if the payee furnishes a taxpayer identification number to the payor at the time of the establishment or acquisition, and the payee does not withdraw more than 69 percent of a reportable interest or dividend payment before the certifications are received within the 30 days. If the payee does not provide the required certifications within 30 days of the establishment or acquisition, the payor must withhold 31 percent of any reportable interest or dividend payments made to the account after its acquisition. For purposes of this section, an account or instrument is considered acquired directly from the payor if the instrument was acquired by the payee without the assistance of a broker or the instrument was acquired directly from a broker who holds the instrument as nominee for the payee (i.e., in street name) and who is considered a payor under § 31.3406(a)-2. For payments made after December 31, 1998, see § 1.6049-5(d)(2)(ii) of this chapter for the application of a 90-day grace period in lieu of the 30-day grace period described in this paragraph (a) if, at the beginning of the 90-day grace period, certain conditions are satisfied. If the grace period provisions of § 1.6049-5(d)(2)(ii) or § 1.1441-1(b)(3)(iv) of this chapter are applied with respect to a new account, the grace period provisions of this paragraph (a) shall not apply to that account.

(b) *Sale of an instrument for a customer by electronic transmission or by mail.*—The special rules set forth in paragraph (a) of this section apply comparably with respect to certification of the taxpayer identification number for the sale of an instrument under section 6045 (as described in § 31.3406(b)(3)-2) through a post-1983 brokerage account (as described in § 31.3406(d)-1(c)(2)) for a customer by electronic transmission or by mail. However, the 30-day rules may apply only if the payee furnishes the payee's taxpayer identification number before the sale occurs. For purposes of applying the 30-day rules under this paragraph (b), a payee's reinvestment of the gross proceeds of the sale into other instruments constitutes a withdrawal.

(c) *Application to foreign payees.*—The rules of paragraphs (a) and (b) of this section also apply to a payee from whom the payor is required to obtain a Form W-8 (or an acceptable substitute) or other evidence of foreign status (pursuant to relevant regulations under an applicable Internal Revenue Code section without regard to the requirement to furnish a taxpayer identifying number, and the certifications described in § § 31.3406(d)-1(b)(3) and 31.3406(d)-2, provided the payee represents orally or otherwise, before or at the time of the acquisition or sale of the instrument or the establishment of the account, that the payee is not a United States citizen or resident. The 30-day rules described in paragraph (a) or (b) of this section may apply only if the payee does not qualify for, or the payor does not apply, the 90-day grace period described in § 1.6049-5(d)(2)(ii) or § 1.1441-1(b)(3)(iv) of this chapter. [Reg. § 31.3406(d)-3.]

☐ [*T.D.* 8637, 12-20-95. *Amended by T.D.* 8734, 10-6-97 (T.D. 8804 delayed the effective date of T.D. 8734 from January 1, 1999, to January 1, 2000; T.D. 8856 further delayed the effective date of T.D. 8734 until January 1, 2001).]

[Reg. § 31.3406(d)-4]

§ 31.3406(d)-4. Special rules for readily tradable instruments acquired through a broker.— (a) *Readily tradable instruments acquired through post-1983 brokerage accounts with a broker who is not a payor.*—(1) *In general.*—If a readily tradable instrument is acquired through a post-1983 brokerage account (as defined in § 31.3406(d)-1(c)(2)) and the broker is not a broker holding a security (including stock) for a customer in street name, the broker must—

(i) Obtain once with respect to each account the certifications described in § 31.3406(d)-2(a) and § 31.3406(d)-1(b) and (c)(2) from the payee (relating to certification regarding payee underreporting and taxpayer identification number, respectively);

(ii) Furnish the payee's taxpayer identification number to the payor; and

(iii) Notify the payor to impose withholding if the payee fails to make either of the required certifications to the broker or if the broker has been notified by the Internal Revenue Service before the acquisition of the instrument that the payee is subject to withholding due to notified payee underreporting under section 3406(a)(1)(C) or that the payee is subject to withholding because the payee's taxpayer identification number is incorrect under section 3406(a)(1)(B)(as described in § 31.3406(d)-5).

(2) *Additional requirements.*—The broker must give the information required by paragraphs (a)(1)(ii) and (iii) of this section to the payor with the transfer instructions for the acquisition (including account registration instructions transmitted by a broker in the case of acquisitions of shares in a mutual fund). A notice including the information described in paragraph (b)(1) of this section fulfills the broker's requirement to give notice to the payor. Once the broker transmits the transfer instructions containing the information required by this section, the broker has no further responsibility to obtain a missing taxpayer identification number or missing certification or to provide additional notices to the payee or payor with respect to the acquisition of the instrument. Upon receiving the notice from a broker, the payor must impose withholding on the account pursuant to § 31.3406(a)-1.

(3) *Transactions entered into through a brokerage account that is not a post-1983 brokerage account.*—If a broker acquires readily tradable instruments for a payee through an account (with the broker) that is not a post-1983 brokerage account (as defined in § 31.3406(d)-1(c)(1)), and the broker is not the payor of the instruments, the broker must furnish the payee's taxpayer identification number to the payor. In addition, if the broker has been notified by the

Internal Revenue Service that the payee is subject to withholding under section 3406 either because of an incorrect taxpayer identification number or due to notified payee underreporting as described in section 3406(a)(1)(B) or (C), respectively, the broker must notify the payor of the instrument to impose withholding with respect to that payee and transmit the information in the manner described in this paragraph (a). After a payor receives a notice from a broker pursuant to section 3406(d)(2)(B) and this paragraph (a), the payor must impose withholding on any accounts of the payee paying reportable interest or dividends as defined in section 3406(b)(2) in accordance with § 31.3406(a)-1.

(4) *Payor must notify payee.*—(i) *Failure to provide certifications.*—If a payor is notified by a broker, as required in paragraph (a)(1) of this section, that a payee is subject to withholding because the payee failed to provide the certifications, as described in § 31.3406(d)-2(a) and § 31.3406(d)-1(b)(3) and (c)(2), and the payor has not received the certifications from the payee, then the payor must notify the payee that withholding has started (or will start) no later than 15 days after the payor makes the first payment to the payee that is subject to withholding under section 3406. A notice that contains the information described in paragraph (b)(2) of this section satisfies the payor's requirement to give notice to the payee. If the broker notifies the payor that the payee failed to make a required certification and the payor has received the certification from the payee, the payor may disregard the notice from the broker.

(ii) *Notified payee underreporting and incorrect taxpayer identification number.*—The payor must notify the payee under this section if the Internal Revenue Service or a broker notifies the payor to withhold either because of an incorrect taxpayer identification number under section 3406(a)(1)(B)(as described in § 31.3406(d)-5) or due to notified payee underreporting under section 3406(a)(1)(C)(as described in § 31.3406(c)-1). If a payor is notified by the Internal Revenue Service or a broker with respect to a readily tradable instrument, the payor may not ignore the notice even if the payee previously provided the payee's taxpayer identification number under penalties of perjury to the payor and even if the payee certified to the payor that the payee is not subject to backup withholding due to a notified payee underreporting. See § 31.3406(d)-5(c)(1) and (2) and (f)(2) for notice requirements under section 3406(a)(1)(B) due to an incorrect taxpayer identification number. See § 31.3406(c)-1(c)(2) for notice requirements under section 3406(a)(1)(C) due to notified payee underreporting.

(b) *Notices.*—(1) *Form of notice by broker to payor.*—A broker who is required under paragraphs (a)(1)(iii) and (2) of this section to notify the payor with respect to a readily tradable instrument may notify the payor in connection with the transfer instructions by means of magnetic media, machine readable document, or any other medium, provided that the notice includes the following information—

(i) The payee's name, address, and taxpayer identification number (if provided to the broker); and

(ii) A statement that the payee is subject to withholding under section 3406(a)(1)(A), (B), (C), or (D) of the Internal Revenue Code, whichever section applies; and

(iii) When applicable, a statement that the broker was notified by the Internal Revenue Service that the payee is subject to withholding under section 3406(a)(1)(B) or (C).

(2) *Form of notice by payor to payee.*—A payor who is required to notify a payee that the payee is subject to withholding must provide notice that is substantially similar to the following—

(i) For a notification concerning a failure to provide a taxpayer identification number in the required manner under section 3406(a)(1)(A) or a failure to make the following certification described in section 3406(a)(1)(D):

Recently, you purchased (identify security acquired). Because of the existence of one or more of the following conditions, payments of interest, dividends, and other reportable amounts that are made to you will be subject to withholding of tax at a 31 percent rate: (specify the condition or conditions, described below, that are applicable)

(1) You failed to provide a taxpayer identification number, or failed to provide this number under penalties of perjury, in connection with the purchase of the acquired security. (An individual's taxpayer identification number is his or her social security number.)

(2) You failed to certify, under penalties of perjury, that you are not subject to withholding due to notified payee underreporting as required under section 3406(a)(1)(D) of the Internal Revenue Code.

If condition (1) applies, you may stop withholding by providing your taxpayer identification number on the enclosed Form W-9, signing the form, and returning it to us. If you do not have a taxpayer identification number, but have applied (or will soon apply) for one, you may so indicate on the Form W-9. Withholding may apply during the 60-day period you are waiting for your taxpayer identification number. You must provide us with your taxpayer identification number promptly after you receive it in order to avoid withholding after the end of the 60-day period or to stop withholding if it has already begun. Certain persons, described on the enclosed Form W-9, are exempt from withholding. Follow the instructions on that form if applicable to you.

If condition (2) applies, you may stop withholding by certifying on the enclosed Form W-9 that you are not subject to withholding due to notified payee underreporting, signing the form, and returning it to us.

If more than one condition applies, you must remove all applicable conditions to stop withholding.

Please address any questions concerning this notice to: [Insert payor identifying information].

(Do not address questions to the broker who purchased the securities for you.)

(ii) For the form of the notice concerning imposition of withholding due to an incorrect taxpayer identification number, see § 31.3406(d)-5(d)(2) and (g)(2).

(iii) For the form of the notice concerning the imposition of withholding due to notified payee underreporting, see § 31.3406(c)-1(d)(2).

(c) *Payor's reliance on information from broker.*— (1) *In general.*—A payor of an instrument acquired by a payee through a broker may rely on the information that the payor receives from the broker pursuant to paragraphs (a) and (b) of this section.

(2) *Amount subject to backup withholding.*— The payor is required to withhold under section 3406 depending on the payor's customary method of making payment on an instrument or instruments owned by a payee. If it is the practice of a payor to combine in one account all readily tradable instruments of the same issue owned by a payee and if only certain of those instruments are subject to withholding, the payor must withhold on the aggregate payment made with respect to all the instruments in the account. Otherwise, the payor must withhold on the payment made on the instrument or instruments with respect to which the payee is subject to withholding. [Reg. § 31.3406(d)-4.]

☐ [*T.D.* 8637, 12-20-95. *Amended by T.D.* 9010, 7-25-2002.]

[Reg. § 31.3406(d)-5]

§ 31.3406(d)-5. Backup withholding when the Service or a broker notifies the payor to withhold because the payee's taxpayer identification number is incorrect.—(a) *Overview.*— Backup withholding under section 3406(a)(1)(B) applies to any reportable payment made with respect to an account of a payee if the Internal Revenue Service or a broker notifies a payor under paragraph (c)(1) or (2) of this section that the payee's name and taxpayer identification number combination ("name/TIN combination") is incorrect and the payor is required under paragraph (c)(3) of this section to identify that account as having the same name/TIN combination. After receiving a notice from the Internal Revenue Service or a broker under paragraph (c)(1) or (2) of this section and identifying an account as having the incorrect name/TIN combination under paragraph (c)(3) of this section, the payor must notify the payee in accordance with paragraph (d) of this section. In addition, under paragraph (e) of this section, the payor must backup withhold on all reportable payments made to such account after the close of the 30th business day after the date that the

payor receives the notice and on or before the close of the 30th calendar day after the date that the payor receives from the payee the certification required under paragraph (f) of this section. Under paragraph (g) of this section, if a payor receives 2 notices from the Internal Revenue Service or broker within 3 calendar years with respect to a payee's account, the payor must notify the payee in accordance with paragraph (g)(2) (rather than paragraph (d)) of this section. In addition, the payor must backup withhold on all reportable payments made with respect to the account after the close of the 30th business day after the date that the payor receives the second notice and on or before the 30th calendar day after the date that the payor receives notification from the Social Security Administration (or the Internal Revenue Service) validating a name/ TIN combination for the account. Paragraph (h) of this section requires a payor to use a corrected name/TIN combination on subsequent information returns.

(b) *Definitions and special rules.*—(1) *Definition of incorrect name/TIN combination.*—An incorrect name/TIN combination is a combination of a name and taxpayer identification number provided on an information return with respect to which the Internal Revenue Service determines that the taxpayer identification number provided is not assigned under section 6109 to the name provided.

(2) *Definition of account.*—The term "account" means any account, instrument, or other relationship with the payor.

(3) *Definition of business day.*—The term "business day" means any day other than a Saturday, Sunday, or legal holiday (within the meaning of section 7503).

(4) *Certain exceptions.*—(i) *In general.*—This section does not apply with respect to any notice received under paragraph (c)(1) or (2) of this section with respect to payments that—

(A) Were made to a fiduciary or nominee account; or

(B) Were not reportable payments (for example, because the payments were made to an exempt recipient).

See § 301.6724-1(f)(3) of this chapter for certain solicitation rules applicable after receipt of a notice under paragraph (c)(1) or (2) of this section with respect to a fiduciary or nominee account.

(ii) *Definition of fiduciary or nominee account.*—A fiduciary or nominee account is an account with respect to which at least one person named in the registration is identified as acting in the capacity as nominee or as administrator, conservator, custodian, receiver, tutor, curator, committee, executor, guardian, trustee, or other fiduciary capacity recognized under governing law.

(c) *Notice regarding an incorrect name/TIN combination.*—(1) *In general.*—If the Internal Revenue Service notifies a payor that a payee's name/TIN combination is incorrect and that the payor must commence backup withholding as required on reportable payments made with respect to accounts of the payee with the same name/TIN combination, the payor must—

(i) Identify under paragraph (c)(3) of this section any account or accounts of the payee having the same name/TIN combination;

(ii) Except as provided in paragraph (g) of this section, notify the payee and backup withhold on reportable payments made to the account or accounts under the rules of paragraphs (d), (e), and (f) of this section. This paragraph (c)(1) also applies if the payor receives notice from a broker under paragraph (c)(2) of this section.

(2) *Additional requirements for payors that are also brokers.*—(i) *In general.*—A broker must notify the payor of an instrument of the information required under paragraph (c)(2)(ii) of this section, if—

(A) The broker (in its capacity as a payor) receives a notice from the Internal Revenue Service under paragraph (c)(1) of this section that a payee's name/TIN combination is incorrect and is required to identify an account of the payee pursuant to paragraph (c)(3) of this section as having the name/TIN combination;

(B) The payee acquires through the same account with the broker a readily tradable instrument with respect to which the broker is not the payor; and

(C) The acquisition of such instrument occurs after the close of the 30th business day after the date that the broker receives that notice (or on any earlier date that the broker chooses to begin applying this paragraph (c)(2)). For purposes of this paragraph (c)(2)(i), with respect to notices under paragraph (c)(1) of this section received on or after September 1, 1992, an acquisition includes a transfer of an instrument out of street name into the name of the registered owner, *i.e.*, the payee.

(ii) *Required information.*—The information required to be provided under this paragraph (c)(2)(ii) is:

(A) The fact that the broker was notified by the Internal Revenue Service that the payee furnished an incorrect name/TIN combination;

(B) The incorrect name/TIN combination; and

(C) The fact that the named payee is subject to backup withholding under section 3406(a)(1)(B). The broker is required to provide this information to the payor of the instrument in connection with the transfer instructions for the acquisition.

(iii) *Termination of obligation to provide information.*—The obligation of a broker to provide information to payors under this paragraph (c)(2) terminates simultaneously with the termination of the broker's obligation to backup withhold (in its capacity as payor) on reportable payments to the account.

(3) *Payor identification of the account or accounts of the payee that have the incorrect taxpayer identification number.*—(i) *In general.*—If an account number or designation is provided in the notice received under paragraph (c)(1) of this section, the payor need only identify any account or accounts corresponding to that number or designation that has the same name/TIN combination provided in the notice. If no account number or designation is provided in the notice received under paragraph (c)(1) of this section, the payor must identify, using reasonable care, all accounts of the payee having the same name/TIN combination provided in the notice. If a payor receives notice from a broker under paragraph (c)(2) of this section with respect to the acquisition of a readily tradable instrument, the payor is not required to identify any other account of the payee.

(ii) *Reasonable care where no account number or designation is provided.*—A payor who satisfies the following two-part facts-and-circumstances test will be considered to have exercised reasonable care for purposes of this paragraph (c)(3).

(A) Part one of the test is satisfied if a payor searches for accounts of the payee on the computer or other recordkeeping system that the payor can reasonably associate with the information return that generated the notice under paragraph (c)(1) of this section. For example, a payor who maintains separate computer or recordkeeping systems for different product lines will have identified and used the appropriate system if the payor searches for accounts of the payee on the computer or recordkeeping system that contains the product line for the type of payments reported on the information return. A payor with the same product line on several nonintegrated computer or record systems will have identified and used the appropriate system if the payor searches for accounts of the payee on any computer or record system that the payor otherwise can reasonably associate with the information return.

(B) Part two of the test is satisfied if the payor inputs the name/TIN combination provided on the notice from the Internal Revenue Service under paragraph (c)(1) of this section into the system that is described in paragraph (c)(3)(ii)(A) of this section. If the system of a payor cannot utilize the name/TIN combination, the payor must input appropriate data or criteria, as determined by the capability of the payor's computer or recordkeeping system.

(iii) *No identification if error is caused by payor.*—A payor may treat an account as not having the incorrect name/TIN combination if the error resulted because the name or taxpayer identification number on such account is not the name or taxpayer identification number that was provided to the payor. This may occur, for example, where a payor transposes numbers in the taxpayer identification number when incorporating it into the payor's business records.

Reg. §31.3406(d)-5(c)(3)(iii)

(4) *Special rules for joint accounts.*—(i) *In general.*—In the case of a joint account, the relevant name/TIN combination for purposes of this section is the name/TIN combination used for information reporting purposes.

(ii) *Transitional rule.*—With respect to notices received under paragraph (c)(1) or (2) of this section prior to September 1, 1993, a payor may treat the name/TIN combination of the first person on a joint account as the relevant name/TIN combination, unless that person is an exempt foreign person and the account registration includes names of persons who are not foreign persons.

(iii) *Optional rule where names are switched.*—A payor may backup withhold under this section on reportable payments made to a joint account if the order of the names (or taxpayer identification numbers) on the account is merely subsequent to receipt of a notice under paragraph (c)(1) or (2) of this section, provided that the name of the person to which the incorrect name/TIN combination originally applies remains on the account.

(5) *Date of receipt.*—For purposes of this section, the date set forth on the notice from the Internal Revenue Service or broker under paragraph (c)(1) or (2) of this section is considered to be the date of receipt of the notice by the payor. However, if the payor demonstrates to the satisfaction of the Internal Revenue Service that the date of actual receipt of the notice is later than the date on the notice, the actual date of receipt is controlling.

(d) *Notice from payors of backup withholding due to an incorrect name/TIN combination.*—(1) *In general.*—Except as provided in paragraph (g) of this section, if a payor receives notice under paragraph (c)(1) or (2) of this section and is required to identify an account as having the incorrect name/TIN combination under paragraph (c)(3) of this section, the payor must send a copy of the notice (or an acceptable substitute notice) to the payee of the account in accordance with the procedures of paragraph (d)(2) of this section.

(2) *Procedures.*—(i) *In general.*—The notice that a payor must send to a payee under paragraph (d)(1) of this section must comply with such procedural requirements as the Internal Revenue Service provides in the Internal Revenue Bulletin such as to form and manner of delivery. A payor must send the notice to the payee within 15 business days after the date that the payor receives the notice from the Internal Revenue Service or a broker under paragraph (c)(1) or (2) of this section.

(ii) *Two or more notices for an account for the same year or received in the same year.*—A payor who receives, under the same payor taxpayer identification number, two or more notices under paragraph (c)(1) or (2) of this section with respect to the same payee's account for the same year, or in the same calendar year, need only send one notice to the payee under this section.

(e) *Period during which backup withholding is required due to notification of an incorrect name/TIN combination.*—(1) *In general.*—Except as provided in paragraph (g) of this section, if a payor receives a notice under paragraph (c)(1) or (2) of this section and is required to identify an account as having the same name/TIN combination under paragraph (c)(3) of this section, the payor must impose backup withholding on all reportable payments made with respect to the account after the close of the 30th business day after the date the payor receives that notice and on or before the close of the 30th calendar day after the day the payor receives from the payee the certification required under paragraph (f) of this section.

(2) *Grace periods.*—(i) *Starting backup withholding.*—A payor may, on an account-by-account basis or in general, choose to begin backup withholding under this paragraph (e) at any time during the 30-business-day period described in paragraph (e)(1) of this section.

(ii) *Stopping backup withholding.*—A payor may, on an account-by-account basis or in general, choose to stop backup withholding under this paragraph (e) at any time within 30 calendar days after the payor receives from the payee the certification required under paragraph (f) of this section.

(3) *Dormant accounts.*—The requirement that a payor backup withhold under this paragraph (e) on reportable payments made with respect to an account terminates no later than the close of the third calendar year ending after the later of—

(i) The date that the last reportable payment was made to that account; or

(ii) The date that the payor received the notice under paragraph (c)(1) or (2) of this section.

(f) *Manner required for payee to furnish certified taxpayer identification number.*—(1) Except as provided in paragraph (g) of this section, in order to prevent backup withholding under paragraph (e) of this section from starting, or to stop it once it has begun, a payee with respect to whom the payor has been notified under paragraph (c)(1) or (2) that the payee's name/TIN combination is incorrect is required on Form W-9 (or an acceptable substitute form) to—

(i) Provide the payee's name and taxpayer identification number; and

(ii) Certify, under penalties of perjury, that the taxpayer identification number being provided is correct.

(2) The certification must be made even if the account is a pre-1984 account and even if the payment to the account is reportable payment other than interest, dividends, patronage dividends, original issue discount, or proceeds of a sale of a security or commodity. In order to prevent backup withholding under paragraph (e) of this section from starting or to stop it once it has begun, a payee is not required to certify,

under penalties of perjury, that the payee is not subject to backup withholding due to notified payee underreporting under section 3406(a)(1)(C). With respect to notices received under paragraph (c)(1) or (2) of this section on or after September 1, 1993, the requirements of this paragraph (f) are not satisfied if a payee provides only an awaiting TIN certification. As a result, a payor must not fail to begin backup withholding under paragraph (e) of this section solely because the payee provided an awaiting TIN certification, or stop once it has begun solely because the payee provided an awaiting TIN certification.

(g) *Receipt of two notices within a three-year period.*—(1) *In general.*—If a payor receives notification under paragraph (c)(1) or (2) of this section twice within three calendar years, and in each case the payor is required to identify the same account as having the incorrect name/TIN combination, the payor must—

(i) Disregard any future certifications (described in paragraph (f) of this section) furnished by the payee with respect to the account until the payor receives notice from the Social Security Administration (or the Internal Revenue Service) validating a name/TIN combination under paragraph (g)(5) of this section;

(ii) Send the notice described in paragraph (g)(2) of this section to the payee (and not the notice required under paragraph (d) of this section) within 15 business days after the date that the payor receives the second notice; and

(iii) Impose backup withholding on the account for the period described in paragraph (g)(3) of this section.

The payor must maintain sufficient records to determine whether the payor has received notices under paragraph (c)(1) or (2) of this section twice within three calendar years with respect to the same account.

(2) *Notice to payee who has provided two incorrect name/TIN combinations within three calendar years.*—The notice to the payee required by paragraph (g)(1) of this section must comply with such procedural requirements as the Internal Revenue Service provides in the Internal Revenue Bulletin such as to form and manner of delivery.

(3) *Period during which backup withholding is required due to a second notice of an incorrect name/taxpayer identification combination within three calendar years.*—(i) *In general.*—If paragraph (g)(1) of this section applies, the payor must backup withhold on all reportable payments made with respect to the account of the payee after the close of the 30th business day after the date that the payor receives the second notice under paragraph (c)(1) or (2) of this section and on or before the close of the 30th calendar day after the date that the payor receives notice from the Social Security Administration (or the Internal Revenue Service) validating a name/TIN combination under paragraph (g)(5) of this section for the account. However, a payor may choose not to

commence backup withholding under this paragraph (g) until January 1, 1992.

(ii) *Grace periods.*—(A) *Starting backup withholding.*—A payor may, on an account-by-account basis or in general, choose to begin backup withholding under this paragraph (g) at any time during the 30-business-day period described in paragraph (g)(3)(i) of this section.

(B) *Stopping backup withholding.*—A payor may, on an account-by-account basis or in general, choose to stop backup withholding under this paragraph (g) at any time within 30 calendar days after the date the payor receives notice from the Social Security Administration (or the Internal Revenue Service) validating a name/TIN combination under paragraph (g)(5) of this section for the account.

(iii) *Dormant accounts.*—The requirement that a payor backup withhold under this paragraph (g) on reportable payments made with respect to an account terminates no later than the close of the third calendar year ending after the later of—

(A) The date that the last reportable payment was made to that account; or

(B) The date that the payor received the second notice under paragraph (c)(1) or (2) of this section.

(4) *Receipt of two notices for the same year or in the same calendar year.*—A payor who receives, under the same payor taxpayer identification number, two or more notices under paragraph (c)(1) or (2) of this section with respect to the same payee's account for the same year, or in the same calendar year, must treat such notices as one notice for purposes of this paragraph (g).

(5) *Notification from the Social Security Administration (or the Internal Revenue Service) validating a name/TIN combination.*—The Social Security Administration (or the Internal Revenue Service) will notify a payor after it validates a name/TIN combination that the payee provides for an account to which paragraph (g)(1) of this section applies. Notification from the Social Security Administration (or the Internal Revenue Service) validating a name/TIN combination satisfies the requirements of this paragraph (g)(5) only if it complies with such procedural requirements as the Internal Revenue Service provides in the Internal Revenue Bulletin such as to form and manner of delivery. In order to obtain notification from the Social Security Administration (or the Internal Revenue Service) validating a name/TIN combination for an account, a payee who receives notice from a payor under paragraph (g)(2) of this section should follow such procedures as the Internal Revenue Service provides in the Internal Revenue Bulletin.

(h) *Payors must use newly provided certified number.*—If a payor receives a certification under paragraph (f) of this section or a notification under paragraph (g)(5) of this section for an account, the payor must use the name/TIN combination provided on such certification or notifi-

Reg. §31.3406(d)-5(h)

cation on information returns for the account for which the due date (without regard to extensions) is more than 30 calendar days after the date that the payor receives the certification or notification. A payor who uses that name/TIN combination on the first such information return satisfies the requirement of section 3406(h)(9) to provide this information to the Internal Revenue Service. If the payor is not required to file any information returns with respect to the account after the date that the payor receives the certification or notification, a payor is deemed to satisfy the requirements of section 3406(h)(9).

(i) *Effective date.*—Except as otherwise provided in this section, the provisions of this section are effective with respect to notices received on or after September 1, 1990, under paragraph (c)(1) or (2) of this section.

(j) *Examples.*—The application of the provisions of this section may be illustrated by the following examples:

Example 1. D opended an account with Bank O prior to 1984 and furnished a taxpayer identification number to O at the time he opened the account. O pays interest on the account at the end of each calendar month, and the account is a pre-1984 account. On October 1, 1990, the Internal Revenue Service notifies Bank O that the name/TIN combination provided by D is incorrect. O timely notifies D as required in paragraph (d)(1) of this section. O does not receive the certification required under paragraph (f) of this section from D. O is required to backup withhold 20 percent of all reportable payments made after November 14, 1990 (which is 30 business days after the date the Internal Revenue Service notified O). Therefore, O is not required to backup withhold on the reportable payment made on October 31, 1990, but is required to backup withhold on the reportable payment made on November 30, 1990. O is required to continue to backup withhold under section 3406(a)(1)(B) until O receives the certification required under paragraph (f) of this section from D (or, if earlier, until backup withholding terminates under paragraph (e)(3) of this section).

Example 2. Assume that same facts as in *Example 1* except that D furnishes a new taxpayer identification number to O on November 1, 1990, but does not certify, under penalties of perjury, that it is his correct taxpayer identification number as required under paragraph (f) of this section. Even though the account is a pre-1984 account, O is required to withhold 20 percent of all reportable payments made after November 14, 1990 (which is 30 business days after the date the Internal Revenue Service notified O), and before the date O receives the certification required under paragraph (f) of this section from D.

Example 3. Assume the same facts as in *Example 2* except that D provides O with the certification required under paragraph (f) of this section on November 20, 1990. D elects pursuant to paragraph (e)(2)(ii) of this section to treat the certification as received on November 20, 1990. Even

though D did not provide the certification to O within 30 business days after the Internal Revenue Service notified O that D provided an incorrect taxpayer identification number, O is not required to backup withhold under section 3406(a)(1)(B) because O did not make any reportable payment to D after 30 business days after notification of an incorrect name/TIN combination and before O received D's certification under paragraph (f) of this section (or, if earlier, until backup withholding terminates under paragraph (e)(3) of this section).

Example 4. Individual F has two post-1983 accounts with Bank R that pay reportable interest: a savings account and a money market account. The money market account was opened in 1986, and the savings account was opened on February 1, 1991. R treats each of these accounts as a separate account on its books and records for business purposes. On October 1, 1990, the Internal Revenue Service notified R pursuant to paragraph (c)(1) of this section that F furnished an incorrect name/TIN combination with respect to the money market account. R timely sends F the notice required under paragraph (d) of this section and receives the certification required under paragraph (f) of this section from F on November 1, 1990. On October 1, 1991, the Internal Revenue Service again notifies R that F furnished an incorrect name/TIN combination with respect to the money market account. Further, R determines from its business records that two notifications of an incorrect name/TIN combination have been received with respect to the money market account within 3 calendar years. R must send F the notice required under paragraph (g)(2) of this section and must commence backup withholding on reportable interest paid on the money market account pursuant to paragraph (g)(3) of this section after November 14, 1991, which is 30 business days after R received the second notice. R must continue to backup withhold under paragraph (g) of this section on the money market account until R receives notification from the Social Security Administration as described in paragraph (g)(5) of this section (or, if earlier, until backup withholding terminates under paragraph (g)(3)(iii) of this section). R is not required to backup withhold on the savings account unless and until it receives notice under paragraph (c)(1) or (2) of this section with respect to the savings account. [Reg. §31.3406(d)-5.]

☐ [*T.D.* 8409, 4-10-92. *Amended by T.D.* 9055, 4-28-2003.]

[Reg. §31.3406(e)-1]

§31.3406(e)-1. Period during which backup withholding is required.—(a) *In general.*—A payor must withhold under section 3406 at a rate of 31 percent on any reportable payment (as defined in section 3406(b)) made to a payee during the period described in this section (irrespective of the number of conditions for imposing withholding under section 3406 that exist with respect to the payee). A payor must continue to withhold under section 3406 until no condition for imposing backup withholding exists with respect to the payee.

(b) *Failure to furnish a taxpayer identification number in the manner required.*—(1) *Start withholding.*—A payor is required to withhold under section 3406(a)(1)(A) at a rate of 31 percent on any reportable payment (as defined in section 3406(b)) at the time the payor pays the reportable payment (as described in §31.3406(a)-4) to a payee if—

(i) The payor has not received the payee's taxpayer identification number in the manner required in §31.3406(d)-1; or

(ii) The payor has received notice from a broker (as required in §31.3406(d)-4(a)(1)(iii)) with respect to a readily tradable instrument that the payee did not furnish a taxpayer identification number to the broker in the manner required in §31.3406(d)-1 and the payor has not received the taxpayer identification number from the payee in this manner.

(2) *Stop withholding.*—The payor must stop withholding under section 3406(a)(1)(A) within 30 days after the payor receives—

(i) The payee's taxpayer identification number in the manner required under §31.3406(d)-1; or

(ii) A statement, in such form and containing such information as is required under applicable regulations, that the payee is not a United States person.

(c) *Notification of an incorrect taxpayer identification number.*—See §31.3406(d)-5(e) and (g)(3) for the period for which withholding is required in the case of notification of an incorrect taxpayer identification number.

(d) *Notified payee underreporting.*—See §31.3406(c)-1(e) for the period for which withholding is required in the case of notified payee underreporting.

(e) *Payee certification failure.*—(1) *Start withholding.*—A payor is required to withhold under section 3406(a)(1)(D) at a rate of 31 percent on any reportable interest or dividend payment (as defined in section 3406(b)(2)) at the time the payor pays such reportable interest or dividend payment (as described in §31.3406(a)-4) to a payee if—

(i) The payor has not received from the payee the certification required in §31.3406(d)-2; or

(ii) The payor has received notice from a broker (as required in §31.3406(d)-4(a)(1)(iii)) with respect to a readily tradable instrument that the payee did not make the required certification and the payor has not received the required certification from the payee.

(2) *Stop withholding.*—The payor must stop withholding under section 3406(a)(1)(D) on any reportable interest or dividend payment within 30 days after the payor receives the certification

from the payee in the manner required by §31.3406(d)-2.

(f) *Rule for determining when the payor receives a taxpayer identification number or certificate from a payee.*—In determining whether a payee has failed to provide a taxpayer identification number or any certification to a payor (including a Form W-8 or substitute form), a payor is required to process the taxpayer identification number or certification within 30 days after the payor receives the taxpayer identification number or certification from the payee or in certain cases, from a broker. Thus, the payor may take up to 30 days to treat the taxpayer identification number or a certificate as having been received. [Reg. §31.3406(e)-1.]

☐ [T.D. 8637, 12-20-95.]

[Reg. §31.3406(f)-1]

§31.3406(f)-1. Confidentiality of information.—(a) *Confidentiality and liability for violation.*—Pursuant to section 3406(f) no person may use any information obtained under section 3406 for any purpose except for the purpose of complying with the requirements of section 3406 or for purposes permitted under section 6103 (subject to the safeguards of section 6103). See section 7431 for civil damages for violating the confidential use of the information (subject to an exception for good faith).

(b) *Permissible use of information.*—(1) *In general.*—A payor or broker may transmit information on a Form W-9, Form W-8, or other acceptable form relating to withholding to the department, institution, or firm (or to any employee therein) responsible for withholding or processing of taxpayer identification numbers, certifications described in §31.3406(h)-3, or other substitute forms. In addition, a broker may notify the payor with respect to a readily tradable instrument of the requirement to withhold and the condition or conditions for imposing withholding (as described in §31.3406(d)-4) that exist with respect to the payee. A payor or broker may, without violating the Internal Revenue Code, close an account of, refuse to open an account for, issue an instrument to, or redeem an instrument for, a person solely because the person fails to furnish the person's taxpayer identification number or documentation of foreign status in the manner required in §31.3406(d)-1 and §31.3406(g)-1, respectively. A payor who closes an account of a payee in the calendar year in which the account was opened and during which no taxpayer identification number or evidence of foreign status was provided for that account will be presumed in the absence of evidence to the contrary to have closed the account without violating section 3406(f) even though the payee is subject to backup withholding under section 3406(a)(1)(A). A payor, except as provided in §§31.3406(d)-3 and 31.3406(g)-3, may not prohibit a payee who fails to furnish the payee's taxpayer identification number in the manner required in §31.3406(d)-1 from withdrawing any funds in the account.

Reg. §31.3406(f)-1(b)(1)

(2) *Window transactions.*—In the case of a window transaction (as defined in §31.3406(b)(2)-3(b)), a payor may, without violating the Internal Revenue Code, refuse to redeem or may refuse to make payment if the payee fails to provide a taxpayer identification number regardless of when the obligation was issued or acquired.

(c) *Specific restrictions on the use of information.*—Except as provided in paragraph (b) of this section, a payor or broker is not permitted to—

(1) Close an account (or instrument) of a payee solely because that payee (or the account of a payee) is subject to withholding under section 3406(a)(1)(A), (B), (C), or (D);

(2) Refuse to open an account or to issue an instrument if the person fails to certify, under penalties of perjury, that the person is not subject to withholding under section 3406(a)(1)(C)(relating to notified payee underreporting);

(3) Use information obtained under section 3406 (including a payee's failure or inability to certify that the payee is not subject to withholding due to notified payee underreporting or the fact that the account is subject to withholding), surcharge an account (i.e., charge an account more than the fee charged a similar account that was not subject to withholding under section 3406), or use that information to determine whether to open or close an account, whether to issue or redeem an instrument, or whether to extend credit to the payee. [Reg. §31.3406(f)-1.]

☐ [*T.D. 8637, 12-20-95.*]

[Reg. §31.3406(g)-1]

§31.3406(g)-1. Exception for payments to certain payees and certain other payments.—
(a) *Exempt recipients.*—(1) *In general.*—A payor of any reportable payment (as defined in section 3406(b)) must not withhold under section 3406 if the payee is—

(i) An organization exempt from taxation under section 501(a) or an individual retirement account;

(ii) The United States or any wholly owned agency or instrumentality thereof;

(iii) A state, the District of Columbia, a possession of the United States, any political subdivision of any of the foregoing, or any wholly owned agency or instrumentality of any one or more of the foregoing;

(iv) A foreign government, a political subdivision of a foreign government, or any wholly owned agency or instrumentality of any one or more of the foregoing (as defined in regulations under section 892); or

(v) An international organization or any wholly owned agency or instrumentality thereof (as defined in section 7701(a)(18)).

(2) *Nonexclusive list.*—Paragraph (a)(1) of this section does not prescribe an exclusive list of payees that are exempt from information reporting and also are exempt from withholding under section 3406.

(b) *Determination of whether a person is described in paragraph (a)(1) of this section.*—The determination of whether a person is a payee described in paragraph (a)(1) of this section must be made as provided in the applicable provisions of section 6049 and the regulations issued thereunder. A payor, even if permitted to treat a person as an exempt recipient without requiring a certificate under the provisions of section 6049, may require a payee, otherwise not required to file a certificate regarding its exempt status, to file a certificate and may treat a payee who fails to file the certificate as a person who is not an exempt recipient. See §31.3406(h)-3 for a description of the Form W-9 or a substitute form prescribed under section 3406 for claiming exempt status.

(c) *Prepaid or advance premium life-insurance contracts.*—A payor of a reportable payment (as defined in section 3406(b)(1)) may, but is not required to, withhold under section 3406 on reportable payments made from January 1, 1984, to December 31, 1996, on prepaid or advance premium life-insurance contracts to a payee who is the owner for tax purposes of the prepaid or advance premium life-insurance contract. For purposes of this exception from backup withholding, a prepaid or advance premium life-insurance contract is one entered into on or before June 30, 1984, by the payee and under which the increment in value of the prepaid or advance premium is used for the payment of premiums during the period in which the exception from backup withholding applies.

(d) *Reportable payments made to nonresident alien individuals.*—A payment of interest to a nonresident alien individual that is described in §1.6049-(8)(a) of this chapter is not subject to withholding under section 3406 if the payor may treat the payee as a foreign beneficial owner or foreign payee under the rules of §1.6049-5(b)(12). (For interest paid to a Canadian nonresident alien individual on or before December 31, 2012, see paragraph (d) of this section as in effect and contained in 26 CFR part 1 revised April 1, 2000.)

(e) *Certain reportable payments made outside the United States by foreign persons, foreign offices of United States banks and brokers, and others.*—For reportable payments made after June 30, 2014, a payor is not required to backup withhold under section 3406 on a reportable payment that is paid and received outside the United States (as defined in §1.6049-4(f)(16)) with respect to an offshore obligation (as defined in §1.6049-5(c)(1)) or on gross proceeds from a sale effected outside the United States (as defined in §1.6045-1(g)(3)(iii)), unless the payor has actual knowledge that the payee is a United States person. Further, no backup withholding is required on a reportable payment of an amount already withheld upon by a participating FFI (as defined in §1.1471-1(b)(91)) or another payor in accordance with the withholding provisions under chapter 3 or 4 of the Code and the regulations under those chapters even if the payee is a known U.S. person. For example, a participating FFI is not required to backup withhold on a reportable payment allocable to its chapter 4 withholding rate pool (as defined in §1.6049-4(f)(5)) of recalcitrant account holders (as described in §1.6049-4(f)(11)), if withholding was applied to the payment (either by the participating FFI or another payor) pursuant to §1.1471-4(b) or §1.1471-2(a). For rules applicable to notional principal contracts, see §1.6041-1(d)(5) of this chapter. For rules applicable to reportable payments made before July 1, 2014, see this paragraph (e) as in effect and contained in 26 CFR part 1 revised April 1, 2013.)

(f) *Effective/applicability date.*—This section applies on or after January 6, 2017. (For payments made after June 30, 2014, and before January 6, 2017, see this section as in effect and contained in 26 CFR part 1, revised April 1, 2016). [Reg. §31.3406(g)-1.]

☐ [*T.D. 8637*, 12-20-95. *Amended by T.D. 8664*, 4-15-96; *T.D. 8734*, 10-6-97; *T.D. 8804*, 12-30-98; *T.D. 8856*, 12-29-99 *T.D. 9136*, 7-12-2004; *T.D. 9584*, 4-17-2012; *T.D. 9658*, 2-28-2014, *T.D. 9699*, 10-24-2014 *and T.D. 9808*, 12-30-2016.]

[Reg. §31.3406(g)-2]

§31.3406(g)-2. Exception for reportable payments for which withholding is otherwise required.—(a) *In general.*—A payor of a reportable payment (as defined in section 3406(b)) must not withhold under section 3406 if the payment is subject to withholding under any other provision of the Internal Revenue Code.

(b) *Payment of wages.*—A payor who is required to make an information return under section 6041 with respect to a payment of wages (as defined in section 3401) because, e.g., the employee makes a certification under section 3402(n)(relating to employees incurring no income tax liability), must not withhold under section 3406 on those wages.

(c) *Distribution from a pension, annuity, or other plan of deferred compensation.*—An amount reportable under section 6047, such as a designated distribution under section 3405, is not a reportable payment subject to withholding under section 3406. See section 3406(b). Designated distributions not subject to withholding under section 3406 include—

(1) Distributions from a pension, annuity, profit-sharing, stock bonus plan, or other plan deferring the receipt of compensation;

(2) Distributions from an individual retirement account or annuity;

(3) Distributions from an owner-employee plan; and

(4) Certain surrenders of life insurance contracts.

(d) *Gambling winnings.*—(1) *In general.*—A payor of a reportable gambling winning must not withhold under section 3406 if tax is required to be withheld from the gambling winning under section 3402(q)(relating to the extension of withholding to certain gambling winnings). If the reportable gambling winning is not required to be withheld upon under section 3402(q), withholding under section 3406 applies to the gambling winning if, and only if, the payee does not furnish a taxpayer identification number to the payor. Section 31.3406(b)(3)-1(b)(3) does not apply to a reportable gambling winning. The payor of a reportable gambling winning is not required to aggregate all such winnings made to a payee during a calendar year, nor is the payor required to determine whether an information return was required to be made with respect to the payee for the preceding year.

(2) *Definition of a reportable gambling winning and determination of amount subject to backup withholding.*—For purposes of withholding under section 3406, a reportable gambling winning is any gambling winning subject to information reporting under section 6041. A gambling winning (other than a winning from bingo, keno, or slot machines) is a reportable gambling winning only if the amount paid with respect to the wager is $600 or more and if the proceeds are at least 300 times as large as the amount wagered. See §1.6041-10 of this chapter to determine whether a winning from bingo, keno, or slot machines is a reportable gambling winning and thus subject to withholding under section 3406. The amount of a reportable gambling winning is—

(i) The amount paid with respect to the amount of the wager reduced, at the option of the payer; by

(ii) The amount of the wager.

(3) *Special rules.*—For special rules for determining the amount of the wager in a wagering transaction with respect to horse racing, dog racing, and jai alai, or amounts paid with respect to identical wagers, see §31.3402(q)-1(c).

(e) *Certain real estate transactions.*—A real estate reporting person (the so-called broker) as defined in section 6045(e)(2) must not withhold under section 3406 on a payment made with respect to a real estate transaction that is subject to reporting under sections 6045(a) and (e) and §1.6045-4 of this chapter.

(f) *Certain payments after an acquisition of accounts or instruments.*—A payor who acquires pre-1984 accounts or instruments described in §31.3406(d)-1(b)(2)(iv) for which the payor does not have a taxpayer identification number or has an obviously incorrect taxpayer identification number as defined in §31.3406(h)-1(b)(2) must start withholding under section 3406(a)(1)(A) and §31.3406(d)-1 on those accounts or instruments no later than sixty days following the date of the payor's acquisition of those accounts or instruments.

(g) *Certain gross proceeds.*—No withholding under section 3406 is required with respect to any portion of the original issue discount on an instrument or security that is subject to withholding under section 3406 as reportable gross proceeds of such instrument or security under section 6045.

(h) *Applicability date.*—The rules apply to reportable gambling winnings paid with respect to a winning event that occurs after November 13, 2017. For rules that apply to payments made with respect to a winning event on or before that date, see § 31.3406(g)-2 as contained in 26 CFR part 31, revised April 1, 2017. [Reg. § 31.3406(g)-2.]

☐ [T.D. 8637, 12-20-95. *Amended by T.D. 9524, 5-6-2011, T.D. 9586, 4-24-2012; T.D. 9807, 12-29-2016 and T.D. 9824, 9-25-2017.]

[Reg. § 31.3406(g)-3]

§ 31.3406(g)-3. Exemption while payee is waiting for a taxpayer identification number.— (a) *In general.*—(1) *Backup withholding not required for 60 days.*—If a payor has received an awaiting-TIN certificate from a payee with respect to an account or instrument receiving reportable interest or dividends as described in section 3406(b)(2), the payor must exempt the payee from withholding under section 3406(a)(1)(A) during the 60-day exemption period to the extent and in the manner described in either paragraph (a)(2) or (3) of this section. The 60-day exemption period means the 60-consecutive-day period beginning with the day the payor receives the awaiting-TIN certificate. The payor must withhold under section 3406 beginning after the 60-day exemption period if the payor has not received a taxpayer identification number from the payee in the manner required in § 31.3406(d)-1. Regardless of whether the payee provides an awaiting-TIN certificate to a payor, the payor is required to withhold under section 3406(a)(1)(D) and § 31.3406(d)-2 on reportable interest or dividend payments as described in § 31.3406(d)-2 if the payee fails to certify, under penalties of perjury, that the payee is not subject to withholding due to notified payee underreporting as required in section 3406(a)(1)(D) and § 31.3406(d)-2.

(2) *Reserve method.*—A payor must not withhold under section 3406 during the 60-day exemption period unless the payee (or a joint payee in the case of a joint account) desires to make a withdrawal of more than $500 of either principal or interest from the account in any single transaction during the period. If a payee (or a joint payee) desires to make a withdrawal of more than $500 during the 60-day exemption period, the payor is required under section 3406 to withhold 31 percent of all reportable payments made during the period and at the time of withdrawal unless the payee reserves 31 percent of all reportable payments made to the account during the period.

(3) *Alternative rule; 7-day grace period.*—(i) *In general.*—A payor who receives an awaiting-TIN certificate may elect, on a payee-by-payee basis or in general, to exempt reportable interest or dividend payments to a payee from withholding under section 3406 applying the rules in paragraph (a)(3)(ii) or (iii) of this section.

(ii) *Withholding on withdrawals.*—Under this paragraph (a)(3)(ii), a payor must obtain a certified taxpayer identification number from the payee within 60 days after the date that the payor receives the awaiting-TIN certification. In addition, the payor must withhold under section 3406 on any withdrawals made after the close of 7 business days after the date the awaiting-TIN certification is received and before the earlier of the date that the payor receives a certified taxpayer identification number from the payee, the date the account is closed (in which case the payor must withhold on any reportable payment made at the time the account or relationship is closed), or the date withholding under section 3406 starts on all reportable payments made to the account, instrument, or relationship. All cash withdrawals in an amount up to the reportable payments made from the day after the date of receipt of the awaiting-TIN certification to the date of withdrawal are treated as reportable payments.

(iii) *Withholding regardless of withdrawals.*—Under this paragraph (a)(3)(iii), a payor must start withholding under section 3406 on the account not later than 7 business days after the date the payor receives the awaiting-TIN certification on reportable payments thereafter made to the account (whether or not the payee makes a cash withdrawal). The payor must withhold under section 3406 until the earlier of the date the payor receives a certified taxpayer identification number from the payee, the date the account is closed, or the date withholding under section 3406 starts on all reportable payments made to the account, instrument, or relationship. The payor must obtain a certified taxpayer identification number from the payee within 60 days after the date that the payor receives the awaiting-TIN certificate or undertake a mailing each year soliciting the certified taxpayer identification number from the payee until the earlier of the calendar year that the certified taxpayer identification number is received, or the calendar year in which the account is closed. However, if the account is closed in December of a calendar year, the mailing must be made after the account is closed and before January 31 of the subsequent calendar year.

(b) *Special rule for readily tradable instruments.*—The 60-day awaiting-TIN exemption described in paragraph (a)(1) of this section applies to payments made with respect to readily tradable instruments only if the payee provides an awaiting-TIN certificate directly to the payor. If a broker acquires a readily tradable instrument through a post-1983 brokerage account (as described in § 31.3406(d)-1(c)(2)) for a payee who has no taxpayer identification number, the broker must advise the payor as required in § 31.3406(d)-4(a)(1) that the payee failed to provide a taxpayer identification number under penalties of perjury, regardless of whether the payee provides an awaiting-TIN certificate to the broker. Once a payor is notified by a broker that a payee failed to provide a taxpayer identification number in the required manner, or that the payee is subject to withholding under section 3406(a)(1)(B) or (C), the payor must impose withholding under section 3406 for the appropriate period described in § 31.3406(e)-1.

(c) *Exceptions.*—(1) *In general.*—The 60-day awaiting-TIN exemption described in paragraph (a) of this section does not apply to—

(i) Window transactions (as defined in § 31.3406(b)(2)-3(b));

(ii) Redemptions of bearer obligations that are subject to reporting under section 6045; or

(iii) Other amounts that are subject to reporting under section 6045 (except as described in paragraph (c)(2) of this section).

(2) *Special rule for amounts subject to reporting under section 6045 other than proceeds of redemptions of bearer obligations.*—If a broker's customer does not provide a taxpayer identification number to the broker, and the broker effects a sale that is subject to reporting under section 6045 (other than a redemption of a bearer obligation), § 31.3406(d)-3(b) applies, whether or not the sale is pursuant to an instruction by electronic transmission, provided the customer furnishes an awaiting-TIN certificate to the broker before the sale. For purposes of this paragraph (c)(2), the 30-day period provided in § 31.3406(d)-3(b) is a 60-day period.

(d) *Awaiting-TIN certificate.*—A payee qualifies for the 60-day awaiting-TIN exemption provided in paragraph (a) of this section if the payee furnishes a written statement to the payor, signed under penalties of perjury, that the payee has not been issued a taxpayer identification number, that the payee has applied for a taxpayer identification number or intends to apply for a number in the near future, and that the payee understands that if the payee does not provide a number to the payor within 60 days, the payor is required under section 3406 to withhold 31 percent of any reportable payment thereafter made to the payee until the payor receives a number, and 31 percent of a withdrawal to the extent of reportable payments made to the payee during the 60-day period, as described in paragraph (a) of this section. Language that is substantially similar to the awaiting-TIN certification on Form W-9 will satisfy the requirements of this paragraph (d).

(e) *Form for awaiting-TIN certificate.*—A payor may use Form W-9 for the awaiting-TIN certificate, or a payor may include language that is substantially similar to the awaiting-TIN certification on Form W-9 in any other document of the payor. See § 31.3406(h)-3, which provides that Form W-9 is the prescribed form but permits use of substitute forms, and specifies the length of time the payor is required to retain the form. If Form W-9 is used, the payee should write "Applied For" in the space reserved for the taxpayer identification number. [Reg. § 31.3406(g)-3.]

□ [*T.D.* 8637, 12-20-95.]

[Reg. § 31.3406(h)-1]

§ 31.3406(h)-1. Definitions.—(a) *In general.*—For purposes of section 3406 and the regulations thereunder, the definitions of this section apply.

(b) *Taxpayer identification number.*—(1) *In general.*—*Taxpayer identification number* means the identifying number assigned to a person under section 6109 (relating to identifying numbers, generally a nine-digit social security number for an individual and a nine-digit employer identification number for a nonindividual, e.g., a corporation, partnership, trust, or estate). An obviously incorrect number is not considered a taxpayer identification number. See § 31.6011(b)-2 and § 301.6109-1 of this chapter for provisions relating to obtaining a taxpayer identification number.

(2) *Obviously incorrect number.*—*Obviously incorrect number* means a number that does not contain nine digits or a number that includes an alpha character as one of the nine digits.

(c) *Broker.*—*Broker* is defined in section 6045(c)(1) and § 1.6045-1(a)(1) of this chapter. If there could be more than one broker with respect to any acquisition, only the broker having the closest contact (as determined under § 1.6045-1(c)(3)(iii) and (iv) of this chapter) with the payee is treated as a broker. In the case of any instrument, the term *broker* does not include any person who is the payor with respect to the instrument as described in § 31.3406(a)-2.

(d) *Readily tradable instrument. Readily tradable instrument.*—means—

(1) Any instrument that is part of an issue any portion of which is traded on an established securities market (within the meaning of section 453(f)(5)); or

(2) Any instrument that is regularly quoted by brokers or dealers making a market.

(e) *Day.*—*Day* means a calendar day unless specified otherwise under any section of the regulations under section 3406. For example, see §§ 31.3406(d)-5(a) and 31.3406(g)-3(a)(2).

(f) *Business day.*—*Business day* means any day other than a Saturday, Sunday, or legal holiday (within the meaning of section 7503). [Reg. § 31.3406(h)-1.]

□ [*T.D.* 8637, 12-20-95. *Amended by T.D.* 9010, 7-25-2002.]

[Reg. § 31.3406(h)-2]

§ 31.3406(h)-2. Special rules.—(a) *Joint accounts.*—(1) *Relevant name and taxpayer identification number combination.*—For purposes of identifying the account subject to withholding under sections 3406(a)(1)(B) and (C), the relevant name and taxpayer identification number combination is that which is used for information reporting purposes.

Reg. § 31.3406(h)-2(a)(1)

(2) *Optional rule for accounts subject to backup withholding under section 3406(a)(1)(B) or (C) where the names are switched.*—See § 31.3406(d)-5(c)(4)(iii) under which a payor may withhold under section 3406(a)(1)(B) as required even though the names or taxpayer identification numbers on the account have been switched. The rules under § 31.3406(d)-5(c)(4)(iii) may be applied comparably by a payor who is required to withhold under section 3406(a)(1)(C).

(3) *Joint foreign payees.*—(i) *In general.*—If the relevant payee listed on a jointly owned account or instrument provides a Form W-8 or documentary evidence described in § 1.1441-1(e)(1)(ii) regarding its foreign status, withholding under section 3406 applies unless every joint payee provides the statement regarding foreign status (under the provisions of chapters 3 or 61 of the Internal Revenue Code and the regulations under those provisions); any one of the joint owners who has not established foreign status provides a taxpayer identification number to the payor in the manner required in § § 31.3406(d)-1 through 31.3406(d)-5; or, in the case of a withholdable payment (as defined in § 1.6049-4(f)(15)), any joint payee does not appear to be an individual as described in § 1.1471-3(f)(7). See § 1.6049-5(d)(2)(iii) of this chapter for corresponding joint payees provisions.

(ii) *Information reporting on an account including foreign payees.*—If any one of the joint payees who has not established foreign status provides a taxpayer identification number under paragraph (a)(3)(i)(B) of this section, that number is the taxpayer identification number that is required to be furnished for purposes of information reporting and withholding under section 3406.

(b) *Backup withholding from an alternative source.*—(1) *In general.*—A payor may not withhold under section 3406 from a source maintained by the payor other than the source with respect to which there exists a liability to withhold under section 3406 with respect to the payee. See section 3403 and § 31.3403-1, which provide that the payor is liable for the amount required to be withheld regardless of whether the payor withholds.

(2) *Exceptions for payments made in property.*—(i) *Backup withholding from alternative source.*—In the case of a payment that is made in property (other than money), the payor must withhold under section 3406, 31 percent of the fair market value of the property determined immediately before or on the date of payment. The payor may withhold under section 3406 from the principal amount being deposited with the payor or from another source maintained by the payee with the payor. The source from which the tax is withheld under section 3406 must be payable to at least one of the persons listed on the account subject to withholding. If the account or source is not payable exclusively to the same person or persons listed on the account

subject to withholding under section 3406, then the payor must obtain a written statement from all other persons to whom the account or source is payable authorizing the payor to withhold under section 3406 from the alternative account or source. A payor that elects to withhold under section 3406 from an alternative source may determine the account or source from which the tax is to be withheld, or may allow the payee to designate the alternative source. A payee may not, however, require a payor to withhold under section 3406 from a specific alternative source. See § 31.3402(q)-1(d), *Example 5,* for methods of withholding on prizes, awards, and gambling winnings paid in property other than cash.

(ii) *Deferral of withholding.*—If the payor cannot locate, using reasonable care (following procedures substantially similar to those set forth in § 31.3406(d)-5(c)(3)(ii)(A) and (B)), an alternative source of cash from which the payor may satisfy its withholding obligation pursuant to paragraph (b)(2)(i) of this section, the payor may defer its obligation to withhold under section 3406, except for reportable payments of property made in connection with prizes, awards, or gambling winnings, until the earlier of—

(A) The date the payor makes a cash payment to the account subject to withholding under section 3406 or cash is otherwise deposited in the account in a sufficient amount to satisfy the obligation in full; or

(B) The close of the fourth calendar year after the obligation arose.

(iii) *Barter exchanges.*—In the case of a barter exchange that issues scrip to, or credits the account of, a member or client of the exchange in payment for property or services, the barter exchange may withhold under section 3406 from—

(A) The scrip or credit, if converted to cash in order to satisfy the deposit requirements of section 6302 and § 31.6302-4; or

(B) Any other source maintained by the exchange for the member or client in the manner described in paragraph (b)(2) of this section.

(c) *Trusts.*—Withholding under section 3406 applies to reportable payments made to a trust if any of the conditions for imposing withholding under section 3406 apply to the trust. Generally, a trust is not a payor and will not be required to withhold under section 3406 on reportable payments that it makes to its beneficiary who is subject to withholding under section 3406. The preceding sentence does not apply, however, to a grantor trust described in § 31.3406(a)-2(b)(1) or (2), which is treated as a payor. The trustee of a trust described in this paragraph (c) may certify that the trust's taxpayer identification number is correct and that the trust is not subject to withholding due to notified payee underreporting, without regard to the status of the beneficiaries of the trust.

(d) *Adjustment of prior withholding by middlemen.*—A middleman payor (as defined in

§ 31.3406(a)-2(b) or in the section on information reporting to which the payment relates) who receives a payment from which tax has been erroneously withheld under section 3406 may seek a refund of the tax withheld by the payor from whom the middleman payor received the payment (referred to as the "upstream payor"). Alternatively, the middleman payor may obtain a refund of the tax by claiming a credit for the amount of tax withheld by the upstream payor against the deposit of any tax imposed by this chapter which the middleman payor is required to withhold and deposit (as described in section 6413 and § 31.6413(a)-2). In either case, the middleman payor must pay or credit the gross amount of the payment (including the tax withheld) to its payee as though it had received the gross amount of the payment from the upstream payor and must withhold under section 3406 only if one of the conditions for imposing backup withholding exists with respect to its payee. If its payee is not subject to withholding under section 3406, the payor must pay or credit the full amount of the payment to the payee, unless, with respect to payments made after December 31, 2000, the payor chooses to apply prior withholding under section 3406 to an amount required to be withheld under another section of the Internal Revenue Code (such as under section 1441) to the extent permitted under procedures prescribed by the Internal Revenue Service (see § 601.601(d)(2) of this chapter). See § 31.6413(a)-3 regarding repayment by a payor of tax erroneously collected from a payee.

(e) *Conversion of amounts paid in foreign currency into United States dollars.*—If a payment is made in a currency other than the United States dollar, the amount subject to withholding under section 3406 is determined by applying the statutory rate of backup withholding to the foreign currency payment and converting the amount withheld into United States dollars on the date of payment at the spot rate (as defined in § 1.988-1(d)(1) of this chapter) or pursuant to a reasonable spot rate convention. For example, a withholding agent may use a month-end spot rate or a monthly average spot rate. A spot rate convention must be used consistently with respect to all non-dollar amounts withheld and from year to year. Such convention cannot be changed without the consent of the Commissioner.

(f) *Coordination with other sections.*—For purposes of section 31, chapter 24 (other than section 3402(n)) of subtitle C of the Internal Revenue Code (relating to employment taxes and collection of income tax at source) and so much of subtitle F (other than section 7205) of the Internal Revenue Code (relating to procedure and administration) as relates to this chapter, and the regulations thereunder—

(1) An amount required to be withheld under section 3406 must be treated as a tax required to be withheld under section 3402;

(2) An amount withheld under section 3406 must be treated as an amount withheld under section 3402;

(3) An amount withheld under section 3406 must be deposited as required under § 31.6302-4;

(4) *Wages* includes the gross amount of any reportable payment (as defined in section 3406(b)) except for purposes of section 6014 (relating to an election by the taxpayer not to compute the tax on his annual return);

(5) *Employee* includes a payee of any reportable payment; and

(6) *Employer* includes a payor who is required to withhold the tax under section 3406 (as defined in § 31.3406(a)-2) with respect to any reportable payment (as defined in section 34069(b)).

(g) *Tax liabilities and penalties.*—A payor is subject to the same civil and criminal penalties for failing to impose withholding under section 3406 as an employer who fails to withhold on a payment of wages. In addition, a broker may be subject to the penalty under section 6705 (failure of a broker to provide notice to a payor).

(h) *To whom payor is liable for amount withheld.*—A payor is not liable to any person for any amount withheld under section 3406. A payor is liable only to the United States for an amount that is required to be withheld as provided in § 31.3403-1.

(i) *Effective/applicability date.*—This section applies to payments made on or after January 6, 2017. (For payments made after June 30, 2014, and before January 6, 2017, see this section as in effect and contained in 26 CFR part 1, revised April 1, 2016.) [Reg. § 31.3406(h)-2.]

☐ [T.D. 8637, 12-20-95. Amended by T.D. 8734, 10-6-97; T.D. 8804, 12-30-98; T.D. 8856, 12-29-99; T.D. 9010, 7-25-2002, T.D. 9658, 2-28-2014 and T.D. 9808, 12-30-2016.]

[Reg. § 31.3406(h)-3]

§ 31.3406(h)-3. Certificates.—(a) *Prescribed form to furnish information under penalties of perjury.*—(1) *In general.*—Except as provided in paragraph (c) of this section, the Form W-9 is the form prescribed under section 3406 on which a payee that is a U.S. person certifies, under penalties of perjury, that—

(i) The taxpayer identification number furnished to the payor is correct (as required in § 31.3406(d)-1 and § 31.3406(d)-5);

(ii) The payee is not subject to withholding due to notified payee underreporting (as required in § 31.3406(d)-2);

(iii) The payee is an exempt recipient (as described in § 31.3406(g)-1); or

(iv) The payee is awaiting receipt of a taxpayer identification number (as described in § 31.3406(g)-3).

(2) *Use of a single or multiple Forms W-9 for accounts of the same Payee.*—A valid Form W-9 must include the name and taxpayer identification number of the payee. Except as provided in

paragraph (b) of this section, the payee must sign under penalties of perjury and date the Form W-9 in order to satisfy the requirements of this section. A payor or broker may require a payee to furnish a separate Form W-9 for each obligation, deposit, certificate, share, membership, contract, or other instrument, or one Form W-9 for all the payee's obligations or relationships with the payor or broker. In addition, a payee of a mutual fund that has a common investment advisor or common principal underwriter with other mutual funds (within the same family of funds) may be permitted, in the discretion of the mutual fund, to provide one Form W-9 with respect to shares acquired or owned in any of the funds.

(b) *Prescribed form to furnish a noncertified taxpayer identification number.*—With respect to accounts or other relationships where the payee is not required to certify, under penalties of perjury, that the taxpayer identification number being furnished is correct, the payor or broker may obtain the taxpayer identification number orally or may use Form W-9, a substitute form, or any other document, but the payee is not required to sign the form.

(c) *Forms prepared by payors or brokers.*—(1) *Substitute forms; in general.*—A payor or broker may prepare and use a form that contains provisions that are substantially similar to those of the official Form W-9. A payor or broker may use any document relating to the transaction, such as the signature card for an account, so long as the certifications are clearly set forth. A payor or broker who uses a substitute form may furnish orally or in writing the instructions for the Form W-9 that relate to the account. A payor or broker may refuse to accept certifications (including the official Form W-9) that are not made on the form or forms provided by the payor or broker. A payor or broker may refuse to accept a certification provided by a payee only if the payor or broker furnishes the payee with an acceptable form immediately upon receipt of an unacceptable form or within 5 business days of receipt of an unacceptable form. An acceptable form for this purpose must contain a notice that the payor or broker has refused to accept the form submitted by the payee and that the payee must submit the acceptable form provided by the payor in order for the payee not to be subject to withholding under section 3406. If the payor or broker requires the payee to furnish a form for each account of the payee, the payor or broker is not required to furnish an acceptable form until the payee furnishes the payor or broker with the payee's account numbers. A payor or broker may use separate substitute forms to have a payee certify under penalties of perjury that—

(i) The payee's taxpayer identification number is correct; and

(ii) The payee is not subject to withholding under section 3406 due to notified payee underreporting.

(2) *Form for exempt recipient.*—A payor or broker may use a substitute form for the payee to certify, under penalties of perjury, that the payee is an exempt recipient (described in §31.3406(g)-1 or described in the respective reporting section), provided the form contains provisions that are substantially similar to those of the official Form W-9 relating to exempt recipients. A certificate must be prepared in accordance with the instructions applicable to exempt recipients on Form W-9, and must set forth fully and clearly the data called for therein. If a payor will treat the payee as an exempt recipient only if the payee files a certificate as to its exempt status, the certificate is valid only if it contains the payee's taxpayer identification number. Thus, a payee must include the payee's taxpayer identification number on a certificate that a payor requires to be made in order to treat the payee as an exempt recipient.

(d) *Special rule for brokers.*—A broker may act as the payee's agent for purposes of furnishing a taxpayer identification number or certification to a payor with respect to any readily tradable instrument (as defined in §31.3406(h)-1(d)) provided the payee provides a taxpayer identification number on Form W-9 or other acceptable substitute form to the broker. The payor may rely on a taxpayer identification number provided by the broker unless certification is required (as described in §31.3406(d)-4) and the broker notifies the payor that the number was not certified.

(e) *Reasonable reliance on certificate.*—(1) *In general.*—A payor is not liable for the tax imposed under section 3406 if the payor's failure to deduct and withhold the tax is due to reasonable reliance, as defined in paragraph (e)(2) of this section, on a Form W-9 (or other acceptable substitute) required by this section.

(2) *Circumstances establishing reasonable reliance.*—For purposes of paragraph (e)(1) of this section, a payor can reasonably rely on a Form W-9 (or other acceptable substitute) unless—

(i) The form does not contain the name and taxpayer identification number of the payee (or does not state, in lieu of a taxpayer identification number, that the payee is awaiting receipt of a taxpayer identification number (i.e., an awaiting-TIN certificate));

(ii) The form is not signed and dated by the payee;

(iii) The form does not contain the statement, when required, that the payee is not subject to withholding due to notified payee underreporting;

(iv) The payee has deleted the jurat or other similar provisions by which the payee certifies or affirms the correctness of the statements contained on the form; or

(v) For purposes of section 3406(a)(1)(C), the payor is required to subject the account to which the form relates to withholding under section 3406(a)(1)(C) under the circumstances described in §31.3406(c)-1(c)(3)(iii).

(f) *Who may sign certificate.*—(1) *In general.*—A Form W-9 or other acceptable substitute form may be signed by any person who is authorized to sign a declaration under penalties of perjury on behalf of the payee as provided in section 6061 and the regulations thereunder (relating to who may sign generally for an individual, which includes certain agents who may sign returns and other documents), section 6062 and the regulations thereunder (relating to who may sign corporate returns), and section 6063 and the regulations thereunder (relating to who may sign partnership returns).

(2) *Notified payee underreporting.*—A payee who has not been notified that he is subject to withholding under section 3406(a)(1)(C) as a result of notified payee underreporting may make the certification related to notified payee underreporting. In addition, a payee who was subject to withholding under section 3406(a)(1)(C) due to notified payee underreporting may certify that he is not subject to withholding under section 3406(a)(1)(C) due to notified payee underreporting if the Internal Revenue Service has provided the payee with written certification that withholding under section 3406(a)(1)(C) due to notified payee underreporting has terminated.

(g) *Retention of certificates.*—(1) *Accounts or instruments that are not pre-1984 accounts and brokerage relationships that are post-1983 brokerage accounts.*—With respect to an account or instrument that is not a pre-1984 account (as described in § 31.3406(d)-1(b)(3)), or with respect to a brokerage relationship that is a post-1983 brokerage account (as described in § 31.3406(d)-1(c)(2)), a payor or broker who receives a Form W-9 or other acceptable substitute form related to withholding under section 3406 must retain the form in its records for 3 years from the date the account is opened or the instrument is purchased. The form may be retained on microfilm or microfiche.

(2) *Accounts or instruments that are pre-1984 accounts and brokerage relationships that are not post-1983 brokerage accounts.*—With respect to a pre-1984 account (as described in § 31.3406(d)-1(b)(1)) or or with respect to a brokerage relationship that is not a post-1983 brokerage account (as described in § 31.3406(d)-1(c)(1)), a payor or broker is not required to retain any Form W-9 or other acceptable substitute form. If, however, the payor or broker requires the payee to file only one Form W-9 or substitute form for all accounts or instruments of the payee, the payor or broker must retain the single form in the manner and for the period of time described in paragraph (g)(1) of this section if that form relates to any account or instrument that is not a pre-1984 account or relates to a post-1983 brokerage account. If a payee has certified that the payee is an exempt recipient described in § 31.3406(g)-1, the payor or broker must retain the form unless the payor or broker can establish the existence of procedures that are reasonably calculated to ensure that a

payee who has so certified is accurately identified in the payor's or broker's records.

(h) *Cross references.*—For the requirement to file an information return (and furnish the related statement) with respect to a reportable payment, particularly if that payment has been subject to withholding under section 3406, see subtitle F, chapter 61, subparts B and C of the Internal Revenue Code. See § 31.6302-4 for the requirement to deposit amounts withheld under section 3406 on either a monthly or semi-weekly basis. See § 31.6011(a)-4(b) for the requirement to file Form 945, Annual Return of Withheld Federal Income Tax, to reflect amounts withheld under section 3406. See § 31.6071(a)-1 for the time for filing the Form 945. [Reg. § 31.3406(h)-3.]

☐ [T.D. 8637, 12-20-95. *Amended by T.D. 8881,* 5-15-2000.]

[Reg. § 31.3406(i)-1]

§ 31.3406(i)-1. Effective date.—Sections 31.3406-0 through 31.3406(i)-1 (except §§ 31.3406(d)-5 and 31.3406(g)-1(c) and except for international transactions) are effective after December 31, 1996, and, optionally, for reportable payments made and transactions occurring on or after December 21, 1995. For the effective date of § 31.3406(d)-5, see § 31.3406(d)-5(i). Section 31.3406(g)-1(c) is effective before January 1, 1997. See §§ 35a.9999-0T through 35a.9999-5 of this chapter for rules that apply to international transactions after December 31, 1996. [Reg. § 31.3406(i)-1.]

☐ [T.D. 8637, 12-20-95.]

[Reg. § 31.3406(j)-1]

§ 31.3406(j)-1. Taxpayer Identification Number (TIN) matching program.—(a) *The matching program.*—Under section 3406(i), the Commissioner has the authority to establish Taxpayer Identification Number (TIN) matching programs. The Commissioner may prescribe in a revenue procedure (see § 601.601(d)(2) of this chapter) or other appropriate guidance the scope and the terms and conditions of participating in any TIN matching program. In general, under a matching program, prior to filing information returns with respect to reportable payments as defined in section 3406(b)(1), a payor of those reportable payments who is entitled to participate in the matching program may contact the Internal Revenue Service (IRS) with respect to the TIN furnished by a payee who has received or is likely to receive a reportable payment. The IRS will inform the payor whether or not a name/TIN combination furnished by the payee matches a name/TIN combination maintained in the data base utilized for the particular matching program. For purposes of this section, the term payor includes an agent designated by the payor to participate in TIN matching on the payor's behalf.

(b) *Notice of incorrect TIN.*—No matching details received by a payor through a matching program will constitute a notice regarding an

Reg. § 31.3406(j)-1(b)

incorrect name/TIN combination under §31.3406(d)-5(c) for purposes of imposing backup withholding under section 3406(a)(1)(B).

(c) *Application of section 3406(f).*—The provisions of section 3406(f), relating to confidentiality of information, apply to any matching details received by a payor through the matching program. A payor may not take into account any such matching details in determining whether to open or close an account with a payee.

(d) *Reasonable cause.*—The IRS will not use either a payor's decision not to participate in an available TIN matching program or the results received by a payor from participation in a TIN matching program implemented under the authority of this section as a basis to assert that the payor lacks reasonable cause under section 6724(a) for the failure to file an information return under section 6721 or to furnish a correct payee statement under section 6722. If the estab-lishment of reasonable cause may be relevant to a substantial number of the participants in a TIN matching program implemented under the authority of this section, the extent to which, if any, a payor may establish reasonable cause by participating in the TIN matching program will be set forth in the guidance establishing the program.

(e) *Definition of account.*—*Account* means any account, instrument, or other relationship with a payor and with respect to which a payor has made or is likely to make a reportable payment as defined in section 3406(b)(1).

(f) *Effective date.*—The last sentence in paragraph (a) of this section is applicable on January 31, 2003. All other provisions of this section are applicable on and after June 18, 1997. [Reg. §31.3406(j)-1.]

☐ [*T.D. 8721, 6-17-97. Amended by T.D. 9041, 1-30-2003 and T.D. 9136, 7-12-2004.*]

>>>→ *Caution: Caution: Reg. §35a.3406-2, below, is effective until December 31, 1996.*

[Reg. §35a.3406-2]

§35a.3406-2. Imposition of backup withholding for notified payee underreporting of reportable interest or dividend payments (Temporary).—(a) *Requirement that a payor backup withhold due to a notified payee underre porting.*—(1) *In general.*—Except as otherwise provided in paragraph (a)(5) of this section, backup withholding under section 3406(a)(1)(C) applies to any reportable interest or dividend payment (as defined in section 3406(b)(2) and paragraph (a)(4) of this section) made to a payee, if the Internal Revenue Service or a broker (as defined in section 3406(h)(5) and paragraph (a)(7) of this section and pursuant to section 3406(d)(2)(B)(ii)(III)) notifies a payor (as defined in section 3406(h)(4) and in paragraph (a)(6) of this section) that the payee is subject to backup withholding due to a notified payee underre-porting (as defined in paragraph (a)(2) of this section). The payor is required under section 3406(c)(4) and paragraph (c)(1) of this section to inform the payee that backup withholding under section 3406(a)(1)(C) has begun. The require-ments for the notice that a payor must send to a payee are set forth in paragraph (c)(2) and (3) of this section. The period for which backup with-holding is required due to a notified payee un-derreporting is described in section 3406(e)(3)(A) and in paragraph (e) of this section. See section 3406(c)(3) and paragraph (g) of this section for the rules regarding how a payee may obtain a determination from the Internal Revenue Service that withholding under section 3406(a)(1)(C) be stopped or not started.

(2) *Definition of notified payee underreport-ing.*—The term "notified payee underreporting" means that the Internal Revenue Service has—

(i) Determined that there was a payee un-derreporting as defined in paragraph (a)(3) of this section,

(ii) Mailed at least four notices to the payee (over a period of at least 120 days) with respect to the underreporting as prescribed in paragraph (f)(1) of this section, and

(iii) Assessed any deficiency attributable to the underreporting in the case of any payee who has filed a return.

(3) *Definition of a payee underreporting.*—The term "payee underreporting" means that the In-ternal Revenue Service has determined, for a taxable year, that—

(i) A payee failed to include in his return of tax under chapter 1 of the Internal Revenue Code for such year any portion of a reportable interest or dividend payment required to be shown on such tax return, or

(ii) A payee may be required to file a return for such year and to include a reportable interest or dividend payment in such return, but failed to file such return.

See paragraph (a)(5) of this section for certain payments to be taken into account in determin-ing whether there is payee underreporting even though those payments may not be defined as reportable interest or dividend payments in par-agraph (a)(4) of this section or even though backup withholding under section 3406(a)(1)(C) may not apply to such payments.

(4) *Definition of a reportable interest or divi-dend payment.*—(i) *In general.*—See section 3406(b)(2), A-2 of §35a.9999-1, A-5 of §35a.9999-3, and A-15 of §35a.9999-2 for the def-inition of reportable interest or dividend payment.

(ii) *Exceptions.*—(A) *Patronage dividends.*—Patronage dividends are treated as reportable interest or dividend payments for purposes of backup withholding under section 3406(a)(1)(C) only if 50 percent or more of the reportable amount is paid in money or by quali-fied check (as defined in section 1388(c)(4)), and then only to the extent that the payment is in money or by qualified check. See the second

>>>→ *Caution: Caution: Reg. §35a.3406-2, below, is effective until December 31, 1996.*

paragraph in A-10 of §35a.9999-3 for an example of how this rule applies.

(B) *Window payments.*—Pursuant to section 3406(b)(7), window payments as defined in A-42 of §35a.9999-1 and A-9 of §35a.9999-2 are not treated as reportable interest or dividend payments for purposes of backup withholding under section 3406(a)(1)(C).

(5) *Reportable interest or dividend payments excluded from backup withholding.*—The following reportable interest or dividend payments are not subject to backup withholding:

(i) *Certain dividends.*—Certain dividend payments as defined in A-9 of §35a.9999-3.

(ii) *Minimal payments.*—Minimal payments as defined in A-19 of §35a.9999-2 if the payor elects not to impose backup withholding on such amounts.

(iii) *Original issue discount.*—Original issue discount as defined in section 1273, unless there is a payment in cash. See A-15 of §35a.9999-2.

(iv) *Payments subject to other withholding.*—Payments already subject to withholding under another provision of the Internal Revenue Code. Reportable minimal payments (to the extent reported on an information return), patronage dividends, original issue discount, and window payments shall be taken into account in determining whether underreporting (as defined in paragraph (a)(3) of this section) has occurred, even though those payments may not be defined as reportable interest or dividend payments under paragraph (a)(4) of this section or even though backup withholding under section 3406(a)(1)(C) may not apply to such payments.

(6) *Definition of payor.*—See section 3406(h)(4), A-41 of §35a.9999-1, and A-1 of §35a.9999-3 for the definition of payor. The term payor includes a broker who holds an instrument in street name.

(7) *Definition of broker.*—See section 3406(h)(5) for the definition of broker.

(b) *Notice to payors and brokers regarding backup withholding.*—(1) *Notice from the Internal Revenue Service.*—The Internal Revenue Service will notify—

(i) Payors to begin backup withholding on reportable interest or dividend payments due to a notified payee underreporting pursuant to section 3406(a)(1)(C); and

(ii) Brokers pursuant to section 3406(c)(5) that a payee is subject to backup withholding under section 3406(a)(1)(C).

(2) *Notice from a broker.*—A broker who receives a notice from the Internal Revenue Service that a payee is subject to backup withholding due to a notified payee underreporting and through whom the payee subsequently acquires a readily tradable instrument (as defined in section 3406(h)(6)) with respect to which the broker is not the payor is required to notify the payor of that instrument that the payee is subject to backup withholding under section 3406(a)(1)(C) in the time and manner provided in A-41 of §35a.9999-1.

(3) *Accounts subject to backup withholding.*—(i) *In general.*—After receiving notice from the Internal Revenue Service or from a broker, as provided in section 3406(d)(2)(B) and paragraphs (b)(1)(i) and (2) of this section, that a payee is subject to backup withholding under section 3406(a)(1)(C), payors are required to withhold 20 percent of all reportable interest or dividend payments subject to backup withholding made with respect to all accounts of the payee.

(ii) *Joint accounts.*—Payors are required to withhold on joint accounts if the payee subject to backup withholding under section 3406(a)(1)(C) is the first person listed on the account at the time the payor receives the notice to begin backup withholding. Backup withholding shall continue to apply to reportable interest and dividend payments made to that account even if the order of the names on the account is subsequently changed, provided that the name of the payee subject to backup withholding remains on the account.

(iii) *Exception.*—Payors are not required to withhold on reportable interest or dividend payments made with respect to an account of the payee that could not be located with reasonable care. The payor will be considered to have exercised reasonable care if the payor uses the name and taxpayer identification number (or names and taxpayer identification numbers if a joint return was filed by the payees) provided on the notice from the Internal Revenue Service or from a broker as prescribed in paragraphs (b)(1)(i) and (2) of this section and in certain circumstances identified in this paragraph (b)(3)(iii) any account numbers provided by the Internal Revenue Service in locating all accounts of a payee or payees. If a payee uses a different name on an account than the name stated on the notice from the Internal Revenue Service or from a broker (for instance, due to marriage or adoption) and the payor can associate both names with the payee using records kept in the ordinary course of business, the payor will be treated as exercising reasonable care if the payor uses both names to locate accounts of the payee. If the taxpayer identification number is not provided to the payor or broker by the Internal Revenue Service, or if the taxpayer identification number provided by the Internal Revenue Service does not match the taxpayer identification number of the payee on the records that the payor or broker maintains in the ordinary course of business, the payor or broker is required to use any account numbers provided by the Internal Revenue Service to identify the payee and that payee's taxpayer identification number. This information

Reg. §35a.3406-2(b)(3)(iii)

⋙→ *Caution: Caution: Reg. §35a.3406-2, below, is effective until December 31, 1996.*

must be used by the payor to locate other accounts of the payee and by the broker to locate the payors with respect to whom the payee subsequently acquires a readily tradable instrument through that broker.

(c) *Notice from payors of backup withholding due to a payee underreporting.*—(1) *In general.*—A payor is required under section 3406(c)(4) to notify the payee in accordance with paragraph (c)(2) of this section that backup withholding has begun because of a notified payee underreporting. Payors who are notified by a broker that a payee is subject to backup withholding under section 3406(a)(1)(C) are also required to send the notice in accordance with paragraph (c)(2) of this section. As a result, the notice requirements provided in A-39 of §35a.9999-1 and in the appendix to §35a.9999-2 shall not apply to those payors notified by a broker that a payee is subject to backup withholding under section 3406(a)(1)(C). The payor must send the notice required by paragraph (c)(2) of this section to the payee no later than 15 days after the date that the payor makes the first payment subject to backup withholding under section 3406(a)(1)(C). The payor must send the notice of backup withholding by first-class mail to the payee at his last known address. Rules similar to the rules in A-17, A-18, A-19, and A-20 of §35a.9999-1 shall apply to the requirement to provide notice by first-class mail.

(2) *Form of the notice to the payee with respect to notified payee underreporting.*—The notice to the payee required by paragraph (c)(1) of this section must state—

(i) That the Internal Revenue Service has given notice that the payee has underreported reportable interest or dividends;

(ii) That, as a result of such underreporting, the payor is required under section 3406(a)(1)(C) of the Internal Revenue Code to withhold 20 percent of reportable interest and dividend payments made to the payee no later than the close of the day 30 days after the date that the payor received the notice;

(iii) The date that the payor received the notice to begin backup withholding under 3406(a)(1)(C);

(iv) That the payee must obtain a determination from the Internal Revenue Service in order to stop the backup withholding under section 3406(a)(1)(C); and

(v) That while he is subject to backup withholding due to payee underreporting, the payee may not certify to a payor making reportable interest or dividend payments (or to a broker acquiring a readily tradable instrument for the payee) that he is not subject to backup withholding under section 3406(a)(1)(C). See section 3406(a)(1)(D) for the backup withholding rules with respect to a payee's failure to make the certification under section 3406(a)(1)(D).

(3) *Exceptions.*—A notice provided to a payee on or before April 23, 1987, will be deemed to satisfy the provisions of paragraph (c)(2) of this section if it informs the payee that the payor has been instructed by the Internal Revenue Service to start backup withholding on reportable interest or dividend payments to the payee. If a payor who has started backup withholding due to notified payee underreporting on or before April 23, 1987, has not provided adequate notice to the payee on or before April 23, 1987, then the payor must provide notice to the payee in the manner prescribed in paragraph (c)(2) of this section by the date that is 45 days after April 23, 1987.

(d) *Notice to stop backup withholding.*—(1) *In general.*—The Internal Revenue Service will provide written certification to the payee that backup withholding is to stop and will notify the payors who were contacted pursuant to paragraph (b) of this section to stop withholding after the Internal Revenue Service makes a determination under paragraph (g) of this section that backup withholding with respect to a payee should stop. The Internal Revenue Service will also notify the brokers who were contacted pursuant to paragraph (b) of this section that the payee is no longer subject to backup withholding under section 3406(a)(1)(C) and that the brokers are no longer obligated to provide notices to payors under paragraph (b)(2) of this section. A broker who receives a certification under this section from the Internal Revenue Service is not required to provide the certification to any payors to which the broker has previously provided the notice required under paragraph (b)(2).

(2) *Date notice to stop withholding will be provided.*—(i) *Underreporting corrected or bona fide dispute.*—If the Internal Revenue Service makes a determination as set forth in paragraph (g)(1)(ii) or (iv) of this section during the 12-month period ending on October 15 of any calendar year, the Internal Revenue Service will provide the certification or notice required by paragraph (d)(1) of this section no later than December 1 of such calendar year.

(ii) *No underreporting or undue hardship.*—If the Internal Revenue Service makes a determination as set forth in paragraph (g)(1)(i) or (iii), the Internal Revenue Service will provide the notices required by paragraph (d)(1) of this paragraph no later than the 45th day after the day on which the Internal Revenue Service makes its determination.

(e) *Period during which withholding is required.*—(1) *In general.*—Upon receiving notice from the Internal Revenue Service after April 23, 1987, to begin backup withholding under section 3406(a)(1)(C) or notification from a broker stating that the payee is subject to backup withholding under section 3406(a)(1)(C), the payor must impose backup withholding on all reportable inter-

>>>→ *Caution: Caution: Reg. §35a.3406-2, below, is effective until December 31, 1996.*

est and dividend payments made to the payee during the period beginning after the close of the 30th day after the day on which the payor receives the notice provided in paragraph (b)(1)(i) or (2) of this section and ending as of the close of the day before the stop date (as described in paragraph (e)(2) of this section). Pursuant to section 3406(e)(5)(C), the payor may elect to begin backup withholding at any time during the 30-day period described in this paragraph.

(2) *Stop date.*—(i) *Underreporting corrected or bona fide dispute.*—In the case of a determination that the underreporting has been corrected or that a bona fide dispute exists (as defined in paragraphs (g)(1)(ii) or (iv) of this section), the stop date is—

(A) January 1 following the 12-month period ending on October 15th of any calendar year in which the determination has been made or, if later,

(B) The day that is 30 days after the earlier of—

(1) The date on which the payor receives written notification from the Internal Revenue Service (under paragraph (d)(2) of this section) that withholding is to stop, or

(2) The date on which the payor receives a copy of the written certification provided to the payee by the Internal Revenue Service that withholding is to stop.

(ii) *No underreporting or undue hardship.*—In the case of a determination that no payee underreporting occurred or that an undue hardship exists or could exist (as defined in paragraph (g)(1)(i) or (iii) of this section), the stop date is the date specified in paragraph (e)(2)(i)(B) of this section.

(iii) *Payor election to shorten or eliminate grace period.*—The payor with respect to any payee may elect to determine the stop date without regard to the grace period provided in section 3406(e)(5)(B) (*i.e.,* without regard to the words "the day that is 30 days after" in paragraph (e)(2)(i)(B) of this section) or by substituting a shorter grace period.

(iv) *Examples.*—The provisions of paragraph (e)(2)(i) may be illustrated by the following examples:

Example (1). The Internal Revenue Service makes a determination by October 15, 1987, that any underreporting with respect to A has been corrected. X, a payor who has been notified to backup withhold on payments of interest to A due to notified payee underreporting, receives written notice from the Internal Revenue Service on December 1, 1987, informing X that A is no longer subject to backup withholding under section 3406(a)(1)(C) and that X must stop backup withholding as of the close of December 31, 1987, or if later, the earlier of the close of the day 30 days after receipt of the notice from the Internal Revenue Service or receipt of the copy of the written certification provided to the payee by the

Internal Revenue Service. The stop date, as provided in paragraph (e)(2)(i)(A) of this section, is January 1, 1988, and the payor must stop backup withholding as of the close of December 31, 1987.

Example (2). Assume the same facts as in *Example (1)* except that X, due to a change of address or for other reasons, does not receive the notice from the Internal Revenue Service to stop backup withholding until December 15, 1987. In addition, A does not provide X with a copy of the certification that was provided to A by the Internal Revenue Service until December 15, 1987. The stop date, as provided in paragraph (e)(2)(i)(B) of this section, is January 14, 1988 (30 days after December 15, 1987), because that date is later than January 1, 1988. However, if a payor elects pursuant to section 3406(e)(5)(C) and paragraph (e)(2)(iii) of this section to determine the stop date without regard to that 30-day grace period, the stop date is January 1, 1987.

Example (3). Assume the same facts as in *Example (2)* except that on December 10, 1987 (rather than on December 15, 1987), A provides X with a copy of the certification from the Internal Revenue Service. The stop date, as provided in paragraph (e)(2)(i)(B) of this section, is January 9, 1988 (30 days after December 10, 1987), because that date is earlier than January 14, 1988 (30 days after the day X received notice from the Internal Revenue Service), but later than January 1, 1988.

(f) *Notice to payees from the Internal Revenue Service.*—(1) *Notice period.*—After the Internal Revenue Service determines that a payee underreporting exists as defined in paragraph (a)(3) of this section, the Internal Revenue Service, pursuant to section 3406(c)(1)(B), will mail to the payee at least four notices over a period of at least 120 days (hereafter referred to as the "notice period") before payors and brokers will be notified that the payee is subject to backup withholding due to a notified payee underreporting as provided in paragraph (b)(1) of this section. The notices may be incorporated with other notices provided to the payee by the Internal Revenue Service.

(2) *Payee subject to withholding.*—After the Internal Revenue Service provides the notices described in paragraph (f)(1) of this section, the Internal Revenue Service will send the notices required by paragraph (b) of this section unless—

(i) A payee obtains a determination under paragraph (g) of this section, or

(ii) In the case of a payee who has filed a tax return, the Internal Revenue Service has not assessed the deficiency attributable to the underreporting.

(3) *Disclosure of names of payors and brokers.*—The Internal Revenue Service pursuant to section 3406(c)(5) may require a payee subject to backup withholding due to a notified payee underreporting to disclose the names of all of his payors of reportable interest or dividend payments and

>>> *Caution: Caution: Reg. §35a.3406-2, below, is effective until December 31, 1996.*

the names of all of the brokers with whom the payee has accounts which may involve reportable interest or dividend payments. To the extent required in the request from the Internal Revenue Service, the payee shall also provide his account numbers and other information necessary to identify the payee's accounts.

(4) *Backup withholding certification.*—Once a payee receives a final notice from the Internal Revenue Service notifying him that his reportable interest or dividend payments are subject to backup withholding due to notified payee underreporting under section 3406(a)(1)(C), the payee shall not certify to any payor or broker, under penalties of perjury, that he is not subject to backup withholding under section 3406(a)(1)(C). See paragraph (k)(2) of this section for the penalties that will apply to a payee who makes a false certification. The payee may not make the certification until the payee receives the certification provided in paragraph (d)(1) of this section from the Internal Revenue Service advising the payee that he is no longer subject to backup withholding under section 3406(a)(1)(C) (as provided in A-33 of § 35a.9999-1). See A-37 of § 35a.9999-1 for the rule applicable to a payor who makes reportable interest or dividend payments to a payee who fails to certify that he is not subject to backup withholding due to notified payee underreporting.

(g) *Determination by the Internal Revenue Service that backup withholding should not start or should be stopped.*—(1) *In general.*—A payee may prevent backup withholding from starting or stop it once it has started if, for the taxable year with respect to which there is a notified payee underreporting and any other taxable years for which there is any payee underreporting, the payee—

(i) Shows that there was no payee underreporting (as provided in paragraph (g)(2) of this section);

(ii) Corrects any payee underreporting (as provided in paragraph (g)(3) of this section);

(iii) Shows that backup withholding will cause or is causing an undue hardship (as defined in paragraph (g)(4) of this section) and that it is unlikely that the payee will underreport interest or dividend payments again; or

(iv) Shows that a bona fide dispute exists as to whether any underreporting has occurred (as provided in paragraph (g)(5) of this section).

(2) *No underreporting.*—A payee may show that no underreporting of interest or dividends exists by presenting receipts or other satisfactory documentation to the Internal Revenue Service showing that all taxes relating to such payments were reported and paid timely or evidence showing that the payee did not have to file a return for the taxable year in question or that the underreporting determination is based upon a factual, clerical, or other mistake.

(3) *Correcting any payee underreporting.*—(i) *Before issuance of a statutory notice of deficiency.*—Before a statutory notice of deficiency is issued to a payee pursuant to section 6212, the payee may correct underreporting by filing a return if one was not previously filed and paying taxes, penalties, and interest due with respect to any underreported interest or dividend payments.

(ii) *After issuance of a statutory notice of deficiency.*—After a statutory notice of deficiency is issued to a payee, the payee may correct underreporting at any time by filing a return if one was not previously filed and paying the entire deficiency and any other taxes including penalties and interest attributable to any payee underreporting of interest or dividend payments. Thus, for example, a payee may correct underreporting after assessment of a deficiency by paying the entire assessment with respect to that deficiency and any other taxes including penalties and interest attributable to any payee underreporting of interest or dividend payments for other taxable years.

(4) *Undue hardship.*—A determination of undue hardship will be based on the overall impact to the payee of having 20 percent of reportable interest and dividend payments withheld. Factors that will be considered in determining whether backup withholding causes undue hardship include, but are not limited to, the following:

(i) Whether estimated tax payments, and other credits for current tax liabilities, or amounts withheld on employee wages or pensions, in addition to backup withholding, would cause significant over-withholding;

(ii) The payee's health, including the payee's ability to pay foreseeable medical expenses;

(iii) The extent of the payee's reliance on interest and dividend payments to meet necessary living expenses and the existence, if any, of other sources of income;

(iv) Whether other income of the payee is limited or fixed (*e.g.*, social security, pension, and unearned income);

(v) The payee's ability to sell or liquidate stocks, bonds, bank accounts, trust accounts, or other assets, and the consequences of doing so;

(vi) Whether the payee reported and timely paid the most recent year's tax liability, including interest and dividend income; and

(vii) Whether the payee has filed a bankruptcy petition with the United States Bankruptcy Court.

In addition to the above factors, the Internal Revenue Service must conclude that it is unlikely that any payee underreporting will occur again.

(5) *Bona fide dispute.*—The Internal Revenue Service may make a determination under this paragraph if there is a dispute between the payee and the Internal Revenue Service on a question of fact or law that is material to a determination under paragraph (g)(1)(i) and, based

⋙→ *Caution: Caution: Reg. §35a.3406-2, below, is effective until December 31, 1996.*

upon all the facts and circumstances, the Internal Revenue Service finds that the dispute is asserted in good faith by the payee and there is a reasonable basis for the payee's position. See the example provided in paragraph (j)(2)(ii) of this section for an illustration of this provision.

(h) *Requests for determinations.*—(1) *In general.*—A payee may request a determination under one or more of the provisions of paragraph (g) of this section. Following its review of a request for a determination under paragraph (g) of this section, the Internal Revenue Service will either provide the payee with a written certification as prescribed in paragraph (d) of this section if the evidence presented warrants the requested determination or will provide the payee with a written notice informing him that a determination was not made.

(2) *Determinations made during the notice period.*—In general, if a determination is made during the notice period as defined in paragraph (f)(1) of this section, then the payee will not be subject to backup withholding due to a notified payee underreporting with respect to any taxable year for which a determination was made.

(3) *Determinations made after the notice period.*—If a determination is made after the notice period, as defined in paragraph (f)(1) of this section, the Internal Revenue Service will provide a notice to payors and brokers, and a certification to the payee as provided in paragraph (d)(1) of this section.

(i) [Reserved].

(j) *Payees filing a joint return.*—(1) *In general.*—For purposes of section 3406(a)(1)(C), if payee underreporting is found to exist with respect to a joint return filed by a husband and wife, then the provisions of this section shall apply to the payees collectively. As a result, both payees will be subject to backup withholding on accounts in their individual names as well as accounts in their joint names. Either or both payees may satisfy the criteria for a determination that no payee underreporting exists, that the underreporting has been corrected, or that a bona fide dispute exists (as provided in paragraphs (g)(1)(i), (ii), or (iv) of this section). Both payees, however, must satisfy the criteria for a determination that backup withholding will cause or is causing undue hardship (as provided in paragraph (g)(1)(iii) of this section).

(2) *Exceptions.*—(i) *Innocent spouse.*—A spouse who files a joint return may obtain a determination that withholding should stop or not start with respect to payments made to his or her individual accounts, if the spouse—

(A) Shows that he or she did not underreport income because he or she is an innocent spouse as described in section 6013(e), or

(B) Shows that there is a bona fide dispute as to whether he or she is an innocent spouse and hence did not underreport income.

(ii) *Example.*—The provisions of paragraph (j)(2)(i) may be illustrated by the following example:

Example. H and W filed a joint return in 1986 on which H failed to include $2,000 of interest income. In 1987, the Internal Revenue Service determined that a payee underreporting exists with respect to H and W for the 1986 tax year. After properly notifying H and W of the underreporting and assessing the tax, the Internal Revenue Service sent notices to payors to begin backup withholding on the joint and individual accounts of H and W and to brokers informing them that H and W are subject to backup withholding under section 3406(a)(1)(C) on their joint and individual accounts. W claims that she is an innocent spouse and requests a determination that she did not underreport interest or dividend income so that her individual accounts will not be subject to backup withholding.

The Internal Revenue Service questions her status as an innocent spouse. If the Internal Revenue Service determines, based upon all the facts and circumstances, that there is a reasonable basis for W's claim to be an innocent spouse and that the claim is made in good faith, W will have a bona fide dispute with the Internal Revenue Service. Consequently, the individual accounts of W will not be subject to further backup withholding due to a notified payee underreporting as provided in paragraph (g)(5) of this section.

The Internal Revenue Service will notify payors to stop backup withholding under section 3406(a)(1)(C) and brokers that W is no longer subject to backup withholding under section 3406(a)(1)(C) on W's individual accounts. Backup withholding will not restart on those accounts unless the Internal Revenue Service ultimately determines that W is not an innocent spouse. In that event the Internal Revenue Service will notify the payors to start backup withholding under section 3406(a)(1)(C) and the brokers that W is subject to backup withholding under section 3406(a)(1)(C) with respect to the individual accounts of W.

(iii) *Divorced or legally separated payee.*—A payee who, at the time of the request for a determination under paragraph (g) of this section, is divorced or legally separated under state law may obtain a determination that undue hardship exists (or would exist) under paragraph (g)(1)(iii) of this section with respect to reportable interest and dividend payments made to his or her individual accounts if the divorced or legally separated payee satisfies the criteria for a determination under paragraph (g)(4) of this section.

(k) *Penalties.*—(1) *Failure to withhold.*—See A-2 of §35a.9999-3 for rules relating to penalties applicable to a payor who fails to withhold on reportable interest and dividend payments made to a payee subject to backup withholding.

Reg. §35a.3406-2(k)(1)

⟫→ *Caution: Caution: Reg. §35a.3406-2, below, is effective until December 31, 1996.*

(2) *False certification.*—(i) *Criminal penalty under section 7205 (b).*—If any individual willfully makes a false certification under section 3406 (d)(1) or (2), then that individual shall, in addition to any other penalty provided by law, upon conviction thereof, be fined not more than $1,000, or imprisoned not more than 1 year, or both.

(ii) *Civil penalty under section 6682.*— (A) *In general.*—In addition to any criminal penalty provided by law, if any individual makes a statement under section 3406 which results in a decrease in the amounts deducted and withheld under chapter 24 of the Internal Revenue Code and, as of the time the statement was made, there was no reasonable basis for the statement, the individual shall pay a penalty of $500 for the statement. The penalty is due upon notice and demand and pursuant to section 6682 collection is not subject to the deficiency procedures of subchapter B of chapter 63 of the Internal Revenue Code. See section 6682.

(B) *Waiver of penalty.*—The payee may obtain a waiver (in whole or part) of the penalty imposed under section 6682(a) and paragraph (k)(2)(ii)(A) of this section if it is established to the satisfaction of the Internal Revenue Service that the taxes imposed under subtitle A of the Internal Revenue Code with respect to the payee for the taxable year in which the false certification was made are equal to or less than the sum of—

(1) The credits against taxes allowed by part IV of subchapter A of chapter 1 of the Internal Revenue Code, and

(2) The payments of estimated tax which are considered payments on account of such taxes.

(C) *Procedure for seeking a waiver.*—To request a waiver under section 6682(b) and paragraph (k)(2)(ii)(B) of this section, the payee must submit to the Internal Revenue Service a written statement with supporting documents to establish all the facts necessary in order to obtain the waiver. The statement must be signed by the person that otherwise would be subject to the penalty imposed by section 6682(a) and paragraph (k)(2)(ii)(A) of this section and must contain a declaration that it is made under penalties of perjury.

(3) *Delay of assessment.*—If a payee institutes or maintains a suit with the United States Tax Court primarily to delay assessment and the payee's position is frivolous or groundless, or the payee unreasonable failed to pursue available administrative remedies, the court may award up to $5,000 in damages under section 6673. The damages will be assessed against and collected from the payee in the same manner as the underlying tax.

(l) Effective date. This section is effective until December 31, 1996. [Temporary Reg. §35a.3406-2.]

☐ [*T.D.* 8137, 4-20-87. *Amended by T.D.* 8637, 12-20-95. *Corrected on* 3-20-96.]

General Provisions Relating to Employment Taxes

See p. 20,601 for regulations not amended to reflect law changes

[Reg. §31.3501(a)-1T]

§31.3501(a)-1T. Question and answer relating to the time employers must collect and pay the taxes on noncash fringe benefits (Temporary).—The following questions and answers relate to the time employers must collect and pay the taxes imposed by subtitle C on noncash fringe benefits:

Q-1: If a noncash fringe benefit constitutes "wages" under section 3121(a), 3306(b), or 3401(a), or constitutes "compensation" under section 3231(e), when must an employer collect and pay the taxes imposed by subtitle C?

A-1: For purposes of an employer's liability to collect and pay the taxes imposed by subtitle C, an employer may deem such fringe benefit to be paid at any time on or after the date on which it is provided, as long as such date is on or before the last day of the calendar quarter in which such benefit is provided. An employer may consider the benefit to be provided in two or more parts for purposes of the preceding sentence. For example, if a fringe benefit with a fair market value of $1,000 is provided on January 1, 1985, the employer could deem $500 paid on February 28, 1985 and $500 paid on March 31, 1985.

With respect to noncash fringe benefits provided during the first calendar quarter of 1985, a special rule applies. Such benefits may be deemed paid at any time on or after the date on which they are provided as long as the date they are deemed paid is on or before the last day of the second calendar quarter of 1985.

In addition, for purposes of §31.6302(c)-1(a)(1)(i), the term "tax" does not include the employer tax under section 3111 with respect to noncash fringe benefits which are deemed by the employer to be paid on the last day of any calendar quarter. For purposes of the first sentence of §31.6302(c)-2(a)(1), the phrase "employer tax imposed after December 31, 1983, under section 3221(a) and (b)" will not include any such employer tax with respect to noncash fringe benefits which are deemed by the employer to be paid on the last day of the quarter; provided that for purposes of deposits required under §31.6302(c)-1(a)(1)(v), such first sentence applies to such noncash fringe benefits.

Notwithstanding anything in this section to the contrary, if an employer in fact withholds, the amount withheld is subject to the general deposit rules.

The manner in which and the time at which the employer withholds amounts from the wages of an employee to pay the taxes imposed under section 3101, 3201, and/or 3402 will generally be left to be determined by the employer and the employee. Any delay in withholding, however, does not affect the employer's obligation, upon the filing of an employment tax return, to pay amounts which would be due under this subtitle if the employer had withheld, with respect to noncash fringe benefits, the amount which would have been required to be withheld if such noncash fringe benefits had been paid in cash on the date the benefits were deemed paid. However, if such amounts are not withheld from the wages of an employee within a reasonable period after payment of the taxes by the employer, payment by the employer may be deemed additional compensation of the employee.

Q-2: Are any fringe benefits excepted from the rules contained in Q/A-1 of this section?

A-2: Yes. The rules contained in Q/A-1 of this section do not apply to the transfer of personal property (both tangible and intangible) of a kind held for investment or to the transfer of real property. Accordingly, an employer is liable for the collection and payment of taxes imposed by this subtitle when such property is transferred. For example, stock transferred in connection with the performance of services is paid, for purposes of this subtitle C, on the date the stock is transferred, i.e., on the date the stock vests pursuant to section 83 (absent a section 83(b) election).

Q-3: What is an example of the application of the rules contained in Q/A-1 of this section with respect to obligations under Chapters 21 and 24 of subtitle C?

A-3: All of employer A's employees received $100 in cash as wages each week from A. In addition, during a calendar quarter, each such employee receives noncash fringe benefits, the fair market value of which is $500. A deems all such noncash fringe benefits to be paid on the last day of the quarter. As of the end of the quarter, no amount has been withheld from the employees' wages with respect to such noncash fringe benefits, and A has "undeposited taxes" (within the meaning of §31.6302(c)-1(a)(1)(i)) of more than $3,000 attributable to amounts actually withheld under section 3102 or section 3402 or due under section 3111 with respect to cash wages of A's employees. The amount which A must deposit within 3 banking days after the end of the quarter will be determined without regard to the noncash fringe benefits deemed paid on the last day of the quarter.

During the month following the quarter, A withholds from its employees with respect to the noncash fringe benefits deemed paid on the last day of the quarter. As A withholds amounts, such amounts become "taxes" subject to §31.6302(c)-1(a)(1)(i). If, as of the date of filing of the return for the period which includes the last

day of the quarter, A has not deposited all amounts with respect to the quarter which are due under section 3111 or which would have been due had A withheld, under sections 3102 and 3402, with respect to noncash fringe benefits, the amount which would have been required to be withheld had such benefits been paid in cash, A shall pay the balance with its return. A must make such payment regardless of whether, at the time the return is filed, he has actually withheld all amounts which he would have been required to withhold had such benefits been paid in cash.

Q-4: If an employee is provided with a noncash fringe benefit and separates from service before the benefit is deemed paid by the employer, is the employer liable for the taxes imposed by subtitle C?

A-4: Yes. The employer's liability is unaffected by his ability to collect the tax from the former employee.

Q-5: If an entity other than the employer provides a noncash fringe benefit to an employee, is that entity considered the employer of such employee with respect to such noncash fringe benefit for any purposes of subtitle C?

A-5: The provision of noncash fringe benefits by an entity to an employee of another employer does not make such entity the employer of such employee with respect to such noncash fringe benefit for any purpose of subtitle C, so long as such noncash fringe benefits are incidental to the provision of wages by the employer to such employee. For example, if two unrelated airlines, A and B, enter into a reciprocal agreement whereby the parents of employees of both airlines are entitled to free flights on both airlines, the fact that A is providing a noncash fringe benefit to the employees of B generally will not make A the employer of such employees for purposes of subtitle C.

Q-6: Do special rules apply to the provision of taxable noncash fringe benefits by a nonemployer under a reciprocal agreement with the employee's employer?

A-6: If the provision of taxable noncash fringe benefits meets the requirements of Q/A-5 of this section, the nonemployer provider of the benefits is not required to withhold. The employer must take the steps necessary to obtain the relevant information from the provider of the benefits in order to enable the employer to satisfy, in a timely manner, its obligations under subtitle C to collect and pay taxes with respect to the noncash fringe benefits provided by the nonemployer.

Q-7: For purposes of subtitle C, how is the fair market value of an employer-provided automobile or other road vehicle during any time period to be determined?

A-7: The value of the availability of an employer-provided automobile or other road vehicle must be determined under the rules provided in §1.61-2T and §1.132-1T. (For purposes of this section, the terms "automobile" and "road vehicle" have the meaning given those terms in Q/

Reg. §31.3501(a)-1T

A-11 of §1.61-2T). For example, assume that an employee adopts the special rule provided in §1.61-2T and that the Annual Lease Value, as defined in §1.61-2T, of an automobile is $2,100. The automobile is provided to employee A on January 1, 1985. As of March 31, A had driven the automobile 1,000 personal miles and 3,000 miles in the course of his employer's business. For the quarter, A would have had wages of $131.25 attributable to his personal use of the automobile computed by subtracting a $393.75 working condition fringe from $525 ($2,100 divided by 4). See section 132(d) and §1.132-1T. During the second quarter of 1985, A drives the automobile only 1,000 miles, all of which are personal. In order to calculate the value of the wages provided to A in the second quarter in the form of the availability of an employer-provided automobile, first A's employer calculates the Annual Lease Value attributable to the first six months of 1985 which is $1,050 ($2,100 divided by 2). Second, A's employer calculates the working condition fringe exclusion which is $630 ($1,050 multiplied by a fraction the numerator of which is A's business mileage (3,000 miles) and the denominator of which is A's total mileage (5,000 miles)). These calculations result in a total inclusion of $420 ($1,050–$630). From the total inclusion of $420, the wages provided in the first quarter, $131.25, are subtracted, leaving $288.75 as the wages includible in the second quarter attributable to the availability to A of the employer-provided automobile.

Q-8: May an employer treat any part of the Annual Lease Value or Daily Lease Value (as defined in §1.61-2T), or the fair market value if the special rule of §1.61-2T is not or cannot be used, of an automobile or other road vehicle made available to an employee as includible in the employee's gross income without regard to whether the employee has used the automobile or other road vehicle in the employer's business?

A-8: No, except as otherwise provided in this Q/A-8, an employer may not include any amount in an employee's income with respect to an employer-provided automobile or other road vehicle unless such inclusion is based on:

(a) Records or a statement submitted by an employee that contain the business and total mileage for the period beginning on January 1, 1985, and ending on the last day of the employer's taxable year that began in 1984, or

(b) Records that satisfy the employer's "adequate contemporaneous record" requirement under section 274(d)(4) and the regulations thereunder for the employer's taxable years beginning after December 31, 1984.

For example, an employer who is subject to (b) of this Q/A-8 may rely on a statement submitted by the employee indicating for the period the number of miles driven by the employee in the employer's business and the total number of miles driven by the employee unless the employer knows or has reason to know the statement submitted is not based on "adequate contemporaneous records". (For purposes of this section, if a road vehicle is available to any person and such availability would be taxable to an employee, miles driven by that person will be considered miles driven by the employee).

Notwithstanding the preceding paragraph of this Q/A-8, an employer may include in an employee's income the value of the availability of an employer-provided road vehicle, calculated without regard to a working condition fringe exclusion based on business mileage if one of the conditions listed in §1.274-6T(f)(1) is satisfied with respect to the relevant period.

In addition, the employer must, before including any amount in an employee's income with respect to an employer-provided road vehicle, take into account other working condition fringe exclusions, such as the security exclusion discussed in §1.132-1T. If proper calculation of an exclusion requires information from the employee and the employee does not respond within a reasonable period of time to a request for that information or produces information which the employer knows or has reason to know is not accurate, the employer may disregard such exclusion in reporting the employee's gross income.

Q-8a. May an employer withhold amounts attributable to noncash fringe benefits on the basis of average wages as permitted under section 3402(h)(1)?

A-8a. In general, yes. In estimating wages under section 3402(h)(1)(A), however, the employer must take into account estimated business use of the benefit (such as an employer-provided road vehicle). In no event, however, may the amount reported by the employer as "wages" for any employee for any quarter be based on an estimation. However, the rules in Q/A-1 of this section regarding permissible delays in actual withholding apply.

Q-9: If an employee purchases any property or service from an employer at a discount and the discount is not excludable under section 132 and any applicable regulations thereunder, when is the noncash fringe benefit provided?

A-9: Such property or service is provided at the time that ownership is transferred, in the case of property, or the time service is rendered, in the case of services. This will be true regardless of when the employee pays for such property or service or the date payment is due or the rate of interest charged prior to payment. The time at which ownership of the property is transferred must be determined under general tax principles.

Q-10: What rules apply with respect to the treatment of the payment of any noncash fringe benefit as the payment of supplemental wages under section 3402?

A-10: An employer may treat the payment of any noncash fringe benefit as the payment of supplemental wages. Thus, if noncash fringe benefits are provided and tax has been withheld from the employee's regular wages, the employer may determine the tax to be withheld with respect to such noncash fringe benefits by using a flat percentage rate of 20 percent, without allowance for exemptions and without reference to any regular payment of wages. For example, assume that during a calendar quarter A receives from his employer a taxable noncash fringe benefit with a fair market value of $1,000. If the requirements specified above are satisfied, A's employer may determine the tax to be withheld with respect to such benefit by using a flat percentage rate of 20 percent. The employer may also determine the tax to be withheld with respect to such benefit by use of the method described in § 31.3402(g)-1(a)(2).

[Reg. § 31.3501(a)-1T.]

☐ [*T.D. 8004, 1-2-85. Amended by T.D. 8009,* 2-15-85.]

[Reg. § 31.3502-1]

§ 31.3502-1. Nondeductibility of taxes in computing taxable income.—For provisions relating to the nondeductibility, in computing taxable income under subtitle A, of the taxes imposed by sections 3101, 3201, and 3211, and of the tax deducted and withheld under chapter 24, see §§ 1.164-2 and 1.275-1 of this chapter (Income Tax Regulations). For provisions relating to the credit allowable to the recipient of the income in respect of the tax deducted and withheld under chapter 24, see § 1.31-1 of this chapter (Income Tax Regulations). [Reg. § 31.3502-1.]

☐ [*T.D. 6354, 1-13-59. Amended by T.D. 6780,* 12-21-64.]

[Reg. § 31.3503-1]

§ 31.3503-1. Tax under chapter 21 or 22 paid under wrong chapter.—If, for any period, an amount is paid as tax—

(a) Under chapter 21 or corresponding provisions of prior law by a person who is not liable for tax for such period under such chapter or prior law, but who is liable for tax for such period under chapter 22 or corresponding provisions of prior law, or

(b) Under chapter 22 or corresponding provisions of prior law by a person who is not liable for tax for such period under such chapter or prior law, but who is liable for tax for such period under chapter 21 or corresponding provisions of prior law,

the amount so paid shall be credited against the tax for which such person is liable and the balance, if any, shall be refunded. Each claim for refund or credit under this section shall be made on Form 843 and in accordance with § 31.6402(a)-2 and the applicable provisions of section 6402(a) and the regulations thereunder in Part 301 of this chapter (Regulations on Procedure and Administration). [Reg. § 31.3503-1.]

☐ [*T.D. 6354, 1-13-59.*]

[Reg. § 31.3504-1]

§ 31.3504-1. Designation of agent by application.—(a) *In general.*—In the event wages as defined in chapter 21 or 24 of the Internal Revenue Code (Code), or compensation as defined in chapter 22 of the Code, of an employee or group of employees, employed by one or more employers, is paid by a fiduciary, agent, or other person ("agent"), or if that agent has the control, receipt, custody, or disposal of (collectively "pays") wages or compensation, the Internal Revenue Service may, subject to the terms and conditions as it deems proper, authorize that agent to perform the acts required of the employer or employers under those provisions of the Code and the regulations that apply, for purposes of the taxes imposed by the chapter or chapters, with respect to wages or compensation paid by the agent. If the agent is authorized by the Internal Revenue Service to perform such acts, all provisions of law (including penalties) and of the regulations applicable to an employer with respect to such acts shall be applicable to the agent. However, each employer for whom the agent acts shall remain subject to all provisions of law (including penalties) and of the regulations applicable to an employer with respect to such acts. Any application to authorize an agent to perform such acts, signed by the agent and the employer, shall be made on the form prescribed by the Internal Revenue Service and shall be filed with the Internal Revenue Service as prescribed in the instructions to the form and other applicable guidance.

(b) *Special rule for home care service recipients.*— (1) *In general.*—In the event an agent is authorized pursuant to paragraph (a) of this section to perform the acts required of an employer under chapters 21 or 24 on behalf of one or more home care service recipients, as defined in paragraph (b)(3) of this section, the Internal Revenue Service may authorize that agent to perform the acts as are required of employers for purposes of the tax imposed by chapter 23 of the Code with respect to wages paid by the agent for home care services, as defined in paragraph (b)(2) of this section, rendered to the home care service recipient. If the agent is authorized by the Internal Revenue Service to perform such acts, all provisions of law (including penalties) and of the regulations applicable to an employer in respect of such acts shall be applicable to the agent. However, each employer for whom the agent acts shall remain subject to all provisions of law (including penalties) and of the regulations applicable to an employer with respect to such acts.

(2) *Home care services.*—For purposes of this section, the term *home care services* includes health care and personal attendant care services rendered to the home care service recipient.

(3) *Home care service recipient.*—For purposes of this section, the term *home care service recipient* means any individual who receives home care services, as defined in paragraph (b)(2) of this section, while enrolled, and for the remainder of the calendar year after ceasing to be enrolled, in a program administered by a Federal, state, or local government agency that provides Federal, state, or local government funds, to pay, in whole or in part, for home care services for that individual.

Reg. § 31.3504-1(b)(3)

(c) *Effective/applicability dates.*—An authorization under paragraph (a) in effect prior to December 12, 2013 continues to be in effect after that date. Paragraph (b) of this section applies to wages paid on or after January 1, 2014. However, pursuant to section 7805(b), taxpayers may rely on paragraph (b) of this section for all taxable years for which a valid designation is in effect under paragraph (a) of this section. [Reg. § 31.3504-1.]

☐ [*T.D. 6354, 1-13-59. Amended by T.D. 7012, 5-14-69 and T.D. 9649, 12-11-2013.*]

[Reg. § 31.3504-2]

§ 31.3504-2. Designation of payor to perform acts of an employer.—(a) *In general.*—A person (as defined in section 7701(a)(1)) that pays wages or compensation ("payor") to the individual(s) performing services for any client pursuant to a service agreement, except as provided in paragraph (d) of this section, is designated to perform the acts required of an employer with respect to the wages or compensation paid. For purposes of this section the term *wages* has the same meaning as the term wages has for purposes of chapters 21, 23, and 24, and the term *compensation* has the same meaning as the term compensation has for purposes of chapter 22. This section is not applicable if the payor has been authorized as an agent of the employer under § 31.3504-1.

(b) *Definitions.*—(1) *Client.*—The term *client* means an individual or entity that enters into a service agreement with the payor.

(2) *Service agreement.*—(i) The term *service agreement* means an agreement pursuant to which the payor —

    (A) Asserts it is the employer (or "co-employer") of the individual(s) performing services for the client;

    (B) Pays wages or compensation to the individual(s) for services the individual(s) perform for the client; and

    (C) Assumes responsibility to collect, report, and pay, or assumes liability for, any taxes applicable under subtitle C of the Code with respect to the wages or compensation paid by the payor to the individual(s) performing services for the client.

    (ii) For purposes of paragraph (b)(2)(i)(A) of this section, the payor may implicitly or explicitly assert it is the employer (or "co-employer") of the individual(s) performing services for the client, including by agreeing to—

    (A) Recruit and hire employees for the client or assign employees as permanent or temporary members of the client's work force, or participate with the client in these actions;

    (B) Hire the client's employees as its own and then provide them back to the client to perform services for the client; or

    (C) File employment tax returns using its own employer identification number that include wages or compensation paid to the individual(s) performing services for the client.

(c) *Effects of designation.*—If a payor is designated to perform the acts required of an employer under this section then the following rules apply—

    (1) A payor must perform the acts required of an employer under each applicable chapter of the Code and the relevant regulations with respect to the wages or compensation paid by such payor. All provisions of law (including penalties) and the regulations applicable to the employer are applicable to the payor so designated with respect to the wages or compensation paid by the payor; and

    (2) Each employer for whom the payor is designated remains subject to all provisions of law (including penalties) and of the regulations applicable to an employer.

(d) *Exceptions.*—A payor is not designated to perform the acts required of an employer under this section for any wages or compensation paid by the payor to the individual(s) performing services for a client if—

    (1) The wages or compensation are reported on a return filed under the client's employer identification number (as defined in section 6109 and the applicable regulations);

    (2) The payor is a common paymaster under sections 3121(s) or 3231(i);

    (3) The payor is the employer of the individual(s) (including an employer within the meaning of section 3401(d)(1)); or

    (4) The payor is treated as an employer under section 3121(a)(2)(A).

(e) *Examples.*—The following examples illustrate the application of this section:

    (1) *Example 1.* Corporation P enters into an agreement with Employer, effective January 1, 2015. Under the agreement, Corporation P hires the Employer's employees as its own employees and provides them back to Employer to perform services for Employer. Corporation P also assumes responsibility to make payment of the individuals' wages and for the collection, reporting, and payment of applicable taxes. For all pay periods in 2015, Employer provides Corporation P with an amount equal to the gross payroll (that is, wage and tax amounts) of the individuals, and Corporation P pays wages (less the applicable withholding) to the individuals performing services for Employer. Corporation P also reports the wage and tax amounts on Form 941, *Employer's QUARTERLY Federal Tax Return,* filed for each quarter of 2015 under Corporation P's employer identification number. Corporation P is not a common paymaster, the employer of the individuals (including an employer within the meaning of section 3401(d)(1)), or treated as the employer of the individual under section 3121(a)(2)(A). Corporation P is designated to perform the acts of an employer with respect to all of the wages Corporation P paid to the individuals performing services for Employer for all quarters of 2015. Employer and Corporation P are each subject to all provisions of law (including penalties) applicable in respect of employers for all quarters of 2015 with respect to such wages.

    (2) *Example 2.* Same facts as *Example 1,* except that Corporation P only reports the wage and tax

amounts on Form 941, *Employer's QUARTERLY Federal Tax Return*, filed for the 1st and 2nd quarters of 2015. Neither Corporation P nor Employer files returns for the 3rd and 4th quarters of 2015. Corporation P is designated to perform the acts of an employer with respect to all of the wages Corporation P paid to the individuals performing services for Employer for all quarters of 2015. Employer and Corporation P are each subject to all provisions of law (including penalties) applicable in respect of employers for all quarters of 2015 with respect to such wages.

(3) *Example 3.* Same facts as *Example 1*, except that neither Corporation P nor Employer reports the wage and tax amounts on Form 941, *Employer's QUARTERLY Federal Tax Return*, for any quarter of 2015. Corporation P is designated to perform the acts of an employer with respect to all of the wages Corporation P paid to the individuals performing services for Employer for all quarters of 2015. Employer and Corporation P are each subject to all provisions of law (including penalties) applicable in respect of employers for all quarters of 2015 with respect to such wages.

(4) *Example 4.* Same facts as *Example 1*, except that Employer provides only net payroll (that is, wages less tax amounts) to Corporation P for each pay period. Corporation P is designated to perform the acts of an employer with respect to all of the wages Corporation P paid to the individuals performing services for Employer for all quarters of 2015. Employer and Corporation P are each subject to all provisions of law (including penalties) applicable in respect of employers for all quarters of 2015 with respect to such wages.

(5) *Example 5.* Same facts as *Example 1*, except that after Corporation P reports the wage and tax amounts on Form 941, *Employer's QUARTERLY Federal Tax Return*, filed for each quarter of 2015 under Corporation P's employer identification number, Corporation P files a claim for refund of the employment taxes it paid for each quarter of 2015 that are related to wages Corporation P paid to the individuals performing services for Employer. The basis for Corporation P's refund claim is that Corporation P is not the employer of the individuals that performed services for Employer. Corporation P is designated to perform the acts of an employer with respect to all of the wages Corporation P paid to the individuals performing services for Employer for all quarters of 2015. Accordingly, Corporation P is not entitled to a refund. Employer and Corporation P are each subject to all provisions of law (including penalties) applicable in respect of employers for all quarters of 2015 with respect to such wages.

(6) *Example 6.* Corporation S enters into an agreement with Employer, effective January 1, 2015. Under the agreement, Corporation S provides payroll services, including payment of wages to individuals performing services for Employer, and assumes responsibility for the collection, reporting, and payment of applicable taxes. For all pay periods in 2015, Employer provides Corporation S with an amount equal to the gross payroll (that is, wage and tax amounts) of the individuals, and Corporation S pays wages (less the applicable withholding) to the individuals performing services for Employer. Corporation S also reports the wage and tax amounts on Form 941, *Employer's QUARTERLY Federal Tax Return*, filed for each quarter of 2015 under Employer's employer identification number. Corporation S is not designated to perform the acts of an employer with respect to all of the wages Corporation S paid to the individuals performing services for Employer for all quarters of 2015. Corporation S did not assert it was the employer and filed Forms 941 using Employer's employer identification number. Accordingly, Corporation S is not liable for the applicable employment taxes under this section. Employer remains subject to all provisions of law (including penalties) applicable in respect of employers for all quarters of 2015 with respect to such wages.

(7) *Example 7.* Corporation T enters into a consulting agreement with Manufacturer effective January 1, 2015, to provide consulting services to Manufacturer. Corporation T is responsible to pay wages to the individuals providing the consulting services to Manufacturer and to collect, report, and pay the applicable taxes. Corporation T has the right to direct and control the individuals as to when and how to perform the consulting services and, thus, is the common law employer of the individuals providing the consulting services. Corporation T is not designated to perform the acts of an employer with respect to all of the wages Corporation T pays to individuals providing consulting services to Manufacturer. However, as the common law employer of the individuals, Corporation T is subject to all provisions of law (including penalties) applicable in respect of employers with respect to such wages.

(8) *Example 8.* On January 1, 2015, Corporation U enters into an agreement with Employer for Employer to farm Corporation U's property. Under the agreement, Corporation U and Employer agree to split the proceeds of the sale of the products grown on the property. Employer hires workers to assist it with the farming. Employer has the right to direct and control the workers as to when and how to perform the services and, thus, is the common law employer of the workers. However, Employer is unable to pay the workers until after the products are sold. Therefore, Corporation U pays wages to the workers and deducts this amount from Employer's share of the profits. Corporation U controls the payment of wages within the meaning of section 3401(d)(1). Corporation U is not designated to perform the acts of an employer with respect to all of the wages Corporation U paid to workers providing services for Employer. How-

ever, as the section 3401(d)(1) employer of the workers performing services for Employer, Corporation U is subject to all provisions of law (including penalties) applicable in respect of employers with respect to such wages.

(9) *Example 9.* Corporation V and Employer execute and submit a Form 2678, *Employer/Payer Appointment of Agent*, to the Service, requesting approval to authorize Corporation V to report, deposit, and pay taxes with respect to wages it pays, as agent of Employer for purposes of Form 941, *Employer's QUARTERLY Federal Tax Return.* The Form 2678 is approved by the Service and effective for all quarters of 2015. Accordingly, Corporation V reports the wages it pays to individuals performing services for Employer and related tax amounts on Form 941 and Schedule R (Form 941), *Allocation Schedule for Aggregate Form 941 Filers*, filed for each quarter of 2015 under Corporation V's employer identification number. Corporation V is not designated under this section to perform the acts of an employer with respect to all of the wages Corporation V paid to the individuals performing services for Employer for all quarters of 2015. However, as an agent authorized under §31.3504-1(a), Corporation V is subject to all provisions of law (including penalties) applicable in respect of employers for all quarters of 2015 with respect to such wages. Employer also remains subject to all provisions of law (including penalties) applicable in respect of employers for all quarters of 2015 with respect to such wages.

(f) *Effective/applicability date.*—These final regulations are effective for wages or compensation paid by a payor in quarters beginning on or after March 31, 2014. [Reg. §31.3504-2.]

☐ [T.D. 9662, 3-28-2014 (*corrected* 5-30-2014).]

[Reg. §31.3505-1]

§31.3505-1. Liability of third parties paying or providing for wages.—(a) *Personal liability in case of direct payment of wages.*—(1) *In general.*—A lender, surety, or other person—

(i) Who is not an employer for purposes of section 3102 (relating to deduction of tax from wages under the Federal Insurance Contributions Act), section 3202 (relating to deduction of tax from compensation under the Railroad Retirement Tax Act), or section 3402 (relating to deduction of income tax from wages) with respect to an employee or group of employees, and

(ii) Who pays wages on or after January 1, 1967, directly to such employee or group of employees, employed by one or more employers, or to an agent on behalf of such employee or employees,

shall be liable in his own person and estate for payment to the United States of an amount equal to the sum of the taxes required to be deducted and withheld from those wages by the employer under subtitle C of the Code and interest from the due date of the employer's return relating to such taxes for the period in which the wages are paid.

(2) *Example.*—The provisions of this paragraph may be illustrated by the following example:

Example. Pursuant to a wage claim of $200, A, a surety company, paid a net amount of $158 to B, an employee of the X Construction Company. This was done in accordance with A's payment bond covering a private construction job on which B was an employee. If X Construction Company fails to make timely payment or deposit of $42.00, the amount of tax required by subtitle C of the Code to be deducted and withheld from a $200 wage payment to B, A becomes personally liable for $42.00 (*i.e.,* an amount equal to the unpaid taxes), plus interest upon this amount from the due date of X's return.

(b) *Personal liability where funds are supplied.*— (1) *In general.*—A lender, surety, or other person who—

(i) Advances funds to or for the account of an employer for the specific purpose of paying wages of the employees of that employer, and

(ii) At the time the funds are advanced, has actual notice or knowledge (within the meaning of section 6323(i)(1)) that the employer does not intend to, or will not be able to, make timely payment or deposit of the amounts of tax required by subtitle C of the Code to be deducted and withheld by the employer from those wages,

shall be liable in his own person and estate for payment to the United States of an amount equal to the sum of the taxes which are required by subtitle C of the Code to be deducted and withheld from wages paid on or after January 1, 1967, and which are not paid over to the United States by the employer, and interest from the due date of the employer's return relating to such taxes. However, the liability of the lender, surety, or other person shall not exceed 25 percent of the amount supplied by him for the payment of wages. The preceding sentence and the second sentence of section 3505(b) limit the liability of a lender, surety, or other person arising solely by reason of section 3505, and they do not limit the liability which the lender, surety or other person may incur to the United States as a third-party beneficiary of an agreement between the lender, surety, or other person and the employer. The liability of a lender, surety, or other person does not include penalties imposed on the taxpayer.

(2) *Examples.*—The provisions of this paragraph may be illustrated by the following examples:

Example (1). D, a savings and loan association, advances $10,000 to Y for the specific purpose of paying the net wages of Y's employees. D advances those funds with knowledge that Y will not be able to make timely payment of the taxes required to be deducted and withheld from these wages by subtitle C of the Code. Y uses the $10,000 to pay the net wages of his employees but fails to remit withholding taxes under subtitle C in the amount of $2,600. D's liability, under this section, is limited to $2,500, 25 percent of the amount supplied for the payment of wages to Y's employees.

Example (2). E, a loan company, advances $15,000 to F, a contractor, for the specific purpose of paying $20,000 of net wages due to F's employees. E advances those funds with knowledge that F will not be able to make timely payment of the taxes required to be deducted and withheld from these wages by subtitle C of the Code. F applies $5,000 of its own funds toward payment of these wages. The amount of tax required to be deducted and withheld from the gross wages is $4,500. The limitation applicable to E's liability is $3,750 (25% of $15,000). However, because E furnished only a portion of the total net wages, E is liable for $3,375 of the taxes required to be deducted and withheld (4,500 × $15,000/$20,000).

(3) *Ordinary working capital loan.*—The provisions of section 3505(b) do not apply in the case of an ordinary working capital loan made to an employer, even though the person supplying the funds knows that part of the funds advanced may be used to make wage payments in the ordinary course of business. Generally, an ordinary working capital loan is a loan which is made to enable the borrower to meet current obligations as they arise. The person supplying the funds is not obligated to determine the specific use of an ordinary working capital loan or the ability of the employer to pay the amounts of tax required by subtitle C of the Code to be deducted and withheld. However, section 3505(b) is applicable where the person supplying the funds has actual notice or knowledge (within the meaning of section 6323(i)(1)) at the time of the advance that the funds, or a portion thereof, are to be used specifically to pay net wages, whether or not the written agreement under which the funds are advanced states a different purpose. Whether or not a lender has actual notice or knowledge that the funds are to be used to pay net wages, or merely that the funds may be so used, depends upon the facts and circumstances of each case. For example, a lender, who has actual notice or knowledge that the withheld taxes will not be paid, will be deemed to have actual notice or knowledge that the funds are to be used specifically to pay net wages where substantially all of the employer's ordinary operating expenses consist of salaries and wages even though funds for other incidental operating expenses may be supplied pursuant to an agreement described as a working capital loan agreement.

(c) *Definition of other person.*—(1) *In general.*—As used in this section, the term "other person" means any person who directly pays the wages or supplies funds for the specific purpose of paying the wages of an employee or group of employees of another employer. It does not include a person acting only as agent of the employer or as agent of the employees.

(2) *Examples.*—The provisions of this paragraph may be illustrated by the following examples:

Example (1). Pursuant to an agreement between L, a labor union, and M, an employer, M makes monthly vacation payments (of a sum equal to a certain percentage of the remuneration paid to each union member employed by M during the previous month) to a union administered pool plan under which each employee's rights are fully vested and nonforfeitable from the time the money is paid by M. Vacation allowances are accumulated by the plan and distributed to eligible employees during their vacations. L, acting merely as a conduit with respect to these payments, would incur no liability under section 3505.

Example (2). N, a construction company, maintains a payroll account with the O Bank in which N deposits its own funds. Pursuant to an automated payroll service agreement between N and O, O prepares payroll checks and earnings statements for each of N's employees reflecting the net pay due each such employee. These checks are delivered to N for signature. After the checks are signed, O distributes them directly to N's employees on the regularly scheduled pay day. O, acting only in the capacity of a disbursing agent of N's funds, would incur no liability under section 3505 with respect to these payroll distributions. However, O may incur liability under section 3505 in the capacity of a lender if it supplies the funds for the payment of wages.

(d) *Payment of taxes and interest.*—(1) *Procedure for payment.*—A lender, surety, or other person may satisfy the personal liability imposed upon him by section 3505 by executing Form 4219 and filing it, accompanied by payment of the amount of tax and interest due the United States, in accordance with the instructions for the form. In the event the lender, surety, or other person does not satisfy the liability imposed by section 3505, the United States may collect the liability by appropriate civil proceeding commenced within 10 years after assessment of the tax against the employer.

(2) *Effect of payment.*—(i) *In general.*—A person paying the amounts of tax required to be deducted and withheld by subtitle C of the Code as a result of section 3505 and this section is not required to pay the employer's portion of the payroll taxes upon those wages, or file an employer's tax return with respect to those wages, or furnish annual wage and tax statements to the employees.

(ii) *Amounts paid by a lender, surety, or other person.*—Any amounts paid by the lender, surety, or other person to the United States pursuant to this section shall be credited against the liability of the employer on whose behalf those payments are made and shall also reduce the total liability imposed upon the lender, surety, or other person under section 3505 and this section.

(iii) *Amounts paid by the employer.*—Any amounts paid to the United States by an employer and applied to his liability under subtitle C of the Code shall reduce the total liability imposed upon that employer by subtitle C. Such payments will also reduce the liability imposed upon a lender, surety, or other person under section 3505 except that such liability shall not be reduced by any portion of an employer's payment applied against the employer's liability under subtitle C which is in excess of the total liability imposed upon the lender, surety, or other person under section 3505. For example, if a lender supplies $1,000 to an employer for the payment of net wages, upon which $300 withholding tax liability is imposed, a part-payment of $25 by the employer which is applied to this liability would reduce the employer's total liability under subtitle C of the Code by that amount, but the liability imposed upon the lender by section 3505(b) in an amount equal to the withholding tax liability of the employer, which is limited to 25 percent of the amount supplied by him, would remain $250. However, if the employer makes another payment of $200 which is applied to his liability for the withholding taxes, the lender's liability under section 3505 attributable to the withholding taxes is reduced by $175 ($225 less $50 (the amount by which the employer's liability exceeds the lender's liability after application of the limitation)). Thus, after the second payment by the employer, the lender's liability under section 3505(b) is $75 ($250 less $175) plus interest due on the underpayment for the period of underpayment to a maximum of $250, 25 percent of the funds supplied.

(3) *Extensions of the period for collection.*—Prior to the expiration of the 10-year period for collection after assessment against the employer, the lender, surety, or other third party may agree in writing with the district director, service center director, or compliance center director to extend the 10-year period for collection. The period so agreed upon may be extended by subsequent agreements in writing made before the expiration of the period previously agreed upon. If any timely proceeding in court for the collection of the tax and any applicable interest is commenced, the period during which such tax and interest may be collected shall be extended and shall not expire until the liability for the tax (or a judgment against the lender, surety, or other third party arising from such liability) is satisfied or becomes unenforceable.

(e) *Returns required by employers and statements for employees.*—This section does not relieve the employer of the responsibilities imposed upon him to file the returns and supply the receipts and statements required under subchapter A, Chapter 61 of the Code (relating to returns and records).

(f) *Time when liability arises.*—The liability under section 3505 and this section of a lender, surety, or other person paying or supplying funds for the payment of wages is incurred on the last day prescribed for the filing of the employer's Federal employment tax return (deter-

mined without regard to any extension of time) in respect of such wages.

(g) *Effective date.*—These regulations are effective on August 1, 1995. [Reg. § 31.3505-1.]

☐ [*T.D.* 7430, 8-19-76. *Amended by T.D.* 8604, 7-31-95.]

[Reg. § 31.3506-1]

§ 31.3506-1. Companion sitting placement services.—(a) *Definitions.*—(1) *Companion sitting placement service.*—For purposes of this section, the term "companion sitting placement service" means a person (whether or not an individual) engaged in the trade or business of placing sitters with individuals who wish to avail themselves of the sitters' services.

(2) *Sitters.*—For purposes of this section, the term "sitters" means individuals who furnish personal attendance, companionship, or household care services to children or to individuals who are elderly or disabled.

(b) *General rule.*—For purposes of subtitle C of the Internal Revenue Code of 1954 (relating to employment taxes), a companion sitting placement service shall not be treated as the employer of its sitters, and the sitters shall not be treated as the employees of the placement service. However, the rule of the preceding sentence shall apply only if the companion sitting placement service neither pays nor receives (directly or through an agent) the salary or wages of the sitters, but is compensated, if at all, on a fee basis by the sitters or the individuals for whom the sitting is performed.

(c) *Individuals deemed self-employed.*—Any individual who, by reason of this section, is deemed not to be the employee of a companion sitting placement service shall be deemed to be self-employed for purposes of the tax on self-employment income (see sections 1401-1403 and the regulations thereunder in part 1 of this chapter (Income Tax Regulations)).

(d) *Scope of rules.*—The rules of this section operate only to remove sitters and companion sitting placement services from the employee-employer relationship when, under §§ 31.3121(d)-1 and 31.3121(d)-2, that relationship would otherwise exist. Thus, if, under §§ 31.3121(d)-1 and 31.3121(d)-2, a sitter is considered to be the employee of the individual for whom the sitting is performed rather than the employee of the companion sitting placement service, this section has no effect upon that employee-employer relationship.

(e) *Examples.*—The provisions of this section may be illustrated by the following examples:

Example (1). X is an agency that places babysitters with individuals who desire babysitting services. X furnishes all the sitters with an instruction manual regarding their conduct and appearance, requires them to file semimonthly reports, and determines the total fee to be charged the individual for whom the sitting is performed. Individuals who need a babysitter contact the agency, are informed of the charges, and, if agreement is reached, a sitter is sent to perform the services. The sitter collects the entire amount of the charges and remits a percentage to X as a fee for the placement. X is a companion sitting placement service within the meaning of paragraph (a)(1) of this section. Therefore, since the agency does not actually pay or receive the wages of the sitters, X is not treated as the employer of the sitters for purposes of this subtitle. The sitters are deemed to be self-employed for the purpose of the tax imposed by section 1401.

Example (2). Assume the same facts as in example (1), except that the individual for whom the sitting is performed pays to X the entire amount of the charges. X retains a percentage and pays the difference to the sitter. Since X actually receives and pays the wages of the sitters, X is the employer of the sitters.

Example (3). As a service to the community a neighborhood association maintains a list of individuals who are available to babysit. Parents in need of a sitter contact the association and are provided with a list of names and telephone numbers. The association charges no fee for the service and takes no action other than compiling the list of sitters and making it available to members of the community. Issues such as hours of work, amount of payment, and the method by which the services are performed are all resolved between the sitter and parent. A, a parent, used the list to hire B to sit for A's child. B performs the services four days a week in A's home and follows specific instructions given by A. Under § 31.3121(d)-1, B is the employee of A rather than the employee of the neighborhood association. Consequently, this section does not apply and B remains the employee of A.

(f) *Effective date.*—This section shall apply to remuneration received after December 31, 1974. [Reg. § 31.3506-1.]

☐ *[T.D. 7691, 4-8-80.]*

[Reg. § 31.3507-1]

§ 31.3507-1. Advance payments of earned income credit.—(a) *General rule.*—(1) *In general.*— Every employer paying wages after June 30, 1979, to an employee with respect to whom an earned income credit advance payment certificate is in effect must, at the time of paying the wages, also pay the employee the advance earned income credit amount of that employee. For the purposes of applying this section and § 31.3507-2—

(i) In the case of an individual who receives wages which are subject to income tax withholding, the term "employee" has the same meaning as set forth in section 3401(c) and the regulations thereunder, and the term "wages" has the same meaning as set forth in sections 3401(a) and 3402(e) and the regulations under those sections; and

(ii) In the case of an individual who does not receive wages which are subject to income

tax withholding, but who receives wages which are subject to employee FICA taxes, the term "employee" has the same meaning as set forth in section 3121(d) and the regulations thereunder and the term "wages" has the same meaning as set forth in section 3121(a) and the regulations thereunder.

An individual not having wages subject to either income tax withholding or employee FICA taxes is not entitled to advance payments of the earned income credit. Moreover, notwithstanding subdivisions (i) and (ii) of this paragraph (a)(1), employers are not required to pay advance earned income credit amounts to agricultural workers paid on a daily basis. For this purpose an "agricultural worker" is an employee who performs "agricultural labor", as that term is defined in section 3121(g) and the regulations thereunder.

(2) *Cross references.*—For determination of the advance earned income credit amount of an employee, see paragraph (b) of this section. For rules relating to the treatment of the payment of an employee's advance earned income credit amount as equivalent to payment by the employer of withholding and FICA taxes, see paragraph (c) of this section. For rules describing the earned income credit advance payment certificate, see § 31.3507-2(a) and (b). For rules relating to the employee's furnishing of the earned income credit advance payment certificate and the payroll periods for which the certificate is effective, see § 31.3507-2(c) and (d).

(b) *Advance earned income credit amount.*—The advance earned income credit amount of an employee is determined, with respect to any payroll period, on the basis of the employee's wages from the employer for the period and in accordance with the advance amount tables prescribed by the Commissioner of Internal Revenue and then in effect for the payroll period. See, however, paragraph (c)(2) of this section. The advance amount paid is reflected on the employee's W-2 form as a separate item (and neither as a reduction of withholding nor an increase in compensation). For purposes of applying this section and § 31.3507-2, the term "payroll period" has the meaning set forth in section 3401(b) and the regulations thereunder. As required by section 3507(c)(2)(A), these advance amount tables must be similar in form to, and coordinated with, the tables prescribed under section 3402 (relating to income tax collected at the source). Sections 3507(c)(2)(B) and 3507(c)(2)(C) provide, respectively, separate rules for the treatment in the advance amount tables of the advance earned income credit of the following two separate classes of employees:

(1) Employees who are not married (within the meaning of section 143), or employees whose spouses do not have an earned income credit advance payment certificate in effect; and

(2) Employees whose spouses have an earned income credit advance payment certificate in effect.

Reg. § 31.3507-1(b)(2)

If during the calendar year an employer has paid an employee amounts of earned income, within the meaning of section 43(c)(2)(A)(i), which in the aggregate equal or exceed $10,000, the employer need not make further payments of advance earned income credit to the employee during that calendar year.

(c) *Payment of advance earned income credit amount as payment of withholding and FICA taxes.*—(1) *In general.*—(i) The provisions of this paragraph (c) apply for all purposes of the Internal Revenue Code of 1954. Payments of advance earned income credit amounts pursuant to paragraph (a)(1) of this section do not constitute the payment of compensation. These payments by the employer are treated as made—

(A) First, from the aggregate amount, with respect to all employees, required to be deducted and withheld for the payroll period under section 3401 (relatinig to income tax withholding);

(B) Second, from the aggregate amount, with respect to all employees, required to be deducted for the payroll period under section 3102 (relating to employee FICA taxes); and

(C) Third, from the aggregate amount of the taxes imposed for the payroll period under section 3111 (relating to employer FICA taxes). For purposes of the requirements of sections 3401, 3102, and 3111, as the case may be, and 6302, amounts equal to the advance earned income credit amounts paid to employees are treated as if paid to the Treasury Department on the day on which the wages (and advance amounts) are paid to the employees. The employer must report the payment and treatment of the advance amounts on the employer's Form 941, 941E, 942, or 943, as the case may be, in accordance with the applicable instructions.

(ii) The provisions of paragraph (c)(1)(i) of this section may be illustrated by the following example:

Example. Employer X has ten employees, each of whom is entitled to advance earned income credit payment of $10. The total of advance amounts paid by the employer to the ten employees for the payroll period is $100. The total of income tax withholding for the payroll period is $90. The total of employee FICA taxes for the payroll period is $61.30, and the total of employer FICA taxes for the payroll period is also $61.30. Under the rules of paragraph (c)(1)(i) of this section, the total of advance amounts paid to employees is treated as if X had paid the Treasury Department on the day X paid the employees' wages: first, the $90 aggregate amount of income tax withholding; and second, $10 of the aggregate amount of employee FICA tax. X remains liable only for $112.60 of the aggregate FICA tax [$51.30 + $61.30 = $112.60].

(2) *Advance payments exceeding taxes due.*—(i) If, for any payroll period, the aggregate amount of advance earned income credit amounts required to be paid by an employer under paragraph (a)(1) of this section exceeds the sum of the amounts for the payroll period referred to in paragraphs (c)(1)(i)(A) through (C) of this section, the employer reduces each advance amount paid for the payroll period by an amount which bears the same ratio to the excess of the advance amounts as the subject advance amount bears to the aggregate of advance amounts for the payroll period. However, this paragraph (c)(2) does not apply if the employer makes the election provided by paragraph (c)(3) of this section.

(ii) The provisions of paragraph (c)(2) of this section may be illustrated by the following example.

Example. Assume the same facts as the example in paragraph (c)(1)(ii) of this section, except that the employer is a state government which does not pay FICA taxes. Under these facts, the advance amounts would be $10 greater than the $90 total of income tax withholding for the payroll period. Assume 10 employees each receiving $10 in advance payments. Under the rule of this paragraph (c)(2), the employer X reduces the amount of the advance amount paid to each employee by 1/10, computed as follows:

$$\frac{\$10}{\$100} = 1/10$$

This is the same result as would be obtained by reducing the advance payment of $10 for each of the ten employees by one-tenth $^{10}/_{100}$ of the $10 excess or $1.00.

(3) *Election to treat excess amounts as advance tax payment.*—In lieu of reducing advance payments under paragraph (c)(2) of this section, an employer may elect under this paragraph (c)(3) to pay in full all advance earned income credit amounts. However, if no election is made, the employer is required to reduce advance amounts paid in accordance with paragraph (c)(2) of this section. The election, if made, applies to all advance earned income credit amounts required to be paid for the payroll period. The employer reflects the election of the employer's Form 941, 941E, 942, or 943, as the case may be, and must specify (with supporting computations) the amount of the excess of the advance amounts paid and the payroll period to which the excess relates. Separate elections may be made for separate payroll periods. The excess of advance amounts paid is treated as an advance payment by the employer of employment taxes described in subdivisions (i) through (iii) of this paragraph (c)(3) and due for the period reported on the Form 941, 941E, 942, or 943 which includes the payroll period during which the excess amounts were paid. The amount of the excess advance payment is applied to the amounts of the employer's liability—

(i) First, for income tax withholding due under section 3401 for the reporting period in which the payment is made;

(ii) Second, for employee FICA taxes due under section 3102 for the reporting period in which the payment is made; and

(iii) Third, for employer FICA taxes due under section 3111 for the reporting period in which the payment is made.

If the amount of the employment taxes (as described) for which the employer remains liable for the reporting period in which the excess payment is made is less than the excess payment, the employer may claim a refund of that portion of the excess amount paid which exceeds the employer's remaining liability for these taxes for the reporting period. This refund may be claimed, in the same manner as a refund of wage withholding taxes paid by the employer under section 3401, on the employer's Form 941, 941E, 942, or 943, as the case may be, for the reporting period. In the absence of a claim for refund, that portion of the excess amount will be applied by the Internal Revenue Service against the employer's liability for employment taxes reported on the employer's Form 941, 941E, 942, or 943, as the case may be, filed for the next reporting period.

(4) *Failure to make advance payments.*—The failure to pay an employee, at the time required by paragraph (a)(1) of this section, all or any part of an advance earned income credit amount as required by this section is treated, for all purposes including penalties, as a failure by the employer as of that time to deduct and withhold under chapter 24 of the Internal Revenue Code of 1954 an amount equal to the advance amount (or part thereof) not paid. This treatment applies to the failure to pay an advance amount to an eligible employee without regard to whether the employee is ultimately not entitled to claim the earned income credit (in full or in part) on a return for the year, so long as the employee has a valid earned income credit advance payment certificate in effect with the employer at the time when the wages were paid. If an employer fails to pay an advance earned income credit amount as required under this section, the advance amount will not be collected by the Internal Revenue Service from the employer if the employer has properly withheld and deposited all income taxes and FICA taxes applicable with respect to the employee. However, such amount may be collected if the employer has not properly withheld and deposited these taxes. [Reg. §31.3507-1.]

☐ [*T.D.* 7766, 1-28-81 (previously issued as Temporary Reg. §38.3507-1 by *T.D.* 7619).]

[Reg. §31.3507-2]

§31.3507-2. Earned income credit advance payment certificates.—(a) *Definition.*—For the purposes of this section and §31.3507-1, an earned income credit advance payment certificate is a statement furnished by an employee to the employer which—

(1) Certifies that the employee reasonably expects to be eligible to receive the earned income credit provided by section 43 for the employee's last taxable year under subtitle A of the Internal Revenue Code of 1954 which begins in the calendar year in which the wages are paid;

(2) Certifies that the employee does not have an earned income credit advance payment

certificate in effect for the calendar year (in which the wages are paid) with respect to the payment of wages by another employer; and

(3) States if the employee's spouse has an earned income credit advance payment certificate in effect with any employer. For the rule for determining if an employee's spouse has a certificate in effect, see paragraph (c)(3) of this section.

(b) *Form and content of earned income credit advance payment certificate.*—(1) *In general.*—Form W-5 (Earned Income Credit Advance Payment Certificate) is the prescribed form for the earned income credit advance payment certificate. The Form W-5 must be prepared in accordance with the instructions applicable thereto and must set forth fully and clearly the data therein called for. In lieu of the prescribed form, a form the provisions of which are identical with those of the prescribed form may be used.

(2) *Invalid certificates.*—A Form W-5 does not meet the requirements of section 3507 or this section and is invalid if it is not completed or signed or contains an alteration or unauthorized addition (as defined in §31.3402(f)(5)-1(b)(1) and (2)). Any earned income credit advance payment certificate which the employee clearly indicates to be false by oral statement or written statement to the employer must be treated by the employer as a certificate which is invalid as of the date of the employee's statement. For purposes of the preceding sentence, the term "employer" includes any individual authorized by the employer to receive earned income credit advance payment certificates or to make payroll distributions. If an employer receives from an employee an invalid certificate, the employer must consider it a nullity with respect to all payments of wages thereafter to the employee and must inform the employee of the certificate's invalidity. The employer is not required to ascertain whether any completed and signed earned income credit advance payment certificate is correct. However, the employer should inform the district director if the employer has reason to believe that the certificate contains any incorrect statement.

(c) *When earned income credit advance payment certificate takes effect.*—(1) *No previous certificate.*—An earned income credit advance payment certificate furnished the employer where no previous certificate is or has been in effect with the employer for that employee for the calendar year takes effect with—

(i) The date of the beginning of the first payroll period ending on or after the date on which the certificate is received by the employer;

(ii) The date of the first payment of wages made without regard to a payroll period on or after the date on which the certificate is received by the employer; or

(iii) The first day of the calendar year for which the certificate is furnished, if that day is later than the otherwise applicable effective date specified in subdivision (i) or (ii) of this paragraph (c)(1).

Reg. §31.3507-2(c)(1)(iii)

(2) *Previous certificate.*—Except as otherwise provided in this paragraph (c)(2), an earned income credit advance payment certificate furnished the employer where a previous certificate is or has been in effect with the employer for that employee for the calendar year takes effect on the date of the first payment of wages made on or after the first status determination date (as defined in paragraph (c)(4) of this section) occurring at least thirty days after the date on which the certificate is received by the employer. However, if the employer so chooses, the employer may treat the certificate as effective on the date of any payment of wages made on or after the date on which the certificate is received by the employer (without regard to any status determination date).

(3) *Certificate of spouse.*—For the sole purpose of applying paragraph (a)(3) of this section, in determining if a certificate is in effect with respect to an employee's spouse, the spouse's certificate is treated as then in effect if the spouse's certificate will be or is reasonably expected to be in effect on the first status determination date following the date on which the employer receives the employee's certificate.

(4) *Status determination date.*—For the purposes of this section, the term "status determination date" means January 1, May 1, July 1, and October 1 of each year.

(d) *Period during which certificate remains in effect; change of status.*—(1) *Period certificate remains in effect.*—An earned income credit advance payment certificate which takes effect during a calendar year continues in effect with respect to the employee only during that calendar year and until revoked by the employee or until another certificate takes effect. See paragraphs (d)(2) and (c)(2) of this section.

(2) *Change of status.*—(i) *Revocation of certificate.*—If, after an employee has furnished an earned income credit advance payment certificate—

(A) The employee no longer wishes to receive advance earned income credit payments; or

(B) There has been a change of circumstances which has the effect of either making the employee ineligible for the earned income credit for the taxable year or causing a certificate to be in effect for the employee's spouse,

then the employee must revoke the certificate previously furnished by furnishing the employer a new certificate (Form W-5 or identical form) in revocation of the earlier certificate. Depending upon the nature of the change of circumstances, the employer may be required, pursuant to the new certificate, to pay further advance earned income credit amounts to the employee (but in different amounts than previously paid to the employer). The Form W-5 (or identical form) must be prepared in accordance with the instructions applicable thereto and must set forth fully and clearly the data therein called for. In the case of revocation due to change of circumstances, the new certificate in revocation must be delivered to the employer within ten days after the employee first learns of the change of circumstances. The new certificate is effective under the rules provided in paragraph (c)(2) of this section for later certificates. A new certificate furnished by an employee which is invalid within the meaning of paragraph (b)(2) of this section is considered a nullity with respect to all payments of wages thereafter to the employee. The prior certificate of the employee remains in effect, unless the employee clearly indicates by an oral or written statement to the employer that the prior certificate is invalid. See paragraph (b)(2) of this section. The employer is not required to ascertain whether any employee has experienced a change of circumstances described in subdivision (i)(B) of this paragraph which necessitates the employee's furnishing a new certificate. However, the employer should inform the district director if the employer has reason to believe that an employee has experienced a change of circumstances as described if the employee does not deliver a new certificate to the employer within the ten day period.

(ii) *Change in spouse's certificate.*—If, after an employee has furnished an earned income credit advance payment certificate stating that a certificate is in effect for the spouse of the employee, the certificate of the spouse is no longer in effect, the employee may furnish the employer with a new certificate which reflects this change of circumstances. [Reg. § 31.3507-2.]

☐ [*T.D.* 7766, 1-28-81 (previously issued as Temporary Reg. § 38.3507-2 by *T.D.* 7619).]

[The next page is 62,351.]

MISCELLANEOUS EXCISE TAXES

Retail Excise Taxes

See p. 20,601 for regulations not amended to reflect law changes

[Reg. §48.0-1]

§48.0-1. Introduction.—The regulations in this part 48 are designated "Manufacturers and Retailers Excise Tax Regulations." The regulations relate to the excise taxes imposed by chapter[s] 31 and 32 of the Internal Revenue Code. Chapter 31 (relating to retail taxes) imposes tax on certain luxury items, special fuels, fuel used in commercial transportation on inland waterways, and heavy trucks and trailers. Chapter 32 (relating to manufacturers taxes) imposes tax on gas guzzler automobiles, highway-type tires, taxable fuel, aviation fuel, coal, certain vaccines, sporting goods, and taxable medical devices. Although chapter 32 also imposes a tax on firearms, this tax is under the jurisdiction of the Bureau of Alcohol, Tobacco, and Firearms. See part 40 of this chapter for regulations relating to returns, payments, and deposits of taxes imposed by chapters 31 and 32 (other than the tax on firearms imposed by section 4181). [Reg. §48.0-1.]

☐ [T.D. 8442, 10-21-92. *Amended by T.D. 8659, 3-13-96 and T.D. 9604, 12-5-2012.*]

[Reg. §48.0-2]

§48.0-2. General definitions and attachment of tax.—(a) *Meaning of terms.*—As used in the regulations in this part, unless otherwise expressly indicated—

(1) The terms defined in the provisions of law contained in the regulations in this part shall have the meanings so assigned to them.

(2) [Reserved]

(3) The term "calendar quarter" means a period of 3 calendar months ending on March 31, June 30, September 30, or December 31.

(4)(i) The term "manufacturer" includes any person who produces a taxable article from scrap, salvage, or junk material, or from new or raw material, by processing, manipulating, or changing the form of an article or by combining or assembling two or more articles. The term also includes a "producer" and an "importer." An "importer" of a taxable article is any person who brings such an article into the United States from a source outside the United States, or who withdraws such an article from a customs bonded warehouse for sale or use in the United States. If the nominal importer of a taxable article is not its beneficial owner (for example, the nominal importer is a customs broker engaged by the beneficial owner), the beneficial owner is the "importer" of the article for purposes of chapter 32 and is liable for tax on his sale or use of the article in the United States. See section 4219 and the regulations thereunder for the circumstances under which sales by persons other than the manufacturer or importer are subject to the manufacturers excise tax.

(ii) Under certain circumstances, as where a person manufactures or produces a taxable article for another person who furnishes materials under an agreement whereby the person who furnished the materials retains title thereto and to the finished article, the person for whom the taxable article is manufactured or produced, and not the person who actually manufactures or produces it, will be considered the manufacturer.

(iii) A manufacturer who sells a taxable article in a knockdown condition is liable for the tax as a manufacturer. Whether the person who buys such component parts and assembles a taxable article from them will also be liable for tax as a further manufacturer of a taxable article will depend on the relative amount of labor, material, and overhead required to assemble the completed article and on whether the article is assembled for a business or personal use. See section 4218 and the regulations thereunder.

(5) The term "sale" means an agreement whereby the seller transfers the property (that is, the title or the substantial incidents of ownership) in goods to the buyer for a consideration called the price, which may consist of money, services, or other things.

(6) The term "taxable article" means any article taxable under section 4041 or chapter 32, Subtitle D, of the Code.

(7) The term "vendor" includes a lessor except that, with respect to the manufacturers excise taxes, this rule applies only where the lessor is also the manufacturer of the article.

(8) The term "purchaser" includes a lessee except that, with respect to the manufacturers excise taxes, this rule applies only where the lessor is also the manufacturer of the article.

(9) The term "exporter" means the person named as shipper or consignor in the export bill of lading.

(10) The term "exportation" means the severance of an article from the mass of things belonging with the United States with the intention of uniting it with the mass of things belonging within some foreign country or within a possession of the United States.

(11) The term "possession of the United States" includes Guam, the Midway Islands, Palmyra, the Panama Canal Zone, the Commonwealth of Puerto Rico, American Samoa, the Virgin Islands, and Wake Island.

(b) *Attachment of tax.*—(1) For purposes of this part, the manufacturers excise tax generally attaches when the title to the article sold passes from the manufacturer to a purchaser, and the retailers excise tax generally attaches when the title to the article sold passes from the retailer to a purchaser.

(2) When title passes is dependent upon the intention of the parties as gathered from the

contract of sale and the attendant circumstances. In the absence of expressed intention, the legal rules of presumption followed in the jurisdiction where the sale is made govern in determining when title passes.

(3) In the case of a sale on credit, the tax attaches whether or not the purchase price is actually collected.

(4) Where a consignor (such as a manufacturer) consigns articles to a consignee (such as a dealer), retaining ownership in them until they are disposed of by the consignee, title does not pass, and the tax does not attach, until sale by the consignee. Where the relationship between a manufacturer and a dealer is that of principal and agent, title does not pass, and the tax does not attach, until sale by the dealer.

(5) In the case of a lease, an installment sale, a conditional sale, or a chattel mortgage arrangement or similar arrangement creating a security interest, a proportionate part of the tax attaches to each payment. See section 4217 and the regulations thereunder for a limitation on the amount of tax payable on lease payments.

(6) In the case of use by the manufacturer, the tax attaches at the time the use begins. [Reg. § 48.0-2.]

☐ [*T.D.* 6408. *Amended by T.D.* 7536, 3-27-78 *and T.D.* 8879, 3-30-2000.]

[Reg. § 48.0-3]

§ 48.0-3. Exemption certificates.—Several sections of the regulations in this part, relating to sales exempt from retailers or manufacturers excise tax, require the retailer or manufacturer (as the case may be) to obtain an exemption certificate from the purchaser to substantiate the exempt character of the sale. Many of these sections also contain specimen forms of acceptable exemption certificates. However, any form of exemption certificate will be acceptable if it includes all the information required to be contained in such a certificate by the pertinent sections of the regulations in this part. If it contains all the required information, a form of exemption certificate that is processed by data processing equipment is acceptable. [Reg. § 48.0-3.]

☐ [*T.D.* 7536, 3-27-78. *Amended by T.D.* 8043, 8-8-85.]

[Reg. § 48.4041-0]

§ 48.4041-0. Applicability of regulations relating to diesel fuel after December 31, 1993.—Sections 48.4041-3 through 48.4041-3 do not apply to sales or uses of diesel fuel after December 31, 1993. For rules relating to the diesel fuel tax imposed by section 4041 after that date, see § 48.4082-4. [Reg. § 48.4041-0.]

☐ [*T.D.* 8659, 3-13-96.]

[Reg. § 48.4041-3]

§ 48.4041-3. Application of tax on sales of special motor fuel for use in motor vehicles and motorboats.—(a) *In general.*—The tax imposed by paragraph (2)(A) of section 4041(a), (or before April 1, 1983, paragraph (1) of section 4041 (b)),

applies to the taxable sale of special motor fuel by any person to an owner, lessee, or other operator of a motor vehicle or motorboat, for use as a fuel in the motor vehicle or motorboat. The tax does not apply to special motor fuel sold for use on or after April 1, 1983, and before October 1, 1988, in an off-highway business use.

(b) *Liability for tax.*—The tax on the taxable sale of special motor fuel is payable by the person who sells the special motor fuel to the owner, lessee, or other operator of a motor vehicle or motorboat.

(c) *Rate of tax.*—(1) *In general.*—Tax is imposed on the sale of special motor fuel at the rate applicable on the date on which the special motor fuel is sold. See § 48.4041-1(b)(2) for rates. The test of taxability at the rates specified in § 48.4041-1(b)(2)(i)(A) and (ii)(A) is whether the fuel is to be used in a motor vehicle or motorboat. For purposes of paragraphs (c)(2) and (3) of this section, the term "qualified business use" has the same meaning as that given to the term "off-highway business use" by section 6421(d)(2).

(2) *Special motor fuel sold for use as a fuel in a motor vehicle.*—Tax at the rates specified in paragraphs (b)(2)(i)(A) and (ii)(A) of § 48.4041-1 applies in the case of the sale of special motor fuel for use as a fuel in a motor vehicle. Tax at the rates specified in that section applies regardless of whether the motor vehicle is a highway vehicle. However, a reduced rate of tax from that imposed by paragraphs (b)(2)(i)(A) of § 48.4041-1 is allowed by paragraph (b)(2)(i)(C) of § 48.4041-1 if special motor fuel is sold for use in a qualified business use. An exemption from the tax imposed by paragraph (b)(2)(ii)(A) of § 48.4041-1 is allowed by paragraph (b)(2)(ii)(C) of § 48.4041-1 if the special motor fuel is sold for use in an off-highway business use.

(3) *Special motor fuel sold for use as fuel in a motorboat.*—Tax at the rates specified in paragraphs (b)(2)(i)(A) and (ii)(A) of § 48.4041-1 applies in the case of the sale of special motor fuel for use as fuel in a motorboat. The qualified business use reduced rate of tax set forth in paragraph (b)(2)(i)(C) of § 48.4041-1 and the off-highway business use exemption set forth in paragraph (b)(2)(ii)(C) of § 48.4041-1 are not applicable to motorboats unless the motorboat is a vessel employed in the fisheries or whaling business. See section 6421(d)(2)(B).

(d) *Example.*—Application of the tax to the sale of special motor fuels may be illustrated by the following example.

Example. The N Company is engaged in the manufacture of ceramic products. It has a vehicle which is used to haul clay from a clay pit to its factory. This vehicle has not been registered for highway use and under the applicable State law is not required to be registered for highway use since none of the hauling of clay is done on public highways. The N Company also uses a ditch digging machine in the vicinity of the clay pit for the construction of drains. A fork lift truck is used to move cartons of merchandise from place to place inside the company's warehouse and to assist in the loading of merchandise onto the company's highway trucks for delivery to purchasers. The highway trucks are registered by the State for use on highways. Special motor fuel is used for the operation of all of these items of equipment. Before April 1, 1983, the special motor fuel sold for use as a fuel in the registered highway trucks is subject to tax at the rate specified in § 48.4041-1(b)(2)(i)(A). On or after January 1, 1979, and before April 1, 1983, the special motor fuel sold for use as a fuel in the unregistered truck used to haul clay from the pit to the factory and in the fork lift truck, assuming both of these are used in qualified business uses, is subject to tax at the rate specified in § 48.4041-1(b)(2)(i)(C). If the unregistered truck and forklift are not used in qualified business uses, then the special motor fuel sold for use in these vehicles is taxable at the rate specified in § 48.4041-1(b)(2)(i)(A) since both are motor vehicles. No tax is payable with respect to the special motor fuel sold for use in the ditch digging machine since that machine is not a motor vehicle. On and after April 1, 1983, and before October 1, 1988, special motor fuel sold for use in the registered trucks is taxable at the rate specified in § 48.4041-1(b)(2)(ii)(A) because the trucks are motor vehicles. On and after April 1, 1983, and before October 1, 1988, special motor fuel sold for use in the unregistered truck and the fork lift, assuming that both vehicles are used in off-highway business uses, is exempt from tax as specified in § 48.4041-1(b)(2)(ii)(C). If the unregistered truck and fork lift are not used in off-highway business uses, then the special motor fuel sold for use in these vehicles is taxable at the rate specified in § 48.4041-1(b)(2)(ii)(A) since both are motor vehicles. No tax is payable with respect to the special motor fuel sold for use in the ditch digging machine since that machine is not a motor vehicle.

(e) *Cross reference.*—(1) For the tax applicable in certain cases based on the use of special motor fuel as a fuel in a motor vehicle or motorboat, see § 48.4041-6.

(2) For the definition of the terms "highway", "motor vehicle", "special motor fuel", and "registered", see paragraphs (a), (c), (f), and (i) of § 48.4041-8. For the definition of the term "off-highway business use", see section 6421(d)(2).

(3) For the exemption from tax with respect to special motor fuel sold for use on a farm for farming purposes or as supplies for vessels, see §§ 48.4041-9 and 48.4041-10, respectively.

(4) For credit or refund of tax paid on special motor fuel resold or used otherwise than for the purpose for which purchased, see section 6427(a). [Reg. § 48.4041-3.]

☐ [*T.D.* 8066, 1-2-86.]

[Reg. § 48.4041-4]

§ 48.4041-4. Application of tax on sales of liquid for use as fuel in aircraft in noncommercial aviation.—(a) *In general.*—The taxes imposed by subparagraphs (1)(A) and (2)(A) of section 4041(c) apply to the taxable sale of any liquid by any person to an owner, lessee, or other operator of an aircraft, for use as a fuel in the aircraft in noncommercial aviation.

(b) *Liability of tax.*—The tax on the taxable sale of any liquid used as fuel in aircraft in noncommercial aviation is payable by the person who sells the liquid to the owner, lessee, or operator of an aircraft in noncommercial aviation.

(c) *Rate of tax.*—Tax is imposed on the sale of liquids used as fuel in aircraft in noncommercial aviation at the rate applicable on the date on which the liquid is sold. See § 48.4041-1(b)(3) for rates.

(d) *Cross references.*—(1) For the tax applicable on the basis of the use of fuel in an aircraft in noncommercial aviation, see § 48.4041-6.

(2) For the definition of the term "noncommercial aviation", see paragraph (j) of § 48.4041-8.

(3) For the exemption of tax with respect to liquids used as fuel in aircraft in noncommercial aviation sold for use on a farm for farming purposes or as supplies for vessels or aircraft, see §§ 48.4041-9 and 48.4041-10, respectively. For tax-free sales if sellers and purchasers are registered, see § 48.4041-11.

(4) For credit or refund of tax paid on fuel used in noncommercial aviation that is resold or used otherwise than for the purpose for which purchased, see section 6427(a).

(e) *Effective date.*—The provisions of this section shall apply to sales or uses occurring before October 1, 1980, and to sales or uses occurring on or after September 1, 1982, and ending before January 1, 1988. [Reg. § 48.4041-4.]

☐ [*T.D.* 8066, 1-2-86.]

[Reg. § 48.4041-5]

§ 48.4041-5. Sales of diesel and special motor fuels and fuel for use in aircraft; rules of general application.—(a) *Taxability of liquid fuel delivered into purchaser's tanks.*—(1) *Fuel supply tanks.*—(i) The sale of diesel fuel to an owner, lessee, or other operator of a diesel-powered highway vehicle, or of special motor fuel to an owner, lessee, or other operator of a motor vehicle or motorboat, or of fuel to an owner, lessee, or other operator of an aircraft used in noncommercial aviation is considered a taxable sale of the liquid fuel if the liquid fuel is delivered by the seller into the fuel supply tank of the vehicle, motorboat, or aircraft. For purposes of this paragraph (a), liquid fuel sold at a location unattended by the seller (such as under a cardlock or meter system) on or after January 2, 1986, is considered to be delivered into the fuel supply tank by the seller except as provided in paragraph (a)(1)(ii) of this section. In this regard, see section 6427(a) for credit or refund of tax if liquid fuel acquired in a transaction subject to tax is used in a nontaxable use.

(ii) If the seller maintains special devices at the unattended location to account accurately for sales of liquid fuel for nontaxable uses (such as assigning a separate "nontaxable" meter or, in a cardlock system, issuing a special "nontaxable" card to a customer who regularly purchases fuel for nontaxable uses), then such sales of liquid fuel shall be considered nontaxable. The seller must maintain sufficient records of such nontaxable sales and include in these records the name of the purchaser, the date of the purchase, and the quantity of fuel purchased in each sale.

(2) *Bulk tanks.*—The sale of diesel fuel to an owner, lessee, or other operator of a diesel-powered highway vehicle, or of special motor fuel to an owner, lessee, or other operator of a motor vehicle or motorboat, or of fuel to an owner, lessee, or other operator of an aircraft used in noncommercial aviation is considered a taxable sale of the liquid fuel if—

(i) The liquid fuel is delivered by the seller into a bulk supply tank (or other container) that is not the fuel supply tank of a vehicle, motorboat, or aircraft; and

(ii) The purchaser furnishes a written statement to the seller before or at the time of the sale stating that the entire quantity of the liquid fuel covered by the sale is for a taxable purpose as a fuel in such a vehicle, motorboat, or aircraft. If the purchaser fails to provide the written statement required by paragraph (a)(2)(ii) of this section, the purchaser is liable for the tax on the later taxable sale or use. If a purchaser acquires both fuel that is to be used for taxable purposes and fuel that is to be used for nontaxable purposes, and the fuel that is to be used for taxable purposes is stored in a different storage tank (or container) from the tank used to store the fuel to be used for nontaxable purposes, the written statement described in paragraph (a)(2)(ii) of this section will relate to the fuel to be used for taxable purposes if proper records are kept by the purchaser that sufficiently identify the tanks (or containers) into which tax-paid fuel is delivered and the quantities of fuel delivered into those tanks (or containers). If only occasional sales for delivery into a bulk storage tank (or other container) are made to a purchaser, a separate statement must be furnished for each order. However, if sales are regularly or frequently made to a purchaser, a written statement covering all orders for a specified period not to exceed 12 calendar quarters is acceptable.

(b) *Sales for resale and to consignees.*—(1) A sale to a dealer for resale is not subject to tax even if it is known at the time of the sale that the liquid fuel will be resold by the dealer for use as a fuel in a diesel-powered highway vehicle, motor vehicle, motorboat, or aircraft.

(2) The tax is payable by the person who makes the taxable sale. If a taxable liquid fuel is consigned to a person for sale and the consignor retains ownership in the liquid fuel until it is disposed of by the consignee, the consignor is the person liable for the tax when a taxable sale of the liquid fuel is made by the consignee. If the consignor transfers ownership in the taxable liquid fuel to the consignee before sale of the liquid fuel by the consignee, the consignee is the person liable for the tax upon a subsequent taxable sale of the liquid. However, if ownership of the liquid fuel is transferred back to the consignor or to another person before a taxable sale is made, as described in paragraph (a) of this section, and thereafter a taxable sale of the liquid fuel is made by such person or by another person acting as the person's agent, such person is liable for the tax. See paragraph (d) of §48.4041-8 for definition of the term "taxable liquid fuel." [Reg. §48.4041-5.]

    ☐ [*T.D.* 8066, 1-2-86. *Amended by T.D.* 8154, 8-24-87.]

[Reg. §48.4041-6]

§48.4041-6. **Application of tax on use of taxable liquid fuel.**—(a) *In general.*—(1) *Diesel fuel.*—(i) If, before April 1, 1983, a person acquires any diesel fuel by any means other than through a transaction subject to tax under section 4041(a)(1) and uses it as a fuel in a diesel powered highway vehicle, the person is liable for a tax under section 4041(a)(2) on the quantity of diesel fuel so used at the appropriate rate set forth in §48.4041-1(b)(1)(i). If a person acquired any diesel fuel through a transaction which is subject to tax at the rate set forth in paragraph (b)(1)(i)(C) or (D) of §48.4041-1, and uses it for a use described in paragraph (b)(1)(i)(A) or (B) of §48.4041-1 the person is liable for an additional tax under section 4041(a)(2) on the quantity of diesel fuel so used. See §48.4041-1(b)(1)(i)(E), (F), or (G) for the applicable rate of tax. See section 6427(a) for credit or refund of tax where diesel fuel acquired in a transaction subject to tax at the rate set forth in paragraph (b)(1)(i)(A) or (B) of §48.4041-1 is used as described in paragraph(b)(1)(i)(C) or (D) of §48.4041-1 or in a nontaxable use.

(ii) On or after April 1, 1983, and before August 1, 1984, if a person acquires any diesel fuel by any means other than through a transaction subject to tax under section 4041(a)(1)(A) and uses it as a fuel in a diesel-powered highway vehicle, the person is liable for a tax under section 4041(a)(1)(B) on the quantity of diesel fuel so used at the appropriate rate set forth in paragraph (b)(1)(ii) of §48.4041-1. If a person acquired any diesel fuel through a transaction for which no tax is imposed by reason of paragraph (b)(1)(ii)(C) of §48.4041-1 and uses it in other than a nontaxable use, the person is liable for a tax under section 4041(a)(1)(B) on the quantity of fuel so used. See paragraph (b)(1)(ii)(D) or (E) or §48.4041-1 for the applicable rate of tax. See section 6427(a) for credit or refund of tax where diesel fuel acquired in a transaction subject to tax at the rate set forth in paragraph (b)(1)(ii)(A) of §48.4041-1 is used as described in paragraph (b)(1)(ii)(C) of §48.4041-1 or in another nontaxable use.

(iii) On or after August 1, 1984, and before October 1, 1988, if a person acquires any diesel fuel by any means other than through a transaction subject to tax under section 4041(a)(1)(A) and uses it as a fuel in a diesel-powered highway vehicle, the person is liable for a tax under section 4041(a)(1)(B) on the quantity of diesel fuel so used at the appropriate rate set forth in paragraph (b)(1)(iii) of § 48.4041-1. If a person acquired any diesel fuel through a transaction for which no tax is imposed by reason of paragraph (b)(1)(iii)(C) of § 48.4041-1 and uses it in other than a nontaxable use, the person is liable for a tax under section 4041(a)(1)(B) on the quantity of fuel so used. See paragraph (b)(1)(iii)(D) of § 48.4041-1 for the applicable rate of tax. See section 6427(a) for credit or refund of tax where diesel fuel acquired in a transaction subject to tax at the rate set forth in paragraph (b)(1)(iii)(A) of § 48.4041-1 is used as described in paragraph (b)(1)(iii)(C) of § 48.4041-1 or in another nontaxable use.

(2) *Special motor fuel.*—(i) On or after January 1, 1979, and before April 1, 1983, if a person acquired any special motor fuel by any means other than through a transaction subject to tax under section 4041(b)(1) and uses it as a fuel in a motor vehicle or motorboat, the person is liable for a tax under section 4041(b)(2) on the quantity of special motor fuel so used at the appropriate rate set forth in § 48.4041-1(b)(2)(i). If a person acquired any special motor fuel through a transaction which is subject to a tax at the rate set forth in paragraph (b)(2)(i)(C) of § 48.4041-1 and uses it in a use other than one for which the reduced rate applies, the person is liable for an additional tax under section 4041(b)(2) on the quantity of special motor fuel so used. See § 48.4041-1(b)(2)(i)(D) or (E) for the applicable rate of tax. See section 6427(a) for credit or refund of tax where special motor fuel acquired in a transaction subject to tax at the rate set forth in paragraph (b)(2)(i)(A) of § 48.4041-1 is used for a purpose described in paragraph (b)(2)(i)(C) of § 48.4041-1 or in a nontaxable use.

(ii) On or after April 1, 1983, and before October 1, 1988, if a person acquired any special motor fuel by any means other than through a transaction subject to tax under section 4041(a)(2)(A) and uses it as a fuel in a motor vehicle or motorboat, the person is liable for a tax under section 4041(a)(2)(B) on the quantity of special motor fuel so used at the appropriate rate set forth in paragraph (b)(2)(ii) of § 48.4041-1. If a person acquired any special motor fuel through a transaction for which no tax is imposed by reason of paragraph (b)(2)(ii)(C) of § 48.4041-1 and uses it in other than a nontaxable use, the person is liable for a tax under section 4041(a)(2)(B) on the quantity of fuel so used. See paragraph (b)(2)(ii)(D) of § 48.4041-1 for the applicable rate of tax. See section 6427(a) for credit or refund of tax where special motor fuel acquired in a transaction subject to tax at the rate set forth in paragraph (b)(2)(ii)(A) of § 48.4041-1 is used for a purpose described in paragraph (b)(2)(ii)(C) of § 48.4041-1 or in another nontaxable use.

(3) *Noncommercial aviation.*—If a person acquires any liquid fuel by any means other than through a transaction subject to tax under section 4041(c)(1)(A) or section 4041(c)(2)(A) and uses it as fuel in an aircraft in noncommercial aviation, the person is liable for a tax under section 4041(c)(1)(B) or section 4041(c)(2)(B) on the quantity of the liquid fuel so used at the appropriate rate set forth in § 48.4041-1(b)(3).

(b) *Bulk purchases by users.*—Taxpayers who purchase taxable liquid fuel in bulk delivered into storage tanks or other containers and use it for taxable or nontaxable purposes or in registered and nonregistered vehicles must maintain adequate records of all fuel used for each purpose to permit verification of the tax paid and of any credits, refunds, or exemptions claimed. [Reg. § 48.4041-6.]

☐ [*T.D.* 8066, 1-2-86.]

[Reg. § 48.4041-7]

§ 48.4041-7. Dual use of taxable liquid fuel.—Tax applies to all taxable liquid fuel sold for use or used as a fuel in the motor which is used to propel a diesel-powered vehicle or in the motor used to propel a motor vehicle, motorboat, or aircraft, even though the motor is also used for a purpose other than the propulsion of the vehicle, motorboat, or aircraft. Thus, if the motor of a diesel-powered highway vehicle or a motorboat operates special equipment by means of a power take-off or power transfer, tax applies to all taxable liquid fuel sold for this use or so used, whether or not the special equipment is mounted on the vehicle or boat. For example, tax applies to diesel fuel sold to operate the mixing unit on a concrete mixer truck of the mixing unit is operated by means of a power take-off from the motor of the vehicle. Similarly, tax applies to all taxable liquid fuel sold for use or used in a motor propelling a fuel oil truck even though the same motor is used to operate the pump (whether or not mounted on the truck) for discharging the fuel into customers' storage tanks. However, tax does not apply to liquid fuel sold for use or used in a separate motor to operate special equipment (whether or not the equipment is mounted on the vehicle). If the taxable liquid fuel used in a separate motor is drawn from the same tank as the one which supplies fuel for the propulsion of the vehicle, a reasonable determination of the quantity of taxable liquid fuel used in such separate motor or during such period is acceptable for purposes of application of the tax. This determination must be based, however, on the operating experience of the person using the taxable liquid fuel, and the taxpayer must maintain records which support the allocation used. Devices to measure the number of miles the vehicle has traveled, such as hubometers, may be used in making a preliminary determination of the number of gallons of fuel used to propel the vehicle. In order to make a final determination of the number of gallons of fuel used to propel the vehicle, there must be added to this preliminary determination the amount of fuel consumed while idling or warming up the motor preparatory to propelling the vehicle. [Reg. § 48.4041-7.]

☐ [*T.D. 8066, 1-2-86.*]

[Reg. § 48.4041-8]

§ 48.4041-8. Definitions.—For purposes of the regulations in this subpart, unless otherwise expressly indicated:

(a) *Highway.*—The term "highway" includes any road (whether a Federal highway, State highway, city street, rural road, or otherwise) in the United States which is not a private roadway.

(b) *Highway vehicle.*—(1) *In general.*—The term "highway vehicle" means any self-propelled vehicle, or any trailer or semi-trailer, designed to perform a function of transporting a load over highways, whether or not also designed to perform other functions, but does not include a vehicle described in paragraph (b)(2) of this section. For purposes of this definition, a vehicle consists of a chassis, or a chassis and a body if the vehicle has a body, but does not include the vehicle's load. Therefore, in determining whether a vehicle is a "highway vehicle", it is immaterial that the vehicle is designed to perform a highway transportation function for only a particular kind of load, such as passengers, furnishings and personal effects (as in a house, office, or utility trailer), a special type of cargo, goods, supplies, or materials, or, except to the extent otherwise provided in paragraph (b)(2)(i) of this section, machinery or equipment specially designed to perform some off-highway task unrelated to highway transportation. In the case of specially designed machinery or equipment, it is also immaterial, except as provided in paragraph (b)(2)(i) of this section, that such machinery or equipment is permanently mounted on the vehicle. For purposes of paragraph (b) of this section, the term "transport" includes the term "tow". A vehicle which is not a highway vehicle within the meaning of this paragraph shall be treated as a non-highway vehicle for purposes of section 4041. Examples of vehicles that are designed to perform a function of transporting a load over the public highways are passenger automobiles, motorcycles, buses, and highway-type trucks, truck tractors, trailers, and semi-trailers.

(2) *Exceptions.*—(i) *Certain specially designed mobile machinery for nontransportation functions.*— A self-propelled vehicle, or trailer or semi-trailer, is not a highway vehicle if it (A) consists of a chassis to which there has been permanently mounted (by welding, bolting, riveting, or other means) machinery or equipment to perform a construction, manufacturing, processing, farming, mining, drilling, timbering, or other operation similar to any one of the foregoing enumerated operations if the operation of the machinery or equipment is unrelated to transportation on or off the public highways, (B) the chassis has been specially designed to serve only as a mobile carriage and mount (and a power source, where applicable) for the particular machinery or equipment involved, whether or not such machinery or equipment is in operation, and (C) by reason of such special design, such chassis could not, without substantial structural modification, be used as a component of a vehicle designed to perform a function of transporting any load other than that particular machinery or equipment or similar machinery or equipment requiring such a specially designed chassis.

(ii) *Certain vehicles specially designed for off-highway transportation.*—A self-propelled vehicle, or a trailer or semi-trailer, is not a highway vehicle if it is (A) specially designed for the primary function of transporting a particular type of load other than over the public highway in connection with a construction, manufacturing, processing, farming, mining, drilling, timbering, or other operation similar to any one of the foregoing enumerated operations, and (B) if by reason of such special design, the use of such vehicle to transport such load over the public highways is substantially limited or substantially impaired. For purposes of applying the rule of clause (b) of this paragraph (b)(2)(ii), account may be taken of whether the vehicle may travel at regular highway speeds, requires a special permit for highway use, is overweight, overheight or overwidth for regular use, and any other relevant considerations. Solely for purposes of determinations under this paragraph (b)(2)(ii), where there is affixed to the vehicle equipment used for loading, unloading, storing, vending, handling, processing, preserving, or otherwise caring for a load transported by the vehicle over the public highways, the functions are related to the transportation of a load over the public highways even though the functions may be performed off the public highways.

(iii) *Certain trailers and semi-trailers specially designed to perform nontransportation functions off the public highways.*—A trailer or semi-trailer is not a highway vehicle if it is specially designed to serve no purpose other than providing an enclosed stationary shelter for the carrying on of a function which is directly connected with and necessary to, and at the off-highway site of, a construction, manufacturing, processing, mining, drilling, farming, timbering, or other operation similar to any one of the foregoing enumerated operations, such as a trailer specially designed to serve as an office for such an operation.

(3) *Optional application.*—For purposes of section 4041, if any rules existing immediately prior to January 13, 1977, would, if applicable, unequivocally resolve an issue involving the definition of a highway vehicle with respect to a period prior to such date, at the option of the taxpayer, such rules existing prior to such date shall be applied to resolve the issue for all periods prior to such date, and the rules of paragraph (b)(1) and (2) of this section, which define the term "highway vehicle", shall not apply with respect to such issue for all periods prior to such date.

(4) *Diesel-powered highway vehicle.*—The term "diesel-powered highway vehicle" means any highway vehicle (within the meaning of paragraph (b)(1) of this section) which is also a motor vehicle (as defined in paragraph (c) of this section) and which uses diesel fuel (as defined in paragraph (e) of this section) for propulsion purposes,

(c) *Motor vehicles.*—The term "motor vehicle" includes all types of vehicles propelled by motor that are designed for carrying or towing loads from one place to another, regardless of the type of load or material carried or towed and whether or not the vehicle is registered or required to be registered for highway use. Included are fork lift trucks used to carry loads at railroad stations, industrial plants, warehouses, etc. The term does not include farm tractors, trench diggers, power shovels, bulldozers, road graders or rollers, and similar equipment which does not carry or tow a load; nor does it include any vehicle which moves exclusively on rails. For periods prior to January 6, 1977, a vehicle which is designed for towing, but not carrying, loads shall not be considered to be a motor vehicle.

(d) *Taxable liquid fuel.*—The term "taxable liquid fuel" (or "taxable liquid") means any liquid which is either—

(1) Diesel fuel as defined in paragraph (e) of this section,

(2) Special motor fuel as defined in paragraph (f) of this section, or

(3) Any liquid fuel used in an aircraft in "noncommercial aviation", as defined in paragraph (h) of this section.

(e) *Diesel fuel.*—The term "diesel fuel" means any liquid (other than a product taxable as gasoline under the provisions of section 4081) which is sold for use or used as a fuel in a diesel-powered highway vehicle.

(f) *Special motor fuel.*—(1) Except as provided in paragraph (f)(2) of this section, *special motor fuel* means any liquid fuel, including—

(i) Any liquefied petroleum gas (such as propane, butane, pentane, or mixtures of the same);

(ii) Liquefied natural gas; or

(iii) Benzol, benezene, naptha, or any other liquid, whether a refined, partly refined, or unrefined product, 10 percent of which has been recovered when the thermometer reads 347° F. (175° C.) or 95 percent of which has been recovered when the thermometer reads 464°F. (240° C.) when subjected to distillation in accordance with the "Standard Method of Test for Distillation of Gasoline, Naptha, Kerosene, and Similar Petroleum Products" (A.S.T.M. designation: D86) of the American Society for Testing Materials, regardless of the trade name under which sold.

(2) The term "special motor fuel" does not include any product taxable under the provisions of section 4081, nor does it include "kerosene, gas oil, or fuel oil", as defined in paragraph (g) of this section.

(g) *Kerosene, gas oil, or fuel oil.*—(1) The term "kerosene, gas oil, or fuel oil" means any product (i) 10 percent of which has not been recovered when the thermometer reads 347° F. (175° C.), and (ii) 95 percent of which has not been recovered when the thermometer reads 464° F. (240° C.), when subjected to distillation in accordance with the "Standard Method of Test for Distillation of Gasoline, Napta, Kerosene, and Similar Petroleum Products" (A.S.T.M. designation: D86) of the American Society for Testing Materials.

(2) Products designated as kerosene, gas oil, or fuel oil which do not fall within the specifications of both paragraphs (g)(1)(i) and (ii) of this section are taxable as special motor fuel if sold or used as a fuel in a motor vehicle or motorboat.

(h) *Fuel used in the aircraft in noncommercial aviation.*—The term "fuel used in an aircraft in noncommercial aviation" means any liquid (including any product taxable under section 4081) that is sold for use or used as a fuel in an aircraft in noncommercial aviation (as defined in paragraph (j) of this section).

(i) *Registered.*—The term "registered", when used with reference to a highway vehicle, means—

(1) Registered for highway use under the laws of any State, District of Columbia, or foreign country, or

(2) Required to be registered for highway use under the law of the State, District of Columbia, or foreign country in which it is operated or situated. Any highway vehicle which is operated under a dealer's tag, license, or permit is considered to be registered. A highway vehicle is not considered to be "registered" solely because there has been issued a special permit for operation of the vehicle at particular times and under specified conditions. However, a highway vehicle which is required to be registered and which also has been issued a special permit for operation of the vehicle under specified conditions, such as carrying an oversized load, is still considered to be "registered".

(j) *Noncommercial aviation.*—The term "noncommercial aviation" means any use of an aircraft, other than in a business of transporting persons or property for compensation or hire by air. The term also includes any use of an aircraft, in a business described in the preceding sentence, which is properly allocable to any transportation exempt from taxes imposed by sections 4261 (transportation of persons) and 4271 (transportation of property) by reason of section 4281 (use of small aircraft on nonestablished lines) or 4282 (transportation of members of affiliated group). [Reg. § 48.4041-8.]

☐[*T.D.* 8066, 1-2-86. *Amended by T.D.* 8609, 8-4-95.]

Reg. § 48.4041-8(j)

[Reg. § 48.4041-9]

§ 48.4041-9. Exemption for farm use.—(a) *In general.*—The tax imposed by section 4041 does not apply to diesel fuel or special motor fuel, or fuel used in noncommercial aviation, sold for use or used on a farm in the United States for farming purposes. The tax applies in the case of diesel fuel delivered into the fuel supply tank of a highway vehicle, or special motor fuel delivered into the fuel supply tank of a motor vehicle or motorboat, even if it is known that the liquid fuel is to be used on a farm for farming purposes. Credit or refund of the tax paid in such case may be claimed as provided by section 6427(c) upon proof that the taxable liquid was used on a farm for farming purposes. A tax-free sale of fuel delivered into the fuel supply tank of an aircraft in noncommercial aviation where such fuel is to be used on the farm for farming purposes may be made only if the requirements of § 48.4041-11 are met. The terms "used on a farm for farming purposes", and related terms, have the same meaning for purposes of the exemption in section 4041(f) and the regulations in this section as these terms are defined in paragraphs (1), (2), and (3) of section 6420(c) and the regulations contained in § 48.6420-4.

(b) *Application of exemption.*—The exemption referred to in paragraph (a) of this section does not apply with respect to diesel fuel or special motor fuel or fuel used in noncommercial aviation sold for use or used for nonfarming purposes, or diesel fuel or special motor fuel or fuel used in noncommercial aviation sold for use or used off a farm, regardless of the nature of the use. Thus, if a vehicle, motorboat, or aircraft is used both on a farm and off the farm, or if it is used on a farm both for farming and nonfarming purposes, the exemption applies only with respect to that portion of the diesel fuel or special motor fuel or fuel used in noncommercial aviation which is sold for use or used "on a farm for farming purposes". For purposes of this exemption, it is immaterial whether or not a vehicle is registered for highway use. However, the actual use of the vehicle and the place where it is used are material. For example, if a truck used on a farm for farming purposes is also used on the highways (even though in connection with operating the farm), tax applies to that diesel fuel or special motor fuel which is sold for use or used in operating the truck on the highways, since the fuel was used off the farm.

(c) *Termination of exemption.*—The exemption referred to in paragraph (a) of this section shall not apply on and after October 1, 1988. [Reg. § 48.4041-9.]

☐ [*T.D.* 8066, 1-2-86.]

[Reg. § 48.4041-10]

§ 48.4041-10. Exemption for use as supplies for vessels or aircraft.—(a) *Application of exemption.*—The tax imposed by section 4041 does not apply to any fuels which are sold for use or used as supplies for vessels or aircraft within the meaning of section 4221(a)(3) and (d)(3), and § 48.4221-4. In the case of a liquid sold for use as fuel in an aircraft, a tax-free sale may be made only if the requirements of § 48.4041-11 are met. For credit or refund of tax paid on fuels which have been sold or used as supplies for vessels or aircraft, see section 6416(b)(2)(B), section 6427, and paragraph (f) of this section.

(b) *Evidence required to establish exemption.*—(1) In order to establish exemption from tax in the case of a sale of fuels for use as supplies for vessels or aircraft, it is necessary that the seller obtain from the owner, charterer, or authorized agent of the vessel or aircraft and retain in its possession a properly executed exemption certificate in the form prescribed by paragraph (c) of this section. If fuel is sold tax free for use as supplies for civil aircraft employed in foreign trade or in trade between the United States and any of its possessions, the exemption certificate must show the name of the country in which the aircraft is registered.

(2) If only occasional sales of fuels are made to a purchaser for use which is exempt from tax as provided in this section, a separate exemption certificate must be furnished for each order. However, if sales are regularly or frequently made to a purchaser for such exempt use, a certificate covering all orders for a specified period not to exceed 12 calendar quarters is acceptable. Such certificates and proper records of invoices, orders, etc., relative to tax-free sales must be kept for inspection by the district director as provided in section 6001. If a seller's records with respect to any sale claimed to be tax free do not include a proper certificate, with supporting invoices and such other evidence as may be necessary to establish the exempt character of the sale, tax is payable by the seller on the sale.

(c) *Acceptable form of exemption certificate.*—The following form of exemption certificate, which must be adhered to in substance, is acceptable for the purposes of this section.
EXEMPTION CERTIFICATE
(For use by purchasers of fuels for use as supplies for certain vessels or aircraft (section 4041(g) of the Internal Revenue Code of 1954).)

(Date) . . . ., 19 . . . .
The undersigned purchaser hereby certifies that he/she is the . . . . . . (owner, charterer, or authorized agent of owner or charterer) of . . . . (Name of company and vessel) and that the fuel specified in the accompanying order, or as specified below or on the reverse side hereof, will be used only as fuel supplies for a vessel belonging to one of the following classes of vessels (including aircraft) to which section 4041(g) of the Internal Revenue Code applies:
(Check class to which vessel belongs):
(1) Vessels (including aircraft) engaged in foreign trade.
(2) Vessels engaged in trade between the Atlantic and Pacific ports of the United States.

(3) Vessels (including aircraft) engaged in trade between the United States and any of its possessions.

(4) Vessels employed in the fisheries or whaling business.

(5) Vessels (including aircraft) of war of the United States or a foreign nation.

The undersigned understands that if the fuels are sold or used otherwise than as stated above and for a taxable purpose specified in section 4041 of the Internal Revenue Code, the undersigned will be liable for the tax upon such sale or use. It is also understood that this certificate may not be used in purchasing fuels, if such fuels are for use as fuels in pleasure vessels, or of any type of aircraft except (1) civil aircraft employed in foreign trade or trade between the United States and any of its possessions, and otherwise entitled to exemption, and (2) aircraft owned by the United States or any foreign country and constituting a part of the armed forces thereof.

The undersigned understands that the fraudulent use of this certificate to secure exemption will subject the undersigned and all others making fraudulent use to a penalty equivalent to the amount of tax due on the sale of the fuel and, upon conviction, to a fine of not more than $10,000, or to imprisonment for not more than 5 years, or both, together with the costs of prosecution. The purchaser also understands that it must be prepared to establish by satisfactory evidence the purpose for which the fuel purchased under this certificate was used.

(Signature)......................

(Address)......................

....

Registration Number if fuel used as supplies for civil aircraft engaged in foreign trade or in trade between the United States and any of its possessions.

(d) *Exemption certificate not obtained prior to filing of seller's excise tax return.*—If the exemption certificate is not obtained prior to the time the seller files a return covering taxes due for the period during which the sale was made, the seller must include the tax on the sale in its return for that period. However, if the certificate is later obtained, a claim for refund of the tax paid on the sale may be filed on Form 843, or a credit for the tax paid may be taken upon a subsequent return as provided by section 6416(b)(2)(B) and § 48.6416(b)-2(c).

(e) *Liability of purchaser.*—The person who purchases fuels tax free as provided in this section is liable for the tax imposed by section 4041 if the person sells or uses such fuel in a sale or use that is not exempt under any provision of law applicable to the taxes imposed by section 4041.

(f) *Credit or refund.*—(1) If diesel fuel or special motor fuel upon which the tax imposed by section 4041(a)(1) or (2), has been paid, is sold or used as supplies for vessels, a credit or refund of the tax is available under section 6416(b)(2)(B) to the retail dealer who paid the tax. As an alterna-

tive, a credit or refund of tax is available under section 6427 to the operator of the vessel who used the fuel. Where the retail dealer claims refund of the tax, the dealer, in accordance with section 6416(a), must reimburse the operator of the vessel for the amount of tax or obtain the written consent of the operator to the filing of such claim.

(2) If aviation fuel upon which the tax imposed by section 4041(c) has been paid is sold or used as supplies for aircraft, credit or refund of the tax is available only as a payment under section 6427 to the operator of the aircraft who uses the fuel or to the person who resells the fuel for such use. [Reg. § 48.4041-10.]

☐ [*T.D.* 8066, 1-2-86.]

[Reg. § 48.4041-11]

§ 48.4041-11. Tax-free sales of fuel for use in noncommercial aviation only if sellers and certain purchasers are registered.—(a) *In general.*— Any sale of liquid fuel for delivery into a fuel supply tank of an aircraft is presumed to be subject to tax under section 4041(c), unless both the seller and purchaser of the liquid fuel are registered as provided in paragraph (b) of this section or are within one of the exceptions provided in paragraph (c) of this section.

(b) *Form of registration.*—Except as provided in paragraph (c) of this section (relating to exceptions for State and local governments, for fuel purchased from customs bonded warehouses or continuous customs custody, and for fuel purchased for use in certain aircraft of the United States or of any foreign nation), tax-free sales under section 4041(c) may be made only if both the seller and the purchaser have registered as required by section 4041(i) and this paragraph (b). If fuel is purchased tax paid for use in noncommercial aviation but is used for a nontaxable purpose, see section 6427(a) for provisions relating to refunds or credits of tax for tax-paid fuels not used for the purpose for which sold. Any person desiring to be registered in order to sell or purchase fuel free of the tax imposed by section 4041(c) must, before making any tax-free sale or purchase, file Form 637A, in duplicate. Form 637A must be filed with the District Director of Internal Revenue for the district in which the principal place of business of the applicant is located (or if the applicant has no principal place of business in the United States, with the Director of International Operations, Internal Revenue Service, Washington, DC 20224). The person who receives a validated Certificate of Registry (Validated Form 637A) is considered to be registered for purposes of selling or purchasing fuel tax free as provided in this section.

(c) *Transactions excepted from registration.*— (1) A State or local government purchasing fuel delivered into a fuel supply tank of an aircraft it operates for its exclusive use may, but is not required to, register as provided in this section.

(2) Any purchaser of aircraft fuel who purchases fuel from any customs bonded ware-

house or from continuous customs custody elsewhere than in a bonded warehouse is not required to register to purchase aircraft fuel from these sources tax free.

(3) Any purchaser of fuel for use in an aircraft which is owned by the United States or any foreign country and constitutes a part of the armed forces thereof is not required to register to purchase aircraft fuel tax free.

(4) The exceptions from registration in paragraphs (c)(1), (2), and (3) of this section do not relieve purchasers from the requirement of furnishing an exemption certificate as required by paragraph (d) of this section.

(d) *Evidence of tax-free sale.*—(1) To establish the right of a purchaser to purchase fuel delivered into the fuel supply tank of an aircraft tax free, the seller must obtain from the purchaser and retain in its possession a certificate, properly executed and signed by or on behalf of the purchaser, containing the following information:

(1) Date of purchase,

(ii) The purchaser's registration number (or the exemption from registration which is relied upon), and

(iii) A brief statement of the intended tax-free use of fuel (for example, by an airline in the business of transporting persons or property for hire).

(2) The following form of certificate which must be adhered to in substance, is acceptable for the purposes of this paragraph.

(Date) . . . . . . , 19 . . . .

The undersigned signifies that he/she, or the . . . . . . (Name of purchaser if other than undersigned) of which the undersigned is . . . . . . (Title) holds Certificate of Registry No. . . . . . . or has not registered because . . . . . . (Brief statement of exception from registration relied upon) delivered into a supply tank of the subject aircraft may be purchased free of tax because the fuel will be used . . . . . . (Brief statement of tax-free use)

The undersigned understands that if the fuel is used otherwise than as stated above and for a purpose taxable under section 4041 of the Internal Revenue Code, the undersigned will be liable for the tax upon such use, and that the undersigned must be prepared to establish by satisfactory evidence the purpose for which the fuel purchased under this certificate was used.

The undersigned also understands that the fraudulent use of this certificate to secure exemption will subject the undersigned and all others making fraudulent use to a penalty equivalent to the amount of tax due on the sale of the fuel and, upon conviction, to a fine of not more than $10,000, or to imprisonment for not more than 5 years, or both, together with the costs of prosecution.

(Signature) . . . .

(Address) . . . .

(3) Except as provided in paragraph (d)(4) of this section, a separate exemption certificate must be furnished for each sale of fuel delivered into a fuel supply tank of an aircraft. If

a portion of the fuel is intended to be used for a nontaxable purpose, the entire amount of the fuel may be sold tax free. Exemption certificates and proper supporting records such as invoices, orders, etc., relative to tax-free sales must be readily accessible for inspection by internal revenue officers and retained as provided in section 6001 of the Code and the regulations thereunder.

(4) If the purchaser of fuel to be used in an aircraft has reasonable grounds to believe that 90 percent or more of the total of the fuel to be purchased by it during a specified period not to exceed 12 calendar quarters will be used in a tax-free use, it may furnish each of its suppliers an exemption certificate covering all purchases for the specified period. The certificate shall be substantially in the same form as the certificate in paragraph (d)(2) of this section, except that in place of the date the purchaser shall specify the period covered by the certificate, and the purchaser shall give a brief explanation of its grounds for belief that 90 percent or more of its total fuel will be used in a tax-free use.

(5) The presumption under section 4041(i) that any liquid delivered into a fuel supply tank of an aircraft is taxable places the duty on the seller of the liquid fuel to use reasonable diligence to satisfy itself that a tax-free sale of fuel to the purchaser is allowed by law. In the absence of circumstances surrounding a sale that would raise a question as to whether a tax-free sale is allowable, the requirement of reasonable diligence is satisfied if the seller receives and retains the required certificate evidencing the right of the purchaser to buy the fuel tax free. However, if the circumstances are such as to indicate the seller has failed to use reasonable diligence, it is not relieved of liability for the tax imposed by section 4041(c). In addition, if the seller fails to obtain and retain the evidence of tax-free sales as required by this paragraph (d), it is not relieved of liability for the tax imposed by section 4041(c). [Reg. § 48.4041-11.]

□ [T.D. 8066, 1-2-86.]

[Reg. § 48.4041-12]

§ 48.4041-12. Sales by United States, etc.— The taxes imposed by section 4041 apply to the sale at retail of taxable liquid fuels by the United States or by any agency or instrumentality of the United States, unless by statute specifically exempted from these taxes. However, the exemptions from these taxes provided by section 4041(f), (g), and (h) and the regulations thereunder contained in this subpart F are available to the extent therein provided. [Reg. § 48.4041-12.]

□ [T.D. 8066, 1-2-86.]

[Reg. § 48.4041-13]

§ 48.4041-13. Other credits or refunds.— (a) *In general.*—For provisions relating to credit or refund of tax paid on taxable liquid fuel resold by the purchaser, or used otherwise than for the purpose for which purchased, see section 6427 and the regulations thereunder contained in Subpart O of this part.

(b) *Tax-paid liquid fuel used by local transit systems.*—For provisions relating to credit or refund in the case of taxable liquid fuel used in vehicles while engaged in furnishing scheduled common carrier public passenger land transportation service along regular routes, see section 6427(b) and the regulations thereunder contained in Subpart O of this part.

(c) *Credit or refund of diesel fuel differential amount.*—For provisions relating to an income tax credit or refund of the increased diesel fuel tax for original purchasers of diesel-powered automobiles and light trucks, see section 6427(g) and the regulations thereunder contained in Subpart O of this part. [Reg. § 48.4041-13.]

☐ [*T.D.* 8066, 1-2-86.]

[Reg. § 48.4041-14]

§ 48.4041-14. Exemption for sale to or use by certain aircraft museums.—(a) *In general.*— (1) The tax imposed by section 4041 does not apply to liquids which are sold for use or used by an aircraft museum in an aircraft or vehicle owned by such museum and used exclusively for the procurement, care, and exhibition of aircraft of the type used for combat or transport in World War II.

(2) In the case of liquid sold for use in a aircraft owned by an aircraft museum and to be used for the purposes described in paragraph (a)(1) of this section, a tax-free sale may be made only if the requirements of § 48.4041-11 are met.

(b) *Cross reference.*—For the definition of aircraft museum, see section 4041(h)(2). [Reg. § 48.4041-14.]

☐ [*T.D.* 8066, 1-2-86.]

[Reg. § 48.4041-15]

§ 48.4041-15. Sales to States or political subdivisions thereof.—(a) *Application of exemption.*—The taxes imposed by section 4041 do not apply in the case of a sale of any liquid by any person for the exclusive use of any State or any political subdivision thereof, the District of Columbia, or in the case of the use of any liquid by any State or any political subdivision thereof, or the District of Columbia, as a fuel in a motor vehicle, motorboat, or aircraft.

(b) *Evidence required to establish exemption.*— Any vendor claiming exemption under this section shall be prepared to produce evidence that will establish the right to exemption from the tax imposed by section 4041. Generally, orders or contracts of a State or a political subdivision thereof, or the District of Columbia, when signed by an authorized officer thereof will be accepted in support of the exemption. However, in the absence of such orders or contracts, a certificate signed by such an authorized officer that the liquid sold was purchased for the exclusive use of a State or political subdivision thereof, or the District of Columbia, will be acceptable. The certificate shall be in substantially the following form:

EXEMPTION CERTIFICATE
(For use by States and local governments. (section 4041(g)(2) of the Internal Revenue Code).)

(Date) _____, 19_____

I hereby certify that I am _____ of _ (State or local government); that I am authorized to execute this certificate; and that
(Check applicable type of certificate)
__ the liquid or liquids specified in the accompanying order, or on the reverse side hereof, (or)
__ all orders placed by the purchaser for the period commencing _____ (Date) and ending _____ (Date) (period not to exceed 12 calendar quarters) are, or will be, purchased from _____ (Name of vendor) for the exclusive use of _____ (Government unit) of _____ (State or local government).
I understand that the exemption from tax in the case of sales of liquids under this exemption certificate is limited to the sale of articles purchased for the exclusive use of a State, etc. I understand that the fraudulent use of this certificate for the purpose of securing this exemption will subject me and all parties making such fraudulent use of this certificate to a fine of not more than $10,000, or to imprisonment for not more than five years, or both, together with costs of prosecution.

_____
(Signature)

_____
(Address)

[Reg. § 48.4041-15.]

☐ [*T.D.* 7536, 3-27-78. Redesignated by *T.D.* 8066, 1-2-86.]

[Reg. § 48.4041-16]

§ 48.4041-16. Sales for export.—(a) *General rule.*—In order for a sale to be exempt from tax under section 4041 as a sale for export, it is necessary that the liquid be (1) identified as having been sold by the retailer for export and (2)

Reg. § 48.4041-16(a)

exported in due course. To establish exemption from tax in the case of a taxable article for export, it is necessary that the retailer maintain adequate records and have in his possession documentary evidence showing that the article was so sold.

(b) *Proof of exportation.*—Exportation may be evidenced by any one of (1) a copy of the export bill of lading issued by the delivering carrier, (2) a certificate by the agent or representative of the export carrier showing actual exportation of the liquid, (3) a certificate of lading signed by a customs officer of the foreign country to which the liquid is exported, or (4) a statement of the foreign consignee showing receipt of the liquid.

(c) *Shipment to possessions of the United States.*—The same provisions as relate to sales for export and proof of exportation will apply to sales for shipment to a possession of the United States, within the meaning of § 48.0-2. [Reg. § 48.4041-16.]

☐ [*T.D. 7536, 3-27-78. Redesignated by T.D. 8066, 1-2-86.*]

[Reg. § 48.4041-17]

§ 48.4041-17. Tax-free retail sales to certain nonprofit educational organizations.—(a) *In general.*—The taxes imposed by section 4041 do not apply in the case of a sale of any liquid by any person to a nonprofit educational organization (as defined in paragraph (b) of this section) for its exclusive use, or in the case of the use of any liquid by such an organization. In the case of a school operated as an activity of an organization described in section 501(c)(3), as referred to in paragraph (b) of this section, the liquid must be sold for the exclusive use of the school, or the liquid must be used exclusively by the school.

(b) *Definition of nonprofit educational organization.*—For purposes of section 4041(g)(4) and this section, the term "nonprofit educational organization" means an organization described in section 170(b)(1)(A)(ii), that is exempt from income tax under section 501(a), whose primary function is the presentation of formal instruction and which normally maintains a regular faculty and curriculum and normally has a regularly enrolled body of pupils or students in attendance at the place where its educational activities are regularly carried on. The term also includes a school operated as an activity of an organization described in section 501(c)(3) which is exempt from income tax under section 501(a), provided such school normally maintains a regular faculty and curriculum and normally has a regularly enrolled body of pupils or students in attendance at the place where its educational activities are regularly carried on.

(c) *Evidence required to establish tax-free sales to a nonprofit educational organization; general rule.*—To establish the right to exemption, the retailer must obtain from the purchaser and retain in its possession a properly executed certificate as set forth in paragraph (d) of this section.

(d) *Forms of exemption certificates.*—The following forms of exemption certificates will be acceptable for the purpose of this section and must be adhered to in substance.

(1) Form of certificate for exemption from retailers excise taxes for use by a nonprofit educational organization, other than a school operated as an activity of a church or other exempt organization that in itself is not a nonprofit educational organization:

EXEMPTION CERTIFICATE

(For use by a nonprofit educational organization (other than a school operated as an activity of a church or other exempt organization that in itself is not a nonprofit educational organization) purchasing articles subject to retailers excise tax for its exclusive use)

(Date) . . . . , 19_____

I hereby certify that I am . . . . (Title) of . . . . (Exempt organization); that I am authorized to execute this certificate; and that the articles specified in the accompanying order or on the reverse side hereof are purchased by such organization exclusively for use in its educational purposes.

I understand that this exemption certificate is for use only by a nonprofit educational organization in the tax-free purchase for its exclusive use of articles subject to the retailers excise tax; and it is agreed that if any article purchased tax free under this exemption certificate is used otherwise, such fact will be reported to the retailer from whom the tax-free purchase was made.

The organization claiming exemption under this certificate has received a determination letter (or a ruling) from the Internal Revenue Service holding the organization to be exempt from income tax as an organization described in section 170(b)(1)(A)(ii) that is exempt from income tax under section 501(a) of the Internal Revenue Code (or has received a determination letter (or ruling) under the corresponding provisions of prior revenue laws). The date of such determination letter (or ruling) is . . . . and such determination letter (or ruling) has not been withdrawn or revoked.

I understand that the fraudulent use of this certificate for the purpose of securing this exemption will subject me and all parties making such fraudulent use of this certificate to a fine of not more than $10,000, or to imprisonment for not more than five years, or both, together with costs of prosecution. . . . .

. . . .
(Signature of authorized individual)

. . . .
(Address)

(2) Form of certificate for exemption from retailers excise taxes for use by a school operated as an activity of a church or other organization described in section 501(c)(3) that in itself is not an educational organization described in section 170(b)(1)(A)(ii) of the Code:

EXEMPTION CERTIFICATE

(For use by or for a school operated as an activity of a church or other organization described in section 501(c)(3) of the Internal Revenue Code of 1954, that is not, in itself, an educational organization described in section 170(b)(1)(A)(ii), purchasing articles subject to retailers excise tax for the exclusive use of the school)

(Date) . . . . , 19____

I hereby certify that I am . . . . (Title) of . . . . (School, church, parish, etc.); that I am authorized to execute this certificate; and that the articles specified in the accompanying order or on the reverse side hereof are purchased by such institution exclusively for use in its educational activities.

I understand that this exemption certificate is for use only by a school operated as an activity of a church or other organization described in section 501(c)(3) of the Internal Revenue Code of 1954, in the tax-free purchase for its exclusive use of articles subject to the retailers excise tax; or by a church, or other organization in the tax-free purchase of any such article for the exclusive use of its school which qualifies for the exemption; and it is agreed that if any article purchased tax free under this exemption certificate is used otherwise, such fact will be reported to the retailer from whom the tax-free purchase was made.

The school operated as an activity of the church or other organization described in section 501(c)(3) of the Internal Revenue Code of 1954, normally maintains a regular faculty and curriculum and normally has a regularly enrolled body of pupils or students in attendance at the place where its educational activities are regularly carried on.

I understand that the fraudulent use of this certificate for the purpose of securing this exemption will subject me and all parties making such fraudulent use of this certificate to a fine of not more than $10,000, or to imprisonment for not more than five years, or both, together with costs of prosecution.

_____
(Signature of authorized individual)

_____
(Address)

(e) *Frequency of certificates.*—Where only occasional sales are made by a retailer to a nonprofit educational organization, as defined in paragraph (b) of this section, a separate exemption certificate should be furnished for each order. However, where sales by the retailer to the educational organization are regularly or frequently made, a certificate covering all orders for a specified period not to exceed 12 calendar quarters will be acceptable. Such certificate and proper records of invoices, orders, etc., relative to tax-free sales must be readily accessible for inspection by internal revenue officers and retained as provided in section 6001 of the Code and the regulations thereunder.

(f) *Prima facie evidence of exempt use.*—The exemption certificate procured by the retailer from the purchasing nonprofit educational organization will be acceptable as prima facie evidence that the article is purchased for the exclusive use of such organization.

(g) *Exemption certificate not obtained prior to filing of retailer's excise tax return.*—If the sale is otherwise exempt but the exemption certificate is not obtained prior to the time the retailer files a return covering taxes due for the period in which the sale was made, the retailer must include the tax on such sale in its return for that period. However, if the certificate is later obtained, a credit may be taken on a subsequent return or a claim for refund of the tax paid on such sale may

Reg. §48.4041-17(g)

be filed, within the period of limitation prescribed by section 6511(b) of the Code and §301.6511(b)-1 of this chapter. [Reg. §48.4041-17.]

☐ *[T.D. 7536, 3-27-78. Redesignated by T.D. 8066, 1-2-86.]*

[Reg. §48.4041-18]

§48.4041-18. Fuels containing alcohol.— (a) *In general.—*(1) *Sale or use after December 31, 1984 and before January 1, 1993.—*Under section 4041(k) the rate of tax applicable to the sale or use after December 31, 1984 and before January 1, 1993, of any liquid fuel described in section 4041(a)(1) or (2) which consists of at least 10% alcohol by volume is:

　(i) 9 cents for each gallon of alcohol mixture sold or used in the case of mixtures described in section 4041(a)(1); or

　(ii) 3 cents for each gallon of alcohol mixture sold or used in the case of mixtures described in section 4041(a)(2). The amount of tax is based upon the total volume of fuel and not merely upon the volume of the nonalcohol components of such fuel. However, see section 4041(b)(2) and §48.4041-19 for rules relating to the complete exemption from taxes imposed by section 4041(a) where at least 85% of the fuel consists of alcohol produced from certain sources.

　(2) *Sale or use after March 31, 1983, and before January 1, 1985.—*For rules relating to the rate of tax imposed on the sale or use after March 31, 1983, and before January 1, 1985 of any liquid fuel described in section 4041(a)(1) or (2) which consists of at least 10% alcohol by volume, see section 4041(k) prior to the enactment of the Tax Reform Act of 1984 (Pub. L. 98-369, 98 Stat. 1007).

　(3) *Sale or use before April 1, 1983.—*No tax is imposed upon the sale or use of any liquid fuel described in section 4041(a)(1) or (a)(2) which consists of at least 10% alcohol if the sale or use occurs after December 31, 1978 and before April 1, 1983.

　(4) *Rate of tax for mixtures which fail to qualify.—*If an alcohol mixture fuel fails to qualify under this section, the entire mixture is taxed at the rate of tax specified under section 4041(a)(1) if the mixture contains diesel fuel, or section 4041(a)(2) if the mixture contains special motor fuel.

(b) *Alcohol mixture fuels qualifying for special tax treatment.—*In order to qualify for the reduced rates of tax described in paragraphs (a)(1) and (a)(2) of this section or the exemption from tax described in paragraph (a)(3) of this section, at least 10% of an alcohol mixture fuel must consist of alcohol as defined in section 4081(c) and §48.4081-2(a)(4) of the regulations. The actual gallonage of each component of the mixture (without adjustment for temperature) shall be used in determining whether the 10 percent alcohol requirement has been met. Further, in determining whether a particular mixture containing less than 10 percent alcohol satisfies this percentage requirement, the District Director shall take into account the existence of any facts and circumstances that establish that but for the commercial and operational realities of the blending process, it may reasonably be concluded that the mixture would have contained at least 10 percent alcohol. A circumstance from which it might be concluded that the mixture would have contained 10 percent alcohol but for its existence is malfunctioning of the meter measuring the amount of a component pumped into a mixture. However, the necessary facts and circumstances will not be found to exist if over a period of time the mixtures blended by a blender show a consistent pattern of failing to contain 10 percent alcohol. In no case will any mixture containing less than 9.802 percent alcohol qualify for the reduced rates set forth in this section. See paragraph (f) of this section for rules relating to information required to be attached to the taxpayer's return of the tax imposed by chapter 31 relating to the alcohol content of the mixture for which tax is paid.

(c) *Later separation.—*If a person separates out the alcohol from a mixture which has been taxed under the rates of section 4041(k), such separation will be treated as a sale of the liquid on the date separated and is subject to tax at the rates set forth under section 4041(a)(1) or (2). The tax liability incurred upon the separation is reduced by the amount of any tax previously imposed under section 4041. Thus, if Y buys 1000 gallons of alcohol mixture fuel taxed at the rate of 3 cents per gallon under section 4041(k) and fuel taxed at the rate of 3 cents per gallon under section 4041(k) and later separates the fuel into 900 gallons of special motor fuel and 100 gallons of alcohol, the separation is treated as a sale of 900 gallons of special motor fuel, taxed at the rate of 9 cents per gallon under section 4041(a), and a sale of 100 gallons of alcohol, exempt from tax under section 4041(b)(2). The tax of $81 on the deemed sale of special motor fuel is reduced by the tax of $30 previously paid on the sale of the alcohol mixture fuel.

(d) *Exemption from tax for alcohol mixture fuels sold or used in an aircraft in noncommercial aviation.—*(1) *In general.—*No tax is imposed upon the sale or use of any liquid fuel described in section 4041(a)(1) or (a)(2) which consists of at least 10% alcohol if such fuel is sold to or used by an owner, lessee or other operator of an aircraft as fuel in such aircraft in noncommercial aviation. See section 4041(c)(4) and the regulations thereunder for the definition of noncommercial aviation.

　(2) *Failure to use alcohol mixture fuel in an aircraft in noncommercial aviation.—*If fuel which is exempt from tax under paragraph (d)(1) of this section is not used as fuel in an aircraft in noncommercial aviation, any other use or sale of such fuel will be considered the use or sale of an alcohol mixture fuel subject to tax according to the rules of this section.

(e) *Refunds relating to diesel, special motor and noncommercial aviation fuels.*—See section 6427 for rules which relate to the allowance of a refund or credit to a person who uses tax-paid diesel, special motor or noncommercial aviation fuels to produce an alcohol mixture fuel.

(f) *Records required to be furnished by the taxpayer.*—A taxpayer making a return of the tax imposed by chapter 31 indicating payment of the tax under section 4041(k) and § 48.4041-18 at the reduced rate must attach a statement to the return indicating the total number of gallons of alcohol mixture fuels containing at least 10 percent alcohol and the total number of gallons of alcohol mixture fuels containing less than 10 percent alcohol but more than 9.802 percent alcohol. However, the taxpayer does not have to specify the precise mixture ratio for every mixture blended for which tax is being paid. For example, the taxpayer pays tax for 10,000 gallons of alcohol mixture fuels. Of these mixtures, 1,000 gallons contain 9.9 percent alcohol, 1,500 gallons contain 9.91 percent alcohol and 7,500 gallons contain 10 percent alcohol. The taxpayer seeks to have all of the mixtures described above qualify for taxation at the reduced rate under the rules of paragraph (b) of this section. The blender must attach a statement to the return of tax filed for these mixtures indicating that of the 10,000 gallons, 7,500 gallons contain at least 10 percent alcohol and 2,500 gallons contain less than 10 percent alcohol.

(g) *Alcohol mixture fuel within the tank of a vehicle.*—(1) *Mixtures within the tank of a vehicle before April 1, 1983.*—If an alcohol mixture fuel is put into the tank of a vehicle prior to April 1, 1983, the fuel is considered used prior to that date. Thus, such fuel will not be subject to the tax described in paragraph (a)(2) of this section and will be exempt from tax according to the provision of paragraph (a)(3) of this section.

(2) *Mixture within the tank of a vehicle before January 1, 1985.*—If an alcohol mixture is put into the tank of a vehicle prior to January 1, 1985, the fuel is considered used prior to that date. Thus, such fuel is subject to the tax described in paragraph (a)(2) of this section. [Reg. § 48.4041-18.]

□ [*T.D. 7658, 12-4-79. Redesignated by T.D. 8066, 1-2-86. Amended by T.D. 8152, 8-20-87.*]

[Reg. § 48.4041-19]

§ 48.4041-19. Exemption for qualified methanol and ethanol fuel.—(a) *In general.*—Under section 4041(b)(2), the tax imposed upon the sale or use of motor fuels under section 4041(a) does not apply to the sale or use of qualified methanol or ethanol fuel.

(b) *Qualified methanol or ethanol fuel defined.*—For purposes of section 4041(b)(2) and this section, qualified methanol or ethanol fuel is liquid motor fuel, 85% of the volume of which consists of alcohol, as defined in section 4081(c) and § 48.4081-2(a)(4) of the regulations as modified by the following sentence. For purposes of sec-

tion 4041(b)(2) and this section, the alcohol contained in a qualified methanol or ethanol fuel may be produced from coal. The actual gallonage of each component of the mixture (without adjustment for temperature) shall be used in determining whether the 85 percent alcohol has been met. Further, in determining whether a particular mixture containing less than 85 percent alcohol satisfies this percentage requirement, the District Director shall take into account the existence of any facts and circumstances, that establish that but for the commercial and operational realities of the blending process, it may reasonably be concluded that the mixture would have contained at least 85 percent alcohol. The necessary facts and circumstances will not be found to exist if over a period of time the mixtures blended by a blender show a consistent pattern of failing to contain 85 percent alcohol.

(c) *Mixtures which do not qualify as qualified methanol or ethanol fuel.*—If a methanol or ethanol fuel does not qualify as qualified methanol or ethanol fuel under this section, the entire mixture is taxed at the rate of tax applicable to sales of special motor fuels under section 4041(a)(2) of the Code.

(d) *Refunds relating to fuels used to produce qualified fuels.*—See section 6427 for rules which relate to the allowance of a refund or credit to a person who uses tax-paid diesel, special motor or noncommercial aviation fuels to produce a qualified methanol or ethanol fuel and section 6416 for rules which relate to the allowance of a refund or credit to a person who uses tax-paid gasoline to produce a qualified methanol or ethanol fuel.

(e) *Later blending.*—If a qualified methanol or ethanol fuel is blended with other motor fuel in a mixture less than 85 percent of which consists of alcohol, the subsequent sale or use of such alcohol mixture fuel is taxable under the provisions of section 4041 or section 4081 subject to the requirements, limitations and exemptions of those sections. Thus, if the alcohol mixture fuel is at least 10% alcohol by volume, sale or use of the fuel is taxed at the rates provided in section 4041(k) or section 4081(c), but if the fuel is less than 10% alcohol, sale or use of the fuel is taxed at the rates provided in section 4041(a) or section 4081(a).

(f) *Effective date.*—Section 4041(b)(2) applies to sales or uses after March 31, 1983, and before October 1, 1988. [Reg. § 48.4041-19.]

□ [*T.D. 8152, 8-20-87.*]

[Reg. § 48.4041-20]

§ 48.4041-20. Partially exempt methanol and ethanol fuel.—(a) *In general.*—Under section 4041(m), the sale or use of partially exempt methanol or ethanol fuel is taxed at the rate of 4^1/$_2$ cents per gallon of fuel sold or used. The amount of tax is based upon the total volume of fuel and not merely upon the nonalcohol portion of the fuel.

Reg. § 48.4041-20(a)

(b) *Partially exempt methanol or ethanol fuel defined.*—For purposes of section 4041(m) and this section, partially exempt methanol or ethanol fuel is liquid motor fuel, 85% of which by volume consists of alcohol, as defined in section 4081 and § 48.4081-2(a)(4) of the regulations, as modified by the following sentence. For purposes of section 4041(m) and this section, the alcohol contained in partially exempt methanol or ethanol fuel must be produced from natural gas. The actual gallonage of each component of the mixture (without adjustment for temperature) shall be used in determining whether the 85 percent alcohol requirement has been met. Further, in determining whether a particular mixture containing less than 85 percent alcohol satisfies this percentage requirement, the District Director shall take into account the existence of any facts and circumstances that establish that but for the commercial and operational realities of the blending process, it may reasonably be concluded that the mixture would have contained at least 85 percent alcohol. The necessary facts and circumstances will not be found to exist if over a period of time the mixtures blended by a blender show a consistent pattern of failing to contain 85 percent alcohol. See paragraph (f) of this section for rules relating to information required to be attached to the taxpayer's return of the tax imposed by chapter 31 relating to the alcohol content of the partially exempt methanol or ethanol fuel for which tax is paid.

(c) *Mixtures which do not qualify as partially exempt methanol or ethanol fuel.*—If methanol or ethanol fuel does not qualify as partially exempt methanol or ethanol fuel under this section, the entire mixture is taxed at the rate of tax applicable under section 4041(a)(2) of the Code.

(d) *Refunds relating to fuels.*—See section 6427 for rules which relate to the allowance of a refund or credit to a person who uses tax-paid diesel, special motor or noncommercial aviation fuel to produce a partially exempt methanol or ethanol fuel and section 6416 for rules which relate to the allowance of a refund or credit to a person who uses tax-paid gasoline to produce a partially exempt methanol or ethanol fuel.

(e) *Later blending.*—If a partially exempt methanol or ethanol fuel is blended with other motor fuel in a mixture less than 85 percent of which consists of alcohol, the subsequent sale or use of such blended motor fuel is taxable under the provisions of section 4041(a) or section 4081(a), subject to the requirements, limitations and exemptions of those sections.

(f) *Records required to be furnished by the taxpayer.*—A taxpayer making a return of the tax imposed by chapter 31 indicating payment of the tax under section 4041(m) and § 48.4041-20 at the reduced rate must attach a statement to the return indicating the total number of gallons of partially exempt methanol or ethanol fuel containing at least 85 percent alcohol and the total number of gallons of partially exempt methanol or ethanol fuel containing less than 85 percent

alcohol, but qualifying for taxation at the reduced rate under the rules of paragraph (b) of this section. However, the taxpayer does not have to specify the precise mixture ratio of every mixture blended for which tax is being paid.

(g) *Effective date.*—Section 4041(m) applies to sales and uses after July 31, 1984. If methanol or ethanol fuel meeting the requirements of paragraph (b) of this section was put into the tank of a vehicle prior to August 1, 1984, the fuel is considered used prior to that date and is subject to the tax described in paragraph (a) of section 4041. [Reg. § 48.4041-20.]

☐ [*T.D. 8152*, 8-20-87.]

[Reg. § 48.4041-21]

§ 48.4041-21. Compressed natural gas (CNG).—(a) *Delivery of CNG into the fuel supply tank of a motor vehicle or motorboat.*—(1) *Imposition of tax.*—Tax is imposed on the delivery of compressed natural gas (CNG) into the fuel supply tank of the propulsion engine of a motor vehicle or motorboat unless tax was previously imposed on the CNG under paragraph (b) of this section.

(2) *Liability for tax.*—If the delivery of the CNG is in connection with a sale, the seller of the CNG is liable for the tax imposed under paragraph (a)(1) of this section. If the delivery of the CNG is not in connection with a sale, the operator of the motor vehicle or motorboat, as the case may be, is liable for the tax imposed under paragraph (a)(1) of this section.

(b) *Bulk sales of CNG.*—(1) *In general.*—Tax is imposed on the sale of CNG that is not in connection with the delivery of the CNG into the fuel supply tank of the propulsion engine of a motor vehicle or motorboat if, by the time of the sale—

(i) The buyer has given the seller a written statement stating that the entire quantity of the CNG covered by the statement is for use by the buyer for a taxable use as a fuel in a motor vehicle or motorboat; and

(ii) The seller has given the buyer a written acknowledgement of receipt of the statement described in paragraph (b)(1)(i) of this section.

(2) *Liability for tax.*—The seller of the CNG is liable for the tax imposed under this paragraph (b).

(c) *Exemptions.*—(1) *In general.*—The taxes imposed under this section do not apply to a delivery or sale of CNG for a use described in section 4041(a)(3)(B), (b)(1), (f), (g), or (h). However, if the person otherwise liable for tax under this section is the seller of the CNG, the exemption under this section applies only if, by the time of sale, the seller receives an unexpired certificate (as described in this paragraph (c)) from the buyer and has no reason to believe any information in the certificate is false.

(2) *Certificate; in general.*—The certificate to be provided by a buyer of CNG is to consist of a statement that is signed under penalties of per-

jury by a person with authority to bind the buyer, should be in substantially the same form as the model certificate provided in paragraph (c)(4) of this section, and should contain all information necessary to complete the model certificate. A new certificate must be given if any information in the current certificate changes. The certificate may be included as part of any business records normally used to document a sale. The certificate expires on the earliest of the following dates:

(i) The date one year after the effective date of the certificate (which may be no earlier than the date it is signed).

(ii) The date a new certificate is provided to the seller.

(iii) The date the seller is notified by the Internal Revenue Service or the buyer that the buyer's right to provide a certificate has been withdrawn.

(3) *Withdrawal of the right to provide a certificate.*—The Internal Revenue Service may withdraw the right of a buyer of CNG to provide a certificate under this paragraph (c) if the buyer uses CNG to which a certificate applies in a taxable use. The Internal Revenue Service may notify any seller to whom the buyer has provided a certificate that the buyer's right to provide a certificate has been withdrawn.

(4) *Model certificate.*

CERTIFICATE OF PERSON BUYING COMPRESSED NATURAL GAS (CNG)
FOR A NONTAXABLE USE
(To support tax-free sales of CNG under section 4041 of the Internal Revenue Code.)

_____

Name, address, and employer identification number of seller
_____ ("Buyer") certifies the following under penalties of perjury:
    Name of buyer
    The CNG to which this certificate relates will be used in a nontaxable use.
    This certificate applies to the following (complete as applicable):
    If this is a single purchase certificate, check here ___ and enter:
1. Invoice or delivery ticket number _____
2. ___ (number of MCFs)
If this is a certificate covering all purchases under a specified account or order number, check here ___ and enter:
1. Effective date _____
2. Expiration date _____
(period not to exceed 1 year after the effective date)
3. Buyer account or order number _____
Buyer will not claim a credit or refund under section 6427 of the Internal Revenue Code for any CNG to which this certificate relates.
Buyer will provide a new certificate to the seller if any information in this certificate changes.
Buyer understands that if Buyer violates the terms of this certificate, the Internal Revenue Service may withdraw Buyer's right to provide a certificate.
Buyer has not been notified by the Internal Revenue Service that its right to provide a certificate has been withdrawn. In addition, the Internal Revenue Service has not notified Buyer that the right to provide a certificate has been withdrawn from a purchaser to which Buyer sells CNG tax free.
Buyer understands that the fraudulent use of this certificate may subject Buyer and all parties making any fraudulent use of this certificate to a fine or imprisonment, or both, together with the costs of prosecution.

_____
Printed or typed name of person signing

_____
Title of person signing

_____
Employer identification number

_____
Address of Buyer

_____
Signature and date signed

(d) *Rate of tax.*—The rate of the tax imposed under this section is the rate prescribed by section 4041(a)(3).

(e) *Effective date.*—This section is effective October 1, 1995. [Reg. § 48.4041-21.]

☐ [*T.D.* 8303, 6-5-90. *Amended by T.D.* 8609, 8-4-95; *T.D.* 8659, 3-13-96; *T.D.* 8879, 3-30-2000 *and T.D.* 9051, 4-1-2003.]

[Reg. § 48.4042-1]

§ 48.4042-1. Tax on fuel used in commercial waterway transportation.—(a) *In general.*—Section 4042(a) imposes an excise tax on the use of liquid fuel in the propulsion system of commercial transportation vessels while traveling on certain inland and intracoastal waterways (*see* § 48.4042-1(f)). The tax applies generally to all types of vessels, including ships, bargers, and tugboats. It is in addition to all other taxes imposed on the sale or use of fuel.

(b) *Amount of tax.*—For the amount of tax, see section 4042(b).

(c) *Person liable for tax.*—The person operating the vessel in which the propulsion fuel is consumed is the user of liquid fuel for purposes of section 4042(a). Thus, a person who operates (or whose employees operate) a vessel is responsible for filing returns and paying the tax. If a vessel owner (or lessee) contracts with an independent contractor to operate the vessel, the independent contractor is the user of liquid fuel for purposes of section 4042(a), regardless of who purchases the fuel.

(d) *Time of use.*—Fuel is not taxed by section 4042(a) when put into a vessel's tanks. For purposes of section 4042(a), fuel is used when it is actually consumed by a vessel's engine.

(e) *Liquid fuels.*—For purposes of the tax imposed under this section, *liquid fuel* means any liquid fuel including gasoline, diesel fuel, special motor fuel, or Bunker C residual fuel oil.

(f) *Commercial waterway transportation.*—(1) *In general.*—For purposes of section 4042(a) and § 48.4042-2(c)(1), the term "commercial waterway transportation" means the use of a vessel on the waterways specified in paragraphs (g)(1) through (27) of this section if—

(i) Use of the vessel is in the business of transporting property for compensation or hire, or

(ii) Use of the vessel is in transporting property in the business of the owner, lessee, or operator of the vessel (whether or not a fee is charged).

Except for the operation of certain fishing vessels, the operation of all vessels satisfying the requirements of paragraphs (f) (1)(i) or (1)(ii) of this section will be deemed "commercial waterway transportation," regardless of whether the vessel is actually engaged in the transportation of property on a particular voyage. Thus, "commercial waterway transportation" includes the operation of vessels while moving empty of cargo, while awaiting passage through locks, while dislodging vessels grounded on a sandbar, while moving to or from a repair facility, while maneuvering around loading and unloading docks, and while fleeting barges into a single tow.

(2) *Fishing vessels exception.*—A vessel does not transport property in the business of the owner, lessee, or operator, for purposes of paragraph (f)(1)(ii) of this section, by merely transporting fish or other aquatic animal life caught on the voyage. The tax imposed by section 4042(a) does not apply to fuel used by a fishing vessel while traveling to a fishing site, while engaged in fishing, or while returning from the fishing site with its catch. However, the tax applies to fuel used by a commercial vessel along the taxable waterways while traveling to pick up aquatic animal life caught by another vessel and while transporting the catch of such other vessel.

(g) *Specified waterways.*—Only fuel used on those waterways specified in section 206 of the Inland Waterways Revenue Act of 1978 (specified waterways) is taxable. The specified waterways are as follows:

(1) Alabama-Coosa Rivers: From junction with the Tombigbee River at river mile (hereinafter referred to as RM) 0 to junction with the Coosa River at RM 314.

(2) Allegheny River: From confluence with the Monongahela River to form the Ohio River at RM 0 to the head of the existing project at East Brady, Pennsylvania, RM 72.

(3) Apalachicola-Chattachoochee and Flint Rivers: Apalachicola River from mouth at Apalachicola Bay (intersection with the Gulf Intracoastal Waterway) RM 0 to junction with Chattachoochee and Flint Rivers at RM 107.8. Chattachoochee River from junction with Apalachicola and Flint Rivers at RM 0 to Columbus, Georgia, at RM 155 and Flint River, from junction with Apalachicola and Chattachoochee Rivers at RM 0 to Bainbridge, Georgia, at RM 28.

(4) Arkansas River (McClellan-Kerr Arkansas River Navigation System): From junction with Mississippi River at RM 0 to port of Catoosa, Oklahoma, at RM 448.2.

(5) Atchafalaya River: From RM 0 at its intersection with the Gulf Intracoastal Waterway at Morgan City, Louisiana, upstream to junction with Red River at RM 116.8

(6) Atlantic Intracoastal Waterway (A.I.W.W.): Two inland water routes approximately paralleling the Atlantic coast between Norfolk, Virginia, and Miami, Florida, for 1,192 miles via both the Albermarle and Chesapeake Canal and Great Dismal Swamp Canal routes. For vessels traveling along the A.I.W.W. no matter how short the distance, the A.I.W.W. includes the main channel, all alternate channels, and all adjoining bays and sounds, regardless of depth. However, vessels merely crossing the A.I.W.W. on route either to a coastal port or to a nonspecified waterway will not be treated as traveling on the A.I.W.W.

(7) Black Warrior-Tombigbee-Mobile Rivers: Black Warrior River System from RM 2.9, Mobile River (at Chickasaw Creek) to confluence with Tombigbee River at RM 45. Tombigbee River (to Demopolis at RM 215.4) to port of Birmingham, RM's 374—411 and upstream to head of navigation on Mulberry Fork (RM 429.6), Locust Fork (RM 407.8), and Sipsey Fork (RM 430.4).

(8) Columbia River (Columbia-Snake Rivers Inland Waterways). From The Dalles at RM 191.5 to Pasco, Washington (McNary Pool), at RM 330, Snake River from RM 0 at the mouth to RM 231.5 at Johnson Bar Landing, Idaho.

(9) Cumberland River: Junction with Ohio River at RM 0 to head of navigation, upstream to Carthage, Tennessee, at RM 313.5

(10) Green and Barren Rivers: Green River from junction with the Ohio River at RM 0 to head of navigation at RM 149.1.

(11) Gulf Intracoastal Waterway (G.I.W.W.): From the mouth of St. Mark's River, Florida, to Brownsville, Texas, 1,134.5 miles. For vessels traveling along the G.I.W.W. no matter how short the distance, the G.I.W.W. includes the main channel, all alternate channels, and all adjoining bays and sounds, regardless of depth. However, vessels merely crossing the G.I.W.W. on route either to a coastal port or to a nonspecified waterway will not be treated as traveling on the G.I.W.W.

(12) Illinois Waterway: Illinois River from junction with the Mississippi River at RM 0 to the Des Plaines River and along the Des Plaines River to Lockport Lock and Dam at RM 291. Chicago Sanitary and Ship Canal from Lockport Lock and Dam at RM 291 to the South Branch Chicago River and along the South Branch Chicago River to Lake Street, Chicago at RM 325.5 near Chicago Harbor. Calumet-Sag Channel from junction with the Chicago Sanitary and Ship Canal to the Little Calumet River and along the Little Calumet and Calumet Rivers to turning basin 5, near the entrance to Lake Calumet, an additional 23.8 RMs. Total waterway distance approximately 350 RMs.

(13) Kanawha River: From junction with Ohio River at RM 0 to RM 90.6 at Deepwater, West Virginia.

(14) Kaskaskia River: From junction with the Mississippi River at RM 0 to RM 36.2 at Fayetteville, Illinois.

(15) Kentucky River: From junction with Ohio River at RM 0 to confluence of Middle and North Forks at RM 258.6.

(16) Lower Mississippi River: From Baton Rouge, Louisiana, RM 233.9 to Cairo, Illinois, RM 953.8.

(17) Upper Mississippi River: From Cairo, Illinois, RM 953.8 to Minneapolis, Minnesota, RM 1,811.4.

(18) Missouri River: From junction with Mississippi River at RM 0 to Sioux City, Iowa, at RM 734.8.

(19) Monongahela River: From junction with Allegheny River to form the Ohio River at RM 0 to junction of the Tygart and West Fork Rivers, Fairmont, West Virginia, at RM 128.7.

(20) Ohio River: From junction with the Mississippi River at RM 0 to junction of the Allegheny and Monongahela Rivers at Pittsburgh, Pennsylvania, at RM 981.

(21) Ouachita-Black Rivers: From the mouth of the Black River at its junction with the Red River at RM 0 to RM 351 at Camden, Arkansas.

(22) Pearl River: From junction of West Pearl River with the Rigolets at RM 0 to Bogalusa, Louisiana, RM 58.

(23) Red River: From RM 0 to the mouth of Cypress Bayou at RM 236.

(24) Tennessee River: From junction with Ohio River at RM 0 to confluence with Holstein and French Rivers at RM 652.

(25) Tennessee-Tombigbee Waterway: From its confluence with the Tennessee River to the Warrior River at Demopolis, Alabama.

(26) White River: From RM 9.8 to RM 255 at Newport, Arkansas.

(27) Willamette River: From RM 21 upstream of Portland, Oregon, to Harrisburg, Oregon, at RM 194. [Reg. § 48.4042-1.]

☐ [*T.D. 7727, 10-27-80. Amended by T.D. 8659, 3-13-96.*]

[Reg. § 48.4042-2]

§ 48.4042-2. **Special rules.**—(a) *Dual use of liquid fuels.*—(1) *Dual use by the propulsion engine.*— The tax imposed by section 4042(a) applies to all taxable liquid used as a fuel in the propulsion system of the vessel, regardless of whether the engine (or other propulsion system) is used for a purpose other than propulsion of the vessel. For purposes of this section, any engines generating movement of a vessel (including bow thrusters used for steering) are part of the propulsion system. The tax does not apply to fuel consumed in engines which are not used to generate movement of a vessel. When the propulsion engine operates special equipment by means of a power take-off or power transfer, the tax applies to all liquid fuel consumed by that engine. For example, the tax applies to all fuel used in the engine operating an alternator, a generator, or pumps, if that engine is used to generate movement of a vessel.

(2) *Common tank.*—If the liquid fuel consumed by a nonpropulsion engine is drawn from the same tank as fuel consumed by a propulsion engine, a reasonable determination of the quantity of fuel used in such a separate engine will be acceptable for purposes of excluding from taxation a portion of the fuel consumed by the vessel. The determination of the amount of fuel consumed by the nonpropulsion engine may be based primarily on the operating experience of the person using the fuel; however, in order to exclude fuel from taxation under the rules set out in this paragraph (a)(2), the taxpayer must maintain records which will support the allocation used.

(b) *Voyages crossing boundaries of the specified waterways.*—Fuel consumed by a vessel traveling along the specified waterways is taxable only to the extent of fuel consumed for propulsion while on the specified waterways. Generally, the operator may calculate the amount of fuel consumed while on the specified waterways during a particular voyage by multiplying total fuel consumed in the propulsion engine by a fraction. The numerator of the fraction is the time spent operating on the specified waterways; the denominator is the total time spent operating on the specified and nonspecified waterways during the voyage. This calculation may not be used when it is unreasonable. It may be determined to be unreasonable by:

Reg. § 48.4042-2(b)

(1) Better evidence of fuel consumed (*e.g.,* readings from an accurate fuel gauge or records from similar voyages); or

(2) The existence of factors causing a substantial discrepancy between the rate of fuel consumption on the specified and nonspecified waterways.

(c) *Records required.*—(1) All operators of vessels used in commercial waterway transportation must maintain records sufficient to establish to the satisfaction of the district director the amount of fuel used for taxable purposes. Those records may include, when relevant to establish liability:

(i) Quantity of fuel and date of acquisition of all liquid fuels acquired for both taxable and nontaxable purposes, whether delivered to storage tanks or tanks on a vessel;

(ii) Date and quantity of fuel pumped into tanks on each vessel;

(iii) Identification number or name of each vessel using fuel; and

(iv) Departure time, departure point, route traveled, destination, and arrival time for each vessel.

(2) Vessel operators seeking a tax exemption provided by section 4042(c) must maintain records which will support any exemption claimed. Where applicable, the records shall contain:

(i) The draft of the vessel on each voyage (for exemption under section 4042(c)(1));

(ii) The type of vessel in which fuel is consumed and the type of vessel in which cargo is transported (for exemption under section 4042(c)(1), (2) or (4); and

(iii) The ultimate use of cargo transported (for exemption under section 4042(c)(3)). [Reg. § 48.4042-2.]

☐ [*T.D.* 7727, 10-27-80. *Amended by T.D.* 8442, 10-21-92.]

[Reg. § 48.4042-3]

§ 48.4042-3. Certain types of commercial waterway transportation excluded.—(a) *Deep draft ocean-going vessels.*—(1) *In general.*—Under section 4042(c)(1), there is no tax imposed by section 4042(a) if:

(i) the vessel was designed primarily for use on the high seas; and

(ii) the vessel has a draft of more than 12 feet on the voyage for which the fuel tax exclusion is sought (*e.g.* 12 feet 1 inch).

(2) *Meaning of "designed primarily for use on the high seas.".*—Section 4042(c)(1) requires a determination of the primacy of the design features rendering the vessel useful for service on the high seas, as opposed to the features which render the vessel useful for service on all less turbulent waters. Thus, whether a ship is "designed primarily for use on the high seas" must be determined from all the facts, including structural features and equipment. If the predominant use of a vessel is on the high seas, it shall be presumed to be "designed primarily for use on

the high seas." If the predominant use of a vessel is on waters other than the high seas, it shall be presumed not to be "designed primarily for use on the high seas."

(3) *Meaning of "high seas.".*—For purposes of this section, "high seas" shall mean waters other than the territorial waters of the United States or any other country. Thus, the high seas shall not include the internal waters of any country, the Great Lakes, harbors, or narrow coastal indentations.

(4) *Twelve foot draft.*—(i) Definition. For purposes of section 4042(c)(1), "draft" shall mean the maximum vertical distance between the mean water line and the bottom of the keel. In cases where a vessel has a skeg or other appendage extending locally below the line of the keel, the draft shall be measured from the deepest appendage. A separate determination of draft must be made for each voyage when the vessel has its greatest load of cargo and fuel. For purposes of this determination, the term "voyage" means a round trip voyage. Therefore, if a vessel travels into the specified waterway system to pick up cargo and has a draft sufficient to qualify for the exclusion when loaded, then for purposes of section 4042(c)(1) the vessel satisfies the 12 foot draft requirement for the entire voyage. Similarly, if a vessel loaded with cargo travels into the specified waterway system with a draft sufficient to qualify for the exclusion provided by section 4042(c)(1), then the fuel consumed on the entire voyage may be excluded, regardless of the vessel's draft after the cargo is unloaded.

(ii) *Example.*—The following example illustrates the application of paragraph (a)(4)(i) of this section:

Example. A ship with a design draft of 20 feet (maximum certified draft when fully loaded) travels into a taxable waterway with only a partial load, such that the draft is 12 feet. The ship unloads and departs the waterway empty. The portion of the fuel consumed for propulsion of the vessel on the specified waterway is taxable because only vessels with a draft greater than 12 feet are eligible for the section 4042(c)(1) exemption from tax.

(b) *Commercial passenger vessels.*—Under section 4042(c)(2), the tax imposed by section 4042(a) does not apply to fuel consumed by vessels used primarily for the transportation of persons. Thus, commercial passenger vessels while being operated as passenger vessels are not subject to tax, even if such vessels in fact transport property in addition to transporting passengers. Similarly, ferry boats carrying passengers are not subject to tax, even if such vessels carry the passengers' automobiles.

(c) *Exemption for State or local governments.*—(1) *In general.*—Under section 4042(c)(3), there is no tax imposed by section 4042(a) if:

(i) The vessel is being used by a State or local government; and

(ii) The vessel is being used in transporting property in the State or local government's business.

(2) *State or local government.*—For purposes of paragraph (c)(1)(i) of this section a "vessel is being used by a State or local government" if it is operated by any State, the District of Columbia, or any political subdivision of a State. If a private party is contracted to haul for a State or local government, the vessel is not "being used by a State or local government." Similarly, if a person other than a State or local government is contracted to supply vessel operators, the fuel consumed by the vessel is not used "by a State or local government," regardless of ownership of the vessel. However, when a local government leases barges and employees of the local government operate the barges, the vessel is being used by the local government.

(3) *Government business.*—The test for whether a vessel is being used "in transporting in a State or local government's business," within the meaning of paragraph (c)(1)(ii) of this section, is whether the ultimate use of the cargo is for a function which is ordinarily carried out by governmental units. For example, when the cargo transported is salt to be spread on icy roads, the vessel is being used "in transporting in a State or local business" because the use to which the cargo will be put (road maintenance) is a function ordinarily performed by governmental units. Fuel consumed in a vessel transporting property for compensation or in furtherance of a business not ordinarily carried out by a governmental unit is not exempt from taxation by section 4042(c)(3).

(d) *Ocean-going barges.*—Under section 4042(c)(4), the tax imposed by section 4042(a) does not apply to fuel consumed by tugs moving exclusively barges released by ocean-going carriers soley to pick up or deliver international cargos. The tax exemption provided by section 4042(c)(4) applies to LASH barges, SEABEE barges, and all other ocean-going barges carried aboard ocean-going vessels. There is no exemption under section 4042(c)(4) while:

(1) One or more of the barges in the tow is not a LASH barge, SEABEE barge, or other ocean-going barge carried aboard an ocean-going vessel; or

(2) One or more of the barges in the tow is not on an international voyage; or

(3) Part of the cargo in the tow is not being transported internationally. [Reg. § 48.4042-3.]

□ [*T.D. 7727*, 10-27-80.]

[Reg. § 145.4051-1]

§ 145.4051-1. Imposition of tax on heavy trucks and trailers sold at retail.—(a) *Imposition of tax.*—(1) *In general.*—Section 4051(a)(1) imposes a tax on the first retail sale (as defined in § 145.4052-1(a)) of the following articles (including in each case parts or accessories therefor sold on or in connection therewith or with the sale thereof):

(i) Automobile truck chassis and bodies;

(ii) Truck trailer and semitrailer chassis and bodies; and

(iii) Tractors of the kind chiefly used for highway transportation in combination with a trailer or semitrailer.

A sale of an automobile truck, truck trailer or semitrailer, shall be considered to be a sale of a chassis and of a body enumerated in this paragraph (a)(1).

(2) *Special rule applicable to chassis and bodies.*—A chassis or body enumerated in paragraph (a)(1) of this section is taxable under section 4051(a)(1) only if such chassis or body is sold for use as a component part of a highway vehicle (as defined in paragraph (d) of § 48.4061(a)-1 (Regulations on Manufacturers and Retailers Excise Taxes)), which is an automobile truck, truck trailer or semitrailer, or a tractor of the kind chiefly used for highway transportation in combination with a trailer or semitrailer. Furthermore, a chassis or body which is not enumerated in paragraph (a)(1) of this section is not taxable under section 4051(a)(1) even though such chassis or body is used as a component part of a highway vehicle (e.g., a chassis or body of a passenger automobile). See paragraphs (e)(1) and (e)(2) of this section for the definitions of a tractor and truck. See paragraphs (e)(1) through (5) of § 145.4052-1 for other provisions applicable to this section. See paragraph (f) of this section, relating to tax-free sales of non-highway vehicles.

(3) *Parts or accessories sold on or in connection with chassis, bodies, etc.*—The tax applies in respect of parts or accessories sold on or in connection with or with the sale of the vehicles specified in section 4051(a)(1). Thus, for example, if at the time the article is sold by the retailer, the part or accessory has been ordered from the retailer, the part or accessory will be considered as sold in connection with and with the sale of the vehicle. The tax applies in such a case whether or not the parts or accessories are billed separately by the retailer. If a taxable chassis, body, or tractor is sold by the retailer, without parts or accessories which are considered equipment essential for the operation or appearance of the taxable article, the sale of such parts or accessories by the retailer to the purchaser of the taxable article will be considered, in the absence of evidence to the contrary, to have been made in connection with the sale of the taxable article even though they are shipped separately, at the same time or on a different date. For example, if a retailer sells to any person a chassis and the bumpers for such chassis, or sells a taxable tractor and the fifth wheel and attachments, the tax applies to such parts or accessories regardless of the method of billing or the time at which the shipments were made. Parts and accessories that are spares or replacements are not subject to tax.

(4) *Exclusions.*—No tax is imposed by section 4051(a)(1) on the sale of automobile truck chassis and bodies, suitable for use with a vehi-

cle which has a gross vehicle weight of 33,000 pounds or less, or truck trailer and semitrailer chassis and bodies, suitable for use with a trailer or semitrailer which has a gross vehicle weight of 26,000 pounds or less. For purposes of this paragraph (a)(4) the term "suitable for use" means practical and commercial fitness for such use. A chassis or body possesses practical fitness for use with a vehicle if it performs its intended function up to a generally acceptable standard of efficiency with the vehicle, and a chassis or body possesses commercial fitness for use with a vehicle if it is generally available for use with the vehicle at a price that is reasonably competitive with other articles that may be used for the same purpose. Thus, a truck chassis which is suitable for use with a vehicle having a gross vehicle weight of 33,000 pounds or less, is not subject to the tax imposed by section 4051(a)(1) regardless of the body actually mounted thereon. A truck trailer or semitrailer chassis suitable for use with a vehicle having a gross vehicle weight of 26,000 pounds or less, is not subject to tax regardless of the body actually mounted thereon. Where an exempt body is mounted on a taxable chassis, or a taxable body is mounted on an exempt chassis, the taxable chassis or body, as the case may be, nevertheless remains subject to such tax, if the resulting vehicle is a highway vehicle as defined in § 48.4061(a)-1.

(b) *Rate of tax.*—With respect to the articles enumerated in paragraph (a)(1) of this section, the rate of tax imposed by section 4051(a)(1) is 12 percent of the price for which the article is sold on or after April 1, 1983. See paragraph (d) of this section relating to vehicles on which a 10 percent tax was imposed under section 4061(a)(1).

(c) *Separate purchase of truck or trailer and parts and accessories therefor.*—(1) *In general.*—If the owner, lessee, or operator of any vehicle, which contains an article taxable under paragraph (a)(1) of this section, installs (or causes to be installed) any part or accessory on such vehicle, and such installation is not later than 6 months after the date such vehicle (as it contains such article) was first placed in service, section 4051(b)(1) imposes a tax on such installation equal to 12 percent of the price of such part or accessory and its installation. For purposes of the tax imposed by section 4051(b)(1) and this paragraph (c)(1) the term "parts and accessories" does not include those parts and accessories which were previously exempt from tax under sections 4061(b)(1) and (2) as in effect prior to January 7, 1983. Thus, for example, articles of general use are exempt from tax. See § 48.4061(b)-2(b). See paragraphs (d)(1) through (4) of § 145.4052-1 for determination of price.

(2) *Placed in service.*—For purposes of paragraph (c)(1) of this section, a vehicle shall be considered placed in service on the date on which the owner of the vehicle took actual possession of the vehicle. This date can be established by the delivery ticket signed by the owner or other comparable document indicating delivery to and acceptance by the owner.

(3) *Exceptions.*—The tax imposed by section 4051(b)(1) and paragraph (c)(1) of this section shall not apply if—

(i) The part or accessory installed is a replacement part or accessory, or

(ii) The aggregate price of the parts and accessories (and their installation) described in paragraph (c)(1) of this section with respect to any vehicle does not exceed $200.

For purposes of paragraph (c)(3)(i) of this section, a part is a replacement part, regardless of when it is ordered, if its use with a vehicle is as a replacement for a part on such vehicle. For purposes of paragraph (c)(3)(ii) of this section, the term "aggregate price of parts and accessories (and their installation)" refers to all purchases and installation charges, not including replacement parts and accessories, made with respect to a vehicle within the 6 month period provided for in paragraph (c)(1) of this section. If the aggregate price of parts and accessories (and their installation) during the 6 month period exceeds $200, the tax imposed under section 4051(b)(1) and paragraph (c)(1) of this section shall apply to the cost of all parts and accessories (and their installation) during such period. For example, a vehicle is purchased and placed in service on July 1, 1983. On August 1, 1983, the owner purchases and has installed parts and accessories at a cost of $150. On September 1, 1983, the owner purchases and has installed parts and accessories at a cost of $300. On September 1, 1983 a tax of $54 will be imposed (12 percent × $450). Any costs of additional parts and accessories installed with respect to the vehicle before January 1, 1984 (and the cost of installation) will also be subject to the 12 percent tax.

(d) *Transitional rule.*—In the case of an article taxable under paragraph (a)(1) of this section, on which a tax was imposed under section 4061(a)(1), the rate of tax set forth in paragraph (b) shall be applied by substituting "2 percent" for "12 percent." For example, if a manufacturer sells a tractor to a dealer on February 1, 1983, for $20,000 (which includes the Federal excise tax), for which a 10 percent tax was paid, and the dealer sells the tractor on April 10, 1983 for $25,000, a tax of 2 percent will be imposed on the $25,000 sales price. See paragraphs (d)(1) through (4) of § 145.4052-1 relating to determination of price.

(e) *Definitions.*—For purposes of this section—

(1) *Tractor.*—(i) The term "tractor" means a highway vehicle primarily designed to tow a vehicle, such as a trailer or semitrailer, but does not carry cargo on the same chassis as the engine. A vehicle equipped with air brakes and/or towing package will be presumed to be primarily designed as a tractor.

(ii) An incomplete chassis cab shall be treated as a tractor if it is equipped with one or more of the following:

(A) A device for supplying pressure from the chassis cab to the brake system (air or hydraulic) of the towed vehicle;

(B) A mechanism for protecting the chassis cab brake system from the effects of a loss of pressure in the brake system of the towed vehicle;

(C) A control linking the brake system of the chassis to the brake system of the towed vehicle;

(D) A control in the cab for operating the towed vehicle's brakes independently of the chassis cab's brakes; or

(E) Any other equipment designed to make it suitable for use as a tractor.

An incomplete chassis cab which is not equipped with any of the devices set forth in paragraphs (e)(1)(ii)(A) through (E) of this section shall be treated as a truck if the purchaser certifies in writing that the vehicle will not be equipped for use as a tractor.

(2) *Truck.*—The term "truck" refers to a highway vehicle that is primarily designed to transport its load on the same chassis as the engine even if it is also equipped to tow a vehicle, such as a trailer or semitrailer.

(3) *Gross vehicle weight.*—(i) For purposes of this section the term "gross vehicle weight" means the maximum total weight of a loaded vehicle. Except as otherwise provided in paragraphs (e)(3)(ii) through (v) of this section, such maximum total weight shall be the gross vehicle weight rating of the article as specified by the manufacturer or established by the seller of the completed article, unless the Commissioner finds that such rating is unreasonable in light of the facts and circumstances in a particular case.

(ii) A seller must specify or establish a weight rating for each chassis, body, or vehicle sold on or after April 1, 1983 if such article requires no additional manufacture other than (A) the addition of readily attachable articles, such as tire or rim assemblies or minor accessories, (B) the performance of minor finishing operations, such as painting, or (C) in the case of a chassis, the addition of a body. If an article is specially equipped to the purchaser's specifications, such specifications may be used to establish the gross vehicle weight of the article.

(iii) A seller shall maintain a record of the gross vehicle weight rating of each truck, trailer and semitrailer sold and excluded from the tax imposed by section 4051(a)(1) by reason of sections 4051(a)(2), (3) and paragraphs (e)(3)(i) through (v) of this section. For this purpose, a record of the serial number of each such article shall be treated as a record of the gross vehicle weight rating of the article if such rating is indicated by the serial number.

(iv) If (A) the seller's rating indicated in a label or identifying device affixed to an article, (B) the rating set forth in the sales invoice or warranty agreement, and (C) the advertised rating for that article (or two or more identical articles) are inconsistent, the highest of such ratings will be considered to be the seller's gross vehicle weight rating specified or established for purposes of the tax imposed by section 4051(a)(1).

(v) The seller's gross vehicle weight rating must take into account, among other things, the strength of the chassis frame and the axle capacity and placement. The Commissioner may exclude from the gross vehicle weight rating any readily attachable parts to the extent the Commissioner finds that the use of such parts in computing the gross vehicle weight rating is unreasonable.

(f) *Tax-free sales.*—With respect to tax-free sales of a chassis or body for use as a component of a vehicle other than a highway vehicle, similar provisions to paragrahs (e)(2)(ii), (iii), and (iv) of § 48.4061(a)-1 shall apply.

(g) *Effective date.*—The provisions of this section shall be effective for articles sold on or after April 1, 1983. [Temporary Reg. § 145.4051-1.]

☐ [*T.D. 7882, 3-30-83. Amended by T.D. 8879, 3-30-2000.*]

[Reg. § 48.4052-1]

§ 48.4052-1. Heavy trucks and trailers; certification requirement.—(a) *In general.*—Tax is not imposed by section 4051 on the sale of an article for resale or leasing in a long-term lease if, by the time of sale, the seller has in good faith accepted from the buyer a statement that the buyer executed in good faith and that is in substantially the same form, and subject to the same conditions, as the certificate described in § 145.4052-1(a)(6) of this chapter, except that the certificate must be signed under penalties of perjury and need not refer to Form 637 or include a registration number.

(b) *References to § 145.4052-1(a)(2) of this chapter.*—References to § 145.4052-1(a)(2) of this chapter appearing in § 145.4052-1 of this chapter apply also to paragraph (a) of this section.

(c) *Effective date.*—This section is applicable after June 30, 1998. In addition, tax is not imposed on a sale occurring after December 31, 1997, and before July 1, 1998, if the conditions of paragraph (a) of this section are satisfied. [Reg. § 48.4052-1.]

☐ [*T.D. 8879, 3-30-2000.*]

[Reg. § 145.4052-1]

§ 145.4052-1. Special rules and definitions.—(a) *First retail sale.*—(1) *General rule.*—For purposes of section 4051(a)(1) and § 145.4051-1, the term "first retail sale" means a taxable sale described in paragraph (a)(2) of this section.

(2) *Taxable sale.*—The sale of an article is a taxable sale unless—

(i) The sale is a tax-free sale under section 4221,

(ii) [Reserved]. For sales after June 30, 1998, see § 48.4052-1 of this chapter,

(iii) There has been a prior taxable sale of the article. Notwithstanding the preceding clause, the sale of a chassis or body of a trailer or semitrailer ("trailer or semitrailer") less than six months after a taxable sale of the article shall be treated as a taxable sale.

(3) *Computation of tax.*—(i) *In general.*—If the sale of an article is a taxable sale under paragraph (a)(2) of this section, the tax shall be computed on the price as determined under paragraph (d) of this section.

(ii) *Exception.*—If the taxable sale of an article is a taxable use of such article under paragraph (c) of this section, the tax shall be computed on the price as determined under paragraph (c) of this section.

(4) *Special rule for tax-paid trailer and semitrailer.*—In the case of a taxable sale of a trailer or semitrailer less than six months after a taxable sale of the article, the seller in the subsequent sale ("the subsequent seller") may claim a credit equal to the amount of tax previously paid by another person ("the previous taxpayer") under section 4051(a)(1) with respect to the prior taxable sale of the article. The credit for such tax will be allowed to the subsequent seller only if the form on which the credit is claimed is accompanied by a statement, signed by the subsequent seller, indicating the amount of the credit being claimed under this paragraph (a)(4) and stating that—

(i) The subsequent seller has not been repaid any portion of such tax by the previous taxpayer,

(ii) The subsequent seller has not provided the previous taxpayer with written consent to allow the previous taxpayer to claim a credit or refund of such tax under section 6416(a), and

(iii) The subsequent seller has records (*e.g.* invoices) substantiating the amount of tax paid by the previous taxpayer with respect to the prior taxable sale of such article.

In no case shall the amount of the credit allowable under this paragraph (a)(4) with respect to an article exceed the tax liability of the subsequent seller with respect to the sale of such article.

(5) *No installment payments of tax.*—If a lease or an installment sale (or another form of sale under which the sales price is paid in installments) is, or is deemed to be, a taxable sale under this section, then the liability for the entire tax arises at the time of the lease or installment sale. No portion of the tax is deferred by reason of the fact that the sales price is paid in installments.

(6) *Certificate.*—A certificate signed by the purchaser, or an officer or employee authorized by the purchaser to sign the certificate, may be accepted by a seller in support of a nontaxable sale to the purchaser. If it is impracticable to furnish a separate certificate for each sale because of the frequency of sales to such purchaser, a certificate covering all orders between given dates (such period not to exceed 12 calendar quarters) will be acceptable. The purchaser may revoke the certificate by sending a written revocation to the seller. The certificate and proper records of invoices, orders, etc., relating to sales made pursuant to such certificate, must be retained by the seller as provided in section 6001 and the regulations thereunder. The certificate shall be substantially in the following form:

EXEMPTION CERTIFICATE

I hereby certify that I am _____
(Title)

of _____, that I am authorized to execute
(Name of purchaser)
this certificate, and that:
(Check appropriate line)

____ the article or articles specified in the accompanying order, or on the reverse side hereof, (or)

____all orders placed by the purchaser for the period commencing _____(Date) (period not to exceed 12 calendar quarters), are purchased either for resale or for lease on a long-term basis.

I have filed Form 637 and have received registration number_____.

I understand that the fraudulent use of this certificate to secure exemption will subject me and all parties making such fraudulent use to a fine of not more than $10,000, or to imprisonment for not more than 5 years, or both, together with costs of prosecution.

_____
(Signature)

_____
(Address)

(b) *Tax treatment of leases.*—(1) *Long-term lease.*—For purposes of this section and § 145.4051-1, the leasing of an article on a long-term basis (as defined in paragraph (d)(6) of this section) will be deemed to be a sale of the article and will be deemed to be a taxable sale unless one of the exceptions contained in paragraph (a)(2) of this section applies. Thus, if a dealer purchases an article tax-free under an exception contained in paragraph (a)(2) of this section and then leases the article on a long-term basis, the leasing of the article will be treated as a taxable sale.

(2) *Short-term lease.*—For purposes of this section and § 145.4051-1, the leasing of an article on a short-term basis (as defined in paragraph (d)(6) of this section) will be deemed to be a taxable use of such article under paragraph (c) of this section and will be deemed to be a taxable sale unless one of the exceptions contained in paragraph (a)(2) of this section applies.

(3) *Computation of tax.*—(i) *Long-term lease by manufacturer, producer, or importer.*—When a manufacturer, producer, or importer is the lessor of an article on a long-term basis (as defined in paragraph (d)(6) of this section) and such lease is deemed to be a taxable sale under paragraph (b)(1) of this section, the tax shall be computed on a presumptive retail sales price as determined under paragraph (d)(4)(i) of this section. The manufacturer, producer, or importer shall be liable for the tax as if the article were sold at retail by such manufacturer, importer, or retailer.

(ii) *Long-term lease by persons other than manufacturer, producer, or importer.*—When a person other than a manufacturer, producer, or importer is the lessor of an article on a long-term basis (as defined in paragraph (d)(6) of this section) and such lease is deemed to be a taxable sale under paragraph (b)(1) of this section, the tax shall be computed on a presumptive retail sales price as determined under paragraph (d)(5)(i) of this section. Such person shall be liable for the tax as if the article were sold at retail by such person.

(c) *Use treated as sale.*—(1) *In general.*—For purposes of this section and § 145.4051-1, the use of an article will be deemed to be a sale of the article. Furthermore, if a person purchases a vehicle for which no tax was imposed under section 4051(a)(1) and thereafter converts such vehicle into an article which would have been taxable under section 4051(a)(1) and uses it, such person shall be liable for the tax as if such article were sold at retail by such person. For example, a truck having a gross vehicle weight rating of 24,000 pounds is sold at retail. The purchaser adds a lift axle, thereby increasing the gross vehicle weight rating to 34,000 pounds. If the purchaser thereafter uses the vehicle the purchaser shall be liable for the tax as if such article were sold at retail.

(2) *Exemption for use in further manufacture.*—The tax on the use of an article to which paragraph (c)(1) of this section applies shall not apply to use of the article by such person as material in the manufacture or production of, or as a component part of, another article to be manufactured or produced by the same user.

(3) *Time of application of tax.*—In the case of taxable use of an article by the seller, the tax attaches at the time such use begins. If tax applies by reason of the sale of an article on or in connection with, or with the sale of another article, the tax attaches at the time of the sale of such other article.

(4) *Events subsequent to taxable use of article.*—Liability for tax incurred on the use of an article is not extinguished or reduced because of any subsequent sale or lease of the article even if such sale or lease would have been exempt if the article had been sold or leased prior to use. If a seller of an article incurs liability for tax on his or her use of an article, and thereafter sells or leases the article in a transaction which otherwise would be subject to tax, liability for tax is not incurred on such sale or lease.

(5) *Computation of tax.*—(i) Except as provided in paragraph (c)(5)(ii) and (c)(5)(iii) of this section, the tax liability incurred on the use of an article shall be computed on the price at which such or similar articles are generally sold in the ordinary course of trade by retailers.

(ii) If the seller of an article regularly sells such articles at retail in arm's length transactions, tax liability on its use of any such article shall be computed on its lowest established retail price for such articles in effect at the time of the taxable use. In establishing such price, there shall be included and excluded, as applicable, the charges and readjustments specified in sections 4216(a), 4216(f), and 6416(b)(1) as in effect at the time the tax liability on the use of the article is incurred. If the seller of an article does not regularly sell such articles at retail in arm's length transactions, a constructive price on which the tax shall be computed will be determined by the Commissioner. This price will be established after considering the selling practices and price structures of sellers of similar articles.

(iii) In the case of any short-term lease (as defined in paragraph (d)(6) of this section) by any person other than a manufacturer, producer, or importer (or related person as defined in paragraph (d)(2)(ii) of this section) of an article that is deemed to be a taxable use of such article under paragraph (b)(2) of this section, the tax imposed by section 4051(a)(1) shall be computed on a price equal to the sum of—

(A) The price (as determined under paragraph (d) of this section) at which such article was sold to the lessor plus the cost of any parts and accessories installed by the lessor (or an agent of the lessor) on such article before the first use of lease by the lessor, plus

(B) The product of the sum described in paragraph (c)(5)(iii)(A) of this section and the presumed markup percentge (as defined in paragraph (d)(7) of this section).

(d) *Determination of price.*—(1) *In general.*—The price for which an article is sold includes the total consideration paid for the article whether that consideration is paid in money, services, or other forms. In addition, there shall be included

Reg. § 145.4052-1(d)(1)

any charge incident to placing the article in condition ready for use. Similar rules to section 4216(a) and the regulations thereunder, relating to charges to be included in the price and excluded from the price, shall apply. For example, charges for transportation, delivery, insurance, and installation (other than installation charges to which section 4051(b) applies), and other expenses actually incurred in connection with the delivery of an article to a purchaser pursuant to a bona fide sale shall be excluded from the price in computing the tax.

(2) *Presumptive retail sales price where tax paid by manufacturer, producer, or importer.*—(i) *In general.*—In the case of a taxable sale (other than a taxable sale described in paragraph (b)(1) of this section) where a manufacturer, producer, importer, or related person is liable for the tax imposed by section 4051, such tax shall be computed on a price equal of the sum of—

(A) The price that would (but for this paragraph (d)(2)) be determined under this paragraph (d), and

(B) The product of the price determined under paragraph (d)(2)(i)(A) of this section and the presumed markup percentage (as defined in paragraph (d)(7) of this section).

(ii) *Related person defined.*—(A) *In general.*—Except as provided in paragraph (d)(2)(ii)(B) of this section, the term "related person" means any person that is a member of the same controlled group (within the meaning of section 5061(e)(3)) as the manufacturer, producer, or importer.

(B) *Exception for permanent retail establishment.*—A person shall not be treated as a related person with respect to the sale of any article if—

(1) Such person sells the article through a permanent retail establishment in the normal course of business of being a retailer, and

(2) Such person has records (*e.g.*, invoices) that substantiate that the article was sold for a price that included a markup equal to or greater than the presumed markup percentage (as defined in paragraph (d)(7) of this section).

(3) *Retail sales price where tax paid by person other than a manufacturer, producer, importer, or related person.*—(i) *In general.*—In the case of a taxable sale (other than a taxable sale defined in paragraph (b)(1) of this section) where a person other than a manufacturer, producer, importer, or related person is liable for the tax imposed by section 4051, such tax shall be computed on a price determined under paragraph (d)(1) of this section.

(ii) *Exception.*—When a person other than a manufacturer, producer, importer, or related person is liable for the tax imposed by section 4051, such tax shall be computed on a price determined under paragraph (d)(2)(i) of this section if—

(A) Such person does not perform any significant activities relating to the processing of the sale of an article,

(B) The principal purpose for processing the sale through such person is to avoid or evade the presumed markup under paragraph (d)(2)(i)(B) of this section, and

(C) Such person does not have records (*e.g.*, invoices) substantiating that the article was sold for a price that included a markup equal to or greater than the presumed markup percentage as defined in paragraph (d)(7) of this section.

(4) *Presumptive retail sales price in the case of a lease by a manufacturer, producer, or importer.*—In the case of any long-term lease (as defined in paragraph (d)(6) of this section) by a manufacturer, producer, importer, or a related person (as defined in paragraph (d)(2)(ii) of this section) of an article that is deemed to be a taxable sale of such article under paragraph (b)(1) of this section, the tax imposed by section 4051(a)(1) shall be computed on a price equal to the sum of—

(i) A constructive sales price established by the Commissioner based on the price at which such article would be sold by a manufacturer, producer, or importer in a sale other than a taxable sale (*e.g.*, a sale to which the exceptions contained in paragraph (a)(2)(ii) of this section apply) on the date the lease is made, and

(ii) The product of the constructive sales price referred to in paragraph (d)(4)(i) of this section and the presumed markup percentage as defined in paragraph (d)(7) of this section.

(5) *Presumptive retail sales price in the case of a long-term lease by any other person.*—In the case of any long-term lease (as defined in paragraph (d)(6) of this section) of an article in which any person other than a manufacturer, producer, or importer (or related person as defined in paragraph (d)(2)(ii) of this section) is the lessor and the long-term lease is deemed to be a taxable sale of such article under paragraph (b)(1) of this section, the tax imposed by section 4051 (a)(1) shall be computed on a price equal to the sum of—

(i) The price (as determined under this paragraph (d)) at which such article was sold to the lessor plus the cost of any parts and accessories installed by the lessor (or an agent of the lessor) on such article before the first use by the lessee or leased in connection with such long-term lease, and

(ii) The product of the sum described in paragraph (d)(5)(i) of this section and the presumed markup percentage as defined in paragraph (d)(7) of this section.

(6) *Long-term and short-term lease defined.*—For purposes of this section, the term "long-term lease" means any lease with a term of one year or more. The term "short-term lease" means any lease with a term of less than one year. In determining a lease term, options to renew shall be taken into account. In addition, two or more successive leases that are part of the same transaction (or a series of related transactions) with

respect to the same or substantially similar article, shall be treated as one lease.

(7) *Presumed markup percentage.*—(i) *In general.*—Except as provided in paragraph (d)(7)(ii) of this section, for purposes of this section the term "presumed markup percentage" shall be four percent.

(ii) *Exceptions.*—For purposes of this section the "presumed markup percentage" for trailers, semitrailers, and remanufactured automobile truck chassis and bodies and tractors shall be zero percent. For purposes of this section an article is a remanufactured article if—

(A) The refurbishing, renovation, or repair of the article causes it to be subject to the tax imposed by section 4051, and

(B) Before remanufacture, such article was previously subject to the tax imposed by section 4051 (or section 4061 prior to its repeal).

(8) *Items excluded from price.*—There shall be excluded from the price—

(i) The amount of tax imposed under sections 4051(a)(1) and (b)(1);

(ii) If stated as a separate charge, the amount of any retail sales tax imposed by any state or political subdivision thereof or the District of Columbia, whether the liability for such tax is imposed on the vendor or vendee; and

(iii) The fair market value (including any tax imposed by section 4071) at retail of any tires (not including any metal rim or rim base). For purposes of this paragraph (d)(8)(iii), fair market value at retail shall be determined by the lowest established price for which the vehicle retailer would sell such tires at retail in the ordinary course of trade. The lowest established price is the lowest price for which the vehicle retailer sells, or offers to sell, a single tire to an independent purchaser who would not ordinarily be expected to buy more than one. If the vehicle retailer has no lowest established price the Commissioner will accept any price provided, under the facts and circumstances, such price is not unreasonable. For vehicles sold on or after April 1, 1983, and before October 15, 1985, a price will not be considered unreasonable if it is no more than an amount equal to 50 percent of the manufacturer's suggested retail price.

(9) *Trade-ins.*—If, in connection with the sale of an article subject to the tax imposed under section 4051(a)(1) or (b)(1) on the price for which sold, a vendor receives from its vendee another article in exchange, the tax on the vendor's sale shall be computed on the basis of the full price of the article sold, unreduced by any amount allowed for the article received from the vendee. For example, where a vehicle costing $20,000 is purchased for $16,000 cash plus a used vehicle valued at $4,000, tax is $2,400 (12 percent × $20,000).

(10) *Sales not at arm's length.*—For purposes of § 145.4051-1 and this section, a sale is considered to be made under circumstances otherwise than at "arm's length" if—

(i) One of the parties is controlled (in law or in fact) by the other, or there is common control, whether or not such control is actually exercised to influence the sale price, or

(ii) The sale is made pursuant to special arrangements between a seller and a purchaser. In the case of an article sold otherwise than at arm's length, and sold at less than the fair market price, the tax imposed under section 4051(a)(1) or (b)(1) shall be computed on the price for which similar articles are sold at retail in the ordinary course of trade, as determined by the Commissioner. Once such a price has been determined, no further adjustment of such price shall be made.

(e) *Examples.*—The provisions of this section may be illustrated by the following examples:

Example (1). M manufactures trucks that are taxable under section 4051. On July 11, 1988, D, a corporation that is a dealer, purchases one truck from M for $50,000. M does not own any stock in D. Prior to this transaction, D gave M a certificate that meets the specifications detailed in paragraph (a)(6) of this section. The certificate states that the truck will be resold or leased on a long-term basis. M's sale to D is not a taxable sale of the truck (within the meaning of paragraph (a)(2) of this section). On July 20, 1988, D resells the truck to a purchaser, P, for $52,000. The additional $2,000 includes the dealer's mark-up, costs of transporting the truck from M to D, and overhead. No parts or accessories were added to the truck. P did not give D a certificate and did not have an agreement with D under which all vehicles purchased were to be resold. The sale of the truck by D to P is a taxable sale within the meaning of paragraph (a)(3) of this section. Therefore, D has a tax liability of $6,240 (12% × $52,000).

Example (2). Assume the same facts as in example (1) except that M owns 80 percent of D's stock. D and M are members of the same controlled group (within the meaning of section 5061(e)(3)). Therefore, D is a related person under paragraph (d)(2)(ii)(A) of this section. On July 20, 1988, D sells the truck to P for $51,000. D does not have records substantiating that the truck was sold for a price that included a markup equal to or greater than the presumed markup percentage. The tax on the sale of the truck to P is determined under paragraph (d)(2)(i) of this section. Therefore, D has a tax liability of $6,240 (12% × ($50,000 + ($50,000 × 4%))).

Example (3). Assume the same facts as in example (1) except that D does not perform any significant activities relating to the sale. Assume further that the principal purpose for processing the sale through D is to avoid the presumed markup and that D did not sell the truck for a price that included a markup equal to or greater then the presumed markup percentage. D, however, is designated the seller of the truck on the invoice. Pursuant to paragraph (d)(3)(ii) of this section, the price of the truck shall be computed on a price determined under paragraph (d)(2)(i).

Reg. § 145.4052-1(e)

Therefore, D, the taxpayer, has a liability of $6,240 [12% × ($50,000 + ($50,000 × 4%))].

Example (4). Assume the same facts as in example (1) except that on July 20, 1988, D leases the truck for a two-year period (*i.e.*, on a long-term basis) to L, a lessee. D's leasing of the truck to L is treated as a taxable sale under paragraph (b)(1) of this section and the tax is computed on the price as determined under paragraph (d)(5)(i) of this section. D has a tax liability of $6,240 [12% × ($50,000 + ($50,000 × 4%))].

Example (5). Assume the same facts as in example (1) except that on July 20, 1988, D leases the truck to L for a six-month period (*i.e.*, a short-term lease). The lease is treated as a use under paragraph (b)(2) of this section. The tax is computed on the price as determined under paragraph (c)(5) of this section. D has a tax liability of $6,240 [12% × ($50,000 + ($50,000 × 4%))].

Example (6). Assume the same facts as in example (1) except that D does not give M a certificate. The sale by M to D is a taxable sale of the truck under paragraph (a)(2) of this section. M's tax liability is $6,240 [12% × ($50,000 + ($50,000 × 4%))]. On July 20, 1988 D leases the truck to L, a lessee. The lease has a two-year term. Since the lease to L occurred after a taxable sale of the truck, paragraph (b)(1) of this section does not apply, and the lease is not treated as a taxable sale under this section.

Example (7). M manufactures trucks that are taxable under section 4051. On July 11, 1988, M leases a truck to a lessee, L. The lease has a two-year term. The lease is treated as a taxable sale under paragraph (b)(1) of this section and the tax is computed on the price as determined under paragraph (d)(4)(i) of this section. The constructive sales price established by the Commissioner, pursuant to paragraph (d)(4)(i) of this section, is $50,000. M has a tax liability of $6,240 [12% × ($50,000 + ($50,000 × 4%))].

Example (8). Assume the same facts as in example (7) except that the lease has a six-month term. The lease is treated as a taxable use under paragraph (b)(2) of this section and the tax is computed under paragraph (c)(5) of this section. The constructive sales price established by the Commissioner, pursuant to paragraph (c)(5)(i) of this section, is $52,000. M has a tax liability of $6,240 (12% × $52,000).

Example (9). M manufactures truck trailers and semitrailers that are taxable under section 4051. On July 5, 1988, D, a dealer, purchases a trailer from M for $10,000. Prior to this transaction, D did not give M a certificate and D did not have an agreement with M to resell all articles purchased. The sale by M to D is a taxable sale of the trailer under paragraph (a)(2) of this section. M has a tax liability of $1,200 (12% × $10,000 + ($10,000 × 0%)).

Example (10). Assume the same facts as in example (9) except that on July 12, 1988, D resells the trailer to P, a purchaser, for $10,500 (the additional $500 includes the dealer's markup, costs of transporting the trailer from M to D, and overhead). P did not give D a certificate and P

did not have an agreement with D that stipulates that all articles purchased were to be leased on a long-term basis or resold. The sale of the trailer by D to P is a taxable sale within the meaning of paragraph (a)(3) of this section. Therefore, D has a tax liability of $1,260 (12% × $10,500). D, however, may file for a credit of $1,200 under section 6402 provided that the requirements of paragraph (a)(4) of this section are met.

(f) *Other rules made applicable.*—For purposes of §145.4051-1 and this section, rules similar to the following provisions shall apply:

(1) Section 48.0-2, relating to general definitions and attachment of tax;

(2) Paragraphs (a)(2) and (3) of §48.4061(a)-1;

(3) The exemptions provided by sections 4063(a) and (d) and the regulations thereunder;

(4) Section 4216(f) and the regulations thereunder, relating to the incorporation of used components; and

(5) Section 4221 and the regulations thereunder, relating to certain tax-free sales.

(g) *Effective date.*—(1) *In general.*—Except as provided below, the provisions of this section shall be effective for articles sold or leased on or after April 1, 1983.

(2) *Certain sales made prior to November 12, 1985.*—If a sale to a lessor before November 12, 1985, was not taxable under §145.4052-1 of the temporary regulations contained in 26 CFR part 145 revised as of April 1, 1983, (the "prior regulations") and it was so treated by the parties, a subsequent sale or lease that was or would have been treated as the first retail sale of the article under the prior regulations will be treated as a taxable sale for purposes of this section. The tax on such subsequent sale will be based on a price determined under paragraph (d) of this section. For example, if an article was sold to a purchaser who intended to lease such article long-term, the sale would not have been taxable under the prior regulations even though the seller did not receive a certificate of the purchaser's intent to lease the vehicle. If such a sale was treated as nontaxable by the parties, and the purchaser leases it long-term on or after October 1, 1987, the lease will be treated as a taxable sale of the article. The tax is to be computed under paragraph (b) (3) (ii) of this section and the price will be computed under paragraph (d) (5).

(3) *Certain sales made after November 11, 1985, and before October 1, 1987.*—(i) *Sales not treated as taxable by purchaser and seller.*—If a sale to a purchaser after November 11, 1985, and before October 1, 1987, was not treated as taxable by the parties, a subsequent sale or lease that was or would have been treated as the first retail sale of the article under the temporary regulations published in the September 13, 1985, issue of the FEDERAL REGISTER (50 FR 37350) ("the interim regulations") will be treated as a taxable sale for the purposes of this section. The tax on a sale or lease after September 30, 1987, will be

Reg. §145.4052-1(f)

based on a price determined under paragraph (d) of this section. For example, if a vehicle was sold on January 3, 1987, to a purchaser who intended to resell the article and who was not in the business of leasing to any extent, the sale would not have been taxable under the interim regulations even though the seller did not receive a certificate indicating the purchaser's intent to resell the article. If such a sale was not treated as a taxable sale by the parties, and the purchaser resells the article, the resale will be treated as a taxable sale of the article under paragraph (a)(2) of this section.

(ii) *Sales treated as first retail sale by purchaser and seller.*—If the sale of an article after November 11, 1985, and before October 1, 1987, was treated as a taxable sale by the parties and tax was paid with respect to the article under the interim regulations, the subsequent sale of the article by the purchaser will not be treated as a taxable sale under paragraph (a)(2) of this section. [Temporary Reg. § 145.4052-1.]

☐ [*T.D. 7882, 3-30-83. Amended by T.D. 8050, 9-13-85; T.D. 8200, 5-11-88; T.D. 8774, 6-26-98 and T.D. 8879, 3-30-2000.*]

Manufacturers Excise Taxes

[Reg. § 48.4061(a)-1]

§ 48.4061(a)-1. Imposition of tax; exclusion for light-duty trucks, etc.—(a) *Imposition of tax.*—(1) *In general.*—Section 4061(a)(1) imposes a tax on the sale by the manufacturer, producer, or importer of the following articles (including in each case parts and accessories therefor sold on or in connection therewith or with the sale thereof):

(i) Automobile truck and bus chassis and bodies;

(ii) Truck and bus trailer and semitrailer chassis and bodies; and

(iii) Tractors of the kind chiefly used for highway transportation in combination with a trailer or semitrailer.

For purposes of this section, a sale of an automobile truck or bus, or a truck or bus trailer or semitrailer, shall be considered to be a sale of a chassis and of a body enumerated in this paragraph (a)(1).

(2) *Special rule applicable to chassis and bodies.*—A chassis or body enumerated in paragraph (a)(1) of this section is taxable under section 4061(a)(1) only if such chassis or body is, within the meaning of paragraph (e) of this section, sold for use as a component part of a highway vehicle (as defined in paragraph (d) of this section), which is an automobile truck or bus, a truck or bus trailer or semitrailer, or a tractor of the kind chiefly used for highway transportation in combination with a trailer or semitrailer. Furthermore, a chassis or body which is not enumerated in paragraph (a)(1) of this section is not taxable under section 4061(a)(1) even though such chassis or body is used as a component part of a higway vehicle (*e.g.*, a chassis or body of a passenger automobile).

(3) *Equipment installed on chassis or bodies.*—(i) For purposes of the tax imposed by section 4061(a)(1), equipment or machinery installed on a taxable chassis or body is considered to be an integral part of the taxable chassis or body if the machinery or equipment contributes toward the highway transportation function of the chassis or body, regardless of whether separate sales of the machinery or equipment would be subject to the tax on automotive parts or accessories imposed by section 4061(b). Therefore, the amount of the sale price of a taxable chassis or body that is attributable to such machinery or equipment must be included in the tax base when computing the tax due on a manufacturer's or importer's sale or use of a taxable chassis or body.

Examples of the type of machinery or equipment that contribute to the highway transportation function of a chassis or body are the following: loading and unloading equipment; towing winches; and all other machinery or equipment contributing to either the maintenance or safety of the vehicle, the preservation of cargo (other than refrigeration units), or the comfort or convenience of the driver or passengers.

(ii) Amounts charged for machinery or equipment that is installed on a taxable chassis or body are not part of the taxable sale price of the chassis or body if (A) such machinery or equipment does not contribute toward the highway transportation function of the chassis or body and (B) the reasonableness of the charge for the machinery or equipment is supportable by adequate records. Examples of such machinery or equipment are the following: equipment designed to spread materials on the highway; machinery or equipment used solely in the operation of mobile amusement rides; television equipment mounted in a mobile television studio; machine shop equipment mounted in a mobile machine shop; and car crushing equipment mounted on the chassis of a mobile car crusher.

(4) *Passenger automobile chassis and bodies, motorcycles, etc.*—No tax is imposed under section 4061(a) on the sale of a motorcycle or, in the case of a sale made after December 10, 1971, on the sale of automobile chassis and bodies not enumerated in paragraph (a)(1) of this section, or of trailer and semitrailer chassis and bodies suitable for use in combination with passenger automobiles. For tax on certain sales made after December 31, 1958, and before December 11, 1971, see paragraph (b)(4) of this section.

(5) *Cross references.*—For additional rules relating to the sale of a chassis or body enumerated in this paragraph for use as a component

part of a highway vehicle, see paragraph (e) of this section. For exclusion of certain light-duty highway vehicles, see paragraph (f) of this section. For provisions relating to the tax-free sale of bodies to certain manufacturers, see section 4063(b) and the regulations thereunder. For other exemptions from the tax imposed under section 4061(a), see sections 4063 and 4221 and the regulations thereunder. For special rules relating to the sale by a manufacturer of a vehicle consisting of a tax-paid chassis and a body manufactured by him, see § 48.4061(a)-5.

(b) *Rate and computation of tax.*—(1) *In general.*—With respect to the articles enumerated in paragraph (a)(1) of this section, the rate of tax imposed by section 4061(a)(1) is:

		Percent
(i)	For articles sold during the period beginning on January 1, 1959, and ending on September 30, 1979	10
(ii)	For articles sold on or after October 1, 1979	5

(2) *Determination of price subject to tax.*—The tax is computed by applying to the price for which the article is sold the rate in effect at the time of the sale. For definition of the term "price" and for application of the tax to leases of articles, see sections 4216 and 4217, respectively, and the regulations thereunder. If an article subject to tax under section 4061(a) has equipment mounted thereon to perform functions other than in connection with the transportation of persons or property, no tax under section 4061(a) attaches to that part of the selling price on the invoice to the customer or can otherwise be established by adequate records. For other rules relating to the sale of parts or accessories in connection with the sale of a chassis, body, or completed unit, see § 48.4061(a)-4. For special rules relating to the determination of selling price when equipment or machinery is permanently installed on a taxable chassis or body, see paragraph (a)(3) of this section.

(3) *Tax on trailers sold before December 11, 1971.*—With respect to sales made after December 31, 1958, and before December 11, 1971, the rate of tax imposed under section 4061(a) on a trailer or semitrailer chassis or body that is a highway vehicle within the meaning of paragraph (d) of this section depends upon a classification of the article. The sale during this period of a trailer or semitrailer chassis or body (other than a house trailer) suitable for use in combination with passenger automobiles is subject to tax as set forth in paragraph (b)(4) of this section. A trailer suitable for use in combination with a passenger automobile which is designed for purposes other than living or sleeping, commonly referred to as a "utility trailer", is an example of a trailer taxable at the 7 percent rate set forth in paragraph (b)(4) of this section. The sale of a trailer or semitrailer chassis or body that is not suitable for use in combination with passenger automobiles is subject to tax as set forth in paragraph (b)(1) of this section.

(4) *Passenger automobile chassis and bodies and related articles sold before December 11, 1971.*—With respect to the sale after December 31, 1958, and before December 11, 1971, of (i) automobile chassis and bodies not enumerated in paragraph (a)(1) of this section or (ii) trailer and semitrailer chassis and bodies suitable for use in combination with passenger automobiles, the tax imposed by section 4061(a) is computed in accordance with paragraph (b)(2) of this section

at the rate of 10 percent for sales prior to June 22, 1965, and at the rate of 7 percent thereafter.

(c) *Liability for tax.*—The tax imposed by section 4061(a) is payable by the manufacturer, producer, or importer making the sale.

(d) *Highway vehicle.*—(1) *Definition.*—For purposes of this subchapter, the term "highway vehicle" means any self-propelled vehicle, or any trailer or semitrailer, designed to perform a function of transporting a load over public highways, whether or not also designed to perform other functions, but does not include a vehicle described in paragraph (d)(2) of this section. For purposes of this definition, a vehicle consists of a chassis, or a chassis and a body if the vehicle has a body, but does not include the vehicle's load. Therefore, in determining whether a vehicle is a "highway vehicle", it is immaterial that the vehicle is designed to perform a highway transportation function for only a particular kind of load, such as passengers, furnishings and personal effects (as in a house, office, or utility trailer), a special type of cargo, goods, supplies, or materials, or, except to the extent otherwise provided in paragraph (d)(2)(i) of this section, machinery or equipment specially designed to perform some off-highway task unrelated to highway transportation. In the case of specially designed machinery or equipment, it is also immaterial, except as provided in paragraph (d)(2)(i) of this section, that such machinery or equipment is permanently mounted on the vehicle. For purposes of paragraph (d) of this section, the term "transport" includes the term "tow", and the term "public highway" includes any road (whether a Federal highway, State highway, city street, or otherwise) in the United States which is not a private roadway. A vehicle which is not a highway vehicle within the meaning of this paragraph shall be treated as a nonhighway vehicle for purposes of this subchapter. Examples of vehicles that are designed to perform a function of transporting a load over the public highways are passenger automobiles, motorcycles, buses, and highway-type trucks, truck tractors, trailers, and semi-trailers.

(2) *Exceptions.*—(i) *Certain specially designed mobile machinery for nontransportation functions.*—A self-propelled vehicle, or trailer or semi-trailer, is not a highway vehicle if it (A) consists of a chassis to which there has been permanently mounted (by welding, bolting, riveting, or other means) machinery or equipment to perform a

construction, manufacturing, processing, farming, mining, drilling, timbering, or operation similar to any one of the foregoing enumerated operations if the operation of the machinery or equipment is unrelated to transportation on or off the public highways, (B) the chassis has been specially designed to serve only as a mobile carriage and mount (and a power source, where applicable) for the particular machinery or equipment involved, whether or not such machinery or equipment is in operation, and (C) by reason of such special design, such chassis could not, without substantial structural modification, be used as a component of a vehicle designed to perform a function of transporting any load other than that particular machinery or equipment or similar machinery or equipment requiring such a specially designed chassis.

(ii) *Certain vehicles specially designed for off-highway transportation.*—A self-propelled vehicle, or a trailer or semi-trailer, is not a highway vehicle if it is (A) specially designed for the primary function of transporting a particular type of load other than over the public highway in connection with a construction, manufacturing, processing, farming, mining, drilling, timbering, or operation similar to any one of the foregoing enumerated operations, and (B) if by reason of such special design, the use of such vehicle to transport such load over the public highways is substantially limited or substantially impaired. For purposes of applying the rule of (B) of this subdivision, account may be taken of whether the vehicle may travel at regular highway speeds, requires a special permit for highway use, is overweight, overheight or overwidth for regular highway use, and any other relevant considerations. Solely for purposes of determinations under this paragraph (d)(2)(ii), where there is affixed to the vehicle equipment used for loading, unloading, storing, vending, handling, processing, preserving, or otherwise caring for a load transported by the vehicle over the public highways, the functions are related to the transportation of a load over the public highways even though such functions may be performed off the public highways.

(iii) *Certain trailers and semi-trailers specially designed to perform non-transportation functions off the public highways.*—A trailer or semi-trailer is not a highway vehicle if it is specially designed to serve no purpose other than providing an enclosed stationary shelter for the carrying on of a function which is directly connected with and necessary [to, and at the off-highway site of, a con-] struction, manufacturing, processing, mining, drilling, farming, timbering, or operation similar to any one of the foregoing enumerated operations such as a trailer specially designed to serve as an office for such an operation.

(3) *Optional application.*—For purposes of this subchapter, if any rules existing immediately prior to January 13, 1977, would, if applicable, unequivocally resolve an issue involving the definition of a highway vehicle with respect to a period prior to such date, at the option of the taxpayer, such rules existing prior to such date shall be applied to resolve the issue for all periods prior to such date, and the rules of paragraph (d)(1) and (2) of this section, which define the term "highway vehicle", shall not apply with respect to such issue for all periods prior to such date.

(4) *Highway vehicles not subject to section 4061 tax.*—Although for purposes of this paragraph (d) passenger automobiles, automobile trailers and semi-trailers, motor homes, motorcycles, light-duty trucks, etc., will be considered to be highway vehicles because they are designed to perform a function of transporting a load over public highways, the tax imposed under section 4061(a) does not apply to the sale of such vehicles because they either are not articles subject to tax under such section or are excluded from tax under section 4061(a)(2). See also paragraphs (a)(4) and (f) of this section. Despite the fact that passenger automobiles, passenger automobile trailers and semi-trailers, motor homes, motorcycles, light-duty trucks, etc., are not subject to the manufacturers excise tax on highway vehicles imposed by section 4061(a), the fact that they are nevertheless considered highway vehicles for purposes of this subchapter can be of material significance in determining the applicability of such excise taxes as the tax imposed by section 4041 (relating to diesel and special motor fuels), the tax imposed by section 4071(a)(1) (relating to tires of the type used on highway vehicles), or the tax imposed by section 4481 (relating to highway use tax on highway motor vehicles). In addition, the definition of the term "highway vehicle" is material in determining the credits or refunds provided by section 6416(b)(2)(I) (relating to diesel fuel used in certain highway vehicles), section 6421(a) (relating to gasoline used for a nonhighway purpose), section 6424 (relating to lubricating oil used otherwise than in a highway motor vehicle), and section 6427(a) (relating to diesel or special motor fuel not used for a taxable purpose).

(e) *Sale of a chassis or body for use as a component of a vehicle other than a highway vehicle.*—(1) *In general.*—Except as otherwise provided in paragraphs (a)(4), (e)(2), or (f) of this section, the sale of a chassis or body shall be deemed to be a sale of a chassis or body enumerated in paragraph (a)(1) of this section if such chassis or body is, in any sense, reasonably suitable for use as a component part of a highway vehicle that is either an automobile truck or bus, a truck or bus trailer or semitrailer, or a tractor of the kind chiefly used for highway transportation in combination with a trailer or semitrailer.

(2) *Exceptions based on unitary concept.*—(i) *Completed vehicles not qualifying as highway vehicles.*—With respect to the sale of a vehicle after January 13, 1977, which would otherwise be treated under paragraph (e)(1) of this section as a sale of a chassis or body enumerated in para-

Reg. § 48.4061(a)-1(e)(2)(i)

graph (a)(1) of this section, the tax imposed under section 4061(a) shall not apply to such sale if the vehicle (considered as a completed unit) is not considered to be a highway vehicle within the meaning of paragraph (d) of this section.

(ii) *Tax-free sales of chassis and bodies.*— With respect to the sale after January 13, 1977 of a chassis or body (not including the sale of a completed vehicle described in paragraph (e)(2)(i) of this section) which would otherwise be treated under paragraph (e)(1) of this section as a sale of a chassis or body enumerated in paragraph (a)(1) of this section, the tax imposed under section 4061(a) shall not apply to such sale if the chassis or body is actually sold for use, or for resale for use, as a component part of a vehicle that is not a highway vehicle within the meaning of paragraph (d) of this section. For purposes of determining the liability of the manufacturer or reseller for the tax imposed under section 4061(a), the test of the preceding sentence will be considered to be met if (A) the purchaser furnishes the statement set forth in paragraph (e)(2)(iv) of this section to the seller before the manufacturer files a return covering excise taxes for the period in which the sale was made, and (B) the manufacturer or reseller complies with the requirements set forth in paragraph (e)(2)(iii) of this section. However, even though the purchaser and manufacturer (or reseller) have complied with the foregoing, the tax imposed under section 4061(a), shall apply to such sale if the manufacturer or reseller has received a written notification (applicable with respect to such sale) from the Internal Revenue Service that sales of a specified type or types of chassis or bodies may not be made tax free pursuant to this paragraph (e)(2)(ii) until further notification. Any such notification issued by the Internal Revenue Service shall be effective only with respect to sales after the manufacturer has received such notification.

(iii) *Requirements to be met.*—In order for a manufacturer or reseller to sell free of tax under paragraph (e)(2)(ii) of this section an otherwise taxable chassis or body, the manufacturer or reseller must—

(A) Retain in his possession the statement required to be furnished by the purchaser and such other evidence as may be furnished by the purchaser to support the tax-free sale. Such evidence shall be retained for at least 3 years from the due date of the tax that would be due if the transaction in question had been a taxable sale; and

(B) Indicate on the invoice with respect to the sale of the chassis or body that the sale of such article is made free of tax under paragraph (e)(2)(ii) of this section.

(iv) *Form of statement.*—In order for an otherwise taxable chassis or body to be sold free of tax under paragraph (e)(2)(ii) of this section, the purchaser must execute and furnish to the manufacturer or reseller a statement that substantially complies with the following form:. . . . . ,19 . . . . . .

Under the penalty of perjury, the undersigned certifies that he, or the . . . . (Name of purchaser if other than the undersigned), of which he is . . . . (Title), is in the business of . . . . (State nature of business), and that the chassis and/or bodies covered by the accompanying order or contract for purchase from . . . . (Name and address of seller) are purchased for (check one) ☐ use, or for ☐ resale for use, as components of the following type or types of nonhighway vehicles:

1. . . . .
2. . . . .
3. . . . .

The undersigned understands that he must be prepared to establish by satisfactory evidence the actual use or disposition of such chassis or bodies and that, upon their use or disposition other than use as components of a nonhighway vehicle, he consents to be treated as the manufacturer of any such chassis or body purchased by him free of the tax imposed by section 4061(a).

The undersigned also understands that he and all guilty parties will, for use of this statement to willfully attempt to evade or defeat the tax imposed under section 4061, be subject, under section 7201, to a fine of not more than $10,000, or imprisonment for not more than 5 years, or both, together with the costs of prosecution.

The undersigned agrees to retain in his possession a copy of this statement for at least 3 years from its date.

. . . .
(Signature)
. . . .
(Address)

(v) *Refund or credit of overpayment.*—If a purchaser furnishes the manufacturer with the statement described in paragraph (e)(2)(iv) of this section after the time the manufacturer has filed a return covering excise taxes for the period in which the sale was made, the manufacturer must include the tax on the sale in his return for the period. However, in such case, if the conditions prescribed in paragraph (e)(2)(iii) of this section are met, a claim for refund of the tax paid on such sale may be filed by the manufacturer on Form 843, or a credit taken on a subsequent return, in accordance with the provisions of sections 6402(a) and 6416(a) and § 48.6416(a)-1.

(vi) *Cross reference.*—For special rules relating to the sale by a manufacturer of a vehicle consisting of a tax-paid chassis and a body manufactured by him, see § 48.4061(a)-5.

(f) *Exclusion of light-duty trucks, buses, and related articles from tax.*—(1) *In general.*—(i) No tax is imposed by section 4061(a)(1) on the sale after December 10, 1971, of the following articles, if suitable for use with a vehicle having a gross vehicle weight of 10,000 pounds or less (as determined under paragraph (f)(3) of this section):

(A) Automobile truck and bus chassis and bodies, and

(B) Truck trailer and semitrailer chassis and bodies, suitable for use with a trailer or semitrailer having a gross vehicle weight of 10,000 pounds or less (as so determined).

(ii) For purposes of this part, a chassis or body is suitable for use with a vehicle having a gross vehicle weight of 10,000 pounds or less (hereafter referred to in this paragraph (f) as a "light-duty vehicle") if such chassis or body is commonly used with such a vehicle or possesses actual, practical, and commercial fitness for such use. A truck or bus chassis, sold after December 10, 1971, which is suitable for use with a light-duty vehicle, is not subject to the tax imposed by section 4061(a)(1) regardless of the body actually mounted thereon. Similarly, a truck trailer or semitrailer chassis sold after such date, suitable for use with a trailer or semitrailer having a gross vehicle weight of 10,000 pounds or less, which trailer or semitrailer is suitable for use in connection with a light-duty towing vehicle, is not subject to such tax regardless of the body actually mounted thereon. A truck or bus body, sold after such date, which is suitable for use with a light-duty vehicle, is not subject to such tax even though it may also be suitable for use with (and is actually a component of) a vehicle having a gross vehicle weight in excess of 10,000 pounds. Similarly, a truck trailer or semitrailer body sold after such date, suitable for use with a trailer or semitrailer having a gross vehicle weight of 10,000 pounds or less, which trailer or semitrailer is suitable for use with a light-duty towing vehicle, is not subject to such tax even though it may also be suitable for use with (and is actually a component of) a trailer or semitrailer having a gross vehicle weight of more than 10,000 pounds, or is used in connection with a vehicle having a gross vehicle weight of more than 10,000 pounds.

(iii) Where an exempt body is mounted on a taxable chassis, or a taxable body is mounted on an exempt chassis, the taxable chassis or taxable body, as the case may be, nevertheless remains subject to such tax, if the resulting vehicle is a highway vehicle as defined in paragraph (d) of this section.

(iv) Where the modification of an article, exempt from tax when sold by the original manufacturer, constitutes further manufacture after the original manufacturer's sale, a tax may be imposed on the subsequent manufacturer's sale or use of the modified article.

(2) *Parts and accessories.*—(i) The sale of a part or accessory which, if sold on December 10, 1971, would be subject to the tax imposed by section 4061(a)(1) as in effect at such time, is not subject to the tax imposed by section 4061(a)(1) as in effect after such date if—

(A) It is sold by the manufacturer on or in connection therewith, or with the sale of, a

vehicle enumerated in paragraph (f)(1)(i) of this section which is not subject to such tax, and

(B) It is not a replacement part (as defined in paragraph (f)(2)(ii) of this section).

(ii) For purposes of this paragraph (f)(2), a part or accessory is considered sold with a vehicle if, as of the time the article is sold by the manufacturer, the part or accessory has been ordered from such manufacturer for use with the vehicle. Thus, for example, original equipment sold after December 10, 1971, with a light-duty vehicle, consisting of parts and accessories which are ordered from the manufacturer of the vehicle not later than the time at which such vehicle is sold by him (whether or not installed as of such time) are not subject to such tax. For purposes of this paragraph (f)(2), a part is a replacement part, regardless of when ordered, if its use with a vehicle is as a replacement for a part of such vehicle. Therefore, spare parts or accessories sold separately or ordered with a light-duty truck are subject to the tax imposed on sales of parts or accessories by section 4061(b)(1), unless they are excluded from tax as articles used interchangeably between truck and passenger vehicles under the provisions of section 4061(b)(2).

(3) *Gross vehicle weight.*—(i) For purposes of paragraph (f)(1) of this section, gross vehicle weight means the maximum total weight of a loaded vehicle. Except as otherwise provided in this paragraph (f)(3), such maximum total weight shall be the gross vehicle weight rating of the article (as manufactured) as specified or established by the manufacturer of the completed article, unless such rating is unreasonable in light of the facts and circumstances in a particular case.

(ii) A manufacturer must specify or establish a weight rating for each chassis, body, or vehicle sold by him after September 22, 1971, if such article requires no additional manufacture other than (A) the addition of readily attachable articles, such as tire or rim assemblies or minor accessories, (B) the performance of minor finishing operations, such as painting, or (C) in the case of a chassis, the addition of a body. If an article is specially manufactured to the purchaser's specifications, such specifications may be used to establish the gross vehicle weight of the article.

(iii) A manufacturer shall maintain a record of the gross vehicle weight rating of each truck, bus, trailer, and semitrailer sold by him and excluded from the tax imposed by section 4061(a)(1) by reason of section 4061(a)(2) and this paragraph (f). For this purpose, a record of the serial number of each such article shall be treated as a record of the gross vehicle weight rating of the article if such rating is indicated by the serial number.

(iv) If (A) the manufacturer's rating indicated in a label or identifying device affixed to an article, (B) the rating set forth in his sales invoice or warranty agreement, and (C) his advertised rating for that article (or two or more identical articles) are inconsistent, the highest of such ratings will be considered to be the manufacturer's gross vehicle weight rating specified or established for purposes of the tax imposed by section 4061(a)(1).

(v) With respect to articles sold after January 31, 1972, the manufacturer's gross vehicle weight rating must take into account the strength of the chassis frame, the axle capacity and placement, and the spring, brake, rim, and tire capacities. The component with the lowest weight rating ordinarily shall be considered determinative of the gross vehicle weight. If the capacity of any of the readily attachable components (springs, brakes, rims, or tires) would otherwise be determinative of a gross vehicle weight rating of 10,000 pounds or less, no readily attachable component will be taken into account in determining such rating unless the rating determined solely on the basis of the chassis frame or the total of the axle ratings is 12,000 pounds or less.

(vi) For purposes of paragraph (f)(3)(v) of this section, the term "total of the axle ratings" means the sum of the maximum load carrying capability (capacity and placement) of the axles (without regard to springs, brakes, rims, and tires) and, in the case of a trailer or semitrailer, the weight, if any, that is to be borne by a vehicle used in combination with the trailer or semitrailer for which gross vehicle weight is determined. [Reg. § 48.4061(a)-1.]

☐ [*T.D. 6648, 4-12-63. Amended by T.D. 6694, 12-4-63; T.D. 6753, 9-8-64; T.D. 7461, 1-12-77 and T.D. 7566, 9-15-78.*]

[Reg. § 48.4061(a)-2]

§ 48.4061(a)-2. Bonding of importers.—
(a) *Authority for requiring bond.*—Section 623 of the Tariff Act of 1930, as amended (19 U.S.C. 1623), provides as follows:

"SEC. 623. *Bonds and other security.* (a) In any case in which bond or other security is not specifically required by law, the Secretary of the Treasury may by regulation or specific instruction require, or authorize collectors of customs to require, such bonds or other security as he, or they, may deem necessary for the protection of the revenue or to assure compliance with any provision of law, regulation, or instruction which the Secretary of the Treasury or the Customs Service may be authorized to enforce.

"(b) Whenever a bond is required or authorized by a law, regulation, or instruction which the Secretary of the Treasury or the Customs Service is authorized to enforce, the Secretary of the Treasury may—

"(1) Except as otherwise specifically provided by law, prescribe the conditions and form of such bond, and fix the amount of penalty thereof, whether for the payment of liquidated damages or of a penal sum: *Provided,* That when a consolidated bond authorized by paragraph 4 of this subsection is taken, the Secretary of the Treasury may fix the penalty of such bond without regard to any other provision of law, regulation, or instruction.

"(2) Provide for the approval of the sureties on such bond, without regard to any general provision of law.

"(3) Authorize the execution of a term bond the conditions of which shall extend to and cover similar cases of importations over such period of time, not to exceed one year, or such longer period as he may fix when in his opinion special circumstances existing in a particular instance require such longer period.

"(4) Authorize, to the extent that he may deem necessary, the taking of a consolidated bond (single entry of term), in lieu of separate bonds to assure compliance with two or more provisions of law, regulations, or instructions which the Secretary of the Treasury or the Customs Service is authorized to enforce. A consolidated bond taken pursuant to the authority contained in this subsection shall have the same force and effect in respect of every provision of law, regulation, or instruction for the purposes for which it is required as though separate bonds had been taken to assure compliance with each such provision.

"(c) The Secretary of the Treasury may authorize the cancellation of any bond provided for in this section, or of any charge that may have been made against such bond, in the event of a breach of any condition of the bond, upon the payment of such lesser amount or penalty or upon such other terms and conditions as he may deem sufficient.

"(d) No condition in any bond taken to assure compliance with any law, regulation, or instruction which the Secretary of the Treasury or the Customs Service is authorized to enforce shall be held invalid on the ground that such condition is not specified in the law, regulation, or instruction authorizing or requiring the taking of such bond.

"(e) The Secretary of the Treasury is authorized to permit the deposit of money or obligations of the United States, in such amount and upon such conditions as he may by regulation prescribe, in lieu of sureties on any bond required or authorized by a law, regulation, or instruction which the Secretary of the Treasury or the Customs Service is authorized to enforce."

(b) *Application for determination whether bond required.*—(1) *Requirement of application.*—(i) *In general.*—Except as otherwise provided in subparagraph (2) of this paragraph, every importer of articles taxable under section 4061(a) shall make application for a determination whether the importer is required to give bond in accordance with the provisions of paragraph (c) of this section. Such application shall be submitted in writing to the district director for the district in which the importer will file returns of any tax under section 4061(a) for which he may incur liability.

(ii) *Form of application.*—No form is prescribed for making the application required under subdivision (i) of this subparagraph, but such application shall include the following information:

(a) The name of the person making the application and the address of his principal place of business, and, if the principal place of business of such person is outside the United States, the address of his principal place of business, office, or agency in the United States.

(b) Information establishing that the person making the application is an importer of articles taxable under section 4061(a).

(c) The kind and approximate number of automobiles, trucks, buses, etc., which the importer may be expected to import during an average calendar quarter and the approximate amount of tax under section 4061(a) for which the importer may be expected to incur liability in respect of such articles.

(d) Whether the importer has filed returns of tax under chapter 31 or chapter 32 within the 2-year period immediately preceding the date on which the application is filed, and, if so, the internal revenue district in which such returns were filed.

(e) Facts pertaining to the importer's assets and liabilities which will aid the district director in determining whether a bond shall be required.

(2) *Exceptions.*—The provisions of subparagraph (1) of this paragraph shall have no application in any case where an article taxable under section 4061(a) is—

(i) Incidentally imported by an individual for his personal use.

(ii) Brought into the United States for export to a foreign country or possession of the United States.

(iii) Admitted to the United States free of duty as an instrument of international traffic.

(iv) Admitted to the United States free of duty as a temporary importation under bond.

(v) Returned to the United States after having been sold in the United States and exported.

(c) *Requirement of bond.*—(1) *In general.*—If the district director determines that a bond is necessary in order to insure payment of the tax under section 4061(a), and to assure compliance with all provisions of the Code and regulations thereunder, with respect to articles imported by any importer required to make application for a determination under paragraph (b) of this section, such bond shall be given by such importer. Such bond shall be submitted, in duplicate, to the district director for the district in which the importer will file returns of any tax under section 4061(a) for which he may incur liability.

(2) *Execution of bond.*—(i) *In general.*—The bond required under this paragraph shall be executed with satisfactory surety. (For provisions as to what will be considered "satisfactory surety", see subparagraph (3) of this paragraph.) Such bond shall be conditioned that the principal shall not engage in any attempt, by himself or by collusion with others, to defraud the United States of any tax under section 4061(a); that he shall render truly and completely all returns, statements, and other documents required of him by law or regulations in respect of such tax; that he shall timely pay all such tax for which he is liable; and in the case of any such tax in respect of an article released from customs custody by reason of such bond, that he shall pay such tax, whether the liability therefor is incurred by him or by some other person as the importer of the articles covered by the bond, unless such other person makes payment of such tax on or before the due date. The bond shall be in an amount which the district director believes to be sufficient to protect the interests of the United States with respect to all articles taxable under section 4061(a) which are released from customs custody by reason of such bond, but in no event shall the bond be in an amount less than the approximate amount of tax under section 4061(a) for which the principal may be expected to incur liability during an average calendar quarter. Such bond shall be signed by the individual, if the principal is an individual; the president, vice president, or other principal officer, if the principal is a corporation; a responsible and duly authorized member or officer having knowledge of its affairs, if the principal is a partnership or other unincorporated organization; or the fiduciary, if the principal is a trust or estate.

(ii) *Cancellation clause.*—The bond required under this paragraph may be accepted with a cancellation clause incorporated therein. Such cancellation clause shall provide that:

(a) Any surety on the bond may at any time give notice to the principal and the district director that he desires to be relieved of liability under said bond after a date named, which shall be at least 60 days after the receipt of notice by the district director.

(b) If the notice is not withdrawn in writing prior to the date named in the notice, the rights of the principal as supported by said bond shall be terminated on such date (unless supported by another bond or bonds). The surety shall, however, remain liable with respect to any tax under section 4061(a) (plus penalties and interest) the liability for which is incurred in respect of articles released from customs custody by reason of the bond.

(c) Said notice may not be given by an agent of the surety, unless it is accompanied by power of attorney duly executed by the surety authorizing the agent to give such notice or by a verified statement that such power of attorney is on file with the Treasury Department.

(iii) *Changes in bond.*—After filing of the bond required under this paragraph, no change may be made in the terms thereof except with the consent of the surety or sureties and subject to the approval of the district director.

(3) *Satisfactory surety.*—(i) *Approved surety company or bonds or notes of the United States.*—For

Reg. §48.4061(a)-2(c)(3)(i)

purposes of subparagraph (2) of this paragraph, a bond shall be considered executed with satisfactory surety if:

(a) It is executed by a surety company holding a certificate of authority from the Secretary as an acceptable surety on Federal bonds; or

(b) It is secured by bonds or notes of the United States as provided in 6 U.S.C. 15 (see 31 CFR Part 225).

(ii) *Other surety acceptable in discretion of district director.*—For purposes of subparagraph (2) of this paragraph, a bond may, in the discretion of the district director, be considered executed with satisfactory surety if, in lieu of being executed or secured as provided in subdivision (i) of this subparagraph, it is—

(a) Executed by a corporate surety (other than a surety company), provided such corporate surety establishes that it is within its corporate powers to act as surety for another corporation or an individual;

(b) Executed by two or more individual sureties, provided such individual sureties meet the conditions contained in subdivision (iii) of this subparagraph;

(c) Secured by a mortgage on real or personal property;

(d) Secured by a certified, cashier's, or treasurer's check drawn on any bank or trust company incorporated under the laws of the United States or any State, Territory, or possession of the United States, or by a United States postal, bank, express, or telegraph money order;

(e) Secured by corporate bonds or stocks, or by bonds issued by a State or political subdivision thereof, of recognized stability; or

(f) Secured by any other acceptable collateral. Collateral shall be deposited with the district director or, in his discretion, with a responsible financial institution acting as escrow agent.

(iii) *Conditions to be met by individual sureties.*—If a bond is executed by two or more individual sureties, the following conditions must be met by each such individual surety:

(a) He must reside within the State in which the principal place of business or legal residence of the primary obligor is located;

(b) He must have property subject to execution of a current market value, above all encumbrances, equal to at least the penalty of the bond;

(c) All real property which he offers as security must be located in the State in which the principal place of business or legal residence of the primary obligor is located;

(d) He must agree not to mortgage, or otherwise encumber, any property offered as security while the bond continues in effect without first securing the permission of the district director; and

(e) He must file with the bond, and annually thereafter so long as the bond continues in effect, an affidavit as to the adequacy of his security, executed on the appropriate form furnished by the district director.

Partners may not act as sureties upon bonds of their partnership. Stockholders of a corporate principal may be accepted as sureties provided their qualifications as such are independent of their holdings of the stock of the corporation.

(iv) *Adequacy of surety.*—No surety or security shall be accepted if it does not adequately protect the interest of the United States.

(4) *New or additional bond.*—The district director may require a new or additional bond under this section in any case where he deems it necessary or desirable in order to protect the interests of the United States.

(d) *Termination of requirement.*—(1) *Application for relief from requirement.*—Any importer who has given bond as required under paragraph (c) of this section may make application for relief from such requirement at any time after the last day of the first month following the close of the calendar quarter in which the bond was given. Any such application shall be submitted to the district director to whom the bond was furnished and shall set forth such facts as will be of assistance to the district director in determining whether the relief shall be granted.

(2) *Relief from requirement.*—In any case where the district director determines that the bond required under paragraph (c) of this section to be given by an importer is no longer necessary to insure payment of any tax under section 4061(a) for which liability may be incurred by such importer, such importer shall no longer be required to give such bond.

(e) *Evidence required for release of imported articles from customs custody.*—(1) *In general.*—Each article taxable under section 4061(a) which arrives in the United States from any foreign country or possession of the United States on or after the first day of the first calendar quarter beginning more than 60 days after the date of publication of this Treasury decision in the Federal Register, and which is imported by any person required under paragraph (b) of this section to make application for a determination whether bond shall be given, shall not, if subject to customs examination and release, be released from customs custody until the evidence prescribed in subparagraph (2)(i) or (ii) of this paragraph has been furnished by such person to the collector of customs.

(2) *Form of evidence.*—The evidence required under subparagraph (1) of this paragraph shall be in the form of a statement, executed, signed, and dated by the district director. Such statement shall show the following:

(i) *Bond required.*—If the importer is required to give bond under this section, the statement shall show—

(a) The total number of articles in respect of which the statement is given.

(b) The model number of each such article.

(c) The name and address of the importer of such articles.

(d) If the articles are to be released from customs custody to a person other than the importer, the name and address of such other person.

(e) That the importer has given a bond which the district director finds sufficient to protect the interests of the United States with respect to any tax under section 4061(a) for which liability may be incurred in respect of such articles.

A statement under this subdivision shall be furnished to the importer by the district director, upon request of the importer, in every case where such importer furnishes the district director with information which establishes to the satisfaction of the district director that the importer has given bond in an amount sufficient to protect the interests of the United States with respect to any tax under section 4061(a) which may become due in respect of the articles to which the request relates, and with such other information as is required under this subdivision to be shown in the statement. Such request, together with such information, shall be submitted by the importer immediately upon receipt by him of notice that articles taxable under section 4061(a) have been exported to his order. A separate request shall be made in respect of each shipment. Each statement given under this subdivision shall be executed in duplicate. The original of such statement shall be furnished by the district director to the importer and the copy shall be retained by the district director.

(ii) *No bond required.*—If the importer is not required to give bond under this section, the statement shall show—

(a) The name and address of the importer.

(b) That bond under this section is not required of such importer.

A statement under this subdivision shall be furnished to the importer by the district director on the date on which the district director determines that the importer is not required to give a bond under this section. Such statement shall be executed in triplicate. The original of such statement and one signed copy shall be furnished by the district director to the importer, and one copy shall be retained by the district director. Additional signed copies of such statement will be furnished by the district director to the importer upon request of the importer. However, once such statement, or a signed copy thereof, has been furnished by the importer to a collector of customs, the requirements imposed by subparagraph (1) of this paragraph are deemed to be satisfied in respect of all articles taxable under section 4061(a) which thereafter arrive in the United States for release to or for the importer in a port under the jurisdiction of such collector of customs, until such time, if any, as such collector of customs receives written notification from the district director or the Commissioner of Customs

that such statement has been withdrawn. [Reg. § 48.4061(a)-2.]

☐ *[T.D. 6499. Amended by T.D. 7517, 11-11-77.]*

[Reg. § 48.4061(a)-3]

§ 48.4061(a)-3. Definitions.—For purposes of the tax imposed by section 4061, unless otherwise expressly indicated:

(a) *Automobile truck.*—The term "automobile truck" includes automobile buses, and truck and bus trailers and semitrailers.

(b) *Other automobile.*—The term "other automobile" means all automobiles other than automobile trucks, and includes trailers and semitrailers suitable for use in connection with passenger automobiles, but does not include house trailers.

(c) *Tractor.*—The term "tractor" means any tractor chiefly used for highway transportation in combination with a trailer or semitrailer. [Reg. § 48.4061(a)-3.]

☐ *[T.D. 6648, 4-12-63.]*

[Reg. § 48.4061(a)-4]

§ 48.4061(a)-4. Parts or accessories sold on or in connection with chassis, bodies, etc.—(a) *In general.*—The tax attaches in respect of parts or accessories for articles specified in section 4061(a) sold on or in connection therewith or with the sale thereof at the rate applicable to the sale of the basic article. The tax attaches in such case whether or not the parts or accessories are billed separately. For the tax applicable to parts or accessories which are not sold on or in connection with the sale of a taxable chassis, body, or tractor, see § 48.4061(b)-1.

(b) *Essential equipment.*—If taxable chassis, bodies, or tractors are sold by the manufacturer, producer, or importer without parts or accessories which are considered equipment essential for the operation or appearance of such articles, the sale of such parts or accessories will be considered, in the absence of evidence to the contrary, to have been made in connection with the sale of the basic article even though they are shipped separately at the same time or on a different date. For example, if a manufacturer sells to any person a chassis and the bumpers for such chassis, or sells a taxable tractor and the fifth wheel and attachments, the tax applies to such parts or accessories at the same rate as on the chassis or tractor regardless of the method of billing or the time at which the shipments were made. [Reg. § 48.4061(a)-4.]

☐ *[T.D. 6648, 4-12-63.]*

[Reg. § 48.4061(a)-5]

§ 48.4061(a)-5. Sale of automobile truck bodies and chassis.—(a) *Sale of completed vehicle.*—An automobile truck (as defined by § 48.4061(a)-3(a)) for purposes of the tax imposed by section 4061(a) consists of two parts, namely, a body and a chassis. Generally, the tax applies to the sale by the manufacturer of each. Thus, if the purchaser of a tax-paid chassis attaches to it a taxable body manufactured by him and sells the completed vehicle, he is liable for tax based on the sale price of the body only. However, in such a case, the tax attaches to the selling price of the entire vehicle unless adequate records are available to show the portion of the total selling price attributable to the body.

(b) *Cross references.*—For special rules relating to the sale of a chassis or body to a purchaser who will use it in the manufacture or assembly of an nonhighway vehicle, see §48.4061(a)-1(e). With respect to bodies sold to a chassis manufacturer, see also section 4063(b) and the regulations thereunder. [Reg. §48.4061(a)-5.]

(1) Parts or accessories sold during the period January 1, 1959, to June 30, 1965, inclusive 8
(2) Parts or accessories sold on or after July 1, 1965 5

The tax is computed by applying to the price for which the part or accessory is sold the rate in effect at the time of the sale. For definition of the term "price" see section 4216 and the regulations thereunder contained in Subpart M of this part.

(c) *Liability for tax.*—The tax imposed by section 4061(b) is payable by the manufacturer, producer, or importer making the sale. [Reg. §48.4061(b)-1.]

☐ [T.D. 6648, 4-12-63. *Amended by T.D.* 6694, 12-4-63, *and T.D.* 6753, 9-8-64.]

[Reg. §48.4061(b)-2]

§48.4061(b)-2. Definition of parts or accessories.—(a) *In general.*—The term "parts or accessories" includes (1) any article the primary use of which is to improve, repair, replace, or serve as a component part of an automobile truck or bus chassis or body, or other automobile chassis or body, or taxable tractor, (2) any article designed to be attached to or used in connection with such chassis, body, or tractor to add to its utility or ornamentation, and (3) any article the primary use of which is in connection with such chassis, body, or tractor, whether or not essential to its operation or use. The term "parts or accessories" includes all articles which have reached such a stage of manufacture as to be commonly known as parts or accessories whether or not fitting operations are required in connection with their installation. An article shall not be deemed to be a taxable part or accessory even though it is designed to be attached to the vehicle or to be primarily used in connection therewith if the article is in effect the load being transported and the primary function of the article is to serve a purpose unrelated to the vehicle as such. For example, a construction derrick attached to a truck is not a taxable part or accessory inasmuch as the derrick is the load of the truck and its use is in connection with construction work at a construction site rather than in connection with the transportation or loading or unloading function of the truck. On the other hand, an article such as a towing cradle or loading or unloading equipment designed to be attached to or to be

☐ [T.D. 6648, 4-12-63.]

[Reg. §48.4061(b)-1]

§48.4061(b)-1. Imposition of tax.—(a) *In general.*—Section 4061(b) imposes a tax on the sale by the manufacturer, producer, or importer of parts or accessories (other than tires and inner tubes and other than automobile radio and television receiving sets) for any of the articles enumerated in section 4061(a) (see paragraph (a) of §48.4061(a)-1).

(b) *Rates of tax.*—Tax is imposed on the sale of parts or accessories for any of the articles enumerated in section 4061(a) at the rates specified below:

Percent

primarily used in connection with a truck is a taxable part or accessory inasmuch as the article contributes to the load-carrying function of the truck. The term "parts or accessories" does not include tires, inner tubes, or automobile radio or television receiving sets, since these articles are expressly exempted by section 4061(b) from the tax. However, the term "parts or accessories" includes tire valves designed for use on tires or tubes for articles taxable under section 4061(a).

(b) *Articles of a general use.*—The term "parts or accessories" does not include articles which are not used primarily in the manufacture, repair, etc., of automobile trucks, other automobiles, or tractors, but have a general use in the manufacture, repair, etc., of various articles. For example, commodities such as ball and roller bearings, bolts, nuts, washers, screws, nails, tacks, rivets, pins, studs, cotters, pipe fittings such as plugs, tees, ells, and elbows, drain cocks, grease cups, oilers, and similar articles are not of themselves parts or accessories unless so constructed as to be used primarily in the manufacture, repair, etc., of automobile trucks, other automobiles, or tractors. On the other hand, parts for automobile parts or accessories are in themselves taxable unless they are articles of a type not specifically designed for use primarily in the automobile field. For example, the tax applies to the sale of gears, flexible shafts, and flexible housings designed as replacement parts for automotive speedometers; as well as replacement parts for automobile engines, transmissions, differentials, steering mechanisms, timers, windshield-wiper motors, and other automobile parts or accessories.

(c) *Materials of a general use.*—(1) *General rule.*—The term "parts or accessories" also does not include material such as glass, cloth, leather, matting linoleum, and other materials sold in rolls or by the foot, such as brake lining, tape, binding, wire, cable, metal and rubber tubing, packing, conduit, and similar material. However, except as provided in subparagraph (2) of this paragraph, when any such material is cut or otherwise transformed by any person into an automobile part or accessory, tax attaches at the time such part or accessory is sold by such person.

(2) *Articles made for immediate installation or repair.*—If in connection with an immediate installation in an automobile truck, other automobile, or tractor an article is produced through the use of special machinery or as a result of specialized skills from lengths or rolls of material, the person producing such article is considered to have manufactured an automobile part or accessory and the tax applies to his sale of such part or accessory. For example, tax applies to the sale of automobile glass cut to size to replace broken glass, or automobile seat covers, automobile floor mats, or fitted truck top covers produced to replace worn seat covers, floor mats, or truck top covers. However, if an article of a minor nature is produced by simple operation from lengths or rolls of material for immediate use by a repairman in the repair of an automobile truck, other automobile, or tractor on which he is then working, the person producing such article is not considered to have manufactured an automobile part or accessory and tax does not apply on his sale of such article. For example, tax does not apply where a wire, hose, or board is cut to size in order to replace a damaged wire, hose, or board of an automobile truck, other automobile, or tractor.

(d) *Examples of articles taxable as parts or accessories.*—Examples of articles which are taxable as parts or accessories are: Automobile air conditioners; baby seats for automobiles; automobile beds; automobile hammocks; automobile clutches; bottle warmers and heating pads designed to operate from an automobile cigarette lighter; automobile radio antennae; automobile license plate frames; automobile clocks; automobile mirrors and mirror brackets; purses for carrying parking meter coins or cases for carrying registration cards when designed for attachment to an automobile; safes primarily designed for use in taxable motor vehicles; electric bulbs primarily designed and adapted for use on automobiles; automobile floor mats; jacks of the mechanical or hydraulic bumper, screw, ratchet, scissors, or other type primarily designed to be carried as accessories in automobiles as distinguised from jacks designed especially for use in garages and repair shops; dollies of the type commonly known as converter dollies which are used as connectors to convert semitrailers to full trailers; tool kits recommended for use with automobiles; automobile seat covers of any construction whether they are ready-made or custom fitted; fitted truck top covers; glass cut to size for installation in automobiles; and automobile bearings, such as automobile crankshaft or connecting rod bearings.

(e) *Effective date.*—This section shall be effective with respect to sales made on or after January 1, 1964. For the definition of parts or accessories applicable to sales thereof prior to such date, see § 48.4061(b)-2 of this chapter (Manufacturers and Retailers Excise Tax Regulations).

(f) *Cross references.*—For provisions relating to the tax imposed upon:

(1) Tires and inner tubes, see section 4071 and the regulations thereunder contained in Subpart H of this part:

(2) Automobile radio and television receiving sets, see section 4141 and the regulations thereunder contained in Subpart J of this part; and

(3) Fare registers and fare boxes for use on buses and automobiles, see section 4191 and the regulations thereunder contained in Subpart L of this part. [Reg. § 48.4061(b)-2.]

☐ [*T.D. 6648, 4-21-63. Amended by T.D. 6655, 5-23-63.*]

[Reg. § 48.4062(a)-1]

§ 48.4062(a)-1. Specific parts or accessories.—Spark plugs, storage batteries, leaf springs, coils, timers, and tire chains, which are suitable for use on or in connection with, or as component parts of, automobile trucks, other automobiles, tractors, or other vehicles enumerated in section 4061(a), are considered parts of, or accessories for, such articles whether or not primarily designed or adapted for such use. [Reg. § 48.4062(a)-1.]

☐ [*T.D. 6648, 4-12-63.*]

[Reg. § 48.4062(b)-1]

§ 48.4062(b)-1. Rebuilt parts or accessories sold on an exchange basis.—The sale price of a rebuilt part or accessory on which the tax is to be computed shall not include the value of a like part or accessory accepted in exchange. The total amount charged in excess of the amount allowed for a like article accepted in an exchange will be the basis for tax. For example, if a rebuilt automobile engine is sold for $100, plus another automobile engine, the tax on the rebuilt engine will be computed on the basis of $100. [Reg. § 48.4062(b)-1.]

☐ [*T.D. 6648, 4-12-63.*]

[Reg. § 48.4063-1]

§ 48.4063-1. Tax-free sales of bodies to chassis manufacturers.—Under the provisions of section 4063(b), the tax imposed by section 4061 (a) shall not apply to bodies sold by the manufacturer thereof to a manufacturer (but not an importer) of automobile trucks (as defined by § 48.4061(a)-3(a)) to be sold by the purchaser. Thus, a manufacturer of automobile truck bodies is permitted to sell such bodies tax free to manufacturers of automobile truck chassis. This section does not apply with respect to the sale of an automobile truck chassis to manufacturers of automobile truck bodies. However, see § 48.4061(a)-1(e) with respect to the sale of an automobile truck chassis for use in the manufacture or assembly of a nonhighway vehicle (within the meaning of § 48.4061(a)-1(d)). In order to effect a tax-free sale of a body as provided in this section both the seller and purchaser must comply with the registration and other requirements of section 4222 and the regulations thereunder. A chassis manufacturer who purchases a body tax free as provided in this section shall, for purposes of application of the tax imposed by section 4061(a), be considered the manufacturer of such body. [Reg. § 48.4063-1.]

☐ [T.D. 6648, 4-12-63. Amended by T.D. 7461, 8-12-77.]

[Reg. § 48.4063-2]

§ 48.4063-2. Tax-free sales of parts or accessories sold for resale on or in connection with the first retail sale of a light-duty truck.—(a) In general.—Under section 4063(e), the 8-percent manufacturers excise tax imposed by section 4061(b) on the sale of truck parts or accessories does not apply to the sale by the manufacturer, producer, or importer of any parts which are to be resold by the purchaser on or in connection with the first retail sale of a light-duty truck as defined in section 4061(a)(2), or which are to be resold by the purchaser to a second purchaser for resale by the second purchaser on or in connection with the first retail sale of a light-duty truck. A tax-free sale is also allowed under section 4063(e) if an ultimate purchaser makes a direct purchase from a manufacturer of a part or accessory for use on or in connection with a substantially contemporaneous purchase of a new light-duty truck.

(b) Evidence required for tax-free sales of light-duty truck parts and accessories.—(1) In general.—The provisions of section 4063(e) do not apply with respect to any sale unless the manufacturer, the first purchaser, and the second purchaser, if any, are all registered as required under section 4222, and unless they comply with all the requirements under that section relating to tax-free sales. To effectuate a tax-free sale directly from the manufacturer, first or second purchaser to an ultimate purchaser, the ultimate purchaser must, in every case, satisfy the provisions of paragraphs (b)(3)(i), (ii) and (iii) of this section. Persons not required to be registered under section 4222(b) may purchase articles tax free by following the same procedures that apply to them in the case of other tax-free sales. See § 48.4222(b)-1.

(2) Revocation or suspension of registration or right to use exemption certificate.—A person's registration and right to sell or purchase articles tax free through the use of an exemption certificate may be revoked or suspended. See § 48.4222(c)-1. Such a revocation or suspension shall be in addition to any other penalties that may apply. Any person who purchases articles tax free and who sells or uses them for a nonexempt purpose shall notify its vendor of the taxable sale or use.

(3) Exemption certificate.—(i) To establish exemption from tax under section 4061(b) in those instances where a sale is made directly to an ultimate purchaser, the manufacturer, first, or second purchaser must obtain (prior to or at the time of sale) from the ultimate purchaser and retain in its possession a properly executed exemption certificate in the form prescribed in paragraph (b)(3)(iii) of this section.

(ii) Where only occasional sales are made, a separate exemption certificate shall be furnished for each order. However, where sales are regularly or frequently made to a purchaser for such exempt use, a certificate covering all sales for a specified period not to exceed 12 calendar quarters will be acceptable. Such certificates and proper records of invoices, orders, etc. relative to tax-free sales must be kept for inspection by the district director as provided in section 6001 and the regulations thereunder.

(iii) The following form of exemption certificate will be acceptable for purposes of this section and must be adhered to in substance.

Exemption Certificate

(For use by ultimate purchaser who purchase[s] parts or accessories from a manufacturer, producer, importer, first or second purchaser for use on or in connection with the first retail sale of a light-duty truck. (Section 4063 of the Internal Revenue Code.))

(Date) . . . . , 19 . . . .
1. I, the undersigned, certify that I am, or the . . . . (Name of company) of which I am . . . . (Position held), is purchasing from the manufacturer, producer, importer, first or second purchaser the parts or accessories specified in section 2 below (or in the purchase order or invoice attached hereto) for use on or in connection with a substantially contemporaneous purchase of a new light-duty truck specified in section 3 below. I also certify that (check applicable type of certificate) . . . . the article or articles specified in the accompanying order, as described below, or . . . . all orders placed by the purchaser for the period commencing . . . . (Date) and ending . . . . (Date) (period not to exceed 12 calendar quarters), will be used only for the above stated tax-exempt purposes and will not be used as a replacement part.

Exemption Certificate

I understand that the willful use of this exemption certificate to evade or defeat the manufacturers excise tax otherwise applicable to these parts or accessories will subject me to a fine of not more than $10,000 or imprisonment for not more than 5 years, or both, together with cost of prosecution.

. . . .

(Signature)

. . . .

(Address)

2. Description of parts and accessories

Type	Quantity	Price	Total
. . . .	. . . .	. . . .	. . . .
. . . .	. . . .	. . . .	. . . .
. . . .	. . . .	. . . .	. . . .

3. Description of new light-duty truck

(a) Type: (b) Quantity,   (c) Serial Number.

(d) GVWR: (e) Date of Sale,   (f) Invoice Number.

(g) Name and Address of Vendor of Vehicle.

(c) *Information; records.*—(1) *Information to be furnished to vendee.*—A vendor (including the manufacturer) selling light-duty truck parts and accessories tax free under section 4063(e) shall indicate to its vendee that the vendee is obtaining the parts or accessories tax free for the purpose of resale (or used) on or in connection with the first retail sale of a light-duty truck. This information may be transmitted by any convenient means, such as coding of sales invoices, provided that the information is presented with sufficient particularity so that the purchaser is informed that the purchaser has obtained the light duty truck parts or accessories tax free.

(2) *Records of vendor.*—A manufacturer or vendor selling light-duty truck parts or accessories tax free under section 4063(e) shall maintain in its records the identity of the purchaser, a signed statement of the exempt purpose for purchasing the light-duty truck parts or accessories, and the quantity of light-duty truck parts or accessories sold tax free to each purchaser.

(3) *Records of vendee.*—A person purchasing light-duty truck parts or accessories tax free under section 4063(e) must maintain sufficient records to establish that the parts or accessories purchased tax free have actually been resold (or used) on or in connection with the first retail sale of a light-duty truck or have been resold to a second purchaser for such a resale by the second purchaser.

(d) *Duty of selling manufacturer to ascertain validity of tax-free sale.*—The selling manufacturer of light-duty truck parts is not relieved of liability under the provisions of section 4063(e) by reason of section 4221(c) for the tax imposed by section 4061(b) if at the time of sale the selling manufacturer has knowledge or reason to believe that the light-duty truck parts or accessories sold by it to the purchaser are not intended for resale (or use) on or in connection with the first retail sale of a light-duty truck. The selling manufacturer is also not relieved of liability if it has knowledge or reason to believe that the purchaser has failed to register, refused to execute an exemption certificate, or that its registration or its right to purchase tax free through the use of an exemption certificate has been revoked or suspended.

(e) *Cross reference.*—For credit or refund, see section 6416(b)(2).

(f) *Effective date.*—Section 4063(e) (relating to light-duty truck parts and accessories) applies to sales on or after December 1, 1978. Light-duty truck parts or accessories sold prior to that date are not exempt from tax under section 4061(b) by reason of section 4063(e). [Reg. § 48.4063-2.]

☐ [*T.D. 7834.*]

[Reg. § 48.4063-3]

§ 48.4063-3. Other tax-free sales.—For provisions relating to tax-free sales of articles referred to in section 4061, see—

(a) Section 4221, relating to certain tax-free sales;

(b) Section 4222, relating to registration; and

(c) Section 4223, relating to special rules pertaining to further manufacture; and the regulations thereunder contained in Subpart N of this part. [Reg. § 48.4063-3.]

☐ [*T.D. 6648, 4-12-63.*]

[Reg. § 48.4064-1]

§ 48.4064-1. Gas guzzler tax.—(a) *General rule.*—(1) *In general.*—Section 4064 imposes on the sale by the manufacturer of an automobile a tax determined in accordance with the tables in section 4064(a)(1) through (7), and in paragraph (a)(2) of this section. The tax is applicable to model types of 1980 and later model year automobiles that have a fuel economy level below the applicable tax-free fuel economy level. Paragraph (b) of this section defines the following terms: sale, manufacturer, automobile, model year, model type, fuel economy, and fuel. Paragraph (c) of this section contains rules relating to the determination of fuel economy. Paragraph (d) of this section contains a special rule for certain small manufacturers. Paragraph (e) of

Reg. § 48.4064-1(a)(1)

this section contains rules relating to the tax-free sales of emergency vehicles.

(2) *Tables.*—(i) In the case of a 1980 model year automobile:

If the fuel economy of the model type in which the automobile falls is:

Miles per gallon:	The tax is—
At least 15	0
At least 14 but less than 15	$200
At least 13 but less than 14	300
Less than 13	550

(ii) In the case of a 1981 model year automobile:

If the fuel economy of the model type in which the automobile falls is:

Miles per gallon:	The tax is—
At least 17	0
At least 16 but less than 17	$200
At least 15 but less than 16	350
At least 14 but less than 15	450
At least 13 but less than 14	550
Less than 13	650

(iii) In the case of a 1982 model year automobile:

If the fuel economy of the model type in which the automobile falls is:

Miles per gallon:	The tax is—
At least 18.5	0
At least 17.5 but less than 18.5	$200
At least 16.5 but less than 17.5	350
At least 15.5 but less than 16.5	450
At least 14.5 but less than 15.5	600
At least 13.5 but less than 14.5	750
At least 12.5 but less than 13.5	950
Less than 12.5	1,200

(iv) In the case of a 1983 model year automobile:

If the fuel economy of the model type in which the automobile falls is:

Miles per gallon:	The tax is—
At least 19	0
At least 18 but less than 19	$350
At least 17 but less than 18	500
At least 16 but less than 17	650
At least 15 but less than 16	800
At least 14 but less than 15	1,000
At least 13 but less than 14	1,250
Less than 13	1,550

(v) In the case of a 1984 model year automobile:

If the fuel economy of the model type in which the automobile falls is:

Miles per gallon:	The tax is—
At least 19.5	0
At least 18.5 but less than 19.5	$450
At least 17.5 but less than 18.5	600
At least 16.5 but less than 17.5	750
At least 15.5 but less than 16.5	950
At least 14.5 but less than 15.5	1,150
At least 13.5 but less than 14.5	1,450
At least 12.5 but less than 13.5	1,750
Less than 12.5	2,150

(vi) In the case of a 1985 model year automobile:

If the fuel economy of the model type in which the automobile falls is:

Miles per gallon:	The tax is—
At least 21	0
At least 20 but less than 21	$500
At least 19 but less than 20	600
At least 18 but less than 19	800
At least 17 but less than 18	1,000
At least 16 but less than 17	1,200
At least 15 but less than 16	1,500
At least 14 but less than 15	1,800
At least 13 but less than 14	2,200
Less than 13	2,650

(vii) In the case of a 1986 or later model year automobile:

If the fuel economy of the model type in which the automobile falls is:

Miles per gallon:	The tax is—
At least 22.5	0
At least 21.5 but less than 22.5	$500
At least 20.5 but less than 21.5	650
At least 19.5 but less than 20.5	850
At least 18.5 but less than 19.5	1,050
At least 17.5 but less than 18.5	1,300
At least 16.5 but less than 17.5	1,500
At least 15.5 but less than 16.5	1,850
At least 14.5 but less than 15.5	2,250
At least 13.5 but less than 14.5	2,700
At least 12.5 but less than 13.5	3,200
Less than 12.5	3,850

(3) *Liability for tax.*—The tax imposed by section 4064 is payable by the manufacturer making the sale. An automobile sold before the time a determination of fuel economy is made for the model type (as defined in paragraph (b)(6) of this section) is subject to tax if it is subsequently determined that the fuel economy level of that model type of automobile is within the taxable range (see paragraph (a)(1) of this section).

(b) *Definitions.*—(1) *Sale.*—Sale includes the use (within the meaning of section 4218) or the first lease (within the meaning of section 4217(e)) of an automobile by the manufacturer.

(2) *Manufacturer.*—The term "manufacturer" has the same meaning assigned to such term under § 48.0-2(a)(4). The term "manufacturer" includes a producer or importer. An importer is a person who imports an automobile whether or not in connection with a trade or business.

(3) *Automobile.*—The term "automobile" means any four-wheeled vehicle—

(i) Propelled by an engine powered by fuel;

(ii) Manufactured primarily for use on public streets, roads, and highways (except any vehicle operated exclusively on a rail or rails);

(iii) Rated at 6,000 pounds gross vehicle weight or less; and

(iv) Requiring no further manufacturing operations to perform its intended function, other than the addition of readily attachable components, such as mirrors or tire and rim assemblies, or minor finishing operations, such as painting. For this purpose, gross vehicle weight means the value specified by the manufacturer as the maximum design loaded weight of a single vehicle. An automobile does not include a nonpassenger automobile as defined in regulations in effect on November 9, 1978 (49 CFR 523.5 (1978)), which were prescribed by the Secretary of Transportation for section 501 of the Motor Vehicle Information and Cost Savings Act (15 U.S.C. 2001). In addition, an automobile does not include the following: any vehicle sold for use and used primarily as an ambulance or combination ambulance-hearse; any vehicle sold for use and used by the United States or by a State or local government primarily for police or other law enforcement purposes; or any vehicle sold for use and used primarily for fire-fighting purposes.

(4) *Model year.*—The term "model year" means the manufacturer's annual production period (as determined by the Administrator of the Environmental Protection Agency) which includes January 1 of any particular calendar year. If the manufacturer has no annual production year, the model year is the calendar year.

Reg. § 48.4064-1(b)(4)

(5) *Model type.*—The term "model type" means a particular class of automobile, as determined by regulations in effect on November 9, 1978 (40 CFR 600.002.79(a)(19) (1978)), which were prescribed by the Administrator of the Environmental Protection Agency.

(6) *Fuel economy.*—The term "fuel economy" means the average number of miles traveled by an automobile per gallon of fuel consumed, rounded to the nearest .1 mile per gallon. The fuel economy for any model type is determined by the Environmental Protection Agency (as determined in accordance with the procedures provided in paragraph (c) of this section). For this purpose, the fuel economy is a combined (urban-highway weighted average) mileage figure estimated in connection with the determination (or redetermination) of general label value (fuel economy information displayed on a sticker that is affixed to new automobiles) mandated under section 506 of the Motor Vehicle Information and Cost Savings Act (15 U.S.C. 2006) and regulations thereunder (40 CFR 600).

(7) *Fuel.*—The term "fuel" means gasoline and diesel fuel.

(c) *Determination of fuel economy.*—For purposes of this section, the fuel economy for any model type is determined (or redetermined) in accordance with the testing and calculation procedures utilized by the Environmental Protection Agency Administrator for model year 1975 (weighted 55 percent urban cycle and 45 percent highway cycle), or any other procedures (yielding comparable results) established by the Administrator. The Environmental Protection Agency's determination (or redetermination) of a model type's fuel economy is made at the time the general label fuel economy value is calculated (or recalculated). This determination (or redetermination) is conclusive for purposes of this section. A redetermination of a model type's fuel economy value shall be effective only with respect to those automobiles for which the manufacturer is required (or is permitted and chooses) under Environmental Protection Agency regulations to affix labels with the recalculated general label fuel economy value.

(d) *Special rule for small manufacturers.*—(1) *In general.*—A small manufacturer (as defined in subparagraph (2)(i) of this paragraph) may apply for a determination that it is not feasible for that manufacturer to meet the statutory tax-free fuel economy level for the model year, with respect to all automobiles produced by that manufacturer, or with respect to a particular model type. For this purpose, the Commissioner (or his delegate) will make a determination of maximum feasible fuel economy level with respect to the automobiles that are the subject of the determination, but only after consultation with the Secretary of Energy, the Secretary of Transportation, and the Administrator of the Environmental Protection Agency (or their delegates) to obtain their views. A finding that it is not feasible for the manufacturer to meet the statutory

tax-free fuel economy level will be made by the Internal Revenue Service if the maximum feasible fuel economy level (as defined in subparagraph (3)(i) of this paragraph) of the automobiles that are the subject of the determination is lower than the statutory tax-free fuel economy level for those automobiles. If it is determined that it is not feasible for a small manufacturer to meet the statutory tax-free fuel economy level, the Secretary (or his delegate) has the discretion to grant to the manufacturer the alternate rate schedule prescribed in paragraph (d)(3)(iii) of this section in lieu of the applicable statutory tax table prescribed in section 4064(a). The decision whether to grant the alternate rate schedule shall be based on the consideration set forth in paragraph (d)(3)(ii) of this section. If a small manufacturer for which an alternate rate schedule under this paragraph (d) is applicable sells an automobile to an importer, the alternate rate schedule applies to the sale by the importer of such automobile if such automobile is of the model year and type to which such alternate schedule applies.

(2) *Definitions.*—(i) *Small manufacturer.*—A small manufacturer is any manufacturer who produced (whether or not in the United States) fewer than 10,000 automobiles in the second model year preceding the affected model year (the model year for which the determination under this paragraph is being made), and who can reasonably be expected to produce (whether or not in the United States) fewer than 10,000 automobiles in the affected model year.

(ii) *Manufacturer.*—For purposes of this paragraph, the term "manufacturer" does not include a person who is only an importer, but does include a producer of automobiles outside the United States who is also an importer.

(iii) *Members of a controlled group.*—For purposes of this paragraph, persons who are members of a controlled group of corporations (as defined in section 1563(a) of the Internal Revenue Code, except that "more than 50 percent" is substituted for "at least 80 percent" each place it appears in section 1563(a)) are treated as one manufacturer.

(3) *Basis for determination.*—(i) *Maximum feasible fuel economy level.*—For purposes of this paragraph, the maximum feasible fuel economy level is determined by taking into account the same factors used in determining the maximum feasible fuel economy level under section 502(e) of the Motor Vehicle Information and Cost Savings Act (as amended) and the regulations thereunder in effect on November 9, 1978. (Those regulations for small manufacturers are prescribed in 49 CFR 525 (1978).) In making this determination, the Commissioner (or his delegate) will consult with the National Highway Traffic Safety Administration of the Department of Transportation.

(ii) *Decision to grant alternate rate schedule.*—In deciding whether to grant an alternate rate schedule, the Secretary (or his delegate) will consider whether the use (in the United States) of the automobile serves an important public policy (*e.g.,* providing public transportation or transportation for the handicapped) that overrides the United States' need to conserve energy. The manufacturer has the burden of demonstrating that the public policy consideration involved overrides the United States' need to conserve energy. The Commissioner (or his delegate), after consultation with the Secretary of Energy, the Secretary of Transportation, and the Administrator of the Environmental Protection Agency (or their delegates), will review the information submitted by the manufacturer and report findings and recommendations to the Secretary (or his delegate).

(iii) *Alternate rate schedule and tax.*—If an alternate rate schedule is granted, the maximum feasible fuel economy level shall be deemed to be the statutory tax-free fuel economy level. Accordingly, a tax is imposed only on automobiles sold that fail to meet the deemed tax-free fuel economy level. The alternate rate schedule shall

be determined by substituting the maximum feasible fuel economy level for the tax-free fuel economy level in the applicable statutory tax table set forth in section 4064(a), and by substituting for the miles per gallon amount prescribed in that applicable table an amount that is the tax-free level decreased by one mile per gallon increments, while keeping the same corresponding tax amount prescribed in that applicable table. The rule for determining an alternate rate schedule may be illustrated by the following example:

Example. Manufacturer X, a small manufacturer of automobiles specifically designed to accommodate disabled passengers, applied for a determination that it is not feasible for X to meet the statutory tax-free fuel economy level for a particular model type of X's 1982 model year automobiles. It was determined that the maximum feasible fuel economy level for that model type was 15 miles per gallon. The Secretary decided to grant X an alternate rate schedule. The alternate rate schedule for the model type would be as follows:

If the fuel economy of the automobile is: Miles per gallon:	The tax is—
At least 15	0
At least 14 but less than 15	$200
At least 13 but less than 14	350
At least 12 but less than 13	450
At least 11 but less than 12	600
At least 10 but less than 11	750
At least 9 but less than 10	950
Less than 9	1,200

Thus, if X's 1982 automobiles of that model year and type attain only 12 miles per gallon (because X fails to modify them to reach the maximum feasible fuel economy level before they are sold), the tax imposed upon the sale of each automobile is $450 (instead of the $1,200 tax (see the applicable statutory tax table set forth in section 4064(a)(3)), which would have been imposed had no alternate rate schedule been prescribed).

(4) *Duration of determination.*—A determination under this paragraph does not apply to more than three model years.

(5) *Requirements for application.*—Each application for a determination under this section must—

(i) Identify the model year or years, and particular model type or types for which a determination is requested;

(ii)(A) In the case of an application for model year 1980, be submitted not later than May 8, 1980;

(B) In the case of an application for model year 1981, be submitted not later than 9 months before the beginning of that model year of March 10, 1980, whichever is later;

(C) In the case of an application for model year 1982 or any subsequent model year, be submitted not later than 9 months before that model year;

(iii) Be submitted in three copies to: Commissioner of Internal Revenue, Attention: Associate Chief Counsel (Technical), 1111 Constitution Avenue, N.W., Washington, D.C. 20224;

(iv) Be written in the English language;

(v) Set forth the full name, address, and title of the official responsible for preparing the application;

(vi) State whether the applicant is a member of a controlled group of corporations (as defined in paragraph (d)(2)(iii) of this section);

(vii) State the total number of automobiles manufactured (whether or not in the United States) by the applicant (or the controlled group of corporations in the case where the applicant is a member of the group) in the second model year immediately preceding each affected model year and the total number of automobiles likely to be manufactured in the affected model year;

(viii) Set forth the same information required by an application pursuant to section 502(c) of the Motor Vehicle Information and Cost Savings Act (as amended) and the regulations thereunder (see 49 CFR 525 (1978)) and state whether or not the applicant under this paragraph has also made an application pursuant to such Act; and

Reg. §48.4064-1(d)(5)(viii)

(ix) Set forth the reasons why an alternate rate schedule should be granted under paragraph (d)(3)(ii) of this section.

(6) *Update of application.*—A manufacturer making an application under this section must update the application when a material change of circumstances occurs or material information not available at the time of applying becomes available. The manufacturer must also furnish any further information that may be required by the Internal Revenue Service.

(7) *Processing of applications.*—If a manufacturer's application is found not to contain the information required by this paragraph, the applicant will be informed of the areas of insufficiency. The application will not receive further consideration until the required information is submitted. Each applicant will be informed in writing whether an application has been granted or denied.

(e) *Tax-free sales of emergency vehicles.*—(1) *In general.*—The tax imposed by section 4064(a) shall not apply to vehicles sold by a manufacturer for use and used (i) primarily as an ambulance or combination ambulance-hearse, (ii) by the United States or by a State or local government primarily for police or other law enforcement purposes, or (iii) primarily for fire-fighting purposes. A vehicle may be sold tax-free by the manufacturer under this paragraph only in those cases where the sale is made directly to a purchaser for an emergency use prescribed in this subparagraph. In order to effect a tax-free sale, the requirements of section 4222 and the regulations thereunder must be met.

(2) *Credit or refund.*—Where tax is paid on the sale of a vehicle, but the vehicle is used or resold for an emergency use prescribed in subparagraph (1) of this paragraph, a claim for refund of the tax paid on such sale may be filed by the manufacturer on Form 8849 (or on such other form as the Commissioner may designate), or a credit may be taken on a subsequent return, in accordance with the provisions of sections 6402(a) and 6416(a) and §48.6416(a)-1. [Reg. §48.4064-1.]

☐ [*T.D. 8036, 4-23-85. Amended by T.D. 8659, 3-13-96.*]

[Reg. §48.4071-1]

§48.4071-1. Imposition and rate of tax.—(a) *Imposition of tax.*—(1) *Imposition of tax before January 1, 1984.*—Section 4071 imposes a tax at the rates set forth in paragraph (b)(1) of this section on tires made wholly or in part of rubber, inner tubes (for tires) made wholly or in part of rubber and tread rubber which are sold by the manufacturer thereof before January 1, 1984.

(2) *Imposition of tax after December 31, 1983.*—Section 4071 imposes a tax at the rates set forth in paragraph (b)(2) of this section on tires of the type used on highway vehicles and made wholly or in part of rubber which are sold by the manufacturer thereof after December 31, 1983.

(3) *Definitions.*—For definitions of the terms "tires," "inner tubes," "tread rubber," "rubber" and "manufacturer," see §48.4072-1 of the regulations.

(b) *Rates and computation of tax.*—(1) *Rates of tax before January 1, 1984.*

(i) *Tires:*

(A) Of the type used on highway vehicles:

(1) For the period July 1, 1965 to December 31, 1980, inclusive—10 cents per pound.

(2) For the period January 1, 1981 to December 31, 1983, inclusive—9.75 cents per pound.

(B) Of the type used on other than highway vehicles:

(1) For the period July 1, 1965 to December 31, 1980, inclusive—5 cents per pound.

(2) For the period January 1, 1981 to December 31, 1983, inclusive—4.875 cents per pound.

(C) Laminated tires for the period July 1, 1965 to December 31, 1983, inclusive—1 cent per pound.

(ii) *Inner tubes:*

For the period July 1, 1965 to December 31, 1983, inclusive—10 cents per pound.

(iii) *Tread Rubber:*

For the period July 1, 1965 to December 31, 1983, inclusive—5 cents per pound.

(2) *Rates of tax on or after January 1, 1984.*—Tires of the type used on highway vehicles:

(i) Tires weighing not more than 40 pounds—0 cents.

(ii) Tires weighing more than 40 pounds but not more than 70 pounds—15 cents for each pound in excess of 40 pounds.

(iii) *Tread Rubber:*

For the period July 1, 1965 to December 31, 1983, inclusive—5 cents per pound.

(2) *Rates of tax on or after January 1, 1984.*—Tires of the type used on highway vehicles:

(i) Tires weighing not more than 40 pounds—0 cents.

(ii) Tires weighing more than 40 pounds but not more than 70 pounds—15 cents for each pound in excess of 40 pounds.

(iii) Tires weighing more than 70 pounds but not more than 90 pounds—$4.50 plus 30 cents for each pound in excess of 70 pounds.

(iv) Tires weighing more than 90 pounds—$10.50 plus 50 cents for each pound in excess of 90 pounds.

(3) *Computation of tax.*—The tax on tires, inner tubes, and tread rubber is computed by applying to the total weight (including a fractional part of a pound) of the article the rate in effect at the time the article is sold. See §48.4071-2, relating to determination of weight.

(c) *Liability for tax.*—The tax imposed by section 4071 is payable by the manufacturer when the manufacturer makes a sale of a taxable article, or as provided in section 4071(b) and § 48.4071-3 for a manufacturer who sells at retail, when the manufacturer delivers a taxable article to a retail store, or to a retail outlet, of the manufacturer.

(d) *Recapped or retreaded tires.*—The recapping or retreading of a tire, whether from shoulder-to-shoulder or bead-to-bead, does not constitute manufacture of a taxable tire. The tax on tires imposed by section 4071 does not apply to the sale of a recapped or retreaded tire, except that a used tire or tire carcass not previously sold in the United States that is recapped or retreaded from shoulder-to-shoulder or bead-to-bead in a foreign country and imported into the United States is subject to the tax imposed by section 4071 when such tire is sold or used by the importer. This paragraph (d) is effective for recapped and retreaded tires sold on or after January 1, 1984. [Reg. § 48.4071-1.]

☐ [*T.D. 7809. Amended by T.D. 8057, and T.D. 8152, 8-20-87.*]

[Reg. § 48.4071-2]

§ 48.4071-2. Determination of weight.—(a) *In general.*—(1) *Tires.*—(i) Metal rims or rim bases are not to be included in determining the total weight of a tire. However, the wire, staples, darts, clips, and other material or fastening devices which form a part of the tire or are required for its use must be included in determining the total weight of the tire. Studs are considered to be part of a tire and are to be included when determining the weight of a tire. In the case of a tubeless tire, the total weight includes the weight of the air valve and stem or any other mechanism that functions as a part of the tire and is used in connection with inflating the tire or maintaining its air pressure.

(ii) When tires are sold with metal rims or rim bases attached, the manufacturer must maintain records that will establish what portion of the total weight of the finished product represents the tire exclusive of the metal rim or rim base.

(2) *Inner tubes.*—The total weight of an inner tube includes the weight of the air valve and stem or any other mechanism attached to the inner tube that is used in connection with inflating the tube or maintaining its air pressure.

(b) *Alternative method of determining the weight of tires after December 1983.*—A manufacturer who has received permission from the Commissioner may, subject to such conditions as the Commissioner may prescribe, determine total weight of tires manufactured and sold by the manufacturer on the basis of the average weight for each type, size, grade, and classification. The average weights must be established in accordance with the method approved by the Commissioner and apply for such periods as the

Commissioner may prescribe. The Commissioner may terminate the approval granted any manufacturer. In the case of the termination of the approval granted any manufacturer, the termination becomes effective 10 days from the date of the receipt by the manufacturer of the notice of termination. A manufacturer may effect termination, as of a specified date, of the privilege to determine total weight in accordance with provisions of this paragraph by giving no less than 10 days' written notice of such intention to the Commissioner. The termination of the approval given a manufacturer does not affect a manufacturer's tax liability for tires sold prior to the effective date of the notice of termination. [Reg. § 48.4071-2.]

☐ [*T.D. 7809. Amended by T.D. 8152, 8-20-87.*]

[Reg. § 48.4071-3]

§ 48.4071-3. Imposition of tax on tires and tubes delivered to manufacturer's retail outlet.—(a) *General rule.*—If, on or after October 1, 1966, a tire or inner tube is delivered by the manufacturer thereof to a retail outlet of the manufacturer, the manufacturer is liable for tax in respect of the tire or tube at the rate set forth in section 4071 in the same manner as if the tire or tube had been sold at the time it was delivered to the retail outlet. The amount of tax payable shall be computed in accordance with the provisions of paragraph (b)(2) of § 48.4071-1, and of § 48.4071-2.

(b) *Definition of retail outlet.*—For purposes of this section, the term "retail outlet" includes the term "retail store." A retail outlet is a facility maintained by a manufacturer for selling tires or tubes at retail. A facility may be a retail outlet even though some sales are made at wholesale at such facility; see paragraph (d)(1) of this section. A facility may also be considered to be a retail outlet for the purposes of this section notwithstanding that its main activity is in another area than selling tires or inner tubes. For example, if a manufacturer operates a facility for both automotive repair and the selling of tires at retail, the facility is considered a retail outlet for the purposes of this section even if the primary activity of the facility is automotive repair. No facility is considered a retail outlet for the purposes of this section if it is determined that less than 15 percent of the taxable tires and inner tubes removed from such facility are sold at retail by such facility. The determination described in the preceding sentence is made on the basis of the experience of a representative period, of at least 12 consecutive calendar months during the 2-year period immediately preceding the first day included in the return period for which tax under section 4071(b) is reported. If a facility has not been in existence during such a 12-month period, the determination is made on the basis of the available experience of the manufacturer. See also paragraph (c)(3) of this section, relating to imposition of tax where a retail outlet is maintained as an adjunct to a production facility or distribution center.

Reg. § 48.4071-3(b)

(c) *Delivery.*—(1) *In general.*—A manufacturer of tires or inner tubes may, at its option, treat either of the following events as constituting delivery to a retail outlet:

(i) Delivery of tires or inner tubes to a common carrier (or, where the tires or tubes are transported by the manufacturer, the placing of the tires or tubes into the manufacturer's over-the-road vehicle) for shipment from the plant in which the tires or tubes are manufactured, or from a regional distribution center of tires and inner tubes, to a retail outlet or to a location in the immediate vicinity of a retail outlet primarily for future delivery to the retail outlet.

(ii) Arrival of the tires or tubes at the retail outlet, or, where shipment is to a location in the immediate vicinity of a retail outlet primarily for future delivery to the retail outlet, the arrival of the tires or tubes at such location.

In its excise tax return for the first return period beginning after September 30, 1966, a manufacturer of tires or inner tubes must elect to determine the date of delivery to retail outlets in accordance with one of the two subdivisions of this paragraph (c)(1) and must determine the dates of all deliveries made to all retail outlets in accordance with the subdivision which the manufacturer has elected to apply. The election may be made in a statement attached to the return for such period. Having elected to treat one of the events listed in subdivision (i) or (ii) of this paragraph (c)(1) as constituting delivery to a retail outlet for purposes of its return for the first return period after September 30, 1966, the manufacturer may not use a different criterion for a subsequent return period unless permission of the district director is obtained in advance.

(2) *Deliveries made in the immediate vicinity of a retail outlet primarily for future delivery to the retail outlet.*—(i) For purposes of this section, any delivery which is made in the immediate vicinity of a retail outlet primarily for future delivery to the retail outlet is deemed to be a delivery to the retail outlet. For the purpose of the preceding sentence, a location is considered to be in the immediate vicinity of a retail outlet if the distance between the location and the retail outlet is sufficiently small so that it is feasible to transport tires and inner tubes between the location and the retail outlet by means of dollies, fork lift trucks, pushcarts, and similar vehicles of the type normally used around the premises of factories and similar establishments, as opposed to highway motor vehicles. For the purpose of the preceding sentence, it is immaterial that a public thoroughfare must be used in order to transport tires or inner tubes to a retail outlet from another location. Tires and inner tubes delivered to a location in the immediate vicinity of a retail outlet are considered to be delivered to the location "primarily for future delivery" to the retail outlet if it is determined that a majority (by number) of the tires and tubes removed from the location are delivered to the retail outlet. The determination described in the preceding sentence is made on

the basis of the experience of a representative period of at least 12 consecutive calendar months during the 2-year period immediately preceding the first day included in the return period for which tax under section 4071(b) is reported. If a facility has not been in existence during such a 12-month period, the determination is made on the basis of the available experience of the manufacturer. If it is determined that the majority of all tires and inner tubes removed from a given location are delivered to a retail outlet of the manufacturer in the immediate vicinity of the location, tax is imposed upon all tires and tubes delivered by the manufacturer to the location, even though all or part of the tires or tubes comprising a particular shipment to the location may be intended for further transportation to a location other than the retail outlet. If it is determined that a majority of all tires and inner tubes removed from a given location are not delivered to a retail outlet of the manufacturer in the immediate vicinity of the location, tax is imposed upon the removal of a tire or inner tube from the location to the premises of the retail outlet. See also paragraph (d)(2) of this section, relating to sales by the manufacturer at facilities other than retail outlets.

(ii) The provisions of this paragraph (c)(2) may be illustrated by the following example:

Example. A manufacturer of tires and tubes whose plant is located in City X operates two facilities in City Y, Warehouse A and Store Q. Store Q is a retail outlet within the meaning of paragraph (b) of this section, and Warehouse A is in the immediate vicinity of Store Q. During the 12-month period ending September 30, 1966, 60 percent of the tires and inner tubes removed from Warehouse A were delivered to Store Q. All tires or inner tubes delivered by the manufacturer to Warehouse A are subject to tax under section 4071(b) and this section (unless, before such delivery, tax was imposed on the same tires and tubes).

(3) *Retail outlet maintained as adjunct of production or distribution facility.*—If a retail outlet is maintained as an adjunct to and in the immediate vicinity of a facility which is not a retail outlet (as, for example, a production plant or a regional distribution center), delivery to the retail outlet is deemed to occur at the earlier of—

(i) The date when a tire or inner tube is removed from the general storage facilities in the facility which is not a retail outlet for transfer to the premises of the retail outlet, or

(ii) The date when a tire or inner tube is designated to be sold by or at the retail outlet.

(d) *Special rules.*—(1) *Retail outlets which also sell at wholesale.*—Tax applies to all shipments of tires and inner tubes delivered to a retail outlet, as defined in paragraph (b)(2) of this section. Thus, for the purposes of section 4071(b) and this section, it is immaterial that all or part of the tires or inner tubes of a particular delivery to a retail outlet are intended for sale at wholesale. See also paragraph (d)(3) of this section.

(2) *Sales by manufacturer at facilities other than retail outlets.*—Sales by the manufacturer of tires and inner tubes at facilities other than retail outlets are subject to tax under section 4071(a).

(3) *Deliveries of tires or tubes on which tax has been previously imposed.*

(i) Tax is not imposed under section 4071(b) and this section on any tire or inner tube in respect of which there was previously imposed a tax under section 4071(a). Similarly, a tire or inner tube is taxed only once under section 4071(b) and this section.

(ii) The provisions of this paragraph (d)(3) may be illustrated by the following example:

Example. A manufacturer has two selling facilities, Store No. 1 and Store No. 2. Only retail sales are made at Store No. 2, which obtains its merchandise from Store No. 1. Assume that, although wholesaling and distribution activities are conducted at Store No. 1, the sale of tires and tubes at retail is conducted at Store No. 1 to the extent that Store No. 1 is a retail outlet within the meaning of paragraph (b) of this section, with the result that tax is imposed on deliveries by the manufacturer of tires and tubes to Store No. 1. Tax is not imposed on a delivery of tires or inner tubes from Store No. 1 to Store No. 2. [Reg. §48.4071-3.]

☐ [T.D. 7809.]

[Reg. §48.4071-4]

§48.4071-4. Original equipment tires on imported articles.—The tax imposed by section 4071(a) applies with respect to tires and inner tubes (other than bicycle tires and inner tubes) that are original equipment for an imported article upon which no tax is imposed under section 4061 if the article is sold on or after December 11, 1971. In such a case, the importer of the article is treated as the manufacturer and vendor of the tires and inner tubes with which the article is equipped. However, the tax imposed by section 4071(a) is not imposed with respect to tires and inner tubes if the imported article is an automobile bus chassis or an automobile bus body. Solely for purposes of this section, the provisions of section 4218 (relating to use by a manufacturer or importer considered a sale) do not apply in cases where an individual imports an article having original equipment tires and tubes and on which article no tax is imposed under section 4061 if the article is imported solely for the individual's personal use and is so used. [Reg. §48.4071-4.]

☐ [T.D. 7809.]

[Reg. §48.4072-1]

§48.4072-1. Definitions.—For purposes of the regulations in this part, unless otherwise expressly indicated:

(a) *Rubber.*—The term "rubber" includes synthetic and substitute rubber.

(b) *Tread rubber.*—The term "tread rubber" means any material (1) which is commonly or commercially known as tread rubber or camelback, or (2) which is a substitute for any material commonly or commercially known as tread rubber or camelback and is of a type used in recapping or retreading tires. The term includes, for example, strips of material, wholly or partially of rubber, natural or synthetic, intended to be vulcanized or otherwise affixed to a tire casing to form the outside perimeter of the tire, smooth or treaded. It also includes treading material produced by reprocessing scrap, salvage, or junk rubber and a continuous rubber ribbon produced through an extrusion process for direct application in recapping or retreading a tire casing. The term does not include rubber in various forms such as strip, slab, pellet, etc. which is used as raw material for the extrusion process. Tread rubber loses its identity as such when it has been used in the recapping or retreading of a tire of a type used on a highway vehicle (without regard to the actual use ultimately made of the tire) or has deteriorated in quality to the point where it is no longer suitable for use in recapping or retreading of a tire. (In the case of such deterioration, see section 6416(b)(2) and §48.6416(b)-2 to secure a refund or credit of the tax paid.)

(c) *Tires of the type used on highway vehicles.*—(1) The term "tires of the type used on highway vehicles", for purposes of §§48.4071-1 through 48.4073-3 means tires of the type used on—

(i) Motor vehicles that are highway vehicles (within the meaning of §48.4061(a)-1(d)), or

(ii) Vehicles of the type used in connection with motor vehicles that are highway vehicles (within the meaning of §48.4061(a)-1(d)). The term "tires of the type used on highway vehicles" does not include bicycle tires. Bicycle tires, however, are included in the term "other tires" as used in section 4071(a)(2).

(2) For purposes of paragraph (c)(1)(i) of this section, tires of the type used on motor vehicles include tires used on motor trucks, buses, passenger automobiles, motor homes, highway tractors, trolley buses or coaches, and motorcycles.

(3) For purposes of paragraph (c)(1)(ii) of this section, tires of the types used on vehicles of the type used in connection with motor vehicles that are highway vehicles include tires used on truck or bus trailers, truck semi-trailers, mobile homes, housetrailers, or utility trailers.

(d) *Inner tubes.*—The term "inner tubes" includes air containers of all types made wholly or in part of rubber and designed and manufactured for use in pneumatic tires.

(e) *Tires.*—The term "tires" includes rubber casings, hoops, and strips or bands of all kinds designed and shaped or built to form the tread of or to fit a vehicle wheel. Tires of either the pneumatic or solid type which fit or form the tread for wheels of any article which is capable of use as a means of transporting a person or burden are taxable as tires. Examples of articles which may be equipped with taxable tires are motor scooters, minibikes, industrial trucks, farm tractors, wheelbarrows, and similar articles. See section 4073(a) and §48.4073-1 with respect to the exemption of tires of certain sizes, and section 4073(b) and §48.4073-2 with respect to the exemption for tires with internal wire fastening.

(f) *Laminated tires.*—For purposes of the tax imposed by section 4071, the term "laminated tires" means tires (1) which are not "tires of the type used on highway vehicles" within the meaning of paragraph (c) of this section, and (2) which consist wholly of scrap rubber from used tire casings with an internal metal fastening agent.

(g) *Manufacturer.*—The term "manufacturer" means manufacturer, producer or importer. A person who converts, by any process, a new tire taxable under section 4071 at one rate of tax into a tire taxable under section 4071 at a different rate (as for example, an off highway-type tire converted into a highway-type tire) is considered to be a manufacturer of the converted tire. If a conversion results in a reduced rate of tax for the converted tire, see section 6416(b)(2) and §48.6416(b)-2 to secure a credit or refund of part of the tax paid. The term "manufactured" includes "produced" and "imported".

(h) *Cross references.*—For other definitions, see §48.0-2. [Reg. §48.4072-1.]

☐ [T.D. 7809.]

[Reg. §48.4073-1]

§48.4073-1. Exemption of tires of certain sizes.—The tax does not apply to sales of tires of all-rubber construction (whether hollow center or solid) if they have no fabric or metal reinforcement and do not exceed either of these measurements:(a) 20 inches in diameter measured to the outside circumferences, and (b) 1³/₄ inches in cross-section. The exemption provided by section 4073(a) is to be determined solely on the measurements of the tire and not on the purpose for which it is designed or used. [Reg. §48.4073-1.]

☐ [T.D. 7809.]

[Reg. §48.4073-2]

§48.4073-2. Exemption of tires with internal wire fastening.—The tax does not apply to sales of tires of any size or dimension manufactured from extruded tiring that is fastened or held

together by means of internal wire or other metallic material. [Reg. §48.4073-2.]

[Reg. §48.4073-3]

§48.4073-3. Exemption of tread rubber used for recapping non-highway tires.—(a) *Sold direct by manufacturer for nontaxable use.*—The tax does not apply to the sale of tread rubber by the manufacturer to any person for use by that person otherwise than in the recapping or retreading of tires of the type used on highway vehicles. In determining whether tread rubber is sold for a taxable or nontaxable use, the type of vehicle on which the recapped or retreaded tire is to be used, or the actual or intended use of the recapped or retreaded tire, is immaterial. The controlling factor is whether the tire resulting from the recapping or retreading is of a type that is used otherwise than on a highway vehicle. For definition of "tires of the type used on highway vehicles", see paragraph (c) of §48.4072-1.

(b) *Sales for resale for nontaxable use.*—No sale of tread rubber may be made tax free for resale even though it is known at the time of the sale that the tread rubber will be resold for use otherwise than in the recapping or retreading of tires of the type used on highway vehicles. However, where the tread rubber is resold for such use, the manufacturer who paid the tax on a sale of the tread rubber may secure a refund or credit in accordance with the provisions of section 6416(b)(2) and §48.6416(b)-2.

(c) *Evidence required to establish exemption.*—(1) To establish the right to sell tread rubber tax free under section 4073(c), the manufacturer must obtain from the purchaser and retain in its possession a properly executed exemption certificate.

(2) Where only occasional sales of tread rubber for exempt use are made to a purchaser, a separate exemption certificate should be furnished for each order. However, where sales are regularly and frequently made to a purchaser for exempt use, a certificate covering all purchases during the period not to exceed 12 calendar quarters is acceptable. The certificates and proper records of invoices, order, etc., relative to tax-free sales must be kept for inspection by the district director as provided in section 6001 and the regulations in Subpart O.

(d) *Acceptable form of exemption certificate.*—The following form of exemption certificate is acceptable for the purposes of this section and must be adhered to in substance:

EXEMPTION CERTIFICATE

(For use by persons who purchase tread rubber from the manufacturer, producer, or importer thereof for use otherwise than in recapping or retreading tires of the type used on highway vehicles (section 4073(c) of the Internal Revenue Code).)

(Date)_____ 19_____

EXEMPTION CERTIFICATE

I, the undersigned, certify that I am the purchaser, or the (Title) _____ of
(Name of purchaser of other than the undersigned) _____
who is the purchaser of: _____ The tread rubber specified in
the accompanying order or contract, or _____ All tread
rubber specified in contracts or orders entered into or placed with (Name of seller)
_____ for the period commencing _____ and
ending _____ (period not to exceed 12 calendar quarters) and that such
tread rubber will not be used in the recapping or retreading of tires of the type used on
highway vehicles, but will be used for the following purposes:

_____
_____
_____
_____

The undersigned understands that if the tread rubber is used for the recapping or
retreading of tires of the type used on highway vehicles, or is sold or otherwise disposed
of, such fact must be promptly reported to the manufacturer. The undersigned also
understands that the fraudulent use of this certificate for the purpose of securing this
exemption will subject the undersigned or any other party making such fraudulent use to
a fine of not more than $10,000, or to imprisonment for not more than 5 years, or both,
together with costs of prosecution. The purchaser also understands that the purchaser
must be prepared to establish by satisfactory evidence the purpose for which the tread
rubber was used.

(Signature) _____

(Address) _____

(e) *Exemption certificate not obtained prior to filing of manufacturer's excise tax return.*—If the sale is otherwise exempt but the exemption certificate is not obtained prior to the time the manufacturer files a return covering taxes due for the period during which the sale was made, the manufacturer must include the tax on the sale in its return for that period. However, if the certificate is later obtained, a claim for refund of the tax paid on the sale may be filed, or a credit for the amount may be taken upon a subsequent return, as provided by section 6416(b)(2) and § 48.6416(b)-2. [Reg. § 48.4073-3.]

□ [T.D. 7809, 2-9-82.]

[Reg. § 48.4073-4]

§ 48.4073-4. Other tax-free sales.—(a) *Cross references.*—For provisions relating to tax-free sales of articles referred to in section 4071, see:

(1) Section 4221, relating to certain tax-free sales, and the regulations thereunder in Subpart H;

(2) Section 4222, relating to registration, and the regulations thereunder in Subpart H;

(3) Section 4223, relating to special rules pertaining to further manufacture, and the regulations thereunder in Subpart H; and

(4) 28 FR 348, January 12, 1963, relating to the authorization of an exemption from the tax imposed by section 4071 by the Secretary of the Treasury under section 4293 for sales of certain tires and inner tubes sold to the American Red Cross on or after March 1, 1963. [Reg. § 48.4073-4.]

□ [T.D. 7809, 2-9-82.]

[Reg. § 48.4081-1]

§ 48.4081-1. Taxable fuel; definitions.—(a) *Overview.*—This section provides definitions for purposes of the tax on taxable fuel imposed by section 4081.

(b) *Definitions.*

Approved terminal or refinery means a terminal or refinery that is operated, respectively, by a taxable fuel registrant that is a terminal operator, or by a taxable fuel registrant that is a refiner.

Aviation gasoline means all special grades of gasoline that are suitable for use in aviation reciprocating engines and covered by ASTM specification D 910 or military specification MIL-G-5572. For availability of ASTM and military specifications, see paragraph (d) of this section.

Blender means any person that produces blended taxable fuel.

Bulk transfer means any transfer of taxable fuel by pipeline or vessel.

Bulk transfer/terminal system means the taxable fuel distribution system consisting of refineries, pipelines, vessels, and terminals. Thus, taxable fuel in a refinery, pipeline, vessel, or terminal is in the bulk transfer/terminal system. Taxable fuel in the fuel supply tank of any engine, or in any tank car, rail car, trailer, truck, or other equipment suitable for ground transportation is not in the bulk transfer/terminal system.

Bus means automobile bus.

Diesel-powered bus means any bus that is propelled by a diesel-powered engine.

Reg. § 48.4081-1(b)

Diesel-powered highway vehicle means a highway vehicle, as defined in §48.4061(a)-1(d), that is propelled by a diesel-powered engine.

Diesel-powered train means any diesel-powered equipment or machinery that rides on rails. Thus, for example, the term includes a locomotive, work train, switching engine, and track maintenance machine.

Enterer generally means the importer of record (under customs law) with respect to the taxable fuel, except that—

(1) If the importer of record is a customs broker engaged by the owner of the taxable fuel, the person for whom the broker is acting is the enterer; and

(2) If there is no importer of record for taxable fuel entered into the United States, the owner of the taxable fuel at the time it is brought into the United States is the enterer.

Entry of taxable fuel into the United States occurs when—

(1) The taxable fuel is brought into the United States and applicable customs law requires that the taxable fuel be entered into the United States for consumption, use, or warehousing; or

(2) The taxable fuel is brought into the United States from Puerto Rico and applicable customs law would require that the taxable fuel be entered into the United States for consumption, use, or warehousing if the taxable fuel were brought into the United States from somewhere other than Puerto Rico.

Excluded liquid means any liquid that—

(1) Contains less than four percent normal paraffins; or

(2) Has a—

(i) Distillation range of 125[degree] F. or less;

(ii) Sulfur content of 10 ppm or less; and

(iii) Minimum color of +27 Saybolt.

Finished gasoline means all products (including gasohol (as defined in §48.4081-6(b)(2))) that are commonly or commercially known or sold as gasoline and are suitable for use as a motor fuel, other than products that have an ASTM octane number of less than 75 as determined by the motor method.

Gasoline means finished gasoline and gasoline blendstocks.

Industrial user means any person that receives gasoline blendstocks by bulk transfer for its own use in the manufacture of any product other than finished gasoline.

Kerosene means any liquid that meets the specifications for kerosene or would meet those specifications but for the presence in the liquid of a dye of the type described in §48.4082-1(b). A liquid meets the specifications for kerosene if it is one of the two grades of kerosene (No. 1-K and No. 2-K) covered by ASTM specification D 3699, or kerosene-type jet fuel covered by ASTM specification D 1655 or military specification MIL-DTL-5624T (Grade JP-5) or MIL-DTL-83133E (Grade JP-8). For availability of ASTM and military specifications, see paragraph (d) of this sec-

tion. However, the term does not include *excluded liquid*.

Position holder means, with respect to taxable fuel in a terminal, the person that holds the inventory position in the taxable fuel, as reflected on the records of the terminal operator. A person holds the inventory position in taxable fuel when that person has a contractual agreement with the terminal operator for the use of storage facilities and terminaling services at a terminal with respect to the taxable fuel. The term also includes a terminal operator that owns taxable fuel in its terminal.

Rack means a mechanism capable of delivering taxable fuel into a means of transport other than a pipeline or vessel.

Refiner means any person that owns, operates, or otherwise controls a refinery.

Refinery means a facility used to produce taxable fuel and from which taxable fuel may be removed by pipeline, by vessel, or at a rack. However, the term does not include a facility where only blended fuel or gasohol (as defined in §48.4081-6(b)(2)), and no other type of taxable fuel, is produced. For this purpose blended fuel is any mixture that, if produced outside the bulk transfer/terminal system, would be blended taxable fuel.

Removal means any physical transfer of taxable fuel, and any use of taxable fuel other than as a material in the production of taxable fuel or special fuels. However, taxable fuel is not removed when it evaporates or is otherwise lost or destroyed.

Sale means—

(1) The transfer of title to, or substantial incidents of ownership in, taxable fuel (other than taxable fuel in a terminal) to the buyer for a consideration, which may consist of money, services, or other property; or

(2) The transfer of the inventory position in the taxable fuel in a terminal if the transferee becomes the position holder with respect to the taxable fuel.

State includes any State, any political subdivision of a State, the District of Columbia, the American Red Cross, and, to the extent provided by section 7871, any Indian tribal government.

Taxable fuel means gasoline, diesel fuel, and kerosene.

Taxable fuel registrant means an enterer, industrial user, refiner, terminal operator, or throughputter that is registered as such under section 4101.

Terminal means a taxable fuel storage and distribution facility that is supplied by pipeline or vessel and from which taxable fuel may be removed at a rack. However, the term does not include any facility at which gasoline blendstocks are used in the manufacture of products other than finished gasoline and from which no gasoline is removed. Also, effective January 2, 1998, the term does not include any facility where finished gasoline, undyed diesel fuel, or undyed kerosene is stored if the facility is operated by a taxable fuel registrant and all such taxable fuel stored at the facility has been previously taxed under section 4081 upon removal from a refinery or terminal.

Terminal operator means any person that owns, operates, or otherwise controls a terminal.

Throughputter means any person that—

(1) Owns taxable fuel within the bulk transfer/terminal system (other than in a terminal); or

(2) Is a position holder.

Vessel means a waterborne taxable fuel transporting vessel.

(c) *Blended taxable fuel, diesel fuel, and gasoline blendstocks; definitions.*—(1) *Blended taxable fuel.*—(i) *In general.*—Except as provided in paragraphs (c)(1)(ii) and (c)(1)(iii) of this section, *blended taxable fuel* means any taxable fuel that is produced outside the bulk transfer/terminal system by mixing—

(A) Taxable fuel with respect to which tax has been imposed under section 4041(a)(1) or 4081(a) (other than taxable fuel for which a credit or payment has been allowed); and

(B) Any other liquid on which tax has not been imposed under section 4081.

(ii) *Exclusion; minor blending.*—A mixture described in paragraph (c)(1)(i) of this section is not blended taxable fuel if, during the calendar quarter in which the blender removes or sells the mixture, all such mixtures removed or sold by the blender contain, in the aggregate, less than 400 gallons of liquid described in paragraph (c)(1)(i)(B) of this section.

(iii) *Exclusion; gasohol.*—Blended taxable fuel does not include any gasohol (as defined in § 48.4081-6(b)(2)) if, disregarding the alcohol, the gasohol is not blended taxable fuel and contains, in addition to permitted amounts of liquids described in paragraph (c)(1)(i)(B) of this section, only gasoline with respect to which—

(A) Tax was imposed under section 4081(a) at a rate described in § 48.4081-6(e) (relating to the gasohol production tax rate and the gasohol tax rate); or

(B) A valid claim is made under section 6427(f).

(2) *Diesel fuel.*—(i) *In general.*—Except as provided in paragraph (c)(2)(ii) of this section, *diesel fuel* means any liquid that, without further processing or blending, is suitable for use as a fuel in a diesel-powered highway vehicle or diesel-powered train. A liquid is suitable for this use if the liquid has practical and commercial fitness for use in the propulsion engine of a diesel-powered highway vehicle or diesel-powered train. A liquid may possess this practical and commercial fitness even though the specified use is not the liquid's predominant use. However, a liquid does not possess this practical and commercial fitness solely by reason of its possible or rare use as a fuel in the propulsion engine of a diesel-powered highway vehicle or diesel-powered train.

(ii) *Exclusion.*—Diesel fuel does not include gasoline, kerosene, excluded liquid, No. 5

and No. 6 fuel oils covered by ASTM specification D 396, or F-76 (Fuel Naval Distillate) covered by military specification MIL-F-16884. For availability of ASTM and military specifications, see paragraph (d) of this section.

(3) *Gasoline blendstocks.*—(i) *In general.*—Except as provided in paragraph (c)(3)(ii) of this section, *gasoline blendstocks* means—

(A) Alkylate;

(B) Butane;

(C) Butene;

(D) Catalytically cracked gasoline;

(E) Coker gasoline;

(F) Ethyl tertiary butyl ether (ETBE);

(G) Hexane;

(H) Hydrocrackate;

(I) Isomerate;

(J) Methyl tertiary butyl ether (MTBE);

(K) Mixed xylene (not including any separated isomer of xylene);

(L) Natural gasoline;

(M) Pentane;

(N) Pentane mixture;

(O) Polymer gasoline;

(P) Raffinate;

(Q) Reformate;

(R) Straight-run gasoline;

(S) Straight-run naphtha;

(T) Tertiary amyl methyl ether (TAME);

(U) Tertiary butyl alcohol (gasoline grade) (TBA);

(V) Thermally cracked gasoline;

(W) Toluene; and

(X) Transmix containing gasoline.

(ii) *Exclusion.*—Gasoline blendstocks does not include any product that cannot, without further processing, be used in the production of finished gasoline. For example, a mixed hydrocarbon stream that is produced in a natural gas processing plant is not a gasoline blendstock if the stream cannot be used to produce finished gasoline without further processing.

(d) *ASTM and military specifications.*—ASTM specifications may be obtained from the American Society for Testing and Materials, 100 Barr Harbor Drive, West Conshohocken, PA 19428. Military specifications may be obtained from the Standardization Document Order Desk, Building 4, Section D, 700 Robbins Avenue, Philadelphia, PA 19111.

(e) *Other definitions.*—For other definitions relating to taxable fuel, see §§ 48.4081-6(b), 48.4082-5(b), 48.4082-6(b), 48.4082-7(b), 48.4101-1(b), 48.6427-9(b), 48.6427-10(b), and 48.6427-11(b).

(f) *Effective date.*—(1) Except as provided in paragraph (f)(2) of this section, this section is applicable after December 31, 1993.

(2) In paragraph (b) of this section the definition of aviation gasoline and the third sentence in the definition of terminal are applicable after January 1, 1998, the definition of kerosene, ex-

cluded liquid, and taxable fuel are applicable after June 30, 1998, and the definition of enterer is applicable to entries of taxable fuel after September 27, 2004. Paragraph (c)(2) of this section is applicable after December 31, 1997. [Reg. § 48.4081-1.]

☐ [T.D. 6433, 12-21-59. *Amended by T.D. 6574, 10-10-61; T.D. 7908, 9-2-83; T.D. 8421, 7-21-92; T.D. 8659, 3-13-96; T.D. 8748, 12-31-97; T.D. 8879, 3-30-2000; T.D. 9051, 4-1-2003; T.D. 9145, 7-29-2004 and T.D. 9346, 7-26-2007.]*

[Reg. § 48.4081-2]

§ 48.4081-2. Taxable fuel; tax on removal at a terminal rack.—(a) *Overview.*—This section provides the general rule that all removals of taxable fuel at a terminal rack are subject to tax and the position holder with respect to the fuel is liable for the tax.

(b) *Imposition of tax.*—Tax is imposed on the removal of taxable fuel from a terminal if the taxable fuel is removed at the rack.

(c) *Liability for tax.*—(1) *In general.*—The position holder with respect to the taxable fuel is liable for the tax imposed under paragraph (b) of this section.

(2) *Joint and several liability of terminal operator; unregistered position holder.*—(i) *In general.*— The terminal operator is jointly and severally liable for the tax imposed under paragraph (b) of this section if—

(A) The position holder with respect to the taxable fuel is a person other than the terminal operator and is not a taxable fuel registrant; and

(B) The terminal operator has not met the conditions of paragraph (c)(2)(ii) of this section.

(ii) *Conditions for avoidance of liability.*—A terminal operator is not liable for tax under this paragraph (c)(2) if, at the time of the removal, the terminal operator—

(A) Is a taxable fuel registrant;

(B) Has an unexpired notification certificate (as described in § 48.4081-5) from the position holder; and

(C) Has no reason to believe that any information in the notification certificate is false.

(3) *Joint and several liability of terminal operator; incorrect information provided.*—The terminal operator is jointly and severally liable for the tax imposed under paragraph (b) of this section if, in connection with the removal of diesel fuel or kerosene that is not dyed and marked in accordance with § 48.4082-1, the terminal operator provides any person (including the position holder with respect to the fuel) with any bill of lading, shipping paper, record, or similar document indicating that the diesel fuel or kerosene is dyed and marked in accordance with § 48.4082-1.

(4) *Example.*—The following example illustrates this paragraph (c) and § 48.4082-1:

Example. (i) TO is a terminal operator and PH is the position holder with respect to, and owner of, 8,000 gallons of diesel fuel stored in TO's terminal. TO and PH are taxable fuel registrants. When the fuel is removed from the terminal at the rack, the fuel is not dyed and marked in accordance with § 48.4082-1, and TO does not provide any person with any paperwork indicating that the fuel is dyed and marked. After the removal from the terminal, PH sells the fuel to individuals for use as heating oil, a nontaxable use.

(ii) Because PH is the position holder of the fuel at the time of the removal from the terminal, PH is liable for the tax imposed by section 4081. The removal is subject to tax because the fuel is not dyed and marked in accordance with § 48.4082-1, and later use of the fuel in a nontaxable use does not make the removal from the terminal exempt from tax.

(iii) Because PH is a taxable fuel registrant and TO did not provide any person with any paperwork indicating that the fuel is dyed and marked, TO is not jointly and severally liable for tax under paragraph (c)(2) or (3) of this section.

(d) *Rate of tax.*—For the rate of tax generally, see section 4081(a). For the rate of tax on gasohol and on gasoline removed for gasohol production, see § 48.4081-6.

(e) *Exemptions.*—For exemptions from the tax imposed under this section, see §§ 48.4081-4 (relating to gasoline blendstocks), 48.4082-1 (relating to dyed diesel fuel and dyed kerosene), 48.4082-5 (relating to diesel fuel and kerosene used in Alaska), 48.4082-6 (relating to aviation-grade kerosene), and 48.4082-7 (relating to kerosene used for a feedstock purpose).

(f) *Effective date.*—This section is applicable after December 31, 1993. [Reg. § 48.4081-2.]

☐ [T.D. 7658, 12-4-79. *Amended by T.D. 8152, 8-30-87; T.D. 8399, 3-3-92; T.D. 8421, 7-21-92; T.D. 8659, 3-13-96 and T.D. 8879, 3-30-2000.]*

[Reg. § 48.4081-3]

§ 48.4081-3. Taxable fuel; taxable events other than removal at the terminal rack.— (a) *Overview.*—Although tax is imposed when taxable fuel is removed from the terminal at the rack, tax also is imposed in certain other situations described in this section.

(b) *Tax on removal from a refinery.*—(1) *Imposition of tax.*—Tax is imposed on the following removals from a refinery:

(i) A removal of taxable fuel by bulk transfer if the refiner or the owner of the taxable fuel immediately before the removal is not a taxable fuel registrant.

(ii) A removal of taxable fuel at the rack.

(iii) After September 30, 1995, a removal of a batch of gasohol from an approved refinery by bulk transfer if the refiner treats itself with respect to the removal as a person that is not registered under section 4101. See § 48.4101-1(a). For the rule providing that no deposit is required in the case of the tax imposed under this paragraph (b)(1)(iii), see § 40.6302(c)-1(f)(4) of this chapter. For the rule allowing inspections of facilities where gasohol is produced, see section 4083.

(2) *Exception for certain refineries.*—The tax imposed under paragraph (b)(1)(ii) of this section does not apply to a removal of taxable fuel if—

(i) The taxable fuel is removed from an approved refinery that is not served by pipeline (other than a pipeline for the receipt of crude oil) or vessel;

(ii) The taxable fuel is received at a facility that is operated by a taxable fuel registrant and is located within the bulk transfer/terminal system;

(iii) The removal from the refinery is by—

(A) Rail car; or

(B) In the case of diesel fuel, a trailer or semi-trailer that is used exclusively for the transport service described in paragraphs (b)(2)(i) and (b)(2)(ii) of this section;

(iv) In the case of taxable fuel removed by rail car, the facility at which the fuel is received is operated by the same person that operates the refinery from which the fuel was removed; and

(v) In the case of diesel fuel removed by a trailer or semi-trailer, the facility at which the fuel is received is less than 20 miles from the refinery from which the diesel fuel was removed.

(3) *Liability for tax.*—The refiner is liable for the tax imposed under paragraph (b)(1) of this section.

(c) *Tax on entry into the United States.*—(1) *Imposition of tax.*—Tax is imposed on the entry of taxable fuel into the United States if—

(i) The entry is by bulk transfer and the enterer is not a taxable fuel registrant; or

(ii) The entry is not by bulk transfer.

(2) *Liability for tax.*—(i) *In general.*—The enterer is liable for the tax imposed under paragraph (c)(1) of this section.

(ii) Joint and several liability of the importer of record. The importer of record with respect to the taxable fuel is jointly and severally liable with the enterer for the tax imposed under paragraph (c)(1) of this section if—

(A) The importer of record is not the enterer of the taxable fuel; and

(B) The enterer is not a taxable fuel registrant.

(iii) Conditions for avoidance of liability. The importer of record is not liable for the tax under paragraph (c)(2)(ii) of this section if, at the time of the entry, the importer of record—

(A) Has an unexpired notification certificate (as described in § 48.4081-5) from the enterer; and

(B) Has no reason to believe that any information in the notification certificate is false.

(iv) *Customs bond.*—The Customs bond posted with respect to the importation of the fuel

will not be charged for the tax imposed on the entry of the fuel if the enterer is a taxable fuel registrant. A Customs bond will not be charged for the tax imposed on the entry of the fuel covered by the bond, if at the time of entry, the surety—

(A) Has an unexpired notification certificate (as described in § 48.4081-5) from the enterer; and

(B) Has no reason to believe that any information in the notification certificate is false.

(d) *Tax on bulk transfers from a terminal by an unregistered position holder.*—(1) *Imposition of tax.*—Tax is imposed on the removal by bulk transfer of taxable fuel from a terminal if the position holder with respect to the taxable fuel is not a taxable fuel registrant.

(2) *Liability for tax.*—(i) *In general.*—The position holder with respect to the taxable fuel is liable for the tax imposed under paragraph (d)(1) of this section.

(ii) *Joint and several liability of terminal operator.*—The terminal operator is jointly and severally liable for the tax imposed under paragraph (d)(1) of this section if—

(A) The position holder with respect to the taxable fuel is a person other than the terminal operator; and

(B) The terminal operator has not met the conditions of paragraph (d)(2)(iii) of this section.

(iii) *Conditions for avoidance of liability.*—A terminal operator is not liable for tax under this paragraph (d)(2) if, at the time of the bulk transfer, the terminal operator—

(A) Is a taxable fuel registrant;

(B) Has an unexpired notification certificate (described in § 48.4081-5) from the position holder; and

(C) Has no reason to believe that any information in the notification certificate is false.

(e) *Tax on bulk transfers not received at an approved terminal or refinery.*—(1) *Imposition of tax.*—Tax on taxable fuel is imposed if—

(i) Taxable fuel is removed by bulk transfer from a refinery or terminal, or entered by bulk transfer into the United States;

(ii) No tax was imposed on such removal or entry under paragraph (b), (c), or (d) of this section; and

(iii) Upon removal from the pipeline or vessel, the taxable fuel is not received at an approved terminal or refinery (or at another pipeline or vessel).

(2) *Liability for tax.*—(i) *In general.*—The owner of the taxable fuel when it is removed from the pipeline or vessel is liable for the tax imposed under paragraph (e)(1) of this section if the owner has not met the conditions of paragraph (e)(2)(ii) of this section.

(ii) *Conditions for avoidance of liability.*—An owner of taxable fuel is not liable for tax under

Reg. § 48.4081-3(e)(2)(ii)

paragraph (e)(2)(i) of this section if, at the time the taxable fuel is removed from the pipeline or vessel, the owner of the taxable fuel—

(A) Is a taxable fuel registrant;

(B) Has an unexpired notification certificate (described in § 48.4081-5) from the operator of the terminal or refinery where the taxable fuel is received; and

(C) Has no reason to believe that any information in the notification certificate is false.

(iii) *Liability of the operator of the facility where the taxable fuel is received.*—The operator of the facility where the taxable fuel is received is liable for the tax imposed under paragraph (e)(1) of this section if the owner of the taxable fuel has met the conditions of paragraph (e)(2)(ii) of this section and is jointly and severally liable for the tax if the owner has not met such conditions.

(f) *Tax on sales within the bulk transfer/terminal system.*—(1) *Imposition of tax.*—Tax is imposed on the sale of taxable fuel located within the bulk transfer/terminal system if the sale is to a person that is not a taxable fuel registrant and tax has not been imposed on such taxable fuel under § 48.4081-2, or paragraph (b), (c), (d), or (e) of this section.

(2) *Exception for certain sales of taxable fuel for export.*—The tax imposed under paragraph (f)(1) of this section does not apply to a sale of taxable fuel if—

(i) The buyer's principal place of business is not within the United States;

(ii) The sale of the fuel occurs as the fuel is delivered into a transport vessel;

(iii) The vessel has a capacity of at least 20,000 barrels of fuel;

(iv) The seller is a taxable fuel registrant and the exporter of record of the fuel; and

(v) The fuel was exported in due course.

(3) *Liability for tax.*—(i) *In general.*—The seller of the taxable fuel is liable for the tax imposed under paragraph (f)(1) of this section if the seller has not met the conditions of paragraph (f)(3)(ii) of this section.

(ii) *Conditions for avoidance of liability.*—A seller is not liable for tax under paragraph (f)(3)(i) of this section if, at the time of the sale, the seller—

(A) Is a taxable fuel registrant;

(B) Has an unexpired notification certificate (described in § 48.4081-5) from the buyer; and

(C) Has no reason to believe that any information in the certificate is false.

(iii) *Liability of the buyer.*—The buyer of the taxable fuel is liable for the tax imposed under paragraph (f)(1) of this section if the seller of the taxable fuel has met the conditions of paragraph (f)(3)(ii) of this section and is jointly and severally liable for the tax if the seller has not met such conditions.

(4) *Example.*—The following example illustrates this paragraph (f) and the definition of the term *sale* in § 48.4081-1:

Example. PH owns one million gallons of untaxed gasoline that is stored in TO's terminal. PH also is the position holder with respect to the gasoline. While the gasoline remains stored in the terminal, PH transfers title to 200,000 gallons of the gasoline to A, a person that is not a taxable fuel registrant. PH continues to hold the inventory position on TO's records with respect to the one million gallons. Because PH continues as the position holder with respect to the gasoline, the transfer of title to the gasoline from PH to A is not a sale of gasoline. Because this transfer of title from PH to A is not a sale of gasoline, the tax imposed under paragraph (f) of this section does not apply to the transfer.

(g) *Tax on removal or sale of blended taxable fuel by the blender.*—(1) *Imposition of tax.*—A tax is imposed on the removal or sale of blended taxable fuel by the blender thereof. Tax is computed on the difference between the total number of gallons of blended taxable fuel removed or sold and the number of gallons of previously taxed taxable fuel used to produce the blended taxable fuel. For this purpose, the alcohol in gasohol is treated as previously taxed taxable fuel.

(2) *Liability for tax.*—(i) *Liability of the blender.*—The blender is liable for the tax imposed under paragraph (g)(1) of this section.

(ii) *Liability of seller of untaxed liquid.*—On and after April 2, 2003, a person that sells any liquid that is used to produce blended taxable fuel is jointly and severally liable for the tax imposed under paragraph (g)(1) of this section on the removal or sale of that blended taxable fuel if the liquid—

(A) Is described in § 48.4081-1(c)(1)(i)(B) (relating to liquids on which tax has not been imposed under section 4081); and

(B) Is sold by that person as gasoline, diesel fuel, or kerosene that has been taxed under section 4081.

(3) *Examples.*—The following examples illustrate the provisions of this paragraph (g) and the definitions of *blended taxable fuel* and *diesel fuel* in § 48.4081-1(c):

Example 1. (i) *Facts.* W is a wholesale distributor of petroleum products and R is a retailer of petroleum products. W sells to R 1,000 gallons of an untaxed liquid (a liquid described in § 48.4081-1(c)(1)(i)(B)) and delivers the liquid into a storage tank (tank) at R's retail facility. However, W's invoice to R states that the liquid is undyed diesel fuel. At the time of the delivery, the tank contains 4,000 gallons of undyed diesel fuel, a taxable fuel that has been taxed under section 4081. The resulting 5,000 gallon mixture is suitable for use as a fuel in a diesel-powered highway vehicle because it has practical and commercial fitness for use in the propulsion engine of a diesel-powered highway vehicle. The mixture does not satisfy the dyeing requirements of §48.4082-1. R sells the mixture from the tank to a construction company for off-highway business use.

(ii) *Analysis*—(A) *Production of blended taxable fuel.* R is a blender within the meaning of §48.4081-1 because R has produced blended taxable fuel, as defined in §48.4081-1, by mixing 1,000 gallons of a liquid that has not been taxed under section 4081 with 4,000 gallons of diesel fuel that has been taxed under section 4081. The mixing occurs outside of the bulk transfer/terminal system and the resulting product is diesel fuel because it is suitable for use as a fuel in a diesel-powered highway vehicle.

(B) *Imposition of tax.* Under paragraph (g)(1) of this section, tax is imposed on R's sale of the 5,000 gallons of blended taxable fuel to the construction company. Even though the blended taxable fuel is sold for off-highway business use, which is a nontaxable use as defined in section 4082(b), the sale is not exempt from tax because the blended taxable fuel does not satisfy the dyeing requirements of §48.4082-1. Tax is computed on 1,000 gallons, which is the difference between the number of gallons of blended taxable fuel R sells (5,000) and the number of gallons of previously taxed taxable fuel used to produce the blended taxable fuel (4,000).

(C) *Liability for tax.* R, as the blender, is liable for this tax under paragraph (g)(2)(i) of this section. W is jointly and severally liable for this tax under paragraph (g)(2)(ii) of this section because the blended taxable fuel is produced using an untaxed liquid that W sold as undyed diesel fuel (that is, as diesel fuel that was taxed under section 4081).

Example 2. (i) *Facts.* W, a wholesale distributor of petroleum products, buys 7,000 gallons of diesel fuel at a terminal rack. The diesel fuel is delivered into a tank trailer. Tax is imposed on the diesel fuel under §48.4081-2 when the diesel fuel is removed at the rack. W then goes to another location where X, the operator of a chemical plant, sells W 1,000 gallons of an untaxed liquid (a liquid described in §48.4081-1(c)(1)(i)(B)). However, X's invoice to W states that the liquid is undyed diesel fuel. This liquid is delivered into the tank trailer already containing the 7,000 gallons of diesel fuel. The resulting 8,000 gallon mixture is suitable for use as a fuel in a diesel-powered highway vehicle because it has practical and commercial fitness for use in the propulsion engine of a diesel-powered highway vehicle. The mixture does not satisfy the dyeing requirements of §48.4082-1. W sells the mixture to R, a retailer of petroleum products, and delivers the mixture into a storage tank at R's retail facility. R sells the mixture to its customers.

(ii) *Analysis*—(A) *Production of blended taxable fuel.* W is a blender within the meaning of §48.4081-1 because W has produced blended taxable fuel, as defined in §48.4081-1, by mixing 1,000 gallons of a liquid that has not been taxed under section 4081 with 7,000 gallons of diesel

fuel that has been taxed under section 4081. The mixing occurs outside of the bulk transfer/terminal system and the resulting product is diesel fuel because it is suitable for use as a fuel in a diesel-powered highway vehicle. Thus, R has bought blended taxable fuel.

(B) *Imposition of tax.* Under paragraph (g)(1) of this section, tax is imposed on W's sale of the 8,000 gallons of blended taxable fuel to R. Tax is computed on 1,000 gallons, which is the difference between the number of gallons of blended taxable fuel W sells (8,000) and the number of gallons of previously taxed taxable fuel used to produce the blended taxable fuel (7,000). No tax is imposed on R's subsequent sale of the blended taxable fuel because tax is imposed only with respect to a removal or sale by the blender.

(C) *Liability for tax.* W, as the blender, is liable for this tax under paragraph (g)(2)(i) of this section. X is jointly and severally liable for this tax under paragraph (g)(2)(ii) of this section because the blended taxable fuel is produced using an untaxed liquid that X sold as undyed diesel fuel (that is, as diesel fuel that was taxed under section 4081). R has no liability for tax because R is not a blender and did not sell any untaxed liquid as a taxed taxable fuel. R only sold taxed taxable fuel, the blended taxable fuel bought from W.

(h) *Rate of tax.*—For the rate of tax generally imposed under this section, see section 4081(a). For the rate of tax on gasohol and on gasoline removed or entered for gasohol production, see §48.4081-6.

(i) *Exemptions.*—For exemptions from the taxes imposed under this section, see §§48.4081-4 (relating to gasoline blendstocks), 48.4082-1 (relating to dyed diesel fuel and dyed kerosene), 48.4082-5 (relating to diesel fuel and kerosene used in Alaska), 48.4082-6 (relating to aviation-grade kerosene), and 48.4082-7 (relating to kerosene used for a feedstock purpose).

(j) Effective/applicability date: This section is applicable January 1, 1994, except that paragraphs (c)(2)(ii) through (iv) of this section are applicable to entries of taxable fuel after September 27, 2004. [Reg. §48.4081-3.]

☐ [*T.D.* 8421, 7-21-92. *Amended by T.D.* 8609, 8-4-95; *T.D.* 8659, 3-13-96; *T.D.* 8879, 3-30-2000; *T.D.* 9051, 4-1-2003; *T.D.* 9145, 7-29-2004 *and T.D.* 9346, 7-26-2007.]

[Reg. §48.4081-4]

§48.4081-4. Gasoline; special rules for gasoline blendstocks.—(a) *Overview.*—This section provides rules exempting from tax certain removals, entries, and sales of gasoline blendstocks. Generally, under prescribed conditions, tax is not imposed on gasoline blendstocks that are not used to produce finished gasoline or that are received at an approved terminal or refinery.

(b) *Nonbulk removals and entries of gasoline blendstocks not used to produce gasoline.*—(1) *Removals and entries not in connection with sales.*—Tax is not imposed under §48.4081-2(b),

48.4081-3(b)(1)(ii), or 48.4081-3(c)(1)(ii) on the removal or entry of gasoline blendstocks not in connection with a sale if—

(i) The person otherwise liable for tax under § 48.4081-2(c)(1) (the position holder), 48.4081-3(b)(3) (the refiner), or 48.4081-3(c)(2) (the enterer) is a taxable fuel registrant; and

(ii) Such person does not use the gasoline blendstocks to produce finished gasoline.

(2) *Removals and entries in connection with sales.*—Tax is not imposed under § 48.4081-2(b), 48.4081-3(b)(1)(ii), or 48.4081-3(c)(1)(ii) on the removal or entry of gasoline blendstocks in connection with a sale if—

(i) The person otherwise liable for tax under § 48.4081-2(c)(1) (the position holder), 48.4081-3(b)(3) (the refiner), or 48.4081-3(c)(2) (the enterer) is a taxable fuel registrant; and

(ii) At the time of the sale, such person has an unexpired certificate (described in paragraph (e) of this section) from the buyer and has no reason to believe any information in the certificate is false.

(3) *Tax on sales after certain nonbulk removals or entries.*—(i) *In general.*—If paragraph (b)(1) or (2) of this section applies to the removal or entry of gasoline blendstocks, tax is imposed on any sale of such blendstocks unless, at the time of the sale, the seller—

(A) Has an unexpired certificate (described in paragraph (e) of this section) from its buyer; and

(B) Has no reason to believe any information in the certificate is false.

(ii) *Liability for tax.*—The seller is liable for the tax imposed under this paragraph (b)(3).

(iii) *Rate of tax.*—For the rate of tax, see section 4081.

(c) *Nonbulk removals and entries of gasoline blendstocks received at an approved terminal or refinery.*—Tax is not imposed under § 48.4081-2(b), 48.4081-3(b)(1)(ii), or 48.4081-3(c)(1)(ii) on the removal or entry of gasoline blendstocks that are received at a terminal or refinery if the person otherwise liable for tax under § 48.4081-2(c)(1) (the position holder), 48.4081-3(b)(3) (the refiner), or 48.4081-3(c)(2) (the enterer)—

(1) Is a taxable fuel registrant;

(2) Has an unexpired notification certificate (described in § 48.4081-5) from the operator of the terminal or refinery where the gasoline blendstocks are received; and

(3) Has no reason to believe that any information in the certificate is false.

(d) *Bulk transfers to a registered industrial user.*—Tax is not imposed under § 48.4081-3(e)(1) if, upon the removal of gasoline blendstocks from a pipeline or vessel, the gasoline blendstocks are received by a taxable fuel registrant that is an industrial user.

(e) *Certificate.*—(1) *In general.*—The certificate to be provided by a buyer of gasoline blendstocks consists of a statement that is signed under penalties of perjury by a person with authority to bind the buyer, is in substantially the same form as the model certificate provided in paragraph (e)(3) of this section, and contains all information necessary to complete such model certificate. A new certificate must be given if any information in the current certificate changes. The certificate may be included as part of any business records normally used to document a sale. The certificate expires on the earliest of the following dates:

(i) The date one year after the effective date of the certificate (which may be no earlier than the date it is signed).

(ii) The date a new certificate is provided to the seller.

(iii) The date the seller is notified by the Internal Revenue Service or the buyer that the buyer's right to provide a certificate has been withdrawn.

(2) *Withdrawal of right to provide certificate.*—The Internal Revenue Service may withdraw the right of a buyer of gasoline blendstocks to provide a certificate under this paragraph (e) if such buyer uses gasoline blendstocks to which a certificate applies in the production of finished gasoline or resells the gasoline blendstocks without obtaining a certificate from its buyer. The Internal Revenue Service may notify any seller to whom the buyer has provided a certificate that the buyer's right to provide a certificate has been withdrawn.

(3) *Model certificate.*

CERTIFICATE OF PERSON BUYING GASOLINE BLENDSTOCKS FOR USE
OTHER THAN IN THE PRODUCTION OF FINISHED GASOLINE
(To support tax-free sales under section 4081 of the Internal Revenue Code.)

_____

Name, address, and employer identification number of seller

The undersigned buyer ("Buyer") hereby certifies the following under penalties of perjury:

The gasoline blendstocks to which this certificate relates will not be used to produce finished gasoline.

This certificate applies to the following (complete as applicable):

If this is a single purchase certificate, check here _____ and enter:

1. Invoice or delivery ticket number_____

2. _____ (number of gallons) of_____ (type of gasoline blendstocks)

If this is a certificate covering all purchases under a specified account or order number, check here_____ and enter:

1. Effective date_____

2. Expiration date_____

(period not to exceed 1 year after the effective date)

3. Type (or types) of gasoline blendstocks_____

4. Buyer account or order number_____

Reg. § 48.4081-4(b)(1)(i)

Buyer will not claim a credit or refund under section 6427(h) of the Internal Revenue Code for any gasoline blendstocks covered by this certificate.

Buyer will provide a new certificate to the seller if any information in this certificate changes.

If Buyer resells the gasoline blendstocks to which this certificate relates, Buyer will be liable for tax unless Buyer obtains a certificate from the purchaser stating that the gasoline blendstocks will not be used to produce finished gasoline and otherwise complies with the conditions of § 48.4081-4(b)(3) of the Manufacturers and Retailers Excise Tax Regulations.

Buyer understands that if Buyer violates the terms of this certificate, the Internal Revenue Service may withdraw Buyer's right to provide a certificate.

Buyer has not been notified by the Internal Revenue Service that its right to provide a certificate has been withdrawn. In addition, the Internal Revenue Service has not notified Buyer that the right to provide a certificate has been withdrawn from a purchaser to which Buyer sells gasoline blendstocks tax free.

Buyer understands that the fraudulent use of this certificate may subject Buyer and all parties making such fraudulent use of this certificate to a fine or imprisonment, or both, together with the costs of prosecution.

_____

Signature and date signed

_____

Printed or typed name of person signing

_____

Title of person signing

_____

Name of Buyer

_____

Employer identification number

_____

Address of Buyer

(f) *Effective date.*—This section is effective January 1, 1994. [Reg. § 48.4081-4.]

☐ [*T.D. 8421, 7-21-92. Amended by T.D. 8659, 3-13-96.*]

[Reg. § 48.4081-5]

§ 48.4081-5. Taxable fuel; notification certificate of taxable fuel registrant.—(a) *Overview.*—This section sets forth requirements for the notification certificate under §§ 48.4081-2(c)(2)(ii), 48.4081-3(c)(2)(iii) and (iv), 48.4081-3(d)(2)(iii), 48.4081-3(e)(2)(iii), 48.4081-3(f)(2)(ii), and 48.4081-4(c) to notify another person of the taxable fuel registrant's registration status.

(b) *Certificate.*—(1) *In general.*—The certificate to be provided by a taxable fuel registrant consists of a statement that is signed under penalties of perjury by a person with authority to bind the registrant, is in substantially the same form as the model provided in paragraph (b)(2) of this section, and contains all information necessary to complete such model. A new certificate must be given if any information in the most recently provided certificate changes. The certificate may be included as part of any business records normally used to document a sale. The certificate expires on the earlier of the following dates:

(i) The date the registrant provides a new certificate.

(ii) The date the recipient of the certificate is notified by either the Internal Revenue Service or the registrant that the registrant's registration has been revoked or suspended.

(2) *Model certificate.*

NOTIFICATION CERTIFICATE OF TAXABLE FUEL REGISTRANT

_____

Name, address, and employer identification number of person receiving certificate

The undersigned taxable fuel registrant ("Registrant") hereby certifies under penalties of perjury that Registrant is registered by the Internal Revenue Service with registration number_____ and that Registrant's registration has not been revoked or suspended by the Internal Revenue Service.

Registrant understands that the fraudulent use of this certificate may subject Registrant and all parties making such fraudulent use of this certificate to a fine or imprisonment, or both, together with the costs of prosecution.

_____

Signature and date signed

_____

Printed or typed name of person signing

_____

Title of person signing

_____

Name of registrant

_____

Employer identification number

_____

Address of registrant

(3) *Use of Form 637 as a notification certificate prohibited.*—A copy of the certificate of registry (Form 637) or letter of registration issued to a registrant by the Internal Revenue Service is not

Reg. § 48.4081-5(b)(3)

a notification certificate described in paragraph (b)(2) of this section.

(c) *Effective date.*—This section is effective January 1, 1994. [Reg. §48.4081-5.]

☐ [T.D. 8421, 7-21-92. *Amended by* T.D. 8659, 3-13-96; T.D. 9145, 7-29-2004 *and* T.D. 9346, 7-26-2007.]

[Reg. §48.4081-6]

§48.4081-6. Gasoline; **gasohol.**— (a) *Overview.*—This section provides rules for determining the applicability of reduced rates of tax on a removal or entry of gasohol or of gasoline used to produce gasohol. Rules are also provided for the imposition of tax on the separation of gasoline from gasohol and the failure to use gasoline that has been taxed at a reduced rate to produce gasohol.

(b) *Explanation of terms.*—(1) *Alcohol.*—(i) *In general; source of the alcohol.*—Except as provided in paragraph (b)(1)(ii) of this section, alcohol means any alcohol that is not a derivative product of petroleum, natural gas, or coal (including peat). Thus, the term includes methanol and ethanol that are not derived from petroleum, natural gas, or coal (including peat). The term also includes alcohol produced either within or outside the United States.

(ii) *Proof and denaturants.*—Alcohol does not include alcohol with a proof of less than 190 degrees (determined without regard to added denaturants). If the alcohol added to a fuel/alcohol mixture (the added alcohol) includes impurities or denaturants, the volume of alcohol in the mixture is determined under the following rules:

(A) The volume of alcohol in the mixture includes the volume of any impurities (other than added denaturants and any fuel with which the alcohol is mixed) that reduce the purity of the added alcohol to not less than 190 proof (determined without regard to added denaturants).

(B) The volume of alcohol in the mixture includes the volume of any approved denaturants that reduce the purity of the added alcohol, but only to the extent that the volume of the approved denaturants does not exceed five percent of the volume of the added alcohol (including the approved denaturants). If the volume of the approved denaturants exceeds five percent of the volume of the added alcohol, the excess over five percent is considered part of the nonalcohol content of the mixture.

(C) For purposes of this paragraph (b)(1)(ii), approved denaturants are any denaturants (including gasoline and nonalcohol fuel denaturants) that reduce the purity of the added alcohol and are added to such alcohol under a formula approved by the Secretary.

(iii) *Products derived from alcohol.*—If alcohol described in paragraphs (b)(1)(i) and (ii) of this section has been chemically transformed in producing another product (that is, the alcohol is no longer present as a separate chemical in the other product) and there is no significant loss in the energy content of the alcohol, any mixture containing the product includes the volume of alcohol used to produce the product. Thus, for example, a mixture of gasoline and ethyl tertiary butyl ether (ETBE), or of gasoline and methyl tertiary butyl ether (MTBE), includes any alcohol described in paragraphs (b)(1)(i) and (ii) of this section that is used to produce the ETBE or MTBE, respectively, in a chemical reaction in which there is no significant loss in the energy content of the alcohol.

(2) *Gasohol.*—(i) *In general.*—(A) Gasohol is a mixture of gasoline and alcohol that is 10 percent gasohol, 7.7 percent gasohol, or 5.7 percent gasohol. The determination of whether a particular mixture is 10 percent gasohol, 7.7 percent gasohol, or 5.7 percent gasohol is made on a batch-by-batch basis. A batch of gasohol is a discrete mixture of gasoline and alcohol.

(B) If a particular mixture is produced within the bulk transfer/terminal system (for example, at a refinery), the determination of whether the mixture is gasohol is made at the time of the taxable removal or entry of the mixture.

(C) If a particular mixture is produced outside the bulk transfer/terminal system (for example, by splash blending after the gasoline has been removed from the terminal at the rack), the determination of whether the mixture is gasohol is made immediately after the mixture is produced. In such a case, the contents of the batch typically correspond to a gasoline meter delivery ticket and an alcohol meter delivery ticket, each of which shows the number of gallons of liquid delivered into the mixture. The volume of each component in a batch (without adjustment for temperature) ordinarily is determined by the number of metered gallons shown on the delivery tickets for the gasoline and alcohol delivered. However, if metered gallons of gasoline and alcohol are added to a tank already containing more than a minor amount of liquid, the determination of whether a batch satisfies the alcohol-content requirement will be made by taking into account the amount of alcohol and non-alcohol fuel contained in the liquid already in the tank. Ordinarily, any amount in excess of 0.5 percent of the capacity of the tank will not be considered minor.

(ii) *10 percent gasohol.*—(A) *In general.*—A batch of gasoline/alcohol mixture is 10 percent gasohol if it contains at least 9.8 percent alcohol by volume, without rounding.

(B) *Batches containing less than 10 percent but at least 9.8 percent alcohol.*—If a batch of mixture contains less than 10 percent alcohol but at least 9.8 percent alcohol, without rounding, only a portion of the batch is considered to be 10 percent gasohol. That portion equals the number of gallons of alcohol in the batch multiplied by 10. Any remaining liquid in the mixture is excess liquid.

(iii) *7.7 percent gasohol.*—(A) *In general.*—A batch of gasoline/alcohol mixture is 7.7 percent gasohol if it contains less than 9.8 percent alcohol but at least 7.55 percent alcohol by volume, without rounding.

(B) *Batches containing less than 7.7 percent but at least 7.55 percent alcohol.*—If a batch of mixture contains less than 7.7 percent alcohol but at least 7.55 percent alcohol, without rounding, only a portion of the batch is considered to be 7.7 percent gasohol. That portion equals the number of gallons of alcohol in the batch multiplied by 12.987. Any remaining liquid in the mixture is excess liquid.

(iv) *5.7 percent gasohol.*—(A) *In general.*—A batch of gasoline/alcohol mixture is 5.7 percent gasohol if it contains less than 7.55 percent alcohol but at least 5.59 percent alcohol by volume, without rounding.

(B) *Batches containing less than 5.7 percent but at least 5.59 percent alcohol.*—If a batch of mixture contains less than 5.7 percent alcohol but at least 5.59 percent alcohol, without rounding, only a portion of the batch is considered to be 5.7 percent gasohol. That portion equals the number of gallons of alcohol in the batch multiplied by 17.544. Any remaining liquid in the mixture is excess liquid.

(v) *Tax on excess liquid.*—If tax was imposed on the excess liquid in any gasohol at the gasohol production tax rate (as defined in paragraph (e)(1) of this section), the excess liquid in the batch is considered to be gasoline with respect to which there is a failure to blend into gasohol for purposes of paragraph (f) of this section. If tax was imposed on the excess liquid at the rate of tax described in section 4081(a), a credit or refund under section 6427(f) is not allowed with respect to the excess liquid.

(vi) *Examples.*—The following examples illustrate this paragraph (b)(2). In these examples, a gasohol blender creates a gasoline/alcohol mixture by pumping a specified amount of gasoline into an empty tank and then adding a specified amount of alcohol.

Example 1. Mixtures containing exactly 10 percent alcohol. The applicable delivery tickets show that the mixture is made with 7200 metered gallons of gasoline and 800 metered gallons of alcohol. Accordingly, the mixture contains 10 percent alcohol (as determined based on the delivery tickets provided to the blender) and qualifies as 10 percent gasohol.

Example 2. Mixtures containing less than 10 percent alcohol but at least 9.8 percent alcohol. The applicable delivery tickets show that the mixture is made with 7205 metered gallons of gasoline and 795 metered gallons of alcohol. Because the mixture contains less than 10 percent alcohol, but more than 9.8 percent alcohol (as determined based on the delivery tickets provided to the blender), 7950 gallons of the mixture qualify as 10 percent gasohol. If tax was imposed on the gasoline in the mixture at the gasohol production rate applicable to 10 percent gasohol, the remaining 50 gallons of the mixture (the excess liquid) are treated as gasoline with respect to which there was a failure to blend into gasohol for purposes of paragraph (f) of this section. If tax was imposed on the gasoline in the mixture at the rate of tax described in section 4081(a), a credit or refund under section 6427(f) is allowed only with respect to 7155 gallons of gasoline.

Example 3. Mixtures containing less than 5.59 percent alcohol. The applicable delivery tickets show that the mixture is made with 7568 metered gallons of gasoline and 436 metered gallons of alcohol. Because the mixture contains only 5.45 percent alcohol (as determined based on the delivery tickets provided to the blender), the mixture does not qualify as gasohol.

(3) *Gasohol blender.*—Gasohol blender means any person that regularly produces gasohol outside of the bulk transfer/terminal system for sale or use in its trade or business.

(4) *Registered gasohol blender.*—Registered gasohol blender means a person that is registered under section 4101 as a gasohol blender.

(c) *Rate of tax on gasoline removed or entered for gasohol production.*—(1) *In general.*—The rate of tax imposed on gasoline under §48.4081-2(b) (relating to tax imposed at the terminal rack), §48.4081-3(b)(1) (relating to tax imposed at the refinery), or §48.4081-3(c)(1) (relating to tax imposed on entries) is the gasohol production tax rate if—

(i) The person liable for tax under §48.4081-2(c)(1) (the position holder), §48.4081-3(b)(3) (the refiner), or §48.4081-3(c)(2) (the enterer) is a taxable fuel registrant and a registered gasohol blender, and such person produces gasohol with the gasoline within 24 hours after removing or entering the gasoline; or

(ii) The gasoline is sold in connection with the removal or entry, the person liable for tax under §48.4081-2(c)(1) (the position holder), §48.4081-3(b)(3) (the refiner), or §48.4081-3(c)(2) (the enterer) is a taxable fuel registrant and the person, at the time of the sale,—

(A) Has an unexpired certificate (as described in paragraph (c)(2) of this section) from the buyer; and

(B) Has no reason to believe that any information in the certificate is false.

Reg. §48.4081-6(c)(1)(ii)(B)

(2) *Certificate.*—(i) *In general.*—The certificate referred to in paragraph (c)(1)(ii)(A) of this section is a statement that is to be provided by a registered gasohol blender that is signed under penalties of perjury by a person with authority to bind the registered gasohol blender, is in substantially the same form as the model certificate provided in paragraph (c)(2)(ii) of this section, and contains all information necessary to complete such model certificate. A new certificate must be given if any information in the current certificate changes. The certificate may be included as part of any business records normally used to document a sale. The certificate expires on the earliest of the following dates:

(A) The date one year after the effective date of the certificate (which may be no earlier than the date it is signed).

(B) The date the registered gasohol blender provides a new certificate to the seller.

(C) The date the seller is notified by the Internal Revenue Service or the gasohol blender that the gasohol blender's registration has been revoked or suspended.

(ii) *Model certificate.*

CERTIFICATE OF REGISTERED GASOHOL BLENDER

(To support sales of gasoline at the gasohol production tax rate under section 4081(c) of the Internal Revenue Code)

Name, address, and employer identification number of seller
_____("Buyer") certifies the following under penalties of perjury:
    Name of buyer
Buyer is registered as a gasohol blender with registration number _____. Buyer's
registration has not been suspended or revoked by the Internal Revenue Service.
The gasoline bought under this certificate will be used by Buyer to produce gasohol (as defined in § 48.4081-6(b) of the Manufacturers and Retailers Excise Tax Regulations) within 24 hours after buying the gasoline.
Type of gasohol Buyer will produce (check one only):
_____10% gasohol
_____7.7% gasohol
_____5.7% gasohol
If the gasohol the Buyer will produce will contain ethanol, check here: _____
This certificate applies to the following (complete as applicable):
If this is a single purchase certificate, check here_____ and enter:
1. Account number _____
2. Number of gallons _____
If this is a certificate covering all purchases under a specified account or order number, check here _____ and enter:
1. Effective date _____
2. Expiration date _____
(period not to exceed 1 year after the effective date)
3. Buyer account or order number _____
Buyer will not claim a credit or refund under section 6427(f) of the Internal Revenue Code for any gasoline covered by this certificate.
Buyer agrees to provide seller with a new certificate if any information on this certificate changes.
Buyer understands that Buyer's registration may be revoked if the gasoline covered by this certificate is resold or is used other than in Buyer's production of the type of gasohol identified above.
Buyer will reduce any alcohol mixture credit under section 40(b) by an amount equal to the benefit of the gasohol production tax rate under section 4081(c) for the gasohol to which this certificate relates.
Buyer understands that the fraudulent use of this certificate may subject Buyer and all parties making any fraudulent use of this certificate to a fine or imprisonment, or both, together with the costs of prosecution.

Printed or typed name of person signing

Title of person signing

Employer identification number

Address of Buyer

Signature and date signed

(iii) *Use of Form 637 or letter of registration as a gasohol blender's certificate prohibited.*—A copy of the certificate of registry (Form 637) or letter of registration issued to a gasohol blender by the Internal Revenue Service is not a gasohol blender's certificate described in paragraph (c)(2)(ii) of this section.

(d) *Rate of tax on gasohol removed or entered.*— The rate of tax imposed on removals or entries of any gasohol under §§ 48.4081-2(b),

48.4081-3(b)(1), and 48.4081-3(c)(1) is the gasohol tax rate. The rate of tax imposed on removals and entries of excess liquid described in paragraph (b)(2) of this section is the rate of tax applicable to gasoline under section 4081(a).

(e) *Tax rates.*—(1) *Gasohol production tax rate.*— The gasohol production tax rate is the applicable rate of tax determined under section 4081(c)(2)(A).

(2) *Gasohol tax rate.*—The gasohol tax rate is the applicable alcohol mixture rate determined under section 4081(c)(4)(A).

(f) *Later separation and failure to blend.*— (1) *Later separation.*—(i) *Imposition of tax.*—A tax is imposed on the removal or sale of gasoline separated from gasohol with respect to which tax was imposed at a rate described in paragraph (e) of this section or with respect to which a credit or payment was allowed or made by reason of section 6427(f)(1).

(ii) *Liability for tax.*—The person that owns the gasohol at the time gasoline is separated from the gasohol is liable for the tax imposed under paragraph (f)(1)(i) of this section.

(iii) *Rate of tax.*—The rate of tax imposed under paragraph (f)(1)(i) of this section is the difference between the rate of tax applicable to gasoline not described in this section and the applicable gasohol production tax rate.

(2) *Failure to blend.*—(i) *Imposition of tax.*— Tax is imposed on the entry, removal, or sale of gasoline (including excess liquid described in paragraph (b)(2) of this section) with respect to which tax was imposed at a gasohol production tax rate if—

(A) The gasoline was not blended into gasohol; or

(B) The gasoline was blended into gasohol but the gasohol production tax rate applicable to the type of gasohol produced is greater than the rate of tax originally imposed on the gasoline.

(ii) *Liability for tax.*—(A) In the case of gasoline with respect to which tax was imposed at the gasohol production tax rate under paragraph (c)(1)(i) of this section, the person liable for the tax imposed by paragraph (f)(2)(i) of this section is the person that was liable for tax on the entry or removal.

(B) In the case of gasoline with respect to which tax was imposed at the gasohol production tax rate under paragraph (c)(1)(ii) of this section, the person that bought the gasoline in connection with the entry or removal is liable for the tax imposed under paragraph (f)(2)(i) of this section.

(iii) *Rate of tax.*—The rate of tax imposed on gasoline described in paragraph (f)(2)(i)(A) of this section is the difference between the rate of tax applicable to gasoline not described in this section and the rate of tax previously imposed on the gasoline. The rate of tax imposed on gasoline described in paragraph (f)(2)(i)(B) of this section is the difference between the gasohol

production tax rate applicable to the type of gasohol produced and the rate of tax previously imposed on the gasoline.

(iv) *Example.*—The following example illustrates this paragraph (f)(2):

Example. (i) A registered gasohol blender bought gasoline in connection with a removal described in paragraph (c)(1)(ii) of this section. Based on the blender's certification (described in paragraph (c)(2) of this section) that the blender would produce 10 percent gasohol with the gasoline, tax at the gasohol production tax rate applicable to 10 percent gasohol was imposed on the removal.

(ii) The blender then produced a mixture by splash blending in a tank holding approximately 8000 gallons of mixture. The applicable delivery tickets show that the mixture was blended by first pumping 7220 metered gallons of gasoline into the empty tank, and then pumping 780 metered gallons of alcohol into the tank. Because the mixture contains 9.75 percent alcohol (as determined based on the delivery tickets provided to the blender) the entire mixture qualifies as 7.7 percent gasohol, rather than 10 percent gasohol.

(iii) Because the 7220 gallons of gasoline were taxed at the gasohol production tax rate applicable to 10 percent gasohol but the gasoline was blended into 7.7 percent gasohol, a failure to blend has occurred with respect to the gasoline. As the person that bought the gasoline in connection with the taxable removal, the blender is liable for the tax imposed under paragraph (f)(2)(i) of this section. The amount of tax imposed is the difference between—

(A) 7220 gallons times the gasohol production tax rate applicable to 7.7 percent gasohol; and

(B) 7220 gallons times the gasohol production tax rate applicable to 10 percent gasohol.

(iv) Because the gasohol does not contain exactly 7.7 percent alcohol, the benefit of the gasohol production tax rate with respect to the alcohol is less than the amount of the alcohol mixture credit under section 40(b) (determined before the application of section 40(c)). Accordingly, the blender may be entitled to claim an alcohol mixture credit for the alcohol used in the gasohol. Under section 40(c), however, the amount of the alcohol mixture credit must be reduced to take into account the benefit provided with respect to the alcohol by the gasohol production tax rate.

(g) *Effective date.*—This section is effective August 7, 1995. [Reg. § 48.4081-6.]

☐ [*T.D.* 8421, 7-21-92. *Amended by T.D.* 8609, 8-4-95; *T.D.* 8659, 3-13-96 *and T.D.* 8879, 3-30-2000.]

[Reg. § 48.4081-7]

§ 48.4081-7. Taxable fuel; conditions for refunds of taxable fuel tax under section 4081(e).—(a) *Overview.*—This section provides reporting requirements and other conditions that a person paying tax to the government under section 4081 must satisfy to receive a refund (but not a credit) under section 4081(e) with respect to taxable fuel on which a prior tax was paid to the government under section 4081. No credit against any tax imposed under the Internal Revenue Code is allowed under this section.

(b) *Conditions to allowance of refund.*—A claim for refund of tax imposed by section 4081 with respect to taxable fuel is allowed under section 4081(e) and this section only if—

(1) A tax imposed by section 4081 with respect to the taxable fuel was paid to the government and not credited or refunded (the "first tax");

(2) After imposition of the first tax, another tax was imposed by section 4081 with respect to the same taxable fuel and was also paid to the government (the "second tax");

(3) The person that paid the second tax to the government has filed a timely claim for re-

fund that contains the information required under paragraph (d) of this section; and

(4) The person that paid the first tax to the government has met the reporting requirements of paragraph (c) of this section.

(c) *Reporting requirements.*—(1) *Reporting by persons paying the first tax.*—Except as provided in paragraph (c)(3) of this section, the person that paid the first tax under § 48.4081-3 (the first taxpayer) must file a report that is in substantially the same form as the model report provided in paragraph (c)(2) of this section (or such other model report as the Commissioner may prescribe) and contains all information necessary to complete such model report (the first taxpayer's report). A first taxpayer's report must be filed with the return to which the report relates (or at such other time, or in such other manner, as prescribed by the Commissioner).

(2) *Model first taxpayer's report.*

FIRST TAXPAYER'S REPORT

1. _____

First Taxpayer's name, address, and employer identification number

2. _____

Name, address, and employer identification number of the buyer of the taxable fuel subject to tax

3. _____

Date and location of removal, entry, or sale

4. _____

Volume and type of taxable fuel removed, entered, or sold

5. Check type of taxable event:

    ____Removal from refinery
    ____Entry into United States
    ____Bulk transfer from terminal by unregistered position holder
    ____Bulk transfer not received at an approved terminal
    ____Sale within the bulk transfer/terminal system
    ____Removal at the terminal rack
    ____Removal or sale by the blender

6. _____

Amount of Federal excise tax paid on account of the removal, entry, or sale

The undersigned taxpayer (the "Taxpayer") has not received, and will not claim, a credit with respect to, or a refund of, the tax on the taxable fuel to which this form relates.

Under penalties of perjury, the Taxpayer declares that Taxpayer has examined this statement, including any accompanying schedules and statements, and, to the best of Taxpayer's knowledge and belief, they are true, correct and complete.

_____

Signature and date signed

_____

Printed or typed name of person signing this report

_____

Title

(3) *Optional reporting for certain taxable events.*—Paragraph (c)(1) of this section does not apply with respect to a tax imposed under § 48.4081-2 (removal at a terminal rack), § 48.4081-3(c)(1)(ii) (nonbulk entries into the United States), or § 48.4081-3(g) (removals or sales by blenders). However, if the person liable for the tax expects that another tax will be imposed under section 4081 with respect to the taxable fuel, that person should (but is not required to) file a first taxpayer's report.

(4) *Information provided to subsequent owners, etc.*—(i) *By person required to file first taxpayer's report.*—A first taxpayer required to file a first taxpayer's report under paragraph (c)(1) of this section must give a copy of the report to—

(A) The person to whom the first taxpayer sells (within the meaning of § 48.4081-1) the taxable fuel within the bulk transfer/terminal system; or

Reg. § 48.4081-7(b)

(B) The owner of the taxable fuel immediately before the imposition of the first tax, if the first taxpayer is not the owner at that time.

(ii) *By person filing optional first taxpayer's report.*—A first taxpayer filing a first taxpayer's report under paragraph (c)(3) of this section should (but is not required to) give a copy of the report to—

(A) The person to whom the first taxpayer sells the taxable fuel; or

(B) The owner of the taxable fuel immediately before the imposition of the first tax, if the first taxpayer is not the owner at that time.

(iii) *By person receiving first taxpayer's report.*—A person that receives a copy of the first taxpayer's report and subsequently sells (within the meaning of § 48.4081-1) the taxable fuel within the bulk transfer/terminal system must give the copy and a statement that satisfies the requirements of paragraph (c)(4)(iv) of this sec-

tion to the buyer. A person that receives a copy of the first taxpayer's report and subsequently sells the taxable fuel outside the bulk transfer/terminal system should (but is not required to) give the copy and a statement that satisfies the requirements of paragraph (c)(4)(iv) of this section to the buyer, if that person expects that another tax will be imposed under section 4081 with respect to the taxable fuel.

(iv) *Form of statement.*—(A) *In general.*—A statement satisfies the requirements of this paragraph (c)(4)(iv) if it is provided at the bottom or on the back of the copy of the first taxpayer's report (or in an attached document). This statement must contain all information necessary to complete the model statement provided in paragraph (c)(4)(iv)(B) of this section (or such other model statement as the Commissioner may prescribe) but need not be in the same format.

(B) *Model statement describing subsequent sale.*

STATEMENT OF SUBSEQUENT SELLER
1.
_____

Name, address, and employer identification number of seller in subsequent sale
2.
_____

Name, address, and employer identification number of buyer in subsequent sale
3.
_____

Date and location of subsequent sale
4.
_____

Volume and type of taxable fuel sold
The undersigned seller (the "Seller") has received the copy of the first taxpayer's report provided with this statement in connection with Seller's purchase of the taxable fuel described in this statement.
Under penalties of perjury, Seller declares that Seller has examined this statement, including any accompanying schedules and statements, and, to the best of Seller's knowledge and belief, they are true, correct and complete.
_____

Signature and date signed
_____

Printed or typed name of person signing this statement
_____

Title

(v) *Sale to multiple buyers.*—If the first taxpayer's report relates to taxable fuel divided among more than one buyer, multiple copies of the first taxpayer's report must be made at the stage that the taxable fuel is divided and each buyer must be given a copy of the report.

(d) *Form and content of claim.*—(1) *In general.*— The following rules apply to claims for refund under section 4081(e):

(i) The claim must be made by the person that paid the second tax to the government and must include all the information described in paragraph (d)(2) of this section.

(ii) The claim must be made on Form 8849 (or such other form as the Commissioner may designate) in accordance with the instructions on the form. The form should be marked *Section 4081(e) Claim* at the top. Section 4081(e) claims must not be included with a claim for a refund under any other provision of the Internal Revenue Code.

(2) *Information to be included in the claim.*— Each claim for a refund under section 4081(e) must contain the following information with respect to the taxable fuel covered by the claim:

(i) Volume and type of taxable fuel.

(ii) Date on which the claimant incurred the tax liability to which this claim relates (the second tax).

(iii) Amount of second tax that claimant paid to the government and a statement that claimant has not included the amount of this tax in the sales price of the taxable fuel to which this claim relates and has not collected that amount from the person that bought the taxable fuel from claimant.

(iv) Name, address, and employer identification number of the person that paid the first tax to the government.

(v) A copy of the first taxpayer's report that relates to the taxable fuel covered by the claim.

(vi) If the taxable fuel covered by the claim was bought other than from the first tax-

Reg. § 48.4081-7(d)(2)(vi)

payer, a copy of the statement of subsequent seller that the claimant received with respect to that taxable fuel.

(e) *Time for filing claim.*—A claim for refund under section 4081(e) may be filed any time after the claimant has filed the return of the second tax and before the end of the period prescribed by section 6511 for the filing of a claim for a refund.

(f) *Examples.*—The following examples illustrate the provisions of this section.

Example 1. (i) A is a taxable fuel registrant that owns 10,000 gallons of gasoline, and on April 5, 1996, is transporting the gasoline by barge on a waterway in the United States. That day, A sells the gasoline to B, a person that is not a taxable fuel registrant. A is liable for tax on the sale under §48.4081-3(f). A pays this tax to the government and attaches to its return of the gasoline tax for the 2nd quarter of 1996 the first taxpayer's report described in paragraph (c) of this section. A also gives a copy of this report to B.

(ii) On April 9, 1996, B sells the gasoline to C, a taxable fuel registrant. B also gives C a copy of the first taxpayer's report and the statement of subsequent seller (required under paragraph (c)(4) of this section). On April 14, 1996, the gasoline is removed from a terminal at the rack. C is the position holder of the gasoline at the time of the removal and thus is liable for tax on the removal under §48.4081-2(c)(1). C pays this tax to the government.

(iii) After C has filed a return of the second tax and before the end of the period prescribed by section 6511 for filing a claim for a refund, C files a claim for a refund of the second tax. The claim is in the form prescribed in paragraph (d)(2) of this section. C includes with its claim a copy of the first taxpayer's report and statement of subsequent seller. Because the conditions to allowance of a refund under paragraph (b) of this section have been met, C is allowed a refund of the second tax.

Example 2. The facts are the same as in *Example 1* except that A does not pay the tax to the government. Because the first tax was not paid to the government as required by paragraph (b)(1) of this section, the conditions to allowance of a refund under paragraph (b) of this section have not been met. Therefore, C is not allowed a refund of the second tax.

(g) *Effective date.*—This section is effective in the case of taxable fuel with respect to which the first tax is imposed after September 30, 1995. [Reg. §48.4081-7.]

☐ [*T.D.* 8421, 7-21-92. *Amended by T.D.* 8609, 8-4-95; *T.D.* 8659, 3-13-96 *and T.D.* 8879, 3-30-2000.]

[Reg. §48.4081-8]

§48.4081-8. Taxable fuel; measurement.—(a) *In general.*—Volumes of taxable fuel may be measured on the basis of actual volumetric gallons or gallons adjusted to 60 degrees Fahrenheit.

(b) *Effective date.*—This section is applicable January 1, 1994. [Reg. §48.4081-8.]

☐ [*T.D.* 8421, 7-21-92. *Amended by T.D.* 8659, 3-13-96; *T.D.* 8879, 3-30-2000 *and T.D.* 8945, 5-17-2001.]

[Reg. §48.4082-1]

§48.4082-1. Diesel fuel and kerosene; exemption for dyed fuel.—(a) *Exemption.*—Tax is not imposed by section 4081 on the removal, entry, or sale of any diesel fuel or kerosene if—

(1) The person otherwise liable for tax is a taxable fuel registrant;

(2) In the case of a removal from a terminal, the terminal is an approved terminal; and

(3) The diesel fuel or kerosene satisfies the dyeing and marking requirements of paragraphs (b), (c), and (d) of this section.

(b) *Dyeing requirements.*—Diesel fuel or kerosene satisfies the dyeing requirement of this paragraph (b) only if the diesel fuel or kerosene contains—

(1) The dye Solvent Red 164 (and no other dye) at a concentration spectrally equivalent to at least 3.9 pounds of the solid dye standard Solvent Red 26 per thousand barrels of diesel fuel or kerosene; or

(2) Any dye of a type and in a concentration that has been approved by the Commissioner.

(c) *Marking requirements.*—[Reserved]

(d) [Reserved]. For further guidance, see §48.4082-1T(d).

(e) *Effective date.*—(1) Except as provided in paragraph (e)(2) of this section, this section is applicable March 14, 1996.

(2) [Reserved]For further guidance, see §48.4082-1T(e)(2). [Reg. §48.4082-1.]

☐ [*T.D.* 8550, 6-28-94. *Amended by T.D.* 8659, 3-13-96; *T.D.* 8879, 3-30-2000 *and T.D.* 9199, 4-25-2005.]

[Reg. §48.4082-1T]

§48.4082-1T. Diesel fuel and kerosene; exemption for dyed fuel (temporary).—(a) through (c) [Reserved]. For further guidance, see §48.4082-1(a) through (c).

(d) *Time and method for adding dye.*—(1) *In general.*—Except as provided by paragraph (d)(6) of this section, diesel fuel or kerosene satisfies the dyeing requirements of this paragraph (d) only if the dye required by §48.4082-1(b) is combined with the diesel fuel or kerosene by means of a mechanical injection system that is approved by the Commissioner for use at the facility where the dyeing occurs. Application for approval must be made in the form and manner required by the Commissioner. Rules similar to the rules of §48.4101-1(g) apply to the Commissioner's action on the applications.

(2) *Mechanical injection system; requirements.*—The Commissioner will approve a mechanical injection system only if—

(i) The system has features that automatically inject an amount of dye that satisfies the concentration requirements of § 48.4082-1(b) into diesel fuel or kerosene as the diesel fuel or kerosene is delivered from the bulk transfer/terminal system into the transport compartment of a truck, trailer, railroad car, or other means of nonbulk transfer;

(ii) The system has calibrated devices that accurately measure and record the amount of dye and the amount of diesel fuel and kerosene that is dispensed for each removal;

(iii) The system has automatic shut-off devices that prevent the removal of more than 100 gallons of undyed diesel fuel or kerosene in the case of a system malfunction;

(iv) The system is secured by either—

(A) Unbroken seals that are issued, installed, and maintained by the terminal operator and secure the measurement devices, shut-off devices, and other access points to the injection system; or

(B) A secured container that controls access to the measurement devices, shut-off devices, and other access points and is secured by an unbroken seal issued, installed, and maintained by the terminal operator;

(v) Each seal securing the system bears a unique identifying number or code and is produced in a manner that provides adequate assurance against duplication; and

(vi) The operator of the facility has written procedures in place for complying with its duty, described in paragraph (d)(4) of this section, to maintain the system's security standards.

(3) *Mechanical injection system; basis for approval.*—In determining whether to approve a mechanical injection system, the Commissioner will take into account the individual circumstances of each facility, including local fire and safety codes, to ensure that the cost of acquiring and maintaining the appropriate levels of security are reasonable for that facility.

(4) *Mechanical injection system; duty of the operator of a mechanical injection system to maintain the system's security standards.*—Each operator of a mechanical injection system must—

(i) Maintain a record for each seal, including its identifying number or code, the location of the seal, the date(s) on which the seal was issued and installed, and the reason for the installation;

(ii) Visually inspect each installed seal not less than once during every 24 hour period to ascertain that each seal and lock mechanism, if applicable, has not been physically altered;

(iii) Check the identifying number or code for each seal against the records maintained by the terminal operator no less frequently than once during each seven day period and record each inspection and verification;

(iv) Promptly notify the Commissioner if inspection of a seal reveals any inconsistency in the records pertaining to that seal, or if the seal has been damaged or removed (other than a

removal authorized by the operator for testing or maintenance);

(v) Maintain a record of each seal that has been replaced to include the seal number or code, the date the seal was issued, the location of the seal, the date the seal was replaced, and the reason the seal was replaced;

(vi) Promptly destroy and replace seals that have been removed from the system;

(vii) Restrict access to unused seal inventory to individuals specifically designated by the operator and maintain a record of such individuals;

(viii) Maintain a record of each installation, inspection, and destruction described in this paragraph (d)(4), including the name of the individual who conducts the installation, inspection, or destruction;

(ix) Make available for the Commissioner's immediate inspection the seals and records described in this paragraph (d)(4); and

(x) Promptly notify the Commissioner if, and when, the dye injection system is placed out of service.

(5) *Mechanical injection system; revocation or suspension of approval.*—The Commissioner may revoke or suspend its approval of a dye injection system if the Commissioner determines that the system does not meet the standards of paragraph (d)(2) of this section or if the operator of the system has not complied with the requirements of paragraph (d)(4) of this section.

(6) *Sales and entries.*—For purposes of determining whether tax is imposed by section 4081 on a sale or entry of diesel fuel or kerosene, such fuel satisfies the dyeing requirements of this paragraph (d) only if the dye required by § 48.4082-1(b) is combined with the fuel before the sale or entry and the seller or enterer has in its records evidence (such as a certificate from the terminal operator providing the fuel) establishing that the dye was combined with the fuel by means of a mechanical injection system. Thus, for example, diesel fuel or kerosene that is entered into the United States by means of nonbulk transfer (such as a railroad car) does not satisfy the requirements of this paragraph (d) if the required dye and marker are combined with diesel fuel or kerosene after the diesel fuel or kerosene has been entered into the United States.

(7) *Cross reference.*—For the penalty relating to mechanical dye injection systems, see section 6715A.

(e) and (e)(1) [Reserved]. For further guidance, see § 48.4082-1(e) and (e)(1).

(2) This section is applicable on October 24, 2005. [Temporary Reg. § 48.4082-1T.]

☐ [*T.D.* 9199, 4-25-2005.]

[Reg. § 48.4082-2]

§ 48.4082-2. Diesel fuel and kerosene; notice required for dyed fuel.—(a) *In general.*—A legible and conspicuous notice stating "*DYED DIESEL FUEL, NONTAXABLE USE ONLY,*

PENALTY FOR TAXABLE USE" must be posted by a seller on any retail pump or other delivery facility where it sells dyed diesel fuel for use by its buyer. A legible and conspicuous notice stating "DYED KEROSENE, NONTAXABLE USE ONLY, PENALTY FOR TAXABLE USE" must be posted by a seller on any retail pump or other delivery facility where it sells dyed kerosene for use by its buyer. Any seller that fails to post the required notice on any retail pump or other delivery facility where it sells dyed fuel is, for purposes of the penalty imposed by section 6715, presumed to know that the fuel will not be used for a nontaxable use.

(b) *Cross reference; terminal operators.*—For the requirement that terminal operators provide a notice with respect to dyed fuel, see § 48.4101-1(h)(3) (relating to terms and conditions of registration for terminal operators).

(c) *Effective date.*—This section is applicable with respect to diesel fuel after December 31, 1993, and with respect to kerosene after June 30, 1998. [Reg. § 48.4082-2.]

☐ [*T.D.* 8659, 3-13-96. *Amended by T.D.* 8685, 11-8-96 *and T.D.* 8879, 3-30-2000.]

[Reg. § 48.4082-3]

§ 48.4082-3. Diesel fuel and kerosene; visual inspection devices.—[Reserved]

☐ [*T.D.* 8659, 3-13-96. *Amended by T.D.* 8879, 3-30-2000.]

[Reg. § 48.4082-4]

§ 48.4082-4. Diesel fuel and kerosene; back-up tax.—(a) *Imposition of tax.*—(1) *In general.*— Tax is imposed by section 4041 on the delivery into the fuel supply tank of the propulsion engine of a diesel-powered highway vehicle (other than a diesel-powered bus) of—

(i) Any diesel fuel or kerosene on which tax has not been imposed by section 4081;

(ii) Any diesel fuel or kerosene for which a credit or payment has been allowed under section 6427; or

(iii) Any liquid (other than taxable fuel) for use as fuel.

(2) *Liability for tax.*—(i) *In general.*—The operator of the highway vehicle into which the fuel is delivered is liable for the tax imposed under paragraph (a)(1) of this section.

(ii) *Joint and several liability of the seller.*— The seller of the fuel is jointly and severally liable for the tax imposed under paragraph (a)(1) of this section if the seller knows or has reason to know that the fuel will not be used in a nontaxable use.

(3) *Rate of tax.*—The rate of tax is the rate imposed on diesel fuel by section 4081(a).

(b) *Tax on diesel fuel and kerosene; buses and trains.*—(1) *In general.*—Tax is imposed by section 4041 on the delivery into the fuel supply tank of the propulsion engine of a diesel-powered bus or a diesel-powered train of—

(i) Any diesel fuel or kerosene on which tax has not been imposed by section 4081;

(ii) Any diesel fuel or kerosene for which a credit or payment has been allowed under section 6427; or

(iii) Any liquid (other than taxable fuel) for use as fuel.

(2) *Liability for tax.*—(i) *In general.*—Except as provided in paragraph (b)(2)(ii) of this section, the operator of the bus or train into which the fuel is delivered is liable for the tax imposed under paragraph (b)(1) of this section.

(ii) *Special rule for certain train operators.*— The person that delivers the fuel into the fuel supply tank of a train, rather than the train operator, is liable for the tax imposed under paragraph (b)(1) of this section if, at the time of the delivery—

(A) The deliverer of the fuel and the operator of the train are both registered as train operators under § 48.4101-1; and

(B) A written agreement between the deliverer of the fuel and the operator requires the deliverer to pay the tax imposed under paragraph (b)(1) of this section.

(3) *Rate of tax.*—(i) *Buses.*—(A) *In general.*— The rate of tax under paragraph (b)(1) of this section is the sum of the rates described in sections 4041(a)(1)(C)(iii)(I) and 4041(d)(1) (the bus rate) if the bus is used to furnish (for compensation) passenger land transportation available to the general public and either such transportation is scheduled and along regular routes or the seating capacity of the bus is at least 20 adults (not including the driver). A bus is available to the general public if the bus is available for hire to more than a limited number of persons, groups, or organizations.

(B) *Other uses.*—The rate of tax under paragraph (b)(1) of this section is the rate of tax imposed on diesel fuel by section 4081(a) if the bus is used for a purpose other than that described in paragraph (b)(3)(i)(A) of this section.

(ii) *Trains.*—The rate of tax under paragraph (b)(1) of this section is the rate prescribed in section 4041 for diesel fuel sold for use in a train (the train rate).

(4) *Cross reference.*—For the registration requirement relating to certain bus and train operators, see § 48.4101-1(c)(2).

(c) *Exemptions.*—The taxes imposed under paragraphs (a) and (b) of this section do not apply to a delivery of any liquid for—

(1) Use on a farm for farming purposes as that term and related terms are defined in § 48.6420-4(a) through (g);

(2) The exclusive use of a State;

(3) Use described in section 4041(h) (relating to use in a vehicle owned by an aircraft museum);

(4) Use in a bus while the bus is engaged in the transportation of students and employees of schools (as defined in the last sentence of section 4221(d)(7)(C));

(5) Use in a qualified local bus (as defined in section 6427(b)(2)(D)) while the bus is engaged in furnishing (for compensation) intracity passenger land transportation that is available to the general public and is scheduled and along regular routes;

(6) Use in a highway vehicle that—

(i) Is not registered (and is not required to be registered) for highway use under the laws of any State or foreign country; and

(ii) Is used in the operator's trade or business or in an activity of the operator described in section 212 (relating to the production of income);

(7) The exclusive use of a nonprofit educational organization, as defined in §48.4221-6(b); or

(8) Use in a highway vehicle that is owned by the United States and is not used on the highway.

(d) *Effective date.*—This section is applicable after December 31, 1993, except that references to kerosene are applicable after June 30, 1998. [Reg. §48.4082-4.]

☐ [*T.D.* 8659, 3-13-96. *Amended by T.D.* 8879, 3-30-2000.]

[Reg. §48.4082-5]

§48.4082-5. Diesel fuel and kerosene; Alaska.—(a) *Application.*—This section applies to diesel fuel or kerosene removed, entered, or sold in Alaska for ultimate sale or use in an exempt area of Alaska.

(b) *Definitions.*

Exempt area of Alaska means the area of Alaska in which the sulfur content requirements for diesel fuel (see section 211(i) of the Clean Air Act (42 U.S.C. 7545(i))) do not apply because the Administrator of the Environmental Protection Agency has granted an exemption under section 211(i)(4) of that Act.

Nontaxable use means a use described in section 4082(b).

Qualified dealer means any person that holds a qualified dealer license from the state of Alaska or has been registered by the district director as a qualified retailer. The district director will register a person as a qualified retailer only if the district director—

(1) Determines that the person, in the course of its trade or business, regularly sells diesel fuel or kerosene for use by its buyer in a nontaxable use; and

(2) Is satisfied with the filing, deposit, payment, and claim history for all federal taxes of the person and any related person.

(c) *Tax-free removals and entries.*—Notwithstanding §48.4082-1, tax is not imposed by section 4081 on the removal or entry of any diesel fuel or kerosene in an exempt area of Alaska if—

(1) The person that would be liable for tax under §48.4081-2 or 48.4081-3 is a taxable fuel registrant and satisfies the requirements of paragraph (e) of this section;

(2) In the case of a removal from a terminal, the terminal is an approved terminal; and

(3) The owner of the diesel fuel or kerosene immediately after the removal or entry holds the fuel for its own use in a nontaxable use or is a qualified dealer.

(d) *Sales after removals and entries.*—(1) *In general.*—Paragraph (c) of this section does not apply with respect to diesel fuel or kerosene that is subsequently sold by a qualified dealer unless—

(i) The fuel is sold in an exempt area of Alaska;

(ii) The buyer purchases the fuel for its own use in a nontaxable use or is a qualified dealer; and

(iii) The seller satisfies the requirements of paragraph (e) of this section.

(2) *Tax imposed at time of sale: liability for tax.*—Notwithstanding §§48.4081-2 and 48.4081-3, in any case in which paragraph (c) of this section does not apply with respect to diesel fuel or kerosene because of a subsequent sale by a qualified dealer, the tax with respect to that fuel is imposed at the time of the subsequent sale and the qualified dealer is liable for the tax.

(3) *Rate of tax.*—For the rate of tax, see section 4081.

(e) *Evidence of tax-free transactions.*—The requirements of section 4082(c)(2) (relating to certification) and this paragraph (e) are satisfied if the person otherwise liable for tax is able to show the district director satisfactory evidence of the exempt nature of the transaction and has no reason to believe that the evidence is false. Satisfactory evidence may include copies of qualified dealer licenses or exemption certificates obtained for state tax purposes.

(f) *Registration.*—With respect to each person that has been registered as a qualified retailer by the district director, the rules of §48.4101-1(g), (h), and (i) apply.

(g) *Cross reference.*—For the tax on previously untaxed diesel fuel or kerosene that is used for a taxable purpose, see §48.4082-4.

(h) *Effective date.*—This section is applicable with respect to diesel fuel removed or entered after December 31, 1996, and with respect to kerosene removed or entered after June 30, 1998. A person registered by the district director as a qualified retailer before April 2, 1998, may be treated, to the extent the district director determines appropriate, as a qualified dealer for the period before that date. [Reg. §48.4082-5.]

☐ [*T.D.* 8693, 12-16-96. *Redesignated and amended by T.D.* 8748, 12-31-97. *Amended by T.D.* 8879, 3-30-2000.]

[Reg. §48.4082-6]

§48.4082-6. Kerosene; exemption for aviation-grade kerosene.—(a) *Overview.*—This section prescribes the conditions under which tax

Reg. §48.4082-6(a)

does not apply to the removal or entry of aviation-grade kerosene that is destined for use as a fuel in an aircraft.

(b) *Definition.*—For purposes of this section, *aviation-grade kerosene* means kerosene-type jet fuel covered by ASTM specification D 1655 or military specification MIL-DTL-5624T (Grade JP-5) or MIL-DTL-83133E (Grade JP-8). For availability of ASTM and military specifications, see § 48.4081-1(d).

(c) *Exemption for certain removals and entries.*— Tax is not imposed under § 48.4081-2(b), 48.4081-3(b)(1)(ii), or 48.4081-3(c)(1)(ii) on the removal or entry of aviation-grade kerosene if—

(1) The person otherwise liable for tax is a taxable fuel registrant;

(2) In the case of a removal from a terminal, the terminal is an approved terminal; and

(3)(i) The person otherwise liable for tax delivers the kerosene into the fuel supply tank of an aircraft and this delivery is not in connection with a sale; or

(ii) The kerosene is sold for use as a fuel in an aircraft and, at the time of the sale, the person otherwise liable for tax has an unexpired certificate (described in paragraph (e) of this section) from the buyer and has no reason to believe any information in the certificate is false.

(d) *Certain later sales.*—(1) *In general.*—Paragraph (c) of this section does not apply with respect to kerosene that is sold as described in paragraph (c)(3)(ii) of this section if there is a later disqualifying sale of the kerosene. A later disqualifying sale is any later sale other than a later sale—

(i) By a person that, at the time of the sale, has an unexpired certificate (described in paragraph (e) of this section) from the buyer and has no reason to believe that any information in the certificate is false; or

(ii) In connection with the delivery of the kerosene into the fuel supply tank of an aircraft.

(2) *Imposition of tax; liability for tax.*—Notwithstanding §§ 48.4081-2 and 48.4081-3, in any case in which paragraph (d)(1) of this section applies, tax is imposed with respect to that kerosene at the time of the first later disqualifying sale and the seller in that sale is liable for the tax.

(3) *Rate of tax.*—For the rate of tax, see section 4081.

(e) *Certificate.*—(1) *In general.*—The certificate described in this paragraph (e) is a statement by a buyer that is signed under penalties of perjury by a person with authority to bind the buyer, is in substantially the same form as the model certificate provided in paragraph (e)(3) of this section, and contains all information necessary to complete the model certificate. A new certificate or notice that the current certificate is invalid must be given if any information in the current certificate changes. The certificate may be included as part of any business records normally used to document a sale. The certificate expires on the earliest of the following dates:

(i) The date one year after the effective date of the certificate (which may be no earlier than the date it is signed).

(ii) The date the buyer provides the seller a new certificate or notice that the current certificate is invalid.

(iii) The date the Internal Revenue Service or the buyer notifies the seller that the buyer's right to provide a certificate has been withdrawn.

(2) *Withdrawal of the right to provide a certificate.*—The Internal Revenue Service may withdraw the right of a buyer of aviation-grade kerosene to provide a certificate under this section if the buyer uses the aviation-grade kerosene to which a certificate relates other than as a fuel in an aircraft or sells the kerosene without first obtaining a certificate from its buyer. The Internal Revenue Service may notify any seller to whom the buyer has provided a certificate that the buyers right to provide a certificate has been withdrawn.

(3) *Model certificate.*

CERTIFICATE OF PERSON BUYING AVIATION-GRADE KEROSENE FOR USE AS A FUEL IN AN AIRCRAFT

(To support tax-free removals and entries of aviation-grade kerosene under section 4082 of the Internal Revenue Code.)

_____ (Buyer) certifies the following under penalties of perjury:
Name of Buyer
The aviation-grade kerosene to which this certificate applies will be used by Buyer as a fuel in an aircraft or resold by Buyer for that use.
This certificate applies to_____ percent of Buyer's purchases from_____ (name, address, and employer identification number of seller) as follows (complete as applicable):
1. A single purchase on invoice or delivery ticket number _____.
2. All purchases between _____ (effective date) and _____ (expiration date) (period not to exceed one year after the effective date) under account or order number(s) _____. If this certificate applies only to Buyer's purchases for certain locations, check here _____ and list the locations.

_____

_____

Buyer is buying the kerosene for (check either or both as applicable):
_____ Buyer's use as a fuel in an aircraft.
_____ Resale for use as a fuel in an aircraft.

Buyer will provide a new certificate to the seller if any information in this certificate changes.

If Buyer sells the aviation-grade kerosene to which this certificate relates and does not deliver it into the fuel supply tank of an aircraft, Buyer will be liable for tax unless Buyer obtains a certificate from its buyer stating that the aviation-grade kerosene will be used as a fuel in an aircraft.

If Buyer violates the terms of this certificate, the Internal Revenue Service may withdraw Buyer's right to provide a certificate.

Buyer has not been notified by the Internal Revenue Service that its right to provide a certificate has been withdrawn.

The fraudulent use of this certificate may subject Buyer and all parties making any fraudulent use of this certificate to a fine or imprisonment, or both, together with the costs of prosecution.

Printed or typed name of person signing
_____

Title of person signing
_____

Employer identification number
_____

Address of Buyer
_____

Signature and date signed

(f) *Effective date.*—This section is applicable after March 30, 2000, except that paragraph (d) of this section is applicable after June 30, 2000. [Reg. § 48.4082-6.]

☐ [T.D. 8879, 3-30-2000.]

[Reg. § 48.4082-7]

§ 48.4082-7. Kerosene; exemption for feedstock purposes.—(a) *Overview.*—This section prescribes the conditions under which tax does not apply to the removal or entry of kerosene for use for a feedstock purpose.

(b) *Definitions.*—The following definitions apply to this section:

Feedstock purpose means the use of kerosene for nonfuel purposes in the manufacture or production of any substance other than gasoline, diesel fuel, or special fuels referred to in section 4041. Thus, for example, kerosene is used for a feedstock purpose when it is used as an ingredient in the production of paint and is not used for a feedstock purpose when it is used to power machinery at a factory where paint is produced.

Feedstock user means a person that uses kerosene for a feedstock purpose.

Registered feedstock user means a feedstock user that is—

(1) Registered under section 4101 as a feedstock user; or

(2) With respect to removals and entries before October 1, 2000, a taxable fuel registrant.

(c) *Exemption for removals and entries.*—Tax is not imposed on the removal or entry of kerosene if—

(1) The person otherwise liable for tax is a taxable fuel registrant;

(2) In the case of a removal from a terminal, the terminal is an approved terminal; and

(3)(i) The person otherwise liable for tax uses the kerosene for a feedstock purpose; or

(ii) The kerosene is sold for use by the buyer for a feedstock purpose and, at the time of the sale, the person otherwise liable for tax has an unexpired certificate (described in paragraph (e) of this section) from the buyer and has no reason to believe any information in the certificate is false.

(d) *Later sale.*—(1) *In general.*—Paragraph (c) of this section does not apply with respect to kerosene that is sold as described in paragraph (c)(3)(ii) of this section if the buyer in that sale (the certifying buyer) sells the kerosene.

(2) *Imposition of tax; liability for tax.*—Notwithstanding §§ 48.4081-2 and 48.4081-3, in any case in which paragraph (d)(1) of this section applies, tax with respect to that kerosene is imposed at the time of the sale by the certifying buyer and the certifying buyer is liable for the tax.

(3) *Rate of tax.*—For the rate of tax, see section 4081.

(e) *Certificate.*—(1) *In general.*—The certificate described in this paragraph (e) is a statement by a buyer that is signed under penalties of perjury by a person with authority to bind the buyer, is in substantially the same form as the model certificate provided in paragraph (e)(2) of this section, and contains all information necessary to complete the model certificate. A new certificate or notice that the current certificate is invalid must be given if any information in the current certificate changes. The certificate may be included as part of any business records normally used to document a sale. The certificate expires on the earliest of the following dates:

(i) The date one year after the effective date of the certificate (which may be no earlier than the date it is signed).

(ii) The date the buyer provides the seller a new certificate or notice that the current certificate is invalid.

(iii) The date the seller is notified by the Internal Revenue Service or the buyer that the buyer's registration has been revoked or suspended.

Reg. § 48.4082-7(e)(1)(iii)

(2) *Model certificate.*

CERTIFICATE OF REGISTERED FEEDSTOCK USER
(To support tax-free removals and entries of kerosene under section 4082 of the Internal Revenue Code.)
_____ (Buyer) certifies the following under penalties of perjury:
Name of Buyer
Buyer is a registered feedstock user with registration number _____. Buyer's registration has not been revoked or suspended.
The kerosene to which this certificate applies will be used by Buyer for a feedstock purpose.
This certificate applies to _____ percent of Buyer's purchases from _____ (name, address, and employer identification number of seller as follows (complete as applicable):
1. A single purchase on invoice or delivery ticket number _____.
2. All purchases between _____ (effective date) and _____ (expiration date) (period not to exceed one year after the effective date) under account or order number(s) _____. If this certificate applies only to Buyer's purchases for certain locations, check here _____ and list the locations.

_____
_____
_____

If Buyer sells the kerosene to which this certificate relates, Buyer will be liable for tax on that sale.
Buyer will provide a new certificate to the seller if any information in this certificate changes.
If Buyer violates the terms of this certificate, the Internal Revenue Service may revoke Buyer's registration.
Buyer understands that the fraudulent use of this certificate may subject Buyer and all parties making any fraudulent use of this certificate to a fine or imprisonment, or both, together with the costs of prosecution.

_____
Printed or typed name of person signing

_____
Title of person signing

_____
Employer identification number

_____
Address of Buyer

_____
Signature and date signed

(f) *Effective date.*—This section is applicable after March 30, 2000, except that paragraph (d) of this section is applicable after June 30, 2000. [Reg. § 48.4082-7.]

☐ [T.D. 8879, 3-30-2000.]

[Reg. § 48.4083-1]

§ 48.4083-1. Taxable fuel; administrative authority.—(a) *In general.*—(1) *Authority to inspect.*—Officers or employees of the IRS designated by the Commissioner, upon presenting appropriate credentials and a written notice to the owner, operator, or agent in charge, are authorized to enter any place and to conduct inspections in accordance with paragraphs (a) through (c) of this section.

(2) *Reasonableness.*—Inspections will be performed in a reasonable manner and at times that are reasonable under the circumstances, taking into consideration the normal business hours of the place to be entered.

(b) *Place of inspection.*—(1) *In general.*—Inspections may be at any place at which taxable fuel is (or may be) produced or stored or at any inspection site where evidence of activities described in section 6715(a) may be discovered. These places may include, but are not limited to—

(i) Any terminal;

(ii) Any fuel storage facility that is not a terminal;

(iii) Any retail fuel facility; or

(iv) Any designated inspection site.

(2) *Designated inspection sites.*—A designated inspection site is any State highway inspection station, weigh station, agricultural inspection station, mobile station, or other location designated by the Commissioner to be used as a fuel inspection site. A designated inspection site will be identified as a fuel inspection site.

(c) *Scope of inspection.*—(1) *Inspection.*—Officers or employees may physically inspect, examine or otherwise search any tank, reservoir, or other container that can or may be used for the production, storage, or transportation of fuel, fuel dyes, or fuel markers. Inspection may also be made of any equipment used for, or in connection with, production, storage, or transportation of fuel, fuel dyes, or fuel markers. This includes any equipment used for the dyeing or marking of fuel. This also includes books and records, if any, that are maintained at the place of inspection and are kept to determine excise tax liability under section 4081.

(2) *Detainment.*—Officers or employees may detain any vehicle or train for the purpose of inspecting its fuel tanks and storage tanks. Detainment will be either on the premises under inspection or at a designated inspection site. Detainment may continue for such reasonable period of time as is necessary to determine the amount and composition of the fuel.

(3) *Removal of samples.*—Officers or employees may take and remove samples of fuel in such quantities as are reasonably necessary to determine the composition of the fuel.

(d) *Refusal to submit to inspection.*—For the penalty for any refusal to permit an entry or inspection authorized by this section, see section 4083(c)(3). This penalty is in addition to any tax that may be imposed by section 4041 or 4081 and any penalty that may be imposed by section 6715.

(e) *Effective date.*—This section is effective January 1, 1994. [Reg. § 48.4083-1.]

☐ [*T.D. 8659, 3-13-96. Amended by T.D. 8685, 11-8-96 and T.D. 8879, 3-30-2000.*]

[Reg. § 48.4091-3]

§ 48.4091-3. Aviation fuel; conditions to allowance of refunds of aviation fuel tax under section 4091(d).—(a) *Overview.*—This section provides the conditions under which a refund of tax imposed by section 4091 is allowable with respect to taxed aviation fuel that is held by a registered aviation fuel producer. No credit against any tax imposed by the Internal Revenue Code is allowed under section 4091(d).

(b) *Conditions to allowance of refund.*—A claim for refund of tax imposed by section 4091 with respect to aviation fuel is allowed under section 4091(d) and this section only if—

(1) A tax imposed by section 4091 with respect to the aviation fuel was paid to the government by an importer or producer (the first producer) and the tax has not been otherwise credited or refunded;

(2) After imposition of the tax, the aviation fuel is acquired by a person that is a registered aviation fuel producer (the second producer);

(3) The second producer has filed a timely claim for refund that contains the information required under paragraph (d) of this section; and

(4) The first producer and any person that owns the fuel after its sale by the first producer and before its purchase by the second producer (a subsequent seller) have met the reporting requirements of paragraph (c) of this section.

(c) *Reporting requirements.*—(1) *In general.*— The reporting requirements of this paragraph (c)(1) are met if the first producer files a report (the first producer's report) that—

(i) Is in substantially the same form as the model report provided in paragraph (c)(2) of this section (or such other model report as the Commissioner may prescribe);

(ii) Contains all information necessary to complete such model report; and

(iii) Is filed at the time and in the manner prescribed by the Commissioner.

(2) *Model first producer's report.*

FIRST PRODUCER'S REPORT

First Producer's name, address, and employer identification number

---

Buyer's name, address, and employer identification number

Date and location of taxable sale

Volume and type of aviation fuel sold

Amount of federal excise tax paid on account of the sale
Under penalties of perjury, First Producer declares that First Producer has examined this statement, including any accompanying schedules and statements, and, to the best of First Producer's knowledge and belief, it is true, correct and complete.

Printed or typed name of the person signing

Title of person signing

Signature and date signed

---

(3) *Information provided to buyers.*—The reporting requirements of this paragraph (c)(3) are met if a first producer that filed a first producer's report under paragraph (c)(1) of this section gives a copy of the report to the person to whom the first producer sells the aviation fuel.

(4) *Statement of subsequent seller.*—(i) *In general.*—The reporting requirements of this paragraph (c)(4) are met if—

(ii)(A) Each subsequent seller gives to its buyer a copy of a statement that provides all information (whether or not in the same format) necessary to complete the model statement prescribed in paragraph (c)(4)(ii) of this section (or such other model statement as the Commissioner may prescribe); and

(B) The statement is provided at the bottom or on the back of the copy of the first producer's report (or in an attached document).

(iii) *Model statement describing subsequent sale.*

Reg. § 48.4091-3(c)(4)(iii)

STATEMENT OF SUBSEQUENT SELLER (AVIATION FUEL)

Name, address, and employer identification number of seller in subsequent sale

Name, address, and employer identification number of buyer in subsequent sale

Date and location of subsequent sale

Volume and type of aviation fuel sold
The undersigned seller (the Seller) has received the copy of the first producer's report provided with this statement in connection with Seller's purchases of the aviation fuel described in this statement.
Under penalties of perjury, Seller declares that Seller has examined this statement, including any accompanying schedules and statements, and, to the best of Seller's knowledge and belief, it is true, correct and complete.

Printed or typed name of person signing

Title of person signing

Signature and date signed

(5) *Sale to multiple buyers.*—If a first producer's report relates to aviation fuel that is divided among more than one buyer, multiple copies of the first producer's report should be made at the stage that the aviation fuel is divided and a copy given to each buyer. The reporting requirements of this paragraph (c) will be met only with respect to the fuel purchased by buyers that are given a copy of the report including any statement required under paragraph (c)(4) of this section.

(d) *Form and content of claim.*—(1) *In general.*—The following rules apply to claims for refund under section 4091(d):

(i) The claim must be made by the second producer and must include all the information described in paragraph (d)(2) of this section.

(ii) The claim must be made on Form 8849 (or such other form as the Commissioner may designate) in accordance with the instructions on the form. The form should be marked *Section 4091(d) Claim* at the top. Section 4091(d) claims must not be included with a claim for a refund under any other provision of the Internal Revenue Code.

(2) *Information to be included in the claim.*—Each claim for a refund under section 4091(d) must contain the following information with respect to the aviation fuel covered by the claim:

(i) Volume and type of aviation fuel.

(ii) Date on which the second producer acquired the aviation fuel to which the claim relates.

(iii) Amount of tax that the first producer paid to the government and a statement that the second producer has not included the amount of that tax in the sales price of the aviation fuel to which the claim relates and has not collected that amount from the person that bought the aviation fuel from the second producer, if any.

(iv) Name, address, and employer identification number of the first producer that paid the tax to the government.

(v) A copy of the first producer's report that relates to the aviation fuel covered by the claim.

(vi) A copy of any statement of a subsequent seller that the second producer received with respect to that aviation fuel.

(e) *Time for filing claim.*—A claim for refund under section 4091(d) may be filed any time after the first producer has filed the return of the tax to which the claim relates and before the end of the period prescribed by section 6511 for the filing of a claim for refund of that tax.

(f) *Effective date.*—This section is applicable with respect to refunds of tax imposed by section 4091 after December 31, 1998. [Reg. § 48.4091-3.]

☐ [*T.D. 8774, 6-26-98. Redesignated by T.D. 8879, 3-30-2000.*]

[Reg. § 48.4101-1]

§ 48.4101-1. Taxable fuel; registration.—(a) *In general.*—(1) This section provides rules relating to registration under section 4101 for purposes of the federal excise tax on taxable fuel imposed by sections 4041(a)(1) and 4081 and the credit or payment allowed to certain ultimate vendors of diesel fuel and kerosene under section 6427.

(2) A person is registered under section 4101 only if the district director has issued a registration letter to the person and the registration has not been revoked or suspended. However, the United States is treated as registered under section 4101.

(3) A refiner that is registered under section 4101 may, with respect to the bulk removal of any batch of gasohol from its refinery, treat itself as a person that is not registered. See § 48.4081-3(b)(1)(iii).

(4) Each business unit that has, or is required to have, a separate employer identification number is treated as a separate person. Thus, two business units (for example, a parent corporation and a subsidiary corporation, or a proprietorship and a related partnership), each of which has a different employer identification number, are two persons.

(5) A registration in effect on December 31, 1993, with respect to the tax on gasoline or diesel fuel is subject to the district director's review, and to revocation or suspension, under the stan-

dards set forth in this section, but remains in effect until the earlier of—

(i) The effective date of a registration issued under paragraph (g)(3) of this section; or

(ii) The effective date of the revocation or suspension of the registration under paragraph (i) of this section.

(6)(i) A person is treated as a taxable fuel registrant if on June 30, 1998, the person—

(A) Is an enterer, refiner, terminal operator, or throughputter with respect to kerosene and is registered under section 4101 as a producer or importer of aviation fuel;

(B) Operates one or more terminals that store kerosene (and no other type of taxable fuel); or

(C) Is a commercial airline, an operator of aircraft in noncommercial aviation, or a fixed base operator and is also a position holder with respect to kerosene.

(ii) A person treated as registered under paragraph (a)(6)(i) of this section is treated as registered from July 1, 1998, until the earlier of—

(A) The date of a subsequent denial of an application for registration under paragraph (g)(2) of this section;

(B) The effective date of a subsequent registration issued under paragraph (g)(3) of this section;

(C) The effective date of a subsequent revocation or suspension of registration under paragraph (i) of this section; or

(D) July 1, 1999.

(b) *Definitions.*—(1) *Applicant.*—An *applicant* is a person that has applied for registration under paragraph (e) of this section.

(2) *Bonded registrant.*—A *bonded registrant* is a person that has given a bond to the district director under paragraph (j) of this section as a condition of registration.

(3) *Gasohol bonding amount.*—The *gasohol bonding amount* is the product of—

(i) The rate of tax applicable to later separation, as described in § 48.4081-6(f)(1)(iii); and

(ii) The total number of gallons of gasoline expected to be bought at the gasohol production tax rate by the gasohol blender during a representative 6-month period (as determined by the district director).

(4) *Penalized for a wrongful act.*—A person has been *penalized for a wrongful act* if the person has—

(i) Been assessed any penalty under chapter 68 of the Internal Revenue Code (or similar provision of the law of any State) for fraudulently failing to file any return or pay any tax, and the penalty has not been wholly abated, refunded, or credited;

(ii) Been assessed any penalty under chapter 68 of the Internal Revenue Code, such penalty has not been wholly abated, refunded, or credited, and the district director determines that the conduct resulting in the penalty is part of a

consistent pattern of failing to deposit, pay, or pay over a substantial amount of tax;

(iii) Been convicted of a crime under chapter 75 of the Internal Revenue Code (or similar provision of the law of any State), or of conspiracy to commit such a crime, and the conviction has not been wholly reversed by a court of competent jurisdiction;

(iv) Been convicted, under the laws of the United States or any State, of a felony for which an element of the offense is theft, fraud, or the making of false statements, and the conviction has not been wholly reversed by a court of competent jurisdiction;

(v) Been assessed any tax under section 4103 and the tax has not been wholly abated, refunded, or credited; or

(vi) Had its registration under section 4101 or 4222 revoked.

(5) *Related person.*—A *related person* is a person that—

(i) Directly or indirectly exercises control over an activity of the applicant if the activity is described in paragraph (c)(1) or (d) of this section;

(ii) Owns, directly or indirectly, five percent or more of the applicant;

(iii) Is under a duty to assure the payment of a tax for which the applicant is responsible;

(iv) Is a member, with the applicant, of a group of organizations (as defined in § 1.52-1(b) of this chapter) that would be treated as a group of trades or businesses under common control for purposes of § 1.52-1 of this chapter; or

(v) Distributed or transferred assets to the applicant in a transaction in which the applicant's basis in the assets is determined by reference to the basis of the assets in the hands of the distributor or transferor.

(6) *Registrant.*—A *registrant* is a person that the district director has, in accordance with paragraph (g)(3) of this section, registered under section 4101 and whose registration has not been revoked or suspended.

(7) *Pipeline operator.*—A *pipeline operator* is any person that operates a pipeline within the bulk transfer/terminal system.

(8) *Vessel operator.*—A *vessel operator* is any person that operates a vessel within the bulk transfer/terminal system. However, for purposes of this definition, *vessel* does not include a deep draft ocean-going vessel (as defined in § 48.4042-3(a)).

(9) *Other definitions.*—For other definitions relating to taxable fuel, see § § 48.4081-1, 48.4081-6(b), 48.4082-5(b), 48.4082-6(b), 48.4082-7(b), 48.6427-9(b), 48.6427-10(b), and 48.6427-11(b).

(c) *Persons required to be registered.*—(1) *In general.*—A person is required to be registered under section 4101 if the person is—

(i) A blender;

(ii) An enterer;

(iii) A pipeline operator;

(iv) A position holder;

(v) A refiner;

(vi) A terminal operator; or

(vii) A vessel operator.

(2) *Bus and train operators.*—Every operator of a bus or train is required to be registered under section 4101 at any time it incurs any liability for tax under section 4041 at the bus rate (as described in § 48.4082-4(b)(3)(i)) or the train rate (as described in § 48.4082-4(b)(3)(ii)).

(3) *Consequences of failing to register.*—For the criminal penalty imposed for failure to register, see section 7232. For the civil penalty imposed for failure to register, see section 7272.

(d) *Persons that may, but are not required to, be registered.*—A person may, but is not required to, be registered under section 4101 if the person is—

(1) A feedstock user;

(2) A gasohol blender;

(3) An industrial user;

(4) A throughputter that is not a position holder;

(5) An ultimate vendor; or

(6) An ultimate vendor (blocked pump).

(e) *Application instructions.*—Application for registration under section 4101 must be made in accordance with the instructions for Form 637 (or such other form as the Commissioner may designate).

(f) *Registration tests.*—(1) *In general.*—(i) *Persons other than ultimate vendors, pipeline operators, and vessel operators.*—Except as provided in paragraph (f)(1)(ii) of this section, the district director will register an applicant only if the district director determines that the applicant meets the following three tests (collectively, the registration tests):

(A) The activity test of paragraph (f)(2) of this section.

(B) The acceptable risk test of paragraph (f)(3) of this section.

(C) The adequate security test of paragraph (f)(4) of this section.

(ii) *Ultimate vendors, pipeline operators, and vessel operators.*—The district director will register an applicant as an ultimate vendor, ultimate vendor (blocked pump), pipeline operator, or vessel operator only if the district director—

(A) Determines that the applicant meets the activity test of paragraph (f)(2) of this section; and

(B) Is satisfied with the filing, deposit, payment, and claim history for all federal taxes of the applicant and any related person.

(2) *The activity test.*—An applicant meets the activity test of this paragraph (f)(2) only if the district director determines that the applicant—

(i) Is, in the course of its trade or business, regularly engaged as an operator of a bus

or train or in the characteristic activity of a person described in paragraph (c)(1) or (d) of this section; or

(ii) Is likely to be (because of such factors as the applicant's business experience, financial standing, or trade connections), in the course of its trade or business, regularly engaged as an operator of a bus or train or in the characteristic activity of a person described in paragraph (c)(1) or (d) of this section within a reasonable time after becoming registered under section 4101.

(3) *Acceptable risk test.*—(i) *In general.*—An applicant meets the acceptable risk test of this paragraph (f)(3) only if—

(A) Neither the applicant nor a related person has been penalized for a wrongful act; or

(B) Even though the applicant or a related person has been penalized for a wrongful act, the district director determines, after review of evidence offered by the applicant, that the registration of the applicant does not create a significant risk of nonpayment or late payment of the tax imposed by sections 4041(a)(1) and 4081.

(ii) *Significant risk of nonpayment or late payment of tax.*—In making the determination described in paragraph (f)(3)(i)(B) of this section, the district director may consider factors such as the following:

(A) The time elapsed since the applicant or related person was penalized for a wrongful act.

(B) The present relationship between the applicant and any related person that was penalized for any wrongful act.

(C) The degree of rehabilitation of the person penalized for any wrongful act.

(D) The amount of bond given by the applicant. In this regard, the district director may accept a bond under paragraph (j) of this section, without regard to the limits on the amount of bond set by paragraph (j)(2) of this section.

(4) *Adequate security test.*—(i) *In general.*—An applicant meets the adequate security test of this paragraph (f)(4) only if the district director determines that the applicant has both adequate financial resources and a satisfactory tax history, or the applicant gives the district director a bond (under the provisions of paragraph (j) of this section).

(ii) *Adequate financial resources.*—(A) *In general.*—An applicant has adequate financial resources only if the district director determines that the applicant is financially capable of paying—

(1) Its expected tax liability under sections 4041(a)(1) and 4081 for a representative 6-month period (as determined by the district director);

(2) In the case of a terminal operator, the expected tax liability under section 4081 of persons other than the terminal operator with respect to taxable fuel removed at the racks of its

terminals during a representative 1-month period (as determined by the district director); and

(3) In the case of a gasohol blender, the gasohol bonding amount.

(B) *Basis for determination.*—The determination under §48.4101-1(f)(4)(ii) must be based on all information relevant to the applicant's financial status.

(iii) *Satisfactory tax history.*—An applicant has a satisfactory tax history only if the district director is satisfied with the filing, deposit, and payment history for all federal taxes of the applicant and any related person.

(g) *Action on the application by the district director.*—(1) *Review of application.*—The district director may investigate the accuracy and completeness of any representations made by an applicant, request any additional relevant information from the applicant, and inspect the applicant's premises during normal business hours without advance notice.

(2) *Denial.*—If the district director determines that an applicant does not meet all of the applicable registration tests described in paragraph (f) of this section, the district director must notify the applicant, in writing, that its application for registration is denied and state the basis for the denial.

(3) *Approval.*—If the district director determines that an applicant meets all of the applicable registration tests described in paragraph (f) of this section, the district director must register the applicant under section 4101 and issue the applicant a letter of registration containing the effective date of the registration. The effective date of the registration must be no earlier than the date on which the district director signs the letter of registration. A copy of an application for registration (Form 637) is not a letter of registration.

(h) *Terms and conditions of registration.*—(1) *Affirmative duties.*—Each registrant must—

(i) Make deposits, file returns, and pay taxes required by the Internal Revenue Code and the regulations;

(ii) Keep records sufficient to show the registrant's tax liability under sections 4041(a)(1) and 4081 and payments or deposits of such liability;

(iii) Make all information reports required under section 4101(d);

(iv) Make available for inspection on demand by the Internal Revenue Service during normal business hours records relevant to a determination of tax liability under sections 4041(a)(1) and 4081; and

(v) Notify the district director of any change (such as a change in ownership) in the information the registrant submitted in connection with its application for registration, or previously submitted under this paragraph (h)(1)(v), within 10 days after the change occurs.

(2) *Prohibited actions.*—A registrant may not—

(i) Sell, lease or otherwise allow another person to use its registration;

(ii) Make any false statement to the district director in connection with a submission under paragraph (h)(1) or (h)(3) of this section;

(iii) Make any false statement on, or violate the terms of, any certificate given to another person to support an exemption from, or a reduced rate of, the tax imposed by section 4081; or

(iv) In the case of an ultimate vendor (blocked pump), deliver kerosene (or allow kerosene to be delivered) into the fuel supply tank of a diesel-powered highway vehicle or diesel-powered train from a blocked pump.

(3) *Additional terms and conditions for terminal operators.*—(i) *Notice required with respect to dyed diesel fuel and dyed kerosene.*—A legible and conspicuous notice stating "DYED DIESEL FUEL, NONTAXABLE USE ONLY, PENALTY FOR TAXABLE USE" must be provided by each terminal operator to any person that receives dyed diesel fuel at a terminal rack of that operator. A legible and conspicuous notice stating "DYED KEROSENE, NONTAXABLE USE ONLY, PENALTY FOR TAXABLE USE" must be provided by each terminal operator to any person that receives dyed kerosene at a terminal rack of that operator. These notices must be provided by the time of the removal and must appear on all shipping papers, bills of lading, and similar documents that are provided by the terminal operator to accompany the removal of the fuel.

(ii) *Records to be maintained relating to removals of diesel fuel or kerosene.*—Each terminal operator must keep the following information with respect to each rack removal of diesel fuel or kerosene at each terminal it operates:

(A) The bill of lading or other shipping document.

(B) The record of whether the fuel was dyed and marked in accordance with §48.4082-1.

(C) The volume and date of the removal.

(D) The identity of the person, such as a common carrier, that physically received the fuel.

(E) Any other information required by the Commissioner.

(iii) *Records to be maintained relating to dye.*—With respect to each of its terminals, a terminal operator must keep records relating to dye inventories and usage.

(iv) [Reserved]. For further guidance, see §48.4101-1T(h)(3)(iv).

(v) *Prohibition on providing incorrect information.*—In connection with the removal of diesel fuel or kerosene that is not dyed and marked in accordance with §48.4082-1, a terminal operator may not provide any person (including the position holder with respect to the fuel) with any bill of lading, shipping paper, or similar docu-

Reg. §48.4101-1(h)(3)(v)

ment indicating that the diesel fuel or kerosene is dyed and marked in accordance with § 48.4082-1.

(i) *Adverse actions by the district director against a registrant.*—(1) *Mandatory revocation or suspension.*—The district director must revoke or suspend the registration of any registrant if the district director determines that the registrant, at any time—

(i) Does not meet one or more of the applicable registration tests under paragraph (f) of this section and has not corrected the deficiency within a reasonable period of time after notification by the district director;

(ii) Has used its registration to evade, or attempt to evade, the payment of any tax imposed by section 4041(a)(1) or 4081, or to postpone or in any manner to interfere with the collection of any such tax, or to make a fraudulent claim for a credit or payment;

(iii) Has aided or abetted another person in evading, or attempting to evade, payment of any tax imposed by section 4041(a)(1) or 4081, or in making a fraudulent claim for a credit or payment; or

(iv) Has sold, leased, or otherwise allowed another person to use its registration.

(2) *Remedial action permitted in other cases.*—If the district director determines that a registrant has, at any time, failed to comply with the terms and conditions of registration under paragraph (h) of this section, made a false statement to the district director in connection with its application for registration or retention of registration, or otherwise used its registration in a manner that creates a significant risk of nonpayment or late payment of tax, then the district director may—

(i) Revoke or suspend the registrant's registration;

(ii) In the case of a registrant other than an ultimate vendor or an ultimate vendor (blocked pump), require the registrant to give a bond under the provisions of paragraph (j) of this section as a condition of retaining its registration; and

(iii) In the case of a registrant other than an ultimate vendor or an ultimate vendor (blocked pump), require the registrant to file monthly or semimonthly returns under § 40.6011(a)-1(b) of this chapter as a condition of retaining its registration.

(3) *Action by the district director to revoke or suspend a registration.*—If the district director revokes or suspends a registration, the district director must so notify the registrant in writing and state the basis for the revocation or suspension. The effective date of the revocation or suspension may not be earlier than the date on which the district director notifies the registrant.

(j) *Bonds.*—(1) *Form.*—Each bond given to the district director as a condition of registration under paragraph (f)(4)(i) or (i)(2)(ii) of this section must be executed in the form prescribed by the district director. Each bond must be—

(i) A public debt obligation of the United States Government;

(ii) An obligation the principal and interest of which are unconditionally guaranteed by the United States Government;

(iii) A bond executed by a surety company listed in Department of the Treasury Circular 570 as an acceptable surety or reinsurer of federal bonds (a surety bond); or

(iv) Any other bond with security (including liens under section 4101(b)(1)(B)) considered acceptable by the district director.

(2) *Amount of bond.*—A bond given under this paragraph (j) must be in an amount that the district director determines will ensure timely collection of the taxes imposed by sections 4041(a)(1) and 4081, taking into account the applicant's financial capabilities, tax history, and expected liability under sections 4041(a)(1) and 4081. The district director may increase or decrease the amount of the required bond to take into account changes in the applicant's financial capabilities, tax history, and expected liability under sections 4041(a)(1) and 4081. However, in no case may the amount of the bond be greater than the amount that the district director determines is equal to—

(i) The applicant's expected tax liability under sections 4041(a)(1) and 4081 for a representative 6-month period (as determined by the district director);

(ii) In the case of a terminal operator, the expected tax liability of persons other than the terminal operator under section 4081 with respect to taxable fuel removed at the racks of its terminals (determined as if all removals of taxable fuel were taxable) during a representative 1-month period (as determined by the district director); and

(iii) In the case of a gasohol blender, the gasohol bonding amount.

(3) *Collection of taxes from a bond.*—If a bonded registrant does not pay the amount of tax it incurs under section 4041(a)(1) or 4081 by the time prescribed in section 6151 for paying that tax, the district director may collect the amount of the unpaid tax (including penalties and interest with respect to that tax) from the bonded registrant's bond.

(4) *Termination of bonds.*—(i) *Surety bonds.*—A surety on a bond may give written notice to the district director and the bonded registrant that the surety desires to be relieved of liability under the bond after a certain date, which date must be at least 60 days after the receipt of the notice by the district director. The surety will be relieved of any liability that the bonded registrant incurs after the date named in the notice. However, the surety remains liable for the amount of tax that the bonded registrant incurred under sections 4041(a)(1) and 4081 during the term of the bond and for penalties and interest with respect to that tax.

(ii) *Other bonds.*—A bond (other than a surety bond) given to the district director may be returned to the bonded registrant only after the earlier of—

(A) The district director's determination that the bonded registrant has paid all taxes that the bonded registrant incurred under sections 4041(a)(1) and 4081 during the period covered by the bond and any penalties and interest with respect to the taxes;

(B) The expiration of the period for assessment of the taxes that the bonded registrant incurred under sections 4041(a)(1) and 4081 taxes during the period covered by the bond, as determined under the provisions of subchapter A of chapter 66 of the Internal Revenue Code; or

(C) The date that the district director receives from the registrant a substitute bond given under this paragraph (j).

(5) *Determination that bond is no longer required.*—If the district director determines that the bonded registrant meets the adequate security test of paragraph (f)(4) of this section without a bond, the registrant is to be released from the obligation to give a bond as a condition of registration under section 4101.

(k) *Cross references.*—For a rule relating to the filing of monthly and semimonthly returns by certain persons that are registered under section 4101, see § 40.6011(a)-1(b)(2) of this chapter. For rules relating to the tax on taxable fuel, see §§ 48.4081-1 through 48.4083-1. For rules relating to claims by registered ultimate vendors, see § 48.6427-9. For rules relating to claims by registered ultimate vendors (blocked pump), see § 48.6427-10.

(l) *Effective dates.*—(1) Except as otherwise provided in this paragraph (l), this section is applicable as of January 1, 1994.

(2) Paragraph (c)(1) of this section (relating to persons required to be registered) is applicable as of January 1, 1995, except that paragraphs (c)(1)(iii) and (c)(1)(vii) of this section are applicable after March 31, 2001.

(3) Paragraph (h)(3)(iii) of this section (relating to certain recordkeeping requirements) is applicable as of July 1, 1996.

(4) References in this section to kerosene are applicable after June 30, 1998.

(5) *Applicability date.*—Paragraph (f)(4)(ii)(B) of this section applies on and after July 6, 2011. [Reg. § 48.4101-1.]

☐ [*T.D. 6434*, 12-21-59. *Amended by T.D. 7908*, 9-2-83; *T.D. 8659*, 3-13-96; *T.D. 8879*, 3-30-2000 (*corrected* 5-5-2000); *9199*, 4-25-2005; *T.D. 9533*, 7-1-2011 *and T.D. 9637*, 9-5-2013.]

[Reg. § 48.4101-2]

§ 48.4101-2. Information reporting.—(a) *In general.*—Each information report under section 4101(d) must be—

(1) Made in the form required by the Commissioner;

(2) Made for a period of one calendar month; and

(3) Filed by the last day of the first month following the month for which the report is made, except that a report relating to any month during 2000 must be filed by February 28, 2001.

(b) *Effective date.*—This section is applicable after March 30, 2000. [Reg. § 48.4101-2.]

☐ [T.D. 8659, 3-13-96. *Amended by T.D. 8879*, 3-30-2000.]

[Reg. § 48.4102-1]

§ 48.4102-1. Inspection of records by State or local tax officers.—(a) *Inspection of records maintained by taxpayer.*—The records that a taxpayer is required to keep with respect to the taxes imposed by section 4081 or 4091 must be open to inspection by any officer of any State or political subdivision thereof, or of the District of Columbia, who is charged with the enforcement or collection of any tax on taxable fuel or aviation fuel.

(b) *Inspection of records maintained by Internal Revenue Service.*—(1) *In general.*—The records maintained by the Internal Revenue Service with respect to the taxes imposed by sections 4081 and 4091 shall, upon the request of an officer (described in paragraph (b)(2) of this section) of a State or political subdivision thereof, or of the District of Columbia, be open to inspection by the officer for purposes of collection or enforcement.

(2) *Requests for inspection.*—Requests for inspection under this paragraph shall be made in writing, signed by any officer of a State, political subdivision, or the District of Columbia, who is charged with the enforcement or collection of any tax on taxable fuel or aviation fuel imposed by the State, political subdivision, or the District of Columbia, and shall be addressed to the director of the Internal Revenue Service Center having custody of the records which it is desired to inspect. Each such request shall state (i) the kind of records (whether pertaining to taxable fuel or aviation fuel) it is desired to inspect, (ii) the period or periods covered by the records involved, (iii) the name of the officer by whom the inspection is to be made, (iv) the name of the representative of the officer who has been designated to make the inspection, (v) by specific reference, the law of the State, political subdivision, or the District of Columbia imposing the tax which the officer is charged with collecting or enforcing, and the law under which the officer is so charged, and (vi) the purpose for which the inspection is to be made. The service center director will notify the person making the request upon approval or disapproval of the request.

(3) *Time and place for inspection.*—In any case where a request for inspection under this paragraph (b) is approved, the inspection shall be made in the office of the service center director having custody of the records which it is desired to inspect, but only in the presence of an internal

revenue officer or employee and during the regular hours of business of the office. [Reg. §48.4102-1.]

☐ [T.D. 6434, 12-21-59. Amended by T.D. 7908, 9-2-83 and T.D. 8659, 3-13-96.]

[Reg. §48.4121-1]

§48.4121-1. **Imposition and rate of tax on coal.**—(a) *Imposition of tax.*—(1) *In general.*—Section 4121(a) imposes a tax on coal mined at any time in this country if the coal is sold or used by the producer after March 31, 1978 (see section 4218 and the regulations under that section for rules relating to the use of coal being treated as a sale of coal). For purposes of this section, the term "producer" means the person in whom is vested ownership of the coal under state law immediately after the coal is severed from the ground, without regard to the existence of any contractual arrangement for the sale or other disposition of the coal or the payment of any royalties between the producer and third parties. The term includes any person who extracts coal from coal waste refuse piles or from the silt waste product which results from the wet washing (or similarly processing) of coal. However, the excise tax does not apply to a producer who sells the silt waste product without extracting the coal from it, or to the producer who uses the silt waste product without extracting the coal from it. Furthermore, the excise tax does not apply to the sale or use of the silt waste product after any coal has been extracted from it.

(2) *Examples.*—Paragraph (a)(1) of this section may be illustrated by the following examples:

Example (1). A, a limited partnership, is the owner of land on which a coal mine is located. A contracts with XYZ Company to extract the coal for a set price per ton. XYZ Company is an independent contractor and has no ownership interest in the coal mined. Under state law, A is the owner of the coal immediately after severance. After XYZ extracts the coal from the mine, A sells the coal. A is the producer of the coal and is responsible for the payment of the excise tax.

Example (2). A, a limited partnership, is the owner of land on which a coal mine is located. A leases the land to XYZ Company, and XYZ Company extracts coal from the mine and sells it. Under state law, XYZ is the owner of the coal immediately after the coal is severed from the ground. XYZ Company is the producer and must pay the excise tax. This is true even though the lease agreement requires XYZ to pay a royalty to A.

Example (3). XYZ Company purchases a coal waste refuse pile from B and extracts the coal from the waste refuse pile and sells the coal. XYZ is the producer and must pay the excise tax.

Example (4). XYZ Company is a producer of coal and operates its own cleaning plant. After wet washing the coal, it sells the coal and the silt waste product. The sale of the coal is subject to the excise tax whereas the sale of the silt is not.

Example (5). Assume the same facts as in example (4) except that before selling the silt waste product XYZ Company extracts a small quantity of finely sized coal from the silt waste product and then sells both the finely sized coal and the silt waste product. The sale of the finely sized coal is subject to the excise tax whereas the sale of the silt is not.

(b) *Rate of tax.*—(1) *Underground mines: surface mines.*—The rate of tax imposed on coal from underground mines located in the United States is the lower of 50 cents per ton (2,000 pounds), or 2 percent of the sale price. The rate of tax imposed on coal from surface mines located in the United States is the lower of 25 cents per ton (2,000 pounds) or 2 percent of the sale price. If a sale or use includes a portion of a ton, the tax is applied proportionally. Thus, if 1200 pounds of coal from an underground mine are sold for $35.00, the tax is 30 cents.

(2) *Combination.*—If a single mine yields coal from both surface and underground mining, the producer must determine the rate (50 cents or 25 cents per ton) for each ton of coal mined: It is presumed that coal is mined from underground mines (50 cents per ton) unless the producer keeps sufficient records to establish to the satisfaction of the Secretary that the coal was mined from a surface mine.

(c) *Exemptions.*—(1) *Lignite or imported coal.*—The excise tax on coal does not apply to lignite or imported coal. Lignite is defined in accordance with the standard specification for classification of coals by rank of the American Society for Testing and Materials (Annual Book of ASTM Standards Part 26, D 388). The procedures specified in D 388 must be followed. If a producer extracts both taxable coal and lignite, then the producer must maintain adequate records to establish the portion of the mineral mined that is exempt from the tax. In determining whether all or a portion of the mineral extracted is lignite, the Service will consider all the facts and circumstances. For example, if a producer sells lignite and coal, the Service will examine all the facts and circumstances, including the contract price, contract specifications, and the amount of lignite extracted as it compares to the amount of lignite sold.

(2) *Other exemptions not applicable.*—There are not exemptions for sales for further manufacture, for export, for use as supplies for vessels or aircraft, for the use of a State or local government, or for the use of a nonprofit educational organization. Furthermore, the Secretary does not have discretion to exempt sales of coal for use of the United States from the tax. There is also no exemption from the coal excise tax when the coal is used in further manufacture of another article that is subject to manufacturers excise tax. For example, if a producer of coal converts coal into gasoline which the producer then sells, the producer is liable for the coal excise tax when the coal is converted into gaso-

line and also liable for the manufacturers excise tax on gasoline when the gasoline is sold.

(d) *Definitions and special rules.*—(1) *Coal produced from surface mine.*—Coal is treated as produced from a surface mine if all of the geological matter (e.g., trees, earth, rock) above the coal is removed before the coal is mined. In addition, both coal mined by auger and coal that is reclaimed from coal waste refuse piles are treated as produced from a surface mine.

(2) *Coal produced from underground mine.*—Coal is treated as produced from an underground mine if it is not produced from a surface mine.

(3) *Coal used by the producer.*—For purposes of this section, the term "coal used by the producer" means use by the producer in other than a mining process. A mining process is determined the same way it is determined for percentage depletion purposes. For example, a producer who mines coal does not "use" the coal and thereby becomes liable for the tax merely because, before selling the coal, the producer breaks it, cleans it, sizes it, or applies one of the other processes listed in section 613(c)(4)(A) of the Code. In such a case, the producer will be liable for the tax only when he sells the coal. On the other hand, a producer who mines coal does become liable for the tax when he uses the coal as fuel, as an ingredient in making coke, or in another process not treated as "mining" under section 613(c).

(4) *Tonnage sold and sales price.*—For purposes of determining both the amount of coal sold by a producer and the sales price of the coal, the point of sale is f.o.b. mine, or f.o.b. cleaning point if the producer cleans the coal before selling it. This is true even if the producer sells the coal on the basis of a delivered price. Accordingly, f.o.b. mine or cleaning point is the point at which the number of tops sold is to be determined for purposes of applying the applicable tonnage rate, and the point at which the sales price is to be determined for purposes of the tax under the 2 percent rate.

(5) *Constructive sale price.*—If a producer uses coal mined by the producer in other than a mining process, a constructive sale price must be used in determining the tax under the 2 percent rate. This constructive price is determined under section 613(c) and 4218(e) of the Code, and is based on sales of like kind and grade of coal by the producer or other producers made f.o.b. mine (if the coal is used without first being cleaned) or f.o.b. cleaning plant (if the coal is cleaned before it is used). Normally, this constructive price will be the same as the constructive price used in determining the producer's percentage depletion deduction. [Reg. §48.4121-1.]

☐ [*T.D.* 7726, 10-6-80, *as amended on* 10-20-80. *Amended by T.D.* 8442, 10-21-92.]

[Reg. §48.4161(a)-1]

§48.4161(a)-1. Imposition and rate of tax; fishing equipment.—(a) *Imposition of tax.*—Section 4161(a) imposes a tax on the sale of the following articles of fishing equipment (including in each case parts or accessories of such articles sold on or in connection therewith or with the sale thereof) by the manufacturer, producer, or importer thereof:

(1) Fishing rods;

(2) Fishing creels;

(3) Fishing reels; and

(4) Artificial lures, baits, and flies.

The tax applies only to those items of fishing equipment specified in section 4161(a) and this paragraph. Therefore, other items of fishing equipment, such as fishing nets, lines, hooks, sinkers, gaffs, etc., are not subject to the tax. Furthermore, the tax applies only to those specified articles of fishing equipment that are designed or constructed for use in the sport of fishing. Accordingly, the tax does not apply to those articles which, although nominally articles that are specified in section 4161(a), are in the nature of toys or novelties that merely simulate articles of a type referred to in section 4161(a), and are not designed or constructed for practical use in the sport of fishing.

(b) *Rate of tax.*—Tax is imposed on the sale of the articles enumerated in section 4161(a) and paragraph (a) of this section at the rate of 10 percent of the price for which such articles are sold. For the definition of the term "price" see section 4216 and the regulations thereunder.

(c) *Liability for tax.*—The tax imposed by section 4161(a) is payable by the manufacturer, producer, or importer making the sale. For determining who is the manufacturer, producer, or importer, see §48.0-2(a)(4). [Reg. §48.4161(a)-1.]

☐ [*T.D.* 7328, 10-10-74. *Amended by T.D.* 8043, 8-8-85.]

[Reg. §48.4161(a)-2]

§48.4161(a)-2. Meaning of terms.—(a) *Fishing rods.*—The term "fishing rods" includes all articles, however designated, that are designed or constructed for use in conjunction with a fishing reel for casting a line and hook in the sport of fishing. The term does not include any article that is neither designed for use in casting, nor suitable for such use. A so-called fishing rod "blank" is not considered to be a "fishing rod" unless the blank contains an affixed handle and reel seat, or is sold in the form of a kit that contains a rod blank, a handle, and a reel seat.

(b) *Fishing creels.*—The term "fishing creels" includes all portable containers, of whatever material made, that are designed for storing and carrying fish from the time they are caught until such time as they are removed form the container for consumption or preservation. The terms does not include any article primarily designed for use in the commercial fishing industry, or an article such as a collapsible wire basket designed to be hung over the side of a boat to keep fish captive and alive in the water.

(c) *Fishing reels.*—The term "fishing reels" includes all mechanical and electrical devices that contain a spool for dispensing and recovering fishing line, and are designed to use with fishing rods in casting and in reeling in hooked fish in the sport of fishing. The term also includes reels designed for use with bows, in the sport of bow-fishing.

(d) *Artificial lures, baits, and flies.*—The term "artificial lures, baits, and flies" includes all artifacts, of whatever materials made, that simulate an article considered edible by fish and are designed to be attached to a line or hook to attract fish so that they may be captured. Thus, the term includes such artifacts as imitation flies, blades, spoons, and spinners, and edible materials that have been processed so as to resemble a different edible article considered more attractive to fish, such as bread crumbs treated so as to simulate salmon eggs, and pork rind cut and dyed to resemble frogs, eels, or tadpoles. [Reg. §48.4161(a)-2.]

☐ [*T.D.* 7328, 10-10-74. *Amended by T.D.* 8043, 8-8-85.]

[Reg. §48.4161(a)-3]

§48.4161(a)-3. Parts and accessories.—(a) *In general.*—The tax attaches with respect to parts and accessories for articles specified in section 4161(a) and §48.4161(a)-1 that are sold on or in connection with such articles, or with the sale thereof, at the same rate applicable to the sale of the basic articles. The tax attaches in such cases whether or not charges for the parts or accessories are billed separately. To be considered a part or accessory for an article specified in section 4161(a), an item must be either essential to the operation of the specified article, or be designed to directly improve the performance of the specified article, or to improve its appearance. For example, a carrying case for a fishing rod is not considered to be a part or accessory for a fishing rod, despite the fact that it is designed for use with the rod, because it is neither essential to the use of the rod, nor does it in any way improve its performance or appearance. A sale of a part or accessory, which would otherwise be considered a sale "on or in connection with" the sale of an article taxable under section 4161(a), is not subject to tax if the part or accessory is sold as a replacement for an identical part or accessory being sold with the taxable article.

(b) *Essential equipment.*—If taxable articles are sold by the manufacturer, producer, or importer thereof, without parts or accessories that are essential for their operation, or are designed directly to improve the performance or appearance of the articles, the separate sale of the parts or accessories to the same vendee will be considered, in the absence of evidence to the contrary, to have been made in connection with the sale of

the basic article, even though the parts or accessories are shipped separately at the same time or on a different date. [Reg. §48.4161(a)-3.]

☐ [*T.D.* 7328, 10-10-74. *Amended by T.D.* 8043, 8-8-85.]

[Reg. §48.4161(a)-4]

§48.4161(a)-4. Use considered sale.—For provisions relating to the tax on use of taxable articles by the manufacturer, producer, or importer thereof, see section 4218 relating to use by a manufacturer being considered a sale, and the regulations thereunder. [Reg. §48.4161(a)-4.]

☐ [*T.D.* 7328, 10-10-74.]

[Reg. §48.4161(a)-5]

§48.4161(a)-5. Tax-free sales.—For provisions relating to the tax-free sales of articles referred to in section 4161(a) see—

(a) Section 4221, relating to certain tax-free sales;

(b) Section 4222, relating to registration;

(c) Section 4223, pertaining to special rules relating to further manufacture; and

(d) Section 4225, relating to exemption of articles manufactured or produced by Indians; and the regulations thereunder. [Reg. §48.4161(a)-5.]

☐ [*T.D.* 7328, 10-10-74.]

[Reg. §48.4161(b)-1]

§48.4161(b)-1. Imposition and rates of tax; bows and arrows.—(a) *Imposition of tax.*—Section 4161(b) imposes a tax on the sale of the following articles by the manufacturer, producer, or importer thereof:

(1) Any bow that has a draw weight of 10 pounds or more;

(2) Any arrow that measures 18 inches overall or more in length;

(3) Any part or accessory (other than a fishing reel) suitable for inclusion in or attachment to a bow or arrow described in subparagraph (1) or (2) of this paragraph; and

(4) Any quiver suitable for use with arrows described in subparagraph (2) of this paragraph.

(b) *Rate of tax.*—The tax is imposed on the sale of articles enumerated in section 4161(b) and paragraph (a) of this section at the rate of 11 percent of the price for which such articles are sold. For definition of the term "price", see section 4216 and the regulations thereunder.

(c) *Liability for tax.*—The tax imposed by section 4161(b) is payable by the manufacturer, producer, or importer making the sale. For determining who is the manufacturer, producer, or importer, see §48.0-2(a)(4). [Reg. §48.4161(b)-1.]

☐ [*T.D.* 7328, 10-10-74. *Amended by T.D.* 8043, 8-8-85.]

[Reg. §48.4161(b)-2]

§48.4161(b)-2. Meaning of terms.—(a) For purposes of the tax imposed by section 4161(b), and unless otherwise expressly indicated:

(1) *Bows.*—The term "bows" includes all articles made of flexible materials, that are designed to be equipped with a string and used for the propelling of arrows in the sport of archery (target shooting), or in hunting or fishing.

(2) *Arrows.*—The term "arrows" includes all articles designed or constructed to be propelled by a bow in the sport of archery (target shooting), or in hunting or fishing. The overall length of an arrow is to be measured from the point of the tip or arrowhead to the end of the arrow nock. In the case of arrows sold by the manufacturer without heads, tips, or nocks, the overall length is to include the length of the shaft plus the length of the nock and head or tip that is normally used with the particular type of arrow shaft.

(b) *Parts and accessories.*—(1) *In general.*— "Parts and accessories" for bows and arrows include all articles (other than fishing reels) suitable for inclusion in, or attachment to, a bow or arrow of the type described in section 4161(b)(1) and paragraph (a) of this section. Examples of parts and accessories for bows are bow handles, bow limbs, bow strings, bow-string silencers, bow stabilizers, arrow rests, bow slings, bow sights, bow levels, bow tip protectors, brush buttons, camouflaged bow covers, and all articles designed to be attached to or included in a bow to assist in aiming or propelling an arrow, or to protect the bow while in use. Examples of parts and accessories for arrows are arrow shafts, nocks, tips, heads, head adapters, and feathers.

(2) *General purpose materials and articles.*— General purpose materials, and articles that are not specifically designed to directly improve the performance or appearance of bows or arrows, or to protect them while in use, are not considered to be "parts and accessories" for bows or arrows, even though such materials may be intended, after further processing, to be included in or attached to bows or arrows. An example of a nontaxable article that is designed for use with a bow, but is neither attached to a bow, nor serves a purpose directly related to the efficient use of a bow, is a carrying case for a bow. Examples of nontaxable general purpose materials or articles are glues and cements, feathers before they are prepared for use with arrows, and bowstring thread before it is processed into bowstrings. Arrow-shaft material is considered to be taxable part for an arrow, unless the manufacturer, producer, or importer can establish that the particular material is unsuitable for use in the manufacture of arrows that are subject to the tax imposed by section 4161(b)(1)(B). In addition, the term "parts and accessories" does not include articles in the nature of expendable supplies, even though such articles are designed to be applied to, or used with, bows or arrows. Examples of such supply materials are bowstring wax, and archery powder.

(c) *Quivers.*—The term "quivers" includes all articles, of whatever material made, that are designed to contain, and to provide ready access to, taxable arrows during the time an archer is engaged in target shooting, hunting, or fishing. The term does not include any article designed solely for storing or transporting arrows during times when the arrows are not in use. [Reg. §48.4161(b)-2.]

☐ [*T.D.* 7328, 10-10-74.]

[Reg. §48.4161(b)-3]

§48.4161(b)-3. Use considered sale.—For provisions relating to the tax on use of taxable articles by the manufacturer, producer, or importer thereof, see section 4218 relating to use by a manufacturer considered a sale, and the regulations thereunder. [Reg. §48.4161(b)-3.]

☐ [*T.D.* 7328, 10-10-74.]

[Reg. §48.4161(b)-4]

§48.4161(b)-4. Tax-free sales.—For provisions relating to tax-free sales of articles referred to in section 4161(b) see—

Section 4221, relating to certain tax-free sales;

(b) Section 4222, relating to registration;

(c) Section 4223, pertaining to special rules relating to further manufacture; and

(d) Section 4225, relating to exemption of articles manufactured or produced by Indians; and the regulations thereunder. [Reg. §48.4161(b)-4.]

☐ [*T.D.* 7328, 10-10-74.]

[Reg. §48.4161(b)-5]

§48.4161(b)-5. Effective date.—The taxes imposed by section 4161(b) are effective with respect to sales made on and after January 1, 1975. [Reg. §48.4161(b)-5.]

☐ [*T.D.* 7328, 10-10-74.]

[Reg. §48.4191-1]

§48.4191-1. Imposition and rate of tax.— (a) *Imposition of tax.*—Under section 4191(a), tax is imposed on the sale of any taxable medical device by the manufacturer, producer, or importer of the device. For the definition of the term *taxable medical device*, see §48.4191-2.

(b) *Rate of tax.*—Tax is imposed on the sale of a taxable medical device at the rate of 2.3 percent of the price for which the device is sold. For the definition of the term *price*, see section 4216 and §§48.4216(a)-1 through 48.4216(e)-3.

(c) *Liability for tax.*—The manufacturer, producer, or importer making the sale of a taxable medical device is liable for the tax imposed by section 4191(a). For rules relating to the determination of who the manufacturer, producer, or importer is for purposes of section 4191, see §48.0-2(a)(4). For the definition of the term *sale*, see §48.0-2(a)(5). For rules relating to the lease of an article by the manufacturer, producer, or importer, see section 4217 and §48.4217-1 through §48.4217-2. For rules relating to the use of an article by the manufacturer, producer, or importer, see section 4218 and §48.4218-1 through §48.4218-5.

(d) *Procedural rules.*—For the procedural rules relating to section 4191, see part 40 of this chapter.

(e) *Tax-free sales for further manufacture or export.*—For rules relating to tax-free sales of taxable medical devices for further manufacture or export, see section 4221 and § 48.4221-1 through § 48.4221-3.

(f) *Payments made on or after January 1, 2013, pursuant to lease, installment sale, or sale on credit contracts.*—For rules relating to the taxability of payments made on or after January 1, 2013, pursuant to a lease, installment sale, or sale on credit contract entered into on or after March 30, 2010, see § 48.4216(c)-1(e)(1). For rules relating to the taxability of payments made on or after January 1, 2013, pursuant to a lease, installment sale, or sale on credit contract entered into before March 30, 2010, see § 48.4216(c)-1(e)(2).

(g) *Effective/applicability date.*—This section applies to sales of taxable medical devices on and after January 1, 2013. [Reg. § 48.4191-1.]

☐ [*T.D.* 9604, 12-5-2012.]

[Reg. § 48.4191-2]

§ 48.4191-2. Taxable medical device.— (a) *Taxable medical device.*—(1) *In general.*—A taxable medical device is any device, as defined in section 201(h) of the Federal Food, Drug, and Cosmetic Act (FFDCA), that is intended for humans. For purposes of this section, a device defined in section 201(h) of the FFDCA that is intended for humans means a device that is listed as a device with the Food and Drug Administration (FDA) under section 510(j) of the FFDCA and 21 CFR part 807, pursuant to FDA requirements.

(2) *Devices that should have been listed with the FDA.*—If a device is not listed as a device with the FDA but the FDA determines that the device should have been listed as a device, the device will be deemed to be listed as a device with the FDA as of the date the FDA notifies the manufacturer or importer in writing that corrective action with respect to listing is required.

(b) *Exemptions.*—(1) *Specific exemptions.*—The term *taxable medical device* does not include eyeglasses, contact lenses, and hearing aids.

(2) *Retail exemption.*—The term *taxable medical device* does not include any device of a type that is generally purchased by the general public at retail for individual use (the retail exemption). A device will be considered to be of a type that is generally purchased by the general public at retail for individual use if it is regularly available for purchase and use by individual consumers who are not medical professionals, and if the design of the device demonstrates that it is not primarily intended for use in a medical institution or office or by a medical professional. Whether a device is of a type described in the preceding sentence is evaluated based on all the relevant facts and circumstances. Factors relevant to this evaluation are enumerated in paragraphs (b)(2)(i) and (ii) of this section. Further, there may be facts and circumstances that are relevant in evaluating whether a device is of a type generally purchased by the general public at retail for individual use in addition to those described in paragraphs (b)(2)(i) and (ii) of this section. The determination of whether a device is of a type that qualifies for the retail exemption is made based on the overall balance of factors relevant to the particular type of device. The fact that a device is of a type that requires a prescription is not a factor in the determination of whether or not the device falls under the retail exemption.

(i) *Regularly available for purchase and use by individual consumers.*—The following factors are relevant in determining whether a device is of a type that is regularly available for purchase and use by individual consumers who are not medical professionals:

(A) Whether consumers who are not medical professionals can purchase the device in person, over the telephone, or over the internet, through retail businesses such as drug stores, supermarkets, or medical supply stores and retailers that primarily sell devices (for example, specialty medical stores, durable medical equipment, prosthetics, orthotics, and supplies (DME-POS) suppliers and similar vendors);

(B) Whether consumers who are not medical professionals can use the device safely and effectively for its intended medical purpose with minimal or no training from a medical professional; and

(C) Whether the device is classified by the FDA under Subpart D of 21 CFR part 890 (Physical Medicine Devices).

(ii) *Primarily for use in a medical institution or office or by a medical professional.*—The following factors are relevant in determining whether a device is designed primarily for use in a medical institution or office or by a medical professional:

(A) Whether the device generally must be implanted, inserted, operated, or otherwise administered by a medical professional;

(B) Whether the cost to acquire, maintain, and/or use the device requires a large initial investment and/or ongoing expenditure that is not affordable for the average individual consumer;

(C) Whether the device is a Class III device under the FDA system of classification;

(D) Whether the device is classified by the FDA under—

(1) 21 CFR part 862 (Clinical Chemistry and Clinical Toxicology Devices), 21 CFR part 864 (Hematology and Pathology Devices), 21 CFR part 866 (Immunology and Microbiology Devices), 21 CFR part 868 (Anesthesiology Devices), 21 CFR part 870 (Cardiovascular Devices), 21 CFR part 874 (Ear, Nose, and Throat Devices), 21 CFR part 876 (Gastroenterology - Urology Devices), 21 CFR part 878 (General and Plastic Surgery Devices), 21 CFR part 882 (Neurological

Devices), 21 CFR part 886 (Ophthalmic Devices), 21 CFR part 888 (Orthopedic Devices), or 21 CFR part 892 (Radiology Devices);

      (2) Subpart B, Subpart D, or Subpart E of 21 CFR part 872 (Dental Devices);

      (3) Subpart B, Subpart C, Subpart D, Subpart E, or Subpart G of 21 CFR part 884 (Obstetrical and Gynecological Devices); or

      (4) Subpart B of 21 CFR part 890 (Physical Medicine Devices); and

      (E) Whether the device qualifies as durable medical equipment, prosthetics, orthotics, and supplies for which payment is available exclusively on a rental basis under the Medicare Part B payment rules, and is an "item requiring frequent and substantial servicing" as defined in 42 CFR 414.222.

      (iii) *Safe Harbor.*—The following devices will be considered to be of a type generally purchased by the general public at retail for individual use:

      (A) Devices that are included in the FDA's online IVD Home Use Lab Tests (Over-the-Counter Tests) database, available at http://www.accessdata.fda.gov/scripts/cdrh/cfdocs/cfIVD/Search.cfm.

      (B) Devices that are described as "OTC" or "over the counter" devices in the relevant FDA classification regulation heading.

      (C) Devices that are described as "OTC" or "over the counter" devices in the FDA's product code name, the FDA's device classification name, or the "classification name" field in the FDA's device registration and listing database, available at http://www.accessdata.fda.gov/scripts/cdrh/cfdocs/cfrl/rl.cfm.

      (D) Devices that qualify as durable medical equipment, prosthetics, orthotics, and supplies, as described in Subpart C of 42 CFR part 414 (Parenteral and Enteral Nutrition) and Subpart D of 42 CFR part 414 (Durable Medical Equipment and Prosthetic and Orthotic Devices), for which payment is available on a purchase basis under Medicare Part B payment rules, and are—

      (1) "Prosthetic and orthotic devices," as defined in 42 CFR 414.202, that do not require implantation or insertion by a medical professional;

      (2) "Parenteral and enteral nutrients, equipment, and supplies" as defined in 42 CFR 411.351 and described in 42 CFR 414.102(b);

      (3) "Customized items," as described in 42 CFR 414.224;

      (4) "Therapeutic shoes," as described in 42 CFR 414.228(c); or

      (5) Supplies necessary for the effective use of durable medical equipment (DME), as described in section 110.3 of chapter 15 of the Medicare Benefit Policy Manual (Centers for Medicare and Medicaid Studies Publication 100-02).

      (iv) *Examples.*—The following examples illustrate the rules of this paragraph (b)(2).

Example 1. X manufactures non-sterile absorbent tipped applicators. X sells the applicators to distributors Y and Z, which, in turn, sell the applicators to medical institutions and offices, medical professionals, and retail businesses. The FDA requires manufacturers of non-sterile absorbent tipped applicators to list the applicators as a device with the FDA. The applicators are classified by the FDA under 21 CFR part 880 (General Hospital and Personal Use Devices) and product code KXF.

Absorbent tipped applicators do not fall within a retail exemption safe harbor set forth in paragraph (b)(2)(iii) of this section. Therefore, the determination of whether the absorbent tipped applicators are devices of a type generally purchased by the general public at retail for individual use must be made on a facts and circumstances basis.

Individual consumers who are not medical professionals can regularly purchase the absorbent tipped applicators at drug stores, supermarkets, cosmetic supply stores or other similar businesses, and can use the applicators safely and effectively for their intended medical purpose without training from a medical professional. Further, the absorbent tipped applicators do not need to be implanted, inserted, operated, or otherwise administered by a medical professional, do not require a large investment and/or ongoing expenditure, are not a Class III device, are not classified by the FDA under a category described in paragraph (b)(2)(ii)(D) of this section, and are not "items requiring frequent and substantial servicing" as defined in 42 CFR 414.222.

Thus, the applicators have multiple factors under paragraph (b)(2)(i) of this section that tend to show they are regularly available for purchase and use by individual consumers and none of the factors under paragraph (b)(2)(ii) of this section tend to show they are designed primarily for use in a medical institution or office or by medical professionals. Based on the totality of the facts and circumstances, the applicators are devices that are of a type that are generally purchased by the general public at retail for individual use.

Example 2. X manufactures adhesive bandages. X sells the adhesive bandages to distributors Y and Z, which, in turn, sell the bandages to medical institutions and offices, medical professionals, and retail businesses. The FDA requires manufacturers of adhesive bandages to list the bandages as a device with the FDA. The adhesive bandages are classified by the FDA under 21 CFR part 880 (General Hospital and Personal Use Devices) and product code KGX.

Adhesive bandages do not fall within a retail exemption safe harbor set forth in paragraph (b)(2)(iii) of this section. Therefore, the determination of whether the adhesive bandages are devices of a type generally purchased by the general public at retail for individual use must be made on a facts and circumstances basis.

Reg. §48.4191-2(b)(2)(iv)

Individual consumers who are not medical professionals can regularly purchase the adhesive bandages at drug stores, supermarkets, or other similar businesses, and can use the adhesive bandages safely and effectively for their intended medical purpose without training from a medical professional. Further, the adhesive bandages do not need to be implanted, inserted, operated, or otherwise administered by a medical professional, do not require a large investment and/or ongoing expenditure, are not Class III devices, are not classified by the FDA under a category described in paragraph (b)(2)(ii)(D) of this section, and are not "items requiring frequent and substantial servicing" as defined in 42 CFR 414.222.

Thus, the adhesive bandages have multiple factors under paragraph (b)(2)(i) of this section that tend to show they are regularly available for purchase and use by individual consumers and none of the factors under paragraph (b)(2)(ii) of this section tend to show they are designed primarily for use in a medical institution or office or by medical professionals. Based on the totality of the facts and circumstances, the adhesive bandages are devices that are of a type that are generally purchased by the general public at retail for individual use.

Example 3. X manufactures snake bite suction kits. X sells the snake bite suction kits to distributors Y and Z, which, in turn, sell the kits to medical institutions and offices, medical professionals, and retail businesses. The FDA requires manufacturers of snake bite suction kits to list the kits as a device with the FDA. The FDA classifies the snake bit suction kits under 21 CFR part 880 (General Hospital and Personal Use Devices) and product code KYP.

Snake bite suction kits do not fall within a retail exemption safe harbor set forth in paragraph (b)(2)(iii) of this section. Therefore, the determination of whether the snake bite suction kits are devices of a type generally purchased by the general public at retail for individual use must be made on a facts and circumstances basis.

Individual consumers who are not medical professionals can regularly purchase the snake bite suction kits at sporting goods stores, camping stores, or other similar retail businesses, and can use the kits safely and effectively for their intended medical purpose without training from a medical professional. Further, the snake bite suction kits do not need to be implanted, inserted, operated, or otherwise administered by a medical professional, do not require a large investment and/or ongoing expenditure, are not Class III devices, are not classified by the FDA under a category described in paragraph (b)(2)(ii)(D) of this section, and are not "items requiring frequent and substantial servicing" as defined in 42 CFR 414.222.

Thus, the snake bite suction kits have multiple factors under paragraph (b)(2)(i) of this section that tend to show they are regularly available for purchase and use by individual consumers and none of the factors under para-

graph (b)(2)(ii) of this section tend to show they are designed primarily for use in a medical institution or office or by medical professionals. Based on the totality of the facts and circumstances, the snake bite suction kits are devices that are of a type that are generally purchased by the general public at retail for individual use.

Example 4. X manufactures denture adhesives. X sells the denture adhesives to distributors Y and Z, which, in turn, sell the adhesives to dental offices and retail businesses. The FDA requires manufacturers of denture adhesives to list the adhesive as a device with the FDA. The FDA classifies the denture adhesives under 21 CFR part 872 (Dental Devices) and product code KXX.

The denture adhesives do not fall within a retail exemption safe harbor set forth in paragraph (b)(2)(iii) of this section. Therefore, the determination of whether the denture adhesives are devices of a type generally purchased by the general public at retail for individual use must be made on a facts and circumstances basis.

Individual consumers who are not medical professionals can regularly purchase the denture adhesives at drug stores, supermarkets, or other similar businesses, and can use the adhesives safely and effectively for their intended medical purpose with minimal or no training from a medical professional. Further, the denture adhesives do not need to be implanted, inserted, operated, or otherwise administered by a medical professional, do not require a large investment and/or ongoing expenditure, are not Class III devices, are not classified by the FDA under a category described in paragraph (b)(2)(ii)(D) of this section, and are not "items requiring frequent and substantial servicing" as defined in 42 CFR 414.222.

Thus, the denture adhesives have multiple factors under paragraph (b)(2)(i) of this section that tend to show they are regularly available for purchase and use by individual consumers and none of the factors under paragraph (b)(2)(ii) of this section tend to show they are designed primarily for use in a medical institution or office or by medical professionals. Based on the totality of the facts and circumstances, the denture adhesives are devices that are of a type that are generally purchased by the general public at retail for individual use.

Example 5. X manufactures mobile x-ray systems. X sells the x-ray systems to distributors Y and Z, which, in turn, sell the systems generally to medical institutions and offices, as well as medical professionals. The FDA requires manufacturers of mobile xray systems to list the systems as a device with the FDA. The FDA classifies the mobile x-ray systems under 21 CFR part 892 (Radiology Devices) and product code IZL.

Mobile x-ray systems do not fall within a retail exemption safe harbor set forth in paragraph (b)(2)(iii) of this section. Therefore, the determination of whether the mobile x-ray systems are devices of a type generally purchased by the general public at retail for individual use must be made on a facts and circumstances basis.

Individual consumers who are not medical professionals can regularly purchase the mobile x-ray systems over the internet. However, individual consumers cannot use the x-ray systems safely and effectively for their intended medical purpose without training from a medical professional. Although the mobile x-ray systems are not Class III devices and are not "items requiring frequent and substantial servicing" as defined in 42 CFR 414.222, they need to be operated by a medical professional, may require a large investment and/or ongoing expenditure, and are classified by the FDA under a category described in paragraph (b)(2)(ii)(D) of this section (21 CFR part 892 (Radiology Devices).

Thus, with regard to the factors under paragraph (b)(2)(i) of this section, the mobile x-ray systems have one factor that tends to show they are regularly available for purchase and use by individual consumers and one factor that tends to show that they are not regularly available for purchase and use by individual consumers. With regard to the factors under paragraph (b)(2)(ii) of this section, the mobile x-ray systems have multiple factors that tend to show they are designed primarily for use in a medical institution or office or by medical professionals. Based on the totality of the facts and circumstances, the mobile x-ray systems are not devices that are of a type that are generally purchased by the general public at retail for individual use.

Example 6. X manufactures pregnancy test kits. X sells the kits to distributors Y and Z, which, in turn, sell the pregnancy test kits to medical institutions and offices, medical professionals, and retail businesses. The FDA requires manufacturers of pregnancy test kits to list the kits as a device with the FDA. The FDA classifies the kits under 21 CFR part 862 (Clinical Chemistry and Clinical Toxicology Devices) and product code LCX.

The pregnancy test kits are included in the FDA's online IVD Home Use Lab Tests (Over-the-Counter Tests) database. Therefore, the over the counter pregnancy test kits fall within the safe harbor set forth in paragraph (b)(2)(iii)(A) of this section. Further, the FDA product code name for LCX is "Kit, Test, Pregnancy, HCG, Over The Counter." Therefore, the pregnancy test kits also fall within the safe harbor set forth in paragraph (b)(2)(iii)(C) of this section. Accordingly, the pregnancy test kits are devices that are of a type that are generally purchased by the general public at retail for individual use.

Example 7. X manufactures blood glucose monitors, blood glucose test strips, and lancets. X sells the blood glucose monitors, test strips, and lancets to distributors Y and Z, which, in turn, sell the monitors, test strips, and lancets to medical institutions and offices, medical professionals, and retail businesses. The FDA requires manufacturers of blood glucose monitors, test strips, and lancets to list the items as devices

with the FDA. The FDA classifies the blood glucose monitors under 21 CFR part 862 (Clinical Chemistry and Clinical Toxicology Devices) and product code NBW. The FDA classifies the test strips under 21 CFR part 862 (Clinical Chemistry and Clinical Toxicology Devices) and product code NBW. The FDA classifies the lancets under 21 CFR part 878 (General and Plastic Surgery Devices) and product code FMK.

The blood glucose monitors and test strips are included in the FDA's online IVD Home Use Lab Tests (Over-the-Counter Tests) database. Therefore, the blood glucose monitors and test strips fall within the safe harbor set forth in paragraph (b)(2)(iii)(A) of this section. Further, the FDA product code name for NBW is "System, Test, Blood Glucose, Over the Counter." Therefore, the blood glucose monitors and test strips also fall within the safe harbor set forth in paragraph (b)(2)(iii)(C) of this section.

In addition, the lancets are supplies necessary for the effective use of DME as described in section 110.3 of chapter 15 of the Medicare Policy Benefit Manual. Therefore, the lancets fall within the safe harbor set forth in paragraph (b)(2)(iii)(D)(5) of this section.

Accordingly, the blood glucose monitors, test strips, and lancets are devices that are of a type that are generally purchased by the general public at retail for individual use.

Example 8. X manufactures single axis endoskeletal knee shin systems, which are used in the manufacture of prosthetic legs. X sells the knee shin systems to Y, a business that makes prosthetic legs. The FDA requires manufacturers of knee shin systems and prosthetic legs to list the items as devices with the FDA. The FDA classifies prosthetic leg components, including knee shin systems, as external limb prosthetic components under Subpart D of 21 CFR part 890.3420 and product code ISH. The FDA classifies prosthetic legs as an external assembled lower limb prosthesis under 21 CFR part 890.3500 and product code ISW / KFX. In addition, the Centers for Medicare and Medicaid Services have assigned the knee shin systems Healthcare Procedure Coding System code L5810.

Prosthetic legs and certain prosthetic leg components, including single axis endoskeletal knee shin systems, fall within the safe harbor for prosthetic and orthotic devices that do not require implantation or insertion by a medical profession that is set forth in paragraph (b)(2)(iii)(D)(1) of this section. Accordingly, both the single axis endoskeletal knee shin systems manufactured by X and the prosthetic legs made by Y are devices that are of a type that are generally purchased by the general public at retail for individual use.

Example 9. X manufactures mechanical and powered wheelchairs. X sells the wheelchairs to distributors Y and Z, which, in turn, sell the wheelchairs to medical institutions and offices, medical professionals, nursing homes, and retail businesses. The FDA requires manufactur-

Reg. §48.4191-2(b)(2)(iv)

ers of manual and powered wheelchairs to list the items as devices with the FDA. The FDA classifies the manual and powered wheelchairs under Subpart D of 21 CFR part 890 (Physical Medicine Devices). The FDA classifies mechanical wheelchairs under product code IOR. The FDA classifies powered wheelchairs under product code product code ITI.

Mechanical and powered wheelchairs do not fall within a retail exemption safe harbor set forth in paragraph (b)(2)(iii) of this section. Therefore, the determination of whether the mechanical and powered wheelchairs are devices of a type generally purchased by the general public at retail for individual use must be made on a facts and circumstances basis.

Individual consumers who are not medical professionals can regularly purchase the wheelchairs in drug stores, medical specialty stores, or DME suppliers, as well as over the internet. In addition, individual consumers can use the wheelchairs safely and effectively for their intended medical purpose with minimal or no training from a medical professional, and the wheelchairs are classified by the FDA under Subpart D of 21 CFR part 890 (Physical Medicine Devices). Further, although the wheelchairs may require a large initial investment and/or ongoing expenditure, they do not need to be implanted, inserted, operated, or otherwise administered by a medical professional, are not Class III devices, are not classified by the FDA under a category described in paragraph (b)(2)(ii)(D) of this section, and are not "items requiring frequent and substantial servicing" as defined in 42 CFR 414.222.

Thus, the wheelchairs have multiple factors under paragraph (b)(2)(i) of this section that tend to show they are regularly available for purchase and use by individual consumers and, at most, only one factor under paragraph (b)(2)(ii) of this section tends to show they are designed primarily for use in a medical institution or office or by medical professionals. Based on the totality of the facts and circumstances, the mechanical and powered wheelchairs are devices that are of a type that are generally purchased by the general public at retail for individual use.

Example 10. X manufactures portable oxygen concentrators. X sells the portable oxygen concentrators to distributors Y and Z, which, in turn, sell the portable oxygen concentrators to medical institutions and offices, medical professionals, and retail businesses. The FDA requires manufacturers of portable oxygen concentrators to list the items as devices with the FDA. The FDA classifies the oxygen regulators under 21 CFR part 868 (Anesthesiology Devices) and product code CAW.

Portable oxygen concentrators do not fall within a retail exemption safe harbor set forth in paragraph (b)(2)(iii) of this section. Therefore, the determination of whether the oxygen concentrators are devices of a type generally purchased by the general public at retail for

individual use must be made on a facts and circumstances basis.

Individual consumers who are not medical professionals can regularly purchase the portable oxygen concentrators in retail pharmacies, medical specialty stores, or DME suppliers, as well as over the internet. In addition, individual consumers can use the portable oxygen concentrators safely and effectively for their intended medical purpose with minimal or no training from a medical professional. Further, although the portable oxygen concentrators are classified by the FDA under a category described in paragraph (b)(2)(ii)(D) of this section, they do not need to be implanted, inserted, operated, or otherwise administered by a medical professional, do not require a large investment and/or ongoing expenditure, are not Class III devices, and are not "items requiring frequent and substantial servicing" as defined in 42 CFR 414.222.

Thus, the portable oxygen concentrators have multiple factors under paragraph (b)(2)(i) of this section that tend to show they are regularly available for purchase and use by individual consumers and only one factor under paragraph (b)(2)(ii) of this section that tends to show they are designed primarily for use in a medical institution or office or by medical professionals. Based on the totality of the facts and circumstances, the portable oxygen concentrators are devices that are of a type that are generally purchased by the general public at retail for individual use.

Example 11. X manufactures urinary ileostomy bags. X sells the urinary ileostomy bags to distributors Y and Z, which, in turn, sell the urinary ileostomy bags to medical institutions and offices, medical professionals, and retail businesses. The FDA requires manufacturers of urinary ileostomy bags to list the items as devices with the FDA. The FDA classifies the urinary ileostomy bags under 21 CFR part 876 (Gastroenterology - Urology Devices) and product code EXH.

The urinary ileostomy bags are "Prosthetic and orthotic devices," as defined in 42 CFR 414.202, that do not require implantation or insertion by a medical professional. Therefore, the urinary ileostomy bags fall within the safe harbor set forth in paragraph (b)(2)(iii)(D)(1) of this section. Accordingly, the urinary ileostomy bags are devices that are of a type that are generally purchased by the general public at retail for individual use.

Example 12. X manufactures nonabsorbable silk sutures. X sells the nonabsorbable silk sutures to distributors Y and Z, which, in turn, sell the nonabsorbable silk sutures to medical institutions and offices, medical professionals, and retail businesses. The FDA requires manufacturers of nonabsorbable silk sutures to list the items as devices with the FDA. The FDA classifies the nonabsorbable silk sutures under 21 CFR part 878 (General and Plastic Surgery Devices) and product code GAP.

Nonabsorbable silk sutures do not fall within a retail exemption safe harbor set forth in paragraph (b)(2)(iii) of this section. Therefore, the determination of whether the nonabsorbable silk sutures are devices of a type generally purchased by the general public at retail for individual use must be made on a facts and circumstances basis.

Individual consumers who are not medical professionals can regularly purchase the nonabsorbable silk sutures over the internet. However, individual consumers cannot use nonabsorbable silk sutures safely and effectively for their intended medical purpose with minimal or no training from a medical professional. Further, although the nonabsorbable silk sutures do not require a large investment and/or ongoing expenditure, are not Class III devices, and are not "items requiring frequent and substantial servicing" as defined in 42 CFR 414.222, the nonabsorbable silk sutures are classified by the FDA under a category described in paragraph (b)(2)(ii)(D) of this section, and they need to be administered by a medical professional.

Thus, with regard to the factors under paragraph (b)(2)(i) of this section, the nonabsorbable silk sutures have one factor that tends to show they are regularly available for purchase and use by individual consumers and one factor that tends to show that they are not regularly available for purchase and use by individual consumers. With regard to the factors under paragraph (b)(2)(ii) of this section, the nonabsorbable silk sutures have multiple factors that tend to show they are designed primarily for use in a medical institution or office or by medical professionals. Based on the totality of the facts and circumstances, the nonabsorbable silk sutures are not devices that are of a type that are generally purchased by the general public at retail for individual use.

Example 13. X manufactures nuclear magnetic resonance imaging (NMRI) systems (also known as magnetic resonance imaging (MRI) systems). X sells the NMRI systems to distributor Y, which, in turn, sells the systems to medical institutions. The FDA requires manufacturers of NMRI systems to list the systems as a device with the FDA. The FDA classifies the magnetic resonance diagnostic device under 21 CFR part 892 (Radiology Devices) and product code LNH.

NMRI systems do not fall within a retail exemption safe harbor set forth in paragraph (b)(2)(iii) of this section. Therefore, the determination of whether the NMRI systems are devices of a type generally purchased by the general public at retail for individual use must be made on a facts and circumstances basis.

Individual consumers who are not medical professionals may be able to regularly purchase the NMRI systems over the internet. However, individual consumers cannot use the NMRI systems safely and effectively for their intended medical purpose without training from a medical professional. Although the NMRI systems are not Class III devices and are not "items

requiring frequent and substantial servicing" as defined in 42 CFR 414.222, they need to be operated by a medical professional, and are of a type classified by the FDA under 21 CFR part 892 (Radiology Devices). Further, the cost to acquire, maintain, and/or use the NMRI systems requires a large initial investment and/or ongoing expenditure that is not affordable for the average consumer.

Thus, with regard to the factors under paragraph (b)(2)(i), the NMRI systems have, at most, one factor that tends to show that they are regularly available for purchase and use by individual consumers and at least one factor that tends to show that they are not regularly available for purchase and use by individual consumers. With regard to the factors under paragraph (b)(2)(ii), the NMRI systems have multiple factors that tend to show they are designed primarily for use in a medical institution or office or by medical professionals. Based on the totality of the facts and circumstances, the NMRI systems are not devices that are of a type that are generally purchased by the general public at retail for individual use.

Example 14. X manufactures therapeutic AC powered adjustable home use beds. X sells the beds to distributors Y and Z, which, in turn, sell the beds to retail businesses. The FDA requires manufacturers of therapeutic AC powered adjustable home use beds to list the items as devices with the FDA. The FDA classifies the therapeutic AC powered adjustable home use beds under 21 CFR part 880 (General Hospital Devices) and product code LLI.

Therapeutic AC powered adjustable home use beds do not fall within a retail exemption safe harbor set forth in paragraph (b)(2)(iii) of this section. Therefore, the determination of whether the beds are devices of a type generally purchased by the general public at retail for individual use must be made on a facts and circumstances basis.

Although the beds may require a large initial investment and/or ongoing expenditure, individual consumers who are not medical professionals can regularly purchase the beds in medical specialty stores or from DME suppliers, as well as over the internet. In addition, individual consumers can use the beds safely and effectively for their intended medical purpose with minimal or no training from a medical professional. Further, the beds are not classified by the FDA under a category described in paragraph (b)(2)(ii)(D) of this section, do not need to be implanted, inserted, operated, or otherwise administered by a medical professional, are not Class III devices, and are not "items requiring frequent and substantial servicing" as defined in 42 CFR 414.222.

Thus, the therapeutic AC powered adjustable home use beds have multiple factors under paragraph (b)(2)(i) of this section that tend to show they are regularly available for purchase and use by individual consumers and, at most, only one factor under paragraph (b)(2)(ii) of this section that tends to show they are designed primarily for use in a medical institution or office or by medical professionals. Based on the totality of the facts and circumstances, the therapeutic AC powered adjustable home use beds are devices that are of a type that are generally purchased by the general public at retail for individual use.

Example 15. X manufactures powered flotation therapy beds. X sells the beds to distributors Y and Z, which, in turn, sell the beds to medical institutions and offices, and medical professionals. The FDA requires manufacturers of powered flotation therapy beds to list the items as devices with the FDA. The FDA classifies the powered flotation therapy beds under 21 CFR part 890 (Physical Medicine Devices) and product code IOQ.

Powered flotation therapy beds do not fall within a retail exemption safe harbor set forth in paragraph (b)(2)(iii) of this section. Therefore, the determination of whether the beds are devices of a type generally purchased by the general public at retail for individual use must be made on a facts and circumstances basis.

Individual consumers who are not medical professionals may be able to regularly purchase the beds over the internet. However, individual consumers cannot use the beds safely and effectively for their intended medical purpose with minimal or no training from a medical professional. Although the powered flotation therapy beds are not Class III devices and are not "items requiring frequent and substantial servicing" as defined in 42 CFR 414.222, they need to be operated or otherwise administered by a medical professional. Further, the cost to acquire, maintain, and/or use the powered flotation therapy beds requires a large initial investment and/or ongoing expenditure that is not affordable for the average consumer.

Thus, with regard to the factors under paragraph (b)(2)(i) of this section, the powered flotation therapy beds have, at most, one factor that tends to show they are regularly available for purchase and use by individual consumers and at least one factor that tends to show they are not regularly available for purchase and use by individual consumers. With regard to the factors under paragraph (b)(2)(ii) of this section, the powered flotation therapy beds have multiple factors that tend to show they are designed primarily for use in a medical institution or office or by medical professionals. Based on the totality of the facts and circumstances, the powered flotation therapy beds are not devices that are of a type that are generally purchased by the general public at retail for individual use.

(c) *Effective/applicability date.*—This section applies to sales of taxable medical devices on and after January 1, 2013. [Reg. § 48.4191-2.]

☐ [*T.D.* 9604, 12-5-2012 (corrected 3-12-2013).]

[Reg. § 48.4216(a)-1]

§ 48.4216(a)-1. Charges to be included in sale price.—(a) *In general.*—The "price" for which an article is sold includes the total consideration paid for the article, whether that consideration is in the form of money, services, or other things. See § 48.0-2(a)(5). However, for purposes of the taxes imposed under chapter 32 certain collateral charges made in connection with the sale of a taxable article must be included in the taxable sale price, whereas others may be excluded. Any charge which is required by a manufacturer, producer, or importer to be paid as a condition of its sale of a taxable article and which is not attributable to an expense falling within one of the exclusions provided in section 4216 or the regulations thereunder is includible in the taxable sale price. It is immaterial for this purpose that the charge may be paid to a person other than the manufacturer, producer, or importer, or that it may be separately billed to the purchaser as a charge earmarked for expenses incurred or to be incurred in his behalf, such as charges for demonstration or display of the article, for sales promotion programs, or otherwise. With respect to the rules relating to exclusion (in the case of sales after December 31, 1960) of charges for local advertising of a manufacturer's products, see section 4216(e) and § 48.4216(e)-1. In the case of sales on credit, a carrying, finance, or service charge is excludable from the sale price if it is reasonably related to the costs of carrying the deferred portion of the sale price (such as interest on the deferred portion of the sale price, expenses of bookkeeping necessary to keep the records of such sales, and expenses of correspondence and other communication in connection with collection).

(b) *Tools and dies.*—Separate charges for tools and dies used in the manufacture or production of a taxable article are to be included, in whole or in part, in the sale price on which the tax is based. It is immaterial whether the charges for such items are billed in a lump sum or are amortized or allocated to each of the taxable articles. If, at the termination of a contract to manufacture taxable articles, the tools and dies used in production pass to the purchaser, only the amount of depreciation of the tools and dies incurred in production, computed on a "production output" basis, should be included in the sale price. If the purchaser furnishes the tools and dies, the amount of the cost thereof, to the extent that such cost has been depreciated in the production of the taxable articles (computed on a "production output" basis), shall be included in determining the sale price of the articles for purposes of computing the tax. This paragraph applies to sales by manufacturers after May 5, 1974.

(c) *Charges for warranty.*—A charge for a warranty of an article which the manufacturer, producer, or importer requires the purchaser to pay in order to obtain the article shall be included in the sale price of the article on which the tax is computed. On the other hand, a charge for a warranty of a taxable article paid at the purchaser's option shall not be included in the sale price for purposes of computing tax thereon.

(d) *Charges for coverings, containers, and packing.*—Any charge by the manufacturer, producer, or importer for coverings and containers of whatever nature used to pack an article for shipment shall be included as part of the sale price for the purpose of computing the tax, whether or not the charges are identified as such on the invoice or are billed separately. Even though there is an agreement that the manufacturer, producer, or importer will repay all or a portion of the charge for the coverings or containers upon the return thereof, the full charge nevertheless shall be included in the sale price. It is immaterial whether the charge made at the time of sale is more or less than the actual value of the covering or container. See paragraph (b)(4) of § 48.6416(b)-1 for provisions relating to the claiming of a credit or refund in the case of a price readjustment due to the return or repossession of a covering or container. Packing charges are to be included in the sale price whether the charges cover normal packing or special packing services, such as for extra protection of the article or for odd-lot quantities. This rule shall apply whether the packing services are initiated by the manufacturer, producer, or importer or are furnished at the request of the purchaser and whether the packing is performed by the manufacturer, producer, or importer or by another person at his request. If the purchaser supplies packing materials, the fair market value of such materials must be included in the tax base when computing tax liability on the sale of the article.

(e) *Taxable and nontaxable articles sold as a unit.*—Where a taxable article and a nontaxable article are sold by the manufacturer as a unit, the tax attaches to that portion of the manufacturer's sale price of the unit which is properly allocable to the taxing article. For example, where a fishing reel (an article subject to tax under section 4161(a)) is equipped with a fishing line (a nontaxable article) and the reel and line are sold as a unit, the tax imposed by section 4161(a) applies only to that portion of the manufacturer's sale price of the unit which is properly allocable to the fishing reel. Normally, the taxable portion of such a unit may be determined by applying to the manufacturer's sale price of the unit the ratio which the manufacturer's separate sale price of the taxable article bears to the sum of the sale prices of both the taxable and nontaxable articles, if such articles are sold separately by the manufacturer. Where the articles (or either one of them) are not sold separately by the manufacturer and do not have established sale prices, the taxable portion is to be determined from a comparison of the actual costs of the articles to the manufacturer. Thus, if the cost of the taxable article represents four-fifths of the total cost of the complete unit, the tax applies to four-fifths of the price charged by the manufacturer for the unit. [Reg. § 48.4216(a)-1.]

☐ [*T.D. 7536, 3-27-78.*]

[Reg. § 48.4216(a)-2]

§ 48.4216(a)-2. Exclusions from sale price.—(a) *Tax.*—(1) *Tax not part of taxable sale price.*—The tax imposed by chapter 32 of the Code on the sale of an article is not part of the taxable sale price of the article. Thus, if a manufacturer computes the tax on a sale price which is determined without regard to the tax, and it charges the proper tax as a separate item, the amount of tax so charged does not become a part of the taxable sale price and no tax is due on the tax so charged. Where no separate charge is made as tax, it will be presumed that the price charged to the purchaser for the article includes the proper tax, and the proper percentage of such price will be allocated to the tax.

(2) *Computation of tax.*—If an article subject to tax at the rate of 10 percent is sold for $100 and an additional item of $10 is billed as tax, $100 is the taxable selling price and $10 is the amount of tax due thereon. However, if the article is sold for $100 with no separate billing or indication of the amount of the tax, it will be presumed that the tax is included in the $100, and a computation will be necessary to determine what portion of the total amount represents the sale price of the article and what portion represents the tax. The computation is as follows:

$$\text{taxable sale price} = \frac{\text{sale price including tax}}{100 + \text{rate of tax}}$$

Thus, if the tax rate is 10 percent and the sale price including tax is $100, the taxable sale price is $90.91 (that is, $100 divided by (100 + 10)), and the tax is 10 percent of $90.91, or $9.09.

(b) *Transportation, delivery, insurance, or installation charges.*—(1) *Charges incurred pursuant to sale.*—Charges for transportation, delivery, insurance, installation, and other expenses actually incurred in connection with the delivery of an article to a purchaser pursuant to a bona fide sale shall be excluded from the sale price in computing the tax. Such charges include all items of transportation, delivery, insurance, installation, and similar expense incurred after shipment to a customer begins, in response to the customer's order, pursuant to a bona fide sale. However, costs of such nature incurred by a manufacturer, producer, or importer in transporting, in the normal course of business and for its benefit and convenience, articles from a factory or port of entry to a warehouse or other facility (regardless of the location of such warehouse or facility) are not considered as being incurred in connection with the delivery of an article to a purchaser pursuant to a bona fide sale, and charges therefor cannot be excluded from the sale price in computing tax liability. Similarly, an allowance granted by a manufacturer as reimbursement for expenses incurred by the purchaser in shipping used articles to the manufacturer for credit against the purchase price of taxable articles shall not be excluded from the sale price when computing tax due on the sale of the taxable articles. In any event, no charge may be excluded from the sale price unless the conditions set forth in subparagraph (2) of this paragraph are complied with. Said conditions are prescribed under the authority granted the Secretary or his delegate in section 4216(a).

(2) *Only actual expenses to be excluded.*— Where a separate charge is made for transportation or other expenses incurred in connection with the delivery of an article to the purchaser pursuant to a bona fide sale, there shall be excluded in arriving at the sale price subject to tax only that portion of the charge which represents the actual expenses incurred for the transportation or other excludible expenses. Where a separate charge is less than the actual expense, the difference is presumed to be included in the billed price. Such difference, together with the separate charge, shall be excluded in arriving at the sale price on which the tax is computed. Similarly, where no separate charge is made but the manufacturer, producer, or importer incurs an expense of the type to which this paragraph has application, the amount of such expense actually incurred shall be excluded from the sale price on which the tax is computed. Where transportation expense is incurred in conjunction with a shipment composed of both taxable and nontaxable articles, only the portion of the expense allocable to the taxable articles shall be excludible. In general, unless the taxpayer establishes to the satisfaction of the district director that another method reasonably apportions such freight expense between taxable and nontaxable articles, such expense should be apportioned on the basis of the relative weights (or, if available, the relative published tariff rates applicable to) the taxable and nontaxable articles. Where it is not feasible to apportion such expense on the basis of relative weights or tariff rates, the expense shall be apportioned on another reasonable basis; for example, in the case of a shipment including both taxable and nontaxable automotive parts which are subject to the same tariff rate, it may be appropriate to apportion the transportation expense on the basis of the relative sale prices. A charge for insurance in connection with the delivery of an article to a purchaser is considered to represent an expense actually incurred only to the extent that an amount equivalent to such charge is paid or payable by the manufacturer to a person authorized to assume such insurance risk.

(3) *Transportation, delivery, or installation services performed by manufacturer.*—For purposes of computing the taxable sale price of articles, it is immaterial whether the transportation, delivery, or other services of the type to which this paragraph has application are performed by a common carrier or independent agency for or on behalf of the manufacturer, producer, or importer, or are performed by the manufacturer, producer, or importer with the use of its own vehicles or other facilities. Thus, where a manufacturer, producer, or importer performs the transportation, delivery, or other services with its equipment, tools, employees, etc., the cost of such services allocable to the sale of the taxable article shall be excluded. In determining whether an expense is an excludible transportation or delivery expense, only those expenses incurred by reason of the fact that the purchaser accepts delivery at some point other than the manufacturer's place of business shall be considered excludible transportation or delivery expenses. All expenses incurred in placing an article packed, ready for shipment on the loading dock at the manufacturer's factory are not excludible transportation or delivery expenses. An allowance granted by the manufacturer, producer, or importer to the purchaser for transportation, delivery, or other expenses incurred or to be incurred by the purchaser in connection with the sale shall be excluded in computing the taxable sale price, if charges for similar expenses would be excludible if incurred by the manufacturer.

(4) *Records in support of exclusion.*—Every manufacturer, producer, or importer making sales of taxable articles shall keep records which will disclose the amount of transportation, delivery, insurance, installation or other expense actually incurred by it in connection with the delivery of a taxable article to a purchaser pursuant to a bona fide sale.

(c) *Other charges.*—A charge or expense not within the scope of paragraph (a) or (b) of this section, whether or not separately stated, may not be excluded in computing the taxable sale price unless it can be shown by adequate records that the charge or expense properly is not to be included as a manufacturing or selling expense or is in no way incidental to placing the article in condition packed ready for shipment. Commissions to manufacturers' agents, or allowances, payments, or adjustments made to, and for the benefit of, persons other than the purchaser may not be excluded or deducted, under any condition, in computing the sale price upon which the tax is computed. [Reg. § 48.4216(a)-2.]

☐ [T.D. 7536, 3-27-78.]

[Reg. § 48.4216(a)-3]

§ 48.4216(a)-3. Other items relating to tax on sale price.—(a) *Exchanges.*—If, in connection with the sale of an article subject to a tax imposed under chapter 32 on the price for which sold, a manufacturer receives from its vendee another article in exchange, the tax on the manufacturer's sale shall be computed on the basis of the amount allowed for the article received from the vendee, plus any additional amount charged the vendee.

(b) *Replacements under warranty.*—If an article, subject to a tax imposed under chapter 32 on the price for which sold, is returned to the manufacturer by reason of the failure of the article under a warranty as to its quality or service, and a new article is given by the manufacturer, free, or at a reduced price, the tax on the new article shall be computed on the actual amount, if any, to be paid to the manufacturer for the new article. See paragraph (b)(2) of § 48.6416(b)-1 for the circumstances under which the allowance made by the manufacturer, producer, or importer upon the return of the first article constitutes a price readjustment of the sale price of the first article and the extent, if any, to which a credit may be allowed, or refund made, of the tax paid by the manufacturer, producer, or importer on the sale of the first article.

(c) *Readjustments in sale price.*—Readjustments in sale price (such as allowable discounts, rebates, bonuses, etc.) cannot be anticipated. The tax must be based upon the original price unless the readjustments have actually been made prior to the close of the period for which the tax upon the sale is returned. However, if the price upon which the tax was computed is subsequently readjusted, credit may be taken against the tax due on a subsequent return or a claim for refund filed as provided by section 6416(b)(1) and the regulations thereunder. [Reg. § 48.4216(a)-3.]

☐ [*T.D. 7536, 3-27-78.*]

[Reg. § 48.4216(b)-1]

§ 48.4216(b)-1. Constructive sale price; scope and application.—(a) *In general.*—Section 4216(b) pertains to those taxes imposed under chapter 32 that are based on the price for which an article is sold, and contains the provisions for constructing a tax base other than the actual sale price of the article, under certain defined conditions.

(b) *Specific applications.*—(1) Section 4216(b)(1) applies to:

(i) Arm's-length sales at retail or on consignment, other than those sales at retail and to retailers to which section 4216(b)(2) and § 48.4216(b)-3 apply; and,

(ii) Sales otherwise than at arm's-length, and at less than fair market price.

(2) Section 4216(b)(2) applies generally to arm's-length sales of an article at retail or to retailers, or both, where the manufacturer also sells the same article to wholesale distributors.

(3) Section 4216(b)(3) provides a formula for determining a constructive sale price for sales of taxable articles between members of an affiliated group of corporations (as "affiliated group" is defined in section 1504(a)) in those instances where the purchasing corporation regularly resells to retailers but does not regularly resell to wholesale distributors, and except for situations where section 4216(b)(4) or (5) applies.

(4) Section 4216(b)(4) provides a special method for computing a constructive sale price for sales of taxable articles between affiliated corporations where the purchasing corporation sells only to retailers, and the normal method of selling within the industry is for manufacturers to sell to wholesale distributors.

(5) Section 4216(b)(5) provides a special method for computing a constructive sale price for sales of articles subject to a tax imposed by section 4061(a) (trucks, buses, tractors, etc.) between affiliated corporations, where the purchasing corporation regularly sells such articles in arm's-length transactions to independent retailers.

(c) *Definitions.*—For purposes of section 4216(b) and the regulations thereunder and unless otherwise indicated:

(1) *Sale at retail.*—A "sale at retail," or a "retail sale," is a sale of an article to a purchaser who intends to use or lease the article rather than resell it. The fact that articles are sold in wholesale lots, or at wholesale prices, will not change the character of such sales as "sales at retail" if the purchaser is not engaged in the business of reselling such articles, and acquires them for the purpose of using them rather than reselling them.

(2) *Retail dealers.*—A "retail dealer," or "retailer," is a person engaged in the business of selling articles at retail.

(3) *Wholesale distributor.*—The term "wholesale distributor" means a person engaged in the business of selling articles to persons engaged in the business of reselling such articles. [Reg. § 48.4216(b)-1.]

☐ [*T.D. 7613, 4-23-79.*]

[Reg. § 48.4216(b)-2]

§ 48.4216(b)-2. Constructive sale price; basic rules.—(a) *In general.*—Section 4216(b)(1) sets forth the conditions that require the Secretary to construct a sale price on which to compute a tax imposed under chapter 32 on the price for which an article is sold. The section requires a constructive sale price to be established where a taxable article is (1) sold at retail, (2) sold while on consignment, or (3) sold otherwise than through an arm's-length transaction at less than fair market price. See § 48.4216(b)-2(c) for the treatment of articles taxable under section 4061(a).

(b) *Sales at retail.*—Section 4216(b)(1)(A) relates to the determination of a constructive sale price for sales of taxable articles sold at arm's length and at retail. In the case of such sales, the constructive sale price is the highest price for which such articles are sold to wholesale distributors, in the ordinary course of trade, by manufacturers or producers thereof, as determined by the Secretary. If the constructive sale price is less than the actual sale price the constructive sale price shall be used as the tax base. If the constructive sale price is not less than the actual sale price, the actual sale price shall be considered as not less than fair market and shall be used as the tax base. In determining the highest price for which articles are sold by manufacturers to wholesale distributors there must be taken into consideration the normal industry practices with respect to section 4216(a) and (f) inclusions and exclusions. However, once a constructive sale price has been determined by the Secretary, no further adjustment of such price shall be made. The provisions of section 4216(b)(1)(A) and this paragraph shall not apply in those instances where the provisions of section 4216(b)(2) and § 48.4216(b)-3 apply.

(c) *Sales of articles taxable under section 4061(a)*.—With respect to sales made after December 31, 1978, in the case of an article the sale of which is taxable under section 4061(a) and which is sold at retail, the tax under this chapter shall be computed on a percentage (as determined by the Secretary but not greater than 100 percent) of the actual selling price based on the highest price for which such articles are sold by manufacturers and producers in the ordinary course of trade. The constructive sale price under this section shall be determined without regard to any individual manufacturer's or producer's cost.

(d) *Sales on consignment*.—As in the case of sales at retail, the constructive sale price for sales on consignment shall be the price for which such articles are sold, in the ordinary course of trade, by manufacturers or producers thereof, as determined by the Secretary. For purposes of section 4216(b)(1)(B) and this paragraph, an article is considered to be sold on consignment if it is sold while it is on consignment to a person which has the right to sell, and does sell, such article in its own name, but never receives title to the article from the manufacturer. Ordinarily, the constructive sale price of an article sold on consignment is the net price received by the manufacturer from the consignee. The provisions of section 4216(b)(1)(B) and this paragraph shall not apply if the provisions of section 4216(b)(2) and § 48.4216(b)-3 apply.

(e) *Sales not at arm's length*.—For purposes of section 4216(b)(1)(C) and this paragraph, a sale is considered to be made under circumstances otherwise than at "arm's length" if:

(1) One of the parties is controlled (in law or in fact) by the other, or there is common control, whether or not such control is actually exercised to influence the sale price, or

(2) The sale is made pursuant to special arrangements between a manufacturer and a purchaser.

In the case of an article sold otherwise than at arm's length, and at less than fair market price, the constructive sale price shall be the price for which such articles are sold, in the ordinary course of trade, by manufacturers or producers thereof, as determined by the Secretary. Once such a constructive sale price has been determined, no further adjustment of such price shall be made. See section 4216(b)(3), (4), and (5), and § 48.4216(b)-4, for specific methods for determining constructive sale prices for inter-company sales under certain defined conditions. [Reg. § 48.4216(b)-2.]

☐ [*T.D.* 7613, 4-23-79.]

[Reg. § 48.4216(b)-3]

§ 48.4216(b)-3. Constructive sale price; special rule for arm's-length sales.—(a) *In general*.—Section 4216(b)(2) provides a special rule under which a manufacturer shall determine a constructive sale price for his sales of taxable articles at retail, and to retail dealers, under certain conditions.

The rule is applicable where:

(1) The manufacturer regularly sells such articles at retail, or to retailers, or both, as the case may be,

(2) The manufacturer also regularly sells such articles to one or more wholesale distributors in arm's-length transactions, and the manufacturer establishes that its prices in such cases are determined without regard to any benefit to be derived under section 4216(b)(2),

(3) The transactions are arm's-length transactions, and

(4) With respect to articles to which the tax imposed by section 4061(a) applies (relating to trucks, buses, tractors, etc.), the normal method of sales for such articles within the industry is not to sell such articles at retail or to retailers, or combinations thereof.

A manufacturer meeting the foregoing requirements shall base its tax liability for sales at retail and sales to retailers on the lower of its actual sale price or the highest price for which it sells the same articles under the same conditions to wholesale distributors.

(b) *Definitions*.—For purposes of section 4216(b)(2) and this section—

(1) *Actual sale price*.—"Actual sale price" means the actual selling price of an article determined in the same manner as sale price is determined for a taxable sale. Accordingly, such price must reflect the inclusions and exclusions set forth in sections 4216(a) and (f), and any price adjustments described in section 6416(b)(1).

(2) *Highest price to wholesale distributors*.—The "highest price" charged wholesale distributors for an article by a manufacturer, producer, or importer thereof, is the highest price at which the manufacturer, producer, or importer sells the article to wholesale distributors, determined without regard to quantity. Such price shall be determined in the same manner as sale price is determined for a taxable sale with respect to sections 4216(a) and (f) inclusions and exclusions; however, since the price is to be a "highest" price, no further adjustment may be made for price readjustments under section 6416(b)(1).

(3) *Regular sales*.—An article is considered to be sold "regularly" at retail or to retailers if sales are made at retail or to retailers periodically and recurringly as a regular part of the seller's business. If a seller makes only isolated or casual sales of an article at retail or to retailers, it is not considered to be selling "regularly" at retail or to retailers. Similarly, a manufacturer is considered to be making regular sales for an article to one or more distributors if it sells the article to at least one distributor periodically and recurringly as a regular part of its business.

(4) *Normal method of sales in industry*.—In the absence of a showing to the Commissioner of Internal Revenue of a more appropriate manner

of determining the normal method of sales within an industry which is practical in application, the normal method of sales within an industry shall be regarded as not being at retail or to retailers, or both, if the industry dollar volume of sales which are at retail or to retailers, or both, is less than half the total industry dollar volume of sales at all levels of distribution by manufacturers, producers, or importers, including sales to other manufacturers, producers, or importers.

(5) *Industry.*—Each of the following categories of articles upon which tax is imposed by section 4061(a) constitutes a separate "industry":

(i) Taxable automobile trucks (consisting of automobile truck bodies and chassis);

(ii) Taxable automobile buses (consisting of automobiles bus bodies and chassis);

(iii) Taxable truck and bus trailers and semitrailers (consisting of chassis and bodies of such trailers and semitrailers); and

(iv) Taxable tractors of the kind chiefly used for highway transportation in combination with a trailer or semitrailer.

(6) *Application of section 4216(b)(2) to certain sales before June 22, 1965.*—In the case of sales before June 22, 1965, of articles then taxable under section 4121 (relating to electric, gas, and oil appliances), section 4216(b)(2) also applied in the case of a sale of such an article to a special dealer. The applicability of section 4216(b)(2) to such a sale may be determined by inserting "or to a special dealer" following "or to a retailer" in so much of section 4216(b)(2) as precedes subparagraph (A); by inserting "or to special dealers" following "retailers" in section 4216(b)(2)(A); and by inserting "(other than special dealers)" after "wholesale distributors" in section 4216(b)(2)(B) and so much of section 4216(b)(2) as follows section 4216(b)(2)(D). A "special dealer" was a distributor of articles taxable under section 4121 who did not maintain a sales force to resell the article whose constructive sale price was established under section 4216(b)(2) but relied on salesmen of the manufacturer, producer, or importer of the article. In the case of sales before June 22, 1965, of articles taxable under section 4191 (relating to business machines) or section 4211 (relating to matches), section 4216(b)(2) was applicable is [in] the same manner as in the case of articles taxable under section 4061(a). With respect to sales after September 30, 1962, section 4216(b)(2)(C) applied only to articles taxable under section 4061(a), 4191, or 4211. Section 4216(b)(2)(C) was applicable to sales before October 1, 1962, of all articles subject to tax under Chapter 32. [Reg. § 48.4216(b)-3.]

□ [*T.D.* 7613, 4-23-79.]

[Reg. § 48.4216(b)-4]

§ 48.4216(b)-4. Constructive sale price; affiliated corporations.—(a) *In general.*—Sections 4216(b)(3), (4) and (5) establish procedures for determining a constructive sale price under section 4216(b)(1)(C) for sales between corporations that are members of the same "affiliated group," as that term is defined in section 1504.

(b) *Sales to which section 4216(b)(3) applies.*—Section 4216(b)(3), which applies to articles sold after December 31, 1969, provides a procedure for determining a constructive sale price under section 4216(b)(1)(C) in those instances where—

(1) A manufacturer, producer or importer regularly sells a taxable article (other than an article subject to a tax imposed by section 4061(a) (trucks, buses, etc.)) to a wholesale distributor which is a member of the same affiliated group as the manufacturer, producer or importer, and

(2) The wholesale distributor regularly sells such article to one or more independent retailers, but does not regularly sell to wholesale distributors.

Under such circumstances the constructive sale price for the article shall be an amount equal to 90 percent of the lowest price for which the distributor regularly sells the article in arm's-length transactions to such independent retailers. Once the constructive sale price has been determined, no adjustment shall be made for sections 4216(a) and (f) inclusions or exclusions or section 6416(b)(1) price readjustments. If both section 4216(b)(3) and section 4216(b)(4) apply with respect to the sale of an article, the constructive sale price for such article shall be the lower of the prices computed under section 4216(b)(3) and section 4216(b)(4).

(c) *Sales to which section 4216(b)(4) applies.*—Section 4216(b)(4), which applies to articles sold after December 31, 1969, provides a procedure for determining a constructive sale price under section 4216(b)(1)(C) in those instances where—

(1) A manufacturer, producer, or importer regularly sells (except for tax-free sales) a taxable article only to a wholesale distributor which is a member of the same affiliated group as the manufacturer, producer, or importer,

(2) The distributor regularly sells (except for tax-free sales) such article only to retail dealers, and

(3) The normal method of sales for such articles within the industry is to sell such articles in arm's-length transactions to wholesale distributors.

Section 4216(b)(4) applies with respect to articles taxable under section 4061(a) (relating to trucks, buses, etc.) only as to sales after December 31, 1969, and before January 1, 1971. Under section 4216(b)(4), the constructive sale price of such article shall be the median price at which the distributor, at the time of the sale by the manufacturer, resells the article to retail dealers, reduced by a percentage of such price equal to the percentage which—

(i) The difference between the median price for which comparable articles are sold to wholesale distributors, in the ordinary course of trade, by manufacturers or producers thereof, and the median price at which such wholesale distributors in arm's-length transactions sell such comparable articles to retailers, is of

Reg. § 48.4216(b)-4(c)(3)(i)

(ii) The median price at which such wholesale distributors in arm's-length transactions sell such comparable articles to retailers.

For purposes of this paragraph, the "median price" for which an article is sold at a particular level of distribution is the price midway between the highest and lowest prices charged vendees at the particular level of distribution. Where only one price is charged at a level of distribution, "median price" is equivalent to "actual price." All sale prices referred to in paragraphs (c) and (d) of this section are prices that must reflect the inclusions and exclusions set forth in sections 4216(a) and (f). However, once a constructive sale price has been determined under these paragraphs, no further adjustment of such price is allowed.

(d) *Application of section 4261(b)(4).*—The application of section 4216(b)(4) and paragraph (c) of this section may be illustrated by the following example:

Example. M, a corporation engaged in the manufacture of article X, sold 100 of such articles at $10.00 per article to a wholesale distributor N, a corporation engaged in the business of selling X articles to independent retail dealers. N is a member of the same affiliated group of corporations as M. M sells X articles only to N. The normal method of manufacturers' sales of X articles in the industry is to sell to independent wholesale distributors. N corporation sells X articles to retailers for $15.00 each. The price for which comparable X articles are sold to wholesale distributors in the ordinary course of trade by manufacturers thereof is $12.00 per article. Wholesale distributors sell X articles to retailers in the ordinary course of trade for $16.00 per article. Under the foregoing facts the constructive sale price determined under section 4216(b)(4) and this paragraph is $11.25, computed as follows:

$$\text{Constructive sale price} = [\$15.00 \text{ minus } [\$15.00 \times \frac{(\$16.00 - \$12.00)}{\$16.00}] = \$11.25.$$

(e) *Sales to which section 4216(b)(5) applies.*—Section 4216(b)(5), which applies to articles sold after December 31, 1970, provides a procedure for determining a constructive sale price under section 4216(b)(1)(C) in those circumstances where—

(1) A manufacturer, producer, or importer of an article subject to a tax imposed by section 4061(a) (trucks, buses, etc.) regularly sells such article to a wholesale distributor that is a member of the same affiliated group of corporations as the manufacturer, producer, or importer, and

(2) Such distributor regularly sells such articles to independent retail dealers.

Under such circumstances the constructive sale price of such article shall be 98¹/₂ percent of the lowest price for which such distributor regularly sells the article in arm's-length transactions to the independent retail dealers. Once the constructive sale price has been determined, no adjustment shall be made for section 4216(a) and (f) inclusions or exclusions or section 6416(b)(1) price readjustments.

(f) *Determination of "lowest price".*—(1) In addition to other considerations, in determining a "lowest price" for purposes of section 4216(b)(1), (3), and (5), and §§48.4216(b)-4(b) and 48.4216(b)-4(e), such price shall be determined—

(i) Without requiring that a given percentage of sales be made at that price (provided that the volume of sales made at that price is great enough to indicate that those sales have not been engaged in primarily to establish a lower tax base), and

(ii) Without including any charge for a fixed amount that the purchaser has an unconditional right to recover on the basis of a contractual arrangement existing at the time of sale.

(2) For purposes of applying section 4216(b)(1) and §48.4216(b)-2, section 4216(b)(6) and this paragraph apply to articles sold after

June 30, 1962. For purposes of applying section 4216(b)(3) and paragraph (b) of this section, section 4216(b)(6) and this paragraph apply to articles sold after December 31, 1969. For purposes of applying section 4216(b)(5) and paragraph (e) of this section, section 4216(b)(6) and this paragraph apply to articles sold after December 31, 1970.

(g) *Definitions.*—For purposes of this section and paragraphs (3), (4), and (5) of section 4216(b), the term "regularly sells" has the same meaning as that accorded the term "regular sales" in subparagraph (3) of §48.4216(b)-3(b), and the term "normal method of sales in the industry" has the same meaning as accorded that term in subparagraph (4) of §48.4216(b)-3(b). [Reg. §48.4216(b)-4.]

☐ [*T.D.* 7613, 4-23-79.]

[Reg. §48.4216(c)-1]

§48.4216(c)-1. Computation of tax on leases and installment sales.—(a) *Leases.*—When a taxable article is leased by a manufacturer, producer, or importer, liability for tax is incurred, except as provided by section 4217(b) and §48.4217-2, on each payment made with respect to such lease. Tax is payable on each lease payment as long as the article is leased by the manufacturer, producer, or importer. The tax payable with respect to each lease payment is a percentage of each payment based on the rate of tax, if any, in effect on the date the lease payment is due. If the article is subsequently sold by the manufacturer, producer, or importer, the tax applies also to such sale, without regard to the tax paid when the article was leased. For definition of the term "lease", see paragraph (a) of §48.4217-1(a).

(b) *Installment sales.*—When a taxable article is sold under an installment payment contract with title reserved in the seller, or under a conditional sale contract, chattel mortgage arrangement or other arrangement creating a security interest with payments to be made in installments, tax shall be computed and paid on each payment made by the purchaser. The tax payable with each payment is a percentage of each payment based on the rate of tax, if any, in effect on the date the payment is due. The part of each payment that is subject to tax is that portion of the payment equal to the percentage of the total charge for the article that is subject to tax. For example, if the total charge for the article is $1,000, and of the total amount charged only 90 percent thereof, or $900, is subject to tax by reason of exclusions, then only 90 percent of the installment payment is subject to tax. If the tax base is a constructive sale price computed under section 4216(b) that is less than the actual sale price of the article, the portion of each payment subject to tax is the percentage of such payment equal to the percentage that the constructive sale price bears to the actual sale price. For example, if an article is sold at retail for $100, and the constructive sale price for such an article computed under the provisions of section 4216(b)(1)(A) is $75, the percentage which the constructive sale price bears to the actual sale price is 75 percent. Accordingly, only 75 percent of each installment payment is subject to tax.

(c) *Sales on credit.*—Where articles are sold on credit under conditions other than those specified in paragraph (b) of this section, the entire tax shall be reported and paid with the return covering the period in which the sale is made, even though the price may not be paid to the manufacturer, producer, or importer until a later date, or not paid at all.

(d) *Effective dates of paragraphs (a) and (b) of this section.*—The rules set forth in paragraphs (a) and (b) of this section are effective as of June 22, 1965. As in effect before June 22, 1965, section 4216(c) required, in the case of a transaction described in section 4216(c)(1), (2), (3), or (4), that there be paid upon each payment with respect to an article that portion of the total tax which was proportionate to the portion of the total amount to be paid represented by such payment.

(e) *Contracts for the lease, installment sale, or sale on credit, of a taxable medical device.*—(1) *General rule.*—Payments made on or after January 1, 2013, pursuant to a contract for the lease, installment sale, or sale on credit of a taxable medical device that was entered into on or after March 30, 2010, are subject to tax under section 4191. The provisions of sections 4216(c) and 4217, paragraphs (a), (b), and (c) of this section, and § 48.4217-2 apply.

(2) *Exception for payments made on or after January 1, 2013, pursuant to written binding contracts entered into prior to March 30, 2010.*—Payments made on or after January 1, 2013, pursuant to a written binding contract for the lease, installment sale, or sale on credit of a taxable medical device that was in effect prior to March 30, 2010, are not subject to tax under

section 4191. This exception includes payments made on or after January 1, 2013, if they are made pursuant to a written binding contract that was entered into prior to March 30, 2010. This exception does not apply to payments made under any contract that is materially modified on or after March 30, 2010. For this purpose, a material modification includes only a modification that materially affects the property to be provided under the contract, the terms of payment under the contract, or the amount payable under the contract. Notwithstanding the foregoing, a material modification does not include a modification to the contract required by applicable Federal, State, or local law.

(3) *Effective/applicability date.*—This section applies on and after January 1, 2013. [Reg. § 48.4216(c)-1.]

☐ [*T.D.* 7536, 3-27-78. *Amended by T.D.* 9604, 12-5-2012 (*corrected* 3-12-2013).]

[Reg. § 48.4216(d)-1]

§ 48.4216(d)-1. Sales of installment accounts.—(a) *In general.*—Except as provided in paragraph (d) of this section, in case of a sale or other disposition by a manufacturer, producer, or importer of an installment account of the type specified in section 4216(c), the tax shall not apply to subsequent installment payments on such account. Instead, there shall be paid an amount equal to the difference between the tax previously paid on such installment account and the total tax computed by applying—

(1) To each installment due before the sale of the installment account, the rate of tax applicable at the time payment thereof was due, and

(2) To each installment, the time for payment of which has not arrived, the rate of tax which, under the provisions of chapter 32 as in effect on the date of the sale of the installment account, is (or is to be) in effect on the date such installment is due.

However, see paragraph (b) of this section if the sale is made in a bankruptcy or insolvency proceeding. The tax due under this paragraph shall be included in the return for the period in which the account is sold.

(b) *Sale in bankruptcy or insolvency proceeding.*—In the case of a sale of an installment account of a manufacturer, producer, or importer pursuant to the order of, or subject to the approval of, a court of competent jurisdiction in a bankruptcy or insolvency proceeding, the amount of tax due shall be computed and paid as provided in paragraph (a) of this section but shall not exceed the amount of tax computed by multiplying (1) the proportionate share of the amount for which such accounts are sold which is allocable to each unpaid installment payment, by (2) the rate of tax which, under the provisions of chapter 32 as in effect on the date of the sale of the installment account, is (or is to be) in effect on the date such payment is due.

(c) *Collection of installment accounts on behalf of the manufacturer.*—Where a manufacturer, producer, or importer retains title to an installment account but turns it over to another person for collection on a fee basis, no sale of such account (or other disposition as contemplated in section 4216(d)) has been made. The tax shall continue to be paid as provided by section 4216(c).

(d) *Returned installment accounts.*—Where an installment account which has been sold or otherwise disposed of is returned to the manufacturer, producer, or importer who sold it under an agreement under which the account was sold, and credit or refund has been allowed under section 6416(b)(5) and the regulations thereunder, the manufacturer, producer, or importer shall pay tax as provided by section 4216(c) and § 48.4216(c)-1 on any subsequent payments made on such returned installment account until such time as there shall have been paid the total tax liability with respect to the account as computed under paragraph (a) of this section.

(e) *Limitation.*—The sum of the amounts payable under this section and § 48.4216(c)-1 on an installment account shall not exceed the total amount of tax which would be payable if such installment account had not been sold or otherwise disposed of (computed as provided in subsection (c)).

(f) *Applicability of paragraphs (a) and (b) of this section.*—The rules set forth in paragraphs (a) and (b) of this section apply in the case of installment accounts sold after June 21, 1965. In the case of installment accounts sold before June 22, 1965, paragraph (b) of this section shall be applied by substituting, in lieu of subparagraph (2) thereof, "the rate of tax, as set forth in chapter 32 of the Code, which applied on the day on which the transaction giving rise to such installment accounts took place." [Reg. § 48.4216(d)-1.]

☐ [*T.D.* 7536, 3-27-78.]

[Reg. § 48.4216(e)-1]

§ 48.4216(e)-1. Exclusion of local advertising charges from sale price.—(a) *In general.*—Section 4216(e) deals with the treatment to be accorded charges made by a manufacturer for, and reimbursements by a manufacturer of expenditures in connection with, the advertising of certain articles subject to excise tax under chapter 32 of the Code. Section 4216(e) provides an exclusion (which is in addition to the exclusions provided by section 4216(a) and the regulations thereunder) in respect of charges for local advertising, as defined in paragraph (b) of this section, for purposes of determining the price for which an article is sold. See paragraph (c) of this section. The exclusion provided by section 4216(e) and paragraph (c) of this section has application only if—

(1) In the case of articles sold during the period January 1, 1961, through December 31, 1962, the advertising is broadcast over a radio or television station, or appears in a newspaper; and

(2) In the case of articles sold on or after January 1, 1963, the advertising is broadcast over a radio or television station, appears in a newspaper or magazine, or is displayed by means of an outdoor advertising sign or poster.

Section 4216(e) also provides an over-all limitation in respect of the sum of the amount of the exclusions from price as charges for local advertising and the amount of the readjustments authorized under section 6416(b)(1) (relating to credits or refunds for price readjustments) in respect of reimbursements by a manufacturer of expenditures for local advertising. See § 48.4216(e)-2. For provisions prohibiting exclusion from price or readjustment of price in respect of charges for, and reimbursements of expenditures for, advertising other than local advertising, see § 48.4216(e)-3.

(b) *Definition of local advertising.*—(1) *In general.*—For purposes of the regulations under sections 4216(e) and 6416(b)(1), the term "local advertising" means advertising which relates to an article with respect to which tax is imposed under chapter 32 of the Code on the price for which sold and which—

(i) Is initiated or obtained by the purchaser or any subsequent vendee,

(ii) Names the article for which the price is determinable under section 4216 and states the location at which such article may be purchased at retail, and

(iii)(a) In the case of articles sold on or after January 1, 1961, and before January 1, 1963, is broadcast over a radio station or television station or appears in a newspaper, or

(b) In the case of articles sold on or after January 1, 1963, is broadcast over a radio station or television station, appears in a newspaper or magazine, or is displayed by means of an outdoor advertising sign or poster.

(2) *Initiating or obtaining advertising.*—For purposes of subparagraph (1) of this paragraph, the advertising must be initiated or obtained by one or more of the persons in the chain of distribution of the article (wholesale distributor, jobber, dealer, etc.) who purchased the article for resale. For purposes of this subparagraph, the manufacturer is not considered to be one of the persons in the chain of distribution of the article. In general, advertising of an article is considered to be initiated or obtained by one or more persons in the chain of distribution of the article if any such person—

(i) Takes an active part in the actual planning and development, or in the arrangements or negotiations leading to the development, of the form and content of the advertising, or

(ii) Contracts for the placement of the advertising.

The participation by the manufacturer of the article in the planning, development, or placement of the advertising is immaterial provided the advertising is in fact initiated or obtained by one or more persons in the chain of distribution of the article. Furthermore, it is immaterial whether or not the advertising is subject to the approval of the manufacturer of the article.

However, if no person in the chain of distribution of the article takes an active part in the actual planning and development, or in the arrangements or negotiations leading to the development, of the form and content of the advertising, but, rather, all such planning, development, arrangements, and negotiations are accomplished by the manufacturer of the article, then such manufacturer is considered to have initiated the advertising, and if he also contracts for the placement of the advertising, such advertising does not qualify as "local advertising".

(3) *Identification of article and sales location.*—To meet the requirements of subparagraph (1) of this paragraph, the advertising must identify the article for which the price is determinable under section 4216 and give the location or locations at which the article may be purchased at retail. All products taxable at the same rate under the same section of chapter 32 of the Code shall be considered to be an "article" for purposes of the preceding sentence. No specific method or means of identification is prescribed. The identification of the article may be made through the use of the name of the manufacturer or the use of an established trade-mark, such as a seal, picture, letter or letters, etc., or a combination thereof. The advertising must identify the particular retail establishment or establishments at which the article may be purchased at retail but need not specify the location of any such establishment in terms of the number by which the premises are designated or the name of the street on which the retail premises are situated. However, the location of the retail premises must be described sufficiently, as, for example, by reference to a particular named shopping area or shopping center, to enable consumers to find the retail establishment.

(4) *Determination of costs of local advertising.*—Where an advertisement identifies more than one article, and all such articles are not taxable, or are not taxable at the same rate under the same section of chapter 32 of the Code, a reasonable allocation of the cost of the advertisement must be made among (i) articles taxable at the same rate under the same section of the Code and (ii) articles which are not taxable under chapter 32 of the Code. For example, in the case of a single page newspaper or magazine advertisement, an allocation of costs reflecting the lineage or space devoted to the specified categories will be considered to reflect a reasonable allocation of the cost of advertising the different articles. As a general rule, only the cost of the "spot" portion identifying the retail establishment is considered "local advertising" in the case of national television or radio programs.

(5) *Meaning of "newspaper".*—The term "newspaper", as used in subparagraph (1) of this paragraph, is limited to those publications which are commonly understood to be newspapers and which are printed and distributed periodically at daily, weekly, or other short intervals for the dissemination of news of a general character and of a general interest. The term does not include handbills, circulars, flyers, or the like, unless printed and distributed as a part of a publication which constitutes a newspaper within the meaning of this subparagraph. Neither does the term include any publication which is issued to supply information on certain subjects of interest to particular groups, unless such publication otherwise qualifies as a newspaper within the meaning of this subparagraph. For purposes of this subparagraph, advertising is not considered to be news of a general character and of a general interest.

(6) *Meaning of "magazine".*—The term "magazine", as used in subparagraph (1) of this paragraph, is limited to those publications which are (i) commonly understood to be magazines, (ii) printed and distributed periodically at least twice a year, and (iii) published for the dissemination of information of a general nature or of special interest to particular groups. The term does not include handbills, circulars, flyers or the like, unless printed and distributed as a part of a publication which constitutes a magazine within the meaning of this subparagraph. For purposes of this subparagraph, advertising is not considered to be information of a general nature or information of special interest to particular groups within the contemplation of subdivision (iii) of this subparagraph.

(7) *Meaning of "outdoor advertising sign or poster".*—The term "outdoor advertising sign or poster", as used in subparagraph (1) of this paragraph, means a sign or poster displaying advertising matter, which is located outside of a roofed enclosure. This term includes both signs or posters on billboards, whether placed on or affixed to land, buildings, or other structures, and those which are displayed on or attached to moving objects, provided the signs or posters are located outside of a roofed enclosure. The term "roofed enclosure" means a roofed structure which is enclosed on more than one-half of its sides by walls, fences, or other barriers.

(c) *Exclusion.*—(1) *Conditions and limitations.*—A charge for local advertising which is required by a manufacturer to be paid as a condition to his sale of an article is not a part of the taxable price of the article, to the extent that such charge meets each of the following conditions and limitations:

(i) Such charge does not exceed 5 percent of the difference between (*a*) an amount which would constitute the taxable price of the article (computed at the time of the sale of the article) if no part of any charge for local advertising were excludable in computing taxable price and (*b*) the amount of any separate charge for the local advertising, whatever the amount of such charge may be.

(ii) Such charge is specifically shown as a separate charge for local advertising of the invoice or statement covering the sale of the article.

Reg. § 48.4216(e)-1(c)(1)(ii)

(iii) Such charge is billed by the manufacturer with the intention on his part of repaying the amount of the charge to the person purchasing the article from him, or to any person who subsequently purchases the article for resale, in reimbursement of costs incurred for local advertising of such article or some other article or articles taxable at the same rate under the same section of the Code. In the absence of evidence to the contrary, the fact of such intention will be assumed in all cases where the manufacturer and his vendees are parties to an advertising plan which calls for such repayments, or the manufacturer can otherwise establish that the vendees to whom he bills such charges understand and expect that such repayments will be made.

(2) *When exclusion ceases to apply.*—To the extent that a charge for local advertising meets the conditions and limitations stated in subparagraph (1) of this paragraph, such charge is excludable in computing the taxable price of the article in respect of which the charge was made. However, the exclusion will cease to apply in respect of any part of such charge which the manufacturer fails to repay, before May 1 of the calendar year following the calendar year in which the article was sold, to the person who purchased the article from him, or to some other person who subsequently purchases the article for resale, in reimbursement of costs incurred for local advertising of such article or some other article or articles taxable at the same rate under the same section of the Code. If, before May 1,

Refrigerators	$10,000
Local advertising charge	500
Total charge	$10,500

At the time of the manufacturer's sale of the refrigerators, it was his intention, in accordance with the agreement between him and the distributor, to make repayment to the distributor of the local advertising charge, to the extent of expenditures by the distributor for radio, television, or newspaper advertising specifically naming refrigerators or other articles taxable at the same rate under section 4111 which were manufactured by the manufacturer, and giving the location of various retail stores within the distributor's territory where such articles may be purchased. Pursuant to such agreement, the selection of the advertising medium to be employed is to be made by the distributor, who is to plan the advertising subject to approval by the manufacturer, and contract for its placement. In this example, the advertising for which the charge is made qualifies as local advertising, the charge is billed to the manufacturer's vendee as a separate charge, the manufacturer intends to repay the charge to his vendee in reimbursement of costs incurred by the vendee for local advertising, and the charge does not exceed 5 percent of $10,000. Accordingly, the manufacturer's charge of $500 for local advertising is not includible in the taxable price of the refrigerators for

such any part of the charge so excluded has not been so repaid, the manufacturer becomes liable for tax on such May 1 in the same manner as if an article taxable under such section of the Code had been sold by him on such May 1 at a taxable price equivalent to that part of the charge not so repaid. However, see paragraph (c)(2) of § 48.6416(b)-1, relating to price readjustments in cases where local advertising charges are not repaid before such May 1 but are subsequently paid over by the manufacturer to his vendees in reimbursement of costs for local advertising. For provisions relating to the method of determining whether a payment by a manufacturer is or is not attributable to an excluded local advertising charge, see paragraph (b)(3) of § 48.4216(e)-2. In any case where the payment is determined to be attributable to such a charge, the date of the sale in connection with which the charge was made shall be determined on a first-in-first-out basis in respect of the vendee to whom the charge was billed by the manufacturer.

(d) *Examples.*—The application of this section may be illustrated by the following examples:

Example (1). During the first calendar quarter of 1961, a manufacturer sold refrigerators to one of his distributors at a total charge of $10,500, exclusive of tax, transportation charges, delivery charges, or other charges which are excludable in computing taxable price pursuant to section 4216(a). This total charge of $10,500 was billed as follows:

purposes of computing and paying the tax imposed by section 4111.

Example (2). Assume the same facts as those stated in Example (1), and assume further that prior to May 1, 1962, the manufacturer has repaid to the distributor, in reimbursement of local advertising expenses incurred by the distributor in connection with refrigerators or other articles taxable at the same rate under section 4111 sold to him by the manufacturer, $400 of the $500 billed as a local advertising charge by the manufacturer in connection with his sale of refrigerators to the distributor in the first quarter of 1961. The manufacturer is liable, as of May 1, 1962, for tax in respect of the $100 which has not been repaid to the distributor. The amount of the tax is determinable at the rate in effect under section 4111 on May 1, 1962, in respect of refrigerators and is includible in the manufacturer's return of tax under such section for the second quarter of 1962.

Example (3). During the first calendar quarter of 1961, a manufacturer sold refrigerators to one of his distributors at a total charge of $11,000, exclusive of tax, transportation charges, delivery charges, or other charges which are excludable in computing taxable price under section 4216(a). This total charge of $11,000 was billed as follows:

Refrigerators	$10,000
Local advertising charge	1,000
Total charge	$11,000

At the time of the manufacturer's sale of the refrigerators, it was his intention, in accordance with the terms of a cooperative advertising plan to which the manufacturer and the distributor were parties, to make repayment to the distributor of the local advertising charge. Pursuant to the plan, the repayment would be made to the extent of expenditures by the distributor for radio, television, or newspaper advertising, initiated or obtained by him, specifically naming refrigerators or other articles taxable at the same rate under section 4111 which were manufactured by the manufacturer, and giving the location of various retail stores within the distributor's territory where such articles may be purchased. In this example, only $500 of the manufacturer's charge of $1,000 for local advertising may be excluded in determining the taxable price of the refrigerators for purposes of reporting and paying the tax imposed by section 4111. The remaining $500 may not be excluded in computing the taxable price of the refrigerators since this is the amount by which the $1,000 local advertising charge exceeds 5 percent of $10,000. Thus, the taxable price of the refrigerators in this example is $10,500.

Example (4). Assume the same facts as those stated in Example (1), except that, pursuant to the agreement between the manufacturer and the distributor, the manufacturer is to contract for the placement of the local advertising. Payment of the $500 local advertising charge is to be made by the manufacturer to the person with whom the advertising is placed in satisfaction of the manufacturer's contractual liability to such person. Under these circumstances, the manufacturer's payment of the $500 charge to the person with whom the advertising is placed does not constitute a refund to the purchaser in reimbursement of costs incurred for local advertising. [Reg. § 48.4216(e)-1.]

☐ [*T.D. 6635. Amended by T.D. 6686 and T.D. 7536, 3-27-78.*]

[Reg. § 48.4216(e)-2]

§ 48.4216(e)-2. Limitation on aggregate of exclusions and price readjustments.—(a) *In general.*—The sum of the amount excluded from taxable price in respect of charges for local advertising, as provided in section 4216(e)(1) and § 48.4216(e)-1, plus the amount of the readjustments for which credits or refunds may be claimed in respect of local advertising, as provided in section 6416(b)(1) and paragraph (c) of § 48.6416(b)-1, is subject to an over-all 5 percent limitation. This limitation applies to each manufacturer, as of the close of each calendar quarter, in respect of all articles taxable under the same section of chapter 32 which were sold by such manufacturer in such quarter (and the preceding quarter or quarters, if any, in the calendar year). For example, a manufacturer selling articles taxable under section 4061 (relating to automobiles,

trucks, buses, etc.), and also selling articles taxable under section 4111 (relating to refrigerators, quick-freeze units, etc.), who makes separate charges for local advertising in connection with his sales, or who makes reimbursement of local advertising expenses to his vendees out of moneys previously included in taxable price, in respect of any one or more articles in each of the two groups must apply the limitation separately in relation to the articles taxable under section 4061 and in relation to the articles taxable under section 4111. However, in such case, no breakdown of the separate articles taxable under section 4061, or of the separate articles taxable under section 4111, is required.

(b) *Computation of over-all 5 percent limitation.*—(1) *In general.*—The limitation prescribed by section 4216(e)(2) (the "over-all 5 percent limitation" referred to in paragraph (a) of this section) as to the total of the exclusions from price and readjustments of price which may be claimed for local advertising in respect of all articles taxable under the same section of chapter 32 of the Code shall be computed as of the close of each calendar quarter of the calendar year. The over-all 5 percent limitation is 5 percent of the difference between (i) the amount which would constitute the total taxable price (computed at the time of sale) of all articles taxable under the same section of chapter 32 of the Code sold by the manufacturer during the elapsed calendar quarters of the calendar year, if no part of any charge for local advertising were excludable in computing taxable price, and (ii) the total of all amounts billed as separate charges for local advertising of such articles (whatever the amount of any single charge or the total of all charges). In making the computations under subdivisions (i) and (ii) of this subparagraph, credits or refunds under section 6416(b) of tax paid on the sale of any such articles are to be disregarded and articles sold tax-free by the manufacturer are to be excluded. The amount by which the over-all 5 percent limitation computed as of the close of a particular calendar quarter in respect of articles taxable under the same section of the Code exceeds the sum of the charges for local advertising excluded in computing the taxable price and the amount of reimbursements for local advertising of such articles made during the elapsed calendar quarters of the calendar year, in respect of which credit or refund has been claimed, represents the unused portion of the over-all 5 percent limitation. Such unused portion is the maximum amount of the reimbursements for local advertising in respect of which credit or refund may be claimed at the close of the particular calendar quarter, subject to the applicable conditions and limitations governing the right to claim a credit or refund in respect of local advertising (see § 48.6416(b)-1). The unused portion of the over-all 5 percent limitation as of the close of the fourth calendar quarter of a calendar year in respect of which credit or refund may not be claimed as of the close of such quarter must be disregarded in computing the over-all 5 percent limitation for any subsequent calendar quarter. Moreover, the amount of any reimbursements for local advertising made by a manufacturer in a calendar year which is in excess of the amount of such reimbursements in respect of which credit or refund may be claimed, within the over-all limitation, as of the close of the calendar year, may not subsequently serve as the basis for a credit or refund.

(2) *Alternative method of computation in certain cases.*—If during the portion of the calendar year ending with the date as of which the over-all 5 percent limitation is being computed the amount of the local advertising charge separately billed by the manufacturer has not, in respect of any sale of any articles taxable under the same section of chapter 32 of the Code, exceeded the amount excludable pursuant to paragraph (c) of § 48.4216(e)-1 in computing taxable price, the over-all 5 percent limitation as of the close of a particular calendar quarter in respect of articles taxable under such section is 5 percent of the total taxable price (computed at the time of the sale) of all such articles sold tax-paid during the calendar year.

(3) *Allocation of amounts paid in reimbursement of expenditures for local advertising.*—If a manufacturer makes contributions to a local advertising program in connection with which he makes excludable local advertising charges, it is necessary that reimbursements by the manufacturer for local advertising be attributed to the charges for local advertising, to the manufacturer's contributions, or allocated between them. Whether an amount paid by a manufacturer in reimbursement of expenses for local advertising is or is not a repayment of a local advertising charge which was excluded from taxable price under section 4216(e)(1) and § 48.4216(e)-1, shall be determined on the basis of an allocation made under the agreement between the manufacturer and his vendee (or any subsequent vendee).

(c) *Examples.*—The application of paragraphs (a) and (b) of this section may be illustrated by the following examples:

Example (1). During the first and second calendar quarters of 1961, a manufacturer makes sales of articles taxable under section 4111 to his distributors. The total charges for such sales, exclusive of the tax, transportation charges, delivery charges, or other charges which are excludable, pursuant to section 4216(a), in computing taxable price, are as follows:

First Quarter

Articles taxable under section 4111	$100,000
Local advertising charges	3,000
Total charge	$103,000

Second Quarter

Articles taxable under section 4111	$150,000
Local advertising charges	4,000
Total charge	$154,000

Assume further that the manufacturer contributes to the advertising plan and that the manufacturer pays $5,500 and $1,000 during the first and second calendar quarters of 1961, respectively, to his distributors in reimbursement of expenses incurred by them for local advertising of the articles purchased from the manufacturer.

Computation as of close of first calendar quarter

1. Amount which would constitute total taxable price (computed at time of sale) if no part of any charge for local advertising were excludable in computing taxable price	$103,000
2. Amounts billed as separate charges for local advertising	3,000
3. Difference	$100,000
4. Over-all 5 percent limitation (5 percent of item 3)	5,000
5. Amount excluded in computing taxable price	3,000
6. Unused portion of limitation	$2,000
7. Allocation, pursuant to agreement, of $5,500 paid to distributors:	
Charges for local advertising	$3,000
Contributions by manufacturer	2,500

Readjustment may be claimed in respect of that portion of the total amount repaid to the distributors which is allocated to the manufacturer's contribution ($2,500) to the extent that such portion does not exceed the unused portion of the over-all 5 percent limitation ($2,000). Accordingly, as of the close of the first calendar quarter the manufacturer may claim credit or refund in respect of a readjustment or price in the amount of $2,000.

Computation as of close of second calendar quarter

1. Amount which would constitute total taxable price (computed at time of sale) if no part of any charge for local advertising were excludable in computing taxable price ($103,000 + $154,000)	$257,000
2. Amounts billed as separate charges for local advertising ($3,000 + $4,000)	7,000
3. Difference	$250,000
4. Over-all 5 percent limitation (5 percent of item 3)	$12,500

5. Amount excluded in computing taxable price ($3,000 + $4,000) plus readjustment claimed at end of first calendar quarter ($2,000) 9,000

6. Unused portion of limitation . . . . $ 3,500

7. Allocation, pursuant to agreement, of $6,500 ($5,500 + $1,000) paid to distributors:

     Charges for local advertising $3,500

     Contributions by manufacturer 3,000

Although the total reimbursements for local advertising expenses attributable to contributions by the manufacturer ($3,000) does not exceed the unused portion of the over-all 5 percent limitation ($3,500), the manufacturer having taken, at the close of the first calendar quarter, a price readjustment in the amount of $2,000 in respect of his contributions is entitled at the close of the second quarter to claim credit or refund in re-

Articles taxable under section 4111 . . . .

Local advertising charges . . . .

         Total charge . . . .

Assume further that the manufacturer contributes to the advertising plan and that the manufacturer pays $3,000 during the first calendar quarter of 1961 to his distributors in reimburse-

spect of a price readjustment in the amount of $1,000 ($3,000 – $2,000).

Example (2). During the first calendar quarter of 1961, a manufacturer sold articles taxable under section 4111 to his distributors at a total charge of $106,000, exclusive of the tax, transportation charges, delivery charges, or other charges which are excludable, pursuant to section 4216(a), in computing taxable price. This total charge of $106,000 was billed as follows:

. . . . $100,000

. . . . 6,000

. . . . $106,000

ment of expenses incurred by them for local advertising of the articles purchased from the manufacturer.

Computation as of close of first calendar quarter

1. Amount which would constitute total taxable price (computed at time of sale) if no part of any charge for local advertising were excludable in computing taxable price $106,000

2. Amounts billed as separate charges for local advertising 6,000

3. Difference $100,000

4. Over-all 5 percent limitation (5 percent of item 3) . . . . $ 5,000

5. Amount excluded in computing taxable price (see paragraph (c) of §48.4216(e)-1) 5,000

6. Unused portion of limitation 0

7. Allocation, pursuant to agreement, of $3,000 paid to distributors:

     Charges for local advertising $2,000

     Contributions by manufacturer 1,000

Credit or refund may not be claimed in respect of that portion of the total amount repaid to the distributors ($3,000) which is allocated to the manufacturer's contribution ($1,000) since the amount excluded in computing taxable price is equal to the over-all 5 percent limitation. [Reg. §48.4216(e)-2.]

☐ [*T.D. 6635. Amended by T.D. 7536, 3-27-78.*]

[Reg. §48.4216(e)-3]

§48.4216(e)-3. No exclusion or readjustment for other advertising charges or reimbursements.—(a) *Exclusions from price.*—No exclusion in computing the taxable price of any article sold by the manufacturer may be allowed in respect of any charge for advertising if, and to the extent that, such charge—

(1) Is for advertising which does not qualify as local advertising within the meaning of section 4216(e)(4) and paragraphs (a) and (b) of §48.4216(e)-1, or

(2) Does not satisfy all of the conditions and limitations stated in section 4216(e)(1) and paragraph (c) of §48.4216(e)-1.

(b) *Readjustments of price.*—No credit or refund under section 6416(b)(1) may be allowed in respect of any amount which was included in the taxable price of an article sold by the manufacturer and which was later paid by him to his

vendee in reimbursement of costs incurred for advertising, if, and to the extent that, the amount so paid—

(1) Is for advertising which does not qualify as local advertising within the meaning of section 4216(e)(4) and paragraph (b) of §48.4216(e)-1, or

(2) Is not within the limitation provided in section or 4216(e)(2), as computed in accordance with §48.4216(e)-2, as of the close of the calendar quarter in which the amount is so paid over or as of the close of any subsequent calendar quarter in the same calendar year. See, however, paragraph (c)(2)(ii) of §48.6416(b)-1, relating to redetermination of price readjustments in cases where local advertising charges ,excluded from taxable price in one calendar year become taxable as of May 1 of the following calendar year. [Reg. §48.4216(e)-3.]

☐ [*T.D. 6635. Amended by T.D. 6686 and T.D. 7536, 3-27-78.*]

[Reg. §48.4216(f)-1]

§48.4216(f)-1. Value of used components excluded from price of certain trucks.—For purposes of the tax imposed by section 4061(a)(1) (relating to trucks, buses, etc.), in determining the price for which an article is sold, the value of any previously used component of such article shall be excluded from the price if the person furnishing the component is the first user of the finished article. For example, where a manufacturer builds a truck for a customer who intends to use, rather than resell the truck, incorporating used parts furnished by the customer, the value of the previously used parts shall not be included in the price for which the truck is considered sold by the manufacturer. [Reg. §48.4216(f)-1.]

☐ [T.D. 7536, 3-27-78.]

[Reg. §48.4217-1]

§48.4217-1. Lease considered as sale.—For purposes of chapter 32 of the Code, the lease of an article by a manufacturer, producer, or importer shall be considered a sale of the article. The term "lease" means a contract or agreement, written or verbal, which gives the lessee an exclusive, continuous right to the possession or use of a particular article for a period of time. The term includes any renewal or extension of a lease or any subsequent lease of the article. However, in the case of the lease of an automobile the sale of which by the manufacturer would be taxable under section 4064, the term includes only the first lease (excluding any renewal or extension of the lease) of such automobile by the manufacturer. [Reg. §48.4217-1.]

☐ [T.D. 7536, 3-27-78. Amended by T.D. 8036, 7-23-85.]

[Reg. §48.4217-2]

§48.4217-2. Limitation on amount of tax applicable to certain leases.—(a) *Conditions for eligibility.*—Section 4217(b) provides for a limitation on the amount of tax that shall apply to the lease, any renewal, or further lease, of an article which, if sold, would be subject to tax on the basis of sale price. Such limitation on the amount of the tax applies with respect to the lease of an article only if, at the time of making the lease, the lessor is engaged in the business of selling in arm's length transactions the same type and model of article. In case of a lease to which section 4217(b) does not apply, tax shall be computed and paid as provided in section 4216(c) and paragraph (a) of §48.4216(c)-1.

(b) *Lessor engaged in business of selling.*—The lessor will be regarded as being engaged in the business of selling in arm's length transactions the same type and model of an article as the one being leased if it periodically and recurringly makes bona fide offers for sale of such articles in the regular course of operation of its business, which offers if accepted would constitute sales at arm's length. Whether the offers are bona fide shall be determined on the basis of the facts in each case, such as sales actually made, the nature of the advertising, sales literature, and other means used to effectuate sales. It is not necessary that the offers for sale be made to the same class of purchasers as those to whom the article is being leased.

(c) *Same type and model of article.*—To qualify as the "same type and model of article", the article offered for sale must be an unused article essentially the same in size, design, and function

as the article being leased. For example, a van-type truck trailer would not be the same type and model as a stake-body of flat-bed truck trailer. Neither would a 25-foot van-type trailer be the same type and model as a 35-foot van-type trailer. Slight differences in appearance or accessories will not render articles dissimilar which are identical in all other respects.

(d) *Basis for tax.*—(1) *Tax payable until total tax is paid.*—In case of a lease of an article to which section 4217(b) applies, tax shall be paid on each lease payment in an amount computed by applying to such lease payment a percentage equal to the rate of tax in effect on the date of the lease payment. Such tax payments shall continue to be made under such lease, or any subsequent lease of the article, until the cumulative total of the tax payments equals the total tax. Lease payments made thereafter with respect to that article shall not be subject to tax. For definition of the term "total tax", see paragraph (e) of this section.

(2) *Changes in tax rates.*—Except as provided in—

(i) Section 701(a)(3) of the Excise Tax Reduction Act of 1965 (79 Stat. 155) in the case of certain reductions in tax rates effective June 22, 1965, or January 1, 1966, and

(ii) Section 401(h)(3) of the Revenue Act of 1971 (85 Stat. 534) in the case of certain reductions in tax rates effective December 11, 1971, if the rate of tax is increased or decreased during a lease period, the new rate shall apply to the lease payments made on and after the date of the change, but the amount of the total tax shall remain the same.

(e) *Total tax.*—For purposes of this section, the term "total tax" means the amount of tax, computed at the rate in effect on the date of the first lease of the article to which section 4217(b) applies, which would be due on the constructive sale price of the article as determined under section 4216(b) and §48.4216(b)-2, as if the article had been sold by a manufacturer at retail on such date.

(f) *Sale of article before total tax becomes payable.*—If the lessor sells the article before the total tax has become payable, the tax payable on the sale shall be the lesser of the following amounts—

(1) The difference between (i) the total tax, and (ii) the aggregate tax applicable to lease payments already received; or

(2) A tax computed, at the rate in effect on the date of the sale, on the price for which the article is sold.

For purposes of subparagraph (2) of this paragraph, the provisions of section 4216(b) for determining a constructive sale price shall not apply if the sale is at arm's length. If the sale is not at arm's length, the tax referred to in subparagraph (2) of this paragraph shall be computed on a constructive sale price as provided in §48.4216(b)-2.

(g) *Sale of article after total tax has become payable.*—If the lessor sells an article after the total tax has become payable, the tax imposed under chapter 32 of the Code shall not apply to such sale.

(h) *Special rules applicable to certain leases entered into before January 1, 1959.*—For purposes of this section, in the case of any lease entered into before, and existing on, January 1, 1959—

(1) Such lease shall be considered to have been entered into on January 1, 1959.

(2) The total tax shall be computed on the fair market value of the article on January 1, 1959.

(3) The lease payments under such lease shall include only payments attributable to periods beginning after December 31, 1958.

(i) *Cross-reference.*—In the case of the lease of an automobile the sale of which by the manufacturer would be taxable under section 4064, the foregoing provisions of this section shall not apply. See section 4217(e) for the rules relating to the payment of the gas guzzler tax. [Reg. §48.4217-2.]

☐ [*T.D. 7536, 3-27-78. Amended by T.D. 8036, 7-23-85.*]

[Reg. §48.4218-1]

§48.4218-1. Tax on use by manufacturer, producer, or importer.—(a) *In general.*—Section 4218 imposes tax in respect of certain uses of articles by the actual manufacturer, producer, or importer thereof. This section also applies in respect of the use of articles by any other person who, pursuant to a provision of chapter 32 of the Code, is considered to be, or is treated as, the manufacturer or producer of the articles. See, for example, section 4223 relating to articles purchased tax free for use in further manufacture.

(b) *Taxable articles in general.*—(1) *Application of tax.*—If the manufacturer, producer, or importer of an article taxable under chapter 32 of the Code (other than an article referred to in paragraph (c), (d), or (e) of this section) uses the article for any purpose other than that indicated in subparagraph (3) or (4) of this paragraph, he shall be liable for tax with respect to the use of such article in the same manner as if the article were sold by him.

(2) *Taxable use in manufacture of nontaxable articles.*—(i) *In general.*—In the case of an article to which subparagraph (1) of this paragraph applies, tax attaches when the manufacturer, producer, or importer of the article uses it as material in the manufacture or production of, or as a component part of, another article which is not taxable under chapter 32 of the Code, regardless of the disposition made of such other article. (See paragraph (c) of §48.4218-5 for computation of tax on such use.)

(ii) *Types of use in manufacture of nontaxable articles.*—Taxable use may consist of the incorporation of a taxable article, such as an electric light bulb, into a nontaxable article, such as a flashlight. Taxable use may also result from the combining of a taxable article (or the components thereof) with a nontaxable article (or the components of a nontaxable article) resulting in a combination end article which itself is not taxable. Although the taxable article may not be a completely separable unit, within the contemplation of the law a taxable article has been produced and incorporated in the combination end article. The following are examples of taxable articles so used:

(a) Household type electric or gas clothes drier incorporated in a combination washer-drier.

(b) Household type electric, gas, or oil cooking range combined either with a range using other means of heating or with a nontaxable space heater.

(c) Taxable radio receiving set incorporated in a combination radio receiver-transmitter or in a combination radio receiver-intercommunication system.

If an automobile part or accessory, radio or television component, or camera lens is used as material in the manufacture or production of, or as a component part of, a taxable article to which subparagraph (1) of this paragraph has application and such article in turn is used in the manufacture or production of, or as a component part of, a nontaxable article, the part or accessory, component, or lens is considered to have been used in the manufacture of the taxable article, and not in the manufacture of the nontaxable article. For example, the use of taxable radio components in the production of a taxable radio receiving set is exempt from tax (see paragraph (d) of this section), but the use of the radio receiving set in the production of a nontaxable combination radio receiver-transmitter is subject to tax. See section 6416(b)(2) or 6416(b)(3) and the regulations thereunder contained in Subpart O for credit or refund of tax paid in respect of such radio receiver if the combination radio receiver-transmitter is by any person exported, sold to a State or local government for its exclusive use, sold to a nonprofit educational organization for its exclusive use, or used or sold for use as supplies for vessels or aircraft.

(3) *Nontaxable use in manufacture of taxable articles.*—The tax on the use of an article to which subparagraph (1) of this paragraph has application shall not apply if the article is used by the manufacturer, producer, or importer thereof as material in the manufacture or production of, or as a component part of, another article taxable under chapter 32 to be manufactured or produced by him. It is immaterial what disposition is made of such other article.

(4) *Gasoline.*—The tax on the use of an article shall not apply in the case of gasoline used on or after October 1, 1961, by any person, for

nonfuel purposes, as a material in the manufacture or production of another article to be manufactured or produced by him. See section 4221 and the regulations thereunder contained in Subpart N. For provisions applicable to use of gasoline by a producer or importer otherwise than in the production of other gasoline, or special motor fuel taxable under section 4041(b), see section 4082(c) and paragraph (c) of § 48.4082-1 contained in Subpart H.

(c) *Tires, inner tubes, and automobile radio or television receiving sets.*—If the manufacturer, producer, or importer of a tire or inner tube taxable under section 4071 (other than a bicycle or inner tube referred to in paragraph (e) of this section), or an automobile radio or television receiving set taxable under section 4141, sells such article on or in connection with the sale of any other article or uses it for any purpose, he shall be liable for tax with respect to such tire, inner tube, or radio or television receiving set in the same manner as if it were sold by him as a separate article. However, tax does not apply where the manufacturer, producer, or importer of the tire, inner tube, or automobile radio or television receiving set sells such article on or in connection with the sale of another article manufactured by him for any of the exempt purposes specified in paragraphs (2) to (5), inclusive, of section 4221(a) and the regulations thereunder contained in Subpart N.

(d) *Automobile parts or accessories, radio or television components, and camera lenses.*—(1) *Application of tax.*—If the manufacturer, producer, or importer of an automobile part or accessory taxable under section 4061(b), a radio or television component taxable under section 4141, or a camera lens taxable under section 4171, uses the article for any purpose other than that indicated in subparagraph (2) of this paragraph, he shall be liable for tax with respect to the use of the article in the same manner as if the article were sold by him. For example, tax applies if the manufacturer, producer, or importer uses the article referred to in this subparagraph for repair or replacement purposes in connection with equipment used by him in the operation of his business.

(2) *Nontaxable use in manufacture of other articles.*—The tax on the use of an article referred to in subparagraph (1) of this paragraph shall not apply if the article is used by the manufacturer, producer, or importer thereof as material in the manufacture or production of, or as a component part of, any other article (whether or not taxable under chapter 32) to be manufactured or produced by him. It is immaterial what disposition is made of such other article.

(e) *Bicycle tires and inner tubes.*—(1) *Application of tax.*—If the manufacturer, producer, or importer of a bicycle tire as defined in section 4221(e)(4)(B) or an inner tube for such tire uses the tire or inner tube for any purpose other than as indicated in subparagraph (2) of this paragraph, he shall be liable for tax with respect to the use of the tire or inner tube in the same manner as if the article were sold by him.

(2) *Nontaxable use in manufacture of other articles.*—The tax on the use of a bicycle tire or inner tube referred to in subparagraph (1) of this paragraph shall not apply if the tire or inner tube is used by the manufacturer, producer, or importer thereof as material in the manufacture or production of, or as a component part of, a new bicycle to be manufactured or produced by him. It is immaterial what disposition is made of the new bicycle. Tax, however, applies in the case of the use of a bicycle tire or inner tube by the manufacturer, producer, or importer thereof in the rebuilding or reconditioning of a used bicycle.

(3) *Effective date.*—The provisions of this paragraph shall apply to the use on or after May 1, 1960, of a bicycle tire or inner tube by the manufacturer, producer, or importer thereof. Liability for tax on the use prior to that date of a bicycle tire or inner tube by the manufacturer, producer, or importer thereof shall be based on the provisions of paragraph (c) of this section which apply to tires and inner tubes in general.

(f) *Use after lease.*—If the manufacturer, producer, or importer of a taxable article leases such article and thereafter uses the article, he incurs liability for tax on such use as provided in these regulations to the same extent as if the article were sold after being leased. See section 4217 and the regulations thereunder in this subpart for application and computation of tax in case of leased articles.

(g) *Time of application of tax.*—In the case of a taxable use of an article by the manufacturer, producer, or importer thereof, the tax attaches at the time such use begins. If tax applies by reason of the sale of an article by the manufacturer, producer, or importer thereof on or in connection with his sale of another article, the tax attaches at the time of the sale of such other article.

(h) *Exemption because of other statutory provisions.*—Tax does not apply on the use of an article by the manufacturer, producer, or importer thereof if under the applicable provisions of the Code the sale of the article for a similar use would not be subject to tax. For example, the use of gasoline by the producer thereof to propel tankers engaged in foreign trade which are owned or leased by the producer would not be subject to tax under section 4218 since a sale for such use would be exempt from tax as provided in section 4221(a)(3). Also, tax need not be paid with respect to the use of an article by the manufacturer, producer, or importer thereof if such use would qualify, under the provisions of section 6416(b), for credit or refund of the tax paid. [Reg. § 48.4218-1.]

☐ [T.D. 6687.]

[Reg. § 48.4218-2]

§ 48.4218-2. Business or personal use of articles.—(a) *Business use.*—Section 4218 applies to the use by a person, in the operation of any business in which he is engaged of a taxable article which has been manufactured, produced, or imported by him or his agent. For example, a person engaged in the operation of a dairy business incurs liability for tax with respect to a truck body manufactured by him and used in the operation of his dairy business.

(b) *Personal use.*—The tax on use of a taxable article does not attach in cases where an individual incidentally manufactures, produces, or imports a taxable article for his personal use or causes a taxable article to be manufactured, produced, or imported for his personal use. [Reg. § 48.4218-2.]

☐ [*T.D. 6687.*]

[Reg. § 48.4218-3]

§ 48.4218-3. Events subsequent to taxable use of article.—Liability for tax incurred on the use of an article is not extinguished or reduced because of any subsequent sale or lease of the article even if such sale or lease would have been exempt if the article had been so sold or leased prior to use. If a manufacturer, producer, or importer of an article incurs liability for tax on his use thereof, and thereafter sells or leases the article in a transaction which otherwise would be subject to tax, liability for tax is not incurred on such sale or lease. [Reg. § 48.4218-3.]

☐ [*T.D. 6687.*]

[Reg. § 48.4218-4]

§ 48.4218-4. Use in further manufacture.—For purposes of section 4218 and § 48.4218-1, an article is used as material in the manufacture or production of, or as a component part of, another article, if it is incorporated in, or is a part or accessory of, the other article. Lubricating oil in the crankcase of a new truck is an example of a taxable article used as material in the manufacture or production of, or as a component part of, another article. In addition, an article (other than gasoline used as a fuel) is considered to be used as material in the manufacture of another article if it is partly or entirely consumed in testing such other article; for example, shells or cartridges used in testing new firearms. Similarly, if an article is partly or wholly consumed in quality testing a production run of like articles (as, for example, an automotive part destroyed in stress testing) such article is also considered to have been used as material in the manufacture of another article. However, if a taxable article that has been used tax free and only partly consumed in testing is later sold, or put to a taxable use, by the manufacturer, tax attaches to such sale or use. An article that is consumed in the manufacturing process other than in testing, so that it is not a physical part of the manufactured article, is not used as material in the manufacture or production of, or as a component part of, such other article. Thus, lubricating oil consumed in operating plant machinery in the course of the manufacture of automobile trucks chasis is not used as material in the manufacture or production of, or as a component part of, the truck chassis. [Reg. § 48.4218-4.]

☐ [*T.D. 6687. Amended by T.D. 7536, 3-27-78.*]

[Reg. § 48.4218-5]

§ 48.4218-5. Computation of tax.—(a) *Tax based on price.*—Except as provided in paragraph (d) of this section, tax liability incurred on the use of an article shall be computed on the price at which such or similar articles are sold in the ordinary course of trade by manufacturers, producers, or importers thereof and in the absence of special arrangements. For additional provisions applicable in computing the tax in the case of the use of an article by a manufacturer or producer who purchased the article free of tax under section 4221(a)(1) for use by him in further manufacture, see section 4223(b) and the regulations thereunder.

(b) *Articles regularly sold by manufacturer.*—If the manufacturer, producer, or importer of an article regularly sells such articles at wholesale in arm's length transactions, tax liability on his use of any such article shall be computed on his lowest established wholesale price for such articles in effect at the time of the taxable use. In establishing such price, there shall be included and excluded, as applicable, the charges and readjustments specified in sections 4216(a), 4216(f), and 6416(b)(1), as in effect at the time tax liability on the use of the article is incurred, and the regulations thereunder contained in this subpart and subpart O. If the manufacturer, producer, or importer of an article does not regularly sell such articles at wholesale in arm's length transactions, a constructive price on which the use tax shall be computed will be determined by the Commissioner. This price will be established after considering the selling practices and price structures of manufacturers, producers, and importers of similar articles.

(c) *Articles governed by section 4218(a) used in manufacture of nontaxable combination articles.*—If the manufacturer, producer, or importer of an article to which section 4218(a) applies does not regularly sell such article separately but uses it as material in the manufacture or production of, or as a component part of, a nontaxable combination article consisting of a taxable and nontaxable article, liabillity for tax on his use shall be computed on the constructive price of the taxable article at the time of use. To determine the constructive price of the taxable article in such case, the combination article is considered to be composed of (1) parts used exclusively in the functioning of the taxable article in the combination, (2) parts used exclusively in the functioning of the nontaxable article in the combination, and (3) parts, called common parts, which serve a dual function in connection with the parts in both subparagraphs (1) and (2) of this paragraph. The ratio which the cost of the parts in subparagraph (1) of this paragraph bears to the sum of the cost of such parts and the parts in subparagraph (2) of this paragraph is applied to the lowest established wholesale price for which like combination articles are at the time of the taxable use being sold by the manufacturer or producer in the ordinary course of trade. The resulting amount is the constructive sale price for the taxable article on which tax is to be computed. The cost of the common parts is allocable to the parts in subparagraphs (1) and (2) of this paragraph in the same ratio, and, therefore, need not be taken into account in the computation since the inclusion and allocation of the cost of such parts in the determination would not result in a different ratio. In determining the lowest established wholesale price for the combination article, there shall be included and excluded, as applicable, the charges and readjustments specified in sections 4216(a), 4216(f), and 6416(b)(1), as in effect at the time tax liability on the use of the taxable article is incurred, and the regulations thereunder contained in this subpart and subpart O of this part. The tax applicable to the use of the article for which a constructive sale price has been computed is not affected by any charges or readjustments of the price for which the nontaxable combination article is sold, whether by reason of the return or repossession of the nontaxable article or its covering or container, or by a bona fide discount, rebate, allowance, or other factor. The application of this subparagraph may be illustrated by the following example:

Example. A manufacturer of a nontaxable washer-drier combination produces and uses an electric clothes drier taxable under section 4121 in the manufacture of the combination article. The lowest established wholesale price of the manufacturer for the washer-drier combination at the time of the taxable use is $150 with respect to identical combinations after including and excluding applicable charges and readjustments. The manufacturer does not regularly sell such drier separately. In the manufacture of the washer-drier the two units are integrated to the extent that certain component parts function both in the operation of the washer and of the drier. The parts used exclusively in the operation of the washer cost $30 and those used exclusively in the operation of the drier cost $20. The taxable cost ratio in this instance is 20/50, or 40 percent. Applying 40 percent to the manufacturer's lowest established wholesale price of $150 for the washer-drier results in $60 as the constructive price for the taxable article in the combination at the time tax liability is incurred. No additional charges or readjustments in connection with, or subsequent to, the sale of the washer-drier combination may affect the tax liability incurred at the time of use.

(d) *Tax based on weight or volume.*—Where liability for tax is incurred on the use of an article subject, if sold, to a tax based on—

(1) the weight of the article (such as a tire), or

(2) the volume of the article (such as gasoline or lubricating oil), the tax due shall be computed on the basis which would be applicable if such article were sold. [Reg. § 48.4218-5.]

☐ [*T.D.* 6687, 11-4-63.]

[Reg. § 48.4219-1]

§ 48.4219-1. Sale of taxable articles by a person other than the manufacturer, producer, or importer.—(a) *General rule.*—If the title to, or ownership of, an article taxable under chapter 32 of the Code is transferred from the manufacturer, producer, or importer thereof, and, under the law, no tax attaches to such transfer, the subsequent sale, lease, or use of such article by the transferee is subject to tax to the same extent and in the same manner as if such transferee were the manufacturer, producer, or importer of the article. The following examples illustrate this rule:

(1) The surviving spouse, child or children, executors or administrators, or other legal representatives, as the case may be, of a deceased manufacturer, producer, or importer of taxable articles, incur liability for tax on all such articles sold by them.

(2) A receiver or trustee in a bankruptcy who under a court order conducts or liquidates the business of a manufacturer, producer, or importer of taxable articles, incurs liability for tax on all taxable articles sold by him, regardless of whether the articles were manufactured, produced, or imported before or after he took charge of the business.

(3) An assignee for the benefit of creditors of a manufacturer, producer, or importer incurs liability for tax with respect to all taxable articles sold by him as such assignee.

(4) If one or more members of a partnership withdraw, or if new partners are admitted, the new partnership so constituted incurs liability for tax on all taxable articles sold by it regardless of when such articles were manufactured, produced, or imported.

(5) A person who acquires title to taxable articles as a result of default of the manufacturer, producer, or importer pursuant to an agreement under the terms of which the articles were pledged as collateral incurs liability of tax with respect to his sale of the articles so acquired.

(6) A person who succeeds to the business of a manufacturer, producer, or importer of taxable articles, such as—

(i) a corporation which results from a consolidation, merger, or reorganization;

(ii) a corporation which acquires the business of an individual or partnership; or

(iii) a stockholder in a corporation who, after its dissolution, continues the business; incurs liability for tax on all taxable articles sold by such person. However, where a manufacturer, producer, or importer sells only his assets, rather than ownership of his business, he incurs liability for tax on the sale of any taxable articles included in such assets.

(b) *Transfer of title to damaged articles.*—If title to a damaged taxable article is transferred by the manufacturer, producer, or importer thereof to a carrier or insurance company in adjustment of a damage claim, such transfer is not considered a taxable sale of the article. If the article is usable, even though damaged, the carrier or insurance company incurs liability for tax on its sale, lease, or use of the article. Where the article has been damaged to the extent that its only value is as scrap, and it is not restored to usable condition, sale thereof by the carrier or insurance company is not subject to tax. [Reg. § 48.4219-1.]

☐ [T.D. 6687, 11-4-63.]

[Reg. § 48.4221-1]

§ 48.4221-1. Tax-free sales; general rule.— (a) *Application of regulations under section 4221.—* (1) *In general.*—The regulations under section 4221 provide rules under which the manufacturer, producer, or importer of an article subject to tax under chapter 32 (or the retailer of an article subject to tax under subchapter A or C of chapter 31) may sell the article tax free under section 4221.

(2) *Limitations.*—The following restrictions must be taken into account in applying the regulations under section 4221:

(i) The exemptions under section 4221(a)(4) and (a)(5) do not apply to the tax imposed by section 4064 (gas guzzler tax).

(ii) The exemptions under section 4221 do not apply to the tax imposed by section 4081 (taxable fuel tax).

(iii) The exemptions under section 4221 do not apply to the tax imposed by section 4091 (aviation fuel tax). For rules relating to tax-free sales of aviation fuel, see section 4092 and the regulations thereunder.

(iv) The exemptions under section 4221 do not apply to the tax imposed by section 4121 (coal tax).

(v) The exemptions under section 4221(a)(3) through (a)(5) do not apply to the tax imposed by section 4131 (vaccine tax). In addition, the exemption under section 4221(a)(2) applies to the vaccine tax only to the extent provided in § 48.4221-3(e) (relating to tax-free sales of vaccine for export).

(vi) The exemptions under section 4221(a) apply only in those cases where the exportation or use referred to is to occur before any other use.

(vii) The exemptions under section 4221(a)(3) through (a)(6) do not apply to the tax imposed by section 4191 (medical device tax).

(b) *Manufacturer relieved of liability in certain cases.*—(1) *General rule.*—Under the provisions of section 4221(c), if an article subject to tax under chapter 32 of the Code is sold free of tax by the manufacturer of the article for an exempt purpose referred to in section 4221(c) and paragraph (b)(2) of this section, the manufacturer shall be relieved of any tax liability under chapter 32 with respect to such sale if the manufacturer in good faith accepts a proper certification by the purchaser that the article or articles will be used by the purchaser in the stated exempt manner. See paragraph (b)(2) of this section for a list of the exempt purposes referred to in section 4221(c).

(2) The following are situations wherein section 4221(c) is applicable with respect to sales made tax free on the assumption that one of the following sections of the Code provides exemption for such sales:

(i) Section 4221(a)(1), to the extent that it relates to sales for further manufacture by a first purchaser (see § 48.4221-2),

(ii) Section 4221(a)(3), relating to supplies for vessels and aircraft (see § 48.4221-4),

(iii) Section 4221(a)(4), relating to sales to State or local governments (see § 48.4221-5),

(iv) Section 4221(a)(5), relating to sales to nonprofit educational organizations (see § 48.4221-6), and

(v) Section 4221(e)(3), relating to the sale of tires used on intercity, local, or school buses (see § 48.4221-8).

(3) *Duty of seller to ascertain validity of tax-free sale.*—If the manufacturer at the time of its sale has reason to believe that the article sold by it is not intended for the exempt purpose indicated by the purchaser, or that the purchaser has failed to register as required, the manufacturer is not considered to have accepted certification from the purchaser in good faith, and is not relieved from liability under the provisions of section 4221(c).

(4) *Information to be furnished to purchaser.*— A manufacturer selling articles free of tax under this section after December 31, 1978, shall indicate to the purchaser that (i) certain articles normally subject to tax are being sold tax free and (ii) the purchaser is obtaining those articles tax free for an exempt purpose under an exemption certificate or its equivalent. The manufacturer may transmit this information by any convenient means, such as coding of sales invoices, provided that the information is presented with sufficient particularity so that the purchaser is informed that he has obtained the articles tax free and—

(i) The purchaser can compute and remit the tax due if an article sold tax free for further manufacture is diverted to a taxable use,

(ii) The manufacturer can remit the tax due with respect to an article purchased tax free for resale for use in further manufacture or for export if, within the 6-month period described in § 48.4221-2(c) or § 48.4221-3(c), the manufacturer does not receive proof that the article has been exported or resold for use in further manufacture, or

(iii) The purchaser can notify the manufacturer if an article otherwise purchased tax free is diverted to a taxable use.

Reg. § 48.4221-1(b)(4)(iii)

(c) *Evidence required in support of tax-free sales.*—(1) *Purchasers required to be registered.*—Every purchaser who is required to be registered (see §48.4222(a)-1) shall furnish to the seller, as evidence in support of each tax-free sale made by the seller to such purchaser, the exempt purpose for which the article or articles are being purchased and the registration number of the purchaser. Such information must be in writing and may be noted on the purchase order or other document furnished by the purchaser to the seller in connection with each sale.

(2) *Purchasers not required to be registered.*—For the evidence which purchasers not required to register must furnish to the seller in support of each tax-free sale made by the seller to such purchasers, see paragraph (b) of §48.4221-3 for sales or resales to a foreign purchaser for export, paragraph (d) of §48.4221-4 for sales of supplies to vessels or aircraft, paragraph (c) of §48.4221-5 for sales to State and local governments, and paragraph (c) of §48.4222(b)-1 for sales and purchases by the United States. [Reg. §48.4221-1.]

☐ [*T.D. 7536, 3-27-78. Amended by T.D. 8036, 7-23-85; T.D. 8659, 3-13-96; T.D. 8879, 3-30-2000 and T.D. 9604, 12-5-2012.*]

[Reg. §48.4221-2]

§48.4221-2. Tax-free sale of articles to be used for, or resold for, further manufacture.—(a) *Further manufacture.*—(1) *In general.*—Under prescribed conditions, an article subject to tax under chapter 32 (other than a tire taxable under section 4071, which is given special treatment under section 4221(e)(2) and §48.4221-7) may be sold tax free by the manufacturer, pursuant to section 4221(a)(1), for use by the purchaser in further manufacture, or for resale by the purchaser to a second purchaser for use by the second purchaser in further manufacture. See section 4221(d)(6) and paragraph (b) of this section for the circumstances under which an article is considered to have been sold for use in further manufacture. See section 6416(b)(3) and §48.6416(b)-3 for the circumstances under which credit or refund is available when tax-paid articles are used in further manufacture.

(2) *Proof of resale for use in further manufacture.*—See section 4221(b)(1) and paragraph (c) of this section for provisions under which the exemption provided in section 4221(a)(1) shall cease to apply in the case of an article sold by the manufacturer to a purchaser for resale to a second purchaser for use in further manufacture unless the manufacturer receives timely proof of resale for further manufacture.

(b) *Circumstances under which an article is considered to have been sold for use in further manufacture.*—(1) An article shall be treated as sold for use in further manufacture if the article is sold for use by the buyer as material in the manufacture or production of, or as a component part of, another article taxable under chapter 32 of the Internal Revenue Code.

(2) An article is used as material in the manufacture or production of, or as a component of, another article if it is incorporated in, or is a part or accessory of, the other article when the other article is sold by the manufacturer. In addition, an article is considered to be used as material in the manufacture of another article if it is consumed in whole or in part in testing such other article. However, an article that is consumed in the manufacturing process other than in testing, so that it is not a physical part of the manufactured article, is not considered to have been used as material in the manufacture of, or as a component part of, another article.

(c) *Proof of resale for further manufacture.*—(1) *Cessation of exemption.*—The exemption provided in section 4221(a)(1) and described in paragraph (a) of this section in respect of an article sold by the manufacturer to a purchaser for resale to a second purchaser for use by the second purchaser in further manufacture shall cease to apply on the first day following the close of the 6-month period which begins on the date of sale of such article by the manufacturer, or the date of shipment of the article by the manufacturer, whichever is earlier, unless, within such 6-month period, the manufacturer receives proof, in the form prescribed by paragraph (c)(2) of this section, that the article was actually resold by the purchaser to a second purchaser for such use. If, on the first day following the close of the 6-month period, such proof has not been received, the manufacturer shall become liable for tax at that time at the rate in effect when the sale was made but otherwise in the same manner as if the article had been sold by it on such first day at a taxable price equivalent to that at which the article was actually sold. If the manufacturer later obtains such proof, it may file a claim for refund or credit of this tax. The payment of this tax by the manufacturer is not considered an overpayment by the subsequent manufacturer or producer for which the subsequent manufacturer or producer is entitled to a credit or refund under section 6416(b)(3). See section 4221(d)(6) and paragraph (b) of this section for the circumstances under which an article is considered to have been sold for use in further manufacture.

(2) *Proof of resale.*—(i) *Certificate of purchaser.*—The proof of resale to be received by the manufacturer, as required under section 4221(b)(1), may consist of either a copy of the invoice of the manufacturer's vendee directed to his purchaser which discloses the certificate of registry number held by each party or a statement described below. In the case of an invoice of manufacturer's vendee, it must appear from such invoice (or by statement attached thereto) that the article was in fact resold for use in further manufacture. In lieu of such an invoice, proof of resale may consist of a statement, executed and signed by the manufacturer's vendee. Such statement shall be in substantially the following form:

STATEMENT OF MANUFACTURER'S VENDEE
(To support tax-free sales of taxable articles to a purchaser for resale to a second purchaser for use in further manufacture (section 4221(a)(1) of the Internal Revenue Code).)

. . . . .Date, 19.

The undersigned, or the (Name of manufacturer's vendee if other than undersigned). . . .
. . . . of which I am (Title). . . . . holds certificate of registry No.. . . . ,
issued by the District Director of Internal Revenue

at. . . . .

The article or articles specified below or on the reverse side thereof were purchased tax free by me, or by (Name of manufacturer's vendee if other than undersigned) . . . .
. . . . , on (Date) . . . . and were thereafter resold to a purchaser who holds certificate of registry No.. . . . . , issued by the District Director of Internal Revenue at . .
. . . . , for use by it as material in the manufacture or production of, or as a component part or parts of, an article or articles taxable under chapter 32 of the Internal Revenue Code, or, if the article or articles are automobile parts or accessories (to which section 4061(b) applies) or gasoline, for use by it as material (for nonfuel uses in the case of gasoline) in the manufacture or production of, or as a component part or parts of, any article or articles.

The undersigned, or (Name of manufacturer's vendee if other than undersigned) . . . . . .
. . . . , has in my/its possession proof of tax-free resale of such article or articles in the form of related purchase orders and sales invoices, and proof of tax-free resale will be retained by me or (Name of manufacturer's vendee if other than undersigned) . . . .
. . . ., for at least 3 years from the date of this statement, and will be made readily available for inspection by Government officers during such 3-year period.

I have not previously executed a statement in respect of such certificate of resale, and I understand that the fraudulent use of this statement may subject me and all parties making such fraudulent use of this statement to a fine of not more than $10,000, or imprisonment for not more than five years, or both, together with the costs of prosecution.

(Signature). . . . .
(Address). . . . .

(ii) *Period covered.*—Any statement executed and signed by the manufacturer's vendee, as provided in subdivision (i) of this paragraph (c)(2), may be executed with respect to any one or more articles purchased tax free from a manufacturer and resold for use in further manufacture within the 6-month period prescribed in section 4221(a)(1) and paragraph (c)(1) of this section. Such statement (or other prescribed proof of resale) must be retained for inspection by the district director as provided in section 6001. [Reg. § 48.4221-2.]

☐ [T.D. 7536, 3-27-78. *Amended by* T.D. 7681, 2-29-80; T.D. 7753, 1-13-81; T.D. 7882, 3-30-83 *and* T.D. 8659, 3-13-96.]

[Reg. § 48.4221-3]

§ 48.4221-3. Tax-free sale of articles for export, or for resale by the purchaser to a second purchaser for export.—(a) *In general.*—(1) An article subject to tax under chapter 32 of the Code may be sold tax free by the manufacturer, pursuant to section 4221(a)(2) and this section, for export, or for resale by the purchaser to a second purchaser for export. See paragraph (a)(10) of § 48.0-2 for the meaning of the term "export". An article may be sold tax free by the manufacturer under the provisions of this section only if the person to whom the manufacturer sells the article intends either to export the article or to resell it to a person who intends to export it. An article may not be sold tax free under the provisions of this section by a manufacturer to a purchaser for resale to a second purchaser which does not intend to export the article itself but plans to resell it to a third purchaser for export. See section 6416(b)(2)(A) and paragraph (b)(1) of § 48.6416(b)-2 for the circumstances under which credit or refund of tax is available where tax-paid articles are exported from the United States.

(2) If an article, otherwise taxable under chapter 32 of the Code—

(i) Is sold tax free by the manufacturer pursuant to section 4221(a)(2) and this section, and

(ii) Is returned subsequently to the United States in an unused and undamaged condition,

then the importer is liable for the tax imposed by chapter 32 on the subsequent sale or use of the article in the United States. The provisions of this paragraph (a)(2) may be illustrated by the following examples:

Example (1). Q, a U.S. motor vehicle manufacturer, previously sold a truck chassis to R, a company in Canada. The sale was tax free under section 4221(a)(2). R mounted a truck body on the truck chassis and sold the completed vehicle to S. Thereafter S sold the completed new vehicle to T who imported the vehicle into the United States and sold it. The sale of the completed truck subjects T to an excise tax liability under section 4061(a)(1) with respect to both the body and the chassis.

Example (2). X, a U.S. manufacturer of trucks, sold a trash collection truck to Y, a company in France. The sale was tax free under section 4221(a)(2). The truck was sold by Y to the City of Nice, France. After initial use, the city determined that the truck was not suited for its needs and resold the truck to X. X returned the truck to the United States where it was resold. The resale of the truck by X does not subject X to an excise tax liability under section 4061(a)(1).

(b) *Sales or resales to a foreign purchaser for export.*—In the case of sales or resales to a foreign purchaser for export, where the first purchaser or the second purchaser is located in a foreign country or possession of the United States, such purchaser is not required to register as provided in section 4222(a) and § 48.4222(a)-1. To establish the right to sell articles tax free for export to a purchaser who is not registered and who is located in a foreign country or a possession of the United States, the manufacturer must obtain from such purchaser at the time title to the article passes or at the time of shipment, whichever is earlier, either:

(1) A written order or contract of sale showing that the manufacturer is to ship the article to a foreign destination; or

(2) Where delivery by the manufacturer is to be made within the United States, a statement from the purchaser showing:

(i) That the article is purchased either to fill existing or future orders for delivery to a foreign destination or for resale to another person engaged in the business of exporting who will export the article, and

(ii) That such article will be transported to its foreign destination in due course prior to use or further manufacture and prior to any resale except for export.

See section 4221(b) and paragraphs (c) and (d) of this section for requirements as to timely proof of exportation and cessation of the exemption for export unless the evidence to show actual exportation has been received by the manufacturer.

(c) *Cessation of exemption.*—The exemption provided in section 4221(a)(2) and paragraph (a) of this section for an article sold by the manufacturer for export or for resale by the purchaser to a second purchaser for export shall cease to apply on the first day following the close of the 6-month period which begins on the date of the sale of the article by the manufacturer, or the date of shipment of the article by the manufacturer, whichever is earlier, unless within the

6-month period the manufacturer receives proof, in the form prescribed by paragraph (d) of this section, that the article was actually exported. If, on the first day following the close of the 6-month period, the proof has not been received, the manufacturer shall become liable for tax at that time at the rate in effect when the sale was made but otherwise in the same manner as if the article had been sold by it on such first day at a taxable price equivalent to that at which the article was actually sold.

(d) *Proof of exportation.*—(1) Exportation may be evidenced by:

(i) A copy of the export bill of lading issued by the delivering carrier,

(ii) A certificate by the agent or representative of the export carrier showing actual exportation of the article,

(iii) A certificate of lading signed by a customs officer of the foreign country to which the article is exported,

(iv) Where the foreign country has no customs administration, a statement of the foreign consignee showing receipt of the article, or

(v) Where a department or agency of the United States Government is unable to furnish any one of the foregoing four types of proof of exportation, a statement or certification on the department or agency stationery, executed by an authorized officer, that the listed or identified articles have, in fact, been exported.

(2) In any case where the manufacturer is not the exporter, the manufacturer must have in its possession a statement from the vendee to whom the manufacturer sold the article stating that the article was in fact exported in due course by the vendee or was sold to another person who in due course exported the article. The statement must state what evidence is available to establish that the article was in fact exported in due course prior to use or further manufacture and prior to resale in the United States other than for export. Such evidence must be that described in paragraph (d)(1) of this section, and the statement must show where such evidence is readily available for inspection by Government officers, and should be in substantially the following form:

STATEMENT OF MANUFACTURER'S VENDEE

(To support tax-free sales of taxable articles to a purchaser for export or for resale to a second purchaser for export (section 4221(a)(2) of the Internal Revenue Code).)

The undersigned, or the (Name of manufacturer's vendee if other than undersigned) . . . . of which I am (Title) . . . . , holds certificate of registry No. . . . , issued by the District Director of Internal Revenue at . . . .

The article or articles specified below or on the reverse side hereof were purchased tax free by me or by (Name of manufacturer's vendee if other than undersigned) . . . . on (Date) . . . . , and were thereafter exported.

The undersigned or (Name of manufacturer's vendee if other than undersigned) . . . . has in my/its possession proof of exportation in respect of such article or articles. The evidence of export available is . . . . and is located at (If other than address below) . . . .

Such proof of exportation will be retained by (Name of manufacturer's vendee) for at least three years from the date of this statement and will be made readily available for inspection by Government officers.

I have not previously executed a statement in respect of the article or articles covered by this statement, and I understand that the fraudulent use of this statement will subject me and all parties making such fraudulent use of this statement to a fine of not more than $10,000, or imprisonment for not more than five years, or both, together with the costs of prosecution.

.................(Signature)
.................(Address)
.................(Date)

(3) The statement executed and signed by the manufacturer's vendee, as provided in paragraph (d)(2) of this section, may be executed with respect to any one or more articles purchased tax free from a manufacturer and exported within the 6-month period prescribed in section 4221(b)(2) and paragraph (c) of this section. Such statement shall be kept for inspection by the district director as provided in section 6001 and the regulations thereunder.

(e) *Vaccines.*—The exemption provided by section 4221(a)(2) applies after August 10, 1993, to the tax imposed on vaccines by section 4131, but only if—

(1) The vaccine is sold by the manufacturer after August 10, 1993; and

(2) In the case of vaccine sold to, or sold for resale to, the United States or any of its agencies or instrumentalities, the United States or such agency or instrumentality notifies the manufacturer that the vaccine is intended for uses other than the vaccination of persons described in 42 U.S.C. 300aa-11(c)(1)(B)(i)(II) (relating to certain U.S. citizens who are vaccinated outside the United States). [Reg. § 48.4221-3.]

☐ *[T.D. 7536, 3-27-78. Amended by T.D. 7729 and T.D. 8561, 8-19-94.]*

[Reg. § 48.4221-4]

§ 48.4221-4. Tax-free sale of articles by the purchaser as supplies for vessels or aircraft.— (a) *Supplies for vessels or aircraft.*—(1) *In general.*—An article subject to tax under chapter 32 may be sold tax free by the manufacturer, pursuant to section 4221(a)(3) and this section, for use by the purchaser as supplies for vessels or aircraft. See paragraph (b) of this section for the meaning of the term "supplies for vessels or aircraft." An article may be sold tax free under the provisions of this section only in those cases where the sale of an article by the manufacturer is made directly to the owner, officer, charterer, or authorized agent of a vessel or aifcraft for use as supplies for the vessel or aircraft. No sale may be made tax free to a dealer for resale for use as supplies for vessels or aircraft, even though it is known at the time of sale by the manufacturer that the article will be so resold. See section 6416(b)(2)(B) and paragraph (b)(2) of § 48.6416(b)-2 for circumstances under which credit or refund of tax is available where taxpaid articles are used, or sold for use, as supplies for vessels or aircraft. An article may not be sold tax free under the provisions of this section by the manufacturer to passengers or members of the crew of a vessel or aircraft.

(2) *Civil aircraft of foreign registry.*—In the case of any article sold by the manufacturer for use by the purchaser as supplies for civil aircraft of foreign registry employed in foreign trade or in trade between the United States and any of its possessions, the provisions of this paragraph apply only if the reciprocity requirements of section 4221(e)(1) are met. See paragraph (c) of this section.

(b) *Meaning of terms.*—(1) *Supplies for vessels or aircraft.*—The term "supplies for vessels or aircraft" means fuel supplies, ships' stores, sea stores, or legitimate equipment on vessels of war of the United States or of any foreign nation, vessels employed in the fisheries or in the whaling business, or vessels actually engaged in foreign trade between the Atlantic and Pacific ports of the United States or between the United States and any of its possessions.

(2) *Fuel supplies, ships' stores, and legitimate equipment.*—The terms "fuel supplies", "ships' stores", and "legitimate equipment" include all articles, materials, supplies, and equipment necessary for the navigation, propulsion, and upkeep of vessels of war of the United States or of any foreign nation, vessels employed in the fisheries or in the whaling business, or vessels actually engaged in foreign trade or in trade between the Atlantic and Pacific ports of the United States or between the United States and any of its possessions, even though such vessels may make intermediate stops in the United States. The term does not include supplies for vessels engaged in trade (i) between domestic ports in the Atlantic Ocean and the Gulf of Mexico, (ii) between domestic ports on the Pacific Ocean, (iii) between domestic ports on the Great Lakes, or (iv) on the inland waterways of the United States.

(3) *Sea stores.*—The term "sea stores" includes any article purchased for use or consumption by the passengers or crew, or both, of a vessel during its voyage.

(4) *Vessels.*—The term "vessels" includes (i) every description of watercraft or other contrivance used, or capable of being used, as a means of transportation on water, (ii) civil aircraft registered in the United States and employed in foreign trade or in trade between the United States and any of its possessions, and (iii) civil aircraft registered in a foreign country and employed in foreign trade or in trade between the United States and any of its possessions.

(5) *Vessels of war of the United States or of any foreign nation.*—The term "vessels of war of the United States or of any foreign nation" includes (i) every description of watercraft or other contri-

vance used, or capable of being used, as a means of transportation on water and constituting equipment of the armed forces (including the U.S. Coast Guard and U.S. National Guard) of the United States or of a foreign nation, and (ii) aircraft owned by the United States or by any foreign nation and constituting equipment of the armed forces thereof. For purposes of this section, vessels or aircraft owned by armed forces are not considered to be equipment of such armed forces while on lease or loan to an organization that is not part of the armed forces.

(6) *Vessels used in fisheries or whaling business.*—The exemption provided by section 4221(a)(3) and paragraph (a) of this section in the case of articles sold for the prescribed use on vessels employed in the fisheries or whaling business is limited to articles sold by the manufacturer for such use on vessels while employed, and to the extent employed, exclusively in the fisheries or in the whaling business. For purposes of this section, vessels engaged in sport fishing are not considered to be employed in the fisheries.

(7) *Civil aircraft.*—The exemption provided by section 4221(a)(3) and paragraph (a) of this section relating to supplies for vessels or aircraft, with respect to civil aircraft, extends only to civil aircraft when employed in foreign trade, or in trade between the United States and any of its possessions. Sales of supplies to civil aircraft when engaged in trade between the Atlantic and the Pacific ports of the United States are not exempt from the tax imposed under chapter 32. See section 4221(e)(1) and paragraph (c) of this section for requirement of reciprocal exemption in the case of a civil aircraft registered in a foreign country.

(8) *Trade.*—The term "trade" includes the transportation of persons or property for hire and the making of the necessary preparations for such transportation. The term "trade" also includes the transportation of property on a vessel or aircraft owned or chartered by the owner of the property in connection with the purchase, sale, or exchange of the property in a commercial business operation. However, a vessel owned or chartered by a company and used in the transportation of personnel or property of such company to or from its business properties located in a foreign country, or in a possession of the United States, is not engaged in "trade".

(c) *Reciprocity required in the case of civil aircraft.*—The exemption provided by section 4221(a)(3) and paragraph (a) of this section with respect to the sales of supplies for civil aircraft registered in a foreign country is further limited in that the privilege of exemption may be granted only if the Secretary of Commerce advises the Secretary of the Treasury that the foreign country allows, or will allow, substantially the same reciprocal privileges. If a foreign country discontinues the allowance of such substantially reciprocal exemption, the exemption allowed by the United States will not apply after the Secretary of the Treasury is notified by the Secretary of Commerce of the discontinuance of the exemption allowed by the foreign country.

(d) *Evidence required to establish exemption.*—(1) *In general.*—The exemption provided in section 4221(a)(3) and paragraph (a) of this section for articles sold for use by the purchaser as supplies for vessels or aircraft applies only (i) if both the manufacturer and purchaser are registered under the provisions of section 4222 or (ii) the purchaser or both the manufacturer and the purchaser are not registered but have satisfied the provisions of paragraph (d)(2) of this section. See paragraph (c) of § 48.4221-1 for the evidence required to establish exemption where the purchaser is registered pursuant to section 4222 and § 48.4222(a)-1.

(2) *Exemption certificates for use in support of tax-free sales of supplies for vessels and aircraft.*—(i) In order to establish exemption from tax under section 4221(a)(3) in those instances where the purchaser or both the manufacturer and purchaser are not registered under section 4222, the manufacturer must obtain (prior to or at the time of the sale) from the owner, chartered, or authorized agent of the vessel or aircraft and retain in the manufacturer's possession a properly executed exemption certificate in the form prescribed by subdivision (iii) of this paragraph (d)(2). If articles are sold tax-free for use as supplies for civil aircraft employed in foreign trade or in trade between the United States and any of its possessions, the exemption certificate must show the name of the country in which the aircraft is registered.

(ii) Where only occasional sales of articles are made to a purchaser for use as supplies for vessels or aircraft, a separate exemption certificate shall be furnished for each order. However, where sales are regularly or frequently made to a purchaser for such exempt use, a certificate covering all orders for a specified period not to exceed 12 calendar quarters will be acceptable. Such certificates and proper records of invoices, orders, etc., relative to tax-free sales must be kept for inspection by the district director as provided in section 6001, and the regulations thereunder.

(iii) *Acceptable form of exemption certificate.*—The following form of exemption certificate will be acceptable for the purposes of this section and must be adhered to in substance:

EXEMPTION CERTIFICATE

(For use by purchasers of articles for use as fuel supplies, ships' stores, sea stores, or legitimate equipment on certain vessels or aircraft (sections 4221 and 4222 of the Internal Revenue Code of 1954).)

(Date) . . . . , 19 .

I, the undersigned purchaser, hereby certify that I am the (Owner, charterer, or authorized agent) . . . . of (Name of company and vessel) . . . . and that:

(Check applicable type of certificate)

. . The article or articles specified in the accompanying order, or on the reverse side hereof, (or)

. . . All orders placed by the purchaser for the period commencing (Date) . . . . and ending (Date) . . . . (period not to exceed 12 calendar quarters),will be used only for fuel supplies, ships' stores, sea stores, or legitimate equipment on a vessel belonging to one of the following classes of vessels to which section 4221 of the Internal Revenue Code applies:

(Check class to which vessel belongs)

. . . . . (1) Vessels engaged in foreign trade.

. . . . . (2) Vessels engaged in trade between the Atlantic and Pacific ports of the United States.

. . . . . (3) Vessels engaged in trade between the United States and any of its possessions.

. . . . . (4) Vessels employed in the fisheries or whaling business.

. . . . . (5) Vessels of war of the United States or a foreign nation.

If the articles are purchased for use on civil aircraft engaged in trade as specified in (1) or (3) above, state the name of the country in which the aircraft is registered: . . . .

I understand that if the articles are used for any purpose other than as stated in this certificate, or are resold or otherwise disposed of, I must report such fact to the manufacturer. I understand that this certificate may not be used in purchasing articles tax free for use as fuel supplies, etc., on pleasure vessels, or on any type of aircraft except (i) civil aircraft employed in foreign trade or trade between the United States and any of its possessions, and (ii) aircraft owned by the United States or any foreign country and constituting a part of the armed forces thereof.

I understand that the fraudulent use of this certificate to secure exemption will subject me and all parties making such fraudulent use of this certificate to a fine of not more than $10,000, or to imprisonment for not more than 5 years, or both, together with costs of prosecution. I also understand that I must be prepared to establish by satisfactory evidence the purpose for which the article was used.

(Signature) . . . .

(Address) . . . .

[Reg. § 48.4221-4.]

☐ [T.D. 7536, 3-27-78.]

[Reg. § 48.4221-5]

§ 48.4221-5. Tax-free sale of articles to States and local governments for their exclusive use.—(a) *In general.*—An article (excluding an automobile subject to tax under section 4064) subject to tax under chapter 32 of the Code may be sold tax free by the manufacturer, pursuant to section 4221(a)(4) and this section, to a State or local government for the exclusive use of such State or local government. See paragraph (b) of this section for the meaning of the term "State or local government." An article may be sold tax free by the manufacturer under this paragraph only in those cases where the sale is made directly to a State or local government for its exclusive use. Accordingly, no sale may be made tax free to a dealer for resale to a State or local government for its exclusive use, even though it is known at the time of sale by the manufacturer that the article will be so resold. A sale of an article to a State or local government for resale is not considered to be a sale for the "exclusive use" of the State or local government, within the meaning of section 4221(a)(4), and, therefore, such sales may not be made tax free. Such sales are not exempt regardless of whether the resales

are made to government employees, or the fact that the article is an item of equipment the employee is required to possess in carrying out his duties. For example, pistols or revolvers may not be sold tax-free to a State or local government for resale to its police officers. See section 6416(b)(2)(C), and paragraph (b)(3) of § 48.6416(b)-2, for the circumstances under which credit or refund of tax is available where tax-paid articles are sold for the exclusive use of a State or local government.

(b) *State or local government.*—The term "State or local government" includes any State, the District of Columbia, and any political subdivision of any of the foregoing.

(c) *Evidence required in support of tax-free sales to States or local governments.*—(1) The evidence required in support of a tax-free sale to the State or local government shall, except as provided in paragraph (c)(2) of this section, consist of a certificate, executed and signed by an officer or employee authorized by the State or local government to execute and sign the certificate. If it is impracticable to furnish a separate certificate for each order or contract because of a frequency of purchases, a certificate covering all orders between given dates (such period not to exceed 12 calendar quarters) will be acceptable. The certifi-

Reg. § 48.4221-5(c)(1)

cates and proper records of invoices, orders, etc., relative to tax-free sales must be retained by the manufacturer as provided in section 6001 and the regulations thereunder. The certificates shall be in substantially the following form:

EXEMPTION CERTIFICATE

(For use by States and local governments (section 4221(a)(4) of the Internal Revenue Code.))

(Date) . . . . , 19 .

I hereby certify that I am . . . . (Title of Officer) of . . . . (State or local government) that I am authorized to execute this certificate; and that:

(Check applicable type of certificate)

. . the article or articles specified in the accompanying order, or on the reverse side hereof, (or) . . . . all orders placed by the purchaser for the period commencing (Date) . . . . and ending (Date) . . . . (period not to exceed 12 calendar quarters), are, or will be, purchased from (Name of manufacturer) . . . . for the exclusive use of (Governmental unit) . . . . of (State or local government) . . . .

I understand that the exemption from tax in the case of sales of articles under this exemption certificate to a State, etc., is limited to the sale of articles purchased for its exclusive use. I understand that the fraudulent use of this certificate for the purpose of securing this exemption will subject me and all parties making such fraudulent use of this certificate to a fine of not more than $10,000, or to imprisonment for not more than 5 years, or both, together with costs of prosecution.

(Signature) . . . .

(Address) . . . .

(2) A purchase order, provided that all of the information required by paragraph (c)(1) of this section is included therein, is acceptable in lieu of a separate exemption certificate.

(d) *Resale of articles purchased tax free by a State or local government.*—If articles purchased tax free for the exclusive use of a State or local government are prior to use by the State or local government resold under circumstances that do not amount to an exclusive use by the State or local government (such as tires that are resold by a volunteer fire department to volunteer firemen), the parties responsible in the State or local government are required to inform the manufacturer, producer, or importer from whom the articles were purchased that they were disposed of in a manner that did not amount to an exclusive use by the State or local government. A willful failure to supply the manufacturer, producer, or importer with the information required by this subparagraph will subject responsible parties to the penalties provided by section 7203. [Reg. § 48.4221-5.]

□ [T.D. 7536, 3-27-78. *Amended by T.D.* 8036, 7-23-85 *and T.D.* 8659, 3-13-96.]

[Reg. § 48.4221-6]

§ 48.4221-6. Tax-free sales of articles to nonprofit educational organizations.—(a) *In general.*—An article (excluding an automobile subject to tax under section 4064) subject to tax under chapter 32 of the Code may be sold tax free by the manufacturer, pursuant to section 4221(a)(5) and this section, to a nonprofit educational organization for its exclusive use. See paragraph (b) of this section for the meaning of the term "nonprofit educational organization". An article may be sold tax free by the manufacturer under this paragraph only in those cases where the sale of an article by the manufacturer is made directly to a nonprofit educational organization for its exclusive use. Accordingly, no sale may be made tax free to a dealer for resale to a nonprofit educational organization for its exclusive use even though it is known at the time of sale by the manufacturer that the article will be so resold. See section 6416(b)(2)(D), and paragraph (b)(4) of § 48.6416(b)-2, for the circumstances under which credit or refund of tax is available where tax-paid articles are sold for the exclusive use of a nonprofit educational organization.

(b) *Nonprofit educational organization.*—The term "nonprofit educational organization" means an organization described in section 170(b)(1)(A)(ii) that is exempt from income tax under section 501(a). Section 170(b)(1)(A)(ii) describes an "educational organization" as one that normally maintains a regular faculty and curriculum and normally has a regularly enrolled body of pupils or students in attendance at the place where its educational activities are regularly carried on. The term also includes a school operated as an activity of an organization described in section 501(c)(3) which is exempt from income tax under section 501(a), provided the primary function of such school is the presentation of formal instruction and provided such school normally maintains a regular faculty and curriculum and normally has a regularly enrolled body of pupils or students in attendance at the place where its educational activities are regularly carried on.

(c) *Evidence required in support of tax-free sales to nonprofit educational organizations.*—Every nonprofit educational organization purchasing tax free under section 4221(a)(5) must furnish the following information to the seller:

(1) The exempt purpose for which the article or articles are being purchased, and

(2) Its registration number, and the district director's office that issued the registration number.

Such information must be in writing and may be noted on the purchase order or other document furnished by the purchaser to the seller in connection with each sale except that a single notification containing the information described in this paragraph may cover all sales by the seller to the purchaser made during a designated period not to exceed 12 successive calendar quarters. See paragraph (c) of § 48.4221-1 for the evidence required to establish exemption. [Reg. § 48.4221-6.]

☐ [T.D. 7536, 3-27-78. Amended by T.D. 7686, 3-18-80 and T.D. 8036, 7-23-85.]

[Reg. § 48.4221-7]

§ 48.4221-7. Tax-free sales of tires and tubes.—(a) In general.—A manufacturer of tires or inner tubes that are taxable under section 4071 may sell such articles tax free if the sale meets the conditions prescribed in section 4221(e)(2) and paragraph (a)(1) and (2) of this section. The following are conditions under which articles taxable under section 4071 may be sold tax free:

(1) The tire or tube is sold for use by the purchaser for sale on or in connection with the sale of another article manufactured or produced by the purchaser; and

(2) The other article is to be sold in a tax-free sale by the purchaser for export, for use as supplies for vessels or aircraft, to a State or local government for its exclusive use, or to a nonprofit educational organization for its exclusive use, or the other article is to be sold by the purchaser for any of such purposes in a sale which would be tax-free but for the fact that the other article is not subject to tax under chapter 32 of the Code.

See section 6416(b)(2)(F) and paragraph (b)(6) of § 48.6416(b)-2 for the circumstances under which credit or refund of tax is available for tax-paid tires or tubes that are resold for the purposes described in this paragraph (a).

(b) Registration requirements.—In order to effect a tax-free sale under section 4221(e)(2)(A), both the manufacturer and purchaser (except for purchasers who are exempt from the registration requirement under § 48.4222(b)-1) must be registered with the District Director of Internal Revenue as required in § 48.4222(a)-1. At the time of sale, the registration number assigned to the purchaser by the district director together with the purpose for which the article was purchased must be shown on (or attached to) the invoice, purchase order, or other document used for the sale.

(c) Proof required in support of tax-free sales of tires and tubes.—(1) Cessation of exemption.—The exemption allowed under section 4221(e)(2)(A) and this section on the sale of a tire or inner tube shall cease to apply unless, within the 6-month period which begins on the date of the tax-free sale by the manufacturer of such article (or, if earlier, on the date of shipment by such manufacturer), the manufacturer receives proof from the purchaser that such article has been used on or in connection with the sale of another article which has been sold for one of the tax-exempt purposes referred to in paragraph (a)(2) of this section. If the manufacturer has not received the required information within such 6-month period, the temporary suspension of the liability for the payment of the tax ceases, and the manufacturer shall include the tax on the sale of the tire or inner tube in his return for the period in which the 6-month period expires. If the required information is received after the expiration of the 6-month period, the manufacturer may file a claim for credit or refund of tax so paid on his sale of the tire or inner tube.

(2) Required information.—The information which the manufacturer must receive within the 6-month period, referred to in paragraph (c)(1) of this section, shall be in substantially the following form:

STATEMENT OF MANUFACTURER'S VENDEE

(To support tax-free sales of tires or inner tubes by the manufacturer thereof for use on or in connection with the sale of another article (section 4221(e)(2) of the Internal Revenue Code))

(Date) . . . . , 19

I certify that I, or the . . . . (Name of purchaser if other than undersigned), of which I am . . . . (Title) am/is in the business of selling . . . . (Products handled) and hold(s) certificate of registry No. . . . . issued by the District Director of Internal Revenue at . . . . ; and that the tires or inner tubes which were purchased or shipped on . . . . , 19 , as specified on the back hereof, have been used on or in connection with the sale of . . . . (Products sold) by such undersigned

Check one

. . . . . for export by . . . . (Name of carrier) to . . . . (Name of foreign country or U.S. possession) and was so exported on (Date) . . . . , 19 (A copy of the bill of lading or other proof of exportation is attached)

. . . . . for use as supplies on . . . . (Name of vessel or aircraft) which is registered in . . . . (Name of country in which vessel or aircraft is registered)

. . . . . to . . . . (Name of State or local government)

. . . . . to . . . . (Name and address of the nonprofit educational organization).

Reg. § 48.4221-7(c)(2)

I understand that the fraudulent use of this certificate for the purpose of substantiating the tax-free sale will subject me and all parties making such fraudulent use of this certificate to revocation of the privilege of purchasing articles tax free and to a fine of not more than $10,000 or to imprisonment for not more than 5 years, or both, together with costs of prosecution.

(Signature) . . . .

(Address) . . . .

[Reg. § 48.4221-7.]

☐ [T.D. 7536, 3-27-78.]

[Reg. § 48.4221-8]

§ 48.4221-8. Tax-free sales of tires, tubes, and tread rubber used on intercity, local, and school buses.—(a) *In general.*—Under section 4221(e)(5), the taxes imposed by section 4071(a)(1), (3) and (4) shall not apply to sales by a manufacturer, producer, or importer of tires of the type used on highway vehicles or inner tubes for tires sold for use by the purchaser on or in connection with a qualified bus, or to the sales by a manufacturer, producer, or importer of tread rubber sold for use by the purchaser in the recapping or retreading of any tire to be used by the purchaser on or in connection with a qualified bus if the requirements of this section are met.

(b) *Meaning of terms.*—(1) *Qualified bus.*— "Qualified bus" means an intercity, local or school bus.

(2) *Intercity or local bus.*—"Intercity or local bus" means any automobile bus which is used predominantly (more than 50 percent) in furnishing (for compensation) passenger land transportation available to the general public if such transportation is scheduled and along regular routes, or if the seating capacity of the bus is at least 20 adults (not including the driver). In determining predominant use, mileage travelled with passengers as well as mileage travelled incidental to such passenger transportation, such as "dead-heading", is counted. Under the first alternative, the size of the bus is not relevant for purposes of determining whether or not the use of the bus qualifies for the exemption. Under the second alternative, for non-scheduled bus operations, such as that provided by charter buses, the exemption is available only if the bus has a passenger seating capacity of at least 20 adults and the transportation is available to the general public. For purposes of determining whether the bus has a seating capacity of at least 20 adults, the bus driver is not included. Service is available to the general public if bus service is used in a passenger transportation business in which service is offered to more than a limited number of persons, groups, or organizations.

(3) *School bus.*—"School bus" means any automobile bus in which "substantially all" (85 percent or more) of the use involves transporting students and employees of a school. Incidental use (deadheading) of the school bus without passengers to or from a point to which students or employees of school are transported is considered to be a use which involves transporting students or employees of schools. A school is any educational organization which normally maintains a regular faculty and curriculum and normally has a regularly enrolled body of pupils or students in attendance at the place where its educational activities are carried on. Tax-exempt schools, taxable schools, and a private contractor who operates a bus for tax-exempt or a taxable school may qualify for the tax exemption if all the requirements of this section are met.

(b) *Registration requirements for tires, tubes, and tread rubber; vendees purchasing tax free.*—The provisions of section 4221(e)(5) do not apply with respect to any sale unless the manufacturer and the vendee are registered as required under section 4222, and unless they comply with all the requirements under that section relating to tax-free sales. See § 48.4222(a)-1. Persons not required to be registered under section 4222(b) may purchase articles tax free by following the same procedures that apply to them in the case of other tax-free sales. See § 48.4222(b)-1. A person's registration and right to sell or purchase articles tax free may be revoked or suspended as provided in § 48.4222(c).1. Such a revocation or suspension shall be in addition to any other penalties that may apply.

(c) *Cross reference.*—For credit or refund, see section 6416(b)(2).

(d) *Information; records.*—(1) *Information to be furnished to purchaser.*—A manufacturer selling tires, tubes, or tread rubber tax free under section 4221(e)(5) shall indicate to the purchaser that the purchaser is obtaining the tires or tubes tax free for the purpose of use on or in connection with a qualified bus, and that the purchaser is obtaining the tread rubber tax free for use in the recapping or retreading of tires to be used by the purchaser on or in connection with a qualified bus. The manufacturer may transmit this information by any convenient means, such as coding of sales invoices, provided that the information is presented with sufficient particularity so that the purchaser is informed that the purchaser has obtained the tires, tubes, and tread rubber tax free.

(2) *Records of manufacturer.*—A manufacturer selling tires, tubes, or tread rubber tax free under section 4221(e)(5) shall maintain in its records the identity of the purchaser, a signed statement of the exempt purpose for purchasing the tires, tubes, or tread rubber, and the quantity of tires, tubes, or tread rubber sold tax free to each purchaser.

(3) *Records of purchaser.*—A person purchasing tires, tubes, or tread rubber tax free under

section 4221(e)(5) must maintain sufficient records to establish that the tires, tubes, or tread rubber purchased tax free has actually been used for that purpose.

(e) *Duty of selling manufacturer to ascertain validity of tax-free sale.*—The selling manufacturer is not relieved of liability under the provisions of section 4221(e)(5) by reason of section 4221(c) for the tax imposed by section 4061(b) if at the time of sale the selling manufacturer has knowledge or reason to believe that the tires, tubes, or tread rubber sold by it to the purchaser are not intended for use on an intercity, local, or school bus, or that the purchaser has failed to register, or that its registration has been revoked or suspended.

(f) *Effective date.*—Section 4221(e)(5) (relating to tires, tubes, and tread rubber) applies to sales on or after December 1, 1978. The sale of tires, tubes, or tread rubber sold prior to that date is not exempt from tax under section 4221(e)(5). [Reg. § 48.4221-8.]

☐ [*T.D. 7834, 9-27-82. Redesignated as Reg. § 48.4221-8 by T.D. 8659, 3-13-96.*]

[Reg. § 48.4222(a)-1]

§ 48.4222(a)-1. Registration.—(a) *General rule.*—Except as provided in § 48.4222(b)-1, tax-free sales under section 4221 may be made only if the manufacturer, first purchaser, and second purchaser, as the case may be, have been registered by the Internal Revenue Service.

(b) *Application instructions.*—Application for registration under section 4222 must be made in accordance with instructions for Form 637 (or such other form as the Commissioner may designate).

(c) *Evidence required in support of tax-free sales.*—See subparagraph (1) of § 48.4221-1(c) for evidence required in support of tax-free sales to purchasers who are required to be registered.

(d) *Failure to register.*—If either the seller or purchaser is not registered as required by this section of the regulations, tax-free sales may not be made, except as indicated in § 48.4222(b)-1.

(e) *Cross references.*—(1) For exceptions to the requirement for registration, see section 4222(b) and § 48.4222(b)-1.

(2) For revocation or suspension of registration, see § 48.4222(c)-1.

(3) For applicability of section 4222 and these regulations to exemptions provided by sections 4063(b), 4182(b), and 4293, see § 48.4222(d)-1. [Reg. § 48.4222(a)-1.]

☐ [*T.D. 7536, 3-27-78. Amended by T.D. 8659, 3-13-96.*]

[Reg. § 48.4222(b)-1]

§ 48.4222(b)-1. Exceptions to the requirement for registration.—(a) *State and local governments.*—The Internal Revenue Service will not register State or local governments under section 4222. To establish the right to sell articles tax free to a State or local government, the manufacturer must obtain the information described in § 48.4221-5(c).

(b) *Sales or resales to foreign purchasers for export.*—Persons whose principal place of business is not within the United States may, but are not required to, register in order to purchase articles tax free for export. To establish the right to sell articles tax free for export to a purchaser who is not registered and who is located in a foreign country or a possession of the United States, the manufacturer must obtain the evidence required by paragraph (b) of § 48.4221-3.

(c) *United States.*—Except as provided in paragraph (b) of § 48.4222(d)-1 (relating to sales to the American Red Cross) the registration requirements of the regulations in this part do not apply to purchases and sales by the United States or any of its agencies or instrumentalities. The evidence required in support of such tax-free purchases and sales is a notation on the purchase order or other document furnished to the seller clearly indicating that the article or articles are being purchased tax free as authorized by Chapter 32 of the Code.

(d) *Supplies for vessels and aircraft.*—An article subject to an excise tax imposed by chapter 32 of the Code may be sold tax free by the manufacturer under the provisions of § 48.4221-4 for use by the purchaser as supplies for a vessel or aircraft if both the manufacturer and the purchaser are registered under the provisions of § 48.4222(a)-1. The article also may, on or after July 1, 1965, be sold tax free for such use even though neither the manufacturer nor the purchaser is so registered if the provisions of paragraph (d) of § 48.4221-4 are satisfied. [Reg. § 48.4222(b)-1.]

☐ [*T.D. 7536, 3-27-78. Amended by T.D. 8659, 3-13-96 and T.D. 8879, 3-30-2000.*]

[Reg. § 48.4222(c)-1]

§ 48.4222(c)-1. Revocation or suspension of registration.—The district director or the Director of International Operations, as the case may be, is authorized to revoke or temporarily suspend, upon written notice, the registration of any person and the right of such person to sell or purchase articles tax free under section 4221 of the Code in any case in which he finds that (1) the registrant is not a bona fide manufacturer, or a purchaser reselling direct to manufacturers or exporters; (2) the registrant is for some other reason not eligible under these regulations to retain a Certificate of Registry; (3) the registrant has used his registration to avoid the payment of any tax imposed by chapter 32 of the Code, or to postpone or interfere in any manner with the collection of such tax; (4) such revocation or suspension is necessary to protect the revenue; or (5) the registrant failed to comply with the requirements of paragraph (c) of § 48.4222(a)-1, relating to the evidence required to support a tax-free sale. The revocation or suspension of registration is in addition to any other penalty

62,470
      Facilities and Services
See p. 20,601 for regulations not amended to reflect law changes

that may apply under the law for any act or failure to act. [Reg. § 48.4222(c)-1.]

☐ [*T.D. 7536, 3-27-78. Amended by T.D. 7753, 1-13-81 and T.D. 7882, 3-30-83.*]

[Reg. § 48.4222(d)-1]

§ 48.4222(d)-1. Registration in the case of certain other exemptions.—The registration procedure set forth in § 48.4222(a)-1 also applies in the following cases:

(a) Tax-free sales on or after March 10, 1980, under section 4064(b)(1) (C) (relating to emergency vehicles). Both the vendor and vendee (other than a State or local government) must be registered.

(b) Tax-free sales under section 4293 to any corporation created by Act of Congress to act in matters of relief under the treaty of Geneva of August 22, 1864 (American Red Cross) for its exclusive use. Both the vendor and the vendee must be registered. [Reg. § 48.4222(d)-1.]

☐ [*T.D. 7536, 3-27-78. Amended by T.D. 7834, 9-27-82; T.D. 8036, 7-23-85 and T.D. 8659, 3-13-96.*]

[Reg. § 48.4223-1]

§ 48.4223-1. Special rules relating to further manufacture.—(a) *Purchasing manufacturer to be treated as the manufacturer.*—For purposes of chapter 32, a manufacturer or producer to whom an article is sold or resold tax free under section 4221(a)(1) of the Code for use by it in further manufacture shall be treated as the manufacturer or producer of such article. If a manufacturer who purchases an article tax free for further manufacture does not use the article for further manufacture, the sale of the article by it, or its use of the article other than in further manufacture, shall, for purposes of the taxes imposed by chapter 32 of the Code, be treated as a sale or use of the article by the manufacturer thereof. See paragraphs (b) and (c) of this section for determination of taxable sale price where an article purchased tax free for further manufacture is resold, or used other than in further manufacture.

(b) *Computation of tax.*—Except as provided in paragraph (c) of this section, the tax liability referred to in paragraph (a) of this section shall be based on the price for which the article was sold by the purchasing manufacturer, or, where the manufacturer uses the article for a purpose

other than which it was purchased, the tax shall be based on the price at which such or similar articles are sold, in the ordinary course of trade by manufacturers, producers, or importers thereof. See section 4218(e) and § 48.4218-5.

(c) *Election.*—(1) Instead of computing the tax as described under paragraph (b) of this section, the purchasing manufacturer who has incurred liability for tax on its sale or use of an article as provided by paragraph (a) of this section may compute the tax incurred under chapter 32 by using as the tax base either the price for which the article was sold to it by the first purchaser, if any, or the price for which such article was sold by the actual manufacturer, producer, or importer of such article. The purchasing manufacturer must have in its possession information upon which to substantiate such basis for tax. For purposes of this paragraph, the price for which the article was sold by the actual manufacturer or by the first purchaser shall be determined as provided in section 4216 and the regulations thereunder. However, such price shall not be adjusted for any discount, rebate, allowance, return, or repossession of a container or covering, or otherwise.

(2) The election under this paragraph shall be in the form of a statement attached to the return reporting the tax applicable to the sale or use of the article which gave rise to such tax liability. Such election, once made, may not be revoked. [Reg. § 48.4223-1.]

☐ [*T.D. 7536, 3-27-78.*]

[Reg. § 48.4225-1]

§ 48.4225-1. Exemption of articles manufactured or produced by Indians.—The exemption provided under section 4225 applies to articles taxable under chapter 32 of the Code that are of native Indian handicraft and are manufactured or produced by Indians on Indian reservations or in Indian schools, or manufactured or produced by Indians who are under the jurisdiction of the United States Government in Alaska. For purposes of this section, Indians who reside on allotments of land adjacent to an Indian reservation and are subject to the supervision, control, and jurisdiction of the Bureau of Indian Affairs are considered to be "Indians on Indian reservations." [Reg. § 48.4225-1.]

☐ [*T.D. 7536, 3-27-78.*]

Facilities and Services

[Reg. § 49.0-1]

§ 49.0-1. Introduction.—The regulations in this part 49 are designated "Facilities and Services Excise Tax Regulations." The regulations relate to the taxes on communications and transportation by air imposed by chapter 33 of the Internal Revenue Code and the taxes on indoor tanning services imposed by section 5000B. See part 40 of this chapter for regulations relating to

returns, payments, and deposits of these taxes. [Reg. § 49.0-1.]

☐ [*T.D. 8442, 10-21-92. Amended by T.D. 9621, 6-10-2013.*]

[Reg. § 49.0-2]

§ 49.0-2. General definitions and use of terms.—As used in the regulations in this part, unless otherwise expressly indicated—

(a) The terms defined in the provisions of law contained in the regulations in this part shall have the meanings so assigned to them.

(b) The Internal Revenue Code of 1954 means the Act approved August 16, 1954 (68A Stat.), entitled "An Act to revise the internal revenue laws of the United States", as amended.

(c) District director means district director of internal revenue. The term also includes the Director of International Operations in all cases where the authority to perform the functions which may be performed by a district director has been delegated to the Director of International Operations.

(d) Calendar quarter means a period of 3 calendar months ending on March 31, June 30, September 30, or December 31. [Reg. § 49.0-2.]

☐ [T.D. 6430, 12-3-59.]

[Reg. § 49.4251-1]

§ 49.4251-1. Imposition of tax.—(a) *In general.*—Section 4251 imposes a tax on amounts paid for general telephone service; toll telephone service; telegraph service; teletypewriter exchange service; wire mileage service; and wire and equipment service. See § 49.4251-2 for rate and application of tax.

Taxable Service	Rate of tax Percent
General telephone service	10
Toll telephone service	10
Telegraph service	10
Teletypewriter exchange service	10
Wire mileage service	10
Wire and equipment service	8

(b) *Amounts paid.*—The term "amounts paid" means the amounts collected for the communication services specified in paragraph (a) of this section, without regard to whether the charge therefor is paid or satisfied in money, service, or other valuable consideration. For additional provisions relating to the term "amounts paid" see the section of the regulations relating to the particular taxable service listed in paragraph (a) of this section.

(c) *Liability for, and return of, tax.*—The taxes imposed by section 4251 are payable by the person paying for the services rendered, and must be paid to the person rendering the services who is required to collect the tax and return and pay over the tax. [Reg. § 49.4251-2.]

☐ [T.D. 6664, 7-15-63. *Amended by T.D. 8442,* 10-21-92.]

[Reg. § 49.4251-3]

§ 49.4251-3. Applicability of sections 4251 to 4254, inclusive.—Except as otherwise provided in this section, the applicability of sections 4251 to 4254, inclusive, as amended and in effect on January 1, 1959, and the regulations in this subpart extends only to amounts paid on or after January 1, 1959, for services rendered on or after such date. In the case of amounts paid pursuant

(b) *Termination of tax on general telephone service.*—(1) Except as otherwise provided in subparagraph (2) of this paragraph, no tax is imposed on amounts paid on or after July 1, 1965, for general telephone service rendered on or after such date.

(2) In the case of amounts paid pursuant to bills rendered on or after July 1, 1965, for general telephone service for which no previous bill was rendered, no tax is imposed on that portion of the amount paid pursuant to such bill or bills as is attributable to general telephone service rendered subsequent to April 30, 1965. However, the tax applies to that portion of the amount paid pursuant to any such bill or bills as is attributable to general telephone service rendered prior to May 1, 1965. The tax also applies to amounts paid for general telephone service pursuant to bills rendered before July 1, 1965, without regard to when the payment is made or the service is rendered. [Reg. § 49.4251-1.]

☐ [T.D. 6664, 7-15-63. *Amended by T.D. 6694,* 12-4-63 *and T.D. 6753,* 9-8-64.]

[Reg. § 49.4251-2]

§ 49.4251-2. Rate and application of tax.—(a) *Rate of tax.*—Tax is imposed on amounts paid for each of the following services rendered at the rate specified below:

to bills rendered on or after January 1, 1959, for services for which no previous bill was rendered, the sections of law and regulations referred to in the preceding sentence are applicable in respect of that portion of the amount paid pursuant to such bill or bills as is attributable to services rendered subsequent to October 31, 1958. For regulations applicable with respect to amounts paid for services rendered prior to November 1, 1958, and amounts paid for services rendered after October 31, 1958, for which a bill was rendered prior to January 1, 1959, see Part 42 of this chapter. See also § § 49.0-3 and 49.0-4, relating to the scope of the regulations and the extent to which prior regulations are superseded. [Reg. § 49.4251-3.]

☐ [T.D. 6664, 7-15-63.]

[Reg. § 49.4251-4]

§ 49.4251-4. Prepaid telephone cards.—(a) *In general.*—In the case of communications services acquired by means of a prepaid telephone card (PTC), the face amount of the PTC is treated as an amount paid for communications services and that amount is treated as paid when the PTC is transferred by any carrier to any person that is not a carrier. This section provides rules for the application of the section 4251 tax to PTCs.

(b) *Definitions.*—The following definitions apply to this section:

Carrier means a telecommunications carrier as defined in 47 U.S.C. 153.

Comparable PTC means a currently available dollar card or tariffed unit card (other than a PTC transferred in bulk or under special circumstances, such as for promotional purposes) that provides the same type and amount of communications services as the PTC to which it is being compared.

Dollar card means a PTC the value of which is designated by the carrier in dollars (even if also designated in units of service), provided that the designated value is not less than the amount for which the PTC is expected to be sold to a holder.

Holder means a person that purchases other than for resale.

Prepaid telephone card (PTC) means a card or similar arrangement that permits its holder to obtain a fixed amount of communications services by means of a code (such as a personal identification number (PIN)) or other access device provided by the carrier and to pay for those services in advance.

Tariff means a schedule of rates and regulations filed by a carrier with the Federal Communications Commission.

Tariffed unit card means a unit card that is transferred by a carrier—

(1) To a holder at a price that does not exceed the designated number of units on the PTC multiplied by the carrier's tariffed price per unit; or

(2) To a transferee reseller subject to a contractual or other arrangement under which the price at which the PTC is sold to a holder will not exceed the designated number of units on the PTC multiplied by the carrier's tariffed price per unit.

Transferee means the first person that is not a carrier to whom a PTC is transferred by a carrier.

Transferee reseller means a transferee that purchases a PTC for resale.

Unit card means a PTC other than a dollar card.

Untariffed unit card means a unit card other than a tariffed unit card.

(c) *Determination of face amount.*—(1) *Dollar card.*—The face amount of a dollar card is the designated dollar value.

(2) *Tariffed unit card.*—The face amount of a tariffed unit card is the designated number of units on the PTC multiplied by the tariffed price per unit.

(3) *Untariffed unit card.*—(i) *Transfer to holder.*—The face amount of an untariffed unit card transferred by a carrier to a holder is the amount for which the carrier sells the PTC to the holder.

(ii) *Transfer to transferee reseller.*—(A) *In general.*—The face amount of an untariffed unit card transferred by a carrier to a transferee reseller is at the option of the carrier—

(1) The highest amount for which the carrier sells a PTC that provides the same type and amount of communications services to a holder that ordinarily would not be expected to buy more than one such PTC at a time (if the carrier makes such sales on a regular and arm's-length basis) or the face amount of a comparable PTC (if the carrier does not make such sales on a regular and arm's-length basis);

(2) 135 percent of the amount for which the carrier sells the PTC to the transferee reseller (including in that amount, in addition to any sum certain fixed at the time of the sale, any contingent amount per unit multiplied by the designated number of units on the PTC); or

(3) If the PTC is of a type that ordinarily is used entirely for domestic communications service, the maximum number of minutes of domestic communications service on the PTC multiplied by the applicable rate.

(B) *Applicable rate.*—The applicable rate under paragraph (c)(3)(ii)(A)(3) of this section with respect to a PTC is $0.30 reduced (but not below $0.20) by $0.01 for each full 20 minutes by which the maximum number of minutes of domestic communications service on the PTC exceeds 40 minutes.

(C) *Sales not at arm's length.*—In the case of a transfer of an untariffed unit card by a carrier to a transferee reseller otherwise than through an arm's-length transaction, the fair market retail value of the PTC shall be substituted for the amount determined in paragraph (c)(3)(ii)(A)(2) of this section.

(4) *Exclusion.*—The amount of any state or local tax imposed on the furnishing or sale of communications services that is separately stated in the bill or on the face of the PTC and the amount of any section 4251 tax separately stated in the bill or on the face of the PTC are disregarded in determining, for purposes of this paragraph (c), the amount for which a PTC is sold.

(d) *Liability for tax.*—(1) *In general.*—Under section 4251(d), the section 4251(a) tax is imposed on the transfer of a PTC by a carrier to a transferee. The person liable for the tax is the transferee. Except as provided in paragraph (d)(2) of this section, the person responsible for collecting the tax is the carrier transferring the PTC to the transferee. If a holder purchases a PTC from a transferee reseller, the amount the holder pays for the PTC is not treated as an amount paid for communications services and thus tax is not imposed on that payment.

(2) *Effect of statement that purchaser is a carrier.*—(i) *On transferor.*—A carrier that transfers a PTC to a purchaser is not responsible for collecting the tax if, at the time of transfer, the transferor carrier has received written notification from the purchaser that the purchaser is a carrier, and the transferor has no reason to believe otherwise. The notification to be provided by the purchaser is a statement, signed under penalties

of perjury by a person with authority to bind the purchaser, that the purchaser is a carrier (as defined in paragraph (b) of this section). The statement is not required to take any particular form.

(ii) *On purchaser.*—If a purchaser that is not a carrier provides the notification described in paragraph (d)(2)(i) of this section to the carrier that transfers a PTC, the purchaser remains liable for the tax imposed on the transfer of the PTC.

(3) *Exemptions.*—Any exemptions available under section 4253 apply to the transfer of a PTC from a carrier to a holder. Section 4253 does not apply to the transfer of a PTC from a carrier to a transferee reseller.

(e) *Examples.*—The following examples illustrate the provisions of this section:

Example 1. Unit card; sold to individual. (i) On May 1, 2000, A, a carrier, sells a card it calls a prepaid telephone card at A's retail store to P, an individual, for P's use in making telephone calls. A provides P with a PIN. The value of the card is not denominated in dollars, but the face of the card is marked 30 minutes. The sales price is $9. A tariff has not been filed for the minutes on the card. The toll telephone service acquired by purchasing the card will be obtained by entering the PIN and the telephone number to be called.

(ii) Because P purchased from a carrier other than for resale, P is a holder. The card provides its holder, P, with a fixed amount of communications services (30 minutes of toll telephone service) to be obtained by means of a PIN, for which P pays in advance of obtaining service; therefore, the card is a PTC. Because the value of the PTC is not designated in dollars and a tariff has not been filed for the minutes on the PTC, the PTC is an untariffed unit card. Because it is transferred by the carrier to the holder, the face amount is the sales price ($9).

(iii) The card is a PTC; thus, under section 4251(d), the face amount is treated as an amount paid for communications services and that amount is treated as paid when the PTC is transferred from A to P. Accordingly, at the time of transfer, P is liable for the 3 percent tax imposed by section 4251(a). The amount of the tax is $0.27 (3% × the $9 face amount). Thus, the total paid by P is $9.27, the $9 sales price plus $0.27 tax. A is responsible for collecting the tax from P.

Example 2. Unit card; given to individual. (i) The facts are the same as in Example 1, except that instead of selling a card, A gives a 30 minute card to P.

(ii) Although the card provides P with a fixed amount of communications services (30 minutes of toll telephone service) to be obtained by means of a PIN, P does not pay for the service. Therefore, the card is not a PTC, even though it is called a prepaid telephone card by A.

(iii) Because the card is not a PTC, section 4251(d) does not apply. Furthermore, no tax is imposed by section 4251(a) because no amount is paid for the communications services.

Example 3. Unit card; adding value. (i) After using the card described in Example 2, P arranges with A by telephone to have 30 minutes of toll telephone service added to the card. The sales price is $9. P is told to continue using the PIN provided with the card.

(ii) Because P purchased from a carrier other than for resale, P is a holder. The arrangement provides its holder, P, with a fixed amount of communications services (30 minutes of toll telephone service) to be obtained by means of a PIN, for which P pays in advance of obtaining service; therefore, the arrangement is a PTC. Because the value of the PTC is not designated in dollars and a tariff has not been filed for the minutes on the PTC, the PTC is an untariffed unit card. Because it is transferred by the carrier to the holder, the face amount is the sales price ($9).

(iii) The arrangement is a PTC; thus, under section 4251(d), the face amount is treated as an amount paid for communications services and that amount is treated as paid when the PTC is transferred from A to P. Accordingly, at the time of transfer, P is liable for the 3 percent tax imposed by section 4251(a). The amount of the tax is $0.27 (3% × the $9 face amount). Thus, the total paid by P is $9.27, the $9 sales price plus $0.27 tax. A is responsible for collecting the tax from P.

Example 4. Dollar card; sold other than for resale. (i) On May 1, 2000, B, a carrier, sells 100,000 cards it calls prepaid telephone cards to Q, an auto dealer, for $50,000. Q will give away a card to each person that visits Q's dealership. B provides Q with a PIN for each card. The face of each card is marked $3. The toll telephone service acquired by purchasing the card will be obtained by entering the PIN and the telephone number to be called.

(ii) Because Q purchased from a carrier other than for resale, Q is a holder. Each card provides its holder, Q, with a fixed amount of communications services ($3 of toll telephone service) to be obtained by means of a PIN, for which Q pays in advance of obtaining service; therefore, each card is a PTC even though Q's visitors do not pay for the cards. The value of each PTC is designated in dollars; therefore, each PTC is a dollar card. Because the PTC is a dollar card, the face amount is the designated dollar value ($3).

(iii) The cards are PTCs; thus, under section 4251(d), the face amount is treated as an amount paid for communications services and that amount is treated as paid when the PTCs are transferred from B to Q. Accordingly, at the time of transfer, Q is liable for the 3 percent tax imposed by section 4251(a). The amount of the tax is $9,000 (3% × the $3 face amount × 100,000 PTCs). Thus, the total paid by Q is $59,000, the $50,000 sales price plus $9,000 tax. B is responsible for collecting the tax from Q.

Example 5. Tariffed unit card; sold to transferee reseller. (i) On May 1, 2000, C, a carrier, sells 1,000 cards it calls prepaid telephone cards to R, a convenience store owner, for $7,000. C provides R with a PIN for each card. The value of the cards is not denominated in dollars, but the face of each card is marked 30 minutes and a tariff of

Reg. §49.4251-4(e)

$0.33 per minute has been filed for the minutes on each card. R agrees that it will sell the cards to individuals for their own use and at a price that does not exceed $0.33 per minute. R actually sells the cards for $9 each (that is, at a price equivalent to $0.30 per minute). The toll telephone service acquired by purchasing the card will be obtained by entering the PIN and the telephone number to be called.

(ii) Because R purchased from a carrier for resale, R is a transferee reseller. Because R's customers will purchase other than for resale, they will be holders. Each card sold by R provides its holder, R's customer, with a fixed amount of communications services (30 minutes of toll telephone service) to be obtained by means of a PIN provided by the carrier, for which R's customer pays in advance of obtaining service; therefore, each card is a PTC. Because the value of each PTC is not designated in dollars and C sells the PTCs to R subject to an arrangement under which the price at which the PTCs are sold to holders will not exceed the designated number of minutes on the PTC multiplied by C's tariffed price per minute, each PTC is a tariffed unit card. Because the PTCs are tariffed unit cards, the face amount of each PTC is $9.90, the designated number of minutes on the PTC multiplied by the tariffed price per minute (30 × $0.33), even though the retail sale price of each card is $9.

(iii) The cards are PTCs; thus, under section 4251(d), the face amount is treated as an amount paid for communications services and that amount is treated as paid when the PTC is transferred from C to R. Accordingly, at the time of transfer, R is liable for the 3 percent tax imposed by section 4251(a). The amount of the tax is $297 (3% × the $9.90 face amount × 1,000 PTCs). Thus, the total paid by R is $7,297, the $7,000 sales price plus $297 tax. C is responsible for collecting the tax from R.

Example 6. Unit card; sold to transferee reseller. (i) On May 1, 2000, D, a carrier, sells 10,000 cards it calls prepaid telephone cards to S, a convenience store owner, for $60,000. D provides S with a PIN for each card. The value of the cards is not denominated in dollars, but the face of each card is marked 30 minutes. A tariff has not been filed for the minutes on each card. S will sell the cards to individuals for their own use for $9 each. D also sells a card that provides 30 minutes of the same type of communications service at its retail store for $9. The toll telephone service acquired by purchasing the card will be obtained by entering the PIN and the telephone number to be called.

(ii) Because S purchased from a carrier for resale, S is a transferee reseller. Because S's customers will purchase other than for resale, they will be holders. Each card sold by S provides its holder, S's customer, with a fixed amount of communications services (30 minutes of toll telephone service) to be obtained by means of a PIN provided by the carrier, for which S's customer pays in advance of obtaining service; therefore,

each card is a PTC. Because the value of each PTC is not designated in dollars and a tariff has not been filed for the minutes on the PTC, each PTC is an untariffed unit card.

(iii) The PTCs are untariffed unit cards transferred by the carrier to a transferee reseller. Thus, the face amount is determined under paragraph (c)(3)(ii) of this section, which permits D to choose from three alternative methods. Under paragraph (c)(3)(ii)(A)(1) of this section, the face amount of each PTC would be $9, the highest amount for which D sells to holders purchasing a single PTC. Alternatively, under paragraph (c)(3)(ii)(A)(2) of this section, the face amount of each PTC would be $8.10, computed as follows: 135% × the $60,000 sales price ÷ 10,000 PTCs. Finally, under paragraph (c)(3)(ii)(A)(3) of this section (assuming the PTCs are of a type that ordinarily is used entirely for domestic communications services), the face amount of each PTC would be $9 ($0.30 × 30 minutes).

(iv) The cards are PTCs; thus, under section 4251(d), the face amount is treated as an amount paid for communications services and that amount is treated as paid when the PTCs are transferred from D to S. Accordingly, at the time of transfer, S is liable for the 3 percent tax imposed by section 4251(a). Assuming that D chooses to determine the face amount as provided in paragraph (c)(3)(ii)(A)(2) of this section, the amount of the tax is $2,430 (3% × the $8.10 face amount × 10,000 PTCs). Thus, the total paid by S is $62,430, the $60,000 sales price plus $2,430 tax. D is responsible for collecting the tax from S.

Example 7. Transfer of card that is not a PTC. (i) On May 1, 2000, E, a carrier, provides a telephone card to T, an individual, for T's use in making telephone calls. E provides T with a PIN. The card provides access to an unlimited amount of communications services. E charges T $0.25 per minute of service, and bills T monthly for services used. The communications services acquired by using the card will be obtained by entering the PIN and the telephone number to be called.

(ii) Although the communications services will be obtained by means of a PIN, T does not receive a fixed amount of communications services. Also, T cannot pay in advance since the amount of T's payment obligation depends upon the number of minutes used. Therefore, the card is not a PTC.

(iii) Because the card is not a PTC, section 4251(d) does not apply. However, the 3 percent tax imposed by section 4251(a) applies to the amounts paid by T to E for the communications services. Accordingly, at the time an amount is paid for communications services, T is liable for tax. E is responsible for collecting the tax from T.

(f) *Effective date.*—This section is applicable with respect to PTCs transferred by a carrier on or after the first day of the first calendar quarter beginning after January 7, 2000. [Reg. § 49.4251-4.]

☐ [*T.D.* 8855, 1-6-2000.]

[Reg. § 49.4252-1]

§ 49.4252-1. General telephone service.— (a) *In general.*—The term "general telephone service" means any telephone or radio telephone service furnished in connection with any fixed or mobile telephone or radio telephone station which may be connected, directly or indirectly, to an exchange operated by a person engaged in the business of furnishing communication service, if by means of such connection communication may be established with any other fixed or mobile telephone or radio telephone station. Such term includes generally the ordinary residential and business or commercial telephone service within a local service area, and includes all types of such service, such as individual line and party line telephones, and extension telephones. Where, in addition to the basic periodic charge for such telephone service within the local service area, there are additional charges, for example, for calls in excess of a certain number or for calls between certain points within the same local service area, the telephone service for which such additional charges are made is included within the term "general telephone service". These additional charges for services within a local service area, generally referred to as "message units", are not considered to be "toll charges". General telephone service, however, is not limited to service furnished within a local service area. Except as otherwise provided in this paragraph, the term includes any service furnished which is telephonic in nature, regardless of the commercial or other name or term by which such service may be known or designated, if the fixed or mobile telephone or radio telephone station used in conjunction with such service may be connected (directly or indirectly) to an exchange whether located within or without the local service area operated by a person engaged in the business of furnishing communication service, and if by means of such connection communication may be established with any other fixed or mobile telephone or radio telephone station. If the described facilities may be connected to such an exchange, the service constitutes general telephone service whether or not it is the practice of the subscriber to the service to make such connection, and whether or not the person engaged in the business of furnishing communication service permits the subscriber to make such connection. General telephone service also includes the use of any private branch exchange (and any fixed or mobile telephone or radio telephone station connected, directly or indirectly, with a private branch exchange), and any tie line or extension line (including an off-premise extension line), which may be connected, directly or indirectly, to an exchange operated by a person engaged in the business of furnishing communication service, if by means of such connection communication may be established with any other fixed or mobile telephone or radio telephone station. However, the term does not include any service which is toll telephone service or wire and equipment service.

For the definition of the term "toll charge", see paragraph (a) of § 49.4252-2. For provisions relating to coin-operatd telephones, see section 4253(a) and § 49.4253-1.

(b) *Amounts paid.*—For purposes of the tax in respect of general telephone service, the term "amounts paid" means the amounts collected for the service, whether the charge is made on a monthly or other periodic basis, or is based on the number of calls made, or is in the form of an assessment as in the case of a mutual telephone system. Where a basic periodic charge is made for the service, with additional charges for all calls or additional calls above a certain number, the additional charges are also subject to the tax. Other rules relating to amounts paid are as follows:

(1) Where the charge for telephone service includes an additional charge for not making payment within a specified time, the total amount paid including the additional charge is the basis for computing the amount of tax due. Similarly, where a discount is allowed for the payment within a specified time of a charge for service rendered, the tax is to be computed on the amount actually paid.

(2) Assessments or charges paid by members or subscribers of a mutual or cooperative telephone company, association, or system for switching services, or for the repair or replacement of instruments, poles, wires, equipment, etc., incidental to ordinary maintenance, are subject to the tax.

(3) All amounts paid by subscribers for private branch exchange service, for the use of switchboard, switching, and other telephone equipment, for the use of trunk line facilities, for tie lines connecting private branch exchanges, and for any extension line, are subject to the tax on general telephone service.

(4) The tax attaches to the total charge made to a hotel or similar subscriber for general telephone service furnished to the hotel or its guests, but no tax attaches to any charge made by the hotel for service rendered in placing the calls for its guests.

(5) In cases where a person leases lines or channels, equipment, and other facilities used in conjunction with general telephone service, the amounts paid by such person for such lines or channels, equipment, and other facilities constitute amounts paid for general telephone service, notwithstanding the fact that the lines or channels, equipment, and other facilities used in conjunction with such service are supplied by different persons or in part by the user of such service.

(c) *Cross reference.*—For other provisions relating to general telephone service, see § 49.4252-4. [Reg. § 49.4252-1.]

☐ [*T.D.* 6664, 7-15-63.]

[Reg. § 49.4252-2]

§ 49.4252-2. Toll telephone service.—(a) *In general.*—The term "toll telephone service" means any telephone or radio telephone message or conversation for which there is a toll charge, and the charge is paid within the United States. A toll charge is a charge made for such a message or conversation to a place beyond the local service area. For the meaning of the term "United States", see paragraph (d) of § 49.4252-4.

(b) *Amounts paid.*—(1) The tax in respect of toll telephone service is imposed on the total amount paid for the service, including any charge, in addition to the basic toll charge, made for "overtime" in connection with a telephone or radio telephone message or conversation.

(2) The tax attaches to the total charge made to a hotel or similar subscriber for toll telephone service furnished to the hotel or its guests, but no tax attaches to any charge made by the hotel for service rendered in placing the calls for its guests.

(c) *Cross reference.*—For provisions relating to toll telephone messages communicated through the use of coin-operated telephones, see section 4253 (a) and § 49.4253-1. For other provisions relating to toll telephone service. see § 49.4252-4. [Reg. § 49.4252-2.]

☐ [T.D. 6664, 7-15-63.]

[Reg. § 49.4252-3]

§ 49.4252-3. Telegraph service.—(a) *In general.*—The term "telegraph service" means a telegraph, cable, or radio dispatch or message for which the charge is paid within the United States. For the meaning of the term "United States", see paragraph (d) of § 49.4252-4.

(b) *Amounts paid.*—A charge made for a telephone toll call used by a telegraph company in effecting delivery of a telegraph message shall be added to the basic charge for the transmission of the telegraph message for the purpose of determining the amount subject to tax. In such case, the telegraph company is not liable for tax on the amount paid by it to the telephone company for the toll call. A charge made for a telephone call which is used to reach a telegraph office for the purpose of sending a telegraph message should not be added to the basic charge for the transmission of the telegraph message, as the telegraph message is considered to begin at the telegraph office.

(c) *Cross reference.*—For provisions relating to telegraph messages communicated through the use of coin-operated telephones, see section 4253(a) and § 49.4253-1. For other provisions relating to telegraph service, see § 49.4252-4. [Reg. § 49.4252-3.]

☐ [T.D. 6664, 7-15-63.]

[Reg. § 49.4252-4]

§ 49.4252-4. Provisions common to telephone and telegraph services.—(a) *In general.*—The tax applies to all amounts paid for services rendered which are incidental to the transmission of a message or conversation. Where dispatches, messages, or conversations are transmitted by telephone, radiotelephone, telegraph, cable, or radio free of any charge whatsoever, no tax attaches, but where the carrier in fact makes some charge for the transmission, either in money, service, or other valuable consideration, such charge is subject to the tax upon the basis of the amount of the charge computed in money or money's worth. The tax is payable by the person paying the transmission charge and is to be collected by the person receiving the payment. If a message, dispatch, or conversation is transmitted "collect", the person who pays the charge therefor is liable for the tax. All telephone and telegraph transmission services when rendered for hire are subject to tax whether or not the agency furnishing such services is a common carrier. For provisions relating to the computation of tax with respect to charges for telephone and telegraph services, see section 4254 and §§ 49.4254-1 and 49.4254-2.

(b) *When transmission begins and ends.*—Transmission begins when the message is delivered by the sender to the carrier, or its agent, and continues until receipt by the addressee or his agent. Thus, an amount paid to a telephone, telegraph, radio, or cable company for messenger service in bringing the recipient of a message to the telephone, or in delivering a dispatch or message, must be included in determining the total amount subject to tax. However, an amount paid for messenger service rendered by a hotel or similar establishment is not to be included in the total charge on which the tax is computed.

(c) *Services rendered under contract.*—(1) Except as an exemption may otherwise be specifically provided for in this part, where, under the provisions of a contract, dispatches, messages, or conversations are transmitted by telephone, radiotelephone, telegraph, cable, or radio in consideration of the payment of a lump sum of money or the performance of services, the amounts paid for such transmissions are subject to tax regardless of whether such dispatches, messages, or conversations relate to the operation of the business of a common carrier and whether they are "on line" or "off line".

(2) Where a telegraph company agrees to transmit over its wires dispatches or messages relating to the business of a carrier free or at reduced rates in consideration of services to be performed by the carrier in transporting men or materials of the telegraph company, all such dispatches or messages are subject to tax.

(d) *Meaning of the term "United States".*—For purposes of section 4252(b) and (c), the term "United States" includes the States and the District of Columbia. Such term also includes inland waters (such as rivers, lakes, bays, etc.) lying wholly within the United States, and, where an international boundary line divides inland waters, such parts of such inland waters as lie within the boundary of the United States, and also the waters known as a marine league from low tide on the coast line. Ships within these limits whether of foreign or domestic registry are considered to be within the United States.

(e) *Exemptions.*—For exemptions from the taxes imposed on amounts paid for telephone and telegraph services, see sections 4253, 4292, 4293, and 4294, and the regulations thereunder contained in this part. [Reg. § 49.4252-4.]

☐ [T.D. 6664, 7-15-63.]

[Reg. § 49.4252-5]

§ 49.4252-5. Teletypewriter exchange service.—(a) *In general.*—The term "teletypewriter exchange service" means any service where a teletypewriter(or similar device) may be connected, directly or indirectly, to an exchange operated by a person engaged in the business of furnishing communication service, if by means of such connection communication may be established with any other teletypewriter (or similar device). If the teletypewriter or similar device used in conjunction with such service may be connected to such an exchange, the service constitutes teletypewriter exchange service whether or not it is the practice of the subscriber to the service to make such connection, and whether or not the person engaged in the business of furnishing communication service permits the subscriber to make such connection.

(b) *Amounts paid.*—In determining the amount of tax due, the amount paid for the service shall include all charges made in connection with the furnishing of any teletypewriter exchange service, such as salaries of operators, if in the employ of the person furnishing such service, charges for equipment, instruments, and other apparatus. In cases where a person leases lines or channels, equipment, and other facilities used in conjunction with teletypewiter exchange service, the amounts paid by such person for such lines or channels, equipment, and other facilities constitute amounts paid for teletypewriter exchange service, notwithstanding the fact that the lines or channels, equipment, and other facilities used in conjunction with such service are supplied by different persons or in part by the user of such service.

(c) *Exemptions.*—For exemptions from the tax imposed on amounts paid for teletypewriter exchange service, see sections 4253, 4292, 4293, and 4294, and the regulations thereunder contained in this part. [Reg. § 49.4252-5.]

☐ [T.D. 6664, 7-15-63.]

[Reg. § 49.4252-6]

§ 49.4252-6. Wire mileage service.—(a) *In general.*—The meaning of the term "wire mileage service" differs depending upon the date on which the service is furnished. For services furnished on or after January 1, 1963, the term means any telephone or radio telephone service not used in the conduct of a trade or business, and any other wire or radio circuit service not used in the conduct of a trade or business, which is not included in § § 49.4252-1 through 49.4252-3, 49.4252-5, and 49.4252-7. The term

"trade or business" as used in this section includes activities of organizations which are conducted with no purpose of gain or profit. For services furnished before January 1, 1963, the term means any telephone or radio telephone service, and any other wire or radio circuit service, which is not included in § § 49.4252-1 through 49.4252-3, 49.4252-5, and 49.4252-7. However, regardless of the date on which the service is furnished, any service which is exempt from tax for any reason specified in section 4253 is not included in wire mileage service. In general, the term means (except as qualified by the preceding sentences of this paragraph) any telephone or radiotelephone service, and any other wire or radio circuit service, which may not be connected, directly or indirectly, to an exchange operated by a person engaged in the business of furnishing communication service. Wire mileage service ordinarily relates to private line or private channel service where lines or channels, equipment, and other facilities are furnished (usually but not necessarily, on a contractual basis) to enable users to communicate between specified locations continuously or for specified periods, as distinguished from the sending of single dispatches, messages, and conversations by telephone, radiotelephone, telegraph, cable, or radio, for which tolls are charged by the carrier. The communications may be telephonic or in code, or may be reproduced at the terminating end in the form of a typewritten page or tape, or picture facsimile. The term "wire mileage service" does not include any service which is used exclusively in furnishing wire and equipment service.

(b) *Examples.*—The following are examples of wire mileage service (except that in the case of services furnished on or after January 1, 1963, wire mileage service does not include any such services used in the conduct of a trade or business):

   (1) Channels and equipment for private telephone service,

   (2) Channels and equipment for private code service,

   (3) Channels and equipment for private teletypewriter or teleprinter service,

   (4) Channels and equipment for program transmission, and

   (5) Channels and equipment for photograph, picture or facsimile transmission, etc.

(c) *Amounts paid.*—In determining the amount of tax due, the amount paid for the service shall include all charges made in connection with the furnishing of any wire mileage service, such as salaries of operators, if in the employ of the person furnishing such service, charges for equipment, instruments, and other apparatus other than station terminal equipment. In cases where a person leases lines or channels, equipment, and other facilities used in conjunction with wire mileage service, the amounts paid by such person for such lines or channels, equipment, and other facilities constitute amounts

Reg. § 49.4252-6(c)

paid for wire mileage service, notwithstanding the fact that the lines or channels, equipment, and other facilities used in conjunction with such service are supplied by different persons or in part by the user of such service.

(d) *Exemptions.*—For exemptions from the tax imposed on amounts paid for wire mileage service, see sections 4253, 4292, 4293, and 4294, and the regulations thereunder contained in this part. [Reg. § 49.4252-6.]

☐ [*T.D.* 6664, 7-15-63.]

[Reg. § 49.4252-7]

§ 49.4252-7. Wire and equipment service.—(a) *In general.*—The term "wire and equipment service" includes stock quotation and information services, burglar alarm or fire alarm service, and all other similar services (whether or not oral transmission is involved). In general, the term relates to wire lines or channels and equipment by means of which information or services are furnished to the subscriber. The phrase "all other similar services" includes innovations in the wire and equipment field. The term does not include teletypewriter exchange service or any service furnished by any means other than wire communication. Tax is imposed on the amounts paid for such wire lines or channels, equipment, and information or services.

(b) *Examples.*—The following are examples of wire and equipment service:

(1) Burglar, fire, or other alarm service where the service consists of wire lines or channels furnished between a remote point and the subscriber's premises, or a police or fire station, or a central station, and over which a signal is transmitted in the case of illegal entry, fire, leakage, etc.

(2) Wire lines or channels furnished between a point of origin and the subscriber's premises over which are given stock and bond market quotations and reports, racing results, baseball scores, and other sporting results, news items, musical programs, weather reports, the time, etc.

(3) Metering services, including wire lines or channels and equipment, furnished between a remote point and the subscriber's premises, over which signals are transmitted so that the subscriber may obtain information as to a given condition at the remote point, such as water level, water pressure, gas pressure, etc.

(4) Remote control wire lines or channels furnished between a remote point and the subscriber's premises over which signals are transmitted which will actuate an instrument at the remote point.

(c) *Amounts paid.*—In determining the amount of tax due, the amount paid for the service shall include all charges made in connection with the furnishing of any wire and equipment services, such as salaries of operators, if in the employ of the person furnishing such service, charges for equipment, instruments, and other apparatus. Where the service rendered includes the furnish-

ing of information or programs such as stock market quotations, baseball scores, racing results, weather reports, or musical programs, etc., any amounts charged for information or programs furnished shall also be included, whether or not individual items are charged or billed separately. In cases where a person leases lines or channels, equipment, and other facilities used in conjunction with wire and equipment service, the amounts paid by such person for such lines or channels, equipment, and other facilities constitute amounts paid for wire and equipment service, notwithstanding the fact that the lines or channels, equipment, and other facilities used in conjunction with such service are supplied by different persons or in part by the user of such service.

(d) *Relationship to wire mileage service.*—The tax on wire mileage service does not apply in respect of any service which is used exclusively in furnishing wire and equipment service. See § 49.4252-6.

(e) *Exemptions.*—For exemptions from the tax imposed on amounts paid for wire and equipment service, see sections 4253, 4292, 4293, and 4294, and the regulations thereunder contained in this part. [Reg. § 49.4252-7.]

☐ [*T.D.* 6664, 7-15-63.]

[Reg. § 49.4253-1]

§ 49.4253-1. Exemption for certain coin-operated service.—(a) *In general.*—Except as provided in paragraph (b) of this section, the tax imposed on amounts paid for general telephone service is not applicable to a single telephone conversation paid for by inserting coins in a public coin-operated telephone. The tax imposed on amounts paid for toll telephone service or telegraph service is not applicable to a single telephone conversation for which a toll charge is made (see paragraph (a) of § 49.4252-2), or to a telegraph message, if the charge for such toll telephone service (including any additional charge for overtime) or telegraph service is less than 25 cents and is paid for by inserting coins in a public coin-operated telephone.

(b) *Exception where service furnished for a guaranteed amount.*—Where a coin-operated telephone service is furnished for a guaranteed amount, the amount paid under such guarantee plus any fixed monthly or other periodic charge is subject to the tax imposed on amounts paid for general telephone service. The tax applies to the full amount of the guarantee whether such amount is paid out of receipts from the coin-box of the telephone or from funds of the subscriber. [Reg. § 49.4253-1.]

☐ [*T.D.* 6664, 7-15-63.]

[Reg. § 49.4253-2]

§ 49.4253-2. Exemption for news services.—(a) *In general.*—The exemption for news services provided by section 4253(b) is applicable to payments for services of the kind listed in section 4251, except general telephone service. The exemption will apply only with respect to payments for services which are utilized exclusively:

(1) In the collection of news for the public press or radio or television broadcasting or in the dissemination of news through the public press or by means of radio or television broadcasting; or

(2) In the collection or dissemination of news by a news ticker service furnishing a general news service similar to that of the public press.

For the exemption to apply, the charge for the services must be billed in writing to the person paying for the services and such person must certify in writing that the services are so utilized.

(b) *Scope of the exemption.*—(1) The exemption applies to amounts charged for messages from any newspaper, press association, radio or television news broadcasting agency, or news ticker service, to any other newspaper, press association, radio or television news broadcasting agency, or news ticker service, or to or from their bona fide correspondents, which messages deal exclusively with the collection of news items for, or the dissemination of news items through, the public press, radio or television broadcasting, or a news ticker service furnishing a general news service similar to that of the public press. The exemption does not extend to messages of an administrative nature such as messages transmitting funds to correspondents, messages to correspondents relating to assignments or hotel accommodations, etc.

(2) The exemption does not extend to the collection and dissemination of information or matters for publication in magazines, periodicals, and trade and scientific publications issued to supply information on certain subjects of interest to particular groups; or to amounts paid by newspapers, press associations, radio or television news broadcasting agencies or networks, or news ticker services, for general telephone service taxable under section 4251. [Reg. §49.4253-2.]

☐ [*T.D.* 6664, 7-15-63.]

[Reg. §49.4253-3]

§49.4253-3. Exemption for certain organizations.—(a) *The American National Red Cross.*—The taxes imposed by section 4251 do not apply to amounts paid for services furnished to the American National Red Cross.

(b) *International organizations.*—The taxes imposed by section 4251 do not apply to amounts paid for services furnished to an international organization. See section 7701(a)(18) for the definition of "international organization". An international organization is designated as such by the President of the United States through an Executive order or orders. When an organization has been designated by the President as entitled to enjoy the privileges, exemptions, and immunities conferred by the International Organizations Immunities Act, or part thereof, including exemption from tax, the exemption applies to the taxes imposed by section 4251 on amounts paid for services unless the President otherwise provides. The exemption is subject to withdrawal or revocation by the President. In case of withdrawal or revocation, unless otherwise provided by the President, the exemption is inapplicable to payments made on or after the date of issuance of the order of withdrawal or the date of revocation.

(c) *Exemption certificate.*—(1) No exemption certificate is required under this section where the payment for the services furnished is made by the American National Red Cross direct to the person furnishing the services. In all other cases the right to exemption under section 4253(c) shall be evidenced by properly executed exemption certificates in substantially the following form:

EXEMPTION CERTIFICATE

. . . . (Date) 19 .

I certify that . . . . (Name of service) have been furnished by . . . . (Telephone, telegraph company, etc.) to . . . . (International Organization, etc.); that the charges of $ . . . . . will be paid from . . . . (International Organization, etc.) funds; and that the charges are exempt from tax under section 4253(c) of the Internal Revenue Code.

. . . .
(Signature of Officer or Employee)

. . . .
(Address) (Title)

NOTE: Penalty for fraudulent use, $10,000 or imprisonment, or both.

(2) See §49.4253-11 for further provisions relating to exemption certificates. [Reg. §49.4253-3.]

☐ [*T.D.* 6664, 7-15-63.]

[Reg. §49.4253-4]

§49.4253-4. Exemption for servicemen in combat zone.—(a) *In general.*—The exemption provided by section 4253(d) is applicable to any payment received for any telephone or radio telephone message or call which originates within a combat zone, as defined in section 112, from a member of the Armed Forces of the United States performing service in such combat zone, if a properly executed certificate of exemption substantially in the form shown in paragraph (c) of this section is furnished to the person receiving such payment.

(b) *Service in combat zone.*—Service is performed in a combat zone only if it is performed in an area which the President of the United States has designated by Executive order, for the purpose of section 112, as an area in which Armed Forces of the United States are or have engaged in combat, and only if it is performed on or after the date designated by the President by Executive order as the date of the commencing of combatant activities in such zone and on or before the date designated by the President by Executive order as the date of the termination of combatant activities in such zone.

(c) *Exemption certificate.*—(1) The exemption certificate shall be in substantially the following form:

EXEMPTION CERTIFICATE
(Overseas Telephone Calls)

. . . . (Date) 19 . . .

I certify that the toll charges of $ . . . . . are for telephone or radio telephone messages originating at . . . . (Point of origin) within a combat zone from . . . . (Name) a member of the Armed Forces of the United States performing service in such combat zone; that the transmission facilities were furnished by . . . . (Name of carrier); and that the charges are exempt from tax under section 4253(d) of the Internal Revenue Code.

. . . .
(Signature of Subscriber)

. . . .
(Address)

NOTE: Penalty for fraudulent use, $10,000 or imprisonment or both.

(2) See §49.4253-11 for further provisions relating to exemption certificates. [Reg. §49.4253-4.]

☐ [*T.D.* 6664, 7-15-63.]

[Reg. §49.4253-5]

§49.4253-5. Exemption for items otherwise taxed.—A dispatch, message, or conversation transmitted by toll telephone, telegraph, or teletypewriter exchange over the combined facilities of several lines or stations of one or more persons is considered to be one dispatch, message, or conversation, and is subject to only one payment of tax under section 4251. [Reg. §49.4253-5.]

☐ [*T.D.* 6664, 7-15-63.]

[Reg. §49.4253-6]

§49.4253-6. Exemption for common carriers and communications companies.—(a) *In general.*—(1) The taxes imposed by section 4251 on amounts paid for wire mileage service and wire and equipment service do not apply to amounts paid for any such services to the extent that the amounts paid are for services utilized by a common carrier, telephone or telegraph company, or television or radio broadcasting station or network in the conduct of its business as such.

(2) The tax imposed by section 4251 on amounts paid for general telephone service does not apply to amounts paid for the use of a continuous telephone or radio telephone line or channel to the extent that the amounts paid are for use by a common carrier, telephone or telegraph company, or television or radio broadcasting station or network in the conduct of its business as such, if such line or channel connects stations between any two of which there would otherwise be a toll charge. A line or channel connects stations between which there would otherwise be a toll charge if the telephone company makes a toll charge for a single message transmitted between the two stations in the case of the ordinary residential and business or commercial telephone service. A line or channel connecting two stations is considered a continuous line or channel if such line or channel does not connect with any switchboard interposed between the two stations, which makes it possible to carry on two or more independent conversations simultaneously. Where a line or channel connects with such a switchboard, the exemption is inapplicable to so much of the amount paid as is attributable to the portion of the line or channel which extends from a station to a switchboard located in the same local service area.

(b) *Exemption inapplicable.*—This particular exemption is not applicable in the case of the taxes imposed on amounts paid for other services by section 4251, even though such services are utilized by the companies described in the conduct of their business as such. [Reg. §49.4253-6.]

☐ [*T.D.* 6664, 7-15-63.]

[Reg. §49.4253-7]

§49.4253-7. Exemption for installation charges.—(a) *In general.*—The taxes imposed by section 4251 do not apply to any amount paid as is properly attributable to the installation of any instrument, wire, pole, switchboard, apparatus, or equipment.

(b) *Maintenance charges subject to tax.*—The exemption provided by section 4253(g) and paragraph (a) of this section is applicable only to amounts paid for installation. Amounts paid for the repair or replacement of instruments, wires, poles, switchboards, apparatus, or equipment, incidental to ordinary maintenance, are subject to tax. [Reg. §49.4253-7.]

☐ [*T.D.* 6664, 7-15-63.]

[Reg. §49.4253-8]

§49.4253-8. Exemption for terminal facilities in case of wire mileage service.—The taxes imposed by section 4251 do not apply to so much of any amount paid for wire mileage service as is paid for, and properly attributable to, the use of any sending or receiving set or device which is station terminal equipment. In general, the term "station terminal equipment" refers to any sending or receiving set or device which is located at the terminals of a line or channel, and does not refer to any such set or device which is otherwise a part of such line or channel. [Reg. §49.4253-8.]

☐ [*T.D.* 6664, 7-15-63.]

[Reg. §49.4253-9]

§49.4253-9. Exemption for certain interior communication systems.—(a) *In general.*—The taxes imposed by section 4251 do not apply to amounts paid for wire mileage service or wire and equipment service, if such service is rendered through the use of an interior communication system.

(b) *Interior communication system.*—The term "interior communication system" means any system:

(1) No part of which is situated off the premises of the subscriber, and which may not be connected, directly or indirectly, with any communication system any part of which is situated off the premises of the subscriber; or

(2) Which is situated exclusively in a vehicle of the subscriber and which is not connected with a communications system.

(c) *Examples.*—The following are examples of interior communication systems:

(1) Burglar, fire, or other alarm service, where the service consists of lines or channels and equipment which are contained solely in the building of the subscriber, and by means of which an alarm is sounded in the building in the case of illegal entry, fire, leakage, etc.

(2) Metering services, including lines or channels and equipment, furnished between two points which are located upon the subscriber's property, and which are not separated by property not owned or leased by the subscriber, over which signals are transmitted so that the subscriber may obtain information as to a given condition at one of the points, such as water level, water pressure, gas pressure, etc. [Reg. §49.4253-9.]

☐ [*T.D.* 6664, 7-15-63.]

[Reg. §49.4253-10]

§49.4253-10. Exemption for certain private communications services.—(a) *In general.*—The tax imposed by section 4251 on amounts paid for general telephone service does not apply to amounts paid for any such service furnished on or after January 1, 1963, to the extent that the amounts paid are for use of any telephone or radio telephone line or channel (including equipment, instruments, and other apparatus furnished exclusively for use in connection with the line or channel) in the conduct of a trade or business when such line or channel is furnished between specified locations in different States or between specified locations in different counties, municipalities, or similar political subdivisions of a State. The term "trade or business" as used in this section includes activities of organizations which are conducted with no purpose of gain or profit. A line or channel is considered to be furnished between specified locations only when the line or channel connects preselected points without the use of switching functions performed by a communications company ex-

change. Where an amount is paid which includes a charge for such a line or channel and also a charge for the service provided by means of switching functions performed by a communications company exchange, the exemption is applicable only to that portion of the amount so paid as is attributable to such a line or channel. The preselected points must be located in different States or in different counties or municipalities of the same State. If the preselected points are located in a State in which the political subdivisions are not denominated as counties or municipalities, then the preselected points must be in different political subdivisions of such State which correspond to counties or municipalities. For purposes of this paragraph the term "municipality" means the largest political subdivision of a State below the level of county or similar subdivision. For the exemption to apply, the charge for the service must be billed in writing to the person paying for the service and such person must certify in writing that the service is for use in the conduct of a trade or business.

(b) *Exemption inapplicable.*—This particular exemption is not applicable in the case of taxes imposed on amounts paid for other services by section 4251, even though such services are utilized in the conduct of a trade or business. [Reg. §49.4253-10.]

☐ [*T.D.* 6664, 7-15-63.]

[Reg. §49.4253-11]

§49.4253-11. Use and retention of exemption certificates.—A separate exemption certificate(as required by §§49.4253-3 and 49.4253-4) shall be furnished for each message paid for as a separate item, but where periodic payments are made, a blanket certificate (for a period not to exceed four calendar quarters) may be accepted as evidence of the right to exemption. An agent of a telegraph, telephone, radio, or cable company should not accept an exemption certificate unless satisfied, on the basis of proper credentials or otherwise, that the person who signed it is the person whom he represents himself to be and that the exemption claimed is allowable under the law. Exemption certificates should be retained with the record of the services rendered for inspection by internal revenue officers as provided in section 6001 and the regulations in Subpart G of this part. [Reg. §49.4253-11.]

☐ [*T.D.* 6664, 7-15-63.]

[Reg. §49.4253-12]

§49.4253-12. Cross reference.—For exemptions applicable to amounts received as payment for services furnished to the government of any State or political subdivision of a State, to the District of Columbia, to the government of the United States, or to certain nonprofit educational organizations, see sections 4292, 4293, and 4294, and the regulations thereunder contained in Subpart F of this part. [Reg. §49.4253-12.]

☐ [*T.D.* 6664, 7-15-63.]

[Reg. §49.4254-1]

§49.4254-1. Computation of tax.—(a) *General rule.*—Except as provided in paragraph (b) of this section, when a bill is rendered to the taxpayer covering charges for general telephone service, toll telephone service, or telegraph service, with respect to which a tax is imposed by section 4251, the amount upon which the tax with respect to such services shall be based shall be the sum of all such charges for such services included in the bill.

(b) *Special rule in certain cases.*—When a bill is rendered to the taxpayer covering charges for general telephone service, toll telephone service, or telegraph service, with respect to which a tax is imposed by section 4251, by a person who groups individual items for purposes of rendering the bill and computing the tax, then the amount on which the tax with respect to each such group shall be based shall be the sum of all items within that group, and the tax on remaining items not included in any such group shall be based on the charge for each item separately. [Reg. §49.4254-1.]

☐ *[T.D. 6664, 7-15-63.]*

[Reg. §49.4254-2]

§49.4254-2. Payment for toll telephone service or telegraph service in coin-operated telephones.—Where the tax on a toll telephone or radio telephone message or conversation, or a telegraph, cable, or radio dispatch or message is paid by inserting coins in a coin-operated telephone, the tax shall be computed to the nearest multiple of 5 cents, and where the tax is midway between multiples of 5 cents, the next highest multiple shall apply. In other words, one-half or a greater fraction of 5 cents shall be treated as 5 cents and a smaller fraction shall be ignored. [Reg. §49.4254-2.]

☐ *[T.D. 6664, 7-15-63.]*

[Reg. §49.4261-1]

§49.4261-1. Imposition of tax; in general.—(a) *Transportation beginning before November 16, 1962.*—Section 4261 imposes a tax equal to 10 percent of the amount paid for taxable transportation of persons by rail, motor vehicles, water, or air which begins before November 16, 1962. For the definition of the term "taxable transportation", see section 4262 and §§49.4262(a)-1 and 49.4262(b)-1. The tax accrues at the time payment is made for the transportation, irrespective of when the transportation is furnished if the transportation actually begins before November 16, 1962.

(b) *Transportation beginning after November 15, 1962.*—Section 4261 imposes a tax equal to 5 percent of the amount paid for the air portion of taxable transportation of persons which begins after November 15, 1962, and before July 1, 1965. For definition of the term "taxable transportation", see section 4262 and §§49.4262(a)-1 and 49.4262(b)-1. The tax accrues at the time payment is made for the transportation, irrespective of when the transportation is furnished if the transportation actually begins after November 15, 1962, and before July 1, 1965.

(c) *In general.*—The purpose of the transportation, whether business or pleasure, is immaterial. It is not necessary that the transportation be between two definite points. If not otherwise exempt, a payment for continuous transportation beginning and ending at the same point is subject to the tax. For the rate of tax with respect to amounts paid for seating and sleeping accommodations in connection with taxable transportation, see §49.4261-9. [Reg. §49.4261-1.]

☐ *[T.D. 6618, 11-13-62. Amended by T.D. 6694, 12-4-63 and T.D. 6753, 9-8-64.]*

[Reg. §49.4261-2]

§49.4261-2. Application of tax.—(a) *Tax on total amount paid.*—The tax is measured by the total amount paid, whether paid at one time or collected at intervals during the course of a continuous transportation, as in the case of a carrier operating under the zone system. For the application of the tax with respect to amount paid for seating or sleeping accommodations in connection with taxable transportation, see §49.4261-9.

(b) *Tax on transportation of each person.*—The tax is determined by the amount paid for transportation with respect to each person. Thus, where a single payment is made for the transportation of two or more persons, the taxability of the payment and the amount of the tax, if any, payable with respect thereto, must be determined on the basis of the portion of the total payment properly allocable to each person transported.

(c) *Charges for nontransportation services.*—Where a payment covers charges for nontransportation services as well as for transportation of a person, such as charges for meals, hotel accommodations, etc., the charges for the nontransportation services may be excluded in computing the tax payable with respect to such payment, provided such charges are separable and are shown in the exact amounts thereof in the records pertaining to the transportation charge. If the charges for nontransportation services are not separable from the charge for transportation of the person, the tax must be computed upon the full amount of the payment. [Reg. §49.4261-2.]

☐ *[T.D. 6430, 12-3-59. Amended by T.D. 6518, 12-21-60 and T.D. 6618, 11-14-62.]*

[Reg. §49.4261-3]

§49.4261-3. Payments made within the United States.—(a) *Transportation beginning and ending in the United States or the 225-mile zone.*—The tax imposed by section 4261(a) applies to payments made within the United States for transportation which begins in the United States or in the 225-mile zone and ends in the United States or in the 225-mile zone. For example, an amount paid within the United States for transportation between New York and Montreal, Canada; between Vancouver, Canada, and Windsor, Canada; or between Nogales, Mexico, and Hermosillo, Mexico, would be fully taxable. See section 4262(c)(2) and paragraph (b) of §49.4262(c)-1 for the definition of the term "225-mile zone."

(b) *Other transportation.*—(1) *Transportation beginning before November 16, 1962.*—In the case of transportation beginning before November 16, 1962 (other than that described in paragraph (a) of this section), for which payment is made in the United States, the tax applies with respect to the amount paid for that portion of such transportation which is directly or indirectly from one port or station in the United States to another port or station in the United States. Transportation that (i) begins in the United States or in the 225-mile zone and ends outside such area, (ii) begins outside the United States or the 225-mile zone and ends inside such area, or (iii) begins outside the United States and ends outside such area is taxable only with respect to such portion of the transportation which is directly or indirectly from one port or station in the United States to another such port or station. Thus, on a trip from Chicago to London, England, with a stopover at New York, for which payment is made in the United States, the tax would apply to the part of the payment which is applicable to the transportation from Chicago to New York.

(2) *Transportation beginning after November 15, 1962.*—In the case of transportation beginning after November 15, 1962 (other than that described in paragraph (a) of this section), for which payment is made in the United States, the tax applies with respect to the amount paid for that portion of such transportation by air which is directly or indirectly from one port or station in the United States to another port or station in the United States, but only if such portion is not a part of "uninterrupted international air transportation" within the meaning of section 4262(c)(3) and paragraph (c) of §49.4262(c)-1. Transportation that

(i) Begins in the United States or the 225-mile zone and ends outside such area,

(ii) Begins outside the United States or the 225-mile zone and ends inside such area, or

(iii) Begins outside the United States and ends outside such area is taxable only with respect to such portion of the transportation by air which is directly or indirectly from one port or station in the United States to another port or station in the United States, but only if such portion is not a part of "uninterrupted international air transportation" within the meaning of section 4262(c)(3) and paragraph (c) of §49.4262(c)-1. Thus, on a trip by air from Chicago to London, England, with a stopover at New York, for which payment is made in the United States, if the portion from Chicago to New York is not a part of "uninterrupted international air transportation" within the meaning of section 4262(c)(3) and paragraph (c) of §49.4262(c)-1, the tax would apply to the part of the payment which is applicable to the transpor-

tation from Chicago to New York. However, if the portion from Chicago to New York is a part of "uninterrupted international air transportation" within the meaning of section 4262(c)(3) and paragraph (c) of §49.4262(c)-1, the tax would not apply.

(c) *Method of computing tax on taxable portion.*—Where a payment is made for transportation which is partially taxable under paragraph (b) of this section—

(1) The tax may be computed on that portion of the total amount paid which the mileage of the taxable portion of the transportation bears to the mileage of the entire trip, or

(2) The tax may be computed on the basis of the applicable local fare for transportation of a like class between the ports or stations referred to in paragraph (b) of this section. Where a uniform fare is charged for transportation between a station and any coastal gateway point of embarkation on a trip to the same international destination, the tax may be computed on the basis of such uniform fare. In the absence of a fare described in this subparagraph, the tax must be determined in accordance with subparagraph (1) of this paragraph. If an international trip includes a leg between coastal gateway points of embarkation for which no additional fare is charged, no tax shall be applicable to such leg of the transportation.

(d) *Cross reference.*—See section 4262(b) and §49.4262(b)-1 for a partial exclusion with respect to amounts paid for certain transportation. [Reg. §49.4261-3.]

☐ [T.D. 6430, 12-3-59. *Amended by T.D.* 6618, 11-14-62.]

[Reg. §49.4261-4]

§49.4261-4. Payments made within the United States; evidence of nontaxability.—(a) *Presumption of taxability.*—The tax imposed by section 4261(a) shall apply to any amount paid within the United States for the transportation of any person, unless the taxpayer establishes in accordance with the provisions of this section that at the time of payment the transportation is not transportation in respect of which tax is imposed by section 4261(a) (see section 4264(d)).

(b) *Through tickets.*—In the case of transportation which is wholly or in part not taxable transportation, the issuance of one ticket (commonly known as a "through ticket") covering such transportation will be sufficient to establish that the amount paid for such transportation is wholly or in part not subject to tax. Thus, if A purchases a through ticket in the United States for transportation by air which begins before November 16, 1962, from Chicago to Edmonton, Canada, with a stopover at Minneapolis, no further evidence will be required to establish that no tax applies with respect to the amount paid for the portion of transportation between Minneapolis and Edmonton. A similar result will be reached if a through ticket is purchased for the same air transportation which begins after November 15, 1962, and the trip is not "uninterrupted international air transportation" within the meaning of section 4262(c)(3) and paragraph (c) of §49.4262(c)-1. See paragraph (d) of this section for the information to be inscribed on all tickets issued for uninterrupted international air transportation.

(c) *Separate tickets.*—Where a separate ticket or order is issued for taxable transportation as defined in section 4262(a)(1) (referred to in this subpart as the "domestic ticket or order"), but the domestic ticket or order is to be used in conjunction with a ticket or order for additional transportation (referred to in this subpart as the "international ticket or order") which changes the tax consequences, unless the domestic ticket or order and the international ticket or order are purchased from a single agency or carrier at the same time, the person making payment for the domestic ticket or order shall at the time of payment exhibit the international ticket or order to the agency or carrier receiving such payment. The agency or carrier which receives the payment for the domestic ticket or order shall inscribe the tickets or orders for the entire journey in the following manner:

(1) The international ticket or order shall be inscribed or stamped with an appropriate legend (for example, "Cannot be reused to obtain any tax exemption on a domestic ticket or order") to show that a domestic ticket or order has been purchased wholly or partially tax free for use in conjunction therewith.

(2) The domestic ticket or order shall be inscribed to show (i) the identity of the agency or carrier which received payment therefor (unless otherwise shown on the ticket or order), (ii) the origin and destination of the additional transportation, (iii) the identity of the carrier furnishing the additional transportation, and (iv) the serial number of the ticket or order covering such additional transportation. If the domestic ticket or order is not large enough to accommodate the prescribed inscription, a statement setting forth the required information shall be attached to such ticket or order.

(d) *Tickets issued for uninterrupted international air transportation.*—All tickets issued for "uninterrupted international air transportation" within the meaning of section 4262(c)(3) and paragraph (c) of §49.4262(c)-1, whether through tickets or separate tickets, must have inscribed thereon, in addition to the other information required in the regulations in this subpart, sufficient information from which may be ascertained the scheduled arrival and departure time at each stopover to which the six-hour scheduled interval requirement of section 4262(c)(3) applies. It will be sufficient, for example, if the airline ticket or tickets show the trip number and the date and time of departure of the aircraft from each such stopover point, provided the published airline schedules show the scheduled time of arrival at each such stopover point. [Reg. §49.4261-4.]

☐ [*T.D.* 6430, 12-3-59. *Amended by T.D.* 6618, 11-14-62.]

[Reg. §49.4261-5]

§49.4261-5. Payments made outside the United States.—(a) *In general.*—The tax imposed by section 4261(b) applies to amounts paid outside the United States for the taxable transportation of persons, but only if such transportation begins and ends in the United States. Thus, in addition to the exclusion provided for certain travel under section 4262(b), the tax imposed by section 4261(b) shall not apply unless the transportation both begins and ends within the United States. Accordingly, the tax does not apply to a payment made outside the United States for one-way or round-trip transportation between a point within the United States and a point outside the United States.

(b) *Transportation between two or more points in the United States.*—(1) For purposes of this section, a payment made outside the United States for transportation between two or more points in the United States is a payment for transportation which begins and ends in the United States, even though additional transportation to or from a point outside the United States is involved in the entire journey, if at the time of making payment for the transportation between two or more points in the United States it is not definitely established, under the rules set forth in §49.4261-6, that such transportation is purchased for use in making the journey from or to a point outside the United States. The fact that the entire journey includes transportation from or to a point outside the United States is not in itself determinative of the liability for tax.

(2) The following examples illustrate the application of this paragraph:

Example (1). W travels from Havana, Cuba, to New York by way of Miami. He purchases in Havana a steamship ticket for his transportation from Havana to Miami and an exchange order for air transportation from Miami to New York. The ticket for the connecting transportation from Havana to Miami, and the order for the transportation from Miami to New York were not appropriately inscribed by the agency or carrier which received the payment for the air transportation involved at the time such payment was received so as to clearly show that the ticket and order were purchased for use in conjunction with each other. Therefore, the agency or carrier which accepts the exchange order and issues the ticket for the transportation from Miami to New York is required to collect the tax which applied to the amount paid outside the United States for such transportation.

Example (2). X travels on a round trip from Montreal, Canada, to Los Angeles by way of New York. He purchases in Montreal air transportation for the round trip between New York and Los Angeles, and uses a private automobile for transportation from Montreal to New York and return to Montreal. The amount paid in Montreal for the round-trip transportation between New York and Los Angeles is a payment for transportation which begins and ends in the United States, and is therefore subject to tax.

(c) *Cross reference.*—See section 4262(b) and § 49.4262(b)-1 for a partial exclusion with respect to amounts paid for certain transportation. [Reg. § 49.4261-5.]

☐ [*T.D.* 6430, 12-3-59.]

[Reg. § 49.4261-6]

§ 49.4261-6. Payments made outside the United States; evidence of nontaxability.— (a) *In general.*—The tax does not apply to a payment made outside the United States for transportation which begins or ends outside the United States. For purposes of the preceding sentence, a payment made outside the United States for transportation between two or more points within the United States (such transportation being referred to hereinafter in this section as "the United States portion"), which is part of transportation from or to a point outside the United States is a payment for transportation which begins or ends outside the United States, where it is definitely established at the time of making payment for the United States portion that such portion is purchased for use in making the journey from or to a point outside the United States. The nontaxable character of the payment made outside the United States for the United States portion shall be established under the rules set forth in paragraphs (b) through (e) of this section.

(b) *Through tickets.*—Where one ticket (commonly known as a "through ticket") is issued to cover all of the United States portion of a journey which begins or ends outside the United States and to cover also the connecting transportation from or to a point outside the United States, no further evidence of the nontaxable character of the transportation covered by such ticket will be required.

(c) *Separate tickets.*—Where separate tickets or orders are issued for the United States portion of a journey which begins or ends outside the United States, the agency or carrier which receives payment for such tickets or orders shall definitely determine at the time of receiving the payment that the United States portion is being purchased for use in conjunction with connecting transportation from or to a point outside the United States, and shall appropriately inscribe the tickets or orders issued outside the United States for the United States portion and for the connecting transportation from or to a point outside the United States to show clearly that such tickets or orders are purchased for use in conjunction with each other. Such tickets or orders shall be inscribed in the following manner:

(1) The ticket or order for the connecting transportation from or to a point outside the United States shall be inscribed or stamped with an appropriate legend (for example, "Not to be used again for purchase of tax-free United States

transportation") to show that the United States portion has been purchased tax free for use in conjunction therewith.

(2) Where the ticket for the United States portion is issued outside the United States, it shall be inscribed to show (i) the identity of the agency or carrier which received payment therefor (unless otherwise shown on the ticket), (ii) the origin and destination of the connecting transportation, (iii) the identity of the carrier furnishing the connecting transportation, and (iv) the serial number of the ticket or order covering such connecting transportation. If the ticket is not large enough to accommodate the prescribed inscription, a statement setting forth the required information shall be attached to such ticket.

(3) Where an order for the United States portion is issued outside the United States, it shall be inscribed to show (i) the origin and destination of the connecting transportation, (ii) the identity of the carrier furnishing the connecting transportation, and (iii) the serial number of the ticket or order covering such connecting transportation.

(d) *Ticket issued pursuant to inscribed order.*—Where the ticket for the United States portion is issued in the United States pursuant to an order which was purchased and properly inscribed outside the United States under the rules set forth in paragraph (c)(3) of this section, liability for payment or collection of tax will not be incurred upon the issuance of the ticket provided the agency or carrier issuing such ticket stamps or inscribes thereon an appropriate legend, for example, "Tax not paid—furnished on order", or "Exempt—order".

(e) *Maintenance of records.*—In any case where a payment for the United States portion is not subject to tax under the rules set forth in this section, the carrier furnishing transportation for the United States portion shall procure and maintain appropriate evidence which will clearly show that the tickets or orders for such transportation were purchased for use in conjunction with connecting transportation from or to a point outside the United States.

(f) *Examples.*—The following are examples of nontaxable transportation:

Example (1). Y travels from London, England, to San Francisco by way of New York. He purchases from an agency or carrier in England all of the transportation involved in such journey, which includes air transportation from London to New York and from New York to San Francisco, for which separate tickets are issued. The agency or carrier which receives the payment for Y's transportation from New York to San Francisco will not be required to collect tax with respect to the payment, provided it determines at the time such payment is received that the transportation in question is being purchased for use in conjunction with the connecting transportation from London to New York and it appropriately inscribes both of the tickets for the journey.

Reg. § 49.4261-6(f)

Example (2). Z travels from Havana, Cuba, to New York by way of Miami. He purchases in Havana a ticket for his transportation by water from Havana to Miami, and later purchases from a travel agency in Havana air transportation from Miami to New York for which the travel agency issues an exchange order. To establish the nontaxable character of the payment for Z's transportation from Miami to New York the travel agency shall determine at the time payment is received by it that the transportation is being purchased for use in conjunction with the connecting transportation from Havana to Miami, and shall make the appropriate inscription on the ticket and the order. The carrier which accepts the exchange order and issues the ticket for the transportation from Miami to New York will not be required to collect tax with respect to the ticket so issued if it appropriately inscribes the ticket as provided in paragraph (d) of this section. [Reg. § 49.4261-6.]

☐ [T.D. 6430, 12-3-59.]

[Reg. § 49.4261-7]

§ 49.4261-7. Examples of payments subject to tax.—The following are examples of payments for transportation which, unless otherwise exempt under section 4263, 4292, 4293, or 4294 are subject to tax:

(a) *Cash fares.*—The tax applies to payments of so-called "cash fares" where no ticket or other evidence of the right to transportation is issued to the passenger.

(b) *Scrip books.*—The tax applies to the amounts paid for scrip books. The tax shall be collected from the purchaser at the time the scrip book is sold, and not when and as the scrip is used for transportation.

(c) *Additional charges.*—Amounts paid as additional charges for changing the class of accommodations, changing the destination or route, extending the time limit of a ticket, as "extra fare", or for exclusive occupancy of a section, etc., are subject to the tax.

(d) *Round-trip tickets.*—An amount of 61 cents or more paid for a round-trip ticket is taxable (1) if the one-way fare of like class is 61 cents or more, or (2) if there is no established one-way fare of like class.

(e) *Commutation or season tickets.*—(1) Amounts paid for commutation or season tickets good for more than one month are subject to tax where the single trip is 30 miles or more. For this purpose the term "30 miles" means 30 constructive miles where the rate for transportation is fixed on the constructive mileage. The tax shall be collected from the purchaser at the time of payment for the commutation or season ticket, and not when and as the ticket is used for transportation.

(2) In the event that a partly used exempt commutation or season ticket is redeemed and the carrier, in determining the amount of the refund, makes a charge at regular rates for the used portion of the ticket, the tax applies to such charge, if the one-way fare is more than 60 cents.

(f) *Prepaid orders, exchange orders, or similar orders.*—The tax applies to the amounts paid for prepaid orders, exchange orders, or similar orders for transportation. Additional amounts paid in procuring transportation in connection with the use of prepaid orders, exchange orders, or similar orders, are likewise subject to tax.

(g) *Combinations of rail, motor vehicle, water, or air transportation.*—The tax applies to the total amount paid for transportation over the lines of a number of connecting carriers; and also with respect to transportation beginning before November 16, 1962, to the total amount paid for any combination of rail, motor vehicle, water, or air transportation, such as rail-air line, air line-motor bus, or motor bus-steamship, etc. For transportation beginning after November 15, 1962, the tax will apply only to any portion of such transportation that is by air.

(h) *Chartered conveyances.*—(1) An amount paid for the charter

(i) Of a special car, train, motor vehicle, aircraft, or boat for transportation which begins before November 16, 1962, or

(ii) Of an aircraft for transportation which begins after November 15, 1962,

provided no charge is made by the charterer to the persons transported, is subject to tax if the amount paid for the charter represents a per capita charge of more than 60 cents for each person actually transported.

(2) The charterer of a conveyance who sells transportation to other persons must collect and account for the tax with respect to all amounts paid to him for transportation which are in excess of 60 cents. In such case, no tax will be due on the amount paid for the charter of the conveyance but it shall be the duty of the owner of the conveyance to advise the charterer of his liability for collecting and accounting for the tax.

(i) *All-expense tours.*—Amounts paid for all-expense tours are subject to tax with respect to that portion representing transportation which is subject to tax. See paragraph (c) of § 49.4261-2 and paragraph (f)(4) of § 49.4261-8.

(j) *Payments remitted to foreign countries by persons in the United States.*—Payments for transportation tickets, prepaid orders, exchange orders, or similar orders are subject to the tax where the payment for such tickets or orders is accomplished by the purchaser either (1) by transmission from within the United States via telegraph or mail of cash, checks, postal or telegraphic money orders, and similar drafts to ticket offices or travel agencies, etc., located in any place without the United States, or (2) by the delivery of the funds to an agency located in the United States for transmission to ticket offices, or travel agencies, etc., without the United States. Such payments are considered to be payments made within the United States. [Reg. § 49.4261-7.]

☐ [T.D. 6430, 12-3-59. *Amended by T.D. 6618,* 11-14-62.]

[Reg. §49.4261-8]

§49.4261-8. Examples of payments not subject to tax.—In addition to a payment specifically exempt under section 4263, 4292, 4293, or 4294, the following are examples of payments not subject to tax:

(a) *Exchange of prepaid order, scrip, etc., for tickets.*—A ticket issued pursuant to an exchange order, prepaid order, airline pilot order, or scrip is not subject to tax where the tax is paid at the time of payment for the order or scrip.

(b) *Caretakers and messengers accompanying freight shipments.*—The tax on the transportation of persons does not apply to amounts paid for transportation of freight that includes also the transportation of caretakers or messengers for which no specific charge as such is made.

(c) *Special baggage transportation equipment.*—An amount paid for special baggage transportation equipment is not subject to the tax on the transportation of persons if separable from the payment for transportation of persons and if shown in the exact amount of the charge on the records covering the taxable transportation payment.

(d) *Circus or show conveyances.*—The amount paid pursuant to a contract for the movement of a circus or show conveyance where the amount covers only the transportation of the performers, laborers, animals, equipment, etc., by such conveyances is not subject to the tax on the transportation of persons imposed by section 4261. However, if the contract payment also covers the issuance to advance agents, bill posters, etc., of circus or show scrip books, or other evidence of the right to transportation, for use on regular passenger conveyances, that portion of the contract payment properly allocable to such scrip books or other evidence is subject to the tax on the transportation of persons.

(e) *Corpses.*—The tax on the transportation of persons does not apply to the amount paid for the transportation of a corpse, but does apply to the amount paid for the transportation of any person accompanying the corpse.

(f) *Miscellaneous charges.*—Where the charge is separable from the payment for the transportation of a person and is shown in the exact amount thereof on the records pertaining to the transportation payment, the tax on the transportation of persons does not apply to the following and similar charges:

(1) Charges for transportation of baggage, including incidental charges such as excess value, storage, transfer, parcel checking, special delivery, etc.

(2) Charges for transportation of an automobile in connection with the transportation of a person.

(3) Charges for bridge or road toll, or a ferry charge of 60 cents or less, made in connection with the transportation beginning before November 16, 1962, of a person by bus. Charges incurred by the carrier which are part of its costs of operation, such as bridge tolls, road tolls, or ferry charges, paid by the carrier on account of the bus and driver, cannot be deducted from the charge made to the passenger in determining the taxable charges for transportation.

(4) Charges for admissions, guides, meals, hotel accommodations, and other nontransportation services, for example, where such items are included in a lump sum payment for an all-expense tour.

(5) Charges in connection with the charter of a land, water, or air conveyance for the transportation of persons beginning before November 16, 1962, or an air conveyance for transportation of persons which begins after November 15, 1962, such as for parking, icing, sanitation, "layover" or "waiting time", movement of equipment in deadhead service, dockage, wharfage, etc.

[Reg. §49.4261-8.]

□ [*T.D.* 6430, 12-3-59. *Amended by T.D.* 6618, 11-14-62.]

[Reg. §49.4261-9]

§49.4261-9. Seats and berths; rate and application of tax.—(a) *Imposition of tax.*—Section 4261(c) imposes a tax at a prescribed rate upon payments of any amount for seating or sleeping accommodations in connection with transportation with respect to which a tax is imposed by section 4261(a) or (b).

(b) *Rate of tax.*—The tax is imposed under section 4261(c) upon the amount paid for seating or sleeping accommodations at the following rates:

(1) 10 percent with respect to amounts paid in connection with taxable transportation by rail, motor vehicle, water, or air which begins before November 16, 1962.

(2) 5 percent with respect to amounts paid in connection with the air portion of any transportation which begins after November 15, 1962.

(c) *Application of other rules to seats and berths.*—The rules and provisions of §§49.4261-1 to 49.4261-6, inclusive, with respect to the tax on payments for transportation imposed by section 4261(a) or (b) are also applicable to the tax on payments for seating or sleeping accommodations. [Reg. §49.4261-9.]

□ [*T.D.* 6430, 12-3-59. *Amended by T.D.* 6618, 11-14-62.]

[Reg. §49.4261-10]

§49.4261-10. By whom paid.—The tax imposed by section 4261 is payable by the person making the taxable payment for transportation or for seats, berths, etc., and is collectible by the person receiving such payment. See section 4264(a) and (c) for special rules relating to payment and collection of tax. [Reg. §49.4261-10.]

□ [*T.D.* 6430, 12-3-59.]

[Reg. §49.4262(a)-1]

§49.4262(a)-1. Taxable transportation.—(a) *In general.*—Unless excluded under section 4262(b) (see §49.4262(b)-1), taxable transportation means—

(1) Transportation which begins in the United States or in that portion of Canada or Mexico which is not more than 225 miles from the nearest point in the continental United States (the "225-mile zone") and ends in the United States or in the 225-mile zone; and

(2) In the case of any other transportation, that portion of such transportation which is directly or indirectly from one port or station in the United States to another port or station in the United States but, with respect to transportation which begins after November 15, 1962, only if such portion is not part of "uninterrupted international air transportation" within the meaning of section 4262(c)(3) and paragraph (c) of §49.4262(c)-1. Transportation from one port or station in the United States to another port or station in the United States occurs whenever a carrier, after leaving any port or station in the United States, makes a regularly scheduled stop at another port or station in the United States irrespective of whether stopovers are permitted or whether passengers disembark.

The provisions of this paragraph are applicable whether the transportation is by rail, motor vehicle, water, or air, or any combination thereof, except that with respect to transportation which begins after November 15, 1962, the tax, if applicable, applies only to the amount paid for that portion of the transportation which is by air.

(b) *Illustrations of taxable transportation under section 4262(a)(1).*—In each of the following examples the transportation is taxable transportation and the amount paid within the United States for such transportation is subject to the tax:

(1) New York to Seattle;

(2) New York to Vancouver, Canada, with a stop at Jasper, Canada;

(3) Chicago to Monterrey, Mexico;

(4) Montreal, Canada, to Toronto, Canada; and

(5) Miami to Los Angeles via Panama.

If in the examples in subparagraphs (1) and (5) of this paragraph, payment for the transportation had been made outside the United States, such payment would nevertheless have been subject to tax since in each case the transportation begins and ends in the United States.

* * *

(c) *Illustrations of taxable transportation under section 4262(a)(2) beginning before November 16, 1962.*—The following examples will illustrate the application of section 4262(a)(2) with respect to transportation beginning before November 16, 1962:

Example (1). A purchases in New York a round-trip ticket for transportation by air from New York to Havana, Cuba, with a stop at Miami. The amount paid for that part of the transportation between New York and Miami on both going and return trips is subject to tax, since such transportation is from one station in the United States to another station in the United States.

Example (2). B purchases a ticket in San Francisco for combination rail and water transportation from San Francisco to New York to Halifax, Canada, to London, England. The amount paid for that part of the transportation between San Francisco and New York is subject to tax, since such transportation is from one station in the United States to another station in the United States. Although Halifax is in the 225-mile zone, the transportation between New York and Halifax is not taxable because it is not transportation from one port in the United States to another port in the United States.

Example (3). C purchases a ticket in Seattle for transportation from Seattle to Lisbon, Portugal, with stops at Vancouver, Edmonton, and Montreal, Canada, and New York. The amount paid for that part of the transportation from Seattle to New York is subject to tax, since it is indirectly from one station in the United States to another station in the United States.

Example (4). E purchases in Chicago a ticket for transportation by air from Chicago to New York to Gander, Newfoundland, to London, England. Only the amount paid for that part of the transportation between Chicago and New York is subject to tax. If, while on the New York-Gander leg of the journey the aircraft is forced to land at Boston, because of weather or other emergency, no tax is imposed by reason of such emergency stop.

Example (5). G charters a plane in New York for transportation to Bogota, Colombia, and pays the charter charges in New York. The plane stops at an airport in Miami for refueling in accordance with its flight plan. The tax attaches with respect to that part of the transportation which is between New York and Miami.

(d) *Illustrations of taxable transportation under section 4262(a)(2) beginning after November 15, 1962.*—The following examples will illustrate the application of section 4262(a)(2) with respect to transportation beginning after November 15, 1962:

Example (1): A purchases in New York a round-trip ticket for transportation by air from New York to Nassau with a schedule stopover of 10 hours in Miami on both the going and return trip. The amount paid for that part of the transportation from New York to Miami on the going trip is subject to tax, since such transportation is from one station in the United States to another station in the United States and the trip is not uninterrupted international air transportation because the scheduled stopover interval in Miami is greater than six hours. The amount paid for the return trip from Miami to New York is subject to tax for the same reason.

Example (2). A purchases a ticket in San Francisco for transportation to London with a stopover in New York. He is to travel by air from San Francisco to New York and from New York to London by water. He is scheduled to stopover in New York for 4 hours. That portion of the total amount paid by A for his transportation applicable to the air transportation between San Francisco and New York is subject to tax since such transportation is from one station in the United States to another station in the United States and is not a part of uninterrupted international air transportation since the complete trip from San Francisco to London is not entirely by air.

Example (3). A purchases a through ticket for air transportation from San Francisco to London with stopovers at Denver, Chicago, Philadelphia, and New York. At each stopover the air carrier has scheduled his arrival and departure within 6 hours. After arriving in Philadelphia, A, for his own convenience, decides to stopover for more than 6 hours. The total amount paid by A for his transportation from San Francisco to New York is subject to tax since the scheduled interval between the beginning or end and the end or beginning of any two segments of the domestic portion of international air transportation exceeded 6 hours. If the stopover interval in Philadelphia is extended for more than 6 hours by the carrier solely for its own convenience such as making repairs to the aircraft, the domestic portion of A's trip will not become taxable, provided A continues his international air transportation no later than on the first available flight offered by the carrier.

Example (4). A purchases a through ticket for transportation by air from Los Angeles to Barbados with stopovers at Houston, Mexico City, Mexico, and Miami. At each stopover, except Mexico City, A's scheduled time of arrival and departure is within six hours. At Mexico City, A's scheduled time of arrival and departure exceeds six hours. The total amount paid by A for his transportation from Los Angeles to Miami, including that part of the transportation to and from Mexico City, is subject to tax since the transportation includes a portion which is indirectly from one port or station in the United States to another port or station in the United States (Houston to Miami via Mexico City) and the scheduled interval in Mexico City between two segments of such portion exceeds six hours. If A's scheduled arrival and departure at each stopover of his transportation which is directly or indirectly between ports or stations in the United States, including that at Mexico City, had been within a six hour interval and A had arrived and departed at each such stopover within that period, the transportation would have qualified as uninterrupted international air transportation and no part of the amount paid for the transportation by air from Los Angeles to Barbados would be subject to tax.

(e) *Illustrations of transportation which is not taxable transportation.*—The following examples will illustrate transportation which is not taxable transportation:

(1) New York to Trinidad with no intervening stops;

(2) Minneapolis to Edmonton, Canada, with a stop at Winnipeg, Canada;

(3) Los Angeles to Mexico City, Mexico, with stops at Tia Juana and Guadalajara, Mexico;

(4) New York to Whitehorse, Yukon Territory, Canada, after November 15, 1962, by air with a scheduled stopover in Chicago of five hours.

Amounts paid for the transportation referred to in examples set forth in subparagraphs (1), (2), and (3) of this paragraph are not subject to the tax regardless of where payment is made, since none of the trips (i) begin in the United States or in the 225-mile zone and end in the United States or in the 225-mile zone, nor (ii) contain a portion of transportation which is directly or indirectly from one port or station in the United States to another port or station in the United States. The amount paid within the United States for the transportation referred to in the example set forth in subparagraph (4) of this paragraph is not subject to tax since the entire trip (including the domestic portion thereof) is "uninterrupted international air transportation" within the meaning of section 4262(c)(3) and paragraph (c) of §49.4262(c)-1. In the event the transportation is paid for outside the United States, no tax is due since the transportation does not begin and end in the United States. [Reg. §49.4262(a)-1.]

☐ [*T.D.* 6430, 12-3-59. *Amended by T.D.* 6618, 11-14-62.]

[Reg. §49.4262(b)-1]

§49.4262(b)-1. Exclusion of certain travel.—(a) *In general.*—Under section 4262(b) taxable transportation does not include that portion of any transportation which meets all four of the following requirements:

(1) Such portion is outside the United States;

(2) Neither such portion nor any segment thereof is directly or indirectly—

(i) Between (a) a point where the route of the transportation leaves or enters the Continental United States, or (b) a port or station in the 225-mile zone, and

(ii) A port or station in the 225-mile zone; (

(3) Such portion—

(i) Begins at either (a) at the point where the route of the transportation leaves the United States, or (b) a port or station in the 225-mile zone, and

(ii) Ends at either (a) the point where the route of the transportation enters the United States, or (b) a port or station in the 225-mile zone; and

(4) A direct line from the point (or the port or station) specified in subparagraph (3)(i) of this paragraph, to the point (or the port or station) specified in subparagraph (3)(ii) of this paragraph, passes through or over a point which is not within 225 miles of the United States.

For purposes of this section, the route of the transportation shall be deemed to leave or enter the United States when it passes over (i) the international boundary line between any part of the United States and a contiguous foreign country, or (ii) a point three nautical miles (3.45 statute miles) from low tide on the coast line.

(b) *Transportation to or from Alaska or Hawaii.*— (1) Under the provisions of section 4262(b) transportation between the continental United States or the 225-mile zone and Alaska or Hawaii will be partially exempt from the tax. The portion of such transportation which (i) is outside the United States, (ii) is not transportation between ports or stations within the continental United States or the 225-mile zone, and (iii) is not transportation between ports or stations within Alaska or Hawaii, meets all the requirements set forth in section 4262(b) and is excluded from taxable transportation.

(2) The provisions of subparagraph (1) of this paragraph may be illustrated by the following examples:

Example (1). A buys a ticket for transportation by air from Seattle to Fairbanks, Alaska, via Ketchikan and Juneau, Alaska, and Whitehorse, Yukon Territory, Canada. The portion of the transportation between the point where the route of the transportation leaves the continental United States and the point where it first enters Alaska (the three-mile limit or the international boundary) is not subject to tax.

Example (2). B purchased combination rail-water transportation beginning before November 16, 1962, from Chicago to Juneau, Alaska, by way of Vancouver, Canada. The portion of the transportation from Vancouver to the point where the route of the transportation enters the three-mile limit off the coast of Alaska is not subject to tax.

Example (3). C purchases a ticket in the United States for transportation by air from Vancouver, Canada, to Honolulu, Hawaii. No part of the route followed by the carrier passes through or over any part of the continental United States. The only part of the payment made by C for this transportation which is subject to the tax is that applicable to the portion of the transportation between the three-mile limit off the coast of Hawaii and the airport in Honolulu.

(c) *Method of computing tax on travel not excluded.*—(1) Where a payment is made for transportation which includes transportation

excluded under the provisions of section 4262(b)—

(i) The tax may be computed on that proportion of the total amount paid which the mileage of the taxable portion of the transportation bears to the mileage of the entire trip, or

(ii) If the taxable portion of the transportation includes transportation from one port or station to another port or station for which an applicable local fare of a like class is available, the tax may be computed on the amount of such local fare, plus an amount equivalent to that proportion of the remainder of the total amount paid which the mileage of the remainder of the taxable portion of the transportation bears to the remainder of the mileage of the entire trip. If the taxable transportation includes a leg from a station to a coastal gateway point of embarkation for which a uniform fare is charged regardless of the gateway point actually used, the tax on such a leg may be computed on the basis of such uniform fare. In the absence of a fare described in this subparagraph, the tax must be determined in accordance with subdivision (i) of this subparagraph. If the taxable portion of the transportation includes a leg between coastal gateway points of embarkation for which no additional fair is charged, no tax shall be applicable to such leg of the transportation.

(2) The basis for determining the proportions described in subdivisions (i) and (ii) of subparagraph (1) of this paragraph shall be the average mileage of the established route traveled by the carrier between given points under normal circumstances.

(d) *Illustration.*—The application of (c) of this section may be illustrated by the following example:

Example. On October 10, 1959, A purchases in San Francisco a ticket for transportation by air to Honolulu, Hawaii. The portion of the transportation which is outside the continental United States and is outside Hawaii is excluded from taxable transportation. The tax applies to that part of the payment made by A which is applicable to the portion of the transportation between the airport in San Francisco and the three-mile limit off the coast of California (a distance of 15 miles) and between the three-mile limit off the coast of Hawaii and the airport in Honolulu (a distance of 5 miles). The part of the payment made by A which is applicable to the taxable portion of his transportation and the tax due thereon are computed in accordance with paragraph (c)(1) as follows:

Mileage of entire trip (San Francisco airport to Honolulu airport)		2400 miles
Mileage in continental United States	15	
Mileage in Hawaii	5	
	20 miles	
Fare from San Francisco to Honolulu		$168.00
Payment for taxable portion ($^{2400}/_{20} \times \$168$)		$ 1.40
Tax due (10% (rate in effect on date of payment) × $1.40)		$ 0.14

(All distances and fares assumed for purposes of this example. If transportation begins after November 15, 1962, the tax applies only to the amount paid for transportation by air and should be computed at the rate of 5 percent.) [Reg. § 49.4262(b)-1.]

☐ *[T.D. 6430, 12-3-59. Amended by T.D. 6618, 11-14-62.]*

[Reg. § 49.4262(c)-1]

§ 49.4262(c)-1. Definitions.—(a) *The continental United States.*—For the purposes of the regulations in this subpart, the term "continental United States" includes only the 48 States existing on July 25, 1956 (the date of the enactment of the Act of July 25, 1956 (Pub. Law 796, 84th Cong., 70 Stat. 644)) and the District of Columbia, including inland waters (such as rivers, lakes, bays, etc.) lying wholly therein, and, where an international boundary line divides inland waters, such parts of such inland waters as lie within the boundary of the United States, and also the waters 3 nautical miles (3.45 statute miles) from low tide on the coast line. For purposes of the regulations in this subpart, the term "continental United States" does not include Alaska or Hawaii for any period either prior or subsequent to their admission into the Union as States.

(b) *The 225-mile zone.*—For purposes of the regulations in this subpart, the term "225-mile zone" means that portion of Canada and Mexico which is not more than 225 miles from the nearest point in the continental United States. Whether any point in Canada or Mexico is more than 225 miles from the continental United States is to be determined by measuring the distance from such point to the nearest point on the boundary of the continental United States.

(c) *Uninterrupted international air transportation.*—(1) For the purpose of the regulations in this subpart, the term "uninterrupted international air transportation" means transportation entirely by air which does not begin in the United States or in the 225-mile zone and end in the United States or in the 225-mile zone provided that

    (i) Where the transportation within the United States involves one stop, the scheduled interval between the beginning or end of the United States portion of such air transportation and the end or beginning of the remainder of the air transportation, and

    (ii) Where the United States portion of such transportation involves two or more stops, the scheduled interval between the beginning or end of one segment and the end or beginning of the continuing segment of such portion

does not exceed six hours. The transportation is considered to be entirely by air even though the passenger may use other means of transportation between two airports provided the scheduled six-hour limitation for his continuing air transportation is complied with. Transportation which otherwise is uninterrupted international air transportation does not cease to be such because of the use of non-air transportation between ports or stations which are outside the United States, provided the non-air transportation is not a part of transportation which is indirectly from one port or station in the United States to another port or station in the United States.

(2) Where the interval between the arrival and departure time at any stopover point in the United States exceeds six hours, such transportation is not uninterrupted international air transportation even though the schedules of the air lines do not make possible a scheduling within the six-hour limit. Where any interval scheduled for six hours or less is increased to exceed six hours, the transportation will continue to be uninterrupted international air transportation if the increase in time is attributable to delays in the arrival or departure of the scheduled air transportation. In such case the transportation shall continue to be uninterrupted international air transportation if the passenger continues his transportation no later than on the first available flight offered by the continuing carrier which affords the passenger substantially the same accommodations as originally purchased. However, if for any other reason such interval at any stopover is increased to more than six hours, the transportation will lose its classification of uninterrupted international air transportation. The tax applicable in such case shall be paid as provided in paragraph (a)(2) of § 49.4264(c)-1. The transportation from the point of origin in the United States to a port or station outside the United States and the 225-mile zone, with a stopover in the United States, must be scheduled before the time the initial transportation commences in order for the United States portion of such transportation to qualify as uninterrupted international air transportation. For example, where transportation by air from Chicago to New York only is scheduled in Chicago and transportation by air from New York to London, England, is scheduled by the passenger after his arrival in New York, the Chicago to New York trip does not qualify as uninterrupted international air transportation even though the passenger may depart on the London flight within six hours after arrival in New York. [Reg. § 49.4262(c)-1.]

☐ *[T.D. 6430, 12-3-59. Amended by T.D. 6618, 11-14-62.]*

[Reg. § 49.4263-1]

§ 49.4263-1. Commutation tickets.—(a) *Tickets for single trips of less than 30 miles.*—Amounts paid for commutation or season tickets or books for single trips of less than 30 miles are exempt from the tax imposed by section 4261, regardless of the length of time for which such tickets or books are valid. The phrase "less than 30 miles" means less than 30 constructive miles in instances where the charge is based on constructive mileage.

(b) *Tickets for one month or less.*—Amounts paid for commutation tickets or books for one month or less are exempt from the tax regardless of the distance of a single trip. [Reg. § 49.4263-1.]

☐ *[T.D. 6430, 12-3-59. Redesignated by T.D. 6618, 11-14-62.]*

[Reg. §49.4263-2]

§49.4263-2. Charges not exceeding 60 cents.—(a) *In general.*—The tax imposed by section 4261 does not apply to transportation payments of 60 cents or less.

(b) *Round trips.*—The exemption is determined by the amount paid for a single one-way trip. Thus, an amount of more than 60 cents paid for round-trip transportation is exempt from the tax, if the regular one-way single fare of like class between the terminal points of the round trip does not exceed 60 cents.

(c) *Charters.*—An amount paid for the charter of a car, train, motor vehicle, aircraft, or boat with respect to transportation beginning before November 16, 1962, or of an aircraft with respect to transportation beginning after November 15, 1962, is exempt from the tax, if the payment represents a per capita charge of sixty cents or less for each person actually transported.

(d) *Seating or sleeping accommodations.*—Any amount paid for seating or sleeping accommodations is not subject to tax under section 4261(c) where the amount of the related payment for transportation is 60 cents or less. However, where the payment for transportation exceeds 60 cents, a payment for seating or sleeping accommodations in connection with such transportation is subject to the tax regardless of the amount thereof. [Reg. §49.4263-2.]

☐ [*T.D. 6430, 12-3-59. Redesignated by T.D. 6618, 11-14-62.*]

[Reg. §49.4263-3]

§49.4263-3. Transportation furnished to certain organizations.—(a) *The American National Red Cross.*—The tax imposed by section 4261 does not apply to amounts paid for transportation or facilities furnished to any corporation created by act of Congress to act in matters of relief under the treaty of Geneva of August 22, 1864 (The American National Red Cross).

(b) *International organizations.*—The tax imposed by section 4261 does not apply to amounts paid for transportation or facilities furnished to an international organization. See section 7701(a)(18) for the definition of "international organization". An international organization is designated as such by the President through an Executive order or orders. When an organization has been designated by the President as entitled to enjoy the privileges, exemptions and immunities conferred by the International Organizations Immunities Act, or part thereof, including exemption from the tax, the exemption applies to amounts so paid unless the President otherwise provides. The exemption is subject to withdrawal or revocation by the President. In case of withdrawal or revocation, unless otherwise provided by the President, the exemption is inapplicable to payments on or after the date of issuance of the order of withdrawal or the date of revocation.

(c) *Evidence of right to exemption.*—The right to exemption under section 4263(b) (and under former section 4263(d)) shall be established by the use of exemption certificate, Form 731. See section 4292 and the regulations thereunder for the rules applicable when the right to exemption is evidenced by exemption certificates. [Reg. §49.4263-3.]

☐ [*T.D. 6430, 12-3-59. Redesignated by T.D. 6618, 11-14-62.*]

[Reg. §49.4263-4]

§49.4263-4. Members of the armed forces.—The tax imposed by section 4261 does not apply to amounts paid for transportation or for seating or sleeping accommodations furnished under special tariffs providing for fares of not more than 2.5 cents per mile applicable to round-trip tickets sold to personnel of the United States Army, Air Force, Navy, Marine Corps, and Coast Guard, including authorized cadets and midshipmen, traveling in uniform of the United States at their own expense when on official leave, furlough, or pass. A person claiming exemption under this section will be required to exhibit to the agent of the carrier a properly executed certificate to show that he is traveling on official leave, furlough, or pass, but the submission of an exemption certificate on Form 731 is not necessary in such case. [Reg. §49.4263-4.]

☐ [*T.D. 6430, 12-3-59. Redesignated by T.D. 6618, 11-14-62.*]

[Reg. §49.4263-5]

§49.4263-5. Small aircraft on nonestablished lines.—(a) *In general.*—Amounts paid for the transportation of persons on a small aircraft of the type sometimes referred to as "air taxis" shall be exempt from the tax imposed under section 4261 provided the aircraft (1) has a gross take-off weight of less than 12,500 pounds determined as provided in paragraph (b) of this section and (2) has a passenger seating capacity of less than 10 adult passengers, including the pilot. The exemption does not apply, however, if the aircraft is operated on an established line.

(b) *Determination of gross take-off weight.*—The term "gross take-off weight of less than 12,500 pounds" means a maximum certificated take-off weight of less than 12,500 pounds. This shall be based on the maximum certificated take-off weight shown in the aircraft operating record or aircraft flight manual which is part of the air worthiness certificate issued by the Federal Aviation Administration.

(c) *Established line.*—The term "operated on an established line" means operated with some degree of regularity between definite points. It does not necessarily mean that strict regularity of schedule is maintained; that the full run is always made; that a particular route is followed; or that intermediate stops are restricted. The term implies that the person rendering the service maintains and exercises control over the direction, route, time, number of passengers carried, etc. [Reg. § 49.4263-5.]

☐ [*T.D. 6430, 12-3-59. Redesignated by T.D. 6618, 11-14-62.*]

[Reg. § 49.4263-6]

§ 49.4263-6. Exemptions applicable with respect to transportation beginning before November 16, 1962.—Section 5(b) of the Tax Rate Extension Act of 1962 repealed the exemptions contained in former section 4263(b) for motor vehicles with seating capacity of less than ten and in former section 4263(c) for fishing trips by boat effective with respect to transportation beginning after November 15, 1962. With respect to transportation which began before November 16, 1962, the tax imposed by section 4261 does not apply with respect to any amount paid for transportation.

(a) By a motor vehicle having a seating capacity of less than ten adult passengers, including the driver, unless such vehicle is operated on an established line, or

(b) By boat where the transportation is for the purpose of fishing from such boat.

In the case of the exemption with respect to a motor vehicle having a seating capacity of less than ten adult passengers, the terms "operated on an established line" means operated with some degree of regularity between definite points. It does not necessarily mean that strict regularity of schedule is maintained; that the full run is always made; that a particular route is followed; or that intermediate stops are restricted. The term implies that the person rendering the service maintains and exercises control over the direction, route, time, number of passengers carried, etc. [Reg. § 49.4263-6.]

☐ [*T.D. 6618, 11-14-62.*]

[Reg. § 49.4264(a)-1]

§ 49.4264(a)-1. Duty to collect the tax; payments made outside the United States.—Where payment is made outside the United States for a prepaid order, exchange order, or similar order for transportation which begins and ends in the United States or for seating or sleeping accommodations in connection therewith, the person furnishing the initial transportation pursuant to such order shall collect all the tax applicable to such transportation or accommodations. See section 4291 and the regulations thereunder for cases where persons receiving payment must collect the tax. [Reg. § 49.4264(a)-1.]

☐ [*T.D. 6430, 12-3-59.*]

[Reg. § 49.4264(b)-1]

§ 49.4264(b)-1. Duty to collect the tax in the case of certain refunds.—(a) *Special rule for collection of tax.*—Section 4264(b) provides a special rule for the collection of the tax where an unused ticket or order (or portion thereof) purchased without payment of tax is presented for refund and, as a result of the use of only a portion of the transportation purchased in connection with

such ticket or order, liability for payment of tax has been incurred. In such a case, the person making the refund shall deduct the amount of the tax due, to the extent available, from the amount which would otherwise be refundable. If the redemption value of the unused ticket or order (or portion thereof) is less than the amount of the tax due on the amount paid for the travel actually performed, the person redeeming the unused ticket or order (or portion thereof) shall make no refund but shall apply the entire amount against the tax due and shall collect any additional tax due or, within 90 days, shall make a report of the amount of the tax remaining uncollected, together with the name and address of the person who sought the refund. The report shall be made to the office of the district director of internal revenue for the district in which the person making such report is located, and a copy of the report shall be furnished to the person presenting the unused ticket or order for redemption.

(b) *Return of tax.*—Any person who has made a collection of tax in accordance with the preceding paragraph shall include such amount in his regular return of taxes required to be collected under section 4291.

(c) *Illustration.*—A carrier receives for redemption a ticket purchased in the United States for transportation from Calgary, Canada, to Edmonton, Canada, which the purchaser bought for use in conjunction with a ticket for non-stop transportation from Seattle to Calgary. The person applying for the refund does not establish to the satisfaction of the carrier that the tax on the Seattle-Calgary ticket has been paid or that the Seattle-Calgary ticket has been redeemed. The carrier, before making any refund for the unused ticket, is required to deduct from the amount otherwise refundable the tax applicable to the amount paid by the purchaser for the transportation from Seattle to Calgary and to report the tax so collected in its quarterly return on Form 720. In the event that the redemption value of the unused Calgary to Edmonton ticket is less than the amount of the tax due on the amount paid for the transportation from Seattle to Calgary, the carrier should not make any refund but should apply against the outstanding tax the entire amount refundable and should either collect the balance of the tax due or make a report, within 90 days, to the office of the district director of internal revenue for the district in which the carrier is located, setting forth the name and address of the person seeking the refund and the amount of the tax remaining uncollected. [Reg. § 49.4264(b)-1.]

☐ [*T.D. 6430, 12-3-59.*]

[Reg. § 49.4264(c)-1]

§ 49.4264(c)-1. Special rule for the payment of tax.—(a) *Rule.*—(1) *In general.*—Except as provided in subparagraph (2) of this paragraph, when any tax imposed by section 4261 is not paid at the time payment for the transportation is made, then to the extent that such tax is not collected under any other provision of law, such tax shall be paid by the person paying for the transportation or by the person using the transportation. The provisions of section 4264(c) apply where the amount paid for transportation is (i) subject to tax at the time such payment is made, but no tax is paid at that time, or (ii) not subject to tax at the time such payment is made, but because of some subsequent event the payment becomes subject to tax. The payment of tax shall be made to the district director of internal revenue for the district in which the taxpayer resides, or to the person from whom the transportation was purchased, within 30 days after whichever of the following first occurs: (a) The rights to the transportation expire, or (b) the transportation becomes subject to tax. Such payment shall be accompanied with an explanation that it is being made in accordance with section 4264(c).

(2) *Transportation no longer qualifying as uninterrupted international air transportation.*—In the case of a payment for transportation beginning after November 15, 1962, which qualifies as "uninterrupted international air transportation" within the meaning of section 4262(c)(3) and paragraph (c) of §49.4262(c)-1 on the date such payment was made and which because of some subsequent event ceases to be uninterrupted international air transportation, to the extent that the tax due is not collected under any other provisions of law, such tax shall be paid by the person paying for the transportation or by the person using the transportation. The payment of the tax shall be made to the air carrier which provides the next continuing portion of the transportation following the occurrence of the event which caused the transportation to cease to be uninterrupted international air transportation and such carrier shall collect the tax at the time the flight is rescheduled or before furnishing the continuing transportation to the passenger, whichever is earlier, unless the carrier has evidence, in writing, that the tax has already been paid to (i) a district director, or (ii) the person to whom the payment for the international air transportation was originally made, or (iii) any person furnishing any portion of such transportation. The provisions of this subparagraph with respect to the responsibility of the continuing carrier to collect the tax due are applicable only if the passenger uses his original ticket or is issued a substitute therefor for the purpose of continuing his transportation. Such provisions are not applicable if the passenger purchases a new ticket to continue his transportation.

(b) *Relationship to other sections.*—Section 4264(c) and this section are not intended in any way to relieve the person receiving the payment for taxable transportation of persons from his duty under section 4291 of collecting the tax at the time such payment is received by him. The provisions of section 4264(c) and this section also do not apply in any case where the tax is col-

lected in the manner provided in section 4264(a) or (b) or in other provisions of law.

(c) *Illustrations.*—The provisions of this section may be illustrated by the following examples:

Example (1). A purchases in New York a round-trip ticket for transportation between New York and London, England, with a stopover in Montreal, Canada. After arriving in Montreal A decides not to continue his trip to London and returns to New York. A is liable for tax with respect to the amount paid for his transportation from New York to Montreal and return. The amount paid for A's transportation became subject to tax at the time he began his return trip to New York, and within 30 days thereafter A must pay the tax to either the person from whom he purchased the ticket or his district director of internal revenue.

Example (2). A purchases in Chicago a ticket for air transportation to begin after November 15, 1962, from Chicago to London with a stopover in New York. A is scheduled to arrive in New York at 4:30 p.m. and depart from New York on the international portion at 7:30 p.m. A arrives in New York on schedule but for his own convenience reschedules his departure on a flight departing at 11:00 p.m. Since A lengthened the interval between the end of the United States portion and the beginning of the international portion beyond the 6-hour limitation, that portion of his international air transportation between Chicago and New York became subject to tax. The carrier furnishing A's transportation from New York to London shall, before furnishing him with any transportation or at the time he reschedules the remaining portion of his trip, whichever is earlier, collect the tax due on the Chicago to New York portion from A unless the carrier has written evidence that such tax has been paid to (i) a district director of internal revenue, or (ii) the person to whom the payment for the international air transportation was originally made, or (iii) any person furnishing any other portion of the international air transportation. [Reg. §49.4264(c)-1.]

☐ [*T.D.* 6430, 12-3-59. *Amended by T.D.* 6618, 11-14-62.]

[Reg. §49.4264(d)-1]

§49.4264(d)-1. Cross reference.—For the rules applicable under section 4264(d) see §49.4261-4 relating to payments made within the United States. [Reg. §49.4264(d)-1.]

☐ [*T.D.* 6430, 12-3-59.]

[Reg. §49.4264(e)-1]

§49.4264(e)-1. Round trips.—(a) *In general.*— For purposes of the regulations in this subpart, a round trip shall be considered to consist of two separate trips, i.e., one trip from the point of departure to the destination and a second trip in returning from the destination. A round trip includes certain journeys in which the same routing is not followed on the return trip from the destination to the point of departure as was taken on the going trip (sometimes referred to as "circle trips"). In the case of a cruise or tour (i.e., transportation to no set destination but with one or more intermediate stops en route) the point farthest from the point of departure will be regarded as the destination for purposes of applying the term "round trip". If a cruise or tour ends at a point other than the one at which it began, the rules of "open jaw" transportation set forth in paragraph (b) of this section apply.

(b) *Open jaw transportation.*—Transportation which qualifies under this paragraph as "open jaw" transportation will be treated in the same manner as a round trip. For purposes of the regulations in this subpart, "open jaw" transportation means (1) transportation from the point of departure to a specified destination and return from the specified destination to a point other than the original point of departure, or (2) transportation from the point of departure to a specified destination and return from a point other than the specified destination to the original point of departure, provided that where the points of the open jaw are in the continental United States or the 225-mile zone, the distance between the points of the open jaw does not exceed the distance of the shorter segment traveled. For example, a trip from New York to New Orleans via Panama would be considered as one trip from New York to Panama and separate trip from Panama to New Orleans, since the distance between the points of the open jaw (i.e., New York and New Orleans) is shorter than the distance between Panama and New Orleans (the shorter of the two segments traveled). Both trips would be nontaxable. On the other hand, transportation from New York to Miami via Bermuda does not qualify as "open jaw" transportation (since the points of the open jaw are in the United States and the distance between them is greater than the shorter segment traveled) and therefore would be considered a single trip from New York to Miami and would be taxable. [Reg. §49.4264(e)-1.]

☐ [*T.D.* 6430, 12-3-59.]

[Reg. §49.4264(f)-1]

§49.4264(f)-1. Transportation outside the northern portion of the Western Hemisphere.—
(a) *Transportation which leaves and re-enters the northern portion of the Western Hemisphere.*—For purposes of the regulations in this subpart, transportation, any part of which is outside the northern portion of the Western Hemisphere (as defined in paragraph (c) of this section) shall, if the route of the transportation leaves and re-enters the northern portion of the Western Hemisphere, be considered to consist of transportation to the point outside such northern portion and of separate transportation thereafter. The amount paid for such transportation will be considered to be a payment made for two trips and the taxability of the payment will be determined accordingly. Thus, an amount paid for transportation from New York to San Francisco with a stop at Caracas, Venezuela, will be considered an

amount paid for a trip from New York to Caracas and for a separate trip from Caracas to San Francisco, neither of which is taxable transportation.

(b) *Transportation beginning before November 16, 1962, by water on a vessel.*—(1) *Special rule.*—Section 4264(f)(2) prior to its amendment by section 5(b) of the Tax Rate Extension Act of 1962 provided a special rule in the case of transportation which begins before November 16, 1962, any part of which is outside the northern portion of the Western Hemisphere, by water on a vessel which makes one or more intermediate stops at ports within the United States on a voyage which (i) begins or ends in the United States, and (ii) ends or begins outside the northern portion of the Western Hemisphere. In such a case, a stop at an intermediate port within the United States at which such vessel is not authorized both to discharge and to take on passengers shall not be considered to be a stop at a port within the United States. A vessel is considered to be authorized both to discharge and to take on passengers at an intermediate port unless there is a legal or other authoritative prohibition of such traffic. For purposes of the preceding sentence, an order issued by the owner or operator of a vessel prohibiting such vessel from either discharging or taking on passengers at the intermediate port is not a legal or other authoritative prohibition of such traffic.

(2) *Illustrations.*—The provisions of this paragraph may be illustrated by the following examples:

Example (1). A purchases a steamship ticket in New York for transportation from New York to Southampton, England. The vessel on which A sails makes an intermediate stop during the course of such voyage at Boston to take on passengers. The vessel is not, however, authorized to discharge passengers at such port. No tax applies to the portion of the transportation between New York and Boston since under section 4264(f)(2) the vessel is not considered to have made a stop at Boston.

Example (2). B purchases a steamship ticket in San Francisco for a voyage from San Francisco to Tokyo, Japan. The vessel on which B travels makes a stop at Honolulu, Hawaii to discharge passengers. The vessel is also permitted to take on passengers in Honolulu. Since the vessel is permitted both to discharge and take on passengers at the stop in Honolulu, the portion of the transportation between San Francisco and Hawaii not excluded under section 4262(b) (i.e., the portion of such transportation between the pier in San Francisco and the three-mile limit off the coast of California and between the three-mile limit off the coast of Hawaii and the pier in Honolulu) is taxable under section 4262(a)(2) as transportation from one port in the United States to another port in the United States.

(c) *Northern portion of the Western Hemisphere.*—For purposes of the regulations in this subpart, the term "northern portion of the Western Hemisphere" means the area lying west of the 30th meridian west of Greenwich, east of the International Date Line, and north of the equator, but not including any country of South America. [Reg. § 49.4264(f)-1.]

☐ [*T.D. 6430, 12-3-59. Amended by T.D. 6618, 11-14-62.*]

[Reg. § 49.4271-1]

§ 49.4271-1. Tax on transportation of property by air.—(a) *Purpose of this section.*—In general, section 4271 of the Internal Revenue Code of 1954, as added by the Airport and Airway Revenue Act of 1970, imposes a tax equal to 5 percent of the amount paid within or without the United States for the transportation of property by air which begins after June 30, 1970, if such transportation begins and ends in the United States. This section sets forth rules as to the general applicability of the tax. This section also sets forth rules as authorized by section 4272(b)(2) which exempt from tax payments for the transportation of property by air in the course of exportation (including shipment to a possession of the United States) by continuous movement, and in due course so exported.

(b) *Imposition of tax.*—(1) The tax imposed by section 4271 applies only to amounts paid to persons engaged in the business of transporting property by air for hire.

(2) The tax imposed by section 4271 does not apply to amounts paid for the transportation of property by air if such transportation is furnished on an aircraft having a maximum certificated takeoff weight (as defined in section 4492(b)) of 6,000 pounds or less, unless such aircraft is operated on an established line. The tax imposed by section 4271 also does not apply to any payment made by one member of an affiliated group (as defined in section 4282(b)) to another member of such group for services furnished in connection with the use of an aircraft if such aircraft is owned or leased by a member of the affiliated group and is not available for hire by persons who are not members of such group.

(3) Since the tax imposed by section 4271 applies only to amounts paid to persons engaged in the business of transporting property by air for hire, the tax applies to amounts paid to an air carrier by a freight forwarder or express company for the transportation of property by air. The tax does not apply to amounts paid by a shipper to a freight forwarder or express company.

(c) *Property exported or imported entirely by air.*—(1) The tax does not apply to amounts paid for transportation entirely by air which begins in the United States and ends outside the United States, or which begins outside the United States and ends in the United States. Transportation of property by air will be considered to begin and end at the points of origin and destination shown on a through airwaybill covering shipment of the property, even though there may be stopovers in the United States (such as, for ex-

ample, to consolidate cargo at a "gateway" city). If a through airwaybill is issued by a person other than a person engaged in the business of transporting property by air for hire (for example, by a freight forwarder), the air carrier may accept an air freight manifest listing the article to be shipped by weight and destination as evidence of the existence of a through airwaybill.

(2) If a through airwaybill covering air transportation from its beginning in the United States to a foreign destination, or from its beginning abroad to a United States destination, has not been issued, then the export or import character of the shipment must be evidenced by a contract or other written evidence clearly showing the beginning point and ending point of the air transportation.

(3) If a through airwaybill has been issued covering air transportation to a foreign destination, but the transportation nevertheless ends in the United States (for example, because the foreign consignee cancels the order before the shipment leaves a gateway city), then the amount paid for air transportation is taxable. In such a case the air carrier must collect the tax from the shipper or other person who paid for the air transportation.

(4) Any transportation of property by air shipped by the Department of Defense through an aerial port of embarkation and debarkation on a U.S. Government bill of lading shall be considered to—

(i) Begin in the United States and end outside the United States if the bill of lading states that the shipment is "For Export", or

(ii) Begin outside the United States and end in the United States if the bill of lading states that the shipment is "Imported by Air".

If a U.S. Government bill of lading stating that a shipment is "For Export" has been issued but the shipment nevertheless ends in the United States, then the amount paid for air transportation is taxable. In such a case the Department of Defense shall notify the air carrier that the shipment is taxable and shall pay the tax to such carrier.

(d) *Exportation involving two or more modes of transportation.*—(1) Even though transportation of property by air begins and ends in the United States, the tax does not apply if the property is being transported in the course of exportation by continuous movement and in due course is so exported, provided the requirements of this paragraph are satisfied. For example, the tax does not apply to air transportation from Chicago to New York if the property is in the course of exportation, by continuous movement, by boat from New York to Europe and in due course is so exported. Delays caused by circumstances beyond the control of the shipper (such as labor disputes or natural disasters) will not interrupt continuous movement. Property arriving at a gateway city by air may be repacked or consolidated with other property without interrupting continuous movement.

(2)(i) Continuous movement in the course of exportation shall be evidenced by (*a*) the execution of the Export Exemption Certificate, Form 1363, and (*b*) proof that exportation has actually occurred.

(ii) Form 1363 may be used in connection with a separate payment otherwise subject to tax or it may be used, with the permission of the district director, as a blanket exemption certificate by a person who expects to make payments for numerous export shipments over an indefinite period of time. If used in connection with a separate payment, the certificate shall be executed, in duplicate, by the shipper or other person making the payment subject to tax. Such person shall retain the duplicate with the shipping papers for at least 3 years from the last day of the month during which the shipment was made from the point of origin, and shall file the original with the carrier at the time of payment of the transportation charge. The carrier receiving the original certificate shall retain it along with the document showing payment of the transportation charge, for a period of at least 3 years from the last day of the month during which the shipment was made from the point of origin.

(iii) Form 1363 may be used as a blanket exemption certificate by a person who demonstrates to the satisfaction of the district director that it is impracticable to execute a separate Form 1363 for each payment. Permission to execute a blanket exemption certificate shall be requested, in writing, from the district director for the district in which is located the principal place of business or principal office or agency of the shipper or other person seeking permission. If permission is granted a separate certificate shall be executed in duplicate, by the shipper or other person making the payments, for each air carrier to be used in making export shipments. Such person shall retain the duplicate together with all shipping papers, and shall file the original with the air carrier with or before payment of the first transportation charge to be covered by the certificate. The air carrier shall retain the original certificate together with all documents showing payment of the transportation charges. Permission to execute a blanket exemption certificate, if granted, shall remain in force until withdrawn by the person who requested such permission or until withdrawn by the district director who granted such permission. Each person shall retain the certificate for at least 3 years after the last day of the month during which the final shipment covered by the certificate was made from the point of origin. Each person shall retain the shipping and payment documents for at least 3 years after the last day of the month during which the shipment was made from the point of origin.

(3) The filing of a properly executed Form 1363 with the carrier suspends liability for the payment of the tax for a period of six months from the date of shipment from the point of origin. If the person who is liable for the tax has not provided evidence to the carrier of the actual exportation of a shipment within such period, then the temporary suspension of the liability for the payment of the tax ceases and the carrier shall collect the tax from the person who paid the carrier for the transportation charge. If, after collection of the tax by the carrier, proof of exportation is subsequently received by the carrier, credit or refund of the tax may be obtained under the terms set forth in section 6415 of the Internal Revenue Code of 1954.

(4) Documentary evidence of the exportation of the property may consist of a copy of export bill of lading, memorandum from the captain of the vessel, customs official, or a foreign consignee, shipper's export declaration, or other evidence sufficient to establish that the property has actually been exported. The person making the payment subject to tax shall furnish the appropriate documentary evidence to the carrier, or a statement that he holds such documentary evidence. In the latter case, the statement must: (i) certify that the property covered by the Export Exemption Certificate, Form 1363 was exported; (ii) identify the evidence of exportation; (iii) specify the foreign destination or the possession of the United States to which the property was shipped; and (iv) show the place where such evidence will be available for inspection by internal revenue officers. Any documentary evidence or statement, as the case may be, shall be retained by the carrier and the person making the payment subject to tax for a period of three years from the last day of the month during which the shipment was made from the point of origin. If the person making the payment subject to tax is not the actual exporter and is unable to obtain documentary evidence of exportation, such person shall obtain from the person having custody of the documentary evidence a statement containing the same facts as listed above for a statement furnished to the carrier by the person liable for the tax. The person making the payment subject to tax shall furnish the original of such statement to the carrier and shall retain a copy in his records. The statement shall be retained for the same three year period as the evidence of exportation is to be retained.

(e) *Definitions.*—(1) *Property.*—The term "property" does not include excess baggage accompanying a passenger travelling on an aircraft operated on an established line.

(2) *Transportation.*—The term "transportation" includes layover or waiting time and movement of the aircraft in deadhead service.

(3) *Taxable transportation.*—The term "taxable transportation" is defined in section 4272.

(f) *Collection of tax.*—The tax imposed by section 4271 shall be paid by the person making the payment subject to tax and shall be collected by the person engaged in the business of transporting property by air for hire who receives such payment, except that in the case of amounts subject to tax which are paid by the U.S. Postal Service, the tax shall not be collected by the

Reg. § 49.4271-1(f)

person engaged in the business of transporting property by air for hire who receives such payment, but instead shall be paid directly by such Service as if it were a collecting agent. [Reg. §49.4271-1.]

☐ [*T.D. 7054, 7-28-70. Amended by T.D. 7190,* 6-28-72; *T.D. 7316, 6-18-74; T.D. 7517, 11-11-77; T.D. 7953, 5-9-84. Redesignated and amended by T.D. 8328, 12-28-90. Amended by T.D. 8442,* 10-21-92.]

[Reg. §49.4291-1]

§49.4291-1. Persons receiving payment must collect tax.—Except as otherwise provided in section 4263(a), every person receiving any payment for facilities or services on which a tax is imposed upon the payor thereof under chapter 33 shall collect the amount of the tax from the person making that payment. Under section 7501, all taxes collected in this manner are held by the collecting agent in trust for the United States. If the person from whom the tax is required to be collected refuses to pay it or if for any reason it is impossible for the collecting agent to collect the tax from that person, the collecting agent is required to report to the Commissioner the name and address of that person, the nature of the facility provided or service rendered, the amount paid therefor, and the date on which paid. Applicable October 1, 2004, this report must be made on or before the report due date. Upon receipt of this report the Commis-

sioner will proceed against the person to whom the facilities were provided or the services rendered to assert the amount of tax due, affording that person the same conference, protest, and appellate rights as are available to other excise taxpayers. In addition, when a field or office audit of a collecting agent's records, or of a taxpayer's records, discloses that the collecting agent failed during prior reporting periods to collect taxes due, the Commissioner may assert those taxes directly against the person to whom the facilities were provided or the services rendered, whether or not the collecting agent had attempted collection or the person liable for the tax had refused payment thereof. For purposes of this section, the report due date is—

(a) In the case of a person using the alternative method of making deposits described in §40.6302(c)-3 of this chapter, the due date of the return on which the item of adjustment relating to the uncollected tax would be reflected if items of adjustment were determined without regard to the limitation in §40.6302(c)-3 of this chapter; and

(b) In any other case, the due date of the return on which the tax would have been reported but for the refusal to pay or inability to collect. [Reg. §49.4291-1.]

☐ [*T.D. 8685, 11-8-96. Amended by T.D. 9051,* 4-1-2003; *T.D. 9149, 8-9-2004 and T.D. 9221,* 8-24-2005.]

Policies Issued by Foreign Insurers

See p. 20,601 for regulations not amended to reflect law changes

[Reg. §46.0-1]

§46.0-1. Amended.—The regulations in this part 46 relate to the taxes on certain insurance policies and self-insured health plans imposed by chapter 34 of the Internal Revenue Code and the tax on the issuer of registration-required obligations not issued in registered form imposed by chapter 39 of the Internal Revenue Code. See part 40 of this chapter for regulations relating to returns, payments, and deposits of taxes imposed by chapters 34 and 39. [Reg. §46.0-1.]

☐ [*T.D. 8442, 10-21-92. Amended by T.D. 9602,* 12-5-2012.]

[Reg. §46.4371-1]

§46.4371-1. Applicability of subpart.—The provisions of this subpart apply only to premiums paid on or after January 1, 1966. See Subpart H, Part 47 of this chapter for provisions relating to premiums paid or charged before January 1, 1966. If any portion of the tax imposed by section 4371 was paid on the basis of the premium charged before January 1, 1966, in accordance with the provisions of §47.4371-2 of this chapter (documentary stamp tax), then, to the extent that such portion was paid by stamp, no further tax is due under the provisions of this subpart. [Reg. §46.4371-1.]

☐ [*T.D. 7023, 1-21-70.*]

[Reg. §46.4371-2]

§46.4371-2. Imposition of tax on policies issued by foreign insurers; scope of tax.— (a) *Certain insurance policies, and indemnity, fidelity, or surety bonds.*—Section 4371(1) imposes a tax upon each policy of insurance (other than those referred to in paragraph (b) of this section), upon each indemnity, fidelity, or surety bond, or upon each certificate, binder, covering note, receipt, memorandum, cablegram, letter, or other instrument by whatever name called, whereby a contract of insurance or an obligation in the nature of an indemnity, fidelity, or surety bond is made, continued, or renewed, if issued—

(1) By a nonresident alien individual, a foreign partnership, or a foreign corporation, as insurer (unless the policy or other instrument is signed or countersigned by an officer or agent of the insurer in a State, Territory, or the District of Columbia in which the insurer is authorized to do business); and either

(2) To or for, or in the name of, a domestic corporation, domestic partnership, or an individual resident of the United States, against or with respect to hazards, risks, losses, or liabilities wholly or partly within the United States; or

(3) To or for, or in the name of, a foreign corporation, foreign partnership, or nonresident individual, engaged in a trade or business within the United States with respect to hazards, risks, or liabilities wholly within the United States.

For definition of the term "indemnity bond," see section 4372(c).

(b) *Life insurance, sickness, and accident policies, and annuity contracts.*—Unless the insurer is subject to tax under section 819, section 4371(2) imposes a tax upon each policy of insurance or annuity contract, or upon each certificate, binder, covering note, receipt, memorandum, cablegram, letter, or other instrument by whatever name called, whereby a contract of insurance or an annuity contract is made, continued, or renewed, if issued—

(1) By a nonresident alien individual, a foreign partnership, or a foreign corporation, as insurer (unless the policy or other instrument is signed or countersigned by an officer or agent of the insurer in a State, Territory, or the District of Columbia in which such insurer is authorized to do business); and

(2) To any person with respect to the life or hazards to the person of a citizen or resident of the United States.

(c) *Reinsurance.*—Section 4371(3) imposes a tax upon each policy of reinsurance, certificate, binder, covering note, receipt, memorandum, cablegram, letter, or other instrument by whatever name called, whereby a contract of reinsurance is made, continued, or renewed, if issued—

(1) By a nonresident alien individual, a foreign partnership, or a foreign corporation, as reinsurer (unless the policy or other instrument is signed or countersigned by an officer or agent of the reinsurer in a State, Territory, or the District of Columbia in which such reinsurer is authorized to do business); and

(2) To any person against, or with respect to, any of the hazards, risks, losses, or liabilities covered by contracts described in section 4371(1) or (2).

(d) *Exempt indemnity bonds.*—The tax imposed by section 4371 does not apply to any indemnity bond described in section 4373(2). [Reg. § 46.4371-2.]

☐ [*T.D.* 7023, 1-21-70.]

[Reg. § 46.4371-3]

§ 46.4371-3. Rate and computation of tax.—(a) *Rate of tax.*—(1) The tax under section 4371(1) is imposed at the rate of 4 cents on each dollar, or fractional part thereof, of the premium payment.

(2) The tax under section 4371(2) and (3) is imposed at the rate of 1 cent on each dollar, or fractional part thereof, of the premium payment.

(b) *Meaning of premium payment.*—For purposes of this subpart, the term "premium payment" means the consideration paid for assuming and carrying the risk or obligation, and includes any additional assessment or charge paid under the contract, whether payable in one sum or installments. [Reg. § 46.4371-3.]

☐ [*T.D.* 7023, 1-21-70.]

[Reg. § 46.4371-4]

§ 46.4371-4. Records required with respect to foreign insurance policies.—(a) Each person required under the provisions of § 46.4374-1 to remit the tax imposed by section 4371 shall keep or cause to be kept accurate records of all policies or other instruments subject to such tax upon which premiums have been paid. Such records must identify each such policy or other instrument in such a manner as to clearly establish the following:(1) The gross premium paid; (2) whether such policy or other instrument is (i) a policy of casualty insurance or an indemnity bond subject to tax under section 4371(1), (ii) a policy of life, sickness, or accident insurance or an annuity contract subject to tax under section 4371(2), or (iii) a policy of reinsurance subject to the tax under section 4371(3); (3) the identity of the insured (as defined in section 4372(d)); (4) the identity of the foreign insurer or reinsurer (as defined in section 4372(a)); and (5) the total premium charged and, if the premium is to be paid in installments, the amount and anniversary date of each such installment.

(b) The records required under the provisions of this section must be kept on file at the place of business or at some other convenient location, for a period of at least 3 years from the date any part of the tax became due or the date any part of the tax is paid, whichever is later, in such manner as to be readily accessible to authorized internal revenue officers or employees. The person having control or possession of a policy or other instrument subject to tax under section 4371 shall retain such policy or other instrument for at least 3 years from the date any part of the tax with respect to such policy was paid. [Reg. § 46.4371-4.]

☐ [*T.D.* 7023, 1-21-70. *Redesignated by T.D.* 8328, 12-28-90.]

[Reg. § 46.4374-1]

§ 46.4374-1. Liability for tax.—(a) *In general.*—Any person who makes, signs, issues, or sells any of the documents and instruments subject to the tax, or for whose use or benefit the same are made, signed, issued, or sold, shall be liable for the tax imposed by section 4371. For purposes of this section, in the case of a reinsurance policy that is subject to the tax imposed by section 4371(3), other than assumption reinsurance, the insured person on the underlying insurance policy, the risk of which is covered in whole or in part by such reinsurance policy, shall not constitute a person for whose use or benefit the reinsurance policy is made, signed, issued, or sold.

(b) *When liability for tax attaches.*—The liability for the tax imposed by section 4371 shall attach at the time the premium payment is transferred to the foreign insurer or reinsurer (including transfers to any bank, trust fund, or similar recipient, designated by the foreign insurer or reinsurer), or to any nonresident agent, solicitor, or broker. A person required to pay tax under this section may remit such tax before the time the tax attaches if he keeps records consistent with such practice.

(c) *Payment of tax.*—The tax imposed by section 4371 shall be paid on the basis of a return by the person who makes payment of the premium to a foreign insurer or reinsurer or to any nonresident agent, solicitor, or broker. If the tax is not paid by the person who paid the premium, the tax imposed by section 4371 shall be paid on the basis of a return by any person who makes, signs, issues, or sells any of the documents or instruments subject to the tax imposed by section 4371, or for whose use or benefit such document or instrument is made, signed, issued, or sold.

(d) *Penalty for failure to pay tax.*—Any person who fails to comply with the requirements of this section with intent to evade the tax shall, in addition to other penalties provided therefor, pay a fine of double the amount of tax. (See section 7270.)

(e) *Effective date.*—This section is applicable for premiums paid on or after November 27, 2002. [Reg. § 46.4374-1.]

☐ [*T.D. 7023, 1-21-70. Amended by T.D. 9024,* 11-26-2002.]

[Reg. § 46.4375-1]

§ 46.4375-1. Fee on issuers of specified health insurance policies.—(a) *In general.*—An issuer of a specified health insurance policy is liable for a fee imposed by section 4375 for policy years ending on or after October 1, 2012, and before October 1, 2019. Paragraph (b) of this section provides definitions that apply for purposes of section 4375 and this section. Paragraph (c) of this section provides rules for calculating the fee under section 4375. Paragraph (d) of this section provides the applicability date. For rules relating to filing the required return and paying the fee, see § § 40.6011(a)-1 and 40.6071(a)-1 of this chapter.

(b) *Definitions.*—The following definitions apply for purposes of section 4375 and this section. See also § 46.4377-1 for additional definitions.

(1) *Specified health insurance policy.*—(i) *In general.*—Except as provided in paragraph (b)(1)(ii) of this section and § 46.4377-1, *specified health insurance policy* means any accident and health insurance policy (including a policy under a group health plan) issued with respect to individuals residing in the United States (as defined in § 46.4377-1(a)(2)), including prepaid health coverage arrangements described in paragraph (b)(2) of this section. *Specified health insurance policy* also includes any policy that provides accident and health coverage to an active employee, former employee, or qualifying beneficiary, as continuation coverage required under the Consolidated Omnibus Budget Reconciliation

Act of 1985 (COBRA) or similar continuation coverage under other Federal law or state law.

(ii) *Exceptions.*—The term *specified health insurance policy* does not include—

(A) Any insurance policy if substantially all of its coverage is of excepted benefits described in section 9832(c);

(B) Any group policy issued to an employer where the facts and circumstances show that the group policy was designed and issued specifically to cover primarily employees who are working and residing outside of the United States (as defined in § 46.4377-1(a)(3));

(C) Any stop loss or indemnity reinsurance policy; or

(D) Any insurance policy to the extent it provides an employee assistance program, disease management program, or wellness program if the program does not provide significant benefits in the nature of medical care or treatment.

(iii) *Stop loss policy.*—For purposes of paragraph (b)(1)(ii) of this section, *stop loss policy* means an insurance policy in which—

(A) The insurer that issues the policy to a person establishing or maintaining a self-insured health plan becomes liable for all, or an agreed upon portion of, losses that person incurs in covering the applicable lives in excess of a specified amount; and

(B) The person establishing or maintaining the self-insured health plan retains its liability to, and its contractual relationship with, the applicable lives covered.

(iv) *Indemnity reinsurance policy.*—For purposes of paragraph (b)(1)(ii) of this section, *indemnity reinsurance policy* means an agreement between two or more insurance companies under which—

(A) The reinsuring company agrees to accept and to indemnify the issuing company for all or part of the risk of loss under policies specified in the agreement; and

(B) The issuing company retains its liability to, and its contractual relationship with, the applicable lives covered.

(2) *Prepaid health coverage arrangement.*—The term *prepaid health coverage arrangement* means an arrangement under which fixed payments or premiums are received as consideration for a person's agreement to provide or arrange for the provision of accident and health coverage to individuals residing in the United States, regardless of how such coverage is provided or arranged to be provided. For example, any hospital or medical service policy or certificate, hospital or medical service plan contract, or health maintenance organization contract is a specified health insurance policy.

(c) *Calculation of fee.*—(1) *In general.*—The amount of the fee for a policy for a policy year is equal to the product of the average number of lives covered under the policy for the policy year (determined in accordance with paragraphs (c)(2) and (c)(3) of this section) and the applicable dollar amount (determined in accordance with paragraph (c)(4) of this section). For purposes of computing the fee under this paragraph (c), in the case of an issuer that determines the average number of lives covered for all policies in effect during a calendar year using the member months method under paragraph (c)(2)(v) of this section or the state form method under paragraph (c)(2)(vi) of this section, the applicable dollar amount with respect to such issuer's policies for such calendar year is the applicable dollar amount for policy years ending on December 31 of such calendar year (determined in accordance with paragraph (c)(4) of this section), except that the applicable dollar amount with respect to such an issuer's policies for calendar year 2019 is the applicable dollar amount for policy years ending on September 30, 2019. For more information, see the examples in paragraphs (c)(2)(iii)(B), (c)(2)(iv)(B), (c)(2)(v)(B), and (c)(2)(vi)(B) of this section.

(2) *Determination of the average number of lives covered under a policy.*—(i) *In general.*—To determine the average number of lives covered under a specified health insurance policy during a policy year, an issuer must use one of the following methods—

(A) The actual count method (described in paragraph (c)(2)(iii) of this section);

(B) The snapshot method (described in paragraph (c)(2)(iv) of this section);

(C) The member months method (described in paragraph (c)(2)(v) of this section); or

(D) The state form method (described in paragraph (c)(2)(vi) of this section).

(ii) *Consistency requirements.*—An issuer must use the same method of calculating the average number of lives covered under a policy consistently for the duration of the year. In addition, for all policies for which a liability is reported on a Form 720, "Quarterly Federal Excise Tax Return," for a particular year, the issuer must use the same method of computing lives covered. An issuer that determines the average number of lives covered by using the actual count method described in paragraph (c)(2)(iii) of this section or the snapshot method described in paragraph (c)(2)(iv) of this section may change its method of computing the average lives covered to the snapshot method or actual count method, respectively, provided that the issuer uses the same method for computing the average lives covered for all policies for which a liability is reported on the Form 720 for that year. For example, an issuer with a policy having a policy year that ends on June 30, Policy A, may determine the average number of lives covered under Policy A for July 1, 2013, to June 30, 2014, using the actual count method if the issuer uses the actual count method for all policies for which a liability will be reported on the Form 720 due by July 31, 2015 (the due date for return that will include the liability for the July 2013 to June 2014 policy year for Policy A). The issuer may change its method for determining the average number

of lives covered under Policy A to the snapshot method for the July 1, 2014, to June 30, 2015, policy year, provided that the snapshot method is used for all policies for which a liability will be reported on the Form 720 due by July 31, 2016 (the due date for return that will 36 include the liability for the July 2014 to June 2015 policy year for Policy A). An issuer that determines the average number of lives covered by using the member months method under paragraph (c)(2)(v) of this section or the state form method under paragraph (c)(2)(vi) of this section must use the same method for calculating lives covered for all policy years for which the fee applies.

(iii) *Actual count method.*—(A) *Calculation method.*—An issuer may determine the average number of lives covered under a policy for a policy year by adding the total number of lives covered for each day of the policy year and dividing that total by the number of days in the policy year.

(B) *Example.*—The following example illustrates the principles of paragraphs (c)(1) and (c)(2)(iii)(A) of this section:

Example. Insurance Company A issues three policies that are in effect during 2014, Group Health Insurance Policy A, which has a policy year from December 1 to November 30, Group Health Insurance Policy B, which has a policy year from March 1 to February 28, and Group Health Insurance Policy C, which has a policy year from January 1 to December 31. To calculate the average number of lives covered for 2014, Insurance Company A must calculate the average number of lives covered for each of its three policies for the policy year that ends in 2014. Insurance Company A chooses to use the actual count method under paragraph (c)(2)(iii)(A) of this section to determine average lives covered for policies having a policy year that ends in 2014. Insurance Company A calculates the sum of lives covered under Policy A for each day of the policy year ending November 30, 2014, as 3,285,000. The average number of lives covered under Policy A for the policy year ending November 30, 2014, is 3,285,000 divided by 365, or 9,000. Insurance Company A calculates the sum of lives covered under Policy B for each day of the policy year ending February 28, 2014, as 547,500. The average number of lives covered under Policy B for the policy year ending on February 28, 2014, is 547,500 divided by 365, or 1,500. Insurance Company A calculates the sum of lives covered under Policy C for each day of the policy year ending December 31, 2014, as 4,380,000. The average number of lives covered under Policy C for the policy year ending December 31, 2014, is 4,380,000 divided by 365, or 12,000. To calculate the section 4375 fee under paragraph (c)(1) of this section for calendar year 2014, Insurance Company A must first determine the applicable dollar amount for each policy under paragraph (c)(4) of this section and multiply that amount by the average number of lives covered for that policy. Insurance Company A then adds the total fees for all three

Reg. §46.4375-1(c)(2)(iii)(B)

policies to determine the total fee under section 4375 that it must pay for calendar year 2014.

(iv) *Snapshot method.*—(A) *Calculation method.*—An issuer may determine the average number of lives covered under a policy for a policy year by adding the totals of lives covered on a date during the first, second, or third month of each quarter (or more dates in each quarter if an equal number of dates is used for each quarter), and dividing that total by the number of dates on which a count is made. For purposes of this paragraph (c)(2)(iv)(A), each date used for the second, third and fourth quarters must be within three days of the date in that quarter that corresponds to the date used for the first quarter, and all dates used must be within the same policy year. If an issuer uses multiple dates for the first quarter, the issuer must use dates in the second, third, and fourth quarters that correspond to each of the dates used for the first quarter or are within three days of such corresponding dates, and all dates used must be within the same policy year. The 30th and 31st day of a month are treated as the last day of the month for purposes of determining the corresponding date for any month that has fewer than 31 days (for example, if either March 30 or March 31 is used as a counting date for a calendar year policy, June 30 is the corresponding date for the second quarter).

(B) *Example.*—The following example illustrates the principles of paragraphs (c)(1) and (c)(2)(iv)(A) of this section:

Example. (i) Insurance Company B issues three policies with 12-month policy years that end in 2014, Group Health Insurance Policy A, which has a policy year from December 1 to November 30, Group Health Insurance Policy B, which has a policy year from March 1 to February 28, and Group Health Insurance Policy C, which has a policy year from January 1 to December 31. To calculate the average number of lives covered for 2014, Insurance Company B must calculate the average number of lives covered for each of its three policies for the policy year that ends in 2014. Insurance Company B chooses to determine the average lives covered using the snapshot method for all policies that have a policy year that ends in 2014 and chooses to count lives covered on a single date of the first month of each quarter of the policy years. Thus, for Policy A, Insurance Company B must count lives covered on a single date falling in each of December 2013, March 2014, June 2014 and September 2014; for Policy B, Insurance Company B must count lives covered on a single date falling in each of March 2014, June 2014, September 2014 and December 2014; and for Policy C, Insurance Company B must count lives covered on a single date falling in each of January 2014, April 2014, July 2014 and October 2014. In addition, the date for each of the second, third, and fourth quarters must fall within three days of the date in such quarter that corresponds to the date used for the first quarter, and must fall within the same policy year.

(ii) On December 6, 2013, Policy A covers 8,900 lives, on March 7, 2014, 9,100 lives, on June 6, 2014, 9,050 lives, and on September 5, 2014, 9,050 lives. Insurance Company B treats the average number of lives covered under Policy A for the policy year ending November 30, 2014, as 36,100 (8,900 + 9,100 + 9,050 + 9,050) divided by 4, or 9,025.

(iii) On March 4, 2013, Policy B covers 1,500 lives, on June 7, 2013, 1,350 lives, on September 6, 2013, 1,400 lives, and on December 6, 2013, 1,550 lives. Insurance Company B treats the average number of lives covered under Policy B for the policy year ending February 28, 2014, as 5,800 (1,500 + 1,350 + 1,400 + 1,550) divided by 4, or 1,450.

(iv) On January 6, 2014, Policy C covers 12,500 lives, on April 4, 2014, 12,250 lives, on July 7, 2014, 12,000 lives, and on October 3, 2014, 11,250 lives. Insurance Company B treats the average number of lives covered under Policy C for the policy year ending December 31, 2014, as 47,750 (12,500 + 12,250 + 12,000 + 11,250) divided by 4, or 12,000.

(v) To calculate the section 4375 fee under paragraph (c)(1) of this section for calendar year 2014, Insurance Company B must first determine the applicable dollar amount for each policy under paragraph (c)(4) of this section and multiply that amount by the number of average lives covered for that policy. Insurance Company B then adds the total fees for all three policies to determine the total fee under section 4375 that it must pay for calendar year 2014.

(v) *Member months method.*—(A) *Calculation method.*—An issuer may determine the average number of lives covered under all policies in effect for a calendar year based on the member months (an amount that equals the sum of the totals of lives covered on pre-specified days in each month of the reporting period) reported on the National Association of Insurance Commissioners (NAIC) Supplemental Health Care Exhibit filed for that calendar year. Under this method, the average number of lives covered under the policies in effect for the calendar year equals the member months divided by 12.

(B) *Example.*—The following example illustrates the principles of paragraphs (c)(1) and (c)(2)(v)(A) of this section:

Example. Insurance Company C chooses to determine the average number of lives covered for all years to which the section 4375 fee applies using the member months method of paragraph (c)(2)(v)(A) of this section. Insurance Company C reports 12,000,000 as its member months on the NAIC Supplemental Health Care Exhibit filed for calendar year 2013. Under the member months method, Insurance Company C calculates the average number of lives covered for all its specified health insurance policies in force during calendar year 2013 by dividing 12,000,000 (member months) by 12 (number of months in the reporting period), which equals

1,000,000. To determine the section 4375 fee it must pay for calendar year 2013, Insurance Company C multiplies 1,000,000 by the applicable dollar amount that is in effect at the end of the calendar year under paragraph (c)(4) of this section.

(vi) *State form method.*—(A) *Calculation method.*—An issuer that is not required to file NAIC annual financial statements may determine the number of lives covered under all policies in effect for the calendar year using a form that is filed with the issuer's state of domicile and a method similar to that described in paragraph (c)(2)(v) of this section, if the form reports the number of lives covered in the same manner as member months are reported on the NAIC Supplemental Health Care Exhibit.

(B) *Example.*—The following example illustrates the principles of paragraphs (c)(1) and (c)(2)(vi)(A) of this section:

Example. Insurance Company D is not required to file the NAIC Supplemental Health Care Exhibit, but files a form with its state of domicile. Insurance Company D chooses to determine the average number of lives covered for all years to which the section 4375 fee applies using the state form method of paragraph (c)(2)(vi)(A) of this section. The state form reports the number of lives covered in the same manner as member months is reported on the NAIC Supplemental Health Care Exhibit. For calendar year 2013, Insurance Company D reports 12,000,000 as its equivalent member months on the state form. Under the state form method, Insurance Company D calculates the average number of lives covered for all of its specified health insurance policies in force during calendar year 2013 by dividing 12,000,000 (equivalent member months) by 12 (number of months in the reporting period), which equals 1,000,000. To determine the section 4375 fee it must pay for calendar year 2013, Insurance Company D multiplies 1,000,000 by the applicable dollar amount that is in effect at the end of the calendar year under paragraph (c)(4) of this section.

(3) *Special rules for the first year and the last year the fee is in effect.*—(i) *Calculation of the average number of lives covered under the policy for the first year the fee is in effect.*—For issuers that determine the average number of lives covered using data reported on the 2012 NAIC Supplemental Health Care Exhibit or a permitted state form that covers the 2012 calendar year, the average number of lives covered under all policies in effect for the 2012 calendar year equals the average number of lives covered for that year (as determined under paragraph (c)(2)(v) or (vi) of this section) multiplied by 1/4. The resulting number is deemed to be the average number of lives covered for policies with policy years ending on or after October 1, 2012, and before January 1, 2013. For policy years beginning before May 14, 2012, and ending on or after October 1, 2012, issuers that determine the average number

of lives covered using the actual count method under paragraph (c)(2)(iii) of this section may calculate the average number of lives covered using data from the period beginning May 14, 2012, through the end of the policy year. For policy years beginning before May 14, 2012, and ending on or after October 1, 2012, issuers that determine the average number of lives covered using the snapshot method under paragraph (c)(2)(iv) of this section may calculate the average number of lives covered using dates from the quarters remaining in the policy year starting on or after May 14, 2012. If an abbreviated year is used, the issuer will divide the number of lives covered by the number of days from May 14, 2012, through the end of the policy year (for the actual count method) or the number of days on which a count was made (for the snapshot method).

(ii) *Calculation of the average number of lives covered under the policy for the last year the fee is in effect.*—For issuers that determine the average number of lives covered using data reported on the 2019 NAIC Supplemental Health Care Exhibit or a permitted state form that covers the 2019 calendar year, the average number of lives covered for all policies in effect during the 2019 calendar year equals the average number of lives covered for that year (as determined under paragraph (c)(2)(v) or (vi) of this section) multiplied by 3/4. The resulting number is deemed to be the average number of lives covered for policies with policy years ending on or after January 1, 2019, and before October 1, 2019.

(iii) *Examples.*—The following examples illustrate the principles of paragraph (c)(3) of this section:

Example 1. Insurance Company E issues Group Health Insurance Policy C, which has a policy year that ends on November 30, 2012. Insurance Company E determines the average number of lives covered under a policy by using the actual count method. Under that method, for that policy year, Insurance Company E calculates the sum of lives covered under Policy C for each day between May 14, 2012, and November 30, 2012, as 10,000. The average number of lives covered under Policy C for that policy year is 10,000 divided by the number of days from May 14, 2012, through November 30, 2012. Alternatively, Insurance Company E could have counted the number of lives covered for the entire policy year and divided the sum by 365.

Example 2. Insurance Company F reports 12,000,000 as its member months on its NAIC Supplemental Health Care Exhibit filed for calendar year 2012. Under the member months method, Insurance Company F calculates the average number of lives covered for 2012 by dividing 12,000,000 (member months) by 12 (number of months in the reporting period), and then multiplying the result (1,000,000) by 1/4, which equals 250,000. Accordingly, the average number of lives covered for policies with policy years ending on or after October 1, 2012, and before January 1, 2013, is 250,000.

Reg. § 46.4375-1(c)(3)(iii)

(4) *Applicable dollar amount.*—For policy years ending on or after October 1, 2012, and before October 1, 2013, the applicable dollar amount is $1. For policy years ending on or after October 1, 2013, and before October 1, 2014, the applicable dollar amount is $2. For any policy year ending in any Federal fiscal year beginning on or after October 1, 2014, the applicable dollar amount is the sum of—

(i) The applicable dollar amount for the policy year ending in the previous Federal fiscal year; plus

(ii) The amount equal to the product of—

(A) The applicable dollar amount for the policy year ending in the previous Federal fiscal year; and

(B) The percentage increase in the projected per capita amount of the National Health Expenditures most recently released by the Department of Health and Human Services before the beginning of the Federal fiscal year.

(d) *Effective/Applicability date.*—This section applies for policies with policy years ending on or after October 1, 2012, and before October 1, 2019. [Reg. § 46.4375-1.]

☐ [T.D. 9602, 12-5-2012.]

[Reg. § 46.4376-1]

§ 46.4376-1. Fee on sponsors of self-insured health plans.—(a) *In general.*—(1) *General rule.*—A plan sponsor of an applicable self-insured health plan is liable for a fee imposed by section 4376 for plans with plan years ending on or after October 1, 2012, and before October 1, 2019. Paragraph (b) of this section provides the definitions that apply for purposes of section 4376 and this section. Paragraph (c) of this section provides the requirements for calculating the fee imposed by section 4376. Paragraph (d) of this section provides the applicability date. For rules relating to filing the required return and paying the fee, see § § 40.6011(a)-1 and 40.6071(a)-1.

(2) [Reserved]

(b) *Definitions.*—The following definitions apply for purposes of section 4376 and this section. See § 46.4377-1 for additional definitions.

(1) *Applicable self-insured health plan.*—(i) *In general.*—Except as provided in paragraph (b)(1)(ii) of this section and § 46.4377-1, *applicable self-insured health plan* means a plan that provides for accident and health coverage (within the meaning of § 46.4377-1(a)) if any portion of the coverage is provided other than through an insurance policy and the plan is established or maintained—

(A) By one or more employers for the benefit of their employees or former employees;

(B) By one or more employee organizations for the benefit of their members or former members;

(C) Jointly by one or more employers and one or more employee organizations for the benefit of employees or former employees;

(D) By a voluntary employees' beneficiary association, as described in section 501(c)(9);

(E) By an organization described in section 501(c)(6); or

(F) By a multiple employer welfare arrangement (as defined in section 3(40) of the Employee Retirement Income Security Act of 1974 (ERISA)), a rural electric cooperative (as defined in section 3(40)(B)(iv) of ERISA), or a rural cooperative association (as defined in section 3(40)(B)(v) of ERISA).

(ii) *Exceptions.*—The term *applicable self-insured health plan* does not include any of the following:

(A) A plan that provides benefits substantially all of which are excepted benefits, as defined in section 9832(c). For example, a health flexible spending arrangement (health FSA) (as described in section 106(c)(2)) that satisfies the requirements to be treated as an excepted benefit under section 9832(c) and § 54.9831-1(c)(3)(v) of this chapter is not an applicable self-insured health plan. A health FSA that is not treated as an excepted benefit under section 9832(c) and § 54.9831-1(c)(3)(v) is an applicable self-insured health plan.

(B) An employee assistance program, disease management program, or wellness program if the program does not provide significant benefits in the nature of medical care or treatment.

(C) A plan that, as demonstrated by the facts and circumstances surrounding the adoption and operation of the plan, was designed specifically to cover primarily employees who are working and residing outside the United States (as defined in § 46.4377-1(a)(3)).

(iii) *Multiple self-insured arrangements established or maintained by the same plan sponsor.*—For purposes of section 4376, two or more arrangements established or maintained by the same plan sponsor that provide for accident and health coverage (within the meaning of § 46.4377-1(a)) other than through an insurance policy and that have the same plan year may be treated as a single applicable self-insured health plan for purposes of calculating the fee imposed by section 4376. For example, if a plan sponsor establishes or maintains a self-insured arrangement providing major medical benefits, and a separate self-insured arrangement with the same plan year providing prescription drug benefits, the two arrangements may be treated as one applicable self- insured health plan so that the same life covered under each arrangement would count as only one covered life under the plan for purposes of calculating the fee. Similarly, if a plan sponsor provides a Health Reimbursement Arrangement (HRA) and another applicable self-insured health plan that provides major medical coverage, the HRA and the major medical plan may be treated as one applicable self-insured health plan if the HRA and the self-insured plan have the same plan year.

(iv) *Examples.*—The following examples illustrate the principle of this paragraph (b)(1):

Example 1. (i) Plan Sponsor D sponsors and maintains three separate plans to provide certain benefits to its employees - Plan 501, Plan 502, and Plan 503.

(ii) Plan 501 is a calendar year plan that provides accident and health benefits, other than through insurance (that is, on a self-insured basis), to employees of Plan Sponsor D. Plan 502 is a calendar year HRA that can be used to pay for qualified accident and medical expenses for employees of Plan Sponsor D and their eligible dependents. Plan 503 provides dental and vision benefits for employees of Plan Sponsor D and eligible dependents, other than through insurance (that is, on a self-insured basis).

(iii) Because Plan 501 and Plan 502 provide accident and health coverage (within the meaning of § 46.4377-1(a)) and are maintained by Plan Sponsor D for the benefit of its employees, Plans 501 and 502 are applicable self-insured health plans that are subject to the fee imposed by section 4376. Because dental and vision benefits are excepted benefits, as defined in section 9832(c), Plan 503 is not an applicable self-insured health plan subject to the section 4376 fee. Under the special rule set forth in § 46.4376-2(b)(1)(iii), Plan Sponsor D may treat Plans 501 and 502 (both self-insured plans with a calendar year plan year) as a single plan for purposes of calculating the fee imposed by section 4376.

Example 2. Same facts as *Example 1*, except Plan 503 is not a Plan that provides dental and vision benefits, but rather a plan that provides accident and health coverage solely to employees who are working and residing outside the United States and does not provide any benefits to employees who are not working and residing outside the United States. Plan 503 is designed specifically to provide coverage to employees working and residing outside the United States because it limits coverage to these employees. Therefore, in accordance with the exception described in § 46.4376-1(b)(1)(ii)(C), Plan 503 is not an applicable self-insured health plan.

(2) *Plan sponsor.*—(i) *In general.*—The term *plan sponsor* means—

(A) The employer, in the case of an applicable self-insured health plan established or maintained by a single employer;

(B) The employee organization, in the case of an applicable self-insured health plan established or maintained by an employee organization;

(C) The joint board of trustees, in the case of a multiemployer plan (as defined in section 414(f));

(D) The committee, in the case of a multiple employer welfare arrangement (as defined in section 3(40) of ERISA);

(E) The cooperative or association that establishes or maintains an applicable self-insured health plan established or maintained by a rural electric cooperative (as defined in section 3(40)(B)(iv) of ERISA) or rural cooperative association (as defined in section 3(40)(B)(v) of ERISA);

(F) The trustee, in the case of an applicable self-insured health plan established or maintained by a voluntary employees' beneficiary association (meaning that the voluntary employees' beneficiary association is not merely serving as a funding vehicle for a plan that is established or maintained by an employer or other person); or

(G) In the case of an applicable self-insured health plan the plan sponsor of which is not described in paragraphs (b)(2)(i)(A) through (F) of this section, the person identified by the terms of the document under which the plan is operated as the plan sponsor, or the person designated by the terms of the document under which the plan is operated as the plan sponsor for section 4376 purposes, provided that designation is made in writing, and that person has consented to the designation in writing, by no later than the date by which the return paying the fee under section 4376 for that plan year is required to be filed, after which date that designation for that plan year may not be changed or revoked, and provided further that a person may be designated as the plan sponsor only if the person is one of the persons establishing or maintaining the plan (for example, one of the employers that establishes or maintains the plan with one or more other employers or employee organizations).

(H) In the case of an applicable self-insured health plan the sponsor of which is not described in paragraphs (b)(2)(i)(A) through (F) of this section, and for which no identification or designation of a plan sponsor has been made pursuant to paragraph (b)(2)(i)(G) of this section, each employer that establishes or maintains the plan (with respect to employees of that employer), each employee organization that establishes or maintains the plan (with respect to members of that employee organization), and each board of trustees, cooperative, or association that establishes or maintains the plan, meaning that each plan sponsor must file a separate Form 720, "Quarterly Federal Excise Tax Return," reflecting its separate liability under section 4376.

(ii) *Examples.*—The following examples illustrate the principles of paragraph (b)(2) of this section:

Example 1. (i) Corporation XYZ is a holding company with no employees that owns all the issued and outstanding shares of Employer X, Employer Y, and Employer Z. Employer X, Employer Y, and Employer Z have established the XYZ Group Health Plan to provide accident and health coverage, provided other than through an insurance policy, for the benefit of their employees. The XYZ Group Health Plan has a calendar year plan year. In addition, there is no plan sponsor identified or designated in the plan document.

(ii) Because the XYZ Group Health Plan provides accident and health coverage other

Reg. § 46.4376-1(b)(2)(ii)

than through an insurance policy, and is established by one or more employers for the benefit of their employees, the XYZ Group Health Plan is an applicable self-insured health plan under section 4376(c)(2)(A) and paragraph (b)(1)(i)(A) of this section. Because a plan sponsor is not identified or designated in the governing plan document, the plan sponsor, for purposes of section 4376, is determined under paragraph (b)(2)(i)(H) of this section as each employer that establishes or maintains the plan (Employer X, Employer Y, and Employer Z), each with respect to its employees covered under the plan. Accordingly, Employer X, Employer Y, and Employer Z each must file a Form 720 reflecting their separate liabilities under section 4376, calculated based on lives covered that are employees of that employer (or spouses, dependents, or other beneficiaries of employees of that employer) and the applicable dollar amount in effect for the plan year.

Example 2. The same facts as *Example 1*, except that the governing plan document designates Employer X as the plan sponsor of the XYZ Group Health Plan for purposes of the fee under section 4376 and Employer X consents to this designation no later than the due date for paying the fee under section 4376. Accordingly, the plan sponsor for purposes of section 4376 is determined under paragraph (b)(2)(i)(G) of this section as Employer X. Employer X must file a Form 720 reflecting liabilities under section 4376, calculated based upon lives covered that are employees of Employer X, Employer Y, or Employer Z, or spouses, dependents, or other beneficiaries of employees of those employers and the applicable dollar amount in effect for the plan year.

(c) *Calculation of fee.*—(1) *In general.*—The amount of the fee for a plan year is equal to the product of the average number of lives covered under the plan for the plan year (determined in accordance with paragraph (c)(2) of this section) and the applicable dollar amount (determined in accordance with paragraph (c)(3) of this section).

(2) *Determination of the average number of lives covered under the plan.*—(i) *In general.*—To determine the average number of lives covered under an applicable self-insured health plan during a plan year, a plan sponsor must use one of the following methods—

(A) The actual count method (described in paragraph (c)(2)(iii) of this section);

(B) The snapshot method (described in paragraph (c)(2)(iv) of this section); or

(C) The Form 5500 method (described in paragraph (c)(2)(v) of this section).

(ii) *Consistency within plan year.*—A plan sponsor must use the same method of calculating the average number of lives covered under the plan consistently for the duration of the plan year. However, a plan sponsor may use a different method from one plan year to the next.

(iii) *Actual count method.*—(A) *In general.*—A plan sponsor may determine the average number of lives covered under a plan for a plan year by adding the totals of lives covered for each day of the plan year and dividing that total by the number of days in the plan year.

(B) *Example.*—The following example illustrates the principles of paragraphs (c)(1) and (c)(2)(iii)(A) of this section:

Example. Employer A is the plan sponsor of the Employer A Self-Insured Health Plan, which has a calendar year plan year. Employer A calculates the sum of lives covered under the plan for each day of the plan year ending December 31, 2013 as 3,285,000. The average number of lives covered under the plan for the plan year ending December 31, 2013, is 3,285,000 divided by 365, or 9,000. To calculate the section 4376 fee for the plan under paragraph (c)(1) of this section for the plan year ending December 31, 2013, Employer A must determine the applicable dollar amount under paragraph (c)(3) of this section and multiply that amount by 9,000.

(iv) *Snapshot method.*—(A) *In general.*—A plan sponsor may determine the average number of lives covered under an applicable self-insured health plan for a plan year by adding the totals of lives covered on a date during the first, second, or third month of each quarter of the plan year (or more dates in each quarter if an equal number of dates is used in each quarter), and dividing that total by the number of dates on which a count was made. For purposes of this paragraph (c)(2)(iv), each date used for the second, third and fourth quarter must be within three days of the date in that quarter that corresponds to the date used for the first quarter, and all dates used must fall within the same plan year. If a plan sponsor uses multiple dates for the first quarter, the plan sponsor must use dates in the second, third, and fourth quarters that correspond to each of the dates used for the first quarter or are within three days of such corresponding dates, and all dates used must fall within the same plan year. The 30th and 31st day of a month are treated as the last day of the month for purposes of determining the corresponding date for any month that has fewer than 31 days (for example, if either March 30 or March 31 is used for a calendar year plan, June 30 is the corresponding date for the second quarter). For purposes of this paragraph (c)(2)(iv), the number of lives covered on a designated date may be determined using either the snapshot factor method described in paragraph (c)(2)(iv)(B) of this section or the snapshot count method described in paragraph (c)(2)(iv)(C) of this section.

(B) *Snapshot factor method.*—Under the snapshot factor method, the number of lives covered on a date is equal to the sum of—

(i) The number of participants with self-only coverage on that date; plus

(ii) The number of participants with coverage other than self-only coverage on the date multiplied by 2.35.

(C) *Snapshot count method.*—Under the snapshot count method, the number of lives covered on a date equals the actual number of lives covered on the designated date.

(D) *Examples.*—The following examples illustrate the principles of paragraphs (c)(1) and (c)(2)(iv) of this section:

Example 1. (i) Employer B is the plan sponsor of the Employer B Self-Insured Health Plan, which has a calendar year plan year. Employer B uses the snapshot method to determine the average number of lives covered under the plan and uses the snapshot count method to determine the number of lives covered on a day in the first month of each calendar quarter of the plan year.

(ii) On January 4, 2013, the Employer B Self-Insured Health Plan covers 2,000 lives, on April 5, 2013, 2,100 lives, on July 5, 2013, 2,050 lives, and on October 4, 2013, 2,050 lives. Under the snapshot method, Employer B must determine the average number of lives covered under the Employer B Self-Insured Health Plan for the plan year ending December 31, 2013, as 8,200 (2,000 + 2,100 + 2,050 + 2,050) divided by 4, or 2,050. To calculate the section 4376 fee under paragraph (c)(1) of this section for the plan year ending December 31, 2013, Employer B must determine the applicable dollar amount under paragraph (c)(3) of this section and multiply that amount by 2,050.

Example 2. (i) Same facts as *Example 1*, except that for the 2014 plan year Employer B determines the number of lives covered that are not covered by self-only coverage using the snapshot factor method (that is, based on the number of participants with coverage other than self-only coverage multiplied by 2.35 (the factor set forth in (c)(2)(iv) of this section)).

(ii) On January 10, 2014, Employer B Self-Insured Health Plan provides self-only coverage to 600 employees and other than self-only coverage to 800 employees. On April 11, 2014, Employer B Self-Insured Health Plan provides self-only coverage to 608 employees and other than self-only coverage to 800 employees. On July 11, 2014 and October 10, 2014, Employer B Self-Insured Health Plan provides self-only coverage to 610 employees and other than self-only coverage to 809 employees.

(iii) Under the snapshot factor method, Employer B must determine the average number of lives covered under the Employer B Self-Insured Health Plan for the plan year ending December 31, 2014 as 9,988 [(600+(800 × 2.35)) + (608 + (800 × 2.35)) + (610 + (809 × 2.35)) + (610 + (809 × 2.35))] divided by 4, or 2,497. To calculate the section 4376 fee under paragraph (c)(1) of this section for the plan year ending December 31, 2014, Employer B must determine the applicable dollar amount under paragraph (c)(3) of this section and multiply that amount by 2,497.

(v) *Form 5500 method.*—(A) *Calculation method.*—A plan sponsor may determine the average number of lives covered under a plan for a plan year based on the number of participants reported on the Form 5500, "Annual Return/Report of Employee Benefit Plan," or the Form 5500-SF, "Short Form Annual Return/Report of Small Employee Benefit Plan," that is filed for the applicable self-insured health plan for that plan year, provided that the Form 5500 or Form 5500-SF is filed no later than the due date for the fee imposed by section 4376 for that plan year. For purposes of this paragraph (c)(2)(v), the average number of lives covered under the plan for the plan year for a plan offering only self-only coverage equals the sum of the total participants covered at the beginning and the end of the plan year, as reported on the Form 5500 or Form 5500-SF for the applicable self-insured health plan, divided by 2. For purposes of this paragraph (c)(2)(v), the average number of lives covered under the plan for the plan year for a plan offering self-only coverage and coverage other than self-only coverage equals the sum of total participants covered at the beginning and the end of the plan year, as reported on the Form 5500 or Form 5500-SF filed for the applicable self-insured health plan.

(B) *Examples.*—The following examples illustrate the principles of paragraphs (c)(1) and (c)(2)(v)(A) of this section:

Example 1. Employer C is the plan sponsor of the Employer C Self-Insured Health Plan, which has a calendar year plan year ending on December 31, 2013. Employer C is required to file a Form 5500 for the plan for the 2013 plan year by July 31, 2014. However, on July 30, 2014, Employer C obtains an automatic 2-1/2 month extension for filing the 2013 Form 5500. Employer C files the 2013 Form 5500 on September 30, 2014 (that is, before the October 15 extended due date). Employer C is not eligible to use the Form 5500 method to determine the average number of lives covered under Plan C for the plan year ending on December 31, 2013, because the 2013 Form 5500 was not filed by the original due date (that is, by July 31, 2014) for the return that reports liability for the fee imposed by section 4376 for the 2013 plan year.

Example 2. Same facts as *Example 1*, except that the Employer C Self-Insured Health Plan has a fiscal year plan year ending on July 31, 2013, and offers only selfonly coverage. Employer C files a Form 5500 for the Employer C Self-Insured Health Plan for the plan year ending July 31, 2013 (the 2012 Form 5500), on the extended due date for filing the 2012 Form 5500 (May 15, 2014). Employer C is eligible to use the Form 5500 method to determine the average number of lives covered under Plan C for the plan year ending on July 31, 2013, because the 2012 Form 5500 had been filed by the due date for the return that reports liability for the fee imposed by section 4376 for that plan year (July 31, 2014).

Reg. § 46.4376-1(c)(2)(v)(B)

Example 3. Same facts as *Example 2*, provided further that the Employer C Self-Insured Health Plan 2012 Form 5500 reports 4,000 plan participants on the first day of the plan year and 4,200 plan participants on the last day of the 2012 plan year. For purposes of calculating the fee under section 4376 using the Form 5500 method, Employer C must treat the number of lives covered for the plan year ending July 31, 2013, as equal to the sum of 4,000 and 4,200 or 8,200, divided by 2, or 4,100. To calculate the section 4376 fee under paragraph (c)(1) of this section for the plan year ending July 31, 2013, Employer C must determine the applicable dollar amount under paragraph (c)(3) of this section and multiply that amount by 4,100.

Example 4. Same facts as *Example 3*, except that the Employer C Self-Insured Health plan offers self-only coverage and family coverage. For purposes of calculating the fee under section 4376 using the Form 5500 method, Employer C must treat the number of lives covered for the plan year ending July 31, 2013, as equal to the sum of 4,000 and 4,200, or 8,200. To calculate the section 4376 fee under paragraph (c)(1) of this section for the plan year ending July 31, 2013, Employer C must determine the applicable dollar amount under paragraph (c)(3) of this section and multiply that amount by 8,200.

(vi) *Special rule for health FSAs and HRAs.*—For purposes of this section, if a plan sponsor does not establish or maintain an applicable self-insured health plan other than a health flexible spending arrangement (health FSA) (as described in section 106(c)(2)) or a health reimbursement arrangement (as described in Notice 2002-45 (2002-2 CB 93)) (HRA), the plan sponsor may treat each participant's health FSA or HRA as covering a single life (and therefore the plan sponsor is not required to include as lives covered any spouse, dependent, or other beneficiary of the individual participant in the health FSA or HRA, as applicable). If a health FSA or HRA that is an applicable self-insured health plan has the same plan sponsor and plan year as another applicable self-insured health plan other than a health FSA or HRA, the two arrangements may be treated as a single plan under paragraph (b)(1)(iii) of this section. However, the special counting rule in this paragraph applies only for purposes of the health FSA or HRA and, therefore, applies only for purposes of the participants in the health FSA or HRA that do not participate in the other applicable self-insured health plan. The participants in the health FSA or HRA that participate in the other applicable self-insured health plan will be counted in accordance with the method applied for counting lives covered under that other plan as described in paragraph (b)(2)(i) of this section. See § 601.601(d)(2) of this chapter.

(vii) *Special rule for lives covered solely by the fully-insured options under an applicable self-insured health plan.*—(A) *In general.*—If an applicable self-insured health plan provides accident

and health coverage through fully-insured options and selfinsured options, the plan sponsor is permitted to disregard the lives that are covered solely under the fully-insured options in determining the lives covered taken into account for the actual count method (described in paragraph (c)(2)(iii) of this section), the snapshot method (described in paragraph (c)(2)(iv) of this section), and the Form 5500 method (described in paragraph (c)(2)(v) of this section).

(B) *Example.*—The following example illustrates the principles of paragraph (c)(2)(vii) of this section:

Example. (i) Employer C is the plan sponsor of the Employer C Health Plan (Plan P). The Plan offers self-only or family health and accident coverage under fully-insured or self-insured options. On June 28, 2015, Employer C files a Form 5500 for Plan P for the plan year ending December 31, 2014 indicating: (1) a total of 4,000 plan participants on the first day of the 2014 plan year; and (2) a total of 4,200 plan participants on the last day of the plan year. Employer C determines that there were 3,000 plan participants (and their families, as applicable) covered under the fully-insured option offered under the plan on the first day of the 2014 plan year, and 2,900 plan participants (and their families, as applicable) covered under the fully-insured option on the last day of the 2014 plan year. Employer C uses the Form 5500 method to calculate the number of lives covered for the 2014 plan year.

(ii) Pursuant to paragraph (c)(2)(vii) of this section, Employer C determines the number of lives covered for the 2014 plan year as: the sum of 1,000 (4,000 total participants on the first day of the plan year - 3,000 participants covered by the specified health insurance policy on the first day of the plan year) and 1,300 (4,200 total participants - 2,900 participants covered by the specified health insurance policy on the first day of the plan year), or 2,300. To calculate the section 4376 fee under paragraph (c)(1) of this section for the 2014 plan year, Employer C must determine the applicable dollar amount under paragraph (c)(3) of this section and multiply that amount by 2,300.

(viii) *Special rule for the first year the fee is in effect.*—Notwithstanding paragraph (c)(2)(i) of this section, for a plan year beginning before July 11, 2012, and ending on or after October 1, 2012, a plan sponsor may determine the average number of lives covered under the plan for the plan year using any reasonable method.

(3) *Applicable dollar amount.*—For a plan year ending on or after October 1, 2012, and before October 1, 2013, the applicable dollar amount is $1. For a plan year ending on or after October 1, 2013, and before October 1, 2014, the applicable dollar amount is $2. For any plan year ending in any Federal fiscal year beginning on or after October 1, 2014, the applicable dollar amount is equal to the sum of—

Reg. § 46.4376-1(c)(2)(vi)

(i) The applicable dollar amount for the plan year ending in the previous Federal fiscal year; plus

(ii) The amount equal to the product of—

(A) The applicable dollar amount for the plan year ending in the previous Federal fiscal year; and

(B) The percentage increase in the projected per capita amount of the National Health Expenditures most recently released by the Department of Health and Human Services before the beginning of the Federal fiscal year.

(4) *Examples.*—The following examples illustrate the principle of paragraph (c)(3) of this section.

Example 1. (Calendar year plan). (i) Plan Sponsor C maintains Plan X which has a calendar year plan year; the plan continues in operation for the entire calendar years 2012 through 2019. Plan X is an applicable self-insured health plan, within the meaning of § 46.4376-1(b)(1), and Plan Sponsor C is liable for the fee imposed by section 4376, determined in accordance with these regulations, beginning with the 2012 plan year - the plan year beginning January 1, 2012, and ending December 31, 2012 - and ending with the 2018 plan year - the plan year beginning January 1, 2018, and ending December 31, 2018. In accordance with § 40.6071(a)-1(c) of this chapter:

(ii) The first Form 720 that must be filed to report and pay the fee imposed by section 4376 for Plan X covers the 2012 plan year (January 1, 2012, through December 31, 2012) and must be filed no later than July 31, 2013, and the fee reported on this form must be calculated by multiplying the average number lives by $1 (the applicable dollar amount in effect for plans with plan years beginning on or after October 1, 2012, and before October 1, 2013); and

(iii) The last Form 720 that must be filed to report and pay the fee imposed by section 4376 for Plan X covers the 2018 plan year (January 1, 2018, through December 31, 2018) and must be filed no later than July 31, 2019, and the fee reported on this form must be calculated using the applicable dollar amount in effect for plan years ending on or after October 1, 2018, and before October 1, 2019.

Example 2. (Fiscal year plan). (i) Plan Sponsor B maintains Plan W, which has a fiscal year plan year ending on July 31; the plan continues in operation for the entire fiscal year plan years from August 1, 2012, through July 31, 2019. Plan W is an applicable self-insured health plan, within the meaning of § 46.4376-1(b)(1), and Plan Sponsor B is liable for the fee imposed by section 4376, determined in accordance with these regulations, beginning with the 2012 plan year - the plan year beginning on August 1, 2012, and ending on July 31, 2013 - and ending with the 2018 plan year - plan year beginning on August 1, 2018, and ending July 31, 2019. In accordance with § 40.6071(a)-1(c) of this chapter:

(ii) The first Form 720 that must be filed to report and pay the fee imposed by section 4376 for Plan X covers the 2012 plan year (August 1, 2012, through July 31, 2013) and must be filed no later than July 31, 2014, and the fee reported on this form must be calculated by multiplying the average number lives by $1 (the applicable dollar amount in effect for plans with plans years beginning on or after October 1, 2012, and before October 1, 2013); and

(iii) The last Form 720 that must be filed to report and pay the fee imposed by section 4376 for Plan X covers the 2018 plan year (August 1, 2018, through July 31, 2019) and must be filed no later than July 31, 2020, and the fee must be calculated using the applicable dollar amount in effect for plan years ending on or after October 1, 2018, and before October 1, 2019.

(d) *Effective/Applicability date.*—This section applies for plan years that end on or after October 1, 2012, and before October 1, 2019. [Reg. § 46.4376-1.]

☐ [*T.D.* 9602, 12-5-2012.]

[Reg. § 46.4377-1]

§ 46.4377-1. Definitions and special rules.— (a) *Definitions.*—The following definitions apply for purposes of sections 4375 and 4376 and § § 46.4375-1 and 46.4376-1.

(1) *Accident and health coverage.*—The term *accident and health coverage* means any coverage that, if provided by an insurance policy, would cause such policy to be a specified health insurance policy (as defined in section 4375(c) and § 46.4375-1(b)(1)). Accident and health coverage also includes coverage for an active employee, a former employee, or a qualifying beneficiary that is continuation coverage required under the Consolidated Omnibus Budget Reconciliation Act of 1985 (COBRA) or similar continuation coverage under other federal law or under state law.

(2) *Individual residing in the United States.*— (i) The term *individual residing in the United States* means an individual with a place of abode in the United States.

(ii) *Determination of place of abode.*—For purposes of paragraph (a)(2) of this section, an issuer or a plan sponsor may rely on the most recent address on file with the issuer or plan sponsor and may treat the primary insured and the primary insured's spouse, dependents, or other beneficiaries covered by the policy as having the same place of abode. For this purpose, the primary insured is the individual covered by the policy whose eligibility for coverage was not due to that individual's status as the spouse, dependent, or other beneficiary of another covered individual.

(3) *United States.*—The term *United States* includes American Samoa, Guam, the Northern Mariana Islands, Puerto Rico, the Virgin Islands, and any other possession of the United States.

(4) *Federal fiscal year.*—The term *Federal fiscal year* means the year beginning on October 1 and ending on the following September 30.

(b) *Treatment of exempt governmental programs.*—(1) *In general.*—The fees imposed by sections 4375 and 4376 do not apply to any covered life under an exempt governmental program as defined in paragraph (b)(2) of this section.

(2) *Exempt governmental program.*—For purposes of this section, *exempt governmental program* means any—

(i) Insurance program established under title XVIII of the Social Security Act;

(ii) Medical assistance program established by title XIX or XXI of the Social Security Act;

(iii) Program established by Federal law for providing medical care (other than through insurance policies) to individuals (or their spouses and dependents) by reason of such individuals being (or having been) members of the Armed Forces of the United States; and

(iv) Program established by Federal law for providing medical care (other than through insurance policies) to members of Indian tribes (as defined in section 4(d) of the Indian Health Care Improvement Act).

(c) *Effective/Applicability date.*—This section applies to all policy and plan years that end on or after October 1, 2012, and before October 1, 2019. [Reg. § 46.4377-1.]

☐ [*T.D. 9602, 12-5-2012.*]

Taxes on Wagering

See p. 20,601 for regulations not amended to reflect law changes

[Reg. § 44.0-1]

§ 44.0-1. Introduction.—(a) *In general.*—The regulations in this part (Part 44, Subchapter D, Chapter I, Title 26 (1954) Code of Federal Regulations) are designated "Wagering Tax Regulations." The regulations relate to the taxes imposed by chapter 35 of the Internal Revenue Code of 1954, as amended, to certain general provisions of chapter 40 of such Code, and to certain related administrative provisions of subtitle F of such Code. Chapter 35 imposes an excise tax on wagers and a special tax to be paid by each person liable for the tax imposed on wagers and by each person engaged in receiving wagers for or on behalf of any person liable for the tax imposed on wagers. References in these regulations to the "Internal Revenue Code" or the "Code" are references to the Internal Revenue Code of 1954, as amended, unless otherwise indicated. References to a section or other provision of law are references to a section or other provision of the Internal Revenue Code, as amended, unless otherwise indicated.

(b) *Division of regulations.*—The regulations in this part (26 CFR Part 44) are divided into five subparts. Subpart A contains provisions relating to the arrangement and numbering of the sections of the regulations in this part, general definitions and use of terms, scope of the regulations, and the extent to which the regulations in this part supersede prior regulations relating to the taxes imposed by chapter 35 of the Internal Revenue Code. Subpart B relates to the tax on wagers. Subpart C relates to the special tax. Subpart D relates to certain miscellaneous and general provisions having application to taxes imposed by chapter 35. Subpart E relates to selected provisions of subtitle F of the Code (Procedure and Administration) which have special application to the taxes imposed by chapter 35 of the Code.

(c) *Arrangement and numbering.*—Each section of the regulations in this part (other than subpart A) is designated by a number composed of the part number followed by a decimal point (44.); the section of the Internal Revenue Code which it interprets; a hyphen (-); and a number identifying the section. By use of these designations one can ascertain the sections of the regulations relating to a provision of the Code. For example, the regulations pertaining to section 4401 of the Code are designated § 44.4401-1, § 44.4401-2, and § 44.4401-3. [Reg. § 44.0-1.]

☐ [*T.D. 6370. Amended by T.D. 7665.*]

[Reg. § 44.0-2]

§ 44.0-2. General definitions and use of terms.—As used in the regulations in this part, unless otherwise expressly indicated—

(a) The terms defined in the provisions of law contained in the regulations in this part shall have the meanings so assigned to them.

(b) The Internal Revenue Code of 1954 means the Act approved August 16, 1954 (68A Stat.), entitled "An Act To revise the internal revenue laws of the United States", as amended.

(c) District director means district director of internal revenue.

(d) The cross references in the regulations in this part to other portions of the regulations, when the word "see" is used, are made only for convenience and shall be given no legal effect. [Reg. § 44.0-2.]

☐ [*T.D. 6370.*]

[Reg. § 44.0-3]

§ 44.0-3. Scope of regulations.—The regulations in this part apply to wagering activity on and after January 1, 1955. [Reg. § 44.0-3.]

☐ [*T.D. 6370.*]

[Reg. §44.0-4]

§44.0-4. Extent to which the regulations in this part supersede prior regulations.—The regulations in this part, with respect to the subject matter within the scope thereof, supersede Regulations 132, 26 CFR (1939) Part 325. [Reg. §44.0-4.]

☐ [T.D. 6370.]

[Reg. §44.4401-1]

§44.4401-1. Imposition of tax.—(a) *In general.*—Section 4401 imposes a tax on all wagers, as defined in section 4421. See §§44.4421 and 44.4421-1 for definition of the term "wager."

(b) *Rate of tax; amount of wager.*—(1) *Rate of tax.*—The tax is imposed at the rate of 10 percent of the amount of any taxable wager.

(2) *Amount of wager.*—(i) The amount of the wager is the amount risked by the bettor, including any charge or fee incident to the placing of the wager as provided in subdivision (iv) of this subparagraph, rather than the amount which he stands to win. Thus, if a bettor bets $5 against a bookmaker's $7 with respect to the outcome of a prize fight, the amount of the wager subject to tax is $5.

(ii) In the case of a "parlay" wager (i.e., a single wager made by a bettor on the outcome of a series of events, usually horse races), the amount of the taxable wager is the amount initially wagered by the bettor irrespective of whether the parlay is successful. In the case of an "if" wager, the amount of the taxable wager is the total of all amounts wagered on each selection of the bettor. For example, A makes a $10 wager on horse R with the understanding that if horse R wins, $5 is to be wagered on horse S and $5 on horse T. If horse R wins, the taxable wager is $20. If horse R loses, the taxable wager is $10. In determining the amount of a taxable wager involving the features of, or a combination of, "parlay" and "if" bets, such as wagers sometimes referred to as a "whipsaw" or an "if and reverse" bet, the rules set forth above relating to "parlay" and "if" bets are to be followed. For example, assume B wagers $10 on horse R with the understanding that if horse R wins, $5 is to be placed as a parlay wager on horses S and T. In such a case, if horse R loses, the taxable wager is $10; if horse R wins, there are two taxable wagers amounting in the aggregate to $15.

(iii) In the case of punchboards with prizes of merchandise, cash, or free plays listed thereon, the amount of the taxable wager is the amount risked by the bettor for all chances taken by him, including the chances taken by the bettor in lieu of the acceptance of an equivalent amount in cash or merchandise.

(iv) In determining the amount of any wager subject to tax there shall be included any charge or fee incident to the placing of the wager. For example, in the case of a wager with respect to a horse race, any amount paid to a bookmaker for the purpose of guaranteeing the bettor a payoff based on actual track odds is to be included as a part of the wager. Similarly, in the case of a lottery, any amount paid to the operator thereof by the bettor for the privilege of making a contribution to the pool or bank is also to be included in the amount of the wager. However, the amount of the wager subject to tax shall not include the amount of the tax where it is established by actual records of the taxpayer that such amount of tax was collected from the bettor as a separate charge. [Reg. §44.4401-1.]

☐ [T.D. 6370.]

[Reg. §44.4401-2]

§44.4401-2. Person liable for tax.—(a) *In general.*—(1) Every person engaged in the business of accepting wagers with respect to a sports event or a contest is liable for the tax on any such wager accepted by him. Every person who operates a wagering pool or lottery conducted for profit is liable for the tax with respect to any wager or contribution placed in such pool or lottery. To be liable for the tax, it is not necessary that the person engaged in the business of accepting wagers or operating a wagering pool or lottery physically receive the wager or contribution. Any wager or contribution received by an agent or employee on behalf of such person shall be considered to have been accepted by and placed with such person.

(2) Any person required to register under section 4412 by reason of having received wagers for or on behalf of another person, but who fails to register the name and place of residence of such other person (hereinafter in this subparagraph referred to as principal), shall be liable for the tax on all wagers received by him during the period in which he has failed to so register the name and place of residence of such principal. Subsequent compliance with section 4412 by the person receiving wagers for another does not relieve him of his liability and duty to pay such tax, nor will the fact that such person incurs liability with respect to the tax on such wagers, relieve his principal of liability for the tax imposed under section 4401 with respect to such wagers. Accordingly, both the person receiving the wagers and his principal shall be liable for the tax on such wagers until the tax is paid. Payment of the tax on such wagers shall not relieve the person receiving wagers of any penalty for failure to register as required by section 4412. This subparagraph has application only to wagers received after September 2, 1958.

(b) *In business of accepting wagers.*—A person is engaged in the business of accepting wagers if he makes it a practice to accept wagers with respect to which he assumes the risk of profit or loss depending upon the outcome of the event or the contest with respect to which the wager is accepted. It is not intended that to be engaged in the business of accepting wagers a person must be either so engaged to the exclusion of all other activities or even primarily so engaged. Thus, for example, an individual may be primarily engaged in business as a salesman, and also for the purpose of the tax be engaged in the business of accepting wagers.

(c) *Lay-offs.*—If a person engaged in the business of accepting wagers or conducting a lottery or betting pool for profit lays off all or part of the wagers placed with him with another person engaged in the business of accepting wagers or conducting a betting pool or lottery for profit, he shall, notwithstanding such lay-off, be liable for the tax on the wagers or contributions initially accepted by him. See § 44.6419-2 for credit and refund provisions applicable with respect to laid-off wagers. [Reg. § 44.4401-2.]

☐ [*T.D.* 6370.]

[Reg. § 44.4401-3]

§ 44.4401-3. When tax attaches.—The tax attaches when (a) a person engaged in the business of accepting wagers with respect to a sports event or a contest, or (b) a person who operates a wagering pool or lottery for profit, accepts a wager or contribution from a bettor. In the case of a wager on credit, the tax attaches whether or not the amount of the wager is actually collected from the bettor. However, if an amount equivalent to the amount of the wager is paid to the bettor prior to the close of the calendar month in which such wager was accepted, either because of the cancellation of the event upon which the wager was placed, or because the wager was cancelled or rescinded by mutual agreement, the wager need not be reported on the taxpayer's return for such month. Where such cancellation or rescission takes place in a month subsequent to the month in which the wager was accepted, credit or refund of the tax paid with respect to such wager may be made subject to the provisions of § 44.6419-1. [Reg. § 44.4401-3.]

☐ [*T.D.* 6370.]

[Reg. § 44.4402-1]

§ 44.4402-1. Exemptions.—(a) *Parimutuel wagering enterprise.*—Section 4402 provides that no tax shall be imposed by section 4401 on any wager placed with, or on any wager placed in a wagering pool conducted by, a parimutuel wagering enterprise licensed under State law.

(b) *Wagering machines.*—(1) *In general.*—Section 4402 provides that no tax shall be imposed by section 4401 on any wager placed in a coin-operated device (as defined in section 4462 as in effect for years beginning before July 1, 1980), or on any amount paid, in lieu of inserting a coin, token, or similar object, to operate a device described in section 4462(a)(2) (as so in effect). These devices include:

(i) So-called "slot" machines that operate by means of the insertion of a coin, token, or similar object and that, by application of the element of chance, may deliver, or entitle the person playing or operating the machine to receive cash, premiums, merchandise, or tokens; and

(ii) Machines that are similar to machines described in paragraph (b)(1)(i) of this section

and are operated without the insertion of a coin, token, or similar object.

(2) *Examples.*—The following devices and machines are examples of the devices referred to in paragraph (b)(1) of this section:

(i) A machine that is operated by means of the insertion of a coin, token, or similar object and that, even though it does not dispense cash or tokens, has the features and characteristics of a gaming device whether or not evidence exists as to actual payoffs.

(ii) A so-called crane machine, claw, digger, or rotary merchandising type device that is operated by the insertion of a coin and adjustment of a control lever for the purpose of removing from the machine, by gripping, pushing, or other manipulation articles such as figurines, lighters, etc., in the machine.

(iii) A pinball machine equipped with a pushbutton for releasing free plays and a meter for recording the plays so released, or equipped with provisions for multiple coin insertion for increasing the odds.

(iv) Pinball machines in connection with which free plays are redeemed in cash, tokens, or merchandise, or prizes are offered to any person for the attainment of designated scores.

(v) A coin-operated machine that displays a poker hand or delivers a ticket with a poker hand symbolized on it that entitles the player to a prize if the poker hand displayed by the machine or symbolized on the ticket constitutes a winning hand. [Reg. § 44.4402-1.]

☐ [*T.D.* 8328, 12-28-90. *Redesignated and amended by T.D.* 8442, 10-21-92.]

[Reg. § 44.4403-1]

§ 44.4403-1. Daily record.—Every person liable for tax under section 4401 shall keep such records as will clearly show as to each day's operations:

(a) The gross amount of all wagers accepted;

(b) The gross amount of each class or type of wager accepted on each separate event, contest, or other wagering medium. For example, in the case of wagers accepted on a horse race, the daily record shall show separately the gross amount of each class or type of wagers (straight bets, parlays, "if" bets, etc.) accepted on each horse in the race. Similarly, in the case of the numbers game, the daily record shall show the gross amount of each class or type of wager accepted on each number.

For additional provisions relating to records, see §§ 44.6001 and 44.6001-1. [Reg. § 44.4403-1.]

☐ [*T.D.* 6370.]

[Reg. § 44.4404-1]

§ 44.4404-1. Territorial extent.—(a) *In general.*—The tax imposed by section 4401 applies to wagers (1) accepted in the United States, or (2) placed by a person who is in the United States (i) with a person who is a citizen or resident of the

United States, or (ii) in a wagering pool or lottery conducted by a person who is a citizen or resident of the United States. All wagers made within the United States are taxable irrespective of the citizenship or place of residence of the parties to the wager. Thus, the tax applies to wagers placed within the United States, even though the person for whom or on whose behalf the wagers are received is located in a foreign country and is not a citizen or resident of the United States. Likewise, a wager accepted outside the United States by a citizen or resident of the United States is taxable if the person making such wager is within the United States at the time the wager is made.

(b) *Examples.*—The following examples illustrate the application of paragraph (a) of this section:

Example (1). A syndicate which maintains its headquarters in a foreign country has representatives in the United States who receive wagers in the United States for or on behalf of such syndicate. For the purposes of section 4404, such wagers are considered as accepted within the United States, the syndicate is considered to be in the business of accepting wagers within the United States, and such wagers are subject to the tax. This is true regardless of the nationality or residence of the members of the syndicate.

Example (2). A Canadian citizen employed in Detroit, Michigan, telephones a horse race bet to a bookmaker who is a United States citizen with his place of business located in Windsor, Canada. The wager is taxable since it is made by a person within the United States with a person who is a United States citizen.

Example (3). A United States citizen while visiting Tijuana, Mexico, makes a wager on the outcome of a horse race with a bookmaker who is also a United States citizen located and doing business in Tijuana. The wager is not taxable since both parties to the wager, though United States citizens, were outside the United States at the time the wager was made. [Reg. § 44.4404-1.]

☐ [*T.D.* 6370.]

[Reg. § 44.4411-1]

§ 44.4411-1. Imposition of tax.—(a) *In general.*—A special tax of $50 per year is required to be paid by each person:

    (1) Who is liable for the tax imposed by section 4401, or

    (2) Who is engaged in receiving wagers for or on behalf of any person who is liable for the tax imposed by section 4401.

(b) *Examples.*—The application of paragraph (a) of this section may be illustrated by the following examples:

Example (1). A, who is engaged in the business of accepting horse race bets, employs ten persons to receive on his behalf wagers which are transmitted by telephone. A also employs a secretary and a bookkeeper. A and each of the ten persons who receive wagers by telephone on behalf of A are liable for the special tax. The secretary and

bookkeeper are not liable for the special tax unless they also receive wagers for A.

Example (2). B operates a numbers game and has an arrangement with ten persons, who are employed in various capacities, such as bootblacks, elevator operators, news dealers, etc., to receive wagers from the public on his behalf. B also employs C to collect from the ten persons referred to the wagers received by them on B's behalf and to deliver such wagers to B. C performs no other services for B. B and the ten persons who receive wagers on his behalf are liable for the special tax. C is not liable for the special tax since he is not engaged in receiving wagers for B.

(c) *Cross references.*—For provisions relating to the payment of the special tax (computation, manner of payment, etc.), see subpart D of this part. [Reg. § 44.4411-1.]

☐ [*T.D.* 6370.]

[Reg. § 44.4412-1]

§ 44.4412-1. Registration.—(a) *In general.*—Every person required to pay the special tax imposed by section 4411 shall register and file a return on Form 11-C. For provisions relating to the general requirement for filing a return, see § 44.6011(a)-1.

(b) *Information to be reported on Form 11-C.*—(1) Every person required to make a return on Form 11-C shall report thereon his full name and place of residence. A person doing business under an alias, style, or trade name shall give his true name, followed by his alias, style, or trade name. In the case of a partnership, association, firm, or company, other than a corporation, the style or trade name shall be given, also the true name of each member and his place of residence. In the case of a corporation, the true name and title of each officer and his place of residence shall be shown.

(2) Each person engaged in the business of accepting wagers on his own account shall report on Form 11-C the name and address of each place where such business will be conducted and the name, address, and number appearing on the special (occupational) stamp of each agent or employee who may receive wagers on his behalf. Thereafter, a return shall be filed on Form 11-C, marked "Supplemental", each time an additional employee or agent is engaged to receive wagers. Such supplemental return shall be filed not later than 10 days after the date such additional employee or agent is engaged to receive wagers and shall show the name, address, and number appearing on the special (occupational) stamp of each such agent or employee. As to a change of address, see § 44.4905-2.

(3) Each agent or employee who receives wagers for or on behalf of a person engaged in the business of accepting wagers on his own account shall report on Form 11-C the name and residence address of each person (i.e., individual, partnership, corporation, etc.) on whose behalf wagers are to be received. Thereafter, the agent

or employee shall file a return on Form 11-C, marked "Supplemental", each time he is engaged or employed to receive wagers for a person or persons other than the person or persons previously reported on Form 11-C. Such supplemental return shall be filed not later than 10 days after the date he is engaged to receive wagers and shall show the name, business address, or, if none, the residence address of the person or persons by whom he is engaged to receive wagers. As to a change of address, see § 44.4905-2.

(c) *Time and place for filing Form 11-C.*—For provisions relating to the time for filing Form 11-C (other than Form 11-C marked "Supplemental"), see § § 44.6071 and 44.6071-1. For provisions relating to the place for filing Form 11-C, see § § 44.6091 and 44.6091-1. [Reg. § 44.4412-1.]

□ [*T.D.* 6370.]

[Reg. § 44.4413-1]

§ 44.4413-1. Certain provisions made applicable.—For regulations under sections 4901, 4902, 4904, 4905, and 4906, as extended and made applicable to the special tax imposed by section 4411 and to the persons upon whom such tax is imposed, see subpart D of this part. [Reg. § 44.4413-1.]

□ [*T.D.* 6370.]

[Reg. § 44.4421-1]

§ 44.4421-1. Definitions.—(a) *Wager.*—The term "wager" means—

(1) Any wager placed with a person engaged in the business of accepting wagers upon the outcome of a sports event or a contest;

(2) Any wager placed in a wagering pool with respect to a sports event or a contest, if such pool is conducted for profit; and

(3) Any wager placed in a lottery conducted for profit.

(b) *Lottery.*—(1) *In general.*—The term "lottery" includes the numbers game, policy, and similar types of wagering. In general, a lottery conducted for profit includes any scheme or method for the distribution of prizes among persons who have paid or promised a consideration for a chance to win such prizes, usually as determined by the numbers or symbols on tickets as drawn from a lottery wheel or other receptacle, or by the outcome of an event, provided such lottery is conducted for profit. The term also includes enterprises commonly known as "policy" or "numbers" and similar types of wagering where the player selects a number, or a combination of numbers, and pays or agrees to pay a certain amount in consideration of which the operator of the lottery, policy, or numbers game agrees to pay a prize or fixed sum of money if the selected number or combination of numbers appear or are published in a manner understood by the parties. For example, the winning number or combination of numbers may appear or be published as a series of numbers in the payoff prices of a series of horse races at a certain race

track, or in the United States Treasury balance reports, or the reports of a stock or commodity exchange. This description is not intended to be restrictive; hence, the substitution of letters or other symbols for numbers, or a different arrangement for determining the winning number or combination of numbers, does not alter the fundamental nature of a game which otherwise would be considered a lottery. The operation of a punch board or a similar gaming device for profit is also considered to be the operation of a lottery.

(2) *Certain games excluded.*—(i) *Cards, dice, etc.*—Section 4421 specifically excludes from the term "lottery" any game of a type in which usually (*a*) the wagers are placed, (*b*) the winners are determined, and (*c*) the distribution of prizes or other property is made, in the presence of all persons placing wagers in such game. Thus, for example, no tax would be payable with respect to wagers made in a bingo or keno game since such a game is usually conducted under circumstances in which the wagers are placed, the winners are determined, and the distribution of prizes is made in the presence of all persons participating in the game. For the same reason, no tax would apply in the case of card games, dice games, or games involving wheels of chance, such as roulette wheels and gambling wheels of a type used at carnivals and public fairs.

(ii) *Drawings conducted by an organization exempt from tax under section 501 or 521.*—Section 4421 specifically excludes from the term "lottery" any drawing conducted by an organization exempt from tax under section 501 or 521 if no part of the net proceeds derived from such drawing inures to the benefit of any private shareholder or individual. For provisions relating to exemption from income tax under section 501 or 521, see the Income Tax Regulations (Part 1 of this chapter).

(c) *Other terms used.*—(1) *Wagering pool.*—A wagering pool conducted for profit includes any scheme or method for the distribution of prizes to one or more winning bettors based upon the outcome of a sports event or a contest, or a combination or series of such events or contests, provided such wagering pool is managed and conducted for the purpose of making a profit.

(2) *Sports event.*—A sports event includes every type of sports event, whether amateur, scholastic, or professional, such as horse racing, auto racing, dog racing, boxing and wrestling matches and exhibitions, baseball, football, and basketball games, tennis and golf matches, track meets, etc.

(3) *Contest.*—A contest includes any type of contest involving speed, skill, endurance, popularity, politics, strength, appearances, etc., such as a general or primary election, the outcome of a nominating convention, a dance marathon, a log-rolling, wood-chopping, weight-lifting, cornhusking, beauty contest, etc.

(4) *Conducted for profit.*—A wagering pool or lottery may be conducted for profit even though a direct profit will not inure from the operation thereof. A wagering pool or lottery operated with the section expectancy of a profit in the form of increased sales, increased attendance, or other indirect benefits is conducted for profit for purposes of the wagering tax. [Reg. § 44.4421-1.]

☐ [T.D. 6370.]

[Reg. § 44.4422-1]

§ 44.4422-1. Doing business in violation of Federal or State law.—Payment of any special tax within the scope of the regulations in this part in nowise authorizes the carrying on of any business in violation of a law of the United States or the law of any State. The special tax stamp is not a license or permit and affords no protection from prosecution for violation of any Federal or State law. See also § 44.4906. [Reg. § 44.4422-1.]

☐ [T.D. 6370.]

Certain Other Excise Taxes

See p. 20,601 for regulations not amended to reflect law changes

[Reg. § 43.0-1]

§ 43.0-1. Introduction.—The regulations in this part 43 are designated "Excise Tax on Transportation by Water." The regulations relate to the taxes on transportation by water imposed by section 4471 of the Internal Revenue Code. See part 40 of this chapter for regulations relating to returns, payments, and deposits of taxes imposed by section 4471. [Reg. § 43.0-1]

☐ [T.D. 8328, 12-28-90. *Redesignated and amended by T.D. 8422, 7-29-92; Amended by T.D. 8442, 10-21-92.*]

[Reg. § 43.4471-1]

§ 43.4471-1. Imposition of tax.—(a) *In general.*—Section 4471 imposes a tax of $3 per passenger on a covered voyage as is defined in section 4472.

(b) *By whom paid.*—The tax is imposed on the person providing the covered voyage (the operator of the vessel). [Reg. § 43.4471-1.]

☐ [T.D. 8314, 10-5-90. *Redesignated and amended by T.D. 8422, 7-29-92.*]

[Reg. § 43.4472-1]

§ 43.4472-1. Definitions.—(a) *In general.*—For definitions of the terms "covered voyage" and "passenger vessel," see sections 4472(1) and (2).

(b) *Voyage.*—For purposes of this section, "voyage" means a journey of a vessel that includes the outward and homeward trips or passages. The voyage commences when the vessel begins to load passengers and continues during the entire ensuing period until the vessel has made one outward and one homeward passage (including intermediate passages, if made). A voyage may be a covered voyage with respect to a passenger even if the passenger does not make both an outward and homeward passage or if the point of first embarkation or disembarkation by the passenger in the United States is an intermediate stop of the vessel.

(c) *Over 1 or more nights.*—A voyage is considered to extend over 1 or more nights if it extends for more than 24 hours.

(d) *Engaged in gambling.*—A passenger is engaged in gambling aboard a vessel if that person is participating as a player in any policy game or other lottery, or any other game of chance, for money or other thing of value, provided that the policy game, other lottery, or game of chance is conducted, sponsored, or operated by the owner or operator of the vessel, as either principal or agent, or by an employee, agent, or franchisee of the owner or operator of the vessel. A passenger is not engaged in gambling aboard a vessel if the passenger participates with other passengers in a casual, "friendly" game of chance that is not conducted, sponsored, or operated by the owner or operator of the vessel or by an employee, agent, or franchisee of the owner or operator.

(e) *Territorial waters.*—For purposes of sections 4471 and 4472, the territorial waters of the United States are those waters within the international boundary line between the United States and any contiguous foreign country or within 3 nautical miles (3.45 statute miles) from low tide on the coastline. No inference is intended as to the extent of the territorial limits for other tax purposes.

(f) *Passenger.*—For purposes of section 4471 and 4472, "passenger" means an individual carried on the vessel except—

(1) The Master; or

(2) A crew member or other individual engaged in the business of the vessel or its owners. A person is engaged in the business of the vessel or its owners if the person is an employee of the vessel or its owners or has a duty, contractual or otherwise, to perform on the vessel on behalf of the vessel or its owners. For example, a person engaged as an entertainer, instructor, or lecturer for the benefit of the passengers is not a passenger, but a person on a promotional trip such as a travel agent or contest winner is a passenger even though the vessel or its owners may derive some future benefit from the promotion. [Reg. § 43.4472-1.]

☐ [T.D. 8422, 7-29-92.]

[Reg. §41.0-1]

§41.0-1. Introduction.—The regulations in this part are designated "Highway Use Tax Regulations." The regulations in this part relate to the tax on the use of certain highway vehicles imposed by section 4481 and to certain associated administrative provisions. [Reg. §41.0-1.]

☐ [*T.D. 6216, 12-6-56. Amended by T.D. 7665, 1-25-80 and T.D. 8879, 3-30-2000.*]

>>> *Caution: Reg. §41.4481-1, below, prior to amendment by T.D. 9698, applies before July 1, 2015.*

[Reg. §41.4481-1]

§41.4481-1. Imposition of tax.—(a) *In general.*—Tax is imposed on the use during a taxable period of any registered highway motor vehicle that (together with the semitrailers and trailers customarily used in connection with highway motor vehicles of the same type as such highway motor vehicle) has a taxable gross weight of at least 55,000 pounds.

(b) *Rate of tax.*—For the rate of tax generally, see section 4481(a). For the rate of tax for certain vehicles used in logging, see section 4483(e). For the rate of tax for certain vehicles base-plated in Canada or Mexico, see section 4483(f). For a special rule for the taxable period in which the tax terminates, see section 4482(d).

(c) *Computation of tax.*—(1) Except as provided in paragraph (c)(2) of this section, the tax on the use of a particular highway motor vehicle a taxable period is computed as follows:

(i) For vehicles with a taxable gross weight of at least 55,000 pounds, but not over 75,000 pounds, add to $100 an amount equal to $22 for each 1,000 pounds (or fraction thereof) in excess of 55,000 pounds; and

(ii) For vehicles with a taxable gross weight over 75,000 pounds, the tax is $550.

(2) If the first taxable use of a particular highway motor vehicle is made after the first month of the taxable period, the tax on the use of such vehicle for such taxable period is computed by multiplying the amount of tax that would be due for a full taxable period as computed under paragraph (c)(1) of this section, by a fraction. Such fraction shall have as its numerator the number of months in the taxable period beginning with the month of first taxable use and as its denominator the number of months in the entire taxable period. For purposes of determining the fraction, any part of a month is counted as a full month. (See example (2) of paragraph (e) of this section.)

(3) If the taxable gross weight of a vehicle increases during the month in which the vehicle is first used in a taxable period, the tax for the vehicle for the taxable period is computed on the basis of the increased weight. If the taxable gross weight of a vehicle increases after the month in which the vehicle was first used in a taxable period, the additional tax liability, if any, that results from the increased weight is calculated according to the following formula:

$$\left[\left(T_1 \times \frac{P}{12}\right) + \left(T_2 \times \frac{R}{12}\right)\right] - T_1.$$

where:

T_1 = Tax imposed for a full taxable period (or partial taxable period as determined under paragraph (c)(2) of this section) at the vehicle's previously reported taxable gross weight.

T_2 = Tax imposed for the same taxable period as used in T_1 at the vehicle's increased taxable gross weight.

P = The number of months in the taxable period during which the vehicle's taxable gross weight was as previously reported for such taxable period. This number does not include the month in which the vehicle's taxable gross weight increased.

R = The number of months remaining in the taxable period including the month in which the vehicle's taxable gross weight was increased.

If tax was imposed for a partial taxable period as determined under paragraph (c)(2) of this section, the additional tax is determined by substituting the number of months in such partial taxable period for "12" in the above formula.

(4) If in any taxable period the taxable gross weight of a highway motor vehicle is decreased, the computation of tax is not affected and no right to credit or refund of any tax paid under section 4481 arises.

(5) If in any taxable period a highway motor vehicle is destroyed or stolen before the first day of the last month in the taxable period, and is not subsequently used during such taxable period, the tax shall be calculated proportionately from the first day of the month in the period in which the first taxable use of the highway motor vehicle occurs to and including the last day of the month in which the highway motor vehicle was destroyed or stolen. Any tax paid under section 4481(a) on such a highway motor vehicle in excess of the tax calculated in the preceding sentence, shall be an overpayment for which a credit or refund of tax may be claimed. For purposes of this paragraph (c)(5), a highway motor vehicle is destroyed if the vehicle is damaged due to an accident or other casualty to such an extent that it is not economical to rebuild.

(6) If the use of a highway motor vehicle during the taxable period is discontinued (for reasons other than destruction or theft as described in paragraph (c)(5) of this section) or is converted to a use which is exempt from the tax imposed by section 4481(a), the computation of the tax is not affected and no right to a credit or refund of any tax paid under section 4481 arises.

(d) *Credit or refund of tax under section 4481(a).*—(1) Any claim for refund of an overpayment of tax under section 4481(a) due to destruction or theft of the vehicle shall be made in accordance with the applicable provisions of this section and § 301.6402-2 (Regulations on Pro-

»»→ *Caution: Reg. §41.4481-1, below, prior to amendment by T.D. 9698, applies before July 1, 2015.*

cedure and Administration) and shall be filed by the person in whose name the vehicle is registered or required to be registered when the vehicle is destroyed or stolen. A claim for refund of the tax imposed by section 4481(a) is to be filed on Form 8849 (or such other form as the Commissioner may designate).

(2) Any person entitled to claim a refund of tax under paragraph (d)(1) of this section may, in lieu of claiming a refund of such tax, claim a credit for such tax on the next Form 2290 required to be filed.

(e) *Examples.*—The application of section 4481 and this section may be illustrated by the following examples:

Example (1). In the taxable period beginning July 1, 1984, the first taxable use of a particular highway motor vehicle, a bus, having a taxable gross weight of 56,000 pounds, occurs on July 10, 1984, at which time the vehicle is registered in the name of X. A tax of $122 ($100 + $22) is imposed on X for the use of such vehicle for such taxable period.

Example (2). On July 1, 1984, X has registered in his name a highway motor vehicle having a taxable gross weight of 60,000 pounds. The vehicle is in "dead storage" until August 10, 1984, at which time X starts using the vehicle on the public highways in carrying on his trucking business. On August 10, 1984, the vehicle is still registered in X's name. Since the first taxable use of this highway motor vehicle during the taxable period occurred on August 10, 1984, X is required to pay a tax of $192.50 ([$100 + (5 × $22)] × $^{11}/_{12}$) for such taxable period.

Example (3). On April 15, 1985, a vehicle with a taxable gross weight of 70,000 pounds and registered in the name of Y is completely destroyed. Y had purchased the vehicle from X who had paid the tax for the taxable period beginning July 1, 1984. Y is entitled to a refund of tax for those full months after destruction in the taxable period ending June 30, 1985. Thus, Y may file a claim for a refund of $71.67—$^2/_{12}$ of the total tax of $430 ($100 + (15 × $22)). [Reg. § 41.4481-1.]

☐ [*T.D. 6216. Amended by T.D. 6743, 6-22-64; T.D. 7409, 3-8-76; T.D. 7505, 8-24-77; T.D. 8027, 5-23-85; T.D. 8159, 9-3-87; T.D. 8177, 3-3-88 and T.D. 8879, 3-30-2000.*]

»»→ *Caution: Reg. §41.4481-1, below, as amended by T.D. 9698, applies on or after July 1, 2015.*

[Reg. § 41.4481-1]

§41.4481-1. Imposition and computation of tax.—(a) *In general.*—Tax is imposed on the use during a taxable period of any registered highway motor vehicle that (together with the semitrailers and trailers customarily used in connection with highway motor vehicles of the same type as such highway motor vehicle) has a taxable gross weight of at least 55,000 pounds.

(b) *Rate of tax.*—For the rate of tax generally, see section 4481(a). For the rate of tax for certain vehicles used in logging, see section 4483(e). For the rate of tax for certain vehicles base-plated in Canada or Mexico, see section 4483(f).

(c) *Computation of tax.*—(1) *In general.*—Except as otherwise provided in this paragraph (c), the tax on the use of a particular highway motor vehicle a taxable period is computed as follows:

(i) For vehicles with a taxable gross weight of at least 55,000 pounds, but not over 75,000 pounds, add to $100 an amount equal to $22 for each 1,000 pounds (or fraction thereof) in excess of 55,000 pounds; and

(ii) For vehicles with a taxable gross weight over 75,000 pounds, the tax is $550.

(2) *Certain prorated taxable periods.*—If the first taxable use of a particular highway motor vehicle is made after the first month of the taxable period, the tax on the use of such vehicle for such taxable period is computed by multiplying the amount of tax that would be due for a full taxable period as computed under paragraph (c)(1) of this section, by a fraction. Such fraction shall have as its numerator the number of months in the taxable period beginning with the

month of first taxable use and as its denominator the number of months in the entire taxable period. For purposes of determining the fraction, any part of a month is counted as a full month. (See example (2) of paragraph (e) of this section.)

(3) *Increase in taxable gross weight during the taxable period.*—If the taxable gross weight of a vehicle increases during the month in which the vehicle is first used in a taxable period, the tax for the vehicle for the taxable period is computed on the basis of the increased weight. If the taxable gross weight of a vehicle increases after the month in which the vehicle was first used in a taxable period, the additional tax liability, if any, that results from the increased weight is calculated according to the following formula:

$$\left[\left(T_1 \times \frac{P}{12} \right) + \left(T_2 \times \frac{R}{12} \right) \right] - T_1.$$

where:

T_1 = Tax imposed for a full taxable period (or partial taxable period as determined under paragraph (c)(2) of this section) at the vehicle's previously reported taxable gross weight.

T_2 = Tax imposed for the same taxable period as used in T_1 at the vehicle's increased taxable gross weight.

P = The number of months in the taxable period during which the vehicle's taxable gross weight was as previously reported for such taxable period. This number does not include the month in which the vehicle's taxable gross weight increased.

R = The number of months remaining in the taxable period including the month in which the vehicle's taxable gross weight was increased.

Reg. §41.4481-1(c)(3)

>>>→ *Caution: Reg. §41.4481-1, below, as amended by T.D. 9698, applies on or after July 1, 2015.*

If tax was imposed for a partial taxable period as determined under paragraph (c)(2) of this section, the additional tax is determined by substituting the number of months in such partial taxable period for "12" in the above formula.

(4) *Prorated taxable period for sold, destroyed, or stolen vehicles.*—(i) *In general.*—The tax on a taxpayer's use of a highway vehicle for a taxable period is determined under paragraph (c)(4)(ii) of this section if—

(A) The vehicle is destroyed or stolen before the first day of the last month in the taxable period and is not later used by the taxpayer during the period; or

(B) The taxpayer sells the vehicle before the first day of the last month in the taxable period and does not later use the vehicle during the period.

(ii) *Computation of tax.*—If the tax on a taxpayer's use of a highway vehicle for a taxable period is determined under this paragraph (c)(4)(ii), the tax is computed by multiplying the amount of tax that would be due for a full taxable period, as computed under paragraph (c)(1) of this section, by a fraction. The fraction has as its numerator the number of months in the period from the first day of the month in the period in which the first taxable use of the highway motor vehicle occurs to and including the last day of the month in which the highway motor vehicle was sold, destroyed, or stolen, and as its denominator the number of months in the entire taxable period. (See paragraph (d) *Example* (3)(i) of this section.)

(iii) *Overpayment.*—If a taxpayer's liability for the tax on the use of a highway vehicle for a taxable period is determined under paragraph (c)(4)(ii) of this section, any tax the taxpayer paid under section 4481(a) on the use of the vehicle for such period in excess of the tax calculated under paragraph (c)(4)(ii) of this section is an overpayment of tax.

(iv) *Definition of destroyed vehicle.*—For purposes of this paragraph (c)(4), a highway motor vehicle is destroyed if the vehicle is damaged due to an accident or other casualty to such an extent that it is not economical to rebuild.

(v) *Form and content of claim.*—A claim for refund of an overpayment described in paragraph (c)(4)(iii) of this section must be made on Form 8849, "Claim for Refund of Excise Taxes" (or such other form as the Commissioner may designate) in accordance with the instructions for that form. A claim for a credit must be made on Form 2290, "Heavy Highway Vehicle Use Tax Return" (or such other form as the Commissioner may designate) in accordance with the instructions for that form. A claim for refund or credit for any vehicle must include—

(A) The vehicle identification number and taxable gross weight of the vehicle;

(B) The date of the sale, destruction, or theft of the vehicle; and

(C) If the vehicle was sold, the name and address of the purchaser of the vehicle.

(vi) *Tax on buyer's use of second-hand vehicles.*—If a vehicle is sold during the taxable period and a credit or refund of the tax imposed by section 4481 is allowable upon the sale under paragraph (c)(4)(iii) of this section, tax is imposed on the use of the vehicle after the sale and before the end of the taxable period. (See paragraph (c)(4)(vii) of this section for the rules regarding the computation of tax after the sale and before the end of the taxable period.)

(vii) *Computation of tax on second-hand vehicles.*—The tax under paragraph (c)(4)(vi) of this section on the use of a vehicle after a sale upon which a credit or refund is allowable is computed by multiplying the amount of tax that would be due for a full taxable period as computed under paragraph (c)(1) of this section by a fraction. The fraction has as its numerator the number of months in the period from the first day of the month in which the first taxable use of the vehicle after the sale occurs (the first day of the month after such month if the first taxable use after the sale occurs in the month of the sale) through the end of the taxable period, and as its denominator the number of months in the entire taxable period. (See paragraph (d) *Example* (3)(ii) of this section.)

(5) *Decrease in taxable gross weight, discontinued use, or converted use.*—The computation of the tax is not affected, and no right to a credit or refund of any tax paid under section 4481 arises, if in any taxable period—

(i) The taxable gross weight of a highway motor vehicle is decreased;

(ii) The use of a highway motor vehicle is discontinued (for reasons other than sale, destruction, or theft as described in paragraph (c)(4) of this section); or

(iii) The highway motor vehicle is converted to a use that is exempt from the tax imposed by section 4481(a).

(d) *Examples.*—The application of §§41.4481-1, 41.4481-2, and 41.4482(c)-1(c) may be illustrated by the following examples:

Example (1). In the taxable period beginning July 1, 1984, the first taxable use of a particular highway motor vehicle, a bus, having a taxable gross weight of 56,000 pounds, occurs on July 10, 1984, at which time the vehicle is registered in the name of X. A tax of $122 ($100 + $22) is imposed on X for the use of such vehicle for such taxable period.

Example (2). On July 1, 1984, X has registered in his name a highway motor vehicle having a taxable gross weight of 60,000 pounds. The vehicle is in "dead storage" until August 10, 1984, at which time X starts using the vehicle on the public highways in carrying on his trucking business. On August 10, 1984, the vehicle is still registered in X's name. Since the first taxable use of this highway motor vehicle during the taxable

>>>→ *Caution: Reg. §41.4481-1, below, as amended by T.D. 9698, applies on or after July 1, 2015.*

period occurred on August 10, 1984, X is required to pay a tax of $192.50 ([$100 + (5 × $22)] × $^{11}/_{12}$) for such taxable period.

Example (3). (i) In July, X uses a vehicle that is registered in X's name and has a taxable gross weight of 70,000 pounds. The vehicle is not a logging vehicle. X pays the $430 of tax imposed by section 4481 for the taxable period. On September 2 of the same calendar year, X sells the vehicle to Y. X's tax is calculated under paragraph (c)(4)(ii) by multiplying the amount of tax that would be due for a full taxable period by a fraction that has as its numerator the number of months in the period from the first day of the month in which X's first taxable use of the highway motor vehicle occurs to and including the last day of the month in which the vehicle was sold, and as its denominator the number of months in the entire taxable period. Thus, X's tax for the period is $107.50 (3/12 of $430), and X may claim a credit or refund of $322.50 ($430.00 - $107.50) in accordance with §41.4481-1(c)(4)(v) after X sells the vehicle.

(ii) On September 23, Y uses the vehicle. Y is liable for tax on the use of the vehicle during the taxable period ending June 30 of the following calendar year. Y's tax is calculated under paragraph (c)(4)(vii) by multiplying the amount of tax that would be due for a full taxable period by a fraction that has as its numerator the number of months in the period from the first day of the month in which Y's first taxable use of the vehicle after the sale occurs (the first day of the month after such month if the first taxable use after the sale occurs in the month of the sale) through the end of the taxable period, and as its denominator the number of months in the entire taxable period. Y's first use of the vehicle occurs in the month of the sale. Accordingly, Y's tax is based on the number of months in the period from the first day of October (the month following the month of the first taxable use) through the end of June, and Y owes a section 4481 tax of $322.50 (9/12 of $430) for the taxable period.

Example 4. Assume the same facts as in *Example* (3)(i), except that on September 2, X sells the vehicle to Dealer, a dealer in highway motor vehicles. X may claim a credit or refund of $322.50. Dealer operates the vehicle exclusively for the purpose of demonstration, which is not a "use" of the vehicle under §41.4482(c)-1(c). On May 2 of the following calendar year, Dealer sells the vehicle to Y. Dealer does not owe a section 4481 tax and may not claim a refund. Y's first taxable use of the vehicle occurs on May 3. Y's first taxable use of the vehicle does not occur in the month of a sale upon which a credit or refund is allowable. Accordingly, Y's tax is calculated under paragraph (c)(2) by multiplying the amount of tax that would be due for a full taxable period by a fraction which has as its numerator the number of months in the taxable period beginning with the month of first taxable use and as its denominator the number of months in the entire taxable period. The numerator is the number of months in the period from the first day of May (the month of Y's first taxable use after the sale) through the end of June, and Y owes a section 4481 tax of $71.67 (2/12 of $430) for the taxable period.

(e) *Effective/applicability date.*—This section applies on and after July 1, 2015. For rules applicable before that date, see 26 CFR 41.4481-1 (revised as of April 1, 2014). [Reg. § 41.4481-1.]

☐ [*T.D. 6216. Amended by T.D. 6743, 6-22-64; T.D. 7409, 3-8-76; T.D. 7505, 8-24-77; T.D. 8027, 5-23-85; T.D. 8159, 9-3-87; T.D. 8177, 3-3-88; T.D. 8879, 3-30-2000 and T.D. 9698, 10-28-2014.*]

>>>→ *Caution: Reg. §41.4481-2, below, prior to amendment by T.D. 9698, applies before July 1, 2015.*

[Reg. § 41.4481-2]

§41.4481-2. Persons liable for tax.—(a) *In general.*—(1)(i) A person is liable for the tax imposed by section 4481 with respect to the use of a highway motor vehicle in a taxable period if the vehicle is registered in the person's name—

(A) At the time of the first use of the vehicle in the taxable period;

(B) In the case of a vehicle under a suspension of tax described in §41.4483-3(a), at the time the use on the public highways during the taxable period exceeds 5,000 miles (7,500 miles for agricultural vehicles);

(C) At the time that an increase in the taxable gross weight of the vehicle results in an additional tax liability (as computed under §41.4481-1(c)(3)) if the increase occurs after the month in which the vehicle was first used in the taxable period; or

(D) At the time of any use during the taxable period that is after the first use during the period, but only to the extent that the tax or any installment payment of the tax has not previously been paid.

(ii) In any case in which more than one person is liable for the tax for a taxable period, the liability of all persons is satisfied to the extent that the tax is paid by any person liable for the tax.

(2) The application of paragraph (a)(1) of this section may be illustrated by the following example:

Example. In the taxable period beginning July 1, 1985, the first taxable use of a particular highway motor vehicle having a taxable gross weight of 60,000 pounds occurs on July 10, 1985, at which time the vehicle is registered in the name of Y. On September 1, 1985, Y sells the vehicle to X who registers and uses the vehicle before the end of such taxable period. Since the vehicle was registered in the name of Y at the time of its first taxable use, Y is liable for the total tax of $210 ($100 + (5 × $22)) imposed on the use of the vehicle for the taxable period. X is also liable for $210 tax or any part thereof, but only to the extent that Y does not pay it. To the

➤➤➤ *Caution: Reg. §41.4481-2, below, prior to amendment by T.D. 9698, applies before July 1, 2015.*

extent that either X or Y pays the tax the other party is relieved of such liability.

(b) *Evidence of prior use of secondhand vehicle.*— Every person who, at any time in the taxable period, acquires and has registered in his name a secondhand highway motor vehicle shall obtain and keep as a part of his records evidence, which he believes to be true, showing whether there was or was not a taxable use of such vehicle at any time in such taxable period prior to the time when the vehicle was registered in his name. Such person shall also obtain and keep as evidence a statement from the transferor as to whether there was in effect, at the time the vehicle was acquired, a suspension under § 41.4483-3(a) of the tax imposed by section 4481(a). The evidence may take the form of a written statement, signed and dated by the person from whom the vehicle was acquired, showing whether there was or was not a prior taxable use of the vehicle and whether there was a suspension of tax in the taxable period. If the vehicle is acquired from a dealer in highway motor vehicles, the statement may be obtained from such dealer or from the person from whom the dealer acquired such vehicle. If evidence is not obtained showing whether there was or was not a prior taxable use of such vehicle and whether there was a suspension of tax in the taxable period, such person shall keep as a part of his records a written statement of the reason why he was unable to obtain such evidence.

(c) *Cross references.*—(1) For provisions relating to interest on underpayments of tax, see § 301.6601-1 of this chapter (Regulations on Procedure and Administration).

(2) For records required to be kept, see § 41.6001-1.

(3) For rules applicable to installment payment of tax for highway use tax liability, see § 41.6156-1.

(4) For rules applicable to time of filing returns, see § 41.6071(a)-1. [Reg. § 41.4481-2.]

☐ [*T.D. 6216. Amended by T.D. 6743, 6-22-64; T.D. 8027, 5-23-85 and T.D. 8879, 3-30-2000.*]

➤➤➤ *Caution: Reg. §41.4481-2, below, as amended by T.D. 9698, applies on or after July 1, 2015.*

[Reg. § 41.4481-2]

§ 41.4481-2. Persons liable for tax.—(a) *In general.*—(1)(i) A person is liable for the tax imposed by section 4481 with respect to the use of a highway motor vehicle in a taxable period if the vehicle is registered in the person's name—

(A) At the time of the first use of the vehicle in the taxable period;

(B) In the case of a vehicle under a suspension of tax described in § 41.4483-3(a), at the time the use on the public highways during the taxable period exceeds 5,000 miles (7,500 miles for agricultural vehicles);

(C) At the time that an increase in the taxable gross weight of the vehicle results in an additional tax liability (as computed under § 41.4481-1(c)(3)) if the increase occurs after the month in which the vehicle was first used in the taxable period; or

(D) At the time of any use during the taxable period that is after the first use during the period, but only to the extent that the tax has not previously been paid.

(ii) In any case in which more than one person is liable for the tax for a taxable period, the liability of all persons is satisfied to the extent that the tax is paid by any person liable for the tax.

(2) If a vehicle is sold during the taxable period and a credit or refund is allowable upon the sale under § 41.4481-1(c)(4)(iii), paragraph (a)(1) of this section is applied with the following modifications:

(i) For purposes of determining the person liable for the tax determined under § 41.4481-1(c)(4)(ii), each reference to a taxable period in paragraph (a)(1) of this section is treated as a reference to the period that begins on the first day of the taxable period in which the vehicle is sold and ends on the date of sale.

(ii) For purposes of determining the person liable for the tax determined under § 41.4481-1(c)(4)(vi), each reference to a taxable period in paragraph (a)(1) of this section is treated as a reference to the period that begins on the date of the sale and ends on the last day of the taxable period in which the vehicle is sold.

(3) The application of paragraph (a) of this section may be illustrated by *Examples* (3) and (4) in § 41.4481-1(d).

(b) *Evidence of prior use of secondhand vehicle.*— Every person who, at any time in the taxable period, acquires and has registered in his name a secondhand highway motor vehicle shall obtain and keep as a part of his records evidence, which he believes to be true, showing whether there was or was not a taxable use of such vehicle at any time in such taxable period prior to the time when the vehicle was registered in his name. Such person shall also obtain and keep as evidence a statement from the transferor as to whether there was in effect, at the time the vehicle was acquired, a suspension under § 41.4483-3(a) of the tax imposed by section 4481(a). The evidence may take the form of a written statement, signed and dated by the person from whom the vehicle was acquired, showing whether there was or was not a prior taxable use of the vehicle and whether there was a suspension of tax in the taxable period. If the vehicle is acquired from a dealer in highway motor vehicles, the statement may be obtained from such dealer or from the person from whom the dealer acquired such vehicle. If evidence is not obtained showing whether there was or was not a prior taxable use of such vehicle and whether there was a suspension of tax in the taxable

≫→ *Caution: Reg. §41.4481-2, below, as amended by T.D. 9698, applies on or after July 1, 2015.*

period, such person shall keep as a part of his records a written statement of the reason why he was unable to obtain such evidence. For provisions relating to penalties for aiding and abetting an understatement of tax liability, see section 6701 of the Internal Revenue Code.

(c) *Effective/applicability date.*—This section applies on and after July 1, 2015. For rules applicable before that date, see 26 CFR 41.4481-2 (revised as of April 1, 2014). [Reg. § 41.4481-2.]

☐ *[T.D. 6216. Amended by T.D. 6743, 6-22-64; T.D. 8027, 5-23-85; T.D. 8879, 3-30-2000 and T.D. 9698, 10-28-2014.]*

[Reg. § 41.4481-3]

§ 41.4481-3. Registration.—(a) For purposes of the regulations in this part, the term "registered" when used in reference to a highway motor vehicle means—

(1) Registered under the law of any State or Territory of the United States, the District of Columbia, or contiguous foreign country, or

(2) Required to be registered under the law of any State or Territory of the United States or contiguous foreign country in which such highway motor vehicle is operated or situated or, in case the vehicle is operated or situated in the District of Columbia, under the law of the District of Columbia.

Any highway motor vehicle which is operated under a dealer's tag, license, or permit is considered to be registered in the name of such dealer. A highway motor vehicle is not considered to be registered solely by reason of the fact that there has been issued a special permit for operation of the vehicle at particular times and under specified conditions.

(b) Any highway motor vehicle which, at any time in the taxable period, is registered both in the name of the owner of the vehicle and in the name of any other person, is considered, for purposes of the regulations in this part, to be registered, at such time, solely in the name of the owner of the vehicle. [Reg. § 41.4481-3.]

☐ *[T.D. 6216. Amended by T.D. 6743, 6-22-64 and T.D. 8159, 9-3-87.]*

[Reg. § 41.4482(a)-1]

§ 41.4482(a)-1. Definition of highway motor vehicle.—(a) *Highway motor vehicle.*—The term "highway motor vehicle" means any vehicle that is both—

(1) A vehicle propelled by means of its own motor, whether such motor is powered by gasoline, diesel fuel, special motor fuels, electricity, or otherwise, and

(2) A "highway vehicle" as defined in § 48.4061(a)-1(d) of this chapter.

(b) *Treatment of certain excluded vehicles.*—Although trailers and semi-trailers used in combination with highway trucks or truck-tractors are not vehicles the use of which is subject to the tax imposed by section 4481(a), trailers and semi-trailers customarily used in combination with highway trucks or truck-tractors are taken into account in determining the taxable gross weight of the highway motor vehicle under § 41.4482(b)-1, which is the base of the tax. [Reg. § 41.4482(a)-1.]

☐ *[T.D. 6216. Amended by T.D. 7461, 1-12-77 and T.D. 8879, 3-30-2000.]*

[Reg. § 41.4482(b)-1]

§ 41.4482(b)-1. Definition of taxable gross weight.—(a) *Actual unloaded weight.*—(1) *In general.*—*Actual unloaded weight* means the empty (or tare) weight of the truck, truck-tractor, or bus, fully equipped for service.

(2) *Trucks and truck-tractors.*—A truck or truck-tractor fully equipped for service includes the body (whether or not designed and adapted primarily for transporting cargo, as for example, concrete mixers); all accessories; all equipment attached to or carried on such truck or truck-tractor for use in connection with the movement of the vehicle by means of its own motor or for use in the maintenance of the vehicle; and a full complement of lubricants, fuel, and water. It does not include the driver, any equipment (not including the body) attached to or carried on the vehicle for use in handling, protecting, or preserving cargo, or any special equipment (such as an air compressor, crane, specialized oilfield machinery, etc.) mounted on the vehicle for use on construction jobs, in oilfield operations, etc.

(3) *Buses.*—A bus fully equipped for service includes the body; all accessories; all equipment attached to or carried on such bus for use in connection with the movement of the vehicle by means of its own motor, for use in the maintenance of the vehicle, or for the accommodation of passengers or others (such as air conditioning equipment and sanitation facilities, etc.); and a full complement of lubricants, fuel, and water. It does not include the driver.

(b) *Determination of taxable gross weight.*—(1) *In general.*—The taxable gross weight of a highway motor vehicle is the sum of the actual unloaded weight of the vehicle fully equipped for service, the actual unloaded weight of any semitrailers or trailers fully equipped for service customarily used in combination with the vehicle, and the weight of the maximum load customarily carried on the vehicle and on any semitrailers or trailers customarily used in combination with the vehicle. In the case of a highway motor vehicle that is registered in at least one State that requires a declaration of gross weight to be stated as a specific amount for any purpose (including proportional or prorate registration or the payment of any other fees or taxes), the taxable gross weight of such vehicle must be no less than the highest gross weight declaration (or combined gross weight declaration in the case of a tractor-trailer or truck-trailer combination) made by the registrant in any State with respect to such vehicle. If a highway motor vehicle is registered in at least one State that requires vehicles to register on the basis of gross weight and such vehicle is not registered in any State that requires a declaration of gross weight to be stated as a specific amount by the registrant, the taxable gross weight of such vehicle must fall within the highest gross weight category of such State for which such vehicle is registered during the taxable period. Declarations of weight made in order to obtain special temporary travel permits which allow a vehicle to, (i) operate in a State in which the vehicle is not registered or prorated, (ii) operate at more than a State's maximum statutory weight limit, or (iii) operate at more than the weight that the vehicle is registered in a State, shall not be considered in determining the taxable gross weight of a vehicle.

(2) *Buses.*—For purposes of the tax imposed by section 4481(a), the taxable gross weight of a bus shall be the sum of the weights referred to in paragraph (b)(1) of this section except that "the weight of the maximum load customarily carried" on a bus shall be equal to 150 pounds times the number of units of seating capacity provided for passengers and driver.

(c) *Examples.*—The provisions of this section may be illustrated by the following examples:

Example (1). A is the owner of a truck-tractor. On January 1, 1985, A registers the truck-tractor in three states—X, Y, and Z. For purposes of registering the vehicle in State X, A declares the gross operating weight of his truck-tractor to be 60,000 pounds. The declaration of the gross weight of the vehicle at 50,000 pounds places A's truck-tractor in the State X registration category of 55,000 to 62,000 pounds gross weight. Thus, the registered weight of A's vehicle in State X is 62,000 pounds. At the same time as A registers the vehicle in State X, A also proportionately registers the vehicle under the IRP in State Y. A uses the same declared gross weight of 60,000 pounds for purposes of the State Y proportional registration. Registration in State Y at this declared gross weight places A's truck-tractor in the State Y gross weight registration category of 58,000 to 68,000 pounds. Finally, A registers the truck-tractor in State Z. Registration of vehicles in State Z is based on the unladen weight of the vehicle. During the taxable period beginning on July 1, 1985, A's truck-tractor is not registered in any other state. For the taxable period beginning on July 1, 1985, A must declare a taxable gross weight of no less than 60,000 pounds for purposes of the tax imposed by section 4481(a) because that is the highest declared gross weight for state registration or other purposes. Should A declare to any State agency a higher gross operating weight with respect to the truck-tractor during the same taxable period (except for a special temporary permit), A would then be liable for additional tax as determined under paragraph (c)(3) of §41.4481-1.

Example (2). Assume the same facts as in example (1), except that on one occasion during the taxable period, A was issued a special 2-day

permit to use his truck-tractor in State Y to haul a load which would give A's unit a total gross weight of 80,000 pounds. A may still declare the taxable gross weight of his unit to be no less than 60,000 pounds because special permits to haul heavier loads on a temporary basis are not considered in determining the taxable gross weight of a vehicle.

Example (3). C owns and has registered in his name 2 trucks which are identical in all respects and which are used to carry the same type of load. The first vehicle is registered only in State X at a registered weight of 73,000 pounds based on a declared gross weight of 70,000 pounds. The second vehicle is registered only in State Y at a registered weight of 68,000 pounds based on a declared gross weight of 65,000 pounds. No other declarations of gross weight are made with respect to either vehicle. For purposes of the Federal heavy vehicle use tax, the taxable gross weight of the vehicle registered in State X may be declared at no less than 70,000 pounds and the taxable gross weight of the vehicle registered in State Y may be declared at no less than 65,000 pounds even though the vehicles are identical. [Reg. §41.4482(b)-1.]

☐ [T.D. 6216, 12-5-56. *Amended by T.D. 6743,* 6-22-64; *T.D. 7011, 5-7-69; T.D. 8027, 5-22-85 and* T.D. 8879, 3-30-2000.]

[Reg. §41.4482(c)-1]

§41.4482(c)-1. Definition of State, taxable period, use, and customarily used.—(a) *State.*— *State* includes any State, any political subdivision of a State, the District of Columbia, and, to the extent provided by section 7871, any Indian tribal government.

(b) *Taxable period.*—For the definition of *taxable period,* see section 4482(c).

(c) *Use.*—The term "use," as used in the regulations in this part with reference to a highway motor vehicle, means the use of the highway motor vehicle on the public highways in the United States, that is, operation of the vehicle, by means of its own motor, on any roadway (whether a Federal highway, State highway, city street, or otherwise) in the United States which is not a private roadway. Thus, for purposes of the tax, there is no use of a highway motor vehicle while the vehicle is in "dead storage." The term "use" does not include operation of a new highway motor vehicle on a public highway in the United States if such operation is merely for the purpose of transporting the vehicle from the point of manufacture or assembly to the consumer, whether direct or with intermediate deliveries to such points as are involved in the distribution process. For example, operation of a new vehicle for the purpose of delivering it from the factory to a branch establishment of the manufacturer, or from the factory or branch establishment to a dealer, distributor, or consumer, does not constitute use of the vehicle within the meaning of the regulations in this part; likewise, the further operation of the vehicle by a dealer or distributor for the purpose of delivering the vehicle to a consumer does not constitute use of the vehicle. Similarly, the operation of a secondhand highway motor vehicle by a dealer or distributor for the purpose of delivering the vehicle to a purchaser does not constitute use of the vehicle within the meaning of the regulations in this part. Furthermore, the term "use" does not include operation of a new or secondhand highway motor vehicle, if such operation is exclusively for the purpose of demonstration of the vehicle by a dealer in, or distributor of, new or secondhand highway motor vehicles. Operation of a highway motor vehicle on a private roadway, or other private property, does not constitute use of the vehicle within the meaning of the regulations in this part.

(d) *Customarily used.*—A semitrailer or trailer is treated as *customarily used* in connection with a highway motor vehicle if the vehicle is equipped to tow the semitrailer or trailer. [Reg. § 41.4482(c)-1.]

☐ [T.D. 6216, 12-6-56. *Amended by T.D.* 6518, 12-20-60; T.D. 6743, 6-22-64; T.D. 7409, 3-5-76; T.D. 7505, 8-24-77; T.D. 8027, 5-22-85; T.D. 8159, 9-3-87 *and T.D.* 8879, 3-30-2000.]

[Reg. § 41.4483-1]

§ 41.4483-1. State exemption.—Use of a highway motor vehicle by a State is exempt from the tax imposed by section 4481. For this purpose, the term *use by a State* means the operation by a State on the public highways in the United States of any highway motor vehicle, whether or not such highway motor vehicle is owned by the State. [Reg. § 41.4483-1.]

☐ [T.D. 6216, 12-6-56. *Amended by T.D.* 8879, 3-30-2000.]

[Reg. § 41.4483-2]

§ 41.4483-2. Exemption for certain transit-type buses.—(a) *In general.*—Use in any taxable period, or part thereof, of any bus of the transit type by any person who is engaged in the operation of a transit system is exempt from the tax, if such person meets the 60-percent passenger fare revenue test provided for in paragraph (e) of this section, for the applicable period prescribed in paragraph (c) of this section as the test period for such person for such system for such taxable period, or part thereof.

(b) *Buses of the transit type.*—The term "transit type," when used in the regulations in this part with reference to a bus, means the type of bus which is designed for the mass transportation of persons within an urban area, as distinguished from the intercity-type bus. A transit-type bus is ordinarily distinguishable from an intercity-type bus by comparison of seats, doors, and baggage facilities. The transit-type bus usually has straight-back seats of the bench type, while the intercity-type bus generally has seats which either can be reclined or are in fact permanently fixed in a reclining position. The transit-type bus is more likely to have an accordion or folding-type door at the front of the bus, and often has a second door in the middle or at the rear for

passengers to leave the bus, as opposed to the emergency-type rear door which may or may not be included in the intercity-type bus. The typical transit-type bus does not have facilities for storing baggage whereas the typical intercity-type bus has facilities for storing baggage in a compartment underneath the floor of the bus or in overhead racks, or both. Other characteristics which may be taken into account in distinguishing a transit-type bus from an intercity-type bus include gear ratios, acceleration and maximum speed, and aisle space for standees. The transit-type bus ordinarily has a lower gear ratio to provide for quick starts and because, in general, buses of this type are operated at low speeds. The intercity-type bus ordinarily has a higher gear ratio and can be operated at much higher speeds. The transit-type bus usually has wider aisles, with overhead straps or bars to accommodate standees.

(c) *Test period.*—(1) In the case of any person who is engaged in the operation of a transit system at any time in the calendar quarter immediately preceding July 1 of any taxable period, the test period for such system for such taxable period shall be such calendar quarter. However, if passenger fare revenue from scheduled service described in paragraph (e) of this section was derived on less than 30 days during such calendar quarter from operation of such system, the test period for such system for such taxable period shall be the last preceding test period for such system. If such system has no preceding test period, then the test period for such system for such taxable period shall be the calendar quarter beginning with July 1 of such taxable period.

(2) Except as otherwise provided in subparagraph (3) of this paragraph, in the case of any person who commences operation of a transit system at any time on or after July 1 of any taxable period, the test period for such system for that part of such taxable period beginning with the first day on which such operation was commenced shall be the calendar quarter in which falls such first day. However, if passenger fare revenue from scheduled service described in paragraph (e) of this section was derived on less than 30 days during such calendar quarter from operation of such system, the test period for such system for such taxable period shall be the following calendar quarter.

(3) In the case of any person who commences operation of a transit system at any time in the last calendar quarter to which the tax imposed by section 4481 applies, such last calendar quarter shall be the test period for such transit system regardless of the number of days in which passenger fare revenue is derived in such calendar quarter.

(d) The term "transit system," as used in the regulations in this part, means any system for furnishing scheduled common carrier public passenger land transportation service along regular routes.

(e) *60-percent passenger fare revenue test.*—For purposes of this section, a person engaged in the operation of a transit system meets the 60-percent passenger fare revenue test, for the applicable test period prescribed in this section, if—

(1) During such test period such person derived passenger fare revenue from the operation of such system, and

(2) At least 60 percent of the total of such passenger fare revenue derived by such person during such test period was attributable to (i) amounts paid for transportation which do not exceed 60 cents, (ii) amounts paid for commutation or season tickets for single trips of less than 30 miles, or (iii) amounts paid for commutation tickets for one month or less. In determining the total of such passenger fare revenue, revenue from sources such as charter fees, rentals of property, advertising receipts, etc., is not taken into account.

(f) *Examples.*—Application of this section may be illustrated by the following examples:

Example (1). The X Transit Company is engaged in the operation of a transit system in the city of A and surrounding area throughout April, May, and June of 1984 and the taxable period beginning July 1, 1984. It derives passenger fare revenue from the operation of such system for 15 days in April and for the entire months of May and June of 1984. On July 1, 1984, the Company is using 60 buses of the transit type and 40 buses of the intercity type. Each of 20 of the transit-type buses and each of 10 of the intercity-type buses has a taxable gross weight of at least 55,000 pounds. (No tax is imposed on the use of either a transit-type bus or an intercity-type bus having a taxable gross weight of less than 55,000 pounds. See §41.4481-1.) Use of the 10 intercity-type buses is subject to the tax for the taxable period beginning with July 1, 1984, since the exemption, if any, applies only to transit-type buses. Use of the 20 transit-type buses is not subject to the tax for such taxable period if at least 60 percent of the total passenger fare revenue derived by the X Transit Company during April, May, and June of 1984 (the test period prescribed in paragraph (c)(1) of this section) from operation of such system was from fares attributable to (i) amounts paid for transportation which do not exceed 60 cents, (ii) amounts paid for commutation or season tickets for single trips of less than 30 miles, or (iii) amounts paid for commutation tickets for one month or less. If the X Transit Company does not meet the 60-percent passenger fare revenue test for April, May, and June of 1984, the tax attaches for the taxable period beginning with July 1, 1984, with respect to the use of each of the 20 transit-type buses having a taxable gross weight of at least 55,000 pounds.

Example (2). Assume the same facts as those stated in Example (1), except that the X Transit Company commences operation of the transit system on July 15, 1984, and derives passenger fare revenue from operation of the system throughout the following August and September. In such case, the test period is July, August, and September of 1984, and if the test is met for this period, no tax is imposed on the use by the Company of any bus of the transit type in the period July 15, 1984, through June 30, 1985.

Example (3). Assume the same facts as those stated in Example (1), except that the X Transit Company commences operation of the transit system on April 15, 1985, and derives passenger fare revenue from operation of the system throughout the following May and June. In such case the test period is April, May, and June of 1985, and if the test is met for this period, no tax is imposed on the use by the Company of any bus of the transit type in the period April 15 through June of 1985 or in the taxable period beginning on July 1, 1985. [Reg. §41.4483-2.]

☐ [T.D. 6216. *Amended by T.D.* 6743, 6-22-64; *T.D.* 8027, 5-23-85 *and T.D.* 8879, 3-30-2000.]

[Reg. §41.4483-3]

§41.4483-3. Exemption for trucks used for 5,000 or fewer miles and agricultural vehicles used for 7,500 or fewer miles on public highways.—(a) *Suspension of tax.*—(1) *In general.*—Liability for the tax imposed by section 4481(a) is suspended during a taxable period if it is reasonable to expect that the vehicle will be used for 5,000 or fewer miles on public highways during such taxable period and the owner furnishes in the time and manner required the information required under paragraph (a)(2) of this section. See paragraph (g) of this section regarding special rules for agricultural vehicles. See §41.4482(c)-1(c) for the meaning of "use" on the public highways.

(2) *Information to be supplied in support of suspension of tax.*—The owner of a highway motor vehicle who reasonably expects that the vehicle will be used for 5,000 or fewer miles on public highways during a taxable period shall furnish on the first Form 2290 filed during the taxable period for such motor vehicle, such information as is required by the Form in order to support the suspension of tax under paragraph (a) of this section.

(b) *Cessation of suspension from tax.*—If a highway motor vehicle on which the tax under section 4481(a) is suspended for a particular taxable period under paragraph (a)(1) of this section is used for more than 5,000 miles on public highways during such taxable period, the owner of the vehicle is liable for the tax for the entire taxable period in accordance with section 4481(a).

(c) *Exemption.*—If at the end of any taxable period during which the tax under section 4481(a) on a highway motor vehicle was suspended under paragraph (a)(1) of this section the vehicle has not been used for more than 5,000 miles on public highways, the vehicle shall be exempt from the tax for that taxable period. The owner of the vehicle shall verify that the vehicle was used for less than 5,000 miles in such ended taxable period on the first Form 2290 filed for the next taxable period.

(d) *Examples.*—The provisions of this section may be illustrated by the following examples:

Example (1). A is the owner of 6 highway motor vehicles, each of which has a taxable gross weight in excess of 55,000 pounds. None of these 6 vehicles are agricultural vehicles. The vehicles are placed in use during July 1984. Because of the nature of his business, A reports on the first Form 2290 filed after June 30, 1984, that he reasonably expects that none of the vehicles will be used for more than 5,000 miles on public highways. Accordingly, the tax imposed by section 4481(a) is suspended for A's 6 vehicles for the taxable period July 1, 1984, through June 30, 1985.

Example (2). Assume the same facts as in example (1) except that during the month of February 1985, the use of one of A's vehicles exceeds 5,000 miles on public highways. A is liable for the full tax for the taxable period July 1, 1984, through June 30, 1985, for that vehicle at the rate set forth in §41.4481-1(b), and must so report on a Form 2290 filed on or before March 31, 1985, the last day of the month following the month in which the use exceeds 5,000 miles.

(e) *Credit or refund of tax for highway motor vehicle used 5,000 or fewer miles.*—(1) If a highway motor vehicle on which the tax imposed by section 4481(a) has been paid for a given taxable period is used for 5,000 or fewer miles on public highways during such taxable period, the person who paid the tax may file a claim for refund of an overpayment of the tax at the end of the taxable period. Claims for refunds of tax made under this paragraph (e) shall be filed in the same manner as claims for refunds filed under §41.4481-1(d). Refunds of tax made under this paragraph (e) shall be without interest.

(2) Any person entitled to claim a refund of tax under paragraph (e)(1) of this section may, in lieu of claiming a refund of such tax, claim credit for such tax on the first Form 2290 filed for the next taxable period.

≫≫→ *Caution: Reg. §41.4483-3(f), below, prior to amendment by T.D. 9698, applies before July 1, 2015.*

(f) *Relief from liability for tax under certain circumstances.*—If the tax imposed by section 4481(a) on a highway motor vehicle is suspended for any taxable period under paragraph (a) of this section and the vehicle is transferred while the suspension is in effect, the transferor will not be liable for any tax on such vehicle for such taxable period if such transferor furnishes a statement to the transferee on which is included the transferor's name, address and taxpayer identification number, the vehicle identification number, the date of transfer of the vehicle, the number of miles the vehicle has been used on the public highways during the taxable period, the odometer reading at the time of the transfer, and the name, address and taxpayer identification number of the transferee. The suspension from tax under paragraph (a) continues until the vehicle is used on the public highways for more than 5,000 miles during the taxable period (including use by the transferor for the portion of the taxable period prior to the transfer). If the transferor has furnished the statement required in this paragraph (f), the transferee and not the transferor is liable for the entire tax under section 4481(a) for the taxable period in which the transfer was made. If the transferor has not furnished such statement to the transferee, then the transferor is also liable for the tax on the use of such vehicle for such taxable period to the extent that the tax or an installment payment of the tax has not been previously paid. See paragraph (b) of this section relating to cessation of suspension from tax and §41.6011(a)-1(a)(3) for a requirement that certain transferees described in this paragraph (f) must file a return.

≫≫→ *Caution: Reg. §41.4483-3(f), below, as amended by T.D. 9698, applies on or after July 1, 2015.*

(f) *Relief from liability for tax under certain circumstances.*—If the tax imposed by section 4481(a) on a highway motor vehicle is suspended for any taxable period under paragraph (a) of this section and the vehicle is transferred while the suspension is in effect, the transferor will not be liable for any tax on such vehicle for such taxable period if such transferor furnishes a statement to the transferee on which is included the transferor's name, address and taxpayer identification number, the vehicle identification number, the date of transfer of the vehicle, the number of miles the vehicle has been used on the public highways during the taxable period, the odometer reading at the time of the transfer, and the name, address and taxpayer identification number of the transferee. The suspension from tax under paragraph (a) continues until the vehicle is used on the public highways for more than 5,000 miles during the taxable period (including use by the transferor for the portion of the taxable period prior to the transfer). If the transferor has furnished the statement required in this paragraph (f), the transferee and not the transferor is liable for the entire tax under section 4481(a) for the taxable period in which the transfer was made. If the transferor has not furnished such statement to the transferee, then the transferor is also liable for the tax on the use of such vehicle for such taxable period (determined in the case of a transfer described in §41.4481-1(c)(4)(i) under §41.4481-1(c)(4)(ii)) to the extent that the tax has not been previously paid. See paragraph (b) of this section relating to cessation of suspension from tax and §41.6011(a)-1(a)(3) for a requirement that certain transferees described in this paragraph (f) must file a return.

(g) *Special rule for agricultural vehicles.*—(1) *In General.*—In applying the provisions of this section to an agricultural vehicle, "7,500" shall be substituted for "5,000" each place it appears in paragraphs (a) through (f) of this section.

(2) *Meaning of terms.*—(i) *Agriculture vehicle.*—An agricultural vehicle is any highway motor vehicle—

(A) Used (or expected to be used) primarily for farming purposes, and

(B) Registered (under the laws of the State or States in which such vehicle is required to be registered) as a highway motor vehicle used for farming purposes.

A highway motor vehicle is used primarily for farming purposes if more than one-half of such vehicle's use (determined on the basis of mileage) during the taxable period is for farming purposes. Further, the highway motor vehicle must be registered (under the laws of the State or States where such vehicle is required to be registered) as a highway motor vehicle used for farming purposes for the entire taxable period in order to qualify as an agricultural vehicle. See §41.4482(a)-(1) for the definition of "highway motor vehicle". A vehicle will be considered to be registered under the laws of the State as a highway motor vehicle used for farming purposes if such vehicle is so registered under a State statute or legally valid regulations. In addition, no special tag or license plate identifying a vehicle as being used for farming purposes is required.

(ii) *Farming purposes.*—For purposes of this section "farming purposes" means the transporting of any farm commodity to or from a farm, or the use directly in agricultural production.

(iii) *Farm commodity.*—A "farm commodity" is any agricultural or horticultural commodity, feed, seed, fertilizer, livestock, bees, poultry, fur-bearing animals, or wildlife. A farm commodity does not include a commodity which has been changed by a processing operation from its raw or natural state. For example, juice which has been extracted from fruits or vegetables is not a farm commodity for purposes of this paragraph (g).

(iv) *Farm.*—The term "farm" includes stock (including feed yards for fattening cattle), dairy, poultry, fruit, fur-bearing animal, and truck farms, plantations, ranches, nurseries, ranges, orchards, and such greenhouses and other similar structures as are used primarily for the raising of any agricultural or horticultural commodity. Greenhouses and other similar structures used primarily for purposes other than the raising of agricultural or horticultural commodities (for example, display, storage, or fabrication of wreaths, corsages, and bouquets) do not constitute "farms".

(v) *Agricultural production.*—(A) *In general.*—A highway motor vehicle is considered to be used directly in agricultural production only if it is used as indicated in the following paragraphs.

(B) *Use of a highway motor vehicle in connection with cultivating, raising and harvesting.*—A highway motor vehicle is considered to be used directly in agricultural production if such vehicle is used in connection with cultivating the soil, or raising or harvesting any agricultural or horticultural commodity, including the raising, shearing, feeding, caring for, training and management of livestock, bees, poultry, and fur-bearing animals and wildlife. A highway motor vehicle which is used in connection with operations such as canning, freezing, packaging, or other processing operations will not be considered to be used directly in agricultural production.

(C) *Use of a highway motor vehicle in connection with planting, cultivation, caring for, cutting, etc., of trees.*—A highway motor vehicle is used directly for agricultural production if it is used in connection with planting, cultivating, caring for, or cutting of trees, or in connection with the preparation (other than milling) of trees for market; but only if such operations are incidental to farming operations. These farming operations include felling trees and cutting them into logs or firewood, but do not include sawing logs into lumber, chipping, or other milling operations. The operations specified in this paragraph (g)(2)(v)(C) will be considered "incidental to farming operations" only if they are a minor nature in comparison with the total farming operations involved. Therefore, a treefarmer or timbergrower may not claim that a highway motor vehicle used in that trade or business is used directly in agricultural production.

(D) *Use of a highway motor vehicle in connection with the operation, management, conservation, improvement, or maintenance of a farm.*—A highway motor vehicle is used directly for agricultural production if it is used in connection with the operation, management, conservation, improvement, or maintenance of a farm and its tools and equipment. Examples of these operations include clearing land, repairing fences and farm buildings, building terraces or irrigation ditches, cleaning tools or farm machinery, painting, and other activities which contribute in any way to the conduct of a farm as such, as distinguished from any other enterprise in which the owner of the highway motor vehicle may be engaged.

(3) *Mileage on farm not counted toward 7,500 mile limit.*—For purposes of this section, the number of miles which a highway motor vehicle is driven on a farm and not on the public highways shall not be taken into account when determining whether the vehicle's mileage is in excess of 7,500 miles. Accurate records should be kept by taxpayers of the number of miles that a highway motor vehicle is operated on a farm.

(h) *Owner.*—For purposes of this section the term "owner" means, with respect to any highway motor vehicle, the person described in section 4481(b).

Reg. §41.4483-3(g)(2)(i)

(i) *Effective/applicability date.*—This section applies on and after July 1, 2015. For rules applicable before that date, see 26 CFR 41.4483-3 (revised as of April 1, 2014). [Reg. § 41.4483-3.]

□ *[T.D. 8027, 5-23-85. Amended by T.D. 8879, 3-30-2000 and T.D. 9698, 10-28-2014.]*

[Reg. § 41.4483-4]

§ 41.4483-4. Application of exemptions.—Any exemption from the tax on the use of a highway motor vehicle has application only with respect to the use of such highway motor vehicle and not with respect to the highway motor vehicle as such. Furthermore, such exemption is subject to those provisions of paragraph (c) of § 41.4481-1 relating to proration of the tax and to the effect of an exempt use of a highway motor vehicle after a taxable use has been made. Thus, if a taxable use is made of a highway motor vehicle at any time in a taxable period, the tax is imposed on the use of such vehicle for such taxable period, computed from the first day of the month in which such taxable use occurred, even though at some time in the same taxable period, before or after such taxable use occurred, the use of the vehicle may have been, or may be, exempt. For example, if a highway motor vehicle is operated exclusively by a State in the period July 1 through September 10 of a taxable period use of such vehicle in such period is exempt from the tax. However, if a taxable use of the vehicle is made on September 11 of such taxable period, the tax imposed on the use of such vehicle for such taxable period is computed from September 1. On the other hand, if a taxable use of the vehicle is made at any time in July of the taxable period, the tax imposed on the use of such vehicle for such taxable period is computed from July 1, even though the vehicle may be operated exclusively by a State in every other month of such period. [Reg. § 41.4483-3.]

□ *[T.D. 6216. Amended by T.D. 6743, 6-22-64. Redesignated T.D. 8027, 5-23-85.]*

[Reg. § 41.4483-6]

§ 41.4483-6. Reduction in tax for trucks used in logging.—(a) *In general.*—The tax imposed by section 4481 shall be reduced by 25 percent in the case of a truck used in logging.

(b) *Truck used in logging.*—The term "truck used in logging" means any highway motor vehicle which—

(1) Is used exclusively during the taxable period for the transportation, to and from a point located on a forested site, of products harvested from such forested site, and

(2) Is registered (under the laws of the State or States in which such vehicle is required to be registered) as a highway motor vehicle used exclusively in the transportation of harvested forest products.

Products harvested from the forested site may include timber which has been processed for commercial use by sawing into lumber, chipping or other milling operations if such processing occurs prior to transportation from the forested site. A vehicle will be considered to be registered under the laws of a state as a highway motor vehicle used exclusively in the transportation of harvested forest products if such vehicle is so registered under a state statute or legally valid regulations. In addition, no special tag or license plate identifying a vehicle as being used in the transportation of harvested forest products is required. [Reg. § 41.4483-6.]

□ *[T.D. 8027, 5-23-85.]*

Environmental Taxes

See p. 20,601 for regulations not amended to reflect law changes

[Reg. § 52.0-1]

§ 52.0-1. Introduction.—The regulations in this part 52 are designated "Environmental Tax Regulations." The regulations relate to the environmental taxes imposed by chapter 38 of the Internal Revenue Code. See part 40 of this chapter for regulations relating to returns, payments, and deposits of taxes imposed by chapter 38. [Reg. § 52.0-1.]

□ *[T.D. 8442, 10-21-92.]*

[Reg. § 52.4681-1]

§ 52.4681-1. Taxes imposed with respect to ozone-depleting chemicals.—(a) *Taxes imposed.*—Sections 4681 and 4682 impose the following taxes with respect to ozone-depleting chemicals (ODCs):

(1) *Tax on ODCs.*—Section 4681(a)(1) imposes a tax on ODCs that are sold or used by the manufacturer or importer thereof. Except as otherwise provided in § 52.4682-1 (relating to the tax on ODCs), the amount of the tax is equal to the product of—

(i) The weight (in pounds) of the ODC;

(ii) The base tax amount (determined under section 4681(b)(1)(B) or (C)) for the calendar year in which the sale or use occurs; and

(iii) The ozone-depletion factor (determined under section 4682(b)) for the ODC.

(2) *Tax on imported taxable products.*—Section 4681(a)(2) imposes a tax on imported taxable products that are sold or used by the importer thereof. Except as otherwise provided in § 52.4682-3 (relating to the tax on imported taxable products), the tax is computed by reference to the weight of the ODCs used as materials in the manufacture of the product. The amount of tax is equal to the tax that would have been imposed on the ODCs under section 4681(a)(1) if the ODCs had been sold in the United States on the date of the sale or use of the imported product. The weight of such ODCs is determined under § 52.4682-3.

(3) *Floor stocks tax.*—(i) *Imposition of tax.*—Section 4682(h) imposes a floor stocks tax on ODCs that—

(A) Are held by any person other than the manufacturer or importer of the ODC on a date specified in paragraph (a)(3)(ii) of this section; and

(B) Are held on such date for sale or for use in further manufacture.

(ii) *Dates on which tax imposed.*—The floor stocks tax is imposed on January 1 of each calendar year after 1989.

(iii) *Amount of tax.*—Except as otherwise provided in § 52.4682-4 (relating to the floor stocks tax), the amount of the floor stocks tax is equal to the excess of—

(A) The tax that would be imposed on the ODC under section 4681(a)(1) if a sale or use of the ODC by its manufacturer or importer occurred on the date the floor stocks tax is imposed (the tentative tax amount), over

(B) The sum of the taxes previously imposed (if any) on the ODC under sections 4681 and 4682.

(b) *Cross-references.*—(1) *Tax on ODCs.*—Additional rules relating to the tax on ODCs are contained in §§ 52.4682-1 and 52.4682-2.

(2) *Tax on imported taxable products.*—Additional rules relating to the tax on imported taxable products are contained in § 52.4682-3.

(3) *Floor stocks tax.*—Additional rules relating to the floor stocks tax are contained in § 52.4682-4.

(4) *Returns, payments, and deposits of tax.*—Rules requiring returns reporting the taxes imposed by sections 4681 and 4682 are contained in part 40 of this chapter. Part 40 of this chapter also provides rules relating to the use of Government depositaries and to the time for filing returns and making payments of tax.

(c) *Definitions of general application.*—The following definitions set forth the meaning of certain terms for purposes of the regulations under sections 4681 and 4682:

(1) *Ozone-depleting chemical.*—The term "ozone-depleting chemical" (ODC) means any chemical listed in section 4682(a)(2).

(2) *United States.*—The term "United States" has the meaning given such term by section 4612(a)(4). Under section 4612(a)(4)—

(i) The term "United States" means the 50 States, the District of Columbia, the Commonwealth of Puerto Rico, any possession of the United States, the Commonwealth of the Northern Mariana Islands, and the Trust Territory of the Pacific Islands; and

(ii) The term includes—

(A) Submarine seabed and subsoil that would be treated as part of the United States (as defined in paragraph (c)(2)(i) of this section) under the principles of section 638 relating to continental shelf areas; and

(B) Foreign trade zones of the United States.

(3) *Manufacture; manufacturer.*—The term "manufacture" when used with respect to any ODC or imported product includes its production, and the term "manufacturer" includes a producer.

(4) *Entry into United States for consumption, use, or warehousing.*—(i) *In general.*—Except as otherwise provided in this paragraph (c)(4), the term "entered into the United States for consumption, use, or warehousing" when used with respect to any goods means—

(A) Brought into the customs territory of the United States (the customs territory) if applicable customs law requires that the goods be entered into the customs territory for consumption, use, or warehousing;

(B) Admitted into a foreign trade zone for any purpose if like goods brought into the customs territory for such purpose would be entered into the customs territory for consumption, use, or warehousing; or

(C) Imported into any other part of the United States (as defined in paragraph (c)(2) of this section) for any purpose if like goods brought into the customs territory for such purpose would be entered into the customs territory for consumption, use, or warehousing.

(ii) *Entry for transportation and exportation.*—Goods entered into the customs territory for transportation and exportation are not goods entered for consumption, use, or warehousing.

(iii) *Entries described in two or more provisions.*—In the case of any goods with respect to which entries are described in two or more provisions of paragraph (c)(4)(i) of this section, only the first such entry is taken into account. Thus, if the admission of goods into a foreign trade zone is an entry into the United States for consumption, use, or warehousing, the subsequent entry of such goods into the customs territory will not be treated as an entry into the United States for consumption, use or warehousing.

(iv) *Certain imported products not entered for consumption, use, or warehousing.*—Imported products that are entered into the United States for consumption, use, or warehousing do not include any imported products that—

(A) Are entered into the customs territory under Harmonized Tariff Schedule (HTS) heading 9801, 9802, 9803, or 9813;

(B) Would, if entered into the customs territory, be entered under any such heading; or

(C) Are brought into the United States by an individual if the product is brought in for use by the individual and is not expected to be used in a trade or business other than a trade or business of performing services as an employee.

(5) *Importer.*—The term "importer" means the person that first sells or uses goods after their entry into the United States for consumption,

use, or warehousing (within the meaning of paragraph (c)(4) of this section).

(6) *Sale.*—The term "sale" means the transfer of title or of substantial incidents of ownership (whether or not delivery to, or payment by, the buyer has been made) for consideration which may include money, services, or property. The determination as to the time a sale occurs shall be made under applicable local law.

(7) *Use.*—(i) *In general.*—Except as otherwise provided in regulations under sections 4681 and 4682, ODCs and imported taxable products are used when they are—

(A) Used as a material in the manufacture of an article, whether by incorporation into such article, chemical transformation, release into the atmosphere, or otherwise; or

(B) Put into service in a trade or business or for production of income.

(ii) *Loss, destruction, packaging, warehousing, and repair.*—The loss, destruction, packaging (including repackaging), warehousing, or repair of ODCs and imported taxable products is not a use of the ODC or product lost, destroyed, packaged, warehoused, or repaired.

(iii) *Cross-references to exceptions.*—For exceptions to the rule contained in paragraph (c)(7)(i) of this section, see—

(A) Section 52.4682-1(b)(2)(iii) (relating to mixture elections), §52.4682-1(b)(2)(iv) (relating to mixtures for export), and §52.4682-1(b)(2)(v) (relating to mixtures for use as a feedstock);

(B) §52.4682-3(c)(2) (relating to the election to treat entry of an imported taxable product as use); and

(C) §52.4682-3(c)(3) (relating to treating sale of an article incorporating an imported taxable product as the first sale or use of the product).

(8) *Pound.*—The term "pound" means a unit of weight that is equal to 16 avoirdupois ounces.

(9) *Post-1990 ODC; post-1989 ODC.*—The term "post-1990 ODC" means any ODC that is listed below Halon-2402 in the table contained in section 4682(a)(2). The term "post-1989 ODC" means any ODC other than a post-1990 ODC.

(d) *Effective date.*—Sections 52.4681-0, 52.4681-1, 52.4682-1, 52.4682-2, 52.4682-3, and 52.4682-4 are effective as of January 1, 1990, and apply to—

(1) Post-1989 ODCs that the manufacturer or importer thereof first sells or uses after December 31, 1989, and post-1990 ODCs that the manufacturer or importer thereof first sells or uses after December 31, 1990;

(2) Imported taxable products that the importer thereof first sells or uses after December 31, 1989 (but, in the case of products first sold or used before January 1, 1991, by taking into account only the post-1989 ODCs used as materials in their manufacture); and

(3) Post-1989 ODCs held for sale or for use in further manufacture by any person other than the manufacturer or importer thereof on January 1, 1990, and post-1989 and post-1990 ODCs that are so held on January 1 of each calendar year after 1990. [Reg. §52.4681-1.]

☐ [*T.D.* 8370, 11-1-91. *Amended by T.D.* 8442, 10-21-92 *and T.D.* 8622, 10-10-95.]

[Reg. §52.4682-1]

§52.4682-1. Ozone-depleting chemicals.—(a) *Overview.*—This section provides rules relating to the tax imposed on ozone-depleting chemicals (ODCs) under section 4681, including rules for identifying taxable ODCs and determining when the tax is imposed, and rules prescribing special treatment for certain ODCs. See §52.4681-1(a)(1) and (c) for general rules and definitions relating to the tax on ODCs.

(b) *Taxable ODCs; taxable event.*—(1) *Taxable ODCs.*—(i) *In general.*—Except as provided in paragraphs (c) through (g) of this section, an ODC is taxable if—

(A) It is listed in section 4682(a)(2) on the date it is sold or used by its manufacturer or importer; and

(B) It is manufactured in the United States or entered into the United States for consumption, use, or warehousing.

(ii) *Storage containers.*—An ODC described in paragraph (b)(1)(i) of this section is taxable without regard to the type or size of storage container in which the ODC is held.

(iii) *Example.*—The application of this paragraph (b)(1) may be illustrated by the following example:
Example. A brings CFC-12, an ODC listed in section 4682(a)(2), into the customs territory and enters the CFC-12 for transportation and exportation. The ODC is not taxable because it is not entered for consumption, use, or warehousing. The ODC also would not be taxable if it were admitted to a foreign trade zone (rather than brought into the customs territory) for transportation and exportation.

(2) *Taxable event.*—(i) *In general.*—(A) *General rule.*—The tax on an ODC is imposed when the ODC is first sold or used (as defined in §52.4681-1(c)(6) and (7)) by its manufacturer or importer.

(B) *Example.*—The application of this paragraph (b)(2)(i) may be illustrated by the following example:
Example. A enters CFC-113, an ODC listed in section 4682(a)(2), into the United States for consumption, use, or warehousing. A warehouses the CFC-113 and then decides to ship the ODC to its factory outside the United States (as defined in §52.4681-1(c)(2)). The CFC-113 is a taxable ODC because the requirements of paragraph (b)(1)(i) of this section have been met. However, tax is not imposed on the ODC because there is no taxable event. A did not sell the ODC and, under §52.4681-1(c)(7), warehousing is not a use.

(ii) *Mixtures.*—Except as provided in paragraphs (b)(2)(iii), (iv), and (v) of this section,

Reg. §52.4682-1(b)(2)(ii)

the creation of a mixture containing two or more ingredients is treated as a taxable use of the ODCs contained in the mixture. For this purpose, a mixture cannot be represented by a chemical formula, and an ODC is contained in a mixture only if the chemical identity of the ODC is not changed. Thus, except as provided in paragraphs (b)(2)(iii), (iv), and (v) of this section—

(A) The tax on the post-1989 ODCs (as defined in §52.4681-1(c)(9)) contained in mixtures created after December 31, 1989, or on the post-1990 ODCs (as defined in §52.4681-1(c)(9)) contained in mixtures created after December 31, 1990, is imposed when the mixture is created and not on any subsequent sale or use of the mixture; and

(B) No tax is imposed under section 4681 on the post-1989 ODCs contained in mixtures created before January 1, 1990, or on the post-1990 ODCs contained in mixtures created before January 1, 1991.

(iii) *Mixture elections.*—(A) *Permitted elections.*—The only elections permitted under this paragraph (b)(2)(iii) are—

(1) An election for the first calendar quarter beginning after December 31, 1989, and all subsequent periods (the 1990 election); and

(2) An election for the first calendar quarter beginning after December 31, 1990, and all subsequent periods (the 1991 election).

(B) *In general.*—A manufacturer or importer may elect to treat the sale or use of mixtures containing ODCs as the first sale or use of the ODCs contained in the mixtures. If a 1990 election is made under this paragraph (b)(2)(iii), the tax on post-1989 ODCs contained in a mixture sold or used after December 31, 1989 (including any such mixture created before January 1, 1990) is imposed on the date of such sale or use. Similarly, if a 1991 election is made under this paragraph (b)(2)(iii), the tax on post-1990 ODCs contained in a mixture sold or used after December 31, 1990 (including any such mixture created before January 1, 1991) is imposed on the date of such sale or use.

(C) *Applicability of elections.*—An election under this paragraph (b)(2)(iii) applies—

(1) In the case of a 1990 election, to all post-1989 ODCs contained in mixtures sold or used by the manufacturer or importer after December 31, 1989 (including any such mixture created before January 1, 1990); and

(2) In the case of a 1991 election, to all post-1990 ODCs contained in mixtures sold or used by the manufacturer or importer after December 31, 1990 (including any such mixture created before January 1, 1991).

(D) *Making the election; revocation.*—An election under this paragraph (b)(2)(iii) shall be made in accordance with the instructions for the return on which the manufacturer or importer reports liability for tax under section 4681. After October 9, 1990, the election may be revoked only with the consent of the Commissioner.

(iv) *Special rule for exports.*—The creation of a mixture for export is not a taxable use of the ODCs contained in the mixture. If a manufacturer or importer sells a mixture for export, §52.4682-5 applies to the ODCs contained in the mixture. See §52.4682-5(e) for rules relating to liability of a purchaser for tax if the mixture is not exported.

(v) *Special rule for use as a feedstock.*—The creation of a mixture for use as a feedstock (within the meaning of paragraph (c) of this section) is not a taxable use of the ODCs contained in the mixture.

(c) *ODCs used as a feedstock.*—(1) *Exemption from tax.*—No tax is imposed on an ODC if the manufacturer or importer of the ODC—

(i) Uses the ODC as a feedstock in the manufacture of another chemical; or

(ii) Sells the ODC in a qualifying sale (within the meaning of paragraph (c)(4) of this section) for use as a feedstock.

(2) *Excess payments.*—(i) *In general.*—Under section 4682(d)(2)(B), a credit or refund is allowed to a person if—

(A) The person uses an ODC as a feedstock; and

(B) The amount of any tax paid with respect to the ODC under section 4681 or 4682 was not determined under section 4682(d)(2)(A).

(ii) *Procedural rules.*—See section 6402 and the regulations thereunder for rules relating to claiming a credit or refund of tax paid with respect to ODCs that are used as a feedstock. A credit against the income tax is not allowed for the amount determined under section 4682(d)(2)(B).

(3) *Definition.*—An ODC is used as a feedstock only if the ODC is entirely consumed (except for trace amounts) in the manufacture of another chemical. Thus, the transformation of an ODC into one or more new compounds (such as the transformation of CFC-113 into chlorotrifluoroethylene (CTFE or 1113), of CFC-113 into CFC-115 and CFC-116, or of carbon tetrachloride into hydrochloric acid during petroleum refining or incineration) is treated as use as a feedstock. On the other hand, the ODCs used in a mixture (including an azeotrope such as R-500 or R-502) are not used as a feedstock.

(4) *Qualifying sale.*—A sale of ODCs for use as a feedstock is a qualifying sale if the requirements of §52.4682-2(b)(1) are satisfied with respect to such sale.

(d) *ODCs used in the manufacture of rigid foam insulation.*—(1) *Phase-in of tax.*—(i) *In general.*—The amount of tax imposed on an ODC is determined under section 4682(g) if the manufacturer or importer of the ODC—

(A) Uses the ODC during 1990, 1991, 1992, or 1993 in the manufacture of rigid foam insulation; or

(B) Sells the ODC in a qualifying sale (within the meaning of paragraph (d)(5) of this section) during 1990, 1991, 1992, or 1993.

(ii) *Amount of tax.*—Under section 4682(g), ODCs described in paragraph (d)(1)(i) of this section are not taxed if sold or used during 1990 and are taxed at a reduced rate if sold or used during 1991, 1992, or 1993.

(2) *Excess payments.*—(i) *In general.*—Under section 4682(g)(3), a credit against income tax or a refund is allowed to a person if—

(A) The person uses an ODC during 1990, 1991, 1992, or 1993 in the manufacture of rigid foam insulation; and

(B) The amount of any tax paid with respect to the ODC under section 4681 or 4682 was not determined under section 4682(g).

(ii) *Procedural rules.*—(A) The amount determined under section 4682(g)(3) shall be treated as a credit described in section 34(a) (relating to credits for gasoline and special fuels) unless a claim for refund has been filed.

(B) See section 6402 and the regulations thereunder for rules relating to claiming a credit or refund of the tax paid with respect to ODCs that are used in the manufacture of rigid foam insulation.

(3) *Definition.*—(i) *Rigid foam insulation.*—The term "rigid foam insulation" means any rigid foam that is designed for use as thermal insulation in buildings, equipment, appliances, tanks, railcars, trucks, or vessels, or on pipes, including any such rigid foam actually used for purposes other than insulation. Information such as test reports on R-values and advertising material reflecting R-value claims for a particular rigid foam may be used to show that such rigid foam is designed for use as thermal insulation.

(ii) *Rigid foam.*—(A) *In general.*—The term "rigid foam" means any closed cell polymeric foam (whether or not rigid) in which chlorofluorocarbons are used to fill voids within the polymer.

(B) *Examples of rigid foam products.*—Rigid foam includes extruded polystyrene foam, polyisocyanurate foam, spray and pour-in-place polyurethane foam, polyethylene foam, phenolic foam, and any other product that the Commissioner identifies as rigid foam in a pronouncement of general applicability. The form of a product identified under this paragraph (d)(3)(ii)(B) does not affect its character as rigid foam. Thus, such products are rigid foam whether in the form of a board, sheet, backer rod, or wrapping, or in a form applied by spraying, pouring, or frothing.

(4) *Use in manufacture.*—An ODC is used in the manufacture of rigid foam insulation if it is incorporated into such product or is expended as a propellant or otherwise in the manufacture or application of such product.

(5) *Qualifying sale.*—A sale of an ODC for use in the manufacture of rigid foam insulation is a qualifying sale if the requirements of § 52.4682-2(b)(2) are satisfied with respect to such sale.

(e) *Halons; phase-in of tax.*—The amount of tax imposed on Halon-1211, Halon-1301, or Halon-2402 (Halons) is determined under section 4682(g) if the manufacturer or importer of Halons sells or uses Halons during 1990, 1991, 1992, or 1993. Under section 4682(g), Halons are not taxed if sold or used during 1990 and are taxed at a reduced rate if sold or used during 1991, 1992, or 1993.

(f) *Methyl chloroform; reduced rate of tax in 1993.*—The amount of tax imposed on methyl chloroform is determined under section 4682(g)(5) if the manufacturer or importer of the methyl chloroform sells or uses it during 1993.

(g) *ODCs used as medical sterilants.*—(1) *Phase-in of tax.*—The amount of tax imposed on an ODC is determined under section 4682(g)(4) if the manufacturer or importer of the ODC—

(i) Uses the ODC during 1993 as a medical sterilant; or

(ii) Sells the ODC in a qualifying sale (within the meaning of paragraph (g)(4) of this section) during 1993.

(2) *Excess payments.*—(i) *In general.*—Under section 4682(g)(4)(B), a credit against income tax (without interest) or a refund of tax (without interest) is allowed to a person if—

(A) The person uses an ODC during 1993 as a medical sterilant; and

(B) The amount of any tax paid with respect to the ODC under section 4681 or 4682 exceeds the amount that would have been determined under section 4682(g)(4).

(ii) *Amount of credit or refund.*—The amount of credit or refund of tax is equal to the excess of—

(A) The tax that was paid with respect to the ODCs under sections 4681 and 4682; over

(B) The tax that would have been imposed under section 4682(g)(4).

(iii) *Procedural rules.*—(A) The amount determined under section 4682(g)(4)(B) and paragraph (g)(2)(ii) of this section is treated as a credit described in section 34(a) (relating to credits for gasoline and special fuels) unless a claim for refund has been filed.

(B) See section 6402 and the regulations under that section for procedural rules relating to claiming a credit or refund of tax.

(3) *Definition of use as a medical sterilant.*—An ODC is used as a medical sterilant if it is used in the manufacture of sterilant gas.

(4) *Qualifying sale.*—A sale of an ODC for use as a medical sterilant is a qualifying sale if

Reg. §52.4682-1(g)(4)

the requirements of §52.4682-2(b)(3) are satisfied with respect to the sale.

(h) *ODCs used as propellants in metered-dose inhalers.*—(1) *Reduced rate of tax.*—The amount of tax imposed on an ODC is determined under section 4682(g)(4) if the manufacturer or importer of the ODC—

(i) Uses the ODC after 1992 as a propellant in a metered-dose inhaler; or

(ii) Sells the ODC in a qualifying sale (within the meaning of paragraph (h)(4) of this section) after 1992.

(2) *Excess payments.*—(i) *In general.*—Under section 4682(g)(4)(B), a credit against income tax (without interest) or a refund of tax (without interest) is allowed to a person if—

(A) The person uses an ODC after 1992 as a propellant in a metered-dose inhaler; and

(B) The amount of any tax paid with respect to the ODC under section 4681 or 4682 exceeds the amount that would have been determined under section 4682(g)(4).

(ii) *Amount of credit or refund.*—The amount of credit or refund of tax is equal to the excess of—

(A) The tax that was paid with respect to the ODCs under sections 4681 and 4682; over

(B) The tax that would have been imposed under section 4682(g)(4).

(iii) *Procedural rules.*—(A) The amount determined under section 4682(g)(4)(B) and paragraph (h)(2)(ii) of this section is treated as a credit described in section 34(a) (relating to credits for gasoline and special fuels) unless a claim for refund has been filed.

(B) See section 6402 and the regulations under that section for procedural rules relating to claiming a credit or refund of tax.

(3) *Definition of metered-dose inhaler.*—A metered-dose inhaler is an aerosol device that delivers a precisely-measured dose of a therapeutic drug.

(4) *Qualifying sale.*—A sale of an ODC for use as a propellant for a metered-dose inhaler is a qualifying sale if the requirements of §52.4682-2(b)(4) are satisfied with respect to the sale.

(i) [Reserved]

(j) *Exports; cross-reference.*—For the treatment of exports of ODCs, see §52.4682-5.

(k) *Recycling.*—[Reserved][Reg. §52.4682-1.]

□ [*T.D.* 8370, 11-1-91. *Amended by T.D.* 8622, 10-10-95.]

[Reg. §52.4682-2]

§52.4682-2. Qualifying sales.—(a) *In general.*—(1) *Special rules applicable to certain sales.*—Special rules apply to sales of ODCs in the following cases:

(i) Under section 4682(d)(2), §52.4682-1(c), and §52.4682-4(b)(2)(v) (relating to ODCs used as a feedstock), ODCs sold in qualifying sales are not taxed.

(ii) Under section 4682(g), §52.4682-1(d), and §52.4682-4(d)(2) (relating to ODCs used in the manufacture of rigid foam insulation), ODCs sold in qualifying sales are not taxed in 1990 and are taxed at a reduced rate in 1991, 1992, and 1993.

(iii) Under section 4682(g)(4) and §52.4682-1(g) (relating to ODCs used as medical sterilants), ODCs sold in qualifying sales are taxed at a reduced rate in 1993.

(iv) Under section 4682(g)(4) and §52.4682-1(h) (relating to ODCs used as propellants in metered-dose inhalers), ODCs sold in qualifying sales are taxed at a reduced rate in years after 1992.

(2) *Qualifying sales.*—A sale of ODCs is not a qualifying sale unless the requirements of this section are satisfied. Although registration with the Internal Revenue Service is not required to establish that a sale of ODCs is a qualifying sale, the certificates required by this section shall be made available for inspection by internal revenue agents and officers.

(b) *Requirements for qualification.*—(1) *Use as a feedstock.*—A sale of ODCs is a qualifying sale for purposes of §§52.4682-1(c) and 52.4682-4(b)(2)(v) if the manufacturer or importer of the ODCs—

(i) Obtains a certificate in substantially the form set forth in paragraph (d)(2) of this section from the purchaser of the ODCs; and

(ii) Relies on the certificate in good faith.

(2) *Use in the manufacture of rigid foam insulation.*—A sale of ODCs is a qualifying sale for purposes of §§52.4682-1(d) and 52.4682-4(d)(2) if the manufacturer or importer of the ODCs—

(i) Obtains a certificate in substantially the form set forth in paragraph (d)(3) of this section from the purchaser of the OCDs; and

(ii) Relies on the certificate in good faith.

(3) *Use as medical sterilants.*—A sale of ODCs is a qualifying sale for purposes of §52.4682-1(g) if the manufacturer or importer of the ODCs—

(i) Obtains a certificate in substantially the form set forth in paragraph (d)(4) of this section from the purchaser of the ODCs; and

(ii) Relies on the certificate in good faith.

(4) *Use as propellants in metered-dose inhalers.*—A sale of ODCs is a qualifying sale for purposes of §§52.4682-1(h) and 52.4682-4(b)(2)(vii) if the manufacturer or importer of the ODCs—

(i) Obtains a certificate in substantially the form set forth in paragraph (d)(5) of this section from the purchaser of the ODCs; and

(ii) Relies on the certificate in good faith.

(c) *Good faith reliance.*—(1) *In general.*—The requirements of paragraph (b) of this section are not satisfied with respect to a sale of ODCs and the sale is not a qualifying sale if at the time of the sale—

(i) The manufacturer or importer has reason to believe that the purchaser will use the ODCs other than for the purpose set forth in the certificate; or

(ii) The Internal Revenue Service has notified the manufacturer or importer that the purchaser's right to provide a certificate has been withdrawn.

(2) *Withdrawal of right to provide a certificate.*—The Internal Revenue Service may withdraw the right of a purchaser to provide a certificate to its supplier if such purchaser uses the ODCs to which its certificate applies other than for the purpose set forth in such certificate, or otherwise fails to comply with the terms of the certificate. The Internal Revenue Service may notify the supplier to whom the purchaser provided the certificate that the purchaser's right to provide a certificate has been withdrawn.

(d) *Certificate.*—(1) *In general.*—(i) *Rules relating to all certificates.*—This paragraph (d) sets forth certificates that satisfy the requirements of paragraphs (b)(1) through (4) of this section. The certificate shall consist of a statement executed and signed under penalties of perjury by a person with authority to bind the purchaser. A cer-

tificate provided under paragraph (d)(2) or (5) of this section may apply to a single purchase or to multiple purchases and need not specify an expiration date. A certificate provided under paragraph (d)(3) or (4) of this section may apply to a single purchase or multiple purchases, and will expire as of December 31, 1993, unless an earlier expiration date is specified in the certificate. A new certificate must be given to the supplier if any information on the current certificate changes. The certificate may be included as part of any business records normally used to document a sale.

(ii) *Special rule relating to certificates executed before January 1, 1992.*—Certificates provided under this paragraph (d)(2) and executed before January 1, 1992, satisfy the requirements of paragraph (b) of this section if they are in substantially the same form as certificates set forth in § 52.4682-2T.

(2) *Certificate relating to ODCs used as a feedstock.*—(i) *ODCs that will be resold for use by the second purchaser as a feedstock.*—If the purchaser will resell the ODCs to a second purchaser for use by such second purchaser as a feedstock, the certificate provided by the purchaser must be in substantially the following form:

CERTIFICATE OF PURCHASER OF CHEMICALS THAT WILL BE RESOLD FOR USE BY THE SECOND PURCHASER AS A FEEDSTOCK

(To support tax-free sales under section 4682(d)(2) of the Internal Revenue Code.)

Date_____

The undersigned purchaser ("Purchaser") hereby certifies the following under penalties of perjury: The following percentage of ozone-depleting chemicals purchased from

_____

(name and address of seller)

will be resold by Purchaser to persons (Second Purchasers) that certify to Purchaser that they are purchasing the ozone-depleting chemicals for use as a feedstock (as defined in § 52.4682-1(c)(3) of the Environmental Tax Regulations).

PRODUCT	PERCENTAGE
CFC-11	_____
CFC-12	_____
CFC-113	_____
CFC-114	_____
CFC-115	_____
Carbon tetrachloride	_____
Methyl chloroform	_____
Other (specify)	_____
_____	

This certificate applies to (check and complete as applicable):

_____All shipments to Purchaser at the following location(s):

_____
_____
_____

_____ All shipments to Purchaser under the following Purchaser account number(s):

_____
_____
_____

_____ All shipments to Purchaser under the following purchase order(s):

_____
_____
_____

_____ One or more shipments to Purchaser identified as follows:

_____
_____
_____

Reg. § 52.4682-2(d)(2)(i)

Purchaser will not claim a credit or refund under section 4682(d)(2)(B) of the Internal Revenue Code for any ozone-depleting chemicals covered by this certificate.

Purchaser understands that any use by Purchaser of the ozone-depleting chemicals to which this certificate applies other than for the purpose set forth in this certificate may result in the withdrawal by the Internal Revenue Service of Purchaser's right to provide a certificate.

Purchaser will retain the business records needed to document the sales covered by this certificate and will make such records available for inspection by Government officers. Purchaser also will retain and make available for inspection by Government officers the certificates of its Second Purchasers.

Purchaser has not been notified by the Internal Revenue Service that its right to provide a certificate has been withdrawn. In addition, the Internal Revenue Service has not notified Purchaser that the right to provide a certificate has been withdrawn from any Second Purchaser who will purchase ozone-depleting chemicals to which this certificate applies.

Purchaser understands that the fraudulent use of this certificate may subject Purchaser and all parties making such fraudulent use of this certificate to a fine or imprisonment, or both, together with the costs of prosecution.

_____

Signature

_____

Printed or typed name of person signing

_____

Title of person signing

_____

Name of Purchaser

_____

Address

_____
_____

Taxpayer Identifying Number

(ii) *ODCs that will be used by the purchaser as a feedstock.*—If the purchaser will use the ODCs as a feedstock, the certificate provided by the purchaser must be in substantially the following form:

CERTIFICATE OF PURCHASER OF CHEMICALS THAT WILL BE USED BY THE PURCHASER AS A FEEDSTOCK
(To support tax-free sales under section 4682(d)(2) of the Internal Revenue Code.)

Date_____

The undersigned purchaser ("Purchaser") hereby certifies the following under penalties of perjury:

The following percentage of ozone-depleting chemicals purchased from

_____

(name and address of seller)

will be used by Purchaser as a feedstock (as defined in § 52.4682-1(c)(3) of the Environmental Tax Regulations).

PRODUCT	PERCENTAGE	KILOGRAMS TO BE TRANSFORMED
CFC-11	_____	_____
CFC-12	_____	_____
CFC-113	_____	_____
CFC-114	_____	_____
CFC-115	_____	_____
Carbon tetrachloride	_____	_____
Methyl chloroform	_____	_____
Other (specify)	_____	_____

This certificate applies to (check and complete as applicable):

_____ All shipments to Purchaser at the following location(s):

_____
_____
_____

_____ All shipments to Purchaser under the following Purchaser account number(s):

_____
_____

Reg. § 52.4682-2(d)(2)(ii)

_____ All shipments to Purchaser under the following purchase order(s):

_____ One or more shipments to Purchaser identified as follows:

Purchaser will not claim a credit or refund under section 4682(d)(2)(B) of the Internal Revenue Code for any ozone-depleting chemicals covered by this certificate.

Purchaser understands that any use of the ozone-depleting chemicals to which this certificate applies other than as a feedstock may result in the withdrawal by the Internal Revenue Service of Purchaser's right to provide a certificate.

Purchaser will retain the business records needed to document the use as a feedstock of the ozone-depleting chemicals to which this certificate applies and will make such records available for inspection by Government officers.

Purchaser has not been notified by the Internal Revenue Service that its right to provide a certificate has been withdrawn.

Purchaser understands that the fraudulent use of this certificate may subject Purchaser and all parties making such fraudulent use of this certificate to a fine or imprisonment, or both, together with the costs of prosecution.

_____
Signature

_____
Printed or typed name of person signing

_____
Title of person signing

_____
Name of Purchaser

_____
Address

_____
Taxpayer Identifying Number

(3) *Certificate relating to ODCs used in the manufacture of rigid foam insulation.—(i) ODCs that will be resold to a second purchaser for use by the second purchaser in the manufacture of rigid foam insulation.—If the purchaser will resell the ODCs* to a second purchaser for use by such second purchaser in the manufacture of rigid foam insulation, the certificate provided by the purchaser must be in substantially the following form:

CERTIFICATE OF PURCHASER OF CHEMICALS THAT WILL BE RESOLD FOR USE BY THE SECOND PURCHASER IN THE MANUFACTURE OF RIGID FOAM INSULATION
(To support tax-free or tax-reduced sales under section 4682(g) of the Internal Revenue Code.)

Effective Date_____
Expiration Date_____
(not after 12/31/93)

The undersigned purchaser ("Purchaser") hereby certifies the following under penalties of perjury:
The following percentage of ozone-depleting chemicals purchased from

_____
(name and address of seller)

will be resold by Purchaser to persons (Second Purchasers) that certify to Purchaser that they are purchasing the ozone-depleting chemicals for use in the manufacture of rigid foam insulation (as defined in §52.4682-1(d)(3) and (4) of the Environmental Tax Regulations).

PRODUCT	PERCENTAGE
CFC-11	_____
CFC-12	_____
CFC-113	_____
CFC-114	_____
CFC-115	_____
Carbon tetrachloride	
Methyl chloroform	
Other (specify)	

This certificate applies to (check and complete as applicable):
____All shipments to Purchaser at the following locations(s):

Reg. §52.4682-2(d)(3)(i)

_____
_____

____All shipments to Purchaser under the following Purchaser account number(s):

_____
_____
_____

____All shipments to Purchaser under the following purchase order(s):

_____
_____
_____

____One or more shipments to Purchaser identified as follows:

_____
_____
_____

Purchaser will not claim a credit or refund under section 4682(g)(3) of the Internal Revenue Code for any ozone-depleting chemicals covered by this certificate.

Purchaser understands that any use by purchaser of the ozone-depleting chemicals to which this certificate applies other than for the purpose set forth in this certificate may result in the withdrawal by the Internal Revenue Service of Purchaser's right to provide a certificate.

Purchaser will retain the business records needed to document the sales covered by this certificate and will make such records available for inspection by Government officers. Purchaser also will retain and make available for inspection by Government officers the certificates of its Second Purchasers.

Purchaser has not been notified by the Internal Revenue Service that its right to provide a certificate has been withdrawn. In addition, the Internal Revenue Service has not notified Purchaser that the right to provide a certificate has been withdrawn from any Second Purchaser who will purchase ozone-depleting chemicals to which this certificate applies.

Purchaser understands that the fraudulent use of this certificate may subject Purchaser and all parties making such fraudulent use of this certificate to a fine or imprisonment, or both, together with the costs of prosecution.

_____
Signature

_____
Printed or typed name of person signing

_____
Title of person signing

_____
Name of Purchaser

_____
Address
_____

_____
Taxpayer Identifying Number

    (ii) *ODCs that will be used by the purchaser in the manufacture of rigid foam insulation.*—If the purchaser will use the ODCs in the manufacture of rigid foam insulation, the certificate provided by the purchaser must be in substantially the following form:

CERTIFICATE OF PURCHASER OF CHEMICALS THAT WILL BE USED BY THE PURCHASER IN THE MANUFACTURE OF RIGID FOAM INSULATION
(To support tax-free or tax-reduced sales under section 4682(g) of the Internal Revenue Code.)

Effective Date_____

Expiration Date_____

(not after 12/31/93)

The undersigned purchaser ("Purchaser") hereby certifies the following under penalties of perjury:

The following percentage of ozone-depleting chemicals purchased from

_____
(name and address of seller)

will be used by Purchaser in the manufacture of rigid foam insulation (as defined in § 52.4682-1(d)(3) and (4) of the Environmental Tax Regulations).

PRODUCT	PERCENTAGE
CFC-11	_____
CFC-12	_____
CFC-113	_____
CFC-114	_____
CFC-115	_____
Carbon tetrachloride	_____

Reg. § 52.4682-2(d)(3)(ii)

Methyl chloroform _____

Other (specify) _____ _____

This certificate applies to (check and complete as applicable):

___All shipments to Purchaser at the following location(s):

_____
_____
_____

___All shipments to Purchaser under the following Purchaser account number(s):

_____
_____
_____

___All shipments to Purchaser under the following purchase order(s):

_____
_____
_____

___One or more shipments to Purchaser identified as follows:

_____
_____
_____

Purchaser will not claim a credit or refund under section 4682(g)(3) of the Internal Revenue Code for any ozone-depleting chemicals covered by this certificate.

Purchaser understands that any use by Purchaser of the ozone-depleting chemicals to which this certificate applies other than in the manufacture of rigid foam insulation may result in the withdrawal by the Internal Revenue Service of Purchaser's right to provide a certificate.

Purchaser will retain the business records needed to document the use in the manufacture of rigid foam insulation of the ozone-depleting chemicals to which this certificate applies and will make such records available for inspection by Government officers.

Purchaser has not been notified by the Internal Revenue Service that its right to provide a certificate has been withdrawn.

Purchaser understands that the fraudulent use of this certificate may subject Purchaser and all parties making such fraudulent use of this certificate to a fine or imprisonment, or both, together with the costs of prosecution.

_____
Signature

_____
Printed or typed name of person signing

_____
Title of person signing

_____
Name of Purchaser

_____
Address
_____

Taxpayer Identifying Number

(4) *Certificate relating to ODCs used as medical sterilants.*—(i) *ODCs that will be resold for use by the second purchaser as medical sterilants.*—If the purchaser will resell the ODCs to a second pur-chaser for use by such second purchaser as medical sterilants, the certificate provided by the purchaser must be in substantially the following form:

CERTIFICATE OF PURCHASER OF CHEMICALS THAT WILL BE RESOLD FOR USE BY THE SECOND PURCHASER AS MEDICAL STERILANTS
(To support tax-reduced sales under
section 4682(g)(4) of the Internal Revenue Code.)

Effective Date _____
Effective Date _____

(not after 12/31/93)

The undersigned purchaser (Purchaser) certifies the following under penalties of perjury:

The following percentage of ozone-depleting chemicals purchased from:

_____

(Name of seller)

_____

(Address of seller)

Reg. §52.4682-2(d)(4)(i)

will be resold by Purchaser to persons (Second Purchasers) that certify to Purchaser that they are purchasing the ozone-depleting chemicals for use as medical sterilants (as defined in § 52.4682-1(g)(3) of the Environmental Tax Regulations).

Product	Percentage
CFC-12	

This certificate applies to (check and complete as applicable):

_____ All shipments to Purchaser at the following location(s):

_____ All shipments to Purchaser under the following Purchaser account number(s):

_____ All shipments to Purchaser under the following purchase order(s):

_____ One or more shipments to Purchaser identified as follows:

Purchaser will not claim a credit or refund under section 4682(g)(4) of the Internal Revenue Code for any ozone-depleting chemicals covered by this certificate.

Purchaser understands that any use by Purchaser of the ozone-depleting chemicals to which this certificate applies other than for the purpose set forth in this certificate may result in the withdrawal by the Internal Revenue Service of Purchaser's right to provide a certificate.

Purchaser will retain the business records needed to document the sales covered by this certificate and will make such records available for inspection by Government officers. Purchaser also will retain and make available for inspection by Government officers the certificates of its Second Purchasers.

Purchaser has not been notified by the Internal Revenue Service that its right to provide a certificate has been withdrawn. In addition, the Internal Revenue Service has not notified Purchaser that the right to provide a certificate has been withdrawn from any Second Purchaser who will purchase ozone-depleting chemicals to which this certificate applies.

Purchaser understands that the fraudulent use of this certificate may subject Purchaser and all parties making such fraudulent use of this certificate to a fine or imprisonment, or both, together with the costs of prosecution.

_____
Name of Purchaser

_____
Address of Purchaser

_____
Taxpayer Identifying Number of Purchaser

_____
Title of person signing

_____
Printed or typed name of person signing

_____
Signature

(ii) *ODCs that will be used by the purchaser as medical sterilants.*—If the purchaser will use the ODCs as medical sterilants, the certificate provided by the purchaser must be in substantially the following form:

**CERTIFICATE OF PURCHASER OF CHEMICALS
THAT WILL BE USED BY THE PURCHASER AS MEDICAL STERILANTS**
(To support tax-reduced sales under
section 4682(g)(4) of the Internal Revenue Code.)

Effective Date _____

Effective Date _____

(not after 12/31/93)

The undersigned purchaser (Purchaser) certifies the following under penalties of perjury:

The following percentage of ozone-depleting chemicals purchased from:

_____
(Name of seller)

_____

Reg. § 52.4682-2(d)(4)(ii)

(Address of seller)

will be used by Purchaser as medical sterilants (as defined in §52.4682-1(g)(3) of the Environmental Tax Regulations).

Product	Percentage
CFC-12	

This certificate applies to (check and complete as applicable):

_____ All shipments to Purchaser at the following location(s):

_____ All shipments to Purchaser under the following Purchaser account number(s):

_____ All shipments to Purchaser under the following purchase order(s):

_____ One or more shipments to Purchaser identified as follows:

Purchaser will not claim a credit or refund under section 4682(g)(4) of the Internal Revenue Code for any ozone-depleting chemicals covered by this certificate.

Purchaser understands that any use by Purchaser of the ozone-depleting chemicals to which this certificate applies other than as medical sterilants may result in the withdrawal by the Internal Revenue Service of Purchaser's right to provide a certificate.

Purchaser will retain the business records needed to document the use as medical sterilants of the ozone-depleting chemicals to which this certificate applies and will make such records available for inspection by Government officers.

Purchaser has not been notified by the Internal Revenue Service that its right to provide a certificate has been withdrawn.

Purchaser understands that the fraudulent use of this certificate may subject Purchaser and all parties making such fraudulent use of this certificate to a fine or imprisonment, or both, together with the costs of prosecution.

Name of Purchaser

Address of Purchaser

Taxpayer Identifying Number of Purchaser

Title of person signing

Printed or typed name of person signing

Signature

(5) *Certificate relating to ODCs used as propellants in metered-dose inhalers.*—(i) *ODCs that will be resold for use by the second purchaser as propellants in metered-dose inhalers.*—If the purchaser will resell the ODCs to a second purchaser for use by such second purchaser as propellants in metered-dose inhalers, the certificate provided by the purchaser must be in substantially the following form:

CERTIFICATE OF PURCHASER OF CHEMICALS THAT WILL BE RESOLD
FOR USE BY THE SECOND PURCHASER AS PROPELLANTS IN METERED-DOSE INHALERS

(To support tax-reduced sales under
section 4682(g)(4) of the Internal Revenue Code.)

Date _____

The undersigned purchaser (Purchaser) certifies the following under penalties of perjury:

The following percentage of ozone-depleting chemicals purchased from:

(Name of seller)

Reg. §52.4682-2(d)(5)(i)

(Address of seller)

will be resold by Purchaser to persons (Second Purchasers) that certify to Purchaser that they are purchasing the ozone-depleting chemicals for use as propellants in metered-dose inhalers (as defined in §52.4682-1(h)(3) of the Environmental Tax Regulations).

Product	Percentage
CFC-11	_____
CFC-12	_____
CFC-114	_____

This certificate applies to (check and complete as applicable):

_____ All shipments to Purchaser at the following location(s):

_____
_____
_____

_____ All shipments to Purchaser under the following Purchaser account number(s):

_____
_____
_____

_____ All shipments to Purchaser under the following purchase order(s):

_____
_____
_____

_____ One or more shipments to Purchaser identified as follows:

_____
_____
_____

Purchaser will not claim a credit or refund under section 4682(g)(4) of the Internal Revenue Code for any ozone-depleting chemicals covered by this certificate.

Purchaser understands that any use by Purchaser of the ozone-depleting chemicals to which this certificate applies other than for the purpose set forth in this certificate may result in the withdrawal by the Internal Revenue Service of Purchaser's right to provide a certificate.

Purchaser will retain the business records needed to document the sales covered by this certificate and will make such records available for inspection by Government officers. Purchaser also will retain and make available for inspection by Government officers the certificates of its Second Purchasers.

Purchaser has not been notified by the Internal Revenue Service that its right to provide a certificate has been withdrawn. In addition, the Internal Revenue Service has not notified Purchaser that the right to provide a certificate has been withdrawn from any Second Purchaser who will purchase ozone-depleting chemicals to which this certificate applies.

Purchaser understands that the fraudulent use of this certificate may subject Purchaser and all parties making such fraudulent use of this certificate to a fine or imprisonment, or both, together with the costs of prosecution.

Name of Purchaser
_____

Address of Purchaser
_____

Taxpayer Identifying Number of Purchaser
_____

Title of person signing
_____

Printed or typed name of person signing
_____

Signature

(ii) *ODCs that will be used by the purchaser as propellants in metered-dose inhalers.*—If the purchaser will use the ODCs as propellants in metered-dose inhalers, the certificate provided by the purchaser must be in substantially the following form:

CERTIFICATE OF PURCHASER OF CHEMICALS THAT WILL BE
USED BY THE PURCHASER AS PROPELLANTS IN METERED-DOSE INHALERS
(To support tax-reduced sales under
section 4682(g)(4) of the Internal Revenue Code.)

Date _____

The undersigned purchaser (Purchaser) certifies the following under penalties of perjury:

The following percentage of ozone-depleting chemicals purchased from:

_____

Reg. §52.4682-2(d)(5)(ii)

(Name of seller) _____

(Address of seller)
will be used by Purchaser as propellants in metered-dose inhalers (as defined in § 52.4682-1(h)(3) of the Environmental Tax Regulations).

Product	Percentage
CFC-11	_____
CFC-12	_____
CFC-114	_____

This certificate applies to (check and complete as applicable):

_____ All shipments to Purchaser at the following location(s):

_____
_____
_____

_____ All shipments to Purchaser under the following Purchaser account number(s):

_____
_____
_____

_____ All shipments to Purchaser under the following purchase order(s):

_____
_____
_____

_____ One or more shipments to Purchaser identified as follows:

_____
_____
_____

Purchaser will not claim a credit or refund under section 4682(g)(4) of the Internal Revenue Code for any ozone-depleting chemicals covered by this certificate.

Purchaser understands that any use by Purchaser of the ozone-depleting chemicals to which this certificate applies other than as propellants in metered-dose inhalers may result in the withdrawal by the Internal Revenue Service of Purchaser's right to provide a certificate.

Purchaser will retain the business records needed to document the use as propellants in metered-dose inhalers of the ozone-depleting chemicals to which this certificate applies and will make such records available for inspection by Government officers.

Purchaser has not been notified by the Internal Revenue Service that its right to provide a certificate has been withdrawn.

Purchaser understands that the fraudulent use of this certificate may subject Purchaser and all parties making such fraudulent use of this certificate to a fine or imprisonment, or both, together with the costs of prosecution.

Name of Purchaser _____

Address of Purchaser _____

Taxpayer Identifying Number of Purchaser _____

Title of person signing _____

Printed or typed name of person signing _____

Signature

[Reg. § 52.4682-2.]

☐ [*T.D.* 8370, 11-1-91. *Amended by T.D.* 8622, 10-10-95.]

[Reg. § 52.4682-3]

§ 52.4682-3. Imported taxable products.—
(a) *Overview; references to Tables; special rule for 1990.*—(1) *Overview.*—This section provides rules relating to the tax imposed on imported taxable products under section 4681, including rules for identifying imported taxable products, determining the weight of the ozone-depleting chemicals (ODCs) used as materials in the manufacture of such products, and computing the amount of tax on such products. See § 52.4681-1(a)(2) and (c) for general rules and definitions relating to the tax on imported taxable products.

(2) *References to Tables.*—When used in this section—

(i) The term "Imported Products Table" (Table) refers to the Table set forth in paragraph (f)(6) of this section; and

(ii) The term "current Imported Products Table" (current Table) used with respect to a product refers to the Table in effect on the date such product is first sold or used by the importer thereof.

Reg. § 52.4682-3(a)(2)(ii)

(3) *Special rule for 1990.*—In the case of products first sold or used before January 1, 1991, post-1990 ODCs (as defined in § 52.4681-1(c)(9)) shall not be taken into account in applying the rules of this section.

(b) *Imported taxable products.*—(1) *In general.*—(i) *Rule.*—Except as provided in paragraph (b)(2) of this section, the term "imported taxable product" means any product that—

(A) Is entered into the United States for consumption, use, or warehousing; and

(B) Is listed in the current Table.

(ii) *Example.*—The application of this paragraph (b)(1) may be illustrated by the following example:

Example. A brings a light truck with a Harmonized Tariff Schedule classification of 8704 into the customs territory and enters the truck for transportation and exportation. Although the truck is listed in the current Table, it is not an imported taxable product because it is not entered for consumption, use, or warehousing. The truck also would not be an imported taxable product if it were admitted to a foreign trade zone (rather than brought into the customs territory) for transportation and exportation.

(2) *Exceptions.*—(i) *In general.*—A product is not treated as an imported taxable product if—

(A) The product is listed in Part I of the current Table and the adjusted tax with respect to the product is *de minimis* (within the meaning of paragraph (b)(2)(ii) of this section); or

(B) The product is listed in Part II of the current Table, the adjusted tax with respect to the product is *de minimis* (within the meaning of paragraph (b)(2)(ii) of this section), and the ODCs (other than methyl chloroform) used as materials in the manufacture of the product were not used for purposes of refrigeration or air conditioning, creating an aerosol or foam, or manufacturing electronic components.

(ii) *De minimis adjusted tax.*—The adjusted tax with respect to a product is *de minimis* if such tax is less than one/tenth of one percent of the importer's cost of acquiring such product. The term "adjusted tax" means the tax that would be imposed under section 4681 on the ODCs used as materials in the manufacture of such product if such ODCs were sold in the United States and the base tax amount were $1.00.

(c) *Taxable event.*—(1) *In general.*—Except as otherwise provided in paragraphs (c)(2) and (3) of this section, the tax on an imported taxable product is imposed when the product is first sold or used (as defined in § 52.4681-1(c)(6) and (7)) by its importer. Thus, for example, imported taxable products that are warehoused or repackaged after entry and then exported without being sold or used in the United States are not subject to tax.

(2) *Election to treat importation as use.*—(i) *In general.*—An importer may elect to treat the entry of products into the United States as the use

of such products. In the case of imported taxable products to which an election under this paragraph (c)(2) applies—

(A) Tax is imposed on the products on the date of entry (as determined under paragraph (c)(2)(ii) of this section) if the products are entered into the United States after the election becomes effective;

(B) Tax is imposed on the products on the date the election becomes effective if the products were entered into the United States after December 31, 1989, and before the election becomes effective; and

(C) No tax is imposed if the products were entered into the United States before January 1, 1990.

(ii) *Date of entry.*—The date of entry is determined by reference to customs law. If the actual date is unknown, the importer may use any reasonable and consistent method to determine the date of entry, provided that such date is within 10 business days of arrival of products in the United States.

(iii) *Applicability of election.*—An election under this paragraph (c)(2) applies to all imported taxable products that are owned (and have not been used) by the importer at the time the election becomes effective and all imported taxable products that are entered into the United States by the importer after the election becomes effective. An election under this paragraph (c)(2) becomes effective at the beginning of the first calendar quarter to which the election applies. After October 9, 1990, the election may be revoked only with the consent of the Commissioner.

(iv) *Making the election.*—An election under this paragraph (c)(2) shall be made in accordance with the instructions for the return on which the importer is required to report liability for tax under section 4681.

(3) *Treating the sale of an article incorporating an imported taxable product as the first sale or use of such product.*—(i) *In general.*—In the case of articles to be sold, an importer may treat the sale of an article manufactured or assembled in the United States as the first sale or use of an imported taxable product incorporated in such article, but only if the importer—

(A) Has consistently treated the sale of similar articles as the first sale or use of similar imported taxable products; and

(B) Has not made an election under paragraph (c)(2) of this section.

(ii) *Similar articles and imported taxable products.*—An importer may establish any reasonable criteria for determining whether articles or imported taxable products are similar for purposes of this paragraph (c)(3).

(iii) *Establishment of consistent treatment.*—An importer has consistently treated the sale of similar articles as the first sale or use of similar imported taxable products only if such treatment is reflected in the computation of tax on the importer's returns for all prior calendar quarters in which such treatment would affect tax liability.

(iv) *Example*.—The application of this paragraph (c)(3) may be illustrated by the following example:

Example. (a) An importer of printed circuits and other electronic components uses those products in assembling television receivers in the United States and also uses the printed circuits in assembling VCRs in the United States. Under the importer's criteria for determining similarity, printed circuits are similar to other printed circuits, but not to the other electronic components. In addition, television receivers are similar to other television receivers, but not to VCRs. The importer has not made an election under paragraph (c)(2) of this section.

(b) Under this paragraph (c)(3), the importer may treat the sale of the television receivers as the first sale or use of the imported printed circuits incorporated into the television receivers. In that case, the tax on the printed circuits would be imposed when the television receivers are sold rather than when the printed circuits are used in assembling the television receivers.

(c) The importer may treat the sale of the television receivers as the first sale or use of the printed circuits incorporated into the television receivers even if the sale of the television receivers is not treated as the first sale or use of the other electronic components incorporated into the television receivers and even if the sale of VCRs is not treated as the first sale or use of the printed circuits incorporated into the VCRs. Under paragraph (c)(3)(i)(A) of this section, however, the importer must have consistently treated the sale of television receivers as the first sale or use of printed circuits incorporated into the receivers. Thus, in the case of television receivers that were assembled before January 1, 1990, and sold after December 31, 1989, the importer must have treated the sale of the television receivers as the first sale or use of the printed circuits incorporated into the television receivers when reporting tax under section 4681 with respect to such printed circuits.

(d) *ODCs used as materials in the manufacture of imported taxable products.*—(1) *ODC weight.*—The tax imposed on an imported taxable product under section 4681 is computed by reference to the weight of the ODCs used as materials in the manufacture of the product (ODC weight). The ODC weight of a product includes the weight of ODCs used as materials in the manufacture of any components of the product.

(2) *ODCs used as materials in the manufacture of a product.*—Except as provided in paragraph (d)(3) of this section, an ODC is used as a material in the manufacture of a product if the ODC is—

(i) Incorporated into the product;

(ii) Released into the atmosphere in the process of manufacturing the product; or

(iii) Otherwise used in the manufacture of the product (but only to the extent the cost of the ODC is properly allocable to the product).

(3) *Protective packaging.*—ODCs used in the manufacture of the protective material in which a product is packaged are not treated as ODCs used as materials in the manufacture of such product.

(4) *Examples.*—The provisions of this paragraph (d) may be illustrated by the following examples:

Example 1. A, a manufacturer located outside the United States, uses ODCs as a solvent to clean the printed circuits it manufactures and as a coolant in the air-conditioning system of the factory in which the printed circuits are manufactured. The ODCs used as a solvent are released into the atmosphere, and, under paragraph (d)(2)(ii) of this section, are used as materials in the manufacture of the printed circuits. The ODCs used as a coolant in the air-conditioning system are also used in the manufacture of the printed circuits. Under paragraph (d)(2)(iii) of this section, these ODCs are used as materials in the manufacture of the printed circuits only to the extent the cost of the ODCs is properly allocable to the printed circuits.

Example 2. B manufactures television receivers outside the United States and wraps them for shipping in a protective packing material manufactured with ODCs. Under paragraph (d)(3) of this section, the ODCs used in the manufacture of the protective packing material are not treated as ODCs used as a material in the manufacture of the television receivers.

(e) *Methods of determining ODC weight; computation of tax.*—(1) *In general.*—This paragraph (e) sets forth the methods to be used for determining the ODC weight of an imported taxable product and a method to be used in computing the tax when the ODC weight cannot be determined. The amount of tax is computed separately for each imported taxable product and the method to be used in determining the ODC weight or otherwise computing the tax is separately determined for each such product. Thus, an importer may use one method in computing the tax on some imported taxable products and different methods in computing the tax on other products. For example, an importer of telephone sets may compute the tax using the exact method described in paragraph (e)(2) of this section for determining the ODC weight of telephone sets supplied by one manufacturer and using the Table method described in paragraph (e)(3) of this section for telephone sets supplied by other manufacturers that have not provided sufficient information to allow the importer to use the exact method.

(2) *Exact method.*—If the importer determines the weight of each ODC used as a material in the manufacture of an imported taxable product and supports that determination with sufficient and reliable information, the ODC weight of the product is the weight so determined.

Reg. §52.4682-3(e)(2)

Under this method, the ODC weight of a mixture is equal to the weight of the ODCs contained in the mixture. Representations by the manufacturer of the product to the importer as to the weight of the ODCs used as materials in the manufacture of the product may be sufficient and reliable information for this purpose. Thus, a letter to the importer signed by the manufacturer may constitute sufficient and reliable information if the letter adequately identifies the product and states the weight of each ODC used as a material in the product's manufacture.

(3) *Table method.*—(i) *In general.*—If the ODC weight of an imported taxable product is not determined using the exact method described in paragraph (e)(2) of this section and the current Table specifies an ODC weight for the product, the ODC weight of the product is the Table ODC weight, regardless of what ODCs were used in the manufacture of the product. In computing the amount of tax, the Table ODC weight shall not be rounded.

(ii) *Special rules.*—(A) *Articles assembled in the United States.*—An importer that assembles finished articles in the United States may compute the amount of tax imposed on the imported taxable products incorporated into the finished article by using the Table ODC weight specified for the article instead of the Table ODC weights specified for the components. In order to compute the tax under this special rule, the importer must determine the actual number of articles manufactured. For example, if an importer manufactures 100 camcorders using imported subassemblies, the importer may compute the amount of tax on the subassemblies by using the Table ODC weight specified for camcorders. Thus, the tax imposed on the subassemblies is equal to the tax that would be imposed on 100 camcorders.

(B) *Combination method.*—This paragraph (e)(3)(ii)(B) applies to an imported taxable product if the current Table specifies weights for two or more ODCs with respect to the product and the importer of the product can determine the weight of any such ODC (and of any ODC used as a substitute for such ODC) and can support such determination with sufficient and reliable information. In determining the ODC weight of any such product, the importer may replace the weight specified in the Table for such ODC with the weight (as determined by the importer) of such ODC and its substitutes. For example, if an importer has sufficient and reliable information to determine the amount of CFC-12 included in a product as a coolant (and to determine that no ODCs have been used as substitutes for CFC-12) but cannot determine the amount of CFC-113 used in manufacturing the product's electronic components, the importer may use the weight specified in the Table for CFC-113 and the actual weight determined by the importer for CFC-12 in determining the ODC weight of the product.

(C) *ODCs used in the manufacture of rigid foam insulation.*—In computing the tax using the method described in this paragraph (e)(3), any ODC for which the Table specifies a weight followed by an asterisk (*) shall be treated as an ODC used in the manufacture of rigid foam insulation (as defined in § 52.4682-1(d)(3) and (4)).

(4) *Value method.*—(i) *General rule.*—If the importer cannot determine the ODC weight of an imported taxable product under the exact method described in paragraph (e)(2) of this section and the Table ODC weight of the product is not specified, the tax imposed on the product under section 4681 is one percent of the entry value of the product.

(ii) *Special rule for mixtures.*—If, in the case of an imported taxable product that is a mixture, the tax was determined under the method described in this paragraph (e)(4), the Commissioner may redetermine the tax based on the ODC weight of the mixture.

(5) *Adjustment for prior taxes.*—(i) *In general.*—If any manufacture with respect to an imported taxable product occurred in the United States or the product incorporates a taxed component or a taxed chemical was used in its manufacture, the product's ODC weight (or value) attributable to manufacture within the United States or to taxed components or taxed chemicals shall be disregarded in computing the tax on such product using a method described in paragraph (e)(2), (3), or (4) of this section.

(ii) *Taxed component.*—The term "taxed component" means any component that previously was subject to tax as an imported taxable product or that would have been so taxed if section 4681 had been in effect for periods before January 1, 1990.

(iii) *Taxed chemical.*—The term "taxed chemical" means any ODC that previously was subject to tax.

(6) *Examples.*—The application of this paragraph (e) may be illustrated by the following examples:

Example 1. A is an importer (as defined in § 52.4681-1(c)(5)) of VCRs. The HTS classification for the VCRs is 8528.10.40. VCRs classified under HTS under HTS heading 8528.10.40 are imported taxable products because they are listed in the Table (contained in paragraph (f)(6) of this section) by name and HTS heading (as described in paragraph (f)(3)(i) of this section). Each VCR is wrapped in protective packing material manufactured with ODCs. A imports and sells 100 VCRs during the first calendar quarter of 1991. A may determine the ODC weight for the VCRs by reference to the Table. The Table ODC weight specified for VCRs classified under HTS heading 8528.10.40 is 0.0586 pound of CFC-113. This weight does not take protective packaging into account. The amount of tax for the first quarter of 1991 is $6.42 (0.0586 (the ODC weight) × 100 (the number of VCRs sold in the quarter) × $1.37

(the base tax amount for CFC-113 in 1991) × 0.8 (the ozone-depletion factor for CFC-113)). If A uses the exact method (as described in paragraph (e)(2) of this section) to determine the ODC weight for the VCRs, A does not take into account the ODCs used in the manufacture of the protective packaging. (Imported protective packaging containing foams made with ODCs other than foams defined in § 52.4682-1(d)(3) is subject to tax, however, if the packaging is sold as packaging or first used as packaging in the United States.)

Example 2. The facts are the same as in *Example 1*, except that A's VCRs are manufactured using methyl chloroform as the solvent instead of CFC-113. If A does not use the exact method to determine the weight of the methyl chloroform used in the manufacture of the VCRs, A must, under paragraphs (e)(3)(i) and (e)(4)(i) of this section, determine the ODC weight by reference to the Table. If A used the Table ODC weight, the computation of tax is the same as in *Example 1*, using the base tax amount and ozone-depletion factor for CFC-113. A does not substitute the base tax amount and ozone-depletion factor of methyl chloroform for those of CFC-113.

Example 3. B imports and sells mixtures of ethylene oxide and CFC-12. The mixture is 88 percent CFC-12 by weight. B also imports and sells R-502. The R-502 is 51 percent CFC-115 by weight. In the first calendar quarter of 1991 B sells 100 pounds of imported ethylene oxide/CFC-12 mixture and 10,000 pounds of imported R-502. The ethylene/CFC-12 mixture and the R-502 are imported taxable products because they are listed in Part I of the Table (contained in paragraph (f)(6) of this section). Under the exact method described in paragraph (e)(2) of this section, B computes the tax based on 88 pounds of CFC-12, the amount of ODCs contained in the imported ethylene oxide mixture, and based on 5100 pounds of CFC-115, the amount of ODCs in the imported R-502.

(f) *Imported Products Table.*—(1) *In general.*— This paragraph (f) contains rules relating to the Imported Products Table (Table) and sets forth the Table. The Table lists all the products that are subject to the tax on imported taxable products and specifies the Table ODC weight of each product for which such a weight has been determined.

(2) *Applicability of Table.*—(i) *In general.*—Except as provided in paragraph (f)(2)(ii) of this section, the Table contained in paragraph (f)(6) of this section is effective on January 1, 1990.

(ii) *Treatment of certain products.*—(A) Products included in a listing that is preceded by a double asterisk (**) in the Table shall not be treated as imported taxable products until October 1, 1990.

(B) Products included in a listing that is preceded by a triple asterisk (***) in the Table shall not be treated as imported taxable products until January 1, 1992.

(3) *Identification of products.*—(i) *In general.*—Each listing in the Table identifies a product by name and includes only products that are described by that name. Most listings (other than listings for mixtures) identify a product by both name and HTS heading. In such cases, a product is included in that listing only if the product is described by that name and the rate of duty on the product is determined by reference to that HTS heading. However, the product is included in that listing even if it is manufactured with or contains a different ODC than the ODC specified in the Table.

(ii) *Electronic items not listed by specific name.*—(A) *In general.*—Part II of the Table contains listings for electronic items that are not included within any other listing in the Table. An imported product is included in these listings only if such imported product—

(1) Is an electronic component listed in chapters 84, 85, or 90 of the Harmonized Tariff Schedule; or

(2) Contains components described in paragraph (f)(3)(ii)(A)(1) of this section and more than 15 percent of the cost of the imported product is attributable to such components.

(B) *Electronic component.*—For purposes of this paragraph (f)(3)(ii), an electronic component is a component whose operation involves the use of nonmechanical amplification or switching devices such as tubes, transistors, and integrated circuits. Such components do not include passive electrical devices such as resistors and capacitors.

(C) *Certain items not included.*—Items such as screws, nuts, bolts, plastic parts, and similar specially fabricated parts that may be used to construct an electronic item are not themselves included in the listing for electronic items not otherwise listed in the Table.

(iii) *Examples.*—The application of this paragraph (f)(3) may be illustrated by the following examples:

Example 1. The Table lists "electronic integrated circuits and microassemblies; HTS heading 8542." A bipolar transistor under HTS heading 8542.11.00.05 is included in this listing because a bipolar transistor is a type of electronic integrated circuit and HTS heading 8542.11.00.05 is included within HTS heading 8542.

Example 2. The Table lists "radios; HTS heading 8527.19," "radio combinations; HTS heading 8527.11" and "radio combinations; HTS heading 8527.31." A radio classified under HTS heading 8527.19 is not included within either listing for radio combinations. However, a radio classified under HTS heading 8527.19.00.20 is included within the listing for radios; HTS heading 8527.19. A radio combination classified under HTS heading 8527.11.20 is included within the listing for radio combinations; HTS heading 8527.11 but not the listing for radio combinations; HTS heading 8527.31. Any radio or radio combination not classified under the

Reg. § 52.4682-3(f)(3)(iii)

HTS heading for any other listing is included in the listing for electronic items not otherwise listed.

(4) *Rules for listing products.*—Products are listed in the Table in accordance with the following rules:

(i) *Listing in Part I.*—A product is listed in Part I of the Table if it is a mixture containing ODCs. In addition, a product other than a mixture containing ODCs will be listed in Part I of a revised Table if the Commissioner has determined that—

(A) The ODC weight of the product is not *de minimis* when the product is produced using the predominant method of manufacturing the product; and

(B) None of the ODCs used as materials in the manufacture of the product under the predominant method are used for purposes of refrigeration or air conditioning, creating an aerosol or foam, or manufacturing electronic components.

(ii) *Listing in Part II.*—A product is listed in Part II of the Table if the Commissioner has determined that the ODCs used as materials in the manufacture of the product under the predominant method are used for purposes of refrigeration or air conditioning, creating an aerosol or foam, or manufacturing electronic components.

(iii) *Listing in Part III.*—A product is listed in Part III of the Table if the Commissioner has determined that the product is not an imported taxable product and the product would otherwise be included within a listing in Part II of the Table. For example, floppy disk drive units are listed in Part III because they are not imported taxable products and they would, but for their listing in Part III, be included within the Part II listing for electronic items not specifically identified.

(5) *Table ODC weight.*—The Table ODC weight of a product is the weight, determined by the Commissioner, of the ODCs that are used as materials in the manufacture of the product under the predominant method of manufacturing. The Table ODC weight is given in pounds per single unit of product unless otherwise specified.

(6) *Table.*—The Table is set forth below:

IMPORTED PRODUCTS TABLE

PART I—Products that are mixtures containing ODCs

Mixtures containing ODCs, including but not limited to:
—anti-static sprays
—automotive products such as "carburetor cleaner," "stop leak," and "oil charge"
—cleaning solvents
—contact cleaners
—degreasers
—dusting sprays
—electronic circuit board coolants
—electronic solvents
—ethylene oxide/CFC-12
—fire extinguisher preparations and charges
—flux removers for electronics
—insect and wasp sprays
—mixtures of ODCs
—propellants
—refrigerants

PART II—Products in which ODCs are used for purposes of refrigeration or air conditioning, creating an aerosol or foam, or manufacturing electronic components

Product Name	Harmonized Tariff Schedule Heading	ODC	ODC Weight
Rigid foam insulation defined in §52.4682-1(d)(3)			
Foams made with ODCs, other than foams defined in §52.4682-1(d)(3)			
Scrap flexible foams made with ODCs			
Medical products containing ODCs:			
surgical staplers			
cryogenic medical instruments			
drug delivery systems			
inhalants			
Dehumidifiers, household	8415.82.00.50	CFC-12	0.344
Chillers:	8415.82.00.65		
charged with CFC-12		CFC-12	1600.
charged with CFC-114		CFC-114	1250.
charged with R-500		CFC-12	1920.
Refrigerator-freezers, household:			

Reg. §52.4682-3(f)(4)

Product Name	Harmonized Tariff Schedule Heading	ODC	ODC Weight
not > 184 liters	8418.10.00.10	CFC-11	1.08*
		CFC-12	0.13
> 184 liters but	8418.10.00.20	CFC-11	1.32*
not > 269 liters		CFC-12	0.26
> 269 liters but	8418.10.00.30	CFC-11	1.54*
not > 382 liters		CFC-12	0.35
> 382 liters	8418.10.00.40	CFC-11	1.87*
		CFC-12	0.35
Refrigerators, household			
not > 184 liters	8418.21.00.10	CFC-11	1.08*
		CFC-12	0.13
> 184 liters but	8418.21.00.20	CFC-11	1.32*
not > 269 liters		CFC-12	0.26
> 269 liters but	8418.21.00.30	CFC-11	1.54*
not > 382 liters		CFC-12	0.35
> 382 liters	8418.21.00.90	CFC-11	1.87*
		CFC-12	0.35
Freezers, household	8418.30	CFC-11	2.*
		CFC-12	0.4
Freezers, household	8418.40	CFC-11	2.*
		CFC-12	0.4
Refrigerating	8418.50	CFC-11	50.*
display counters		CFC-12	260.
not > 227 kg			
Icemaking machines:	8418.69		
charged with CFC-12		CFC-12	1.4
charged with R-502		CFC-115	3.39
Drinking water coolers:	8418.69		
charged with CFC-12		CFC-12	0.21
charged with R-500		CFC-12	0.22
Centrifugal chillers, hermetic:	8418.69		
charged with CFC-12		CFC-12	1600.
charged with CFC-114		CFC-114	1250.
charged with R-500		CFC-12	1920.
Reciprocating chillers:	8418.69		
charged with CFC-12		CFC-12	200.
Mobile refrigeration systems:	8418.99		
containers		CFC-12	15.
trucks		CFC-12	11.
trailers		CFC-12	20.
Refrigeration condensing units:			
not > 746W	8418.99.00.05	CFC-12	0.3
> 746W but not > 2.2KW	8418.99.00.10	CFC-12	1.
> 2.2KW but not > 7.5KW	8418.99.00.15	CFC-12	3.
> 7.5KW but not > 22.3KW	8418.99.00.20	CFC-12	8.5
> 22.3 KW	8418.99.00.25	CFC-12	17.
Fire extinguishers, charged w/ODCs	8424		
Electronic typewriters and word processors	8469	CFC-113	0.2049
Electronic calculators	8470.10	CFC-113	0.0035
Electronic calculators w/printing device	8470.21	CFC-113	0.0057
Electronic calculators	8470.29	CFC-113	0.0035
Account machines	8470.40	CFC-113	0.1913
Cash registers	8470.50	CFC-113	0.1913
Digital automatic data processing machines w/ cathode ray tube, not included in subheading 8471.20.00.90	8471.20	CFC-113	0.3663
Laptops, notebooks, and pocket computers	8471.20.00.90	CFC-113	0.03567
Digital processing units w/entry value:			
not > $100K	8471.91	CFC-113	0.498
> $100K	8471.91	CFC-113	27.6667
Combined input/output units (terminals)	8471.92	CFC-113	0.36
Keyboards	8471.92	CFC-113	0.0742
Display units	8471.92	CFC-113	0.0386
Printer units	8471.92	CFC-113	0.1558
Input or output units	8471.92	CFC-113	0.1370
Hard magnetic disk drive units not included in subheading 8471.93.10 for a disk of a diameter:			

Reg. §52.4682-3(f)(6)

Product Name	Harmonized Tariff Schedule Heading	ODC	ODC Weight
not > 9 cm (3½ inches)	8471.93	CFC-113	0.2829
> 9 cm (3½ inches) but not > 21 cm (8¼ inches)	8471.93	CFC-113	1.1671
Nonmagnetic storage units w/entry value > $1,000	8471.93	CFC-113	2.7758
Magnetic disk drive units for a disk of a diameter over 21 cm (8¼ inches)	8471.93.10	CFC-113	4.0067
Power supplies	8471.99.30	CFC-113	0.0655
Electronic office machines	8472	CFC-113	0.0010
Populated cards for digital processing units in subheading 8471.91 w/value:			
not > $100K	8473.30	CFC-113	0.1408
> $100K	8473.30	CFC-113	4.82
Automatic goods-vending machines with refrigerating device	8476.11	CFC-12	0.45
Microwave ovens with electronic controls, with capacity of:	8516.5		
0.99 cu. ft. or less		CFC-113	0.03
1.0 through 1.3 cu. ft.		CFC-113	0.0441
1.31 cu. ft. or greater		CFC-113	0.0485
Microwave oven combinations with electronic controls	8516.60.40.60	CFC-113	0.0595
Telephone sets w/entry value:			
not > $11.00	8517.10	CFC-113	0.0225
> $11.00	8517.10	CFC-113	0.1
Teleprinters and teletypewriters	8517.20	CFC-113	0.1
Switching equipment not included in subheading 8517.30.20	8517.30	CFC-113	0.1267
Private branch exchange switching equipment	8517.30.20	CFC-113	0.0753
Modems	8517.40	CFC-113	0.0225
Intercoms	8517.81	CFC-113	0.0225
Facsimile machines	8517.82	CFC-113	0.0225
Loudspeakers, microphones, headphones, and electric sound amplifier sets, not included in subheading 8518.30.10	8518	CFC-113	0.0022
Telephone handsets	8518.30.10	CFC-113	0.0420
Turntables, record players, cassette players, and other sound reproducing apparatus	8519	CFC-113	0.0022
Magnetic tape recorders and other sound recording apparatus, not included in subheading 8520.20	8520	CFC-113	0.0022
Telephone answering machines	8520.20	CFC-113	0.1
Color video recording/reproducing apparatus	8521.10.00.20	CFC-113	0.0586
Videodisc players	8521.90	CFC-113	0.0106
Cordless handset telephones	8525.20.50	CFC-113	0.1
Cellular communication equipment	8525.20.60	CFC-113	0.4446
TV cameras	8525.30	CFC-113	1.4230
Camcorders	8525.30	CFC-113	0.0586
Radio combinations	8527.11	CFC-113	0.0022
Radios	8527.19	CFC-113	0.0014
Motor vehicle radios with or w/o tape player	8527.21	CFC-113	0.0021
Radio combinations	8527.31	CFC-113	0.0022
Radios	8527.32	CFC-113	0.0014
Tuners w/o speaker	8527.39.00.20	CFC-113	0.0022
Television receivers	8528	CFC-113	0.0386
VCRs	8528.10.40	CFC-113	0.0586
Home satellite earth stations	8528.10.80.55	CFC-113	0.0106
Electronic assemblies for HTS headings 8525, 8527, & 8528	8529.90	CFC-113	0.0816
Indicator panels incorporating liquid crystal devices or light emitting diodes	8531.20	CFC-113	0.0146
Printed circuits	8534	CFC-113	0.001
Computerized numerical controls	8537.10.00.30	CFC-113	0.1306
Diodes, crystals, transistors and other similar discrete semiconductor devices	8541	CFC-113	0.0001
Electronic integrated circuits and microassemblies	8542	CFC-113	0.0002
Signal generators	8543.20	CFC-113	0.6518

Reg. §52.4682-3(f)(6)

Product Name	Harmonized Tariff Schedule Heading	ODC	ODC Weight
Avionics	8543.90.40	CFC-113	0.9150
Signal generators subassemblies	8543.90.80	CFC-113	0.1265
Insulated or refrigerated railway freight cars	8606	CFC-11	100.*
Passenger automobiles:	8703		
foams (interior)		CFC-11	0.8
foams (exterior)		CFC-11	0.7
with charged a/c		CFC-12	2.
without charged a/c		CFC-12	0.2
electronics		CFC-113	0.5
Light trucks:	8704		
foams (interior)		CFC-11	0.6
foams (exterior)		CFC-11	0.1
with charged a/c		CFC-12	2.
without charged a/c		CFC-12	0.2
electronics		CFC-113	0.4
** Heavy trucks and tractors, GVW 33,001 lbs or more:	8704		
foams (interior)		CFC-11	0.6
foams (exterior)		CFC-11	0.1
with charged a/c		CFC-12	3.
without charged a/c		CFC-12	0.2
electronics		CFC-113	0.4
Motorcycles with seat foamed with ODCs	8711	CFC-11	0.04
Bicycles with seat foamed with ODCs	8712	CFC-11	0.04
Seats foamed with ODCs	8714.95	CFC-11	0.04
Aircraft	8802	CFC-12	0.25 lb/1000 lbs Operating Empty Weight (OEW)
			30.0 lbs/1000 lbs
		CFC-13	OEW
Optical fibers	9001	CFC-12	0.005 lb/thousand feet
Electronics cameras	9006	CFC-113	0.01
Photocopiers	9009	CFC-113	0.0426
Avionics	9014.20	CFC-113	0.915
Electronic drafting machines	9017	CFC-113	0.12
Complete patient	9018.19.80	CFC-12	0.94
monitoring systems		CFC-113	3.4163
Complete patient monitoring systems; subassemblies thereof	9018.19.80.60	CFC-113	1.932
Physical or chemical			
analysis instruments	9027	CFC-12	0.0003
		CFC-113	0.0271
Oscilloscopes	9030	CFC-11	0.49
		CFC-12	0.5943
		CFC-113	0.2613
Foam chairs	9401	CFC-11	0.3
Foam sofas	9401	CFC-11	0.75
Foam mattresses	9404.21	CFC-11	1.6
Electronic games and electronic components thereof	9504	CFC-113	
Electronic items not otherwise listed in the Table:			
included in HTS chapters 84, 85, 90		CFC-113	0.0004 pound/ $1.00 of entry value
*** not included in HTS chapters 84, 85, 90		CFC-113	0.0004 pound/ $1.00 of entry value

PART III—Products that are not Imported Taxable Products

Product Name	Harmonized Tariff Schedule Heading
Room air conditioners	8415.10.00.6
Dishwashers	8422.11
Clothes washers	8450.11
Clothes dryers	8451.21
Floppy disk drive units	8471.93
Transformers and inductors	8504
Toasters	8516.72
Unrecorded media	8523
Recorded media	8524

Product Name	Harmonized Tariff Schedule Heading
Capacitors	8532
Resistors	8533
Switching apparatus	8536
Cathode tubes	8540

* See paragraph (e)(3)(ii)(C) of this section. Denotes an ODC used in the manufacture of rigid foam insulation.
** See paragraph (f)(2)(ii)(A) of this section. Denotes products for which the effective date is October 1, 1990.
*** See paragraph (f)(2)(ii)(B) of this section. Denotes products for which the effective date is January 1, 1992.

(g) *Requests for modification of Table.*—(1) *In general.*—Any manufacturer or importer of a product may request that the Secretary modify the Table in any of the following respects:

(i) Adding a product to the Table and specifying its Table ODC weight.

(ii) Removing a product from the Table.

(iii) Changing or specifying the Table ODC weight of a product.

(2) *Form of request.*—The Secretary will consider a request for modification that includes the following:

(i) The name, address, taxpayer identifying number, and principal place of business of the requester.

(ii) For each product with respect to which a modification is requested:

(A) The name of the product;

(B) The HTS heading or subheading;

(C) The type of modification requested;

(D) The Table ODC weight that should be specified for the product if the request related to adding a product or changing or specifying its Table ODC weight; and

(E) The data supporting the request.

(3) *Address.*—The address for submission of requests under this paragraph (g) is: Internal Revenue Service, P.O. Box 7604, Ben Franklin Station, Attn: CC:CORP:T:R (Imported Products Table), room 5228, Washington, D.C. 20044.

(4) *Public inspection and copying.*—Requests submitted under this paragraph (g) will be available in the Internal Revenue Service Freedom of Information Reading Room for public inspection and copying. [Reg. § 52.4682-3.]

☐ [*T.D.* 8370, 11-1-91.]

[Reg. § 52.4682-4]

§ 52.4682-4. Floor stocks tax.—(a) *Overview.*—This section provides rules for identifying ozone-depleting chemical (ODCs) that are subject to the floor stocks tax imposed by section 4682(h)(1), determining the person that is liable for the tax, and computing the amount of the tax. See § 52.4681-1(a)(3) and (c) for general rules and definitions relating to the floor stocks tax.

(b) *Identifying rules.*—(1) *ODCs subject to floor stocks tax; ODCs held for sale or for use in further manufacture.*—(i) *In general.*—The floor stocks tax is imposed only on an ODC that is held for sale or for use in further manufacture on the date the tax is imposed. This paragraph (b)(1) provides rules for identifying ODCs held for sale or for use in further manufacture.

(ii) *Held for sale.*—(A) *In general.*—For purposes of determining whether an ODC is held for sale, the term "sale" shall have the meaning set forth in § 52.4681-1(c)(6). ODCs held for sale include ODCs that will be sold in connection with the provision of services or in connection with the sale of a manufactured article and, in such cases, include ODCs that will be sold without the statement of a separate charge for those ODCs.

(B) *ODCs held by a government.*—An ODC that is held by a government for its own use is not held for sale even if the ODC will be transferred between agencies or other subdivisions that have or are required to have different employer identification numbers.

(iii) *Held for use in further manufacture.*—Except as otherwise provided in paragraph (b)(2)(v) of this section, an ODC is held for use in further manufacture if—

(A) The ODC will be used as a material (within the meaning of paragraph (b)(1)(iv) of this section) in the manufacture of an article; and

(B) Such article will be held for sale.

(iv) *Use as material.*—(A) *In general.*—Except as provided in paragraph (b)(1)(iv)(B) of this section, an ODC will be used as a material in the manufacture of an article if the ODC will be—

(1) Incorporated into the article; or

(2) Released into the atmosphere in the process of manufacturing the article.

(B) *ODCs used in equipment.*—For purposes of the floor stocks tax, an ODC is not used as a material in the manufacture of an article if the ODC is (or will be) contained in equipment used in such manufacture and the ODC will be used for its intended purpose without being released from such equipment. Thus, ODCs that are (or will be) used as coolants in a factory's air-conditioning system are not used as materials in the manufacture of articles produced in the factory.

(v) *Storage containers.*—The floor stocks tax is imposed on an ODC without regard to the type or size of the storage container in which the ODC is held. Thus, the tax may apply to an ODC whether it is in a 14-ounce can or a 30-pound tank.

(vi) *Examples.*—The provisions of this paragraph (b)(1) may be illustrated by the following examples:

Example 1. A, a manufacturer of air conditioners, holds an ODC for use in air conditioners that it will manufacture and sell. A holds the ODC for use in further manufacture.

Example 2. B, a manufacturer of electronic components, holds an ODC for use as a solvent to clean printed circuits that it will sell to computer manufacturers. B holds the ODC for use in further manufacture.

Example 3. C, an automobile dealer, holds an ODC for use in charging air conditioners installed in automobiles that it sells to retail customers. C does not hold the ODC for use in further manufacture. C does, however, hold the ODC for sale, even if the customers are not separately charged for ODCs used in the automobile air conditioners.

Example 4. D operates an air-conditioning repair service and holds an ODC for use in repairing air conditioners for its customers. D holds the ODC for sale even if the customers are not separately charged for ODCs used in the repairs.

Example 5. E, a grocery-store chain, holds an ODC for use in its refrigeration units. E does not hold the ODC for sale or for use in further manufacture.

Example 6. F, a bank, holds an ODC for use in its fire extinguishers to protect the computer system. F does not hold the ODC for sale or for use in further manufacture.

Example 7. G, a government agency, holds an ODC for use in the refrigeration equipment of its various units. The units have separate employer identification numbers. The ODC is stored in a central warehouse until needed by a unit and then transferred to the unit upon request. G does not hold the ODC for sale or for use in further manufacture.

(2) Except as otherwise provided in paragraphs (d)(2) and (d)(3) of this section, the floor stocks tax is not imposed on any ODC in any year in which the base tax amount does not increase.

(i) *Mixtures.*—(A) *Tax imposed on January 1, 1990.*—In the case of the floor stocks tax imposed on January 1, 1990, the tax is not imposed on an ODC that has been mixed with any other ingredients.

(B) *Taxes imposed after 1990.*—(1) *In general.*—In the case of the floor stocks tax imposed on January 1 of a calendar year after 1990, the tax is not imposed on an ODC that has been mixed with any other ingredients, but only if it is established that such ingredients contribute to the accomplishment of the purpose for which the mixture will be used. A mixture is not exempt from tax under this paragraph (b)(2)(i)(B), however, if it contains only an ODC and an inert ingredient that doe snot contribute to the accomplishment of the purpose for which the mixture will be used.

(2) *Exception.*—In the case of a floor stocks tax imposed on or after January 1, 1992, a mixture is not exempt from floor stocks tax under this paragraph (b)(2)(i)(B) if it contains only ODCs and one or more stabilizers. For this

purpose, the term "stabilizer" means an ingredient needed to maintain the chemical integrity of the ODC.

(C) *Examples.*—The provisions of this paragraph (b)(2)(i) may be illustrated by the following examples:

Example 1. The floor stocks tax is not imposed on the ODCs contained in refrigerants such as R-500 and R-502 because such products are mixtures of ODCs and other chemicals that contribute to the accomplishment of the purpose for which the mixture will be used.

Example 2. The floor stocks tax is not imposed on the ODCs contained in automotive products used for checking for leaks because such products are a mixture of ODCs and small amounts of dyes and oils that contribute to the accomplishment of the purpose for which the mixture will be used.

Example 3. The floor stocks tax is not imposed on Halon 1301 pressurized with nitrogen. Although nitrogen is an inert ingredient, it contributes to the accomplishment of the purpose for which the mixture will be used.

Example 4. On January 1, 1993, the floor stocks tax is imposed on methyl chloroform that is stabilized to prevent hydrolization or chemical reaction during transportation or use, unless the stabilized methyl chloroform has also been mixed with other ingredients that contribute to the accomplishment of the purpose for which the mixture will be used.

(ii) *Manufactured articles.*—The floor stocks tax is not imposed on an ODC that is contained in a manufactured article in which the ODC will be used for its intended purpose without being released from such article. For example, the tax is not imposed on the ODCs contained in the cooling coils of a refrigerator even if the refrigerator is held for sale. However, the tax is imposed on a can of ODC used to recharge an air conditioning unit because the ODC must be expelled from the can in order to be used. Similarly, beginning in 1991, the tax is imposed on Halons contained in a fire extinguisher held for sale because such ODCs must be expelled from the fire extinguisher in order to be used.

(iii) *Recycled ODCs.*—The floor stocks tax is not imposed on ODCs that have been reclaimed or recycled. For example, the tax is not imposed on an ODC that is held for use in further manufacture after being used as a solvent and recycled.

(iv) *ODCs held by the manufacturer or importer.*—The floor stocks tax is not imposed on ODCs held by their manufacturer or importer.

(v) *ODCs used as a feedstock.*—(A) *In general.*—The floor stocks tax is not imposed on any ODC that was sold in a qualifying sale for use as a feedstock (as defined in §52.4682-1(c)).

(B) *Post-1989 ODCs sold before January 1, 1990; post-1990 ODCs sold before January 1,*

Reg. §52.4682-4(b)(2)(v)(B)

1991.—A post-1989 ODC that was sold by its manufacturer or importer before January 1, 1990, or a post-1990 ODC that was sold by its manufacturer or importer before January 1, 1991, shall be treated, for purposes of this paragraph (b)(2)(v), as an ODC that was sold in a qualifying sale for purposes of §52.4682-1(c) if the ODC will be used as a feedstock (within the meaning of §52.4682-1(c)(3)).

(vi) *ODCs to be exported.*—(A) *In general.*—The floor stocks tax is not imposed on any ODC that was sold in a qualifying sale for export (as defined in §52.4682-5(d)(1)).

(B) *ODCs sold before January 1, 1993.*—An ODC that was sold by its manufacturer or importer before January 1, 1993, is treated, for purposes of this paragraph (b)(2)(vi), as an ODC that was sold in a qualifying sale for export for purposes of §52.4682-5(d)(1) if the ODC will be exported.

(vii) *ODCs used as propellants in metered-dose inhalers; years after 1992.*—(A) *In general.*—The floor stocks tax is not imposed on January 1 of calendar years after 1992 on any ODC that was sold in a qualifying sale for use as a propellant in a metered-dose inhaler (as defined in §52.4682-1(h)).

(B) *ODCs sold before January 1, 1993.*—An ODC that was sold by its manufacturer or importer before January 1, 1993, is treated, for purposes of this paragraph (b)(2)(vii), as an ODC that was sold in a qualifying sale for purposes of §52.4682-1(h) if the ODC will be used as a propellant in a metered-dose inhaler (within the meaning of §52.4682-1(h)).

(viii) *ODCs used as medical sterilants; 1993.*—The floor stocks tax is not imposed in 1993 on any ODC held for use as a medical sterilant (as defined in §52.4682-1(g)).

(c) *Person liable for tax.*—(1) *In general.*—The person liable for the floor stocks tax on an ODC is the person that holds the ODC on a date on which the tax is imposed. The person who holds the ODC is the person who has title to the ODC (whether or not delivery to such person has been made) as of the first moment of such date. The person who has title at such time is determined under applicable local law.

(2) *Special rule.*—Each business unit that has, or is required to have, its own employer identification number is treated as a separate person for purposes of the floor stocks tax. For example, a chain of automotive parts stores that has one employer identification number is one person for purposes of the floor stocks tax, and a parent corporation and subsidiary corporation that each have a different employer identification number are two persons for purposes of the floor stocks tax.

(d) *Computation of tax; tentative tax amount.*—(1) *In general.*—(i) *Generally applicable rules.*—This paragraph (d) provides rules for determining the tentative tax amount and the amount of the floor stocks tax. Section 52.4681-1(a)(3) provides that the amount of the floor stocks tax on an ODC is determined by reference to a tentative tax amount. The tentative tax amount is the amount of tax that would be imposed on the ODC under section 4681(a)(1) if a sale of the ODC by the manufacturer or importer had occurred on the date the floor stocks tax is imposed. The amount of the floor stocks tax imposed on the ODCs contained in a nonexempt mixture is computed on the basis of the weight of the ODCs in that mixture.

(ii) *Floor stocks tax imposed on post-1989 ODCs on January 1, 1990.*—The floor stocks tax imposed on post-1989 ODCs (as defined in §52.4681-1(c)(9)) on January 1, 1990, is equal to the tentative tax amount. See paragraph (d)(2) of this section for rules relating to the floor stocks tax imposed on ODCs used in the manufacture of rigid foam insulation. See paragraph (d)(3) of this section for rules relating to the floor stocks tax imposed on Halons.

(iii) *Floor stocks tax imposed on post-1990 ODCs on January 1, 1991.*—The floor stocks tax imposed on post-1990 ODCs (as defined in §52.4681-1(c)(9)) on January 1, 1991, is equal to the tentative tax amount.

(iv) *Other floor stocks taxes.*—(A) *In general.*—The following rules apply for floor stocks taxes imposed on post-1989 ODCs after January 1, 1990, and on post-1990 ODCs after January 1, 1991:

(1) The tentative tax amount is determined, except as provided in paragraph (d)(2), (3), or (4) of this section, by reference to the rate of tax prescribed in section 4681(b)(1)(B) and the ozone-depletion factors prescribed in section 4682(b).

(2) The amount of the floor stocks tax on an ODC is equal to the amount by which the tentative tax amount exceeds the amount of taxes previously imposed on the ODC.

(B) *Example.*—The application of this paragraph (d)(1)(iv) may be illustrated by the following example:

Example. The floor stocks tax imposed on one pound of CFC-12 held for sale on January 1, 1992, is $0.30 (the amount by which $1.67, the tentative tax, exceeds $1.37, the tax previously imposed on CFC-12).

(2) *ODCs used in the manufacture of rigid foam insulation; 1990, 1991, 1992, and 1993.*—(i) *In general.*—In the case of an ODC that was sold in a qualifying sale for purposes of §52.4682-1(d) (relating to use in the manufacture of rigid foam insulation) the tentative tax amount is determined under section 4682(g) for purposes of computing the floor stocks tax imposed on the ODC on January 1 of 1990, 1991, 1992 or 1993. For purposes of computing the floor stocks tax imposed on the ODC on January 1, 1990, the tentative tax amount is zero. The floor stocks tax is not imposed on ODCs for use in the manufacture of rigid foam insulation in 1992 and 1993.

(ii) *Post-1989 ODCs sold before January 1, 1990; post-1990 ODCs sold before January 1, 1991.*—A post-1989 ODC that was sold by its manufacturer or importer before January 1, 1990, or a post-1990 ODC that was sold by its manufacturer or importer before January 1, 1991, shall be treated, for purposes of paragraphs (d)(2) and (e) of this section, as an ODC that was sold in a qualifying sale for purposes of §52.4682-1(d) if the ODC will be used in the manufacture of rigid foam insulation (within the meaning of §52.4682-1(d)(3) and (4)).

(3) *Halons; 1990, 1991, 1992, and 1993.*—In the case of Halon-1211, Halon-1301, or Halon-2402 (Halons), the tentative tax amount is determined under section 4682(g) for purposes of computing the floor stocks tax imposed on Halons on January 1 of 1990, 1991, 1992, or 1993. For purposes of computing the floor stocks tax imposed on Halons on January 1, 1990, the tentative tax amount is zero. The floor stocks tax is not imposed on Halons in 1992 and 1993.

(4) *Methyl chloroform; 1993.*—In the case of methyl chloroform, the tentative tax amount is determined under section 4682(g)(5) for purposes of computing the floor stocks tax imposed on January 1, 1993.

(e) *De minimis exception.*—(1) *1990 and 1992.*—In the case of the floor stocks tax imposed on January 1 of 1990 or 1992, a person is liable for the tax only if, on the date the tax is imposed, the person holds at least 400 pounds of post-1989 ODCs that are not described in paragraph (d)(2) or (3) of this section and are otherwise subject to tax.

(2) *1991.*—In the case of the floor stocks tax imposed on January 1, 1991, a person is liable for the tax only if, on such date, the person holds at least 400 pounds of ODCs subject to the 1991 floor stocks tax. For this purpose, ODCs subject to the 1991 floor stocks tax are—

(i) Post-1990 ODCs that are subject to tax; and

(ii) Post-1989 ODCs that are described in paragraph (d)(2) or (3) of this section and are otherwise subject to tax.

(3) *1993.*—In the case of the floor stocks tax imposed on January 1, 1993, a person is liable for the tax only if, on such date, the person holds at least 400 pounds of ODCs that are not described in paragraph (d)(2) or (3) of this section and are otherwise subject to tax.

(4) *1994.*—In the case of the floor stocks tax imposed on January 1, 1994, a person is liable for the tax only if, on such date, the person holds—

(i) At least 400 pounds ODCs that are not described in paragraph (d)(2) or (d)(3) of this section and are otherwise subject to tax;

(ii) At least 200 pounds of ODCs that are described in paragraph (d)(2) of this section and are otherwise subject to tax; or

(iii) At least 20 pounds of ODCs that are described in paragraph (d)(3) of this section and are otherwise subject to tax.

(5) *Calendar years after 1994.*—In the case of the floor stocks tax imposed on January 1 of 1995 and each following calendar year, a person is liable for the tax only if, on such date, the person holds—

(i) At least 400 pounds of ODCs that are not described in paragraph (d)(3) or (d)(4) of this section and are otherwise subject to tax;

(ii) At least 50 pounds of ODCs that are described in paragraph (d)(3) of this section and are otherwise subject to tax; or

(iii) At least 1000 pounds of ODCS that are described in paragraph (d)(4) of this section and are otherwise subject to tax.

(6) *Examples.*—The rules of this paragraph (e) may be illustrated by the following examples:

Example 1. On January 1, 1990, A holds for sale 300 pounds of CFC-12 (a post-1989 ODC not described in paragraph (d)(2) or (d)(3) of this section) and 500 pounds of R-500 (a mixture). A does not hold at least 400 pounds of ODCs that are taken into account under paragraph (e)(1) of this section and, under paragraph (b)(2)(i) of this section, mixtures are not subject to the floor stocks tax. Thus, A is not liable for the floor stocks tax imposed on January 1, 1990.

Example 2. On January 1, 1990, B holds for sale 250 pounds of CFC-12 and 250 pounds of CFC-113 (post-1989 ODCs not described in paragraph (d)(2) or (3) of this section). B holds 500 pounds of ODCs that are taken into account under paragraph (e)(1) of this section. Thus, B is liable for the floor stocks tax imposed on January 1, 1990, because B holds at least 400 pounds of ODCs for sale.

Example 3. On January 1, 1990, C holds 200 pounds of post-1990 ODCs and 500 pounds of post-1989 ODCs for use in further manufacture. C will use 300 pounds of the post-1989 ODCs in the manufacture of rigid foam insulation (as defined in §52.4682-1(d)(3) and (4)). The remainder of the ODCs are not described in paragraph (d)(2) or (3) of this section. Under paragraph (e)(1) of this section, post-1990 ODCs and ODCs that will be used in the manufacture of rigid foam insulation are disregarded in determining whether the *de minimis* exception is applicable in 1990. Thus, C holds only 200 pounds of ODCs that are taken into account under paragraph (e)(1) of this section and is not liable for the floor stocks tax imposed on January 1, 1990.

Example 4. (a) The facts are the same as in *Example 3*, except that the ODCs are held on January 1, 1991. Under paragraph (e)(2) of this section, the 200 pounds of post-1990 ODCs and the 300 pounds of post-1989 ODCs that will be used in the manufacture of rigid foam insulation are taken into account in determining whether the *de minimis* exception is applicable in 1991. Under paragraph (b)(2) of this section, the remaining 200 pounds of post-1989 ODCs are [is] not taken into account because the base tax amount applicable to post-1989 ODCs does not increase in 1991. Thus, C holds 500 pounds of ODCs that are taken into account under paragraph (e)(2) of this section and is liable for the floor stocks tax imposed on January 1, 1991.

(b) The amount of the floor stocks tax imposed on the 200 pounds of post-1990 ODCs and the 300 pounds of post-1989 ODCs that will be used in the manufacture of rigid foam insulation is equal to the tentative tax amount because those ODCs were not previously subject to tax.

Example 5. (a) On January 1, 1994, D holds for sale 300 pounds of CFC-113 (an ODC not described in paragraph (d)(2) or (d)(3) of this section) and 25 pounds of Halon-1301 (an ODC described in paragraph (d)(3) of this section). D is liable for the floor stocks tax imposed on January 1, 1994, because 25 pounds of Halon-1301 exceeds the de minimis amount specified in paragraph (e)(4)(iii) of this section. The 300 pounds of CFC-113 is less than the amount specified in paragraph (e)(4)(i) of this section. Nevertheless, tax is imposed on both the 25 pounds of Halon-1301 and the 300 pounds of CFC-113.

(b) The amount of the floor stocks tax is determined separately for the 300 pounds of CFC-113 and the 25 pounds of Halon-1301 and is equal to the difference between the tentative tax amount and the amount of tax previously imposed on those ODCS. For Halon-1301, for example, the tax is determined as follows. The tentative tax amount is $1,087.50 ($4.35 (the base tax amount in 1994) x 10 (the ozone-depletion factor for Halon-1301) x 25 (the number of pounds held)). The tax previously imposed on the Halon-1301 is $6.28 ($3.35 (the base tax amount in 1993) x 10 (the ozone-depletion factor for Halon-1301) x 0.75 percent (the applicable percentage determined under section 4682(g)(2)(A)) x 25 (the number of pounds held)). Thus, the floor stocks tax imposed on the 25 pounds of Halon-1301 in 1994 is $1,081.22, the difference between $1,087.50 (the tentative tax amount) and $6.28 (the tax previously imposed).

(f) *Inventory.*—(1) *In general.*—If, on the date on which the floor stocks tax is imposed, a person holds ODCs for sale or for use in further manufacture and the ODCs were not manufactured or imported by such person, the following rules apply:

(i) The person shall prepare an inventory of all such ODCs that the person holds on the date on which the tax is imposed.

(ii) The inventory shall be taken as of the first moment of the date on which the tax is imposed, but work-back or work-forward inventories will be acceptable if supported by adequate commercial records of receipt, use, and disposition of ODCs held for sale or for use in further manufacture.

(iii) The person must maintain records of the inventory and make such records available for inspection and copying by internal revenue agents and officers. Records of the inventory are not to be filed with the Internal Revenue Service.

(2) *Circumstances in which an inventory is not required.*—The inventory requirement of paragraph (f)(1) of this section does not apply to any person holding, on a date on which floor stocks tax is imposed, only ODCs that are not subject to tax by reason of a statutory exemption (*e.g.*, use as a feedstock) or regulatory exclusion other than the *de minimis* exception provided by paragraph (e) of this section (*e.g.*, mixtures). In addition, any person that holds ODCs subject to the floor stocks tax and also holds ODCs that are nontaxable under the provisions of paragraph (b)(2) of this section, is not required to inventory the nontaxable ODCs. However, any person that holds any ODCs that either are subject to the floor stocks tax or would be subject to the floor stocks tax but for the *de minimis* exception must inventory those ODCs.

(3) *Examples.*—The rules of this paragraph (f) may be illustrated by the following examples:

Example 1. On January 1, 1990, A holds for sale 300 pounds of CFC-12 (a post-1989 ODC not described in paragraph (d)(2) or (d)(3) of this section) and 500 pounds of R-500 (a mixture). As required by paragraph (f)(1) of this section, A must prepare an inventory of the CFC-12 A holds for sale on that date even though, under paragraph (e)(1) of this section, the 300 pounds of CFC-12 is not taken into account because it is *de minimis.* However, as provided in paragraph (f)(2) of this section, A is not required to inventory the R-500 because, under paragraph (b)(2) of this section, mixtures are not subject to the floor stocks tax.

Example 2. On January 1, 1991, B holds for sale 1,000 pounds of CFC-12 (a post-1989 ODC not described in paragraph (d)(2) or (d)(3) of this section). As provided under paragraph (f)(2) of this section, B is not required to prepare an inventory because CFC-12 is not subject to the floor stocks tax in 1991.

(g) *Time for paying tax.*—The floor stocks tax imposed under section 4682(h) shall be paid without assessment or notice. In the case of the floor stocks tax imposed on January 1, 1990, the tax shall be paid by April 1, 1990. In the case of floor stocks taxes imposed after January 1, 1990, the tax shall be paid by June 30 of the year in which the tax is imposed. [Reg. § 52.4682-4.]

☐ [*T.D.* 8370, 11-1-91. *Amended by T.D.* 8622, 10-10-95.]

[Reg. § 52.4682-5]

§ 52.4682-5. Exports.—(a) *Overview.*—This section provides rules relating to the tax imposed under section 4681 on ozone-depleting chemicals (ODCs) that are exported. In general, tax is not imposed on ODCs that a manufacturer or importer sells for export, or for resale by the purchaser to a second purchaser for export, if the procedural requirements set forth in paragraph (d) of this section are met. The tax benefit of this exemption is limited, however, to the manufacturer's or importer's exemption amount. Thus, if the tax that would otherwise be imposed under section 4681 on ODCs that a manufacturer or importer sells for export exceeds this exemption amount, a tax equal to the excess is imposed on the ODCS. The exemption amount, which is determined separately for post-1989 ODCs and post-1990 ODCs, is calculated for each calendar year in accordance with the rules of paragraph (c) of this section. This section also provides rules under which a tax imposed under section 4681 on exported ODCs may be credited or refunded, subject to the same limit on tax benefits, if the procedural requirements set forth in paragraph (f) of this section are met. See §52.4681-1(c) for definitions relating to the tax on ODCs.

(b) *Exemption or partial exemption from tax.*—(1) *In general.*—Except as provided in paragraph (b)(2) of this section, no tax is imposed on an ODC if the manufacturer or importer of the ODC sells the ODC in a qualifying sale for export (within the meaning of paragraph (d)(1) of this section).

(2) *Tax imposed if exemption amount exceeded.*—(i) *Post-1989 ODCs.*—The tax imposed on post-1989 ODCs that a manufacturer or importer sells in qualifying sales for export during a calendar year is equal to the excess (if any) of—

(A) The tax that would be imposed on the ODCs but for section 4682(d)(3) and this section; over

(B) The post-1989 ODC exemption amount for the calendar year determined under paragraph (c)(1) of this section.

(ii) *Post-1990 ODCs.*—The tax imposed on post-1990 ODCs that a manufacturer or importer sells in qualifying sales for export during a calendar year is equal to the excess (if any) of—

(A) The tax that would be imposed on the ODCs but for section 4682(d)(3) and this section; over

(B) The post-1990 ODC exemption amount for the calendar year determined under paragraph (c)(2) of this section.

(iii) *Allocation of tax.*—(A) *Post-1989 ODCs.*—The tax (if any) determined under paragraph (b)(2)(i) of this section may be allocated among the post-1989 ODCs on which it is imposed in any manner, provided that the amount allocated to any post-1989 ODC does not exceed the tax that would be imposed on such ODC but for section 4682(d)(3) and this section.

(B) *Post-1990 ODCs.*—The tax (if any) determined under paragraph (b)(2)(ii) of this section may be allocated among the post-1990 ODCs on which it is imposed in any manner, provided that, the amount allocated to any post-1990 ODC does not exceed the tax that would be imposed on such ODC but for section 4682(d)(3) and this section.

(c) *Exemption amount.*—(1) *Post-1989 ODC exemption amount.*—A manufacturer's or importer's post-1989 ODC exemption amount for a calendar year is the sum of the following amounts:

(i) The 1986 export percentage of the aggregate tax that would (but for section 4682(d), section 4682(g), and this section) be imposed under section 4681 on the maximum quantity,

determined without regard to additional production allowances, of post-1989 ODCs that the person is permitted to manufacture during the calendar year under rules prescribed by the Environmental Protection Agency (40 CFR part 82).

(ii) The aggregate tax that would (but for section 4682(d), section 4682(g), and this section) be imposed under section 4681 on post-1989 ODCs that the person manufactures during the calendar year under any additional production allowance granted by the Environmental Protection Agency.

(iii) The aggregate tax that would (but for section 4682(d), section 4682(g), and this section) be imposed under section 4681 on post-1989 ODCs imported by the person during the calendar year.

(2) *Post-1990 ODC exemption amount.*—A manufacturer's or importer's post-1990 ODC exemption amount for a calendar year is the sum of the following amounts:

(i) The 1989 export percentage of the aggregate tax that would (but for section 4682(d), section 4682(g), and this section) be imposed under section 4681 on the maximum quantity, determined without regard to additional production allowances, of post-1990 ODCs the person is permitted to manufacture during the calendar year under rules prescribed by the Environmental Protection Agency.

(ii) The aggregate tax that would (but for section 4682(d), section 4682(g), and this section) be imposed under section 4681 on post-1990 ODCs that the person manufactures during the calendar year under any additional production allowance granted by the Environmental Protection Agency.

(iii) The aggregate tax that would (but for section 4682(d), section 4682(g), and this section) be imposed under section 4681 on post-1990 ODCs imported by the person during the calendar year.

(3) *Definitions.*—(i) *1986 export percentage.*—See section 4682(d)(3)(B)(ii) for the meaning of the term *1986 export percentage.*

(ii) *1989 export percentage.*—See section 4682(d)(3)(C) for the meaning of the term *1989 export percentage.*

(d) *Procedural requirements relating to tax-free sales for export.*—(1) *Qualifying sales.*—(i) *In general.*—A sale of ODCs is a qualifying sale for export if—

(A) The seller is the manufacturer or importer of the ODCs and the purchaser is a purchaser for export or for resale to a second purchaser for export;

(B) At the time of the sale, the seller and the purchaser are registered with the Internal Revenue Service; and

(C) At the time of the sale, the seller—

(1) Has an unexpired certificate in substantially the form set forth in paragraph (d)(3)(ii) of this section from the purchaser; and

(2) Relies on the certificate in good faith.

(ii) *Qualifying resale.*—A sale of ODCs is a qualifying resale for export if—

Reg. §52.4682-5(d)(1)(ii)

(A) The seller acquired the ODCs in a qualifying sale for export and the purchaser is a second purchaser for export;

(B) At the time of the sale, the seller and the purchaser are registered with the Internal Revenue Service; and

(C) At the time of the sale, the seller—

(1) Has an unexpired certificate in substantially the form set forth in paragraph (d)(3)(ii)(A) of this section from the purchaser of the ODCs; and

(2) Relies on the certificate in good faith.

(iii) *Special rule relating to sales made before July 1, 1993.*—If a sale for export made before July 1, 1993, satisfies all the requirements of paragraph (d)(1)(i) or (ii) of this section other than those relating to registration, the sale will be treated as a qualifying sale (or resale) for export. Thus, a sale made before July 1, 1993, may be a qualifying sale (or resale) even if the parties to the sale are not registered and the required certificate does not contain statements regarding registration.

(iv) *Registration.*—Application for registration is made on Form 637 (or any other form designated for the same use by the Commissioner) according to the instructions applicable to the form. A person is registered only if the district director has issued that person a letter of registration and it has not been revoked or suspended. The effective date of the registration must be no earlier than the date on which the district director signs the letter of registration. Each business unit that has, or is required to have, a separate employer identification number is treated as a separate person.

(2) *Good faith reliance.*—The requirements of paragraph (d)(1) of this section are not satisfied with respect to a sale of ODCs and the sale is not a qualifying sale (or resale) if, at the time of the sale—

(i) The seller has reason to believe that the ODCs are not purchased for export; or

(ii) The Internal Revenue Service has notified the seller that the purchaser's registration has been revoked or suspended.

(3) *Certificate.*—(i) *In general.*—The certificate required under paragraph (d)(1) of this section consists of a statement executed and signed under penalties of perjury by a person with authority to bind the purchaser, in substantially the same form as model certificates provided in paragraph (d)(1)(3)(ii) of this section, and containing all information necessary to complete such model certificate. A new certificate must be given if any information in the current certificate changes. The certificate may be included as part of any business records normally used to document a sale. The certificate expires on the earliest of the following dates—

(A) The date one year after the effective date of the certificate;

(B) The date the purchaser provides a new certificate to the seller; or

(C) The date the seller is notified by the Internal Revenue Service or the purchaser that the purchaser's registration has been revoked or suspended.

(ii) *Model certificates.*—(A) *ODCs sold for export by the purchaser.*—If the purchaser will export the ODCS, the certificate must be in substantially the following form:

CERTIFICATE OF PURCHASER OF CHEMICALS
FOR EXPORT BY THE PURCHASER

(To support tax-free sales under
section 4682(d)(3) of the Internal Revenue Code.)

Effective Date _____

Expiration Date _____
(not more than one year after effective date)

The undersigned purchaser (Purchaser) certifies the following under penalties of perjury:
Purchaser is registered with the Internal Revenue Service as a purchaser of ozone-depleting chemicals for export under registration number _____. Purchaser's registration has not been suspended or revoked by the Internal Revenue Service.

The following percentage of ozone-depleting chemicals purchased from:

_____
(Name of seller)

_____
(Address of seller)

_____
(Taxpayer identifying number of seller)
are purchased for export by Purchaser.

Product	Percentage
CFC-11	_____
CFC-12	_____
CFC-113	_____
CFC-114	_____
CFC-115	_____
Halon-1211	_____
Halon-1301	_____

Reg. § 52.4682-5(d)(1)(ii)(A)

Halon-2402 _____
Carbon tetrachloride _____
Methyl chloroform _____

Other (specify) _____ _____

This certificate applies to (check and complete as applicable):

_____ All shipments to Purchaser at the following location(s):
_____
_____
_____

_____ All shipments to Purchaser under the following Purchaser account number(s):
_____
_____
_____

_____ All shipments to Purchaser under the following purchase order(s):
_____
_____
_____

_____ One or more shipments to Purchaser identified as follows:
_____
_____
_____

Purchaser understands that Purchaser will be liable for tax imposed under section 4681 if Purchaser does not export the ODCs to which this certificate applies.

Purchaser understands that any use of the ODCs to which this certificate applies other than for export may result in the revocation of Purchaser's registration.

Purchaser will retain the business records needed to document the export of the ozone-depleting chemicals to which this certificate applies and will make such records available for inspection by Government officers.

Purchaser has not been notified by the Internal Revenue Service that its registration has been revoked or suspended.

Purchaser understands that the fraudulent use of this certificate may subject Purchaser and all parties making such fraudulent use of this certificate to a fine or imprisonment, or both, together with the costs of prosecution.

_____
Name of Purchaser

_____
Address of Purchaser

_____
Taxpayer Identifying Number of Purchaser

_____
Title of person signing

_____
Printed or typed name of person signing

_____
Signature

(B) *ODCs sold by the purchaser for resale for export by the second purchaser.*—If the purchaser will resell the ODCs to a second purchaser for export by the second purchaser, the certificate must be in substantially the following form:

CERTIFICATE OF PURCHASER OF CHEMICALS FOR RESALE FOR EXPORT BY THE SECOND PURCHASER

(To support tax-free sales under section 4682(d)(3) of the Internal Revenue Code.)

Effective Date _____
Expiration Date _____
(not more than one year after effective date)

The undersigned purchaser (Purchaser) certifies the following under penalties of perjury:

Purchaser is registered with the Internal Revenue Service as a purchaser of ozone-depleting chemicals for export under registration number _____. Purchaser's registration has not been suspended or revoked by the Internal Revenue Service.

The following percentage of ozone-depleting chemicals purchased from:

_____
(Name of seller)

Reg. §52.4682-5(d)(3)(ii)(B)

_____

(Address of seller)

_____

(Taxpayer identifying number of seller)

will be resold by Purchaser to persons (Second Purchasers) that certify to Purchaser that they are (1) registered with the Internal Revenue Service as purchasers of ozone-depleting chemicals for export and (2) purchasing the ozone-depleting chemicals for export.

Product	Percentage
CFC-11	_____
CFC-12	_____
CFC-113	_____
CFC-114	_____
CFC-115	_____
Halon-1211	_____
Halon-1301	_____
Halon-2402	_____
Carbon tetrachloride	_____
Methyl chloroform	_____
Other (specify) _____	_____

This certificate applies to (check and complete as applicable):

_____ All shipments to Purchaser at the following location(s):

_____
_____
_____

_____ All shipments to Purchaser under the following Purchaser account number(s):

_____
_____
_____

_____ All shipments to Purchaser under the following purchase order(s):

_____
_____
_____

_____ One or more shipments to Purchaser identified as follows:

_____
_____
_____

Purchaser understands that Purchaser will be liable for tax imposed under section 4681 if Purchaser does not resell the ODCs to which this certificate applies to a Second Purchaser for export or export those ODCs.

Purchaser understands that any use of the ODCs to which this certificate applies other than for resale to Second Purchasers for export may result in the revocation of Purchaser's registration.

Purchaser will retain the business records needed to document the sales to Second Purchasers for export covered by this certificate and will make such records available for inspection by Government officers. Purchaser also will retain and make available for inspection by Government officers the certificates of its Second Purchasers.

Purchaser has not been notified by the Internal Revenue Service that its registration has been revoked or suspended. In addition, the Internal Revenue Service has not notified Purchaser of the revocation or suspension of the registration of any Second Purchaser who will purchase ozone-depleting chemicals to which this certificate applies.

Purchaser understands that the fraudulent use of this certificate may subject Purchaser and all parties making such fraudulent use of this certificate to a fine or imprisonment, or both, together with the costs of prosecution.

_____

Name of Purchaser

_____

Address of Purchaser

_____

Taxpayer Identifying Number of Purchaser

_____

Title of person signing

_____

Printed or typed name of person signing

_____

Signature

(4) _Documentation of export._—(i) _After December 31, 1992._—After December 31, 1992, to document the exportation of any ODCs, a person must have the evidence required by the Environmental Protection Agency as proof that the ODCs were exported.

Reg. §52.4682-5(d)(4)(i)

(ii) *Before January 1, 1993.*—Before January 1, 1993, to document the exportation of any ODCs, a person must have evidence substantially similar to that required by the Environmental Protection Agency as proof that the ODCs were exported.

(e) *Purchaser liable for tax.*—(1) *Purchaser in qualifying sale.*—The purchaser of ODCs in a qualifying sale for export is treated as the manufacturer of the ODC and is liable for any tax imposed under section 4681 (determined without regard to exemptions for qualifying sales under this section or § 52.4682-1) when it sells or uses the ODCs if that purchaser does not—

(i) Export the ODCs and document the exportation of the ODCs in accordance with paragraph (d)(4) of this section; or

(ii) Sell the ODCs in a qualifying resale for export.

(2) *Purchaser in qualifying resale.*—The purchaser of ODCs in a qualifying resale for export is treated as the manufacturer of the ODC and is liable for any tax imposed under section 4681 (determined without regard to exemptions for qualifying sales under this section or § 52.4682-1) when it sells or uses the ODCs if that purchaser does not export the ODCs and document the exportation of the ODCs in accordance with paragraph (d)(4) of this section.

(f) *Credit or refund.*—(1) *In general.*—Except as provided in paragraph (f)(2) of this section, a manufacturer or importer that meets the conditions of paragraph (f)(3) of this section is allowed a credit or refund (without interest) of the tax it paid to the government under section 4681 on ODCs that are exported. Persons other than manufacturers and importers of ODCs cannot file claims for credit or refund of tax imposed under section 4681 on ODCs that are exported.

(2) *Limitation.*—The amount of credits or refunds of tax under this paragraph (f) is limited—

(i) In the case of tax paid on post-1989 ODCs sold during a calendar year, to the amount (if any) by which the post-1989 exemption amount for the year exceeds the tax benefit provided to such post-1989 ODCs under paragraph (b) of this section; and

(ii) In the case of tax paid on post-1990 ODCs sold during a calendar year, to the amount (if any) by which the post-1990 exemption amount for the year exceeds the tax benefit provided to such post-1990 ODCs under paragraph (b) of this section.

(3) *Conditions to allowance of credit or refund.*—The conditions of this paragraph (f)(3) are met if the manufacturer or importer—

(i) Documents the exportation of the ODCs in accordance with paragraph (d)(4) of this section; and

(ii) Establishes that it has—

(A) Repaid or agreed to repay the amount of the tax to the person that exported the ODC; or

(B) Obtained the written consent of the exporter to the allowance of the credit or the making of the refund.

(4) *Procedural rules.*—See section 6402 and the regulations under that section for procedural rules relating to filing a claim for credit or refund of tax.

(g) *Examples.*—The following examples illustrate the provisions of this section. In each example, the sales are qualifying sales for export (within the meaning of paragraph (d)(1) of this section), all registration, certification, and documentation requirements of this section are met, and the ODCs sold for export are exported:

Example 1. (i) *Facts.* D, a corporation, manufactures CFC-11, a post-1989 ODC, and does not manufacture or import any other ODCs. In 1993, D manufactures 100,000 pounds of CFC-11, the maximum quantity D is allowed to manufacture in 1993 under EPA regulations. D has no additional production allowance from EPA for 1993. In 1993, the tax on CFC-11 is $3.35 per pound. D's 1986 export percentage for post-1989 ODCs is 50%. In 1993, D sells 80,000 pounds of CFC-11 in qualifying sales for export. The remainder of D's production is not exported.

(ii) *Components of limit on tax benefit.* Under paragraph (c)(1) of this section, D's exemption amount for 1993 is equal to the sum of—

(A) D's 1986 export percentage multiplied by the aggregate tax that would (but for section 4682(d), section 4682(g), and § 52.4682-5) be imposed under section 4681 on the maximum quantity of post-1989 ODCs D is permitted to manufacture during 1993;

(B) The aggregate tax that would (but for section 4682(d), section 4682(g), and § 52.4682-5) be imposed under section 4681 on post-1989 ODCs that D manufactures during 1993 under an additional production allowance; and

(C) The aggregate tax that would (but for section 4682(d), section 4682(g), and § 52.4682-5) be imposed under section 4681 on post-1989 ODCs imported by D during 1993.

(iii) *Limit on tax benefit.* The amounts described in paragraphs (ii)(B) and (C) of this *Example 1* are equal to zero. Thus, D's 1993 exemption amount is $167,500 (50% of $335,000 (the tax that would otherwise be imposed on 100,000 pounds of CFC-11 in 1993)).

(iv) *Application of limit on tax benefit.* Under paragraph (b)(2) of this section, the tax imposed

Reg. § 52.4682-5(g)

on the CFC-11 D sells for export is equal to the excess of the tax that would have been imposed on those ODCs but for section 4682(d) and §52.4682-5, over D's 1993 exemption amount. But for §52.4682-5, $268,000 ($3.35 × 80,000) of tax would have been imposed on the CFC-11 sold for export. Thus, $100,500 ($268,000 – $167,500) of tax is imposed on the CFC-11 sold for export.

Example 2. (i) *Facts.* E, a corporation, manufactures CFC-11, a post-1989 ODC, and does not manufacture or import any other ODCs. In 1993, E manufactures 100,000 pounds of CFC-11, the maximum quantity E is allowed to manufacture in 1993 under EPA regulations. E has no additional production allowance for 1993. In 1993, the tax on CFC-11 is $3.35 per pound. E's 1986 export percentage for post-1989 ODCs is 50%. In 1993, E sells 45,000 pounds of CFC-11 tax free in qualifying sales for export and pays tax under section 4681 on an additional 35,000 pounds of exported CFC-11. The remainder of E's production is not exported.

(ii) *Limit on tax benefit.* E's 1993 exemption amount is $167,500, (50% of $335,000 (the tax that would otherwise be imposed on 100,000 pounds of CFC-11 in 1993)). The credit or refund allowed to E under paragraph (f) of this section is limited under paragraph (f)(2) of this section to the amount by which E's 1993 exemption amount exceeds E's 1993 tax benefit under paragraph (b) of this section.

(iii) *Application of limit on tax benefit.* Because E sold 45,000 pounds of CFC-11 tax free in qualifying sales for export in 1993, E's 1993 tax benefit under paragraph (b) of this section is $150,750 ($3.35 × 45,000). Thus, the credit or refund allowed to E under paragraph (f) of this section is limited to $16,750 ($167,500 – $150,750).

Example 3. (i) *Facts.* F, a corporation, manufactures CFC-11, a post-1989 ODC, and does not manufacture any other ODCs. F also imports CFC-11. In 1993, F manufactures 60,000 pounds of CFC-11 (100,000 pounds is the maximum quantity F is allowed to manufacture in 1993 under EPA regulations) and imports 40,000 pounds. F has no additional production allowance from EPA for 1993. In 1993, the tax on CFC-11 is $3.35 per pound. F's 1986 export percentage for post-1989 ODCs is 50%. In 1993, F sells 45,000 pounds of CFC-11 tax free in qualifying sales for export and pays tax under section 4681 on an additional 35,000 pounds of exported CFC-11. The remainder of F's production is not exported.

(ii) *Limit on tax benefit.* F's 1993 exemption amount is $301,500, ($167,500 (50% of $335,000 (the tax that would otherwise be imposed on 100,000 pounds of CFC-11 in 1993) plus $134,000 (the tax that would otherwise be imposed on the 40,000 pounds imported)). The credit or refund allowed to F under paragraph (f) of this section is limited under paragraph (f)(2) of this section to the amount by which F's 1993 exemption amount exceeds F's 1993 tax benefit under paragraph (b) of this section.

(iii) *Application of limit on tax benefit.* Because F sold 45,000 pounds of CFC-11 tax free in qualifying sales for export in 1993, F's 1993 tax benefit under paragraph (b) of this section is $150,750 ($3.35 × 45,000). Thus, the credit or refund allowed to F under paragraph (f) of this section is limited to $150,750 ($301,500 – $150,750). The limitation does not affect F's credit or refund because the tax F paid on exported ODCs is only $117,250 ($3.35 × 35,000).

(h) *Effective date.*—This section is effective January 1, 1993. [Reg. §52.4682-5.]

☐ [*T.D.* 8622, 10-10-95.]

Registration-Required Obligations

See p. 20,601 for regulations not amended to reflect law changes

[Reg. §46.4701-1]

§46.4701-1. Tax on issuer of registration-required obligation not in registered form.— (a) *In general.*—Section 4701 imposes a tax (determined under paragraph (c) of this section) on any person (referred to as the issuer) who issues an obligation that—

(1) is a registration-required obligation, and

(2) is not issued in registered form.

(b) *Definitions.*—(1) *Person.*—The term "person" includes all governmental entities.

(2) *Obligations.*—The term "obligation" includes bonds, debentures, notes, certificates and other evidences of indebtedness regardless of how denominated.

(3) *Registration-required obligation.*—The term "registration-required obligation" has the

same meaning as when used in section 163(f) (and the regulations thereunder) which relates to the denial of a deduction for interest on certain obligations not in registered form. However, the term "registration-required obligation" does not include any obligation which would otherwise be exempt from Federal income tax under section 103(a) or any other provision of law.

(4) *Registered form.*—The term "registered form" has the same meaning as when used in section 103(j) (and the regulations thereunder) which relates to obligations which must be in registered form to be tax-exempt.

(5) *Issuer.*—Except as provided in §1.163-5T(d) (relating to pass-through certificates) and §1.163-5T(e) (relating to REMICs), the "issuer" is the person whose interest deduction would be disallowed solely by reason of section 163(f)(1).

(6) *Date of issuance.*—(i) For obligations intended to be offered to the public, the term "date of issuance" means the date the obligation is first sold to the public at the issue price.

(ii) For an obligation which is privately placed, the term "date of issuance" is the date the obligation is first sold by the issuer.

(7) *Issue price.*—See section 1273(b) and the regulations thereunder for the definition of "issue price".

(c) *Rate and computation of tax.*—The tax under section 4701(a) is imposed in an amount equal to the product of—

(1) 1 percent of the principal amount of the obligation, multiplied by

(2) the number of calendar years (or portions thereof) during the period beginning on the date of issuance of the obligation and ending on the date of maturity.

For purposes of this paragraph, the term "principal amount" for a discounted obligation is the issue price, and for all other obligations, including obligations sold at a premium, the term "principal amount" is the stated redemption price at maturity.

(d) *Payment of tax.*—Every person who incurs liability for the tax imposed by section 4701 is required to file a return in accordance with section 6011 and §46.6011(a)-1 relating to the general requirement of a return, statement or list.

(e) *Effective date.*—The provisions of this section shall apply to obligations issued after December 31, 1982, unless issued on the exercise of a warrant or the conversion of a convertible obligation if the warrant or obligation was offered or sold outside the United States without registration under the Securities Act of 1933 and was issued before August 10, 1982. See section 310(d)(3) of the Tax Equity and Fiscal Responsibility Act of 1982. [Reg. §46.4701-1.]

☐ [*T.D. 8102, 9-19-86. Amended by T.D. 8300, 5-9-90.*]

General Provisions Relating to Occupational Taxes

See p. 20,601 for regulations not amended to reflect law changes

[Reg. §44.4901-1]

§44.4901-1. Payment of special tax.— (a) *Condition precedent to carrying on business.*— No persons shall engage in the business of accepting wagers subject to the tax imposed by section 4401 until he has filed a return on Form 11-C and paid the special tax imposed by section 4411. Likewise, no person shall engage in receiving wagers for or on behalf of any person engaged in the business of accepting wagers until he has filed a return on Form 11-C and paid the special tax imposed by section 4411. For provisions relating to the tax imposed by section 4401 and the special tax imposed by section 4411, see Subparts B and C of this part, respectively.

(b) *Computation of special tax.*—(1) Section 4411 imposes a special tax of $50 per year which is required to be paid by each person who is liable for the tax imposed by section 4401 (tax on wagers) or who is engaged in receiving wagers for or on behalf of any person who is liable for the tax imposed by section 4401. A person engaged both in accepting wagers on his own account and in receiving wagers or or on behalf of some other person is required to purchase but one special tax stamp.

(2) The tax year begins July 1 and ends June 30 of the following calendar year. Persons commencing business between August 1 and June 30 (both dates inclusive) shall pay a proportionate part of the annual tax. "Commencing business" means the initial acceptance by a person of a wager subject to the tax imposed by section 4401 or the initial receiving of a taxable wager by an agent or employee for or on behalf of some other person. Persons in business for only a portion of a month are liable for tax for the full month, i.e., a person first becoming subject to the special tax on, for example, the 20th day of a month, is liable for tax for the entire month.

(c) *Tax payment evidenced by special tax stamp.*— (1) Upon receipt of a return on Form 11-C, together with remittance of the full amount of tax due, the district director will issue a special tax stamp as evidence of payment of the special tax.

(2) District directors will distinctly write or print on the stamp before it is delivered or mailed to the taxpayer the following information: (i) The taxpayer's registered name, and (ii) the business or office address of the taxpayer if he has one; if not, the residence address. Special tax stamps will be transmitted by ordinary mail, unless it is requested that they be transmitted by registered mail in which case additional cost to cover registry fee shall be remitted with the return.

(3) District directors and their collection officers are forbidden to issue receipts in lieu of stamps representing the payment of special taxes.

(d) *Cross references.*—For provisions relating to registration and information required to be reported on Form 11-C, see §44.4412-1. For other provisions relating to Form 11-C, see §§44.6011(a)-1 (relating to returns), 44.6071-1 (time for filing returns and other documents), and 44.6091-1 (place for filing returns or other documents). [Reg. §44.4901-1.]

☐ [*T.D. 6530, 1-19-61. Amended by T.D. 6774, 12-1-64 and T.D. 7279, 6-21-73.*]

[Reg. §44.4902-1]

§44.4902-1. Partnership liability.—Any number of persons doing business in copartnership shall be required to pay but one special tax. The district director may issue a special tax stamp to a copartnership in a firm or trade name, provided the names and addresses of all members of the partnership are disclosed on Form 11-C. [Reg. § 44.4902-1.]

☐ [*T.D. 6530, 1-19-61.*]

[Reg. § 44.4905-1]

§ 44.4905-1. Change of ownership.— (a) *Changes through death.*—Whenever any person who has paid the special tax imposed by section 4411 dies, the surviving spouse or child, or executor or administrator, or other legal representative, may carry on such business for the remainder of the term for which such special tax has been paid without any additional payment, subject to the conditions hereinafter stated. If the surviving spouse or child, or executor or administrator, or other legal representative of the deceased taxpayer continues the business, such person shall within 30 days after the date of the death of the taxpayer execute a return on Form 11-C. Such return shall show the name of the deceased taxpayer, together with all other data required to be reported on Form 11-C (see § 44.4412-1), and the stamp issued to such taxpayer shall be submitted with the return for proper notation by the district director.

(b) *Changes from other causes.*—A receiver or trustee in bankruptcy may continue the business under the stamp issued to the taxpayer at the place and for the period for which the special tax was paid. An assignee for the benefit of creditors may continue business under his assignor's special tax stamp without incurring additional special tax liability. In such cases the change shall be registered with the district director in a manner similar to that required by paragraph (a) of this section.

(c) *Changes in firm.*—When one or more members of a firm partnership withdraw, the business may be continued by the remaining partner or partners under the same special tax stamp for the remainder of the period for which the stamp was issued to the old firm. The change shall, however, be registered in the same manner as required in paragraph (a) of this section. If new partners are taken into a firm the new firm so constituted may not carry on business under the special tax stamp of the old firm. The new firm shall make a return on Form 11-C and pay the special tax imposed by section 4411 reckoned from the first day of the month in which it began business, even though the name of such firm be the same as that of the old. If the members of a partnership, which has paid the special tax, form a corporation to continue the business a new special tax stamp must be obtained in the name of the corporation.

(d) *Change in corporation.*—If a corporation changes its name, no additional tax is due, provided the change in name is registered with the district director in the manner required by paragraph (a) of this section. An increase in the capital stock of a corporation does not create a new special tax liability if the laws of the State under which it is incorporated permit such increase without the formation of a new corporation. A stockholder in a corporation, who after its dissolution continues the business, incurs liability for the special tax imposed by section 4411 unless he already has a special tax stamp obtained in respect of activities conducted as a sole proprietor. [Reg. § 44.4905-1.]

☐ [*T.D. 6530, 1-19-61. Amended by T.D. 7279, 6-21-73.*]

[Reg. § 44.4905-2]

§ 44.4905-2. Change of address.— (a) *Procedure by taxpayer.*—(1) *After June 30, 1963.*—Whenever, after June 30, 1963, a taxpayer changes his business or residence address to a location other than that specified in his last return on Form 11-C, he shall register the change with the district director from whom the special tax stamp was purchased by filing a new return, Form 11-C, designated "Supplemental Return", setting forth the new address and the date of change. He shall so register the change of address before:

(i) He engages in any wagering activity at the new address, or

(ii) The termination of a 30-day period which begins on the day after the date of such change,

whichever occurs first. The taxpayer's special tax stamp shall accompany the supplemental return for proper notation by the district director. As to liability in case of failure to register a change of address, see § 44.4905-3.

(2) *Before July 1, 1963.*—Whenever, before July 1, 1963, a taxpayer changes his business or residence address to a location other than that specified in his last return of Form 11-C, he shall, within 30 days after the date of such change, register the change with the district director from whom the special tax stamp was purchased by filing a new return, Form 11-C, designated "Supplemental Return", setting forth the new address and the date of change. The taxpayer's special tax stamp shall accompany the supplemental return for proper notation by the district director. As to liability in case of failure to register a change of address, see § 44.4905-3.

(b) *Procedure by district director; removal within district.*—When registration of a change of address within the same district is made by a taxpayer in the manner specified in paragraph (a) of this section, the district director, if necessary, will enter on his records the new address and the date of change. If the information disclosed on the supplemental return is such as to require a change on the face of the special tax stamp, the district director will make the proper change and return the stamp to the taxpayer.

(c) *Procedure by district director; removal to another district.*—In case of removal of the taxpayer's office or principal place of business (or residence address, if he has no office or principal place of business) to another district, the district director, after noting the transfer on his records, shall transmit the special tax stamp to the district director for the district to which such office or business was removed. The latter will make an entry on his records, as in the case of an original registration in his district, correct the address on the stamp, if necessary, and note also thereon his name, title, date, and district, and then forward the stamp to the taxpayer. [Reg. § 44.4905-2.]

☐ [*T.D.* 6530, 1-19-61. *Amended by T.D.* 7279, 6-21-73.]

[Reg. § 44.4905-3]

§ 44.4905-3. Liability for failure to register change or removal.—Any person succeeding to and carrying on a business for which the special tax imposed by section 4411 has been paid, and any taxpayer changing his residence address or

his place of business, without registering such change as provided in § § 44.4905-1 and 44.4905-2 shall be liable to an additional tax, and to the penalty prescribed in section 6651 for failure to make a return. (For regulations under section 6651, see the Regulations on Procedure and Administration(Part 301 of this chapter).) [Reg. § 44.4905-3.]

☐ [*T.D.* 6530, 1-19-61.]

[Reg. § 44.4906-1]

§ 44.4906-1. Cross reference.—For provisions relating to the applicability of Federal and State laws, see section 4422 and § 44.4422-1. [Reg. § 44.4906-1.]

☐ [*T.D.* 6530, 1-19-61.]

Public Charities

[Reg. § 56.4911-0]

§ 56.4911-0. Outline of regulations under section 4911.—Immediately following is an outline of the regulations under section 4911 of the Internal Revenue Code relating to an excise tax on electing public charities' excess lobbying expenditures.

§ 56.4911-0. Outline of regulations under section 4911.

§ 56.4911-1. Tax on excess lobbying expenditures.
  (a) In general.
  (b) Excess lobbying expenditures.
  (c) Nontaxable amounts.
    (1) Lobbying nontaxable amount.
    (2) Grass roots nontaxable amount.
  (d) Examples.

§ 56.4911-2. Lobbying expenditures, direct lobbying communications, and grass roots lobbying communications.
  (a) Lobbying expenditures.
    (1) In general.
    (2) Overview of § 56.4911 and the definitions of "direct lobbying communication" and "grass roots lobbying communication".
  (b) Influencing legislation: direct and grass roots lobbying communications defined.
    (1) Direct lobbying communication.
    (2) Grass roots lobbying communication.
    (3) Exceptions to the definition of influencing legislation.
    (4) Examples.
    (5) Special rule for certain mass media advertisements.
  (c) Exceptions to the definitions of direct lobbying communication and grass roots lobbying communication.
    (1) Nonpartisan analysis, study, or research exception.
    (2) Examinations and discussions of broad social, economic, and similar problems.

    (3) Requests for technical advice.
    (4) Communications pertaining to "self-defense" by the organization.
  (d) Definitions.
    (1) Legislation.
    (2) Action.
    (3) Legislative body.
    (4) Administrative bodies.

§ 56.4911-3. Expenditures for direct and/or grass roots lobbying communications.
  (a) Definition of term "expenditures for".
    (1) In general.
    (2) Allocation of mixed purpose expenditures.
    (3) Allocation of mixed lobbying.
  (b) Examples.
  (c) Certain transfers treated as lobbying expenditures.
    (1) Transfer earmarked for grass roots purposes.
    (2) Transfer earmarked for direct and grass roots lobbying.
    (3) Certain transfers to noncharities that lobby.

§ 56.4911-4. Exempt purpose expenditures.
  (a) Application.
  (b) Included expenditures.
  (c) Excluded expenditures.
  (d) Certain transfers treated as exempt purpose expenditures.
  (e) Transfers not exempt purpose expenditures.
  (f) Definitions.
  (g) Example.

§ 56.4911-5. Communications with members.
  (a) In general.
  (b) Communications (directed only to members) that are not lobbying communications.
  (c) Communications (directed only to members) that are direct lobbying communications.

Reg. § 56.4911-0

(d) Communications (directed only to members) that are grass roots lobbying communications.

(e) Written communications directed to members and nonmembers.

(1) In general.

(2) Direct lobbying directly encouraged.

(3) Grass roots expenditure if grass roots lobbying directly encouraged.

(4) No direct encouragement of direct lobbying or of grass roots lobbying.

(f) Definitions and special rules.

(1) Member; general rule.

(2) Member; special rule.

(3) Member; affiliated group of organizations.

(4) Member; limited affiliated group of organizations.

(5) Subscriber.

(6) Directly encourages.

(7) Percentages of total distribution.

(8) Reasonable allocation rule.

§ 56.4911-6. *Records of lobbying and grass roots expenditures.*

(a) Records of lobbying expenditures.

(b) Records of grass roots expenditures.

§ 56.4911-7. *Affiliated group of organizations.*

(a) Affiliation between two organizations.

(1) In general.

(2) Organizations not described in section 501(c)(3).

(3) Action on legislative issues.

(b) Interlocking governing boards.

(1) In general.

(2) Majority or quorum.

(3) Votes required under governing instrument or local law.

(4) Representatives constituting less than 15% of governing board.

(5) Representatives.

(c) Governing instrument.

(d) Three or more organizations affiliated.

(1) Two controlled organizations affiliated.

(2) Chain rule.

(e) Affiliated group of organizations.

(1) Defined.

(2) Multiple membership.

(3) Taxable year of affiliated group.

(4) Electing member organization.

(5) Election of member's year as group's taxable year.

(f) Examples.

§ 56.4911-8. *Excess lobbying expenditures of affiliated group.*

(a) Application.

(b) Affiliated group treated as one organization.

(c) Tax imposed on excess lobbying expenditures of affiliated group.

(d) Liability for tax.

(1) Electing organizations.

(2) Tax based on excess lobbying expenditures.

(3) Tax based on excess grass roots expenditures.

(4) Tax based on exempt purpose expenditures.

(5) Taxable year for which liable.

(6) Organization a member of more than one affiliated group.

(e) Former member organization.

§ 56.4911-9. *Application of section 501(h) to affiliated groups of organizations.*

(a) Scope.

(b) Determination required.

(c) Member organizations that are not electing organizations.

(d) Filing of information relating to affiliated group of organizations.

(1) Scope.

(2) In general.

(3) Additional information required.

(4) Information required of electing member organization.

(e) Example.

(f) Cross reference.

§ 56.4911-10. *Members of a limited affiliated group of organizations.*

(a) Scope.

(b) Members of limited affiliated group.

(c) Controlling and controlled organizations.

(d) Expenditures of controlling organization.

(1) Scope.

(2) Expenditures for direct lobbying.

(3) Grass roots expenditures.

(4) Exempt purpose expenditures.

(e) Expenditures of controlled member.

(f) Reports of members of limited affiliated groups.

(1) Controlling member organization's additional information on annual return.

(2) Reports of controlling members to other members.

(3) Reports of controlled member organizations.

(g) National legislative issues.

(h) Examples.

§ 56.6001-1. *Notice or regulations requiring records, statements, and special returns.*

(a) In general.

(b) Cross references.

§ 56.6011-1. *General requirement of return, statement, or list.* [Reg. § 56.4911-0.]

☐ [T.D. 8308, 8-30-90.]

[Reg. § 56.4911-1]

§ 56.4911-1. Tax on excess lobbying expenditures.—(a) *In general.*—Section 4911(a) imposes an excise tax of 25 percent on the excess lobbying expenditures (as defined in paragraph (b) of this section) for a taxable year of an organization for which the expenditure test election under section 501(h) is in effect (an "electing public charity"). An electing public charity's annual limit on expenditures for influencing legislation (i.e., the amount of lobbying expenditures on which no tax is due) is the lobbying nontaxable amount or, on expenditures for influencing legislation through grass roots lobbying, the grass roots nontaxable amount (see paragraph (c) of this section). For rules concerning the application of the excise tax imposed by section 4911(a) to the members of an affiliated group of organizations (as defined in §56.4911-7(e)), see §56.4911-8.

(b) *Excess lobbying expenditures.*—For any taxable year for which the expenditure test election under section 501(h) is in effect, the amount of an electing public charity's excess lobbying expenditures is the greater of—

(1) The amount by which the organization's lobbying expenditures (within the meaning of §56.4911-2(a)) exceed the organization's lobbying nontaxable amount, or

(2) The amount by which the organization's grass roots expenditures (within the meaning of §56.4911-2(a)) exceed the organization's grass roots nontaxable amount.

(c) *Nontaxable amounts.*—(1) *Lobbying nontaxable amount.*—Under section 4911(c)(2), the lobbying nontaxable amount for any taxable year for which the expenditure test election is in effect is the lesser of—

(i) $1,000,000, or

(ii) To the extent of the electing public charity's exempt purpose expenditures (within the meaning of §56.4911-4) for that year, the sum of 20 percent of the first $500,000 of such expenditures, plus 15 percent of the second $500,000 of such expenditures, plus 10 percent of the third $500,000 of such expenditures, plus 5 percent of the remainder of such expenditures.

(2) *Grass roots nontaxable amount.*—Under section 4911(c)(4), an electing public charity's grass roots nontaxable amount for any taxable year is 25 percent of its lobbying nontaxable amount for that year.

(d) *Examples.*—The provisions of this section are illustrated by the examples in §1.501(h)-3. [Reg. §56.4911-1.]

☐ [T.D. 8308, 8-30-90.]

[Reg. §56.4911-2]

§56.4911-2. Lobbying expenditures, direct lobbying communications, and grass roots lobbying communications.—(a) *Lobbying expenditures.*—(1) *In general.*—An electing public charity's lobbying expenditures for a year are the sum of its expenditures during that year for direct lobbying communications ("direct lobbying expenditures") plus its expenditures during that year for grass roots lobbying communications ("grass roots expenditures").

(2) *Overview of §56.4911-2 and the definitions of "direct lobbying communication" and "grass roots lobbying communication".*—Paragraph (b)(1) of

this section defines the term "direct lobbying communication." Paragraph (b)(2) of this section provides the general definition of the term "grass roots lobbying communication." (But also see paragraph (b)(5) of this section (special rebuttable presumption regarding certain paid mass media communications) and §56.4911-5 (special, more lenient, definitions for certain communications from an electing public charity to its bona fide members)). Paragraph (b)(3) of this section lists and cross-references various exceptions to the definitions set forth in paragraphs (b)(1) and (2) (the text of the exceptions, along with relevant definitions and examples, is generally set forth in paragraph (c)). Paragraph (b)(4) of this section contains numerous examples illustrating the application of paragraphs (b)(1), (2) and (3). As mentioned above, paragraph (b)(5) of this section sets forth the special rebuttable presumption regarding a limited number of paid mass media communications about highly publicized legislation. Paragraph (d) of this section contains definitions of (and examples illustrating) various terms used in this section.

(b) *Influencing legislation: direct and grass roots lobbying communications defined.*—(1) *Direct lobbying communication.*—(i) *Definition.*—A direct lobbying communication is any attempt to influence any legislation through communication with:

(A) Any member or employee of a legislative body; or

(B) Any government official or employee (other than a member or employee of a legislative body) who may participate in the formulation of the legislation, but only if the principal purpose of the communication is to influence legislation.

(ii) *Required elements.*—A communication with a legislator or government official will be treated as a direct lobbying communication under this §56.4911-2(b)(1) if, but only if, the communication:

(A) Refers to specific legislation (see paragraph (d)(1) of this section for a definition of the term "specific legislation"); and

(B) Reflects a view on such legislation.

(iii) *Special rule for referenda, ballot initiatives or similar procedures.*—Solely for purposes of this section 4911, where a communication refers to and reflects a view on a measure that is the subject of a referendum, ballot initiative or similar procedure, the general public in the state or locality where the vote will take place constitutes the legislative body, and individual members of the general public are, for purposes of this paragraph (b)(1), legislators. Accordingly, if such a communication is made to one or more members of the general public in that state or locality, the communication is a direct lobbying communication (unless it is nonpartisan analysis, study or research (see paragraph (c)(1) of this section).

(2) *Grass roots lobbying communication.*—(i) *Definition.*—A grass roots lobbying communi-

cation is any attempt to influence any legislation through an attempt to affect the opinions of the general public or any segment thereof.

(ii) *Required elements.*—A communication will be treated as a grass roots lobbying communication under this §56.4911-2(b)(2)(ii) if, but only if, the communication:

(A) Refers to specific legislation (see paragraph (d)(1) of this section for a definition of the term "specific legislation");

(B) Reflects a view on such legislation; and

(C) Encourages the recipient of the communication to take action with respect to such legislation (see paragraph (b)(2)(iii) of this section for the definition of encouraging the recipient to take action).

For special, more lenient rules regarding an organization's communications directed only or primarily to bona fide members of the organization, see §56.4911-5. For special rules regarding certain paid mass media advertisements about highly publicized legislation, see paragraph (b)(5) of this section. For special rules regarding lobbying on referenda, ballot initiatives and similar procedures, see paragraph (b)(1)(iii) of this section)).

(iii) *Definition of encouraging recipient to take action.*—For purposes of this section, encouraging a recipient to take action with respect to legislation means that the communication:

(A) States that the recipient should contact a legislator or an employee of a legislative body, or should contact any other government official or employee who may participate in the formulation of legislation (but only if the principal purpose of urging contact with the government official or employee is to influence legislation);

(B) States the address, telephone number, or similar information of a legislator or an employee of a legislative body;

(C) Provides a petition, tear-off postcard or similar material for the recipient to communicate with a legislator or an employee of a legislative body, or with any other government official or employee who may participate in the formulation of legislation (but only if the principal purpose of so facilitating contact with the government official or employee is to influence legislation); or

(D) Specifically identifies one or more legislators who will vote on the legislation as: opposing the communication's view with respect to the legislation; being undecided with respect to the legislation; being the recipient's representative in the legislature; or being a member of the legislative committee or subcommittee that will consider the legislation. Encouraging the recipient to take action under this paragraph (b)(2)(iii)(D) does not include naming the main sponsor(s) of the legislation for purposes of identifying the legislation.

(iv) *Definition of directly encouraging recipient to take action.*—Communications described in one or more of paragraphs (b)(2)(iii) (A) through (C) of this section not only "encourage," but also "directly encourage" the recipient to take action with respect to legislation. Communications described in paragraph (b)(2)(iii)(D) of this section, however, do not directly encourage the recipient to take action with respect to legislation. Thus, a communication would encourage the recipient to take action with respect to legislation, but not *directly* encourage such action, if the communication does no more than identify one or more legislators who will vote on the legislation as: opposing the communication's view with respect to the legislation; being undecided with respect to the legislation; being the recipient's representative in the legislature; or being a member of the legislative committee or subcommittee that will consider the legislation. Communications that encourage the recipient to take action with respect to legislation but that do not *directly* encourage the recipient to take action with respect to legislation may be within the exception for nonpartisan analysis, study or research (see paragraph (c)(1) of this section) and thus not be grass roots lobbying communications.

(v) *Subsequent lobbying use of nonlobbying communications or research materials.*—(A) *Limited effect of application.*—Even though certain communications or research materials are initially not grass roots lobbying communications under the general definition set forth in paragraph (b)(2)(ii) of this section, subsequent use of the communications or research materials for grass roots lobbying may cause them to be treated as grass roots lobbying communications. This paragraph (b)(2)(v) does not cause any communications or research materials to be considered direct lobbying communications.

(B) *Limited scope of application.*—Under this paragraph (b)(2)(v), only "*advocacy* communications or research materials" are potentially treated as grass roots lobbying communications. Communications or research materials that are not "*advocacy* communications or research materials" are not treated as grass roots lobbying communications under this paragraph (b)(2)(v). "Advocacy communications or research materials" are any communications or materials that both refer to and reflect a view on specific legislation but that do not, in their initial format, contain a direct encouragement for recipients to take action with respect to legislation.

(C) *Subsequent use in lobbying.*—Where advocacy communications or research materials are subsequently accompanied by a direct encouragement for recipients to take action with respect to legislation, the advocacy communications or research materials themselves are treated as grass roots lobbying communications unless the organization's primary purpose in undertaking or preparing the advocacy communications or research materials was not for use in lobbying. In such a case, all expenses of preparing and distributing the advocacy communications or research materials will be treated as grass roots expenditures.

(D) *Time limit on application of subsequent use rule.*—The characterization of expenditures as grass roots lobbying expenditures under paragraph (b)(2)(v)(C) shall apply only to expenditures paid less than six months before the first use of the advocacy communications or research materials with a direct encouragement to action.

(E) *Safe harbor in determining "Primary Purpose".*—The primary purpose of the organization in undertaking or preparing advocacy communications or research materials will not be considered to be for use in lobbying if, prior to or contemporaneously with the use of the advocacy communications or research materials with the direct encouragement to action, the organization makes a substantial nonlobbying distribution of the advocacy communications or research materials (without the direct encouragement to action). Whether a distribution is substantial will be determined by reference to all of the facts and circumstances, including the normal distribution pattern of similar nonpartisan analyses, studies or research by that and similar organizations.

(F) *Special rule for partisan analysis, study or research.*—In the case of advocacy communications or research materials that are not nonpartisan analysis, study or research, the nonlobbying distribution thereof will not be considered "substantial" unless that distribution is at least as extensive as the lobbying distribution thereof.

(G) *Factors considered in determining primary purpose.*—Where the nonlobbying distribution of advocacy communications or research materials is not substantial, all of the facts and circumstances must be weighed to determine whether the organization's primary purpose in preparing the advocacy communications or research materials was for use in lobbying. While not the only factor, the extent of the organization's nonlobbying distribution of the advocacy communications or research materials is particularly relevant, especially when compared to the extent of their distribution with the direct encouragement to action. Another particularly relevant factor is whether the lobbying use of the advocacy communications or research materials is by the organization that prepared the document, a related organization, or an unrelated organization. Where the subsequent lobbying distribution is made by an unrelated organization, clear and convincing evidence (which must include evidence demonstrating cooperation or collusion between the two organizations) will be required to establish that the primary purpose for preparing the communication was for use in lobbying.

(H) *Examples.*—The provisions of this paragraph (b)(2)(v) are illustrated by the following examples:

Example (1). Assume a nonlobbying "report" (that is not nonpartisan analysis, study or research) is prepared by an organization, but distributed to only 50 people. The report, in that format, refers to and reflects a view on specific legislation but does not contain a direct encouragement for the recipients to take action with respect to legislation. Two months later, the organization sends the report to 10,000 people along with a letter urging recipients to write their Senators about the legislation discussed in the report. Because the report's nonlobbying distribution is not as extensive as its lobbying distribution, the report's nonlobbying distribution is not substantial for purposes of this paragraph (b)(2)(v). Accordingly, the organization's primary purpose in preparing the report must be determined by weighing all of the facts and circumstances. In light of the relatively minimal nonlobbying distribution and the fact that the lobbying distribution is by the preparing organization rather than by an unrelated organization, and in the absence of evidence to the contrary, both the report and the letter are grass roots lobbying communications. Assume that all costs of preparing the report were paid within the six months preceding the mailing of the letter. Accordingly, all of the organization's expenditures for preparing and mailing the two documents are grass roots lobbying expenditures.

Example (2). Assume the same facts as in Example (1), except that the costs of the report are paid over the two month period of January and February. Between January 1 and 31, the organization pays $1,000 for the report. In February, the organization pays $500 for the report. Further assume that the report is first used with a direct encouragement to action on August 1. Six months prior to August 1 is February 1. Accordingly, no costs paid for the report before February 1 are treated as grass roots lobbying expenditures under the subsequent use rule. Under these facts, the subsequent use rule treats only the $500 paid for the report in February as grass roots lobbying expenditures.

(3) *Exceptions to the definition of influencing legislation.*—In many cases, a communication is not a direct or grass roots lobbying communication under paragraph (b)(1) or (b)(2) of this section if it falls within one of the exceptions listed in paragraph (c) of this section. See paragraph (c)(1), *Nonpartisan analysis, study or research;* paragraph (c)(2), *Examinations and discussions of broad social, economic and similar problems;* paragraph (c)(3), *Requests for technical advice;* and paragraph (c)(4), *Communications pertaining to self-defense by the organization.* In addition, see § 56.4911-5, which provides special rules regarding the treatment of certain lobbying communications directed in whole or in part to members of an electing public charity.

(4) *Examples.*—This paragraph (b)(4) provides examples to illustrate the rules set forth in this section regarding direct and grass roots lobbying. The expenditure test election under section 501(h) is assumed to be in effect for all organizations discussed in the examples in this paragraph (b)(4). In addition, it is assumed that

Reg. §56.4911-2(b)(4)

the special rules of §56.4911-5, regarding certain of a public charity's communications with its members, do not apply to any of the examples in this paragraph (b)(4).

(i) *Direct lobbying.*—The provisions of this section regarding direct lobbying communications are illustrated by the following examples:

Example (1). Organization P's employee, X, is assigned to approach members of Congress to gain their support for a pending bill. X drafts and P prints a position letter on the bill. P distributes the letter to members of Congress. Additionally, X personally contacts several members of Congress or their staffs to seek support for P's position on the bill. The letter and the personal contacts are direct lobbying communications.

Example (2). Organization M's president writes a letter to the Congresswoman representing the district in which M is headquartered, requesting that the Congresswoman write an administrative agency regarding proposed regulations recently published by that agency. M's president also requests that the Congresswoman's letter to the agency state the Congresswoman's support of M's application for a particular type of permit granted by the agency. The letter written by M's president is not a direct lobbying communication.

Example (3). Organization Z prepares a paper on a particular state's environmental problems. The paper does not reflect a view on any specific pending legislation or on any specific legislative proposal that Z either supports or opposes. Z's representatives give the paper to a state legislator. Z's paper is not a direct lobbying communication.

Example (4). State X enacts a statute that requires the licensing of all day care providers. Agency B in State X is charged with preparing rules to implement the bill enacted by State X. One week after enactment of the bill, organization C sends a letter to Agency B providing detailed proposed rules that organization C suggests to Agency B as the appropriate standards to follow in implementing the statute on licensing of day care providers. Organization C's letter to Agency B is not a lobbying communication.

Example (5). Organization B researches, prepares and prints a code of standards of minimum safety requirements in an area of common electrical wiring. Organization B sells the code of standards booklet to the public and it is widely used by professionals in the installation of electrical wiring. A number of states have codified all, or part, of the code of standards as mandatory safety standards. On occasion, B lobbies state legislators for passage of the code of standards for safety reasons. Because the primary purpose of preparing the code of standards was the promotion of public safety and the standards were specifically used in a profession for that purpose, separate from any legislative requirement, the research, preparation, printing and public distribution of the code of standards is not an expenditure for a direct (or grass roots) lobbying communication. Costs, such as trans-portation, photocopying, and other similar expenses, incurred in lobbying state legislators for passage of the code of standards into law are expenditures for direct lobbying communications.

Example (6). On the organization's own initiative, representatives of Organization F present written testimony to a Congressional committee. The news media report on the testimony of Organization F, detailing F's opposition to a pending bill. The testimony is a direct lobbying communication but is not a grass roots lobbying communication.

Example (7). Organization R's monthly newsletter contains an editorial column that refers to and reflects a view on specific pending bills. R sends the newsletter to 10,000 nonmember subscribers. Senator Doe is among the subscribers. The editorial column in the newsletter copy sent to Senator Doe is not a direct lobbying communication because the newsletter is sent to Senator Doe in her capacity as a subscriber rather than her capacity as a legislator. (Note, though, that the editorial column may be a grass roots lobbying communication if it encourages recipients to take action with respect to the pending bills it refers to and on which it reflects a view).

Example (8). Assume the same facts as in Example (7), except that one of Senator Doe's staff members sees Senator Doe's copy of the editorial and writes to R requesting additional information. R responds with a letter that refers to and reflects a view on specific legislation. R's letter is a direct lobbying communication unless it is within one of the exceptions set forth in paragraph (c) of this section (such as the exception for nonpartisan analysis, study or research). (R's letter is not within the scope of the exception for responses to written requests from a legislative body or committee for technical advice (see paragraph (c)(3) of this section) because the letter is not in response to a written request from a legislative body or committee).

(ii) *Grass roots lobbying.*—The provisions of this section regarding grass roots lobbying communications are illustrated in paragraph (b)(4)(ii) (A) of this section by examples of communications that are not grass roots lobbying communications and in paragraph (b)(4)(ii)(B) by examples of communications that are grass roots lobbying communications. The provisions of this section are further illustrated in paragraph (b)(4)(ii)(C), with particular regard to the exception for nonpartisan analysis, study, or research:

(A) *Communications that are not grass roots lobbying communications.*

Example (1). Organization L places in its newsletter an article that asserts that lack of new capital is hurting State W's economy. The article recommends that State W residents either invest more in local businesses or increase their savings so that funds will be available to others interested in making investments. The article is an attempt to influence opinions with respect to a general problem that might receive legislative attention and is distributed in a manner so as to reach and influence many individuals. However, the article does not refer to specific legislation that is pending in a legislative body, nor does the article refer to a specific legislative proposal the organization either supports or opposes. The article is not a grass roots lobbying communication.

Example (2). Assume the same facts as Example (1), except that the article refers to a bill pending in State W's legislature that is intended to provide tax incentives for private savings. The article praises the pending bill and recommends that it be enacted. However, the article does not encourage readers to take action with respect to the legislation. The article is not a grass roots lobbying communication.

Example (3). Organization B sends a letter to all persons on its mailing list. The letter includes an update on numerous environmental issues with a discussion of general concerns regarding pollution, proposed federal regulations affecting the area, and several pending legislative proposals. The letter endorses two pending bills and opposes another pending bill, but does not name any legislator involved (other than the sponsor of one bill, for purposes of identifying the bill), nor does it otherwise encourage the reader to take action with respect to the legislation. The letter is not a grass roots lobbying communication.

Example (4). A pamphlet distributed by organization Z discusses the dangers of drugs and encourages the public to send their legislators a coupon, printed with the statement "I support a drug-free America." The term "drug-free America" is not widely identified with any of the many specific pending legislative proposals regarding drug issues. The pamphlet does not refer to any of the numerous pending legislative proposals, nor does the organization support or oppose a specific legislative proposal. The pamphlet is not a grass roots lobbying communication.

Example (5). A pamphlet distributed by organization B encourages readers to join an organization and "get involved in the fight against drugs." The text states, in the course of a discussion of several current drug issues, that organization B supports a specific bill before Congress that would establish an expanded drug control program. The pamphlet does not encourage readers to communicate with legislators about the bill (such as by including the names of undecided or opposed legislators). The pamphlet is not a grass roots lobbying communication.

Example (6). Organization E, an environmental organization, routinely summarizes in each edition of its newsletter the new environment-related bills that have been introduced in Congress since the last edition of the newsletter. The newsletter identifies each bill by a bill number and the name of the legislation's sponsor. The newsletter also reports on the status of previously introduced environment-related bills. The summaries and status reports do not encourage recipients of the newsletter to take action with respect to legislation, as described in paragraphs (b)(2)(iii) (A) through (D) of this section. Although the summaries and status reports refer to specific legislation and often reflect a view on such legislation, they do not encourage the newsletter recipients to take action with respect to such legislation. The summaries and status reports are not grass roots lobbying communications.

Example (7). Organization B prints in its newsletter a report on pending legislation that B supports, the Family Equity bill. The report refers to and reflects a view on the Family Equity bill, but does not directly encourage recipients to take action. Nor does the report specifically identify any legislator as opposing the communication's view on the legislation, as being undecided, or as being a member of the legislative committee or subcommittee that will consider the legislation. However, the report does state the following:

Rep. Doe (D-Ky.) and Rep. Roe (R-Ma.), both ardent supporters of the Family Equity bill, spoke at B's annual convention last week. Both encouraged B's efforts to get the Family Equity bill enacted and stated that they thought the bill could be enacted even over a presidential veto. B's legislative affairs liaison questioned others, who seemed to agree with that assessment. For example, Sen. Roe (I-Ca.) said that he thinks the bill will pass with such a large majority, "the President won't even consider vetoing it".

Assume the newsletter, and thus the report, is sent to individuals throughout the U.S., including some recipients in Kentucky, Massachusetts and California. Because the report is distributed nationally, the mere fact that the report identifies several legislators by party and state as part of its discussion does not mean the report specifically identifies the named legislators as the Kentucky, Massachusetts and California recipients' representatives in the legislature for purposes of paragraph (b)(2)(iii) of this section. The report is not a grass roots lobbying communication.

(B) *Communications that are grass roots communications.*

Example (1). A pamphlet distributed by organization Y states that the "President's plan for a drug-free America," which will establish a drug control program, should be passed. The pamphlet encourages readers to "write or call your senators and representatives and tell them to vote for the President's plan." No legislative proposal formally bears the name "President's plan for a drug-free America," but that and similar terms have been widely used in connection with specific legislation pending in Congress that was initially proposed by the President. Thus, the pamphlet refers to specific legislation, reflects a view on the legislation, and encourages readers to take action with respect to the legislation. The pamphlet is a grass roots lobbying communication.

Reg. §56.4911-2(b)(4)(ii)(B)

Example (2). Assume the same facts as in Example (1), except that the pamphlet does not encourage the public to write or call representatives, but does list the members of the committee that will consider the bill. The pamphlet is a grass roots lobbying communication.

Example (3). Assume the same facts as in Example (1), except that the pamphlet encourages readers to "write the President to urge him to make the bill a top legislative priority" rather than encouraging readers to communicate with members of Congress. The pamphlet is a grass roots lobbying communication.

Example (4). Organization B, a nonmembership organization, includes in one of three sections of its newsletter an endorsement of two pending bills and opposition to another pending bill and also identifies several legislators as undecided on the three bills. The section of the newsletter devoted to the three pending bills is a grass roots lobbying communication.

Example (5). Organization D, a nonmembership organization, sends a letter to all persons on its mailing list. The letter includes an extensive discussion concluding that a significant increase in spending for the Air Force is essential in order to provide an adequate defense of the nation. Prior to a concluding fund raising request, the letter encourages readers to write their Congressional representatives urging increased appropriations to build the B-1 bomber. The letter is a grass roots lobbying communication.

Example (6). The President nominates X for a position in the President's cabinet. Organization Y disagrees with the views of X and does not believe X has the necessary administrative capabilities to effectively run a cabinet-level department. Accordingly, Y sends a general mailing requesting recipients to write to four Senators on the Senate Committee that will consider the nomination. The mailing is a grass roots lobbying communication.

Example (7). Organization F mails letters requesting that each recipient contribute money to or join F. In addition, the letters express F's opposition to a pending bill that is to be voted upon by the U.S. House of Representatives. Although the letters are form letters sent as a mass mailing, each letter is individualized to report to the recipient the name of the recipient's congressional representative. The letters are grass roots lobbying communications.

Example (8). Organization C sends a mailing that opposes a specific legislative proposal and includes a postcard addressed to the President for the recipient to sign stating opposition to the proposal. The letter requests that the recipient send to C a contribution as well as the postcard opposing the proposal. C states in the letter that it will deliver all the postcards to the White House. The letter is a grass roots lobbying communication.

(C) *Additional examples.*
Example (1). The newsletter of an organization concerned with drug issues is circulated primarily to individuals who are not members of the organization. A story in the newsletter reports on the prospects for passage of a specifically identified bill, stating that the organization supports the bill. The newsletter story identifies certain legislators as undecided, but does not state that readers should contact the undecided legislators. The story does not provide a full and fair exposition sufficient to qualify as nonpartisan analysis, study or research. The newsletter story is a grass roots lobbying communication.

Example (2). Assume the same facts as in Example (1), except that the newsletter story provides a full and fair exposition sufficient to qualify as nonpartisan analysis, study or research. The newsletter story is *not* a grass roots lobbying communication because it is within the exception for nonpartisan analysis, study or research (since it does not *directly* encourage recipients to take action).

Example (3). Assume the same facts as in Example (2), except that the newsletter story explicitly asks readers to contact the undecided legislators. Because the newsletter story directly encourages readers to take action with respect to the legislation, the newsletter story is not within the exception for nonpartisan analysis, study or research. Accordingly, the newsletter story is a grass roots lobbying communication.

Example (4). Assume the same facts as in Example (1), except that the story does not identify any undecided legislators. The story is not a grass roots lobbying communication.

Example (5). X organization places an advertisement that specifically identifies and opposes a bill that X asserts would harm the farm economy. The advertisement is not a mass media communication described in paragraph (b)(5)(ii) of this section and does not directly encourage readers to take action with respect to the bill. However, the advertisement does state that Senator Y favors the legislation. Because the advertisement refers to and reflects a view on specific legislation, and also encourages the readers to take action with respect to the legislation by specifically identifying a legislator who opposes X's views on the legislation, the advertisement is a grass roots lobbying communication.

Example (6). Assume the same facts as in Example (5), except that instead of identifying Senator Y as favoring the legislation, the advertisement identifies the "junior Senator from State Z" as favoring the legislation. The advertisement is a grass roots lobbying communication.

Example (7). Assume the same facts as in Example (5), except that instead of identifying Senator Y as favoring the legislation, the advertisement states: "Even though this bill will have a devastating effect upon the farm economy, most of the Senators from the Farm Belt states are inexplicably in favor of the bill." The advertisement does not specifically identify one or more legislators as opposing the advertisement's view on the bill in question. Accordingly, the advertisement is not a grass roots lobbying communication because it does not encourage readers to take action with respect to the legislation.

Example (8). Organization V trains volunteers to go door-to-door to seek signatures for petitions to be sent to legislators in favor of a specific bill. The volunteers are wholly unreimbursed for their time and expenses. The volunteers' costs (to the extent any are incurred) are not lobbying or exempt purpose expenditures made by V (but the volunteers may not deduct their out-of-pocket expenditures (see section 170(f)(6)). When V asks the volunteers to contact others and urge them to sign the petitions, V encourages those volunteers to take action in favor of the specific bill. Accordingly, V's costs of soliciting the volunteers' help and its costs of training the volunteers are grass roots expenditures. In addition, the costs of preparing, copying, distributing, etc. the petitions (and any other materials on the same specific subject used in the door-to-door signature gathering effort), are grass roots expenditures.

(5) *Special rule for certain mass media advertisements.*—(i) *In general.*—A mass media advertisement that is not a grass roots lobbying communication under the three-part grass roots lobbying definition contained in paragraph (b)(2) of this section may be a grass roots lobbying communication by virtue of paragraph (b)(5)(ii) of this section. The special rule in paragraph (b)(5)(ii) generally applies only to a limited type of paid advertisements that appear in the mass media.

(ii) *Presumption regarding certain paid mass media advertisements about highly publicized legislation.*—If within two weeks before a vote by a legislative body, or a committee (but not a subcommittee) thereof, on a highly publicized piece of legislation, an organization's paid advertisement appears in the mass media, the paid advertisement will be presumed to be a grass roots lobbying communication, but only if the paid advertisement both reflects a view on the general subject of such legislation and either: refers to the highly publicized legislation; or encourages the public to communicate with legislators on the general subject of such legislation. An organization can rebut this presumption by demonstrating that the paid advertisement is a type of communication regularly made by the organization in the mass media without regard to the timing of legislation (that is, a customary course of business exception) or that the timing of the paid advertisement was unrelated to the upcoming legislative action. Notwithstanding the fact that an organization successfully rebuts the presumption, a mass media communication described in this paragraph (b)(5)(ii) is a grass roots lobbying communication if the communication would be a grass roots lobbying communication under the rules contained in paragraph (b)(2) of this section.

(iii) *Definitions.*—(A) *Mass media.*—For purposes of this paragraph (b)(5), the term "mass media" means television, radio, billboards and general circulation newspapers and magazines. General circulation newspapers and magazines do not include newspapers or magazines published by an organization for which the expenditure test election under section 501(h) is in effect, except where both: the total circulation of the newspaper or magazine is greater than 100,000; and fewer than one-half of the recipients are members of the organization (as defined in § 56.4911-5(f)).

(B) *Paid advertisement.*—For purposes of this paragraph (b)(5), where an electing public charity is itself a mass media publisher or broadcaster, all portions of that organization's mass media publications or broadcasts are treated as paid advertisements in the mass media, except those specific portions that are advertisements paid for by another person. The term "mass media" is defined in paragraph (b)(5)(iii)(A).

(C) *Highly publicized.*—For purposes of this paragraph (b)(5), "highly publicized" means frequent coverage on television and radio, and in general circulation newspapers, during the two weeks preceding the vote by the legislative body or committee. In the case of state or local legislation, "highly publicized" means frequent coverage in the mass media that serve the state or local jurisdiction in question. Even where legislation receives frequent coverage, it is "highly publicized" only if the pendency of the legislation or the legislation's general terms, purpose, or effect are known to a significant segment of the general public (as opposed to the particular interest groups directly affected) in the area in which the paid mass media advertisement appears.

(iv) *Examples.*—The special rule of this paragraph (b)(5) is illustrated by the following examples. The expenditure test election under section 501(h) is assumed to be in effect for all organizations discussed in the examples in this paragraph (b)(5)(iv):

Example (1). Organization X places a television advertisement advocating one of the President's major foreign policy initiatives, as outlined by the President in a series of speeches and as drafted into proposed legislation. The initiative is popularly known as "the President's World Peace Plan," and is voted upon by the Senate four days after X's advertisement. The advertisement concludes: "SUPPORT THE PRESIDENT'S WORLD PEACE PLAN!" The President's plan and position are highly publicized during the two weeks before the Senate vote, as evidenced by: coverage of the plan on several nightly television network news programs; more than one article about the plan on the front page of a majority of the country's ten largest daily general circulation newspapers; and an editorial about the plan in four of the country's ten largest daily general circulation newspapers. Although the advertisement does not encourage readers to contact legislators or other government officials, the advertisement does refer to specific legislation and reflect a view on

Reg. § 56.4911-2(b)(5)(iv)

the general subject of the legislation. The communication is presumed to be a grass roots lobbying communication.

Example (2). Assume the same facts as in Example (1), except that the advertisement appears three weeks before the Senate's vote on the plan. Because the advertisement appears more than two weeks before the legislative vote, the advertisement is *not* within the scope of the special rule for mass media communications on highly publicized legislation. Accordingly, the advertisement is a grass roots lobbying communication only if it is described in the general definition contained in paragraph (b)(2) of this section. Because the advertisement does not encourage recipients to take action with respect to the legislation in question, the advertisement is not a grass roots lobbying communication.

Example (3). Organization Y places a newspaper advertisement advocating increased government funding for certain public works projects the President has proposed and that are being considered by a legislative committee. The advertisement explains the President's proposals and concludes: "SUPPORT FUNDING FOR THESE VITAL PROJECTS!" The advertisement does not encourage readers to contact legislators or other government officials nor does it name any undecided legislators, but it does name the legislation being considered by the committee. The President's proposed funding of public works, however, is not highly publicized during the two weeks before the vote: there has been little coverage of the issue on nightly television network news programs, only one front-page article on the issue in the country's ten largest daily general circulation newspapers, and only one editorial about the issue in the country's ten largest daily general circulation newspapers. Two days after the advertisement appears, the committee votes to approve funding of the projects. Although the advertisement appears less than two weeks before the legislative vote, the advertisement is *not* within the scope of the special rule for mass media communications on highly publicized legislation because the issue of funding for public works projects is not highly publicized. Thus, the advertisement is a grass roots lobbying communication only if it is described in the general definition contained in paragraph (b)(2) of this section. Because the advertisement does not encourage recipients to take action with respect to the legislation in question, the advertisement is not a grass roots lobbying communication.

Example (4). Organization P places numerous advertisements in the mass media about a bill being considered by the State Assembly. The bill is highly publicized, as evidenced by numerous front-page articles, editorials and letters to the editor published in the state's general circulation daily newspapers, as well as frequent coverage of the bill by the television and radio stations serving the state. The advertisements run over a three week period and, in addition to showing pictures of a family being robbed at gunpoint, say: "The State Assembly is consider-

ing a bill to make gun ownership illegal. This outrageous legislation would violate your constitutional rights and the rights of other law-abiding citizens. If this legislation is passed, you and your family will be criminals if you want to exercise your right to protect yourselves." The advertisements refer to and reflect a view on a specific bill but do not encourage recipients to take action. Sixteen days after the last advertisement runs, a State Assembly committee votes to defeat the legislation. None of the advertisements is a grass roots lobbying communication.

Example (5). Assume the same facts as in Example (4), except that it is publicly announced prior to the advertising campaign that the committee vote is scheduled for five days after the last advertisement runs. Because of public pressure resulting from the advertising campaign, the bill is withdrawn and no vote is ever taken. None of the advertisements is a grass roots lobbying communication.

(c) *Exceptions to the definitions of direct lobbying communication and grass roots lobbying communication.*—(1) *Nonpartisan analysis, study, or research exception.*—(i) *In general.*—Engaging in nonpartisan analysis, study, or research and making available to the general public or a segment or members thereof or to governmental bodies, officials, or employees the results of such work constitute neither a direct lobbying communication under §56.4911-2(b)(1) nor a grass roots lobbying communication under §56.4911-2(b)(2).

(ii) *Nonpartisan analysis, study, or research.*—For purposes of this section, "nonpartisan analysis, study, or research" means an independent and objective exposition of a particular subject matter, including any activity that is "educational" within the meaning of §1.501(c)(3)-1(d)(3). Thus, "nonpartisan analysis, study, or research" may advocate a particular position or viewpoint so long as there is a sufficiently full and fair exposition of the pertinent facts to enable the public or an individual to form an independent opinion or conclusion. The mere presentation of unsupported opinion, however, does not qualify as "nonpartisan analysis, study, or research".

(iii) *Presentation as part of a series.*—Normally, whether a publication or broadcast qualifies as "nonpartisan analysis, study, or research" will be determined on a presentation-by-presentation basis. However, if a publication or broadcast is one of a series prepared or supported by an electing organization and the series as a whole meets the standards of paragraph (c)(1)(ii) of this section, then any individual publication or broadcast within the series is not a direct or grass roots lobbying communication even though such individual broadcast or publication does not, by itself, meet the standards of paragraph (c)(1)(ii) of this section. Whether a broadcast or publication is considered part of a series will ordinarily depend upon all the facts and circumstances of each particular situation. However, with respect to broadcast activities, all broadcasts within any period of six consecutive months will ordinarily be eligible to be considered as part of a series. If an electing organization times or channels a part of a series which is described in this paragraph (c)(1)(iii) in a manner designed to influence the general public or the action of a legislative body with respect to a specific legislative proposal, the expenses of preparing and distributing such part of the analysis, study, or research will be expenditures for a direct or grass roots lobbying communication, as the case may be.

(iv) *Making available results of nonpartisan analysis, study, or research.*—An organization may choose any suitable means, including oral or written presentations, to distribute the results of its nonpartisan analysis, study, or research, with or without charge. Such means include distribution of reprints of speeches, articles and reports; presentation of information through conferences, meetings and discussions; and dissemination to the news media, including radio, television and newspapers, and to other public forums. For purposes of this paragraph (c)(1)(iv), such communications may not be limited to, or be directed toward, persons who are interested solely in one side of a particular issue.

(v) *Subsequent lobbying use of certain analysis, study or research.*—Even though certain analysis, study or research is initially within the exception for nonpartisan analysis, study or research, subsequent use of that analysis, study or research for grass roots lobbying may cause that analysis, study or research to be treated as a grass roots lobbying communication that is not within the exception for nonpartisan analysis, study or research. This paragraph (c)(1)(v) does not cause any analysis, study or research to be considered a direct lobbying communication. For rules regarding when analysis, study or research is treated as a grass roots lobbying communication that is not within the scope of the exception for nonpartisan analysis, study or research, see paragraph (b)(2)(v) of this section.

(vi) *Directly encouraging action by recipients of a communication.*—A communication that reflects a view on specific legislation is not within the nonpartisan analysis, study, or research exception of this paragraph (c)(1) if the communication directly encourages the recipient to take action with respect to such legislation. For purposes of this section, a communication directly encourages the recipient to take action with respect to legislation if the communication is described in one or more of paragraphs (b)(2)(iii)(A) through (C) of this section. As described in paragraph (b)(2)(iv) of this section, a communication would encourage the recipient to take action with respect to legislation, but not *directly* encourage such action, if the communication does no more than specifically identify one or more legislators who will vote on the legislation as: opposing the communication's view with respect to the legislation; being undecided with respect to the legislation; being the recipi-

ent's representative in the legislature; or being a member of the legislative committee or subcommittee that will consider the legislation.

(vii) *Examples.*—The provisions of this paragraph (c)(1) may be illustrated by the following examples:

Example (1). Organization M establishes a research project to collect information for the purpose of showing the dangers of the use of pesticides in raising crops. The information collected includes data with respect to proposed legislation, pending before several State legislatures, which would ban the use of pesticides. The project takes favorable positions on such legislation without producing a sufficiently full and fair exposition of the pertinent facts to enable the public or an individual to form an independent opinion or conclusion on the pros and cons of the use of pesticides. This project is not within the exception for nonpartisan analysis, study, or research because it is designed to present information merely on one side of the legislative controversy.

Example (2). Organization N establishes a research project to collect information concerning the dangers of the use of pesticides in raising crops for the ostensible purpose of examining and reporting information as to the pros and cons of the use of pesticides in raising crops. The information is collected and distributed in the form of a published report which analyzes the effects and costs of the use and nonuse of various pesticides under various conditions on humans, animals and crops. The report also presents the advantages, disadvantages, and economic cost of allowing the continued use of pesticides unabated, of controlling the use of pesticides, and of developing alternatives to pesticides. Even if the report sets forth conclusions that the disadvantages as a result of using pesticides are greater than the advantages of using pesticides and that prompt legislative regulation of the use of pesticides is needed, the project is within the exception for nonpartisan analysis, study, or research since it is designed to present information on both sides of the legislative controversy and presents a sufficiently full and fair exposition of the pertinent facts to enable the public or an individual to form an independent opinion or conclusion.

Example (3). Organization O establishes a research project to collect information on the presence or absence of disease in humans from eating food grown with pesticides and the presence or absence of disease in humans from eating food not grown with pesticides. As part of the research project, O hires a consultant who prepares a "fact sheet" which calls for the curtailment of the use of pesticides and which addresses itself to the merits of several specific legislative proposals to curtail the use of pesticides in raising crops which are currently pending before State Legislatures. The "fact sheet" presents reports of experimental evidence tending to support its conclusions but omits any reference to reports of experimental evidence

Reg. §56.4911-2(c)(1)(vii)

tending to dispute its conclusions. O distributes ten thousand copies to citizens' groups. Expenditures by O in connection with this work of the consultant are not within the exception for nonpartisan analysis, study, or research.

Example (4). P publishes a bimonthly newsletter to collect and report all published materials, ongoing research, and new developments with regard to the use of pesticides in raising crops. The newsletter also includes notices of proposed pesticide legislation with impartial summaries of the provisions and debates on such legislation. The newsletter does not encourage recipients to take action with respect to such legislation, but is designed to present information on both sides of the legislative controversy and does present such information fully and fairly. It is within the exception for nonpartisan analysis, study, or research.

Example (5). X is satisfied that A, a member of the faculty of Y University, is exceptionally well qualified to undertake a project involving a comprehensive study of the effects of pesticides on crop yields. Consequently, X makes a grant to A to underwrite the cost of the study and of the preparation of a book on the effect of pesticides on crop yields. X does not take any position on the issues or control the content of A's output. A produces a book which concludes that the use of pesticides often has a favorable effect on crop yields, and on that basis argues against pending bills which would ban the use of pesticides. A's book contains a sufficiently full and fair exposition of the pertinent facts, including known or potential disadvantages of the use of pesticides, to enable the public or an individual to form an independent opinion or conclusion as to whether pesticides should be banned as provided in the pending bills. The book does not directly encourage readers to take action with respect to the pending bills. Consequently, the book is within the exception for nonpartisan analysis, study, or research.

Example (6). Assume the same facts as Example (2), except that, instead of issuing a report, X presents within a period of 6 consecutive months a two-program television series relating to the pesticide issue. The first program contains information, arguments, and conclusions favoring legislation to restrict the use of pesticides. The second program contains information, arguments, and conclusions opposing legislation to restrict the use of pesticides. The programs are broadcast within 6 months of each other during commensurate periods of prime time. X's programs are within the exception for nonpartisan analysis, study, or research. Although neither program individually could be regarded as nonpartisan, the series of two programs constitutes a balanced presentation.

Example (7). Assume the same facts as in Example (6), except that X arranged for televising the program favoring legislation to restrict the use of pesticides at 8:00 on a Thursday evening and for televising the program opposing such legislation at 7:00 on a Sunday morning. X's presentation is not within the exception for non-

partisan analysis, study, or research, since X disseminated its information in a manner prejudicial to one side of the legislative controversy.

Example (8). Organization Z researches, writes, prints and distributes a study on the use and effects of pesticide X. A bill is pending in the U.S. Senate to ban the use of pesticide X. Z's study leads to the conclusion that pesticide X is extremely harmful and that the bill pending in the U.S. Senate is an appropriate and much needed remedy to solve the problems caused by pesticide X. The study contains a sufficiently full and fair exposition of the pertinent facts, including known or potential advantages of the use of pesticide X, to enable the public or an individual to form an independent opinion or conclusion as to whether pesticides should be banned as provided in the pending bill. In its analysis of the pending bill, the study names certain undecided senators on the Senate committee considering the bill. Although the study meets the three-part test for determining whether a communication is a grass roots lobbying communication, the study is within the exception for nonpartisan analysis, study or research, because it does not directly encourage recipients of the communication to urge a legislator to oppose the bill.

Example (9). Assume the same facts as in Example (8), except that, after stating support for the pending bill, the study concludes: "You should write to the undecided committee members to support this crucial bill." The study is not within the exception for nonpartisan analysis, study or research because it directly encourages the recipients to urge a legislator to support a specific piece of legislation.

Example (10). Organization X plans to conduct a lobbying campaign with respect to illegal drug use in the United States. It incurs $5,000 in expenses to conduct research and prepare an extensive report primarily for use in the lobbying campaign. Although the detailed report discusses specific pending legislation and reaches the conclusion that the legislation would reduce illegal drug use, the report contains a sufficiently full and fair exposition of the pertinent facts to enable the public or an individual to form an independent conclusion regarding the effect of the legislation. The report does not encourage readers to contact legislators regarding the legislation. Accordingly, the report does not, in and of itself, constitute a lobbying communication.

Copies of the report are available to the public at X's office, but X does not actively distribute the report or otherwise seek to make the contents of the report available to the general public. Whether or not X's distribution is sufficient to meet the requirement in §56.4911-2(c)(1)(iv) that a nonpartisan communication be made available, X's distribution is not substantial (for purposes of §56.4911-2(b)(2)(v)(E)) in light of all of the facts and circumstances, including the normal distribution pattern of similar nonpartisan reports. X then mails copies of the report, along with a letter, to 10,000 individuals on X's mailing list. In the letter, X requests that individuals contact legislators urging passage of the legislation discussed in the report. Because X's research and report were primarily undertaken by X for lobbying purposes and X did not make a substantial distribution of the report (without an accompanying lobbying message) prior to or contemporaneously with the use of the report in lobbying, the report is a grass roots lobbying communication that is not within the exception for nonpartisan analysis, study or research.

Example (11). Assume the same facts as in Example (10), except that before using the report in the lobbying campaign, X sends the research and report (without an accompanying lobbying message) to universities and newspapers. At the same time, X also advertises the availability of the report in its newsletter. This distribution is similar in scope to the normal distribution pattern of similar nonpartisan reports. In light of all of the facts and circumstances, X's distribution of the report is substantial. Because of X's substantial distribution of the report, X's primary purpose will be considered to be other than for use in lobbying and the report will not be considered a grass roots lobbying communication. Accordingly, only the expenditures for copying and mailing the report to the 10,000 individuals on X's mailing list, as well as for preparing and mailing the letter, are expenditures for grass roots lobbying communications.

Example (12). Organization M pays for a bumper sticker that reads: "STOP ABORTION: Vote *NO* on Prop. X!" M also pays for a 30-second television advertisement and a billboard that similarly advocate opposition to Prop. X. In light of the limited scope of the communications, none of the communications is within the exception for nonpartisan analysis, study or research. First, none of the communications rises to the level of analysis, study or research. Second, none of the communications is nonpartisan because none contains a sufficiently full and fair exposition of the pertinent facts to enable the public or an individual to form an independent opinion or conclusion. Thus, each communication is a direct lobbying communication.

(2) *Examinations and discussions of broad social, economic, and similar problems.*—Examinations and discussions of broad social, economic, and similar problems are neither direct lobbying communications under §56.4911-2(b)(1) nor grass roots lobbying communications under §56.4911-2(b)(2) even if the problems are of the type with which government would be expected to deal ultimately. Thus, under §56.4911-2(b)(1) and (2), lobbying communications do not include public discussion, or communications with members of legislative bodies or governmental employees, the general subject of which is also the subject of legislation before a legislative body, so long as such discussion does not address itself to the merits of a specific legislative proposal and so long as such discussion does not directly encourage recipients to take action with respect to legislation. For example, this para-

graph (c)(2) excludes from grass roots lobbying under §56.4911-2(b)(2) an organization's discussions of problems such as environmental pollution or population growth that are being considered by Congress and various State legislatures, but only where the discussions are not directly addressed to specific legislation being considered, and only where the discussions do not directly encourage recipients of the communication to contact a legislator, an employee of a legislative body, or a government official or employee who may participate in the formulation of legislation.

(3) *Requests for technical advice.*—A communication is not a direct lobbying communication under §56.4911-2(b)(1) if the communication is the providing of technical advice or assistance to a governmental body, a governmental committee, or a subdivision of either in response to a written request by the body, committee, or subdivision, as set forth in §53.4945-2(d)(2).

(4) *Communications pertaining to "self-defense" by the organization.*—A communication is not a direct lobbying communication under §56.4911-2(b)(1) if either:

(i) The communication is an appearance before, or communication with, any legislative body with respect to a possible action by the body that might affect the existence of the electing public charity, its powers and duties, its tax-exempt status, or the deductibility of contributions to the organization, as set forth in §53.4945-2(d)(3);

(ii) The communication is by a member of an affiliated group of organizations (within the meaning of §56.4911-7(e)), and is an appearance before, or communication with, a legislative body with respect to a possible action by the body that might affect the existence of any other member of the group, its powers and duties, its tax-exempt status, or the deductibility of contributions to it;

(iii) The communication is by an electing public charity more than 75 percent of the members of which are other organizations that are described in section 501(c)(3), and is an appearance before, or communication with, any legislative body with respect to a possible action by the body which might affect the existence of one or more of the section 501(c)(3) member organizations, their powers, duties, or tax-exempt status, or the deductibility (under section 170) of contributions to one or more of the section 501(c)(3) member organizations, but only if the principal purpose of the appearance or communication is to defend the section 501(c)(3) member organizations (rather than the nonsection 501(c)(3) member organizations); or

(iv) The communication is by an electing public charity that is a member of a limited affiliated group of organizations under §56.4911-10, and is an appearance before, or communication with, the Congress of the United States with respect to a possible action by the Congress that might affect the existence of any

Reg. §56.4911-2(c)(4)(iv)

member of the limited affiliated group, its powers and duties, tax-exempt status, or the deductibility of contributions to it.

(v) Under the self-defense exception of paragraphs (c)(4)(i) through (iv) of this section, a charity may communicate with an entire legislative body, with committees or subcommittees of a legislative body, with individual legislators, with legislative staff members, or with representatives of the executive branch who are involved with the legislative process, so long as such communication is limited to the prescribed subjects. Similarly, under the self-defense exception, a charity may make expenditures in order to initiate legislation if such legislation concerns only matters which might affect the existence of the charity, its powers and duties, its tax-exempt status, or the deductibility of contributions to such charity. For examples illustrating the application and scope of the self-defense exception of this paragraph (c)(4), see § 53.4945-2(d)(3)(ii).

(d) *Definitions.*—For purposes of section 4911 and the regulations thereunder—

(1) *Legislation.*—(i) *In general.*—"Legislation" includes action by the Congress, any state legislature, any local council, or similar legislative body, or by the public in a referendum, ballot initiative, constitutional amendment, or similar procedure. "Legislation" includes a proposed treaty required to be submitted by the President to the Senate for its advice and consent from the time the President's representative begins to negotiate its position with the prospective parties to the proposed treaty.

(ii) *Definition of specific legislation.*—For purposes of paragraphs (b)(1) and (b)(2) of this section, "specific legislation" includes both legislation that has already been introduced in a legislative body and a specific legislative proposal that the organization either supports or opposes. In the case of a referendum, ballot initiative, constitutional amendment, or other measure that is placed on the ballot by petitions signed by a required number or percentage of voters, an item becomes "specific legislation" when the petition is first circulated among voters for signature.

(iii) *Examples.*—The terms "legislation" and "specific legislation" are illustrated using the following examples:

Example (1). A nonmembership organization includes in its newsletter an article about problems with the use of pesticide X that states in part: "Legislation that is pending in Congress would prohibit the use of this very dangerous pesticide. Fortunately, the legislation will probably be passed. Write your congressional representatives about this important issue." This is a grass roots lobbying communication that refers to and reflects a view on specific legislation and that encourages recipients to take action with respect to that legislation.

Example (2). An organization based in State A notes in its newsletter that State Z has passed a bill to accomplish a stated purpose and then says that State A should pass such a bill.

The organization urges readers to write their legislators in favor of such a bill. No such bill has been introduced into the State A legislature. The organization has referred to and reflected a view on a specific legislative proposal and has also encouraged readers to take action thereon.

(2) *Action.*—The term "action" in paragraph (d)(1)(i) of this section is limited to the introduction, amendment, enactment, defeat or repeal of acts, bills, resolutions, or similar items.

(3) *Legislative body.*—"Legislative body" does not include executive, judicial, or administrative bodies.

(4) *Administrative bodies.*—"Administrative bodies" includes school boards, housing authorities, sewer and water districts, zoning boards, and other similar Federal, State, or local special purpose bodies, whether elective or appointive. Thus, for example, for purposes of section 4911, the term "any attempt to influence any legislation" does not include attempts to persuade an executive body or department to form, support the formation of, or to acquire property to be used for the formation or expansion of, a public park or equivalent preserves (such as public recreation areas, game, or forest preserves, and soil demonstration areas) established or to be established by act of Congress, by executive action in accordance with an act of Congress, or by a State, municipality or other governmental unit described in section 170(c)(1), as compared with attempts to persuade a legislative body, a member thereof, or other governmental official or employee, to promote the appropriation of funds for such an acquisition or other legislative authorization of such an acquisition. Therefore, for example, an organization would not be influencing legislation for purposes of section 4911, if it proposed to a Park Authority that it purchase a particular tract of land for a new park, even though such an attempt would necessarily require the Park Authority eventually to seek appropriations to support a new park. However, in such a case, the organization would be influencing legislation, for purposes of section 4911, if it provided the Park Authority with a proposed budget to be submitted to a legislative body, unless such submission is described by one of the exceptions set forth in paragraph (c) of this section. [Reg. § 56.4911-2.]

☐ [*T.D.* 8308, 8-30-90.]

[Reg. § 56.4911-3]

§ 56.4911-3. Expenditures for direct and/or grass roots lobbying communications.—(a) *Definition of term "expenditures for".*—(1) *In general.*—This § 56.4911-3 contains allocation rules regarding what portion of a lobbying communication's costs is a direct lobbying expenditure, what portion is a grass roots expenditure and what portion is, in certain cases, a nonlobbying expenditure. Except as otherwise indicated in this paragraph(a), all costs of preparing a direct or grass roots lobbying communication are included as expenditures for direct or grass roots lobbying. Expenditures for a direct or grass roots lobbying communication ("lobbying expenditures") include amounts paid or incurred as current or deferred compensation for an employee's services attributable to the direct or grass roots lobbying communication, and the allocable portion of administrative, overhead, and other general expenditures attributable to the direct or grass roots lobbying communication. For example, except as otherwise provided in this paragraph (a), all expenditures for researching, drafting, reviewing, copying, publishing and mailing a direct or grass roots lobbying communication, as well as an allocable share of overhead expenses, are included as expenditures for direct or grass roots lobbying.

(2) *Allocation of mixed purpose expenditures.*—(i) *Nonmembership communications.*—Except as provided in paragraph (a)(2)(ii) of this section, lobbying expenditures for a communication that also has a bona fide nonlobbying purpose must include all costs attributable to those parts of the communication that are on the same specific subject as the lobbying message. All costs attributable to those parts of the communication that are not on the same specific subject as the lobbying message are not included as lobbying expenditures for allocation purposes. Whether or not a portion of a communication is on the same specific subject as the lobbying message will depend on the surrounding facts and circumstances. In general, a portion of a communication will be on the same specific subject as the lobbying message if that portion discusses an activity or specific issue that would be directly affected by the specific legislation that is the subject of the lobbying message. Moreover, discussion of the background or consequences of the specific legislation, or discussion of the background or consequences of an activity or specific issue affected by the specific legislation, is also considered to be on the same specific subject as the lobbying communication.

(ii) *Membership communications.*—In the case of lobbying expenditures for a communication that also has a bona fide nonlobbying purpose and that is sent only or primarily to members, an electing public charity must make a reasonable allocation between the amount expended for the lobbying purpose and the amount expended for the nonlobbying purpose. An electing public charity that includes as a lobbying expenditure only the amount expended for the specific sentence or sentences that encourage the recipient to take action with respect to legislation has not made a reasonable allocation. For purposes of this paragraph, a communication is sent only or primarily to members if more than half of the recipients of the communication are members of the electing public charity making the communication within the meaning of § 56.4911-5. See § 56.4911-5 for separate rules on communications sent only or primarily to members. Nothing in this paragraph (a) shall change any allocation required by § 56.4911-5.

(3) *Allocation of mixed lobbying.*—If a communication (to which § 56.4911-5 does not apply) is both a direct lobbying communication and a grass roots lobbying communication, the communication will be treated as a grass roots lobbying communication except to the extent that the electing public charity demonstrates that the communication was made primarily for direct lobbying purposes, in which case a reasonable allocation shall be made between the direct and the grass roots lobbying purposes served by the communication.

(b) *Examples.*—The provisions of paragraph (a) of this section are illustrated by the following examples. Except where otherwise explicitly stated, the expenditure test election under section 501(h) is assumed to be in effect for all organizations discussed in the examples in this paragraph (b). See § 56.4911-5 for special rules applying to the member communications described in some of the following examples.

Example (1). Organization R makes the services of E, one of its paid executives, available to S, an organization described in section 501(c)(4) of the Code. E works for several weeks to assist S in developing materials that urge voters to contact their congressional representatives to indicate their support for specific legislation. In performing this work, E uses office space and clerical assistance provided by R. R pays full salary and benefits to E during this period and receives no reimbursement from S for these payments or for the other facilities and assistance provided. All expenditures of R, including allocable office and overhead expenses, that are attributable to this assignment are grass roots expenditures because E was engaged in an attempt to influence legislation.

Example (2). An organization distributes primarily to nonmembers a pamphlet with two articles on unrelated subjects. The total cost of preparing, printing and mailing the pamphlet is $11,000, $1,000 for preparation and $10,000 for printing and mailing. The cost of preparing one article, a nonlobbying communication, is $600. The article is printed on three of the four pages in the pamphlet. The cost of preparing the second article, a grassroots lobbying communication that addresses only one specific subject, is $400. This article is printed on one page of the four page pamphlet. In this situation, $400 of preparation costs and $2,500 (25% of $10,000) of printing and mailing costs are expenditures for a grass roots lobbying communication.

Example (3). Assume the same facts as in Example (2), except that the pamphlet is distributed only to members. In addition, assume the second article states that the recipient members should contact their congressional representatives. The organization allocates $400 of preparation costs and $2,500 of printing and mailing costs as expenditures for direct lobbying (see § 56.4911-5(c)). The allocation is reasonable for purposes of § 56.4911-3(a)(2)(ii).

Example (4). Organization J places a full-page advertisement in a newspaper. The advertisement urges passage of pending legislation to build three additional nuclear powered submarines, and states that readers should write their Congressional representatives in favor of the legislation. The advertisement also provides a general description of J's purposes and activities, invites readers to become members of J and asks readers to contribute money to J. Except for the cost of the portion of the advertisement describing J's purposes and activities and the portion specifically seeking members and contributions, the entire cost of the advertisement is an expenditure for a grass roots lobbying communication, because the entire advertisement, except for the lines specifically describing J and specifically seeking members and contributions, is on the same specific subject as the grass roots lobbying message.

Example (5). Assume the same facts as in Example (4), except that J places in the newspaper two separate half-page advertisements instead of one full-page advertisement. One of the two advertisements discusses the need for three additional nuclear powered submarines and urges readers to write their Congressional representatives in favor of the pending legislation to build the three submarines. The other advertisement contains only the membership and fundraising appeals, along with a general description of J's purposes and activities. The half-page advertisement urging readers to write to Congress is a grass roots lobbying communication and all of J's expenditures for producing and placing that advertisement are expenditures for a grass roots lobbying communication. J's expenditures for the other half-page advertisement are not expenditures for a grass roots or direct lobbying communication.

Example (6). Assume the same facts as in Example (4), except that the communication by J is in a letter mailed only to members of J, rather than in a newspaper advertisement, and the invitation to become a member of J is an invitation to join a new membership category. In addition, assume that the communication states that the member recipients should ask nonmembers to write their Congressional representatives. J allocates one-half of the cost of the mailing as an expenditure for a grass roots lobbying communication (see §56.4911-5(d)). Because the communication had both bona fide nonlobbying (e.g., membership solicitation and fundraising) purposes as well as lobbying purposes, J's allocation of one-half of the cost of the communication to grass roots lobbying and one-half to nonlobbying is reasonable for purposes of §56.4911-3(a)(2)(ii).

Example (7). A particular monthly issue of organizations X's newsletter, which is distributed mainly to nonmembers of X, has three articles of equal length. The first article is a grass roots lobbying communication, the sole specific subject of which is pending legislation to help protect seals from being slaughtered in certain foreign countries. The second article discusses the rapid decline in the world's whale population, particularly because of the illegal hunting of whales by foreign countries. The third article deals with air pollution and the acid rain problem in North America. Because the first article is a grass roots lobbying communication, all of the costs allocable to that article (e.g., one-third of the newsletter's printing and mailing costs) are lobbying expenditures. The second article is not a lobbying communication and the pending legislation relating to seals addressed in the first article does not affect the illegal whale hunting activities. Because the second and third articles are not lobbying communications and are also not on the same specific subject as the first article, no portion of the costs attributable to those articles is a grass roots lobbying expenditure.

Example (8). Organization T, a nonmembership organization, prepares a three page document that is mailed to 3,000 persons on T's mailing list. The first two pages of the three page document, titled "The Need for Child Care," support the need for additional child care programs, and include statistics on the number of children living in homes where both parents work or in homes with a single parent. The two pages also make note of the inadequacy of the number of day care providers to meet the needs of these parents. The third page of the document, titled "H.R. 1," indicates T's support of H.R. 1, a bill pending in the U.S. House of Representatives. The document states that H.R. 1 will provide for $10,000,000 in additional subsidies to child care providers, primarily for those providers caring for lower income children. The third page of the document also notes that H.R. 1 includes new federal standards regulating the quality of child care providers. The document ends with T's request that recipients contact their congressional representative in support of H.R. 1. The entire three page document is on the same specific subject, and, therefore, all expenditures of preparing and distributing the three page document are grass roots lobbying expenditures.

Example (9). Assume the same facts as in Example (8), except that the document has a fourth page. The fourth page does not refer to the general need for child care or the specific need for additional child care providers. Instead, the fourth page advocates that a particular federal agency commence, under its existing statutory authority, licensing of day care providers in order to promote safe and effective child care. The cost of the fourth page is not a lobbying expenditure.

Example (10). Assume the same facts as in Example (8), except that T is a membership organization, 75 percent of the recipients of the three page document are members of T, and 25 percent of the recipients are nonmembers and are not subscribers within the meaning of §56.4911-5(f)(5). Assume also that the document states that readers should write to Congress, but does not state that the readers should urge nonmembers to write to Congress. T treats the document as having a bona fide nonlobbying purpose, the purpose of educating its members about the need for child care. Accordingly, T allocates one-half of the cost of preparing and distributing the document as a lobbying expenditure (see § 56.4911-5(e)(2)(i)), of which 75 percent is a direct lobbying expenditure (see § 56.4911-5(e)(2)(iii)) and 25 percent is a grass roots lobbying expenditure (see § 56.4911-5(e)(2)(ii)). The remaining one-half is allocated as a nonlobbying expenditure. T's allocation is reasonable for purposes of § 56.4911-3(a)(2)(ii) and is correct for purposes of § 56.4911-5(e).

Example (11). Assume the same facts as in Example (10), except that T allocates one percent of the cost of preparing and distributing the document as a lobbying expenditure (for purposes of § 56.4911-5(e)(2)) and 99 percent as a nonlobbying expenditure. T's allocation is based upon the fact that out of 200 lines in the document, only two lines state that the recipient should contact legislators about the pending legislation. T's allocation is unreasonable for purposes of § 56.4911-3(a)(2)(ii).

Example (12). Organization F, a nonmembership organization, sends a one page letter to all persons on its mailing list. The only subject of the letter is the organization's opposition to a pending bill allowing private uses of certain national parks. The letter requests recipients to send letters opposing the bill to their congressional representatives. A second one page letter is sent in the same envelope. The second letter discusses the broad educational activities and publications of the organization in all areas of environmental protection and ends by requesting the recipient to make a financial contribution to organization F. Since the separate second letter is on a different subject from the lobbying letter, and the letters are of equal length, 50 percent of the mailing costs must be allocated as an expenditure for a grass roots lobbying communication.

Example (13). Assume the same facts as in Example (12), except that F is a membership organization and the letters in question are sent primarily (90 percent) to members. The other 10 percent of the recipients are nonmembers and are not subscribers within the meaning of § 56.4911-5(f)(5). Assume also that the first letter does not state that readers should urge nonmembers to write to legislators. F allocates one-half of the mailing costs as a lobbying expenditure, of which 90 percent is a direct lobbying expenditure and 10 percent is a grass roots lobbying expenditure (see § 56.4911-5(e)(2)). F's allocation is reasonable for purposes of § 56.4911-3(a)(2)(ii) and is correct for purposes of § 56.4911-5.

(c) *Certain transfers treated as lobbying expenditures.*—(1) *Transfer earmarked for grass roots purposes.*—A transfer is a grass roots expenditure to the extent that it is earmarked (as defined in § 56.4911-4(f)(4)) for grass roots lobbying purposes and is not described in § 56.4911-4(e).

(2) *Transfer earmarked for direct and grass roots lobbying.*—A transfer that is earmarked for direct lobbying purposes or for direct lobbying and grass roots lobbying purposes is treated as a grass roots expenditure in full except to the ex-

tent the transferor demonstrates that all or part of the amounts transferred were expended for direct lobbying purposes, in which case that part of the amounts transferred is a direct lobbying expenditure by the transferor. This paragraph (c)(2) shall not apply to any expenditure described in § 56.4911-4(e).

(3) *Certain transfers to noncharities that lobby.*—(i) *Limited application of paragraph (c)(3).*—(A) *In general.*—This paragraph (c)(3) applies only to transfers for less than fair market value from an electing public charity to any noncharity that makes lobbying expenditures. A noncharity is any entity that is not described in section 501(c)(3). In order for this paragraph to apply, the electing public charity must transfer to a noncharity more in value than it receives in return. For example, this paragraph does not apply to an electing public charity's fair market value payment of rent to a landlord. However, this paragraph does apply where an electing public charity and a noncharity share office space and the electing public charity pays more than fair market value rent to the noncharity. Similarly, this paragraph applies where an electing public charity sells goods or services to a noncharity for less than fair market value. See paragraphs (c)(3)(i)(B), (C) and (D) of this section for exceptions where non-fair market value transfers are not covered by this paragraph (c)(3). See paragraph (c)(3)(i)(E) of this section to determine the amount of any non-fair market value transfer covered by this paragraph (c)(3). See paragraph (c)(3)(ii) of this section for the rules that apply to transfers governed by this paragraph (c)(3).

(B) *Exception for controlled grants.*—Notwithstanding paragraph (c)(3)(i)(A) of this section, this paragraph (c)(3) does not apply where an electing public charity makes a grant to a noncharity that is a controlled grant (as defined in § 56.49114(f)(3)).

(C) *Exception for transfers that artificially inflate exempt purpose expenditures.*—Notwithstanding paragraph (c)(3)(i)(A) of this section, this paragraph (c)(3) does not apply where an electing public charity makes a grant to a noncharity that is an expenditure described in § 56.4911-4(e) (relating to grants that artificially inflate exempt purpose expenditures).

(D) *Exception for substantially related activity.*—Notwithstanding paragraph (c)(3)(i)(A) of this section, this paragraph (c)(3) does not apply where an electing public charity, in the course of an activity that is substantially related to the accomplishment of the electing public charity's exempt purposes, makes goods or services widely available for less than fair market value to individual members of the general public and those goods or services are actually purchased (or consumed for no charge) by a substantial number of wholly unrelated individual members of the general public for less than fair market value. For purposes of the preceding sentence, the term "individual member of the general public" does not include any person or entity directly or indirectly affiliated with the electing public charity in question. The following example illustrates this paragraph (c)(3)(i)(D):

Example. Organization P is an educational organization dedicated to preserving the environment. One of P's activities is educating the public about the benefits of installing cost-effective passive solar energy systems, thereby helping to preserve the environment. P charges for its extensive literature and advice, but the charges are less than the fair market value of the literature and advice. P makes its literature and advice widely available to individual members of the general public by advertising in various media and by pamphlets distributed in various areas. P annually provides its literature and advice for less than fair market value to 500 wholly unrelated families, businesses, and tax-exempt organizations. Several of the businesses and tax-exempt organizations make lobbying expenditures within the meaning of section 4911. P's provision of its goods and services to these entities is not covered by this paragraph (c)(3) (and thus does not give rise to a lobbying expenditure by P under paragraph (c)(3)(ii)).

(E) *Determination of amount of transfer governed by paragraph (c)(3).*—Where an electing public charity receives nothing of value in return for its transfer, the amount of the transfer governed by this paragraph (c)(3) is the greater of the fair market value or the cost of the goods or services transferred to the noncharity. Where the noncharity transfers something of value to the electing public charity in return for the charity's transfer, but that payment is less than the fair market value of the charity's transfer to the noncharity, the amount of the transfer governed by this paragraph (c)(3) is the excess of: first, the greater of the fair market value or cost of the goods or services transferred to the noncharity over, second, the value of the amount transferred to the charity. For example, if an electing public charity transfers $10,000 of goods and services to a noncharity that makes lobbying expenditures in return for payment by the noncharity of $2,000, the amount of the transfer governed by this paragraph (c)(3) is $8,000.

(ii) *Rules governing transfers to which paragraph (c)(3) applies.*—A transfer to which this paragraph (c)(3) applies is treated in whole or in part as a grass roots and/or direct lobbying expenditure by the transferor in accordance with paragraphs (c)(3)(ii)(A), (B) and (C) of this section. In applying those paragraphs, the expenditures of the transferee will be determined as if the regulations under section 4911 applied to the transferee. This paragraph (c)(3) discusses only when certain transfers are lobbying expenditures by the transferor. This paragraph does not address other issues that may arise when an electing public charity makes a noncontrolled grant to a noncharity. Nothing in this paragraph (c)(3) shall be used to interpret issues relating to noncontrolled grants by charities to noncharities, such as whether the noncontrolled grant is con-

sistent with the continued tax-exempt status of the electing public charity.

(A) *Transfers treated as grass roots expenditures.*—The transfer is treated as a grass roots expenditure to the extent of the lesser of two amounts: the amount of the transfer and the amount of the transferee's grass roots expenditures.

(B) *Transfers treated as direct lobbying expenditures.*—If the transfer is greater than the transferee's grass roots expenditures, the excess is treated as a direct lobbying expenditure, but only to the extent of the transferee's direct lobbying expenditures. (If, however, the transfer is less than the transferee's grass roots expenditures, none of the transfer is a direct lobbying expenditure).

(C) *Transfers treated as non-lobbying.*—If the transfer is greater than the sum of the transferee's grass roots and direct lobbying expenditures, the excess of the transfer over those lobbying expenses is not a lobbying expenditure.

(iii) *Example.*—The following example illustrates the application of this paragraph (c)(3):

Example. Organization C, an electing public charity, shares employee E with N, a noncharity that makes lobbying expenditures. N's grass roots expenditures are $5,000 and its direct lobbying expenditures are $25,000. Each organization pays one-half of the $100,000 in direct and overhead costs associated with E. E devotes one-quarter of his time to C and three-quarters of his time to N. In substance, this arrangement is a transfer (for less than fair market value) from C to N in the amount of $25,000 (one-quarter of the $100,000 of direct and overhead costs associated with E's work). Accordingly, C is treated as having made a $5,000 grass roots expenditure (the lesser of N's grass roots expenditures ($5,000) or the amount of the transfer ($25,000)). C is also treated as having made a $20,000 direct lobbying expenditure (the lesser of N's direct lobbying expenditures ($25,000) or the remaining amount of the transfer ($20,000)). [Reg. § 56.4911-3.]

☐ [*T.D.* 8308, 8-30-90.]

[Reg. § 56.4911-4]

§ 56.4911-4. Exempt purpose expenditures.—(a) *Application.*—This section provides rules under section 4911(e) for determining an electing public charity's "exempt purpose expenditures" for a taxable year for purposes of section 4911(c)(2) and § 56.4911-1(c)(2). Those two sections generally define an electing public charity's lobbying limit (lobbying nontaxable amount) as a sliding scale percentage of the organization's exempt purpose expenditures. In determining an electing public charity's exempt purpose expenditures, no expenditure shall be counted twice by an organization.

(b) *Included expenditures.*—Amounts paid or incurred by an organization that are exempt purpose expenditures include—

(1) Amounts paid or incurred to accomplish a purpose enumerated in section 170(c)(2)(B), including (but not limited to) the amount of any transfer made by the organization (other than a transfer described in paragraph (e) of this section) to another organization to accomplish the transferor's exempt purposes, and including amounts expended by an organization out of transfers (other than a transfer described in paragraph (e) of this section) for which the organization is the transferee,

(2) Amounts paid or incurred as current or deferred compensation for an employee's services for a purpose enumerated in section 170(c)(2)(B),

(3) The allocable portion of administrative overhead, and other general expenditures attributable to the accomplishment of a purpose enumerated in section 170(c)(2)(B),

(4) Lobbying expenditures (as defined in §56.4911-2(a)) whether or not for a purpose enumerated in section 170(c)(2)(B),

(5) Amounts paid or incurred for activities described in §56.4911-2(c),

(6) Amounts paid or incurred for activities described in §56.4911-5 that are not lobbying expenditures,

(7) A reasonable allowance for exhaustion, wear and tear, obsolescence or amortization, of assets to the extent used for one or more of the purposes described in paragraphs (b)(1) through (6) of this section, computed on a straight-line basis (for this purpose, an allowance for depreciation will be treated as reasonable if based on a useful life that would satisfy section 312(k)(3)(A) as in effect on January 1, 1985), and

(8) Fundraising expenditures (but see section 4911(e)(1)(C) and paragraphs (c)(3) and (4) of this section).

(c) *Excluded expenditures.*—Notwithstanding paragraph (b) of this section, exempt purpose expenditures do not include—

(1) Amounts paid or incurred that are neither expenditures to accomplish a purpose enumerated in section 170(c)(2)(B), lobbying expenditures (as defined in §56.4911-2(a)), nor expenditures described in paragraph (b)(5), (6) or (8) of this section,

(2) The amount of any transfer described in paragraph (e) of this section,

(3) Amounts paid to or incurred for a separate fundraising unit (as defined in paragraph (f)(2) of this section) of an organization or of an affiliated organization (see §56.4911-7(a)),

(4) Amounts paid to or incurred for any person not an employee, or any organization not an affiliated organization, if paid or incurred primarily for fundraising, but only if such person or organization engages in fundraising, fundraising counselling or the provision of similar advice or services,

(5) Amounts paid or incurred that are properly chargeable to a capital account, determined in accordance with the principles that apply under section 263 or, as applicable, section 263A, with respect to an unrelated trade or business,

(6) Amounts paid or incurred for a tax that is not imposed in connection with the organization's efforts to accomplish a purpose described in section 170(c)(2)(B), such as taxes imposed under sections 511(a)(1) and 4911(a), and

(7) Amounts paid or incurred for the production of income. For purposes of this section, amounts are paid or incurred for the production of income if they are paid or incurred for a purpose or activity that is not substantially related (aside from the need of the organization for income or funds or the use it makes of the profits derived) to the exercise or performance by the organization of its charitable, educational or other purpose or function constituting the basis for its exemption under section 501. For example, the costs of managing an endowment are amounts that are paid or incurred for the production of income and are thus not exempt purpose expenditures. Fundraising expenditures are not, for purposes of this section, amounts that are paid or incurred for the production of income. Instead, the determination of whether fundraising costs are exempt purpose expenditures must be made with reference to section 4911(e)(1)(C) and paragraphs (b)(8), (c)(3) and (c)(4) of this section.

(d) *Certain transfers treated as exempt purpose expenditures.*—(1) An organization's transfer will be treated as an exempt purpose expenditure under paragraph (b)(1) of this section if it is—

(i) Described in either paragraph (d)(2) or (d)(3) of this section, and

(ii) Not described in paragraph (e) of this section.

(2) A transfer is described in this paragraph (d)(2) if it is made to an organization described in section 501(c)(3) in furtherance of the transferor's exempt purposes and is not earmarked for any purpose other than a purpose described in section 170(c)(2)(B). Thus, a payment of dues by a local or state organization to, respectively, a state or national organization that is described in section 501(c)(3) is considered an exempt purpose expenditure of the transferor to the extent it is not otherwise earmarked.

(3) A transfer is described in this paragraph (d)(3) if it is a controlled grant (as defined in paragraph (f)(3) of this section), but only to the extent of the amounts that are paid or incurred by the transferee that would be exempt purpose expenditures if paid or incurred by the transferor.

(e) *Transfers not exempt purpose expenditures.*—(1) An organization's transfer is described in this paragraph (e) if it is described in one of paragraphs (e)(2) through (e)(4).

(2) A transfer is described in this paragraph (e)(2) if it is made to a member of any affiliated group (as defined in §56.4911-7(e)) of which the transferor is a member.

(3) A transfer is described in this paragraph (e)(3) if the Commissioner determines that the

transfer artificially inflates the amount of the transferor's or transferee's exempt purpose expenditures. In general, the Commissioner will make that determination if a substantial purpose of a transfer is to inflate those exempt purpose expenditures. A transfer described in this paragraph will not be considered an exempt purpose expenditure of the transferor, but will be an exempt purpose expenditure of the transferee to the extent that the transferee expends the transfer in the active conduct of its charitable activities or attempts to influence legislation. Standards similar to those found in §53.4942(b)-1(b) may be applied in determining whether the transferee has expended amounts in the "active conduct" of its charitable activities or attempts to influence legislation.

(4) A transfer is described in this paragraph (e)(4) if it is not a controlled grant and is made to an organization not described in section 501(c)(3) that does not attempt to influence legislation.

(f) *Definitions.*—(1) For purposes of paragraph (c) of this section, "fundraising" includes—

(i) Soliciting dues or contributions from members of the organization, from persons whose dues are in arrears, or from the general public,

(ii) Soliciting grants from businesses or other organizations, including organizations described in section 501(c)(3), or

(iii) Soliciting grants from a governmental unit referred to in section 170(c)(1), or any agency or instrumentality thereof.

(2) For purposes of paragraph (c) of this section, a separate fundraising unit of any organization must consist of either two or more individuals a majority of whose time is spent on fundraising for the organization, or any separate accounting unit of the organization that is devoted to fundraising. For purposes of paragraph (c) of this section, amounts paid to or incurred for a separate fundraising unit include all amounts incurred for the creation, production, copying, and distribution of the fundraising portion of a separate fundraising unit's communication. (For example, an electing public charity that has a separate fundraising unit may not count the cost of postage for a separate fundraising unit's fundraising communication as an exempt purpose expenditure even though, under the electing public charity's accounting system, that cost is attributable to the mailroom rather than to the separate fundraising unit).

(3) For purposes of this section, a "controlled grant" is a grant made by an eligible organization described in §1.501(h)-2(b) to an organization not described in section 501(c)(3) that meets the following requirements:

(i) The donor limits the grant to a specific project of the recipient that is in furtherance of the donor's (nonlobbying) exempt purposes; and

(ii) The donor maintains records to establish that the grant is used in furtherance of the donor's (nonlobbying) exempt purposes.

(4) A transfer, including a grant or payment of dues, is "earmarked" for a specific purpose—

(i) To the extent that the transferor directs the transferee to add the amount transferred to a fund established to accomplish the purpose, or

(ii) To the extent of the amount transferred or, if less, the amount agreed upon to be expended to accomplish the purpose, if there exists an agreement, oral or written, whereby the transferor may cause the transferee to expend amounts to accomplish the purpose or whereby the transferee agrees to expend an amount to accomplish the purpose.

(g) *Example.*—The provisions of this section are illustrated by the following example:

Example. Organization X is an exempt organization described in section 501(c)(3) that is organized for the purpose of rehabilitating alcoholics. X elected to be subject to the provisions of section 501(h) in 1981. For 1981, X had the following expenditures that are included in its exempt purpose expenditures to the extent indicated.

Description	Total	Includible
Cost of real estate purchased for use as half-way house for alcoholics, attributable to the following:		
Land	$30,000	$-0-
Building	200,000	-0-
Depreciation 40-year useful life	-0-	5,000
Expenses of operating its half-way house	170,000	170,000
Administrative expenses of the organization allocated to the operation of its half-way house	95,000	95,000
Depreciation and allowances for equipment	10,000	10,000
Expenses related to attempts to influence legislation (lobbying expenditures)	40,000	40,000
Amounts paid to Z by the Organization for fundraising	35,000	-0-
Total	$580,000	$320,000

Note.—For 1981, X's exempt purpose expenditures total $320,000. The $35,000 paid by X to Z for fundraising is not included in the exempt purpose expenditures total. All lobbying expenses are included in full. Only depreciation computed on a straight-line basis is included in exempt purpose expenditures.

[Reg. §56.4911-4.]   □[T.D. 8308, 8-30-90.]

Reg. §56.4911-4(e)(4)

[Reg. §56.4911-5]

§56.4911-5. Communications with members.

(a) *In general.*—For purposes of section 4911, expenditures for certain communications between an organization and its members ("membership communications") are treated more leniently than are communications to non-members. This §56.4911-5 contains rules about the more lenient treatment. In certain cases, this section provides that expenditures for a membership communication are not lobbying expenditures even though those expenditures would be lobbying expenditures if the communication were to nonmembers. In other cases, this section provides that expenditures for a membership communication are direct lobbying expenditures even though those expenditures would be grass roots expenditures if the communication were to nonmembers. Paragraphs (b), (c) and (d) of this section set forth the more lenient rules that apply for communications that are directed only to members. Paragraph(e) of this section sets forth the more lenient rules that apply for communications that are directed primarily, but not solely, to members. Paragraph (f) of this section sets forth certain definitions and special rules.

(b) *Communications (directed only to members) that are not lobbying communications.*—Expenditures for a communication that refers to, and reflects a view on, specific legislation are not lobbying expenditures if the communication satisfies the following requirements:

(1) The communication is directed only to members of the organization;

(2) The specific legislation the communication refers to, and reflects a view on, is of direct interest to the organization and its members;

(3) The communication does not directly encourage the member to engage in direct lobbying (whether individually or through the organization); and

(4) The communication does not directly encourage the member to engage in grass roots lobbying (whether individually or through the organization).

(c) *Communications (directed only to members) that are direct lobbying communications.*—Expenditures for a communication that refers to, and reflects a view on, specific legislation and that satisfies the requirements of paragraphs (b)(1), (b)(2), and (b)(4) of this section, but does not satisfy the requirements of paragraph (b)(3) of this section, are treated as expenditures for direct lobbying.

(d) *Communications (directed only to members) that are grass roots lobbying communications.*—Expenditures for a communication that refers to, and reflects a view on, specific legislation and that satisfies the requirements of paragraphs (b)(1) and (b)(2) of this section, but does not satisfy the requirements of paragraph (b)(4) of this section, are treated as grass roots expenditures (whether or not the communication satis-

fies the requirements of paragraph (b)(3) of this section).

(e) *Written communications directed to members and nonmembers.*—(1) *In general.*—Expenditures for any written communication that is designed primarily for members of an organization (but not directed only to members) and that refers to, and reflects a view on, specific legislation of direct interest to the organization and its members, are treated as expenditures for direct or grass roots lobbying in accordance with paragraph (e)(2), (e)(3) or (e)(4) of this section. For purposes of this section, a communication is designed primarily for members of an organization if more than half of the recipients of the communication are members of the organization.

(2) *Direct lobbying directly encouraged.*—(i) *Lobbying expenditure amount.*—If a written communication described in paragraph (e)(1) of this section directly encourages readers to engage individually or through the organization in direct lobbying but does not directly encourage them to engage in grass roots lobbying, the cost of the communication is allocated between expenditures for direct lobbying and grass roots expenditures in accordance with paragraphs (e)(2)(ii) and (iii) of this section. The portion of the cost to be allocated includes all costs of preparing all the material with respect to which readers are urged to engage in direct lobbying plus the mechanical and distribution costs attributable to the lineage devoted to this material (see §1.512(a)-1(f)(6)).

(ii) *Grass roots amount.*—The amount allocable as a grass roots expenditure for a communication described in paragraph (e)(1) of this section is the amount calculated in paragraph (e)(2)(i) of this section multiplied by the sum of the nonmember subscribers percentage and the all other distribution percentage, both as defined in paragraph (f)(7) of this section. Solely for purposes of the allocation described in this paragraph (e)(2)(ii), the nonmember subscribers percentage is treated as zero unless it is greater than 15% of total distribution.

(iii) *Direct lobbying amount.*—The amount allocable as an expenditure for direct lobbying for a communication described in paragraph (e)(1) of this section is the excess of the amount described in paragraph (e)(2)(i) of this section over the amount described in paragraph (e)(2)(ii) of this section.

(3) *Grass roots expenditure if grass roots lobbying directly encouraged.*—If a written communication described in paragraph (e)(1) of this section directly encourages readers to engage individually or collectively (whether through the organization or otherwise) in grass roots lobbying (whether or not it also encourages readers to engage in direct lobbying), the grass roots expenditure includes all the costs of preparing all the material with respect to which readers are urged to engage in grass roots lobbying plus the mechanical and distribution costs attributable to

the lineage devoted to this material (see § 1.512(a)-1(f)(6)).

(4) *No direct encouragement of direct lobbying or of grass roots lobbying.*—If a written communication described in paragraph (e)(1) of this section does not directly encourage readers to engage in either direct lobbying or grass roots lobbying, expenditures for the communication are not lobbying expenditures.

(f) *Definitions and special rules.*—For purposes of the regulations under section 4911—

(1) *Member; general rule.*—A person is a member of an electing public charity if the person—

(i) Pays dues or makes a contribution of more than a nominal amount,

(ii) Makes a contribution of more than a nominal amount of time, or

(iii) Is one of a limited number of "honorary" or "life" members who have more than a nominal connection with the electing public charity and who have been chosen for a valid reason (such as length of service to the organization or involvement in activities forming the basis of the electing public charity's exemption) unrelated to the electing public charity's dissemination of information to its members.

(2) *Member; special rule.*—A person not a member of an electing public charity within the meaning of paragraph (f)(1) of this section may be treated as a member if the electing public charity demonstrates to the satisfaction of the Internal Revenue Service that there is a good reason for its membership requirements not meeting the requirements of such paragraph (f)(1), and that its membership requirements do not operate to permit an abuse of the rules described in this section.

(3) *Member; affiliated group of organizations.*—For purposes of this section, a person who is a member of an organization that is a member of an affiliated group of organizations (within the meaning of § 56.4911-7(e)) is treated as a member of each organization in the affiliated group.

(4) *Member; limited affiliated group of organizations.*—For purposes of this section, a person who is a member of an organization that is a member of a limited affiliated group of organizations (within the meaning of § 56.4911-10(b)) is treated as a member of each organization in the limited affiliated group, but only to the extent that the communication relates to a national legislative issue (within the meaning of § 56.4911-10(g)).

(5) *Subscriber.*—A person is a subscriber to a written communication if—

(i) The person is a member of the publishing organization and the membership dues expressly include the right to receive the written communication, or

(ii) The person has affirmatively expressed a desire to receive the written communication and has paid more than a nominal amount for the communication.

(6) *Directly encourages.*—(i) *Direct lobbying.*—(A) *In general.*—For purposes of this section, a communication directly encourages a recipient to engage in direct lobbying, whether individually or through the organization, if the communication:

(1) States that the recipient should contact a legislator or an employee of a legislative body, or should contact any other government official or employee who may participate in the formulation of legislation (but only if the principal purpose of urging contact with the government official or employee is to influence legislation);

(2) States the address, telephone number, or similar information of a legislator or an employee of a legislative body; or

(3) Provides a petition, tear-off postcard or similar material for the recipient to communicate his or her views to a legislator or an employee of a legislative body, or to any other government official or employee who may participate in the formulation of legislation (but only if the principal purpose of so facilitating contact with the government official or employee is to influence legislation).

(B) *"Self-defense" exception for communications with members.*—Notwithstanding the provisions of paragraph (f)(6)(i)(A) of this section, for purposes of paragraphs (b)(3), (e)(2)(i), (e)(3) and (e)(4) of this section, a communication that directly encourages a member to engage in direct lobbying activities that are described in section 4911(d)(2)(C) and that would not be attempts to influence legislation if engaged in directly by the organization is treated as a communication that does not directly encourage a member to engage in direct lobbying.

(ii) *Grass roots lobbying.*—For purposes of paragraphs (b)(4), (e)(3) and (e)(4) of this section, a communication directly encourages recipients to engage individually or collectively (whether through the organization or otherwise) in grass roots lobbying if the communication:

(A) States that the recipient should encourage any nonmember to contact a legislator or an employee of a legislative body, or to contact any other government official or employee who may participate in the formulation of legislation (but only if the principal purpose of urging contact with the government official or employee is to influence legislation);

(B) States that the recipient should provide to any nonmember the address, telephone number, or similar information of a legislator or an employee of a legislative body; or

(C) Provides (or requests that the recipient provide to nonmembers) a petition, tear-off postcard or similar material for the recipient (or nonmember) to use to ask any nonmember to communicate views to a legislator or an employee of a legislative body, or to any other government official or employee who may participate in the formulation of legislation, but only if the principal purpose of so facilitating contact with the government official or employee is to influence legislation. For purposes of this paragraph (f)(6)(ii)(C), a petition is provided for the recipient to use to ask any nonmember to communicate views if, for example, the petition has an entire page of preprinted signature blocks. Similarly, for purposes of this paragraph (f)(6)(ii)(C), where a communication is distributed to a single member and provides several tear-off postcards addressed to a legislator, the postcards are presumed to be provided for the member to use to ask a nonmember to communicate with the legislator.

(7) *Percentages of total distribution.*—With respect to a communication described in paragraph (e)(1) of this section—

(i) "Member percentage" means the percentage of total distribution that represents distribution of a single copy to any member;

(ii) "Nonmember subscribers percentage" means the percentage of total distribution that represents distribution to nonmember subscribers (including libraries); and

(iii) "All other distribution percentage" means 100% reduced by the sum of the member percentage and the nonmember subscribers percentage.

(8) *Reasonable allocation rule.*—In the case of lobbying expenditures for a communication that also has a bona fide nonlobbying purpose and that is sent only or primarily to members, an electing public charity must make a reasonable allocation between the amount expended for the lobbying purpose and the amount expended for the nonlobbying purpose. See §56.4911-3(a)(2)(ii). [Reg. §56.4911-5.]

☐ [T.D. 8308, 8-30-90.]

[Reg. §56.4911-6]

§56.4911-6. Records of lobbying and grass roots expenditures.—(a) *Records of lobbying expenditures.*—An electing public charity must keep a record of its lobbying expenditures for the taxable year. Lobbying expenditures of which an organization must keep a record include the following:

(1) Expenditures for grass roots lobbying, as described in paragraph (b) of this section;

(2) Amounts directly paid or incurred for direct lobbying, including payments to another organization earmarked for direct lobbying, fees and expenses paid to individuals or organizations for direct lobbying, and printing, mailing, and other direct costs of reproducing and distributing materials used in direct lobbying;

(3) The portion of amounts paid or incurred as current or deferred compensation for an employee's services for direct lobbying;

(4) Amounts paid for out-of-pocket expenditures incurred on behalf of the organization and for direct lobbying, whether or not incurred by an employee;

(5) The allocable portion of administrative, overhead, and other general expenditures attributable to direct lobbying;

(6) Expenditures for publications or for communications with members to the extent the expenditures are treated as expenditures for direct lobbying under §56.4911-5; and

(7) Expenditures for direct lobbying of a controlled organization (within the meaning of §56.4911-10(c)) to the extent included by a controlling organization (within the meaning of §56.4911-10(c)) in its lobbying expenditures.

(b) *Records of grass roots expenditures.*—An electing public charity must keep a record of its grass roots expenditures for the taxable year. Grass roots expenditures of which an organization must keep a record include the following:

(1) Amounts directly paid or incurred for grass roots lobbying, including payments to other organizations earmarked for grass roots lobbying, fees and expenses paid to individuals or organizations for grass roots lobbying, and the printing, mailing, and other direct costs of reproducing and distributing materials used in grass roots lobbying;

(2) The portion of amounts paid or incurred as current or deferred compensation for an employee's services for grass roots lobbying;

(3) Amounts paid for out-of-pocket expenditures incurred on behalf of the organization and for grass roots lobbying, whether or not incurred by an employee;

(4) The allocable portion of administrative, overhead and other general expenditures attributable to grass roots lobbying;

(5) Expenditures for publications or communications that are treated as expenditures for grass roots lobbying under §56.4911-5; and

(6) Expenditures for grass roots lobbying of a controlled organization (within the meaning of §56.4911-10(c)) to the extent included by a controlling organization (within the meaning of §56.4911-10(c)) in its grass roots expenditures. [Reg. §56.4911-6.]

☐ [T.D. 8308, 8-30-90.]

[Reg. §56.4911-7]

§56.4911-7. Affiliated group of organizations.—(a) *Affiliation between two organizations.*—Sections 4911(f)(1) through (3) contain a limited anti-abuse rule for groups of affiliated organizations. In general, the rule operates to prevent numerous organizations from being created for the purpose of avoiding the sliding-scale percentage limitation on an electing public charity's lobbying expenditures (as well as avoiding the $1,000,000 cap on a single electing public charity's lobbying expenditures). This is generally accomplished by treating the members of an affiliated group as a single organization for purposes of measuring both lobbying expenditures and permitted lobbying expenditures. The anti-abuse rule is implemented by this §56.4911-7 and §§56.4911-8 and -9. This §56.4911-7 defines the term "affiliated group of organizations" and defines the taxable year of an affiliated group of organizations. Section 56.4911-8 provides rules concerning the exempt purpose expenditures, lobbying expenditures and grass roots expenditures of an affiliated group of organizations, as well as rules concerning the application of the excise tax imposed by section 4911(a) on excess lobbying expenditures by the group. Section 56.4911-9 provides rules concerning the application of the section 501(h) lobbying expenditure limits to members of an affiliated group of organizations. (For additional rules for members of a limited affiliated group of organizations (generally, organizations that are affiliated solely by reason of governing instrument provisions that extend control solely with respect to national legislation), see section 4911(f)(4) and §56.4911-10).

(1) *In general.*—For purposes of the regulations under section 4911, two organizations are affiliated, subject to the limitation described in paragraph (a)(2) of this section, if one organization is able to control action on legislative issues by the other by reason of interlocking governing boards (see paragraph (b) of this section) or by reason of provisions of the governing instruments of the controlled organization (see paragraph (c) of this section). The ability of the controlling organization to control action on legislative issues by the controlled organization is sufficient to establish that the organizations are affiliated; it is not necessary that the control be exercised.

(2) *Organizations not described in section 501(c)(3).*—Two organizations, neither of which is described in section 501(c)(3), are affiliated only if there exists at least one organization described in section 501(c)(3) that is affiliated with both organizations.

(3) *Action on legislative issues.*—For purposes of this section, the term "action on legislative issues" includes taking a position in the organization's name on legislation, authorizing any person to take a position in the organization's name on legislation, or authorizing any lobbying expenditures. The phrase does not include actions taken merely to correct unauthorized actions taken in the organization's name.

(b) *Interlocking governing boards.*—(1) *In general.*—Two organizations have interlocking governing boards if one organization (the controlling organization) has a sufficient number of representatives (within the meaning of paragraph (b)(5) of this section) on the governing board of the second organization (the controlled organization) so that by aggregating their votes, the representatives of the controlling organization can cause or prevent action on legislative issues by the controlled organization. If two organizations have interlocking governing boards, the organizations are affiliated without regard to how or whether the representatives of the controlling organization vote on any particular matter.

(2) *Majority or quorum.*—Except as provided in paragraph (b)(3) or (4) of this section, the number of representatives of an organization (the controlling organization) who are members of the governing board of a second organization (the controlled organization) will be presumed sufficient to cause or prevent action on legislative issues by the controlled organization if that number either—

(i) Constitutes a majority of incumbents on the governing board, or

(ii) Constitutes a quorum, or is sufficient to prevent a quorum, for acting on legislative issues.

(3) *Votes required under governing instrument or local law.*—Except as provided in paragraph (b)(4) of this section, if under the governing documents of an organization (the controlled organization), it can be determined that a lesser number of votes than the number described in paragraph (b)(2) of this section is necessary or sufficient to cause or to prevent action on legislative issues, the number of representatives of the controlling organization who are members of the governing board of the controlled organization will be considered sufficient to cause or prevent action on legislative issues if it equals or exceeds that number.

(4) *Representatives constituting less than 15% of governing board.*—Notwithstanding paragraph (b)(2) or (3) of this section, if the number of representatives of one organization is less than 15 percent of the incumbents on the governing board of a second organization, the two organizations are not affiliated by reason of interlocking governing boards.

(5) *Representatives.*—(i) This paragraph (b)(5) describes members of the governing board of one organization (the controlled organization) who are considered representatives of a second organization (the controlling organization). Under this paragraph (b)(5), a member of the governing board of a controlled organization may be a representative of more than one controlling organization. A person with no authority to vote on any issue being considered by the governing board is not a representative of any organization.

(ii) A board member of one organization (the controlled organization) is a representative of a second organization (the controlling organization) if the controlling organization has specifically designated that person to be a board member of the controlled organization. For purposes of this paragraph (b)(5)(ii) and paragraph (b)(5)(iii) of this section, a board member of the controlled organization is specifically designated by the controlling organization if the board member is selected by virtue of the right of the controlling organization, under the governing instruments of the controlled organization, either to designate a person to be a member of the controlled organization's governing board, or to select a person for a position that entitles the holder of that position to be a member of the controlled organization's governing board.

(iii) A board member of one organization who is specifically designated by a second organization, a majority of the governing board of which is made up of representatives of a third organization, is a representative of the third organization as well as being a representative of the second organization pursuant to paragraph (b)(5)(ii) of this section.

(iv) A board member of one organization who is also a member of the governing board of a second organization is a representative of the second organization.

(v) A board member of one organization who is an officer or paid executive staff member of a second organization is a representative of the second organization. Although titles are significant in determining whether a person is a member of the executive staff of an organization, any employee of an organization who possesses authority commonly exercised by an executive is considered an executive staff member for purposes of this paragraph (b)(5)(v).

(c) *Governing instrument.*—One organization (the "controlling" organization) is affiliated with a second organization (the "controlled" organization) by reason of the governing instruments of the controlled organization if the governing instruments of the controlled organization limit the independent action of the controlled organization on legislative issues by requiring it to be bound by decisions of the other organization on legislative issues.

(d) *Three or more organizations affiliated.*—(1) *Two controlled organizations affiliated.*—If a controlling organization described in this section is affiliated with each of two or more controlled organizations described in this section, then the controlled organizations are affiliated with each other.

(2) *Chain rule.*—If one organization is a controlling organization described in this section with respect to a second organization and that second organization is a controlling organization with respect to a third organization, then the first organization is affiliated with the third.

(e) *Affiliated group of organizations.*—(1) *Defined.*—For purposes of the regulations under section 4911, an affiliated group of organizations is a group of organizations—

(i) Each of which is affiliated with every other member for at least thirty days of the taxable year of the affiliated group (determined without regard to the election provided for in paragraph (e)(5) of this section),

(ii) Each of which is an eligible organization (within the meaning of § 1.501(h)-2(b)(1)), and

(iii) At least one of which is an electing member organization (within the meaning of paragraph (e)(4) of this section).

Each organization in a group of organizations that satisfies the requirements of the preceding

sentence is a member of the affiliated group of organizations for the taxable year of the affiliated group.

(2) *Multiple membership.*—For any taxable year of an organization, it may be a member of two or more affiliated groups of organizations.

(3) *Taxable year of affiliated group.*—If all members of an affiliated group have the same taxable year, that taxable year is the taxable year of the affiliated group. If the members of an affiliated group do not all have the same taxable year, the taxable year of the affiliated group is the calendar year, unless the election under paragraph (e)(5) of this section is made.

(4) *Electing member organization.*—For purposes of the regulations under section 4911, an "electing member organization" is an organization to which the expenditure test election under section 501(h) applies on at least one day of the taxable year of the affiliated group of which it is a member. For purposes of the preceding sentence (and notwithstanding § 1.501(h)-2(a)), the expenditure test is not considered to apply to the organization on any day before the date on which it files the Form 5768 making the expenditure test election.

(5) *Election of member's year as group's taxable year.*—The taxable year of an affiliated group may be determined according to the provisions of this paragraph (e)(5) if all of the members of the affiliated group so elect. Under this paragraph (e)(5), each member organization shall apply the provisions of section 501(h) and 4911, and the regulations thereunder (unless the regulations provide otherwise), by treating its own taxable year as the taxable year of the affiliated group. The election may be made by an electing member organization by attaching to its annual return a statement from itself and every other member of the affiliated group that contains: the organization's name, address, and employer identification number; and its signed consent to the election provided for in this paragraph (e)(5). The election must be made no later than the due date of the first annual return of any electing member for its taxable year for which the member is liable for tax under section 4911(a), determined under § 56.4911-8(d). The election may not be made or revoked after the due date of the return referred to in the preceding sentence except upon such terms and conditions as the Commissioner may prescribe.

(f) *Examples.*—The provisions of this section are illustrated by the following examples.

Example (1). M, N, and O are eligible organizations within the meaning of § 1.501(h)-2(b)(1). Each has a governing board made up of nine members. Five members on the board of N are also members of the board of M. N designates five individuals from among its board, officers, and executive staff members to serve on the board of O. M is affiliated with N, N is affiliated with O, and M is affiliated with O.

Reg. § 56.4911-7(f)

Example (2). X, an eligible organization, has a board consisting of 10 members. Five unaffiliated tax-exempt organizations each designate two individuals to serve on the governing board of X. A simple majority of the board of X is a quorum and may establish X's position on legislative issues. X is not affiliated with any of the five autonomous organizations by reason of interlocking governing boards.

Example (3). P and Q are eligible organizations. The governing instruments of Q state that it will not take a position on legislation if P disapproves of the position. In addition, there is regular correspondence between P and Q with regard to positions on legislation. P is affiliated with Q regardless of whether P has ever vetoed a position taken by Q.

Example (4). The governing board of organization R resolves to adopt the position taken on legislative issues by organization S. R and S are eligible organizations and do not have interlocking governing boards. The governing instruments of R do not mention organization S and do not indicate that R is to be bound by the decisions of legislation of any organization. R and S are not affiliated.

Example (5). Organization Z is bound, under the terms of its governing instruments, by the legislative positions of organization Y. Organization Y, however, is bound, under the terms of its governing instruments, by the legislative positions of organization X. Organization X is affiliated with Y and Z; Y is affiliated with X and Z; and Z is affiliated with X and Y.

Example (6). Organizations T and U have interlocking boards of directors. T is the controlling organization. Organization V is bound, under the terms of its governing instruments, by the legislative positions of U. T and V are affiliated because T may cause or prevent action on legislative issues by U, and V is bound by U's action. If U were the controlling organization, T and V would be affiliated as two organizations controlled by the same organization.

Example (7). Organization A is described in section 501(c)(4). It is affiliated, as the controlling organization, with organizations K and L, both of which are described in section 501(c)(3) and are eligible to elect under section 501(h). If K elects under section 501(h), K and L are an affiliated group of organizations. Even though A is affiliated with K and L, A is not a member of that affiliated group of organizations because A is not an eligible organization within the meaning of §1.501(h)-2(b)(1) (see §56.4911-7(e)(1) for the definition of which affiliated organizations may be members of an affiliated group of organizations).

Example (8). G, H, I, and J are eligible organizations. G, H, and I have elected the expenditure test under section 501(h). The governing board of J has nine members. Under the governing instruments of J, organizations G, H, and I each designate three members of the governing board of J. Also under the governing instruments of J,

action on legislative issues requires the approval of any seven board members. Because the three representatives of G may prevent action on legislative issues, J is affiliated with G. Similarly, J is affiliated with each of H and I. However, under none of the rules of affiliation is G affiliated with H, or H with I, or I with G. Therefore J is a member of one affiliated group comprising G and J, of another group comprising H and J, and of a third group comprising I and J.

Example (9). Organizations C, D, and E have been affiliated for many years and have all elected the expenditure test. Each has a taxable year ending July 31. For every day of the year ending July 31, 1992, they were eligible organizations, electing member organizations, and affiliated with each other. On no day of that year were they affiliated with any other eligible organization having a different taxable year. Therefore, the year ending July 31, 1992, is the taxable year of the affiliated group comprising C, D, and E. [Reg. §56.4911-7.]

☐ [T.D. 8308, 8-30-90.]

[Reg. §56.4911-8]

§56.4911-8. Excess lobbying expenditures of affiliated group.—(a) *Application.*—This section provides rules concerning the exempt purpose expenditures, lobbying expenditures, and grass roots expenditures of an affiliated group of organizations, and the application of the excise tax imposed by section 4911(a) on the excess lobbying expenditures of the group.

(b) *Affiliated group treated as one organization.*— Under section 4911(f), an affiliated group of organizations is treated as a single organization for purposes of the tax imposed by section 4911(a). For any taxable year of the affiliated group, the group's lobbying expenditures, grass roots expenditures, and exempt purpose expenditures are equal to the sum of the lobbying expenditures, grass roots expenditures, and exempt purpose expenditures, respectively, paid or incurred by each member during the taxable year of the affiliated group. The lobbying and grass roots nontaxable amounts for the affiliated group for a taxable year are determined under section 4911(c)(2) and (4) and §56.4911-1(c) and are based on the sum of the exempt purpose expenditures described in the preceding sentence. The lobbying and grass roots ceiling amounts for the affiliated group for a taxable year are calculated under §1.501(h)-3(c)(3) and (6) based upon the nontaxable amounts determined pursuant to the preceding sentence.

(c) *Tax imposed on excess lobbying expenditures of affiliated group.*—The excise tax under section 4911(a) is imposed for a taxable year of an affiliated group if the group has excess lobbying expenditures. For any taxable year of an affiliated group, the group's excess lobbying expenditures are the greater of—

(1) The amount by which the group's lobbying expenditures exceed the group's lobbying nontaxable amount, or

(2) The amount by which the group's grass roots expenditures exceed the group's grass roots nontaxable amount.

(d) *Liability for tax.*—(1) *Electing organizations.*—As provided in this paragraph (d), an electing member organization is liable for all or a portion of the excise tax imposed by section 4911(a) on the excess lobbying expenditures of an affiliated group of organizations. An organization that is liable under this paragraph (d) is not liable for any excise tax under section 4911 based on its own excess lobbying expenditures. A member of the affiliated group that is not an electing member organization is not liable for any portion of the excise tax that is imposed with respect to the affiliated group.

(2) *Tax based on excess lobbying expenditures.*—If the excise tax imposed by section 4911(a) on the excess lobbying expenditures of an affiliated group of organizations is based upon the amount described in paragraph (c)(1) of this section, and at least one electing member has made lobbying expenditures, each electing member organization is liable for a portion of the tax equal to the amount of the tax multiplied by a fraction, the numerator of which is the electing member organization's lobbying expenditures paid or incurred during the taxable year of the affiliated group, and the denominator of which is the sum of the lobbying expenditures of all electing member organizations in the group paid or incurred during the taxable year of the affiliated group.

(3) *Tax based on excess grass roots expenditures.*—If the excise tax imposed by section 4911(a) on the excess lobbying expenditures of an affiliated group of organizations is based upon the amount described in paragraph (c)(2) of this section, and at least one electing member has made grass roots expenditures, each electing member organization is liable for a portion of the tax equal to the amount of the tax multiplied by the fraction described in paragraph (d)(2) of this section, except that "grass roots expenditures" is substituted for "lobbying expenditures."

(4) *Tax based on exempt purpose expenditures.*—If the excise tax imposed by section 4911(a) on the excess lobbying expenditures of an affiliated group of organizations is based upon the amount described in paragraph (c)(2) of this section, and if paragraphs (d)(2) and (d)(3) of this section do not apply because no electing organization has made lobbying or grass roots expenditures, respectively, each electing member organization is liable for a portion of the tax equal to the amount of tax multiplied by a fraction the numerator of which is the electing member organization's exempt purpose expenditures and the denominator of which is the exempt purpose expenditures of all the electing member organizations in the affiliated group.

(5) *Taxable year for which liable.*—An electing member organization that is liable for all or a portion of the excise tax imposed by section 4911(a) on the excess lobbying expenditures of an affiliated group of organizations is liable for the tax as if the tax were imposed for its taxable year with which or within which ends the taxable year of the affiliated group.

(6) *Organization a member of more than one affiliated group.*—If, under this paragraph (d), an organization is liable for its taxable year for two or more excise taxes imposed by section 4911(a) on the excess lobbying expenditures of two or more affiliated groups, then the organization is liable only for the greater of the two or more taxes.

(e) *Former member organization.*—An electing member organization that ceases to be a member of an affiliated group of organizations, the taxable year of which is different from its own, must thereafter determine its liability under §56.4911-1 for the excise tax imposed by section 4911(a) as if its taxable year were the taxable year of the affiliated group of which it was formerly a member. An organization to which this paragraph (e) applies that is liable for the excise tax imposed by section 4911(a) is liable for the tax as if the tax were imposed for its taxable year within which ends the taxable year of the affiliated group of which it was formerly a member. The Commissioner may, at the Commissioner's discretion, permit an organization to disregard the rules of this paragraph (e) and to determine any liability under section 4911(a) based upon its own taxable year. [Reg. §56.4911-8.]

☐ [*T.D.* 8308, 8-30-90.]

[Reg. §56.4911-9]

§56.4911-9. Application of section 501(h) to affiliated groups of organizations.—(a) *Scope.*—This section provides rules concerning the application of the limitations of section 501(h) to members of an affiliated group of organizations (as defined in §56.4911-7(e)(1)).

(b) *Determination required.*—For each taxable year of an affiliated group of organizations, the calculations described in §1.501(h)-3(b)(1)(i) and (ii) must be made, based on the expenditures of the group. If, for a taxable year of an affiliated group, it is determined that the sum of the affiliated group's lobbying or grass roots expenditures for the group's base years exceeds 150 percent of the sum of the group's corresponding nontaxable amounts for the base years, then under section 501(h), each member organization that is an electing member organization (as defined in §56.4911-7(e)(4)) at any time in the taxable year of the affiliated group shall be denied tax exemption beginning with its first taxable year beginning after the end of such taxable year of the affiliated group. Thereafter, exemption shall be denied unless (pursuant to §1.501(h)-3(d)) the organization reapplies and is recognized as exempt as an organization described in section 501(c)(3). For purposes of this section, the term "base years" generally means the taxable year of the affiliated group for which a determination is made and the group's three preceding taxable years. Base years, however, do not include any year preceding the first year in which at least one member of the group was treated as described in section 501(c)(3).

(c) *Member organizations that are not electing organizations.*—An organization that is a member of an affiliated group of organizations but that is not an electing member organization remains subject to the "substantial part test" described in section 501(c)(3) with respect to its activities involving attempts to influence legislation.

(d) *Filing of information relating to affiliated group of organizations.*—(1) *Scope.*—The filing requirements described in this paragraph (d) apply to each member of an affiliated group of organizations for the taxable year of the member with which, or within which, ends the taxable year of the affiliated group.

(2) *In general.*—Each member of an affiliated group of organizations shall provide to every other member of the group, before the first day of the second month following the close of the affiliated group's taxable year, its name, identification number, and the information required under § 1.6033-2(a)(2)(ii) (k) for its expenditures during the group's taxable year and for prior taxable years of the group that are base years under paragraph (b). For groups electing under § 56.4911-7(e)(5) to have each member file information with respect to the group based on its taxable year, each member shall provide the information required by the preceding sentence by treating each taxable year of any member of the group as a taxable year for the group.

(3) *Additional information required.*—In addition to the information required by § 1.6033-2(a)(2)(ii) (k), each member of an affiliated group of organizations must provide on its annual return the group's taxable year and, if the election under § 56.4911-7(e)(5) is made, the name, identification number, and taxable year identifying the return with which its consent to the election was filed.

(4) *Information required of electing member organization.*—In addition to the information required by § 1.6033-2(a)(2)(ii) (k) and paragraph (d)(3) of this section, each electing member organization (as defined in § 56.4911-7(e)(4)) must provide on its annual return—

(i) The name and identification number of each member of the group, and

(ii) The appropriate calculation described in § 56.4911-8(d), if the organization is an electing member organization liable for all or any portion of the excise tax imposed by section 4911(a).

(e) *Example.*—The provisions of this section may be illustrated by the following example:

Example. (1) M, N, and O are affiliated organizations under § 56.4911-7(a). M's taxable year ends November 30, N's, January 31, and O's, June 30. On June 20, 1979, O files Form 5768 to elect to be governed by the expenditure test. M files Form 5768 in December of 1979. Neither M nor O revokes the election, and no organization makes the election provided for in § 56.4911-7(e)(5). M, N, and O constitute an affiliated group of organizations, the first taxable year of which is the calendar year 1979.

(2) Because the organizations did not elect under § 56.4911-7(e)(5) to use their own taxable years as the group's taxable years, the expenditures of the affiliated group for its first taxable year are the expenditures made by M, N, and O during calendar year 1979, and are reported by M, N, and O on their returns for their taxable years within which falls December 31, 1979. M reports the expenditures of the affiliated group for 1979 on its return for its taxable year ending November 30, 1980; and O, on its return for its taxable year ending June 30, 1980. N is not an electing member (as defined in § 56.4911-7(e)(4)). Accordingly, under paragraph (d)(3)(i) of this section, it reports the name and identification number of each member of the group.

(3) The following tables summarize the expenditures by the affiliated group for the calendar years indicated. None of the group's lobbying expenditures for its taxable years 1979 through 1982 were grass roots expenditures.

Table I. Group's Expenditures

Year	Exempt Purpose Expenditures (EPE)	Calculation	Lobbying Nontaxable Amount (LNTA)	Lobbying Expenditures (LE)
1979	$400,000	(20% × $400,000 =)	$80,000	$100,000
1980	$300,000	(20% × $300,000 =)	$60,000	$100,000
1981	$600,000	(20% × $500,000 + 15% x $100,000 =)	$115,000	$120,000
1982	$500,000	(20% × $500,000 =)	$100,000	$220,000
Totals:	$1,800,000		$355,000	$540,000

Table II. Expenditures of M and O

	Exempt Purpose Expenditures M	Exempt Purpose Expenditures O	Lobbying Nontaxable Amount M	Lobbying Nontaxable Amount O	Lobbying Expenditures M	Lobbying Expenditures O	M plus O
1979	125,000	100,000	25,000	20,000	60,000	20,000	80,000
1980	100,000	50,000	20,000	10,000	40,000	40,000	80,000
1981	250,000	100,000	50,000	20,000	60,000	40,000	100,000
1982	200,000	100,000	40,000	20,000	160,000	40,000	200,000

Reg. §56.4911-9(c)

(4) For the affiliated group's taxable years 1979, 1980, 1981, and 1982, the group has excess lobbying expenditures. Under section 4911(f)(1)(B) and §56.4911-8(d), M and O, as electing member organizations, are liable for a portion of the 25 percent excise tax imposed on the group's excess lobbying expenditures, based on their respective shares of the lobbying expenditures of all electing member organizations. For 1979, the excess lobbying expenditures are $20,000 ($100,000 – $80,000). The tax is 25% of $20,000 or $5,000; M must pay $3,750 {($60,000/$80,000) × $5,000 = $3,750)}, and O must pay $1,250 {($20,000/$80,000)× $5,000 = $1,250}. For 1980, the tax is $10,000 and each must pay $5,000. For 1981, the tax is $1,250, of which M must pay $750 and O must pay $500. For 1982, the tax is $30,000. M must pay $24,000 and O must pay $6,000. M and O are not liable for any separate 4911 excise tax that otherwise would have been imposed on their separate excess lobbying expenditures.

(5) Under §56.4911-9(b), the group must make the calculation described in §1.501(h)-3(b)(1) for each of the group's taxable years 1979 through 1982. The following illustrates only the required calculation for the group's taxable year 1982. For its taxable year 1982, the group must determine whether it normally has made lobbying expenditures in excess of its lobbying ceiling amount. The determination takes into account the group's expenditures in base years 1979 through 1982. The sum of the group's lobbying expenditures for the base years ($540,000) exceeds 150% of the sum of the group's lobbying nontaxable amounts for the base years (150%× $355,000 = $532,500). Therefore, for its taxable year 1982, the group normally has made lobbying expenditures in excess of its lobbying ceiling amount. Under section 501(h) and §56.4911-9(b), M is not exempt from tax under section 501(a) as an organization described in section 501(c)(3) for its taxable year beginning December 1, 1983, and O is not exempt for its year beginning July 1, 1983. Whether N's lobbying expenditures disqualify it for tax exemption at any time after January 1, 1979, is determined under the substantial part test of section 501(c)(3).

(f) *Cross reference.*—For other provisions relating to members of an affiliated group of organizations, see §§56.4911-2(c)(4)(ii), 56.4911-4(c)(2), 56.4911-4(e), and 56.4911-5(f)(3). [Reg. §56.4911-9.]

☐ [*T.D.* 8308, 8-30-90.]

[Reg. §56.4911-10]

§56.4911-10. Members of a limited affiliated group of organizations.—(a) *Scope.*—This section provides additional rules for members of a limited affiliated group of organizations, as defined in paragraph (b) of this section (relating generally to organizations that are affiliated solely by reason of provisions of their governing instruments that extend control solely with respect to national legislation). Except as otherwise provided in this section, §§56.4911-8 and 56.4911-9 do not apply to members of a limited affiliated group. Thus, as modified by this section, the regulations under sections 501(h) and 4911 apply to electing members of a limited affiliated group individually. For example, §§56.4911-2 through -4, which, by their terms, include amounts described in paragraph (d) of this section, are used in applying sections 501(h) and 4911 to controlling member organizations(within the meaning of paragraph (c) of this section). Except as otherwise provided in this section, members of a limited affiliated group that are not electing organizations are subject to the substantial part test.

(b) *Members of limited affiliated group.*—For purposes of section 4911, a limited affiliated group consists of two or more organizations that meet the following requirements:

(1) Each organization is a member of an affiliated group of organizations as defined in §56.4911-7(e);

(2) No two members of the affiliated group described in paragraph (b)(1) of this section are affiliated by reason of interlocking governing boards under §56.4911-7(b); and

(3) No member of the affiliated group described in paragraph (b)(1) of this section is, under its governing instrument, bound by decisions of one or more of the other such members on legislative issues other than national legislative issues.

Each organization in a group of organizations that satisfies the requirements of the preceding sentence is a member of the limited affiliated group.

(c) *Controlling and controlled organizations.*— For purposes of this section, a member of a limited affiliated group is a controlling member organization if it controls one or more of the other members of the limited affiliated group, and a member of a limited affiliated group is a controlled member organization if it is controlled by one or more of the other members of the limited affiliated group. For purposes of the preceding sentence, whether an organization controls a second organization shall be determined by whether the second organization is bound, under its governing instruments, by actions taken by the first organization on national legislative issues.

(d) *Expenditures of controlling organization.*— (1) *Scope.*—This paragraph (d) applies to a controlling member organization that has the expenditure test election in effect for its taxable year. This paragraph (d) applies whether or not the

Reg. §56.4911-10(d)(1)

organization is also a controlled member organization. In determining a controlling member organization's expenditures, no expenditure shall be counted twice.

(2) *Expenditures for direct lobbying.*—A controlling member organization for which the expenditure test election is in effect shall include in its direct lobbying expenditures for its taxable year the direct lobbying expenditures (as defined in §§56.4911-2 and -3) paid or incurred with respect to national legislative issues during such year by each organization that is a member of the limited affiliated group and is controlled (within the meaning of paragraph (c) of this section) by such controlling member organization.

(3) *Grass roots expenditures.*—A controlling member organization for which the expenditure test election is in effect shall include in its grass roots expenditures for its taxable year the grass roots expenditures (as defined in §§56.4911-2 and -3) paid or incurred with respect to national legislative issues during such year by each organization that is a member of the limited affiliated group and is controlled (within the meaning of paragraph (c) of this section) by such controlling member organization.

(4) *Exempt purpose expenditures.*—The exempt purpose expenditures of a controlling member organization do not include the exempt purpose expenditures (other than lobbying expenditures described in paragraphs (d)(2) and (d)(3) of this section) of any organization that is a controlled member organization with respect to it.

(e) *Expenditures of controlled member.*—A controlled member organization that is an electing organization but that does not control (within the meaning of paragraph (c) of this section) any organization in the limited affiliated group shall apply sections 501(h) and 4911 and the regulations thereunder without regard to the expenditures of any other member of the limited affiliated group.

(f) *Reports of members of limited affiliated groups.*—(1) *Controlling member organization's additional information on annual return.*—In addition to the information required by §1.6033-2(a)(2)(ii)(k), each controlling member organization for which the expenditure test election is in effect must provide on its annual return the name and identification number of each member of the limited affiliated group.

(2) *Reports of controlling members to other members.*—Each controlling member organization for which an expenditure test election is in effect must notify each member that it controls of its taxable year in order for the controlled organization to prepare the report required by paragraph (f)(3) of this section. Such notification must be made before the beginning of the second month after the close of each taxable year of the controlling member for which the election is in effect.

(3) *Reports of controlled member organization.*—Every controlled member organization (whether or not the expenditure test election is in effect with respect to it) shall provide to each member of the limited affiliated group that controls it, before the first day of the second month following the close of the taxable year of each such controlling organization, its name, identification number, and the lobbying expenditures and grass roots expenditures on national legislative issues incurred by the controlled member organization.

(g) *National legislative issues.*—The term "national legislative issue" means legislation, limited to action by the Congress of the United States or by the public in any national procedure. If an issue is both national and local, it is characterized as a national legislative issue if the contemplated legislation is Congressional legislation.

(h) *Examples.*—The provisions of this section are illustrated by the following examples:

Example (1). State X has an income tax law that uses definitions contained in the Internal Revenue Code as it may be amended from time to time. Legislation to change a definition in the Internal Revenue Code is pending in Congress. This is a national legislative issue even though Congressional action may affect state law.

Example (2). Organization M takes a position favoring approval by Congress of a proposed amendment to the United States Constitution. This is a national legislative issue. After approval by Congress and submission to the states for ratification, the proposed amendment ceases to be a national legislative issue.

Example (3). N, O, and P are organizations described in section 501(c)(3) that do not have interlocking governing boards, within the meaning of §56.4911-7(b). N has elected the expenditure test under section 501(h). By virtue of the governing instruments of O and P, any decision made by N on national legislative issues (such as issues concerning action on acts, bills, resolutions, or similar items by Congress) binds both O and P. Under their governing instruments, O and P are not bound on any other issues. Therefore, N, O, and P constitute a limited affiliated group. If P sends a series of letters and pamphlets to members of Congress in support of bill V, their cost will be included in N's and P's expenditures for direct lobbying and in N's and P's exempt purposes expenditures, but will not be included in O's lobbying expenditures. If N hires a lobbyist to solicit support for bill V, the cost of hiring the lobbyist will be includable only in N's lobbying expenditures. Any lobbying expenditures incurred by either O or P on any issue that is not a national legislative issue will not be included in N's lobbying expenditures.

Example (4). Y is an electing organization and a member of a limited affiliated group of organizations. Y controls organizations A, B, and C with respect to national legislative issues but is not controlled by any other organization. Y's taxable year is the calendar year. During 1982, A dissolves on March 15th and D, also controlled by Y with respect to national legislative issues, is established on May 1st. For 1982 the limited affiliated group comprises Y, A, B, C, and D.

Example (5). P, Q, R, and S are electing organizations. The governing instruments of Q require it to adopt the positions on national legislative issues adopted by P. R is similarly bound by Q's positions. R and S have interlocking governing boards, within the meaning of § 56.4911-7(b), but S's governing instruments do not require it to adopt the position of any other organization on any legislative issues. Under § 56.4911-7(e)(1), P, Q, R, and S are members of an affiliated group. Applying paragraph (b) of this section, it is determined that (1) P, Q, R and S are members of an affiliated group; and (2) R and S are affiliated by reason of interlocking governing boards. Accordingly, P, Q, R and S are not a limited affiliated group. Similarly, P, Q, and R do not constitute a limited affiliated group because they are members of an affiliated group comprising P, Q, R, and S, two of whose members, R and S, are affiliated by reason of interlocking governing boards.

Example (6). T, U, V, and W are electing organizations. The governing instruments of U and V require them to adopt the positions on national legislative issues adopted by T, but do not require them to adopt the positions of any organization on any other legislative issues. The governing documents of W require it to adopt the positions of V on all legislative issues. Applying paragraph (b) of this section, it is determined that (1) T, U, V, and W are all members of an affiliated group; (2) no two of T, U, V, and W are affiliated by reason of interlocking governing boards; but (3) W is bound, under its governing instrument, by decisions of V on legislative issues that are not national legislative issues. Accordingly, T, U, V, and W do not constitute a limited affiliated group. Similarly, T, U, and V do not constitute a limited affiliated group. T, U, V, and W are an affiliated group under § 56.4911-7. [Reg. § 56.4911-10.]

☐ [T.D. 8308, 8-30-90.]

Private Foundations and Certain Other Tax-Exempt Organizations

PRIVATE FOUNDATIONS

See p. 20,601 for regulations not amended to reflect law changes

[Reg. § 53.4940-1]

§ 53.4940-1. Excise tax on net investment income.—(a) *In general.*—For taxable years beginning after September 30, 1977, section 4940 imposes an excise tax of 2 percent of the net investment income (as defined in section 4940(c) and paragraph (c) of this section) of a tax-exempt private foundation (as defined in section 509). For taxable years beginning after December 31, 1969, and before October 1, 1977, the tax imposed by section 4940 is 4 percent of the net investment income. This tax will be reported on the form the foundation is required to file under section 6033 for the taxable year and will be paid annually at the time prescribed for filing such annual return (determined without regard to any extension of time for filing). In addition, an excise tax is imposed in the manner prescribed in paragraph (b) of this section on certain non-exempt private foundations (including certain non-exempt charitable trusts). Except as provided in the succeeding sentence, this tax is to be reported by means of a schedule attached to the organization's income tax return.

For taxable years ending on or after December 31, 1975, the tax imposed by section 4940(b) and paragraph (b) of this section on a trust described in section 4947(a)(1) which is a private foundation shall be reported on Form 5227. The tax imposed by section 4940(b) and this section is to be paid annually at the time the organization is required to pay its income taxes imposed under Subtitle A. Except as otherwise provided herein, no exclusions or deductions from gross investment income or credits against tax are allowable under this section.

(b) *Taxable foundations.*—(1) The excise tax imposed under section 4940 on private foundations which are not exempt from taxation under section 501(a) is equal to:

   (i) The amount (if any) by which the sum of

      (A) The tax on net investment income imposed under section 4940(a), computed as if such private foundation were exempt from taxation under section 501(a) and described in section 501(c)(3) for the taxable year, plus

      (B) The amount of the tax which would have been imposed under section 511 for such taxable year if such private foundation had been exempt from taxation under section 501(a), exceeds

      (ii) The tax imposed under subtitle A on such private foundation for the taxable year.

(2) The provisions of this paragraph may be illustrated by the following examples:

Example (1). Assume that the tax liability under subtitle A for private foundation X, which is not exempt from taxation under section 501(a) for 1970, is $10,000. Had X been exempt under section 501(a) for 1970, the tax imposed under section 4940(a) would have been $4,000 and the tax imposed under section 511 would have been $7,000. The excess of the sum of the taxes which would have been imposed under sections 4940(a) and 511 ($11,000) over the tax that was imposed under subtitle A ($10,000) is $1,000, the amount of the tax imposed on such organization under section 4940(b).

Example (2). Assume the facts stated in Example (1), except that the tax liability under subtitle A is $15,000 rather than $10,000. Because the sum of the taxes which would have been imposed under sections 4940(a) and 511 ($11,000) does not exceed the tax that was imposed under subtitle A ($15,000), there is no tax imposed under section 4940(b) with respect to such foundation.

(c) *Net investment income defined.*—(1) *In general.*—For purposes of section 4940(a), "net investment income" of a private foundation is the amount by which:

(i) The sum of the gross investment income (as defined in section 4940(c)(2) and paragraph (d) of this section) and the capital gain net income (net capital gain for taxable years beginning before January 1, 1977) (within the meaning of section 4940(c)(4) and paragraph (f) of this section) exceeds

(ii) The deductions allowed by section 4940(c)(3) and paragraph (e) of this section.

Except to the extent inconsistent with the provisions of this section, net investment income shall be determined under the principles of subtitle A.

(2) *Tax-exempt income.*—For purposes of computing net investment income under section 4940, the provisions of section 103 (relating to interest on certain governmental obligations) and section 265 (relating to expenses and interest relating to tax-exempt income) and the regulations thereunder shall apply.

(d) *Gross investment income.*—(1) *In general.*—For purposes of paragraph (c) of this section, "gross investment income" means the gross amounts of income from interest, dividends, rents, and royalties (including overriding royalties) received by a private foundation from all sources, but does not include such income to the extent included in computing the tax imposed by section 511. Under this definition, interest, dividends, rents, and royalties derived from assets devoted to charitable activities are includible in gross investment income. Therefore, for example, interest received on a student loan would be includible in the gross investment income of a private foundation making such loan. For purposes of paragraph (c) of this section, gross investment income also includes the items of investment income described in § 1.512(b)-1(a).

(2) *Certain estate and trust disbursements.*—In the case of a distribution from an estate or a trust described in section 4947(a)(1) or (2), such distribution shall not retain its character in the hands of the distributee for purposes of computing the tax under section 4940; except that, in the case of a distribution from a trust described in section 4947(a)(2), the income of such trust attributable to transfers in trust after May 26, 1969, shall retain its character in the hands of a distributee private foundation for purposes of section 4940

(unless such income is taken into account because of the application of section 671).

(3) *Treatment of certain distributions in redemption of stock.*—For purposes of applying section 302(b)(1), any distribution made to a private foundation by a disqualified person (as defined in section 4946(a)), in redemption of stock held by such private foundation in a business enterprise shall be treated as not essentially equivalent to a dividend if all of the following conditions are satisfied: (i) such redemption is of stock which was owned by a private foundation on May 26, 1969 (or which is acquired by a private foundation under the terms of a trust which was irrevocable on May 26, 1969, or under the terms of a will executed on or before such date, which is in effect on such date and at all times thereafter, or would have passed under such a will but before that time actually passes under a trust which would have met the test of this subdivision but for the fact that the trust was revocable (but was not in fact revoked)); (ii) such foundation is required to dispose of such property in order not to be liable for tax under section 4943 (relating to taxes on excess business holdings); and (iii) such foundation receives in return an amount which equals or exceeds the fair market value of such property at the time of such disposition or at the time a contract for such disposition was previously executed in a transaction which would not constitute a prohibited transaction (within the meaning of section 503(b) or the corresponding provisions of prior law). In the case of a disposition before January 1, 1975, section 4943 shall be applied without taking section 4943(c)(4) into account. A distribution which otherwise qualifies under section 302 as a distribution in part or full payment in exchange for stock shall not be treated as essentially equivalent to a dividend because it does not meet the requirements of this subparagraph.

(e) *Deductions.*—(1) *In general.*—(i) For purposes of computing net investment income, there shall be allowed as a deduction from gross investment income all the ordinary and necessary expenses paid or incurred for the production or collection of gross investment income or for the management, conservation, or maintenance of property held for the production of such income, determined with the modifications set forth in subparagraph (2) of this paragraph. Such expenses include that portion of a private foundation's operating expenses which is paid or incurred for the production or collection of gross investment income. Taxes paid or incurred under this section are not paid or incurred for the production or collection of gross investment income. A private foundation's operating expenses include compensation of officers, other salaries and wages of employees, outside professional fees, interest, and rent and taxes upon property used in the foundation's operations. Where a private foundation's officers or employees engage in activities on behalf of the foundation for both investment purposes and for exempt purposes, compensation and salaries paid to such officers or employees must be allocated between the investment activities and the exempt activities. To the extent a private foundation's expenses are taken into account in computing the tax imposed by section 511, they shall not be deductible for purposes of computing the tax imposed by section 4940.

(ii) Where only a portion of property produces, or is held for the production of, income subject to the section 4940 excise tax, and the remainder of the property is used for exempt purposes, the deductions allowed by section 4940(c)(3) shall be apportioned between the exempt and nonexempt uses.

(iii) No amount is allowable as a deduction under this section to the extent it is paid or incurred for purposes other than those described in subdivision (i) of this subparagraph. Thus, for example, the deductions prescribed by the following sections are not allowable: (1) the charitable deduction prescribed under sections 170 and 642(c); (2) the net operating loss deduction prescribed under section 172; and (3) the special deductions prescribed under Part VIII, subchapter B, chapter 1.

(2) *Deduction modifications.*—The following modifications shall be made in determining deductions otherwise allowable under this paragraph:

(i) The depreciation deduction shall be allowed, but only on the basis of the straight line method provided in section 167(b)(1).

(ii) The depletion deduction shall be allowed, but such deduction shall be determined without regard to section 613, relating to percentage depletion.

(iii) The basis to be used for purposes of the deduction allowed for depreciation or depletion shall be the basis determined under the rules of Part II of subchapter O of chapter 1, subject to the provisions of section 4940(c)(3)(B), and without regard to section 4940(c)(4)(B), relating to the basis for determining gain, or section 362(c). Thus, a private foundation must reduce the cost or other substituted or transferred basis by an amount equal to the straight line depreciation or cost depletion, without regard to whether the foundation deducted such depreciation or depletion during the period prior to its first taxable year beginning after December 31, 1969. However, where a private foundation has previously taken depreciation or depletion deductions in excess of the amount which would have been taken had the straight line or cost method been employed, such excess depreciation or depletion also shall be taken into account to reduce basis. If the facts necessary to determine the basis of property in the hands of the donor or the last preceding owner by whom it was not acquired by gift are unknown to a donee private foundation, then the original basis to such foundation of such property shall be determined under the rules of § 1.1015-1(a)(3).

(iv) The deduction for expenses paid or incurred in any taxable year for the production of gross investment income earned as an incident to a charitable function shall be no greater than the income earned from such function which is includible as gross investment income for such year. For example, where rental income is incidentally realized in 1971 from historic buildings held open to the public, deductions for amounts paid or incurred in 1971 for the production of such income shall be limited to the amount of rental income includible as gross investment income for 1971.

(f) *Capital gain and losses.*—(1) *General rule.*—In determining capital gain net income (net capital gain for taxable years beginning before January 1, 1977) for purposes of the tax imposed by section 4940, there shall be taken into account only capital gains and losses from the sale or other disposition of property held by a private foundation for investment purposes (other than program-related investments, as defined in section 4944(c)), and property used for the production of income included in computing the tax imposed by section 511 except to the extent gain or loss from the sale or other disposition of such property is taken into account for purposes of such tax. For taxable years beginning after December 31, 1972, property shall be treated as held for investment purposes even though such property is disposed of by the foundation immediately upon its receipt, if it is property of a type which generally produces interest, dividends, rents, royalties, or capital gains through appreciation (for example, rental real estate, stock, bonds, mineral interests, mortgages, and securities). Under this subparagraph, gains and losses from the sale or other disposition of property used for the exempt purposes of the private foundation are excluded. For example, gain or loss on the sale of the buildings used for the exempt activities of a private foundation would not be subject to the section 4940 tax. Where the foundation uses property for its exempt purposes, but also incidentally derives income from such property which is subject to the tax imposed by section 4940(a), any gain or loss resulting from the sale or other disposition of such property is not subject to the tax imposed by section 4940(a). For example, if a tax-exempt private foundation maintains buildings of a historical nature and keeps them open for public inspection, but requires a number of its employees to live in these buildings and charges the employees rent, the rent would be subject to the tax imposed by section 4940(a), but any gain or loss resulting from the sale of such property would not be subject to such tax. However, where the foundation uses property for both exempt purposes and (other than incidentally) for investment purposes (for example, a building in which the foundation's charitable and investment activities are carried on), that portion of any gain or loss from the sale or other disposition of such property which is allocable to the investment use of such property must be taken into account in computing net capital gain for such taxable year. For purposes of this paragraph, a distribution of property for purposes described in section 170(c)(1) or (2)(B) which is a qualifying distribution under section 4942 shall not be treated as a sale or other disposition of property.

(2) *Basis.*—(i) The basis for purposes of determining gain from the sale or other disposition of property shall be the greater of:

(A) Fair market value on December 31, 1969, plus or minus all adjustments after December 31, 1969, and before the date of disposition under the rules of part II of subchapter O of chapter 1, provided that the property was held by the private foundation on December 31, 1969, and continuously thereafter to the date of disposition, or

(B) Basis as determined under the rules of part II of subchapter O of chapter 1,

subject to the provisions of section 4940(c)(3)(B) (and without regard to section 362(c)).

(ii) For purposes of determining loss from the sale or other disposition of property, basis as determined in subdivision (i) (B) of this subparagraph shall apply.

(3) *Losses.*—Where the sale or other disposition of property referred to in section 4940(c)(4)(A) results in a capital loss, such loss may be subtracted from capital gains from the sale or other disposition of other such property during the same taxable year, such excess may not be deducted from gross investment income under section 4940(c)(3) in any taxable year, nor may such excess be used to reduce gains in either prior or future taxable years, regardless of whether the foundation is a corporation or a trust.

(4) *Examples.*—The provisions of this paragraph may be illustrated by the following examples:

Example (1). A private foundation holds certain depreciable real property on December 31, 1969, having a basis of $102,000. The fair market value of such property on that date was $100,000. For its taxable year 1970 the foundation was allowed depreciation for such property of $5,100 on the straight-line method, the allowable amount computed on the $102,000 basis. The property was sold on January 1, 1971, for $100,000. Because fair market value on December 31, 1969, less straight-line depreciation of $5,100 ($94,900) is less than basis as determined by part II of subchapter O of chapter 1, $96,900 ($102,000 less $5,100), a gain of $3,100 is recognized (*i.e.,* sales price of $100,000 less the greater of the two possible bases).

Example (2). Assume the same facts in Example (1), except that the sale price was $95,000. Because the sale price was $1,900 less than the basis for loss ($96,900 as determined by the application of subparagraph (2)(ii) of this paragraph), there is a capital loss of $1,900 which may be deducted against capital gains for 1971 (if any) in determining capital gain net income (for taxable years beginning after December 31, 1976).

Example (3). A private foundation holds certain depreciable real property on December 31, 1969, having a basis of $102,000. The fair market value of such property on that date was $110,000. For its taxable year 1970 the foundation was allowed depreciation for such property of $5,100 on the straight line method, the allowable amount computed on the $102,000 basis. The property was sold on January 1, 1971, for $100,000. Fair market value on December 31, 1969, less straight line depreciation of $5,100 ($104,900) exceeds basis as determined by part II of subchapter O of chapter 1, $96,900 ($102,000 less $5,100), and will be used for purposes of determining gain. Because basis for purposes of determining gain exceeds sale price, there is no gain. There is no loss because basis for purposes of determining loss ($96,900) is less than sale price. [Reg. § 53.4940-1.]

☐ [T.D. 7250, 12-29-72. *Amended by* T.D. 7407, 3-3-76; T.D. 7606, 3-29-79; T.D. 7728, 10-31-80 *and* T.D. 8423, 7-28-92.]

[Reg. § 53.4941(a)-1]

§ 53.4941(a)-1. Imposition of initial taxes.— (a) *Tax on self-dealer.*—(1) *In general.*—Section 4941(a)(1) of the Code imposes an excise tax on each act of self-dealing between a disqualified person (as defined in section 4946(a)) and a private foundation. Except as provided in subparagraph (2) of this paragraph, this tax shall be imposed on a disqualified person even though he had no knowledge at the time of the act that such act constituted self-dealing. Notwithstanding the preceding two sentences, however, a transaction between a disqualified person and a private foundation will not constitute an act of self-dealing if—

(i) The transaction is a purchase or sale of securities by a private foundation through a stockbroker where normal trading procedures on a stock exchange or recognized over-the-counter market are followed;

(ii) Neither the buyer nor the seller of the securities nor the agent of either knows the identity of the other party involved; and

(iii) The sale is made in the ordinary course of business, and does not involve a block of securities larger than the average daily trading volume of that stock over the previous four weeks.

However, the preceding sentence shall not apply to a transaction involving a dealer who is a disqualified person acting as a principal or to a transaction which is an act of self-dealing pursuant to section 4941(d)(1)(B) and § 53.4941(d)-2(c)(1). Tax imposed by section 4941(a)(1) is at the rate of 5 percent of the amount involved (as defined in section 4941(e)(2) and § 53.4941(e)-1(b)) with respect to the act of self-dealing for each year or partial year in the taxable period (as defined in section 4941(e)(1)) and shall be paid by any disqualified person (other than a foundation manager acting only in the capacity of a foundation manager) who participates in the act of self-dealing. However, if a foundation manager is also acting as a self-dealer, he may be liable for both the tax imposed by section 4941(a)(1) and the tax imposed by section 4941(a)(2).

(2) *Government officials.*—In the case of a government official (as defined in section 4946(c)), the tax shall be imposed upon such government offical who participates in an act of self-dealing, only if he knows that such act is an act of self-dealing. See paragraph (b)(3) of this section for a definition of "knowing".

(3) *Participation.*—For purposes of this paragraph, a disqualified person shall be treated as participating in an act of self-dealing in any case in which he engages or takes part in the transaction by himself or with others, or directs any person to do so.

(b) *Tax on foundation manager.*—(1) *In general.*—Section 4941(a)(2) of the Code imposes an excise tax on the participation of any foundation manager in the act of self-dealing between a disqualified person and a private foundation. This tax is imposed only in cases in which the following circumstances are present:

(i) A tax is imposed by section 4941(a)(1),

(ii) Such participating foundation manager knows that the act is an act of self-dealing, and

(iii) The participation by the foundation manager is willful and is not due to reasonable cause.

The tax imposed by section 4941(a)(2) is at the rate of 2½ percent of the amount involved with respect to the act of self-dealing for each year or partial year in the taxable period and shall be paid by any foundation manager described in subdivisions (ii) and (iii) of this subparagraph.

(2) *Participation.*—The term "participation" shall include silence or inaction on the part of a foundation manager where he is under a duty to speak or act, as well as any affirmative action by such manager. However, a foundation manager will not be considered to have participated in an act of self-dealing where he has opposed such act in a manner consistent with the fulfillment of his responsibilities to the private foundation.

(3) *Knowing.*—For purposes of section 4941, a person shall be considered to have participated in a transaction "knowing" that it is an act of self-dealing only if—

(i) He has actual knowledge of sufficient facts so that, based solely upon such facts, such transaction would be an act of self-dealing,

(ii) He is aware that such an act under these circumstances may violate the provisions of federal tax law governing self-dealing, and

(iii) He negligently fails to make reasonable attempts to ascertain whether the transaction is an act of self-dealing, or he is in fact aware that it is such an act.

For purposes of this part, and chapter 42, the term "knowing" does not mean "having reason to know". However, evidence tending to show that a person has reason to know of a particular fact or particular rule is relevant in determining whether he had actual knowledge of such fact or rule. Thus, for example, evidence tending to show that a person has reason to know of sufficient facts so that, based solely upon such facts, a transaction would be an act of self-dealing is relevant in determining whether he has actual knowledge of such facts.

(4) *Willful.*—Participation by a foundation manager shall be deemed willful if it is voluntary, conscious, and intentional. No motive to avoid the restrictions of the law or the incurrence of any tax is necessary to make the participation willful. However, participation by a foundation manager is not willful if he does not know that the transaction in which he is participating is an act of self-dealing.

(5) *Due to reasonable cause.*—A foundation manager's participation is due to reasonable cause if he has exercised his responsibility on behalf of the foundation with ordinary business care and prudence.

(6) *Advice of counsel.*—If a person, after full disclosure of the factual situation to legal counsel (including house counsel), relies on the advice of such counsel expressed in a reasoned written legal opinion that an act is not an act of self-dealing under section 4941, although such act is subsequently held to be an act of self-dealing, the person's participation in such act will ordinarily not be considered "knowing" or "willful" and will ordinarily be considered "due to reasonable cause" within the meaning of section 4941(a)(2). For purposes of this subparagraph, a written legal opinion will be considered "reasoned" even if it reaches a conclusion which is subsequently determined to be incorrect so long as such opinion addresses itself to the facts and applicable law. However, a written legal opinion will not be considered "reasoned" it if does nothing more than recite the facts and express a conclusion. However, the absence of advice of counsel with respect to an act shall not, by itself, give rise to any inference that a person participated in such act knowingly, willfully, or without reasonable cause.

(c) *Burden of proof.*—For provisions relating to the burden of proof in cases involving the issue whether a foundation manager or a government official has knowingly participated in an act of self-dealing, see section 7454(b). [Reg. §53.4941(a)-1.]

☐ [*T.D. 7270, 4-16-73. Amended by T.D. 7299, 12-21-73.*]

[Reg. §53.4941(b)-1]

§53.4941(b)-1. Imposition of additional taxes.—(a) *Tax on self-dealer.*—Section 4941(b)(1) of the Code imposes an excise tax in any case in which an initial tax is imposed by section 4941(a)(1) on an act of self-dealing by a disqualified person with a private foundation and the act is not corrected within the taxable period (as defined in §53.4941(e)-1(a)). The tax imposed by section 4941(b)(1) is at the rate of 200 percent of the amount involved and shall be paid by any disqualified person (other than a foundation manager acting only in the capacity of a foundation manager) who participated in the act of self-dealing.

(b) *Tax on foundation manager.*—Section 4941(b)(2) of the Code imposes an excise tax to be paid by a foundation manager in any case in which a tax is imposed by section 4941(b)(1) and the foundation manager refused to agree to part or all of the correction of the self-dealing act. The tax imposed by section 4941(b)(2) is at the rate of 50 percent of the amount involved and shall be paid by any foundation manager who refused to agree to part or all of the correction of the self-dealing act. For the limitations on liability of a foundation manager, see § 53.4941(c)-1(b). [Reg. § 53.4941(b)-1.]

☐ [*T.D. 7270, 4-16-73. Amended by T.D. 8084, 5-1-86.*]

[Reg. § 53.4941(c)-1]

§ 53.4941(c)-1. Special rules.—(a) *Joint and several liability.*—(1) In any case where more than one person is liable for the tax imposed by any paragraph of section 4941(a) or (b), all such persons shall be jointly and severally liable for the taxes imposed under such paragraph with respect to such act of self-dealing.

(2) The provisions of this paragraph may be illustrated by the following example:

Example. A and B, who are managers of private foundation X, lend one of the foundation's paintings to G, a disqualified person, for display in G's office, in a transaction which gives rise to liability for tax under section 4941(a)(2) (relating to tax on foundation managers). An initial tax is imposed on both A and B with respect to the act of lending the foundation's painting to G. A and B are jointly and severally liable for the tax.

(b) *Limits on liability for management.*—(1) The maximum aggregate amount of tax collectible under section 4941(a)(2) from all foundation managers with respect to any one act of self-dealing shall be $10,000, and the maximum aggregate amount of tax collectible under section 4941(b)(2) from all foundation managers with respect to any one act of self-dealing shall be $10,000.

(2) The provisions of this paragraph may be illustrated by the following example:

Example. A, a disqualified person with respect to private foundation Y, sells certain real estate having a fair market value of $500,000 to Y for $500,000 in cash. B, C, and D, all the managers of foundation Y, authorized the purchase on Y's behalf knowing that such purchase was an act of self-dealing. The actions of B, C, and D in approving the purchase were willful and not due to reasonable cause. Initial taxes are imposed upon the foundation managers under subsections (a)(2) and (c)(2) of section 4941. The tax to be paid by the foundation managers is $10,000 (the lesser of $10,000 or 2½% of the amount

involved). The managers are jointly and severally liable for this $10,000, and the sum may be collected by the Internal Revenue Service from any one of them. [Reg. § 53.4941(c)-1.]

☐ [*T.D. 7270, 4-16-73.*]

[Reg. § 53.4941(d)-1]

§ 53.4941(d)-1. Definition of self-dealing.— (a) *In general.*—For purposes of section 4941, the term "self-dealing" means any direct or indirect transaction described in § 53.4941(d)-2. For purposes of this section it is immaterial whether the transaction results in a benefit or a detriment to the private foundation. The term "self-dealing" does not, however, include a transaction between a private foundation and a disqualified person where the disqualified person status arises only as a result of such transaction. For example, the bargain sale of property to a private foundation is not a direct act of self-dealing if the seller becomes a disqualified person only by reason of his becoming a substantial contributor as a result of the bargain element of the sale. For the effect of section 4942, 4943, 4944, and 4945 upon an act of self-dealing which also results in the imposition of tax under one or more of such sections, see the regulations under those sections.

(b) *Indirect self-dealing.*—(1) *Certain business transactions.*—The term "indirect self-dealing" shall not include any transaction described in § 53.4941(d)-2 between a disqualified person and an organization controlled by a private foundation (within the meaning of subparagraph (5) of this paragraph) if—

(i) The transaction results from a business relationship which was established before such transaction constituted an act of self-dealing (without regard to this paragraph),

(ii) The transaction was at least as favorable to the organization controlled by the foundation as an arm's-length transaction with an unrelated person, and

(iii) Either—

(*a*) The organization controlled by the foundation could have engaged in the transaction with someone other than a disqualified person only at a severe economic hardship to such organization, or

(*b*) Because of the unique nature of the product or services provided by the organization controlled by the foundation, the disqualified person could not have engaged in the transaction with anyone else, or could have done so only by incurring severe economic hardship. See example (2) of subparagraph (8) of this paragraph.

(2) *Grants to intermediaries.*—The term "indirect self-dealing" shall not include a transaction engaged in with a government official by an intermediary organization which is a recipient of a grant from a private foundation and which is not controlled by such foundation (within the meaning of subparagraph (5) of this paragraph) if the private foundation does not earmark the

use of the grant for any named government official and there does not exist an agreement, oral or written, whereby the grantor foundation may cause the selection of the government official by the intermediary organization. A grant by a private foundation is earmarked if such grant is made pursuant to an agreement, either oral or written, that the grant will be used by any named individual. Thus, a grant by a private foundation shall not constitute an indirect act of self-dealing even though such foundation had reason to believe that certain government officials would derive benefits from such grant so long as the intermediary organization exercises control, in fact, over the selection process and actually makes the selection completely independently of the private foundation. See example (3) of subparagraph (8) of this paragraph.

(3) *Transactions during the administration of an estate or revocable trust.*—The term "indirect self-dealing" shall not include a transaction with respect to a private foundation's interest or expectancy in property (whether or not encumbered) held by an estate (or revocable trust, including a trust which has become irrevocable on a grantor's death), regardless of when title to the property vests under local law, if—

(i) The administrator or executor of an estate or trustee of a revocable trust either—

(a) Possesses a power of sale with respect to the property,

(b) Has the power to reallocate the property to another beneficiary, or

(c) Is required to sell the property under the terms of any option subject to which the property was acquired by the estate (or revocable trust);

(ii) Such transaction is approved by the probate court having jurisdiction over the state (or by another court having jurisdiction over the estate (or trust) or over the private foundation);

(iii) Such transaction occurs before the estate is considered terminated for Federal income tax purposes pursuant to paragraph (a) of §1.641(b)-3 of this chapter (or in the case of a revocable trust, before it is considered subject to section 4947);

(iv) The estate (or trust) receives an amount which equals or exceeds the fair market value of the foundation's interest or expectancy in such property at the time of the transaction, taking into account the terms of any option subject to which the property was acquired by the estate (or trust); and

(v) With respect to transactions occurring after April 16, 1973, the transaction either—

(a) Results in the foundation receiving an interest or expectancy at least as liquid as the one it gave up,

(b) Results in the foundation receiving an asset related to the active carrying out of its exempt purposes, or

(c) Is required under the terms of any option which is binding on the estate (or trust).

(4) *Transactions with certain organizations.*—A transaction between a private foundation and an organization which is not controlled by the foundation (within the meaning of subparagraph (5) of this paragraph), and which is not described in section 4946(a)(1)(E), (F), or (G) because persons described in section 4946(a)(1)(A), (B), (C), or (D) own no more than 35 percent of the total combined voting power or profits or beneficial interest of such organization, shall not be treated as an indirect act of self-dealing between the foundation and such disqualified persons solely because of the ownership interest of such persons in such organization.

(5) *Control.*—For purposes of this paragraph, an organization is controlled by a private foundation if the foundation or one or more of its foundation managers (acting only in such capacity) may, only by aggregating their votes or positions of authority, require the organization to engage in a transaction which if engaged in with the private foundation would constitute self-dealing. Similarly, for purposes of this paragraph, an organization is controlled by a private foundation in the case of such a transaction between the organization and a disqualified person, if such disqualified person, together with one or more persons who are disqualified persons by reason of such person's relationship (within the meaning of section 4946(a)(1)(C) through (G)) to such disqualified person, may, only by aggregating their votes or positions of authority with that of the foundation, require the organization to engage in such a transaction. The "controlled" organization need not be a private foundation; for example, it may be any type of exempt or nonexempt organization including a school, hospital, operating foundation, or social welfare organization. For purposes of this paragraph, an organization will be considered to be controlled by a private foundation or by a private foundation and disqualified persons referred to in the second sentence of this subparagraph if such persons are able, in fact, to control the organization (even if their aggregate voting power is less then 50 percent of the total voting power of the organization's governing body) or if one or more of such persons has the right to exercise veto power over the actions of such organization relevant to any potential acts of self-dealing. A private foundation shall not be regarded as having control over an organization merely because it exercises expenditure responsibility (as defined in section 4945(d)(4) and (h)) with respect to contributions to such organization. See example (6) of subparagraph (8) of this paragraph.

(6) *Certain transactions involving limited amounts.*—The term "indirect self-dealing" shall not include any transaction between a disqualified person and an organization controlled by a private foundation (within the meaning of subparagraph (5) of this paragraph) or between two disqualified persons where the foundation's assets may be affected by the transaction if—

(i) The transaction arises in the normal and customary course of a retail business engaged in with the general public,

(ii) In the case of a transaction between a disqualified person and an organization controlled by a private foundation, the transaction is at least as favorable to the organization controlled by the foundation as an arm's-length transaction with an unrelated person, and

(iii) The total of the amounts involved in such transactions with respect to any one such disqualified person in any one taxable year does not exceed $5,000.

See example (7) of subparagraph (8) of this paragraph.

(7) *Applicability of statutory exceptions to indirect self-dealing.*—The term "indirect self-dealing" shall not include a transaction involving one or more disqualified persons to which a private foundation is not a party, in any case in which the private foundation, by reason of section 4941(d)(2), could itself engage in such a transaction. Thus, for example, even if a private foundation has control (within the meaning of subparagraph (5) of this paragraph) of a corporation, the corporation may pay to a disqualified person except a government official, reasonable compensation for personal services.

(8) *Examples.*—The provisions of this paragraph may be illustrated by the following examples:

Example (1). Private foundation P owns the controlling interest of the voting stock of corporation X and, as a result of such interest, elects a majority of the board of directors of X. Two of the foundation managers, A and B, who are also directors of corporation X, form corporation Y for the purpose of building and managing a country club. A and B receive a total of 40 percent of Y's stock, making Y a disqualified person with respect to P under section 4946(a)(1)(E). In order to finance the construction and operation of the country club, Y requested and received a loan in the amount of $4,000,000 from X. The making of the loan by X to Y shall constitute an indirect act of self-dealing between P and Y.

Example (2). Private foundation W owns the controlling interest of the voting stock of corporation X, a manufacturer of certain electronic computers. Corporation Y, a disqualified person with respect to W, owns the patent for, and manufactures, one of the essential component parts used in the computers. X has been making regular purchases of the patented component from Y since 1965, subject to the same terms as all other purchasers of such component parts. X could not buy similar components from another source. Consequently, X would suffer severe economic hardship if it could not continue to purchase these components from Y, since it would then be forced to develop a computer which could be constructed with other components. Under these circumstances, the continued purchase by X from Y of these components shall

not be an indirect act of self-dealing between W and Y.

Example (3). Private foundation Y made a grant to M University, an organization described in section 170(b)(1)(A)(ii), for the purpose of conducting a seminar to study methods for improving the administration of the judicial system. M is not controlled by Y within the meaning of subparagraph (5) of this paragraph. In conducting the seminar, M made payments to certain government officials. By the nature of the grant, Y had reason to believe that government officials would be compensated for participation in the seminar. M, however, had completely independent control over the selection of such participants. Thus, such grant by Y shall not constitute an indirect act of self-dealing with respect to the government officials.

Example (4). A, a substantial contributor to P, a private foundation, bequeathed one-half of his estate to his spouse and one-half of his estate to P. Included in A's estate is a one-third interest in AB, a partnership. The other two-thirds interest in AB is owned by B, a disqualified person with respect to P. The one-third interest in AB was subject to an option agreement when it was acquired by the estate. The executor of A's estate sells the one-third interest in AB to B pursuant to such option agreement at the price fixed in such option agreement in the sale which meets the requirements of subparagraph (3) of this paragraph. Under these circumstances, the sale does not constitute an indirect act of self-dealing between B and P.

Example (5). A bequeathed $100,000 to his wife and a piece of unimproved real estate of equivalent value to private foundation Z, of which A was the creator and a foundation manager. Under the laws of State Y, to which the estate is subject, title to the real estate vests in the foundation upon A's death. However, the executor has the power under State law to reallocate the property to another beneficiary. During a reasonable period for administration of the estate, the executor exercises this power and distributes the $100,000 cash to the foundation and the real estate to A's wife. The probate court having jurisdiction over the estate approves the executor's action. Under these circumstances, the executor's action does not constitute an indirect act of self-dealing between the foundation and A's wife.

Example (6). Private foundation P owns 20 percent of the voting stock of corporation W. A, a substantial contributor with respect to P, owns 16 percent of the voting stock of corporation W. B, A's son, owns 15 percent of the voting stock of the corporation W. The terms of the voting stock are such that P, A, and B could vote their stock in a block to elect a majority of the board of directors of W. W is treated as controlled by P (within the meaning of subparagraph (5) of this paragraph) for purposes of this example. A and B also own 50 percent of the stock of corporation Y, making Y a disqualified person with respect to P under section 4946(a)(1)(E). W makes a loan to Y of $1,000,000. The making of this loan by W to Y shall constitute an indirect act of self-dealing between P and Y.

Example (7). A, a disqualified person with respect to private foundation P, enters into a contract with corporation M, which is also a disqualified person with respect to P. P owns 20 percent of M's stock, and controls M within the meaning of subparagraph (5) of this paragraph. M is in the retail department store business. Purchases by A of goods sold by M in the normal and customary course of business at retail or higher prices are not indirect acts of self-dealing so long as the total of the amounts involved in all of such purchases by A in any one year does not exceed $5,000. [Reg. § 53.4941(d)-1.]

☐ [*T.D.* 7270, 4-16-73.]

[Reg. § 53.4941(d)-2]

§ 53.4941(d)-2. Specific acts of self-dealing.— Except as provided in § 53.4941(d)-3 or § 53.4941(d)-4—

(a) *Sale or exchange of property.*—(1) *In general.*—The sale or exchange of property between a private foundation and a disqualified person shall constitute an act of self-dealing. For example, the sale of incidental supplies by a disqualified person to a private foundation shall be an act of self-dealing regardless of the amount paid to the disqualified person for the incidental supplies. Similarly, the sale of stock or other securities by a disqualified person to a private foundation in a "bargain sale" shall be an act of self-dealing regardless of the amount paid for such stock or other securities. An installment sale may be subject to the provisions of both section 4941(d)(1)(A) and section 4941(d)(1)(B).

(2) *Mortgaged property.*—For purposes of subparagraph (1) of this paragraph, the transfer of real or personal property by a disqualified person to a private foundation shall be treated as a sale or exchange if the foundation assumes a mortgage or similar lien which was placed on the property prior to the transfer, or takes subject to a mortgage or similar lien which a disqualified person placed on the property with the 10-year period ending on the date of transfer. For purposes of this subparagraph, the term "similar lien" shall include, but is not limited to, deeds of trust and vendors' liens, but shall not include any other lien if such lien is insignificant in relation to the fair market value of the property transferred.

(b) *Leases.*—(1) *In general.*—Except as provided in subparagraphs (2) and (3) of this paragraph, the leasing of property between a disqualified person and a private foundation shall constitute an act of self-dealing.

(2) *Certain leases without charge.*—The leasing of property by a disqualified person to a private foundation shall not be an act of self-dealing if the lease is without charge. For purposes of this subparagraph, a lease shall be considered to be without charge even though the private foundation pays for janitorial ser-vices, utilities, or other maintenance costs it incurs for the use of the property, so long as the payment is not made directly or indirectly to a disqualified person.

(3) *Certain leases of office space.*—For taxable years beginning after December 31, 1979, the leasing of office space by a disqualified person to a private foundation shall not be an act of self-dealing if—

(i) The leased space is in a building in which there are other tenants who are not disqualified persons,

(ii) The lease is pursuant to a binding lease which was in effect on October 9, 1969, or pursuant to renewals of such a lease,

(iii) The execution of the lease was not a prohibited transaction (within the meaning of section 503(b) or the corresponding provisions of prior law) at the time of such execution, and

(iv) The terms of the lease (or any renewal) reflect an arm's length transaction. A lease or renewal of such lease is described in this subparagraph (3) only if it satisfies the requirements of § 53.4941(d)-4(c)(1) and (2), applied without regard to the December 31, 1979 deadline described therein.

(c) *Loans.*—(1) *In general.*—Except as provided in subparagraphs (2), (3), and (4) of this paragraph, the lending of money or other extension of credit between a private foundation and a disqualified person shall constitute an act of self-dealing. Thus, for example, an act of self-dealing occurs where a third party purchases property and assumes a mortgage, the mortgagee of which is a private foundation, and subsequently the third party transfers the property to a disqualified person who either assumes liability under the mortgage or takes the property subject to the mortgage. Similarly, except in the case of the receipt and holding of a note pursuant to a transaction described in § 53.4941(d)-1(b)(3), an act of self-dealing occurs where a note, the obligor of which is a disqualified person, is transferred by a third party to a private foundation which becomes the creditor under the note.

(2) *Loans without interest.*—Subparagraph (1) of this paragraph shall not apply to the lending of money or other extension of credit by a disqualified person to a private foundation if the loan or other extension of credit is without interest or other charge.

(3) *Certain evidences of future gifts.*—The making of a promise, pledge, or similar arrangement to a private foundation by a disqualified person, whether evidenced by an oral or written agreement, a promissory note, or other instrument of indebtedness, to the extent motivated by charitable intent and unsupported by consideration, is not an extension of credit (within the meaning of this paragraph) before the date of maturity.

(4) *General banking functions.*—Under section 4941(d)(2)(E) the performance by a bank or trust company which is a disqualified person of

trust functions and certain general banking services for a private foundation is not an act of self-dealing, where the banking services are reasonable and necessary to carrying out the exempt purposes of the private foundation, if the compensation paid to the bank or trust company, taking into account the fair interest rate for the use of the funds by the bank or trust company, for such services is not excessive. The general banking services allowed by this subparagraph are:

(i) Checking accounts, as long as the bank does not charge interest on any overwithdrawals,

(ii) Savings accounts, as long as the foundation may withdraw its funds on no more than 30 days' notice without subjecting itself to a loss of interest on its money for the time during which the money was on deposit, and

(iii) Safekeeping activities.

See example (3) of § 53.4941(d)-3(c)(2).

(d) *Furnishing goods, services, or facilities.*— (1) *In general.*—Except as provided in subparagraph (2) or (3) of this paragraph (or § 53.4941(d)-3(b)), the furnishing of goods, services, or facilities between a private foundation and a disqualified person shall constitute an act of self-dealing. This subparagraph shall apply, for example, to the furnishing of goods, services, or facilities such as office space, automobiles, auditoriums, secretarial help, meals, libraries, publications, laboratories, or parking lots. Thus, for example, if a foundation furnishes personal living quarters to a disqualified person (other than a foundation manager or employee) without charge, such furnishing shall be an act of self-dealing.

(2) *Furnishing of goods, services, or facilities to foundation managers and employees.*—The furnishing of goods, services, or facilities such as those described in subparagraph (1) of this paragraph to a foundation manager in recognition of his services as a foundation manager, or to another employee (including an individual who would be an employee but for the fact that he receives no compensation for his services) in recognition of his services in such capacity, is not an act of self-dealing if the value of such furnishing (whether or not includible as compensation in his gross income) is reasonable and necessary to the performance of his tasks in carrying out the exempt purposes of the foundation and, taken in conjunction with any other payment of compensation or payment or reimbursement of expenses to him by the foundation, is not excessive. For example, if a foundation furnishes meals and lodging which are reasonable and necessary (but not excessive) to a foundation manager by reason of his being a foundation manager, then, without regard to whether such meals and lodging are excludable from gross income under section 119 as furnished for the convenience of the employer, such furnishing is not an act of self-dealing. For the effect of section 4945(d)(5) upon

an expenditure for unreasonable administrative expenses, see § 53.4945-6(b)(2).

(3) *Furnishing of goods, services, or facilities by a disqualified person without charge.*—The furnishing of goods, services, or facilities by a disqualified person to a private foundation shall not be an act of self-dealing if they are furnished without charge. Thus, for example, the furnishing of goods such as pencils, stationery, or other incidental supplies, or the furnishing of facilities such as a building, by a disqualified person to a foundation shall be allowed if such supplies or facilities are furnished without charge. Similarly, the furnishing of services (even though such services are not personal in nature) shall be permitted if such furnishing is without charge. For purposes of this subparagraph, a furnishing of goods shall be considered without charge even though the private foundation pays for transportation, insurance, or maintenance costs it incurs in obtaining or using the property, so long as the payment is not made directly or indirectly to the disqualified person.

(e) *Payment of compensation.*—The payment of compensation (or payment or reimbursement of expenses) by a private foundation to a disqualified person shall constitute an act of self-dealing. See, however, § 53.4941(d)-3(c) for the exception for the payment of compensation by a foundation to a disqualified person for personal services which are reasonable and necessary to carry out the exempt purposes of the foundation.

(f) *Transfer or use of the income or assets of a private foundation.*—(1) *In general.*—The transfer to, or use by or for the benefit of, a disqualified person of the income or assets of a private foundation shall constitute an act of self-dealing. For purposes of the preceding sentence, the purchase or sale of stock or other securities by a private foundation shall be an act of self-dealing if such purchase or sale is made in an attempt to manipulate the price of the stock or other securities to the advantage of a disqualified person. Similarly, the indemnification (of a lender) or guarantee (of repayment) by a private foundation with respect to a loan to a disqualified person shall be treated as a use for the benefit of a disqualified person of the income or assets of the foundation (within the meaning of this subparagraph). In addition, if a private foundation makes a grant or other payment which satisfies the legal obligation of a disqualified person, such grant or payment shall ordinarily constitute an act of self-dealing to which this subparagraph applies. However, if a private foundation makes a grant or payment which satisfies a pledge, enforceable under local law, to an organization described in section 501(c)(3), which pledge is made on or before April 16, 1973, such grant or payment shall not constitute an act of self-dealing to which this subparagraph applies so long as the disqualified person obtains no substantial benefit, other than the satisfaction of his obligation, from such grant or payment.

(2) *Certain incidental benefits.*—The fact that a disqualified person receives an incidental or tenuous benefit from the use by a foundation of its income or assets will not, by itself, make such use an act of self-dealing. Thus, the public recognition a person may receive, arising from the charitable activities of a private foundation to which such person is a substantial contributor, does not in itself result in an act of self-dealing since generally the benefit is incidental and tenuous. For example, a grant by a private foundation to a section 509(a)(1), (2), or (3) organization will not be an act of self-dealing merely because such organization is located in the same area as a corporation which is a substantial contributor to the foundation, or merely because one of the section 509(a)(1), (2), or (3) organization's officers, directors, or trustees is also a manager of or a substantial contributor to the foundation. Similarly, a scholarship or a fellowship grant to a person other than a disqualified person, which is paid or incurred by a private foundation in accordance with a program which is consistent with—

(i) The requirements of the foundation's exempt status under section 501(c)(3),

(ii) The requirements for the allowance of deductions under section 170 for contributions made to the foundation, and

(iii) The requirements of section 4945(g)(1),

will not be an act of self-dealing under section 4941(d)(1) merely because a disqualified person indirectly receives an incidental benefit from such grant. Thus, a scholarship or a fellowship grant made by a private foundation in accordance with a program to award scholarships or fellowship grants to the children of employees of a substantial contributor shall not constitute an act of self-dealing if the requirements of the preceding sentence are satisfied. For an example of the kind of scholarship program with an employment nexus that meets the above requirements, see § 53.4945-4(b)(5) (Example 1).

(3) *Non-compensatory indemnification of foundation managers against liability for defense in civil proceedings.*—(i) Except as provided in § 53.4941(d)-3(c), section 4941(d)(1) shall not apply to the indemnification by a private foundation of a foundation manager, with respect to the manager's defense in any civil judicial or civil administrative proceeding arising out of the manager's performance of services (or failure to perform services) on behalf of the foundation, against all expenses (other than taxes, including taxes imposed by chapter 42, penalties, or expenses of correction) including attorneys' fees, judgments and settlement expenditures if—

(A) Such expenses are reasonably incurred by the manager in connection with such proceeding; and

(B) The manager has not acted willfully and without reasonable cause with respect to the act or failure to act which led to such proceeding or to liability for tax under chapter 42.

(ii) Similarly, except as provided in § 53.4941(d)-3(c), section 4941(d)(1) shall not apply to premiums for insurance to make or to reimburse a foundation for an indemnification payment allowed pursuant to this paragraph (f)(3). Neither shall an indemnification or payment of insurance allowed pursuant to this paragraph (f)(3) be treated as part of the compensation paid to such manager for purposes of determining whether the compensation is reasonable under chapter 42.

(4) *Compensatory indemnification of foundation managers against liability for defense in civil proceedings.*—(i) The indemnification by a private foundation of a foundation manager for compensatory expenses shall be an act of self-dealing under this paragraph unless when such payment is added to other compensation paid to such manager the total compensation is reasonable under chapter 42. A compensatory expense for purposes of this paragraph (f) is—

(A) Any penalty, tax (including a tax imposed by chapter 42), or expense of correction that is owed by the foundation manager;

(B) Any expense not reasonably incurred by the manager in connection with a civil judicial or civil administrative proceeding arising out of the manager's performance of services on behalf of the foundation; or

(C) Any expense resulting from an act or failure to act with respect to which the manager has acted willfully and without reasonable cause.

(ii) Similarly, the payment by a private foundation of the premiums for an insurance policy providing liability insurance to a foundation manager for expenses described in this paragraph (f)(4) shall be an act of self-dealing under this paragraph (f) unless when such premiums are added to other compensation paid to such manager the total compensation is reasonable under chapter 42.

(5) *Insurance Allocation.*—A private foundation shall not be engaged in an act of self-dealing if the foundation purchases a single insurance policy to provide its managers both the noncompensatory and the compensatory coverage discussed in this paragraph (f), provided that the total insurance premium is allocated and that each manager's portion of the premium attributable to the compensatory coverage is included in that manager's compensation for purposes of determining reasonable compensation under chapter 42.

(6) *Indemnification.*—For purposes of this paragraph (f), the term *indemnification* shall include not only reimbursement by the foundation for expenses that the foundation manager has already incurred or anticipates incurring but also direct payment by the foundation of such expenses as the expenses arise.

(7) *Taxable Income.*—The determination of whether any amount of indemnification or insurance premium discussed in this paragraph (f) is

Reg. §53.4941(d)-2(f)(7)

included in the manager's gross income for individual income tax purposes is made on the basis of the provisions of chapter 1 and without regard to the treatment of such amount for purposes of determining whether the manager's compensation is reasonable under chapter 42.

(8) *De minimis items.*—Any property or service that is excluded from income under section 132(a)(4) may be disregarded for purposes of determining whether the recipient's compensation is reasonable under chapter 42.

(9) *Examples.*—The provisions of this paragraph may be illustrated by the following examples:

Example (1). M, a private foundation, makes a grant of $50,000 to the governing body of N City for the purpose of alleviating the slum conditions which exist in a particular neighborhood of N. Corporation P, a substantial contributor to M, is located in the same area in which the grant is to be used. Although the general improvement of the area may constitute an incidental and tenuous benefit to P, such benefit by itself will not constitute an act of self-dealing.

Example (2). Private foundation X established a program to award scholarship grants to the children of employees of corporation M, a substantial contributor to X. After disclosure of the method of carrying out such program, X received a determination letter from the Internal Revenue Service stating that X is exempt from taxation under section 501(c)(3), that contributions to X are deductible under section 170, and that X's scholarship program qualifies under section 4945(g)(1). A scholarship grant to a person not a disqualified person with respect to X paid or incurred by X in accordance with such program shall not be an indirect act of self-dealing between X and M.

Example (3). Private foundation Y owns voting stock in corporation Z, the management of which includes certain disqualified persons with respect to Y. Prior to Z's annual stockholder meeting, the management solicits and receives the foundation's proxies. The transfer of such proxies in and of itself shall not be an act of self-dealing.

Example (4). A, a disqualified person with respect to private foundation S, contributes certain real estate to S for the purpose of building a neighborhood recreation center in a particular underprivileged area. As a condition of the gift, S agrees to name the recreation center after A. Since the benefit to A is only incidental and tenuous, the naming of the recreation center, by itself, will not be an act of self-dealing.

(g) *Payment to a government official.*—Except as provided in section 4941(d)(2)(G) or §53.4941(d)-3(e), the agreement by a private foundation to make any payment of money or other property to a government official, as defined in section 4946(c), shall constitute an act of self-dealing. For purposes of this paragraph, an individual who is otherwise described in section 4946(c) shall be treated as a government official

while on leave of absence from the government without pay. [Reg. §53.4941(d)-2.]

☐ [*T.D. 7270, 4-16-73. Amended by T.D. 7938, 1-30-84 and T.D. 8639, 12-19-95.*]

[Reg. §53.4941(d)-3]

§53.4941(d)-3. Exceptions to self-dealing.—
(a) *General rule.*—In general, a transaction described in section 4941(d)(2)(B), (C), (D), (E), (F), (G), or (H) is not an act of self-dealing. Section 4941(d)(2)(B), (C), and (H) provide limited exceptions to certain specific transactions, as described in paragraphs (b)(2), (b)(3), (c)(2), and (d)(3) of §53.4941(d)-2.

(b) *Furnishing of goods, services, or facilities to a disqualified person.*—(1) *In general.*—Under section 4941(d)(2)(D), the furnishing of goods, services, or facilities by a private foundation to a disqualified person shall not be an act of self-dealing if such goods, services, or facilities are made available to the general public on at least as favorable a basis as they are made available to the disqualified person. This subparagraph shall not apply, however, in the case of goods, services or facilities furnished later than May 16, 1973, unless such goods, services or facilities are functionally related, within the meaning of section 4942(j)(5), to the exercise or performance by a private foundation of its charitable, educational, or other purpose or function constituting the basis for its exemption under section 501(c)(3).

(2) *General public.*—For purposes of this paragraph, the term "general public" shall include those persons who, because of the particular nature of the activities of the private foundation, would be reasonably expected to utilize such goods, services, or facilities. This paragraph shall not apply, however, unless there are a substantial number of persons other than disqualified persons who are actually utilizing such goods, services or facilities. Thus, a private foundation which furnishes recreational or park facilities to the general public may furnish such facilities to a disqualified person provided they are furnished to him on a basis which is not more favorable than that on which they are furnished to the general public. Similarly, the sale of a book or magazine by a private foundation to disqualified persons shall not be an act of self-dealing if the publication of the book or magazine is functionally related to a charitable or educational activity of the foundation and the book or magazine is made available to the disqualified persons and the general public at the same price. In addition, if the terms of the sale require, for example, payment within 60 days from the date of delivery of the book or magazine, such terms are consistent with normal commercial practices, and payment is made within the 60-day period, the transaction shall not be treated as a loan or other extension of credit under §53.4941(d)-2(c)(1).

(c) *Payment of compensation for certain personal services.*—(1) *In general.*—Under section

4941(d)(2)(E), except in the case of a government official (as defined in section 4946(c)), the payment of compensation (and the payment or reimbursement of expenses, including reasonable advances for expenses anticipated in the immediate future) by a private foundation to a disqualified person for the performance of personal services which are reasonable and necessary to carry out the exempt purpose of the private foundation shall not be an act of self-dealing if such compensation (or payment or reimbursement) is not excessive. For purposes of this subparagraph the term "personal services" includes the services of a broker serving as agent for the private foundation, but not the services of a dealer who buys from the private foundation as principal and resells to third parties. For the determination whether compensation is excessive, see § 1.162-7 of this chapter (Income Tax Regulations). This paragraph applies without regard to whether the person who receives the compensation (or payment or reimbursement) is an individual. The portion of any payment which represents payment for property shall not be treated as payment of compensation (or payment or reimbursement of expenses) for the performance of personal services for purposes of this paragraph. For rules with respect to the performance of general banking services, see § 53.4941(d)-2(c)(4). Further, the making of a cash advance to a foundation manager or employee for expenses on behalf of the foundation is not an act of self-dealing, so long as the amount of the advance is reasonable in relation to the duties and expense requirements of the foundation manager. Except where reasonably allowable pursuant to subdivision (iii) of this subparagraph, such advances shall not ordinarily exceed $500. For example, if a foundation makes an advance to a foundation manager to cover anticipated out-of-pocket current expenses for a reasonable period (such as a month) and the manager accounts to the foundation under a periodic reimbursement program for actual expenses incurred, the foundation will not be regarded as having engaged in an act of self-dealing—

(i) When it makes the advance,

(ii) When it replenishes the funds upon receipt of supporting vouchers from the foundation manager, or

(iii) If it temporarily adds to the advance to cover extraordinary expenses anticipated to be incurred in fulfillment of a special assignment (such as long distance travel).

(2) *Examples.*—The provisions of this paragraph may be illustrated by the following examples:

Example (1). M, a partnership, is a firm of ten lawyers engaged in the practice of law. A and B, partners in M, serve as trustees to private foundation W and, therefore, are disqualified persons. In addition, A and B own more than 35 percent of the profits interest in M, thereby making M a disqualified person. M performs various legal services for W from time to time as such services are requested. The payment of compensation by W to M shall not constitute an act of self-dealing if the services performed are reasonable and necessary for the carrying out of W's exempt purposes and the amount paid by W for such services is not excessive.

Example (2). C, a manager of private foundation X, owns an investment counseling business. Acting in his capacity as an investment counselor, C manages X's investment portfolio for which he receives an amount which is determined to be not excessive. The payment of such compensation to C shall not constitute an act of self-dealing.

Example (3). M, a commercial bank, serves as a trustee for private foundation Y. In addition to M's duties as trustee, M maintains Y's checking and savings accounts and rents a safety deposit box to Y. The use of the funds by M and the payment of compensation by Y to M for such general banking services shall be treated as the payment of compensation for the performance of personal services which are reasonable and necessary to carry out the exempt purposes of Y if such compensation is not excessive.

Example (4). D, a substantial contributor to private foundation Z, owns a factory which manufactures microscopes. D contracts with Z to manufacture 100 microscopes for Z. Any payment to D under the contract shall constitute an act of self-dealing, since such payment does not constitute the payment of compensation for the performance of personal services.

(d) *Certain transactions between a foundation and a corporation.*—(1) *In general.*—Under section 4941(d)(2)(F), any transaction between a private foundation and a corporation which is a disqualified person will not be an act of self-dealing if such transaction is engaged in pursuant to a liquidation, merger, redemption, recapitalization, or other corporate adjustment, organization, or reorganization, so long as all the securities of the same class as that held (prior to such transaction) by the foundation are subject to the same terms and such terms provide for receipt by the foundation of no less than fair market value. For purposes of this paragraph, all of the securities are not "subject to the same terms" unless, pursuant to such transaction, the corporation makes a bona fide offer on a uniform basis to the foundation and every other person who holds such securities. The fact that a private foundation receives property, such as debentures, while all other persons holding securities of the same class receive cash for their interests, will be evidence that such offer was not made on a uniform basis. This paragraph may apply even if no other person holds any securities of the class held by the foundation. In such event, however, the consideration received by holders of other classes of securities, or the interests retained by holders of such other classes, when considered in relation to the consideration received by the foundation, must indicate that the foundation received at least as favorable treatment in relation to its interests as the holders of any other class of securities. In addition, the foundation must receive no less than the fair market value of its interests.

(2) *Examples.*—The provisions of this paragraph may be illustrated by the following examples:

Example (1). Private foundation X owns 50 percent of the Class A preferred stock of corporation M, which is a disqualified person with respect to X. The terms of such securities provide that the stock may be called for redemption at any time by M at 105 percent of the face amount of the stock. M exercises this right and calls all the Class A preferred stock by paying 105 percent of the face amount in cash. At the time of the redemption of the Class A preferred stock, it is determined that the fair market value of the preferred stock is equal to its face amount. In such case, the redemption by M of the preferred stock of X is not an act of self-dealing.

Example (2). Private foundation Y, which is on a calendar year basis, acquires 60 percent of the Class A preferred stock of corporation N by will on January 10, 1970. N, which is also on a calendar year basis, is a disqualified person with respect to Y. In 1971, N offers to redeem all of the Class A preferred stock for a consideration equal to 100 percent of the face amount of such stock by the issuance of debentures. The offer expires January 2, 1972. Both Y and all other holders of the Class A preferred stock accept the offer and enter into the transaction on January 2, 1972, at which time it is determined that the fair market value of the debentures is no less than the fair market value of the preferred stock. The transaction on January 2, 1972, shall not be treated as an act of self-dealing for 1972. However, because under § 53.4941(e)-1(e)(1)(i) an act of self-dealing occurs on the first day of each taxable year or portion of a taxable year that an extension of credit from a foundation to a disqualified person goes uncorrected, if such debentures are held by Y after December 31, 1972, except as provided in § 53.4941(d)-4(c)(4), such extension of credit shall not be excepted from the definition of an act of self-dealing by reason of the January 2, 1972, transaction. See § 53.4941(d)-4(c)(4) for rules indicating that under certain circumstances such debentures could be held by Y until December 31, 1979.

(e) *Certain payments to government officials.*—Under section 4941(d)(2)(G), in the case of a government official, in addition to the exceptions provided in section 4941(d)(2)(B), (C), and (D), section 4941(d)(1) shall not apply to—

(1) A prize or award which is not includible in gross income under section 74(b), if the government official receiving such prize or award is selected from the general public;

(2) A scholarship or a fellowship grant which is excludable from gross income under section 117(a) and which is to be utilized for study at an educational institution described in section 151(e)(4);

(3) Any annuity or other payment (forming part of a stock-bonus, pension, or profit sharing plan) by a trust which constitutes a qualified trust under section 401;

(4) Any annuity or other payment under a plan which meets the requirements of section 404(a)(2);

(5) Any contribution or gift (other than a contribution or gift of money) to, or services or facilities made available to, any government official, if the aggregate value of such contributions, gifts, services, and facilities does not exceed $25 during any calendar year;

(6) Any payment made under 5 U.S.C. chapter 41 (relating to government employees' training programs);

(7) Any payment or reimbursement of traveling expenses (including amounts expended for meals and lodging, regardless of whether the government official is "away from home" within the meaning of section 162(a)(2), and including reasonable advances for such expenses anticipated in the immediate future) for travel solely from one point in the United States to another in connection with one or more purposes described in section 170(c)(1) or (2)(B), but only if such payment or reimbursement does not exceed the actual cost of the transportation involved plus an amount for all other traveling expenses not in excess of 125 percent of the maximum amount payable under 5 U.S.C. 5702(a) for like travel by employees of the United States;

(8) Any agreement to employ or make a grant to a government official for any period after the termination of his government service if such agreement is entered into within 90 days prior to such termination;

(9) If a government official attends or participates in a conference sponsored by a private foundation, the allocable portion of the cost of such conference and other non-monetary benefits (for example, benefits of a professional, intellectual, or psychological nature, or benefits resulting from the publication or the distribution to participants of a record of the conference), as well as the payment or reimbursement of expenses (including reasonable advances for expenses anticipated in connection with such a conference in the near future), received by such government official as a result of such attendance or participation shall not be subject to section 4941(d)(1), so long as the conference is in furtherance of the exempt purposes of the foundation; or

(10) In the case of any government official who was on leave of absence without pay on December 31, 1969, pursuant to a commitment entered into on or before such date for the purpose of engaging in certain activities for which such individual was to be paid by one or more private foundations, any payment of compensation (or payment or reimbursement of expenses, including reasonable advances for expenses anticipated in the immediate future) by such private foundations to such individual for any continuous period after December 31, 1969, and

prior to January 1, 1971, during which such individual remains on leave of absence to engage in such activities. A commitment is considered entered into on or before December 31, 1969, if on or before such date, the amount and nature of the payments to be made and the name of the individual receiving such payments were entered on the records of the payor, or were otherwise adequately evidenced, or the notice of the payment to be received was communicated to the payee orally or in writing. [Reg. §53.4941(d)-3.]

☐ [T.D. 7270, 4-16-73. *Amended by T.D. 7938,* 1-30-84.]

[Reg. §53.4941(d)-4]

§53.4941(d)-4. **Transitional rules.**— (a) *Certain transactions involving securities acquired by a foundation before May 27, 1969.*—(1) *In general.*—Under section 101(l)(2)(A) of the Tax Reform Act of 1969 (83 Stat. 533), any transaction between a private foundation and a corporation which is a disqualified person shall not be an act of self-dealing if such transaction is pursuant to the terms of securities of such corporation, if such terms were in existence at the time such securities were acquired by the foundation, and if such securities were acquired by the foundation before May 27, 1969.

(2) *Example.*—The provisions of this paragraph may be illustrated by the following example:

Example. Private foundation X purchased preferred stock of corporation M, a disqualified person with respect to X, on March 15, 1969. The terms of such securities on such date provided that the stock could be called by M at any time if M paid the outstanding shareholders cash equal to 105 percent of the face amount of the stock. If M exercises this right and calls the stock owned by X on February 15, 1970, such call shall not constitute an act of self-dealing even if such price is not equivalent to fair market value on such date and even if not all of the securities of that class are called.

(b) *Disposition of certain business holdings.*— (1) *In general.*—Under section 101(l)(2)(B) of the Tax Reform Act of 1969 (83 Stat. 533), the sale, exchange, or other disposition of property which is owned by a private foundation on May 26, 1969, to a disqualified person shall not be an act of self-dealing if the foundation is required to dispose of such property in order not to be liable for tax under section 4943 (determined without regard to section 4943(c)(2)(C) and as if every disposition by the foundation were made to disqualified persons) and if such disposition satisfies the requirements of subparagraph (2) of this paragraph. For purposes of applying this paragraph in the case of a disposition completed before January 1, 1975, or after October 4, 1976, and before January 1, 1977, the amount of excess business holdings is determined under section 4943(c) without taking subsection (c)(4) into account.

(2) *Terms of the disposition.*—Subparagraph (1) of this paragraph shall not apply unless—

(i) The private foundation receives an amount which equals or exceeds the fair market value of the business holdings at the time of disposition or at the time a contract for such disposition was previously executed; and

(ii) At the time with respect to which subdivision (i) of this subparagraph is applied, the transaction would not have constituted a prohibited transaction within the meaning of section 503(b) or the corresponding provisions of prior law if such provisions had been applied at such time.

(3) *Property received under a trust or will.*— For purposes of this paragraph, property shall be considered as owned by a private foundation on May 26, 1969, if such property is acquired by such foundation under the terms of a will executed on or before such date, under the terms of a trust which was irrevocable on such date, or under the terms of a revocable trust executed on or before such date if the property would have passed under a will which would have met the requirements of this subparagraph but for the fact that a grantor dies without having revoked the trust. An amendment or republication of a will which was executed on or before May 26, 1969, does not prevent any interest in a business enterprise which was to pass under the terms of such will (which terms were in effect on May 26, 1969, and at all times thereafter) from being treated as owned by a private foundation on or before May 26, 1969, solely because—

(i) There is a reduction in the interest in the business enterprise which the foundation was to receive under the terms of the will (for example, if the foundation is to receive the residuary estate and one class of stock is disposed of by the decedent during his lifetime or by a subsequent codicil),

(ii) Such amendment or republication is necessary in order to comply with section 508(e) and the regulations thereunder,

(iii) There is a change in the executor of the will, or

(iv) There is any other change which does not otherwise change the rights of the foundation with respect to such interest in the business enterprise.

However, if under such amendment or republication there is an increase of the interest in the business enterprise which the foundation was to receive under the terms of the will in effect on May 26, 1969, such increase shall not be treated as owned by the private foundation on or before May 26, 1969, but under such circumstances the interest which would have been acquired before such increase shall be treated as owned by the private foundation on or before May 26, 1969.

(4) *Examples.*—The provisions of this paragraph may be illustrated by the following examples:

Example (1). On May 26, 1969, private foundation X owns 10 percent of corporation Y's voting stock, which is traded on the New York Stock Exchange. Disqualified persons with respect to X own an additional 40 percent of such voting stock. X is on a calendar year basis. Prior to January 1, 1975, X privately sold its entire 10 percent for cash to B, a disqualified person, at the price quoted on the stock exchange at the close of the day less commissions. Since the 10 percent owned by X would constitute excess business holdings without the application of section 4943(c)(2)(C) or (4), the disposition will not constitute an act of self-dealing.

Example (2). Assume the facts as stated in Example (1), except that the only stock of corporation Y which X owns is 1.5 percent of Y's voting stock. Since the 1.5 percent owned by X would constitute excess business holdings without the application of section 4943(c)(2)(C) or (4), the disposition of the stock to B for cash will not constitute an act of self-dealing.

Example (3). Assume the facts as stated in Example (1), except that B, instead of paying cash as consideration for the stock, issued a 10-year secured promissory note as consideration for the stock. The issuance of such promissory note will not be treated as an act of self-dealing until taxable years beginning after December 31, 1979, unless such issuance would have been a prohibited transaction under section 503(b), or unless the transaction does not remain throughout its life at least as favorable as an arm's-length contract negotiated currently. See paragraph (c) of this section.

(c) *Existing leases and loans.*—(1) *In general.*— Under section 101(l)(2)(C) of the Tax Reform Act of 1969 (83 Stat. 533), the leasing of property or the lending of money (or other extension of credit) between a disqualified person and a private foundation pursuant to a binding contract which was in effect on October 9, 1969 (or pursuant to a renewal or modification of such a contract, as described in subparagraph (2) of this paragraph), shall not be an act of self-dealing until taxable years beginning after December 31, 1979, if—

(i) At the time the contract was executed, such contract was not a prohibited transaction (within the meaning of section 503(b) or the corresponding provisions of prior law), and

(ii) The leasing or lending of money (or other extension of credit) remains throughout the term of the lease or extension of credit at least as favorable as a current arm's-length transaction with an unrelated person.

(2) *Renewal or modification of existing contracts.*—A renewal or a modification of an existing contract is referred to in subparagraph (1) of this paragraph only if any modifications of the terms of such contract are not substantial and the relative advantages of the modified contract compared with contracts entered into at arm's-length with an unrelated person at the time of the renewal or modification are at least as favorable to the private foundation as the relative advantages of the original contract compared with contracts entered into at arm's-length with an unrelated person at the time of execution of the original contract. Such renewal or modification need not be provided for in the original contract; it may take place before or after the expiration of the original contract and at any time before the first day of the first taxable year of the private foundation beginning after December 31, 1979. Where, in a normal commercial setting, an unrelated party in the position of a private foundation could be expected to insist upon a renegotiation or termination of a binding contract, the private foundation must so act. Thus, for example, if a disqualified person leases office space from a private foundation on a month-to-month basis, and a party in the position of the private foundation could be expected to renegotiate the rent required in such contract because of a rise in the fair market value of such office space, the private foundation must so act in order to avoid participation in an act of self-dealing. Where the private foundation has no right to insist upon renegotiation, an act of self-dealing shall occur if the terms of the contract become less favorable to the foundation than an arm's-length contract negotiated currently, unless—

(i) The variation from current fair market value is *de minimis*, or

(ii) The contract is renegotiated by the foundation and the disqualified person so that the foundation will receive no less than fair market value.

For purposes of subdivision (i) of this subparagraph *de minimis* ordinarily shall be no more than one-half of 1 percent in the rate of return in the case of a loan, or 10 percent of the rent in the case of a lease.

(3) *Example.*—The provisions of subparagraphs (1) and (2) of this paragraph may be illustrated by the following example.

Example. Under a binding contract entered into on January 1, 1964, X, a private foundation, leases a building for 10 years from Z, a disqualified person. At the time the contract was executed, the lease was not a "prohibited transaction" within the meaning of section 503(b), since the rent charged X was only 50 percent of the rent which would have been charged in an arm's-length transaction with an unrelated person. On January 1, 1974, X renewed the lease for 5 additional years. The terms of the renewal agreement provided for a 20 percent increase in the amount of rent charged X. However, at the time of such renewal, the rent which would have been charged in an arm's-length transaction had also increased by 20 percent from that of 1964. The renewal agreement shall not be treated as an act of self-dealing.

(4) *Certain exchanges of stock or securities for bonds, debentures or other indebtedness.*—(i) In the case of a transaction described in paragraph (a) or (b) of this section or paragraph (d) of § 53.4941(d)-3, where a bond, debenture, or other indebtedness of a disqualified person is acquired

by a private foundation in exchange for stock or securities which it held on October 9, 1969, and at all times thereafter, such indebtedness shall be treated as an extension of credit pursuant to a binding contract in effect on October 9, 1969, to which this paragraph applies. Thus, so long as the extension of credit remains at least as favorable as an arm's-length transaction with an unrelated person and neither the acquisition of the securities which were exchanged for the indebtedness nor the exchange of such securities for the indebtedness was a prohibited transaction within the meaning of section 503(b) (or the corresponding provisions of prior law) at the time of such acquisition, such extension of credit shall not be an act of self-dealing until taxable years beginning after December 31, 1979.

(ii) The provisions of this subparagraph may be illustrated by the following examples:

Example (1). Assume the facts as stated in Example (2) of §53.4941(d)-3(d)(2), except that the preferred stock was held by Y on October 9, 1969, and at all times thereafter until the redemption occurred on January 2, 1972. In addition, assume that the acquisition of the preferred stock was not a prohibited transaction within the meaning of section 503(b) at the time of such acquisition and the exchange of the preferred stock for the debentures would not have been a prohibited transaction within the meaning of section 503(b). For 1973 through 1979, the extension of credit arising from the holding of the debentures is not an act of self-dealing so long as the extension of credit remains at least as favorable as an arm's-length transaction with an unrelated person. See, however, Example (3) of §53.4941(e)-1(e)(1)(ii).

Example (2). Assume the same facts as stated in Example (1) of §53.4941(d)-4(b)(4), except that private foundation X sold its entire 10 percent of corporation Y's voting stock in exchange for Y's secured notes which mature on December 31, 1985. For taxable years beginning before January 1, 1980, the extension of credit arising from the holding of such notes by X is not an act of self-dealing so long as the extension of credit remains at least as favorable as an arm's-length transaction with an unrelated person and neither the acquisition of the securities which were exchanged for the indebtedness nor the exchange of such securities for the indebtedness was a prohibited transaction within the meaning of section 503(b) (or the corresponding provisions of prior law). Under §53.4941(e)-1, a new extension of credit occurs on the first day of each taxable year in which an indebtedness is outstanding; therefore, if the secured notes are held by X after December 31, 1979, a new extension of credit not excepted from the definition of an act of self-dealing will occur on the first day of the first taxable year beginning after December 31, 1979, and on the first day of each succeeding taxable year in which X holds such secured notes.

(d) *Sharing of goods, services, or facilities before January 1, 1980.*—(1) Under section 101(l)(2)(D)

of the Tax Reform Act of 1969 (83 Stat. 533), the use (other than leasing) of goods, services, or facilities which are shared by a private foundation and a disqualified person shall not be an act of self-dealing until taxable years beginning after December 31, 1979, if—

(i) The use is pursuant to an arrangement in effect before October 9, 1969, and at all times thereafter;

(ii) The arrangement was not a prohibited transaction (within the meaning of section 503(b) or the corresponding provisions of prior law) at the time it was made; and

(iii) The arrangement would not be a prohibited transaction if section 503(b) continued to apply.

For purposes of this paragraph, such arrangement need not be a binding contract.

(2) The provisions of this paragraph may be illustrated by the following example:

Example. In 1964 X, a private foundation, and B, a disqualified person, arranged for the sharing of computer time in B's son's company for a 10-year period commencing January 1, 1965. B's son has the unilateral right to terminate the arrangement at any time. X uses the computer facilities in connection with an analysis of its grant-making activities, while B's use is related to his business affairs. Both X and B make reasonable fixed payments to the computer company based on the number of hours of computer use and comparable to fees charged in arm's length transactions with unrelated parties. The company imposes a maximum limit per month on the sum of the number of hours for which X and B use the computer facilities. Under these circumstances, the sharing of computer time is not an act of self-dealing.

(e) *Use of certain property acquired before October 9, 1969.*—(1) Under section 101(l)(2)(E) of the Tax Reform Act of 1969 (83 Stat. 533), the use of property in which a private foundation and a disqualified person have a joint or common interest will not be an act of self-dealing if the interests of both in such property were acquired before October 9, 1969.

(2) The provisions of this paragraph may be illustrated by the following example:

Example. Prior to October 9, 1969, C, a disqualified person, gave beachfront property to private foundation X for use as a recreational facility for underprivileged, inner-city children during the summer months. However, C retained the right to use such property for his life. The use of such property by C or X is not an act of self-dealing.

(f) *Disposition of leased property.*—(1) *In general.*—Under section 101(l)(2)(F) of the Tax Reform Act of 1969, as amended by the Tax Reform Act of 1976 (90 Stat. 1713), the sale, exchange or other disposition (other than by lease) to a disqualified person of property being leased to the disqualified person by a private foundation is not an act of self-dealing if—

(i) The private foundation is leasing substantially all of the property to the disqualified person under a lease to which paragraph (c) of this section applies;

(ii) The disposition occurs after October 4, 1976, and before January 1, 1978; and

(iii) The disposition satisfies the requirements of paragraph (f)(2) of this section.

(2) *Terms of disposition.*—Paragraph (f)(1) of this section applies only if—

(i) The private foundation receives an amount that equals or exceeds the fair market value of the property either at the time of the disposition or at the time (after June 30, 1976) the contract for such disposition was executed;

(ii) In computing the fair market value of the property, no diminution of that value results from the fact that the property is subject to any lease to disqualified persons; and

(iii) At the time with respect to which subdivision (f)(2)(i) of this section is applied, the transaction would not have constituted a prohibited transaction within the meaning of section 503(b) or the corresponding provisions of prior law if those provisions had been applied at the time of the transaction. [Reg. § 53.4941(d)-4.]

☐ [*T.D. 7270, 4-16-73. Amended by T.D. 7678, 2-25-80.*]

[Reg. § 53.4941(e)-1]

§ 53.4941(e)-1. Definitions.—(a) *Taxable period.*—(1) *In general.*—For purposes of any act of self-dealing, the term "taxable period" means the period beginning with the date on which the act of self-dealing occurs and ending on the earliest of:

(i) The date of mailing of a notice of deficiency under section 6212 with respect to the tax imposed by section 4941(a)(1),

(ii) The date on which the correction of the act of self-dealing is completed, or

(iii) The date on which the tax imposed by section 4941(a)(1) is assessed.

(2) *Date of occurrence.*—An act of self-dealing occurs on the date on which all the terms and conditions of the transaction and the liabilities of the parties have been fixed. Thus, for example, if a private foundation gives a disqualified person a binding option on June 15, 1971, to purchase property owned by the foundation at any time before June 15, 1972, the act of self-dealing has occurred on June 15, 1971. Similarly, in the case of a conditional sales contract, the act of self-dealing shall be considered as occurring on the date the property is transferred subject only to the condition that the buyer make payment for receipt of such property.

(3) *Special rule.*—Where a notice of deficiency referred to in subparagraph (1)(i) of this paragraph is not mailed because a waiver of the restrictions on assessment and collection of a deficiency has been accepted, or because the deficiency is paid, the date of filing of the waiver or

the date of such payment, respectively, shall be treated as the end of the taxable period.

(4) *Examples.*—The provisions of this paragraph may be illustrated by the following examples:

Example (1). On July 16, 1970, F, a manager of private foundation X acting on behalf of the foundation, knowing his act to be one of self-dealing, willfully and without reasonable cause engaged in an act of self-dealing by selling certain real estate to A, a disqualified person. On March 25, 1973, the Internal Revenue Service mailed a notice of deficiency to A with respect to the tax imposed on the sale under section 4941(a)(1). The taxable period with respect to the act of self-dealing for both A and F is July 16, 1970, through March 25, 1973.

Example (2). Assume the facts as stated in Example (1), except that the act of self-dealing is corrected by A on March 17, 1971. The taxable period with respect to the act of self-dealing for both A and F is July 16, 1970, through March 17, 1971.

Example (3). Assume the facts as stated in Example (1), except that on August 20, 1972, A files a waiver of the restrictions on assessment and collection of the tax imposed on the sale under section 4941(a)(1) which is accepted. The taxable period with respect to the act of self-dealing for both A and F is July 16, 1970, through August 20, 1972.

(b) *Amount involved.*—(1) *In general.*—Except as provided in subparagraph (2) of this paragraph, for purposes of any act of self-dealing, the term "amount involved" means the greater of the amount of money and the fair market value of the other property given or the amount of money and the fair market value of the other property received.

(2) *Exceptions.*—(i) In the case of the payment of compensation for personal services to persons other than government officials, the amount involved shall be only the excess compensation paid by the private foundation.

(ii) Where the use of money or other property is involved, the amount involved shall be the greater of the amount paid for such use or the fair market value of such use for the period for which the money or other property is used. Thus, for example, in the case of a lease of a building by a private foundation to a disqualified person, the amount involved is the greater of the amount of rent received by the private foundation from the disqualified person or the fair rental value of the building for the period such building is used by the disqualified person.

(iii) In cases in which a transaction would not have been an act of self-dealing had the private foundation received fair market value, the amount involved is the excess of the fair market value of the property transferred by the private foundation over the amount which the private foundation receives, but only if the parties have made a good faith effort to determine fair market value. For purposes of this subdivision a good faith effort to determine fair market value shall ordinarily have been made where—

(a) The person making the valuation is not a disqualified person with respect to the foundation and is both competent to make the valuation and not in a position, whether by stock ownership or otherwise, to derive an economic benefit from the value utilized, and

(b) The method utilized in making the valuation is a generally accepted method for valuing comparable property, stock, or securities for purposes of arm's-length business transactions where valuation is a significant factor.

See section 4941(d)(2)(F) and §§ 53.4941(d)-1(b)(3), 53.4941(d)-3(d)(1) and 53.4941(d)-4(b). Thus, for example, if a corporation which is a disqualified person with respect to a private foundation recapitalizes in a transaction which would be described in section 4941(d)(2)(F) but for the fact that the private foundation receives new stock worth only $95,000 in exchange for the stock which it previously held in the corporation and which has a fair market value of $100,000 at the time of the recapitalization, the amount involved would be $5,000 ($100,000 − $95,000) if there had been a good faith attempt to value the stock. Similarly, if an estate enters into a transaction with a disqualified person with respect to a foundation and such transaction would be described in § 53.4941(d)-1(b)(3) but for the fact that the estate receives less than fair market value for the property exchanged, the amount involved is the excess of the fair market value of the property the estate transfers to the disqualified person over the money and the fair market value of the property received by the estate.

(3) *Time for determining fair market value.*— The fair market value of the property or the use thereof, as the case may be, shall be determined as of the date on which the act of self-dealing occurred in the case of the initial taxes imposed by section 4941(a) and shall be the highest fair market value during the taxable period in the case of the additional taxes imposed by section 4941(b).

(4) *Examples.*—The provisions of this paragraph may be illustrated by the following examples:

Example (1). A, a disqualified person with respect to private foundation M, uses an airplane owned by M on June 15 and June 16, 1970, for a two-day trip to New York City on personal business and pays M $500 for the use of such airplane. The fair rental value for the use of the airplane for those two days is $3,000. For purposes of section 4941(a), the amount involved with respect to the act of self-dealing is $3,000.

Example (2). On April 10, 1970, B, a manager of private foundation P, borrows $100,000 from P at 6 percent interest per annum. Both principal and interest are to be paid one year from the date of the loan. The fair market value of the use of the money on April 10, 1970, is 10 percent per annum. Six months later, B and P terminate the loan, and B repays the $100,000 principal plus $3,000 ($100,000 × 6 percent for one-half year) interest. For purposes of section 4941(a), the amount involved with respect to the act of self-dealing is $5,000 ($100,000 × 10 percent for one-half year) for each year or partial year in the taxable period.

Example (3). C, a substantial contributor to private foundation S, leases office space in a building owned by S for $3,600 for 1 year beginning on January 1, 1971. The fair rental value of the building for a one-year lease on January 1, 1971, is $5,600. On December 31, 1971, the lease is terminated. For purposes of section 4941(a), the amount involved with respect to the act of self-dealing is $5,600 for each year or partial year in the taxable period.

Example (4). D, a disqualified person with respect to private foundation T, purchases 100 shares of stock from T for $5,000 on June 15, 1982. The fair market value of the 100 shares of stock on that date is $4,800. D sells the 100 shares of stock on December 20, 1983, for $6,000. On December 27, 1983, a notice of deficiency with respect to the taxes imposed under subsections (a) and (b) of section 4941 is mailed to D and the taxable period ends. D fails to correct during the taxable period. Between June 15, 1982, and the end of the taxable period, the stock was quoted on the New York Stock Exchange at a high of $67 per share. The amount involved with respect to the tax imposed under subsection (a) is $5,000, and the amount involved with respect to the tax imposed under subsection (b) for failure to correct is $6,700 (100 shares at $67 per share), the highest fair market value during the taxable period.

Example (5). Corporation M, a disqualified person with respect to private foundation V, redeems all of its Class B common stock, some of which is held by V. The redemption of V's stock would be described in section 4941(d)(2)(F) but for the fact that V receives only $95,000 in exchange for stock which has a fair market value of $100,000 at the time of the transaction. The $95,000 value of V's stock, which is not publicly traded, was determined by investment bankers in accordance with accepted methods of valuation that would be utilized if the M stock held by V were to be offered for sale to the public. Therefore, the amount involved with respect to the transaction will ordinarily be limited to $5,000 ($100,000 − $95,000).

(c) *Correction.*—(1) *In general.*—Correction shall be accomplished by undoing the transaction which constituted the act of self-dealing to the extent possible, but in no case shall the resulting financial position of the private foundation be worse than that which it would be if the disqualified person were dealing under the highest fiduciary standards. For example, where a disqualified person sells property to a private foundation for cash, correction may be accomplished by recasting the transaction in the form of a gift by returning the cash to the foundation. Subparagraphs (2) through (6) of this paragraph

Reg. § 53.4941(e)-1(c)(1)

illustrate the minimum standards of correction in the case of certain specific acts of self-dealing. Principles similar to the principles contained in such subparagraphs shall be applied with respect to other acts of self-dealing. Any correction pursuant to this paragraph and section 4941 shall not be an act of self-dealing.

(2) *Sales by foundation.*—(i) In the case of a sale of property by a private foundation to a disqualified person for cash, undoing the transaction includes, but is not limited to, requiring rescission of the sale where possible. However, in order to avoid placing the foundation in a position worse than that in which it would be if rescission were not required, the amount returned to the disqualified person pursuant to the rescission shall not exceed the lesser of the cash received by the private foundation or the fair market value of property received by the disqualified person. For purposes of the preceding sentence, fair market value shall be the lesser of the fair market value at the time of the act of self-dealing or the fair market value at the time of rescission. In addition to rescission, the disqualified person is required to pay over to the private foundation any net profits he realized after the original sale with respect to the property he received from the sale. Thus, for example, the disqualified person must pay over to the foundation any income derived by him from the property he received from the original sale to the extent such income during the correction period exceeds the income derived by the foundation during the correction period from the cash which the disqualified person originally paid to the foundation.

(ii) If, prior to the end of the correction period, the disqualified person resells the property in an arm's-length transaction to a bona fide purchaser who is not the foundation or another disqualified person, no rescission is required. In such case, the disqualified person must pay over to the foundation the excess (if any) of the greater of the fair market value of such property on the date on which correction of the act of self-dealing occurs or the amount realized by the disqualified person from such arm's length resale over the amount which would have been returned to the disqualified person pursuant to subdivision (i) of this subparagraph if rescission had been required. In addition, the disqualified person is required to pay over to the foundation any net profits he realized, as described in subdivision (i) of this subparagraph.

(iii) *Examples.*—The provisions of this subparagraph may be illustrated by the following examples:

Example (1). On July 1, 1970, private foundation M sold a painting to A, a disqualified person, for $5,000, in a transaction not within any of the exceptions to self-dealing. The fair market value of the painting on such date was $6,000. On March 25, 1971, the painting is still owned by A and has a fair market value of $7,200. A did not derive any income as a result of purchasing the painting. In order to correct the act of self-dealing under this subparagraph on March 25, 1971, the sale must be rescinded by the return of the painting to M. However, pursuant to such rescission, M must not pay A more than $5,000, the original consideration received by M.

Example (2). Assume the facts as stated in Example (1), except that A sold the painting on December 15, 1970, in an arm's-length transaction to C, a bona fide purchaser who is not a disqualified person, for $6,100. In addition, assume that the fair market value of the painting on March 25, 1971, is $7,600. In order to correct the act of self-dealing under this subparagraph on March 25, 1971, A must pay M $2,600 ($7,600, the fair market value at the time of correction, less $5,000, the amount which would have been returned to A if rescission had been required). Since the painting was sold to C in an arm's-length transaction prior to correction, no rescission is required.

(3) *Sales to foundation.*—(i) In the case of a sale of property to a private foundation by a disqualified person for cash, undoing the transaction includes, but is not limited to, requiring rescission of the sale where possible. However, in order to avoid placing the foundation in a position worse than that in which it would be if rescission were not required, the amount received from the disqualified person pursuant to the rescission shall be the greatest of the cash paid to the disqualified person, the fair market value of the property at the time of the original sale, or the fair market value of the property at the time of rescission. In addition to rescission, the disqualified person is required to pay over to the private foundation any net profits he realized after the original sale with respect to the consideration he received from the sale. Thus, for example, the disqualified person must pay over to the foundation any income derived by him from the cash he received from the original sale to the extent such income during the correction period exceeds the income derived by the foundation during the correction period from the property which the disqualified person originally transferred to the foundation.

(ii) If, prior to the end of the correction period, the foundation resells the property in an arm's-length transaction to a bona fide purchaser who is not a disqualified person, no rescission is required. In such case, the disqualified person must pay over to the foundation the excess (if any) of the amount which would have been received from the disqualified person pursuant to subdivision (i) of this subparagraph, if rescission had been required over the amount realized by the foundation upon resale of the property. In addition, the disqualified person is required to pay over to the foundation any net profits he realized, as described in subdivision (i) of this subparagraph.

(iii) *Examples.*—The provisions of this subparagraph may be illustrated by the following examples:

Example (1). On February 10, 1972, D, a disqualified person with respect to private foundation P, sells 100 shares of X stock to P for $2,500 in a transaction which does not fall within any of the exceptions to self-dealing. The fair market value of the 100 shares of X stock on February 10, 1972, is $3,200. On June 1, 1973, the 100 shares of X stock have a fair market value of $2,900. From February 10, 1972, through June 1, 1973, P has received dividends of $90 from the stock, and D has received interest of $300 from the $2,500 which D received as consideration for the stock. In order to correct the act of self-dealing under this subparagraph on June 1, 1973, the sale must be rescinded by the return of the stock to D. However, pursuant to such rescission, D must pay $3,200, the fair market value of the stock on the date of sale. In addition, D must pay P $210, the amount of income derived by D during the correction period from the $2,500 received from P ($300) minus the income derived by P during the correction period from the stock sold to P ($90).

Example (2). Assume the facts as stated in Example (1), except that on September 1, 1972, P sells the 100 shares of X stock to E, a bona fide purchaser who is not a disqualified person, in an arm's length transaction for $2,750. Assume further that P has not received any dividends from the stock prior to the sale to E, but that P receives interest of $260 from the $2,750 received as consideration for the stock for the period from September 1, 1972, to June 1, 1973. In order to correct the act of self-dealing under this subparagraph on June 1, 1973, D must pay P $450 ($3,200, the amount which would have been received from D if rescission had been required, less $2,750, the amount realized by P from the sale to E). In addition, D must pay P $40, the amount of income derived by D during the correction period from the $2,500 received from P ($300) minus the income derived by P during the correction period from the stock sold to P ($260 from the $2,750 received as consideration for the stock). Since the stock was sold to E in an arm's length transaction prior to correction, no rescission is required.

(4) *Use of property by a disqualified person.*— (i) In the case of the use by a disqualified person of property owned by a private foundation, undoing the transaction includes, but is not limited to, terminating the use of such property. In addition to termination, the disqualified person must pay the foundation—

(a) The excess (if any) of the fair market value of the use of the property over the amount paid by the disqualified person for such use until such termination, and

(b) The excess (if any) of the amount which would have been paid by the disqualified person for the use of the property on or after the date of such termination, for the period such disqualified person would have used the property (without regard to any further extensions or renewals of such period) if such termination had not occurred, over the fair market value of such use for such period.

In applying (a) of this subdivision the fair market value of the use of property shall be the higher of the rate (that is, fair rental value per period in the case of use of property other than money or fair interest rate in the case of use of money) at the time of the act of self-dealing (within the meaning of paragraph (e)(1) of this section) or such rate at the time of correction of such act of self-dealing. In applying (b) of this subdivision the fair market value of the use of property shall be the rate at the time of correction.

(ii) The provisions of this subparagraph may be illustrated by the following examples:

Example (1). On January 1, 1972, private foundation S rented the third story of its office building to A, a disqualified person, for one year at an annual rent of $10,000, in a transaction not within any of the exceptions to self-dealing. Both S and A are on the calendar year basis. The fair rental value of such office space for a one-year period on January 1, 1972, is $12,000. On June 30, 1972, the fair rental value of such office space for a one-year period is $13,000. In order to correct the act of self-dealing under this subparagraph on June 30, 1972, A must terminate his use of the property. In addition, A must pay S $1,500, the excess of $6,500 (the fair rental value for six months as of June 30, 1972) over $5,000 (the amount paid to S from January 1, 1972, to June 30, 1972).

Example (2). On January 1, 1972, private foundation R rented the fourth story of its office building to B, a disqualified person, for one year at an annual rent of $10,000, in a transaction not included in any of the exceptions to self-dealing. Both R and B are on the calendar year basis. On January 1, 1973, B continues to rent the office space as a periodic tenant paying his rent monthly at an annual rate of $10,000. The fair rental value of such office space for a one-year period on January 1, 1972, is $12,000, and as of January 1, 1973, is $1,250 per month. As of December 31, 1973, the fair rental value of such office space is $14,000 for a one-year period and $1,200 on a monthly basis. In order to correct his acts of self-dealing (within the meaning of paragraph (e)(1) of this section) under this subparagraph on December 31, 1973, B must terminate his use of the property. In addition, B must pay R $9,000, $4,000 for his use of the property for 1972 (the excess of $14,000, the fair rental value for one year as of December 31, 1973, over $10,000, the amount B paid R for his use of the property for 1972) and $5,000 for his use of the property for 1973 (the excess of $15,000, the fair rental value for 12 months as of January 1, 1973, over $10,000, the amount B paid R for his use of the property for 1973).

Example (3). B, a substantial contributor to private foundation T, leases office space in a building owned by T for $5,000 for one year beginning on November 10, 1972, in a transaction not included in any of the exceptions to self-dealing. The fair rental value of the building for a one-year period on November 10, 1972, is $4,000. On May 10, 1973, the fair rental value of the building for the remaining period of the lease is $2,200. In order to correct the acts of self-dealing under this subparagraph on May 10, 1973, B and T must terminate the lease. In addition, B must pay T $300 (the excess of $2,500, the amount which would have been paid by B for the remaining period of the lease if it had not been terminated, over $2,200, the fair rental value at the time of correction for the remaining period of the lease).

(5) *Use of property by a private foundation.*— (i) In the case of the use by a private foundation of property owned by a disqualified person, undoing the transaction includes, but is not limited to, terminating the use of such property. In addition to termination, the disqualified person must pay the foundation—

(a) The excess (if any) of the amount paid to the disqualified person for such use until such termination over the fair market value of the use of the property, and

(b) The excess (if any) of the fair market value of the use of the property, for the period the foundation would have used the property (without regard to any further extensions or renewals of such period) if such termination had not occurred, over the amount which would have been paid to the disqualified person on or after the date of such termination for such use for such period.

In applying (a) of this subdivision the fair market value of the use of property shall be the lesser of the rate (that is, fair rental value per period in the case of use of property other than money or fair interest rate in the case of use of money) at the time of the act of self-dealing (within the meaning of paragraph (e)(1) of this section) or such rate at the time of correction of such act of self-dealing. In applying (b) of this subdivision the fair market value of the use of property shall be the rate at the time of correction.

(ii) The provisions of this subparagraph may be illustrated by the following examples:

Example (1). On July 1, 1972, private foundation X leases office space in a building owned by C, a disqualified person, for one year at an annual rent of $6,000. Both X and C are on the calendar year basis. The fair rental value of such office space for a one-year period as of July 1, 1972, is $4,200. As of January 1, 1973, the fair rental value of such office space for a one-year period is $5,400, and as of June 30, 1973, the fair rental value of such office space for a one-year period is $4,800. In order to correct his acts of self-dealing (within the meaning of paragraph (e)(1) of this section) under this subparagraph on June 30, 1973, C must terminate X's use of the property. In addition, C must pay X $1,500, $900 (the excess of $3,000, the amount paid to C from July 1, 1972, through December 31, 1972, over $2,100, the fair rental value for six months as of July 1, 1972) plus $600 (the excess of $3,000, the amount paid to C from January 1, 1973, through June 30, 1973, over $2,400, the fair rental value for six months as of June 30, 1973).

Example (2). On April 1, 1973, D, a disqualified person with respect to private founda-tion Y, loans $100,000 to Y at 6 percent interest per annum. Both principal and interest are to be paid on April 1, 1978. The fair market value of the use of the money on April 1, 1973, is 9 percent per annum. On April 1, 1974, D and Y terminate the loan. On such date, the fair market value of the use of $100,000 is 10 percent per annum. In order to correct the act of self-dealing on April 1, 1974, in addition to the termination of the loan from D to Y, D must pay Y $16,000, the excess of $40,000 ($100,000 × 10 percent, the fair market value of the use determined at the time of correction, from April 1, 1974, to April 1, 1978) over $24,000 (the amount of interest Y would have paid to D from April 1, 1974, to April 1, 1978, if the loan from D to Y had not been terminated).

(6) *Payment of compensation to a disqualified person.*—In the case of the payment of compensation by a private foundation to a disqualified person for the performance of personal services which are reasonable and necessary to carry out the exempt purpose of such foundation, undoing the transaction requires that the disqualified person pay to the foundation any amount which is excessive. However, termination of the employment or independent contractor relationship is not required.

(7) *Special rule for correction of valuation errors.*—(i) In the case of a transaction described in paragraph (b)(2)(iii) of this section, a "correction" of the act of self-dealing shall ordinarily be deemed to occur if the foundation is paid an amount of money equal to the amount involved (as defined in paragraph (b)(2)(iii) of this section) plus such additional amounts as are necessary to compensate it for the loss of the use of the money or other property during the period commencing on the date of the act of self-dealing and ending on the date the transaction is corrected pursuant to this subparagraph.

(ii) The provisions of this subparagraph may be illustrated by the following example:

Example. Assume the same facts as in Example (5) of paragraph (b)(4) of this section. Such transaction shall be considered as corrected by a payment of $5,000 by M to V, together with an additional payment to V of an amount equal to the interest which V could have obtained on $5,000 for the period commencing on the date of the redemption and ending on the date the act is corrected.

(d) *Cross reference.*—For rules relating to taxable events that are corrected within the correction period, defined in section 4963(e), see section 4961(a), and the regulations thereunder.

(e) *Act of self-dealing.*—(1) *Number of acts; use of money or property.*—(i) *In general.*—If a transaction between a private foundation and a disqualified person is determined to be self-dealing (as defined in section 4941(d)), for purposes of section 4941 there is generally one act of self-dealing. For the date on which such act is treated as occurring, see paragraph (a)(2) of this section. If, however, such transaction relates to the leasing of property, the lending of money or other extension of credit, other use of money or property, or payment of compensation, the transaction will generally be treated (for purposes of section 4941 but not section 507 or 6684) as giving rise to an act of self-dealing on the day the transaction occurs plus an act of self-dealing on the first day of each taxable year or portion of a taxable year which is within the taxable period and which begins after the taxable year in which the transaction occurs.

(ii) *Examples.*—The provisions of this subparagraph may be illustrated by the following examples:

Example (1). On August 31, 1970, X, a private foundation, sells a building to A, a disqualified person with respect to X. A is on the calendar year basis. Under these circumstances, the transaction between A and X is one act of self- dealing which is treated for purposes of section 4941 as occurring on August 31, 1970.

Example (2). Assume the facts as stated in Example (1), except that, instead of selling the building to A, X leases the building to A for a term of four years beginning July 31, 1970, at an annual rental of $12,000. The fair rental value of the building is also $12,000 per annum as of July 31, 1970, and throughout the next four years. This transaction is corrected on September 30, 1973, in accordance with paragraph (c)(4) of this section. Under these circumstances, the transaction between A and X constitutes four separate acts of self-dealing, which are treated for purposes of section 4941 as occurring on July 31, 1970, January 1, 1971, January 1, 1972, and January 1, 1973. Consequently, there are four taxable periods. The first taxable period is from July 31, 1970, to September 30, 1973; the second is from January 1, 1971, to September 30, 1973; the third is from January 1, 1972, to September 30, 1973; and the fourth is from January 1, 1973, to September 30, 1973. For purposes of the initial taxes in section 4941(a), the amount involved is $5,000 for the first taxable period, $12,000 for the second, $12,000 for the third, and $9,000 for the fourth. The initial taxes to be paid by A are thus $1,000 ($5,000 × 5% × 4 taxable years or partial taxable years in the taxable period) for the first act; $1,800 ($12,000 × 5% × 3) for the second act; $1,200 ($12,000 × 5% × 2) for the third act; and $450 ($9,000 × 5% × 1) for the fourth act.

Example (3). Assume the facts as stated in Example (1) of §53.4941(d)-4(c)(4)(ii). If the debentures are held by Y after December 31, 1979, the extension of credit will not be excepted from the definition of an act of self-dealing, because a new act of self-dealing will be treated (for purposes of section 4941) as occurring on January 1, 1980.

(2) *Number of acts; joint participation by disqualified persons.*—(i) *In general.*—If joint participation in a transaction by two or more disqualified persons constitutes self-dealing (such as a joint sale of property to a private foundation or joint use of its money or property), such transaction shall generally be treated as a separate act of self-dealing with respect to each disqualified person for purposes of section 4941. For purposes of section 507 and, in the case of a foundation manager, section 6684, however, such transaction shall be treated as only one act of self-dealing. For purposes of this subparagraph, an individual and one or more members of his family (within the meaning of section 4946(d)) shall be treated as one person, regardless of whether a member of the family is a disqualified person not only by reason of section 4946(a)(1)(D) but also by reason of another subparagraph of section 4946(a)(1). However, the liability imposed on a disqualified person and one or more members of his family for joint participation in an act of self-dealing shall be joint and several in accordance with section 4941(c)(1) and §53.4941(c)-1(a).

(ii) *Examples.*—The provisions of this subparagraph may be illustrated by the following examples:

Example (1). Private foundation X permits A, a substantial contributor to X, and her spouse, H, to use an automobile owned by X and normally used in its foundation activities to travel from State Z to State Y for a vacation on December 1, 1971. The automobile is then returned to X until December 21, 1971, when X again permits them to use the automobile to return to their home in State Z. Under these circumstances, there is one act of self-dealing on December 1, 1971, and a second act of self-dealing on December 21, 1971.

Example (2). Assume the facts as stated in Example (1), except that B joined A and H on their vacation and travelled with them both to and from State Y. B is a disqualified person with respect to X, but he is not related by blood or marriage to A or H. Assume also that X is not paid for the use of its automobile, but that the fair rental value during the taxable period is $300 (or $100 per person) for a one-way trip between State Y and State Z. Under these circumstances, there are four acts of self-dealing, two with respect to A and H and two with respect to B. The amount involved with respect to A and H is $200 for each act, and the amount involved with respect to B is $100 for each act.

(f) *Fair market value.*—For purposes of §§ 53.4941(a)-1 through 53.4941(f)-1, fair market value shall be determined pursuant to the provisions of §53.4942(a)-2(c)(4). [Reg. §53.4941(e)-1.]

☐ [*T.D. 7270, 4-16-73. Amended by T.D. 8084, 5-1-86.*]

[Reg. § 53.4941(f)-1]

§ 53.4941(f)-1. Effective dates.—(a) *In general.*—Except as provided in paragraph (b) of this section, §§ 53.4941(a)-1 through 53.4941(e)-1 shall apply to all acts of self-dealing engaged in after December 31, 1969.

(b) *Transitional rules.*—(1) *Commitments made prior to January 1, 1970, between private foundations and government officials.*—Section 4941 shall not apply to a payment for one or more purposes described in section 170(c)(1) or (2)(B) made on or after January 1, 1970, by a private foundation to a government official, if such payment is made pursuant to a commitment entered into prior to such date, but only if such commitment was made in accordance with the foundation's usual practices and is reasonable in amount in light of the purposes of the payment. For purposes of this subparagraph, a commitment will be considered entered into prior to January 1, 1970, if prior to such date, the amount and nature of the payments to be made and the name of the payee were entered on the records of the payor, or were otherwise adequately evidenced, or the notice of the payment to be received was communicated to the payee in writing.

(2) *Special transitional rule.*—In the case of an act of self-dealing engaged in prior to July 5, 1971, section 4941(a)(1) shall not apply if—

(i) The participation (as defined in § 53.4941(a)-1(a)(3)) by the disqualified person in such act is not willful and is due to reasonable cause (as defined in § 53.4941(a)-1(b)(4) and (5)),

(ii) The transaction would not be a prohibited transaction if section 503(b) applied, and

(iii) The act is corrected (within the meaning of § 53.4941(e)-1(c)) within a period ending [insert 90 days after date on which final regulations under section 4941 are filed by the Federal Register], extended (prior to the expiration of the original period) by any period which the Commissioner determines is reasonable and necessary (within the meaning of § 53.4941(e)-1(d)) to bring about correction of the act of self-dealing. [Reg. § 53.4941(f)-1.]

☐ [T.D. 7270, 4-16-73.]

[Reg. § 53.4942(a)-1]

§ 53.4942(a)-1. Taxes for failure to distribute income.—(a) *Imposition of tax.*—(1) *Initial tax.*—Except as provided in paragraph (b) of this section, section 4942(a) imposes an excise tax of 15 percent on the undistributed income (as defined in paragraph (a) of § 53.4942(a)-2) of a private foundation for any taxable year which has not been distributed before the first day of the second (or any succeeding) taxable year following such taxable year (if such first day falls within the taxable period as defined in paragraph (c)(1) of this section). For purposes of section 4942 and this section, the term "distributed" means distributed as qualifying distributions under section 4942(g). See paragraph (d)(2) of § 53.4942(a)-3 with respect to correction of deficient distributions for prior taxable years.

(2) *Additional tax.*—In any case in which an initial excise tax is imposed by section 4942(a) on the undistributed income of a private foundation for any taxable year, section 4942(b) imposes an additional excise tax on any portion of such income remaining undistributed at the close of the correction period (as defined in paragraph (c)(1) of this section). The tax imposed by section 4942(b) is equal to 100 percent of the amount

remaining undistributed at the close of the taxable period.

(3) *Payment of tax.*—Payment of the excise taxes imposed by section 4942(a) or (b) is in addition to, and not in lieu of, making the distribution of such undistributed income as required by section 4942. See section 507(a)(2) and the regulations thereunder.

(4) *Examples.*—The provisions of this paragraph may be illustrated by the following examples:

Example (1). M, a private foundation which uses the calendar year as its taxable year, has at the end of 1981, $50,000 of undistributed income (as defined in paragraph (a) of § 53.4942(a)-2) for 1981. As of January 1, 1983, $40,000 is still undistributed. On August 15, 1983, a notice of deficiency with respect to the excise taxes imposed by section 4942(a) and (b) is mailed to M under section 6212(a) and the taxable period ends. Thus, under these facts, an initial excise tax of $6,000 (15 percent of $40,000) is imposed upon M. An additional excise tax of $40,000 (100 percent of $40,000) is imposed by section 4942(b). Under section 4961(a), however, if the undistributed income is reduced to zero during the correction period, this latter tax will not be assessed, and if assessed, it will be abated, and if collected, it will be credited or refunded as an overpayment.

Example (2). Assume the facts as stated in example (1), except that the notice of deficiency is mailed to M on September 7, 1984, and as of January 1, 1984, only $10,000 of the $50,000 of undistributed income with respect to 1981 is undistributed. Therefore, initial excise taxes of $6,000 (15 percent of $40,000, M's undistributed income from 1981, as of January 1, 1983) and $1,500 (15 percent of $10,000, M's undistributed income from 1981 as of January 1, 1984) are imposed by section 4942(a). If the $10,000 remains undistributed as of September 7, 1984, the end of the taxable period, an additional excise tax of $10,000 (100 percent of $10,000, M's undistributed income from 1981, as of September 7, 1984) is imposed by section 4942(b).

(b) *Exceptions.*—(1) *In general.*—The initial excise tax imposed by section 4942(a) shall not apply to the undistributed income of a private foundation—

(i) For any taxable year for which it is an operating foundation (as defined in section 4942(j)(3) and the regulations thereunder), or

(ii) To the extent that the foundation failed to distribute any amount solely because of incorrect valuation of assets under paragraph (c)(4) of § 53.4942(a)-2, if—

(a) The failure to value the assets properly was not willful and was due to reasonable cause.

(b) Such amount is distributed as qualifying distributions (within the meaning of paragraph (a) of § 53.4942(a)-3) by the foundation during the allowable distribution period (as defined in paragraph (c)(2) of this section),

(c) The foundation notifies the Commissioner that such amount has been distributed (within the meaning of subdivision (ii) (b) of this subparagraph) to correct such failure, and

(d) Such distribution is treated under paragraph (d)(2) of § 53.4942(a)-3 as made out of the undistributed income for the taxable year for which a tax would (except for this subdivision) have been imposed by section 4942.

(2) *Improper valuation.*—For purposes of subparagraph (1)(ii) of this paragraph, failure to value an asset properly shall be regarded as "not willful" and "due to reasonable cause" whenever, under all the facts and circumstances, the foundation can show that it has made all reasonable efforts in good faith to value such an asset in accordance with the provisions of paragraph (c)(4) of § 53.4942(a)-2. If a foundation, after full disclosure of the factual situation, obtains a bona fide appraisal of the fair market value of an asset by a person qualified to make such an appraisal (whether or not such a person is a disqualified person with respect to the foundation), and such foundation relies upon such appraisal, then failure to value the asset properly shall ordinarily be regarded as "not willful" and "due to reasonable cause". Notwithstanding the preceding sentence, the failure to obtain such a bona fide appraisal shall not, by itself, give rise to any inference that a foundation's failure to value an asset properly was willful or not due to reasonable cause.

(3) *Example.*—The provisions of this paragraph may be illustrated by the following example:

Example. In 1976 M, a private foundation which was established in 1975 and which uses the calendar year as the taxable year, incorrectly values its assets under paragraph (c)(4) of § 53.4942(a) in a manner which is not willful and is due to reasonable cause. As a result of the incorrect valuation of assets, $20,000 which should be distributed with respect to 1976 is not distributed, and as of January 1, 1978, such amount is still undistributed. On March 29, 1978, a notice of deficiency with respect to the excise taxes imposed by section 4942(a) and (b) is mailed to M under section 6212(a). On May 5, 1978 (within the allowable distribution period), M makes a qualifying distribution of $20,000 which is treated under paragraph (d)(2) of § 53.4942(a)-3 as made out of M's undistributed income for 1976. M notifies the Commissioner of its action. Under the stated facts, an initial excess tax of $3,000 (15 percent of $20,000) would (except for the exception contained in subparagraph (1)(ii) of this paragraph) have been imposed by section 4942(a), but since all of the requirements of this subparagraph are satisfied no tax is imposed by section 4942(a).

(c) *Certain periods.*—For purposes of this section—

(1) *Taxable period.*—(i) The term "taxable period" means, with respect to the undistributed income of a private foundation for any taxable year, the period beginning with the first day of the taxable year and ending on the earlier of:

(A) The date of mailing of a notice of deficiency under section 6212(a) with respect to the initial excise tax imposed under section 4942(a), or

(B) The date on which the initial excise tax imposed under section 4942(a) is assessed.

For example, assume M, a private foundation which uses the calendar year as the taxable year, has $15,000 of undistributed income for 1981. A notice of deficiency is mailed to M under section 6212(a) on June 1, 1983. With respect to the undistributed income of M for 1981, the taxable period began on January 1, 1981, and ended on June 1, 1983.

(ii) Where a notice of deficiency referred to in subdivision (i) of this subparagraph is not mailed because there is a waiver of the restrictions on assessment and collection of a deficiency, or because the deficiency is paid, the date of filing of the waiver or the date of such payment, respectively, shall be treated as the end of the taxable period.

(2) *Allowable distribution period.*—(i) The term "allowable distribution period" means the period beginning with the first day of the first taxable year following the taxable year in which the incorrect valuation of foundation assets (described in paragraph (b)(1)(ii) of this section) occurred and ending 90 days after the date of mailing of a notice of deficiency under section 6212(a) with respect to the initial excise tax imposed by section 4942(a). This period shall be extended by any period in which a deficiency cannot be assessed under section 6213(a), and any other period which the Commissioner determines is reasonable and necessary to permit a distribution of undistributed income under section 4942.

(ii) Where a notice of deficiency referred to in subdivision (i) of this subparagraph is not mailed because there is a waiver of the restrictions on assessment and collection of a deficiency, or because the deficiency is paid, the date of filing of the waiver or the date of such payment, respectively, shall be treated as the end of the allowable distribution period.

(3) *Cross reference.*—For rules relating to taxable events that are corrected within the correction period, defined in section 4963(e), see section 4961(a) and the regulations thereunder.

(4) *Examples.*—The provisions of this paragraph may be illustrated by the following examples:

Example (1). In 1975 M, a private foundation which uses the calendar year as the taxable year, made an error in valuing its assets which was not willful and was due to reasonable cause. The error caused M not to distribute $25,000 that should have been distributed with respect to 1975. On March 1, 1978, a notice of deficiency with respect to the excise taxes imposed by section 4942(a) and (b) was mailed to M under section 6212(a). With respect to the undistributed income for 1975, the "taxable period" is the period from January 1, 1975, through March 1, 1978, and the "allowable distribution period" is the period from January 1, 1976, through May 30, 1978 (90 days after the mailing of the notice of deficiency).

Example (2). Assume the facts as stated in example (1), except that the Commissioner determines that it is reasonable and necessary to extend the period for distribution through June 15, 1978. Thus, the "allowable distribution period" is from January 1, 1976, through June 15, 1978.

(d) *Effective date.*—Except as otherwise specifically provided, section 4942 and the regulations thereunder shall only apply with respect to taxable years beginning after December 31, 1969. [Reg. § 53.4942(a)-1.]

☐ *[T.D. 7256, 2-2-73. Amended by T.D. 8084, 5-1-86.]*

[Reg. § 53.4942(a)-2]

§ 53.4942(a)-2. Computation of undistributed income.—(a) *Undistributed income.*—For purposes of section 4942, the term "undistributed income" means, with respect to any private foundation for any taxable year as of any time, the amount by which—

(1) The distributable amount (as defined in paragraph (b) of this section) for such taxable year, exceeds

(2) The qualifying distributions (as defined in § 53.4942(a)-3) made before such time out of such distributable amount.

(b) *Distributable amount.*—(1) *In general.*—For purposes of paragraph (a) of this section, the term "distributable amount" means—

(i) For taxable years beginning before January 1, 1982, an amount equal to the greater of the minimum investment return (as defined in paragraph (c) of this section) or the adjusted net income (as defined in paragraph (d) of this section); and

(ii) For taxable years beginning after December 31, 1981, an amount equal to the minimum investment return (as defined in paragraph (c) of this section),

reduced by the sum of the taxes imposed on such private foundation for such taxable year under subtitle A of the Code and section 4940, and increased by the amounts received from trusts described in subparagraph (2) of this paragraph.

(2) *Certain trust amounts.*—(i) *In general.*—The distributable amount shall be increased by the income portion (as defined in subdivision (ii) of this subparagraph) of distributions from trusts described in section 4947(a)(2) with respect to amounts placed in trust after May 26, 1969. If such distributions are made with respect to amounts placed in trust both on or before and after May 26, 1969, such distributions shall be allocated between such amounts to determine the extent to which such distributions shall be included in the foundation's distributable amount. For rules relating to the segregation of

amounts placed in trust on or before May 26, 1969, from amounts placed in trust after such date and to the allocation of income derived from such amounts, see paragraph (c)(5) of § 53.4947-1.

(ii) *Income portion of distributions to private foundations.*—For purposes of subdivision (i) of this subparagraph, the income portion of a distribution from a section 4947(a)(2) trust to a private foundation in a particular taxable year of such foundation shall be the greater of:

(a) The amount of such distribution which is treated as income (within the meaning of section 643(b)) of the trust, or

(b) The guaranteed annuity, or fixed percentage of the fair market value of the trust property (determined annually), which the private foundation is entitled to receive for such year, regardless of whether such amount is actually received in such year or in any prior or subsequent year.

(iii) *Limitation.*—Notwithstanding subdivisions (i) and (ii) of this subparagraph, a private foundation shall not be required to distribute a greater amount for any taxable year than would have been required (without regard to this subparagraph) for such year had the corpus of the section 4947(a)(2) trust to which the distribution described in subdivision (ii) of this subparagraph is attributable been taken into account by such foundation as an asset described in paragraph (c)(1)(i) of this section.

(c) *Minimum investment return.*—(1) *In general.*—For purposes of paragraph (b) of this section, the "minimum investment return" for any private foundation for any taxable year is the amount determined by multiplying—

(i) The excess of the aggregate fair market value of all assets of the foundation, other than those described in subparagraph (2) or (3) of this paragraph, over the amount of the acquisition indebtedness with respect to such assets (determined under section 514(c)(1), but without regard to the taxable year in which the indebtedness was incurred), by

(ii) The applicable percentage (as defined in subparagraph (5) of this paragraph) for such year.

For purposes of subdivision (i) of this subparagraph, the aggregate fair market value of all assets of the foundation shall include the average of the fair market values on a monthly basis of securities for which market quotations are readily available (within the meaning of subparagraph (4)(i)(a) of this paragraph), the average of the foundation's cash balances on a monthly basis (less the cash balances excluded from the computation of the minimum investment return by operation of subparagraph (3)(iv) of this paragraph), and the fair market value of all other assets (except those assets described in subparagraph (2) or (3) of this paragraph) for the period of time during the year for which such assets are held by the foundation. Any determination of the fair market value of an asset required pursuant to the provisions of this subparagraph shall be made in accordance with the rules of subparagraph (4) of this paragraph.

(2) *Certain assets excluded.*—For purposes of this paragraph, the assets taken into account in determining minimum investment return shall not include the following:

(i) Any future interest (such as a vested or contingent remainder, whether legal or equitable) of a foundation in the income or corpus of any real or personal property, other than a future interest created by the private foundation, after December 31, 1969, until all intervening interests in, and rights to the actual possession or enjoyment of, such property have expired, or, although not actually reduced to the foundation's possession, until such future interest has been constructively received by the foundation, as where it has been credited to the foundation's account, set apart for the foundation, or otherwise made available so that the foundation may acquire it at any time or could have acquired it if notice of intention to acquire had been given;

(ii) The assets of an estate until such time as such assets are distributed to the foundation or, due to a prolonged period of administration, such estate is considered terminated for Federal income tax purposes by operation of paragraph (a) of §1.641(b)-3 of this chapter (Income Tax Regulations);

(iii) Any present interest of a foundation in any trust created and funded by another person (see, however, paragraph (b)(2) of this section with respect to amounts received from certain trusts described in section 4947(a)(2));

(iv) Any pledge to the foundation of money or property (whether or not the pledge may be legally enforced); and

(v) Any assets used (or held for use) directly in carrying out the foundation's exempt purpose.

(3) *Assets used (or held for use) in carrying out the exempt purpose.*—(i) *In general.*—For purposes of subparagraph (2)(v) of this paragraph, an asset is "used (or held for use) directly in carrying out the foundation's exempt purpose" only if the asset is actually used by the foundation in the carrying out of the charitable, educational, or other similar purpose which gives rise to the exempt status of the foundation, or if the foundation owns the asset and establishes to the satisfaction of the Commissioner that its immediate use for such exempt purpose is not practical (based on the facts and circumstances of the particular case) and that definite plans exist to commence such use within a reasonable period of time. Consequently, assets which are held for the production of income or for investment (for example, stocks, bonds, interest-bearing notes, endowment funds, or, generally, leased real estate) are not being used (or held for use) directly in carrying out the foundation's exempt purpose, even though the income from such assets is used to carry out such exempt purpose. Whether an asset is held for the production of income or for investment rather than used (or held for use)

directly by the foundation to carry out its exempt purpose is a question of fact. For example, an office building used for the purpose of providing offices for employees engaged in the management of endowment funds of the foundation is not being used (or held for use) directly by the foundation to carry out its charitable, educational, or other similar exempt purpose. However, where property is used both for charitable, educational, or other similar exempt purposes and for other purposes, if such exempt use represents 95 percent or more of the total use, such property shall be considered to be used exclusively for a charitable, educational, or other similar exempt purpose. If such exempt use of such property represents less than 95 percent of the total use, reasonable allocation between such exempt and nonexempt use must be made for purposes of this paragraph. Property acquired by the foundation to be used in carrying out its charitable, educational, or other similar exempt purpose may be considered as used (or held for use) directly to carry out such exempt purpose even though the property, in whole or in part, is leased for a limited period of time during which arrangements are made for its conversion to the use for which it was acquired, provided such income-producing use of the property does not exceed a reasonable period of time. Generally, one year shall be deemed to be a reasonable period of time for purposes of the immediately preceding sentence. For treatment of the income derived from such income-producing use, see paragraph (d)(2)(viii) of this section. Where the income-producing use continues beyond a reasonable period of time, the property shall not be deemed to be used by the foundation to carry out its charitable, educational, or other similar exempt purpose, but, instead, as of the time the income-producing use becomes unreasonable, such property shall be treated as disposed of within the meaning of paragraph (d)(2)(iii)(*b*) of this section to the extent that the acquisition of the property was taken into account as a qualifying distribution (within the meaning of paragraph (a)(2) of §53.4942(a)-3 for any taxable year. If, subsequently, the property is used by the foundation directly in carrying out its charitable, educational, or other similar exempt purpose, a qualifying distribution in the amount of its then fair market value, determined in accordance with the rules contained in subparagraph (4) of this paragraph, shall be deemed to have been made as of the time such exempt use begins.

(ii) *Illustrations.*—Examples of assets which are "used (or held for use) directly in carrying out the foundation's exempt purpose" include, but are not limited to, the following:

(a) Administrative assets, such as office equipment and supplies which are used by employees or consultants of the foundation, to the extent such assets are devoted to and used directly in the administration of the foundation's charitable, educational, or other similar exempt activities;

(b) Real estate or the portion of a building used by the foundation directly in its charitable, educational, or other similar exempt activities;

(c) Physical facilities used in such activities, such as paintings or other works of art owned by the foundation which are on public display, fixtures and equipment in classrooms, and research facilities and related equipment, which under the facts and circumstances serve a useful purpose in the conduct of such activities;

(d) Any interest in a functionally related business (as defined in subdivision (iii) of this subparagraph) or in a program-related investment (as defined in section 4944(c));

(e) The reasonable cash balances (as described in subdivision (iv) of this subparagraph) necessary to cover current administrative expenses and other normal and current disbursements directly connected with the foundation's charitable, educational, or other similar exempt activities; and

(f) Any property leased by a foundation in carrying out its charitable, educational, or other similar exempt purpose at no cost (or at a nominal rent) to the lessee or for a program-related purpose (within the meaning of section 4944(c)), such as the leasing of renovated apartments to low-income tenants at a low rental as part of the lessor-foundation's program for rehabilitating a blighted portion of a community. For treatment of the income derived from such use, see paragraph (d)(2)(viii) of this section.

(iii) *Functionally related business.*—(a) *In general.*—The term "functionally related business" means—

(1) A trade or business which is not an unrelated trade or business (as defined in section 513), or

(2) An activity which is carried on within a larger aggregate of similar activities or within a larger complex of other endeavors which is related (aside from the need of the organization for income or funds or the use it makes of the profits derived) to the charitable, educational, or other similar exempt purpose of the organization.

(b) *Examples.*—The provisions of this subdivision may be illustrated by the following examples:

Example (1). X, a private foundation, maintains a community of historic value which is open to the general public. For the convenience of the public, X, through a wholly owned, separately incorporated, taxable entity, maintains a restaurant and hotel in such community. Such facilities are within the larger aggregate of activities which makes available for public enjoyment the various buildings of historic interest and which is related to X's exempt purpose. Thus, the operation of the restaurant and hotel under such circumstances constitutes a functionally related business.

Example (2). Y, a private foundation, as part of its medical research program under section 501(c)(3), publishes a medical journal in carrying out its exempt purpose. Space in the journal is sold for commercial advertising. Notwithstanding the fact that the advertising activity may be subject to the tax imposed by section 511, such activity is within a larger complex of endeavors which makes available to the scientific community and the general public developments with respect to medical research and is therefore a functionally related business.

(iv) *Cash held for charitable, etc. activities.*—For purposes of subdivision (ii) (e) of this subparagraph, the reasonable cash balance which a private foundation needs to have on hand to cover expenses and disbursements described in such subdivision will generally be deemed to be an amount, computed on an annual basis, equal to one and one-half percent of the fair market value of all assets described in subparagraph (1)(i) of this paragraph, without regard to subdivision (ii)(e) of this subparagraph. However, if the Commissioner is satisfied that under the facts and circumstances an amount in addition to such one and one-half percent is necessary for payment of such expenses and disbursements, then such additional amount may also be excluded from the amount of assets described in subparagraph (1)(i) of this paragraph. All remaining cash balances, including amounts necessary to pay any tax imposed by section 511 or any section of chapter 42 of the Code except section 4940, are to be included in the assets described in subparagraph (1)(i) of this paragraph.

(4) *Valuation of assets.*—(i) *Certain securities.*—(a) For purposes of subparagraph (1)(i) of this paragraph, a private foundation may use any reasonable method to determine the fair market value on a monthly basis of securities for which market quotations are readily available, as long as such method is consistently used. For purposes of this subparagraph, market quotations are readily available if a security is:

(1) Listed on the New York Stock Exchange, the American Stock Exchange, or any city or regional exchange in which quotations appear on a daily basis, including foreign securities listed on a recognized foreign national or regional exchange;

(2) Regularly traded in the national or regional over-the-counter market, for which published quotations are available; or

(3) Locally traded, for which quotations can readily be obtained from established brokerage firms.

(b) For purposes of this subdivision, commonly accepted methods of valuation must be used in making an appraisal. Valuations made in accordance with the principles stated in the regulations under section 2031 constitute acceptable methods of valuation. This paragraph (c)(4)(i)(b) applies only for taxable years beginning before January 1, 1976. See section

4942(e)(2)(B) and paragraph (c)(4)(i)(c) of this section for special valuation rules that apply for subsequent taxable years.

(c) For purposes of this subdivision (i) and with respect to taxable years beginning after December 31, 1975, if the private foundation can show that the value of securities determined on the basis of market quotations as provided by subdivision (i)(a) does not reflect the fair market value thereof because—

(1) The securities constitute a block of securities so large in relation to the volume of actual sales on the existing market that it could not be liquidated in a reasonable time without depressing the market,

(2) The securities are securities in a closely held corporation and sales are few or of a sporadic nature, and/or

(3) The sale of the securities would result in a forced or distress sale because the securities could not be offered to the public for sale without first being registered under the Securities Act of 1933 or because of other factors,

then the price at which the securities could be sold as such outside the usual market, as through an underwriter, may be a more accurate indication of value than market quotations. On the other hand, if the securities to be valued represent a controlling interest, either actual or effective, in a going business, the price at which other lots change hands may have little relation to the true value of the securities. No decrease in the fair market value of any given class of securities determined on the basis of market quotations as provided by subdivision (i)(a) shall be allowed except as authorized by this subdivision, and no such decrease shall in the aggregate exceed 10 percent of the fair market value of such class of securities so determined on the basis of market quotations and without regard to this subdivision.

(d) In the case of securities described in subdivision (i)(a) of this subparagraph, which are held in trust for, or on behalf of, a foundation by a bank or other financial institution which values such securities periodically by use of a computer, a foundation may determine the correct value of such securities by use of such computer pricing system, provided the Commissioner has accepted such computer pricing system as a valid method for valuing securities for Federal estate tax purposes.

(e) This subdivision may be illustrated by the following examples:

Example (1). U, a private foundation, owns 1,000 shares of the stock of M Corporation. M stock is regularly traded on the New York Stock Exchange. U consistently follows a practice of valuing its 1,000 shares of M stock on the last trading day of each month based upon the quoted closing price for M stock. U's method of valuing its M Corporation stock is permissible under the rules contained in subdivision (i)(a) of this subparagraph.

Example (2). Assume the facts as stated in example (1), except that U consistently follows a practice of valuing its 1,000 shares of M stock by taking the mean of the closing prices for M stock on the first and last trading days of each month and the trading day nearest the 15th day of each month. U's method of valuing its M stock is permissible under the rules contained in subdivision (i)(a) of this subparagraph.

Example (3). Assume the facts as stated in example (1), except that U consistently follows a practice of valuing its M stock by taking the mean of the highest and lowest quoted prices for the stock on the last trading day of each month. U's method of valuing its M stock is permissible under the rules contained in subdivision (1)[(i)](a) of this subparagraph.

Example (4). V, a private foundation, owns 1,000 shares of the stock of N Corporation. N stock is regularly traded in the national over-the-counter market and published quotations of the bid and asked prices for the stock are available. V consistently follows a practice of valuing its 1,000 shares of N stock on the first trading day of each month by taking the mean of the bid and asked prices on that day. V's method of valuing its N Corporation stock is permissible under the rules contained in subdivision (i)(a) of this subparagraph.

Example (5). W, a private foundation, owns 1,000 shares of the stock of O Corporation. O stock is locally traded and quotations can readily be obtained from established brokerage firms. W consistently follows a practice of valuing its O stock on the 15th day of each month by obtaining a bona fide quotation of bid and asked prices for the stock from an established brokerage firm and taking the mean of such prices on that day. If a quotation is unavailable on the regular valuation date, W values its O stock based upon a bona fide quotation on the first day thereafter on which such a quotation is available. W's method of valuing its O Corporation stock is permissible under the rules contained in subdivision (i)(a) of this subparagraph.

(ii) *Cash.*—In order to determine the amount of a foundation's cash balances, the foundation shall value its cash on a monthly basis by averaging the amount of cash on hand as of the first day of each month and as of the last day of each month.

(iii) *Common trust funds.*—If a private foundation owns a participating interest in a common trust fund (as defined in section 584) established and administered under a plan providing for the periodic valuation of participating interests during the fund's taxable year and the reporting of such valuations to participants, the value of the foundation's interest in the common trust fund based upon the average of the valuations reported to the foundation during its taxable year will ordinarily constitute an acceptable method of valuation.

(iv) *Other assets.*—(a) Except as otherwise provided in subdivision (iv)(b) of this subparagraph, the fair market value of assets other than those described in subdivisions (i) through (iii)

Reg. §53.4942(a)-2(c)(4)(iv)(a)

of this subparagraph shall be determined annually. Thus, the fair market value of securities other than those described in subdivision (i) of this subparagraph shall be determined in accordance with this subdivision (a). If, however, a private foundation owns voting stock of an issuer of unlisted securities and has, or together with disqualified persons or another private foundation has, effective control of the issuer (within the meaning of § 53.4943-3(b)(3)(ii)), then to the extent that the issuer's assets consist of shares of listed securities issues, such assets shall be valued monthly on the basis of market quotations or in accordance with section 4942(e)(2)(B), if applicable. Thus, for example, if a private foundation and a disqualified person together own all of the unlisted voting stock of a holding company which in turn holds a portfolio of securities of issues which are listed on the New York Stock Exchange, in determining the net worth of the holding company, the underlying portfolio securities are to be valued monthly by reference to market quotations for their issues unless a decrease in such value is authorized in accordance with section 4942(e)(2)(B). Such determination may be made by employees of the private foundation or by any other person, without regard to whether such person is a disqualified person with respect to the foundation. A valuation made pursuant to the provisions of this subdivision, if accepted by the Commissioner, shall be valid only for the taxable year for which it is made. A new valuation made in accordance with these provisions is required for the succeeding taxable year.

(b) If the requirements of this subdivision are met, the fair market value of any interest in real property, including any improvements thereon, may be determined on a five-year basis. Such value must be determined by means of a certified, independent appraisal made in writing by a qualified person who is neither a disqualified person with respect to, nor an employee of, the private foundation. The appraisal is certified only if it contains a statement at the end thereof to the effect that, in the opinion of the appraiser, the values placed on the assets appraised were determined in accordance with valuation principles regularly employed in making appraisals of such property using all reasonable valuation methods. The foundation shall retain a copy of the independent appraisal for its records. If a valuation made pursuant to the provisions of this subdivision in fact falls within the range of reasonable values for the appraised property, such valuation may be used by the foundation for the taxable year for which the valuation is made and for each of the succeeding four taxable years. Any valuation made pursuant to the provisions of this subdivision may be replaced during the five-year period by a subsequent five-year valuation made in accordance with the rules set forth in this subdivision, or with an annual valuation made in accordance with subdivision (iv)(a) of this subparagraph, and the most recent such valuation of such assets shall be used in computing the foundation's minimum investment return. In the case of a foundation organized before May 27, 1969, a valuation made in accordance with this subdivision applicable to the foundation's first taxable year beginning after December 31, 1972 and the four succeeding taxable years must be made no later than the last day of such first taxable year. In the case of a foundation organized after May 26, 1969, a valuation made in accordance with this subdivision applicable to the foundation's first taxable year beginning after February 5, 1973, and the succeeding four taxable years must be made no later than the last day of such first taxable year. Any subsequent valuation made in accordance with this subdivision must be made no later than the last day of the first taxable year for which such new valuation is applicable. A valuation, if properly made in accordance with the rules set forth in this subdivision, will not be disturbed by the Commissioner during the five-year period for which it applies even if the actual fair market value of such property changes during such period.

(c) For purposes of this subdivision, commonly accepted methods of valuation must be used in making an appraisal. Valuations made in accordance with the principles stated in the regulations under section 2031 constitute acceptable methods of valuation. The term "appraisal," as used in this subdivision, means a determination of fair market value and is not to be construed in a technical sense peculiar to particular property or interests therein, such as, for example, mineral interests in real property.

(v) *Definition of "securities".*—For purposes of this subparagraph, the term "securities" includes, but it is not limited to, common and preferred stocks, bonds, and mutual fund shares.

(vi) *Valuation date.*—(a) In the case of an asset which is required to be valued on an annual basis as provided in subdivision (iv) (a) of this subparagraph, such asset may be valued as of any day in the private foundation's taxable year to which such valuation applies, provided the foundation follows a consistent practice of valuing such asset as of such date in all taxable years.

(b) A valuation described in subdivision (iv) (b) of this subparagraph may be made as of any day in the first taxable year of the private foundation to which such valuation is to be applied.

(vii) *Assets held for less than a taxable year.*—For purposes of this paragraph, any asset described in subparagraph (1)(i) of this paragraph which is held by a foundation for only part of a taxable year shall be taken into account for purposes of determining the foundation's minimum investment return for such taxable year by multiplying the fair market value of such asset (as determined pursuant to this subparagraph) by a fraction, the numerator of which is the number of days in such taxable year that the foundation held such asset and the denominator of which is the number of days in such taxable year.

(5) *Applicable percentage.*—(i) *In general.*—For purposes of paragraph (c)(1)(ii) of this section, except as provided in paragraph (c)(5)(ii) or (iii) of this section, the applicable percentage is:

(a) Six percent for a taxable year beginning in 1970 or 1971;

(b) Five and a half percent for a taxable year beginning in 1972;

(c) Five and one-quarter percent for a taxable year beginning in 1973;

(d) Six percent for a taxable year beginning in 1974 or 1975; and

(e) Five percent for taxable years beginning after Dec. 31, 1975.

(ii) *Transitional rule.*—In the case of organizations organized before May 27, 1969 (including organizations deemed to be so organized by virtue of the provisions of paragraph (e)(2) of this section), section 4942 shall, for all purposes other than the determination of the minimum investment return under section 4942(j)(3)(B)(ii), for taxable years—

(a) Beginning before January 1, 1972, apply without regard to section 4942(e),

(b) Beginning in 1972, apply with an applicable percentage of $4^{1}/_{8}$ percent,

(c) Beginning in 1973, apply with an applicable percentage of $4^{3}/_{8}$ percent, and

(d) Beginning in 1974, apply with an applicable percentage of $5^{1}/_{2}$ percent.

(iii) *Short taxable periods.*—In any case in which a taxable year referred to in this subparagraph is a period less than 12 months, the applicable percentage to be applied to the amount determined under the provisions of subparagraph (1) of this paragraph shall be equal to the applicable percentage for the calendar year in which the short taxable period began multiplied by a fraction, the numerator of which is the number of days in such short taxable period and the denominator of which is 365.

(d) *Adjusted net income.*—(1) *Definition.*—For purposes of paragraph (b) of this section, the term "adjusted net income" means the excess (if any) of—

(i) The gross income for the taxable year (including gross income from any unrelated trade or business) determined with the income modifications provided by subparagaph (2) of this paragraph, over

(ii) The sum of the deductions (including deductions directly connected with the carrying on of any unrelated trade or business), determined with the deduction modifications provided by subparagraph (4) of this paragraph, which would be allowed to a corporation subject to the tax imposed by section 11 for the taxable year.

In computing the income includible under this paragraph as gross income and the deductions allowable under this paragraph from such income, the principles of subtitle A of the Code shall apply except to the extent such principles

conflict with section 4942 and the regulations thereunder (without regard to this sentence). Except as otherwise provided in this paragraph, no exclusions or deductions from gross income or credits against tax are allowable under this paragraph. For purposes of subdivision (i) of this subparagraph, the term "gross income" does not include gifts, grants, or contributions received by the private foundation but does include income from a functionally related business (as defined in paragraph (c)(3)(iii) of this section).

(2) *Income modifications.*—The income modifications referred to in subparagraph (1)(i) of this paragraph are as follows:

(i) Section 103 (relating to interest on certain governmental obligations) shall not apply. Hence, interest which would have been excluded from gross income by section 103 shall be included in gross income.

(ii) Capital gains and losses from the sale or other disposition of property shall be taken into account only in an amount equal to any net short-term capital gain (as defined in section 1222(5)) for the taxable year. Long-term capital gain or loss is not included in the computation of adjusted net income. Similarly, net section 1231 gains shall be excluded from the computation of adjusted net income. However, net section 1231 losses shall be included in the computation of adjusted net income, if such losses are otherwise described in subparagraph (1)(ii) of this paragraph. Any net short-term capital loss for a given taxable year shall not be taken into account in computing adjusted net income for such year or in computing net short-term capital gain for purposes of determining adjusted net income for prior or future taxable years regardless of whether the foundation is a corporation or a trust.

(iii) The following amounts shall be included in gross income for the taxable year—

(a) Amounts received or accrued as repayments of amounts which were taken into account as a qualifying distribution within the meaning of paragraph (a)(2)(i) of § 53.4942(a)-3 for any taxable year;

(b) Notwithstanding subdivision (ii) of this subparagraph, gross amounts received or accrued from the sale or other disposition of property to the extent that the acquisition of such property was taken into account as a qualifying distribution (within the meaning of paragraph (a)(2)(ii) of § 53.4942(a)-3) for any taxable year; and

(c) Any amount set aside under paragraph (b) of § 53.4942(a)-3 to the extent it is determined that such amount is not necessary for the purposes for which it was set aside.

(iv) Any distribution received by a private foundation from a disqualified person in redemption of stock held by such private foundation if a business enterprise shall be treated as not essentially equivalent to a dividend under section 302(b)(1) if all of the following conditions are satisfied:

Reg. § 53.4942(a)-2(d)(2)(iv)

(a) Such redemption is of stock which was owned by a private foundation on May 26, 1969 (or which is acquired by a private foundation under the terms of a trust which was irrevocable on May 26, 1969, or under the terms of a will executed on or before such date which are in effect on such date and at all times thereafter);

(b) Such foundation is required to dispose of such property in order not to be liable for tax under section 4943 (relating to taxes on excess business holdings) applied, in the case of a disposition before January 1, 1975, without taking section 4943(c)(4) into account; and

(c) Such foundation receives in return an amount which equals or exceeds the fair market value of such property at the time of such disposition or at the time a contract for such disposition was previously executed in a transaction which would not constitute a prohibited transaction (within the meaning of section 503(b) or the corresponding provisions of prior law).

(v) If, as of the date of distribution of property for purposes described in section 170(c)(1) or (2)(B), the fair market value of such property exceeds its adjusted basis, such excess shall not be deemed an amount includible in gross income.

(vi) The income received by a private foundation from an estate during the period of administration of such estate shall not be included in such foundation's gross income, unless, due to a prolonged period of administration, such estate is considered terminated for Federal income tax purposes by operation of paragraph (a) of §1.641(b)-3 of this chapter (Income Tax Regulations).

(vii) Distributions received by a private foundation from a trust created and funded by another person shall not be included in the foundation's gross income. However, with respect to distributions from certain trusts described in section 4947(a)(2), see paragraph (b)(2) of this section.

(viii) Gross income shall include all amounts derived from, or in connection with, property held by the foundation, even though the fair market value of such property may not be included in such foundation's assets for purposes of determining minimum investment return by operation of paragraph (c)(3) of this section.

(ix) Gross income shall include amounts treated in a preceding taxable year as a "qualifying distribution" by operation of paragraph (c) of §53.4942(a)-3 where such amounts are not redistributed by the close of the donee organization's succeeding taxable year in accordance with the rules prescribed in such paragraph (c). In such cases, such amounts shall be included in the donor foundation's gross income for such foundation's first taxable year beginning after the close of the donee organization's first taxable year following the donee organization's taxable year of receipt.

(x) For taxable years ending after October 4, 1976, section 4942(f)(2)(D) states that section 483 (relating to imputed interest on deferred payments) does not apply to payments made pursuant to a binding contract entered into in a taxable year beginning before January 1, 1970. Amounts that are not treated as imputed interest because of section 4942(f)(2)(D) and this subdivision will represent gain or loss from the sale of property. If the gain or loss is long term capital gain or loss, section 4942(f)(2)(B) excludes the gain or loss from the computation of the foundation's gross income. If, in a taxable year beginning after December 31, 1969, there is a substantial change in the terms of a contract entered into in a taxable year beginning before January 1, 1970, then any payment made pursuant to the changed contract is not considered a payment made pursuant to a contract entered into in a taxable year beginning before January 1, 1970. Whether or not a change in the terms of a contract (for example, a change relating to time of payment, sales price, or obligations under the contract) is a substantial change is determined by applying the rules under section 483 and §1.483-1(b)(4). As used in this subdivision, a binding contract includes an irrevocable written option.

(3) *Adjusted basis.*—(i) *In general.*—For purposes of subparagraph (2)(ii) of this paragraph, the adjusted basis for purposes of determining gain from the sale or other disposition of property shall be determined in accordance with the rules set forth in subdivision (ii) of this subparagraph and the adjusted basis for purposes of determining loss from such disposition shall be determined in accordance with the rules set forth in subdivision (iii) of this subparagraph. Further, the provisions of this subparagraph do not apply for any purpose other than for purposes of subparagraph (2)(ii) of this paragraph. For example, the determination of gain pursuant to the provisions of section 341 is determined without regard to this subparagraph.

(ii) *Gain from sale or other disposition.*—The adjusted basis for purposes of determining gain from the sale or other disposition of property shall be the greater of:

(a) The fair market value of such property on December 31, 1969, plus or minus all adjustments after December 31, 1969, and before the date of sale or other disposition under the rules of Part II, subchapter O, chapter 1 of the Code, provided that the property was held by the private foundation on December 31, 1969, and continuously thereafter to such date of sale or other disposition; or

(b) The adjusted basis as determined under the rules of Part II, subchapter O, chapter 1 of the Code, subject to the provisions of section 4940(c)(3)(B) and the regulations thereunder (and without regard to section 362(c)). With respect to assets acquired prior to December 31, 1969, which were subject to depreciation or depletion, for purposes of determining the adjustments to be made to basis between the date of acquisition and December 31, 1969, an amount equal to straight-line depreciation or cost depletion shall be taken into account. In addition, in determining such adjustments to basis, if any other adjustments would have been made during such period (such as a change in useful life based upon additional data or a change in facts), such adjustments shall also be taken into account.

(iii) *Loss from sale or other disposition.*—For purposes of determining loss from the sale or other disposition of property, adjusted basis as determined in subdivision (ii)(*b*) of this subparagraph shall apply.

(iv) *Examples.*—The provisions of this subparagraph may be illustrated by the following examples:

Example (1). A private foundation, which uses the cash receipts and disbursements method of accounting, purchased certain depreciable real property on December 1, 1969. On December 31, 1969, the fair market value of such property was $100,000 and its adjusted basis (determined under the provisions of this subparagraph) was $102,000. The property was sold on January 2, 1970, for $105,000. Because fair market value on December 31, 1969, $100,000, is less than the adjusted basis as determined by Part II, subchapter O, chapter 1 of the Code, $102,000, a short-term gain of $3,000 is recognized (*i.e.*, sale price of $105,000 less the greater of the two possible bases) for purposes of subparagraph (2)(ii) of this paragraph.

Example (2). Assume the facts as stated in example (1), except that the sale price was $95,000. Because the sale price was $7,000 less than the adjusted basis for loss ($102,000 as determined by the application of subdivision (iii) of this subparagraph), there is a capital loss of $7,000 which may be deducted against short-term capital gains for 1970 (if any) in determining net short-term capital gain.

Example (3). A private foundation, which uses the cash receipts and disbursements method of accounting, purchased unimproved land on December 1, 1969. On December 31, 1969, the fair market value of such property was $110,000 and its adjusted basis (determined under the provisions of this subparagraph) was $102,000. The property was sold on January 2, 1970, for $105,000. Since the fair market value on December 31, 1969, $110,000, exceeds the adjusted basis as determined by Part II, subchapter O, chapter 1 of the Code, $102,000, such fair market value will be used for purposes of determining gain. However, because the adjusted basis for purposes of determining gain exceeds the sale price, there is no gain. Furthermore, because the adjusted basis for purposes of determining loss, $102,000, is less than the sale price, there is no loss.

(4) *Deduction modifications.*—(i) *In general.*— For purposes of computing adjusted net income under subparagraph (1) of this paragraph, no deduction shall be allowed other than all the ordinary and necessary expenses paid or incurred for the production or collection of gross income or for the management, conservation, or maintenance of property held for the production of such income, except as provided in subdivision (ii) of this subparagraph. Such expenses include that portion of a private foundation's operating expenses which is paid or incurred for the production or collection of gross income. Operating expenses include compensation of officers, other salaries and wages of employees, interest, rent, and taxes. Where only a portion of the property produces (or is held for the production of) income subject to the provisions of section 4942, and the remainder of the property is used for charitable, educational, or other similar exempt purposes, the deductions allowed by this subparagraph shall be apportioned between the exempt and non-exempt uses. Similarly, where the deductions with respect to property used for a charitable, educational, or other similar exempt purpose exceed the income derived from such property, such excess shall not be allowed as a deduction, but may be treated as a qualifying distribution described in paragraph (a)(2)(ii) of § 53.4942(a)-3. Furthermore, this subdivision does not allow deductions which are not paid or incurred for the purposes herein prescribed. Thus, for example, the deductions prescribed by the following sections are not allowable: (*a*) The charitable contributions deduction prescribed under sections 170 and 642(c); (*b*) the net operating loss deduction prescribed under section 172; and (*c*) the special deductions prescribed under Part VIII, subchapter B, chapter 1 of the Code.

(ii) *Special rules.*—For purposes of computing adjusted net income under subparagraph (1) of this paragraph: (*a*) The allowances for depreciation and depletion as determined under section 4940(c)(3)(B) and the regulations thereunder shall be taken into account, and (*b*) section 265 (relating to expenses and interest relating to tax-exempt interest) shall not apply.

(e) *Certain transitional rules.*—(1) *In general.*— In the case of organizations organized before May 27, 1969, section 4942 shall—

(i) Not apply to an organization to the extent its income is required to be accumulated pursuant to the mandatory terms (as in effect on May 26, 1969, and at all times thereafter) of an instrument executed before May 27, 1969, with respect to the transfer of income producing property to such organization, except that section 4942 shall apply to such organization if the organization would have been denied exemption had section 504(a) not been repealed, or would have had its deductions under section 642(c) limited had section 681(c) not been repealed. In applying the preceding sentence, in addition to the limitations contained in section 504(a) or 681(c) before its repeal, section 504(a)(1) or 681(c)(1) shall be treated as not applying to an organization to the extent its income is required to be accumulated pursuant to the mandatory terms (as in effect on January 1, 1951, and at all times thereafter) of an instrument executed before January 1, 1951, with respect to the transfer of income producing property to such organization before such date, if such transfer was irrevocable on such date; and

(ii) Not apply to an organization which is prohibited by its governing instrument or other instrument from distributing capital or corpus to the extent the requirements of section 4942 are inconsistent with such prohibition.

(2) *Certain existing organizations.*—For purposes of this section, an organization will be deemed to be organized prior to May 27, 1969, if it is either a testamentary trust created under the will of an individual who died prior to such date or an inter vivos trust which was in existence and irrevocable prior to such date, even though it is not funded until after May 26, 1969. Similarly, a split-interest trust, as described in section 4947(a)(2) (without regard to section 4947(a)(2)(C)), which became irrevocable prior to May 27, 1969, and which is treated as a private foundation under section 4947(a)(1) subsequent to such date, likewise shall be treated as an organization organized prior to such date. See section 507(b)(2) and the regulations thereunder with respect to the applicability of transitional rules where there has been a merger of two or more private foundations or a reorganization of a private foundation.

(3) *Limitation.*—With respect to taxable years beginning after December 31, 1971, subparagraph (1)(i) and (ii) of this paragraph shall apply only for taxable years during which there is pending any judicial proceeding by the private foundation which is necessary to reform, or to excuse such foundation from compliance with, its governing instrument or any other instrument (as in effect on May 26, 1969) in order to comply with the provisions of section 4942, and in the case of subparagraph (1)(i) of this paragraph for all taxable years following the taxable year in which such judicial proceeding is terminated during which the governing instrument or any other instrument does not permit compliance with such provisions. Thus, the exception described in subparagraph (1)(ii) of this paragraph applies after 1971 only for taxable years during which such judicial proceeding is pending. Accordingly, beginning with the first taxable year following the taxable year in which such judicial proceeding is terminated, such foundation will be required to meet the requirements of section 4942 and the regulations thereunder (and be subject to the taxes provided upon failure to do so) except to the extent such foundation is required to accumulate income as described in subparagraph (1)(i) of this paragraph, even if the governing instrument continues to prohibit invasion of capital or corpus. In any case where a foundation's governing instrument or any other instrument requires accumulation of income as described in subparagraph (1)(i) of this paragraph beginning with the first taxable year following the taxable year in which such judicial proceeding is terminated, the distributable amount (as defined in paragraph (b) of this section) for such foundation shall be reduced by the amount of the income required to be accumu-

lated. Therefore, if the foundation's adjusted net income for any taxable year equals or exceeds its minimum investment return for such year, the accumulation provision will be given full effect. However, if the minimum investment return exceeds the adjusted net income for any taxable year, the foundation will be required to distribute such excess for such year. For purposes of this paragraph, a judicial proceeding will be treated as pending only if the foundation is diligently pursuing its judicial remedies and there is no unreasonable delay in such proceeding for which the private foundation is responsible.

(4) *Examples.*—The provisions of this paragraph may be illustrated by the following examples:

Example (1). X, a private foundation organized in 1930, is required by the mandatory terms of its governing instrument to accumulate 25 percent of its adjusted net income and to add such accumulations to corpus. The instrument also prohibits distribution of corpus for any purpose. On July 13, 1971, X instituted an action in the appropriate State court to reform the instrument by deleting the accumulation and corpus provisions described above. If the court's final order reforms the accumulation provision to allow distributions of income sufficient to avoid the imposition of a tax under section 4942, then section 4942 applies to X, regardless of the court's action with respect to the corpus provision. However, if the court rules that the accumulation provision may not be reformed, section 4942 applies to X only to the extent provided for in subparagraph (3) of this paragraph, regardless of the court's action with respect to the corpus provision.

Example (2). Private foundation Y was created by the will of A who died in 1940. Y's governing instrument requires that 40 percent of Y's adjusted net income be added to corpus each year. In an action commenced prior to December 31, 1971, a court of competent jurisdiction ruled that this accumulation provision must be complied with. In Y's succeeding taxable year its adjusted net income is $120,000, and its minimum investment return is $140,000. Thus, Y is required to accumulate $48,000 (40 percent of $120,000) and shall be allowed to do so. Therefore, Y's distributable amount for such taxable year shall be the greater of its adjusted net income ($120,000) or its minimum investment return ($140,000), reduced by the amount of the income required to be accumulated ($48,000) and the taxes imposed by subtitle A of the Code and section 4940 and increased by any trust distributions described in paragraph (b)(2) of this section. Accordingly, Y's distributable amount for such taxable year is $92,000 ($140,000 reduced by $48,000), before other adjustments. If Y's minimum investment return had been $120,000 instead of $140,000, its distributable amount for such taxable year would have been $72,000 ($120,000 reduced by $48,000), before other adjustments. Similarly, if Y's minimum investment return had been $100,000 instead of $140,000, its distributable amount for such taxable year would also have been $72,000, before other adjustments. [Reg. § 53.4942(a)-2.]

☐ [*T.D. 7256, 2-2-73. Amended by T.D. 7486, 5-12-77, T.D. 7594, 2-5-79, T.D. 7610, 4-10-79, T.D. 7715, 8-25-80, T.D. 7849, 11-9-82 and T.D. 7878, 3-21-83.*]

[Reg. § 53.4942(a)-3]

§ 53.4942(a)-3. Qualifying distributions defined.—(a) *In general.*—(1) *Distributions generally.*—For purposes of section 4942 and the regulations thereunder, the amount of a qualifying distribution of property (as defined in subparagraph(2) of this paragraph) is the fair market value of such property as of the date such qualifying distribution is made. The amount of an organization's qualifying distributions will be determined solely on the cash receipts and disbursements method of accounting described in section 466(c)(1).

(2) *Definition.*—The term "qualifying distribution" means:

(i) Any amount (including program related investments, as defined in section 4944(c), and reasonable and necessary administrative expenses) paid to accomplish one or more purposes described in section 170(c)(1) or (2)(B), other than any contribution to:

(*a*) A private foundation which is not an operating foundation (as defined in section 4942(j)(3)), except as provided in paragraph (c) of this section;

(*b*) An organization controlled (directly or indirectly) by the contributing private foundation or one or more disqualified persons with respect to such foundation, except as provided in paragraph (c) of this section; or

(*c*) An organization described in section 4942(g)(4)(A)(i) or (ii), if paid by a private foundation that is not an operating foundation;

(ii) Any amount paid to acquire an asset used (or held for use) directly in carrying out one or more purposes described in section 170(c)(1) or (2)(B). See paragraph (c)(3) of § 53.4942(a)-2 for the definition of "used (or held for use)"; or

(iii) Any amount set aside within the meaning of paragraph (b) of this section.

(3) *Control.*—For purposes of subparagraph (2)(i)(*b*) of this paragraph, an organization is "controlled" by a foundation or one or more disqualified persons with respect to the foundation if any of such persons may, by aggregating their votes or positions of authority, require the donee organization to make an expenditure, or prevent the donee organization from making an expenditure, regardless of the method by which the control is exercised or exercisable. "Control" of a donee organization is determined without regard to any conditions imposed upon the donee as part of the distribution or any other restrictions accompanying the distribution as to the manner in which the distribution is to be used, unless such conditions or restrictions are described in paragraph (a)(8) of § 1.507-2 of this chapter (Income Tax Regulations). In general, it is the donee, not the distribution, which must be "controlled" by the distributing private foundation for the provisions of subparagraph (2)(i)(*b*) of this paragraph to apply. Thus, the furnishing of support to an organization and the consequent imposition of budgetary procedures upon that organization with respect to such support shall not in itself be treated as subjecting that organization to the distributing foundation's control within the meaning of this subparagraph. Such "budgetary procedures" include expenditure responsibility requirements under section 4945(d)(4). The "controlled" organization need not be a private foundation; it may be any type of exempt or nonexempt organization including a school, hospital, operating foundation, or social welfare organization.

(4) *Borrowed funds.*—(i) *In general.*—For purposes of this paragraph, if a private foundation borrows money in a particular taxable year to make expenditures for a specific charitable, educational, or other similar purpose, a qualifying distribution out of such borrowed funds will, except as otherwise provided in subdivision (ii) of this subparagraph, be deemed to have been made only at the time that such borrowed funds are actually distributed for such exempt purpose.

(ii) *Funds borrowed before 1970.*—(*a*) If a private foundation has borrowed money in a taxable year beginning before January 1, 1970, or subsequently borrows money pursuant to a written commitment which was binding as of the last day of such taxable year, to make expenditures for a specific charitable, educational, or other similar exempt purpose, if such borrowed funds are in fact expended for such purpose in any taxable year, and if such loan is thereafter repaid, in whole or in part, in a taxable year beginning after December 31, 1969, then, at the election of the foundation as provided in subdivision (ii) (*b*) of this subparagraph, a qualifying distribution will be deemed to have been made at such time or times that such loan principal is so repaid rather than at the earlier time that the borrowed funds were actually distributed for such exempt purpose.

(*b*) The election described in subdivision (ii)(*a*) of this subparagraph is to be made by attaching a statement to the form the private foundation is required to file under section 6033 for the first taxable year beginning after December 31, 1969 in which a repayment of loan principal is made. Such statement shall be made a part of such form and shall be attached to such form in each succeeding taxable year in which any repayment of loan principal is made. The statement shall set forth the name and address of the lender, the amount borrowed, the specific use made of such borrowed funds, and the private foundation's election to treat repayments of loan principal as qualifying distributions.

(iii) *Interest.*—Any payment of interest with respect to a loan described in subdivision (i) or (ii) of this subparagraph shall be treated as a deduction under paragraph (d)(1)(ii) of § 53.4942(a)-2 in the taxable year in which it is made.

(5) *Changes in use of an asset.*—If an asset not used (or held for use) directly in carrying out one or more purposes described in section 170(c)(1) or (2)(B) is subsequently converted to such a use, the foundation may treat such conversion as a qualifying distribution. The amount of such qualifying distribution shall be the fair market value of the converted asset as of the date of its conversion. For purposes of the preceding sentence, fair market value shall be determined by making a valuation of the converted asset as of the date of its conversion in accordance with the rules set forth in paragraph (c)(4) of § 53.4942(a)-2.

(6) *Certain foreign organizations.*—(i) *In general.*—A distribution for purposes described in section 170(c)(2)(B) to a foreign organization, which has not received a ruling or determination letter that it is an organization described in section 509(a)(1), (a)(2), or (a)(3) or in section 4942(j)(3), will be treated as a distribution made to an organization described in section 509(a)(1), (a)(2), or (a)(3) (other than an organization described in section 4942(g)(4)(A)(i) or (ii)) or in section 4942(j)(3) if the distributing foundation has made a good faith determination that the donee organization is an organization described in section 509(a)(1), (a)(2), or (a)(3) (other than an organization described in section 4942(g)(4)(A)(i) or (ii)) or in section 4942(j)(3). A determination ordinarily will be considered a good faith determination if the determination is based on current written advice received from a qualified tax practitioner concluding that the donee is an organization described in section 509(a)(1), (a)(2), or (a)(3) (other than an organization described in section 4942(g)(4)(A)(i) or (ii)) or in section 4942(j)(3), and if the foundation reasonably relied in good faith on the written advice in accordance with the requirements of § 1.6664-4(c)(1) of this chapter. The written advice must set forth sufficient facts concerning the operations and support of the donee organization for the Internal Revenue Service to determine that the donee organization would be likely to qualify as an organization described in section 509(a)(1), (a)(2), or (a)(3) (other than an organization described in section 4942(g)(4)(A)(i) or (ii)) or in section 4942(j)(3) as of the date of the written advice. For purposes of this section, except as provided in the next sentence, written advice will be considered current if, as of the date of distribution, the relevant law on which the advice is based has not changed since the date of the written advice and the factual information on which the advice is based is from the donee's current or prior taxable year (or annual accounting period if the donee does not have a taxable year for United States federal tax purposes). Written advice that a donee met the public support test under section 170(b)(1)(A)(vi) or section 509(a)(2) for a test period of five years will be treated as current for purposes of distributions to the donee during the two taxable years (or, as applicable, annual accounting periods) of the donee immediately following the end of the five-year test period.

(ii) *Definitions.*—For purposes of this paragraph (a)(6)—

(a) The term "foreign organization" means any organization that is not described in section 170(c)(2)(A).

(b) The term "qualified tax practitioner" means an attorney, a certified public accountant, or an enrolled agent, within the meaning of 31 CFR 10.2 and 10.3, who is subject to the requirements in 31 CFR part 10.

(7) *Payment of tax.*—The payment of any tax imposed under chapter 42 of the Code shall not be treated as a qualifying distribution.

(8) *Examples.*—The provisions of this paragraph may be illustrated by the following examples:

Example (1). M, a private foundation which uses the calendar year as the taxable year, makes the following payments in 1970: (i) a payment of $44,000 to five employees for conducting a foundation program of educational grants for research and study; (ii) $20,000 for various items of overhead, 10 percent of which is attributable to the activities of the employees mentioned in payment (i) of this example and the other 90 percent of which is attributable to administrative expenses which were not paid to accomplish any section 170(c)(1) or (2)(B) purpose; and (iii) a $100,000 general purpose grant paid to an educational institution described in section 170(b)(1)(A)(ii) which is not controlled by M or any disqualified persons with respect to M. Payments (i) and (ii) of this example are qualifying distributions to the extent of $46,000 ($44,000 of salaries and 10 percent of the overhead, both of which are reasonable administrative expenses paid to accomplish section 170(c)(1) or (2)(B) purposes). Payment (iii) of this example is also a qualifying distribution, since it is a contribution for section 170(c)(2)(B) purposes to an organization which is not described in subparagraph (2)(i)(a) or (b) of this paragraph. The other 90 percent of payment (ii) of this example may constitute items of deduction under paragraph (d)(1)(ii) of § 53.4942(a)-2 if such items otherwise qualify under such paragraph.

Example (2). On February 21, 1972, N, a private foundation which uses the calendar year as the taxable year, pays $500,000 for real property on which it plans to build hospital facilities to be used for medical care and education. The real property produces no income and the hospital facilities will not be constructed until 1974 according to the set-aside plan submitted to and approved by the Commissioner pursuant to paragraph (b) of this section. The purchase of the land is a qualifying distribution under subparagraph (2)(ii) of this paragraph. If, however, the property were used to produce rental income for more than a reasonable period of time before construction of the hospital is begun, then as of the time such rental use becomes unreasonable (i) such purchase would no longer constitute a qualifying distribution under subparagraph (2)(ii) of this paragraph and (ii) the amount of the qualifying distribution would be included in N's gross income. See paragraphs (c)(3)(i) and (d)(2)(iii)(b) of §53.4942(a)-2.

Example (3). In 1971, X, a private foundation engaged in holding paintings and exhibiting them to the public, purchases an additional building to be used to exhibit the paintings. Such expenditure is a qualifying distribution under subparagraph (2)(ii) of this paragraph. In 1975, X sells the building. Under paragraph (d)(2)(iii)(b) of §53.4942(a)-2, all of the proceeds of the sale (less direct costs of the sale) are included in X's gross income for 1975.

Example (4). In January 1969, M, a private foundation which uses the calendar year as the taxable year, borrows $10 million to give to N, a private college, for the construction of a science center. M borrowed the money from X, a commercial bank. M is to repay X at the rate of $1.1 million per year ($1 million principal plus $0.1 million interest) for 10 years beginning in January, 1973. M distributed $5 million of the borrowed funds to N in February 1969, and the other $5 million in March 1970. M files a statement with the form it is required to file under section 6033 for 1973 which contains the information required by subparagraph (4)(ii)(b) of this paragraph. Pursuant to M's election, each repayment of loan principal constitutes a qualifying distribution in the year of repayment. Accordingly, the distribution of $5 million to N in March 1970 will not be treated as a qualifying distribution. Each payment of interest ($0.1 million annually) with respect to M's loan from X is treated as a deduction under paragraph (d)(1)(ii) of §53.4942(a)-2 in the taxable year in which it is made.

Example (5). Private foundation Y engages in providing care for the aged. Y makes a distribution of cash to H, a hospital described in section 170(b)(1)(A)(iii) which is not controlled by Y or any disqualified person with respect to Y. The distribution is made subject to the conditions that H will invest the money as a separate fund which will bear a name commemorating the creator of Y and will use the income from such fund only for H's exempt hospital purposes which relate to care for the aged. Under these circumstances, the distribution from Y to H is a qualifying distribution pursuant to subparagraph (2)(i) of this paragraph.

(b) *Certain set-asides.*—(1) *In general.*—An amount set aside for a specific project that is for one or more of the purposes described in section 170(c)(1) or (2)(B) may be treated as a qualifying distribution in the year in which set aside (but not in the year in which actually paid), if the requirements of section 4942(g)(2) and this paragraph (b) are satisfied. The requirements of this

paragraph (b) are satisfied if the private foundation establishes to the satisfaction of the Commissioner that the amount set aside will be paid for the specific project within 60 months after it is set aside, and

(i) The set-aside satisfies the suitability test described in subparagraph (2) of this paragraph, or

(ii) With respect to a set-aside made in a taxable year beginning after December 31, 1974, the private foundation satisfies the cash distribution test described in subparagraph (3) of this paragraph.

If the suitability test or cash distribution test is otherwise satisfied, the 60 month period for paying the amount set aside may, for good cause shown, be extended by the Commissioner.

(2) *Suitability test.*—The suitability test is satisfied if the private foundation establishes to the satisfaction of the Commissioner that the specific project for which the amount is set aside is one that can be better accomplished by the set-aside than by the immediate payment of funds. Specific projects than can be better accomplished by the use of a set-aside include, but are not limited to, projects in which relatively long-term grants or expenditures must be made in order to assure the continuity of particular charitable projects or program-related investments (as defined in section 4944(c)) or where grants are made as part of a matching-grant program. Such projects include, for example, a plan to erect a building to house the direct charitable, educational, or other similar exempt activity of the private foundation (such as a museum building in which paintings are to be hung), even though the exact location and architectural plans have not been finalized; a plan to purchase an additional group of paintings offered for sale only as a unit that requires an expenditure of more than one year's income; or a plan to fund a specific research program that is of such magnitude as to require an accumulation of funds before beginning the research, even though not all of the details of the program have been finalized.

(3) *Cash distribution test; in general.*—The cash distribution test is satisfied if—

(i) The specific project for which the amount is set aside will not be completed before the end of the taxable year in which the set-aside is made,

(ii) The private foundation actually distributes, in cash or its equivalent and for one or more of the purposes described in section 170(c)(1) or (2)(B), the "start-up period minimum amount" described in subparagraph (4) of this paragraph during the private foundation's start-up period, and

(iii) The private foundation actually distributes, in cash or its equivalent and for one or more of the purposes described in section 170(c)(1) or (2)(B), the "full-payment period minimum amount" described in subparagraph (5) of this paragraph in each taxable year of the private foundation's full-payment period.

For purposes of the cash distribution test, an amount set aside will be treated as distributed in the year in which actually paid and not in the year in which set aside.

(4) *Minimum distribution required during start-up period.*—(i) *Start-up period.*—For private foundations created before January 1, 1972, the start-up period is the four taxable years immediately preceding the taxable year beginning in calendar year 1976. For private foundations created after December 31, 1971 (or for organizations that first become private foundations after that date), the start-up period is the four taxable years following the taxable year in which the private foundation was created (or otherwise became a private foundation). For purposes of this subparagraph (4), a private foundation will be considered "created" in the taxable year in which the private foundation's distributable amount (as determined under section 4942(d)) first exceeds $500.

(ii) *Start-up period minimum amount.*—The amount that a private foundation must actually distribute in cash or its equivalent during the private foundation's start-up period is not less than the sum of—

(a) Twenty percent of the private foundation's distributable amount (as determined under section 4942(d)) for the first taxable year of the start-up period,

(b) Forty percent of the private foundation's distributable amount for the second taxable year of the start-up period,

(c) Sixty percent of the private foundation's distributable amount for the third taxable year of the start-up period, and

(d) Eighty percent of the private foundation's distributable amount for the fourth taxable year of the start-up period.

(iii) *Timing of distributions.*—The requirement that a private foundation distribute the start-up period minimum amount during the start-up period is a requirement that such amount be distributed before the end of the start-up period, and is not a requirement that any portion of such amount be distributed in any one taxable year of the start-up period.

(iv) *Distribution actually made during start-up period.*—In general, only a distribution actually made during the start-up period is taken into account in determining whether a private foundation has distributed the start-up period minimum amount. However, in the case of a private foundation created after December 31, 1971 (or an organization that first became a private foundation after that date), a distribution actually made during the taxable year in which the foundation was created (the year immediately preceding the first taxable year of the private foundation's start-up period) may be treated as a distribution actually made during the start-up period. In addition, a distribution actually made by a private foundation within $5^1/2$ months after the end of the start-up period

will be treated as a distribution actually made during the start-up period if—

(a) The private foundation was unable to determine the distributable amount for the fourth taxable year of the start-up period until after the end of such period, and

(b) The private foundation actually made distributions prior to the end of the start-up period based upon a reasonable estimate of the private foundation's distributable amount for the fourth taxable year of the start-up period.

(v) *Examples.*—The provisions of this subparagraph (4) may be illustrated by the following examples:

Example (1). F, a private foundation created on January 1, 1975, uses the calendar year as its taxable year. The start-up period for F is January 1, 1976 through December 31, 1979. F has distributable amounts under section 4942(d) for taxable years 1976 through 1979 in the following amounts: 1976, $100,000; 1977, $120,000; 1978, $150,000; 1979, $200,000. F's start-up period minimum amount is the sum of the following amounts: 20% of $100,000 ($20,000); 40% of $120,000 ($48,000); 60% of $150,000 ($90,000); and 80% of $200,000 ($160,000); which equals $318,000. Thus F is required to actually distribute at least $318,000 in cash or its equivalent during the start-up period.

Example (2). F, a private foundation created in 1969, uses the calendar year as its taxable year. F's start-up period is the calendar years 1972 through 1975. F makes two cash distributions in 1972. The first distribution is made on account of a set-aside made in 1969. Under section 4942(g), that distribution is treated as a qualifying distribution made in 1969. The second distribution is treated under section 4942(h) as made out of F's undistributed income for 1971. In addition, F makes a cash distribution in 1976 that is treated under section 4942(h) as made out of F's undistributed income for 1975. In determining whether F has distributed its start-up period minimum amount within the start-up period, the 1972 distributions are both taken into account because they were actually made during F's start-up period. The 1976 distribution is not taken into account, however, because that distribution was not actually made during F's start-up period.

(5) *Minimum distribution required during full-payment period.*—(i) *Full-payment period.*—A private foundation's full-payment period includes each taxable year that begins after the end of the private foundation's start-up period.

(ii) *Full-payment period minimum amount.*—The amount that a private foundation must actually distribute in cash or its equivalent in a taxable year of the private foundation's full-payment period is not less than 100 percent of the private foundation's distributable amount determined under section 4942(d) (without regard to section 4942(i)) with respect to the taxable year.

Reg. §53.4942(a)-3(b)(4)

(iii) *Carryover of distributions in excess of full-payment period minimum amount.*—If, in a taxable year beginning after December 31, 1975, a private foundation distributes an amount in excess of the full-payment period minimum amount for the taxable year, the excess shall be used to reduce the full-payment period minimum amount in the taxable years in the adjustment period. The amount of the excess distribution used to reduce the full-payment period minimum amount in each successive taxable year of the adjustment period shall be equal to the amount of such excess less the sum of the full-payment period minimum amounts for all prior taxable years in the adjustment period to which the excess was previously applied. The taxable years in the adjustment period are the five taxable years immediately following the taxable year in which the excess distribution is made. Any distribution in excess of the full-payment period minimum amount made during a taxable year of the adjustment period shall not be taken into account under this subparagraph (iii) until any earlier excess has been completely applied against full-payment period minimum amounts during its adjustment period.

(iv) *Distributions actually made during a taxable year.*—Except as described in subdivision (ii) of subparagraph (6), only a distribution actually made during a taxable year of the full-payment period is taken into account in determining whether a private foundation has distributed the full-payment period minimum amount for such year.

(v) *Examples.*—The provisions of this subparagraph (5) may be illustrated by the following examples:

Example (1). F, a private foundation created on January 1, 1973, uses the calendar year as its taxable year. F has a start-up period of January 1, 1974, through December 31, 1977, and a full-payment period that includes every taxable year beginning after December 31, 1977. F's distributable amount (as determined under section 4942(d)) for 1978 is $500,000. Thus, F's full-payment period minimum amount for 1978 is $500,000. During 1978 F distributes $100,000 in cash to Charity X and $400,000 in cash to Charity Y on account of a set-aside made in 1973. F has distributed its full-payment period minimum amount for 1978 because it has made actual cash distributions during that year which total $500,000. However, F has made qualifying distributions (as determined under section 4942(g)) with respect to 1978 of only $100,000. In order to avoid liability for the tax on undistributed income under section 4942(a), F must distribute or set aside an additional $400,000 before January 1, 1980.

Example (2). Assume the facts as stated in Example (1) except that in 1978 F makes cash distributions totaling $600,000. Since the total cash distributions made in 1978 ($600,000) exceed the full-payment period minimum amount for 1978 ($500,000), there exists a $100,000 excess which must be used by F to reduce its full-

payment period minimum amounts for the years 1979-1983 (the taxable years in the adjustment period with respect to the 1978 excess). Therefore, if F's distributable amount (as determined under section 4942(d)) for 1979 is $500,000, F's full-payment period minimum amount for 1979 is $400,000 ($500,000 − $100,000).

(6) *Failure to distribute minimum amounts.*—(i) *In general.*—If a private foundation fails to actually distribute the start-up period minimum amount during the start-up period or, except as described in subdivision (ii) of this subparagraph (6), if a private foundation fails to actually distribute the full-payment period minimum amount during a taxable year of the full-payment period, then any set-aside made by the private foundation during the start-up period (if the failure relates to the start-up period) or during the taxable year (if the failure relates to the full-payment period) that was not approved by the Commissioner under the suitability test described in subparagraph (2) of this paragraph will not be treated as a qualifying distribution. Further, any set-aside made after the year of such a failure to so distribute a minimum amount will be treated as a qualifying distribution only if the Commissioner approves the set-aside under the suitability test. In any case in which a set-aside ceases to be treated as a qualifying distribution as a result of a failure to distribute the full-payment period minimum amount, a private foundation may be assessed a deficiency under section 4942(a) within the period described in section 6501(n)(3).

(ii) *Correction of certain failures to distribute.*—If a private foundation's failure to distribute the full-payment period minimum amount during a taxable year of the full-payment period was not willful and was due to reasonable cause, the private foundation may correct the failure to so distribute. Correction will be achieved if the private foundation distributes within the correction period cash or its equivalent in an amount not less than the difference between the full-payment period minimum amount for the taxable year and the amount actually distributed during the taxable year. The correction period is the correction period as defined in section 4962(e), determined with respect to the earliest occurring taxable event (as defined in section 4962(e)(2)(A)) that would result if the failure to distribute a full-payment period minimum amount were not corrected. The additional distribution will be treated for purposes of subparagraph (5) of this paragraph as made during the taxable year with respect to which the failure occurred. If a private foundation fails to distribute the full-payment period minimum amount during a taxable year of the full-payment period because such amount can be determined only after the end of the taxable year, no "willful failure to distribute" the full-payment period minimum amount will occur if the private foundation makes an additional distribution within 5¹/₂ months after the end of the taxable year.

(7) *Approval and information requirements.*— (i) *Suitability test.*—If an amount is set aside under the suitability test of section 4942(g)(2)(B)(i) and subparagraph (2) of this paragraph, the private foundation must apply for the Commissioner's approval of the set-aside before the end of the taxable year in which the amount is set aside. The Commissioner will either approve or disapprove the set-aside in writing. An otherwise proper set-aside will not be treated as a qualifying distribution under this paragraph (b) with respect to a taxable year if the Commissioner's approval is not sought before the end of the taxable year in which the amount is actually set aside. To obtain approval by the Commissioner for a set-aside under the suitability test, the private foundation must write to Commissioner of Internal Revenue, Attention: OP:E:EO:T, 1111 Constitution Avenue, N.W., Washington, D.C. 20224, and include—

(a) A statement describing the nature and purposes of the specific project and the amount of the set-aside for which approval is requested;

(b) A statement describing the amounts and approximate dates of any planned additions to the set-aside after its initial establishment;

(c) A statement of the reasons why the project can be better accomplished by a set-aside than by the immediate payment of funds;

(d) A detailed description of the project, including estimated costs, sources of any future funds expected to be used for completion of the project, and the location or locations (general or specific) of any physical facilities to be acquired or constructed as part of the project; and

(e) A statement by an appropriate foundation manager (as defined in section 4946(b)) that the amounts to be set aside will actually be paid for the specific project within a specified period of time that ends not more than 60 months after the date of the first set-aside, or a statement showing good cause why the period for paying the amount set aside should be extended (including a showing that the proposed project could not be divided into two or more projects covering periods of no more than 60 months each) and setting forth the extension of time required.

(ii) *Cash distribution test.*—If an amount is set aside under the cash distribution test of section 4942(g)(2)(B)(ii) and subparagraphs (3), (4), and (5) of this paragraph, then for taxable years ending after April 2, 1984, the private foundation must submit an attachment with the return required by section 6033 for the taxable year in which the amount is set aside and for certain subsequent taxable years. For the taxable year in which the amount is set aside the attachment must include—

(a) A statement describing the nature and purposes of the specific project for which amounts are to be set aside;

(b) A statement that the amounts set aside for the specific project will actually be paid

for the specific project within a specified period of time that ends not more than 60 months after the date of the set-aside;

(c) A statement that the project will not be completed before the end of the taxable year of the private foundation in which the set-aside is made;

(d) A statement showing the distributable amounts determined under section 4942(d) for any past taxable years in the private foundation's start-up and full-payment periods; and

(e) A statement showing the aggregate amount of actual payments made in cash or its equivalent, for purposes described in section 170(c)(1) or (2)(B), during each taxable year in the private foundation's start-up and full-payment periods. This statement should include a detailed description of any payments that are to be treated, pursuant to the rules of subparagraphs (4)(iv) and (6)(ii) of this paragraph (b), as distributed during a taxable year prior to the taxable year in which such payments were actually made and, in addition, should explain the circumstances that justify the application of those rules.

For the five taxable years following the taxable year in which the amount is set aside (or, if longer, for each taxable year in the extended period for paying the amount set aside), the attachment must include the statements required by (d) and (e) of this subdivision (ii). The submission of the statement required by (b) of this subdivision (ii) will satisfy the requirement of section 4942(g)(2)(B) and subparagraph (1) of this paragraph (b) that the private foundation establish to the satisfaction of the Commissioner that the amount set aside will be paid for the specific project within 60 months after it is set aside.

(8) *Evidence of set-aside.*—A set-aside that is approved by the Commissioner or which satisfies the cash distribution test shall be evidenced by the entry of a dollar amount on the books and records of a private foundation as a pledge or obligation to be paid at a future date or dates. Any amount which is set aside shall be taken into account for purposes of determining the private foundation's minimum investment return under §53.4942(a)-2(c)(1), and any income attributable to such set-aside shall be taken into account in computing adjusted net income under §53.4942(a)-2(d).

(9) *Contingent set-aside.*—In the event a private foundation is involved in litigation and may not distribute assets or income because of a court order, the private foundation may (except as provided in §53.4942(a)-2(e)(1)(i) or (ii)) seek and obtain a set-aside for a purpose described in §53.4942(a)-3(a)(2). The amount to be set aside shall be equal to that portion of the private foundation's distributable amount which is attributable to the assets or income that are held pursuant to court order and which, but for the court order precluding the distribution of such assets or income, would have been distributed. In the event

that the litigation encompasses more than one taxable year, the private foundation may seek additional contingent set-asides. Such amounts must actually be distributed by the last day of the taxable year following the taxable year in which the litigation is terminated. Amounts not distributed by the close of the appropriate taxable year shall be treated as described in § 53.4942(a)-2(d)(2)(iii)(c) for the succeeding taxable year.

(c) *Certain contributions to section 501(c)(3) organizations.*—(1) *In general.*—For purposes of this section, the term "qualifying distribution" includes (in the year in which it is paid) a contribution to an exempt organization described in section 501(c)(3) and described in paragraph (a)(2)(i)(*a*) or (*b*) of this section if—

(i) Not later than the close of the first taxable year after the donee organization's taxable year in which such contribution is received, such donee organization makes a distribution equal to the full amount of such contribution and such distribution is a qualifying distribution (within the meaning of paragraph (a) of this section, without regard to this paragraph) which is treated under paragraph (d) of this section as a distribution out of corpus (or would be so treated if such section 501(c)(3) organization were a private foundation which is not an operating foundation); and

(ii) The private foundation making the contribution obtains adequate records or other sufficient evidence from such donee organization (such as a statement by an appropriate officer, director, or trustee of such donee organization) showing (except as otherwise provided in this subparagraph) (*a*) that the qualifying distribution described in subdivision (i) of this subparagraph has been made by such organization, (*b*) the name and addresses of the recipients of such distribution and the amount received by each, and (*c*) that the distribution is treated as a distribution out of corpus under graph (d) of this section (or would be so treated if the donee organization were a private foundation which is not an operating foundation).

Where a distribution is for an administrative expense which is part of a section 170(c)(1) or (2)(B) expenditure or is part of another section 170(c)(1) or (2)(B) expenditure that cannot reasonably be separately accounted for, the provisions of subdivision (ii) of this subparagraph may be satisfied by the submission by the donee organization of a statement setting forth the general purpose for which such expenditure was made and that the amount was distributed as a qualifying distribution described in subdivision (ii)(*c*) of this subparagraph.

(2) *Distribution requirements.*—(i) In order for a donee organization to meet the distribution requirements of subparagraph (1)(i) of this paragraph, it must, not later than the close of the first taxable year after its taxable year in which any contributions are received, distribute (within the meaning of this subparagraph) an amount equal in value to the contributions received in such

prior taxable year and have no remaining undistributed income for such prior taxable year. In the event that a donee organization redistributes less than an amount equal to the total contributions from donor organizations which are required to be redistributed by such donee organization by the close of the first taxable year following the taxable year in which such contributions were received, amounts treated as redistributions of such contributions shall be deemed to have been made pro rata out of all such contributions, regardless of any earmarking or identification made by such donee organization with respect to the source of such distributions. See paragraph (d)(2)(ix) of § 53.4942(a)-2 for the treatment of amounts deemed not to have so redistributed. For purposes of this paragraph, the term "contributions" means all contributions, whether of cash or property, and the fair market value of contributed property determined as of the date of the contribution must be used in determining whether an amount equal in value to the contributions received has been redistributed.

(ii) For purposes of this paragraph, the characterization of qualifying distributions made during the taxable year (i.e., whether out of the prior year's undistributed income, the current year's undistributed income, or corpus) is to be made as of the close of the taxable year in question, except to the extent that a different characterization is effected by means of the election provided for by paragraph (d)(2) of this section or by subdivision (iv) of this subparagraph. Once it is determined that a qualifying distribution is attributable to corpus, such distribution will first be charged to distributions which are required to be redistributed under this paragraph.

(iii) All amounts contributed to a specific exempt organization described in section 501(c)(3) and in paragraph (a)(2)(i)(*a*) or (*b*) of this section within any one taxable year of such organization shall be treated (with respect to the contributing private foundation) as one "contribution". If subparagraph (1)(i) or (ii) of this paragraph is not completely satisfied with respect to such contribution within the meaning of such subparagraph, only that portion of such contribution which was redistributed (within the meaning of subparagraph (1)(i) and (ii) of this paragraph) shall be treated as a qualifying distribution.

(iv) In order to satisfy distribution requirements under section 170(b)(1)(E)(ii) or this paragraph, a donee organization may elect to treat as a current distribution out of corpus any amount distributed in a prior taxable year which was treated as a distribution out of corpus under paragraph (d)(1)(iii) of this section provided that (*a*) such amount has not been availed of for any other purpose, such as a carryover under paragraph (e) of this section or a redistribution under this paragraph for a prior year, (*b*) such corpus distribution occurred within the preceding 5 years, and (*c*) such amount is not later availed of for any other purpose. Such election must be made by attaching a statement to the return the foundation is required to file under section 6033 with respect to the taxable year for which such election is to apply. Such statement must contain a declaration by an appropriate foundation manager (within the meaning of section 4946(b)(1)) that the foundation is making an election under this subdivision and it must specify that the distribution was treated under paragraph (d)(1)(iii) of this section as a distribution out of corpus in a designated prior taxable year (or years).

(3) *Examples.*—The provisions of subparagraphs (1) and (2) of this paragraph may be illustrated by the following examples. It is assumed in these examples that all private foundations described use the calendar year as the taxable year.

Example (1). In 1972 M, a private foundation, makes a contribution out of 1971 income to X, another private foundation which is not an operating foundation. The contribution is the only one received by X in 1972. In 1973 X makes a qualifying distribution to an art museum maintained by an operating foundation in an amount equal to the amount of the contribution received from M. X also distributes all of its undistributed income for 1972 and 1973 for other purposes described in section 170(c)(2)(B). Under the provisions of paragraph (d) of this section, such distribution to the museum is treated as a distribution out of corpus. Thus, M's contribution to X is a qualifying distribution out of M's 1971 income provided M obtains adequate records or other sufficient evidence from X showing the nature and amount of the distribution made by X, the identity of the recipient, and the fact that the distribution is treated as made out of corpus. If X's qualifying distributions during 1973 had been equal only to M's contribution to X and X's undistributed income for 1972, X could have made an election under paragraph (d)(2) of this section to treat the amount distributed in excess of its 1972 undistributed income as a distribution out of corpus and in that manner satisfied the requirements of this paragraph.

Example (2). Assume the facts stated in example (1), except that X is a private college described in section 170(b)(1)(A)(ii) which is controlled by disqualified persons with respect to M and that the records which X furnishes to M show that the distribution would have been treated as made out of corpus if X were a private nonoperating foundation. Under these circumstances, result is the same as in example (1).

Example (3). Assume the facts stated in example (1), except that X makes a distribution to the museum equal only to one-half of the contribution from M, that the remainder of such contribution is added to X's funds and used to pay charitable administrative expenses, and that the records obtained by M from X are not sufficient to show the amounts distributed or the identities of the recipients of the distributions. The contribution by M to X will be a qualifying distribution only to the extent that M can obtain (i) other

sufficient evidence (such as statements from officers or employees of X or from the museum) showing the facts required by subparagraph (1)(ii)(*a*), (*b*), and (*c*) of this paragraph and (ii) a statement from X setting forth that the remainder of the contribution was used for charitable administrative expenses which constituted qualifying distributions described in paragraph (a)(2)(i) of this section.

Example (4). X and Y are private nonoperating foundations. A is an exempt organization which is not described in section 501(c)(3) but which supervises and conducts a program described in section 170(c)(2)(B). Y, but not X, controls A within the meaning of paragraph (a)(3) of this section. In 1972, X and Y each makes a grant to A of $100, specifically designated for use in the operation of A's section 170(c)(2)(B) program. X has made a qualifying distribution to A because the distribution is one described in paragraph (a)(2)(i) of this section. However, because A is controlled by Y, Y's grant of $100 to A does not constitute a qualifying distribution within the meaning of such paragraph (a)(2)(i). Furthermore, because A is not an exempt organization described in section 501(c)(3), Y's grant to A does not constitute a qualifying distribution by operation of the provisions of this paragraph.

Example (5). N, a private nonoperating foundation, had distributable amounts of $100 in 1970 and $125 in 1971. In 1970 N received total contributions of $540: $150 from Y, a public charity; $70 from Z, a private foundation; $140 from Q, a private foundation, subject to the requirement that N earmark the amount and distribute it before distributing Z's contribution; and, $180 from R, also a private foundation. However, R specifically instructed N that such contribution did not have to be redistributed because R already had made enough qualifying distributions to avoid all section 4942 taxes. N is not controlled by Y, Z, Q, or R, and N made no qualifying distributions in 1970. By the close of 1971, N had made qualifying distributions of $420, earmarking $140 as having been a distribution of Q's contribution, but had made no election under paragraph (d)(2) of this section to have any amount distributed which was in excess of N's 1970 undistributed income treated as distributed out of corpus. Therefore, the first $225 of qualifying distributions made in 1971 (the sum of $100 and $125, N's distributable amounts for 1970 and 1971, respectively) are treated as amounts described in paragraph (d)(1)(i) and (ii) of this section. Since Y's contribution is a contribution from a public charity and does not have to be "redistributed" and since R specifically instructed N that its contribution need not be "redistributed", the remaining $195 of qualifying distributions will be treated as distributed pro rata from Z's and Q's contributions, regardless of N's earmarking. Accordingly, of Z's original qualifying distribution of $70 only $65 ($195 multiplied by $70, Z's contribution, over $210, the total ($70 plus $140) of Z's and Q's contributions) will be treated as redistributed by N. Similarly, of Q's original qualifying distribution of

$140 only $130 ($195 multiplied by $140 over $210) will be treated as redistributed by N. Thus, Z's gross income for 1972 will be increased by $5 ($70 less the $65 actually redistributed), and Q's gross income for 1972 will be increased by $10 ($140 less the $130 actually redistributed).

(4) *Limitation.*—A contribution by a private foundation to a donee organization which the donee uses to make payments to another organization (the secondary donee) shall not be regarded as a contribution by the private foundation to the secondary donee if the distributing foundation does not earmark the use of the contribution for any named secondary donee and does not retain power to cause the selection of the secondary donee by the organization to which such foundation has made the contribution. For purposes of this subparagraph, a contribution described herein shall not be regarded as a contribution by the foundation to the secondary donee even though such foundation has reason to believe that certain organizations would derive benefits from such contribution so long as the original donee organization exercises control, in fact, over the selection process and actually makes the selection completely independently of such foundation.

(5) *Transitional rule.*—(i) For purposes of this paragraph, a contribution to a private foundation which is not an operating foundation and which is not controlled (directly or indirectly) by the distributing foundation or one or more disqualified persons with respect to the distributing foundation will be treated as a contribution to an operating foundation if—

(a) Such contribution is made pursuant to a written commitment which was binding on May 26, 1969, and at all times thereafter,

(b) Such contribution is made for one or more of the purposes described in section 170(c)(1) or (2)(B), and

(c) Such contribution is to be paid out to the donee private foundation on or before December 31, 1974.

(ii) For purposes of this subparagraph, a written commitment will be considered to have been binding prior to May 27, 1969, only if the amount and nature of the contribution and the name of the donee foundation were entered in the records of the distributing foundation, or were otherwise adequately evidenced, prior to May 27, 1969, or notice of the contribution was communicated in writing to such donee prior to May 27, 1969.

(d) *Treatment of qualifying distributions.*—(1) *In general.*—Except as provided in subparagraph (2) of this paragraph, any qualifying distribution

made during a taxable year shall be treated as made—

(i) First out of the undistributed income (as defined in paragraph (a) of §53.4942(a)-2) of the immediately preceding taxable year (if the private foundation was subject to the initial excise tax imposed by section 4942(a) for such preceding taxable year) to the extent thereof;

(ii) Second out of the undistributed income for the taxable year to the extent thereof; and

(iii) Then out of corpus.

(2) *Election.*—In the case of any qualifying distribution which (under subparagraph (1) of this paragraph) is not treated as made out of the undistributed income of the immediately preceding taxable year, the foundation may elect to treat any portion of such distribution as made out of the undistributed income of a designated prior taxable year or out of corpus. Such election must be made by filing a statement with the Commissioner during the taxable year in which such qualifying distribution is made or by attaching a statement to the return the foundation is required to file under section 6033 with respect to the taxable year in which such qualifying distribution was made. Such statement must contain a declaration by an appropriate foundation manager (within the meaning of section 4946(b)(1)) that the foundation is making an election under this subparagraph, and it must specify whether the distribution is made out of the undistributed income of a designated prior taxable year (or years) or is made out of corpus. In any case where the election described in this subparagraph is made during the taxable year in which the qualifying distribution is made, such election may be revoked in whole or in part by filing a statement with the Commissioner during such taxable year revoking such election in whole or in part or by attaching a statement to the return the foundation is required to file under section 6033 with respect to the taxable year in which the qualifying distribution was made revoking such election in whole or in part. Such statement must contain a declaration by an appropriate foundation manager (within the meaning of section 4946(b)(1)) that the foundation is revoking an election under this subparagraph in whole or in part, and it must specify the election or part thereof being revoked.

(3) *Examples.*—The provisions of this paragraph may be illustrated by the following examples:

Example (1). M, a private foundation which was created in 1968 and which uses the calendar year as the taxable year, has distributable amounts and qualifying distributions for 1970 through 1976 as follows:

Year	1970	1971	1972	1973	1974	1975	1976
Distributable amount	$100	$100	$100	$100	$100	$100	$100
Qualifying distribution	$0	$100	$250	$100	$100	$100	$100

In 1971 the qualifying distribution of $100 is treated under subparagraph (1)(i) of this paragraph as made out of the $100 of undistributed income for 1970. The qualifying distribution of $250 in 1972 is treated as made: (i) $100 out of the undistributed income for 1971 under subparagraph (1)(i) of this paragraph; (ii) $100 out of the undistributed income for 1972 under subparagraph (1)(ii) of this paragraph; and (iii) $50 out of corpus in 1972 under subparagraph (1)(iii) of this paragraph. The qualifying distribution of $100 in each of the years 1973 through 1976 is treated as made out of the undistributed income for each of those respective years under subparagraph (1)(ii) of this paragraph. See paragraph (e) of this section for rules relating to the carryover of qualifying distributions out of corpus.

Example (2). M, a private foundation which uses the calendar year as the taxable year, has undistributed income of $300 for 1981, $200 for 1982, and $400 for 1983. On January 14, 1983, M makes its first qualifying distribution in 1983 when it sets aside (within the meaning of paragraph (b) of this section) $700 for construction of a hospital. On February 24, 1983 a notice of deficiency with respect to the excise taxes imposed by section 4942(a) and (b) in regard to M's undistributed income for 1981 is mailed to M under section 6212(a). M notifies the Commissioner in writing on March 24, 1983, that it is making an election under subparagraph (2) of this paragraph to have its distribution of January 14th applied first against its undistributed income for 1982, next against its undistributed income for 1981, and last against its undistributed income for 1983. Thus, $200 of the $700 qualifying distribution is treated as made out of the undistributed income for 1982; $300, out of undistributed income for 1981; and $200 ($700 less the sum of $200 and $300), out of the undistributed income for 1983. Thus, an initial excise tax of $45 (15 percent of $300) is imposed under section 4942 (a). Since M made the election described above, the $300 (treated as distributed out of undistributed income for 1981) corrects (within the meaning of section 4963(d)(2)) the taxable act because the undistributed income for 1981 is reduced to zero. Furthermore, correction is effected within the correction period (as defined in section 4963(e)(1) and §53.4963-1(e)). Therefore, under the provisions of section 4961(a), the additional tax imposed by section 4942(b) will not be assessed.

(e) *Carryover of excess qualifying distributions.*— (1) *In general.*—If in any taxable year for which an organization is subject to the initial excise tax imposed by section 4942(a) there is created an excess of qualifying distributions (as determined under subparagraph (2) of this paragraph), such excess may be used to reduce distributable amounts in any taxable year of the adjustment period (as defined [in] subparagraph (3) of this paragraph). For purposes of section 4942, includ-

ing paragraph (d) of this section, the distributable amount for a taxable year in the adjustment period shall be reduced to the extent of the lesser of (i) the excess of qualifying distributions made in prior taxable years to which such adjustment period applies or (ii) the remaining undistributed income at the close of such taxable year after applying any qualifying distributions made in such taxable year to the distributable amount for such taxable year (determined without regard to this paragraph). If during any taxable year of the adjustment period there is created another excess of qualifying distributions, such excess shall not be taken into account until any earlier excess of qualifying distributions has been completely applied against distributable amounts during its adjustment period.

(2) *Excess qualifying distributions.*—An excess of qualifying distributions is created for any taxable year beginning after December 31, 1969, if—

(i) The total qualifying distributions treated (under paragraph (d) of this section) as made out of the undistributed income for such taxable year or as made out of corpus with respect to such taxable year (other than amounts distributed by an organization in satisfaction of section 170(b)(1)(E)(ii) or paragraph (c) of this section, or applied to a prior taxable year by operation of the elections contained in paragraphs (c)(2)(iv) and (d)(2) of this section), exceeds

(ii) The distributable amount for such taxable year (determined without regard to this paragraph).

(3) *Adjustment period.*—For purposes of this paragraph, the taxable years in the adjustment period are the five taxable years immediately following the taxable year in which the excess of qualifying distributions is created. Thus, an excess (within the meaning of subparagraph (2) of this paragraph) for any one taxable year can not be carried over beyond the succeeding five taxable years. However, if during any taxable year in the adjustment period an organization ceases to be subject to the initial excise tax imposed by section 4942(a), any portion of the excess of qualifying distributions, which prior to such taxable year has not been applied against distributable amounts, may not be carried over to such taxable year or subsequent taxable years in the adjustment period, even if during any of such taxable years the organization again becomes subject to the initial excise tax imposed by section 4942(a).

(4) *Examples.*—The provisions of this paragraph may be illustrated by the following examples:

Example (1). (i) F, a private foundation which was created in 1967 and which uses the calendar year as the taxable year, has distributable amounts and qualifying distributions for 1970 through 1976 as follows:

Year	1970	1971	1972	1973	1974	1975	1976
Distributable amount	$100	$100	$100	$100	$100	$100	$100
Qualifying distribution	$0	$250	$70	$140	$60	$75	$105

(ii) The qualifying distributions made in 1971 will be treated under paragraph (d) of this section as $100 made out of the undistributed income for 1970, then as $100 made out of the undistributed income for 1971, and finally as $50 out of corpus in 1971. Since the total qualifying distributions for 1971 ($150) exceed the distributable amount for 1971 ($100), there exists a $50 excess of qualifying distributions which F may use to reduce its distributable amounts for the years 1972 through 1976 (the taxable years in the adjustment period with respect to the 1971 excess). Therefore, the $100 distributable amount for 1972 is reduced by $30 (the lesser of the 1971 excess ($50) and the remaining undistributed income at the close of 1972 ($30), after the qualifying distributions of $70 for 1972 were applied to the original distributable amount for 1972 of $100). Since the distributable amount for 1972 was reduced to $70, there is no remaining undistributed income for 1972. Accordingly, the qualifying distributions made in 1973 will be treated as $100 made out of the undistributed income for 1973 and as $40 out of corpus in 1973. Since this amount ($140) exceeds the distributable amount for 1973 ($100), there exists a $40 excess which F may use to reduce its distributable amounts for the years 1974 through 1978 (the taxable years in the adjustment period with respect to the 1973 excess). However, in accordance with subparagraph (1) of this paragraph such excess may not be used to reduce F's distributable amounts for the years 1974 through 1976 until the excess created in 1971 has been completely applied against distributable amounts during such years. The distributable amount for 1974 is reduced by $40 (the lesser of the unused portion of the 1971 excess ($20) plus the 1973 excess ($40) and the remaining undistributed income at the close of 1974 ($40), after the qualifying distributions of $60 for 1974 were applied to the original distributable amount for 1974 of $100). The distributable amount for 1975 is reduced by $20 (the lesser of the unused portion of the 1973 excess of qualifying distributions ($20) and the remaining undistributed income at the close of 1975 ($25), after the qualifying distributions of $75 for 1975 were applied to the original distributable amount for 1975 of $100). Consequently, qualifying distributions made in 1976 will be treated as made first out of the $5 of remaining undistributed income for 1975 and then as $100 made out of the undistributed income for 1976.

Example (2). Assume the facts as stated in example (1), except that in 1974 F receives a contribution of $300 from G, a private foundation which controls F (within the meaning of paragraph (a)(3) of this section), and F distributes such contribution in 1975 in satisfaction of paragraph (c) of this section. Under these circumstances, there would be no excess of qualifying distributions for 1975 with respect to such distribution, since such distribution is excluded from the computation of an excess of qualifying distributions by operation of subparagraph (2)(i) of this paragraph.

Example (3). Assume the facts as stated in example (1), except that in 1972 F is treated as an operating foundation (as such term is defined in section 4942(j)(3)). In accordance with subparagraph (3) of this paragraph since F is not subject to the initial excise tax imposed by section 4942(a) for 1972, the 1971 excess can not be carried forward to 1972 or any subsequent year in the adjustment period with respect to the 1971 excess, even if F is subsequently treated as a private nonoperating foundation for any year during the period 1973 through 1976.

(f) *Effective/applicability date and transition relief.*—Paragraphs (a)(2)(i) and (a)(6) of this section are effective on and apply with respect to distributions made after September 25, 2015. However, foundations may continue to rely on the provisions of paragraph (a)(6) of this section as contained in 26 CFR part 53, revised April 1, 2015, with respect to distributions made on or before December 24, 2015 pursuant to a good faith determination made in accordance with such provisions. Also, foundations may continue to rely on the provisions of paragraph (a)(6) of this section as contained in 26 CFR part 53, revised April 1, 2015, with respect to distributions pursuant to a written commitment made on or before September 25, 2015 and pursuant to a good faith determination made on or before such date in accordance with such provisions if the committed amount is distributed within five years of such date. [Reg. § 53.4942(a)-3.]

☐ [*T.D. 7256, 2-7-73. Amended by T.D. 7486, 5-12-77, T.D. 7849, 11-9-82, T.D. 7938, 1-30-84 T.D. 8084, 5-1-86 and T.D. 9740, 9-23-2015.*]

[Reg. § 53.4942(b)-1]

§ 53.4942(b)-1. Operating foundations.—(a) *Operating foundation defined.*—(1) *In general.*—For purposes of section 4942 and the regulations thereunder, the term "operating foundation" means any private foundation which, in addition to satisfying the assets test, the endowment test or the support test set forth in § 53.4942(b)-2(a), (b) and (c), makes qualifying distributions (within the meaning of § 53.4942(a)-3(a)(2)) directly for the active conduct of activities constituting its charitable, educational, or other similar exempt purpose equal in value to—

(i) For taxable years beginning before January 1, 1982, substantially all of the foundation's adjusted net income (as defined in § 53.4942(a)-2(d)); and

(ii) For taxable years beginning after December 31, 1981, substantially all of the lesser of the foundation's adjusted net income (as defined in § 53.4942(a)-2(d)) or minimum investment return (as defined in § 53.4942(a)-2(c)). If the foundation's qualifying distributions exceed its minimum investment return (but are less than the foundation's adjusted net income) substantially all of such qualifying distributions must be made directly for the active conduct of activities constituting its charitable, educational or other similar exempt purpose. However, if the foundation's minimum investment return is less than its adjusted net income and the foundation's qualifying distributions equal or exceed such adjusted net income, only that portion of the qualifying distributions equal to substantially all of the foundation's adjusted net income must be made directly for the active conduct of activities constituting its charitable, educational or other similar exempt purpose.

(2) *Certain elderly care facilities described in section 4942(j)(6).*—(i) *In general.*—For purposes of the distribution requirements of section 4942 (but no other provision of the Internal Revenue Code) and for taxable years beginning after December 31, 1969, the term "operating foundation" includes a private foundation which—

(A) On or before May 26, 1969, and continuously thereafter to the close of the taxable year, operates and maintains, as its principal functional purpose, residential facilities for the long-term care, comfort, maintenance, or education of permanently and totally disabled persons, elderly persons, needy widows, or children, and

(B) Satisfies the endowment test set forth in § 53.4942(b)-2(b).

(ii) *Principal functional purpose.*—For purposes of section 4942(j)(6) and this subparagraph (2), an organization's "principal functional purpose" is operating and maintaining residential facilities for the long-term care, comfort, maintenance, or education of permanently and totally disabled persons, elderly persons, needy widows, or children, if it is organized for the principal purpose of operating and maintaining such residential facilities and is primarily engaged directly in the operation and maintenance of those facilities. An organization will be treated as being primarily engaged directly in the operation and maintenance of the described residential facilities if at least 50% of the qualifying distributions (as defined in § 53.4942(a)-3(a)(2)) normally made by the organization are expended for the operation and maintenance of the facilities.

(b) *Active conduct of activities constituting the exempt purpose.*—(1) *In general.*—For purposes of this section, except as provided in subparagraph (2) or (3) of this paragraph, qualifying distributions are not made by a foundation "directly for the active conduct of activities constituting its charitable, educational, or other similar exempt purpose" unless such qualifying distributions are used by the foundation itself, rather than by or through one or more grantee organizations which receive such qualifying distributions directly or indirectly from such foundation. Thus, grants made to other organizations to assist them in conducting activities which help to accomplish their charitable, educational, or other

similar exempt purpose are considered an indirect, rather than direct, means of carrying out activities constituting the charitable, educational, or other similar exempt purpose of the grantor foundation, regardless of the fact that the exempt activities of the grantee organization may assist the grantor foundation in carrying out its own exempt activities. However, amounts paid to acquire or maintain assets which are used directly in the conduct of the foundation's exempt activities, such as the operating assets of a museum, public park, or historic site, are considered direct expenditures for the active conduct of the foundation's exempt activities. Likewise, administrative expenses (such as staff salaries and traveling expenses) and other operating costs necessary to conduct the foundation's exempt activities (regardless of whether they are "directly for the active conduct" of such exempt activities) shall be treated as qualifying distributions expended directly for the active conduct of such exempt activities if such expenses and costs are reasonable in amount. Conversely, administrative expenses and operating costs which are not attributable to exempt activities, such as expenses in connection with the production of investment income, are not treated as such qualifying distributions. Expenses attributable to both exempt and nonexempt activities shall be allocated to each such activity on a reasonable and consistently applied basis. Any amount set aside by a foundation for a specific project, such as the acquisition and restoration, or construction, of additional buildings or facilities which are to be used by the foundation directly for the active conduct of the foundation's exempt activities, shall be deemed to be qualifying distributions expended directly for the active conduct of the foundation's exempt activities if the initial setting aside of the funds constitutes a set-aside within the meaning of paragraph (b) of § 53.4942(a)-3.

(2) *Payments to individual beneficiaries.*—(i) *In general.*—If a foundation makes or awards grants, scholarships, or other payments to individual beneficiaries (including program related investment within the meaning of section 4944(c) made to individuals or corporate enterprises) to support active programs conducted to carry out the foundation's charitable, educational, or other similar exempt purpose, such grants, scholarships, or other payments will be treated as qualifying distributions made directly for the active conduct of exempt activities for purposes of paragraph (a) of this section only if the foundation, apart from the making or awarding of the grants, scholarships, or other payments, otherwise maintains some significant involvement (as defined in subdivision (ii) of this subparagraph) in the active programs in support of which such grants, scholarships, or other payments were made or awarded. Whether the making or awarding of grants, scholarships, or other payments constitutes qualifying distributions made directly for the active conduct of the foundation's exempt activities is to be determined on

the basis of the facts and circumstances of each particular case. The test applied is a qualitative, rather than a strictly quantitative, one. Therefore, if the foundation maintains a significant involvement (as defined in subdivision (ii) of this subparagraph) it will not fail to meet the general rule of subparagraph (1) of this paragraph solely because more of its funds are devoted to the making or awarding of grants, scholarships, or other payments than to the active programs which such grants, scholarships, or other payments support. However, if a foundation does no more than select, screen, and investigate applicants for grants or scholarships, pursuant to which the recipients perform their work or studies alone or exclusively under the direction of some other organization, such grants or scholarships will not be treated as qualifying distributions made directly for the active conduct of the foundation's exempt activities. The administrative expenses of such screening and investigation (as opposed to the grants or scholarships themselves) may be treated as qualifying distributions made directly for the active conduct of the foundation's exempt activities.

(ii) *Definition.*—For purposes of this subparagraph, a foundation will be considered as maintaining a "significant involvement" in a charitable, educational, or other similar exempt activity in connection with which grants, scholarships, or other payments are made or awarded if—

(A) An exempt purpose of the foundation is the relief of poverty or human distress, and its exempt activities are designed to ameliorate conditions among a poor or distressed class of persons or in an area subject to poverty or national disaster (such as providing food or clothing to indigents or residents of a disaster area), the making or awarding of the grants or other payments to accomplish such exempt purpose is direct and without the assistance of an intervening organization or agency, and the foundation maintains a salaried or voluntary staff of administrators, researchers, or other personnel who supervise and direct the activities described in this subdivision (A) on a continuing basis; or

(B) The foundation has developed some specialized skills, expertise, or involvement in a particular discipline or substantive area (such as scientific or medical research, social work, education, or the social sciences), it maintains a salaried staff of administrators, researchers, or other personnel who supervise or conduct programs or activities which support and advance the foundation's work in its particular area of interest, and, as a part of such programs or activities, the foundation makes or awards grants, scholarships, or other payments to individuals to encourage and further their involvement in the foundation's particular area of interest and in some segment of the programs or activities carried on by the foundation (such as grants under which the recipients, in addition to independent study, attend classes, seminars, or conferences sponsored or conducted by the foundation, or grants to engage in social work or scientific research projects which are under the general direction and supervision of the foundation).

(3) *Payment of section 4940 tax.*—For purposes of section 4942(j)(3)(A) and (B)(ii), payment of the tax imposed upon a foundation under section 4940 shall be considered a qualifying distribution which is made directly for the active conduct of activities constituting the foundation's charitable, educational, or other similar exempt purpose.

(c) *Substantially all.*—For purposes of this section, the term "substantially all" shall mean 85 percent or more. Thus, if a foundation makes qualifying distributions directly for the active conduct of activities constituting its charitable, educational, or other similar exempt purpose in an amount equal to at least 85 percent of its adjusted net income, it will be considered as satisfying the income test described in this section even if it makes grants to organizations or engages in other activities with the remainder of its adjusted net income and with other funds. In determining whether the amount of qualifying distributions made directly for the active conduct of such exempt activities equals at least 85 percent of a foundation's adjusted net income, a foundation is not required to trace the source of such expenditures to determine whether they were derived from income or from contributions.

(d) *Examples.*—The provisions of this section may be illustrated by the following examples. It is assumed that none of the organizations described in these examples is described in section 509(a)(1), (2), or (3).

Example (1). N, an exempt museum described in section 501(c)(3), was founded by the gift of an endowment from a single contributor. N uses 90 percent of its adjusted net income to operate the museum. If N satisfies one of the tests set forth in § 53.4942(b)-2 it may be classified as an operating foundation since substantially all of the qualifying distributions made by N are used directly for the active conduct of N's exempt activities within the meaning of paragraph (b)(1) of this section.

Example (2). M, an exempt organization described in section 501(c)(3), was created to improve conditions in a particular urban ghetto. M receives its funds primarily from a limited number of wealthy contributors interested in helping carry out its exempt purpose. M's program consists of making a survey of the problems of the ghetto to determine the areas in which its funds may be applied most effectively. Approximately 10 percent of M's adjusted net income is used to conduct this survey. The balance of its income is used to make grants to other nonprofit organizations doing work in the ghetto in those areas determined to have the greatest likelihood of resulting in improved conditions. Under these circumstances, since only 10 percent of M's adjusted net income may be considered as consti-

tuting qualifying distributions made directly for the active conduct of M's exempt activities, M cannot qualify as an operating foundation.

Example (3). Assume the facts as stated in example (2), except that M uses the remaining 90 percent of its adjusted net income for the following purposes: (1) M maintains a salaried staff of social workers and researchers who analyze its surveys and make recommendations as to methods for improving ghetto conditions; (2) M makes grants to independent social scientists who assist in these analyses and recommendations; (3) M publishes periodic reports indicating the results of its surveys and recommendations; (4) M makes grants to social workers and others who act as advisors to nonprofit organizations, as well as small business enterprises, functioning in the community (these advisors acting under the general direction of M attempt to implement M's recommendations through their advice and assistance to the nonprofit organizations and small business enterprises); and (5) M makes grants to other social scientists who study and report on the success of the various enterprises which attempt to implement M's recommendations. Under these circumstances, M satisfies the requirements of paragraph (b)(2) of this section, and the various grants it makes constitute qualifying distributions made directly for the active conduct of its exempt activities. Thus, if M satisfies one of the tests set forth in §53.4942(b)-2 it may be classified as an operating foundation.

Example (4). P, an exempt educational organization described in section 501(c)(3), was created for the purpose of training teachers for institutions of higher education. Each year P awards a substantial number of fellowships to students for graduate study leading towards their M.A. or Ph. D. degrees. The applicants for these fellowships are carefully screened by P's staff, and only those applicants who indicate a strong interest in teaching in colleges or universities are chosen. P publishes and circulates various pamphlets encouraging a development of interests in college teaching and describing its fellowships. P also conducts annual summer seminars which are attended by its fellowship recipients, its staff, consultants and other interested parties. The purpose of these seminars is to foster and encourage the development of college teaching. P publishes a report of the seminar proceedings along with related studies written by those who attended. Despite the fact that a substantial portion of P's adjusted net income is devoted to granting fellowships, its commitment to encouraging individuals to become teachers at institutions of higher learning, its maintenance of a staff and programs designed to further this purpose, and the granting of fellowships to encourage involvement both in its own seminars and in its exempt purpose indicate a significant involvement by P beyond the mere granting of fellowships. Thus, the fellowship grants made by P constitute qualifying distributions made directly for the active conduct of P's exempt activities within the meaning of paragraph (b)(2) of this section.

Example (5). Q, an exempt organization described in section 501(c)(3), is composed of professional organizations interested in different branches of one academic discipline. Q trains its own professional staff, conducts its own program of research, selects research topics, screens and investigates grant recipients, makes grants to those selected, and sets up and conducts conferences and seminars for the grantees. Q has particular knowledge and skill in the given discipline, carries on activities to advance its study of that discipline, and makes grants to individuals to enable them to participate in activities which it conducts in carrying out its exempt purpose. Under these circumstances, Q's grants constitute qualifying distributions made directly for the active conduct of Q's exempt activities within the meaning of paragraph (b)(2) of this section.

Example (6). R, an exempt medical research organization described in section 501(c)(3), was created to study and perform research concerning heart disease. R has its own research center in which it carries on a broad number of research projects in the field of heart disease with its own professional staff. Physicians and scientists who are interested in special projects in this area present the plans for their projects to R. The directors of R study these plans and decide if the project is feasible and will further the work being done by R. If it is, R makes a grant to the individual to enable him to carry out his project, either at R's facilities or elsewhere. Reports of the progress of the project are made periodically to R, and R exercises a certain amount of supervision over the project. The resulting findings of these projects are usually published by R. Under these circumstances, the grants made by R constitute qualifying distributions made directly for the active conduct of R's exempt activities within the meaning of paragraph (b)(2) of this section.

Example (7). S, an exempt organization described in section 501(c)(3), maintains a large library of manuscripts and other historical reference material relating to the history and development of the region in which the collection is located. S makes a limited number of annual grants to enable post-doctoral scholars and doctoral candidates to use its library. Sometimes S obtains the right to publish the scholar's work, although this is not a prerequisite to the receipt of a grant. The primary criterion for selection of grant recipients is the usefulness of the library's resources to the applicant's field of study. Under these circumstances, the grants made by S constitute qualifying distributions made directly for the active conduct of S's exempt activities within the meaning of paragraph (b)(2) of this section.

Example (8). T, an exempt charitable organization described in section 501(c)(3), was created by the members of one family for the purpose of relieving poverty and human suffering. T has a large salaried staff of employees who operate offices in various areas throughout the country. Its employees make gifts of foods and clothing to poor persons in the area serviced by each office. On occasion, T also provides temporary relief in the form of food and clothing to persons in areas

stricken by natural disasters. If conditions improve in one poverty area, T transfers the resources of the office in that area to another poverty area. Under these circumstances, the gifts of food and clothing made by T constitute qualifying distributions made directly for the active conduct of T's exempt activities within the meaning of paragraph (b)(2) of this section.

Example (9). U, an exempt scientific organization described in section 501(c)(3), was created for the principal purpose of studying the effects of early childhood brain damage. U conducts an active and continuous research program in this area through a salaried staff of scientists and physicians. As part of its research program, U awards scholarships to young people suffering mild brain damage to enable them to attend special schools equipped to handle such problems. The recipients are periodically tested to determine the effect of such schooling upon them. Under these circumstances, the scholarships awarded by U constitute qualifying distributions made directly for the active conduct of U's exempt activities within the meaning of paragraph (b)(2) of this section.

Example (10). O, an exempt charitable organization described in section 501(c)(3), was created for the purpose of giving scholarships to children of the employees by X Corporation who meet the standards set by O. O not only screens and investigates each applicant to make sure that he complies with the academic and financial requirements set for scholarship recipients, but also administers an examination which each applicant must take—90 percent of O's adjusted net income is used in awarding these scholarships to the chosen applicants. O does not conduct any activities of an educational nature as its own. Under these circumstances, O is not using substantially all of its adjusted net income directly for the active conduct of its exempt activities within the meaning of paragraph (b) of this section. Thus, O is not an operating foundation because it fails to satisfy the income test set forth in paragraph (a) of this section. [Reg. § 53.4942(b)-1.]

☐ [*T.D. 7249, 12-29-72. Amended by T.D. 7718, 9-3-80 and T.D. 7878, 3-21-83.*]

[Reg. § 53.4942(b)-2]

§ 53.4942(b)-2. Alternative tests.—(a) *Assets test.*—(1) *In general.*—A private foundation will satisfy the assets test under the provisions of this paragraph if substantially more than half of the foundation's assets:

(i) Are devoted directly (A) to the active conduct of activities constituting the foundation's charitable, educational, or other similar exempt purpose, (B) to functionally related businesses (as defined in paragraph (c)(3)(iii) of § 53.4942(a)-2), or (C) to any combination thereof;

(ii) Are stock of a corporation which is controlled by the foundation (within the meaning of section 368(c)) and substantially all the assets of which (within the meaning of paragraph (c) of § 53.4942(b)-1) are so devoted; or

(iii) Are in part assets which are described in subdivision (i) of this subparagraph and in part stock which is described in subdivision (ii) of this subparagraph.

(2) *Qualifying assets.*—(i) *In general.*—For purposes of subparagraph (1) of this paragraph, an asset is "devoted directly to the active conduct of activities constituting the foundation's charitable, educational, or other similar exempt purpose" only if the asset is actually used by the foundation directly for the active conduct of activities constituting its charitable, educational, or other similar exempt purpose. Thus, such assets as real estate, physical facilities or objects (such as museum assets, classroom fixtures and equipment, and research facilities), and intangible assets (such as patents, copyrights and trademarks) will be considered qualifying assets for purposes of this paragraph to the extent they are used directly for the active conduct of the foundation's exempt activities. However, assets which are held for the production of income, for investment, or for some other similar use (for example, stocks, bonds, interest-bearing notes, endowment funds, or, generally, leased real estate) are not devoted directly to the active conduct of the foundation's exempt activities, even though the income derived from such assets is used to carry out such exempt activities. Whether an asset is held for the production of income, for investment, or for some other similar use rather than being used for the active conduct of the foundation's exempt activities is a question of fact. For example, an office building used for the purpose of providing offices for employees engaged in the management of endowment funds of the foundation is not devoted to the active conduct of the foundation's exempt activities. However, where property is used both for exempt purposes and for other purposes, if such exempt use represents 95 percent or more of the total use, such property shall be considered to be used exclusively for an exempt purpose. Property acquired by a foundation to be used in carrying out the foundation's exempt purpose may be considered as devoted directly to the active conduct of such purpose even though the property, in whole or in part, is leased for a limited period of time during which arrangements are made for its conversion to the use for which it was acquired, provided such income-producing use of the property does not exceed a reasonable period of time. Generally, one year shall be deemed to be a reasonable period of time for purposes of the immediately preceding sentence. Similarly, where property is leased by a foundation in carrying out its exempt purpose and where the rental income derived from such property by the foundation is less than the amount which would be required to be charged in order to recover the cost of purchase and maintenance of such property (taking into account the deductions permitted by paragraph (d)(4) of § 53.4942(a)-2), such property shall be considered devoted directly to the active conduct of the foundation's exempt activities.

Reg. § 53.4942(b)-2(a)(2)(i)

(ii) *Limitations.*—(A) Assets which are held for the purpose of extending credit or making funds available to members of a charitable class (including any interest in a program related-investment, except as provided in paragraph (b)(2) of § 53.4942(b)-1) are not considered assets devoted directly to the active conduct of activities constituting the foundation's charitable, educational, or other similar exempt purpose. For example, assets which are set aside in special reserve accounts to guarantee student loans made by lending institutions will not be considered assets devoted directly to the active conduct of the foundation's exempt activities.

(B) Any amount set aside by a foundation within the meaning of paragraph (b)(1) of § 53.4942(b)-1 shall not be treated as an asset devoted directly to the active conduct of the foundation's exempt activities.

(3) *Assets held for less than a taxable year.*—For purposes of this paragraph, any asset which is held by a foundation for part of a taxable year shall be taken into account for such taxable year by multiplying the fair market value of such asset (as determined pursuant to subparagraph (4) of this paragraph) by a fraction, the numerator of which is the number of days in such taxable year that the foundation held such asset and the denominator of which is the number of days in such taxable year.

(4) *Valuation.*—For purposes of this paragraph, all assets shall be valued at their fair market value. Fair market value shall be determined in accordance with the rules set forth in paragraph (c)(4) of § 53.4942(a)-2, except in the case of assets which are devoted directly to the active conduct of the foundation's exempt activities and for which neither a ready market nor standard valuation methods exist (such as historical objects or buildings, certain works of art, and botanical gardens). In such cases, the historical cost (unadjusted for depreciation) shall be considered equal to fair market value unless the foundation demonstrates that fair market value is other than cost. In any case in which the foundation so demonstrates that the fair market value of an asset is other than historical cost, such substituted valuation may be used for the taxable year for which such new valuation is demonstrated and for each of the succeeding four taxable years if the valuation methods and procedures prescribed by paragraph (c)(4)(iv)(B) of § 53.4942(a)-2 are followed.

(5) *Substantially more than half.*—For purposes of this paragraph, the term "substantially more than half" shall mean 65 percent or more.

(6) *Examples.*—The provisions of this paragraph may be illustrated by the following examples. It is assumed that none of the organizations described in these examples is described in section 509(a)(1), (2), or (3).

Example (1). W, an exempt organization described in section 501(c)(3), is devoted to the maintenance and operation of a historic area for the benefit of the general public. W has acquired and erected facilities for lodging and other visitor accommodations in such area, which W operates through a wholly owned, separately incorporated, taxable entity. These facilities comprise substantially all of the subsidiary's assets. The operation of such accommodations constitutes a functionally related business within the meaning of paragraph (c)(3)(iii) of § 53.4942(a)-2. Under these circumstances, the stock of the subsidiary will be considered as part of W's assets which may be taken into account by W in determining whether it satisfies the assets test described in this paragraph.

Example (2). M, an exempt conservation organization described in section 501(c)(3), is devoted to acquiring, preserving, and otherwise making available for public use geographically diversified areas of natural beauty. M has acquired and erected facilities for lodging and other visitor accommodations in national park areas. The operation of such accommodations constitutes a functionally related business within the meaning of paragraph (c)(3)(iii) of § 53.4942(a)-2. Therefore, M's assets which are directly devoted to such visitor accommodations may be taken into account by M in determining whether it satisfies the assets test described in this paragraph.

Example (3). P, an exempt organization described in section 501(c)(3), is devoted to acquiring and restoring historic houses. To insure that the restored houses will be kept in the restored condition, and to make the houses more readily available for public display, P rents the houses rather than sells them once they have been restored. The rental income derived by P is substantially less than the amount which would be required to be charged in order to recover the cost of purchase, restoration, and maintenance of such houses. Therefore, such houses may be taken into account by P in determining whether it satisfies the assets test described in this paragraph.

Example (4). Z, an exempt organization described in section 501(c)(3), is devoted to improving the public's understanding of Renaissance art. Z's principal assets are a number of paintings of this period which it circulates on an active and continuing basis to museums and schools for public display. These paintings constitute 80 percent of Z's assets. Under these circumstances, although Z does not have a building in which it displays these paintings, such paintings are devoted directly to the active conduct of activities constituting Z's exempt purpose. Therefore, Z has satisfied the assets test described in this paragraph.

(b) *Endowment test.*—(1) *In general.*—A foundation will satisfy the endowment test under the provisions of this paragraph if it normally makes qualifying distributions (within the meaning of paragraph (a)(2) of § 53.4942(a)-3) directly for the active conduct of activities constituting its charitable, educational, or other similar exempt purpose in an amount not less than two-thirds of its minimum investment return (as defined in para-

graph (c) of §53.4942(a)-2). In determining whether the amount of such qualifying distributions is not less than an amount equal to two-thirds of the foundation's minimum investment return, the foundation is not required to trace the source of such expenditures to determine whether they were derived from investment income or from contributions.

(2) *Definitions.*—For purposes of this paragraph, the phrase "directly for the active conduct of activities constituting the foundation's charitable, educational, or other similar exempt purpose" shall have the same meaning as in paragraph (b) of §53.4942(b)-1.

(3) *Example.*—This paragraph may be illustrated by the following example:

Example. X, an exempt organization described in section 501(c)(3) and not described in section 509(a)(1), (2), or (3), was created on July 15, 1970. X uses the cash receipts and disbursements method of accounting. For 1971, the fair market value of X's assets not described in paragraph (c)(2) or (3) of §53.4942(a)-2 is $400,000. X makes qualifying distributions for 1971 directly for the active conduct of its exempt activities of $17,000. For 1971 two-thirds of X's minimum investment return is $16,000 (6 percent × $400,000 = $24,000; ²/₃ × $24,000 = $16,000). Under these circumstances, X has satisfied the endowment test described in this paragraph for 1971. However, if X's qualifying distributions for 1971 directly for the active conduct of its exempt activities were only $15,000, X would not satisfy the endowment test for 1971, unless the fair market value of its assets not described in paragraph (c)(2) or (3) of §53.4942(a)-2 were no greater than $375,000 (6 percent × $375,000 = $22,500; ²/₃ × $22,500 = $15,000).

(c) *Support test.*—(1) *In general.*—A foundation will satisfy the support test under the provisions of this paragraph if:

(i) Substantially all of its support (other than gross investment income as defined in section 509(e)) is normally received from the general public and from five or more exempt organizations which are not described in section 4946(a)(1)(H) with respect to each other or the recipient foundation;

(ii) Not more than 25 percent of its support (other than gross investment income) is normally received from any one such exempt organization; and

(iii) Not more than half of its support is normally received from gross investment income.

(2) *Definitions and special rules.*—For purposes of this paragraph—

(i) *Support.*—The term "support" shall have the same meaning as in section 509(d).

(ii) *Substantially all.*—The term "substantially all" shall have the same meaning as in paragraph (c) of §53.4942(b)-1.

(iii) *Support from exempt organizations.*—The support received from any one exempt organization may be counted towards satisfaction of the support test described in this paragraph only if the foundation receives support from no fewer than five exempt organizations. For example, a foundation which normally receives 20 percent of its support (other than gross investment income) from each of five exempt organizations may qualify under this paragraph even though it receives no support from the general public. However, if a foundation normally received 10 percent of its support from each of three exempt organizations and the balance of its support from sources other than exempt organizations, such support could not be taken into account in determining whether the foundation had satisfied the support test set forth in this paragraph.

(iv) *Support from the general public.*—"Support" received from an individual, or from a trust or corporation (other than an exempt organization), shall be taken into account as support from the general public only to the extent that the total amount of the support received from any such individual, trust, or corporation during the period for determining the normal sources of the foundation's support (as set forth in §53.4942(b)-3) does not exceed one percent of the foundation's total support (other than gross investment income) for such period. In applying this one-percent limitation, all support received by the foundation from any person and from any other person or persons standing in a relationship to such person which is described in section 4946(a)(1)(C) through (G) and the regulations thereunder shall be treated as received from one person. For purposes of this paragraph, support received from a governmental unit described in section 170(c)(1) shall be treated as support received from the general public, but shall not be subject to the one-percent limitation. [Reg. §53.4942(b)-2.]

☐ [*T.D.* 7249, 12-29-72.]

[Reg. §53.4942(b)-3]

§53.4942(b)-3. **Determination of compliance with operating foundation tests.**—(a) *In general.*—A foundation may satisfy the income test and either the assets, endowment, or support test by satisfying such tests for any three taxable years during a four-year period consisting of the taxable year in question and the three immediately preceding taxable years or on the basis of an aggregation of all pertinent amounts of income or assets held, received, or distributed during such four-year period. A foundation may not use one method for satisfying the income test described in paragraph (a) of §53.4942(b)-1 and another for satisfying either the assets, endowment, or support test described in §53.4942(b)-2. Thus, if a foundation satisfies the income test on the three-out-of-four-year basis for a particular taxable year, it may not use the aggregation method for satisfying either the assets, endowment, or support test for such particular taxable

year. However, the fact that a foundation has chosen one method for satisfying the tests under §§ 53.4942(b)-1 and 53.4942(b)-2 for one taxable year will not preclude it from satisfying such tests for a subsequent taxable year by the alternate method. If a foundation fails to satisfy the income test and either the assets, endowment, or support test for a particular taxable year under either the three-out-of-four-year method or the aggregation method, it shall be treated as a nonoperating foundation for such taxable year and for all subsequent taxable years until it satisfies the tests set forth in §§ 53.4942(b)-1 and 53.4942(b)-2 for a taxable year occurring after the taxable year in which it was treated as a nonoperating foundation.

(b) *New organizations.*—(1) *In general.*—Except as provided in subparagraph (2) of this paragraph, an organization organized after December 31, 1969, will be treated as an operating foundation only if it has satisfied the tests set forth in §§ 53.4942(b)-1 and 53.4942(b)-2 for its first taxable year of existence. If an organization satisfies such tests for its first taxable year, it will be treated as an operating foundation from the beginning of such taxable year. If such is the case, the organization will be treated as an operating foundation for its second and third taxable years of existence only if it satisfies the tests set forth in §§ 53.4942(b)-1 and 53.4942(b)-2 by the aggregation method for all such taxable years that it has been in existence.

(2) *Special rule.*—An organization organized after December 31, 1969, will be treated as an operating foundation prior to the end of its first taxable year if such organization has made a good faith determination that it is likely to satisfy the income test set forth in paragraph (a) of § 53.4942(b)-1 and one of the tests set forth in § 53.4942(b)-2 for such first taxable year pursuant to subparagraph (1) of this paragraph. Such a "good faith determination" ordinarily will be considered as made where the determination is based on an affidavit or opinion of counsel of such organization that such requirements will be satisfied. Such an affidavit or opinion must set forth sufficient facts concerning the operations and support of such organization for the Commissioner to be able to determine that such organization is likely to satisfy such requirements. An organization which, pursuant to this subparagraph, has been treated as an operating foundation for its first taxable year, but actually fails to qualify as an operating foundation under subparagraph (1) of this paragraph for such taxable year, will be treated as a private foundation which is not an operating foundation as of the first day of its second taxable year for purposes of making any determination under the internal revenue laws with respect to such organization. The preceding sentence shall not apply if such organization establishes to the satisfaction of the Commissioner that it is likely to qualify as an operating foundation on the basis of its second, third and fourth taxable years. Thus, if such an

organization fails to qualify as an operating foundation in its second, third, and fourth taxable year after having failed in its first taxable year, it will be treated as a private foundation which is not an operating foundation as of the first day of such second, third or fourth taxable year in which it fails to qualify as an operating foundation, except as otherwise provided by paragraph (d) of this section. Such status as a private foundation which is not an operating foundation will continue until such time as the organization is able to satisfy the tests set forth in §§ 53.4942(b)-1 and 53.4942(b)-2 by either the three-out-of-four-year method or the aggregation method. For the status of grants or contributions made to such an organzation with respect to sections 170 and 4942, see paragraph (d) of this section.

(c) *Transitional rule for existing organizations.*—An organization organized before December 31, 1969 (including organizations deemed to be so organized by virtue of the principles of paragraph (e)(2) of § 53.4942(a)-2), but which is unable to satisfy the tests under §§ 53.4942(b)-1 and 53.4942(b)-2 for its first taxable year beginning after December 31, 1969 on the basis of its operations for taxable years prior to such taxable year by either the three-out-of-four-year method or the aggregation method, will be treated as a new organization for purposes of paragraph (b) of this section only if:

(1) The organization changes its methods of operation prior to its first taxable year beginning after December 31, 1972 to conform to the requirements of §§ 53.4942(b)-1 and 53.4942(b)-2;

(2) The organization has made a good faith determination (within the meaning of paragraph (b)(2) of the section) that it is likely to satisfy the tests set forth in §§ 53.4942(b)-1 and 53.4942(b)-2 prior to its first taxable year beginning after December 31, 1972 on the basis of its income or assets held, received, or distributed during its taxable years beginning in 1970 through 1972; and

(3) Such good faith determination is attached to the return the organization is required to file under section 6033 for its taxable year beginning in 1972.

(d) *Treatment of contributions.*—(1) *In general.*—The status of grants or contributions made to an operating foundation with respect to sections 170 and 4942 will not be affected until notice of change of status of such organization is made to the public (such as by publication in the Internal Revenue Bulletin), unless the grant or contribution was made after:

(i) The act or failure to act that resulted in the organization's inability to satisfy the requirements of §§ 53.4942(b)-1 and 53.4942(b)-2, and the grantor or contributor was responsible for, or was aware of, such act or failure to act, or

(ii) The grantor or contributor acquired knowledge that the Commissioner has given notice to such organization that it would be deleted from classification as an operating foundation.

(2) *Exception.*—For purposes of subparagraph (1)(i) of this paragraph, a grantor or contributor will not be considered to be responsible for, or aware of, the act or failure to act that resulted in the grantee organization's inability to satisy the requirements of §§53.4942(b)-1 and 53.4942(b)-2 if such grantor or contributor has made his grant or contribution in reliance upon a written statement by the grantee organization that such grant or contribution would not result in the inability of such grantee organization to qualify as an operating foundation. Such a statement must be signed by a foundation manager (as defined in section 4946(b)) of the grantee organization and must set forth sufficient facts concerning the operations and support of such grantee organization to assure a reasonably prudent man that his grant or contribution will not result in the grantee organization's inability to qualify as an operating foundation. [Reg. §53.4942(b)-3.]

☐ [T.D. 7249, 12-29-72.]

[Reg. §53.4943-1]

§53.4943-1. General rule; purpose.—Generally, under section 4943, the combined holdings of a private foundation and all disqualified persons (as defined in section 4946(a)) in any corporation conducting a business which is not substantially related (aside from the need of the foundation for income or funds or the use it makes of the profits derived) to the exempt purposes of the foundation are limited to 20 percent of the voting stock in such corporation. In addition, the combined holdings of a private foundation and all disqualified persons in any unincorporated business (other than a sole proprietorship) which is not substantially related (aside from the need of the foundation for income or funds or the use it makes of the profits derived) to the exempt purposes of such foundation are limited to 20 percent of the beneficial or profits interest in such business. In the case of a sole proprietorship which is not substantially related (within the meaning of the preceding sentence), section 4943 provides that a private foundation shall have no permitted holdings. These general provisions are subject to a number of exceptions and special provisions which will be described in following sections. [Reg. §53.4943-1.]

☐ [T.D. 7946, 7-5-77.]

[Reg. §53.4943-2]

§53.4943-2. Imposition of tax on excess business holdings of private foundations.—(a) *Imposition of initial tax.*—(1) *In general.*—(i) *Initial tax.*—Section 4943(a)(1) imposes an initial excise tax (the "initial tax") on the excess business holdings of a private foundation for each taxable year of the foundation which ends during the taxable period defined in section 4943(d)(2). The amount of such tax is equal to 5 percent of the total value of all the private foundation's excess business holdings in each of its business enterprises. In determining the value of

the excess business holdings of the foundation subject to tax under section 4943, the rules set forth in §§20.2031-1 through 20.2031-3 of this chapter (Estate Tax Regulations) shall apply.

(ii) *Disposition of certain excess business holdings within ninety days.*—In any case in which a private foundation acquires excess business holdings, other than as a result of a purchase by the foundation, the foundation shall not be subject to the taxes imposed by section 4943, but only if it disposes of an amount of its holdings so that it no longer has such excess business holdings within 90 days from the date on which it knows, or has reason to know, of the event which caused it to have such excess business holdings. Similarly, a private foundation shall not be subject to the taxes imposed by section 4943 because of its purchase of holdings where it did not know, or have reason to know of prior acquisitions by disqualified persons, but only if the foundation disposes of its excess holdings within the 90-day period described previously, and its purchase would not have created excess business holding but for such prior acquisitions by disqualified persons. In determining whether for purposes of this (ii) the foundation has disposed of such excess business holdings during such 90-day period, any disposition of holdings by a disqualified person during such period shall be disregarded.

(iii) *Extension of ninety day period.*—The period described in paragraph (a)(1)(ii) of this section, during which no tax shall be imposed under section 4943, shall be extended to include the period during which a foundation is prevented by federal or state securities laws from disposing of such excess business holdings.

(iv) *Effect of disposition subject to material restrictions.*—If a private foundation disposes of an interest in a business enterprise but imposes any material restrictions or conditions that prevent the transferee from freely and effectively using or disposing of the transferred interest, then the transferor foundation will be treated as owning such interest until all such restrictions or conditions are eliminated (regardless of whether the transferee is treated for other purposes of the Code as owning such interest from the date of the transfer). However, a restriction or condition imposed in compliance with federal or state securities laws, or in accordance with the terms or conditions of the gift or bequest through which such interest was acquired by the foundation, shall not be considered a material restriction or condition imposed by a private foundation.

(v) *Foundation knowledge of acquisitions made by disqualified persons.*—(A) For purposes of paragraph (a)(1)(ii) of this section, whether a private foundation will be treated as knowing, or having reason to know, of the acquisition of holdings by a disqualified person will depend on the facts and circumstances of each case. Factors which will be considered relevant to a determination that a private foundation did not know or had no reason to know of an acquisition are: the

fact that it did not discover acquisitions made by disqualified persons through the use of procedures reasonably calculated to discover such holdings; the diversity of foundation holdings; and the existence of large numbers of disqualified persons who have little or no contact with the foundation or its managers.

(B) The provisions of paragraph (a)(1)(v)(A) of this section may be illustrated by the following example:

Example. By the fifteenth day of the fifth month after the close of each taxable year, the F Foundation sends to each foundation manager, substantial contributor, person holding more than a 20% interest (as described in section 4946(a)(1)(C)) in a substantial contributor, and foundation described in section 4946(a)(1)(H), a questionnaire asking such persons to list all holdings, actual or constructive, in each business enterprise in which F had holdings during the taxable year in excess of those permitted by the 2 percent *de minimis* rule of section 4943(c)(2)(C). In preparing the list of such enterprises, F takes into account its constructive holdings only if, during the taxable year, F (along with all related foundations described in section 4946(a)(1)(H)) owned over 2% of the voting stock, profits interest or beneficial interest in the entity actually owning the holdings constructively held by F. The questionnaire asks each such person to list the holdings in such enterprises of any persons who, because of their relationship to such disqualified person, were themselves disqualified persons (*i.e.*, members of the family (as defined in section 4946(d)), and any corporations, partnerships, trusts and estates described in section 4946(a)(1)(E) through (G) in which such person, or members of his family, had an interest). The questionnaire asks that constructive holdings be listed only if, during the taxable year, the disqualified person owned over 2% of the voting stock, profits interests or beneficial interest in the entity actually owning the holdings constructively held by such person. (Thus a disqualified person owning less than 2% of a mutual fund is not required to list his attributed share of all the securities in the portfolio of the fund.) If no response to the questionnaire is received, the foundation seeks the information requested by the questionnaire by mailing a second (but not a third) questionnaire. If a questionnaire which is returned to the foundation indicates that certain information was unavailable to the person completing the questionnaire, the foundation seeks that information directly. For example, if a disqualified person indicates that he could not find out whether a corporation described in section 4946(a)(1)(E) had holdings in the enterprise listed in the questionnaire, the foundation seeks to obtain this information directly from the corporation by mailing it a questionnaire. In such a case, F may be found not to have reason to know of the acquisition of holdings by a disqualified person.

(vi) *Holdings acquired other than by purchase.*—See section 4943(c)(6) and § 53.4943-6

for rules relating to the acquisition of certain holdings other than by purchase by the foundation or a disqualified person.

(2) *Special rules.*—In applying subparagraph (1) of this paragraph, the tax imposed by section 4943(a)(1)—

(i) Shall be imposed on the last day of the private foundation's taxable year, but

(ii) The amount of such tax and the value of the excess business holdings subject to such tax shall be determined with respect to the foundation's holdings (based upon voting power, profits or beneficial interest, or value, whichever is applicable) in any business enterprise as of that day during the foundation's taxable year when the foundation's excess holdings in such enterprise were the greatest.

In applying subdivision (ii) of this subparagraph, if a foundation's excess business holdings in a business enterprise which constitute such foundation's greatest excess holdings in such enterprise for any taxable year are maintained for 2 or more days during such taxable year, the value of such excess holdings which is subject to tax under section 4943(a)(1) shall be the greatest value of such excess holdings in such enterprise as of any day on which such greatest excess holdings are maintained during such taxable year.

(3) *Examples.*—The provisions of this paragraph may be illustrated by the following examples:

Example (1). Y is a private foundation reporting on a calendar year basis. On January 1, 1973, Y has 20 shares of common stock in corporation N, of which five shares constitute excess business holdings. On June 1, 1973, Y disposes of such five shares; however, because of additional acquisitions of N common stock on such date by disqualified persons with respect to Y, the remaining 15 shares of N common stock held by Y now constitute excess business holdings. There are no further acquisitions or dispositions of N common stock during 1973 by Y or its disqualified persons. Although Y's greatest holdings in N during 1973 are held between January 1, 1973, and May 31, 1973, Y's greatest excess holdings in N during 1973 are held between June 1, 1973, and December 31, 1973. Therefore, the tax specified in section 4943(a)(1) shall be computed on the basis of the greatest value of such greatest excess holdings as of any day between June 1 and December 31, 1973.

Example (2). X is a private foundation reporting on a calendar year basis. On January 1, 1972, X has 100 shares of common stock in M corporation which are excess business holdings. On such date each share of M common stock has a fair market value of $100. On February 28, 1972, in an effort to dispose of such excess business holdings, X sells 70 shares of M common stock for $120 per share (the fair market value of each share on such date) to A, an individual who is not a disqualified person within the meaning of section 4946(a). The value of $120 per share is the

highest fair market value between January 1 and February 28, 1972. X disposes of no more stock in M for the remainder of calendar year 1972. On December 31, 1972, the fair market value of each share of M common stock is $80. X calculates its tax on its excess business holdings in M for 1972 as follows:

100 shares of M common stock times $120 fair market value per share as of Feb. 28, 1972	$12,000
$12,000 multiplied by rate of tax (percent)	5
Amount of tax on X foundation's excess business holdings for 1972	$ 600

Example (3). Assume the same facts as in Example (2) except that the sale of X to A occurs on January 7, 1973, when the fair market value of each share of M corporation common stock equals $70. A value of $100 per share is the highest fair market value of the M common stock between January 1 and January 7, 1973. On May 9, 1973, X for the first time has excess business holdings in N corporation in the form of 200 shares of N common stock. The value per share of N common stock on May 9, 1973, equals $200. X makes no disposition of the N common stock during 1973, and the value of each share of N common stock as of December 31, 1973 equals $250 (the highest value of N common stock during 1973). X calculates its tax on its excess business holdings in both M and N for 1973 as follows:

100 shares of M common stock times $100 fair market value per share	$10,000
200 shares of N common stock times $250 fair market value per share	$50,000
Total	$60,000
$60,000 multiplied by rate of tax (percent)	5
Amount of tax on X foundation's excess business holdings for 1973	$3,000

(b) *Additional tax.*—In any case in which the initial tax is imposed under section 4943(a) with respect to the holdings of a private foundation in any business enterprise, if, at the close of the taxable period (as defined in section 4943(d)(2) and §53.4943-9) with respect to such holdings the foundation still has excess business holdings in such enterprise, there is imposed a tax under section 4943(b) equal to 200 percent of the value of such excess holdings as of the last day of the taxable period. [Reg. §53.4943-2.]

☐ [T.D. 7496, 7-5-77. *Amended by* T.D. 8084, 5-1-86.]

[Reg. §53.4943-3]

§53.4943-3. Determination of excess business holdings.—(a) *Excess business holdings.*—(1) *In general.*—For purposes of section 4943, the term "excess business holdings" means, with respect to the holdings of any private foundation in any business enterprise (as described in section 4943(d)(4)), the amount of stock or other interest in the enterprise which, except as provided in §53.4943-2(a)(1), the foundation, or a disqualified person, would have to dispose of, or cause the disposition of, to a person other than a disqualified person (as defined in section 4946(a)) in order for the remaining holdings of the foundation in such enterprise to be permitted holdings (as defined in paragraphs (b) and (c) of this section). If a private foundation is required by section 4943 and the regulations thereunder to dispose of certain shares of a class of stock in a particular period of time and other shares of the same class of stock in a shorter period of time, any stock disposed of shall be charged first against those dispositions which must be made in such shorter period.

(2) *Example.*—The provisions of this paragraph may be illustrated by the following example:

Example. Corporation X has outstanding 100 shares of voting stock, with each share entitling the holder thereof to one vote. F, a private foundation, possesses 20 shares of X voting stock representing 20 percent of the voting power in X. Assume that the permitted holdings of F in X under paragraph (b)(1) of this section are 11 percent of the voting stock in X. F, therefore, possesses voting stock in X representing a percentage of voting stock in excess of the percentage permitted by such paragraph. Such excess percentage is 9 percent of the voting stock in X, determined by subtracting the percentage of voting stock representing the permitted holdings of F in X (i.e., 11 percent) from the percentage of voting stock held by F in X (i.e., 20 percent) (20%–11%=9%). The excess business holdings of F in X are an amount of voting stock representing such excess percentage, or 9 shares of X voting stock (9 percent of 100).

(b) *Permitted holdings in an incorporated business enterprise.*—(1) *In general.*—(i) *Permitted holdings defined.*—Except as otherwise provided in section 4943(c)(2) and (4), the permitted holdings of any private foundation in an incorporated business enterprise (including a real estate investment trust, as defined in section 856) are—

(A) 20 percent of the voting stock in such enterprise reduced (but not below zero) by

(B) The percentage of voting stock in such enterprise actually or constructively owned by all disqualified persons.

(ii) *Voting stock.*—For purposes of this section, the percentage of voting stock held by any person in a corporation is normally determined by reference to the power of stock to vote for the election of directors, with treasury stock and stock which is authorized but unissued being disregarded. Thus, for example, if a private foundation holds 20 percent of the shares of one class of stock in a corporation, which class is entitled to elect three directors, and such foundation holds no stock in the other class of stock, which is entitled to elect five directors, such

foundation shall be treated as holding 7.5 percent of the voting stock because the class of stock it holds has 37.5 percent of such voting power, by reason of being able to elect three of the eight directors, and the foundation holds one-fifth of the shares of such class (20 percent of 37.5 percent is 7.5 percent). The fact that extraordinary corporate action (*e.g.*, charter or by-law amendments) by a corporation may require the favorable vote of more than a majority of the directors, or of the outstanding voting stock, of such corporation shall not alter the determination of voting power of stock in such corporation in accordance with the two preceding sentences.

(2) *Nonvoting stock as permitted holdings.*—(i) *In general.*—In addition to those holdings permitted by paragraph (b)(1) of this section, the permitted holdings of a private foundation in an incorporated business enterprise shall include any share of nonvoting stock in such enterprise held by the foundation in any case in which all disqualified persons hold, actually or constructively, no more than 20 percent (35 percent where third persons have effective control as defined in paragraph (b)(3)(ii) of this section) of the voting stock in such enterprise. All equity interests which do not have voting power attributable to them shall, for purposes of section 4943, be classified as nonvoting stock. For this purpose, evidences of indebtedness (including convertible indebtedness), and warrants and other options or rights to acquire stock shall not be considered equity interests.

(ii) *Stock with contingent voting rights and convertible nonvoting stock.*—Stock carrying voting rights which will vest only when conditions, the occurrence of which are indeterminate, have been met, such as preferred stock which gains such voting rights only if no dividends are paid thereon, will be treated as nonvoting stock until the conditions have occurred which cause the voting rights to vest. When such rights vest, the stock will be treated as voting stock that was acquired other than by purchase, but only if the private foundation or disqualified persons had no control over whether the conditions would occur. Similarly, nonvoting stock which may be converted into voting stock will not be treated as voting stock until such conversion occurs. For special rules where stock is acquired other than by purchase, see section 4943(c)(6) and the regulations thereunder.

(iii) *Example.*—The provisions of this paragraph (2) may be illustrated by the following example:

Example. Assume that F, a private foundation, holds 10 percent of the single class of voting stock of corporation X, and owns 20 shares of nonvoting stock in X. Assume further that A and B, the only disqualified persons with respect to F, hold 10 percent of the voting stock of X. Under the provisions of paragraph (b)(1) of this section, the 10 percent of X voting stock held by F will be classified as permitted holdings of F in X since 20 percent less the percentage of voting stock held

by A and B in X is 10 percent. In addition, under the provisions of this (2), the 20 shares of X nonvoting stock will qualify as permitted holdings of F in X since the percentage of voting stock held by A and B in X is no greater than 20 percent.

(3) *Thirty-five-percent rule where third person has effective control of enterprise.*—(i) *In general.*—Except as provided in section 4943(c)(4), paragraph (b)(1) of this section shall be applied by substituting 35 percent for 20 percent if—

(A) The private foundation and all disqualified persons together do not hold, actually or constructively, more than 35 percent of the voting stock in the business enterprise, and

(B) The foundation establishes to the satisfaction of the Commissioner that effective control (as defined in paragraph (b)(3)(ii) of this section) of the business enterprise is in one or more persons (other than the foundation itself) who are not disqualified persons.

(ii) *"Effective control" defined.*—For purposes of this subparagraph, the term "effective control" means the possession, directly or indirectly, of the power to direct or cause the direction of the management and policies of a business enterprise, whether through the ownership of voting stock, the use of voting trusts, or contractual arrangements, or otherwise. It is the reality of control which is decisive and not its form or the means by which it is exercisable. Thus, where a minority interest held by individuals who are not disqualified persons has historically elected the majority of a corporation's directors, effective control is in the hands of those individuals.

(4) *Two percent de minimis rule.*—(i) *In general.*—Under section 4943(c)(2)(C), a private foundation is not treated as having excess business holdings in any incorporated business enterprise in which it (together with all other private foundations (including trusts described in section 4947(a)(2)) which are described in section 4946(a)(1)(H)) actually or constructively owns not more than 2 percent of the voting stock and not more than 2 percent in value of all outstanding shares of all classes of stock. If, however, the private foundation, together with all other private foundations which are described in section 4946(a)(1)(H), actually or constructively owns more than 2 percent of either the voting stock or the value of the outstanding shares of all classes of stock in any incorporated business enterprise, all the stock in such business enterprise classified as excess business holding under section 4943 is treated as excess business holdings. For purposes of this paragraph, any stock owned by a private foundation which is treated as held by a disqualified person under section 4943(c)(4)(B), (5), or (6) shall be treated as actually owned by the private foundation. See paragraph (b)(1) of §53.4941(d)-4 for the determination of excess business holdings without regard to section 4943(c)(2)(C) for purposes

of applying section 101(C)(2)(B) of the Tax Reform Act of 1969 (83 Stat. 533).

(ii) *Examples.*—The provisions of this subparagraph may be illustrated by the following examples:

Example (1). F, a private foundation, owns 1 percent of the single class of voting stock and 1 percent in value of all the outstanding shares of all classes of stock in X corporation. No other private foundation described in section 4946(a)(1)(H) owns any stock in X. All of the stock owned by F in X would be excess business holdings under section 4943(c)(1) if section 4943(c)(2)(C) were inapplicable. F owns no other shares of stock in X. Since F owns no more than 2 percent of the voting stock and no more than 2 percent in value of all outstanding shares of all classes of stock in X, under section 4943(c)(2)(C) none of the stock in X owned by F is treated as excess business holdings.

Example (2). Assume the facts as stated in Example (1), except that F and T, a controlled private foundation under section 4946(a)(1)(H), together own 1 percent of all the voting stock and 1 percent in value of all the outstanding shares of all classes of stock in X. All of the stock in X owned by F and T would be excess business holdings under section 4943(c)(1) if section 4943(c)(2)(C) were inapplicable. Since F and T together own no more than 2 percent of the voting stock and no more than 2 percent in value of all outstanding shares of all classes of stock in X, under section 4943(c)(2)(C) none of the stock in X owned by either F or T is treated as excess business holdings.

Example (3). Assume the facts as stated in Example (1), except that F owns 3 percent of the voting stock in X, 2 percent of which is treated as held by P, a disqualified person of F, under section 4943(c)(4)(B). Under subdivision (i) of this subparagraph, the 2 percent of the stock in X owned by F which is treated as held by P under section 4943(c)(4)(B) is treated as actually owned by F for purposes of section 4943(c)(2)(C). Consequently, all of the X stock owned by F is treated as excess business holdings under section 4943(c)(2)(C). However, only 1 percent of the stock in X is subject to tax under section 4943(a), since the other 2 percent is treated as owned by a disqualified person under section 4943(c)(4)(B) for purposes of determining the tax upon F under section 4943(a).

(c) *Permitted holdings in an unincorporated business enterprise.*—(1) *In general.*—The permitted holdings of a private foundation in any business enterprise which is not incorporated shall, subject to the provisions of subparagraphs (2), (3), and (4) of this paragraph, be determined under the principles of paragraph (b) of this section.

(2) *Partnership or joint venture.*—In the case of a partnership (including a limited partnership) or joint venture, the terms "profits interest" and "capital interest" shall be substituted for "voting stock" and "nonvoting stock," respectively, wherever those terms appear in para-

graph (b) of this section. The interest in profits of such foundation (or such disqualified person) shall be determined in the same manner as its distributive share of partnership taxable income. See section 704(b) (relating to the determination of the distributive share by the income or loss ratio) and the regulations thereunder. In the absence of a provision in the partnership agreement, the capital interest of such foundation (or such disqualified person) in a partnership shall be determined on the basis of its interest in the assets of the partnership which would be distributable to such foundation (or such disqualified person) upon its withdrawal from the partnership, or upon liquidation of the partnership, whichever is the greater.

(3) *Sole proprietorship.*—For purposes of section 4943, a private foundation shall have no permitted holdings in a sole proprietorship. In the case of a transfer by a private foundation of a portion of a sole proprietorship, see paragraph (c)(2) of this section (relating to permitted holdings in partnerships). For the treatment of a private foundation's ownership of a sole proprietorship prior to May 26, 1969, see §53.4943-4.

(4) *Trusts and other unincorporated business enterprises.*—(i) *In general.*—In the case of any unincorporated business enterprise which is not described in paragraph (c)(2) or (3) of this section, the term "beneficial interest" shall be substituted for "voting stock" wherever the term appears in paragraph (b) of this section. Any and all references to nonvoting stock in paragraph (b) of this section shall be inapplicable with respect to any unincorporated business enterprise described in this subparagraph.

(ii) *Trusts.*—For purposes of section 4943, the beneficial interest of a private foundation or any disqualified person in a trust shall be the beneficial remainder interest of such foundation or person determined as provided in paragraph (b) of §53.4943-8.

(iii) *Other unincorporated business enterprises.*—For purposes of section 4943, the beneficial interest of a private foundation or any disqualified person in an unincorporated business enterprise (other than a trust or an enterprise described in paragraph (c)(2) or (3) of this section) includes any right to receive a portion of distributions of profits of such enterprise, and, if the portion of distributions is not fixed by an agreement among the participants, any right to receive a portion of the assets (if any) upon liquidation of the enterprise, except as a creditor or employee. For purposes of this subparagraph, a right to receive distributions of profits includes a right to receive any amount from such profits (other than as a creditor or employee), whether as a sum certain or as a portion of profits realized by the enterprise. Where there is no agreement fixing the rights of the participants in such enterprise, the interest of such foundation (or such disqualified person) in such enterprise shall be determined by dividing the amount of all

equity investments or contributions to the capital of the enterprise made or obligated to be made by such foundation (or such disqualified person) by the amount of all equity investments or contributions to capital made or obligated to be made by all participants in the enterprise.

(d) *Examples.*—The provisions of this section may be illustrated by the following examples:

(i) Determination of voting stock percentages:

(a) Total number of outstanding votes in X	100
(b) Total number of votes in X held by F	30
(c) Total number of votes in X held by A and B	10
(d) Percentage of voting stock in X held by F (item (b) divided by item (a)) (percent)	30
(e) Percentage of voting stock in X held by A and B (item (c) divided by item (a)) (percent) . .	10

(ii) Determination of permitted holdings of voting stock:

(a) Percentage of voting stock in X held by A and B (percent)	10
(b) Permitted holdings of voting stock by F in X (20% less item (a)) (percent)	10

(iii) Determination of excess business holdings:

(a) Percentage of voting stock in X held by F (percent)	30
(b) Permitted holdings of voting stock by F in X (percent)	10
(c) Item (a) less item (b) (percent)	20
(d) Excess business holdings of F in X (i.e., an amount of X voting stock representing a percentage of voting stock equivalent to that in item (c)) (shares)	20

Example (2). F, a private foundation, is a partner in P partnership. In addition, A and B, the only disqualified persons with respect to F, are partners in P. The partnership agreement of P contains no provisions regarding the sharing of profits by, and the respective capital interests of, the partners.

(i) Assume that, under section 704(b), F's distributive share of P taxable income is determined to be 20 percent. In addition, assume that under such section, A and B are determined to have a 4-percent distributive share each of P taxable income. Accordingly, F holds a 20-percent profits interest in P, and A and B hold an 8-percent profits interest in P. Assuming that the provisions of section 4943(c)(2)(B) do not apply, the permitted holdings of F in P are 12 percent of the profits interest in P, determined by subtracting the percentage of the profits interest held by A and B in P (i.e., 8 percent) from 20 percent. (20 percent − 8 percent = 12 percent.) F, therefore, holds a percentage of the profits interest in P in excess of the percentage permitted by §53.4943-3(b)(1). The excess business holdings of F in P are a percentage of the profits interest in P equivalent to such excess percentage, or 8 percent of the profits interest in P, determined by subtracting the permitted holdings of F in P (i.e., 12 percent) from the percentage of the profits interest held by F in P (i.e., 20 percent) (20 percent − 12 percent = 8 percent).

(ii) Assume that, under the partnership agreement, F would be entitled to a distribution of 20 percent of P's assets upon F's withdrawal from P and to a distribution of 30 percent of P's assets upon the liquidation of P. F, therefore, holds a 30-percent capital interest in P; that is, the greater of the percentage of the assets of P distributable to F upon F's withdrawal from P, or the percentage of such assets distributable to F upon the liquidation of P. Since the percentage of the profits interest held by A and B in P is less than 20 percent, such 30-percent capital interest

Example (1). Corporation X has outstanding 100 shares of voting stock, with each share entitling the holder thereof to one vote. Assume that F, a private foundation, possesses 30 shares of X voting stock, and that A and B, the only disqualified persons with respect to F, together own 10 shares of X voting stock. The excess business holdings of F in X are 20 shares of X voting stock, determined as follows:

will be included in the permitted holdings of F in P. [Reg. §53.4943-3.]

☐ [*T.D.* 7496, 7-5-77.]

[Reg. §53.4943-4]

§53.4943-4. Present   holdings.— (a) *Introduction.*—(1) *Section 4943(c)(4) in general.*—(i) Paragraph(4) of section 4943(c) prescribes transition rules for a private foundation which, but for such paragraph, would have excess business holdings on May 26, 1969. Section 4943(c)(4) provides such a foundation with protection from the initial tax on excess business holdings in two ways. First, the entire interest of such a foundation in any business enterprise in which such a foundation, but for section 4943(c)(4), would have had excess business holdings on May 26, 1969, is treated under section 4943(c)(4)(B) as held by disqualified persons for a certain period of time (the "first phase"). The effect of such treatment is to prevent a private foundation from being subject to the initial tax with respect to its May 26, 1969, interest during the first phase holding period and also to prevent the foundation from purchasing any additional business holdings in such business enterprise during such period (unless the combined holdings of the foundation and all disqualified persons fall below the 20 percent (or 35 percent, if applicable) figure prescribed by section 4943(c)(2)). Second, section 4943(c)(4)(A)(i) initially increases the percentage of permitted holdings of such a foundation to a percentage equal to the difference between—

(A) The percentage of combined holdings of the foundation and all disqualified persons in such business enterprise on May 26, 1969 (subject to a 50 percent maximum), and

(B) The percentage of holdings of all disqualified persons.

The percentage referred to in paragraph (a)(1)(i)(A) of this section is referred to in this

section as the "substituted level". This "substituted level" is then reduced by the "downward ratchet rule" prescribed by section 4943(c)(4)(A)(ii) and paragraph (d)(3) of this section for certain dispositions by such foundation or by disqualified persons. The primary purpose of the substituted level is to indicate what the permitted holdings in such business enterprise will be immediately after the expiration of the first phase holding period. Thereafter, the permitted holdings of a private foundation itself are further limited to a maximum 25 percent interest in such business enterprise by section 4943(c)(4)(D) as soon as the combined holdings of all disqualified persons in such business enterprise exceed 2 percent (of the voting stock). If the combined holdings of all disqualified persons at no time exceed 2 percent (of the voting stock) during the 15 years following the first phase (the "second phase"), then the substituted level is reduced to a 35 percent maximum after the second phase.

(ii) Paragraph (a)(1)(i) of this section may be illustrated by the following example:

Example. On May 26, 1969, private foundation P held a 5 percent interest in corporation X (voting stock and value). On such date disqualified persons held a 16 percent interest in X (voting stock and value). Assume that except for section 4943(c)(4), P would have had a 1 percent interest in X which would have constituted excess business holdings. Therefore, section 4943(c)(4)(B) applies and P's 5 percent interest in X is treated as held by a disqualified person during the 10-year period beginning May 26, 1969. Since the entire 21 percent held by P and disqualified persons is now treated as held by disqualified persons, P's substituted level is 21 percent and its permitted holdings is zero (21% − 21%). However, P has no excess business holdings in X, because during the 10-year period P is not treated as holding such interest. The only change in the interest in X occurs on January 2, 1972, when P disposes of 2 percent of its interest in X to A, an unrelated person. Since the interest held by P and all disqualified persons (21% − 2% = 19%) has decreased below 20 percent, P's substituted level is reduced to 20 percent and its permitted holdings are 1 percent (20% − 19%) on such date. Therefore, if the other interests in X do not change, P will not have excess business holdings if P purchases no more than an additional 1 percent interest in X.

(2) *Interaction of provisions of section 4943(c)(4), (5), and (6).*—During the first phase, a private foundation may acquire additional interests in a business enterprise, other than by purchase, which are entitled to be treated as held by disqualified persons for varying holding periods under section 4943(c)(5) or (6) (relating respectively to certain holdings acquired pursuant to the terms of a trust or will in effect on May 26, 1969, and to the 5-year period to dispose of certain gifts, bequests, etc.). In any case, holdings which the private foundation disposes of shall be charged first against those holdings which it

must dispose of in the shortest period in order to avoid the initial tax thereon. Further, acquisitions of a private foundation under a pre-May 27, 1969, will or trust described in section 4943(c)(5) are treated in a manner similar to the treatment of interests actually held by a private foundation on May 26, 1969. See §§ 53.4943-5 and 53.4943-6.

(b) *Present holdings in general.*—(1) Section 4943(c)(4)(B) provides that any interest in a business enterprise held by a private foundation on May 26, 1969, if the foundation on such date has excess business holdings (determined without regard to section 4943(c)(4)), shall (while held by the foundation) be treated as held by a disqualified person during a first phase. Therefore, no interest of a private foundation shall be treated as held by a disqualified person under section 4943(c)(4)(B) and this section unless:

(i) The private foundation was an entity (not including a revocable trust) in existence on May 26, 1969, even though it was not then treated as a private foundation under section 509 or section 4947;

(ii) Such interest was actually or constructively owned by such entity on such date; and

(iii) Without regard to section 4943(c)(4) such entity had on such date an interest (considered in connection with the interests actually or constructively owned by all disqualified persons with respect to such entity on that date in the same business enterprise, determined as if the entity were then a private foundation) which exceeded the permitted holdings prescribed by section 4943(c)(2) or (3).

(See, however, section 4943(c)(5) and § 53.4943-5 for similar treatment for certain interests acquired by a private foundation under the terms of a trust or a will which were in effect on May 26, 1969.) If a private foundation owns an interest described by section 4943(c)(4)(B), then the length of the first phrase for such an interest is prescribed by paragraph (c) of this section and shall not be affected by any interest acquired by the private foundation or any disqualified person in such business enterprise after May 26, 1969. In addition, the amount of permitted holdings in such business enterprise is prescribed by paragraph (d) of this section. An interest constructively held by a private foundation (or a disqualified person) on May 26, 1969, shall not cease to be an interest to which section 4943(c)(4) applies merely because it is later distributed to such foundation (or to such disqualified person). Nor shall an interest directly held by a private foundation (or disqualified person) on May 26, 1969, cease to be treated as an interest to which section 4943(c)(4) applies to the extent it remains actually or constructively held by such foundation (or such disqualified person) upon transfer of such interest, such as upon the incorporation of a sole proprietorship.

(2) The provisions of this paragraph may be illustrated by the following example:

Example. A, a nonprofit research organization described in section 501(c)(3), was organized

in 1966. On May 26, 1969, A held 50 percent of the stock of corporation B. For its taxable years 1970, 1971, and 1972, A is classified as an organization described in section 509(a)(2). However, for 1973 and subsequent years, A fails to satisfy the gross investment income limitation of section 509(a)(2)(B), and is thus classified as a private foundation. In such a case, section 4943(c)(4) applies, and a disqualified person shall be treated as holding A's stock in B during a first phase that begins on May 26, 1969.

(c) *First phase holding periods.*—(1) *In general.*— If, on May 26, 1969, a private foundation has excess business holdings in any business enterprise (determined with regard to the 20 or 35 percent permitted holdings of section 4943(c)(2)), then all interests which such foundation holds, actually or constructively, in such enterprise on May 26, 1969, shall (while held by such foundation) be deemed held by a disqualified person during the following periods:

(i) The 20-year period beginning on May 26, 1969, if the private foundation holds, actually or constructively, more than 95 percent of the voting stock (or more than a 95 percent profits or beneficial interest in the case of an unincorporated enterprise) in such enterprise on such date;

(ii) Except as provided in paragraph (c)(1)(i) of this section, the 15-year period beginning on May 26, 1969, if the private foundation and all disqualified persons hold, actually or constructively on such date, more than 75 percent of the voting stock (or more than a 75 percent profits or beneficial interest in the case of any unincorporated enterprise) or 75 percent of the value of all outstanding shares of all classes of stock in such enterprise (or more than a 75 percent profits and capital interest in the case of a partnership or joint venture); or

(iii) The 10-year period beginning on May 26, 1969, in any case not described in paragraph (c)(1)(i) or (ii) of this section.
The 20-year, 15-year, or 10-year period described in this subdivision (whichever applies) shall, for purposes of section 4943 and this section, be known as the "first phase".

(2) *Sole proprietorships.*—The 20-year period described in paragraph (c)(1) of this section shall apply with respect to any interest which a private foundation holds in a sole proprietorship on May 26, 1969. See paragraph (b) of this section for the effect of converting such an enterprise to a corporate, partnership, or other form.

(3) *Suspension of first-phase periods.*—The 20-year, 15-year, or 10-year period described in paragraph (c)(1) of this section shall be suspended during the pendency of any judicial proceeding which is brought and diligently litigated by the private foundation and which is necessary to reform, or to excuse the foundation from compliance with, its governing instrument or any other instrument (as in effect on May 26, 1969) in order to allow disposition of any excess business holdings held by the foundation on May 26, 1969.

(4) *Election to shorten the period during which certain holdings of private foundations are treated as held by disqualified persons.*—If, on May 26, 1969, the combined holdings of a private foundation and all disqualified persons in any one business enterprise are such as to make applicable the 15-year period referred to in paragraph (c)(1)(ii) of this section, and if, on such date, the foundation's holdings do not exceed 95 percent of the voting stock in such enterprise, then such 15-year period is shortened to the 10-year period referred to in paragraph (c)(1)(iii), if at any time before January 1, 1971, one or more individuals—

(i) Who are substantial contributors (as described in section 507(d)(2)), or members of the family within the meaning of section 4946(d) of one or more substantial contributors, to such private foundation, and

(ii) Who on May 26, 1969, held in the aggregate more than 15 percent of the voting stock in the enterprise,

made an election in the manner described in 26 CFR 143.6 (rev. as of Apr. 1, 1974).

(5) *Examples.*—The provisions of this paragraph (c) may be illustrated by the following examples:

Example (1). Assume that F, a private foundation, owns, on May 26, 1969, 50 shares of voting stock in corporation X representing 50 percent of the voting power in X and 25 percent of the value of all outstanding shares of all classes of stock in X. Assume further that A and B, the only disqualified persons with respect to F, own five shares each of voting stock in X on such date. The 10 shares of voting stock in X owned by A and B together represent 10 percent of the voting power in X and 5 percent of the value of all outstanding shares of all classes of stock in X. Under the provisions of §53.4943-3, the excess business holdings of F in X (determined without regard to section 4943(c)(4)) as of such date are, therefore, 40 percent of X voting stock. Accordingly, since the combined holdings of F, A, and B in X are, on such date, less than 75 percent of the voting stock in X and less than 75 percent of the value of all outstanding shares of all classes of stock in X, under the provisions of section 4943(c)(4)(B)(iii), all holdings of F in X (*i.e.*, 50 percent of X voting stock) will be treated as held by a disqualified person through May 25, 1979.

Example (2). Assume the facts as stated in Example (1), except that F, on December 15, 1969, purchases an additional 10 shares of voting stock in X respresenting 10 percent of X voting power. Assume, further, that there were no other transactions in the stock in X during 1969. While the 50 percent of X voting stock held by F on May 26, 1969, will be deemed held by a disqualified person through May 25, 1979, the additional 10 shares of X voting stock acquired by purchase by F on December 15, 1969, will not be deemed to be so held. Accordingly, since, under the provisions of §53.4943-3, such 10 shares represent excess business holding of F in X, such 10 shares

will be subject to the imposition of tax under the provisions of section 4943(a).

Example (3). Assume the facts as stated in Example (1), except that F, on December 15, 1971, acquires an additional 10 shares of voting stock in X (representing 10 percent of X voting power) under the terms of a will which was executed before May 26, 1969, to which section 4943(c)(5) applies. While the 50 percent of X voting stock held by F on May 26, 1969, will be deemed held by a disqualified person through May 25, 1979, the additional 10 percent of X voting stock acquired by F on December 15, 1971, will, under the provisions of section 4943(c)(5), be deemed held by a disqualified person through December 14, 1981. See § 53.4943-5.

Example (4). Assume that F, a private foundation, owns on May 26, 1969, 50 shares of voting stock in corporation Y representing 50 percent of the voting power in Y. Assume further that C and D, the only disqualified persons with respect to F, own on such date 15 shares each of Y voting stock and that the 30 shares of Y voting stock owned by C and D together represent 30 percent of the voting power in Y. Under the provisions of § 53.4943-3 the excess business holdings of F in Y (determined without regard to section 4943(c)(4)) as of such date are, therefore, 50 percent of Y voting stock. Accordingly, since the combined holdings of F, C, and D in Y represent, on such date, more than 75 percent of the voting stock in Y, under the provisions of section 4943(c)(4)(B)(ii), all holdings of F in Y, (*i.e.*, 50 percent of Y voting stock) will be treated as held by a disqualified person through May 25, 1984.

Example (5). M, a private foundation, owns on May 26, 1969, sole proprietorship S. Since, under the provisions of § 53.5954-3, M's ownership of S constitutes excess business holdings (determined without regard to section 4943(c)(4)) as of May 26, 1969, and since M's interest in S is greater than 95 percent on such date, under the provisions of this paragraph a disqualified person will be treated as the owner of S for the 20-year period beginning on such date. If S is later incorporated, that percentage of the interest in S retained by M, even though less than a 95-percent interest, shall continue to be treated as held by a disqualified person through May 25, 1989.

Example (6). A and B, individuals, together own on May 26, 1969, 40 shares of voting stock in corporation X representing 40 percent of the voting power in X and 20 percent of the value of all outstanding shares of all classes of stock in X. A and B are both disqualified persons with respect to F, a private foundation, which owns no stock in X on May 26, 1969. On January 1, 1973, A and B donate the 40 shares of X voting stock held by them to F. Since F had no excess business holdings on May 26, 1969, section 4943(c)(4) does not apply. See however, section 4943(c)(6) and § 53.4943-6.

Example (7). Assume the facts as stated in Example (6), except that F, on May 26, 1969,

owns 50 shares of voting stock in X, representing 50 percent of the voting power in X and 25 percent of the value of all outstanding shares of all classes of stock in X. Under the provisions of this paragraph, the 50 shares of X voting stock held by F on May 26, 1969 shall be treated in accordance with the provisions of section 4943(c)(4), while the 40 shares of X voting stock acquired by F on January 1, 1973 shall be treated in accordance with the provisions of section 4943(c)(6). See § 53.4943-6.

(d) *Permitted holdings under section 4943(c)(4).*—(1) *In general.*—The permitted holdings of a private foundation to which section 4943(c)(4) applies in a business enterprise shall be as follows:

(i) The excess of the substituted combined voting level over the disqualified person voting level, and separately,

(ii) The excess of the substituted combined value level over the disqualified person value level.

(2) *Definitions.*—For purposes of paragraph (d) of this section—

(i) The term "disqualified person voting level" on any given date means the percentage of voting stock held by all disqualified persons together on such date (including stock deemed held by such a person by reason of section 4943(c)(4), (5), or (6)).

(ii) The term "disqualified person value level" on any given date means the percentage of the total value of all outstanding shares of all classes of stock in a business enterprise held by all disqualified persons together on such date (including stock deemed held by such a person by reason of section 4943(c)(4), (5), or (6)).

(iii) The term "foundation voting level" prior to the second phase is equal to zero. After the first phase, such term on any given date means the lowest percentage of voting stock held by a private foundation (without regard to section 4943(c)(4)(B)) in a business enterprise on May 26, 1969, and at all times thereafter up to such date. See section 4943(c)(5) and § 53.4943-5 for the effect of interests acquired pursuant to the terms of certain wills or trusts in effect on May 26, 1969.

(iv) The term "foundation value level" prior to the second phase is equal to zero. After the first phase, such term on any given date means the lowest percentage of the total value of all outstanding shares of all classes of stock held by a private foundation (without regard to section 4943(c)(4)(B)) in a business enterprise on May 26, 1969, and at all times thereafter up to such date. See section 4943(c)(5) and § 53.4943-5 for the effect of interests acquired pursuant to the terms of certain wills or trusts in effect on May 26, 1969.

(v) The term "substituted combined voting level" means the lowest percentage to which the sum of the foundation voting level plus the disqualified person voting level has been reduced since May 26, 1969, by paragraph (d)(4) of

this section (the "downward ratchet rule"), subject to the following modifications:

(A) In no event shall such substituted level exceed 50 percent; and

(B) Such substituted level shall be increased (but not above 50 percent) in accordance with section 4943(c)(5) and § 53.4943-5 for certain interests acquired by such foundation pursuant to the terms of a will or trust in effect on May 26, 1969.

(vi) The term "substituted combined value level" means the lowest percentage to which the sum of the foundation value level plus the disqualified person value level has been reduced since May 26, 1969, by paragraph (d)(4) of this section (the "downward ratchet rule"), subject to the following modifications:

(A) In no event shall such substituted level exceed 50 percent; and

(B) Such substituted level shall be increased (but not above 50 percent) in accordance with section 4943(c)(5) and § 53.4943-5 for certain interests acquired by such foundation pursuant to the terms of a will or trust in effect on May 26, 1969.

(vii) In the case of an interest in a partnership or joint venture, definitions (i) through (iv) of this subparagraph shall be applied by substituting "profit interests" for "voting stock" and "all partnership interests" for "all outstanding shares of all classes of stock."

(viii) In the case of an interest in a business enterprise other than a corporation, partnership or joint venture, definitions (i) through (iv) of this subparagraph shall be applied by substituting "beneficial remainder interests" for "voting stock" and "all beneficial remainder interests" for "all outstanding shares of all classes of stock."

(ix) Each level defined in paragraph (d)(2)(iii), (iv), (v), and (vi) as of any date shall be carried over to the subsequent date subject to any adjustments prescribed for such level.

(3) *Permitted holdings—First phase.*—Since during the first phase the substituted combined voting level generally does not exceed the disqualified person voting level, and the substituted combined value level generally does not exceed the disqualified person value level, the permitted holdings during the first phase are generally equal to zero. The permitted holdings during the first phase exceed zero only where the 20 percent (or 35 percent) limitation on the downward ratchet rule contained in paragraph (d)(4)(ii)(B) of this section applies.

(4) *Downward ratchet rule.*—(i) *In general.*—Except as provided in paragraph (d)(4)(ii) of this section and section 4943(c)(5)—

(A) *Scope of rule.*—In general, when the percentage of the holdings in a business enterprise held by a private foundation and all disqualified persons together to which section 4943(c)(4) applies decreases, or when the percentage of the holdings of the private foundation alone in such business enterprise decreases, such

holdings may not be increased (except as provided under section 4943(c)(5) or (6)). This so-called "downward ratchet rule" is designed to prevent the private foundation from purchasing additional holdings in the business enterprise until the substituted combined voting level is reduced to the 20-percent (or 35 percent) figure prescribed by section 4943(c)(2).

(B) *Levels affected.*—Under the downward ratchet rule any decrease after May 26, 1969, in the percentage of holdings comprising either the substituted combined voting level, the substituted combined value level, the foundation voting level or the foundation value level shall cause the respective level to be decreased to such decreased percentage for purposes of determining the foundation's permitted holdings.

(C) *Implementation of reductions.*—Thus, if at any time the sum of the foundation voting level and the disqualified person voting level is less than the immediately preceding substituted combined voting level, the substituted level shall be decreased so that it equals such sum. For example, if on May 26, 1969, a foundation and all disqualified persons together have holdings in a business enterprise equal to 50 percent, on such date the substituted combined voting level and the disqualified person voting level equal 50 percent (since such holdings of the foundation are treated as held by a disqualified person). If the private foundation or a disqualified person on May 27, 1969, sold 2 percent of such holdings to a nondisqualified person, the disqualified person voting level would be decreased to 48 percent (50% − 2%), causing the substituted combined voting level to be decreased to 48 percent. As a further example, assume that on May 26, 1969, a foundation and all disqualified persons together have holdings in a business enterprise equal to 50 percent, and when the first phase expires on May 26, 1979, the substituted combined voting level is still 50 percent, the foundation voting level is 10 percent, and the disqualified person voting level is 40 percent. If a disqualified person thereafter sells 2 percent to a nondisqualified person so that the sum of the disqualified person voting level (40% − 2% = 38%) and the foundation voting level (10%) equals 48 percent (38% + 10%), then the substituted combined voting level is decreased to 48 percent. Similarly, if at any time the sum of the foundation value level and the disqualified person value level is less than the immediately preceding substituted combined value level, the substituted combined value level shall be decreased so that it equals such sum.

(D) *Restrictions on increases in levels.*—In addition, none of the four levels referred to in paragraph (d)(4)(i)(B) of this section may be adjusted upward to reflect any increase in the holdings comprising such level, except as provided in section 4943(c)(5) and § 53.4943-5. As a result, any transfer of May 26, 1969, holdings from a disqualified person to a private foundation shall not increase the foundation voting level or the foundation value level (unless the transfer quali-

fies under section 4943(c)(5)), and thus may reduce the substituted combined value level (and, where appropriate, the substituted combined voting level). Thus, in the last preceding example, if the disqualified person, instead of selling the 2 percent interest to a nondisqualified person, had sold such interest to the foundation, the substituted combined voting level would still be reduced to 48 percent, since the disqualified person voting level would be reduced by 2 percent (to 38%) but the foundation voting level would not be increased by 2 percent (remaining at 10%). However, any transfer of May 26, 1969, holdings from a private foundation to a disqualified person under section 101(1)(2)(B) of the Tax Reform Act of 1969, shall reduce the foundation value level (and, where appropriate, the foundation voting level), but will not reduce the substituted combined value level or the substituted combined voting level. The disqualified person voting level and disqualified person value level are correspondingly increased, not being limited to interests held since May 26, 1969. In addition, a transfer of May 26, 1969, holdings from one disqualified person to another, for example, by bequest, shall not reduce the substituted combined voting level nor the substituted combined value level.

(ii) *Exceptions.*—(A) *One percent de minimis rule.*—If after May 26, 1969, there are one or more decreases in the holdings comprising any of the four levels referred to in paragraph (d)(4)(i)(B) of this section during any taxable year of a private foundation, and if such decreases are attributable to issuances of stock (or such issuances coupled with redemptions), then, unless the aggregate of such decreases equals or exceeds 1 percent, the determination of whether there is a decrease in such level for purposes of this paragraph (d)(4) shall be made only at the close of such taxable year. If, however, the aggregate of such decreases equals or exceeds 1 percent, such level shall be decreased at that time as if the previous sentence had never applied.

(B) *Twenty percent (or 35 percent) floor.*—In no event shall the downward ratchet rule contained in paragraph (d)(4)(i) of this section decrease the substituted combined voting level or the substituted combined value level below 20 percent, or, for purposes of section 4943(c)(2)(B), below 35 percent.

(iii) *Special rules.*—(A) *Change of foundation managers.*—In the case of a foundation manager (as defined in section 4946(b)) who on May 26, 1969, owns holdings in a business enterprise and who is replaced by another foundation manager, the decrease in the substituted combined voting or value levels shall be limited to the excess, if any, of the departing foundation manager's holdings over his successor's holdings.

(B) *Termination of private foundation status under section 507.*—If an organization gives the notification described in section 507(b)(1)(B)(ii) of the commencement of a 60-month termination period and fails to meet

the requirements of section 509(a)(1), (2) or (3) for the entire period, then such organization will be treated as a private foundation during the entire 60-month period for purposes of this paragraph (d)(4) and section 4946(a)(1)(H). For example, X, a private foundation gives notification of the commencement of a 60-month termination commencing on January 1, 1972. X and Y, another private foundation, are effectively controlled by the same persons within the meaning of section 4946(a)(1)(H). X and Y hold 25 percent each of the voting stock of Z corporation on May 26, 1969, so that the substituted combined voting level for X or Y is 50 percent on such date. If X meets the requirements of section 509(a)(1), (2), or (3) for the entire 60-month period, section 4946(a)(1)(H) is inapplicable to X, and, under the downward ratchet rule, the substituted combined voting level for Y is decreased by 25 percent. On the other hand, if X meets the requirements of section 509(a)(2) for its taxable years 1972 and 1973, but fails to meet the requirements of section 509(a)(1), (2), or (3) in 1974, 1975, and 1976, then solely for purposes of section 4943(c)(4)(A)(ii) and this paragraph (d)(4), X will be treated as a disqualified person with respect to Y, and Y will be treated as a disqualified person with respect to X, for taxable years 1972 through 1976 pursuant to section 4946(a)(1)(H). Thus, for purposes of section 4943(c)(4)(A)(ii), the substituted combined voting level for X or Y will not be decreased by reason of the fact that X was attempting to terminate under section 507(b)(1)(B), and assuming no other transactions, such level will remain at 50 percent.

(iv) *Examples.*—The provisions of this paragraph (d)(4) may be illustrated by the following examples:

Example (1). F, a private foundation, owns on May 26, 1969, 50 shares of voting stock in corporation X respresenting 50 percent of the voting stock in X and 25 percent of the value of all outstanding shares of all classes of stock in X. A and B, the only disqualified persons with respect to F, together own, on such date, 2 shares of voting stock in X representing 2 percent of the voting stock in X and 1 percent of the value of all outstanding shares of all classes of stock in X. In addition, on such date, F owns 30 shares of nonvoting stock in X, representing 30 percent of the value of all outstanding shares of all classes of stock in X, and A and B together own 15 shares of nonvoting stock in X representing 15 percent of the value of all outstanding shares of all classes of stock in X. The provisions of section 4943(c)(4)(B)(iii) apply and during the 10-year period beginning on May 26, 1969, a disqualified person is deemed to hold all interests of F in X. Assume that on February 1, 1972, F sells to C, an unrelated individual, 12 shares of voting stock in X representing 12 percent of the voting stock in X and 6 percent of the value of all outstanding shares of all classes of stock in X.

(i) Beginning on May 26, 1969, the disqualified person voting level is 52 percent, the

foundation voting level is zero, and the substituted combined voting level is 50 percent; the disqualified person value level is 71 percent, the foundation value level is zero, and the substituted combined value level is 50 percent.

(ii) Beginning on February 1, 1972, the disqualified person voting level is 40 percent (52% − 12%), the foundation voting level is zero, and the substituted combined voting level is 40 percent; the disqualified person value level is 65 percent (71% − 6%), the foundation value level is zero and the substituted combined value level is 50 percent.

Example (2). F, a private foundation on the calendar year basis, holds, on May 26, 1969, 30 percent of the voting stock in corporation Y. C and D, the only disqualified persons with respect to F, together hold, on such date, 10 percent of the voting stock in Y. The provisions of section 4943(c)(4)(B)(iii) apply with respect to F, and disqualified persons are deemed to hold all interests of F in Y for the 10-year period beginning on May 26, 1969, so that the substituted combined voting level as of such date is 40 percent. On February 1, 1973, a stock issuance by Y causes the combined holdings of voting power by F, C, and D in Y to decrease by 0.3 percent. On June 1, 1973, another issuance causes such combined holdings to decrease by 0.5 percent. In September 1, 1973, an unrelated stock redemption by Y causes such combined holdings to increase by 0.4 percent. Under this paragraph the determination whether there is a decrease in the substituted combined voting level for purposes of the downward ratchet rule shall not be made before January 1, 1974, since the aggregate of the decreases occurring on February 1 and June 1 of 1973 is less than 1 percent (0.3% + 0.5%). Therefore, the substituted combined voting level as of January 1, 1974, is 39.6 percent (40% − [(0.3% + 0.5%) − 0.4%]).

Example (3). Assume the facts as stated in Example (2), except that, on October 1, 1973, a stock issuance by Y causes the combined holdings of voting power by F, C, and D in Y to decrease by 0.3 percent. Since the aggregate of the decreases occurring on February 1, June 1, and October 1, of 1973 exceeds 1 percent, the determination whether there is a decrease in the substituted combined voting level shall be made as of October 1, 1973. At that time the substituted combined voting level shall be reduced to 39.2 percent (40% − 0.3% − 0.5%), the lowest actual combined holdings during the period that the *de minimis* rule was in effect.

(5) *Permitted holdings—Second phase.*—(i) *In general.*—For purposes of section 4943 and this section, the term "second phase" means the 15-year period immediately following the first phase. Upon the expiration of the first phase with respect to an interest to which section 4943(c)(4) applies, such interest shall no longer be treated as held by a disqualified person under section 4943(c)(4)(B). During the second phase, the manner of determining the permitted holdings of a private foundation to which section

4943(c)(4) applies shall be the same as applicable to the first phase, except that a 25 percent maximum shall apply under certain conditions specified in paragraph (d)(5)(ii) of this section. For these purposes the substituted combined voting level and the substituted combined value level in effect for the foundation at the end of the first phase shall be carried over to the second phase. The substituted levels are carried over because although there is a decrease in the disqualified person levels (since holdings are no longer treated as held by disqualified persons under section 4943(c)(4)(B)), a corresponding increase in the foundation levels occurs. For example, if a private foundation on May 26, 1969, held 10 percent of the voting stock in a corporation and disqualified persons held 40 percent of the voting stock, both the disqualified person voting level and the substituted combined voting level equal 50 percent (10% + 40%). Assuming no transactions during the first phase, on May 26, 1979, the disqualified person voting level would be decreased to 40 percent (50% − 10%), but the foundation voting level would be increased to 10 percent so that the substituted combined voting level would remain at 50 percent. In addition, the downward ratchet rule of paragraph (d)(4) of this section shall continue to apply, to prevent the foundation and disqualified persons from purchasing any additional interest in the same enterprise until the substituted combined voting level decreases below 20 percent.

(ii) *25 percent maximum on foundation holdings.*—If, or as soon as, the disqualified person voting level exceeds 2 percent after the expiration of the first phase, the permitted holdings shall not thereafter exceed 25 percent of the voting stock or 25 percent of the value of all outstanding shares of all classes of stock, even though the holdings of the foundation and all disqualified persons combined do not exceed the substituted level. Solely for purposes of determining whether the 25 percent limitation of this subdivision (ii) applies, the disqualified person voting level shall not be treated as exceeding 2 percent solely as a result of the holdings of a private foundation which are treated as held by a disqualified person by reason of section 4943(c)(5) or (6). For example, where under the constructive ownership rules for trusts in § 53.4943-8(b), a private foundation is deemed to own more than 2 percent of the voting stock of a business enterprise but such stock is treated as held by a disqualified person under section 4943(c)(5), the determination of the substituted percentage for permitted holdings in the second phase will be as if the foundation owned the stock held by the trust. Similarly, where a private foundation is the only remainder beneficiary of a trust that is a disqualified person under section 4946(a)(1)(H), the disqualified person voting level shall not be treated as exceeding 2 percent solely as a result of the holdings of such a trust.

(6) *Permitted holdings—Third phase.*—For purposes of section 4943 and this section, the term "third phase" means the entire period fol-

lowing the second phase. During the third phase the manner of determining the permitted holdings of a private foundation to which section 4943(c)(4) applies shall be the same as applicable to the second phase under paragraph (d)(5) of this section (including the carryover of levels from the earlier phase). However, if the 25 percent limit of paragraph (d)(5)(ii) of this section never applied during the second phase, the substituted combined voting level and the substituted combined value level each shall not exceed 35 percent during the third phase.

(7) *Examples.*—The provisions of this paragraph may be illustrated by the following examples:

Example (1). F, a private foundation, owns, on May 26, 1969, 30 shares of voting stock in corporation Z representing 30 percent of the voting power in Z and 15 percent of the value of all outstanding shares of all classes of stock in Z, and owns, on such date, 10 shares of nonvoting stock in Z representing 10 percent of the value of all outstanding shares of all classes of stock in Z. E and G, the only disqualified persons with respect to F, own, on such date, 5 shares each of nonvoting stock in Z. The 10 shares of nonvoting stock in Z owned by E and G together represent 10 percent of the value of all outstanding shares of all classes of stock in Z. Assume further that F cannot meet the requirements for the 35 percent test of section 4943(c)(2)(B). For purposes of applying section 4943(c)(4)(B) and this paragraph, F has excess business holdings in Z (determined without regard to section 4943(c)(4)), because under section 4943(c)(2)(A) F's permitted holdings are 20 percent (20% − 0%) of the voting stock since disqualified persons have no holdings of voting stock. Therefore, section 4943(c)(4)(B) and this paragraph apply, and a disqualified person is treated as holding F's shares of both voting and nonvoting stock in Z for the 10-year period through May 25, 1979. Thus, since all holdings by F in Z are treated as held by a disqualified person during the first phase, F cannot be subject to tax under section 4943(a) on its May 26, 1969, holdings prior to the termination of the first phase, regardless of whether or not disqualified persons purchase additional shares of Z during the first phase.

Example (2). Assume the same facts as in Example (1), and further assume that there were no transactions in the stock of Z during the first phase (May 26, 1969 through May 25, 1979). During the first phase the permitted holdings by F in Z for both the voting stock and the value is zero. The disqualified person voting level and the substituted combined voting level are each 30 percent, and the disqualified person value level and the substituted combined value level are each 35 percent (15% + 10% + 10%). The substituted levels are carried over into the second phase. The disqualified person voting level on May 26, 1979, the beginning of the second phase, is zero, because the voting shares held by F are no longer treated as held by a disqualified person. Therefore, F's permitted holdings

such date are 30 percent of the voting stock, because such percentage is equal to the excess of the substituted combined voting level (30%) over the disqualified person voting level (0%). The disqualified person value level on May 26, 1979, is 10 percent, because the voting and nonvoting shares held by F are no longer treated as held by a disqualified person. Therefore, F's permitted holdings on such date are 25 percent of the value of Z stock, because such percentage is equal to the excess of the substituted combined value level (35%) over the disqualified person value level (10%) as of such date.

Example (3). Assume the facts as stated in Example (2), except that E and G acquire, on February 1, 1970, 10 shares of Z voting stock representing 10 percent of the voting power in Z and 5 percent of the value of all outstanding shares of all classes of stock in Z. During the first phase such permitted holdings remain zero, and prior to May 25, 1979, the substituted combined voting level and substituted combined value level remain 30 and 35 percent, respectively, because such levels may not be increased by acquisitions by disqualified persons. However, the disqualified person voting level and the disqualified person value level are each increased to 40 percent (30% + 10%) and 40 percent (35% + 5%) respectively. During the first phase the excess of the disqualified person voting level over the substituted combined voting level (40% − 30%) and the excess of the disqualified person value level over the substituted combined value level (40% − 35%) indicate how much stock F must dispose of during the first phase to avoid the initial tax when it expires. On May 25, 1979, the last day of the first phase, F disposes of 12 shares of Z voting stock, representing 12 percent of the voting power in Z and 6 percent of the value of all such outstanding shares. The disposition by F reduces the interest F owns to 18 percent (30% − 12%) of the voting power, and 19 percent (25% − 6%) of the value of all outstanding shares of all classes of stock, in Z. Since the disqualified person voting level decreases to 28 percent (40% − 12%), the substituted combined voting level as of May 25, 1979, accordingly is decreased to 28 percent under the downward ratchet rule. Similarly, the substituted combined value level is decreased to 34 percent, as the disqualified person value level as of such date is 34 percent (40% − 6%). On May 26, 1979, the disqualified person voting level is 10 percent (28% − 18%), and the disqualified person value level is 15 percent (34% − 19%), since the shares owned by F are no longer treated as held by a disqualified person as of such date. Accordingly, on May 26, 1979, the permitted holdings by F in Z are 18 percent of the voting power in Z, because such percentage is equal to the excess of the substituted combined voting level (28%) over the disqualified person voting level (10%) as of such date. Similarly, the permitted holdings of F in Z by value are 19 percent (34% − 15%). If F had not disposed of the 12 shares, then on May 26, 1979, F's permitted holdings in voting power and value

would be 20 percent (30% – 10%) and 20 percent (35% – 15%), respectively.

Example (4). F, a private foundation, owns on May 26, 1969, 35 shares of voting stock in corporation Y representing 35 percent of the voting stock in Y and 17.5 percent of the value of all classes of stock in Y, and owns on such date 45 shares of nonvoting stock representing 22.5 percent of the value of all outstanding shares of all classes of stock in Y. No disqualified person with respect to F owns, on such date, any stock in Y. Assume further that Y cannot meet the requirements of the 35 percent test of section 4943(c)(2)(B). For purposes of applying section 4943(c)(4)(B) and this paragraph, F has excess business holdings in Y (determined without regard to section 4943(c)(4)), because under section 4943(c)(2)(A) F's permitted holdings are 20 percent (20% – 0%) of the voting stock since disqualified persons have no holdings of voting stock. Therefore, section 4943(c)(4)(B) and this paragraph apply, and a disqualified person is treated as holding F's shares of both voting and nonvoting stock in Y for the 10-year period through May 25, 1979. During the first phase the permitted holdings by F in Y of both the voting stock and of value are zero. The disqualified person voting level and the substituted combined voting level are each 35 percent, and the disqualified person value level and the substituted combined value level are each 40 percent (17.5% + 22.5%). The substituted levels are carried over into the second phase. The disqualified person voting level and value level on May 26, 1979, are both zero, because the shares held by F are no longer treated as held by a disqualified person. Therefore, F's permitted holdings on such date are 35 percent of the voting power (35% – 0%) and 40 percent of the value (40% – 0%). Assume that on February 1, 1981, A, a disqualified person, acquires 6 percent of the voting stock in Y representing 3 percent of the value of all outstanding shares of all classes of stock in Y. The permitted holdings by F in Z on February 1, 1981, are thus reduced to 25 percent of the voting stock (the lesser of the separate 25% second phase limitation or 29% (35% substituted combined voting level minus 6% disqualified person voting level)) and 25 percent of the value (the lesser of the separate 25% second phase limitation or 37% (40% substituted combined value level minus 3% disqualified person value level)). But see paragraph (d)(8) of this section for limitations on restrictions with respect to nonvoting stock.

Example (5). Assume the same facts as in Example (4) except that A does not acquire the 6 shares of voting stock until February 1, 1996 (in the third phase), rather on February 1, 1981. Thus, F's permitted holdings in Y would remain at 35 percent of the voting stock and 40 percent of the value during the second phase, which expired on May 25, 1994. Assume that on May 25, 1994, the last day of the second phase, F disposes of 10 shares of nonvoting stock representing 5 percent of the value of all outstanding shares in Y to meet the 35 percent third phase

limit. In accordance with the downward ratchet rule, the substituted combined value level and F's permitted holdings in Y would be reduced to 35 percent of value. On February 1, 1996, F's permitted holdings in Y would be reduced to 25 percent of the voting stock (the lesser of the separate 25% third phase limitation or 29% (35% substituted combined voting level minus 6% disqualified person level)) and 25 percent of the value (the lesser of the separate 25% third phase limitation or 32% (35% substituted combined value level minus 3% disqualified person value level)). But see paragraph (d)(8) of this section for limitations on restrictions with respect to nonvoting stock.

(8) *Special rule where all holdings are permitted under section 4943(c)(2).*—(i) Since section 4943(c)(4) and this paragraph provide transitional rules for foundations which would otherwise have had excess business holdings on May 26, 1969, no holdings shall cease to be permitted holdings under this paragraph where such holdings would be permitted holdings under section 4943(c)(2) and § 53.4943-3. Thus, for example, where the substituted combined voting level has been reduced to 20 percent, the provisions of § 53.4943-3(b)(2) concerning nonvoting stock as permitted holdings generally apply.

(ii) The provisions of this paragraph (d)(8) may be illustrated by the following example:

Example. (A) F, a private foundation, owns, on May 26, 1969, 40 shares of voting stock in corporation X respresenting 40 percent of the voting stock in X and 20 percent of the value of all outstanding shares of all classes of stock in X, and owns, on such date, 60 shares of nonvoting stock in X, representing 30 percent of the value of all outstanding shares of all classes of stock in X. A, the only disqualified person with respect to F, owns, on such date, 10 shares of voting stock in X, representing 10 percent of the voting stock in X and 5 percent of the value of all outstanding shares of all classes of stock in X. Under section 4943(c)(4)(B)(iii), a disqualified person is deemed the owner of all holdings by F in X for the 10-year period beginning on May 26, 1969.

(B) Assume that the only transaction in X stock during the first phase is the disposition of 30 shares of voting stock by F on May 1, 1975. The voting stock held by F is permitted holdings under § 53.4943-3 and under such section since all disqualified persons together do not own more than 20 percent of the voting stock in X, all nonvoting stock held by F shall also be treated as permitted holdings. Therefore, all the stock held by F is permitted holdings.

(C) Assume that on May 1, 1975, F had disposed of only 15 shares of voting stock and also had disposed of 35 shares of nonvoting stock. On May 26, 1979, at the beginning of the second phase, this paragraph (d)(8) would not apply since F would have excess business holdings under § 53.4943-3. Under the provisions of this section, the permitted holdings by F in X on such date are 25 percent of the voting stock (35%

substituted combined voting level minus 10% disqualified person voting level) and 25 percent of the value (30% substituted combined value level minus 5% disqualified person value level).

(9) *Special rule for certain private foundations.*—In the case of a private foundation—

(i) Which was incorporated before January 1, 1951;

(ii) Substantially all of the assets of which on May 26, 1969, consisted of more than 90 percent of the stock of an incorporated business enterprise which is licensed and regulated, the sales or contracts of which are regulated, and the professional representatives of which are licensed, by State regulatory agencies in at least 10 States;

(iii) Which acquired such stock solely by gift, devise, or bequest;

(iv) Which does not purchase any stock or other interest in such enterprise after May 26, 1969, and does not acquire any stock or other interest in any other business enterprise which constitutes excess business holdings under §53.4943-3; and

(v) Which, in the last 5 taxable years ending on or before December 31, 1970, expended substantially all of its adjusted net income (as defined in section 4942(f)) for the purpose or function for which it is organized and operated;

paragraph (d)(1) through (5) of this section (permitted holdings during the first and second phase) shall be applied with respect to the holdings of such foundation in such incorporated business enterprise by substituting "51 percent" for "50 percent," and section 4943(c)(4)(D) (third phase) shall not apply with respect to such holdings. For purposes of the preceding sentence, stock of such enterprise in a trust created before May 27, 1969, of which the foundation is the remainder beneficiary shall be deemed to be held by such foundation on May 26, 1969, if such foundation held (without regard to such trust) more than 20 percent of the stock of such enterprise on May 26, 1969.

(10) *Special rule for changes in the relative values of stock of different classes.*—(i) In the case of a corporation that has more than one class of stock outstanding, if the percentage of value held by the private foundation, its disqualified persons, or both, increases over a period of time solely as a result of changes in the relative values of the stock of different classes, then the foundation value level, the disqualified person value level, and the substituted combined value level, as defined in paragraph (d)(2) of this section, shall be adjusted to reflect such increase. An increase in the percentage of value held shall not be considered to have occurred solely as a result of changes in the relative values of the stock of different classes if:

(A) There has been any increase during the period in the percentage of any class of stock held by the private foundation, its disqualified persons, or both, or

(B) There has been any issuance, redemption, or purchase by the issuing corporation of any stock during the period.

See §53.4943-6(d) for rules relating to increases caused by readjustments.

(ii) *Example.*—The provisions of this paragraph (b)[d](10) may be illustrated by the following example:

Example. (i) At all times since May 26, 1969, F, a private foundation, has held 25% (500,000 shares) of the outstanding class of voting stock of X corporation. No disqualified person with respect to F holds any voting stock of X. In addition X has had outstanding since May 26, 1969, a class of non-voting preferred stock, none of which is held by F or a disqualified person. X is an active business corporation and third parties do not have effective control of X. On May 26, 1969, the voting stock (2 million shares outstanding) was trading for $5 a share on the New York Stock Exchange. The non-voting preferred stock, not publicly traded, was valued at $1 million. The total value of all outstanding stock was $11 million ($10 million voting stock plus $1 million non-voting preferred). On May 26, 1969, F held 22.73% of the value of X's outstanding stock ($2.5 million/$11 million).

(ii) On October 31, 1982, X's voting stock is trading for $20 a share and the nonvoting stock is valued at $3 million. At all times during the period May 26, 1969, through October 31, 1982, F has held 25 percent of the voting stock and none of the nonvoting stock of X. No stock of X is owned by disqualified persons. No stock of X has been issued, redeemed or purchased by X during this period. On October 13, 1982, the total value of X's outstanding stock is $43 million ($40 million voting stock and $3 million nonvoting stock) and F holds 23.26 percent of the value of X's outstanding stock ($10 million/$43 million). F's foundation value level and the substituted combined value level are increased from 22.73 percent to 23.26 percent to reflect this change.

(iii) On November 1, 1982, X corporation distributes the stock of Y corporation, a wholly-owned subsidiary, to X's shareholders. Y is a business enterprise. Under this paragraph (d)(10), all of F's stock in X is permitted holdings under section 4943(c)(4) even though the percentage of value held by F has increased from 22.73 percent on May 26, 1969, to 23.26 percent on November 1, 1982. F's permitted holdings in Y will be determined by reference to F's permitted holdings in X under §53.4943-7. Therefore, assuming no prohibited transaction occurs, F's permitted holdings in Y stock equal 25 percent of Y's voting stock and, separately, 23.26 percent of the value of all of Y's outstanding stock. [Reg. §53.4943-4.]

☐ [*T.D.* 7496, 7-5-77. *Amended by T.D.* 7944, 2-21-84.]

[Reg. §53.4943-5]

§53.4943-5. Present holdings acquired by trust or a will.—(a) *Interests to which section 4943(c)(5) applies.*—(1) *In general.*—Section 4943(c)(5) provides that section 4943(c)(4) (other than the 20-year first phase holding period) applies to an interest in a business enterprise acquired after May 26, 1969 by a private foundation under the terms of a trust which was

irrevocable on May 26, 1969, or under the terms of a will executed on or before May 26, 1969, which were in effect on May 26, 1969, and at all times thereafter, as if such interest were held on May 26, 1969. However the first phase holding period prescribed by § 53.4943-4(c)(1)(ii) or (iii) shall commence for such an interest on the date of distribution to the foundation. Unlike section 4943(c)(4) and § 53.4943-4, section 4943(c)(5) and this section treat only the interest so acquired (and not the entire interest held by the foundation in such enterprise on the date of distribution) as held by a disqualified person during a first phase holding period. (See, however, section 4943(c)(6) and paragraph (b)(2) of § 53.4943-6 for the treatment of other holdings of the foundation in the same enterprise if an interest to which section 4943(c)(5) applies is acquired from a person who was not a disqualified person prior to the acquisition.) In addition, section 4943(c)(5) and this section shall not apply if after the acquisition of such an interest the foundation would not have excess business holdings (determined without regard to section 4943(c)(4), (5), or (6)).

(2) *After-acquired interests.*—Section 4943(c)(5) and this section shall not apply to any interest acquired after May 26, 1969, by an estate or trust, other than by reason of the death of the decedent. For example, where a foundation is a residuary beneficiary under the terms of a will executed before May 26, 1969, and the residue of the estate consists of cash, then stock subsequently purchased with this cash for distribution to the foundation will not be treated as an interest acquired under the terms of a will executed on or before May 26, 1969.

(3) *Certain revocable trusts.*—If an interest in a business enterprise actually passes to a private foundation under a trust which would have met the tests referred to in paragraph (a)(1) of this section but for the fact that the trust was revocable (even though it was not in fact revoked) and such interest would have passed to such foundation under a will that meets those tests but for the fact that the grantor died without having revoked the trust, then for purposes of section 4943(c)(5) and this section, such an interest shall be treated as having been acquired by the foundation under the will.

(4) *Modification of will.*—(i) *In general.*—For purposes of section 4943(c)(5) and this section, an amendment or republication of a will which was executed on or before May 26, 1969, does not prevent any interest in a business enterprise which was to pass under the terms (which were in effect on May 26, 1969, and at all times thereafter) of such will from being treated as a present holding under section 4943(c)(4) or (5)—

(A) Solely because there is a reduction in the interest in the business enterprise which the foundation was to receive under the terms of the will (for example, if the foundation is to receive the residuary estate, and if one class of stock is disposed of by the decedent during his lifetime or by a subsequent codicil);

(B) Solely because such amendment or republication is necessary in order to comply with section 508(e) and the regulations thereunder;

(C) Solely because there is a change in the executor of the will; or

(D) Solely because of any other change which does not otherwise change the rights of the foundation with respect to such interest in the business enterprise.

However, if under such amendment or republication there is an increase in the interest in the business enterprise which the foundation was to receive under the terms of the will in effect on May 26, 1969, such increase shall not be treated as present holdings under section 4943(c)(4) or (5). Under such circumstances the interest which would have been acquired before such increase shall remain present holdings. See section 4943(c)(6) and § 53.4943-6 with respect to the treatment of such increase in holdings of a private foundation.

(ii) *Examples.*—The provisions of this paragraph (a)(4) may be illustrated by the following examples:

Example (1). On May 9, 1985, A modifies by codicil his will which was in effect on May 26, 1969, and was unchanged until such modification. The purpose of the codicil was, in the event of A's death, to increase the number of shares in X Corporation that would pass to the W foundation from 70 percent of all the voting power and value to 80 percent. Under these facts, if A dies without further modifying the terms of the will which apply to W's interest in X, section 4943(c)(5) will apply to 70 percent of the X voting power and value and section 4943(c)(6) will apply to 10 percent of the X voting power and value, since 10 percent of the X voting power and value would not pass under a provision of the will which was in effect on May 26, 1969, and at all times thereafter. Accordingly, if the stock is distributed to W on July 6, 1988, then, assuming that on May 26, 1969, W and all disqualified persons owned less than 75% of the voting stock in X, an amount of such stock representing 70 percent of X voting power and value shall be treated as held by a disqualified person through July 5, 1998, and an amount of such stock representing 10 percent of X voting power and value shall be treated as held by a disqualified person through July 5, 1993.

Example (2). Assume the facts as stated in Example (1), except that the sole purpose of the codicil was to change the executor of the will. Under paragraph (a)(4)(i) of this section, such codicil will not prevent the X voting stock which was bequeathed to W from being treated as held by a disqualified person through July 5, 1998.

(b) *Holding periods.*—(1) *In general.*—An interest to which section 4943(c)(5) applies shall be entitled to a 15-year holding period starting on the date of distribution only if the interests actually or constructively owned by a private foundation and all disqualified persons on May 26, 1969, in a business enterprise exceed 75 percent of the voting stock (or of the profits or beneficial interest) or 75 percent of the value of all outstanding shares of all classes of stock (or of the profits and capital interest) in such enterprise. For purposes of the preceding sentence, interests held by the foundation on May 26, 1969, shall be deemed to include an interest to which section 4943(c)(5) applies and which has been acquired (on or before the date of distribution for the interest in question) from a person who was not a disqualified person on May 26, 1969. Therefore, if under the terms of a will in effect on May 26, 1969, and at all times thereafter, a private foundation is created on July 1, 1975, and receives 76 percent of the voting stock of a business enterprise on that date, such stock shall be treated as held by a disqualified person until June 30, 1990. Any interest to which section 4943(c)(5) applies but which is not entitled to a 15-year holding period shall be entitled to a 10-year holding period starting on the date of distribution. For purposes of this paragraph the date of distribution shall be deemed to occur no later than the date on which the trust or estate is considered to be terminated under § 1.641(b)-3 of this chapter (Income Tax Regulations).

(2) *Constructive ownership prior to date of distribution.*—To the extent that an interest to which section 4943(c)(5) applies is constructively held by a private foundation under section 4943(d)(1) and § 53.4943-8 prior to the date of distribution, it shall be treated as held by a disqualified person prior to such date by reason of section 4943(c)(5). In addition, in the case of a foundation's interest in a trust which was irrevocable on May 26, 1969, and to which both sections 4943(c)(4) and (c)(5) apply, the first phase holding period for such interest shall end with whichever such period under section 4943(c)(4) or (5) ends later. For example, if under the terms of such a trust, 96 percent of the voting stock in a business enterprise was constructively held by a private foundation on May 26, 1969, and was distributed to such foundation on June 30, 1970, such interest is entitled to a 20-year holding period beginning on May 26, 1969.

(c) *Permitted holdings.*—(1) *In general.*—The permitted holdings of a private foundation which has an interest in a business enterprise to which section 4943(c)(5) applies shall be determined in accordance with the rules of paragraph (d) of § 53.4943-4. The levels referred to in such paragraph shall be adjusted to take into account the acquisition of such an interest as if it were treated as held by a disqualified person from May 26, 1969, until the date of acquisition. See also § 53.4943-6(b)(2) for the special rule for interests held by a private foundation at the time it acquires a section 4943(c)(5) interest from a nondisqualified person. Thus, for example, if on June 30, 1975, the disqualified person voting level and the substituted combined voting level in corporation X with respect to foundation F are 45 percent, and a nondisqualified person's 10 percent voting interest in X is acquired by F on July 1, 1975, in a transaction to which section 4943(c)(5) applies, the above-mentioned levels shall be increased to 55 and 50 percent respectively, on July 1, 1975. However, if such interest had been acquired from a person who was a disqualified person on May 26, 1969, rather than from a nondisqualified person, no adjustments in such levels would have taken place on July 1, 1975. In such a case, though, at the beginning of the second phase on July 1, 1985, the foundation voting level would be increased by 10 percent, and the disqualified person voting level decreased by 10 percent (assuming that none of the acquired stock had been disposed of prior to such date).

(2) *Separate phases.*—The phases for each interest to which section 4943(c)(5) applies start independently from those for any other interest of the foundation in the same enterprise to which section 4943(c)(4) or (5) applies. Therefore, until an interest enters its own second phase, the 25 percent limit described in paragraph (d)(5) of § 53.4943-4 shall not apply to such interest since such interest (and any subsequently acquired section 4943(c)(5) interest in the first phase) is still treated as held by a disqualified person for purposes of that 25 percent limit. In addition, if such an interest enters its second phase and at such time all disqualified persons together do not have holdings in excess of 2 percent of the voting stock in the same business enterprise, then the 25 percent limit of section 4943(c)(4)(D)(i) shall not then apply to such interest, even though such limit may have been applicable to an interest with an earlier second phase. Moreover, the 35 percent limit of section 4943(c)(4)(D)(ii) shall cause only interests which have entered the third phase to become excess business holdings, taking into account, however, interests in prior phases in determining the holdings subject to such limit.

(3) *Examples.*—The provisions of this paragraph may be illustrated by the following examples: (After each example is a chart setting forth the chronological changes in the various levels referred to in paragraph (d) of § 53.4943-4.)

Example (1). On May 26, 1969, F, a private foundation, owns no stock in M Corporation, and A, a disqualified person owns 40 percent of the voting stock (voting power and value) in M. A dies on May 1, 1971, leaving 30 percent of the voting stock in M to F and leaving the other 10 percent to a disqualified person. Distribution is made on June 1, 1972, and assume that section 4943(c)(5) applies. No transactions in the stock of M, other than those described in this example, occur. On May 26, 1969, the substituted combined voting level is 40 percent, the disqualified person voting level is deemed to be 40 percent, and the permitted holdings by F in M is deemed

to be 0 percent (40% – 40%). On May 1, 1971 (the date that F acquired the M stock by reason of its constructive ownership of A's estate), the various levels remain unchanged. On May 1, 1971, the 30 percent interest is treated as held by a disqualified person for a period extending through May 31, 1982. On June 1, 1981, F disposes of 6 percent of the voting stock to a nondisqualified person. The substituted combined voting level and the disqualified person voting level thereby are reduced to 34 percent (40% – 6%) each. On June 1, 1982, at the beginning of the second phase, the foundation voting level increases to 24 percent (30% – 6%) and the

disqualified person voting level is reduced to 10 percent (34% – 24%). The substituted combined voting level as of June 1, 1982, remains at 34 percent. The permitted holdings as of such date are 24 percent (34% – 10%). If F had not disposed of any holdings prior to June 1, 1982, F's permitted holdings would have been 25 percent, the lesser of 25 percent (the limitation of section 4943(c)(4)(D)(i)), or 30 percent (40% – 10%). Since on such date the 30 percent interest would no longer have been treated as held by a disqualified person, F would have had excess business holdings of 5 percent (30% – 25%).

Date	F owns	Interest treated as held by disqualified person	Disqualified persons own	Foundation voting level	Substituted combined voting level	Disqualified person voting level	Permitted holdings	Comments
5/26/69	0%	0%	40%	0%	40%	40%	0%	
5/1/71	+30%	+30%	–30%					A dies.
Do.	30%	30%	10%	0%	40%	40%	0%	
6/1/72	30%	30%	10%	0%	40%	40%	0%	Distribution.
6/1/81	– 6%	– 6%			– 6%	– 6%		F sells 6%.
6/1/81	24%	24%	10%	0%	34%	34%	0%	
6/1/82	–24%			+24%		–24%	+24%	2d phase
Do.	24%	0%	10%	24%	34%	10%	24%	begins.

Example (2). (i) On May 26, 1969, F, a private foundation, owns 30 percent of the voting stock of N Corporation (voting power and value) and disqualified persons own 20 percent of the voting stock of N Corporation. On May 1, 1971, B, a disqualified person, dies leaving 15 percent of the voting stock to F. Assume that distribution was made on June 1, 1972, and that section 4943(c)(5) applies. On May 26, 1969, the substituted combined voting level and the disqualified person voting levels are each 50 percent and the permitted holdings are 0 percent (50% – 50%). On May 1, 1971, and June 1, 1972, these levels remain unchanged. On May 1, 1971, the 15 percent interest is treated as held by a disqualified person for a period extending through May 31, 1982.

(ii) On July 1, 1978, F sells 6 percent of the F stock to a nondisqualified person, thereby reducing the disqualified person voting level and the substituted combined voting level to 44 percent (50% – 6%). On May 26, 1979, at the beginning of the second phase for F's 1969 holdings, the foundation voting level is 24 percent (30% – 6%), the substituted combined voting level is still 44 percent, and the disqualified person voting level is 20 percent (44% – 24%). The permitted holdings are 24 percent (44% – 20%). In addition F's 24 percent holdings do not exceed the 25 percent limitation of section 4943(c)(4)(D)(i) and paragraph (d)(5)(ii) of § 53.4943-4.

(iii) On August 1, 1981, F sells 16 percent of the N stock to a nondisqualified person, thereby

reducing the foundation voting level to 8 percent (24% – 16%), and reducing the substituted combined voting level to 28 percent (44% – 16%). The disqualified person voting level remains at 20 percent. On June 1, 1982, at the beginning of the second phase for F's holdings acquired by will, the substituted combined voting level is still 28 percent, the foundation voting level is 23 percent (8% + 15%), the disqualified person voting level is 5 percent (20% – 15%), and the permitted holdings are 23 percent (28% – 5%).

(iv) If F had not disposed of the 6 percent on July 1, 1978, then on May 26, 1979, at the beginning of the second phase for F's 1969 holdings, F's permitted holdings would have been 25 percent, the lesser of 25 percent (the limitation of section 4943(c)(4)(D)(i)), or 30 percent (50% – 20%). Since F's 30 percent interest would no longer have been treated as held by a disqualified person on May 26, 1979, F would have had excess business holdings of 5 percent (30% – 25%). Similarly, if F had not disposed of the 16 percent interest on August 1, 1981 (but had disposed of the 6 percent interest), on July 1, 1982, at the beginning of the second phase for F's holdings acquired by will, F's permitted holdings would have been 25 percent, the lesser of 25 percent (under section 4943(c)(4)(D)(i)), or 39 percent (44% – 5%). Since as of such date F's entire holdings of 39 percent would no longer have been treated as held by a disqualified person, F would have had excess business holdings of 14 percent (39% – 25%).

Date	F owns	F's interest 1969	F's interest 1971	Interest treated as held by disqualified person	Disqualified persons own	Foundation voting level	Substituted combined voting level	Disqualified person voting level	Permitted holdings	Comments
5/26/69	30%	30%		30%	20%	0%	50%	50%	0%	
5/1/71	+15%		+15%	+15%	−15%					B dies
5/1/71	45%	30%	15%	45%	5%	0%	50%	50%	0%	
6/1/72	45%	30%	15%	45%	5%	0%	50%	50%	0%	Distribution
7/1/78	−6%	−6%		−6%			−6%	−6%		F sells 6%
7/1/78	39%	24%	15%	39%	5%	0%	44%	44%	0%	
										2nd phase for 24%
5/26/79				−24%		+24%		−24%	+24%	
5/26/79	39%	24%	15%	15%	5%	24%	44%	20%	24%	
8/1/81	−16%	−16%				−16%	−16%		−16%	F sells 16%
8/1/81	23%	8%	15%	15%	5%	8%	28%	20%	8%	
7/1/82				−15%		+15%		−15%	+15%	All in 2nd phase
7/1/82	23%	8%	15%	0%	5%	23%	28%	5%	23%	

Example (3). (i) On May 26, 1969, F, a private foundation owns 5 percent of the voting stock of O Corporation (voting power and value), and disqualified persons own 45 percent of the voting stock. C, a disqualified person, dies on May 1, 1971, and leaves 41 percent of the voting stock of O to F. Assume that distribution is made on June 1, 1972, and that section 4943(c)(5) applies. On May 26, 1969, the substituted combined voting level and the disqualified person voting level are 50 percent and the permitted holdings are 0 percent (50% – 50%). On May 1, 1971, and June 1, 1972, the various levels remain unchanged. On May 1, 1971, the 41 percent interest is treated as held by a disqualified person for a period extending through May 31, 1982. On May 26, 1979, at the beginning of the second phase for F's 1969 holdings of 5 percent, the 5 percent is no longer treated as held by a disqualified person, the foundation voting level is 5 percent, the disqualified person voting level is reduced to 45 percent (50% – 5%), and the substituted combined voting level remains at 50 percent. On such date F's permitted holdings are 5 percent (50% – 45%). Since the 41 percent interest is treated as held by a disqualified person, the interest treated as held by F (5%) does not exceed the 25 percent limitation of section 4943(c)(4)(D)(i).

(ii) On August 1, 1981, F sells 22 percent of the O stock to a nondisqualified person, thereby reducing the foundation voting level to 0 percent. Since the reductions are first applied to the 1969 holdings of 5 percent, 17 percent (22% – 5%) applies to the 41 percent interest, reducing such interest to 24 percent (41% – 17%), and reducing the disqualified person voting level to 28 percent (45% – 17%). The substituted combined voting level is reduced to 28 percent (0% + 28%). On June 1, 1982, at the beginning of the second phase for F's holdings acquired by will, the substituted combined voting level remains at 28 percent, the foundation voting level is 24 percent the disqualified person voting level is reduced to 4 percent (28% – 24%).

(iii) If F had not disposed of the 22 percent interest prior to June 1, 1982, F's permitted holdings would have been 25 percent, the lesser of 25 percent (under section 4943(c)(4)(D)(i)), or 46 percent (50% – 4%). Since as of such date, F's entire holdings of 46 percent would no longer have been treated as held by a disqualified person, F would have had excess business holdings of 21 percent (46% – 25%).

Date	F owns	F's interest 1969	F's interest 1971	Interest treated as held by disqualified person	Disqualified persons own	Foundation voting level	Substituted combined voting level	Disqualified person voting level	Permitted holdings	Comments
5/26/69	5%	5%		5%	45%	0%	50%	50%	0%	
5/1/71	+41%		+41%	+41%	−41%					C dies
5/1/71	46%	5%	41%	46%	4%	0%	50%	50%	0%	
6/1/72	46%	5%	41%	46%	4%	0%	50%	50%	0%	Distribution
5/26/79				−5%		+5%		−5%	+5%	2nd phase for 5%
5/26/79	46%	5%	41%	41%	4%	5%	50%	45%	5%	
8/1/81	−22%	−5%	−17%	−17%		−5%	−22%	−17%	−5%	F sells 22%
8/1/81	24%	0%	24%	24%	4%	0%	28%	28%	0%	
6/1/82				−24%		+24%		−24%	+24%	2nd phase for 24%
6/1/82	24%	0%	24%	0%	4%	24%	28%	4%	24%	

Example (4). (i) On May 26, 1969, F, a private foundation, owns 30 percent of the voting stock in P Corporation (voting power and value), and disqualified persons own 20 percent. On May 1,

1971, D, a disqualified person, dies leaving 18 percent of the voting stock to F. Assume that distribution was made on June 1, 1972, and that section 4943(c)(5) applies. On May 26, 1969, the substituted combined voting level and the disqualified person voting level are each 50 percent and the permitted holdings are 0 percent (50% – 50%). On May 1, 1971, and June 1, 1972, these levels remain unchanged. On May 1, 1971, the 18 percent interest is treated as held by a disqualified person for a period extending through May 31, 1982. On May 26, 1979, the foundation voting level increases to 30 percent, the disqualified person voting level decreases to 20 percent (50% – 30%), and the permitted holdings are 30 percent (50% – 20%). On June 1, 1982, the foundation voting level increases to 48 percent, the disqualified person voting level decreases to 2 percent and the permitted holdings are 48 percent (50% – 2%). Since at no time during the second phase for F's 1969 holdings did all disqualified persons together have holdings in ex-cess of 2 percent of the voting stock of P, the 25 percent limitation of section 4943(c)(4)(D)(i) did not apply to F's 1969 holdings.

(ii) On July 1, 1993, F disposes of 16 percent of the stock in P, thereby reducing the substituted combined voting level to 34 percent (50% – 16%), and reducing the permitted holdings to 32 percent (34% – 2%). If F had not disposed of the 16 percent of the stock of P prior to May 26, 1994, on such date, under section 4943(c)(4)(D)(ii), F's substituted combined voting level for its 1969 holdings would have been 35 percent, and the permitted holdings would have been 33 percent (35% – 2%). Since none of F's holdings of 48 percent would have been treated as held by a disqualified person on such date (the beginning of the third phase for F's 1969 holdings), F would have had excess business holdings of 15 percent, the lesser of 30 percent (F's 1969 holdings in the third phase), or 15 percent (the excess of F's 48 percent holdings over the permitted holdings of 33 percent).

Date	F owns	F's interest 1969	F's interest 1971	Interest treated as held by disqualified person	Disqualified persons own	Foundation voting level	Substituted combined voting level	Disqualified person voting level	Permitted holdings	Comments
5/26/69	30%	30%		30%	20%	0%	50%	50%	0%	
5/1/71	+18%		+18%	+18%	–18%					D dies
5/1/71	48%	30%	18%	48%	2%	0%	50%	50%	0%	
6/1/72	48%	30%	18%	48%	2%	0%	50%	50%	0%	Distribution
5/26/79				–30%		+30%		–30%	+30%	2nd phase for 30%
5/26/79	48%	30%	18%	18%	2%	30%	50%	20%	30%	
6/1/82				–18%		+18%		–18%	+18%	2nd phase for 18%
6/1/82	48%	30%	18%	0%	2%	48%	50%	2%	48%	
7/1/93	–16%	–16%				–16%	–16%		–16%	F disposes of 16%
7/1/93	32%	14%	18%	0%	2%	32%	34%	2%	32%	
5/26/94	32%	14%	18%	0%	2%	32%	34%	2%	32%	3rd phase for 14%
6/1/97	32%	14%	18%	0%	2%	32%	34%	2%	32%	3rd phase for 18%

Example (5). (i) On May 26, 1969, F, a private foundation, owns 5 percent of the voting stock in Q Corporation (voting power and value), and disqualified persons own 45 percent. On May 1, 1971, E, a disqualified person, dies leaving 43 percent of the voting stock to F. Assume that distribution was made on June 1, 1972, and that section 4943(c)(5) applies. On May 26, 1969, the substituted combined voting level and the disqualified person voting level are each 50 percent and the permitted holdings are 0 percent (50% – 50%). On May 1, 1971, and June 1, 1972, these levels remain unchanged. On May 1, 1971, the 43 percent interest is treated as held by a disqualified person for a period extending through May 31, 1982. On May 26, 1979, the foundation voting level increases to 5 percent, the disqualified person voting level decreases to 45 percent, and the permitted holdings are 5 percent (50% – 45%). On June 1, 1982, the foundation voting level increases to 48 percent, the disqualified person voting level decreases to 2 percent, and the permitted holdings are 48 percent (50% – 2%). At no time during the second phase for F's 1969 holdings did all disqualified persons together have holdings in excess of 2 percent of the voting stock of Q. Therefore, the 25 percent limitation of section 4943(c)(4)(D)(i) did not apply.

(ii) On July 1, 1993, F sells 6 percent of the stock in Q to a nondisqualified person. This reduces the substituted combined voting level to 44 percent and reduces the permitted holdings to 42 percent (44% – 2%). If F had not disposed of the 6 percent of the stock in 1993, on May 26, 1994, at the beginning of the third phase for F's 1969 holdings, F would have had 5 percent excess business holdings. The excess business holdings are 5 percent because although the excess business holdings computed for the third phase are 15 percent (the excess of F's actual holdings (48%) over the permitted holdings of 33 percent (35% – 2%)), only 5 percent of the holdings are in this phase and subject to the 35 percent combined holdings limitation.

(iii) On July 1, 1995, F sells 10 percent of the stock in Q, thereby reducing the substituted combined voting level to 34 percent and reducing the permitted holdings to 32 percent (34% – 2%). If F had not disposed of the 10 percent of the stock, on June 1, 1997, at the beginning of the

third phase for F's acquired holdings, F would have had 9 percent excess business holdings (the excess of F's total holdings in the third phase (42%) over the permitted holdings of 33 percent (35% − 2%)).

Date	F owns	F's interest 1969	F's interest 1971	Interest treated as held by disqualified person	Disqualified persons own	Foundation voting level	Substituted combined voting level	Disqualified person voting level	Permitted holdings	Comments
5/26/69	5%	5%		5%	45%	0%	50%	50%	0%	
5/1/71	+43%		+43%	+43%	−43%					E dies
5/1/71	48%	5%	43%	48%	2%	0%	50%	50%	0%	
6/1/72	48%	5%	43%	48%	2%	0%	50%	50%	0%	Distribution 2nd phase for 5%
5/26/79				−5%		+ 5%		− 5%	+ 5%	
5/26/79	48%	5%	43%	43%	2%	5%	50%	45%	5%	2nd phase for 43%
6/1/82				−43%		+43%		−43%	+43%	
6/1/82	48%	5%	43%	0%	2%	48%	50%	2%	48%	F sells 6%
7/1/93	− 6%	− 5%	− 1%			− 6%	− 6%		− 6%	
7/1/93	42%	0%	42%	0%	2%	42%	44%	2%	42%	F sells 10%
7/1/95	−10%		−10%			−10%	−10%		−10%	
7/1/95	32	0%	32%	0%	2%	32%	34%	2%	32%	3rd phase for 32%
6/1/97	32%	0%	32%	0%	2%	32%	34%	2%	32%	

Example (6). (i) On May 26, 1969, F, a private foundation, owns 30 percent of the voting stock in R Corporation (voting power and value), and disqualified persons own 20 percent. On August 1, 1978, F disposes of 6 percent of the stock to a nondisqualified person. On May 1, 1981, G, a disqualified person, dies leaving 15 percent of the voting stock to F. Assume that distribution was made on June 1, 1982, and that section 4943(c)(5) applies. On May 26, 1969, the substituted combined voting level and the disqualified person voting level are each 50 percent, and the permitted holdings are 0 percent (50% − 50%). On August 1, 1978, these levels decrease to 44 percent (50% − 6%). On May 26, 1979, the foundation voting level increases to 24 percent (30% − 6%), the disqualified person voting level decreases to 20 percent (44% − 24%), and the permitted holdings are 24 percent (44% − 20%). If F had not disposed of the 6 percent of the stock prior to May 26, 1979, on May 26, 1979, the beginning of the second phase for F's 1969 holdings, F's permitted holdings would have been 25 percent, the lesser of 25 percent (under section 4943(c)(4)(W)(i)) or 30 percent (50% − 20%). Since the 30 percent interest would no longer have been treated as held by a disqualified person on such a date, F would have had excess business holdings of 5 percent (30% − 25%).

(ii) On May 1, 1981, and June 1, 1982 (assuming F had disposed of the 6 percent hold-ings), the foundation voting level, the disqualified person voting level, the substituted combined voting level and permitted holdings remain respectively 24 percent, 20 percent, 44 percent and 24 percent. On May 1, 1981, the 15 percent interest is treated as held by a disqualified person for a period extending through May 31, 1992. On July 1, 1991, F sells 16 percent of the voting stock in R to a nondisqualified person, thereby reducing the substituted combined voting level to 28 percent (44% − 16%), and reducing the foundation voting level to 8 percent (24% − 16%). The disqualified person voting level remains at 20 percent. On June 1, 1992, at the beginning of the second phase of F's holdings acquired by will, the substituted combined voting level remains at 28 percent, the foundation voting level increases to 23 percent (8% + 15%) and the disqualified person voting level decreases to 5 percent (20% − 15%). The permitted holdings on such date are 23 percent (28% − 5%). If F had not disposed of the 16 percent interest prior to June 1, 1992, F's permitted holdings would have been 25 percent, the lesser of 25 percent (under section 4943(c)(4)(D)(i)) or 39 percent (44% − 5%). Since as of such date, F's entire holdings of 39 percent would no longer have been treated as held by a disqualified person, F would have had excess business holdings of 14 percent (39% − 25%).

Date	F owns	F's interest 1969	F's interest 1981	Interest treated as held by disqualified person	Disqualified persons own	Foundation voting level	Substituted combined voting level	Disqualified person voting level	Permitted holdings	Comments
5/26/69	30%	30%		30%	20%	0%	50%	50%	0%	
8/1/78	– 6%	– 6%		– 6%			– 6%	– 6%		F disposes of 6%
8/1/78	24%	24%		24%	20%	0%	44%	44%	0%	
5/26/79				–24%		+24%		–24%	+24%	2nd phase for 24%
5/26/79	24%	24%		0%	20%	24%	44%	20%	24%	
5/1/81	+15%		+15%	+15%	–15%					G dies
5/1/81	39%	24%	15%	15%	5%	24%	44%	20%	24%	
6/1/82	39%	24%	15%	15%	5%	24%	44%	20%	24%	Distribution
7/1/91	–16%	–16%				–16%	–16%		–16%	F disposes of 16%
7/1/91	23%	8%	15%	15%	5%	8%	28%	20%	8%	
6/1/92				–15%		+15%		–15%	+15%	2nd phase of 15%
6/1/92	23%	8%	15%	0%	5%	23%	28%	5%	23%	

Example (7). (i) On May 26, 1969, F, a private foundation, owns 5 percent of the voting stock in S Corporation (voting power and value), and disqualified persons own 45 percent. On May 1, 1980, H, a disqualified person, dies leaving 41 percent of the voting stock to F. Assume that distribution is made on June 1, 1981, and that section 4943(c)(5) applies. On May 26, 1969, the substituted combined voting level and disqualified person voting levels are each 50 percent. On May 26, 1979, the disqualified person voting level decreases to 45 percent, the foundation voting level increases to 5 percent, and the permitted holdings are 5 percent (50% – 45%). On May 1, 1980, and June 1, 1981, the levels remain the same. Since the 41 percent holdings are treated as held by a disqualified person for the period beginning on May 1, 1980, and extending through May 31, 1991, F's remaining holdings of 5 percent do not exceed the 25 percent limitation of section 4943(c)(4)(D)(i).

(ii) On August 1, 1990, F sells 22 percent of the voting stock of S to a nondisqualified person, reducing the 5 percent foundation voting level to zero, leaving 17 percent (22% – 5%) to reduce the disqualified person voting level to 28 percent (45% – 17%) so that the substituted combined voting level equals 28 percent (50% – 22%). On June 1, 1991, the beginning of the second phase for the remaining 24 percent (41% – 17%) of F's holdings acquired by will, the foundation voting level increases from zero to 24 percent, the disqualified person voting level decreases to 4 percent (28% – 24%), the substituted combined voting level remains at 28 percent, and the permitted holdings equal 24 percent (28% – 4%).

(iii) If F had not disposed of the 22 percent holdings prior to June 1, 1991, F's permitted holdings would have been 25 percent, the lesser of 25 percent (under section 4943 (c)(4)(D)(i)) or 46 percent (50% – 4%). Since as of such date, F's entire holdings of 46 percent would no longer have been treated as held by a disqualified person, F would have had excess business holdings of 21 percent (46% – 25%).

Date	F owns	F's interest 1969	F's interest 1980	Interest treated as held by disqualified person	Disqualified persons own	Foundation voting level	Substituted combined voting level	Disqualified person voting level	Permitted holdings	Comments
5/26/69	5%	5%		5%	45%	0%	50%	50%	0%	
5/26/69				– 5%		+ 5%		– 5%	+ 5%	2nd phase for 5%
5/26/69	5%	5%		0%	45%	5%	50%	45%	5%	
5/1/80	+41%		+41%	+41%	–41%					H dies
5/1/80	46%	5%	41%	41%	4%	5%	50%	45%	5%	
6/1/81	46%	5%	41%	41%	4%	5%	50%	45%	5%	Distribution
8/1/90	–22%	– 5%	–17%	–17%		– 5%	–22%	–17%	– 5%	F disposes of 22%
8/1/90	24%	0%	24%	24%	4%	0%	28%	28%	0%	
6/1/91				–24%		+24%		–24%	+24%	2nd phase for 24%
6/1/91	24%	0%	24%	0%	4%	24%	28%	4%	24%	

[Reg. § 53.4943-5.] ☐ [*T.D.* 7496, 7-5-77.]

Reg. § 53.4943-5(c)(3)

[Reg. § 53.4943-6]

§ 53.4943-6. Five-year period to dispose of gifts, bequests, etc.—(a) *In general.*—(1) *Application.*—(i) Paragraph (6) of section 4943(c) prescribes transition rules for a private foundation, which, but for such paragraph, would have excess business holdings as a result of a change in the holdings in a business enterprise after May 26, 1969 (other than by purchase by such private foundation or by a disqualified person) to the extent that section 4943(c)(5) (relating to certain holdings acquired under a pre-May 27, 1969, will or trust) does not apply.

(ii) Subparagraph (A) of section 4943(c)(6) applies where, immediately prior to a change in holdings described in paragraph (a)(1)(i) of this section, the foundation has no excess business holdings in such enterprise (determined without regard to section 4943(c)(4), (5), or (6)). In such a case, the entire interest of the foundation in such enterprise (immediately after such change) shall (while held by the foundation) be treated as held by a disqualified person (rather than by the foundation) during the five-year period beginning on the date of such change.

(iii) Subparagraph (B) of section 4943(c)(6) applies where the foundation has excess business holdings in such enterprise (determined without regard to section 4943(c)(4), (5), or (6)) immediately prior to a change in holdings described in paragraph (a)(1)(i) of this section. In such a case, the interest of the foundation in such enterprise (immediately after such change) shall (while held by the foundation) be treated as held by a disqualified person (rather than the foundation) during the five-year period beginning on the date of such change, except that if and as soon as any holdings in such enterprise become excess business holdings during such period (determined without regard to such change (and the resulting application of section 4943(c)(6) to the foundation's interest in such enterprise)), such holdings shall no longer be treated as held by a disqualified person under this section, but shall constitute excess business holdings subject to the initial tax. In applying the preceding sentence, if holdings of the foundation which (but for such change in holdings (and the resulting application of section 4943(c)(6) to the foundation's interest in such enterprise)) would be subject to the 25 percent limit prescribed by section 4943(c)(4)(D) after the expiration of the first phase, such holdings shall be treated as subject to such percentage limitation for purposes of determining excess business holdings. For example, if a private foundation in 1978 has present holdings of 28 percent in a business enterprise to which section 4943(c)(4) applies, and such holdings would exceed the 25 percent limit of section 4943(c)(4)(D)(i) on May 26, 1979, a gift of 5 percent to the foundation in 1978 of an interest in such enterprise shall not prevent the 3 percent (28% – 25%) excess over the 25 percent limit from constituting excess business holdings on May 26, 1979, if on such date disqualified persons hold more than a 2 percent interest in such enterprise (and no other transaction has taken place).

(2) *Acquisitions that are not purchases.*—Section 4943(c)(6) does not apply if a change in holdings in a business enterprise is the result of a purchase by the private foundation or a disqualified person. For purposes of subparagraph (a) of this paragraph, the term "purchase" shall not include any acquisition by gift, devise, bequest, legacy, or intestate succession. Paragraph (d) of this section provides rules for the treatment of increases in holdings received in a readjustment (as defined in § 53.4943-7(d)(1)).

(3) *Examples.*—The provisions of paragraph (a) of this section may be illustrated by the following examples:

Example (1). On January 4, 1985, A, an individual, makes a contribution to F, a private foundation, of 200 shares of X Corporation common stock. Assume that F had no X stock before January 4, 1985, and under section 4943(c)(1) the receipt of the X stock by F would cause some or all of the 200 shares of the X stock to be classified as excess business holdings. Under the provisions of section 4943(c)(6)(A) and this paragraph (a), since the contribution of the X stock to F is a gift and not a purchase, the X stock in F's hands is treated as held by disqualified persons and not by F through January 3, 1990.

Example (2). Assume the facts as stated in Example (1) except that F receives the X stock as a bequest pursuant to the terms of A's will executed on April 1, 1980. A dies on June 3, 1984, and the stock is distributed to F on February 16, 1985. As in Example (1), the bequest of X to F is not a purchase under this paragraph (a). Consequently, the X stock in F's hands is treated as held by disqualified persons and not by F through February 15, 1990.

Example (3). On February 1, 1980, F, a private foundation, owns 15 percent of the voting stock of X Corporation, and disqualified persons own 4 percent of the voting stock of X Corporation. On February 2, 1980, B, a nondisqualified person, contributes 8 percent of the voting stock of X to F in a transaction to which section 4943(c)(5) does not apply. Assuming that the 35 percent limit of section 4943(c)(2)(B) does not apply under the provisions of section 4943(c)(6)(A) and paragraph (a) of this section the 23 percent voting stock owned by F on such date is treated as held by a disqualified person through February 1, 1985, since F would have had excess business holdings of 7 percent as a result of the contribution (23% actual holdings less 16% (20% – 4%) permitted holdings). On March 1, 1984, C, another nondisqualified person, contributes 6 percent of the voting stock of X Corporation to F. But for this second contribution and the resulting application of section 4943(c)(6) to F's interest in X, F would have excess business holdings of 7 percent (23% – 16%) within the five-year period beginning on the date of such contribution. Accordingly, under section 4943(c)(6)(B) and paragraph (a) of this section, all 29 percent (6% + 23%) of the

stock held by F on March 1, 1984, will be treated as held by a disqualified person until March 1, 1989, except that 7 percent will cease to be so treated on February 2, 1985. If prior to February 2, 1985, no further transactions occurred in the stock of X, F would have excess business holdings of 7 percent subject to the initial tax, since the amount still treated as held by disqualified persons (29% – 7%) plus the amount actually held by disqualified persons (4%) already exceed 20 percent.

(b) *Special rules for acquisitions by will or trust.*—(1) *In general.*—In the case of an acquisition of holdings in a business enterprise by a private foundation pursuant to the terms of a will or trust, the five-year period described in section 4943(c)(6) and in this section shall not commence until the date on which the distribution of such holdings from the estate or trust to the foundation occurs. See § 53.4943-5(b)(1) for rules relating to the determination of the date of distribution under the terms of a will or trust. For purposes of this subparagraph, holdings in a business enterprise will not be treated as acquired by a private foundation pursuant to the terms of a will where the holdings in the business enterprise were not held by the decedent. Thus, in the case of after-acquired property, this subparagraph shall not apply, the five-year period described in section 4943(c)(6) and this section shall commence on the date of acquisition of such holdings by the estate, and such five-year period may expire prior to the date of distribution of such holdings from the estate. To the extent that an interest to which section 4943(c)(6) and this paragraph (b)(1) apply is constructively held by a private foundation under section 4943(d)(1) and § 53.4943-8 prior to the date of distribution, it shall be treated as held by a disqualified person prior to such date by reason of section 4943(c)(6). See § 53.4943-8 for rules relating to constructive holdings held in an estate or trust for the benefit of the foundation.

(2) *Special rule for section 4943(c)(5) interests acquired from a nondisqualified person.*—(i) In the case of holdings of a private foundation in a business enterprise to which section 4943(c)(5) (relating to certain holdings acquired under a pre-May 27, 1969, will or trust) applies which are acquired from a nondisqualified person, the interest of the foundation in such enterprise (immediately after such acquisition) shall (while held by the foundation) be treated as held by a disqualified person (rather than the foundation) under section 4943(c)(6)(B) and paragraph (a)(1)(iii) of this section from the date of acquisition until the end of the fifth year following the date of distribution of such holdings. Thereafter, only the holdings to which section 4943(c)(5) and § 53.4943-5(a)(1) apply shall continue to be treated as held by a disqualified person until the end of the first phase with respect thereto.

(ii) The provisions of paragraph (b)(2)(i) of this section may be illustrated by the following examples:

Example (1). On May 26, 1969, F, a private foundation, owns 5 percent of the voting stock of Corporation X and no disqualified persons own any stock in X. On June 30, 1977, a nondisqualified person bequeaths to F 33 percent of the voting stock in X to which section 4943(c)(5) applies. This 33 percent interest is distributed to F on August 17, 1978. Under section 4943(c)(6)(A) the entire 38 percent (5% + 33%) of the X voting stock shall be treated as held by a disqualified person from June 30, 1977 (the date the 33 percent interest is contructively acquired by F) until August 17, 1983 (five years after the date of distribution of the 33 percent interest to F). However, assuming that the 35 percent limit of section 4943(c)(2)(B) does not apply, the substituted combined voting level on June 30, 1977 is only 33 percent because there was no interest to which section 4943(c)(4) or (5) applied immediately before that date and thus there was no substituted combined voting level at that time. In that case, since the 3-phase holding period is only available for the interest acquired by will (33%) under section 4943(c)(5), the substituted combined voting level on June 30, 1977 is only 33 percent, not 38 percent. Assuming that the substituted combined voting level remains 33 percent at all relevant times, and prior to August 17, 1983, no further transactions occur in the stock of X, F on that date would have excess business holdings of 5 percent subject to the initial tax. The amount treated as held by disqualified persons at that time (33%) would equal the substituted combined voting level at that time (33%), and thus permitted holdings would be zero. Under section 4943(c)(5) the 33 percent interest will continue to be treated as held by a disqualified person until August 17, 1988 (10 years after the date of distribution).

Example (2). On May 26, 1969, F, a private foundation, owns 29 percent of the stock (voting power and value) of Corporation X, and on June 30, 1977, a nondisqualified person bequeaths to F 23 percent of the stock (voting power and value) in X to which section 4943(c)(5) does apply. This 23 percent interest is distributed to F on August 17, 1978. Disqualified persons hold no stock of X. Although the substituted combined voting and value levels cannot exceed 50 percent on May 26, 1979 (at the start of the second phase with respect to the 29 percent interest), under section 4943(c)(6)(B) the entire 52 percent (29% + 23%) of the X voting stock shall be treated as held by a disqualified person from June 30, 1977 (the date the 23% interest is constructively acquired by F) until August 17, 1983 (five years after the date of distribution of the 23% interest to F). On June 1, 1980, during such second phase, D, a disqualified person, purchases 3 percent of the X stock (voting power and value). On such date, but for the acquisition by F of the 23 percent interest, F would have had excess business holdings of 4 percent. The purchase by D of more than 2 percent of the voting stock of X causes the 25 percent limit of section 4943(c)(4)(D)(i) to apply to the 29 percent interest (29% – 25% = 4%). Thus, on June 1, 1980, 4 percent of the X voting stock

held by F since May 27, 1969, shall cease to be treated as held by a disqualified person under section 4943(c)(6)(B) and become excess business holdings subject to the initial tax. See §53.4943-2(a)(1)(ii) for the 90-day period in which to dispose of these excess business holdings resulting from the purchase by the disqualified person.

(c) *Exceptions.*—(1) Section 4943(c)(6) and this section shall not apply to any transfer of holdings in a business enterprise by one private foundation to another private foundation which is related to the first foundation within the meaning of section 4946(a)(1)(H).

(2) Section 4943(c)(6) and this section shall not apply to an increase in the holdings of a private foundation in a business enterprise that is part of a plan whereby disqualified persons will purchase additional holdings in the same enterprise during the five-year period beginning on the date of such change, *e.g.*, to maintain control of such enterprise, since such increase shall be treated as caused in part by the purchase of such additional holdings.

(3) The purchase of holdings by an entity whose holdings are treated as constructively owned by a foundation, its disqualified persons, or both, under section 4943(d)(1) shall be treated as a purchase by a disqualified person if the foundation, its disqualified persons or both have effective control of the entity or otherwise can control the purchase. For example, if a foundation is the beneficiary of a specific bequest of $20,000 and its consent is required for the estate to make a purchase using such cash, then a purchase by the estate using such cash would be treated as a purchase by a disqualified person. Similarly, if an executor of an estate is a disqualified person with respect to a private foundation, any purchase by the estate would be treated as a purchase by a disqualified person.

(4) If a private foundation, its disqualified persons, or both, hold an interest in specific property under the terms of a will or trust, and if the private foundation, its disqualified persons, or both, consent or otherwise agree to the substitution of holdings in a business enterprise for such specific property, such holdings shall be treated as required by purchase by a disqualified person. For example, if a private foundation is the beneficiary of a specific bequest of $20,000 and the private foundation agrees to accept certain of the estate's holdings in a business enterprise in satisfaction of such specific bequest, such holdings will be treated as acquired by purchase by a disqualified person even if such holdings were held by the decedent.

(d) *Readjustments and distributions.*—(1) *General rule.*—Except as otherwise provided in subparagraph (2) of this paragraph, any increase in holdings in a business enterprise that is the result of a readjustment (as defined in §53.4943-7(d)(1)) shall be treated as acquired other than by purchase. However, holdings that are attributable to holdings owned by the private foundation that would have been excess busi-

ness holdings except for the fact that such holdings were treated as held by a disqualified person prior to the readjustment shall in no event be treated as held by a disqualified person after the date on which the holdings to which the change is attributable would have ceased to be treated as held by a disqualified person.

(2) *Exceptions.*—Any increase in holdings in a business enterprise that is the result of a readjustment (as defined in §53.4943-7(d)(1)), including any change resulting from application of the rule in §53.4943-8(c)(3), shall be treated as occurring by purchase by a disqualified person:

(i) To the extent the increase is attributable to holdings that were excess business holdings prior to the readjustment, and separately

(ii) To the full extent of the increase if the readjustment includes a prohibited transaction, unless the foundation establishes to the satisfaction of the Commissioner that effective control of all parties to the transaction was, at the time of the transaction, in one or more persons (other than the foundation) who are not disqualified persons with respect to the foundation. See §53.4943-7(d)(2) for the definition of prohibited transaction.

(3) *Section 4943(c)(6) holdings.*—If, immediately prior to a readjustment (as defined in §53.4943-7(d)(1)), a private foundation has holdings in a business enterprise that are treated under section 4943(c)(6) as held by a disqualified person, then any holdings in a business enterprise that are received in the readjustment in exchange for such section 4943(c)(6) holdings shall be treated as the holdings surrendered in the exchange to the same extent as provided in §53.4943-7 with respect to exchanges involving holdings to which section 4943(c)(4) or (5) applies. Rules similar to those in §53.4943-7(a)(2) shall be applied to determine when holdings are treated as surrendered or received in a readjustment for purposes of this paragraph.

(4) *Redemption by a corporation that is a disqualified person.*—If a foundation holds an interest in a corporation that is a disqualified person, an increase in the holdings of the private foundation, its disqualified persons, or both, as a result of a redemption or a purchase of stock of the disqualified person corporation by such corporation shall not be treated as acquired by purchase by a disqualified person based solely on the status of the corporation as a disqualified person.

(5) *One percent rule for redemptions.*—If the holdings of a foundation, its disqualified persons, or both, in a business enterprise are increased as a result of one or more redemptions during any taxable year then, unless the aggregate of such increases equals or exceeds one percent of the outstanding voting stock or one percent of the value of all outstanding shares of all classes of stock, the determination of whether such increases cause the foundation to have excess business holdings shall be made only at the close of the private foundation's taxable year.

The five-year period described in section 4943(c)(6) or the 90-day period described in § 53.4943-2(a)(1)(ii), whichever is applicable, shall begin on the last day of such taxable year. If, however, the aggregate of such increases equals or exceeds one percent of the outstanding voting stock or one percent of the value of all outstanding shares of all classes of stock, the determination of whether such increases cause the foundation to have excess business holdings shall be made, and the applicable five-year or 90-day period shall begin, as of the date the increases, in the aggregate, equal or exceed one percent.

(6) *Examples.*—The provisions of this paragraph are illustrated in § 53.4943-7(f) and by the following examples:

Example (1). (i) F, a private foundation, holds 20% of the voting stock of X corporation, an active business enterprise. No disqualified person with respect to F holds any X stock. In 1980, X redeems 10% of its outstanding shares, increasing F's holdings to 22% of the X stock. Assume the redemption by X is not a prohibited transaction.

(ii) All of F's holdings before the redemption are permitted holdings under section 4943(c)(2). There is no effective control of X by third parties so that 35% permitted holdings rule is inapplicable. F's holdings after the redemption exceed the permitted holdings under section 4943(c)(2) (20%). Because the increase is attributable to stock that was permitted holdings prior to the readjustment, and the readjustment does not involve a prohibited transaction, the 2% increase in F's holdings of X stock is treated as acquired other than by purchase. Therefore, under section 4943(c)(6) and this section, F will have 5 years from the date of the redemption to dispose of the 2% excess.

Example (2). (i) Assume the same facts as in *Example (1)* except that the 20% of X stock held by F was donated by X corporation, was worth more than $5,000 and represented 20% of the contributions received by the foundation through the end of the taxable year in which the gift of stock was made.

(ii) X corporation is a disqualified person with respect to F under section 4946(a)(1)(A). Under subparagraph (4), the redemption of X stock is not treated as a purchase by a disqualified person merely because X is a disqualified person with respect to F. Therefore the rules of this paragraph apply as if the redemption were made by a corporation which is not a disqualified person. The analysis and result are the same as in *Example (1).*

Example (3). (i) On May 1, 1990, F, a private foundation, received a donation of 40% of the stock of X corporation, a business enterprise. Neither F nor any disqualified person with respect to F holds any other interest in X. On June 1, 1992, the X corporation redeemed F's 40% interest in exchange for 100% of the stock of Y corporation, a wholly-owned subsidiary of X.

Assume the redemption by X is not a prohibited transaction.

(ii) Under section 4943(c)(6), the X stock acquired by gift is treated as held by disqualified persons through April 30, 1995. Under subparagraph (3) of this paragraph (d), 40% of the 100% interest in Y received in exchange for F's 40% interest in X is treated as F's 40% interest in X and is therefore treated as held by disqualified persons through April 30, 1995. In addition, under subparagraph (1) of this paragraph (d), the 60% interest in Y that represents an increase in holdings above the 40% held before the readjustment will be treated as acquired other than by purchase. However, F's 20% interest in X in excess of the 20% permitted holdings under 4943(c)(2) would have been excess business holdings if such interest had not been treated as held by a disqualified person on June 1, 1992. Therefore, to the extent of a 30% interest in Y (*i.e.,* the portion of the increased holdings in Y attributable to F's 20% holdings in X) the increased holdings will be treated as held by disqualified persons only through April 30, 1995, since this is the latest date on which F's original 40% interest in X would have been treated as held by disqualified persons. The remaining 30% interest in Y will be treated as held by disqualified persons for five years from the date of the exchange (through May 31, 1997).

(e) *Constructive holdings.*—Any change in holdings in a business enterprise that occurs because a corporation ceases to be actively engaged in a trade or business, thus causing its holdings to be constructively owned by its shareholders, shall be treated as acquired other than by purchase.

(f) *Certain transactions treated as purchases; cross references.*—For the application of section 4943(c)(6) to holdings that were not an interest in a business enterprise when acquired but that subsequently become holdings in a business enterprise, see § 53.4943-10(d)(2). [Reg. § 53.4943-6.]

□ [*T.D. 7496, 7-5-77. Amended by T.D. 7944, 2-21-84.*]

[Reg. § 53.4943-7]

§ 53.4943-7. Special rules for readjustments involving grandfathered holdings.—(a) *General rules.*—(1) *Readjustments.*—Except to the extent provided in paragraph (b) of this section, if a private foundation, its disqualified persons, or both together have holdings in a corporation to which section 4943(c)(4) or (5) applies, stock of a corporation received by the foundation, its disqualified persons, or both together in a readjustment(as defined in paragraph (d)(1) of this section) in exchange for such holdings to which section 4943(c)(4) or (5) applies shall be treated, for purposes of section 4943(c)(4) or (5), as the stock surrendered in the exchange.

(2) *No exchange necessary.*—Paragraph (a)(1) of this section shall apply to all readjustments even if no exchange occurs. For purposes of this section, all stock held (directly or indirectly)

before a readjustment in any corporation involved in the readjustment shall be treated as stock surrendered in the readjustment and all stock held (directly or indirectly) after the readjustment in any corporation involved in the readjustment shall be treated as stock received in the readjustment in exchange for the stock treated as surrendered.

(b) *Exceptions and limitations.*—(1) *Limitation on increases in percentage of voting stock.*—(i) If the percentage of voting stock in a business enterprise owned (directly or indirectly) by a private foundation by reason of its ownership of stock received in an exchange described in paragraph (a) of this section exceeds the greatest percentage of voting stock in any business enterprise owned (directly or indirectly) by the private foundation prior to such exchange by reason of its ownership of the stock surrendered by it in the exchange, then—

(A) That portion of the stock received by the private foundation in the exchange which represents such excess is to be treated as an increase in the holdings of the private foundation in accordance with § 53.4943-6(d), and

(B) Only the remaining portion of the stock received by the private foundation in the exchange shall be treated as the stock surrendered by the private foundation in the exchange.

(ii) If the sum of the percentage of voting stock in a business enterprise owned (directly or indirectly) by disqualified persons by reason of their ownership of stock received in an exchange described in paragraph (a) of this section plus the percentage of voting stock in the business enterprise owned (directly or indirectly) by the private foundation by reason of its ownership of stock received in the exchange and treated as the stock surrendered under paragraph (b)(1)(i) of this section exceeds the greatest percentage of voting stock in any business enterprise owned (directly or indirectly) by the private foundation and its disqualified person in combination by reason of their ownership of the stock surrendered by them in the exchange, then—

(A) That portion of the stock received by the disqualified persons in the exchange which represents such excess is to be treated as an increase in the holdings of the disqualified persons in accordance with § 53.4943-6(d), and

(B) Only the remaining portion of the stock received by the disqualified persons in the exchange is to be treated as the stock surrendered by the disqualified persons in the exchange.

(2) *Limitation on increase in percentage of value.*—(i) If the percentage of value of all outstanding shares of all classes of stock in a business enterprise owned (directly or indirectly) by a private foundation by reason of its ownership of stock received in an exchange described in paragraph (a) of this section exceeds the greatest percentage of such value in any business enterprise owned (directly or indirectly) by the pri-

vate foundation prior to such exchange by reason of its ownership of the stock surrendered by it in the exchange, then—

(A) That portion of the stock received by the private foundation in the exchange which represents such excess is to be treated as an increase in the holdings of the private foundation in accordance with § 53.4943-6(d), and

(B) Only the remaining portion of the stock received by the private foundation in the exchange shall be treated as the stock surrendered by the private foundation in the exchange.

(ii) If the sum of the percentage of value of all outstanding shares of all classes of stock in a business enterprise owned (directly or indirectly) by disqualified persons by reason of their ownership of stock received in an exchange described in paragraph (a) of this section plus the percentage of such value in the business enterprise owned (directly or indirectly) by the private foundation by reason of its ownership of stock received in the exchange and treated as the stock surrendered under paragraph (b)(2)(i) of this section exceeds the greatest percentage of such value in any business enterprise owned (directly or indirectly) by the private foundation and its disqualified persons in combination prior to the exchange by reason of their ownership of the stock surrendered by them in the exchange, then—

(A) That portion of the stock received by the disqualified persons in the exchange which represents such excess is to be treated as an increase in the holdings of the disqualified persons in accordance with § 53.4943-6(d), and

(B) Only the remaining portion of the stock received by the disqualified persons in the exchange is to be treated as the stock surrendered by the disqualified persons in the exchange.

(3) *Increases in percentage of both voting stock and value.*—(i) If, as the result of an exchange described in paragraph (a) of this section, a private foundation has excesses determined under both paragraphs (b)(1)(i) and (b)(2)(i) of this section, then—

(A) That portion of the stock received by the private foundation in the exchange that represents the larger excess is to be treated as an increase in the holdings of the private foundation in accordance with § 53.4943-6(d), and

(B) Only the remaining portion of the stock received by the private foundation in the exchange is to be treated as the stock surrendered by the private foundation in the exchange.

(ii) If as the result of an exchange described in paragraph (a) of this section, disqualified persons have excesses determined under both paragraphs (b)(1)(ii) and (b)(2)(ii) of this section, then—

(A) That portion of the stock received by the disqualified persons in the exchange that represents the larger excess is to be treated as an increase in the holdings of the disqualified persons in accordance with § 53.4943-6(d), and

Reg. § 53.4943-7(b)(3)(ii)(A)

(B) Only the remaining portion of the stock received by disqualified persons in the exchange is to be treated as the stock surrendered by disqualified persons in the exchange.

(4) *Exception for prohibited transactions.*—If a readjustment includes a prohibited transaction, as defined in paragraph (d)(2) of this section, then this paragraph shall be applied substituting, for purposes of paragraph (b)(1) and (b)(2), the lowest percentage of voting power or value owned prior to the exchange in any business enterprise involved in the readjustment to which the exchange relates for the greatest percentage of voting power or value in any business enterprise owned by reason of ownership of the stock surrendered in the exchange.

(5) *Voting and value levels.*—After an exchange described in paragraph (a) of this section, the private foundation voting and value levels, and the substituted combined voting and value levels (as defined in §53.4943-4(d)(2)) shall be the lesser of each respective level immediately prior to the exchange with respect to the stock surrendered in the exchange and each such respective level determined immediately after the exchange by taking into account only the stock received in the exchange that is treated under this paragraph as the stock surrendered in the exchange. If the stock of more than one corporation is surrendered in exchange for stock of one corporation, the highest of each voting or value level determined immediately prior to the exchange with respect to the stock of the corporations surrendered in the exchange shall be treated as such level immediately prior to the exchange.

(6) *Determination of phases.*—(i) *In general.*—Stock received in an exchange described in paragraph (a) of this section that is treated as stock surrendered in the exchange under this paragraph shall be treated as subject to the same first, second, and third phases that were applicable to the stock surrendered for it. For purposes of determining the applicable phases, stock received in an exchange shall be treated as received in exchange for particular holdings of stock surrendered based on the terms of the exchange. Where only a portion of the stock received is treated as the stock surrendered, such portion of the stock received shall be treated as exchanged for particular holdings of stock surrendered in the same proportions as the total stock received was exchanged for particular holdings of stock surrendered. For example, if 20 shares of X stock owned by a private foundation, subject to a first phase beginning on January 1, 1978 and ending on December 31, 1987, are exchanged for 20 shares of Y stock, and 40 shares of X stock owned by the private foundation, subject to a first phase beginning on June 1, 1980 and ending on May 31, 1990, are exchanged for 40 shares of Y stock, then ¹/₃ of the Y stock received by the private foundation is treated as received in exchanged [sic] for X stock having the January 1, 1978—December 31, 1987 first phase and ²/₃ of the Y stock received by the

private foundation is treated as received in exchange for the X stock having the June 1, 1980—May 31, 1990 first phase. If only 30 shares of the Y stock received by the private foundation are treated as the stock surrendered, then ¹/₃ (10 Y shares) will be subject to the January 1, 1978—December 31, 1987 first phase and ²/₃ (20 Y shares) will be subject to the June 1, 1980—May 31, 1990 first phase.

(ii) *Transitional rule.*—In any case in which holdings subject to section 4943(c)(4) or 4943(c)(5) have been consolidated prior to May 22, 1984, then the longest first phase applicable to any of the holdings surrendered in the consolidation shall be applied to the holdings received by the foundation in the consolidation that are treated as the holdings surrendered in the consolidation. For purposes of this clause, a consolidation is any readjustment that results in a reduction in the number of entities in which the foundation has direct holdings.

(c) *Plan to dispose of excess business holdings.*—(1) Notwithstanding §53.4943-4(d)(4)(i)(D) (relating to restrictions on increases in levels) and paragraphs (a) and (b) of this section, if a readjustment occurs under an approved plan to dispose of stock to which section 4943(c)(4) or (5) applies, in order to meet the requirements of section 4943(c)(4) (*i.e.*, to meet the reduced limits that will be applicable after the first phase holding period described in §53.4943-4(c)) or to meet the requirements of section 4943(c)(2), all of the stock received in the readjustment shall be treated as held by disqualified persons through the end of the longest first phase holding period applicable to stock surrendered in the readjustment. The foundation and substituted combined voting and value levels shall not be increased on account of the readjustment.

(2) For purposes of this paragraph, a plan is an approved plan only if it is approved by the Commissioner and may be subject to such conditions as the Commissioner determines. A plan must be approved prior to any exchange or distribution pursuant to the plan except for a showing of good cause such as a business emergency.

(d) *Definitions.*—(1) *Readjustments.*—For purposes of this section, the term "readjustment" includes, but is not limited to—

(i) A merger or consolidation;

(ii) A recapitalization;

(iii) An acquisition of stock or assets;

(iv) A transfer of assets;

(v) A change in identity, form, or place of organization, however effected;

(vi) A redemption;

(vii) A distribution of assets or of stock, including a distribution to which section 301, 302, 331, or 355 applies or a distribution of stock of the distributing corporation.

(2) *Prohibited transaction.*—A prohibited transaction is any transaction involving a private foundation that has holdings in a business enterprise which—

(i) Acquires stock (or similar interest in the case of an unincorporated entity) or assets of a business enterprise or redeems its own stock (or similar interest in the case of an unincorporated entity) using cash or other property transferred to the acquiring business enterprise (e.g., as a contribution to capital) by the private foundation, its disqualified persons, or both;

(ii) Acquires stock (or similar interest in the case of an unincorporated entity) or assets of a business enterprise or redeems its own stock (or similar interest in the case of an unincorporated entity) using the proceeds of a loan made to, or guaranteed by, the private foundation, its disqualified persons, or both;

(iii) Acquires 40 percent or more of the voting stock (or similar interest in the case of an unincorporated entity), 40 percent or more of the value of all outstanding shares of all classes of stock (or similar interest in the case of an unincorporated entity), or 40 percent or more of the assets of a business enterprise if the acquiring business enterprise's net assets used in its trade or business prior to such acquisition are insubstantial when compared to the net assets acquired or when compared to the net assets of the business enterprise, the stock (or similar interest in the case of an unincorporated entity) of which was acquired. For this purpose, an insubstantial ratio means a ratio that is 15% or less; or

(iv) Is used as a device to acquire or expand excess business holdings. The determination of whether a business enterprise is used as a device to acquire or expand excess business holdings shall be determined based on all the facts and circumstances. A business enterprise shall be presumed to have been used as a device to acquire or expand excess business holdings if it acquires 40 percent or more of the voting stock (or similar interest in the case of an unincorporated entity), 40 percent or more of the value of all outstanding shares of all classes of stock (or similar interest in the case of an unincorporated entity), or 40 percent or more of the assets of a business enterprise if the consideration for the acquisition consists primarily of nonvoting stock (or similar interest in the case of an unincorporated entity) of the acquiring business enterprise.

(3) *Corporation involved in a readjustment.*—A corporation shall be treated as involved in a readjustment if, as part of the readjustment, any stock of the corporation is issued or redeemed, or any stock or assets of the corporation are distributed, exchanged, purchased, sold, acquired, or otherwise transferred.

(e) *Application to unincorporated business enterprise.*—The rules of this section shall apply equally to partnerships and other unincorporated business enterprises, applying the rules and substitutions provided in §53.4943-3(c)(2), (3), and (4).

(f) *Examples.*—The provisions of this section and §53.4943-6(d) are illustrated by the following examples, which assume no prohibited transactions are involved unless otherwise stated:

Example (1). (i) F, a private foundation, has owned 80% of the one outstanding class of stock of X corporation since 1965. The X stock is subject to section 4943(c)(4) with a first phase ending on May 25, 1984. On January 1, 1982, X merges with Y corporation to form Z corporation. X, Y and Z are active business corporations. F owns no Y stock. No disqualified person with respect to F owns any stock in X, Y, or Z. After the merger, F owns 25% of the one outstanding class of Z stock. Third parties do not control Z so that the 35% permitted holdings rule under section 4943(c)(2) is inapplicable.

(ii) F's percentages of voting power and value in Z after the merger (25%) are less than F's percentages of voting power and value in X before the merger (80%). Therefore, under paragraph (a)(1) of this section, all of F's holdings in Z are treated as the X stock surrendered. Therefore, the Z stock is treated as subject to section 4943(c)(4) with a first phase ending on May 25, 1984. Under the downward ratchet of paragraph (a)(5) of this section, the foundation voting and value levels and the substituted combined voting and value levels are reduced to 25%.

Example (2). (i) F, a private foundation, owns 100% of the one outstanding class of stock in X corporation and 30% of the one outstanding class of stock in Y corporation. F has held this stock continuously since 1960, and no disqualified person has ever owned any stock in X or Y. Under section 4943(c)(4), F's holdings in X are treated as held by disqualified persons through the end of the first phase on May 25, 1989, and F's holdings in Y are permitted holdings during the second phase, which began on May 26, 1979. On January 1, 1985, X and Y consolidate, forming a new corporation Z. In the consolidation, F acquires 50% of the one class of outstanding stock of Z, 40% in exchange for F's 100% interest in X and 10% in exchange for F's 30% interest in Y. Unrelated parties hold the remaining 50% of Z.

(ii) F's percentages of voting power and value in Z after the merger (50%) are less than F's percentages of voting power and value in X before the merger (100%). Thus, under paragraph (a)(1) of this section, the 50% interest in Z held by F is treated as the stock surrendered in the exchange for purposes of section 4943(c)(4). Under paragraph (b)(6) of this section, the 10% interest in Z received for the Y stock is subject to the same second phase period as the surrendered Y stock. The 40% interest in Z received for the X stock is subject to the same first phase period as the surrendered X stock.

Example (3). (i) F, a private foundation, owns 50% of the one class of outstanding stock in X corporation which F has held continuously since 1935. No disqualified person with respect to F owns any stock in X. Neither F nor any disqualified person with respect to F owns any stock in Y corporation. On July 1, 1982, X and Y enter into an agreement to consolidate their businesses in a

reorganization to which section 368(a)(1)(A) will apply. As a result of the contemplated consolidation, F will own 60% of the voting stock in Z, the resulting corporation. In addition, parties unrelated to F will own the remaining 40% of the Z voting stock and 100% of a new issue of nonvoting preferred stock in Z. Assume for purposes of this example, that the 60% of the voting stock to be held by F in Z will represent 50% of the fair market value of the outstanding Z stock.

(ii) Under the provisions of paragraph (b)(1) of this section, that portion of the Z stock held by F which represents a percentage of voting power equivalent to that held by F in X immediately prior to the consolidation (i.e., 50%) will be treated as the X stock held by F on May 26, 1969, for purposes of section 4943(c)(4). Therefore, 50% of the Y stock will be treated as subject to a second phase ending on May 25, 1994. The remaining portion of the Z voting stock held by F (10%) is subject to the provisions of § 53.4943-6(d)(1). F will have five years from the date of the merger in which to dispose of 10% of the Z stock without incurring the tax on excess business holdings.

Example (4). (i) F, a private foundation, owns 80% of the one class of outstanding stock in X corporation, an active business corporation. F has held this stock continuously since 1960 and no disqualified person with respect to F owns any stock in X. X has two operating divisions, one which manufactures shoes and the other which manufactures refrigerators. On January 1, 1978, in a section 351(a) exchange, X transferred all of the assets of its shoe manufacturing division to Y, a corporation which X has formed for this purpose, and receives 100% of the stock of Y so that Y is a wholly-owned subsidiary of X. X then transfers all of the Y stock to F in exchange for all of F's holdings of X stock in a distribution to which section 355 applies.

(ii) Under paragraph (b)(1) of this section, 80% of the Y stock is treated as the X stock surrendered in the exchange for purposes of section 4943(c)(4). The 80% is treated under § 53.4943-4(c) as held by disqualified persons through May 25, 1984, which constitutes the 15-year first phase holding period applicable to the 80% holding in X. The 80% of the Y stock must be reduced to the permitted holdings allowed during the second and third phase as provided by section 4943(c)(4)(D) in the same manner as F's holdings of X stock would have had to have been reduced.

(iii) Under § 53.4943-6(d)(1), the remaining 20% of Y stock is treated as held by a disqualified person for five years from the date of the exchange. F will have five years from the date of the exchange in which to dispose of 20% of the Y stock without incurring the tax on excess business holdings.

Example (5). (i) X corporation, an active business corporation, has outstanding 1,000 shares of one class of stock, of which 600 shares have been held by F1, a private foundation; 100 shares have

been held by F2, another private foundation; and 100 shares have been held by D, a disqualified person with respect to both F1 and F2. Unrelated parties hold the remaining 200 shares. F1 and F2 are disqualified persons with respect to each other under section 4946(a)(1)(H). Thus, F1 holds 60% of the X stock (600/1000); F2 and D each hold 10% (100/1000); and the foundation group (F1, F2 and D) holds 80% of X (800/1000). The holdings of F1 and F2 were acquired on January 1, 1980 pursuant to a pre-1969 will and are subject to section 4943(c)(5). There have been no changes in holdings since January 1, 1980.

(ii) On January 1, 1985, pursuant to a plan to dispose of excess business holdings approved by the Commissioner under paragraph (c) of this section, X redeems for cash the 600 shares held by F1. After the redemption, D and F2 each hold 25% of X (100/400). F1 no longer holds any X stocks. The foundation group's holdings (F1, F2 and D) have decreased from 80% to 50% while holdings of unrelated parties have increased from 20% to 50%. At the same time F2's and D's holdings each have increased from 10% to 25%.

(iii) Notwithstanding the increase in F2's and D's holdings, under paragraph (c) of this section, all of the X stock held by F2 will be treated as held by a disqualified person through the end of the first phase (December 31, 1994). However, the foundation voting and value levels do not increase. Therefore, after the end of the first phase, F2's holdings in X may not exceed 10 percent (if the combined holdings of F1, F2 and D exceed the permitted holdings under section 4943(c)(2)).

Example (6). (i) X corporation, an active business corporation, has outstanding 1,000 shares of its one class of stock. Since 1960, 100 shares (10%) have been held by F, a private foundation, and 350 shares (35%) have been held by D, a disqualified person with respect to F. All of the stock held by F is permitted holdings under section 4943(c)(4) and the substituted combined voting and value levels are 45% (10% + 35%). Because of disagreements concerning management of X between D and A, an unrelated party who holds 300 shares (30%) of the X stock, X redeems all of A's shares on December 1, 1981.

(ii) After the redemption, F holds 14.3% (100/700) of the X stock and D holds 50% (350/700), for combined holdings of 64.3%. Because the combined holdings exceed the substituted combined voting level (45%) by more than F's entire holdings, all of the F stock is excess business holdings. However, all of F's stock will be treated as acquired other than by purchase under § 53.4943-6(d)(1) and therefore will be treated under section 4943(c)(6) and this section, as held by a disqualified person for five years from the date of the redemption (through November 30, 1986). If the combined holdings of F and its disqualified person are reduced to 45 percent by the end of the five year period, F may retain a portion of its holdings in X (limited to no more than the foundation voting and value level of 10 percent).

Example (7). Assume the same facts as in *Example (6)*, except that D loaned the money to X that was used to redeem A's shares. Under these facts, the increased holdings result from a prohibited transaction described in paragraph (d)(2) of this section. Therefore, all of F's stock will be treated as acquired by purchase by a disqualified person under § 53.4943-6(d)(2). F will have 90 days after the redemption in which to dispose of its holdings or to reduce its holdings and the combined holdings to the levels held prior to the redemption as discussed in *Example (6).*

Example (8). (i) F, a private foundation, has held 100% of the outstanding stock of X corporation since 1960. F also holds 15% of the voting stock of Y corporation. Both X and Y are active business corporations. X has $1 million in net assets used in its trade or business and Y has $6.7 million used in its trade or business. On June 1, 1985, Y is merged into X. After the merger F holds 25% of the voting stock of X. No person other than F controls X after the merger.

(ii) Because more than 40% of Y was acquired and the net assets of X, the acquiring corporation, used in its trade or business prior to the merger represent less than 15% of the net assets of Y used in its trade or business, the merger is a prohibited transaction described in paragraph (d)(2)(iii). Therefore, only 15% of the stock of X is treated, pursuant to paragraph (b), as the stock held by F prior to the redemption. F's holding of 5% (the excess of F's 25% holdings over the 20% permitted holdings in X (determined under section 4943(c)(2)) are treated as purchased by a disqualified person pursuant to § 53.4943-6(d)(2). F will have 90 days after June 1, 1985, in which to dispose of the 5% excess holdings. [Reg. § 53.4943-7.]

☐ [*T.D.* 7944, 2-21-84.]

[Reg. § 53.4943-8]

§ 53.4943-8. Business holdings; constructive ownership.—(a) *Constructive ownership.*—(1) *In general.*—For purposes of section 4943, in computing the holdings in a business enterprise of a private foundation, or a disqualified person (as defined in section 4946), any stock or other interest owned, directly or indirectly, by or for a corporation, partnership, estate or trust shall be considered as being owned proportionately by or for its shareholders, partners, or beneficiaries except as otherwise provided in paragraphs (b), (c) and (d) of this section. Any interest in a business enterprise actually or constructively owned by a shareholder of a corporation, a partner of a partnership, or a beneficiary of an estate or trust shall not be considered as constructively held by the corporation, partnership, trust or estate. Further, if any corporation, partnership, estate or trust has a warrant or other option to acquire an interest in a business enterprise, such interest is not deemed to be constructively owned by such entity until the option is exercised. (See paragraph (b)(2) of § 53.4943-3 for rules that options are not stock for purposes of determining excess business holdings.)

(2) *Powers of appointment.*—Any interest in business enterprise over which a foundation or a disqualified person has a power of appointment exercisable in favor of the foundation or a disqualified person shall be considered owned by the foundation or disqualified person holding such power of appointment.

(3) *Determination of extent of constructive ownership.*—If an interest in a business enterprise owned by a corporation is constructively owned by a shareholder, each shareholder's proportion of ownership is generally computed on the basis of the voting stock each shareholder has in the corporation. In determining holdings permitted under section 4943(c)(4) and (5), each shareholder's proportion of ownership in the business enterprise shall also be computed on the basis of value, taking into account both voting and nonvoting stock held by the shareholder.

(4) *Nonvoting stock.*—If a private foundation, its disqualified persons, or both, own (directly or constructively) nonvoting stock of a parent corporation, the holdings of which are treated as constructively owned by its shareholders by reason of section 4943(d)(1) and this section, such nonvoting stock shall be treated as nonvoting stock of any corporation in which the parent corporation holds an interest for purposes of the limitation on the holding of nonvoting stock under section 4943(c)(2)(A) and § 53.4943-3(b)(2).

(5) *Interests held by certain disqualified persons.*—In the case of an entity that is a disqualified person (other than an entity described in section 4946(a)(1)(H)), the holdings of which are treated as constructively owned by its shareholders, partners, or beneficiaries, for purposes of determining the total holdings of disqualified persons the holdings of the entity shall be considered held by a disqualified person only to the extent such holdings are treated as constructively owned by disqualified persons who are shareholders, partners, or beneficiaries of the entity. In the case of an entity described in section 4946(a)(1)(H) or an entity, the holdings of which are not treated as constructively owned by its shareholders, partners, or beneficiaries, all holdings of such entity shall be treated as held by a disqualified person if and only if the entity itself is a disqualified person.

(b) *Estates and trusts.*—(1) *In general.*—Any interest actually or constructively owned by an estate or trust is deemed constructively owned, in the case of an estate, by its beneficiaries or, in the case of a trust, by its remainder beneficiaries except as provided in paragraphs (b)(2), (3) and (4) of this section (relating to certain split-interest trusts described in section 4947(a)(2), to trusts of qualified pension, profit-sharing, and stock bonus plans described in section 401(a) and to revocable trusts). Thus, if a trust owns 100 percent of the stock of a corporation A, and if, on an actuarial basis, W's life interest in the trust is 15 percent, Y's life interest is 25 percent, and Z's remainder interest is 60 percent, under this para-

graph (b), Z will be considered to be the owner of 100 percent of the stock of corporation A. See §53.4943-4, §53.4943-5 and §53.4943-6 for rules relating to certain actual or constructive holdings of a foundation being treated as held by a disqualified person. For the treatment of certain property acquired by an estate or trust after May 26, 1969, see paragraph (a)(2) of §53.4943-5.

(2) *Split-interest trusts.*—(i) *Amounts transferred in trust after May 26, 1969.*—In the case of an interest in a business enterprise which was transferred to a trust described in section 4947(a)(2) after May 26, 1969, for the benefit of a private foundation, no portion of such interest shall be considered as owned by the private foundation—

(A) If the foundation holds only an income interest in the trust, or

(B) If the foundation holds only a remainder interest in the trust (unless the foundation can exercise primary investment discretion with respect to such interest)

until such trust ceases to be so described. See section 4947(a)(2) and (b)(3) and the regulations thereunder for rules relating to such trusts. See also sections 4946(a)(1)(G) and (H) and the regulations thereunder relating to when a trust described in this paragraph (b)(2) is itself a disqualified person.

(ii) *Amounts transferred in trust on or before May 26, 1969.*—In the case of an interest in a business enterprise which was transferred to a trust described in section 4947(a)(2) (without regard to section 4947(a)(2)(C)) on or before May 26, 1969, for the benefit of a private foundation, no portion of such interest shall be considered as owned by the foundation until it is actually distributed to the foundation or until the trust ceases to be so described. See section 4943(c)(5) and §53.4943-5 for rules relating to certain trusts which were irrevocable on May 26, 1969.

(3) *Employee benefit trusts.*—An interest in a business enterprise owned by a trust described in section 401(a) (pension and profit-sharing plans) shall not be considered as owned by its beneficiaries, unless disqualified persons (within the meaning of section 4946) control the investment of the trust assets.

(4) *Revocable trusts.*—An interest in a business enterprise owned by a revocable trust shall be treated as owned by the grantor of such trust.

(5) *Estates.*—For purposes of applying section 4943(d)(1) to estates, the term "beneficiary" includes any person (including a private foundation) entitled to receive property of a decedent pursuant to a will or pursuant to laws of descent and distribution. However, a person shall no longer be considered a beneficiary of an estate when all the property to which he is entitled has been received by him, when he no longer has a claim against the estate and when there is only a remote possibility that it will be necessary for the estate to seek the return of property or to seek payment from him by contribution or otherwise

to satisfy claims against the estate or expenses of administration. When pursuant to the preceding sentence, a person (including a private foundation) ceases to be a beneficiary, stock or another interest in a business enterprise owned by the estate shall not thereafter be considered owned by such person. If any person is the constructive owner of an interest in a business enterprise actually held by an estate, the date of death of the testator or decedent intestate shall be the first day on which such person shall be considered a constructive owner of such interest. See §53.4943-5 for rules relating to wills executed on or before May 26, 1969.

(c) *Corporation actively engaged in a trade or business.*—(1) *In general.*—Except as provided in paragraphs (c)(2) and (3) of this section, any interest (whether or not in a separate entity) owned by a corporation which is actively engaged in a trade or business shall not be deemed to be constructively owned by such corporation's shareholders.

(2) *Actively engaged in a trade or business.*— For purposes of paragraph (c)(1) of this section—

(i) A corporation shall not be considered to be actively engaged in a trade or business if the corporation is not a business enterprise by reason of section 4943(d)(3)(A) or (B) and §53.4943-10(b) or (c);

(ii) In the case of a corporation which owns passive holdings and is actively engaged in a trade or business, such corporation shall not be considered to be actively engaged in a trade or business if the net assets used in such trade or business are insubstantial when compared to passive holdings.

(3) *Exceptions.*—If a corporation has been involved in a prohibited transaction, any interest in a business enterprise owned by such corporation shall be treated as constructively owned by its shareholders, whether or not such corporation is actively engaged in a trade or business. For a definition of prohibited transaction, see §53.4943-7(d)(2).

(4) *Affiliated group.*—In applying this paragraph to the common parent in an affiliated group (as defined in §53.4943-10(c)(3)(ii)), the assets and activities of the affiliated group shall be treated as the assets and activities of the common parent.

(d) *Partnerships.*—Any interest in a business enterprise which is owned by a partnership shall be deemed to be constructively owned by the partners in such partnerships.

(e) *Examples.*—The provisions of this section are illustrated by the following examples.

Example (1). F, a private foundation, directly owns voting stock of X, a holding company described in section 4943(d)(3)(B). That stock represents 40% of the voting power in X and 20% of the value of all outstanding shares of all classes of stock in X. F also owns nonvoting stock in X that represents 10% of the value of all outstanding shares of all classes of stock in X. D, a dis-

qualified person, owns voting stock of X that represents 40% of the voting power in X and 20% of the value. D does not own any nonvoting stock in X. X corporation's only holding is stock of Y corporation. The Y voting stock held by X represents 50% of the voting power in Y and 25% of the value of all outstanding shares of all classes of stock in Y. X also owns nonvoting stock in Y that represents 25% of the value of all outstanding shares of all classes of stock in Y. Under paragraph (a)(3) of this section, F and D each constructively owns 20% of the voting power in Y through their voting interest in X (40% of X's 50% in Y). F also constructively owns 15% of the value of all outstanding shares of all classes of stock in Y through F's interest in X (F's 30% of the value of X multiplied by X's 50% of the value of Y), while D constructively owns 10% of the value of Y (D's 20% of the value of X multiplied by X's 50% of the value of Y).

Example (2). (i) F, a private foundation, owns 50% of the one class of nonvoting stock of X corporation, a corporation described in section 4943(d)(3)(B) and paragraph (c)(2)(i) above. D, a disqualified person with respect to F as described in section 4946(a)(1)(A), owns 40% of the one class of voting stock of X. X corporation is a disqualified person with respect to F because D owns more than 35% of the voting of X. (See section 4946(a)(1)(E).) On January 1, 1980, X purchases for cash 40% of the only class of stock of Y corporation, a retail clothing store, from unrelated third parties.

(ii) Under paragraph (a)(4) of this section, F is treated as owning nonvoting stock of Y. Although X is a disqualified person, its holdings are not treated as held by disqualified persons except as constructive holdings. Therefore, the "deemed" nonvoting stock in Y is a permitted holding because D, a disqualified person with respect to F, constructively owns only 16% of the voting stock of Y (less than 20% permitted under section 4943(c)(2)).

Example (3). (i) The facts are the same as in *Example (2),* except that X purchases 100% of the stock of Y corporation. Under paragraph (a)(4) of this section, F is treated as owning nonvoting stock of Y. The "deemed" nonvoting stock in Y is not a permitted holding because D, a disqualified person with respect to F, constructively owns 40% of the voting stock of Y.

Example (4). (i) D, a disqualified person with respect to F, owns 40% of the one class of stock in X corporation, an active business. X is a disqualified person with respect to F. X acquires 40% of the voting stock in Y corporation. Under paragraph (a)(5) of this section, the holdings of X in Y are treated as held by a disqualified person. F cannot hold any Y stock, voting or nonvoting. [Reg. § 53.4943-8.]

☐ [*T.D. 7496, 7-5-77. Amended by T.D. 7944,* 2-21-84.]

[Reg. § 53.4943-9]

§ 53.4943-9. Business holdings; certain periods.—(a) *Taxable period.*—(1) *In general.*—For

purposes of section 4943, the term "taxable period" means, with respect to any excess business holdings of a private foundation in a business enterprise, the period beginning with the first day on which there are such excess business holdings and ending on there on the earliest of:

(i) The date of mailing of a notice of deficiency under section 6212 with respect to the tax imposed on the holdings by section 4943(a);

(ii) The date on which the excess is eliminated; or

(iii) The date on which the tax imposed by section 4943(a) is assessed.

For example, M, a private foundation, first has excess business holdings in X, a corporation, on February 5, 1972. A notice of deficiency is mailed under section 6212 to M on June 1, 1974. With respect to M's excess business holdings in X, the taxable period begins on February 5, 1972, and ends on June 1, 1974.

(2) *Special rule.*—Where a notice of deficiency referred to in subparagraph (1)(i) of this paragraph is not mailed because there is a waiver of the restrictions on assessment and collection of a deficiency, or because the deficiency is paid, the date of filing of the waiver or the date of such payment, respectively, shall be treated as the end of the taxable period.

(3) *Suspension of taxable period for 90 days.*—In any case in which a private foundation has excess business holdings solely because of the acquisition of an interest in a business enterprise to which paragraph (a)(1)(ii) or (iii) of § 53.4943-2 applies, the taxable period described in paragraph (a) of this section shall be suspended for the 90-day period (as extended) starting with the date on which the foundation knows or has reason to know of the acquisition, provided that at the end of such period the foundation has disposed of such excess holdings.

(b) *Cross reference.*—For rules relating to taxable events that are corrected within the correction period, defined in section 4963(e), see section 4961(a) and the regulations thereunder.

(c) *Correction.*—For purposes of section 4943, correction shall be considered as made when no interest in the enterprise held by the foundation is classified as an excess business holding under section 4943(c)(1). In any case where the private foundation has excess business holdings which are constructively held for it under section 4943(c)(1), correction shall be considered made when either a corporation, partnership, estate, or trust in which holdings in such enterprise are constructively held for the foundation or a disqualified person, the foundation itself, or a disqualified person disposes of a sufficient interest in the enterprise so that no interest in the enterprise held by the foundation is classified as excess business holdings under section 4943(c)(1). [Reg. § 53.4943-9.]

☐ [*T.D. 7496, 7-5-77. Amended by T.D. 8084,* 5-1-86.]

[Reg. §53.4943-10]

§53.4943-10. Business enterprise; definition.—(a) *In general.*—(1) Except as provided in paragraph (b) or (c) of this section, under section 4943(d)(4) the term "business enterprise" includes the active conduct of a trade or business, including any activity which is regularly carried on for the production of income from the sale of goods or the performance of services and which constitutes an unrelated trade or business under section 513. For purposes of the preceding sentence, where an activity carried on for profit constitutes an unrelated trade or business, no part of such trade or business shall be excluded from the classification of a business enterprise merely because it does not result in a profit.

(2) Notwithstanding paragraph (a)(1) of this section, a bond or other evidence of indebtedness does not constitute a holding in a business enterprise unless such bond or evidence of indebtedness is otherwise determined to be an equitable interest in such enterprise. Similarly, a leasehold interest in real property does not constitute an interest in a business enterprise, even though rent payable under such lease is dependent, in whole or in part, upon the income or profits derived by another from such property, unless such leasehold interest constitutes an interest in the income or profits of an unrelated trade or business under section 513.

(b) *Certain program-related activities.*—For purposes of section 4943(d)(4) the term "business enterprise" does not include a functionally related business as defined in section 4942(j)(5). See §53.4942(a)-2(c)(3)(iii). In addition, business holdings do not include program-related investments (such as investments in small businesses in central cities or in corporations to assist in neighborhood renovation) as defined in section 4944(c) and the regulations thereunder.

(c) *Income derived from passive sources.*—(1) *In general.*—For purposes of section 4943(d)(4), the term "business enterprise" does not include a trade or business at least 95 percent of the gross income of which is derived from passive sources; except that if in the taxable year in question less than 95 percent of the income of a trade or business is from passive sources, the foundation may, in applying this 95 percent test, substitute for the passive source gross income in such taxable year the average gross income from passive sources for the 10 taxable years immediately preceding the taxable year in question (or for such shorter period as the entity has been in existence). Thus, stock in a passive holding company is not to be considered a holding in a business enterprise even if the company is controlled by the foundation. Instead, the foundation is treated as owning its proportionate share of any interests in a business enterprise held by such company under section 4943(d)(1).

(2) *Gross income from passive sources.*—Gross income from passive sources, for purposes of this paragraph, includes the items excluded by sections 512(b)(1) (relating to dividends, interest,

and annuities), 512(b)(2) (relating to royalties), 512(b)(3) (relating to rent) and 512(b)(5) (relating to gains or losses from the disposition of certain property). Any income classified as passive under this paragraph does not lose its character merely because section 512(b)(4) or 514 (relating to unrelated debt-financed income) applies to such income. In addition, income from passive sources includes income from the sale of goods (including charges or costs passed on at cost to purchasers of such goods or income received in settlement of a dispute concerning or in lieu of the exercise of the right to sell such goods) if the seller does not manufacture, produce, physically receive or deliver, negotiate sales of, or maintain inventories in such goods. Thus, for example, where a corporation purchases a product under a contract with the manufacturer, resells it under contract at a uniform markup in price, and does not physically handle the product, the income derived from that markup meets the definition of passive income for purposes of this paragraph. On the other hand, income from individually negotiated sales, such as those made by a broker, would not meet such definition even if the broker did not physically handle the goods.

(3) *Affiliated group.*—(i) For a common parent corporation in an affiliated group, substitute "consolidated gross income" in subparagraph (1) of this paragraph.

(ii) For purposes of this section, the term "affiliated group" shall have the same meaning as in section 1504(a), without regard to section 1504(b) through (e).

(iii) Section 53.4943-11(d) provides a transitional rule for certain parent corporations.

(d) *Application of section 4943(c)(6).*—(1) *Program related activities.*—If a private foundation holds an interest which is not an interest in a business enterprise because of paragraph (b) of this section (relating to program related activities), and such interest later becomes an interest in a business enterprise solely by reason of failing to meet the requirements of such paragraph (b), such interest will then be subject to section 4943(c)(6) (regardless of when it was originally acquired) and will be treated as having been acquired other than by purchase for purposes of section 4943(c)(6).

(2) *Passive holdings, etc.*—(i) Except as provided in subdivision (ii), if a private foundation holds an interest that is not an interest in a business enterprise, and the interest later becomes an interest in a business enterprise (other than by reason of a readjustment as defined in §53.4943-7(d)(1)), the interest will be treated as having been acquired by purchase by a disqualified person at the time the interest becomes an interest in a business enterprise. The treatment of an interest that becomes an interest in a business enterprise by reason of a readjustment shall be determined under §53.4943-6 and §53.4943-7.

(ii) If a private foundation establishes that the events which caused an interest not originally a business enterprise to become a business

Reg. §53.4943-10

enterprise were not effectively controlled by the private foundation, then such interest shall be treated as acquired other than by purchase from the time of the change for purposes of section 4943(c)(6).

(iii) See §53.4943-3(b)(4)(ii) for the definition of effective control.

(e) *Sole proprietorship.*—For purposes of section 4943 and the regulations thereunder, the term "sole proprietorship" means any business enterprise (as defined in paragraphs (a), (b), and (c)) of this section—

(1) Which is actually and directly owned by a private foundation,

(2) In which the foundation has a 100 percent equity interest, and

(3) Which is not held by a corporation, trust, or other business entity for such foundation.

A foundation may be considered to own a sole proprietorship even though the foundation is itself a corporation or a trust. However, a sole proprietorship which is owned by a foundation shall cease to be treated as a sole proprietorship when the foundation no longer has a 100-percent interest in the equity of the business enterprise. Thus, if and when a foundation sells a 10-percent interest in a sole proprietorship, such business enterprise shall be treated as a partnership under section 4943 and the regulations thereunder. [Reg. §53.4943-10.]

☐ [*T.D. 7496, 7-5-77. Amended by T.D. 7944, 2-21-84.*]

[Reg. §53.4943-11]

§53.4943-11. Effective/applicability date.— (a) *In general.*—Section 4943 and §§53.4943-1 through 53.4943-11 shall take effect for taxable years beginning after December 31, 1969, except as otherwise provided by such sections.

(b) *Special transitional rule.*—In the case of any acquisition of excess holdings prior to February 2, 1973, section 4943(a)(1) shall not apply if correction occurs (within the meaning of paragraph (c) of §53.4943-9) within a period ending 90 days after July 5, 1977, extended (prior to the expiration of the original period) by any period which the Commissioner determines is reasonable and necessary (within the meaning of paragraph (b) of §53.4943-9) to bring about such correction.

(c) *Special transitional rule for aquisition by will, etc.*—(i) The rule in §53.4943-6(b)(1) whereby holdings not held by a decedent are not treated as acquired under a will shall not apply to acquisitions of after-acquired property of a decedent's estate occurring on or before May 22, 1984.

(ii) The rule in §53.4943-6(b)(1) treating a purchase by an estate as a purchase by a disqualified person where the executor is a disqualified person shall not apply to purchases occurring on or before May 22, 1984.

(d) *Special transitional rule for affiliated groups.*—If on or before May 22, 1984, a foundation holds an interest in a common parent corporation in an affiliated group, as defined in §53.4943-10(c)(3)(ii), the foundation may elect to have both §53.4943-8(c)(4) and §53.4943-10(c)(3) not apply to such common parent corporation. No election may be made to have only one section not apply. Such election shall be made by the governing body of the private foundation at any time prior to February 22, 1985.

(e) *Special transitional rule for changes to a business enterprise.*—Any interest that is not an interest in a business enterprise which becomes an interest in a business enterprise under §53.4943-10(d)(2) prior to May 22, 1984, will be treated as having been acquired other than by purchase for purposes of section 4943(c)(6).

(f) *Special transitional rule for private foundations that qualified as Type III supporting organizations before August 17, 2006.*—The present holdings of a private foundation that qualified as a Type III supporting organization under section 509(a)(3) immediately before August 17, 2006, and that was reclassified as a private foundation under section 509(a) on or after August 17, 2006, solely as a result of the rules enacted by section 1241 of the Pension Protection Act of 2006, Public Law 109-280 (120 Stat. 780), will be determined using the same rules that apply to Type III supporting organizations under section 4943(f)(7).

(g) *Special transitional rule for Type III supporting organizations created as trusts before November 20, 1970.*—A trust that qualifies as a Type III supporting organization under section 509(a)(3) and meets the requirements of §1.509(a)-4(i)(9) of this chapter will be treated as a "functionally integrated Type III supporting organization" for purposes of section 4943(f)(3)(A). [Reg. §53.4943-11.]

☐ [*T.D. 7496, 7-5-77. Amended by T.D. 7944, 2-21-84 and T.D. 9605, 12-21-2012.*]

[Reg. §53.4944-1]

§53.4944-1. Initial taxes.—(a) *On the private foundation.*—(1) *In general.*—If a private foundation(as defined in section 509) invests any amount in such a manner as to jeopardize the carrying out of any of its exempt purposes, section 4944(a)(1) of the Code imposes an excise tax on the making of such investment. This tax is to be paid by the private foundation and is at the rate of 5 percent of the amount so invested for each taxable year (or part thereof) in the taxable period (as defined in section 4944(e)(1)). The tax imposed by section 4944(a)(1) and this paragraph shall apply to investments of either income or principal.

(2) *Jeopardizing investments.*—(i) Except as provided in section 4944(c), §53.4944-3, §53.4944-6(a), and subdivision (ii) of this subparagraph, an investment shall be considered to jeopardize the carrying out of the exempt purposes of a private foundation if it is determined that the foundation managers, in making such investment, have failed to exercise ordinary business care and prudence, under the facts and circumstances prevailing at the time of making

the investment, in providing for the long- and short-term financial needs of the foundation to carry out its exempt purposes. In the exercise of the requisite standard of care and prudence the foundation managers may take into account the expected return (including both income and appreciation of capital), the risks of rising and falling price levels, and the need for diversification within the investment portfolio (for example, with respect to type of security, type of industry, maturity of company, degree of risk and potential for return). The determination whether the investment of a particular amount jeopardizes the carrying out of the exempt purposes of a foundation shall be made on an investment by investment basis, in each case taking into account the foundation's portfolio as a whole. No category of investments shall be treated as a *per se* violation of section 4944. However, the following are examples of types or methods of investment which will be closely scrutinized to determine whether the foundation managers have met the requisite standard of care and prudence: Trading in securities on margin, trading in commodity futures, investments in working interests in oil and gas wells, the purchase of "puts" and "calls", and "straddles," the purchase of warrants, and selling short. The determination whether the investment of any amount jeopardizes the carrying out of a foundation's exempt purposes is to be made as of the time that the foundation makes the investment and not subsequently on the basis of hindsight. Therefore, once it has been ascertained that an investment does not jeopardize the carrying out of a foundation's exempt purposes, the investment shall never be considered to jeopardize the carrying out of such purposes, even though, as a result of such investment, the foundation subsequently realizes a loss. The provisions of section 4944 and the regulations thereunder shall not exempt or relieve any person from compliance with any Federal or State law imposing any obligation, duty, responsibility, or other standard of conduct with respect to the operation or administration of an organization or trust to which section 4944 applies. Nor shall any State law exempt or relieve any person from any obligation, duty, responsibility, or other standard of conduct provided in section 4944 and the regulations thereunder.

(ii)(*a*) Section 4944 shall not apply to an investment made by any person which is later gratuitously transferred to a private foundation. If such foundation furnishes any consideration to such person upon the transfer, the foundation will be treated as having made an investment (within the meaning of section 4944(a)(1)) in the amount of such consideration.

(*b*) Section 4944 shall not apply to an investment which is acquired by a private foundation solely as a result of a corporate reorganization within the meaning of section 368(a).

(iii) For purposes of section 4944, a private foundation which, after December 31, 1969, changes the form or terms of an investment (regardless of whether subdivision (ii) of this sub-

paragraph applies to such investment), will be considered to have entered into a new investment on the date of such change, except as provided in subdivision (ii)(*b*) of this subparagraph. Accordingly, a determination, under subdivision (i) of this subparagraph, whether such change in the investment jeopardizes the carrying out of the foundation's exempt purposes shall be made at such time.

(iv) It is not intended that the taxes imposed under chapter 42 be exclusive. For example, if a foundation purchases a sole proprietorship in a business enterprise within the meaning of section 4943(d)(4), in addition to tax under section 4943, the foundation may be liable for tax under section 4944 if the investment jeopardizes the carrying out of any of its exempt purposes.

(b) *On the management.*—(1) *In general.*—In any case in which a tax is imposed by section 4944(a)(1) and paragraph (a) of this section, section 4944(a)(2) of the Code imposes on the participation of any foundation manager in the making of the investment, knowing that it is jeopardizing the carrying out of any of the foundation's exempt purposes, a tax equal to 5 percent of the amount so invested for each taxable year of the foundation (or part thereof) in the taxable period (as defined in section 4944(e)(1)), subject to the provisions of section 4944(d) and § 53.4944-4, unless such participation is not willful and is due to reasonable cause. The tax imposed under section 4944(a)(2) shall be paid by the foundation manager.

(2) *Definitions and special rules.*—(i) *Knowing.*—For purposes of section 4944, a foundation manager shall be considered to have participated in the making of an investment "knowing" that it is jeopardizing the carrying out of any of the foundation's exempt purposes only if—

(*a*) He has actual knowledge of sufficient facts so that, based solely upon such facts, such investment would be a jeopardizing investment under paragraph (a)(2) of this section,

(*b*) He is aware that such an investment under these circumstances may violate the provisions of federal tax law governing jeopardizing investments, and

(*c*) He negligently fails to make reasonable attempts to ascertain whether the investment is a jeopardizing investment, or he is in fact aware that it is such an investment.

For purposes of this part and chapter 42, the term "knowing" does not mean "having reason to know". However, evidence tending to show that a foundation manager has reason to know of a particular fact or particular rule is relevant in determining whether he had actual knowledge of such fact or rule. Thus, for example, evidence tending to show that a foundation manager has reason to know of sufficient facts so that, based solely upon such facts, an investment would be a jeopardizing investment is relevant in determining whether he has actual knowledge of such facts.

Reg. § 53.4944-1(a)(2)(ii)(a)

(ii) *Willful.*—A foundation manager's participation in a jeopardizing investment is willful if it is voluntary, conscious, and intentional. No motive to avoid the restrictions of the law or the incurrence of any tax is necessary to make such participation willful. However, a foundation manager's participation in a jeopardizing investment is not willful if he does not know that it is a jeopardizing investment under paragraph (a)(2) of this section.

(iii) *Due to reasonable cause.*—A foundation manager's actions are due to reasonable cause if he has exercised his responsibility on behalf of the foundation with ordinary business care and prudence.

(iv) *Participation.*—The participation of any foundation manager in the making of an investment shall consist of any manifestation of approval of the investment.

(v) *Advice of counsel.*—If a foundation manager, after full disclosure of the factual situation to legal counsel (including house counsel), relies on the advice of such counsel expressed in a reasoned written legal opinion that a particular investment would not jeopardize the carrying out of any of the foundation's exempt purposes (because, as a matter of law, the investment is excepted from such classification, for example, as a program-related investment under section 4944(c)), then although such investment is subsequently held to be a jeopardizing investment under paragraph (a)(2) of this section, the foundation manager's participation in such investment will ordinarily not be considered "knowing" or "willful" and will ordinarily be considered "due to reasonable cause" within the meaning of section 4944(a)(2). In addition, if a foundation manager, after full disclosure of the factual situation to qualified investment counsel, relies on the advice of such counsel, such advice being derived in a manner consistent with generally accepted practices of persons who are such a qualified investment counsel and being expressed in writing that a particular investment will provide for the long-and short-term financial needs of the foundation under paragraph (a)(2) of this section, then although such investment is subsequently held not to provide for such long-and short-term financial needs, the foundation manager's participation in failing to provide for such long- and short-term financial needs will ordinarily not be considered "knowing" or "willful" and will ordinarily be considered "due to reasonable cause" within the meaning of section 4944(a)(2). For purposes of this subdivision, a written legal opinion will be considered "reasoned" even if it reaches a conclusion which is subsequently determined to be incorrect so long as such opinion addresses itself to the facts and applicable law. However, a written legal opinion will not be considered "reasoned" if it does nothing more than recite the facts and express a conclusion. However, the absence of advice of legal counsel or qualified investment counsel with respect to the investment shall not, by itself, give rise to any inference that a foundation manager participated in such investment knowingly, willfully, or without reasonable cause.

(vi) *Cross reference.*—For provisions relating to the burden of proof in cases involving the issue whether a foundation manager has knowingly participated in the making of a jeopardizing investment, see section 7454(b).

(c) *Examples.*—The provisions of this section may be illustrated by the following examples:

Example (1). A is a foundation manager of B, a private foundation with assets of $100,000. A approves the following three investments by B after taking into account with respect to each of them B's portfolio as a whole: (1) an investment of $5,000 in the common stock of corporation X; (2) an investment of $10,000 in the common stock of corporation Y; and (3) an investment of $8,000 in the common stock of corporation Z. Corporation X has been in business a considerable time, its record of earnings is good and there is no reason to anticipate a diminution of its earnings. Corporation Y has a promising product, has had earnings in some years and substantial losses in others, has never paid a dividend, and is widely reported in investment advisory services as seriously undercapitalized. Corporation Z has been in business a short period of time and manufactures a product that is new, is not sold by others, and must compete with a well-established alternative product that serves the same purpose. Z's stock is classified as a high-risk investment by most investment advisory services with the possibility of substantial long-term appreciation but with little prospect of a current return. A has studied the records of the three corporations and knows the foregoing facts. In each case the price per share of common stock purchased by B is favorable to B. Under the standards of paragraph (a)(2)(i) of this section, the investment of $10,000 in the common stock of Y and the investment of $8,000 in the common stock of Z may be classified as jeopardizing investments, while the investment of $5,000 in the common stock of X will not be so classified. B would then be liable for an initial tax of $500 (*i.e.,* 5% of $10,000) for each year (or part thereof) in the taxable period for the investment in Y, and an initial tax of $400 (*i.e.,* 5% of $8,000) for each year (or part thereof) in the taxable period for the investment in Z. Further, A had actual knowledge that the investments in the common stock of Y and Z were jeopardizing investments and would be, therefore, liable for the same amount of initial taxes as B.

Example (2). Assume the facts as stated in Example (1), except that: (1) in the case of corporation Y, B's investment will be made for new stock to be issued by Y and there is reason to anticipate that B's investment, together with investments required by B to be made concurrently with its own, will satisfy the capital needs of corporation Y and will thereby overcome the

Reg. §53.4944-1(c)

difficulties that have resulted in Y's uneven earnings record; and (2) in the case of corporation Z, the management has a demonstrated capacity for getting new businesses started successfully and Z has received substantial orders for its new product. Under the standards of paragraph (a)(2)(i) of this section, neither the investment in Y nor the investment in Z will be classified as a jeopardizing investment and neither A nor B will be liable for an initial tax on either of such investments.

Example (3). D is a foundation manager of E, a private foundation with assets of $200,000. D was hired by E to manage E's investments after a careful review of D's training, experience and record in the field of investment management and advice indicated to E that D was well qualified to provide professional investment advice in the management of E's investment assets. D, after careful research into how best to diversify E's investments, provide for E's long-term financial needs, and protect against the effects of long-term inflation, decides to allocate a portion of E's investment assets to unimproved real estate in selected areas of the country where population patterns and economic factors strongly indicate continuing growth at a rapid rate. D determines that the short-term financial needs of E can be met through E's other investments. Under the standards of paragraph (a)(2)(i) of this section, the investment of a portion of E's investment assets in unimproved real estate will not be classified as a jeopardizing investment and neither D nor E will be liable for an initial tax on such investment. [Reg. § 53.4944-1.]

☐ [*T.D. 7240, 12-28-72. Amended by T.D. 7299, 12-21-73.*]

[Reg. § 53.4944-2]

§ 53.4944-2. Additional taxes.—(a) *On the private foundation.*—Section 4944(b)(1) of the Code imposes an excise tax in any case in which an initial tax is imposed by section 4944(a)(1) and § 53.4944-1(a) on the making of a jeopardizing investment by a private foundation and such investment is not removed from jeopardy within the taxable period (as defined in section 4944(e)(1)). The tax imposed under section 4944(b)(1) is to be paid by the private foundation and is at the rate of 25 percent of the amount of the investment. This tax shall be imposed upon the portion of the investment which has not been removed from jeopardy within the taxable period.

(b) *On the management.*—Section 4944(b)(2) of the Code imposes an excise tax in any case in which an additional tax is imposed by section 4944(b)(1) and paragraph (a) of this section and a foundation manager has refused to agree to part or all of the removal of the investment from jeopardy. The tax imposed under section 4944(b)(2) is at the rate of 5 percent of the amount of the investment, subject to the provisions of section 4944(d) and § 53.4944-4. This tax is to be paid by any foundation manager who has refused to agree to the removal of part or all

of the investment from jeopardy, and shall be imposed upon the portion of the investment which has not been removed from jeopardy within the taxable period.

(c) *Examples.*—The provisions of this section may be illustrated by the following examples:

Example (1). X is a foundation manager of Y, a private foundation. On the advice of X, Y invests $5,000 in the common stock of corporation M. Assume that both X and Y are liable for the taxes imposed by section 4944(a) on the making of the investment. Assume further that no part of the investment is removed from jeopardy within the taxable period and that X refused to agree to such removal. Y will be liable for an additional tax of $1,250 (*i.e.*, $5,000 × 25%). X will be liable for an additional tax of $250 (*i.e.*, $5,000 × 5%).

Example (2). Assume the facts as stated in Example (1), except that X is not liable for the tax imposed by section 4944(a)(2) for his participation in the making of the investment, because such participation was not willful and was due to reasonable cause. X will nonetheless be liable for the tax of $250 imposed by section 4944(b)(2) since an additional tax has been imposed upon Y and since X refused to agree to the removal of the investment from jeopardy.

Example (3). Assume the facts as stated in Example (1), except that Y removes $2,000 of the investment from jeopardy within the taxable period, with X refusing to agree to the removal from jeopardy of the remaining $3,000 of such investment. Y will be liable for an additional tax of $750, imposed upon the portion of the investment which has not been removed from jeopardy within the taxable period (*i.e.*, $3,000 × 25%). Further, X will be liable for an additional tax of $150, also imposed upon the same portion of the investment (*i.e.*, $3,000 × 5%). [Reg. § 53.4944-2.]

☐ [*T.D. 7240, 12-28-72. Amended by T.D. 8084, 5-1-86.*]

[Reg. § 53.4944-3]

§ 53.4944-3. Exception for program-related investments.—(a) *In general.*—(1) For purposes of section 4944 and § § 53.4944-1 through 53.4944-6, a "program-related investment" shall not be classified as an investment which jeopardizes the carrying out of the exempt purposes of a private foundation. A "program-related investment" is an investment which possesses the following characteristics:

(i) The primary purpose of the investment is to accomplish one or more of the purposes described in section 170(c)(2)(B);

(ii) No significant purpose of the investment is the production of income or the appreciation of property; and

(iii) No purpose of the investment is to accomplish one or more of the purposes described in section 170(c)(2)(D).

(2)(i) An investment shall be considered as made primarily to accomplish one or more of the purposes described in section 170(c)(2)(B) if it

significantly furthers the accomplishment of the private foundation's exempt activities and if the investment would not have been made but for such relationship between the investment and the accomplishment of the foundation's exempt activities. For purposes of section 4944 and §§ 53.4944-1 through 53.4944-6, the term "purposes described in section 170(c)(2)(B)" shall be treated as including purposes described in section 170(c)(2)(B) whether or not carried out by organizations described in section 170(c).

(ii) An investment in an activity described in section 4942(j)(4)(B) and the regulations thereunder shall be considered, for purposes of this paragraph, as made primarily to accomplish one or more of the purposes described in section 170(c)(2)(B).

(iii) In determining whether a significant purpose of an investment is the production of income or the appreciation of property, it shall be relevant whether investors solely engaged in the investment for profit would be likely to make the investment on the same terms as the private foundation. However, the fact that an investment produces significant income or capital appreciation shall not, in the absence of other factors, be conclusive evidence of a significant purpose involving the production of income or the appreciation of property.

(iv) An investment shall not be considered as made to accomplish one or more of the purposes described in section 170(c)(2)(D) if the recipient of the investment appears before, or communicates to, any legislative body with respect to legislation or proposed legislation of direct interest to such recipient, provided that the expense of engaging in such activities would qualify as a deduction under section 162.

(3)(i) Once it has been determined that an investment is "program-related" it shall not cease to qualify as a "program-related investment" provided that changes, if any, in the form or terms of the investment are made primarily for exempt purposes and not for any significant purpose involving the production of income or the appreciation of property. A change made in the form or terms of a program-related investment for the prudent protection of the foundation's investment shall not ordinarily cause the investment to cease to qualify as program-related. Under certain conditions, a program-related investment may cease to be program-related because of a critical change in circumstances, as, for example, where it is serving an illegal purpose or the private purpose of the foundation or its managers. For purposes of the preceding sentence, an investment which ceases to be program-related because of a critical change in circumstances shall in no event subject the foundation making the investment to the tax imposed by section 4944(a)(1) before the thirtieth day after the date on which such foundation (or any of its managers) has actual knowledge of such critical change in circumstances.

(ii) If a private foundation changes the form or terms of an investment, and if, as a result of the application of subdivision (i) of this subparagraph, such investment no longer qualifies as program-related, the determination whether the investment jeopardizes the carrying out of exempt purposes shall be made pursuant to the provisions of § 53.4944-1(a)(2).

(b) *Examples.*—The provisions of this section may be illustrated by the following examples:

Example (1). X is a small business enterprise located in a deteriorated urban area and owned by members of an economically disadvantaged minority group. Conventional sources of funds are unwilling or unable to provide funds to X on terms it considers economically feasible. Y, a private foundation, makes a loan to X bearing interest below the market rate for commercial loans of comparable risk. Y's primary purpose for making the loan is to encourage the economic development of such minority groups. The loan has no significant purpose involving the production of income or the appreciation of property. The loan significantly furthers the accomplishment of Y's exempt activities and would not have been made but for such relationship between the loan and Y's exempt activities. Accordingly, the loan is a program-related investment even though Y may earn income from the investment in an amount comparable to or higher than earnings from conventional portfolio investments.

Example (2). Assume the facts as stated in Example (1), except that after the date of execution of the loan Y extends the due date of the loan. The extension is granted in order to permit X to achieve greater financial stability before it is required to repay the loan. Since the change in the terms of the loan is made primarily for exempt purposes and not for any significant purpose involving the production of income or the appreciation of property, the loan shall continue to qualify as a program-related investment.

Example (3). X is a small business enterprise located in a deteriorated urban area and owned by members of an economically disadvantaged minority group. Conventional sources of funds are unwilling to provide funds to X at reasonable interest rates unless it increases the amount of its equity capital. Consequently, Y, a private foundation, purchases shares of X's common stock. Y's primary purpose in purchasing the stock is to encourage the economic development of such minority group, and no significant purpose involves the production of income or the appreciation of property. The investment significantly furthers the accomplishment of Y's exempt activities and would not have been made but for such relationship between the investment and Y's exempt activities. Accordingly, the purchase of the common stock is a program-related investment, even though Y may realize a profit if X is successful and the common stock appreciates in value.

Example (4). X is a business enterprise which is not owned by low-income persons or minority group members, but the continued operation of X is important to the economic well-being of a

deteriorated urban area because X employs a substantial number of low-income persons from such area. Conventional sources of funds are unwilling or unable to provide funds to X at reasonable rates. Y, a private foundation, makes a loan to X at an interest rate below the market rate for commercial loans of comparable risk. The loan is made pursuant to a program run by Y to assist low-income persons by providing increased economic opportunities and to prevent community deterioration. No significant purpose of the loan involves the production of income or the appreciation of property. The investment significantly furthers the accomplishment of Y's exempt activities and would not have been made but for such relationship between the loan and Y's exempt activities. Accordingly, the loan is a program-related investment.

Example (5). X is a business enterprise which is financially secure and the stock of which is listed and traded on a national exchange. Y, a private foundation, makes a loan to X at an interest rate below the market rate in order to induce X to establish a new plant in a deteriorated urban area which, because of the high risks involved, X would be unwilling to establish absent such inducement. The loan is made pursuant to a program run by Y to enhance the economic development of the area by, for example, providing employment opportunities for low-income persons at the new plant, and no significant purpose involves the production of income or the appreciation of property. The loan significantly furthers the accomplishment of Y's exempt activities and would not have been made but for such relationship between the loan and Y's exempt activities. Accordingly, even though X is large and established, the investment is program-related.

Example (6). X is a business enterprise which is owned by a nonprofit community development corporation. When fully operational, X will market agricultural products, thereby providing a marketing outlet for low-income farmers in a depressed rural area. Y, a private foundation, makes a loan to X bearing interest at a rate less than the rate charged by financial institutions which have agreed to lend funds to X if Y makes the loan. The loan is made pursuant to a program run by Y to encourage economic redevelopment of depressed areas, and no significant purpose involves the production of income or the appreciation of property. The loan significantly furthers the accomplishment of Y's exempt activities and would not have been made but for such relationship between the loan and Y's exempt activities. Accordingly, the loan is a program-related investment.

Example (7). X, a private foundation, invests $100,000 in the common stock of corporation M. The dividends received from such investment are later applied by X in furtherance of its exempt purposes. Although there is a relationship between the return on the investment and the accomplishment of X's exempt activities, there is no relationship between the investment *per se*

and such accomplishment. Therefore, the investment cannot be considered as made primarily to accomplish one or more of the purposes described in section 170(c)(2)(B) and cannot qualify as program-related.

Example (8). S, a private foundation, makes an investment in T, a business corporation, which qualifies as a program-related investment under section 4944(c) at the time that it is made. All of T's voting stock is owned by S. T experiences financial and management problems which, in the judgment of the foundation, require changes in management, in financial structure or in the form of the investment. The following three methods of resolving the problems appear feasible to S, but each of the three methods would result in reduction of the exempt purposes for which the program-related investment was initially made:

(a) *Sale of stock or assets.* The foundation sells its stock to an unrelated person. Payment is made in part at the time of sale; the balance is payable over an extended term of years with interest on the amount outstanding. The foundation receives a purchase-money mortgage.

(b) *Lease.* The corporation leases its assets for a term of years to an unrelated person, with an option in the lessee to buy the assets. If the option is exercised, the terms of payment are to be similar to those described in (a) of this example.

(c) *Management contract.* The corporation enters into a management contract which gives broad operating authority to one or more unrelated persons for a term of years. The foundation and the unrelated persons are obligated to contribute toward working capital requirements. The unrelated persons will be compensated by a fixed fee or a share of profits, and they will receive an option to buy the stock held by S or the assets of the corporation. If the option is exercised, the terms of payment are to be similar to those described in (a) of this example.

Each of the three methods involves a change in the form or terms of a program-related investment for the prudent protection of the foundation's investment. Thus, under § 53.4944-3(a)(3)(i), none of the three transactions (nor any debt instruments or other obligations held by S as a result of engaging in one of these transactions) would cause the investment to cease to qualify as program-related.

Example (9). X is a socially and economically disadvantaged individual. Y, a private foundation, makes an interest-free loan to X for the primary purpose of enabling X to attend college. The loan has no significant purpose involving the production of income or the appreciation of property. The loan significantly furthers the accomplishment of Y's exempt activities and would not have been made but for such relationship between the loan and Y's exempt activities. Accordingly, the loan is a program-related investment.

Example (10). Y, a private foundation, makes a high-risk investment in low-income housing, the

indebtedness with respect to which is insured by the Federal Housing Administration. Y's primary purpose in making the investment is to finance the purchase, rehabilitation, and construction of housing for low-income persons. The investment has no significant purpose involving the production of income or the appreciation of property. The investment significantly furthers the accomplishment of Y's exempt activities and would not have been made but for such relationship between the investment and Y's exempt activities. Accordingly, the investment is program-related.

Example 11. X is a business enterprise that researches and develops new drugs. X's research demonstrates that a vaccine can be developed within ten years to prevent a disease that predominantly affects poor individuals in developing countries. However, neither X nor other commercial enterprises like X will devote their resources to develop the vaccine because the potential return on investment is significantly less than required by X or other commercial enterprises to undertake a project to develop new drugs. Y, a private foundation, enters into an investment agreement with X in order to induce X to develop the vaccine. Pursuant to the investment agreement, Y purchases shares of the common stock of S, a subsidiary corporation that X establishes to research and develop the vaccine. The agreement requires S to distribute the vaccine to poor individuals in developing countries at a price that is affordable to the affected population, although, the agreement does not preclude S from selling the vaccine to other individuals at a market rate. The agreement also requires S to publish the research results, disclosing substantially all information about the results that would be useful to the interested public. S agrees that the publication of its research results will be made as promptly after the completion of the research as is reasonably possible without jeopardizing S's right to secure patents necessary to protect its ownership or control of the results of the research. The expected rate of return on Y's investment in S is less than the expected market rate of return for an investment of similar risk. Y's primary purpose in making the investment is to fund scientific research in the public interest. No significant purpose of the investment involves the production of income or the appreciation of property. The investment significantly furthers the accomplishment of Y's exempt activities and would not have been made but for such relationship between the investment and Y's exempt activities. Accordingly, Y's purchase of the common stock of S is a program-related investment.

Example 12. Q, a developing country, produces a substantial amount of recyclable solid waste materials that are currently disposed of in landfills and by incineration, contributing significantly to environmental deterioration in Q. X is a new business enterprise located in Q. X's only activity will be collecting recyclable solid waste materials in Q and delivering those materials to recycling centers that are inaccessible to a major-

ity of the population. If successful, the recycling collection business would prevent pollution in Q caused by the usual disposition of solid waste materials. X has obtained funding from only a few commercial investors who are concerned about the environmental impact of solid waste disposal. Although X made substantial efforts to procure additional funding, X has not been able to obtain sufficient funding because the expected rate of return is significantly less than the acceptable rate of return on an investment of this type. Because X has been unable to attract additional investors on the same terms as the initial investors, Y, a private foundation, enters into an investment agreement with X to purchase shares of X's common stock on the same terms as X's initial investors. Although there is a high risk associated with the investment in X, there is also the potential for a high rate of return if X is successful in the recycling business in Q. Y's primary purpose in making the investment is to combat environmental deterioration. No significant purpose of the investment involves the production of income or the appreciation of property. The investment significantly furthers the accomplishment of Y's exempt activities and would not have been made but for such relationship between the investment and Y's exempt activities. Accordingly, Y's purchase of the X common stock is a program-related investment.

Example 13. Assume the facts as stated in *Example 12,* except that X offers Y shares of X's common stock in order to induce Y to make a below-market rate loan to X. X previously made the same offer to a number of commercial investors. These investors were unwilling to provide loans to X on such terms because the expected return on the combined package of stock and debt was below the expected market return for such a package based on the level of risk involved, and they were also unwilling to provide loans on other terms X considers economically feasible. Y accepts the stock and makes the loan on the same terms that X offered to the commercial investors. Y's primary purpose in making the investment is to combat environmental deterioration. No significant purpose of the investment involves the production of income or the appreciation of property. The investment significantly furthers the accomplishment of Y's exempt activities and would not have been made but for such relationship between the investment and Y's exempt activities. Accordingly, the loan accompanied by the acceptance of common stock is a program-related investment.

Example 14. X is a business enterprise located in V, a rural area in State Z. X employs a large number of poor individuals in V. A natural disaster occurs in V, causing significant damage to the area. The business operations of X are harmed because of damage to X's equipment and buildings. X has insufficient funds to continue its business operations and conventional sources of funds are unwilling or unable to provide loans to X on terms it considers economically feasible. In order to enable X to continue its business operations, Y, a private foundation,

Reg. §53.4944-3(b)

makes a loan to X bearing interest below the market rate for commercial loans of comparable risk. Y's primary purpose in making the loan is to provide relief to the poor and distressed. No significant purpose of the loan involves the production of income or the appreciation of property. The loan significantly furthers the accomplishment of Y's exempt activities and would not have been made but for such relationship between the loan and Y's exempt activities. Accordingly, the loan is a program-related investment.

Example 15. Y, a private foundation, makes loans bearing interest below the market rate for commercial loans of comparable risk to poor individuals who live in W, a developing country, to enable them to start small businesses such as a roadside fruit stand. Conventional sources of funds were unwilling or unable to provide such loans on terms they consider economically feasible. Y's primary purpose in making the loans is to provide relief to the poor and distressed. No significant purpose of the loans involves the production of income or the appreciation of property. The loans significantly further the accomplishment of Y's exempt activities and would not have been made but for such relationship between the loans and Y's exempt activities. Accordingly, the loans to the poor individuals who live in W are program-related investments.

Example 16. X is a limited liability company treated as a partnership for federal income tax purposes. X purchases coffee from poor farmers residing in a developing country, either directly or through farmer-owned cooperatives. To fund the provision of efficient water management, crop cultivation, pest management, and farm management training to the poor farmers by X, Y, a private foundation, makes a loan to X bearing interest below the market rate for commercial loans of comparable risk. The loan agreement requires X to use the proceeds from the loan to provide the training to the poor farmers. X would not provide such training to the poor farmers absent the loan. Y's primary purpose in making the loan is to educate poor farmers about advanced agricultural methods. No significant purpose of the loan involves the production of income or the appreciation of property. The loan significantly furthers the accomplishment of Y's exempt activities and would not have been made but for such relationship between the loan and Y's exempt activities. Accordingly, the loan is a program-related investment.

Example 17. X is a social welfare organization that is recognized as an organization described in section 501(c)(4). X was formed to develop and encourage interest in painting, sculpture, and other art forms by, among other things, conducting weekly community art exhibits. X needs to purchase a large exhibition space to accommodate the demand for exhibition space within the community. Conventional sources of funds are unwilling or unable to provide funds to X on terms it considers economically feasible. Y, a private foundation, makes a loan to X at an interest rate below the market rate for commercial loans of comparable risk to fund the purchase of the new space. Y's primary purpose in making the loan is to promote the arts. No significant purpose of the loan involves the production of income or the appreciation of property. The loan significantly furthers the accomplishment of Y's exempt activities and would not have been made but for such relationship between the loan and Y's exempt activities. Accordingly, the loan is a program-related investment.

Example 18. X is a non-profit corporation that provides child care services in a low-income neighborhood, enabling many residents of the neighborhood to be gainfully employed. X meets the requirements of section 501(k) and is recognized as an organization described in section 501(c)(3). X's current child care facility has reached capacity and has a long waiting list. X has determined that the demand for its services warrants the construction of a new child care facility in the same neighborhood. X is unable to obtain a loan from conventional sources of funds including B, a commercial bank because of X's credit record. Pursuant to a deposit agreement, Y, a private foundation, deposits $h in B, and B lends an identical amount to X to construct the new child care facility. The deposit agreement requires Y to keep $h on deposit with B during the term of X's loan and provides that if X defaults on the loan, B may deduct the amount of the default from the deposit. To facilitate B's access to the funds in the event of default, the agreement requires that the funds be invested in instruments that allow B to access them readily. The deposit agreement also provides that Y will earn interest at a rate of t% on the deposit. The t% rate is substantially less than Y could otherwise earn on this sum of money, if Y invested it elsewhere. The loan agreement between B and X requires X to use the proceeds from the loan to construct the new child care facility. Y's primary purpose in making the deposit is to further its educational purposes by enabling X to provide child care services within the meaning of section 501(k). No significant purpose of the deposit involves the production of income or the appreciation of property. The deposit significantly furthers the accomplishment of Y's exempt activities and would not have been made but for such relationship between the deposit and Y's exempt activities. Accordingly, the deposit is a program-related investment.

Example 19. Assume the same facts as stated in *Example 18,* except that instead of making a deposit of $h into B, Y enters into a guarantee agreement with B. The guarantee agreement provides that if X defaults on the loan, Y will repay the balance due on the loan to B. B was unwilling to make the loan to X in the absence of Y's guarantee. X must use the proceeds from the loan to construct the new child care facility. At the same time, X and Y enter into a reimbursement agreement whereby X agrees to reimburse Y for any and all amounts paid to B under the guarantee agreement. The signed guarantee and

reimbursement agreements together constitute a "guarantee and reimbursement arrangement." Y's primary purpose in entering into the guarantee and reimbursement arrangement is to further Y's educational purposes. No significant purpose of the guarantee and reimbursement arrangement involves the production of income or the appreciation of property. The guarantee and reimbursement arrangement significantly furthers the accomplishment of Y's exempt activities and would not have been made but for such relationship between the guarantee and reimbursement arrangement and Y's exempt activities. Accordingly, the guarantee and reimbursement arrangement is a program-related investment.

(c) *Effective/applicability date.*—Paragraphs (a)(2)(ii) and (b), *Examples 11* through *19* of this section, apply on or after April 25, 2016. [Reg. §53.4944-3.]

☐ [*T.D. 7240, 12-28-72. Amended by T.D. 9762, 4-21-2016.*]

[Reg. §53.4944-4]

§53.4944-4. Special rules.—(a) *Joint and several liability.*—In any case where more than one foundation manager is liable for the tax imposed under section 4944(a)(2) or (b)(2) with respect to any one jeopardizing investment, all such foundation managers shall be jointly and severally liable for the tax imposed under each such paragraph with respect to such investment.

(b) *Limits on liability for management.*—With respect to any one jeopardizing investment, the maximum aggregate amount of tax collectible under section 4944(a)(2) from all foundation managers shall not exceed $5,000, and the maximum aggregate amount of tax collectible under section 4944(b)(2) from all foundation managers shall not exceed $10,000.

(c) *Examples.*—The provisions of this section may be illustrated by the following examples:

Example (1). A, B, and C are foundation managers of X, a private foundation. Assume that A, B, and C are liable for both initial and additional taxes under sections 4944(a)(2) and 4944(b)(2), respectively, for the following investments by X: an investment of $5,000 in the common stock of corporation M, and an investment of $10,000 in the common stock of corporation N. A, B, and C will be jointly and severally liable for the following initial taxes under section 4944(a)(2): a tax of $250 (*i.e.,* 5% of $5,000) for each year (or part thereof) in the taxable period (as defined in section 4944(e)(1)) for the investment in M, and a tax of $500 (*i.e.,* 5% of $10,000) for each year (or part thereof) in the taxable period for the investment in N. Further, A, B, and C will be jointly and severally liable for the following additional taxes under section 4944(b)(2): a tax of $250 (*i.e.,* 5% of $5,000) for the investment in M, and a tax of $500 (*i.e.,* 5% of $10,000) for the investment in N.

Example (2). Assume the facts as stated in Example (1), except that X has invested $500,000 in

the common stock of M, and $1,000,000 in the common stock of N. A, B, and C will be jointly and severally liable for the following initial taxes under section 4944(a)(2): a tax of $5,000 for the investment in M and a tax of $5,000 for the investment in N. Further, A, B, and C will be jointly and severally liable for the following additional taxes under section 4944(b)(2): a tax of $10,000 for the investment in M, and a tax of $10,000 for the investment in N. [Reg. §53.4944-4.]

☐ [*T.D. 7240, 12-28-72.*]

[Reg. §53.4944-5]

§53.4944-5. Definitions.—(a) *Taxable period.*—(1) *In general.*—For purposes of section 4944, the term "taxable period" means, with respect to any investment which jeopardizes the carrying out of a private foundation's exempt purposes, the period beginning with the date on which the amount is so invested and ending on the earliest of:

(i) The date of mailing of a notice of deficiency under section 6212 with respect to the tax imposed on the making of the investment by section 4944(a)(1);

(ii) The date on which the amount invested is removed from jeopardy; or

(iii) The date on which the tax imposed by section 4944(a)(1) is assessed.

(2) *Special rule.*—Where a notice of deficiency referred to in subparagraph (1)(i) of this paragraph is not mailed because there is a waiver of the restrictions on assessment and collection of a deficiency, or because the deficiency is paid, the date of filing of the waiver or the date of such payment, respectively, shall be treated as the end of the taxable period.

(b) *Removal from jeopardy.*—An investment which jeopardizes the carrying out of a private foundation's exempt purposes shall be considered to be removed from jeopardy when—

(1) The foundation sells or otherwise disposes of the investment, and

(2) The proceeds of such sale or other disposition are not themselves investments which jeopardize the carrying out of such foundation's exempt purposes.

A change by a private foundation in the form or terms of a jeopardizing investment shall result in the removal of the investment from jeopardy if, after such change, the investment no longer jeopardizes the carrying out of such foundation's exempt purposes. For purposes of section 4944, the making by a private foundation of one jeopardizing investment and a subsequent exchange by the foundation of such investment for another jeopardizing investment will be treated as only one jeopardizing investment, except as provided in §53.4944-6(b) and (c). For the treatment of a jeopardizing investment which is removed from jeopardy or otherwise transferred by a private foundation by the making of a grant or by bargain-sale, see sections 4941 and 4945 and the regulations thereunder. A jeopardizing invest-

ment cannot be removed from jeopardy by a transfer from a private foundation to another private foundation which is related to the transferor foundation within the meaning of section 4946(a)(1)(H)(i) or (ii), unless the investment is a program-related investment in the hands of the transferee foundation.

(c) *Examples.*—The provisions of this section may be illustrated by the following examples:

Example (1). X, a private foundation on the calendar year basis, makes a $1,000 jeopardizing investment on January 1, 1970. X thereafter sells the investment for $1,000 on January 3, 1971. The taxable period is from January 1, 1970, to January 3, 1971. X will be liable for an initial tax of $100, that is, a tax of 5 percent of the amount of the investment for each year (or part thereof) in the taxable period.

Example (2). Assume that both C and D are investments which jeopardize exempt purposes. X, a private foundation, purchases C in 1971 and later exchanges C for D. Such exchange does not constitute a removal of C from jeopardy. In addition, no new taxable period will arise with respect to D, since, for purposes of section 4944, only one jeopardizing investment has been made.

Example (3). Assume the facts as stated in Example (2), except that X sells C for cash and later reinvests such cash in D. Two separate investments jeopardizing exempt purposes have resulted. Since the cash received in the interim is not of a jeopardizing nature, the amount invested in C has been removed from jeopardy and, thus, the taxable period with respect to C has been terminated. The subsequent reinvestment of such cash in D gives rise to a new taxable period with respect to D.

(d) *Cross reference.*—For rules relating to taxable events that are corrected within the correction period, defined in section 4963(e), see section 4961(a) and the regulations thereunder. [Reg. § 53.4944-5.]

☐ [*T.D.* 7240, 12-28-72. *Amended by T.D.* 8084, 5-1-86.]

[Reg. § 53.4944-6]

§ 53.4944-6. Special rules for investments made prior to January 1, 1970.—(a) Except as provided in paragraph (b) or (c) of this section, an investment made by a private foundation prior to January 1, 1970, shall not be subject to the provisions of section 4944.

(b) If the form or terms of an investment made by a private foundation prior to January 1, 1970, are changed (other than as described in paragraph (c) of this section) on or after such date, the provisions of § 53.4944-1(a)(2)(iii) shall apply with respect to such investment.

(c) In the case of an investment made by a private foundation prior to January 1, 1970, which is exchanged on or after such date for another investment, for purposes of section 4944 the foundation will be considered to have made a new investment on the date of such exchange,

unless the post-1969 investment is described in § 53.4944-1(a)(2)(ii)(*b*). Accordingly, a determination, under § 53.4944-1(a)(2)(i), whether the investment jeopardizes the carrying out of the foundation's exempt purposes shall be made as such time. [Reg. § 53.4944-6.]

☐ [*T.D.* 7240, 12-28-72.]

[Reg. § 53.4945-1]

§ 53.4945-1. Taxes on taxable expenditures.—(a) *Imposition of initial taxes.*—(1) *Tax on private foundation.*—Section 4945(a)(1) of the Code imposes an excise tax on each taxable expenditure(as defined in section 4945(d)) of a private foundation. This tax is to be paid by the private foundation and is at the rate of 10 percent of the amount of each taxable expenditure.

(2) *Tax on foundation manager.*—(i) *In general.*—Section 4945(a)(2) of the Code imposes, under certain circumstances, an excise tax on the agreement of any foundation manager to the making of a taxable expenditure by a private foundation. This tax is imposed only in cases in which the following circumstances are present:

(*a*) A tax is imposed by section 4945(a)(1),

(*b*) Such foundation manager knows that the expenditure to which he agrees is a taxable expenditure, and

(*c*) Such agreement is willful and is not due to reasonable cause. However, the tax with respect to any particular expenditure applies only to the agreement of those foundation managers who are authorized to approve, or to exercise discretion in recommending approval of, the making of the expenditure by the foundation and to those foundation managers who are members of a group (such as the foundation's board of directors or trustees) which is so authorized. For the definition of the term "foundation manager", see section 4946(b) and the regulations thereunder.

(ii) *Agreement.*—The agreement of any foundation manager to the making of a taxable expenditure shall consist of any manifestation of approval of the expenditure which is sufficient to constitute an exercise of the foundation manager's authority to approve, or to exercise discretion in recommending approval of, the making of the expenditure by the foundation, whether or not such manifestation of approval is the final or decisive approval on behalf of the foundation.

(iii) *Knowing.*—For purposes of section 4945, a foundation manager shall be considered to have agreed to an expenditure "knowing" that it is a taxable expenditure only if—

(*a*) He has actual knowledge of sufficient facts so that, based solely upon such facts, such expenditure would be a taxable expenditure,

(*b*) He is aware that such an expenditure under these circumstances may violate the provisions of federal tax law governing taxable expenditures, and

(c) He negligently fails to make reasonable attempts to ascertain whether the expenditure is a taxable expenditure, or he is in fact aware that it is such an expenditure.

For purposes of this part and chapter 42, the term "knowing" does not mean "having reason to know". However, evidence tending to show that a foundation manager has reason to know of a particular fact or particular rule is relevant in determining whether he had actual knowledge of such fact or rule. Thus, for example, evidence tending to show that a foundation manager has reason to know of sufficient facts so that, based solely upon such facts, an expenditure would be a taxable expenditure is relevant in determining whether he has actual knowledge of such facts.

(iv) Willful.—A foundation manager's agreement to a taxable expenditure is willful if it is voluntary, conscious, and intentional. No motive to avoid the restrictions of the law or the incurrence of any tax is necessary to make an agreement willful. However, a foundation manager's agreement to a taxable expenditure is not willful if he does not know that it is a taxable expenditure.

(v) Due to reasonable cause.—A foundation manager's actions are due to reasonable cause if he has exercised his responsibility on behalf of the foundation with ordinary business care and prudence.

(vi) Advice of counsel.—If a foundation manager, after full disclosure of the factual situation to legal counsel (including house counsel), relies on the advice of such counsel expressed in a reasoned written legal opinion that an expenditure is not a taxable expenditure under section 4945 (or that expenditures conforming to certain guidelines are not taxable expenditures), although such expenditure is subsequently held to be a taxable expenditure (or that certain proposed reporting procedures with respect to an expenditure will satisfy the tests of section 4945(h), although such procedures are subsequently held not to satisfy such section), the foundation manager's agreement to such expenditure (or to grants made with provisions for such reporting procedures which are taxable solely because of such inadequate reporting procedures) will ordinarily not be considered "knowing" or "willful" and will ordinarily be considered "due to reasonable cause" within the meaning of section 4945(a)(2). For purposes of the subdivision, a written legal opinion will be considered "reasoned" even if it reaches a conclusion which is subsequently determined to be incorrect so long as such opinion addresses itself to the facts and applicable law. However, a written legal opinion will not be considered "reasoned" if it does nothing more than recite the facts and express a conclusion. However, the absence of advice of counsel with respect to an expenditure shall not, by itself, give rise to any inference that a foundation manager agreed to the making of the expenditure knowingly, willfully, or without reasonable cause.

(vii) Rate and incidence of tax.—The tax imposed under section 4945(a)(2) is at the rate of $2^1/_2$ percent of the amount of each taxable expenditure to which the foundation manager has agreed. This tax shall be paid by the foundation manager.

(viii) Cross reference.—For provisions relating to the burden of proof in cases involving the issue whether a foundation manager has knowingly agreed to the making of a taxable expenditure, see section 7454(b).

(b) Imposition of additional taxes.—(1) *Taxes on private foundation.*—Section 4945(b)(1) of the Code imposes an excise tax in any case in which an initial tax is imposed under section 4945(a)(1) on a taxable expenditure of a private foundation and the expenditure is not corrected within the taxable period (as defined in section 4945(i)(2)). The tax imposed under section 4945(b)(1) is to be paid by the private foundation and is at the rate of 100 percent of the amount of each taxable expenditure.

(2) Tax on foundation manager.—Section 4945(b)(2) of the Code imposes an excise tax in any case in which a tax is imposed under section 4945(b)(1) and a foundation manager has refused to agree to part or all of the correction of the taxable expenditure. The tax imposed under section 4945(b)(2) is at the rate of 50 percent of the amount of the taxable expenditure. This tax is to be paid by any foundation manager who has refused to agree to part or all of the correction of the taxable expenditure.

(c) Special rules.—(1) *Joint and several liability.*—In any case where more than one foundation manager is liable for the tax imposed under section 4945(a)(2) or (b)(2) with respect to the making of a taxable expenditure, all such foundation managers shall be jointly and severally liable for the tax imposed under such paragraph with respect to such taxable expenditure.

(2) Limits on liability for management.—The maximum aggregate amount of tax collectible under section 4945(a)(2) from all foundation managers with respect to any one taxable expenditure shall be $5,000, and the maximum aggregate amount of tax collectible under section 4945(b)(2) from all foundation managers with respect to any one taxable expenditure shall be $10,000.

(3) Examples.—The provisions of this paragraph may be illustrated by the following examples:

Example (1). A, B, and C comprise the board of directors of Foundation M. They vote unanimously in favor of a grant of $100,000 to D, a business associate of each of the directors. The grant is to be used by D for travel and educational purposes and is not made in accordance with the requirements of section 4945(g). Each director knows that D was selected as the recipient of the grant solely because of his friendship with the directors and is aware that some grants made for travel, study, or other similar purposes

may be taxable expenditures. Also, none of the directors makes any attempt to consult counsel, or to otherwise determine, whether this grant is a taxable expenditure. Initial taxes are imposed under paragraphs (1) and (2) of section 4945(a). The tax to be paid by the foundation is $10,000 (10 percent of $100,000). The tax to be paid by the board of directors is $2,500 (2¹/₂ percent of $100,000). A, B, and C are jointly and severally liable for this $2,500 and this sum may be collected by the Service from any one of them.

Example (2). Assume the same facts as in example (1). Further assume that within the taxable period A makes a motion to correct the taxable expenditure at a meeting of the board of directors. The motion is defeated by a two-to-one vote, A voting for the motion and B and C voting against it. In these circumstances an additional tax is imposed on the private foundation in the amount of $100,000 (100 percent of $100,000). The additional tax imposed on B and C is $10,000 (50 percent of $100,000 subject to a maximum of $10,000). B and C are jointly and severally liable for the $10,000, and this sum may be collected by the Service from either of them.

(d) *Correction.*—(1) *In general.*—Except as provided in paragraph (d)(2) or (3) of this section, correction of a taxable expenditure shall be accomplished by recovering part or all of the expenditure to the extent recovery is possible, and, where full recovery cannot be accomplished, by any additional corrective action which the Commissioner may prescribe. Such additional corrective action is to be determined by circumstances of each particular case and may include the following:

(i) Requiring that any unpaid funds due the grantee be withheld;

(ii) Requiring that no further grants be made to the particular grantee;

(iii) In addition to other reports that are required, requiring periodic (*e.g.,* quarterly) reports from the foundation with respect to all expenditures of the foundation (such reports shall be equivalent in detail to the reports required by section 4945(h)(3) and § 53.4945-5(d));

(iv) Requiring improved methods of exercising expenditure responsibility;

(v) Requiring improved methods of selecting recipients of individual grants; and

(vi) Requiring such other measures as the Commissioner may prescribe in a particular case. The foundation making the expenditure shall not be under any obligation to attempt to recover the expenditure by legal action if such action would in all probability not result in the satisfaction of execution on a judgment.

(2) *Correction for inadequate reporting.*—If the expenditure is taxable only because of a failure to obtain a full and complete report as required by section 4945(h)(2) or because of a failure to make a full and detailed report as required by section 4945(h)(3), correction may be accomplished by obtaining or making the report in question. In addition, if the expenditure is taxa-

ble only because of a failure to obtain a full and complete report as required by section 4945(h)(2) and an investigation indicates that no grant funds have been diverted to any use not in furtherance of a purpose specified in the grant, correction may be accomplished by exerting all reasonable efforts to obtain the report in question and reporting the failure to the Internal Revenue Service, even though the report is not finally obtained.

(3) *Correction for failure to obtain advance approval.*—Where an expenditure is taxable under section 4945(d)(3) only because of a failure to obtain advance approval of procedures with respect to grants as required by section 4945(g), correction may be accomplished by obtaining approval of the grant making procedures and establishing to the satisfaction of the Commissioner that:

(i) no grant funds have been diverted to any use not in furtherance of a purpose specified in the grant;

(ii) the grant making procedures instituted would have been approved if advance approval of such procedures had been properly requested; and

(iii) where advance approval of grant making procedures is subsequently required, such approval will be properly requested.

(e) *Certain periods.*—(1) *Taxable period.*—For purposes of section 4945, the term "taxable period" means, with respect to any taxable expenditure, the period beginning with the date on which the taxable expenditure occurs and ending on the earlier of:

(i) The date of mailing of a notice of deficiency under section 6212 with respect to the tax imposed on taxable expenditures by section 4945(a)(1); or

(ii) The date on which the tax imposed by section 4945(a)(1) is assessed.

(2) *Cross reference.*—For rules relating to taxable events that are corrected within the correction period, defined in section 4963(e), see section 4961(a) and the regulations thereunder. [Reg. § 53.4945-1.]

☐ [*T.D.* 7215, 10-30-72. *Amended by T.D.* 7299, 12-21-73, *T.D.* 7527, 12-23-77 *and T.D.* 8084, 5-1-86.]

[Reg. § 53.4945-2]

§ 53.4945-2. **Propaganda influencing legislation.**—(a) *Propaganda influencing legislation, etc.*—(1) *In general.*—Under section 4945(d)(1) the term "taxable expenditure" includes any amount paid or incurred by a private foundation to carry on propaganda, or otherwise to attempt, to influence legislation. An expenditure is an attempt to influence legislation if it is for a direct or grass roots lobbying communication, as defined in § 56.4911-2 (without reference to §§ 56.4911-2(b)(3) and 56.4911-2(c) and § 56.4911-3. See, however, paragraph (d) of this section for exceptions to the general rule of this paragraph (a)(1).

(2) *Expenditures for membership communications.*—Section 56.4911-5, which provides special rules for electing public charities' communications with their members, does not apply to private foundations. Thus, whether a private foundation's communications with its members (assuming it has any) are lobbying communications is determined solely under §56.4911-2 and without reference to §56.4911-5. However, where a private foundation makes a grant to an electing public charity, §56.4911-5 applies to the electing public charity's communications with its own members. Therefore, in the limited context of determining whether a private foundation's grant to an electing public charity is a taxable expenditure under section 4945, the §56.4911-5 membership rules apply. For example, if the grant is specifically earmarked for a communication from the electing public charity to its members and the communication is, because of §56.4911-5, a nonlobbying communication, the grant is not a taxable expenditure under section 4945.

(3) *Jointly funded projects.*—A private foundation will not be treated as having paid or incurred any amount to attempt to influence legislation merely because it makes a grant to another organization upon the condition that the recipient obtain a matching support appropriation from a governmental body. In addition, a private foundation will not be treated as having made taxable expenditures of amounts paid or incurred in carrying on discussions with officials of governmental bodies provided that:

(i) The subject of such discussions is a program which is jointly funded by the foundation and the government or is a new program which may be jointly funded by the foundation and the government,

(ii) The discussions are undertaken for the purpose of exchanging data and information on the subject matter of the program, and

(iii) Such discussions are not undertaken by foundation managers in order to make any direct attempt to persuade governmental officials or employees to take particular positions on specific legislative issues other than such program.

(4) *Certain expenditures by recipients of program-related investments.*—Any amount paid or incurred by a recipient of a program-related investment (as defined in §53.4944-3) in connection with an appearance before, or communication with, any legislative body with respect to legislation or proposed legislation of direct interest to such recipient shall not be attributed to the investing foundation, if—

(i) The foundation does not earmark its funds to be used for any activities described in section 4945(d)(1) and

(ii) A deduction under section 162 is allowable to the recipient for such amount.

(5) *Grants to public organizations.*—(i) *In general.*—A grant by a private foundation to an or-

ganization described in section 509(a)(1), (2) or (3) does not constitute a taxable expenditure by the foundation under section 4945(d), other than under section 4945(d)(1), if the grant by the private foundation is not earmarked to be used for any activity described in section 4945(d)(2) or (5), is not earmarked to be used in a manner which would violate section 4945(d)(3) or (4), and there does not exist an agreement, oral or written, whereby the grantor foundation may cause the grantee to engage in any such prohibited activity or to select the recipient to which the grant is to be devoted. For purposes of this paragraph (a)(5)(i), a grant by a private foundation is earmarked if the grant is given pursuant to an agreement, oral or written, that the grant will be used for specific purposes. For the expenditure responsibility requirements with respect to organizations other than those described in section 509(a)(1), (2), or (3), see §53.4945-5. For rules for determining whether grants to public charities are taxable expenditures under section 4945(d)(1), see paragraphs (a)(2), (a)(6) and (a)(7) of this section.

(ii) *Certain "public" organizations.*—For purposes of this section, an organization shall be considered a section 509(a)(1) organization if it is treated as such under subparagraph (4) of §53.4945-5(a).

(6) *Grants to public organizations that attempt to influence legislation.*—(i) *General support grant.*—A general support grant by a private foundation to an organization described in section 509(a)(1), (2), or (3) (a "public charity" for purposes of paragraphs (a)(6) and (7) of this section) does not constitute a taxable expenditure under section 4945(d)(1) to the extent that the grant is not earmarked, within the meaning of §53.4945-2(a)(5)(i), to be used in an attempt to influence legislation. The preceding sentence applies without regard to whether the public charity has made the election under section 501(h).

(ii) *Specific project grant.*—A grant by a private foundation to fund a specific project of a public charity is not a taxable expenditure by the foundation under section 4945(d)(1) to the extent that—

(A) The grant is not earmarked, within the meaning of §53.4945-2(a)(5)(i), to be used in an attempt to influence legislation, and

(B) The amount of the grant, together with other grants by the same private foundation for the same project for the same year, does not exceed the amount budgeted, for the year of the grant, by the grantee organization for activities of the project that are not attempts to influence legislation. If the grant is for more than one year, the preceding sentence applies to each year of the grant with the amount of the grant measured by the amount actually disbursed by the private foundation in each year or divided equally between years, at the option of the private foundation. The same method of measuring the annual amount must be used in all years of a grant. This paragraph (a)(6)(ii) applies without

regard to whether the public charity has made the election under section 501(h).

(iii) *Reliance upon grantee's budget.*—For purposes of determining the amount budgeted by a prospective grantee for specific project activities that are not attempts to influence legislation under paragraph (a)(6)(ii) of this section, a private foundation may rely on budget documents or other sufficient evidence supplied by the grantee organization (such as a signed statement by an authorized officer, director or trustee of such grantee organization) showing the proposed budget of the specific project, unless the private foundation doubts or, in light of all the facts and circumstances, reasonably should doubt the accuracy or reliability of the documents.

(7) *Grants to organizations that cease to be described in 501(c)(3).*—(i) *Not taxable expenditure; conditions.*—A grant to a public charity (as defined in paragraph (a)(6)(i) of this section) that thereafter ceases to be an organization described in section 501(c)(3) by reason of its attempts to influence legislation is not a taxable expenditure if—

(A) The grant meets the requirements of paragraph (a)(6) of this section,

(B) The recipient organization had received a ruling or determination letter, or an advance ruling or determination letter, that it is described in sections 501(c)(3) and 509(a),

(C) Notice of a change in the recipient organization's status has not been made to the public (such as by publication in the Internal Revenue Bulletin), and the private foundation has not acquired knowledge that the Internal Revenue Service has given notice to the recipient organization that it will be deleted from such status, and

(D) The recipient organization is not controlled directly or indirectly by the private foundation. A recipient organization is controlled by a private foundation for this purpose if the private foundation and disqualified persons (defined in section 4946(a)(1)(A) through (H)) with reference to the private foundation, by aggregating their votes or positions of authority, can cause or prevent action on legislative issues by the recipient.

(ii) *Examples.*—The provisions of paragraphs (a)(6) and (a)(7) of this section are illustrated by the following examples:

Example (1). W, a private foundation, makes a general support grant to Z, a public charity described in section 509(a)(1). Z informs W that, as an insubstantial portion of its activities, Z attempts to influence the State legislature with regard to changes in the mental health laws. The use of the grant is not earmarked by W to be used in a manner that would violate section 4945(d)(1). Even if the grant is subsequently devoted by Z to its legislative activities, the grant by W is not a taxable expenditure under section 4945(d).

Example (2). X, a private foundation, makes a specific project grant to Y University for the purpose of conducting research on the potential environmental effects of certain pesticides. X does not earmark the grant for any purpose that would violate section 4945(d)(1) and there is no oral or written agreement or understanding whereby X may cause Y to engage in any activity described in section 4945(d)(1), (2), or (5), or to select any recipient to which the grant may be devoted. Further, X determines, based on budget information supplied by Y, that Y's budget for the project does not contain any amount for attempts to influence legislation. X has no reason to doubt the accuracy or reliability of the budget information. Y uses most of the funds for the research project; however, Y expends a portion of the grant funds to send a representative to testify at Congressional hearings on a specific bill proposing certain pesticide control measures. The portion of the grant funds expended with respect to the Congressional hearings is not treated as a taxable expenditure by X under section 4945(d)(1).

Example (3). M, a private foundation, makes a specific project grant of $150,000 to P, a public charity described in section 509(a)(1). In requesting the grant from M, P stated that the total budgeted cost of the project is $200,000, and that of this amount $20,000 is allocated to attempts to influence legislation related to the project. M relies on the budget figures provided by P in determining the amount P will spend on influencing legislation and M has no reason to doubt the accuracy or reliability of P's budget figures. In making the grant, M did not earmark any of the funds from the grant to be used for attempts to influence legislation. M's grant of $150,000 to P will not constitute a taxable expenditure under section 4945(d)(1) because M did not earmark any of the funds for attempts to influence legislation and because the amount of its grant ($150,000) does not exceed the amount allocated to specific project activities that are not attempts to influence legislation ($200,000 − $20,000 = $180,000).

Example (4). Assume the same facts as in example (3), except that M's grant letter to P provides that M has the right to renegotiate the terms of the grant if there is a substantial deviation from those terms. This additional fact does not make M's grant a taxable expenditure under section 4945(d)(1).

Example (5). Assume the same facts as in example (3), except that M made a specific project grant of $200,000 to P. Part of M's grant of $200,000 will constitute a taxable expenditure under section 4945(d)(1). The amount of the grant ($200,000) exceeds by $20,000 the amount P allocated to specific project activities that are not attempts to influence legislation ($180,000). M has made a taxable expenditure of $20,000.

Example (6). Assume the same facts as [in]example (3), except that M made a specific project grant of $180,000, and received from P an enforceable commitment that grant funds would not be used in connection with attempts to influ-

ence legislation. M's grant is not a taxable expenditure under section 4945(d)(1).

Example (7). Assume the same facts as in example (3), except that M directed P to hire A, an individual, to expend $20,000 from the grant to engage in direct lobbying (within the meaning of §56.4911-2(b)) and grass roots lobbying (within the meaning of §56.4911-2(c)). P does not expend any other grant funds for lobbying activities. The $20,000 that is earmarked for direct lobbying and grass roots lobbying is a taxable expenditure under section 4945(d)(1).

Example (8). R, a public charity described in section 509(a)(1), requested N, a private foundation, to make a general purpose grant to it to aid R in carrying out its exempt purpose. In making this request, R notified N that it had elected the expenditure test under section 501(h) and that it expected to attempt to influence legislation in areas related to its exempt purpose. Since its formation, R generally has had exempt purpose expenditures (as defined in §56.4911-4) in excess of $7,000,000 in each of its taxable years, and has budgeted in excess of $7,000,000 of exempt purpose expenditures for the year of the grant. N made a grant of $200,000 to R. N did not earmark the funds for R's attempt to influence legislation. The general purpose grant by N does not constitute a taxable expenditure under section 4945(d)(1).

Example (9). Assume the same facts as in example (8), except that N learns that R has had excess lobbying expenditures (within the meaning of §56.4911-1(b)) in some prior years. N also learns that in no year has [sic] R's lobbying or grass roots expenditures (within the meaning of §56.4911-2(a) and (c)) exceeded the corresponding ceiling amount (within the meaning of §1.501(h)-3(c)(3) and (6)). N then makes the grant to R. After receiving the grant, R spends a large portion of its funds on influencing legislation and, as a consequence, is denied exemption from tax, as an organization described in section 501(c)(3), under section 501(h) and §1.501(h)-3. No disqualified person with respect to N controlled, in whole or in part, R's attempts to influence legislation. The general purpose grant will not constitute a taxable expenditure under section 4945(d)(1).

Example (10). X, a private foundation, makes a specific project grant to Y, a public charity described in section 509(a). In requesting the grant, Y stated that it planned to use the funds to purchase a computer for purposes of computerizing its research files and that the grant will not be used to influence legislation. Two years after X makes the grant, X discovers that Y has also used the computer for purposes of maintaining and updating the mailing list for Y's lobbying newsletter. Because X did not earmark any of the grant funds to be used for attempts to influence legislation and because X had no reason to doubt the accuracy or reliability of Y's documents representing that the grant would not be used to influence legislation, X's grant is not treated as a taxable expenditure.

Example (11). G, a private foundation, makes a specific project grant of $300,000 to L, a public charity described in section 509(a)(1) for a three-year specific project studying child care problems. L provides budget material indicating that the specific project will expend $200,000 in each of three years. L's budget materials indicate that attempts to influence legislation will amount to $10,000 in the first year, $20,000 in the second year and $100,000 in the third year. G intends to pay its $300,000 grant over three years as follows: $200,000 in the first year, $50,000 in the second year and $50,000 in the third year. The amount of the grant actually disbursed by G in the first year of the grant exceeds the nonlobbying expenditures of L in that year. However, because the amount of the grant in each of the three years, when divided equally among the three years ($100,000 for each year), is not more than the nonlobbying expenditures of L on the specific project for any of the three years, none of the grant is treated as a taxable expenditure under section 4945(d)(1).

Example (12). P, a private foundation, makes a $120,000 specific project grant to C, a public charity described in section 509(a) for a three-year project. P intends to pay its grant to C in three equal annual installments of $40,000. C provides budget material indicating that the specific project will expend $100,000 in each of three years. C's budget materials, which P reasonably does not doubt, indicate that the project's attempts to influence legislation will amount to $50,000 in each of the three years. After P pays the first annual installment to C, but before P pays the second installment to C, reliable information comes to P's attention that C has spent $90,000 of the project's $100,000 first-year budget on attempts to influence legislation. This information causes P to doubt the accuracy and reliability of C's budget materials. Because of the information, P does not pay the second-year installment to C. P's payment of the first installment of $40,000 is not a taxable expenditure under section 4945(d)(1) because the grant in the first year is not more than the nonlobbying expenditures C projected in its budget materials that P reasonably did not doubt.

Example (13). Assume the same facts as in example (12), except that P pays the second-year installment of $40,000 to C. In the project's second year, C once again spends $90,000 of the project's $100,000 annual budget in attempts to influence legislation. Because P doubts or reasonably should doubt the accuracy or reliability of C's budget materials when P makes the second-year grant payment, P may not rely upon C's budget documents at that time. Accordingly, although none of the $40,000 paid in the first installment is a taxable expenditure, only $10,000 ($100,000 minus $90,000) of the second-year grant payment is not a taxable expenditure. The remaining $30,000 of the second installment is a taxable expenditure within the meaning of section 4945(d)(1).

Example (14). B, a private foundation, makes a specific project grant to C, a public

charity described in section 509(a), of $40,000 for the purpose of conducting a study on the effectiveness of seat belts in preventing traffic deaths. B did not earmark any of the grant for attempts to influence legislation. In requesting the grant from B, C submitted a budget of $100,000 for the project. The budget contained expenses for postage and mailing, computer time, advertising, consulting services, salaries, printing, advertising, and similar categories of expenses. C also submitted to B a statement, signed by an officer of C, that 30% of the budgeted funds would be devoted to attempts to influence legislation within the meaning of section 4945. B has no reason to doubt the accuracy of the budget figures or the statement. B may rely on the budget figures and signed statement provided by C in determining the amount C will spend on influencing legislation. B's grant to C will not constitute a taxable expenditure under section 4945(d)(1), because the amount of the grant does not exceed the amount allocated to specific project activities that are not attempts to influence legislation.

(b) [Reserved]

(c) [Reserved]

(d) *Exceptions.*—(1) *Nonpartisan analysis, study, or research.*—(i) *In general.*—A communication is not a lobbying communication, for purposes of §53.4945-2(a)(1), if the communication constitutes engaging in nonpartisan analysis, study or research and making available to the general public or a segment or members thereof or to governmental bodies, officials, or employees the results of such work. Accordingly, an expenditure for such a communication does not constitute a taxable expenditure under section 4945(d)(1) and §53.4945-2(a)(1).

(ii) *Nonpartisan analysis, study, or research.*—For purposes of section 4945(e), "nonpartisan analysis, study, or research" means an independent and objective exposition of a particular subject matter, including any activity that is "educational" within the meaning of §1.501(c)(3)-1(d)(3). Thus, "nonpartisan analysis, study, or research" may advocate a particular position or viewpoint so long as there is a sufficiently full and fair exposition of the pertinent facts to enable the public or an individual to form an independent opinion or conclusion. On the other hand, the mere presentation of unsupported opinion does not qualify as "nonpartisan analysis, study, or research".

(iii) *Presentation as part of a series.*—Normally, whether a publication or broadcast qualifies as "nonpartisan analysis, study, or research" will be determined on a presentation-by-presentation basis. However, if a publication or broadcast is one of a series prepared or supported by a private foundation and the series as a whole meets the standards of subdivision (ii) of this subparagraph, then any individual publication or broadcast within the series will not result in a taxable expenditure even though such individual broadcast or publication does not, by itself, meet

the standards of subdivision (ii) of this subparagraph. Whether a broadcast or publication is considered part of a series will ordinarily depend on all the facts and circumstances of each particular situation. However, with respect to broadcast activities, all broadcasts within any period of 6 consecutive months will ordinarily be eligible to be considered as part of a series. If a private foundation times or channels a part of a series which is described in this subdivision in a manner designed to influence the general public or the action of a legislative body with respect to a specific legislative proposal in violation of section 4945(d)(1), the expenses of preparing and distributing such part of the analysis, study, or research will be a taxable expenditure under this section.

(iv) *Making available results of analysis, study, or research.*—A private foundation may choose any suitable means, including oral or written presentations, to distribute the results of its nonpartisan analysis, study, or research, with or without charge. Such means include distribution of reprints of speeches, articles and reports (including the report required under section 6056); presentation of information through conferences, meetings and discussions; and dissemination to the news media, including radio, television and newspapers, and to other public forums. For purposes of this paragraph (d)(1)(iv), such communications may not be limited to, or be directed toward, persons who are interested solely in one side of a particular issue.

(v) *Subsequent lobbying use of certain analysis, study or research.*—(A) *In general.*—Even though certain analysis, study or research is initially within the exception for nonpartisan analysis, study or research, subsequent use of that analysis, study or research for grass roots lobbying may cause that analysis, study or research to be treated as a grass roots lobbying communication that is not within the exception for nonpartisan analysis, study or research. This paragraph (d)(1)(v) of this section does not cause any analysis, study or research to be considered a direct lobbying communication. For rules regarding when analysis, study or research is treated as a grass roots lobbying communication that is not within the scope of the exception for nonpartisan analysis, study or research, see §56.4911-2(b)(2)(v).

(B) *Special rule for grants to public charities.*—This paragraph (d)(1)(v)(B) of this section applies where a public charity uses a private foundation grant to finance, in whole or in part, a nonlobbying communication that is subsequently used in lobbying, causing the public charity's expenditures for the communication to be treated as lobbying expenditures under the subsequent use rule. In such a case, the private foundation's grant will ordinarily not be characterized as a lobbying expenditure by virtue of the subsequent use rule. The only situations where the private foundation's grant will be treated as a lobbying expenditure under the sub-

sequent use rule are where the private foundation's primary purpose in making the grant to the public charity was for lobbying or where, at the time of making the grant, the private foundation knows (or in light of all the facts and circumstances reasonably should know) that the public charity's primary purpose in preparing the communication to be funded by the grant is for use in lobbying.

(vi) *Directly encouraging action by recipients of a communication.*—A communication that reflects a view on specific legislation is not within the nonpartisan analysis, study or research exception of this § 53.4945-2(d)(1) if the communication directly encourages the recipient to take action with respect to such legislation. For purposes of this section, a communication directly encourages the recipient to take action with respect to legislation if the communication is described in one or more of § 56.4911-2(b)(2)(iii)(A) through (C). As described in § 56.4911-2(b)(2)(iv), a communication would encourage the recipient to take action with respect to legislation, but not *directly* encourage such action, if the communication does no more than specifically identify one or more legislators who will vote on the legislation as: opposing the communication's view with respect to the legislation; being undecided with respect to the legislation; being the recipient's representative in the legislature; or being a member of the legislative committee or subcommittee that will consider the legislation.

(vii) *Examples.*—The provisions of this paragraph may be illustrated by the following examples:

Example (1). M, a private foundation, establishes a research project to collect information for the purpose of showing the dangers of the use of pesticides in raising crops. The information collected includes data with respect to proposed legislation, pending before several State legislatures, which would ban the use of pesticides. The project takes favorable positions on such legislation without producing a sufficiently full and fair exposition of the pertinent facts to enable the public or an individual to form an independent opinion or conclusion on the pros and cons of the use of pesticides. This project is not within the exception for nonpartisan analysis, study, or research because it is designed to present information merely on one side of the legislative controversy.

Example (2). N, a private foundation, establishes a research project to collect information concerning the dangers of the use of pesticides in raising crops for the ostensible purpose of examining and reporting information as to the pros and cons of the use of pesticides in raising crops. The information is collected and distributed in the form of a published report which analyzes the effects and costs of the use and nonuse of various pesticides under various conditions on humans, animals and crops. The report also presents the advantages, disadvantages, and economic cost of allowing the continued use of pesticides unabated, of controlling the use of

pesticides, and of developing alternatives to pesticides. Even if the report sets forth conclusions that the disadvantages as a result of using pesticides are greater than the advantages of using pesticides and that prompt legislative regulation of the use of pesticides is needed, the project is within the exception for nonpartisan analysis, study or research since it is designed to present information on both sides of the legislative controversy and presents a sufficiently full and fair exposition of the pertinent facts to enable the public or an individual to form an independent opinion or conclusion. ·

Example (3). O, a private foundation, establishes a research project to collect information on the presence or absence of disease in humans from eating food grown with pesticides and the presence or absence of disease in humans from eating food not grown with pesticides. As part of the research project, O hires a consultant who prepares a "fact sheet" which calls for the curtailment of the use of pesticides and which addresses itself to the merits of several specific legislative proposals to curtail the use of pesticides in raising crops which are currently pending before State Legislatures. The "fact sheet" presents reports of experimental evidence tending to support its conclusions but omits any reference to reports of experimental evidence tending to dispute its conclusions. O distributes ten thousand copies to citizens' groups. Expenditures by O in connection with this work of the consultant are not within the exception for nonpartisan analysis, study, or research.

Example (4). P publishes a bi-monthly newsletter to collect and report all published materials, ongoing research, and new developments with regard to the use of pesticides in raising crops. The newsletter also includes notices of proposed pesticide legislation with impartial summaries of the provisions and debates on such legislation. The newsletter does not encourage recipients to take action with respect to such legislation, but is designed to present information on both sides of the legislative controversy and does present such information fully and fairly. It is within the exception for nonpartisan analysis, study, or research.

Example (5). X is satisfied that A, a member of the faculty of Y University, is exceptionally well qualified to undertake a project involving a comprehensive study of the effects of pesticides on crop yields. Consequently, X makes a grant to A to underwrite the cost of the study and of the preparation of a book on the effect of pesticides on crop yields. X does not take any position on the issues or control the content of A's output. A produces a book which concludes that the use of pesticides often has a favorable effect on crop yields, and on that basis argues against pending bills which would ban the use of pesticides. A's book contains a sufficiently full and fair exposition of the pertinent facts, including known or potential disadvantages of the use of pesticides, to enable the public or an individual to form an independent opinion or conclusion as to whether pesticides should be

banned as provided in the pending bills. The book does not directly encourage readers to take action with respect to the pending bills. Consequently, the book is within the exception for nonpartisan analysis, study, or research.

Example (6). Assume the same facts as Example (2), except that, instead of issuing a report, X presents within a period of 6 consecutive months a two-program television series relating to the pesticide issue. The first program contains information, arguments, and conclusions favoring legislation to restrict the use of pesticides. The second program contains information, arguments, and conclusions opposing legislation to restrict the use of pesticides. The programs are broadcast within 6 months of each other during commensurate periods of prime time. X's programs are within the exception for nonpartisan analysis, study, or research. Although neither program individually could be regarded as nonpartisan, the series of two programs constitutes a balanced presentation.

Example (7). Assume the same facts as Example (6), except that X arranged for televising the program favoring legislation to restrict the use of pesticides at 8:00 p.m. on a Thursday evening and for televising the program opposing such legislation at 7:00 a.m. on a Sunday morning. X's presentation is not within the exception for nonpartisan analysis, study, or research, since X disseminated its information in a manner prejudicial to one side of the legislative controversy.

Example (8). Organization Z researches, writes, prints and distributes a study on the use and effects of pesticide X. A bill is pending in the U.S. Senate to ban the use of pesticide X. Z's study leads to the conclusion that pesticide X is extremely harmful and that the bill pending in the U.S. Senate is an appropriate and much needed remedy to solve the problems caused by pesticide X. The study contains a sufficiently full and fair exposition of the pertinent facts, including known or potential advantages of the use of pesticide X, to enable the public or an individual to form an independent opinion or conclusion as to whether pesticides should be banned as provided in the pending bills. In its analysis of the pending bill, the study names certain undecided Senators on the Senate committee considering the bill. Although the study meets the three part test for determining whether a communication is a grass roots lobbying communication, the study is within the exception for nonpartisan analysis, study or research, because it does not directly encourage recipients of the communication to urge a legislator to opppose the bill.

Example (9). Assume the same facts as in Example (8), except that, after stating support for the pending bill, the study concludes: "You should write to the undecided commitee members to support this crucial bill." The study is not within the exception for nonpartisan analysis, study or research because it directly encourages the recipients to urge a legislator to support a specific piece of legislation.

Example (10). Organization X plans to conduct a lobbying campaign with respect to illegal drug use in the United States. It incurs $5,000 in expenses to conduct research and prepare an extensive report primarily for use in the lobbying campaign. Although the detailed report discusses specific pending legislation and reaches the conclusion that the legislation would reduce illegal drug use, the report contains a sufficiently full and fair exposition of the pertinent facts to enable the public or an indiviudal to form an independent conclusion regarding the effect of the legislation. The report does not encourage readers to contact legislators regarding the legislation. Accordingly, the report does not, in and of itself, constitute a lobbying communication.

Copies of the report are available to the public at X's office, but X does not actively distribute the report or otherwise seek to make the contents of the report available to the general public. Whether or not X's distribution is sufficient to meet the requirement in §53.4945-2(d)(1)(iv) that a nonpartisan communication be made available, X's distribution is not substantial (for purposes of §§53.4945-2(d)(1)(v) and 56.4911-2(b)(2)(v) in light of all of the facts and circumstances, including the normal distribution pattern of similar nonpartisan reports. X then mails copies of the report, along with a letter, to 10,000 individuals on X's mailing list. In the letter, X requests that individuals contact legislators urging passage of the legislation discussed in the report. Because X's research and report were primarily undertaken by X for lobbying purposes and X did not make a substantial distribution of the report (without an accompanying lobbying message) prior to or contemporaneously with the use of the report in lobbying, the report is a grass roots lobbying communication that is not within the exception for nonpartisan analysis, study or research. Thus, the expenditures for preparing and mailing both the report and the letter are taxable expenditures under section 4945.

Example (11). Assume the same facts as in Example (10), except that before using the report in the lobbying campaign, X sends the research and report (without an accompanying lobbying message) to universities and newspapers. At the same time, X also advertises the availability of the report in its newsletter. This distribution is similar in scope to the normal distribution pattern of similar nonpartisan reports. In light of all of the facts and circumstances, X's distribution of the report is substantial. Because of X's substantial distribution of the report, X's primary purpose will be considered to be other than for use in lobbying and the report will not be considered a grass roots lobbying communication. Accordingly, only the expenditures for copying and mailing the report to the 10,000 individuals on X's mailing list, as well as for preparing and mailing the letter, are expenditures for grass roots lobbying communications, and are thus taxable expenditures under section 4945.

Example (12). Organization M pays for a bumper sticker that reads: "STOP ABORTION:

Vote *NO* on Prop. X!" M also pays for a 30-second television advertisement and a billboard that similarly advocate opposition to Prop. X. In light of the limited scope of the communications, none of the communications is within the exception for nonpartisan analysis, study or research. First, none of the communications rises to the level of analysis, study or research. Second, none of the communications is nonpartisan because none contains a sufficiently full and fair exposition of the pertinent facts to enable the public or an individual to form an independent opinion or conclusion. Thus, each communication is a lobbying communication.

(2) *Technical advice or assistance.*—(i) *In general.*—Amounts paid or incurred in connection with providing technical advice or assistance to a governmental body, a governmental committee, or a subdivision of either of the foregoing, in response to a written request by such body, committee, or subdivision do not constitute taxable expenditures for purposes of this section. Under this exception, the request for assistance or advice must be made in the name of the requesting governmental body, committee or subdivision rather than an individual member thereof. Similarly, the response to such request must be available to every member of the requesting body, committee or subdivision. For example, in the case of a written response to a request for technical advice or assistance from a Congressional committee, the response will be considered available to every member of the requesting committee if the response is submitted to the person making such request in the name of the committee and it is made clear that the response is for the use of all the members of the committee.

(ii) *Nature of technical advice or assistance.*—"Technical advice or assistance" may be given as a result of knowledge or skill in a given area. Because such assistance or advice may be given only at the express request of a governmental body, committee or subdivision, the oral or written presentation of such assistance or advice need not qualify as nonpartisan analysis, study or research. The offering of opinions or recommendations will ordinarily qualify under this exception only if such opinions or recommendations are specifically requested by the governmental body, committee or subdivision or are directly related to the materials so requested.

(iii) *Examples.* The provisions of this subparagraph may be illustrated by the following examples:

Example (1). A Congressional committee is studying the feasibility of legislation to provide funds for scholarships to United States students attending schools abroad. X, a private foundation which has engaged in a private scholarship program of this type, is asked, in writing, by the committee to describe the manner in which it selects candidates for its program. X's response disclosing its methods of selection constitutes technical advice or assistance.

Example (2). Assume the same facts as Example (1), except that X's response not only includes a description of its own grant-making procedures, but also its views regarding the wisdom of adopting such a program. Since such views are directly related to the subject matter of the request for technical advice or assistance, expenditures paid or incurred with respect to the presentation of such views would not constitute taxable expenditures. However, expenditures paid or incurred with respect to a response which is not directly related to the subject matter of the request for technical advice or assistance would constitute taxable expenditures unless the presentation can qualify as the making available of nonpartisan analysis, study or research.

Example (3). Assume the same facts as Example (1), except that X is requested, in addition, to give any views it considers relevant. A response to this request giving opinions which are relevant to the committee's consideration of the scholarship program but which are not necessarily directly related to X's scholarship program, such as discussions of alternative scholarship programs and their relative merits, would qualify as "technical advice or assistance", and expenditures paid or incurred with respect to such response would not constitute taxable expenditures.

Example (4). A, an official of the State Department, makes a written request in his official capacity for information from Foundation Y relating to the economic development of Country M and for the opinions of Y as to the proper position of the United States in pending negotiations with M concerning a proposed treaty involving a program of economic and technical aid to M. Y's furnishing of such information and opinions constitutes technical advice or assistance.

Example (5). In response to a telephone inquiry from Senator X's staff, organization B sends Senator X a report concluding that the Senate should not advise and consent to the nomination of Z to serve as a Supreme Court Justice. Because the request was not in writing, and also because the request was not from the Senate itself or from a committee or subcommittee, B's report is not within the scope of the exception for responses to requests for technical advice. Accordingly, B's report is a lobbying communication unless the report is within the scope of the exception for nonpartisan analysis, study or research.

Example (6). Assume the same facts as in Example (5), except that B's report is sent in response to a written request that Senator X sends to B. The request from Senator X is a request from the Senator as an individual member of the Senate rather than from the Senate itself or from a committee or subcommittee. Accordingly, B's report is not within the scope of the exception for responses to requests for technical advice and is a lobbying communication unless the report is within the scope of the exception for nonpartisan analysis, study or research.

Reg. §53.4945-2(d)(2)(ii)

Example (7). Assume the same facts as in Example (6), except that B's report is sent in response to a written request from the Senate committee that is considering the nomination for an evaluation of the nominee's legal writings and a recommendation as to whether the candidate is or is not qualified to serve on the Supreme Court. The report is within the scope of the exception for responses to requests for technical advice and is not a lobbying communication.

(3) *Decisions affecting the powers, duties, etc., of a private foundation.*—(i) *In general.*—Paragraph (c) of this section does not apply to any amount paid or incurred in connection with an appearance before, or communication with, any legislative body with respect to a possible decision of such body which might affect the existence of the private foundation, its powers and duties, its tax-exempt status, or the deductibility of contributions to such foundation. Under this exception, a foundation may communicate with the entire legislative body, committees or subcommittees of such legislative body, individual congressmen or legislators, members of their staffs, or representatives of the executive branch, who are involved in the legislative process, if such communication is limited to the prescribed subjects. Similarly, the foundation may make expenditures in order to initiate legislation if such legislation concerns only matters which might affect the existence of the private foundation, its powers and duties, its tax-exempt status, or the deductibility of contributions to such foundation.

(ii) *Examples.* The provisions of this subparagraph may be illustrated by the following examples:

Example (1). A bill is being considered by Congress which would, if enacted, restrict the power of a private foundation to engage in transactions with certain related persons. Under the proposed bill a private foundation would lose its exemption from taxation if it engages in such transactions. W, a private foundation, writes to the Congressional committee considering the bill, arguing that the enactment of such a bill would not be advisable, and subsequently appears before such committee to make its arguments. In addition, W requests that the Congressional committee consider modification of the 2 percent *de minimis* rule of section 4943(c)(2)(C). Expenditures paid or incurred with respect to such submissions do not constitute taxable expenditures since they are made with respect to a possible decision of Congress which might affect the existence of the private foundation, its powers and duties, its tax-exempt status, or the deduction of contributions to such foundation.

Example (2). A bill being considered in a State legislature is designed to implement the requirements of section 508(e) of the Internal Revenue Code of 1954. Under such section, a private foundation is required to make certain amendments to its governing instrument. X, a private foundation, makes a submission to the legislature which proposes alternative measures which might be taken in lieu of the proposed bill. X also arranges to have its president contact certain State legislators with regard to this bill. Expenditures paid or incurred in making such submission and in contacting the State legislators do not constitute taxable expenditures since they are made with respect to a possible decision of such State legislature which might affect the existence of the private foundation, its powers and duties, its tax-exempt status, or the deduction of contributions to such foundation.

Example (3). A bill is being considered by a State legislature under which the State would assume certain responsibilities for nursing care of the aged. Y, a private foundation which hitherto has engaged in such activities, appears before the State legislature and contends that such activities can be better performed by privately supported organizations. Expenditures paid or incurred with respect to such appearance are not made with respect to possible decisions of the State legislature which might affect the existence of the private foundation, its powers and duties, its tax-exempt status, or the deduction of contributions to such foundation, but rather merely affect the scope of the private foundation's future activities.

Example (4). A State legislature is considering the annual appropriations bill. Z, a private foundation which had hitherto performed contract research for the State, appears before the appropriations committee in order to attempt to persuade the committee of the advisability of continuing the program. Expenditures paid or incurred with respect to such appearance are not made with respect to possible decisions of the State legislature which might affect the existence of the private foundation, its powers and duties, its tax-exempt status, or the deduction of contributions to such foundation, but rather merely affect the scope of the private foundation's future activities.

(4) *Examinations and discussions of broad social, economic, and similar problems.*—Examinations and discussions of broad social, economic, and similar problems are neither direct lobbying communications under § 56.4911-2(b)(1) nor grass roots lobbying communications under § 56.4911-2(b)(2) even if the problems are of the type with which government would be expected to deal ultimately. Thus, under § 56.4911-2(b)(1) and (2), lobbying communications do not include public discussion, or communications with members of legislative bodies or governmental employees, the general subject of which is also the subject of legislation before a legislative body, so long as such discussion does not address itself to the merits of a specific legislative proposal and so long as such discussion does not directly encourage recipients to take action with respect to legislation. For example, this paragraph (d)(4) excludes from grass roots lobbying under § 56.4911-2(b)(2) an organization's discussions of problems such as environmental pollution or population growth that are being

considered by Congress and various State legislatures, but only where the discussions are not directly addressed to specific legislation being considered, and only where the discussions do not directly encourage recipients of the communication to contact a legislator, an employee of a legislative body, or a government official or employee who may participate in the formulation of legislation. [Reg. § 53.4945-2.]

□ [*T.D. 7215, 10-30-72. Amended by T.D. 8308, 8-30-90.*]

[Reg. § 53.4945-3]

§ 53.4945-3. Influencing elections and carrying on voter registration drives.—(a) *Expenditures to influence elections or carry on voter registration drives.*—(1) *In general.*—Under section 4945(d)(2), the term "taxable expenditure" includes any amount paid or incurred by a private foundation to influence the outcome of any specific public election or to carry on, directly or indirectly, any voter registration drive, unless such amount is paid or incurred by an organization described in section 4945(f). However, for treatment of non-earmarked grants to public organizations, see § 53.4945-2(a)(5) and for treatment of certain earmarked grants to organizations described in section 4945(f), see paragraph (b)(2) of this section.

(2) *Influencing the outcome of a specific public election.*—For purposes of this section, an organization shall be considered to be influencing the outcome of any specific public election if it participates or intervenes, directly or indirectly, in any political campaign on behalf of or in opposition to any candidate for public office. The term "candidate for public office" means an individual who offers himself, or is proposed by others, as a contestant for an elective public office, whether such office be national, State or local. Activities which constitute participation or intervention in a political campaign on behalf of or in opposition to a candidate include, but are not limited to:

(i) Publishing or distributing written or printed statements or making oral statements on behalf of or in opposition to such a candidate;

(ii) Paying salaries or expenses of campaign workers; and

(iii) Conducting or paying the expenses of conducting a voter registration drive limited to the geographic area covered by the campaign.

(b) *Nonpartisan activities carried on by certain organizations.*—(1) *In general.*—If an organization meets the requirements described in section 4945(f), an amount paid or incurred by such organization shall not be considered a taxable expenditure even though the use of such amount is otherwise described in section 4945(d)(2). Such requirements are:

(i) The organization is described in section 501(c)(3) and exempt from taxation under section 501(a);

(ii) The activities of the organization are nonpartisan, are not confined to one specific

election period, and are carried on in five or more States;

(iii) The organization expends at least 85 percent of its income directly for the active conduct (within the meaning of section 4942(j)(3) and the regulations thereunder) of the activities constituting the purpose or function for which it is organized and operated;

(iv) The organization receives at least 85 percent of its support (other than gross investment income as defined in section 509(e)) from exempt organizations, the general public, governmental units described in section 170(c)(1), or any combination of the foregoing; the organization does not receive more than 25 percent of its support (other than gross investment income) from any one exempt organization (for this purpose treating private foundations which are described in section 4946(a)(1)(H) with respect to each other as one exempt organization); and not more than half of the support of the organization is received from gross investment income; and

(v) Contributions to the organization for voter registration drives are not subject to conditions that they may be used only in specified States, possessions of the United States, or political subdivisions or other areas of any of the foregoing, or the District of Columbia, or that they may be used in only one specific election period.

(2) *Grants to section 4945(f) organizations.*—If a private foundation makes a grant to an organization described in section 4945(f) (whether or not such grantee is a private foundation as defined in section 509(a)), such grant will not be treated as a taxable expenditure under section 4945(d)(2) or (4). Even if a grant to such an organization is earmarked for voter registration purposes generally, such a grant will not be treated as a taxable expenditure under section 4945(d)(2) or (4) as long as such earmarking does not violate section 4945(f)(5).

(3) *Period for determining support.*—(i) *In general.*—The determination whether an organization meets the support test in section 4945(f)(4) for any taxable year is to be made by aggregating all amounts of support received by the organization during the taxable year and the immediately preceding four taxable years. However, the support received in any taxable year which begins before January 1, 1970, shall be excluded.

(ii) *New organizations and organizations with no preceding taxable years beginning after December 31, 1969.*—Except as provided in subparagraph (4) of this paragraph, in the case of a new organization or an organization with no taxable years that begin after December 31, 1969, and immediately precede the taxable year in question, the requirements of the support test in section 4945(f)(4) will be considered as met for the taxable year if such requirements are met by the end of the taxable year.

(iii) *Organization with three or fewer preceding taxable years.*—In the case of an organization which has been in existence for at least one but

fewer than four preceding taxable years beginning after December 31, 1969, the determination whether such organization meets the requirements of the support test in section 4945(f)(4) for the taxable year is to be made by taking into account all the support received by such organization during the taxable year and during each preceding taxable year beginning after December 31, 1969.

(4) *Advance rulings.*—An organization will be given an advance ruling that it is an organization described in section 4945(f) for its first taxable year of operation beginning after [insert date these final regulations are filed by the Office of the Federal Register] or for its first taxable year of operation beginning after December 31, 1969, if it submits evidence establishing that it can reasonably be expected to meet the tests under section 4945(f) for such taxable year. An organization which, pursuant to this subparagraph, has been treated as an organization described in section 4945(f) for a taxable year (without withdrawal of such treatment by notification from the Internal Revenue Service during such year), but which actually fails to meet the requirements of section 4945(f) for such taxable year, will not be treated as an organization described in section 4945(f) as of the first day of its next taxable year (for purposes of making any determination under the internal revenue laws with respect to such organization) and until such time as the organization does meet the requirements of section 4945(f). For purposes of section 4945, the status of grants or contributions with respect to grantors or contributors to such organization will not be affected until notice of change of status of such organization is made to the public (such as by publication in the Internal Revenue Bulletin). The preceding sentence shall not apply, however, if the grantor or contributor was responsible for, or was aware of, the fact that the organization did not satisfy section 4945(f) at the end of the taxable year with respect to which the organization had obtained an advance ruling or a determination letter that it was a section 4945(f) organization, or acquired knowledge that the Internal Revenue Service had given notice to such organization that it would be deleted from classification as a section 4945(f) organization. [Reg. § 53.4945-3.]

☐ [*T.D.* 7215, 10-30-72.]

[Reg. § 53.4945-4]

§ 53.4945-4. Grants to individuals.— (a) *Grants to individuals.*—(1) *In general.*—Under section 4945(d)(3) the term "taxable expenditure" includes any amount paid or incurred by a private foundation as a grant to an individual for travel, study, or other similar purposes by such individual unless the grant satisfies the requirements of section 4945(g). Grants to individuals which are not taxable expenditures because made in accordance with the requirements of section 4945(g) may result in the imposition of excise taxes under other provisions of chapter 42.

(2) *"Grants" defined.*—For purposes of section 4945, the term "grants" shall include, but is not limited to, such expenditures as scholarships, fellowships, internships, prizes, and awards. Grants shall also include loans for purposes described in section 170(c)(2)(B) and "program related investments" (such as investments in small businesses in central cities or in businesses which assist in neighborhood renovation). Similarly, "grants" include such expenditures as payments to exempt organizations to be used in furtherance of such recipient organizations' exempt purposes whether or not such payments are solicited by such recipient organizations. Conversely, "grants" do not ordinarily include salaries or other compensation to employees. For example, "grants" do not ordinarily include educational payments to employees which are includible in the employees' incomes pursuant to section 61. In addition, "grants" do not ordinarily include payments (including salaries, consultants' fees and reimbursement for travel expenses such as transportation, board, and lodging) to persons (regardless of whether such persons are individuals) for personal services in assisting a foundation in planning, evaluating or developing projects or areas of program activity by consulting, advising, or participating in conferences organized by the foundation.

(3) *Requirements for individual grants.*— (i) *Grants for other than section 4945(d)(3) purposes.*—A grant to an individual for purposes other than those described in section 4945(d)(3) is not a taxable expenditure within the meaning of section 4945(d)(3). For example, if a foundation makes grants to indigent individuals to enable them to purchase furniture, such grants are not taxable expenditures within the meaning of section 4945(d)(3) even if the requirements of section 4945(g) are not met.

(ii) *Grants for section 4945(d)(3) purposes.*— Under section 4945(g), a grant to an individual for travel, study, or other similar purposes is not a "taxable expenditure" only if:

(a) The grant is awarded on an objective and nondiscriminatory basis (within the meaning of paragraph (b) of this section);

(b) The grant is made pursuant to a procedure approved in advance by the Commissioner; and

(c) It is demonstrated to the satisfaction of the Commissioner that:

(1) The grant constitutes a scholarship or fellowship grant which is excluded from gross income under section 117(a) and is to be utilized for study at an educational institution described in section 151(e)(4);

(2) The grant constitutes a prize or award which is excluded from gross income under section 74(b), and the recipient of such prize or award is selected from the general public (within the meaning of section 4941(d)(2)(G)(i) and the regulations thereunder); or

(3) The purpose of the grant is to achieve a specific objective, produce a report or other similar product, or improve or enhance a literary, artistic, musical, scientific, teaching, or other similar capacity, skill, or talent of the grantee.

If a grant is made to an individual for a purpose described in section 4945(g)(3) and such grant otherwise meets the requirements of section 4945(g), such grant shall not be treated as a taxable expenditure even if it is a scholarship or a fellowship grant which is not excludable from income under section 117 or if it is a prize or award which is includible in income under section 74.

(iii) *Renewals.*—A renewal of a grant which satisfied the requirements of subdivision (ii) of this subparagraph shall not be treated as a grant to an individual which is subject to the requirements of this section, if—

(a) The grantor has no information indicating that the original grant is being used for any purpose other than that for which it was made,

(b) Any reports due at the time of the renewal decision pursuant to the terms of the original grant have been furnished, and

(c) Any additional criteria and procedures for renewal are objective and nondiscriminatory.

For purposes of this section, an extension of the period over which a grant is to be paid shall not itself be regarded as a grant or a renewal of a grant.

(4) *Certain designated grants.*—(i) *In general.*—A grant by a private foundation to another organization, which the grantee organization uses to make payments to an individual for purposes described in section 4945(d)(3), shall not be regarded as a grant by the private foundation to the individual grantee if the foundation does not earmark the use of the grant for any named individual and there does not exist an agreement, oral or written, whereby such grantor foundation may cause the selection of the individual grantee by the grantee organization. For purposes of this subparagraph, a grant described herein shall not be regarded as a grant by the foundation to an individual grantee even though such foundation has reason to believe that certain individuals would derive benefits from such grant so long as the grantee organization exercises control, in fact, over the selection process and actually makes the selection completely independently of the private foundation.

(ii) *Certain grants to "public charities".*—A grant by a private foundation to an organization described in section 509(a)(1), (2), or (3), which the grantee organization uses to make payments to an individual for purposes described in section 4945(d)(3), shall not be regarded as a grant by the private foundation to the individual grantee (regardless of the application of subdivision (i) of this subparagraph) if the grant is made for a project which is to be undertaken under the supervision of the section 509(a)(1), (2), or (3) organization and such grantee organization controls the selection of the individual grantee. This subdivision shall apply regardless of whether the name of the individual grantee was first proposed by the private foundation, but only if there is an objective manifestation of the section 509(a)(1), (2), or (3) organization's control over the selection process, although the selection need not be made completely independently of the private foundation. For purposes of this subdivision, an organization shall be considered a section 509(a)(1) organization if it is treated as such under subparagraph (4) of § 53.4945-5(a).

(iii) *Grants to governmental agencies.*—If a private foundation makes a grant to an organization described in section 170(c)(1) (regardless of whether it is described in section 501(c)(3)) and such grant is earmarked for use by an individual for purposes described in section 4945(d)(3), such grant is not subject to the requirements of section 4945(d)(3) and (g) and this section (regardless of the application of subdivision (i) of this subparagraph) if the section 170(c)(1) organization satisfies the Commissioner in advance that its grant-making program:

(a) Is in furtherance of a purpose described in section 170(c)(2)(B),

(b) Requires that the individual grantee submit reports to it which would satisfy paragraph (c)(3) of this section, and

(c) Requires that the organization investigate jeopardized grants in a manner substantially similar to that described in paragraph (c)(4) of this section.

(iv) *Examples.*—The provisions of this subparagraph may be illustrated by the following examples:

Example (1). M, a university described in section 170(b)(1)(A)(ii), requests that P, a private foundation, grant it $100,000 to enable M to obtain the services of a particular scientist for a research project in a special field of biochemistry in which he has exceptional qualifications and competence. P, after determining that the project deserves support, makes the grant to M to enable it to obtain the services of this scientist. M is authorized to keep the funds even if it is unsuccessful in attempting to employ the scientist. Under these circumstances P will not be treated as having made a grant to the individual scientist for purposes of section 4945(d)(3) and (g), since the requirements of subdivision (i) of this subparagraph have been satisfied. Even if M were not authorized to keep the funds if it is unsuccessful in attempting to employ the scientist, P would not be treated as having made a grant to the individual scientist for purposes of section 4945(d)(3) and (g), since it is clear from the facts and circumstances that the selection of the particular scientist was made by M and thus the requirements of subdivision (ii) of this subparagraph would have been satisfied.

Example (2). Assume the same facts as Example (1), except that there are a number of

scientists who are qualified to administer the research project, P suggests the name of the particular scientist to be employed by M, and M is not authorized to keep the funds if it is unsuccessful in attempting to employ the particular scientist. For purposes of section 4945(d)(3) and (g), P will be treated as having made a grant to the individual scientist whose name it suggested, since it is clear from the facts and circumstances that selection of the particular scientist was made by P.

Example (3). X, a private foundation, is aware of the exceptional research facilities at Y University, an organization described in section 170(b)(1)(A)(ii). Officials of X approach officials of Y with an offer to give Y a grant of $100,000 if Y will engage an adequately qualified physicist to conduct a specific research project. Y's officials accept this proposal, and it is agreed that Y will administer the funds. After examining the qualifications of several research physicists, the officials of Y agree that A, whose name was first suggested by officials of X and who first suggested the specific research project to X, is uniquely qualified to conduct the project. X's grant letter provides that X has the right to renegotiate the terms of the grant if there is a substantial deviation from such terms, such as breakdown of Y's research facilities or termination of the conduct of the project by an adequately qualified physicist. Under these circumstances, X will not be treated as having made a grant to A for purposes of section 4945(d)(3) and (g), since the requirements of subdivision (ii) of this subparagraph have been satisfied.

Example (4). Professor A, a scholar employed by University Y, an organization described in section 170(b)(1)(A)(ii), approaches Foundation X to determine the availability of grant funds for a particular research project supervised or conducted by Professor A relevant to the program interests of Foundation X. After learning that Foundation X would be willing to consider the project if University Y were to submit the project to X, Professor A submits his proposal to the appropriate administrator of University Y. After making a determination that it should assume responsibility for the project, that Professor A is qualified to conduct the project, and that his participation would be consistent with his other faculty duties, University Y formally adopts the grant proposal and submits it to Foundation X. The grant is made to University Y which, under the terms of the grant, is responsible for the expenditure of the grant funds and the grant project. In such a case, and even if Foundation X retains the right to renegotiate the terms of the grant if the project ceases to be conducted by Professor A, the grant shall not be regarded as a grant by Foundation X to Professor A since University Y has retained control over the selection process within the meaning of subdivision (ii) of this subparagraph.

(5) *Earmarked grants to individuals.*—A grant by a private foundation to an individual, which

meets the requirements of section 4945(d)(3) and (g), is a taxable expenditure by such foundation under section 4945(d) only if—

(i) The grant is earmarked to be used for any activity described in section 4945(d)(1), (2), or (5), or is earmarked to be used in a manner which would violate section 4945(d)(3) or (4),

(ii) There is an agreement, oral or written, whereby such grantor foundation may cause the grantee to engage in any such prohibited activity and such grant is in fact used in a manner which violates section 4945(d), or

(iii) The grant is made for a purpose other than a purpose described in section 170(c)(2)(B).

For purposes of this subparagraph, a grant by a private foundation is earmarked if such grant is given pursuant to an agreement, oral or written, that the grant will be used for specific purposes.

(b) *Selection of grantees on "an objective and nondiscriminatory basis".*—(1) *In general.*—For purposes of this section, in order for a foundation to establish that its grants to individuals are made on an objective and nondiscriminatory basis, the grants must be awarded in accordance with a program which, if it were a substantial part of the foundation's activities, would be consistent with:

(i) The existence of the foundation's exempt status under section 501(c)(3);

(ii) The allowance of deductions to individuals under section 170 for contributions to the granting foundation; and

(iii) The requirements of subparagraphs (2), (3), and (4) of this paragraph.

(2) *Candidates for grants.*—Ordinarily, selection of grantees on an objective and nondiscriminatory basis requires that the group from which grantees are selected be chosen on the basis of criteria reasonably related to the purposes of the grant. Furthermore, the group must be sufficiently broad so that the giving of grants to members of such group would be considered to fulfill a purpose described in section 170(c)(2)(B). Thus, ordinarily the group must be sufficiently large to constitute a charitable class. However, selection from a group is not necessary where taking into account the purposes of the grant, one or several persons are selected because they are exceptionally qualified to carry out these purposes or it is otherwise evident that the selection is particularly calculated to effectuate the charitable purpose of the grant rather than to benefit particular persons or a particular class of persons. Therefore, consistent with the requirements of this subparagraph, the foundation may impose reasonable restrictions on the group of potential grantees. For example, selection of a qualified research scientist to work on a particular project does not violate the requirements of section 4945(d)(3) merely because the foundation selects him from a group of three scientists who are experts in that field.

(3) *Selection from within group of potential grantees.*—The criteria used in selecting grant re-

cipients from the potential grantees should be related to the purpose of the grant. Thus, for example, proper criteria for selecting scholarship recipients might include (but are not limited to) the following: prior academic performance; performance on tests designed to measure ability and aptitude for college work; recommendations from instructors; financial need; and the conclusions which the selection committee might draw from a personal interview as to the individual's motivation, character, ability and potential.

(4) *Persons making selections.*—The person or group of persons who select recipients of grants should not be in a position to derive a private benefit, directly or indirectly, if certain potential grantees are selected over others.

(5) *Examples.*—The provisions of this paragraph may be illustrated by the following examples:

Example (1). X Company employs 100,000 people of whom 1,000 are classified by the company as executives. The company has organized the X Company Foundation which, as its sole activity, provides 100 four-year college scholarships per year for children of the company's employees. Children of all employees (other than disqualified persons with respect to the foundation) who have worked for the X Company for at least two years are eligible to apply for these scholarships. In previous years, the number of children eligible to apply for such scholarships has averaged 2,000 per year. Selection of scholarship recipients from among the applicants is made by three prominent educators, who have no connection (other than as members of the selection committee) with the company, the foundation or any of the employees of the company. The selections are made on the basis of the applicants' prior academic performance, performance on certain tests designed to measure ability and aptitude for college work, and financial need. No disproportionate number of scholarships has been granted to relatives of executives of X Company. Under these circumstances, the operation of the scholarship program by the X Company Foundation: (1) is consistent with the existence of the foundation's exempt status under section 501(c)(3) and with the allowance of deductions under section 170 for contributions to the foundation; (2) utilizes objective and nondiscriminatory criteria in selecting scholarship recipients from among the applicants; and (3) utilizes a selection committee which appears likely to make objective and nondiscriminatory selections of grant recipients.

Example (2). Assume the same facts as Example (1), except that the foundation establishes a program to provide 20 college scholarships per year for members of a certain ethnic minority. All members of this minority group (other than disqualified persons with respect to the foundation) living in State Z are eligible to apply for these scholarships. It is estimated that at least 400 persons will be eligible to apply for these scholarships each year. Under these circumstances, the operation of this scholarship program by the foundation: (1) is consistent with the existence of the foundation's exempt status under section 501(c)(3) and with the allowance of deductions under section 170 for contributions to the foundation; (2) utilizes objective and nondiscriminatory criteria in selecting scholarship recipients from among the applicants; and (3) utilizes a selection committee which appears likely to make objective and nondiscriminatory selections of grant recipients.

(c) *Requirements of a proper procedure.*—(1) *In general.*—Section 4945(g) requires that grants to individuals must be made pursuant to a procedure approved in advance. To secure such approval, a private foundation must demonstrate to the satisfaction of the Commissioner that—

(i) Its grant procedure includes an objective and nondiscriminatory selection process (as described in paragraph (b) of this section);

(ii) Such procedure is reasonably calculated to result in performance by grantees of the activities that the grants are intended to finance; and

(iii) The foundation plans to obtain reports to determine whether the grantees have performed the activities that the grants are intended to finance.

No single procedure or set of procedures is required. Procedures may vary depending upon such factors as the size of the foundation, the amount and purpose of the grants and whether one or more recipients are involved.

(2) *Supervision of scholarship and fellowship grants.*—Except as provided in subparagraph (5) of this paragraph, with respect to any scholarship or fellowship grants, a private foundation must make arrangements to receive a report of the grantee's courses taken (if any) and grades received (if any) in each academic period. Such a report must be verified by the educational institution attended by the grantee and must be obtained at least once a year. In cases of grantees whose study at an educational institution does not involve the taking of courses but only the preparation of research papers or projects, such as the writing of a doctoral thesis, the foundation must receive a brief report on the progress of the paper or project at least once a year. Such a report must be approved by the faculty member supervising the grantee or by another appropriate university official. Upon completion of a grantee's study at an educational institution, a final report must also be obtained.

(3) *Grants described in section 4945(g)(3).*—With respect to a grant made under section 4945(g)(3), the private foundation shall require reports on the use of the funds and the progress made by the grantee toward achieving the purposes for which the grant was made. Such reports must be made at least once a year. Upon completion of the undertaking for which the grant was made, a final report must be made describing the grantee's accomplishments with respect to the grant and accounting for the funds received under such grant.

Reg. §53.4945-4(c)(3)

(4) *Investigation of jeopardized grants.*—(i) Where the reports submitted under this paragraph or other information (including the failure to submit such reports) indicates that all or any part of a grant is not being used in furtherance of the purposes of such grant, the foundation is under a duty to investigate. While conducting its investigation, the foundation must withhold further payments to the extent possible until any delinquent reports required by this paragraph have been submitted and where required by subdivision (ii) or (iii) of this subparagraph.

(ii) In cases in which the grantor foundation determines that any part of a grant has been used for improper purposes and the grantee has not previously diverted grant funds to any use not in furtherance of a purpose specified in the grant, the foundation will not be treated as having made a taxable expenditure solely because of the diversion so long as the foundation—

(a) Is taking all reasonable and appropriate steps either to recover the grant funds or to insure the restoration of the diverted funds and the dedication (consistent with the requirements of (b)(1) and (2) of this subdivision) of other grant funds held by the grantee to the purposes being financed by the grant, and

(b) Withholds any further payments to the grantee after the grantor becomes aware that a diversion may have taken place (hereinafter referred to as "further payments") until it has—

(1) Received the grantee's assurances that future diversions will not occur, and

(2) Required the grantee to take extraordinary precautions to prevent future diversions from occurring.

If a foundation is treated as having made a taxable expenditure under this subparagraph in a case to which this subdivision applies, then unless the foundation meets the requirements of (a) of this subdivision the amount of the taxable expenditure shall be the amount of the diversion plus the amount of any further payments to the same grantee. However, if the foundation complies with the requirements of (a) of this subdivision but not the requirements of (b) of this subdivision, the amount of the taxable expenditure shall be the amount of such further payments.

(iii) In cases where a grantee has previously diverted funds received from a grantor foundation, and the grantor foundation determines that any part of a grant has again been used for improper purposes, the foundation will not be treated as having made a taxable expenditure solely by reason of such diversion so long as the foundation—

(a) Is taking all reasonable and appropriate steps to recover the grant funds or to insure the restoration of the funds and the dedication (consistent with the requirements of (b)(2) and (3) of this subdivision) of other grant funds held by the grantee to the purposes being financed by the grant, and

(b) Withholds further payments until—

(1) Such funds are in fact so recovered or restored,

(2) It has received the grantee's assurances that future diversions will not occur, and

(3) It requires the grantee to take extraordinary precautions to prevent future diversions from occurring.

If a foundation is treated as having made a taxable expenditure under this subparagraph in a case to which this subdivision applies, then unless the foundation meets the requirements of (a) of this subdivision, the amount of the taxable expenditure shall be the amount of the diversion plus the amount of any further payments to the same grantee. However, if the foundation complies with requirements of (a) of this subdivision, but fails to withhold further payments until the requirements of (b) of this subdivision are met, the amount of the taxable expenditure shall be the amount of such further payments.

(iv) The phrase "all reasonable and appropriate steps" in subdivisions (ii) and (iii) of this subparagraph includes legal action where appropriate but need not include legal action if such action would in all probability not result in the satisfaction of execution on a judgment.

(5) *Supervision of certain scholarship and fellowship grants.*—Subparagraphs (2) and (4) of this paragraph shall be considered satisfied with respect to scholarship or fellowship grants under the following circumstances:

(i) The scholarship or fellowship grants are described in section 4945(g)(1);

(ii) The grantor foundation pays the scholarship or fellowship grants to an educational institution described in section 151(e)(4); and

(iii) Such educational institution agrees to use the grant funds to defray the recipient's expenses or to pay the funds (or a portion thereof) to the recipient only if the recipient is enrolled at such educational institution and his standing at such educational institution is consistent with the purposes and conditions of the grant.

(6) *Retention of records.*—A private foundation shall retain records pertaining to all grants to individuals for purposes described in section 4945(d)(3). Such records shall include:

(i) All information the foundation secures to evaluate the qualification of potential grantees;

(ii) Identification of grantees (including any relationship of any grantee to the foundation sufficient to make such grantee a disqualified person of the private foundation within the meaning of section 4946(a)(1));

(iii) Specification of the amount and purpose of each grant; and

(iv) The follow-up information which the foundation obtains in complying with subparagraphs (2), (3) and (4) of this paragraph.

Reg. §53.4945-4(c)(4)

(7) *Example.*—The provisions of paragraphs (b) and (c) of this section may be illustrated by the following example:

Example. The X Foundation grants ten scholarships each year to graduates of high schools in its area to permit the recipients to attend college. It makes the availability of its scholarships known by oral or written communications each year to the principals of three major high schools in the area. The foundation obtains information from each high school on the academic qualifications, background, and financial need of applicants. It requires that each applicant be recommended by two of his teachers or by the principal of his high school. All application forms are reviewed by the foundation officer responsible for making the awards and scholarships are granted on the basis of the academic qualifications and financial need of the grantees. The foundation obtains annual reports on the academic performance of the scholarship recipient from the college or university which he attends. It maintains a file on each scholarship awarded, including the original application, recommendations, a record of the action taken on the application, and the reports on the recipient from the institution which he attends. The described procedures of the X Foundation for the making of grants to individuals qualify for Internal Revenue Service approval under section 4945(g). Furthermore, if the X Foundation's scholarship program meets the requirements of subparagraph (5) of this paragraph, X Foundation will not have to obtain reports on the academic performance of the scholarship recipients.

(d) *Submission of grant procedure.*—(1) *Contents of request for approval of grant procedures.*—A request for advance approval of a foundation's grant procedures must fully describe the foundation's procedures for awarding grants and for ascertaining that such grants are used for the proper purposes. The approval procedure does not contemplate specific approval of particular grant programs but instead one-time approval of a system of standards, procedures, and follow-up designed to result in grants which meet the requirements of section 4945(g). Thus, such approval shall apply to a subsequent grant program as long as the procedures under which it is conducted do not differ materially from those described in the request to the Commissioner. The request must contain the following items:

(i) A statement describing the selection process. Such statement shall be sufficiently detailed for the Commissioner to determine whether the grants are made on an objective and nondiscriminatory basis under paragraph (b) of this section.

(ii) A description of the terms and conditions under which the foundation ordinarily makes such grants, which is sufficient to enable the Commissioner to determine whether the grants awarded under such procedures would meet the requirements of paragraph (1), (2), or (3) of section 4945(g).

(iii) A detailed description of the private foundation's procedure for exercising supervision over grants, as described in paragraph (c)(2) and (3) of this section.

(iv) A description of the foundation's procedures for review of grantee reports, for investigation where diversion of grant funds from their proper purposes is indicated, and for recovery of diverted grant funds, as described in paragraph (c)(4) of this section.

(2) *Place of submission.*—Request for approval of grant procedures shall be submitted to the District Director.

(3) *Internal Revenue Service action on request for approval of grant procedures.*—If, by the 45th day after a request for approval of grant procedures has been properly submitted to the Internal Revenue Service, the organization has not been notified that such procedures are not acceptable, such procedures shall be considered as approved from the date of submission until receipt of actual notice from the Internal Revenue Service that such procedures do not meet the requirements of this section. If a grant to an individual for a purpose described in section 4945(d)(3) is made after notification to the organization by the Internal Revenue Service that the procedures under which the grant is made are not acceptable, such grant is a taxable expenditure under this section.

(e) *Effective dates.*—(1) *In general.*—This section shall apply to all grants to individuals for travel, study or other similar purposes which are made by private foundations more than 90 days after October 30, 1972.

(2) *Transitional rules.*—(i) *Grants committed prior to January 1, 1970.*—Section 4945(d)(3) and (g) and this section shall not apply to a grant for section 170(c)(2)(B) purposes made on or after January 1, 1970, if the grant was made pursuant to a commitment entered into prior to such date, but only if such commitment was made in accordance with the foundation's usual practices and is reasonable in amount in light of the purposes of the grant. For purposes of this subdivision, a commitment will be considered entered into prior to January 1, 1970, if prior to such date, the amount and nature of the payments to be made and the name of the payee were entered on the records of the payor, or were otherwise adequately evidenced, or the notice of the payment to be received was communicated to the payee in writing.

(ii) *Grants awarded on or after January 1, 1970.*—In the case of a grant awarded on or after January 1, 1970, but prior to the expiration of 90 days after October 30, 1972, and paid within 48 months after the award of such grant, the requirements of section 4945(g) that an individual grant be awarded on an objective and nondiscriminatory basis pursuant to a procedure approved in advance by the Commissioner will be deemed satisfied if the grantor utilizes any procedure in good faith in awarding a grant to an

Reg. § 53.4945-4(e)(2)(ii)

individual which, in fact, is reasonably calculated to provide objectivity and nondiscrimination in the awarding of such grant and to result in a grant which complies with the conditions of section 4945(g)(1), (2) or (3). [Reg. § 53.4945-4.]

☐ [*T.D.* 7215, 10-30-72.]

[Reg. § 53.4945-5]

§ 53.4945-5. Grants to organizations.— (a) *Grants to nonpublic organizations.*—(1) *In general.*—Under section 4945(d)(4) the term "taxable expenditure" includes any amount paid or incurred by a private foundation as a grant to an organization (other than an organization described in section 509(a)(1), (a)(2), or (a)(3) (other than an organization described in section 4942(g)(4)(A)(i) or (ii)) or in section 4940(d)(2)), unless the private foundation exercises expenditure responsibility with respect to such grant in accordance with section 4945(h). However, the granting foundation does not have to exercise expenditure responsibility with respect to amounts granted to organizations described in section 4945(f).

(2) *"Grants" described.*—For a description of the term "grants", see § 53.4945-4(a)(2).

(3) *Section 509(a)(1), (2), and (3) organizations.*—See section 508(b) and the regulations thereunder for rules relating to when a grantor may rely on a potential grantee's characterization of its status as set forth in the notice described in section 508(b).

(4) *Certain "public" organizations.*—For purposes of this section, an organization will be treated as a section 509(a)(1) organization if:

(i) It qualifies as such under paragraph (a) of § 1.509(a)-2 of this chapter;

(ii) It is an organization described in section 170(c)(1) or 511(a)(2)(B), even if it is not described in section 501(c)(3); or

(iii) It is a foreign government, or any agency or instrumentality thereof, or an international organization designated as such by Executive Order under 22 U.S.C. 288, even if it is not described in section 501(c)(3).

However, any grant to an organization referred to in this subparagraph must be made exclusively for charitable purposes as described in section 170(c)(2)(B).

(5) *Certain foreign organizations.*—(i) *In general.*—If a private foundation makes a grant to a foreign organization, which does not have a ruling or determination letter that it is an organization described in section 509(a)(1), (a)(2), or (a)(3) or in section 4940(d)(2), the grant will nonetheless be treated as a grant made to an organization described in section 509(a)(1), (a)(2), or (a)(3) (other than an organization described in section 4942(g)(4)(A)(i) or (ii)) or in section 4940(d)(2) if the grantor private foundation has made a good faith determination that the grantee organization is an organization described in section 509(a)(1), (a)(2), or (a)(3) (other than an organization described in section 4942(g)(4)(A)(i) or (ii)) or in

section 4940(d)(2). A determination ordinarily will be considered a good faith determination if the determination is based on current written advice received from a qualified tax practitioner concluding that the grantee is an organization described in section 509(a)(1), (a)(2), or (a)(3) (other than an organization described in section 4942(g)(4)(A)(i) or (ii)) or in section 4940(d)(2), and if the foundation reasonably relied in good faith on the written advice in accordance with the requirements of § 1.6664-4(c)(1) of this chapter. The written advice must set forth sufficient facts concerning the operations and support of the grantee organization for the Internal Revenue Service to determine that the grantee organization would be likely to qualify as an organization described in section 509(a)(1), (a)(2), or (a)(3) (other than an organization described in section 4942(g)(4)(A)(i) or (ii)) or in section 4940(d)(2) as of the date of the written advice. For purposes of these rules, except as provided in the next sentence, written advice will be considered current if, as of the date of the grant payment, the relevant law on which the advice is based has not changed since the date of the written advice and the factual information on which the advice is based is from the grantee's current or prior taxable year (or annual accounting period if the grantee does not have a taxable year for United States federal tax purposes). Written advice that a grantee met the public support test under section 170(b)(1)(A)(vi) or section 509(a)(2) for a test period of five years will be treated as current for purposes of grant payments to the grantee during the two taxable years (or, as applicable, annual accounting periods) of the grantee immediately following the end of the five-year test period. See paragraphs (b)(5) and (6) of this section for additional rules relating to foreign organizations.

(ii) *Definitions.*—For purposes of this paragraph (a)(5)—

(a) The term "foreign organization" means any organization that is not described in section 170(c)(2)(A).

(b) The term "qualified tax practitioner" means an attorney, a certified public accountant, or an enrolled agent, within the meaning of 31 CFR 10.2 and 10.3, who is subject to the requirements in 31 CFR part 10.

(6) *Certain earmarked grants.*—(i) *In general.*—A grant by a private foundation to a grantee organization which the grantee organization uses to make payments to another organization (the secondary grantee) shall not be regarded as a grant by the private foundation to the secondary grantee if the foundation does not earmark the use of the grant for any named secondary grantee and there does not exist an agreement, oral or written, whereby such grantor foundation may cause the selection of the secondary grantee by the organization to which it has given the grant. For purposes of this subdivision, a grant described herein shall not be regarded as a grant by the foundation to the secondary grantee even though such foundation

has reason to believe that certain organizations would derive benefits from such grant so long as the original grantee organization exercises control, in fact, over the selection process and actually makes the selection completely independently of the private foundation.

(ii) *To governmental agencies.*—If a private foundation makes a grant to an organization described in section 170(c)(1) and such grant is earmarked for use by another organization, the granting foundation need not exercise expenditure responsibility with respect to such grant if the section 170(c)(1) organization satisfies the Commissioner in advance that:

(a) Its grantmaking program is in furtherance of a purpose described in section 170(c)(2)(B), and

(b) The section 170(c)(1) organization exercises "expenditure responsibility" in a manner that would satisfy this section if it applied to such section 170(c)(1) organization. However, with respect to such grant, the granting foundation must make the reports required by section 4945(h)(3) and paragraph (d) of this section, unless such grant is earmarked for use by an organization described in section 509(a)(1), (a)(2), or (a)(3) (other than an organization described in section 4942(g)(4)(A)(i) or (ii)), or in section 4940(d)(2).

(b) *Expenditure responsibility.*—(1) *In general.*—A private foundation is not an insurer of the activity of the organization to which it makes a grant. Thus, satisfaction of the requirements of sections 4945(d)(4) and (h) and of subparagraph (3) or (4) of this paragraph, will ordinarily mean the grantor foundation will not have violated section 4945(d)(1) or (2). A private foundation will be considered to be exercising "expenditure responsibility" under section 4945(h) as long as it exerts all reasonable efforts and establishes adequate procedures—

(i) To see that the grant is spent solely for the purpose for which made,

(ii) To obtain full and complete reports from the grantee on how the funds are spent, and

(iii) To make full and detailed reports with respect to such expenditures to the Commissioner.

In cases in which pursuant to paragraph (a)(6) of this section a grant is considered made to a secondary grantee rather than the primary grantee, the grantor foundation's obligation to obtain reports from the grantee pursuant to section 4945(h)(2) and this section will be satisfied if appropriate reports are obtained from the secondary grantee. For rules relating to expenditure responsibility with respect to transfers of assets described in section 507(b)(2), see section 507(b)(2) and the regulations thereunder.

(2) *Pre-grant inquiry.*—(i) Before making a grant to an organization with respect to which expenditure responsibility must be exercised under this section, a private foundation should conduct a limited inquiry concerning the poten-

tial grantee. Such inquiry should be complete enough to give a reasonable man assurance that the grantee will use the grant for the proper purposes. The inquiry should concern itself with matters such as: (a) the identity, prior history and experience (if any) of the grantee organization and its managers; and (b) any knowledge which the private foundation has (based on prior experience or otherwise) of, or other information which is readily available concerning, the management, activities, and practices of the grantee organization. The scope of the inquiry might be expected to vary from case to case depending upon the size and purpose of the grant, the period over which it is to be paid, and the prior experience which the grantor has had with respect to the capacity of the grantee to use the grant for the proper purposes. For example, if the grantee has made proper use of all prior grants to it by the grantor and filed the required reports substantiating such use, no further pre-grant inquiry will ordinarily be necessary. Similarly, in the case of an organization, such as a trust described in section 4947(a)(2), which is required by the terms of its governing instrument to make payments to a specified organization exempt from taxation under section 501(a), a less extensive pre-grant inquiry is required than in the case of a private foundation possessing discretion with respect to the distribution of funds.

(ii) The provisions of this subparagraph may be illustrated by the following examples:

Example (1). Officials of M, a newly established organization which is described in section 501(c)(4), request a grant from X Foundation to be used for a proposed program to combat drug abuse by establishing neighborhood clinics in certain ghetto areas of a city. Before making a grant to M, X makes an inquiry concerning the identity, prior history and experience of the officials of M. X obtains information pertaining to the officials of M from references supplied by these officials. Since one of the references indicated that A, an official of M, has an arrest record, police records are also checked and A's probation officer is interviewed. The inquiry also shows M has no previous history of administering grants and that the officials of M have had no experience in administering programs of this nature. However, in the opinion of X's managers, M's officials (including A who appears to be fully rehabilitated after having been convicted of a narcotics violation several years ago) are well qualified to conduct this program since they are members of the communities in which the clinics are to be established and are more likely to be trusted by drug users in these communities than are outsiders. Under these circumstances X has complied with the requirements of this subparagraph and a grant to M for its proposed program will not be treated as a taxable expenditure solely because of the operation of this subparagraph.

Example (2). Foundation Y wishes to make a grant to Foundation R for use in R's scholarship program. Y has made similar grants to R

annually for the last several years and knows that R's managers have observed the terms of the previous grants and have made all requested reports with respect to such grants. No changes in R's management have occurred during the past several years. Under these circumstances, Y has enough information to have such assurance as a reasonable man would require that the grant to R will be used for proper purposes. Consequently, Y is under no obligation to make any further pre-grant inquiry pursuant to this subparagraph.

Example (3). S Foundation requests a grant from Z Foundation for use in S's program of providing medical research fellowships. S has been engaged in this program for several years and has received large numbers of grants from other foundations. Z's managers know that the reputations of S and of S's officials are good. Z's managers also have been advised by managers of W Foundation that W had recently made a grant to S and that W's managers were satisfied that such grant has been used for the purposes for which it was made. Under these circumstances Z has enough information to have such assurance as a reasonable man would require that the grant to S will be used for proper purposes. Consequently, Z is under no obligation to make any further pre-grant inquiry pursuant to this subparagraph.

(3) *Terms of grants.*—Except as provided in subparagraph (4) of this paragraph, in order to meet the expenditure responsibility requirements of section 4945(h), a private foundation must require that each grant to an organization, with respect to which expenditure responsibility must be exercised under this section, be made subject to a written commitment signed by an appropriate officer, director or trustee of the grantee organization. Such commitment must include an agreement by the grantee—

(i) To repay any portion of the amount granted which is not used for the purposes of the grant,

(ii) To submit full and complete annual reports on the matter in which the funds are spent and the progress made in accomplishing the purposes of the grant, except as provided in paragraph (c)(2) of this section,

(iii) To maintain records of receipts and expenditures and to make its books and records available to the grantor at reasonable times, and

(iv) Not to use any of the funds—

(a) To carry on propaganda, or otherwise to attempt, to influence legislation (within the meaning of section 4945(d)(1)),

(b) To influence the outcome of any specific public election, or to carry on, directly or indirectly, any voter registration drive (within the meaning of section 4945(d)(2)),

(c) To make any grant which does not comply with the requirements of section 4945(d)(3) or (4), or

(d) To undertake any activity for any purpose other than one specified in section 170(c)(2)(B).

The agreement must also clearly specify the purposes of the grant. Such purposes may include contributing for capital endowment, for the purchase of capital equipment, or for general support provided that neither the grants nor the income therefrom may be used for purposes other than those described in section 170(c)(2)(B).

(4) *Terms of program-related investments.*—In order to meet the expenditure responsibility requirements of section 4945(h), with regard to the making of a program-related investment (as defined in section 4944 and the regulations thereunder), a private foundation must require that each such investment with respect to which expenditure responsibility must be exercised under section 4945(d)(4) and (h) and this section be made subject to a written commitment signed by an appropriate officer, director or trustee of the recipient organization. Such commitment must specify the purpose of the investment and must include an agreement by the organization—

(i) To use all the funds received from the private foundation (as determined under paragraph (c)(3) of this section) only for the purposes of the investment and to repay any portion not used for such purposes, provided that, with respect to equity investments, such repayment shall be made only to the extent permitted by applicable law concerning distributions to holders of equity interests,

(ii) At least once a year during the existence of the program-related investment, to submit full and complete financial reports of the type ordinarily required by commercial investors under similar circumstances and a statement that it has complied with the terms of the investment,

(iii) To maintain books and records adequate to provide information ordinarily required by commercial investors under similar circumstances and to make such books and records available to the private foundation at reasonable times, and

(iv) Not to use any of the funds—

(a) To carry on propaganda, or otherwise to attempt, to influence legislation (within the meaning of section 4945(d)(1)),

(b) To influence the outcome of any specific public election, or to carry on, directly or indirectly, any voter registration drive (within the meaning of section 4945(d)(2)), or

(c) With respect to any recipient which is a private foundation (as defined in section 509(a)), to make any grant which does not comply with the requirements of section 4945(d)(3) or (4).

(5) *Certain grants to foreign organizations.*—With respect to a grant to a foreign organization (other than an organization described in section 509(a)(1), (a)(2), or (a)(3) (other than an organization described in section 4942(g)(4)(A)(i) or (ii)) or in section 4940(d)(2) or treated as so described pursuant to paragraph (a)(4) or (5) of this section), paragraph (b)(3)(iv) or (b)(4)(iv) of this section shall be deemed satisfied if the agreement referred to in paragraph (b)(3) or (4) of this

section imposes restrictions on the use of the grant substantially equivalent to the limitations imposed on a domestic private foundation under section 4945(d). Such restrictions may be phrased in appropriate terms under foreign law or custom and ordinarily will be considered sufficient if an affidavit or opinion of counsel (of the grantor or grantee) or written advice of a qualified tax practitioner is obtained stating that, under foreign law or custom, the agreement imposes restrictions on the use of the grant substantially equivalent to the restrictions imposed on a domestic private foundation under paragraph (b)(3) or (4) of this section.

(6) *Special rules for grants by foreign private foundations.*—With respect to activities in jurisdictions other than those described in section 170(c)(2)(A), the failure of a foreign private foundation which is described in section 4948(b) to comply with subparagraph (3) or (4) of this paragraph with respect to a grant to an organization shall not constitute an act or failure to act which is a prohibited transaction (within the meaning of section 4948(c)(2)).

(7) *Expenditure responsibility with respect to certain transfers of assets described in section 507.*— (i) *Transfers of assets described in section 507(b)(2).*—For rules relating to the extent to which the expenditure responsibility rules contained in sections 4945(d)(4) and (h) and this section apply to transfers of assets described in section 507(b)(2), see §§ 1.507-3(a)(7), 1.507-3(a)(8)(ii)(f), and 1.507-3(a)(9).

(ii) *Certain other transfers of assets.*—For rules relating to the extent to which the expenditure responsibility rules contained in sections 4945(d)(4) and (h) and this section apply to certain other transfers of assets described in § 1.507-3(b), see § 1.507-3(b) of this chapter.

(8) *Restrictions on grants (other than program-related investments) to organizations not described in section 501(c)(3).*—For other restrictions on certain grants (other than program-related investments) to organizations which are not described in section 501(c)(3), see § 53.4945-6(c).

(c) *Reports from grantees.*—(1) *In general.*—In the case of grants described in section 4945(d)(4), except as provided in subparagraph (2) of this paragraph, the granting private foundation shall require reports on the use of the funds, compliance with the terms of the grant, and the progress made by the grantee toward achieving the purposes for which the grant was made. The grantee shall make such reports as of the end of its annual accounting period within which the grant or any portion thereof is received and all such subsequent periods until the grant funds are expended in full or the grant is otherwise terminated. Such reports shall be furnished to the grantor within a reasonable period of time after the close of the annual accounting period of the grantee for which such reports are made. Within a reasonable period of time after the close of its annual accounting period during which the

use of the grant funds is completed, the grantee must make a final report with respect to all expenditures made from such funds (including salaries, travel, and supplies) and indicating the progress made toward the goals of the grant. The grantor need not conduct any independent verification of such reports unless it has reason to doubt their accuracy or reliability.

(2) *Capital endowment grants to exempt private foundations.*—If a private foundation makes a grant described in section 4945(d)(4) to a private foundation which is exempt from taxation under section 501(a) for endowment, for the purchase of capital equipment, or for other capital purposes, the grantor foundation shall require reports from the grantee on the use of the principal and the income (if any) from the grant funds. The grantee shall make such reports annually for its taxable year in which the grant was made and the immediately succeeding two taxable years. Only if it is reasonably apparent to the grantor that, before the end of such second succeeding taxable year, neither the principal, the income from the grant funds, nor the equipment purchased with the grant funds has been used for any purpose which would result in liability for tax under section 4945(d), the grantor may then allow such reports to be discontinued.

(3) *Grantees' accounting and record-keeping procedures.*—(i) A private foundation grantee exempt from taxation under section 501(a) (or the recipient of a program-related investment) need not segregate grant funds physically nor separately account for such funds on its books unless the grantor requires such treatment of the grant funds. If such a grantee neither physically segregates grant funds nor establishes separate accounts on its books, grants received within a given taxable year beginning after December 31, 1969, shall be deemed, for purposes of section 4945, to be expended before grants received in a succeeding taxable year. In such case expenditures of grants received within any such taxable year shall be prorated among all such grants. In accounting for grant expenditures, private foundations may make the necessary computations on a cumulative annual basis (or, where appropriate, as of the date for which the computations are made). The rules set forth in the preceding three sentences shall apply to the extent they are consistent with the available records of the grantee and with the grantee's treatment of qualifying distributions under section 4942(h) and the regulations thereunder. The records of expenditures, as well as copies of the reports submitted to the grantor, must be kept for at least 4 years after completion of the use of the grant funds.

(ii) For rules relating to accounting and record-keeping requirements for grantees other than those described in subdivision (i) of this subparagraph, see §§ 53.4945-5(b)(8) and 53.4945-6(c).

(4) *Reliance on information supplied by grantee.*—A private foundation exercising expen-

diture responsibility with respect to its grants may rely on adequate records or other sufficient evidence supplied by the grantee organization (such as a statement by an appropriate officer, director or trustee of such grantee organization) showing, to the extent applicable, the information which the grantor must report to the Internal Revenue Service in accordance with paragraph (d)(2) of this section.

(d) *Reporting to Internal Revenue Service by grantor.*—(1) *In general.*—To satisfy the report-making requirements of section 4945(h)(3), a granting foundation must provide the required information on its annual information return, required to be filed by section 6033, for each taxable year with respect to each grant made during the taxable year which is subject to the expenditure responsibility requirements of section 4945(h). Such information must also be provided on such return with respect to each grant subject to such requirements upon which any amount or any report is outstanding at any time during the taxable year. However, with respect to any grant made for endowment or other capital purposes, the grantor must provide the required information only for any taxable year for which the grantor must require a report from the grantee under paragraph (c)(2) of this section. The requirements of this subparagraph with respect to any grant may be satisfied by submission with the foundation's information return of a report received from the grantee, if the information required by subparagraph (2) of this paragraph is contained in such report.

(2) *Contents of report.*—The report required by this paragraph shall include the following information:

(i) The name and address of the grantee,

(ii) The date and amount of the grant,

(iii) The purpose of the grant,

(iv) The amounts expended by the grantee (based upon the most recent report received from the grantee),

(v) Whether the grantee has diverted any portion of the funds (or the income therefrom in the case of an endowment grant) from the purpose of the grant (to the knowledge of the grantor),

(vi) The dates of any reports received from the grantee, and

(vii) The date and results of any verification of the grantee's reports undertaken pursuant to and to the extent required under paragraph (c)(1) of this section by the grantor or by others at the direction of the grantor.

(3) *Record-keeping requirements.*—In addition to the information included on the information return, a granting foundation shall make available to the Internal Revenue Service at the foundation's principal office each of the following items:

(i) A copy of the agreement covering each "expenditure responsibility" grant made during the taxable year,

(ii) A copy of each report received during the taxable year from each grantee on any "expenditure responsibility" grant, and

(iii) A copy of each report made by the grantor's personnel or independent auditors of any audits or other investigations made during the taxable year with respect to any "expenditure responsibility" grant.

(4) *Reports received after the close of grantor's accounting year.*—Data contained in reports required by this paragraph, which reports are received by a private foundation after the close of its accounting year but before the due date of its information return for that year need not be reported on such return, but may be reported on the grantor's information return for the year in which such reports are received from the grantee.

(e) *Violations of expenditure responsibility requirements.*—(1) *Diversions by grantee.*—(i) Any diversion of grant funds (including the income therefrom in the case of an endowment grant) by the grantee to any use not in furtherance of a purpose specified in the grant may result in the diverted portion of such grant being treated as a taxable expenditure of the grantor under section 4945(d)(4). However, for purposes of this section, the fact that a grantee does not use any portion of the grant funds as indicated in the original budget projection shall not be treated as a diversion if the use to which the funds are committed is consistent with the purpose of the grant as stated in the grant agreement and does not result in a violation of the terms of such agreement required to be included by paragraph (b)(3) or (b)(4) of this section.

(ii) In any event, a grantor will not be treated as having made a taxable expenditure under section 4945(d)(4) solely by reason of a diversion by the grantee, if the grantor has complied with subdivision (iii)(*a*) and (*b*) or (iv)(*a*) and (*b*) of this subparagraph, whichever is applicable.

(iii) In cases in which the grantor foundation determines that any part of a grant has been used for improper purposes and the grantee has not previously diverted grant funds, the foundation will not be treated as having made a taxable expenditure solely by reason of the diversion so long as the foundation—

(*a*) Is taking all reasonable and appropriate steps either to recover the grant funds or to insure the restoration of the diverted funds and the dedication (consistent with the requirements of (*b*)(1) and (2) of this subdivision) of the other grant funds held by the grantee to the purposes being financed by the grant, and

(*b*) Withholds any further payments to the grantee after the grantor becomes aware that a diversion may have taken place (hereinafter referred to as "further payments") until it has—

(*1*) Received the grantee's assurances that future diversions will not occur, and

(2) Required the grantee to take extraordinary precautions to prevent future diversions from occurring.

If a foundation is treated as having made a taxable expenditure under this subparagraph in a case to which this subdivision applies, then unless the foundation meets the requirements of *(a)* of this subdivision the amount of the taxable expenditure shall be the amount of the diversion (for example, the income diverted in the case of an endowment grant, or the rental value of capital equipment for the period of time for which diverted) plus the amount of any further payments to the same grantee. However, if the foundation complies with the requirements of *(a)* of this subdivision but not the requirements of *(b)* of this subdivision, the amount of the taxable expenditures shall be the amount of such further payments.

(iv) In cases where a grantee has previously diverted funds received from a grantor foundation, and the grantor foundation determines that any part of a grant has again been used for improper purposes, the foundation will not be treated as having made a taxable expenditure solely by reason of such diversion so long as the foundation—

(a) Is taking all reasonable and appropriate steps to recover the grant funds or to insure the restoration of the diverted funds and the dedication (consistent with the requirements of *(b)(2)* and *(3)* of this subdivision) of other grant funds held by the grantee to the purposes being financed by the grant, except that if, in fact, some or all of the diverted funds are not so restored or recovered, then the foundation must take all reasonable and appropriate steps to recover all of the grant funds, and

(b) Withholds further payments until—

(1) Such funds are in fact so recovered or restored,

(2) It has received the grantee's assurances that future diversions will not occur, and

(3) It requires the grantee to take extraordinary precautions to prevent future diversions from occurring.

If a foundation is treated as having made a taxable expenditure under this subparagraph in a case to which this subdivision applies, then unless the foundation meets the requirements of *(a)* of this subdivision, the amount of the taxable expenditure shall be the amount of the diversion plus the amount of any further payments to the same grantee. However, if the foundation complies with the requirements of *(a)* of this subdivision, but fails to withhold further payments until the requirements of *(b)* of this subdivision are met, the amount of the taxable expenditure shall be the amount of such further payments.

(v) The phrase "all reasonable and appropriate steps" (as used in subdivisions (iii) and (iv) of this subparagraph) includes legal action where appropriate but need not include legal action if such action would in all probability not result in the satisfaction of execution on a judgment.

(2) *Grantee's failure to make reports.*—A failure by the grantee to make the reports required by paragraph (c) of this section (or the making of inadequate reports) shall result in the grant's being treated as a taxable expenditure by the grantor unless the grantor:

(i) Has made the grant in accordance with paragraph (b) of this section,

(ii) Has complied with the reporting requirements contained in paragraph (d) of this section,

(iii) Makes a reasonable effort to obtain the required report, and

(iv) Withholds all future payments on this grant and on any other grant to the same grantee until such report is furnished.

(3) *Violations by the grantor.*—In addition to the situations described in subparagraphs (1) and (2) of this paragraph, a grant which is subject to the expenditure responsibility requirements of section 4945(h) will be considered a taxable expenditure of the granting foundation if the grantor—

(i) Fails to make a pre-grant inquiry as described in paragraph (b)(2) of this section,

(ii) Fails to make the grant in accordance with a procedure consistent with the requirements of paragraph (b)(3) or (4) of this section, or

(iii) Fails to report to the Internal Revenue Service as provided in paragraph (d) of this section.

(f) *Effective dates.*—(1) *In general.*—This section shall apply to all grants which are subject to the expenditure responsibility requirements of section 4945(d)(4) and (h) and which are made by private foundations more than 90 days after October 30, 1972.

(2) *Transitional rules.*—(i) *Certain grants awarded prior to May 27, 1969.*—Section 4945(d)(4) and (h) and this section shall not apply to a grant to a private foundation which is not controlled, directly or indirectly, by the grantor foundation or one or more disqualified persons (as defined in section 4946) with respect to the grantor foundation, provided that such grant—

(a) Is made pursuant to a written commitment which was binding on May 26, 1969, and at all times thereafter,

(b) Is made for one or more of the purposes described in section 170(c)(2)(B), and

(c) Is to be paid out to such grantee foundation on or before December 31, 1974.

(ii) *Grants or expenditures committed prior to January 1, 1970.*—Except as provided in paragraph (e)(2)(i) of §53.4945-4, section 4945 shall not apply to a grant or an expenditure for section 170(c)(2)(B) purposes made on or after January 1, 1970, if the grant or expenditure was made pursuant to a commitment entered into prior to such date, but only if (in the case of a grant or an expenditure other than an unlimited general-

purpose grant to an organization) such commitment is reasonable in amount in light of the purposes of the grant. For purposes of this subdivision, a commitment will be considered entered into prior to January 1, 1970, if prior to such date, the amount and nature of the payments to be made and the name of the payee were entered on the records of the payor, or were otherwise adequately evidenced, or the notice of the payment to be received was communicated to the payee in writing.

(iii) *Grants awarded on or after January 1, 1970.*—Paragraphs (b), (c), and (d) of this section shall not apply to grants awarded on or after January 1, 1970, but prior to the expiration of 90 days after October 30, 1972, if the grantor has made reasonable efforts, and has established adequate procedures such as a prudent man would adopt in managing his own property, to see that the grant is spent solely for the purpose for which made, to obtain full and complete reports from the grantee on how the funds are spent, and to make full and detailed reports with respect to such grant to the Commissioner. With respect to any return filed with the Internal Revenue Service before the expiration of 90 days after October 30, 1972, the grantor may treat reports which satisfy the requirements of the statement to be attached to Form 4720 for the year 1970 under "Specific Instructions—Question B" (items (1) through (5)) as satisfying the grantor reporting requirements with respect to "expenditure responsibility" grants. In the case of a private foundation required to file an annual return for a taxable year ending after January 1, 1970, and before December 31, 1970, the reporting requirements imposed by section 4945(h)(3) for such period shall be regarded as satisfied if such reports are made on the annual return for its first taxable year beginning after December 31, 1969.

(3) *Effective/applicability date of paragraphs (a)(1), (a)(5), (a)(6)(ii), and (b)(5) and transition relief.*—Paragraphs (a)(1), (a)(5), (a)(6)(ii), and (b)(5) of this section are effective on and apply with respect to grants paid after September 25, 2015. However, foundations may continue to rely on paragraph (a)(5) as contained in 26 CFR part 53, revised April 1, 2015, with respect to grants paid on or before December 24, 2015 pursuant to a good faith determination made in accordance with such provisions. Also, foundations may continue to rely on paragraph (a)(5) as contained in 26 CFR part 53, revised April 1, 2015, with respect to grants paid pursuant to a written commitment made on or before September 25, 2015 and pursuant to a good faith determination made on or before such date in accordance with such provisions if the committed amount is paid out within five years of such date. [Reg. § 53.4945-5.]

☐ [*T.D. 7215, 10-30-72. Amended by T.D. 7233, 12-20-72 T.D. 7290, 11-16-73 and T.D. 9740, 9-23-2015.*]

[Reg. § 53.4945-6]

§ 53.4945-6. Expenditures for noncharitable purposes.—(a) *In general.*—Under section 4945(d)(5) the term "taxable expenditure" includes any amount paid or incurred by a private foundation for any purpose other than one specified in section 170(c)(2)(B). Thus, ordinarily only an expenditure for an activity which, if it were a substantial part of the organization's total activities, would cause loss of tax exemption is a taxable expenditure under section 4945(d)(5). For purposes of this section and §§ 53.4945-1 through 53.4945-5, the term "purposes described in section 170(c)(2)(B)" shall be treated as including purposes described in section 170(c)(2)(B) whether or not carried out by an organization described in section 170(c).

(b) *Particular expenditures.*—(1) The following types of expenditures ordinarily will not be treated as taxable expenditures under section 4945(d)(5):

(i) Expenditures to acquire investments entered into for the purpose of obtaining income or funds to be used in furtherance of purposes described in section 170(c)(2)(B),

(ii) Reasonable expenses with respect to investments described in subdivision (i) of this subparagraph,

(iii) Payment of taxes,

(iv) Any expenses which qualify as deductions in the computation of unrelated business income tax under section 511,

(v) Any payment which constitutes a qualifying distribution under section 4942(g) or an allowable deduction under section 4940,

(vi) Reasonable expenditures to evaluate, acquire, modify, and dispose of program-related investments, or

(vii) Business expenditures by the recipient of a program-related investment.

(2) Conversely, any expenditures for unreasonable administrative expenses, including compensation, consultant fees, and other fees for services rendered, will ordinarily be taxable expenditures under section 4945(d)(5) unless the foundation can demonstrate that such expenses were paid or incurred in the good faith belief that they were reasonable and that the payment or incurrence of such expenses in such amounts was consistent with ordinary business care and prudence. The determination of whether an expenditure is unreasonable shall depend upon the facts and circumstances of the particular case.

(c) *Grants to "noncharitable" organizations.*—(1) *In general.*—Since a private foundation cannot make an expenditure for a purpose other than a purpose described in section 170(c)(2)(B), a private foundation may not make a grant to an organization other than an organization described in section 501(c)(3) unless

(i) The making of the grant itself constitutes a direct charitable act or the making of a program-related investment, or

(ii) Through compliance with the requirements of subparagraph (2) of this paragraph, the grantor is reasonably assured that the grant will be used exclusively for purposes described in section 170(c)(2)(B).

For purposes of this paragraph, an organization treated as a section 509(a)(1) organization under § 53.4945-5(a)(4) shall be treated as an organization described in section 501(c)(3).

(2) *Grants other than transfers of assets described in § 1.507-3(c)(1).*—(i) If a private foundation makes a grant which is not a transfer of assets pursuant to any liquidation, merger, redemption, recapitalization, or other adjustment, organization or reorganization to any organization other than an organization described in section 501(c)(3) (except an organization described in section 509(a)(4)), the grantor is reasonably assured (within the meaning of subparagraph (1)(ii) of this paragraph) that the grant will be used exclusively for purposes described in section 170(c)(2)(B) only if the grantee organization agrees to maintain and, during the period in which any portion of such grant funds remain unexpended, does continuously maintain the grant funds (or other assets transferred) in a separate fund dedicated to one or more purposes described in section 170(c)(2)(B). The grantor of a grant described in this paragraph must also comply with the expenditure responsibility provisions contained in sections 4945(d) and (h) and § 53.4945-5.

(ii) For purposes of this paragraph, a foreign organization which does not have a ruling or determination letter that it is an organization described in section 501(c)(3) (other than section 509(a)(4)) will be treated as an organization described in section 501(c)(3) (other than section 509(a)(4)) if in the reasonable judgment of a foundation manager of the transferor private foundation, the grantee organization is an organization described in section 501(c)(3) (other than section 509(a)(4)). The term "reasonable judgment" shall be given its generally accepted legal sense within the outlines developed by judicial decisions in the law of trusts.

(3) *Transfers of assets described in § 1.507-3(c)(1).*—If a private foundation makes a transfer of assets (other than a transfer described in subparagraph (1)(i) of this paragraph) pursuant to any liquidation, merger, redemption, recapitalization, or other adjustment, organization, or reorganization to any person, the transferred assets will not be considered used exclusively for purposes described in section 170(c)(2)(B) unless the assets are transferred to a fund or organization described in section 501(c)(3) (other than an organization described in section 509(a)(4)) or treated as so described under section 4947(a)(1). [Reg. § 53.4945-6.]

☐ [*T.D.* 7215, 10-30-72. *Amended by T.D.* 7233, 12-20-72.]

[Reg. § 53.4946-1]

§ 53.4946-1. Definitions and special rules.— (a) *Disqualified person.*—(1) For purposes of chapter 42 and the regulations thereunder, the following are disqualified persons with respect to a private foundation—

(i) All substantial contributors to the foundation, as defined in section 507(d)(2) and the regulations thereunder,

(ii) All foundation managers of the foundation as defined in section 4946(b)(1) and paragraph (f)(1)(i) of this section,

(iii) An owner of more than 20 percent of—

(a) The total combined voting power of a corporation,

(b) The profits interest of a partnership,

(c) The beneficial interest of a trust or unincorporated enterprise, which is (during such ownership) a substantial contributor to the foundation, as defined in section 507(d)(2) and the regulations thereunder,

(iv) A member of the family, as defined in section 4946(d) and paragraph (h) of this section, of any of the individuals described in subdivision (i), (ii), or (iii) of this subparagraph,

(v) A corporation of which more than 35 percent of the total combined voting power is owned by persons described in subdivision (i), (ii), (iii), or (iv) of this subparagraph,

(vi) A partnership of which more than 35 percent of the profits interest is owned by persons described in subdivision (i), (ii), (iii), or (iv) of this subparagraph, and

(vii) A trust, estate, or unincorporated enterprise of which more than 35 percent of the beneficial interest is owned by persons described in subdivision (i), (ii), (iii), or (iv) of this subparagraph.

(2) For purposes of subparagraphs (1)(iii)(*b*) and (vi) of this paragraph, the profits interest of a partner shall be equal to his distributive share of income of the partnership, as determined under section 707(b)(3) and the regulations thereunder as modified by section 4946(a)(4).

(3) For purposes of subparagraph (1)(iii)(*c*) and (vii) of this paragraph, the beneficial interest in an unincorporated enterprise (other than a trust or estate) includes any right to receive a portion of distributions from profits of such enterprise, and, if the portion of distributions is not fixed by an agreement among the participants, any right to receive a portion of the assets (if any) upon liquidation of the enterprise, except as a creditor or employee. For purposes of this subparagraph, a right to receive distributions of profits includes a right to receive any amount from such profits other than as creditor or employee, whether as a sum certain or as a portion of profits realized by the enterprise. Where there is no agreement fixing the rights of the participants in such enterprise, the fraction of the respective interests of each participant in such enterprise shall be determined by dividing the amount of all investments or contributions to the

capital of the enterprise made or obligated to be made by such participant by the amount of all investments or contributions to capital made or obligated to be made by all of them.

(4) For purposes of subparagraph (1)(iii)(c) and (vii) of this paragraph, a person's beneficial interest in a trust shall be determined in proportion to the actuarial interest of such person in the trust.

(5) For purposes of subparagraph (1)(iii)(a) and (v) of this paragraph, the term "combined voting power" includes voting power represented by holdings of voting stock, actual or constructive (under section 4946(a)(3)), but does not include voting rights held only as a director or trustee.

(6) For purposes of subparagraph (1)(iii)(a) and (v) of this paragraph, the term "voting power" includes outstanding voting power and does not include voting power obtainable but not obtained, such as, for example, voting power obtainable by converting securities or nonvoting stock into voting stock or by exercising warrants or options to obtain voting stock, and voting power which will vest in preferred stockholders only if and when the corporation has failed to pay preferred dividends for a specified period of time or has otherwise failed to meet specified requirements. Similarly, for purposes of subparagraph (1) (iii) (b) and (c), (vi), and (vii) of this paragraph, the terms "profits interest" and "beneficial interest" include any such interest that is outstanding, but do not include any such interest that is obtainable but has not been obtained.

(7) For purposes of sections 170(b)(1)(E)(iii), 507(d)(1), 508(d), 509(a)(1) and (3), and chapter 42, the term "disqualified person" shall not include an organization which is described in section 509(a)(1), (2), or (3), or any other organization which is wholly owned by such section 509(a)(1), (2), or (3) organization.

(8) For purposes of section 4941 only, the term "disqualified person" shall not include any organization which is described in section 501(c)(3) (other than an organization described in section 509(a)(4)).

(b) *Section 4943.*—(1) For purposes of section 4943 only, the term "disqualified person" includes a private foundation—

(i) Which is effectively controlled (within the meaning of §1.482-1(a)(3) of this chapter), directly or indirectly, by the same person or persons (other than a bank, trust company, or similar organization acting only as a foundation manager) who control the private foundation in question, or

(ii) Substantially all the contributions to which were made, directly or indirectly, by persons described in subdivision (i), (ii), (iii), or (iv) of paragraph (a)(1) of this section who made, directly or indirectly, substantially all of the contributions to the private foundation in question.

(2) For purposes of subparagraph (1)(ii) of this paragraph, one or more persons will be considered to have made substantially all of the contributions to a private foundation, if such

persons have contributed or bequeathed at least 85 percent (and each such person has contributed or bequeathed at least 2 percent) of the total contributions and bequests (within the meaning of section 507(d)(2) and the regulations thereunder) which have been received by such private foundation during its entire existence.

(3) *Examples.*—The provisions of this paragraph may be illustrated by the following examples:

Example (1). A, a private foundation, has a board of directors made up of X, Y, Z, M, N, and O. Foundation B's board of directors is made up of Y, M, N, and O. The board of directors in each case has plenary power to determine the manner in which the foundation is operated. For purposes of section 4943, foundation A is a disqualified person with respect to foundation B, and foundation B is a disqualified person with respect to foundation A.

Example (2). Private foundation A has received contributions of $100,000 throughout its existence: $35,000 from X, $51,000 from Y (who is X's father), and $14,000 from Z (an unrelated person). Private foundation B has received $100,000 in contributions during its existence: $50,000 from X and $50,000 from W, X's wife.

For purposes of section 4943, private foundation A is a disqualified person with respect to private foundation B, and private foundation B is a disqualified person with respect to private foundation A.

(c) *Section 4941.*—For purposes of section 4941, a government official, as defined in section 4946(c) and paragraph (g) of this section, is a disqualified person.

(d) *Attribution of stockholdings.*—(1) For purposes of paragraph (a)(1)(iii)(a) and (v) of this section, indirect stockholdings shall be taken into account under section 267(c) and the regulations thereunder. However, for purposes of this paragraph—

(i) Section 267(c)(4) shall be treated as though it provided that the members of the family of an individual are the members within the meaning of section 4946(d) and paragraph (h) of this section; and

(ii) Any stockholdings which have been counted once (whether by reason of actual or constructive ownership) in applying section 4946(a)(1)(E) shall not be counted a second time. For purposes of paragraph (a)(1)(v) of this section, section 267(c) shall be applied without regard to section 267(c)(3), and stock constructively owned by an individual by reason of the application of section 267(c)(2) shall not be treated as owned by him if he is described in section 4946(a)(1)(D) but not also in section 4946(a)(1)(A), (B), or (C).

(2) *Examples.*—The provisions of this paragraph may be illustrated by the following examples:

Example (1). D is a substantial contributor to private foundation Y. D owns 20 percent of the

outstanding stock of corporation P. E, D's wife, owns none of the outstanding stock of P. F, E's father, owns 10 percent of the outstanding stock of P. E. is treated under section 507(d)(2) as a substantial contributor to Y. E is also treated under section 267(c)(2) as owning both D's 20 percent and F's 10 percent of P, but E is treated as owning nothing for purposes of section 4946(a)(1)(E) because D's 20 percent and F's 10 percent have already been taken into account once (because of their actual ownership of the stock of P) for such purposes. Hence, corporation P is not a disqualified person under section 4946(a)(1)(E) with respect to private foundation Y because persons described in section 4946(a)(1)(A), (B), (C), and (D) own only 30 percent of the stock of P.

Example (2). I, a substantial contributor to private foundation X, is the son of J. I owns 100 percent of the stock of corporation R, which in turn owns 18 percent of the stock of corporation S. J owns 18 percent of the stock of S. I constructively owns 36 percent of the stock of S (J's 18 percent plus R's 18 percent). Both J's actual holdings and R's actual holdings are counted in determining I's constructive holdings because this does not result in counting either of the holdings more than once for purposes of section 4946(a)(1)(E). Therefore, S is a disqualified person with respect to private foundation X, since I, a substantial contributor, constructively owns more than 35 percent of S's stock.

(e) *Attribution of profits or beneficial interests.*—(1) For purposes of paragraph (a)(1)(iii)(*b*), (iii)(*c*), (vi), and (vii) of this section, ownership of profits or beneficial interests shall be taken into account as though such ownership related to stockholdings, if such stockholdings would be taken into account under section 267(c) and the regulations thereunder, except that section 267(c)(3) shall not apply to attribute the ownership of one partner to another solely by reason of such partner relationship. However, for purposes of this paragraph—

(i) Section 267(c)(4) shall be treated as though it provided that the members of the family of an individual are the members within the meaning of section 4946(d) and paragraph (h) of this section; and

(ii) Any profits interest or beneficial interest which has been counted once (whether by reason of actual or constructive ownership) in applying section 4946(a)(1)(F) or (G) shall not be counted a second time.

For purposes of paragraph (a)(1)(vi) and (vii) of this section, profits or beneficial interests constructively owned by an individual by reason of the application of section 267(c)(2) shall not be treated as owned by him if he is described in section 4946(a)(1)(D) but not in section 4946(a)(1)(A), (B) or (C).

(2) *Example.*—The provisions of this paragraph may be illustrated by the following example:

Example. Partnership S is a substantial contributor to private foundation X. Trust T, of which G is sole beneficiary, owns 12 percent of the profits interest of S. G's husband, H, owns 10 percent of the profits interest of S. H is a disqualified person with respect to X (under section 4946(a)(1)(C)) because he is considered to own 22 percent of the profits interest of S (10 percent actual ownership, plus G's 12 percent constructively under section 267(c)(2)). G is a disqualified person with respect to X (under section 4946(a)(1)(C)) because she is considered to own 22 percent of the profits interest of S (12 percent constructively by reason of her beneficial interest in trust T, plus 10 percent constructively under section 267(c)(2) by reason of being a member of the family of H).

(f) *Foundation manager.*—(1) For purposes of chapter 42 and the regulations thereunder, the term "foundation manager" means—

(i) An officer, director, or trustee of a foundation (or a person having powers or responsibilities similar to those of officers, directors, or trustees of the foundation), and

(ii) With respect to any act or failure to act, any employee of the foundation having final authority or responsibility (either officially or effectively) with respect to such act or failure to act.

(2) For purposes of subparagraph (1)(i) of this paragraph, a person shall be considered an officer of a foundation if—

(i) He is specifically so designated under the certificate of incorporation, by-laws, or other constitutive documents of the foundation; or

(ii) He regularly exercises general authority to make administrative or policy decisions on behalf of the foundation.

With respect to any act or failure to act, any person described in subdivision (ii) of this subparagraph who has authority merely to recommend particular administrative or policy decisions, but not to implement them without approval of a superior, is not an officer. Moreover, such independent contractors as attorneys, accountants, and investment managers and advisors, acting in their capacities as such, are not officers within the meaning of subparagraph (1)(i) of this paragraph.

(3) For purposes of subparagraph (1)(ii) of this paragraph, an individual rendering services to a private foundation shall be considered an employee of the foundation only if he is an employee within the meaning of section 3121(d)(2).

(4) Since the definition of the term "disqualified person" contained in section 4946(a)(1)(B) incorporates only so much of the definition of the term "foundation manager" as is found in section 4946(b)(1) and subparagraph (1)(i) of this paragraph, any references, in section 4946 and this section, to "disqualified persons" do not constitute references to persons who are "foundation managers" solely by reason of the definition of that term contained in section 4946(b)(2) and subparagraph (1)(ii) of this paragraph.

(g) *Government official.*—(1) *In general.*—Except as provided in subparagraph (3) of this paragraph, for purposes of section 4941 and paragraph (c) of this section, the term "government official" means, with respect to an act of self-dealing described in section 4941, an individual who, at the time of such act, is described in subdivision (i), (ii), (iii), (iv), or (v) of this subparagraph (other than a "special Government employee" as defined in 18 U.S.C. 202(a)):

(i)*(a)* An individual who holds an elective public office in the executive or legislative branch of the Government of the United States.

(b) An individual who holds an office in the executive or judicial branch of the Government of the United States, appointment to which was made by the President.

(ii) An individual who holds a position in the executive, legislative or judicial branch of the Government of the United States—

(a) Which is listed in schedule C of rule VI of the Civil Service Rules, or

(b) The compensation for which is equal to or greater than the lowest rate prescribed for GS-16 of the General Schedule under 5 U.S.C. 5332.

(iii) An individual who holds a position under the House of Representatives or the Senate of the United States, as an employee of either of such bodies, who receives gross compensation therefrom at an annual rate of $15,000 or more.

(iv) The holder of an elective or appointive public office in the executive, legislative, or judicial branch of the government of a State, possession of the United States, or political subdivision or other area of any of the foregoing, or of the District of Columbia, for which the gross compensation is at an annual rate of $15,000 or more, who is described in subparagraph (2) of this paragraph.

(v) The holder of a position as personal or executive assistant or secretary to any individual described in subdivision (i), (ii), (iii) or (iv) of this subparagraph.

(2) *Public office.*—(i) *Definition.*—In defining the term "public office" for purposes of section 4946(c)(5) and subparagraph (1)(iv) of this paragraph, such term must be distinguished from mere public employment. Although holding a public office is one form of public employment, not every position in the employ of a State or other governmental subdivision (as described in section 4946(c)(5)) constitutes a "public office." Although a determination whether a public employee holds a public office depends on the facts and circumstances of the case, the essential element is whether a significant part of the activities of a public employee is the independent performance of policymaking functions. In applying this subparagraph, several factors may be considered as indications that a position in the executive, legislative, or judicial branch of the government of a State, possession of the United States, or political subdivision or other area of any of the foregoing, or of the District of Columbia, constitutes a "public office." Among such factors to be considered in addition to that set forth above, are that the office is created by the Congress, a State constitution, or the State legislature, or by a municipality or other governmental body pursuant to authority conferred by the Congress, State constitution, or State legislature, and the powers conferred on the office and the duties to be discharged by such office are defined either directly or indirectly by the Congress, State constitution, or State legislature, or through legislative authority.

(ii) *Illustrations.*—The following are illustrations of positions of public employment which do not involve policymaking functions within the meaning of subdivision (i) of this subparagraph and which are thus not a "public office" for purposes of section 4946(c)(5) and subparagraph (1)(iv) of this paragraph:

(a) The chancellor, president, provost, dean, and other officers of a State university who are appointed, elected, or otherwise hired by a State Board of Regents or equivalent public body and who are subject to the direction and supervision of such body;

(b) Professors, instructors, and other members of the faculty of a State educational institution who are appointed, elected, or otherwise hired by the officers of the institution or by the State Board of Regents or equivalent public body;

(c) The superintendent of public schools and other public school officials who are appointed, elected, or otherwise hired by a Board of Education or equivalent public body and who are subject to the direction and supervision of such body;

(d) Public school teachers who are appointed, elected, or otherwise hired by the superintendent of public schools or by a Board of Education or equivalent public body;

(e) Physicians, nurses, and other professional person associated with public hospitals and State boards of health who are appointed, elected, or otherwise hired by the governing board or officers of such hospitals or agencies; and

(f) Members of police and fire departments, except for those department heads who, under the facts and circumstances of the case, independently perform policymaking functions as a significant part of their activities.

(3) *Certain government officials on leave of absence.*—For purposes of this paragraph, an individual who is otherwise described in section 4946(c) and this paragraph who was on leave of absence without pay on December 31, 1969, from his position or office pursuant to a commitment entered into on or before such date to engage in certain activities for which he is paid by one or more private foundations, is not to be treated as holding such position or office for any continuous period after December 31, 1969, and prior to January 1, 1971, during which such individual remains on leave of absence to engage in the same activities for which he is paid by such

foundations. For purposes of this subparagraph, a commitment is considered entered into on or before December 31, 1969, if on or before such date, the amount and nature of the payments to be made and the name of the individual receiving such payments were entered on the records of the payor, or were otherwise adequately evidenced, or the notice of the payment to be received was communicated to the payee orally or in writing.

(h) *Members of the family.*—For purposes of this section, the members of the family of an individual include only—

(1) His spouse,

(2) His ancestors,

(3) His lineal descendants, and

(4) Spouses of his lineal descendants.

For example, a brother or sister of an individual is not a member of his family for purposes of this section. However, for example, the wife of a grandchild of an individual is a member of his family for such purposes. For purposes of this paragraph, a legally adopted child of an individual shall be treated as a child of such individual by blood. [Reg. § 53.4946-1.]

☐ [*T.D.* 7241, 12-28-71.]

[Reg. § 53.4947-1]

§ 53.4947-1. Application of tax.—(a) *In general.*—Section 4947 subjects trusts which are not exempt from taxation under section 501(a), all or part of the unexpired interests in which are devoted to one or more of the purposes described in section 170(c)(2)(B), and which have amounts in trust for which a deduction was allowed under section 170, 545(b)(2), 556(b)(2), 642(c), 2055, 2106(a)(2), or 2522 to the same requirements and restrictions as are imposed on private foundations. The basic purpose of section 4947 is to prevent these trusts from being used to avoid the requirements and restrictions applicable to private foundations. For purposes of this section, a trust shall be presumed (in the absence of proof to the contrary) to have amounts in trust for which a deduction was allowed under section 170, 545(b)(2), 556(b)(2), 642(c), 2055, 2106(a)(2), or 2522 if a deduction would have been allowable under one of these sections. Also for purposes of this section and § 53.4947-2, the term "purposes described in section 170(c)(2)(B)" shall be treated as including purposes described in section 170(c)(1).

(b) *Charitable trusts.*—(1) *General rule.*—(i) For purposes of this section and § 53.4947-2, a "charitable trust," within the meaning of section 4947(a)(1), is a trust which is not exempt from taxation under section 501(a), all of the unexpired interests in which are devoted to one or more of the purposes described in section 170(c)(2)(B), and for which a deduction was allowed under section 170, 545(b)(2), 556(b)(2), 642(c), 2055, 2106(a)(2) or 2522 (or the corresponding provisions of prior law). A trust is one for which a deduction was allowed under section 642(c), within the meaning of section

4947(a)(1), once a deduction is allowed under section 642(c) to the trust for any amount paid or permanently set aside. (See section 642(c) and § 1.642-4 for the limitation on such deduction in certain cases.) A charitable trust (as defined in this paragraph) shall be treated as an organization described in section 501(c)(3) and, if it is determined under section 509 that the trust is a private foundation, then Part II of subchapter F of chapter 1 of the Code (other than section 508(a), (b) and (c)) and chapter 42 shall apply to the trust. However, the charitable trust is not treated as an organization described in section 501(c)(3) for purposes of exemption from taxation under section 501(a). Thus, the trust is subject to the excise tax on its investment income under section 4940(b) rather than the tax imposed by section 4940(a). For purposes of satisfying the organizational test described in § 1.501(c)(3)-1(b) when a charitable trust seeks an exemption from taxation under section 501(a), a charitable trust (as defined in this paragraph) shall be considered organized on the day it first becomes subject to section 4947(a)(1). However, for purposes of the special and transitional rules in sections 4940(c)(4)(B), 4942(f)(4), 4943(c)(4)(A)(i) and (B) and section 101(1)(2)(A), (B), (C), and (D), and (1)(3) of the Tax Reform Act of 1969, a charitable trust (as defined in this paragraph) shall be considered organized on the first day it has amounts in trust for which a deduction was allowed (within the meaning of paragraph (a) of this section) under section 170, 545(b)(2), 556(b)(2), 642(c), 2055, 2106(a)(2), or 2522. Thus, under this rule, a trust may be treated as a private foundation in existence on a date governing one of the applicable special and transitional rules even though the trust did not otherwise become subject to the provisions of chapter 42 until a later date.

(ii) The provisions of paragraph (b)(1) of this section may be illustrated by the following examples:

Example (1). On January 30, 1970, X creates an inter vivos trust under which M receives 50 percent and N receives 50 percent of the trust's income for 10 years, and upon the termination of which, at the end of the 10-year period, the corpus is to be distributed to O. M, N and O are all organizations described in section 501(c)(3) and X is allowed a deduction under section 170 for the value of all interests placed in trust. The trustees of the trust do not give notice to the Internal Revenue Service under the provisions of section 508(a), and the trust will therefore not be exempt from taxation under section 501(a). The trust is a charitable trust within the meaning of section 4947(a)(1) from the date of its creation.

Example (2). On March 1, 1971, Y creates a charitable remainder annuity trust described in section 664(d)(1) under which Z, Y's son, receives $10,000 per year for life, remainder to be held in trust for P, an organization described in section 501(c)(3). Y is allowed a deduction under section 170 for the present value of the remainder interest to P. During Z's lifetime, the trust is a split-interest trust described in section

Reg. § 53.4947-1(b)(1)(ii)

4947(a)(2) and paragraph (c) of this section. Upon the death of Z, all unexpired interests (consisting of P's remainder interest) will be devoted to section 170(c)(2)(B) purposes. Except as provided in § 53.4947-1(b)(2)(iv) (relating to a reasonable period of settlement) the trust will be treated as a charitable trust within the meaning of section 4947(a)(1) from the date of the death of Z unless the trustees of the trust apply for recognition of section 501(c)(3) status under the provisions of section 508(a).

(2) *Scope of application of section 4947(a)(1).*— (i) *In general.*—Subject to paragraph (b)(2)(ii) through (vii) of this section, section 4947(a)(1) applies to nonexempt trusts in which all unexpired interests are charitable. For purposes of this section, the term "charitable" when used to describe an interest or beneficiary refers to the purposes described in section 170(c)(2)(B). An estate from which the executor or administrator is required to distribute all of the net assets in trust to such beneficiaries will not be considered a charitable trust under section 4947(a)(1) during the period of estate administration or settlement, except as provided in paragraph (b)(2)(ii) of this section. A charitable trust created by will shall be considered a charitable trust under section 4947(a)(1) as of the date of death of the decedent-grantor, except as provided in paragraph (b)(2)(v) of this section (relating to trusts which wind up). For the circumstances under which segregated amounts are treated as charitable trusts, see § 53.4947-1(c)(3)(iii).

(ii) *Estates.*—(A) When an estate from which the executor or administrator is required to distribute all of the net assets in trust for charitable beneficiaries, or free of trust to such beneficiaries, is considered terminated for Federal income tax purposes under § 1.641(b)-3 (a), then the estate will be treated as a charitable trust under section 4947(a)(1) between the date on which the estate is considered terminated under § 1.641(b)-3 (a) and the date final distribution of all of the net assets is made to or for the benefit of the charitable beneficiaries. This (ii) does not affect the determination of the tax liability under subtitle A of the beneficiaries of the estates.

(B) The provisions of this (ii) may be illustrated by the following example:

Example. X bequeaths his entire estate, including 100 percent of the stock of a wholly-owned corporation, to M, an organization described in section 501(c)(3), under a will which gives his executor authority to hold the stock and manage the corporation for a period of up to 10 years for the benefit of M prior to its ultimate disposition. A deduction for the charitable bequest was allowed to X's estate under section 2055. The executor is vested with a full range of powers, including the power of sale. Upon the death of X, his executor distributes X's assets to M except for the stock of the corporation, which he holds for 5 years prior to its disposition. The continued holding of the stock of the corporation by the executor after the expiration of a reasona-

ble time for performance of all the ordinary duties of administration causes the estate to be considered terminated for Federal income tax purposes pursuant to § 1.641(b)-3 (a) and thereby subjects it to the provisions of section 4947(a)(1) from the date of such termination to the date of final disposition of the stock of the corporation.

(iii) *Certain split-interest trusts which wind up.*—A split-interest trust (as defined in paragraph (c) of this section) in which all of the unexpired interests are charitable remainder interests and in which the charitable beneficiaries have become entitled to distributions of corpus in trust or free of trust shall continue to be treated as a split-interest trust under section 4947(a)(2) until the date on which final distribution of all the net assets is made. However, if after the expiration of any intervening interests the trust is considered terminated for Federal income tax purposes under § 1.641(b)-3 (b), then the trust will be treated as a charitable trust under section 4947(a)(1), rather than a split-interest trust under section 4947(a)(2), between the date on which the trust is considered terminated under § 1.641(b)-3 (b) and the date on which such final distribution of all of the net assets is made to or for the benefit of the charitable remainder beneficiaries. This (iii) does not affect the determination of the tax liability under subtitle A of the beneficiaries of the trusts.

(iv) *Split-interest trusts which become charitable trusts.*—(A) A split-interest trust (as defined in paragraph (c) of this section) in which all of the unexpired interests are charitable remainder interests and in which some or all of the charitable beneficiaries are not entitled to distributions of corpus within the meaning of paragraph (b)(2)(iii) of this section shall continue to be treated as a split-interest trust under section 4947(a)(2) rather than a charitable trust under section 4947(a)(1) for a reasonable period of settlement after the expiration of the noncharitable interest. Thus, a split-interest trust which under its terms is to continue to hold assets for charitable beneficiaries after the expiration of the noncharitable interest rather than distributing them as in paragraph (b)(2)(iii) of this section is given a reasonable period of settlement before being treated as a charitable trust. For purposes of this paragraph, the term "reasonable period of settlement" means that period reasonably required (or if shorter, actually required) by the trustee to perform the ordinary duties of administration necessary for the settlement of the trust. These duties include, for example, the collection of assets, the payment of debts, taxes, and distributions, and the determination of the rights of the subsequent beneficiaries.

(B) This (iv) may be illustrated by the following example:

Example. On January 15, 1971, A creates a charitable remainder annuity trust described in section 664(d)(1) under which the trustees are required to distribute $10,000 a year to B, A's wife, for life, remainder to be held in trust for the use of M, an organization described in section

501(c)(3). A is allowed a deduction under section 170 for the amount of the charitable interest, and the trust is, therefore, treated as a split-interest trust under section 4947(a)(2) from the date of its creation. B dies on February 10, 1975. On April 15, 1975, the trustees complete performance of the ordinary duties of administration necessary for the settlement of the trust brought about by the death of B. These duties include, for example, an accounting for and payment to the estate of B of amounts accrued by B while alive during 1975. However, the trustees do not distribute the corpus to M by April 15, 1975. The trust shall continue to be treated as a split-interest trust under section 4947(a)(2) until April 15, 1975. After April 15, 1975, the trust shall be treated as a charitable trust under section 4947(a)(1).

(v) *Certain revocable and testamentary trusts which wind up.*—A revocable trust that becomes irrevocable upon the death of the decedent-grantor, or a trust created by will, from which the trustee is required to distribute all of the net assets in trust for or free of trust to charitable beneficiaries is not considered a charitable trust under section 4947(a)(1) for a reasonable period of settlement (within the meaning of paragraph (b)(2)(iv) of this section) after becoming irrevocable. After that period the trust is considered a charitable trust under section 4947(a)(1).

(vi) *Revocable trusts which become charitable trusts.*—A revocable trust that becomes irrevocable upon the death of the decedent-grantor in which all of the unexpired interests are charitable and under the terms of the governing instrument of which the trustee is required to hold some or all of the net assets in trust after becoming irrevocable solely for charitable beneficiaries is not considered a trust under section 4947(a)(1) for a reasonable period of settlement (within the meaning of paragraph (b)(2)(iv) of this section) after becoming irrevocable except that section 4941 may apply if the requirements of §53.4941(d)-1(b)(3) are not met. After that period, the trust is considered a charitable trust under section 4947(a)(1).

(vii) *Trust devoted to 170(c) purposes.*—(A) A trust all of the unexpired interests in which are devoted to section 170(c)(3) or (5) purposes together with section 170(c)(2)(B) purposes shall be considered a charitable trust except that payments under the terms of the governing instrument to an organization described in section 170(c)(3) or (5) shall not be considered a violation of section 4945(d)(5) or any other provisions of chapter 42 and shall be considered qualifying distributions under section 4942.

(B) *Example.*—The application of paragraph (b)(2)(vii) of this section may be illustrated by the following example:

Example. On January 30, 1970, H creates an *inter vivos* trust under the terms of the governing instrument of which M, an organization described in section 170(c)(3), and N, an organi-

zation described in section 501(c)(3), are each to receive 50 percent of the income for a period of 10 years. At the end of the 10-year period, the corpus is to be distributed to O, an organization also described in section 501(c)(3). H is allowed a deduction under section 170 for the value of all interests placed in trust. The payments to M do not constitute a violation of section 4945(d)(5) or any other provision of chapter 42 and constitute qualifying distributions under section 4942. However, except as provided in the previous sentence, the trust shall be considered a charitable trust.

(3) *Charitable trusts described in section 509(a)(3).*—For purposes of section 509(a)(3)(A), a charitable trust shall be treated as if organized on the day on which it first becomes subject to section 4947(a)(1). However, for purposes of applying §§1.509(a)-4(d)(2)(iv)(*a*), and 1.509(a)-4(i)(1)(ii) and (iii)(*c*) the previous relationship between the charitable trust and the section 509(a)(1) or (2) organizations it benefits or supports may be considered. If the charitable trust otherwise meets the requirements of section 509(a)(3), it may obtain recognition of its status as a section 509(a)(3) organization by requesting a ruling from the Internal Revenue Service. For the special rules pertaining to the application of the organizational test to organizations terminating their private foundation status under the 12-month or 60-month termination period provided under section 507(b)(1)(B) by becoming "public" under section 509(a)(3), see the regulations under section 507(b)(1).

(c) *Split-interest trusts.*—(1) *General rule.*—(i) *Definition.*—For purposes of this section and §53.4947-2, a "split-interest trust," within the meaning of section 4947(a)(2), is a trust which is not exempt from taxation under section 501(a), not all of the unexpired interests in which are devoted to one or more of the purposes described in section 170(c)(2)(B), and which has amounts in trust for which a deduction was allowed (within the meaning of paragraph (a) of this section) under section 170, 545(b)(2), 556(b)(2), 642(c), 2055, 2106(a)(2), or 2522. A trust is one which has amounts in trust for which a deduction was allowed under section 642(c) within the meaning of section 4947(a)(2) once a deduction is allowed under section 642(c) to the trust for any amount permanently set aside. This (i) also includes any trust which is not treated as a charitable trust by operation of paragraph (b)(2)(iii) or (iv) of this section (relating to split-interest trusts in the process of winding up or during a reasonable period of settlement). Section 4947(a)(1) shall apply to a trust described in this (i) (without regard to section 4947(a)(2)(A), (B), or (C)) from the first date upon which the provisions of paragraph (b)(2)(iii) or (iv) of this section are satisfied. For the circumstances under which a trust all of the unexpired interests in which are devoted to section 170(c)(3) or (5) purposes together with section 170(c)(2)(B) purposes is considered a charitable trust, see §53.4947-1(b)(2)(vii).

Reg. §53.4947-1(c)(1)(i)

(ii) *Applicability of statutory rules.*—A split-interest trust is subject to the provisions of section 507 (except as provided in paragraph (e) of this section), 508(e) (to the extent applicable to a split-interest trust), 4941, 4943 (except as provided in section 4947(b)(3)), 4944 (except as provided in section 4947(b)(3)), and 4945 in the same manner as if such trust were a private foundation.

(iii) *Special rules.*—A newly created trust shall, for purposes of section 4947(a)(2), be treated as having amounts in trust for which a deduction was allowed under section 170, 545(b)(2), 556(b)(2), 642(c), 2055, 2106(a)(2), or 2522 from the date of its creation, even if a deduction was allowed for such amounts only at a later date. For purposes of this (iii), the date of creation of a charitable remainder trust shall be determined by applying the rules in § 1.664-1(a)(4).

(2) *Exception for amounts payable to income beneficiaries.*—(i) Under section 4947(a)(2)(A), paragraph (c)(1)(ii) of this section does not apply to any amounts payable under the terms of a split-interest trust to income beneficiaries unless a deduction was allowed under section 170(f)(2)(B), 2055(e)(2)(B), or 2522(c)(2)(B) with respect to income interest of any such beneficiary. See § 1.170A-6(c), § 20.2055-2(e)(2), and § 25.2522(c)-3(c)(2) for rules regarding the allowance of these deductions. However, section 4947(a)(2)(A) does not apply when the value of all interests in property transferred in trust are deductible under section 170, 545(b)(2), 556(b)(2), 642(c), 2055, 2106(a)(2), or 2522.

(ii) The application of this subparagraph may be illustrated by the following examples:

Example (1). H creates a charitable remainder unitrust (described in section 664(d)(2)) which is required annually to pay W, H's wife, 5 percent of the net fair market value of the trust assets, valued annually, for her life; and to pay the remainder to Y, a section 501(c)(3) organization. A deduction under section 170(f)(2)(A) was allowed with respect to the remainder interest of Y. Under section 4947(a)(2)(A), each annual amount which becomes payable to W during her life is not subject to paragraph (c)(1)(ii) of this section on or after the date upon which it becomes so payable and the payment of each amount to W is not an act of self-dealing under section 4941(d)(1) and does not violate any other provision of chapter 42. However, except as provided in the preceding sentence, the trust is subject to paragraph (c)(1)(ii) of this section in the same manner as any other split-interest trust.

Example (2). H bequeaths the residue of his estate in trust for the benefit of S, his son, and Y, an organization described in section 501(c)(3). A guaranteed annuity interest of $10,000 is to be paid to S for 20 years. A guaranteed annuity interest of $5,000 which meets the requirements contained in § 20.2055-2(e)(2)(v)(a) is also to be paid to Y for 20 years. Upon termination of the 20-year term, the corpus is to be distributed to Z,

another organization described in section 501(c)(3). The trust is a charitable remainder annuity trust as described in section 664(d)(1) and the regulations thereunder, and a deduction under section 2055(e)(2)(A) was allowed with respect to the remainder interest of Z. A deduction was also allowed under section 2055(e)(2)(B) with respect to the guaranteed annuity interest of Y. The assets in the trust are not segregated under section 4947(a)(2)(B) and paragraph (c)(3) of this section. Under section 4947(a)(2)(A), each payment of $10,000 to S is not subject to section 4947(a)(2) and paragraph (c)(1)(ii) of this section. The payment of each amount to S is not an act of self-dealing under section 4941(d)(1) and does not violate any other provision of chapter 42. However, except as provided in the preceding sentence, the trust is subject to section 4947(a)(2) and paragraph (c)(1)(ii) of this section in the same manner as any other split-interest trust.

Example (3). H creates a trust under which the trustees are required to pay over an annuity interest of $20,000 to W, H's wife, for her life. A guaranteed annuity interest of $10,000 which meets the requirements contained in § 25.2522(c)-3 (c)(2)(v) is also to be paid to X, an organization described in section 501(c)(3), for the life of W. Upon the death of W, the corpus of the trust, which consists of office buildings M and N, is to be distributed to S, H's son. He received a deduction under section 2522(c)(2)(B) for the value of X's income interest in the trust. The assets in the trust are not segregated under section 4947(a)(2)(B) and paragraph (c)(3) of this section. Under section 4947(a)(2)(A), each payment of $20,000 to W is not subject to section 4947(a)(2) and paragraph (c)(1)(ii) of this section. The payment of each amount to W is not an act of self-dealing under section 4941(d)(1) and does not violate any other provision of chapter 42. However, except as provided in the preceding sentence, the trust is subject to paragraph (c)(1)(ii) of this section in the same manner as any other split-interest trust. See example (1) of paragraph (c)(3)(v) of this section for the application of section 4947(a)(2)(B) to a similar trust where the trustees segregate the assets of the trust.

(3) *Exception for certain segregated amounts.*—(i) *In general.*—Under section 4947(a)(2)(B), paragraph (c)(1)(ii) of this section does not apply to assets held in trust (together with the income and capital gains derived from the assets), which are segregated from other assets held in trust for which a deduction was allowed for an income or remainder interest under section 170, 545(b)(2), 556(b)(2), 642(c), 2055, 2106(a)(2), or 2522.

(ii) *Segregation of amounts.*—Amounts will generally be considered segregated (within the meaning of section 4947(a)(2)(B)) if:

(A) assets with respect to which no deduction was allowed (for an income or remainder interest) under section 170, 545(b)(2), 556(b)(2), 642(c), 2055, 2106(a)(2), or 2522, are separately accounted for under section 4947(a)(3) and paragraph (c)(4) of this section from assets

for which such a deduction was allowed for any income or remainder interest and,

(B) by reason of the separate accounting the trust can be treated as two separate trusts, one of which is devoted exclusively to noncharitable income and remainder interests and the other of which is a charitable trust described in section 4947(a)(1) or a split-interest trust described in section 4947(a)(2).

Under these circumstances, only the "trust" which is devoted exclusively to noncharitable income and remainder interests will be considered a segregated amount which, under section 4947(a)(2)(B), is not subject to section 4947(a)(2) and paragraph (c)(1)(ii) of this section.

(iii) *Exclusively charitable amounts.*—If, under section 4947(a)(2)(B),

(A) an amount held in trust which is devoted exclusively to noncharitable income and remainder interests is segregated from

(B) an amount held in trust which is devoted exclusively to charitable income and remainder interests,

then for purposes of this section the amount described in paragraph (c)(3)(iii)(B) of this section will be treated as a charitable trust which is subject to the provisions of section 4947(a)(1).

(iv) *Charitable and noncharitable amounts.*—If, under section 4947(a)(2)(B),

(A) an amount held in trust which is devoted exclusively to noncharitable income and remainder interests is segregated from

(B) an amount held in trust which is devoted to both charitable income or remainder interests and noncharitable income or remainder interests,

then for purposes of this section the amount described in paragraph (c)(3)(iv)(B) of this section will be treated as a split-interest trust which is subject to the provisions of section 4947(a)(2).

(v) *Examples.*—The application of paragraph (c)(3) of this section may be illustrated by the following examples:

Example (1). H creates a trust under which the trustees are required to pay over annually 5 percent of the net fair market value of M building, valued to W, H's wife, for life, remainder to S, H's son. The other asset in the trust is N building, with respect to which the trustees are required to pay over annually 5 percent of the net fair market value of the building, valued annually, to X, a section 501(c)(3) organization, for a period of 15 years, remainder to S. Each asset is separately accounted for under section 4947(a)(3) and paragraph (c)(4) of this section. H received a deduction under section 2522 for the value of X's income interest in N building. Under these circumstances, M building is considered segregated (within the meaning of section 4947(a)(2)(B)) from N building and is not subject to section 4947(a)(2). The remainder interest of S in N building is not considered segregated from the income interest of X in N building, since both are interests in the same

asset. N building is considered held in a split-interest trust which is subject to section 4947(a)(2) and paragraph (c)(1)(ii) of this section.

Example (2). H transfers $50,000 in trust to pay $2,500 per year to Z, a section 501(c)(3) organization, for a term of 20 years, remainder to S, H's son. H is allowed a deduction under section 2522 for the present value of Z's income interest. The income interest of Z in the trust asset cannot be segregated (within the meaning of section 4947(a)(2)(B)) from the remainder interest of S since both are interests in the same asset. Therefore, the entire trust is subject to section 4947(a)(2) and paragraph (c)(1)(ii) of this section.

(4) *Accounting for segregated amounts.*—(i) *General rule.*—Under section 4947(a)(2)(B), a trust with respect to which amounts are segregated within the meaning of paragraph (c)(3) of this section must separately account for the various income, deduction, and other items properly attributable to each segregated amount in the books of account and separately account to each of the beneficiaries of the trust.

(ii) *Method.*—Separate accounting shall be made—

(A) According to the method regularly employed by the trust, if the method is reasonable, and

(B) In all other cases in a manner which, in the opinion of the Commissioner, is reasonable.

A method of separate accounting will be considered "regularly employed" by a trust when the method has been consistently followed in prior taxable years or when a trust which has never before maintained segregated amounts initiates a reasonable method of separate accounting for its segregated amounts and consistently follows such method thereafter. The trust shall keep permanent records and other data relating to the segregated amounts as are necessary to enable the district director to determine the correctness of the application of the rules prescribed in paragraph (c)(3) and (4) of this section.

(5) *Amounts transferred in trust before May 27, 1969.*—(i) *General rule.*—Under section 4947(a)(2)(C), paragraph (c)(1)(ii) of this section does not apply to any amounts transferred in trust before May 27, 1969. For purposes of this (5), an amount shall be considered to be transferred in trust only when the transfer is one which meets the requirements for the allowance of a deduction under section 170, 545(b)(2), 556(b)(2), 642(c), 2055, 2106(a)(2), or 2522 (or the corresponding provisions of prior law). Income and capital gains which are derived at any time from amounts transferred in trust before May 27, 1969, shall also be excluded from the application of paragraph (c)(1)(ii) of this section. If an asset which was transferred in trust before May 27, 1969, is sold or exchanged after May 26, 1969, any asset received by the trust upon the sale or exchange shall be treated as an asset which was transferred in trust before May 27, 1969.

Reg. §53.4947-1(c)(5)(i)

(ii) *Requirement for separate accounting for amounts transferred in trust before May 27, 1969.*—If:

(A) Amounts are transferred in trust after May 26, 1969, and the trust to which the amounts are transferred also contains

(B) Amounts transferred in trust before May 27, 1969,

the general rule of paragraph (c)(5)(i) of this section applicable to the amounts described in paragraph (c)(5)(ii)(B) of this section will apply only if the amounts described in paragraph (c)(5)(ii)(A) of this section (together with all income and capital gains derived therefrom) are separately accounted for (within the meaning of paragraph (c)(4) of this section) from the amounts described in paragraph (c)(5)(ii)(B) of this section, together with all income and capital gains derived therefrom. For the application of section 508(e) to a trust with respect to which amounts were transferred both before and after May 27, 1969, see section 508(e) and the regulations thereunder.

(iii) *Exception for certain testamentary trusts.*—(A) Amounts transferred in trust before May 27, 1969 include amounts transferred in trust after May 26, 1969 when the transfer is made under the terms of a testamentary trust created by the will of a decedent who died before May 27, 1969, (regardless of whether the executors or the testamentary trustees are required to execute testamentary trusts by court order under applicable local law). Amounts transferred in trust before May 27, 1969, also include amounts transferred to a testamentary trust created by the will of a decedent who died after May 26, 1969 if the will was executed before May 27, 1969 and no dispositive provision of the will was amended (within the meaning of §20.2055-2(e)(4) and (5)) by the decedent by codicil or otherwise, after May 26, 1969, and the decedent was on May 27, 1969, and at all times thereafter under a mental disability (as defined in §1.642(c)-2(b)(3)(ii)) to amend the will by codicil or otherwise.

(B) The provisions of this (iii) may be illustrated by the following example:

Example. X executed a will in 1960 which provided for the creation of a testamentary trust which meets the description of a split-interest trust under section 4947(a)(2). X died on April 15, 1969. Under the provisions of his will, the probate court permitted certain property in X's estate to be transferred to the testamentary trust at fixed intervals over a period of two years during the administration of the estate. Section 4947(a)(2) does not apply to any amount described in this example, including the amounts transferred after May 26, 1969, because, for purposes of section 4947(a)(2)(C), each such transfer will be treated as an amount transferred in trust before May 27, 1969, within the meaning of section 4947(a)(2)(C).

(6) *Scope of application of section 4947(a)(2).*—(i) *In general.*—Subject to paragraph (c)(6)(ii),

(iii), and (iv) of this section, section 4947(a)(2) applies to trusts in which some but not all unexpired interests are charitable. An estate from which the executor or administrator is required to distribute all of the net assets in trust or free of trust to both charitable and noncharitable beneficiaries will not be considered to be a split-interest trust under section 4947(a)(2) during the period of estate administration or settlement, except as provided in paragraph (c)(6)(ii) of this section. A split-interest trust created by will shall be considered a split-interest trust under section 4947(a)(2) as of the date of death of the decedent-grantor, except as provided in paragraph (c)(6)(iv) of this section.

(ii) *Estates.*—(A) When an estate from which the executor or administrator is required to distribute all of the net assets in trust or free of trust to both charitable and noncharitable beneficiaries is considered terminated for Federal income tax purposes under §1.641(b)-3 (a), then the estate will be treated as a split-interest trust under section 4947(a)(2) (or a charitable trust under section 4947(a)(1), if applicable) between the date on which the estate is considered terminated under §1.641(b)-3 (a) and the date on which final distribution of the net assets to the last remaining charitable beneficiary is made. This (ii) does not affect the determination of the tax liability under subtitle A of either charitable or noncharitable beneficiaries of the estates.

(B) The provisions of this (ii) may be illustrated by the following example:

Example. X dies on January 15, 1973 and bequeaths $10,000 to M, an organization described in section 501(c)(3), and the residue of his estate to W, his wife. A deduction for the charitable bequest was allowed to X's estate under section 2055. Substantially all of X's estate consists of 100 percent of the stock of a wholly owned corporation, certain liquid assets such as marketable stocks and securities and bank accounts, and X's home, automobile, and other personal property. X's will gives the executor a full range of powers, including the power to sell the stock of the wholly owned corporation. After the death of X, his executor continues to manage the wholly owned corporation while attempting to sell the stock of the corporation. During this period, the executor makes no distributions to M. On May 24, 1978, the Internal Revenue Service determines under §1.641(b)-3(a) that the administration of the estate has been unduly prolonged and the estate is considered terminated as of that date for Federal income tax purposes. X's estate will be treated as a split-interest trust described in section 4947(a)(2) between May 24, 1978 and the date on which the $10,000 bequest to M is satisfied. X's estate will therefore be subject to the applicable private foundation provisions during that period and, for example, a sale of the house by the estate to any disqualified person (as defined in section 4946) will be an act of self-dealing under section 4941.

(iii) *Revocable trusts which become split-interest trusts.*—A revocable trust that becomes irrevocable upon the death of the decedent-grantor under the terms of the governing instrument of which the trustee is required to hold some or all of its net assets in trust after becoming irrevocable for both charitable and noncharitable beneficiaries is not considered a split-interest trust under section 4947(a)(2) for a reasonable period of settlement after becoming irrevocable except that section 4941 may apply if the requirements of § 53.4941(d)-1(b)(3) are not met.

After that period, the trust is considered a split-interest trust under section 4947(a)(2). For purposes of this (iii), the term "reasonable period of settlement" means that period reasonably required (or if shorter, actually required) by the trustee to perform the ordinary duties of administration necessary for the settlement of the trust. These duties include, for example, the collection of assets, the payment of debts, taxes, and distributions, and the determination of rights of the subsequent beneficiaries.

(iv) *Certain revocable and testamentary trusts which wind up.*—A revocable trust that becomes irrevocable upon the death of the decedent-grantor, or a trust created by will, from which the trustee is required to distribute all of the net assets in trust or free of trust to both charitable and noncharitable beneficiaries is not considered a split-interest trust under section 4947(a)(2) for a reasonable period of settlement (within the meaning of paragraph (c)(6)(iii) of this section) after becoming irrevocable. After that period, the trust is considered a split-interest trust under section 4947(a)(2) (or a charitable trust under section 4947(a)(1), if applicable).

(d) *Cross references; Governing instrument requirements and charitable deduction limitations.*— For the application of section 642(c)(6) (relating to section 170 limitations on charitable deductions of non-exempt private foundation trusts) to a trust described in section 4947(a)(1), see § 1.642(c)-4. For the denial of a deduction under section 170, 545(b)(2), 556(b)(2), 642(c), 2055, 2106(a)(2), or 2522 for a gift, a bequest, or an amount paid to (and the denial of a deduction under section 642(c) for an amount set aside in) a trust described in section 4947(a)(1) or (2) that fails to meet the applicable governing instrument requirements of section 508(e) by the end of the taxable year of the trust, see section 508(d)(2) and § 1.508-2(b). Since a charitable remainder trust (as defined in section 664) is not exempt under section 501(a), it is subject to section 4947(a)(2), and thus to the governing instrument requirements of section 508(e) to the extent they are applicable.

(e) *Application of section 507(a).*—(1) *General rule.*—The provisions of section 507(a) shall not apply to a trust described in section 4947(a)(1) or (2) by reason of any payment to a beneficiary that is directed by the terms of the governing instrument of the trust and is not discretionary

with the trustee or, in the case of a discretionary payment, by reason of, or following, the expiration of the last remaining charitable interest in the trust.

(2) *Examples.*—The provisions of this (e) may be illustrated by the following examples:

Example (1). H creates a section 4947(a)(1) trust under which the income is to be paid for 15 years to R, a section 501(c)(3) organization. Upon the expiration of 15 years, the trust is to terminate and distribute all of its assets to S, another section 501(c)(3) organization. Distribution of the corpus of the trust to S will not be considered a termination of the trust's private foundation status within the meaning of section 507(a).

Example (2). H creates a trust under which X, a section 501(c)(3) organization, receives $20,000 per year for a period of 20 years, remainder to S, H's son. H is allowed a deduction under section 2522 for the present value of X's interest.

When the final payment to X has been made at the end of the 20-year period in accordance with the terms of the trust, the provisions of section 4947(a)(2) will cease to apply to the trust because the trust no longer retains any amounts for which the deduction under section 2522 was allowed. However, the final payment to X will not be considered a termination of the trust's private foundation status within the meaning of section 507(a).

Example (3). J creates a charitable remainder annuity trust described in section 664(d)(1) under which S, J's son, receives $10,000 per year for life, remainder to be distributed outright to P, an organization described in section 501(c)(3). J is allowed a deduction under section 170 for the value of the remainder interest placed in trust for the benefit of P, and the provisions of section 4947(a)(2) apply to the trust. At the death of S, the trust will terminate and all assets will be distributed to P. However, such final distribution to P will not be considered a termination of the trust's private foundation status within the meaning of section 507(a). [Reg. § 53.4947-1.]

☐ [*T.D.* 7431, 8-20-76.]

[Reg. § 53.4947-2]

§ 53.4947-2. Special rules.—(a) *Limit to segregated amounts.*—If any amounts held in trust are segregated within the meaning of § 53.4947-1(c)(3), the value of the net assets for purposes of section 507(c)(2) and (g) shall be limited to the segregated amounts with respect to which a deduction under section 170, 545(b)(2), 556(b)(2), 642(c), 2055, 2106(a)(2), or 2522 was allowed. See the regulations under section 507(c)(2) and (g).

(b) *Applicability of sections 4943 and 4944 to split-interest trusts.*—(1) *General rule.*—Under section 4947(b)(3), sections 4943 and 4944 do not apply to a split-interest trust described in section 4947(a)(2) if:

(i) all the income interest (and none of the remainder interest) of the trust is devoted solely to one or more of the purposes described in

section 170(c)(2)(B) and all amounts in the trust for which a deduction was allowed under section 170, 545(b)(2), 556(b)(2), 642(c), 2055, 2106(a)(2), or 2522 have an aggregated value (at the time for which the deduction was allowed) of not more than 60 percent of the aggregate fair market value of all amounts in the trust (after the payment of estate taxes and all other liabilities), or

(ii) a deduction was allowed under section 170, 545(b)(2), 556(b)(2), 642(c), 2055, 2106(a)(2) or 2522 for amounts payable under the terms of the trust to every remainder beneficiary, but not to any income beneficiary.

This (1) shall apply to a trust described in paragraph (b)(1)(ii) of this section only if all amounts payable under the terms of the trust to every remainder beneficiary are to be devoted solely to one or more of the purposes described in section 170(c)(2)(B). After the expiration of all income interests in a trust described in paragraph (b)(1)(ii) of this section, the trust shall become subject to section 4947(a)(1) under § 53.4947-1(b)(2), and section 4947(b)(3) shall no longer apply to the trust. A pooled income fund described in section 642(c)(5) will generally meet the requirements of paragraph (b)(1)(ii) of this section, as will a charitable remainder trust described in section 664(d)(1), if in either case it does not make payments to any income beneficiary described in section 170(c).

(2) *Definitions.*—(i) For purposes of section 4947(b)(3)(A), the term "income interest" shall include an interest in property transferred in trust which is in the form of a guaranteed annuity interest or unitrust interest as described in § 1.170A-6(c), § 20.2055-2(e)(2) or § 25.2522(c)-3(c)(2) and the term "remainder interest" shall include an interest which succeeds an "income interest" within the meaning of this (i).

(ii) For purposes of section 4947(b)(3)(B), the term "income beneficiary" shall include a recipient of payments described in section 642(c)(5)(F) from a pooled income fund, payments described in section 664(d)(1)(A) from a charitable remainder annuity trust, or payments described in section 664(d)(2)(A) or (3) from a charitable remainder unitrust. The term "remainder beneficiary" shall include a beneficiary of a remainder interest described in section 642(c)(5) or 664(d)(1)(C) or (2)(C).

(c) *Effective date.*—Except as otherwise provided in §§ 53.4947-1 and 53.4947-2 and the regulations under sections 508(d) and (e), §§ 53.4947-1 and 53.4947-2 shall take effect on January 1, 1970. [Reg. § 53.4947-2.]

☐ [*T.D.* 7431, 8-20-76.]

[Reg. § 53.4948-1]

§ 53.4948-1. Application of taxes and denial of exemption with respect to certain foreign organizations.—(a) *Tax on income of certain foreign organizations.*—(1) In lieu of the tax imposed by section 4940 and the regulations thereunder,

there is hereby imposed for each taxable year beginning after December 31, 1969, on the gross investment income (within the meaning of section 4940(c)(2) and the regulations thereunder) derived from sources within the United States (within the meaning of section 861 and the regulations thereunder) by every foreign organization which is a private foundation (within the meaning of section 509 and the regulations thereunder) and exempt from taxation under section 501(a) for the taxable year a tax equal to 4 percent of such income, except as provided in subparagraph (3) of this paragraph. The tax (if any) will be reported on the form the foundation is required to file under section 6033 for the taxable year, and will be paid annually at the time prescribed for filing such annual return (determined without regard to any extension of time for filing). For purposes of this section, the term "foreign organization" means any organization which is not described in section 170(c)(2)(A).

(2) With respect to the deduction and withholding of tax imposed by section 4948(a), see section 1443(b) and the regulations thereunder.

(3) Whenever there exists a tax treaty between the United States and a foreign country, and a foreign private foundation subject to section 4948(a) is a resident of such country or is otherwise entitled to the benefits of such treaty (whether or not such benefits are available to all residents), if the treaty provides that any item or items (or all items with respect to an organization exempt from income taxation) of gross investment income (within the meaning of section 4940(c)(2)) shall be exempt from income tax, such item or items shall not be taken into account by such foundation in computing the tax to be imposed under section 4948(a) for any taxable year for which the treaty is effective.

(b) *Certain sections inapplicable.*—Section 507 (relating to termination of private foundation status), section 508 (relating to special rules with respect to section 501(c)(3) organizations), and chapter 42 (other than section 4948) of the Code shall not apply to any foreign organization which from the date of its creation has received at least 85 percent of its support (as defined in section 509(d), other than section 509(d)(4)) from sources outside the United States. For purposes of this paragraph, gifts, grants, contributions, or membership fees directly or indirectly from a United States person (as defined in section 7701(a)(30)) are from sources within the United States.

(c) *Denial of exemption to foreign organizations engaged in prohibited transactions.*—(1) *In general.*—A foreign private foundation described in section 4948(b) and paragraph (b) of this section shall not be exempt from taxation under section 501(a) if it has engaged in a prohibited transaction (within the meaning of subparagraph (2) of this paragraph) after December 31, 1969.

(2) *Prohibited transactions.*—(i) For purposes of this section, the term "prohibited transaction" means any act or failure to act (other than with

respect to section 4942(e), relating to minimum investment return) which would subject a foreign private foundation described in paragraph (b) of this section, or a disqualified person (as defined in section 4946) with respect thereto, to liability for a penalty under section 6684 (relating to assessable penalties with respect to liability for tax under chapter 42) or a tax under section 507 (relating to termination of private foundation status) if such foreign private foundation were a domestic private foundation.

(ii) For purposes of subdivision (i) of this subparagraph—

(a) Approval by an appropriate foreign government of grants by the foreign private foundation to individuals is sufficient to satisfy the requirements of section 4945(g) and the regulations thereunder.

(b) In determining whether a grantee of the foreign organization is a private foundation which is not an operating foundation for purposes of section 4942(g)(1)(A)(ii) or is an organization which is not described in section 509(a)(1), (2), or (3) for purposes of section 4945(d)(4) and (h), a determination made by such foreign organization will be accepted if such determination is made in good faith after a reasonable effort to identify the status of its grantee.

(iii) For purposes of subdivision (i) of this subparagraph, in order for an act or failure to act (without regard to section 4942(e)) to be treated as a prohibited transaction under section 4948(c)(2) by reason of the application of section 6684(1), there must have been a prior act or failure to act (without regard to section 4942(e)), which—

(a) Would have resulted in liability for tax under chapter 42 (other than section 4940 or 4948(a)) if the foreign private foundation had been a domestic private foundation, and

(b) Had been the subject of a warning from the Commissioner that a second act or failure to act (without regard to section 4942(e)) would result in a prohibited transaction. The second act or failure to act (with respect to which a warning described in subparagraph (3)(i) of this paragraph is given) need not be related to the prior act or failure to act with respect to which a warning from the Commissioner was given under (b) of this subdivision.

(3) *Taxable years affected.*—(i) Except as provided in subdivision (ii) of this subparagraph, a foreign private foundation described in paragraph (b) of this section shall be denied exemption from taxation under section 501(a) by reason of subparagraph (1) of this paragraph for all taxable years beginning with the taxable year during which it is notified by the Commissioner that it has engaged in a prohibited transaction. The Commissioner shall publish such notice in the FEDERAL REGISTER on the day on which he so notifies such foreign private foundation. In the case of an act or failure to act (without regard to section 4942(e)) which would result in a penalty under section 6684(1) if the foreign private foundation were a domestic private foundation,

before giving notice under this subdivision the Commissioner shall warn such foreign private foundation that such act or failure to act may be treated as a prohibited transaction. However, such act or failure to act will not be treated as a prohibited transaction if it is corrected (within the meaning of chapter 42 and the regulations thereunder) within 90 days after the making of such warning.

(ii)(a) Any foreign private foundation described in paragraph (b) of this section which is denied exemption from taxation under section 501(a) by reason of subparagraph (1) of this paragraph may, with respect to the second taxable year following the taxable year in which notice is given under subdivision (i) of this subparagraph (or any taxable year subsequent to such second taxable year), file a request for exemption from taxation under section 501(a) on Form 1023. In addition to the information generally required of an organization requesting exemption as an organization described in section 501(a), a request under this subdivision must contain or have attached to it a written declaration, made under the penalties of perjury, by a principal officer of such organization authorized to make such declaration, that the organization will not knowingly again engage in a prohibited transaction.

(b) If the Commissioner is satisfied that such organization will not knowingly again engage in a prohibited transaction and that the organization has satisfied all other requirements under section 501, the organization will be so notified in writing. In such case the organization shall not, with respect to taxable years beginning with the taxable year with respect to which a request under this subdivision is filed, be denied exemption from taxation under section 501(a) by reason of any prohibited transaction which was engaged in before the date on which notice was given under subdivision (i) of this subparagraph. Section 4948(c) provides that an organization denied exemption under such section will not be exempt from taxation under section 501(a) for the taxable year in which notice of loss of exemption is given and at least one immediately subsequent taxable year.

(d) *Disallowance of certain charitable deductions.*—No gift, bequest, legacy, devise, or transfer shall be allowed as a deduction under section 170, 545(b)(2), 556(b)(2), 642(c), 2055, 2106(a)(2), or 2522, if made:

(1) To a foreign private foundation described in paragraph (b) of this section after the date on which the Commissioner publishes notice under paragraph (c)(3)(i) of this section that he has notified such organization that it has engaged in a prohibited transaction, and

(2) In a taxable year of such organization for which it is not exempt from taxation under section 501(a) by reason of paragraph (c)(1) of this section.

For purposes of this paragraph, a bequest, legacy, devise, or transfer under section 2055 or 2106(a)(2) shall be treated as made on the date of death of the decedent. For example, assume that

Reg. § 53.4948-1(d)(2)

an individual gives money to a foreign private foundation described in section 4948(b) in January 1970, January 1971, and January 1972. The organization has a taxable year from June 1 through May 31. In February 1970, notice is duly published that the foreign organization has engaged in a prohibited transaction. In December 1970, the organization duly submits a request for exemption under paragraph (c)(3)(ii)(a) of this section which is granted for the taxable year ending May 31, 1972. The January 1970 gift is allowable as a deduction under section 2522

since it was made before the notice (February 1970). The January 1971 gift is not allowable as a deduction because the taxable year ending May 31, 1971, is a nonexempt year (the first taxable year subsequent to the taxable year of the notice) for the foreign organization. The January 1972 gift is allowable as a deduction under section 2522 because the taxable year ending May 31, 1972, is an exempt year for the organization. [Reg. § 53.4948-1.]

☐ [T.D. 7218, 11-9-72.]

BLACK LUNG BENEFIT TRUSTS

[Reg. § 53.4951-1]

§ 53.4951-1. Black lung trusts—taxes on self-dealing.—(a) *In general.*—Section 4951 contains provisions that correspond to provisions of section 4941 (relating to taxes on foundation self-dealing) and section 4946 (relating to definitions and special rules). Regulations and rulings under these corresponding provisions apply to section 4951 where appropriate.

(b) *Transfer of property to trust.*—A transfer of personal property without consideration to a trust for which a deduction is allowable under section 192 does not constitute a sale or exchange for purposes of section 4951 unless the property is subject to a mortgage or similar lien within section 4951(d)(2)(A). The transfer to a trust of a note or other evidence of indebtedness constitutes an extension of credit to the obligor for purposes of section 4951(d)(1)(B).

(c) *Deposits.*—A time or demand deposit made with a bank or credit union that is a trustee or other disqualified person with respect to a trust constitutes a lending of money for purposes of section 4951(d)(1)(B) even though the deposit is of a kind generally authorized for investments by the trust.

(d) *Trustee.*—The term "trustee" as used in section 4951(e)(5)(B) includes any person having powers or responsibilities with respect to a trust similar to those of trustees.

(e) *Misallocation of insurance premium.*—Under section 501(c)(21)(A)(ii) and § 1.501(c)(21)-1(d), a trust may pay a portion of a premium for insurance which covers both black lung liabilities and other liabilities, so long as the requirements of

section 501(c)(21)(A)(i) concerning allocation of the total premium are met. However, if an insurance company misallocates the total premium in a manner which benefits a disqualified person, the amount of misallocation constitutes a use of trust assets for the benefit of the disqualified person within section 4951(d)(1)(D). For these purposes, it is irrelevant whether the combination of insurance is sold under one policy or more than one policy.

(f) *Effective date.*—Section 4951 applies with respect to acts that occur after December 31, 1977, in and for trust taxable years beginning after December 31, 1977. [Reg. § 53.4951-1.]

☐ [T.D. 7644, 9-6-79.]

[Reg. § 53.4952-1]

§ 53.4952-1. Black lung trusts—taxes on taxable expenditures.—(a) *In general.*—Section 4952 contains provisions that generally correspond to provisions of section 4945 (relating to taxes on taxable expenditures by private foundations) and section 4946 (relating to definitions and special rules). Regulations and rulings under these corresponding provisions apply to section 4952 where appropriate. See section 4952(e)(1) for the definition of "correction".

(b) *Unauthorized investments.*—The term "taxable expenditure" in section 4952(d) includes an investment that is not authorized under section 501(c)(21)(B)(ii).

(c) *Effective date.*—Section 4952 applies with respect to expenditures made after December 31, 1977, in and for trust taxable years beginning after December 31, 1977. [Reg. § 53.4952-1.]

☐ [T.D. 7644, 9-6-79.]

TAXES ON POLITICAL EXPENDITURES

[Reg. § 53.4955-1]

§ 53.4955-1. Tax on political expenditures.—(a) *Relationship between section 4955 excise taxes and substantive standards for exemption under section 501(c)(3).*—The excise taxes imposed by section 4955 do not affect the substantive standards for tax exemption under section 501(c)(3). under which an organization is described in section 501(c)(3) only if it does not participate or inter-

vene in any political campaign on behalf of any candidate for public office.

(b) *Imposition of initial taxes on organization managers.*—(1) *In general.*—The excise tax under section 4955(a)(2) on the agreement of any organization manager to the making of a political expenditure by a section 501(c)(3) organization is imposed only in cases where—

(i) A tax is imposed by section 4955(a)(1);

(ii) The organization manager knows that the expenditure to which the manager agrees is a political expenditure; and

(iii) The agreement is willful and is not due to reasonable cause.

(2) *Type of organization managers covered.*— *(i) In general.*—The tax under section 4955(a)(2) is imposed only on those organization managers who are authorized to approve, or to exercise discretion in recommending approval of, the making of the expenditure by the organization and on those organization managers who are members of a group (such as the organization's board of directors or trustees) which is so authorized.

(ii) *Officer.*—For purposes of section 4955(f)(2)(A), a person is an officer of an organization if—

(A) That person is specifically so designated under the certificate of incorporation, bylaws, or other constitutive documents of the foundation; or

(B) That person regularly exercises general authority to make administrative or policy decisions on behalf of the organization. Independent contractors, acting in a capacity as attorneys, accountants, and investment managers and advisors, are not officers. With respect to any expenditure, any person described in this paragraph (b)(2)(ii)(B) who has authority merely to recommend particular administrative or policy decisions, but not to implement them without approval of a superior, is not an officer.

(iii) *Employee.*—For purposes of section 4955(f)(2)(B), an individual rendering services to an organization is an employee of the organization only if that individual is an employee within the meaning of section 3121(d)(2). With respect to any expenditure, an employee (other than an officer, director, or trustee of the organization) is described in section 4955(f)(2)(B) only if he or she has final authority or responsibility (either officially or effectively) with respect to such expenditure.

(3) *Type of agreement required.*—An organization manager agrees to the making of a political expenditure if the manager manifests approval of the expenditure which is sufficient to constitute an exercise of the organization manager's authority to approve, or to exercise discretion in recommending approval of, the making of the expenditure by the organization. The manifestation of approval need not be the final or decisive approval on behalf of the organization.

(4) Knowing—

(i) *General rule.*—For purposes of section 4955, an organization manager is considered to have agreed to an expenditure *knowing* that it is a political expenditure only if—

(A) The manager has actual knowledge of sufficient facts so that, based solely upon these facts, the expenditure would be a political expenditure;

(B) The manager is aware that such an expenditure under these circumstances may violate the provisions of federal tax law governing political expenditures; and

(C) The manager negligently fails to make reasonable attempts to ascertain whether the expenditure is a political expenditure, or the manager is aware that it is a political expenditure.

(ii) *Amplification of general rule.*—For purposes of section 4955, knowing does not mean having reason to know. However, evidence tending to show that an organization manager has reason to know of a particular fact or particular rule is relevant in determining whether the manager had actual knowledge of the fact or rule. Thus, for example, evidence tending to show that an organization manager has reason to know of sufficient facts so that, based solely upon those facts, an expenditure would be a political expenditure is relevant in determining whether the manager has actual knowledge of the facts.

(5) *Willful.*—An organization manager's agreement to a political expenditure is willful if it is voluntary, conscious, and intentional. No motive to avoid the restrictions of the law or the incurrence of any tax is necessary to make an agreement willful. However, an organization manager's agreement to a political expenditure is not willful if the manager does not know that it is a political expenditure.

(6) *Due to reasonable cause.*—An organization manager's actions are due to reasonable cause if the manager has exercised his or her responsibility on behalf of the organization with ordinary business care and prudence.

(7) *Advice of counsel.*—An organization manager's agreement to an expenditure is ordinarily not considered knowing or willful and is ordinarily considered due to reasonable cause if the manager, after full disclosure of the factual situation to legal counsel (including house counsel), relies on the advice of counsel expressed in a reasoned written legal opinion that an expenditure is not a political expenditure under section 4955 (or that expenditures conforming to certain guidelines are not political expenditures). For this purpose, a written legal opinion is considered reasoned even if it reaches a conclusion which is subsequently determined to be incorrect, so long as the opinion addresses itself to the facts and applicable law. A written legal opinion is not considered reasoned if it does nothing more than recite the facts and express a conclusion. However, the absence of advice of counsel with respect to an expenditure does not, by itself, give rise to any inference that an organization manager agreed to the making of the expenditure knowingly, willfully, or without reasonable cause.

(8) *Cross reference.*—For provisions relating to the burden of proof in cases involving the issue of whether an organization manager has

Reg. §53.4955-1(b)(8)

knowingly agreed to the making of a political expenditure, see section 7454(b).

(c) Amplification of political expenditure definition

(1) *General rule.*—Any expenditure that would cause an organization that makes the expenditure to be classified as an action organization by reason of § 1.501(c)(3)-1(c)(3)(iii) of this chapter is a political expenditure within the meaning of section 4955(d)(1).

(2) *Other political expenditures.*—(i) For purposes of section 4955(d)(2), an organization is effectively controlled by a candidate or prospective candidate only if the individual has a continuing, substantial involvement in the day-to-day operations or management of the organization. An organization is not effectively controlled by a candidate or a prospective candidate merely because it is affiliated with the candidate, or merely because the candidate knows the directors, officers, or employees of the organization. The effectively controlled test is not met merely because the organization carries on its research, study, or other educational activities with respect to subject matter or issues in which the individual is interested or with which the individual is associated.

(ii) For purposes of section 4955(d)(2), a determination of whether the primary purpose of an organization is promoting the candidacy or prospective candidacy of an individual for public office is made on the basis of all the facts and circumstances. The factors to be considered include whether the surveys, studies, materials, etc. prepared by the organization are made available only to the candidate or are made available to the general public; and whether the organization pays for speeches and travel expenses for only one individual, or for speeches or travel expenses of several persons. The fact that a candidate or prospective candidate utilizes studies, papers, materials, etc., prepared by the organization (such as in a speech by the candidate) is not to be considered as a factor indicating that the organization has a purpose of promoting the candidacy or prospective candidacy of that individual where such studies, papers, materials, etc. are not made available only to that individual.

(iii) Expenditures for voter registration, voter turnout, or voter education constitute other expenses, treated as political expenditures by reason of section 4955(d)(2)(E), only if the expenditures violate the prohibition on political activity provided in section 501(c)(3).

(d) *Abatement, refund, or no assessment of initial tax.*—No initial (first-tier) tax will be imposed under section 4955(a), or the initial tax will be abated or refunded, if the organization or an organization manager establishes to the satisfaction of the IRS that—

(1) The political expenditure was not willful and flagrant; and

(2) The political expenditure was corrected.

(e) Correction.—(1) *Recovery of Expenditure.*—For purposes of section 4955(f)(3) and this section, correction of a political expenditure is accomplished by recovering part or all of the expenditure to the extent recovery is possible, and, where full recovery cannot be accomplished, by any additional corrective action which the Commissioner may prescribe. The organization making the political expenditure is not under any obligation to attempt to recover the expenditure by legal action if the action would in all probability not result in the satisfaction of execution on a judgment.

(2) *Establishing safeguards.*—Correction of a political expenditure must also involve the establishment of sufficient safeguards to prevent future political expenditures by the organization. The determination of whether safeguards are sufficient to prevent future political expenditures by the organization is made by the District Director.

(f) *Effective date.*—This section is effective December 5, 1995. [Reg. § 53.4955-1.]

☐ [*T.D.* 8628, 12-4-95.]

EXCESS BENEFIT TRANSACTIONS

(3) Contemporaneous substantiation.

   (i) Reporting of benefit.

     (A) In general.

     (B) Failure to report due to reasonable cause.

     (ii) Other written contemporaneous evidence.

   (4) Examples.

§ 53.4958-5 Transaction in which the amount of the economic benefit is determined in whole or in part by the revenues of one or more activities of the organization.—[Reserved]

§ 53.4958-6 Rebuttable presumption that a transaction is not an excess benefit transaction.

   (a) In general.

   (b) Rebutting the presumption.

   (c) Requirements for invoking rebuttable presumption.

    (1) Approval by an authorized body.

     (i) In general.

     (ii) Individuals not included on authorized body.

     (iii) Absence of conflict of interest.

    (2) Appropriate data as to comparability.

     (i) In general.

     (ii) Special rule for compensation paid by small organizations.

     (iii) Application of special rule for small organizations.

     (iv) Examples.

    (3) Documentation.

   (d) No presumption with respect to non-fixed payments until amounts are determined.

    (1) In general.

    (2) Special rule for certain non-fixed payments subject to a cap.

   (e) No inference from absence of presumption.

   (f) Period of reliance on rebuttable presumption.

§ 53.4958-7 Correction.

   (a) In general.

   (b) Form of correction.

    (1) Cash or cash equivalents.

    (2) Anti-abuse rule.

    (3) Special rule relating to nonqualified deferred compensation.

    (4) Return of specific property.

     (i) In general.

     (ii) Payment not equal to correction amount.

     (iii) Disqualified person may not participate in decision.

   (c) Correction amount.

   (d) Correction where contract has been partially performed.

   (e) Correction in the case of an applicable tax-exempt organization that has ceased to exist, or is no longer tax-exempt.

    (1) In general.

    (2) Section 501(c)(3) organizations.

    (3) Section 501(c)(4) organizations.

   (f) Examples.

§ 53.4958-8 Special rules.

   (a) Substantive requirements for exemption still apply.

   (b) Interaction between section 4958 and section 7611 rules for church tax inquiries and examinations.

   (c) Other substantiation requirements.

[Reg. § 53.4958-0.]

  ☐ [T.D. 8978, 1-22-2002.]

[Reg. § 53.4958-1]

§ 53.4958-1. Taxes on excess benefit transactions.—(a) *In general.*—Section 4958 imposes excise taxes on each excess benefit transaction (as defined in section 4958(c) and § 53.4958-4) between an applicable tax-exempt organization (as defined in section 4958(e) and § 53.4958-2) and a disqualified person (as defined in section 4958(f)(1) and § 53.4958-3). A disqualified person who receives an excess benefit from an excess benefit transaction is liable for payment of a section 4958(a)(1) excise tax equal to 25 percent of the excess benefit. If an initial tax is imposed by section 4958(a)(1) on an excess benefit transaction and the transaction is not corrected (as defined in section 4958(f)(6) and § 53.4958-7) within the taxable period (as defined in section 4958(f)(5) and paragraph (c)(2)(ii) of this section), then any disqualified person who received an excess benefit from the excess benefit transaction on which the initial tax was imposed is liable for an additional tax of 200 percent of the excess benefit. An organization manager (as defined in section 4958(f)(2) and paragraph (d) of this section) who participates in an excess benefit transaction, knowing that it was such a transaction, is liable for payment of a section 4958(a)(2) excise tax equal to 10 percent of the excess benefit, unless the participation was not willful and was due to reasonable cause. If an organization manager also receives an excess benefit from an excess benefit transaction, the manager may be liable for both taxes imposed by section 4958(a).

(b) *Excess benefit defined.*—An excess benefit is the amount by which the value of the economic benefit provided by an applicable tax-exempt organization directly or indirectly to or for the use of any disqualified person exceeds the value of the consideration (including the performance of services) received for providing such benefit.

(c) *Taxes paid by disqualified person.*—(1) *Initial tax.*—Section 4958(a)(1) imposes a tax equal to 25 percent of the excess benefit on each excess benefit transaction. The section 4958(a)(1) tax shall be paid by any disqualified person who received an excess benefit from that excess benefit transaction. With respect to any excess benefit transaction, if more than one disqualified person is liable for the tax imposed by section 4958(a)(1), all such persons are jointly and severally liable for that tax.

(2) *Additional tax on disqualified person.*—(i) *In general.*—Section 4958(b) imposes a tax

equal to 200 percent of the excess benefit in any case in which section 4958(a)(1) imposes a 25-percent tax on an excess benefit transaction and the transaction is not corrected (as defined in section 4958(f)(6) and §53.4958-7) within the taxable period (as defined in section 4958(f)(5) and paragraph (c)(2)(ii) of this section). If a disqualified person makes a payment of less than the full correction amount under the rules of §53.4958-7, the 200-percent tax is imposed only on the unpaid portion of the correction amount (as described in §53.4958-7(c)). The tax imposed by section 4958(b) is payable by any disqualified person who received an excess benefit from the excess benefit transaction on which the initial tax was imposed by section 4958(a)(1). With respect to any excess benefit transaction, if more than one disqualified person is liable for the tax imposed by section 4958(b), all such persons are jointly and severally liable for that tax.

(ii) *Taxable period.*—*Taxable period* means, with respect to any excess benefit transaction, the period beginning with the date on which the transaction occurs and ending on the earlier of—

(A) The date of mailing a notice of deficiency under section 6212 with respect to the section 4958(a)(1) tax; or

(B) The date on which the tax imposed by section 4958(a)(1) is assessed.

(iii) *Abatement if correction during the correction period.*—For rules relating to abatement of taxes on excess benefit transactions that are corrected within the correction period, as defined in section 4963(e), see sections 4961(a), 4962(a), and the regulations thereunder. The abatement rules of section 4961 specifically provide for a 90-day correction period after the date of mailing a notice of deficiency under section 6212 with respect to the section 4958(b) 200-percent tax. If the excess benefit is corrected during that correction period, the 200-percent tax imposed shall not be assessed, and if assessed the assessment shall be abated, and if collected shall be credited or refunded as an overpayment. For special rules relating to abatement of the 25-percent tax, see section 4962.

(d) *Tax paid by organization managers.*—(1) *In general.*—In any case in which section 4958(a)(1) imposes a tax, section 4958(a)(2) imposes a tax equal to 10 percent of the excess benefit on the participation of any organization manager who knowingly participated in the excess benefit transaction, unless such participation was not willful and was due to reasonable cause. Any organization manager who so participated in the excess benefit transaction must pay the tax.

(2) *Organization manager defined.*—(i) *In general.*—An organization manager is, with respect to any applicable tax-exempt organization, any officer, director, or trustee of such organization, or any individual having powers or responsibilities similar to those of officers, directors, or trustees of the organization, regardless of title. A person is an officer of an organization if that person—

(A) Is specifically so designated under the certificate of incorporation, by-laws, or other constitutive documents of the organization; or

(B) Regularly exercises general authority to make administrative or policy decisions on behalf of the organization. A contractor who acts solely in a capacity as an attorney, accountant, or investment manager or advisor, is not an officer. For purposes of this paragraph (d)(2)(i)(B), any person who has authority merely to recommend particular administrative or policy decisions, but not to implement them without approval of a superior, is not an officer.

(ii) *Special rule for certain committee members.*—An individual who is not an officer, director, or trustee, yet serves on a committee of the governing body of an applicable tax-exempt organization (or as a designee of the governing body described in §53.4958-6(c)(1)) that is attempting to invoke the rebuttable presumption of reasonableness described in §53.4958-6 based on the committee's (or designee's) actions, is an organization manager for purposes of the tax imposed by section 4958(a)(2).

(3) *Participation.*—For purposes of section 4958(a)(2) and this paragraph (d), participation includes silence or inaction on the part of an organization manager where the manager is under a duty to speak or act, as well as any affirmative action by such manager. An organization manager is not considered to have participated in an excess benefit transaction, however, where the manager has opposed the transaction in a manner consistent with the fulfillment of the manager's responsibilities to the applicable tax-exempt organization.

(4) *Knowing.*—(i) *In general.*—For purposes of section 4958(a)(2) and this paragraph (d), a manager participates in a transaction knowingly only if the person—

(A) Has actual knowledge of sufficient facts so that, based solely upon those facts, such transaction would be an excess benefit transaction;

(B) Is aware that such a transaction under these circumstances may violate the provisions of Federal tax law governing excess benefit transactions; and

(C) Negligently fails to make reasonable attempts to ascertain whether the transaction is an excess benefit transaction, or the manager is in fact aware that it is such a transaction.

(ii) *Amplification of general rule.*—*Knowing* does not mean having reason to know. However, evidence tending to show that a manager has reason to know of a particular fact or particular rule is relevant in determining whether the manager had actual knowledge of such a fact or rule. Thus, for example, evidence tending to show that a manager has reason to know of sufficient facts so that, based solely upon such facts, a transaction would be an excess benefit transaction is relevant in determining whether the manager has actual knowledge of such facts.

(iii) *Reliance on professional advice.*—An organization manager's participation in a transaction is ordinarily not considered knowing within the meaning of section 4958(a)(2), even though the transaction is subsequently held to be an excess benefit transaction, to the extent that, after full disclosure of the factual situation to an appropriate professional, the organization manager relies on a reasoned written opinion of that professional with respect to elements of the transaction within the professional's expertise. For purposes of section 4958(a)(2) and this paragraph (d), a written opinion is reasoned even though it reaches a conclusion that is subsequently determined to be incorrect so long as the opinion addresses itself to the facts and the applicable standards. However, a written opinion is not reasoned if it does nothing more than recite the facts and express a conclusion. The absence of a written opinion of an appropriate professional with respect to a transaction shall not, by itself, however, give rise to any inference that an organization manager participated in the transaction knowingly. For purposes of this paragraph, appropriate professionals on whose written opinion an organization manager may rely, are limited to—

    (A) Legal counsel, including in-house counsel;

    (B) Certified public accountants or accounting firms with expertise regarding the relevant tax law matters; and

    (C) Independent valuation experts who—

        (1) Hold themselves out to the public as appraisers or compensation consultants;

        (2) Perform the relevant valuations on a regular basis;

        (3) Are qualified to make valuations of the type of property or services involved; and

        (4) Include in the written opinion a certification that the requirements of paragraphs (d)(4)(iii)(C)(*1*) through (*3*) of this section are met.

    (iv) *Satisfaction of rebuttable presumption of reasonableness.*—An organization manager's participation in a transaction is ordinarily not considered knowing within the meaning of section 4958(a)(2), even though the transaction is subsequently held to be an excess benefit transaction, if the appropriate authorized body has met the requirements of § 53.4958-6(a) with respect to the transaction.

    (5) *Willful.*—For purposes of section 4958(a)(2) and this paragraph (d), participation by an organization manager is willful if it is voluntary, conscious, and intentional. No motive to avoid the restrictions of the law or the incurrence of any tax is necessary to make the participation willful. However, participation by an organization manager is not willful if the manager does not know that the transaction in which the manager is participating is an excess benefit transaction.

    (6) *Due to reasonable cause.*—An organization manager's participation is due to reasonable cause if the manager has exercised responsibility on behalf of the organization with ordinary business care and prudence.

    (7) *Limits on liability for management.*—The maximum aggregate amount of tax collectible under section 4958(a)(2) and this paragraph (d) from organization managers with respect to any one excess benefit transaction is $10,000.

    (8) *Joint and several liability.*—In any case where more than one person is liable for a tax imposed by section 4958(a)(2), all such persons shall be jointly and severally liable for the taxes imposed under section 4958(a)(2) with respect to that excess benefit transaction.

    (9) *Burden of proof.*—For provisions relating to the burden of proof in cases involving the issue of whether an organization manager has knowingly participated in an excess benefit transaction, see section 7454(b) and § 301.7454-2 of this chapter. In these cases, the Commissioner bears the burden of proof.

    (e) *Date of occurrence.*—(1) *In general.*—Except as otherwise provided, an excess benefit transaction occurs on the date on which the disqualified person receives the economic benefit for Federal income tax purposes. When a single contractual arrangement provides for a series of compensation or other payments to (or for the use of) a disqualified person over the course of the disqualified person's taxable year (or part of a taxable year), any excess benefit transaction with respect to these aggregate payments is deemed to occur on the last day of the taxable year (or if the payments continue for part of the year, the date of the last payment in the series).

    (2) *Special rules.*—In the case of benefits provided pursuant to a qualified pension, profit-sharing, or stock bonus plan, the transaction occurs on the date the benefit is vested. In the case of a transfer of property that is subject to a substantial risk of forfeiture or in the case of rights to future compensation or property (including benefits under a nonqualified deferred compensation plan), the transaction occurs on the date the property, or the rights to future compensation or property, is not subject to a substantial risk of forfeiture. However, where the disqualified person elects to include an amount in gross income in the taxable year of transfer pursuant to section 83(b), the general rule of paragraph (e)(1) of this section applies to the property with respect to which the section 83(b) election is made. Any excess benefit transaction with respect to benefits under a deferred compensation plan which vest during any taxable year of the disqualified person is deemed to occur on the last day of such taxable year. For the rules governing the timing of the reasonableness determination for deferred, contingent, and certain other noncash compensation, see § 53.4958-4(b)(2).

(3) *Statute of limitations rules.*—See sections 6501(e)(3) and (l) and the regulations thereunder for statute of limitations rules as they apply to section 4958 excise taxes.

(f) *Effective date for imposition of taxes.*—(1) *In general.*—The section 4958 taxes imposed on excess benefit transactions or on participation in excess benefit transactions apply to transactions occurring on or after September 14, 1995.

(2) *Existing binding contracts.*—The section 4958 taxes do not apply to any transaction occurring pursuant to a written contract that was binding on September 13, 1995, and at all times thereafter before the transaction occurs. A written binding contract that is terminable or subject to cancellation by the applicable tax-exempt organization without the disqualified person's consent (including as the result of a breach of contract by the disqualified person) and without substantial penalty to the organization, is no longer treated as a binding contract as of the earliest date that any such termination or cancellation, if made, would be effective. If a binding written contract is materially changed, it is treated as a new contract entered into as of the date the material change is effective. A material change includes an extension or renewal of the contract (other than an extension or renewal that results from the person contracting with the applicable tax-exempt organization unilaterally exercising an option expressly granted by the contract), or a more than incidental change to any payment under the contract. [Reg. § 53.4958-1.]

☐ [*T.D.* 8978, 1-22-2002.]

[Reg. § 53.4958-2]

§ 53.4958-2. Definition of applicable tax-exempt organization.—(a) *Organizations described in section 501(c)(3) or (4) and exempt from tax under section 501(a).*—(1) *In general.*—An applicable tax-exempt organization is any organization that, without regard to any excess benefit, would be described in section 501(c)(3) or (4) and exempt from tax under section 501(a). An applicable tax-exempt organization also includes any organization that was described in section 501(c)(3) or (4) and was exempt from tax under section 501(a) at any time during a five-year period ending on the date of an excess benefit transaction (the lookback period).

(2) *Exceptions from definition of applicable tax-exempt organization.*—(i) *Private foundation.*—A private foundation as defined in section 509(a) is not an applicable tax-exempt organization for section 4958 purposes.

(ii) *Governmental unit or affiliate.*—A governmental unit or an affiliate of a governmental unit is not an applicable tax-exempt organization for section 4958 purposes if it is—

(A) Exempt from (or not subject to) taxation without regard to section 501(a); or

(B) Relieved from filing an annual return pursuant to the authority of § 1.6033-2(g)(6).

(3) *Organizations described in section 501(c)(3).*—An organization is described in section 501(c)(3) for purposes of section 4958 only if the organization—

(i) Provides the notice described in section 508; or

(ii) Is described in section 501(c)(3) and specifically is excluded from the requirements of section 508 by that section.

(4) *Organizations described in section 501(c)(4).*—An organization is described in section 501(c)(4) for purposes of section 4958 only if the organization—

(i) Has applied for and received recognition from the Internal Revenue Service as an organization described in section 501(c)(4); or

(ii) Has filed an application for recognition under section 501(c)(4) with the Internal Revenue Service, has filed an annual information return as a section 501(c)(4) organization under the Internal Revenue Code or regulations promulgated thereunder, or has otherwise held itself out as being described in section 501(c)(4) and exempt from tax under section 501(a).

(5) *Effect of non-recognition or revocation of exempt status.*—An organization is not described in paragraph (a)(3) or (4) of this section during any period covered by a final determination or adjudication that the organization is not exempt from tax under section 501(a) as an organization described in section 501(c)(3) or (4), so long as that determination or adjudication is not based upon participation in inurement or one or more excess benefit transactions. However, the organization may be an applicable tax-exempt organization for that period as a result of the five-year lookback period described in paragraph (a)(1) of this section.

(6) *Examples.*—The following examples illustrate the principles of this section, which defines an applicable tax-exempt organization for purposes of section 4958:

Example 1. O is a nonprofit corporation formed under state law. O filed its application for recognition of exemption under section 501(c)(3) within the time prescribed under section 508(a). In its application, O described its plans for purchasing property from some of its directors at prices that would exceed fair market value. After reviewing the application, the IRS determined that because of the proposed property purchase transactions, O failed to establish that it met the requirements for an organization described in section 501(c)(3). Accordingly, the IRS denied O's application. While O's application was pending, O engaged in the purchase transactions described in its application at prices that exceeded the fair market values of the properties. Although these transactions would constitute excess benefit transactions under section 4958, because the IRS never recognized O as an organization described in section 501(c)(3), O was never an applicable tax-exempt organization under section 4958. Therefore, these transactions are not subject to the excise taxes provided in section 4958.

Example 2. O is a nonprofit corporation formed under state law. O files its application for recognition of exemption under section 501(c)(3) within the time prescribed under section 508(a). The IRS issues a favorable determination letter in Year 1 that recognizes O as an organization described in section 501(c)(3). Subsequently, in Year 5 of O's operations, O engages in certain transactions that constitute excess benefit transactions under section 4958 and violate the proscription against inurement under section 501(c)(3) and § 1.501(c)(3)-1(c)(2). The IRS examines the Form 990, "Return of Organization Exempt From Income Tax", that O filed for Year 5. After considering all the relevant facts and circumstances in accordance with § 1.501(c)(3)-1(f), the IRS concludes that O is no longer described in section 501(c)(3) effective in Year 5. The IRS does not examine the Forms 990 that O filed for its first four years of operations and, accordingly, does not revoke O's exempt status for those years. Although O's tax-exempt status is revoked effective in Year 5, under the *lookback* rules in paragraph (a)(1) of this section and § 53.4958-3(a)(1) of this chapter, during the five-year period prior to the excess benefit transactions that occurred in Year 5, O was an applicable tax-exempt organization and O's directors were disqualified persons as to O. Therefore, the transactions between O and its directors during Year 5 are subject to the applicable excise taxes provided in section 4958.

(b) *Special rules.*—(1) *Transition rule for lookback period.*—In the case of any excess benefit transaction occurring before September 14, 2000, the lookback period described in paragraph (a)(1) of this section begins on September 14, 1995, and ends on the date of the transaction.

(2) *Certain foreign organizations.*—A foreign organization, recognized by the Internal Revenue Service or by treaty, that receives substantially all of its support (other than gross investment income) from sources outside of the United States is not an organization described in section 501(c)(3) or (4) for purposes of section 4958. [Reg. § 53.4958-2.]

☐ [*T.D.* 8978, 1-22-2002 *and T.D.* 9390, 3-27-08.]

[Reg. § 53.4958-3]

§ 53.4958-3. Definition of disqualified person.—(a) *In general.*—(1) *Scope of definition.*— Section 4958(f)(1) defines *disqualified person,* with respect to any transaction, as any person who was in a position to exercise substantial influence over the affairs of an applicable tax-exempt organization at any time during the five-year period ending on the date of the transaction (the lookback period). Paragraph (b) of this section describes persons who are defined to be disqualified persons under the statute, including certain family members of an individual in a position to exercise substantial influence, and certain 35-percent controlled entities. Paragraph (c) of this section describes persons in a position to exercise

substantial influence over the affairs of an applicable tax-exempt organization by virtue of their powers and responsibilities or certain interests they hold. Paragraph (d) of this section describes persons deemed not to be in a position to exercise substantial influence. Whether any person who is not described in paragraph (b), (c) or (d) of this section is a disqualified person with respect to a transaction for purposes of section 4958 is based on all relevant facts and circumstances, as described in paragraph (e) of this section. Paragraph (f) of this section describes special rules for affiliated organizations. Examples in paragraph (g) of this section illustrate these categories of persons.

(2) *Transition rule for lookback period.*—In the case of any excess benefit transaction occurring before September 14, 2000, the lookback period described in paragraph (a)(1) of this section begins on September 14, 1995, and ends on the date of the transaction.

(b) *Statutory categories of disqualified persons.*— (1) *Family members.*—A person is a disqualified person with respect to any transaction with an applicable tax-exempt organization if the person is a member of the family of a person who is a disqualified person described in paragraph (a) of this section (other than as a result of this paragraph) with respect to any transaction with the same organization. For purposes of the following sentence, a legally adopted child of an individual is treated as a child of such individual by blood. A person's family is limited to—

(i) Spouse;

(ii) Brothers or sisters (by whole or half blood);

(iii) Spouses of brothers or sisters (by whole or half blood);

(iv) Ancestors;

(v) Children;

(vi) Grandchildren;

(vii) Great grandchildren; and

(viii) Spouses of children, grandchildren, and great grandchildren.

(2) *Thirty-five percent controlled entities.*— (i) *In general.*—A person is a disqualified person with respect to any transaction with an applicable tax-exempt organization if the person is a 35-percent controlled entity. A 35-percent controlled entity is—

(A) A corporation in which persons described in this section (except in paragraphs (b)(2) and (d) of this section) own more than 35 percent of the combined voting power;

(B) A partnership in which persons described in this section (except in paragraphs (b)(2) and (d) of this section) own more than 35 percent of the profits interest; or

(C) A trust or estate in which persons described in this section (except in paragraphs (b)(2) and (d) of this section) own more than 35 percent of the beneficial interest.

(ii) *Combined voting power.*—For purposes of this paragraph (b)(2), combined voting power includes voting power represented by holdings of voting stock, direct or indirect, but does not include voting rights held only as a director, trustee, or other fiduciary.

(iii) *Constructive ownership rules.*— (A) *Stockholdings.*—For purposes of section 4958(f)(3) and this paragraph (b)(2), indirect stockholdings are taken into account as under section 267(c), except that in applying section 267(c)(4), the family of an individual shall include the members of the family specified in section 4958(f)(4) and paragraph (b)(1) of this section.

(B) *Profits or beneficial interest.*—For purposes of section 4958(f)(3) and this paragraph (b)(2), the ownership of profits or beneficial interests shall be determined in accordance with the rules for constructive ownership of stock provided in section 267(c) (other than section 267(c)(3)), except that in applying section 267(c)(4), the family of an individual shall include the members of the family specified in section 4958(f)(4) and paragraph (b)(1) of this section.

(c) *Persons having substantial influence.*—A person who holds any of the following powers, responsibilities, or interests is in a position to exercise substantial influence over the affairs of an applicable tax-exempt organization:

(1) *Voting members of the governing body.*— This category includes any individual serving on the governing body of the organization who is entitled to vote on any matter over which the governing body has authority.

(2) *Presidents, chief executive officers, or chief operating officers.*—This category includes any person who, regardless of title, has ultimate responsibility for implementing the decisions of the governing body or for supervising the management, administration, or operation of the organization. A person who serves as president, chief executive officer, or chief operating officer has this ultimate responsibility unless the person demonstrates otherwise. If this ultimate responsibility resides with two or more individuals (e.g., co-presidents), who may exercise such responsibility in concert or individually, then each individual is in a position to exercise substantial influence over the affairs of the organization.

(3) *Treasurers and chief financial officers.*—This category includes any person who, regardless of title, has ultimate responsibility for managing the finances of the organization. A person who serves as treasurer or chief financial officer has this ultimate responsibility unless the person demonstrates otherwise. If this ultimate responsibility resides with two or more individuals who may exercise the responsibility in concert or individually, then each individual is in a position to exercise substantial influence over the affairs of the organization.

(4) *Persons with a material financial interest in a provider-sponsored organization.*—For purposes of section 4958, if a hospital that participates in a provider-sponsored organization (as defined in section 1855(e) of the Social Security Act, 42 U.S.C. 1395w-25) is an applicable tax-exempt organization, then any person with a material financial interest (within the meaning of section 501(o)) in the provider-sponsored organization has substantial influence with respect to the hospital.

(d) *Persons deemed not to have substantial influence.*—A person is deemed not to be in a position to exercise substantial influence over the affairs of an applicable tax-exempt organization if that person is described in one of the following categories:

(1) *Tax-exempt organizations described in section 501(c)(3).*—This category includes any organization described in section 501(c)(3) and exempt from tax under section 501(a).

(2) *Certain section 501(c)(4) organizations.*— Only with respect to an applicable tax-exempt organization described in section 501(c)(4) and § 53.4958-2(a)(4), this category includes any other organization so described.

(3) *Employees receiving economic benefits of less than a specified amount in a taxable year.*—This category includes, for the taxable year in which benefits are provided, any full-or part-time employee of the applicable tax-exempt organization who—

(i) Receives economic benefits, directly or indirectly from the organization, of less than the amount referenced for a highly compensated employee in section 414(q)(1)(B)(i);

(ii) Is not described in paragraph (b) or (c) of this section with respect to the organization; and

(iii) Is not a substantial contributor to the organization within the meaning of section 507(d)(2)(A), taking into account only contributions received by the organization during its current taxable year and the four preceding taxable years.

(e) *Facts and circumstances govern in all other cases.*—(1) *In general.*—Whether a person who is not described in paragraph (b), (c) or (d) of this section is a disqualified person depends upon all relevant facts and circumstances.

(2) *Facts and circumstances tending to show substantial influence.*—Facts and circumstances tending to show that a person has substantial influence over the affairs of an organization include, but are not limited to, the following—

(i) The person founded the organization;

(ii) The person is a substantial contributor to the organization (within the meaning of section 507(d)(2)(A)), taking into account only contributions received by the organization during its current taxable year and the four preceding taxable years;

(iii) The person's compensation is primarily based on revenues derived from activities of the organization, or of a particular department or function of the organization, that the person controls;

(iv) The person has or shares authority to control or determine a substantial portion of the organization's capital expenditures, operating budget, or compensation for employees;

(v) The person manages a discrete segment or activity of the organization that represents a substantial portion of the activities, assets, income, or expenses of the organization, as compared to the organization as a whole;

(vi) The person owns a controlling interest (measured by either vote or value) in a corporation, partnership, or trust that is a disqualified person; or

(vii) The person is a non-stock organization controlled, directly or indirectly, by one or more disqualified persons.

(3) *Facts and circumstances tending to show no substantial influence.*—Facts and circumstances tending to show that a person does not have substantial influence over the affairs of an organization include, but are not limited to, the following—

(i) The person has taken a bona fide vow of poverty as an employee, agent, or on behalf, of a religious organization;

(ii) The person is a contractor (such as an attorney, accountant, or investment manager or advisor) whose sole relationship to the organization is providing professional advice (without having decision-making authority) with respect to transactions from which the contractor will not economically benefit either directly or indirectly (aside from customary fees received for the professional advice rendered);

(iii) The direct supervisor of the individual is not a disqualified person;

(iv) The person does not participate in any management decisions affecting the organization as a whole or a discrete segment or activity of the organization that represents a substantial portion of the activities, assets, income, or expenses of the organization, as compared to the organization as a whole; or

(v) Any preferential treatment a person receives based on the size of that person's contribution is also offered to all other donors making a comparable contribution as part of a solicitation intended to attract a substantial number of contributions.

(f) *Affiliated organizations.*—In the case of multiple organizations affiliated by common control or governing documents, the determination of whether a person does or does not have substantial influence shall be made separately for each applicable tax-exempt organization. A person may be a disqualified person with respect to transactions with more than one applicable tax-exempt organization.

(g) *Examples.*—The following examples illustrate the principles of this section. A finding that a person is a disqualified person in the following examples does not indicate that an excess benefit transaction has occurred. If a person is a disqualified person, the rules of section 4958(c) and §53.4958-4 apply to determine whether an excess benefit transaction has occurred. The examples are as follows:

Example 1. N, an artist by profession, works part-time at R, a local museum. In the first taxable year in which R employs N, R pays N a salary and provides no additional benefits to N except for free admission to the museum, a benefit R provides to all of its employees and volunteers. The total economic benefits N receives from R during the taxable year are less than the amount referenced for a highly compensated employee in section 414(q)(1)(B)(i). The part-time job constitutes N's only relationship with R. N is not related to any other disqualified person with respect to R. N is deemed not to be in a position to exercise substantial influence over the affairs of R. Therefore, N is not a disqualified person with respect to R in that year.

Example 2. The facts are the same as in *Example 1*, except that in addition to the salary that R pays N for N's services during the taxable year, R also purchases one of N's paintings for x. The total of N's salary plus x exceeds the amount referenced for highly compensated employees in section 414(q)(1)(B)(i). Consequently, whether N is in a position to exercise substantial influence over the affairs of R for that taxable year depends upon all of the relevant facts and circumstances.

Example 3. Q is a member of K, a section 501(c)(3) organization with a broad-based public membership. Members of K are entitled to vote only with respect to the annual election of directors and the approval of major organizational transactions such as a merger or dissolution. Q is not related to any other disqualified person of K. Q has no other relationship to K besides being a member of K and occasionally making modest donations to K. Whether Q is a disqualified person is determined by all relevant facts and circumstances. Q's voting rights, which are the same as granted to all members of K, do not place Q in a position to exercise substantial influence over K. Under these facts and circumstances, Q is not a disqualified person with respect K.

Example 4. E is the headmaster of Z, a school that is an applicable tax-exempt organization for purposes of section 4958. E reports to Z's board of trustees and has ultimate responsibility for supervising Z's day-to-day operations. For example, E can hire faculty members and staff, make changes to the school's curriculum and discipline students without specific board approval. Because E has ultimate responsibility for supervising the operation of Z, E is in a position to exercise substantial influence over the affairs of Z. Therefore, E is a disqualified person with respect to Z.

Example 5. Y is an applicable tax-exempt organization for purposes of section 4958 that de-

cides to use bingo games as a method of generating revenue. Y enters into a contract with B, a company that operates bingo games. Under the contract, B manages the promotion and operation of the bingo activity, provides all necessary staff, equipment, and services, and pays Y q percent of the revenue from this activity. B retains the balance of the proceeds. Y provides no goods or services in connection with the bingo operation other than the use of its hall for the bingo games. The annual gross revenue earned from the bingo games represents more than half of Y's total annual revenue. B's compensation is primarily based on revenues from an activity B controls. B also manages a discrete activity of Y that represents a substantial portion of Y's income compared to the organization as a whole. Under these facts and circumstances, B is in a position to exercise substantial influence over the affairs of Y. Therefore, B is a disqualified person with respect to Y.

Example 6. The facts are the same as in *Example 5*, with the additional fact that P owns a majority of the stock of B and is actively involved in managing B. Because P owns a controlling interest (measured by either vote or value) in and actively manages B, P is also in a position to exercise substantial influence over the affairs of Y. Therefore, under these facts and circumstances, P is a disqualified person with respect to Y.

Example 7. A, an applicable tax-exempt organization for purposes of section 4958, owns and operates one acute care hospital. B, a for-profit corporation, owns and operates a number of hospitals. A and B form C, a limited liability company. In exchange for proportional ownership interests, A contributes its hospital, and B contributes other assets, to C. All of A's assets then consist of its membership interest in C. A continues to be operated for exempt purposes based almost exclusively on the activities it conducts through C. C enters into a management agreement with a management company, M, to provide day to day management services to C. Subject to supervision by C's board, M is given broad discretion to manage C's day to day operation and has ultimate responsibility for supervising the management of the hospital. Because M has ultimate responsibility for supervising the management of the hospital operated by C, A's ownership interest in C is its primary asset, and C's activities form the basis for A's continued exemption as an organization described in section 501(c)(3), M is in a position to exercise substantial influence over the affairs of A. Therefore, M is a disqualified person with respect to A.

Example 8. T is a large university and an applicable tax-exempt organization for purposes of section 4958. L is the dean of the College of Law of T, a substantial source of revenue for T, including contributions from alumni and foundations. L is not related to any other disqualified person of T. L does not serve on T's governing body or have ultimate responsibility for managing the university as whole. However, as dean of the College of Law, L plays a key role in faculty hiring and determines a substantial portion of the capital expenditures and operating budget of the College of Law. L's compensation is greater than the amount referenced for a highly compensated employee in section 414(q)(1)(B)(i) in the year benefits are provided. L's management of a discrete segment of T that represents a substantial portion of the income of T (as compared to T as a whole) places L in a position to exercise substantial influence over the affairs of T. Under these facts and circumstances L is a disqualified person with respect to T.

Example 9. S chairs a small academic department in the College of Arts and Sciences of the same university T described in *Example 8*. S is not related to any other disqualified person of T. S does not serve on T's governing body or as an officer of T. As department chair, S supervises faculty in the department, approves the course curriculum, and oversees the operating budget for the department. S's compensation is greater than the amount referenced for a highly compensated employee in section 414(q)(1)(B)(i) in the year benefits are provided. Even though S manages the department, that department does not represent a substantial portion of T's activities, assets, income, expenses, or operating budget. Therefore, S does not participate in any management decisions affecting either T as a whole, or a discrete segment or activity of T that represents a substantial portion of its activities, assets, income, or expenses. Under these facts and circumstances, S does not have substantial influence over the affairs of T, and therefore S is not a disqualified person with respect to T.

Example 10. U is a large acute-care hospital that is an applicable tax-exempt organization for purposes of section 4958. U employs X as a radiologist. X gives instructions to staff with respect to the radiology work X conducts, but X does not supervise other U employees or manage any substantial part of U's operations. X's compensation is primarily in the form of a fixed salary. In addition, X is eligible to receive an incentive award based on revenues of the radiology department. X's compensation is greater than the amount referenced for a highly compensated employee in section 414(q)(1)(B)(i) in the year benefits are provided. X is not related to any other disqualified person of U. X does not serve on U's governing body or as an officer of U. Although U participates in a provider-sponsored organization (as defined in section 1855(e) of the Social Security Act), X does not have a material financial interest in that organization. X does not receive compensation primarily based on revenues derived from activities of U that X controls. X does not participate in any management decisions affecting either U as a whole or a discrete segment of U that represents a substantial portion of its activities, assets, income, or expenses. Under these facts and circumstances, X does not have substantial influence over the affairs of U, and therefore X is not a disqualified person with respect to U.

Example 11. W is a cardiologist and head of the cardiology department of the same hospital U

described in *Example 10*. The cardiology department is a major source of patients admitted to U and consequently represents a substantial portion of U's income, as compared to U as a whole. W does not serve on U's governing board or as an officer of U. W does not have a material financial interest in the provider-sponsored organization (as defined in section 1855(e) of the Social Security Act) in which U participates. W receives a salary and retirement and welfare benefits fixed by a three-year renewable employment contract with U. W's compensation is greater than the amount referenced for a highly compensated employee in section 414(q)(1)(B)(i) in the year benefits are provided. As department head, W manages the cardiology department and has authority to allocate the budget for that department, which includes authority to distribute incentive bonuses among cardiologists according to criteria that W has authority to set. W's management of a discrete segment of U that represents a substantial portion of its income and activities (as compared to U as a whole) places W in a position to exercise substantial influence over the affairs of U. Under these facts and circumstances, W is a disqualified person with respect to U.

Example 12. M is a museum that is an applicable tax-exempt organization for purposes of section 4958. D provides accounting services and tax advice to M as a contractor in return for a fee. D has no other relationship with M and is not related to any disqualified person of M. D does not provide professional advice with respect to any transaction from which D might economically benefit either directly or indirectly (aside from fees received for the professional advice rendered). Because D's sole relationship to M is providing professional advice (without having decision-making authority) with respect to transactions from which D will not economically benefit either directly or indirectly (aside from customary fees received for the professional advice rendered), under these facts and circumstances, D is not a disqualified person with respect to M.

Example 13. F is a repertory theater company that is an applicable tax-exempt organization for purposes of section 4958. F holds a fund-raising campaign to pay for the construction of a new theater. J is a regular subscriber to F's productions who has made modest gifts to F in the past. J has no relationship to F other than as a subscriber and contributor. F solicits contributions as part of a broad public campaign intended to attract a large number of donors, including a substantial number of donors making large gifts. In its solicitations for contributions, F promises to invite all contributors giving $z or more to a special opening production and party held at the new theater. These contributors are also given a special number to call in F's office to reserve tickets for performances, make ticket exchanges, and make other special arrangements for their convenience. J makes a contribution of $z to F, which makes J a substantial contributor within the meaning of section 507(d)(2)(A), taking into account only contributions received by F during its current and the four preceding taxable years. J receives the benefits described in F's solicitation. Because F offers the same benefit to all donors of $z or more, the preferential treatment that J receives does not indicate that J is in a position to exercise substantial influence over the affairs of the organization. Therefore, under these facts and circumstances, J is not a disqualified person with respect to F.

[Reg. §53.4958-3.]

☐ [*T.D.* 8978, 1-22-2002.]

[Reg. §53.4958-4]

§53.4958-4. Excess benefit transaction.— (a) *Definition of excess benefit transaction.*—(1) *In general.*—An *excess benefit transaction* means any transaction in which an economic benefit is provided by an applicable tax-exempt organization directly or indirectly to or for the use of any disqualified person, and the value of the economic benefit provided exceeds the value of the consideration(including the performance of services) received for providing the benefit. Subject to the limitations of paragraph (c) of this section (relating to the treatment of economic benefits as compensation for the performance of services), to determine whether an excess benefit transaction has occurred, all consideration and benefits (except disregarded benefits described in paragraph (a)(4) of this section) exchanged between a disqualified person and the applicable tax-exempt organization and all entities the organization controls(within the meaning of paragraph (a)(2)(ii)(B) of this section) are taken into account. For example, in determining the reasonableness of compensation that is paid (or vests, or is no longer subject to a substantial risk of forfeiture) in one year, services performed in prior years may be taken into account. The rules of this section apply to all transactions with disqualified persons, regardless of whether the amount of the benefit provided is determined, in whole or in part, by the revenues of one or more activities of the organization. For rules regarding valuation standards, see paragraph (b) of this section. For the requirement that an applicable tax-exempt organization clearly indicate its intent to treat a benefit as compensation for services when paid, see paragraph (c) of this section.

(2) *Economic benefit provided indirectly.*— (i) *In general.*—A transaction that would be an excess benefit transaction if the applicable tax-exempt organization engaged in it directly with a disqualified person is likewise an excess benefit transaction when it is accomplished indirectly. An applicable tax-exempt organization may provide an excess benefit indirectly to a disqualified person through a controlled entity or through an intermediary, as described in paragraphs (a)(2)(ii) and (iii) of this section, respectively.

(ii) *Through a controlled entity.*—(A) *In general.*—An applicable tax-exempt organization

may provide an excess benefit indirectly through the use of one or more entities it controls. For purposes of section 4958, economic benefits provided by a controlled entity will be treated as provided by the applicable tax-exempt organization.

(B) *Definition of control.*—(1) *In general.*—For purposes of this paragraph, *control* by an applicable tax-exempt organization means—

(i) In the case of a stock corporation, ownership (by vote or value) of more than 50 percent of the stock in such corporation;

(ii) In the case of a partnership, ownership of more than 50 percent of the profits interests or capital interests in the partnership;

(iii) In the case of a nonstock organization (i.e., an entity in which no person holds a proprietary interest), that at least 50 percent of the directors or trustees of the organization are either representatives (including trustees, directors, agents, or employees) of, or directly or indirectly controlled by, an applicable tax-exempt organization; or

(iv) In the case of any other entity, ownership of more than 50 percent of the beneficial interest in the entity.

(2) *Constructive ownership.*—Section 318 (relating to constructive ownership of stock) shall apply for purposes of determining ownership of stock in a corporation. Similar principles shall apply for purposes of determining ownership of interests in any other entity.

(iii) *Through an intermediary.*—An applicable tax-exempt organization may provide an excess benefit indirectly through an intermediary. An intermediary is any person (including an individual or a taxable or tax-exempt entity) who participates in a transaction with one or more disqualified persons of an applicable tax-exempt organization. For purposes of section 4958, economic benefits provided by an intermediary will be treated as provided by the applicable tax-exempt organization when—

(A) An applicable tax-exempt organization provides an economic benefit to an intermediary; and

(B) In connection with the receipt of the benefit by the intermediary—

(1) There is evidence of an oral or written agreement or understanding that the intermediary will provide economic benefits to or for the use of a disqualified person; or

(2) The intermediary provides economic benefits to or for the use of a disqualified person without a significant business purpose or exempt purpose of its own.

(iv) *Examples.*—The following examples illustrate when economic benefits are provided indirectly under the rules of this paragraph (a)(2):

Example 1. K is an applicable tax-exempt organization for purposes of section 4958. L is a wholly-owned taxable subsidiary of K. J is employed by K, and is a disqualified person with respect to K. K pays J an annual salary of $ 12m, and reports that amount as compensation during calendar year 2001. Although J only performed services for K for nine months of 2001, J performed equivalent services for L during the remaining three months of 2001. Taking into account all of the economic benefits K provided to J, and all of the services J performed for K and L, $12m does not exceed the fair market value of the services J performed for K and L during 2001. Therefore, under these facts, K does not provide an excess benefit to J directly or indirectly.

Example 2. F is an applicable tax-exempt organization for purposes of section 4958. D is an entity controlled by F within the meaning of paragraph (a)(2)(ii)(B) of this section. T is the chief executive officer (CEO) of F. As CEO, T is responsible for overseeing the activities of F. T's duties as CEO make him a disqualified person with respect to F. T's compensation package with F represents the maximum reasonable compensation for T's services as CEO. Thus, any additional economic benefits that F provides to T without T providing additional consideration constitute an excess benefit. D contracts with T to provide enumerated consulting services to D. However, the contract does not require T to perform any additional services for D that T is not already obligated to perform as F's chief executive officer. Therefore, any payment to T pursuant to the consulting contract with D represents an indirect excess benefit that F provides through a controlled entity, even if F, D, or T treats the additional payment to T as compensation.

Example 3. P is an applicable tax-exempt organization for purposes of section 4958. S is a taxable entity controlled by P within the meaning of paragraph (a)(2)(ii)(B) of this section. V is the chief executive officer of S, for which S pays V $w in salary and benefits. V also serves as a voting member of P's governing body. Consequently, V is a disqualified person with respect to P. P provides V with $x representing compensation for the services V provides P as a member of its governing body. Although $x represents reasonable compensation for the services V provides directly to P as a member of its governing body, the total compensation of $w + $x exceeds reasonable compensation for the services V provides to P and S collectively. Therefore, the portion of total compensation that exceeds reasonable compensation is an excess benefit provided to V.

Example 4. G is an applicable tax-exempt organization for section 4958 purposes. F is a disqualified person who was last employed by G in a position of substantial influence three years ago. H is an entity engaged in scientific research and is unrelated to either F or G. G makes a grant to H to fund a research position. H subsequently advertises for qualified candidates for the research position. F is among several highly qualified candidates who apply for the research position. H hires F. There was no evidence of an oral or written agreement or understanding with

G that H will use G's grant to provide economic benefits to or for the use of F. Although G provided economic benefits to H, and in connection with the receipt of such benefits, H will provide economic benefits to or for the use of F, H acted with a significant business purpose or exempt purpose of its own. Under these facts, G did not provide an economic benefit to F indirectly through the use of an intermediary.

(3) *Exception for fixed payments made pursuant to an initial contract.*—(i) *In general.*—Except as provided in paragraph (a)(3)(iv) of this section, section 4958 does not apply to any fixed payment made to a person pursuant to an initial contract.

(ii) *Fixed payment.*—(A) *In general.*—For purposes of paragraph (a)(3)(i) of this section, *fixed payment* means an amount of cash or other property specified in the contract, or determined by a fixed formula specified in the contract, which is to be paid or transferred in exchange for the provision of specified services or property. A fixed formula may incorporate an amount that depends upon future specified events or contingencies, provided that no person exercises discretion when calculating the amount of a payment or deciding whether to make a payment (such as a bonus). A specified event or contingency may include the amount of revenues generated by (or other objective measure of) one or more activities of the applicable tax-exempt organization. A fixed payment does not include any amount paid to a person under a reimbursement (or similar) arrangement where discretion is exercised by any person with respect to the amount of expenses incurred or reimbursed.

(B) *Special rules.*—Amounts payable pursuant to a qualified pension, profit-sharing, or stock bonus plan under section 401(a), or pursuant to an employee benefit program that is subject to and satisfies coverage and nondiscrimination rules under the Internal Revenue Code (e.g., sections 127 and 137), other than nondiscrimination rules under section 9802, are treated as fixed payments for purposes of this section, regardless of the applicable tax-exempt organization's discretion with respect to the plan or program. The fact that a person contracting with an applicable tax-exempt organization is expressly granted the choice whether to accept or reject any economic benefit is disregarded in determining whether the benefit constitutes a fixed payment for purposes of this paragraph.

(iii) *Initial contract.*—For purposes of paragraph (a)(3)(i) of this section, *initial contract* means a binding written contract between an applicable tax-exempt organization and a person who was not a disqualified person within the meaning of section 4958(f)(1) and §53.4958-3 immediately prior to entering into the contract.

(iv) *Substantial performance required.*—Paragraph (a)(3)(i) of this section does not apply to any fixed payment made pursuant to the initial contract during any taxable year of the person contracting with the applicable tax-exempt organization if the person fails to perform substantially the person's obligations under the initial contract during that year.

(v) *Treatment as a new contract.*—A written binding contract that provides that the contract is terminable or subject to cancellation by the applicable tax-exempt organization (other than as a result of a lack of substantial performance by the disqualified person, as described in paragraph (a)(3)(iv) of this section) without the other party's consent and without substantial penalty to the organization is treated as a new contract as of the earliest date that any such termination or cancellation, if made, would be effective. Additionally, if the parties make a material change to a contract, it is treated as a new contract as of the date the material change is effective. A material change includes an extension or renewal of the contract (other than an extension or renewal that results from the person contracting with the applicable tax-exempt organization unilaterally exercising an option expressly granted by the contract), or a more than incidental change to any amount payable under the contract. The new contract is tested under paragraph (a)(3)(iii) of this section to determine whether it is an initial contract for purposes of this section.

(vi) *Evaluation of non-fixed payments.*—Any payment that is not a fixed payment (within the meaning of paragraph (a)(3)(ii) of this section) is evaluated to determine whether it constitutes an excess benefit transaction under section 4958. In making this determination, all payments and consideration exchanged between the parties are taken into account, including any fixed payments made pursuant to an initial contract with respect to which section 4958 does not apply.

(vii) *Examples.*—The following examples illustrate the rules governing fixed payments made pursuant to an initial contract. Unless otherwise stated, assume that the person contracting with the applicable tax-exempt organization has performed substantially the person's obligations under the contract with respect to the payment. The examples are as follows:

Example 1. T is an applicable tax-exempt organization for purposes of section 4958. On January 1, 2002, T hires S as its chief financial officer by entering into a five-year written employment contract with S. S was not a disqualified person within the meaning of section 4958(f)(1) and §53.4958-3 immediately prior to entering into the January 1, 2002, contract (initial contract). S's duties and responsibilities under the contract make S a disqualified person with respect to T (see §53.4958-3(c)(3)). Under the initial contract, T agrees to pay S an annual salary of $200,000, payable in monthly installments. The contract provides that, beginning in 2003, S's annual salary will be adjusted by the increase in the Consumer Price Index (CPI) for

the prior year. Section 4958 does not apply because S's compensation under the contract is a fixed payment pursuant to an initial contract within the meaning of paragraph (a)(3) of this section. Thus, for section 4958 purposes, it is unnecessary to evaluate whether any portion of the compensation paid to S pursuant to the initial contract is an excess benefit transaction.

Example 2. The facts are the same as in *Example 1,* except that the initial contract provides that, in addition to a base salary of $200,000, T may pay S an annual performance-based bonus. The contract provides that T's governing body will determine the amount of the annual bonus as of the end of each year during the term of the contract, based on the board's evaluation of S's performance, but the bonus cannot exceed $100,000 per year. Unlike the base salary portion of S's compensation, the bonus portion of S's compensation is not a fixed payment pursuant to an initial contract, because the governing body has discretion over the amount, if any, of the bonus payment. Section 4958 does not apply to payment of the $200,000 base salary (as adjusted for inflation), because it is a fixed payment pursuant to an initial contract within the meaning of paragraph (a)(3) of this section. By contrast, the annual bonuses that may be paid to S under the initial contract are not protected by the initial contract exception. Therefore, each bonus payment will be evaluated under section 4958, taking into account all payments and consideration exchanged between the parties.

Example 3. The facts are the same as in *Example 1,* except that in 2003, T changes its payroll system, such that T makes biweekly, rather than monthly, salary payments to its employees. Beginning in 2003, T also grants its employees an additional two days of paid vacation each year. Neither change is a material change to S's initial contract within the meaning of paragraph (a)(3)(v) of this section. Therefore, section 4958 does not apply to the base salary payments to S due to the initial contract exception.

Example 4. The facts are the same as in *Example 1,* except that on January 1, 2003, S becomes the chief executive officer of T and a new chief financial officer is hired. At the same time, T's board of directors approves an increase in S's annual base salary from $200,000 to $240,000, effective on that day. These changes in S's employment relationship constitute material changes of the initial contract within the meaning of paragraph (a)(3)(v) of this section. As a result, S is treated as entering into a new contract with T on January 1, 2003, at which time S is a disqualified person within the meaning of section 4958(f)(1) and §53.4958-3. T's payments to S made pursuant to the new contract will be evaluated under section 4958, taking into account all payments and consideration exchanged between the parties.

Example 5. J is a performing arts organization and an applicable tax-exempt organization for purposes of section 4958. J hires W to become the chief executive officer of J. W was not a disqualified person within the meaning of section 4958(f)(1) and §53.4958-3 immediately prior to entering into the employment contract with J. As a result of this employment contract, W's duties and responsibilities make W a disqualified person with respect to J (see §53.4958-3(c)(2)). Under the contract, J will pay W $x (a specified amount) plus a bonus equal to 2 percent of the total season subscription sales that exceed $100z. The $x base salary is a fixed payment pursuant to an initial contract within the meaning of paragraph (a)(3) of this section. The bonus payment is also a fixed payment pursuant to an initial contract within the meaning of paragraph (a)(3) of this section, because no person exercises discretion when calculating the amount of the bonus payment or deciding whether the bonus will be paid. Therefore, section 4958 does not apply to any of J's payments to W pursuant to the employment contract due to the initial contract exception.

Example 6. Hospital B is an applicable tax-exempt organization for purposes of section 4958. Hospital B hires E as its chief operating officer. E was not a disqualified person within the meaning of section 4958(f)(1) and §53.4958-3 immediately prior to entering into the employment contract with Hospital B. As a result of this employment contract, E's duties and responsibilities make E a disqualified person with respect to Hospital B (see §53.4958-3(c)(2)). E's initial employment contract provides that E will have authority to enter into hospital management arrangements on behalf of Hospital B. In E's personal capacity, E owns more than 35 percent of the combined voting power of Company X. Consequently, at the time E becomes a disqualified person with respect to B, Company X also becomes a disqualified person with respect to B (see §53.4958-3(b)(2)(i)(A)). E, acting on behalf of Hospital B as chief operating officer, enters into a contract with Company X under which Company X will provide billing and collection services to Hospital B. The initial contract exception of paragraph (a)(3)(i) of this section does not apply to the billing and collection services contract, because at the time that this contractual arrangement was entered into, Company X was a disqualified person with respect to Hospital B. Although E's employment contract (which is an initial contract) authorizes E to enter into hospital management arrangements on behalf of Hospital B, the payments made to Company X are not made pursuant to E's employment contract, but rather are made by Hospital B pursuant to a separate contractual arrangement with Company X. Therefore, even if payments made to Company X under the billing and collection services contract are fixed payments (within the meaning of paragraph (a)(3)(ii) of this section), section 4958 nonetheless applies to payments made by Hospital B to Company X because the billing and collection services contract itself does not constitute an initial contract under paragraph (a)(3)(iii) of this section. Accordingly, all payments made to Company X under the billing and collection services contract will be evaluated under section 4958.

Example 7. Hospital C, an applicable tax-exempt organization, enters into a contract with Company Y, under which Company Y will provide a wide range of hospital management services to Hospital C. Upon entering into this contractual arrangement, Company Y becomes a disqualified person with respect to Hospital C. The contract provides that Hospital C will pay Company Y a management fee of *x* percent of adjusted gross revenue (i.e., gross revenue increased by the cost of charity care provided to indigents) annually for a five-year period. The management services contract specifies the cost accounting system and the standards for *indigents* to be used in calculating the cost of charity care. The cost accounting system objectively defines the direct and indirect costs of all health care goods and services provided as charity care. Because Company Y was not a disqualified person with respect to Hospital C immediately before entering into the management services contract, that contract is an initial contract within the meaning of paragraph (a)(3)(iii) of this section. The annual management fee paid to Company Y is determined by a fixed formula specified in the contract, and is therefore a fixed payment within the meaning of paragraph (a)(3)(ii) of this section. Accordingly, section 4958 does not apply to the annual management fee due to the initial contract exception.

Example 8. The facts are the same as in *Example 7*, except that the management services contract also provides that Hospital C will reimburse Company Y on a monthly basis for certain expenses incurred by Company Y that are attributable to management services provided to Hospital C (e.g., legal fees and travel expenses). Although the management fee itself is a fixed payment not subject to section 4958, the reimbursement payments that Hospital C makes to Company Y for the various expenses covered by the contract are not fixed payments within the meaning of paragraph (a)(3)(ii) of this section, because Company Y exercises discretion with respect to the amount of expenses incurred. Therefore, any reimbursement payments that Hospital C pays pursuant to the contract will be evaluated under section 4958.

Example 9. X, an applicable tax-exempt organization for purposes of section 4958, hires C to conduct scientific research. On January 1, 2003, C enters into a three-year written employment contract with X (initial contract). Under the terms of the contract, C is required to work full-time at X's laboratory for a fixed annual salary of $90,000. Immediately prior to entering into the employment contract, C was not a disqualified person within the meaning of section 4958(f)(1) and § 53.4958-3, nor did C become a disqualified person pursuant to the initial contract. However, two years after joining X, C marries D, who is the child of X's president. As D's spouse, C is a disqualified person within the meaning of section 4958(f)(1) and § 53.4958-3 with respect to X. Nonetheless, section 4958 does not apply to X's salary payments to C due to the initial contract exception.

Example 10. The facts are the same as in *Example 9*, except that the initial contract included a below-market loan provision under which C has the unilateral right to borrow up to a specified dollar amount from X at a specified interest rate for a specified term. After C's marriage to D, C borrows money from X to purchase a home under the terms of the initial contract. Section 4958 does not apply to X's loan to C due to the initial contract exception.

Example 11. The facts are the same as in *Example 9*, except that after C's marriage to D, C works only sporadically at the laboratory, and performs no other services for X. Notwithstanding that C fails to perform substantially C's obligations under the initial contract, X does not exercise its right to terminate the initial contract for nonperformance and continues to pay full salary to C. Pursuant to paragraph (a)(3)(iv) of this section, the initial contract exception does not apply to any payments made pursuant to the initial contract during any taxable year of C in which C fails to perform substantially C's obligations under the initial contract.

(4) *Certain economic benefits disregarded for purposes of section 4958.*—The following economic benefits are disregarded for purposes of section 4958—

(i) *Nontaxable fringe benefits.*—An economic benefit that is excluded from income under section 132, except any liability insurance premium, payment, or reimbursement that must be taken into account under paragraph (b)(1)(ii)(B)(2) of this section;

(ii) *Expense reimbursement payments pursuant to accountable plans.*—Amounts paid under reimbursement arrangements that meet the requirements of § 1.62-2(c) of this chapter;

(iii) *Certain economic benefits provided to a volunteer for the organization.*—An economic benefit provided to a volunteer for the organization if the benefit is provided to the general public in exchange for a membership fee or contribution of $75 or less per year;

(iv) *Certain economic benefits provided to a member of, or donor to, the organization.*—An economic benefit provided to a member of an organization solely on account of the payment of a membership fee, or to a donor solely on account of a contribution for which a deduction is allowable under section 170 (charitable contribution), regardless of whether the donor is eligible to claim the deduction, if—

(A) Any non-disqualified person paying a membership fee or making a charitable contribution above a specified amount to the organization is given the option of receiving substantially the same economic benefit; and

(B) The disqualified person and a significant number of non-disqualified persons make a payment or charitable contribution of at least the specified amount;

(v) *Economic benefits provided to a charitable beneficiary.*—An economic benefit provided to a

person solely because the person is a member of a charitable class that the applicable tax-exempt organization intends to benefit as part of the accomplishment of the organization's exempt purpose; and

(vi) *Certain economic benefits provided to a governmental unit.*—Any transfer of an economic benefit to or for the use of a governmental unit defined in section 170(c)(1), if the transfer is for exclusively public purposes.

(5) *Exception for certain payments made pursuant to an exemption granted by the Department of Labor under ERISA.*—Section 4958 does not apply to any payment made pursuant to, and in accordance with, a final individual prohibited transaction exemption issued by the Department of Labor under section 408(a) of the Employee Retirement Income Security Act of 1974 (88 Stat. 854) (ERISA) with respect to a transaction involving a plan (as defined in section 3(3) of ERISA) that is an applicable tax exempt organization.

(b) *Valuation standards.*—(1) *In general.*—This section provides rules for determining the value of economic benefits for purposes of section 4958.

(i) *Fair market value of property.*—The value of property, including the right to use property, for purposes of section 4958 is the fair market value (i.e., the price at which property or the right to use property would change hands between a willing buyer and a willing seller, neither being under any compulsion to buy, sell or transfer property or the right to use property, and both having reasonable knowledge of relevant facts).

(ii) *Reasonable compensation.*—(A) *In general.*—The value of services is the amount that would ordinarily be paid for like services by like enterprises (whether taxable or tax-exempt) under like circumstances (i.e., reasonable compensation). Section 162 standards apply in determining reasonableness of compensation, taking into account the aggregate benefits (other than any benefits specifically disregarded under paragraph (a)(4) of this section) provided to a person and the rate at which any deferred compensation accrues. The fact that a compensation arrangement is subject to a cap is a relevant factor in determining the reasonableness of compensation. The fact that a State or local legislative or agency body or court has authorized or approved a particular compensation package paid to a disqualified person is not determinative of the reasonableness of compensation for purposes of section 4958.

(B) *Items included in determining the value of compensation for purposes of determining reasonableness under section 4958.*—Except for economic benefits that are disregarded for purposes of section 4958 under paragraph (a)(4) of this section, compensation for purposes of determining reasonableness under section 4958 includes all economic benefits provided by an applicable tax-exempt organization in exchange for the performance of services. These benefits include, but are not limited to—

(1) All forms of cash and noncash compensation, including salary, fees, bonuses, severance payments, and deferred and noncash compensation described in § 53.4958-1(e)(2);

(2) Unless excludable from income as a *de minimis* fringe benefit pursuant to section 132(a)(4), the payment of liability insurance premiums for, or the payment or reimbursement by the organization of—

(i) Any penalty, tax, or expense of correction owed under section 4958;

(ii) Any expense not reasonably incurred by the person in connection with a civil judicial or civil administrative proceeding arising out of the person's performance of services on behalf of the applicable tax-exempt organization; or

(iii) Any expense resulting from an act or failure to act with respect to which the person has acted willfully and without reasonable cause; and

(3) All other compensatory benefits, whether or not included in gross income for income tax purposes, including payments to welfare benefit plans, such as plans providing medical, dental, life insurance, severance pay, and disability benefits, and both taxable and nontaxable fringe benefits (other than fringe benefits described in section 132), including expense allowances or reimbursements (other than expense reimbursements pursuant to an accountable plan that meets the requirements of § 1.62-2(c)), and the economic benefit of a below-market loan (within the meaning of section 7872(e)(1)). (For this purpose, the economic benefit of a below-market loan is the amount deemed transferred to the disqualified person under section 7872(a) or (b), regardless of whether section 7872 otherwise applies to the loan).

(C) *Inclusion in compensation for reasonableness determination does not govern income tax treatment.*—The determination of whether any item listed in paragraph (b)(1)(ii)(B) of this section is included in the disqualified person's gross income for income tax purposes is made on the basis of the provisions of chapter 1 of Subtitle A of the Internal Revenue Code, without regard to whether the item is taken into account for purposes of determining reasonableness of compensation under section 4958.

(2) *Timing of reasonableness determination.*—(i) *In general.*—The facts and circumstances to be taken into consideration in determining reasonableness of a fixed payment (within the meaning of paragraph (a)(3)(ii) of this section) are those existing on the date the parties enter into the contract pursuant to which the payment is made. However, in the event of substantial non-performance, reasonableness is determined based on all facts and circumstances, up to and including circumstances as of the date of payment. In

Reg. §53.4958-4(b)(2)(i)

the case of any payment that is not a fixed payment under a contract, reasonableness is determined based on all facts and circumstances, up to and including circumstances as of the date of payment. In no event shall circumstances existing at the date when the payment is questioned be considered in making a determination of the reasonableness of the payment. These general timing rules also apply to property subject to a substantial risk of forfeiture. Therefore, if the property subject to a substantial risk of forfeiture satisfies the definition of fixed payment (within the meaning of paragraph (a)(3)(ii) of this section), reasonableness is determined at the time the parties enter into the contract providing for the transfer of the property. If the property is not a fixed payment, then reasonableness is determined based on all facts and circumstances up to and including circumstances as of the date of payment.

(ii) *Treatment as a new contract.*—For purposes of paragraph (b)(2)(i) of this section, a written binding contract that provides that the contract is terminable or subject to cancellation by the applicable tax-exempt organization without the other party's consent and without substantial penalty to the organization is treated as a new contract as of the earliest date that any such termination or cancellation, if made, would be effective. Additionally, if the parties make a material change to a contract (within the meaning of paragraph (a)(3)(v) of this section), it is treated as a new contract as of the date the material change is effective.

(iii) *Examples.*—The following examples illustrate the timing of the reasonableness determination under the rules of this paragraph (b)(2):

Example 1. G is an applicable tax-exempt organization for purposes of section 4958. H is an employee of G and a disqualified person with respect to G. H's new multi-year employment contract provides for payment of a salary and provision of specific benefits pursuant to a qualified pension plan under section 401(a) and an accident and health plan that meets the requirements of section 105(h)(2). The contract provides that H's salary will be adjusted by the increase in the Consumer Price Index (CPI) for the prior year. The contributions G makes to the qualified pension plan are equal to the maximum amount G is permitted to contribute under the rules applicable to qualified plans. Under these facts, all items comprising H's total compensation are treated as fixed payments within the meaning of paragraph (a)(3)(ii) of this section. Therefore, the reasonableness of H's compensation is determined based on the circumstances existing at the time G and H enter into the employment contract.

Example 2. The facts are the same as in *Example 1,* except that the multi-year employment contract provides, in addition, that G will transfer title to a car to H under the condition that if H fails to complete *x* years of service with G, title to the car will be forfeited back to G. All relevant information about the type of car to be provided (including the make, model, and year) is included in the contract. Although ultimate vesting of title to the car is contingent on H continuing to work for G for *x* years, the amount of property to be vested (i.e., the type of car) is specified in the contract, and no person exercises discretion regarding the type of property or whether H will retain title to the property at the time of vesting. Under these facts, the car is a fixed payment within the meaning of paragraph (a)(3)(ii) of this section. Therefore, the reasonableness of H's compensation, including the value of the car, is determined based on the circumstances existing at the time G and H enter into the employment contract.

Example 3. N is an applicable tax-exempt organization for purposes of section 4958. On January 2, N's governing body enters into a new one-year employment contract with K, its executive director, who is a disqualified person with respect to N. The contract provides that K will receive a specified amount of salary, contributions to a qualified pension plan under section 401(a), and other benefits pursuant to a section 125 cafeteria plan. In addition, the contract provides that N's governing body may, in its discretion, declare a bonus to be paid to K at any time during the year covered by the contract. K's salary and other specified benefits constitute fixed payments within the meaning of paragraph (a)(3)(ii) of this section. Therefore, the reasonableness of those economic benefits is determined on the date when the contract was made. However, because the bonus payment is not a fixed payment within the meaning of paragraph (a)(3)(ii) of this section, the determination of whether any bonus awarded to N is reasonable must be made based on all facts and circumstances (including all payments and consideration exchanged between the parties), up to and including circumstances as of the date of payment of the bonus.

(c) *Establishing intent to treat economic benefit as consideration for the performance of services.*—(1) *In general.*—An economic benefit is not treated as consideration for the performance of services unless the organization providing the benefit clearly indicates its intent to treat the benefit as compensation when the benefit is paid. Except as provided in paragraph (c)(2) of this section, an applicable tax-exempt organization (or entity controlled by an applicable tax-exempt organization, within the meaning of paragraph (a)(2)(ii)(B) of this section) is treated as clearly indicating its intent to provide an economic benefit as compensation for services only if the organization provides written substantiation that is contemporaneous with the transfer of the economic benefit at issue. If an organization fails to provide this contemporaneous substantiation, any services provided by the disqualified person will not be treated as provided in consideration for the economic benefit for purposes of determining the reasonableness of the transaction. In no event shall an economic benefit that a dis-

qualified person obtains by theft or fraud be treated as consideration for the performance of services.

(2) *Nontaxable benefits.*—For purposes of section 4958(c)(1)(A) and this section, an applicable tax-exempt organization is not required to indicate its intent to provide an economic benefit as compensation for services if the economic benefit is excluded from the disqualified person's gross income for income tax purposes on the basis of the provisions of chapter 1 of Subtitle A of the Internal Revenue Code. Examples of these benefits include, but are not limited to, employer-provided health benefits and contributions to a qualified pension, profit-sharing, or stock bonus plan under section 401(a), and benefits described in sections 127 and 137. However, except for economic benefits that are disregarded for purposes of section 4958 under paragraph (a)(4) of this section, all compensatory benefits (regardless of the Federal income tax treatment) provided by an organization in exchange for the performance of services are taken into account in determining the reasonableness of a person's compensation for purposes of section 4958.

(3) *Contemporaneous substantiation.*— (i) *Reporting of benefit.*—(A) *In general.*—An applicable tax-exempt organization provides contemporaneous written substantiation of its intent to provide an economic benefit as compensation if—

(1) The organization reports the economic benefit as compensation on an original Federal tax information return with respect to the payment (e.g., Form W-2, "Wage and Tax Statement", or Form 1099, "Miscellaneous Income") or with respect to the organization (e.g., Form 990, "Return of Organization Exempt From Income Tax"), or on an amended Federal tax information return filed prior to the commencement of an Internal Revenue Service examination of the applicable tax-exempt organization or the disqualified person for the taxable year in which the transaction occurred (as determined under § 53.4958-1(e)); or

(2) The recipient disqualified person reports the benefit as income on the person's original Federal tax return (e.g., Form 1040, "U.S. Individual Income Tax Return"), or on the person's amended Federal tax return filed prior to the earlier of the following dates—

(i) Commencement of an Internal Revenue Service examination described in paragraph (c)(3)(i)(A)(1) of this section; or

(ii) The first documentation in writing by the Internal Revenue Service of a potential excess benefit transaction involving either the applicable tax-exempt organization or the disqualified person.

(B) *Failure to report due to reasonable cause.*—If an applicable tax-exempt organization's failure to report an economic benefit as required under the Internal Revenue Code is due to reasonable cause (within the meaning of

§ 301.6724-1 of this chapter), then the organization will be treated as having clearly indicated its intent to provide an economic benefit as compensation for services. To show that its failure to report an economic benefit that should have been reported on an information return was due to reasonable cause, an applicable tax-exempt organization must establish that there were significant mitigating factors with respect to its failure to report (as described in § 301.6724-1(b) of this chapter), or the failure arose from events beyond the organization's control (as described in § 301.6724-1(c) of this chapter), and that the organization acted in a responsible manner both before and after the failure occurred (as described in § 301.6724-1(d) of this chapter).

(ii) *Other written contemporaneous evidence.*—In addition, other written contemporaneous evidence may be used to demonstrate that the appropriate decision-making body or an officer authorized to approve compensation approved a transfer as compensation for services in accordance with established procedures, including but not limited to—

(A) An approved written employment contract executed on or before the date of the transfer;

(B) Documentation satisfying the requirements of § 53.4958-6(a)(3) indicating that an authorized body approved the transfer as compensation for services on or before the date of the transfer; or

(C) Written evidence that was in existence on or before the due date of the applicable Federal tax return described in paragraph (c)(3)(i)(A)(1) or (2) of this section (including extensions but not amendments), of a reasonable belief by the applicable tax-exempt organization that a benefit was a nontaxable benefit as defined in paragraph (c)(2) of this section.

(4) *Examples.*—The following examples illustrate the requirement that an organization contemporaneously substantiate its intent to provide an economic benefit as compensation for services, as defined in paragraph (c) of this section:

Example 1. G is an applicable tax-exempt organization for purposes of section 4958. G hires an individual contractor, P, who is also the child of a disqualified person of G, to design a computer program for it. G executes a contract with P for that purpose in accordance with G's established procedures, and pays P $1,000 during the year pursuant to the contract. Before January 31 of the next year, G reports the full amount paid to P under the contract on a Form 1099 filed with the Internal Revenue Service. G will be treated as providing contemporaneous written substantiation of its intent to provide the $1,000 paid to P as compensation for the services P performed under the contract by virtue of either the Form 1099 filed with the Internal Revenue Service reporting the amount, or by virtue of the written contract executed between G and P.

Reg. § 53.4958-4(c)(4)

Example 2. G is an applicable tax-exempt organization for purposes of section 4958. D is the chief operating officer of G, and a disqualified person with respect to G. D receives a bonus at the end of the year. G's accounting department determines that the bonus is to be reported on D's Form W-2. Due to events beyond G's control, the bonus is not reflected on D's Form W-2. As a result, D fails to report the bonus on D's individual income tax return. G acts to amend Forms W-2 affected as soon as G is made aware of the error during an Internal Revenue Service examination. G's failure to report the bonus on an information return issued to D arose from events beyond G's control, and G acted in a responsible manner both before and after the failure occurred. Thus, because G had reasonable cause (within the meaning § 301.6724-1 of this chapter) for failing to report D's bonus, G will be treated as providing contemporaneous written substantiation of its intent to provide the bonus as compensation for services when paid.

Example 3. H is an applicable tax-exempt organization and J is a disqualified person with respect to H. J's written employment agreement provides for a fixed salary of $y. J's duties include soliciting funds for various programs of H. H raises a large portion of its funds in a major metropolitan area. Accordingly, H maintains an apartment there in order to provide a place to entertain potential donors. H makes the apartment available exclusively to J to assist in the fundraising. J's written employment contract does not mention the use of the apartment. H obtains the written opinion of a benefits compensation expert that the rental value of the apartment is not includable in J's income by reason of section 119, based on the expectation that the apartment will be used for fundraising activities. Consequently, H does not report the rental value of the apartment on J's Form W-2, which otherwise correctly reports J's taxable compensation. J does not report the rental value of the apartment on J's individual Form 1040. Later, the Internal Revenue Service correctly determines that the requirements of section 119 were not satisfied. Because of the written expert opinion, H has written evidence of its reasonable belief that use of the apartment was a nontaxable benefit as defined in paragraph (c)(2) of this section. That evidence was in existence on or before the due date of the applicable Federal tax return. Therefore, H has demonstrated its intent to treat the use of the apartment as compensation for services performed by J.

[Reg. § 53.4958-4.]

☐ [T.D. 8978, 1-22-2002 (*corrected* 3-18-2002).]

[Reg. § 53.4958-5]

§ 53.4958-5. Transaction in which the amount of the economic benefit is determined in whole or in part by the revenues of one or more activities of the organization.—[Reserved]

☐ [T.D. 8978, 1-22-2002.]

[Reg. § 53.4958-6]

§ 53.4958-6. Rebuttable presumption that a transaction is not an excess benefit transaction.—(a) *In general.*—Payments under a compensation arrangement are presumed to be reasonable, and a transfer of property, or the right to use property, is presumed to be at fair market value, if the following conditions are satisfied—

(1) The compensation arrangement or the terms of the property transfer are approved in advance by an authorized body of the applicable tax-exempt organization (or an entity controlled by the organization with the meaning of § 53.4958-4(a)(2)(ii)(B)) composed entirely of individuals who do not have a conflict of interest (within the meaning of paragraph (c)(1)(iii) of this section) with respect to the compensation arrangement or property transfer, as described in paragraph (c)(1) of this section;

(2) The authorized body obtained and relied upon appropriate data as to comparability prior to making its determination, as described in paragraph (c)(2) of this section; and

(3) The authorized body adequately documented the basis for its determination concurrently with making that determination, as described in paragraph (c)(3) of this section.

(b) *Rebutting the presumption.*—If the three requirements of paragraph (a) of this section are satisfied, then the Internal Revenue Service may rebut the presumption that arises under paragraph (a) of this section only if it develops sufficient contrary evidence to rebut the probative value of the comparability data relied upon by the authorized body. With respect to any fixed payment (within the meaning of § 53.4958-4(a)(3)(ii)), rebuttal evidence is limited to evidence relating to facts and circumstances existing on the date the parties enter into the contract pursuant to which the payment is made (except in the event of substantial nonperformance). With respect to all other payments (including non-fixed payments subject to a cap, as described in paragraph (d)(2) of this section), rebuttal evidence may include facts and circumstances up to and including the date of payment. See § 53.4958-4(b)(2)(i).

(c) *Requirements for invoking rebuttable presumption.*—(1) *Approval by an authorized body.*—(i) *In general.*—An authorized body means—

(A) The governing body (i.e., the board of directors, board of trustees, or equivalent controlling body) of the organization;

(B) A committee of the governing body, which may be composed of any individuals permitted under State law to serve on such a committee, to the extent that the committee is permitted by State law to act on behalf of the governing body; or

(C) To the extent permitted under State law, other parties authorized by the governing body of the organization to act on its behalf by following procedures specified by the governing

body in approving compensation arrangements or property transfers.

(ii) *Individuals not included on authorized body.*—For purposes of determining whether the requirements of paragraph (a) of this section have been met with respect to a specific compensation arrangement or property transfer, an individual is not included on the authorized body when it is reviewing a transaction if that individual meets with other members only to answer questions, and otherwise recuses himself or herself from the meeting and is not present during debate and voting on the compensation arrangement or property transfer.

(iii) *Absence of conflict of interest.*—A member of the authorized body does not have a conflict of interest with respect to a compensation arrangement or property transfer only if the member—

(A) Is not a disqualified person participating in or economically benefitting from the compensation arrangement or property transfer, and is not a member of the family of any such disqualified person, as described in section 4958(f)(4) or §53.4958-3(b)(1);

(B) Is not in an employment relationship subject to the direction or control of any disqualified person participating in or economically benefitting from the compensation arrangement or property transfer;

(C) Does not receive compensation or other payments subject to approval by any disqualified person participating in or economically benefitting from the compensation arrangement or property transfer;

(D) Has no material financial interest affected by the compensation arrangement or property transfer; and

(E) Does not approve a transaction providing economic benefits to any disqualified person participating in the compensation arrangement or property transfer, who in turn has approved or will approve a transaction providing economic benefits to the member.

(2) *Appropriate data as to comparability.*—(i) *In general.*—An authorized body has appropriate data as to comparability if, given the knowledge and expertise of its members, it has information sufficient to determine whether, under the standards set forth in §53.4958-4(b), the compensation arrangement in its entirety is reasonable or the property transfer is at fair market value. In the case of compensation, relevant information includes, but is not limited to, compensation levels paid by similarly situated organizations, both taxable and tax-exempt, for functionally comparable positions; the availability of similar services in the geographic area of the applicable tax-exempt organization; current compensation surveys compiled by independent firms; and actual written offers from similar institutions competing for the services of the disqualified person. In the case of property, relevant information includes, but is not limited to, current independent appraisals of the value of all

property to be transferred; and offers received as part of an open and competitive bidding process.

(ii) *Special rule for compensation paid by small organizations.*—For organizations with annual gross receipts (including contributions) of less than $1 million reviewing compensation arrangements, the authorized body will be considered to have appropriate data as to comparability if it has data on compensation paid by three comparable organizations in the same or similar communities for similar services. No inference is intended with respect to whether circumstances falling outside this safe harbor will meet the requirement with respect to the collection of appropriate data.

(iii) *Application of special rule for small organizations.*—For purposes of determining whether the special rule for small organizations described in paragraph (c)(2)(ii) of this section applies, an organization may calculate its annual gross receipts based on an average of its gross receipts during the three prior taxable years. If any applicable tax-exempt organization is controlled by or controls another entity (as defined in §53.4958-4(a)(2)(ii)(B)), the annual gross receipts of such organizations must be aggregated to determine applicability of the special rule stated in paragraph (c)(2)(ii) of this section.

(iv) *Examples.*—The following examples illustrate the rules for appropriate data as to comparability for purposes of invoking the rebuttable presumption of reasonableness described in this section. In all examples, compensation refers to the aggregate value of all benefits provided in exchange for services. The examples are as follows:

Example 1. Z is a university that is an applicable tax-exempt organization for purposes of section 4958. Z is negotiating a new contract with Q, its president, because the old contract will expire at the end of the year. In setting Q's compensation for its president at $600x per annum, the executive committee of the Board of Trustees relies solely on a national survey of compensation for university presidents that indicates university presidents receive annual compensation in the range of $100x to $700x; this survey does not divide its data by any criteria, such as the number of students served by the institution, annual revenues, academic ranking, or geographic location. Although many members of the executive committee have significant business experience, none of the members has any particular expertise in higher education compensation matters. Given the failure of the survey to provide information specific to universities comparable to Z, and because no other information was presented, the executive committee's decision with respect to Q's compensation was not based upon appropriate data as to comparability.

Example 2. The facts are the same as *Example 1*, except that the national compensation survey divides the data regarding compensation for university presidents into categories based on

various university-specific factors, including the size of the institution (in terms of the number of students it serves and the amount of its revenues) and geographic area. The survey data shows that university presidents at institutions comparable to and in the same geographic area as Z receive annual compensation in the range of $200x to $300x. The executive committee of the Board of Trustees of Z relies on the survey data and its evaluation of Q's many years of service as a tenured professor and high-ranking university official at Z in setting Q's compensation at $275x annually. The data relied upon by the executive committee constitutes appropriate data as to comparability.

Example 3. X is a tax-exempt hospital that is an applicable tax-exempt organization for purposes of section 4958. Before renewing the contracts of X's chief executive officer and chief financial officer, X's governing board commissioned a customized compensation survey from an independent firm that specializes in consulting on issues related to executive placement and compensation. The survey covered executives with comparable responsibilities at a significant number of taxable and tax-exempt hospitals. The survey data are sorted by a number of different variables, including the size of the hospitals and the nature of the services they provide, the level of experience and specific responsibilities of the executives, and the composition of the annual compensation packages. The board members were provided with the survey results, a detailed written analysis comparing the hospital's executives to those covered by the survey, and an opportunity to ask questions of a member of the firm that prepared the survey. The survey, as prepared and presented to X's board, constitutes appropriate data as to comparability.

Example 4. The facts are the same as *Example 3,* except that one year later, X is negotiating a new contract with its chief executive officer. The governing board of X obtains information indicating that the relevant market conditions have not changed materially, and possesses no other information indicating that the results of the prior year's survey are no longer valid. Therefore, X may continue to rely on the independent compensation survey prepared for the prior year in setting annual compensation under the new contract.

Example 5. W is a local repertory theater and an applicable tax-exempt organization for purposes of section 4958. W has had annual gross receipts ranging from $400,000 to $800,000 over its past three taxable years. In determining the next year's compensation for W's artistic director, the board of directors of W relies on data compiled from a telephone survey of three other unrelated performing arts organizations of similar size in similar communities. A member of the board drafts a brief written summary of the annual compensation information obtained from this informal survey. The annual compensation information obtained in the telephone survey is appropriate data as to comparability.

(3) *Documentation.*—(i) For a decision to be documented adequately, the written or electronic records of the authorized body must note—

(A) The terms of the transaction that was approved and the date it was approved;

(B) The members of the authorized body who were present during debate on the transaction that was approved and those who voted on it;

(C) The comparability data obtained and relied upon by the authorized body and how the data was obtained; and

(D) Any actions taken with respect to consideration of the transaction by anyone who is otherwise a member of the authorized body but who had a conflict of interest with respect to the transaction.

(ii) If the authorized body determines that reasonable compensation for a specific arrangement or fair market value in a specific property transfer is higher or lower than the range of comparability data obtained, the authorized body must record the basis for its determination. For a decision to be documented concurrently, records must be prepared before the later of the next meeting of the authorized body or 60 days after the final action or actions of the authorized body are taken. Records must be reviewed and approved by the authorized body as reasonable, accurate and complete within a reasonable time period thereafter.

(d) *No presumption with respect to non-fixed payments until amounts are determined.*—(1) *In general.*—Except as provided in paragraph (d)(2) of this section, in the case of a payment that is not a fixed payment (within the meaning of §53.4958-4(a)(3)(ii)), the rebuttable presumption of this section arises only after the exact amount of the payment is determined, or a fixed formula for calculating the payment is specified, and the three requirements for the presumption under paragraph (a) of this section subsequently are satisfied. See §53.4958-4(b)(2)(i).

(2) *Special rule for certain non-fixed payments subject to a cap.*—If the authorized body approves an employment contract with a disqualified person that includes a non-fixed payment (such as a discretionary bonus) subject to a specified cap, the authorized body may establish a rebuttable presumption with respect to the non-fixed payment at the time the employment contract is entered into if—

(i) Prior to approving the contract, the authorized body obtains appropriate comparability data indicating that a fixed payment of up to a certain amount to the particular disqualified person would represent reasonable compensation;

(ii) The maximum amount payable under the contract (taking into account both fixed and non-fixed payments) does not exceed the amount referred to in paragraph (d)(2)(i) of this section; and

(iii) The other requirements for the rebuttable presumption of reasonableness under paragraph (a) of this section are satisfied.

(e) *No inference from absence of presumption.*— The fact that a transaction between an applicable tax-exempt organization and a disqualified person is not subject to the presumption described in this section neither creates any inference that the transaction is an excess benefit transaction, nor exempts or relieves any person from compliance with any Federal or state law imposing any obligation, duty, responsibility, or other standard of conduct with respect to the operation or administration of any applicable tax-exempt organization.

(f) *Period of reliance on rebuttable presumption.*— Except as provided in paragraph (d) of this section with respect to non-fixed payments, the rebuttable presumption applies to all payments made or transactions completed in accordance with a contract, provided that the provisions of paragraph (a) of this section were met at the time the parties entered into the contract. [Reg. §53.4958-6.]

☐ [*T.D. 8978, 1-22-2002.*]

[Reg. §53.4958-7]

§53.4958-7. Correction.—(a) *In general.*—An excess benefit transaction is corrected by undoing the excess benefit to the extent possible, and taking any additional measures necessary to place the applicable tax-exempt organization involved in the excess benefit transaction in a financial position not worse than that in which it would be if the disqualified person were dealing under the highest fiduciary standards. Paragraph (b) of this section describes the acceptable forms of correction. Paragraph (c) of this section defines the correction amount. Paragraph (d) of this section describes correction where a contract has been partially performed. Paragraph (e) of this section describes correction where the applicable tax-exempt organization involved in the transaction has ceased to exist or is no longer tax-exempt. Paragraph(f) of this section provides examples illustrating correction.

(b) *Form of correction.*—(1) *Cash or cash equivalents.*—Except as provided in paragraphs (b)(3) and (4) of this section, a disqualified person corrects an excess benefit only by making a payment in cash or cash equivalents, excluding payment by a promissory note, to the applicable tax-exempt organization equal to the correction amount, as defined in paragraph (c) of this section.

(2) *Anti-abuse rule.*—A disqualified person will not satisfy the requirements of paragraph (b)(1) of this section if the Commissioner determines that the disqualified person engaged in one or more transactions with the applicable tax-exempt organization to circumvent the requirements of this correction section, and as a result, the disqualified person effectively transferred property other than cash or cash equivalents.

(3) *Special rule relating to nonqualified deferred compensation.*—If an excess benefit transaction results, in whole or in part, from the vesting (as described in §53.4958-1(e)(2)) of benefits provided under a nonqualified deferred compensation plan, then, to the extent that such benefits have not yet been distributed to the disqualified person, the disqualified person may correct the portion of the excess benefit resulting from the undistributed deferred compensation by relinquishing any right to receive the excess portion of the undistributed deferred compensation (including any earnings thereon).

(4) *Return of specific property.*—(i) *In general.*—A disqualified person may, with the agreement of the applicable tax-exempt organization, make a payment by returning specific property previously transferred in the excess benefit transaction. In this case, the disqualified person is treated as making a payment equal to the lesser of—

(A) The fair market value of the property determined on the date the property is returned to the organization; or

(B) The fair market value of the property on the date the excess benefit transaction occurred.

(ii) *Payment not equal to correction amount.*—If the payment described in paragraph (b)(4)(i) of this section is less than the correction amount (as described in paragraph (c) of this section), the disqualified person must make an additional cash payment to the organization equal to the difference. Conversely, if the payment described in paragraph (b)(4)(i) of this section exceeds the correction amount (as described in paragraph (c) of this section), the organization may make a cash payment to the disqualified person equal to the difference.

(iii) *Disqualified person may not participate in decision.*—Any disqualified person who received an excess benefit from the excess benefit transaction may not participate in the applicable tax-exempt organization's decision whether to accept the return of specific property under paragraph (b)(4)(i) of this section.

(c) *Correction amount.*—The correction amount with respect to an excess benefit transaction equals the sum of the excess benefit (as defined in §53.4958-1(b)) and interest on the excess benefit. The amount of the interest charge for purposes of this section is determined by multiplying the excess benefit by an interest rate, compounded annually, for the period from the date the excess benefit transaction occurred (as defined in §53.4958-1(e)) to the date of correction. The interest rate used for this purpose must be a rate that equals or exceeds the applicable Federal rate (AFR), compounded annually, for the month in which the transaction occurred. The period from the date the excess benefit transaction occurred to the date of correction is used to determine whether the appropriate AFR is the Federal short-term rate, the Federal midterm rate, or the Federal long-term rate. See section 1274(d)(1)(A).

(d) *Correction where contract has been partially performed.*—If the excess benefit transaction arises under a contract that has been partially performed, termination of the contractual relationship between the organization and the disqualified person is not required in order to correct. However, the parties may need to modify the terms of any ongoing contract to avoid future excess benefit transactions.

(e) *Correction in the case of an applicable tax-exempt organization that has ceased to exist, or is no longer tax-exempt.*—(1) *In general.*—A disqualified person must correct an excess benefit transaction in accordance with this paragraph where the applicable tax-exempt organization that engaged in the transaction no longer exists or is no longer described in section 501(c)(3) or (4) or exempt from tax under section 501(a).

(2) *Section 501(c)(3) organizations.*—In the case of an excess benefit transaction with a section 501(c)(3) applicable tax-exempt organization, the disqualified person must pay the correction amount, as defined in paragraph (c) of this section, to another organization described in section 501(c)(3) and exempt from tax under section 501(a) in accordance with the dissolution clause contained in the constitutive documents of the applicable tax-exempt organization involved in the excess benefit transaction, provided that—

(i) The organization receiving the correction amount is described in section 170(b)(1)(A) (other than in section 170(b)(1)(A)(vii) and (viii)) and has been in existence and so described for a continuous period of at least 60 calendar months ending on the correction date;

(ii) The disqualified person is not also a disqualified person (as defined in § 53.4958-3) with respect to the organization receiving the correction amount; and

(iii) The organization receiving the correction amount does not allow the disqualified person (or persons described in § 53.4958-3(b) with respect to that person) to make or recommend any grants or distributions by the organization.

(3) *Section 501(c)(4) organizations.*—In the case of an excess benefit transaction with a section 501(c)(4) applicable tax-exempt organization, the disqualified person must pay the correction amount, as defined in paragraph (c) of this section, to a successor section 501(c)(4) organization or, if no tax-exempt successor, to any organization described in section 501(c)(3) or (4) and exempt from tax under section 501(a), provided that the requirements of paragraphs (e)(2)(i) through (iii) of this section are satisfied (except that the requirement that the organization receiving the correction amount is described in section 170(b)(1)(A) (other than in section 170(b)(1)(A)(vii) and (viii)) shall not apply if the organization is described in section 501(c)(4)).

(f) *Examples.*—The following examples illustrate the principles of this section describing the requirements of correction:

Example 1. W is an applicable tax-exempt organization for purposes of section 4958. D is a disqualified person with respect to W. W employed D in 1999 and made payments totaling $12t to D as compensation throughout the taxable year. The fair market value of D's services in 1999 was $7t. Thus, D received excess compensation in the amount of $5t, the excess benefit for purposes of section 4958. In accordance with § 53.4958-1(e)(1), the excess benefit transaction with respect to the series of compensatory payments during 1999 is deemed to occur on December 31, 1999, the last day of D's taxable year. In order to correct the excess benefit transaction on June 30, 2002, D must pay W, in cash or cash equivalents, excluding payment with a promissory note, $5t (the excess benefit) plus interest on $5t for the period from the date the excess benefit transaction occurred to the date of correction (i.e., December 31, 1999, to June 30, 2002). Because this period is not more than three years, the interest rate D must use to determine the interest on the excess benefit must equal or exceed the short-term AFR, compounded annually, for December, 1999 (5.74%, compounded annually).

Example 2. X is an applicable tax-exempt organization for purposes of section 4958. B is a disqualified person with respect to X. On January 1, 2000, B paid X $6v for Property F. Property F had a fair market value of $10v on January 1, 2000. Thus, the sales transaction on that date provided an excess benefit to B in the amount of $4v. In order to correct the excess benefit on July 5, 2005, B pays X, in cash or cash equivalents, excluding payment with a promissory note, $4v (the excess benefit) plus interest on $4v for the period from the date the excess benefit transaction occurred to the date of correction (i.e., January 1, 2000, to July 5, 2005). Because this period is over three but not over nine years, the interest rate B must use to determine the interest on the excess benefit must equal or exceed the mid-term AFR, compounded annually, for January, 2000 (6.21%, compounded annually).

Example 3. The facts are the same as in *Example 2*, except that B offers to return Property F. X agrees to accept the return of Property F, a decision in which B does not participate. Property F has declined in value since the date of the excess benefit transaction. On July 5, 2005, the property has a fair market value of $9v. For purposes of correction, B's return of Property F to X is treated as a payment of $9v, the fair market value of the property determined on the date the property is returned to the organization. If $9v is greater than the correction amount ($4v plus interest on $4v at a rate that equals or exceeds 6.21%, compounded annually, for the period from January 1, 2000, to July 5, 2005), then X may make a cash payment to B equal to the difference.

Example 4. The facts are the same as in *Example 3*, except that Property F has increased in value since January 1, 2000, the date the excess benefit

transaction occurred, and on July 5, 2005, has a fair market value of $13v$. For purposes of correction, B's return of Property F to X is treated as a payment of $10v$, the fair market value of the property on the date the excess benefit transaction occurred. If $10v$ is greater than the correction amount ($4v$ plus interest on $4v$ at a rate that equals or exceeds 6.21%, compounded annually, for the period from January 1, 2000, to July 5, 2005), then X may make a cash payment to B equal to the difference.

Example 5. The facts are the same as in *Example 2.* Assume that the correction amount B paid X in cash on July 5, 2005, was $5.58v$. On July 4, 2005, X loaned $5.58v$ to B, in exchange for a promissory note signed by B in the amount of $5.58v$, payable with interest at a future date. These facts indicate that B engaged in the loan transaction to circumvent the requirement of this section that (except as provided in paragraph (b)(3) or (4) of this section), the correction amount must be paid only in cash or cash equivalents. As a result, the Commissioner may determine that B effectively transferred property other than cash or cash equivalents, and therefore did not satisfy the correction requirements of this section.

[Reg. § 53.4958-7.]

☐ [*T.D.* 8978, 1-22-2002.]

[Reg. § 53.4958-8]

§ 53.4958-8. Special rules.—(a) *Substantive requirements for exemption still apply.*—Section 4958 does not affect the substantive standards for tax exemption under section 501(c)(3) or (4), including the requirements that the organization be organized and operated exclusively for exempt purposes, and that no part of its net earnings inure to the benefit of any private shareholder or individual. Thus, regardless of whether a particular transaction is subject to excise taxes under section 4958, existing principles and rules may be implicated, such as the limitation on private benefit. For example, transactions that are not subject to section 4958 because of the initial contract exception described in § 53.4958-4(a)(3) may, under certain circumstances, jeopardize the organization's tax-exempt status.

(b) *Interaction between section 4958 and section 7611 rules for church tax inquiries and examinations.*—The procedures of section 7611 will be used in initiating and conducting any inquiry or examination into whether an excess benefit transaction has occurred between a church and a disqualified person. For purposes of this rule, the reasonable belief required to initiate a church tax inquiry is satisfied if there is a reasonable belief that a section 4958 tax is due from a disqualified person with respect to a transaction involving a church. See § 301.7611-1 Q&A 19 of this chapter.

(c) *Other substantiation requirements.*—These regulations, in § 53.4958-4(c)(3), set forth specific substantiation rules. Compliance with the specific substantiation rules of that section does not relieve applicable tax-exempt organizations of

other rules and requirements of the Internal Revenue Code, regulations, Revenue Rulings, and other guidance issued by the Internal Revenue Service (including the substantiation rules of sections 162 and 274, or § 1.6001-1(a) and (c) of this chapter). [Reg. § 53.4958-8.]

☐ [*T.D.* 8978, 1-22-2002.]

[Reg. § 53.4959-1]

§ 53.4959-1. Taxes on failures by hospital organizations to meet section 501(r)(3).—(a) *Excise tax for failure to meet the section 501(r)(3) requirements.*—(1) *In general.*—If a hospital organization (as defined in § 1.501(r)-1(b)(18)) fails to meet the requirements of section 501(r)(3) separately with respect to a hospital facility it operates in any taxable year, there is imposed on the hospital organization a tax equal to $50,000. If a hospital organization operates multiple hospital facilities and fails to meet the requirements of section 501(r)(3) with respect to more than one facility it operates, the $50,000 tax is imposed on the hospital organization separately for each hospital facility's failure. The tax is imposed for each taxable year that a hospital facility fails to meet the requirements of section 501(r)(3).

(2) *Examples.*—The following examples illustrate this paragraph (a):

Example 1. (i) U is a hospital organization that operates only one hospital facility, V. In Year 1, V conducts a community health needs assessment (CHNA) and adopts an implementation strategy to meet the health needs identified through the CHNA. In Years 2 and 3, V does not conduct a CHNA. V fails to conduct a CHNA by the last day of Year 4. Accordingly, U has failed to meet the requirements of section 501(r)(3) with respect to V in Year 4 because V has failed to conduct a CHNA in Years 2, 3, and 4. U is subject to a tax equal to $50,000 for Year 4.

(ii) V also fails to conduct a CHNA by the last day of Year 5. Accordingly, U has failed to meet the requirements of section 501(r)(3) with respect to V in Year 5 because V has failed to conduct a CHNA in Years 3, 4, and 5. U is subject to a tax equal to $50,000 for Year 5.

Example 2. P is a hospital organization that operates only one hospital facility, Q. In Year 1, Q conducts a CHNA and adopts an implementation strategy to meet the health needs identified through the CHNA. In Years 2 and 3, Q does not conduct a CHNA. In Year 4, Q conducts a CHNA but does not adopt an implementation strategy to meet the health needs identified through that CHNA by the 15th day of the fifth month of Year 5. Accordingly, P has failed to meet the requirements of section 501(r)(3) with respect to Q in Year 4 because Q has failed to adopt an implementation strategy by the 15th day of the fifth month after the end of the taxable year in which Q conducted its CHNA. P is subject to a tax equal to $50,000 for Year 4.

Example 3. R is a hospital organization that operates two hospital facilities, S and T. In Year 1, S and T each conduct a CHNA and adopt an implementation strategy to meet the health

needs identified through the CHNA. In Years 2 and 3, S and T do not conduct a CHNA. S and T each fail to conduct a CHNA by the last day of Year 4. Accordingly, R has failed to meet the requirements of section 501(r)(3) with respect to both S and T in Year 4. R is subject to a tax equal to $100,000 ($50,000 for S's failure plus $50,000 for T's failure) for Year 4.

(b) *Interaction with other provisions.*—(1) *Correction.*—Unless a hospital organization's failure to meet the requirements of section 501(r)(3) involves an omission or error that is described in and corrected in accordance with § 1.501(r)-2(b) (and is thus not considered a failure), a failure to meet the requirements of section 501(r)(3) will result in a tax being imposed on the organization under this section, notwithstanding the organization's correction and disclosure of the failure in accordance with the guidance described in § 1.501(r)-2(c).

(2) *Interaction with other taxes.*—The tax imposed by this section is in addition to any tax imposed by § 1.501(r)-2(d) or as a result of revocation of a hospital organization's section 501(c)(3) status.

(c) *Effective/applicability date.*—Paragraph (a) of this section applies on and after December 29, 2014. [Reg. § 53.4959-1.]

☐ [*T.D.* 9708, 12-29-2014 (*corrected* 3-10-2015).]

ABATEMENT OF FIRST AND SECOND TIER TAXES

[Reg. § 53.4961-1]

§ 53.4961-1. Abatement of second tier taxes for correction within correction period.—If any taxable event is corrected during the correction period for the event, then any second tier tax imposed with respect to the event shall not be assessed. If the tax has been assessed, it shall be abated. If the tax has been collected, it shall be credited or refunded as an overpayment. For purposes of this section, the tax imposed includes interest, additions to the tax and additional amounts. For definitions of the terms "second tier tax," "taxable event," "correct," and "correction period," see § 53.4963-1. [Reg. § 53.4961-1.]

☐ [*T.D.* 8084, 5-1-86.]

[Reg. § 53.4961-2]

§ 53.4961-2. Court proceedings to determine liability for second tier tax.—(a) *Introduction.*—Under section 4961(b) and (c), the period of limitations on collection may be suspended and assessment or collection of first or second tier tax may be prohibited during the pendency of administrative and judicial proceedings conducted to determine a taxpayer s liability for second tier tax. This section provides rules relating to the suspension of the limitations period and the prohibitions on assessment and collection. In addition, this section describes the administrative and judicial proceedings to which these rules apply.

(b) *Initial proceeding.*—(1) *Defined.*—For purposes of subpart K, an initial proceeding means a proceeding described in subparagraph (2) or (3).

(2) Tax Court proceeding before assessment A proceeding is described in this subparagraph (2) if it is a proceeding with respect to the taxpayer's liability for second tier tax and is commenced in accordance with section 6213(a).

(3) *Refund proceeding commenced before correction period ends.*—A proceeding is described in this subparagraph (3) if it is a proceeding commenced under section 7422, in accordance with the provisions of § 53.4963-1(e)(4) and (5) (relating to prerequisites to extension of the correction period during certain refund proceedings), and with respect to the taxpayer's liability for second tier tax.

(c) *Supplemental proceeding.*—(1) *Jurisdiction.*—If a determination in an initial proceeding that a taxpayer is liable for a second tier tax has become final, the court in which the initial proceeding was commenced shall have jurisdiction to conduct any necessary supplemental proceeding to determine whether the taxable event was corrected during the correction period.

(2) *Time for beginning proceeding.*—The time for beginning a supplemental proceeding begins on the day after a determination in an initial proceeding becomes final and ends on the 96th day after the last day of the correction period.

(d) *Restriction on assessment during Tax Court proceeding.*—If a supplemental proceeding described in section 4961(b) and § 53.4961-2(c) is commenced in the Tax Court, the provisions of the second and third sentences of section 6213(a) and the first and third sentences of § 301.6213-1(a)(2) apply with respect to a deficiency in second tier tax until the decision of the Tax Court in the supplemental proceeding is final.

(e) *Suspension of period of collection for second tier tax.*—(1) *Scope.*—Except as provided in subparagraph (6), this paragraph (e) applies to the second tier tax assessed with respect to a taxable event if a claim described in subparagraph (2) is filed.

(2) *Claim for refund.*—A claim for refund is described in this subparagraph (2) if, no later than 90 days after the day on which the second tier tax is assessed with respect to a taxable event, the taxpayer—

(i) Pays the full amount of first tier tax for the taxable period, and

(ii) Files a claim for refund of the amount paid.

(3) *Collection prohibited.*—No levy or proceeding in court for the collection of the second tier tax shall be made, begun, or prosecuted until the end of the collection prohibition period de-

scribed in subparagraph (5). Notwithstanding section 7421(a), the collection by levy or proceeding may be enjoined during the collection prohibition period by a proceeding in the proper court.

(4) *Suspension of running of period of limitation on collection.*—With respect to a second tier tax to which this paragraph (e) applies, the running of the period of limitations provided in section 6502 (relating to collection of tax by levy or by a proceeding in court) shall be suspended for the collection prohibition period described in subparagraph (5).

(5) *Collection prohibition period.*—The collection prohibition period begins on the day the second tier tax is assessed and ends on the latest of:

(i) The day a decision in a refund proceeding commenced before the 91st day after denial of the claim described in subparagraph (2) of this paragraph (including any supplemental proceeding under § 53.4961-2(c)) becomes final;

(ii) The 90th day after the claim referred to in subparagraph (2) is denied; or

(iii) The 90th day after the second tier tax is assessed.

(6) *Jeopardy collection.*—If the Secretary makes a finding that the collection of the second tier tax is in jeopardy, nothing in this paragraph (e) shall prevent the immediate collection of such tax.

(f) *Finality.*—(1) *Tax Court proceeding.*—For purposes of this subpart K, section 7481 applies in determining when a decision in a Tax Court proceeding becomes final.

(2) *Refund proceeding.*—For purposes of this subpart K, § 301.7422-1 applies in determining when a decision in a refund proceeding becomes final. [Reg. § 53.4961-2.]

☐ [*T.D.* 8084, 5-1-86.]

[Reg. § 53.4963-1]

§ 53.4963-1. Definitions.—(a) *First tier tax.*—For purposes of this subpart K, the term "first tier tax" means any tax imposed by subsection (a) of section 4941, 4942, 4943, 4944, 4945, 4951, 4952, 4955, 4958, 4971, or 4975. A first tier tax may also be referred to as an "initial tax" in parts 53 and 54.

(b) *Second tier tax.*—For purposes of this subpart K, the term "second tier tax" means any tax imposed by subsection (b) of section 4941, 4942, 4943, 4944, 4945, 4951, 4952, 4955, 4958, 4971, or 4975. A second tier tax may also be referred to as an "additional tax" in parts 53 and 54.

(c) *Taxable event.*—For purposes of this subpart K, the term "taxable event" means any act, or failure to act, giving rise to liability for tax under section 4941, 4942, 4943, 4944, 4945, 4951, 4952, 4955, 4958, 4971, or 4975.

(d) *Correct.*—(1) *In general.*—Except as provided in subparagraph (2), the term "correct"

has the same meaning for purposes of this subpart K as in the section which imposes the second tier tax or the regulations thereunder.

(2) *Special rules.*—The term "correct" means—

(i) For a second tier tax imposed by section 4942(b), reducing the amount of the undistributed income to zero,

(ii) For a second tier tax imposed by section 4943(b), reducing the amount of the excess business holdings to zero, and

(iii) For a second tier tax imposed by section 4944(b), removing the investment from jeopardy.

(e) *Correction period.*—(1) *In general.*—The correction period with respect to any taxable event shall begin with the date on which the taxable event occurs and shall end 90 days after the date of mailing of a notice of deficiency under section 6212 with respect to the second tier tax imposed with respect to the taxable event.

(2) *Extensions of correction period.*—The correction period referred to in subparagraph (1) of this paragraph shall be extended by any period in which a deficiency cannot be assessed under section 6213(a). In addition, the correction period referred to in subparagraph (1) of this paragraph (e) shall be extended in accordance with subparagraphs (3), (4), and (5) of this paragraph except that subparagraph (4) or (5) shall not operate to extend a correction period with respect to which a taxpayer has filed a petition with the United States Tax Court for redetermination of a deficiency within the time prescribed by section 6213(a).

(3) *Extensions by Commissioner.*—The correction period referred to in subparagraph (1) of this paragraph may be extended by any period which the Commissioner determines is reasonable and necessary to bring about correction (including, for taxes imposed by section 4975, equitable relief sought by the Secretary of Labor) of the taxable event. The Commissioner ordinarily will not extend the correction period unless the following factors are present:

(i) The taxpayer on whom the second tier tax is imposed, the Secretary of Labor (for taxes imposed by section 4975), or an appropriate State officer (as defined in section 6104(c)(2)) is actively seeking in good faith to correct the taxable event;

(ii) Adequate corrective action cannot reasonably be expected to result during the unextended correction period;

(iii) For taxes imposed by section 4975, the Secretary of Labor requests the extension because subdivision (ii) applies; and

(iv) For taxes imposed by chapter 42 (other than taxes imposed by section 4940), the taxable event appears to have been an isolated occurrence so that it appears unlikely that similar taxable events will occur in the future.

(4) *Extension for payment of first tier tax.*—If, within the unextended correction period, the tax-

payer pays the full amount of the first tier tax imposed with respect to the taxable event the Commissioner shall extend the correction period to the later of—

(i) Ninety days after the payment of the first tier tax, or

(ii) The last day of the correction period determined without regard to this paragraph.

(5) *Extensions for filing claim for refund or refund suit.*—If prior to the expiration of the correction period (including extensions) a claim for refund is filed with respect to payment of the full amount of the first tier tax imposed with respect to the taxable event, the Commissioner shall extend the correction period during the pendency of the claim plus an additional 90 days. If within that time a suit or proceeding referred to in section 7422(g) with respect to the claim is filed, the Commissioner shall extend the correction period until the determination in the suit for refund (determined without regard to a supplemental proceeding under section 4961(b)) is final, determined under § 301.7422-2(a).

(6) *End of correction period if waiver accepted.*—If the notice of deficiency referred to in paragraph (1) is not mailed because there is a waiver of the restrictions on assessment and col-

lection of the deficiency or because the deficiency is paid, the correction period will end with the end of the collection prohibition period described in § 53.4961-2(e)(5).

(7) *Date on which taxable event occurs.*—For purposes of subparagraph (1), the taxable event shall be treated as occurring—

(i) Under section 4942, on the first day of the taxable year for which there is undistributed income,

(ii) Under section 4943, on the first day on which there are excess business holdings,

(iii) Under section 4971, on the last day of the plan year in which there is an accumulated funding deficiency, and

(iv) In all other cases, the date on which the event occurred.

(f) *Effective date.*—The provisions of this subpart K are effective with respect to second tier taxes assessed after December 24, 1980. The preceding sentence shall not be construed to permit the assessment of a tax in a case to which, on December 24, 1980, the doctrine of res judicata applied. [Reg. § 53.4963-1.]

☐ [*T.D.* 8084, 5-1-86. *Amended by T.D.* 8628, 12-4-95 *and T.D.* 8920, 1-9-2001.]

TAX SHELTER TRANSACTIONS

[Reg. § 53.4965-1]

§ 53.4965-1. Overview.—(a) *Entity-level excise tax.*—Section 4965 imposes two excise taxes with respect to certain tax shelter transactions to which tax-exempt entities are parties. Section 4965(a)(1) imposes an entity-level excise tax on certain tax-exempt entities that are parties to "prohibited tax shelter transactions," as defined in section 4965(e). See § 53.4965-2 for the discussion of covered tax-exempt entities. See § 53.4965-3 for the definition of prohibited tax shelter transactions. See § 53.4965-4 for the definition of tax-exempt party to a prohibited tax shelter transaction. The entity-level excise tax under section 4965(a)(1) is imposed on a specified percentage of the entity's net income or proceeds that are attributable to the transaction for the relevant tax year (or a period within that tax year). The rate of tax depends on whether the entity knew or had reason to know that the transaction was a prohibited tax shelter transaction at the time the entity became a party to the transaction. See § 53.4965-7(a) for the discussion of the entity-level excise tax under section 4965(a)(1). See § 53.4965-6 for the discussion of "knowing or having reason to know." See § 53.4965-8 for the definition of net income and proceeds and the standard for allocating net income and proceeds that are attributable to a prohibited tax shelter transaction to various periods.

(b) *Manager-level excise tax.*—Section 4965(a)(2) imposes a manager-level excise tax on "entity managers," as defined in section 4965(d), of tax-

exempt entities who approve the entity as a party (or otherwise cause the entity to be a party) to a prohibited tax shelter transaction and know or have reason to know, at the time the tax-exempt entity enters into the transaction, that the transaction is a prohibited tax shelter transaction. See § 53.4965-5 for the definition of entity manager and the meaning of "approving or otherwise causing," and § 53.4965-6 for the discussion of "knowing or having reason to know." See § 53.4965-7(b) for the discussion of the manager-level excise tax under section 4965(a)(2).

(c) *Effective/applicability dates.*—See § 53.4965-9 for the discussion of the relevant effective and applicability dates. [Reg. § 53.4965-1.]

☐ [*T.D.* 9492, 7-2-2010.]

[Reg. § 53.4965-2]

§ 53.4965-2. Covered tax-exempt entities.— (a) *In general.*—Under section 4965(c), the term "tax-exempt entity" refers to entities that are described in sections 501(c), 501(d), or 170(c) (other than the United States), Indian tribal governments (within the meaning of section 7701(a)(40)), and tax-qualified pension plans, individual retirement arrangements and similar tax-favored savings arrangements that are described in sections 4979(e)(1), (2) or (3), 529, 457(b), or 4973(a). The tax-exempt entities referred to in section 4965(c) are divided into two broad categories, non-plan entities and plan entities.

(b) *Non-plan entities.*—Non-plan entities are—
(1) Entities described in section 501(c);

(2) Religious or apostolic associations or corporations described in section 501(d);

(3) Entities described in section 170(c), including states, possessions of the United States, the District of Columbia, political subdivisions of states and political subdivisions of possessions of the United States (but not including the United States); and

(4) Indian tribal governments within the meaning of section 7701(a)(40).

(c) *Plan entities.*—Plan entities are—

(1) Entities described in section 4979(e)(1) (qualified plans under section 401(a), including qualified cash or deferred arrangements under section 401(k) (including a section 401(k) plan that allows designated Roth contributions));

(2) Entities described in section 4979(e)(2) (annuity plans described in section 403(a));

(3) Entities described in section 4979(e)(3) (annuity contracts described in section 403(b), including a section 403(b) arrangement that allows Roth contributions);

(4) Qualified tuition programs described in section 529;

(5) Eligible deferred compensation plans under section 457(b) that are maintained by a governmental employer as defined in section 457(e)(1)(A);

(6) Arrangements described in section 4973(a) which include—

(i) Individual retirement plans defined in section 408(a) and (b), including—

(A) Simplified employee pensions (SEPs) under section 408(k);

(B) Simple individual retirement accounts (SIMPLEs) under section 408(p);

(C) Deemed individual retirement accounts or annuities (IRAs) qualified under a qualified plan (deemed IRAs) under section 408(q); and

(D) Roth IRAs under section 408A.

(ii) Arrangements described in section 220(d) (Archer Medical Savings Accounts (MSAs));

(iii) Arrangements described in section 403(b)(7) (custodial accounts treated as annuity contracts);

(iv) Arrangements described in section 530 (Coverdell education savings accounts); and

(v) Arrangements described in section 223(d) (health savings accounts (HSAs)).

(d) *Effective/applicability dates.*—See § 53.4965-9 for the discussion of the relevant effective and applicability dates. [Reg. § 53.4965-2.]

☐ [*T.D.* 9492, 7-2-2010 (*corrected* 8-3-2010).]

[Reg. § 53.4965-3]

§ 53.4965-3. Prohibited tax shelter transactions.—(a) *In general.*—Under section 4965(e), the term *prohibited tax shelter transaction* means—

(1) Listed transactions within the meaning of section 6707A(c)(2), including subsequently listed transactions described in paragraph (b) of this section; and

(2) Prohibited reportable transactions, which consist of the following reportable transactions within the meaning of section 6707A(c)(1)—

(i) Confidential transactions, as described in § 1.6011-4(b)(3) of this chapter; or

(ii) Transactions with contractual protection, as described in § 1.6011-4(b)(4) of this chapter.

(b) *Subsequently listed transactions.*—A subsequently listed transaction for purposes of section 4965 is a transaction that is identified by the Secretary as a listed transaction after the tax-exempt entity has entered into the transaction and that was not a prohibited reportable transaction (within the meaning of section 4965(e)(1)(C) and paragraph (a)(2) of this section) at the time the entity entered into the transaction.

(c) *Cross-reference.*—The determination of whether a transaction is a listed transaction or a prohibited reportable transaction for section 4965 purposes shall be made under the law applicable to section 6707A(c)(1) and (c)(2).

(d) *Effective/applicability dates.*—See § 53.4965-9 for the discussion of the relevant effective and applicability dates. [Reg. § 53.4965-3.]

☐ [*T.D.* 9492, 7-2-2010.]

[Reg. § 53.4965-4]

§ 53.4965-4. Definition of tax-exempt party to a prohibited tax shelter transaction.—(a) *In general.*—For purposes of sections 4965 and 6033(a)(2), a tax-exempt entity is a party to a prohibited tax shelter transaction if the entity—

(1) Facilitates a prohibited tax shelter transaction by reason of its tax-exempt, tax indifferent or tax-favored status; or

(2) Is identified in published guidance, by type, class or role, as a party to a prohibited tax shelter transaction.

(b) Published guidance may identify which tax-exempt entities, by type, class or role, will not be treated as a party to a prohibited tax shelter transaction.

(c) *Example.*—The following example illustrates the principle of paragraph (a)(1) of this section:

Example. A tax-exempt entity enters into a transaction (Transaction A) with an S corporation. Transaction A is the same as or substantially similar to the transaction identified by the Secretary as a listed transaction in Notice 2004-30 (2004-1 CB 828). The tax-exempt entity's role in Transaction A is similar to the role of the tax-exempt party, as described in Notice 2004-30. Under the terms of the transaction, as described in Notice 2004-30, the tax-exempt entity receives the S corporation stock and purports to aid the S corporation and its shareholders in avoiding taxable income. The tax-exempt entity facilitates Transaction A by reason of its tax-exempt, tax indifferent or tax-favored status. Accordingly, the tax-exempt entity is a party to Transaction A

for purposes of sections 4965 and 6033(a)(2). See § 601.601(d)(2)(ii)(*b*) of this chapter.

(d) *Effective/applicability dates.*—See § 53.4965-9 for the discussion of the relevant effective and applicability dates. [Reg. § 53.4965-4.]

☐ [T.D. 9492, 7-2-2010.]

[Reg. § 53.4965-5]

§ 53.4965-5. **Entity managers and related definitions.**—(a) *Entity manager of a non-plan entity.*—(1) *In general.*—Under section 4965(d)(1), an *entity manager of a non-plan entity* is—

(i) A person with the authority or responsibility similar to that exercised by an officer, director, or trustee of an organization (that is, the non-plan entity); and

(ii) With respect to any act, the person who has final authority or responsibility (either individually or as a member of a collective body) with respect to such act.

(2) *Definition of officer.*—For purposes of paragraph (a)(1)(i) of this section, a person is considered to be an officer of the non-plan entity (or to have similar authority or responsibility) if the person—

(i) Is specifically designated as such under the certificate of incorporation, bylaws, or other constitutive documents of the non-plan entity; or

(ii) Regularly exercises general authority to make administrative or policy decisions on behalf of the non-plan entity.

(3) *Exception for acts requiring approval by a superior.*—With respect to any act, any person is not described in paragraph (a)(2)(ii) of this section if the person has authority merely to recommend particular administrative or policy decisions, but not to implement them without approval of a superior.

(4) *Delegation of authority.*—A person is an entity manager of a non-plan entity within the meaning of paragraph (a)(1)(ii) of this section if, with respect to any prohibited tax shelter transaction, such person has been delegated final authority or responsibility with respect to such transaction (including by transaction type or dollar amount) by a person described in paragraph (a)(1)(i) of this section or the governing board of the entity. For example, an investment manager is an entity manager with respect to a prohibited tax shelter transaction if the non-plan entity's governing body delegated to the investment manager the final authority to make certain investment decisions and, in the exercise of that authority, the manager committed the entity to the transaction. To be considered an entity manager of a non-plan entity within the meaning of paragraph (a)(1)(ii) of this section, a person need not be an employee of the entity. A person is not described in paragraph (a)(1)(ii) of this section if the person is merely implementing a decision made by a superior.

(b) *Entity manager of a plan entity.*—(1) *In general.*—Under section 4965(d)(2), an *entity manager*

of a plan entity is the person who approves or otherwise causes the entity to be a party to the prohibited tax shelter transaction.

(2) *Special rule for plan participants and beneficiaries who have investment elections.*—(i) *Fully self-directed plans or arrangements.*—In the case of a fully self-directed qualified plan, IRA, or other savings arrangement (including a case where a plan participant or beneficiary is given a list of prohibited investments, such as collectibles), if the plan participant or beneficiary selected a certain investment and, therefore, approved the plan entity to become a party to a prohibited tax shelter transaction, the plan participant or the beneficiary is an entity manager.

(ii) *Plans or arrangements with limited investment options.*—In the case of a qualified plan, IRA, or other savings arrangement where a plan participant or beneficiary is offered a limited number of investment options from which to choose, the person responsible for determining the pre-selected investment options is an entity manager and the plan participant or the beneficiary generally is not an entity manager.

(c) *Meaning of "approves or otherwise causes".*—(1) *In general.*—A person is treated as approving or otherwise causing a tax-exempt entity to become a party to a prohibited tax shelter transaction if the person has the authority to commit the entity to the transaction, either individually or as a member of a collective body, and the person exercises that authority.

(2) *Collective bodies.*—If a person shares the authority described in paragraph (c)(1) of this section as a member of a collective body (for example, board of trustees or committee), the person will be considered to have exercised such authority if the person voted in favor of the entity becoming a party to the transaction. However, a member of the collective body will not be treated as having exercised the authority described in paragraph (c)(1) of this section if he or she voted against a resolution that constituted approval or an act that caused the tax-exempt entity to be a party to a prohibited tax shelter transaction, abstained from voting for such approval, or otherwise failed to vote in favor of such approval.

(3) *Exceptions.*—(i) *Successor in interest.*—If a tax-exempt entity that is a party to a prohibited tax shelter transaction is dissolved, liquidated, or merged into a successor entity, an entity manager of the successor entity will not, solely by reason of the reorganization, be treated as approving or otherwise causing the successor entity to become a party to a prohibited tax shelter transaction, provided that the reorganization of the tax-exempt entity does not result in a material change to the terms of the transaction. For purposes of this paragraph (c)(3)(i), a material change includes an extension or renewal of the agreement (other than an extension or renewal that results from another party to the transaction unilaterally exercising an option granted by the

agreement) or a more than incidental change to any payment under the agreement. A change for the sole purpose of substituting the successor entity for the original tax-exempt party is not a material change.

(ii) *Exercise or nonexercise of options.*— Nonexercise of an option pursuant to a transaction involving the tax-exempt entity generally will not constitute an act of approving or causing the entity to be a party to the transaction. If, pursuant to a transaction involving the tax-exempt entity, the entity manager exercises an option (such as a repurchase option), the entity manager will not be subject to the entity manager-level tax if the exercise of the option does not result in the tax-exempt entity becoming a party to a second transaction that is a prohibited tax shelter transaction.

(4) *Example.*—The following example illustrates the principles of paragraph (c)(3)(ii) of this section:

Example. In a sale-in, lease-out (SILO) transaction described in Notice 2005-13 (2005-1 CB 630), X, which is a non-plan entity, has purported to sell property to Y, a taxable entity and lease it back for a term of years. At the end of the basic lease term, X has the option of "repurchasing" the property from Y for a predetermined purchase price, with funds that have been set aside at the inception of the transaction for that purpose. The entity manager, by deciding to exercise or not exercise the "repurchase" option is not approving or otherwise causing the non-plan entity to become a party to a second prohibited tax shelter transaction. See § 601.601(d)(2)(ii)(b) of this chapter.

(5) *Coordination with the reason-to-know standard.*—The determination that an entity manager approved or caused a tax-exempt entity to be a party to a prohibited tax shelter transaction, by itself, does not establish liability for the section 4965(a)(2) tax. For rules on determining whether an entity manager knew or had reason to know that the transaction was a prohibited tax shelter transaction, see § 53.4965-6(b).

(d) *Effective/applicability dates.*—See § 53.4965-9 for the discussion of the relevant effective and applicability dates. [Reg. § 53.4965-5.]

☐ [T.D. 9492, 7-2-2010 (corrected 8-3-2010).]

[Reg. § 53.4965-6]

§ 53.4965-6. Meaning of "knows or has reason to know".—(a) *Attribution to the entity.*—An entity will be treated as knowing or having reason to know for section 4965 purposes if one or more of its entity managers knew or had reason to know that the transaction was a prohibited tax shelter transaction at the time the entity manager(s) approved the entity as (or otherwise caused the entity to be) a party to the transaction. The entity shall be attributed the knowledge or reason to know of any entity manager described in § 53.4965-5(a)(1)(i) even if that entity manager does not approve the entity as (or otherwise cause the entity to be) a party to the transaction.

(b) *Determining whether an entity manager knew or had reason to know.*—(1) *In general.*—Whether an entity manager knew or had reason to know that a transaction is a prohibited tax shelter transaction is based on all facts and circumstances. In order for an entity manager to know or have reason to know that a transaction is a prohibited tax shelter transaction, the entity manager must have knowledge of sufficient facts that would lead a reasonable person to conclude that the transaction is a prohibited tax shelter transaction. An entity manager will be considered to have "reason to know" if a reasonable person in the entity manager's circumstances would conclude that the transaction was a prohibited tax shelter transaction based on all the facts reasonably available to the manager at the time of approving the entity as (or otherwise causing the entity to be) a party to the transaction. Factors that will be considered in determining whether a reasonable person in the entity manager's circumstances would conclude that the transaction was a prohibited tax shelter transaction include, but are not limited to—

(i) The presence of tax shelter indicia (see paragraph (b)(2) of this section);

(ii) Whether the entity manager received a disclosure statement prior to the consummation of the transaction indicating that the transaction may be a prohibited tax shelter transaction (see paragraph (b)(3) of this section); and

(iii) Whether the entity manager made appropriate inquiries into the transaction (see paragraph (b)(4) of this section).

(2) *Tax-shelter indicia.*—The presence of indicia that a transaction is a tax shelter will be treated as an indication that the entity manager knew or had reason to know that the transaction was a prohibited tax shelter transaction. Tax shelter indicia include but are not limited to—

(i) The transaction is extraordinary for the entity considering prior investment activity;

(ii) The transaction promises an economic return for the organization that is exceptional considering the amount invested by, the participation of, or the absence of risk to the organization; or

(iii) The transaction is of significant size relative to the receipts of the entity.

(3) *Effect of disclosure statements.*—Receipt by an entity manager of a statement, including a statement described in section 6011(g), in advance of a transaction that the transaction may be a prohibited tax shelter transaction (or a statement that a partnership, hedge fund or other investment conduit may engage in a prohibited tax shelter transaction in the future) is a factor relevant in the determination of whether the entity manager knew or had reason to know that the transaction is a prohibited transaction. However, an entity manager will not be treated as knowing or having reason to know that the

transaction was a prohibited tax shelter transaction solely because the entity manager receives such a disclosure.

(4) *Appropriate inquiries.*—What inquiries are appropriate will be determined from the facts and circumstances of each case. For example, if one or more tax shelter indicia are present or if an entity manager receives a disclosure statement described in paragraph (b)(3) of this section, an entity manager has a responsibility to inquire further whether the transaction is a prohibited tax shelter transaction.

(c) *Reliance on professional advice.*—(1) *In general.*—An entity manager is not required to obtain the advice of a professional tax advisor to establish that the entity manager made appropriate inquiries. Moreover, not seeking professional advice, by itself, shall not give rise to an inference that the entity manager had reason to know that a transaction is a prohibited tax shelter transaction.

(2) *Reliance on written opinion of professional tax advisor.*—An entity manager may establish that he or she did not have a reason to know that a transaction was a prohibited tax shelter transaction at the time the tax-exempt entity entered into the transaction if the entity manager reasonably, and in good faith, relied on the written opinion of a professional tax advisor. Reliance on the written opinion of a professional tax advisor establishes that the entity manager did not have reason to know if, taking into account all the facts and circumstances, the reliance was reasonable and the entity manager acted in good faith. For example, the entity manager's education, sophistication, and business experience will be relevant in determining whether the reliance was reasonable and made in good faith. In no event will an entity manager be considered to have reasonably relied in good faith on an opinion unless the requirements of this paragraph (c)(2) are satisfied. The fact that these requirements are satisfied, however, will not necessarily establish that the entity manager reasonably relied on the opinion in good faith. For example, reliance may not be reasonable or in good faith if the entity manager knew, or reasonably should have known, that the advisor lacked knowledge in the relevant aspects of Federal tax law.

(i) *All facts and circumstances considered.*—The advice must be based upon all pertinent facts and circumstances and the law as it relates to those facts and circumstances. The requirements of this paragraph (c)(2) are not satisfied if the entity manager fails to disclose a fact that it knows, or reasonably should know, is relevant to determining whether the transaction is a prohibited tax shelter transaction.

(ii) *No unreasonable assumptions.*—The advice must not be based on unreasonable factual or legal assumptions (including assumptions as to future events) and must not unreasonably rely on the representations, statements, findings, or agreements of the entity manager or any other

person (including another party to the transaction or a material advisor within the meaning of sections 6111 and 6112).

(iii) *"More likely than not" opinion.*—The written opinion of the professional tax advisor must apply the appropriate law to the facts and, based on this analysis, must conclude that the transaction was not a prohibited tax shelter transaction at a "more likely than not" level of certainty at the time the entity manager approved the entity (or otherwise caused the entity) to be a party to the transaction.

(3) *Special rule.*—An entity manager's reliance on a written opinion of a professional tax advisor will not be considered reasonable if the advisor is, or is related to a person who is, a material advisor with respect to the transaction within the meaning of sections 6111 and 6112.

(d) *Subsequently listed transactions.*—An entity manager will not be treated as knowing or having reason to know that a transaction (other than a prohibited reportable transaction as defined in section 4965(e)(1)(C) and § 53.4965-3(a)(2)) is a prohibited tax shelter transaction if the entity enters into the transaction before the date on which the transaction is identified by the Secretary as a listed transaction.

(e) *Effective/applicability dates.*—See § 53.4965-9 for the discussion of the relevant effective and applicability dates. [Reg. § 53.4965-6.]

☐ [*T.D. 9492, 7-2-2010.*]

[Reg. § 53.4965-7]

§ 53.4965-7. Taxes on prohibited tax shelter transactions.—(a) *Entity-level taxes.*—(1) *In general.*—Entity-level excise taxes apply to non-plan entities (as defined in § 53.4965-2(b)) that are parties to prohibited tax shelter transactions.

(i) *Prohibited tax shelter transactions other than subsequently listed transactions.*—(A) *Amount of tax if the entity did not know and did not have reason to know.*—If the tax-exempt entity did not know and did not have reason to know that the transaction was a prohibited tax shelter transaction at the time the entity entered into the transaction, the tax is the highest rate of tax under section 11 multiplied by the greater of—

(1) The entity's net income with respect to the prohibited tax shelter transaction (after taking into account any tax imposed by Subtitle D, other than by this section, with respect to such transaction) for the taxable year; or

(2) 75 percent of the proceeds received by the entity for the taxable year that are attributable to such transaction.

(B) *Amount of tax if the entity knew or had reason to know.*—If the tax-exempt entity knew or had reason to know that the transaction was a prohibited tax shelter transaction at the time the entity entered into the transaction, the tax is the greater of—

(1) 100 percent of the entity's net income with respect to the transaction (after taking

into account any tax imposed by Subtitle D, other than by this section, with respect to such transaction) for the taxable year; or

    (2) 75 percent of the proceeds received by the entity for the taxable year that are attributable to such transaction.

    (ii) *Subsequently listed transactions.*— (A) *In general.*—In the case of a subsequently listed transaction (as defined in section 4965(e)(2) and §53.4965-3(b)), the tax-exempt entity's income and proceeds attributable to the transaction are allocated between the period before the transaction became listed and the period beginning on the date the transaction became listed. See §53.4965-8 for the standard for allocating net income or proceeds to various periods. The tax for each taxable year is the highest rate of tax under section 11 multiplied by the greater of—

    (1) The entity's net income with respect to the subsequently listed transaction (after taking into account any tax imposed by Subtitle D, other than by this section, with respect to such transaction) for the taxable year that is allocable to the period beginning on the later of the date such transaction is identified by the Secretary as a listed transaction or the first day of the taxable year; or

    (2) 75 percent of the proceeds received by the entity for the taxable year that are attributable to such transaction and allocable to the period beginning on the later of the date such transaction is identified by the Secretary as a listed transaction or the first day of the taxable year.

    (B) *No increase in tax.*—The 100 percent tax under section 4965(b)(1)(B) and §53.4965-7(a)(1)(i)(B) does not apply to any subsequently listed transaction (as defined in section 4965(e)(2) and §53.4965-3(b)) entered into by a tax-exempt entity before the date on which the transaction is identified by the Secretary as a listed transaction.

    (2) *Taxable year.*—The excise tax imposed under section 4965(a)(1) applies for the taxable year in which the entity becomes a party to the prohibited tax shelter transaction and any subsequent taxable year for which the entity has net income or proceeds attributable to the transaction. A taxable year for tax-exempt entities is the calendar year or fiscal year, as applicable, depending on the basis on which the tax-exempt entity keeps its books for Federal income tax purposes. If a tax-exempt entity has not established a taxable year for Federal income tax purposes, the entity's taxable year for the purpose of determining the amount and timing of net income and proceeds attributable to a prohibited tax shelter transaction will be deemed to be the annual period the entity uses in keeping its books and records.

    (b) *Manager-level taxes.*—(1) *Amount of tax.*—If any entity manager approved or otherwise caused the tax-exempt entity to become a party to a prohibited tax shelter transaction and knew

or had reason to know that the transaction was a prohibited tax shelter transaction, such entity manager is liable for the $20,000 tax. See §53.4965-5(d) for the meaning of approved or otherwise caused. See §53.4965-6 for the meaning of knew or had reason to know.

    (2) *Timing of the entity manager tax.*—If a tax-exempt entity enters into a prohibited tax shelter transaction during a taxable year of an entity manager, then the entity manager that approved or otherwise caused the tax-exempt entity to become a party to the transaction is liable for the entity manager tax for that taxable year if the entity manager knew or had reason to know that the transaction was a prohibited tax shelter transaction.

    (3) *Example.*—The application of paragraph (b)(2) of this section is illustrated by the following example:

    Example. The entity manager's taxable year is the calendar year. On December 1, 2006, the entity manager approved or otherwise caused the tax-exempt entity to become a party to a transaction that the entity manager knew or had reason to know was a prohibited tax shelter transaction. The tax-exempt entity entered into the transaction on January 31, 2007. The entity manager is liable for the entity manager level tax for the entity manager's 2007 taxable year, during which the tax-exempt entity entered into the prohibited tax shelter transaction.

    (4) *Separate liability.*—If more than one entity manager approved or caused a tax-exempt entity to become a party to a prohibited tax shelter transaction while knowing (or having reason to know) that the transaction was a prohibited tax shelter transaction, then each such entity manager is separately (that is, not jointly and severally) liable for the entity manager-level tax with respect to the transaction.

    (c) *Effective/applicability dates.*—See §53.4965-9 for the discussion of the relevant effective and applicability dates. [Reg. §53.4965-7.]

    ☐ [*T.D.* 9492, 7-2-2010.]

[Reg. §53.4965-8]

    §53.4965-8. Definition of net income and proceeds and standard for allocating net income or proceeds to various periods.—(a) *In general.*—For purposes of section 4965(a), the amount and the timing of the net income and proceeds attributable to the prohibited tax shelter transaction will be computed in a manner consistent with the substance of the transaction. In determining the substance of listed transactions, the IRS will look to, among other items, the listing guidance and any subsequent guidance published in the Internal Revenue Bulletin relating to the transaction.

    (b) *Definition of net income and proceeds.*— (1) *Net income.*—A tax-exempt entity's net income attributable to a prohibited tax shelter transaction is its gross income derived from the transaction reduced by those deductions that are

attributable to the transaction and that would be allowed by chapter 1 of the Internal Revenue Code if the tax-exempt entity were treated as a taxable entity for this purpose, and further reduced by taxes imposed by Subtitle D, other than by this section, with respect to the transaction.

(2) *Proceeds.*—(i) *Tax-exempt entities that facilitate the transaction by reason of their tax-exempt, tax indifferent or tax-favored status.*—Solely for purposes of section 4965, in the case of a tax-exempt entity that is a party to the transaction by reason of § 53.4965-4(a)(1) of this chapter, the term *proceeds* means the gross amount of the tax-exempt entity's consideration for facilitating the transaction, not reduced for any costs or expenses attributable to the transaction. Published guidance with respect to a particular prohibited tax shelter transaction may designate additional amounts as proceeds from the transaction for section 4965 purposes.

(ii) *Treatment of gifts and contributions.*—To the extent not otherwise included in the definition of proceeds in paragraph (b)(2)(i) of this section, any amount that is a gift or a contribution to a tax-exempt entity and is attributable to a prohibited tax shelter transaction will be treated as proceeds for section 4965 purposes, unreduced by any associated expenses.

(c) *Allocation of net income and proceeds.*—(1) *In general.*—For purposes of section 4965(a), the net income and proceeds attributable to a prohibited tax shelter transaction must be allocated in a manner consistent with the tax-exempt entity's established method of accounting for Federal income tax purposes. If the tax-exempt entity has not established a method of accounting for Federal income tax purposes, solely for purposes of section 4965(a) the tax-exempt entity must use the cash receipts and disbursements method of accounting (cash method) provided for in section 446 of the Internal Revenue Code to determine the amount and timing of net income and proceeds attributable to a prohibited tax shelter transaction.

(2) *Special rule.*—If a tax-exempt entity has established a method of accounting other than the cash method, the tax-exempt entity may nevertheless use the cash method of accounting to determine the amount of the net income and proceeds—

(i) Attributable to a prohibited tax shelter transaction entered into prior to the effective date of section 4965(a) tax and allocable to pre- and post-effective date periods; or

(ii) Attributable to a subsequently listed transaction and allocable to pre- and post-listing periods.

(d) *Transition year rules.*—In the case of the taxable year that includes August 16, 2006 (the transition year), the IRS will treat the period beginning on the first day of the transition year and ending on August 15, 2006, and the period beginning on August 16, 2006, and ending on the last day of the transition year as short taxable years. This treatment is solely for purposes of allocating net income or proceeds under section 4965. The tax-exempt entity continues to file tax returns for the full taxable year, does not file tax returns with respect to these deemed short taxable years and does not otherwise take the short taxable years into account for Federal tax purposes. Accordingly, the net income or proceeds that are properly allocated to the transition year in accordance with this section will be treated as allocable to the period—

(1) Ending on or before August 15, 2006 (and accordingly not subject to tax under section 4965(a)) to the extent such net income or proceeds would have been properly taken into account in accordance with this section by the tax-exempt entity in the deemed short year ending on August 15, 2006; and

(2) Beginning after August 15, 2006 (and accordingly subject to tax under section 4965(a)) to the extent such income or proceeds would have been properly taken into account in accordance with this section by the tax-exempt entity in the short year beginning August 16, 2006.

(e) *Allocation to pre- and post-listing periods.*—If a transaction other than a prohibited reportable transaction (as defined in section 4965(e)(1)(C) and § 53.4965-3(a)(2)) to which the tax-exempt entity is a party is subsequently identified in published guidance as a listed transaction during a taxable year of the entity (the listing year) in which it has net income or proceeds attributable to the transaction, the net income or proceeds are allocated between the pre- and post-listing periods. The IRS will treat the period beginning on the first day of the listing year and ending on the day immediately preceding the date of the listing, and the period beginning on the date of the listing and ending on the last day of the listing year as short taxable years. This treatment is solely for purposes of allocating net income or proceeds under section 4965. The tax-exempt entity continues to file tax returns for the full taxable year, does not file tax returns with respect to these deemed short taxable years and does not otherwise take the short taxable years into account for Federal tax purposes. Accordingly, the net income or proceeds that are properly allocated to the listing year in accordance with this section will be treated as allocable to the period—

(1) Ending before the date of the listing (and accordingly not subject to tax under section 4965(a)) to the extent such net income or proceeds would have been properly taken into account in accordance with this section by the tax-exempt entity in the deemed short year ending on the day immediately preceding the date of the listing; and

(2) Beginning on the date of the listing (and accordingly subject to tax under section 4965(a)) to the extent such income or proceeds would have been properly taken into account in accordance with this section by the tax-exempt entity in the short year beginning on the date of the listing.

(f) *Examples.*—The following examples illustrate the allocation rules of this section:

Example 1. (i) In 1999, X, a calendar year non-plan entity using the cash method of accounting, entered into a lease-in/lease-out transaction (LILO) substantially similar to the transaction described in Notice 2000-15 (2000-1 CB 826) (describing Rev. Rul. 99-14 (1999-1 CB 835), superseded by Rev. Rul. 2002-69 (2002-2 CB 760)). In 1999, X purported to lease property to Y pursuant to a "head lease," and Y purported to lease the property back to X pursuant to a "sublease" of a shorter term. In form, X received $268M as an advance payment of head lease rent. Of this amount, $200M had been, in form, financed by a nonrecourse loan obtained by Y. X deposited the $200M with a "debt payment undertaker." This served to defease both a portion of X's rent obligation under its sublease and Y's repayment obligation under the nonrecourse loan. Of the remainder of the $268M advance head lease rent payment, X deposited $54M with an "equity payment undertaker." This served to defease the remainder of X's rent obligation under the sublease as well as the exercise price of X's end-of-sublease term purchase option. This amount inures to the benefit of Y and enables Y to recover its investment in the transaction and a return on that investment. In substance, the $54M is a loan from Y to X. X retained the remaining $14M of the advance head lease rent payment. In substance, this represents a fee for X's participation in the transaction. See §601.601(d)(2)(ii)(*b*) of this chapter.

(ii) According to the substance of the transaction, the head lease, sublease and nonrecourse debt will be ignored for Federal income tax purposes. Therefore, any net income or proceeds resulting from these elements of the transaction will not be considered net income or proceeds attributable to the LILO transaction for purposes of section 4965(a). The $54M deemed loan from Y to X and the $14M fee are not ignored for Federal income tax purposes.

(iii) Under X's established cash basis method of accounting, any net income received in 1999 and attributable to the LILO transaction is allocated to X's December 31, 1999, tax year for purposes of section 4965. The $14M fee received in 1999, which constitutes proceeds of the transaction, is likewise allocated to that tax year. Because the 1999 tax year is before the effective date of the section 4965 tax, X will not be subject to any excise tax under section 4965 for the amounts received in 1999.

(iv) Any earnings on the amount deposited with the equity payment undertaker that constitute gross income to X will be reduced by X's original issue discount deductions with respect to the deemed loan from Y, in determining X's net income from the transaction.

Example 2. B, a non-plan entity using the cash method of accounting, has an annual accounting period that ends on December 31, 2006. B entered into a prohibited tax shelter transaction on March 15, 2006. On that date, B received a payment of $600,000 as a fee for its involvement in the transaction. B received no other proceeds or income attributable to this transaction in 2006. Under B's method of accounting, the payment received by B on March 15, 2006, is taken into account in the deemed short year ending on August 15, 2006. Accordingly, solely for purposes of section 4965, the payment is treated as allocable solely to the period ending on or before August 15, 2006, and is not subject to the excise tax imposed by section 4965(a).

Example 3. The facts are the same as in *Example 2*, except that B received an additional payment of $400,000 on September 30, 2006. Under B's method of accounting, the payment received by B on September 30, 2006, is taken into account in the deemed short year beginning on August 16, 2006. Accordingly, solely for purposes of section 4965, the $400,000 payment is treated as allocable to the period beginning after August 15, 2006, and is subject to the excise tax imposed by section 4965(a).

Example 4. C, a non-plan entity using the cash method of accounting, has an annual accounting period that ends on December 31. C entered into a prohibited tax shelter transaction on May 1, 2005. On March 15, 2007, C received a payment of $580,000 attributable to the transaction. On June 1, 2007, the transaction is identified by the IRS in published guidance as a listed transaction. On June 15, 2007, C received an additional payment of $400,000 attributable to the transaction. Under C's method of accounting, the payments received on March 15, 2007, and June 15, 2007, are taken into account in 2007. The IRS will treat the period beginning on January 1, 2007, and ending on May 31, 2007, and the period beginning on June 1, 2007, and ending on December 31, 2007, as short taxable years. The payment received by C on March 15, 2007, is taken into account in the deemed short year ending on May 31, 2007. Accordingly, solely for purposes of section 4965, the payment is treated as allocable solely to the pre-listing period, and is not subject to the excise tax imposed by section 4965(a). The payment received by C on June 15, 2007, is taken into account in the deemed short year beginning on June 1, 2007. Accordingly, solely for purposes of section 4965, the payment is treated as allocable to the post-listing period, and is subject to the excise tax imposed by section 4965(a).

(g) *Effective/applicability dates.*—See §53.4965-9 for the discussion of the relevant effective and applicability dates. [Reg. §53.4965-8.]

☐ [*T.D.* 9492, 7-2-2010 (*corrected* 8-3-2010).]

[Reg. §53.4965-9]

§53.4965-9. Effective/applicability dates.—(a) *In general.*—The taxes under section 4965(a) and §53.4965-7 are effective for taxable years ending after May 17, 2006, with respect to transactions entered into before, on or after that date, except that no tax under section 4965(a) applies with respect to income or proceeds that are properly allocable to any period ending on or before August 15, 2006.

(b) *Applicability of the regulations.*—As of July 6, 2010, except as provided in paragraph (c) of

this section, §§ 53.4965-1 through 53.4965-8 of this chapter will apply to taxable years ending after July 6, 2007. A tax-exempt entity may rely on the provisions of §§ 53.4965-1 through 53.4965-8 for taxable years ending on or before July 6, 2007.

(c) *Effective/applicability date with respect to certain knowing transactions.*—(1) *Entity-level tax.*—The 100 percent tax under section 4965(b)(1)(B) and § 53.4965-7(a)(1)(i)(B) does not apply to prohibited tax shelter transactions entered into by a tax-exempt entity on or before May 17, 2006.

(2) *Manager-level tax.*—The IRS will not assert that an entity manager who approved or caused a tax-exempt entity to become a party to a prohibited tax shelter transaction is liable for the entity manager tax under section 4965(b)(2) and § 53.4965-7(b)(1) with respect to the transaction if the tax-exempt entity entered into such transaction prior to May 17, 2006. [Reg. § 53.4965-9.]

☐ [*T.D.* 9492, 7-2-2010.]

Qualified Pension, Etc., Plans

See p. 20,601 for regulations not amended to reflect law changes

[Reg. § 54.4971-1]

§ 54.4971-1. General rules relating to excise tax on failure to meet minimum funding standards.—

(a) [Reserved]

(b) [Reserved]

(c) *Additional tax.*—Section 4971(b) imposes an excise tax in any case in which an initial tax is imposed under section 4971(a) on an accumulated funding deficiency and the accumulated funding deficiency is not corrected within the taxable period (as defined in section 4971(c)(3)). The additional tax is 100 percent of the accumulated funding deficiency to the extent not corrected.

(d) [Reserved]

(e) *Definition of taxable period.*—(1) *In general.*—For purposes of any accumulated funding deficiency, the term "taxable period" means the period beginning with the end of the plan year in which there is an accumulated funding deficiency and ending on the earlier of:

(i) The date of mailing of a notice of deficiency under section 6212 with respect to the tax imposed by section 4971(a), or

(ii) The date on which the tax imposed by section 4971(a) is assessed.

(2) *Special rule.*—Where a notice of deficiency referred to in paragraph (e)(1)(i) of this section is not mailed because a waiver of the restrictions on assessment and collection of a deficiency has been accepted or because the deficiency is paid, the date of filing of the waiver or the date of such payment, respectively, shall be treated as the end of the taxable period. [Reg. § 54.4971-1.]

☐ [*T.D.* 8084, 5-1-86.]

[Reg. § 54.4971(c)-1]

§ 54.4971(c)-1. Taxes on failure to meet minimum funding standards; definitions.—(a) *In general.*—This section sets forth definitions that apply for purposes of applying the rules of section 4971.

(b) *Accumulated funding deficiency.*—(1) *Multiemployer plans.*—With respect to a multiemployer plan defined in section 414(f), the term *accumulated funding deficiency* has the meaning given to that term by section 431. A plan's accumulated funding deficiency for a plan year takes into account all charges and credits to the funding standard account under section 412 for plan years before the first plan year for which section 431 applies to the plan.

(2) *CSEC plans.*—With respect to a CSEC plan (that is, a plan that fits within the definition of a CSEC plan in section 414(y) for plan years beginning on or after January 1, 2014 and for which the election under section 414(y)(3)(A) has not been made), the term *accumulated funding deficiency* means the CSEC accumulated funding deficiency determined under section 433. A plan's CSEC accumulated funding deficiency for a plan year takes into account all charges and credits to the funding standard account under section 412 for plan years before the first plan year for which section 433 applies to the plan.

(c) *Unpaid minimum required contribution.*—(1) *In general.*—The term *unpaid minimum required contribution* means, with respect to any plan year, the portion of the minimum required contribution under section 430 for the plan year for which contributions have not been made on or before the due date for the plan year under section 430(j)(1). The unpaid minimum required contribution is determined after taking into account the interest adjustment to contributions under § 1.430(j)-1(b)(4) and any offsets from use of the funding balances under § 1.430(f)-1(d).

(2) *Accumulated funding deficiency for pre-effective plan year.*—For purposes of this section, a plan's accumulated funding deficiency under section 412 for the pre-effective plan year is treated as an unpaid minimum required contribution for that plan year until correction is made under the rules of paragraph (d)(2) of this section.

(d) *Correct.*—(1) *Accumulated funding deficiency.*—With respect to an accumulated funding deficiency for a plan year that is described in

paragraph (b) of this section, the term *correct* means to contribute, to or under the plan, the amount necessary to reduce the accumulated funding deficiency as of the end of that plan year to zero. To reduce the deficiency to zero, the contribution must include interest at the plan's valuation interest rate for the period between the end of that plan year and the date of the contribution (determined taking into account the rules of section 431(c)(8) or section 433(c)(9), as applicable).

(2) *Unpaid minimum required contribution.*— (i) *In general.*—With respect to an unpaid minimum required contribution for a plan year, the term *correct* means to contribute, to or under the plan, an amount that, when discounted to the valuation date for the plan year for which the unpaid minimum required contribution is due at the appropriate rate of interest, equals or exceeds the unpaid minimum required contribution. For this purpose, the appropriate rate of interest is the plan's effective interest rate for the plan year for which the unpaid minimum required contribution is due except to the extent that the payments are subject to additional interest as provided under section 430(j)(3) or (4).

(ii) *Pre-PPA accumulated funding deficiency.*—With respect to the accumulated funding deficiency under section 412 for the pre-effective plan year that is described in paragraph (c)(2) of this section, the term *correct* means to contribute, to or under the plan, the amount of that accumulated funding deficiency increased with interest from the end of the pre-effective plan year to the date of the contribution at the plan's valuation interest rate for the pre-effective plan year.

(iii) *Ordering rule.*—For purposes of section 4971 and this section, a contribution is attributable first to the earliest plan year of any unpaid minimum required contribution for which correction has not yet been made.

(3) *Corrective action of certain retroactive plan amendments.*—Certain retroactive plan amendments that meet the requirements of section 412(d)(2) may reduce the minimum required contribution for a plan year, which would reduce the accumulated funding deficiency or the amount of the unpaid minimum required contribution for a plan year.

(e) *Taxable period.*—(1) *In general.*—The term *taxable period* means the period beginning with the end of the plan year in which there is an accumulated funding deficiency or unpaid minimum required contribution, whichever is applicable, and ending on the earlier of:'

(i) The date of mailing of a notice of deficiency under section 6212 with respect to the tax imposed by section 4971(a); or

(ii) The date on which the tax imposed by section 4971(a) is assessed.

(2) *Special rule.*—Where a notice of deficiency referred to in paragraph (e)(1)(i) of this section is not mailed because a waiver of the restrictions on assessment and collection of a deficiency has been accepted or because the deficiency is paid, the date of filing of the waiver or the date of such payment, respectively, is treated as the end of the taxable period.

(f) *Single-employer plan.*—The term *single-employer plan* means a plan to which the minimum funding requirements of section 412 apply that is not a multiemployer plan as described in section 414(f). The term *single-employer plan* includes a multiple employer plan to which section 413(c) applies, other than a CSEC plan as described in paragraph (b)(2) of this section.

(g) *Examples.*—The following examples illustrate the rules of this section.

Example 1. (i) Plan A, a single-employer defined benefit plan, has a calendar year plan year and a January 1 valuation date. The sponsor of Plan A has a calendar taxable year. Plan A has no funding shortfall as of January 1, 2008, and Plan A has no unpaid minimum required contributions for 2008 or any earlier plan year. The minimum required contribution for the 2009 plan year is $250,000. The plan sponsor makes one contribution for 2009 on July 1, 2009 in the amount of $200,000, and the sponsor does not make an election to use the prefunding balance or funding standard carryover balance to offset the minimum required contribution for 2009. The effective interest rate for Plan A for the 2009 plan year is 5.90%.

(ii) The contribution paid July 1, 2009 is discounted for 6 months (to the valuation date) at the effective interest rate ($200,000 ÷ $1.0590^{(6/12)}$ = $194,349). The unpaid minimum required contribution for the 2009 plan year is $250,000 minus $194,349, or $55,651. The excise tax due under section 4971(a) is 10% of the unpaid minimum required contribution, or $5,565.

Example 2. (i) The facts are the same as in *Example 1.* The plan sponsor makes an additional contribution of $175,000 on December 31, 2010.

(ii) Under the ordering rule in paragraph (d)(2)(iii) of this section, the contribution made on December 31, 2010 is applied first to correct the unpaid minimum required contribution for 2009. The portion of the contribution paid December 31, 2010 that is required to eliminate the unpaid minimum required contribution for 2009 (taking into account the 2009 effective interest rate for the 24 months between January 1, 2009 and the payment date of December 31, 2010), is $55,651 multiplied by $1.059^{(24/12)}$ or $62,412. The remaining payment of $112,588 ($175,000 minus $62,412) is applied to the contribution required for the 2010 plan year.

Example 3. (i) Plan B, a single-employer defined benefit plan, has a calendar year plan year. The sponsor of Plan B has a calendar taxable year. Plan B has an accumulated funding deficiency of $100,000 as of December 31, 2007, including additional interest due to late required installments during 2007. The valuation interest rate for the 2007 plan year is 7.5%.

(ii) In accordance with paragraph (c)(2) of this section, the accumulated funding deficiency under section 412 as of December 31, 2007 is considered an unpaid minimum required contribution until it is corrected. Pursuant to paragraph (d)(2)(ii) of this section, the amount needed to correct that accumulated funding deficiency is $100,000 plus interest at the valuation interest rate of 7.5% for the period between December 31, 2007 and the date of payment of the contribution.

(iii) The funding shortfall as of January 1, 2008 is calculated as the difference between the funding target and the value of assets as of that date. The assets are not adjusted by the amount of the accumulated funding deficiency. The fact that the contribution was not made for the 2007 plan year means that the January 1, 2008 funding shortfall is larger than it would have been otherwise.

Example 4. (i) The facts are the same as in *Example 3.* The minimum required contribution for the 2008 plan year is $125,000, but the plan sponsor does not make any required contributions for 2008.

(ii) The total unpaid minimum required contribution as of December 31, 2008 is the sum of the $100,000 accumulated funding deficiency under section 412 from 2007 and the $125,000 unpaid minimum required contribution for 2008, or $225,000. The section 4971(a) excise tax applies to the aggregate unpaid minimum required contributions for all plan years that remain unpaid as of the end of 2008. In this case, there is an unpaid minimum required contribution of $100,000 for the 2007 plan year and an unpaid minimum required contribution of $125,000 for the 2008 plan year. The section 4971(a) excise tax is 10% of the aggregate of those unpaid amounts, $22,500.

Example 5. (i) The facts are the same as in *Example 4,* except that the plan sponsor makes a contribution of $150,000 on December 31, 2008. No additional contributions are paid through September 15, 2009. Required installments of $25,000 each are due April 15, 2008, July 15, 2008, October 15, 2008, and January 15, 2009. Plan B's effective interest rate for the 2008 plan year is 5.75%.

(ii) In accordance with paragraph (c)(2) of this section, the accumulated funding deficiency under section 412 as of December 31, 2007 is treated as an unpaid minimum required contribution until it is corrected.

(iii) The December 31, 2008 contribution is first applied to the 2007 accumulated funding deficiency under section 412 that is treated as an unpaid minimum required contribution. Accordingly, the amount needed to correct the 2007 unpaid required minimum contribution ($100,000 multiplied by 1.075, or $107,500) is applied to eliminate this unpaid minimum required contribution for the 2007 plan year.

(iv) The remaining $42,500 December 31, 2008 contribution ($150,000 minus $107,500) is then applied to the 2008 minimum required contribution. This amount is first allocated to the re-

quired installment due April 15, 2008. In accordance with § 1.430(j)-1(b)(4)(ii) of this chapter, the adjustment for interest on late required installments is increased by 5 percentage points for the period of underpayment. Therefore, $25,000 of the remaining December 31, 2008 contribution is discounted using an interest rate of 10.75% for the $8^{1}/_{2}$-month period between the payment date of December 31, 2008 and the required installment due date of April 15, 2008, and at the 5.75% effective interest rate for the $3^{1}/_{2}$ months between April 15, 2008 and January 1, 2008. This portion of the December 31, 2008 contribution results in an adjusted amount of $22,880 (that is, $25,000 ÷ $1.1075^{(8.5/12)}$ ÷ $1.0575^{(3.5/12)}$) as of January 1, 2008.

(v) The remaining December 31, 2008 contribution is then applied to the required installment due July 15, 2008. The $17,500 balance of the December 31, 2008 contribution ($150,000 minus $107,500 minus $25,000) is paid after the due date for the second required installment. Accordingly, the remaining $17,500 contribution is adjusted using an interest rate of 10.75% for the $5^{1}/_{2}$-month period between the payment date of December 31, 2008 and the required installment due date of July 15, 2008, and at the 5.75% effective interest rate for the $6^{1}/_{2}$ months between July 15, 2008 and January 1, 2008. This portion of the December 31, 2008 contribution results in an adjusted amount of $16,202 (that is, $17,500 ÷ $1.1075^{(5.5/12)}$ ÷ $1.0575^{(6.5/12)}$) as of January 1, 2008.

(vi) The remaining unpaid minimum required contribution for 2008 is $125,000 minus the interest-adjusted amounts of $22,880 and $16,202 applied towards the 2008 minimum required contribution as determined in paragraphs (iv) and (v) of this *Example 5.* This results in an unpaid minimum required contribution of $85,918 for 2008. The section 4971(a) excise tax is 10% of the unpaid minimum required contribution, or $8,592.

Example 6. (i) Plan C, a single-employer defined benefit plan, has a calendar year plan year and a January 1 valuation date, and has no funding standard carryover balance or prefunding balance as of January 1, 2008. Plan C's sponsor has a calendar taxable year. The minimum required contributions for Plan C are $100,000 for the 2008 plan year, $110,000 for the 2009 plan year, $125,000 for the 2010 plan year, and $135,000 for the 2011 plan year. No contributions for these plan years are made until September 15, 2012, at which time the plan sponsor contributes $273,000 (which is exactly enough to correct the unpaid minimum required contributions for the 2008 and 2009 plan years).

(ii) The excise tax under section 4971(a) for the 2008 taxable year is 10% of the aggregate unpaid minimum required contributions for all plan years remaining unpaid as of the end of any plan year ending within the 2008 taxable year. Accordingly, the excise tax for the 2008 taxable year is $10,000 (that is, 10% of $100,000). The excise tax for the 2009 taxable year is $21,000 (that is, 10% of the sum of $100,000 and $110,000) and the

excise tax for the 2010 taxable year is $33,500 (that is, 10% of the sum of $100,000, $110,000, and $125,000).

(iii) The contribution made on September 15, 2012 is applied to correct the unpaid minimum required contributions for the 2008 and 2009 plan years by the deadline for making contributions for the 2011 plan year. Therefore, the excise tax under section 4971(a) for the 2011 taxable year is based only on the remaining unpaid minimum required contributions for the 2010 and 2011 plan years, or $26,000 (that is, 10% of the sum of $125,000 and $135,000).

(iv) The plan sponsor may also be required to pay an excise tax of 100% under section 4971(b), if the unpaid minimum required contributions are not corrected by the end of the taxable period.

(h) *Effective/applicability dates and transition rules.*—(1) *Statutory effective date.*—(i) *In general.*—In general, the amendments made to section 4971 by section 114 of the Pension Protection Act of 2006, Public Law 109-280, 120 Stat. 780 (2006), as amended (PPA '06), apply to taxable years beginning on or after January 1, 2008, but only with respect to a plan year that—

(A) Begins on or after January 1, 2008; and

(B) Ends with or within any such taxable year.

(ii) *Plans with delayed PPA '06 effective dates.*—In the case of a plan for which the effective date of section 430 for purposes of determining the minimum required contribution is delayed in accordance with sections 104 through 106 of PPA '06, the amendments made to section 4971 by section 114 of PPA '06 apply to taxable years beginning on or after January 1, 2008, but only with respect to a plan year—

(A) To which section 430 applies to determine the minimum required contribution of the plan; and

(B) That ends with or within any such taxable year.

(2) *Effective date of regulations.*—This section is effective for taxable years beginning on or after the statutory effective date described in paragraph (h)(1) of this section, but in no event does this section apply to taxable years ending before April 15, 2008.

(3) *Pre-effective plan year.*—For purposes of this section, the pre-effective plan year for a plan is the plan year described in § 1.430(a)-1(h)(5) of this chapter. Thus, except for plans with a delayed effective date under paragraph (h)(1)(ii) of this section, the pre-effective plan year for a plan is the last plan year beginning before January 1, 2008. [Reg. § 54.4971(c)-1.]

☐ [T.D. 9732, 9-8-2015.]

[Reg. § 54.4972-1]

§ 54.4972-1. Tax on excess contributions to plans benefiting self-employed individuals.—(a) *In general.*—Section 4972 imposes a tax of 6 percent on the amount of the excess contributions (as defined in section 4972(b) and paragraph (c) of this section) under certain qualified plans (as defined in paragraph (b) of this section) for each taxable year beginning after December 31, 1975, of the employer who maintains such plan. Partnerships and sole proprietors are to report this tax by filing Form 5330 (or other designated form) and the tax is to be paid annually at the time prescribed for filing such return (determined without regard to any extension of time for filing).

(b) *Employers to whom section applies.*—The tax under section 4972 is imposed on employers who maintain a qualified plan during their taxable year. For this purpose, the term "qualified plan" means a pension or profit-sharing plan which includes a trust described in section 401(a), an annuity plan described in section 403(a), or a bond purchase plan described in section 405(a). In addition to being a qualified plan, the plan must provide contributions or benefits for employees some or all of whom are employees within the meaning of section 401(c)(1). For this purpose, the plan does not have to provide contributions or benefits for employees who are employees within the meaning of section 401(c)(1) during the taxable year; it is sufficient that the plan so provided in a prior taxable year.

(c) *Excess contributions.*—(1) *In general.*—For a taxable year of an employer for purposes of section 4972 and this section, the term "excess contributions" means—

(i) The amount (if any) by which the sum of—

(A) The amount (if any) determined under section 4972(b)(2) and paragraph (d) of this section, plus

(B) The amount (if any) determined under section 4972(b)(3) and paragraph (e) of this section, plus

(C) The amount (if any) determined under section 4972(b)(4) and paragraph (f) of this section, exceeds

(ii) The amount (if any) of any correcting distributions (as defined in section 4972(b)(5) and paragraph (g) of this section) made in all prior taxable years beginning after December 31, 1975.

(2) *Contributions allocable to insurance.*—For purposes of section 4972(b) and this section, the amount of any contribution made under the plan which is allocable to the purchase of life, accident, health, or other insurance is not taken into account. The amount of any contribution which is allocable to the cost of insurance protection is determined in accordance with the provisions of paragraph (g) of § 1.404(e)-1A and paragraph (b) of § 1.72-16.

(d) *Contributions by owner-employees.*—(1) *General rule.*—In the case of a plan which provides contributions or benefits for employees some or all of whom are owner-employees, within the

meaning of section 401(c)(3), the amount determined under section 4972(b)(2) and this paragraph for the employer's taxable year is the amount computed separately with respect to each owner-employee equal to the sum of—

(i) The excess (if any) of—

(A) The amount contributed under the plan by each owner-employee as an employee (that is, each owner-employee's contributions within the meaning of section 401(c)(5)(B)) for such taxable year of the employer, over

(B) The amount permitted under section 4972(c) and paragraph (h) of this section to be contributed by each owner-employee as an employee for such taxable year of the employer, and

(ii) The amount determined under section 4972(b)(2) and this paragraph for the immediately preceding taxable year of the employer, reduced by the excess (if any) of the amount described in subdivision (i)(B) of this subparagraph over the amount described in subdivision (i)(A) of this subparagraph for such taxable year of the employer.

(2) *Rollover amounts.*—The provisions of section 4972(c) and paragraph (d) of this section are not applicable to amounts contributed on behalf of an owner-employee in a rollover contribution described in section 402(a)(5), 403(a)(4), 408(d)(3), or 409(b)(3)(C).

(3) *Examples.*—The provisions of this paragraph may be illustrated by the following examples:

Example (1). (i) A and B are the only owner-employees covered under the X Employees' trust. The X Partnership, the X Trust, and the X Plan all use the calendar year as their annual accounting period, at all relevant times. The amount determined under section 4972(b)(2) for 1975 is 0 because this section does not apply to contributions made for taxable years beginning before January 1, 1976. In calendar year 1976, A contributes $2,500 and B contributes $2,500 to the trust. The amount permitted to be contributed to the trust for 1976 with respect to A as an employee is $1,800 and with respect to B as an employee is $2,200.

(ii) The amount determined under this paragraph for 1976 with respect to A is $700, computed as follows: the sum of the excess of the amount contributed by A ($2,500) over the amount permitted to be contributed by A ($1,800), and the amount determined under this paragraph for A in 1975 (0).

(iii) The amount determined under this paragraph for 1976 with respect to B is $300, computed as follows: the sum of the excess of the amount contributed by B ($2,500) over the amount permitted to be contributed by B ($2,200), and the amount determined under this paragraph for B in 1975 (0).

(iv) The amount determined under section 4972(b)(2) and this paragraph for 1976 with respect to the employer, X Partnership, is $1,000, the sum of the amounts determined separately

under this paragraph with respect to A ($700) and B ($300). The tax under section 4972 for 1976 on the X Partnership (assuming that no other events affecting the determination of the tax under section 4972 occur) is 6 percent of $1,000 or $60.

Example (2). (i) Assume the facts stated in Example (1). In calendar year 1977, A contributes $1,500 and B contributes $2,300 to the trust. Assume that the amount permitted to be contributed to the trust for 1977, under section 4972(c) for A and B is $2,500 each.

(ii) The amount determined under this paragraph for 1977 with respect to A is 0, computed as follows: the sum of 0 (the excess of the amount contributed by A ($1,500) over the amount permitted to be contributed ($2,500)) and $700, the amount determined under this paragraph for A in 1976, reduced by $1,000 (the amount permitted to be contributed by A ($2,500) over the amount contributed by A ($1,500)).

(iii) The amount determined under this paragraph for 1977 with respect to B is $100, computed as follows: the sum of 0 (the excess of the amount contributed by B ($2,300) over the amount permitted to be contributed $2,500)) and $300, the amount determined under this paragraph for B in 1976, reduced by $200 (the amount permitted to be contributed ($2,500) by B over the amount contributed by B ($2,300)).

(iv) The amount determined under section 4972(b) and this paragraph for 1977 with respect to the employer, X Partnership, is $100, the sum of the amounts determined separately under this paragraph with respect to A ($0) and B ($100). The tax imposed under section 4972 for 1977 on the X Partnership (assuming that no other events affecting the determination of the tax under section 4972 occur) is 6 percent of $100, or $6.

(e) *Defined benefit plans.*—(1) *General rule.*—In the case of a defined benefit plan (as defined in section 414(j) and the regulations thereunder), the amount determined under section 4972(b)(3) and this paragraph for the taxable year of the employer is the amount contributed under the plan by the employer during the taxable year plus the amounts, if any, contributed by the employer during any prior taxable year beginning after December 31, 1975, if—

(i) As of the close of the taxable year, the full funding limitation of the plan (determined under section 412(c)(7) and the regulations thereunder) is 0, and

(ii) Such amounts contributed have not been deductible by the employer for the taxable year or for any prior taxable year beginning after December 31, 1975.

See section 404 and the regulations thereunder for the determination of the amount deductible by the employer for the taxable year. If the amounts contributed by the employer exceed the amounts which have been deductible, the amount determined under this paragraph shall not exceed the amounts which have not been deductible. For purposes of this paragraph, the

determination of both the amounts contributed and the amounts deductible by the employer for any relevant taxable year includes amounts contributed and deductible on behalf of any employee covered under the plan, including common-law employees and other self-employed individuals who are not owner-employees in addition to owner-employees. The determination of whether the full funding limitation is zero shall be made taking into account all the plan assets unreduced by any deduction carryover under section 404(a)(1)(D). The determination of whether the full funding limitation is zero as of the close of the employer's taxable year shall be made with respect to the plan year ending with or within the employer's taxable year. Consequently, if an employer whose taxable year is the calendar year establishes and maintains a defined benefit plan whose plan year begins on July 1 and ends on June 30, the full funding limitation for that plan will be determined with respect to the plan year ending on June 30 within the calendar taxable year including that June 30.

(2) *Illustration.*—The provisions of this paragraph may be illustrated by the following example:

Example. (i) The X Partnership ("X") adopts the Y Defined Plan ("Y Plan") on January 1, 1977. The taxable year of X is the calendar year. The Y Plan also has a calendar plan year. For 1977, $25,000 is contributed to the Y plan by X. Assume that for 1979, (1) only $10,000 is deductible by X for 1977 under section 404 and (2) the full funding limitation of the Y Plan (determined under section 412(c)(7)) on December 31, 1977, is greater than zero. For 1978, X makes no additional contributions to the Y Plan. Assume that for 1978, (1) no amount is deductible by X under section 404 and (2) the full funding limitation of the Y Plan (determined under section 412(c)(7)) on December 31, 1978, is zero. The amount determined under section 4972(b)(3) and this paragraph for the 1978 taxable year is $15,000, computed as follows: the difference between (A) the sum of the amounts contributed by X for taxable year 1978 (0), and the amounts contributed by X for taxable year 1977 ($25,000) and (B) the sum of the amount deductible for taxable year 1978 (0) and the amount deductible for taxable year 1977 ($10,000). The tax imposed under section 4972 for 1978 on X (assuming that no other events affecting the determination of the tax under section 4972 occur) is 6 percent of $15,000 or $900.

(ii) For 1979, X makes no additional contributions to the Y Plan. Assume that for 1979, (1) the full funding limitation of the Y Plan determined under section 412(c)(7) is greater than zero. Assume further that $10,000 of the amounts contributed for 1977 is deductible by X for 1979 under section 404. There is no amount determined under section 4972(b)(3) and this paragraph for 1979 because the condition described in subparagraph (1)(i) of this paragraph is not satisfied.

(iii) For 1980, X makes no additional contributions to the Y Plan. Assume that for 1980, (1) no amount is deductible under section 404 and (2) the full funding limitation of the Y Plan (determined under section 412(c)(7)) on December 31, 1980, is zero. The amount determined under section 4972(b)(3) and this paragraph for the 1980 taxable year is $5,000 computed as follows: the difference between (A) $25,000, the sum of the amounts contributed by X for taxable years 1980 (0), 1979 (0), 1978 (0), and 1977 ($25,000) and (B) $20,000, the sum of the amounts deductible for taxable years 1980 (0), 1979 ($10,000), 1978 (0), and 1977 ($10,000). The tax imposed under section 4972 for 1980 on X (assuming that no other events affecting the determination of the tax under section 4972 occur) is 6 percent of $5,000, or $300.

(f) *Defined contribution plans.*—(1) *General rule.*—In the case of a defined contribution plan (as defined in section 414(i) and the regulations thereunder), the amount determined under section 4972(b)(4) and this paragraph for the taxable year of the employer is equal to the portion of the amounts contributed under the plan by the employer during the taxable year plus the amounts contributed by the employer during any prior taxable year beginning after December 31, 1975, which has not been deductible by the employer for the taxable year or for any such prior taxable year. For purposes of this paragraph, the determination of both the amounts contributed and the amounts deductible by the employer for any relevant taxable year includes amounts contributed and deductible on behalf of any employee covered under the plan, including common-law employees and other self-employed individuals who are not owner-employees in addition to owner-employees.

(2) *Illustration.*—The provisions of this paragraph may be illustrated by the following example:

Example. (i) The X Partnership ("X") adopts the Z Defined Conribution Plan and Trust ("Z Plan") on January 1, 1976. X's taxable year and the plan year of Z are both calendar years. For 1976, X contributes $40,000, of which $30,000 is deductible under section 404 for taxable year 1976. The amount determined under section 4972(b)(4) and this paragraph for 1976 is $10,000 (the difference between (A) $40,000, the amount contributed by X for taxable year 1976 and (B) $30,000, the amount deductible for taxable year 1976).

(ii) For 1977, X contributes $25,000, and the amounts deductible by X under section 404 for taxable year 1977 is $30,000 ($5,000 for the contribution carryover from 1976 and $25,000 with respect to the 1977 contribution). The amount determined under section 4972(b)(4) and this paragraph for 1977 is $5,000, computed as follows: The difference between (A) $65,000, the sum of the amounts contributed by X for taxable year 1976 ($40,000) and the amounts contributed by X for taxable year 1977 ($25,000), and (B) $60,000, the sum of the amounts deductible for

taxable year 1976 ($30,000) and the amounts deductible for taxable year 1977 ($30,000).

(g) *Correcting distribution.*—(1) *General rule.*— For purposes of section 4972(b) and this paragraph, the term "correcting distribution" means, for the taxable year of the employer, the sum of—

(i) In the case of a contribution made as an employee by an owner-employee, within the meaning of section 401 (c)(3), to a defined benefit or defined contribution plan, the amount, or any part thereof, determined under section 4972(b)(2) and paragraph (d) of this section which is distributed to the owner-employee who contributed such amount to the plan;

(ii) In the case of a defined benefit plan, the amount, or any part thereof, determined under section 4972(b)(3) and paragraph (e) of this section which is distributed from the plan to the employer, and

(iii) In the case of a defined contribution plan, the amount, or any part thereof, determined under section 4972(b)(4) and paragraph (f) of this section which is distributed to (A) the employer or (B) to the employee for whom such amount was contributed.

If, for any employer taxable year in which a defined contribution plan is maintained, there is a correcting distribution to an employee which could be from amounts described in subparagraph (1)(i) and (iii) of this paragraph for such employee, then such correcting distribution shall be deemed to be made first from amounts described in such subparagraph (1)(i) and then from amounts described in such subparagraph (1)(iii) for purposes of this section and section 72. For the income tax treatment of such distributions to employees, see section 72 and the regulations thereunder. Any such distributions to employees shall not be subject to the tax imposed by section 4975 nor result in the defined contribution plan failing to satisfy the exclusive benefit requirement of section 401(a), solely by reason of being a correcting distribution within the meaning of this paragraph. If, for any employer taxable year in which a defined benefit or defined contribution plan is maintained, there is a correcting distribution described in subparagraph (1)(ii) or (iii) of this paragraph to the employer maintaining the plan, such distribution shall not be subject to the tax imposed by section 4975 nor result in the plan's failing to satisfy the exclusive benefit or the definitely determinable requirements under section 401(a). If, for any employer taxable year in which a money purchase pension plan is maintained, a correcting distribution described in subparagraph (1)(iii) of this paragraph is made to an employee who has not yet become eligible to receive retirement benefits under the plan, the qualification of the pension plan (and trust) under section 401(a) may be adversely affected. See § 1.401-1(b)(1)(i). A correcting distribution described in subparagraph (1)(iii) of this paragraph to an owner-employee prior to age 59½ must be precluded under the plan. See section 401(d)(4).

(2) *Illustration.*—The provisions of this paragraph may be illustrated by the following example:

Example. (i) A and B who are over the age of 59½ and who are owner-employees covered under the X Employees' Defined Contribution Plan and Profit-Sharing Trust ("Plan Y"). The X Partnership ("X") and Plan Y are on calendar years. In calendar year 1976, A contributes $2,500 and B contributes $2,500 to Plan Y. The amount permitted to be contributed to Plan Y for 1976 with respect to A as an employee is $1,800 and with respect to B as an employee is $2,200. X contributes to Plan Y $5,000 on behalf of A and $5,000 on behalf of B. Of this amount, assume that $2,700 is deductible with respect to A and $3,300 is deductible with respect to B by X under section 404. The amount determined under section 4972(b)(2) and paragraph (d) of this section (the excess owner-employee contributions made by A and B to Plan Y) for taxable year 1976 is $1,000, computed as follows: the sum of (A) for A, $700, the difference between his own contributions ($2,500) and the amount permitted to be contributed by A ($1,800) and (B) for B, $300, the difference between his own contributions ($2,500) and the amount permitted to be contributed by B ($2,200). The amount determined under section 4972(b)(4) and paragraph (f) of this section (the excess contributions made by X to Plan Y) for taxable year 1976 is $4,000, computed as follows: the sum of (A) by X for A, $2,300, the difference between contributions by X ($5,000) and the amount deductible by X for A ($2,700) and (B) by X for B, $1,700, the difference between contributions by X for B ($5,000) and the amount deductible by X for B ($3,300). During 1976, there is no correcting distribution, within the meaning of section 4972 and this paragraph, because there are no distributions to A, B, or X.

(ii) Assume that, for taxable year 1977, the amounts determined under sections 4972(b)(2) and 4972(b)(4) remain the same as for taxable year 1976, that is, $1,000 ($700 for A and $300 for B) and $4,000 ($2,700 by X for A and $1,300 by X for B), respectively. Assume further that, in 1977, Plan Y distributes $3,000 to A and $1,000 to B. The amount determined under section 4972(b)(5) and this paragraph (the correcting distribution for Plan Y) for taxable year 1977 is $4,000, computed and attributed as follows: the sum of (A) $3,000 with respect to A, the amount of the distribution to A applied first to A's $700 amount described in subparagraph (1)(i) of this paragraph and next to A's $2,300 amount described in subparagraph (1)(iii) of this paragraph and (B) $1,000 with respect to B, the amount of the distribution to B applied first to B's $300 amount described in subparagraph (1)(i) of this paragraph and next to B's $1,700 amount described in subparagraph (1)(iii) of this paragraph. For purposes of computing the excess contributions for taxable year 1977, the correcting distribution of $4,000 would not be taken into account because only correcting distributions for prior years are considered. However, for taxable year

1978 the correcting distribution of $4,000 would be taken into account.

(iii) Assume that, for taxable year 1978, there are no additional amounts determined under sections 4972(b)(2) and 4972(b)(4) and that Plan Y distributes $900 to B. The amount determined under section 4972(b)(5) and this paragraph (the correcting distribution for Plan Y) for the 1978 taxable year is $900, computed and attributed as follows: the amount of the distribution to B, $900, applied to B's $1,000 amount described in subparagraph (1)(iii) of this paragraph. For purposes of computing the excess contributions for taxable year 1978, the correcting distribution of $900 would not be taken into account. However, for taxable year 1979, the correcting distribution of $900 would be taken into account.

(h) *Amount permitted to be contributed by owner-employee.*—(1) *General rule.*—Except as provided in subparagraph (2), for purposes of section 4972(b)(2) and paragraph (d), the amount permitted to be contributed under a plan by an owner-employee as an employee for any taxable year of the employer is the smallest of the following—

(i) $2,500,

(ii) 10 percent of the earned income (as defined in section 401(c)(2)) for such taxable year derived by the owner-employee from the trade or business with respect to which the plan is established, or

(iii) The amount of the contribution which would be contributed by the owner-employee (as an employee) if such contribution were made at the rate of contributions which is permitted to be made by employees who are not owner-employees during such taxable year.

(2) *Special rule.*—In the case of a taxable year of the employer in which there are no employees other than owner-employees, the amount permitted to be contributed under a plan by an owner-employee (as an employee) is zero.

(i) *Special rules and cross references.*—(1) *Time of contributions.*—For purposes of this section, time of employer contributions made with respect to any taxable year shall take into account the rules specified in section 404(a)(6), relating to time when contributions deemed made.

(2) *Disallowance of deduction.*—For disallowance of deduction for taxes paid under this section, see section 275(a)(6).

(3) *Certain annuity contracts.*—For a special rule relating to owner-employee contributions for premiums on annuity, etc. contracts, see § 1.401(e)-4(a).

(4) *Disqualification for excess contributions.*—For plan qualification requirements relating to excess contributions, see section 401(d)(5). [Reg. § 54.4972-1.]

☐ [*T.D.* 7759, 1-16-81.]

[Reg. § 54.4974-1]

§ 54.4974-1. Excise tax on accumulations in individual retirement accounts or annuities.—(a) *General rule.*—A tax equal to 50 percent of the amount by which the minimum amount required to be distributed from an individual retirement account or annuity described in section 408 during the taxable year of the payee under paragraph (b) of this section exceeds the amount actually distributed during the taxable year is imposed by section 4974 on the payee.

(b) *Minimum amount required to be distributed.*—For purposes of this section, the minimum amount required to be distributed is the amount required under § 1.408-2(b)(6)(v) to be distributed in the taxable year described in paragraph (a) of this section.

(c) *Examples.*—The application of this section may be illustrated by the following examples.

Example (1). In 1975, the minimum amount required to be distributed under § 1.408-2(b)(6)(v) to A under his individual retirement account is $100. Only $60 is actually distributed to A in 1975. Under section 4974, A would have an excise tax liability of $20 [50% of ($100−60)].

Example (2). Although no distribution is required under § 1.408-2(b)(6)(v) to be made in 1986, H, a married individual born on February 1, 1921, who has established and maintained an individual retirement account decides to begin receiving distributions from the account beginning in 1986. H's wife, W, was born on March 6, 1921. H and W are calendar year taxpayers. H decides to receive his interest in the account over the joint life and last survivor expectancy of himself and his wife. On January 1, 1986, the balance in H's account is $10,000; H and W, based on their nearest birthdates, are 65; and the joint life and last survivor expectancy of H and his wife is 22.0 years (see Table II of § 1.72-9). His annual payments during the following years (none of which were required) were determined by dividing the balance in the account on the first day of each year by the joint life and last survivor expectancy reduced by the number of whole years elapsed since the distributions were to commence.

Date	Life expectancy minus whole years elapsed	Account balance at beginning of each year	Annual payment
1-1-86	22.0	$10,000	$455
1-1-87	21.0	$10,118	$482
1-1-88	20.0	$10,214	$511
1-1-89	19.0	$10,285	$541
1-1-90	18.0	$10,329	$574
1-1-91	17.0	$10,340	$608

For 1986, 1987, 1989, and 1990, the amount required to be distributed under § 1.408-2(b)(6)(v) is zero. Thus, H would have no excise tax liability under section 4974 for these years. In 1991, the year H attains age 70½, the amount required to be distributed from the account under § 1.408-2(b)(6)(v) is $565, determined by dividing $10,340 (the account balance as of January 1, 1991) by 18.3 years (the joint life and last survi-

vor expectancy of H and W, assuming they are both still living, as of January 1, 1991). If W should die after December 31, 1990, the joint life and last survivor expectancy determined on January 1, 1991 (18.3 years) would not be redetermined. Because the amount distributed from the account in 1991 ($608) exceeds the amount required to be distributed from the account in 1991 ($565), H has no excise tax liability under section 4974 for 1991.

Example (3). Assume the same facts as in example (2) except that W dies in 1988. For 1988, 1989, and 1990, the amount required to be distributed under §1.408-2(b)(6)(v) is zero. Thus, H would have no excise tax liability under section 4974 for these years. In 1991, the amount required to be distributed under §1.408-2(b)(6)(v) is $855, determined by dividing $10,340 (the account balance as of January 1, 1991) by 12.1 years (the life expectancy of H as of January 1, 1991). Because the amount distributed from the account in 1991 ($608) is less than the amount required to be distributed from the account in 1991 ($855), H has an excise tax liability of $123.50 under section 4974 for 1991 [50% of ($855–$608)]. [Reg. §54.4974-1.]

☐ [*T.D.* 7714, 8-7-80.]

[Reg. §54.4974-2]

§54.4974-2. Excise tax on accumulations in qualified retirement plans.—

Q-1. Is any tax imposed on a payee under any qualified retirement plan or any eligible deferred compensation plan (as defined in section 457(b)) to whom an amount is required to be distributed for a taxable year if the amount distributed during the taxable year is less than the required minimum distribution?

A-1. Yes, if the amount distributed to a payee under any qualified retirement plan or any eligible deferred compensation plan (as defined in section 457(b)) for a calendar year is less than the required minimum distribution for such year, an excise tax is imposed on such payee under section 4974 for the taxable year beginning with or within the calendar year during which the amount is required to be distributed. The tax is equal to 50 percent of the amount by which such required minimum distribution exceeds the actual amount distributed during the calendar year. Section 4974 provides that this tax shall be paid by the payee. For purposes of section 4974, the term *required minimum distribution* means the minimum distribution amount required to be distributed pursuant to section 401(a)(9), 403(b)(10), 408(a)(6), 408(b)(3), or 457(d)(2), as the case may be, and the regulations thereunder. Except as otherwise provided in A-6 of this section, the required minimum distribution for a calendar year is the required minimum distribution amount required to be distributed during the calendar year. A-6 of this section provides a special rule for amounts required to be distributed by an employee's (or individual's) required beginning date.

Q-2. For purposes of section 4974, what is a qualified retirement plan?

A-2. For purposes of section 4974, each of the following is a qualified retirement plan—

(a) A plan described in section 401(a) which includes a trust exempt from tax under section 501(a);

(b) An annuity plan described in section 403(a);

(c) An annuity contract, custodial account, or retirement income account described in section 403(b);

(d) An individual retirement account described in section 408(a) (including a Roth IRA described in section 408A);

(e) An individual retirement annuity described in section 408(b) (including a Roth IRA described in section 408A); or

(f) Any other plan, contract, account, or annuity that, at any time, has been treated as a plan, account, or annuity described in paragraphs (a) through (e) of this A-2, whether or not such plan, contract, account, or annuity currently satisfies the applicable requirements for such treatment.

Q-3. If a payee's interest under a qualified retirement plan is in the form of an individual account, how is the required minimum distribution for a given calendar year determined for purposes of section 4974?

A-3. (a) *General rule.* If a payee's interest under a qualified retirement plan is in the form of an individual account and distribution of such account is not being made under an annuity contract purchased in accordance with A-4 of §1.401(a)(9)-6, the amount of the required minimum distribution for any calendar year for purposes of section 4974 is the required minimum distribution amount required to be distributed for such calendar year in order to satisfy the minimum distribution requirements in §1.401(a)(9)-5 as provided in the following (whichever is applicable)—

(1) Section 401(a)(9) and §§1.401(a)(9)-1 through 1.401(a)(9)-5 and 1.401(a)(9)-7 through 1.401(a)(9)-9 in the case of a plan described in section 401(a) which includes a trust exempt under section 501(a) or an annuity plan described in section 403(a);

(2) Section 403(b)(10) and §1.403(b)-6(e) (in the case of an annuity contract, custodial account, or retirement income account described in section 403(b));

(3) Section 408(a)(6) or (b)(3) and §1.408-8 (in the case of an individual retirement account or annuity described in section 408(a) or (b)); or

(4) Section 457(d) in the case of an eligible deferred compensation plan (as defined in section 457(b)).

(b) *Default provisions.* Unless otherwise provided under the qualified retirement plan (or, if applicable, the governing instrument of the qualified retirement plan), the default provisions in A-4(a) of §1.401(a)(9)-3 apply in determining the required minimum distribution for purposes of section 4974.

(c) *Five-year rule.* If the 5-year rule in section 401(a)(9)(B)(ii) applies to the distribution to a payee, no amount is required to be distributed for any calendar year to satisfy the applicable enumerated section in paragraph (a) of this A-3 until the calendar year which contains the date 5 years after the date of the employee's death. For the calendar year which contains the date 5 years after the employee's death, the required minimum distribution amount required to be distributed to satisfy the applicable enumerated section is the payee's entire remaining interest in the qualified retirement plan.

Q-4. If a payee's interest in a qualified retirement plan is being distributed in the form of an annuity, how is the amount of the required minimum distribution determined for purposes of section 4974?

A-4. If a payee's interest in a qualified retirement plan is being distributed in the form of an annuity (either directly from the plan, in the case of a defined benefit plan, or under an annuity contract purchased from an insurance company), the amount of the required minimum distribution for purposes of section 4974 will be determined as follows:

(a) *Permissible annuity distribution option.* A permissible annuity distribution option is an annuity contract (or, in the case of annuity distributions from a defined benefit plan, a distribution option) which specifically provides for distributions which, if made as provided, would for every calendar year equal or exceed the minimum distribution amount required to be distributed to satisfy the applicable section enumerated in paragraph (a) of A-2 of this section for every calendar year. If the annuity contract (or, in the case of annuity distributions from a defined benefit plan, a distribution option) under which distributions to the payee are being made is a permissible annuity distribution option, the required minimum distribution for a given calendar year will equal the amount which the annuity contract (or distribution option) provides is to be distributed for that calendar year.

(b) *Impermissible annuity distribution option.* An impermissible annuity distribution option is an annuity contract (or, in the case of annuity distributions from a defined benefit plan, a distribution option) under which distributions to the payee are being made that specifically provides for distributions which, if made as provided, would for any calendar year be less than the minimum distribution amount required to be distributed to satisfy the applicable section enumerated in paragraph (a) of A-3 of this section. If the annuity contract (or, in the case of annuity distributions from a defined benefit plan, the distribution option) under which distributions to the payee are being made is an impermissible annuity distribution option, the required minimum distribution for each calendar year will be determined as follows:

(1) If the qualified retirement plan under which distributions are being made is a defined benefit plan, the minimum distribution amount required to be distributed each year will be the amount which would have been distributed under the plan if the distribution option under which distributions to the payee were being made was the following permissible annuity distribution option:

(i) In the case of distributions commencing before the death of the employee, if there is a designated beneficiary under the impermissible annuity distribution option for purposes of section 401(a)(9), the permissible annuity distribution option is the joint and survivor annuity option under the plan for the lives of the employee and the designated beneficiary that provides for the greatest level amount payable to the employee determined on an annual basis. If the plan does not provide such an option or there is no designated beneficiary under the impermissible distribution option for purposes of section 401(a)(9), the permissible annuity distribution option is the life annuity option under the plan payable for the life of the employee in level amounts with no survivor benefit.

(ii) In the case of distributions commencing after the death of the employee, if there is a designated beneficiary under the impermissible annuity distribution option for purposes of section 401(a)(9), the permissible annuity distribution option is the life annuity option under the plan payable for the life of the designated beneficiary in level amounts. If there is no designated beneficiary, the 5-year rule in section 401(a)(9)(B)(ii) applies. See paragraph (b)(3) of this A-4. The determination of whether or not there is a designated beneficiary and the determination of which designated beneficiary's life is to be used in the case of multiple beneficiaries will be made in accordance with §1.401(a)(9)-4 and A-7 of §1.401(a)(9)-5. If the defined benefit plan does not provide for distribution in the form of the applicable permissible distribution option, the required minimum distribution for each calendar year will be an amount as determined by the Commissioner.

(2) If the qualified retirement plan under which distributions are being made is a defined contribution plan and the impermissible annuity distribution option is an annuity contract purchased from an insurance company, the minimum distribution amount required to be distributed each year will be the amount that would have been distributed in the form of an annuity contract under the permissible annuity distribution option under the plan determined in accordance with paragraph (b)(1) of this A-4 for defined benefit plans. If the defined contribution plan does not provide the applicable permissible annuity distribution option, the required minimum distribution for each calendar year will be the amount that would have been distributed under an annuity described in paragraph (b)(2)(i) or (ii) of this A-4 purchased with the employee's or individual's account used to purchase the annuity contract that is the impermissible annuity distribution option.

(i) In the case of distributions commencing before the death of the employee, if there is a

Reg. §54.4974-2

designated beneficiary under the impermissible annuity distribution option for purposes of section 401(a)(9), the annuity is a joint and survivor annuity for the lives of the employee and the designated beneficiary which provides level annual payments and which would have been a permissible annuity distribution option. However, the amount of the periodic payment which would have been payable to the survivor will be the applicable percentage under the table in A-2(c) of §1.401(a)(9)-6 of the amount of the periodic payment which would have been payable to the employee or individual. If there is no designated beneficiary under the impermissible distribution option for purposes of section 401(a)(9), the annuity is a life annuity for the life of the employee with no survivor benefit which provides level annual payments and which would have been a permissible annuity distribution option.

(ii) In the case of a distribution commencing after the death of the employee, if there is a designated beneficiary under the impermissible annuity distribution option for purposes of section 401(a)(9), the annuity option is a life annuity for the life of the designated beneficiary which provides level annual payments and which would have been a permissible annuity distribution option. If there is no designated beneficiary, the 5-year rule in section 401(a)(9)(B)(ii) applies. See paragraph (b)(3) of this A-4. The amount of the payments under the annuity contract will be determined using the interest rate and actuarial tables prescribed under section 7520 determined using the date determined under A-3 of §1.401(a)(9)-3 when distributions are required to commence and using the age of the beneficiary as of the beneficiary's birthday in the calendar year that contains that date. The determination of whether or not there is a designated beneficiary and the determination of which designated beneficiary's life is to be used in the case of multiple beneficiaries will be made in accordance with §1.401(a)(9)-4 and A-7 of §1.401(a)(9)-5.

(3) If the 5-year rule in section 401(a)(9)(B)(ii) applies to the distribution to the payee under the contract (or distribution option), no amount is required to be distributed to satisfy the applicable enumerated section in paragraph (a) of this A-4 until the calendar year which contains the date 5 years after the date of the employee's death. For the calendar year which contains the date 5 years after the employee's death, the required minimum distribution amount required to be distributed to satisfy the applicable enumerated section is the payee's entire remaining interest in the annuity contract (or under the plan in the case of distributions from a defined benefit plan).

(4) If the plan provides that the required beginning date for purposes of section 401(a)(9) for all employees is April 1 of the calendar year following the calendar year in which the employee attained age 70½ in accordance with paragraph A-2(e) of §1.401(a)(9)-2, the required minimum distribution for each calendar year for an employee who is not a 5-percent owner for purposes of this section will be the lesser of the amount determined based on the required beginning date as set forth in A-2(a) of §1.401(a)(9)-2 or the required beginning date under the plan. Thus, for example, if an employee dies after attaining age 70½, but before April 1 of the calendar year following the calendar year in which the employee retired, and there is no designated beneficiary as of September 30 of the year following the employee's year of death, required minimum distributions for calendar years after the calendar year containing the employee's date of death may be based on either the applicable distribution period provided under either the 5-year rule of A-1 of §1.401(a)(9)-3 or the employee's remaining life expectancy as set forth in A-5(c)(3) of §1.401(a)(9)-5.

Q-5. If there is any remaining benefit with respect to an employee (or IRA owner) after any calendar year in which the entire remaining benefit is required to be distributed under section 401(a)(9), what is the amount of the required minimum distribution for each calendar year subsequent to such calendar year?

A-5. If there is any remaining benefit with respect to an employee (or IRA owner) after the calendar year in which the entire remaining benefit is required to be distributed, the required minimum distribution for each calendar year subsequent to such calendar year is the entire remaining benefit.

Q-6. With respect to which calendar year is the excise tax under section 4974 imposed in the case in which the amount not distributed is an amount required to be distributed by April 1 of a calendar year (by the employee's or individual's required beginning date)?

A-6. In the case in which the amount not paid is an amount required to be paid by April 1 of a calendar year, such amount is a required minimum distribution for the previous calendar year, i.e., for the employee's or the individual's first distribution calendar year. However, the excise tax under section 4974 is imposed for the calendar year containing the last day by which the amount is required to be distributed, i.e., the calendar year containing the employee's or individual's required beginning date, even though the preceding calendar year is the calendar year for which the amount is required to be distributed. There is also a required minimum distribution for the calendar year which contains the employee's or individual's required beginning date. Such distribution is also required to be made during the calendar year which contains the employee's or individual's required beginning date.

Q-7. Are there any circumstances when the excise tax under section 4974 for a taxable year may be waived?

A-7. (a) *Reasonable cause.* The tax under section 4974(a) may be waived if the payee described in section 4974(a) establishes to the satisfaction of the Commissioner the following—

(1) The shortfall described in section 4974(a) in the amount distributed in any taxable year was due to reasonable error; and

(2) Reasonable steps are being taken to remedy the shortfall.

(b) *Automatic waiver.* The tax under section 4974 will be automatically waived, unless the Commissioner determines otherwise, if—

(1) The payee described in section 4974(a) is an individual who is the sole beneficiary and whose required minimum distribution amount for a calendar year is determined under the life expectancy rule described in § 1.401(a)(9)-3 A-3 in the case of an employee's or individual's death before the employee's or individual's required beginning date; and

(2) The employee's or individual's entire benefit to which that beneficiary is entitled is distributed by the end of the fifth calendar year following the calendar year that contains the employee's or individual's date of death. [Reg. § 54.4974-2.]

☐ [*T.D. 8987, 4-16-2002 (corrected 5-20-2002). Amended by T.D. 9130, 6-14-2004 and T.D. 9340, 7-23-2007.*]

[Reg. § 54.4975-1]

§ 54.4975-1. General rules relating to excise tax on prohibited transactions.—(a) *Scope.*—This section provides general rules for the imposition of the excise taxes on prohibited transactions.

(b) *Initial tax.*—Section 4975(a) imposes an initial tax on each prohibited transaction. The initial tax is 5 percent of the amount involved with respect to the prohibited transaction for each year (or part thereof) in the taxable period.

(c) *Additional tax.*—Section 4975(b) imposes an excise tax in any case in which an initial tax is imposed under section 4975(a) on a prohibited transaction and the prohibited transaction is not corrected within the taxable period (as defined in paragraph (d) of this section). The additional tax is 100 percent of the amount involved with respect to the prohibited transaction.

(d) *Taxable period.*—(1) *In general.*—For purposes of any prohibited transaction, the term "taxable period" means the period beginning with the date on which the prohibited transaction occurs and ending on the earliest of:

(i) The date of mailing of a notice of deficiency under section 6212 with respect to the tax imposed by section 4975(a);

(ii) The date on which correction of the prohibited transaction is completed; or

(iii) The date on which the tax imposed by section 4975(a) is assessed.

(2) *Special rule.*—Where a notice of deficiency referred to in paragraph (d)(1)(i) of this section is not mailed because a waiver of the restrictions on assessment and collection of a deficiency has been accepted or because the deficiency is paid, the date of filing of the waiver or the date of such payment, respectively, shall be

treated as the end of the taxable period. [Reg. § 54.4975-1.]

☐ [*T.D. 8084, 5-1-86.*]

[Reg. § 54.4975-6]

§ 54.4975-6. Statutory exemptions for office space or services and certain transactions involving financial institutions.—(a) *Exemption for office space or services.*—(1) *In general.*—Section 4975(d)(2) exempts from the excise taxes imposed by section 4975 payment by a plan to a disqualified person, including a fiduciary, for office space or any service (or a combination of services), if (i) such office space or service is necessary for the establishment or operation of the plan; (ii) such office space or service is furnished under a contract or arrangement which is reasonable; and (iii) no more than reasonable compensation is paid for such office space or service. However, section 4975(d)(2) does not contain an exemption for acts described in section 4975(c)(1)(E) (relating to fiduciaries dealing with the income or assets of plans in their own interest or for their own account) or acts described in section 4975(c)(1)(F) (relating to fiduciaries receiving consideration for their own personal account from any party dealing with a plan in connection with a transaction involving the income or assets of the plan). Such acts are separate transactions not described in section 4975(d)(2). See § § 54.4975-6(a)(5) and 54.4975-6(a)(6) for guidance as to whether transactions relating to the furnishing of office space or services by fiduciaries to plans involve acts described in section 4975(c)(1)(E).

Section 4975(d)(2) does not contain an exemption from other provisions of the Code, such as section 401, or other provisions of law which may impose requirements or restrictions relating to the transactions which are exempt under section 4975(d)(2). See, for example, the general fiduciary responsibility provisions of section 404 of the Employee Retirement Income Security Act of 1974 (the Act) (88 Stat. 877). The provisions of section 4975(d)(2) are further limited by the flush language at the end of section 4975(d) (relating to transactions with owner-employees and related persons).

(2) *Necessary service.*—A service is necessary for the establishment or operation of a plan within the meaning of section 4975(d)(2) and § 54.4975-6(a)(1)(i) if the service is appropriate and helpful to the plan obtaining the service in carrying out the purposes for which the plan is established or maintained. A person providing such a service to a plan (or a person who is a disqualified person solely by reason of a relationship to such a service provider described in section 4975(e)(2)(F), (G), (H), or (I)) may furnish goods which are necessary for the establishment or operation of the plan in the course of, and incidental to, the furnishing of such service to the plan.

(3) *Reasonable contract or arrangement.*—No contract or arrangement is reasonable within the

meaning of section 4975(d)(2) and § 54.4975-6(a)(1)(ii) if it does not permit termination by the plan without penalty to the plan on reasonably short notice under the circumstances to prevent the plan from becoming locked into an arrangement that has become disadvantageous. A long-term lease which may be terminated prior to its expiration (without penalty to the plan) on reasonably short notice under the circumstances is not generally an unreasonable arrangement merely because of its long term. A provision in a contract or other arrangement which reasonably compensates the service provider or lessor for loss upon early termination of the contract, arrangement or lease is not a penalty. For example, a minimal fee in a service contract which is charged to allow recoupment of reasonable start-up costs is not a penalty.

Similarly, a provision in a lease for a termination fee that covers reasonably foreseeable expenses related to the vacancy and reletting of the office space upon early termination of the lease is not a penalty. Such a provision does not reasonably compensate for loss if it provides for payments in excess of actual loss or if it fails to require mitigation of damages.

(4) *Reasonable compensation.*—Section 4975(d)(2) and § 54.4975-6(a)(1)(iii) permit a plan to pay a disqualified person reasonable compensation for the provision of office space or services described in section 4975(d)(2). Paragraph (e) of this section contains regulations relating to what constitutes reasonable compensation for the provision of services.

(5) *Transactions with fiduciaries.*—(i) *In general.*—If the furnishing of office space or a service involves an act described in section 4975(c)(1)(E) or (F) (relating to acts involving conflicts of interest by fiduciaries), such an act constitutes a separate transaction which is not exempt under section 4975(d)(2). The prohibitions of sections 4975(c)(1)(E) and (F) supplement the other prohibitions of section 4975(c)(1) by imposing on disqualified persons who are fiduciaries a duty of undivided loyalty to the plans for which they act. These prohibitions are imposed upon fiduciaries to deter them from exercising the authority, control, or responsibility which makes such persons fiduciaries when they have interests which may conflict with the interests of the plans for which they act. In such cases, the fiduciaries have interests in the transactions which may affect the exercise of their best judgment as fiduciaries. Thus, a fiduciary may not use the authority, control, or responsibility which makes such person a fiduciary to cause a plan to pay an additional fee to such fiduciary (or to a person in which such fiduciary has an interest which may affect the exercise of such fiduciary's best judgment as a fiduciary) to provide a service. Nor may a fiduciary use such authority, control, or responsibility to cause a plan to enter into a transaction involving plan assets whereby such fiduciary (or a person in which such fiduciary has an interest which may affect the exercise of such fiduciary's best judgment as a fiduciary)

will receive consideration from a third party in connection with such transaction.

A person in which a fiduciary has an interest which may affect the exercise of such fiduciary's best judgment as a fiduciary includes, for example, a person who is a disqualified person by reason of a relationship to such fiduciary described in section 4975(e)(2)(E), (F), (G), (H), or (I).

(ii) *Transactions not described in section 4975(c)(1)(E).*—A fiduciary does not engage in an act described in section 4975(c)(1)(E) if the fiduciary does not use any of the authority, control or responsibility which makes such person a fiduciary to cause a plan to pay additional fees for a service furnished by such fiduciary or to pay a fee for a service furnished by a person in which such fiduciary has an interest which may affect the exercise of such fiduciary's best judgment as a fiduciary. This may occur, for example, when one fiduciary is retained on behalf of a plan by a second fiduciary to provide a service for an additional fee. However, because the authority, control or responsibility which makes a person a fiduciary may be exercised "in effect" as well as in form, mere approval of the transaction by a second fiduciary does not mean that the first fiduciary has not used any of the authority, control or responsibility which makes such person a fiduciary to cause the plan to pay the first fiduciary an additional fee for a service.

(iii) *Services without compensation.*—If a fiduciary provides services to a plan without the receipt of compensation or other consideration (other than reimbursement of direct expenses properly and actually incurred in the performance of such services within the meaning of paragraph (e)(4) of this section), the provision of such services does not, in and of itself, constitute an act described in section 4975(c)(1)(E) or (F). The allowance of a deduction to an employer under section 162 or 212 for the expense incurred in furnishing office space or services to a plan established or maintained by such employer does not constitute compensation or other consideration.

(6) *Examples.*—The provisions of § 54.4975-6(a)(5) may be illustrated by the following examples:

Example (1). E, an employer whose employees are covered by plan P, is a fiduciary of P. I has a professional investment adviser in which E has no interest which may affect the exercise of E's best judgment as a fiduciary. E causes P to retain I to provide certain kinds of investment advisory services of a type which causes I to be a fiduciary of P under section 4975(e)(3)(B). Thereafter, I proposes to perform for additional fees portfolio evaluation services in addition to the services currently provided. The provision of such services is arranged by I and approved on behalf of the plan by E. I has not engaged in an act described in section 4975(c)(1)(E), because I did not use any of the authority, control or responsibility which makes I a fiduciary (the provision of in-

vestment advisory services) to cause the plan to pay I additional fees for the provision of the portfolio evaluation services. E has not engaged in an act which is described in section 4975(c)(1)(E). E, as the fiduciary who has the responsibility to be prudent in his selection and retention of I and the other investment advisers of the plan, has an interest in the purchase by the plan of portfolio evaluation services. However, such an interest is not an interest which may affect the exercise of E's best judgment as a fiduciary.

Example (2). D, a trustee of plan P with discretion over the management and disposition of plan assets, relies on the advice of C, a consultant to P, as to the investment of plan assets, thereby making C a fiduciary of the plan. On January 1, 1978, C recommends to D that the plan purchase an insurance policy from U, an insurance company which is not a disqualified person with respect to P. C thoroughly explains the reasons for the recommendation and makes a full disclosure concerning the fact that C will receive a commission from U upon the purchase of the policy by P. D considers the recommendation and approves the purchase of the policy by P. C receives a commission. Under such circumstances, C has engaged in an act described in section 4975(c)(1)(E) (as well as section 4975(c)(1)(F)) because C is in fact exercising the authority, control or responsibility which makes C a fiduciary to cause the plan to purchase the policy. However, the transaction is exempt from the prohibited transaction provisions of section 4975(c)(1) if the requirements of Prohibited Transaction Exemption 77-9 are met.

Example (3). Assume the same facts as in Example (2) except that the nature of C's relationship with the plan is not such that C is a fiduciary of P. The purchase of the insurance policy does not involve an act described in section 4975(c)(1)(E) or (F), because such sections only apply to acts by fiduciaries.

Example (4). E, an employer whose employees are covered by plan P, is a fiduciary with respect to P. A, who is not a disqualified person with respect to P, persuades E that the plan needs the services of a professional investment adviser and that A should be hired to provide the investment advice. Accordingly, E causes P to hire A to provide investment advice of the type which makes A a fiduciary under § 54.4975-9(c)(1)(ii)(B). Prior to the expiration of A's first contract with P, A persuades E to cause P to renew A's contract with P to provide the same services for additional fees in view of the increased costs in providing such services. During the period of A's second contract, A provides additional investment advice services for which no additional charge is made. Prior to the expiration of A's second contract, A persuades E to cause P to renew his contract for additional fees in view of the additional services A is providing. A has not engaged in an act described in section 4975(c)(1)(E), because A has not used any of the authority, control or responsibility which makes A a fiduciary (the provision of investment ad-

vice) to cause the plan to pay additional fees for A's services.

Example (5). F, a trustee of plan P with discretion over the management and disposition of plan assets, retains C to provide administrative services to P of the type which makes C a fiduciary under section 4975(e)(3)(C). Thereafter, C retains F to provide, for additional fees, actuarial and various kinds of administrative services in addition to the services F is currently providing to P. Both F and C have engaged in an act described in section 4975(c)(1)(E). F, regardless of any intent which he may have had at the time he retained C, has engaged in such an act because F has, in effect, exercised the authority, control or responsibility which makes F a fiduciary to cause the plan to pay F additional fees for the services. C, whose continued employment by P depends on F, has also engaged in such an act, because C has an interest in the transaction which might affect the exercise of C's best judgment as a fiduciary. As a result, C has dealt with plan assets in his own interest under section 4975(c)(1)(E).

Example (6). F, a fiduciary of plan P with discretionary authority respecting the management of P, retains S, the son of F, to provide for a fee various kinds of administrative services necessary for the operation of the plan. F has engaged in an act described in section 4975(c)(1)(E), because S is a person in whom F has an interest which may affect the exercise of F's best judgment as a fiduciary. Such act is not exempt under section 4975(d)(2) irrespective of whether the provision of the services by S is exempt.

Example (7). T, one of the trustees of plan P, is president of bank B. The bank proposes to provide administrative services to P for a fee. T physically absents himself from all consideration of B's proposal and does not otherwise exercise any of the authority, control or responsibility which makes T a fiduciary to cause the plan to retain B. The other trustees decide to retain B. T has not engaged in an act described in section 4975(c)(1)(E). Further, the other trustees have not engaged in an act described in section 4975(c)(1)(E) merely because T is on the board of trustees of P. This fact alone would not make them have an interest in the transaction which might affect the exercise of their best judgment as fiduciaries.

(b) *Exemption for bank deposits.*—(1) *In general.*—Section 4975(d)(4) exempts from the excise taxes imposed by section 4975 investment of all or a part of a plan's assets in deposits bearing a reasonable rate of interest in a bank or similar financial institution supervised by the United States or a State, even though such bank or similar financial institution is a fiduciary or other disqualified person with respect to the plan, if the conditions of either § 54.4975-6(b)(2) or § 54.4975-6(b)(3) are met. Section 4975(d)(4) provides an exemption from section 4975(c)(1)(E) (relating to fiduciaries dealing with the income or assets of plans in their own interest or for their own account), as well as sections

4975(c)(1)(A) throught (D), because section 4975(d)(4) contemplates a bank or similar financial institution causing a plan for which it acts as a fiduciary to invest plan assets in its own deposits if the requirements of section 4975(d)(4) are met. However, it does not provide an exemption from section 4975(c)(1)(F) (relating to fiduciaries receiving consideration for their own personal account from any party dealing with a plan in connection with a transaction involving the income or assets of the plan). The receipt of such consideration is a separate transaction not described in the exemption. Section 4975(d)(4) does not contain an exemption from other provisions of the Code, such as section 401, or other provisions of law which may impose requirements or restrictions relating to the transactions which are exempt under section 4975(d)(4). See, for example, the general fiduciary responsibility provisions of section 404 of the Act. The provisions of section 4975(d)(4) are further limited by the flush language at the end of section 4975(d) (relating to transactions with owner-employees and related persons).

(2) *Plan covering own employees.*—Such investment may be made if the plan is one which covers only the employees of the bank or similar financial institution, the employees of any of its affiliates, or the employees of both.

(3) *Other plans.*—(i) *General rule.*—Such investment may be made if the investment is expressly authorized by a provision of the plan or trust instrument or if the investment is expressly authorized (or made) by a fiduciary of the plan (other than the bank or similar financial institution or any of its affiliates) who has authority to make such investments, or to instruct the trustee or other fiduciary with respect to investments, and who has no interest in the transaction which may affect the exercise of such authorizing fiduciary's best judgment as a fiduciary so as to cause such authorization to constitute an act described in section 4975(c)(1)(E) or (F). Any authorization to make investments contained in a plan or trust instrument will satisfy the requirement of express authorization for investments made prior to November 1, 1977.

Effective November 1, 1977, in the case of a bank or similar financial institution that invests plan assets in deposits in itself or its affiliates under an authorization contained in a plan or trust instrument, such authorization must name such bank or similar financial institution and must state that such bank or similar financial institution may make investments in deposits which bear a reasonable rate of interest in itself (or in an affiliate).

(ii) *Example.*—B, a bank, is the trustee of plan P's assets. The trust instruments give the trustee the right to invest plan assets in its discretion. B invests in the certificates of deposit of bank C, which is a fiduciary of the plan by virtue of performing certain custodial and administrative services. The authorization is sufficient for the plan to make such investment under section

4975(d)(4). Further, such authorization would suffice to allow B to make investments in deposits in itself prior to November 1, 1977. However, subsequent to October 31, 1977, B may not invest in deposits in itself, unless the plan or trust instrument specifically authorizes it to invest in deposits of B.

(4) *Definitions.*—(i) The term "bank or similar financial institution" includes a bank (as defined in section 581), a domestic building and loan association (as defined in section 7701(a)(19)), and a credit union (as defined in section 101(6) of the Federal Credit Union Act).

(ii) A person is an affiliate of a bank or similar financial institution if such person and such bank or similar financial institution would be treated as members of the same controlled group of corporations or as members of two or more trades or businesses under common control within the meaning of section 414(b) or (c) and the regulations thereunder.

(iii) The term "deposits" includes any account, temporary or otherwise, upon which a reasonable rate of interest is paid, including a certificate of deposit issued by a bank or similar financial institution.

(c) *Exemption for ancillary bank services.*—(1) *In general.*—Section 4975(d)(6) exempts from the excise taxes imposed by section 4975 the provision of certain ancillary services by a bank or similar financial institution (as defined in § 54.4975-6(b)(4)(i)) supervised by the United States or a State to a plan for which it acts as a fiduciary if the conditions in § 54.4975-6(c)(2) are met. Such ancillary services include services which do not meet the requirements of section 4975(d)(2), because the provision of such services involves an act described in section 4975(c)(1)(E) (relating to fiduciaries dealing with the income or assets of plans in their own interest or for their own account) by the fiduciary bank or similar financial institution. Section 4975(d)(6) provides an exemption from section 4975(c)(1)(E), because section 4975(d)(6) contemplates the provision of such ancillary services without the approval of a second fiduciary (as described in § 54.4975-6(a)(5)(ii)) if the conditions of § 54.4975-6(c)(2) are met. Thus, for example, plan assets held by a fiduciary bank which are reasonably expected to be needed to satisfy current plan expenses may be placed by the bank in a non-interest-bearing checking account in the bank if the conditions of § 54.4975-6(c)(2) are met, notwithstanding the provisions of section 4975(d)(4) (relating to investments in bank deposits). However, section 4975(d)(6) does not provide an exemption for an act described in section 4975(c)(1)(F) (relating to fiduciaries receiving consideration for their own personal account from any party dealing with a plan in connection with a transaction involving the income or assets of the plan). The receipt of such consideration is a separate transaction not described in section 4975(d)(6). Section 4975(d)(6) does not contain an exemption from other provisions of the Code, such as section 401, or other

provisions of law which may impose requirements or restrictions relating to the transactions which are exempt under section 4975(d)(6). See, for example, the general fiduciary responsibility provisions of section 404 of the Act. The provisions of section 4975(d)(6) are further limited by the flush language at the end of section 4975(d) (relating to transactions with owner-employees and related persons).

(2) *Conditions.*—Such service must be provided:

(i) At not more than reasonable compensation;

(ii) Under adequate internal safeguards which assure that the provision of such service is consistent with sound banking and financial practice, as determined by Federal or State supervisory authority; and

(iii) Only to the extent that such service is subject to specific guidelines issued by the bank or similar financial institution which meet the requirements of §54.4975-6(c)(3).

(3) *Specific guidelines.*—[Reserved]

(d) *Exemption for services as a fiduciary.*—[Reserved]

(e) *Compensation for services.*—(1) *In general.*—Section 4975(d)(2) refers to the payment of reasonable compensation by a plan to a disqualified person for services rendered to the plan. Section 4975(d)(10) and §§54.4975-6(e)(2) through 54.4975-6(e)(5) clarify what constitutes reasonable compensation for such services.

(2) *General rule.*—Generally, whether compensation is "reasonable" under sections 4975(d)(2) and (10) depends on the particular facts and circumstances of each case.

(3) *Payments to certain fiduciaries.*—Under sections 4975(d)(2) and (10), the term "reasonable compensation" does not include any compensation to a fiduciary who is already receiving full-time pay from an employer or association of employers (any of whose employees are participants in the plan) or from an employee organization (any of whose members are participants in the plan), except for the reimbursement of direct expenses properly and actually incurred and not otherwise reimbursed. The restrictions of this paragraph (e)(3) do not apply to a disqualified person who is not a fiduciary.

(4) *Certain expenses not direct expenses.*—An expense is not a direct expense to the extent it would have been sustained had the service not been provided or if it represents an allocable portion of overhead costs.

(5) *Expense advances.*—Under sections 4975(d)(2) and (10), the term "reasonable compensation", as applied to a fiduciary or an employee of a plan, includes an advance to such a fiduciary or employee by the plan to cover direct expenses to be properly and actually incurred by such person in the performance of such person's duties with the plan if:

(i) The amount of such advance is reasonable with respect to the amount of the direct expense which is likely to be properly and actually incurred in the immediate future (such as during the next month); and

(ii) The fiduciary or employee accounts to the plan at the end of the period covered by the advance for the expenses properly and actually incurred.

(6) *Excessive compensation.*—Under sections 4975(d)(2) and (10), any compensation which would be considered excessive under §1.162-7 (relating to compensation for personal services which constitutes an ordinary and necessary trade or business expense) will not be "reasonable compensation". Depending upon the facts and circumstances of the particular situation, compensation which is not excessive under §1.162-7 may, nevertheless, not be "reasonable compensation" within the meaning of sections 4975(d)(2) and (10). [Reg. §54.4975-6.]

☐ [T.D. 7491, 6-13-77.]

[Reg. §54.4975-7]

§54.4975-7. Other statutory exemptions.—(a) [Reserved]

(b) *Loans to employee stock ownership plans*—

(1) *Definitions.*—When used in this paragraph (b) and §54.4975-11, the terms listed below have the following meanings:

(i) *ESOP.*—The term "ESOP" refers to an employee stock ownership plan that meets the requirements of section 4975(e)(7) and §54.4975-11. It is not synonymous with "stock bonus plan." A stock bonus plan must, however, be an ESOP to engage in an exempt loan. The qualification of an ESOP under section 401(a) and §54.4975-11 will not be adversely affected merely because it engages in a non-exempt loan.

(ii) *Loan.*—The term "loan" refers to a loan made to an ESOP by a disqualified person or a loan to an ESOP which is guaranteed by a disqualified person. It includes a direct loan of cash, a purchase-money transaction, and an assumption of the obligation of an ESOP. "Guarantee" includes an unsecured guarantee and the use of assets of a disqualified person as collateral for a loan, even though the use of assets may not be a guarantee under applicable state law. An amendment of a loan in order to qualify as an exempt loan is not a refinancing of the loan or the making of another loan.

(iii) *Exempt loan.*—The term "exempt loan" refers to a loan that satisfies the provisions of this paragraph (b). A "non-exempt loan" is one that fails to satisfy such provisions.

(iv) *Publicly traded.*—The term "publicly traded" refers to a security that is listed on a national securities exchange registered under section 6 of the Securities Exchange Act of 1934 (15 U.S.C. 78f) or that is quoted on a system sponsored by a national securities association

registered under section 15A(b) of the Securities Exchange Act (15 U.S.C. 78o).

(v) *Qualifying employer security.*—The term "qualifying employer security" refers to a security described in § 54.4975-12.

(2) *Statutory exemption.*—(i) *Scope.*—Section 4975(d)(3) provides an exemption from the excise tax imposed under section 4975(a) and (b) by reason of section 4975(c)(1)(A) through (E). Section 4975(d)(3) does not provide an exemption from the imposition of such tax by reason of section 4975(c)(1)(F), relating to fiduciaries receiving consideration for their own personal account from any party dealing with a plan in connection with a transaction involving the income or assets of the plan.

(ii) *Special scrutiny of transaction.*—The exemption under section 4975(d)(3) includes within its scope certain transactions in which the potential for self-dealing by fiduciaries exists and in which the interests of fiduciaries may conflict with the interests of participants. To guard against these potential abuses, the Internal Revenue Service will subject these transactions to special scrutiny to ensure that they are primarily for the benefit of participants and their beneficiaries. Although the transactions need not be arranged and approved by an independent fiduciary, fiduciaries are cautioned to exercise scrupulously their discretion in approving them. For example, fiduciaries should be prepared to demonstrate compliance with the net effect test and the arm's-length standard under paragraph (b)(3)(ii) and (iii) of this section. Also, fiduciaries should determine that the transaction is truly arranged primarily in the interest of participants and their beneficiaries rather than, for example, in the interest of certain selling shareholders.

(3) *Primary benefit requirement.*—(i) *In general.*—An exempt loan must be primarily for the benefit of the ESOP participants and their beneficiaries. All the surrounding facts and circumstances, including those described in paragraph (b)(3)(ii) and (iii) of this section, will be considered in determining whether the loan satisfies this requirement. However, no loan will satisfy the requirement unless it satisfies the requirements of paragraph (b)(4), (5), and (6) of this section.

(ii) *Net effect on plan assets.*—At the time that a loan is made, the interest rate for the loan and the price of securities to be acquired with the loan proceeds should not be such that plan assets might be drained off.

(iii) *Arm's-length standard.*—The terms of a loan, whether or not between independent parties, must, at the same time the loan is made, be at least as favorable to the ESOP as the terms of a comparable loan resulting from arm's-length negotiations between independent parties.

(4) *Use of loan proceeds.*—The proceeds of an exempt loan must be used within a reasonable time after their receipt by the borrowing ESOP only for any or all of the following purposes:

(i) To acquire qualifying employer securities.

(ii) To repay such loan.

(iii) To repay a prior exempt loan. A new loan, the proceeds of which are so used, must satisfy the provisions of this paragraph (b).

Except as provided in paragraph (b)(9) and (10) of this section or as otherwise required by applicable law, no security acquired with the proceeds of an exempt loan may be subject to a put, call, or other option, or buy-sell or similar arrangement while held by and when distributed from a plan, whether or not the plan is then an ESOP.

(5) *Liability and collateral of ESOP for loan.*—An exempt loan must be without recourse against the ESOP. Furthermore, the only assets of the ESOP that may be given as collateral on an exempt loan are qualifying employer securities of two classes: those acquired with the proceeds of the loan and those that were used as collateral on a prior exempt loan repaid with the proceeds of the current exempt loan. No person entitled to payment under the exempt loan shall have any right to assets of the ESOP other than:

(i) Collateral given for the loan,

(ii) Contributions (other than contributions of employer securities) that are made under and ESOP to meet its obligations under the loan, and

(iii) Earnings attributable to such collateral and the investment of such contributions.

The payments made with respect to an exempt loan by the ESOP during a plan year must not exceed an amount equal to the sum of such contributions and earnings received during or prior to the year less such payments in prior years. Such contributions and earnings must be accounted for separately in the books of account of the ESOP until the loan is repaid.

(6) *Default.*—In the event of default upon an exempt loan, the value of plan assets transferred in satisfaction of the loan must not exceed the amount of default. If the lender is a disqualified person, a loan must provide for a transfer of plan assets upon default only upon and to the extent of the failure of the plan to meet the payment schedule of the loan. For purposes of this subparagraph (6), the making of a guarantee does not make a person a lender.

(7) *Reasonable rate of interest.*—The interest rate of a loan must not be in excess of a reasonable rate of interest. All relevant factors will be considered in determining a reasonable rate of interest, including the amount and duration of the loan, the security and guarantee (if any) involved, the credit standing of the ESOP and the guarantor (if any), and the interest rate prevailing for comparable loans. When these factors are considered, a variable interest rate may be reasonable.

(8) *Release from encumbrance.*—(i) *General rule.*—In general, an exempt loan must provide for the release from encumbrance under this subdivision (i) of plan assets used as collateral for the loan. For each plan year during the duration of the loan, the number of securities released must equal the number of encumbered securities held immediately before release for the current plan year multiplied by a fraction. The numerator of the fraction is the amount of principal and interest paid for the year. The denominator of the fraction is the sum of the numerator plus the principal and interest to be paid for all future years. See §54.4975-7(b)(8)(iv). The number of future years under the loan must be definitely ascertainable and must be determined without taking into account any possible extensions or renewal periods. If the interest rate under the loan is variable, the interest to be paid in future years must be computed by using the interest rate applicable as of the end of the plan year. If collateral includes more than one class of securities, the number of securities of each class to be released for a plan year must be determined by applying the same fraction to each class.

(ii) *Special rule.*—A loan will not fail to be exempt merely because the number of securities to be released from encumbrance is determined solely with reference to principal payments. However, if release is determined with reference to principal payments only, the following three additional rules apply. The first rule is that the loan must provide for annual payments of principal and interest at a cumulative rate that is not less rapid at any time than level annual payments of such amounts for 10 years. The second rule is that interest included in any payment is disregarded only to the extent that it would be determined to be interest under standard loan amortization tables. The third rule is that this subdivision (ii) is not applicable from the time that, by reason of a renewal, extension, or refinancing, the sum of the expired duration of the exempt loan, the renewal period, the extension period, and the duration of a new exempt loan exceeds 10 years.

(iii) *Caution against plan disqualification.*—Under an exempt loan, the number of securities released from encumbrance may vary from year to year. The release of securities depends upon certain employer contributions and earnings under the ESOP. Under §54.4975-11(d)(2) actual allocations to participants' accounts are based upon assets withdrawn from the suspense account. Nevertheless, for purposes of applying the limitations under section 415 to these allocations, under §54.4975-11(a)(8)(ii) contributions used by the ESOP to pay the loan are treated as annual additions to participants' accounts. Therefore, particular caution must be exercised to avoid exceeding the maximum annual additions under section 415. At the same time, release from encumbrance in annual varying amounts may reflect a failure on the part of the employer to make substantial and recurring contributions to the ESOP which will lead to loss of qualifica-

tion under section 401(a). The Internal Revenue Service will observe closely the operation of ESOP's that release encumbered securities in varying annual amounts, particularly those that provide for the deferral of loan payments or for balloon payments.

(iv) *Illustration.*—The general rule under paragraph (b)(8)(i) of this section operates as illustrated in the following example:

Example. Corporation X establishes an ESOP that borrows $750,000 from a bank. X guarantees the loan, which is for 15 years at 5% interest and is payable in level annual amounts of $72,256.72. Total payments on the loan are $1,083,850.80. The ESOP uses the entire loan proceeds to acquire 15,000 shares of X stock which is used as collateral for the loan. The number of securities to be released for the first year is 1,000 shares, i.e., 15,000 shares × $72,256.72/$1,083,850.80 = 15,000 shares × 1/15. The number of securities to be released for the second year is 1,000 shares, i.e., 14,000 shares × $72,256.72/$1,011,594.08 = 14,000 shares × 1/14. If all loan payments are made as originally scheduled, the number of securities released in each succeeding year of the loan will also be 1,000.

(9) *Right of first refusal.*—Qualifying employer securities acquired with proceeds of an exempt loan may, but need not, be subject to a right of first refusal. However, any such right must meet the requirements of this subparagraph (9). Securities subject to such right must be stock or an equity security, or a debt security convertible into stock or an equity security. Also, the securities must not be publicly traded at the time the right may be exercised. The right of first refusal must be in favor of the employer, the ESOP, or both in any order of priority. The selling price and other terms under the right must not be less favorable to the seller than the greater of the value of the security determined under §54.4975-11(d)(5), or the purchase price and other terms offered by a buyer, other than the employer or the ESOP, making a good faith offer to purchase the security. The right of first refusal must lapse no later than 14 days after the security holder gives written notice to the holder of the right that an offer by a third party to purchase the security has been received.

(10) *Put option.*—A qualifying employer security acquired with the proceeds of an exempt loan by an ESOP after September 30, 1976, must be subject to a put option if it is not publicly traded when distributed or if it is subject to a trading limitation when distributed. For purposes of this subparagraph (10), a "trading limitation" on a security is a restriction under any Federal or state securities law, any regulation thereunder, or an agreement, not prohibited by this paragraph (b), affecting the security which would make the security not as freely tradable as one not subject to such restriction. The put option must be exercisable only by a participant, by the participant's donees, or by a person (includ-

ing an estate or its distributee) to whom the security passes by reason of a participant's death. (Under this subparagraph (10), "participant" means a participant and beneficiaries of the participant under the ESOP.) The put option must permit a participant to put the security to the employer. Under no circumstances may the put option bind the ESOP. However, it may grant the ESOP an option to assume the rights and obligations of the employer at the time that the put option is exercised. If it is known at the time a loan is made that Federal or state law will be violated by the employer's honoring such put option, the put option must permit the security to be put, in a manner consistent with such law, to a third party (e.g., an affiliate of the employer or a shareholder other than the ESOP) that has substantial net worth at the time the loan is made and whose net worth is reasonably expected to remain substantial.

(11) *Duration of put option.*—(i) *General rule.*—A put option must be exercisable at least during a 15-month period which begins on the date the security subject to the put option is distributed by the ESOP.

(ii) *Special rule.*—In the case of a security that is publicly traded without restriction when distributed but ceases to be so traded within 15 months after distribution, the employer must notify each security holder in writing on or before the tenth day after the date the security ceases to be so traded that for the remainder of the 15-month period the security is subject to a put option. The number of days between such tenth day and the date on which notice is actually given, if later than the tenth day, must be added to the duration of the put option. The notice must inform distributees of the terms of the put options that they are to hold. Such terms must satisfy the requirements of paragraph (b)(10) through (12) of this section.

(12) *Other put option provisions.*—(i) *Manner of exercise.*—A put option is exercised by the holder notifying the employer in writing that the put option is being exercised.

(ii) *Time excluded from duration of put option.*—The period during which a put option is exercisable does not include any time when a distributee is unable to exercise it because the party bound by the put option is prohibited from honoring it by applicable Federal or state law.

(iii) *Price.*—The price at which a put option must be exercisable is the value of the security, determined under §54.4975-11(d)(5).

(iv) *Payment terms.*—The provisions for payment under a put option must be reasonable. The deferral of payment is reasonable if adequate security and a reasonable interest rate are provided for any credit extended and if the cumulative payments at any time are no less than the aggregate of reasonable periodic payments as of such time. Periodic payments are reasonable if annual installments, beginning with 30 days after the date the put option is exercised,

are substantially equal. Generally, the payment period may not end more than 5 years after the date the put option is exercised. However, it may be extended to a date no later than the earlier of 10 years from the date the put option is exercised or the date the proceeds of the loan used by the ESOP to acquire the security subject to the put option are entirely repaid.

(v) *Payment restrictions.*—Payment under a put option may be restricted by the terms of a loan, including one used to acquire a security subject to a put option, made before November 1, 1977. Otherwise, payment under a put option must not be restricted by the provisions of a loan or any other arrangement, including the terms of the employer's articles of incorporation, unless so required by applicable state law.

(13) *Other terms of loan.*—An exempt loan must be for a specific term. Such loan may not be payable at the demand of any person, except in the case of default.

(14) *Status of plan as ESOP.*—To be exempt, a loan must be made to a plan that is an ESOP at the time of such loan. However, a loan to a plan formally designated as an ESOP at the time of the loan that fails to be an ESOP because it does not comply with section 401(a) of the Code or §54.4975-11 will be exempt as of the time of such loan if the plan is amended retroactively under section 401(b) or §54.4975-11(a)(4).

(15) *Special rules for certain loans.*—(i) *Loans made before January 1, 1976.*—A loan made before January 1, 1976, or made afterwards under a binding agreement in effect on January 1, 1976 (or under renewals permitted by the terms of the agreement on that date) is exempt for the entire period of the loan if it otherwise satisfies the provisions of this paragraph (b) for such period, even though it does not satisfy the following provisions of this section: the last sentence of paragraph (b)(4) and all of paragraph (b)(5), (6), (8)(i) and (ii), and (9) through (13), inclusive.

(ii) *Loans made after December 31, 1975, but before November 1, 1977.*—A loan made after December 31, 1975, but before November 1, 1977 or made afterwards under a binding agreement in effect on November 1, 1977 (or under renewals permitted by the terms of the agreement on that date) is exempt for the entire period of the loan if it otherwise satisfies the provisions of this paragraph (b) for such period even though it does not satisfy the following provisions of this section: paragraph (b)(6) and (9) and the three additional rules listed in paragraph (b)(8)(ii).

(iii) *Release rule.*—Notwithstanding paragraph (b)(15)(i) and (ii) of this section, if the proceeds of a loan are used to acquire securities after November 1, 1977, the loan must comply by such date with the provisions of paragraph (b)(8) of this section.

(iv) *Default rule.*—Notwithstanding paragraph (b)(15)(i) and (ii) of this section, a loan by a disqualified person other than a guarantor

must meet the requirements of paragraph (b)(6) of this section. A loan will meet these requirements if it is retroactively amended before November 1, 1977 to meet these requirements.

(v) *Put option rule.*—With respect to a security distributed before November 1, 1977, the put option provisions of paragraph (b)(10), (11), and (12) of this section will be deemed satisfied as of the date the security is distributed if by December 31, 1977, the security is subject to a put option satisfying such provisions. For purposes of satisfying such provisions, the security will be deemed distributed on the date the put option is issued. However, the put option provisions need not be satisfied with respect to a security that is not owned on November 1, 1977 by a person in whose hands a put option must be exercisable. [Reg. § 54.4975-7.]

☐ [*T.D.* 7506, 8-30-77.]

[Reg. § 54.4975-9]

§ 54.4975-9. Definition of "Fiduciary".—
(a) [Reserved]

(b) [Reserved]

(c) *Investment advice.*—(1) A person shall be deemed to be rendering "investment advice" to an employee benefit plan, within the meaning of section 4975(e)(3)(B) and this paragraph, only if:

(i) Such person renders advice to the plan as to the value of securities or other property, or makes recommendations as to the advisability of investing in, purchasing, or selling securities or other property; and

(ii) Such person either directly or indirectly (e.g., through or together with any affiliate)—

(A) Has discretionary authority or control, whether or not pursuant to agreement, arrangement or understanding, with respect to purchasing or selling securities or other property for the plan; or

(B) Renders any advice described in paragraph (c)(1)(i) of this section on a regular basis to the plan pursuant to a mutual agreement, arrangement or understanding, written or otherwise, between such person and the plan or a fiduciary with respect to the plan, that such services will serve as a primary basis for investment decisions with respect to plan assets, and that such person will render individualized investment advice to the plan based on the particular needs of the plan regarding such matters as, among other things, investment policies or strategy, overall portfolio composition, or diversification of plan investments.

(2) A person who is a fiduciary with respect to a plan by reason of rendering investment advice (as defined in paragraph (c)(1) of this section) for a fee or other compensation, direct or indirect, with respect to any moneys or other property of such plan, or having any authority or responsibility to do so, shall not be deemed to be a fiduciary regarding any assets of the plan with respect to which such person does not have any discretionary authority, discretionary control or discretionary responsibility, does not exercise any authority or control, does not render investment advice (as defined in paragraph (c)(1) of this section) for a fee or other compensation, and does not have any authority or responsibility to render such investment advice, provided that nothing in this paragraph shall be deemed to:

(i) Exempt such person from the provisions of section 405(a) of the Employee Retirement Income Security Act of 1974 concerning liability for fiduciary breaches by other fiduciaries with respect to any assets of the plan; or

(ii) Exclude such person from the definition of the term "disqualified person" (as set forth in section 4975(e)(2)) with respect to any assets of the plan.

(d) *Execution of securities transactions.*—(1) A person who is a broker or dealer registered under the Securities Exchange Act of 1934, a reporting dealer who makes primary markets in securities of the United States Government or of an agency of the United States Government and reports daily to the Federal Reserve Bank of New York its positions with respect to such securities and borrowings thereon, or a bank supervised by the United States or a State, shall not be deemed to be a fiduciary, within the meaning of section 4975(e)(3), with respect to an employee benefit plan solely because such person executes transactions for the purchase or sale of securities on behalf of such plan in the ordinary course of its business as a broker, dealer, or bank, pursuant to instructions of a fiduciary with respect to such plan, if:

(i) Neither the fiduciary nor any affiliate of such fiduciary is such broker, dealer, or bank; and

(ii) The instructions specify (A) the security to be purchased or sold, (B) a price range within which such security is to be purchased or sold, or, if such security is issued by an open-end investment company registered under the Investment Company Act of 1940 (15 U.S.C. 80a-1, et seq.), a price which is determined in accordance with Rule 22c-1 under the Investment Company Act of 1940 (17 CFR 270.22c-1), (C) a time span during which such security may be purchased or sold (not to exceed five business days), and (D) the minimum or maximum quantity of such security which may be purchased or sold within such price range, or, in the case of a security issued by an open-end investment company registered under the Investment Company Act of 1940, the minimum or maximum quantity of such security which may be purchased or sold, or the value of such security in dollar amount which may be purchased or sold, at the price referred to in paragraph (d)(1)(ii)(B) of this section.

(2) A person who is a broker-dealer, reporting dealer, or bank which is a fiduciary with respect to an employee benefit plan solely by reason of the possession or exercise of discretionary authority or discretionary control in the management of the plan or the management or

Reg. § 54.4975-9(d)(2)

disposition of plan assets in connection with the execution of a transaction for the purchase or sale of securities on behalf of such plan which fails to comply with the provisions of paragraph (d)(1) of this section, shall not be deemed to be a fiduciary regarding any assets of the plan with respect to which such broker-dealer, reporting dealer or bank does not have any discretionary authority, discretionary control or discretionary responsibility, does not exercise any authority or control, does not render investment advice (as defined in paragraph (c)(1) of this section) for a fee or other compensation, and does not have any authority or responsibility to render such investment advice, provided that nothing in this paragraph shall be deemed to:

(i) Exempt such broker-dealer, reporting dealer, or bank from the provisions of section 405(a) of the Employee Retirement Income Security Act of 1974 concerning liability for fiduciary breaches by other fiduciaries with respect to any assets of the plan; or

(ii) Exclude such broker-dealer, reporting dealer, or bank from the definition of the term "disqualified person" (as set forth in section 4975(e) (2)) with respect to any assets of the plan.

(e) *Affiliate and control.*—(1) For purposes of paragraphs (c) and (d) of this section, an "affiliate" of a person shall include:

(i) Any person directly or indirectly, through one or more intermediaries, controlling, controlled by, or under common control with such person;

(ii) Any officer, director, partner, employee or relative (as defined in section 4975(e)(6)) of such person; and

(iii) Any corporation or partnership of which such person is an officer, director or partner.

(2) For purposes of this paragraph, the term "control" means the power to exercise a controlling influence over the management or policies of a person other than an individual. [Reg. § 54.4975-9.]

☐ [*T.D. 7386*, 10-28-75.]

[Reg. § 54.4975-11]

§ 54.4975-11. "ESOP" requirements.—(a) *In general.*—(1) *Type of plan.*—To be an "ESOP" (employee stock ownership plan), a plan described in section 4975(e)(7)(A) must meet the requirements of this section. See section 4975(e)(7)(B).

(2) *Designation as ESOP.*—To be an ESOP, a plan must be formally designated as such in the plan document.

(3) *Continuing loan provisions under plan.*— (i) *Creation of protections and rights.*—The terms of an ESOP must formally provide participants with certain protections and rights with respect to plan assets acquired with the proceeds of an exempt loan. These protections and rights are those referred to in the third sentence of § 54.4975-7(b)(4), relating to put, call, or other options and to buy-sell or similar arrangements,

and in § 54.4975-7(b)(10), (11), and (12), relating to put options.

(ii) *"Nonterminable" protections and rights.*—The terms of an ESOP must also formally provide that these protections and rights are nonterminable. Thus, if a plan holds or has distributed securities acquired with the proceeds of an exempt loan and either the loan is repaid or the plan ceases to be an ESOP, these protections and rights must continue to exist under the terms of the plan. However, the protections and rights will not fail to be nonterminable merely because they are not exercisable under § 54.4975-7(b)(11) and (12)(ii). For example, if, after a plan ceases to be an ESOP, securities acquired with the proceeds of an exempt loan cease to be publicly traded, the 15-month period prescribed by § 54.4975-7(b)(11) includes the time when the securities are publicly traded.

(iii) *No incorporation by reference of protections and rights.*—The formal requirements of paragraph (a)(3)(i) and (ii) of this section must be set forth in the plan. Mere reference to the third sentence of § 54.4975-7(b)(4) and to the provisions of § 54.4975-7(b)(10), (11), and (12) is not sufficient.

(iv) *Certain remedial amendments.*—Notwithstanding the limits under paragraph (a)(4) and (10) of this section on the retroactive effect of plan amendments, a remedial plan amendment adopted before December 31, 1979, to meet the requirements of paragraph (a)(3)(i) and (ii) of this section is retroactively effective as of the later of the date on which the plan was designated as an ESOP or November 1, 1977.

(4) *Retroactive amendment.*—A plan meets the requirements of this section as of the date that it is designated as an ESOP if it is amended retroactively to meet, and in fact does meet, such requirements at any of the following times:

(i) 12 months after the date on which the plan is designated as an ESOP;

(ii) 90 days after a determination letter is issued with respect to the qualification of the plan as an ESOP under this section, but only if the determination is requested by the time in paragraph (a)(4)(i) of this section; or

(iii) A later date approved by the district director.

(5) *Addition to other plan.*—An ESOP may form a portion of a plan the balance of which includes a qualified pension, profit-sharing, or stock bonus plan which is not an ESOP. A reference to an ESOP includes an ESOP that forms a portion of another plan.

(6) *Conversion of existing plan to an ESOP.*— If an existing pension, profit-sharing, or stock bonus plan is converted into an ESOP, the requirements of section 404 of the Employee Retirement Income Security Act of 1974 (ERISA) (88 Stat. 877), relating to fiduciary duties, and section 401(a) of the Code, relating to requirements for plans established for the exclusive benefit of employees, apply to such conversion. A conver-

sion may constitute a termination of an existing plan. For definition of a termination, see the regulations under section 411(d)(3) of the Code and section 4041(f) of ERISA.

(7) *Certain arrangements barred.*—(i) *Buy-sell agreements.*—An arrangement involving an ESOP that creates a put option must not provide for the issuance of put options other than as provided under §54.4975-7(b)(10), (11), and (12). Also, as ESOP must not otherwise obligate itself to acquire securities from a particular security holder at an indefinite time determined upon the happening of an event such as the death of the holder.

(ii) *Integrated plans.*—A plan designated as an ESOP after November 1, 1977, must not be integrated directly or indirectly with contributions or benefits under Title II of the Social Security Act or any other State or Federal law. ESOP's established and integrated before such date may remain integrated. However, such plans must not be amended to increase the integration level or the integration percentage. Such plans may in operation continue to increase the level of integration if under the plan such increase is limited by reference to a criterion existing apart from the plan.

(8) *Effect of certain ESOP provisions on section 401(a) status.*—(i) *Exempt loan requirements.*—An ESOP will not fail to meet the requirements of section 401(a)(2) merely because it gives plan assets as collateral for an exempt loan under §54.4975-7(b)(5) or uses plan assets under §54.4975-7(b)(6) to repay an exempt loan in the event of default.

(ii) *Individual annual contribution limitation.*—An ESOP will not fail to meet the requirements of section 401(a)(16) merely because annual additions under section 415(c) are calculated with respect to employer contributions used to repay an exempt loan rather than with respect to securities allocated to participants.

(iii) *Income pass-through.*—An ESOP will not fail to meet the requirements of section 401(a) merely because it provides for the current payment of income under paragraph (f)(3) of this section.

(9) *Transitional rules for ESOP's established before November 1, 1977.*—A plan established before November 1, 1977 that otherwise satisfies the provisions of this section constitutes an ESOP if it is amended by December 31, 1977, to comply from November 1, 1977 with this section even though before November 1, 1977 the plan did not satisfy paragraphs (c) and (d)(2), (4), and (5) of this section.

(10) *Additional transitional rules.*—Notwithstanding paragraph (a)(9) of this section, a plan established before November 1, 1977 that otherwise satisfies the provisions of this section constitutes an ESOP if by December 31, 1977, it is amended to comply from November 1, 1977 with this section even though before such date the

plan did not satisfy the following provisions of this section:

(i) Paragraph (a)(3) and (8)(iii);

(ii) The last sentence of paragraph (d)(3); and

(iii) Paragraph (f)(3).

(b) *Plan designed to invest primarily in qualifying employer securities.*—A plan constitutes an ESOP only if the plan specifically states that it is designed to invest primarily in qualifying employer securities. Thus, a stock bonus plan or a money purchase pension plan constituting an ESOP may invest part of its assets in other than qualifying employer securities. Such plan will be treated the same as other stock bonus plans or money purchase pension plans qualified under section 401(a) with respect to those investments.

(c) *Suspense account.*—All assets acquired by an ESOP with the proceeds of an exempt loan under section 4975(d)(3) must be added to and maintained in a suspense account. They are to be withdrawn from the suspense account by applying §54.4975-7(b)(8) and (15) as if all securities in the suspense account were encumbered. Such assets acquired before November 1, 1977, must be withdrawn by applying §54.4975-7(b)(8) or the provision of the loan that controls release from encumbrance. Assets in such suspense accounts are assets of the ESOP. Thus, for example, such assets are subject to section 401(a)(2).

(d) *Allocations to accounts of participants.*— (1) *In general.*—Except as provided in this section, amounts contributed to an ESOP must be allocated as provided under §1.401-1(b)(ii) and (iii) of this chapter, and securities acquired by an ESOP must be accounted for as provided under §1.402(a)-1(b)(2)(ii) of this chapter.

(2) *Assets withdrawn from suspense account.*— As of the end of each plan year, the ESOP must consistently allocate to the participants' accounts non-monetary units representing participants' interests in assets withdrawn from the suspense account.

(3) *Income.*—Income with respect to securities acquired with the proceeds of an exempt loan must be allocated as income of the plan except to the extent that the ESOP provides for the use of income from such securities to repay the loan. Certain income may be distributed currently under paragraph (f)(3) of this section.

(4) *Forfeitures.*—If a portion of a participant's account is forfeited, qualifying employer securities allocated under paragraph (d)(2) of this section must be forfeited only after other assets. If interests in more than one class of qualifying employer securities have been allocated to the participant's account, the participant must be treated as forfeiting the same proportion of each such class.

(5) *Valuation.*—For purposes of §54.4975-7(b)(9) and (12) and this section, valuations must be made in good faith and based on all relevant factors for determining the fair mar-

ket value of securities. In the case of a transaction between a plan and a disqualified person, value must be determined as of the date of the transaction. For all other purposes under this subparagraph (5), value must be determined as of the most recent valuation date under the plan. An independent appraisal will not in itself be a good faith determination of value in the case of a transaction between a plan and a disqualified person. However, in other cases, a determination of fair market value based on at least an annual appraisal independently arrived at by a person who customarily makes such appraisals and who is independent of any party to a transaction under § 54.4975-7(b)(9) and (12) will be deemed to be a good faith determination of value.

(e) *Multiple plans.*—(1) *General rule.*—An ESOP may not be considered together with another plan for purposes of applying section 401(a)(4) and (5) or section 410(b) unless—

(i) The ESOP and such other plan exist on November 1, 1977, or

(ii) Paragraph (e)(2) of this section is satisfied.

(2) *Special rule for combined ESOP's.*—Two or more ESOP's, one or more of which does not exist on November 1, 1977, may be considered together for purposes of applying section 401(a)(4) and (5) or section 410(b) only if the proportion of qualifying employer securities to total plan assets is substantially the same for each ESOP and—

(i) The qualifying employer securities held by all ESOP's are all of the same class; or

(ii) The ratios of each class held to all such securities held is substantially the same for each plan.

(3) *Amended coverage, contribution, or benefit structure.*—For purposes of paragraph (e)(1)(i) of this section, if the coverage, contribution, or benefit structure of a plan that exists on November 1, 1977 is amended after that date, as of the effective date of the amendment, the plan is no longer considered to be a plan that exists on November 1, 1977.

(f) *Distribution.*—(1) *In general.*—Except as provided in paragraph (f)(2) and (3) of this section, with respect to distributions, a portion of an ESOP consisting of a stock bonus plan or a money purchase pension plan is not to be distinguished from other such plans under section 401(a). Thus, for example, benefits distributable from the portion of an ESOP consisting of a stock bonus plan are distributable only in stock of the employer. Also, benefits distributable from the money-purchase portion of the ESOP may be, but are not required to be, distributable in qualifying employer securities.

(2) *Exempt loan proceeds.*—If securities acquired with the proceeds of an exempt loan available for distribution consist of more than one class, a distributee must receive substantially the same proportion of each such class. However, as indicated in paragraph (f)(1) of this sec-

tion, benefits distributable from the portion of an ESOP consisting of a stock bonus plan are distributable only in stock of the employer.

(3) *Income.*—Income paid with respect to qualifying employer securities acquired by an ESOP in taxable years beginning after December 31, 1974, may be distributed at any time after receipt by the plan to participants on whose behalf such securities have been allocated. However, under an ESOP that is a stock bonus plan, income held by the plan for a 2-year period or longer must be distributed under the general rules described in paragraph (f)(1) of this section. (See the last sentence of section 803(h), Tax Reform Act of 1976). [Reg. § 54.4975-11.]

☐ [*T.D. 7506,* 8-30-77. *Amended by T.D. 7571,* 11-16-78.]

[Reg. § 54.4975-12]

§ 54.4975-12. Definition of the term "qualifying employer security".—(a) *In general.*—For purposes of section 4975(e)(8) and this section, the term "qualifying employer security" means an employer security which is:

(1) Stock or otherwise an equity security, or

(2) A bond, debenture, note, or certificate or other evidence of indebtedness which is described in paragraphs (1), (2), and (3) of section 503(e).

(b) *Special rule.*—In determining whether a bond, debenture, note, or certificate or other evidence of indebtedness is described in paragraphs (1), (2), and (3) of section 503(e), any organization described in section 401(a) shall be treated as an organization subject to the provisions of section 503. [Reg. § 54.4975-12.]

☐ [*T.D. 7506,* 8-30-77.]

[Reg. § 141.4975-13]

§ 141.4975-13. Definition of "amount involved" and "correction." (Temporary).—Until superseded by permanent regulations under sections 4975(f), (4) and (5), § 53.4941(e)-1 of this chapter (Foundation Excise Tax Regulations) will be controlling to the extent such regulations describe terms appearing both in section 4941(e) and section 4975(f). [Temporary Reg. § 141.4975-13.]

☐ [*T.D. 7425,* 8-5-76. *Amended by T.D. 8084,* 5-1-86.]

[Reg. § 54.4975-14]

§ 54.4975-14. Election to pay an excise tax for certain pre-1975 prohibited transactions.—(a) *In general.*—Section 2003(c)(1)(B) of the Employee Retirement Income Security Act of 1974 (88 Stat. 978) provides an election to pay an excise tax by certain persons involved prior to 1975 in prohibited transactions within the meaning of section 503(b) or (g).

(b) *Effect of election.*—If a valid election is made under this section with respect to a particular transaction, any loss of exemption under section 501(a) because of a prohibited transaction

within the meaning of section 503(b) or (g) shall not apply. Instead, the person who made the election referred to in this section shall be subject to the taxes which would have been imposed by section 4975(a) or (b) as though section 4975 had imposed a tax in respect of the transaction. (However, section 4975(f)(1), relating to joint and several liability, shall not apply to any person who has not made an election under this section, and interest for late payment of tax shall not begin to accrue until after the date of the election.) Such an election is irrevocable. However, the making of the election does not affect the application of section 6501 for purposes of assessment and collection of tax and section 6511 for purposes of filing a claim for credit or refund with respect to taxpayers and to taxable years of taxpayers whose tax liability is or may be affected by reason of the nonapplication of a denial of exempt status.

(c) *Method of election.*—A person shall make the election referred to in this section by filing the form issued for such purpose by the Internal Revenue Service, including therein the information required by such form and the instructions issued with respect thereto, and by paying the tax which the taxpayer indicates is due at the time the return is filed. To be valid the election must be made prior to the later of December 6, 1976, or 120 days after the date of notification referred to in § 1.503(a)-1(b) of this chapter (Income Tax Regulations), relating to loss of exemption for certain prohibited transactions. If there has been no notification of loss of exemption, the election may be made at any time. However, these limitations do not preclude an agreement between the disqualified person and the district director to extend the time within which the election is permitted.

(d) *Computation of section 4975 excise tax.*—To the extent applicable, and solely for purposes associated with the payment of a section 4975 excise tax under the election referred to in this section, § 53.4941(e)-1 of this chapter (Foundation Excise Tax Regulations) is controlling. [Reg. § 54.4975-14.]

☐ [*T.D.* 7489, 5-26-77.]

[Reg. § 54.4975-15]

§ 54.4975-15. Other transitional rules.—
(a) [Reserved]

(b) [Reserved]

(c) [Reserved]

(d) *Provision of certain services until June 30, 1977.*—(1) *In general.*—Section 2003(c)(2)(D) of the Employee Retirement Income Security Act of 1974 (the Act) (88 Stat. 979) provides that section 4975 shall not apply to the provision of services before June 30, 1977, between a plan and a disqualified person if the three requirements contained in section 2003(c)(2)(D) of the Act are met. The first requirement is that such services must be provided either (i) under a binding contract in effect on July 1, 1974 (or pursuant to a renewal or modification of such contract); or (ii) by a dis-

qualified person who ordinarily and customarily furnished such services on June 30, 1974. The second requirement is that the services be provided on terms that remain at least as favorable to the plan as an arm's-length transaction with an unrelated party would be. For this purpose, such services are provided on terms that remain at least as favorable to the plan as an arm's-length transaction with an unrelated party would be if, at the time of execution (or renewal) of such binding contract, the contract (or renewal) is on terms at least as favorable to the plan as an arm's-length transaction with an unrelated party would be. However, if in a normal commercial setting an unrelated party in the position of the plan could be expected to insist upon a renegotiation or termination of a binding contract, the plan must so act. Thus, for example, if a disqualified person provides services to a plan on a month-to-month basis, and a party in the position of the plan could be expected to renegotiate the price paid under such contract because of a decline in the fair market value of such services, the plan must so act in order to avoid participation in a prohibited transaction. The third requirement is that the provision of services must not be, or have been, at the time of such provision a prohibited transaction within the meaning of section 503(b) or the corresponding provisions of prior law. If these three requirements are met, section 4975 will apply neither to services provided before June 30, 1977 (both to customers to whom such services were being provided on June 30, 1974, and to new customers) nor to the receipt of compensation therefor. Thus, if these three requirements are met, section 4975 will not apply until June 30, 1977, to the provision of services to a plan by a disqualified person (including a fiduciary) even if such services could not be furnished pursuant to the exemption provisions of sections 4975(d)(2) or (6) and § 54.4975-6. For example, if the three requirements of section 2003(c)(2)(D) of the Act are met, a person serving as fiduciary to a plan who already receives full-time pay from an employer or an association of employers, whose employees are participants in such plan, or from an employee organization whose members are participants in such plan, may continue to receive reasonable compensation from the plan for services rendered to the plan before June 30, 1977. Similarly, until June 30, 1977, a plan consultant who may be a fiduciary because of the nature of the consultative and administrative services being provided may, if these three requirements are met, continue to cause the sale of insurance to the plan and continue to receive commissions for such sales from the insurance company writing the policy. Further, if the three requirements of section 2003(c)(2)(D) of the Act are met, a securities broker-dealer who renders investment advice to a plan for a fee, thereby becoming a fiduciary, may furnish other services to the plan, such as brokerage services, and receives compensation therefor. Also, if a registered representative of such a broker-dealer were a fiduciary, the registered representative may

receive compensation, including commissions, for brokerage services performed before June 30, 1977.

(2) *Persons deemed to be June 30, 1974, service providers.*—A disqualified person with respect to a plan which did not, on June 30, 1974, ordinarily and customarily furnish a particular service, will nevertheless be considered to have ordinarily and customarily furnished such service on June 30, 1974, for purposes of this section and section 2003(c)(2)(D) of the Act, if either of the following conditions are met:

(i) At least 50 percent of the outstanding beneficial interests of such disqualified person are owned directly or through one or more intermediaries by the same person or persons who owned, directly or through one or more intermediaries, at least 50 percent of the outstanding beneficial interests of a person who ordinarily and customarily furnished such service on June 30, 1974; or

(ii) Control or the power to exercise a controlling influence over the management and policies of such disqualified person is possessed, directly or through one or more intermediaries, by the same person or persons who possessed, directly or through one or more intermediaries, control or the power to exercise a controlling influence over the management and policies of a person who ordinarily and customarily furnished such service on June 30, 1974. For purposes of this paragraph (d)(2) a person shall be deemed to be an "intermediary" of another person if at least 50 percent of the outstanding beneficial interests of such person are owned by such other person, directly or indirectly, or if such other person controls or has the power to exercise a controlling influence over the management and policies of such person.

(3) *Examples.*—The principles of §54.4975-15(d)(2) may be illustrated by the following examples.

Example (1). A owns 50 percent of the outstanding beneficial interest of ABC Partnership which ordinarily and customarily furnished certain services on June 30, 1974. On July 2, 1974, ABC Partnership was incorporated into ABC Corporation with one class of stock outstanding. A owns 50 percent of the shares of such stock. ABC Corporation furnishes the same services that were furnished by ABC Partnership on June 30, 1974. ABC Corporation will be deemed to have ordinarily and customarily furnished such services on June 30, 1974, for purposes of section 2003(c)(2)(D) of the Act.

Example (2). A and B together own 100 percent of the beneficial interests of AB Partnership, which ordinarily and customarily furnished certain services on June 30, 1974. On September 1, 1974, AB Partnership was incorporated into AB Corporation with one class of stock outstanding. A and B each own 20 percent of such outstanding class of stock and together have control over the management and policies of AB Corporation. AB Corporation furnishes the same services that

were furnished by AB Partnership on June 30, 1974. AB Corporation will be deemed to have ordinarily and customarily furnished such services on June 30, 1974, for purposes of section 2003(c)(2)(D) of the Act.

Example (3). On June 30, 1974, M Corporation was ordinarily and customarily furnishing certain services. On that date, X, Y and Z together owned 50 percent of all classes of the outstanding shares of M Corporation. On January 28, 1975, all of the shareholders of M Corporation exchanged their shares in M Corporation for shares of a new N Corporation. As a result of that exchange, X, Y and Z together own 50 percent of the common stock of N Corporation, the only class of N Corporation stock outstanding after the exchange. N Corporation furnishes the services formerly furnished by M Corporation. N Corporation will be deemed to have ordinarily and customarily furnished such services on June 30, 1974, for purposes of section 2003(c)(2)(D) of the Act.

Example (4). I Corporation ordinarily and customarily furnished certain services on June 30, 1974. On November 3, 1975, I corporation organizes a wholly owned subsidiary, S Corporation, which furnishes the same services ordinarily and customarily furnished by I Corporation on June 30, 1974. S Corporation will be deemed to have ordinarily and customarily furnished such services on June 30, 1974, for purposes of section 2003(c)(2)(D) of the Act.

Example (5). X Corporation, wholly-owned and controlled by A, ordinarily and customarily furnished certain services on June 30, 1974. Y Corporation did not perform such services on that date. On January 2, 1976, X Corporation is merged into Y Corporation and, although A received less than 50 percent of the total outstanding shares of Y Corporation, after such merger A has control over the management and policies of Y Corporation. Y Corporation furnishes the same services that were formerly furnished by X Corporation. Y Corporation will be deemed to have ordinarily and customarily furnished such services on June 30, 1974, for purposes of section 2003(c)(2)(D) of the Act. [Reg. §54.4975-15.]

☐ [*T.D.* 7491, 6-21-77.]

[Reg. §54.4976-1T]

§54.4976-1T. Questions and answers relating to taxes with respect to welfare benefit funds. (Temporary)

Q-1: What does section 4976 provide?

A-1: Section 4976 imposes a tax on employers who provide disqualified benefits through a welfare benefit fund. The tax imposed is equal to 100 percent of the disqualified benefit.

Q-2: What constitutes a disqualified benefit?

A-2: A disqualified benefit is (a) any post-retirement medical or life insurance benefit provided with respect to a key employee (as defined in section 419A(d)(3)) through a welfare benefit fund if a separate account is required to be established for such employee under section 419A(d) and the cost for such coverage is not charged

against or paid from such separate account; (b) any post-retirement medical or life insurance benefit provided through a welfare benefit fund with respect to an individual in whose favor discrimination is prohibited unless the plan of which the fund is a part meets the requirements of section 505(b) with respect to that benefit; and (c) any portion of the fund which reverts to the benefit of the employer. A post-retirement medical or life insurance benefit provided with respect to a key employee will not constitute a disqualified benefit even though such benefit is not provided through a separate account if the cost of such benefit is paid by the employer in the taxable year in which the benefit is provided and there is not (and there is not required to be) a separate account with an outstanding credit balance maintained for the key employee.

Q-3: What is the effective date of section 4976?

A-3: (a) Generally, section 4976 applies to disqualified benefits provided by a welfare benefit fund after December 31, 1985. However, a disqualified benefit, as defined in section 4976(b)(1) or (2), is not subject to section 4976(a) if it is provided from "existing reserves for post-retirement medical or life insurance benefits" that are within the transition rule set forth in section 512(a)(3)(E)(iii) and Q&A-4 of §1.512(a)-5T (or would be if such transition rule applied to such welfare benefit fund). For example, if a welfare benefit fund in existence on July 18, 1984, provides an individual in whose favor discrimination is prohibited with a post-retirement life insurance benefit after December 31, 1985, that does not meet the requirements of section 505(b) and if the welfare benefit fund received no contributions after July 18, 1984, then the disqualified benefit provided by the fund is not subject to section 4976(a).

(b) A welfare benefit fund will be able to avoid the application of section 4976(b)(1) and (2) if the employer withdraws from such fund, before April 7, 1986, any amounts that are not attributable to "existing reserves for post-retirement medical or life insurance benefits" because they were neither actually set aside nor treated as actually set aside under Q&A-4 of §1.512(a)-5T, on July 18, 1984. The employer making such a withdrawal must include the amount in income for the first taxable year ending after July 18, 1984, or, to the extent that the withdrawn amount is attributable to the following taxable year, for such following taxable year. Such a withdrawal will not be treated as an impermissible distribution or reversion under section 501(c)(9), and will not be treated as a disqualified benefit under section 4976(b)(3). Of course, to the extent that the welfare benefit fund contains amounts that are attributable to "existing reserves" but are not within the transition rule set forth in Q&A-4 of §1.512(a)-5T (as applied to welfare benefit funds), for example, because such amounts exceed the amounts that could have been accumulated under the principles set forth in Revenue Rulings 69-382, 1969-2 C.B. 28; 69-478, 1969-2 C.B. 29; and 73-599, 1973-2 C.B. 40, the fund will

not be able to avoid the application of section 4976(b)(1) and (2) under this paragraph.

(c) In the case of a plan which is maintained pursuant to one or more collective bargaining agreements (1) between employee representatives and one or more employers and (2) which are in effect on July 1, 1985 (or ratified on or before that date), the provision does not apply to disqualified benefits provided in years beginning before the termination of the last of the collective bargaining agreements pursuant to which the plan is maintained (determined without regard to any extension of the contract agreed to after July 1, 1985). For purposes of the preceding sentence, any plan amendment made pursuant to a collective bargaining agreement relating to the plan which amends the plan solely to conform to any requirement added under section 511 of the Tax Reform Act 1984 (i.e., requirements under sections 419, 419A, 512(a)(3)(E), and 4976) shall not be treated as a termination of such collective bargaining agreement. [Temporary Reg. §54.4976-1T.]

□ [T.D. 8073, 1-29-86.]

[Reg. §54.4977-1T]

§54.4977-1T. Questions and answers relating to the election concerning lines of business in existence on January 1, 1984 (Temporary).—The following questions and answers relate to the election by employers under section 4977 of the Internal Revenue Code of 1954, as added by section 531(e)(1) of the Tax Reform Act of 1984 (98 Stat. 886), to treat all employees of any line of business in existence on January 1, 1984, as employees of one of those lines of business for purposes of section 132(a)(1) and (2):

Q-1: What does section 4977 provide with respect to the exclusion from gross income of certain fringe benefits?

A-1: In general, section 4977 provides an elective grandfather rule that allows an employer under certain circumstances to treat employees of all lines of business which were in existence on January 1, 1984, as employees of one of those lines of business for purposes of section 132(a)(1) and (2), but not for purposes of section 132(g)(2).

Q-2: Under what circumstances does the elective grandfather rule of section 4977 apply?

A-2: If—

(a) an election under section 4977 is in effect with respect to an employer for any calendar year, and

(b) on and after January 1, 1984, at least 85 percent of the employees of the employer in all of its lines of business which existed on January 1, 1984, were entitled to employee discounts or services provided by the employer in one line of business,

then all employees of any line of business of the employer which was in existence on January 1, 1984, are treated, for purposes of section 132(a)(1) and (2) (but not for purposes of section 132(g)(2)) as employees of the one line of business referred to in (b) of this Q/A-2.

Q-3: How does an employer make the election provided for in section 4977?

A-3: An employer must file a statement with the director of the service center with which the employer's tax returns are filed. The statement must indicate that the employer is electing to apply the provisions of section 4977 to one or more of the employer's lines of business and must contain the following information:

(a) The employer's name, address, and taxpayer identification number;

(b) A description of all of the employer's lines of business in existence on January 1, 1984; and

(c) For each line of business which is to have as an employee for purposes of section 132(a)(1) and (2) an individual who but for the election under section 4977 would not be treated as an employee for purposes of section 132(a)(1) and (2)—

(1) a description of the no-additional-cost service or qualified employee discount (including, with respect to discounts, the percentage discount) to be offered to employees pursuant to section 4977 in such line of business, and

(2) with respect to employees in all of the employer's lines of business in existence on January 1, 1984, the number of such employees and the number entitled to the described fringe benefit. Such numbers may be determined as of a date which does not precede the date the election is filed by more than 30 days.

Q-4: In order to make a timely section 4977 election, when must an employer file the election statement?

A-4: Except as otherwise provided in the second sentence of this answer, the employer must file the election statement before the end of the calendar year preceding the year for which the election is to apply. For calendar year 1985, however, the employer has until March 31, 1985, to file the election statement. However, the Commissioner may, in his discretion, extend the March 31, 1985 deadline to a later date.

Q-5: Does section 4977 apply to all calendar years following the calendar year in which the election is made?

A-5: Yes, unless the employer revokes the election.

Q-6: When is a revocation effective?

A-6: A revocation is effective with respect to the calendar year following the calendar year in which it is filed.

Q-7: If an employer does not make a timely section 4977 election with respect to 1985, will the employer be entitled to make an election with respect to any subsequent year?

A-7: No.

Q-8: If an employer revokes a section 4977 election, is the employer entitled to elect the application of section 4977 for subsequent years?

A-8: No. [Temporary Reg. § 54.4977-1T.]

☐ [*T.D.* 8004, 1-2-85.]

[Reg. § 54.4978-1T]

§ 54.4978-1T. Questions and answers relating to the tax on certain dispositions by employee stock ownership plans and certain cooperatives (Temporary).

Q-1: What does section 4978 provide?

A-1: Section 4978 imposes a tax (as determined under section 4978(b) and Q&A-2 of this section) on the amount realized on the disposition of any qualified securities, if:

(a) An employee stock ownership plan or eligible worker-owned cooperative acquires any qualified securities in a sale to which section 1042 applies;

(b) Such plan or cooperative disposes of any qualified securities during the 3-year period after the date on which any qualified securities were acquired in the sale to which section 1042 applies; and

(c) Either (1) the percentage of the total outstanding shares of the class of employer securities of which the disposed qualified securities are a part held by such plan or cooperative after such disposition is less than the percentage of the total outstanding shares of such class of employer securities held immediately after the sale to which section 1042 applies, or (2) the value of the employer securities held by such plan or cooperative immediately after such disposition is less than 30 percent of the total value of all employer securities outstanding at that time. For purposes of this section, the following terms have the same meanings given to such terms by the identified provisions: "employee stock ownership plan" (section 4975(e)(7)); "qualified securities" (section 1042(b)(1)); "eligible worker-owned cooperative" (section 1042(b)(2)); "employer securities" (section 409(l)). For purposes of determining what constitutes a disposition to which section 4978 applies, see Q&A-3 of this section.

Q-2: What is the amount of tax imposed under section 4978?

A-2: Section 4978 imposes a tax of 10 percent of the amount realized on the disposition of qualified securities. The amount realized that is subject to tax under section 4978 shall not exceed that portion of the amount realized that is allocable to qualified securities acquired within the 3-year period prior to the date of disposition and to which section 1042 applied ("restricted qualified securities"). In determining the amount realized (except as otherwise provided in Q&A-3 of this section), any disposition of employer securities with respect to which the condition contained in provision (c) of Q&A-1 is met shall be treated, first, as a disposition of restricted qualified securities (on a first in, first out basis) and, thereafter, as a disposition of any other employer securities. Thus, for example, if a plan disposes of more employer securities than the number of restricted qualified securities held by the plan at that time and immediately after such disposition the value of the employer securities held by the plan is less than 30 percent of the total value of all outstanding employer securities, the portion

of the total amount realized that is allocable to restricted qualified securities subject to tax under section 4978 is determined by multiplying the total amount realized on the disposition by a fraction, the numerator of which is the total value of restricted qualified securities included in the disposition and the denominator of which is the total value of employer securities in the disposition.

Q-3: What constitutes a "disposition" under section 4978?

A-3: (a) Under section 4978, the term "disposition" includes any sale, exchange, or distribution. However, in the case of any exchange of qualified securities for stock of another corporation in any reorganization described in section 368(a)(1), such exchange shall not be treated as a disposition for purposes of section 4978.

(b) Section 4978 shall not apply to any disposition of qualified securities which is made by reason of:

(1) The death of the employee;

(2) The retirement of the employee after the employee has attained 59 $\frac{1}{2}$ years of age;

(3) The disability of the employee (within the meaning of section 72(m)(5)); or

(4) The separation of the employee from service for any period which results in a 1-year break in service (within the meaning of section 411(a)(6)(A)).

Any disposition of employer securities within this paragraph and any disposition of employer securities with respect to which the condition contained in provision (c) of Q&A-1 of this section is not met shall be treated, first, as a disposition of securities that are not restricted qualified securities and, thereafter, as a disposition of restricted qualified securities (on a first-in, first-out basis).

(c) If restricted qualified securities held by an employee stock ownership plan or eligible worker-owned cooperative no longer meet the definition of qualified securities ("old restricted qualified securities") as a result of a transaction changing (1) the status of a corporation as an employer, or as a member of a controlled group of corporations including the employer, or (2) the existence of employer securities of the type described in section 409(l)(1), the disposition of such securities shall not be treated as a disposition of restricted qualified securities to which the tax under section 4978 is imposed if, within 90 days after such disposition, securities meeting the requirements of section 409(l) ("new restricted qualified securities") that are of equal value to the old restricted qualified securities (at the time of the disposition of the old restricted qualified securities) are substituted for such old restricted qualified securities. However, for purposes of determining the tax imposed under section 4978, old restricted qualified securities shall not be treated as if they retained their status as restricted qualified securities and new restricted qualified securities derived from the disposition of old restricted qualified securities pursuant to the preceding sentence shall be treated as restricted qualified securities for the remaining

portion of the period during which the disposition of the old restricted qualified securities would have been subject to tax under section 4978.

Q-4: To whom does the tax under section 4978 apply?

A-4: The tax under section 4978 is imposed on the domestic corporation (or corporations) or the eligible worker-owned cooperative that made the written statement of consent as described in section 1042(a)(2)(B) and Q&A-2 of §1.1042-1T with respect to the disposition of the restricted qualified securities.

Q-5: When does section 4978, as enacted by the Tax Reform Act of 1984, become effective?

A-5: Section 4978 applies to the disposition of qualified securities acquired in a sale to which section 1042 applies. See Q&A-6 of §1.1042-1T for the effective date of section 1042. [Temporary Reg. §54.4978-1T.]

☐ [*T.D. 8073, 1-29-86.*]

[Reg. §54.4979-0]

§54.4979-0. Excise tax on certain excess contributions and excess aggregate contributions; table of contents.—This section contains the captions that appear in §54.4979-1.

§54.4979-1. Excise tax on certain excess contributions and excess aggregate contributions.

(a) In general.

  (1) General rule.

  (2) Liability for tax.

  (3) Due date and form for payment of tax.

  (4) Special rule for simplified employee pensions.

(b) Definitions.

  (1) Excess aggregate contributions.

  (2) Excess contributions.

  (3) Plan.

(c) No tax when excess distributed within 2½ months of close of year or additional employer contributions made.

  (1) General rule.

  (2) Tax treatment of distributions.

  (3) Income.

  (4) Example.

(d) Effective date.

  (1) General rule.

  (2) Section 403(b) annuity contracts.

  (3) Collectively bargained plans and plans of state or local governments.

  (4) Plan years beginning before January 1, 1992.

[Reg. §54.4979-0.]

☐ [*T.D.* 8357, 8-8-91. *Amended by T.D.* 8581, 12-22-94.]

[Reg. §54.4979-1]

§54.4979-1. Excise tax on certain excess contributions and excess aggregate contributions.—(a) *In general.*—(1) *General rule.*—In the case of any plan (as defined in paragraph (b)(3) of this section), there is imposed a tax for the employer's taxable year equal to 10 percent of the sum of:

(i) Any excess contributions under a plan for the plan year ending in the taxable year; and

(ii) Any excess aggregate contributions under the plan for the plan year ending in the taxable year.

(2) *Liability for tax.*—The tax imposed by paragraph (a)(1) of this section is to be paid by the employer. In the case of a collectively bargained plan to which section 413(b) applies, all employers who are parties to the collective bargaining agreement and whose employees are participants in the plan are jointly and severally liable for the tax.

(3) *Due date and form for payment of tax.*—(i) The tax described in paragraph (a)(1) of this section is due on the last day of the 15th month after the close of the plan year to which the excess contributions or excess aggregate contributions relate.

(ii) An employer that owes the tax described in paragraph (a)(1) of this section must file the form prescribed by the Commissioner for the payment of the tax.

(4) *Special rule for simplified employee pensions.*—(i) An employer that maintains a simplified employee pension (SEP) as defined in section 408(k) that accepts elective contributions is exempt from the tax of section 4979 and paragraph (a)(1) of this section if it notifies its employees of the fact and tax consequences of excess contributions within 2^1/$_2$ months following the plan year for which excess contributions are made. The notification must meet the standards of paragraph (a)(4)(ii) of this section.

(ii) The employer's notification to each affected employee of the excess SEP contributions must specifically state, in a manner calculated to be understood by the average plan participant: the amount of the excess contributions attributable to that employee's elective deferrals; the calendar year for which the excess contributions were made; that the excess contributions are includible in the affected employee's gross income for the specified calendar year; and that failure to withdraw the excess contributions and income attributable thereto by the due date (plus extensions) for filing the affected employee's tax return for the preceding calendar year may result in significant penalties.

(iii) If an employer does not notify its employees by the last day of the 12-month period following the year of excess SEP contributions, the SEP will no longer be considered to meet the requirements of section 408(k)(6).

(b) *Definitions.*—The following is a list of terms and definitions to be used for purposes of section 4979 and this section:

(1) *Excess aggregate contributions.*—The term "excess aggregate contribution" has the meaning set forth in § 1.401(m)-5 of this Chapter. For purposes of determining excess aggregate contributions under an annuity contract described in

section 403(b), the contract is treated as a plan described in section 401(a).

(2) *Excess contributions.*—The term "excess contributions" has the meaning set forth in sections 401(k)(8)(B), 408(k)(6)(C)(ii), and 501(c)(18). See, e.g., § 1.401(k)-6 of this Chapter.

(3) *Plan.*—The term "plan" means:

(i) A plan described in section 401(a) that includes a trust exempt from tax under section 501(a);

(ii) Any annuity plan described in section 403(a);

(iii) Any annuity contract described in section 403(b);

(iv) A simplified employee pension of an employer that satisfies the requirements of section 408(k); and

(v) A plan described in section 501(c)(18). The term includes any plan that at any time has been determined by the Secretary to be one of the types of plans described in this paragraph (b)(3).

(c) *No tax when excess distributed within 2½ months of close of year or additional employer contributions made.*—(1) *General rule.*—No tax is imposed under this section on any excess contribution or excess aggregate contribution, as the case may be, to the extent the contribution (together with any income allocable thereto) is corrected before the close of the first 2^1/$_2$ months of the following plan year (6 months in the case of a plan that includes an eligible automatic contribution arrangement within the meaning of section 414(w)). The extension to 6 months applies to a distribution of excess contributions or excess aggregate contributions for a plan year beginning on or after January 1, 2010, only where all the eligible NHCEs and eligible HCEs (both as defined in § 1.401(k)-6 of this Chapter) are covered employees under an eligible automatic contribution arrangement within the meaning of section 414(w) for the entire plan year (or the portion of the plan year that the eligible NHCEs and eligible HCEs are eligible employees under the plan)). Qualified nonelective contributions and qualified matching contributions taken into account under § 1.401(k)-2(a)(6) of this Chapter or qualified nonelective contributions or elective contributions taken into account under § 1.401(m)-2(a)(6) of this Chapter for a plan year may permit a plan to avoid excess contributions or excess aggregate contributions, respectively, even if made after the close of the 2^1/$_2$ month (or 6 month) period for distributing excess contributions or excess aggregate contributions without the excise tax. See § 1.401(k)-2(b)(1)(i) and (5)(i) of this Chapter for methods to avoid excess contributions, and § 1.401(m)-2(b)(1)(i) of the Chapter for methods to avoid excess aggregate contributions.

(2) *Tax treatment of distributions.*—See § 1.401(k)-2(b)(3)(ii) and (2)(vi) of this Chapter for rules for determining the tax consequences to a participant of a distribution or recharacteriza-

tion of excess contributions and income allocable thereto, including a special rule for de minimis distributions. See § 1.401(m)-2(b)(2)(vi) of this Chapter for rules for determining the tax consequences to a participant of a distribution of excess aggregate contributions and income allocable thereto.

(3) *Income.*—See § 1.401(k)-2(b)(2)(iv) of this Chapter for rules for determining income allocable to excess contributions. See § 1.401(m)-2(b)(2)(iv) of this Chapter for rules for determining income allocable to excess aggregate contributions.

(4) *Example.*—The provisions of this paragraph (c) are illustrated by the following example.

Example. (i) Employer X maintains Plan Y, a calendar year profit-sharing plan that includes a qualified cash or deferred arrangement. Under the plan, failure to satisfy the actual deferral percentage test may only be corrected by distributing the excess contributions or making qualified nonelective contributions (QNECs).

(ii) On December 31, 1990, X determines that Y does not satisfy the actual deferral percentage test for the 1990 plan year, and that excess contributions for the year equal $5,000. On March 1, 1991, Y distributes $2,000 of these excess contributions. On May 30, 1991, X distributes another $2,000 of excess contributions. On December 17, 1991, X contributes QNECs for certain nonhighly compensated employees, thereby eliminating the remainder of the excess contributions for 1990.

(iii) X has incurred a tax liability under section 4979 for 1990 equal to 10 percent of the excess contributions that were in the plan as of December 31, 1990. However, this tax is not imposed on the $2,000 distributed on March 1, 1991, or the amount corrected by QNECs. X must pay an excise tax of $200, 10 percent of the $2,000 of excess contributions distributed after March 15, 1991. This tax must be paid by March 31, 1992.

(d) *Effective date.*—(1) *General rule.*—Except as provided in paragraphs (d)(2) through (4), this section is effective for plan years beginning after December 31, 1986.

(2) *Section 403(b) annuity contracts.*—In the case of an annuity contract under section 403(b), this section applies to plan years beginning after December 31, 1988.

(3) *Collectively bargained plans and plans of state or local governments.*—For plan years beginning before January 1, 1993, the provisions of this section do not apply to a collectively bargained plan that automatically satisfies the requirements of section 410(b). See §§ 1.401(a)(4)-1(c)(5) and 1.410(b)-2(b)(7) of this chapter. In the case of a plan (including a collectively bargained plan) maintained by a state or local government, the provisions of this section do not apply for plan years beginning before the later of January 1, 1996, or 90 days after the opening of the first legislative session beginning on or after January 1, 1996, of the governing body with authority to amend the plan, if that body does not meet continuously. For purposes of this paragraph (d)(3), the term *governing body with authority to amend the plan* means the legislature, board, commission, council, or other governing body with authority to amend the plan.

(4) *Plan years beginning before January 1, 1992.*—For plan years beginning before January 1, 1992, a reasonable interpretation of the rules set forth in section 4979, as in effect during those years, may be relied upon in determining whether the excise tax is due for those years. [Reg. § 54.4979-1.]

☐ [T.D. 8357, 8-8-91. *Amended by* T.D. 8581, 12-22-94; T.D. 9169, 12-28-2004 *and* T.D. 9447, 2-23-2009.]

[Reg. § 54.4980B-0]

§ 54.4980B-0. Table of contents.—This section contains first a list of the section headings and then a list of the questions in each section in §§ 54.4980B-1 through 54.4980B-10.

LIST OF SECTIONS

§ 54.4980B-1 COBRA in general.

§ 54.4980B-2 Plans that must comply.

§ 54.4980B-3 Qualified beneficiaries.

§ 54.4980B-4 Qualifying events.

§ 54.4980B-5 COBRA continuation coverage.

§ 54.4980B-6 Electing COBRA continuation coverage.

§ 54.4980B-7 Duration of COBRA continuation coverage.

§ 54.4980B-8 Paying for COBRA continuation coverage.

§ 54.4980B-9 Business reorganizations and employer withdrawals from multiemployer plans.

§ 54.4980B-10 Interaction of FMLA and COBRA.

LIST OF QUESTIONS

§ 54.4980B-1 COBRA in general.

Q-1: What are the health care continuation coverage requirements contained in section 4980B of the Internal Revenue Code and in ERISA?

Q-2: What standard applies for topics not addressed in §§ 54-4980B-1 through 54.4980B-10?

§ 54.4980B-2 Plans that must comply.

Q-1: For purposes of section 4980B, what is a group health plan?

Q-2: For purposes of section 4980B, what is the employer?

Q-3: What is a multiemployer plan?

Q-4: What group health plans are subject to COBRA?

Q-5: What is a small-employer plan?

Q-6: How is the number of group health plans that an employer or employee organization maintains determined?

Q-7: What is the plan year?

Q-8: How do the COBRA continuation coverage requirements apply to cafeteria plans and other flexible benefit arrangements?

Q-9: What is the effect of a group health plan's failure to comply with the requirements of section 4980B(f)?

Q-10: Who is liable for the excise tax if a group health plan fails to comply with the requirements of section 4980B(f)?

Q-11: If a person is liable for the excise tax under section 4980B, what form must the person file and what is the due date for the filing and payment of the excise tax?

§ 54.4980B-3 Qualified beneficiaries.

Q-1: Who is a qualified beneficiary?

Q-2: Who is an employee and who is a covered employee?

Q-3: Who are the similarly situated nonCOBRA beneficiaries?

§ 54.4980B-4 Qualifying events.

Q-1: What is a qualifying event?

Q-2: Are the facts surrounding a termination of employment (such as whether it was voluntary or involuntary) relevant in determining whether the termination of employment is a qualifying event?

§ 54.4980B-5 COBRA continuation coverage.

Q-1: What is COBRA continuation coverage?

Q-2: What deductibles apply if COBRA continuation coverage is elected?

Q-3: How do a plan's limits apply to COBRA continuation coverage?

Q-4: Can a qualified beneficiary who elects COBRA continuation coverage ever change from the coverage received by that individual immediately before the qualifying event?

Q-5: Aside from open enrollment periods, can a qualified beneficiary who has elected COBRA continuation coverage choose to cover individuals (such as newborn children, adopted children, or new spouses) who join the qualified beneficiary's family on or after the date of the qualifying event?

§ 54.4980B-6 Electing COBRA continuation coverage.

Q-1: What is the election period and how long must it last?

Q-2: Is a covered employee or qualified beneficiary responsible for informing the plan administrator of the occurrence of a qualifying event?

Q-3: During the election period and before the qualified beneficiary has made an election, must coverage be provided?

Q-4: Is a waiver before the end of the election period effective to end a qualified beneficiary's election rights?

Q-5: Can an employer or employee organization withhold money or other benefits owed to a qualified beneficiary until the qualified beneficiary either waives COBRA continuation coverage, elects and pays for such coverage, or allows the election period to expire?

Q-6: Can each qualified beneficiary make an independent election under COBRA?

§ 54.4980B-7 Duration of COBRA continuation coverage.

Q-1: How long must COBRA continuation coverage be made available to a qualified beneficiary?

Q-2: When may a plan terminate a qualified beneficiary's COBRA continuation coverage due to coverage under another group health plan?

Q-3: When may a plan terminate a qualified beneficiary's COBRA continuation coverage due to the qualified beneficiary's entitlement to Medicare benefits?

Q-4: When does the maximum coverage period end?

Q-5: How does a qualified beneficiary become entitled to a disability extension?

Q-6: Under what circumstances can the maximum coverage period be expanded?

Q-7: If health coverage is provided to a qualified beneficiary after a qualifying event without regard to COBRA continuation coverage (for example, as a result of state or local law, the Uniformed Services Employment and Reemployment Rights Act of 1994 (38 U.S.C. 4315), industry practice, a collective bargaining agreement, severance agreement, or plan procedure), will such alternative coverage extend the maximum coverage period?

Q-8: Must a qualified beneficiary be given the right to enroll in a conversion health plan at the end of the maximum coverage period for COBRA continuation coverage?

§ 54.4980B-8 Paying for COBRA continuation coverage.

Q-1: Can a group health plan require payment for COBRA continuation coverage?

Q-2: When is the applicable premium determined and when can a group health plan increase the amount it requires to be paid for COBRA continuation coverage?

Q-3: Must a plan allow payment for COBRA continuation coverage to be made in monthly installments?

Q-4: Is a plan required to allow a qualified beneficiary to choose to have the first payment for COBRA continuation coverage applied prospectively only?

Q-5: What is timely payment for COBRA continuation coverage?

§ 54.4980B-9 Business reorganizations and employer withdrawals from multiemployer plans.

Q-1: For purposes of this section, what are a business reorganization, a stock sale, and an asset sale?

Q-2: In the case of a stock sale, what are the selling group, the acquired organization, and the buying group?

Q-3: In the case of an asset sale, what are the selling group and the buying group?

Q-4: Who is an M & A qualified beneficiary?

Q-5: In the case of a stock sale, is the sale a qualifying event with respect to a covered employee who is employed by the acquired organization before the sale and who continues to be

employed by the acquired organization after the sale, or with respect to the spouse or dependent children of such a covered employee?

Q-6: In the case of an asset sale, is the sale a qualifying event with respect to a covered employee whose employment immediately before the sale was associated with the purchased assets, or with respect to the spouse or dependent children of such a covered employee who are covered under a group health plan of the selling group immediately before the sale?

Q-7: In a business reorganization, are the buying group and the selling group permitted to allocate by contract the responsibility to make COBRA continuation coverage available to M & A qualified beneficiaries?

Q-8: Which group health plan has the obligation to make COBRA continuation coverage available to M & A qualified beneficiaries in a business reorganization?

Q-9: Can the cessation of contributions by an employer to a multiemployer group health plan be a qualifying event?

Q-10: If an employer stops contributing to a multiemployer group health plan, does the multiemployer plan have the obligation to make COBRA continuation coverage available to a qualified beneficiary who was receiving coverage under the multiemployer plan on the day before the cessation of contributions and who is, or whose qualifying event occurred in connection with, a covered employee whose last employment prior to the qualifying event was with the employer that has stopped contributing to the multiemployer plan?

§ 54.4980B-10 Interaction of FMLA and COBRA.

Q-1: In what circumstances does a qualifying event occur if an employee does not return from leave taken under FMLA?

Q-2: If a qualifying event described in Q & A-1 of this section occurs; when does it occur, and how is the maximum coverage period measured?

Q-3: If an employee fails to pay the employee portion of premiums for coverage under a group health plan during FMLA leave or declines coverage under a group health plan during FMLA leave, does this affect the determination of whether or when the employee has experienced a qualifying event?

Q-4: Is the application of the rules in Q & A-1 through Q & A-3 of this section affected by a requirement of state or local law to provide a period of coverage longer than that required under FMLA?

Q-5: May COBRA continuation coverage be conditioned upon reimbursement of the premiums paid by the employer for coverage under a group health plan during FMLA leave?

[Reg. § 54.4980B-0.]

☐ [*T.D.* 8812, 2-2-99. *Amended by T.D.* 8928, 1-9-2001 *and T.D.* 9457, 9-4-2009.]

[Reg. § 54.4980B-1]

§ 54.4980B-1. COBRA in general.—The COBRA continuation coverage requirements are described in general in the following questions-and-answers:

Q-1: What are the health care continuation coverage requirements contained in section 4980B of the Internal Revenue Code and in ERISA?

A-1: (a) Section 4980B provides generally that a group health plan must offer each qualified beneficiary who would otherwise lose coverage under the plan as a result of a qualifying event an opportunity to elect, within the election period, continuation coverage under the plan. The continuation coverage requirements were added to section 162 by the Consolidated Omnibus Budget Reconciliation Act of 1985 (COBRA), Public Law 99-272 (100 Stat. 222), and moved to section 4980B by the Technical and Miscellaneous Revenue Act of 1988, Public Law 100-647 (102 Stat. 3342). Continuation coverage required under section 4980B is referred to in §§ 54.4980B-1 through 54.4980B-10 as COBRA continuation coverage.

(b) COBRA also added parallel continuation coverage requirements to Part 6 of Subtitle B of Title I of the Employee Retirement Income Security Act of 1974 (ERISA) (29 U.S.C. 1161-1168), which is administered by the U.S. Department of Labor. If a plan does not comply with the COBRA continuation coverage requirements, the Internal Revenue Code imposes an excise tax on the employer maintaining the plan (or on the plan itself), whereas ERISA gives certain parties—including qualified beneficiaries who are participants or beneficiaries within the meaning of Title I of ERISA, as well as the Department of Labor—the right to file a lawsuit to redress the noncompliance. The rules in §§ 54.4980B-1 through 54.4980B-10 apply for purposes of section 4980B and generally also for purposes of the COBRA continuation coverage requirements in Title I of ERISA. However, certain provisions of the COBRA continuation coverage requirements (such as the definitions of group health plan, employee, and employer) are not identical in the Internal Revenue Code and Title I of ERISA. In those cases in which the statutory language is not identical, the rules in §§ 54.4980B-1 through 54.4980B-10 nonetheless apply to the COBRA continuation coverage requirements of Title I of ERISA, except to the extent those rules are inconsistent with the statutory language of Title I of ERISA.

(c) A group health plan that is subject to section 4980B (or the parallel provisions under ERISA) is referred to as being subject to COBRA. (See Q&A-4 of § 54.4980B-2). A qualified beneficiary can be required to pay for COBRA continuation coverage. The term *qualified beneficiary* is defined in Q&A-1 of § 54.4980B-3. The term *qualifying event* is defined in Q&A-1 of § 54.4980B-4. COBRA continuation coverage is described in § 54.4980B-5. The election procedures are described in § 54.4980B-6. Duration of COBRA con-

Reg. § 54.4980B-1

tinuation coverage is addressed in §54.4980B-7, and payment for COBRA continuation coverage is addressed in §54.4980B-8. Section 54.4980B-9 contains special rules for how COBRA applies in connection with business reorganizations and employer withdrawals from a multiemployer plan, and §54.4980B-10 addresses how COBRA applies for individuals who take leave under the Family and Medical Leave Act of 1993. Unless the context indicates otherwise, any reference in §§54.4980B-1 through §54.4980B-10 to COBRA refers to section 4980B (as amended) and to the parallel provisions of ERISA.

Q-2: What standard applies for topics not addressed in §§54.4980B-1 through 54.4980B-10?

A-2: For purposes of section 4980B, for topics relating to the COBRA continuation coverage requirements of section 4980B that are not addressed in §§54.4980B-1 through 54.4980B-10 (such as methods for calculating the applicable premium), plans and employers must operate in good faith compliance with a reasonable interpretation of the statutory requirements in section 4980B.

[Reg. §54.4980B-1.]

☐ [T.D. 8812, 2-2-99 (corrected 3-24-99). *Amended by T.D. 8928, 1-9-2001.*]

[Reg. §54.4980B-2]

§54.4980B-2. Plans that must comply.—The following questions-and-answers apply in determining which plans must comply with the COBRA continuation coverage requirements:

Q-1: For purposes of section 4980B, what is a group health plan?

A-1: (a) For purposes of section 4980B, a group health plan is a plan maintained by an employer or employee organization to provide health care to individuals who have an employment-related connection to the employer or employee organization or to their families. Individuals who have an employment-related connection to the employer or employee organization consist of employees, former employees, the employer, and others associated or formerly associated with the employer or employee organization in a business relationship (including members of a union who are not currently employees). Health care is provided under a plan whether provided directly or through insurance, reimbursement, or otherwise, and whether or not provided through an on-site facility (except as set forth in paragraph (d) of this Q & A-1), or through a cafeteria plan (as defined in section 125) or other flexible benefit arrangement. (See paragraphs (b) through (e) in Q & A-8 of this section for rules regarding the application of the COBRA continuation coverage requirements to certain health flexible spending arrangements.) For purposes of this Q & A-1, insurance includes not only group insurance policies but also one or more individual insurance policies in any arrangement that involves the provision of health care to two or more employees. A plan maintained by an employer or employee organization is any plan of, or contributed to (directly or indirectly) by, an employer or employee organization. Thus, a group health plan is maintained by an employer or employee organization even if the employer or employee organization does not contribute to it if coverage under the plan would not be available at the same cost to an individual but for the individual's employment-related connection to the employer or employee organization. These rules are further explained in paragraphs (b) through (d) of this Q & A-1. An exception for qualified long-term care services is set forth in paragraph (e) of this Q & A-1, and for medical savings accounts in paragraph (f) of this Q & A-1. See Q & A-6 of this section for rules to determine the number of group health plans that an employer or employee organization maintains.

(b) For purposes of §§54.4980B-1 through 54.4980B-10, *health care* has the same meaning as *medical care* under section 213(d). Thus, health care generally includes the diagnosis, cure, mitigation, treatment, or prevention of disease, and any other undertaking for the purpose of affecting any structure or function of the body. Health care also includes transportation primarily for and essential to health care as described in the preceding sentence. However, health care does not include anything that is merely beneficial to the general health of an individual, such as a vacation. Thus, if an employer or employee organization maintains a program that furthers general good health, but the program does not relate to the relief or alleviation of health or medical problems and is generally accessible to and used by employees without regard to their physical condition or state of health, that program is not considered a program that provides health care and so is not a group health plan. For example, if an employer maintains a spa, swimming pool, gymnasium, or other exercise/fitness program or facility that is normally accessible to and used by employees for reasons other than relief of health or medical problems, such a facility does not constitute a program that provides health care and thus is not a group health plan. In contrast, if an employer maintains a drug or alcohol treatment program or a health clinic, or any other facility or program that is intended to relieve or alleviate a physical condition or health problem, the facility or program is considered to be the provision of health care and so is considered a group health plan.

(c) Whether a benefit provided to employees constitutes health care is not affected by whether the benefit is excludable from income under section 132 (relating to certain fringe benefits). For example, if a department store provides its employees discounted prices on all merchandise, including health care items such as drugs or eyeglasses, the mere fact that the discounted prices also apply to health care items will not cause the program to be a plan providing health care, so long as the discount program would normally be accessible to and used by employees without regard to health needs or physical condition. If, however, the employer maintaining the discount program is a health clinic, so that

the program is used exclusively by employees with health or medical needs, the program is considered to be a plan providing health care and so is considered to be a group health plan.

(d) The provision of health care at a facility that is located on the premises of an employer or employee organization does not constitute a group health plan if—

(1) The health care consists primarily of first aid that is provided during the employer's working hours for treatment of a health condition, illness, or injury that occurs during those working hours;

(2) The health care is available only to current employees; and

(3) Employees are not charged for the use of the facility.

(e) A plan does not constitute a group health plan subject to COBRA if substantially all of the coverage provided under the plan is for qualified long-term care services (as defined in section 7702B(c)). For this purpose, a plan is permitted to use any reasonable method in determining whether substantially all of the coverage provided under the plan is for qualified long-term care services.

(f) Under section 106(b)(5), amounts contributed by an employer to a medical savings account (as defined in section 220(d)) are not considered part of a group health plan subject to COBRA. Thus, a plan is not required to make COBRA continuation coverage available with respect to amounts contributed by an employer to a medical savings account. A high deductible health plan does not fail to be a group health plan subject to COBRA merely because it covers a medical savings account holder.

Q-2: For purposes of section 4980B, what is the employer?

A-2: (a) For purposes of section 4980B, employer refers to—

(1) A person for whom services are performed;

(2) Any other person that is a member of a group described in section 414(b), (c), (m), or (o) that includes a person described in paragraph (a)(1) of this Q & A-2; and

(3) Any successor of a person described in paragraph (a)(1) or (2) of this Q & A-2.

(b) An employer is a successor employer if it results from a consolidation, merger, or similar restructuring of the employer or if it is a mere continuation of the employer. See paragraph (c) in Q & A-8 of § 54.4980B-9 for rules describing the circumstances in which a purchaser of substantial assets is a successor employer to the employer selling the assets.

Q-3: What is a multiemployer plan?

A-3: For purposes of §§ 54.4980B-1 through 54.4980B-10, a multiemployer plan is a plan to which more than one employer is required to contribute, that is maintained pursuant to one or more collective bargaining agreements between one or more employee organizations and more than one employer, and that satisfies such other requirements as the Secretary of Labor may prescribe by regulation. Whenever reference is

made in §§ 54.4980B-1 through 54.4980B-10 to a plan of or maintained by an employer or employee organization, the reference includes a multiemployer plan.

Q-4: What group health plans are subject to COBRA?

A-4: (a) All group health plans are subject to COBRA except group health plans described in paragraph (b) of this Q&A-4. Group health plans described in paragraph (b) of this Q&A-4 are referred to in §§ 54.4980B-1 through 54.4980B-10 as excepted from COBRA.

(b) The following group health plans are excepted from COBRA—

(1) Small-employer plans (see Q&A-5 of this section);

(2) Church plans (within the meaning of section 414(e)); and

(3) Governmental plans (within the meaning of section 414(d)).

(c) The COBRA continuation coverage requirements generally do not apply to group health plans that are excepted from COBRA. However, a small-employer plan otherwise excepted from COBRA is nonetheless subject to COBRA with respect to qualified beneficiaries who experience a qualifying event during a period when the plan is not a small-employer plan (see paragraph (g) of Q&A-5 of this section).

(d) Although governmental plans are not subject to the COBRA continuation coverage requirements, group health plans maintained by state or local governments are generally subject to parallel continuation coverage requirements that were added by section 10003 of COBRA to the Public Health Service Act (42 U.S.C. 300bb-1 through 300bb-8), which is administered by the U.S. Department of Health and Human Services. Federal employees and their family members covered under the Federal Employees Health Benefit Program are covered by generally similar, but not parallel, temporary continuation of coverage provisions enacted by the Federal Employees Health Benefits Amendments Act of 1988. See 5 U.S.C. 8905a.

Q-5: What is a small-employer plan?

A-5: (a) Except in the case of a multiemployer plan, a *small-employer plan* is a group health plan maintained by an employer (within the meaning of Q&A-2 of this section) that normally employed fewer than 20 employees (within the meaning of paragraph (c) of this Q&A-5) during the preceding calendar year. In the case of a multiemployer plan, a *small-employer plan* is a group health plan under which each of the employers contributing to the plan for a calendar year normally employed fewer than 20 employees during the preceding calendar year. See Q & A-6 of this section for rules to determine the number of plans that an employer or employee organization maintains. The rules of this paragraph (a) are illustrated in the following example:

Example. (i) Corporation S employs 12 employees, all of whom work and reside in the United States. S maintains a group health plan for its

employees and their families. S is a wholly-owned subsidiary of P. In the previous calendar year, the controlled group of corporations including P and S employed more than 19 employees, although the only employees in the United States of the controlled group that includes P and S are the 12 employees of S.

(ii) Under § 1.414(b)-1 of this chapter, foreign corporations are not excluded from membership in a controlled group of corporations. Consequently, the group health plan maintained by S is not a small-employer plan during the current calendar year because the controlled group including S normally employed at least 20 employees in the preceding calendar year.

(b) An employer is considered to have normally employed fewer than 20 employees during a particular calendar year if, and only if, it had fewer than 20 employees on at least 50 percent of its typical business days during that year.

(c) All full-time and part-time common law employees of an employer are taken into account in determining whether an employer had fewer than 20 employees; however, an individual who is not a common law employee of the employer is not taken into account. Thus, the following individuals are not counted as employees for purposes of this Q&A-5 even though they are referred to as employees for all other purposes of §§ 54.4980B-1 through 54.4980B-10—

(1) Self-employed individuals (within the meaning of section 401(c)(1));

(2) Independent contractors (and their employees and independent contractors); and

(3) Directors (in the case of a corporation).

(d) In determining the number of the employees of an employer, each full-time employee is counted as one employee and each part-time employee is counted as a fraction of an employee, determined in accordance with paragraph (e) of this Q & A-5.

(e) An employer may determine the number of its employees on a daily basis or a pay period basis. The basis used by the employer must be used with respect to all employees of the employer and must be used for the entire year for which the number of employees is being determined. If an employer determines the number of its employees on a daily basis, it must determine the actual number of full-time employees on each typical business day and the actual number of part-time employees and the hours worked by each of those part-time employees on each typical business day. Each full-time employee counts as one employee on each typical business day and each part-time employee counts as a fraction, with the numerator of the fraction equal to the number of hours worked by that employee and the denominator equal to the number of hours that must be worked on a typical business day in order to be considered a full-time employee. If an employer determines the number of its employees on a pay period basis, it must determine the actual number of full-time employees employed during that pay period and the actual number of part-time employees employed and the hours worked by each of those

part-time employees during the pay period. For each day of that pay period, each full-time employee counts as one employee and each part-time employee counts as a fraction, with the numerator of the fraction equal to the number of hours worked by that employee during that pay period and the denominator equal to the number of hours that must be worked during that pay period in order to be considered a full-time employee. The determination of the number of hours required to be considered a full-time employee is based upon the employer's employment practices, except that in no event may the hours required to be considered a full-time employee exceed eight hours for any day or 40 hours for any week.

(f) In the case of a multiemployer plan, the determination of whether the plan is a small-employer plan on any particular date depends on which employers are contributing to the plan on that date and on the workforce of those employers during the preceding calendar year. If a plan that is otherwise subject to COBRA ceases to be a small-employer plan because of the addition during a calendar year of an employer that did not normally employ fewer than 20 employees on a typical business day during the preceding calendar year, the plan ceases to be excepted from COBRA immediately upon the addition of the new employer. In contrast, if the plan ceases to be a small-employer plan by reason of an increase during a calendar year in the workforce of an employer contributing to the plan, the plan ceases to be excepted from COBRA on the January 1 immediately following the calendar year in which the employer's workforce increased.

(g) A small-employer plan is generally excepted from COBRA. If, however, a plan that has been subject to COBRA (that is, was not a small-employer plan) becomes a small-employer plan, the plan remains subject to COBRA for qualifying events that occurred during the period when the plan was subject to COBRA. The rules of this paragraph (g) are illustrated by the following examples:

Example 1. An employer maintains a group health plan. The employer employed 20 employees on more than 50 percent of its working days during 2001, and consequently the plan is not excepted from COBRA during 2002. Employee E resigns and does not work for the employer after January 31, 2002. Under the terms of the plan, E is no longer eligible for coverage upon the effective date of the resignation, that is, February 1, 2002. The employer does not hire a replacement for E. E timely elects and pays for COBRA continuation coverage. The employer employs 19 employees for the remainder of 2002, and consequently the plan is not subject to COBRA in 2003. The plan must nevertheless continue to make COBRA continuation coverage available to E during 2003 until the obligation to make COBRA continuation coverage available ceases under the rules of § 54.4980B-7. The obligation could continue until August 1, 2003, the date that is 18 months after the date of E's qualifying event, or longer if E is eligible for a disability extension.

Example 2. The facts are the same as in *Example 1.* The employer continues to employ 19 employees throughout 2003 and 2004 and consequently the plan continues to be excepted from COBRA during 2004 and 2005. Spouse *S* is covered under the plan because *S* is married to one of the employer's employees. On April 1, 2002, *S* is divorced from that employee and ceases to be eligible for coverage under the plan. The plan is subject to COBRA during 2002 because *X* normally employed 20 employees during 2001. *S* timely notifies the plan administrator of the divorce and timely elects and pays for COBRA continuation coverage. Even though the plan is generally excepted from COBRA during 2003, 2004, and 2005, it must nevertheless continue to make COBRA continuation coverage available to *S* during those years until the obligation to make COBRA continuation coverage available ceases under the rules of §54.4980B-7. The obligation could continue until April 1, 2005, the date that is 36 months after the date of *S*'s qualifying event.

Example 3. The facts are the same as in *Example 2.* *C* is a dependent child of one of the employer's employees and is covered under the plan. A dependent child is no longer eligible for coverage under the plan upon the attainment of age 23. *C* attains age 23 on November 16, 2005. The plan is excepted from COBRA with respect to *C* during 2005 because the employer normally employed fewer than 20 employees during 2004. Consequently, the plan is not obligated to make COBRA continuation coverage available to *C* (and would not be obligated to make COBRA continuation coverage available to *C* even if the plan later became subject to COBRA again).

Q-6: How is the number of group health plans that an employer or employee organization maintains determined?

A-6: (a) The rules of this Q & A-6 apply in determining the number of group health plans that an employer or employee organization maintains. All references elsewhere in §§54.4980B-1 through 54.4980B-10 to a group health plan are references to a group health plan as determined under Q & A-1 of this section and this Q & A-6. Except as provided in paragraph (b) or (c) of this Q & A-6, all health care benefits, other than benefits for qualified long-term care services (as defined in section 7702B(c)), provided by a corporation, partnership, or other entity or trade or business, or by an employee organization, constitute one group health plan, unless—

(1) It is clear from the instruments governing an arrangement or arrangements to provide health care benefits that the benefits are being provided under separate plans; and

(2) The arrangement or arrangements are operated pursuant to such instruments as separate plans.

(b) A multiemployer plan and a nonmultiemployer plan are always separate plans.

(c) If a principal purpose of establishing separate plans is to evade any requirement of law,

then the separate plans will be considered a single plan to the extent necessary to prevent the evasion.

(d) The significance of treating an arrangement as two or more separate group health plans is illustrated by the following examples:

Example 1. (i) Employer *X* maintains a single group health plan, which provides major medical and prescription drug benefits. Employer *Y* maintains two group health plans; one provides major medical benefits and the other provides prescription drug benefits.

(ii) *X*'s plan could comply with the COBRA continuation coverage requirements by giving a qualified beneficiary experiencing a qualifying event with respect to *X*'s plan the choice of either electing both major medical and prescription drug benefits or not receiving any COBRA continuation coverage under *X*'s plan. By contrast, for *Y*'s plans to comply with the COBRA continuation coverage requirements, a qualified beneficiary experiencing a qualifying event with respect to each of *Y*'s plans must be given the choice of electing COBRA continuation coverage under either the major medical plan or the prescription drug plan or both.

Example 2. If a joint board of trustees administers one multiemployer plan, that plan will fail to qualify for the small-employer plan exception if any one of the employers whose employees are covered under the plan normally employed 20 or more employees during the preceding calendar year. However, if the joint board of trustees maintains two or more multiemployer plans, then the exception would be available with respect to each of those plans in which each of the employers whose employees are covered under the plan normally employed fewer than 20 employees during the preceding calendar year.

Q-7: What is the plan year?

A-7: (a) The *plan year* is the year that is designated as the plan year in the plan documents.

(b) If the plan documents do not designate a plan year (or if there are no plan documents), then the plan year is determined in accordance with this paragraph (b).

(1) The plan year is the deductible/limit year used under the plan.

(2) If the plan does not impose deductibles or limits on an annual basis, then the plan year is the policy year.

(3) If the plan does not impose deductibles or limits on an annual basis, and either the plan is not insured or the insurance policy is not renewed on an annual basis, then the plan year is the employer's taxable year.

(4) In any other case, the plan year is the calendar year.

Q-8: How do the COBRA continuation coverage requirements apply to cafeteria plans and other flexible benefit arrangements?

A-8: (a)(1) The provision of health care benefits does not fail to be a group health plan merely because those benefits are offered under a cafete-

ria plan (as defined in section 125) or under any other arrangement under which an employee is offered a choice between health care benefits and other taxable or nontaxable benefits. However, the COBRA continuation coverage requirements apply only to the type and level of coverage under the cafeteria plan or other flexible benefit arrangement that a qualified beneficiary is actually receiving on the day before the qualifying event. See paragraphs (b) through (e) of this Q & A-8 for rules limiting the obligations of certain health flexible spending arrangements.

(2) The rules of this paragraph (a) are illustrated by the following example:

Example: (i) Under the terms of a cafeteria plan, employees can choose among life insurance coverage, membership in a health maintenance organization (HMO), coverage for medical expenses under an indemnity arrangement, and cash compensation. Of these available choices, the HMO and the indemnity arrangement are the arrangements providing health care. The instruments governing the HMO and indemnity arrangements indicate that they are separate group health plans. These group health plans are subject to COBRA. The employer does not provide any group health plan outside of the cafeteria plan. *B* and *C* are unmarried employees. *B* has chosen the life insurance coverage, and *C* has chosen the indemnity arrangement.

(ii) *B* does not have to be offered COBRA continuation coverage upon terminating employment, nor is a subsequent open enrollment period for active employees required to be made available to *B*. However, if *C* terminates employment and the termination constitutes a qualifying event, *C* must be offered an opportunity to elect COBRA continuation coverage under the indemnity arrangement. If *C* makes such an election and an open enrollment period for active employees occurs while *C* is still receiving the COBRA continuation coverage, *C* must be offered the opportunity to switch from the indemnity arrangement to the HMO (but not to the life insurance coverage because that does not constitute coverage provided under a group health plan).

(b) If a health flexible spending arrangement (health FSA), within the meaning of section 106(c)(2), satisfies the two conditions in paragraph (c) of this Q & A-8 for a plan year, the obligation of the health FSA to make COBRA continuation coverage available to a qualified beneficiary who experiences a qualifying event in that plan year is limited in accordance with paragraphs (d) and (e) of this Q & A-8, as illustrated by an example in paragraph (f) of this Q & A-8. To the extent that a health FSA is obligated to make COBRA continuation coverage available to a qualified beneficiary, the health FSA must comply with all the applicable rules of §§ 54.4980B-1 through 54.4980B-10, including the rules of Q & A-3 in § 54.498OB-5 (relating to limits).

(c) The conditions of this paragraph (c) are satisfied if—

(1) Benefits provided under the health FSA are excepted benefits within the meaning of sections 9831 and 9832; and

(2) The maximum amount that the health FSA can require to be paid for a year of COBRA continuation coverage under Q & A-1 of § 54.4980B-8 equals or exceeds the maximum benefit available under the health FSA for the year.

(d) If the conditions in paragraph (c) of this Q & A-8 are satisfied for a plan year, then the health FSA is not obligated to make COBRA continuation coverage available for any subsequent plan year to any qualified beneficiary who experiences a qualifying event during that plan year.

(e) If the conditions in paragraph (c) of this Q & A-8 are satisfied for a plan year, the health FSA is not obligated to make COBRA continuation coverage available for that plan year to any qualified beneficiary who experiences a qualifying event during that plan year unless, as of the date of the qualifying event, the qualified beneficiary can become entitled to receive during the remainder of the plan year a benefit that exceeds the maximum amount that the health FSA is permitted to require to be paid for COBRA continuation coverage for the remainder of the plan year. In determining the amount of the benefit that a qualified beneficiary can become entitled to receive during the remainder of the plan year, the health FSA may deduct from the maximum benefit available to that qualified beneficiary for the year (based on the election made under the health FSA for that qualified beneficiary before the date of the qualifying event) any reimbursable claims submitted to the health FSA for that plan year before the date of the qualifying event.

(f) The rules of paragraphs (b), (c), (d), and (e) of this Q & A-8 are illustrated by the following example:

Example. (i) An employer maintains a group health plan providing major medical benefits and a group health plan that is a health FSA, and the plan year for each plan is the calendar year. Both the plan providing major medical benefits and the health FSA are subject to COBRA. Under the health FSA, during an open season before the beginning of each calendar year, employees can elect to reduce their compensation during the upcoming year by up to $1200 per year and have that same amount contributed to a health flexible spending account. The employer contributes an additional amount to the account equal to the employee's salary reduction election for the year. Thus, the maximum amount available to an employee under the health FSA for a year is two times the amount of the employee's salary reduction election for the year. This amount may be paid to the employee during the year as reimbursement for health expenses not covered by the employer's major medical plan (such as deductibles, copayments, prescription drugs, or eyeglasses). The employer determined, in accordance with section 4980B(f)(4), that a reasonable estimate of the cost of providing coverage for

similarly situated nonCOBRA beneficiaries for 2002 under this health FSA is equal to two times their salary reduction election for 2002 and, thus, that two times the salary reduction election is the applicable premium for 2002.

(ii) Because the employer provides major medical benefits under another group health plan, and because the maximum benefit that any employee can receive under the health FSA is not greater than two times the employee's salary reduction election for the plan year, benefits under this health FSA are excepted benefits within the meaning of sections 9831 and 9832. Thus, the first condition of paragraph (c) of this Q & A-8 is satisfied for the year. The maximum amount that a plan can require to be paid for coverage (outside of coverage required to be made available due to a disability extension) under Q & A-1 of §54.4980B-8 is 102 percent of the applicable premium. Thus, the maximum amount that the health FSA can require to be paid for coverage for the 2002 plan year is 2.04 times the employee's salary reduction election for the plan year. Because the maximum benefit available under the health FSA is 2.0 times the employee's salary reduction election for the year, the maximum benefit available under the health FSA for the year is less than the maximum amount that the health FSA can require to be paid for coverage for the year. Thus, the second condition in paragraph (c) of this Q & A-8 is also satisfied for the 2002 plan year. Because both conditions in paragraph (c) of this Q & A-8 are satisfied for 2002, with respect to any qualifying event occurring in 2002, the health FSA is not obligated to make COBRA continuation coverage available for any year after 2002.

(iii) Whether the health FSA is obligated to make COBRA continuation coverage available in 2002 to a qualified beneficiary with respect to a qualifying event that occurs in 2002 depends upon the maximum benefit that would be available to the qualified beneficiary under COBRA continuation coverage for that plan year. *Case 1*: Employee *B* has elected to reduce *B*'s salary by $1200 for 2002. Thus, the maximum benefit that *B* can become entitled to receive under the health FSA during the entire year is $2400. *B* experiences a qualifying event that is the termination of *B*'s employment on May 31, 2002. As of that date, *B* had submitted $300 of reimbursable expenses under the health FSA. Thus, the maximum benefit that *B* could become entitled to receive for the remainder of 2002 is $2100. The maximum amount that the health FSA can require to be paid for COBRA continuation coverage for the remainder of 2002 is 102 percent times 1/12 of the applicable premium for 2002 times the number of months remaining in 2002 after the date of the qualifying event. In *B*'s case, the maximum amount that the health FSA can require to be paid for COBRA continuation coverage for 2002 is 2.04 times $1200, or $2448. One-twelfth of $2448 is $204. Because seven months remain in the plan year, the maximum amount that the health FSA can require to be paid for *B*'s coverage for the remainder of the year is seven

times $204, or $1428. Because $1428 is less than the maximum benefit that *B* could become entitled to receive for the remainder of the year ($2100), the health FSA is required to make COBRA continuation coverage available to *B* for the remainder of 2002 (but not for any subsequent year).

(iv) *Case 2*: The facts are the same as in *Case 1* except that *B* had submitted $1000 of reimbursable expenses as of the date of the qualifying event. In that case, the maximum benefit available to *B* for the remainder of the year would be $1400 instead of $2100. Because the maximum amount that the health FSA can require to be paid for *B*'s coverage is $1428, and because the $1400 maximum benefit for the remainder of the year does not exceed $1428, the health FSA is not obligated to make COBRA continuation coverage available to *B* in 2002 (or any later year). (Of course, the administrator of the health FSA is permitted to make COBRA continuation coverage available to every qualified beneficiary in the year that the qualified beneficiary's qualifying event occurs in order to avoid having to determine the maximum benefit available for each qualified beneficiary for the remainder of the plan year.)

Q-9: What is the effect of a group health plan's failure to comply with the requirements of section 4980B(f)?

A-9: Under section 4980B(a), if a group health plan subject to COBRA fails to comply with section 4980B(f), an excise tax is imposed. Moreover, non-tax remedies may be available if the plan fails to comply with the parallel requirements in ERISA, which are administered by the Department of Labor.

Q-10: Who is liable for the excise tax if a group health plan fails to comply with the requirements of section 4980B(f)?

A-10: (a) In general, the excise tax is imposed on the employer maintaining the plan, except that in the case of a multiemployer plan (see Q & A-3 of this section for a definition of multiemployer plan) the excise tax is imposed on the plan.

(b) In certain circumstances, the excise tax is also imposed on a person involved with the provision of benefits under the plan (other than in the capacity of an employee), such as an insurer providing benefits under the plan or a third party administrator administering claims under the plan. In general, such a person will be liable for the excise tax if the person assumes, under a legally enforceable written agreement, the responsibility for performing the act to which the failure to comply with the COBRA continuation coverage requirements relates. Such a person will be liable for the excise tax notwithstanding the absence of a written agreement assuming responsibility for complying with COBRA if the person provides coverage under the plan to a similarly situated nonCOBRA beneficiary (see Q&A-3 of §54.4980B-3 for a definition of similarly situated nonCOBRA beneficiaries) and the employer or plan adminis-

trator submits a written request to the person to provide to a qualified beneficiary the same coverage that the person provides to the similarly situated nonCOBRA beneficiary. If the person providing coverage under the plan to a similarly situated nonCOBRA beneficiary is the plan administrator and the qualifying event is a divorce or legal separation or a dependent child's ceasing to be covered under the generally applicable requirements of the plan, the plan administrator will also be liable for the excise tax if the qualified beneficiary submits a written request for coverage.

Q-11: If a person is liable for the excise tax under section 4980B, what form must the person file and what is the due date for the filing and payment of the excise tax?

A-11: (a) *In general.* See §§ 54.6011-2 and 54.6151-1.

(b) *Due date for filing of return by employers or other persons responsible for benefits under a group health plan.* See § 54.6071-1(a)(1).

(c) *Due date for filing of return by multiemployer plans.* See § 54.6071-1(a)(2).

(d) *Effective/applicability date.* In the case of an employer or other person mentioned in paragraph (b) of this Q & A-11, the rules in this Q & A-11 are effective for taxable years beginning on or after January 1, 2010. In the case of a plan mentioned in paragraph (c) of this Q & A-11, the rules in this Q & A-11 are effective for plan years beginning on or after January 1, 2010.
[Reg. § 54.4980B-2.]

☐ [*T.D. 8812, 2-2-99. Amended by T.D. 8928, 1-9-2001 and T.D. 9457, 9-4-2009.*]

[Reg. § 54.4980B-3]

§ 54.4980B-3. Qualified beneficiaries.—The determination of who is a qualified beneficiary, an employee, or a covered employee, and of who are the similarly situated nonCOBRA beneficiaries is addressed in the following questions-and-answers:

Q-1: Who is a qualified beneficiary?

A-1: (a)(1) Except as set forth in paragraphs (c) through (f) of this Q&A-1, a qualified beneficiary is—

(i) Any individual who, on the day before a qualifying event, is covered under a group health plan by virtue of being on that day either a covered employee, the spouse of a covered employee, or a dependent child of the covered employee; or

(ii) Any child who is born to or placed for adoption with a covered employee during a period of COBRA continuation coverage.

(2) In the case of a qualifying event that is the bankruptcy of the employer, a covered employee who had retired on or before the date of substantial elimination of group health plan coverage is also a qualified beneficiary, as is any spouse, surviving spouse, or dependent child of such a covered employee if, on the day before the bankruptcy qualifying event, the spouse, surviving spouse, or dependent child is a beneficiary under the plan.

(3) In general, an individual (other than a child who is born to or placed for adoption with a covered employee during a period of COBRA continuation coverage) who is not covered under a plan on the day before the qualifying event cannot be a qualified beneficiary with respect to that qualifying event, and the reason for the individual's lack of actual coverage (such as the individual's having declined participation in the plan or failed to satisfy the plan's conditions for participation) is not relevant for this purpose. However, if the individual is denied or not offered coverage under a plan under circumstances in which the denial or failure to offer constitutes a violation of applicable law (such as the Americans with Disabilities Act, 42 U.S.C. 12101-12213, the special enrollment rules of section 9801, or the requirements of section 9802 prohibiting discrimination in eligibility to enroll in a group health plan based on health status), then, for purposes of §§ 54.4980B-1 through 54.4980B-10, the individual will be considered to have had the coverage that was wrongfully denied or not offered.

(4) Paragraph (b) of this Q&A-1 describes how certain family members are not qualified beneficiaries even if they become covered under the plan; paragraphs (c), (d), and (e) of this Q&A-1 place limits on the general rules of this paragraph (a) concerning who is a qualified beneficiary; paragraph (f) of this Q&A-1 provides when an individual who has been a qualified beneficiary ceases to be a qualified beneficiary; paragraph (g) of this Q&A-1 defines *placed for adoption*; and paragraph (h) of this Q&A-1 contains examples.

(b) In contrast to a child who is born to or placed for adoption with a covered employee during a period of COBRA continuation coverage, an individual who marries any qualified beneficiary on or after the date of the qualifying event and a newborn or adopted child (other than one born to or placed for adoption with a covered employee) are not qualified beneficiaries by virtue of the marriage, birth, or placement for adoption or by virtue of the individual's status as the spouse or the child's status as a dependent of the qualified beneficiary. These new family members do not themselves become qualified beneficiaries even if they become covered under the plan. (For situations in which a plan is required to make coverage available to new family members of a qualified beneficiary who is receiving COBRA continuation coverage, see Q&A-5 of § 54.4980B-5, paragraph (c) in Q&A-4 of § 54.4980B-5, and section 9801(f)(2).)

(c) An individual is not a qualified beneficiary if, on the day before the qualifying event referred to in paragraph (a) of this Q&A-1, the individual is covered under the group health plan by reason of another individual's election of COBRA continuation coverage and is not already a qualified beneficiary by reason of a prior qualifying event.

(d) A covered employee can be a qualified beneficiary only in connection with a qualifying event that is the termination, or reduction of

hours, of the covered employee's employment, or that is the bankruptcy of the employer.

(e) An individual is not a qualified beneficiary if the individual's status as a covered employee is attributable to a period in which the individual was a nonresident alien who received from the individual's employer no earned income (within the meaning of section 911(d)(2)) that constituted income from sources within the United States (within the meaning of section 861(a)(3)). If, pursuant to the preceding sentence, an individual is not a qualified beneficiary, then a spouse or dependent child of the individual is not considered a qualified beneficiary by virtue of the relationship to the individual.

(f) A qualified beneficiary who does not elect COBRA continuation coverage in connection with a qualifying event ceases to be a qualified beneficiary at the end of the election period (see Q&A-1 of §54.4980B-6). Thus, for example, if such a former qualified beneficiary is later added to a covered employee's coverage (e.g., during an open enrollment period) and then another qualifying event occurs with respect to the covered employee, the former qualified beneficiary does not become a qualified beneficiary by reason of the second qualifying event. If a covered employee who is a qualified beneficiary does not elect COBRA continuation coverage during the election period, then any child born to or placed for adoption with the covered employee on or after the date of the qualifying event is not a qualified beneficiary. Once a plan's obligation to make COBRA continuation coverage available to an individual who has been a qualified beneficiary ceases under the rules of §54.4980B-7, the individual ceases to be a qualified beneficiary.

(g) For purposes of §§54.4980B-1 through 54.4980B-10, *placement for adoption* or *being placed for adoption* means the assumption and retention by the covered employee of a legal obligation for total or partial support of a child in anticipation of the adoption of the child. The child's placement for adoption with the covered employee terminates upon the termination of the legal obligation for total or partial support. A child who is immediately adopted by the covered employee without a preceding placement for adoption is considered to be placed for adoption on the date of the adoption.

(h) The rules of this Q&A-1 are illustrated by the following examples:

Example 1. (i) B is a single employee who voluntarily terminates employment and elects COBRA continuation coverage under a group health plan. To comply with the requirements of section 9801(f), the plan permits a covered employee who marries to have her or his spouse covered under the plan. One month after electing COBRA continuation coverage, B marries and chooses to have B's spouse covered under the plan.

(ii) B's spouse is not a qualified beneficiary. Thus, if B dies during the period of COBRA continuation coverage, the plan does not have to

offer B's surviving spouse an opportunity to elect COBRA continuation coverage.

Example 2. (i) C is a married employee who terminates employment. C elects COBRA continuation coverage for C but not C's spouse, and C's spouse declines to elect such coverage. C's spouse thus ceases to be a qualified beneficiary. At the next open enrollment period, C adds the spouse as a beneficiary under the plan.

(ii) The addition of the spouse during the open enrollment period does not make the spouse a qualified beneficiary. The plan thus will not have to offer the spouse an opportunity to elect COBRA continuation coverage upon a later divorce from or death of C.

Example 3. (i) Under the terms of a group health plan, a covered employee's child, upon attaining age 19, ceases to be a dependent eligible for coverage.

(ii) At that time, the child must be offered an opportunity to elect COBRA continuation coverage. If the child elects COBRA continuation coverage, the child marries during the period of the COBRA continuation coverage, and the child's spouse becomes covered under the group health plan, the child's spouse is not a qualified beneficiary.

Example 4. (i) D is a single employee who, upon retirement, is given the opportunity to elect COBRA continuation coverage but declines it in favor of an alternative offer of 12 months of employer-paid retiree health benefits. At the end of the election period, D ceases to be a qualified beneficiary and will not have to be given another opportunity to elect COBRA continuation coverage (at the end of those 12 months or at any other time). D marries E during the period of retiree health coverage and, under the terms of that coverage, E becomes covered under the plan.

(ii) If a divorce from or death of D will result in E's losing coverage, E will be a qualified beneficiary because E's coverage under the plan on the day before the qualifying event (that is, the divorce or death) will have been by reason of D's acceptance of 12 months of employer-paid coverage after the prior qualifying event (D's retirement) rather than by reason of an election of COBRA continuation coverage.

Example 5. (i) The facts are the same as in *Example 4*, except that, under the terms of the plan, the divorce or death does not cause E to lose coverage so that E continues to be covered for the balance of the original 12-month period.

(ii) E does not have to be allowed to elect COBRA continuation coverage because the loss of coverage at the end of the 12-month period is not caused by the divorce or death, and thus the divorce or death does not constitute a qualifying event. See Q&A-1 of §54.4980B-4.

Q-2: Who is an employee and who is a covered employee?

A-2: (a)(1) For purposes of §§54.4980B-1 through 54.4980B-10 (except for purposes of Q&A-5 in §54.4980B-2, relating to the exception from COBRA for plans maintained by an em-

ployer with fewer than 20 employees), an *employee* is any individual who is eligible to be covered under a group health plan by virtue of the performance of services for the employer maintaining the plan or by virtue of membership in the employee organization maintaining the plan. Thus, for purposes of §§ 54.4980B-1 through 54.4980B-10 (except for purposes of Q&A-5 in § 54.4980B-2), the following individuals are employees if their relationship to the employer maintaining the plan makes them eligible to be covered under the plan—

(i) Self-employed individuals (within the meaning of section 401(c)(1));

(ii) Independent contractors (and their employees and independent contractors); and

(iii) Directors (in the case of a corporation).

(2) Similarly, whenever reference is made in §§ 54.4980B-1 through 54.4980B-10 (except in Q&A-5 of § 54.4980B-2) to an employment relationship (such as by referring to the termination of employment of an employee or to an employee's being employed by an employer), the reference includes the relationship of those individuals who are employees within the meaning of this paragraph (a). See paragraph (c) in Q&A-5 of § 54.4980B-2 for a narrower meaning of employee solely for purposes of Q&A-5 of § 54.4980B-2.

(b) For purposes of §§ 54.4980B-1 through 54.4980B-10, a *covered employee* is any individual who is (or was) provided coverage under a group health plan (other than a plan that is excepted from COBRA on the date of the qualifying event; see Q&A-4 of § 54.4980B-2) by virtue of being or having been an employee. For example, a retiree or former employee who is covered by a group health plan is a covered employee if the coverage results in whole or in part from her or his previous employment. An employee (or former employee) who is merely eligible for coverage under a group health plan is generally not a covered employee if the employee (or former employee) is not actually covered under the plan. In general, the reason for the employee's (or former employee's) lack of actual coverage (such as having declined participation in the plan or having failed to satisfy the plan's conditions for participation) is not relevant for this purpose. However, if the employee (or former employee) is denied or not offered coverage under circumstances in which the denial or failure to offer constitutes a violation of applicable law (such as the Americans with Disabilities Act, 42 U.S.C. 12101 through 12213, the special enrollment rules of section 9801, or the requirements of section 9802 prohibiting discrimination in eligibility to enroll in a group health plan based on health status), then, for purposes of §§ 54.4980B-1 through 54.4980B-10, the employee (or former employee) will be considered to have had the coverage that was wrongfully denied or not offered.

Q-3: Who are the similarly situated nonCOBRA beneficiaries?

A-3: For purposes of §§ 54.4980B-1 through 54.4980B-10, *similarly situated nonCOBRA beneficiaries* means the group of covered employees, spouses of covered employees, or dependent children of covered employees receiving coverage under a group health plan maintained by the employer or employee organization who are receiving that coverage for a reason other than the rights provided under the COBRA continuation coverage requirements and who, based on all of the facts and circumstances, are most similarly situated to the situation of the qualified beneficiary immediately before the qualifying event. [Reg. § 54.4980B-3.]

☐ [*T.D.* 8812, 2-2-99. *Amended by T.D.* 8928, 1-9-2001.]

[Reg. § 54.4980B-4]

§ 54.4980B-4. Qualifying events.—The determination of what constitutes a qualifying event is addressed in the following questions-and-answers:

Q-1: What is a qualifying event?

A-1: (a) A *qualifying event* is an event that satisfies paragraphs (b), (c), and (d) of this Q&A-1. Paragraph (e) of this Q&A-1 further explains a reduction of hours of employment, paragraph (f) of this Q&A-1 describes the treatment of children born to or placed for adoption with a covered employee during a period of COBRA continuation coverage, and paragraph (g) of this Q&A-1 contains examples. See Q & A-1 through Q & A-3 of § 54.4980B-10 for special rules in the case of leave taken under the Family and Medical Leave Act of 1993 (29 U.S.C. 2601-2619).

(b) An event satisfies this paragraph (b) if the event is any of the following—

(1) The death of a covered employee;

(2) The termination (other than by reason of the employee's gross misconduct), or reduction of hours, of a covered employee's employment;

(3) The divorce or legal separation of a covered employee from the employee's spouse;

(4) A covered employee's becoming entitled to Medicare benefits under Title XVIII of the Social Security Act (42 U.S.C. 1395-1395ggg);

(5) A dependent child's ceasing to be a dependent child of a covered employee under the generally applicable requirements of the plan; or

(6) A proceeding in bankruptcy under Title 11 of the United States Code with respect to an employer from whose employment a covered employee retired at any time.

(c) An event satisfies this paragraph (c) if, under the terms of the group health plan, the event causes the covered employee, or the spouse or a dependent child of the covered employee, to lose coverage under the plan. For this purpose, to *lose coverage* means to cease to be covered under the same terms and conditions as in effect immediately before the qualifying event. Any increase in the premium or contribution that must be paid by a covered employee (or the spouse or dependent child of a covered em-

ployee) for coverage under a group health plan that results from the occurrence of one of the events listed in paragraph (b) of the Q&A-1 is a loss of coverage. In the case of an event that is the bankruptcy of the employer, *lose coverage* also means any substantial elimination of coverage under the plan, occurring within 12 months before or after the date the bankruptcy proceeding commences, for a covered employee who had retired on or before the date of the substantial elimination of group health plan coverage or for any spouse, surviving spouse, or dependent child of such a covered employee if, on the day before the bankruptcy qualifying event, the spouse, surviving spouse, or dependent child is a beneficiary under the plan. For purposes of this paragraph (c), a loss of coverage need not occur immediately after the event, so long as the loss of coverage occurs before the end of the maximum coverage period (see Q&A-4 and Q&A-6 of § 54.4980B-7). However, if neither the covered employee nor the spouse or a dependent child of the covered employee loses coverage before the end of what would be the maximum coverage period, the event does not satisfy this paragraph (c). If coverage is reduced or eliminated in anticipation of an event (for example, an employer's eliminating an employee's coverage in anticipation of the termination of the employee's employment, or an employee's eliminating the coverage of the employee's spouse in anticipation of a divorce or legal separation), the reduction or elimination is disregarded in determining whether the event causes a loss of coverage.

(d) An event satisfies this paragraph (d) if it occurs while the plan is subject to COBRA. Thus, an event will not satisfy this paragraph (d) if it occurs while the plan is excepted from COBRA (see Q&A-4 of § 54.4980B-2). Even if the plan later becomes subject to COBRA, it is not required to make COBRA continuation coverage available to anyone whose coverage ends as a result of an event during a year in which the plan is excepted from COBRA. For example, if a group health plan is excepted from COBRA as a small- employer plan during the year 2001 (see Q&A-5 of § 54.4980B-2) and an employee terminates employment on December 31, 2001, the termination is not a qualifying event and the plan is not required to permit the employee to elect COBRA continuation coverage. This is the case even if the plan ceases to be a small-employer plan as of January 1, 2002. Also, the same result will follow even if the employee is given three months of coverage beyond December 31 (that is, through March of 2002), because there will be no qualifying event as of the termination of coverage in March. However, if the employee's spouse is initially provided with the three-month coverage through March 2002, but the spouse divorces the employee before the end of the three months and loses coverage as a result of the divorce, the divorce will constitute a qualifying event during 2002 and so entitle the spouse to elect COBRA continuation coverage.

See Q&A-7 of § 54.4980B-7 regarding the maximum coverage period in such a case.

(e) A reduction of hours of a covered employee's employment occurs whenever there is a decrease in the hours that a covered employee is required to work or actually works, but only if the decrease is not accompanied by an immediate termination of employment. This is true regardless of whether the covered employee continues to perform services following the reduction of hours of employment. For example, an absence from work due to disability, a temporary layoff, or any other reason (other than due to leave that is FMLA leave; see § 54.4980B-10) is a reduction of hours of a covered employee's employment if there is not an immediate termination of employment. If a group health plan measures eligibility for the coverage of employees by the number of hours worked in a given time period, such as the preceding month or quarter, and an employee covered under the plan fails to work the minimum number of hours during that time period, the failure to work the minimum number of required hours is a reduction of hours of that covered employee's employment.

(f) The qualifying event of a qualified beneficiary who is a child born to or placed for adoption with a covered employee during a period of COBRA continuation coverage is the qualifying event giving rise to the period of COBRA continuation coverage during which the child is born or placed for adoption. If a second qualifying event has occurred before the child is born or placed for adoption (such as the death of the covered employee), then the second qualifying event also applies to the newborn or adopted child. See Q&A-6 of § 54.4980B-7.

(g) The rules of this Q&A-1 are illustrated by the following examples, in each of which the group health plan is subject to COBRA:

Example 1. (i) An employee who is covered by a group health plan terminates employment (other than by reason of the employee's gross misconduct) and, beginning with the day after the last day of employment, is given 3 months of employer-paid coverage under the same terms and conditions as before that date. At the end of the three months, the coverage terminates.

(ii) The loss of coverage at the end of the three months results from the termination of employment and, thus, the termination of employment is a qualifying event.

Example 2. (i) An employee who is covered by a group health plan retires (which is a termination of employment other than by reason of the employee's gross misconduct) and, upon retirement, is required to pay an increased amount for the same group health coverage that the employee had before retirement.

(ii) The increase in the premium or contribution required for coverage is a loss of coverage under paragraph (c) of this Q&A-1 and, thus, the retirement is a qualifying event.

Example 3. (i) An employee and the employee's spouse are covered under an employer's group

Reg. § 54.4980B-4

health plan. The employee retires and is given identical coverage for life. However, the plan provides that the spousal coverage will not be continued beyond six months unless a higher premium for the spouse is paid to the plan.

(ii) The requirement for the spouse to pay a higher premium at the end of the six months is a loss of coverage under paragraph (c) of this Q&A-1. Thus, the retirement is a qualifying event and the spouse must be given an opportunity to elect COBRA continuation coverage.

Example 4. (i) *F* is a covered employee who is married to *G*, and both are covered under a group health plan maintained by *F*'s employer. *F* and *G* are divorced. Under the terms of the plan, the divorce causes *G* to lose coverage. The divorce is a qualifying event, and *G* elects COBRA continuation coverage, remarries during the period of COBRA continuation coverage, and *G*'s new spouse becomes covered under the plan. (See Q&A-5 in § 54.4980B-5, paragraph (c) in Q&A-4 of § 54.4980B-5, and section 9801(f)(2).) *G* dies. Under the terms of the plan, the death causes *G*'s new spouse to lose coverage under the plan.

(ii) *G*'s death is not a qualifying event because *G* is not a covered employee.

Example 5. (i) An employer maintains a group health plan for both active employees and retired employees (and their families). The coverage for active employees and retired employees is identical, and the employer does not require retirees to pay more for coverage than active employees. The plan does not make COBRA continuation coverage available when an employee retires (and is not required to because the retired employee has not lost coverage under the plan). The employer amends the plan to eliminate coverage for retired employees effective January 1, 2002. On that date, several retired employees (and their spouses and dependent children) have been covered under the plan since their retirement for less than the maximum coverage period that would apply to them in connection with their retirement.

(ii) The elimination of retiree coverage under these circumstances is a deferred loss of coverage for those retirees (and their spouses and dependent children) under paragraph (c) of this Q&A-1 and, thus, the retirement is a qualifying event. The plan must make COBRA continuation coverage available to them for the balance of the maximum coverage period that applies to them in connection with the retirement.

Q-2: Are the facts surrounding a termination of employment (such as whether it was voluntary or involuntary) relevant in determining whether the termination of employment is a qualifying event?

A-2: Apart from facts constituting gross misconduct, the facts surrounding the termination or reduction of hours are irrelevant in determining whether a qualifying event has occurred. Thus, it does not matter whether the employee voluntarily terminated or was discharged. For example, a strike or a lockout is a termination or reduction of hours that constitutes a qualifying event if the strike or lockout results in a loss of coverage as described in paragraph (c) of Q&A-1 of this section. Similarly, a layoff that results in such a loss of coverage is a qualifying event. [Reg. § 54.4980B-4.]

☐ [T.D. 8812, 2-2-99. *Amended by* T.D. 8928, 1-9-2001.]

[Reg. § 54.4980B-5]

§ 54.4980B-5. COBRA continuation coverage.—The following questions-and-answers address the requirements for coverage to constitute COBRA continuation coverage:

Q-1: What is COBRA continuation coverage?

A-1: (a) If a qualifying event occurs, each qualified beneficiary (other than a qualified beneficiary for whom the qualifying event will not result in any immediate or deferred loss of coverage) must be offered an opportunity to elect to receive the group health plan coverage that is provided to similarly situated nonCOBRA beneficiaries (ordinarily, the same coverage that the qualified beneficiary had on the day before the qualifying event). See Q & A-3 of § 54.4980B-3 for the definition of similarly situated nonCOBRA beneficiaries. This coverage is COBRA continuation coverage. If coverage is modified for similarly situated nonCOBRA beneficiaries, then the coverage made available to qualified beneficiaries is modified in the same way. If the continuation coverage offered differs in any way from the coverage made available to similarly situated nonCOBRA beneficiaries, the coverage offered does not constitute COBRA continuation coverage and the group health plan is not in compliance with COBRA unless other coverage that does constitute COBRA continuation coverage is also offered. Any elimination or reduction of coverage in anticipation of an event described in paragraph (b) of Q & A-1 of § 54.4980B-4 is disregarded for purposes of this Q & A-1 and for purposes of any other reference in §§ 54.4980B-1 through 54.4980B-10 to coverage in effect immediately before (or on the day before) a qualifying event. COBRA continuation coverage must not be conditioned upon, or discriminate on the basis of lack of, evidence of insurability.

(b) In the case of a qualified beneficiary who is a child born to or placed for adoption with a covered employee during a period of COBRA continuation coverage, the child is generally entitled to elect immediately to have the same coverage that dependent children of active employees receive under the benefit packages under which the covered employee has coverage at the time of the birth or placement for adoption. Such a child would be entitled to elect coverage different from that elected by the covered employee during the next available open enrollment period under the plan. See Q&A-4 of this section.

Q-2: What deductibles apply if COBRA continuation coverage is elected?

A-2: (a) Qualified beneficiaries electing COBRA continuation coverage generally are subject

to the same deductibles as similarly situated nonCOBRA beneficiaries. If a qualified beneficiary's COBRA continuation coverage begins before the end of a period prescribed for accumulating amounts toward deductibles, the qualified beneficiary must retain credit for expenses incurred toward those deductibles before the beginning of COBRA continuation coverage as though the qualifying event had not occurred. The specific application of this rule depends on the type of deductible, as set forth in paragraphs (b) through (d) of this Q&A-2. Special rules are set forth in paragraph (e) of this Q&A-2, and examples appear in paragraph (f) of this Q&A-2.

(b) If a deductible is computed separately for each individual receiving coverage under the plan, each individual's remaining deductible amount (if any) on the date COBRA continuation coverage begins is equal to that individual's remaining deductible amount immediately before that date.

(c) If a deductible is computed on a family basis, the remaining deductible for the family on the date that COBRA continuation coverage begins depends on the members of the family electing COBRA continuation coverage. In computing the family deductible that remains on the date COBRA continuation coverage begins, only the expenses of those family members receiving COBRA continuation coverage need be taken into account. If the qualifying event results in there being more than one family unit (for example, because of a divorce), the family deductible may be computed separately for each resulting family unit based on the members in each unit. These rules apply regardless of whether the plan provides that the family deductible is an alternative to individual deductibles or an additional requirement.

(d) Deductibles that are not described in paragraph (b) or (c) of this Q&A-2 must be treated in a manner consistent with the principles set forth in those paragraphs.

(e) If a deductible is computed on the basis of a covered employee's compensation instead of being a fixed dollar amount and the employee remains employed during the period of COBRA continuation coverage, the plan is permitted to choose whether to apply the deductible by treating the employee's compensation as continuing without change for the duration of the COBRA continuation coverage at the level that was used to compute the deductible in effect immediately before the COBRA continuation coverage began, or to apply the deductible by taking the employee's actual compensation into account. In applying a deductible that is computed on the basis of the covered employee's compensation instead of being a fixed dollar amount, for periods of COBRA continuation coverage in which the employee is not employed by the employer, the plan is required to compute the deductible by treating the employee's compensation as continuing without change for the duration of the COBRA continuation coverage either at the level that was used to compute the deductible in effect immediately before the COBRA continuation

coverage began or at the level that was used to compute the deductible in effect immediately before the employee's employment was terminated.

(f) The rules of this Q&A-2 are illustrated by the following examples; in each example, deductibles under the plan are determined on a calendar year basis:

Example 1. (i) A group health plan applies a separate $100 annual deductible to each individual it covers. The plan provides that the spouse and dependent children of a covered employee will lose coverage on the last day of the month after the month of the covered employee's death. A covered employee dies on June 11, 2001. The spouse and the two dependent children elect COBRA continuation coverage, which will begin on August 1, 2001. As of July 31, 2001, the spouse has incurred $80 of covered expenses, the older child has incurred no covered expenses, and the younger one has incurred $120 of covered expenses (and therefore has already satisfied the deductible).

(ii) At the beginning of COBRA continuation coverage on August 1, the spouse has a remaining deductible of $20, the older child still has the full $100 deductible, and the younger one has no further deductible.

Example 2. (i) A group health plan applies a separate $200 annual deductible to each individual it covers, except that each family member is treated as having satisfied the individual deductible once the family has incurred $500 of covered expenses during the year. The plan provides that upon the divorce of a covered employee, coverage will end immediately for the employee's spouse and any children who do not remain in the employee's custody. A covered employee with four dependent children is divorced, the spouse obtains custody of the two oldest children, and the spouse and those children all elect COBRA continuation coverage to begin immediately. The family had accumulated $420 of covered expenses before the divorce, as follows: $70 by each parent, $200 by the oldest child, $80 by the youngest child, and none by the other two children.

(ii) The resulting family consisting of the spouse and the two oldest children accumulated a total of $270 of covered expenses, and thus the remaining deductible for that family could be as high as $230 (because the plan would not have to count the incurred expenses of the covered employee and the youngest child). The remaining deductible for the resulting family consisting of the covered employee and the two youngest children is not subject to the rules of this Q&A-2 because their coverage is not COBRA continuation coverage.

Example 3. Each year a group health plan pays 70 percent of the cost of an individual's psychotherapy after that individual's first three visits during the year. A qualified beneficiary whose election of COBRA continuation coverage takes effect beginning August 1, 2001 and who has already made two visits as of that date need only

Reg. §54.4980B-5

pay for one more visit before the plan must begin to pay 70 percent of the cost of the remaining visits during 2001.

Example 4. (i) A group health plan has a $250 annual deductible per covered individual. The plan provides that if the deductible is not satisfied in a particular year, expenses incurred during October through December of that year are credited toward satisfaction of the deductible in the next year. A qualified beneficiary who has incurred covered expenses of $150 from January through September of 2001 and $40 during October elects COBRA continuation coverage beginning November 1, 2001.

(ii) The remaining deductible amount for this qualified beneficiary is $60 at the beginning of the COBRA continuation coverage. If this individual incurs covered expenses of $50 in November and December of 2001 combined (so that the $250 deductible for 2001 is not satisfied), the $90 incurred from October through December of 2001 are credited toward satisfaction of the deductible amount for 2002.

Q-3: How do a plan's limits apply to COBRA continuation coverage?

A-3: (a) Limits are treated in the same way as deductibles (see Q&A-2 of this section). This rule applies both to limits on plan benefits (such as a maximum number of hospital days or dollar amount of reimbursable expenses) and limits on out-of-pocket expenses (such as a limit on copayments, a limit on deductibles plus copayments, or a catastrophic limit). This rule applies equally to annual and lifetime limits and applies equally to limits on specific benefits and limits on benefits in the aggregate under the plan.

(b) The rule of this Q&A-3 is illustrated by the following examples; in each example limits are determined on a calendar year basis:

Example 1. (i) A group health plan pays for a maximum of 150 days of hospital confinement per individual per year. A covered employee who has had 20 days of hospital confinement as of May 1, 2001 terminates employment and elects COBRA continuation coverage as of that date.

(ii) During the remainder of the year 2001 the plan need only pay for a maximum of 130 days of hospital confinement for this individual.

Example 2. (i) A group health plan reimburses a maximum of $20,000 of covered expenses per family per year, and the same $20,000 limit applies to unmarried covered employees. A covered employee and spouse who have no children divorce on May 1, 2001, and the spouse elects COBRA continuation coverage as of that date. In 2001, the employee had incurred $5,000 of expenses and the spouse had incurred $8,000 before May 1.

(ii) The plan can limit its reimbursement of the amount of expenses incurred by the spouse on and after May 1 for the remainder of the year to $12,000 ($20,000 – $8,000 = $12,000). The remaining limit for the employee is not subject to the rules of this Q&A-3 because the employee's coverage is not COBRA continuation coverage.

Example 3. (i) A group health plan pays for 80 percent of covered expenses after satisfaction of a $100-per-individual deductible, and the plan pays for 100 percent of covered expenses after a family has incurred out-of-pocket costs of $2,000. The plan provides that upon the divorce of a covered employee, coverage will end immediately for the employee's spouse and any children who do not remain in the employee's custody. An employee and spouse with three dependent children divorce on June 1, 2001, and one of the children remains with the employee. The spouse elects COBRA continuation coverage as of that date for the spouse and the other two children. During January through May of 2001, the spouse incurred $600 of covered expenses and each of the two children in the spouse's custody after the divorce incurred covered expenses of $1,100. This resulted in total out-of-pocket costs for these three individuals of $800 ($300 total for the three deductibles, plus $500 for 20 percent of the other $2,500 in incurred expenses [$600 + $1,100 + $1,100 = $2,800; $2,800 – $300 = $2,500]).

(ii) For the remainder of 2001, the resulting family consisting of the spouse and two children has an out-of-pocket limit of $1,200 ($2,000 – $800 = $1,200). The remaining out-of-pocket limit for the resulting family consisting of the employee and one child is not subject to the rules of this Q&A-3 because their coverage is not COBRA continuation coverage.

Q-4: Can a qualified beneficiary who elects COBRA continuation coverage ever change from the coverage received by that individual immediately before the qualifying event?

A-4: (a) In general, a qualified beneficiary need only be given an opportunity to continue the coverage that she or he was receiving immediately before the qualifying event. This is true regardless of whether the coverage received by the qualified beneficiary before the qualifying event ceases to be of value to the qualified beneficiary, such as in the case of a qualified beneficiary covered under a region-specific health maintenance organization (HMO) who leaves the HMO's service region. The only situations in which a qualified beneficiary must be allowed to change from the coverage received immediately before the qualifying event are as set forth in paragraphs (b) and (c) of this Q&A-4 and in Q&A-1 of this section (regarding changes to or elimination of the coverage provided to similarly situated nonCOBRA beneficiaries).

(b) If a qualified beneficiary participates in a region-specific benefit package (such as an HMO or an on-site clinic) that will not service her or his health needs in the area to which she or he is relocating (regardless of the reason for the relocation), the qualified beneficiary must be given, within a reasonable period after requesting other coverage, an opportunity to elect alternative coverage that the employer or employee organization makes available to active employees. If the employer or employee organization makes group health plan coverage available to similarly situated nonCOBRA beneficiaries that can be extended in the area to which the qualified benefi-

ciary is relocating, then that coverage is the alternative coverage that must be made available to the relocating qualified beneficiary. If the employer or employee organization does not make group health plan coverage available to similarly situated nonCOBRA beneficiaries that can be extended in the area to which the qualified beneficiary is relocating but makes coverage available to other employees that can be extended in that area, then the coverage made available to those other employees must be made available to the relocating qualified beneficiary. The effective date of the alternative coverage must be not later than the date of the qualified beneficiary's relocation, or, if later, the first day of the month following the month in which the qualified beneficiary requests the alternative coverage. However, the employer or employee organization is not required to make any other coverage available to the relocating qualified beneficiary if the only coverage the employer or employee organization makes available to active employees is not available in the area to which the qualified beneficiary relocates (because all such coverage is region-specific and does not service individuals in that area).

(c) If an employer or employee organization makes an open enrollment period available to similarly situated active employees with respect to whom a qualifying event has not occurred, the same open enrollment period rights must be made available to each qualified beneficiary receiving COBRA continuation coverage. An open enrollment period means a period during which an employee covered under a plan can choose to be covered under another group health plan or under another benefit package within the same plan, or to add or eliminate coverage of family members.

(d) The rules of this Q&A-4 are illustrated by the following examples:

Example 1. (i) *E* is an employee who works for an employer that maintains several group health plans. Under the terms of the plans, if an employee chooses to cover any family members under a plan, all family members must be covered by the same plan and that plan must be the same as the plan covering the employee. Immediately before *E*'s termination of employment (for reasons other than gross misconduct), *E* is covered along with *E*'s spouse and children by a plan. The coverage under that plan will end as a result of the termination of employment.

(ii) Upon *E*'s termination of employment, each of the four family members is a qualified beneficiary. Even though the employer maintains various other plans and options, it is not necessary for the qualified beneficiaries to be allowed to switch to a new plan when *E* terminates employment.

(iii) COBRA continuation coverage is elected for each of the four family members. Three months after *E*'s termination of employment there is an open enrollment period during which similarly situated active employees are offered an opportunity to choose to be covered under a new plan or to add or eliminate family coverage.

(iv) During the open enrollment period, each of the four qualified beneficiaries must be offered the opportunity to switch to another plan (as though each qualified beneficiary were an individual employee). For example, each member of *E*'s family could choose coverage under a separate plan, even though the family members of employed individuals could not choose coverage under separate plans. Of course, if each family member chooses COBRA continuation coverage under a separate plan, the plan can require payment for each family member that is based on the applicable premium for individual coverage under that separate plan. See Q&A-1 of §54.4980B-8.

Example 2. (i) The facts are the same as in *Example 1*, except that *E*'s family members are not covered under *E*'s group health plan when *E* terminates employment.

(ii) Although the family members do not have to be given an opportunity to elect COBRA continuation coverage, *E* must be allowed to add them to *E*'s COBRA continuation coverage during the open enrollment period. This is true even though the family members are not, and cannot become, qualified beneficiaries (see Q&A-1 of §54.4980B-3).

Q-5: Aside from open enrollment periods, can a qualified beneficiary who has elected COBRA continuation coverage choose to cover individuals (such as newborn children, adopted children, or new spouses) who join the qualified beneficiary's family on or after the date of the qualifying event?

A-5: (a) Yes. Under section 9801, employees eligible to participate in a group health plan (whether or not participating), as well as former employees participating in a plan (referred to in those rules as participants), are entitled to special enrollment rights for certain family members upon the loss of other group health plan coverage or upon the acquisition by the employee or participant of a new spouse or of a new dependent through birth, adoption, or placement for adoption, if certain requirements are satisfied. Employees not participating in the plan also can obtain rights for self-enrollment under those rules. Once a qualified beneficiary is receiving COBRA continuation coverage (that is, has timely elected and made timely payment for COBRA continuation coverage), the qualified beneficiary has the same right to enroll family members under those special enrollment rules as if the qualified beneficiary were an employee or participant within the meaning of those rules. However, neither a qualified beneficiary who is not receiving COBRA continuation coverage nor a former qualified beneficiary has any special enrollment rights under those rules.

(b) In addition to the special enrollment rights described in paragraph (a) of this Q&A-5, if the plan covering the qualified beneficiary provides that new family members of active employees can become covered (either automatically or

upon an appropriate election) before the next open enrollment period, then the same right must be extended to the new family members of a qualified beneficiary.

(c) If the addition of a new family member will result in a higher applicable premium (for example, if the qualified beneficiary was previously receiving COBRA continuation coverage as an individual, or if the applicable premium for family coverage depends on family size), the plan can require the payment of a correspondingly higher amount for the COBRA continuation coverage. See Q&A-1 of § 54.4980B-8.

(d) The right to add new family members under this Q&A-5 is in addition to the rights that newborn and adopted children of covered employees may have as qualified beneficiaries; see Q&A-1 in § 54.4980B-3.

[Reg. § 54.4980B-5.]

☐ [*T.D.* 8812, 2-2-99. *Amended by T.D.* 8928, 1-9-2001.]

[Reg. § 54.4980B-6]

§ 54.4980B-6. Electing COBRA continuation coverage.—The following questions-and-answers address the manner in which COBRA continuation coverage is elected:

Q-1: What is the election period and how long must it last?

A-1: (a) A group health plan can condition the availability of COBRA continuation coverage upon the timely election of such coverage. An election of COBRA continuation coverage is a timely election if it is made during the election period. The election period must begin not later than the date the qualified beneficiary would lose coverage on account of the qualifying event. (See paragraph (c) of Q&A-1 of § 54.4980B-4 for the meaning of *lose coverage*.) The election period must not end before the date that is 60 days after the later of—

(1) The date the qualified beneficiary would lose coverage on account of the qualifying event; or

(2) The date notice is provided to the qualified beneficiary of her or his right to elect COBRA continuation coverage.

(b) An election is considered to be made on the date it is sent to the plan administrator.

(c) The rules of this Q&A-1 are illustrated by the following example:

Example. (i) An unmarried employee without children who is receiving employer-paid coverage under a group health plan voluntarily terminates employment on June 1, 2001. The employee is not disabled at the time of the termination of employment nor at any time thereafter, and the plan does not provide for the extension of the required periods (as is permitted under paragraph (b) of Q & A-4 of § 54.4980B-7).

(ii) *Case 1:* If the plan provides that the employer-paid coverage ends immediately upon the termination of employment, the election period must begin not later than June 1, 2001, and must not end earlier than July 31, 2001. If notice of the right to elect COBRA continuation cover-

age is not provided to the employee until June 15, 2001, the election period must not end earlier than August 14, 2001.

(iii) *Case 2:* If the plan provides that the employer-paid coverage does not end until 6 months after the termination of employment, the employee does not lose coverage until December 1, 2001. The election period can therefore begin as late as December 1, 2001, and must not end before January 30, 2002.

(iv) *Case 3:* If employer-paid coverage for 6 months after the termination of employment is offered only to those qualified beneficiaries who waive COBRA continuation coverage, the employee loses coverage on June 1, 2001, so the election period is the same as in Case 1. The difference between Case 2 and Case 3 is that in Case 2 the employee can receive 6 months of employer-paid coverage and then elect to pay for up to an additional 12 months of COBRA continuation coverage, while in Case 3 the employee must choose between 6 months of employer-paid coverage and paying for up to 18 months of COBRA continuation coverage. In all three cases, COBRA continuation coverage need not be provided for more than 18 months after the termination of employment (see Q & A-4 of § 54.4980B-7), and in certain circumstances might be provided for a shorter period (see Q & A-1 of § 54.4980B-7).

Q-2: Is a covered employee or qualified beneficiary responsible for informing the plan administrator of the occurrence of a qualifying event?

A-2: (a) In general, the employer or plan administrator must determine when a qualifying event has occurred. However, each covered employee or qualified beneficiary is responsible for notifying the plan administrator of the occurrence of a qualifying event that is either a dependent child's ceasing to be a dependent child under the generally applicable requirements of the plan or a divorce or legal separation of a covered employee. The group health plan is not required to offer the qualified beneficiary an opportunity to elect COBRA continuation coverage if the notice is not provided to the plan administrator within 60 days after the later of—

(1) The date of the qualifying event; or

(2) The date the qualified beneficiary would lose coverage on account of the qualifying event.

(b) For purposes of this Q&A-2, if more than one qualified beneficiary would lose coverage on account of a divorce or legal separation of a covered employee, a timely notice of the divorce or legal separation that is provided by the covered employee or any one of those qualified beneficiaries will be sufficient to preserve the election rights of all of the qualified beneficiaries.

Q-3: During the election period and before the qualified beneficiary has made an election, must coverage be provided?

A-3: (a) In general, each qualified beneficiary has until 60 days after the later of the date the qualifying event would cause her or him to lose coverage or the date notice is provided to the qualified beneficiary of her or his right to elect

COBRA continuation coverage to decide whether to elect COBRA continuation coverage. If the election is made during that period, coverage must be provided from the date that coverage would otherwise have been lost (but see Q&A-4 of this section). This can be accomplished as described in paragraph (b) or (c) of this Q&A-3.

(b) In the case of an indemnity or reimbursement arrangement, the employer or employee organization can provide for plan coverage during the election period or, if the plan allows retroactive reinstatement, the employer or employee organization can terminate the coverage of the qualified beneficiary and reinstate her or him when the election (and, if applicable, payment for the coverage) is made. Claims incurred by a qualified beneficiary during the election period do not have to be paid before the election (and, if applicable, payment for the coverage) is made. If a provider of health care (such as a physician, hospital, or pharmacy) contacts the plan to confirm coverage of a qualified beneficiary during the election period, the plan must give a complete response to the health care provider about the qualified beneficiary's COBRA continuation coverage rights during the election period. For example, if the plan provides coverage during the election period but cancels coverage retroactively if COBRA continuation coverage is not elected, then the plan must inform a provider that a qualified beneficiary for whom coverage has not been elected is covered but that the coverage is subject to retroactive termination. Similarly, if the plan cancels coverage but then retroactively reinstates it once COBRA continuation coverage is elected, then the plan must inform the provider that the qualified beneficiary currently does not have coverage but will have coverage retroactively to the date coverage was lost if COBRA continuation coverage is elected. (See paragraph (c) of Q&A-5 in § 54.4980B-8 for similar rules that a plan must follow in confirming coverage during a period when the plan has not received payment but that is still within the grace period for a qualified beneficiary for whom COBRA continuation coverage has been elected.)

(c)(1) In the case of a group health plan that provides health services (such as a health maintenance organization or a walk-in clinic), the plan can require with respect to a qualified beneficiary who has not elected and paid for COBRA continuation coverage that the qualified beneficiary choose between—

(i) Electing and paying for the coverage; or

(ii) Paying the reasonable and customary charge for the plan's services, but only if a qualified beneficiary who chooses to pay for the services will be reimbursed for that payment within 30 days after the election of COBRA continuation coverage (and, if applicable, the payment of any balance due for the coverage).

(2) In the alternative, the plan can provide continued coverage and treat the qualified beneficiary's use of the facility as a constructive election. In such a case, the qualified beneficiary is obligated to pay any applicable charge for the coverage, but only if the qualified beneficiary is informed that use of the facility will be a constructive election before using the facility.

Q-4: Is a waiver before the end of the election period effective to end a qualified beneficiary's election rights?

A-4: If, during the election period, a qualified beneficiary waives COBRA continuation coverage, the waiver can be revoked at any time before the end of the election period. Revocation of the waiver is an election of COBRA continuation coverage. However, if a waiver of COBRA continuation coverage is later revoked, coverage need not be provided retroactively (that is, from the date of the loss of coverage until the waiver is revoked). Waivers and revocations of waivers are considered made on the date they are sent to the employer, employee organization, or plan administrator, as applicable.

Q-5: Can an employer or employee organization withhold money or other benefits owed to a qualified beneficiary until the qualified beneficiary either waives COBRA continuation coverage, elects and pays for such coverage, or allows the election period to expire?

A-5: No. An employer, and an employee organization, must not withhold anything to which a qualified beneficiary is otherwise entitled (by operation of law or other agreement) in order to compel payment for COBRA continuation coverage or to coerce the qualified beneficiary to give up rights to COBRA continuation coverage (including the right to use the full election period to decide whether to elect such coverage). Such a withholding constitutes a failure to comply with the COBRA continuation coverage requirements. Furthermore, any purported waiver obtained by means of such a withholding is invalid.

Q-6: Can each qualified beneficiary make an independent election under COBRA?

A-6: Yes. Each qualified beneficiary (including a child who is born to or placed for adoption with a covered employee during a period of COBRA continuation coverage) must be offered the opportunity to make an independent election to receive COBRA continuation coverage. If the plan allows similarly situated active employees with respect to whom a qualifying event has not occurred to choose among several options during an open enrollment period (for example, to switch to another group health plan or to another benefit package under the same group health plan), then each qualified beneficiary must also be offered an independent election to choose during an open enrollment period among the options made available to similarly situated active employees with respect to whom a qualifying event has not occurred. If a qualified beneficiary who is either a covered employee or the spouse of a covered employee elects COBRA continuation coverage and the election does not specify whether the election is for self- only coverage, the election is deemed to include an elec-

tion of COBRA continuation coverage on behalf of all other qualified beneficiaries with respect to that qualifying event. An election on behalf of a minor child can be made by the child's parent or legal guardian. An election on behalf of a qualified beneficiary who is incapacitated or dies can be made by the legal representative of the qualified beneficiary or the qualified beneficiary's estate, as determined under applicable state law, or by the spouse of the qualified beneficiary. (See also Q&A-5 of § 54.4980B-7 relating to the independent right of each qualified beneficiary with respect to the same qualifying event to receive COBRA continuation coverage during the disability extension.) The rules of this Q&A-6 are illustrated by the following examples; in each example each group health plan is subject to COBRA:

Example 1. (i) Employee H and H's spouse are covered under a group health plan immediately before H's termination of employment (for reasons other than gross misconduct). Coverage under the plan will end as a result of the termination of employment.

(ii) Upon H's termination of employment, both H and H's spouse are qualified beneficiaries and each must be allowed to elect COBRA continuation coverage. Thus, H might elect COBRA continuation coverage while the spouse declines to elect such coverage, or H might elect COBRA continuation coverage for both of them. In contrast, H cannot decline COBRA continuation coverage on behalf of H's spouse. Thus, if H does not elect COBRA continuation coverage on behalf of the spouse, the spouse must still be allowed to elect COBRA continuation coverage.

Example 2. (i) An employer maintains a group health plan under which all employees receive employer-paid coverage. Employees can arrange to cover their families by paying an additional amount. The employer also maintains a cafeteria plan, under which one of the options is to pay part or all of the employee share of the cost for family coverage under the group health plan. Thus, an employee might pay for family coverage under the group health plan partly with before-tax dollars and partly with after-tax dollars.

(ii) If an employee's family is receiving coverage under the group health plan when a qualifying event occurs, each of the qualified beneficiaries must be offered an opportunity to elect COBRA continuation coverage, regardless of how that qualified beneficiary's coverage was paid for before the qualifying event.

[Reg. § 54.4980B-6.]

☐ [T.D. 8812, 2-2-99. *Amended by* T.D. 8928, 1-9-2001.]

[Reg. § 54.4980B-7]

§ 54.4980B-7. Duration of COBRA continuation coverage.—The following questions-and-answers address the duration of COBRA continuation coverage:

Q-1: How long must COBRA continuation coverage be made available to a qualified beneficiary?

A-1: (a) Except for an interruption of coverage in connection with a waiver, as described in Q & A-4 of § 54.4980B-6, COBRA continuation coverage that has been elected for a qualified beneficiary must extend for at least the period beginning on the date of the qualifying event and ending not before the earliest of the following dates—

(1) The last day of the maximum coverage period (see Q & A-4 of this section);

(2) The first day for which timely payment is not made to the plan with respect to the qualified beneficiary (see Q & A-5 in § 54.4980B-8);

(3) The date upon which the employer or employee organization ceases to provide any group health plan (including successor plans) to any employee;

(4) The date, after the date of the election, upon which the qualified beneficiary first becomes covered under any other group health plan, as described in Q & A-2 of this section;

(5) The date, after the date of the election, upon which the qualified beneficiary first becomes entitled to Medicare benefits, as described in Q & A-3 of this section; and

(6) In the case of a qualified beneficiary entitled to a disability extension (see Q & A-5 of this section), the later of—

(i) Either 29 months after the date of the qualifying event, or the first day of the month that is more than 30 days after the date of a final determination under Title II or XVI of the Social Security Act (42 U.S.C. 401-433 or 1381-1385) that the disabled qualified beneficiary whose disability resulted in the qualified beneficiary's being entitled to the disability extension is no longer disabled, whichever is earlier; or

(ii) The end of the maximum coverage period that applies to the qualified beneficiary without regard to the disability extension.

(b) However, a group health plan can terminate for cause the coverage of a qualified beneficiary receiving COBRA continuation coverage on the same basis that the plan terminates for cause the coverage of similarly situated nonCOBRA beneficiaries. For example, if a group health plan terminates the coverage of active employees for the submission of a fraudulent claim, then the coverage of a qualified beneficiary can also be terminated for the submission of a fraudulent claim. Notwithstanding the preceding two sentences, the coverage of a qualified beneficiary can be terminated for failure to make timely payment to the plan only if payment is not timely under the rules of Q&A-5 in § 54.4980B-8.

(c) In the case of an individual who is not a qualified beneficiary and who is receiving coverage under a group health plan solely because of the individual's relationship to a qualified beneficiary, if the plan's obligation to make COBRA continuation coverage available to the qualified beneficiary ceases under this section, the plan is

not obligated to make coverage available to the individual who is not a qualified beneficiary.

Q-2: When may a plan terminate a qualified beneficiary's COBRA continuation coverage due to coverage under another group health plan?

A-2: (a) If a qualified beneficiary first becomes covered under another group health plan (including for this purpose any group health plan of a governmental employer or employee organization) after the date on which COBRA continuation coverage is elected for the qualified beneficiary and the other coverage satisfies the requirements of paragraphs (b), (c), and (d) of this Q&A-2, then the plan may terminate the qualified beneficiary's COBRA continuation coverage upon the date on which the qualified beneficiary first becomes covered under the other group health plan (even if the other coverage is less valuable to the qualified beneficiary). By contrast, if a qualified beneficiary first becomes covered under another group health plan on or before the date on which COBRA continuation coverage is elected, then the other coverage cannot be a basis for terminating the qualified beneficiary's COBRA continuation coverage.

(b) The requirement of this paragraph (b) is satisfied if the qualified beneficiary is actually covered, rather than merely eligible to be covered, under the other group health plan.

(c) The requirement of this paragraph (c) is satisfied if the other group health plan is a plan that is not maintained by the employer or employee organization that maintains the plan under which COBRA continuation coverage must otherwise be made available.

(d) The requirement of this paragraph (d) is satisfied if the other group health plan does not contain any exclusion or limitation with respect to any preexisting condition of the qualified beneficiary (other than such an exclusion or limitation that does not apply to, or is satisfied by, the qualified beneficiary by reason of the provisions in section 9801 (relating to limitations on preexisting condition exclusion periods in group health plans)).

(e) The rules of this Q&A-2 are illustrated by the following examples:

Example 1. (i) Employer X maintains a group health plan subject to COBRA. C is an employee covered under the plan. C is also covered under a group health plan maintained by Employer Y, the employer of C's spouse. C terminates employment (for reasons other than gross misconduct), and the termination of employment causes C to lose coverage under X's plan (and, thus, is a qualifying event). C elects to receive COBRA continuation coverage under X's plan.

(ii) Under these facts, X's plan cannot terminate C's COBRA continuation coverage on the basis of C's coverage under Y's plan.

Example 2. (i) Employer W maintains a group health plan subject to COBRA. D is an employee covered under the plan. D terminates employment (for reasons other than gross misconduct), and the termination of employment causes D to lose coverage under W's plan (and, thus, is a

qualifying event). D elects to receive COBRA continuation coverage under W's plan. Later D becomes employed by Employer V and is covered under V's group health plan. D's coverage under V's plan is not subject to any exclusion or limitation with respect to any preexisting condition of D.

(ii) Under these facts, W can terminate D's COBRA continuation coverage on the date D becomes covered under V's plan.

Example 3. (i) The facts are the same as in *Example 2*, except that D becomes employed by V and becomes covered under V's group health plan before D elects COBRA continuation coverage under W's plan.

(ii) Because the termination of employment is a qualifying event, D must be offered COBRA continuation coverage under W's plan, and W is not permitted to terminate D's COBRA continuation coverage on account of D's coverage under V's plan because D first became covered under V's plan before COBRA continuation coverage was elected for D.

Q-3: When may a plan terminate a qualified beneficiary's COBRA continuation coverage due to the qualified beneficiary's entitlement to Medicare benefits?

A-3: (a) If a qualified beneficiary first becomes entitled to Medicare benefits under Title XVIII of the Social Security Act (42 U.S.C. 1395-1395ggg) after the date on which COBRA continuation coverage is elected for the qualified beneficiary, then the plan may terminate the qualified beneficiary's COBRA continuation coverage upon the date on which the qualified beneficiary becomes so entitled. By contrast, if a qualified beneficiary first becomes entitled to Medicare benefits on or before the date that COBRA continuation coverage is elected, then the qualified beneficiary's entitlement to Medicare benefits cannot be a basis for terminating the qualified beneficiary's COBRA continuation coverage.

(b) A qualified beneficiary becomes entitled to Medicare benefits upon the effective date of enrollment in either part A or B, whichever occurs earlier. Thus, merely being eligible to enroll in Medicare does not constitute being entitled to Medicare benefits.

Q-4: When does the maximum coverage period end?

A-4: (a) Except as otherwise provided in this Q & A-4, the maximum coverage period ends 36 months after the qualifying event. The maximum coverage period for a qualified beneficiary who is a child born to or placed for adoption with a covered employee during a period of COBRA continuation coverage is the maximum coverage period for the qualifying event giving rise to the period of COBRA continuation coverage during which the child was born or placed for adoption. Paragraph (b) of this Q & A-4 describes the starting point from which the end of the maximum coverage period is measured. The date that the maximum coverage period ends is described in paragraph (c) of this Q & A-4 in a case where the qualifying event is a termination of employ-

ment or reduction of hours of employment, in paragraph (d) of this Q & A-4 in a case where a covered employee becomes entitled to Medicare benefits under Title XVIII of the Social Security Act (42 U.S.C. 1395-1395ggg) before experiencing a qualifying event that is a termination of employment or reduction of hours of employment, and in paragraph (e) of this Q & A-4 in the case of a qualifying event that is the bankruptcy of the employer. See Q & A-8 of §54.4980B-2 for limitations that apply to certain health flexible spending arrangements. See also Q & A-6 of this section in the case of multiple qualifying events. Nothing in §§54.4980B-1 through 54.4980B-10 prohibits a group health plan from providing coverage that continues beyond the end of the maximum coverage period.

(b)(1) The end of the maximum coverage period is measured from the date of the qualifying event even if the qualifying event does not result in a loss of coverage under the plan until a later date. If, however, coverage under the plan is lost at a later date and the plan provides for the extension of the required periods, then the maximum coverage period is measured from the date when coverage is lost. A plan provides for the extension of the required periods if it provides both—

(i) That the 30-day notice period (during which the employer is required to notify the plan administrator of the occurrence of certain qualifying events such as the death of the covered employee or the termination of employment or reduction of hours of employment of the covered employee) begins on the date of the loss of coverage rather than on the date of the qualifying event; and

(ii) That the end of the maximum coverage period is measured from the date of the loss of coverage rather than from the date of the qualifying event.

(2) In the case of a plan that provides for the extension of the required periods, whenever the rules of §§54.4980B-1 through 54.4980B-10 refer to the measurement of a period from the date of the qualifying event, those rules apply in such a case by measuring the period instead from the date of the loss of coverage.

(c) In the case of a qualifying event that is a termination of employment or reduction of hours of employment, the maximum coverage period ends 18 months after the qualifying event if there is no disability extension, and 29 months after the qualifying event if there is a disability extension. See Q & A-5 of this section for rules to determine if there is a disability extension. If there is a disability extension and the disabled qualified beneficiary is later determined to no longer be disabled, then a plan may terminate the COBRA continuation coverage of an affected qualified beneficiary before the end of the disability extension; see paragraph (a)(6) in Q & A-1 of this section.

(d)(1) If a covered employee becomes entitled to Medicare benefits under Title XVIII of the Social Security Act (42 U.S.C. 1395-1395ggg)

before experiencing a qualifying event that is a termination of employment or reduction of hours of employment, the maximum coverage period for qualified beneficiaries other than the covered employee ends on the later of—

(i) 36 months after the date the covered employee became entitled to Medicare benefits; or

(ii) 18 months (or 29 months, if there is a disability extension) after the date of the covered employee's termination of employment or reduction of hours of employment.

(2) See paragraph (b) of Q & A-3 of this section regarding the determination of when a covered employee becomes entitled to Medicare benefits.

(e) In the case of a qualifying event that is the bankruptcy of the employer, the maximum coverage period for a qualified beneficiary who is the retired covered employee ends on the date of the retired covered employee's death. The maximum coverage period for a qualified beneficiary who is the spouse, surviving spouse, or dependent child of the retired covered employee ends on the earlier of—

(1) The date of the qualified beneficiary's death; or

(2) The date that is 36 months after the death of the retired covered employee.

Q-5: How does a qualified beneficiary become entitled to a disability extension?

A-5: (a) A qualified beneficiary becomes entitled to a disability extension if the requirements of paragraphs (b), (c), and (d) of this Q&A-5 are satisfied with respect to the qualified beneficiary. If the disability extension applies with respect to a qualifying event, it applies with respect to each qualified beneficiary entitled to COBRA continuation coverage because of that qualifying event. Thus, for example, the 29-month maximum coverage period applies to each qualified beneficiary who is not disabled as well as to the qualified beneficiary who is disabled, and it applies independently with respect to each of the qualified beneficiaries. See Q&A-1 in §54.4980B-8, which permits a plan to require payment of an increased amount during the disability extension.

(b) The requirement of this paragraph (b) is satisfied if a qualifying event occurs that is a termination, or reduction of hours, of a covered employee's employment.

(c) The requirement of this paragraph (c) is satisfied if an individual (whether or not the covered employee) who is a qualified beneficiary in connection with the qualifying event described in paragraph (b) of this Q&A-5 is determined under Title II or XVI of the Social Security Act (42 U.S.C. 401-433 or 1381-1385) to have been disabled at any time during the first 60 days of COBRA continuation coverage. For this purpose, the period of the first 60 days of COBRA continuation coverage is measured from the date of the qualifying event described in paragraph (b) of this Q & A-5 (except that if a loss of coverage would occur at a later date in the absence of an election for COBRA continuation coverage and if the plan provides for the extension of the re-

quired periods (as described in paragraph (b) of Q & A-4 of this section) then the period of the first 60 days of COBRA continuation coverage is measured from the date on which the coverage would be lost). However, in the case of a qualified beneficiary who is a child born to or placed for adoption with a covered employee during a period of COBRA continuation coverage, the period of the first 60 days of COBRA continuation coverage is measured from the date of birth or placement for adoption. For purposes of this paragraph (c), an individual is determined to be disabled within the first 60 days of COBRA continuation coverage if the individual has been determined under Title II or XVI of the Social Security Act to have been disabled before the first day of COBRA continuation coverage and has not been determined to be no longer disabled at any time between the date of that disability determination and the first day of COBRA continuation coverage.

(d) The requirement of this paragraph (d) is satisfied if any of the qualified beneficiaries affected by the qualifying event described in paragraph (b) of this Q&A-5 provides notice to the plan administrator of the disability determination on a date that is both within 60 days after the date the determination is issued and before the end of the original 18-month maximum coverage period that applies to the qualifying event.

Q-6: Under what circumstances can the maximum coverage period be expanded?

A-6: (a) The maximum coverage period can be expanded if the requirements of Q&A-5 of this section (relating to the disability extension) or paragraph (b) of this Q&A-6 are satisfied.

(b) The requirements of this paragraph (b) are satisfied if a qualifying event that gives rise to an 18-month maximum coverage period (or a 29-month maximum coverage period in the case of a disability extension) is followed, within that 18-month period (or within that 29-month period, in the case of a disability extension), by a second qualifying event (for example, a death or a divorce) that gives rise to a 36-month maximum coverage period. (Thus, a termination of employment following a qualifying event that is a reduction of hours of employment cannot be a second qualifying event that expands the maximum coverage period; the bankruptcy of an employer also cannot be a second qualifying event that expands the maximum coverage period.) In such a case, the original 18-month period (or 29-month period, in the case of a disability extension) is expanded to 36 months, but only for those individuals who were qualified beneficiaries under the group health plan in connection with the first qualifying event and who are still qualified beneficiaries at the time of the second qualifying event. No qualifying event (other than a qualifying event that is the bankruptcy of the employer) can give rise to a maximum coverage period that ends more than 36 months after the date of the first qualifying event (or more than 36 months after the date of the loss of coverage, in the case of a plan that provides for the extension of the required periods; see para-

graph (b) in Q & A-4 of this section). For example, if an employee covered by a group health plan that is subject to COBRA terminates employment (for reasons other than gross misconduct) on December 31, 2000, the termination is a qualifying event giving rise to a maximum coverage period that extends for 18 months to June 30, 2002. If the employee dies after the employee and the employee's spouse and dependent children have elected COBRA continuation coverage and on or before June 30, 2002, the spouse and dependent children (except anyone among them whose COBRA continuation coverage had already ended for some other reason) will be able to receive COBRA continuation coverage through December 31, 2003. See Q & A-8(b) of § 54.4980B-2 for a special rule that applies to certain health flexible spending arrangements.

Q-7: If health coverage is provided to a qualified beneficiary after a qualifying event without regard to COBRA continuation coverage (for example, as a result of state or local law, the Uniformed Services Employment and Reemployment Rights Act of 1994 (38 U.S.C. 4315), industry practice, a collective bargaining agreement, severance agreement, or plan procedure), will such alternative coverage extend the maximum coverage period?

A-7: (a) No. The end of the maximum coverage period is measured solely as described in Q&A-4 and Q&A-6 of this section, which is generally from the date of the qualifying event.

(b) If the alternative coverage does not satisfy all the requirements for COBRA continuation coverage, or if the amount that the group health plan requires to be paid for the alternative coverage is greater than the amount required to be paid by similarly situated nonCOBRA beneficiaries for the coverage that the qualified beneficiary can elect to receive as COBRA continuation coverage, the plan covering the qualified beneficiary immediately before the qualifying event must offer the qualified beneficiary receiving the alternative coverage the opportunity to elect COBRA continuation coverage. See Q&A-1 of § 54.4980B-6.

(c) If an individual rejects COBRA continuation coverage in favor of alternative coverage, then, at the expiration of the alternative coverage period, the individual need not be offered a COBRA election. However, if the individual receiving alternative coverage is a covered employee and the spouse or a dependent child of the individual would lose that alternative coverage as a result of a qualifying event (such as the death of the covered employee), the spouse or dependent child must be given an opportunity to elect to continue that alternative coverage, with a maximum coverage period of 36 months measured from the date of that qualifying event.

Q-8: Must a qualified beneficiary be given the right to enroll in a conversion health plan at the end of the maximum coverage period for COBRA continuation coverage?

A-8: If a qualified beneficiary's COBRA continuation coverage under a group health plan ends

as a result of the expiration of the maximum coverage period, the group health plan must, during the 180-day period that ends on that expiration date, provide the qualified beneficiary the option of enrolling under a conversion health plan if such an option is otherwise generally available to similarly situated nonCOBRA beneficiaries under the group health plan. If such a conversion option is not otherwise generally available, it need not be made available to qualified beneficiaries.

[Reg. § 54.4980B-7.]

☐ [*T.D.* 8812, 2-2-99. *Amended by T.D.* 8928, 1-9-2001.]

[Reg. § 54.4980B-8]

§ 54.4980B-8. Paying for COBRA continuation coverage.—The following questions-and-answers address paying for COBRA continuation coverage:

Q-1: Can a group health plan require payment for COBRA continuation coverage?

A-1: (a) Yes. For any period of COBRA continuation coverage, a group health plan can require the payment of an amount that does not exceed 102 percent of the applicable premium for that period. (See paragraph (b) of this Q&A-1 for a rule permitting a plan to require payment of an increased amount due to the disability extension.) The *applicable premium* is defined in section 4980B(f)(4). A group health plan can terminate a qualified beneficiary's COBRA continuation coverage as of the first day of any period for which timely payment is not made to the plan with respect to that qualified beneficiary (see Q&A-1 of § 54.4980B-7). For the meaning of *timely payment*, see Q&A-5 of this section.

(b) A group health plan is permitted to require the payment of an amount that does not exceed 150 percent of the applicable premium for any period of COBRA continuation coverage covering a disabled qualified beneficiary (for example, whether single or family coverage) if the coverage would not be required to be made available in the absence of a disability extension. (See Q&A-5 of § 54.4980B-7 for rules to determine whether a qualified beneficiary is entitled to a disability extension.) A plan is not permitted to require the payment of an amount that exceeds 102 percent of the applicable premium for any period of COBRA continuation coverage to which a qualified beneficiary is entitled without regard to the disability extension. Thus, if a qualified beneficiary entitled to a disability extension experiences a second qualifying event within the original 18-month maximum coverage period, then the plan is not permitted to require the payment of an amount that exceeds 102 percent of the applicable premium for any period of COBRA continuation coverage. By contrast, if a qualified beneficiary entitled to a disability extension experiences a second qualifying event after the end of the original 18-month maximum coverage period, then the plan may require the payment of an amount that is up to 150 percent of the applicable premium for the remainder of

the period of COBRA continuation coverage (that is, from the beginning of the 19th month through the end of the 36th month) as long as the disabled qualified beneficiary is included in that coverage. The rules of this paragraph (b) are illustrated by the following examples; in each example the group health plan is subject to COBRA:

Example 1. (i) An employer maintains a group health plan. The plan determines the cost of covering individuals under the plan by reference to two categories, individual coverage and family coverage, and the applicable premium is determined for those two categories. An employee and members of the employee's family are covered under the plan. The employee experiences a qualifying event that is the termination of the employee's employment. The employee's family qualifies for the disability extension because of the disability of the employee's spouse. (Timely notice of the disability is provided to the plan administrator.) Timely payment of the amount required by the plan for COBRA continuation coverage for the family (which does not exceed 102 percent of the cost of family coverage under the plan) was made to the plan with respect to the employee's family for the first 18 months of COBRA continuation coverage, and the disabled spouse and the rest of the family continue to receive COBRA continuation coverage through the 29th month.

(ii) Under these facts, the plan may require payment of up to 150 percent of the applicable premium for family coverage in order for the family to receive COBRA continuation coverage from the 19th month through the 29th month. If the plan determined the cost of coverage by reference to three categories (such as employee, employee-plus-one-dependent, employee-plus-two-or- more-dependents) or more than three categories, instead of two categories, the plan could still require, from the 19th month through the 29th month of COBRA continuation coverage, the payment of 150 percent of the cost of coverage for the category of coverage that included the disabled spouse.

Example 2. (i) The facts are the same as in *Example 1,* except that only the covered employee elects and pays for the first 18 months of COBRA continuation coverage.

(ii) Even though the employee's disabled spouse does not elect or pay for COBRA continuation coverage, the employee satisfies the requirements for the disability extension to apply with respect to the employee's qualifying event. Under these facts, the plan may not require the payment of more than 102 percent of the applicable premium for individual coverage for the entire period of the employee's COBRA continuation coverage, including the period from the 19th month through the 29th month. If COBRA continuation coverage had been elected and paid for with respect to other nondisabled members of the employee's family, then the plan could not require the payment of more than 102 percent of the applicable premium for family coverage (or for any other appropriate category

of coverage that might apply to that group of qualified beneficiaries under the plan, such as employee-plus-one-dependent or employee-plus-two-or-more-dependents) for those family members to continue their coverage from the 19th month through the 29th month.

(c) A group health plan does not fail to comply with section 9802(b) (which generally prohibits an individual from being charged, on the basis of health status, a higher premium than that charged for similarly situated individuals enrolled in the plan) with respect to a qualified beneficiary entitled to the disability extension merely because the plan requires payment of an amount permitted under paragraph (b) of this Q & A-1.

Q-2: When is the applicable premium determined and when can a group health plan increase the amount it requires to be paid for COBRA continuation coverage?

A-2: (a) The applicable premium for each determination period must be computed and fixed by a group health plan before the determination period begins. A determination period is any 12-month period selected by the plan, but it must be applied consistently from year to year. The determination period is a single period for any benefit package. Thus, each qualified beneficiary does not have a separate determination period beginning on the date (or anniversaries of the date) that COBRA continuation coverage begins for that qualified beneficiary.

(b) During a determination period, a plan can increase the amount it requires to be paid for a qualified beneficiary's COBRA continuation coverage only in the following three cases:

(1) The plan has previously charged less than the maximum amount permitted under Q&A-1 of this section and the increased amount required to be paid does not exceed the maximum amount permitted under Q&A-1 of this section;

(2) The increase occurs during the disability extension and the increased amount required to be paid does not exceed the maximum amount permitted under paragraph (b) of Q&A-1 of this section; or

(3) A qualified beneficiary changes the coverage being received (see paragraph (c) of this Q&A-2 for rules on how the amount the plan requires to be paid may or must change when a qualified beneficiary changes the coverage being received).

(c) If a plan allows similarly situated active employees who have not experienced a qualifying event to change the coverage they are receiving, then the plan must also allow each qualified beneficiary to change the coverage being received on the same terms as the similarly situated active employees. (See Q&A-4 in § 54.4980B-5.) If a qualified beneficiary changes coverage from one benefit package (or a group of benefit packages) to another benefit package (or another group of benefit packages), or adds or eliminates coverage for family members, then the following rules apply. If the change in coverage is to a benefit package, group of benefit

packages, or coverage unit (such as family coverage, self-plus-one-dependent, or self-plus-two-or-more-dependents) for which the applicable premium is higher, then the plan may increase the amount that it requires to be paid for COBRA continuation coverage to an amount that does not exceed the amount permitted under Q&A-1 of this section as applied to the new coverage. If the change in coverage is to a benefit package, group of benefit packages, or coverage unit (such as individual or self-plus-one- dependent) for which the applicable premium is lower, then the plan cannot require the payment of an amount that exceeds the amount permitted under Q&A-1 of this section as applied to the new coverage.

Q-3: Must a plan allow payment for COBRA continuation coverage to be made in monthly installments?

A-3: Yes. A group health plan must allow payment for COBRA continuation coverage to be made in monthly installments. A group health plan is permitted to also allow the alternative of payment for COBRA continuation coverage being made at other intervals (for example, weekly, quarterly, or semiannually).

Q-4: Is a plan required to allow a qualified beneficiary to choose to have the first payment for COBRA continuation coverage applied prospectively only?

A-4: No. A plan is permitted to apply the first payment for COBRA continuation coverage to the period of coverage beginning immediately after the date on which coverage under the plan would have been lost on account of the qualifying event. Of course, if the group health plan allows a qualified beneficiary to waive COBRA continuation coverage for any period before electing to receive COBRA continuation coverage, the first payment is not applied to the period of the waiver.

Q-5: What is timely payment for COBRA continuation coverage?

A-5: (a) Except as provided in this paragraph (a) or in paragraph (b) or (d) of this Q&A-5, timely payment for a period of COBRA continuation coverage under a group health plan means payment that is made to the plan by the date that is 30 days after the first day of that period. Payment that is made to the plan by a later date is also considered timely payment if either—

(1) Under the terms of the plan, covered employees or qualified beneficiaries are allowed until that later date to pay for their coverage for the period; or

(2) Under the terms of an arrangement between the employer or employee organization and an insurance company, health maintenance organization, or other entity that provides plan benefits on the employer's or employee organization's behalf, the employer or employee organization is allowed until that later date to pay for coverage of similarly situated nonCOBRA beneficiaries for the period.

(b) Notwithstanding paragraph (a) of this Q&A-5, a plan cannot require payment for any

Reg. § 54.4980B-8

period of COBRA continuation coverage for a qualified beneficiary earlier than 45 days after the date on which the election of COBRA continuation coverage is made for that qualified beneficiary.

(c) If, after COBRA continuation coverage has been elected for a qualified beneficiary, a provider of health care (such as a physician, hospital, or pharmacy) contacts the plan to confirm coverage of a qualified beneficiary for a period for which the plan has not yet received payment, the plan must give a complete response to the health care provider about the qualified beneficiary's COBRA continuation coverage rights, if any, described in paragraphs (a), (b), and (d) of this Q&A-5. For example, if the plan provides coverage during the 30- and 45-day grace periods described in paragraphs (a) and (b) of this Q&A-5 but cancels coverage retroactively if payment is not made by the end of the applicable grace period, then the plan must inform a provider with respect to a qualified beneficiary for whom payment has not been received that the qualified beneficiary is covered but that the coverage is subject to retroactive termination if timely payment is not made. Similarly, if the plan cancels coverage if it has not received payment by the first day of a period of coverage but retroactively reinstates coverage if payment is made by the end of the grace period for that period of coverage, then the plan must inform the provider that the qualified beneficiary currently does not have coverage but will have coverage retroactively to the first date of the period if timely payment is made. (See paragraph (b) of Q&A-3 in §54.4980B-6 for similar rules that the plan must follow in confirming coverage during the election period.)

(d) If timely payment is made to the plan in an amount that is not significantly less than the amount the plan requires to be paid for a period of coverage, then the amount paid is deemed to satisfy the plan's requirement for the amount that must be paid, unless the plan notifies the qualified beneficiary of the amount of the deficiency and grants a reasonable period of time for payment of the deficiency to be made. For this purpose, as a safe harbor, 30 days after the date the notice is provided is deemed to be a reasonable period of time. An amount is not significantly less than the amount the plan requires to be paid for a period of coverage if and only if the shortfall is no greater than the lesser of the following two amounts:

(1) Fifty dollars (or such other amount as the Commissioner may provide in a revenue ruling, notice, or other guidance published in the Internal Revenue Bulletin (see §601.601(d)(2)(ii) of this chapter)); or

(2) 10 percent of the amount the plan requires to be paid.

(e) Payment is considered made on the date on which it is sent to the plan.

[Reg. §54.4980B-8.]

☐ [*T.D.* 8812, 2-2-99. *Amended by T.D.* 8928, 1-9-2001.]

[Reg. §54.4980B-9]

§54.4980B-9. Business reorganizations and employer withdrawals from multiemployer plans.

The following questions-and-answers address who has the obligation to make COBRA continuation coverage available to affected qualified beneficiaries in the context of business reorganizations and employer withdrawals from multiemployer plans:

Q-1: For purposes of this section, what are a business reorganization, a stock sale, and an asset sale?

A-1: For purposes of this section:

(a) A *business reorganization* is a stock sale or an asset sale.

(b) A *stock sale* is a transfer of stock in a corporation that causes the corporation to become a different employer or a member of a different employer. (See Q & A-2 of §54.4980B-2, which defines *employer* to include all members of a controlled group of corporations.) Thus, for example, a sale or distribution of stock in a corporation that causes the corporation to cease to be a member of one controlled group of corporations, whether or not it becomes a member of another controlled group of corporations, is a stock sale.

(c) An *asset sale* is a transfer of substantial assets, such as a plant or division or substantially all the assets of a trade or business.

(d) The rules of §1.414(b)-1 of this chapter apply in determining what constitutes a controlled group of corporations, and the rules of §§1.414(c)-1 through 1.41(c)-5 of this chapter apply in determining what constitutes a group of trades or businesses under common control.

Q-2: In the case of a stock sale, what are the selling group, the acquired organization, and the buying group?

A-2: In the case of a stock sale—

(a) The *selling group* is the controlled group of corporations, or the group of trades or businesses under common control, of which a corporation ceases to be a member as a result of the stock sale;

(b) The *acquired organization* is the corporation that ceases to be a member of the selling group as a result of the stock sale; and

(c) The *buying group* is the controlled group of corporations, or the group of trades or businesses under common control, of which the acquired organization becomes a member as a result of the stock sale. If the acquired organization does not become a member of such a group, the *buying group* is the acquired organization.

Q-3: In the case of an asset sale, what are the selling group and the buying group?

A-3: In the case of an asset sale—

(a) The *selling group* is the controlled group of corporations or the group of trades or businesses under common control that includes the corporation or other trade or business that is selling the assets; and

(b) The *buying group* is the controlled group of corporations or the group of trades or businesses under common control that includes the corporation or other trade or business that is buying the assets.

Q-4: Who is an M & A qualified beneficiary?

A-4: (a) Asset sales: In the case of an asset sale, an individual is an M & A qualified beneficiary if the individual is a qualified beneficiary whose qualifying event occurred prior to or in connection with the sale and who is, or whose qualifying event occurred in connection with, a covered employee whose last employment prior to the qualifying event was associated with the assets being sold.

(b) Stock sales: In the case of a stock sale, an individual is an M & A qualified beneficiary if the individual is a qualified beneficiary whose qualifying event occurred prior to or in connection with the sale and who is, or whose qualifying event occurred in connection with, a covered employee whose last employment prior to the qualifying event was with the acquired organization.

(c) In the case of a qualified beneficiary who has experienced more than one qualifying event with respect to her or his current right to COBRA continuation coverage, the qualifying event referred to in paragraphs (a) and (b) of this Q & A-4 is the first qualifying event.

Q-5: In the case of a stock sale, is the sale a qualifying event with respect to a covered employee who is employed by the acquired organization before the sale and who continues to be employed by the acquired organization after the sale, or with respect to the spouse or dependent children of such a covered employee?

A-5: No. A covered employee who continues to be employed by the acquired organization after the sale does not experience a termination of employment as a result of the sale. Accordingly, the sale is not a qualifying event with respect to the covered employee, or with respect to the covered employee's spouse or dependent children, regardless of whether they are provided with group health coverage after the sale, and neither the covered employee, nor the covered employee's spouse or dependent children, become qualified beneficiaries as a result of the sale.

Q-6: In the case of an asset sale, is the sale a qualifying event with respect to a covered employee whose employment immediately before the sale was associated with the purchased assets, or with respect to the spouse or dependent children of such a covered employee who are covered under a group health plan of the selling group immediately before the sale?

A-6: (a) Yes, unless—

(1) The buying group is a successor employer under paragraph (c) of Q & A-8 of this section or Q & A-2 of § 54.4980B-2, and the covered employee is employed by the buying group immediately after the sale; or

(2) The covered employee (or the spouse or any dependent child of the covered employee) does not lose coverage (within the meaning of paragraph (c) in Q & A-1 of § 54.4980B-4) under a group health plan of the selling group after the sale.

(b) Unless the conditions in paragraph (a)(1) or (2) of this Q & A-6 are satisfied, such a covered employee experiences a termination of employment with the selling group as a result of the asset sale, regardless of whether the covered employee is employed by the buying group or whether the covered employee's employment is associated with the purchased assets after the sale. Accordingly, the covered employee, and the spouse and dependent children of the covered employee who lose coverage under a plan of the selling group in connection with the sale, are M & A qualified beneficiaries in connection with the sale.

Q-7: In a business reorganization, are the buying group and the selling group permitted to allocate by contract the responsibility to make COBRA continuation coverage available to M & A qualified beneficiaries?

A-7: Yes. Nothing in this section prohibits a selling group and a buying group from allocating to one or the other of the parties in a purchase agreement the responsibility to provide the coverage required under §§ 54.4980B-1 through 54.4980B-10. However, if and to the extent that the party assigned this responsibility under the terms of the contract fails to perform, the party who has the obligation under Q & A-8 of this section to make COBRA continuation coverage available to M & A qualified beneficiaries continues to have that obligation.

Q-8: Which group health plan has the obligation to make COBRA continuation coverage available to M & A qualified beneficiaries in a business reorganization?

A-8: (a) In the case of a business reorganization (whether a stock sale or an asset sale), so long as the selling group maintains a group health plan after the sale, a group health plan maintained by the selling group has the obligation to make COBRA continuation coverage available to M & A qualified beneficiaries with respect to that sale. This Q & A-8 prescribes rules for cases in which the selling group ceases to provide any group health plan to any employee in connection with the sale. Paragraph (b) of this Q & A-8 contains these rules for stock sales, and paragraph (c) of this Q & A-8 contains these rules for asset sales. Neither a stock sale nor an asset sale has any effect on the COBRA continuation coverage requirements applicable to any group health plan for any period before the sale.

(b)(1) In the case of a stock sale, if the selling group ceases to provide any group health plan to any employee in connection with the sale, a group health plan maintained by the buying group has the obligation to make COBRA continuation coverage available to M & A qualified beneficiaries with respect to that stock sale. A group health plan of the buying group has this obligation beginning on the later of the following two dates and continuing as long as the buying group continues to maintain a group health plan (but subject to the rules in § 54.4980B-7, relating to the duration of COBRA continuation coverage)—

(i) The date the selling group ceases to provide any group health plan to any employee; or

(ii) The date of the stock sale.

(2) The determination of whether the selling group's cessation of providing any group health

Reg. § 54.4980B-9

plan to any employee is in connection with the stock sale is based on all of the relevant facts and circumstances. A group health plan of the buying group does not, as a result of the stock sale, have an obligation to make COBRA continuation coverage available to those qualified beneficiaries of the selling group who are not M & A qualified beneficiaries with respect to that sale.

(c)(1) In the case of an asset sale, if the selling group ceases to provide any group health plan to any employee in connection with the sale and if the buying group continues the business operations associated with the assets purchased from the selling group without interruption or substantial change, then the buying group is a successor employer to the selling group in connection with that asset sale. A buying group does not fail to be a successor employer in connection with an asset sale merely because the asset sale takes place in connection with a proceeding in bankruptcy under Title 11 of the United States Code. If the buying group is a successor employer, a group health plan maintained by the buying group has the obligation to make COBRA continuation coverage available to M & A qualified beneficiaries with respect to that asset sale. A group health plan of the buying group has this obligation beginning on the later of the following two dates and continuing as long as the buying group continues to maintain a group health plan (but subject to the rules in §54.4980B-7, relating to the duration of COBRA continuation coverage)—

(i) The date the selling group ceases to provide any group health plan to any employee; or

(ii) The date of the asset sale.

(2) The determination of whether the selling group's cessation of providing any group health plan to any employee is in connection with the asset sale is based on all of the relevant facts and circumstances. A group health plan of the buying group does not, as a result of the asset sale, have an obligation to make COBRA continuation coverage available to those qualified beneficiaries of the selling group who are not M & A qualified beneficiaries with respect to that sale.

(d) The rules of Q & A-1 through Q & A-7 of this section and this Q & A-8 are illustrated by the following examples; in each example, each group health plan is subject to COBRA:

Stock Sale Examples

Example 1. (i) Selling Group S consists of three corporations, A, B, and C. Buying Group P consists of two corporations, D and E. P enters into a contract to purchase all the stock of C from S effective July 1, 2002. Before the sale of C, S maintains a single group health plan for the employees of A, B, and C (and their families). P maintains a single group health plan for the employees of D and E (and their families). Effective July 1, 2002, the employees of C (and their families) become covered under P's plan. On

June 30, 2002, there are 48 qualified beneficiaries receiving COBRA continuation coverage under S's plan, 15 of whom are M & A qualified beneficiaries with respect to the sale of C. (The other 33 qualified beneficiaries had qualifying events in connection with a covered employee whose last employment before the qualifying event was with either A or B.)

(ii) Under these facts, S's plan continues to have the obligation to make COBRA continuation coverage available to the 15 M & A qualified beneficiaries under S's plan after the sale of C to P. The employees who continue in employment with C do not experience a qualifying event by virtue of P's acquisition of C. If they experience a qualifying event after the sale, then the group health plan of P has the obligation to make COBRA continuation coverage available to them.

Example 2. (i) Selling Group S consists of three corporations, A, B, and C. Each of A, B, and C maintains a group health plan for its employees (and their families). Buying Group P consists of two corporations, D and E. P enters into a contract to purchase all of the stock of C from S effective July 1, 2002. As of June 30, 2002, there are 14 qualified beneficiaries receiving COBRA continuation coverage under C's plan. C continues to employ all of its employees and continues to maintain its group health plan after being acquired by P on July 1, 2002.

(ii) Under these facts, C is an acquired organization and the 14 qualified beneficiaries under C's plan are M & A qualified beneficiaries. A group health plan of S (that is, either the plan maintained by A or the plan maintained by B) has the obligation to make COBRA continuation coverage available to the 14 M & A qualified beneficiaries. S and P could negotiate to have C's plan continue to make COBRA continuation coverage available to the 14 M & A qualified beneficiaries. In such a case, neither A's plan nor B's plan would make COBRA continuation coverage available to the 14 M & A qualified beneficiaries unless C's plan failed to fulfill its contractual responsibility to make COBRA continuation coverage available to the M & A qualified beneficiaries. C's employees (and their spouses and dependent children) do not experience a qualifying even in connection with P's acquisition of C, and consequently no plan maintained by either P or S has any obligation to make COBRA continuation coverage available to C's employees (or their spouses or dependent children) in connection with the transfer of stock in C from S to P.

Example 3. (i) The facts are the same as in *Example 2*, except that C ceases to employ two employees on June 30, 2002, and those two employees never become covered under P's plan.

(ii) Under these facts, the two employees experience a qualifying event on June 30, 2002 because their termination of employment causes a loss of group health coverage. A group health

plan of S (that is, either the plan maintained by A or the plan maintained by B) has the obligation to make COBRA continuation coverage available to the two employees (and to any spouse or dependent child of the two employees who loses coverage under C's plan in connection with the termination of employment of the two employees) because they are M & A qualified beneficiaries with respect to the sale of C.

Example 4. (i) Selling Group S consists of three corporations, A, B, and C. Buying Group P consists of two corporations, D and E. P enters into a contract to purchase all of the stock of C from S effective July 1, 2002. Before the sale of C, S maintains a single group health plan for the employees of A, B, and C (and their families). P maintains a single group health plan for the employees of D and E (and their families). Effective July 1, 2002, the employees of C (and their families) become covered under P's plan. On June 30, 2002, there are 25 qualified beneficiaries receiving COBRA continuation coverage under S's plan, 20 of whom are M & A qualified beneficiaries with respect to the sale of C. (The other five qualified beneficiaries had qualifying events in connection with a covered employee whose last employment before the qualifying event was with either A or B.) S terminates its group health plan effective June 30, 2002 and begins to liquidate the assets of A and B and to lay off the employees of A and B.

(ii) Under these facts, S ceases to provide a group health plan to any employee in connection with the sale of C to P. Thus, beginning July 1, 2002 P's plan has the obligation to make COBRA continuation coverage available to the 20 M & A qualified beneficiaries, but P is not obligated to make COBRA continuation coverage available to the other 5 qualified beneficiaries with respect to S's plan as of June 30, 2002 or to any of the employees of A or B whose employment is terminated by S (or to any of those employees' spouses or dependent children).

Asset Sale Examples

Example 5. (i) Selling Group S provides group health plan coverage to employees at each of its operating divisions. S sells the assets of one of its divisions to Buying Group P. Under the terms of the group health plan covering the employees at the division being sold, their coverage will end on the date of the sale. P hires all but one of those employees, gives them the same positions that they had with S before the sale, and provides them with coverage under a group health plan. Immediately before the sale, there are two qualified beneficiaries receiving COBRA continuation coverage under a group health plan of S whose qualifying events occurred in connection with a covered employee whose last employment prior to the qualifying event was associated with the assets sold to P.

(ii) These two qualified beneficiaries are M & A qualified beneficiaries with respect to the asset sale to P. Under these facts, a group health plan of S retains the obligation to make COBRA continuation coverage available to these two M & A

qualified beneficiaries. In addition, the one employee P does not hire as well as all of the employees P hires (and the spouses and dependent children of these employees) who were covered under a group health plan of S on the day before the sale are M & A qualified beneficiaries with respect to the sale. A group health plan of S also has the obligation to make COBRA continuation coverage available to these M & A qualified beneficiaries.

Example 6. (i) Selling Group S provides group health plan coverage to employees at each of its operating divisions. S sells substantially all of the assets of all of its divisions to Buying Group P, and S ceases to provide any group health plan to any employee on the date of the sale. P hires all but one of S's employees on the date of the asset sale by S, gives those employees the same positions that they had with S before the sale, and continues the business operations of those divisions without substantial change or interruption. P provides these employees with coverage under a group health plan. Immediately before the sale, there are 10 qualified beneficiaries receiving COBRA continuation coverage under a group health plan of S whose qualifying events occurred in connection with a covered employee whose last employment prior to the qualifying event was associated with the assets sold to P.

(ii) These 10 qualified beneficiaries are M & A qualified beneficiaries with respect to the asset sale to P. Under these facts, P is a successor employer described in paragraph (c) of this Q & A-8. Thus, a group health plan of P has the obligation to make COBRA continuation coverage available to these 10 M & A qualified beneficiaries.

(iii) The one employee that P does not hire and the family members of that employee are also M & A qualified beneficiaries with respect to the sale. A group health plan of P also has the obligation to make COBRA continuation coverage available to these M & A qualified beneficiaries.

(iv) The employees who continue in employment in connection with the asset sale (and their family members) and who were covered under a group health plan of S on the day before the sale are not M & A qualified beneficiaries because P is a successor employer to S in connection with the asset sale. Thus, no group health plan of P has any obligation to make COBRA continuation coverage available to these continuing employees with respect to the qualifying event that resulted from their losing coverage under S's plan in connection with the asset sale.

Example 7. (i) Selling Group S provides group health plan coverage to employees at each of its two operating divisions. S sells the assets of one of its divisions to Buying Group P1. Under the terms of the group health plan covering the employees at the division being sold, their coverage will end on the date of the sale. P1 hires all but one of those employees, gives them the same positions that they had with S before the sale, and provides them with coverage under a group health plan.

Reg. §54.4980B-9

(ii) Under these facts, a group health plan of S has the obligation to make COBRA continuation coverage available to M & A qualified beneficiaries with respect to the sale to P1. (If an M & A qualified beneficiary first became covered under P1's plan after electing COBRA continuation coverage under S's plan, then S's plan could terminate the COBRA continuation coverage once the M & A qualified beneficiary became covered under P1's plan, provided that the remaining conditions of Q & A-2 of §54.49890B-7 were satisfied.)

(iii) Several months after the sale to P1, S sells the assets of its remaining division to Buying Group P2 and S ceases to provide any group health plan to any employee on the date of that sale. Thus, under Q & A-1 of §54.4980B-7, S ceases to have an obligation to make COBRA continuation coverage available to any qualified beneficiary on the date of the sale to P2. P1 and P2 are unrelated organizations.

(iv) Even if it was foreseeable that S would sell its remaining division to an unrelated third party after the sale to P1, under these facts the cessation of S to provide any group health plan to any employee on the date of the sale to P2 is not in connection with the asset sale to P1. Thus, even after the date S ceases to provide any group health plan to any employee, no group health plan of P1. has any obligation to make COBRA continuation coverage available to M & A qualified beneficiaries with respect to the asset sale to P1 by S. If P2 is a successor employer under the rules of paragraph (c) of this Q & A-8 and maintains one or more group health plans after the sale, then a group health plan of P2 would have an obligation to make COBRA continuation coverage available to M & A qualified beneficiaries with respect to the asset sale to P2 by S (but in such a case employees of S before the sale who continued working for P2 after the sale would not be M & A qualified beneficiaries). However, even in such a case, no group health plan of P2 would have an obligation to make COBRA continuation coverage available to M & A qualified beneficiaries with respect to the asset sale to P1 by S. Thus, under these facts, after S has ceased to provide any group health plan to any employee, no plan has an obligation to make COBRA continuation coverage available to M & A qualified beneficiaries with respect to the asset sale to P1.

Example 8. (i) Selling Group S provides group health plan coverage to employees at each of its operating divisions. S sells substantially all of the assets of all of its divisions to Buying Group P. P hires most of S's employees on the date of the purchase of S's assets, retains those employees in the same positions that they had with S before the purchase, and continues the business operations of those divisions without substantial change or interruption. P provides these employees with coverage under a group health plan. S continues to employ a few employees for the principal purpose of winding up the affairs of S in preparation for liquidation. S continues to provide coverage under a group health plan to these few remaining employees for several weeks after the date of the sale and then ceases to provide any group health plan to any employee.

(ii) Under these facts, the cessation by S to provide any group health plan to any employee is in connection with the asset sale to P. Because of this, and because P continued the business operations associated with those assets without substantial change or interruption, P is a successor employer to S with respect to the asset sale. Thus, a group health plan of P has the obligation to make COBRA continuation coverage available to M & A qualified beneficiaries with respect to the sale beginning on the date that S ceases to provide any group health plan to any employee. (A group health plan of S retains this obligation for the several weeks after the date of the sale until S ceases to provide any group health plan to any employee.)

Q-9: Can the cessation of contributions by an employer to a multiemployer group health plan be a qualifying event?

A-9: The cessation of contributions by an employer to a multiemployer group health plan is not itself a qualifying event, even though the cessation of contributions may cause current employees (and their spouses and dependent children) to lose coverage under the multiemployer plan. An event coinciding with the employer's cessation of contributions (such as a reduction of hours of employment in the case of striking employees) will constitute a qualifying event if it otherwise satisfies the requirements of Q & A-1 of §54.4980B-4.

Q-10: If an employer stops contributing to a multiemployer group health plan, does the multiemployer plan have the obligation to make COBRA continuation coverage available to a qualified beneficiary who was receiving coverage under the multiemployer plan on the day before the cessation of contributions and who is, or whose qualifying event occurred in connection with, a covered employee whose last employment prior to the qualifying event was with the employer that has stopped contributing to the multiemployer plan?

A-10: (a) In general, yes. (See Q & A-3 of §54.4980B-2 for a definition of *multiemployer plan*.) If, however, the employer that stops contributing to the multiemployer plan makes group health plan coverage available to (or starts contributing to another multiemployer plan that is a group health plan with respect to) a class of the employer's employees formerly covered under the multiemployer plan, the plan maintained by the employer (or the other multiemployer plan), from that date forward, has the obligation to make COBRA continuation coverage available to any qualified beneficiary who was receiving coverage under the multiemployer plan on the day before the cessation of contributions and who is, or whose qualifying event occurred in connection with, a covered employee whose last employment prior to the qualifying event was with the employer.

(b) The rules of Q & A-9 of this section and this Q & A-10 are illustrated by the following examples; in each example, each group health plan is subject to COBRA:

Example 1. (i) Employer Z employs a class of employees covered by a collective bargaining agreement and participating in multiemployer group health plan M. As required by the collective bargaining agreement, Z has been making contributions to M. Z experiences financial difficulties and stops making contributions to M but continues to employ all of the employees covered by the collective bargaining agreement. Z's cessation of contributions to M causes those employees (and their spouses and dependent children) to lose coverage under M. Z does not make group health plan coverage available to any of the employees covered by the collective bargaining agreement.

(ii) After Z stops contributing to M, M continues to have the obligation to make COBRA continuation coverage available to any qualified beneficiary who experienced a qualifying event that preceded or coincided with the cessation of contributions to M and whose coverage under M on the day before the qualifying event was due to an employment affiliation with Z. The loss of coverage under M for those employees of Z who continue in employment (and the loss of coverage for their spouses and dependent children) does not constitute a qualifying event.

Example 2. (i) The facts are the same as in *Example 1* except that B, one of the employees covered under M before Z stops contributing to M, is transferred into management. Z maintains a group health plan for managers and B becomes eligible for coverage under the plan on the day of B's transfer.

(ii) Under these facts, Z does not make group health plan coverage available to a class of employees formerly covered under M after B becomes eligible under Z's group health plan for managers. Accordingly, M continues to have the obligation to make COBRA continuation coverage available to any qualified beneficiary who experienced a qualifying event that preceded or coincided with the cessation of contributions to M and whose coverage under M on the day before the qualifying event was due to an employment affiliation with Z.

Example 3. (i) Employer Y employs two classes of employees—skilled and unskilled laborers—covered by a collective bargaining agreement and participating in multiemployer group health plan M. As required by the collective bargaining agreement, Y has been making contributions to M. Y stops making contributions to M but continues to employ all the employees covered by the collective bargaining agreement. Y's cessation of contributions to M causes those employees (and their spouses and dependent children) to lose coverage under M. Y makes group health plan coverage available to the skilled laborers immediately after their coverage ceases under M, but Y does not make group health plan coverage available to any of the unskilled laborers.

(ii) Under these facts, because Y makes group health plan coverage available to a class of employees previously covered under M immediately after both classes of employees lose coverage under M, Y alone has the obligation to make COBRA continuation coverage available to any qualified beneficiary who experienced a qualifying event that preceded or coincided with the cessation of contributions to M and whose coverage under M on the day before the qualifying event was due to an employment affiliation with Y, regardless of whether the employment affiliation was as a skilled or unskilled laborer. However, the loss of coverage under M for those employees of Y who continue in employment (and the loss of coverage for their spouses and dependent children) does not constitute a qualifying event.

Example 4. (i) Employer X employs a class of employees covered by a collective bargaining agreement and participating in multiemployer group health plan M. As required by the collective bargaining agreement, X has been making contributions to M. X experiences financial difficulties and is forced into bankruptcy by its creditors. X continues to employ all of the employees covered by the collective bargaining agreement. X also continues to make contributions to M until the current collective bargaining agreement expires, on June 30, 2001, and then X stops making contributions to M. X's employees (and their spouses and dependent children) lose coverage under M effective July 1, 2001. X does not enter into another collective bargaining agreement covering the class of employees covered by the expired collective bargaining agreement. Effective September 1, 2001, X establishes a group health plan covering the class of employees formerly covered by the collective bargaining agreement. The group health plan also covers their spouses and dependent children.

(ii) Under these facts, M has the obligation to make COBRA continuation coverage available from July 1, 2001 until August 31, 2001, and the group health plan established by X has the obligation to make COBRA continuation coverage available from September 1, 2001 until the obligation ends (see Q & A-1 of §54.4980B-7) to any qualified beneficiary who experienced a qualifying event that preceded or coincided with the cessation of contributions to M and whose coverage under M on the day before the qualifying event was due to an employment affiliation with X. The loss of coverage under M for those employees of X who continue in employment (and the loss of coverage for their spouses and dependent children) does not constitute a qualifying event.

Example 5. (i) Employer W employs a class of employees covered by a collective bargaining agreement and participating in multiemployer group health plan M. As required by the collective bargaining agreement, W has been making contributions to M. The employees covered by the collective bargaining agreement vote to decertify their current employee representative effective January 1, 2002 and vote to certify a

new employee representative effective the same date. As a consequence, on January 1, 2002 they cease to be covered under M and commence to be covered under multiemployer group health plan N.

(ii) Effective January 1, 2002, N has the obligation to make COBRA continuation coverage available to any qualified beneficiary who experienced a qualifying event that preceded or coincided with the cessation of contributions to M and whose coverage under M on the day before the qualifying event was due to an employment affiliation with W. The loss of coverage under M for those employees of W who continue in employment (and the loss of coverage for their spouses and dependent children) does not constitute a qualifying event.

[Reg. § 54.4980B-9.]

☐ [*T.D.* 8928, 1-9-2001.]

[Reg. § 54.4980B-10]

§ 54.4980B-10. Interaction of FMLA and CO-BRA.—The following questions-and-answers address how the taking of leave under the Family and Medical Leave Act of 1993 (FMLA) (29 U.S.C. 2601-2619) affects the COBRA continuation coverage requirements:

Q-1: In what circumstances does a qualifying event occur if an employee does not return from leave taken under FMLA?

A-1: (a) The taking of leave under FMLA does not constitute a qualifying event. A qualifying event under Q & A-1 of § 54.4980B-4 occurs, however, if—

(1) An employee (or the spouse or a dependent child of the employee) is covered on the day before the first day of FMLA leave (or becomes covered during the FMLA leave) under a group health plan of the employee's employer;

(2) The employee does not return to employment with the employer at the end of the FMLA leave; and

(3) The employee (or the spouse or a dependent child of the employee) would, in the absence of COBRA continuation coverage, lose coverage under the group health plan before the end of the maximum coverage period.

(b) However, the satisfaction of the three conditions in paragraph (a) of this Q & A-1 does not constitute a qualifying event if the employer eliminates, on or before the last day of the employee's FMLA leave, coverage under a group health plan for the class of employees (while continuing to employ that class of employees) to which the employee would have belonged if the employee had not taken FMLA leave.

Q-2: If a qualifying event described in Q & A-1 of this section occurs, when does it occur, and how is the maximum coverage period measured?

A-2: A qualifying event described in Q & A-1 of this section occurs on the last day of FMLA leave. (The determination of when FMLA leave ends is not made under the rules of this section. See the FMLA regulations, 29 CFR Part 825 (§ § 825.100-825.800).) The maximum coverage period (see Q & A-4 of § 54.4980B-7) is measured from the date of the qualifying event (that is, the

last day of FMLA leave). If, however, coverage under the group health plan is lost at a later date and the plan provides for the extension of the required periods (see paragraph (b) of Q & A-4 of § 54.4980B-7), then the maximum coverage period is measured from the date when coverage is lost. The rules of this Q & A-2 are illustrated by the following examples:

Example 1. (i) Employee B is covered under the group health plan of Employer X on January 31, 2001. B takes FMLA leave beginning February 1, 2001. B's last day of FMLA leave is 12 weeks later, on April 25, 2001, and B does not return to work with X at the end of the FMLA leave. If B does not elect COBRA continuation coverage, B will not be covered under the group health plan of X as of April 26, 2001.

(ii) B experiences a qualifying event on April 25, 2001, and the maximum coverage period is measured from that date. (This is the case even if, for part or all of the FMLA leave, B fails to pay the employee portion of premiums for coverage under the group health plan of X and is not covered under X's plan. See Q & A-3 of this section.)

Example 2. (i) Employee C and C's spouse are covered under the group health plan of Employer Y on August 15, 2001. C takes FMLA leave beginning August 16, 2001. C informs Y less than 12 weeks later, on September 28, 2001, that C will not be returning to work. Under the FMLA regulations, 29 CFR Part 825 (§ § 825.100-825.800), C's last day of FMLA leave is September 28, 2001. C does not return to work with Y at the end of the FMLA leave. If C and C's spouse do not elect COBRA continuation coverage, they will not be covered under the group health plan of Y as of September 29, 2001.

(ii) C and C's spouse experience a qualifying event on September 28, 2001, and the maximum coverage period (generally 18 months) is measured from that date. (This is the case even if, for part or all of the FMLA leave, C fails to pay the employee portion of premiums for coverage under the group health plan of Y and C or C's spouse is not covered under Y's plan. See Q & A-3 of this section.)

Q-3: If an employee fails to pay the employee portion of premiums for coverage under a group health plan during FMLA leave or declines coverage under a group health plan during FMLA leave, does this affect the determination of whether or when the employee has experienced a qualifying event?

A-3: No. Any lapse of coverage under a group health plan during FMLA leave is irrelevant in determining whether a set of circumstances constitutes a qualifying event under Q & A-1 of this section or when such a qualifying event occurs under Q & A-2 of this section.

Q-4: Is the application of the rules in Q & A-1 through Q & A-3 of this section affected by a requirement of state or local law to provide a period of coverage longer than that required under FMLA?

A-4: No. Any state or local law that requires coverage under a group health plan to be maintained during a leave of absence for a period

longer than that required under FMLA (for example, for 16 weeks of leave rather than for the 12 weeks required under FMLA) is disregarded for purposes of determining when a qualifying event occurs under Q & A-1 through Q & A-3 of this section.

Q-5: May COBRA continuation coverage be conditioned upon reimbursement of the premiums paid by the employer for coverage under a group health plan during FMLA leave?

A-5: No. The U.S. Department of Labor has published rules describing the circumstances in which an employer may recover premiums it pays to maintain coverage, including family coverage, under a group health plan during FMLA leave from an employee who fails to return from leave. See 29 CFR 825.213. Even if recovery of premiums is permitted under 29 CFR 825.213, the right to COBRA continuation coverage cannot be conditioned upon the employee's reimbursement of the employer for premiums the employer paid to maintain coverage under a group health plan during FMLA leave.

[Reg. § 54.4980B-10.]

☐ [*T.D.* 8928, 1-9-2001.]

[Reg. § 54.4980D-1]

§ 54.4980D-1. Requirement of return and time for filing of the excise tax under section 4980D.

Q-1: If a person is liable for the excise tax under section 4980D, what form must the person file and what is the due date for the filing and payment of the excise tax?

A-1: (a) *In general.* See § § 54.6011-2 and 54.6151-1.

(b) *Due date for filing of return by employers.* See § 54.6071-1(b)(1).

(c) *Due date for filing of return by multiemployer plans or multiple employer health plans.* See § 54.6071-1(b)(2).

(d) *Effective/applicability date.* In the case of an employer or other person mentioned in paragraph (b) of this Q & A-1, the rules in this Q & A-1 are effective for taxable years beginning on or after January 1, 2010. In the case of a plan mentioned in paragraph (c) of this Q & A-1, the rules in this Q & A-1 are effective for plan years beginning on or after January 1, 2010. [Reg. § 54.4980D-1.]

☐ [*T.D.* 9457, 9-4-2009.]

[Reg. § 54.4980E-1]

§ 54.4980E-1. Requirement of return and time for filing of the excise tax under section 4980E.

Q-1: If a person is liable for the excise tax under section 4980E, what form must the person file and what is the due date for the filing and payment of the excise tax?

A-1: (a) *In general.* See § § 54.6011-2, 54.6151-1 and 54.6071-1(c).

(b) *Effective/applicability date.* The rules in this Q & A-1 are effective for plan years beginning on or after January 1, 2010. [Reg. § 54.4980E-1.]

☐ [*T.D.* 9457, 9-4-2009.]

[Reg. § 54.4980F-1]

§ 54.4980F-1. Notice requirements for certain pension plan amendments significantly reducing the rate of future benefit accrual.—The following questions and answers concern the notification requirements imposed by 4980F of the Internal Revenue Code and section 204(h) of ERISA relating to a plan amendment of an applicable pension plan that significantly reduces the rate of future benefit accrual or that eliminates or significantly reduces an early retirement benefit or retirement-type subsidy.

List of Questions

Q-1. What are the notice requirements of section 4980F(e) of the Internal Revenue Code and section 204(h) of ERISA?

Q-2. What are the differences between section 4980F and section 204(h)?

Q-3. What is an "applicable pension plan" to which section 4980F and section 204(h) apply?

Q-4. What is "section 204(h) notice" and what is a "section 204(h) amendment"?

Q-5. For which amendments is section 204(h) notice required?

Q-6. What is an amendment that reduces the rate of future benefit accrual or reduces an early retirement benefit or retirement-type subsidy for purposes of determining whether section 204(h) notice is required?

Q-7. What plan provisions are taken into account in determining whether an amendment is a section 204(h) amendment?

Q-8. What is the basic principle used in determining whether a reduction in the rate of future benefit accrual or a reduction in an early retirement benefit or retirement-type subsidy is significant for purposes of section 4980F and section 204(h)?

Q-9. When must section 204(h) notice be provided?

Q-10. To whom must section 204(h) notice be provided?

Q-11. What information is required to be provided in a section 204(h) notice?

Q-12. What special rules apply if participants can choose between the old and new benefit formulas?

Q-13. How may section 204(h) notice be provided?

Q-14. What are the consequences if a plan administrator fails to provide section 204(h) notice?

Q-15. What are some of the rules that apply with respect to the excise tax under section 4980F?

Q-16. How do section 4980F and section 204(h) apply when a business is sold?

Reg. § 54.4980F-1

Q-17. How are amendments to cease accruals and terminate a plan treated under section 4980F and section 204(h)?

Q-18. What are the effective dates of section 4980F, section 204(h), as amended by EGTRRA, and these regulations?

Questions and Answers

Q-1. What are the notice requirements of section 4980F(e) of the Internal Revenue Code and section 204(h) of ERISA?

A-1. (a) *Requirements of Internal Revenue Code section 4980F(e) and ERISA section 204(h)*. Section 4980F of the Internal Revenue Code (section 4980F) and section 204(h) of the Employee Retirement Income Security Act of 1974, as amended (ERISA), 29 U.S.C. 1054(h) (section 204(h)) each generally requires notice of an amendment to an applicable pension plan that either provides for a significant reduction in the rate of future benefit accrual or that eliminates or significantly reduces an early retirement benefit or retirement-type subsidy. The notice is required to be provided to plan participants and alternate payees who are applicable individuals (as defined in Q&A-10 of this section), to certain employee organizations, and to contributing employers under a multiemployer plan (as described in Q&A-10(a) of this section). The plan administrator must generally provide the notice before the effective date of the plan amendment. Q&A-9 of this section sets forth the time frames for providing notice, Q&A-11 of this section sets forth the content requirements for the notice, and Q&A-12 of this section contains special rules for cases in which participants can choose between the old and new benefit formulas.

(b) *Other notice requirements*. Other provisions of law may require that certain parties be notified of a plan amendment. See, for example, sections 102 and 104 of ERISA, and the regulations thereunder, for requirements relating to summary plan descriptions and summaries of material modifications.

Q-2. What are the differences between section 4980F and section 204(h)?

A-2. The notice requirements of section 4980F generally are parallel to the notice requirements of section 204(h), as amended by the Economic Growth and Tax Relief Reconciliation Act of 2001, Public Law 107-16 (115 Stat. 38) (2001) (EGTRRA). However, the consequences of the failure to satisfy the requirements of the two provisions differ: section 4980F imposes an excise tax on a failure to satisfy the notice requirements, while section 204(h)(6), as amended by EGTRRA, contains a special rule with respect to an egregious failure to satisfy the notice requirements. See Q&A-14 and Q&A-15 of this section. Except to the extent specifically indicated, these regulations apply both to section 4980F and to section 204(h).

Q-3. What is an "applicable pension plan" to which section 4980F and section 204(h) apply?

A-3. (a) *In general*. Section 4980F and section 204(h) apply to an applicable pension plan. For purposes of section 4980F, an *applicable pension plan* means a defined benefit plan qualifying under section 401(a) or 403(a) of the Internal Revenue Code, or an individual account plan that is subject to the funding standards of section 412 of the Internal Revenue Code. For purposes of section 204(h), an *applicable pension plan* means a defined benefit plan that is subject to part 2 of subtitle B of title I of ERISA, or an individual account plan that is subject to such part 2 and to the funding standards of section 412 of the Internal Revenue Code. Accordingly, individual account plans that are not subject to the funding standards of section 412 of the Internal Revenue Code, such as profit-sharing and stock bonus plans and contracts under section 403(b) of the Internal Revenue Code, are not applicable pension plans to which section 4980F or section 204(h) apply. Similarly, a defined benefit plan that neither qualifies under section 401(a) or 403(a) of the Internal Revenue Code nor is subject to part 2 of subtitle B of title I of ERISA is not an applicable pension plan. Further, neither a governmental plan (within the meaning of section 414(d) of the Internal Revenue Code), nor a church plan (within the meaning of section 414(e) of the Internal Revenue Code) with respect to which no election has been made under section 410(d) of the Internal Revenue Code is an applicable pension plan.

(b) *Section 204(h) notice not required for small plans covering no employees*. Section 204(h) notice is not required for a plan under which no employees are participants covered under the plan, as described in § 2510.3-3(b) of the Department of Labor regulations, and which has fewer than 100 participants.

Q-4. What is "section 204(h) notice" and what is a "section 204(h) amendment"?

A-4. (a) *Section 204(h) notice* is notice that complies with section 4980F(e) of the Internal Revenue Code, section 204(h)(1) of ERISA, and this section.

(b) A *section 204(h) amendment* is an amendment for which section 204(h) notice is required under this section.

Q-5. For which amendments is section 204(h) notice required?

A-5. (a) *Significant reduction in the rate of future benefit accrual*. Section 204(h) notice is required for an amendment to an applicable pension plan that provides for a significant reduction in the rate of future benefit accrual.

(b) *Early retirement benefits and retirement- type subsidies*. Section 204(h) notice is also required for an amendment to an applicable pension plan that provides for the significant reduction of an early retirement benefit or retirement-type subsidy. For purposes of this section, *early retirement benefit* and *retirement-type subsidy* mean early retirement benefits and retirement-type subsidies within the meaning of section 411(d)(6)(B)(i).

(c) *Elimination or cessation of benefits*. For purposes of this section, the terms *reduce* or *reduction* include eliminate or cease or elimination or cessation.

Reg. §54.4980F-1

(d) *Delegation of authority to Commissioner*. The Commissioner may provide in revenue rulings, notices, or other guidance published in the Internal Revenue Bulletin (see § 601.601(d)(2) of this chapter) that section 204(h) notice need not be provided for plan amendments otherwise described in paragraph (a) or (b) of this Q&A-5 that the Commissioner determines to be necessary or appropriate, as a result of changes in the law, to maintain compliance with the requirements of the Internal Revenue Code (including requirements for tax qualification), ERISA, or other applicable federal law.

Q-6. What is an amendment that reduces the rate of future benefit accrual or reduces an early retirement benefit or retirement-type subsidy for purposes of determining whether section 204(h) notice is required?

A-6. (a) *In general*. For purposes of determining whether section 204(h) notice is required, an amendment reduces the rate of future benefit accrual or reduces an early retirement benefit or retirement-type subsidy only as provided in paragraph (b) or (c) of this Q&A-6.

(b) *Reduction in rate of future benefit accrual*—(1) *Defined benefit plans*. For purposes of section 4980F and section 204(h), an amendment to a defined benefit plan reduces the rate of future benefit accrual only if it is reasonably expected that the amendment will reduce the amount of the future annual benefit commencing at normal retirement age (or at actual retirement age, if later) for benefits accuring for a year. For this purpose, the annual benefit commencing at normal retirement age is the benefit payable in the form in which the terms of the plan express the accrued benefit (or, in the case of a plan in which the accrued benefit is not expressed in the form of an annual benefit commencing at normal retirement age, the benefit payable in the form of a single life annuity commencing at normal retirement age that is the actuarial equivalent of the accrued benefit expressed under the terms of the plan, as determined in accordance with section 411(c)(3) of the Internal Revenue Code).

(2) *Individual account plans*. For purposes of section 4980F and section 204(h), an amendment to an individual account plan reduces the rate of future benefit accrual only if it is reasonably expected that the amendment will reduce the amount of contributions or forfeitures allocated for any future year. Changes in the investments or investment options under an individual account plan are not taken into account for this purpose.

(3) *Determination of rate of future benefit accrual*. The rate of future benefit accrual for purposes of this paragraph (b) is determined without regard to optional forms of benefit within the meaning of § 1.411(d)-4, Q&A-1(b) of this chapter (other than the annual benefit described in paragraph (b)(1) of this Q&A-6). The rate of future benefit accrual is also determined without regard to ancillary benefits and other rights or features as defined in § 1.401(a)(4)-4(e) of this chapter.

(c) *Reduction of early retirement benefits or retirement-type subsidies*. For purposes of section 4980F and section 204(h), an amendment reduces an early retirement benefit or retirement-type subsidy only if it is reasonably expected that the amendment will eliminate or reduce an early retirement benefit or retirement-type subsidy.

Q-7. What plan provisions are taken into account in determining whether an amendment is a section 204(h) amendment?

A-7. (a) *Plan provisions taken into account*— (1) *In general*. All plan provisions that may affect the rate of future benefit accrual, early retirement benefits, or retirement-type subsidies of participants or alternate payees must be taken into account in determining whether an amendment is a section 204(h) amendment. For example, plan provisions that may affect the rate of future benefit accrual include the dollar amount or percentage of compensation on which benefit accruals are based; the definition of service or compensation taken into account in determining an employee's benefit accrual; the method of determining average compensation for calculating benefit accruals; the definition of normal retirement age in a defined benefit plan; the exclusion of current participants from future participation; benefit offset provisions; minimum benefit provisions; the formula for determining the amount of contributions and forfeitures allocated to participants' accounts in an individual account plan; in the case of a plan using permitted disparity under section 401(I) of the Internal Revenue Code, the amount of disparity between the excess benefit percentage or excess contribution percentage and the base benefit percentage or base contribution percentage (all as defined in section 401(I) of the Internal Revenue Code); and the actuarial assumptions used to determine contributions under a target benefit plan (as defined in § 1.401(a)(4)-8(b)(3)(i) of this chapter). Plan provisions that may affect early retirement benefits or retirement-type subsidies include the right to receive payment of benefits after severance from employment and before normal retirement age and actuarial factors used in determining optional forms for distribution of retirement benefits.

(2) *Provisions incorporated by reference in plan*. If all or a part of a plan's rate of future benefit accrual, or an early retirement benefit or retirement-type subsidy provided under the plan, depends on provisions in another document that are referenced in the plan document, a change in the provisions of the other document is an amendment of the plan.

(b) *Plan provisions not taken into account*—(1) *In general*. Plan provisions that do not affect the rate of future benefit accrual of participants or alternate payees are not taken into account in determining whether there has been a reduction in the rate of future benefit accrual.

(2) *Interaction with section 411(d)(6)*. Any benefit that is not a section 411(d)(6) protected benefit as described in § § 1.411(d)-3(g)(14) and 1.411(d)-4, Q&A-1(d) of this chapter, or that is a

Reg. § 54.4980F-1

section 411(d)(6) protected benefit that may be eliminated or reduced as permitted under §1.411(d)-3(c), (d), or (f), or under §1.411(d)-4, Q&A-2(a)(2), (a)(3), (b)(1), or (b)(2)(ii) through (b)(2)(xi) of this chapter, is not taken into account in determining whether an amendment is a section 204(h) amendment. Thus, for example, provisions relating to the right to make after-tax deferrals are not taken into account.

(c) *Examples.* The following examples illustrate the rules in this Q&A-7:

Example 1. (i) *Facts.* A defined benefit plan provides a normal retirement benefit equal to 50% of highest 5-year average pay multiplied by a fraction (not in excess of one), the numerator of which equals the number of years of participation in the plan and the denominator of which is 20. A plan amendment is adopted that changes the numerator or denominator of that fraction.

(ii) *Conclusion.* The plan amendment must be taken into account in determining whether there has been a reduction in the rate of future benefit accrual.

Example 2. (i) *Facts.* Plan C is a multiemployer defined benefit plan subject to several collective bargaining agreements. The specific benefit formula under Plan C that applies to an employee depends on the hourly rate of contribution of the employee's employer, which is set forth in the provisions of the collective bargaining agreements that are referenced in the Plan C document. Collective Bargaining Agreement A between Employer B and the union representing employees of Employer B is renegotiated to provide that the hourly contribution rate for an employee of B who is subject to the Collective Bargaining Agreement A will decrease. That decrease will result in a decrease in the rate of future benefit accrual for employees of B.

(ii) *Conclusion.* Under paragraph (a)(2) of this Q&A-7, the change to Collective Bargaining Agreement A is a plan amendment that is a section 204(h) amendment if the reduction in the rate of future benefit accrual is significant.

Q-8. What is the basic principle used in determining whether a reduction in the rate of future benefit accrual or a reduction in an early retirement benefit or retirement-type subsidy is significant for purposes of section 4980F and section 204(h)?

A-8. (a) *General rule.* Whether an amendment reducing the rate of future benefit accrual or eliminating or reducing an early retirement benefit or retirement-type subsidy provides for a reduction that is significant for purposes of section 4980F (and section 204(h) of ERISA) is determined based on reasonable expectations taking into account the relevant facts and circumstances at the time the amendment is adopted, or, if earlier, at the effective date of the amendment.

(b) *Application for determining significant reduction in the rate of future benefit accrual.* For a defined benefit plan, the determination of whether an amendment provides for a significant reduction in the rate of future benefit accrual is made by comparing the amount of the annual benefit commencing at normal retirement age (or at actual retirement age, if later), as determined under Q&A-6(b)(1) of this section, under the terms of the plan as amended with the amount of the annual benefit commencing at normal retirement age (or at actual retirement age, if later), as determined under Q&A-6(b)(1) of this section, under the terms of the plan prior to amendment. For an individual account plan, the determination of whether an amendment provides for a significant reduction in the rate of future benefit accrual is made in accordance with Q&A-6(b)(2) of this section by comparing the amounts to be allocated in the future to participants' accounts under the terms of the plan as amended with the amounts to be allocated in the future to participants' accounts under the terms of the plan prior to amendment. An amendment to convert a money purchase pension plan to a profit-sharing or other individual account plan that is not subject to section 412 of the Internal Revenue Code is, in all cases, deemed to be an amendment that provides for a significant reduction in the rate of future benefit accrual.

(c) *Application to certain amendments reducing early retirement benefits or retirement-type subsidies.* Section 204(h) notice is not required for an amendment that reduces an early retirement benefit or retirement-type subsidy if the amendment is permitted under the third sentence of section 411(d)(6)(B) of the Internal Revenue Code and paragraphs (c), (d), and (f) of §1.411(d)-3 of this chapter (relating to the elimination or reduction of benefits or subsidies which create significant burdens or complexities for the plan and plan participants unless the amendment adversely affects the rights of any participant in a more than de minimis manner). However, in determining whether an amendment reducing a retirement-type subsidy constitutes a significant reduction because it reduces a retirement-type subsidy as permitted under §1.411(d)-3(e)(6) of this chapter, the amendment is treated in the same manner as an amendment that limits the retirement-type subsidy to benefits that accrue before the applicable amendment date (as defined at §1.411(d)-3(g)(4) of this chapter) with respect to each participant or alternate payee to whom the reduction is reasonably expected to apply.

(d) *Plan amendments reflecting a change in statutorily mandated minimum present value rules.* If a defined benefit plan offers a distribution to which the minimum present value rules of section 417(e)(3) apply (other than a payment to which section 411(a)(13)(A) applies) and the plan is amended to reflect the changes to the applicable interest rate and applicable mortality table in section 417(e)(3) made by the Pension Protection Act of 2006, Public Law 109-780 (120 Stat. 780) (PPA '06) (and no change is made in the dates on which the payment will be made), no section 204(h) notice is required to be provided.

(e) *Examples.* The following examples illustrate the rules in this Q&A-8:

Example 1. (i) *Facts.* Pension Plan A is a defined benefit plan that provides a rate of benefit ac-

crual of 1% of highest-5 years pay multiplied by years of service, payable annually for life commencing at normal retirement age (or at actual retirement age, if later). An amendment to Plan A is adopted on August 1, 2009, effective January 1, 2010, to provide that any participant who separates from service after December 31, 2009, and before January 1, 2015, will have the same number of years of service he or she would have had if his or her service continued to December 31, 2014.

(ii) *Conclusion.* In this example, the effective date of the plan amendment is January 1, 2010. While the amendment will result in a reduction in the annual rate of future benefit accrual from 2011 through 2014 (because, under the amendment, benefits based upon an additional 5 years of service accrue on January 1, 2010, and no additional service is credited after January 1, 2010 until January 1, 2015), the amendment does not result in a reduction that is significant because the amount of the annual benefit commencing at normal retirement age (or at actual retirement age, if later) under the terms of the plan as amended is not under any conditions less than the amount of the annual benefit commencing at normal retirement age (or at actual retirement age, if later) to which any participant would have been entitled under the terms of the plan had the amendment not been made.

Example 2. (i) *Facts.* The facts are the same as in *Example 1,* except that the 2009 amendment does not alter the plan provisions relating to a participant's number of years of service, but instead amends the plan's provisions relating to early retirement benefits. Before the amendment, the plan provides for distributions before normal retirement age to be actuarially reduced, but, if a participant retires after attainment of age 55 and completion of 10 years of service, the applicable early retirement reduction factor is 3% per year for the years between the ages 65 and 62 and 6% per year for the ages from 62 to 55. The amendment changes these provisions so that an actuarial reduction applies in all cases, but, in accordance with section 411(d)(6)(B), provides that no participant's early retirement benefit will be less than the amount provided under the plan as in effect on December 31, 2009 with respect to service before January 1, 2010. For participant X, the reduction is significant.

(ii) *Conclusion.* The amendment will result in a reduction in a retirement-type subsidy provided under Plan A (i.e., Plan A's early retirement subsidy). Section 204(h) notice must be provided to participant X and any other participant for whom the reduction is significant and the notice must be provided at least 45 days before January 1, 2010 (or by such other date as may apply under Q&A-9 of this section).

Example 3. (i) *Facts.* The facts are the same as in *Example 2,* except that, for participant X, the change does not go into effect for any annuity commencement date before January 1, 2011. Participant X continues employment through January 1, 2011.

(ii) *Conclusion.* The conclusion is the same as in *Example 2.* Taking into account the rule in the second sentence of Q&A-8(c) of this section, the reduction that occurs for participant X on January 1, 2011, is treated as the same reduction that occurs under *Example 2.* Accordingly, assuming that the reduction is significant, section 204(h) notice must be provided to participant X at least 45 days before the January 1, 2010 effective date of the amendment (or by such other date as may apply under Q&A-9 of this section).

Q-9. When must section 204(h) notice be provided?

A-9. (a) *45-day general rule.* Except as otherwise provided in this Q&A-9, section 204(h) notice must be provided at least 45 days before the effective date of any section 204(h) amendment. See paragraph (e) of this Q&A-9 for special rules for amendments permitting participant choice.

(b) *15-day rule for small plans.* Except for amendments described in paragraphs (d)(2) and (g) of this Q&A-9, section 204(h) notice must be provided at least 15 days before the effective date of any section 204(h) amendment in the case of a small plan. For purposes of this section, a small plan is a plan that the plan administrator reasonably expects to have, on the effective date of the section 204(h) amendment, fewer than 100 participants who have an accrued benefit under the plan.

(c) *15-day rule for multiemployer plans.* Except for amendments described in paragraphs (d)(2) and (g) of this Q&A-9, section 204(h) notice must be provided at least 15 days before the effective date of any section 204(h) amendment in the case of a multiemployer plan. For purposes of this section, a multiemployer plan means a multiemployer plan as defined in section 414(f) of the Internal Revenue Code.

(d) *Special timing rule for business transactions*— (1) *15-day rule for section 204(h) amendment in connection with an acquisition or disposition.* Except for amendments described in paragraphs (d)(2) and (g) of this Q&A-9, if a section 204(h) amendment is adopted in connection with an acquisition or disposition, section 204(h) notice must be provided at least 15 days before the effective date of the section 204(h) amendment.

(2) *Later notice permitted for a section 204(h) amendment significantly reducing early retirement benefit or retirement-type subsidies in connection with certain plan transfers, mergers, or consolidations.* If a section 204(h) amendment is adopted with respect to liabilities that are transferred to another plan in connection with a transfer, merger, or consolidation of assets or liabilities as described in section 414(l) of the Internal Revenue Code and §1.414(l)-1 of this chapter, the amendment is adopted in connection with an acquisition or disposition, and the amendment significantly reduces an early retirement benefit or retirement-type subsidy, but does not significantly reduce the rate of future benefit accrual, then section 204(h) notice must be provided no later than 30 days after the effective date of the section 204(h) amendment.

Reg. §54.4980F-1

(3) *Definition of acquisition or disposition.* For purposes of this paragraph (d), see § 1.410(b)-2(f) of this chapter for the definition of acquisition or disposition.

(e) *Timing rule for amendments permitting participant choice.* In general, section 204(h) notice of a section 204(h) amendment that provides applicable individuals with a choice between the old and the new benefit formulas (as described in Q&A-12 of this section) must be provided in accordance with the time period applicable under paragraphs (a) through (d) of this Q&A-9. See Q&A-12 of this section for additional guidance regarding section 204(h) notice in connection with participant choice.

(f) *Special timing rule for certain plans maintained by commercial airlines.* See section 402 of PPA '06 for a special rule that applies to certain plans maintained by an employer that is a commercial passenger airline or the principal business of which is providing catering services to a commercial passenger airline. Under this special rule, section 204(h) notice must be provided at least 15 days before the effective date of the amendment.

(g) *Special timing rules relating to certain section 204(h) amendments that reduce section 411(d)(6) protected benefits*—(1) *Plan amendments permitted to reduce prior accruals.* This paragraph (g) generally provides special rules with respect to a plan amendment that would not violate section 411(d)(6) even if the amendment were to reduce section 411(d)(6) protected benefits, which are limited to accrued benefits that are attributable to service before the applicable amendment date. For example, this paragraph (g) applies to amendments that are permitted to be effective retroactively under section 412(d)(2) of the Code (section 412(c)(8) for plan years beginning before January 1, 2008), section 418D of the Code, section 418E of the Code, section 4281 of ERISA, or section 1107 of PPA '06. See, generally, § 1.411(d)-3(a)(1).

(2) *General timing rule for amendments to which this paragraph (g) applies.* For an amendment to which this paragraph (g) applies, the amendment is effective on the first date on which the plan is operated as if the amendment were in effect. Thus, except as otherwise provided in this paragraph (g), a section 204(h) notice for an amendment to which paragraph (a) of this section applies that is adopted after the effective date of the amendment must be provided, with respect to any applicable individual, at least 45 days before (or such other date as may apply under paragraph (b), (c), (d), or (f) of this Q&A-9) the date the amendment is put into operational effect.

(3) *Special rules for section 204(h) notices provided in connection with other disclosure requirements*—(i) *In general.* Notwithstanding the requirements in this Q&A-9 and Q&A-11 of this section, if a plan provides one of the notices in paragraph (g)(3)(ii) of this Q&A-9, in accordance with the applicable timing and content rules for such notice, the plan is treated as timely providing a section 204(h)

notice with respect to a section 204(h) amendment.

(ii) *Notice requirements.* The notices in this paragraph (g)(3)(ii) are—

(A) A notice required under any revenue ruling, notice, or other guidance published under the authority of the Commissioner in the Internal Revenue Bulletin to affected parties in connection with a retroactive plan amendment described in section 412(d)(2) (section 412(c)(8) for plan years beginning before January 1, 2008);

(B) A notice required under section 101(j) of ERISA if an amendment is adopted to comply with the benefit limitation requirements of section 206(g) of ERISA (section 436 of the Code);

(C) A notice required under section 432(b)(3)(D) of the Code for an amendment adopted to comply with the benefit restrictions under section 432(f)(2);

(D) A notice required under section 418D, or section 4244A(b) of ERISA, for an amendment that reduces or eliminates accrued benefits attributable to employer contributions with respect to a multiemployer plan in reorganization;

(E) A notice required under section 418E, or section 4245(e) of ERISA, relating to the effects of the insolvency status for a multiemployer plan; and

(F) A notice required under section 4281 of ERISA for an amendment of a multiemployer plan reducing benefits pursuant to section 4281(c) of ERISA.

(4) *Delegation of authority to Commissioner.* The Commissioner may provide special rules under section 4980F, in revenue rulings, notices, or other guidance published in the Internal Revenue Bulletin (see § 601.601(d)(2)(ii)(b) of this chapter), that the Commissioner determines to be necessary or appropriate with respect to a section 204(h) amendment—

(A) That applies to benefits accrued before the applicable amendment date but that does not violate section 411(d)(6); or

(B) For which there is a required notice relating to a reduction in benefits and such notice has timing and content requirements similar to a section 204(h) notice with respect to a significant reduction in the rate of future benefit accruals.

Q-10. To whom must section 204(h) notice be provided?

A-10. (a) *In general.* Section 204(h) notice must be provided to each applicable individual, to each employee organization representing participants who are applicable individuals, and, for plan years beginning after December 31, 2007, to each employer that has an obligation to contribute (within the meaning of section 4212(a) of ERISA) to a multiemployer plan. A special rule is provided in paragraph (d) of this Q&A-10.

(b) *Applicable individual.* Applicable individual means each participant in the plan, and any alternate payee, whose rate of future benefit accrual under the plan is reasonably expected to be significantly reduced, or for whom an early retirement benefit or retirement-type subsidy under the plan may reasonably be expected to be

significantly reduced, by the section 204(h) amendment. The determination is made with respect to individuals who are reasonably expected to be participants or alternate payees in the plan at the effective date of the section 204(h) amendment.

(c) *Alternate payee.* Alternate payee means a beneficiary who is an alternate payee (within the meaning of section 414(p)(8) of the Internal Revenue Code) under an applicable qualified domestic relations order (within the meaning of section 414(p)(1)(A) of the Internal Revenue Code).

(d) *Designees.* Section 204(h) notice may be provided to a person designated in writing by an applicable individual or by an employee organization representing participants who are applicable individuals, instead of being provided to that applicable individual or employee organization. Any designation of a representative made through an electronic method that satisfies standards similar to those of Q&A-13(c)(1) of this section satisfies the requirement that a designation be in writing.

(e) *Facts and circumstances test.* Whether a participant or alternate payee is an applicable individual is determined on a typical business day that is reasonably proximate to the time the section 204(h) notice is provided (or at the latest date for providing section 204(h) notice, if earlier), based on all relevant facts and circumstances.

(f) *Examples.* The following examples illustrate the rules in this Q&A-10:

Example 1. (i) *Facts.* A defined benefit plan requires an individual to complete 1 year of service to become a participant who can accrue benefits, and participants cease to accrue benefits under the plan at severance from employment with the employer. There are no alternate payees and employees are not represented by an employee organization. On November 18, 2004, the plan is amended effective as of January 1, 2005 to reduce significantly the rate of future benefit accrual. Section 204(h) notice is provided on November 1, 2004.

(ii) *Conclusion.* Section 204(h) notice is only required to be provided to individuals who, based on the facts and circumstances on November 1, 2004, are reasonably expected to have completed at least 1 year of service and to be employed by the employer on January 1, 2005.

Example 2. (i) *Facts.* The facts are the same as in Example 1, except that the sole effect of the plan amendment is to alter the pre-amendment plan provisions under which benefits payable to an employee who retires after 20 or more years of service are unreduced for commencement before normal retirement age. The amendment requires 30 or more years of service in order for benefits commencing before normal retirement age to be unreduced, but the amendment only applies for future benefit accruals.

(ii) *Conclusion.* Section 204(h) notice is only required to be provided to individuals who, on January 1, 2005, have completed at least 1 year of service but less than 30 years of service, are employed by the employer, have not attained normal retirement age, and will have completed 20 or more years of service before normal retirement age if their employment continues to normal retirement age.

Example 3. (i) *Facts.* A plan is amended to reduce significantly the rate of future benefit accrual for all current employees who are participants. Based on the facts and circumstances, it is reasonable to expect that the amendment will not reduce the rate of future benefit accrual of former employees who are currently receiving benefits or of former employees who are entitled to deferred vested benefits.

(ii) *Conclusion.* The plan administrator is not required to provide section 204(h) notice to any former employees.

Example 4. (i) *Facts.* The facts are the same as in Example 3, except that the plan covers two groups of alternate payees. The alternate payees in the first group are entitled to a certain percentage or portion of the former spouse's accrued benefit and, for this purpose, the accrued benefit is determined at the time the former spouse begins receiving retirement benefits under the plan. The alternate payees in the second group are entitled to a certain percentage or portion of the former spouse's accrued benefit and, for this purpose, the accrued benefit was determined at the time the qualified domestic relations order was issued by the court.

(ii) *Conclusion.* It is reasonable to expect that the benefits to be received by the second group of alternate payees will not be affected by any reduction in a former spouse's rate of future benefit accrual. Accordingly, the plan administrator is not required to provide section 204(h) notice to the alternate payees in the second group.

Example 5. (i) *Facts.* A plan covers hourly employees and salaried employees. The plan provides the same rate of benefit accrual for both groups. The employer amends the plan to reduce significantly the rate of future benefit accrual of the salaried employees only. At that time, it is reasonable to expect that only a small percentage of hourly employees will become salaried in the future.

(ii) *Conclusion.* The plan administrator is not required to provide section 204(h) notice to the participants who are currently hourly employees.

Example 6. (i) *Facts.* A plan covers employees in Division M and employees in Division N. The plan provides the same rate of benefit accrual for both groups. The employer amends the plan to reduce significantly the rate of future benefit accrual of employees in Division M. At that time, it is reasonable to expect that in the future only a small percentage of employees in Division N will be transferred to Division M.

(ii) *Conclusion.* The plan administrator is not required to provide section 204(h) notice to the participants who are employees in Division N.

Reg. §54.4980F-1

Example 7. (i) *Facts.* The facts are the same facts as in *Example 6,* except that at the time the amendment is adopted, it is expected that thereafter Division N will be merged into Division M in connection with a corporate reorganization (and the employees in Division N will become subject to the plan's amended benefit formula applicable to the employees in Division M).

(ii) *Conclusion.* In this case, the plan administrator must provide section 204(h) notice to the participants who are employees in Division M and to the participants who are employees in Division N.

Example 8. (i) *Facts.* A plan is amended to reduce significantly the rate of future benefit accrual for all current employees who are participants. The plan amendment will be effective on January 1, 2004. The plan will provide the notice to applicable individuals on October 31, 2003. In determining which current employees are applicable individuals, the plan administrator determines that October 1, 2003, is a typical business day that is reasonably proximate to the time the section 204(h) notice is provided.

(ii) *Conclusion.* In this case, October 1, 2003 is a typical business day that satisfies the requirements of Q&A-10(e) of this section.

Q-11. What information is required to be provided in a section 204(h) notice?

A-11. (a) *Explanation of notice requirements*— (1) *In general.* Section 204(h) notice must include sufficient information to allow applicable individuals to understand the effect of the plan amendment. In order to satisfy this rule, a plan administrator providing section 204(h) notice must generally satisfy paragraphs (a)(2), (a)(3), (a)(4), (a)(5), and (a)(6) of this Q&A-11. See paragraph (g)(3) of Q&A-9 of this section for special rules relating to section 204(h) notices provided in connection with certain other written notices. See also paragraph (g)(4) of Q&A-9 of this section for a delegation of authority to the Commissioner to provide special rules.

(2) *Information in section 204(h) notice.* The information in a section 204(h) notice must be written in a manner calculated to be understood by the average plan participant and to apprise the applicable individual of the significance of the notice.

(3) *Required narrative description of amendment*— (i) *Reduction in rate of future benefit accrual.* In the case of an amendment reducing the rate of future benefit accrual, the notice must include a description of the benefit or allocation formula prior to the amendment, a description of the benefit or allocation formula under the plan as amended, and the effective date of the amendment.

(ii) *Reduction in early retirement benefit or retirement-type subsidy.* In the case of an amendment that reduces an early retirement benefit or retirement-type subsidy (other than as a result of an amendment reducing the rate of future benefit accrual), the notice must describe how the early retirement benefit or retirement-type subsidy is calculated from the accrued benefit before the

amendment, how the early retirement benefit or retirement-type subsidy is calculated from the accrued benefit after the amendment, and the effective date of the amendment. For example, if, for a plan with a normal retirement age of 65, the change is from an unreduced normal retirement benefit at age 55 to an unreduced normal retirement benefit at age 60 for benefits accrued in the future, with an actuarial reduction to apply for benefits accrued in the future to the extent that the early retirement benefit begins before age 60, the notice must state the change and specify the factors that apply in calculating the actuarial reduction (for example, a 5% per year reduction applies for early retirement before age 60).

(4) *Sufficient information to determine the approximate magnitude of reduction*—(i) *General rule*—(A) Section 204(h) notice must include sufficient information for each applicable individual to determine the approximate magnitude of the expected reduction for that individual. Thus, in any case in which it is not reasonable to expect that the approximate magnitude of the reduction for each applicable individual will be reasonably apparent from the description of the amendment provided in accordance with paragraph (a)(3) of this Q&A-11, further information is required. The further information may be provided by furnishing additional narrative information or in other information that satisfies this paragraph of this section.

(B) To the extent any expected reduction is not uniformly applicable to all participants, the notice must either identify the general classes of participants to whom the reduction is expected to apply, or by some other method include sufficient information to allow each applicable individual receiving the notice to determine which reductions are expected to apply to that individual.

(ii) *Illustrative examples*—(A) *Requirement generally.* The requirement to include sufficient information for each applicable individual to determine the approximate magnitude of the expected reduction for that individual under (a)(4)(i)(A) of this Q&A-11 is deemed satisfied if the notice includes one or more illustrative examples showing the approximate magnitude of the reduction in the examples, as provided in this paragraph (a)(4)(ii). Illustrative examples are in any event required to be provided for any change from a traditional defined benefit formula to a cash balance formula or a change that results in a period of time during which there are no accruals (or minimal accruals) with regard to normal retirement benefits or an early retirement subsidy (a wear-away period).

(B) *Examples must bound the range of reductions.* Where an amendment results in reductions that vary (either among participants, as would occur for an amendment converting a traditional defined benefit formula to a cash balance formula, or over time as to any individual participant, as would occur for an amendment that results in a wear-away period), the illustrative example(s) provided in accordance with this paragraph (a)(4)(ii) must show the approximate range of the

reductions. However, any reductions that are likely to occur in only a de minimis number of cases are not required to be taken into account in determining the range of the reductions if a narrative statement is included to that effect and examples are provided that show the approximate range of the reductions in other cases. Amendments for which the maximum reduction occurs under identifiable circumstances, with proportionately smaller reductions in other cases, may be illustrated by one example illustrating the maximum reduction, with a statement that smaller reductions also occur. Further, assuming that the reduction varies from small to large depending on service or other factors, two illustrative examples may be provided showing the smallest likely reduction and the largest likely reduction.

(C) *Assumptions used in examples.* The examples provided under this paragraph (a)(4)(ii) are not required to be based on any particular form of payment (such as a life annuity or a single sum), but may be based on whatever form appropriately illustrates the reduction. The examples generally may be based on any reasonable assumptions (for example, assumptions relating to the representative participant's age, years of service, and compensation, along with any interest rate and mortality table used in the illustrations, as well as salary scale assumptions used in the illustrations for amendments that alter the compensation taken into account under the plan), but the section 204(h) notice must identify those assumptions. However, if a plan's benefit provisions include a factor that varies over time (such as a variable interest rate), the determination of whether an amendment is reasonably expected to result in a wear-away period must be based on the value of the factor applicable under the plan at a time that is reasonably close to the date section 204(h) notice is provided, and any wear-away period that is solely a result of a future change in the variable factor may be disregarded. For example, to determine whether a wear-away occurs as a result of a section 204(h) amendment that converts a defined benefit plan to a cash balance pension plan that will credit interest based on a variable interest factor specified in the plan, the future interest credits must be projected based on the interest rate applicable under the variable factor at the time section 204(h) notice is provided.

(D) *Individual statements.* This paragraph (a)(4)(ii) may be satisfied by providing a statement to each applicable individual projecting what that individual's future benefits are reasonably expected to be at various future dates and what that individual's future benefits would have been under the terms of the plan as in effect before the section 204(h) amendment, provided that the statement includes the same information required for examples under paragraphs (a)(4)(ii)(A) through (C) of this Q&A-11, including showing the approximate range of the reductions for the individual if the reductions vary over time and identification of the assumptions used in the projections.

(5) *No false or misleading information.* A section 204(h) notice may not include materially false or misleading information (or omit information so as to cause the information provided to be misleading).

(6) *Additional information when reduction not uniform*—(i) *In general.* If an amendment by its terms affects different classes of participants differently (e.g., one new benefit formula will apply to Division A and another to Division B), then the requirements of paragraph (a) of this Q&A-11 apply separately with respect to each such general class of participants. In addition, the notice must include sufficient information to enable an applicable individual who is a participant to understand which class he or she is a member of.

(ii) *Option for different section 204(h) notices.* If a section 204(h) amendment affects different classes of applicable individuals differently, the plan administrator may provide to differently affected classes of applicable individuals a section 204(h) notice appropriate to those individuals. Such section 204(h) notice may omit information that does not apply to the applicable individuals to whom it is furnished, but must identify the class or classes of applicable individuals to whom it is provided.

(b) *Examples.* The following examples illustrate the requirements paragraph (a) of this Q&A-11. In each example, it is assumed that the actual notice provided is written in a manner calculated to be understood by the average plan participant and to apprise the applicable individual of the significance of the notice in accordance with paragraph (a)(2) of this Q&A-11. The examples are as follows:

Example 1. (i) *Facts.* Plan A provides that a participant is entitled to a normal retirement benefit of 2% of the participant's average pay over the 3 consecutive years for which the average is the highest (highest average pay) multiplied by years of service. Plan A is amended to provide that, effective January 1, 2004, the normal retirement benefit will be 2% of the participant's highest average pay multiplied by years of service before the effective date, plus 1% of the participant's highest average pay multiplied by years of service after the effective date. The plan administrator provides notice that states: "Under the Plan's current benefit formula, a participant's normal retirement benefit is 2% of the participant's average pay over the 3 consecutive years for which the average is the highest multiplied by the participant's years of service. This formula is being changed by a plan amendment. Under the Plan as amended, a participant's normal retirement benefit will be the sum of 2% of the participant's average pay over the 3 consecutive years for which the average is the highest multiplied by years of service before the January 1, 2004 effective date, plus 1% of the participant's average pay over the 3 consecutive years for which the average is the highest multiplied by the participant's years of service after December 31, 2003. This change is effective on January 1, 2004." The notice does not contain any additional information.

(ii) *Conclusion.* The notice satisfies the requirements of paragraph (a) of this Q&A-11.

Example 2. (i) *Facts.* Plan B provides that a participant is entitled to a normal retirement benefit at age 64 of 2.2% of the participant's career average pay multiplied by years of service. Plan B is amended to cease all accruals, effective January 1, 2004. The plan administrator provides notice that includes a description of the old benefit formula, a statement that, after December 31, 2003, no participant will earn any further accruals, and the effective date of the amendment. The notice does not contain any additional information.

(ii) *Conclusion.* The notice satisfies the requirements of paragraph (a) of this Q&A-11.

Example 3. (i) *Facts.* Plan C provides that a participant is entitled to a normal retirement benefit at age 65 of 2% of career average compensation multiplied by years of service. Plan C is amended to provide that the normal retirement benefit will be 1% of average pay over the 3 consecutive years for which the average is the highest multiplied by years of service. The amendment only applies to accruals for years of service after the amendment, so that each employee's accrued benefit is equal to the sum of the benefit accrued as of the effective date of the amendment plus the accrued benefit equal to the new formula applied to years of service beginning on or after the effective date. The plan administrator provides notice that describes the old and new benefit formulas and also explains that for an individual whose compensation increases over the individual's career such that the individual's highest 3-year average exceeds the individual's career average, the reduction will be less or there may be no reduction. The notice does not contain any additional information.

(ii) *Conclusion.* The notice satisfies the requirements of paragraph (a) of this Q&A-11.

Example 4. (i) *Facts.* (A) Plan D is a defined benefit pension plan under which each participant accrues a normal retirement benefit, as a life annuity beginning at the normal retirement age of 65, equal to the participant's number of years of service multiplied by 1.5 percent multiplied by the participant's average pay over the 3 consecutive years for which the average is the highest. Plan D provides early retirement benefits for former employees beginning at or after age 55 in the form of an early retirement annuity that is actuarially equivalent to the normal retirement benefit, with the reduction for early commencement based on reasonable actuarial assumptions that are specified in Plan D. Plan D provides for the suspension of benefits of participants who continue in employment beyond normal retirement age, in accordance with section 203(a)(3)(B) of ERISA and regulations thereunder issued by the Department of Labor. The pension of a participant who retires after age 65 is calculated under the same normal retirement benefit formula, but is based on the participant's service credit and highest 3-year pay at the time of late

retirement with any appropriate actuarial increases.

(B) Plan D is amended, effective July 1, 2005, to change the formula for all future accruals to a cash balance formula under which the opening account balance for each participant on July 1, 2005, is zero, hypothetical pay credits equal to 5 percent of pay are credited to the account thereafter, and hypothetical interest is credited monthly based on the applicable interest rate under section 417(e)(3) of the Internal Revenue Code at the beginning of the quarter. Any participant who terminates employment with vested benefits can receive an actuarially equivalent annuity (based on the same reasonable actuarial assumptions that are specified in Plan D) commencing at any time after termination of employment and before the plan's normal retirement age of 65. The benefit resulting from the hypothetical account balance is in addition to the benefit accrued before July 1, 2005 (taking into account only service and highest 3-year pay before July 1, 2005), so that it is reasonably expected that no wear-away period will result from the amendment. The plan administrator expects that, as a general rule, depending on future pay increases and future interest rates, the rate of future benefit accrual after the conversion is higher for participants who accrue benefits before approximately age 50 and after approximately age 70, but is lower for participants who accrue benefits between approximately age 50 and age 70.

(C) The plan administrator of Plan D announces the conversion to a cash balance formula on May 16, 2005. The announcement is delivered to all participants and includes a written notice that describes the old formula, the new formula, and the effective date.

(D) In addition, the notice states that the Plan D formula before the conversion provided a normal retirement benefit equal to the product of a participant's number of years of service multiplied by 1.5 percent multiplied by the participant's average pay over the 3 years for which the average is the highest (highest 3-year pay). The notice includes an example showing the normal retirement benefit that will be accrued after June 30, 2005 for a participant who is age 49 with 10 years of service at the time of the conversion. The plan administrator reasonably believes that such a participant is representative of the participants whose rate of future benefit accrual will be reduced as a result of the amendment. The example estimates that, if the participant continues employment to age 65, the participant's normal retirement benefit for service from age 49 to age 65 will be $657 per month for life. The example assumes that the participant's pay is $50,000 at age 49. The example states that the estimated $657 monthly pension accrues over the 16-year period from age 49 to age 65 and that, based on assumed future pay increases, this amount annually would be 9.1 percent of the participant's highest 3-year pay at age 65, which over the 16 years from age 49 to age 65 averages 0.57 percent

per year multiplied by the participant's highest 3-year pay. The example also states that the sum of the monthly annuity accrued before the conversion in the 10-year period from age 39 to age 49 plus the $657 monthly annuity estimated to be accrued over the 16-year period from age 49 to age 65 is $1,235 and that, based on assumed future increases in pay, this would be 17.1 percent of the participant's highest 3-year pay at age 65, which over the employee's career from age 39 to age 65 averages 0.66 percent per year multiplied by the participant's highest 3-year pay. The notice also includes two other examples with similar information, one of which is intended to show the circumstances in which a small reduction may occur and the other of which shows the largest reduction that the plan administrator thinks is likely to occur. The notice states that the estimates are based on the assumption that pay increases annually after June 30, 2005, at a 4 percent rate. The notice also specifies that the applicable interest rate under section 417(e) for hypothetical interest credits after June 30, 2005 is assumed to be 6 percent, which is the section 417(e) of the Internal Revenue Code applicable interest rate under the plan for 2005.

(ii) *Conclusion.* The information in the notice, as described in paragraph (i)(C) and (i)(D) of this *Example 4*, satisfies the requirements of paragraph (a)(3) of this Q&A-11 with respect to applicable individuals who are participants. The requirements of paragraph (a)(4) of this Q&A-11 are satisfied because, as noted in paragraph (i)(D) of this *Example 4*, the notice describes the old formula and describes the estimated future accruals under the new formula in terms that can be readily compared to the old formula, i.e., the notice states that the estimated $657 monthly pension accrued over the 16-year period from age 49 to age 65 averages 0.57 percent of the participant's highest 3-year pay at age 65. The requirement in paragraph (a)(4)(ii) of this Q&A-11 that the examples include sufficient information to be able to determine the approximate magnitude of the reduction would also be satisfied if the notice instead directly stated the amount of the monthly pension that would have accrued over the 16-year period from age 49 to age 65 under the old formula.

Example 5. (i) *Facts.* The facts are the same as in *Example 4*, except that, under the plan as in effect before the amendment, the early retirement pension for a participant who terminates employment after age 55 with at least 20 years of service is equal to the normal retirement benefit without reduction from age 65 to age 62 and reduced by only 5 percent per year for each year before age 62. As a result, early retirement benefits for such a participant constitute a retirement-type subsidy. The plan as in effect after the amendment provides an early retirement benefit equal to the sum of the early retirement benefit payable under the plan as in effect before the amendment taking into account only service and highest 3-year pay before July 1, 2005, plus an early retirement annuity that is actuarially equivalent to the account balance for service after June 30,

2005. The notice provided by the plan administrator describes the old early retirement annuity, the new early retirement annuity, and the effective date. The notice includes an estimate of the early retirement annuity payable to the illustrated participant for service after the conversion if the participant were to retire at age 59 (which the plan administrator believes is a typical early retirement age) and elect to begin receiving an immediate early retirement annuity. The example states that the normal retirement benefit expected to be payable at age 65 as a result of service from age 49 to age 59 is $434 per month for life beginning at age 65 and that the early retirement annuity expected to be payable as a result of service from age 49 to age 59 is $270 per month for life beginning at age 59. The example states that the monthly early retirement annuity of $270 is 38 percent less than the monthly normal retirement benefit of $434, whereas a 15 percent reduction would have applied under the plan as in effect before the amendment. The notice also includes similar information for examples that show the smallest and largest reduction that the plan administrator thinks is likely to occur in the early retirement benefit. The notice also specifies the applicable interest rate, mortality table, and salary scale used in the example to calculate the early retirement reductions.

(ii) *Conclusion.* The information in the notice, as described in paragraphs (i)(C) and (D) of *Example 4* and paragraph (i) of this *Example 5*, satisfies the requirements of paragraph (a)(3) of this Q&A-11 with respect to applicable individuals who are participants. The requirements of paragraph (a)(4) of this Q&A-11 are satisfied because, as noted in paragraph (i) of this *Example 5*, the notice describes the early retirement subsidy under the old formula and describes the estimated early retirement pension under the new formula in terms that can be readily compared to the old formula, i.e., the notice states that the monthly early retirement pension of $270 is 38 percent less than the monthly normal retirement benefit of $434, whereas a 15 percent reduction would have applied under the plan as in effect before the amendment. The requirements of paragraph (a)(4)(ii) of this Q&A-11 that the examples include sufficient information to be able to determine the approximate magnitude of the reduction would also be satisfied if the notice instead directly stated the amount of the monthly early retirement pension that would be payable at age 59 under the old formula.

Q-12. What special rules apply if participants can choose between the old and new benefit formulas?

A-12. In any case in which an applicable individual can choose between the benefit formula (including any early retirement benefit or retirement-type subsidy) in effect before the section 204(h) amendment (old formula) or the benefit formula in effect after the section 204(h) amendment (new formula), section 204(h) notice has not been provided unless the applicable individual has been provided the information required under Q&A-11 of this section, and has also been

provided sufficient information to enable the individual to make an informed choice between the old and new benefit formulas. The information required under Q&A-11 of this section must be provided by the date otherwise required under Q&A-9 of this section. The information sufficient to enable the individual to make an informed choice must be provided within a period that is reasonably contemporaneous with the date by which the individual is required to make his or her choice and that allows sufficient advance notice to enable the individual to understand and consider the additional information before making that choice.

Q-13. How may section 204(h) notice be provided?

A-13. (a) *Delivering section 204(h) notice.* A plan administrator (including a person acting on behalf of the plan administrator, such as the employer or plan trustee) must provide section 204(h) notice through a method that results in actual receipt of the notice or the plan administrator must take appropriate and necessary measures reasonably calculated to ensure that the method for providing section 204(h) notice results in actual receipt of the notice. Section 204(h) notice must be provided either in the form of a paper document or in an electronic form that satisfies the requirements of paragraph (c) of this Q&A-13. First class mail to the last known address of the party is an acceptable delivery method. Likewise, hand delivery is acceptable. However, the posting of notice is not considered provision of section 204(h) notice. Section 204(h) notice may be enclosed with or combined with other notice provided by the employer or plan administrator (for example, a notice of intent to terminate under title IV of ERISA). Except as provided in paragraph (c) of this Q&A-13, a section 204(h) notice is deemed to have been provided on a date if it has been provided by the end of that day. When notice is delivered by first class mail, the notice is considered provided as of the date of the United States postmark stamped on the cover in which the document is mailed.

(b) *Example.* The following example illustrates the provisions of paragraph (a) of this Q&A-13:

Example. (i) *Facts.* Plan A is amended to reduce significantly the rate of future benefit accrual effective January 1, 2005. Under Q&A-9 of this section, section 204(h) notice is required to be provided at least 45 days before the effective date of the amendment. The plan administrator causes section 204(h) notice to be mailed to all affected participants. The mailing is postmarked November 16, 2004.

(ii) *Conclusion.* Because section 204(h) notice is given 45 days before the effective date of the plan amendment, it satisfies the timing requirement of Q&A-9 of this section.

(c) *New technologies*—(1) *General rule.* A section 204(h) notice may be provided to an applicable individual through an electronic method (other than an oral communication or a recording of an oral communication), provided that all of the following requirements are satisfied:

(i) Either the notice is actually received by the applicable individual or the plan administrator takes appropriate and necessary measures reasonably calculated to ensure that the method for providing section 204(h) notice results in actual receipt of the notice by the applicable individual.

(ii) The section 204(h) notice is delivered using an electronic medium (other than an oral communication or a recording of an oral communication) under an electronic system that satisfies the applicable notice requirements of § 1.401(a)-21.

(iii) *Special effective date.* For plan years beginning prior to January 1, 2007, Q&A-13 of this section, as it appeared in the April 1, 2006 edition of 26 CFR part 1, applies.

(2) *Examples.* The following examples illustrate the requirement in paragraph (c)(1)(i) of this Q&A-13. In these examples, it is assumed that the notice satisfies the requirements in paragraphs (c)(1)(ii) of this section. The examples are as follows:

Example 1. (i) *Facts.* On July 1, 2003, M, a plan administrator of Company N's plan, sends notice intended to constitute section 204(h) notice to A, an employee of Company N and a participant in the plan. The notice is sent through e-mail to A's e-mail address on Company N's electronic information system. Accessing Company N's electronic information system is not an integral part of A's duties. M sends the e-mail with a request for a computer-generated notification that the message was received and opened. M receives notification indicating that the e-mail was received and opened by A on July 9, 2003.

(ii) *Conclusion.* With respect to A, although M has failed to take appropriate and necessary measures reasonably calculated to ensure that the method for providing section 204(h) notice results in actual receipt of the notice, M satisfies the requirement of paragraph (c)(1)(i) of this Q&A-13 on July 9, 2003, which is when A actually receives the notice.

Example 2. (i) *Facts.* On August 1, 2003, O, a plan administrator of Company P's plan, sends a notice intended to constitute section 204(h) notice of ERISA to B, who is an employee of Company P and a participant in Company P's plan. The notice is sent through e-mail to B's e-mail address on Company P's electronic information system. B has the ability to effectively access electronic documents from B's e-mail address on Company P's electronic information system and accessing the system is an integral part of B's duties.

(ii) *Conclusion.* Because access to the system is an integral part of B's duties, O has taken appropriate and necessary measures reasonably calculated to ensure that the method for providing section 204(h) notice results in actual receipt of the notice. Thus, regardless of whether B actually accesses B's email on that date, O satisfies the requirement of paragraph (c)(1)(i) of this Q&A-13 on August 1, 2003, with respect to B.

Q-14. What are the consequences if a plan administrator fails to provide section 204(h) notice?

A-14. (a) *Egregious failures*—(1) *Effect of egregious failure to provide section 204(h) notice.* Section 204(h)(6)(A) of ERISA provides that, in the case of any egregious failure to meet the notice requirements with respect to any plan amendment, the plan provisions are applied so that all applicable individuals are entitled to the greater of the benefit to which they would have been entitled without regard to the amendment, or the benefit under the plan with regard to the amendment. For a special rule applicable in the case of a plan termination, see Q&A-17(b) of this section.

(2) *Definition of egregious failure.* For purposes of section 204(h) of ERISA and this Q&A-14, there is an egregious failure to meet the notice requirements if a failure to provide required notice is within the control of the plan sponsor and is either an intentional failure or a failure, whether or not intentional, to provide most of the individuals with most of the information they are entitled to receive. For this purpose, an intentional failure includes any failure to promptly provide the required notice or information after the plan administrator discovers an unintentional failure to meet the requirements. A failure to give section 204(h) notice is deemed not to be egregious if the plan administrator reasonably determines, taking into account section 4980F, section 204(h), these regulations, other administrative pronouncements, and relevant facts and circumstances, that the reduction in the rate of future benefit accrual resulting from an amendment is not significant (as described in Q&A-8 of this section), or that an amendment does not significantly reduce an early retirement benefit or retirement-type subsidy.

(3) *Example.* The following example illustrates the provisions of this paragraph (a):

Example. (i) *Facts.* Plan A is amended to reduce significantly the rate of future benefit accrual effective January 1, 2003. Section 204(h) notice is required to be provided 45 days before January 1, 2003. Timely section 204(h) notice is provided to all applicable individuals (and to each employee organization representing participants who are applicable individuals), except that the employer intentionally fails to provide section 204(h) notice to certain participants until May 16, 2003.

(ii) *Conclusion.* The failure to provide section 204(h) notice is egregious. Accordingly, for the period from January 1, 2003 through June 30, 2003 (which is the date that is 45 days after May 16, 2003), all participants and alternate payees are entitled to the greater of the benefit to which they would have been entitled under Plan A as in effect before the amendment or the benefit under the plan as amended.

(b) *Effect of non-egregious failure to provide section 204(h) notice.* If an egregious failure has not occurred, the amendment with respect to which section 204(h) notice is required may become

effective with respect to all applicable individuals. However, see section 502 of ERISA for civil enforcement remedies. Thus, where there is a failure, whether or not egregious, to provide section 204(h) notice in accordance with this section, individuals may have recourse under section 502 of ERISA.

(c) *Excise taxes.* See section 4980F and Q&A-15 of this section for excise taxes that may apply to a failure to notify applicable individuals of a pension plan amendment that provides for a significant reduction in the rate of future benefit accrual or eliminates or significantly reduces an early retirement benefit or retirement-type subsidy, regardless of whether or not the failure is egregious.

Q-15. What are some of the rules that apply with respect to the excise tax under section 4980F?

A-15. (a) *Person responsible for excise tax.* In the case of a plan other than a multiemployer plan, the employer is responsible for reporting and paying the excise tax. In the case of a multiemployer plan, the plan is responsible for reporting and paying the excise tax.

(b) *Excise tax inapplicable in certain cases.* Under section 4980F(c)(1) of the Internal Revenue Code, no excise tax is imposed on a failure for any period during which it is established to the satisfaction of the Commissioner that the employer (or other person responsible for the tax) exercised reasonable dilligence, but did not know that the failure existed. Under section 4980F(c)(2) of the Internal Revenue Code, no excise tax applies to a failure to provide section 204(h) notice if the employer (or other person responsible for the tax) exercised reasonable diligence and corrects the failure within 30 days after the employer (or other person responsible for the tax) first knew, or exercising reasonable diligence would have known, that such failure existed. For purposes of section 4980F(c)(1) of the Internal Revenue Code, a person has exercised reasonable diligence, but did not know that the failure existed if and only if—

(1) The person exercised reasonable diligence in attempting to deliver section 204(h) notice to applicable individuals by the latest date permitted under this section; and

(2) At the latest date permitted for delivery of section 204(h) notice, the person reasonably believes that section 204(h) notice was actually delivered to each applicable individual by that date.

(c) *Example.* The following example illustrates the provisions of paragraph (b) of this Q&A-15:

Example. (i) *Facts.* Plan A is amended to reduce significantly the rate of future benefit accrual. The employer sends out a section 204(h) notice to all affected participants and other applicable individuals and to any employee organization representing applicable individuals, including actual delivery by hand to employees at work-sites and by first-class mail for any other applicable individual and to any employee organization representing applicable individuals. However,

although the employer exercises reasonable diligence in seeking to deliver the notice, the notice is not delivered to any participants at one worksite due to a failure of an overnight delivery service to provide the notice to appropriate personnel at that site for them to timely hand deliver the notice to affected employees. The error is discovered when the employer subsequently calls to confirm delivery. Appropriate section 204(h) notice is then promptly delivered to all affected participants at the worksite.

(ii) *Conclusion*. Because the employer exercised reasonable diligence, but did not know that a failure existed, no excise tax applies, assuming that participants at the worksite receive section 204(h) notice within 30 days after the employer first knew, or exercising reasonable diligence would have known, that the failure occurred.

Q-16. How do section 4980F and section 204(h) apply when a business is sold?

A-16. (a) *Generally*. Whether section 204(h) notice is required in connection with the sale of a business depends on whether a plan amendment is adopted that significantly reduces the rate of future benefit accrual or significantly reduces an early retirement benefit or retirement-type subsidy.

(b) *Examples*. The following examples illustrate the rules of this Q&A-16:

Example 1. (i) *Facts*. Corporation Q maintains Plan A, a defined benefit plan that covers all employees of Corporation Q, including employees in its Division M. Plan A provides that participating employees cease to accrue benefits when they cease to be employees of Corporation Q. On January 1, 2006, Corporation Q sells all of the assets of Division M to Corporation R. Corporation R maintains Plan B, which covers all of the employees of Corporation R. Under the sale agreement, employees of Division M become employees of Corporation R on the date of the sale (and cease to be employees of Corporation Q), Corporation Q continues to maintain Plan A following the sale, and the employees of Division M become participants in Plan B.

(ii) *Conclusion*. No section 204(h) notice is required because no plan amendment was adopted that reduced the rate of future benefit accrual. The employees of Division M who become employees of Corporation R ceased to accrue benefits under Plan A because their employment with Corporation Q terminated.

Example 2. (i) *Facts*. Subsidiary Y is a wholly owned subsidiary of Corporation S. Subsidiary Y maintains Plan C, a defined benefit plan that covers employees of Subsidiary Y. Corporation S sells all of the stock of Subsidiary Y to Corporation T. At the effective date of the sale of the stock of Subsidiary Y, in accordance with the sale agreement between Corporation S and Corporation T, Subsidiary Y amends Plan C so that all benefit accruals cease.

(ii) *Conclusion*. Section 204(h) notice is required to be provided because Subsidiary Y adopted a plan amendment that significantly reduced the rate of future benefit accrual in Plan C.

Example 3. (i) *Facts*. As a result of an acquisition, Corporation U maintains two defined benefit plans: Plan D covers employees of Division N and Plan E covers the rest of the employees of Corporation U. Plan E provides a significantly lower rate of future benefit accrual than Plan D. Plan D is merged with Plan E, and all of the employees of Corporation U will accrue benefits under the merged plan in accordance with the benefit formula of former Plan E.

(ii) *Conclusion*. Section 204(h) notice is required.

Example 4. (i) *Facts*. The facts are the same as in *Example 3*, except that the rate of future benefit accrual in Plan E is not significantly lower. In addition, Plan D has a retirement-type subsidy that Plan E does not have and the Plan D employees' rights to the subsidy under the merged plan are limited to benefits accrued before the merger.

(ii) *Conclusion*. Section 204(h) notice is required for any participants or beneficiaries for whom the reduction in the retirement-type subsidy is significant (and for any employee organization representing such participants).

Example 5. (i) *Facts*. Corporation V maintains several plans, including Plan F, which covers employees of Division P. Plan F provides that participating employees cease to accrue further benefits under the plan when they cease to be employees of Corporation V. Corporation V sells all of the assets of Division P to Corporation W, which maintains Plan G for its employees. Plan G provides a significantly lower rate of future benefit accrual than Plan F. Plan F is merged with Plan G as part of the sale, and employees of Division P who become employees of Corporation W will accrue benefits under the merged plan in accordance with the benefit formula of former Plan G.

(ii) *Conclusion*. No section 204(h) notice is required because no plan amendment was adopted that reduces the rate of future benefit accrual or eliminates or significantly reduces an early retirement benefit or retirement-type subsidy. Under the terms of Plan F as in effect prior to the merger, employees of Division P cease to accrue any further benefits (including benefits with respect to early retirement benefits and any retirement-type subsidy) under Plan F after the date of the sale because their employment with Corporation V terminated.

Q-17. How are amendments to cease accruals and terminate a plan treated under section 4980F and section 204(h)?

A-17. (a) *General rule*—(1) *Rule*. An amendment providing for the cessation of benefit accruals on a specified future date and for the termination of a plan is subject to section 4980F and section 204(h).

(2) *Example*. The following example illustrates the rule of paragraph (a)(1) of this Q&A-17:

Example. (i) *Facts*. An employer adopts an amendment that provides for the cessation of benefit accruals under a defined benefit plan on December 31, 2003, and for the termination of

the plan pursuant to title IV of ERISA as of a proposed termination date that is also December 31, 2003. As part of the notice of intent to terminate required under title IV in order to terminate the plan, the plan administrator gives section 204(h) notice of the amendment ceasing accruals, which states that benefit accruals will cease "on December 31, 2003 whether or not the plan is terminated on that date." However, because all the requirements of title IV for a plan termination are not satisfied, the plan cannot be terminated until a date that is later than December 31, 2003.

(ii) *Conclusion.* Nonetheless, because section 204(h) notice was given stating that the plan was amended to cease accruals on December 31, 2003, section 204(h) does not prevent the amendment to cease accruals from being effective on December 31, 2003. The result would be the same had the section 204(h) notice informed the participants that the plan was amended to provide for a proposed termination date of December 31, 2003 and to provide that "benefit accruals will cease on the proposed termination date whether or not the plan is terminated on that date." However, neither section 4980F nor section 204(h) would be satisfied with respect to the December 31, 2003 effective date if the section 204(h) notice had merely stated that benefit accruals would cease. "on the termination date" or "on the proposed termination date."

(3) *Additional requirements under title IV of ERISA.* See 29 CFR 4041.23(b)(4) and 4041.43(b)(5) for special rules applicable to plans terminating under title IV of ERISA.

(b) *Terminations in accordance with title IV of ERISA.* A plan that is terminated in accordance with title IV of ERISA is deemed to have satisfied section 4980F and section 204(h) not later than the termination date (or date of termination, as applicable) established under section 4048 of ERISA. Accordingly, neither section 4980F nor section 204(h) would in any event require that any additional benefits accrue after the effective date of the termination.

(c) *Amendment effective before termination date of a plan subject to title IV of ERISA.* To the extent that an amendment providing for a significant reduction in the rate of future benefit accrual or a significant reduction in an early retirement benefit or retirement-type subsidy has an effective date that is earlier than the termination date (or date of termination, as applicable) established under section 4048 of ERISA, that amendment is subject to section 4980F and section 204(h). Accordingly, the plan administrator must provide section 204(h) notice (either separately, with, or as part of the notice of intent to terminate) with respect to such an amendment.

Q-18. What are the effective dates of section 4980F, section 204(h), as amended by EGTRRA, and these regulations?

A-18. (a) *Statutory effective date*—(1) *General rule.* Section 4980F and section 204(h), as amended by EGTRRA, apply to plan amendments taking effect on or after June 7, 2001 (stat-

utory effective date), which is the date of enactment of EGTRRA.

(2) *Transition rule.* For amendments applying after the statutory effective date in paragraph (a)(1) of this Q&A-18 and prior to the regulatory effective date in paragraph (c) of this Q&A-18, the requirements of section 4980F(e)(2) and (3) of the Internal Revenue Code and section 204(h), as amended by EGTRRA, are treated as satisfied if the plan administrator makes a reasonable, good faith effort to comply with those requirements.

(3) *Special notice rule*—(i) *In general.* Notwithstanding Q&A-9 of this section, section 204(h) notice is not required by section 4980F(e) of the Internal Revenue Code or section 204(h), as amended by EGTRRA, to be provided prior to September 7, 2001 (the date that is three months after the date of enactment of EGTRRA).

(ii) *Reasonable notice.* The requirements of section 4980F and section 204(h), as amended by EGTRRA, do not apply to any plan amendment that takes effect on or after June 7, 2001 if, before April 25, 2001, notice was provided to participants and beneficiaries adversely affected by the plan amendment (and their representatives) which was reasonably expected to notify them of the nature and effective date of the plan amendment. For purposes of this paragraph (a)(3)(ii), notice that complies with § 1.411(d)-6 of this chapter, as it appeared in the April 1, 2001 edition of 26 CFR part 1, is deemed to be notice which was reasonably expected to notify participants and beneficiaries adversely affected by the plan amendment (and their representatives) of the nature and effective date of the plan amendment.

(4) *Special effective date for certain section 204(h) amendments made by plans of commercial airlines.* Section 402 of PPA '06 applies to section 204(h) amendments adopted in plan years ending after August 17, 2006.

(5) *Special effective date for rule relating to contributing employers.* Section 502(c) of PPA '06, which amended section 4980F(e)(1) of the Internal Revenue Code, applies to section 204(h) amendments adopted in plan years beginning after December 31, 2007.

(b) *Regulatory effective date*—(1) *General effective date.* Except as otherwise provided in this paragraph (b) of this section, Q&A-1 through Q&A-18 of this section apply to amendments with an effective date that is on or after September 1, 2003.

(2) *Effective date for Q&A-7(a)(2).* Q&A-7(a)(2) of this section applies to amendments with an effective date that is on or after January 1, 2004.

(3) *Effective dates for Q&A-9(g)(1), (g)(3), and (g)(4)*—(i) *General effective date.* Except as otherwise provided in Q&A-18(b)(3)(ii) or (b)(3)(iii) of this section, Q&A-9(g)(1), (g)(3), and (g)(4) of this section apply to amendments that are effective on or after January 1, 2008.

(ii) *Effective dates for Q&A-9(g)(2) and Q&A-7(b).* Except as otherwise provided in Q&A-18(b)(3)(iii) of this section, Q&A-9(g)(2) and Q&A-7(b) of this section apply to section

204(h) amendments adopted in plan years begin-ning after July 1, 2008.

(iii) *Special rules for section 204(h) amendments to an applicable defined benefit plan.* Except as other-wise provided in paragraph (b)(3)(i) or (b)(3)(ii) of this Q&A-18, with respect to any section 204(h) notice provided in connection with a sec-tion 204(h) amendment to an applicable defined benefit plan within the meaning of section 411(a)(13)(C)(i) to limit distributions as permit-ted under section 411(a)(13)(A) for distributions made after August 17, 2006, that is made pursu-ant to section 701 of PPA '06, paragraphs (g)(1) and (g)(2) of Q&A-9 of this section apply to amendments that are effective after December 21, 2006. For such an amendment that is effective not later than December 31, 2008, section 204(h) notice does not fail to be timely if the notice is provided at least 30 days, rather than 45 days, before the date that the amendment is first effective.

(c) *Amendments taking effect prior to June 7, 2001.* For rules applicable to amendments taking effect prior to June 7, 2001, see § 1.411(d)-6 of this chapter, as it appeared in the April 1, 2001 edi-tion of 26 CFR part 1. [Reg. § 54.4980F-1.]

☐ [*T.D.* 9052, 4-8-2003 (*corrected* 5-6-2003). *Amended by T.D.* 9219, 8-11-2005; *T.D.* 9294, 10-19-2006 *and T.D.* 9472, 11-23-2009.]

[Reg. § 54.4980G-0]

§ 54.4980G-0. Table of contents.—This section contains the questions for § § 54.4980G-1, 54.4980G-2, 54.4980G-3, 54.4980G-4, and 54.4980G-5.

§ 54.4980G-1 Failure of employer to make comparable health savings account contributions.

Q-1: What are the comparability rules that ap-ply to employer contributions to Health Savings Accounts (HSAs)?

Q-2: What are the categories of HDHP cover-age for purposes of applying the comparability rules?

Q-3: What is the testing period for making comparable contributions to employees' HSAs?

Q-4: How is the excise tax computed if em-ployer contributions do not satisfy the compara-bility rules for a calendar year?

§ 54.4980G-2 Employer contribution defined.

Q-1: Do the comparability rules apply to amounts rolled over from an employee's HSA or Archer Medical Savings Account (Archer MSA)?

Q-2: If an employee requests that his or her employer deduct after-tax amounts from the em-ployee's compensation and forward these amounts as employee contributions to the em-ployee's HSA, do the comparability rules apply to these amounts?

§ 54.4980G-3 Definition of employee for comparabil-ity testing.

Q-1: Do the comparability rules apply to con-tributions that an employer makes to the HSAs of independent contractors or self-employed individuals?

Q-2: May a sole proprietor who is an eligible individual contribute to his or her own HSA without contributing to the HSAs of his or her employees who are eligible individuals?

Q-3: Do the comparability rules apply to con-tributions by a partnership to a partner's HSA?

Q-4: How are members of controlled groups treated when applying the comparability rules?

Q-5: What are the categories of employees for comparability testing?

Q-6: Are employees who are included in a unit of employees covered by a collective bargaining agreement comparable participating employees?

Q-7: Is an employer permitted to make compa-rable contributions only to the HSAs of compara-ble participating employees who have coverage under the employer's HDHP?

Q-8: If an employee and his or her spouse are eligible individuals who work for the same em-ployer and one employee-spouse has family cov-erage for both employees under the employer's HDHP, must the employer make comparable contributions to the HSAs of both employees?

Q-9: Does an employer that makes HSA con-tributions only for one class of non-collectively bargained employees who are eligible individu-als, but not for another class of non-collectively bargained employees who are eligible individu-als (for example, management v. non-manage-ment) satisfy the requirement that the employer make comparable contributions?

Q-10: If an employer contributes to the HSAs of former employees who are eligible individu-als, do the comparability rules apply to these contributions?

Q-11: Is an employer permitted to make com-parable contributions only to the HSAs of com-parable participating former employees who have coverage under the employer's HDHP?

Q-12: If an employer contributes only to the HSAs of former employees who are eligible indi-viduals with coverage under the employer's HDHP, must the employer make comparable contributions to the HSAs of former employees who are eligible individuals with coverage under the employer's HDHP because of an elec-tion under a COBRA continuation provision (as defined in section 9832(d)(1))?

Q-13: How do the comparability rules apply if some employees have HSAs and other employ-ees have Archer MSAs?

§ 54.4980G-4 Calculating comparable contributions.

Q-1: What are comparable contributions?

Q-2: How does an employer comply with the comparability rules when some non-collectively bargained employees who are eligible individu-als do not work for the employer during the entire calendar year?

Q-3: How do the comparability rules apply to employer contributions to employees' HSAs if some non-collectively bargained employees work full-time during the entire calendar year, and other non-collectively bargained employees work full-time for less than the entire calendar year?

Q-4: May an employer make contributions for the entire year to the HSAs of its employees who are eligible individuals at the beginning of the calendar year (i.e., on a pre-funded basis) instead of contributing on a pay-as-you-go or on a look-back basis?

Q-5: Must an employer use the same contribution method as described in Q & A-2 and Q & A-4 of this section for all employees for any month during the calendar year?

Q-6: How does an employer comply with the comparability rules if an employee has not established an HSA at the time the employer contributes to its employees' HSAs?

Q-7: If an employer bases its contributions on a percentage of the HDHP deductible, how is the correct percentage or dollar amount computed?

Q-8: Does an employer that contributes to the HSA of each comparable participating employee in an amount equal to the employee's HSA contribution or a percentage of the employee's HSA contribution (matching contributions) satisfy the rule that all comparable participating employees receive comparable contributions?

Q-9: If an employer conditions contributions by the employer to an employee's HSA on an employee's participation in health assessments, disease management programs or wellness programs and makes the same contributions available to all employees who participate in the programs, do the contributions satisfy the comparability rules?

Q-10: If an employer makes additional contributions to the HSAs of all comparable participating employees who have attained a specified age or who have worked for the employer for a specified number of years, do the contributions satisfy the comparability rules?

Q-11: If an employer makes additional contributions to the HSAs of all comparable participating employees who are eligible to make the additional contributions (HSA catch-up contributions) under section 223(b)(3), do the contributions satisfy the comparability rules?

Q-12: If an employer's contributions to an employee's HSA result in non-comparable contributions, may the employer recoup the excess amount from the employee's HSA?

Q-13: What constitutes a reasonable interest rate for purposes of making comparable contributions?

Q-14: How does an employer comply with the comparability rules if an employee has not established an HSA by December 31st?

Q-15: For any calendar year, may an employer accelerate part or all of its contributions for the entire year to the HSAs of employees who have incurred, during the calendar year, qualified medical expenses (as defined in section 223(d)(2)) exceeding the employer's cumulative HSA contributions at that time?

Q-16: What is the effective date for the rules in Q & A-14 and Q & A-15 of this section?

§ 54.4980G-5 HSA comparability rules and cafeteria plans and waiver of excise tax.

Q-1: If an employer makes contributions through a section 125 cafeteria plan to the HSA of each employee who is an eligible individual, are the contributions subject to the comparability rules?

Q-2: If an employer makes contributions through a cafeteria plan to the HSA of each employee who is an eligible individual in an amount equal to the amount of the employee's HSA contribution or a percentage of the amount of the employee's HSA contribution (i.e., matching contributions), are the contributions subject to the section 4980G comparability rules?

Q-3: If under the employer's cafeteria plan, employees who are eligible individuals and who participate in health assessments, disease management programs or wellness programs receive an employer contribution to an HSA and the employees have the right to elect to make pre-tax salary reduction contributions to their HSAs, are the contributions subject to the comparability rules?

Q-4: May all or part of the excise tax imposed under section 4980G be waived?

[Reg. § 54.4980G-0.]

☐ [*T.D.* 9277, 7-28-2006 (*corrected* 9-12-2006). Amended by T.D. 9393, 4-16-2008.]

[Reg. § 54.4980G-1]

§ 54.4980G-1. Failure of employer to make comparable health savings account contributions.

Q-1: What are the comparability rules that apply to employer contributions to Health Savings Accounts (HSAs)?

A-1: If an employer makes contributions to any employee's HSA, the employer must make comparable contributions to the HSAs of all comparable participating employees. See Q & A-1 in § 54.4980G-4 for the definition of comparable contributions. Comparable participating employees are eligible individuals (as defined in section 223(c)(1)) who are in the same category of employees and who have the same category of high deductible health plan (HDHP) coverage. See sections 4980G(b) and 4980E(d)(3). See section 223(c)(2) and (g) for the definition of an HDHP. See also Q & A-5 in § 54.4980G-3 for the categories of employees and Q & A-2 of this section for the categories of HDHP coverage. But see Q & A-6 in § 54.4980G-3 for treatment of collectively bargained employees and Q & A-1 in § 54.4980G-6 for the rules allowing larger comparable contributions to nonhighly compensated employees.

Q-2: What are the categories of HDHP coverage for purposes of applying the comparability rules?

A-2: (a) *In general.* Generally, the categories of coverage are self-only HDHP coverage and family HDHP coverage. Family HDHP coverage means any coverage other than self-only HDHP coverage. The comparability rules apply separately to self-only HDHP coverage and family HDHP coverage. In addition, if an HDHP has family coverage options meeting the descrip-

tions listed in paragraph (b) of this Q & A-2, each such coverage option may be treated as a separate category of coverage and the comparability rules may be applied separately to each category. However, if the HDHP has more than one category that provides coverage for the same number of individuals, all such categories are treated as a single category for purposes of the comparability rules. Thus, the categories of "employee plus spouse" and "employee plus dependent," each providing coverage for two individuals, are treated as the single category "self plus one" for comparability purposes. See, however, the final sentence of paragraph (a) of Q & A-1 of § 54.4980G-4 for a special rule that applies if different amounts are contributed for different categories of family coverage. See also § 54.4980G-6 for the rules allowing larger comparable contributions to nonhighly compensated employees.

(b) *HDHP Family coverage categories.* The coverage categories are—

(1) Self plus one;

(2) Self plus two; and

(3) Self plus three or more.

(c) *Examples.* The rules of this Q & A-2 are illustrated by the following examples:

Example 1. Employer A maintains an HDHP and contributes to the HSAs of eligible employees who elect coverage under the HDHP. The HDHP has self-only coverage and family coverage. Thus, the categories of coverage are self-only and family coverage. Employer A contributes $750 to the HSA of each eligible employee with self-only HDHP coverage and $1,000 to the HSA of each eligible employee with family HDHP coverage. Employer A's contributions satisfy the comparability rules.

Example 2. (i) Employer B maintains an HDHP and contributes to the HSAs of eligible employees who elect coverage under the HDHP, The HDHP has the following coverage options:

(A) Self-only;

(B) Self plus spouse;

(C) Self plus dependent;

(D) Self plus spouse plus one dependent;

(E) Self plus two dependents; and

(F) Self plus spouse and two or more dependents.

(ii) The self plus spouse category and the self plus dependent category constitute the same category of HDHP coverage (self plus one) and Employer B must make the same comparable contributions to the HSAs of all eligible individuals who are in either the self plus spouse category of HDHP coverage or the self plus dependent category of HDHP coverage. Likewise, the self plus spouse plus one dependent category and the self plus two dependents category constitute the same category of HDHP coverage (self plus two) and Employer B must make the same comparable contributions to the HSAs of all eligible individuals who are in either the self plus spouse plus one dependent category of

HDHP coverage or the self plus two dependents category of HDHP coverage.

Example 3. (i) Employer C maintains an HDHP and contributes to the HSAs of eligible employees who elect coverage under the HDHP. The HDHP has the following coverage options:

(A) Self-only;

(B) Self plus one;

(C) Self plus two; and

(D) Self plus three or more.

(ii) Employer C contributes $500 to the HSA of each eligible employee with self-only HDHP coverage, $750 to the HSA of each eligible employee with self plus one HDHP coverage, $900 to the HSA of each eligible employee with self plus two HDHP coverage and $1,000 to the HSA of each eligible employee with self plus three or more HDHP coverage. Employer C's contributions satisfy the comparability rules.

Q-3: What is the testing period for making comparable contributions to employees' HSAs?

A-3: To satisfy the comparability rules, an employer must make comparable contributions for the calendar year to the HSAs of employees who are comparable participating employees. See section 4980G(a). See Q & A-3 and Q & A-4 in § 54.4980G-4 for a discussion of HSA contribution methods.

Q-4: How is the excise tax computed if employer contributions do not satisfy the comparability rules for a calendar year?

A-4: (a) *Computation of tax.* If employer contributions do not satisfy the comparability rules for a calendar year, the employer is subject to an excise tax equal to 35% of the aggregate amount contributed by the employer to HSAs for that period.

(b) *Example.* The following example illustrates the rules in paragraph (a) of this Q & A-4:

Example. During the 2007 calendar year, Employer D has 8 employees who are eligible individuals with self-only coverage under an HDHP provided by Employer D. The deductible for the HDHP is $2,000. For the 2007 calendar year, Employer D contributes $2,000 each to the HSAs of two employees and $1,000 each to the HSAs of the other six employees, for total HSA contributions of $10,000. Employer D's contributions do not satisfy the comparability rules. Therefore, Employer D is subject to an excise tax of $3,500 (35% of $10,000) for its failure to make comparable contributions to its employees' HSAs.

Q-5: If a person is liable for the excise tax under section 4980G, what form must the person file and what is the due date for the filing and payment of the excise tax?

A-5: (a) *In general.* § § 54.6011-2, 54.6151-1 and 54.6071-1(d).

(b) *Effective/applicability date.* The rules in this Q & A-5 are effective for employer contributions made for calendar years beginning on or after January 1, 2010.

[Reg. § 54.4980G-1.]

☐ [*T.D.* 9277, 7-28-2006. *Amended by T.D.* 9457, 9-4-2009.]

Reg. § 54.4980G-1

[Reg. § 54.4980G-2]

§ 54.4980G-2. Employer contribution defined.

Q-1: Do the comparability rules apply to amounts rolled over from an employee's HSA or Archer Medical Savings Account (Archer MSA)?

A-1: No. The comparability rules do not apply to amounts rolled over from an employee's HSA or Archer MSA.

Q-2: If an employee requests that his or her employer deduct after-tax amounts from the employee's compensation and forward these amounts as employee contributions to the employee's HSA, do the comparability rules apply to these amounts?

A-2: No. Section 106(d) provides that amounts contributed by an employer to an eligible employee's HSA shall be treated as employer-provided coverage for medical expenses and are excludible from the employee's gross income up to the limit in section 223(b). After-tax employee contributions to an HSA are not subject to the comparability rules because they are not employer contributions under section 106(d).

[Reg. § 54.4980G-2.]

☐ [*T.D. 9277, 7-28-2006.*]

[Reg. § 54.4980G-3]

§ 54.4980G-3. Failure of employer to make comparable health savings account contributions.

Q-1: Do the comparability rules apply to contributions that an employer makes to the HSAs of independent contractors or self-employed individuals?

A-1: No. The comparability rules apply only to contributions that an employer makes to the HSAs of employees.

Q-2: May a sole proprietor who is an eligible individual contribute to his or her own HSA without contributing to the HSAs of his or her employees who are eligible individuals?

A-2: (a) *Sole proprietor not an employee.* Yes. The comparability rules apply only to contributions made by an employer to the HSAs of employees. Because a sole proprietor is not an employee, the comparability rules do not apply to contributions the sole proprietor makes to his or her own HSA. However, if a sole proprietor contributes to any employee's HSA, the sole proprietor must make comparable contributions to the HSAs of all comparable participating employees. In determining whether the comparability rules are satisfied, contributions that a sole proprietor makes to his or her own HSA are not taken into account.

(b) *Example.* The following example illustrates the rules in paragraph (a) of this Q & A-2:

Example. In a calendar year, B, a sole proprietor is an eligible individual and contributes $1,000 to B's own HSA. B also contributes $500 for the same calendar year to the HSA of each employee who is an eligible individual. The comparability rules are not violated by B's $1,000 contribution to B's own HSA.

Q-3: Do the comparability rules apply to contributions by a partnership to a partner's HSA?

A-3: (a) *Partner not an employee.* No. Contributions by a partnership to a bona fide partner's HSA are not subject to the comparability rules because the contributions are not contributions by an employer to the HSA of an employee. The contributions are treated as either guaranteed payments under section 707(c) or distributions under section 731. However, if a partnership contributes to the HSAs of any employee who is not a partner, the partnership must make comparable contributions to the HSAs of all comparable participating employees.

(b) *Example.* The following example illustrates the rules in paragraph (a) of this Q & A-3:

Example. (i) Partnership X is a limited partnership with three equal individual partners, A (a general partner), B (a limited partner), and C (a limited partner). C is to be paid $300 annually for services rendered to Partnership X in her capacity as a partner without regard to partnership income (a section 707(c) guaranteed payment). D and E are the only employees of Partnership X and are not partners in Partnership X. A, B, C, D, and E are eligible individuals and each has an HSA. During Partnership X's Year 1 taxable year, which is also a calendar year, Partnership X makes the following contributions—

(A) A $300 contribution to each of A's and B's HSAs which are treated as section 731 distributions to A and B;

(B) A $300 contribution to C's HSA in lieu of paying C the guaranteed payment directly; and

(c) A $200 contribution to each of D's and E's HSAs, who are comparable participating employees.

(ii) Partnership X's contributions to A's and B's HSAs are section 731 distributions, which are treated as cash distributions. Partnership X's contribution to C's HSA is treated as a guaranteed payment under section 707(c). The contribution is not excludible from C's gross income under section 106(d) because the contribution is treated as a distributive share of partnership income for purposes of all Code sections other than sections 61(a) and 162(a), and a guaranteed payment to a partner is not treated as compensation to an employee. Thus, Partnership X's contributions to the HSAs of A, B, and C are not subject to the comparability rules. Partnership X's contributions to D's and E's HSAs are subject to the comparability rules because D and E are employees of Partnership X and are not partners in Partnership X. Partnership X's contributions satisfy the comparability rules.

Q-4: How are members of controlled groups treated when applying the comparability rules?

A-4: All persons or entities treated as a single employer under section 414 (b), (c), (m), or (o) are treated as one employer. See sections 4980G(b) and 4980E(e).

Q-5: What are the categories of employees for comparability testing?

A-5: (a) *Categories.* The categories of employees for comparability testing are as follows (but see Q & A-6 of this section for the treatment of collectively bargained employees and Q & A-1 of § 54.4980G-6 for a special rule for contributions made to the HSAs of nonhighly compensated employees)—

(1) Current full-time employees;

(2) Current part-time employees; and

(3) Former employees (except for former employees with coverage under the employer's HDHP because of an election under a COBRA continuation provision (as defined in section 9832(d)(1)).

(b) *Part-time and full-time employees.* For purposes of section 4980G, part-time employees are customarily employed for fewer than 30 hours per week and full-time employees are customarily employed for 30 or more hours per week. See sections 4980G(b) and 4980E(d)(4)(A) and (B).

(c) *In general.* Except as provided in Q & A-6 of this section, the categories of employees in paragraph (a) of this Q & A-5 are the exclusive categories of employees for comparability testing. An employer must make comparable contributions to the HSAs of all comparable participating employees (eligible individuals who are in the same category of employees with the same category of HDHP coverage) during the calendar year without regard to any classification other than these categories. For example, full-time eligible employees with self-only HDHP coverage and part-time eligible employees with self-only HDHP coverage are separate categories of employees and different amounts can be contributed to the HSAs for each of these categories. But see § 54.4980G-6 for a special rule for contributions made to the HSAs of nonhighly compensated employees.

Q-6: Are employees who are included in a unit of employees covered by a collective bargaining agreement comparable participating employees?

A-6: (a) *In general.* No. Collectively bargained employees who are covered by a bona fide collective bargaining agreement between employee representatives and one or more employers are not comparable participating employees, if health benefits were the subject of good faith bargaining between such employee representatives and such employer or employers. Former employees covered by a collective bargaining agreement also are not comparable participating employees.

(b) *Examples.* The following examples illustrate the rules in paragraph (a) of this Q & A-6. The examples read as follows:

Example 1. Employer A offers its employees an HDHP with a $1,500 deductible for self-only coverage. Employer A has collectively bargained and non-collectively bargained employees. The collectively bargained employees are covered by a collective bargaining agreement under which

health benefits were bargained in good faith. In the 2007 calendar year, Employer A contributes $500 to the HSAs of all eligible non-collectively bargained employees with self-only coverage under Employer A's HDHP. Employer A does not contribute to the HSAs of the collectively bargained employees. Employer A's contributions to the HSAs of non-collectively bargained employees satisfy the comparability rules. The comparability rules do not apply to collectively bargained employees.

Example 2. Employer B offers its employees an HDHP with a $1,500 deductible for self-only coverage. Employer B has collectively bargained and non-collectively bargained employees. The collectively bargained employees are covered by a collective bargaining agreement under which health benefits were bargained in good faith. In the 2007 calendar year and in accordance with the terms of the collective bargaining agreement, Employer B contributes to the HSAs of all eligible collectively bargained employees. Employer B does not contribute to the HSAs of the non-collectively bargained employees. Employer B's contributions to the HSAs of collectively bargained employees are not subject to the comparability rules because the comparability rules do not apply to collectively bargained employees. Accordingly, Employer B's failure to contribute to the HSAs of the non-collectively bargained employees does not violate the comparability rules.

Example 3. Employer C has two units of collectively bargained employees - unit Q and unit R - each covered by a collective bargaining agreement under which health benefits were bargained in good faith. In the 2007 calendar year and in accordance with the terms of the collective bargaining agreement, Employer C contributes to the HSAs of all eligible collectively bargained employees in unit Q. In accordance with the terms of the collective bargaining agreement, Employer C makes no HSA contributions for collectively bargained employees in unit R. Employer C's contributions to the HSAs of collectively bargained employees are not subject to the comparability rules because the comparability rules do not apply to collectively bargained employees.

Example 4. Employer D has a unit of collectively bargained employees that are covered by a collective bargaining agreement under which health benefits were bargained in good faith. In accordance with the terms of the collective bargaining agreement, Employer D contributes an amount equal to a specified number of cents per hour for each hour worked to the HSAs of all eligible collectively bargained employees. Employer D's contributions to the HSAs of collectively bargained employees are not subject to the comparability rules because the comparability rules do not apply to collectively bargained employees.

Q-7: Is an employer permitted to make comparable contributions only to the HSAs of compara-

ble participating employees who have coverage under the employer's HDHP?

A-7: (a) *Employer-provided HDHP coverage.* If during a calendar year, an employer contributes to the HSA of any employee who is an eligible individual covered under an HDHP provided by the employer, the employer is required to make comparable contributions to the HSAs of all comparable participating employees with coverage under any HDHP provided by the employer. An employer that contributes only to the HSAs of employees who are eligible individuals with coverage under the employer's HDHP is not required to make comparable contributions to HSAs of employees who are eligible individuals but are not covered under the employer's HDHP.

(b) *Non-employer provided HDHP coverage.* An employer that contributes to the HSA of any employee who is an eligible individual with coverage under any HDHP that is not an HDHP provided by the employer, must make comparable contributions to the HSAs of all comparable participating employees whether or not covered under the employer's HDHP. An employer that makes a reasonable good faith effort to identify all comparable participating employees with non-employer provided HDHP coverage and makes comparable contributions to the HSAs of such employees satisfies the requirements in paragraph (b) of this Q & A-7.

(c) *Examples.* The following examples illustrate the rules in this Q & A-7. None of the employees in the following examples are covered by a collective bargaining agreement. The examples read as follows:

Example 1. In a calendar year, Employer E offers an HDHP to its full-time employees. Most full-time employees are covered under Employer E's HDHP and Employer E makes comparable contributions only to these employees' HSAs. Employee W, a full-time employee of Employer E and an eligible individual, is covered under an HDHP provided by the employer of W's spouse and not under Employer E's HDHP. Employer E is not required to make comparable contributions to W's HSA.

Example 2. In a calendar year, Employer F does not offer an HDHP. Several full-time employees of Employer F, who are eligible individuals, have HSAs. Employer F contributes to these employees' HSAs. Employer F must make comparable contributions to the HSAs of all full-time employees who are eligible individuals.

Example 3. In a calendar year, Employer G offers an HDHP to its full-time employees. Most full-time employees are covered under Employer G's HDHP and Employer G makes comparable contributions to these employees' HSAs and also to the HSAs of full-time employees who are eligible individuals and who are not covered under Employer G's HDHP. Employee S, a full-time employee of Employer G and a comparable participating employee, is covered under an HDHP provided by the employer of S's spouse and not under Employer G's HDHP. Employer

G must make comparable contributions to S's HSA.

Q-8: If an employee and his or her spouse are eligible individuals who work for the same employer and one employee-spouse has family coverage for both employees under the employer's HDHP, must the employer make comparable contributions to the HSAs of both employees?

A-8: (a) *In general.* If the employer makes contributions only to the HSAs of employees who are eligible individuals covered under its HDHP where only one employee-spouse has family coverage for both employees under the employer's HDHP, the employer is not required to contribute to the HSAs of both employee-spouses. The employer is required to contribute to the HSA of the employee-spouse with coverage under the employer's HDHP, but is not required to contribute to the HSA of the employee-spouse covered under the employer's HDHP by virtue of his or her spouse's coverage. However, if the employer contributes to the HSA of any employee who is an eligible individual with coverage under an HDHP that is not an HDHP provided by the employer, the employer must make comparable contributions to the HSAs of both employee-spouses if they are both eligible individuals. If an employer is required to contribute to the HSAs of both employee-spouses, the employer is not required to contribute amounts in excess of the annual contribution limits in section 223(b).

(b) *Examples.* The following examples illustrate the rules in paragraph (a) of this Q & A-8. None of the employees in the following examples are covered by a collective bargaining agreement. The examples read as follows:

Example 1. In a calendar year, Employer H offers an HDHP to its full-time employees. Most full-time employees are covered under Employer H's HDHP and Employer H makes comparable contributions only to these employees' HSAs. T and U are a married couple. Employee T, who is a full-time employee of Employer H and an eligible individual, has family coverage under Employer H's HDHP for T and T's spouse. Employee U, who is also a full-time employee of Employer H and an eligible individual, does not have coverage under Employer H's HDHP except as the spouse of Employee T. Employer H is required to make comparable contributions to T's HSA, but is not required to make comparable contributions to U's HSA.

Example 2. In a calendar year, Employer J offers an HDHP to its full-time employees. Most full-time employees are covered under Employer J's HDHP and Employer J makes comparable contributions to these employees' HSAs and to the HSAs of full-time employees who are eligible individuals but are not covered under Employer J's HDHP. R and S are a married couple. Employee S, who is a full-time employee of Employer J and an eligible individual, has family coverage under Employer J's HDHP for S and S's spouse. Employee R, who is also a full-time employee of Employer J and an eligible individ-

ual, does not have coverage under Employer J's HDHP except as the spouse of Employee S. Employer J must make comparable contributions to S's HSA and to R's HSA.

Q-9: Does an employer that makes HSA contributions only for one class of non-collectively bargained employees who are eligible individuals, but not for another class of non-collectively bargained employees who are eligible individuals (for example, management v. non-management) satisfy the requirement that the employer make comparable contributions?

A-9: (a) *Different classes of employees.* No. If the two classes of employees are comparable participating employees, the comparability rules are not satisfied. The only categories of employees for comparability purposes are current full-time employees, current part-time employees, and former employees. Collectively bargained employees are not comparable participating employees. But see Q & A-1 in § 54.4980G-5 on contributions made through a cafeteria plan. See § 54.4980G-6 for a special rule for contributions made to the HSAs of nonhighly compensated employees.

(b) *Examples.* The following examples illustrate the rules in paragraph (a) of this Q & A-9. None of the employees in the following examples are covered by a collective bargaining agreement. The examples read as follows:

Example 1. In a calendar year, Employer K maintains an HDHP covering all management and non-management employees. Employer K contributes to the HSAs of non-management employees who are eligible individuals covered under its HDHP. Employer K does not contribute to the HSAs of its management employees who are eligible individuals covered under its HDHP. The comparability rules are not satisfied.

Example 2. All of Employer L's employees are located in city X and city Y. In a calendar year, Employer L maintains an HDHP for all employees working in city X only. Employer L does not maintain an HDHP for its employees working in city Y. Employer L contributes $500 to the HSAs of city X employees who are eligible individuals with coverage under its HDHP. Employer L does not contribute to the HSAs of any of its city Y employees. The comparability rules are satisfied because none of the employees in city Y are covered under an HDHP of Employer L. (However, if any employees in city Y were covered by an HDHP of Employer L, Employer L could not fail to contribute to their HSAs merely because they work in a different city.)

Example 3. Employer M has two divisions - division N and division O. In a calendar year, Employer M maintains an HDHP for employees working in division N and division O. Employer M contributes to the HSAs of division N employees who are eligible individuals with coverage under its HDHP. Employer M does not contribute to the HSAs of division O employees who are eligible individuals covered under its HDHP. The comparability rules are not satisfied.

Q-10: If an employer contributes to the HSAs of former employees who are eligible individuals, do the comparability rules apply to these contributions?

A-10: (a) *Former employees.* Yes. The comparability rules apply to contributions an employer makes to former employees' HSAs. Therefore, if an employer contributes to any former employee's HSA, it must make comparable contributions to the HSAs of all comparable participating former employees (former employees who are eligible individuals with the same category of HDHP coverage). However, an employer is not required to make comparable contributions to the HSAs of former employees with coverage under the employer's HDHP because of an election under a COBRA continuation provision (as defined in section 9832(d)(1)). See Q & A-5 and Q & A-12 of this section. The comparability rules apply separately to former employees because they are a separate category of covered employee. See Q & A-5 of this section. Also, former employees who were covered by a collective bargaining agreement immediately before termination of employment are not comparable participating employees. See Q & A-6 of this section.

(b) *Locating former employees.* An employer making comparable contributions to former employees must take reasonable actions to locate any missing comparable participating former employees. In general, such actions include the use of certified mail, the Internal Revenue Service Letter Forwarding Program or the Social Security Administration's Letter Forwarding Service.

(c) *Examples.* The following examples illustrate the rules in paragraph (a) of this Q & A-10. None of the employees in the following examples are covered by a collective bargaining agreement. The examples read as follows:

Example 1. In a calendar year, Employer N contributes $1,000 for the calendar year to the HSA of each current employee who is an eligible individual with coverage under any HDHP. Employer N does not contribute to the HSA of any former employee who is an eligible individual. Employer N's contributions satisfy the comparability rules.

Example 2. In a calendar year, Employer O contributes to the HSAs of current employees and former employees who are eligible individuals covered under any HDHP. Employer O contributes $750 to the HSA of each current employee with self-only HDHP coverage and $1,000 to the HSA of each current employee with family HDHP coverage. Employer O also contributes $300 to the HSA of each former employee with self-only HDHP coverage and $400 to the HSA of each former employee with family HDHP coverage. Employer O's contributions satisfy the comparability rules.

Q-11: Is an employer permitted to make comparable contributions only to the HSAs of com-

Reg. § 54.4980G-3

parable participating former employees who have coverage under the employer's HDHP?

A-11: If during a calendar year, an employer contributes to the HSA of any former employee who is an eligible individual covered under an HDHP provided by the employer, the employer is required to make comparable contributions to the HSAs of all former employees who are comparable participating former employees with coverage under any HDHP provided by the employer. An employer that contributes only to the HSAs of former employees who are eligible individuals with coverage under the employer's HDHP is not required to make comparable contributions to the HSAs of former employees who are eligible individuals and who are not covered under the employer's HDHP. However, an employer that contributes to the HSA of any former employee who is an eligible individual with coverage under an HDHP that is not an HDHP of the employer, must make comparable contributions to the HSAs of all former employees who are eligible individuals whether or not covered under an HDHP of the employer.

Q-12: If an employer contributes only to the HSAs of former employees who are eligible individuals with coverage under the employer's HDHP, must the employer make comparable contributions to the HSAs of former employees who are eligible individuals with coverage under the employer's HDHP because of an election under a COBRA continuation provision (as defined in section 9832(d)(1))?

A-12: No. An employer that contributes only to the HSAs of former employees who are eligible individuals with coverage under the employer's HDHP is not required to make comparable contributions to the HSAs of former employees who are eligible individuals with coverage under the employer's HDHP because of an election under a COBRA continuation provision (as defined in section 9832(d)(1)).

Q-13: How do the comparability rules apply if some employees have HSAs and other employees have Archer MSAs?

A-13: (a) *HSAs and Archer MSAs.* The comparability rules apply separately to employees who have HSAs and employees who have Archer MSAs. However, if an employee has both an HSA and an Archer MSA, the employer may contribute to either the HSA or the Archer MSA, but not to both.

(b) *Example.* The following example illustrates the rules in paragraph (a) of this Q & A-13:

Example. In a calendar year, Employer P contributes $600 to the Archer MSA of each employee who is an eligible individual and who has an Archer MSA. Employer P contributes $500 for the calendar year to the HSA of each employee who is an eligible individual and who has an HSA. If an employee has both an Archer MSA and an HSA, Employer P contributes to the employee's Archer MSA and not to the employee's HSA. Employee X has an Archer MSA and an HSA. Employer P contributes $600 for the calendar year to X's Archer MSA but does not contrib-

ute to X's HSA. Employer P's contributions satisfy the comparability rules.

[Reg. § 54.4980G-3.]

☐ [*T.D. 9277, 7-28-2006. Amended by T.D. 9457, 9-4-2009.*]

[Reg. § 54.4980G-4]

§ 54.4980G-4. Calculating comparable contributions.

Q-1: What are comparable contributions?

A-1: (a) *Definition.* Contributions are comparable if, for each month in a calendar year, the contributions are either the same amount or the same percentage of the deductible under the HDHP for employees who are eligible individuals with the same category of coverage on the first day of that month. Employees with self-only HDHP coverage are tested separately from employees with family HDHP coverage. Similarly, employees with different categories of family HDHP coverage may be tested separately. See Q & A-2 in § 54.4980G-1. An employer is not required to contribute the same amount or the same percentage of the deductible for employees who are eligible individuals with one category of HDHP coverage that it contributes for employees who are eligible individuals with a different category of HDHP coverage. For example, an employer that satisfies the comparability rules by contributing the same amount to the HSAs of all employees who are eligible individuals with family HDHP coverage is not required to contribute any amount to the HSAs of employees who are eligible individuals with self-only HDHP coverage, or to contribute the same percentage of the self-only HDHP deductible as the amount contributed with respect to family HDHP coverage. However, the contribution with respect to the self plus two category may not be less than the contribution with respect to the self plus one category and the contribution with respect to the self plus three or more category may not be less than the contribution with respect to the self plus two category. But see Q & A-1 of § 54.4980G-6 for a special rule for contributions made to the HSAs of nonhighly compensated employees.

(b) *Examples.* The following examples illustrate the rules in paragraph (a) of this Q & A-1. None of the employees in the following examples are covered by a collective bargaining agreement. The examples read as follows:

Example 1. In the 2007 calendar year, Employer A offers its full-time employees three health plans, including an HDHP with self-only coverage and a $2,000 deductible. Employer A contributes $1,000 for the calendar year to the HSA of each employee who is an eligible individual electing the self-only HDHP coverage. Employer A makes no HSA contributions for employees with family HDHP coverage or for employees who do not elect the employer's self-only HDHP. Employer A's HSA contributions satisfy the comparability rules.

Example 2. In the 2007 calendar year, Employer B offers its employees an HDHP with a $3,000

deductible for self-only coverage and a $4,000 deductible for family coverage. Employer B contributes $1,000 for the calendar year to the HSA of each employee who is an eligible individual electing the self-only HDHP coverage. Employer B contributes $2,000 for the calendar year to the HSA of each employee who is an eligible individual electing the family HDHP coverage. Employer B's HSA contributions satisfy the comparability rules.

Example 3. In the 2007 calendar year, Employer C offers its employees an HDHP with a $1,500 deductible for self-only coverage and a $3,000 deductible for family coverage. Employer C contributes $1,000 for the calendar year to the HSA of each employee who is an eligible individual electing the self-only HDHP coverage. Employer C contributes $1,000 for the calendar year to the HSA of each employee who is an eligible individual electing the family HDHP coverage. Employer C's HSA contributions satisfy the comparability rules.

Example 4. In the 2007 calendar year, Employer D offers its employees an HDHP with a $1,500 deductible for self-only coverage and a $3,000 deductible for family coverage. Employer D contributes $1,500 for the calendar year to the HSA of each employee who is an eligible individual electing the self-only HDHP coverage. Employer D contributes $1,000 for the calendar year to the HSA of each employee who is an eligible individual electing the family HDHP coverage. Employer D's HSA contributions satisfy the comparability rules.

Example 5. (i) In the 2007 calendar year, Employer E maintains two HDHPs. Plan A has a $2,000 deductible for self-only coverage and a $4,000 deductible for family coverage. Plan B has a $2,500 deductible for self-only coverage and a $4,500 deductible for family coverage. For the calendar year, Employer E makes contributions to the HSA of each full-time employee who is an eligible individual covered under Plan A of $600 for self-only coverage and $1,000 for family coverage. Employer E satisfies the comparability rules, if it makes either of the following contributions for the 2007 calendar year to the HSA of each full-time employee who is an eligible individual covered under Plan B—

(A) $600 for each full-time employee with self-only coverage and $1,000 for each full-time employee with family coverage; or

(B) $750 for each employee with self-only coverage and $1,125 for each employee with family coverage (the same percentage of the deductible Employer E contributes for full-time employees covered under Plan A, 30% of the deductible for self-only coverage and 25% of the deductible for family coverage).

(ii) Employer E also makes contributions to the HSA of each part-time employee who is an eligible individual covered under Plan A of $300 for self-only coverage and $500 for family coverage. Employer E satisfies the comparability rules, if it makes either of the following contributions for the 2007 calendar year to the HSA of each part-

time employee who is an eligible individual covered under Plan B—

(A) $300 for each part-time employee with self-only coverage and $500 for each part-time employee with family coverage; or

(B) $375 for each part-time employee with self-only coverage and $563 for each part-time employee with family coverage (the same percentage of the deductible Employer E contributes for part-time employees covered under Plan A, 15% of the deductible for self-only coverage and 12.5% of the deductible for family coverage).

Example 6. (i) In the 2007 calendar year, Employer F maintains an HDHP. The HDHP has the following coverage options—

(A) A $2,500 deductible for self-only coverage;

(B) A $3,500 deductible for self plus one dependent (self plus one);

(C) A $3,500 deductible for self plus spouse (self plus one);

(D) A $3,500 deductible for self plus spouse and one dependent (self plus two); and

(E) A $3,500 deductible for self plus spouse and two or more dependents (self plus three or more).

(ii) Employer F makes the following contributions for the calendar year to the HSA of each full-time employee who is an eligible individual covered under the HDHP—

(A) $750 for self-only coverage;

(B) $1,000 for self plus one dependent;

(C) $1,000 for self plus spouse;

(D) $1,500 for self plus spouse and one dependent; and

(E) $2,000 for self plus spouse and two or more dependents.

(iii) Employer F's HSA contributions satisfy the comparability rules.

Example 7. (i) In a calendar year, Employer G offers its employees an HDHP and a health flexible spending arrangement (health FSA). The health FSA reimburses employees for medical expenses as defined in section 213(d). Some of Employer G's employees have coverage under the HDHP and the health FSA, some have coverage under the HDHP and their spouse's FSA, and some have coverage under the HDHP and are enrolled in Medicare. For the calendar year, Employer G contributes $500 to the HSA of each employee who is an eligible individual. No contributions are made to the HSAs of employees who have coverage under Employer G's health FSA or under a spouse's health FSA or who are enrolled in Medicare.

(ii) The employees who have coverage under a health FSA (whether Employer H's or their spouse's FSA) or who are covered under Medicare are not eligible individuals. Specifically, the employees who have coverage under the health FSA or under a spouse's health FSA are not comparable participating employees because they are not eligible individuals under section 223(c)(1). Similarly, the employees who are enrolled in Medicare are not comparable participating employees because they are not eligible

individuals under section 223(b)(7) and (c)(1). Therefore, employees who have coverage under the health FSA or under a spouse's health FSA and employees who are enrolled in Medicare are excluded from comparability testing. See sections 4980G(b) and 4980E. Employer G's contributions satisfy the comparability rules.

Q-2: How does an employer comply with the comparability rules when some non-collectively bargained employees who are eligible individuals do not work for the employer during the entire calendar year?

A-2: (a) *In general.* In determining whether the comparability rules are satisfied, an employer must take into account all full-time and part-time employees who were employees and eligible individuals for any month during the calendar year. (Full-time and part-time employees are tested separately. See Q & A-5 in §54.4980G-3.) There are two methods to comply with the comparability rules when some employees who are eligible individuals do not work for the employer during the entire calendar year; contributions may be made on a pay-as-you-go basis or on a look-back basis. See Q & A-9 through Q & A-11 in §54.4980G-3 for the rules regarding comparable contributions to the HSAs of former employees.

(b) *Contributions on a pay-as-you-go basis.* An employer may comply with the comparability rules by contributing amounts at one or more dates during the calendar year to the HSAs of employees who are eligible individuals as of the first day of the month, if contributions are the same amount or the same percentage of the HDHP deductible for employees who are eligible individuals as of the first day of the month with the same category of coverage and are made at the same time. Contributions made at the employer's usual payroll interval for different groups of employees are considered to be made at the same time. For example, if salaried employees are paid monthly and hourly employees are paid bi-weekly, an employer may contribute to the HSAs of hourly employees on a bi-weekly basis and to the HSAs of salaried employees on a monthly basis. An employer may change the amount that it contributes to the HSAs of employees at any point. However, the changed contribution amounts must satisfy the comparability rules.

(c) *Examples.* The following examples illustrate the rules in paragraph (b) of this Q & A-2: The examples read as follows:

Example 1. (i) Beginning on January 1st, Employer H contributes $50 per month on the first day of each month to the HSA of each employee who is an eligible individual on that date. Employer H does not contribute to the HSAs of former employees. In mid-March of the same year, Employee X, an eligible individual, terminates employment after Employer H has contributed $150 to X's HSA. After X terminates employment, Employer H does not contribute additional amounts to X's HSA. In mid-April of the same year, Employer H hires Employee Y, an

eligible individual, and contributes $50 to Y's HSA in May and $50 in June. Effective in July of the same year, Employer H stops contributing to the HSAs of all employees and makes no contributions to the HSA of any employee for the months of July through December. In August, Employer H hires Employee Z, an eligible individual. Employer H does not contribute to Z's HSA. After Z is hired, Employer H does not hire additional employees. As of the end of the calendar year, Employer H has made the following HSA contributions to its employees' HSAs—

(A) Employer H contributed $150 to X's HSA;

(B) Employer H contributed $100 to Y's HSA;

(C) Employer H did not contribute to Z's HSA; and

(D) Employer H contributed $300 to the HSA of each employee who was an eligible individual and employed by Employer J from January through June.

(ii) Employer H's contributions satisfy the comparability rules.

Example 2. In a calendar year, Employer J offers its employees an HDHP and contributes on a monthly pay-as-you-go basis to the HSAs of employees who are eligible individuals with coverage under Employer J's HDHP. In the calendar year, Employer J contributes $50 per month to the HSA of each of employee with self-only HDHP coverage and $100 per month to the HSA of each employee with family HDHP coverage. From January 1st through March 31st of the calendar year, Employee X is an eligible individual with self-only HDHP coverage. From April 1st through December 31st of the calendar year, X is an eligible individual with family HDHP coverage. For the months of January, February and March of the calendar year, Employer J contributes $50 per month to X's HSA. For the remaining months of the calendar year, Employer J contributes $100 per month to X's HSA. Employer J's contributions to X's HSA satisfy the comparability rules.

(d) *Contributions on a look-back basis.* An employer may also satisfy the comparability rules by determining comparable contributions for the calendar year at the end of the calendar year, taking into account all employees who were eligible individuals for any month during the calendar year and contributing the same percentage of the HDHP deductible or the same dollar amount to the HSAs of all employees with the same category of coverage for that month.

(e) *Examples.* The following examples illustrate the rules in paragraph (d) of this Q & A-2. The examples read as follows:

Example 1. In a calendar year, Employer K offers its employees an HDHP and contributes on a look-back basis to the HSAs of employees who are eligible individuals with coverage under Employer K's HDHP. Employer K contributes $600 ($50 per month) for the calendar year to the HSA of each employee with self-only HDHP coverage and $1,200 ($100 per month) for the calendar year to the HSA of each employee with family HDHP coverage. From January 1st

through June 30th of the calendar year, Employee Y is an eligible individual with family HDHP coverage. From July 1st through December 31st, Y is an eligible individual with self-only HDHP coverage. Employer K contributes $900 on a look-back basis for the calendar year to Y's HSA ($100) per month for the months of January through June and $50 per month for the months of July through December). Employer K's contributions to Y's HSA satisfy the comparability rules.

Example 2. On December 31st, Employer L contributes $50 per month on a look-back basis to each employee's HSA for each month in the calendar year that the employee was an eligible individual. In mid-March of the same year, Employee T, an eligible individual, terminated employment. In mid-April of the same year, Employer L hired Employee U, who becomes an eligible individual as of May 1st and works for Employer L through December 31st. On December 31st, Employer L contributes $150 to Employee T's HSA and $400 to Employee U's HSA. Employer L's contributions satisfy the comparability rules.

(f) Periods and dates for making contributions. With both the pay-as-you go method and the look-back method, an employer may establish, on a reasonable and consistent basis, periods for which contributions will be made (for example, a quarterly period covering three consecutive months in a calendar year) and the dates on which such contributions will be made for that designated period (for example, the first day of the quarter or the last day of the quarter in the case of an employer who has established a quarterly period for making contributions). An employer that makes contributions on a pay-as-you-go basis for a period covering more than one month will not fail to satisfy the comparability rules because an employee who terminates employment prior to the end of the period for which contributions were made has received more contributions on a monthly basis than employees who have worked the entire period. In addition, an employer that makes contributions on a pay-as-you-go basis for a period covering more than one month must make HSA contributions for any comparable participating employees hired after the date of initial funding for that period.

(g) *Example.* The following example illustrates the rules in paragraph (f) of this Q & A-2:

Example. Employer M has established, on a reasonable and consistent basis, a quarterly period for making contributions to the HSAs of eligible employees on a pay-as-you-go basis. Beginning on January 1st, Employer M contributes $150 for the first three months of the calendar year to the HSA of each employee who is an eligible individual on that date. On January 15th, Employee V, an eligible individual, terminated employment after Employer M has contributed $150 to V's HSA. On January 15th, Employer M hired Employee W, who becomes an eligible individual as of February 1st. On April 1st, Employer M has contributed $100 to W's HSA for

the two months (February and March) in the quarter period that Employee W was an eligible employee. Employer M's contributions satisfy the comparability rules.

(h) *Maximum contribution permitted for all employees who are eligible individuals during the last month of the taxable year.* An employer may contribute up to the maximum annual contribution amount for the calendar year (based on the employees' HDHP coverage) to the HSAs of all employees who are eligible individuals on the first day of the last month of the employees' taxable year, including employees who worked for the employer for less than the entire calendar year and employees who became eligible individuals after January 1st of the calendar year. For example, such contribution may be made on behalf of an eligible individual who is hired after January 1st or an employee who becomes an eligible individual after January 1st. Employers are not required to provide more than a pro-rata contribution based on the number of months that an individual was an eligible individual and employed by the employer during the year. However, if an employer contributes more than a pro-rata amount for the calendar year to the HSA of any eligible individual who is hired after January 1st of the calendar year or any employee who becomes an eligible individual any time after January 1st of the calendar year, the employer must contribute that same amount on an equal and uniform basis to the HSAs of all comparable participating employees (as defined in Q & A-1 in § 54.4980G-1) who are hired or become eligible individuals after January 1st of the calendar year. Likewise, if an employer contributes the maximum annual contribution amount for the calendar year to the HSA of any eligible individual who is hired after January 1st of the calendar year or any employee who becomes an eligible individual any time after January 1st of the calendar year, the employer must contribute the maximum annual contribution amount on an equal and uniform basis to the HSAs of all comparable participating employees (as defined in Q & A-1 in § 54.4980G-1) who are hired or become eligible individuals after January 1st of the calendar year. An employer who makes the maximum calendar year contribution or more than a pro-rata contribution to the HSAs of employees who become eligible individuals after the first day of the calendar year or eligible individuals who are hired after the first day of the calendar year will not fail to satisfy comparability merely because some employees will have received more contributions on a monthly basis than employees who worked the entire calendar year.

(i) *Examples.* The following examples illustrate the rules in paragraph (h) in this Q & A-2. In the following examples, no contributions are made through a section 125 cafeteria plan and none of the employees are covered by a collective bargaining agreement.

Example 1. On January 1, 2010, Employer Q contributes $1,000 for the calendar year to the HSAs of employees who are eligible individuals with family HDHP coverage. In mid-March of

the same year, Employer Q hires Employee A, an eligible individual with family HDHP coverage. On April 1, 2010, Employer Q contributes $1,000 to the HSA of Employee A. In September of the same year, Employee B becomes an eligible individual with family HDHP coverage. On October 1, 2010, Employer G contributes $1,000 to the HSA of Employee B. Employer Q does not make any other contributions for the 2010 calendar year. Employer Q's contributions satisfy the comparability rules.

Example 2. For the 2010 calendar year, Employer R only has two employees, Employee C and Employee D. Employee C, an eligible individual with family HDHP coverage, works for Employer R for the entire calendar year. Employee D, an eligible individual with family HDHP coverage works for Employer R from July 1st through December 31st. Employer R contributes $1,200 for the calendar year to the HSA of Employee C and $600 to the HSA of Employee D. Employer R does not make any other contributions for the 2010 calendar year. Employer R's contributions satisfy the comparability rules.

(j) *Effective/applicability date.* The rules in paragraphs (h) and (i) of Q & A-2 are effective for employer contributions made for calendar years beginning on or after January 1, 2010.

Q-3: How do the comparability rules apply to employer contributions to employees' HSAs if some non-collectively bargained employees work full-time during the entire calendar year, and other non-collectively bargained employees work full-time for less than the entire calendar year?

A-3: Employer contributions to the HSAs of employees who work full-time for less than twelve months satisfy the comparability rules if the contribution amount is comparable when determined on a month-to-month basis. For example, if the employer contributes $240 to the HSA of each full-time employee who works the entire calendar year, the employer must contribute $60 to the HSA of each full-time employee who works on the first day of each three months of the calendar year. The rules set forth in this Q & A-2 apply to employer contributions made on a pay-as-you-go basis or on a look-back basis as described in Q & A-3 of this section. See sections 4980G(b) and 4980E(d)(2)(B).

Q-4: May an employer make contributions for the entire year to the HSAs of its employees who are eligible individuals at the beginning of the calendar year (on a pre-funded basis) instead of contributing on a pay-as-you-go or on a look-back basis?

A-4: (a) *Contributions on a pre-funded basis.* Yes. An employer may make contributions for the entire year to the HSAs of its employees who are eligible individuals at the beginning of the calendar year. An employer that pre-funds the HSAs of its employees will not fail to satisfy the comparability rules because an employee who terminates employment prior to the end of the calendar year has received more contributions on a monthly basis than employees who work

the entire calendar year. See Q & A-12 of this section. Under section 223(d)(1)(E), an account beneficiary's interest in an HSA is nonforfeitable. An employer must make comparable contributions for all employees who are comparable participating employees for any month during the calendar year, including employees who are eligible individuals hired after the date of initial funding. An employer that makes HSA contributions on a pre-funded basis may also contribute on a pre-funded basis to the HSAs of employees who are eligible individuals hired after the date of initial funding. Alternatively, an employer that has pre-funded the HSAs of comparable participating employees may contribute to the HSAs of employees who are eligible individuals hired after the date of initial funding on a pay-as-you-go basis or on a look-back basis. An employer that makes HSA contributions on a pre-funded basis must use the same contribution method for all employees who are eligible individuals hired after the date of initial funding.

(b) *Example.* The following example illustrates the rules in paragraph (a) of this Q & A-4:

Example. (i) On January 1, Employer N contributes $1,200 for the calendar year on a pre-funded basis to the HSA of each employee who is an eligible individual. In mid-May, Employer N hires Employee B, who becomes an eligible individual as of June 1st. Therefore, Employer N is required to make comparable contributions to B's HSA beginning in June. Employer N satisfies the comparability rules with respect to contributions to B's HSA if it makes HSA contributions in any one of the following ways—

(A) Pre-funding B's HSA by contributing $700 to B's HSA;

(B) Contributing $100 per month on a pay-as-you-go basis to B's HSA; or

(C) Contributing to B's HSA at the end of the calendar year taking into account each month that B was an eligible individual and employed by Employer M.

(ii) If Employer M hires additional employees who are eligible individuals after initial funding, it must use the same contribution method for these employees that it used to contribute to B's HSA.

Q-5: Must an employer use the same contribution method as described in Q & A-2 and Q & A-4 of this section for all employees who were comparable participating employees for any month during the calendar year?

A-5: Yes. If an employer makes comparable HSA contributions on a pay-as-you-go basis, it must do so for each employee who is a comparable participating employee as of the first day of the month. If an employer makes comparable contributions on a look-back basis, it must do so for each employee who was a comparable participating employee for any month during the calendar year. If an employer makes HSA contributions on a pre-funded basis, it must do so for all employees who are comparable participating employees at the beginning of the calendar year and must make comparable HSA

contributions for all employees who are comparable participating employees for any month during the calendar year, including employees who are eligible individuals hired after the date of initial funding. See Q & A-4 of this section for rules regarding contributions for employees hired after initial funding.

Q-6: How does an employer comply with the comparability rules if an employee has not established an HSA at the time the employer contributes to its employees' HSAs?

A-6: (a) *Employee has not established an HSA at the time the employer funds its employees' HSAs.* If an employee has not established an HSA at the time the employer funds its employees' HSAs, the employer complies with the comparability rules by contributing comparable amounts plus reasonable interest to the employee's HSA when the employee establishes the HSA, taking into account each month that the employee was a comparable participating employee. See Q & A-13 of this section for rules regarding reasonable interest.

(b) *Example.* The following example illustrates the rules in paragraph (a) of this Q & A-6:

Example. Beginning on January 1st, Employer O contributes $500 per calendar year on a pay-as-you-go basis to the HSA of each employee who is an eligible individual. Employee C is an eligible individual during the entire calendar year but does not establish an HSA until March. Notwithstanding C's delay in establishing an HSA, Employer O must make up the missed HSA contributions plus reasonable interest for January and February by April 15th of the following calendar year.

Q-7: If an employer bases its contributions on a percentage of the HDHP deductible, how is the correct percentage or dollar amount computed?

A-7: (a) *Computing HSA contributions.* The correct percentage is determined by rounding to the nearest 1/100th of a percentage point and the dollar amount is determined by rounding to the nearest whole dollar.

(b) *Example.* The following example illustrates the rules in paragraph (a) of this Q & A-7:

Example. In this *Example,* assume that each HDHP provided by Employer P satisfies the definition of an HDHP for the 2007 calendar year. In the 2007 calendar year, Employer P maintains two HDHPs. Plan A has a deductible of $3,000 for self-only coverage. Employer P contributes $1,000 for the calendar year to the HSA of each employee covered under Plan A. Plan B has a deductible of $3,500 for self-only coverage. Employer P satisfies the comparability rules if it makes either of the following contributions for the 2007 calendar year to the HSA of each employee who is an eligible individual with self-only coverage under Plan B—

(i) $1,000; or

(ii) $1,167 (33.33% of the deductible rounded to the nearest whole dollar amount).

Q-8: Does an employer that contributes to the HSA of each comparable participating employee in an amount equal to the employee's HSA contribution or a percentage of the employee's HSA contribution (matching contributions) satisfy the rule that all comparable participating employees receive comparable contributions?

A-8: No. If all comparable participating employees do not contribute the same amount to their HSAs and, consequently, do not receive comparable contributions to their HSAs, the comparability rules are not satisfied, notwithstanding that the employer offers to make available the same contribution amount to each comparable participating employee. But see Q & A-1 in §54.4980G-5 on contributions to HSAs made through a cafeteria plan.

Q-9: If an employer conditions contributions by the employer to an employee's HSA on an employee's participation in health assessments, disease management programs or wellness programs and makes the same contributions available to all employees who participate in the programs, do the contributions satisfy the comparability rules?

A-9: No. If all comparable participating employees do not elect to participate in all the programs and consequently, all comparable participating employees do not receive comparable contributions to their HSAs, the employer contributions fail to satisfy the comparability rules. But see Q & A-1 in §54.4980G-5 on contributions made to HSAs through a cafeteria plan.

Q-10: If an employer makes additional contributions to the HSAs of all comparable participating employees who have attained a specified age or who have worked for the employer for a specified number of years, do the contributions satisfy the comparability rules?

A-10: No. If all comparable participating employees do not meet the age or length of service requirement, all comparable participating employees do not receive comparable contributions to their HSAs and the employer contributions fail to satisfy the comparability rules.

Q-11: If an employer makes additional contributions to the HSAs of all comparable participating employees who are eligible to make the additional contributions (HSA catch-up contributions) under section 223(b)(3), do the contributions satisfy the comparability rules?

A-11: No. If all comparable participating employees are not eligible to make the additional HSA contributions under section 223(b)(3), all comparable participating employees do not receive comparable contributions to their HSAs, and the employer contributions fail to satisfy the comparability rules.

Q-12: If an employer's contributions to an employee's HSA result in non-comparable contributions, may the employer recoup the excess amount from the employee's HSA?

A-12: No. An employer may not recoup from an employee's HSA any portion of the employer's contribution to the employee's HSA. Under section 223(d)(1)(E), an account beneficiary's interest in an HSA is nonforfeitable. However, an employer may make additional HSA contributions to satisfy the comparability rules.

Reg. §54.4980G-4

An employer may contribute up until April 15th following the calendar year in which the non-comparable contributions were made. An employer that makes additional HSA contributions to correct non-comparable contributions must also contribute reasonable interest. However, an employer is not required to contribute amounts in excess of the annual contribution limits in section 223(b). See Q & A-13 of this section for rules regarding reasonable interest.

Q-13: What constitutes a reasonable interest rate for purposes of making comparable contributions?

A-13: The determination of whether a rate of interest used by an employer is reasonable will be based on all of the facts and circumstances. If an employer calculates interest using the Federal short-term rate as determined by the Secretary in accordance with section 1274(d), the employer is deemed to use a reasonable interest rate.

Q-14: Does an employer fail to satisfy the comparability rules for a calendar year if the employer fails to make contributions with respect to eligible employees because the employee has not established an HSA or because the employer does not know that the employee has established an HSA?

A-14: (a) *In general.* An employer will not fail to satisfy the comparability rules for a calendar year (Year 1) merely because the employer fails to make contributions with respect to an eligible employee because the employee has not established an HSA or because the employer does not know that the employee has established an HSA, if —

(1) The employer provides timely written notice to all such eligible employees that it will make comparable contributions for Year 1 for eligible employees who, by the last day of February of the following calendar year (Year 2), both establish an HSA and notify the employer (in accordance with a procedure specified in the notice) that they have established an HSA; and

(2) For each such eligible employee who establishes an HSA and so notifies the employer on or before the last day of February of Year 2, the employer contributes to the HSA for Year 1 comparable amounts (taking into account each month that the employee was a comparable participating employee) plus reasonable interest by April 15th of Year 2.

(b) *Notice.* The notice described in paragraph (a) of this Q & A-14 must be provided to each eligible employee who has not established an HSA by December 31 of Year 1 or if the employer does not know if the employee established an HSA. The employer may provide the notice to other employees as well. However, if an employee has earlier notified the employer that he or she has established an HSA, or if the employer has previously made contributions to that employee's HSA, the employer may not condition making comparable contributions on receipt of any additional notice from that employee. For each calendar year, a notice is deemed to be timely if the employer provides the notice no

earlier than 90 days before the first HSA employer contribution for that calendar year and no later than January 15 of the following calendar year.

(c) *Model notice.* Employers may use the following sample language as a basis in preparing their own notices.

Notice to Employees Regarding Employer Contributions to HSAs:

This notice explains how you may be eligible to receive contributions from [employer] if you are covered by a High Deductible Health Plan (HDHP). [Employer] provides contributions to the Health Savings Account (HSA) of each employee who is [insert employer's eligibility requirements for HSA contributions] ("eligible employee"). If you are an eligible employee, you must do the following in order to receive an employer contribution:

(1) establish an HSA on or before the last day in February of [insert year after the year for which the contribution is being made] and;

(2) notify [insert name and contact information for appropriate person to be contacted] of your HSA account information on or before the last day in February of [insert year after year for which the contribution is being made]. [Specify the HSA account information that the employee must provide (e.g., account number, name and address of trustee or custodian, etc.) and the method by which the employee must provide this account information (e.g., in writing, by e-mail, on a certain form, etc.)].

If you establish your HSA on or before the last day of February in [insert year after year for which the contribution is being made] and notify [employer] of your HSA account information, you will receive your HSA contributions, plus reasonable interest, for [insert year for which contribution is being made] by April 15 of [insert year after year for which contribution is being made]. If, however, you do not establish your HSA or you do not notify us of your HSA account information by the deadline, then we are not required to make any contributions to your HSA for [insert applicable year]. You may notify us that you have established an HSA by sending an [e-mail or] a written notice to [insert name, title and, if applicable, e-mail address]. If you have any questions about this notice, you can contact [insert name and title] at [insert telephone number or other contact information].

(e) *Electronic delivery.* An employer may furnish the notice required under this section electronically in accordance with § 1.401(a)-21 of this chapter.

(f) *Examples.* The following examples illustrate the rules in this Q & A-14:

Example 1. In a calendar year, Employer Q contributes to the HSAs of current employees who are eligible individuals covered under any

HDHP. For the 2009 calendar year, Employer Q contributes $50 per month on the first day of each month, beginning January 1st, to the HSA of each employee who is an eligible employee on that date. For the 2009 calendar year, Employer Q provides written notice satisfying the content requirements of this Q & A-14 on October 16, 2008 to all employees regarding the availability of HSA contributions for eligible employees. For eligible employees who are hired after October 16, 2008, Employer Q provides such a notice no later than January 15, 2010. Employer Q's notice satisfies the notice timing requirements in paragraph (a)(1) of this Q & A-14.

Example 2. Employer R's written cafeteria plan permits employees to elect to make pre-tax salary reduction contributions to their HSAs. Employees making this election have the right to receive cash or other taxable benefits in lieu of their HSA pretax contribution. Employer R automatically contributes a non-elective matching contribution to the HSA of each employee who makes a pre-tax HSA contribution. Because Employer R's HSA contributions are made through the cafeteria plan, the comparability requirements do not apply to the HSA contributions made by Employer R. Consequently, Employer R is not required to provide written notice to its employees regarding the availability of this matching HSA contribution. See Q & A-1 in 54.4980G- 5 for treatment of HSA contributions made through a cafeteria plan.

Example 3. In a calendar year, Employer S maintains an HDHP and only contributes to the HSAs of eligible employees who elect coverage under its HDHP. For the 2009 calendar year, Employer S employs ten eligible employees and all ten employees have elected coverage under Employer S's HDHP and have established HSAs. For the 2009 calendar year, Employer S makes comparable contributions to the HSAs of all ten employees. Employer S satisfies the comparability rules. Thus, Employer S is not required to provide written notice to its employees regarding the availability of HSA contributions for eligible employees.

Example 4. In a calendar year, Employer T contributes to the HSAs of current full-time employees with family coverage under any HDHP. For the 2009 calendar year, Employer T provides timely written notice satisfying the content requirements of this section to all employees regardless of HDHP coverage. Employer T makes identical monthly contributions to all eligible employees (meaning full time employees with family HDHP coverage) that establish HSAs. Employer T contributes comparable amounts (taking into account each month that the employee was a comparable participating employee) plus reasonable interest to the HSAs of the eligible employees that establish HSAs and provide the necessary information after the end of the year but on or before the last day of February, 2010. Employer T makes no contribution to the HSAs of employees that do not establish an HSA or that do not provide the necessary information on or before the last day of Febru-

ary, 2010. Employer T satisfies the comparability requirements.

Example 5. For the 2009 calendar year, Employer V contributes to the HSAs of current full time employees with family coverage under any HDHP. Employer V has 500 current full time employees. As of the date for Employer V's first HSA contribution for the 2009 calendar year, 450 eligible employees have established HSAs. Employer V provides timely written notice satisfying the content requirements of this section only to those 50 eligible employees who have not established HSAs. Employer V makes identical quarterly contributions to the 450 eligible employees who established HSAs. By April 15, 2010, Employer V contributes comparable amounts to the other eligible employees who establish HSAs and provide the necessary information on or before the last day of February, 2010. Employer V makes no contribution to the HSAs of eligible employees that do not establish an HSA or that do not provide the necessary information on or before the last day of February, 2010. Employer V satisfies the comparability rules.

Q-15: For any calendar year, may an employer accelerate part or all of its contributions for the entire year to the HSAs of employees who have incurred, during the calendar year, qualified medical expenses (as defined in section 223(d)(2)) exceeding the employer's cumulative HSA contributions at that time?

A-15: (a) *In general.* Yes. For any calendar year, an employer may accelerate part or all of its contributions for the entire year to the HSAs of employees who have incurred, during the calendar year, qualified medical expenses exceeding the employer's cumulative HSA contributions at that time. If an employer accelerates contributions to the HSA of any such eligible employee, all accelerated contributions must be available throughout the calendar year on an equal and uniform basis to all such eligible employees. Employers must establish reasonable uniform methods and requirements for accelerated contributions and the determination of medical expenses.

(b) *Satisfying comparability.* An employer that accelerates contributions to the HSAs of its employees will not fail to satisfy the comparability rules because employees who incur qualifying medical expenses exceeding the employer's cumulative HSA contributions at that time have received more contributions in a given period than comparable employees who do not incur such expenses, provided that all comparable employees receive the same amount or the same percentage for the calendar year. Also, an employer that accelerates contributions to the HSAs of its employees will not fail to satisfy the comparability rules because an employee who terminates employment prior to the end of the calendar year has received more contributions on a monthly basis than employees who work the entire calendar year. An employer is not required to contribute reasonable interest on either accelerated or non-accelerated HSA contri-

butions. But see Q & A-6 and Q & A-12 of this section for when reasonable interest must be paid.

Q-16: What is the effective date for the rules in Q & A-14 and Q & A-15 of this section?

A-16: These regulations apply to employer contributions made for calendar years beginning on or after January 1, 2009.
[Reg. § 54.4980G-4.]

☐ [*T.D. 9277, 7-28-2006 (corrected 9-12-2006). Amended by T.D. 9393, 4-16-2008 and T.D. 9457, 9-4-2009.*]

[Reg. § 54.4980G-5]

§ 54.4980G-5. HSA comparability rules and cafeteria plans and waiver of excise tax.

Q-1: If an employer makes contributions through a section 125 cafeteria plan to the HSA of each employee who is an eligible individual, are the contributions subject to the comparability rules?

A-1: (a) *In general.* No. The comparability rules do not apply to HSA contributions that an employer makes through a section 125 cafeteria plan. However, contributions to an HSA made through a cafeteria plan are subject to the section 125 nondiscrimination rules (eligibility rules, contributions and benefits tests and key employee concentration tests). See section 125(b), (c) and (g) and the regulations thereunder.

(b) *Contributions made through a section 125 cafeteria plan.* Employer contributions to employees' HSAs are made through a section 125 cafeteria plan and are subject to the section 125 cafeteria plan nondiscrimination rules and not the comparability rules if under the written cafeteria plan, the employees have the right to elect to receive cash or other taxable benefits in lieu of all or a portion of an HSA contribution (meaning that all or a portion of the HSA contributions are available as pre-tax salary reduction amounts), regardless of whether an employee actually elects to contribute any amount to the HSA by salary reduction.

Q-2: If an employer makes contributions through a cafeteria plan to the HSA of each employee who is an eligible individual in an amount equal to the amount of the employee's HSA contribution or a percentage of the amount of the employee's HSA contribution (matching contributions), are the contributions subject to the section 4980G comparability rules?

A-2: No. The comparability rules do not apply to HSA contributions that an employer makes through a section 125 cafeteria plan. Thus, where matching contributions are made by an employer through a cafeteria plan, the contributions are not subject to the comparability rules of section 4980G. However, contributions, including matching contributions, to an HSA made under a cafeteria plan are subject to the section 125 nondiscrimination rules (eligibility rules, contributions and benefits tests and key employee concentration tests). See Q & A-1 of this section.

Q-3: If under the employer's cafeteria plan, employees who are eligible individuals and who participate in health assessments, disease management programs or wellness programs receive an employer contribution to an HSA and the employees have the right to elect to make pre-tax salary reduction contributions to their HSAs, are the contributions subject to the comparability rules?

A-3: (a) *In general.* No. The comparability rules do not apply to employer contributions to an HSA made through a cafeteria plan. See Q & A-1 of this section.

(b) *Examples.* The following examples illustrate the rules in this § 54.4980G-5. The examples read as follows:

Example 1. Employer A's written cafeteria plan permits employees to elect to make pre-tax salary reduction contributions to their HSAs. Employees making this election have the right to receive cash or other taxable benefits in lieu of their HSA pre-tax contribution. The section 125 cafeteria plan nondiscrimination rules and not the comparability rules apply because the HSA contributions are made through the cafeteria plan.

Example 2. Employer B's written cafeteria plan permits employees to elect to make pre-tax salary reduction contributions to their HSAs. Employees making this election have the right to receive cash or other taxable benefits in lieu of their HSA pre-tax contribution. Employer B automatically contributes a non-elective matching contribution or seed money to the HSA of each employee who makes a pre-tax HSA contribution. The section 125 cafeteria plan nondiscrimination rules and not the comparability rules apply to Employer B's HSA contributions because the HSA contributions are made through the cafeteria plan.

Example 3. Employer C's written cafeteria plan permits employees to elect to make pre-tax salary reduction contributions to their HSAs. Employees making this election have the right to receive cash or other taxable benefits in lieu of their HSA pre-tax contribution. Employer C makes a non-elective contribution to the HSAs of all employees who complete a health risk assessment and participate in Employer C's wellness program. Employees do not have the right to receive cash or other taxable benefits in lieu of Employer C's non-elective contribution. The section 125 cafeteria plan nondiscrimination rules and not the comparability rules apply to Employer C's HSA contributions because the HSA contributions are made through the cafeteria plan.

Example 4. Employer D's written cafeteria plan permits employees to elect to make pre-tax salary reduction contributions to their HSAs. Employees making this election have the right to receive cash or other taxable benefits in lieu of their HSA pre-tax contribution. Employees participating in the plan who are eligible individuals receive automatic employer contributions to their HSAs. Employees make no election with respect to Employer D's contribution and do not have the right to receive cash or other taxable

benefits in lieu of Employer D's contribution, but are permitted to make their own pre-tax salary reduction contributions to fund their HSAs. The section 125 cafeteria plan nondiscrimination rules and not the comparability rules apply to Employer D's HSA contributions because the HSA contributions are made through the cafeteria plan.

Q-4: May all or part of the excise tax imposed under section 4980G be waived?

A-4: In the case of a failure which is due to reasonable cause and not to willful neglect, all or a portion of the excise tax imposed under section 4980G may be waived to the extent that the payment of the tax would be excessive relative to the failure involved. See sections 4980G(b) and 4980E(c).

[Reg. § 54.4980G-5.]

□ [T.D. 9277, 7-28-2006.]

[Reg. § 54.4980G-6]

§ 54.4980G-6. Special rule for contributions made to the HSAs of nonhighly compensated employees.

Q-1: May an employer make larger contributions to the HSAs of nonhighly compensated employees than to the HSAs of highly compensated employees?

A-1: Yes. Employers may make larger HSA contributions for nonhighly compensated employees who are comparable participating employees than for highly compensated employees who are comparable participating employees. See Q & A-1 in § 54.4980G-1 for the definition of comparable participating employee. For purposes of this section, highly compensated employee is defined under section 414(q). Nonhighly compensated employees are employees that are not highly compensated employees. The comparability rules continue to apply with respect to contributions to the HSAs of all nonhighly compensated employees. Employers must make comparable contributions for the calendar year to the HSA of each nonhighly compensated employee who is a comparable participating employee.

Q-2: May an employer make larger contributions to the HSAs of highly compensated employees than to the HSAs of nonhighly compensated employees?

A-2: (a) *In general.* No. Employer contributions to HSAs for highly compensated employees who are comparable participating employees may not be larger than employer HSA contributions for nonhighly compensated employees who are comparable participating employees. The comparability rules continue to apply with respect to contributions to the HSAs of all highly compensated employees. Employers must make comparable contributions for the calendar year to the HSA of each highly compensated comparable participating employee. See Q & A-1 in § 54.4980G-1 for the definition of comparable participating employee.

(b) *Examples.* The following examples illustrate the rules in Q & A-1 and Q & A-2 of this section.

No contributions are made through a section 125 cafeteria plan and none of the employees in the following examples are covered by a collective bargaining agreement. All of the employees in the following examples have the same HDHP deductible for the same category of coverage.

Example 1. In 2010, Employer A contributes $1,000 for the calendar year to the HSA of each full-time nonhighly compensated employee who is an eligible individual with self-only HDHP coverage. Employer A makes no contribution to the HSA of any full-time highly compensated employee who is an eligible individual with self-only HDHP coverage. Employer A's HSA contributions for calendar year 2010 satisfy the comparability rules.

Example 2. In 2010, Employer B contributes $2,000 for the calendar year to the HSA of each full-time nonhighly compensated employee who is an eligible individual with self-only HDHP coverage. Employer B also contributes $1,000 for the calendar year to the HSA of each full-time highly compensated employee who is an eligible individual with self-only HDHP coverage. Employer B's HSA contributions for calendar year 2010 satisfy the comparability rules.

Example 3. In 2010, Employer C contributes $1,000 for the calendar year to the HSA of each full-time nonhighly compensated employee who is an eligible individual with self-only HDHP coverage. Employer C contributes $2,000 for the calendar year to the HSA of each full-time highly compensated employee who is an eligible individual with self-only HDHP coverage. Employer C's HSA contributions for calendar year 2010 do not satisfy the comparability rules.

Example 4. In 2010, Employer D contributes $1,000 for the calendar year to the HSA of each full-time nonhighly compensated employee who is an eligible individual with self-only HDHP coverage. Employer D also contributes $1,000 to the HSA of each full-time highly compensated employee who is an eligible individual with self-only HDHP coverage. In addition, the employer contributes an additional $500 to the HSA of each nonhighly compensated employee who participates in a wellness program. The nonhighly compensated employees did not receive comparable contributions, and, therefore, Employer D's HSA contributions for calendar year 2010 do not satisfy the comparability rules.

Example 5. In 2010, Employer E contributes $1,000 for the calendar year to the HSA of each full-time non-management nonhighly compensated employee who is an eligible individual with family HDHP coverage. Employer E also contributes $500 for the calendar year to the HSA of each full-time management nonhighly compensated employee who is an eligible individual with family HDHP coverage. The nonhighly compensated employees did not receive comparable contributions, and, therefore, Employer E's HSA contributions for calendar year 2010 do not satisfy the comparability rules.

Q-3: May an employer make larger HSA contributions for employees with self plus two

HDHP coverage than employees with self plus one HDHP coverage even if the employees with self plus two are all highly compensated employees and the employees with self plus one are all nonhighly compensated employees?

A-3: (a) Yes. Q & A-1 in § 54.4980G-4 provides that an employer's contribution with respect to the self plus two category of HDHP coverage may not be less than the contribution with respect to the self plus one category and the contribution with respect to the self plus three or more category may not be less than the contribution with respect to the self plus two category. Therefore, the comparability rules are not violated if an employer makes a larger HSA contribution for the self plus two category of HDHP coverage than to self plus one coverage, even if the employees with self plus two coverage are all highly compensated employees and the employees with self plus one coverage are all nonhighly compensated employees. Likewise, the comparability rules are not violated if an employer makes a larger HSA contribution for the self plus three category of HDHP coverage than to self plus two coverage, even if the employees with self plus three coverage are all highly compensated employees and the employees with self plus two coverage are all nonhighly compensated employees.

(b) *Example.* The following example illustrates the rules in paragraph (a) of this Q & A-3. In the following example, no contributions are made through a section 125 cafeteria plan and none of the employees are covered by a collective bargaining agreement.

Example. In 2010, Employer F contributes $1,000 for the calendar year to the HSA of each full-time employee who is an eligible individual with self plus one HDHP coverage. Employer F contributes $1,500 for the calendar year to the HSA of each employee who is an eligible individual with self plus two HDHP coverage. The deductible for both the self plus one HDHP and the self plus two HDHP is $2,000. Employee A, an eligible individual, is a nonhighly compensated employee with self plus one coverage. Employee B, an eligible individual, is a highly compensated employee with self plus two coverage. For the 2010 calendar year, Employer F contributes $1,000 to Employee A's HSA and $1,500 to Employee B's HSA. Employer F's HSA contributions satisfy the comparability rules.

Q-4: What is the effective date for the rules in this section?

A-4: The rules in this section are effective for employer contributions made for calendar years beginning on or after January 1, 2010.

[Reg. § 54.4980G-6.]

☐ [*T.D.* 9457, 9-4-2009.]

[Reg. § 54.4980G-7]

§ 54.4980G-7. Special comparability rules for qualified HSA distributions contributed to

HSAs on or after December 20, 2006 and before January 1, 2012.

Q-1: How do the comparability rules of section 4980G apply to qualified HSA distributions under section 106(e)(2)?

A-1: The comparability rules of section 4980G do not apply to amounts contributed to employee HSAs through qualified HSA distributions. However, in order to satisfy the comparability rules, if an employer offers qualified HSA distributions, as defined in section 106(e)(2), to any employee who is an eligible individual covered under any HDHP, the employer must offer qualified HSA distributions to all employees who are eligible individuals covered under any HDHP. However, if an employer offers qualified HSA distributions only to employees who are eligible individuals covered under the employer's HDHP, the employer is not required to offer qualified HSA distributions to employees who are eligible individuals but are not covered under the employer's HDHP.

Q-2: What is the effective date for the rules in this section?

A-2: The rules in this section are effective for are effective for employer contributions made for calendar years beginning on or after January 1, 2010.

[Reg. § 54.4980G-7.]

☐ [*T.D.* 9457, 9-4-2009.]

[Reg. § 54.4980H-0]

§ 54.4980H-0. Table of contents.—This section lists the table of contents for §§ 54.4980H-1 through 54.4980H-6.

§ 54.4980H-1 Definitions.

  (a) Definitions.

    (1) Administrative period.

    (2) Advance credit payment.

    (3) Affordable Care Act.

    (4) Applicable large employer.

    (5) Applicable large employer member.

    (6) Applicable premium tax credit.

    (7) Bona fide volunteer.

    (8) Calendar month.

    (9) Church, or a convention or association of churches.

    (10) Collective bargaining agreement.

    (11) Cost-sharing reduction.

    (12) Dependent.

    (13) Educational organization.

    (14) Eligible employer-sponsored plan.

    (15) Employee.

    (16) Employer.

    (17) Employment break period.

    (18) Exchange.

    (19) Federal poverty line.

    (20) Form W-2 wages.

    (21) Full-time employee.

    (22) Full-time equivalent employee (FTE).

    (23) Government entity.

    (24) Hour of service.

    (25) Initial measurement period.

[Reg. § 54.4980H-0.]

☐ [*T.D.* 9655, 2-10-2014.]

[Reg. § 54.4980H-1]

§ 54.4980H-1. Definitions.—(a) *Definitions.*— The definitions in this section apply only for purposes of this section and §§ 54.4980H-2 through 54.4980H-6.

(1) *Administrative period.*—The term *administrative period* means an optional period, selected by an applicable large employer member, of no longer than 90 days beginning immediately following the end of a measurement period and ending immediately before the start of the associated stability period. The administrative period also includes the period between a new employee's start date and the beginning of the initial measurement period, if the initial measurement period does not begin on the employee's start date.

(2) *Advance credit payment.*—The term *advance credit payment* means an advance payment of the premium tax credit as provided in Affordable Care Act section 1412 (42 U.S.C. 18082).

(3) *Affordable Care Act.*—The term *Affordable Care Act* means the Patient Protection and Affordable Care Act, Public Law 111-148 (124 Stat. 119 (2010)), and the Health Care and Education Reconciliation Act of 2010, Public Law 111-152 (124 Stat. 1029 (2010)), as amended by the Medicare and Medicaid Extenders Act of 2010, Public Law 111-309 (124 Stat. 3285 (2010)), the Comprehensive 1099 Taxpayer Protection and Repayment of Exchange Subsidy Overpayments Act of 2011, Public Law 112-9 (125 Stat. 36 (2011)), the Department of Defense and Full-Year Continuing Appropriations Act, 2011, Public Law 112-10 (125 Stat. 38 (2011)), and the 3% Withholding Repeal and Job Creation Act, Public Law 112-56 (125 Stat. 711 (2011)).

(4) *Applicable large employer.*—The term *applicable large employer* means, with respect to a calendar year, an employer that employed an average of at least 50 full-time employees (including full-time equivalent employees) on business days during the preceding calendar year. For rules relating to the determination of applicable large employer status, see § 54.4980H-2.

(5) *Applicable large employer member.*—The term *applicable large employer member* means a person that, together with one or more other persons, is treated as a single employer that is an applicable large employer. For this purpose, if a person, together with one or more other persons, is treated as a single employer that is an applicable large employer on any day of a calendar month, that person is an applicable large employer member for that calendar month. If the applicable large employer comprises one person, that one person is the applicable large employer member. An applicable large employer member does not include a person that is not an employer or only an employer of employees with no hours of service for the calendar year. For rules for government entities, and churches, or

conventions or associations of churches, see § 54.4980H-2(b)(4).

(6) *Applicable premium tax credit.*—The term *applicable premium tax credit* means any premium tax credit that is allowed or paid under section 36B and any advance payment of such credit.

(7) *Bona fide volunteer.*—The term *bona fide volunteer* means an employee of a government entity or an organization described in section 501(c) that is exempt from taxation under section 501(a) whose only compensation from that entity or organization is in the form of—

(i) Reimbursement for (or reasonable allowance for) reasonable expenses incurred in the performance of services by volunteers, or

(ii) Reasonable benefits (including length of service awards), and nominal fees, customarily paid by similar entities in connection with the performance of services by volunteers.

(8) *Calendar month.*—The term *calendar month* means one of the 12 full months named in the calendar, such as January, February, or March.

(9) *Church or a convention or association of churches.*—The term *church or a convention or association of churches* has the same meaning as provided in § 1.170A-9(b).

(10) *Collective bargaining agreement.*—The term *collective bargaining agreement* means an agreement that the Secretary of Labor determines to be a collective bargaining agreement, provided that the health benefits provided under the collective bargaining agreement are the subject of good faith bargaining between employee representatives and one or more employers, and the agreement between employee representatives and one or more employers satisfies section 7701(a)(46).

(11) *Cost-sharing reduction.*—The term *cost-sharing reduction* means a cost-sharing reduction and any advance payment of the reduction as defined under section 1402 of the Affordable Care Act and 45 CFR 155.20.

(12) *Dependent.*—The term *dependent* means a child (as defined in section 152(f)(1) but excluding a stepson, stepdaughter or an eligible foster child (and excluding any individual who is excluded from the definition of dependent under section 152 by operation of section 152(b)(3))) of an employee who has not attained age 26. A child attains age 26 on the 26th anniversary of the date the child was born. A child is a dependent for purposes of section 4980H for the entire calendar month during which he or she attains age 26. Absent knowledge to the contrary, applicable large employer members may rely on an employee's representation about that employee's children and the ages of those children. The term *dependent* does not include the spouse of an employee.

(13) *Educational organization.*—The term *educational organization* means an entity described in § 1.170A-9(c)(1), whether or not described in sec-

tion 501(c)(3) and tax-exempt under section 501(a). Thus, the term *educational organization* includes taxable entities, tax-exempt entities and government entities.

(14) *Eligible employer-sponsored plan.*—The term *eligible employer-sponsored plan* has the same meaning as provided under section 5000A(f)(2) and the regulations thereunder and any other applicable guidance.

(15) *Employee.*—The term *employee* means an individual who is an employee under the common-law standard. See § 31.3401(c)-1(b). For purposes of this paragraph (a)(15), a leased employee (as defined in section 414(n)(2)), a sole proprietor, a partner in a partnership, a 2-percent S corporation shareholder, or a worker described in section 3508 is not an employee.

(16) *Employer.*—The term *employer* means the person that is the employer of an employee under the common-law standard. See § 31.3121(d)-1(c). For purposes of determining whether an employer is an applicable large employer, all persons treated as a single employer under section 414(b), (c), (m), or (o) are treated as a single employer. Thus, all employees of a controlled group of entities under section 414(b) or (c), an affiliated service group under section 414(m), or an entity in an arrangement described under section 414(o), are taken into account in determining whether the members of the controlled group or affiliated service group together are an applicable large employer. For purposes of determining applicable large employer status, the term *employer* also includes a predecessor employer (see paragraph (a)(36) of this section) and a successor employer.

(17) *Employment break period.*—The term *employment break period* means a period of at least four consecutive weeks (disregarding special unpaid leave), measured in weeks, during which an employee of an educational organization is not credited with hours of service for an applicable large employer.

(18) *Exchange.*—The term *Exchange* means an Exchange as defined in 45 CFR 155.20.

(19) *Federal poverty line.*—The term *federal poverty line* means for a plan year any of the poverty guidelines (updated periodically in the **Federal Register** by the Secretary of Health and Human Services under the authority of 42 U.S.C. 9902(2)) in effect within six months before the first day of the plan year of the applicable large employer member's health plan, as selected by the applicable large employer member.

(20) *Form W-2 wages.*—The term *Form W-2 wages* with respect to an employee refers to the amount of wages as defined under section 3401(a) for the applicable calendar year (required to be reported in Box 1 of the Form W-2 (Wage and Tax Statement)) received from an applicable large employer.

(21) *Full-time employee.*—(i) *In general.*—The term *full-time employee* means, with respect to a calendar month, an employee who is employed an average of at least 30 hours of service per week with an employer. For rules on the determination of whether an employee is a full-time employee, including a description of the look-back measurement method and the monthly measurement method, see § 54.4980H-3. The look-back measurement method for identifying full-time employees is available only for purposes of determining and computing liability under section 4980H and not for the purpose of determining status as an applicable large employer under § 54.4980H-2.

(ii) *Monthly equivalency.*—Except as otherwise provided in paragraph (a)(21)(iii) of this section, 130 hours of service in a calendar month is treated as the monthly equivalent of at least 30 hours of service per week, and this 130 hours of service monthly equivalency applies for both the look-back measurement method and the monthly measurement method for determining full-time employee status.

(iii) *Determination of full-time employee status using weekly rule under the monthly measurement method.*—Under the optional weekly rule set forth in § 54.4980H-3(c)(3), full-time employee status for certain calendar months is based on hours of service over four weekly periods and for certain other calendar months is based on hours of service over five weekly periods. With respect to a month with four weekly periods, an employee with at least 120 hours of service is a full-time employee, and with respect to a month with five weekly periods, an employee with at least 150 hours of service is a full-time employee. For purposes of this rule, the seven continuous calendar days that constitute a week (for example Sunday through Saturday) must be consistently applied for all calendar months of the calendar year.

(22) *Full-time equivalent employee (FTE).*—The term *full-time equivalent employee*, or *FTE*, means a combination of employees, each of whom individually is not treated as a full-time employee because he or she is not employed on average at least 30 hours of service per week with an employer, who, in combination, are counted as the equivalent of a full-time employee solely for purposes of determining whether the employer is an applicable large employer. For rules on the method for determining the number of an employer's full-time equivalent employees, or FTEs, see § 54.4980H-2(c).

(23) *Government entity.*—The term *government entity* means the government of the United States, any State or political subdivision thereof, any Indian tribal government (as defined in section 7701(a)(40)) or subdivision of an Indian tribal government (determined in accordance with section 7871(d)), or any agency or instrumentality of any of the foregoing.

(24) *Hour of service.*—(i) *In general.*—The term *hour of service* means each hour for which

an employee is paid, or entitled to payment, for the performance of duties for the employer; and each hour for which an employee is paid, or entitled to payment by the employer for a period of time during which no duties are performed due to vacation, holiday, illness, incapacity (including disability), layoff, jury duty, military duty or leave of absence (as defined in 29 CFR 2530.200b-2(a)). For the rules for determining an employee's hours of service, see § 54.4980H-3.

(ii) *Excluded hours.*—(A) *Bona fide volunteers.*—The term *hour of service* does not include any hour for services performed as a bona fide volunteer.

(B) *Work-study program.*—The term *hour of service* does not include any hour for services to the extent those services are performed as part of a Federal Work-Study Program as defined under 34 CFR 675 or a substantially similar program of a State or political subdivision thereof.

(C) *Services outside the United States.*—The term *hour of service* does not include any hour for services to the extent the compensation for those services constitutes income from sources without the United States (within the meaning of sections 861 through 863 and the regulations thereunder).

(iii) *Service for other applicable large employer members.*—In determining hours of service and status as a full-time employee for all purposes under section 4980H, an hour of service for one applicable large employer member is treated as an hour of service for all other applicable large employer members for all periods during which the applicable large employer members are part of the same group of employers forming an applicable large employer.

(25) *Initial measurement period.*—The term *initial measurement period* means a period selected by an applicable large employer member of at least three consecutive months but not more than 12 consecutive months used by the applicable large employer as part of the look-back measurement method in § 54.4980H-3(d).

(26) *Limited non-assessment period for certain employees.*—References to the *limited non-assessment period for certain employees* refers to the limited period during which an employer will not be subject to an assessable payment under section 4980H(a), and in certain cases section 4980H(b), with respect to an employee as set forth in—

(i) Section 54.4980H-2(b)(5) (regarding the transition rule for an employer's first year as an applicable large employer),

(ii) Section 54.4980H-3(c)(2) (regarding the application of section 4980H for the three full calendar month period beginning with the first full calendar month in which an employee is first otherwise eligible for an offer of coverage under the monthly measurement method),

(iii) Section 54.4980H-3(d)(2)(iii) (regarding the application of section 4980H during the initial three full calendar months of employment for an employee reasonably expected to be a full-time employee at the start date, under the look-back measurement method),

(iv) Section 54.4980H-3(d)(3)(iii) (regarding the application of section 4980H during the initial measurement period to a new variable hour employee, seasonal employee or part-time employee determined to be employed on average at least 30 hours of service per week, under the look-back measurement method),

(v) Section 54.4980H-3(d)(3)(vii) (regarding the application of section 4980H following an employee's change in employment status to a full-time employee during the initial measurement period, under the look-back measurement method), and

(vi) Section 54.4980H-4(c) and § 54.4980H-5(c) (regarding the application of section 4980H to the calendar month in which an employee's start date occurs on a day other than the first day of the calendar month).

(27) *Minimum essential coverage.*—The term *minimum essential coverage*, or *MEC*, has the same meaning as provided in section 5000A(f) and any regulations or other guidance thereunder.

(28) *Minimum value.*—The term *minimum value* has the same meaning as provided in section 36B(c)(2)(C)(ii) and any regulations or other guidance thereunder.

(29) *Month.*—The term *month* means—

(i) A *calendar month* as defined in paragraph (a)(8) of this section, or

(ii) The period that begins on any date following the first day of a calendar month and that ends on the immediately preceding date in the immediately following calendar month (for example, from February 2 to March 1 or from December 15 to January 14).

(30) *New employee.*—Under the look-back measurement method, the term *new employee* means an employee who has been employed by an applicable large employer for less than one complete standard measurement period; for treatment of the employee as a new employee or continuing employee under the look-back measurement method following a period for which no hours of service are earned, see the rehire and continuing employee rules at § 54.4980H-3(d)(6). Under the monthly measurement method, the term *new employee* means an employee who either has not previously been employed by the applicable large employer or has previously been employed by the applicable large employer but is treated as a new employee under the rehire and continuing employee rules at § 54.4980H-3(c)(4).

(31) *Ongoing employee.*—The term *ongoing employee* means an employee who has been employed by an applicable large employer member for at least one complete standard measurement period. For the treatment of an ongoing employee as a new employee or continuing employee following a period for which no hours of

service are earned, see the rehire and continuing employee rules at § 54.4980H-3(d)(6).

(32) *Part-time employee.*—The term *part-time employee* means a new employee who the applicable large employer member reasonably expects to be employed on average less than 30 hours of service per week during the initial measurement period, based on the facts and circumstances at the employee's start date. Whether an employer's determination that a new employee is a part-time employee is reasonable is based on the facts and circumstances at the employee's start date. Factors to consider in determining a new employee's full-time employee status are set forth in § 54.4980H-3(d)(2)(ii).

(33) *Period of employment.*—The term *period of employment* means the period of time beginning on the first date for which an employee is credited with an hour of service for an applicable large employer (including any member of that applicable large employer) and ending on the last date on which the employee is credited with an hour of service for that applicable large employer, both dates inclusive. An employee may have one or more periods of employment with the same applicable large employer.

(34) *Person.*—The term *person* has the same meaning as provided in section 7701(a)(1) and the regulations thereunder.

(35) *Plan year.*—A *plan year* must be twelve consecutive months, unless a short plan year of less than twelve consecutive months is permitted for a valid business purpose. A *plan year* is permitted to begin on any day of a year and must end on the preceding day in the immediately following year (for example, a plan year that begins on October 15, 2015, must end on October 14, 2016). A calendar year *plan year* is a period of twelve consecutive months beginning on January 1 and ending on December 31 of the same calendar year. Once established, a plan year is effective for the first plan year and for all subsequent plan years, unless changed, provided that such change will only be recognized if made for a valid business purpose. A change in the plan year is not permitted if a principal purpose of the change in plan year is to circumvent the rules of section 4980H or these regulations.

(36) *Predecessor employer.*—[Reserved]

(37) *Qualified health plan.*—The term *qualified health plan* means a qualified health plan as defined in Affordable Care Act section 1301(a) (42 U.S.C. 18021(a)), but does not include a catastrophic plan described in Affordable Care Act section 1302(e) (42 U.S.C. 18022(e)).

(38) *Seasonal employee.*—The term *seasonal employee* means an employee who is hired into a position for which the customary annual employment is six months or less.

(39) *Seasonal worker.*—The term *seasonal worker* means a worker who performs labor or services on a seasonal basis as defined by the Secretary of Labor, including (but not limited to)

workers covered by 29 CFR 500.20(s)(1), and retail workers employed exclusively during holiday seasons. Employers may apply a reasonable, good faith interpretation of the term *seasonal worker* and a reasonable good faith interpretation of 29 CFR 500.20(s)(1) (including as applied by analogy to workers and employment positions not otherwise covered under 29 CFR 500.20(s)(1)).

(40) *Section 1411 Certification.*—The term *Section 1411 Certification* means the certification received as part of the process established by the Secretary of Health and Human Services under which an employee is certified to the employer under section 1411 of the Affordable Care Act as having enrolled for a calendar month in a qualified health plan with respect to which an applicable premium tax credit or cost-sharing reduction is allowed or paid with respect to the employee.

(41) *Section 4980H(a) applicable payment amount.*—The term *section 4980H(a) applicable payment amount* means, with respect to any calendar month, 1/12 of $2,000, adjusted for inflation in accordance with section 4980H(c)(5) and any applicable guidance thereunder.

(42) *Section 4980H(b) applicable payment amount.*—The term *section 4980H(b) applicable payment amount* means, with respect to any calendar month, 1/12 of $3,000, adjusted for inflation in accordance with section 4980H(c)(5) and any applicable guidance thereunder.

(43) *Self-only coverage.*—The term *self-only coverage* means health insurance coverage provided to only one individual, generally the employee.

(44) *Special unpaid leave.*—The term *special unpaid leave* means—

(i) Unpaid leave that is subject to the Family and Medical Leave Act of 1993 (FMLA), Public Law 103-3, 29 U.S.C. 2601 et seq.;

(ii) Unpaid leave that is subject to the Uniformed Services Employment and Reemployment Rights Act of 1994 (USERRA), Public Law 103-353, 38 U.S.C. 4301 et seq.; or

(iii) Unpaid leave on account of jury duty.

(45) *Stability period.*—The term *stability period* means a period selected by an applicable large employer member that immediately follows, and is associated with, a standard measurement period or an initial measurement period (and, if elected by the employer, the administrative period associated with that standard measurement period or initial measurement period), and is used by the applicable large employer member as part of the look-back measurement method in § 54.4980H-3(d).

(46) *Standard measurement period.*—The term *standard measurement period* means a period of at least three but not more than 12 consecutive months that is used by an applicable large employer member as part of the look-back measure-

ment method in § 54.4980H-3(d). See § 54.4980H-3(d)(1)(ii) for rules on the use of payroll periods that include the beginning and end dates of the measurement period.

(47) *Start date.*—The term *start date* means the first date on which an employee is required to be credited with an hour of service with an employer. For rules relating to when, following a period for which an employee does not earn an hour of service, that employee may be treated as a new employee with a new start date rather than a continuing employee, see the rehire and continuing employee rules at § 54.4980H-3(c)(4) and § 54.4980H-3(d)(6).

(48) *United States.*—The term *United States* means United States as defined in section 7701(a)(9).

(49) *Variable hour employee-.*—(i) *In general.*—The term *variable hour employee* means an employee if, based on the facts and circumstances at the employee's start date, the applicable large employer member cannot determine whether the employee is reasonably expected to be employed on average at least 30 hours of service per week during the initial measurement period because the employee's hours are variable or otherwise uncertain.

(ii) *Factors.*—(A) *In general.*—Factors to consider in determining whether it can be determined that the employee is reasonably expected to be (or reasonably expected not to be) employed on average at least 30 hours of service per week during the initial measurement period include, but are not limited to, whether the employee is replacing an employee who was a full-time employee or a variable hour employee, the extent to which the hours of service of employees in the same or comparable positions have actually varied above and below an average of 30 hours of service per week during recent measurement periods, and whether the job was advertised, or otherwise communicated to the new employee or otherwise documented (for example, through a contract or job description) as requiring hours of service that would average at least 30 hours of service per week, less than 30 hours of service per week, or may vary above and below an average of 30 hours of service per week. These factors are only relevant for a particular new employee if the employer has no reason to anticipate that the facts and circumstances related to that new employee will be different. In all cases, no single factor is determinative. For purposes of determining whether an employee is a variable hour employee, the applicable large employer member may not take into account the likelihood that the employee may terminate employment with the applicable large employer (including any member of the applicable large employer) before the end of the initial measurement period.

(B) *Additional factors for an employee hired by an employer for temporary placement at an unrelated entity.*—In the case of an individual who, under all the facts and circumstances, is the employee of an entity (referred to solely for purposes of this paragraph (a)(49) as a "temporary staffing firm") that hired such individual for temporary placement at an unrelated entity that is not the common law employer, additional factors to consider to determine whether the employee is reasonably expected to be (or reasonably expected not to be) employed by the temporary staffing firm on average at least 30 hours of service per week during the initial measurement period include, but are not limited to, whether other employees in the same position of employment with the temporary staffing firm, as part of their continuing employment, retain the right to reject temporary placements that the temporary staffing firm offers the employee; typically have periods during which no offer of temporary placement is made; typically are offered temporary placements for differing periods of time; and typically are offered temporary placements that do not extend beyond 13 weeks.

(C) *Educational organizations.*—An employer that is an educational organization cannot take into account the potential for, or likelihood of, an employment break period in determining its expectation of future hours of service.

(iii) *Application only for look-back measurement method.*—The term *variable hour employee* is used as a category of employees under the look-back measurement method and is not relevant to the monthly measurement method.

(50) *Week.*—The term *week* means any period of seven consecutive calendar days applied consistently by the applicable large employer member.

(b) *Effective/applicability date.*—This section is applicable for periods after December 31, 2014. [Reg. § 54.4980H-1.]

☐ [*T.D.* 9655, 2-10-2014.]

[Reg. § 54.4980H-2]

§ 54.4980H-2. Applicable large employer and applicable large employer member.—(a) *In general.*—Section 4980H applies to an applicable large employer and to all of the applicable large employer members that comprise that applicable large employer.

(b) *Determining applicable large employer status.*—(1) *In general.*—An employer's status as an applicable large employer for a calendar year is determined by taking the sum of the total number of full-time employees (including any seasonal workers) for each calendar month in the preceding calendar year and the total number of FTEs (including any seasonal workers) for each calendar month in the preceding calendar year, and dividing by 12. The result, if not a whole number, is then rounded to the next lowest whole number. If the result of this calculation is less than 50, the employer is not an applicable large employer for the current calendar year. If the result of this calculation is 50 or more, the employer is an applicable large employer for the

current calendar year, unless the seasonal worker exception in paragraph (b)(2) of this section applies.

(2) *Seasonal worker exception.*—If the sum of an employer's full-time employees and FTEs exceeds 50 for 120 days or less during the preceding calendar year, and the employees in excess of 50 who were employed during that period of no more than 120 days are seasonal workers, the employer is not considered to employ more than 50 full-time employees (including FTEs) and the employer is not an applicable large employer for the current calendar year. In the case of an employer that was not in existence on any business day during the preceding calendar year, if the employer reasonably expects that the sum of its full-time employees and FTEs for the current calendar year will exceed 50 for 120 days or less during the calendar year, and that the employees in excess of 50 who will be employed during that period of no more than 120 days will be seasonal workers, the employer is not an applicable large employer for the current calendar year. For purposes of this paragraph (b)(2) only, four calendar months may be treated as the equivalent of 120 days. The four calendar months and the 120 days are not required to be consecutive.

(3) *Employers not in existence in preceding calendar year.*—An employer not in existence throughout the preceding calendar year is an applicable large employer for the current calendar year if the employer is reasonably expected to employ an average of at least 50 full-time employees (taking into account FTEs) on business days during the current calendar year and it actually employs an average of at least 50 full-time employees (taking into account FTEs) on business days during the calendar year. An employer is treated as not having been in existence throughout the prior calendar year only if the employer was not in existence on any business day in the prior calendar year. See paragraph (b)(2) of this section for the application of the seasonal worker exception to employers not in existence in the preceding calendar year.

(4) *Special rules for government entities, churches, and conventions and associations of churches.*—[Reserved]

(5) *Transition rule for an employer's first year as an applicable large employer.*—With respect to an employee who was not offered coverage by the employer at any point during the prior calendar year, if the applicable large employer offers coverage to the employee on or before April 1 of the first calendar year for which the employer is an applicable large employer, the employer will not be subject to an assessable payment under section 4980H by reason of its failure to offer coverage to the employee for January through March of that year, provided that this relief applies only with respect to potential liability under section 4980H(b) (for January through March of the first calendar year for which the employer is an applicable large employer) if the coverage offered by April 1 provides minimum value. If the em-

ployer does not offer coverage to the employee by April 1, the employer may be subject to a section 4980H(a) assessable payment with respect January through March of the first calendar year for which the employer is an applicable large employer in addition to any later calendar months for which coverage was not offered. If the employer offers coverage to the employee by April 1 that does not provided minimum value, the employer may be subject to a section 4980H(b) assessable payment with respect to the employee for January through March of the first calendar year for which the employer is an applicable large employer in addition to any later calendar months for which coverage does not provide minimum value or is not affordable. This rule applies only during the first year that an employer is an applicable large employer (and would not apply if, for example, the employer falls below the 50 full-time employee (plus FTE) threshold for a subsequent calendar year and then increases employment and becomes an applicable large employer again).

(c) *Full-time equivalent employees (FTEs).*—(1) *In general.*—In determining whether an employer is an applicable large employer, the number of FTEs it employed during the preceding calendar year is taken into account. All employees (including seasonal workers) who were not employed on average at least 30 hours of service per week for a calendar month in the preceding calendar year are included in calculating the employer's FTEs for that calendar month.

(2) *Calculating the number of FTEs.*—The number of FTEs for each calendar month in the preceding calendar year is determined by calculating the aggregate number of hours of service for that calendar month for employees who were not full-time employees (but not more than 120 hours of service for any employee) and dividing that number by 120. In determining the number of FTEs for each calendar month, fractions are taken into account; an employer may round the number of FTEs for each calendar month to the nearest one hundredth.

(d) *Examples.*—The following examples illustrate the rules of paragraphs (a) through (c) of this section. In these examples, hours of service are computed following the rules set forth in § 54.4980H-3, and references to years refer to calendar years unless otherwise specified. The employers in *Example 2* through *Example 6* are each the sole applicable large employer member of the applicable large employer, as determined under section 414(b), (c), (m), and (o).

Example 1 (Applicable large employer/controlled group). (i) *Facts.* For all of 2015 and 2016, Corporation Z owns 100 percent of all classes of stock of Corporation Y and Corporation X. Corporation Z has no employees at any time in 2015. For every calendar month in 2015, Corporation Y has 40 full-time employees and Corporation X has 60 full-time employees. Corporations Z, Y, and X are a controlled group of corporations under section 414(b).

(ii) *Conclusion*. Because Corporations Z, Y and X have a combined total of 100 full-time employees during 2015, Corporations Z, Y, and X together are an applicable large employer for 2016. Each of Corporations Z, Y and X is an applicable large employer member for 2016.

Example 2 (Applicable large employer with FTEs). (i) *Facts*. During each calendar month of 2015, Employer W has 20 full-time employees each of whom averages 35 hours of service per week, 40 employees each of whom averages 90 hours of service per calendar month, and no seasonal workers.

(ii) *Conclusion*. Each of the 20 employees who average 35 hours of service per week count as one full-time employee for each calendar month. To determine the number of FTEs for each calendar month, the total hours of service of the employees who are not full-time employees (but not more than 120 hours of service per employee) are aggregated and divided by 120. The result is that the employer has 30 FTEs for each calendar month (40 × 90 = 3,600, and 3,600 ÷ 120 = 30). Because Employer W has 50 full-time employees (the sum of 20 full-time employees and 30 FTEs) during each calendar month in 2015, and because the seasonal worker exception is not applicable, Employer W is an applicable large employer for 2016.

Example 3 (Seasonal worker exception). (i) *Facts*. During 2015, Employer V has 40 full-time employees for the entire calendar year, none of whom are seasonal workers. In addition, Employer V also has 80 seasonal workers who are full-time employees and who work for Employer V from September through December 2015. Employer V has no FTEs during 2015.

(ii) *Conclusion*. Before applying the seasonal worker exception, Employer V has 40 full-time employees during each of eight calendar months of 2015, and 120 full-time employees during each of four calendar months of 2015, resulting in an average of 66.67 full-time employees for the year. However, Employer V's workforce exceeded 50 full-time employees (counting seasonal workers) for no more than four calendar months (treated as the equivalent of 120 days) in calendar year 2015, and the number of full-time employees would be less than 50 during those months if seasonal workers were disregarded. Accordingly, because after application of the seasonal worker exception described in paragraph (b)(2) of this section Employer V is not considered to employ more than 50 full-time employees, Employer V is not an applicable large employer for 2016.

Example 4 (Seasonal workers and other FTEs). (i) *Facts*. Same facts as *Example 3*, except that Employer V has 20 FTEs in August, some of whom are seasonal workers.

(ii) *Conclusion*. The seasonal worker exception described in paragraph (b)(2) of this section does not apply if the number of an employer's full-time employees (including seasonal workers) and FTEs exceeds 50 for more than 120 days during the calendar year. Because Employer V

has at least 50 full-time employees for a period greater than four calendar months (treated as the equivalent of 120 days) during 2015, the exception described in paragraph (b)(2) of this section does not apply. Employer V averaged 68 full-time employees in 2015: [(40 × 7) + (60 × 1) + (120 × 4)] ÷ 12 = 68.33, and accordingly, Employer V is an applicable large employer for calendar year 2016.

Example 5 (New employer). (i) *Facts*. Corporation S is incorporated on January 1, 2016. On January 1, 2016, Corporation S has three employees. However, prior to incorporation, Corporation S's owners purchased a factory intended to open within two calendar months of incorporation and to employ approximately 100 full-time employees. By March 15, 2016, Corporation S has more than 75 full-time employees.

(ii) *Conclusion*. Because Corporation S can reasonably be expected to employ on average at least 50 full-time employees on business days during 2016, and actually employs an average of at least 50 full-time employees on business days during 2016, Corporation S is an applicable large employer (and an applicable large employer member) for calendar year 2016.

Example 6 (First year as applicable large employer). (i) *Facts*. As of January 1, 2015, Employer R has been in existence for several years and did not average 50 or more full-time employees (including FTEs) on business days during 2014. Employer R averages 50 or more full-time employees on business days during 2015, so that for 2016 Employer R is an applicable large employer, for the first time. For all the calendar months of 2016, Employer R has the same 60 full-time employees. Employer R offered 20 of those full-time employees healthcare coverage during 2015, and offered those same employees coverage providing minimum value for 2016. With respect to the 40 full-time employees who were not offered coverage during 2015, Employer R offers coverage providing minimum value for calendar months April 2016 through December 2016.

(ii) *Conclusion*. For the 40 full-time employees not offered coverage during 2015 and offered coverage providing minimum value for the calendar months April 2016 through December 2016, the failure to offer coverage during the calendar months January 2016 through March 2016 will not result in an assessable payment under section 4980H with respect to those employees for those three calendar months. For those same 40 full-time employees, the offer of coverage during the calendar months April 2016 through December 2016 may result in an assessable payment under section 4980H(b) with respect to any employee for any calendar month for which the offer is not affordable and for which Employer R has received a Section 1411 Certification. For the other 20 full-time employees, the offer of coverage during 2016 may result in an assessable payment under section 4980H(b) for any calendar month if the offer is not affordable and Employer R has received a Section 1411 Certification with respect to the employee who

Reg. §54.4980H-2(d)

received the offer of coverage. For all calendar months of 2016, Employer R will not be subject to an assessable payment under section 4980H(a).

(e) *Additional guidance.*—With respect to an employer's status as an applicable large employer, the Commissioner may prescribe additional guidance of general applicability, published in the Internal Revenue Bulletin (see § 601.601(d)(2)(ii)(b) of this chapter).

(f) *Effective/applicability date.*—This section is applicable for periods after December 31, 2014. [Reg. § 54.4980H-2.]

☐ [*T.D.* 9655, 2-10-2014.]

[Reg. § 54.4980H-3]

§ 54.4980H-3. Determining full-time employees.—(a) *In general.*—This section sets forth the rules for determining hours of service and status as a full-time employee for purposes of section 4980H. These regulations provide two methods for determining full-time employee status—the monthly measurement method, set forth in paragraph (c) of this section, and the look-back measurement method, set forth in paragraph (d) of this section. The monthly measurement method applies for purposes of determining and calculating liability under section 4980H(a) and (b), as well as, with respect to paragraph (c)(1) of this section, determination of applicable large employer status (except with respect to the weekly rule under the monthly measurement method). The look-back measurement method applies solely for purposes of determining and calculating liability under section 4980H(a) and (b) (and not for purposes of determining status as an applicable large employer). See § 54.4980H-1(a)(21) for the definition of full-time employee. The rules set forth in this section prescribe the minimum standards for determining status as a full-time employee for purposes of section 4980H; treatment of additional employees as full-time employees for other purposes does not affect section 4980H liability if those employees are not full-time employees under the look-back measurement method or the monthly measurement method.

(b) *Hours of service.*—(1) *In general.*—The following rules on the calculation of hours of service apply for purposes of applying both the look-back measurement method and the monthly measurement method.

(2) *Hourly employees calculation.*—Under the look-back measurement method and the monthly measurement method, for employees paid on an hourly basis, an employer must calculate actual hours of service from records of hours worked and hours for which payment is made or due.

(3) *Non-hourly employees calculation.*—(i) *In general.*—Except as otherwise provided, under the look-back measurement method and the monthly measurement method, for employees paid on a non-hourly basis, an employer must

calculate hours of service by using one of the following methods:

(A) Using actual hours of service from records of hours worked and hours for which payment is made or due;

(B) Using a days-worked equivalency whereby the employee is credited with eight hours of service for each day for which the employee would be required to be credited with at least one hour of service in accordance with paragraph (b)(2) of this section; or

(C) Using a weeks-worked equivalency whereby the employee is credited with 40 hours of service for each week for which the employee would be required to be credited with at least one hour of service in accordance with paragraph (b)(2) of this section.

(ii) *Change in method.*—An employer must use one of the three methods in paragraph (b)(3)(i) of this section for calculating the hours of service for non-hourly employees. An employer is not required to use the same method for all non-hourly employees, and may apply different methods for different categories of non-hourly employees, provided the categories are reasonable and consistently applied. Similarly, an applicable large employer member is not required to apply the same methods as other applicable large employer members of the same applicable large employer for the same or different categories of non-hourly employees, provided that in each case the categories are reasonable and consistently applied by the applicable large employer member. An employer may change the method of calculating the hours of service of non-hourly employees (or of one or more categories of non-hourly employees) for each calendar year.

(iii) *Prohibited use of equivalencies.*—The number of hours of service calculated using the days-worked or weeks-worked equivalency must reflect generally the hours actually worked and the hours for which payment is made or due. An employer is not permitted to use the days-worked equivalency or the weeks-worked equivalency if the result is to substantially understate an employee's hours of service in a manner that would cause that employee not to be treated as a full-time employee, or if the result is to understate the hours of service of a substantial number of employees (even if no particular employee's hours of service are understated substantially and even if the understatement would not cause the employee to not be treated as a full-time employee). For example, as to the former, an employer may not use a days-worked equivalency in the case of an employee who generally works three 10-hour days per week, because the equivalency would substantially understate the employee's hours of service as 24 hours of service per week, which would result in the employee being treated as not a full-time employee.

(c) *Monthly measurement method.*—(1) *In general.*—Under the monthly measurement method,

an applicable large employer member determines each employee's status as a full-time employee by counting the employee's hours of service for each calendar month. See § 54.4980H-1(a)(21) for the definition of full-time employee. This paragraph (c)(1) (except with respect to the weekly rule) applies for purposes of the determination of status as an applicable large employer; paragraphs (c)(2) through (4) of this section do not apply for purposes of the determination of status as an applicable large employer. For rules regarding the use of the look-back measurement method and the monthly measurement method for different categories of employees, see paragraph (e) of this section.

(2) *Employee first otherwise eligible for an offer of coverage.*—The rule in this paragraph (c)(2) applies with respect to an employee who, in a calendar month, first becomes otherwise eligible to be offered coverage under a group health plan of an employer using the monthly measurement method with respect to that employee. For purposes of this paragraph (c)(2), an employee is otherwise eligible to be offered coverage under a group health plan for a calendar month if, pursuant to the terms of the plan as in effect for that calendar month, the employee meets all conditions to be offered coverage under the plan for that calendar month, other than the completion of a waiting period, within the meaning of § 54.9801-2, and an employee is first otherwise eligible if the employee has not previously been eligible or otherwise eligible for an offer of coverage under a group health plan of the employer during the employee's period of employment. An employer is not subject to an assessable payment under section 4980H(a) with respect to an employee for each calendar month during the period of three full calendar months beginning with the first full calendar month in which the employee is otherwise eligible for an offer of coverage under a group health plan of the employer, provided that the employee is offered coverage no later than the first day of the first calendar month immediately following the three-month period if the employee is still employed on that day. If the coverage for which the employee is otherwise eligible during the three-month period, and which the employee actually is offered on the day following that three-month period if still employed, provides minimum value, the employer also will not be subject to an assessable payment under section 4980H(b) with respect to that employee for the three-month period. This rule cannot apply more than once per period of employment of an employee. If an employee terminates employment and returns under circumstances that would constitute a rehire as set forth in paragraph (c)(4) of this section, the rule in this paragraph (c)(2) may apply again.

(3) *Use of weekly periods.*—With respect to a category of employees for whom an employer uses the monthly measurement method, an employer may determine full-time employee status

for a calendar month based on hours of service over a period that:

(i) begins on the first day of the week that includes the first day of the calendar month, provided that the period over which hours of service are measured does not include the week in which falls the last day of the calendar month (unless that week ends with the last day of the calendar month, in which case it is included); or

(ii) begins on the first day of the week immediately subsequent to the week that includes the first day of the calendar month (unless the week begins on the first day of the calendar month, in which case it is included), provided the period over which hours of service are measured includes the week in which falls the last day of the calendar month.

(4) *Employees rehired after termination of employment or resuming service after other absence.*—(i) *Treatment as a new employee after a period of absence for employees of employers other than educational organizations.*—Except as provided in paragraph (c)(4)(ii) of this section (related to rules for employers that are educational organizations), an employee who resumes providing services to (or is otherwise credited with an hour of service for) an applicable large employer after a period during which the individual was not credited with any hours of service may be treated as having terminated employment and having been rehired, and therefore may be treated as a new employee upon the resumption of services only if the employee did not have an hour of service for the applicable large employer for a period of at least 13 consecutive weeks immediately preceding the resumption of services. The rule set forth in this paragraph (c)(4)(i) applies solely for the purpose of determining whether the employee, upon the resumption of services, is treated as a new employee or as a continuing employee, and does not determine whether the employee is treated as a continuing full-time employee (for example, an employee on leave) or a terminated employee for some or all of the period during which no hours of service are credited.

(ii) *Treatment as a new employee after a period of absence for employees of educational organizations.*—With respect to an employer that is an educational organization, an employee who resumes providing services to (or is otherwise credited with an hour of service for) an applicable large employer after a period during which the individual was not credited with any hours of service may be treated as having terminated employment and having been rehired, and therefore may be treated as a new employee upon the resumption of services, only if the employee did not have an hour of service for the applicable large employer for a period of at least 26 consecutive weeks immediately preceding the resumption of services. The rule set forth in this paragraph (c)(4)(ii) applies solely for the purpose of determining whether the employee, upon the resumption of services, is treated as a new employee or as a continuing employee, and does

not determine whether the employee is treated as a continuing full-time employee (for example, an employee on leave) or a terminated employee for some or all of the period during which no hours of service are credited.

(iii) *Averaging method for special unpaid leave and employment break periods.*—The averaging method for periods of special unpaid leave and employment break periods does not apply under the monthly measurement method, regardless of whether the employer is (or is not) an educational organization.

(iv) *Treatment of continuing employee.*—The rule set forth in paragraph (c)(2) of this section applies to an employee treated as a continuing employee in the same way that it applies to an employee who has not experienced a period with no hours of service. A continuing employee treated as a full-time employee is treated as offered coverage upon resumption of services if the employee is offered coverage as of the first day that employee is credited with an hour of service, or, if later, as soon as administratively practicable. For this purpose, offering coverage by no later than the first day of the calendar month following resumption of services is deemed to be as soon as administratively practicable.

(v) *Rule of parity.*—For purposes of determining the period after which an employee may be treated as having terminated employment and having been rehired, an applicable large employer may choose a period, measured in weeks, of at least four consecutive weeks during which the employee was not credited with any hours of service that exceeds the number of weeks of that employee's period of employment with the applicable large employer immediately preceding the period that is shorter than 13 weeks (for an employee of an educational organization employer, a period that is shorter than 26 weeks).

(vi) *International transfers.*—An employer may treat an employee as having terminated employment if the employee transfers to a position at the same applicable large employer (including a different applicable large employer member that is part of the same applicable large employer) if the position is anticipated to continue indefinitely or for at least 12 months and if substantially all of the compensation will constitute income from sources without the United States (within the meaning of sections 861 through 863 and the regulations thereunder). With respect to an employee transferring from a position that was anticipated to continue indefinitely or for at least 12 months and in which substantially all of the compensation for the hours of service constitutes income from sources without the United States (within the meaning of sections 861 through 863 and the regulations thereunder) to a position at the same applicable large employer (including a different applicable large employer member that is part of the same applicable large employer) with respect to which substantially all of the compensation will consti-

tute U.S. source income, the employer may treat that employee as a new hire to the extent consistent with the rules related to rehired employees as set forth in paragraph (c)(4) of this section.

(5) *Examples.*—The following examples illustrate the rules of paragraphs (c)(1) through (4) of this section. In each example, the employer is an applicable large employer with 200 full-time employees (including FTEs) that uses the monthly measurement method to identify full-time employees and offers coverage only to employees who are full-time employees (and their dependents).

Example 1 (Monthly measurement method - employee first otherwise eligible for an offer of coverage). (i) *Facts.* Employer Z uses the monthly measurement method. Employer Z hires Employee A on January 1, 2016. For each calendar month in 2016, Employee A averages 20 hours of service per week and is not eligible (or otherwise eligible) for an offer of coverage under the group health plan of Employer Z. Effective January 1, 2017, Employee A is promoted to a position that is eligible for an offer of coverage under a group health plan of Employer Z, following completion of a 90-day waiting period. For January 2017 through March 2017, Employee A meets all of the conditions for eligibility under the group health plan, other than completion of the waiting period. The coverage that would have been offered to Employee A under the terms of the plan, but for the waiting period, during those three months would have provided minimum value. Effective April 1, 2017, Employer Z offers Employee A coverage that provides minimum value. Employee A averages 40 hours of service per week for each calendar month in 2017.

(ii) *Conclusion.* Because Employer Z offers minimum value coverage to Employee A no later than the first day following the period of three full calendar months beginning with the first full calendar month in which Employee A is otherwise eligible for an offer of coverage under a group health plan of Employer Z, Employer Z is not subject to an assessable payment for January 2017 through March 2017 under section 4980H by reason of its failure to offer coverage to Employee A during those months. For calendar months after March 2017, an offer of minimum value coverage may result in an assessable payment under section 4980H(b) with respect to Employee A for any month for which the offer is not affordable and for which Employer Z has received a Section 1411 Certification. Employer Z is not subject to an assessable payment under section 4980H by reason of its failure to offer coverage to Employee A during each month of 2016 because for each month of 2016, Employee A was not a full-time employee.

Example 2 (Rehire rules under monthly measurement method for employers that are not educational organizations). (i) *Facts.* Same as *Example 1*, except that Employee A has zero hours of service during a nine week period of unpaid leave (that constitutes special unpaid leave) beginning on June 25, 2017, and ending on August 26, 2017. As

a result of the nine week period during which Employee A has zero hours of service, Employee A averages less than 30 hours of service per week for July 2017 and August 2017. Employee A averages more than 30 hours of service per week for each month between and including September 2017 through December 2017. Employer Z does not use the rule of parity, set forth in paragraph (c)(4)(v) of this section, and Employer Z is not an educational organization.

(ii) *Conclusion.* Because Employee A resumes providing services for Employer Z after a period during which the employee was not credited with any hours of service of less than 13 consecutive weeks, Employer Z may not treat Employee A as having terminated employment and having been rehired. Therefore, Employer Z may not treat Employee A as a new employee upon the resumption of services, and, accordingly, Employer Z may not apply the rule set forth in paragraph (c)(2) of this section. Although the nine consecutive weeks of zero hours of service constitute special unpaid leave, the averaging method for periods of special unpaid leave does not apply under the monthly measurement method. Therefore, Employer Z may treat Employee A as a non-full-time employee for July 2017 and August 2017.

Example 3 (Use of weekly rule). (i) *Facts.* Employer Y uses the monthly measurement method in combination with the weekly rule for purposes of determining whether an employee is a full-time employee for a particular calendar month. For purposes of applying the weekly rule, Employer Y uses the period of Sunday through Saturday as a week and includes the week that includes the first day of a calendar month and excludes the week that includes the last day of a calendar month (except in any case in which the last day of the calendar month occurs on a Saturday). Employer Y measures hours of service for the five weeks from Sunday, December 27, 2015, through Saturday, January 30, 2016, to determine an employee's full-time employee status for January 2016, for the four weeks from Sunday, January 31, 2016, through Saturday, February 27, 2016, to determine an employee's status for February 2016, and the four weeks from Sunday, February 28, 2016, through Saturday, March 26, 2016, to determine an employee's status for March 2016. For January 2016, Employer Y treats an employee as a full-time employee if the employee has at least 150 hours of service (30 hours per week × 5 weeks). For February 2016 and March 2016, Employer Y treats an employee as a full-time employee if the employee has at least 120 hours of service (30 hours per week × 4 weeks).

(ii) *Conclusion.* Employer Y has correctly applied the weekly rule as part of the monthly measurement method for determining each employee's status as a full-time employee for the months January, February, and March 2016.

(d) *Look-back measurement method.*—(1) *Ongoing employees.*—(i) *In general.*—Under the look-back measurement method for ongoing employ-

ees, an applicable large employer determines each ongoing employee's full-time employee status by looking back at the standard measurement period. The applicable large employer member determines the months in which the standard measurement period starts and ends, provided that the determination must be made on a uniform and consistent basis for all employees in the same category (see paragraph (d)(1)(v) of this section for a list of permissible categories). For example, if an applicable large employer member chooses a standard measurement period of 12 months, the applicable large employer member could choose to make it the calendar year, a non-calendar plan year, or a different 12-month period, such as one that ends shortly before the start of the plan's annual open enrollment period. If the applicable large employer member determines that an employee was employed on average at least 30 hours of service per week during the standard measurement period, then the applicable large employer member must treat the employee as a full-time employee during a subsequent stability period, regardless of the employee's number of hours of service during the stability period, so long as he or she remains an employee.

(ii) *Use of payroll periods.*—For payroll periods that are one week, two weeks, or semimonthly in duration, an employer is permitted to treat as a measurement period a period that ends on the last day of the payroll period preceding the payroll period that includes the date that would otherwise be the last day of the measurement period, provided that the measurement period begins on the first day of the payroll period that includes the date that would otherwise be the first day of the measurement period. An employer may also treat as a measurement period a period that begins on the first day of the payroll period that follows the payroll period that includes the date that would otherwise be the first day of the measurement period, provided that the measurement period ends on the last day of the payroll period that includes the date that would otherwise be the last day of the measurement period. For example, an employer using the calendar year as a measurement period could exclude the entire payroll period that included January 1 (the beginning of the year) if it included the entire payroll period that included December 31 (the end of that same year), or, alternatively, could exclude the entire payroll period that included December 31 of a calendar year if it included the entire payroll period that included January 1 of that calendar year.

(iii) *Employee determined to be employed an average of at least 30 hours of service per week.*—An employee who was employed on average at least 30 hours of service per week during the standard measurement period must be treated as a full-time employee for a stability period that begins immediately after the standard measurement period and any applicable administrative period. The stability period must be at least six consecu-

tive calendar months but no shorter in duration than the standard measurement period.

(iv) *Employee determined not to be employed on average at least 30 hours of service per week.*—If an employee was not employed an average of at least 30 hours of service per week during the standard measurement period, the applicable large employer member may treat the employee as not a full-time employee during the stability period that follows, but is not longer than, the standard measurement period. The stability period must begin immediately after the end of the measurement period and any applicable administrative period.

(v) *Permissible employee categories.*—Different applicable large employer members of the same applicable large employer may use measurement periods and stability periods that differ either in length or in their starting or ending dates. In addition, subject to the rules governing the relationship between the length of the measurement period and the stability period, applicable large employer members may use measurement periods and stability periods that differ either in length or in their starting and ending dates for—

(A) Collectively bargained employees and non-collectively bargained employees,

(B) Each group of collectively bargained employees covered by a separate collective bargaining agreement,

(C) Salaried employees and hourly employees, and

(D) Employees whose primary places of employment are in different States.

(vi) *Optional administrative period.*—An applicable large employer member may provide for an administrative period that begins immediately after the end of a standard measurement period and that ends immediately before the associated stability period; however, any administrative period between the standard measurement period and the stability period for ongoing employees may neither reduce nor lengthen the measurement period or the stability period. The administrative period following the standard measurement period may last up to 90 days. To prevent this administrative period from creating a period during which coverage is not available, the administrative period must overlap with the prior stability period, so that, during any such administrative period applicable to ongoing employees following a standard measurement period, ongoing employees who are enrolled in coverage because of their status as full-time employees based on a prior measurement period must continue to be covered through the administrative period. Applicable large employer members may use administrative periods that differ in length for the categories of employees identified in paragraph (d)(1)(v) of this section.

(vii) *Change in employment status.*—Except as provided in paragraph (f)(2) of this section, if an ongoing employee experiences a change in employment status before the end of a stability period, the change will not affect the application of the classification of the employee as a full-time employee (or not a full-time employee) for the remaining portion of the stability period. For example, if an ongoing employee in a certain position of employment is not treated as a full-time employee during a stability period because the employee's hours of service during the prior measurement period were insufficient for full-time-employee treatment, and the employee experiences a change in employment status that involves an increased level of hours of service, the treatment of the employee as a non-full-time employee during the remainder of the stability period is unaffected. Similarly, if an ongoing employee in a certain position of employment is treated as a full-time employee during a stability period because the employee's hours of service during the prior measurement period were sufficient for full-time-employee treatment, and the employee experiences a change in employment status that involves a lower level of hours of service, the treatment of the employee as a full-time employee during the remainder of the stability period is unaffected.

(viii) *Example.*—The following example illustrates the application of paragraph (d)(1) of this section:

(A) *Facts.*—Employer Z is an applicable large employer member and computes hours of service following the rules in this paragraph (d)(1). Employer Z chooses to use a 12-month stability period that begins January 1 and a 12-month standard measurement period that begins October 15. Consistent with the terms of Employer Z's group health plan, only employees classified as full-time employees using the lookback measurement method are eligible for coverage. Employer Z chooses to use an administrative period between the end of the standard measurement period (October 14) and the beginning of the stability period (January 1) to determine which employees were employed on average 30 hours of service per week during the measurement period, notify them of their eligibility for the plan for the calendar year beginning on January 1 and of the coverage available under the plan, answer questions and collect materials from employees, and enroll those employees who elect coverage in the plan. Previously-determined full-time employees already enrolled in coverage continue to be offered coverage through the administrative period. Employee A and Employee B have been employed by Employer Z for several years, continuously from their start date. Employee A was employed on average 30 hours of service per week during the standard measurement period that begins October 15, 2015, and ends October 14, 2016, and for all prior standard measurement periods. Employee B also was employed on average 30 hours of service per week for all prior standard measurement periods, but averaged less than 30 hours of service per week during the standard

measurement period that begins October 15, 2015, and ends October 14, 2016.

(B) *Conclusions*.—Because Employee A was employed for the entire standard measurement period that begins October 15, 2015, and ends October 14, 2016, Employee A is an ongoing employee with respect to the stability period running from January 1, 2017, through December 31, 2017. Because Employee A was employed on average 30 hours of service per week during that standard measurement period, Employee A is offered coverage for the entire 2017 stability period (including the administrative period from October 15, 2017, through December 31, 2017). Because Employee A was employed on average 30 hours of service per week during the prior standard measurement period, Employee A is offered coverage for the entire 2016 stability period and, if enrolled, would continue such coverage during the administrative period from October 15, 2016, through December 31, 2016. Because Employee B was employed for the entire standard measurement period that begins October 15, 2015, and ends October 14, 2016, Employee B is also an ongoing employee with respect to the stability period in 2017. Because Employee B was not a full-time employee based on hours of service during this standard measurement period, Employee B is not offered coverage for the stability period in 2017 (including the administrative period from October 15, 2017, through December 31, 2017). However, because Employee B was employed on average 30 hours of service per week during the prior standard measurement period, Employee B is offered coverage through the end of the 2016 stability period and, if enrolled, would continue such coverage during the administrative period from October 15, 2016, through December 31, 2016. Employer Z complies with the standards of paragraph (d)(1) of this section because the standard measurement period is no longer than 12 months, the stability period for ongoing employees who are full-time employees based on hours of service during the standard measurement period is not shorter than the standard measurement period, the stability period for ongoing employees who are not full-time employees based on hours of service during the standard measurement period is no longer than the standard measurement period, and the administrative period is no longer than 90 days.

(2) *New non-variable hour, new non-seasonal and new non-part-time employees*.—(i) *In general*.— For a new employee who is reasonably expected at the employee's start date to be a full-time employee (and is not a seasonal employee), an applicable large employer member determines such employee's status as a full-time employee based on the employee's hours of service for each calendar month. If the employee's hours of service for the calendar month equal or exceed an average of 30 hours of service per week, the employee is a full-time employee for that calendar month. Once a new employee who is reasonably expected at the employee's start date to be a full-time employee (and is not a seasonal em-

ployee) becomes an ongoing employee, the rules set forth in paragraph (d)(1) of this section apply for determining full-time employee status.

(ii) *Factors for determining full-time employee status*.—Whether an employer's determination that a new employee (who is not a seasonal employee) is a full-time employee or is not a full-time employee is reasonable is based on the facts and circumstances at the employee's start date. Factors to consider in determining whether a new employee who is not a seasonal employee is reasonably expected at the employee's start date to be a full-time employee include, but are not limited to, whether the employee is replacing an employee who was (or was not) a full-time employee, the extent to which hours of service of ongoing employees in the same or comparable positions have varied above and below an average of 30 hours of service per week during recent measurement periods, and whether the job was advertised, or otherwise communicated to the new hire or otherwise documented (for example, through a contract or job description), as requiring hours of service that would average 30 (or more) hours of service per week or less than 30 hours of service per week. In all cases, no single factor is determinative. An educational organization employer cannot take into account the potential for, or likelihood of, an employment break period in determining its expectation of future hours of service.

(iii) *Application of section 4980H to initial full three calendar months of employment*.—Notwithstanding paragraph (d)(2)(i) of this section, with respect to an employee who is reasonably expected at his or her start date to be a full-time employee (and is not a seasonal employee), the employer will not be subject to an assessable payment under section 4980H(a) for any calendar month of the three-month period beginning with the first day of the first full calendar month of employment if, for the calendar month, the employee is otherwise eligible for an offer of coverage under a group health plan of the employer, provided that the employee is offered coverage by the employer no later than the first day of the fourth full calendar month of employment if the employee is still employed on that day. If the offer of coverage for which the employee is otherwise eligible during the first three full calendar months of employment, and which the employee actually is offered by the first day of the fourth month if still employed, provides minimum value, the employer also will not be subject to an assessable payment under section 4980H(b) with respect to that employee for the first three full calendar months of employment. For purposes of this paragraph (d)(2)(iii), an employee is otherwise eligible to be offered coverage under a group health plan for a calendar month if, pursuant to the terms of the plan as in effect for that calendar month, the employee meets all conditions to be offered coverage under the plan for that calendar month, other than the completion of a waiting period, within the meaning of § 54.9801-2.

Reg. § 54.4980H-3(d)(2)(iii)

(3) *New variable hour employees, new seasonal employees, and new part-time employees.*—(i) *In general.*—For new variable hour employees, new seasonal employees, and new part-time employees, applicable large employer members are permitted to determine whether the new employee is a full-time employee using an initial measurement period of no less than three consecutive months and no more than 12 consecutive months (as selected by the applicable large employer member) that begins on the employee's start date or on any date up to and including the first day of the first calendar month following the employee's start date (or on the first day of the first payroll period starting on or after the employee's start date, if later, as set forth in paragraph (d)(3)(ii) of this section). The applicable large employer member measures the new employee's hours of service during the initial measurement period and determines whether the employee was employed on average at least 30 hours of service per week during this period. The stability period for such employees must be the same length as the stability period for ongoing employees.

(ii) *Use of payroll periods.*—An applicable large employer member may apply the payroll period rule set forth in paragraph (d)(1)(ii) of this section for purposes of determining an initial measurement period, provided that the initial measurement period must begin on the start date or any date during the period beginning with the employee's start date and ending with the later of the first day of the first calendar month following the employee's start date and the first day of the first payroll period that starts after the employee's start date. As set forth in paragraph (d)(1)(ii) of this section, the use of payroll periods for purposes of determining the initial measurement period applies for payroll periods that are one week, two weeks, or semimonthly in duration.

(iii) *Employees determined to be employed on average at least 30 hours of service per week.*—If a new variable hour employee, new seasonal employee, or new part-time employee has on average at least 30 hours of service per week during the initial measurement period, the applicable large employer member must treat the employee as a full-time employee during the stability period that begins after the initial measurement period (and any associated administrative period). The stability period must be a period of at least six consecutive calendar months that is no shorter in duration than the initial measurement period. The stability period must begin immediately after the end of the measurement period and any applicable administrative period. With respect to an employee who has on average at least 30 hours of service per week during the initial measurement period, the employer will not be subject to an assessable payment under section 4980H(a) for any calendar month during the initial measurement period and any associated administrative period if, for the calendar month, the employee is otherwise eligible for an offer of coverage under a group health plan of the employer, provided that the employee is offered coverage by the employer no later than the first day of the associated stability period if the employee is still employed on that day. If the offer of coverage for which the employee is otherwise eligible during the initial measurement period, and which the employee actually is offered by the first day of the stability period if still employed, provides minimum value, the employer also will not be subject to an assessable payment under section 4980H(b) with respect to that employee during the initial measurement period and any associated administrative period. For purposes of this paragraph (d)(3)(iii), an employee is otherwise eligible to be offered coverage under a group health plan for a month if, pursuant to the terms of the plan as in effect for that calendar month, the employee meets all conditions to be offered coverage under the plan for that month, other than the completion of a waiting period, within the meaning of § 54.9801-2.

(iv) *Employees determined not to be employed on average at least 30 hours of service per week.*—If a new variable hour employee, new seasonal employee, or new part-time employee does not have on average at least 30 hours of service per week during the initial measurement period, the applicable large employer member may treat the employee as not a full-time employee during the stability period that follows the initial measurement period. Except as provided in paragraph (d)(4)(iv) of this section, the stability period for such employees must not be more than one month longer than the initial measurement period and must not exceed the remainder of the first entire standard measurement period (plus any associated administrative period) for which a variable hour employee, seasonal employee, or part-time employee has been employed. The stability period must begin immediately after the end of the measurement period and any applicable administrative period.

(v) *Permissible differences in measurement or stability periods for different categories of employees.*—Subject to the rules governing the relationship between the length of the measurement period and the stability period, with respect to a new variable hour employee, new seasonal employee, or new part-time employee, applicable large employer members may use measurement periods and stability periods that differ either in length or in their starting and ending dates for the categories of employees identified in paragraph (d)(1)(v) of this section.

(vi) *Optional administrative period.*—(A) *In general.*—Subject to the limits in paragraph (d)(3)(vi)(B) of this section, an applicable large employer member may apply an administrative period in connection with an initial measurement period and before the start of the stability period. This administrative period must not ex-

ceed 90 days in total. For this purpose, the administrative period includes all periods between the start date of a new variable hour employee, new seasonal employee, or new part-time employee and the date the employee is first offered coverage under the applicable large employer member's group health plan, other than the initial measurement period. Thus, for example, if the applicable large employer member begins the initial measurement period on the first day of the first month following a new employee's start date, the period between the employee's start date and the first day of the next month must be taken into account in applying the 90-day limit on the administrative period. Similarly, if there is a period between the end of the initial measurement period and the date the employee is first offered coverage under the plan, that period must be taken into account in applying the 90-day limit on the administrative period. Applicable large employer members may use administrative periods that differ in length for the categories of employees identified in paragraph (d)(1)(v) of this section.

(B) *Limit on combined length of initial measurement period and administrative period.*—In addition to the specific limits on the initial measurement period (which must not exceed 12 months) and the administrative period (which must not exceed 90 days), there is a limit on the combined length of the initial measurement period and the administrative period applicable to a new variable hour employee, new seasonal employee, or new part-time employee. Specifically, the initial measurement period and administrative period together cannot extend beyond the last day of the first calendar month beginning on or after the first anniversary of the employee's start date. For example, if an applicable large employer member uses a 12-month initial measurement period for a new variable hour employee, and begins that initial measurement period on the first day of the first calendar month following the employee's start date, the period between the end of the initial measurement period and the offer of coverage to a new variable hour employee who is a full-time employee based on hours of service during the initial measurement period must not exceed one month.

(vii) *Change in employment status during the initial measurement period.*—(A) *In general.*—If a new variable hour employee, new seasonal employee, or new part-time employee experiences a change in employment status before the end of the initial measurement period such that, if the employee had begun employment in the new position or status, the employee would have reasonably been expected to be employed on average at least 30 hours of service per week (or, if applicable, would not have been a seasonal employee and would have been expected to be employed on average at least 30 hours of service per week), the rules set forth in the remainder of this paragraph (d)(3)(vii) apply. With respect to an employee described in this paragraph (d)(3)(vii) and subject to the rules in the next sentence, the employer will not be subject to an assessable payment under section 4980H for the period before the first day of the fourth full calendar month following the change in employment status (or, if earlier and the employee averages 30 or more hours of service per week during the initial measurement period, the first day of the first month following the end of the initial measurement period (including any optional administrative period associated with the initial measurement period)). An employer will not be subject to an assessable payment under section 4980H(a) with respect to an employee described in this paragraph (d)(3)(vii) for any calendar month during the period described in the prior sentence if, for the calendar month, the employee is otherwise eligible for an offer of coverage under a group health plan of the employer, provided that the employee is offered coverage by the employer no later than the end of the period described in the prior sentence if the employee is still employed on that date; if the offer of coverage for which the employee is otherwise eligible during the period described in the prior sentence, and which the employee is actually offered by the first day after the end of that period if still employed, provides minimum value, the employer also will not be subject to an assessable payment under section 4980H(b) with respect to that employee during that period. For purposes of this paragraph (d)(3)(vii), an employee is otherwise eligible to be offered coverage under a group health plan for a calendar month if, pursuant to the terms of the plan as in effect for that calendar month, the employee meets all conditions to be offered coverage under the plan for that calendar month, other than the completion of a waiting period, within the meaning of § 54.9801-2.

(B) *Example.*—The following example illustrates the provisions of paragraph (d)(3)(vii) of this section. In the following example, the applicable large employer member has 200 full-time employees and offers all of its full-time employees (and their dependents) the opportunity to enroll in minimum essential coverage under an eligible employer-sponsored plan. The coverage is affordable within the meaning of section 36B(c)(2)(C)(i) (or is treated as affordable under one of the affordability safe harbors described in § 54.4980H-5) and provides minimum value.

Example (Change in employment status from variable hour employee to full-time employee). (i) *Facts.* For new variable hour employees, Employer Z uses a 12-month initial measurement period that begins on the start date and applies an administrative period from the end of the initial measurement period through the end of the first calendar month beginning on or after the end of the initial measurement period. For new variable hour employees, Employer Z offers coverage no later than the first day of the fourteenth month after the start date if an employee averages 30 or more hours of service per week

during the initial measurement period. Employer Z hires Employee A on May 10, 2015. Employee A's initial measurement period runs from May 10, 2015, through May 9, 2016, with the optional administrative period ending June 30, 2016. At Employee A's May 10, 2015, start date, Employee A is a variable hour employee. On September 15, 2015, Employer Z promotes Employee A to a position that can reasonably be expected to average at least 30 hours of service per week. For October 2015 through December 2015, Employee A is otherwise eligible for an offer of coverage that provides minimum value, and, on January 1, 2016, Employee A is offered coverage by the employer that provides minimum value.

(ii) *Conclusion.* Employer Z will not be subject to an assessable payment under section 4980H(a) with respect to Employee A for October 2015, November 2015, or December 2015, because for each of those months Employee A is otherwise eligible for an offer of coverage and because Employee A is offered coverage by January 1, 2016 (the date that is the earlier of the first day of the fourth calendar month following the change in employment status (January 1, 2016) or the first day of the calendar month after the end of the initial measurement period plus the optional administrative period (July 1, 2016)). Because the coverage offered on January 1, 2016, provides minimum value, Employer Z also will not be subject to an assessable payment under section 4980H(b) with respect to Employee A for October 2015, November 2015, or December 2015.

(4) *Transition from new variable hour employee, new seasonal employee, or new part-time employee to ongoing employee.*—(i) *In general.*—Once a new variable hour employee, new seasonal employee, or new part-time employee has been employed for an entire standard measurement period, the applicable large employer member must test the employee for full-time employee status, beginning with that standard measurement period, at the same time and under the same conditions as apply to other ongoing employees. Accordingly, for example, an applicable large employer member with a calendar year standard measurement period that also uses a one-year initial measurement period beginning on the employee's start date would test a new employee whose start date is April 12 for full-time employee status first based on the initial measurement period (April 12 of the year including the start date through April 11 of the following year) and again based on the calendar year standard measurement period (if the employee continues in employment for that entire standard measurement period) beginning on January 1 of the year after the start date.

(ii) *Employee determined to be employed an average of at least 30 hours of service per week.*—An employee who was employed an average of at least 30 hours of service per week during an initial measurement period or standard measurement period must be treated as a full-time employee for the entire associated stability period. This is the case even if the employee was employed an average of at least 30 hours of service per week during the initial measurement period but was not employed an average of at least 30 hours of service per week during the overlapping or immediately following standard measurement period. In that case, the applicable large employer member may treat the employee as not a full-time employee only after the end of the stability period associated with the initial measurement period. Thereafter, the applicable large employer member must determine the employee's status as a full-time employee in the same manner as it determines such status in the case of its other ongoing employees as described in paragraph (d)(1) of this section.

(iii) *Employee determined not to be employed an average of at least 30 hours of service per week.*—If the employee was not employed an average of at least 30 hours of service per week during the initial measurement period, but was employed at least 30 hours of service per week during the overlapping or immediately following standard measurement period, the employee must be treated as a full-time employee for the entire stability period that corresponds to that standard measurement period (even if that stability period begins before the end of the stability period associated with the initial measurement period). Thereafter, the applicable large employer member must determine the employee's status as a full-time employee in the same manner as it determines such status in the case of its other ongoing employees as described in paragraph (d)(1) of this section.

(iv) *Treatment during periods between stability periods.*—If there is a period between the end of the stability period associated with the initial measurement period and the beginning of the stability period associated with the first full standard measurement period during which an employee is employed, the treatment as a full-time employee or not a full-time employee that applies during the stability period associated with the initial measurement period continues to apply until the beginning of the stability period associated with the first full standard measurement period during which the employee is employed.

(5) *Examples.*—The following examples illustrate the look-back measurement methods described in paragraphs (d)(1), (d)(3) and (d)(4) of this section. In all of the following examples, the applicable large employer member has 200 full-time employees and offers all of its full-time employees (and their dependents) the opportunity to enroll in minimum essential coverage under an eligible employer-sponsored plan. The coverage is affordable within the meaning of section 36B(c)(2)(C)(i) (or is treated as affordable coverage under one of the affordability safe harbors described in § 54.4980H-5) and provides minimum value. In *Example 1* through *Example 8*, the new employee is a new variable hour em-

ployee, and the employer has chosen to use a 12-month standard measurement period for ongoing employees starting October 15 and a 12-month stability period associated with that standard measurement period starting January 1. (Thus, during the administrative period from October 15 through December 31 of each calendar year, the employer continues to offer coverage to employees who qualified for coverage for that entire calendar year based upon having an average of at least 30 hours of service per week during the prior standard measurement period.) In *Example 9* and *Example 10*, the new employee is a new variable hour employee, and the employer uses a six-month standard measurement period, starting each May 1 and November 1, with six-month stability periods associated with those standard measurement periods starting January 1 and July 1. In *Example 12, Example 13*, and *Example 14*, the employer is in the trade or business of providing temporary workers to numerous clients that are unrelated to the employer and to one another; the employer is the common law employer of the temporary workers based on all of the facts and circumstances; the employer offers health plan coverage only to full-time employees (including temporary workers who are full-time employees) and their dependents; and the employer uses a 12-month initial measurement period for new variable hour employees that begins on the start date and applies an administrative period from the end of the initial measurement period through the end of the first calendar month beginning after the end of the initial measurement period.

Example 1 (12-Month initial measurement period followed by 1+ partial month administrative period). (i) *Facts.* For new variable hour employees, Employer Z uses a 12-month initial measurement period that begins on the start date and applies an administrative period from the end of the initial measurement period through the end of the first calendar month beginning on or after the end of the initial measurement period. Employer Z hires Employee A on May 10, 2015. Employee A's initial measurement period runs from May 10, 2015, through May 9, 2016. Employee A has an average of 30 hours of service per week during this initial measurement period. Employer Z offers coverage that provides minimum value to Employee A for a stability period that runs from July 1, 2016, through June 30, 2017. For each calendar month during the period beginning with June 2015 and ending with June 2016, Employee A is otherwise eligible for an offer of coverage with respect to the coverage that is offered to Employee A on July 1, 2016.

(ii) *Conclusion.* Employer Z uses an initial measurement period that does not exceed 12 months; an administrative period totaling not more than 90 days; and a combined initial measurement period and administrative period that does not last beyond the final day of the first calendar month beginning on or after the one-year anniversary of Employee A's start date. Accordingly, Employer Z complies with the standards for the initial measurement period and

stability periods for a new variable hour employee. Employer Z will not be subject to an assessable payment under section 4980H(a) with respect to Employee A for any calendar month from June 2015 through June 2016 because, for each month during that period, Employee A is otherwise eligible for an offer of coverage and because coverage is offered no later than the end of the initial measurement period plus the associated administrative period (July 1, 2016). Employer Z will not be subject to an assessable payment under section 4980H(b) with respect to Employee A for any calendar month from June 2015 through June 2016 because the coverage Employer Z offers to Employee A provides minimum value. Employer Z will not be subject to an assessable payment under section 4980H(a) or (b) with respect to Employee A for May 2015 because an applicable large employer member is not subject to an assessable payment under section 4980H with respect to an employee for the calendar month in which falls the employee's start date if the start date is on a date other than the first day of the calendar month. Employer Z must test Employee A again based on the period from October 15, 2015, through October 14, 2016 (Employer Z's first standard measurement period that begins after Employee A's start date).

Example 2 (11-Month initial measurement period followed by 2+ partial month administrative period). (i) *Facts.* Same as *Example 1,* except that Employer Z uses an 11-month initial measurement period that begins on the start date and applies an administrative period from the end of the initial measurement period until the end of the second calendar month beginning after the end of the initial measurement period. Employee A's initial measurement period runs from May 10, 2015, through April 9, 2016. The administrative period associated with Employee A's initial measurement period ends on June 30, 2016. Employee A has an average of 30 hours of service per week during this initial measurement period.

(ii) *Conclusion.* Same as *Example 1.*

Example 3 (11-Month initial measurement period preceded by partial month administrative period and followed by 2-month administrative period). (i) *Facts.* Same as *Example 1,* except that Employer Z uses an 11-month initial measurement period that begins on the first day of the first calendar month beginning after the start date and applies an administrative period that runs from the end of the initial measurement period through the end of the second calendar month beginning on or after the end of the initial measurement period. Employee A's initial measurement period runs from June 1, 2015, through April 30, 2016. The administrative period associated with Employee A's initial measurement period ends on June 30, 2016. Employee A has an average of 30 hours of service per week during this initial measurement period.

(ii) *Conclusion.* Same as *Example 1.*

Example 4 (12-Month initial measurement period preceded by partial month administrative period and followed by 2-month administrative period). (i)

Facts. For new variable hour employees, Employer Z uses a 12-month initial measurement period that begins on the first day of the first month following the start date and applies an administrative period that runs from the end of the initial measurement period through the end of the second calendar month beginning on or after the end of the initial measurement period. Employer Z hires Employee A on May 10, 2015. Employee A's initial measurement period runs from June 1, 2015, through May 31, 2016. Employee A has an average of 30 hours of service per week during this initial measurement period. Employer Z offers coverage to Employee A for a stability period that runs from August 1, 2016, through July 31, 2017.

(ii) *Conclusion.* Employer Z does not satisfy the standards for the look-back measurement method in paragraph (d)(3)(vi)(B) of this section because the combination of the initial partial month delay, the 12-month initial measurement period, and the two month administrative period means that the coverage offered to Employee A does not become effective until after the first day of the second calendar month following the first anniversary of Employee A's start date. Accordingly, Employer Z is potentially subject to an assessable payment under section 4980H for each full calendar month during the initial measurement period and associated administrative period.

Example 5 (Continuous full-time employee). (i) *Facts.* Same as *Example 1*; in addition, Employer Z tests Employee A again based on Employee A's hours of service from October 15, 2015, through October 14, 2016 (Employer Z's first standard measurement period that begins after Employee A's start date), determines that Employee A has an average of 30 hours of service per week during that period, and offers Employee A coverage for July 1, 2017, through December 31, 2017. (Employee A already has an offer of coverage for the period of January 1, 2017, through June 30, 2017, because that period is covered by the initial stability period following the initial measurement period, during which Employee A was determined to be a full-time employee.)

(ii) *Conclusion.* Employer Z is not subject to any payment under section 4980H for any calendar month during 2017 with respect to Employee A.

Example 6 (Initially full-time employee, becomes non-full-time employee). (i) *Facts.* Same as *Example 1*; in addition, Employer Z tests Employee A again based on Employee A's hours of service from October 15, 2015, through October 14, 2016 (Employer Z's first standard measurement period that begins after Employee A's start date), and determines that Employee A has an average of 28 hours of service per week during that period. Employer Z continues to offer coverage to Employee A through June 30, 2017 (the end of the stability period based on the initial measurement period during which Employee A was determined to be a full-time employee), but does not offer coverage to Employee A for the period of July 1, 2017, through December 31, 2017.

(ii) *Conclusion.* Employer Z is not subject to any payment under section 4980H for any calendar month during 2017 with respect to Employee A.

Example 7 (Initially non-full-time employee). (i) *Facts.* Same as *Example 1*, except that Employee A has an average of 28 hours of service per week during the initial measurement period (May 10, 2015, through May 9, 2016), and Employer Z does not offer coverage to Employee A for any calendar month in 2016.

(ii) *Conclusion.* From Employee A's start date through the end of 2016, Employer Z is not subject to any payment under section 4980H with respect to Employee A, because Employer Z complies with the standards for the measurement and stability periods for a new variable hour employee with respect to Employee A and because under those standards, Employee A is not a full-time employee for any month during 2016.

Example 8 (Initially non-full-time employee, becomes full-time employee). (i) Facts. Same as *Example 7*; in addition, Employer Z tests Employee A again based on Employee A's hours of service from October 15, 2015, through October 14, 2016 (Employer Z's first standard measurement period that begins after Employee A's start date), determines that Employee A has an average of 30 hours of service per week during this standard measurement period, and offers coverage to Employee A for 2017.

(ii) *Conclusion.* Employer Z is not subject to any payment under section 4980H for any calendar month during 2017 with respect to Employee A.

Example 9 (Initially full-time employee). (i) *Facts.* For new variable hour employees, Employer Y uses a six-month initial measurement period that begins on the start date and applies an administrative period that runs from the end of the initial measurement period through the end of the first full calendar month beginning after the end of the initial measurement period. Employer Y hires Employee B on May 10, 2015. Employee B's initial measurement period runs from May 10, 2015, through November 9, 2015, during which Employee B has an average of 30 hours of service per week. Employer Y offers coverage that provides minimum value to Employee B for a stability period that runs from January 1, 2016, through June 30, 2016. For each calendar month during the period from June 2015 through December 2015, Employee B is otherwise eligible for an offer of coverage with respect to the coverage that is offered to Employee B on January 1, 2016.

(ii) *Conclusion.* Employer Y uses an initial measurement period that does not exceed 12 months; an administrative period totaling not more than 90 days; and a combined initial measurement period and administrative period that does not extend beyond the final day of the first calendar month beginning on or after the one-

year anniversary of Employee B's start date. Employer Y complies with the standards for the measurement and stability periods for a new variable hour employee with respect to Employee B. Employer Y is not subject to an assessable payment under section 4980H(a) with respect to Employee B for any calendar month from June 2015 through December 2015 because, for each month during that period, Employee B is otherwise eligible for an offer of coverage and because Employee B is offered coverage no later than the end of the initial measurement period plus the associated administrative period (January 1, 2016). Employer Y is not subject to an assessable payment under section 4980H(b) with respect to Employee B for any calendar month from June 2015 through December 2015 because the coverage Employer Y offers to Employee B no later than January 1, 2016, provides minimum value. Employer Y is not subject to an assessable payment under section 4980H(a) or (b) with respect to Employee B for May 2015 because an applicable large employer member is not subject to an assessable payment under section 4980H with respect to an employee for the calendar month in which falls the employee's start date if the start date is on a date other than the first day of the calendar month. Employer Y must test Employee B again based on Employee B's hours of service during the period from November 1, 2015, through April 30, 2016 (Employer Y's first standard measurement period that begins after Employee B's start date).

Example 10 (Initially full-time employee, becomes non-full-time employee). (i) *Facts.* Same as *Example 9*; in addition, Employer Y tests Employee B again based on Employee B's hours of service during the period from November 1, 2015, through April 30, 2016 (Employer Y's first standard measurement period that begins after Employee B's start date), during which period Employee B has an average of 28 hours of service per week. Employer Y continues to offer coverage to Employee B through June 30, 2016 (the end of the initial stability period based on the initial measurement period during which Employee B has an average of 30 hours of service per week), but does not offer coverage to Employee B from July 1, 2016, through December 31, 2016.

(ii) *Conclusion.* Employer Y is not subject to any payment under section 4980H with respect to Employee B for any calendar month during 2016.

Example 11 (Seasonal employee, 12-month initial measurement period; 1+ partial month administrative period). (i) *Facts.* Employer X offers health plan coverage only to full-time employees (and their dependents). Employer X uses a 12-month initial measurement period for new seasonal employees that begins on the start date and applies an administrative period from the end of the initial measurement period through the end of the first calendar month beginning after the end of the initial measurement period. Employer X hires Employee C, a ski instructor, on November 15, 2015, with an anticipated season during

which Employee C will work running through March 15, 2016. Employee C's initial measurement period runs from November 15, 2015, through November 14, 2016.

(ii) *Conclusion.* Employer X determines that Employee C is a seasonal employee because Employee C is hired into a position for which the customary annual employment is six months or less. Accordingly, Employer X may treat Employee C as a seasonal employee during the initial measurement period.

Example 12 (Variable hour employee; temporary staffing firm). (i) *Facts.* Employer W hires Employee D on January 1, 2015, in a position under which Employer W will offer assignments to Employee D to provide services in temporary placements at clients of Employer W, and employees of Employer W in the same position as Employee D, as part of their continuing employment, retain the right to reject an offer of placement. Employees of Employer W in the same position of employment as Employee D typically perform services for a particular client for 40 hours of service per week for a period of less than 13 weeks, and for each employee there are typically periods in a calendar year during which Employer W does not have an assignment to offer the employee. At the time Employee D is hired by Employer W, Employer W has no reason to anticipate that Employee D's position of employment will differ from the typical employee in the same position.

(ii) *Conclusion.* Employer W cannot determine whether Employee D is reasonably expected to average at least 30 hours of service per week for the 12-month initial measurement period. Accordingly, Employer W may treat Employee D as a variable hour employee during the initial measurement period.

Example 13 (Variable hour employee; temporary staffing firm). (i) *Facts.* Employer V hires Employee E on January 1, 2015, in a position under which Employer V will offer assignments to Employee E to provide services in temporary placements at clients of Employer V. Employees of Employer V in the same position of employment as Employee E typically are offered assignments of varying hours of service per week (so that some weeks of the assignment typically result in more than 30 hours of service per week and other weeks of the assignment typically result in less than 30 hours of service per week). Although a typical employee in the same position of employment as Employee E rarely fails to have an offer of an assignment for any period during the calendar year, employees of Employer V in the same position of employment, as part of their continuing employment, retain the right to reject an offer of placement, and typically refuse one or more offers of placement and do not perform services for periods ranging from four to twelve weeks during a calendar year. At the time Employee E is hired by Employer V, Employer V has no reason to anticipate that Employee E's position of employment will differ from the typical employee in the same position.

Reg. §54.4980H-3(d)(5)

(ii) *Conclusion.* Employer V cannot determine whether Employee E is reasonably expected to average at least 30 hours of service per week for the 12-month initial measurement period. Accordingly, Employer V may treat Employee E as a variable hour employee during the initial measurement period.

Example 14 (Variable hour employee; temporary staffing firm). (i) *Facts.* Employer T hires Employee F on January 1, 2015, in a position under which Employer T will offer assignments to Employee F to provide services in temporary placements at clients of Employer T. Employees of Employer T in the same position typically are offered assignments of 40 or more hours of service per week for periods expected to last for periods of three months to 12 months, subject to a request for renewal by the client. Employees of Employer T in similar positions to Employee F are typically offered and take new positions immediately upon cessation of a placement. At the time Employee F is hired by Employer T, Employer T has no reason to anticipate that Employee F's position of employment will differ from the typical employee in the same position.

(ii) *Conclusion.* Employer T must assume that Employee F will be employed by Employer T and available for an offer of temporary placement for the entire initial measurement period. Under that assumption, Employer T would reasonably determine that Employee F is reasonably expected to average at least 30 hours of service per week for the 12-month initial measurement period. Accordingly, Employer T may not treat Employee F as a variable hour employee during the initial measurement period.

Example 15 (Variable hour employee). (i) *Facts.* Employee G is hired on an hourly basis by Employer S to fill in for employees who are absent and to provide additional staffing at peak times. Employer S expects that Employee G will average 30 hours of service per week or more for Employee G's first few months of employment, while assigned to a specific project, but also reasonably expects that the assignments will be of unpredictable duration, that there will be periods of unpredictable duration between assignments, that the hours per week required by subsequent assignments will vary, and that Employee G will not necessarily be available for all assignments.

(ii) *Conclusion.* Employer S cannot determine whether Employee G is reasonably expected to average at least 30 hours of service per week for the initial measurement period. Accordingly, Employer S may treat Employee G as a variable hour employee during the initial measurement period.

Example 16 (Period between initial stability period and standard stability period). (i) *Facts.* Employer R uses an 11-month initial measurement period for new variable hour, new seasonal, and new part-time employees with an administrative period that lasts from the end of the initial measurement period through the last day of the first calendar month beginning on or after the first anniversary of the employee's start date. Employer R uses a standard measurement period of October 15 through October 14, and an administrative period of October 15 through December 31. Employee H is hired as a variable hour employee on October 20, 2015, with an initial measurement period of October 20, 2015, through September 19, 2016, and an administrative period lasting through November 30, 2016. Employee H is a full-time employee based on the hours of service in the initial measurement period, and Employee H's stability period for the initial measurement period is December 1, 2016, through November 30, 2017. Employee H's first full standard measurement period begins on October 15, 2016, with an associated stability period beginning on January 1, 2018. The standard measurement period beginning on October 15, 2015, does not apply to Employee H because Employee H is not hired until October 20, 2015.

(ii) *Conclusion.* For the period after the stability period associated with the initial measurement period and before the stability period associated with Employee H's first full standard measurement period (that is December 1, 2017, through December 31, 2017), Employer R must treat Employee H as a full-time employee because the treatment as a full-time employee (or not a full-time employee) that applies during the stability period associated with the initial measurement period continues to apply until the beginning of the stability period associated with the first full standard measurement period during which the employee is employed.

(6) *Employees rehired after termination of employment or resuming service after other absence.*— (i) *Treatment as a new employee after a period of absence for employees of employers other than educational organizations.*—(A) *In general.*—The rules in this paragraph (d)(6)(i) apply to employers that are not educational organizations. For rules relating to employers that are educational organizations, see paragraph (d)(6)(ii) of this section. An employee who resumes providing services to (or is otherwise credited with an hour of service for) an applicable large employer that is not an educational organization after a period during which the employee was not credited with any hours of service may be treated as having terminated employment and having been rehired, and therefore may be treated as a new employee upon the resumption of services, only if the employee did not have an hour of service for the applicable large employer for a period of at least 13 consecutive weeks immediately preceding the resumption of services. The rule set forth in this paragraph (d)(6)(i) applies solely for the purpose of determining whether the employee, upon the resumption of services, is treated as a new employee or as a continuing employee, and does not determine whether the employee is treated as a continuing full-time employee or a terminated employee during the period during which no hours of service are credited.

(B) *Averaging method for special unpaid leave.*—For purposes of applying the look-back

measurement method described in paragraph (d) of this section to an employee who is not treated as a new employee under paragraph (d)(6)(i) of this section, the employer determines the employee's average hours of service for a measurement period by computing the average after excluding any special unpaid leave during that measurement period and by using that average as the average for the entire measurement period. Alternatively, for purposes of determining the employee's average hours of service for the measurement period, the employer may choose to treat the employee as credited with hours of service for any periods of special unpaid leave during that measurement period at a rate equal to the average weekly rate at which the employee was credited with hours of service during the weeks in the measurement period that are not part of a period of special unpaid leave. There is no limit on the number of hours of service required to be excluded or credited (as the case may be) with respect to special unpaid leave. For purposes of this paragraph (d)(6)(i)(B), in computing the average weekly rate, employers are permitted to use any reasonable method if applied on a consistent basis. In addition, if an employee's average weekly rate under this paragraph (d)(6)(i)(B) is computed for a measurement period and that measurement period is shorter than six months, the six-month period ending with the close of the measurement period is used to compute the average hours of service.

(C) *Averaging rules for employment break periods for employers other than educational organizations.*—The averaging rule for employment break periods described in paragraph (d)(6)(ii)(B) of this section applies only to educational organizations and does not apply to other employers.

(ii) *Treatment as a new employee after a period of absence for employees of employers that are educational organizations.*—(A) *In general.*—The rules of this paragraph (d)(6)(ii) apply only to employers that are educational institutions. An employee who resumes providing services to (or is otherwise credited with an hour of service for) an applicable large employer that is an educational organization after a period during which the employee was not credited with any hours of service may be treated as having terminated employment and having been rehired, and therefore may be treated as a new employee upon the resumption of services, only if the employee did not have an hour of service for the applicable large employer for a period of at least 26 consecutive weeks immediately preceding the resumption of services. The rule set forth in this paragraph (d)(6)(ii)(A) applies solely for the purpose of determining whether the employee, upon the resumption of services, is treated as a new employee or as a continuing employee, and does not determine whether the employee is treated as a continuing full-time employee or a terminated employee during the period during which no hours of service are credited.

(B) *Averaging method for special unpaid leave and employment break periods.*—For purposes of applying the look-back measurement method described in paragraph (d) of this section to an employee who is not treated as a new employee under paragraph (d)(6)(ii)(A) of this section, an educational organization employer determines the employee's average hours of service for a measurement period by computing the average after excluding any special unpaid leave and any employment break period during that measurement period and by using that average as the average for the entire measurement period. Alternatively, for purposes of determining the employee's average hours of service for the measurement period, the employer may choose to treat the employee as credited with hours of service for any periods of special unpaid leave and any employment break period during that measurement period at a rate equal to the average weekly rate at which the employee was credited with hours of service during the weeks in the measurement period that are not part of a period of special unpaid leave or an employment break period. Notwithstanding the preceding two sentences, no more than 501 hours of service during employment break periods in a calendar year are required to be excluded (under the first sentence) or credited (under the second sentence) by an educational organization, provided that this 501-hour limit does not apply to hours of service required to be excluded or credited in respect of special unpaid leave. In applying the preceding sentence, an employer that uses the method described in the first sentence of this paragraph (d)(6)(ii)(B) determines the number of hours excluded by multiplying the average weekly rate for the measurement period (determined as in the second sentence of this paragraph (d)(6)(ii)(B)) by the number of weeks in the employment break period. For purposes of this paragraph (d)(6)(ii)(B), in computing the average weekly rate, employers are permitted to use any reasonable method if applied on a consistent basis. In addition, if an employee's average weekly rate under this paragraph (d)(6)(ii)(B) is being computed for a measurement period and that measurement period is shorter than six months, the six-month period ending with the close of the measurement period is used to compute the average hours of service.

(iii) *Treatment of continuing employee.*— Under the look-back measurement method, an employee treated as a continuing employee retains, upon resumption of services, the status that employee had with respect to the application of any stability period (for example, if the continuing employee returns during a stability period in which the employee is treated as a full-time employee, the employee is treated as a full-time employee upon return and through the end of that stability period). For purposes of the preceding sentence, a continuing employee treated as a full-time employee is treated as offered coverage upon resumption of services if the employee is offered coverage as of the first day that

Reg. § 54.4980H-3(d)(6)(iii)

employee is credited with an hour of service, or, if later, as soon as administratively practicable. For this purpose, offering coverage by no later than the first day of the calendar month following resumption of services is deemed to be as soon as administratively practicable. If a continuing employee returns during a stability period in which the employee is treated as a full-time employee and the employer previously made the employee an offer of coverage with respect to the entire stability period and the employee declined the offer, the employer will continue to be treated as having offered coverage for that stability period and the employer need not make a new offer of coverage for the remainder of the ongoing stability period due to the employee's resumption of services.

(iv) *Rule of parity.*—For purposes of determining the period after which an employee may be treated as having terminated employment and having been rehired, an applicable large employer may choose a period, measured in weeks, of at least four consecutive weeks during which the employee was not credited with any hours of service that exceeds the number of weeks of that employee's period of employment with the applicable large employer immediately preceding the period and that is shorter than 13 weeks (for an employee of an educational organization employer, a period that is shorter than 26 weeks). For purposes of the preceding sentence, the duration of the immediately preceding period of employment is determined after application to that period of employment of the averaging methods described in paragraphs (d)(6)(i)(B) and (d)(6)(ii)(B) of this section (relating to employment break periods and special unpaid leave), if applicable.

(v) *International transfers.*—An employer may treat an employee as having terminated employment if the employee transfers to a position at the same applicable large employer (including a different applicable large employer member that is part of the same applicable large employer) if the position is anticipated to continue indefinitely or for at least 12 months and if substantially all of the compensation will constitute income from sources without the United States (within the meaning of sections 861 through 863 and the regulations thereunder). With respect to an employee transferring from a position that was anticipated to continue indefinitely or for at least 12 months and in which substantially all of the compensation for the hours of service constitutes income from sources without the United States (within the meaning of sections 861 through 863 and the regulations thereunder) to a position at the same applicable large employer (including a different applicable large employer member that is part of the same applicable large employer) with respect to which substantially all of the compensation will constitute U.S. source income, the employer may treat that employee as a new hire to the extent consistent with the rules related to rehired employees in paragraph (d)(6) of this section.

(vi) *Anti-abuse rule.*—For purposes of this paragraph (d)(6), any hour of service is disregarded if the hour of service is credited, or the services giving rise to the crediting of the hour of service are requested or required of the employee, for a purpose of avoiding or undermining the application of the employee rehire rules under paragraph (d)(6) of this section, or the application of the averaging method for employment break periods under paragraph (d)(6)(ii)(B) of this section. For example, if an employee of an educational organization would otherwise have a period with no hours of service to which the rules under paragraph (d)(6)(ii)(B) of this section would apply, but for the employer's request or requirement that the employee perform one or more hours of service for a purpose of avoiding the application of those rules, any such hours of service for the week are disregarded, and the rules under paragraph (d)(6)(ii)(B) of this section will apply.

(vii) *Examples.*—The following examples illustrate the provisions of paragraph (d)(6) of this section. All employers in these examples are applicable large employer members with 200 full-time employees (including full-time equivalent employees), each is in a different applicable large employer group, and each determines full-time employee status under the look-back measurement method. None of the periods during which an employee is not credited with an hour of service for an employer involve special unpaid leave or the employee being credited with hours of service for any applicable large employer member in the same applicable large employer as the employer.

Example 1. (i) *Facts.* As of April 1, 2015, Employee A has been an employee of Employer Z (which is not an educational organization) for 10 years. On April 1, 2015, Employee A terminates employment and is not credited with an hour of service until June 1, 2015, when Employer Z rehires Employee A and Employee A continues as an employee through December 31, 2015, which is the close of the measurement period as applied by Employer Z.

(ii) *Conclusion.* Because the period for which Employee A is not credited with any hours of service is not longer than Employee A's prior period of employment and is less than 13 weeks, Employee A is not treated as having terminated employment and been rehired for purposes of determining whether Employee A is treated as a new employee upon resumption of services. Therefore, Employee A's hours of service prior to termination are required to be taken into account for purposes of the measurement period, and Employee A's period with no hours of service is taken into account as a period of zero hours of service during the measurement period.

Example 2. (i) *Facts.* Same facts as *Example 1*, except that Employee A is rehired on December 1, 2015.

(ii) *Conclusion.* Because the period during which Employee A is not credited with an hour

of service for Employer Z exceeds 13 weeks, Employee A is treated as having terminated employment on April 1, 2015, and having been rehired as a new employee on December 1, 2015, for purposes of determining Employee A's full-time employee status. Because Employee A is treated as a new employee, Employee A's hours of service prior to termination are not taken into account for purposes of the measurement period, and the period between termination and rehire with no hours of service is not taken into account in the new measurement period that begins after the employee is rehired.

Example 3. (i) *Facts.* Employee B is employed by Employer Y, an educational organization. Employee B is employed for 38 hours of service per week on average from September 7, 2014, through May 23, 2015, and then does not provide services (and is not otherwise credited with an hour of service) during the summer break when the school is generally not in session. Employee B resumes providing services for Employer Y on September 7, 2015, when the new school year begins.

(ii) *Conclusion.* Because the period from May 24, 2015 through September 5, 2015 (a total of 15 weeks), during which Employee B is not credited with an hour of service does not exceed 26 weeks, and also does not exceed the number of weeks of Employee B's immediately preceding period of employment, Employee B is not treated as having terminated employment on May 24, 2015, and having been rehired on September 6, 2015. Also, for purposes of determining Employee B's average hours of service per week for the measurement period, Employee B is credited, under the averaging method for employment break periods applicable to educational organizations, as having an average of 38 hours of service per week for the 15 weeks between May 24, 2015 and September 5, 2015, during which Employee B otherwise was credited with no hours of service. However, Employer Y is not required to credit more than 501 hours of service for the employment break period (15 weeks x 38 hours = 570 hours).

Example 4. (i) *Facts.* Same facts as *Example 3,* except that Employee B does not resume providing services for Employer Y until December 5, 2015.

(ii) *Conclusion.* Because the period from May 24, 2015 through December 5, 2015, exceeds 26 weeks, Employee B may be treated as having terminated employment on May 24, 2015, and having been rehired on December 5, 2015. Because Employee B is treated as a new employee on December 5, 2015, Employee B's hours of service prior to termination are not taken into account for purposes of the measurement period, and the period between termination and rehire with no hours of service is not taken into account in the new measurement period that begins after Employee B is rehired. The averaging method for employment break periods applicable to educational organizations does not apply because Employee B is treated as a new employee rather

than a continuing employee as of the date of resumption of services.

(e) *Use of the look-back measurement method and the monthly measurement method for different categories of employees.*—Different applicable large employer members of the same applicable large employer may use different methods of determining full-time employee status (that is, either the monthly measurement method or the look-back measurement method). In addition, an applicable large employer member may use either the monthly measurement method or the look-back measurement method for each of the categories of employees set forth in paragraphs (d)(1)(v) and (d)(3)(v) of this section, and is not required to use the same method for all categories.

(f) *Changes in employment status resulting in a change in full-time employee determination method.*—(1) *Change in employment status from a position to which a look-back measurement method applies to a position to which the monthly measurement method applies, or vice versa.*—(i) *Change from look-back measurement method to monthly measurement method.*—For an employee transferring from a position under which the look-back measurement method is used to determine the employee's status as a full-time employee, to a position under which the monthly measurement method is used to determine the employee's status as a full-time employee, the following rules apply:

(A) For an employee who at the time of the change of position is in a stability period under which the employee is treated as a full-time employee, the employer must continue to treat the employee as a full-time employee through the end of the stability period;

(B) For an employee who at the time of the change of position is in a stability period under which the employee is not treated as a full-time employee, the employer may continue to treat the employee as not a full-time employee through the end of the stability period, or may apply the monthly measurement method set forth in paragraph (c) of this section through the end of the stability period beginning with any calendar month including the calendar month in which the change in employment status occurs or any subsequent calendar month;

(C) For the stability period associated with the measurement period during which the change in employment status occurs, the employer must treat the employee as a full-time employee for any calendar month during which the employee either would be treated as a full-time employee under the stability period that would have applied based on the measurement period in which the change in employment status occurred or would be treated as a full-time employee under the monthly measurement method; and

(D) For any calendar month subsequent to the stability period identified in paragraph (f)(1)(i)(C) of this section, the monthly

measurement method applies for determination of the employee's status as a full-time employee.

(ii) *Change from monthly measurement method to look-back measurement method.*—For an employee who is transferring from a position under which the monthly measurement method is used to determine the employee's status as a full-time employee, to a position under which a look-back measurement method is used to determine the employee's status as a full-time employee, the following rules apply:

(A) For the remainder of the applicable stability period during which the change in employment status occurs, the employer must continue to use the monthly measurement method to determine the employee's status as a full-time employee unless the employee's hours of service prior to the change in employment status would have resulted in the employee being treated as a full-time employee during the stability period in which the change in employment status occurs, in which case the employer must treat the employee as a full-time employee for that stability period;

(B) For the applicable stability period following the measurement period during which the change in employment status occurs, the employer must treat the employee as a full-time employee for any calendar month during which the employee either would be treated as a full-time employee based on the measurement period during which the change in employment status occurs or would be treated as a full-time employee under the monthly measurement method; and

(C) For any calendar month subsequent to the stability period identified in paragraph (f)(1)(ii)(B) of this section, the look-back measurement method applies for determination of the employee's status as a full-time employee.

(iii) *Examples.*—The following examples illustrate the rules of this paragraph (f). In each example, the employer is an applicable large employer with 200 full-time employees (including FTEs). For each example, the employer uses the monthly measurement method for determining whether a salaried employee is a full-time employee, and the look-back measurement method for determining whether an hourly employee is a full-time employee with a measurement period from October 15 through October 14 of the following calendar year, and a stability period from January 1 through December 31. In each case, the relevant employee has been employed continuously for several years.

Example 1 (Look-back measurement method to monthly measurement method). Employee A is an hourly employee. Based on Employee A's hours of service from October 15, 2015, through October 14, 2016, Employee A is treated as a full-time employee from January 1, 2017, through December 31, 2017. On July 1, 2017, Employee A transfers from a position as an hourly employee to a position as a salaried employee. For the months July 2017 through December 2017, Employee A

must be treated as a full-time employee. Employee A is employed for hours of service from October 15, 2016, through October 14, 2017, such that under the applicable look-back measurement method Employee A would be treated as a full-time employee for the period of January 1, 2018, through December 31, 2018. Accordingly, Employee A must be treated as a full-time employee for the calendar year 2018. For calendar year 2019, the determination of whether Employee A is a full-time employee is made under the monthly measurement method.

Example 2 (Look-back measurement method to monthly measurement method). Same facts as *Example 1*, except that based on Employee A's hours of service from October 15, 2015, through October 14, 2016, Employee A is not treated as a full-time employee from January 1, 2017, through December 31, 2017. For the months July 2017 through December 2017, Employer Z may either treat Employee A as not a full-time employee or apply the monthly measurement method to determine Employee A's status as a full-time employee. Employee A is employed for hours of service from October 15, 2016, through October 14, 2017, such that under the applicable look-back measurement method Employee A would be treated as a full-time employee for the period of January 1, 2018, through December 31, 2018. Employee A must be treated as a full-time employee for the calendar year 2018. For calendar year 2019, the determination of whether Employee A is a full-time employee is made under the monthly measurement method.

Example 3 (Look-back measurement method to monthly measurement method). Same facts as *Example 1*, except that Employee A is employed for hours of service from October 15, 2016, through October 14, 2017, such that under the applicable look-back measurement method Employee A would not be treated as a full-time employee for the period of January 1, 2018, through December 31, 2018. For the calendar year 2018, Employer Z must treat Employee A as a full-time employee only for calendar months during which Employee A would be a full-time employee under the monthly measurement method. For calendar year 2019, the determination of whether Employee A is a full-time employee is made under the monthly measurement method.

Example 4 (Monthly measurement method to look-back measurement method). Employee B is a salaried employee of Employer Y. On July 1, 2017, Employee B transfers to an hourly employee position. Based on Employee B's hours of service from October 15, 2015, through October 14, 2016, Employee B would have been treated as a full-time employee for the stability period from January 1, 2017, through December 31, 2017, had the look-back measurement method applicable to hourly employees applied to Employee B for the entire stability period. For the calendar months January 2017 through June 2017 (prior to Employee B's change to hourly employee status), Employee B's status as a full-time employee is determined using the monthly measurement method. For the calendar months July 2017

through December 2017, Employer Y must treat Employee B as a full-time employee because Employee B would have been treated as a full-time employee during that portion of the stability period had the look-back measurement method applied to Employee B for that entire stability period. Employee B is employed for hours of service from October 15, 2016, through October 14, 2017, such that under the applicable look-back measurement method Employee B would be treated as a full-time employee for the period January 1, 2018, through December 31, 2018. Accordingly, Employee B must be treated as a full-time employee for the calendar year 2018. For calendar year 2019, the determination of whether Employee B is a full-time employee is made under the applicable look-back measurement method.

Example 5 (Monthly measurement method to look-back measurement method). Same facts as *Example 4*, except that based on Employee B's hours of service from October 15, 2015, through October 14, 2016, Employee B would not have been treated as a full-time employee from January 1, 2017, through December 31, 2017. For the calendar months of 2017, Employer Y applies the monthly measurement method to determine Employee B's status as a full-time employee. Employee B is employed for hours of service from October 15, 2016, through October 14, 2017, such that under the applicable look-back measurement method Employee B would be treated as a full-time employee for the period January 1, 2018, through December 31, 2018. Accordingly, Employee B must be treated as a full-time employee for the calendar year 2018. For calendar year 2019, the determination of whether Employee B is a full-time employee is made under the applicable look-back measurement method.

Example 6 (Monthly measurement method to look-back measurement method). Same facts as *Example 4*, except that Employee B is employed for hours of service from October 15, 2016, through October 14, 2017, such that under the applicable look-back measurement method Employee B would not be treated as a full-time employee for the period of January 1, 2018, through December 31, 2018. For the calendar year 2018, Employer Y must treat Employee B as a full-time employee only for calendar months during which Employee B would be a full-time employee under the monthly measurement method.

(2) *Special rule for certain employees to whom minimum value coverage has been continuously offered.*—(i) *In general.*—Notwithstanding the rules in paragraphs (e) and (f) of this section, an employer using the look-back measurement method to determine the full-time employee status of an employee may apply the monthly measurement method to that employee beginning on the first day of the fourth full calendar month following the calendar month in which the employee experiences a change in employment status such that, if the employee had begun employment in the new position or status, the employee would have reasonably been expected not to be em-

ployed on average at least 30 hours of service per week (for example, the employee has changed to a part-time position of only 20 hours of service per week). This rule only applies with respect to an employee to whom the applicable large employer member offered minimum value coverage by the first day of the calendar month following the employee's initial three full calendar months of employment through the calendar month in which the change in employment status described in this paragraph (f)(2) occurs, and only if the employee actually averages less than 30 hours of service per week for each of the three full calendar months following the change in employment status. For the three full calendar months between the employee's change in employment status and the application of the monthly measurement method, the employee's full-time employee status is determined based on the employee's status during the applicable stability period(s). Under this rule, an employer may apply the monthly measurement method to an employee even if the employer does not apply the monthly measurement method to the other employees in the same category of employees under paragraph (d)(1)(v) or (d)(3)(v) of this section (for example, under this method an employer could apply the monthly measurement method to an hourly employee, even if the employer uses the look-back measurement method to determine full-time employee status of all other hourly employees). The employer may continue to apply the monthly measurement method through the end of the first full measurement period (and any associated administrative period) that would have applied had the employee remained under the applicable look-back measurement method.

(ii) *Examples.*—The following examples illustrate the rule of paragraphs (f)(2) of this section. In each example, the employer is an applicable large employer with 200 full-time employees (including FTEs).

Example 1 (New variable hour employee, no delay in coverage, becomes non-full-time employee). (i) *Facts.* Employer Z, an applicable large employer, uses the look-back measurement method to determine the full-time employee status for all of its employees. On May 10, 2015, Employer Z hired Employee A who is a variable hour employee. Although Employee A is a new variable hour employee, so that Employer Z could wait until the end of an initial measurement period to offer coverage to Employee A without an assessable payment under section 4980H with respect to Employee A, Employer Z offers coverage that provides minimum value to Employee A on September 1, 2015. For its ongoing employees, Employer Z has chosen to use a 12-month standard measurement period starting October 15 and a 12-month stability period associated with that standard measurement period starting January 1. Employee A continues in employment with Employer Z for over five years and averages more than 30 hours of service per week for all measurement periods through the measurement period ending October 14, 2020. On February 12, 2021, Employee A experiences a change in position of employment with Employer Z to a position under which Employer Z reasonably expects Employee A to average less than 30 hours of service per week. For the calendar months after February 2021, Employee A averages less than 30 hours of service per week. Employer Z offered Employee A coverage that provided minimum value continuously from September 1, 2015, through May 31, 2021. Effective June 1, 2021, Employer Z elects to apply the monthly measurement method to determine Employee A's status as a full-time employee for the remainder of the stability period ending December 31, 2021, and the calendar year 2022 (which is through the end of the first full measurement period following the change in employment status plus the associated administrative period). Applying the stability period beginning January 1, 2021, Employer Z treats Employee A as a full-time employee for each calendar month from January 2021 through May 2021. Applying the monthly measurement method, for each calendar month from June 2021 through December 2022, Employer Z treats Employee A as not a full-time employee.

(ii) *Conclusion.* Because Employer Z offered coverage that provided minimum value to Employee A from no later than the first day of the fourth full calendar month following Employee A's start date through the calendar month in which the change in employment status occurred, and because Employee A did not average 30 hours of service per week for any of the three calendar months immediately following Employee A's change in employment status to an employee not reasonably expected to average 30 hours of service per week, Employer Z may use the monthly measurement method to determine the full-time employee status of Employee A beginning on the first day of the fourth month following the change in employment status (June 1, 2021) through the end of the first full measurement period (plus any associated administrative period) immediately following the change in employment status (December 31, 2022). Because Employee A did not average at least 30 hours of service per week for any calendar month from June 2021 through December 2022, Employer Z has properly treated Employee A as not a full-time employee for those calendar months.

Example 2 (New full-time employee, no delay in coverage, becomes non-full-time employee). (i) *Facts.* Same facts as *Example 1*, except that at Employee A's start date, Employer Z reasonably expects that Employee A will average at least 30 hours of service per week. Accordingly, Employer Z offers coverage to Employee A beginning on September 1, 2015, and offers coverage continuously to Employee A for all calendar months through May 2021.

(ii) *Conclusion.* Same as *Example 1.*

(g) *Nonpayment or late payment of premiums.*—An applicable large employer member will not be treated as failing to offer to a full-time employee (and his or her dependents) the opportunity to enroll in minimum essential coverage under an eligible employer-sponsored plan for an employee whose coverage under the plan is terminated during the coverage period solely due to the employee failing to make a timely payment of the employee portion of the premium. This treatment continues only through the end of the coverage period (typically the plan year). For this purpose, the rules in § 54.4980B-8, Q&A-5(a), (c), (d) and (e) apply under this section to the payment for coverage with respect to a full-time employee in the same manner that they apply to payment for COBRA continuation coverage under § 54.4980B-8.

(h) *Additional guidance.*—With respect to the determination of full-time employee status, including determination of hours of service, the Commissioner may prescribe additional guidance of general applicability, published in the Internal Revenue Bulletin (see § 601.601(d)(2)(ii)(b) of this chapter).

(i) *Effective/applicability date.*—This section is applicable for periods after December 31, 2014. [Reg. § 54.4980H-3.]

☐ [*T.D.* 9655, 2-10-2014.]

[Reg. § 54.4980H-4]

§ 54.4980H-4. Assessable payments under section 4980H(a).—(a) *In general.*—If an applicable large employer member fails to offer to its full-time employees (and their dependents) the opportunity to enroll in minimum essential coverage under an eligible employer-sponsored plan for any calendar month, and the applicable large employer member has received a Section 1411 Certification with respect to at least one full-time employee, an assessable payment is imposed. For the calendar month, the applicable large employer member will owe an assessable payment equal to the product of the section 4980H(a) applicable payment amount and the number of full-time employees of the applicable large employer member (other than employees in a limited non-assessment period for certain employees and as adjusted in accordance with paragraph (e) of this section). For purposes of this paragraph (a), an applicable large employer member is treated as offering such coverage to its full-time employees (and their dependents) for a calendar month if, for that month, it offers such coverage to all but five percent (or, if greater, five) of its full-time employees (provided that an employee is treated as having been offered coverage only if the employer also offers coverage to that employee's dependents). For purposes of the preceding sentence, an employee in a limited non-assessment period for certain employees is not included in the calculation.

(b) *Offer of coverage.*—(1) *In general.*—An applicable large employer member will not be treated as having made an offer of coverage to a full-time employee for a plan year if the employee does not have an effective opportunity to elect to enroll in the coverage at least once with respect to the plan year, or does not have an effective opportunity to decline to enroll if the coverage offered does not provide minimum value or requires an employee contribution for any calendar month of more than 9.5 percent of a monthly amount determined as the federal poverty line for a single individual for the applicable calendar year, divided by 12. For this purpose, the applicable federal poverty line is the federal poverty line for the 48 contiguous states and the District of Columbia. Whether an employee has an effective opportunity to enroll or to decline to enroll is determined based on all the relevant facts and circumstances, including adequacy of notice of the availability of the offer of coverage, the period of time during which acceptance of the offer of coverage may be made, and any other conditions on the offer. An employee's election of coverage from a prior year that continues for the next plan year unless the employee affirmatively elects to opt out of the plan constitutes an offer of coverage for purposes of section 4980H.

(2) *Offer of coverage on behalf of another entity.*—For purposes of section 4980H, an offer of coverage by one applicable large employer member to an employee for a calendar month is treated as an offer of coverage by all applicable large employer members for that calendar month. In addition, an offer of coverage made to an employee on behalf of a contributing employer under a multiemployer or single employer Taft-Hartley plan or multiple employer welfare arrangement (MEWA) is treated as made by the employer. For an offer of coverage to an employee performing services for an employer that is a client of a staffing firm, in cases in which the staffing firm is not the common law employer of the individual and the staffing firm makes an offer of coverage to the employee on behalf of the client employer under a plan established or maintained by the staffing firm, the offer is treated as made by the client employer for purposes of section 4980H only if the fee the client employer would pay to the staffing firm for an employee enrolled in health coverage under the plan is higher than the fee the client employer would pay the staffing firm for the same employee if that employee did not enroll in health coverage under the plan.

(c) *Partial calendar month.*—If an applicable large employer member fails to offer coverage to a full-time employee for any day of a calendar month, that employee is treated as not offered coverage during that entire month, regardless of whether the employer uses the payroll period rule set forth in §54.4980H-3(d)(1)(ii) or the weekly rule set forth in §54.4980H-3(c)(3) to determine full-time employee status for the calendar month. However, in a calendar month in which the employment of a full-time employee terminates, if the employee would have been offered coverage for the entire calendar month had the employee been employed for the entire calendar month, the employee is treated as having been offered coverage for that entire calendar

month. In addition, an applicable large employer member is not subject to an assessable payment under section 4980H with respect to an employee for the calendar month in which the employee's start date occurs if the start date is on a date other than the first day of the calendar month, and, in addition, with respect to the calendar month in which the start date occurs, such an employee is not included for purposes of the calculation of any potential liability under section 4980H(a).

(d) *Application to applicable large employer member.*—The liability for an assessable payment under section 4980H(a) for a calendar month with respect to a full-time employee applies solely to the applicable large employer member that was the employer of that employee for that calendar month. For an employee who was an employee of more than one applicable large employer member of the same applicable large employer during a calendar month, the liability for the assessable payment under section 4980H(a) for a calendar month applies to the applicable large employer member for whom the employee has the greatest number of hours of service for that calendar month (if the employee has an equal number of hours of service for two or more applicable large employer members of the same applicable large employer for the calendar month, those applicable large employer members can treat one of those members as the employer of that employee for that calendar month for purposes of this section, and if the members do not select one member, or select in an inconsistent manner, the IRS will select a member to be treated as the employer of that employee for purposes of the assessable payment determination). For a calendar month, an applicable large employer member may be liable for an assessable payment under section 4980H(a) or under section 4980H(b), but will not be liable for an assessable payment under both section 4980H(a) and section 4980H(b).

(e) *Allocated reduction of 30 full-time employees.*—For purposes of the liability calculation under paragraph (a) of this section, with respect to each calendar month, an applicable large employer member's number of full-time employees is reduced by that member's allocable share of 30. The applicable large employer member's allocation is equal to 30 allocated ratably among all members of the applicable large employer on the basis of the number of full-time employees employed by each applicable large employer member during the calendar month (after application of the rules of paragraph (d) of this section addressing employees who work for more than one applicable large employer member during a calendar month). If an applicable large employer member's total allocation is not a whole number, the allocation is rounded to the next highest whole number. This rounding rule may result in the aggregate reduction for the entire group of applicable large employer members exceeding 30.

(f) *Example.*—The following example illustrates the provisions of paragraphs (a) and (e) of this section.

Example. (i) *Facts.* Applicable large employer member Z and applicable large employer member Y are the two members of an applicable large employer. Applicable large employer member Z employs 40 full-time employees in each calendar month of 2017. Applicable large employer member Y employs 35 full-time employees in each calendar month of 2017. Assume that for 2017, the applicable payment amount for a calendar month is $2,000 divided by 12. Applicable large employer member Z does not sponsor an eligible employer-sponsored plan for any calendar month of 2017, and receives a Section 1411 Certification for 2017 with respect to at least one of its full-time employees. Applicable large employer member Y sponsors an eligible employer-sponsored plan under which all of its full-time employees are eligible for minimum essential coverage.

(ii) *Conclusion.* Pursuant to section 4980H(a) and this section, applicable large employer member Z is subject to an assessable payment under section 4980H(a) for 2017 of $48,000, which is equal to 24 × $2,000 (40 full-time employees reduced by 16 (its allocable share of the 30-employee offset ((40/75) × 30 = 16)) and then multiplied by $2,000). Applicable large employer member Y is not subject to an assessable payment under section 4980H(a) for 2017.

(g) *Additional guidance.*—With respect to assessable payments under section 4980H(a), the Commissioner may prescribe additional guidance of general applicability, published in the Internal Revenue Bulletin (see §601.601(d)(2)(ii)(b) of this chapter).

(h) *Effective/applicability date.*—This section is applicable for periods after December 31, 2014. [Reg. §54.4980H-4.]

☐ [*T.D.* 9655, 2-10-2014.]

[Reg. §54.4980H-5]

§54.4980H-5. Assessable payments under section 4980H(b).—(a) *In general.*—If an applicable large employer member offers to its full-time employees (and their dependents) the opportunity to enroll in minimum essential coverage under an eligible employer-sponsored plan for any calendar month (including an offer of coverage to all but five percent or less (or, if greater, five or less) of its full-time employees (provided that an employee is treated as having been offered coverage only if the employer also offers coverage to that employee's dependents)) and the applicable large employer member has received a Section 1411 Certification with respect to one or more full-time employees of the applicable large employer member, then there is imposed on the applicable large employer member an assessable payment equal to the product of the number of full-time employees of the applicable large employer member for which it has received a Section 1411 Certification (minus the number of those employees in a limited non-assessment period for certain employees and the number of other employees who were offered the opportunity to enroll in minimum essential coverage under an eligible employer-sponsored plan that satisfied minimum value and met one or more of the affordability safe harbors described in paragraph (e) of this section) and the section 4980H(b) applicable payment amount. Notwithstanding the foregoing, the aggregate amount of assessable payment determined under this paragraph (a) with respect to all employees of an applicable large employer member for any calendar month may not exceed the product of the section 4980H(a) applicable payment amount and the number of full-time employees of the applicable large employer member during that calendar month (reduced by the applicable large employer member's ratable allocation of the 30 employee reduction under §54.4980H-4(e)).

(b) *Offer of coverage.*—For purposes of this section, the same rules with respect to an offer of coverage for purposes of section 4980H(a) apply. See §54.4980H-4.

(c) *Partial calendar month.*—If an applicable large employer member fails to offer coverage to a full-time employee for any day of a calendar month, that employee is treated as not offered coverage during that entire month, regardless of whether the employer uses the payroll period rule set forth in §54.4980H-3(d)(1)(ii) or the weekly rule set forth in §54.4980H-3(c)(3) to determine full-time employee status for the calendar month. However, in a calendar month in which a full-time employee's employment terminates, if the employee would have been offered coverage if the employee had been employed for the entire month, the employee is treated as having been offered coverage during that month. Also, an applicable large employer member is not subject to an assessable payment under section 4980H with respect to an employee for the calendar month in which the employee's start date occurs if the start date is on a date other than the first day of the calendar month.

(d) *Applicability to applicable large employer member.*—The liability for an assessable payment under section 4980H(b) for a calendar month with respect to a full-time employee applies solely to the applicable large employer member that was the employer of that employee for that calendar month. For an employee who was a full-time employee of more than one applicable large employer member during that calendar month, the liability for the assessable payment under section 4980H(b) for a calendar month applies to the applicable large employer member for whom the employee has the greatest number of hours of service for that calendar month (if the employee has an equal number of hours of service for two or more applicable large employer members for the calendar month, those applicable large employer members can treat one of those members as the employer of that employee for that calendar month for purposes of this paragraph (d), and if the members do not select one member, or select in an inconsistent manner, the IRS will select a member to be treated as the employer of that employee for purposes of the assessable payment determination). For a calendar month, an applicable large employer member may be liable for an assessable payment under section 4980H(a) or under section 4980H(b), but will not be liable for an assessable payment under both section 4980H(a) and section 4980H(b).

(e) *Affordability.*—(1) *In general.*—An employee who is offered coverage by an applicable large employer member may be eligible for an applicable premium tax credit or cost-sharing reduction if that offer of coverage is not affordable within the meaning of section 36B(c)(2)(C)(i) and the regulations thereunder.

(2) *Affordability safe harbors for section 4980H(b) purposes.*—The affordability safe harbors set forth in paragraph (e)(2)(ii) through (iv) of this section apply solely for purposes of section 4980H(b), so that an applicable large employer member that offers minimum essential coverage providing minimum value will not be subject to an assessable payment under section 4980H(b) with respect to any employee receiving the applicable premium tax credit or cost-sharing reduction for a period for which the coverage is determined to be affordable under the requirements of an affordability safe harbor. This rule applies even if the applicable large employer member's offer of coverage that meets the requirements of an affordability safe harbor is not affordable for a particular employee under section 36B(c)(2)(C)(i) and an applicable premium tax credit or cost-sharing reduction is allowed or paid with respect to that employee.

(i) *Conditions of using an affordability safe harbor.*—An applicable large employer member may use one or more of the affordability safe harbors described in this paragraph (e)(2) only if the employer offers its full-time employees and their dependents the opportunity to enroll in minimum essential coverage under an eligible employer-sponsored plan that provides minimum value with respect to the self-only coverage offered to the employee. Use of any of the safe harbors is optional for an applicable large employer member, and an applicable large employer member may choose to apply the safe harbors for any reasonable category of employees, provided it does so on a uniform and consistent basis for all employees in a category. Reasonable categories generally include specified job categories, nature of compensation (hourly or salary), geographic location, and similar bona fide business criteria. An enumeration of employees by name or other specific criteria having substantially the same effect as an enumeration by name is not considered a reasonable category.

(ii) *Form W-2 safe harbor-.*—(A) *Full-year offer of coverage.*—An employer will not be sub-

ject to an assessable payment under section 4980H(b) with respect to a full-time employee if that employee's required contribution for the calendar year for the employer's lowest cost self-only coverage that provides minimum value during the entire calendar year (excluding COBRA or other continuation coverage except with respect to an active employee eligible for continuation coverage) does not exceed 9.5 percent of that employee's Form W-2 wages from the employer (and any other member of the same applicable large employer that also pays wages to that employee) for the calendar year. Application of this safe harbor is determined after the end of the calendar year and on an employee-by-employee basis, taking into account the Form W-2 wages and the required employee contribution for that year. In addition, to qualify for this safe harbor, the employee's required contribution must remain a consistent amount or percentage of all Form W-2 wages during the calendar year (or during the plan year for plans with non-calendar year plan years) so that an applicable large employer member is not permitted to make discretionary adjustments to the required employee contribution for a pay period. A periodic contribution that is based on a consistent percentage of all Form W-2 wages may be subject to a dollar limit specified by the employer.

(B) *Adjustment for partial-year offer of coverage.*—For an employee not offered coverage for an entire calendar year, the Form W-2 safe harbor is applied by adjusting the Form W-2 wages to reflect the period for which coverage was offered, then determining whether the employee's required contribution for the employer's lowest cost self-only coverage that provides minimum value, totaled for the periods during which coverage was offered, does not exceed 9.5 percent of the adjusted amount of Form W-2 wages. To adjust Form W-2 wages for this purpose, the Form W-2 wages are multiplied by a fraction equal to the number of calendar months for which coverage was offered over the number of calendar months in the employee's period of employment with the employer during the calendar year. For this purpose, if coverage is offered during at least one day during the calendar month, or the employee is employed for at least one day during the calendar month, the entire calendar month is counted in determining the applicable fraction.

(iii) *Rate of pay safe harbor.*—An applicable large employer member satisfies the rate of pay safe harbor with respect to an hourly employee for a calendar month if the employee's required contribution for the calendar month for the applicable large employer member's lowest cost self-only coverage that provides minimum value does not exceed 9.5 percent of an amount equal to 130 hours multiplied by the lower of the employee's hourly rate of pay as of the first day of the coverage period (generally the first day of the plan year) or the employee's lowest hourly rate of pay during the calendar month. An applicable large employer member satisfies the rate of pay safe harbor with respect to a non-hourly employee for a calendar month if the employee's required contribution for the calendar month for the applicable large employer member's lowest cost self-only coverage that provides minimum value does not exceed 9.5 percent of the employee's monthly salary, as of the first day of the coverage period (instead of 130 multiplied by the hourly rate of pay); provided that if the monthly salary is reduced, including due to a reduction in work hours, the safe harbor is not available, and, solely for purposes of this paragraph (e)(2)(iii), an applicable large employer member may use any reasonable method for converting payroll periods to monthly salary. For this purpose, if coverage is offered during at least one day during the calendar month, the entire calendar month is counted both for purposes of determining the assumed income for the calendar month and for determining the employee's share of the premium for the calendar month.

(iv) *Federal poverty line safe harbor.*—An applicable large employer member satisfies the federal poverty line safe harbor with respect to an employee for a calendar month if the employee's required contribution for the calendar month for the applicable large employer member's lowest cost self-only coverage that provides minimum value does not exceed 9.5 percent of a monthly amount determined as the federal poverty line for a single individual for the applicable calendar year, divided by 12. For this purpose, if coverage is offered during at least one day during the calendar month, the entire calendar month is counted both for purposes of determining the monthly amount for the calendar month and for determining the employee's share of the premium for the calendar month. For this purpose, the applicable federal poverty line is the federal poverty line for the State in which the employee is employed.

(v) *Examples.*—The following examples illustrate the application of the affordability safe harbors described in this paragraph (e)(2). In each example, each employer is an applicable large employer member with 200 full-time employees (including full-time equivalent employees).

Example 1 (Form W-2 wages safe harbor). (i) *Facts.* Employee A is employed by Employer Z consistently from January 1, 2015, through December 31, 2015. In addition, Employer Z offers Employee A and his dependents minimum essential coverage during that period that provides minimum value. The employee contribution for self-only coverage is $100 per calendar month, or $1,200 for the calendar year. For 2015, Employee A's Form W-2 wages with respect to employment with Employer Z are $24,000.

(ii) *Conclusion.* Because the employee contribution for 2015 is less than 9.5 percent of Employee A's Form W-2 wages for 2015, the coverage offered is treated as affordable with respect to Employee A for 2015 ($1,200 is 5 percent of $24,000).

Example 2 (Form W-2 wages safe harbor). (i) *Facts.* Employee B is employed by Employer Y from January 1, 2015, through September 30, 2015. In addition, Employer Y offers Employee B and his dependents minimum essential coverage during that period that provides minimum value. The employee contribution for self-only coverage is $100 per calendar month, or $900 for Employee B's period of employment. For 2015, Employee B's Form W-2 wages with respect to employment with Employer Y are $18,000. For purposes of applying the affordability safe harbor, the Form W-2 wages are multiplied by 9/9 (9 calendar months of coverage offered over 9 months of employment during the calendar year) or 1. Accordingly, affordability is determined by comparing the adjusted Form W-2 wages ($18,000) to the employee contribution for the period for which coverage was offered ($900).

(ii) *Conclusion.* Because the employee contribution for 2015 is less than 9.5 percent of Employee B's adjusted Form W-2 wages for 2015, the coverage offered is treated as affordable with respect to Employee B for 2015 ($900 is 5 percent of $18,000).

Example 3 (Form W-2 wages safe harbor). (i) *Facts.* Employee C is employed by Employer X from May 15, 2015, through December 31, 2015. In addition, Employer X offers Employee C and her dependents minimum essential coverage during the period from August 1, 2015, through December 31, 2015, that provides minimum value. The employee contribution for self-only coverage is $100 per calendar month, or $500 for Employee C's period of employment. For 2015, Employee C's Form W-2 wages with respect to employment with Employer X are $15,000. For purposes of applying the affordability safe harbor, the Form W-2 wages are multiplied by 5/8 (5 calendar months of coverage offered over 8 months of employment during the calendar year). Accordingly, affordability is determined by comparing the adjusted Form W-2 wages ($9,375 or $15,000 × 5/8) to the employee contribution for the period for which coverage was offered ($500).

(ii) *Conclusion.* Because the employee contribution of $500 is less than 9.5 percent of $9,375 (Employee C's adjusted Form W-2 wages for 2015), the coverage offered is treated as affordable with respect to Employee C for 2015 ($500 is 5.33 percent of $9,375).

Example 4 (Rate of pay safe harbor). (i) *Facts.* Employer W offers its full-time employees and their dependents minimum essential coverage that provides minimum value. For the 2016 calendar year, Employer W is using the rate of pay safe harbor to establish premium contribution amounts for full-time employees paid at a rate of $7.25 per hour (the minimum wage in Employer W's jurisdiction) for each calendar month of the entire 2016 calendar year. Employer W can apply the affordability safe harbor by using an assumed monthly income amount that is based on an assumed 130 hours of service multiplied by $7.25 per hour ($942.50 per calendar month). To satisfy the safe harbor, Employer W would set the employee monthly contribution amount at a rate that does not exceed 9.5 percent of the assumed monthly income of $942.50. Employer W sets the employee contribution for self-only coverage at $85 per calendar month for 2016.

(ii) *Conclusion*. Because $85 is less than 9.5 percent of the employee's assumed monthly income at a $7.25 rate of pay, the coverage offered is treated as affordable under the rate of pay safe harbor for each calendar month of 2016 ($85 is 9.01 percent of $942.50).

Example 5 (Rate of pay safe harbor). (i) *Facts.* Employee E is employed by Employer V from May 1, 2015, through December 31, 2015. Employer V offers Employee E and her dependents minimum essential coverage from May 1, 2015, through December 31, 2015, that provides minimum value. The employee contribution for self-only coverage is $100 per calendar month. From May 1, 2015, through October 31, 2015, Employee E is paid at a rate of $10 per hour. From November 1, 2015, through December 31, 2015, Employee E is paid at a rate of $12 per hour. For purposes of applying the affordability safe harbor for the calendar months May 2015 through October 2015, Employer V may assume that Employee E earned $1,300 per calendar month (130 hours of service multiplied by $10 (which is the lower of the employee's hourly rate of pay at the beginning of the coverage period ($10) and the lowest hourly rate of pay for the calendar month ($10)). Accordingly, affordability is determined by comparing the assumed income ($1,300 per month) to the employee contribution ($100 per calendar month). For the calendar months November 2015 through December 2015, Employer V may assume that Employee E earned $1,300 per calendar month (130 hours of service multiplied by $10 (which is the lower of the employee's hourly rate of pay at the beginning of the coverage period ($10) and the lowest hourly rate of pay for the calendar month ($12)). Accordingly, affordability is determined by comparing the assumed income ($1,300 per month) to the employee contribution ($100 per calendar month).

(ii) *Conclusion*. Because $100 is less than 9.5 percent of Employee E's assumed monthly income for each calendar month from May 2015 through December 2015, the coverage offered is treated as affordable with respect to Employee E

for May 2015 through December 2015 ($100 is 7.69 percent of $1,300).

Example 6 (Federal poverty line safe harbor). (i) *Facts.* Employee F is employed by Employer T from January 1, 2015, through December 31, 2015. In addition, Employer T offers Employee F and his dependents minimum essential coverage during that period that provides minimum value. Employer T uses the look-back measurement method. Under that measurement method as applied by Employer T, Employee F is treated as a full-time employee for the entire calendar year 2015. Employee F is regularly credited with 35 hours of service per week but is credited with only 20 hours of service during the month of March 2015 and only 15 hours of service during the month of August 2015. Assume for this purpose that the federal poverty line for 2015 for an individual is $11,670. With respect to Employee F, Employer T sets the monthly employee contribution for employee single-only coverage for each calendar month of 2015 at $92.39 (9.5 percent of $11,670, divided by 12).

(ii) *Conclusion*. Regardless of Employee F's actual wages for any calendar month in 2015, including the months of March 2015 and August 2015, when Employee F has lower wages because of significantly lower hours of service, the coverage under the plan is treated as affordable with respect to Employee F, because the employee contribution does not exceed 9.5 percent of the federal poverty line.

(f) *Additional guidance.*—With respect to assessable payments under section 4980H(b), including the determination of whether an offer of coverage is affordable for purposes of section 4980H, the Commissioner may prescribe additional guidance of general applicability, published in the Internal Revenue Bulletin (see § 601.601(d)(2)(ii)(b) of this chapter).

(g) *Effective/applicability date.*—This section is applicable for periods after December 31, 2014. [Reg. § 54.4980H-5.]

☐ [*T.D.* 9655, 2-10-2014.]

[Reg. § 54.4980H-6]

§ 54.4980H-6. Administration and procedure.—(a) *In general.*—[Reserved]

(b) *Effective/applicability date.*—This section is applicable for periods after December 31, 2014. [Reg. § 54.4980H-6.]

☐ [*T.D.* 9655, 2-10-2014.]

Qualified Investment Entities

See p. 20,601 for regulations not amended to reflect law changes

[Reg. § 55.4981-1]

§ 55.4981-1. Imposition of excise tax on certain real estate investment trust taxable income not distributed during the taxable year; taxable years ending on or before January 1, 1987.— Section 4981, as in effect before amendment by the Tax Reform Act of 1986, imposes an excise

tax on a real estate investment trust if the deduction for dividends paid for the taxable year does not equal at least 75 percent of its real estate investment trust taxable income (computed as provided in section 4981, as in effect before amendment by the Tax Reform Act of 1986) for the taxable year. For purposes of section 4981, as in effect before amendment by the Tax Reform Act of 1986, the deduction for dividends paid is computed without regard to capital gains dividends(as defined in section 857(b)(3)(C)) and without regard to any dividends actually paid after the close of the taxable year. Thus, dividends considered as paid during the taxable year under section 858 are disregarded. Deficiency dividends(as defined in section 860(f)) paid with respect to the taxable year are also disregarded. The return referred to in the last sentence of section 4981, as in effect before amendment by the Tax Reform Act of 1986, is the income tax return. Section 4981, as in effect before amendment by the Tax Reform Act of 1986, applies only to taxable years beginning after December 31, 1979, and ending before January 1, 1987, for which the taxpayer is taxable under part II of subchapter M of chapter 1 of subtitle A as a real estate investment trust. [Reg. § 55.4981-1.]

☐ [T.D. 7767, 2-3-81. *Amended by* T.D. 7936, 1-17-84, *and* T.D. 8180, 2-29-88.]

[Reg. § 55.4981-2]

§ 55.4981-2. Imposition of excise tax with respect to certain undistributed income of real estate investment trusts; calendar years beginning after December 31, 1986.—Section 4981, as amended by the Tax Reform Act of 1986, imposes an excise tax on a real estate investment trust in the amount of four percent of the excess, if any, of the required distribution for a calendar year over the distributed amount for such calendar year. Section 4981, as so amended, applies only to calendar years that begin after December 31, 1986. For provisions relating to the imposition of an excise tax with respect to certain undistributed income of real estate investment trusts for taxable years ending before January 1, 1987, see § 55.4981-1. [Reg. § 55.4981-2.]

☐ [T.D. 8180, 2-29-88.]

[Reg. § 54.4981A-1T]

§ 54.4981A-1T. Tax on excess distributions and excess accumulations (Temporary).—The following questions and answers relate to the tax on excess distributions and excess accumulations under section 4981A of the Internal Revenue Code of 1986, as added by section 1133 of the Tax Reform Act of 1986 (Pub. L. 99-514) (TRA '86).

Table of Contents

a. General Provisions and Excess Distributions
b. Special Grandfather Rules
c. Special Rules
d. Excess Accumulations

a. General Provisions and Excess Distributions

a-1: Q. What changes were made by section 1133 of TRA '86 regarding excise taxes applicable to distributions from qualified employer plans and individual retirement plans?

A. Section 1133 of TRA '86 added section 4981A to the Code. Section 4981A imposes an excise tax of 15 percent on (a) excess distributions, as defined in section 4981A(c)(1) and Q&A a-2 of this section, and (b) excess accumulations, as defined in section 4981A(d)(3) and Q&A d-2

of this section. The excise tax on excess distributions generally applies to excess distributions made after December 31, 1986 (see Q&A c-6 of this section). The excise tax on excess accumulations applies to estates of decedents dying after December 31, 1986 (see Q&A d-11 of this section). Excess distributions are certain distributions from qualified employer plans and individual retirement plans. Excess accumulations are certain amounts held on the date of death of an employee or individual by qualified plans and individual retirement plans.

a-2: Q. How are excess distributions defined?

A. Excess distributions are generally defined as the excess of the aggregate amount of distributions received by or with respect to an individual during a calendar year over the greater of (a) $150,000 (unindexed) or (b) $112,500 (indexed as provided in Q&A a-9 of this section beginning in 1988 for cost-of-living increases). Certain individuals may elect to have the portion of their excess distributions that is subject to tax determined under a "special grandfather" rule that is described below (see Q&A b-1 through b-14 of this section).

a-3: Q. Distributions from what plans and arrangements are taken into account in applying section 4981A?

A. (a) *General rule.* Section 4981A applies to distributions under any qualified employer plan or individual retirement plan described in section 4981A(e). For this purpose, a qualified employer plan means any—

(1) Qualified pension, profit-sharing or stock bonus plan described in section 401(a) that includes a trust exempt from tax under section 501(a);

(2) Annuity plan described in section 403(a);

(3) Annuity contract, custodial account, or retirement income account described in section 403(b)(1), 403(b)(7) or 403(b)(9); and

(4) Qualified bond purchase plan described in section 405(a) prior to that section's repeal by section 491(a) of the Tax Reform Act of 1984 (TRA '84).

(b) *Individual retirement plan.* An individual retirement plan is defined in section 7701(a)(37) and means any individual retirement account described in section 408(a) or individual retirement annuity described in section 408(b). Also, an individual retirement plan includes a retirement bond described in section 409(a) prior to that section's repeal by section 491(b) of the Tax Reform Act of 1984 (TRA '84).

(c) *Other distributions.* (1) Distributions under any plan, contract or account that has at any time been treated as a qualified employer plan or individual retirement plan described in paragraph (a) or (b) of this Q&A a-3 will be treated for purposes of section 4981A as distributions from a qualified employer plan or individual retirement plan whether or not such plan, contract, or account satisfies the applicable qualification requirements at the time of the distribution.

(2)(i) For purposes of this paragraph (c), an employer plan will be considered to have been treated as a qualified employer plan if any employer maintaining the plan has at any time filed an income tax return and claimed deductions that would be allowable under section 404 (and that were not disallowed) only if the plan was a qualified employer plan under section 401(a) or 403(a). Similarly, if an income tax return has been filed at any time with respect to the trust (or plan or insurance company), and the income of the trust (insurance company, etc.) is reported (and is not disallowed) based on the trust (or plan) being treated as a qualified employer plan described in section 401(a), or 403(a) or (b), then the employer plan is considered to have been treated as a qualified employer plan.

(ii) For purposes of this paragraph (c), an individual retirement plan (IRA) will be considered to have been treated as a qualified IRA if any contributions to the IRA were either deducted (or designated as a nondeductible contribution described in section 408(o)) on a filed individual income tax return or excluded from an individual's gross income on a filed income tax return because such contributions were reported as regular contributions or rollover contributions (such as those described in section 402(a)(5), 403(a)(4), 403(b)(8) or 408(d)(3)) to an IRA described in section 408(a) or (b) (or section 409 of pre-1984 law). Similar treatment applies to an employer contribution to a simplified employee pension described in section 408(k), if such contribution is deducted on an employer's filed income tax return, including a self-employed individual's return.

a-4: Q. Which distributions with respect to an individual under a qualified employer plan or an individual retirement plan are excluded from consideration for purposes of determining an individual's excess distributions?

A. (a) *Exclusions.* In determining the extent to which an individual has excess distributions for a calendar year, the following distributions are disregarded—

(1) Any distribution received by any person with respect to an individual as a result of the death of that individual.

(2) Any distribution with respect to an individual that is received by an alternate payee under a qualified domestic relations order within the meaning of section 414(p) that is includible in the income of the alternate payee.

(3) Any distribution with respect to an individual that is attributable to the individual's investment in the contract as determined under the rules of section 72(f). This would include, for example, distributions that are excluded from gross income under section 72 because they are treated as a recovery of after-tax employee contributions from a qualified employer plan or nondeductible contributions from an individual retirement plan.

(4) Any portion of a distribution to the extent that it is not included in gross income by reason of a rollover contribution described in section 402(a)(5), 403(a)(4), 403(b)(8), or 408(d)(3).

(5) Any health coverage or any distribution of medical benefits provided under an arrangement described in section 401(h) to the extent that the coverage or distribution is excludable under section 104, 105, or 106.

(b) *Alternate payee.* Any distributions to an alternate payee described in paragraph (a)(2) of this Q&A a-4 must be taken into account by such alternate payee for purposes of calculating the excess distributions received by (or excess accumulations held by) the alternate payee.

a-5: Q. If an annuity contract that represents an irrevocable commitment to provide an employee's benefits under the plan is distributed to an individual, how are the distribution of such annuity contract and distributions of amounts under such a contract taken into account for purposes of calculating excess distributions?

A. Except to the extent that the value of an annuity contract is includible in income in the year the contract is distributed or any subsequent year, the distribution of an annuity contract (including a group annuity contract) in satisfaction of plan liabilities is disregarded for purposes of calculating excess distributions. Any amounts that are actually distributed under the contract to the individual (to the extent not excluded under Q&A a-4 of this section) or are otherwise includible in income with respect to the contract (*e.g.,* by reason of the inclusion in income of the value of the annuity contract in the year of the contract's distribution or any subsequent year) are taken into account for purposes of calculating excess distributions for the calendar year during which such amounts are received or otherwise includible in income. For purposes of this Q&A a-5, the term "plan" means any qualified employer plan or individual retirement plan specified in section 4981A(e) and Q&A a-3 of this section.

a-6: Q. Are minimum distributions required under section 401(a)(9), 408(a)(6), 408(b)(3) or 403(b)(10) taken into account to determine excess distributions?

A. Yes. Distributions received during a calendar year are taken into account in determining an individual's excess distributions for such calendar year even though such distributions are required under section 401(a)(9), 408(a)(6), 408(b)(3) or 403(b)(10). For example, minimum distributions under section 401(a)(9) received during the 1987 calendar year for calendar years 1985 and 1986 will be subject to section 4981A as distributions for 1987.

a-7: Q. Are distributions of excess deferrals permitted under section 402(g)(2), or distributions of excess contributions or excess aggregate contributions permitted under section 401(k) or (m), or distributions of IRA contributions permitted under section 408(d)(4) or (5) taken into account for purposes of calculating excess distributions?

A. No. Distributions of excess deferrals, excess contributions, excess aggregate contributions, distributions of IRA contributions, and income allocable to such contributions or deferrals, that

Reg. §54.4981A-1T

are made in accordance with the provisions of sections 402(g)(2), 401(k)(8), 401(m)(6), or 408(d)(4) or (5) are not taken into account for purposes of calculating excess distributions.

a-8: Q. What distributions from qualified employer plans or individual retirement plans are taken into account in determining an individual's excess distributions?

A. With the exception of distributions noted above in Q&As a-4, a-5, and a-7 of this section, all distributions from qualified employer plans or individual retirement plans must be taken into account in determining an individual's excess distributions for the calendar year in which such distributions are received. In general, all such distributions are taken into account whether or not they are currently includible in income. Thus, for example, net unrealized appreciation in employer securities described in section 402(a) is taken into account in the year distributed. However, health coverage or distributions of medical benefits provided under an arrangement described in section 401(h) that are excludable from income under section 104, 105, or 106 are not subject to section 4981A. In addition, distributions that are excludable from income because they are rolled over to a plan or an individual retirement account are not taken into account. (See Q&A a-4(a)(4) and (5) of this section). Amounts that are includible in income for a calendar year are treated as distributions and, thus, are taken into account even if the amounts are not actually distributed during such year. Thus, deemed distributions to provide insurance coverage includible in income under section 72 (PS-58 amounts), loan amounts treated as deemed distributions under section 72(p), and amounts includible under section 402(b) or section 403(c) by reason of the employer plan or individual retirement plan not being qualified during the year are taken into account.

a-9: Q. Will the dollar threshold amount used to determine an individual's excess distributions be adjusted for inflation in calendar years after 1987?

A. Beginning in 1988, the $112,500 threshold amount is adjusted to reflect post-1986 cost-of-living increases (COLAs) at the same time and in the same manner as the adjustment described in section 415(d). The threshold amount is adjusted even though the distribution is from a defined contribution plan that is subject to a freeze on COLAs because the defined benefit plan limit is below $120,000 (see section 415(c)(1)(A)). However, the $150,000 threshold amount is not adjusted to reflect such increases.

b. Special Grandfather Rule

b-1: Q. How are benefits accrued before TRA '86 treated under the excise tax provisions described in section 4981A?

A. (a) *Grandfather amount.* Certain eligible individuals may elect to use a special grandfather rule that exempts from the excise tax the portion of distributions treated as a recovery of such individual's total benefits accrued on or before

August 1, 1986 (grandfather amount). However, distributions that are treated as a recovery of the grandfather amount are taken into account in determining the extent to which other distributions are excess distributions (see Q&A b-4 of this section). Under this special grandfather rule, the grandfather amount equals the value of an individual's total benefits (as described in Q&As b-8 and b-9 of this section) in all qualified employer plans and individual retirement plans on August 1, 1986. An individual's benefits in such plans include amounts determinable on August 1, 1986, that are payable to the individual under a qualified domestic relations order within the meaning of section 414(p)(QDRO). However, QDRO benefits that, when distributed, are includible in the income of the alternate payee are not included in the employee's grandfathered amount. Further, plan benefits that are attributable to a deceased individual and that are payable to an eligible individual as a beneficiary are generally not included in determining the eligible individual's grandfather amount. Procedures for determining the grandfather amount are described in Q&As b-11 through b-14 of this section.

(b) *Recovery of grandfather amount.* The portion of any distribution made after August 1, 1986, that is treated as a recovery of a grandfather amount depends on which of two grandfather recovery methods the individual elects. The two alternative methods are described in Q&As b-11 through b-14 of this section. The amount of the distribution for a year that is treated as a recovery of a grandfather amount in a year is applied to reduce the individual's unrecovered grandfather amount for future years (*i.e.,* the individual's accrued benefits as described in Q&As b-8 and b-9 on August 1, 1986, reduced by previous distributions treated as a recovery of a grandfather amount) on a dollar for dollar basis until the individual's unrecovered grandfather amount has been reduced to zero. When the individual's grandfather amount has been reduced to zero, the special grandfather rule ceases to apply and the entire amount of any subsequent excess distributions received is subject to the 15 percent excise tax.

b-2: Q. Who may elect to use the special grandfather rules?

A. Any individual whose accrued benefits as described in Q&As b-8 and b-9 of this section in all qualified plans and individual retirement plans on August 1, 1986 (initial grandfather amount) have a value of at least $562,500 may elect to use the special grandfather rule.

b-3: Q. How does an eligible individual make a valid election to use the special grandfather rule?

A. (a) *Form of election.* An individual who is eligible to use the special grandfather rule must affirmatively elect to use that rule. The election is made on a Form 5329 filed with the individual's income tax return (Form 1040, etc.) for a taxable year beginning after December 31, 1986, and before January 1, 1989 (*i.e.,* the 1987 or 1988 taxable year).

Reg. §54.4981A-1T

(b) *Information required.* The individual must report the following information on the Form 5329:

(1) The individual's initial grandfather amount.

(2) The grandfather recovery method to be used.

(3) Such other information as is required by the Form 5329.

(c) *Deadline for election.* The deadline for filing such election is the due date, calculated with extensions, for filing the individual's 1988 income tax return. If an individual dies before the expiration of such deadline, an election, or the revocation of a prior election, may be made as part of the final income tax return filed on behalf of such deceased individual by the deceased individual's personal representative. An election or revocation of a prior election may also be filed before the expiration of such deadline with Schedule S (Form 706). See Q&A c-7 of this section.

(d) *Revocation of election.* Elections filed before the deadline may be revoked by filing an amended income tax return for any applicable year. A change in the grandfather recovery method is considered a revocation of a prior election and an amended Form 5329 must be filed for any prior year in which a different grandfather recovery method was used. Thus, a change in the election may require a change in the 1987 tax return. An individual must refile for 1987 based on the new election if additional tax is owed. However, an election (or nonelection) is irrevocable after the filing deadline for the taxable year beginning in 1988 has passed. Thus, an individual who has not made an election by the last day plus extensions for filing the 1988 return may not do so through an amended return.

(e) *Subsequent years.* (1) Any eligible individual who has elected the special grandfather rule must attach to the individual's income tax return for all subsequent taxable years in which the individual receives excess distributions (determined without regard to the grandfather rule) a copy of the Form 5329 on which the individual elected the grandfather rule. A copy of the Form 5329 on which the individual (or the individual's personal representative) elected the grandfather rule must also be filed with Schedule S (Form 706) unless the initial election is filed with such schedule.

(2) The individual must also make such other reports in the form and at the time as the Commissioner may prescribe. See Q&A c-7 of this section for the applicable reporting requirements if the individual or the individual's estate is liable for any tax on excess distributions or an excess accumulation under section 4981A(a) or (d).

b-4: Q. How do individuals who have elected to use the special grandfather rule determine the extent to which their distributions for any calendar year are excess distributions?

A. (a) *Excess distributions under grandfather rule, threshold amount.* Individuals who elect to use the special grandfather rule are not eligible to use the $150,000 threshold amount in computing their excess distributions for any calendar year. Instead, such electing individuals must compute their excess distributions for a calendar year using a $112,500 (indexed for cost-of-living increases) threshold amount. The rule of this paragraph (a) applies for all calendar years, including the calendar year in which an individual's unrecovered grandfather amount has been reduced to zero and all subsequent calendar years. Once the indexed amount has increased to $150,000 or more, the threshold amount will be the same for all individuals.

(b) *Base for excise tax under grandfather rule.* Although the portion of any distribution that is treated as a recovery of an individual's grandfather amount is not subject to the excise tax, such portion must be taken into account in determining the extent to which the individual has excess distributions for a calendar year. The effect of this rule is that the amount against which the 15 percent excise tax is applied for any calendar year during which a grandfather amount is recovered equals the individual's distributions for such year reduced by the greater of (1) the applicable threshold amount for such year or (2) the grandfather amount recovered for such year. (See the examples in Q&A b-14 of this section.)

b-5: Q. How is the value of an individual's total accrued benefits on August 1, 1986, calculated for purposes of determining (a) whether an individual is eligible to elect the special grandfather rule and (b) the amount of any electing individual's initial grandfather amount under such rule?

A. (a) *Introduction.* The value of an individual's total accrued benefits on August 1, 1986, is the sum of the values of the individual's accrued benefits on such date under all qualified employer plans or individual retirement plans, as determined under this Q&A b-5. If such value exceeds $562,500, the individual may elect the special grandfather rule. In such case, the value so determined may be applied against distributions as determined under this section, whether or not such distributions are from the same plan or IRA for which such grandfather amount is determined. For purposes of determining the value of accrued benefits on August 1, 1986, an annuity contract or an individual's interest in a group annuity contract described in Q&A a-5 of this section is treated as an accrued benefit under the qualified retirement plan or IRA from which it was distributed and an IRA is treated as a defined contribution plan.

(b) *Defined benefit plan*—(1) *General rule.* The amount of an individual's accrued benefit on August 1, 1986, under a defined benefit plan is determined as of that date under the provisions of the plan based on the individual's service and compensation on that date. The present value of such benefit is determined by an actuarial valuation of such accrued benefit performed as of August 1, 1986. Alternatively, accrued benefits may be determined as of July 31, 1986. In such case, the applicable rules are applied by substi-

Reg. §54.4981A-1T

tuting the July 31 date for the August 1 date in the applicable provisions. (See Q&A b-9 of this section for rules for determining the amount of benefits and values and the actuarial assumptions to be used in such determination.)

(2) *Alternative method.* Alternatively, the present value of an individual's accrued benefit on August 1, 1986, may be determined using the following method:

(i) Determine the amount of the individual's actual accrued benefit (prior benefit) on the valuation date that immediately precedes August 1, 1986 (prior date). The valuation date for purposes of using this alternative method is the valuation date used for purposes of section 412. In making this determination, plan amendments that are adopted after that prior date are disregarded.

(ii) Determine the amount of the individual's adjusted accrued benefit (adjusted prior benefit) on the prior date by reducing the prior benefit in paragraph (b)(2)(i) of this Q&A b-5 by the amount of distributions that reduce the accrued benefit or transfers from the plan and by increasing the prior benefit in paragraph (b)(2)(i) of this Q&A b-5 by any increase in benefit resulting from either transfers to the plan or plan amendments that were made (or, in the case of a plan amendment, both adopted and effective) after the prior valuation date, but on or before August 1, 1986.

(iii) Determine the amount of the individual's actual accrued benefit (future benefit) on the valuation date immediately following August 1, 1986 (next date). In making this determination, plan amendments, etc. that are either adopted or effective after August 1 are disregarded.

(iv) Determine the amount of the individual's adjusted accrued benefit (adjusted future benefit) on the next date by increasing the future benefit in paragraph (b)(2)(iii) of this Q&A b-5 by the amount of any distributions that reduce the accrued benefit or transfers from the plan and by reducing the future benefit in paragraph (b)(2)(iii) of this Q&A b-5 by the amount of any transfer to the plan that was made after August 1, 1986, but on or before the next valuation date to the amount in paragraph (b)(2)(iii) of this Q&A b-5.

(v) Calculate the weighted average of paragraphs (b)(2)(ii) and (b)(2)(iv) of this Q&A b-5, where the weights applied are the number of complete calendar months separating the applicable prior date and the applicable next date, respectively, and August 1, 1986.

(vi) Determine the actuarial present value of the benefit in paragraph (b)(2)(v) of this Q&A b-5 as of August 1, 1986, using the methods and assumptions described in Q&A b-9 of this section.

The grandfather amount on August 1, 1986, attributable to the accrued benefits under the defined benefit plan is equal to the amount determined in paragraph (b)(2)(vi) of this Q&A b-5.

(3) *Certain insurance plans treated as defined contribution plans.* (i) Accrued benefits not in pay status under a plan satisfying the requirements of section 411(b)(1)(F) are determined under the rules in paragraph (c) of this Q&A b-5 for defined contribution plans. For purposes of applying paragraph (c) of this Q&A b-5 to such benefits, the cash surrender value of the contract is substituted for the account balance. If accrued benefits are in pay status under such a plan, the rules of this paragraph (b) apply to such benefits.

(ii) Accrued benefits not in pay status that are attributable to voluntary employee contributions (including rollover amounts) to a defined benefit plan are determined under the rules in paragraph (c) of this Q&A b-5 as if the account balance attributable thereto is under a defined contribution plan. If such benefits are in pay status and are used to fund the benefit under the defined benefit plan, the rules of this paragraph (b) apply to such benefits.

(c) *Defined contribution plan*—(1) *General rule.* The value of an individual's accrued benefit on August 1, 1986, under a defined contribution plan (including IRAs) is the value of the individual's account balance on such date (or on the immediately preceding day). Paragraph (b)(3) of this Q&A b-5 requires that benefits derived from certain insured plans and from voluntary contributions to a defined benefit plan be determined under the rules of this paragraph (c).

(2) *Alternative method.* Alternatively, if a valuation was not performed as of August 1, 1986 (or as of the immediately preceding day), the value of an individual's accrued benefit may be determined as follows:

(i) Determine the value of the individual's account balance on the valuation date immediately preceding August 1, 1986 (prior valuation date).

(ii) Determine the value of the individual's adjusted account balance on the prior valuation date by subtracting (or adding, respectively) the amount of any distribution, including a transfer to another plan or a forfeiture from the account balance (or the amount of any allocation to the account balance, including a transfer from another plan, rollover received or forfeiture from another account) that was made after the prior valuation date but on or before August 1, 1986, from (or to) the amount in paragraph (c)(2)(i) of this Q&A b-5.

(iii) Determine the value of the individual's account balance on the valuation date immediately following August 1, 1986 (next valuation date).

(iv) Determine the value of the individual's adjusted account balance on the next valuation date by adding (or subtracting, respectively) the amount of any distribution, of a type described in paragraph (c)(2)(ii) of this Q&A b-5 (or the amount of any allocation to the account balance, of a type described in paragraph (c)(2)(ii) of this Q&A b-5), that was made after August 1, 1986, but on or before the next valuation date to (or from) the amount in paragraph (c)(2)(iii) of this Q&A b-5.

Reg. §54.4981A-1T

(v) Calculate the weighted average of paragraphs (c)(2)(ii) and (c)(2)(iv) of this Q&A b-5, where the weights applied are the number of complete calendar months separating the applicable valuation date and the applicable next [valuation] date, respectively, and August 1, 1986.

The grandfather amount on August 1, 1986, attributable to the account balance in the defined contribution plan or the individual retirement plan is the amount in paragraph (c)(2)(v) of this Q&A b-5.

b-6: Q. For purposes of determining the value of accrued benefits in a defined contribution plan or a defined benefit plan on August 1, 1986, are nonvested benefits taken into account?

A. Yes. All accrued benefits, whether or not vested, are taken into account.

b-7: Q. To what extent are benefits payable with respect to an individual under a qualified employer plan or an individual retirement plan not taken into account for purposes of calculating the individual's grandfather amount?

A. (a) *Exclusions.* The following benefits payable with respect to an individual are not taken into account for purposes of this calculation:

(1) Benefits attributable to investment in the contract as defined in section 72(f). However, amounts attributable to deductible employee contributions (as defined in section 72(o)(5)(A)) are considered part of the accrued benefit.

(2) Amounts that are determinable on August 1, 1986, as payable to an alternate payee who is required to include such amounts in gross income (a spouse or former spouse) under a qualified domestic relations order (QDRO) within the meaning of section 414(p).

(3) Amounts that are attributable to IRA contributions that are distributed pursuant to section 408(d)(4) or (5).

(b) *Alternate payee.* Under a QDRO described in paragraph (a)(2) of this Q&A b-7, amounts are considered part of the accrued benefit of the alternate payee for purposes of calculating the value of the alternate payee's accrued benefit on August 1, 1986. Similarly, such amounts are used by the alternate payee to compute excess distributions.

b-8: Q. What adjustments to the grandfather amount are necessary to take into account rollovers from one qualified employer plan or individual retirement plan to another such plan?

A. (a) *Rollovers outstanding on valuation date.* Generally, rollovers between plans result in adjustment to the grandfather amount under the rules in Q&A b-5 of this section. However, if a rollover amount is distributed from one plan on or before an applicable valuation date of such plan and is rolled over into the receiving plan after the receiving plan's applicable valuation date and if these events result in an inappropriate duplication or omission of the rollover amount, then an adjustment to the grandfather amount must be made to remove the duplication or omission. The Commissioner may provide necessary rules concerning this adjustment.

(b) *Valuation.* If the rollover amount described in paragraph (a) of this Q&A b-8 is in a form of property other than cash, the property of which the outstanding rollover consists is valued as of the date the rollover contribution is received by the transferee qualified employer plan or individual retirement plan and that value is the amount of the rollover. If the outstanding rollover is in the form of cash, the amount of the cash is the amount of the rollover.

b-9: Q. What is the form of the grandfather benefit under a defined benefit plan and how is it valued?

A. (a) *Benefit form.* The grandfather amount under a defined benefit plan is determined on the basis of the form of benefit (including any subsidized form of benefit such as a subsidized early retirement benefit or a subsidized joint and survivor annuity) provided under the plan as of August 1, 1986 that has the greatest present value as determined in paragraph (b) of this b-9. If the plan provides a subsidized joint and survivor annuity, for purposes of determining the grandfather amount, it will be assumed that an unmarried individual is married and that the individual's spouse is the same age as the individual. Assumptions as to future withdrawals, future salary increases or future cost-of-living increases are not permitted.

(b) *Value of grandfather amount.* The grandfather amount under a defined benefit plan is the present value of the individual's benefit form determined under paragraph (a) of this Q&A b-9. Thus, the benefit form is reduced to reflect its value on the applicable valuation date. The present value of the benefit form on August 1, 1986, or the applicable date, is computed using the factors specified under the terms of the plan as in effect on August 1, 1986, to calculate a single sum distribution if the plan provides for such a distribution. If the plan does not provide for such a distribution form, such present value is computed using the interest rate and mortality assumptions specified in § 20.2031-7 of the Estate Tax Regulations.

b-10: Q. Is the plan administrator (or trustee) of a qualified plan (or individual retirement account) required to report to an individual the value of the individual's benefit under the plan as of August 1, 1986?

A. (a) *Request required.* No report is required unless the individual requests a report and the request is received before April 15, 1989. If requested, the plan administrator (or trustee or issuer) must report to such individual the value of the individual's benefit under the plan as of August 1, 1986, determined in accordance with Q&A a-5 through a-10 of this section. Such report must be made within a reasonable time after the individual's request but not later than July 15, 1989.

(b) *Other rules.* Alternate payees must make their own request for valuation reports. Any report furnished to an employee who has an alternate payee with respect to the plan must include the separate values attributable to each such in-

Reg. § 54.4981A-1T

dividual. Any report furnished to an alternate payee must include only the value attributable to the alternate payee. Reports may be furnished to individuals even if no request is made. Individuals must keep records of the reports received from plans or IRAs in order to substantiate all grandfather amounts.

(c) *Authority.* The rules in this Q&A are provided under the authority in section 6047(d).

b-11: Q. How is the portion of a distribution that is treated as a recovery of an individual's grandfather amount as described in b-1 of this section to be calculated?

A. (a) *General rule.* All distributions received between August 1 and December 31, 1986, inclusive, are treated as a recovery of a grandfather amount. The portion of distributions received after December 31, 1986, that is treated as a recovery of the grandfather amount is determined under either the discretionary method or the attained age method. An amount that is treated as a recovery of grandfather benefits is applied to reduce the initial grandfather amount that was calculated as of August 1, 1986, on a dollar for dollar basis until the unrecovered amount has been reduced to zero. No other recalculation of the grandfather amount is to be made for a date after August 1, 1986.

(b) *Methods, etc.* The grandfather amount may be recovered by an individual under either the discretionary method or the attained age method. After the individual's total grandfather amount is treated as recovered under either method, the tax on excess distributions and excess accumulations is determined without regard to any grandfather amount.

b-12: Q. Under the discretionary method, what portion of each distribution is treated as a return of the individual's grandfather amount?

A. (a) *Initial percentage.* Under the discretionary method, unless the individual elects in accordance with paragraph (b) below, 10 percent of the total distributions that the individual receives during any calendar year is treated as a recovery of the grandfather amount.

(b) *Acceleration.* The individual may elect to accelerate the rate of recovery to 100 percent of the total aggregate distributions received during a calendar year commencing with any calendar year, including 1987 (acceleration election). In such case, the rate of recovery is accelerated to 100 percent for the calendar year with respect to which the election is made and for all subsequent calendar years.

(c) *Election.* To recover the grandfather amount using the discretionary method, an individual must elect to use such method when making the election to use the special grandfather rule on the Form 5329. (See Q&A b-3 of this section.) The acceleration election must be made for the individual's taxable year beginning with or within the first calendar year for which such election is made and must be filed with the individual's income tax return for that year. Such acceleration election may also be made or revoked retroactively on an amended return for such year. How-

ever, the acceleration election may not be made after the individual's death other than with the individual's final income tax return or with a return for a prior year for which a return was not filed before the individual's death. Thus, the acceleration election may not be made on an amended return filed after the individual's death for a year for which a return was filed before the individual's death. The preceding two sentences shall not apply to deaths occurring in 1987 or 1988. The estate is entitled to use the remaining grandfather amount to determine if there is an excess accumulation. See Q&A d-3 of this section. The acceleration election shall be made on such form and in such manner as the Commissioner prescribes in a manner consistent with the rules of this section.

b-13: Q. Under the attained age method, what portion of each distribution is treated as a return of the individual's grandfather amount?

A. Under the attained age method, the portion of total distributions received during any year that is treated as a recovery of an individual's grandfather amount is calculated by multiplying the individual's aggregate distributions for a calendar year by a fraction. The numerator of the fraction is the difference between the individual's attained age in completed months on August 1, 1986, and the individual's attained age in months at age 35 (420 months). The denominator of the fraction is the difference between the individual's attained age in completed months on December 31 of the calendar year and the individual's attained age in months at age 35 (420 months). An individual whose 35th birthday is after August 1, 1986, may not use the attained age method.

b-14: Q. How is the 15 percent tax with respect to excess distributions for a calendar year calculated by an individual who has elected to use the special grandfather rule?

A. The calculation of the excise tax may be illustrated by the following examples:

Example 1. (a) An individual (A) who participates in two retirement plans, a qualified defined contribution plan and a qualified defined benefit plan, has a total value of accrued benefits on August 1, 1986 under both plans of $1,000,000. Because this amount exceeds $562,000, A is eligible to elect to use the special grandfather rule to calculate the portion of subsequent distributions that are exempt from tax. A elects to use the discretionary grandfather recovery method and attaches a valid election to the 1987 income tax return. A does not elect to accelerate the rate of recovery for 1987. On October 1, 1986, A receives a distribution of $200,000. On February 1, 1987, A receives a distribution of $45,000 and, on November 1, 1987, receives a distribution of $200,000. The 15 percent excise tax applicable to aggregate distributions in 1987 is calculated as follows:

(1) Value of grandfather amount on

    8/1/86 . . . . $1,000,000

(2) Grandfather amounts recovered in

    1986 but after 8/1/86 . . . . $200,000

(3) Value of grandfather amount on
12/31/86 ((1) – (2)) $800,000

(4) Grandfather recovery percentage . . 10%

(5) Distributions between 1/1/87 and
12/31/87 ($45,000 + $200,000) $245,000

(6) Portion of (5) exempt from tax ((4) ×
(5)) $24,500

(7) Amount potentially subject to tax ((5)
– (6)) $220,500

(8) Portion of aggregate distributions in
excess of $112,500 ($45,000 + $200,000
– $112,500) $132,500

(9) Amount subject to tax (lesser of (7)
and (8)) $132,500

(10) Amount of tax (15% of (9)) $19,875

(11) Remaining undistributed value of
grandfather amount as of 12/31/87
((3) – (6)) $775,500

(b) In 1988, A receives no distributions from either plan. On February 1, 1989, A receives a distribution of $300,000 and on December 31, 1989, receives a distribution of $75,000. A makes a valid acceleration election for the 1989 taxable year, whereby A accelerates the rate of grandfather recovery that will apply for calendar years after 1988 to 100 percent. Assume the annual threshold amount for the 1989 calendar year is $125,000 (i.e., 112,500 indexed). The 15 percent excess tax applicable to distributions in 1989 is calculated as follows:

(1) Value of grandfather amount on
1/1/89 . . . . $775,500

(2) Grandfather recovery percentage
designated for 1989 calendar year . 100%

(3) Distributions between 1/1/89 and
12/31/89 ($300,000 + $75,000) $375,000

(4) Portion of (3) exempt from tax (2) ×
(3) $375,000

(5) Amount potentially subject to tax ((3)
– (4)) $0

(6) Portion of aggregate distributions in
excess of $125,000 ($300,000 + $75,000
– $125,000) $250,000

(7) Amount subject to tax (lesser of (5)
and (6)) $0

(8) Amount of tax (15% of (7)) $0

(9) Remaining undistributed value of
grandfather amount as of 12/31/89
((1) – (4)) $400,500

The entire amount of any distribution for subsequent calendar years will be treated as a recovery of the grandfather amount and applied against the grandfather amount until the unrecovered grandfather amount is reduced to zero.

Example 2. The facts are the same as in *Example 1* except that A elects to use the attained age recovery method and A makes a valid election for the 1987 taxable year. Further assume that A's attained age in months on August 1, 1986 is 462 months and on December 31, 1987 is 476 months. The 15 percent excise tax applicable to aggregate distributions in 1987 is calculated as follows:

(1) Value of grandfather amount on
8/1/86 . . . . $1,000,000

(2) Grandfather amounts recovered in
1986 but after 8/1/86 . . . . $200,000

(3) Value of grandfather amount on
12/31/86 ((1) – (2)) $800,000

(4) Completed months of age in excess of
420 on 8/1/86 42

(5) Completed months of age in excess of
420 on 12/31/87 56

(6) Grandfather fraction as of 12/31/86
((4) divided by (5)) . . . . $^{3}/_{4}$

(7) Distributions between 1/1/87 and
12/31/87 ($45,000 + $200,000) $245,000

(8) Portion of (7) exempt from tax ((6) ×
(7)) $183,750

(9) Amount potentially subject to tax ((7)
– (8)) $61,250

(10) Portion of aggregate distributions in
excess of $112,500 ($45,000 + $200,000
– $112,500) $132,500

(11) Amount subject to tax (lesser of (9)
and (10)) $61,250

(12) Amount of tax (15% of (11)) $9,187

(13) Unrecovered grandfather amount as
of 12/31/87 ((3) – (8)) $616,250

c. Special Rules

c-1: Q. How is the excise tax computed if a person elects special tax treatment under section 402 or 403 for a lump sum distribution?

A. (a) *General rule*—(1) *Conditions.* Section 4981A(c)(4) provides for a special tax computation that applies to an individual in a calendar year if the individual receives distributions that include a lump sum distribution and the individual makes certain elections under section 402 or 403 with respect to that lump sum distribution (lump sum election).

(2) *Lump sum election.* A lump sum election includes an election of (i) 5-year income averaging under section 402(e)(4)(B); (ii) phaseout capital gains treatment under sections 402(a)(2) or 403(a)(2) prior to their repeal by section 1122(b) of TRA '86 and as permitted under section 1122(h)(4) of TRA '86; (iii) grandfathered long-term capital gains under sections 402(a)(2) and 403(a)(2) prior to such repeal and as permitted by section 1122(h)(3) of TRA '86; and (iv) grandfathered 10-year income averaging under section 402(e) (including such treatment under a section 402(e)(4)(L) election) prior to amendment by section 1122(a) of TRA '86 and as permitted by section 1122(h)(3)(A)(ii) and (5) of the TRA '86.

(3) *Special tax computation.* (i) If the conditions in paragraph (a)(1) of this Q&A c-1 are satisfied for a calendar year, the rules of this subparagraph (a)(3) apply for purposes of determining whether there are excess distributions and tax under section 4981A.

(ii) All distributions are divided into two categories. These two categories are the lump sum distribution and other distributions. Whether or not a particular distribution is a distribution subject to section 4981A and is in either category is determined under the rules in section 4981A and this section. Thus, the exclusions under section 4981A(c)(2) and Q&A a-4(a) of this section apply here. For example, a distribution that is a tax-free recovery of employee contributions is not in either category.

Reg. §54.4981A-1T

(iii) The excise tax under section 4981A(c)(1) is computed in the normal manner except that (A) it is the sum of the otherwise applicable taxes determined separately for the two categories of excess distributions and (B) a different amount (threshold amount) is subtracted from the distributions in each category in determining the amount of the excess distributions. The threshold amount that is subtracted from the portion of the distributions that is not part of the lump sum distribution is the applicable threshold amount, determined without regard to section 4981A(c)(4) and the lump sum election. Thus, the threshold amount subtracted from the amount in this category is either the $150,000 amount or the $112,500 amount (indexed). The threshold amount that is subtracted from the amount of the lump sum distribution is 5 times the applicable threshold amount as described above. Thus, the threshold amount subtracted from the lump sum distribution is $750,000 or 5 times $112,500 indexed (initially $562,500).

(b) *Grandfather rule.*—(1) *In general.* This paragraph (b) provides special rules where an individual makes both the grandfather election described in section 4981A(c)(5) and the lump sum election described in paragraph (a) of this Q&A c-1. See Q&A b-11 through 14 for other rules that apply to such grandfather election.

(2) *Discretionary method.* If the individual uses the discretionary method, described in Q&As b-11 and 12 of this section, the applicable threshold amount is $112,500 (indexed). Under this method, the grandfather amount is recovered at a 10 percent or 100 percent rate in any calendar year and is offset separately against distributions in each category of distributions at the appropriate rate. If, for any calendar year, distributions are received in both categories and the total of the appropriate percentage (10 percent or 100 percent) of the distributions in each category exceed the unrecovered grandfathered amount, then such grandfather amount must be recovered ratably from the distributions in each category. This rule applies even if the distributions in one category are less than the threshold amount for that category and the distributions in the other category exceed the threshold amount for that category.

(3) *Attained age method.* If the individual uses the attained age method, described in Q&As b-11 and 13 of this section, the threshold amount is $112,500 (indexed). Under this method, to determine the portion of the distributions in each category that is treated as a recovery of the grandfather amount, the fraction described in Q&A b-13 of this section is applied separately to the distributions in each category of distributions. If, for any calendar year, distributions are received in both categories and the total of the amounts of the distributions in each category that are treated as a recovery of the grandfather amount exceeds the unrecovered grandfather amount, then such grandfather amount must be recovered ratably from the distributions in each category. This rule applies even if the distributions in one category are less than the threshold

amount for that category and the distributions in the other category exceed the threshold amount for that category.

(c) *Amount in lump sum category.* All amounts received from the employer that are required to be distributed to the individual in order to make a lump sum election described in paragraph (a) of this Q&A c-1 are included in the lump sum category. Amounts are in the lump sum category even though they are not subject to income tax under the election. Thus, for example, the following amounts would be in the lump sum category: (1) Appreciation on employer securities received as part of a distribution for which a lump sum treatment is elected; and (2) amounts that are phased out when section 1122 of TRA '86 is elected. However, accumulated deductible employee contributions under the plan (within the meaning of section 72(o)(5)) are in the nonlump sum category.

(d) *Examples.* The rules in this Q&A c-1 are illustrated by the following examples:

Example (1). (a) On January 1, 199X, individual A who is age 65 and is a calendar year taxpayer receives a lump sum distribution described in section 402(e)(4)(A) from a qualified employer plan (Plan X). A receives no other distribution in 199X. A elects 5-year income averaging under section 402(e)(4)(B) and also elects section 402(e)(4)(L) treatment (treating pre-74 participation as post-1973 participation) on A's income tax return for 199X. Thus, A also makes the lump sum election described in paragraph (a)(2), above. For 199X, the $112,500 threshold amount indexed is $125,000. A does not make a grandfather election so that A's threshold amount is $150,000.

(b) A's distribution from Plan X consists of cash in the amount of $800,000. A has a section 72(f) investment in the contract. A has over the years made after-tax contributions to Plan X of $50,000. A's distributions subject to section 4981A equal $750,000 because of the exclusion of A's $50,000 after-tax contributions.

(c) A's distributions consist solely of amounts in the lump sum category. A's threshold amount equals $750,000 under the rules of this paragraph (a)(iii), above, (5 times $150,000). Because A's threshold amount ($750,000) equals the amount of A's distribution from Plan X ($750,000) no part of A's distribution from Plan X is treated as an excess distribution subject to the 15-percent excise tax.

Example (2). (a) Assume the same facts as in *Example (1)*, except that A receives an additional distribution from an individual retirement plan described in section 408(a) (IRA Y) in 199X of $150,000. A has made no nondeductible contributions to IRA Y and all of the $150,000 is a distribution subject to section 4981A.

(b) A's distributions consist of two categories, the lump sum category (Plan X $750,000) and the other than lump sum category (IRA Y $150,000). A separate threshold amount is subtracted from A's IRA Y distribution. This threshold amount equals $150,000 under the rules of this paragraph (a)(3), above, the same initial threshold amount that is applied against the lump sum prior to the multiplication by 5). Because A's threshold amount ($150,000) equals the amount of A's distribution from IRA Y ($150,000), no part of A's distribution from IRA Y would be treated as an excess distribution subject to the 15-percent excise tax.

Example (3). (a) Assume the same facts as in *Example (2),* except that A's distribution is $825,000 from Plan X, before reduction of $50,000 for employee contributions, instead of $800,000, so that A's distribution subject to section 4981A from Plan X is $775,000. A made a valid grandfather election. Therefore, the applicable threshold amount is $125,000 ($112,500 indexed for 199X). A's unrecovered grandfather amount as of the end of the year preceding 199X is $1,000,000 (A had a benefit under another retirement plan (Plan Z) on August 1, 1986, and A's account balance under Plan Z, which is a stock bonus plan, is $6,000,000 on January 1, 199X.) A also made a valid election of the discretionary method to recover A's grandfather amount.

(b) If A recovers A's grandfather amount in 199X at the 10 percent rate, 10 percent of A's distributions that are in the lump sum category (Plan X $775,000) is treated as a recovery of A's grandfather amount. Similarly, 10 percent of A's distributions that are in the other than lump sum category (IRA Y $150,000) is treated as a recovery of A's grandfather amount. Thus, A's grandfather amount is reduced by $92,500 ($77,500 Plan X and $15,000 IRA Y) for the 199X calendar year and is $907,500 on January 1 of the year following 199X. Because the amounts of the distributions in each category that are treated as a recovery of grandfather amount are less than the applicable threshold amount for each category ($625,000 Plan X, $125,000 IRA Y), the recovery of the grandfather amount does not affect the calculations of the 199X excise tax.

(c) Because A's distribution from IRA Y of $150,000 exceeds A's threshold amount of $125,000 ($112,500 indexed) applicable to nonlump sum distributions by $25,000 and A's distribution subject to section 4981A from Plan X of $775,000 exceeds A's threshold amount of $625,000 (5 × $125,000) applicable to lump sums by $150,000, A is subject to the 15-percent excise tax. A's tax under section 4981A is $26,250 (15 percent of $25,000 plus 15 percent of $150,000).

Example (4). (a) Assume the same facts as in *Example (3)* except that A makes a valid acceleration election under the discretionary method with respect to A's grandfather amount of $1,000,000 for calendar year 199X.

(b) Because A's grandfather amount on January 1, 199X ($1,000,000) equals or exceeds A's distribution subject to section 4981A ($925,000) for 199X, no part of A's distribution from Plan X or IRA Y would be treated as excess distribution subject to the 15-percent excise tax.

(c) A's distributions subject to 4981A from Plan X of $775,000 and from IRA Y of $150,000 are offset 100 percent by A's grandfather amount

of $1,000,000. Therefore, A's grandfather amount on January 1 of the year following 199X is $75,000 ($1,000,000 minus $925,000). This $75,000 would be required to be offset 100 percent against any distributions received in that year.

Example (5). (a) Assume the same facts as in *Example (4),* except that A's distribution subject to section 4981A from Plan X, after reduction of the $50,000 for employee contributions, is $1,000,000 and from IRA Y is $125,000 (equal to the threshold amount), totaling $1,125,000.

(b) Because the sum of the amount received in the lump sum category and the other than lump sum category of distributions is greater than the grandfather amount ($1,000,000), the grandfather amount must be allocated to each separate category on the basis of the ratio of the amount received in each category to the sum of these amounts. Thus, $888,889 ($1,000,000 × ($1,000,000 divided by $1,125,000)) is allocated to the lump-sum category and $111,111 ($1,000,000 × ($125,000 divided by $1,125,000)) is allocated to the other than lump sum category. A's distributions of $1,000,000 in the lump sum category are reduced by $888,889, the greater of $625,000 (the threshold amount) or $888,889 (grandfather amount), and equal $111,111. A's excise tax is $16,666 (15 percent of $111,000). A owes no excess distribution tax on the $125,000 received from IRA Y because it is fully offset by the threshold amount of $125,000.

(c) Because A's distribution subject to section 4981A for the year of $1,125,000 ($1,000,000 plus $125,000) exceeds A's grandfather amount on January 1, 199X of $1,000,000, A's grandfather amount is zero for all subsequent calendar years.

c-2: Q. Must retirement plans be amended to limit future benefit accruals so that the amounts that are distributed would not be subject to an excise tax under section 4981A?

A. No. A qualified employer plan need not be amended to reduce future benefits so that the amount of annual aggregate distributions are not subject to tax under section 4981A. Section 415 does, however, require plan provisions that limit the accrual of benefits and contributions to specified amounts. The operation of the excise tax of section 4981A is independent of plan qualification requirements limiting benefits and contributions under qualified plans.

c-3: Q. Is a plan amendment reducing accrued benefits a permitted method of avoiding the excise tax?

A. No. Accrued benefits may not be reduced to avoid the imposition of the excise tax. Such reduction would violate employer plan qualification requirements, including section 411(d)(6).

c-4: Q. To what extent is the 15 percent section 4981A tax reduced by the 10 percent section 72(t) tax?

A. (a) *General rule.* The 15 percent tax on excess distributions may be offset by the 10 percent tax on early distributions to the extent that the 10 percent tax is applied to excess distributions. For example, assume that individual (A), age 56, receives a distribution of $200,000 from a qualified employer plan (Plan X) during calendar year 1987. Further, assume that the entire distribution is subject to the 10-percent tax of section 72(t). A tax of $20,000 (10% of $200,000) is imposed on the distribution under section 72(t). Assuming that the distribution is not a lump sum distribution eligible for special tax treatment under section 402, part of the distribution is subject to tax under section 4981A. If A does not elect the special grandfather rule, A's dollar limitation is $150,000 and the amount of the $200,000 distribution that is an excess distribution is $50,000 ($200,000 − $150,000). The 15 percent tax is $7,500 (15% of $50,000). The portion of the $20,000 section 72(t) tax on early distributions that is attributable to the excess distribution is $5,000 (10% of $50,000). This amount is credited against the section 4981A tax. Therefore, the total tax imposed on the distribution under both provisions is $22,500 ($20,000 + ($7,500-$5,000)).

(b) *Example.* (1) If some, but not all, distributions made for a calendar year are subject to the section 72(t) tax, the offset is applied only to the extent that the section 72(t) tax applies to amounts that exceed the applicable threshold amount for that calendar year. For example, assume that during 1987 individual B receives a distribution of $40,000 that is not subject to the 10 percent section 72(t) tax and a separate distribution of $160,000 that is subject to the 10 percent section 72(t) tax. A tax of $16,000 (10% of $160,000) is imposed by section 72(t). Excess distributions for the year, assuming B does not elect the special grandfather rule, are $50,000 ($40,000 + $160,000-$150,000). The tax under section 4981A is $7,500 (15% of $50,000). For purposes of determining the extent to which the 10 percent tax is applied to excess distributions, the only amounts subject to the 10 percent tax that are taken into account are distributions in excess of $150,000 (or if greater, the $112,500 (indexed) threshold for the year). The amount of distributions for 1987 to which the 10 percent tax is applicable ($160,000) exceeds $150,000 by $10,000. Thus, the portion of the section 72(t) tax of $16,000 that is attributable to excess distributions equals $1,000 (10 percent of $10,000). This amount is credited against the section 4981A tax. The total tax payable under the provisions of sections 72(t) and 4981A is $18,500 ($16,000 + ($7,500-$1,000)).

(c) *Net unrealized appreciation.* A distribution consisting of net unrealized appreciation of employer securities that is excluded from gross income is not subject to section 72(t) and, therefore, there is no section 72(t) tax on such distribution that may be used to offset the tax on excess distributions.

c-5: *Q.* If a distribution that is subject to both the 10 percent tax on early distributions from qualified plans imposed under section 72(t) and the 15 percent tax on excess distributions imposed under section 4981A is received by an individual who elects to calculate the 15 percent tax using the special grandfather rule, how is the

offset of the 10 percent tax imposed under section 72(t) calculated?

A. The section 4981A tax is reduced only by the amount of the 10 percent tax that is attributable to the portion of the distribution to which the section 4981A tax applies. For example, assume that (a) an individual (A), age 57, receives during 199X a distribution from a qualified plan of $325,000 that is subject to the 10 percent section 72(t) tax; (b) the distribution is not a lump sum distribution and is subject to the 15 percent excise tax imposed by section 4981A; (c) A has elected to use the special grandfather rule; and (d) A accelerates the rate of recovery of the remaining grandfather amount of $250,000 so that only $75,000 of this distribution is subject to the section 4981A tax. Thus, the section 4981A tax is $11,250 (15% of $75,000). The portion of the section 72(t) 10 percent tax that is offset against the section 4981A tax of $11,250 is limited to $7,500 (10% of $75,000), the section 72(t) tax on the amount of distributions after taking into account the reduction under the grandfather rule.

c-6: *Q.* When do distributions become subject to the excise tax under section 4981A?

A. (a) *General rule.* Excess distributions made after December 31, 1986, are subject to the excise tax under section 4981A.

(b) *Transitional rule—*(1) *Termination.* Distributions prior to January 1, 1988, made on account of certain terminations of a qualified employer plan are not subject to tax under section 4981A. For a plan termination to be eligible for this transitional rule, the plan termination must occur before January 1, 1987. For purposes of applying the rules of section 4981A (except the reporting requirements), any such distribution is treated as if made on December 31, 1986. The distribution of an annuity contract is not an excepted distribution. See Q&A a-5 of this section.

(2) *Lump sum distributions.* A lump sum distribution that an individual who separates from service in 1986 receives in calendar year 1987 before March 16 is treated as a distribution received in 1986 if such individual elects to treat it as received in 1986 under the provisions of section 1124 of TRA '86. Thus, such a qualifying section 1124 distribution is not subject to tax under section 4981A for 1987. For purposes of applying the rules of section 4981A, the amount attributable to such distribution is included in the individual's August 1, 1986 accrued benefit and such distribution is treated as if made on December 31, 1986.

(3) *Grandfather amount recovery.* If an individual described in this paragraph elects the special grandfather rule, the entire amount of distributions described in subparagraph (1) or (2) of this paragraph (b) is treated as a recovery of the individual's grandfather amount because it is treated as received on December 31, 1986. Thus, the individual's outstanding grandfather amount as of the date of the distribution is reduced by the amount of such distribution.

c-7: Q. How is the tax on excess distributions or on excess accumulations under section 4981A reported?

A. (a) *Tax on excess distributions.* An individual liable for tax on account of excess distributions under section 4981A must complete Form 5329 and attach it to his income tax return for the taxable year beginning with or within the calendar year during which the excess distributions are received. The amount of the tax is reported on such form and in such manner as prescribed by the Commissioner.

(b) *Tax on excess accumulations*—(1) *General rule.* If, with respect to the estate of any individual, there is a tax under section 4981A(d) on account of the individual's excess accumulations, the amount of such tax is reported on Schedule S (Form 706 or 706NR). Schedule S must be filed on or before the due date under section 6075 including extensions, for filing the estate tax return. The tax under section 4981A(d) must be paid by the otherwise applicable due date for paying the estate tax imposed by chapter 11 even if, pursuant to section 6018(a), no return is otherwise required with respect to the estate tax imposed by chapter 11.

(2) *Earliest due date.* Notwithstanding paragraph (b)(1) of this c-7, the due date for filing Schedule S (Form 706) and paying the tax on excess accumulations under section 4981A(d) is not earlier than February 1, 1988. Thus, with respect to the estates of individuals dying in January through April of 1987, the due date for filing Schedule S (Form 706) and paying any tax owed under section 4981A(d) is not earlier than February 1, 1988 even if the due date for filing the Schedule 706 and paying the estate tax imposed by chapter 11 is an earlier date. Further, no interest or penalties will be charged for failure to pay any tax on excess accumulations under section 4981A before January 31, 1988.

c-8: Q. Does the fact that the benefits under a qualified retirement plan or individual retirement account are community property affect the determination of the excise tax under section 4981A?

A. Generally, no. The operation of community property law is disregarded in determining the amount of aggregate annual distributions. Thus, the excise tax under section 4981A is computed without regard to the spouse's community property interest in the individual's or decedent's distributions or accumulation. Also, any reporting to the individual by a trustee, must be done on an aggregate basis without regard to the community property law.

d. *Excess Accumulations*

d-1: Q. To what extent does section 4981A increase the estate tax imposed by chapter 11 with respect to the estates of any decedents?

A. Section 4981A(d) provides that the estate tax imposed by chapter 11 with respect to the estate of any decedent is increased by an amount equal to 15 percent of the decedent's excess accumulation. See Q&A d-2 through d-7 of this section for rules for determining the decedent's excess accumulation. See Q&A d-8 of this section concerning credits under section 2010 through 2016. See Q&A d-9 of this section for examples illustrating the determination of the increase in estate tax under section 4981A(d).

d-2: Q. How is the amount of a decedent's excess accumulation determined?

A. (a) *General rule.* A decedent's excess accumulation is the excess of (1) the aggregate value of the decedent's interests in all qualified employer plans and individual retirement plans (decedent's aggregate interest) as of the date of the decedent's death over (2) an amount equal to the present value of a hypothetical life annuity determined under Q&A d-7 of this section. If the personal representative for the individual's estate elects to value the property in the gross estate under section 2032, the applicable valuation date prescribed by section 2032 shall be substituted for the decedent's date of death.

(b) *Other rules.* See Q&A d-3 and d-4 of this section if the decedent or, where appropriate, the decedent's personal representative validly elects the special grandfather rule and has any unused grandfather benefit as of the date of his death. See Q&A d-5 and d-6 of this section to determine the decedent's aggregate interest.

d-3: Q. Does the special grandfather rule apply for purposes of determining the amount of the decedent's excess accumulation?

A. Yes. If a decedent prior to death (or the decedent's personal representative after death) makes an election that satisfied the procedures in Q&A b-3 of this section, the special grandfather rule applies.

d-4: Q. How is the decedent's excess accumulation determined if the special grandfather rule applies?

A. If the special grandfather rule applies, the decedent's excess accumulation is the excess of (a) the decedent's aggregate interest (determined under Q&A d-5 of this section) over (b) the greater of (1) the decedent's remaining unrecovered grandfather amount as of the date of the decedent's death, or (2) an amount equal to the present value of a hypothetical life annuity under Q&A d-7 of this section.

d-5: Q. How is the value of the decedent's aggregate interest as of the applicable valuation date under Q&A d-2 determined?

A. (a) *Method of valuation.* The value of the decedent's aggregate interest on the decedent's date of death is determined in a manner consistent with the valuation of such interests for purposes of determining the individual's gross estate for purposes of chapter 11. If the personal representative for an individual's estate subject to estate tax elects to value the property in the gross estate under section 2032, the decedent's aggregate interest is valued in a manner consistent with the rules prescribed by section 2032 (and other relevant estate tax sections). No adjustments provided in chapter 11 in valuing the gross estate are made. Thus, there is no adjustment under section 2057 (relating to the sale of certain employer securities).

Reg. §54.4981A-1T

(b) *Amounts included.* Generally, all amounts payable to beneficiaries of the decedent under any qualified employer plan (including amounts payable to a surviving spouse under a qualified joint and survivor annuity or qualified preretirement survivor annuity) or individual retirement plan, whether or not otherwise included in valuing the decedent's gross estate, are considered to be part of the decedent's interest in such plan.

(c) *Rollover after death.* If any amount is distributed from a qualified employer plan or individual retirement plan within the 60-day period ending on the decedent's date of death and is rolled over to an IRA after such date but within 60 days of the date distributed, the decedent's aggregate interest is increased by the amount rolled over, valued as of the date received by the IRA.

d-6: Q. Are there any reductions in the decedent's aggregate interest?

A. The decedent's aggregate interest is reduced by the following:

(a) *Amount payable to alternate payee.* The amount of any portion of the deceased individual's interest in a qualified employer plan that is payable to an alternate payee in whose income the amount is includible under a qualified domestic relations order within the meaning of section 414(p) (QDRO). However, such portion must be taken into account in determining the excess distribution or the excess accumulation upon the death of such alternate payee for purposes of determining if there is a tax under section 4981A(a) or an increase in the estate tax under section 4981A(d) with respect to such alternate payee.

(b) *Investment in the contract.* The amount of the deceased individual's unrecovered investment, within the meaning of section 72(f), in any qualified employer plan or individual retirement plan.

(c) *Life insurance proceeds.* The excess of any amount payable by reason of the death of the individual under a life insurance contract held under a qualified employer plan over the cash surrender value of such contract immediately before the death of such individual (the amount excludable from income by reason of section 101(a)). Amounts excludable from gross income because of section 101(b) do not reduce the decedent's aggregate interest.

(d) *Interest as a beneficiary.* The amount of the deceased individual's interest in a qualified retirement plan or individual retirement plan by reason of the death of another individual.

d-7: Q. How is the present value of the hypothetical life annuity determined?

A. (a) *General rule.* The hypothetical life annuity is a single life annuity contract that provides for equal annual annuity payments commencing on the decedent's date of death for the life of an individual whose age is the same as the decedent's determined as of the date of the decedent's death. The amount of each annual payment is equal to the greater of $150,000 (unindexed) and $112,500 (as indexed until the

date of death). If the decedent elected (or the decedent's personal representative elects) the special grandfather rule, the amount of each annual payment is $112,500 (as indexed until the date of death) even if there is no remaining grandfather amount.

(b) *Determination of age.* The decedent's age as of the decedent's date of death for purposes of valuing the hypothetical life annuity is the decedent's attained age (in whole years) as of the decedent's date of death. For example, if the decedent was born on February 2, 1930, and died on August 3, 1990, the decedent's age for purposes of valuing the hypothetical life annuity is 60.

(c) *Interest rate assumptions.* The present value of the single life annuity described above must then be calculated using the interest rate and mortality assumptions in § 20.2031-7 of the Estate Tax Regulations in effect on the date of death.

d-8: Q. Are any credits, deductions, exclusions, etc. that apply for estate tax purposes allowable as an offset against the excise tax under section 4981A(d) for excess accumulations?

A. No. No credits, deductions, exclusions, etc. that apply for estate tax purposes are allowed to offset the tax imposed under section 4981A(d). Thus, no credits under section 2010 through 2016 or other reductions permitted by Chapter 11 are allowable against the tax under section 4981A(d) for excess accumulations. For example, no credits are allowable for the unified credit against the estate tax, for state death taxes, or for gift taxes.

d-8A: Q. Is the estate liable for the the excise tax of 15 percent on the amount of the decedent's excess accumulations?

A. Yes. In all events, the estate is liable for the excise tax of 15 percent on the amount of the decedent's excess accumulations. Transferee liability rules under chapter 11 do apply, however. Similarly, the reimbursement provisions of section 2205 also apply. Additionally, the rules generally applicable for purposes of determining the apportionment of the estate tax apply to the apportionment of the excise tax under section 4981A(d). Thus, the decedent's will or the applicable state apportionment law may provide that the executor is entitled to recover the tax imposed under section 4981A(d) attributable to any property from the beneficiary entitled to receive such property. However, absent such a provision in the decedent's will or in the applicable state apportionment law, the executor is not entitled to recover the tax imposed under section 4981A(d) attributable to any property from the beneficiary entitled to receive such property.

d-9: Q. How is the additional tax computed with respect to a decedent's estate under section 4981A(d)?

A. The determination of the additional tax under section 4981A(d) is illustrated by the following examples:

Example 1. (a) An individual (A) dies on February 1, 199X at age 70 and 9 months. As of A's date of death, A has an interest in a defined benefit plan described in section 401(a) (Plan X). Plan X has never provided for employee contributions. A has no section 72(f) investment in Plan X. A does not have any interest in any other qualified employer plan or individual retirement plan. The alternate valuation date in section 2032 does not apply. A did not elect to have the special grandfather rule apply. A's interest in Plan X is the form of a qualified joint and survivor annuity. The value of the remaining payments under the joint and survivor annuity as of A's date of death (determined under D-5) is $2,000,000.

(b) Because A is age 70 and 9 months on A's date of death, A's life expectancy as of A's date of death is calculated using age 70 (A's attained age in whole years on A's date of death). The factor from Table A of § 20.2031-7(f) used to determine the present value of a single life annuity for an individual age 70 is 6.0522. The greater of $150,000 or $112,500 indexed for 199X is $150,000. The present value of the hypothetical single life annuity is $907,830 ($150,000 × 6.0522).

(c) The amount of A's excess accumulation is $1,092,170, determined as follows: $2,000,000 (value of A's interest in Plan X) minus $907,830 (value of hypothetical single life annuity contract) equals $1,092,170.

(d) The increase in the estate tax under section 4981A(d) is $163,825 (15 percent of $1,092,170).

Example 2. (a) The facts are the same as in *Example 1,* except that A's interest in Plan X consists of the following:

(1) $2,000,000, value of employer-provided portion of a qualified joint and survivor annuity determined as of A's date of death using the interest and mortality assumptions in § 20.2031-7.

(2) $200,000, proceeds of a term life insurance contract (no cash surrender value before death).

(3) $100,000, amount (employer-provided portion) payable to A's former spouse pursuant to a QDRO.

(4) $100,000, amount of A's investment in Plan X.

(b) The value of A's interest in Plan X for purposes of calculating A's excess accumulation is still $2,000,000. The proceeds of the term life insurance contract, the amount payable under the QDRO, and the amount of A's investment in Plan X are excluded from such value.

Example 3. (a) The facts are the same as in *Example 1,* except that A elected the special grandfather rule. A's initial grandfather amount was $1,100,000. As of A's date of death, A had received $500,000 in distributions that were treated as a return of A's grandfather amount. Thus, A's unused grandfather amount is $600,000 ($1,100,000 − $500,000). In 199X, assume that $112,500 indexed is still $112,500.

(b) A's excess retirement accumulation is determined as follows: $2,000,000 minus the greater of (1) $600,000 or (2) the present value of a period certain annuity of $112,500 a year for 16 years. The present value of a single life annuity

of $112,500 a year for an individual age 70 is determined as follows: $112,500 × 6.0522 = $680,827.25. $680,827.25 is greater than $600,000. Thus the amount of the excess retirement accumulation is $1,319,173 ($2,000,000 minus $680,827).

(c) The additional estate tax under section 4981A(d) is $197,875 (15 percent of $1,319,173).

Example 4. (a) The facts are the same as in *Example 3* except that, as of A's date of death, A received $90,000 in distributions that were treated as a return of A's grandfather amount. Thus, A's unused granfather amount is $1,010,000 ($1,100,000 − $90,000).

(b) A's excess retirement accumulation is determined as follows: $2,000,000 minus the greater of (1) $1,010,000 (A's unused grandfather amount) or (2) $680,827.25 (the present value of a single life annuity of $112,500 a year for an individual age 70). A's unused grandfather amount is greater than the present value of the hypothetical life annuity. Thus, the amount of the excess retirement accumulation is $990,000 ($2,000,000 − $1,010,000).

(c) The additional estate tax under section 4981A(d) is $148,500 (15 percent of $990,000).

d-10: Q. If a surviving spouse rolls over a distribution from a qualified retirement plan or an individual retirement plan of the decedent to an individual retirement plan (IRA) established in the spouse's own name, is any distribution in a calendar year from the IRA receiving such rollover included in determining the spouse's excess distribution or excess accumulation in such calendar year?

A. (a) *General rule.* If a surviving spouse rolls over a distribution from a qualified retirement plan or an individual retirement plan of the decedent to an individual retirement plan (IRA) established in the spouse's own name with the rollover contribution and no other contributions or transfers are made to the IRA receiving the rollover contribution, distributions from such IRA will be excluded in determining the spouse's excess distributions and the value of the IRA will be excluded in determining the spouse's excess accumulation. If the surviving spouse rolls over a distribution from a qualified retirement plan or IRA of the decedent to an IRA for which the spouse has prior contributions or makes additional contributions to the IRA receiving the distribution, distributions from the IRA will be included in determining the amount of the excess distributions received by the spouse for the calendar year of the distribution and the value of the IRA at the applicable valuation date will be included in determining the spouse's excess accumulation.

(b) *Special rules.* The rule in paragraph (a) of this Q&A d-10 also applies if a surviving spouse elects to treat an inherited IRA (described in section 408(d)(3)(C)(ii)) as the spouse's own IRA as long as the surviving spouse makes no further contributions to such IRA.

(c) *Other beneficiaries.* Rules similar to the rules in paragraphs (a) & (b) shall apply to an individ-

Reg. § 54.4981A-1T

ual who elected to treat an IRA as subject to the distribution requirements of section 408(a)(6), prior to amendment by section 521(b) of TRA '84, under § 1.408-2(b)(7)(ii) of the Income Tax Regulations.

d-11: Q. To what estates does the excise tax under section 4981A(d) apply?

A. The excise tax under section 4981A(d) applies to estates of decedents dying after December 31, 1986.

d-12: Q. Is the aggregate interest reduced by distributions described in paragraph (b)(1) of Q&A c-6 of this section (distributions prior to January 1, 1988, made on account of certain terminations of a qualified employer plan) which are made after the individual's death.

A. Yes, the value of the individual's aggregate interest determined under Q&A d-5 of this section is reduced by distributions described in paragraph (b)(1) of Q&A c-6 of this section which are made after the individual's death. [Temporary Reg. § 54.4981A-1T.]

☐ [*T.D.* 8165, 12-9-87.]

[Reg. § 55.4982-1]

§ 55.4982-1. Imposition of excise tax on undistributed income of regulated investment companies.—Section 4982 imposes an excise tax on a regulated investment company in the amount of four percent of the excess, if any, of the required distribution for a calendar year over the distributed amount for such calendar year. Section 4982 applies only to calendar years beginning after December 31, 1986. [Reg. § 55.4982-1.]

☐ [*T.D.* 8180, 2-29-88.]

Maintenance of Minimum Essential Coverage

See p. 20,601 for regulations not amended to reflect law changes

[Reg. § 1.5000A-0]

§ 1.5000A-0. Table of contents.—This section lists the captions contained in §§ 1.5000A-1 through 1.5000A-5.

(2) Exemption certification.

(b) Member of health care sharing ministries.

(1) In general.

(2) Health care sharing ministry.

(c) Exempt noncitizens.

(1) In general.

(2) Exempt noncitizens.

(d) Incarcerated individuals.

(1) In general.

(2) Incarcerated.

(e) Individuals with no affordable coverage.

(1) In general.

(2) Required contribution percentage.

(i) In general.

(ii) Indexing.

(iii) Plan year.

(3) Individuals eligible for coverage under eligible employer-sponsored plans.

(i) Eligibility.

(A) In general.

(B) Multiple eligibility.

(C) Special rule for post-employment coverage.

(ii) Required contribution for individuals eligible for coverage under an eligible employer-sponsored plan.

(A) Employees.

(B) Individuals related to employees.

(C) Required contribution for part-year period.

(D) Employer contributions to health reimbursement arrangements.

(E) Wellness program incentives.

(iii) Examples.

(4) Individuals ineligible for coverage under eligible employer-sponsored plans.

(i) Eligibility for coverage other than an eligible employer-sponsored plan.

(ii) Required contribution for individuals ineligible for coverage under eligible employer-sponsored plans.

(A) In general.

(B) Applicable plan.

(1) In general.

(2) Lowest cost bronze plan does not cover all individuals included in the taxpayer's nonexempt family.

(i) In general.

(ii) Optional simplified method for applicable plan identification.

(C) Wellness program incentives.

(D) Credit allowable under section 36B.

(E) Required contribution for part-year period.

(iii) Examples.

(f) Household income below filing threshold.

(1) In general.

(2) Applicable filing threshold.

(i) In general.

(ii) Certain dependents.

(3) Manner of claiming the exemption.

(g) Members of Indian tribes.

(h) Individuals with hardship exemption certification.

(1) In general.

(2) Hardship exemption certification.

(3) Hardship exemption without hardship exemption certification.

(i) [Reserved]

(j) Individuals with certain short coverage gaps.

(1) In general.

(2) Short coverage gap.

(i) In general.

(ii) Coordination with other exemptions.

(iii) More than one short coverage gap during calendar year.

(3) Continuous period.

(i) In general.

(ii) Continuous period straddling more than one taxable year.

(4) Examples.

§ 1.5000A-4 *Computation of shared responsibility payment.*

(a) In general.

(b) Monthly penalty amount.

(1) In general.

(2) Flat dollar amount.

(i) In general.

(ii) Applicable dollar amount.

(iii) Special applicable dollar amount for individuals under age 18.

(iv) Indexing of applicable dollar amount.

(3) Excess income amount.

(i) In general.

(ii) Income percentage.

(c) Monthly national average bronze plan premium.

(d) Examples.

§ 1.5000A-5 *Administration and procedure.*

(a) In general.

(b) Special rules.

(1) Waiver of criminal penalties.

(2) Limitations on liens and levies.

(3) Authority to offset against overpayment.

(c) Effective/applicability date. [Reg. § 1.5000A-0.]

☐ [*T.D.* 9632, 8-27-2013 (*corrected* 12-24-2013) and T.D. 9705, 11-21-2014.]

[Reg. § 1.5000A-1]

§ 1.5000A-1. Maintenance of minimum essential coverage and liability for the shared responsibility payment.—(a) *In general.*—For each month during the taxable year, a nonexempt individual must have minimum essential coverage or pay the shared responsibility payment. For a month, a nonexempt individual is an individual in existence for the entire month who is not an exempt individual described in § 1.5000A-3.

(b) *Coverage under minimum essential coverage.*—(1) *In general.*—An individual has minimum essential coverage for a month in which the individual is enrolled in and entitled to receive benefits under a program or plan identified as minimum essential coverage in § 1.5000A-2 for at least one day in the month.

(2) *Special rule for United States citizens or residents residing outside the United States or residents of territories.*—An individual is treated as having minimum essential coverage for a month—

(i) If the month occurs during any period described in section 911(d)(1)(A) or section 911(d)(1)(B) that is applicable to the individual; or

(ii) If, for the month, the individual is a bona fide resident of a possession of the United States (as determined under section 937(a)).

(c) *Liability for shared responsibility payment.*— (1) *In general.*—A taxpayer is liable for the shared responsibility payment for a month for which—

(i) The taxpayer is a nonexempt individual without minimum essential coverage; or

(ii) A nonexempt individual for whom the taxpayer is liable under paragraph (c)(2) or (c)(3) of this section does not have minimum essential coverage.

(2) *Liability for dependents.*—(i) *In general.*— For a month when a nonexempt individual does not have minimum essential coverage, if the nonexempt individual is a dependent (as defined in section 152) of another individual for the other individual's taxable year including that month, the other individual is liable for the shared responsibility payment attributable to the dependent's lack of coverage. An individual is a dependent of a taxpayer for a taxable year if the individual satisfies the definition of dependent under section 152, regardless of whether the taxpayer claims the individual as a dependent on a Federal income tax return for the taxable year. If an individual may be claimed as a dependent by more than one taxpayer in the same calendar year, the taxpayer who properly claims the individual as a dependent for the taxable year is liable for the shared responsibility payment attributable to the individual. If more than one taxpayer may claim an individual as a dependent in the same calendar year but no one claims the individual as a dependent, the taxpayer with priority under the rules of section 152 to claim the individual as a dependent is liable for the shared responsibility payment for the individual.

(ii) *Special rules for dependents adopted or placed in foster care during the taxable year.*— (A) *Taxpayers adopting an individual.*—If a taxpayer adopts a nonexempt dependent (or accepts a nonexempt dependent who is an eligible foster child as defined in section 152(f)(1)(C)) during the taxable year and is otherwise liable for the nonexempt dependent under paragraph (c)(2)(i) of this section, the taxpayer is liable under paragraph (c)(2)(i) of this section for the nonexempt dependent only for the full months in the taxable year that follow the month in which the adoption or acceptance occurs.

(B) *Taxpayers placing an individual for adoption.*—If a taxpayer who is otherwise liable for a nonexempt dependent under paragraph (c)(2)(i) of this section places (or, by operation of law, must place) the nonexempt dependent for adoption or foster care during the taxable year, the taxpayer is liable under paragraph (c)(2)(i) of this section for the nonexempt dependent only for the full months in the taxable year that precede the month in which the adoption or foster care placement occurs.

(C) *Examples.*—The following examples illustrate the provisions of this paragraph (c)(2)(ii). In each example the taxpayer's taxable year is a calendar year.

Example 1. Taxpayers adopting a child. (i) E and F, married individuals filing a joint return, initiate proceedings for the legal adoption of a 2-year old child, G, in January 2016. On May 15, 2016, G becomes the adopted child (within the meaning of section 152(f)(1)(B)) of E and F, and resides with them for the remainder of 2016. Prior to the adoption, G resides with H, an unmarried individual, with H providing all of G's support. For 2016 G meets all requirements under section 152 to be E and F's dependent, and not H's dependent.

(ii) Under paragraph (c)(2) of this section, E and F are not liable for a shared responsibility payment attributable to G for January through May of 2016, but are liable for a shared responsibility payment attributable to G, if any, for June through December of 2016. H is not liable for a shared responsibility payment attributable to G for any month in 2016, because G is not H's dependent for 2016 under section 152.

Example 2. Taxpayers placing a child for adoption. (i) The facts are the same as *Example 1*, except the legal adoption occurs on August 15, 2016, and, for 2016, G meets all requirements under section 152 to be H's dependent, and not E and F's dependent.

(ii) Under paragraph (c)(2) of this section, H is liable for a shared responsibility payment attributable to G, if any, for January through July of 2016, but is not liable for a shared responsibility payment attributable to G for August through December of 2016. E and F are not liable for a shared responsibility payment attributable to G for any month in 2016, because G is not E and F's dependent for 2016 under section 152.

(3) *Liability of individuals filing a joint return.*—Married individuals (within the meaning of section 7703) who file a joint return for a taxable year are jointly liable for any shared responsibility payment for a month included in the taxable year.

(d) *Definitions.*—The definitions in this paragraph (d) apply to this section and §§ 1.5000A-2 through 1.5000A-5.

(1) *Affordable Care Act.*—Affordable Care Act refers to the Patient Protection and Affordable Care Act, Public Law 111-148 (124 Stat. 119

(2010)), and the Health Care and Education Reconciliation Act of 2010, Public Law 111-152 (124 Stat. 1029 (2010)), as amended.

(2) *Employee.*—*Employee* includes former employees.

(3) *Exchange.*—*Exchange* has the same meaning as in 45 CFR 155.20.

(4) *Family.*—A taxpayer's family means the individuals for whom the taxpayer properly claims a deduction for a personal exemption under section 151 for the taxable year.

(5) *Family coverage.*—*Family coverage* means health insurance that covers more than one individual.

(6) *Group health insurance coverage.*—*Group health insurance coverage* has the same meaning as in section 2791(b)(4) of the Public Health Service Act (42 U.S.C. 300gg-91(b)(4)).

(7) *Group health plan.*—*Group health plan* has the same meaning as in section 2791(a)(1) of the Public Health Service Act (42 U.S.C. 300gg-91(a)(1)).

(8) *Health insurance coverage.*—*Health insurance coverage* has the same meaning as in section 2791(b)(1) of the Public Health Service Act (42 U.S.C. 300gg-91(b)(1)).

(9) *Health insurance issuer.*—*Health insurance issuer* has the same meaning as in section 2791(b)(2) of the Public Health Service Act (42 U.S.C. 300gg-91(b)(2)).

(10) *Household income.*—(i) *In general.*—*Household income* means the sum of—

(A) A taxpayer's modified adjusted gross income; and

(B) The aggregate modified adjusted gross income of all other individuals who—

(1) Are included in the taxpayer's family under paragraph (d)(4) of this section; and

(2) Are required to file a Federal income tax return for the taxable year.

(ii) *Modified adjusted gross income.*—*Modified adjusted gross income* means adjusted gross income (within the meaning of section 62) increased by—

(A) Amounts excluded from gross income under section 911; and

(B) Tax-exempt interest the taxpayer receives or accrues during the taxable year.

(11) *Individual market.*—*Individual market* has the same meaning as in section 1304(a)(2) of the Affordable Care Act (42 U.S.C. 18024(a)(2)).

(12) *Large and small group market.*—*Large group market* and *small group market* have the same meanings as in section 1304(a)(3) of the Affordable Care Act (42 U.S.C. 18024(a)(3)).

(13) *Month.*—*Month* means calendar month.

(14) *Qualified health plan.*—*Qualified health plan* has the same meaning as in section 1301(a) of the Affordable Care Act (42 U.S.C. 18021(a)).

(15) *Rating area.*—*Rating area* has the same meaning as in § 1.36B-1(n).

(16) *Self-only coverage.*—*Self-only coverage* means health insurance that covers one individual.

(17) *Shared responsibility family.*—*Shared responsibility family* means, for a month, all nonexempt individuals for whom the taxpayer (and the taxpayer's spouse, if the taxpayer is married and files a joint return with the spouse) is liable for the shared responsibility payment under paragraph (c) of this section.

(18) *State.*—*State* means each of the 50 states and the District of Columbia. [Reg. § 1.5000A-1.]

☐ [*T.D. 9632, 8-27-2013 (corrected 12-24-2013).*]

[Reg. § 1.5000A-2]

§ 1.5000A-2. Minimum essential coverage.—(a) *In general.*—*Minimum essential coverage* means coverage under a government-sponsored program (described in paragraph (b) of this section), an eligible employer-sponsored plan (described in paragraph (c) of this section), a plan in the individual market (described in paragraph (d) of this section), a grandfathered health plan (described in paragraph (e) of this section), or other health benefits coverage (described in paragraph (f) of this section). Minimum essential coverage does not include coverage described in paragraph (g) of this section. All terms defined in this section apply for purposes of this section and § 1.5000A-1 and § § 1.5000A-3 through 1.5000A-5.

(b) *Government-sponsored program.*—(1) *In general.*—Except as provided in paragraph (2), *government-sponsored program* means any of the following:

(i) *Medicare.*—The Medicare program under part A of Title XVIII of the Social Security Act (42 U.S.C.1395c and following sections);

(ii) *Medicaid.*—The Medicaid program under Title XIX of the Social Security Act (42 U.S.C. 1396 and following sections);

(iii) *Children's Health Insurance Program.*—The Children's Health Insurance Program (CHIP) under Title XXI of the Social Security Act (42 U.S.C 1397aa and following sections);

(iv) *TRICARE.*—Medical coverage under chapter 55 of Title 10, U.S.C., including coverage under the TRICARE program;

(v) *Veterans programs.*—The following health care programs under chapter 17 or 18 of Title 38, U.S.C.:

(A) The medical benefits package authorized for eligible veterans under 38 U.S.C. 1710 and 38 U.S.C. 1705;

(B) The Civilian Health and Medical Program of the Department of Veterans Affairs (CHAMPVA) authorized under 38 U.S.C. 1781; and

(C) The comprehensive health care program authorized under 38 U.S.C. 1803 and 38 U.S.C. 1821 for certain children of Vietnam Veterans and Veterans of covered service in Korea who are suffering from spina bifida.

(vi) *Peace Corp program.*—A health plan under section 2504(e) of Title 22, U.S.C. (relating to Peace Corps volunteers); and

(vii) *Nonappropriated Fund Health Benefits Program.*—The Nonappropriated Fund Health Benefits Program of the Department of Defense, established under section 349 of the National Defense Authorization Act for Fiscal Year 1995 (Public Law No. 103-337; 10 U.S.C. 1587 note).

(2) *Certain health care coverage not minimum essential coverage under a government-sponsored program.*—Government-sponsored program does not mean any of the following:

(i) Optional coverage of family planning services under section 1902(a)(10)(A)(ii)(XXI) of the Social Security Act (42 U.S.C. 1396a(a)(10)(A)(ii)(XXI));

(ii) Optional coverage of tuberculosis-related services under section 1902(a)(10)(A)(ii)(XII) of the Social Security Act (42 U.S.C. 1396a(a)(10)(A)(ii)(XII));

(iii) Coverage of pregnancy-related services under section 1902(a)(10)(A)(i)(IV) and (a)(10)(A)(ii)(IX) of the Social Security Act (42 U.S.C. 1396a(a)(10)(A)(i)(IV), (a)(10)(A)(ii)(IX));

(iv) Coverage limited to treatment of emergency medical conditions in accordance with 8 U.S.C. 1611(b)(1)(A), as authorized by section 1903(v) of the Social Security Act (42 U.S.C. 1396b(v));

(v) Coverage for medically needy individuals under section 1902(a)(10)(C) of the Social Security Act (42 U.S.C. 1396a(a)(10)(C)) and 42 CFR 435.300 and following sections;

(vi) Coverage authorized under section 1115(a) of the Social Security Act (42 U.S.C. 1315(a));

(vii) Coverage under section 1079(a), 1086(c)(1), or 1086(d)(1) of title 10, U.S.C., that is solely limited to space available care in a facility of the uniformed services for individuals excluded from TRICARE coverage for care from private sector providers; and

(viii) Coverage under sections 1074a and 1074b of title 10, U.S.C., for an injury, illness, or disease incurred or aggravated in the line of duty for individuals who are not on active duty.

(c) *Eligible employer-sponsored plan.*—(1) *In general.*—Eligible employer-sponsored plan means, with respect to any employee:

(i) Group health insurance coverage offered by, or on behalf of, an employer to the employee that is—

(A) A governmental plan (within the meaning of section 2791(d)(8) of the Public Health Service Act (42 U.S.C.300gg-91(d)(8)));

(B) Any other plan or coverage offered in the small or large group market within a State; or

(C) A grandfathered health plan (within the meaning of paragraph (e) of this section) offered in a group market; or

(ii) A self-insured group health plan under which coverage is offered by, or on behalf of, an employer to the employee.

(2) *Government-sponsored program generally not an eligible employer-sponsored plan.*—Except for the program identified in paragraph (b)(1)(vii) of this section, a government-sponsored program described in paragraph (b) of this section is not an eligible employer-sponsored plan.

(d) *Plan in the individual market.*—(1) *In general.*—Plan in the individual market means health insurance coverage offered to individuals in the individual market within a state, other than short-term limited duration insurance within the meaning of section 2791(b)(5) of the Public Health Service Act (42 U.S.C. 300gg-91(b)(5)).

(2) *Qualified health plan offered by an Exchange.*—A qualified health plan offered by an Exchange is a plan in the individual market. If a territory of the United States elects to establish an Exchange under section 1323(a)(1) and (b) of the Affordable Care Act (42 U.S.C. 18043(a)(1), (b)), a qualified health plan offered by that Exchange is a plan in the individual market.

(e) *Grandfathered health plan.*—Grandfathered health plan means any group health plan or group health insurance coverage to which section 1251 of the Affordable Care Act (42 U.S.C. 18011) applies.

(f) *Other coverage that qualifies as minimum essential coverage.*—Minimum essential coverage includes any plan or arrangement recognized by the Secretary of Health and Human Services, in coordination with the Secretary of the Treasury, as minimum essential coverage.

(g) *Excepted benefits not minimum essential coverage.*—Minimum essential coverage does not include any coverage that consists solely of excepted benefits described in section 2791(c)(1), (c)(2), (c)(3), or (c)(4) of the Public Health Service Act (42 U.S.C. § 300gg-91(c)). [Reg. § 1.5000A-2.]

☐ [*T.D.* 9632, 8-27-2013 (*corrected* 12-24-2013) and T.D. 9705, 11-21-2014.]

[Reg. § 1.5000A-3]

§ 1.5000A-3. Exempt individuals.—
(a) *Members of recognized religious sects.*—(1) *In general.*—An individual is an exempt individual for a month that includes a day on which the individual has in effect a religious conscience exemption certification described in paragraph (a)(2) of this section.

(2) *Exemption certification.*—A religious conscience exemption certification is issued by an Exchange in accordance with the requirements of section 1311(d)(4)(H) of the Affordable Care Act (42 U.S.C. 18031(d)(4)(H)), 45 CFR 155.605(c), and 45 CFR 155.615(b) and certifies that an individual is—

(i) A member of a recognized religious sect or division of the sect that is described in section 1402(g)(1); and

(ii) An adherent of established tenets or teachings of the sect or division as described in that section.

(b) *Member of health care sharing ministries.*— (1) *In general.*—An individual is an exempt individual for a month that includes a day on which the individual is a member of a health care sharing ministry.

(2) *Health care sharing ministry.*—For purposes of this section, *health care sharing ministry* means an organization—

(i) That is described in section 501(c)(3) and is exempt from tax under section 501(a);

(ii) Members of which share a common set of ethical or religious beliefs and share medical expenses among themselves in accordance with those beliefs and without regard to the state in which a member resides or is employed;

(iii) Members of which retain membership even after they develop a medical condition;

(iv) That (or a predecessor of which) has been in existence at all times since December 31, 1999;

(v) Members of which have shared medical expenses continuously and without interruption since at least December 31, 1999; and

(vi) That conducts an annual audit performed by an independent certified public accounting firm in accordance with generally accepted accounting principles and makes the annual audit report available to the public upon request.

(c) *Exempt noncitizens.*—(1) *In general.*—An individual is an exempt individual for a month that the individual is an exempt noncitizen.

(2) *Exempt noncitizens.*—For purposes of this section, an individual is an exempt noncitizen for a month if the individual—

(i) Is not a U.S. citizen or U.S. national for any day during the month; and

(ii) Is either—

(A) A nonresident alien (within the meaning of section 7701(b)(1)(B)) for the taxable year that includes the month; or

(B) An individual who is not lawfully present (within the meaning of 45 CFR 155.20) on any day in the month.

(d) *Incarcerated individuals.*—(1) *In general.*— An individual is an exempt individual for a month that includes a day on which the individual is incarcerated.

(2) *Incarcerated.*—For purposes of this section, the term *incarcerated* means confined, after the disposition of charges, in a jail, prison, or similar penal institution or correctional facility.

(e) *Individuals with no affordable coverage.*— (1) *In general.*—An individual is an exempt individual for a month in which the individual lacks affordable coverage. For purposes of this paragraph (e), an individual lacks affordable coverage in a month if the individual's required contribution (determined on an annual basis) for minimum essential coverage for the month exceeds the required contribution percentage (as defined in paragraph (e)(2) of this section) of the individual's household income. For purposes of this paragraph (e), an individual's household income is increased by any amount of the required contribution made through a salary reduction arrangement that is excluded from gross income.

(2) *Required contribution percentage.*—(i) *In general.*—Except as provided in paragraph (e)(2)(ii) of this section, the required contribution percentage is 8 percent.

(ii) *Indexing.*—For plan years beginning in any calendar year after 2014, the required contribution percentage is the percentage determined by the Department of Health and Human Services that reflects the excess of the rate of premium growth between the preceding calendar year and 2013 over the rate of income growth for the period.

(iii) *Plan year.*—For purposes of this paragraph (e), *plan year* means the eligible employer-sponsored plan's regular 12-month coverage period, or for a new employee or an individual who enrolls during a special enrollment period, the remainder of a 12-month coverage period.

(3) *Individuals eligible for coverage under eligible employer-sponsored plans.*—(i) *Eligibility.*— (A) *In general.*—Except as provided in paragraph (e)(3)(i)(B) of this section, an employee or related individual (as defined in paragraph (e)(3)(ii)(B) of this section) is treated as eligible for coverage under an eligible employer-sponsored plan for a month during a plan year if the employee or related individual could have enrolled in the plan for any day in that month during an open or special enrollment period, regardless of whether the employee or related individual is eligible for any other type of minimum essential coverage.

(B) *Multiple eligibility.*—For purposes of this paragraph (e)(3), an employee eligible for coverage under an eligible employer-sponsored plan offered by the employee's employer is not treated as eligible as a related individual for coverage under an eligible employer-sponsored plan (for example, an eligible employer-sponsored plan offered by the employer of the employee's spouse) for any month included in the plan year of the eligible employer-sponsored plan offered by the employee's employer.

(C) *Special rule for post-employment coverage.*—A former employee or an individual related to a former employee, who may enroll in continuation coverage required under Federal law or a state law that provides comparable continuation coverage, or in retiree coverage under an eligible employer-sponsored plan, is eligible for coverage under an eligible employer-sponsored plan only if the individual enrolls in the coverage.

(ii) *Required contribution for individuals eligible for coverage under an eligible employer-sponsored plan.*—(A) *Employees.*—In the case of an employee who is eligible to purchase coverage under an eligible employer-sponsored plan sponsored by the employee's employer, the required contribution is the portion of the annual premium that the employee would pay (whether through salary reduction or otherwise) for the lowest cost self-only coverage.

(B) *Individuals related to employees.*—In the case of an individual who is eligible for coverage under an eligible employer-sponsored plan because of a relationship to an employee and for whom a personal exemption deduction under section 151 is claimed on the employee's Federal income tax return (related individual), the required contribution is the portion of the annual premium that the employee would pay (whether through salary reduction or otherwise) for the lowest cost family coverage that would cover the employee and all related individuals who are included in the employee's family and are not otherwise exempt under § 1.5000A-3.

(C) *Required contribution for part-year period.*—For each individual described in paragraph (e)(3)(ii)(A) or (e)(3)(ii)(B) of this section, affordability under this paragraph (e)(3) is determined separately for each employment period that is less than a full calendar year or for the portions of an employer's plan year that fall in different taxable years of the individual. Coverage under an eligible employer-sponsored plan is affordable for a part-year period if the annualized required contribution for self-only coverage (in the case of the employee) or family coverage (in the case of a related individual) under the plan for the part-year period does not exceed the required contribution percentage of the individual's household income for the taxable year. The annualized required contribution is the required contribution determined under paragraph (e)(3)(ii)(A) or (e)(3)(ii)(B) of this section for the part-year period times a fraction, the numerator of which is 12 and the denominator of which is the number of months in the part-year period during the individual's taxable year. Only full calendar months are included in the computation under this paragraph (e)(3)(ii)(C).

(D) *Employer contributions to health reimbursement arrangements.*—Amounts newly made available for the current plan year under a health reimbursement arrangement that an employee may use to pay premiums, or may use to pay cost-sharing or benefits not covered by the primary plan in addition to premiums, are counted toward the employee's required contribution if the health reimbursement arrangement would be integrated, as that term is used in Notice 2013-54 (2013-40 IRB 287) or in any successor published guidance (see § 601.601(d) of this chapter), with

an eligible employer-sponsored plan for an employee enrolled in the plan. The eligible employer-sponsored plan and the health reimbursement arrangement must be offered by the same employer. Employer contributions to a health reimbursement arrangement count toward an employee's required contribution only to the extent the amount of the annual contribution is required under the terms of the plan or otherwise determinable within a reasonable time before the employee must decide whether to enroll in the eligible employer-sponsored plan.

(E) *Employer contributions to cafeteria plans.*—Amounts made available for the current plan year under a cafeteria plan, within the meaning of section 125, are taken into account in determining an employee's or a related individual's required contribution if:

(1) The employee may not opt to receive the amount as a taxable benefit;

(2) The employee may use the amount to pay for minimum essential coverage; and

(3) The employee may use the amount exclusively to pay for medical care, within the meaning of section 213.

(F) *Wellness program incentives.*—Nondiscriminatory wellness program incentives, within the meaning of § 54.9802-1(f) of this chapter, offered by an eligible employer-sponsored plan that affect premiums are treated as earned in determining an employee's required contribution for purposes of affordability of an eligible employer-sponsored plan to the extent the incentives relate exclusively to tobacco use. Wellness program incentives that do not relate to tobacco use or that include a component unrelated to tobacco use are treated as not earned for this purpose. For purposes of this section, the term *wellness program incentive* has the same meaning as the term *reward* in § 54.9802-1(f)(1)(i) of this chapter.

(G) *Opt-out arrangements.*—[Reserved]

(iii) *Examples.*—The following examples illustrate the application of this paragraph (e)(3). Unless stated otherwise, in each example, each individual's taxable year is a calendar year, the individual is ineligible for any other exemptions described in this section for a month, the rate of premium growth has not exceeded the rate of income growth since 2013, and the individual's employer offers a single plan that uses a calendar plan year and is an eligible employer-sponsored plan as described in § 1.5000A-2(c).

Example 1. Unmarried employee with no dependents. Taxpayer A is an unmarried individual with no dependents. In November 2015, A is eligible to enroll in self-only coverage under a plan offered by A's employer for calendar year 2016. If A enrolls in the coverage, A is required to pay $5,000 of the total annual premium. In 2016, A's household income is $60,000. Under paragraph (e)(3)(ii)(A) of this section, A's required contribution is $5,000, the portion of the annual premium A pays for self-only coverage. Under paragraph (e)(1) of this section, A lacks affordable coverage for 2016 because A's required contribution ($5,000) is greater than 8% of A's household income ($4,800).

Example 2. Married employee with dependents. Taxpayers B and C are married and file a joint return for 2016. B and C have two children, D and E. In November 2015, B is eligible to enroll in self-only coverage under a plan offered by B's employer for calendar year 2016 at a cost of $5,000 to B. C, D, and E are eligible to enroll in family coverage under the same plan for 2016 at a cost of $20,000 to B. B, C, D, and E's household income for 2016 is $90,000. Under paragraph (e)(3)(ii)(A) of this section, B's required contribution is B's share of the cost for self-only coverage, $5,000. Under paragraph (e)(1) of this section, B has affordable coverage for 2016 because B's required contribution ($5,000) does not exceed 8% of B's household income ($7,200). Under paragraph (e)(3)(ii)(B) of this section, the required contribution for C, D, and E is B's share of the cost for family coverage, $20,000. Under paragraph (e)(1) of this section, C, D, and E lack affordable coverage for 2016 because their required contribution ($20,000) exceeds 8% of their household income ($7,200).

Example 3. Plan year is a fiscal year. (i) Taxpayer F is an unmarried individual with no dependents. In June 2015, F is eligible to enroll in self-only coverage under a plan offered by F's employer for the period July 2015 through June 2016 at a cost to F of $4,750. In June 2016, F is eligible to enroll in self-only coverage under a plan offered by F's employer for the period July 2016 through June 2017 at a cost to F of $5,000. In 2016, F's household income is $60,000.

(ii) Under paragraph (e)(3)(ii)(C) of this section, F's annualized required contribution for the period January 2016 through June 2016 is $4,750 ($2,375 paid for premiums in 2016 × 12/6). Under paragraph (e)(1) of this section, F has affordable coverage for January 2016 through June 2016 because F's annualized required contribution ($4,750) does not exceed 8% of F's household income ($4,800).

(iii) Under paragraph (e)(3)(ii)(C) of this section, F's annualized required contribution for the period July 2016 to December 2016 is $5,000 ($2,500 paid for premiums in 2016 × 12/6). Under paragraph (e)(1) of this section, F lacks affordable coverage for July 2016 through December 2016 because F's annualized required contribution ($5,000) exceeds 8% of F's household income ($4,800).

Example 4. Eligibility for coverage under an eligible employer-sponsored plan and under government sponsored coverage. Taxpayer G is unmarried and has one child, H. In November 2015, H is eligible to enroll in family coverage under a plan offered by G's employer for 2016. H is also eligible to enroll in the CHIP program for 2016. Under paragraph (e)(3)(i) of this section, H is treated as eligible for coverage under an eligible employer-sponsored plan for each month in 2016, notwithstanding that H is eligible to enroll in government sponsored coverage for the same period.

(4) *Individuals ineligible for coverage under eligible employer-sponsored plans.*—(i) *Eligibility for coverage other than an eligible employer-sponsored plan.*—An individual is treated as ineligible for coverage under an eligible employer-sponsored plan for a month that is not described in paragraph (e)(3)(i) of this section.

(ii) *Required contribution for individuals ineligible for coverage under eligible employer-sponsored plans.*—(A) *In general.*—In the case of an individual who is ineligible for coverage under an eligible employer-sponsored plan, the required contribution is the premium for the applicable plan, reduced by the maximum amount of any credit allowable under section 36B for the taxable year, determined as if the individual was covered for the entire taxable year by a qualified health plan offered through the Exchange serving the rating area where the individual resides.

(B) *Applicable plan.*—(1) *In general.*— Except as provided in paragraph (e)(4)(ii)(B)(2) of this section, *applicable plan* means the single lowest cost bronze plan available in the individual market through the Exchange serving the rating area in which the individual resides (without regard to whether the individual purchased a qualified health plan through the Exchange) that would cover all individuals in the individual's nonexempt family. For purposes of this paragraph (e)(4), an individual's *nonexempt family* means the family (as defined in § 1.5000A-1(d)(4)) that includes the individual, excluding any family members who are otherwise exempt under section 1.5000A-3 or are treated as eligible for coverage under an eligible employer-sponsored plan under paragraph (e)(3)(i) of this section. The premium for the applicable plan takes into account rating factors (for example, an individual's age or tobacco use) that an Exchange would use to determine the cost of coverage.

(2) *Lowest cost bronze plan does not cover all individuals included in the taxpayer's nonexempt family.*—(i) *In general.*—If the Exchange serving the rating area where the individual resides does not offer a single bronze plan covering all individuals included in the individual's nonexempt family, the premium for the applicable plan is the sum of the premiums for the lowest cost bronze plans that are offered through the Exchanges serving the rating areas where one or more of the individuals reside that would cover in the aggregate all the individuals in the individual's nonexempt family. For instance, coverage offered through the Exchange in a rating area might not cover a family member living in different rating area or a single policy might not cover all the members in a taxpayer's household.

(ii) *Optional simplified method for applicable plan identification.*—[Reserved]

Reg. § 1.5000A-3(e)(4)(ii)(B)(2)(ii)

(C) *Wellness program incentives.*— [Reserved]

(D) *Credit allowable under section 36B.*— For purposes of paragraph (e)(4)(ii)(A) of this section, *maximum amount of any credit allowable under section 36B* means the maximum amount of the credit that would be allowable to the individual, or to the taxpayer who can properly claim the individual as a dependent, under section 36B if all members of the individual's nonexempt family enrolled in a qualified health plan through the Exchange serving the rating area where the individual resides.

(E) *Required contribution for part-year period.*—For each individual, affordability under paragraph (e)(4) of this section is determined separately for each period described in paragraph (e)(4)(ii)(E) of this section that is less than a 12-month period. Coverage under a plan is affordable for a part-year period if the annualized required contribution for coverage under the plan for the part-year period does not exceed the required contribution percentage of the individual's household income for the taxable year. The annualized required contribution is the required contribution determined under paragraph (e)(4)(ii)(A) of this section for the part-year period times a fraction, the numerator of which is 12 and the denominator of which is the number of months in the part-year period during the individual's taxable year. Only full calendar months are included in the computation under this paragraph (e)(4)(ii)(D).

(iii) *Examples.*—The following examples illustrate the provisions of this paragraph (e)(4). Unless stated otherwise, in each example the taxpayer's taxable year is a calendar year, the rate of premium growth has not exceeded the rate of income growth since 2013, and the taxpayer is ineligible for any of the exemptions described in paragraphs (a) through (d) and (f) through (j) of this section for a month.

Example 1. Unmarried individual with no dependents. (i) Taxpayer G is an unmarried individual with no dependents. G is ineligible to enroll in any minimum essential coverage other than coverage in the individual market for all months in 2016. The annual premium for the lowest cost bronze self-only plan in G's rating area (G's applicable plan) is $5,000. The adjusted annual premium for the second lowest cost silver self-only plan in G's rating area (G's applicable benchmark plan within the meaning of §1.36B-3(f)) is $5,500. In 2016 G's household income is $40,000, which is 358% of the Federal poverty line for G's family size for the taxable year.

(ii) Under paragraph (e)(4)(ii)(C) of this section, the credit allowable under section 36B is determined pursuant to section 36B. With household income at 358% of the Federal poverty line, G's applicable percentage is 9.5. Because each month in 2016 is a coverage month (within the meaning of §1.36B-3(c)), G's maximum credit allowable under section 36B is the excess of G's

premium for the applicable benchmark plan over the product of G's household income and G's applicable percentage ($1,700). Therefore, under paragraph (e)(4)(ii)(A) of this section, G's required contribution is $3,300. Under paragraph (e)(1) of this section, G lacks affordable coverage for 2016 because G's required contribution ($3,300) exceeds 8% of G's household income ($3,200).

Example 2. Family. (i) In 2016 Taxpayers M and N are married and file a joint return. M and N have two children, P and Q. M, N, P, and Q are ineligible to enroll in minimum essential coverage other than coverage in the individual market for a month in 2016. The annual premium for M, N, P, and Q's applicable plan is $20,000. The adjusted annual premium for M, N, P, and Q's applicable benchmark plan (within the meaning of §1.36B-3(f)) is $25,000. M and N's household income is $80,000, which is 347% of the Federal poverty line for a family size of 4 for the taxable year.

(ii) Under paragraph (e)(4)(ii)(C) of this section, the credit allowable under section 36B is determined pursuant to section 36B. With household income at 347% of the Federal poverty line, the applicable percentage is 9.5. Because each month in 2016 is a coverage month (within the meaning of §1.36B-3(c)), the maximum credit allowable under section 36B is the excess of the premium for the applicable benchmark plan over the product of the household income and the applicable percentage ($17,400). Therefore, under paragraph (e)(4)(ii)(A) of this section, the required contribution for M, N, P, and Q is $2,600. Under paragraph (e)(1) of this section, M, N, P, and Q have affordable coverage for 2016 because their required contribution ($2,600) does not exceed 8% of their household income ($6,400).

Example 3. Family with some members eligible for government-sponsored coverage. (i) In 2016 Taxpayers U and V are married and file a joint return. U and V have two children, W and X. U and V are ineligible to enroll in minimum essential coverage other than coverage in the individual market for all months in 2016; however, W and X are eligible for coverage under CHIP for 2016. The annual premium for U, V, W, and X's applicable plan is $20,000. The adjusted annual premium for the second lowest cost silver plan that would cover U and V (the applicable benchmark plan within the meaning of §1.36B-3(f)) is $12,500. U and V's household income is $50,000, which is 217% of the Federal poverty line for a family size of 4 for the taxable year. W and X do not enroll in CHIP coverage.

(ii) Under paragraph (e)(4)(ii)(C) of this section, the credit allowable under section 36B is determined pursuant to section 36B. With household income at 217% of the Federal poverty line, the applicable percentage is 6.89. Each month in 2016 is a coverage month (within the meaning of §1.36B-3(c)) for U and V, but no months in 2016 are coverage months for W and X because they are eligible for CHIP coverage. The maximum credit allowable under section 36B is the excess of the premium for the applicable benchmark plan over the product of the household income and the applicable percentage ($9,055). Therefore, under paragraph (e)(4)(ii)(A) of this section, the required contribution is $10,945. Under paragraph (e)(1) of this section, U, V, W, and X lack affordable coverage for 2016 because their required contribution ($10,945) exceeds 8% of their household income ($4,000).

Example 4. Family with some members enrolled in government-sponsored minimum essential coverage. The facts are the same as *Example 3,* except W and X enroll in CHIP coverage on January 1, 2016. Under paragraph (e)(4)(ii)(B), U, V, W, and X are members of U and V's nonexempt family for 2016. Therefore, the annual premium for the applicable plan is the same as in *Example 3* ($20,000). The maximum credit allowable under section 36B is also the same as in *Example 3* ($9,055). Under paragraph (e)(4)(ii)(A) of this section, the required contribution is $10,945. Under paragraph (e)(1) of this section, U and V lack affordable coverage for 2016 because their required contribution ($10,945) exceeds 8% of their household income ($4,000).

(f) *Household income below filing threshold.*—(1) *In general.*—An individual is an exempt individual for any taxable year for which the individual's household income is less than the applicable filing threshold.

(2) *Applicable filing threshold.*—(i) *In general.*—For purposes of this section, *applicable filing threshold* means the amount of gross income that would trigger an individual's requirement to file a Federal income tax return under section 6012(a)(1).

(ii) *Certain dependents.*—The applicable filing threshold for an individual who is properly claimed as a dependent by another taxpayer is equal to the other taxpayer's applicable filing threshold.

(3) *Manner of claiming the exemption.*—A taxpayer is not required to file a Federal income tax return solely to claim the exemption described in this paragraph (f). If a taxpayer has a household income below the applicable filing threshold and nevertheless files a Federal income tax return, the taxpayer may claim the exemption described in this paragraph (f) on the return.

(g) *Members of Indian tribes.*—An individual is an exempt individual for a month that includes a day on which the individual is a member of an Indian tribe. For purposes of this section, *Indian tribe* means a group or community described in section 45A(c)(6).

(h) *Individuals with hardship exemption certification.*—(1) *In general.*—Except as provided in paragraph (h)(3) of this section, an individual is an exempt individual for a month that includes a day on which the individual has in effect a hardship exemption certification described in paragraph (h)(2) of this section.

(2) *Hardship exemption certification.*—A hardship exemption certification is issued by an Exchange under section 1311(d)(4)(H) of the Affordable Care Act (42 U.S.C. 18031(d)(4)(H)), 45 CFR 155.605(g)(1), (g)(2), (g)(4) and (g)(6), 45 CFR 155.610(i), and 45 CFR 155.615(f), and certifies that an individual has suffered a hardship (as that term is defined in 45 CFR 155.605(g)) affecting the capability to obtain minimum essential coverage.

(3) *Hardship exemption without hardship exemption certification.*—An individual may claim an exemption without obtaining a hardship exemption certification described in paragraph (h)(2) of this section for any month that includes a day on which the individual meets the requirements of any hardship for which:

(i) The Secretary of HHS issues guidance of general applicability describing the hardship and indicating that an exemption for such hardship can be claimed on a Federal income tax return pursuant to guidance published by the Secretary; and

(ii) The Secretary issues published guidance of general applicability, see § 601.601(d)(2) of this chapter, allowing an individual to claim the hardship exemption on a return without obtaining a hardship exemption from an Exchange.

(i) [Reserved]

(j) *Individuals with certain short coverage gaps.*—(1) *In general.*—An individual is an exempt individual for a month the last day of which is included in a short coverage gap.

(2) *Short coverage gap.*—(i) *In general.*—*Short coverage gap* means a continuous period of less than three months in which the individual is not covered under minimum essential coverage. If the individual does not have minimum essential coverage for a continuous period of three or more months, none of the months included in the continuous period are treated as included in a short coverage gap.

(ii) *Coordination with other exemptions.*—For purposes of this paragraph (j), an individual is treated as having minimum essential coverage for a month in which an individual is exempt under any of paragraphs (a) through (h) of this section.

(iii) *More than one short coverage gap during calendar year.*—If a calendar year includes more than one short coverage gap, the exemption provided by this paragraph (j) only applies to the earliest short coverage gap.

(3) *Continuous period.*—(i) *In general.*—Except as provided in paragraph (j)(3)(ii) of this section, the number of months included in a continuous period is determined without regard to the calendar years in which months included in that period occur. For purposes of paragraph (j) of this section, a continuous period begins no earlier than January 1, 2014.

(ii) *Continuous period straddling more than one taxable year.*—If an individual does not have

Reg. § 1.5000A-3(j)(3)(ii)

minimum essential coverage for a continuous period that begins in one taxable year and ends in the next, for purposes of applying this paragraph (j) to the first taxable year, the months in the second taxable year included in the continuous period are disregarded. For purposes of applying this paragraph (j) to the second taxable year, the months in the first taxable year included in the continuous period are taken into account.

(4) *Examples.*—The following examples illustrate the provisions of this paragraph (j). Unless stated otherwise, in each example the taxpayer's taxable year is a calendar year and the taxpayer is ineligible for any of the exemptions described in paragraphs (a) through (h) of this section for a month.

Example 1. Short coverage gap. Taxpayer D has minimum essential coverage in 2016 from January 1 through March 2. After March 2, D does not have minimum essential coverage until D enrolls in an eligible employer-sponsored plan effective June 15. Under § 1.5000A-1(b), for purposes of section 5000A, D has minimum essential coverage for January, February, March, and June through December. D's continuous period without coverage is 2 months, April and May. April and May constitute a short coverage gap under paragraph (j)(2)(i) of this section.

Example 2. Continuous period of 3 months or more. The facts are the same as in *Example 1*, except D's coverage is not effective until July 1. D's continuous period without coverage is 3 months, April, May, and June. Under paragraph (j)(2)(i) of this section, April, May, and June are not included in a short coverage gap.

Example 3. Short coverage gap following exempt period. Taxpayer E is incarcerated from January 1 through June 2. E enrolls in an eligible employer-sponsored plan effective September 15. Under paragraph (d) of this section, E is exempt for the period January through June. Under paragraph (j)(2)(ii) of this section, E is treated as having minimum essential coverage for this period, and E's continuous period without minimum essential coverage is 2 months, July and August. July and August constitute a short coverage gap under paragraph (j)(2)(i) of this section.

Example 4. Continuous period covering more than one taxable year. Taxpayer F, an unmarried individual with no dependents, has minimum essential coverage for the period January 1 through October 15, 2016. F is without coverage until February 15, 2017. F files his Federal income tax return for 2016 on March 10, 2017. Under paragraph (j)(3)(ii) of this section, November and December of 2016 are treated as a short coverage gap. However, November and December of 2016 are included in the continuous period that includes January 2017. The continuous period for 2017 is not less than 3 months and, therefore, January is not a part of a short coverage gap.

Example 5. Enrollment following loss of coverage. The facts are the same as in *Example 4* except F loses coverage on June 15, 2017. F enrolls in

minimum essential coverage effective September 15, 2017. The continuous period without minimum essential coverage in July and August of 2017 is two months and, therefore, is a short coverage gap. Because January 2017 was not part of a short coverage gap, the earliest short coverage gap occurring in 2017 is the gap that includes July and August.

Example 6. Multiple coverage gaps. (i) The facts are the same as in *Example 5* except F has minimum essential coverage for November 2016. Under paragraph (j)(3)(ii) of this section, December 2016 is treated as a short coverage gap.

(ii) December 2016 is included in the continuous period that includes January 2017. This continuous period is two months and, therefore, January 2017 is the earliest month in 2017 that is included in a short coverage gap. Under paragraph (j)(2)(iii) of this section, the exemption under this paragraph (j) applies only to January 2017. Thus, the continuous period without minimum essential coverage in July and August of 2017 is not a short coverage gap. [Reg. § 1.5000A-3.]

☐ [*T.D.* 9632, 8-27-2013 (*corrected* 12-24-2013). Amended by T.D. 9705, 11-21-2014 *and T.D.* 9804, 12-14-2016.]

[Reg. § 1.5000A-4]

§ 1.5000A-4. Computation of shared responsibility payment.—(a) *In general.*—For each taxable year, the shared responsibility payment imposed on a taxpayer in accordance with § 1.5000A-1(c) is the lesser of—

(1) The sum of the monthly penalty amounts; or

(2) The sum of the monthly national average bronze plan premiums for the shared responsibility family.

(b) *Monthly penalty amount.*—(1) *In general.*— *Monthly penalty amount* means, for a month that a nonexempt individual is not covered under minimum essential coverage, 1/12 multiplied by the greater of—

(i) The flat dollar amount; or

(ii) The excess income amount.

(2) *Flat dollar amount.*—(i) *In general.*—*Flat dollar amount* means the lesser of—

(A) The sum of the applicable dollar amounts for all individuals included in the taxpayer's shared responsibility family; or

(B) 300 percent of the applicable dollar amount (determined without regard to paragraph (b)(2)(iii) of this section) for the calendar year with or within which the taxable year ends.

(ii) *Applicable dollar amount.*—Except as provided in paragraphs (b)(2)(iii) and (b)(2)(iv) of this section, the applicable dollar amount is—

(A) $95 in 2014;

(B) $325 in 2015; or

(C) $695 in 2016.

(iii) *Special applicable dollar amount for individuals under age 18.*—If an individual has not attained the age of 18 before the first day of a month, the applicable dollar amount for the individual is equal to one-half of the applicable dollar amount (as expressed in paragraph (b)(2)(ii) of this section) for the calendar year in which the month occurs. For purposes of this paragraph (b)(2)(iii), an individual attains the age of 18 on the anniversary of the date when the individual was born. For example, an individual born on March 1, 1999, attains the age of 18 on March 1, 2017.

(iv) *Indexing of applicable dollar amount.*— In any calendar year after 2016, the applicable dollar amount is $695 as increased by the product of $695 and the cost-of-living adjustment determined under section 1(f)(3) for the calendar year. For purposes of this paragraph (b)(2)(iv), the cost-of-living adjustment is determined by substituting "calendar year 2015" for "calendar year 1992" in section 1(f)(3)(B). If any increase under this paragraph (b)(2)(iv) is not a multiple of $50, the increase is rounded down to the next lowest multiple of $50.

(3) *Excess income amount.*—(i) *In general.*— *Excess income amount* means the product of—

(A) The excess of the taxpayer's household income over the taxpayer's applicable filing threshold (as defined in § 1.5000A-3(f)(2)); and

(B) The income percentage.

(ii) *Income percentage.*—For purposes of this section, *income percentage* means—

(A) 1.0 percent for taxable years beginning in 2013;

(B) 1.0 percent for taxable years beginning in 2014;

(C) 2.0 percent for taxable years beginning in 2015; or

(D) 2.5 percent for taxable years beginning after 2015.

(c) *Monthly national average bronze plan premium.*—*Monthly national average bronze plan premium* means, for a month for which a shared responsibility payment is imposed, 1/12 of the annual national average premium for qualified health plans that have a bronze level of coverage, would provide coverage for the taxpayer's shared responsibility family members who do not have minimum essential coverage for the month, and are offered through Exchanges for plan years beginning in the calendar year with or within which the taxable year ends.

(d) *Examples.*—The following examples illustrate the provisions of this section. In each example the taxpayer's taxable year is a calendar year and all members of the taxpayer's shared responsibility family are ineligible for any of the exemptions described in § 1.5000A-3 for a month.

Example 1. Unmarried taxpayer without minimum essential coverage. (i) In 2016, Taxpayer G is an unmarried individual with no dependents. G does not have minimum essential coverage for any month in 2016. G's household income is $120,000. G's applicable filing threshold is $12,000. The annual national average bronze plan premium for G is $5,000.

(ii) For each month in 2016, under paragraph (b)(2)(ii) of this section, G's applicable dollar amount is $695. Under paragraph (b)(2)(i) of this section, G's flat dollar amount is $695 (the lesser of $695 and $2,085 ($695 x 3)). Under paragraph (b)(3) of this section, G's excess income amount is $2,700 (($120,000 - $12,000) × 0.025). Therefore, under paragraph (b)(1) of this section, the monthly penalty amount is $225 (the greater of $58 ($695/12) or $225 ($2,700/12)).

(iii) The sum of the monthly penalty amounts is $2,700 ($225 × 12). The sum of the monthly national average bronze plan premiums is $5,000 ($5,000/12 × 12). Therefore, under paragraph (a) of this section, the shared responsibility payment imposed on G for 2016 is $2,700 (the lesser of $2,700 or $5,000).

Example 2. Part-year coverage. The facts are the same as in *Example 1*, except G has minimum essential coverage for January through June. The sum of the monthly penalty amounts is $1,350 ($225 × 6). The sum of the monthly national average bronze plan premiums is $2,500 ($5,000/12 × 6). Therefore, under paragraph (a) of this section, the shared responsibility payment imposed on G for 2016 is $1,350 (the lesser of $1,350 or $2,500).

Example 3. Family without minimum essential coverage. (i) In 2016, Taxpayers H and J are married and file a joint return. H and J have three children: K, age 21, L, age 15, and M, age 10. No member of the family has minimum essential coverage for any month in 2016. H and J's household income is $250,000. H and J's applicable filing threshold is $24,000. The annual national average bronze plan premium for a family of 5 (3 adults, 2 children) is $15,000.

(ii) For each month in 2016, under paragraphs (b)(2)(ii) and (b)(2)(iii) of this section, the applicable dollar amount is $2,780 (($695 x 3 adults) + (($695/2) × 2 children)). Under paragraph (b)(2)(i) of this section, the flat dollar amount is $2,085 (the lesser of $2,780 and $2,085 ($695 × 3)). Under paragraph (b)(3) of this section, the excess income amount is $5,650 (($250,000 - $24,000) × 0.025). Therefore, under paragraph (b)(1) of this section, the monthly penalty amount is $470.83 (the greater of $173.75 ($2,085/12) or $470.83 ($5,650/12)).

(iii) The sum of the monthly penalty amounts is $5,650 ($470.83 × 12). The sum of the monthly national average bronze plan premiums is $15,000 ($15,000/12 × 12). Therefore, under paragraph (a) of this section, the shared responsibility payment imposed on H and J for 2016 is $5,650 (the lesser of $5,650 or $15,000).

Example 4. Change in shared responsibility family during the year. (i) The facts are the same as in *Example 3*, except J has minimum essential coverage for January through June. The annual national average bronze plan premium for a family of 4 (2 adults, 2 children) is $10,000.

(ii) For the period January through June 2016, under paragraphs (b)(2)(ii) and (b)(2)(iii) of this section the applicable dollar amount is $2,085 (($695 × 2 adults) + (($695/2) × 2 children)). Under paragraph (b)(2)(i) of this section, the flat dollar amount is $2,085 (the lesser of $2,085 or $2,085 ($695 × 3)).

(iii) For the period July through December 2016, the applicable dollar amount is $2,780 (($695 × 3 adults) + (($695/2) × 2 children)). Under paragraph (b)(2) of this section, the flat dollar amount is $2,085 (the lesser of $2,780 or $2,085 ($695 × 3)). Under paragraph (b)(3) of this section, the excess income amount is $5,650 (($250,000 - $24,000) × 0.025). Therefore, under paragraph (b)(1) of this section, for January through June the monthly penalty amount is $470.83 (the greater of $173.75 ($2,085/12) or $470.83 ($5,650/12)). The monthly penalty amount for July through December is $470.83 (the greater of $173.75 ($2,085/12) or $470.83 ($5,650/12)).

(iv) The sum of the monthly penalty amounts is $5,650 ($470.83 × 12). The sum of the monthly national average bronze plan premiums is $12,500 ((($10,000/12) × 6) + (($15,000/12) × 6)). Therefore, under paragraph (a) of this section, the shared responsibility payment imposed on H and J for 2016 is $5,650 (the lesser of $5,650 or $12,500).

Example 5. Eighteenth birthday during the year. (i) In 2016 Taxpayers S and T are married and file a joint return. S and T have one child, U, who turns 18 years old on June 28. S, T, and U do not enroll in, and as a result are not eligible to receive benefits under, affordable employer-sponsored coverage offered by T's employer for 2016. S and T's household income is $60,000. S and T's applicable filing threshold is $24,000. The annual national average bronze plan premium for a family of 3 (2 adults, 1 child) is $11,000.

(ii) For the period January through June 2016, under paragraphs (b)(2)(ii) and (b)(2)(iii) of this section, the applicable dollar amount is $1,737.50 (($695 × 2 adults) + ($695/2) × 1 child)). Under paragraph (b)(2) of this section, the flat dollar amount is $1,737.50 (the lesser of $1,737.50 or $2,085 ($695 × 3)).

(iii) For the period July through December 2016, the applicable dollar amount is $2,085 ($695 × 3). Under paragraph (b)(2)(i) of this section, the flat dollar amount is $2,085 (the lesser of $2,085 or $2,085 ($695 x 3)). Under paragraph (b)(3) of this section, the excess income amount is $900 (($60,000 - $24,000) × 0.025). Therefore, under paragraph (b)(1) of this section, for January through June the monthly penalty amount is $144.79 (the greater of $144.79 ($1,737.50/12) or $75 ($900/12)). The monthly penalty amount for July through December is $173.75 (the greater of $173.75 ($2,085/12) or $75 ($900/12)).

(iv) The sum of the monthly penalty amounts is $1,911.24 (($144.79 × 6) + ($173.75 × 6)). The

sum of the monthly national average bronze plan premiums is $11,000 ($11,000/12 × 12). Therefore, under paragraph (a) of this section, the shared responsibility payment imposed on S and T for 2016 is $1,911.24 (the lesser of $1,911.24 or $11,000). [Reg. § 1.5000A-4.]

☐ [*T.D. 9632,* 8-27-2013 (*corrected* 12-24-2013) and T.D. 9705, 11-21-2014.]

[Reg. § 1.5000A-5]

§ 1.5000A-5. **Administration and procedure.**—(a) *In general.*—A taxpayer's liability for the shared responsibility payment for a month must be reported on the taxpayer's Federal income tax return for the taxable year that includes the month. The period of limitations for assessing the shared responsibility payment is the same as that prescribed by section 6501 for the taxable year to which the Federal income tax return on which the shared responsibility payment is to be reported relates. The shared responsibility payment is payable upon notice and demand by the Secretary, and except as provided in paragraph (b) of this section, is assessed and collected in the same manner as an assessable penalty under subchapter B of chapter 68 of the Internal Revenue Code. The shared responsibility payment is not subject to deficiency procedures of subchapter B of chapter 63 of the Internal Revenue Code. Interest on this payment accrues in accordance with the rules in section 6601.

(b) *Special rules.*—Notwithstanding any other provision of law—

(1) *Waiver of criminal penalties.*—In the case of a failure by a taxpayer to timely pay the shared responsibility payment, the taxpayer is not subject to criminal prosecution or penalty for the failure.

(2) *Limitations on liens and levies.*—If a taxpayer fails to pay the shared responsibility payment imposed by this section and § § 1.5000A-1 through 1.5000A-4, the Secretary will not file notice of lien on any property of the taxpayer, or levy on any property of the taxpayer for the failure.

(3) *Authority to offset against overpayment.*—Nothing in this section prohibits the Secretary from offsetting any liability for the shared responsibility payment against any overpayment due the taxpayer, in accordance with section 6402(a) and its corresponding regulations.

(c) *Effective/applicability date.*—This section and § § 1.5000A-1 through 1.5000A-4 apply for months beginning after December 31, 2013. [Reg. § 1.5000A-5.]

☐ [*T.D. 9632,* 8-27-2013.]

Cosmetic Services

See p. 20,601 for regulations not amended to reflect law changes

[Reg. §49.5000B-1]

§49.5000B-1. Indoor tanning services.— (a) *Overview.*—This section provides rules for the tax imposed by section 5000B on any indoor tanning service.

(b) *Imposition of tax.*—(1) *General rule.*—Tax is imposed by section 5000B at the time of payment for any indoor tanning service.

(2) *Undesignated payment cards—In general.*— Payment for indoor tanning services is made when an undesignated payment card is redeemed, in whole or in part, to pay for indoor tanning services (and not when a payment is made to purchase the undesignated payment card).

(c) *Definitions.*—(1) The term *indoor tanning service* means a service employing any electronic product designed to incorporate one or more ultraviolet lamps and intended for the irradiation of an individual by ultraviolet radiation, with wavelengths in air between 200 and 400 nanometers, to induce skin tanning. The term does not include phototherapy service performed by, and on the premises of, a licensed medical professional (such as a dermatologist, psychologist, or registered nurse).

(2) The term *other goods and services* includes, but is not limited to, protective eyewear, footwear, towels, and tanning lotions; manicures, pedicures, and other cosmetic or spa treatments; and access to sport or exercise facilities.

(3) The term *phototherapy service* means a service that exposes an individual to specific wavelengths of light for the treatment of—

(i) Dermatological conditions (such as acne, psoriasis, and eczema);

(ii) Sleep disorders;

(iii) Seasonal affective disorder or other psychiatric disorder;

(iv) Neonatal jaundice;

(v) Wound healing; or

(vi) Other medical condition determined by a licensed medical professional to be treatable by exposing the individual to specific wavelengths of light.

(4) The term *provider* means a person that provides an indoor tanning service as defined in paragraph (c)(1) of this section.

(5) The term *qualified physical fitness facility* means a facility—

(i) In which the predominant business or activity is providing equipment and services to its members for purposes of exercise and physical fitness (determined by taking into consideration all of the facts and circumstances, such as the cost of the equipment, variety of services offered, actual usage of services by customers, revenue generated by different services, and how the entity holds itself out to the public through advertising or other means);

(ii) In which providing indoor tanning services is not a substantial part of the business or activity; and

(iii) That does not sell indoor tanning services for a fee to the public or otherwise offer different pricing options to its members based in whole or in part on access to indoor tanning services.

(6) The term *undesignated payment card* means a gift certificate, gift card, or similar item that can be redeemed for goods or services that may, but do not necessarily, include indoor tanning services.

(d) *Application of tax.*—(1) *Tax on total amount paid for indoor tanning services.*—(i) *In general.*— The tax is imposed on the total amount paid for indoor tanning services, including any amount paid by insurance. The total amount paid is presumed to include the tax if the tax is not separately stated.

(ii) *Free services and reduced rates.*—The tax does not apply to indoor tanning services that are provided free of charge. Indoor tanning services are provided free of charge if no one pays anything of value to the provider of the service for the indoor tanning service. Thus, for example, tax is not imposed on the redemption of a promotional coupon for indoor tanning services if the coupon is provided at no cost and at no obligation to purchase anything. If indoor tanning services are provided at a reduced rate, the tax applies to the amount actually paid for the services.

(iii) *Bonus points.*—The redemption of benefits such as "bonus points" under a loyalty program or similar program or promotion is not a payment for indoor tanning services. Thus, for example, in a promotion that entitles a customer to a "free" tan with the purchase of four tans, tax is not imposed on the redemption of the fifth tan because the amount paid for the four tans included a reduced price for the fifth tan.

(iv) *Other fees.*—Fees for starting, joining, registering, enrolling, and similar fees paid to a provider to join a monthly (or other periodic) membership program that provides indoor tanning services are amounts paid for indoor tanning services. Similarly, amounts paid to a provider that temporarily suspend a periodic membership program are amounts paid for indoor tanning services.

(2) *Charges for other goods and services; tanning services separately stated.*—If a payment covers charges for indoor tanning services as well as other goods and services, the charges for other goods and services may be excluded in computing the tax payable on the amount paid, if the charges—

(i) Are separable (regardless of the manner of invoicing the charges);

(ii) Do not exceed the fair market value of such other goods and services; and

(iii) Are shown in the exact amounts in the provider's records pertaining to the indoor tanning services charge.

(3) *Charges for other goods and services; tanning services bundled.*—This paragraph (d)(3) applies if paragraph (d)(2) of this section does not apply. If a provider offers indoor tanning services (whether of a specified or unlimited amount, including "free" or reduced-rate indoor tanning services) bundled with other goods and services, the payment for the bundled services includes an amount paid for indoor tanning services. The tax applies to that portion of the amount paid to the provider that is reasonably attributable to indoor tanning services. The amount reasonably attributable to indoor tanning services may be determined by—

(i) Applying to the total amount paid a ratio determined by comparing—

(A) The provider's charge for indoor tanning services not in bundled services or, if the provider only charges for indoor tanning services as part of bundled services, the fair market value of similar indoor tanning services (based on the amount charged by comparable providers in the same geographic area); to

(B) The charge determined in paragraph (d)(3)(i)(A) of this section plus the provider's charge for the other goods and services in the bundled services or, if the provider only charges for other goods and services as part of bundled services, the fair market value of similar goods and services (based on the amount charged by comparable providers in the same geographic area); or

(ii) Any other method allowed in guidance published in the Internal Revenue Bulletin.

(4) *Exemption; qualified physical fitness facilities.*—No portion of a payment to a qualified physical fitness facility (within the meaning of paragraph (c)(5) of this section) that includes access to indoor tanning services is treated as a payment for indoor tanning services.

(e) *Person liable for the tax.*—(1) *General rule.*—The person who pays for the indoor tanning service is deemed to be the person on whom the service is performed for purposes of collecting the tax. Thus, the person paying for the indoor tanning service is liable for the tax at the time of payment.

(2) *Undesignated payment cards.*—(i) *In general.*—In the case of a payment made with an undesignated payment card (as defined in paragraph (c)(6) of this section), the person who redeems the card, in whole or in part, to pay specifically for indoor tanning services is the person who pays for the indoor tanning services. Thus, the person who redeems an undesignated payment card, in whole or in part, to pay specifically for indoor tanning services is liable for the tax at the time such payment is made (as described in paragraph (b)(2) of this section).

(ii) *Alternative treatment.*—The Treasury Department and IRS may provide additional options for the treatment of undesignated payment cards in guidance published in the Internal Revenue Bulletin.

(3) *Tax not collected at time of payment.*—If the person paying for the indoor tanning services does not pay the tax to the person receiving the payment for the services at the time of payment for the services, the person receiving the payment is liable for the tax.

(f) *Persons receiving payment must collect tax.*—Every person receiving a payment for indoor tanning services on which a tax is imposed under this section must collect the amount of the tax from the person making that payment.

(g) *Examples.*—The following examples illustrate the application of section 5000B and this section.

Example 1: Imposition of tax; general rule. (i) P is a nail salon that also provides indoor tanning service incidental to its primary business of providing nail salon services. P advertises a price of $15.00 (exclusive of the tax imposed by section 5000B) for one 10-minute indoor tanning service. During a period when the tax is 10 percent of the amount paid, P calculates the section 5000B tax on $15.00 as provided by paragraph (d)(1) of this section. Thus, the tax is $1.50 ($15.00 X 10%). The person paying for the service is liable for the tax when that person pays for the services. If P does not collect the tax from the person at the time of the payment for the services, P is liable for the tax.

(ii) The facts are the same as in paragraph (i) of this example except that P's advertised price of $15.00 includes the tanning tax. In this case, the tax is $1.36 ($15.00 X 10%/110%) under the second sentence of paragraph (d)(1) of this section.

Example 2: Charges for other goods and services; tanning services separately stated. P provides indoor tanning services and other goods and services. On July 1, 2013, A, an individual, pays P for one 10-minute indoor tanning service and one pair of protective eyewear. P charges $15.00 for the 10-minute indoor tanning service and $2.00 for a pair of protective eyewear. The $2.00 charge for the protective eyewear does not exceed its fair market value. The invoice from P is $17.00 (exclusive of the tax imposed by section 5000B) and separately states the cost of the protective eyewear. Because the cost of the protective eyewear is separately stated, P calculates the section 5000B tax on $15.00 as provided by paragraph (d)(2) of this section. A is liable for the tax when A pays for the services. If P does not collect the tax from A at the time A pays for the services, P is liable for the tax.

Example 3: Charges for other goods and services; tanning services bundled. P provides indoor tanning services and other goods and services and offers bundled services. On July 1, 2013, A, an individual, buys bundled service from P that includes 10 swimming lessons, the use of towels while on P's premises, one pair of protective eyewear, and 2 "free" 10-minute indoor tanning services. P charges $252.00 (exclusive of the tax imposed by section 5000B) for the bundled services. If these services are purchased separately, P charges (exclusive of the tax imposed by section 5000B) $25.00 per swimming lesson, $15.00 for a 10-minute indoor tanning service, $2.00 for the protective eyewear, and does not charge for the use of towels while on P's premises. As determined under paragraph (d)(3) of this section, the section 5000B tax applies to the amount reasonably attributable to the indoor tanning service, which is $26.81 (($30.00/$282.00) x $252.00).

Example 4: Person liable for the tax. On July 1, 2013, A buys bundled services (described in *Example 3*) from P as a gift for B. Under paragraph (e)(1) of this section, A is deemed to be the person on whom the indoor tanning services are performed for purposes of collecting the tax. Therefore, under paragraph (b)(1) of this section, A is liable for the tax when A pays for the services. The tax will be computed under the rules of paragraph (d)(3) of this section. If A does not pay the tax at the time A pays for the services, P is liable for the tax.

Example 5: Undesignated payment cards. (i) P operates a spa that provides a variety of cosmetic goods and services, including indoor tanning services. On July 1, 2013, A buys a gift certificate in the amount of $100.00 from P as a gift for B. The gift certificate may be redeemed by B for B's choice among several services offered by P, including indoor tanning services. On July 15, 2013, B partially redeems the gift certificate to pay for one 10-minute indoor tanning service.

(ii) Under paragraph (b)(2) of this section, a payment for indoor tanning services is made, and the tax under section 5000B is imposed, on July 15, 2013, when B partially redeems the gift certificate to pay for one indoor tanning service. Under paragraph (e)(2) of this section, B is the person who pays for the indoor tanning services. Therefore, B is liable for the tax, computed under the rules of paragraph (d) of this section, and pays the tax by permitting P to debit the amount of the tax from the balance of the gift certificate or by paying the amount of the tax to P in cash. If B does not pay the tax at the time B partially redeems the gift certificate to pay for the indoor tanning services, P is liable for the tax.

Example 6: Charges for other goods and services; tanning services bundled; amount attributable to tanning services. On July 1, 2013, A pays $1,000.00 (exclusive of the tax imposed by section 5000B) to spa P for the right to use the following equipment and services during the month of July: up to four massages or facials, unlimited use of a sauna, steam room, showers, and towel service, and unlimited indoor tanning services. If the

services are purchased separately, P charges (exclusive of the tax imposed by section 5000B) $150.00 for unlimited indoor tanning services during the month of July, and $900.00 for the other equipment and services during the month of July, not including indoor tanning services. Under paragraph (b) of this section, A has made a payment for indoor tanning services and the tax will be computed under the rules of paragraph (d)(3) of this section. As determined under paragraph (d)(3) of this section, the section 5000B tax applies to the amount reasonably attributable to the indoor tanning services, which is $142.86 (($150.00/$1050.00) x $1000.00). If A does not pay the tax at the time A pays for the bundled services, P is liable for the tax.

Example 7: Payments to qualified physical fitness facilities. P operates a fullservice gym facility that offers fitness classes, multiple exercise machines (such as treadmills, stationary bicycles, weight training machines, and free weights), and has as its predominant business providing these facilities, equipment, and services to members for purposes of exercise and physical fitness. P provides its members with access to indoor tanning services, comprised of two tanning beds that meet the definition of indoor tanning services under paragraph (c)(1) of this section. P generally charges its members a fee for monthly usage of its facilities, equipment, and services, but also offers short-term or free trial memberships and allows non-members to purchase individual or a series of exercise classes. P does not charge any fee for the indoor tanning services, does not offer indoor tanning services separately from its other services, and has no membership tier or category that differs from others based on access to the indoor tanning services. P holds itself out to the public through advertising and marketing as providing equipment and services to improve physical fitness. On July 1, 2013, A pays a membership fee to P in return for use of P's facility during the month of July. Under paragraph (d)(4) of this section, no portion of A's membership fee payment is treated as a payment made for indoor tanning services, because A is a qualified physical fitness facility under paragraph (c)(5) of this section. Therefore, no liability for tax arises under section 5000B.

(h) *Effective/applicability date.*—This section applies to amounts paid on or after June 11, 2013. For rules that apply before that date, see 26 CFR part 49 (revised as of April 1, 2013). [Reg. § 49.5000B-1.]

☐ [*T.D.* 9621, 6-10-2013.]

Tax on Certain Foreign Procurement

[Reg. § 1.5000C-0]

§ 1.5000C-0. Outline of regulation provisions for section 5000C.—This section lists the captions contained in §§ 1.5000C-1 through 1.5000C-7.

§ 1.5000C-1 Tax on specified Federal procurement payments.

(a) Overview.
(b) Imposition of tax.
(c) Definitions.
(d) Exemptions.
   (1) Simplified acquisitions.
   (2) Emergency acquisitions.
   (3) Certain personal service contracts.

(4) Certain foreign humanitarian assistance contracts.

(5) Certain international agreements.

(6) Goods manufactured or produced or services provided in the United States.

(7) Goods manufactured or produced or services provided in a country that is a party to an international procurement agreement.

(e) Country in which goods are manufactured or produced or services provided.

(1) Goods manufactured or produced.

(2) Provision of services.

(3) Allocation of total contract price to determine the nonexempt amount.

(4) Reduction or elimination of withholding by an acquiring agency.

§1.5000C-2 Withholding on specified Federal procurement payments.

(a) In general.

(b) Steps in determining the obligation to withhold under section 5000C.

(1) Determine whether the payment is pursuant to a contract for goods or services.

(2) Determine whether the payment is made pursuant to a contract with a U.S. person.

(3) Determine whether the payment is for purchases under the simplified acquisition procedures.

(4) Determine whether the payment is for emergency acquisitions.

(5) Determine whether the payment is for personal services under the simplified acquisition threshold.

(6) Determine whether the payment is pursuant to a foreign humanitarian assistance contract.

(7) Determine whether the foreign contracting party is entitled to relief pursuant to an international agreement.

(8) Determine whether the contract is for goods manufactured or produced or services provided in the United States or in a foreign country that is a party to an international procurement agreement.

(9) Compute amounts to withhold.

(10) Deposit and report amounts withheld.

(c) Determining whether the contracting party is a U.S. person.

(1) In general.

(2) Determination based on Taxpayer Identification Number (TIN).

(3) Determination based on the Form W-9.

(4) Contracting party treated as a foreign contracting party.

(d) Withholding when a foreign contracting party submits a Section 5000C Certificate.

(1) In general.

(2) Exemption for a foreign contracting party entitled to the benefit of relief pursuant to certain international agreements.

(3) Exemption when goods are manufactured or produced or services provided in the United States, or in a foreign country that is a party to an international procurement agreement.

(4) Information required for Section 5000C Certificate.

(5) Validity period of Section 5000C Certificate.

(6) Change in circumstances.

(7) Form W-14.

(8) Time for submitting Section 5000C Certificate.

(e) Offset for underwithholding or overwithholding.

(1) In general.

(2) Underwithholding.

(3) Overwithholding.

§1.5000C-3 Payment and returns of tax withheld by the acquiring agency.

(a) In general.

(b) Deposit rules.

(1) Acquiring agency with a chapter 3 deposit requirement treats amounts withheld as under chapter 3.

(2) Acquiring agency with no chapter 3 filing obligation deposits withheld amounts monthly.

(c) Return requirements.

(1) In general.

(2) Classified or confidential contracts.

(d) Special arrangement for certain contracts.

§1.5000C-4 Requirement for the foreign contracting party to file a return and pay tax, and procedures for the contracting party to seek a refund.

(a) In general.

(b) Tax obligation of foreign contracting party independent of withholding.

(c) Return of tax by the foreign contracting party.

(d) Time and manner of paying tax.

(e) Refund requests when amount withheld exceeds tax liability.

§1.5000C-5 Anti-abuse rule.

§1.5000C-6 Examples.

§1.5000C-7 Effective/applicability date. [Reg. §1.5000C-0.]

☐ [*T.D.* 9782, 8-17-2016.]

[Reg. §1.5000C-1]

§1.5000C-1. Tax on specified Federal procurement payments.—(a) *Overview.*—This section provides definitions and general rules relating to the imposition of, and exemption from, the tax on specified Federal procurement payments under section 5000C. Section 1.5000C-2 provides rules concerning withholding under section 5000C(d)(1), including the steps that must be taken to determine the obligation to withhold and whether an exemption from withholding applies. Section 1.5000C-3 provides the time and manner for depositing the amounts withheld under section 5000C and the related reporting requirements. Section 1.5000C-4 contains the rules that apply to a foreign contracting party that must pay and report the tax under section 5000C when the tax obligation under section 5000C is not fully satisfied by withholding, as well as procedures by which a contracting party may seek a refund when the amount withheld exceeds its tax liability under section 5000C.

Section 1.5000C-5 contains an anti-abuse rule. Section 1.5000C-6 contains examples illustrating the principles of §§ 1.5000C-1 through 1.5000C-4. Finally, § 1.5000C-7 contains the effective/applicability date for §§ 1.5000C-1 through 1.5000C-7.

(b) *Imposition of tax.*—Except as otherwise provided, section 5000C imposes on any foreign contracting party a tax equal to 2 percent of the amount of a specified Federal procurement payment. In general, the tax imposed under section 5000C applies to specified Federal procurement payments received pursuant to contracts entered into on and after January 2, 2011. Specified Federal procurement payments received by a nominee or agent on behalf of a contracting party are considered to be received by that contracting party. The tax imposed under section 5000C is to be applied in a manner consistent with U.S. obligations under international agreements. Payments for the purchase or lease of land or an interest in land are not subject to the tax imposed under section 5000C.

(c) *Definitions.*—Solely for purposes of section 5000C and §§ 1.5000C-1 through 1.5000C-7, the following definitions apply:

(1) The term *acquiring agency* means the U.S. government department, agency, independent establishment, or corporation described in paragraph (c)(7) of this section that is a party to the contract. To the extent that a U.S. government department or agency, other than the acquiring agency, is making the payments pursuant to the contract, that department or agency is also considered to be the acquiring agency.

(2) The term *contract* has the same meaning as provided in 48 CFR 2.101, and thus does not include a grant agreement or a cooperative agreement within the meaning of 31 U.S.C. 6304 and 6305, respectively. A contract may include an agreement that is not executed under the Federal Acquisition Regulations (FAR), 48 CFR Chapter 1.

(3) The term *contract ratio* refers to the nonexempt amount over the total contract price.

(4) The term *contracting party* means any person that is a party to a contract with the U.S. government that is entered into on or after January 2, 2011. See § 1.5000C-1(b) for situations involving a nominee or agent.

(5) The term *foreign contracting party* means a contracting party that is a foreign person.

(6) The term *foreign person* means any person other than a United States person (as defined in section 7701(a)(30)).

(7) The term *Government of the United States* or *U.S. government* means the executive departments specified in 5 U.S.C. 101, the military departments specified in 5 U.S.C. 102, the independent establishments specified in 5 U.S.C. 104(1), and wholly owned government corporations specified in 31 U.S.C. 9101(3). Unless otherwise specified in 5 U.S.C. 101, 102, or 104(1), or 31 U.S.C. 9101(3), the term Government of the United States or U.S. government does not include any quasi-governmental entities or instrumentalities of the U.S. government.

(8) The term *international procurement agreement* means the World Trade Organization Government Procurement Agreement within the meaning of 48 CFR 25.400(a)(1) and any free trade agreement to which the United States is a party that includes government procurement obligations that provide appropriate competitive government procurement opportunities to U.S. goods, services, and suppliers. A party to an international procurement agreement is a signatory to the agreement and does not include a country that is merely an observer with respect to the agreement.

(9) The term *nonexempt amount* means the portion of the contract price allocated to nonexempt goods and nonexempt services.

(10) The term *nonexempt goods* means goods manufactured or produced in a foreign country that is not a party to an international procurement agreement with the United States.

(11) The term *nonexempt services* means services provided in a foreign country that is not a party to an international procurement agreement with the United States.

(12) The term *outlying areas* has the same meaning as set forth in 48 CFR 2.101(b), which includes Puerto Rico, the Northern Mariana Islands, American Samoa, Guam, the Virgin Islands, Baker Island, Howland Island, Jarvis Island, Johnston Atoll, Kingman Reef, Midway Islands, Navassa Island, Palmyra Atoll, and Wake Atoll.

(13) The term *qualified income tax treaty* means a U.S. income tax treaty in force that contains a nondiscrimination provision that applies to the tax imposed under section 5000C and prohibits taxation that is more burdensome on a foreign national than a U.S. national (or in the case of certain income tax treaties, taxation that is more burdensome on a foreign citizen than a U.S. citizen), regardless of its residence.

(14) The term *Section 5000C Certificate* means a written statement that includes the information described in § 1.5000C-2(d) that the foreign contracting party submits to an acquiring agency for the purposes of demonstrating that the foreign contracting party is eligible for certain exemptions from withholding (in whole or in part) under section 5000C with respect to a contract. The term may also include any form that the Internal Revenue Service may prescribe as a substitute for the Section 5000C Certificate, such as Form W-14, "Certificate of Foreign Contracting Party Receiving Federal Procurement Payments."

(15) The term *specified Federal procurement payment* means any payment made pursuant to a contract with a foreign contracting party that is for goods manufactured or produced or services provided in a foreign country that is not a party to an international procurement agreement with the United States. For purposes of the prior sentence, a foreign country does not include an outlying area.

(16) The term *Taxpayer Identification Number* or *TIN* means the identifying number assigned to a person under section 6109, as defined in section 7701(a)(41).

(17) The term *total contract price* means the total cost to the U.S. Government of the goods and services procured under a contract and paid to the contracting party.

(d) *Exemptions.*—The tax imposed under paragraph (b) of this section does not apply to the payments made in the following situations. For the exemptions in paragraphs (d)(5), (6) and (7) of this section, see § 1.5000C-2(d) for the procedures to eliminate withholding by an acquiring agency.

(1) *Simplified acquisitions.*—Payments for purchases under the simplified acquisition procedures that do not exceed the simplified acquisition threshold as described in 48 CFR 2.101.

(2) *Emergency acquisitions.*—Payments made pursuant to a contract if the contract is—

(i) Awarded under the "unusual and compelling urgency" authority of 48 CFR 6.302-2, or

(ii) Entered into under the emergency acquisition flexibilities as defined in 48 CFR part 18.

(3) *Certain personal service contracts.*—Payments for services provided by, and under contracts with, a single individual in which the payments do not (and will not) exceed on an annual calendar year basis the simplified acquisition threshold as described in 48 CFR 2.101 for all years of the contract. Payments that satisfy this exemption remain exempt if the contract is later renegotiated so that future payments under the contract do not meet this exemption.

(4) *Certain foreign humanitarian assistance contracts.*—Payments made by the U.S. government pursuant to a contract with a foreign contracting party to obtain goods or services described in or authorized under 7 U.S.C. 1691, *et seq.*, 22 U.S.C. 2151, *et seq.*, 22 U.S.C 2601 *et seq.*, 22 U.S.C. 5801 *et seq.*, 22 U.S.C. 5401 *et seq.*, 10 U.S.C. 402, 10 U.S.C. 404, 10 U.S.C. 407, 10 U.S.C. 2557, and 10 U.S.C. 2561, if the acquiring agency determines that the payment is for the purpose of providing foreign humanitarian assistance.

(5) *Certain international agreements.*—Payments made by the U.S. government pursuant to a contract with a foreign contracting party when the payments are entitled to relief from the tax imposed under section 5000C pursuant to an international agreement with the United States, including relief pursuant to a nondiscrimination provision of a qualified income tax treaty, because the foreign contracting party is entitled to the benefit of that provision.

(6) *Goods manufactured or produced or services provided in the United States.*—A payment made pursuant to a contract to the extent that the payment is for goods manufactured or produced or services provided in the United States.

(7) *Goods manufactured or produced or services provided in a country that is a party to an international procurement agreement.*—A payment made pursuant to a contract to the extent the payment is for goods manufactured or produced or services provided in a country that is a party to an international procurement agreement, as defined in paragraph (c)(8) of this section.

(e) *Country in which goods are manufactured or produced or services provided.*—(1) *Goods manufactured or produced.*—Solely for purposes of section 5000C, goods are manufactured or produced in the country (or countries)—

(i) Where property has been substantially transformed into the goods that are procured pursuant to a contract; or

(ii) Where there has been assembly or conversion of component parts (involving activities that are substantial in nature and generally considered to constitute the manufacture or production of property) into the final product that constitutes the goods procured pursuant to a contract.

(2) *Provision of services.*—Solely for purposes of section 5000C, services are considered to be provided in the country where the individuals performing the services are physically located when they perform their duties pursuant to the contract.

(3) *Allocation of total contract price to determine the nonexempt amount.*—If, pursuant to a contract, goods are manufactured or produced, or services are provided, in multiple countries and only a portion of the goods manufactured or produced, or the services provided, pursuant to the contract are nonexempt goods or nonexempt services, a foreign contracting party may use a reasonable allocation method to determine the nonexempt amount. A reasonable allocation method would include taking into account the proportionate costs (including the cost of labor and raw materials) incurred to manufacture or produce the goods in each country, or taking into account the proportionate costs incurred to provide the services in each country.

(4) *Reduction or elimination of withholding by an acquiring agency.*—For procedures to reduce or eliminate withholding by an acquiring agency based on where goods are manufactured or produced or where services are provided, including as a result of an allocation under this paragraph (e), see § 1.5000C-2(d). [Reg. § 1.5000C-1.]

☐ [*T.D.* 9782, 8-17-2016.]

[Reg. § 1.5000C-2]

§ 1.5000C-2. Withholding on specified Federal procurement payments.—(a) *In general.*— Except as otherwise provided in this section, every acquiring agency making a specified Federal procurement payment on which tax is imposed under section 5000C and § § 1.5000C-1 through 1.5000C-7 must deduct and withhold an amount equal to 2 percent of the payment. For rules relating to the liability of a foreign contracting party with respect to specified Federal procurement payments not fully withheld upon at source, see § 1.5000C-4. An acquiring agency may rely upon any information furnished by a contracting party under this section unless the acquiring agency has reason to know that the information is incorrect or unreliable. An acquiring agency has reason to know that the information is incorrect or unreliable if it has knowledge of relevant facts or statements contained in the submitted information such that a reasonably prudent person in the position of the acquiring agency would know that the information provided is incorrect or unreliable.

(b) *Steps in determining the obligation to withhold under section 5000C.*—An acquiring agency generally determines its obligation to withhold under section 5000C according to the steps described in this paragraph (b). See, however, paragraph (e) of this section for situations in which withholding may be increased in the case of underwithholding, or may be decreased in the case of overwithholding.

(1) *Determine whether the payment is pursuant to a contract for goods or services.*—The acquiring agency determines whether it is making a payment pursuant to a contract for goods or services. To the extent that the acquiring agency is making a payment for any other purpose, it does not have an obligation to withhold under section 5000C on the payment.

(2) *Determine whether the payment is made pursuant to a contract with a U.S. person.*—The acquiring agency determines whether the payment is made pursuant to a contract with a person considered to be a United States person (U.S. person) in accordance with paragraph (c) of this section. If the other contracting party is a U.S. person, the acquiring agency does not have an obligation to withhold under section 5000C on the payment.

(3) *Determine whether the payment is for purchases under the simplified acquisition procedures.*—The acquiring agency determines whether the payment is for purchases under the simplified acquisitions procedures that do not exceed the simplified acquisition threshold as described in 48 CFR 2.101. If it is, the acquiring agency does not have an obligation to withhold under section 5000C on the payment.

(4) *Determine whether the payment is for emergency acquisitions.*—The acquiring agency determines whether the payment is made for certain emergency acquisitions within the meaning of §1.5000C-1(d)(2). If it is, the acquiring agency does not have an obligation to withhold under section 5000C on the payment.

(5) *Determine whether the payment is for personal services under the simplified acquisition threshold.*—The acquiring agency determines whether payments for services under contracts with a single individual do not exceed the simplified acquisition threshold as described in 48 CFR 2.101 on an annual basis for all years of the contract. If that is the case, the acquiring agency does not have an obligation to withhold under section 5000C on the payment.

(6) *Determine whether the payment is pursuant to a foreign humanitarian assistance contract.*—The acquiring agency determines whether the payment is made pursuant to a foreign humanitarian assistance contract described in §1.5000C-1(d)(4). If it is, the acquiring agency does not have an obligation to withhold under section 5000C on the payment.

(7) *Determine whether the foreign contracting party is entitled to relief pursuant to an international agreement.*—If the foreign contracting party submits a Section 5000C Certificate in accordance with paragraph (d) of this section representing that the foreign contracting party is entitled to relief from the tax imposed under section 5000C pursuant to an international agreement with the United States (such as relief pursuant to the nondiscrimination provision of a qualified income tax treaty), the acquiring agency does not have an obligation to withhold under section 5000C on the payment.

(8) *Determine whether the contract is for goods manufactured or produced or services provided in the United States or in a foreign country that is a party to an international procurement agreement.*—If the foreign contracting party submits a Section 5000C Certificate in accordance with paragraph (d) of this section that represents that the contract is for goods manufactured or produced or services provided in the United States, or in a foreign country that is a party to an international procurement agreement, the acquiring agency does not have an obligation to withhold. If the Section 5000C Certificate provides that payments under the contract are only partially exempt from withholding under section 5000C, the acquiring agency must withhold to the extent described in paragraph (b)(8) of this section.

(9) *Compute amounts to withhold.*—If, after evaluating each step described in this paragraph (b), the acquiring agency determines that it has an obligation to withhold, the acquiring agency computes the amount of withholding by multiplying the amount of the payment by 2 percent, unless the foreign contracting party has provided a Section 5000C Certificate or the payment is only in part for goods or services. In cases in which the Section 5000C Certificate demonstrates that the exemption in Step 8 applies, the acquiring agency generally computes the amount of withholding by multiplying the amount of the payment by the contract ratio provided on the most recent Section 5000C Certificate, the product of which is multiplied by 2 percent. However, in cases in which the exemption in Step 8 applies and the requirements of paragraph (d)(4)(iii)(B)(2) of this section are met, the acquiring agency computes the amount of withholding based on the payment for the specifically identified items, which may be identified by the contract line item number, or CLIN. In the case in which the payment is only in part for goods or services, the acquiring agency reduces the amount of the payment subject to the tax to the extent it is for something other than goods or services. The acquiring agency withholds the computed amount from the payment.

Reg. §1.5000C-2(b)(9)

(10) *Deposit and report amounts withheld.*— The acquiring agency deposits and reports the amounts determined in the prior step in accordance with § 1.5000C-3.

(c) *Determining whether the contracting party is a U.S. person.*—(1) *In general.*—An acquiring agency must rely on the provisions of this paragraph (c) to determine the status of the contracting party as a U.S. person for purposes of withholding under section 5000C.

(2) *Determination based on Taxpayer Identification Number (TIN).*—An acquiring agency must treat a contracting party as a U.S. person if the U.S. government information system (such as the System for Award Management (SAM)) indicates that the contracting party is a corporation (for example, because the name listed in SAM contains the term "Corporation," "Inc.," or "Corp.") and that it has a TIN that begins with two digits other than "98" (a limited liability company or LLC is not treated as a corporation for purposes of this paragraph (c)(2)). Further, an acquiring agency must treat a contracting party as a U.S. person if the acquiring agency has access to a U.S. government information system that indicates that the contracting party is an individual with a TIN that begins with a digit other than "9".

(3) *Determination based on the Form W-9.*— An acquiring agency must treat a contracting party as a U.S. person if the person has submitted to it a valid Form W-9, "Request for Taxpayer Identification Number (TIN) and Certificate" (or valid substitute form described in § 31.3406(h)-3(c)(2) of this chapter), signed under penalties of perjury.

(4) *Contracting party treated as a foreign contracting party.*—If an acquiring agency cannot determine that a contracting party is a U.S. person based on application of paragraph (c)(2) or (3) of this section, then the contracting party is treated as a foreign contracting party for purposes of this section.

(d) *Withholding when a foreign contracting party submits a Section 5000C Certificate.*—(1) *In general.*—Unless the acquiring agency has reason to know that the information is incorrect or unreliable, the acquiring agency may rely on a claim that a foreign contracting party is entitled to an exemption (in whole or in part) from withholding on payments pursuant to a contract if the foreign contracting party provides a Section 5000C Certificate to the acquiring agency as prescribed in this paragraph (d). When a Section 5000C Certificate is furnished, the acquiring agency does not withhold, or must reduce the amount of withholding, on payments made to a foreign person if the certificate establishes that the foreign person is wholly or partially exempt from withholding. An acquiring agency may establish a system for a foreign contracting party to electronically furnish a Section 5000C Certificate.

(2) *Exemption for a foreign contracting party entitled to the benefit of relief pursuant to certain international agreements.*—An acquiring agency does not withhold on payments pursuant to a contract with a foreign contracting party when the payment is entitled to relief from the tax imposed under section 5000C pursuant to an international agreement, including relief pursuant to a nondiscrimination provision of a qualified income tax treaty, because the foreign contracting party is entitled to the benefit of that agreement and the foreign contracting party has submitted a Section 5000C Certificate that includes all of the information described in paragraphs (d)(4)(i) and (ii) of this section.

(3) *Exemption when goods are manufactured or produced or services provided in the United States, or in a foreign country that is a party to an international procurement agreement.*—An acquiring agency does not withhold on payments pursuant to a contract with a foreign contracting party to the extent that the payments are for goods manufactured or produced or services provided in the United States or in a foreign country that is a party to an international procurement agreement with the United States, provided that the foreign contracting party has submitted a Section 5000C Certificate that includes all of the information described in paragraphs (d)(4)(i) and (iii) of this section. If the Section 5000C Certificate provides that the payment is only partially exempt from withholding under section 5000C, the acquiring agency must withhold to the extent that the payment is not exempt.

(4) *Information required for Section 5000C Certificate.*—(i) *In general.*—The Section 5000C Certificate must be signed under penalties of perjury by the foreign contracting party and contain—

(A) The name of the foreign contracting party, country of organization (if applicable), and permanent residence address of the foreign contracting party;

(B) The mailing address of the foreign contracting party (if different than the permanent residence address);

(C) The TIN assigned to the foreign contracting party (if any);

(D) The identifying or reference number on the contract (if known);

(E) The name and address of the acquiring agency;

(F) A statement that the person signing the Section 5000C Certificate is the foreign contracting party listed in paragraph (d)(4)(i)(A) of this section (or is authorized to sign on behalf of the foreign contracting party);

(G) A statement that the foreign contracting party is not acting as an agent or nominee for another foreign person with respect to the goods manufactured or produced or services provided under the contract;

(H) A statement that the foreign contracting party agrees to pay an amount equal to any tax (including any applicable penalties and interest) due under section 5000C that the acquiring agency does not withhold under section 5000C;

(I) A statement that the foreign contracting party acknowledges and understands the rules in §1.5000C-4 relating to procedural obligations related to section 5000C; and

(J) A statement that the foreign contracting party has not engaged in a transaction (or series of transactions) with a principal purpose of avoiding the tax imposed under section 5000C as defined in §1.5000C-5.

(ii) *Additional information required for claiming an exemption based on certain international agreements with the United States.*—In addition to the information required by paragraph (d)(4)(i) of this section, a foreign contracting party claiming an exemption from withholding in reliance on a provision of an international agreement with the United States, including a qualified income tax treaty, must provide—

(A) The name of the international agreement under which the foreign contracting party is claiming benefits;

(B) The specific provision of the international agreement relied upon (for example, the nondiscrimination article of a qualified income tax treaty); and

(C) The basis on which it is entitled to the benefits of that provision (for example, because the foreign contracting party is a corporation organized in a foreign country that has in force a qualified income tax treaty with the United States that covers all nationals, regardless of their residence).

(iii) *Additional required information for claiming exemption based on country where goods are manufactured or services provided.*—(A) *In general.*—In addition to the information required by paragraph (d)(4)(i) of this section, a foreign contracting party claiming an exemption from withholding (in whole or in part) because payments will be pursuant to a contract for goods manufactured or produced or services provided in the United States, or a foreign country that is party to an international procurement agreement, must describe on the Section 5000C Certificate the relevant goods or services and the country (or countries) in which they are manufactured or produced, or are provided, and must include the name of the international procurement agreement or agreements (if relevant).

(B) *Information on allocation to exempt and nonexempt amounts.*—(1) *In general.*—In situations in which a foreign contracting party claims the exemption in paragraph (d)(3) of this section with respect to only a portion of the payments received under the contract, the Section 5000C Certificate must include an explanation of the method used by the foreign contracting party to allocate the total contract price among the countries, as described in §1.5000C-1(e)(3), if applicable. In general, the Section 5000C Certificate also must include the total contract price and the nonexempt amount; however, when necessary, an estimate of the total contract price or the nonexempt amount may be used. For example, total contract price may be estimated when a Section 5000C Certificate is being completed with respect to payments to be made pursuant to a cost-reimbursement

contract that is paid on the basis of actual incurred costs and the total amount of such costs is not known at the time the certificate is provided.

(2) *Specific identification of exempt items.*—If agreed to by the acquiring agency, the Section 5000C Certificate may identify specific exempt and nonexempt amounts. For example, specific contract line items (such as a contract line item number or CLIN) identified in the contract may be listed on the Section 5000C Certificate as exempt and nonexempt amounts (in whole or in part), as applicable. When this paragraph applies, and whether or not the contract identifies exempt and nonexempt amounts, a foreign contracting party must provide the information required by paragraphs (d)(4)(iii)(A) and (d)(4)(iii)(B)(1) of this section, on the Section 5000C Certificate to explain why the contract line items are eligible for an exemption; however, the foreign contracting party is not required to include information about the total contract price under this paragraph. In these circumstances, only one Section 5000C Certificate is required to be provided identifying the exempt and nonexempt contract line items that relate to the contract (for example, a spreadsheet may be attached to the Section 5000C Certificate that identifies the contract line items with an explanation for the treatment as exempt or nonexempt).

(5) *Validity period of Section 5000C Certificate.*—Except as otherwise provided in paragraph (d)(6) of this section, the Section 5000C Certificate is valid for the term of the contract.

(6) *Change in circumstances.*—A foreign contracting party must submit a revised Section 5000C Certificate within 30 days of a change in circumstances that causes the information in a Section 5000C Certificate held by the acquiring agency to be incorrect with respect to the acquiring agency's determination of whether to withhold or the amount of withholding under Section 5000C. An acquiring agency must request a new Section 5000C Certificate from a contracting party in circumstances in which it knows (or has reason to know) that a previously submitted Section 5000C Certificate becomes incorrect or unreliable. An acquiring agency may request an updated Section 5000C Certificate at any time, including when other documentation is required under the contract, such as the annual representations and certifications required in 48 CFR 4.1201. See §1.5000C-6, *Example 6,* for an illustration of this paragraph (6).

(7) *Form W-14.*—A foreign contracting party may choose to use Form W-14, "Certificate of Foreign Contracting Party Receiving Federal Procurement Payments" (or other form that the IRS may prescribe), as its Section 5000C Certificate, provided that it includes all the necessary information required by this paragraph (d).

(8) *Time for submitting Section 5000C Certificate.*—A contracting party must submit the Section 5000C Certificate (such as Form W-14 or Form W-9) as early as practicable (for example,

Reg. §1.5000C-2(d)(8)

when the offer for the contract is submitted to the U.S. government). In all cases, however, the Section 5000C Certificate must be submitted to the acquiring agency no later than the date of execution of the contract.

(e) *Offset for underwithholding or overwithholding.*—(1) *In general.*—If the foreign contracting party discovers that amounts withheld on prior payments either were insufficient or in excess of the amount required to satisfy its tax liability under section 5000C, the foreign contracting party may request the acquiring agency to increase or decrease the amount of withholding on future payments for which withholding is required under section 5000C. The request must be in writing, signed under penalties of perjury, contain the amount by which the foreign contracting party requests to increase or decrease future amounts withheld under section 5000C, and explain the reason for the request. The request may be submitted in conjunction with an original or updated Section 5000C Certificate.

(2) *Underwithholding.*—Upon receipt of a request described in paragraph (e)(1) of this section, acquiring agencies may increase the amount of withholding under this paragraph to correct underwithholding only if the payment for which the increase is applied is otherwise subject to withholding under section 5000C and made before the date that Form 1042, "Annual Withholding Tax Return for U.S. Source Income of Foreign Persons," is required to be filed (not including extensions) with respect to the payment for which the underwithholding occurred. Amounts withheld under this paragraph must be deposited and reported in the time and manner as prescribed by § 1.5000C-3. *See* § 1.5000C-4 for procedures for a foreign contracting party that must pay tax due when its tax liability under section 5000C was not fully satisfied by withholding by an acquiring agency.

(3) *Overwithholding.*—Upon receipt of a request described in paragraph (e)(1) of this section, acquiring agencies may decrease the amount of withholding on subsequent payments made to the foreign contracting party that are otherwise subject to withholding under section 5000C provided that the payment for which the decrease is applied is made on or before the date on which Form 1042, "Annual Withholding Tax Return for U.S. Source Income of Foreign Persons," is required to be filed (not including extensions) with respect to the payment for which the overwithholding occurred. *See* § 1.5000C-4(e) for procedures for foreign contracting parties to file a claim for refund for the overwithheld amount under section 5000C. [Reg. § 1.5000C-2.]

☐ [*T.D.* 9782, 8-17-2016.]

[Reg. § 1.5000C-3]

§ 1.5000C-3. Payment and returns of tax withheld by the acquiring agency.—(a) *In general.*— This section provides administrative procedures that acquiring agencies must follow to satisfy their obligations to deposit and report amounts withheld under § 1.5000C-2. An acquiring

agency with a section 5000C withholding obligation must increase the amount it deducts and withholds under chapter 3 for fixed or determinable annual or periodical income (FDAP income) by the amount it must withhold under § 1.5000C-2. Accordingly, this section generally applies the administrative provisions of chapter 3 for FDAP income relating to the deposit, payment, and reporting for amounts withheld under § 1.5000C-2, and contains some variation from those provisions to take into account the nature of the tax imposed under section 5000C.

(b) *Deposit rules.*—(1) *Acquiring agency with a chapter 3 deposit requirement treats amounts withheld as under chapter 3.*—If an acquiring agency has a chapter 3 deposit obligation for a period, it must treat any amount withheld under § 1.5000C-2 as an additional amount of tax withheld under chapter 3 for purposes of the deposit rules of § 1.6302-2. Thus, depending on the combined amount withheld under chapter 3 and § 1.5000C-2, an acquiring agency subject to this paragraph (b)(1) must make monthly deposits, quarter-monthly deposits, or annual deposits under the rules in § 1.6302-2. To the extent provided in forms, instructions, or publications prescribed by the Internal Revenue Service (IRS), acquiring agencies must deposit all withheld amounts by *electronic funds transfer*, as that term is defined in § 31.6302-1(h)(4)(i) of this chapter.

(2) *Acquiring agency with no chapter 3 filing obligation deposits withheld amounts monthly.*—If an acquiring agency has no chapter 3 deposit obligation to which the deposit rules of § 1.6302-2 apply for a calendar month, it must make monthly deposits of the amounts withheld under the rules in this paragraph (b)(2). Thus, an acquiring agency with no chapter 3 deposit obligations and that has withheld any amount under § 1.5000C-2 during any calendar month must deposit that amount by the 15th day of the month following the payment. To the extent provided in forms, instructions, or publications prescribed by the Internal Revenue Service (IRS), acquiring agencies must deposit all withheld amounts by *electronic funds transfer*, as that term is defined in § 31.6302-1(h)(4)(i) of this chapter.

(c) *Return requirements.*—(1) *In general.*—Except as provided in paragraph (c)(2) of this section, an acquiring agency that withholds an amount pursuant to section 5000C generally must file Form 1042-S, "Foreign Person's U.S. Source Income Subject to Withholding," and Form 1042, "Annual Withholding Tax Return for U.S. Source Income of Foreign Persons," each year, or other such forms as the IRS may prescribe, to report information related to amounts withheld under section 5000C. The acquiring agency must prepare a Form 1042-S for each contracting party reporting the amount withheld under section 5000C for the preceding calendar year. The Form 1042 must show the aggregate amounts withheld under section 5000C that were required to be reported on Forms 1042-S (including those amounts withheld under section 5000C for which a Form 1042-S is not required to be filed pursuant to paragraph (c)(2) of this section). The Form 1042 must also include the information required by the form and accompanying instructions. Further, any forms required under this paragraph (c) are due at the same time, at the same place, and eligible for the same extended due dates and may be amended in the same manner as Form 1042 and Form 1042-S (or such other forms as the IRS may prescribe related to chapter 3). The acquiring agency must furnish a copy of the Form 1042-S (or such other form as the IRS may prescribe for the same purpose) to the contracting party for whom the form is prepared on or before March 15 of the calendar year following the year in which the amount subject to reporting under section 5000C was paid. It must be filed with a transmittal form as provided in the instructions for Form 1042-S and to the transmittal form. Section 5000C Certificates or other statements or information as prescribed by § 1.5000C-2 that are provided to the acquiring agency are not required to be attached to the Form 1042 filed with the IRS. However, an acquiring agency that is required to file Form 1042 must retain a copy of Form 1042, Form 1042-S, the Section 5000C Certificates, or other statements or information prescribed by § 1.5000C-2 for at least three years from the original due date of Form 1042 or the date it was filed, whichever is later. An acquiring agency that is not required to file Form 1042 must retain any Section 5000C Certificates or other statements or information as prescribed by § 1.5000C-2 for at least three years from the date the Form 1042 would have been due had the acquiring agency had an obligation to file.

(2) *Classified or confidential contracts.*—An acquiring agency is not required to report information otherwise required by this section on Form 1042-S for payments made pursuant to classified or confidential contracts (as described in section 6050M(e)(3)), unless the acquiring agency determines that the information reported on the Form 1042-S does not compromise the safeguarding of classified information or national security.

(d) *Special arrangement for certain contracts.*—In limited circumstances, the IRS may authorize the amount otherwise required to be withheld under section 5000C to be deposited in the time and manner mutually agreed upon by the acquiring agency and the foreign contracting party. In these circumstances, the IRS may in its sole discretion also modify any reporting or return requirements of the acquiring agency or the foreign contracting party. [Reg. § 1.5000C-3.]

☐ [*T.D. 9782, 8-17-2016.*]

[Reg. § 1.5000C-4]

§ 1.5000C-4. Requirement for the foreign contracting party to file a return and pay tax, and procedures for the contracting party to seek a refund.—(a) *In general.*—For purposes of subtitle F of the Internal Revenue Code ("Procedure and Administration"), the tax imposed under section 5000C on foreign persons is treated as a tax imposed under subtitle A. Except as provided elsewhere in the regulations under section 5000C, forms, or accompanying instructions, the tax imposed on foreign contracting parties under section 5000C is administered in a manner similar to gross basis income taxes. This section provides procedures that a foreign contracting party must follow to satisfy its obligations to report and deposit tax due under § 1.5000C-1 as well as procedures for contracting parties to seek a refund of amounts overwithheld.

(b) *Tax obligation of foreign contracting party independent of withholding.*—A foreign contracting party subject to tax under section 5000C and § § 1.5000C-1 through 1.5000C-7 remains liable for the tax unless its tax obligation was fully satisfied by withholding by an acquiring agency in accordance with § § 1.5000C-2 and 1.5000C-3.

(c) *Return of tax by the foreign contracting party.*—If the tax liability under § 1.5000C-1 relating to a payment is not fully satisfied by withholding in accordance with § § 1.5000C-2 and 1.5000C-3 (including as a result of the use of an estimated nonexempt amount or estimated total contract price in computing the contract ratio), a foreign contracting party subject to tax under § 1.5000C-1 during a calendar year must make a return of tax on, for example, Form 1120-F, "U.S. Income Tax Return of a Foreign Corporation," or such other form as the Internal Revenue Service (IRS) may prescribe to report the amount of tax due under section 5000C (required return). A foreign contracting party with no other U.S. tax filing obligation other than with respect to its liability for the tax imposed under section 5000C must file its required return on or before the fifteenth day of the sixth month following the close of its taxable year. The required return must include the information required by the form and accompanying instructions. The required return must be filed at the place and time (including any extension of time to file) provided by the form and accompanying instructions. Penalties for failure to file contained in Subtitle F can apply to foreign contracting parties who fail to file the required return. A foreign contracting party must attach copies of all Forms 1042-S, "Foreign Person's U.S. Source Income Subject to Withholding," received from acquiring agencies (if any) to the required return.

(d) *Time and manner of paying tax.*—A foreign contracting party must pay the tax imposed under section 5000C in the manner provided and in the time prescribed in the required return and accompanying instructions. In general, the foreign contracting party must pay the tax at the time that the required return is due, excluding extensions. To the extent provided in forms, instructions, or publications prescribed by the IRS, each foreign contracting party must deposit tax due under section 5000C by *electronic funds transfer*, as that term is defined in § 31.6302-1(h)(4)(i) of this chapter. A foreign contracting party that fails to pay tax in the time and manner prescribed in this section (or under forms, instructions, or publications prescribed by the IRS under this section) may be subject to penalties and interest under Subtitle F.

(e) *Refund requests when amount withheld exceeds tax liability.*—After taking into account any offsets pursuant to §1.5000C-2(e)(3), if the acquiring agency has overwithheld amounts under section 5000C and has made a deposit of the amounts under §1.5000C-3(b), the contracting party may claim a refund of the amount overwithheld pursuant to the procedures described in chapter 65. The contracting party's claim for refund must meet the requirements of section 6402 and the regulations thereunder, as applicable, and must be filed before the expiration of the period of limitations on refund in section 6511 and the regulations thereunder. In general, the contracting party making a refund claim must file the required return to claim a refund, stating the grounds upon which the claim is based. A Section 5000C Certificate and a copy of the Form 1042-S received from the acquiring agency must be attached to the required return. For purposes of this section, an amount is overwithheld if the amount withheld from the payment pursuant to section 5000C and §§1.5000C-1 through 1.5000C-7 exceeds the contracting party's tax liability under §1.5000C-1, regardless of whether the overwithholding was in error or appeared correct when it occurred. A U.S. person may seek a refund under this paragraph (e) even if it was treated as a foreign person under the rules in §1.5000C-2 (for example, because it neither had a taxpayer identification number on file in the System for Award Management nor submitted Form W-9, "Request for Taxpayer Identification Number (TIN) and Certification," to the acquiring agency). [Reg. §1.5000C-4.]

☐ [*T.D.* 9782, 8-17-2016.]

[Reg. §1.5000C-5]

§1.5000C-5. **Anti-abuse rule.**—If a foreign person engages in a transaction (or series of transactions) with a principal purpose of avoiding the tax imposed under section 5000C, the transaction (or series of transactions) may be disregarded or the arrangement may be recharacterized (including disregarding an intermediate entity), in accordance with its substance. If this section applies, the foreign person remains liable for any tax (including any tax obligation unsatisfied as a result of underwithholding) and the Internal Revenue Service retains all other rights and remedies under any applicable law available to collect any tax imposed on the foreign contracting party by section 5000C. [Reg. §1.5000C-5.]

☐ [*T.D.* 9782, 8-17-2016.]

[Reg. §1.5000C-6]

§1.5000C-6. **Examples.**—The rules of §§1.5000C-1 through 1.5000C-4 are illustrated by the following examples. For purposes of the examples: All contracts are executed with acquiring agencies on or after January 2, 2011, and are for the provision of either goods or services; none of the exemptions described in §1.5000C-1(d) apply, unless otherwise explicitly stated; the acquiring agencies have no other

withholding obligations under chapter 3 of the Code and have no other contracts subject to section 5000C; the foreign contracting parties do not have any U.S. source income or a U.S. tax return filing obligation other than a tax return filing obligation that arises based on the facts described in the particular example; and none of the contracts are classified or confidential contracts as described in section 6050M(e)(3).

Example 1. U.S. person not subject to tax; no withholding. (i) *Facts.* Company A Inc., a domestic corporation and the contracting party, enters into a contract with Agency L, the acquiring agency. Before making its first payment under the contract (for example, on the date of execution of the contract), pursuant to the first step in §1.5000C-2(b), Agency L determines that the contract will be for services. Under the second step, Agency L reviews Company A Inc.'s record in the System for Award Management (SAM) and determines that Company A is a corporation and is considered to be a U.S. person because Agency L's records demonstrate that Company A Inc. is a business entity treated as a corporation for tax purposes that has a TIN that does not begin with "98."

(ii) *Analysis.* Company A Inc. is a U.S. person and thus is not subject to the tax under section 5000C. Moreover, because Company A Inc. is a corporation for tax purposes that has a TIN that does not begin with "98," Agency L is able to determine that it has no obligation to withhold any amounts under section 5000C on the payment made to Company A Inc. For purposes of section 5000C, Company A Inc. could also establish that it is a U.S. person by providing a Form W-9, "Request for Taxpayer Identification Number (TIN) and Certification," to Agency L. Company A Inc. does not need to file a Section 5000C Certificate to demonstrate its eligibility for an exemption from withholding.

Example 2. Foreign national entitled to the benefit of a nondiscrimination provision of a treaty; no withholding. (i) *Facts.* Company B, a foreign contracting party and a national of Country T, provides goods to Agency M, the acquiring agency. Company B determines that it is exempt from tax under section 5000C because it is entitled to the benefit of the nondiscrimination article of a qualified income tax treaty between the United States and Country T. Company B submits a Section 5000C Certificate to Agency M when the contract is executed. Company B uses Form W-14, "Certificate of Foreign Contracting Party Receiving Federal Procurement Payments," and properly fills the relevant sections stating the name of the treaty, the specific article relied upon, and the basis on which it is entitled to the benefits of that article. Following the steps in §1.5000C-2, Agency M determines that the nondiscrimination provision of the Country T-United States income tax treaty applies to exempt Company B from the tax imposed under section 5000C. Agency M makes one lump sum payment of $50 million to Company B pursuant to the contract.

(ii) *Analysis.* Company B has no liability for tax under section 5000C because it is entitled to the benefit of a nondiscrimination article of a qualified income tax treaty. Because Company B submitted a Section 5000C Certificate meeting the requirements in § 1.5000C-2 and Agency M does not have reason to know that the submitted information is incorrect or unreliable, Agency M is not required to withhold under section 5000C. Agency M must retain the Section 5000C Certificate for at least three years pursuant to § 1.5000C-3(c)(1) from the due date for the Form 1042 (if it were required).

Example 3. Foreign treaty beneficiary does not submit Section 5000C Certificate; withholding required. (i) *Facts.* The facts are the same as in *Example 2,* except that Company B does not submit a Section 5000C Certificate to Agency M before Agency M makes the $50 million payment.

(ii) *Analysis.* Company B is not subject to tax under section 5000C, but Agency M must nevertheless withhold on the payment made to Company B because Agency M did not receive a Section 5000C Certificate from Company B in the time and manner required pursuant to § 1.5000C-2(d). Agency M must withhold $1 million (2 percent of $50 million) on the payment, and deposit that amount under the rules in § 1.5000C-3 no later than the 15th day of the month following the month in which the payment was made. Agency M must also complete Forms 1042, "Annual Withholding Tax Return for U.S. Source Income of Foreign Persons," and 1042-S, "Foreign Person's U.S. Source Income Subject to Withholding," on or before the date specified on those forms and the accompanying instructions. Agency M must furnish copies of Form 1042-S to Company B. Agency M must retain a copy of the Form 1042 and the Form 1042-S for 3 years from the due date for the Form 1042 pursuant to § 1.5000C-3(c)(1). As Company B is not liable for the tax, it may later file a claim for refund pursuant to the procedures described in chapter 65.

Example 4. Foreign contracting party partially exempt from tax under section 5000C when goods are manufactured in different countries. (i) *Facts.* Company C, a foreign contracting party, provides goods to Agency N in 2015. The terms of the contract require that payment be made to Company C by Agency N in two $5 million installments in 2015. Company C has a TIN that begins with "98" and is not entitled to relief pursuant to an international agreement with the United States, such as relief pursuant to a nondiscrimination provision of a qualified income tax treaty. Some of the goods are manufactured in Country R, which is a party to an international procurement agreement with the United States, with the remainder being manufactured in Country S, a country that is not a party to an international procurement agreement with the United States. Company C uses a reasonable allocation method based on the information available to it at the time in accordance with § 1.5000C-1(e)(3) to estimate that $3 million is the nonexempt amount that is allocated to the goods produced in Country S. Company C submits a valid and complete Section 5000C Certificate to Agency N in the time and manner required by §§ 1.5000C-1

through 1.5000C-7 that provides that the nonexempt amount is $3 million. In 2015, Agency N pays Company C in two installments pursuant to the terms of the contract.

(ii) *Analysis.* Using a reasonable allocation method to determine the estimated nonexempt amount, Company C determines that pursuant to section 5000C and §§ 1.5000C-1 through 1.5000C-7, tax of $30,000 (2 percent of the $5 million payment, or $100,000 multiplied by a fraction, the numerator of which is the estimated nonexempt amount, $3 million, and the denominator of which is the estimated total contract price, or $10 million) is imposed on each payment made to Company C. Because Company C has timely submitted a Section 5000C Certificate explaining the basis for this allocation, Agency N withholds $30,000 on each payment made to Company C. Agency N must deposit each $30,000 withholding tax under the rules in § 1.5000C-3 no later than the 15th day of the month following the month in which each payment is made. Agency N must also complete Forms 1042 and 1042-S and furnish copies of Form 1042-S to Company C. Agency N must retain a copy of the Form 1042 and the Form 1042-S for at least three years from the due date for the Form 1042 pursuant to § 1.5000C-3(c)(1). Provided that Agency N properly withholds on the nonexempt portion as required under section 5000C and §§ 1.5000C-1 through 1.5000C-7 and that Company C's estimate of the nonexempt amount is the actual nonexempt amount, Company C does not have an additional tax liability or a U.S. tax return filing obligation as a result of receiving the payments.

Example 5. Foreign contracting party liable for additional tax under Section 5000C not fully withheld upon due to errors on the Section 5000C Certificate. (i) *Facts.* The facts are the same as in *Example 4,* except that the Section 5000C Certificate submitted to Agency N by Company C erroneously provides that the estimated nonexempt amount is $1.5 million instead of $3 million. As a result, Agency N only withholds $15,000 (2 percent of the $5 million payment multiplied by a fraction (the numerator of which is the estimated nonexempt amount stated on the Section 5000C Certificate, $1.5 million, and the denominator of which is the estimated total contract price, or $10 million)) on each payment made to Company C. Agency N neither discovered nor had reason to know that the information on the Section 5000C Certificate was incorrect or unreliable. After both payments have been made and after the filing due date for Form 1042 for 2015, Company C determines that the estimated nonexempt amount should have been stated as $3 million on the Section 5000C Certificate.

(ii) *Analysis.* The tax imposed under section 5000C on Company C as a result of the receipt of specified Federal procurement payments is $60,000 and this amount has not been fully satisfied by withholding by Agency N. Accordingly, Company C must remit additional tax of $30,000 ($60,000 tax liability less $30,000 amounts already withheld by Agency N) and file its required return, a Form 1120-F, "U.S. Income Tax

Return of a Foreign Corporation," for 2015 to report this tax liability, as required by § 1.5000C-4. Company C must explain its corrected allocation method in its Form 1120-F. Company C must also attach a copy of the Form 1042-S it received from Agency N to Form 1120-F.

Example 6. Foreign contracting party submits revised Section 5000C Certificate due to change in circumstances. (i) *Facts.* The facts are the same as in *Example 4*, except that, after the first payment, Company C changes its business so that all of the goods manufactured with respect to the second payment are manufactured in Country R. Prior to the second payment, Company C submits a revised Section 5000C Certificate indicating this change in circumstance pursuant to § 1.5000C-2(d)(6).

(ii) *Analysis.* Agency N withholds $30,000 on the first payment made to Company C and does not withhold on the second payment. Company C does not have an additional tax liability or a U.S. tax return filing obligation as a result of receiving the payments. [Reg. § 1.5000C-6.]

☐ [*T.D.* 9782, 8-17-2016.]

[Reg. § 1.5000C-7]

§ 1.5000C-7. Effective/applicability date.—Section 5000C applies to specified Federal procurement payments received pursuant to contracts entered into on and after January 2, 2011. Sections 1.5000C-1 through 1.5000C-7 apply on and after November 16, 2016. Contracting parties and acquiring agencies may rely upon the rules in the regulations before such date. If a foreign contracting party fully satisfies its tax and filing obligations under section 5000C with respect to any payments received in tax years ending before November 16, 2016 on or before the later of November 16, 2016 or the due date for the foreign person's income tax return for the year in which the payment was received in a manner consistent with the final regulations, penalties will not be asserted on the foreign contracting parties with respect to those payments or returns. [Reg. § 1.5000C-7.]

☐ [*T.D.* 9782, 8-17-2016.]

Branded Prescription Drug Fee

See p. 20,601 for regulations not amended to reflect law changes

[Reg. § 51.1]

§ 51.1. Overview.—(a) The regulations in this part 51 are designated "Branded Prescription Drug Fee Regulations."

(b) The regulations in this part 51 provide guidance on the annual fee imposed on covered entities engaged in the business of manufacturing or importing branded prescription drugs by section 9008 of the Patient Protection and Affordable Care Act (ACA), Public Law 111-148 (124 Stat. 119 (2010)), as amended by section 1404 of the Health Care and Education Reconciliation Act of 2010 (HCERA), Public Law 111-152 (124 Stat. 1029 (2010)). All references in these regulations to section 9008 are references to section 9008 of the ACA, as amended by section 1404 of HCERA. Unless otherwise indicated, all other section references are to sections in the Internal Revenue Code. All references to "fee" in these regulations are references to the fee imposed by section 9008.

(c) Section 9008(b)(4) sets an applicable fee amount for each year, beginning with 2011, that will be apportioned among covered entities with aggregate branded prescription drug sales of over $5 million to government programs or pursuant to coverage under such programs. Generally, each covered entity is liable for a fee in each fee year that is based on its sales of branded prescription drugs in the sales year that corresponds to the fee year in an amount determined by the Internal Revenue Service (IRS) under the rules of this part. [Reg. § 51.1.]

☐ [*T.D.* 9684, 7-24-2014.]

[Reg. § 51.2]

§ 51.2. Explanation of terms.—(a) *In general.*—This section explains the terms used in this part for purposes of the fee imposed by section 9008 on branded prescription drugs.

(b) *Agencies.*—The term *Agencies* means—

(1) The Centers for Medicare and Medicaid Services of the Department of Health and Human Services (CMS);

(2) The Department of Veterans Affairs (VA); and

(3) The Department of Defense (DOD).

(c) *Branded prescription drug.*—(1) *In general.*—The term *branded prescription drug* means—

(i) Any prescription drug the application for which was submitted under section 505(b) of the Federal Food, Drug, and Cosmetic Act (21 U.S.C. 355(b)) (FFDCA); or

(ii) Any biological product the license for which was submitted under section 351(a) of the Public Health Service Act (42 U.S.C. 262(a)).

(2) *Prescription drug.*—The term *prescription drug* means any drug that is subject to section 503(b) of the FFDCA.

(d) *Branded prescription drug sales.*—The term *branded prescription drug sales* means sales of branded prescription drugs to any government program or pursuant to coverage under any such government program. However, the term does not include sales of orphan drugs.

(e) *Covered entity.*—(1) *In general.*—The term *covered entity* means any manufacturer or importer with gross receipts from branded prescription drug sales including—

(i) A single-person covered entity; or

(ii) A controlled group.

(2) *Single-person covered entity.*—The term *single-person covered entity* means a covered entity that is not affiliated with a controlled group.

(3) *Controlled group.*—The term *controlled group* means a group of two or more persons, including at least one person that is a covered entity, that is treated as a single employer under section 52(a), 52(b), 414(m), or 414(o).

(4) *Special rules for controlled groups.*—For purposes of paragraph (e)(3) of this section (related to controlled groups)—

(i) A foreign entity subject to tax under section 881 is included within a group under section 52(a) or 52(b); and

(ii) A person is treated as being a member of a controlled group if it is a member of the group on the end of the day on December 31st of the sales year.

(5) *Covered entity status.*—(i) *Rule.*—An entity's status as a covered entity begins in the first fee year in which the entity has branded prescription drug sales and continues each subsequent fee year until there are no remaining branded prescription drug sales for that entity to be taken into account as described in §51.5(c) or used to calculate the adjustment amount described in §51.5(e).

(ii) *Example.*—The following example illustrates the rule of paragraph (e)(5)(i) of this section:

(A) *Facts.*—Entity A is a manufacturer with gross receipts of more than $5 million from branded prescription drugs sales in 2011. Entity A does not have any gross receipts from branded prescription drug sales before or after 2011.

(B) *Analysis.*—Entity A is a covered entity beginning in 2011 because it had gross receipts from branded prescription drug sales in 2011. For the 2011 fee year, Entity A does not owe a fee because the 2011 fee is based on sales data from the 2009 sales year. For the 2012 fee year, Entity A does not owe a fee because the 2012 fee is based on sales data from the 2010 sales year. Entity A continues to be a covered entity for the 2012 fee year because its branded prescription drug sales from the 2011 sales year have not yet been taken into account as described in §51.5(c) and used to calculate the adjustment amount described in §51.5(e). For the 2013 fee year, Entity A continues to be a covered entity because a portion of its branded prescription drug sales from the 2011 sales year are taken into account as described in §51.5(c) for purposes of computing the 2013 fee. For the 2013 fee year, Entity A is also liable for the adjustment amount described in §51.5(e) for the difference between its 2012 fee computed using sales data from the 2010 sales year, which is $0, and what the 2012 fee would have been using sales data from the 2011 sales year. For the 2014

fee year, Entity A continues to be a covered entity because a portion of its branded prescription drug sales for the 2011 sales year are used to calculate the adjustment amount described in §51.5(e). Therefore, for the 2014 fee year, Entity A will receive an adjustment amount for the difference between its 2013 fee computed using sales data from the 2011 sales year, and what the 2013 fee would have been using sales data from the 2012 sales year, which is $0. After the 2014 fee year, there are no remaining branded prescription drug sales to be taken into account as described in §51.5(c) or used to calculate the adjustment amount described in §51.5(e) for Entity A. Accordingly, Entity A is not a covered entity after the 2014 fee year.

(f) *Designated entity.*—(1) *In general.*—The term *designated entity* means the person within a controlled group that is designated to act for the controlled group regarding the fee by—

(i) Filing Form 8947, "Report of Branded Prescription Drug Information";

(ii) Receiving IRS communications about the fee for the group;

(iii) Filing an error report for the group, if applicable, as described in §51.7; and

(iv) Paying the fee to the government.

(2) *Selection of designated entity.*—(i) *Controlled group selection of a designated entity.*—Except as provided in paragraph (f)(2)(ii) of this section, the controlled group may select a person as the designated entity by filing Form 8947 in accordance with the form instructions. The designated entity must state under penalties of perjury that all members of the controlled group have consented to the selection of the designated entity. The designated entity must maintain a record of all member consents. Each member of a controlled group must maintain a record of its consent to the controlled group's selection of the designated entity.

(ii) *Requirement for affiliated groups; agent for the group.*—If the controlled group, without regard to foreign corporations included under section 9008(d)(2)(B), is also an affiliated group whose common parent files a consolidated return for federal income tax purposes, the designated entity is the agent for the group (within the meaning of §1.1502-77 of this title).

(iii) *IRS selection of a designated entity.*—Except as provided in paragraph (f)(2)(ii) of this section, if a controlled group does not select a designated entity as provided in paragraph (f)(2)(i) of this section, the IRS will select a member of the controlled group as the designated entity for the controlled group. If the IRS selects the designated entity, then all members of that controlled group will be deemed to have consented to the IRS's selection of the designated entity.

(g) *Fee year.*—The term *fee year* means the calendar year in which the fee for a particular sales year must be paid to the government.

(h) *Government programs.*—The term *government programs* (collectively "Programs"), means—

(1) The Medicare Part B program;

(2) The Medicare Part D program;

(3) The Medicaid program;

(4) Any program under which branded prescription drugs are procured by the Department of Veterans Affairs;

(5) Any program under which branded prescription drugs are procured by the Department of Defense; and

(6) The TRICARE retail pharmacy program.

(i) *Manufacturer or importer.*—The term *manufacturer or importer* means the person identified in the Labeler Code of the National Drug Code (NDC) for a branded prescription drug.

(j) *NDC.*—The term *NDC* means the National Drug Code. The NDC is a unique identifier that is assigned to all drug products approved by the Food and Drug Administration (FDA), including a branded prescription drug. The Labeler Code is the first five numeric characters of the NDC or the first six numeric characters when the available five-character code combinations are exhausted.

(k) *Orphan drugs.*—(1) *In general.*—Except as provided in paragraph (k)(2) of this section, the term *orphan drug* means any branded prescription drug for which any person claimed a section 45C credit and that credit was allowed for any taxable year.

(2) *Exclusions.*—The term *orphan drug* does not include—

(i) Any drug for which there has been a final assessment or court order disallowing the full section 45C credit taken for the drug; or

(ii) Any drug for any sales year after the calendar year in which the FDA approved the drug for marketing for any indication other than the treatment of a rare disease or condition for which a section 45C credit was allowed, regardless of whether a section 45C credit was allowed for the drug before, in the same year as, or after this FDA designation.

(3) *FDA marketing approval for treatment of another rare disease or condition.*—If a drug has prior FDA marketing approval for the treatment of a rare disease or condition for which a section 45C credit was allowed, and the FDA subsequently gives the drug marketing approval for the treatment of another rare disease or condition for which another section 45C credit was also allowed, the drug retains its status as an orphan drug provided the FDA has never approved the drug for marketing for any indication other than the treatment of a rare disease or condition for which a section 45C credit was allowed.

(4) *Examples.*—The following examples illustrate the rules of this paragraph (k):

Example 1: Allowance of section 45C credit and later FDA marketing approval of drug for an indica- tion other than the treatment of a rare disease or condition. (i) *Facts.* Drug A is a branded prescription drug that was not on the market before 2011. In 2011, a covered entity claimed a section 45C credit for its qualified clinical testing expenses related to Drug A. There was no final IRS assessment or court order that disallowed the full credit for Drug A. In 2012, the FDA approved Drug A for marketing for an indication other than the treatment of the rare disease or condition for which the section 45C credit was allowed and this indication was not for another rare disease or condition for which a section 45C was allowed.

(ii) *Analysis.* In 2011 and 2012, Drug A is an orphan drug because: first, it was a branded prescription drug for which a person claimed a section 45C credit and for which that credit was allowed for a taxable year; second, there was not a final assessment or court order disallowing the full credit taken for the drug; and third, before 2012, the FDA did not approve the drug for marketing for any indication other than the treatment of a rare disease or condition for which a section 45C credit was allowed. However, Drug A is not an orphan drug for the 2013 sales year or later sales years because in 2012 the FDA approved Drug A for marketing for an indication other than the treatment of the rare disease or condition for which the section 45C credit was allowed and this indication was not for treatment of another rare disease or condition for which a section 45C credit was allowed.

Example 2: FDA marketing approval of drug for an indication other than the treatment of a rare disease or condition and later allowance of section 45C credit. (i) Facts. Drug B is a branded prescription drug that was not on the market before 2011. In 2011, FDA approved Drug B for marketing for the treatment of a rare disease or condition and also approved Drug B for marketing for an indication other than the treatment of a rare disease or condition. In 2012, a covered entity claimed a section 45C credit for its qualified clinical testing expenses related to Drug B. There was no final IRS assessment or court order that disallowed the full credit for Drug B.

(ii) *Analysis.* In 2011, Drug B is not an orphan drug because no section 45C credit was allowed and because the FDA approved Drug B for an indication other than the treatment of a rare disease or condition. In 2012, although the covered entity was allowed a section 45C credit for its qualified clinical testing expenses related to Drug B and there was no final IRS assessment or court order that disallowed the full credit, Drug B still is not an orphan drug because the FDA had approved the drug in 2011 for marketing for an indication other than the treatment of a rare disease or condition for which a section 45C credit was allowed in 2012. Thus, Drug B is not an orphan drug for the 2012 sales year or later sales years.

Example 3: Allowance of section 45C credit and subsequent allowance of section 45C credit with no intervening FDA marketing approval of drug for an indication other than the treatment of a rare disease or condition for which a section 45C credit was allowed. (i) *Facts.* Drug C is a branded prescription drug that was not on the market before 2010. In 2010, a covered entity claimed a section 45C credit for its qualified clinical testing expenses related to Drug C. In 2012, a covered entity claimed an additional section 45C credit for its qualified clinical testing expenses related to Drug C for marketing for the treatment of a rare disease or condition different than the one for which the section 45C credit was claimed in 2010. There was no final IRS assessment or court order that disallowed the full credit for Drug C in 2010 or 2012. The FDA has not approved Drug C for an indication other than the treatment of a rare disease or condition for which a section 45C was allowed.

(ii) *Analysis.* In 2010 and 2011, Drug C is an orphan prescription drug because: first, it was a branded prescription drug for which a person claimed a section 45C credit and for which that credit was allowed for a taxable year; second, there was not a final assessment or court order disallowing the full credit taken for the drug; and third, FDA had not approved the drug for marketing for any indication other than the treatment of a rare disease or condition for which a section 45C credit was allowed. In 2012, Drug C retains its orphan drug status because another section 45C credit was allowed and the FDA did not approve Drug C for marketing for any indication other than- the treatment of another rare disease or condition for which a section 45C credit was allowed. Thus, Drug C is an orphan drug for the 2013 sales year.

(l) *Sales taken into account.*—The term *sales taken into account* means branded prescription drug sales after application of the percentage adjustment table in section 9008(b)(2) (relating to annual sales less than $400,000,001). See §51.5(a)(3).

(m) *Sales year.*—The term *sales year* means the second calendar year preceding the fee year. Thus, for example, for the fee year of 2014, the sales year is 2012. [Reg. §51.2.]

☐ [T.D. 9684, 7-24-2014. *Amended by* T.D. 9823, 7-24-2017.]

[Reg. §51.3]

§51.3. Information requested from covered entities.—(a) *In general.*—Annually, each covered entity may submit a completed Form 8947, "Report of Branded Prescription Drug Information," in accordance with the instructions for the form. Generally, the form solicits information from covered entities on NDCs, orphan drugs, designated entities, rebates, and other information specified by the form or its instructions.

(b) *Due date.*—Form 8947 must be filed by the date prescribed in guidance in the Internal Revenue Bulletin. [Reg. §51.3.]

☐ [T.D. 9684, 7-24-2014.]

[Reg. §51.4]

§51.4. Information provided by the Agencies.—(a) *In general.*—For each sales year, the IRS will compile a list of branded prescription drugs by NDC using the data submitted on Forms 8947 and in error reports submitted as part of the dispute resolution process (described in §51.7) and, after applying appropriate due diligence, will provide this list to the Agencies. The Agencies will provide data to the IRS on branded prescription drug sales that occurred during the sales year by Program and NDC. The Agencies will provide data for use in preparing the preliminary fee calculation (described in §§51.5 and 51.6) and may revise or supplement that data following review of error reports submitted as part of the dispute resolution process. The calculation methodology for calculating the sales amounts for each Program, including any reasonable estimation techniques and assumptions that the Agencies expect to use, is described in this section.

(b) *Medicare Part D.*—(1) *In general.*—CMS will determine branded prescription drug sales under Medicare Part D by aggregating the ingredient cost reported in the "Ingredient Cost Paid" field on the Prescription Drug Event (PDE) records at the NDC level, reduced by discounts, rebates, and other price concessions provided by the covered entity, for each sales year. CMS will only include PDE data that Part D sponsors have submitted by the PDE submission deadline (within 6 months after the end of the sales year) and that CMS has approved for inclusion in the Part D payment reconciliation.

(2) *Discounts, rebates, and other price concessions.*—(i) *In general.*—For purposes of paragraph (b)(1) of this section, the term *discounts, rebates, and other price concessions* means:

(A) Any direct and indirect remuneration (DIR) (within the meaning of paragraph (b)(2)(ii) of this section), which includes any DIR reported on the PDE records at the 3 point of sale and any DIR reported on a Detailed DIR Report (within the meaning of a paragraph (b)(2)(iii) of this section); and

(B) Any coverage gap discount amount (within the meaning of paragraph (b)(2)(iv) of this section).

(ii) *Direct and indirect remuneration.*—For purposes of paragraph (b)(2)(i)(A) of this section, the term *direct and indirect remuneration* (DIR) has the same meaning as found in the definition of *actually paid* in 42 CFR 423.308.

(iii) *Detailed DIR Report.*—For purposes of paragraph (b)(2)(i)(A) of this section, the term *Detailed DIR Report* means the report containing any DIR (within the meaning of paragraph (b)(2)(ii) of this section) that is collected yearly from Part D sponsors at the NDC level.

(iv) *Coverage gap discount amount.*—For purposes of paragraph (b)(2)(i)(B) of this section, the term *coverage gap discount amount* means a 50-percent manufactured-paid discount on certain drugs under the Coverage Gap Discount Program described in section 1860D-14A of the Social Security Act.

(c) *Medicare Part B.*—(1) *In general.*—CMS will determine branded prescription drug sales under Medicare Part B using the following two data sources:

(i) CMS will use data reported by manufacturers pursuant to section 1847A(c) of the Social Security Act to calculate the annual weighted average sales price (ASP) for each Healthcare Common Procedure Coding System (HCPCS) code for the sales year.

(ii) CMS will use the Medicare Part B National Summary Data File located at http://www.cms.gov/NonIdentifiableDataFiles/03_PartBNationalSummaryDataFile.asp to obtain the number of allowed billing units per HCPCS code for claims incurred during the sales year.

(2) *Calculation.*—(i) *In general.*—Using the data described in paragraph (c)(1) of this section, CMS will determine branded prescription drugs sales under Medicare Part B as described in paragraphs (c)(3), (4), and (5) of this section. CMS reports sales amounts per HCPCS billing code, not per NDC. Therefore, a covered entity's total Part B sales amounts for all NDCs in a given HCPCS billing code appears under only one NDC in each HCPCS billing code and the covered entity's remaining NDCs in the HCPCS billing code are listed with a sales amount of zero.

(ii) *Example of a Part B sales report*:

HCPCS	NDC	Part B amount
J9876	12345-6789-01	$789,000
	12345-6789-02	0
	12345-6789-03	0
	12345-6800-80	0
	12345-6800-90	0

(3) *HCPCS code; single entity.*—For each HCPCS code consisting solely and exclusively of branded prescription drugs (as identified by their respective NDCs) manufactured by a single entity, CMS will multiply the annual weighted ASP by the total number of allowed billing units paid during the sales year to determine the total sales for all NDCs associated with the HCPCS code attributed to Medicare Part B.

(4) *HCPCS code; multiple manufacturers and/or multiple drugs.*—(i) *Step one.*—For each HCPCS code consisting of a mixture of branded prescription drugs made by different manufacturers and/or a mixture of branded prescription and generic drugs, CMS will determine—

(A) The annual weighted ASP for the HCPCS code;

(B) The total number of allowed billing units paid by Medicare Part B for each HCPCS code during the sales year;

(C) The names of the entities engaged in manufacturing each NDC assigned to the HCPCS code; and

(D) Those entities (if any) identified in paragraph (c)(4)(i)(C) of this section that are manufacturing branded prescription drugs assigned to the HCPCS code.

(ii) *Step two.*—Using the information from paragraph (c)(4)(i) of this section, CMS will then do the following:

(A) Calculate the proportion of sales, expressed as a percentage, attributed to each NDC assigned to the HCPCS code by determining the percentage of total sales reported to CMS by each manufacturer of NDC(s) that are assigned to the HCPCS code. For example, if HCPCS code JXXXX contains three drugs with a total of $310,000 sales reported by manufacturers to CMS for the sales year, and $100,000 was reported for Drug A, $200,000 was reported for Drug B, and $10,000 was reported for Drug C, the proportion of sales attributed to each NDC will be 32.26 percent for Drug A, 64.52 percent for Drug B, and 3.22 percent for Drug C; and

(B) For each NDC, multiply the product of the annual weighted ASP and the total allowed billing units paid by Medicare Part B for the HCPCS code by the proportion of sales calculated in paragraph (c)(4)(ii)(A) of this section to determine the sales reportable to the IRS (that is, percentage x (annual weighted ASP x allowed units) = total sales reported to IRS for the NDC). The sales for each manufacturer's NDCs assigned to a HCPCS code are summed and the total sales for each manufacturer's NDCs in a HCPCS code will be reported to the IRS.

(5) *HCPCS code; unable to establish a reliable proportion of sales.*—If CMS is unable to establish a reliable proportion of sales attributable to each NDC assigned to the HCPCS code using the method described in paragraph (c)(4)(ii)(A) of this section, CMS will use Medicare Part D utilization percentages in lieu of the proportion of sales determined under paragraph (c)(4)(ii)(A) of this section to perform the calculation described in paragraph (c)(4)(ii)(B) of this section.

(d) *Medicaid.*—(1) CMS will determine the branded prescription drug sales for Medicaid as the per-unit Average Manufacturer Price (AMP) less the Unit Rebate Amounts (URA) that CMS calculates based on manufacturer-reported pricing data multiplied by the number of units reported billed by states to manufacturers. This data will be based on the data reported to CMS for the sales year by covered entities and the states for drugs paid for by the states in the Medicaid Drug Rebate Program for the sales year. The data will include all branded prescription drug units for which the states bill rebates to covered entities under the Medicaid Drug Rebate Program. This program includes, but is not limited to, units paid for under various health care plans such as fee for service, managed care organizations, and drugs administered in a non-retail setting such as drugs administered in a physician's office, clinic, hospital or other setting. The Medicaid Drug Rebate Program's calculated branded prescription drug fee does not include state-only pharmaceutical program sales or rebates.

(2) For any covered entity identified in the first five (or six) digits of an NDC during any of the four quarters of a sales year, CMS will use the following methodology to derive the sales figures that account for third-party payers, such as Medicare Part B:

(i) Report total dollars per NDC for AMP minus URA multiplied by the units reported by a state or states.

(ii) Determine the percentage of the total amount reimbursed that is the Medicaid amount of that reimbursement. For example, if the total amount reimbursed is $100,000, and the Medicaid amount reimbursed is $20,000, then the percentage is 20 percent.

(iii) Multiply the percentage of the Medicaid amount of that reimbursement (in the example in paragraph (d)(2)(ii) of this section, 20 percent) by the dollar figure derived from paragraph (d)(2)(i) of this section (AMP minus URA multiplied by units) to get the new adjusted sales dollar totals.

(e) *Department of Veterans Affairs.*—VA will determine branded prescription drug sales to VA by providing, by NDC, the total amount paid (net of refunds and rebates, when they are associated with a specific NDC) for each branded prescription drug procured by VA for its beneficiaries during the sales year. For this purpose, a drug is procured on the invoice (billing) date. The basis of this information will be national procurement data reported during the sales year by VA's Pharmaceutical Prime Vendor to the VA Pharmacy Benefits Management Service and National Acquisition Center. VA sales data includes the Industrial Funding Fee and the Cost Recovery Fee because these amounts are part of the price VA pays to its Pharmaceutical Prime Vendor to procure a drug.

(f) *Department of Defense.*—DOD will determine branded prescription drug sales to DOD (for DOD programs other than the TRICARE retail pharmacy program) by providing, by Labeler Code, the manufacturer's name, the NDC, brand name, and the amount paid (net of rebates and or refunds) for each branded prescription drug procured by DOD (for DOD programs other than the TRICARE retail pharmacy program) during the sales year. For DOD programs other than the TRICARE retail pharmacy program, a drug is procured based upon the date it was ordered. DOD includes the Industrial Funding Fee and the Cost Recovery Fee in its drug sales data because these amounts are part of the price DOD pays to procure a drug.

(g) *TRICARE.*—DOD will determine branded prescription drug sales to DOD for the TRICARE retail pharmacy program by providing, by Labeler Code, the manufacturer's name, the NDC, brand name, and the amount paid (net of rebates or refunds) for each branded prescription drug procured by DOD through the TRICARE retail pharmacy program during the sales year. For the TRICARE retail pharmacy program, a drug is procured based upon the date it was dispensed. The amount paid is based on the submitted ingredient cost paid, aggregated by NDC, for eligible TRICARE retail pharmacy claims submitted during the program year, minus any refunds or rebates for the corresponding claims. [Reg. §51.4.]

☐ [T.D. 9684, 7-24-2014 (*corrected* 9-25-2014).]

[Reg. §51.5]

§51.5. Fee calculation.—(a) *Fee components.*— (1) *In general.*—For every fee year, the IRS will calculate a covered entity's total fee as described in this section. The IRS will determine a covered entity's total fee by applying, if applicable, the adjustment amount described in paragraph (e) of this section to the entity's allocated fee described in paragraph (d) of this section.

(2) *Calculation of branded prescription drug sales.*—Each covered entity's allocated fee for any fee year is equal to an amount that bears the same ratio to the applicable amount as the covered entity's branded prescription drug sales taken into account during the sales year bears to the aggregate branded prescription drug sales of all covered entities taken into account during the sales year.

(3) *Applicable amount.*—The applicable amounts for fee years are—

Fee year	Applicable amount
2011	$2,500,000,000
2012	$2,800,000,000
2013	$2,800,000,000
2014	$3,000,000,000
2015	$3,000,000,000
2016	$3,000,000,000

Fee year	Applicable amount
2017	$4,000,000,000
2018	$4,100,000,000
2019 and thereafter	$2,800,000,000

(4) *Sales taken into account.*—A covered entity's branded prescription drug sales taken into account during any calendar year are as follows:

Covered entity's branded prescription drug sales during the calendar year that are:	Percentage of branded prescription drug sales taken into account is
Not more than $5,000,000	0 percent
More than $5,000,000 but not more than $125,000,000	10 percent
More than $125,000,000 but not more than $225,000,000	40 percent
More than $225,000,000 but not more than $400,000,000	75 percent
More than $400,000,000	100 percent

(b) *Determination of branded prescription drug sales.*—The IRS will compile each covered entity's branded prescription drug sales for each Program by NDC. Each NDC will be attributed to the covered entity identified in the Labeler Code as of the end of the day on December 31st of the sales year. For a covered entity that is a controlled group, this includes all NDCs in which a member of the covered entity is identified. For this purpose, the IRS may revise the list of NDCs as a result of information received in the dispute resolution process, and the data the IRS uses to produce the final fee calculation will include any revisions provided by the Agencies at the completion of the dispute resolution process. Each covered entity's branded prescription drug sales will be reduced by its Medicaid state supplemental rebate amounts in the following manner. If CMS has Medicaid state supplemental rebate information for a sales year, CMS will report to the IRS branded prescription drug sales for Medicaid net of Medicaid state supplemental rebates. If CMS does not have complete Medicaid state supplemental rebate information for a sales year, the IRS will reduce the branded prescription drug sales that CMS reported for Medicaid by Medicaid state supplemental rebates reported by the covered entities on Form 8947.

(c) *Determination of sales taken into account.*—(1) For each sales year and for each covered entity, the IRS will calculate sales taken into account. The resulting number is the numerator of the ratio described in paragraph (d)(1) of this section.

(2) For each sales year, the IRS will calculate the aggregate branded prescription drug sales taken into account for all covered entities. The resulting number is the denominator of the ratio described in paragraph (d)(2) of this section.

(d) *Allocated fee calculation.*—For each covered entity for each fee year, the IRS will calculate the entity's allocated fee by multiplying the applicable amount from paragraph (a)(2) of this section by a fraction—

(1) The numerator of which is the covered entity's branded prescription drug sales taken into account during the sales year (described in paragraph (c)(1) of this section); and

(2) The denominator of which is the aggregate branded prescription drug sales taken into account for all covered entities during the same year (described in paragraph (c)(2) of this section).

(e) *Adjustment amount.*—(1) *In general.*—In addition to the allocated fee computed under paragraph (d) of this section, the IRS will also automatically calculate for each covered entity an adjustment amount. An adjustment amount reflects the difference between the allocated fee determined for the covered entity in the immediately preceding fee year, using data from the second calendar year preceding that fee year, and what the allocated fee would have been for that entity for the immediately preceding fee year using data from the calendar year immediately preceding that fee year. For example, for 2014, the adjustment amount for a covered entity will be the difference between the entity's 2013 allocated fee, using 2011 data, and what the 2013 allocated fee would have been using 2012 data. Although the adjustment reflects a revision of the prior year's fee based on data from the year immediately preceding the prior fee year, the adjustment is only taken into account by adding it to or subtracting it from the allocated fee computed under paragraph (d) of this section for the current fee year to arrive at the total fee for the current fee year. An adjustment amount is treated as a component of the current year's fee. For purposes of section 6601, any increase in the allocated fee computed under paragraph (d) of this section for the current fee year resulting from any adjustment amount, along with the remainder of the fee, is treated as a fee liability due on the due date for the current year's fee. For purposes of sections 6511 and 6611, any adjustment amount that decreases the allocated fee computed under paragraph (d) of this section for the current fee year is treated as a payment towards the current fee liability made on the due date of the current fee year.

(2) *Amounts paid to a covered entity because of an adjustment amount.*—If a covered entity's adjustment amount reduces the fee computed under paragraph (d) of this section below zero and results in an amount due to the covered entity for the fee year, the IRS will pay this amount due to the covered entity. A covered entity does not file Form 843, Claim for Refund and Request for Abatement, to receive this amount owed to a covered entity. [Reg. §51.5.]

☐ [*T.D.* 9684, 7-24-2014.]

[Reg. §51.6]

§51.6. Notice of preliminary fee calculation.—(a) *Content of notice.*—For each sales year, the IRS will make a preliminary calculation of the fee for each covered entity as described in §51.5. The IRS will notify each covered entity of its preliminary fee calculation for that sales year. The notification to a covered entity of its preliminary fee calculation will include—

(1) The covered entity's allocated fee;

(2) The covered entity's branded prescription drug sales, by NDC, by Program;

(3) The covered entity's branded prescription drug sales taken into account after application of §51.5(a)(4);

(4) The aggregate branded prescription drug sales taken into account for all covered entities;

(5) The covered entity's adjustment amount calculated as described in §51.5(e); and

(6) A reference to the fee dispute resolution procedures set forth in guidance published in the Internal Revenue Bulletin.

(b) *Time of notice.*—The IRS will send each covered entity notice of its preliminary fee calculation by the date prescribed in guidance published in the Internal Revenue Bulletin. [Reg. §51.6.]

☐ [*T.D.* 9684, 7-24-2014.]

[Reg. §51.7]

§51.7. Dispute resolution process.—(a) *In general.*—Upon receipt of its preliminary fee calculation, each covered entity will have an opportunity to dispute this calculation by submitting to the IRS an error report as described in this section. The IRS will provide its final determination with respect to error reports no later than the time the IRS provides a covered entity with a final fee calculation.

(b) *Error report information.*—To assert that there have been one or more errors in the drug sales data reported by a Program, the mathematical calculation of the fee, the rebate data, the listing of an NDC for an orphan drug, or any other error, a covered entity must submit an error report with each asserted error reported on a separate line. The report must include the following information—

(1) Entity name, address, and Employer Identification Number (EIN) as previously reported on the Form 8947;

(2) The name, telephone number, fax number, and e-mail address (if available) of one or more employees or representatives of the entity with whom the IRS may discuss the claimed errors. If the representative is not an employee of the covered entity who is authorized under section 6103 or designated on Form 8947 to discuss the information reported on Form 8947 with the IRS, a Form 2848, "Power of Attorney and Declaration of Representative," must be filed with the error report;

(3) For an error in the drug sales data reported by a Program, the name of the Program that reported the data, the NDC, the specific amount of sales data disputed, the proposed corrected amount, an explanation of why the Agency should use the proposed corrected data instead, and documentation of any Program drug sales data or other information used to establish the existence of any errors.

(4) For a mathematical calculation error, the specific calculation element(s) that the entity disputes and its proposed corrected calculation;

(5) For a rebate data error, the NDC for the drug to which it relates; a discussion of whether the data used in the preliminary fee calculation matches previously reported Form 8947 data on rebates; and, if the data used in the preliminary fee calculation does match the Form 8947 data, an explanation of why the Form 8947 data was erroneous and why the IRS should use the proposed corrected data instead;

(6) For the listing of an NDC for an orphan drug, the name and NDC of the orphan drug; a discussion of whether the data used in the preliminary fee calculation matches previously reported Form 8947 data on orphan drugs; and, if the data used in the preliminary fee calculation does match the Form 8947 data, an explanation of why the Form 8947 data was erroneous and why the IRS should use the proposed corrected data instead;

(7) For any other asserted error, an explanation of the nature of the error, how the error affects the fee calculation, an explanation of how the entity established that an error occurred, the proposed correction to the error, and an explanation of why the IRS or Agency should use the proposed corrected data instead;

(8) If an entity is using data to establish the existence of an error and that data was not reported on Form 8947 or contained in the notification of the preliminary fee calculation, a description of what the data is, how the entity acquired the data, and who maintains it; and

(9) Documentation of any rebate and orphan drug data, or other information used to establish the existence of any errors.

(c) *Form, manner, and timing of submission.*—Each covered entity must submit its error report(s) in the form and manner that is prescribed in guidance published in the Internal Revenue Bulletin. This guidance will also prescribe the date by which each covered entity must submit its report(s).

(d) *Finality.*—A covered entity must assert any basis for contesting its preliminary fee calculation during the dispute resolution period. In the interest of providing finality to the fee calculation process, the IRS will not accept an error report after the end of the dispute resolution period or alter the final fee calculation on the basis of information provided after the end of the dispute resolution period. [Reg. §51.7.]

☐ [*T.D.* 9684, 7-24-2014.]

[Reg. §51.8]

§51.8. Notification and payment of fee.—
(a) *Notification of final fee calculation.*—No later than August 31st of each fee year, the IRS will send each covered entity its final fee calculation for that year. In any fee year, the IRS will base its final fee calculation on data provided to it by the Agencies as adjusted pursuant to the dispute resolution process. The notification to a covered entity of its final fee calculation will include—

(1) The covered entity's allocated fee;

(2) The covered entity's adjustment amount calculated as described in §51.5;

(3) The covered entity's branded prescription drug sales, by NDC, by Program;

(4) The covered entity's branded prescription drug sales taken into account after application of §51.5(a)(4);

(5) The aggregate branded prescription drug sales taken into account for all covered entities; and

(6) The final determination with respect to error reports.

(b) *Differences in preliminary fee calculation and final fee calculation.*—A covered entity's final fee calculation may differ from the covered entity's preliminary fee calculation because of changes made pursuant to the dispute resolution process described in §51.7. Even if a covered entity did not file an error report described in §51.7, a covered entity's final fee may differ from a covered entity's preliminary fee because of a change in data reported by the Agencies after resolution of error reports, including a change in the aggregate prescription drug sales figure. A change in aggregate prescription drug sales data can affect each covered entity's fee because each covered entity's fee is a fraction of the aggregate fee collected from all covered entities. A covered entity's final fee may also differ from its preliminary fee calculation because the data used in the preliminary fee calculation may have contained inaccurate branded prescription drug sales information that was corrected or updated at the conclusion of the dispute resolution process.

(c) *Payment of final fee.*—Each covered entity must pay its final fee by September 30th of the fee year. For a controlled group, the payment

must be made using the designated entity's EIN as reported on Form 8947. The fee must be paid by electronic funds transfer as required by §51.6302-1. There is no tax return to be filed for the fee.

(d) *Joint and several liability.*—In the case of a controlled group that is liable for the fee, all members of the controlled group are jointly and severally liable for the fee. Accordingly, if a controlled group's fee is not paid, the IRS will separately assess each member of the group for the full amount of the controlled group's fee. [Reg. §51.8.]

☐ [*T.D.* 9684, 7-24-2014.]

[Reg. §51.9]

§51.9. Tax treatment of fee.—(a) *Treatment as an excise tax.*—The fee imposed by section 9008 is treated as an excise tax for purposes of subtitle F of the Internal Revenue Code (Code) (sections 6001-7874). Thus, references in subtitle F to "taxes imposed by this title," "internal revenue tax," and similar references, are also references to the fee imposed by section 9008. For example, the fee imposed by section 9008 is assessed (section 6201), collected (sections 6301, 6321, and 6331), enforced (section 7402 and 7403), subject to examination and summons (section 7602), and subject to confidentiality rules (section 6103) in the same manner as taxes imposed by the Code.

(b) *Deficiency procedures.*—The deficiency procedures of sections 6211-6216 do not apply to the fee imposed by section 9008.

(c) *Limitation on assessment.*—The IRS must assess the amount of the fee for any fee year within three years of September 30th of that fee year.

(d) *Application of section 275.*—The fee is treated as a tax described in section 275(a)(6) (relating to taxes for which no deduction is allowed). [Reg. §51.9.]

☐ [*T.D.* 9684, 7-24-2014.]

[Reg. §51.10]

§51.10. Refund claims.—Any claim for a refund of the fee must be made by the person that paid the fee to the government and must be made on Form 843, "Claim for Refund and Request for Abatement," in accordance with the instructions for that form. [Reg. §51.10.]

☐ [*T.D.* 9684, 7-24-2014.]

[Reg. §51.11]

§51.11. Applicability date.—(a) Except as otherwise provided in this section, §§51.1 through 51.10 apply on and after July 28, 2014.

(b) Section 51.2(e)(3) applies on and after July 24, 2017. [Reg. §51.11.]

☐ [*T.D.* 9684, 7-24-2014. *Amended by T.D.* 9823, 7-24-2017.]

Health Insurance Providers Fee

See p. 20,601 for regulations not amended to reflect law changes

[Reg. § 57.1]

§ 57.1. Overview.—(a) The regulations in this part are designated "Health Insurance Providers Fee Regulations."

(b) The regulations in this part provide guidance on the annual fee imposed on covered entities engaged in the business of providing health insurance by section 9010 of the Patient Protection and Affordable Care Act (PPACA), Public Law 111-148 (124 Stat. 119 (2010)), as amended by section 10905 of PPACA, and as further amended by section 1406 of the Health Care and Education Reconciliation Act of 2010, Public Law 111-152 (124 Stat. 1029 (2010)) (collectively, the Affordable Care Act or ACA). All references to section 9010 in this part 57 are references to section 9010 of the ACA. Unless otherwise indicated, all other references to subtitles, chapters, subchapters, and sections are references to subtitles, chapters, subchapters and sections in the Internal Revenue Code and the related regulations.

(c) Section 9010(e)(1) sets an applicable fee amount for each year, beginning with 2014, that will be apportioned among covered entities with aggregate net premiums written over $25 million for health insurance for United States health risks. Generally, each covered entity is liable for a fee in each fee year that is based on its net premiums written during the data year in an amount determined by the Internal Revenue Service (IRS) under the rules of this part. [Reg. § 57.1.]

☐ [*T.D.* 9643, 11-26-2013.]

[Reg. § 57.2]

§ 57.2. Explanation of terms.—(a) *In general.*—This section explains the terms used in this part 57 for purposes of the fee.

(b) *Covered entity.*—(1) *In general.*—Except as provided in paragraph (b)(2) of this section, the term *covered entity* means any entity with net premiums written for health insurance for United States health risks in the fee year if the entity is—

(i) A health insurance issuer within the meaning of section 9832(b)(2), defined in section 9832(b)(2) as an insurance company, insurance service, or insurance organization that is licensed to engage in the business of insurance in a State and that is subject to State law that regulates insurance (within the meaning of section 514(b)(2) of the Employee Retirement Income Security Act of 1974 (ERISA));

(ii) A health maintenance organization within the meaning of section 9832(b)(3), defined in section 9832(b)(3) as—

(A) A Federally qualified health maintenance organization (as defined in section 1301(a) of the Public Health Service Act);

(B) An organization recognized under State law as a health maintenance organization; or

(C) A similar organization regulated under State law for solvency in the same manner and to the same extent as such a health maintenance organization;

(iii) An insurance company subject to tax under part I or II of subchapter L, or that would be subject to tax under part I or II of subchapter L but for the entity being exempt from tax under section 501(a);

(iv) An entity that provides health insurance under Medicare Advantage, Medicare Part D, or Medicaid; or

(v) A multiple employer welfare arrangement (MEWA), within the meaning of section 3(40) of ERISA, to the extent not fully insured, provided that for this purpose a covered entity does not include a MEWA that with respect to the plan year ending with or within the section 9010 data year satisfies the requirements for exemption from reporting under 29 CFR 2520.101-2(c)(2)(ii)(A), (B), or (C).

(2) *Exclusions.*—(i) *Self-insured employer.*—The term *covered entity* does not include any entity (including a voluntary employees' beneficiary association under section 501(c)(9) (VEBA)) that is part of a self-insured employer plan to the extent that such entity self-insures its employees' health risks. The term *self-insured employer* means an employer that sponsors a self-insured medical reimbursement plan within the meaning of § 1.105-11(b)(1)(i) of this chapter. Self-insured medical reimbursement plans include plans that do not involve shifting risk to an unrelated third party as described in § 1.105-11(b)(1)(ii) of this chapter. A self-insured medical reimbursement plan may use an insurance company or other third party to provide administrative or bookkeeping functions. For purposes of this section, the term *self-insured employer* does not include a MEWA.

(ii) *Governmental entity.*—The term *covered entity* does not include any governmental entity. For this purpose, the term *governmental entity* means—

(A) The government of the United States;

(B) Any State or a political subdivision thereof (as defined for purposes of section 103) including, for example, a State health department or a State insurance commission;

(C) Any Indian tribal government (as defined in section 7701(a)(40)) or a subdivision thereof (determined in accordance with section 7871(d)); or

(D) Any agency or instrumentality of any of the foregoing.

(iii) *Certain nonprofit corporations.*—The term *covered entity* does not include any entity—

(A) That is incorporated as a nonprofit corporation under a State law;

(B) No part of the net earnings of which inures to the benefit of any private shareholder or individual (within the meaning of §§ 1.501(a)-1(c) and 1.501(c)(3)-1(c)(2) of this chapter);

(C) No substantial part of the activities of which is carrying on propaganda, or otherwise attempting, to influence legislation (within the meaning of § 1.501(c)(3)-1(c)(3)(ii) of this chapter) (or which is described in section 501(h)(3) and is not denied exemption under section 501(a) by reason of section 501(h));

(D) That does not participate in, or intervene in (including the publishing or distributing of statements), any political campaign on behalf of (or in opposition to) any candidate for public office (within the meaning of § 1.501(c)(3)-1(c)(3)(iii) of this chapter); and

(E) More than 80 percent of the gross revenues of which is received from government programs that target low-income, elderly, or disabled populations under titles XVIII, XIX, and XXI of the Social Security Act.

(iv) *Certain voluntary employees' beneficiary associations (VEBAs).*—The term *covered entity* does not include any entity that is described in section 501(c)(9) that is established by an entity (other than by an employer or employers) for purposes of providing health care benefits. This exclusion applies to a VEBA that is established by a union or established pursuant to a collective bargaining agreement and having a joint board of trustees (such as in the case of a multiemployer plan within the meaning of section 3(37) of ERISA or a single-employer plan described in section 302(c)(5) of the Labor Management Relations Act, 29 U.S.C. 186(c)(5)). This exclusion does not apply to a MEWA.

(3) *Application of exclusions.*—(i) *Test year.*—An entity qualifies for an exclusion described in paragraphs (b)(2)(i) through (iv) of this section if it so qualifies in its test year. The term *test year* means either the entire data year or the entire fee year.

(ii) *Consistency rule.*—For purposes of paragraph (b)(3)(i) of this section, an entity must use the same test year as it used in its first fee year beginning after December 31, 2014, and in each subsequent fee year. Thus, for example, if an entity used the 2014 data year as its test year for the 2015 fee year, that entity must use the data year as its test year for each subsequent fee year.

(iii) *Special rule for fee year as test year.*—For purposes of paragraph (b)(3) of this section, any entity that uses the fee year as its test year but ultimately does not qualify for an exclusion described in paragraphs (b)(2)(i) through (iv) of this section for that entire fee year must use the

data year as its test year for each subsequent fee year.

(4) *State.*—Solely for purposes of paragraph (b) of this section, the term *State* means any of the 50 States, the District of Columbia, or any of the possessions of the United States, including American Samoa, Guam, the Northern Mariana Islands, Puerto Rico, and the Virgin Islands.

(c) *Controlled groups.*—(1) *In general.*—The term *controlled group* means a group of two or more persons, including at least one person that is a covered entity, that is treated as a single employer under section 52(a), 52(b), 414(m), or 414(o).

(2) *Treatment of controlled group.*—A controlled group (as defined in paragraph (c)(1) of this section) is treated as a single covered entity for purposes of the fee.

(3) *Special rules.*—For purposes of paragraph (c)(1) of this section (related to controlled groups)—

(i) A foreign entity subject to tax under section 881 is included within a controlled group under section 52(a) or (b); and

(ii) A person is treated as being a member of the controlled group if it is a member of the group at the end of the day on December 31st of the data year. However, a person's net premiums written are included in net premiums written for the controlled group only if the person would qualify as a covered entity in the fee year if the person were not a member of the controlled group.

(d) *Data year.*—The term *data year* means the calendar year immediately before the fee year. Thus, for example, 2013 is the data year for fee year 2014.

(e) *Designated entity.*—(1) *In general.*—The term *designated entity* means the person within a controlled group that is designated to act on behalf of the controlled group regarding the fee with respect to—

(i) Filing Form 8963, "Report of Health Insurance Provider Information";

(ii) Receiving IRS communications about the fee for the group;

(iii) Filing a corrected Form 8963 for the group, if applicable, as described in § 57.6; and

(iv) Paying the fee for the group to the government.

(2) *Selection of designated entity.*—(i) *In general.*—Except as provided in paragraph (e)(2)(ii) of this section, each controlled group must select a designated entity by having that entity file the Form 8963 in accordance with the form instructions. The designated entity must state under penalties of perjury that all persons that provide health insurance for United States health risks that are members of the group have consented to the selection of the designated entity. Each member of a controlled group must maintain a record of its consent to the controlled group's selection

of the designated entity. The designated entity must maintain a record of all member consents.

(ii) *Requirement for consolidated groups; common parent.*—If a controlled group, without regard to foreign corporations included under section 9010(c)(3)(B), is also an affiliated group the common parent of which files a consolidated return for Federal income tax purposes, the designated entity is the agent for the group (within the meaning of § 1.1502-77 of this chapter) for the data year.

(iii) *Failure to select a designated entity.*— Excepted as provided in paragraph (e)(2)(ii) of this section, if a controlled group fails to select a designated entity as provided in paragraph (e)(2)(i) of this section, then the IRS will select a member of the controlled group to be the designated entity. If the IRS selects the designated entity, then all members of the controlled group that provide health insurance for a United States health risk will be deemed to have consented to the IRS's selection of the designated entity.

(f) *Fee.*—The term *fee* means the fee imposed by section 9010 on each covered entity engaged in the business of providing health insurance.

(g) *Fee year.*—The term *fee year* means the calendar year in which the fee must be paid to the government. The first fee year is 2014.

(h) *Health insurance.*—(1) *In general.*—Except as provided in paragraph (h)(2) of this section, the term *health insurance* generally has the same meaning as the term *health insurance coverage* in section 9832(b)(1)(A), defined to mean benefits consisting of medical care (provided directly, through insurance or reimbursement, or otherwise) under any hospital or medical service policy or certificate, hospital or medical service plan contract, or health maintenance organization contract, when these benefits are offered by an entity that is one of the types of entities described in paragraph (b)(1)(i) through (b)(1)(v) of this section. The term *health insurance* includes limited scope dental and vision benefits under section 9832(c)(2)(A) and retiree-only health insurance.

(2) *Exclusions.*—The term *health insurance* does not include—

(i) Coverage only for accident, or disability income insurance, or any combination thereof, within the meaning of section 9832(c)(1)(A);

(ii) Coverage issued as a supplement to liability insurance within the meaning of section 9832(c)(1)(B);

(iii) Liability insurance, including general liability insurance and automobile liability insurance, within the meaning of section 9832(c)(1)(C);

(iv) Workers' compensation or similar insurance within the meaning of section 9832(c)(1)(D);

(v) Automobile medical payment insurance within the meaning of section 9832(c)(1)(E);

(vi) Credit-only insurance within the meaning of section 9832(c)(1)(F);

(vii) Coverage for on-site medical clinics within the meaning of section 9832(c)(1)(G);

(viii) Other insurance coverage that is similar to the insurance coverage in paragraph (h)(2)(i) through (vii) of this section under which benefits for medical care are secondary or incidental to other insurance benefits, within the meaning of section 9832(c)(1)(H), to the extent such insurance coverage is specified in regulations under section 9832(c)(1)(H);

(ix) Benefits for long-term care, nursing home care, home health care, community-based care, or any combination thereof, within the meaning of section 9832(c)(2)(B), and such other similar, limited benefits to the extent such benefits are specified in regulations under section 9832(c)(2)(C);

(x) Coverage only for a specified disease or illness within the meaning of section 9832(c)(3)(A);

(xi) Hospital indemnity or other fixed indemnity insurance within the meaning of section 9832(c)(3)(B);

(xii) Medicare supplemental health insurance (as defined under section 1882(g)(1) of the Social Security Act), coverage supplemental to the coverage provided under chapter 55 of title 10, United States Code, and similar supplemental coverage provided to coverage under a group health plan, within the meaning of section 9832(c)(4);

(xiii) Coverage under an employee assistance plan, a disease management plan, or a wellness plan, if the benefits provided under the plan constitute excepted benefits under section 9832(c)(2) (or do not otherwise provide benefits consisting of health insurance under paragraph (h)(1) of this section);

(xiv) Student administrative health fee arrangements, as defined in paragraph (h)(3);

(xv) Travel insurance, as defined in paragraph (h)(4) of this section; or

(xvi) Indemnity reinsurance, as defined in paragraph (h)(5)(i) of this section.

(3) *Student administrative health fee arrangement.*—For purposes of paragraph (h)(2)(xiv) of this section, the term *student administrative health fee arrangement* means an arrangement under which an educational institution, other than through an insured arrangement, charges student administrative health fees to students on a periodic basis to help cover the cost of student health clinic operations and care delivery (regardless of whether the student uses the clinic and regardless of whether the student purchases any available student health insurance coverage).

(4) *Travel insurance.*—For purposes of paragraph (h)(2)(xv) of this section, the term *travel insurance* means insurance coverage for personal risks incident to planned travel, which may include, but is not limited to, interruption or cancellation of trip or event, loss of baggage or

Reg. §57.2(h)(4)

personal effects, damages to accommodations or rental vehicles, and sickness, accident, disability, or death occurring during travel, provided that the health benefits are not offered on a stand-alone basis and are incidental to other coverage. For this purpose, the term *travel insurance* does not include major medical plans that provide comprehensive medical protection for travelers with trips lasting 6 months or longer, including, for example, those working overseas as an expatriate or military personnel being deployed.

(5) *Reinsurance.*—(i) *Indemnity reinsurance.*—For purposes of paragraphs (h)(2)(xvi) and (k) of this section, the term *indemnity reinsurance* means an agreement between one or more reinsuring companies and a covered entity under which—

(A) The reinsuring company agrees to accept, and to indemnify the issuing company for, all or part of the risk of loss under policies specified in the agreement; and

(B) The covered entity retains its liability to, and its contractual relationship with, the individuals whose health risks are insured under the policies specified in the agreement.

(ii) *Assumption reinsurance.*—For purposes of paragraph (k) of this section, the term *assumption reinsurance* means reinsurance for which there is a novation and the reinsurer takes over the entire risk of loss pursuant to a new contract.

(i) *Located in the United States.*—The term *located in the United States* means present in the United States (within the meaning of paragraph (m) of this section) under section 7701(b)(7) (for presence in the 50 States and the District of Columbia) or § 1.937-1(c)(3)(i) of this chapter (for presence in a possession of the United States).

(j) *NAIC.*—The term *NAIC* means the National Association of Insurance Commissioners.

(k) *Net premiums written.*—The term *net premiums written* means premiums written, including reinsurance premiums written, reduced by reinsurance ceded, and reduced by ceding commissions and medical loss ratio (MLR) rebates with respect to the data year. For this purpose, MLR rebates are computed on an accrual basis in determining net premiums written. Because indemnity reinsurance within the meaning of paragraph (h)(5)(i) of this section is not health insurance under paragraph (h)(1) of this section, the term *net premiums written* does not include premiums written for indemnity reinsurance and is not reduced by indemnity reinsurance ceded. However, in the case of assumption reinsurance within the meaning of paragraph (h)(5)(ii) of this section, the term *net premiums written* does include premiums written for assumption reinsurance and is reduced by assumption reinsurance premiums ceded.

(l) *SHCE.*—The term *SHCE* means the Supplemental Health Care Exhibit. The SHCE is a form published by the NAIC that most covered entities are required to file annually under State law.

(m) *United States.*—For purposes of paragraph (i) of this section, the term *United States* means the 50 States, the District of Columbia, and any possession of the United States, including American Samoa, Guam, the Northern Mariana Islands, Puerto Rico, and the Virgin Islands.

(n) *United States health risk.*—The term *United States health risk* means the health risk of any individual who is—

(1) A United States citizen;

(2) A resident of the United States (within the meaning of section 7701(b)(1)(A)); or

(3) Located in the United States (within the meaning of paragraph (i) of this section) during the period such individual is so located. [Reg. § 57.2.]

☐ [*T.D. 9643, 11-26-2013. Amended by T.D. 9711, 2-23-2015 and T.D. 9830, 2-22-2018.*]

[Reg. § 57.3]

§ 57.3. Reporting requirements and associated penalties.—(a) *Reporting requirement.*—(1) *In general.*—Annually, each covered entity, including each controlled group that is treated as a single covered entity, must report its net premiums written for health insurance of United States health risks during the data year to the IRS by April 15th of the fee year on Form 8963, "Report of Health Insurance Provider Information," in accordance with the instructions for the form. A covered entity that has net premiums written during the data year is subject to this reporting requirement even if it does not have any amount taken into account as described in § 57.4(a)(4). If an entity is not in the business of providing health insurance for any United States health risk in the fee year, it is not a covered entity and does not have to report.

(2) *Manner of reporting.*—The IRS may provide rules in guidance published in the Internal Revenue Bulletin for the manner of reporting by a covered entity under this section, including rules for reporting by a designated entity on behalf of a controlled group that is treated as a single covered entity.

(3) *Disclosure of reported information.*—Pursuant to section 9010(g)(4), the information reported on each original and corrected Form 8963 will be open for public inspection or available upon request.

(b) *Penalties.*—(1) *Failure to report.*—(i) *In general.*—A covered entity that fails to timely submit a report containing the information required by paragraph (a) of this section is liable for a failure to report penalty in the amount described in paragraph (b)(1)(ii) of this section in addition to its fee liability and any other applicable penalty, unless the failure is due to reasonable cause as defined in paragraph (b)(1)(iii) of this section.

(ii) *Amount.*—The amount of the failure to report penalty described in paragraph (b)(1)(i) of this section is—

(A) $10,000, plus

(B) The lesser of—

(1) An amount equal to $1,000 multiplied by the number of days during which such failure continues; or

(2) The amount of the covered entity's fee for which the report was required.

(iii) *Reasonable cause.*—The failure to report penalty described in paragraph (b)(1)(i) of this section is waived if the failure is due to reasonable cause. A failure is due to reasonable cause if the covered entity exercised ordinary business care and prudence and was nevertheless unable to submit the report within the prescribed time. In determining whether the covered entity was unable to submit the report timely despite the exercise of ordinary business care and prudence, the IRS will consider all the facts and circumstances surrounding the failure to submit the report.

(iv) *Treatment of penalty.*—The failure to report penalty described in this paragraph (b)(1)—

(A) Is treated as a penalty under subtitle F;

(B) Must be paid on notice and demand by the IRS and in the same manner as a tax under the Internal Revenue Code; and

(C) Is a penalty for which only civil actions for refund under procedures of subtitle F apply.

(2) Accuracy-related penalty.—(i) *In general.*—A covered entity that understates its net premiums written for health insurance of United States health risks in the report required under paragraph (a)(1) of this section is liable for an accuracy-related penalty in the amount described in paragraph (b)(2)(ii) of this section, in addition to its fee liability and any other applicable penalty.

(ii) *Amount.*—The amount of the accuracy-related penalty described in paragraph (b)(2)(i) of this section is the excess of—

(A) The amount of the covered entity's fee for the fee year that the IRS determines should have been paid in the absence of any understatement; over

(B) The amount of the covered entity's fee for the fee year that the IRS determined based on the understatement.

(iii) *Understatement.*—An understatement of a covered entity's net premiums written for health insurance of United States health risks is the difference between the amount of net premiums written that the covered entity reported and the amount of net premiums written that the IRS determines the covered entity should have reported.

(iv) *Treatment of penalty.*—The accuracy-related penalty is subject to the provisions of subtitle F that apply to assessable penalties imposed under chapter 68.

(3) Controlled groups.—Each member of a controlled group that is required to provide information to the controlled group's designated entity for purposes of the report required to be submitted by the designated entity on behalf of the controlled group is jointly and severally liable for any penalties described in this paragraph (b) for any reporting failures by the designated entity. [Reg. § 57.3.]

☐ [*T.D.* 9643, 11-26-2013.]

[Reg. § 57.4]

§ 57.4. Fee calculation.—(a) *Fee components.*—(1) *In general.*—For every fee year, the IRS will calculate a covered entity's allocated fee as described in this section.

(2) Calculation of net premiums written.—Each covered entity's allocated fee for any fee year is equal to an amount that bears the same ratio to the applicable amount as the covered entity's net premiums written for health insurance of United States health risks during the data year taken into account bears to the aggregate net premiums written for health insurance of United States health risks of all covered entities during the data year taken into account.

(3) Applicable amount.—The applicable amounts for fee years are—

Fee year	Applicable amount
2014	$ 8,000,000,000
2015	$ 11,300,000,000
2016	$ 11,300,000,000
2017	$ 13,900,000,000
2018	$ 14,300,000,000
2019 and thereafter	The applicable amount in the preceding fee year increased by the rate of premium growth (within the meaning of section 36B(b)(3)(A)(ii)).

(4) Net premiums written taken into account.—(i) *In general.*—A covered entity's net premiums written for health insurance of United States health risks during any data year are taken into account as follows:

Covered entity's net premiums written during the data year that are:	Percentage of net premiums written taken into account is:
Not more than $25,000,000	0
More than $25,000,000 but not more than $50,000,000	50
More than $50,000,000	100

(ii) *Controlled groups.*—In the case of a controlled group, paragraph (a)(4)(i) of this section applies to all net premiums written for health insurance of United States health risks during the data year, in the aggregate, of the entire controlled group, except that any net premiums written by any member of the controlled group that is a nonprofit corporation meeting the requirements of § 57.2(b)(2)(iii) or a voluntary employees' beneficiary association meeting the requirements of § 57.2(b)(2)(iv) are not taken into account.

Reg. § 57.4(a)(4)(ii)

(iii) *Partial exclusion for certain exempt activities.*—After the application of paragraph (a)(4)(i) of this section, if the covered entity (or any member of a controlled group treated as a single covered entity) is exempt from Federal income tax under section 501(a) and is described in section 501(c)(3), (4), (26), or (29) as of December 31st of the data year, then only 50 percent of its remaining net premiums written for health insurance of United States health risks that are attributable to its exempt activities (and not to activities of an unrelated trade or business as defined in section 513) during the data year are taken into account. If an entity to which this partial exclusion applies is a member of a controlled group, then the partial exclusion applies to that entity after first applying paragraph (a)(4)(i) on a pro rata basis to all members of the controlled group.

(b) *Determination of net premiums written.*—(1) *In general.*—The IRS will determine net premiums written for health insurance of United States health risks for each covered entity based on the Form 8963, "Report of Health Insurance Provider Information," submitted by each covered entity, together with any other source of information available to the IRS. Other sources of information that the IRS may use to determine net premiums written for each covered entity include the SHCE, which supplements the annual statement filed with the NAIC pursuant to State law, the annual statement itself or the Accident and Health Policy Experience filed with the NAIC, the MLR Annual Reporting Form filed with the Center for Medicare & Medicaid Services' Center for Consumer Information and Insurance Oversight of the U.S. Department of Health and Human Services, or any similar statements filed with the NAIC, with any State government, or with the Federal government pursuant to applicable State or Federal requirements.

(2) *Presumption for United States health risks.*—For any covered entity that files the SHCE with the NAIC, the entire amount reported on the SHCE as direct premiums written will be considered to be for health insurance of United States health risks as described in § 57.2(n) (subject to any applicable exclusions for amounts that are not health insurance as described in § 57.2(h)(2)) unless the covered entity can demonstrate otherwise.

(c) *Determination of amounts taken into account.*—(1) For each fee year and for each covered entity, the IRS will calculate the net premiums written for health insurance of United States health risks taken into account during the data year. The resulting number is the numerator of the fraction described in paragraph (d)(1) of this section.

(2) For each fee year, the IRS will calculate the aggregate net premiums written for health insurance of United States health risks taken into account for all covered entities during the data year. The resulting number is the denominator of the fraction described in paragraph (d)(2) of this section.

(d) *Allocated fee calculated.*—For each covered entity for each fee year, the IRS will calculate the covered entity's allocated fee by multiplying the applicable amount from paragraph (a)(3) of this section by a fraction—

(1) The numerator of which is the covered entity's net premiums written for health insurance of United States health risks during the data year taken into account (described in paragraph (c)(1) of this section); and

(2) The denominator of which is the aggregate net premiums written for health insurance of United States health risks for all covered entities during the data year taken into account (described in paragraph (c)(2) of this section). [Reg. § 57.4.]

☐ [*T.D.* 9643, 11-26-2013.]

[Reg. § 57.5]

§ 57.5. Notice of preliminary fee calculation.—(a) *Content of notice.*—Each fee year, the IRS will make a preliminary calculation of the fee for each covered entity as described in § 57.4. The IRS will notify each covered entity of its preliminary fee calculation for that fee year. The notification to a covered entity of its preliminary fee calculation will include—

(1) The covered entity's allocated fee;

(2) The covered entity's net premiums written for health insurance of United States health risks;

(3) The covered entity's net premiums written for health insurance of United States health risks taken into account after the application of § 57.4(a)(4);

(4) The aggregate net premiums written for health insurance of United States health risks taken into account for all covered entities; and

(5) Instructions for how to submit a corrected Form 8963, "Report of Health Insurance Provider Information," to correct any errors through the error correction process.

(b) *Timing of notice.*—The IRS will specify in other guidance published in the Internal Revenue Bulletin the date by which it will send each covered entity a notice of its preliminary fee calculation. [Reg. § 57.5.]

☐ [*T.D.* 9643, 11-26-2013.]

[Reg. § 57.6]

§ 57.6. Error correction process.—(a) *In general.*—Upon receipt of its preliminary fee calculation, each covered entity must review this calculation during the error correction period. If the covered entity identifies one or more errors in its preliminary fee calculation, the covered entity must timely submit to the IRS a corrected Form 8963, "Report of Health Insurance Provider Information," during the error correction period. The corrected Form 8963 will replace the original Form 8963 for all purposes, including for the purpose of determining whether an accuracy-related penalty applies, except that a covered entity remains subject to the failure to report penalty if it fails to timely submit the original Form 8963. In the case of a controlled group, if the preliminary fee calculation for the controlled group contains one or more errors, the corrected Form 8963 must include all of the required information for the entire controlled group, including members that do not have corrections.

(b) *Time and manner.*—The IRS will specify in other guidance published in the Internal Revenue Bulletin the time and manner by which a covered entity must submit a corrected Form 8963. The IRS will provide its final determination regarding the covered entity's submission no later than the time the IRS provides a covered entity with a final fee calculation.

(c) *Finality.*—Covered entities must assert any basis for contesting their preliminary fee calculation during the error correction period. In the interest of providing finality to the fee calculation process, the IRS will not accept a corrected Form 8963 after the end of the error correction period or alter final fee calculations on the basis of information provided after the end of the error correction period. [Reg. §57.6.]

☐ [*T.D. 9643, 11-26-2013.*]

[Reg. §57.7]

§57.7. Notification and fee payment.— (a) *Content of notice.*—Each fee year, the IRS will make a final calculation of the fee for each covered entity as described in §57.4. The IRS will base its final fee calculation on each covered entity's original or corrected Form 8963, "Report of Health Insurance Provider Information," as adjusted by other sources of information described in §57.4(b)(1). The notification to a covered entity of its final fee calculation will include-

(1) The covered entity's allocated fee;

(2) The covered entity's net premiums written for health insurance of United States health risks;

(3) The covered entity's net premiums written for health insurance of United States health risks taken into account after the application of §57.4(a)(4);

(4) The aggregate net premiums written for health insurance of United States health risks taken into account for all covered entities; and

(5) The final determination on the covered entity's corrected Form 8963, "Report of Health Insurance Provider Information," if any.

(b) *Timing of notice.*—The IRS will send each covered entity a notice of its final fee calculation by August 31st of the fee year.

(c) *Differences in preliminary fee calculation and final calculation.*—A covered entity's final fee calculation may differ from the covered entity's preliminary fee calculation because of changes made pursuant to the error correction process described in §57.6 or because the IRS discovered additional information relevant to the fee calcu-

lation through other information sources as described in §57.4(b)(1). Even if a covered entity did not file a corrected Form 8963 described in §57.6, a covered entity's final fee may differ from a covered entity's preliminary fee because of information discovered about that covered entity through other information sources. In addition, a change in aggregate net premiums written for health insurance of United States health risks can affect every covered entity's fee because each covered entity's fee is equal to a fraction of the aggregate fee collected from all covered entities.

(d) *Payment of final fee.*—Each covered entity must pay its final fee by September 30th of the fee year. For a controlled group, the payment must be made using the designated entity's Employer Identification Number as reported on Form 8963. The fee must be paid by electronic funds transfer as required by §57.6302-1. There is no tax return to be filed with the payment of the fee.

(e) *Controlled groups.*—In the case of a controlled group that is liable for the fee, all members of the controlled group are jointly and severally liable for the fee. Accordingly, if a controlled group's fee is not paid, the IRS may separately assess each member of the controlled group for the full amount of the controlled group's fee. [Reg. §57.7.]

☐ [*T.D. 9643, 11-26-2013.*]

[Reg. §57.8]

§57.8. Tax treatment of fee.—(a) *Treatment as an excise tax.*—The fee is treated as an excise tax for purposes of subtitle F (sections 6001-7874). Thus, references in subtitle F to "taxes imposed by this title," "internal revenue tax," and similar references, are also references to the fee. For example, the fee is assessed (section 6201), collected (sections 6301, 6321, and 6331), enforced (section 7602), and subject to examination and summons (section 7602) in the same manner as taxes imposed by the Code.

(b) *Deficiency procedures.*—The deficiency procedures of sections 6211-6216 do not apply to the fee.

(c) *Limitation on assessment.*—The IRS must assess the amount of the fee for any fee year within three years of September 30th of that fee year.

(d) *Application of section 275.*—The fee is treated as a tax described in section 275(a)(6) (relating to taxes for which no deduction is allowed). [Reg. §57.8.]

☐ [*T.D. 9643, 11-26-2013.*]

[Reg. §57.9]

§57.9. Refund claims.—Any claim for a refund of the fee must be made by the entity that paid the fee to the government and must be made on Form 843, "Claim for Refund and Request for Abatement," in accordance with the instructions for that form. [Reg. §57.9.]

☐ [*T.D. 9643, 11-26-2013.*]

[Reg. §57.10]

§57.10. Effective/applicability date.—(a) *In general.*—Except as provided in paragraph (b), §§57.1 through 57.9 apply to any fee that is due on or after September 30, 2014.

(b) *Paragraphs (b)(3) and (c)(3)(ii) of §57.2.*—Paragraphs (b)(3) and (c)(3)(ii) of §57.2 apply on February 22, 2018. [Reg. §57.10.]

☐ [*T.D. 9643, 11-26-2013. Amended by T.D. 9711, 2-23-2015 and T.D. 9830, 2-22-2018.*]

ALCOHOL, TOBACCO, AND CERTAIN OTHER EXCISE TAXES

Greenmail

See p. 20,601 for regulations not amended to reflect law changes

[Reg. §156.5881-1]

§156.5881-1. Imposition of excise tax on greenmail.—(a) *In general.*—Section 5881 of the Code imposes a tax equal to 50 percent of the gain or other income realized by any person on the receipt of greenmail, whether or not the gain or other income is recognized.

(b) *Transactions occurring on or after March 31, 1988.*—For transactions occurring on or after March 31, 1988, greenmail is defined as any consideration transferred by a corporation (or any person acting in concert with the corporation) to directly or indirectly acquire stock of the corporation from any shareholder if:

(1) The transferring shareholder has held the stock (as determined under section 1223) for less than two years before entering into the agreement to transfer the stock,

(2) The shareholder, any person acting in concert with the shareholder, or any person related to the shareholder or to a person acting in concert with the shareholder made or threatened to make a public tender offer for stock of the corporation at some time during the two-year period ending on the date of the acquisition of the stock by the corporation, and

(3) The acquisition is pursuant to an offer that was not made on the same terms to all shareholders.

(c) *Transactions occurring before March 31, 1988.*—For transactions occurring before March 31, 1988, greenmail has the same meaning as in paragraph (b) of this section, except that it does not include any consideration transferred by any person acting in concert with the corporation described in that paragraph.

(d) *Effective date.*—Generally, section 5881 of the Code applies to consideration received after December 22, 1987, in taxable years ending after that date. However, section 5881 does not apply to any acquisition of stock pursuant to a written binding contract in effect on December 15, 1987, and at all times thereafter before the acquisition. [Reg. §156.5881-1.]

☐ [*T.D. 8379, 12-17-91.*]

Structured Settlement Factoring Transactions

See p. 20,601 for regulations not amended to reflect law changes

[Reg. §157.5891-1]

§157.5891-1. Imposition of excise tax on structured settlement factoring transactions.—(a) *In general.*—Section 5891 imposes on any person who acquires, directly or indirectly, structured settlement payment rights in a structured settlement factoring transaction a tax equal to 40 percent of the factoring discount with respect to such factoring transaction.

(b) *Exceptions for certain approved transactions.*—(1) *In general.*—The excise tax shall not apply to a structured settlement factoring transaction if the transfer of structured settlement payment rights is approved in advance in a qualified order.

(2) *Qualified order dispositive.*—A qualified order shall be treated as dispositive for purposes of this exception.

(c) *Definitions.*—(1) *Applicable state statute means*—

(i) A statute that is enacted by the state in which the payee of the structured settlement is domiciled and provides for the entry of an order, judgment, or decree described in paragraph (c)(4)(i) of this section; or

(ii) If there is no such statute, a statute that—

(A) Is enacted by the state in which either the party to the structured settlement (including an assignee under a qualified assignment under section 130) or the person issuing the funding asset for the structured settlement is domiciled or has its principal place of business; and

(B) Provides for the entry of such an order, judgment, or decree.

(2) *Applicable state court means*, with respect to any applicable state statute, a court of the state that enacted such statute. If the payee of the

structured settlement is not domiciled in the state that enacted the statute, the term also includes a court of the state in which the payee is domiciled.

(3) *Factoring discount* means an amount equal to the excess of—

(i) The aggregate undiscounted amount of structured settlement payments being acquired in the structured settlement factoring transaction; over

(ii) The total amount actually paid by the acquirer to the person from whom such structured settlement payments are acquired.

(4) *Qualified order* means a final order, judgment, or decree that—

(i) Finds that the transfer of structured settlement payment rights does not contravene any Federal or state statute, or the order of any court or responsible administrative authority, and is in the best interest of the payee, taking into account the welfare and support of the payee's dependents; and

(ii) Is issued under the authority of an applicable state statute by an applicable state court, or is issued by the responsible administrative authority (if any) which has exclusive jurisdiction over the underlying action or proceeding which was resolved by means of the structured settlement.

(5) *Responsible administrative authority* means the administrative authority that had jurisdiction over the underlying action or proceeding that was resolved by means of the structured settlement.

(6) *State* includes the Commonwealth of Puerto Rico and any possession of the United States.

(7) *Structured settlement* means an arrangement—

(i) that is established by—

(A) Suit or agreement for the periodic payment of damages excludable from the gross income of the recipient under section 104(a)(2); or

(B) Agreement for the periodic payment of compensation under any workers' compensation law excludable from the gross income of the recipient under section 104(a)(1); and

(ii) Under which the periodic payments are—

(A) Of the character described in section 130(c)(2)(A) and (B); and

(B) Payable by a person who is a party to the suit or agreement or to the workers' compensation claim or by a person who has assumed the liability for such periodic payments under a qualified assignment in accordance with section 130.

(8) *Structured settlement factoring transaction* means a transfer of structured settlement payment rights (including portions of structured settlement payments) made for consideration by means of sale, assignment, pledge, or other form of encumbrance or alienation for consideration other than—

(i) The creation or perfection of a security interest in structured settlement payment rights under a blanket security agreement entered into with an insured depository institution in the absence of any action to redirect the structured settlement payments to such institution (or agent or successor thereof) or otherwise to enforce such blanket security interest as against the structured settlement payment rights; or

(ii) A subsequent transfer of structured settlement payment rights acquired in a structured settlement factoring transaction.

(9) *Structured settlement payment rights* means rights to receive payments under a structured settlement.

(d) *Coordination with other provisions of the Internal Revenue Code.*—(1) *In general.*—If the applicable requirements of sections 72, 104(a)(1), 104(a)(2), 130, and 461(h) were satisfied at the time the structured settlement involving structured settlement payment rights was entered into, the subsequent occurrence of a structured settlement factoring transaction shall not affect the application of the provisions of such sections to the parties to the structured settlement (including an assignee under a qualified assignment under section 130) in any taxable year.

(2) *No withholding of tax.*—The provisions of section 3405 regarding withholding of tax shall not apply to the person making the payments in the event of a structured settlement factoring transaction.

(e) *Effective dates.*—This section applies to structured settlement factoring transactions entered into on or after July 8, 2004. For structured settlement factoring transactions entered into before July 8, 2004, see § 157.5891-1T of this chapter (2003-1 C.B. 564. See § 601.601(d)(2) of this chapter.), as it appeared in the April 1, 2003, edition of 26 CFR part 157. [Reg. § 157.5891-1.]

☐ [*T.D.* 9134, 7-7-2004.]

[The next page is 64,601.]

PROCEDURE AND ADMINISTRATION

Information and Returns
RETURNS AND RECORDS
Records, Statements and Special Returns

See p. 20,601 for regulations not amended to reflect law changes

[Reg. § 1.6001-1]

§ 1.6001-1. **Records.**—(a) *In general.*—Except as provided in paragraph (b) of this section, any person subject to tax under subtitle A of the Code (including a qualified State individual income tax which is treated pursuant to section 6361(a) as if it were imposed by chapter 1 of subtitle A), or any person required to file a return of information with respect to income, shall keep such permanent books of account or records, including inventories, as are sufficient to establish the amount of gross income, deductions, credits, or other matters required to be shown by such person in any return of such tax or information.

(b) *Farmers and wage-earners.*—Individuals deriving gross income from the business of farming, and individuals whose gross income includes salaries, wages, or similar compensation for personal services rendered, are required with respect to such income to keep such records as will enable the district director to determine the correct amount of income subject to the tax. It is not necessary, however, that with respect to such income individuals keep the books of account or records required by paragraph (a) of this section. For rules with respect to the records to be kept in substantiation of traveling and other business expenses of employees, see § 1.162-17.

(c) *Exempt organizations.*—In addition to such permanent books and records as are required by paragraph (a) of this section with respect to the tax imposed by section 511 on unrelated business income of certain exempt organizations, every organization exempt from tax under section 501(a) shall keep such permanent books of account or records, including inventories, as are sufficient to show specifically the items of gross income, receipts and disbursements. Such organizations shall also keep such books and records as are required to substantiate the information required by section 6033. See section 6033 and §§ 1.6033-1 through -3.

(d) *Notice by district director requiring returns, statements, or the keeping of records.*—The district director may require any person, by notice served upon him, to make such returns, render such statements, or keep such specific records as will enable the district director to determine whether or not such person is liable for tax under subtitle A of the Code, including qualified State individual income taxes, which are treated pursuant to section 6361(a) as if they were imposed by chapter 1 of subtitle A.

(e) *Retention of records.*—The books or records required by this section shall be kept at all times available for inspection by authorized internal revenue officers or employees, and shall be retained so long as the contents thereof may become material in the administration of any internal revenue law [Reg. § 1.6001-1.]

☐ [*T.D.* 6364, 2-13-59. *Amended by T.D.* 7122, 6-7-71; *T.D.* 7577, 12-19-78 *and T.D.* 8308, 8-30-90.]

[Reg. § 20.6001-1]

§ 20.6001-1. **Persons required to keep records and render statements.**—(a) It is the duty of the executor to keep such complete and detailed records of the affairs of the estate for which he acts as will enable the district director to determine accurately the amount of the estate tax liability. All documents and vouchers used in preparing the estate tax return (§ 20.6018-1) shall be retained by the executor so as to be available for inspection whenever required.

(b) In addition to filing an estate tax return (see § 20.6018-1) and, if applicable, a preliminary notice (see § 20.6036-1), the executor shall furnish such supplemental data as may be necessary to establish the correct estate tax. It is therefore the duty of the executor (1) to furnish, upon requests, copies of any documents in his possession (or on file in any court having jurisdiction over the estate) relating to the estate, appraisal lists of any items included in the gross estate, copies of balance sheets or other financial statements obtainable by him relating to the value of stock, and any other information obtainable by him that may be found necessary in the determination of the tax, and (2) to render any written statement, containing a declaration that it is made under penalties of perjury, of facts within his knowledge which the district director may require for the purpose of determining whether a tax liability exists and, if so, the extent thereof. Failure to comply with such a request will render the executor liable to penalties (see section 7269), and proceedings may be instituted in the proper court of the United States to secure compliance therewith (see section 7604).

(c) Persons having possession or control of any records or documents containing or supposed to contain any information concerning the estate, or having knowledge of or information about any fact or facts which have a material bearing upon the liability, or the extent of liability, of the estate for the estate tax, shall, upon request of the district director, make disclosure thereof. Failure on the part of any person to comply with such request will render him liable to penalties (section 7269), and compliance with the request may be enforced in the proper court of the United States (section 7604).

(d) Upon notification from the Internal Revenue Service, a corporation (organized or created in the United States) or its transfer agent is required to furnish the following information pertaining to stocks or bonds registered in the name of a nonresident decedent (regardless of citizenship): (1) The name of the decedent as registered; (2) the date of the decedent's death; (3) the decedent's residence and his place of death; (4) the names and addresses of executors, attorneys, or other representatives of the estate, within and without the United States; and (5) a description of the securities, the number of shares or bonds and the par values thereof. [Reg. § 20.6001-1.]

☐ [*T.D. 6296, 6-23-58. Amended by T.D. 7238, 12-28-72.*]

[Reg. § 25.6001-1]

§ 25.6001-1. Records required to be kept.— (a) *In general.*—Every person subject to taxation under chapter 12 of the Internal Revenue Code of 1954 shall for the purpose of determining the total amount of his gifts, keep such permanent books of account or records as are necessary to establish the amount of his total gifts (limited as provided by section 2503(b)), together with the deductions allowable in determining the amount of his taxable gifts, and the other information required to be shown in a gift tax return. All documents and vouchers used in preparing the gift tax return (see § 25.6019-1) shall be retained by the donor so as to be available for inspection whenever required.

(b) *Supplemental data.*—In order that the Internal Revenue Service may determine the correct tax the donor shall furnish such supplemental data as may be deemed necessary by the Internal Revenue Service. It is, therefore, the duty of the donor to furnish, upon request, copies of all documents relating to his gift or gifts, appraisal lists of any items included in the total amount of gifts, copies of balance sheets or other financial statements obtainable by him relating to the value of stock constituting the gift, and any other information obtainable by him that may be necessary in the determination of the tax. See section 2512 and the regulations issued thereunder. For every policy of life insurance listed on the return, the donor must procure a statement from the insurance company on Form 712 and file it with the internal revenue officer with whom the return is filed. If specifically requested by an internal revenue officer, the insurance company shall file this statement direct with the internal revenue officer. [Reg. § 25.6001-1.]

☐ [*T.D. 6334, 11-14-58. Amended by T.D. 7012, 5-14-69 and T.D. 7517, 11-11-77.*]

[Reg. § 31.6001-1]

§ 31.6001-1. Records in general.—(a) *Form of records.*—The records required by the regulations in this part shall be kept accurately, but no particular form is required for keeping the records. Such forms and systems of accounting shall be used as will enable the district director to ascertain whether liability for tax is incurred and, if so, the amount thereof.

(b) *Copies of returns, schedules, and statements.*— Every person who is required, by the regulations in this part or by instructions applicable to any form prescribed thereunder, to keep any copy of any return, schedule, statement, or other document, shall keep such copy as a part of his records.

(c) *Records of claimants.*—Any person (including an employee) who, pursuant to the regulations in this part, claims a refund, credit, or abatement, shall keep a complete and detailed record with respect to the tax, interest, addition to the tax, additional amount, or assessable penalty to which the claim relates. Such record shall include any records required of the claimant by paragraph (b) of this section and by § § 31.6001-2 to 31.6001-5, inclusive, which relate to the claim.

(d) *Records of employees.*—While not mandatory (except in the case of claims), it is advisable for each employee to keep permanent, accurate records showing the name and address of each employer for whom he performs services as an employee, the dates of beginning and termination of such services, the information with respect to himself which is required by the regulations in this subpart to be kept by employers, and the receipts furnished in accordance with the provisions of § 31.6051-1.

(e) *Place and period for keeping records.*—(1) All records required by the regulations in this part shall be kept, by the person required to keep them, at one or more convenient and safe locations accessible to internal revenue officers, and shall at all times be available for inspection by such officers.

(2) Except as otherwise provided in the following sentence, every person required by the regulations in this part to keep records in respect of a tax (whether or not such person incurs liability for such tax) shall maintain such records for at least four years after the due date of such tax for the return period to which the records relate, or the date such tax is paid, whichever is the later. The records of claimants required by paragraph (c) of this section shall be maintained for a period of at least four years after the date the claim is filed.

(f) *Cross references.*—See § § 31.6001-2 to 31.6001-5, inclusive, for additional records required with respect to the Federal Insurance Contributions Act, the Railroad Retirement Tax Act, the Federal Unemployment Tax Act, and the collection of income tax at source on wages, respectively. [Reg. § 31.6001-1.]

☐ [*T.D. 6354, 1-13-59.*]

[Reg. § 41.6001-1]

§ 41.6001-1. Records.—(a) *Records to be kept.*— Every person in whose name a highway motor vehicle having a taxable gross weight of at least 55,000 pounds is registered or required to be registered at any time during the taxable period shall keep records sufficient to enable the Commissioner to determine whether such person is liable for the tax and, if so, the amount thereof. See § 41.4482(b)-1 for the definition of taxable gross weight. Such records shall show with respect to each such vehicle:

(1) A description of the vehicle (including serial number or manufacturer's number) in sufficient detail to permit positive identification of the vehicle.

(2) The weight of the loads carried by the vehicle in such form as is required under the laws of any State in which the vehicle is registered or required to be registered, in order to permit verification of such vehicle's taxable gross weight.

(3) The date on which such person acquired such vehicle and the name and address of the person from whom the vehicle was acquired.

(4) The first month of each taxable period in which occurred a taxable use of each such vehicle while the vehicle was registered in the name of such person; information showing whether such vehicle was operated, while registered in the name of such person, in any prior month in such taxable period; and if such vehicle was so operated, evidence establishing that such operation was not a taxable use.

(5) The date of sale or other transfer to another of any such vehicle, together with the name and address of the person to whom transferred.

(6) In the case of any such vehicle disposed of otherwise than by sale or other transfer (including disposition by theft or destruction), the date and method of disposition of the vehicle.

(7) In the case of a secondhand highway motor vehicle acquired at any time in the taxable period, evidence showing whether there was a prior taxable use in such taxable period of the highway motor vehicle (see paragraph (b) of § 41.4481-2) or whether there was a suspension of tax in effect (see § 41.4483-3).

(8) A copy of each return, schedule, statement, or other document filed, pursuant to the regulations in this part or in accordance with the instructions applicable to any form prescribed thereunder, by the person required to keep such records.

(b) *Transit systems.*—Every person engaged in the operation of a transit system who claims exemption from tax with respect to a transit-type bus shall keep records sufficient to show, with respect to each taxable period, whether it meets the 60-percent passenger fare revenue test (see paragraph (e) of § 41.4483-2) for the period prescribed as the test period (see paragraph (c) of § 41.4483-2) for such system for such taxable period.

(c) *Exemption for vehicles used 5,000 miles or less.*—The owner of a highway motor vehicle who reasonably expects the vehicle to be exempt from the tax under section 4481(a) by reason of § 41.4483-3(c) for a given taxable period shall keep records which indicate the reason that the use of the vehicle is not expected to exceed 5,000 miles on public highways.

(d) *Records of claimants.*—Any person claiming refund, credit, or abatement of the tax, interest, additional amount, addition to the tax, or assessable penalty, shall keep a complete and detailed record with respect to the claim.

(e) *Place and period for keeping records.*—(1) All records required by the regulations in this part shall be kept, by the person required to keep them, at a convenient and safe location within the United States which is accessible to internal revenue officers. Such records shall at all times be available for inspection by such officers. If such person has a principal place of business in the United States, the records shall be kept at such place of business.

(2) Records required by paragraph (a) of this section shall be maintained for a period of at least 3 years after the date the tax becomes due or the date the tax is paid, whichever is the later. Records required by paragraphs (b) and (c) of this section shall be maintained for a period of at least 3 years after the end of the taxable period for which such exemption applies. Records required by paragraph (d) of this section (including any record required by paragraphs (a), (b), or (c) of this section which relates to a claim) shall be maintained for a period of at least 3 years after the date the claim is filed. [Reg. § 41.6001-1.]

☐ [*T.D. 6216, 12-6-56. Amended by T.D. 6743, 6-22-64 and T.D. 8027, 5-23-85; T.D. 8879, 3-30-2000 and T.D. 9698, 10-28-2014.*]

[Reg. § 44.6001-1]

§ 44.6001-1. Record requirements.—(a) *In general.*—(1) In addition to all other records required pursuant to § 44.4403-1, every person required to pay tax under section 4401 shall keep such records as will clearly show as to each day's operation:

(i) Separately, the gross amount of wagers—

(a) Accepted directly by the taxpayer or at any registered place of business of the taxpayer (other than laid-off wagers),

(b) Accepted for his account by agents at any place other than a registered place of business of the taxpayer (other than laid-off wagers), and

(c) Accepted as laid-off wagers from persons subject to the tax on wagers;

(ii) With respect to wagers laid off with others, the name, address, and registration number of each person with whom the laid-off wagers were placed, and the gross amount laid off with each such person, showing separately the gross amount of laid-off wagers with respect to each event, contest, or other wagering medium, as, for example, the gross amount laid off on each horse in a race; and

(iii) The gross amount of tax collected from or charged to bettors as a separate item.

(2) If a taxpayer has any agents or employees receiving wagers on his behalf, he shall maintain a separate record showing the name and address of each agent or employee, the period of employment, and the number of the special tax stamp issued to each agent or employee.

(3) A duplicate copy of each return required by §44.6011(a)-1 shall be retained as part of the taxpayer's records.

(b) *Records of agent or employee.*—Every person who is engaged in receiving for or on behalf of another person (at any place other than a registered place of business of such other person) wagers of a type subject to the tax imposed by section 4401 shall keep a record showing for each day (1) the gross amount of such wagers received by him, (2) the amount, if any, retained as a commission or as compensation for receiving such wagers, and (3) the amount turned over to the person on whose behalf the wagers were received, and the name and address of such person.

(c) *Record of claimants.*—Any person claiming a credit or refund shall keep a complete and detailed record of each overpayment and of each laid-off wager for which credit is taken or refund is claimed, including a copy of the certificate required under paragraph (d) of §44.6419-2.

(d) *Place for keeping records.*—Every person required to pay the tax imposed by section 4401 shall keep or cause to be kept, at his office or principal place of business, or, if he has no office or principal place of business, at his residence or some other convenient or safe location, all such records as are required pursuant to paragraphs (a) and (c) of this section and §§44.4403 and 44.4403-1.

(e) *Period for retaining records.*—All records required by the regulations in this part shall at all times be available for inspection by internal revenue officers. Records required by §44.4403-1 and by paragraph (a) of this section shall be maintained for a period of at least three years from the date the tax became due. Records required by paragraph (b) of this section shall be maintained for a period of at least three years from the date the wager was received. Records required by paragraph (c) of this section shall be maintained for a period of at least three years from the date any credit is taken or refund is claimed. [Reg. §44.6001-1.]

☐ [T.D. 6370, 4-4-59. *Amended by* T.D. 6568, 8-15-61.]

[Reg. §53.6001-1]

§53.6001-1. Notice or regulations requiring records, statements, and special returns.—(a) *In general.*—Any person subject to tax under chapter 42, Subtitle D, of the Code shall keep such complete and detailed records as are sufficient to enable the district director to determine accurately the amount of liability under chapter 42.

(b) *Notice by district director requiring returns, statements, or the keeping of records.*—The district director may require any person, by notice served upon him, to make such returns, render such statements, or keep such specific records as will enable the district director to determine whether or not such person is liable for tax under chapter 42.

(c) *Retention of records.*—The records required by this section shall be kept at all times available for inspection by authorized internal revenue officers or employees, and shall be retained so long as the contents thereof may become material in the administration of any internal revenue law. [Reg. §53.6001-1.]

☐ [T.D. 7368, 7-15-75.]

[Reg. §55.6001-1]

§55.6001-1. Notice or regulations requiring records, statements and special returns.—(a) *In general.*—Any person subject to tax under chapter 44 of the Code shall keep such complete and detailed records as are sufficient to enable the district director to determine accurately the amount of liability under chapter 44.

(b) *Notice by district director requiring returns, statements, or the keeping of records.*—The district director may require any person, by notice served upon him, to make such returns, render such statements, or keep such specific records as will enable the district director to determine whether or not such person is liable for tax under chapter 44.

(c) *Retention of records.*—The records required by this section shall be kept at all times available for inspection by authorized internal revenue officers or employees, and shall be retained so long as the contents thereof may become material in the administration of any internal revenue law. [Reg. §55.6001-1.]

☐ [T.D. 7767, 2-3-81.]

[Reg. §56.6001-1]

§56.6001-1. Notice or regulations requiring records, statements, and special returns.—(a) *In general.*—The provisions of §53.6001-1 shall apply to any person subject to tax under chapter 41, Subtitle D, of the Code, by treating each reference to chapter 42 in §53.6001-1 as a reference to chapter 41.

(b) *Cross references.*—See §56.4911-6 for general information on records of lobbying expenditures. See §§56.4911-9(d) and 56.4911-10(f) for information that members of an affiliated group and a limited affiliated group, respectively, are to provide to other members of the group and to the Internal Revenue Service. [Reg. §56.6001-1.]

☐ [T.D. 8308, 8-30-90.]

[Reg. §156.6001-1]

§156.6001-1. Notice or regulations requiring records, statements, and special returns.—(a) *In general.*—Any person subject to tax under chapter 54 (Greenmail) of the Code shall keep such complete and detailed records as are sufficient to enable the district director to determine accurately the amount of liability under chapter 54.

(b) *Notice by district director requiring returns, statements, or the keeping of records.*—The district director may require any person, by notice served upon him, to make such returns, render such statements, or keep such specific records as will enable the district director to determine whether or not the person is liable for tax under chapter 54 of the Code.

(c) *Retention of records.*—The records required by this section shall be kept at all times available for inspection by authorized internal revenue officers or employees, and shall be retained so long as the contents thereof may become material in the administration of any internal revenue law. [Reg. § 156.6001-1.]

☐ [*T.D.* 8379, 12-17-91.]

[Reg. §157.6001-1]

§157.6001-1. Records, statements, and special returns.—(a) *In general.*—Any person subject to tax under chapter 55 (Structured Settlement Factoring Transactions) of the Internal Revenue Code must keep such complete and detailed records as are sufficient to enable the Internal Revenue Service (IRS) to determine accurately the amount of liability under chapter 55.

(b) *Notice by the IRS requiring returns, statements, or the keeping of records.*—The IRS may require any person, by notice served upon him, to make such returns, render such statements, or keep such specific records as will enable the IRS to determine whether or not the person is liable for tax under chapter 55.

(c) *Retention of records.*—The records required by this section must be kept at all times available for inspection by the IRS, and shall be retained so long as the contents thereof may become material in the administration of any internal revenue law. [Reg. § 157.6001-1.]

☐ [*T.D.* 9134, 7-7-2004.]

[Reg. §301.6001-1]

§301.6001-1. Notice or regulations requiring records, statements, and special returns.—For provisions requiring records, statements, and special returns, see the regulations relating to the particular tax. [Reg. § 301.6001-1.]

☐ [*T.D.* 6498, 10-24-60.]

[Reg. §1.6001-2]

§1.6001-2. Returns.—For rules relating to returns required to be made by every individual, estate or trust which is liable for one or more qualified State individual income taxes as defined in section 6362 for a taxable year, see paragraph (b) of §301.6361-1 of this chapter (Regulations on Procedure and Administration). [Reg. § 1.6001-2.]

☐ [*T.D.* 7577, 12-19-78.]

[Reg. §31.6001-2]

§31.6001-2. Additional records under Federal Insurance Contributions Act.—(a) *In general.*—(1) Every employer liable for tax under the Federal Insurance Contributions Act shall keep records of all remuneration, whether in cash or in a medium other than cash, paid to his employees after 1954 for services (other than agricultural labor which constitutes or is deemed to constitute employment, domestic service in a private home of the employer, or service not in the course of the employer's trade or business) performed for him after 1936. Such records shall show with respect to each employee receiving such remuneration—

(i) The name, address, and account number of the employee and such additional information with respect to the employee as is required by paragraph (c) of §31.6011(b)-2 when the employee does not advise the employer what his account number and name are as shown on an account number card issued to the employee by the Social Security Administration.

(ii) The total amount and date of each payment of remuneration (including any sum withheld therefrom as tax or for any other reason) and the period of services covered by such payment.

(iii) The amount of each such remuneration payment which constitutes wages subject to tax. See §§31.3121(a)-1 to 31.3121(a)(12)-1, inclusive.

(iv) The amount of employee tax, or any amount equivalent to employee tax, collected with respect to such payment, and, if collected at a time other than the time such payment was made, the date collected. See paragraph (b) of §31.3102-1 for provisions relating to collection of amounts equivalent to employee tax.

(v) If the total remuneration payment (subdivision (ii) of this subparagraph) and the amount thereof which is taxable (subdivision (iii) of this subparagraph) are not equal, the reason therefor.

(2) Every employer shall keep records of the details of each adjustment or settlement of taxes under the Federal Insurance Contributions Act made pursuant to the regulations in this part. The employer shall keep as a part of his records a copy of each statement furnished pursuant to paragraph (c) of §31.6011(a)-1.

(3) Every employer shall keep records of all remuneration in the form of tips received by his employees after 1965 in the course of their employment and reported to him pursuant to section 6053(a). The employer shall keep as part of his records employee statements of tips furnished him pursuant to section 6053(a) (unless the information disclosed by such statements is recorded on another document retained by the employer pursuant to subparagraph (1) of this

paragraph) and copies of employer statements furnished employees pursuant to section 6053(b).

(b) *Agricultural labor, domestic service, and service not in the course of employer's trade or business.*—(1) Every employer who pays cash remuneration after 1954 for the performance for him after 1950 of agricultural labor which constitutes or is deemed to constitute employment, of domestic, service in a private home of the employer not on a farm operated for profit, or of service not in the course of his trade or business shall keep records of all such cash remuneration with respect to which he incurs, or expects to incur, liability for the taxes imposed by the Federal Insurance Contributions Act, or with respect to which amounts equivalent to employee tax are deducted pursuant to section 3102(a). See §§ 31.3101-3, 31.3111-3, and 31.3121(a)-2 for provisions relating, respectively, to the liability for employee tax which is incurred when wages are received, the liability for employer tax which is incurred when wages are paid, and the time when wages are paid and received. Such records shall show with respect to each employee receiving such cash remuneration—

(i) The name of the employee.

(ii) The account number of each employee to whom wages for such services are paid, within the meaning of § 31.3121(a)-2, and such additional information as is required by paragraph (c) of § 31.6011(b)-2 when the employee does not advise the employer what his account number and name are as shown on an account number card issued to the employee by the Social Security Administration.

(iii) The amount of such cash remuneration paid to the employee (including any sum withheld therefrom as tax or for any other reason) for agricultural labor which constitutes or is deemed to constitute employment, for domestic service in a private home of the employer not on a farm operated for profit, or for service not in the course of the employer's trade or business; the calendar month in which such cash remuneration was paid; and the character of the services for which such cash remuneration was paid. When the employer incurs liability for the taxes imposed by the Federal Insurance Contributions Act with respect to any such cash remuneration which he did not previously expect would be subject to the taxes, the amount of any such cash remuneration not previously made a matter of record shall be determined by the employer to the best of his knowledge and belief.

(iv) The amount of employee tax, or any amount equivalent to employee tax, collected with respect to such cash remuneration and the calendar month in which collected. See paragraph (b) of § 31.3102-1 for provisions relating to collection of amounts equivalent to employee tax.

(v) To the extent material to a determination of tax liability, the number of days during each calendar year after 1956 on which agricultural labor which constitutes or is deemed to

constitute employment is performed by the employee for cash remuneration computed on a time basis.

(2) Every person to whom a "crew leader", as that term is defined in section 3121(i), furnishes individuals for the performance of agricultural labor after December 31, 1958, shall keep records of the name; permanent mailing address, or if none, present address; and identification number, if any, of such "crew leader". [Reg. § 31.6001-2.]

☐ [*T.D.* 6516, 12-20-60. *Amended by T.D.* 7001, 1-23-69.]

[Reg. § 41.6001-2]

§ 41.6001-2. **Proof of payment for state registration purposes.**—(a) *In general.*—This section sets forth the circumstances under which a State must require proof of payment of the tax imposed by section 4481(a), and the required manner in which such proof of payment is to be received by the State as a condition of issuing a registration for a highway motor vehicle. A State must either comply with the provisions of this section or, in the alternative, comply with such other rules regarding the satisfaction of this proof of payment requirement as may be prescribed by the Commissioner (by Revenue Procedure or otherwise), in order to avoid a reduction of Federal-aid highway funds apportioned under 23 U.S.C. 104(b)(4). For purposes of this section, the rules of section 7502 and § 301.7502-1 of this chapter (relating to timely mailing treated as timely filing) determine when an application for registration is considered to be received by a State.

(b) *Proof of payment required.*—(1) *In general.*— A State to which an application is made to register a highway motor vehicle must receive from the registrant proof of payment of the tax imposed by section 4481(a) (or proof of suspension of such tax under § 41.4483-3) unless otherwise provided in this paragraph (b)(1), or paragraph (b)(2) or (5) of this section. See paragraph (c) of this section for the meaning of "proof of payment". Such proof of payment must be received by the State before the State issues a registration for such vehicle unless the State is using a system of registration provided in paragraph (b)(3) of this section. The term "proof of payment", when used in this section, shall be considered to refer in appropriate cases to proof of suspension of the tax imposed by section 4481(a). Except as provided in paragraph (b)(4) of this section, any proof of payment presented to a State must relate to tax paid (or suspended under § 41.4483-3) for the taxable period which includes the date that the State receives the application for registration. A "base state" must be presented proof of payment when issuing an "apportioned plate" under the International Registration Plan (IRP) (or similar agreement) for a highway motor vehicle, but no proof of payment of the tax imposed by section 4481(a) is required to be presented to the other states for which the vehicle is proportionally registered and which are listed on the

IRP cab card issued by the base state. Further, a State is not required to receive proof of payment in order to issue special temporary travel permits which allow a vehicle to, (i) operate in a State in which the vehicle is not registered (including proportional or prorate registration), (ii) operate at more than the State's maximum statutory weight limit, or (iii) operate at more than the weight that the vehicle is registered in a State. Further, a State may register a highway motor vehicle without proof of payment if the person registering the vehicle presents the original or a photocopy of a bill of sale (or other document evidencing transfer) indicating that the vehicle was purchased by the owner either as a new or used vehicle during the preceding 60 days before the date that the State receives the application for registration of such vehicle.

(ii) [Reserved].

(2) *States required to receive proof of payment with respect to vehicles subject to tax.*— (i) *Registration in States that register vehicles on the basis of gross weight.*—A State that registers vehicles on the basis of gross weight must require proof of payment with respect to any highway motor vehicle that has a declared gross weight in that State of 55,000 pounds or more. If no declaration of a specific gross weight is made with respect to a highway motor vehicle registered on the basis of gross weight, then the State must require proof of payment with respect to such vehicle if the minimum weight of the registered weight category for such vehicle is 55,000 pounds or more. No such proof of payment is required for any vehicle that does not have a declared gross weight in that State of 55,000 pounds or more.

(ii) *Registration in States that register vehicles other than on the basis of gross weight.*—A State that registers vehicles other than on the basis of gross weight must require proof of payment in order to register a highway motor vehicle unless the State receives a written statement stating that during the taxable period which includes the date on which the State receives the application for registration, such vehicle had a taxable gross weight of less than 55,000 pounds. The written statement must state the number of vehicles being registered that have a taxable gross weight of less than 55,000 pounds and must be signed by the person registering the vehicles. A State may register a highway motor vehicle without receiving either proof of payment or a written statement as described above if such vehicle has an unladen weight of 8,000 pounds or less. However, the State must require proof of payment when issuing a "base plate" registration for a vehicle if a gross weight declaration of 55,000 pounds or more is made to the State with respect to such vehicle in order to proportionally register the vehicle in another State under the IRP.

(iii) *State may require additional proof.*— Nothing contained in this section shall prohibit a State from refusing to register a highway motor vehicle without additional proof that the vehicle is not subject to tax under section 4481(a) even though the person registering the vehicle submits a written statement declaring that the taxable gross weight of such vehicle is less than 55,000 pounds.

(3) *Suspension registration system.*—A State may issue a registration with respect to any or all highway motor vehicles subject to tax under section 4481(a)without receiving proof of payment if such vehicles are registered under a "suspension" registration system. Registration of a vehicle subject to tax under a suspension system must be on the condition that, (i) the State receive proof of payment with respect to such vehicle no later than 4 months (or any lesser time to be determined by the State) after the beginning of the vehicle's registration period, and (ii) the State's system provides for the automatic suspension (*e.g*, through the use of computer-generated notices) of such vehicle's registration if no proof of payment is received within the required time. Following such a suspension of registration, the State must not allow the vehicle to be registered until valid proof of payment is received. A State may either register all vehicles subject to tax under section 4481(a) in the manner described in this paragraph (b)(3) or adopt this manner of registration only in situations which the State deems appropriate. A State that registers vehicles other than on the basis of gross weight may also register vehicles not subject to tax under a suspension registration system for purposes of receiving the written statement described in paragraph (b)(2)(ii).

(4) *Registration during certain months.*—In the case of a highway motor vehicle subject to tax under section 4481(a) for which a State receives an application for registration during the months of July, August or September, proof of payment for the immediately preceding taxable period may be used to verify payment of the tax imposed by section 4481(a).

(ii) [Reserved].

(5) *Registration in a State several times during the taxable period.*—A State is required to receive proof of payment with respect to a highway motor vehicle subject to tax under section 4481(a) only once during a taxable period. Thus, in the case of a State that allows a highway motor vehicle to be registered on a quarterly basis, rather than annually, proof of payment will be required to be presented to the State only once during the taxable period. The State may designate any one of the four quarterly registration periods as the time for submitting proof of payment.

(6) *Proof of payment records.*—See 23 CFR Part 669 for a description of the supporting documentation and records that will be required by the Federal Highway Administration (FHWA) in order to allow the FHWA to verify that the State is in compliance with the rules of this section.

Reg. § 41.6001-2(b)(6)

➤➤➤ *Caution: Reg. §41.6001-2(c), below, prior to amendment by T.D. 9698, applies before July 1, 2015.*

(c) *Proof of payment.*—(1) *In general.*—(i) The proof of payment required in paragraph (b) of this section shall consist of a receipted Schedule 1 (Form 2290) that is returned by the Internal Revenue Service to a taxpayer who files a return of tax under section 4481(a) and pays the amount of tax (or installment thereof) due with such return. A photocopy of such receipted Schedule 1 shall also serve as proof of payment. Such Schedule 1 shall serve as proof of suspension of such tax under § 41.4483-3 for the number of vehicles entered in that part of the Schedule 1 designated for vehicles for which tax has been suspended. Except as provided in paragraph (c)(1)(ii) of this section, the vehicle identification number of the vehicle being registered must appear on the Schedule 1 (or an attached page) in order for the Schedule 1 to be a valid proof of payment for such vehicle.

(ii) With respect to taxable periods beginning before July 1, 2000, if a receipted Schedule 1 is submitted as proof of payment for the registration of one or more highway motor vehicles and—

(A)*(1)* The total of the number of vehicles on such Schedule 1 for which tax has not been suspended under § 41.4483-3 exceeds 21, or

(2) The total of the number of vehicles on such Schedule 1 for which tax has been suspended under § 41.4483-3 exceeds 9, and

(B) The name of the taxpayer appearing on such Schedule 1 is one of the names in which such vehicles are sought to be registered, such Schedule 1 shall be accepted as proof of payment in support of the registration of a number of vehicles equal to or less than such total and a list of the vehicles (or their vehicle identification numbers) is not required as part of such proof of payment.

(iii) With respect to taxable periods beginning before July 1, 2000, if a Schedule 1 which does not include a list of vehicle identification numbers is submitted as proof of payment for the registration of one or more highway motor vehicles and the name of the taxpayer appearing on such Schedule 1 is not one of the names in which such vehicles are sought to be registered then such Schedule 1 shall be accepted as proof of payment in support of the registration of a number of vehicles equal to or less than the total number of vehicles on such Schedule 1 provided the Schedule 1 is accompanied by a written statement executed by the taxpayer. Such written statement shall contain the vehicle identification numbers of the vehicles sought to be registered and a statement that the tax under section 4481(a) has been paid with respect to such vehicles for the taxable period. The statement must be signed by the taxpayer whose name appears on the Schedule 1.

(2) *Acceptable substitute for receipted Schedule 1.*—(i) *General rule.*—For purposes of this section, a State shall accept as proof of payment a photocopy of the Form 2290 (with the Schedule 1 attached) which was filed with the Internal Revenue Service for the vehicle being registered with sufficient documentation of payment of tax due at the time the Form 2290 was filed (such as a photocopy of both sides of a cancelled check). This substitute proof of payment may be used to register a vehicle when, for example, the receipted Schedule 1 has been lost, or when at the time required for registration of a vehicle, a receipted Schedule 1 has not been received by a taxpayer who has filed a Form 2290 with respect to such vehicle. The rules of paragraph (c)(1)(ii) of this section regarding the circumstances in which a list of vehicle identification numbers is not required as part of a valid proof of payment, apply to a non-receipted Schedule 1 received by a State with a Form 2290 as a substitute proof of payment under this paragraph (c)(2).

(ii) [Reserved]. For further guidance, see § 41.6001-2T(c)(2)(ii).

➤➤➤ *Caution: Reg. §41.6001-2(c), below, as amended by T.D. 9698, applies on or after July 1, 2015.*

(c) *Proof of payment.*—(1) *In general.*—The proof of payment required in paragraph (b) of this section consists of a receipted Schedule 1 (Form 2290 "Heavy Highway Vehicle Use Tax Return") that is returned by the Internal Revenue Service, by mail or electronically, to a taxpayer that files a return of tax under section 4481(a), meets the requirements of § 41.6011(a)-1, and pays the amount of tax due with such return. A photocopy of such receipted Schedule 1 also serves as proof of payment. Such Schedule 1 serves as proof of suspension of such tax under § 41.4483-3 for the number of vehicles entered in that part of the Schedule 1 designated for vehicles for which tax has been suspended. The vehicle identification number of the vehicle being registered must appear on the Schedule 1 (or an attached page) in order for the Schedule 1 to be a valid proof of payment for such vehicle.

(2) *Acceptable substitute for receipted Schedule 1.*—For purposes of this section, a State must accept as proof of payment a photocopy of the Form 2290 (with the Schedule 1 attached) that was filed with the Internal Revenue Service for the vehicle being registered with sufficient documentation of payment of tax due at the time the Form 2290 was filed (such as a photocopy of both sides of a cancelled check). This substitute proof of payment may be used to register a vehicle when, for example, the receipted Schedule 1 has been lost, or when at the time required for registration of a vehicle, a receipted Schedule 1 has not been received by a taxpayer who has filed a Form 2290 with respect to such vehicle.

(d) *Examples.*—The application of this section may be illustrated by the following examples:

Example (1). A applies to register a 3-axle single unit truck in State R, a member of the International Registration Plan, on November 1, 1985. State R registers vehicles based on unladen weight. At the same time, A applies for a proportional registration under the IRP to use the truck in State S. State S does not register vehicles on the basis of unladen weight. For purposes of the proportional registration in State S, A declares the gross weight of his truck at 50,000 pounds. A does not register the truck in any other states. A's truck has a taxable gross weight, as determined under § 41.4482(b)-1, of less than 55,000 pounds and therefore is not subject to tax under section 4481(a). A submits a written statement along with his application for registration in State R. The written statement states that A's vehicle has a taxable gross weight of less than 55,000 pounds and is signed by A. State R may register A's truck and issue a proportional registration for A to use his truck in State S without receiving proof of payment.

Example (2). Assume the same facts as in example (1) except that A applies for proportional registration under the IRP in State S and declares the truck to have a gross weight of 60,000 pounds. The taxable gross weight of A's truck, as determined under § 41.4482(b)-1 is 60,000 pounds. State R may not register A's truck unless it receives proof of payment within the meaning of paragraph (c) of this section.

Example (3). On October 10, 1985, C applies to register 9 vehicles in State U and declares the gross weight of each vehicle to be 70,000 pounds. C has not applied for registration in any other states. At the time of applying for registration, C presents a photocopy of a receipted Schedule 1 (Form 2290) that shows a total of 9 vehicles which are subject to tax under section 4481(a) and for which tax is not suspended under § 41.4483-3(a). The vehicle identification numbers of the vehicles that C is seeking to register must be listed on the Schedule 1 in order for State U to register the vehicles.

(e) *Effective/applicability date.*—Paragraph (c) of this section applies to registrations of highway motor vehicles pursuant to applications that are received by a State on or after July 1, 2015. The rules of section 7502 and § 301.7502-1 of this chapter (relating to timely mailing treated as timely filing) determine when an application for registration is considered to be received by a State. For rules applicable to applications before that date, see 26 CFR 41.6001-2 (revised as of April 1, 2014). [Reg. § 41.6001-2.]

☐ [*T.D.* 8027, 5-23-85. *Amended by T.D.* 8879, 3-30-2000; *T.D.* 9537, 7-15-2011 *and T.D.* 9698 10-28-2014.]

[Reg. § 31.6001-3]

§ 31.6001-3. Additional records under Railroad Retirement Tax Act.—(a) *Records of employers.*—(1) Every employer liable for tax under the Railroad Retirement Tax Act shall keep records of all remuneration (whether in money or in something which may be used in lieu of money), other than tips, paid to his employees after 1954 for services rendered to him (including "time

lost") after 1954. Such records shall show with respect to each employee—

(i) The name and address of the employee.

(ii) The total amount and date of each payment of remuneration to the employee (including any sum withheld therefrom as tax or for any other reason) and the period of service (including any period of absence from active service) covered by such payment.

(iii) The amount of such remuneration payment with respect to which the tax is imposed.

(iv) The amount of employee tax collected with respect to such payment, and, if collected at a time other than the time such payment was made, the date collected.

(v) If the total payment of remuneration (paragraph (a)(1)(ii) of this section) and the amount thereof with respect to which the tax is imposed (paragraph (a)(1)(iii) of this section) are not equal, the reason therefor.

(2) The employer shall keep records of the details of each adjustment or settlement of taxes under the Railroad Retirement Tax Act made pursuant to the regulations in this part.

(b) *Records of employee representatives.*—Every individual liable for employee representative tax under the Railroad Retirement Tax Act shall keep records of all remuneration (whether in money or in something which may be used in lieu of money) paid to him after 1954 for services rendered (including "time lost") by him as an employee representative after 1954. Such records shall show—

(1) The name and address of each employee organization employing him.

(2) The total amount and date of each payment of remuneration for services rendered as an employee representative (including any sum withheld therefrom as tax or for any other reason) and the period of service (including any period of absence from active service) covered by such payment.

(3) The amount of such remuneration payment with respect to which the employee representative tax is imposed.

(4) If the total payment of remuneration (paragraph (a)(2) of this section) and the amount thereof with respect to which the employee representative tax is imposed (paragraph (a)(3) of this section) are not equal, the reason therefor. [Reg. § 31.6001-3.]

[Reg. § 41.6001-3]

§ 41.6001-3. Proof of payment for entry into the United States.—(a) *In general.*—(1) Except as otherwise provided in paragraph (a)(2) of this section, proof of payment of the tax imposed by section 4481(a) must be presented to United States Customs officials with respect to any highway motor vehicle subject to the tax imposed by section 4481(a) that has a base for registration purposes in a contiguous foreign country upon entry of such vehicle into the United States during any taxable period to which this section applies. Such proof of payment must relate to tax paid (or suspended under §41.4483-3) for the taxable period that includes the date of entry into the United States. See paragraph (c) of this section for the definition of the term "proof of payment."

(2) No proof of payment is required upon entry of a highway motor vehicle described in paragraph (a)(1) of this section into the United States if, as of the date of such entry, the period of time for filing a return of the tax imposed on such vehicle by section 4481(a) for the taxable period that includes the date of such entry has not expired and a written declaration is presented to United States Customs officials. Such declaration must state that, as of the date of such entry, the period of time for filing a return of the tax imposed on such vehicle by section 4481(a) for the taxable period that includes the date of such entry has not expired. The written declaration must include (1) the name, address, and taxpayer identification number of the person liable under §41.4481-2 for the tax imposed on such vehicle; (2) the vehicle identification number of such vehicle; (3) the date on which such vehicle was first used on the public highways in the United States during the taxable period (or a statement that the current entry is the first use on the public highways in the United States during the taxable period); (4) an acknowledgement by the person liable for the tax imposed on such vehicle that the willful use of the declaration to evade or defeat the tax otherwise applicable under section 4481(a) will subject such person to a fine or imprisonment or both; and (5) the signature of the person liable for the tax imposed on such vehicle. A copy of the written declaration shall be retained in the records of the person liable for the tax imposed on such vehicle under the rules of §41.6001-1. See §41.6071(a)-1 for rules regarding the time for filing a return of the tax imposed by section 4481(a).

(b) *Failure to provide proof of payment.*—If, upon attempting to enter the United States, the operator of a highway motor vehicle described in paragraph (a) of this section is unable to present proof of payment of the tax imposed by section 4481(a), or documentation described in paragraph (a)(2) of this section, with respect to such vehicle, then such vehicle may be denied entry into the United States.

(c) *Proof of payment.*—(1) *In general.*—For purposes of this section, the proof of payment required in paragraph (a) of this section shall consist of a receipted Schedule 1 (Form 2290) that is returned by the Internal Revenue Service to a taxpayer that files a return of tax under section 4481(a) and pays the amount of tax (or installment thereof) due with such return. A photocopy of such receipted Schedule 1 shall also serve as proof of payment. Such proof of payment shall also serve as proof of suspension of the tax under §41.4483-3 for the number of vehicles entered in that part of the Schedule 1 designated for vehicles for which tax has been suspended. The vehicle identification number of any vehicle for which a return is being filed, whether tax is being paid with respect to such vehicle or tax is suspended on such vehicle, must appear on the Schedule 1 (or an attached page) in order for the Schedule 1 to be a valid proof of payment for such vehicle.

(2) *Acceptable substitute for receipted Schedule 1.*—For purposes of this section, a photocopy of the Form 2290 (with the Schedule 1 attached) that is filed with the Internal Revenue Service for a vehicle being entered into the United States with sufficient documentation of payment of tax due at the time the Form 2290 is filed (such as a photocopy of both sides of a cancelled check) shall be accepted as proof of payment. No documentation of payment of tax is required with the substitute proof of payment if at the time the Form 2290 is filed the tax imposed by section 4481(a) is suspended under §41.4483-3 with respect to the vehicle entering the United States. This substitute proof of payment may be used to enter a vehicle into the United States when, for example, the receipted Schedule 1 has been lost, or if the taxpayer that filed a Form 2290 with respect to such vehicle has not received a receipted Schedule 1 at the time such vehicle enters the United States.

(d) *Taxable periods to which this section applies.*—This section shall apply to any taxable period beginning on or after July 1, 1987. [Reg. §41.6001-3.]

☐ [T.D. 8159, 9-3-87. *Amended by* T.D. 8177, 3-3-88.]

[Reg. §31.6001-4]

§31.6001-4. Additional records under Federal Unemployment Tax Act.—(a) *Records of employers.*—Every employer liable for tax under the Federal Unemployment Tax Act for any calendar year shall, with respect to each such year, keep such records as are necessary to establish—

(1) The total amount of remuneration (including any sum withheld therefrom as tax or for any other reason) paid to his employees during the calendar year for services performed after 1938.

(2) The amount of such remuneration which constitutes wages subject to the tax. See §31.3306(b)-1 through §31.3306(b)(8)-1.

(3) The amount of contributions paid by him into each State unemployment fund, with respect to services subject to the law of such State, showing separately (i) payments made and neither deducted nor to be deducted from the remuneration of his employees, and (ii) payments made and deducted or to be deducted from the remuneration of his employees.

(4) The information required to be shown on the prescribed return and the extent to which the employer is liable for the tax.

(5) If the total remuneration paid (subparagraph (1) of this paragraph) and the amount thereof which is subject to the tax (subparagraph (2) of this paragraph) are not equal, the reason therefor.

(6) To the extent material to a determination of tax liability, the dates, in each calendar quarter, on which each employee performed services not in the course of the employer's trade or business, and the amount of cash remuneration paid at any time for such services performed within such quarter. See § 31.3306(c)(3)-1.

The term "remuneration," as used in this paragraph, includes all payments whether in cash or in a medium other than cash, except that the term does not include payments in a medium other than cash for services not in the course of the employer's trade or business. See § 31.3306(b)(7)-1.

(b) *Records of persons who are not employers.*— Any person who employs individuals in employment (see § 31.3306(c)-1 to § 31.3306(c)-3, inclusive) during any calendar year but who considers that he is not an employer subject to the tax (see § 31.3306(a)-1) shall, with respect to each such year, be prepared to establish by proper records (including, where necessary, records of the number of employees employed each day) that he is not an employer subject to the tax. [Reg. § 31.6001-4.]

☐ [*T.D. 6516, 12-20-60. Amended by T.D. 6658, 6-27-63.*]

[Reg. § 31.6001-5]

§ 31.6001-5. Additional records in connection with collection of income tax at source on wages.—(a) Every employer required under section 3402 to deduct and withhold income tax upon the wages of employees shall keep records of all remuneration paid to (including tips reported by) such employees. Such records shall show with respect to each employee—

(1) The name and address of the employee, and, after December 31, 1962, the account number of the employee.

(2) The total amount and date of each payment of remuneration (including any sum withheld therefrom as tax or for any other reason) and the period of services covered by such payment.

(3) The amount of such remuneration payment which constitutes wages subject to withholding.

(4) The amount of tax collected with respect to such remuneration payment and, if collected at a time other than the time such payment was made, the date collected.

(5) If the total remuneration payment (subparagraph (2) of this paragraph) and the amount thereof which is taxable (subparagraph (3) of this paragraph) are not equal, the reason therefor.

(6) Copies of any statements furnished by the employee pursuant to paragraph (b)(12) of § 31.3401(a)-1 of Subpart E of the regulations in this part (relating to permanent residents of the Virgin Islands).

(7) Copies of any statements furnished by the employee pursuant to § § 31.3401(a)(6)-1 and 31.3401(a)(7)-1, relating to nonresident alien individuals.

(8) Copies of any statements furnished by the employee pursuant to § 31.3401(a)(8)(A)-1 of Subpart E of the regulations in this part (relating to residence or physical presence in a foreign country).

(9) Copies of any statements furnished by the employee pursuant to § 31.3401(a)(8)(C)-1 of Subpart E of the regulations in this part (relating to citizens resident in Puerto Rico).

(10) The fair market value and date of each payment of noncash remuneration, made to an employee after August 9, 1955, for services performed as a retail commission salesman, with respect to which no income tax is withheld by reason of § 31.3402(j)-1 of Subpart E of the regulations in this part.

[Subparagraph (11) was deleted by T.D. 7888.—CCH.]

(12) In the case of the employer for whom services are performed, with respect to payments made directly by him after December 31, 1955, under an accident or health plan (as defined in section 105 and the regulations thereunder)—

(i) The beginning and ending dates of each period of absence from work for which any such payment was made; and

(ii) Sufficient information to establish the amount and weekly rate of each such payment.

(13) The withholding exemption certificates (Forms W-4 and W-4E) filed with the employer by the employee.

(14) The agreement, if any, between the employer and the employee for the withholding of additional amounts of tax pursuant to § 31.3402(i)-1 of Subpart E of the regulations in this part.

(15) To the extent material to a determination of tax liability, the dates, in each calendar quarter, on which the employee performed services not in the course of the employer's trade or business, and the amount of cash remuneration paid at any time for such services performed within such quarter. See § 31.3401(a)(4)-1 of Subpart E of the regulations in this part.

(16) In the case of tips received by an employee after 1965 in the course of his employment, copies of any statements furnished by the employee pursuant to section 6053(a) unless the information disclosed by such statements is recorded on another document retained by the employer pursuant to the provisions of this paragraph.

(17) Any request of an employee under section 3402(h)(3) and § 31.3402(h)(3)-1 to have the amount of tax to be withheld from his wages computed on the basis of his cumulative wages, and any notice of revocation thereof.

The term "remuneration," as used in this paragraph, includes all payments whether in cash or in a medium other than cash, except that the term does not include payments in a medium other than cash for services not in the course of the employer's trade or business, and does not include tips received by an employee in any medium other than cash or in cash if such tips amount to less than $20 for any calendar month. See §§ 31.3401(a)(11)-1 and 31.3401(a)(16)-1, respectively.

(b) The employer shall keep records of the details of each adjustment or settlement of income tax withheld under section 3402 made pursuant to the regulations in this part. [Reg. § 31.6001-5.]

☐ [T.D. 6155, 12-29-55 and T.D. 6354, 1-13-59. Amended by T.D. 6606, 8-24-62; T.D. 6908, 12-30-66; T.D. 7001, 1-17-69; T.D. 7048, 6-23-70; T.D. 7053, 7-20-70 and T.D. 7888, 4-22-83.]

[Reg. § 31.6001-6]

§ 31.6001-6. Notice by district director requiring returns, statements, or the keeping of records.—The district director may require any person, by notice served upon him, to make such returns, render such statements, or keep such specific records as will enable the district director to determine whether or not such person is liable for any of the taxes to which the regulations in this part have application. [Reg. § 31.6001-6.]

☐ [T.D. 6472, 6-22-60.]

Tax Returns or Statements

[Reg. § 1.6011-1]

§ 1.6011-1. General requirement of return, statement, or list.—(a) *General rule.*—Every person subject to any tax, or required to collect any tax, under subtitle A of the Code, shall make such returns or statements as are required by the regulations in this chapter. The return or statement shall include therein the information required by the applicable regulations or forms.

(b) *Use of prescribed forms.*—Copies of the prescribed return forms will so far as possible be furnished taxpayers by district directors. A taxpayer will not be excused from making a return, however, by the fact that no return form has been furnished to him. Taxpayers not supplied with the proper forms should make application therefor to the district director in ample time to have their returns prepared, verified, and filed on or before the due date with the internal revenue office where such returns are required to be filed. Each taxpayer should carefully prepare his return and set forth fully and clearly the information required to be included therein. Returns which have not been so prepared will not be accepted as meeting the requirements of the Code. In the absence of a prescribed form, a statement made by a taxpayer disclosing his gross income and the deductions therefrom may be accepted as a tentative return, and, if filed within the prescribed time, the statement so made will relieve the taxpayer from liability for the addition to tax imposed for the delinquent filing of the return, provided that without unnecessary delay such a tentative return is supplemented by a return made on the proper form.

(c) *Tax withheld on nonresident aliens and foreign corporations.*—For requirements respecting the return of the tax required to be withheld under chapter 3 of the Code on nonresident aliens and foreign corporations and tax-free covenant bonds, see § 1.1461-2. [Reg. § 1.6011-1.]

☐ [T.D. 6364, 2-13-59. Amended by T.D. 6922, 6-16-67.]

[Reg. § 20.6011-1]

§ 20.6011-1. General requirement of return, statement, or list.—(a) *General rule.*—Every person made liable for any tax imposed by subtitle B of the Code shall make such returns or statements as are required by the regulations in this part. The return or statement shall include therein the information required by the applicable regulations or forms.

(b) *Use of prescribed forms.*—Copies of the forms prescribed by §§ 20.6018-1 and 20.6036-1 may be obtained from district directors. The fact that an executor has not been furnished with copies of these forms will not excuse him from making a return or, if applicable, from filing a preliminary notice. Application for a form shall be made to the district director in ample time for the executor to have the form prepared, verified, and filed with the appropriate internal revenue office on or before the date prescribed for the filing thereof (see §§ 20.6071-1 and 20.6075-1). The executor shall carefully prepare the return and, if applicable, the preliminary notice so as to set forth fully and clearly the data called for therein. A return or, if applicable, a preliminary notice which has not been so prepared will not be accepted as meeting the requirements of §§ 20.6018-1 through 20.6018-4 and § 20.6036-1. [Reg. § 20.6011-1.]

☐ [T.D. 6296, 6-23-58. Amended by T.D. 7238, 12-28-72.]

[Reg. § 25.6011-1]

§ 25.6011-1. General requirement of return, statement, or list.—(a) *General rule.*—Every person made liable for any tax imposed by chapter 12 of the Code shall make such returns or statements as are required by the regulations in this part. The return or statement shall include therein the information required by the applicable regulations or forms.

(b) *Use of prescribed forms.*—Copies of the forms prescribed by paragraph (b) of § 25.6001-1 and § 25.6019-1 may be obtained from district directors and directors of service centers. The fact that a person required to file a form has not been furnished with copies of a form will not excuse him from the making of a gift tax return, or from the furnishing of the evidence for which the forms are to be used. Application for a form should be made to the district director or director of a service center in ample time to enable the person whose duty it is to file the form to have the form prepared, verified, and filed on or before the date prescribed for the filing thereof. [Reg. § 25.6011-1.]

☐ [*T.D.* 6334, 11-14-58. *Amended by T.D.* 7012, 5-14-69.]

[Reg. § 53.6011-1]

§ 53.6011-1. General requirement of return, statement, or list.—(a) Every private foundation liable for tax under section 4940 or 4948(a) shall file an annual return with respect to such tax on the form prescribed by the Internal Revenue Service for such purpose and shall include therein the information required by such form and the instructions issued with respect thereto.

(b) Every person liable for tax imposed by section 4941(a), 4942(a), 4943(a), 4944(a), 4945(a), 4955(a), 4958(a), 4959 or 4965(a), and every private foundation and every trust described in section 4947(a)(2) which has engaged in an act of self-dealing (as defined in section 4941(d)) (other than an act giving rise to no tax under section 4941(a)) shall file an annual return on Form 4720 and shall include therein the information required by such form and the instructions issued with respect thereto. In the case of any tax imposed by sections 4941(a), 4942(a), 4943(a), and 4944(a), the annual return shall be filed with respect to each act (or failure to act) for each year (or part thereof) in the taxable period (as defined in sections 4941(e)(1), 4942(j)(1), 4943(d)(2), and 4944(e)(1)). In the case of a tax imposed by section 4945(a), 4955(a), 4958(a), or 4965(a), the annual return shall be filed with respect to each act for the year in which such act giving rise to liability occurred. In the case of a tax imposed by section 4959 on a hospital organization (as defined in § 1.501(r)-1(b)(18)), the annual return must include the required information for each of the organization's hospital facilities that failed to meet the requirements of section 501(r)(3) for the taxable year.

(c) If a Form 4720 is filed by a private foundation or trust described in section 4947(a)(2) with respect to a transaction to which other persons are required to file under paragraph (b) of this section, such persons may by their signature designate such organization's Form 4720 (to the extent applicable) as their return for purposes of compliance with this paragraph. However, this paragraph shall not apply to a person whose taxable year is other than the taxable year of the foundation or trust.

(d) For taxable years ending on or after December 31, 1975, every trust described in section 4947(a)(2) which is subject to any of the provisions of Chapter 42 as if it were a private foundation shall file an annual return on Form 5227. For taxable years beginning after December 31, 1980, every trust described in section 4947(a)(1) which is a private foundation shall file an annual return on Form 990-PF.

(e) For taxable years beginning after December 31, 1977, every person liable for tax under section 4951, 4952, or 4953 (relating to taxes on self-dealing, taxable expenditures, and excess contributions involving black lung benefit trusts) shall file an annual return with respect to the tax on the form prescribed by the Internal Revenue Service for that purpose. The person liable for the tax shall include the information required by the form and its related instructions. [Reg. § 53.6011-1.]

☐ [*T.D.* 7368, 7-15-75. *Amended by T.D.* 7407, 3-3-76; *T.D.* 7838, 10-5-82; *T.D.* 8026, 5-17-85; *T.D.* 8628, 12-4-95; *T.D.* 8705, 12-31-96; *T.D.* 9334, 7-5-2007; *T.D.* 9629, 8-14-2013 *and T.D.* 9708, 12-29-2014.]

[Reg. § 54.6011-1]

§ 54.6011-1. General requirement of return, statement, or list.—(a) *Minimum funding standards or excess contributions for self-employed individuals and section 403(b)(7)(A) custodial accounts.*—Any employer or individual liable for tax under section 4971, 4972 or 4973(a)(2) (for a custodial account under section 403(b)(7)(A)) shall file an annual return on Form 5330 and shall include therein the information required by such form and the instructions issued with respect thereto.

(b) *Tax on prohibited transactions.*—Every disqualified person (as defined in section 4975(e)(2)) liable for the tax imposed under section 4975(a) with respect to a prohibited transaction shall file an annual return on Form 5330 and shall include therein the information required by such form and the instructions issued with respect thereto. The annual return on Form 5330 shall be filed with respect to each prohibited transaction and for each taxable year (or part thereof) of the disqualified person in the taxable period (as defined in section 4975(f)(2)) beginning on the date on which such prohibited transaction occurs.

(c) *Entity manager tax on prohibited tax shelter transactions.*—(1) *In general.*—Any entity manager of a tax-exempt entity described in section 4965(c)(4), (c)(5), (c)(6), or (c)(7) who is liable for tax under section 4965(a)(2) shall file a return on Form 5330, "Return of Excise Taxes Related to Employee Benefit Plans," on or before the 15th day of the fifth month following the close of such entity manager's taxable year during which the entity entered into the prohibited tax shelter transaction, and shall include therein the information required by such form and the instructions issued with respect thereto.

(2) *Transition rule.*—A Form 5330, "Return of Excise Taxes Related to Employee Benefit Plans," for an excise tax under section 4965 that was due on or before October 4, 2007, will be deemed to have been filed on the due date if it was filed by October 4, 2007, and if the section 4965 tax that was required to be reported on that Form 5330 was paid by October 4, 2007.

(d) *Effective/applicability date.*—Paragraph (c) of this section is applicable on July 6, 2007. [Reg. § 54.6011-1.]

☐ [*T.D.* 7838, 10-5-82. *Amended by T.D.* 9334, 7-5-2007 *and T.D.* 9492, 7-2-2010 (*corrected* 8-3-2010).]

[Reg. § 54.6011-1T]

§ 54.6011-1T. General requirement of return, statement, or list (temporary).—(a) *Tax on reversions of qualified plan assets to employer.*—Every employer liable for the tax imposed under section 4980(a) with respect to an employer reversion (as defined in section 4980(c)(2)) shall file a quarterly return on Form 5330 and shall include therein the information required by such form and the instructions issued with respect thereto. The quarterly return on Form 5330 shall be filed with respect to employer reversions from each qualified plan (as defined in section 4980(c)(1)).

(b) *[Reserved].*

[Temporary Reg. § 54.6011-1T.]

☐ [*T.D.* 8133, 4-1-87. *Amended by T.D.* 9334, 7-5-2007 (*corrected* 8-15-2007) *and T.D.* 9492, 7-2-2010.]

[Reg. § 54.6011-2]

§ 54.6011-2. General requirement of return, statement, or list.—Effective for any Form 8928 that is due on or after January 1, 2010, any person liable for tax under section 4980B, 4980D, 4980E, or 4980G of the Code shall file a return with respect to the tax on Form 8928. The return must include the information required by Form 8928 and the instructions issued with respect to it. [Reg. § 54.6011-2.]

☐ [*T.D.* 9457, 9-4-2009.]

[Reg. § 55.6011-1]

§ 55.6011-1. General requirement of return, statement, or list.—Every person liable for tax under Chapter 44 shall file an annual return with respect to the tax on the form prescribed by the Internal Revenue Service for such purpose and shall include therein the information required by the form and the instructions issued with respect thereto. For calendar years beginning after December 31, 1986, the return, which must be made on a calendar year basis, shall be filed by a real estate investment trust on Form 8612 and by a regulated investment company on Form 8613. [Reg. § 55.6011-1.]

☐ [*T.D.* 7767, 2-3-81. *Amended by T.D.* 8180, 2-29-88.]

[Reg. § 56.6011-1]

§ 56.6011-1. General requirement of return, statement, or list.—Every organization liable for the tax imposed by section 4911(a) shall file an annual return with respect to the tax on the form prescribed by the Internal Revenue Service for that purpose and shall include the information required by the form and its instructions. [Reg. § 56.6011-1.]

☐ [*T.D.* 8308, 8-30-90.]

[Reg. § 156.6011-1]

§ 156.6011-1. General requirement of return, statement or list.—Every person liable for tax under section 5881 of the Code shall file a return with respect to the tax on the form prescribed by the Internal Revenue Service (Form 8725). Each such person shall include therein the information required by the form and the instructions issued with respect thereto. [Reg. § 156.6011-1.]

☐ [*T.D.* 8379, 12-17-91.]

[Reg. § 157.6011-1]

§ 157.6011-1. General requirement of return, statement, or list.—Every person liable for tax under section 5891 must file a return with respect to the tax in accordance with the forms and instructions provided by the Internal Revenue Service. [Reg. § 157.6011-1.]

☐ [*T.D.* 9134, 7-7-2004.]

[Reg. § 301.6011-1]

§ 301.6011-1. General requirement of return, statement or list.—(a) For provisions requiring returns, statements, or lists, see the regulations relating to the particular tax.

(b) The Internal Revenue Service may prescribe in forms, instructions, or other appropriate guidance the information or documentation required to be included with any return or any statement required to be made or other document required to be furnished under any provision of the internal revenue laws or regulations. [Reg. § 301.6011-1.]

☐ [*T.D.* 9040, 1-30-2003.]

[Reg. § 1.6011-2]

§ 1.6011-2. Returns, etc., of DISC's and former DISC's.—(a) *Records and information.*—Every DISC and former DISC (as defined in section 992(a)) must comply with section 6001 and the regulations thereunder, relating to required records, statements, and special returns. Thus, for example, a DISC is required to maintain the books of account or records described in § 1.6001-1(a). In addition, every DISC must furnish to each of its shareholders on or before the last day of the second month following the close of the taxable year of the DISC a copy of Schedule K (Form 1120-DISC) disclosing the amounts of actual distributions and deemed distributions from the DISC to such shareholder for the taxable year of the DISC. In the case of a deficiency distribution to meet qualification requirements, see § 1.992-3(a)(4) for requirements that distribution be designated in the form of a communication sent to a shareholder and service center at the time of distribution.

(b) *Returns.*—(1) *Requirement of return.*—Every DISC (as defined in section 992(a)(1)) shall make a return of income. A former DISC (as defined in section 992(a)(3)) shall also make a return of income in addition to any other return required. The return required of a DISC or former DISC under this section shall be made on Form 1120-DISC. The provisions of § 1.6011-1 shall apply with respect to a DISC and former DISC. A former DISC should indicate clearly on Form 1120-DISC that it is making a return of income as a former DISC (for example, by labeling at the top of the Form 1120-DISC "Former DISC"). In the case of a former DISC, those items on the form which pertain to the computation of taxable income shall not be completed, but Schedules J, K, L, and M must be completed. Except as otherwise specifically provided in the Code or regulations, the return of a DISC or former DISC is considered to be an income tax return.

(2) *Existence of DISC.*—A corporation which is a DISC and which is in existence during any portion of a taxable year is required to make a return for that fractional part of its taxable year during which it was in existence. [Reg. § 1.6011-2.]

☐ [*T.D.* 7533, 2-14-78.]

[Reg. § 301.6011-2]

§ 301.6011-2. Required use of magnetic media.—(a) *Meaning of terms.*—The following definitions apply for purposes of this section:

(1) *Magnetic media.*—The term *magnetic media* means any media permitted under applicable regulations, revenue procedures or publications, or, in the case of returns filed with the Social Security Administration, Social Security Administration publications. These generally include magnetic tape, tape cartridge, and diskette, as well as other media (such as electronic filing) specifically permitted under the applicable regulations, procedures, or publications.

(2) *Machine-readable paper form.*—The term "machine-readable paper form" means—

(i) Optical-scan paper form; or

(ii) Any other machine-readable paper form permitted under applicable regulations, revenue procedures, or Social Security Administration publications.

(3) *Person.*—The term "person" includes any person that is required to file a return that is described in paragraph (b) of this section. Thus, the term "person" includes the United States, a State, the District of Columbia, a foreign government, a political subdivision of a State or of a foreign government, or an international organization. In addition, in the case of an affiliated group of corporations filing a consolidated return, each member of the affiliated group is a separate person.

(b) *Returns required on magnetic media.*—(1) If the use of Form 1042-S, 1094 series, 1095-B, 1095-C, 1098, 1098-E, 1098-T, 1099 series, 5498, 8027, W-2G, or other form treated as a form specified in this paragraph (b)(1) is required by the applicable regulations or revenue procedures for the purpose of making an information return, the information required by the form must be submitted on magnetic media, except as otherwise provided in paragraph (c) of this section. Returns on magnetic media must be made in accordance with applicable revenue procedures or publications (see § 601.601(d)(2)(ii)(*b*) of this chapter). Pursuant to these procedures, the consent of the Commissioner of Internal Revenue (or other authorized officer or employee of the Internal Revenue Service) to a magnetic medium must be obtained by submitting Form 4419 (Application for Filing Information Returns Magnetically/Electronically) prior to submitting a return described in this paragraph (b)(1) on the magnetic medium.

(2) If the use of Form W-2 (Wage and Tax Statement), Form 499R-2/W-2PR (Withholding Statement (Puerto Rico)), Form W-2VI (U.S. Virgin Islands Wage and Tax Statement), Form W-2GU (Guam Wage and Tax Statement), Form W-2AS (American Samoa Wage and Tax Statement), or other form treated as a form specified in this paragraph (b)(2) is required for the purpose of making an information return, the information required by the form must be submitted on magnetic media, except as otherwise provided in paragraph (c) of this section. Returns described in this paragraph (b)(2) must be made in accordance with applicable Social Security Administration procedures or publications (which may be obtained from the local office of the Social Security Administration).

(3) The Commissioner may prescribe by revenue procedure that additional forms are treated, for purposes of this section, as forms specified in paragraph (b)(1) or (b)(2) of this section.

(c) *Exceptions.*—(1) *Low-volume filers/250-threshold.*—(i) *In general.*—No person is required to file information returns on magnetic media unless the person is required to file 250 or more returns during the calendar year. Persons filing fewer than 250 returns during the calendar year may make the returns on the prescribed paper form, or, alternatively, such persons may make returns on magnetic media in accordance with paragraph (b) of this section.

(ii) *Machine-readable forms.*—Returns made on a paper form under this paragraph (c)(1) shall be machine-readable if applicable revenue procedures provide for a machine-readable paper form.

(iii) *No aggregation.*—Each type of information return described in paragraphs (b)(1) and (2) of this section is considered a separate return for purposes of this paragraph (c)(1). Therefore, the 250-threshold applies separately to each type of form required to be filed.

(iv) *Examples.*—The provisions of paragraph (c)(1)(iii) of this section are illustrated by the following examples:

Example 1. For the calendar year ending December 31, 1998, Company X is required to file 200 returns on Form 1099-INT and 350 returns on Form 1099-MISC. Company X is not required to file Forms 1099-INT on magnetic media but is required to file Forms 1099-MISC on magnetic media.

Example 2. During the calendar year ending December 31, 1998, Company Y has 275 employees in Puerto Rico and 50 employees in American Samoa. Company Y is required to file Forms 499R-2/W-2PR on magnetic media but is not required to file Forms W-2AS on magnetic media.

Example 3. For the calendar year ending December 31, 1998, Company Z files 300 original returns on Form 1099-DIV and later files 70 corrected returns on Form 1099-DIV. Company Z is required to file the original returns on magnetic media. However, Company Z is not required to file the corrected returns on magnetic media because the corrected returns fall under the 250-threshold. See § 301.6721-1(a)(2)(ii).

(2) *Waiver.*—(i) The Commissioner may waive the requirements of this section if hardship is shown in a request for waiver filed in accordance with this paragraph (c)(2)(i). The principal factor in determining hardship will be the amount, if any, by which the cost of filing the information returns in accordance with this section exceeds the cost of filing the returns on other media. Notwithstanding the foregoing, if an employer is required to make a final return on Form 941, or a variation thereof, and expedited filing of Forms W-2, Forms 499R-2/W-2PR, Forms W-2VI, Forms W-2GU, or Form W-2AS is required, the unavailability of the specifications for magnetic media filing will be treated as creating a hardship (see § 31.6071(a)-1(a)(3)(ii) of this chapter). A request for waiver must be made in accordance with applicable revenue procedures or publications (see § 601.601(d)(2)(ii)(*b*) of this chapter). Pursuant to these procedures, a request for waiver should be filed at least 45 days before the due date of the information return in order for the Service to have adequate time to respond to the request for waiver. The waiver will specify the type of information return and the period to which it applies and will be subject to such terms and conditions regarding the method of reporting as may be prescribed by the Commissioner.

(ii) The Commissioner may prescribe rules that supplement the provisions of paragraph (c)(2)(i) of this section.

(d) *Paper form returns.*—Returns submitted on paper forms (whether or not machine-readable) permitted under paragraph (c) of this section shall be in accordance with applicable Internal Revenue Service or Social Security Administration procedures.

(e) *Applicability of current procedures.*—Until procedures are prescribed which further implement the mandatory filing on magnetic media provided by this section, a return to which this section applies shall be made in the manner and shall be subject to the requirements and conditions (including the requirement of applying for consent to the magnetic medium) prescribed in the regulations, revenue procedures and Social Security Administration publications relating to the filing of such return on magnetic media.

(f) *Failure to file.*—If a person fails to file an information return on magnetic media when required to do so by this section, the person is deemed to have failed to file the return. In addition, if a person making returns on a paper form under paragraph (c) of this section fails to file a return on machine-readable paper form when required to do so by this section, the person is deemed to have failed to file the return. See sections 6652, 6693, and 6721 for penalties for failure to file certain returns. See also section 6724 and the regulations under section 6721 for the specific rules and limitations regarding the penalty imposed under section 6721 for failure to file on magnetic media.

(g) *Effective dates.*—(1) Except as otherwise provided in paragraph (g)(2) or (3) of this section, this section applies to returns required to be filed after December 31, 1986.

(2) Paragraphs (a)(1), (b)(1), (b)(2), (c)(1)(i), (c)(1)(iii), (c)(1)(iv), (c)(2), (d), (e), and (f) of this section are effective for information returns required to be filed after December 31, 1996. For information returns required to be filed after December 31, 1989, and before January 1, 1997, see section 6011(e).

(3) This section applies to returns on Forms 1098-E, "Student Loan Interest Statement," and 1098-T, "Tuition Statement," filed after December 31, 2003. [Reg. § 301.6011-2.]

☐ [*T.D.* 8081, 3-20-86. *Amended by T.D.* 8097, 8-25-86; *T.D.* 8140, 5-15-87; *T.D.* 8636, 12-20-95; *T.D.* 8772, 6-29-98; *T.D.* 8992, 4-26-2002; *T.D.* 9029, 12-18-2002, *T.D.* 9660, 3-5-2014 *and T.D.* 9804, 12-14-2016.]

[Reg. § 1.6011-3]

§ 1.6011-3. Requirement of statement from payees of certain gambling winnings.—(a) *General rule.*—Except as provided in paragraph (c) of this section, any person receiving a payment with respect to a wager in a sweepstakes, wagering pool, lottery, or other wagering transaction (including a parimutuel pool with respect to horse races, dog races, or jai alai) shall make a statement to the payer of such winnings upon the payer's demand. Such statements shall accompany the payer's return made with respect to the payment as required pursuant to section 3402(q) or 6041, as the case may be.

(b) *Contents of statement.*—The statement referred to in paragraph (a) shall contain information (in addition to that required under section 6041 (c)) as to the amount, if any, of winnings from identical wagers to which the recipient is entitled. If any person other than the recipient is entitled to all or a portion of the payment, the statement shall also include information as to the amount, if any, of winnings from identical wagers to which each such person is entitled. The statement shall be provided on Form W-2G or, if persons other than the recipient are entitled to all or a portion of such payment, on Form 5754.

(c) *Exception.*—The requirement of paragraph (a) of this section does not apply with respect to any payment of winnings—

(i) From a slot machine play, or a bingo or keno game,

(ii) Which is subject to withholding under section 3402(q) without regard to the existence of winnings from identical wagers, or

(iii) For which no return of information under section 6041 is required of the payer.

(d) *Meaning of terms.*—For purposes of this section, the terms "sweepstakes", "wagering pool", "lottery," "other wagering transaction" and "identical wagers" shall have the same meaning as ascribed to them under § 31.3402(q)-1. [Reg. § 1.6011-3.]

☐ [T.D. 7919, 10-11-83.]

[Reg. § 301.6011-3]

§ 301.6011-3. Required use of magnetic media for partnership returns.—(a) *Partnership returns required on magnetic media.*—If a partnership with more than 100 partners is required to file a partnership return pursuant to § 1.6031(a)-1 of this chapter, the information required by the applicable forms and schedules must be filed on magnetic media, except as otherwise provided in paragraph (b) of this section. Returns filed on magnetic media must be made in accordance with applicable revenue procedures or publications. In prescribing revenue procedures or publications, the Commissioner may determine that partnerships will be required to use any one form of magnetic media filing. For example, the Commissioner may determine that partnerships with more than 100 partners must file their partnership returns electronically. In filing its return, a partnership must register to participate in the magnetic media filing program in the manner prescribed by the Internal Revenue Service in applicable revenue procedures or publications.

(b) *Waiver.*—The Commissioner may waive the requirements of this section if hardship is shown in a request for waiver filed in accordance with this paragraph (b). A determination of hardship will be based upon all of the facts and circumstances. One factor in determining hardship will be the reasonableness of the incremental cost to the partnership of complying with the magnetic media filing requirements. Other factors, such as equipment breakdowns or destruction of magnetic media filing equipment, also may be considered. A request for waiver must be made in accordance with applicable revenue procedures or publications. The waiver will specify the type of partnership return and the period to which it applies. The waiver will also be subject to such terms and conditions regarding the method of filing as may be prescribed by the Commissioner.

(c) *Failure to file.*—If a partnership fails to file a partnership return on magnetic media in the manner required and when required to do so by this section, the partnership will be deemed to have failed to file the return in the manner prescribed for purposes of the information return penalty under section 6721. See § 301.6724-1(c)(3) for rules regarding the waiver of penalties for undue economic hardship relating to filing returns on magnetic media.

(d) *Meaning of terms.*—The following definitions apply for purposes of this section:

(1) *Magnetic media.*—The term *magnetic media* means any magnetic media permitted under applicable regulations, revenue procedures, or publications. These generally include magnetic tape, tape cartridge, and diskette, as well as other media (such as electronic filing) specifically permitted under the applicable regulations, procedures, or publications.

(2) *Partnership.*—The term *partnership* means a partnership as defined in § 1.761-1(a) of this chapter.

(3) *Partner.*—The term *partner* means a member of a partnership as defined in section 7701(a)(2).

(4) *Partnership return.*—The term *partnership return* means a form in Series 1065 (including Form 1065, U.S. Partnership Return of Income, and Form 1065-B, U.S. Return of Income for Electing Large Partnerships), along with the corresponding Schedules K-1 and all other related forms and schedules that are required to be attached to the Series 1065 form.

(5) *Partnerships with more than 100 partners.*—A partnership has more than 100 partners if, over the course of the partnership's taxable year, the partnership had more than 100 partners, regardless of whether a partner was a partner for the entire year or whether the partnership had over 100 partners on any particular day in the year. For purposes of this paragraph (d)(5), however, only those persons having a direct interest in the partnership must be considered partners for purposes of determining the number of partners during the partnership's taxable year.

(e) *Examples.*—The following examples illustrate the provisions of paragraph (d)(5) of this section. In the examples, the partnerships utilize the calendar year, and the taxable year in question is 2000:

Example 1. Partnership P had five general partners and 90 limited partners on January 1, 2000. On March 15, 2000, 10 more limited partners acquired an interest in P. On September 29, 2000, the 10 newest partners sold their individual partnership interests to C, a corporation which was one of the original 90 limited partners. On December 31, 2000, P had the same five general partners and 90 limited partners it had on January 1, 2000. P had a total of 105 partners over the course of partnership taxable year 2000. Therefore, P must file its 2000 partnership return on magnetic media.

Example 2. Partnership Q is a general partnership that had 95 partners on January 1, 2000. On March 15, 2000, 10 partners sold their individual partnership interests to corporation D, which was not previously a partner in Q. On September 29, 2000, corporation D sold one-half of its partnership interest in equal shares to five individuals, who were not previously partners in Q. On December 31, 2000, Q had a total of 91 partners, and on no date in the year did Q have more than 100 partners. Over the course of the year, however, Q had 101 partners. Therefore, Q must file its 2000 partnership return on magnetic media.

Example 3. Partnership G is a general partnership with 100 partners on January 1, 2000. There are no new partners added to G in 2000. One of G's partners, A, is a partnership with 53 partners. A is one partner, regardless of the number of partners A has. Therefore, G has 100 partners and is not required to file its 2000 partnership return on magnetic media.

(f) *Effective date.*—In general, this section applies to partnership returns for taxable years ending on or after December 31, 2000. However, electing large partnerships under section 775 and partnerships using foreign addresses on their Series 1065 forms are not required to file using magnetic media for taxable years ending before January 1, 2001. [Reg. § 301.6011-3.]

☐ [T.D. 8843, 11-10-99.]

[Reg. § 1.6011-4]

§ 1.6011-4. Requirement of statement disclosing participation in certain transactions by taxpayers.—(a) *In general.*—Every taxpayer that has participated, as described in paragraph (c)(3) of this section, in a reportable transaction within the meaning of paragraph (b) of this section and who is required to file a tax return must file within the time prescribed in paragraph (e) of this section a disclosure statement in the form prescribed by paragraph (d) of this section. The fact that a transaction is a reportable transaction shall not affect the legal determination of whether the taxpayer's treatment of the transaction is proper.

(b) *Reportable transactions.*—(1) *In general.*—A reportable transaction is a transaction described in any of the paragraphs (b)(2) through (7) of this section. The term transaction includes all of the factual elements relevant to the expected tax treatment of any investment, entity, plan, or arrangement, and includes any series of steps carried out as part of a plan.

(2) *Listed transactions.*—A listed transaction is a transaction that is the same as or substantially similar to one of the types of transactions that the Internal Revenue Service (IRS) has determined to be a tax avoidance transaction and identified by notice, regulation, or other form of published guidance as a listed transaction.

(3) *Confidential transactions.*—(i) *In general.*—A confidential transaction is a transaction that is offered to a taxpayer under conditions of confidentiality and for which the taxpayer has paid an advisor a minimum fee.

(ii) *Conditions of confidentiality.*—A transaction is considered to be offered to a taxpayer under conditions of confidentiality if the advisor who is paid the minimum fee places a limitation on disclosure by the taxpayer of the tax treatment or tax structure of the transaction and the limitation on disclosure protects the confidentiality of that advisor's tax strategies. A transaction is treated as confidential even if the conditions of confidentiality are not legally binding on the taxpayer. A claim that a transaction is proprietary or exclusive is not treated as a limitation on disclosure if the advisor confirms to the taxpayer that there is no limitation on disclosure of the tax treatment or tax structure of the transaction.

(iii) *Minimum fee.*—For purposes of this paragraph (b)(3), the minimum fee is—

(A) $250,000 for a transaction if the taxpayer is a corporation;

(B) $50,000 for all other transactions unless the taxpayer is a partnership or trust, all of the owners or beneficiaries of which are corporations (looking through any partners or beneficiaries that are themselves partnerships or trusts), in which case the minimum fee is $250,000.

(iv) *Determination of minimum fee.*—For purposes of this paragraph (b)(3), in determining the minimum fee, all fees for a tax strategy or for services for advice (whether or not tax advice) or for the implementation of a transaction are taken into account. Fees include consideration in whatever form paid, whether in cash or in kind, for services to analyze the transaction (whether or not related to the tax consequences of the transaction), for services to implement the transaction, for services to document the transaction, and for services to prepare tax returns to the extent return preparation fees are unreasonable in light of the facts and circumstances. For purposes of this paragraph (b)(3), a taxpayer also is treated as paying fees to an advisor if the taxpayer knows or should know that the amount it pays will be paid indirectly to the advisor, such as through a referral fee or fee-sharing arrangement. A fee does not include amounts paid to a person, including an advisor, in that person's capacity as a party to the transaction. For example, a fee does not include reasonable charges for the use of capital or the sale or use of property. The IRS will scrutinize carefully all of the facts and circumstances in determining whether consideration received in connection with a confidential transaction constitutes fees.

(v) *Related parties.*—For purposes of this paragraph (b)(3), persons who bear a relationship to each other as described in section 267(b) or 707(b) will be treated as the same person.

(4) *Transactions with contractual protection.*—(i) *In general.*—A transaction with contractual protection is a transaction for which the taxpayer or a related party (as described in section 267(b) or 707(b)) has the right to a full or partial refund of fees (as described in paragraph (b)(4)(ii) of this section) if all or part of the intended tax

consequences from the transaction are not sustained. A transaction with contractual protection also is a transaction for which fees (as described in paragraph (b)(4)(ii) of this section) are contingent on the taxpayer's realization of tax benefits from the transaction. All the facts and circumstances relating to the transaction will be considered when determining whether a fee is refundable or contingent, including the right to reimbursements of amounts that the parties to the transaction have not designated as fees or any agreement to provide services without reasonable compensation.

(ii) *Fees.*—Paragraph (b)(4)(i) of this section only applies with respect to fees paid by or on behalf of the taxpayer or a related party to any person who makes or provides a statement, oral or written, to the taxpayer or related party (or for whose benefit a statement is made or provided to the taxpayer or related party) as to the potential tax consequences that may result from the transaction.

(iii) *Exceptions.*—(A) *Termination of transaction.*—A transaction is not considered to have contractual protection solely because a party to the transaction has the right to terminate the transaction upon the happening of an event affecting the taxation of one or more parties to the transaction.

(B) *Previously reported transaction.*—If a person makes or provides a statement to a taxpayer as to the potential tax consequences that may result from a transaction only after the taxpayer has entered into the transaction and reported the consequences of the transaction on a filed tax return, and the person has not previously received fees from the taxpayer relating to the transaction, then any refundable or contingent fees are not taken into account in determining whether the transaction has contractual protection. This paragraph (b)(4) does not provide any substantive rules regarding when a person may charge refundable or contingent fees with respect to a transaction. See Circular 230, 31 CFR Part 10, for the regulations governing practice before the IRS.

(5) *Loss transactions.*—(i) *In general.*—A loss transaction is any transaction resulting in the taxpayer claiming a loss under section 165 of at least—

(A) $10 million in any single taxable year or $20 million in any combination of taxable years for corporations;

(B) $10 million in any single taxable year or $20 million in any combination of taxable years for partnerships that have only corporations as partners (looking through any partners that are themselves partnerships), whether or not any losses flow through to one or more partners; or

(C) $2 million in any single taxable year or $4 million in any combination of taxable years for all other partnerships, whether or not any losses flow through to one or more partners;

(D) $2 million in any single taxable year or $4 million in any combination of taxable years for individuals, S corporations, or trusts, whether or not any losses flow through to one or more shareholders or beneficiaries; or

(E) $50,000 in any single taxable year for individuals or trusts, whether or not the loss flows through from an S corporation or partnership, if the loss arises with respect to a section 988 transaction (as defined in section 988(c)(1) relating to foreign currency transactions).

(ii) *Cumulative losses.*—In determining whether a transaction results in a taxpayer claiming a loss that meets the threshold amounts over a combination of taxable years as described in paragraph (b)(5)(i) of this section, only losses claimed in the taxable year that the transaction is entered into and the five succeeding taxable years are combined.

(iii) *Section 165 loss.*—(A) For purposes of this section, in determining the thresholds in paragraph (b)(5)(i) of this section, the amount of a section 165 loss is adjusted for any salvage value and for any insurance or other compensation received. See § 1.165-1(c)(4). However, a section 165 loss does not take into account offsetting gains, or other income or limitations. For example, a section 165 loss does not take into account the limitation in section 165(d) (relating to wagering losses) or the limitations in sections 165(f), 1211, and 1212 (relating to capital losses). The full amount of a section 165 loss is taken into account for the year in which the loss is sustained, regardless of whether all or part of the loss enters into the computation of a net operating loss under section 172 or a net capital loss under section 1212 that is a carryback or carryover to another year. A section 165 loss does not include any portion of a loss, attributable to a capital loss carryback or carryover from another year, that is treated as a deemed capital loss under section 1212.

(B) For purposes of this section, a section 165 loss includes an amount deductible pursuant to a provision that treats a transaction as a sale or other disposition, or otherwise results in a deduction under section 165. A section 165 loss includes, for example, a loss resulting from a sale or exchange of a partnership interest under section 741 and a loss resulting from a section 988 transaction.

(6) *Transactions of interest.*—A transaction of interest is a transaction that is the same as or substantially similar to one of the types of transactions that the IRS has identified by notice, regulation, or other form of published guidance as a transaction of interest.

(7) [*Reserved*].

(8) *Exceptions.*—(i) *In general.*—A transaction will not be considered a reportable transaction, or will be excluded from any individual category of reportable transaction under paragraphs (b)(3) through (7) of this section, if the Commissioner makes a determination by

published guidance that the transaction is not subject to the reporting requirements of this section. The Commissioner may make a determination by individual letter ruling under paragraph (f) of this section that an individual letter ruling request on a specific transaction satisfies the reporting requirements of this section with regard to that transaction for the taxpayer who requests the individual letter ruling.

(ii) *Special rule for RICs.*—For purposes of this section, a regulated investment company (RIC) as defined in section 851 or an investment vehicle that is owned 95 percent or more by one or more RICs at all times during the course of the transaction is not required to disclose a transaction that is described in any of paragraphs (b)(3) through (5) and (b)(7) of this section unless the transaction is also a listed transaction or a transaction of interest.

(c) *Definitions.*—For purposes of this section, the following definitions apply:

(1) *Taxpayer.*—The term *taxpayer* means any person described in section 7701(a)(1), including S corporations. Except as otherwise specifically provided in this section, the term *taxpayer* also includes an affiliated group of corporations that joins in the filing of a consolidated return under section 1501.

(2) *Corporation.*—When used specifically in this section, the term *corporation* means an entity that is required to file a return for a taxable year on any 1120 series form, or successor form, excluding S corporations.

(3) *Participation.*—(i) *In general.*—(A) *Listed transactions.*—A taxpayer has participated in a listed transaction if the taxpayer's tax return reflects tax consequences or a tax strategy described in the published guidance that lists the transaction under paragraph (b)(2) of this section. A taxpayer also has participated in a listed transaction if the taxpayer knows or has reason to know that the taxpayer's tax benefits are derived directly or indirectly from tax consequences or a tax strategy described in published guidance that lists a transaction under paragraph (b)(2) of this section. Published guidance may identify other types or classes of persons that will be treated as participants in a listed transaction. Published guidance also may identify types or classes of persons that will not be treated as participants in a listed transaction.

(B) *Confidential transactions.*—A taxpayer has participated in a confidential transaction if the taxpayer's tax return reflects a tax benefit from the transaction and the taxpayer's disclosure of the tax treatment or tax structure of the transaction is limited in the manner described in paragraph (b)(3) of this section. If a partnership's, S corporation's or trust's disclosure is limited, and the partner's, shareholder's, or beneficiary's disclosure is not limited, then the partnership, S corporation, or trust, and not the partner, shareholder, or beneficiary, has participated in the confidential transaction.

(C) *Transactions with contractual protection.*—A taxpayer has participated in a transaction with contractual protection if the taxpayer's tax return reflects a tax benefit from the transaction and, as described in paragraph (b)(4) of this section, the taxpayer has the right to the full or partial refund of fees or the fees are contingent. If a partnership, S corporation, or trust has the right to a full or partial refund of fees or has a contingent fee arrangement, and the partner, shareholder, or beneficiary does not individually have the right to the refund of fees or a contingent fee arrangement, then the partnership, S corporation, or trust, and not the partner, shareholder, or beneficiary, has participated in the transaction with contractual protection.

(D) *Loss transactions.*—A taxpayer has participated in a loss transaction if the taxpayer's tax return reflects a section 165 loss and the amount of the section 165 loss equals or exceeds the threshold amount applicable to the taxpayer as described in paragraph (b)(5)(i) of this section. If a taxpayer is a partner in a partnership, shareholder in an S corporation, or beneficiary of a trust and a section 165 loss as described in paragraph (b)(5) of this section flows through the entity to the taxpayer (disregarding netting at the entity level), the taxpayer has participated in a loss transaction if the taxpayer's tax return reflects a section 165 loss and the amount of the section 165 loss that flows through to the taxpayer equals or exceeds the threshold amounts applicable to the taxpayer as described in paragraph (b)(5)(i) of this section. For this purpose, a tax return is deemed to reflect the full amount of a section 165 loss described in paragraph (b)(5) of this section allocable to the taxpayer under this paragraph (c)(3)(i)(D), regardless of whether all or part of the loss enters into the computation of a net operating loss under section 172 or net capital loss under section 1212 that the taxpayer may carry back or carry over to another year.

(E) *Transactions of interest.*—A taxpayer has participated in a transaction of interest if the taxpayer is one of the types or classes of persons identified as participants in the transaction in the published guidance describing the transaction of interest.

(F) *[Reserved].*

(G) *Shareholders of foreign corporations.*— (1) *In general.*—A reporting shareholder of a foreign corporation participates in a transaction described in paragraphs (b)(2) through (5) and (b)(7) of this section if the foreign corporation would be considered to participate in the transaction under the rules of this paragraph (c)(3) if it were a domestic corporation filing a tax return that reflects the items from the transaction. A reporting shareholder of a foreign corporation participates in a transaction described in paragraph (b)(6) of this section only if the published guidance identifying the transaction includes the reporting shareholder among the types or classes of persons identified as participants. A reporting shareholder (and any successor in interest) is considered to participate in a transaction under this paragraph (c)(3)(i)(G) only for its first taxable year with or within which ends the first taxable year of the foreign corporation in which the foreign corporation participates in the transaction, and for the reporting shareholder's five succeeding taxable years.

(2) *Reporting shareholder.*—The term *reporting shareholder* means a United States shareholder (as defined in section 951(b)) in a controlled foreign corporation (as defined in section 957) or a 10 percent shareholder (by vote or value) of a qualified electing fund (as defined in section 1295).

(ii) *Examples.*—The following examples illustrate the provisions of paragraph (c)(3)(i) of this section:

Example 1. Notice 2003-55 (2003-2 CB 395), which modified and superseded Notice 95-53 (1995-2 CB 334) (see §601.601(d)(2) of this chapter), describes a lease stripping transaction in which one party (the transferor) assigns the right to receive future payments under a lease of tangible property and treats the amount realized from the assignment as its current income. The transferor later transfers the property subject to the lease in a transaction intended to qualify as a transferred basis transaction, for example, a transaction described in section 351. The transferee corporation claims the deductions associated with the high basis property subject to the lease. The transferor's and transferee corporation's tax returns reflect tax positions described in Notice 2003-55. Therefore, the transferor and transferee corporation have participated in the listed transaction. In the section 351 transaction, the transferor will have received stock with low value and high basis from the transferee corporation. If the transferor subsequently transfers the high basis/low value stock to a taxpayer in another transaction intended to qualify as a transferred basis transaction and the taxpayer uses the stock to generate a loss, and if the taxpayer knows or has reason to know that the tax loss claimed was derived indirectly from the lease stripping transaction, then the taxpayer has participated in the listed transaction. Accordingly, the taxpayer must disclose the transaction and the manner of the taxpayer's participation in the transaction under the rules of this section. For purposes of this example, if a bank lends money to the transferor, transferee corporation, or taxpayer for use in their transactions, the bank has not participated in the listed transaction because the bank's tax return does not reflect tax consequences or a tax strategy described in the listing notice (nor does the bank's tax return reflect a tax benefit derived from tax consequences or a tax strategy described in the listing notice) nor is the bank described as a participant in the listing notice.

Example 2. XYZ is a limited liability company treated as a partnership for tax purposes. X, Y, and Z are members of XYZ. X is an individual, Y is an S corporation, and Z is a partnership. XYZ enters into a confidential transaction under paragraph (b)(3) of this section. XYZ and X are bound by the confidentiality agreement, but Y and Z are not bound by the agreement. As a result of the transaction, XYZ, X, Y, and Z all reflect a tax benefit on their tax returns. Because XYZ's and X's disclosure of the tax treatment and tax structure are limited in the manner described in paragraph (b)(3) of this section and their tax returns reflect a tax benefit from the transaction, both XYZ and X have participated in the confidential transaction. Neither Y nor Z has participated in the confidential transaction because they are not subject to the confidentiality agreement.

Example 3. P, a corporation, has an 80% partnership interest in PS, and S, an individual, has a 20% partnership interest in PS. P, S, and PS are calendar year taxpayers. In 2006, PS enters into a transaction and incurs a section 165 loss (that does not meet any of the exceptions to a section 165 loss identified in published guidance) of $12 million and offsetting gain of $3 million. On PS' 2006 tax return, PS includes the section 165 loss and the corresponding gain. PS must disclose the transaction under this section because PS' section 165 loss of $12 million is equal to or greater than $2 million. P is allocated $9.6 million of the section 165 loss and $2.4 million of the offsetting gain. P does not have to disclose the transaction under this section because P's section 165 loss of $9.6 million is not equal to or greater than $10 million. S is allocated $2.4 million of the section 165 loss and $600,000 of the offsetting gain. S must disclose the transaction under this section because S's section 165 loss of $2.4 million is equal to or greater than $2 million.

(4) *Substantially similar.*—The term *substantially similar* includes any transaction that is expected to obtain the same or similar types of tax consequences and that is either factually similar or based on the same or similar tax strategy. Receipt of an opinion regarding the tax consequences of the transaction is not relevant to the determination of whether the transaction is the same as or substantially similar to another transaction. Further, the term *substantially similar* must be broadly construed in favor of disclosure. For example, a transaction may be substantially similar to a listed transaction even though it involves different entities or uses different Internal Revenue Code provisions. (See for example, Notice 2003-54 (2003-2 CB 363), describing a transaction substantially similar to the transactions in Notice 2002-50 (2002-2 CB 98), and Notice 2002-65 (2002-2 CB 690).) The following examples illustrate situations where a transaction is the same as or substantially similar to a listed transaction under paragraph (b)(2) of this section. (Such transactions may also be reportable transactions under paragraphs (b)(3) through (7) of this section.) See §601.601(d)(2)(ii)(*b*) of this chapter. The following examples illustrate the provisions of this paragraph (c)(4):

Example 1. Notice 2000-44 (2000-2 CB 255) (see §601.601(d)(2)(ii)(*b*) of this chapter), sets

Reg. §1.6011-4(c)(4)

forth a listed transaction involving offsetting options transferred to a partnership where the taxpayer claims basis in the partnership for the cost of the purchased options but does not adjust basis under section 752 as a result of the partnership's assumption of the taxpayer's obligation with respect to the options. Transactions using short sales, futures, derivatives or any other type of offsetting obligations to inflate basis in a partnership interest would be the same as or substantially similar to the transaction described in Notice 2000-44. Moreover, use of the inflated basis in the partnership interest to diminish gain that would otherwise be recognized on the transfer of a partnership asset would also be the same as or substantially similar to the transaction described in Notice 2000-44. See § 601.601(d)(2)(ii)(b).

Example 2. Notice 2001-16 (2001-1 CB 730) (see § 601.601(d)(2)(ii)(*b*) of this chapter), sets forth a listed transaction involving a seller (X) who desires to sell stock of a corporation (T), an intermediary corporation (M), and a buyer (Y) who desires to purchase the assets (and not the stock) of T. M agrees to facilitate the sale to prevent the recognition of the gain that T would otherwise report. Notice 2001-16 describes M as a member of a consolidated group that has a loss within the group or as a party not subject to tax. Transactions utilizing different intermediaries to prevent the recognition of gain would be the same as or substantially similar to the transaction described in Notice 2001-16. An example is a transaction in which M is a corporation that does not file a consolidated return but which buys T stock, liquidates T, sells assets of T to Y, and offsets the gain on the sale of those assets with currently generated losses. See § 601.601(d)(2)(ii)(*b*).

(5) *Tax.*—The term *tax* means Federal income tax.

(6) *Tax benefit.*—A tax benefit includes deductions, exclusions from gross income, nonrecognition of gain, tax credits, adjustments (or the absence of adjustments) to the basis of property, status as an entity exempt from Federal income taxation, and any other tax consequences that may reduce a taxpayer's Federal income tax liability by affecting the amount, timing, character, or source of any item of income, gain, expense, loss, or credit.

(7) *Tax return.*—The term *tax return* means a Federal income tax return and a Federal information return.

(8) *Tax treatment.*—The tax treatment of a transaction is the purported or claimed Federal income tax treatment of the transaction.

(9) *Tax structure.*—The tax structure of a transaction is any fact that may be relevant to understanding the purported or claimed Federal income tax treatment of the transaction.

(d) *Form and content of disclosure statement.*—A taxpayer required to file a disclosure statement under this section must file a completed Form 8886, "Reportable Transaction Disclosure Statement" (or a successor form), in accordance with this paragraph (d) and the instructions to the form. The Form 8886 (or a successor form) is the disclosure statement required under this section. The form must be attached to the appropriate tax return(s) as provided in paragraph (e) of this section. If a copy of a disclosure statement is required to be sent to the Office of Tax Shelter Analysis (OTSA) under paragraph (e) of this section, it must be sent in accordance with the instructions to the form. To be considered complete, the information provided on the form must describe the expected tax treatment and all potential tax benefits expected to result from the transaction, describe any tax result protection (as defined in § 301.6111-3(c)(12) of this chapter) with respect to the transaction, and identify and describe the transaction in sufficient detail for the IRS to be able to understand the tax structure of the reportable transaction and the identity of all parties involved in the transaction. An incomplete Form 8886 (or a successor form) containing a statement that information will be provided upon request is not considered a complete disclosure statement. If the form is not completed in accordance with the provisions in this paragraph (d) and the instructions to the form, the taxpayer will not be considered to have complied with the disclosure requirements of this section. If a taxpayer receives one or more reportable transaction numbers for a reportable transaction, the taxpayer must include the reportable transaction number(s) on the Form 8886 (or a successor form). See § 301.6111-3(d)(2) of this chapter.

(e) *Time of providing disclosure.*—(1) *In general.*—The disclosure statement for a reportable transaction must be attached to the taxpayer's tax return for each taxable year for which a taxpayer participates in a reportable transaction. In addition, a disclosure statement for a reportable transaction must be attached to each amended return that reflects a taxpayer's participation in a reportable transaction. A copy of the disclosure statement must be sent to OTSA at the same time that any disclosure statement is first filed by the taxpayer pertaining to a particular reportable transaction. If a reportable transaction results in a loss which is carried back to a prior year, the disclosure statement for the reportable transaction must be attached to the taxpayer's application for tentative refund or amended tax return for that prior year. In the case of a taxpayer that is a partnership, an S corporation, or a trust, the disclosure statement for a reportable transaction must be attached to the partnership, S corporation, or trust's tax return for each taxable year in which the partnership, S corporation, or trust participates in the transaction under the rules of paragraph (c)(3)(i) of this section. If a taxpayer who is a partner in a partnership, a shareholder in an S corporation, or a beneficiary of a trust receives a timely Schedule K-1 less than 10 calendar days before the due date of the taxpayer's return (including extensions) and, based on receipt of the timely Schedule K-1, the taxpayer determines that the taxpayer participated in a reportable transaction within the meaning of paragraph (c)(3) of this section, the disclosure statement will not be considered late if the taxpayer discloses the reportable transaction by filing a disclosure statement with OTSA within 60 calendar days after the due date of the taxpayer's return (including extensions). The Commissioner in his discretion may issue in published guidance other provisions for disclosure under § 1.6011-4.

(2) *Special rules.*—(i) *Listed transactions and transactions of interest.*—In general, if a transaction becomes a listed transaction or a transaction of interest after the filing of a taxpayer's tax return (including an amended return) reflecting the taxpayer's participation in the listed transaction or transaction of interest and before the end of the period of limitations for assessment of tax for any taxable year in which the taxpayer participated in the listed transaction or transaction of interest, then a disclosure statement must be filed, regardless of whether the taxpayer participated in the transaction in the year the transaction became a listed transaction or a transaction of interest, with OTSA within 90 calendar days after the date on which the transaction became a listed transaction or a transaction of interest. The Commissioner also may determine the time for disclosure of listed transactions and transactions of interest in the published guidance identifying the transaction.

(ii) *Loss transactions.*—If a transaction becomes a loss transaction because the losses equal or exceed the threshold amounts as described in paragraph (b)(5)(i) of this section, a disclosure statement must be filed as an attachment to the taxpayer=s tax return for the first taxable year in which the threshold amount is reached and to any subsequent tax return that reflects any amount of section 165 loss from the transaction.

(3) *Multiple disclosures.*—The taxpayer must disclose the transaction in the time and manner provided for under the provisions of this section regardless of whether the taxpayer also plans to disclose the transaction under other published guidance, for example, § 1.6662-3(c)(2).

(4) *Example.*—The following example illustrates the application of this paragraph (e):

Example. In January of 2008, F, a calendar year taxpayer, enters into a transaction that at the time is not a listed transaction and is not a transaction described in any of the paragraphs (b)(3) through (7) of this section. All the tax benefits from the transaction are reported on F's 2008 tax return filed timely in April 2009. On May 2, 2011, the IRS publishes a notice identifying the transaction as a listed transaction described in paragraph (b)(2) of this section. Upon issuance of the May 2, 2011 notice, the transaction becomes a reportable transaction described in paragraph (b) of this section. The period of limitations on assessment for F's 2008 taxable year is still open. F is required to file Form 8886

for the transaction with OTSA within 90 calendar days after May 2, 2011.

(f) *Rulings and protective disclosures.*—(1) *Rulings.*—If a taxpayer requests a ruling on the merits of a specific transaction on or before the date that disclosure would otherwise be required under this section, and receives a favorable ruling as to the transaction, the disclosure rules under this section will be deemed to have been satisfied by that taxpayer with regard to that transaction, so long as the request fully discloses all relevant facts relating to the transaction which would otherwise be required to be disclosed under this section. If a taxpayer requests a ruling as to whether a specific transaction is a reportable transaction on or before the date that disclosure would otherwise be required under this section, the Commissioner in his discretion may determine that the submission satisfies the disclosure rules under this section for the taxpayer requesting the ruling for that transaction if the request fully discloses all relevant facts relating to the transaction which would otherwise be required to be disclosed under this section. The potential obligation of the taxpayer to disclose the transaction under this section will not be suspended during the period that the ruling request is pending.

(2) *Protective disclosures.*—If a taxpayer is uncertain whether a transaction must be disclosed under this section, the taxpayer may disclose the transaction in accordance with the requirements of this section and comply with all the provisions of this section, and indicate on the disclosure statement that the disclosure statement is being filed on a protective basis. The IRS will not treat disclosure statements filed on a protective basis any differently than other disclosure statements filed under this section. For a protective disclosure to be effective, the taxpayer must comply with these disclosure regulations by providing to the IRS all information requested by the IRS under this section.

(g) *Retention of documents.*—(1) In accordance with the instructions to Form 8886 (or a successor form), the taxpayer must retain a copy of all documents and other records related to a transaction subject to disclosure under this section that are material to an understanding of the tax treatment or tax structure of the transaction. The documents must be retained until the expiration of the statute of limitations applicable to the final taxable year for which disclosure of the transaction was required under this section. (This document retention requirement is in addition to any document retention requirements that section 6001 generally imposes on the taxpayer.) The documents may include the following:

(i) Marketing materials related to the transaction;

(ii) Written analyses used in decision-making related to the transaction;

(iii) Correspondence and agreements between the taxpayer and any advisor, lender, or

Reg. § 1.6011-4(g)(1)(iii)

other party to the reportable transaction that relate to the transaction;

    (iv) Documents discussing, referring to, or demonstrating the purported or claimed tax benefits arising from the reportable transaction; and documents, if any, referring to the business purposes for the reportable transaction.

    (2) A taxpayer is not required to retain earlier drafts of a document if the taxpayer retains a copy of the final document (or, if there is no final document, the most recent draft of the document) and the final document (or most recent draft) contains all the information in the earlier drafts of the document that is material to an understanding of the purported tax treatment or tax structure of the transaction.

    (h) *Effective/applicability date.*—(1) *In general.*— This section applies to transactions entered into on or after August 3, 2007. However, this section applies to transactions of interest entered into on or after November 2, 2006. Paragraph (f)(1) of this section applies to ruling requests received on or after November 1, 2006. Otherwise, the rules that apply with respect to transactions entered into before August 3, 2007, are contained in §1.6011-4 in effect prior to August 3, 2007. (See 26 CFR part 1 revised as of April 1, 2007).

    (2) *[Reserved].*
[Reg. §1.6011–4.]

    ☐ *[T.D. 9046, 2-28-2003. Amended by T.D. 9108, 12-29-2003; T.D. 9295, 11-1-2006 and T.D. 9350, 7-31-2007 (corrected 5-10-2010).]*

[Reg. §20.6011-4]

§20.6011-4. Requirement of statement disclosing participation in certain transactions by taxpayers.—(a) *In general.*—If a transaction is identified as a *listed transaction* or a *transaction of interest* as defined in §1.6011-4 of this chapter by the Commissioner in published guidance (see §601.601(d)(2)(ii)(b) of this chapter), and the listed transaction or transaction of interest involves an estate tax under chapter 11 of subtitle B of the Internal Revenue Code, the transaction must be disclosed in the manner stated in such published guidance.

    (b) *Effective/applicability date.*—This section applies to listed transactions entered into on or after January 1, 2003. This section applies to transactions of interest entered into on or after November 2, 2006. [Reg. §20.6011–4.]

    ☐ *[T.D. 9046, 2-28-2003. Amended by T.D. 9350, 7-31-2007.]*

[Reg. §25.6011-4]

§25.6011-4. Requirement of statement disclosing participation in certain transactions by taxpayers.—(a) *In general.*—If a transaction is identified as a *listed transaction* or a *transaction of interest* as defined in §1.6011-4 of this chapter by the Commissioner in published guidance (see §601.601(d)(2)(ii)(b) of this chapter), and the listed transaction or transaction of interest involves a gift tax under chapter 12 of subtitle B of the Internal Revenue Code, the transaction must

be disclosed in the manner stated in such published guidance.

    (b) *Effective/applicability date.*—This section applies to listed transactions entered into on or after January 1, 2003. This section applies to transactions of interest entered into on or after November 2, 2006. [Reg. §25.6011–4.]

    ☐ *[T.D. 9046, 2-28-2003. Amended by T.D. 9350, 7-31-2007.]*

[Reg. §26.6011-4]

§26.6011-4. Requirement of statement disclosing participation in certain transactions by taxpayers.—(a) *In general.*—If a transaction is identified as a *listed transaction* or a *transaction of interest* as defined in §1.6011-4 of this chapter by the Commissioner in published guidance, and the listed transaction or transaction of interest involves a tax on generation-skipping transfers under chapter 13 of subtitle B of the Internal Revenue Code, the transaction must be disclosed in the manner stated in such published guidance.

    (b) *Effective/applicability date.*—This section applies to listed transactions and transactions of interest entered into on or after November 14, 2011. [Reg. §26.6011–4.]

    ☐ *[T.D. 9556, 11-10-2011.]*

[Reg. §31.6011-4]

§31.6011-4. Requirement of statement disclosing participation in certain transactions by taxpayers.—(a) *In general.*—If a transaction is identified as a *listed transaction* or a *transaction of interest* as defined in §1.6011-4 of this chapter by the Commissioner in published guidance (see §601.601(d)(2)(ii)(b) of this chapter), and the listed transaction or transaction of interest involves an employment tax under chapters 21 through 25 of subtitle C of the Internal Revenue Code, the transaction must be disclosed in the manner stated in such published guidance.

    (b) *Effective/applicability date.*—This section applies to listed transactions entered into on or after January 1, 2003. This section applies to transactions of interest entered into on or after November 2, 2006. [Reg. §31.6011–4.]

    ☐ *[T.D. 9046, 2-28-2003. Amended by T.D. 9350, 7-31-2007.]*

[Reg. §53.6011-4]

§53.6011-4. Requirement of statement disclosing participation in certain transactions by taxpayers.—(a) *In general.*—If a transaction is identified as a *listed transaction* or a *transaction of interest* as defined in §1.6011-4 of this chapter by the Commissioner in published guidance (see §601.601(d)(2)(ii)(b) of this chapter), and the listed transaction or transaction of interest involves an excise tax under chapter 42 of subtitle D of the Internal Revenue Code (relating to private foundations and certain other tax-exempt organizations), the transaction must be disclosed in the manner stated in such published guidance.

(b) *Effective/applicability date.*—This section applies to listed transactions entered into on or after January 1, 2003. This section applies to transactions of interest entered into on or after November 2, 2006. [Reg. § 53.6011–4.]

☐ [*T.D.* 9046, 2-28-2003. *Amended by T.D.* 9350, 7-31-2007.]

[Reg. § 54.6011-4]

§ 54.6011-4. Requirement of statement disclosing participation in certain transactions by taxpayers.—(a) *In general.*—If a transaction is identified as a *listed transaction* or a *transaction of interest* as defined in § 1.6011-4 of this chapter by the Commissioner in published guidance (see § 601.601(d)(2)(ii)(*b*) of this chapter), and the listed transaction or transaction of interest involves an excise tax under chapter 43 of subtitle D of the Internal Revenue Code (relating to qualified pension, etc., plans) the transaction must be disclosed in the manner stated in such published guidance.

(b) *Effective/applicability date.*—This section applies to listed transactions entered into on or after January 1, 2003. This section applies to transactions of interest entered into on or after November 2, 2006. [Reg. § 54.6011–4.]

☐ [*T.D.* 9046, 2-28-2003. *Amended by T.D.* 9350, 7-31-2007.]

[Reg. § 56.6011-4]

§ 56.6011-4. Requirement of statement disclosing participation in certain transactions by taxpayers.—(a) *In general.*—If a transaction is identified as a *listed transaction* or a *transaction of interest* as defined in § 1.6011-4 of this chapter by the Commissioner in published guidance (see § 601.601(d)(2) of this chapter), and the listed transaction or transaction of interest involves an excise tax under chapter 41 of subtitle D of the Internal Revenue Code (relating to public charities), the transaction must be disclosed in the manner stated in such published guidance.

(b) *Effective/applicability date.*—This section applies to listed transactions entered into on or after January 1, 2003. This section applies to transactions of interest entered into on or after November 2, 2006. [Reg. § 56.6011–4.]

☐ [*T.D.* 9046, 2-28-2003. *Amended by T.D.* 9350, 7-31-2007.]

[Reg. § 1.6011-5]

§ 1.6011-5. Required use of magnetic media for corporate income tax returns.—The return of a corporation that is required to be filed on magnetic media under § 301.6011-5 of this chapter must be filed in accordance with Internal Revenue Service revenue procedures, publications, forms, or instructions, including those posted electronically. (See § 601.601(d)(2) of this chapter). [Reg. § 1.6011-5.]

☐ [*T.D.* 9363, 11-9-2007.]

[Reg. § 301.6011-5]

§ 301.6011-5. Required use of magnetic media for corporate income tax returns.—(a) *Corporate income tax returns required on magnetic media.*—(1) A corporation required to file a corporate income tax return on Form 1120, "U.S. Corporation Income Tax Return," under § 1.6012-2 of this chapter must file its corporate income tax return on magnetic media if the corporation is required by the Internal Revenue Code or regulations to file at least 250 returns during the calendar year. Returns filed on magnetic media must be made in accordance with applicable revenue procedures, publications, forms, or instructions. In prescribing revenue procedures, publications, forms, or instructions, the Commissioner may direct the type of magnetic media filing. (See § 601.601(d)(2) of this chapter).

(2) All members of a controlled group of corporations must file their corporate income tax returns on magnetic media if the aggregate number of returns required to be filed by the controlled group of corporations is at least 250.

(b) *Waiver.*—The Commissioner may grant waivers of the requirements of this section in cases of undue hardship. A request for waiver must be made in accordance with applicable revenue procedures or publications. The waiver also will be subject to the terms and conditions regarding the method of filing as may be prescribed by the Commissioner.

(c) *Failure to file.*—If a corporation fails to file a corporate income tax return on magnetic media when required to do so by this section, the corporation is deemed to have failed to file the return. (See section 6651 for the addition to tax for failure to file a return). In determining whether there is reasonable cause for failure to file the return, § 301.6651-1(c) and rules similar to the rules in § 301.6724-1(c)(3) (undue economic hardship related to filing information returns on magnetic media) will apply.

(d) *Meaning of terms.*—The following definitions apply for purposes of this section:

(1) *Magnetic media.*—The term *magnetic media* means any magnetic media permitted under applicable regulations, revenue procedures, or publications. These generally include magnetic tape, tape cartridge, and diskette, as well as other media, such as electronic filing, specifically permitted under the applicable regulations, procedures, publications, forms, or instructions. (See § 601.601(d)(2) of this chapter).

(2) *Corporation.*—The term *corporation* means a corporation as defined in section 7701(a)(3).

(3) *Controlled group of corporations.*—The term *controlled group of corporations* means a group of corporations as defined in section 1563(a).

(4) *Corporate income tax return.*—The term *corporate income tax return* means a Form 1120,

Reg. § 301.6011-5(d)(4)

"U.S. Corporation Income Tax Return," along with all other related forms, schedules, and statements that are required to be attached to the Form 1120, and all members of the Form 1120 series of returns, including amended and superseding returns.

(5) *Determination of 250 returns.*—For purposes of this section, a corporation or controlled group of corporations is required to file at least 250 returns if, during the calendar year ending with or within the taxable year of the corporation or the controlled group, the corporation or the controlled group is required to file at least 250 returns of any type, including information returns (for example, Forms W-2, Forms 1099), income tax returns, employment tax returns, and excise tax returns. In the case of a short year return, a corporation is required to file at least 250 returns if, during the calendar year which includes the short taxable year of the corporation, the corporation is required to file at least 250 returns of any type, including information returns (for example, Forms W-2, Forms 1099), income tax returns, employment tax returns, and excise tax returns. If the corporation is a member of a controlled group, the determination of the number of returns includes all returns required to be filed by all members of the controlled group during the calendar year ending with or within the taxable year of the controlled group.

(e) *Example.*—The following example illustrates the provisions of paragraph (d)(5) of this section:

Example. The taxable year of Corporation X, a fiscal year taxpayer with assets in excess of $10 million, ends on September 30. During the calendar year ending December 31, 2007, X was required to file one Form 1120, "U.S. Corporation Income Tax Return," 100 Forms W-2, "Wage and Tax Statement," 146 Forms 1099-DIV, "Dividends and Distributions," one Form 940, "Employer's Annual Federal Unemployment (FUTA) Tax Return," and four Forms 941, "Employer's Quarterly Federal Tax Return." Because X is required to file 252 returns during the calendar year that ended within its taxable year ending September 30, 2008, X is required to file its Form 1120 electronically for its taxable year ending September 30, 2008.

(f) *Effective/applicability dates.*—This section applies to corporate income tax returns for corporations that report total assets at the end of the corporation's taxable year that equal or exceed $10 million on Schedule L of their Form 1120, for taxable years ending on or after December 31, 2006, except for the application of the short year rules in paragraph (d)(5) of this section, which is applicable for taxable years ending on or after November 13, 2007. [Reg. § 301.6011-5.]

☐ [*T.D.* 9363, 11-9-2007.]

[Reg. § 1.6011-6]

§ 1.6011-6. [Reserved]

☐ [*T.D.* 9518, 3-28-2011.]

[Reg. § 301.6011-6]

§ 301.6011-6. Statement of series and series organizations.—[Reserved].

☐ [*T.D.* 9518, 3-28-2011.]

[Reg. § 1.6011-7]

§ 1.6011-7. Specified tax return preparers required to file individual income tax returns using magnetic media.—Individual income tax returns that are required to be filed on magnetic media by tax return preparers under section 6011(e)(3) and § 301.6011-7 of this chapter must be filed in accordance with Internal Revenue Service regulations, revenue procedures, revenue rulings, publications, forms or instructions, including those posted electronically. [Reg. § 1.6011-7.]

☐ [*T.D.* 9518, 3-28-2011.]

[Reg. § 301.6011-7]

§ 301.6011-7. Specified tax return preparers required to file individual income tax returns using magnetic media.—(a) *Definitions.*— (1) *Magnetic media.*—For purposes of this section, the term *magnetic media* has the same meaning as in § 301.6011-2(a)(1).

(2) *Individual income tax return.*—The term *individual income tax return* means any return of tax imposed by subtitle A on individuals, estates, and trusts.

(3) *Specified tax return preparer.*—The term *specified tax return preparer* means any person who is a tax return preparer, as defined in section 7701(a)(36) and § 301.7701-15, unless that person reasonably expects to file 10 or fewer individual income tax returns in a calendar year. If a person who is a tax return preparer is a member of a firm, that person is a specified tax return preparer unless the person's firm members in the aggregate reasonably expect to file 10 or fewer individual income tax returns in a calendar year. Solely for the 2011 calendar year, a person will not be considered a specified tax return preparer if that person reasonably expects, or if the person is a member of a firm, the firm's members in the aggregate reasonably expect, to file fewer than 100 individual income tax returns in the 2011 calendar year. Solely for purposes of this section, a person is considered a member of a firm if the person is an employee, agent, member, partner, shareholder, or other equity holder of the firm.

(4) *File or Filed.*—(i) For purposes of section 6011(e)(3) and these regulations only, an individual income tax return is considered to be "filed" by a tax return preparer or a specified tax return preparer if the preparer submits the individual income tax return to the IRS on the taxpayer's behalf, either electronically (by e-file or other magnetic media) or in non-electronic (paper) form. Submission of an individual income tax return by a tax return preparer or a specified tax return preparer in non-electronic form includes the transmission, sending, mailing or otherwise

delivering of the paper individual income tax return to the IRS by the preparer, any member, employee, or agent of the preparer, or any member, employee, or agent of the preparer's firm.

(ii) An individual income tax return will not be considered to be filed, as defined in paragraph (a)(4)(i) of this section, by a tax return preparer or specified tax return preparer if the tax return preparer or specified tax return preparer who prepared the return obtains, on or prior to the date the individual income tax return is filed, a handsigned and dated statement from the taxpayer (by either spouse if a joint return) that states the taxpayer chooses to file the individual income tax return in paper format, and that the taxpayer, and not the preparer, will submit the paper individual income tax return to the IRS. The IRS may provide guidance through forms, instructions or other appropriate guidance regarding how tax return preparers and specified tax return preparers can document a taxpayer's choice to file an individual income tax return in paper format.

(iii) The rules contained in this section do not alter or affect a taxpayer's obligation to file returns under any other provision of law. The definition of file or filed by a tax return preparer or specified tax return preparer contained in paragraph (a)(4)(i) of this section applies only for the purposes of section 6011(e)(3) and these regulations and does not apply for any other purpose under any other provision of law.

(b) *Magnetic media filing requirement.*—Except as provided in paragraphs (a)(4)(ii) and (c) of this section, any individual income tax return prepared by a specified tax return preparer in a calendar year must be filed on magnetic media if the return is filed by the specified tax return preparer.

(c) *Exclusions.*—The following exclusions apply to the magnetic media filing requirement in this section:

(1) *Undue hardship waiver.*—The IRS may grant a waiver of the requirement of this section in cases of undue hardship. An undue hardship waiver may be granted upon application by a specified tax return preparer consistent with instructions provided in published guidance and as prescribed in relevant forms and instructions. A determination of undue hardship will be based upon all facts and circumstances. The undue hardship waiver provided to a specified tax return preparer may apply to a series or class of individual income tax returns or for a specified period of time, subject to the terms and conditions regarding the method of filing prescribed in such waiver.

(2) *Administrative exemptions.*—The IRS may provide administrative exemptions from the requirement of this section for certain classes of specified tax return preparers, or regarding certain types of individual income tax returns, as the IRS determines necessary to promote effective and efficient tax administration. The IRS may provide administrative exemptions and any

criteria or procedures necessary to claim an administrative exemption through forms, instructions, or other appropriate guidance.

(d) *Reasonably expect to file.*—(1) *In general.*—The determination of whether a tax return preparer reasonably expects, or if the preparer is a member of a firm, the firm's members in the aggregate reasonably expect, to file 10 or fewer individual income tax returns (or, in the case of the 2011 calendar year, fewer than 100 individual income tax returns) is made by adding together all of the individual income tax returns the tax return preparer and, if the preparer is a member of a firm, the firm's members reasonably expect to prepare and file in the calendar year. In making this determination, individual income tax returns that the tax return preparer reasonably expects will not be subject to the magnetic media filing requirement under paragraph (a)(4)(ii) of this section or are excluded from the requirement under (c)(2) of this section are not to be counted. Individual income tax returns excluded from the magnetic media filing requirement under paragraph (c)(1) of this section are to be counted for purposes of making this determination.

(2) *Time for making determination of reasonable expectations.*—The determination regarding reasonable expectations is made separately for each calendar year in order to ascertain whether the magnetic media filing requirement applies to a tax return preparer for that year. For each calendar year, the determination of whether a tax return preparer and the preparer's firm reasonably expect to file 10 or fewer individual income tax returns (or, in the case of the 2011 calendar year, fewer than 100 individual income tax returns) is made based on all relevant, objective, and demonstrable facts and circumstances prior to the time the tax return preparer and the preparer's firm first file an individual income tax return during the calendar year.

(e) *Examples.*—The following examples illustrate the rules of paragraphs (a) through (d) of this section.

Example 1. Tax Return Preparer A is an accountant who recently graduated from college with an accounting degree and has opened his own practice. A has not prepared individual income tax returns for compensation in the past and does not plan to focus his practice on individual income tax return preparation. A intends instead to focus his practice on providing specialized accounting services to certain health care service providers. A has no plans to, and does not, employ or engage any other tax return preparers. A estimates that he may be asked by some clients to prepare and file their individual income tax returns for compensation, but A expects that the number of people who do ask him to provide this service will be no more than seven in 2012. In fact, A actually prepares and files six paper Forms 1040 (U.S. Individual Income Tax Return) in 2012. Due to a growing client base, and based upon his experience in

2012, A expects that the number of individual income tax returns he will prepare and file in 2013 will at least double, estimating he will prepare and file 12 Form 1040 returns in 2013. A does not qualify as a specified tax return preparer for 2012 because A reasonably expects to file 10 or fewer returns (seven) in 2012. Consequently, A is not required to electronically file the individual income tax returns he prepares and files in 2012. A's expectation is reasonable based on his business projections, individual income tax return filing history, and staffing decisions. A is a specified tax return preparer in 2013, however, because based on those same factors A reasonably expects to file more than 10 individual income tax returns (12) during that calendar year. A, therefore, must electronically file all individual income tax returns that A prepares and files in 2013 that are not otherwise excluded from the electronic filing requirement.

Example 2. Same facts as in *Example 1*, except three of Tax Return Preparer A's clients specifically chose to have A prepare their individual income tax returns in paper format in 2012 with the clients mailing their respective returns to the IRS. A expects that these three clients will similarly choose to have him prepare their returns in paper format in 2013, with the clients being responsible for mailing their returns to the IRS. A is not required to electronically file these three returns in 2013 because the taxpayers chose to file their returns in paper format. A obtained a hand-signed and dated statement from each of those taxpayers, indicating that they chose to file their returns in paper format. These three individual income tax returns are not counted in determining how many individual income tax returns A reasonably expects to file in 2013. Because the total number of individual income tax returns A reasonably expects to file in 2013 (nine) does not exceed 10, A is not a specified tax return preparer for calendar year 2013, and A is not required to electronically file any individual income tax return that he prepares and files in 2013.

Example 3. Tax Return Preparer B is a solo general practice attorney in a small county. Her practice includes the preparation of wills and assisting executors in administering estates. As part of her practice, B infrequently prepares and files Forms 1041 (U.S. Income Tax Return for Estates and Trusts) for executors. In the past three years, she prepared and filed an average of five Forms 1041 each year and never exceeded more than seven Forms 1041 in any year. Based on B's prior experience and her estimate for 2012, made prior to the time she first files an individual income tax return in 2012, she reasonably expects to prepare and file no more than five Forms 1041 in 2012. Due to the unforeseen deaths of several of her clients in late 2011, B actually prepares and files 12 Forms 1041 in 2012. B does not find out about these deaths until after she has already filed the first Form 1041 in 2012 for another client. B is not required to electronically file these returns in 2012. She does not qualify as a specified tax return preparer for

calendar year 2012 because prior to the time she filed the first Form 1041 in 2012, she reasonably expected to file 10 or fewer individual income tax returns in 2012.

Example 4. Same facts as *Example 3*, except, in addition to the five Forms 1041 that she expects to prepare and file in 2012, Tax Return Preparer B also expects to prepare and file 10 paper Forms 1040 (U.S. Individual Income Tax Return) in 2012, based upon the requests that she has received from some of her clients. Because the total number of individual income tax returns B reasonably expects to file in 2012 (fifteen) exceeds 10, B is a specified tax return preparer for calendar year 2012, and B must electronically file all individual income tax returns that B prepares and files in 2012 that are not otherwise excluded from the electronic filing requirement.

Example 5. Firm X consists of two tax return preparers, Tax Return Preparer C who owns Firm X, and Tax Return Preparer D who is employed by C in Firm X. Based upon the firm's experience over the past three years, C and D reasonably expect to file nine and ten individual income tax returns for compensation, respectively, in 2012. Both C and D must electronically file the individual income tax returns that they prepare in 2012, unless the returns are otherwise excluded from the electronic filing requirement, because they are members of the same firm and the aggregated total of individual income tax returns that they reasonably expect to file in 2012 (nineteen), exceeds 10 individual income tax returns.

(f) *Additional guidance.*—The IRS may implement the requirements of this section through additional guidance, including by revenue procedures, notices, publications, forms and instructions, including those issued electronically.

(g) *Effective /applicability date.*—This section is effective on March 30, 2011, and applicable to individual income tax returns filed after December 31, 2010. [Reg. § 301.6011-7.]

☐ [*T.D.* 9518, 3-28-2011.]

[Reg. § 1.6011-8]

§ 1.6011-8. Requirement of income tax return for taxpayers who claim the premium tax credit under section 36B.—(a) *Requirement of return.*—Except as otherwise provided in this paragraph (a), a taxpayer who receives the benefit of advance payments of the premium tax credit under section 36B must file an income tax return for that taxable year on or before the due date for the return (including extensions of time for filing) and reconcile the advance credit payments. However, if advance credit payments are made for coverage of an individual for whom no taxpayer claims a personal exemption deduction, the taxpayer who attests to the Exchange to the intention to claim a personal exemption deduction for the individual as part of the determination that the taxpayer is eligible for advance credit payments must file a tax return and reconcile the advance credit payments.

(b) *Effective/applicability date.*—Except as otherwise provided, this section applies for taxable years beginning after December 31, 2016. Paragraph (a) of §1.6011-8 as contained in 26 CFR part I edition revised as of April 1, 2016, applies to taxable years ending after December 31, 2013, and beginning before January 1, 2017. [Reg. §1.6011-8.]

☐ [*T.D.* 9590, 5-18-2012. *Amended by T.D.* 9745, 12-16-2015 *and T.D.* 9804, 12-14-2016.]

[Reg. §31.6011(a)-1]

§31.6011(a)-1. Returns under Federal Insurance Contributions Act.—(a) *Requirement.*—(1) *In general.*—Except as otherwise provided in paragraphs (a)(3) and (a)(5) of this section and in §31.6011(a)-5 every employer is required to make a return for the first calendar quarter in which the employer pays wages, other than wages for agricultural labor, subject to the tax imposed by the Federal Insurance Contributions Act, and is required to make a return for each subsequent calendar quarter (whether or not wages are paid therein) until the employer has filed a final return in accordance with §31.6011(a)-6. Except as otherwise provided in §31.6011(a)-8 and in paragraphs (a)(3), (a)(4), and (a)(5) of this section, Form 941, "Employer's QUARTERLY Federal Tax Return," is the form prescribed for making the return required by this paragraph (a)(1). Such return shall not include wages for agricultural labor required to be reported on any return prescribed by paragraph (a)(2) of this section. The return shall include wages received by an employee in the form of tips only to the extent of the tips reported by the employee to the employer in a written statement furnished to the employer pursuant to section 6053(a).

(2) *Employers of agricultural workers.*—Every employer who pays wages for agricultural labor with respect to taxes imposed by the Federal Insurance Contributions Act must make a return for the first calendar year in which the employer pays such wages and for each subsequent calendar year (whether or not wages are paid) until the employer has filed a final return in accordance with §31.6011(a)-6. Form 943, "Employer's Annual Federal Tax Return for Agricultural Employees," is the form prescribed for making the annual return required by this section, except that, if the employer's principal place of business is in Puerto Rico, or if the employer has employees who are subject to income tax withholding for Puerto Rico, the return must be made on Form 943-PR, "Planilla para la Declaración ANUAL de la Contribución Federal del Patrono de Empleados Agrícolas." However, Form 943 is the form prescribed for making such return in the case of every employer of agricultural workers who is required pursuant to §31.6011(a)-4 to make a return of income tax withheld from wages.

(3) *Employers of domestic workers.*—Schedule H (Form 1040), "Household Employment Taxes," is the form prescribed for use by every employer in making a return as required under paragraph (a)(1) of this section in respect of wages, as defined in the Federal Insurance Contributions Act, paid by the employer in any calendar year for domestic service as defined in section 3510. Schedule H (Form 1040) is generally filed as an attachment to an income tax return; however, if the employer does not otherwise have an obligation to file an income tax return, Schedule H (Form 1040) may be filed as a separate return. If, however, the employer is required under paragraph (a)(1) of this section to make a return on Form 941, "Employer's QUARTERLY Federal Tax Return," or under paragraph (a)(2) of this section to make a return on Form 943, "Employer's Annual Federal Tax Return For Agricultural Employees," or under paragraph (a)(5) of this section to make a return on Form 944, "Employer's ANNUAL Federal Tax Return," the employer may choose instead to report wages with respect to domestic workers on such Form 941, Form 943, or Form 944. If such wages are included on Form 941, Form 943, or Form 944, the employer must also include Federal unemployment tax for the employee(s) on Form 940, "Employer's Annual Federal Unemployment (FUTA) Tax Return," under the provisions of §31.6011(a)-3.

(4) *Employers in Puerto Rico, the U.S. Virgin Islands, Guam, American Samoa, or the Commonwealth of the Northern Mariana Islands.*—Except as otherwise provided in paragraph (a)(5), Form 941-PR, "Planilla para la Declaracion Federal TRIMESTRAL del Patrono," is the form prescribed for use in making the return required under paragraph (a)(1) of this section in the case of every employer whose principal place of business is in Puerto Rico, or if the employer has employees who are subject to income tax withholding for Puerto Rico. Except as otherwise provided in paragraph (a)(5), Form 941-SS, "Employer's QUARTERLY Federal Tax Return (American Samoa, Guam, the Commonwealth of the Northern Mariana Islands, and the U.S. Virgin Islands)," is the form prescribed for use in making the return required under paragraph (a)(1) of this section in the case of every employer whose principal place of business is in the U.S. Virgin Islands, Guam, American Samoa, or the Commonwealth of the Northern Mariana Islands, or if the employer has employees who are subject to income tax withholding for these U.S. possessions. Form 944 (or Form 944, as described under paragraph (a)(5) of this section, if the IRS notified the employer that Form 944 must be filed in lieu of Form 941) is the form prescribed for making the return in the case of every employer who is required pursuant to §31.6011(a)-4 to make a return of income tax withheld from wages.

(5) *Employers in the Employers' Annual Federal Tax Program (Form 944).*—(i) *In general.*—Employers notified of their qualification for the Employers' Annual Federal Tax Program (Form 944) are required to file Form 944, "Employer's ANNUAL Federal Tax Return," instead of Form

941 (or Form 941-SS or Form 941-PR under paragraph (a)(4) of this section) to make a return as required by paragraph (a)(1) of this section. Upon proper request by the employer, the IRS will notify employers in writing of their qualification for the Employers' Annual Federal Tax Program (Form 944). The IRS will notify employers when they no longer qualify for the Employers' Annual Federal Tax Program (Form 944) and must file Forms 941 instead. Qualified employers are those with an estimated annual employment tax liability (that is, social security, Medicare, and withheld Federal income taxes) of $1,000 or less for the entire calendar year, except employers required under—

(A) Paragraph (a)(2) of this section to make a return on Form 943, "Employer's Annual Federal Tax Return For Agricultural Employees"; or

(B) Paragraph (a)(3) of this section to make a return on Schedule H (Form 1040), "Household Employment Taxes."

(ii) *Requests to opt in or opt out of the Employers' Annual Federal Tax Program (Form 944).*— The IRS has established procedures in Revenue Procedure 2009-51 published in the Internal Revenue Bulletin for employers to follow to request to participate in the Employers' Annual Federal Tax Program (Form 944) (to opt in) and to request to be removed from the Employers' Annual Federal Tax Program (Form 944) after becoming a participant in order to file Forms 941 instead (to opt out). The IRS will notify employers that their filing requirements have changed to Form 944 or Forms 941. Employers must follow the procedures in Revenue Procedure 2009-51 or its successor to request to opt in or opt out of the Employers' Annual Federal Tax Program (Form 944).

(b) *When to report wages.*—Wages with respect to which taxes are imposed by the Federal Insurance Contributions Act shall be reported in the return of such taxes required under this section or §31.6011(a)-5 for the return period in which they are actually paid unless they were constructively paid in a prior return period, in which case such wages shall be reported only in the return for such prior period. However, if such wages are deemed to be paid in a later return period, they shall be reported only in the return for such later period. See §31.3121(a)-2 relating to the time when wages are paid or deemed to be paid.

(c) *Adjustments and refunds.*—For rules applicable to adjustments and refunds of employment taxes, see sections 6205, 6402, 6413, and 6414, and the applicable regulations.

(d) *Returns by employees in respect of tips.*—If—

(1) An employee, during a calendar year, is paid wages in the form of tips which are subject to the tax under section 3101, and

(2) Any portion of the tax under section 3101 in respect of such wages can not be collected by the employer from wages (exclusive of tips) of such employee or from funds turned over by the employee to the employer,
the employee shall make a return for the calendar year in respect of the employee tax not collected by the employer. Except as otherwise provided in this subparagraph, the return shall be made on Form 1040. The form to be used by residents of the Virgin Islands, Guam, or American Samoa is Form 1040SS. In the case of a resident of Puerto Rico who is not required to make a return of income under section 6012(a), the form to be used is Form 1040SS, except that Form 1040PR shall be used if it is furnished by the Internal Revenue Service to such resident for use in lieu of Form 1040SS.

(e) *Time and place for filing returns.*—For provisions relating to the time and place for filing returns, see §§31.6071(a)-1 and 31.6091-1, respectively.

(f) *Wages paid in nonconvertible foreign currency.*—For provisions relating to returns filed by certain employers who pay wages in nonconvertible foreign currency, see §301.6316-7 of this chapter (Regulations on Procedure and Administration).

(g) *Returns by employees in respect of Additional Medicare Tax.*—An employee who is paid wages, as defined in section 3121(a), subject to the tax under section 3101(b)(2)(Additional Medicare Tax), must make a return for the taxable year in respect of such tax. The return shall be made on Form 1040, "U.S. Individual Income Tax Return." The form to be used by residents of the U.S. Virgin Islands, Guam, American Samoa, or the Northern Mariana Islands is Form 1040-SS, "U.S. Self-Employment Tax Return (Including Additional Child Tax Credit for Bona Fide Residents of Puerto Rico)." The form to be used by residents of Puerto Rico is either Form 1040-SS or Form 1040-PR, "Planilla para la Declaración de la Contribución Federal sobre el Trabajo por Cuenta Propia (Incluyendo el Crédito Tributario Adicional por Hijos para Residentes Bona Fide de Puerto Rico)."

(h) *Effective/applicability dates.*—Paragraphs (a)(1) and (a)(5)(i) of this section apply to taxable years beginning on or after December 30, 2008. Paragraph (a)(4) of this section applies to taxable years beginning on or after January 1, 2012. Paragraph (a)(5)(ii) of this section applies to taxable years beginning on or after January 1, 2010. The rules of paragraph (a)(1) of this section that apply to taxable years beginning before December 30, 2008, are contained in §31.6011(a)-1 as in effect prior to December 30, 2008. The rules of paragraph (a)(4) of this section that apply to taxable years beginning before January 1, 2012, are contained in §31.6011(a)-1 as in effect prior to January 1, 2012. The rules of paragraph (a)(5)(ii) of this section that apply to taxable years beginning before January 1, 2010, but on or after December 30, 2008, are contained in §31.6011(a)-1T as in effect on or after December 30, 2008. The rules of paragraph (a)(5) of this section that apply to taxable years beginning before December 30, 2008, are contained in §31.6011(a)-1T as in effect prior to December 30, 2008. Paragraph (g) of this section applies to taxable years beginning on or after November 29, 2013. [Reg. §31.6011(a)-1.]

☐ [T.D. 6516, 12-20-60. Amended by T.D. 7001, 1-17-69; T.D. 7200, 8-15-72; T.D. 7351, 4-16-75; T.D. 7396, 1-12-76; T.D. 9239, 12-30-2005; T.D. 9405, 6-30-2008; T.D. 9440, 12-24-2008; T.D. 9566, 12-9-2011 and T.D. 9645, 11-26-2013 (corrected 1-28-2014).]

[Reg. §31.6011(a)-2]

§31.6011(a)-2. Returns under Railroad Retirement Tax Act.—(a) *Requirement.*—(1) *Employers.*—Every employer shall make a return for the first return period after 1954 within which compensation taxable under the Railroad Retirement Tax Act is paid to his employee or employees for services rendered after 1954, and for each subsequent return period (whether or not taxable compensation is paid therein) until he has filed a final return in accordance with §31.6011(a)-6. For calendar years after 1975, the return period shall be the calendar year; for calendar years prior to 1976, the return period shall be the calendar quarter. Form CT-1 is the form prescribed for making the return required under this paragraph. One original and a duplicate of each return on Form CT-1 shall be filed with the director of the service center.

(2) *Employee representatives.*—Every employee representative shall make a return for the first calendar quarter after 1954 within which he is paid taxable compensation for services rendered after 1954 as an employee representative, and for each subsequent calendar quarter (whether or not he is paid taxable compensation therein) until he has filed a final return in accordance with §31.6011(a)-6. Form CT-2 is the form prescribed for making the return required under this subparagraph. One original and a duplicate of each return on Form CT-2 shall be filed with the director of the service center.

(b) *When to report compensation.*—(1) *In general.*—Except as otherwise provided in subparagraph (2) of this paragraph, compensation taxable under the Railroad Retirement Tax Act shall be reported in the return required under this section for the period in which it is deemed, under paragraph (d) of §31.3231(e)-1 to be paid, unless under such section the compensation may be deemed to be paid in more than one return period, in which case it shall be reported only in the return for the first return period in which it is deemed to be paid.

(2) *Pre-1976 returns of employers required by State law to pay compensation on weekly basis.*—(i) *In general.*—If any employer is required by the laws of any State to pay compensation weekly in any calendar year prior to 1976, the return of tax with respect to such compensation may, at the election of such employer, cover all payroll weeks which, or the major part of which, fall within the period for which a return of tax is required by paragraph (a)(1) of this section. This provision shall not apply, however, to any payroll week which falls in two calendar years. Any employer who elects to file a return as provided in this subparagraph shall notify the district director in writing of such election and shall include therein a statement setting forth the facts which entitle him to make the election. Such notice shall be in duplicate and shall be attached to the original and duplicate of the return for the first period to which such election applies. Any election so made shall be binding upon the employer with respect to all returns subsequently made by him until the director of the service center authorizes or directs the employer to make a return on a different basis. For the purpose of determining the time when compensation is deemed to be paid in accordance with paragraph (d) of §31.3231(e)-1 and of determining the due date of a return in accordance with paragraph (b) of §31.6071(a)-1, the calendar month following the period covered by the return of an employer making such election is the same calendar month which would be determinative for such purposes if the employer had not made the election.

(ii) *Prior elections.*—An election made by an employer, pursuant to the provisions of 26 CFR (1939) 410.501(b) (Regulations 100) or of 26 CFR (1939) 411.601(b) (Regulations 114), which is in force and effect at the time the employer makes his first return under this section shall satisfy the requirements of paragraph (b)(2)(i) of this section with respect to the making of an election and shall be binding upon the employer with respect to all returns made by him under this section until the director of the service center authorizes or directs the employer to make a return on a different basis.

(iii) *Example.*—Employer X is required by State law to pay his employees within 6 days after the compensation is earned. In compliance with the State law, employer X, for services rendered to him for the payroll week of June 27 to July 2, 1955, pays his employees on the last-named date. June 1955 is the last month of a period for which a return of tax is required by paragraph (a)(1) of this section. Employer X may elect to include in the return required by paragraph (a)(1) of this section for the period April 1 to June 30, 1955, the compensation paid to his employees for the payroll week of June 27 to July 2, 1955, inclusive, although the compensation for July 1 and 2 falls within another period for which a return is required by paragraph (a)(1) of this section. If, in this example, the payroll week ended on July 5, 1955, the compensation paid for the payroll week of June 29 to July 5 would be included in the return period in which July falls although the compensation earned for June 29 and 30 fell in a prior return period under the general rule.

(c) *Time and place for filing returns.*—For provisions relating to the time and place for filing returns, see §§31.6071(a)-1 and 31.6091-1, respectively.

(d) *Returns by employees and employee represent-atives in respect of Additional Medicare Tax.*—An employee or employee representative who is paid compensation, as defined in section 3231(e), subject to the tax under sections 3201(a) (as calculated under section 3101(b)(2)) or section 3211(a) (as calculated under section 3101(b)(2)) (Additional Medicare Tax), must make a return for the taxable year in respect of such tax. The return shall be made on Form 1040, "U.S. Individual Income Tax Return." The form to be used by residents of the U.S. Virgin Islands, Guam, American Samoa, or the Northern Mariana Islands is Form 1040-SS, "U.S. Self-Employment Tax Return (Including Additional Child Tax Credit for Bona Fide Residents of Puerto Rico)." The form to be used by residents of Puerto Rico is either Form 1040-SS or Form 1040-PR, "Planilla para la Declaración de la Contribución Federal sobre el Trabajo por Cuenta Propia (Incluyendo el Crédito Tributario Adicional por Hijos para Residentes Bona Fide de Puerto Rico)."

(e) *Effective/applicability date.*—Paragraph (d) of this section applies to taxable years beginning on or after November 29, 2013. [Reg. § 31.6011(a)-2.]

☐ [*T.D.* 6516, 12-20-60. *Amended by T.D.* 7396, 1-13-76 *and T.D.* 9645, 11-26-2013.]

[Reg. § 31.6011(a)-3]

§ 31.6011(a)-3. Returns under Federal Unemployment Tax Act.—(a) *Requirement.*—Every person shall make a return of tax under the Federal Unemployment Tax Act for each calendar year with respect to which he is an employer as defined in § 31.3306(a)-1. Except as otherwise provided in § 31.6011(a)-8, Form 940 is the form prescribed for use in making the return.

(b) *When to report wages.*—Wages taxable under the Federal Unemployment Tax Act shall be reported in the return required under this section for the return period in which they are actually paid unless they were constructively paid in a prior return period, in which case such wages shall be reported only in the return for such prior period.

(c) *Time and place for filing returns.*—For provisions relating to the time and place for filing returns, see §§ 31.6071(a)-1 and 31.6091-1, respectively. [Reg. § 31.6011(a)-3.]

☐ [*T.D.* 6516, 12-20-60. *Amended by T.D.* 7200, 8-15-72.]

[Reg. § 31.6011(a)-4]

§ 31.6011(a)-4. Returns of income tax withheld.—(a) *Withheld from wages.*—(1) *In general.*—Except as otherwise provided in paragraphs (a)(2), (a)(3), (a)(4), and (b) of this section, and in § 31.6011(a)-5, every person required to make a return of income tax withheld from wages pursuant to section 3402 shall make a return for the first calendar quarter in which the person is

required to deduct and withhold such tax and for each subsequent calendar quarter, whether or not wages are paid therein, until the person has filed a final return in accordance with § 31.6011(a)-6. Except as otherwise provided in paragraphs (a)(2), (a)(3), (a)(4), and (b) of this section, and in § 31.6011(a)-8, Form 941, "Employer's QUARTERLY Federal Tax Return," is the form prescribed for making the return required under this paragraph (a)(1).

(2) *Wages paid for domestic service.*—Schedule H (Form 1040), "Household Employment Taxes," is the form prescribed for making the return required under paragraph (a)(1) of this section with respect to income tax withheld, pursuant to an agreement under section 3402(p), from wages paid for domestic service as defined in section 3510. Schedule H (Form 1040) is generally filed as an attachment to an income tax return; however, if the employer does not otherwise have an obligation to file an income tax return, Schedule H (Form 1040) may be filed as a separate return. The preceding sentence shall not apply in the case of an employer who has chosen under § 31.6011(a)-1(a)(3) to use Form 941, "Employer's QUARTERLY Federal Tax Return," Form 943, "Employer's Annual Tax Return for Agricultural Employees," or Form 944, "Employer's ANNUAL Federal Tax Return," as the return with respect to such payments for purposes of the Federal Insurance Contributions Act. For the requirements relating for Schedule H (Form 1040) with respect to qualified State individual income taxes, see § 301.6361-1(d)(3)(iv).

(3) *Wages paid for agricultural labor.*—Every person shall make a return of income tax withheld, pursuant to an agreement under section 3402(p), from wages paid for agricultural labor for the first calendar year in which he is required (by reason of such agreement) to deduct and withhold such tax and for each subsequent calendar year (whether or not wages for agricultural labor are paid therein) until he has filed a final return in accordance with § 31.6011(a)-6. Form 943 is the form prescribed for making the return required under this subparagraph. For the requirements relating to Form 943 with respect to qualified State individual income taxes, see paragraph (d)(3)(iv) of § 301.6361-1.

(4) *Employers in the Employers' Annual Federal Tax Program (Form 944).*—(i) *In general.*—Employers notified of their qualification for the Employers' Annual Federal Tax Program (Form 944) are required to file Form 944, "Employer's ANNUAL Federal Tax Return," instead of Form 941 to make a return of income tax withheld from wages pursuant to section 3402. Upon proper request by the employer, the IRS will notify employers in writing of their qualification for the Employers' Annual Federal Tax Program (Form 944). The IRS will notify employers when they no longer qualify for the Employers' Annual Federal Tax Program (Form 944) and must file Forms 941 instead. Qualified employers are

those with an estimated annual employment tax liability (that is, social security, Medicare, and withheld federal income taxes) of $1,000 or less for the entire calendar year, except employers required under—

(A) Paragraph (a)(3) of this section to make a return on Form 943, "Employer's Annual Federal Tax Return For Agricultural Employees"; or

(B) Paragraph (a)(2) of this section to make a return on Schedule H (Form 1040), "Household Employment Taxes."

(ii) *Request to opt in or opt out of the Employers' Annual Federal Tax Program (Form 944).*— The IRS established procedures in Revenue Procedure 2009-51 published in the Internal Revenue Bulletin for employers to follow to request to participate in the Employers' Annual Federal Tax Program (Form 944) (to opt in) and to request to be removed from the Employers' Annual Federal Tax Program (Form 944) after becoming a participant in order to file Forms 941 instead (to opt out). The IRS will notify employers that their filing requirements have changed to Form 944 or Forms 941. Employers must follow the procedures in Revenue Procedure 2009-51 or its successor to opt in or opt out of the Employers' Annual Federal Tax Program (Form 944).

(b) *Withheld from nonpayroll payments.*—Every person required to withhold tax from nonpayroll payments for calendar year 1994 must make a return for calendar year 1994 and for any subsequent calendar year in which the person is required to withhold such tax until the person makes a final return in accordance with §31.6011(a)-6. Every person not required to withhold tax from nonpayroll payments for calendar year 1994 must make a return for the first calendar year after 1994 in which the person is required to withhold such tax and for any subsequent calendar year in which the person is required to withhold such tax until the person makes a final return in accordance with §31.6011(a)-6. Form 945, Annual Return of Withheld Federal Income Tax, is the form prescribed for making the return required under this paragraph (b). Nonpayroll payments are—

(1) Certain gambling winnings subject to withholding under section 3402(q);

(2) Retirement pay for services in the Armed Forces of the United States subject to withholding under section 3402;

(3) Certain annuities as described in section 3402(o)(1)(B);

(4) Pensions, annuities, IRAs, and certain other deferred income subject to withholding under section 3405; and

(5) Reportable payments subject to backup withholding under section 3406.

(c) *Time and place for filing returns.*—For provisions relating to the time and place for filing returns, see §§31.6071(a)-1 and 31.6091-1, respectively.

(d) *Effective/applicability dates.*—Paragraphs (a)(1) and (a)(4)(i) of this section apply to taxable years beginning on or after December 30, 2008.

Paragraph (a)(4)(ii) of this section applies to taxable years beginning on or after January 1, 2010. The rules of paragraph (a)(1) of this section that apply to taxable years beginning before December 30, 2008, are contained in §31.6011(a)-4 as in effect prior to December 30, 2008. The rules of paragraph (a)(4)(ii) of this section that apply to taxable years beginning before January 1, 2010, but on or after December 30, 2008, are contained in §31.6011(a)-4T as in effect on or after December 30, 2008. The rules of paragraph (a)(4) of this section that apply to taxable years beginning before December 30, 2008, are contained in §31.6011(a)-4T as in effect prior to December 30, 2008. [Reg. §31.6011(a)-4.]

☐ [*T.D.* 6354, 1-13-59. *Amended by T.D.* 7096, 3-17-71; *T.D.* 7200, 8-15-72; *T.D.* 7351, 4-16-75; *T.D.* 7577, 12-19-78; *T.D.* 7580, 12-20-78; *T.D.* 8504, 12-22-93; *T.D.* 8624, 10-13-95; *T.D.* 8672, 5-29-96; *T.D.* 9239, 12-30-2005; *T.D.* 9405, 6-30-2008 *T.D.* 9440, 12-24-2008; *T.D.* 9524, 5-6-2011, *T.D.* 9566, 12-9-2011 *and T.D.* 9586, 4-24-2012.]

[Reg. §31.6011(a)-5]

§31.6011(a)-5. Monthly returns.—(a) *In general.*—(1) *Requirement.*—The provisions of this section are applicable in respect of the taxes reportable on returns required pursuant to §31.6011(a)-1 or §31.6011(a)-4. An employer (or other person) who is required by §31.6011(a)-1 or §31.6011(a)-4 to make quarterly or annual returns on any such form shall, in lieu of making such quarterly or annual returns, make returns of such taxes in accordance with the provisions of this section if the employer is so notified in writing by the IRS. Every employer (or other person) notified by the IRS shall make a return for the calendar month in which the notice is received, for each of the prior calendar months in the return period, and for each calendar month afterwards (whether or not wages are paid in any such month) until the employer has filed a final return or is required to make quarterly or annual returns pursuant to notification as provided in paragraph (a)(2) of this section. Each return required under this section shall be made on the form prescribed for making the return which would otherwise be required of the employer (or other person) under the provisions of §31.6011(a)-1 or §31.6011(a)-4, except that, if some other form is furnished by the IRS for use in lieu of such prescribed form, the return shall be made on such other prescribed form. The IRS may notify any employer (or other person)—

(i) Who by reason of notification as provided in §301.7512-1, is required to comply with the provisions of such §301.7512-1; or

(ii) Who failed to—

(A) Make any return required pursuant to §31.6011(a)-1 or §31.6011(a)-4;

(B) Pay tax reportable on any such form; or

(C) Deposit any such tax as required under the provisions of §31.6302-1.

(2) *Termination of requirement.*—The IRS, in its discretion, may notify the employer in writing that the employer shall discontinue the filing of

monthly returns under this section. If the employer is so notified, the IRS will provide the employer with instructions for filing the final monthly return. Afterwards, the employer shall make quarterly or annual returns in accordance with the provisions of § 31.6011(a)-1 or § 31.6011(a)-4.

(b) *Information returns on Form W-3 and Social Security Administration copies of Form W-2.*—See § 31.6051-2 for requirements with respect to information returns on Form W-3 and Social Security Administration copies of Form W-2.

(c) *Time and place for filing returns.*—For provisions relating to the time and place for filing returns, see § § 31.6071(a)-1 and 31.6091-1, respectively. [Reg. § 31.6011(a)-5.]

☐ [*T.D. 6354, 1-13-59. Amended by T.D. 7351, 4-16-75; T.D. 7580, 12-20-78; T.D. 8637, 12-20-95; T.D. 9061, 6-10-2003 and T.D. 9405, 6-30-2008.*]

[Reg. § 31.6011(a)-6]

§ 31.6011(a)-6. Final returns.—(a) *In general.*—(1) *Federal Insurance Contributions Act; income tax withheld from wages and nonpayroll payments.*—An employer (or other person) who is required to make a return on a particular form pursuant to § 31.6011(a)-1, § 31.6011(a)-4, or § 31.6011(a)-5, and who in any return period ceases to pay wages or nonpayroll payments in respect of which he is required to make a return on that form, must make the return for the period as a final return. Each return made as a final return shall be marked "Final return" by the person filing the return. Every such person filing a final return (other than a final return on Form 942 or Form 943) must furnish information showing the date of the last payment of wages (as defined in section 3121(a) or section 3401(a)), and, if appropriate, the date of the last payment of nonpayroll payments defined in § 31.6011(a)-4(b). If (i) for any return period an employer makes a final return on a particular form, and (ii) after the close of such period the employer pays wages, as defined in section 3121(a) or section 3401(a), in respect of which the same or a different return form is prescribed, such employer shall make returns on the appropriate return form. For example, if an employer who has filed a final return on Form 941 pays wages only for domestic service in his private home not on a farm operated for profit, the employer is required to make returns on Form 942 in respect of such wages.

(2) *Railroad Retirement Tax Act.*—(i) *Form CT-1.*—An employer required to make returns on Form CT-1 who in any return period ceases to pay taxable compensation shall make the return on Form CT-1 for such period as a final return. Such return shall be marked "Final return" by the person filing the return, and such person shall furnish information showing the date of the last payment of taxable compensation. An employer who has only temporarily ceased to pay taxable compensation shall continue to file returns on Form CT-1.

(ii) *Form CT-2.*—An employee representative required to make returns on Form CT-2 who in any calendar quarter ceases to be paid taxable compensation for services as an employee representative shall make the return on Form CT-2 for such quarter as a final return. Such return shall be marked "Final return" by the person filing the return, and such person shall furnish information showing the date of the last payment of taxable compensation. An employee representative who only temporarily ceases to be paid taxable compensation for services as an employee representative shall continue to file returns on Form CT-2.

(3) *Federal Unemployment Tax Act.*—An employer required to make a return on Form 940 for a calendar year in which he ceases to be an employer, as defined in § 31.3306(a)-1, because of the discontinuance, sale, or other transfer of his business, shall make such return as a final return. Such return shall be marked "Final return" by the person filing the return.

(b) *Statement to accompany final return.*—There shall be executed as a part of each final return, except in the case of a final return on Form 942, a statement showing the address at which the records required by the regulations in this part will be kept, the name of the person keeping such records, and, if the business of an employer has been sold or otherwise transferred to another person, the name and address of such person and the date on which such sale or other transfer took place. If no such sale or transfer occurred or the employer does not know the name of the person to whom the business was sold or transferred, that fact should be included in the statement. Such statement shall include any information required by this section as to the date of the last payment of wages or compensation. If the statement is executed as a part of a final return on Form CT-1 or Form CT-2, such statement shall be furnished in duplicate.

(c) *Time and place for filing returns.*—For provisions relating to the time and place for filing returns, see § § 31.6071(a)-1 and 31.6091-1, respectively. [Reg. § 31.6011(a)-6.]

☐ [*T.D. 6354, 1-13-59. Amended by T.D. 7396, 1-12-76 and T.D. 8637, 12-20-95.*]

[Reg. § 31.6011(a)-7]

§ 31.6011(a)-7. Execution of returns.—(a) *In general.*—Each return required under the regulations in this part, together with any prescribed copies or supporting data, shall be filled in and disposed of in accordance with the forms, instructions, and regulations applicable thereto. The return shall be carefully prepared so as fully and accurately to set forth the data required to be furnished therein. Returns which have not been so prepared will not be accepted as meeting the requirements of the regulations in this part. The return may be made by an agent in the name of the person required to make the return if an acceptable power of attorney is filed with the district director and if such return includes all taxes required to be reported by such person on such return for the period covered by the return. Only one return on any one prescribed form for a return period shall be filed by or for a taxpayer. Any supplemental return made on such form in accordance with § 31.6205-1 shall constitute a part of the return which it supplements. Except as may be provided under procedures authorized by the Commissioner with respect to taxes imposed by the Railroad Retirement Tax Act, consolidated returns of two or more employers are not permitted, as for example, returns of a parent and a subsidiary corporation. For provisions relating to the filing of returns of the taxes imposed by the Federal Insurance Contributions Act and of income tax withheld under section 3402 in the case of governmental employers, see § 31.3122 and § 31.3404-1.

(b) *Use of prescribed forms.*—(1) *In general.*— Copies of the prescribed return forms will so far as possible be regularly furnished taxpayers by the Internal Revenue Service. A taxpayer will not be excused from making a return, however, by the fact that no return form has been furnished to him. Taxpayers not supplied with the proper forms should make application therefor to an internal revenue office in ample time to have their returns prepared, verified, and filed on or before the due date with the internal revenue office with which they are required to file their returns. See §§ 31.6071(a)-1 and 31.6091-1, relating, respectively, to the time and place for filing returns. In the absence of a prescribed return form, a statement made by a taxpayer disclosing the aggregate amount of wages or compensation reportable on such form for the period in respect of which a return is required and the amount of taxes due may be accepted as a tentative return. If filed within the prescribed time, the statement so made will relieve the taxpayer from liability for the addition to tax imposed for the delinquent filing of the return, provided that without unnecessary delay such tentative return is supplemented by a return made on the proper form. For additions to the tax in case of failure to file a return within the prescribed time, see the provisions of § 301.6651-1 of this chapter (Regulations on Procedure and Administration).

(2) *Permission for use of magnetic tape.*—In any case where the use of Form W-2 is required for the purpose of making a return or reporting information, such requirement may be satisfied by submitting the information required by such form on magnetic tape or other approved media, provided that the prior consent of the Commissioner of Social Security (or other authorized officer or employee thereof) has been obtained.

(c) *Signing and verification.*—For provisions relating to the signing of returns, see § 31.6061-1.

For provisions relating to the verifying of returns, see § 31.6065(a)-1.

(d) *Reporting of identifying numbers.*—For provisions relating to the reporting of identifying numbers on returns required under the regulations in this part, see § 31.6109-1. [Reg. § 31.6011(a)-7.]

☐ [*T.D.* 6354, 1-13-59. *Amended by T.D.* 6472, 6-22-60; *T.D.* 6606, 8-24-62; *T.D.* 6883, 5-2-66; *T.D.* 7276, 5-4-73; *T.D.* 7396, 1-12-76 *and T.D.* 7580, 12-20-78.]

[Reg. § 31.6011(a)-8]

§ 31.6011(a)-8. Composite return in lieu of specified form.—The Commissioner may authorize the use, at the option of the employer, of a composite return in lieu of any form specified in this part for use by an employer, subject to such conditions, limitations, and special rules governing the preparation, execution, filing, and correction thereof as the Commissioner may deem appropriate. Such composite return shall consist of a form prescribed by the Commissioner and an attachment or attachments of magnetic tape or other approved media. Notwithstanding any provisions in this part to the contrary, a single form and attachment may comprise the returns of more than one employer. To the extent that the use of a composite return has been authorized by the Commissioner, references in this part to a specific form for use by the employer shall be deemed to refer also to a composite return under this section. [Reg. § 31.6011(a)-8.]

☐ [*T.D.* 7200, 8-15-72.]

[Reg. § 31.6011(a)-9]

§ 31.6011(a)-9. Instructions to forms control as to which form is to be used.—Notwithstanding provisions in this part which specify the use of a particular form for a return or other document required by this part, the use of a different form may be required by the latter form's instructions. In such case, the latter form shall be completed in accordance with its instructions. [Reg. § 31.6011(a)-9.]

☐ [*T.D.* 7351, 4-16-75.]

[Reg. § 31.6011(a)-10]

§ 31.6011(a)-10. Instructions to forms may waive filing requirement in case of no liability tax returns.—Notwithstanding provisions in this part which require that a tax return be filed, the instructions to the form on which a return of tax is otherwise required by this part to be made may waive such requirement with respect to a particular class or classes of no liability tax returns. Returns in a class for which such requirement has been so waived need not be made. [Reg. § 31.6011(a)-10.]

☐ [*T.D.* 8229, 9-14-88.]

[Reg. § 40.0-1]

§ 40.0-1. Introduction.—(a) *In general.*—The regulations in this part 40 are designated "Excise

Tax Procedural Regulations." The regulations set forth administrative provisions relating to the excise taxes imposed by chapters 31, 32, 33, 34, 36, 38, 39, and 49 (except for the chapter 32 tax imposed by section 4181 (firearms tax) and the chapter 36 taxes imposed by sections 4461 (harbor maintenance tax) and 4481 (heavy vehicle use tax)), and to floor stocks taxes imposed on articles subject to any of these taxes. Chapter 31 relates to retail excise taxes; chapter 32 to manufacturers' excise taxes; chapter 33 to taxes imposed on communications services and air transportation; chapter 34 to taxes imposed on certain insurance policies; chapter 36 to taxes imposed on transportation by water; chapter 38 to environmental taxes; chapter 39 to taxes imposed on registration-required obligations; and chapter 49 to taxes imposed on indoor tanning services. References in this part to "taxes" also include references to the fees imposed by sections 4375 and 4376. See parts 43, 46, 48, 49, and 52 of this chapter for regulations relating to the imposition of tax.

(b) *References to forms.*—Any reference to a form in this part is also a reference to any other form designated for the same use by the Commissioner after October 22, 1992.

(c) *Definition of semimonthly period.*—The term "semimonthly period" means the first 15 days of a calendar month (the "first semimonthly period") or the portion of a calendar month following the 15th day of the month (the "second semimonthly period").

(d) *Effective/applicability date.*—This part applies to returns that relate to periods beginning after March 31, 2013. For rules that apply before that date, see 26 CFR part 40 (revised as of April 1, 2013). [Reg. § 40.0-1.]

☐ [*T.D. 8442, 10-21-92. Amended by T.D. 8887, 6-7-2000; T.D. 8963, 8-8-2001; T.D. 9486, 6-11-2010; T.D. 9602, 12-5-2012 and T.D. 9621, 6-10-2013.*]

[Reg. § 40.6011(a)-1]

§ 40.6011(a)-1. Returns.—(a) *In general.*— (1) *Return required.*—The return of any tax to which this part 40 applies must be made on Form 720, *Quarterly Federal Excise Tax Return,* according to the instructions applicable to the form. The requirement for filing a return under this part 40 applies separately to each tax listed by IRS Number on Form 720. Except as provided in this paragraph (a)(1), an entry must be made on the line for the IRS Number in order to file a return of the tax corresponding to that number. The entry on an IRS Number line of the word "none," "zero," or comparable entry clearly indicating a denial of liability constitutes a return of that tax. The entry of the word "none" across the return or in the summary portion, provided it clearly indicates a denial of liability for all taxes, constitutes a return of all taxes listed on Form 720.

(2) *Period covered by return.*—(i) *In general.*— Except as provided in paragraphs (b) and (c) of this section, the return must be made for a period of one calendar quarter. A return must be filed for the first calendar quarter in which liability for tax is incurred (or in which tax must be collected and paid over) and for each subsequent calendar quarter, whether or not liability is incurred (or tax must be collected and paid over) during that subsequent quarter, until a final return under § 40.6011(a)-2 is filed. In the case of one-time filings (as defined in § 40.6011(a)-2(b)) and returns of floor stocks taxes under § 40.6011(a)-2(c), a first return is also a final return.

(ii) *First return.*—A person's return is a first return if the person was not required under this part 40 to file a return (other than a final return) for the preceding period.

(iii) *Floor stocks tax return.*—A return reporting liability for a floor stocks tax described in § 40.0-1(a) is a return for the calendar quarter in which the tax payment is due and not the calendar quarter in which the liability for tax is incurred.

(3) *Person required to file the return.*—Except in the case of a tax required to be collected and paid over, the person incurring liability for tax must file the return. In the case of a tax required to be collected and paid over, the person required to collect the tax (and not the person incurring liability) must file the return.

(b) *Monthly and semimonthly returns.*—(1) *In general.*—If the district director determines that any person that is required under this section to file returns has failed to comply in a timely manner with the requirements of this part 40 relating to returns, payments, and deposits of tax, that person will be required, if so notified in writing by the district director, to make a return for a monthly or semimonthly period (as defined in § 40.0-1(c)). Each person so notified by the district director must make a return for the calendar month or semimonthly period in which the notice is received and for each calendar month or semimonthly period thereafter until the person has filed a final return or until the person is notified by the district director to resume making quarterly returns.

(2) *Certain persons liable for tax on taxable fuel.*—The district director may require a person to make a return of tax for a monthly or semimonthly period in the manner prescribed in paragraph (b)(1) of this section if the person—

(i) Is a bonded registrant (as defined in § 48.4101-1(b) of this chapter) at any time during the period;

(ii) has been registered under section 4101 for less than one year at the beginning of the period;

(iii) Meets the acceptable risk test of § 48.4101-1(f)(3) of this chapter by reason of § 48.4101-1(f)(3)(i)(B) of this chapter at any time during the period;

(iv) Has failed to comply with the applicable provisions of § 48.4101-1(h) of this chapter (relating to the terms and conditions of registration);

(v) Is liable for tax under §48.4082-4(a) of this chapter (relating to the back-up tax on diesel fuel and kerosene) at any time during the period; or

(vi) Is liable for tax under section 4081 (relating to the tax on taxable fuel) at any time during the period and is not registered under section 4101 at that time.

(c) *Fees on health insurance policies and self-insured health plans.*—(1) *In general.*—A return that reports liability imposed by section 4375 or 4376 is a return for policies or plans with policy or plan years ending in the previous calendar year, and, for issuers that determine the average number of lives covered under a policy for purposes of section 4375 using the member months method under §46.4375-1(c)(2)(v) or the state form method under §46.4375-1(c)(2)(vi) of this chapter, the return is for all policies in effect during the previous calendar year. The second sentence of paragraph (a)(2)(i) of this section (relating to filing quarterly returns regardless of whether liability is incurred) does not apply to a person that files a Form 720, "Quarterly Federal Excise Tax Return," only to report liability imposed by section 4375 or 4376.

(2) *Applicability date.*—This paragraph (c) applies to returns that report liability imposed by section 4375 or 4376. [Reg. §40.6011(a)-1.]

☐ [T.D. 8442, 10-21-92. *Amended by T.D. 8659,* 3-13-96; T.D. 8685, 11-8-96; T.D. 8748, 12-31-97; T.D. 8879, 3-30-2000; T.D. 8887, 6-7-2000; T.D. 8963, 8-8-2001 *and T.D. 9602, 12-5-2012.*]

[Reg. §41.6011(a)-1]

§41.6011(a)-1. Returns.—(a) *In general.*— (1) A person that is liable for tax under §41.4481-2(a)(1)(i)(A), (B), or (C) must file a return for the taxable period with respect to the tax imposed by section 4481.

(2) A person that is liable for tax under §41.4481-2(a)(1)(i)(D) must file a return for a taxable period with respect to the tax imposed by section 4481 if the Commissioner notifies the person that the tax for the taxable period has not been paid in full.

(3) A transferee of a vehicle that receives a statement described in the first sentence of §41.4483-3(f) must file a return with the statement attached.

(4) A person that is liable for tax under §41.4481-2(a)(1)(i)(A), (B), (C), or (D), after taking into account the modification required under §41.4481-2(a)(2), is treated as liable for tax by the same provision of §41.4481-2(a)(1)(i) for purposes of this section and must file a return.

(b) *Form 2290.*—The return required under paragraph (a) of this section is Form 2290, "Heavy Highway Vehicle Use Tax Return," or such other return as the Commissioner may prescribe. The return is made in accordance with the instructions applicable to the form.

(c) *Required use of electronic filing.*—(1) *In general.*—A person that files any return reporting 25 or more vehicles must file the return electronically, as prescribed by the Commissioner. For this purpose, the number of vehicles reported on a return is the total number of vehicles for which tax is reported and does not include vehicles for which a suspension of tax is claimed.

(2) *Examples.*—The application of this paragraph (c) may be illustrated by the following examples:

Example 1. A has 100 vehicles registered in its name, all of which have a taxable gross weight in excess of 55,000 pounds. Seventy-five of the vehicles are in use on July 1. Twenty-five are in dead storage as described in §41.4482(c)-1(c). The vehicles in dead storage are not in use and they are not listed on the Schedule 1. A files Form 2290 electronically for the 75 vehicles in use on July 1 and receives a receipted Schedule 1. On August 23 of the same calendar year, A uses the remaining 25 vehicles. A does not file Form 2290 electronically but uses a paper Form 2290. A has failed to meet the requirements of section 4481(e) for the remaining 25 vehicles.

Example 2. Assume the same facts as in *Example* 1 except that on August 23, A uses 15 of the vehicles that were not used in July. The remaining 10 vehicles are not used in August. A does not file Form 2290 electronically but uses a paper Form 2290. A has correctly filed a return as required by section 4481(e).

(d) *Effective/applicability date.*—Paragraphs (a)(4) and (c) of this section apply to returns filed on and after July 1, 2015. For rules applicable before that date, see 26 CFR 41.6011(a)-1 (revised as of April 1, 2014). [Reg. §41.6011(a)-1.]

☐ [T.D. 6216. *Amended by T.D. 6743, 6-22-64;* T.D. 8879, 3-30-2000 *and T.D. 9698, 10-28-2014.*]

[Reg. §44.6011(a)-1]

§44.6011(a)-1. Returns.—(a) *In general.*— Every person required to pay the tax on wagers imposed by section 4401 of the Code shall make for each month, from the daily records required by §§44.4403-1 and 44.6001-1, a return on Form 730 in accordance with the instructions and regulations applicable thereto. A return shall be made for each month whether or not liability has been incurred for that month. If the taxpayer ceases operations which make him liable for the tax, the last return shall be marked "Final Return".

(b) *Return on Form 11-C.*—Every person required to pay the special tax imposed by section 4411 shall make a return on Form 11-C in accordance with the instructions and regulations applicable thereto. [Reg. §44.6011(a)-1.]

☐ [T.D. 6370, 4-4-59.]

[Reg. §46.6011(a)-1]

§46.6011(a)-1. Returns.—(a) *In general.*—Liability for tax imposed under section 4371, 4501(a) or 4701 shall be reported on Form 720. Except as provided in paragraph (b) of this section, a return on Form 720 shall be filed for a period of one calendar quarter. Every person required to make a return on Form 720 for a return period ended December 31, 1954, shall make a return for each subsequent calendar quarter, month, or semimonthly period (whether or not liability was incurred for any tax reportable on such return for such return period) until he has filed a final return in accordance with § 46.6011(a)-2. Every person not required to make a return on Form 720 for a return period ended December 31, 1954, shall make a return for the first calendar quarter thereafter in which he incurs liability for tax imposed under section 4371, 4501(a) or 4701 and shall make a return for each subsequent calendar quarter, month, or semimonthly period until he has filed a final return in accordance with § 46.6011(a)-2.

(b) *Monthly and semimonthly returns.*—(1) *Requirement.*—If the district director determines that any taxpayer who is required to make deposit of taxes under the provisions of § 46.6302(c)-1 has failed to make deposits of such taxes, such taxpayer shall be required, if so notified in writing by the district director, to file a monthly or semimonthly return on Form 720, except that, if some other form is furnished by the district director for use in lieu of Form 720, the return shall be made on such other form. Every person so notified by the district director shall make a return for the calendar month or semimonthly period (as defined in § 46.6302(c)-1(b)(1)) in which the notice is received and for each calendar month or semimonthly period thereafter until he has filed a final return or is required to make returns on the basis of a different return period pursuant to notification as provided in subparagraph (2) of this paragraph.

(2) *Change of requirement.*—The district director, in his discretion, may notify the taxpayer in writing that he is required to make a quarterly or monthly return, if he has been filing returns for a semimonthly period, or is required to make a quarterly or semimonthly return, if he has been filing monthly returns.

(3) *Return for period change takes effect.*—If a taxpayer who has been filing quarterly returns receives notice to file a monthly or semimonthly return or a taxpayer who has been filing monthly returns receives notice to file a semimonthly return, the first return required pursuant to the notice shall be made for the month or semimonthly period in which the notice is received and all prior months or semimonthly periods which are not includible in a prior period for which the taxpayer is required to file a return. If a taxpayer who has been filing monthly or semimonthly returns receives notice to file a quarterly return, the last month or semimonthly period for which a return shall be made is the last month or semimonthly period of the calendar quarter in which such notice is received. If a taxpayer who has been filing semimonthly returns receives notice to file a monthly return, the

last semimonthly period for which a return shall be made is the last semimonthly period of the month in which such notice is received.

(c) *Signing and verification of returns.*—For provisions relating to the signing and verification of returns, see §§ 46.6061-1 and 46.6065, respectively.

(d) *Time and place for filing returns.*—For provisions relating to the time and place for filing returns, see §§ 46.6071(a)-1 and 46.6091-1, respectively. [Reg. § 46.6011(a)-1.]

☐ [T.D. 6461, 5-6-60. *Amended by T.D. 6915*, 3-29-67; *T.D. 7023, 1-21-70 and T.D. 8102*, 9-19-86.]

[Reg. § 49.6011(a)-1]

§ 49.6011(a)-1. Returns.—(a) *In general.*—Liability for tax imposed under chapter 33 of the Code shall be reported on Form 720. Except as provided in paragraph (b) of this section, a return on Form 720 shall be filed for a period of one calendar quarter. Every person required to make a return on Form 720 for the return period ended December 31, 1958, shall make a return for each subsequent calendar quarter, month, or semimonthly period (whether or not liability was incurred for any tax reportable on the return for such return period) until he has filed a final return in accordance with § 49.6011(a)-2. Every person not required to make a return on Form 720 for the return period ended December 31, 1958, shall make a return for the first calendar quarter thereafter in which he incurs liability for tax imposed under chapter 33, and shall make a return for each subsequent calendar quarter, month, or semimonthly period until he has filed a final return in accordance with § 49.6011(a)-2. Each return required under the regulations in this part, together with any prescribed copies, records, or supporting data, shall be filled in and disposed of in accordance with the forms, instructions, and regulations applicable thereto.

(b) *Monthly and semimonthly returns.*—(1) *Requirement.*—If the district director determines that any person who is required to make deposit of taxes under the provisions of § 49.6302(c)-1 has failed to make deposits of such taxes, such person shall be required, if so notified in writing by the district director, to file a monthly or semimonthly return on Form 720, except that, if some other form is furnished by the district director for use in lieu of Form 720, the return shall be made on such other form. Every person so notified by the district director shall make a return for the calendar month or semimonthly period (as defined in § 49.6302(c)-1 (b)) in which the notice is received and for each calendar month or semimonthly period thereafter until he has filed a final return or is required to make returns on the basis of a different return period pursuant to notification as provided in subparagraph (2) of this paragraph.

(2) *Change of requirement.*—The district director, in his discretion, may notify the person in writing that he is required to make a quarterly or

monthly return, if he has been filing returns for a semimonthly period, or is required to make a quarterly or semimonthly return, if he has been filing monthly returns.

(3) *Return for period change takes effect.*—If a person who has been filing quarterly returns receives notice to file a monthly or semimonthly return or a person who has been filing monthly returns receives notice to file a semimonthly return, the first return required pursuant to the notice shall be made for the month or semimonthly period in which the notice is received and all prior months or semimonthly periods which are not includible in a prior period for which the person is required to file a return. If a person who has been filing monthly or semimonthly returns receives notice to file a quarterly return, the last month or semimonthly period for which a return shall be made is the last month or semimonthly period of the calendar quarter in which such notice is received. If a person who has been filing semimonthly returns receives notice to file a monthly return, the last semimonthly period for which a return shall be made is the last semimonthly period of the month in which such notice is received. [Reg. § 49.6011(a)-1.]

☐ [*T.D. 6915, 3-28-67.*]

[Reg. § 40.6011(a)-2]

§ 40.6011(a)-2. Final returns.—(a) *In general.*—(1) *Permanent cessation of operations.*—Any person that is required under § 40.6011(a)-1 to make returns and that permanently ceases all operations with respect to which liability for tax was incurred (or with respect to which tax had to be collected and paid over) must make a final return in accordance with the instructions applicable to the form on which the return is made. A person does not make a final return if only a temporary or partial cessation of such operations occurs and must continue to file returns as required under § 40.6011(a)-1.

(2) *Change in law without cessation of operations.*—Any person that is required under § 40.6011(a)-1 to make returns must make a final return in accordance with the instructions applicable to the form on which the return is made if, by reason of a change in law, that person is no longer liable for any tax (or, in the case of a collected tax, is no longer responsible for collecting and paying over any tax). For example, if the tax on a product is changed from a retail tax to a manufacturers tax, a retailer formerly liable for the tax but now buying the product tax-paid from its supplier must make a final return (assuming that the retailer has no other tax liability reportable on the return).

(b) *Special rule for one-time filings.*—(1) *In general.*—A first return is also a final return if it is a one-time filing. A return is a one-time filing if the person reporting tax does not engage in any activity with respect to which tax is reportable on the return in the course of a trade or business.

(2) *Deposits not required.*—See § 40.6302(c)-1(e)(2) for a rule providing that no deposit of taxes reported on a one-time filing is required.

(c) *Special rule for floor stocks taxes.*—A first return reporting only floor stocks taxes under this part 40 is also a final return. [Reg. § 40.6011(a)-2.]

☐ [*T.D. 8442, 10-21-92. Amended by T.D. 8685, 11-8-96 and T.D. 8963, 8-8-2001.*]

[Reg. § 46.6011(a)-2]

§ 46.6011(a)-2. Final returns.—(a) *In general.*—Any person who is required to make a return on Form 720 pursuant to § 46.6011(a)-1, and who in any return period ceases operations in respect of which he is required to make a return on such form, shall make such return for such period as a final return. Each return made as a final return shall be marked "Final Return" by the person filing the return. A person who has only temporarily ceased to incur liability for tax required to be reported on Form 720, because of temporary or seasonal suspension of his business or for other reasons, shall not make a final return but shall continue to file returns.

(b) *Statement to accompany final return.*—There shall be executed as a part of each final return a statement showing the address at which the records required by the regulations in this part will be kept, the name of the person keeping such records, and, if the business of a taxpayer has been sold or otherwise transferred to another person, the name and address of such person and the date on which such sale or transfer took place. If no such sale or transfer occurred or the taxpayer does not know the name of the person to whom the business was sold or transferred, that fact should be included in the statement. [Reg. § 46.6011(a)-2.]

☐ [*T.D. 6461, 5-6-60.*]

[Reg. § 49.6011(a)-2]

§ 49.6011(a)-2. Final returns.—(a) *In general.*—Any person who is required to make a return on Form 720 pursuant to § 49.6011(a)-1, and who in any return period ceases operations in respect of which he is required to make a return on such form, shall make his return for that period as a final return. Each return made as a final return shall be marked "Final Return" by the person filing the return. A person who has only temporarily ceased to incur liability for tax required to be reported on Form 720, because of temporary or seasonal suspension of his business or for other reasons, shall not make a final return but shall continue to file returns.

(b) *Statement to accompany final return.*—There shall be executed as a part of each final return a statement showing the address at which the records required by the regulations in this part will be kept, the name of the person keeping such records, and, if the business of a person required to make a return on Form 720 has been sold or otherwise transferred to another person,

Reg. § 49.6011(a)-2(b)

the name and address of such other person and the date on which the sale or transfer took place. If no sale or transfer occurred or the person required to make a return on Form 720 does not know the name of the person to whom the business was sold or transferred, that fact should be included in the statement. [Reg. § 49.6011(a)-2.]

☐ [T.D. 6915, 3-28-67.]

[Reg. § 31.6011(b)-1]

§ 31.6011(b)-1. Employers' identification numbers.—(a) *Requirement of application.*—(1) *In general.*—(i) *Before October 1, 1962.*—Except as provided in paragraph (b) of this section, every employer who on any day after December 31, 1954, and before October 1, 1962, has in his employ one or more individuals in employment for wages subject to the taxes imposed by the Federal Insurance Contributions Act, but who prior to such day neither has been assigned an identification number nor has applied therefor, shall make an application on Form SS-4 for an identification number.

(ii) *On or after October 1, 1962.*—Except as provided in paragraph (b) of this section, every employer who on any day after September 30, 1962, has in his employ one or more individuals in employment for wages which are subject to the taxes imposed by the Federal Insurance Contributions Act or which are subject to the withholding of income tax from wages under section 3402, but who prior to such day neither has been assigned an identification number nor has applied therefor, shall make an application on Form SS-4 for an identification number.

(iii) *Method of application.*—The application, together with any supplementary statement, shall be prepared in accordance with the form, instructions, and regulations applicable thereto, and shall set forth fully and clearly the data therein called for. Form SS-4 may be obtained from any district director or director of a service center or any district office of the Social Security Administration. The application shall be filed with the internal revenue officer designated in the instructions applicable to Form SS-4, or with the nearest district office of the Social Security Administration. The application shall be signed by (a) the individual, if the employer is an individual; (b) the president, vice president, or other principal officer, if the employer is a corporation; (c) a responsible and duly authorized member or officer having knowledge of its affairs, if the employer is a partnership or other unincorporated organization; or (d) the fiduciary, if the employer is a trust or estate. An identification number will be assigned to the employer in due course upon the basis of the information reported on the application required under this section.

(2) *Time for filing Form SS-4.*—The application for an identification number shall be filed on or before the seventh day after the first payment of wages to which reference is made in subparagraph (1) of this paragraph. For provisions relating to the time when wages are paid, see § 31.3121(a)-2 and paragraph (b) of § 31.3402(a)-1.

(b) *Employers who are assigned identification numbers without application.*—An identification number may be assigned, without application by the employer, in the case of an employer who has in his employ only employees who are engaged exclusively in the performance of domestic service in his private home not on a farm operated for profit (see § 31.3121(a)(7)-1). If an identification number is so assigned, the employer is not required to make an application on Form SS-4 for the number.

(c) *Crew leaders.*—Any person who, as a crew leader within the meaning of section 3121(o), furnishes individuals to perform agricultural labor for another person shall, on or before the first date on which he furnishes such individuals to perform such labor for such other person, advise such other person of his name, permanent mailing address, or if none, present address, and identification number, if any.

(d) *Use of identification number.*—The identification number assigned to an employer (other than a household employer referred to in paragraph (b) of this section) shall be shown in the employer's records, and shall be shown in his claims to the extent required by the applicable forms, regulations, and instructions. For provisions relating to the inclusion of identification numbers in returns, statements on Form W-2, and depositary receipts, see § 31.6109-1. [Reg. § 31.6011(b)-1.]

☐ [T.D. 6354, 1-13-59. *Amended by T.D. 6606,* 8-24-62 *and T.D. 7012, 5-14-89.*]

[Reg. § 31.6011(b)-2]

§ 31.6011(b)-2. Employees' account numbers.—(a) *Requirement of application.*—(1) *In general.*—(i) *Before November 1, 1962.*—Every employee who on any day after December 31, 1954, and before November 1, 1962, is in employment for wages subject to the taxes imposed by the Federal Insurance Contributions Act, but who prior to such day has neither secured an account number nor made application therefor, shall make an application on Form SS-5 for an account number.

(ii) *On or after November 1, 1962.*—Every employee who on any day after October 31, 1962, is in employment for wages which are subject to the taxes imposed by the Federal Insurance Contributions Act or which are subject to the withholding of income tax from wages under section 3402, but who prior to such day has neither secured an account number nor made application therefor, shall make an application on Form SS-5 for an account number.

(iii) *Method of application.*—The application shall be prepared in accordance with the form, instructions, and regulations applicable thereto, and shall set forth fully and clearly the data therein called for. The employee shall file the application with any district office of the Social Security Administration or, if the employee is not working within the United States, with the district office of the Social Security Administration at Baltimore, Maryland. Form SS-5 may be obtained from any district office of the Social Security Administration or from any district director. An account number will be assigned to the employee by the Social Security Administration in due course upon the basis of information reported on the application required under this section. A card showing the name and account number of the employee to whom an account number has been assigned will be furnished to the employee by the Social Security Administration.

(2) *Time for filing Form SS-5.*—The application shall be filed on or before the seventh day after the occurrence of the first day of employment to which reference is made in subparagraph (1) of this paragraph, unless the employee leaves the employ of his employer before such seventh day, in which case the application shall be filed on or before the date on which the employee leaves the employ of his employer.

(3) *Changes and corrections.*—Any employee may have his account number changed at any time by applying to a district office of the Social Security Administration and showing good reasons for a change. With that exception, only one account number will be assigned to an employee. Any employee whose name is changed by marriage or otherwise, or who has stated incorrect information on Form SS-5, should report such change or correction to a district office of the Social Security Administration. Copies of the form for making such reports may be obtained from any district office of the Administration.

(b) *Duties of employee with respect to his account number.*—(1) *Information to be furnished to employer.*—An employee shall, on the day on which he enters the employ of any employer for wages, comply with the provisions of subdivision (i), (ii), (iii), or (iv) of this subparagraph, except that, if the employee's services for the employer consist solely of agricultural labor, domestic service in a private home of the employer not on a farm operated for profit, or service not in the course of the employer's trade or business, the employee shall comply with such provisions on the first day on which wages are paid to him by such employer, within the meaning of § 31.3121(a)-2:

(i) *Employee who has account number card.*—If the employee has been issued an account number card by the Social Security Administration and has the card available, the employee shall show it to the employer.

(ii) *Employee who has number but card not available.*—If the employee does not have available the account number card issued to him by the Social Security Administration but knows what his account number is, and what his name is, exactly as shown on such card, the employee

shall advise the employer of such number and name. Care must be exercised that the employer is correctly advised of such number and name.

(iii) *Employee who has receipt acknowledging application.*—If the employee does not have an account number card but has available a receipt issued to him by an office of the Social Security Administration acknowledging that an application for an account number has been received, the employee shall show such receipt to the employer.

(iv) *Employee who is unable to furnish number or receipt.*—If an employee is unable to comply with the requirement of subdivision (i), (ii), or (iii) of this subparagraph, the employee shall furnish to the employer a statement in writing, signed by the employee, setting forth the date of the statement, the employee's full name, present address, date and place of birth, father's full name, mother's full name before marriage, and the employee's sex, including a statement as to whether the employee has previously filed an application on Form SS-5 and, if so, the date and place of such filing. The information required by this subdivision shall be furnished on Form SS-5, if a copy of Form SS-5 is available. The furnishing of such a Form SS-5 or other statement by the employee to the employer does not relieve the employee of his obligation to make an application on Form SS-5 and file it with a district office of the Social Security Administration as required by paragraph (a) of this section. The foregoing provisions of this subdivision are not applicable to an employee engaged exclusively in the performance of domestic service in a private home of his employer not on a farm operated for profit, or in the performance of agricultural labor, if the services are performed for an employer other than an employer required to file returns of the taxes imposed by the Federal Insurance Contributions Act with the office of the United States Internal Revenue Service in Puerto Rico. However, such employee shall advise the employer of his full name and present address.

For provisions relating to the duties of an employer when furnished the information required by subdivision (i), (ii), (iii), or (iv) of this subparagraph, see paragraph (c) of this section.

(2) *Additional information to be furnished by employee to employer.*—Every employee who, on the day on which he is required to comply with subdivision (i), (ii), (iii), or (iv) of subparagraph (1) of this paragraph, has an account number card but for any reason does not show such card to the employer on such day shall promptly thereafter show the card to the employer. An employee who does not have an account number card on such day shall, upon receipt of an account number card from the Social Security Administration, promptly show such card to the employer, if he is still in the employ of that employer. If the employee has left the employ of the employer when the employee receives an account number card from the Social Security Administration, he shall promptly advise the

Reg. §31.6011(b)-2(b)(2)

employer of his account number and name exactly as shown on such card. The account number originally assigned to an employee (or the number as changed in accordance with paragraph (a)(3) of this section) shall be used by the employee as required by this paragraph even though he enters the employ of other employers.

(3) *Furnishing of account number by employee to employer.*—See § 31.6109-1 for additional provisions relating to the furnishing of an account number by the employee to his employer.

(c) *Duties of employer with respect to employees' account numbers.*—(1) *Employee who shows account number.*—Upon being shown the account number card issued to an employee by the Social Security Administration, the employer shall enter the account number and name, exactly as shown on the card, in the employer's records, returns, statements for employees, and claims to the extent required by the applicable forms, regulations, and instructions.

(2) *Employee who does not show account number card.*—With respect to an employee who, on the day on which he is required to comply with subdivision (i), (ii), (iii), or (iv) of paragraph (b)(1) of this section, does not show the employer an account number card issued to the employee by the Social Security Administration, the employer shall request such employee to show him such card. If the card is not shown, the employer shall comply with the applicable provisions of subdivision (i), (ii), (iii), (iv), or (v) of this subparagraph:

(i) *Employee who has not applied for account number.*—If the employee has not been assigned an account number and has not made application therefor with a district office of the Social Security Administration, the employer shall inform the employee of his duties under this section.

(ii) *Employee who has account number.*—If the employee advises the employer of his number and name as shown on his account number card, as provided in paragraph (b)(1)(ii) of this section, the employer shall enter such number and name in his records.

(iii) *Employee who has receipt for application.*—If the employee shows the employer, as provided in paragraph (b)(1)(iii) of this section, a receipt issued to him by an office of the Social Security Administration acknowledging that an application for an account number has been received from the employee, the employer shall enter in his records with respect to such employee the name and address of the employee exactly as shown on the receipt, the expiration date of the receipt, and the address of the issuing office. The receipt shall be retained by the employee.

(iv) *Employee who furnishes Form SS-5 or statement.*—If the employee furnishes information to the employer as provided in paragraph (b)(1)(iv) of this section, the employer shall retain such information for use as provided in subparagraph (3)(ii) of this paragraph.

(v) *Household or agricultural employees.*—If the employee advises the employer of his full name and present address in accordance with those provisions of paragraph (b)(1)(iv) of this section which are applicable in the case of employees engaged exclusively in the performance of domestic service in a private home of the employer not on a farm operated for profit, or agricultural labor, the employer shall enter such name and address in his records.

(3) *Account number unknown when return is filed.*—In any case in which the employee's account number is for any reason unknown to the employer at the time the employer's return is filed for any return period with respect to which the employer is required to report the wages paid to such employee—

(i) *If employee has shown receipt for application.*—If the employee has shown to the employer, as provided in paragraph (b)(1)(iii) of this section, a receipt issued to him by an office of the Social Security Administration acknowledging that an application for an account number has been received from the employee, the employer shall enter on the return, with the entry with respect to the employee, the name and address of the employee exactly as shown on the receipt, the expiration date of the receipt, and the address of the issuing office.

(ii) *If employee furnished Form SS-5 or statement.*—If the employee has furnished information to the employer as provided in paragraph (b)(1)(iv) of this section, the employer shall prepare a copy of the Form SS-5 or statement furnished by the employee and attach the copy to the return.

(iii) *If employee did not furnish receipt, Form SS-5, or statement.*—If neither subdivision (i) nor (ii) of this subparagraph is applicable, the employer shall, except as provided in subparagraph (4) of this paragraph, attach to the return a Form SS-5 or statement, signed by the employer, setting forth as fully and clearly as practicable the employee's full name, his present or last known address, date and place of birth, father's full name, mother's full name before marriage, the employee's sex, and a statement as to whether an application for an account number has previously been filed by the employee and, if so, the date and place of such filing. The employer shall also insert in such Form SS-5 or statement an explanation of why he has not secured from the employee the information referred to in paragraph (b)(1)(iv) of this section, and shall insert the word "Employer" as part of his signature.

(4) *Household or agricultural employees.*—The provisions of subparagraph (3)(iii) of this paragraph are not applicable with respect to an employee engaged exclusively in the performance of domestic service in a private home of his employer not on a farm operated for profit, or in the performance of agricultural labor, if the ser-

vices are performed for an employer other than an employer required to file returns of the taxes imposed by the Federal Insurance Contributions Act with the office of the United States Internal Revenue Service in Puerto Rico. If any such employee has not furnished to the employer the information required by paragraph (b)(1)(i), (ii), or (iii) of this section prior to the time the employer's return is filed for any return period with respect to which the employer is required to report wages paid to such employee, the employer shall enter the word "Unknown" in the account number column of the return and (i) file with the return a statement showing the employee's full name and present or last known address, or (ii) enter such address on the return form immediately below the name of the employee.

(5) *Where to obtain Form SS-5.*—Employers may obtain copies of Form SS-5 from any district office of the Social Security Administration or from any district director.

(6) *Prospective employees.*—While not mandatory, it is suggested that the employer advise any prospective employee who does not have an account number of the requirements of paragraphs (a) and (b) of this section. [Reg. § 31.6011(b)-2.]

☐ [*T.D.* 6354, 1-13-59. *Amended by T.D.* 6606, 8-24-62.]

[Reg. § 301.6011(g)-1]

§ 301.6011(g)-1. Disclosure by taxable party to the tax-exempt entity.—(a) *Requirement of disclosure.*—(1) *In general.*—Except as provided in paragraph (d)(2) of this section, any taxable party (as defined in paragraph (c) of this section) to a prohibited tax shelter transaction (as defined in section 4965(e) and § 53.4965-3 of this chapter) must disclose by statement to each tax-exempt entity (as defined in section 4965(c) and § 53.4965-2 of this chapter) that the taxable party knows or has reason to know is a party to such transaction (as defined in paragraph (b) of this section) that the transaction is a prohibited tax shelter transaction.

(2) *Determining whether a taxable party knows or has reason to know.*—Whether a taxable party knows or has reason to know that a tax-exempt entity is a party to a prohibited tax shelter transaction is based on all the facts and circumstances. If the taxable party knows or has reason to know that a prohibited tax shelter transaction involves a tax-exempt, tax indifferent or tax-favored entity, relevant factors for determining whether the taxable party knows or has reason to know that a specific tax-exempt entity is a party to the transaction include—

(i) The extent of the efforts made to determine whether a tax-exempt entity is facilitating the transaction by reason of its tax-exempt, tax indifferent or tax-favored status (or is identified in published guidance, by type, class or role, as a party to the transaction); and

(ii) If a tax-exempt entity is facilitating the transaction by reason of its tax-exempt, tax indifferent or tax-favored status (or is identified in published guidance, by type, class or role, as a party to the transaction), the extent of the efforts made to determine the identity of the tax-exempt entity.

(b) *Definition of tax-exempt party to a prohibited tax shelter transaction.*—For purposes of section 6011(g), a tax-exempt entity is a party to a prohibited tax shelter transaction if the entity is defined as such under § 53.4965-4 of this chapter.

(c) *Definition of taxable party.*—(1) *In general.*— For purposes of this section, the term *taxable party* means—

(i) A person who has entered into and participates or expects to participate in the transaction under § § 1.6011-4(c)(3)(i)(A), (B), or (C), 20.6011-4, 25.6011-4, 31.6011-4, 53.6011-4, 54.6011-4, or 56.6011-4 of this chapter; or

(ii) A person who is designated as a taxable party by the Secretary in published guidance.

(2) *Special rules.*—(i) *Certain listed transactions.*—If a transaction that was otherwise not a prohibited tax shelter transaction becomes a listed transaction after the filing of a person's tax return (including an amended return) reflecting either tax consequences or a tax strategy described in the published guidance listing the transaction (or a tax benefit derived from tax consequences or a tax strategy described in the published guidance listing the transaction), the person is a taxable party beginning on the date the transaction is described as a listed transaction in published guidance.

(ii) *Persons designated as non-parties.*—Published guidance may identify which persons, by type, class or role, will not be treated as a party to a prohibited tax shelter transaction for purposes of section 6011(g).

(d) *Time for providing disclosure statement.*— (1) *In general.*—A taxable party to a prohibited tax shelter transaction must make the disclosure required by this section to each tax-exempt entity that the taxable party knows or has reason to know is a party to the transaction within 60 days after the last to occur of—

(i) The date the person becomes a taxable party to the transaction within the meaning of paragraph (c) of this section;

(ii) The date the taxable party knows or has reason to know that the tax-exempt entity is a party to the transaction within the meaning of paragraph (b) of this section; or

(iii) July 6, 2010.

(2) *Termination of a disclosure obligation.*—A person shall not be required to provide the disclosure otherwise required by this section if the person does not know or have reason to know that the tax-exempt entity is a party to the transaction within the meaning of paragraph (b) of this section on or before the first date on which the transaction is required to be disclosed by the

person under §§1.6011-4, 20.6011-4, 25.6011-4, 31.6011-4, 53.6011-4, 54.6011-4, or 56.6011-4 of this chapter.

(3) Disclosure is not required with respect to any prohibited tax shelter transaction entered into by a tax-exempt entity on or before May 17, 2006.

(e) *Frequency of disclosure.*—One disclosure statement is required per tax-exempt entity per transaction. See paragraph (h) of this section for rules relating to designation agreements.

(f) *Form and content of disclosure statement.*— The statement disclosing to the tax-exempt entity that the transaction is a prohibited tax shelter transaction must be a written statement that—

(1) Identifies the type of prohibited tax shelter transaction (including the published guidance citation for a listed transaction); and

(2) States that the tax-exempt entity's involvement in the transaction may subject either it or its entity manager(s) or both to excise taxes under section 4965 and to disclosure obligations under section 6033(a) of the Internal Revenue Code.

(g) *To whom disclosure is made.*—The disclosure statement must be provided—

(1) In the case of a non-plan entity as defined in §53.4965-2(b) of this chapter, to—

(i) Any entity manager of the tax-exempt entity with authority or responsibility similar to that exercised by an officer, director or trustee of an organization; or

(ii) If a person described in paragraph (g)(1)(i) of this section is not known, to the primary contact on the transaction.

(2) In the case of a plan entity as defined in §53.4965-2(c) of this chapter, including a fully self-directed qualified plan, IRA, or other savings arrangement, to any entity manager of the plan entity who approved or otherwise caused the entity to become a party to the prohibited tax shelter transaction.

(h) *Designation agreements.*—If more than one taxable party is required to disclose a prohibited tax shelter transaction under this section, the taxable parties may designate by written agreement a single taxable party to disclose the transaction. The transaction must then be disclosed in accordance with this section. The designation of one taxable party to disclose the transaction does not relieve the other taxable parties of their obligation to disclose the transaction to a tax-exempt entity that is a party to the transaction in accordance with this section, if the designated taxable party fails to disclose the transaction to the tax-exempt entity in a timely manner.

(i) *Penalty for failure to provide disclosure statement.*—See section 6707A for the penalty applicable to the failure to disclose a prohibited tax shelter transaction in accordance with this section.

(j) *Effective date/applicability date.*—This section will apply with respect to transactions entered

into by a tax-exempt entity after May 17, 2006. [Reg. §301.6011(g)-1.]

☐ [*T.D.* 9492, 7-2-2010.]

[Reg. §1.6012-1]

§1.6012-1. Individuals required to make returns of income.—(a) *Individual citizen or resident.*—(1) *In general.*—Except as provided in subparagraph (2) of this paragraph, an income tax return must be filed by every individual for each taxable year beginning before January 1, 1973, during which he receives $600 or more of gross income, and for each taxable year beginning after December 31, 1972, during which he receives $750 or more of gross income, if such individual is—

(i) A citizen of the United States, whether residing at home or abroad,

(ii) A resident of the United States even though not a citizen thereof, or

(iii) An alien bona fide resident of Puerto Rico or any section 931 possession, as defined in §1.931-1(c)(1), during the entire taxable year.

(2) *Special rules.*—(i) For taxable years beginning before January 1, 1970, an individual who is described in subparagraph (1) of this paragraph and who has attained the age of 65 before the close of his taxable year must file an income tax return only if he receives $1,200 or more of gross income during his taxable year.

(ii) For taxable years beginning after December 31, 1969, and before January 1, 1973, an individual described in subparagraph (1) of this paragraph (other than an individual referred to in section 142(b))—

(a) Who is not married (as determined by applying section 143(a) and the regulations thereunder) must file an income tax return only if he receives $1,700 or more of gross income during his taxable year, except that if such an individual has attained the age of 65 before the close of his taxable year an income tax return must be filed by such individual only if he receives $2,300 or more of gross income during his taxable year.

(b) Who is entitled to make a joint return under section 6013 and the regulations thereunder must file an income tax return only if his gross income received during his taxable year, when combined with the gross income of his spouse received during his taxable year, is $2,300 or more. However, if such individual or his spouse has attained the age of 65 before the close of the taxable year an income tax return must be filed by such individual only if their combined gross income is $2,900 or more. If both the individual and his spouse have attained the age of 65 before the close of the taxable year such return must be filed only if their combined gross income is $3,500 or more. However, this subdivision (ii)(b) shall not apply if the individual and his spouse did not have the same household as their home at the close of their taxable year, if such spouse files a separate return for a taxable year which includes any part of such individual's taxable year, or if any other taxpayer is entitled to an exemption for such individual or his spouse under section 151(e) for such other taxpayer's taxable year beginning in the calendar year in which such individual's taxable year begins. For example, a married student more than half of whose support is furnished by his father must file an income tax return if he receives $600 or more of gross income during his taxable year.

(iii) For taxable years beginning after December 31, 1972, an individual described in subparagraph (1) of this paragraph (other than an individual referred to in section 142(b))—

(a) Who is not married (as determined by applying section 143(a) and the regulations thereunder) must file an income tax return only if he receives $1,750 or more of gross income during his taxable year, except that if such an individual has attained the age of 65 before the close of his taxable year an income tax return must be filed by such individual only if he receives $2,500 or more of gross income during his taxable year.

(b) Who is entitled to make a joint return under section 6013 and the regulations thereunder must file an income tax return only if his gross income received during his taxable year, when combined with the gross income of his spouse received during his taxable year, is $2,500 or more. However, if such individual or his spouse has attained the age of 65 before the close of the taxable year an income tax return must be filed by such individual only if their combined gross income is $3,250 or more. If both the individual and his spouse attain the age of 65 before the close of the taxable year such return must be filed only if their combined gross income is $4,000 or more. However, this subdivision (iii)(b) shall not apply if the individual and his spouse did not have the same household as their home at the close of their taxable year, if such spouse files a separate return for a taxable year which includes any part of such individual's taxable year, or if any other taxpayer is entitled to an exemption for the taxpayer or his spouse under section 151(e) for such other taxpayer's taxable year beginning in the calendar year in which such individual's taxable year begins. For example, a married student more than half of whose support is furnished by his father must file an income tax return if he receives $750 or more of gross income during the taxable year.

(iv) For purposes of section 6012(a)(1)(A)(ii) and subdivisions (ii)(b) and (iii)(b) of this subparagraph, an individual and his spouse are considered to have the same household as their home at the close of a taxable year if the same household constituted the principal place of abode of both the individual and his spouse at the close of such taxable year (or on the date of death, if the individual or his spouse died within the taxable year). The individual and his spouse will be considered to have the same household as their home at the close of the taxable year notwithstanding a temporary absence from the household due to special circumstances, as, for example, in the case of a nonpermanent failure on the part of the individual and his spouse to have a common abode by reason of illness, education, business, vacation, or military service. For example, A, a calendar-year individual under 65 years of age, is married to B, also under 65 years of age, and is a member of the Armed Forces of the United States. During 1970 A is transferred to an overseas base. A and B give up their home, which they had jointly occupied until that time; B moves to the home of her parents for the duration of A's absence. They fully intend to set up a new joint household upon A's return. Neither A nor B must file a return for 1970 if their combined gross income for the year is less than $2,300 and if no other taxpayer is entitled to a dependency exemption for A or B under section 151(e).

(v) In the case of a short taxable year referred to in section 443(a)(1), an individual described in subparagraph (1) of this paragraph shall file an income tax return if his gross income received during such short taxable year equals or exceeds his own personal exemption allowed by section 151(b) (prorated as provided in section 443(c)) and, when applicable, his additional exemption for age 65 or more allowed by section 151(c)(1) (prorated as provided in section 443(c)).

(vi) For rules relating to returns required to be made by every individual who is liable for one or more qualified State individual income taxes, as defined in section 6362, for a taxable year, see paragraph (b) of §301.6361-1 of this chapter (Regulations on Procedure and Administration).

(vii) For taxable years beginning after December 31, 1978, an individual who receives payments during the calendar year in which the taxable year begins under section 3507 (relating to advance payment of earned income credit) must file an income tax return.

(viii) For rules relating to returns required of taxpayers who receive advance payments of the premium tax credit under section 36B, see §1.6011-8(a).

(3) *Earned income from without the United States and gain from sale of residence.*—For the purpose of determining whether an income tax return must be filed for any taxable year beginning after December 31, 1957, gross income shall be computed without regard to the exclusion provided for in section 911 (relating to earned income from sources without the United States). For the purpose of determining whether an income tax return must be filed for any taxable year ending after December 31, 1963, gross income shall be computed without regard to the exclusion provided for in section 121 (relating to sale of residence by individual who has attained age 65). In the case of an individual claiming an exclusion under section 121, he shall attach Form 2119 to the return required under this paragraph and in the case of an individual claiming an exclusion under section 911, he shall attach Form 2555 to the return required under this paragraph.

(4) *Return of income of minor.*—A minor is subject to the same requirements and elections for making returns of income as are other individuals. Thus, for example, for a taxable year beginning after December 31, 1972, a return must be made by or for a minor who has an aggregate of $1,750 of gross income from funds held in trust for him and from his personal services, regardless of the amount of his taxable income. The return of a minor must be made by the minor himself or must be made for him by his guardian or other person charged with the care of the minor's person or property. See paragraph (b)(3) of §1.6012-3. See §1.73-1 for inclusion in the minor's gross income of amounts received for his personal services. For the amount of tax which is considered to have been properly assessed against the parent, if not paid by the child, see section 6201(c) and paragraph (c) of §301.6201-1 of this chapter (Regulations on Procedure and Administration).

(5) *Returns made by agents.*—The return of income may be made by an agent if, by reason of disease or injury, the person liable for the making of the return is unable to make it. The return may also be made by an agent if the taxpayer is unable to make the return by reason of continuous absence from the United States (including Puerto Rico as if a part of the United States) for a period of at least 60 days prior to the date prescribed by law for making the return. In addition, a return may be made by an agent if the taxpayer requests permission, in writing, of the district director for the internal revenue district in which is located the legal residence or principal place of business of the person liable for the making of the return, and such district director determines that good cause exists for permitting the return to be so made. However, assistance in the preparation of the return may be rendered under any circumstances. Whenever a return is made by an agent it must be accompanied by a power of attorney (or copy thereof) authorizing him to represent his principal in making, executing, or filing the return. A Form 2848, when properly completed, is sufficient. In addition, where one spouse is physically unable by reason of disease or injury to sign a joint return, the other spouse may, with the oral consent of the one who is incapacitated, sign the incapacitated spouse's name in the proper place on the return followed by the words "By . . . . Husband (or Wife)," and by the signature of the signing spouse in his own right, provided that a dated statement signed by the spouse who is signing the return is attached to and made a part of the return stating—

(i) The name of the return being filed,

(ii) The taxable year,

(iii) The reason for the inability of the spouse who is incapacitated to sign the return, and

(iv) That the spouse who is incapacitated consented to the signing of the return.

The taxpayer and his agent, if any, are responsible for the return as made and incur liability for the penalties provided for erroneous, false, or fraudulent returns.

(6) *Form of return.*—Form 1040 is prescribed for general use in making the return required under this paragraph. Form 1040A is an optional short form which, in accordance with paragraph (a)(7) of this section, may be used by certain taxpayers. A taxpayer otherwise entitled to use Form 1040A as his return for any taxable year may not make his return on such form if he elects not to take the standard deduction provided in section 141, and in such case he must make his return on Form 1040. For taxable years beginning before January 1, 1970, a taxpayer entitled under section 6014 and §1.6014-1 to elect not to show his tax on his return must, if he desires to exercise such election, make his return on Form 1040A. Form 1040W is an optional short form which, in accordance with paragraph (a)(8) of this section, may be used only with respect to taxable years beginning after December 31, 1958 and ending before December 31, 1961.

(7)(i) *Use of Form 1040A.*—Form 1040A may be filed only by those individuals entitled to use such form as provided by and in accordance with the instructions for such form.

(ii) *Computation and payment of tax.*—Unless a taxpayer is entitled to elect under section 6014 and §1.6014-1 not to show the tax on Form 1040A and does so elect, he shall compute and show on his return on Form 1040A the amount of the tax imposed by subtitle A of the Code and shall, without notice and demand therefor, pay any unpaid balance of such tax not later than the date fixed for filing the return.

(iii) *Change of election to use Form 1040A.*—A taxpayer who has elected to make his return on Form 1040A may change such election. Such change of election shall be within the time and subject to the conditions prescribed in section 144(b) and §1.144-2 relating to change of election to take, or not to take the standard deduction.

(iv) *Status benefits not allowable.*—The status of a taxpayer as head of household as defined in section 1(b)(2), or as a surviving spouse, as defined in section 2(b), shall not be considered in determining the tax liability of a taxpayer filing Form 1040A.

(8) *Use of Form 1040W for certain taxable years.*—(i) *In general.*—An individual may use Form 1040W as his return for any taxable year beginning after December 31, 1958, and ending before December 31, 1961, in which the gross income of the individual, regardless of the amount thereof—

(a) Consists entirely of remuneration for personal services performed as an employee (whether or not such remuneration constitutes wages as defined in section 3401(a)), dividends, or interest, and

(b) Does not include more than $200 from dividends and interest.

For purposes of determining whether gross income from dividends and interest exceeds $200, dividends from domestic corporations are taken into account to the extent that they are includible in gross income. For purposes of this subparagraph, any reference to Form 1040 in §§ 1.4-2, 1.142-1, and 1.144-1 and this section shall also be deemed a reference to Form 1040W.

(ii) *Change of election to use Form 1040W.*— A taxpayer who has elected to make his return on Form 1040W may change such election. Such change of election shall be within the time and subject to the conditions prescribed in section 144(b) and § 1.144-2, relating to change of election to take, or not to take, the standard deduction.

(iii) *Joint return of husband and wife on Form 1040W.*—A husband and wife, eligible under section 6013 and the regulations thereunder to file a joint return for the taxable year, may, subject to the provisions of this subparagraph, make a joint return on Form 1040W for any taxable year beginning after December 31, 1958, and ending before December 31, 1961, in which the aggregate gross income of the spouses (regardless of amount) consists entirely of remuneration for personal services performed as an employee (whether or not such remuneration constitutes wages as defined in section 3401(a)), dividends, or interest, and does not include more than $200 from dividends and interest. For purposes of determining whether gross income from sources to which the $200 limitation applies exceeds such amount in cases where both spouses receive dividends from domestic corporations, the amount of such dividends received by each spouse is taken into account to the extent that such dividends are includible in gross income. See section 116 and §§ 1.116-1 and 1.116-2. If a joint return is made by husband and wife on Form 1040W, the liability for the tax shall be joint and several.

(9) *Items of tax preference.*—For a taxable year ending after December 31, 1969, an individual shall attach Form 4625 to the return required by this paragraph if during the year the individual—

(i) has items of tax preference (described in section 57) in excess of its minimum tax exemption (determined under § 1.58-1) or

(ii) uses a net operating loss carryover from a prior taxable year in which it deferred minimum tax under section 56(b).

(b) *Return of nonresident alien individual.*—(1) *Requirement of return.*—(i) *In general.*—Except as otherwise provided in subparagraph (2) of this paragraph, every nonresident alien individual (other than one treated as a resident under section 6013(g) or (h)) who is engaged in trade or business in the United States at any time during the taxable year or who has income which is subject to taxation under subtitle A of the Code shall make a return on Form 1040NR. For this purpose it is immaterial that the gross income for the taxable year is less than the minimum amount specified in section 6012(a) for making a

return. Thus, a nonresident alien individual who is engaged in a trade or business in the United States at any time during the taxable year is required to file a return on Form 1040NR even though (a) he has no income which is effectively connected with the conduct of a trade or business in the United States, (b) he has no income from sources within the United States, or (c) his income is exempt from income tax by reason of an income tax convention or any section of the Code. However, if the nonresident alien individual has no gross income for the taxable year, he is not required to complete the return schedules but must attach a statement to the return indicating the nature of any exclusions claimed and the amount of such exclusions to the extent such amounts are readily determinable.

(ii) *Treaty income.*—If the gross income of a nonresident alien individual includes treaty income, as defined in paragraph (b)(1) of § 1.871-12, a statement shall be attached to the return on Form 1040NR showing with respect to that income—

(a) The amounts of tax withheld,

(b) The names and post office addresses of withholding agents, and

(c) Such other information as may be required by the return form, or by the instructions issued with respect to the form, to show the taxpayer's entitlement to the reduced rate of tax under the tax convention.

(2) *Exceptions.*—(i) *Return not required when tax is fully paid at source.*—A nonresident alien individual (other than one treated as a resident under section 6013(g) or (h)) who at no time during the taxable year is engaged in a trade or business in the United States is not required to make a return for the taxable year if his tax liability for the taxable year is fully satisfied by the withholding of tax at source under chapter 3 of the Code. This subdivision does not apply to a nonresident alien individual who has income for the taxable year which is treated under section 871(c) or (d) and § 1.871-9 (relating to students or trainees) or § 1.871-10 (relating to real property income) as income which is effectively connected for the taxable year with the conduct of a trade or business in the United States by that individual, or to a nonresident alien individual making a claim under § 301.6402-3 of this chapter (Procedure and Administration Regulations) for the refund of an overpayment of tax for the taxable year. In addition, this subdivision does not apply to a nonresident alien individual who has income for the taxable year that is treated under section 871(b)(1) as effectively connected with the conduct of a trade or business within the United States by reason of the operation of section 897. For purposes of this subdivision, some of the items of income from sources within the United States upon which the tax liability will not have been fully satisfied by the withholding of tax at source under chapter 3 of the Code are:

(a) Interest upon so-called tax-free covenant bonds upon which, in accordance with section 1451 and §1.1451-1, a tax of only 2 percent is required to be withheld at the source,

(b) In the case of bonds or other evidences of indebtedness issued after September 28, 1965, amounts described in section 871(a)(1)(C),

(c) Capital gains described in section 871(a)(2) and paragraph (d) of §1.871-7, and

(d) Accrued interest received in connection with the sale of bonds between interest dates, which, in accordance with paragraph (h) of §1.1441-4, is not subject to withholding of tax at the source.

(ii) *Return of individual for taxable year of change of U.S. citizenship or residence.*—(a) If an alien individual becomes a citizen or resident of the United States during the taxable year and is a citizen or resident of the United States on the last day of such year, he must make a return of Form 1040 for the taxable year. However, a separate schedule is required to be attached to this return to show the income tax computation for the part of the taxable year during which the alien was neither a citizen nor resident of the United States, unless an election under section 6013(g) or (h) is in effect for the alien. A Form 1040NR, clearly marked "Statement" across the top, may be used as such a separate schedule.

(b) If an individual abandons his U.S. citizenship or residence during the taxable year and is not a citizen or resident of the United States on the last day of such year, he must make a return on Form 1040NR for the taxable year, even if an election under section 6013(g) was in effect for the taxable year preceding the year of abandonment. However, a separate schedule is required to be attached to this return to show the income tax computation for the part of the taxable year during which the individual was a citizen or resident of the United States. A Form 1040, clearly marked "Statement" across the top, may be used as such a separate schedule.

(c) A return is required under this subdivision (ii) only if the individual is otherwise required to make a return for the taxable year.

(iii) *Beneficiaries of estates or trusts.*—A nonresident alien individual who is a beneficiary of an estate or trust which is engaged in trade or business in the United States is not required to make a return for the taxable year merely because he is deemed to be engaged in trade or business within the United States under section 875(2). However, such nonresident alien beneficiary will be required to make a return if he otherwise satisfies the conditions of subparagraph (1)(i) of this paragraph for making a return.

(iv) *Certain alien residents of Puerto Rico.*—This paragraph does not apply to a nonresident alien individual who is a bona fide resident of Puerto Rico during the taxable year. See section 876 and paragraph (a)(1)(iii) of this section.

(3) *Representative or agent for nonresident alien individual.*—(i) *Cases where power of attorney is not*

required.—The responsible representative or agent within the United States of a nonresident alien individual shall make on behalf of his nonresident alien principal a return of, and shall pay the tax on, all income coming within his control as representative or agent which is subject to the income tax under subtitle A of the Code. The agency appointment will determine how completely the agent is substituted for the principal for tax purposes. Any person who collects interest or dividends on deposited securities of a nonresident alien individual, executes ownership certificates in connection therewith, or sells such securities under special instructions shall not be deemed merely by reason of such acts to be the responsible representative or agent of the nonresident alien individual. If the responsible representative or agent does not have a specific power of attorney from the nonresident alien individual to file a return in his behalf, the return shall be accompanied by a statement to the effect that the representative or agent does not possess specific power of attorney to file a return for such individual but that the return is being filed in accordance with the provisions of this subdivision.

(ii) *Cases where power of attorney is required.*—Whenever a return of income of a nonresident alien individual is made by an agent acting under a duly authorized power of attorney for that purpose, the return shall be accompanied by the power of attorney in proper form, or a copy thereof, specifically authorizing him to represent his principal in making, executing, and filing the income tax return. Form 2848 may be used for this purpose. The agent, as well as the taxpayer, may incur liability for the penalties provided for erroneous, false, or fraudulent returns. For the requirements regarding signing of returns, see §1.6061-1. The rules of paragraph (e) of §601.504 of this chapter (Statement of Procedural Rules) shall apply under this subparagraph in determining whether a copy of a power of attorney must be certified.

(iii) *Limitation.*—A return of income shall be required under this subparagraph only if the nonresident alien individual is otherwise required to make a return in accordance with this paragraph.

(4) *Disallowance of deductions and credits.*—For provisions disallowing deductions and credits when a return of income has not been filed by or on behalf of a nonresident alien individual, see section 874(a) and the regulations thereunder.

(5) *Effective date.*—This paragraph shall apply for taxable years beginning after December 31, 1966, except that it shall not be applied to require (i) the filing of a return for any taxable year ending before January 1, 1974, which, pursuant to instructions applicable to the return, is not required to be filed or (ii) the amendment of a return for such a taxable year which, pursuant to such instructions, is required to be filed. For corresponding rules applicable to taxable years

beginning before January 1, 1967, see 26 CFR 1.6012-1(b) (Rev. as of Jan. 1, 1967).

(c) *Cross reference.*—For returns by fiduciaries for individuals, estates, and trusts, see § 1.6012-3. [Reg. § 1.6012-1.]

☐ [T.D. 6364, 2-13-59. *Amended by T.D.* 6455, 3-1-60; *T.D.* 6533, 1-18-61; *T.D.* 6581, 12-5-61; *T.D.* 6777, 12-15-64; *T.D.* 6817, 4-7-65; *T.D.* 6856, 10-19-65; *T.D.* 6885, 6-1-66; *T.D.* 7069, 11-10-70; *T.D.* 7269, 4-12-73; *T.D.* 7274, 5-4-73; *T.D.* 7332, 12-20-74; *T.D.* 7564, 9-11-78; *T.D.* 7577, 12-19-78; *T.D.* 7670, 1-30-80; *T.D.* 7683, 3-12-80; *T.D.* 8000, 12-26-84; *T.D.* 8113, 12-18-86, *T.D.* 9391, 4-4-2008, *and T.D.* 9590, 5-18-2012.]

[Reg. § 301.6012-1]

§ 301.6012-1. Persons required to make returns of income.—For provisions with respect to persons required to make returns of income, see §§ 1.6012-1 to 1.6012-4, inclusive, of this chapter (Income Tax Regulations). [Reg. § 301.6012-1.]

☐ [T.D. 6498, 10-24-60.]

[Reg. § 1.6012-2]

§ 1.6012-2. Corporations required to make returns of income.—(a) *In general.*—(1) *Requirement of return.*—Except as provided in paragraphs (e) and (g)(1) of this section with respect to charitable and other organizations having unrelated business income and to certain foreign corporations, respectively, every corporation, as defined in section 7701(a)(3), subject to taxation under subtitle A of the Code shall make a return of income regardless of whether it has taxable income or regardless of the amount of its gross income.

(2) *Existence of corporation.*—A corporation in existence during any portion of a taxable year is required to make a return. If a corporation was not in existence throughout an annual accounting period (either calendar year or fiscal year), the corporation is required to make a return for that fractional part of a year during which it was in existence. A corporation is not in existence after it ceases business and dissolves, retaining no assets, whether or not under State law it may thereafter be treated as continuing as a corporation for certain limited purposes connected with winding up its affairs, such as for the purpose of suing and being sued. If the corporation has valuable claims for which it will bring suit during this period, it has retained assets and therefore continues in existence. A corporation does not go out of existence if it is turned over to receivers or trustees who continue to operate it. If a corporation has received a charter but has never perfected its organization and has transacted no business and has no income from any source, it may upon presentation of the facts to the district director be relieved from the necessity of making a return. In the absence of a proper showing of such facts to the district director, a corporation will be required to make a return.

(3) *Form of return.*—The return required of a corporation under this section shall be made on Form 1120 unless the corporation is of a type for which a special form is prescribed. The special forms of returns and schedules required of particular types of corporations are set forth in paragraphs (b) to (g), inclusive, of this section.

(4) *Disclosure of uncertain tax positions.*—A corporation required to make a return under this section shall attach Schedule UTP, Uncertain Tax Position Statement, or any successor form, to such return, in accordance with forms, instructions, or other appropriate guidance provided by the IRS.

(5) *Effective/applicability date.*—Paragraph (a)(4) of this section applies to returns filed for tax years beginning on or after January 1, 2010.

(b) *Personal holding companies.*—A personal holding company, as defined in section 542, including a foreign corporation within the definition of such section, shall attach Schedule PH, Computation of U.S. Personal Holding Company Tax, to the return required by paragraph (a) or (g), as the case may be, of this section.

(c) *Insurance companies.*—(1) *Domestic life insurance companies.*—(i) *In general.*—A life insurance company subject to tax under section 801 shall make a return on Form 1120-L, "U.S. Life Insurance Company Income Tax Return." Except as provided in paragraph (c)(4) of this section, such company shall file with its return—

(A) A copy of its annual statement which shows the reserves used by the company in computing the taxable income reported on its return; and

(B) A copy of Schedule A (real estate) and of Schedule D (bonds and stocks), or any successor thereto, of such annual statement.

(ii) *Mutual savings banks.*—Mutual savings banks conducting life insurance business and meeting the requirements of section 594 are subject to partial tax computed on Form 1120, "U.S. Corporation Income Tax Return," and partial tax computed on Form 1120-L. The Form 1120-L is attached as a schedule to Form 1120, together with the annual statement and schedules required to be filed with Form 1120-L.

(2) *Domestic nonlife insurance companies.*—Every domestic insurance company other than a life insurance company shall make a return on Form 1120-PC, "U.S. Property and Casualty Insurance Company Income Tax Return." This includes organizations described in section 501(m)(1) that provide commercial-type insurance and organizations described in section 833. Except as provided in paragraph (c)(4) of this section, such company shall file with its return a copy of its annual statement (or a pro forma annual statement), including the underwriting and investment exhibit (or any successor thereto) for the year covered by such return.

(3) *Foreign insurance companies.*—The provisions of paragraphs (c)(1) and (c)(2) of this sec-

tion concerning the returns and statements of insurance companies subject to tax under section 801 or section 831 also apply to foreign insurance companies subject to tax under those sections, except that the copy of the annual statement required to be submitted with the return shall, in the case of a foreign insurance company that is not required to file an annual statement, be a copy of the pro forma annual statement relating to the United States business of such company.

(4) *Exception for insurance companies filing their Federal income tax returns electronically.*—If an insurance company described in paragraph (c)(1), (c)(2), or (c)(3) of this section files its Federal income tax return electronically, it should not include on or with such return its annual statement (or pro forma annual statement), or any portion thereof. Such statement must be available at all times for inspection by authorized Internal Revenue Service officers or employees and retained for so long as such statements may be material in the administration of any internal revenue law. See § 1.6001-1(e).

(5) *Definition.*—For purposes of this section, the term annual statement means the annual statement, the form of which is approved by the National Association of Insurance Commissioners (NAIC), which is filed by an insurance company for the year with the insurance departments of States, Territories, and the District of Columbia. The term annual statement also includes a pro forma annual statement if the insurance company is not required to file the NAIC annual statement.

(d) *Affiliated groups.*—For the forms to be used by affiliated corporations filing a consolidated return, see § 1.1502-75.

(e) *Charitable and other organizations with unrelated business income.*—Every organization described in section 511(a)(2) which is subject to the tax imposed by section 511(a)(1) on its unrelated business taxable income shall make a return on Form 990-T for each taxable year if it has gross income, included in computing unrelated business taxable income for such taxable year, of $1,000 or more. The filing of a return of unrelated business income does not relieve the organization of the duty of filing other required returns.

(f) *Subchapter T cooperatives.*—(1) *In general.*— For taxable years ending on or after December 31, 2007, a cooperative organization described in section 1381 (including a farmers' cooperative exempt from tax under section 521) is required to make a return, whether or not it has taxable income and regardless of the amount of its gross income, on Form 1120-C, "U.S. Income Tax Return for Cooperative Associations," or such other form as may be designated by the Commissioner.

(2) *Farmers' cooperatives.*—For taxable years ending before December 31, 2007, a farmers' cooperative organization described in section 521(b)(1) (including a farmers' cooperative that is not exempt from tax under section 521) is required to make a return on Form 990-C, "Farmers' Cooperative Association Income Tax Return."

(3) *Effective/applicability date.*—This paragraph (f) is applicable on or after July 13, 2007.

(g) *Returns by foreign corporations.*—(1) *Requirement of return.*—(i) *In general.*—Except as otherwise provided in subparagraph (2) of this paragraph, every foreign corporation which is engaged in trade or business in the United States at any time during the taxable year or which has income which is subject to taxation under subtitle A of the Code (relating to income taxes) shall make a return on Form 1120-F. Thus, for example, a foreign corporation which is engaged in trade or business in the United States at any time during the taxable year is required to file a return on Form 1120-F even though (*a*) it has no income which is effectively connected with the conduct of a trade or business in the United States, (*b*) it has no income from sources within the United States, or (*c*) its income is exempt from income tax by reason of an income tax convention or any section of the Code. However, if the foreign corporation has no gross income for the taxable year, it is not required to complete the return schedules but must attach a statement to the return indicating the nature of any exclusions claimed and the amount of such exclusions to the extent such amounts are readily determinable.

(ii) *Treaty income.*—If the gross income of a foreign corporation includes treaty income, as defined in paragraph (b)(1) of § 1.871-12, a statement shall be attached to the return on Form 1120-F showing with respect to that income—

(*a*) The amounts of tax withheld,

(*b*) The names and post office addresses of withholding agents, and

(*c*) Such other information as may be required by the return form or by the instructions issued with respect to the form, to show the taxpayer's entitlement to the reduced rate of tax under the tax convention.

(iii) *Balance sheet and reconciliation of income.*—At the election of the taxpayer, the balance sheets and reconciliation of income, as shown on Form 1120-F, may be limited to—

(*a*) The assets of the corporation located in the United States and to its other assets used in the trade or business conducted in the United States, and

(*b*) Its income effectively connected with the conduct of a trade or business in the United States and its other income from sources within the United States.

(2) *Exceptions.*—(i) *Return not required when tax is fully paid at source.*—(*a*) *In general.*—A foreign corporation which at no time during the taxable year is engaged in a trade or business in the United States is not required to make a return for the taxable year if its tax liability for the taxable year is fully satisfied by the withholding

of tax at source under chapter 3 of the Code. For purposes of this subdivision, some of the items of income from sources within the United States upon which the tax liability will not have been fully satisfied by the withholding of tax at source under chapter 3 of the Code are:

(1) Interest upon so-called tax-free covenant bonds upon which, in accordance with section 1451 and § 1.1451-1, a tax of only 2 percent is required to be withheld at source,

(2) In the case of bonds or other evidence of indebtedness issued after September 25, 1965, amounts described in section 881(a)(3),

(3) Accrued interest received in connection with the sale of bonds between interest dates, which, in accordance with paragraph (h) of § 1.1441-4, is not subject to withholding of tax at source.

(b) *Corporations not included.*—This subdivision (i) shall not apply—

(1) To a foreign corporation which has income for the taxable year which is treated under section 882(d) or (e) and § 1.882-2 as income which is effectively connected for the taxable year with the conduct of a trade or business in the United States by that corporation,

(2) To a foreign corporation making a claim under § 301.6402-3 of this chapter (Procedure and Administration Regulations) for the refund of an overpayment of tax for the taxable year, or

(3) To a foreign corporation described in paragraph (c)(2)(i) of § 1.532-1 whose accumulated taxable income for the taxable year is determined under paragraph (b)(2) of § 1.535-1.

(ii) *Beneficiaries of estates or trusts.*—A foreign corporation which is a beneficiary of an estate or trust which is engaged in trade or business in the United States is not required to make a return for the taxable year merely because it is deemed to be engaged in trade or business within the United States under section 875(2). However, such foreign corporation will be required to make a return if it otherwise satisfies the conditions of subparagraph (1)(i) of this paragraph for making a return.

(iii) *Special returns and schedules.*—The provisions of paragraphs (b) through (f) of this section shall apply to a foreign corporation except that a foreign corporation which is an insurance company to which paragraph (c)(3) of this section applies shall make a return on Form 1120-F and not on Form 1120. If a foreign corporation which is an insurance company to which paragraph (c)(1) or (2) of this section applies has income for the taxable year from sources within the United States which is not effectively connected for that year with the conduct of a trade or business in the United States by that corporation, the corporation shall attach to its return on Form 1120L or 1120M, as the case may be, a separate schedule showing the nature and amount of the items of such income, the rate of

tax applicable thereto, and the amount of tax withheld therefrom under chapter 3 of the code.

(3) *Representative or agent for foreign corporation.*—(i) *Cases where power of attorney is not required.*—The responsible representative or agent within the United States of a foreign corporation shall make on behalf of his principal a return of, and shall pay the tax on, all income coming within his control as representative or agent which is subject to the income tax under subtitle A of the code. The agency appointment will determine how completely the agent is substituted for the principal for tax purposes. Any person who collects interest or dividends on deposited securities of a foreign corporation, executes ownership certificates in connection therewith, or sells such securities under special instructions shall not be deemed merely by reason of such acts to be the responsible representative or agent of the foreign corporation. If the responsible representative or agent does not have a specific power of attorney from the foreign corporation to file a return in its behalf, the return shall be accompanied by a statement to the effect that the representative or agent does not possess specific power of attorney to file a return for such corporation but that the return is being filed in accordance with the provisions of this subdivision.

(ii) *Cases where power of attorney is required.*—Whenever a return of income of a foreign corporation is made by an agent acting under a duly authorized power of attorney for that purpose, the return shall be accompanied by the power of attorney in proper form, or a copy thereof specifically authorizing him to represent his principal in making, executing, and filing the income tax return. Form 2848 may be used for this purpose. The agent, as well as the taxpayer, may incur liability for the penalties provided for erroneous, false, or fraudulent returns. For the requirements regarding signing of returns, see § 1.6062-1. The rules of paragraph (e) of § 601.504 of this chapter (Statement of Procedural Rules) shall apply under this subparagraph in determining whether a copy of a power of attorney must be certified.

(iii) *Limitation.*—A return of income shall be required under this subparagraph only if the foreign corporation is otherwise required to make a return in accordance with this paragraph.

(4) *Disallowance of deductions and credits.*—For provisions disallowing deductions and credits when a return of income has not been filed by or on behalf of a foreign corporation, see section 882(c)(2) and the regulations thereunder, and paragraph (b)(2) and (3) of § 1.535-1.

(5) *Effective date.*—This paragraph shall apply for taxable years beginning after December 31, 1966, except that it shall not be applied to require (i) the filing of a return for any taxable year ending before January 1, 1974, which, pursuant to instructions applicable to the return, is

Reg. § 1.6012-2(g)(5)

not required to be filed or (ii) the amendment of a return for such a taxable year which, pursuant to such instructions, is required to be filed. For corresponding rules applicable to taxable years beginning before January 1, 1967, see 26 CFR 1.6012-2(g) (Rev. as of Jan. 1, 1967).

(h) *Electing small business corporations.*—An electing small business corporation, whether or not subject to the tax imposed by section 1378, shall make a return on Form 1120-S. See also section 6037 and the regulations thereunder.

(i) *Hospital organizations with noncompliant hospital facilities.*—Every hospital organization (as defined in §1.501(r)-1(b)(18)) that is subject to the tax imposed by §1.501(r)-2(d) shall make a return on Form 990-T. The filing of a return to pay the tax described in §1.501(r)-2(d) does not relieve the organization of the duty of filing other required returns.

(j) *Items of tax preference.*—(1) *In general.*—Every corporation required to make a return under this section and having items of tax preference (described in section 57 and the regulations thereunder) in any amount shall file the required form relating to such items as part of such return.

(2) *Organizations with unrelated business income and foreign corporations.*—Regardless of the provisions of paragraphs (e) and (g) of this section, any organization described in either such paragraph having items of tax preference (described in section 57 and the regulations thereunder) in any amount entering into the computation of unrelated business income is required to make a return on form 990-T or form 1120F, respectively, and to attach the required form as part of such return.

(k) *Other provisions.*—For returns by fiduciaries for corporations, see §1.6012-3. For information returns by corporations regarding payments of dividends, see §§1.6042-1 to 1.6042-3, inclusive; regarding corporate dissolutions or liquidations, see §1.6043-1; regarding distributions in liquidation, see §1.6043-2; regarding payments of patronage dividends, see §§1.6044-1 to 1.6044-4, inclusive; and regarding certain payments of interest, see §§1.6049-1 and 1.6049-2. For information returns of officers, directors, and shareholders of foreign personal holding companies, as defined in section 552, see §§1.6035-1 and 1.6035-2. For returns as to formation or reorganization of foreign corporations, see §§1.6046-1 to 1.6046-3, inclusive.

(l) *Effective/applicability date.*—Paragraph (c) of this section applies to any taxable year beginning on or after May 30, 2006. However, taxpayers may apply paragraph (c) of this section to any original Federal income tax return (including any amended return filed on or before the due date (including extensions) of such original return) timely filed on or after May 30, 2006. For taxable years beginning before May 30, 2006, see §1.6012-2 as contained in 26 CFR part 1 in effect on April 1, 2006. [Reg. §1.6012-2.]

□ [T.D. 6364, 2-13-59. *Amended by* T.D. 6427, 12-2-59; T.D. 6523, 12-28-60; T.D. 6533, 1-18-61; T.D. 6628, 12-27-62; T.D. 6960, 6-24-68; T.D. 7244, 12-29-72; T.D. 7293, 11-27-73; T.D. 7332, 12-20-74; T.D. 7564, 9-11-78; T.D. 7579, 12-19-78; T.D. 7838, 10-5-82; T.D. 9264, 5-26-2006; T.D. 9329, 6-13-2007; T.D. 9336, 7-27-2007; T.D. 9510, 12-13-2010 *and* T.D. 9708, 12-29-2014.]

[Reg. §1.6012-3]

§1.6012-3. **Returns by fiduciaries.**—(a) *For estates and trusts.*—(1) *In general.*—Every fiduciary, or at least one of the joint fiduciaries, must make a return of income on form 1041 (or by use of a composite return pursuant to §1.6012-5) and attach the required form if the estate or trust has items of tax preference (as defined in section 57 and the regulations thereunder) in any amount—

(i) For each estate for which he acts if the gross income of such estate for the taxable year is $600 or more;

(ii) For each trust for which he acts, except a trust exempt under section 501(a), if such trust has for the taxable year any taxable income, or has for the taxable year gross income of $600 or more regardless of the amount of taxable income; and

(iii) For each estate and each trust for which he acts, except a trust exempt under section 501(a), regardless of the amount of income for the taxable year, if any beneficiary of such estate or trust is a nonresident alien.

(iv) For each trust electing to be taxed as, or as part of, an estate under section 645 for which a trustee acts, and for each related estate joining in a section 645 election for which an executor acts, if the aggregate gross income of the electing trust(s) and related estate, if any, joining in the election for the taxable year is $600 or more. (For the respective filing requirements of the trustee of each electing trust and executor of any related estate, see §1.645-1).

(2) *Wills and trust instruments.*—At the request of the Internal Revenue Service, a copy of the will or trust instrument (including any amendments), accompanied by a written declaration of the fiduciary under the penalties of perjury that it is a true and complete copy, shall be filed together with a statement by the fiduciary indicating the provisions of the will or trust instrument (including any amendments) which, in the fiduciary's opinion, determine the extent to which the income of the estate or trust is taxable to the estate or trust, the beneficiaries, or the grantor, respectively.

(3) *Domiciliary and ancillary representatives.*—In the case of an estate required to file a return under subparagraph (1) of this paragraph, having both domiciliary and ancillary representatives, the domiciliary and ancillary representatives must each file a return on Form 1041. The domiciliary representative is required to include in the return rendered by him as such domiciliary representative the entire income of the estate. The return of the ancillary representa-

tive shall be filed with the district director for his internal revenue district and shall show the name and address of the domiciliary representative, the amount of gross income received by the ancillary representative, and the deductions to be claimed against such income, including any amount of income properly paid or credited by the ancillary representative to any legatee, heir, or other beneficiary. If the ancillary representative for the estate of a nonresident alien is a citizen or resident of the United States, and the domiciliary representative is a nonresident alien, such ancillary representative is required to render the return otherwise required of the domiciliary representative.

(4) *Two or more trusts.*—A trustee of two or more trusts must make a separate return for each trust, even though such trusts were created by the same grantor for the same beneficiary or beneficiaries.

(5) *Trusts with unrelated business income.*— Every fiduciary for a trust described in section 511(b)(2) which is subject to the tax on its unrelated business taxable income by section 511(b)(1) shall make a return on Form 990-T for each taxable year if the trust has gross income, included in computing unrelated business taxable income for such taxable year, of $1,000 or more. The filing of a return of unrelated business income does not relieve the fiduciary of such trusts from the duty of filing other required returns.

(6) *Charitable remainder trusts.*—Every fiduciary for a charitable remainder annuity trust (as defined in § 1.664-2) or a charitable remainder unitrust (as defined in § 1.664-3) shall make a return on Form 1041-B for each taxable year of the trust even though it is nonexempt because it has unrelated business taxable income. The return on Form 1041-B shall be made in accordance with the instructions for the form and shall be filed with the designated Internal Revenue office on or before the 15th day of the fourth month following the close of the taxable year of the trust. A copy of the instrument governing the trust, accompanied by a written declaration of the fiduciary under the penalties of perjury that it is a true and complete copy, shall be attached to the return for the first taxable year of the trust.

(7) *Certain trusts described in section 4947(a)(1).*—For taxable years beginning after December 31, 1980, in the case of a trust described in section 4947(a)(1) which has no taxable income for a taxable year, the filing requirements of Section 6012 and this section shall be satisfied by the filing, pursuant to § 53.6011-1 of this chapter (Foundation Excise Tax Regulations) and § 1.6033-2(a), by the fiduciary of such trust of—

(i) Form 990-PF if such trust is treated as a private foundation, or

(ii) Form 990 if such trust is not treated as a private foundation.

When the provisions of this paragraph (7) are met, the fiduciary shall not be required to file Form 1041.

(8) *Estates and trusts liable for qualified tax.*— In the case of an estate or trust which is liable for one or more qualified State individual income taxes, as defined in section 6362, for a taxable year, see paragraph (b) of § 301.6361-1 of this chapter (Regulations on Procedure and Administration) for rules relating to returns required to be made.

(9) *A trust any portion of which is treated as owned by the grantor or another person pursuant to sections 671 through 678.*—In the case of a trust any portion of which is treated as owned by the grantor or another person under the provisions of subpart E (section 671 and following) part I, subchapter J, chapter 1 of the Internal Revenue Code see § 1.671-4.

(10) *Hospital organizations organized as trusts with noncompliant hospital facilities.*—Every fiduciary for a hospital organization (as defined in § 1.501(r)-1(b)(18)) organized as a trust described in section 511(b)(2) that is subject to the tax imposed by § 1.501(r)-2(d) shall make a return on Form 990-T. The filing of a return to pay the tax described in § 1.501(r)-2(d) does not relieve the organization of the duty of filing other required returns.

(b) *For other persons.*—(1) *Decedents.*—The executor or administrator of the estate of a decedent, or other person charged with the property of a decedent, shall make the return of income required in respect of such decedent. For the decedent's taxable year which ends with the date of his death, the return shall cover the period during which he was alive. For the filing of returns of income for citizens and alien residents of the United States, and alien residents of Puerto Rico, see paragraph (a) of § 1.6012-1. For the filing of a joint return after death of spouse, see paragraph (d) of § 1.6013-1.

(2) *Nonresident alien individuals.*—(i) *In general.*—A resident or domestic fiduciary or other person charged with the care of the person or property of a nonresident alien individual shall make a return for that individual and pay the tax unless—

(a) The nonresident alien individual makes a return of, and pays the tax on, his income for the taxable year,

(b) A responsible representative or agent in the United States of the nonresident alien individual makes a return of, and pays the tax on, the income of such alien individual for the taxable year, or

(c) The nonresident alien individual has appointed a person in the United States to act as his agent for the purpose of making a return of income and, if such fiduciary is required to file a Form 1041 for an estate or trust of which such alien individual is a beneficiary, such fiduciary attaches a copy of the agency appointment to his return on Form 1041.

Reg. § 1.6012-3(b)(2)(i)(c)

(ii) *Income to be returned.*—A return of income shall be required under this subparagraph only if the nonresident alien individual is otherwise required to make a return in accordance with paragraph (b) of §1.6012-1. The provisions of that paragraph shall apply in determining the form of return to be used and the income to be returned.

(iii) *Disallowance of deductions and credits.*—For provisions disallowing deductions and credits when a return of income has not been filed by or on behalf of a nonresident alien individual, see section 874 and the regulations thereunder.

(iv) *Alien resident of Puerto Rico.*—This subparagraph shall not apply to the return of a nonresident alien individual who is a bona fide resident of Puerto Rico during the entire taxable year. See §1.876-1.

(v) *Cross reference.*—For requirements of withholding tax at source on nonresident alien individuals and of returns with respect to such withheld taxes, see §§1.1441-1 to 1.1465-1, inclusive.

(3) *Persons under a disability.*—A fiduciary acting as the guardian of a minor, or as the guardian or committee of an insane person, must make the return of income required in respect of such person unless, in the case of a minor, the minor himself makes the return or causes it to be made.

(4) *Corporations.*—A receiver, trustee in dissolution, trustee in bankruptcy, or assignee, who, by order of a court of competent jurisdiction, by operation of law or otherwise, has possession of or holds title to all or substantially all the property or business of a corporation, shall make the return of income for such corporation in the same manner and form as corporations are required to make such returns. Such return shall be filed whether or not the receiver, trustee, or assignee is operating the property or business of the corporation. A receiver in charge of only a small part of the property of a corporation, such as a receiver in mortgage foreclosure proceedings involving merely a small portion of its property, need not make the return of income. See also §1.6041-1, relating to returns regarding information at source; §§1.6042-1 to 1.6042-3, inclusive, relating to returns regarding payments of dividends; §§1.6044-1 to 1.6044-4, inclusive, relating to returns regarding payments of patronage dividends; §§1.6049-1 and 1.6049-2, relating to returns regarding certain payments of interest.

(5) *Individuals in receivership.*—A receiver who stands in the place of an individual must make the return of income required in respect of such individual. A receiver of only part of the property of an individual need not file a return, and the individual must make his own return.

(c) *Joint fiduciaries.*—In the case of joint fiduciaries, a return is required to be made by only one

of such fiduciaries. A return made by one of joint fiduciaries shall contain a statement that the fiduciary has sufficient knowledge of the affairs of the person for whom the return is made to enable him to make the return, and that the return is, to the best of his knowledge and belief, true and correct.

(d) *Other provisions.*—For the definition of the term "fiduciary", see section 7701(a)(6) and the regulations thereunder. For information returns required to be made by fiduciaries under section 6041, see §1.6041-1. As to further duties and liabilities of fiduciaries, see section 6903 and §301.6903-1 of this chapter (Regulations on Procedure and Administration). [Reg. §1.6012-3.]

☐ [*T.D. 6031, 7-8-58 and T.D. 6364, 2-13-59. Amended by T.D. 6628, 12-27-62; T.D. 6972, 9-11-68; T.D. 7200, 8-15-72; T.D. 7202, 8-22-72; T.D. 7332, 12-20-74; T.D. 7407, 3-3-76; T.D. 7564, 9-11-78; T.D. 7577, 12-19-78; T.D. 7608, 4-3-79; T.D. 7796, 11-23-81; T.D. 7838, 10-5-82; T.D. 8026, 5-17-85; T.D. 8633, 12-20-95; T.D. 9032, 12-23-2002 and T.D. 9708, 12-29-2014.]*

[Reg. §1.6012-4]

§1.6012-4. Miscellaneous returns.—For returns by regulated investment companies of tax on undistributed capital gain designated for special treatment under section 852(b)(3)(D), see §1.852-9. For returns with respect to tax withheld on nonresident aliens and foreign corporations and on tax-free covenant bonds, see §§1.1461-1 to 1.1465-1, inclusive. For returns of tax on transfers to avoid income tax, see §1.1494-1. For the requirement of an annual report by persons completing a Government contract, see 26 CFR (1939) 17.16 (Treasury Decision 4906, approved June 23, 1939), and 26 CFR (1939) 16.15 (Treasury Decision 4909, approved June 28, 1939), as made applicable to section 1471 of the 1954 Code by Treasury Decision 6091, approved August 16, 1954 (19 F.R. 5167, C.B. 1954-2, 47). See also §1.1471-1. [Reg. §1.6012-4.]

☐ [*T.D. 6364, 2-13-59. Amended by T.D. 7332, 12-20-74.*]

[Reg. §1.6012-5]

§1.6012-5. Composite return in lieu of specified form.—The Commissioner may authorize the use, at the option of a person required to make a return, of a composite return in lieu of any form specified in this part for use by such a person, subject to such conditions, limitations, and special rules governing the preparation, execution, filing, and correction thereof as the Commissioner may deem appropriate. Such composite return shall consist of a form prescribed by the Commissioner and an attachment or attachments of magnetic tape or other approved media. Notwithstanding any provisions in this part to the contrary, a single form and attachment may comprise the returns of more than one such person. To the extent that the use of a composite return has been authorized by the Commissioner, references in this part to a specific form for use by such a person shall be deemed to refer also to a composite return under this section. [Reg. §1.6012-5.]

☐ [*T.D. 7200, 8-15-72.*]

[Reg. §1.6012-6]

§1.6012-6. **Returns by political organizations.**—(a) *Requirement of return.*—(1) [Reserved]. For further guidance, see §1.6012-6T(a)(1).

(2) *Taxable years beginning after December 31, 1971, and before January 1, 1975.*—For taxable years beginning after December 31, 1971, and before January 1, 1975, any political organization which would be described in section 527(e)(1) if such section applied to such years shall not be required to make a return if such organization would not be required to make a return under paragraph (a)(1) of this section.

(b) *Form of return.*—The return required by an organization or fund upon which a tax is imposed by section 527(b) shall be made on Form 1120-POL. [Reg. §1.6012-6.]

☐ [*T.D. 7516, 11-1-77. Amended by T.D. 9821, 7-18-2017.*]

[Reg. §1.6012-6T]

§1.6012-6T. **Returns by political organizations (temporary).**—(a) *Requirement of return.*—(1) *In general.*—For taxable years beginning after December 31, 1974, every political organization described in section 527(e)(1), and every fund described in section 527(f)(3) or section 527(g), and every organization described in section 501(c) and exempt from taxation under section 501(a) shall, if a tax is imposed on such an organization or fund by section 527(b), make a return of income on or before the fifteenth day of the fourth month following the close of the taxable year.

(2) [Reserved]. For further guidance, see §1.6012-6(a)(2).

(b) [Reserved]. For further guidance, see §1.6012-6(b).

(c) *Applicability date.*—This section applies to returns filed after July 20, 2017. Section 1.6012-6 (as contained in 26 CFR part 1, revised April 2017) applies to returns filed before July 20, 2017.

(d) *Expiration date.*—The applicability of this section will expire on or before July 17, 2020. [Temporary Reg. §1.6012-6T.]

☐ *T.D. 9821, 7-18-2017.*]

[Reg. §1.6013-1]

§1.6013-1. **Joint returns.**—(a) *In general.*—(1) A husband and wife may elect to make a joint return under section 6013(a) even though one of the spouses has no gross income or deductions. For rules for determining whether individuals occupy the status of husband and wife for purposes of filing a joint return, see paragraph (a) of §1.6013-4. For any taxable year with respect to which a joint return has been filed, separate returns shall not be made by the spouses after the time for filing the return of either has expired. See, however, paragraph (d)(5) of this section for the right of an executor to file a late separate return for a deceased spouse and thereby disaffirm a timely joint return made by the surviving spouse.

(2) A joint return of a husband and wife (if not made by an agent of one or both spouses) shall be signed by both spouses. The provisions of paragraph (a)(5) of §1.6012-1, relating to returns made by agents, shall apply where one spouse signs a return as agent for the other, or where a third party signs a return as agent for one or both spouses.

(b) *Nonresident alien.*—A joint return shall not be made if either the husband or wife at any time during the taxable year is a nonresident alien, unless an election is in effect for the taxable year under section 6013(g) or (h) and the regulations thereunder.

(c) *Different taxable years.*—Except as otherwise provided in this section, a husband and wife shall not file a joint return if they have different taxable years.

(d) *Joint return after death.*—(1) Section 6013(a)(2) provides that a joint return may be made for the survivor and the deceased spouse or for both deceased spouses if the taxable years of such spouses begin on the same day and end on different days only because of the death of either or both. Thus, if a husband and wife make their returns on a calendar year basis, and the wife dies on August 1, 1956, a joint return may be made with respect to the calendar year 1956 of the husband and the taxable year of the wife beginning on January 1, 1956, and ending with her death on August 1, 1956. Similarly, if husband and wife both make their returns on the basis of a fiscal year beginning on July 1 and the wife dies on October 1, 1956, a joint return may be made with respect to the fiscal year of the husband beginning on July 1, 1956, and ending on June 30, 1957, and with respect to the taxable year of the wife beginning on July 1, 1956, and ending with her death on October 1, 1956.

(2) The provision allowing a joint return to be made for the taxable year in which the death of either or both spouses occurs is subject to two limitations. The first limitation is that if the surviving spouse remarries before the close of his taxable year, he shall not make a joint return with the first spouse who died during the taxable year. In such a case, however, the surviving spouse may make a joint return with his new spouse provided the other requirements with respect to the filing of a joint return are met. The second limitation is that the surviving spouse shall not make a joint return with the deceased spouse if the taxable year of either spouse is a fractional part of the year under section 443(a)(1) resulting from a change of accounting period. For example, if a husband and wife make their returns on the calendar year basis and the wife dies on March 1, 1956, and thereafter the husband receives permission to change his annual accounting period to a fiscal year beginning July

Reg. §1.6013-1(d)(2)

1, 1956, no joint return shall be made for the short taxable year ending June 30, 1956. Similarly, if a husband and wife who make their returns on a calendar year basis receive permission to change to a fiscal year beginning July 1, 1956, and the wife dies on June 1, 1956, no joint return shall be made for the short taxable year ending June 30, 1956.

(3) Section 6013(a)(3) provides for the method of making a joint return in the case of the death of one spouse or both spouses. The general rule is that, in the case of the death of one spouse, or of both spouses, the joint return with respect to the decedent may be made only by his executor or administrator, as defined in paragraph (c) of §1.6013-4. An exception is made to this general rule whereby, in the case of the death of one spouse, the joint return may be made by the surviving spouse with respect to both him and the decedent if all the following conditions exist:

(i) No return has been made by the decedent for the taxable year in respect of which the joint return is made;

(ii) No executor or administrator has been appointed at or before the time of making such joint return; and

(iii) No executor or administrator is appointed before the last day prescribed by law for filing the return of the surviving spouse.

These conditions are to be applied with respect to the return for each of the taxable years of the decedent for which a joint return may be made if more than one such taxable year is involved. Thus, in the case of husband and wife on the calendar year basis, if the wife dies in February 1957, a joint return for the husband and wife for 1956 may be made if the conditions set forth in this subparagraph are satisfied with respect to such return. A joint return also may be made by the survivor for both himself and the deceased spouse for the calendar year 1957 if it is separately determined that the conditions set forth in this subparagraph are satisfied with respect to the return for such year. If, however, the deceased spouse should, prior to her death, make a return for 1956, the surviving spouse may not thereafter make a joint return for himself and the deceased spouse for 1956.

(4) If an executor or administrator is appointed at or before the time of making the joint return or before the last day prescribed by law for filing the return of the surviving spouse, the surviving spouse cannot make a joint return for himself and the deceased spouse whether or not a separate return for the deceased spouse is made by such executor or administrator. In such a case, any return made solely by the surviving spouse shall be treated as his separate return. The joint return, if one is to be made, must be made by both the surviving spouse and the executor or administrator. In determining whether an executor or administrator is appointed before the last day prescribed by law for filing the return of the surviving spouse, an extension of time for making the return is included.

(5) If the surviving spouse makes the joint return provided for in subparagraph (3) of this paragraph and thereafter an executor or administrator of the decedent is appointed, the executor or administrator may disaffirm such joint return. This disaffirmance, in order to be effective, must be made within one year after the last day prescribed by law for filing the return of the surviving spouse (including any extension of time for filing such return) and must be made in the form of a separate return for the taxable year of the decedent with respect to which the joint return was made. In the event of such proper disaffirmance the return made by the survivor shall constitute his separate return, that is, the joint return made by him shall be treated as his return and the tax thereon shall be computed by excluding all items properly includible in the return of the deceased spouse. The separate return made by the executor or administrator shall constitute the return of the deceased spouse for the taxable year.

(6) The time allowed the executor or administrator to disaffirm the joint return by the making of a separate return does not establish a new due date for the return of the deceased spouse. Accordingly, the provisions of sections 6651 and 6601, relating to delinquent returns and delinquency in payment of tax, are applicable to such return made by the executor in disaffirmance of the joint return.

(e) *Return of surviving spouse treated as joint return.*—For provisions relating to the treatment of the return of a surviving spouse as a joint return for each of the next two taxable years following the year of the death of the spouse, see section 2 and §1.2-2. [Reg. §1.6013-1.]

☐ [*T.D.* 6364, 2-13-59. *Amended by T.D.* 7274, 5-4-73 *and T.D.* 7670, 1-30-80.]

[Reg. §301.6013-1]

§301.6013-1. Joint returns of income tax by husband and wife.—For provisions with respect to joint returns of income tax by husband and wife, see §§1.6013-1 to 1.6013-7, inclusive, of this chapter (Income Tax Regulations). [Reg. §301.6013-1.]

☐ [*T.D.* 6498, 10-24-60. *Amended by T.D.* 7670, 1-30-80.]

[Reg. §1.6013-2]

§1.6013-2. Joint return after filing separate return.—(a) *In general.*—(1) Where an individual has filed a separate return for a taxable year for which a joint return could have been made by him and his spouse under section 6013(a), and the time prescribed by law for filing the return for such taxable year has expired, such individual and his spouse may, under conditions hereinafter set forth, make a joint return for such taxable year. The joint return filed pursuant to section 6013(b) shall constitute the return of the husband and wife for such year, and all payments, credits, refunds, or other repayments, made or allowed with respect to the separate return of either spouse are to be taken into account in determining the extent to which the tax based on the joint return has been paid.

(2) If a joint return is made under section 6013(b), any election, other than the election to file a separate return, made by either spouse in his separate return for the taxable year with respect to the treatment of any income, deduction, or credit of such spouse shall not be changed in the making of the joint return where such election would have been irrevocable if the joint return had not been made. Thus, if one spouse has made an irrevocable election to adopt and use the last-in, first-out inventory method under section 472, this election may not be changed upon making the joint return under section 6013(b).

(3) A joint return made under section 6013(b) after the death of either spouse shall, with respect to the decedent, be made only by his executor or administrator. Thus, where no executor or administrator has been appointed, a joint return cannot be made under section 6013(b).

(4) A nonresident alien treated as a resident under section 6013(g) or (h) for any taxable year ending on or after December 31, 1975, but before December 31, 1978, and the alien's United States citizen or resident spouse may file a joint return for that taxable year, even though one or both of the spouses have previously filed separate returns for that taxable year. In this case, the rule in paragraph (a)(3) of this section does not apply.

(b) *Limitations with respect to making of election.*—A joint return shall not be made under section 6013(b)(1) with respect to a taxable year—

(1) Beginning on or before July 30, 1996, unless there is paid in full at or before the time of the filing of the joint return the amount shown as tax upon such joint return; or

(2) After the expiration of three years from the last day prescribed by law for filing the return for such taxable year determined without regard to any extension of time granted to either spouse; or

(3) After there has been mailed to either spouse, with respect to such taxable year, a notice of deficiency under section 6212, if the spouse, as to such notice, files a petition with the Tax Court of the United States within the time prescribed in section 6213; or

(4) After either spouse has commenced a suit in any court for the recovery of any part of the tax for such taxable year; or

(5) After either spouse has entered into a closing agreement under section 7121 with respect to such taxable year, or after any civil or criminal case arising against either spouse with respect to such taxable year has been compromised under section 7122.

(c) *When return deemed filed; assessment and collection; credit or refund.*—(1) For the purpose of section 6501, relating to the period of limitations upon assessment and collection, and section 6651, relating to delinquent returns, a joint return made under section 6013(b) shall be deemed to have been filed, giving due regard to any extension of time granted to either spouse, on the following date:

(i) Where both spouses filed separate returns, prior to making the joint return under section 6013(b), on the date the last separate return of either spouse was filed for the taxable year, but not earlier than the last date prescribed by law for the filing of the return of either spouse;

(ii) Where only one spouse was required and did file a return prior to the making of the joint return under section 6013(b), on the date of the filing of the separate return, but not earlier than the last day prescribed by law for the filing of such return; or

(iii) Where both spouses were required to file a return, but only one spouse did so file, on the date of the filing of the joint return under section 6013(b).

(2) For the purpose of section 6511, relating to refunds and credits, a joint return made under section 6013(b) shall be deemed to have been filed on the last date prescribed by law for filing the return for such taxable year, determined without regard to any extension of time granted to either spouse for filing the return or paying the tax.

(d) *Additional time for assessment.*—In the case of a joint return made under section 6013 (b), the period of limitations provided in sections 6501 and 6502 shall not be less than one year after the date of the actual filing of such joint return. The expiration of the one year is to be determined without regard to the rules provided in paragraph (c)(1) of this section, relating to the application of sections 6501 and 6651 with respect to a joint return made under section 6013(b).

(e) *Additions to the tax and penalties.*—(1) Where the amount shown as the tax by the husband and wife on a joint return made under section 6013(b) exceeds the aggregate of the amounts shown as tax on the separate return of each spouse, and such excess is attributable to negligence, intentional disregard of rules and regulations, or fraud at the time of the making of such separate return, there shall be assessed, collected, and paid in the same manner as if it were a deficiency an additional amount as provided by the following:

(i) If any part of such excess is attributable to negligence, or intentional disregard of rules and regulations, at the time of the making of such separate return, but without any intent to defraud, this additional amount shall be 5 percent of the total amount of the excess.

(ii) If any part of such excess is attributable to fraud with intent to evade tax at the time of the making of such separate return, this additional amount shall be 50 percent of the total amount of the excess. The latter addition is in lieu of the 50 percent addition to the tax provided in section 6653(b).

(2) For purposes of section 7206(1) and (2) and section 7207 (relating to criminal penalties in the case of fraudulent returns), the term "return" includes a separate return filed by a spouse with respect to a taxable year for which a joint return is made under section 6013(b) after the filing of a separate return. [Reg. § 1.6013-2.]

☐ [T.D. 6364, 2-13-59. *Amended by T.D. 7670,* 1-30-80 *and T.D. 8725, 7-21-97.*]

[Reg. § 1.6013-3]

§ 1.6013-3. Treatment of joint return after death of either spouse.—For purposes of section 21 (relating to change in rates during a taxable year), section 443 (relating to returns for a period of less than 12 months), and section 7851(a)(1)(A) (relating to the applicability of certain provisions of the Internal Revenue Code of 1954 and the Internal Revenue Code of 1939), where the husband and wife have different taxable years because of death of either spouse, the joint return shall be treated as if the taxable years of both ended on the date of the closing of the surviving spouse's taxable year. Thus, in cases where the Internal Revenue Code of 1939 otherwise would apply to the taxable year of the decedent spouse and the Internal Revenue Code of 1954 would apply to the taxable year of the surviving spouse, this provision makes the Internal Revenue Code of 1954 applicable to the taxable years of both spouses if a joint return is filed. [Reg. § 1.6013-3.]

☐ [T.D. 6364, 2-13-59.]

[Reg. § 1.6013-4]

§ 1.6013-4. Applicable rules.—(a) *Status as husband and wife.*—For the purpose of filing a joint return under section 6013, the status as husband and wife of two individuals having taxable years beginning on the same day shall be determined—

(1) If the taxable year of each individual is the same, as of the close of such year; and

(2) If the close of the taxable year is different by reason of the death of one spouse, as of the time of such death.

An individual legally separated from his spouse under a decree of divorce or of separate maintenance shall not be considered as married. However, the mere fact that spouses have not lived together during the course of the taxable year shall not prohibit them from making a joint return. A husband and wife who are separated under an interlocutory decree of divorce retain the relationship of husband and wife until the decree becomes final. The fact that the taxpayer and his spouse are divorced or legally separated at any time after the close of the taxable year shall not deprive them of their right to file a joint return for such taxable year under section 6013.

(b) *Computation of income, deductions, and tax.*—If a joint return is made, the gross income and adjusted gross income of husband and wife on the joint return are computed in an aggregate

amount and the deductions allowed and the taxable income are likewise computed on an aggregate basis. Deductions limited to a percentage of the adjusted gross income, such as the deduction for charitable, etc., contributions and gifts, under section 170, will be allowed with reference to such aggregate adjusted gross income. A similar rule is applied in the case of the limitation of section 1211(b) on the allowance of losses resulting from the sale or exchange of capital assets (see § 1.1211-1). Although there are two taxpayers on a joint return, there is only one taxable income. The tax on the joint return shall be computed on the aggregate income and the liability with respect to the tax shall be joint and several. For computation of tax in the case of a joint return, see § 1.2-1. For tax in the case of a joint return of husband and wife electing to pay the optional tax under section 3, see § 1.3-1. For the election not to show on a joint return the amount of tax due in connection therewith, see paragraph (c) of § 1.6014-1 and paragraph (d) of § 1.6014-2. For separate computations of the self-employment tax of each spouse on a joint return, see paragraph (b) of § 1.6017-1.

(c) *Definition of executor or administrator.*—For purposes of section 6013 the term "executor or administrator" means the person who is actually appointed to such office and not a person who is merely in charge of the property of the decedent.

(d) *Return signed under duress.*—If an individual asserts and establishes that he or she signed a return under duress, the return is not a joint return. The individual who signed such return under duress is not jointly and severally liable for the tax shown on the return or any deficiency in tax with respect to the return. The return is adjusted to reflect only the tax liability of the individual who voluntarily signed the return, and the liability is determined at the applicable rates in section 1(d) for married individuals filing separate returns. Section 6212 applies to the assessment of any deficiency in tax on such return. [Reg. § 1.6013-4.]

☐ [T.D. 6364, 2-13-59. *Amended by T.D. 7102,* 3-23-71 *and T.D. 9003, 7-17-2002.*]

[Reg. § 1.6013-6]

§ 1.6013-6. Election to treat nonresident alien individual as resident of the United States.—(a) *Election for special treatment.*—(1) *In general.*—Two individuals who are husband and wife at the close of a taxable year ending on or after December 31, 1975, may make an election under this section for that taxable year if, at the close of that year, one spouse is a citizen or resident of the United States and the other spouse is a nonresident alien. The effect of the election is that each spouse is treated as a resident of the United States for purposes of chapters 1, 5, and 24 and sections 6012, 6013, 6072, and 6091 of the Code for the entire taxable year. An election made under this section is in effect for the taxable year for which made and for all subsequent years of the husband and wife, except—

(i) Any taxable year for which the election is suspended, as described in paragraph (a)(3) of this section, and

(ii) Any taxable year for which the election is terminated in accordance with paragraph (b) of this section and all subsequent taxable years.

A husband and wife may not make an election if an election previously made under this section by either spouse has been terminated under paragraph (b) of this section.

(2) *Particular rules.*—(i) As used in paragraph (a)(3) of this section, the term "United States spouse" means any married individual who is a citizen or resident of the United States at any time during a taxable year.

(ii) An individual's residence is determined by application of the principles of §§ 301.7701(b)-1 through 301.7701(b)-9 of this chapter relating to what constitutes residence in the United States by an alien individual.

(iii) Whether two individuals are married at the close of a taxable year is determined by application of the rules in § 1.6013-4(a).

(iv) The provisions of section 879 and the regulations thereunder shall not apply for any taxable year for which an election under this section is in effect.

(v) An individual who makes an election under this section may not, for United States income tax purposes, claim under any United States income tax treaty not to be a U.S. resident. The relationship of U.S. income tax treaties and the election under this section is illustrated by the following example.

Example. H, a U.S. citizen, is married to W, a nonresident alien of the United States and a domiciliary of country X. H and W maintain their only permanent home in country X. W receives both U.S. source and country X source interest during the taxable year. The interest is not effectively connected with a permanent establishment or a fixed base in any country. H and W make the section 6013(g) election. Under article ii (1) of the United States—country X Income Tax Convention interest derived and beneficially owned by a resident of one contracting state is exempt from tax in the other contracting state. Article 4(1) of the treaty provides that an individual is a resident of a contracting state if subject to tax in that country by reason of the individual's domicile, residence, or citizenship. Under article 4(1) of the treaty, W is a resident of country X by virtue of her domicile in country X and also of the United States by virtue of the section 6013(g) election. Article 4(2) of the treaty provides that if an individual is a resident of both the United States and country X by reason of article 4(1), the individual shall be deemed to be a resident of the contracting state in which he or she has a permanent home available. Because W's sole permanent home is in country X, under article 4(2) of the treaty W is treated as a resident of country X for purposes of the treaty. Because W has elected under section 6013(g) to be treated as a U.S. resident (and thus to be taxed on world-wide income), W may not, for U.S. income tax purposes, claim under the treaty not to be a U.S. resident. W, therefore, is subject to U.S. income tax on the interest. For purposes of country X income tax, W is considered a resident of country X under the treaty.

(3) *Suspension of election.*—(i) An election made under this section is suspended and is not in effect for a taxable year subsequent to the first taxable year for which made if neither spouse is a United States spouse during that subsequent taxable year. Thus, for example, the election is in suspense if both spouses are nonresident aliens for the entire taxable year.

(ii) If either spouse dies during any taxable year for which the election under this section is in effect, other than the first taxable year for which the election is to be in effect, the taxable year shall include, solely for purposes of this paragraph (a)(3), only those days during the taxable year on which both spouses are alive. Thus, for example, if the United States spouse dies during the taxable year, the election is not suspended for that year even if the surviving nonresident alien spouse never acquires United States citizenship or residency. Similarly, if the nonresident alien spouse dies during the taxable year, the election is not suspended for that year even if the surviving United States spouse subsequently abandons United States citizenship or residency. However, if neither spouse was a United States spouse at any time during the period of the taxable year when both spouses were alive, the election is suspended for that year even if the surviving spouse subsequently acquires United States citizenship or residency. For the effect of the death of either spouse on the status of the election in subsequent taxable years, see paragraph (b)(2) of this section.

(4) *Time and manner of making an election.*— (i) A husband and wife shall make the election under this section by attaching a statement to a joint return for the first taxable year for which the election is to be in effect. The election must be made before the expiration of the period prescribed by section 6511(a) (or section 6511(c) if the period is extended by agreement) for making a claim for credit or refund. If either or both spouses die after the close of the taxable year but before the joint return is filed, the election may be made by the executor, administrator, or other person charged with the property of the deceased spouse. If the election is made with a joint amended return, the amended return should be made on Form 1040 or 1040A, the word "Amended" should be written clearly on the front of the return, and an amended return also must be filed for each subsequent taxable year as to which a return previously has been filed by either spouse.

(ii) The statement must contain a declaration that the election is being made and that the requirements of paragraph (a)(1) of this section are met for the taxable year. The statement must also contain the name, address, and taxpayer identifying number of each spouse. If the elec-

Reg. § 1.6013-6(a)(4)(ii)

tion is being made on behalf of a deceased spouse, the statement must contain the name and address of the executor, administrator, or other person making the election on behalf of the deceased spouse. The statement must be signed by both persons making the election.

(b) *Termination of election.*—(1) *Revocation.*— (i) An election under this section shall terminate if either spouse revokes the election. An election that is revoked terminates as of the first taxable year for which the last day prescribed by section 6072(a) and 6081(a) for filing the return of tax has not yet occurred.

(ii) Revocation of the election is made by filing a statement of revocation in the following manner. If the spouse revoking the election is required to file a return under section 6012, the statement is filed by attaching it to the return for the first taxable year to which the revocation applies. If the spouse revoking the election is not required to file a return under section 6012, but files a claim for refund under section 6511, the statement is filed by attaching it to the claim for refund. If the spouse revoking the election is not required to file a return and does not file a claim for refund, the statement is filed by submitting it to the service center director with whom was filed the most recent joint return of the spouses. The revocation may, if the revoking spouse dies after the close of the first taxable year to which the revocation applies but before the return, claim for refund, or statement of revocation is filed, be made by the executor, administrator or other person charged with the property of the deceased spouse.

(iii) A revocation of the election is effective as of a particular taxable year if it is filed on or before the last day prescribed by section 6072(a) and 6081(a) for filing the return of tax for that taxable year. However, the revocation is not final until that last day.

(iv) The statement of revocation must contain a declaration that the election under this section is being revoked. The statement must also contain the name, address, and taxpayer identifying number of each spouse. If the revocation is being made on behalf of a deceased spouse, the statement must contain the name and address of the executor, administrator, or other person revoking the election on behalf of the deceased spouse. The statement must also include a list of the States, foreign countries, and possessions of the United States which have community property laws and in which—

(A) Each spouse is domiciled, or

(B) Real property is located from which either of the spouses receives income.

The statement must be signed by the person revoking the election.

(2) *Death.*—An election under this section shall terminate if either spouse dies. An election that terminates on account of death terminates as of the first taxable year of the surviving spouse following the taxable year in which the death occurred. However, if the surviving spouse is a citizen or resident of the United States who is entitled to the benefits of section 2, the election terminates as of the first taxable year following the last taxable year for which the surviving spouse is entitled to the benefits of section 2. If both spouses die within the same taxable year, the election terminates as of the first day after the close of the taxable year in which the deaths occurred.

(3) *Legal separation.*—An election under this section terminates if the spouses legally separate under a decree of divorce or of separate maintenance. An election that terminates on account of legal separation terminates as of the close of the taxable year preceding the taxable year in which the separation occurs. The rules in § 1.6013-4(a) are relevant in determining whether two spouses are legally separated.

(4) *Inadequate records.*—An election under this section may be terminated by the Commissioner if it is determined that either spouse has failed to keep adequate records. An election that is terminated on account of inadequate records terminates as of the close of the taxable year preceding the taxable year for which the Commissioner determines that the election should be terminated. Adequate records are the books, records, and other information reasonably necessary to ascertain the amount of liability for taxes under chapters 1, 5, and 24 of the code of either spouse for the taxable year. Adequate records also include the granting of access to the books and records.

(c) *Illustrations.*—The application of this section is illustrated by the following examples. In each case the individual's taxable year is the calendar year and the spouses are not legally separated.

Example (1). W, a U.S. citizen for the entire taxable year 1979, is married to H, a nonresident alien individual. W and H may make the section 6013(g) election for 1979 by filing the statement of election with a joint return. If W and H make the election, income from sources within and without the United States received by W and H in 1979 and subsequent years must be included in gross income for each taxable year unless the election later is terminated or suspended. While W and H must file a joint return for 1979, joint or separate returns may be filed for subsequent years.

Example (2). H and W are husband and wife and are both nonresident alien individuals. In June 1980 H becomes a U.S. resident and remains a resident for the balance of the year. H and W may make the section 6013(g) election for 1980. If H and W make the election, income from sources within and without the United States received by H and W for the entire taxable year 1980 and subsequent years must be included in gross income for each taxable year, unless the election later is terminated or suspended.

Example (3). W, a U.S. resident on December 31, 1981, is married to H, a nonresident alien. W and H make the section 6013(g) election and file joint returns for 1981 and succeeding years. On January 10, 1987, W becomes a nonresident alien. H has remained a nonresident alien. W and H may file a joint return or separate returns for 1987. As neither W nor H is a U.S. resident at any time during 1988, their election is suspended for 1988. If W and H have U.S. source or foreign source income effectively connected with the conduct of a U.S. trade or business in 1988, they must file separate returns as nonresident aliens. W becomes a U.S. resident again on January 5, 1990. Their election no longer is in suspense. Income from sources within and without the United States received by W or H in the years their election is not suspended must be included in gross income for each taxable year.

Example (4). H, a U.S. citizen for the entire taxable year 1979, is married to W, who is not a U.S. citizen. While W believes that she is a U.S. resident, H and W make the section 6013(g) election for 1979 to cover the possibility that later it would be determined that she is a nonresident alien during 1979. The election for 1979 will not be considered evidence that W was a nonresident alien in prior years. Income from sources within and without the United States received by H and W in 1979 and subsequent years must be included in gross income for each taxable year, unless the election later is terminated or suspended. [Reg. § 1.6013-6.]

☐ [*T.D. 7670, 1-30-80. Amended by T.D. 7842,* 11-2-85 *and T.D. 8411, 4-24-92.*]

[Reg. § 1.6013-7]

§ 1.6013-7. Joint return for year in which nonresident alien becomes resident of the United States.—(a) *Election for special treatment.*—(1) *In general.*—Two individuals who are husband and wife at the close of a taxable year ending on or after December 31, 1975, may make an election under this section for that taxable year if one spouse is a citizen or resident of the United States on the last day of that taxable year and the other spouse is a nonresident alien at the beginning of that taxable year and a citizen or resident of the United States at the close of that taxable year. Two married individuals who are nonresident aliens at the beginning of a taxable year and who are U.S. citizens or residents on the last day of that taxable year qualify for the election. The effect of the election is that each spouse is treated as a resident of the United States for purposes of chapters 1, 5, and 24 and sections 6012, 6013, 6072, and 6091 of the Code for all of that taxable year. A husband and wife may not make an election if an election has previously been made under this section by either spouse.

(2) *Particular rules.*—The rules in subdivisions (ii) through (v) of § 1.6013-6(a)(2) are applicable to this section.

(3) *Time and manner of making an election.*—A husband and wife shall make the election under this section in accordance with the rules in § 1.6013-6(a)(4).

(b) *Section 6013(g) election in effect.*—If an election under section 6013(g) is in effect for a year subsequent to the first taxable year for which made and during that subsequent year the husband and wife meet the requirements of section 6013(h) and paragraph (a)(1) of this section, then the election under section 6013(g) shall apply to that subsequent taxable year. A separate election under section 6013(h) is not required for that subsequent taxable year. [Reg. § 1.6013-7.]

☐ [*T.D. 7670, 1-30-80.*]

[Reg. § 301.6014-1]

§ 301.6014-1. Income tax return—Tax not computed by taxpayer.—For provisions relating to the election not to show on an income tax return the amount of tax due in connection therewith, see § § 1.6014-1 and 1.6014-2 of this chapter (Income Tax Regulations). [Reg. § 301.6014-1.]

☐ [*T.D. 6498, 10-24-60. Amended by T.D. 7102,* 3-23-71.]

[Reg. § 1.6014-2]

§ 1.6014-2. Tax not computed by taxpayer for taxable years beginning after December 31, 1969.—(a) *In general.*—An individual subject to the tax imposed by section 1 of the Code may, in accordance with the instructions applicable to the income tax return to be filed, elect, for any taxable year beginning after December 31, 1969, not to show on his income tax return for such year the amount of tax due in connection with such return.

(b) *Restriction on making an election.*—The election pursuant to this section shall not be made by an individual who does not file his return (or amended return) making such election on or before the date prescribed in section 6072(a) for the filing of the original return (determined without regard to any extension of time).

(c) *Effect of election.*—(1) A taxpayer who, in accordance with the provisions of this section, elects not to show the tax on his income tax return is not required to pay the unpaid balance of such tax at the time he files the return. In such case, the tax will be computed for the taxpayer by the Internal Revenue Service, and a notice will be mailed to the taxpayer stating the amount of tax due. Where it is determined that a refund of tax is due, the Internal Revenue Service will send such refund to the taxpayer. See paragraph (c) of § 301.6402-3 of this chapter (Regulations on Procedure and Administration). The computation of tax by the Internal Revenue Service shall be treated for purposes of this chapter as if made by the taxpayer, and such computation or the issuance of a notice or refund pursuant thereto shall not relieve the taxpayer of liability for any deficiency (although the deficiency is based upon an amount of tax different from that computed for the taxpayer by the Internal Revenue Service) or affect the rights of the Internal Revenue Service with respect to any subsequent audit or other review of the taxpayer's return.

(2) Where the election provided for in this section is made by a taxpayer who takes the

standard deduction and who has adjusted gross income of less than $10,000, such election constitutes an election to pay the tax imposed by section 3.

(3) A taxpayer who makes an election under section 6014 shall not be precluded from claiming—

(i) Status as a head of household or a surviving spouse;

(ii) The credit under section 31 (relating to tax withheld on wages);

(iii) The credit under section 37 (relating to retirement income);

(iv) The credit under section 38 (relating to investment in certain depreciable property);

(v) The credit under section 39 (relating to certain uses of gasoline and lubricating oil);

(vi) The credit under section 41 (relating to contributions to candidates for public office);

(vii) The credit under section 42 (relating to personal exemptions);

(viii) The credit under section 43 (relating to earned income);

(ix) The credit under section 44 (relating to purchase of new principal residence); or

(x) The credit under section 45 (relating to overpayments of tax).

(d) *Joint returns.*—(1) A husband and wife who file a joint return may elect not to show the tax on such return in accordance with the rules prescribed in paragraphs (a) and (b) of this section.

(2) The tax computed for a husband and wife who elect pursuant to this section not to show their tax on their joint income tax return shall be the lesser of the following amounts:

(i) A tax computed as though the return of income constituted a joint return, or

(ii) If sufficient information is provided for the taxable income of each spouse to be determined, a tax computed as though the return of income constituted the separate returns of the spouses.

(e) *Married individuals filing separate returns.*—This section shall apply to married individuals filing separate returns unless otherwise provided in the instructions accompanying a return. The instructions may require the taxpayer to attach to his return a statement to the effect that his tax and the tax of his spouse were determined in accordance with the rules of sections 141(d) and 142(a).

(f) *Revocation of election.*—An election pursuant to this section may be revoked on an amended return (whether such return is filed before or after the date prescribed in section 6072(a) for filing the original return). [Reg. § 1.6014-2.]

☐ [*T.D. 7102, 3-23-71. Amended by T.D. 7298, 12-21-73 and T.D. 7391, 12-1-75.*]

Reg. § 1.6014-2(c)(3)

[Reg. § 1.6015-0]

§ 1.6015-0. Table of contents.—This section lists captions contained in §§ 1.6015-1 through 1.6015-9.

(iii) Knowledge of the source not sufficient.

(iv) Factors supporting actual knowledge.

(v) Abuse exception.

(3) Disqualified asset transfers.

(i) In general.

(ii) Disqualified asset defined.

(iii) Presumption.

(4) Examples.

(d) Allocation.

(1) In general.

(2) Allocation of erroneous items.

(i) Benefit on the return.

(ii) Fraud.

(iii) Erroneous items of income.

(iv) Erroneous deduction items.

(3) Burden of proof.

(4) General allocation method.

(i) Proportionate allocation.

(ii) Separate treatment items.

(iii) Child's liability.

(iv) Allocation of certain items.

(A) Alternative minimum tax.

(B) Accuracy-related and fraud penalties.

(5) Examples.

(6) Alternative allocation methods.

(i) Allocation based on applicable tax rates.

(ii) Allocation methods provided in subsequent published guidance.

(iii) Example.

§ 1.6015-4 Equitable relief.

§ 1.6015-5 Time and manner for requesting relief.

(a) Requesting relief.

(b) Time period for filing a request for relief.

(1) In general.

(2) Definitions.

(i) Collection activity.

(ii) Section 6330 notice.

(3) Requests for relief made before commencement of collection activity.

(4) Examples.

(5) Premature requests for relief.

(c) Effect of a final administrative determination.

§ 1.6015-6 Nonrequesting spouse's notice and opportunity to participate in administrative proceedings.

(a) In general.

(b) Information submitted.

(c) Effect of opportunity to participate.

§ 1.6015-7 Tax Court review.

(a) In general.

(b) Time period for petitioning the Tax Court.

(c) Restrictions on collection and suspension of the running of the period of limitations.

(1) Restrictions on collection under § 1.6015-2 or 1.6015-3.

(2) Waiver of the restrictions on collection.

(3) Suspension of the running of the period of limitations.

(i) Relief under § 1.6015-2 or 1.6015-3.

(ii) Relief under § 1.6015-4.

(4) Definitions.

(i) Levy.

(ii) Proceedings in court.

(iii) Assessment to which the election relates.

§ 1.6015-8 Applicable liabilities.

(a) In general.

(b) Liabilities paid on or before July 22, 1998.

(c) Examples.

§ 1.6015-9 Effective date.

[Reg. § 1.6015-0.]

☐ [T.D. 9003, 7-17-2002.]

[Reg. § 1.6015-1]

§ 1.6015-1. Relief from joint and several liability on a joint return.—(a) *In general.*—(1) An individual who qualifies and elects under section 6013 to file a joint Federal income tax return with another individual is jointly and severally liable for the joint Federal income tax liabilities for that year. A spouse or former spouse may be relieved of joint and several liability for Federal income tax for that year under the following three relief provisions:

(i) Innocent spouse relief under § 1.6015-2.

(ii) Allocation of deficiency under § 1.6015-3.

(iii) Equitable relief under § 1.6015-4.

(2) A requesting spouse may submit a single claim electing relief under both or either §§ 1.6015-2 and 1.6015-3, and requesting relief under § 1.6015-4. However, equitable relief under § 1.6015-4 is available only to a requesting spouse who fails to qualify for relief under §§ 1.6015-2 and 1.6015-3. If a requesting spouse elects the application of either § 1.6015-2 or 1.6015-3, the Internal Revenue Service will consider whether relief is appropriate under the other elective provision and, to the extent relief is unavailable under either, under § 1.6015-4. If a requesting spouse seeks relief only under § 1.6015-4, the Secretary may not grant relief under § 1.6015-2 or 1.6015-3 in the absence of an affirmative election made by the requesting spouse under either of those sections. If in the course of reviewing a request for relief only under § 1.6015-4, the IRS determines that the requesting spouse may qualify for relief under § 1.6015-2 or 1.6015-3 instead of § 1.6015-4, the Internal Revenue Service will correspond with the requesting spouse to see if the requesting spouse would like to amend his or her request to elect the application of § 1.6015-2 or 1.6015-3. If the requesting spouse chooses to amend the claim for relief, the requesting spouse must submit an affirmative election under § 1.6015-2 or

Reg. § 1.6015-1(a)(2)

1.6015-3. The amended claim for relief will relate back to the original claim for purposes of determining the timeliness of the claim.

(3) Relief is not available for liabilities that are required to be reported on a joint Federal income tax return but are not income taxes imposed under Subtitle A of the Internal Revenue Code (e.g., domestic service employment taxes under section 3510).

(b) *Duress.*—For rules relating to the treatment of returns signed under duress, see § 1.6013-4(d).

(c) *Prior closing agreement or offer in compromise.*—(1) *In general.*—A requesting spouse is not entitled to relief from joint and several liability under § 1.6015-2, 1.6015-3, or 1.6015-4 for any tax year for which the requesting spouse has entered into a closing agreement with the Commissioner that disposes of the same liability that is the subject of the claim for relief. In addition, a requesting spouse is not entitled to relief from joint and several liability under § 1.6015-2, 1.6015-3, or 1.6015-4 for any tax year for which the requesting spouse has entered into an offer in compromise with the Commissioner. For rules relating to the effect of closing agreements and offers in compromise, see sections 7121 and 7122, and the regulations thereunder.

(2) *Exception for agreements relating to TEFRA partnership proceedings.*—The rule in paragraph (c)(1) of this section regarding the unavailability of relief from joint and several liability when the liability to which the claim for relief relates was the subject of a prior closing agreement entered into by the requesting spouse, shall not apply to an agreement described in section 6224(c) with respect to partnership items (or any penalty, addition to tax, or additional amount that relates to adjustments to partnership items) that is entered into while the requesting spouse is a party to a pending partnership-level proceeding conducted under the provisions of subchapter C of chapter 63 of subtitle F of the Internal Revenue Code (TEFRA partnership proceeding). If, however, a requesting spouse enters into a closing agreement pertaining to any penalty, addition to tax, or additional amount that relates to adjustments to partnership items, at a time when the requesting spouse is not a party to a pending TEFRA partnership proceeding (e.g., in connection with an affected items proceeding), then the provisions of paragraph (c)(1) shall apply. Similarly, if a requesting spouse enters into a closing agreement with respect to both partnership items (including affected items) and nonpartnership items, while the requesting spouse is a party to a pending TEFRA partnership proceeding, the provisions of paragraph (c)(1) shall apply to the portion of the closing agreement that relates to nonpartnership items and the provisions of this paragraph (c)(2) shall apply to the remainder of the closing agreement.

(3) *Examples.*—The following examples illustrate the rules of this paragraph (c):

Example 1. H and W file joint returns for taxable years 2002-2004, on which they claim losses attributable to H's limited partnership interest in Partnership A. In January 2006, the Internal Revenue Service commences an audit under the provisions of subchapter C of chapter 63 of subtitle F of the Internal Revenue Code (TEFRA partnership proceeding) regarding Partnership A's 2002-2004 taxable years, and sends H and W a notice under section 6223(a)(1). In September 2007, H files a bankruptcy petition under chapter 7 of the Bankruptcy Code and receives a discharge in April 2008. In August 2008, H and W enter into a closing agreement with the Internal Revenue Service, in which H and W agree to the disallowance of some of the claimed losses from Partnership A for taxable years 2002 through 2007. W may not later claim relief from joint and several liability under section 6015 as to the disallowed losses attributable to Partnership A for taxable years 2002 to 2007. This is because at the time W entered into the closing agreement, H's partnership items attributable to Partnership A had converted to nonpartnership items as a result of H's filing of the bankruptcy petition. The conversion of H's items also terminated W's status as a partner in the TEFRA partnership proceeding regarding Partnership A. Consequently, the closing agreement did not pertain to partnership items and W was not a party to a pending partnership-level proceeding regarding Partnership A when she entered into the closing agreement. Accordingly, the exception in paragraph (c)(2) of this section for agreements relating to TEFRA partnership proceedings does not apply.

Example 2. H and W file a joint return for taxable year 2002, on which they claim $25,000 in losses attributable to H's general partnership interest in Partnership B. In November 2003, the Service proposes a deficiency in tax relating to H's and W's 2002 joint return arising from omitted taxable interest income in the amount of $2,000 that is attributable to H. In July 2005, the Internal Revenue Service commences a TEFRA partnership proceeding regarding Partnership B's 2002 and 2003 taxable years, and sends H and W a notice under section 6223(a)(1). In March 2006, H and W enter into a closing agreement with the Service. The closing agreement provides for the disallowance of the claimed losses from Partnership B in excess of H's and W's out-of-pocket expenditures relating to Partnership B for taxable year 2002 and any subsequent year(s) in which H and W claimed losses from Partnership B. In addition, H and W agree to the imposition of the accuracy-related penalty under section 6662 with respect to the disallowed losses attributable to partnership B. In the closing agreement, H and W also agree to the deficiency resulting from the omitted interest income for taxable year 2002. W may not later claim relief from joint and several liability under section 6015 as to the deficiency in tax attributable to the omitted income of $2,000 for taxable year 2002, because this portion of the closing agreement pertains to nonpartnership items. In contrast, W may claim relief from joint and several liability as to the disallowed losses and accuracy-related penalty attributable to Partnership B for taxable year 2002 or any subsequent year(s). This is because this portion of the closing agreement pertains to partnership and affected items and was entered into at a time when W was a party to the pending partnership-level proceeding regarding Partnership B. Consequently, W never had the opportunity to raise the innocent spouse defense in the course of that TEFRA partnership proceeding. (See § 1.6015-5(b)(5) relating to premature claims).

(d) *Fraudulent scheme.*—If the Secretary establishes that a spouse transferred assets to the other spouse as part of a fraudulent scheme, relief is not available under section 6015, and section 6013(d)(3) applies to the return. For purposes of this section, a fraudulent scheme includes a scheme to defraud the Service or another third party, including, but not limited to, creditors, ex-spouses, and business partners.

(e) *Res judicata and collateral estoppel.*—A requesting spouse is barred from relief from joint and several liability under section 6015 by res judicata for any tax year for which a court of competent jurisdiction has rendered a final decision on the requesting spouse's tax liability if relief under section 6015 was at issue in the prior proceeding, or if the requesting spouse meaningfully participated in that proceeding and could have raised relief under section 6015. A requesting spouse has not meaningfully participated in a prior proceeding if, due to the effective date of section 6015, relief under section 6015 was not available in that proceeding. Also, any final decisions rendered by a court of competent jurisdiction regarding issues relevant to section 6015 are conclusive and the requesting spouse may be collaterally estopped from relitigating those issues.

(f) *Community property laws.*—(1) *In general.*— In determining whether relief is available under § 1.6015-2, 1.6015-3, or 1.6015-4, items of income, credits, and deductions are generally allocated to the spouses without regard to the operation of community property laws. An erroneous item is attributed to the individual whose activities gave rise to such item. See § 1.6015-3(d)(2).

(2) *Example.*—The following example illustrates the rule of this paragraph (f):

Example. (i) H and W are married and have lived in State A (a community property state) since 1987. On April 15, 2003, H and W file a joint Federal income tax return for the 2002 taxable year. In August 2005, the Internal Revenue Service proposes a $17,000 deficiency with respect to the 2002 joint return. A portion of the deficiency is attributable to $20,000 of H's unreported interest income from his individual bank account. The remainder of the deficiency is attributable to $30,000 of W's disallowed business expense deductions. Under the laws of State A, H and W each own 1/2 of all income earned and property acquired during the marriage.

(ii) In November 2005, H and W divorce and W timely elects to allocate the deficiency. Even though the laws of State A provide that 1/2 of the interest income is W's, for purposes of relief under this section, the $20,000 unreported interest income is allocable to H, and the $30,000 disallowed deduction is allocable to W. The community property laws of State A are not considered in allocating items for this purpose.

(g) *Scope of this section and §§ 1.6015-2 through 1.6015-9.*—This section and §§ 1.6015-2 through 1.6015-9 do not apply to any portion of a liability for any taxable year for which a claim for credit or refund is barred by operation of law or rule of law.

(h) *Definitions.*—(1) *Requesting spouse.*—A requesting spouse is an individual who filed a joint return and elects relief from Federal income tax liability arising from that return under § 1.6015-2 or 1.6015-3, or requests relief from Federal income tax liability arising from that return under § 1.6015-4.

(2) *Nonrequesting spouse.*—A nonrequesting spouse is the individual with whom the requesting spouse filed the joint return for the year for which relief from liability is sought.

(3) *Item.*—An item is that which is required to be separately listed on an individual income tax return or any required attachments. Items include, but are not limited to, gross income, deductions, credits, and basis.

(4) *Erroneous item.*—An erroneous item is any item resulting in an understatement or deficiency in tax to the extent that such item is omitted from, or improperly reported (including improperly characterized) on an individual income tax return. For example, unreported income from an investment asset resulting in an understatement or deficiency in tax is an erroneous item. Similarly, ordinary income that is improperly reported as capital gain resulting in an understatement or deficiency in tax is also an erroneous item. In addition, a deduction for an expense that is personal in nature that results in an understatement or deficiency in tax is an erroneous item of deduction. An erroneous item is also an improperly reported item that affects the liability on other returns (e.g., an improper net operating loss that is carried back to a prior year's return). Penalties and interest are not erroneous items. Rather, relief from penalties and interest will generally be determined based on the proportion of the total erroneous items from which the requesting spouse is relieved. If a penalty relates to a particular erroneous item, see § 1.6015-3(d)(4)(iv)(B).

(5) *Election or request.*—A qualifying election under § 1.6015-2 or 1.6015-3, or request under § 1.6015-4, is the first timely claim for relief from joint and several liability for the tax year for which relief is sought. A qualifying election also includes a requesting spouse's second election to seek relief from joint and several liability for the same tax year under § 1.6015-3 when the additional qualifications of paragraphs (h)(5)(i) and (ii) of this section are met—

Reg. § 1.6015-1(h)(5)

(i) The requesting spouse did not qualify for relief under § 1.6015-3 when the Internal Revenue Service considered the first election solely because the qualifications of § 1.6015-3(a) were not satisfied; and

(ii) At the time of the second election, the qualifications for relief under § 1.6015-3(a) are satisfied.

(i) [Reserved]

(j) *Transferee liability.*—(1) *In general.*—The relief provisions of section 6015 do not negate liability that arises under the operation of other laws. Therefore, a requesting spouse who is relieved of joint and several liability under § 1.6015-2, 1.6015-3, or 1.6015-4 may nevertheless remain liable for the unpaid tax (including additions to tax, penalties, and interest) to the extent provided by Federal or state transferee liability or property laws. For the rules regarding the liability of transferees, see sections 6901 through 6904 and the regulations thereunder. In addition, the requesting spouse's property may be subject to collection under Federal or state property laws.

(2) *Example.*—The following example illustrates the rule of this paragraph (j):

Example. H and W timely file their 1998 joint income tax return on April 15, 1999. H dies in March 2000, and the executor of H's will transfers all of the estate's assets to W. In July 2001, the Internal Revenue Service assesses a deficiency for the 1998 return. The items giving rise to the deficiency are attributable to H. W is relieved of the liability under section 6015, and H's estate remains solely liable. The Internal Revenue Service may seek to collect the deficiency from W to the extent permitted under Federal or state transferee liability or property laws.

[Reg. § 1.6015-1.]

☐ [*T.D.* 9003, 7-17-2002.]

[Reg. § 1.6015-2]

§ 1.6015-2. Relief from liability applicable to all qualifying joint filers.—(a) *In general.*—A requesting spouse may be relieved of joint and several liability for tax (including additions to tax, penalties, and interest) from an understatement for a taxable year under this section if the requesting spouse elects the application of this section in accordance with § § 1.6015-1(h)(5) and 1.6015-5, and—

(1) A joint return was filed for the taxable year;

(2) On the return there is an understatement attributable to erroneous items of the nonrequesting spouse;

(3) The requesting spouse establishes that in signing the return he or she did not know and had no reason to know of the understatement; and

(4) It is inequitable to hold the requesting spouse liable for the deficiency attributable to the understatement.

(b) *Understatement.*—The term *understatement* has the meaning given to such term by section 6662(d)(2)(A) and the regulations thereunder.

(c) *Knowledge or reason to know.*—A requesting spouse has knowledge or reason to know of an understatement if he or she actually knew of the understatement, or if a reasonable person in similar circumstances would have known of the understatement. For rules relating to a requesting spouse's actual knowledge, see § 1.6015-3(c)(2). All of the facts and circumstances are considered in determining whether a requesting spouse had reason to know of an understatement. The facts and circumstances that are considered include, but are not limited to, the nature of the erroneous item and the amount of the erroneous item relative to other items; the couple's financial situation; the requesting spouse's educational background and business experience; the extent of the requesting spouse's participation in the activity that resulted in the erroneous item; whether the requesting spouse failed to inquire, at or before the time the return was signed, about items on the return or omitted from the return that a reasonable person would question; and whether the erroneous item represented a departure from a recurring pattern reflected in prior years' returns (e.g., omitted income from an investment regularly reported on prior years' returns).

(d) *Inequity.*—All of the facts and circumstances are considered in determining whether it is inequitable to hold a requesting spouse jointly and severally liable for an understatement. One relevant factor for this purpose is whether the requesting spouse significantly benefitted, directly or indirectly, from the understatement. A significant benefit is any benefit in excess of normal support. Evidence of direct or indirect benefit may consist of transfers of property or rights to property, including transfers that may be received several years after the year of the understatement. Thus, for example, if a requesting spouse receives property (including life insurance proceeds) from the nonrequesting spouse that is beyond normal support and traceable to items omitted from gross income that are attributable to the nonrequesting spouse, the requesting spouse will be considered to have received significant benefit from those items. Other factors that may also be taken into account, if the situation warrants, include the fact that the requesting spouse has been deserted by the nonrequesting spouse, the fact that the spouses have been divorced or separated, or that the requesting spouse received benefit on the return from the understatement. For guidance concerning the criteria to be used in determining whether it is inequitable to hold a requesting spouse jointly and severally liable under this section, see Rev. Proc. 2000-15 (2000-1 C.B. 447), or other guidance published by the Treasury and IRS (see § 601.601(d)(2) of this chapter).

(e) *Partial relief.*—(1) *In general.*—If a requesting spouse had no knowledge or reason to know of only a portion of an erroneous item, the requesting spouse may be relieved of the liability attributable to that portion of that item, if all other requirements are met with respect to that portion.

(2) *Example.*—The following example illustrates the rules of this paragraph (e):

Example. H and W are married and file their 2004 joint income tax return in March 2005. In April 2006, H is convicted of embezzling $2 million from his employer during 2004. H kept all of his embezzlement income in an individual bank account, and he used most of the funds to support his gambling habit. H and W had a joint bank account into which H and W deposited all of their reported income. Each month during 2004, H transferred an additional $10,000 from the individual account to H and W's joint bank account. W paid the household expenses using this joint account, and regularly received the bank statements relating to the account. W had no knowledge or reason to know of H's embezzling activities. However, W did have knowledge and reason to know of $120,000 of the $2 million of H's embezzlement income at the time she signed the joint return because that amount passed through the couple's joint bank account. Therefore, W may be relieved of the liability arising from $1,880,000 of the unreported embezzlement income, but she may not be relieved of the liability for the deficiency arising from $120,000 of the unreported embezzlement income of which she knew and had reason to know.

[Reg. § 1.6015-2.]

☐ [*T.D.* 9003, 7-17-2002.]

[Reg. § 1.6015-3]

§ 1.6015-3. Allocation of deficiency for individuals who are no longer married, are legally separated, or are not members of the same household.—(a) *Election to allocate deficiency.*—A requesting spouse may elect to allocate a deficiency if, as defined in paragraph (b) of this section, the requesting spouse is divorced, widowed, or legally separated, or has not been a member of the same household as the nonrequesting spouse at any time during the 12-month period ending on the date an election for relief is filed. For purposes of this section, the marital status of a deceased requesting spouse will be determined on the earlier of the date of the election or the date of death in accordance with section 7703(a)(1). Subject to the restrictions of paragraph (c) of this section, an eligible requesting spouse who elects the application of this section in accordance with §§ 1.6015-1(h)(5) and 1.6015-5 generally may be relieved of joint and several liability for the portion of any deficiency that is allocated to the nonrequesting spouse pursuant to the allocation methods set forth in paragraph (d) of this section. Relief may be available to both spouses filing the joint return if each spouse is eligible for and elects the application of this section.

(b) *Definitions.*—(1) *Divorced.*—A determination of whether a requesting spouse is divorced for purposes of this section will be made in accordance with section 7703 and the regulations thereunder. Such determination will be made as of the date the election is filed.

(2) *Legally separated.*—A determination of whether a requesting spouse is legally separated for purposes of this section will be made in accordance with section 7703 and the regulations thereunder. Such determination will be made as of the date the election is filed.

(3) *Members of the same household.*—(i) *Temporary absences.*—A requesting spouse and a nonrequesting spouse are considered members of the same household during either spouse's temporary absences from the household if it is reasonable to assume that the absent spouse will return to the household, and the household or a substantially equivalent household is maintained in anticipation of such return. Examples of temporary absences may include, but are not limited to, absence due to incarceration, illness, business, vacation, military service, or education.

(ii) *Separate dwellings.*—A husband and wife who reside in the same dwelling are considered members of the same household. In addition, a husband and wife who reside in two separate dwellings are considered members of the same household if the spouses are not estranged or one spouse is temporarily absent from the other's household within the meaning of paragraph (b)(3)(i) of this section.

(c) *Limitations.*—(1) *No refunds.*—Relief under this section is only available for unpaid liabilities resulting from understatements of liability. Refunds are not authorized under this section.

(2) *Actual knowledge.*—(i) *In general.*—If, under section 6015(c)(3)(C), the Secretary demonstrates that, at the time the return was signed, the requesting spouse had actual knowledge of an erroneous item that is allocable to the nonrequesting spouse, the election to allocate the deficiency attributable to that item is invalid, and the requesting spouse remains liable for the portion of the deficiency attributable to that item. The Service, having both the burden of production and the burden of persuasion, must establish, by a preponderance of the evidence, that the requesting spouse had actual knowledge of the erroneous item in order to invalidate the election.

(A) *Omitted income.*—In the case of omitted income, knowledge of the item includes knowledge of the receipt of the income. For example, assume W received $5,000 of dividend income from her investment in X Co. but did not report it on the joint return. H knew that W received $5,000 of dividend income from X Co. that year. H had actual knowledge of the erroneous item (i.e., $5,000 of unreported dividend income from X Co.), and no relief is available under this section for the deficiency attributable to the dividend income from X Co. This rule

Reg. § 1.6015-3(c)(2)(i)(A)

applies equally in situations where the other spouse has unreported income although the spouse does not have an actual receipt of cash (e.g., dividend reinvestment or a distributive share from a flow-through entity shown on Schedule K-1, "Partner's Share of Income, Credits, Deductions, etc.").

(B) *Deduction or credit.*—(1) *Erroneous deductions in general.*—In the case of an erroneous deduction or credit, knowledge of the item means knowledge of the facts that made the item not allowable as a deduction or credit.

(2) *Fictitious or inflated deduction.*—If a deduction is fictitious or inflated, the IRS must establish that the requesting spouse actually knew that the expenditure was not incurred, or not incurred to that extent.

(ii) *Partial knowledge.*—If a requesting spouse had actual knowledge of only a portion of an erroneous item, then relief is not available for that portion of the erroneous item. For example, if H knew that W received $1,000 of dividend income and did not know that W received an additional $4,000 of dividend income, relief would not be available for the portion of the deficiency attributable to the $1,000 of dividend income of which H had actual knowledge. A requesting spouse's actual knowledge of the proper tax treatment of an item is not relevant for purposes of demonstrating that the requesting spouse had actual knowledge of an erroneous item. For example, assume H did not know W's dividend income from X Co. was taxable, but knew that W received the dividend income. Relief is not available under this section. In addition, a requesting spouse's knowledge of how an erroneous item was treated on the tax return is not relevant to a determination of whether the requesting spouse had actual knowledge of the item. For example, assume that H knew of W's dividend income, but H failed to review the completed return and did not know that W omitted the dividend income from the return. Relief is not available under this section.

(iii) *Knowledge of the source not sufficient.*—Knowledge of the source of an erroneous item is not sufficient to establish actual knowledge. For example, assume H knew that W owned X Co. stock, but H did not know that X Co. paid dividends to W that year. H's knowledge of W's ownership in X Co. is not sufficient to establish that H had actual knowledge of the dividend income from X Co. In addition, a requesting spouse's actual knowledge may not be inferred when the requesting spouse merely had reason to know of the erroneous item. Even if H's knowledge of W's ownership interest in X Co. indicates a reason to know of the dividend income, actual knowledge of such dividend income cannot be inferred from H's reason to know. Similarly, the IRS need not establish that a requesting spouse knew of the source of an erroneous item in order to establish that the requesting spouse had actual knowledge of the item itself. For example, assume H knew that W received $1,000, but he did not know the source of the $1,000. W and H omit the $1,000 from their joint return. H has actual knowledge of the item giving rise to the deficiency ($1,000), and relief is not available under this section.

(iv) *Factors supporting actual knowledge.*—To demonstrate that a requesting spouse had actual knowledge of an erroneous item at the time the return was signed, the IRS may rely upon all of the facts and circumstances. One factor that may be relied upon in demonstrating that a requesting spouse had actual knowledge of an erroneous item is whether the requesting spouse made a deliberate effort to avoid learning about the item in order to be shielded from liability. This factor, together with all other facts and circumstances, may demonstrate that the requesting spouse had actual knowledge of the item, and the requesting spouse's election would be invalid with respect to that entire item. Another factor that may be relied upon in demonstrating that a requesting spouse had actual knowledge of an erroneous item is whether the requesting spouse and the nonrequesting spouse jointly owned the property that resulted in the erroneous item. Joint ownership is a factor supporting a finding that the requesting spouse had actual knowledge of an erroneous item. For purposes of this paragraph, a requesting spouse will not be considered to have had an ownership interest in an item based solely on the operation of community property law. Rather, a requesting spouse who resided in a community property state at the time the return was signed will be considered to have had an ownership interest in an item only if the requesting spouse's name appeared on the ownership documents, or there otherwise is an indication that the requesting spouse asserted dominion and control over the item. For example, assume H and W live in State A, a community property state. After their marriage, H opens a bank account in his name. Under the operation of the community property laws of State A, W owns 1/2 of the bank account. However, W does not have an ownership interest in the account for purposes of this paragraph (c)(2)(iv) because the account is not held in her name and there is no other indication that she asserted dominion and control over the item.

(v) *Abuse exception.*—If the requesting spouse establishes that he or she was the victim of domestic abuse prior to the time the return was signed, and that, as a result of the prior abuse, the requesting spouse did not challenge the treatment of any items on the return for fear of the nonrequesting spouse's retaliation, the limitation on actual knowledge in this paragraph (c) will not apply. However, if the requesting spouse involuntarily executed the return, the requesting spouse may choose to establish that the return was signed under duress. In such a case, § 1.6013-4(d) applies.

(3) *Disqualified asset transfers.*—(i) *In general.*—The portion of the deficiency for which a requesting spouse is liable is increased (up to the

entire amount of the deficiency) by the value of any disqualified asset that was transferred to the requesting spouse. For purposes of this paragraph (c)(3), the value of a disqualified asset is the fair market value of the asset on the date of the transfer.

(ii) *Disqualified asset defined.*—A disqualified asset is any property or right to property that was transferred from the nonrequesting spouse to the requesting spouse if the principal purpose of the transfer was the avoidance of tax or payment of tax (including additions to tax, penalties, and interest).

(iii) *Presumption.*—Any asset transferred from the nonrequesting spouse to the requesting spouse during the 12-month period before the mailing date of the first letter of proposed deficiency (e.g., a 30-day letter or, if no 30-day letter is mailed, a notice of deficiency) is presumed to be a disqualified asset. The presumption also applies to any asset that is transferred from the nonrequesting spouse to the requesting spouse after the mailing date of the first letter of proposed deficiency. The presumption does not apply, however, if the requesting spouse establishes that the asset was transferred pursuant to a decree of divorce or separate maintenance or a written instrument incident to such a decree. If the presumption does not apply, but the Internal Revenue Service can establish that the purpose of the transfer was the avoidance of tax or payment of tax, the asset will be disqualified, and its value will be added to the amount of the deficiency for which the requesting spouse remains liable. If the presumption applies, a requesting spouse may still rebut the presumption by establishing that the principal purpose of the transfer was not the avoidance of tax or payment of tax.

(4) *Examples.*—The following examples illustrate the rules in this paragraph (c):

Example 1. Actual knowledge of an erroneous item. (i) H and W file their 2001 joint Federal income tax return on April 15, 2002. On the return, H and W report W's self-employment income, but they do not report W's self-employment tax on that income. H and W divorce in July 2003. In August 2003, H and W receive a 30-day letter from the Internal Revenue Service proposing a deficiency with respect to W's unreported self-employment tax on the 2001 return. On November 4, 2003, H files an election to allocate the deficiency to W. The erroneous item is the self-employment income, and it is allocable to W. H knows that W earned income in 2001 as a self-employed musician, but he does not know that self-employment tax must be reported on and paid with a joint return.

(ii) H's election to allocate the deficiency to W is invalid because, at the time H signed the joint return, H had actual knowledge of W's self-employment income. The fact that H was unaware of the tax consequences of that income (i.e., that an individual is required to pay self-employment tax on that income) is not relevant.

Example 2. Actual knowledge not inferred from a requesting spouse's reason to know. (i) H has long been an avid gambler. H supports his gambling habit and keeps all of his gambling winnings in an individual bank account, held solely in his name. W knows about H's gambling habit and that he keeps a separate bank account, but she does not know whether he has any winnings because H does not tell her, and she does not otherwise know of H's bank account transactions. H and W file their 2001 joint Federal income tax return on April 15, 2002. On October 31, 2003, H and W receive a 30-day letter proposing a $100,000 deficiency relating to H's unreported gambling income. In February 2003, H and W divorce, and in March 2004, W files an election under section 6015(c) to allocate the $100,000 deficiency to H.

(ii) While W may have had reason to know of the gambling income because she knew of H's gambling habit and separate account, W did not have actual knowledge of the erroneous item (i.e., the gambling winnings). The Internal Revenue Service may not infer actual knowledge from W's reason to know of the income. Therefore, W's election to allocate the $100,000 deficiency to H is valid.

Example 3. Actual knowledge and failure to review return. (i) H and W are legally separated. In February 1999, W signs a blank joint Federal income tax return for 1998 and gives it to H to fill out. The return was timely filed on April 15, 1999. In September 2001, H and W receive a 30-day letter proposing a deficiency relating to $100,000 of unreported dividend income received by H with respect to stock of ABC Co. owned by H. W knew that H received the $100,000 dividend payment in August 1998, but she did not know whether H reported that payment on the joint return.

(ii) On January 30, 2002, W files an election to allocate the deficiency from the 1998 return to H. W claims she did not review the completed joint return, and therefore, she had no actual knowledge that there was an understatement of the dividend income. W's election to allocate the deficiency to H is invalid because she had actual knowledge of the erroneous item (dividend income from ABC Co.) at the time she signed the return. The fact that W signed a blank return is irrelevant. The result would be the same if W had not reviewed the completed return or if W had reviewed the completed return and had not noticed that the item was omitted.

Example 4. Actual knowledge of an erroneous item of income. (i) H and W are legally separated. In June 2004, a deficiency is proposed with respect to H's and W's 2002 joint Federal income tax return that is attributable to $30,000 of unreported income from H's plumbing business that should have been reported on a Schedule C. No Schedule C was attached to the return. At the time W signed the return, W knew that H had a plumbing business but did not know whether H received any income from the business. W's election to allocate to H the deficiency attributable to the $30,000 of unreported plumbing income is valid.

(ii) Assume the same facts as in paragraph (i) of this *Example 5* except that, at the time W

Reg. § 1.6015-3(c)(4)

signed the return, W knew that H received $20,000 of plumbing income. W's election to allocate to H the deficiency attributable to the $20,000 of unreported plumbing income (of which W had actual knowledge) is invalid. W's election to allocate to H the deficiency attributable to the $10,000 of unreported plumbing income (of which W did not have actual knowledge) is valid.

(iii) Assume the same facts as in paragraph (i) of this *Example 5* except that, at the time W signed the return, W did not know the exact amount of H's plumbing income. W did know, however, that H received at least $8,000 of plumbing income. W's election to allocate to H the deficiency attributable to $8,000 of unreported plumbing income (of which W had actual knowledge) is invalid. W's election to allocate to H the deficiency attributable to the remaining $22,000 of unreported plumbing income (of which W did not have actual knowledge) is valid.

(iv) Assume the same facts as in paragraph (i) of this *Example 5* except that H reported $26,000 of plumbing income on the return and omitted $4,000 of plumbing income from the return. At the time W signed the return, W knew that H was a plumber, but she did not know that H earned more than $26,000 that year. W's election to allocate to H the deficiency attributable to the $4,000 of unreported plumbing income is valid because she did not have actual knowledge that H received plumbing income in excess of $26,000.

(v) Assume the same facts as in paragraph (i) of this *Example 5* except that H reported only $20,000 of plumbing income on the return and omitted $10,000 of plumbing income from the return. At the time W signed the return, W knew that H earned at least $26,000 that year as a plumber. However, W did not know that, in reality, H earned $30,000 that year as a plumber. W's election to allocate to H the deficiency attributable to the $6,000 of unreported plumbing income (of which W had actual knowledge) is invalid. W's election to allocate to H the deficiency attributable to the $4,000 of unreported plumbing income (of which W did not have actual knowledge) is valid.

Example 5. Actual knowledge of a deduction that is an erroneous item. (i) H and W are legally separated. In February 2005, a deficiency is asserted with respect to their 2002 joint Federal income tax return. The deficiency is attributable to a disallowed $1,000 deduction for medical expenses H claimed he incurred. At the time W signed the return, W knew that H had not incurred any medical expenses. W's election to allocate to H the deficiency attributable to the disallowed medical expense deduction is invalid because W had actual knowledge that H had not incurred any medical expenses.

(ii) Assume the same facts as in paragraph (i) of this *Example 6* except that, at the time W

signed the return, W did not know whether H had incurred any medical expenses. W's election to allocate to H the deficiency attributable to the disallowed medical expense deduction is valid because she did not have actual knowledge that H had not incurred any medical expenses.

(iii) Assume the same facts as in paragraph (i) of this *Example 6* except that the Internal Revenue Service disallowed $400 of the $1,000 medical expense deduction. At the time W signed the return, W knew that H had incurred some medical expenses but did not know the exact amount. W's election to allocate to H the deficiency attributable to the disallowed medical expense deduction is valid because she did not have actual knowledge that H had not incurred medical expenses (in excess of the floor amount under section 213(a)) of more than $600.

(iv) Assume the same facts as in paragraph (i) of this *Example 6* except that H claims a medical expense deduction of $10,000 and the Internal Revenue Service disallows $9,600. At the time W signed the return, W knew H had incurred some medical expenses but did not know the exact amount. W also knew that H incurred medical expenses (in excess of the floor amount under section 213(a)) of no more than $1,000. W's election to allocate to H the deficiency attributable to the portion of the overstated deduction of which she had actual knowledge ($9,000) is invalid. W's election to allocate the deficiency attributable to the portion of the overstated deduction of which she had no knowledge ($600) is valid.

Example 6. Disqualified asset presumption. (i) H and W are divorced. In May 1999, W transfers $20,000 to H, and in April 2000, H and W receive a 30-day letter proposing a $40,000 deficiency on their 1998 joint Federal income tax return. The liability remains unpaid, and in October 2000, H elects to allocate the deficiency under this section. Seventy-five percent of the net amount of erroneous items are allocable to W, and 25% of the net amount of erroneous items are allocable to H.

(ii) In accordance with the proportionate allocation method (see paragraph (d)(4) of this section), H proposes that $30,000 of the deficiency be allocated to W and $10,000 be allocated to himself. H submits a signed statement providing that the principal purpose of the $20,000 transfer was not the avoidance of tax or payment of tax, but he does not submit any documentation indicating the reason for the transfer. H has not overcome the presumption that the $20,000 was a disqualified asset. Therefore, the portion of the deficiency for which H is liable ($10,000) is increased by the value of the disqualified asset ($20,000). H is relieved of liability for $10,000 of the $30,000 deficiency allocated to W, and remains jointly and severally liable for the remaining $30,000 of the deficiency (assuming that H does not qualify for relief under any other provision).

Reg. § 1.6015-3(c)(4)

Example 7. Disqualified asset presumption inapplicable. On May 1, 2001, H and W receive a 30-day letter regarding a proposed deficiency on their 1999 joint Federal income tax return relating to unreported capital gain from H's sale of his investment in Z stock. W had no actual knowledge of the stock sale. The deficiency is assessed in November 2001, and in December 2001, H and W divorce. According to a decree of divorce, H must transfer 1/2 of his interest in mutual fund A to W. The transfer takes place in February 2002. In August 2002, W elects to allocate the deficiency to H. Although the transfer of 1/2 of H's interest in mutual fund A took place after the 30-day letter was mailed, the mutual fund interest is not presumed to be a disqualified asset because the transfer of H's interest in the fund was made pursuant to a decree of divorce.

Example 8. Overcoming the disqualified asset presumption. (i) H and W are married for 25 years. Every September, on W's birthday, H gives W a gift of $500. On February 28, 2002, H and W receive a 30-day letter from the Internal Revenue Service relating to their 1998 joint individual Federal income tax return. The deficiency relates to H's Schedule C business, and W had no knowledge of the items giving rise to the deficiency. H and W are legally separated in June 2003, and, despite the separation, H continues to give W $500 each year for her birthday. H is not required to give such amounts pursuant to a decree of divorce or separate maintenance.

(ii) On January 27, 2004, W files an election to allocate the deficiency to H. The $1,500 transferred from H to W from February 28, 2001 (a year before the 30-day letter was mailed) to the present is presumed disqualified. However, W may overcome the presumption that such amounts were disqualified by establishing that such amounts were birthday gifts from H and that she has received such gifts during their entire marriage. Such facts would show that the amounts were not transferred for the purpose of avoidance of tax or payment of tax.

(d) *Allocation.*—(1) *In general.*—(i) An election to allocate a deficiency limits the requesting spouse's liability to that portion of the deficiency allocated to the requesting spouse pursuant to this section.

(ii) Only a requesting spouse may receive relief. A nonrequesting spouse who does not also elect relief under this section remains liable for the entire amount of the deficiency. Even if both spouses elect to allocate a deficiency under this section, there may be a portion of the deficiency that is not allocable, for which both spouses remain jointly and severally liable.

(2) *Allocation of erroneous items.*—For purposes of allocating a deficiency under this section, erroneous items are generally allocated to the spouses as if separate returns were filed, subject to the following four exceptions:

(i) *Benefit on the return.*—An erroneous item that would otherwise be allocated to the nonrequesting spouse is allocated to the requesting spouse to the extent that the requesting spouse received a tax benefit on the joint return.

(ii) *Fraud.*—The Internal Revenue Service may allocate any item between the spouses if the Internal Revenue Service establishes that the allocation is appropriate due to fraud by one or both spouses.

(iii) *Erroneous items of income.*—Erroneous items of income are allocated to the spouse who was the source of the income. Wage income is allocated to the spouse who performed the services producing such wages. Items of business or investment income are allocated to the spouse who owned the business or investment. If both spouses owned an interest in the business or investment, the erroneous item of income is generally allocated between the spouses in proportion to each spouse's ownership interest in the business or investment, subject to the limitations of paragraph (c) of this section. In the absence of clear and convincing evidence supporting a different allocation, an erroneous income item relating to an asset that the spouses owned jointly is generally allocated 50% to each spouse, subject to the limitations in paragraph (c) of this section and the exceptions in paragraph (c)(2)(iv) of this section. For rules regarding the effect of community property laws, see § 1.6015-1(f) and paragraph (c)(2)(iv) of this section.

(iv) *Erroneous deduction items.*—Erroneous deductions related to a business or investment are allocated to the spouse who owned the business or investment. If both spouses owned an interest in the business or investment, an erroneous deduction item is generally allocated between the spouses in proportion to each spouse's ownership interest in the business or investment. In the absence of clear and convincing evidence supporting a different allocation, an erroneous deduction item relating to an asset that the spouses owned jointly is generally allocated 50% to each spouse, subject to the limitations in paragraph (c) of this section and the exceptions in paragraph (d)(4) of this section. Deduction items unrelated to a business or investment are also generally allocated 50% to each spouse, unless the evidence shows that a different allocation is appropriate.

(3) *Burden of proof.*—Except for establishing actual knowledge under paragraph (c)(2) of this section, the requesting spouse must prove that all of the qualifications for making an election under this section are satisfied and that none of the limitations (including the limitation relating to transfers of disqualified assets) apply. The requesting spouse must also establish the proper allocation of the erroneous items.

(4) *General allocation method.*—(i) *Proportionate allocation.*—(A) The portion of a deficiency allocable to a spouse is the amount that bears the same ratio to the deficiency as the net amount of erroneous items allocable to the spouse bears to the net amount of all erroneous items. This calculation may be expressed as follows:

Reg. §1.6015-3(d)(4)(i)(A)

$$X = (\text{deficiency}) \quad \times \quad \frac{\text{net amount of erroneous items allocable to the spouse}}{\text{net amount of all erroneous items}}$$

where X=the portion of the deficiency allocable to the spouse.

(B) The proportionate allocation applies to any portion of the deficiency other than—

(1) Any portion of the deficiency attributable to erroneous items allocable to the nonrequesting spouse of which the requesting spouse had actual knowledge;

(2) Any portion of the deficiency attributable to separate treatment items (as defined in paragraph (d)(4)(ii) of this section);

(3) Any portion of the deficiency relating to the liability of a child (as defined in paragraph (d)(4)(iii) of this section) of the requesting spouse or nonrequesting spouse;

(4) Any portion of the deficiency attributable to alternative minimum tax under section 55;

(5) Any portion of the deficiency attributable to accuracyrelated or fraud penalties;

(6) Any portion of the deficiency allocated pursuant to alternative allocation methods authorized under paragraph (d)(6) of this section.

(ii) *Separate treatment items.*—Any portion of a deficiency that is attributable to an item allocable solely to one spouse and that results from the disallowance of a credit, or a tax or an addition to tax (other than tax imposed by section 1 or section 55) that is required to be included with a joint return (a separate treatment item) is allocated separately to that spouse. If such credit or tax is attributable in whole or in part to both spouses, then the IRS will determine on a case by case basis how such item will be allocated. Once the proportionate allocation is made, the liability for the requesting spouse's separate treatment items is added to the requesting spouse's share of the liability.

(iii) *Child's liability.*—Any portion of a deficiency relating to the liability of a child of the requesting and nonrequesting spouse is allocated jointly to both spouses. For purposes of this paragraph, a child does not include the taxpayer's stepson or stepdaughter, unless such child was legally adopted by the taxpayer. If the child is the child of only one of the spouses, and the other spouse had not legally adopted such child, any portion of a deficiency relating to the liability of such child is allocated solely to the parent spouse.

(iv) *Allocation of certain items.*—(A) *Alternative minium tax.*—Any portion of a deficiency relating to the alternative minimum tax under section 55 will be allocated appropriately.

(B) *Accuracy-related and fraud penalties.*—Any accuracyrelated or fraud penalties under section 6662 or 6663 are allocated to the spouse whose item generated the penalty.

(5) *Examples.*—The following examples illustrate the rules of this paragraph (d). In each example, assume that the requesting spouse or spouses qualify to elect to allocate the deficiency, that any election is timely made, and that the deficiency remains unpaid. In addition, unless otherwise stated, assume that neither spouse has actual knowledge of the erroneous items allocable to the other spouse. The examples are as follows:

Example 1. Allocation of erroneous items. (i) H and W file a 2003 joint Federal income tax return on April 15, 2004. On April 28, 2006, a deficiency is assessed with respect to their 2003 return. Three erroneous items give rise to the deficiency—

(A) Unreported interest income, of which W had actual knowledge, from H's and W's joint bank account;

(B) A disallowed business expense deduction on H's Schedule C; and

(C) A disallowed Lifetime Learning Credit for W's postsecondary education, paid for by W.

(ii) H and W divorce in May 2006, and in September 2006, W timely elects to allocate the deficiency. The erroneous items are allocable as follows:

(A) The interest income would be allocated 1/2 to H and 1/2 to W, except that W has actual knowledge of it. Therefore, W's election to allocate the portion of the deficiency attributable to this item is invalid, and W remains jointly and severally liable for it.

(B) The business expense deduction is allocable to H.

(C) The Lifetime Learning Credit is allocable to W.

Example 2. Proportionate allocation. (i) W and H timely file their 2001 joint Federal income tax return on April 15, 2002. On August 16, 2004, a $54,000 deficiency is assessed with respect to their 2001 joint return. H and W divorce on October 14, 2004, and W timely elects to allocate the deficiency. Five erroneous items give rise to the deficiency—

(A) A disallowed $15,000 business deduction allocable to H;

(B) $20,000 of unreported income allocable to H;

(C) A disallowed $5,000 deduction for educational expense allocable to H;

(D) A disallowed $40,000 charitable contribution deduction allocable to W; and

(E) A disallowed $40,000 interest deduction allocable to W.

	W's items
$40,000	charitable deduction
$40,000	interest deduction
$80,000	

(iii) The ratio of erroneous items allocable to W to the total erroneous items is 2/3 ($80,000/$120,000). W's liability is limited to $36,000 of the deficiency (2/3 of $54,000). The Internal Revenue Service may collect up to $36,000 from W and up to $54,000 from H (the total amount collected, however, may not exceed $54,000). If H also made an election, there would be no remaining joint and several liability, and the Internal Revenue Service would be permitted to collect $36,000 from W and $18,000 from H.

Example 3. Proportionate allocation with joint erroneous item. (i) On September 4, 2001, W elects to allocate a $3,000 deficiency for the 1998 tax year to H. Three erroneous items give rise to the deficiency—

(A) Unreported interest in the amount of $4,000 from a joint bank account;

H's items
$2,000 business deduction
Total allocable items: $8,000

(iii) The ratio of erroneous items allocable to W to the total erroneous items is 3/4 ($6,000/$8,000). W's liability is limited to $1,500 of the deficiency (3/4 of $2,000) allocated to her. The Internal Revenue Service may collect up to $2,500 from W (3/4 of the total allocated deficiency plus $1,000 of the deficiency attributable to the joint bank account interest) and up to $3,000 from H (the total amount collected, however, cannot exceed $3,000).

(iv) Assume H also elects to allocate the 1998 deficiency. H is relieved of liability for 3/4 of the deficiency, which is allocated to W. H's relief totals $1,500 (3/4 of $2,000). H remains liable for $1,500 of the deficiency (1/4 of the allocated deficiency plus $1,000 of the deficiency attributable to the joint bank account interest).

Example 4. Separate treatment items (STIs). (i) On September 1, 2006, a $28,000 deficiency is assessed with respect to H's and W's 2003 joint return. The deficiency is the result of 4 erroneous items—

W's share of allocable items
3/4 ($24,000/$32,000)

(v) W's liability for the portion of the deficiency subject to proportionate allocation is limited to $9,000 (3/4 of $12,000) and H's liability for such portion is limited to $3,000 (1/4 of $12,000).

W's share of total deficiency
$9,000 allocated deficiency
$14,000 self-employment tax
$23,000

(ii) In total, there are $120,000 worth of erroneous items, of which $80,000 are attributable to W and $40,000 are attributable to H.

	H's items
$15,000	business deduction
$20,000	unreported income
$5,000	education deduction
$40,000	

(B) A disallowed deduction for business expenses in the amount of $2,000 attributable to H's business; and

(C) Unreported wage income in the amount of $6,000 attributable to W's second job.

(ii) The erroneous items total $12,000. Generally, income, deductions, or credits from jointly held property that are erroneous items are allocable 50% to each spouse. However, in this case, both spouses had actual knowledge of the unreported interest income. Therefore, W's election to allocate the portion of the deficiency attributable to this item is invalid, and W and H remain jointly and severally liable for this portion. Assume that this portion is $1,000. W may allocate the remaining $2,000 of the deficiency.

W's items
$6,000 wage income

(A) A disallowed Lifetime Learning Credit of $2,000 attributable to H;

(B) A disallowed business expense deduction of $8,000 attributable to H;

(C) Unreported income of $24,000 attributable to W; and

(D) Unreported self-employment tax of $14,000 attributable to W.

(ii) H and W both elect to allocate the deficiency.

(iii) The $2,000 Lifetime Learning Credit and the $14,000 self-employment tax are STIs totaling $16,000. The amount of erroneous items included in computing the proportionate allocation ratio is $32,000 ($24,000 unreported income and $8,000 disallowed business expense deduction). The amount of the deficiency subject to proportionate allocation is reduced by the amount of STIs ($28,000 − $16,000 = $12,000).

(iv) Of the $32,000 of proportionate allocation items, $24,000 is allocable to W, and $8,000 is allocable to H.

H's share of allocable items
1/4 ($8,000/$32,000)

(vi) After the proportionate allocation is completed, the amount of the STIs is added to each spouse's allocated share of the deficiency.

H's share of total deficiency
$3,000 allocated deficiency
$2,000 Lifetime Learning Credit
$5,000

Reg. §1.6015-3(d)(5)

(vii) Therefore, W's liability is limited to $23,000 and H's liability is limited to $5,000.

Example 5. Requesting spouse receives a benefit on the joint return from the nonrequesting spouse's erroneous item. (i) In 2001, H reports gross income of $4,000 from his business on Schedule C, and W reports $50,000 of wage income. On their 2001 joint Federal income tax return, H deducts $20,000 of business expenses resulting in a net loss from his business of $16,000. H and W divorce in September 2002, and on May 22, 2003, a $5,200 deficiency is assessed with respect to their 2001 joint return. W elects to allocate the deficiency. The deficiency on the joint return results from a disallowance of all of H's $20,000 of deductions.

(ii) Since H used only $4,000 of the disallowed deductions to offset gross income from his business, W benefitted from the other $16,000 of the disallowed deductions used to offset her wage income. Therefore, $4,000 of the disallowed deductions are allocable to H and $16,000 of the disallowed deductions are allocable to W. W's liability is limited to $4,160 (4/5 of $5,200). If H also elected to allocate the deficiency, H's election to allocate the $4,160 of the deficiency to W would be invalid because H had actual knowledge of the erroneous items.

Example 6. Calculation of requesting spouse's benefit on the joint return when the nonrequesting spouse's erroneous item is partially disallowed. Assume the same facts as in Example 6, except that H deducts $18,000 for business expenses on the joint return, of which $16,000 are disallowed. Since H used only $2,000 of the $16,000 disallowed deductions to offset gross income from his business, W received benefit on the return from the other $14,000 of the disallowed deductions used to offset her wage income. Therefore, $2,000 of the disallowed deductions are allocable to H and $14,000 of the disallowed deductions are allocable to W. W's liability is limited to $4,550 (7/8 of $5,200).

(6) *Alternative allocation methods.*— (i) *Allocation based on applicable tax rates.*—If a deficiency arises from two or more erroneous items that are subject to tax at different rates (e.g., ordinary income and capital gain items), the deficiency will be allocated after first separating the erroneous items into categories according to their applicable tax rate. After all erroneous items are categorized, a separate allocation is made with respect to each tax rate category using the proportionate allocation method of paragraph (d)(4) of this section.

(ii) *Allocation methods provided in subsequent published guidance.*—Additional alternative methods for allocating erroneous items under section 6015(c) may be prescribed by the Treasury and IRS in subsequent revenue rulings, revenue procedures, or other appropriate guidance.

(iii) *Example.*—The following example illustrates the rules of this paragraph (d)(6):

Example. Allocation based on applicable tax rates. H and W timely file their 1998 joint Federal income tax return. H and W divorce in 1999. On July 13, 2001, a $5,100 deficiency is assessed with respect to H's and W's 1998 return. Of this deficiency, $2,000 results from unreported capital gain of $6,000 that is attributable to W and $4,000 of capital gain that is attributable to H (both gains being subject to tax at the 20% marginal rate). The remaining $3,100 of the deficiency is attributable to $10,000 of unreported dividend income of H that is subject to tax at a marginal rate of 31%. H and W both timely elect to allocate the deficiency, and qualify under this section to do so. There are erroneous items subject to different tax rates; thus, the alternative allocation method of this paragraph (d)(6) applies. The three erroneous items are first categorized according to their applicable tax rates, then allocated. Of the total amount of 20% tax rate items ($10,000), 60% is allocable to W and 40% is allocable to H. Therefore, 60% of the $2,000 deficiency attributable to these items (or $1,200) is allocated to W. The remaining 40% of this portion of the deficiency ($800) is allocated to H. The only 31% tax rate item is allocable to H. Accordingly, H is liable for $3,900 of the deficiency ($800+$3,100), and W is liable for the remaining $1,200.

[Reg. § 1.6015-3.]

☐ [*T.D. 9003, 7-17-2002.*]

[Reg. § 1.6015-4]

§ 1.6015-4. Equitable relief.—(a) A requesting spouse who files a joint return for which a liability remains unpaid and who does not qualify for full relief under § 1.6015-2 or 1.6015-3 may request equitable relief under this section. The Internal Revenue Service has the discretion to grant equitable relief from joint and several liability to a requesting spouse when, considering all of the facts and circumstances, it would be inequitable to hold the requesting spouse jointly and severally liable.

(b) This section may not be used to circumvent the limitation of § 1.6015-3(c)(1) (i.e., no refunds under § 1.6015-3). Therefore, relief is not available under this section to obtain a refund of liabilities already paid, for which the requesting spouse would otherwise qualify for relief under § 1.6015-3.

(c) For guidance concerning the criteria to be used in determining whether it is inequitable to hold a requesting spouse jointly and severally liable under this section, see Rev. Proc. 2000-15 (2000-1 C.B. 447), or other guidance published by the Treasury and IRS (see § 601.601(d)(2) of this chapter). [Reg. § 1.6015-4.]

☐ [*T.D. 9003, 7-17-2002.*]

[Reg. § 1.6015-5]

§ 1.6015-5. Time and manner for requesting relief.—(a) *Requesting relief.*—To elect the application of § 1.6015-2 or 1.6015-3, or to request equitable relief under § 1.6015-4, a requesting spouse must file Form 8857, "Request for Innocent Spouse Relief" (or other specified form); submit a written statement containing the same information required on Form 8857, which is signed under penalties of perjury; or submit information in the manner prescribed by the Treasury and IRS in forms, relevant revenue rulings, revenue procedures, or other published guidance (see § 601.601(d)(2) of this chapter).

(b) *Time period for filing a request for relief.*— (1) *In general.*—To elect the application of § 1.6015-2 or 1.6015-3, or to request equitable relief under § 1.6015-4, a requesting spouse must file Form 8857 or other similar statement with the Internal Revenue Service no later than two years from the date of the first collection activity against the requesting spouse after July 22, 1998, with respect to the joint tax liability.

(2) *Definitions.*—(i) *Collection activity.*—For purposes of this paragraph (b), collection activity means a section 6330 notice; an offset of an overpayment of the requesting spouse against a liability under section 6402; the filing of a suit by the United States against the requesting spouse for the collection of the joint tax liability; or the filing of a claim by the United States in a court proceeding in which the requesting spouse is a party or which involves property of the requesting spouse. Collection activity does not include a notice of deficiency; the filing of a Notice of Federal Tax Lien; or a demand for payment of tax. The term *property of the requesting spouse*, for purposes of this paragraph (b), means property in which the requesting spouse has an ownership interest (other than solely through the operation of community property laws), including property owned jointly with the nonrequesting spouse.

(ii) *Section 6330 notice.*—A section 6330 notice refers to the notice sent, pursuant to section 6330, providing taxpayers notice of the Service's intent to levy and of their right to a collection due process (CDP) hearing.

(3) *Requests for relief made before commencement of collection activity.*—An election or request for relief may be made before collection activity has commenced. For example, an election or request for relief may be made in connection with an audit or examination of the joint return or a demand for payment, or pursuant to the CDP hearing procedures under section 6320 in connection with the filing of a Notice of Federal Tax Lien. For more information on the rules regarding collection due process for liens, see the Treasury regulations under section 6320. However, no request for relief may be made before the date specified in paragraph (b)(5) of this section.

(4) *Examples.*—The following examples illustrate the rules of this paragraph (b):

Example 1. On January 11, 2000, a section 6330 notice is mailed to H and W regarding their 1997 joint Federal income tax liability. The Internal Revenue Service levies on W's employer on June 5, 2000. The Internal Revenue Service levies on H's employer on July 10, 2000. An election or request for relief must be made by January 11,

2002, which is two years after the Internal Revenue Service sent the section 6330 notice.

Example 2. The Internal Revenue Service offsets an overpayment against a joint liability for 1995 on January 12, 1998. The offset only partially satisfies the liability. The Internal Revenue Service takes no other collection actions. On July 24, 2001, W elects relief with respect to the unpaid portion of the 1995 liability. W's election is timely because the Internal Revenue Service has not taken any collection activity after July 22, 1998; therefore, the two-year period has not commenced.

Example 3. Assume the same facts as in *Example 2*, except that the Internal Revenue Service sends a section 6330 notice on January 22, 1999. W's election is untimely because it is filed more than two years after the first collection activity after July 22, 1998.

Example 4. H and W do not remit full payment with their timely filed joint Federal income tax return for the 1989 tax year. No collection activity is taken after July 22, 1998, until the United States files a suit against both H and W to reduce the tax assessment to judgment and to foreclose the tax lien on their jointly-held business property on July 1, 1999. H elects relief on October 2, 2000. The election is timely because it is made within two years of the filing of a collection suit by the United States against H.

Example 5. W files a Chapter 7 bankruptcy petition on July 10, 2000. On September 5, 2000, the United States files a proof of claim for her joint 1998 income tax liability. W elects relief with respect to the 1998 liability on August 20, 2002. The election is timely because it is made within two years of the date the United States filed the proof of claim in W's bankruptcy case.

(5) *Premature requests for relief.*—The Internal Revenue Service will not consider premature claims for relief under § 1.6015-2, 1.6015-3, or 1.6015-4. A premature claim is a claim for relief that is filed for a tax year prior to the receipt of a notification of an audit or a letter or notice from the IRS indicating that there may be an outstanding liability with regard to that year. Such notices or letters do not include notices issued pursuant to section 6223 relating to TEFRA partnership proceedings. A premature claim is not considered an election or request under § 1.6015-1(h)(5).

(c) *Effect of a final administrative determination.*—(1) *In general.*—A requesting spouse is entitled to only one final administrative determination of relief under § 1.6015-1 for a given assessment, unless the requesting spouse properly submits a second request for relief that is described in § 1.6015-1(h)(5).

(2) *Example.*—The following example illustrates the rule of this paragraph (c):

Example. In January 2001, W becomes a limited partner in partnership P, and in February 2001, she starts her own business from which she earns $100,000 of net income for the year. H and W file a joint return for tax year 2001, on which

Reg. § 1.6015-5(c)(2)

they claim $20,000 in losses from their investment in P, and they omit W's self-employment tax. In March 2003, the Internal Revenue Service commences an audit under the provisions of subchapter C of chapter 63 of subtitle F of the Internal Revenue Code (TEFRA partnership proceeding) and sends H and W a notice under section 6223(a)(1). In September 2003, the Internal Revenue Service audits H's and W's 2001 joint return regarding the omitted self-employment tax. H may file a claim for relief from joint and several liability for the self-employment tax liability because he has received a notification of an audit indicating that there may be an outstanding liability on the joint return. However, his claim for relief regarding the TEFRA partnership proceeding is premature under paragraph (b)(5) of this section. H will have to wait until the Internal Revenue Service sends him a notice of computational adjustment or assesses the liability resulting from the TEFRA partnership proceeding before he files a claim for relief with respect to any such liability. The assessment relating to the TEFRA partnership proceeding is separate from the assessment for the self-employment tax; therefore, H's subsequent claim for relief for the liability from the TEFRA partnership proceeding is not precluded by his previous claim for relief from the self-employment tax liability under this paragraph (c).

[Reg. § 1.6015-5.]

☐ [*T.D.* 9003, 7-17-2002 (*corrected* 8-23-2002).]

[Reg. § 1.6015-6]

§ 1.6015-6. Nonrequesting spouse's notice and opportunity to participate in administrative proceedings.—(a) *In general.*—(1) When the Internal Revenue Service receives an election under § 1.6015-2 or 1.6015-3, or a request for relief under § 1.6015-4, the Internal Revenue Service must send a notice to the nonrequesting spouse's last known address that informs the nonrequesting spouse of the requesting spouse's claim for relief. For further guidance regarding the definition of last known address, see § 301.6212-2 of this chapter. The notice must provide the nonrequesting spouse with an opportunity to submit any information that should be considered in determining whether the requesting spouse should be granted relief from joint and several liability. A nonrequesting spouse is not required to submit information under this section. Upon the request of either spouse, the Internal Revenue Service will share with one spouse the information submitted by the other spouse, unless such information would impair tax administration.

(2) The Internal Revenue Service must notify the nonrequesting spouse of the Service's preliminary and final determinations with respect to the requesting spouse's claim for relief under section 6015.

(b) *Information submitted.*—The Internal Revenue Service will consider all of the information (as relevant to each particular relief provision)

that the nonrequesting spouse submits in determining whether relief from joint and several liability is appropriate, including information relating to the following—

(1) The legal status of the requesting and nonrequesting spouses' marriage;

(2) The extent of the requesting spouse's knowledge of the erroneous items or underpayment;

(3) The extent of the requesting spouse's knowledge or participation in the family business or financial affairs;

(4) The requesting spouse's education level;

(5) The extent to which the requesting spouse benefitted from the erroneous items;

(6) Any asset transfers between the spouses;

(7) Any indication of fraud on the part of either spouse;

(8) Whether it would be inequitable, within the meaning of §§ 1.6015-2(d) and 1.6015-4, to hold the requesting spouse jointly and severally liable for the outstanding liability;

(9) The allocation or ownership of items giving rise to the deficiency; and

(10) Anything else that may be relevant to the determination of whether relief from joint and several liability should be granted.

(c) *Effect of opportunity to participate.*—The failure to submit information pursuant to paragraph (b) of this section does not affect the nonrequesting spouse's ability to seek relief from joint and several liability for the same tax year. However, information that the nonrequesting spouse submits pursuant to paragraph (b) of this section is relevant in determining whether relief from joint and several liability is appropriate for the nonrequesting spouse should the nonrequesting spouse also submit an application for relief. [Reg. § 1.6015-6.]

☐ [*T.D.* 9003, 7-17-2002.]

[Reg. § 1.6015-7]

§ 1.6015-7. Tax Court review.—(a) *In general.*—Requesting spouses may petition the Tax Court to review the denial of relief under § 1.6015-1.

(b) *Time period for petitioning the Tax Court.*—Pursuant to section 6015(e), the requesting spouse may petition the Tax Court to review a denial of relief under § 1.6015-1 within 90 days after the date notice of the Service's final determination is mailed by certified or registered mail (90-day period). If the IRS does not mail the requesting spouse a final determination letter within 6 months of the date the requesting spouse files an election under § 1.6015-2 or 1.6015-3, the requesting spouse may petition the Tax Court to review the election at any time after the expiration of the 6-month period, and before the expiration of the 90-day period. The Tax Court also may review a claim for relief if Tax Court jurisdiction has been acquired under another section of the Internal Revenue Code such as section 6213(a) or 6330(d).

(c) *Restrictions on collection and suspension of the running of the period of limitations.*—(1) *Restrictions on collection under §1.6015-2 or 1.6015-3.*—Unless the Internal Revenue Service determines that collection will be jeopardized by delay, no levy or proceeding in court shall be made, begun, or prosecuted against a requesting spouse electing the application of §1.6015-2 or 1.6015-3 for the collection of any assessment to which the election relates until the expiration of the 90-day period described in paragraph (b) of this section, or if a petition is filed with the Tax Court, until the decision of the Tax Court becomes final under section 7481. For more information regarding the date on which a decision of the Tax Court becomes final, see section 7481 and the regulations thereunder. Notwithstanding the above, if the requesting spouse appeals the Tax Court's decision, the Internal Revenue Service may resume collection of the liability from the requesting spouse on the date the requesting spouse files the notice of appeal, unless the requesting spouse files an appeal bond pursuant to the rules of section 7485. Jeopardy under this paragraph (c)(1) means conditions exist that would require an assessment under section 6851 or 6861 and the regulations thereunder.

(2) *Waiver of the restrictions on collection.*—A requesting spouse may, at any time (regardless of whether a notice of the Service's final determination of relief is mailed), waive the restrictions on collection in paragraph (c)(1) of this section.

(3) *Suspension of the running of the period of limitations.*—(i) *Relief under §1.6015-2 or 1.6015-3.*—The running of the period of limitations in section 6502 on collection against the requesting spouse of the assessment to which an election under §1.6015-2 or 1.6015-3 relates is suspended for the period during which the Internal Revenue Service is prohibited by paragraph (c)(1) of this section from collecting by levy or a proceeding in court and for 60 days thereafter. However, if the requesting spouse signs a waiver of the restrictions on collection in accordance with paragraph (c)(2) of this section, the suspension of the period of limitations in section 6502 on collection against the requesting spouse will terminate on the date that is 60 days after the date the waiver is filed with the Internal Revenue Service.

(ii) *Relief under §1.6015-4.*—If a requesting spouse seeks only equitable relief under §1.6015-4, the restrictions on collection of paragraph (c)(1) of this section do not apply. Accordingly, the request for relief does not suspend the running of the period of limitations on collection.

(4) *Definitions.*—(i) *Levy.*—For purposes of this paragraph (c), levy means an administrative levy or seizure described by section 6331.

(ii) *Proceedings in court.*—For purposes of this paragraph (c), proceedings in court means suits filed by the United States for the collection of Federal tax. Proceedings in court does not

refer to the filing of pleadings and claims and other participation by the Internal Revenue Service or the United States in suits not filed by the United States, including Tax Court cases, refund suits, and bankruptcy cases.

(iii) *Assessment to which the election relates.*—For purposes of this paragraph (c), the assessment to which the election relates is the entire assessment of the deficiency to which the election relates, even if the election is made with respect to only part of that deficiency. [Reg. §1.6015-7.]

☐ [*T.D.* 9003, 7-17-2002.]

[Reg. §1.6015-8]

§1.6015-8. Applicable liabilities.—(a) *In general.*—Section 6015 applies to liabilities that arise after July 22, 1998, and to liabilities that arose prior to July 22, 1998, that were not paid on or before July 22, 1998.

(b) *Liabilities paid on or before July 22, 1998.*—A requesting spouse seeking relief from joint and several liability for amounts paid on or before July 22, 1998, must request relief under section 6013(e) and the regulations thereunder.

(c) *Examples.*—The following examples illustrate the rules of this section:

Example 1. H and W file a joint Federal income tax return for 1995 on April 15, 1996. There is an understatement on the return attributable to an omission of H's wage income. On October 15, 1998, H and W receive a 30-day letter proposing a deficiency on the 1995 joint return. W pays the outstanding liability in full on November 30, 1998. In March 1999, W files Form 8857, requesting relief from joint and several liability under section 6015(b). Although W's liability arose prior to July 22, 1998, it was unpaid as of that date. Therefore, section 6015 is applicable.

Example 2. H and W file their 1995 joint Federal income tax return on April 15, 1996. On October 14, 1997, a deficiency of $5,000 is assessed regarding a disallowed business expense deduction attributable to H. On June 30, 1998, the Internal Revenue Service levies on the $3,000 in W's bank account in partial satisfaction of the outstanding liability. On August 31, 1998, W files a request for relief from joint and several liability. The liability arose prior to July 22, 1998. Section 6015 is applicable to the $2,000 that remained unpaid as of July 22, 1998, and section 6013(e) is applicable to the $3,000 that was paid prior to July 22, 1998. [Reg. §1.6015-8.]

☐ [*T.D.* 9003, 7-17-2002.]

[Reg. §1.6015-9]

§1.6015-9. Effective date.—Sections 1.6015-0 through 1.6015-9 are applicable for all elections under §1.6015-2 or 1.6015-3 or any requests for relief under §1.6015-4 filed on or afte July 18, 2002. [Reg. §1.6015-9.]

☐ [*T.D.* 9003, 7-17-2002.]

[Reg. §1.6017-1]

§1.6017-1. Self-employment tax returns.—
(a) *In general.*—(1) Every individual, other than
a nonresident alien, having net earnings from
self-employment, as defined in section 1402, of
$400 or more for the taxable year shall make a
return of such earnings. For purposes of this
section, an individual who is a resident of the
Virgin Islands, Puerto Rico, or (for any taxable
year beginning after 1960) Guam or American
Samoa is not to be considered a nonresident
alien individual. See paragraph(d) of
§1.1402(b)-1. A return is required under this section if an individual has self-employment income, as defined in section 1402(b), even though
he may not be required to make a return under
section 6012 for purposes of the tax imposed by
section 1 or 3. Provisions applicable to returns
under section 6012(a) shall be applicable to returns under this section.

(2) Except as otherwise provided in this
subparagraph, the return required by this section
shall be made on Form 1040. The form to be used
by residents of the Virgin Islands, Guam, or
American Samoa is Form 1040SS. In the case of a
resident of Puerto Rico who is not required to
make a return of income under section 6012(a),
the form to be used is Form 1040SS, except that
Form 1040PR shall be used if it is furnished by
the Internal Revenue Service to such resident for
use in lieu of Form 1040SS.

(b) *Joint returns.*—(1) In the case of a husband
and wife filing a joint return under section 6013,
the tax on self-employment income is computed
on the separate self-employment income of each
spouse, and not on the aggregate of the two
amounts. The requirement of section 6013(d)(3)
that in the case of a joint return the tax is computed on the aggregate income of the spouses is
not applicable with respect to the tax on self-
employment income. Where the husband and
wife each has net earnings from self-employment of $400 or more, it will be necessary for
each to complete separate schedules of the computation of self-employment tax with respect to
the net earnings of each spouse, despite the fact
that a joint return is filed. If the net earnings
from self-employment of either the husband or
the wife are less than $400, such net earnings are
not subject to the tax on self-employment income, even though they must be shown on the
joint return for purposes of the tax imposed by
section 1 or 3.

(2) Except as otherwise expressly provided,
section 6013 is applicable to the return of the tax
on self-employment income; therefore, the liability with respect to such tax in the case of a joint
return is joint and several.

(c) *Social security account numbers.*—(1) Every
individual making a return of net earnings from
self-employment for any period commencing
before January 1, 1962, is required to show
thereon his social security account number, or, if
he has no such account number, to make application therefor on Form SS-5 before filing such
return. However, the failure to apply for or receive a social security account number will not
excuse the individual from the requirement that
he file such return on or before the due date
thereof. Form SS-5 may be obtained from any
district office of the Social Security Administration or from any district director. The application
shall be filed with a district office of the Social
Security Administration or, in the case of an
individual not in the United States, with the
district office of the Social Security Administration at Baltimore, Maryland. An individual who
has previously secured a social security account
number as an employee shall use that account
number on his return of net earnings from self-
employment.

(2) For provisions applicable to the securing
of identifying numbers and the reporting thereof
on returns and schedules for periods commencing after December 31, 1961, see §1.6109-1.

(d) *Declaration of estimated tax with respect to
taxable years beginning after December 31, 1966.*—
For taxable years beginning after December 31,
1966, section 6015 provides that the term "estimated tax" includes the amount which an individual estimates as the amount of self-
employment tax imposed by chapter 2 for the
taxable year. Thus, individuals upon whom self-
employment tax is imposed by section 1401 must
make a declaration of estimated tax if they meet
the requirements of section 6015(a), except as
otherwise provided under section 6015(i). [Reg.
§1.6017-1.]

☐ [*T.D.* 6364, 2-13-59. *Amended by T.D.* 6691,
12-2-63 *and T.D.* 7427, 8-9-76.]

[Reg. §301.6017-1]

§301.6017-1. Self-employment tax returns.—
For provisions relating to the requirement of self-
employment tax returns, see §1.6017-1 of this
chapter (Income Tax Regulations). [Reg.
§301.6017-1.]

☐ [*T.D.* 6498, 10-24-60.]

[Reg. §20.6018-1]

§20.6018-1. Returns.—(a) *Estates of citizens or
residents.*—A return must be filed on Form 706
for the estate of every citizen or resident of the
United States whose gross estate exceeded
$60,000 in value on the date of his death. The
value of the gross estate at the date of death
governs with respect to the filing of the return
regardless of whether the value of the gross estate is, at the executor's election, finally determined as of a date subsequent to the date of
death pursuant to the provisions of section 2032.
Duplicate copies of the return are not required to
be filed. For the contents of the return, see
§20.6018-3.

(b) *Estates of nonresidents not citizens.*—(1) *In
general.*—Except as provided in subparagraph (2)
of this paragraph, a return must be filed on Form
706 or Form 706NA for the estate of every nonresident not a citizen of the United States if the
value of that part of the gross estate situated in

the United States on the date of his death exceeded $30,000 in the case of a decedent dying on or after November 14, 1966, or $2,000 in the case of a decedent dying before November 14, 1966. Under certain conditions the return may be made only on Form 706. See the instructions on Form 706NA for circumstances under which that form may not be used. Duplicate copies of the return are not required to be filed. For the contents of the return, see § 20.6018-3. For the determination of the gross estate situated in the United States, see §§ 20.2103-1 and 20.2104-1.

(2) *Certain estates of decedents dying on or after November 14, 1966.*—In the case of an estate of a nonresident not a citizen of the United States dying on or after November 14, 1966—

(i) *Transfers subject to the tax imposed by section 2107(a).*—If the transfer of the estate is subject to the tax imposed by section 2107(a) (relating to expatriation to avoid tax), any amounts includible in the decedent's gross estate under section 2107(b) are to be added to the value on the date of his death of that part of his gross estate situated in the United States, for purposes of determining under subparagraph (1) of this paragraph whether his gross estate exceeded $30,000 on the date of his death.

(ii) *Transfers subject to a Presidential proclamation.*—If the transfer of the estate is subject to tax pursuant to a Presidential proclamation made under section 2108(a) (relating to Presidential proclamations of the application of pre-1967 estate tax provisions), the return must be filed on Form 706 or Form 706NA if the value on the date of the decedent's death of that part of his gross estate situated in the United States exceeded $2,000.

(c) *Place for filing.*—See § 20.6091-1 for the place where the return shall be filed.

(d) *Time for filing.*—See § 20.6075-1 for the time for filing the return. [Reg. § 20.6018-1.]

☐ [*T.D.* 7296, 12-11-73.]

[Reg. § 20.6018-2]

§ 20.6018-2. Returns; person required to file return.—It is required that the duly qualified executor or administrator shall file the return. If there is more than one executor or administrator, the return must be made jointly by all. If there is no executor or administrator appointed, qualified and acting within the United States, every person in actual or constructive possession of any property of the decedent situated in the United States is constituted an executor for purposes of the tax (see § 20.2203-1), and is required to make and file a return. If in any case the executor is unable to make a complete return as to any part of the gross estate, he is required to give all the information he has as to such property, including a full description, and the name of every person holding a legal or beneficial interest in the property. If the executor is unable to make a return as to any property, every person holding a legal or beneficial interest therein

shall, upon notice from the district director, make a return as to that part of the gross estate. For delinquency penalty for failure to file return, see section 6651 and § 301.6651-1 of this chapter (Regulations on Procedure and Administration). For criminal penalties for failure to file a return and filing a false or fraudulent return, see sections 7203, 7206, 7207, and 7269. [Reg. § 20.6018-2.]

☐ [*T.D.* 6296, 6-23-58.]

[Reg. § 20.6018-3]

§ 20.6018-3. Returns; contents of returns.—(a) *Citizens or residents.*—The return of an estate of a decedent who was a citizen or resident of the United States at the time of his death must contain an itemized inventory by schedule of the property constituting the gross estate and lists of the deductions under the proper schedules. The return shall set forth (1) the value of the gross estate (see §§ 20.2031-1 through 20.2044-1), (2) the deductions claimed (see §§ 20.2052-1 through 20.2056(e)-3), (3) the taxable estate (see § 20.2051-1), and (4) the gross estate tax, reduced by any credits (see §§ 20.2011-1 through 20.2014-6) against the tax. In listing upon the return the property constituting the gross estate (other than household and personal effects for which see § 20.2031-6), the description of it shall be such that the property may be readily identified for the purpose of verifying the value placed on it by the executor.

(b) *Nonresidents not citizens.*—The return of an estate of a decedent who was not a citizen or resident of the United States at the time of his death must contain the following information: (1) An itemized list of that part of the gross estate situated in the United States (see §§ 20.2103-1 and 20.2104-1); (2) in the case of an estate the transfer of which is subject to the tax imposed by section 2107(a) (relating to expatriation to avoid tax), a list of any amounts with respect to stock in a foreign corporation which are includible in the gross estate under section 2107(b), together with an explanation of how the amounts were determined; (3) an itemized list of any deductions claimed (see §§ 20.2106-1 and 20.2106-2); (4) the amount of the taxable estate (see § 20.2106-1); and (5) the gross estate tax, reduced by any credits against the tax (see § 20.2102-1). For the disallowance of certain deductions if the return does not disclose that part of the gross estate not situated in the United States, see §§ 20.2106-1 and 20.2106-2.

(c) *Provisions applicable to returns described in paragraphs (a) and (b) of this section.*—(1) A legal description shall be given of each parcel of real estate, and, if located in a city, the name of the street and number, its area, and, if improved, a short statement of the character of the improvements.

(2) A description of bonds shall include the number held, principal amount, name of obligor, date of maturity, rate of interest, date or dates on which interest is payable, series number if there

is more than one issue, and the principal exchange upon which listed, or the principal business office of the obligor, if unlisted. A description of stocks, shall include number of shares, whether common or preferred, and, if preferred, what issue, par value, quotation at which returned, exact name of corporation, and, if the stock is unlisted, the location of the principal business office and State in which incorporated and the date of incorporation, or if the stock is listed, the principal exchange upon which sold. A description of notes shall include name of maker, date on which given, date of maturity, amount of principal, amount of principal unpaid, rate of interest and whether simple or compound, date to which interest has been paid and amount of unpaid interest. A description of the seller's interest in land contracts shall include name of buyer, date of contract, description of property, sale price, initial payment, amounts of installment payments, unpaid balance of principal and accrued interest, interest rate and date prior to decedent's death to which interest had been paid.

(3) A description of bank accounts shall disclose the name and address of depository, amount on deposit, whether a checking, savings, or a time-deposit account, rate of interest, if any payable, amount of interest accrued and payable, and serial number. A description of life insurance shall give the name of the insurer, number of policy, name of the beneficiary, and the amount of the proceeds.

(4) In describing an annuity, the name and address of the grantor of the annuity shall be given, or, if the annuity is payable out of a trust or other funds, such a description as will fully identify it. If the annuity is payable for a term of years, the duration of the term and the date on which it began shall be given, and if payable for the life of a person other than the decedent, the date of birth of such person shall be stated. If the executor has not included in the gross estate the full value of an annuity or other payment described in section 2039, he shall nevertheless fully describe the annuity and state its total purchase price and the amount of the contribution made by each person (including the decedent's employer) toward the purchase price. If the executor believes that any part of the annuity or other payment is excludable from the gross estate under the provisions of section 2039, or for any other reason, he shall state in the return the reason for his belief.

(5) Judgments should be described by giving the title of the cause and the name of the court in which rendered, date of judgment, name and address of the judgment debtor, amount of judgment, and rate of interest to which subject, and by stating whether any payments have been made thereon, and, if so, when and in what amounts.

(6) If, pursuant to section 2032, the executor elects to have the estate valued at a date or dates subsequent to the time of the decedent's death, there must be set forth on the return: (i) An itemized description of all property included in the gross estate on the date of the decedent's death, together with the value of each item as of that date; (ii) an itemized disclosure of all distributions, sales, exchanges, and other dispositions of any property during the 6-month (1 year, if the decedent died on or before December 31, 1970) period after the date of the decedent's death, together with the dates thereof; and (iii) the value of each item of property in accordance with the provisions of section 2032 (see § 20.2032-1). Interest and rents accrued at the date of the decedent's death and dividends declared to stockholders of record on or before the date of the decedent's death and not collected at that date are to be shown separately. (See also paragraph (e) of § 20.6018-4 with respect to documents required to be filed with the return.)

(7) All transfers made by the decedent within 3 years before the date of his death of a value of $1,000 or more and all transfers (other than outright transfers not in trust) made by the decedent at any time during his life of a value of $5,000 or more, except bona fide sales for an adequate and full consideration in money or money's worth, must be disclosed in the return, whether or not the executor regards the transfers as subject to the tax. If the executor believes that such a transfer is not subject to the tax, a brief statement of the pertinent facts shall be made. [Reg. § 20.6018-3.]

☐ [*T.D. 7238, 12-28-72 and T.D. 7295, 12-11-73.*]

[Reg. § 20.6018-4]

§ 20.6018-4. Returns; documents to accompany the return.—(a) A certified copy of the will, if the decedent died testate, must be submitted with the return, together with copies of such other documents as are required in Form 706 and in the applicable sections of these regulations. There may also be filed copies of any documents which the executor may desire to submit in explanation of the return.

(b) In the case of an estate of a nonresident citizen, the executor shall also file the following documents with the return: (1) A copy of any inventory of property and schedule of liabilities, claims against the estate and expenses of administration filed with the foreign court of probate jurisdiction, certified by a proper official of the court; and (2) a copy of any return filed under any applicable foreign inheritance, estate, legacy, or succession tax act, certified by a proper official of the foreign tax department.

(c) In the case of an estate of a nonresident not a citizen of the United States, the executor must also file with the return, but only if deductions are claimed or the transfer of the estate is subject to the tax imposed by section 2107(a) (relating to expatriation to avoid tax), a copy of the inventory of property filed under the foreign death duty act; or, if no such inventory was filed, a certified copy of the inventory filed with the foreign court of probate jurisdiction.

(d) For every policy of life insurance listed on the return, the executor must procure a statement, on Form 712, by the company issuing the policy and file it with the return.

(e) If, pursuant to section 2032, the executor elects to have the estate valued at a date or dates subsequent to the time of the decedent's death, the executor shall file with the return evidence in support of any statements made by him in the return as to distributions, sales, exchanges, or other dispositions of property during the 6-month (1 year, if the decedent died on or before December 31, 1970) period which followed the decedent's death. If the court having jurisdiction over the estate makes an order or decree of distribution during that period, a certified copy thereof must be submitted as part of the evidence. The district director, or the director of a service center, may require the submission of such additional evidence as is deemed necessary.

(f) In any case where a transfer, by trust or otherwise, was made by a written instrument, a copy thereof shall be filed with the return if (1) the property is included in the gross estate, or (2) the executor pursuant to the provisions of paragraph (c)(7) of § 20.6018-3 has made a disclosure of the transfer on the return but has not included its value in the gross estate in the belief that it is not so includible. If the written instrument is of public record, the copy shall be certified, or if it is not of record, the copy shall be verified. If the decedent was a nonresident not a citizen at the time of his death, the copy may be either certified or verified.

(g) If the executor contends that the value of property transferred by the decedent within a period of three years ending with the date of the decedent's death should not be included in the gross estate because he considers that the transfer was not made in contemplation of death, he shall file with the return (1) a copy of the death certificate, and (2) a statement, containing a declaration that it is made under the penalties of perjury, of all the material facts and circumstances, including those directly or indirectly indicating the decedent's motive in making the transfer and his mental and physical condition at that time. However, this data need not be furnished with respect to transfers of less than $1,000 in value unless requested by the district director. [Reg. § 20.6018-4.]

☐ [T.D. 6296, 6-23-58. *Amended by T.D. 7238,* 12-28-72 *and T.D. 7296,* 12-11-73.]

[Reg. § 25.6019-1]

§ 25.6019-1. Persons required to file returns.—(a) *Gifts made after December 31, 1981.*— Subject to section 2523(i)(2), an individual citizen or resident of the United States who in any calendar year beginning after December 31, 1981, makes any transfer by gift other than a transfer that, under section 2503(b) or (e) (relating, respectively, to certain gifts of $10,000 per donee and the exclusion for payment of certain educational and medical expenses), is not included in the total amount of gifts for that year, or a transfer of an interest with respect to which a marital deduction is allowed for the value of the entire interest under section 2523 (other than a marital deduction allowed by reason of section 2523(f), regarding qualified terminable interest property for which a return must be filed in order to make the election under that section), must file a gift tax return on Form 709 for that calendar year.

(b) *Gifts made after December 31, 1976, and before January 1, 1982.*—An individual citizen or resident of the United States who makes a transfer by gift within any calendar year beginning after December 31, 1976, and before January 1, 1982, must file a gift tax return on Form 709 for any calendar quarter in which the sum of the taxable gifts made during that calendar quarter, plus all other taxable gifts made during the year (for which a return has not yet been required to be filed), exceeds $25,000. If the aggregate transfers made in a calendar year after 1976 and before 1982 that must be reported do not exceed $25,000, only one return must be filed for the calendar year and it must be filed by the due date for a fourth quarter gift tax return (April 15).

(c) *Gifts made after December 31, 1970, and before January 1, 1977.*—An individual citizen or resident of the United States who makes a transfer by gift within any calendar year beginning after December 31, 1970, and before January 1, 1977, must file a gift tax return on Form 709 for the calendar quarter in which any portion of the value of the gift, or any portion of the sum of the values of the gifts to such donee during that calendar year, is not excluded from the total amount of taxable gifts for that year, and must also make a return for any subsequent quarter within the same taxable year in which any additional gift is made to the same donee.

(d) *Gifts by nonresident alien donors.*—The rules contained in paragraphs (a) through (c) of this section also apply to a nonresident not a citizen of the United States provided that, under section 2501(a)(1) and § 25.2511-3, the transfer is subject to the gift tax.

(e) *Miscellaneous provisions.*—Only individuals are required to file returns and not trusts, estates, partnerships, or corporations. Duplicate copies of the return are not required to be filed. See §§ 25.6075-1 and 25.6091-1 for the time and place for filing the gift tax return. For delinquency penalties for failure to file or pay the tax, see section 6651 and § 301.6651-1 of this chapter (Procedure and Administration Regulations). For criminal penalties for failure to file a return and filing a false or fraudulent return, see sections 7203, 7206, and 7207.

(f) *Return required even if no tax due.*—The return is required even though, because of the deduction authorized by section 2522 (charitable deduction) or the unified credit under section 2505, no tax may be payable on the transfer.

(g) *Deceased donor.*—If the donor dies before filing his return, the executor of his will or the administrator of his estate shall file the return. If the donor becomes legally incompetent before filing his return, his guardian or committee shall file the return.

(h) *Ratification of return.*—The return shall not be made by an agent unless by reason of illness, absence, or nonresidence, the person liable for the return is unable to make it within the time prescribed. Mere convenience is not sufficient reason for authorizing an agent to make the return. If by reason of illness, absence or nonresidence, a return is made by an agent, the return must be ratified by the donor or other person liable for its filing within a reasonable time after such person becomes able to do so. If the return filed by the agent is not so ratified, it will not be considered the return required by the statute. Supplemental data may be submitted at the time of ratification. The ratification may be in the form of a statement executed under the penalties of perjury and filed with the internal revenue officer with whom the return was filed, showing specifically that the return made by the agent has been carefully examined and that the person signing ratifies the return as the donor's. If a return is signed by an agent, a statement fully explaining the inability of the donor must accompany the return. [Reg. § 25.6019-1.]

☐ [*T.D.* 6334, 11-14-58. *Amended by T.D.* 7012, 5-14-69; *T.D.* 7238, 12-28-72 *and T.D.* 8522, 2-28-94.]

[Reg. § 25.6019-2]

§ 25.6019-2. Returns required in case of consent under section 2513.—Except as otherwise provided in this section, the provisions of § 25.6019-1 (other than paragraph (d) of § 25.6019-1) apply with respect to the filing of a gift tax return or returns in the case of a husband and wife who consent (see § 25.2513-1) to the application of section 2513. If both spouses are (without regard to the provisions of section 2513) required under the provisions of § 25.6019-1 to file returns, returns must be filed by both spouses. If only one of the consenting spouses is (without regard to the provisions of section 2513) required under § 25.6019-1 to file a return, a return must be filed by that spouse. In the latter case if, after giving effect to the provisions of section 2513, the other spouse is considered to have made a gift not excluded from the total amount of such other spouse's gifts for the taxable year by reason of section 2503(b) or (e) (relating, respectively, to certain gifts of $10,000 per donee and the exclusion for certain educational or medical expenses), a return must also be filed by such other spouse. Thus, if during a calendar year beginning after December 31, 1981, the first spouse made a gift of $18,000 to a child (the gift not being either a future interest in property or an amount excluded under section 2503(e)) and the other spouse made no gifts, only the first spouse is required to file a return for that calendar year. However, if the other spouse had made a gift in excess of $2,000 to the same child during the same calendar year or if the gift made by the first spouse had amounted to $21,000, each

spouse would be required to file a return if the consent is signified as provided in section 2513. [Reg. § 25.6019-2.]

☐ [*T.D.* 6334, 11-14-58. *Amended by T.D.* 7238, 12-28-72 *and T.D.* 8522, 2-28-94.]

[Reg. § 25.6019-3]

§ 25.6019-3. Contents of return.—(a) *In general.*—The return must set forth each gift made during the calendar year (or calendar quarter with respect to gifts made after December 31, 1970, and before January 1, 1982) that under sections 2511 through 2515 is to be included in computing taxable gifts; the deductions claimed and allowable under sections 2521 through 2524; and the taxable gifts made for each of the preceding reporting periods. (See § 25.2504-1.) In addition the return shall set forth the fair market value of all gifts not made in money, including gifts resulting from sales and exchanges of property made for less than full and adequate consideration in money or money's worth, giving, as of the date of the sale or exchange, both the fair market value of the property sold or exchanged and the fair market value of the consideration received by the donor. If a donor contends that his retained power over property renders the gift incomplete (see § 25.2511-2) and hence not subject to tax as of the calendar quarter or calendar year of the initial transfer, the transaction should be disclosed in the return for the calendar quarter or calendar year of the initial transfer and evidence showing all relevant facts, including a copy of the instrument of transfer, shall be submitted with the return. The instructions printed on the return should be carefully followed. A certified or verified copy of each document required by the instructions printed on the return form shall be filed with the return. Any additional documents the donor may desire to submit may be submitted with the return.

(b) *Disclosure of transfers coming within provisions of section 2516.*—Section 2516 provides that certain transfers of property pursuant to written property settlements between husband and wife are deemed to be transfers for full and adequate consideration in money or money's worth if divorce occurs within 2 years. In any case where a husband and wife enter into a written agreement of the type contemplated by section 2516 and the final decree of divorce is not granted on or before the due date for the filing of a gift tax return for the calendar year (or calendar quarter with respect to periods beginning after December 31, 1970, and ending before January 1, 1982) in which the agreement became effective (see § 25.6075-1), then, except to the extent § 25.6019-1 provides otherwise, the transfer must be disclosed by the transferor upon a gift tax return filed for the calendar year (or calendar quarter) in which the agreement becomes effective, and a copy of the agreement must be attached to the return. In addition, a certified copy of the final divorce decree shall be furnished the internal revenue officer with whom the return was filed not later than 60 days after the divorce is granted. Pending receipt of evidence that the final decree of divorce has been granted (but in no event for a period of more than 2 years from the effective date of the agreement), the transfer will tentatively be treated as made for a full and adequate consideration in money or money's worth. [Reg. § 25.6019-3.]

   ☐ [*T.D. 6334, 11-14-58. Amended by T.D. 7012, 5-14-69; T.D. 7238, 12-28-72 and T.D. 8522, 2-28-94.*]

[Reg. § 25.6019-4]

§ 25.6019-4. Description of property listed on return.—The properties comprising the gifts made during the calendar year (or calendar quarter with respect to gifts made after December 31, 1970, and before January 1, 1982) must be listed on the return and described in a manner that they may be readily identified. Thus, there should be given for each parcel of real estate a legal description, its area, a short statement of the character of any improvements, and, if located in a city, the name of the street and number. Description of bonds shall include the number transferred, principal amount, name of obligor, date of maturity, rate of interest, date or dates on which interest is payable, series number where there is more than one issue, and the principal exchange upon which listed, or the principal business office of the obligor, if unlisted. Description of stocks shall include number of shares, whether common or preferred, and, if preferred, what issue thereof, par value, quotation at which returned, exact name of corporation, and, if the stock is unlisted, the location of the principal business office, the State in which incorporated and the date of incorporation, or if the stock is listed, the principal exchange upon which sold. Description of notes shall include name of maker, date on which given, date of maturity, amount of principal, amount of principal unpaid, rate of interest and whether simple or compound, and date to which interest has been paid. If the gift or property includes accrued income thereon to the date of the gift, the amount of such accrued income shall be separately set forth. Description of the seller's interest in land contracts transferred shall include name of buyer, date of contract, description of property, sale price, initial payment, amounts of installment payments, unpaid balance of principal, interest rate, and date prior to gift to which interest has been paid. Description of life insurance policies shall show the name of the insurer and the number of the policy. In describing an annuity, the name and address of the issuing company shall be given, or, if payable out of a trust or other fund, such a description as will fully identify the trust or fund. If the annuity is payable for a term of years, the duration of the term and the date on which it began shall be given, and if payable for the life of any person, the date of birth of that person shall be stated. Judgments shall be described by giving the title of the cause and the name of the court in which rendered, date of judgment, name and address of judgment debtor, amount of judg-

ment, rate of interest to which subject, and by stating whether any payments have been made thereon, and, if so, when and in what amounts. [Reg. § 25.6019-4.]

   ☐ [*T.D. 6334, 11-14-58. Amended by T.D. 7238, 12-28-72 and T.D. 8522, 2-28-94.*]

[Reg. § 301.6020-1]

§ 301.6020-1. Returns prepared or executed by the Commissioner or other internal revenue officers.—(a) *Preparation of returns.*—(1) *In general.*—If any person required by the Internal Revenue Code (Code) or by the regulations to make a return fails to make such return, it may be prepared by the Commissioner or other authorized Internal Revenue Officer or employee provided such person consents to disclose all information necessary for the preparation of such return. The return upon being signed by the person required to make it shall be received by the Commissioner as the return of such person.

   (2) *Responsibility of person for whom return is prepared.*—A person for whom a return is prepared in accordance with paragraph (a)(1) of this section shall for all legal purposes remain responsible for the correctness of the return to the same extent as if the return had been prepared by him.

   (b) *Execution of returns.*—(1) *In general.*—If any person required by the Code or by the regulations to make a return (other than a declaration of estimated tax required under section 6654 or 6655) fails to make such return at the time prescribed therefore, or makes, willfully or otherwise, a false, fraudulent or frivolous return, the Commissioner or other authorized Internal Revenue Officer or employee shall make such return from his own knowledge and from such information as he can obtain through testimony or otherwise. The Commissioner or other authorized Internal Revenue Officer or employee may make the return by gathering information and making computations through electronic, automated or other means to make a determination of the taxpayer's tax liability.

   (2) *Form of the return.*—A document (or set of documents) signed by the Commissioner or other authorized Internal Revenue Officer or employee shall be a return for a person described in paragraph (b)(1) of this section if the document (or set of documents) identifies the taxpayer by name and taxpayer identification number, contains sufficient information from which to compute the taxpayer's tax liability, and purports to be a return. A Form 13496, "IRC Section 6020(b) Certification," or any other form that an authorized Internal Revenue Officer or employee signs and uses to identify a set of documents containing the information set forth in this paragraph as a section 6020(b) return, and the documents identified, constitute a return under section 6020(b). A return may be signed by the name or title of an Internal Revenue Officer or employee being handwritten, stamped, typed, printed or otherwise mechanically affixed to the return, so

long as that name or title was placed on the document to signify that the Internal Revenue Officer or employee adopted the document as a return for the taxpayer. The document and signature may be in written or electronic form.

(3) *Status of returns.*—Any return made in accordance with paragraph (b)(1) of this section and signed by the Commissioner or other authorized Internal Revenue Officer or employee shall be good and sufficient for all legal purposes except insofar as any Federal statute expressly provides otherwise. Furthermore, the return shall be treated as the return filed by the taxpayer for purposes of determining the amount of the addition to tax under sections 6651(a)(2) and (3).

(4) *Deficiency procedures.*—For deficiency procedures in the case of income, estate, and gift taxes, see §§ 6211 through 6216, inclusive, and §§ 301.6211-1 through 301.6215-1, inclusive.

(5) *Employment status procedures.*—For pre-assessment procedures in employment taxes cases involving worker classification, see section 7436 (proceedings for determination of employment status).

(6) *Examples.*—The application of this paragraph (b) is illustrated by the following examples:

Example 1. Individual A, a calendar-year taxpayer, fails to file his 2003 return. Employee X, an Internal Revenue Service (IRS) employee, opens an examination related to A's 2003 taxable year. At the end of the examination, X completes a Form 13496, "IRC Section 6020(b) Certification," and attached to it the documents listed on the form. Those documents explain examination changes and provide sufficient information to compute A's tax liability. The Form 13496 provides that the IRS employee identified on the form certifies that the attached pages constitute a return under section 6020(b). When X signs the certification package, the package constitutes a return under paragraph (b) of this section because the package identifies A by name, contains A's taxpayer identifying number (TIN), has sufficient information to compute A's tax liability, and contains a statement stating that it constitutes a return under section 6020(b). In addition, the IRS will determine the amount of the additions to tax under section 6651(a)(2) by treating the section 6020(b) return as the return filed by the taxpayer. Likewise, the IRS will determine the amount of any addition to tax under section 6651(a)(3), which arises only after notice and demand for payment, by treating the section 6020(b) return as the return filed by the taxpayer.

Example 2. Same facts as in *Example 1*, except that, after performing the examination, X does not compile any examination documents together as a related set of documents. X also does not sign and complete the Form 13496 nor associate the forms explaining examination changes with any other document. Because X did not sign any document stating that it constitutes a return

under section 6020(b) and the documents otherwise do not purport to be a section 6020(b) return, the documents do not constitute a return under section 6020(b). Therefore, the IRS cannot determine the section 6651(a)(2) addition to tax against nonfiler A for A's 2003 taxable year on the basis of those documents.

Example 3. Individual C, a calendar-year taxpayer, fails to file his 2003 return. The IRS determines through its automated internal matching programs that C received reportable income and failed to file a return. The Service, again through its automated systems, generates a Letter 2566, "30 Day Proposed Assessment (SFR-01) 910 SC/CG." This letter contains C's name, TIN, and has sufficient information to compute C's tax liability. Contemporaneous with the creation of the Letter 2566, the IRS, through its automated system, electronically creates and stores a certification stating that the electronic data contained as part of C's account constitutes a valid return under section 6020(b) as of that date. Further, the electronic data includes the signature of the IRS employee authorized to sign the section 6020(b) return upon its creation. Although the signature is stored electronically, it can appear as a printed name when the IRS requests a paper copy of the certification. The electronically created information, signature, and certification is a return under section 6020(b). The IRS will treat that return as the return filed by the taxpayer in determining the amount of the section 6651(a)(2) addition to tax with respect to C's 2003 taxable year. Likewise, the IRS will determine the amount of any addition to tax under section 6651(a)(3), which arises only after notice and demand for payment, by treating the section 6020(b) return as the return filed by the taxpayer.

Example 4. Corporation M, a quarterly taxpayer, fails to file a Form 941, "Employer's Quarterly Federal Tax Return," for the second quarter of 2004. Q, a IRS employee authorized to sign returns under section 6020(b), prepares a Form 941 by hand, stating Corporation M's name, address, and TIN. Q completes the Form 941 by entering line item amounts, including the tax due, and then signs the document. The Form 941 that Q prepared and signed constitutes a section 6020(b) return because the Form 941 purports to be a return under section 6020(b), the form contains M's name and TIN, and it includes sufficient information to compute M's tax liability for the second quarter of 2004.

(c) *Cross references.*—(1) For provisions that a return executed by the Commissioner or other authorized internal revenue officer or employee will not start the running of the period of limitations on assessment and collection, see section 6501(b)(3) and § 301.6501(b)-1(e).

(2) For determining the period of limitations on collection after assessment of a liability on a return executed by the Commissioner or other authorized internal revenue officer or employee, see section 6502 and § 301.6502-1.

(3) For additions to the tax and additional amounts for failure to file returns, see section

6651 and §301.6651-1, and section 6652 and §301.6652-1, respectively.

(4) For additions to the tax for failure to pay tax, see section 6651 and §301.6651-1.

(5) For criminal penalties for willful failure to make returns, see sections 7201, 7202 and 7203.

(6) For criminal penalties for willfully making false or fraudulent returns, see sections 7206 and 7207.

(7) For civil penalties for filing frivolous income tax returns, see section 6702.

(8) For authority to examine books and witnesses, see section 7602 and §301.7602-1.

(d) *Effective/Applicability date.*—This section is applicable on February 20, 2008. [Reg. §301.6020-1.]

☐ [*T.D.* 9380, 2-19-2008.]

[Reg. §301.6021-1]

§301.6021-1. Listing by district directors of taxable objects owned by nonresidents of internal revenue districts.—Whenever there are in any internal revenue district any articles subject to tax, which are not owned or possessed by or under the care or control of any person within such district, and of which no list has been transmitted to the district director, as required by law or by regulations prescribed pursuant to law, the district director, or other authorized internal revenue officer or employee, shall enter the premises where such articles are situated, shall make such inspection of the articles as may be necessary, and shall make lists of the same according to the forms prescribed. Such lists, being subscribed by the district director or other authorized internal revenue officer or employee, shall be sufficient lists of such articles for all purposes. [Reg. §301.6021-1.]

☐ [*T.D.* 6498, 10-24-60.]

[Reg. §1.6031(a)-1]

§1.6031(a)-1. Return of partnership income.—(a) *Domestic partnerships.*—(1) *Return required.*—Except as provided in paragraphs (a)(3) and (c) of this section, every domestic partnership must file a return of partnership income under section 6031 (partnership return) for each taxable year on the form prescribed for the partnership return. The partnership return must be filed for the taxable year of the partnership regardless of the taxable years of the partners. For taxable years of a partnership and of a partner, see section 706 and §1.706-1. For the rules governing partnership statements to partners and nominees, see §1.6031(b)-1T. For the rules requiring the disclosure of certain transactions, see §1.6011-4T.

(2) *Content of return.*—The partnership return must contain the information required by the prescribed form and the accompanying instructions.

(3) *Special rule.*—(i) A partnership that has no income, deductions, or credits for federal income tax purposes for a taxable year is not required to file a partnership return for that year.

(ii) The Commissioner may, in guidance published in the Internal Revenue Bulletin (see §601.601(d)(2)(ii)(*b*) of this chapter), provide for an exception to partnership reporting under section 6031 and for conditions for the exception, if all or substantially all of a partnership's income is derived from the holding or disposition of tax-exempt obligations (as defined in section 1275(a)(3) and §1.1275-1(e)) or shares in a regulated investment company (as defined in section 851(a)) that pays exempt-interest dividends (as defined in section 852(b)(5)).

(4) *Failure to file.*—For the consequences of a failure to comply with the requirements of section 6031(a) and this paragraph (a), see sections 6229(a), 6231(f), 6698, and 7203.

(b) *Foreign partnerships.*—(1) *General rule.*—(i) *Filing requirement.*—A foreign partnership is not required to file a partnership return, if the foreign partnership does not have gross income that is (or is treated as) effectively connected with the conduct of a trade or business within the United States (ECI) and does not have gross income (including gains) derived from sources within the United States (U.S.-source income). Except as provided in paragraphs (b)(2) and (3) of this section, a foreign partnership that has ECI or has U.S.-source income that is not ECI must file a partnership return for its taxable year in accordance with the rules for domestic partnerships in paragraph (a) of this section.

(ii) *Special rule.*—For purposes of this paragraph (b)(1) and paragraph (b)(3)(iii) of this section, a foreign partnership will not be considered to have derived income from sources within the United States solely because a U.S. partner marks to market his pro rata share of PFIC stock held by the foreign partnership pursuant to an election under section 1296.

(2) *Foreign partnerships with de minimis U.S.-source income and de minimis U.S. partners.*—A foreign partnership (other than a withholding foreign partnership, as defined in §1.1441-5(c)(2)(i)) that has $20,000 or less of U.S.-source income and has no ECI during its taxable year is not required to file a partnership return if, at no time during the partnership taxable year, one percent or more of any item of partnership income, gain, loss, deduction, or credit is allocable in the aggregate to direct United States partners. The United States partners must directly report their shares of the allocable items of partnership income, gain, loss, deduction, and credit.

(3) *Filing obligations for certain other foreign partnerships with no ECI.*—(i) *General requirements for modified filing obligations.*—A foreign partnership will be subject to the modified filing obligations in paragraphs (b)(3)(ii) and (iii) of this section if, in addition to satisfying the requirements contained in paragraph 5(b)(3)(ii) and (iii) of this section—

Reg. §1.6031(a)-1(b)(3)(i)

(A) The partnership is not a withholding foreign partnership as defined in § 1.1441-5(c)(2)(i);

(B) Forms 1042 and 1042-S are filed by the partnership with respect to the amounts subject to reporting under § 1.1461-1(b) and (c), unless the partnership is not required to file such returns under § 1.1461-1(b)(2) and (c)(4), in which case Forms 1042 and 1042-S must be filed by another withholding agent or agents; and

(C) The tax liability of the partners with respect to such amounts has been fully satisfied by the withholding of tax at the source, if applicable, under chapter 3 of the Internal Revenue Code.

(ii) *Foreign partnerships with U.S.-source income but no U.S. partners.*—A foreign partnership that has U.S.-source income is not required to file a partnership return if the partnership has no ECI and no United States partners at any time during the partnership's taxable year.

(iii) *Foreign partnerships with U.S.-source income and U.S. partners.*—Except as provided in paragraph (b)(2) of this section, a foreign partnership with one or more United States partners that has U.S.-source income but no ECI must file a partnership return. However, such a foreign partnership need not file Statements of Partner's Share of Income, Credit, Deduction, Etc. (Schedules K-1) for any partners other than its direct United States partners and its passthrough partners (whether U.S. or foreign) through which United States partners hold an interest in the foreign partnership. Schedules K-1 that are not excepted from filing under this paragraph (b)(3)(iii) must contain the same information required of a domestic partnership filing under paragraph (a) of this section.

(4) *Information or returns required of partners who are United States persons.*—(i) *In general.*—If a United States person is a partner in a partnership that is not required to file a partnership return, the district director or director of the relevant service center may require that person to render the statements or provide the information necessary to verify the accuracy of the reporting by that person of any items of partnership income, gain, loss, deduction, or credit.

(ii) *Controlled foreign partnerships.*—Certain United States persons who are partners in a foreign partnership controlled (within the meaning of section 6038(e)(1)) by United States persons may be required to provide information with respect to the partnership under section 6038.

(5) *Certain partnership elections.*—For a partnership that is not otherwise required to file a partnership return, if an election that can only be made by the partnership under section 703 (affecting the computation of taxable income derived from a partnership) is to be made by or for the partnership, a return on the form prescribed for the partnership return must be filed for the partnership. Unless otherwise provided in the

form or the accompanying instructions, a return filed solely to make an election need only contain a written statement citing paragraph (b)(5)(ii) of this section, listing the name and address of the partnership making the election, and clearly identifying the specific election being made. A return filed under paragraph (b)(5)(ii) of this section solely to make an election is not a partnership return. Thus, such a return is not a return filed under section 6031(a) for purposes of sections 6501 (except regarding the specific election issue), 6231(a)(1)(A), and 6233. The return must be signed by—

(i) Each partner that is a partner in the partnership at the time the election is made; or

(ii) Any partner of the partnership who is authorized (under local law or the partnership's organizational documents) to make the election and who represents to having such authorization under penalties of perjury.

(6) *Exclusion for certain organizations.*—The return requirement of section 6031 and this section does not apply to the International Telecommunications Satellite Organization, the International Maritime Satellite Organization, or any organization that is a successor of either.

(c) *Partnerships excluded from the application of subchapter K of the Internal Revenue Code.*—(1) *Wholly excluded.*—(i) *Year of election.*—An eligible partnership as described in § 1.761-2(a) that elects to be excluded from all the provisions of subchapter K of chapter 1 of the Internal Revenue Code in the manner specified by § 1.761-2(b)(2)(i) must timely file the form prescribed for the partnership return for the taxable year for which the election is made. In lieu of the information otherwise required, the return must contain or be accompanied by the information required by § 1.761-2(b)(2)(i).

(ii) *Subsequent years.*—Except as otherwise provided in paragraph (c)(1)(i) of this section, an eligible partnership that elects to be wholly excluded from the application of subchapter K is not required to file a partnership return.

(2) *Deemed excluded.*—An eligible partnership that is deemed to have elected exclusion from the application of subchapter K beginning with its first taxable year, as specified in § 1.761-2(b)(2)(ii), is not required to file a partnership return.

(d) *Definitions.*—(1) *Partnership.*—For the meaning of the term *partnership*, see § 1.761-1(a).

(2) *United States person.*—In applying this section, a United States person is a person described in section 7701(a)(30); the government of the United States, a State, or the District of Columbia (including an agency or instrumentality thereof); or a corporation created or organized in Guam, the Commonwealth of Northern Mariana Islands, the U.S. Virgin Islands, and American Samoa, if the requirements of section 881(b)(1)(A), (B), and (C) are met for such corporation. The term does not include an alien indi-

vidual who is a resident of Puerto Rico, Guam, the Commonwealth of Northern Mariana Islands, the U.S. Virgin Islands, or American Samoa, as determined under § 301.7701(b)-1(d) of this chapter.

(3) *United States partner.*—In applying this section, a United States partner is any United States person who holds a direct or indirect interest in the partnership.

(4) *Indirect interest.*—An indirect interest is any interest held through one or more passthrough partners, as defined in section 6231(a)(9).

(e) *Procedural requirements.*—(1) *Place for filing.*—The return of a partnership must be filed with the service center prescribed in the relevant IRS revenue procedure, publication, form, or instructions to the form (see § 601.601(d)(2)).

(2) [Reserved]. For further guidance, see § 1.6031(a)-1T(e)(2).

(3) *Magnetic media filing.*—For magnetic media filing requirements with respect to partnerships, see section 6011(e)(2) and the regulations thereunder.

(f) *Effective dates.*—This section applies to taxable years of a partnership beginning after December 31, 1999, except that —

(1) Paragraph (b)(3) of this section applies to taxable years of a foreign partnership beginning after December 31, 2000; and

(2) Paragraph (a)(3)(ii) of this section applies to taxable years of a partnership beginning on or after November 5, 2003. [Reg. § 1.6031(a)-1.]

☐ [*T.D.* 8841, 11-10-99. *Amended by T.D.* 9000, 6-14-2002; *T.D.* 9094, 11-5-2003; *T.D.* 9123, 4-30-2004, *T.D.* 9177, 2-10-2005 *and T.D.* 9821, 7-18-2017.]

[Reg. § 1.6031(a)-1T]

§ 1.6031(a)-1T. Return of partnership income (temporary).—(a) through (d) [Reserved]. For further guidance, see § 1.6031(a)-1(a) through (d).

(e)(1) [Reserved]. For further guidance, see § 1.6031(a)-1(e)(1).

(2) *Time for filing.*—The return of a partnership must be filed on or before the date prescribed by section 6072(b).

(f) *Applicability date.*—This section applies to returns filed on or after July 20, 2017. Section 1.6031(a)-1 (as contained in 26 CFR part 1, revised April 2017) applies to returns filed before July 20, 2017.

(g) *Expiration date.*—The applicability of this section will expire on or before July 17, 2020. [Temporary Reg. § 1.6031(a)-1T.]

☐ *T.D.* 9821, 7-18-2017.]

[Reg. § 301.6031(a)-1]

§ 301.6031(a)-1. Return of partnership income.—For provisions relating to the requirement of returns of partnership income, see § 1.6031(a)-1 of this chapter. [Reg. § 301.6031(a)-1.]

☐ [*T.D.* 8841, 11-10-99.]

[Reg. § 1.6031(b)-1T]

§ 1.6031(b)-1T. Statements to partners (temporary).—(a) *Statement required to be furnished to partners.*—(1) *In general.*—Except as provided in this paragraph (a)(1) and paragraph (a)(2)(ii) of this section, any partnership required under section 6031(a) and the regulations thereunder to file a partnership return for a taxable year shall furnish to every person who was a partner (within the meaning of section 7701(a)(2)) at any time during the taxable year a written statement containing the information described in paragraph (a)(3) of this section. This section shall not apply to a real estate mortgage investment conduit (REMIC) treated as a partnership under subtitle F of the Code by reason of section 860F(e). For the reporting requirements applicable to REMICs see § 1.6031(b)-2T.

(2) *Special rules applicable to partnership interests held by nominees.*—(i) *Statements furnished to nominees.*—For any partnership taxable year beginning after October 22, 1986, a partnership shall provide a person that holds (directly or indirectly) an interest in such partnership as a nominee on behalf of another person at any time during such year with a statement under paragraph (a)(1) of this section with respect to such interest if—

(A) Such nominee has not furnished the statement required under § 1.6031(c)-1T(a)(1)(i) to the partnership with respect to such other person;

(B) Such nominee either holds legal title to such partnership interest in its own name or is identified in a statement provided to the partnership pursuant to § 1.6031(c)-1T(a)(1)(i) by another nominee as the person on whose behalf such other nominee holds such interest; and

(C) Such nominee is not a person described in § 1.6031(c)-1T(a)(2) (relating to the special rule for clearing agencies).

In such case, the partnership shall assume, for purposes of this section, that the nominee is the beneficial owner of the partnership interest.

(ii) *Statements not required to be furnished to partners holding partnership interests through nominees.*—A partnership shall not be required to furnish a statement under paragraph (a)(1) of this section to a partner with respect to any portion of such partner's interest in the partnership that is owned through a nominee if—

(A) Such nominee has not furnished (or is not required to furnish under § 1.6031(c)-1T(a)(2)), a statement to the partnership under § 1.6031(c)-1T(a)(1)(i) with respect to such partner; and

(B) Such partner has not furnished (or is not required to furnish) a statement to the partnership under § 1.6031(c)-1T(a)(3), with respect to such interest in the partnership.

Reg. § 1.6031(b)-1T(a)(2)(ii)(B)

(3) *Contents of statement.*—The statement required under paragraph (a)(1) of this section shall include the following information:

(i) The partner's distributive share of partnership income, gain, loss, deduction, or credit required to be shown on the partnership return (or, for taxable years beginning before January 1, 1987, the partner's distributive share of partnership income, gain, loss, deduction, or credit shown on the partnership return); and

(ii) To the extent provided by form or the accompanying instructions, any additional information that may be required to apply particular provisions of subtitle A of the Code to the partner with respect to items related to the partnership.

(b) *Time for furnishing statement.*—The statement required to be furnished by the partnership under paragraph (a)(1) of this section shall be furnished on or before the day on which the partnership return for that taxable year is required to be filed (determined with regard to extensions). For partnership returns the due date for which (determined without regard to extensions) is before January 1, 1987, the statement required to be furnished by the partnership under paragraph (a)(1) of this section shall be furnished on or before the day on which the partnership return is filed.

(c) *Statement may be provided to agent.*—If a partner designates another person, such as an attorney or an investment advisor, as the partner's (or nominee's) agent in dealing with the partnership, the partnership may provide the statement required under paragraph (a)(1) of this section with respect to such partner to such other person instead of the partner.

(d) *Penalties.*—For penalties for failure to comply with the requirements of section 6031(b) and paragraph (a) of this section, see section 6722(a).

(e) *Effective date.*—Except as otherwise provided in this section, the provisions of this section apply to partnership taxable years beginning after September 3, 1982. [Temporary Reg. § 1.6031(b)-1T.]

☐ [*T.D.* 8225, 9-6-88.]

[Reg. § 1.6031(b)-2T]

§ 1.6031(b)-2T. REMIC reporting requirements(temporary).—[Reserved].—

[Reg. § 1.6031(c)-1T]

§ 1.6031(c)-1T. Nominee reporting of partnership information (temporary).—(a) *Statements required to be furnished to partnership.*—(1) *Statement from nominee.*—(i) *In general.*—Except as otherwise provided in this section, any person who holds, directly or indirectly, an interest in a partnership (required under section 6031(a) and the regulations thereunder to file a partnership return for a taxable year) as a nominee on behalf of another person at any time during the partnership taxable year shall furnish to the partnership a written statement (or statements) for that

taxable year with respect to such other person containing the information described in paragraph (a)(1)(ii) of this section.

(ii) *Contents of statement.*—The statement required under paragraph (a)(1)(i) of this section shall, except as otherwise provided in paragraph (a)(4) of this section, include the following information:

(A) The name, address, and taxpayer identification number of the nominee;

(B) The name, address, and taxpayer identification number of such other person;

(C) Whether such other person is—

(1) A person that is not a United States person;

(2) A foreign government, an international organization, or any wholly-owned agency or instrumentality of either of the foregoing; or

(3) A tax-exempt entity (within the meaning of section 168(h)(2));

(D) A description of any interest in the partnership held by the nominee on behalf of such other person at the beginning of the partnership taxable year;

(E) A description of any interest in the partnership that the nominee acquires (within the meaning of paragraph (g)(1) of this section) on behalf of such other person during the partnership taxable year, the method of acquisition (e.g., purchase, exchange, acquisition at death, gift, or commencement of nominee relationship) and acquisition cost (within the meaning of paragraph (g)(2) of this section) of such interest, and the date of the acquisition of such interest; and

(F) A description of any interest in the partnership that the nominee transfers (within the meaning of paragraph (g)(5) of this section) on behalf of such other person during the partnership taxable year, the net proceeds from the transfer (within the meaning of paragraph (g)(6) of this section) of such interest, and the date of the transfer of such interest.

A description of a partnership interest must include sufficient detail to enable the partnership to furnish to such other person the statement required under § 1.6031(b)-1T(a).

(2) *Special rule for clearing agencies.*—A clearing agency registered pursuant to the provisions of section 17A of the Securities Exchange Act of 1934 (or its nominee) that holds an interest in a partnership as a nominee on behalf of another person shall not be required to furnish any statement described in paragraph (a)(1)(i) of this section with respect to such interest.

(3) *Special rule for brokers and financial institutions.*—(i) *Additional statement required.*—Any broker (within the meaning of paragraph (g)(3) of this section) or financial institution (within the meaning of paragraph (g)(4) of this section) that holds an interest in a partnership indirectly through a nominee described in paragraph (a)(2) of this section at any time during a partnership taxable year shall furnish (in addition to any

statement (or statements) required under paragraph (a)(1)(i) of this section) to the partnership a written statement (or statements) containing the information described in paragraph (a)(3)(ii) of this section with respect to any interest in such partnership that it holds (directly or indirectly) for its own account at any time during such partnership taxable year.

(ii) *Contents of statement.*—The statement required under paragraph (a)(3)(i) of this section shall, except as otherwise provided in paragraph (a)(4) of this section, include the following information:

(A) The name, address, and taxpayer identification number of the broker or financial institution;

(B) Whether such broker or financial institution is a person that is not a United States person;

(C) A description of any interest in the partnership held by the broker or financial institution for its own account at the beginning of the partnership taxable year;

(D) A description of any interest in the partnership that the broker or financial institution acquires for its own account during the partnership taxable year, the method of acquisition and acquisition cost of such interest, and the date of the acquisition of such interest; and

(E) A description of any interest in the partnership that the broker or financial institution transfers for its own account during the partnership taxable year, the net proceeds from the transfer of such interest, and the date of the transfer of such interest.

A description of a partnership interest held by a broker or financial institution for its own account must include sufficient detail to enable the partnership to furnish to the broker or financial institution the statement required under § 1.6031(b)-1T(a).

(4) *Exception.*—(i) *In general.*—Except as otherwise provided in this paragraph (a)(4), any statement required under paragraph (a)(1)(i) or (3)(i) of this section for a taxable year is not required to include—

(A) That part of the information described in paragraph (a)(1)(ii)(E) and (3)(ii)(D) of this section regarding the method of acquisition and acquisition cost; or

(B) That part of the information described in paragraph (a)(1)(ii)(F) and (3)(ii)(E) of this section regarding the net proceeds from the transfer;

to the extent that, prior to the beginning of the partnership taxable year, the partnership has provided the nominee with a written statement that the nominee need not provide such information to the partnership, and the partnership has not modified or revoked such statement. For purposes of the preceding sentence, the modification or revocation of a statement furnished to a nominee is effective for a partnership taxable year if and only if the partnership notifies the nominee of such modification or revocation by a written statement more than 60 days before the beginning of the partnership taxable year. The nominee shall retain a copy of any statement that is furnished to it by the partnership under this paragraph (a)(4) in the nominee's records so long as the contents thereof may become material in the administration of any internal revenue law.

(ii) *Effect of election under section 754.*—Paragraph (a)(4)(i)(A) of this section shall not apply to a partnership taxable year if—

(A) The partnership has an election in effect under section 754 (relating to optional adjustment to basis of partnership property) for such taxable year; and

(B) The nominee knows or has reason to know of such election more than 60 days before the beginning of such taxable year.

(5) *Examples.*—The following examples illustrate the application of this paragraph (a):

Example (1). B, a broker, holds 50 units of interest in Partnership P, a calendar year partnership, in street name for customer A, the beneficial owner. B holds the units on behalf of A at all times during 1989. B must furnish a statement to P for calendar year 1989 under paragraph (a)(1)(i) of this section that includes the information required under paragraph (a)(1)(ii)(A) through (D) of this section. The description of the partnership interest held by B on A's behalf on January 1, 1989, must identify the number of units of P held by B on A's behalf at that time (50), and the class of the partnership interest (including the Committee on Uniform Security Identification Procedures (CUSIP) number of the partnership interest, if known).

Example (2). The facts are the same as in example (1), except that pursuant to A's instructions, B sells 25 of A's units of interest in P on August 1, 1989, receiving net proceeds from the transfer of $500. In addition to the information described in example (1), the statement that B must furnish to P must include the class of the partnership interest transferred (including the CUSIP number of the partnership interest, if known), the number of units transferred (25), the net proceeds from the transfer ($500), and the date of the transfer (August 1, 1989).

Example (3). The facts are the same as in example (1), except that A is not the beneficial owner, but rather holds the units as a nominee on behalf of C, the beneficial owner, at all times during 1989. In addition to the statement that B must furnish to P (as described in Example (1) of this paragraph (a)(5)), A must furnish a statement to P for calendar year 1989 under paragraph (a)(1)(i) of this section that includes the information required under paragraph (a)(1)(ii)(A) through (D) of this section. If both A and B provide P with the statement required under paragraph (a)(1)(i) of this section, P must provide C with the statement required under § 1.6031(b)-1T(a)(1).

(b) *Time for furnishing statements.*—A nominee may furnish to the partnership any statement required under paragraph (a) of this section annually, quarterly, monthly, or on any other basis, provided that all statements required to be furnished under paragraph (a) of this section for a partnership taxable year shall be furnished on or before the last day of the first month following the close of such partnership taxable year.

(c) *Use of magnetic media.*—A nominee required to furnish a written statement under paragraph (a) of this section, may, in lieu of furnishing such written statement, furnish the required information on magnetic tape or by other media if the partnership and the nominee so agree.

(d) *Use of single document.*—Any person who holds interests in a partnership as a nominee on behalf of more than one other person during the partnership taxable year may, in lieu of furnishing to the partnership a separate statement for each such other person, furnish to the partnership a single document which includes, for each such other person, the information described in paragraph (a)(1)(ii) of this section. To the extent that a single document is used, references in this section to the statement required under paragraph (a)(1)(i) of this section shall be deemed to refer also to the information included in a single document under this paragraph (d).

(e) *Retention of information.*—The nominee shall retain a copy of any statement that is furnished to the partnership under this section in the nominee's records so long as the contents thereof may become material in the administration of any internal revenue law.

(f) *Use of agent.*—If a partnership has designated another person, such as a clearing organization, as the partnership's agent for purposes of receiving the statements required under paragraph (a) of this section, such statements may be furnished to that other person instead of the partnership. If a nominee has designated another person as its agent for purposes of furnishing to the partnership (or its agent) the statements required under paragraph (a) of this section, that other person may furnish such statements to the partnership (or its agent) on behalf of the nominee.

(g) *Meaning of terms.*—For purposes of this section, the following terms have the meanings set forth below:

(1) The term "acquires" means—

(i) A purchase or other acquisition of a partnership interest; or

(ii) The commencement of a nominee relationship, including the substitution of one nominee for another.

(2) The term "acquisition cost" means the sum of any money paid and the fair market value of any property (other than money) transferred to acquire a partnership interest increased by any expenses paid or incurred with respect to the acquisition (such as broker's fees or commissions).

(3) The term "broker" shall have the meaning set forth in paragraph (a)(1) of § 1.6045-1.

(4) The term "financial institution" means a financial institution such as a bank, mutual savings bank, savings and loan association, building and loan association, cooperative bank, homestead association, credit union, industrial loan association or bank, or other similar organization.

(5) The term "transfer" means—

(i) A sale, exchange, or other disposition of a partnership interest; or

(ii) The termination of a nominee relationship, including the substitution of one nominee for another.

(6) The term "net proceeds from the transfer" means the sum of any money and the fair market value of any property (other than money) received in connection with a transfer of a partnership interest reduced by any expenses paid or incurred with respect to the transfer (such as broker's fees or commissions).

(7) The term "person" includes the United States, a State, the District of Columbia, a foreign government, a political subdivision of a State or foreign government, or an international organization.

(h) *Statement required by nominees that do not comply with § 1.6031(c)-1T(a).*—(1) *In general.*—Any person that—

(i) Holds an interest in a partnership as a nominee (other than a nominee described in paragraph (a)(3) of this section) on behalf of another person at any time during the partnership taxable year;

(ii) Does not furnish to such partnership the statement required under paragraph (a)(1)(i) of this section for such other person with respect to such interest in the partnership; and

(iii) Receives from such partnership the statement described in paragraph (a)(1) of § 1.6031(b)-1T with respect to such interest in the partnership;

shall furnish to such other person a written statement containing the information described in paragraph (h)(2) of this section with respect to such interest in the partnership.

(2) *Contents of statement.*—The statement required under paragraph (h)(1) of this section shall contain the following information:

(i) The distributive share of partnership income, gain, loss, deduction, or credit required to be shown on the partnership return that is allocable to such interest in the partnership; and

(ii) Any additional information that may be required to apply particular provisions of subtitle A of the Code to the beneficial owner of such interest in the partnership in connection with items related to the partnership.

(3) *Time for furnishing statements.*—A nominee shall furnish the statement required under paragraph (h)(1) of this section within 30 days after receiving the statement described in paragraph (a) of § 1.6031(b)-1T.

(i) *REMICs.*—This section shall not apply with respect to any interest in a real estate mortgage investment conduit (REMIC) treated as a partnership under subtitle F of the Code by reason of section 860F(e). For the nominee reporting requirements with respect to REMICs see § 1.6031(c)-2T.

(j) *Penalties.*—[Reserved].

(k) *Effective date.*—(1) *In general.*—Except as otherwise provided in paragraph (k)(2) of this section, the provisions of this section shall apply to partnership taxable years beginning after October 22, 1986.

(2) *Transitional rule for taxable years beginning before January 1, 1989.*—For partnership taxable years beginning before January 1, 1989,—

(i) Any statement that a nominee is required to furnish to a partnership under paragraph (a)(1) of this section shall not be required to include the following information:

(A) The information described in paragraph (a)(1)(ii)(C) of this section;

(B) That part of the information described in paragraph (a)(1)(ii)(E) of this section regarding the method of acquisition and acquisition cost of a partnership interest; or

(C) That part of the information described in paragraph (a)(1)(ii)(F) of this section regarding the net proceeds from the transfer of a partnership interest.

(ii) A broker or financial institution shall not be required to furnish the additional statement described in paragraph (a)(3)(i) of this section. [Temporary Reg. § 1.6031(c)-1T.]

☐ [*T.D.* 8225, 9-6-88.]

[Reg. § 1.6031(c)-2T]

§ 1.6031(c)-2T. Nominee reporting of REMIC information (temporary).—[Reserved]

[Reg. § 1.6032-1]

§ 1.6032-1. Returns of banks with respect to common trust funds.—[Reserved]. For further guidance, see § 1.6032-1T. [Reg. § 1.6032-1.]

☐ [*T.D.* 6364, 2-13-59. *Amended by T.D.* 7564, 9-11-78, *T.D.* 7935, 1-12-84 *and T.D.* 9821, 7-18-2017.]

[Reg. § 1.6032-1T]

§ 1.6032-1T. Returns of banks with respect to common trust funds.—(a) Every bank (as defined in section 581) maintaining a common trust fund shall make a return of income of the common trust fund, regardless of the amount of its taxable income. Member banks of an affiliated group that serve as co-trustees with respect to a common trust fund must act jointly in making a return for the fund. If a bank maintains more than one common trust fund, a separate return shall be made for each. No particular form is prescribed for making the return under this section, but Form 1065 may be used if it is designated by the bank as the return of a common trust fund. The return shall be made for the taxable year of the common trust fund and shall be filed on or before the date prescribed by section 6072(b) with the service center prescribed in the relevant IRS revenue procedure, publication, form, or instructions to the form (see § 601.601(d)(2) of this chapter). Such return shall state specifically with respect to the fund the items of gross income and the deductions allowed by subtitle A of the Code, shall include each participant's name and address, the participant's proportionate share of taxable income or net loss (exclusive of gains and losses from sales or exchanges of capital assets), the participant's proportionate share of gains and losses from sales or exchanges of capital assets, and the participant's share of items which enter into the determination of the tax imposed by section 56. See §§ 1.584-2 and 1.58-5. If the common trust fund is maintained by two or more banks that are members of the same affiliated group, the return must also identify the member bank in the group that has contributed each participant's property or money to the fund. A copy of the plan of the common trust fund must be filed with the return. If, however, a copy of such plan has once been filed with a return, it need not again be filed if the return contains a statement showing when and where it was filed. If the plan is amended in any way after such copy has been filed, a copy of the amendment must be filed with the return for the taxable year in which the amendment was made. For the signing of a return of a bank with respect to common trust funds, see § 1.6062-1, relating to the manner prescribed for the signing of a return of a corporation.

(b) This section applies to returns filed on or after July 20, 2017. Section 1.6032-1 (as contained in 26 CFR part 1, revised April 2017) applies to taxable years beginning before July 20, 2017.

(c) The applicability of this section will expire on or before July 17, 2020. [Temporary Reg. § 1.6032-1T.]

☐ *T.D.* 9821, 7-18-2017.]

[Reg. § 301.6032-1]

§ 301.6032-1. Returns of banks with respect to common trust funds.—For provisions relating to requirement of returns of banks with respect to common trust funds, see § 1.6032-1 of this chapter (Income Tax Regulations). [Reg. § 301.6032-1.]

☐ [*T.D.* 6498, 10-24-60.]

[Reg. § 1.6033-1]

§ 1.6033-1. Returns by exempt organizations; taxable years beginning before January 1, 1970.—[The text of Reg. § 1.6033-1, relating to returns by exempt organizations for taxable years beginning before 1970, is no longer reproduced by CCH. Present rules are contained in Reg. § 1.6033-2.]

[Reg. § 301.6033-1]

§ 301.6033-1. Returns by exempt organizations.—For provisions relating to the requirement of returns by exempt organizations, see

§1.6033-1 of this chapter (Income Tax Regulations). [Reg. §301.6033-1.]

☐ [T.D. 6498, 10-24-60.]

[Reg. §1.6033-2]

§1.6033-2. Return by exempt organizations (taxable years beginning after December 31, 1969) and returns by certain nonexempt organizations (taxable years beginning after December 31, 1980).—(a) *In general.*—(1) Except as provided in section 6033(a)(3) and paragraph (g) of this section, every organization exempt from taxation under section 501(a) shall file an annual information return specifically setting forth its items of gross income, gross receipts and disbursements, and such other information as may be prescribed in the instructions, issued with respect to the return. Except as provided in paragraph (d) of this section, such return shall be filed annually regardless of whether such organization is chartered by, or affiliated or associated with, any central, parent, or other organization.

(2)(i) Except as otherwise provided in this paragraph and paragraph (g) of this section, every organization exempt from taxation under section 501(a), and required to file a return under section 6033 and this section (including, for taxable years ending before December 31, 1972, private foundations, as defined in section 509(a)), other than an organization described in section 401(a) or 501(d), shall file its annual return on Form 990. For taxable years ending on or after December 31, 1972, every private foundation shall file Form 990-PF as its annual information return. For taxable years beginning after December 31, 1977, every section 501(c)(21) black lung trust shall file an annual information return on Form 990-BL or any other form prescribed by the Internal Revenue Service for that purpose.

(ii) The information generally required to be furnished by an organization exempt under section 501(a) is:

(a) Its gross income for the year. For this purpose, gross income includes tax-exempt income, but does not include contributions, gifts, grants, and similar amounts received. Whether an item constitutes a contribution, gift, grant, or similar amount depends upon all the surrounding facts and circumstances. The computation of gross income shall be made by subtracting the cost of goods sold from all receipts other than gross contributions, gifts, grants and similar amounts received and nonincludible dues and assessments from members and affiliates.

(b) To the extent not included in gross income, its dues and assessments from members and affiliates for the year.

(c) Its expenses incurred within the year attributable to gross income.

(d) Its disbursements (including prior years' accumulations) made within the year for the purposes for which it is exempt.

(e) A balance sheet showing its assets, liabilities, and net worth as of the beginning and end of such year. Detailed information relating to the assets, liabilities, and net worth shall be furnished on the schedule provided for this purpose on the return required by this section. Such schedule shall be supplemented by attachments where appropriate.

(f) The total of the contributions, gifts, grants and similar amounts received by it during the taxable year, and the names and addresses of all persons who contributed, bequeathed, or devised $5,000 or more (in money or other property) during the taxable year. In the case of a private foundation (as defined in section 509(a)), the names and addresses of all persons who became substantial contributors (as defined in section 507(d)(2)) during the taxable year shall be furnished. In addition, for its first taxable year beginning after December 31, 1969, each private foundation shall furnish the names and addresses of all persons who became substantial contributors before such taxable year. For special rules with respect to contributors and donors, see subdivision (iii) of this subparagraph.

(g) The names and addresses of all officers, directors, or trustees (or any person having responsibilities or powers similar to those of officers, directors or trustees) of the organization, and, in the case of a private foundation, all persons who are foundation managers, within the meaning of section 4946(b)(1). Organizations must also attach a schedule showing the names and addresses and/or total numbers of key employees, highly compensated employees, and independent contractors as prescribed by publication, form, or instructions.

(h) A schedule showing the compensation and other payments made to each person whose name is required to be listed pursuant to paragraph (a)(2)(ii)(g) of this section during the calendar year ending within the organization's annual accounting period, or during such other period as prescribed by publication, form, or instructions.

(i) For any taxable year ending on or after December 31, 1971, such information as is required by Forms 4848 and 4849 and, only with respect to any such taxable year ending before December 31, 1972, such information as is required by Form 2950. Such forms are required by this section to be filed by an organization exempt from tax under section 501(a) which is an employer who maintains a funded pension or annuity plan for its employees. See paragraph (g) of this section for exceptions from filing. Form 4849 need not be filed by the organization if the fiduciary for the plan has given written notification to the organization that such form will be filed as an attachment to Form 990-P filed by the fiduciary. Form 4848 (and Form 4849 if required to be filed by the organization) shall be filed as a separate return on or before the due date for Form 990. For rules relating to the extension of time for filing, see section 6081 and the regulations thereunder and the instructions for Form 4848. A central organization which files Form 990 as a group return under paragraph (d) of this section may also file Form 4848 as a group return. The rules provided by paragraph (d) of this section with respect to a group return filed on

Form 990 shall apply to a group return filed on Form 4848. Unless otherwise expressly provided therein, an authorization to include a local organization in a group for purposes of filing Form 990 as a group return shall be treated as an authorization to include such local organization in a group for purposes of filing Form 4848 as a group return. A group return on Form 4848 shall be filed in accordance with this section and the instructions to Form 4848 and shall be considered the return of each local organization included therein. In addition to the information required to be furnished by Forms 4848 and 4849, the district director may require any further information that he considers necessary to determine qualification of the plan under section 401 or the taxability under section 403(b) of a beneficiary under an annuity purchased by a section 501(c)(3) organization.

(j) In the case of a private foundation liable for tax imposed under Chapter 42, such information as is required by Form 4720.

(k) Its lobbying expenditures, grass roots expenditures, exempt purpose expenditures, lobbying nontaxable amount, and grass roots nontaxable amount for the taxable year and for prior taxable years that are base years (within the meaning of §1.501(h)-3(c)(7)), if the organization has an election under section 501(h) in effect for the taxable year. An organization that is a member of an affiliated group of organizations (as defined in §56.4911-7(e)) but that is not a member of a limited affiliated group (as defined in §56.4911-10(b)) shall report this information based on the expenditures of all members of the group during the taxable year of the group that ends with or within the member's taxable year and for prior taxable years of the group that are base years (within the meaning of §56.4911-9(b)). For additional information required to be furnished by members of an affiliated group of organizations, and by controlling members in a limited affiliated group, see §§56.4911-9(d) and 56.4911-10(f)(1), respectively.

(l) In the case of a hospital organization (as defined in §1.501(r)-1(b)(18)) described in section 501(c)(3) during the taxable year—

(1) A copy of its audited financial statements for the taxable year (or, in the case of an organization the financial statements of which are included in consolidated financial statements with other organizations, such consolidated financial statements);

(2) Either a copy of the most recently adopted implementation strategy, within the meaning of §1.501(r)-3(c), for each hospital facility it operates or the URL of each Web page where it has made each such implementation strategy widely available on a Web site within the meaning of §1.501(r)-1(b)(29) along with or as part of the report documenting the community health needs assessment (CHNA) to which the implementation strategy relates;

(3) For each hospital facility it operates, a description of the actions taken during the taxable year to address the significant health needs identified through its most recently conducted CHNA, within the meaning of §1.501(r)-3(b), or, if no actions were taken with respect to one or more of these health needs, the reason(s) why no actions were taken; and

(4) The amount of the excise tax imposed on the organization under section 4959 during the taxable year.

(iii) *Special rules.*—In providing the names and addresses of contributors and donors under subdivision (ii)(f) of this subparagraph—

(a) An organization described in section 501(c)(3) which meets the 33⅓ percent-of-support test of the regulations under section 170(b)(1)(A)(vi) (without regard to whether such organization otherwise qualifies as an organization described in section 170(b)(1)(A)) is required to provide the name and address of a person who contributed, bequeathed, or devised $5,000 or more during the year only if his amount is in excess of 2 percent of the total contributions, bequests and devises received by the organization during the year.

(b) An organization other than a private foundation is required to report only the names and addresses of contributors of whom it has actual knowledge. For instance, an organization need not require an employer who withholds contributions from the compensation of employees and pays over to the organization periodically the total amounts withheld, to specify the amounts paid over with respect to a particular employee. In such case, unless the organization has actual knowledge that a particular employee gave more than $5,000 (and in excess of 2 percent if (a) of this subdivision is applicable), the organization need report only the name and address of the employer, and the total amount paid over by him.

(c) Separate and independent gifts made by one person in a particular year need be aggregated to determine if his contributions and bequests exceed $5,000 (and in excess of 2 percent if (a) of this subdivision is applicable), only if such gifts are of $1,000 or more.

(d)(1) Organizations described in section 501(c)(8) or (10) (and, for taxable years beginning after December 31, 1970, organizations described in section 501(c)(7)) that receive contributions or bequests to be used exclusively for purposes described in section 170(c)(4), 2055(a)(3), or 2522(a)(3), must attach a schedule with respect to all gifts which aggregate more than $1,000 from any one person showing the name of the donor, the amount of the contribution or bequest, the specific purpose for which such amount was received, and the specific use to which such amount was put. In the case of an amount set aside for such purposes, the organization shall indicate the manner in which such amount is held (for instance, whether such amount is commingled with amounts held for other purposes). If the contribution or bequest was transferred to another organization, the schedule must include the name of the transferee organization, a description of the nature of such organization, and a description of the relationship between the transferee and transferor organizations.

(2) For taxable years beginning after December 31, 1970, such organizations must also attach a statement showing the total dollar amount of contributions and bequests received for such purposes which are $1,000 or less.

(iv) *Listing of States.*—A private foundation is required to attach to its return required by this section a list of all States—

(a) to which the organization reports in any fashion concerning its organization, assets, or activities, or

(b) with which the organization has registered (or which it has otherwise notified in any manner) that it intends to be, or is, a charitable organization or a holder of property devoted to a charitable purpose.

(3)(i) For taxable years beginning after December 31, 1969, and ending before December 31, 1971, every employee's trust described in section 401(a) which is exempt from taxation under section 501(a) shall file an annual return on Form 990-P. The return shall include the information required by paragraph (b)(5)(ii) of § 1.401-1. For such years, in addition, the trust must file the information required to be filed by the employer pursuant to the provisions of § 1.404(a)-2, unless the employer has notified the trustee in writing that he has filed or will timely file such information. If the trustee has received such notification from the employer, then such notification, or a copy thereof, shall be retained by the trust as a part of its records.

(ii) For taxable years ending on or after December 31, 1971, and before December 31, 1975, every employee's trust described in section 401(a) which is exempt from taxation under section 501(a) shall file an annual return on Form 990-P. The trust shall furnish such information as is required by such form and the instructions issued with respect thereto.

(4) For taxable years beginning after December 31, 1980, trusts described in section 4947(a)(1) and nonexempt private foundations shall comply with the requirements of section 6033 and this section in the same manner as organizations described in section 501(c)(3) which are exempt from tax under section 501(a). This section shall be applied for taxable years beginning after December 31, 1980 as if trusts described in section 4947(a)(1) and nonexempt private foundations were described in section 501(c)(3). Therefore, for purposes of this section, all references to exempt organizations shall include section 4947(a)(1) trusts and nonexempt private foundations and all references to private foundations shall include section 4947(a)(1) trusts that would be private foundations if they were described in section 501(c)(3) and all nonexempt private foundations. Similarly, for purposes of paragraph (a)(2)(ii)(d), the purposes for which a section 4947(a)(1) trust or a nonexempt private foundation is organized shall be treated as the purposes for which it is exempt. For pur-

poses of this section, the term "nonexempt private foundation" means a taxable organization (other than a section 4947(a)(1) trust) that is a private foundation. See section 509(b) and § 1.509(b)-1. See also section 642(c)(6) and § 1.642(c)-4.

(b) *Accounting period for filing return.*—A return required by this section shall be on the basis of the established annual accounting period of the organization. If the organization has no such established accounting period, such return shall be on the basis of the calendar year.

(c) *Returns when exempt status not established.*—An organization claiming an exempt status under section 501(a) prior to the establishment of such exempt status under section 501 and § 1.501(a)-1, shall file a return required by this section in accordance with the instructions applicable thereto. In such case the organization must indicate on such return that it is being filed in the belief that the organization is exempt under section 501(a), but that the Internal Revenue Service has not yet recognized such exemption.

(d) *Group returns.*—(1) A central, parent, or like organization (referred to in this paragraph as "central organization"), exempt under section 501(a) and described in section 501(c) (other than a private foundation), although required to file a separate annual return for itself under section 6033 and paragraph (a) of this section, may file annually, in addition to such separate annual return, a group return on Form 990. Such group return may be filed for two or more of the local organizations, chapters, or the like (referred to in this paragraph as "local organizations") which are (i) affiliated with such central organization at the close of its annual accounting period, (ii) subject to the general supervision or control of the central organization, and (iii) exempt from taxation under the same paragraph of section 501(c) of the Code, although the local organizations are not necessarily exempt under the paragraph under which the central organization is exempt. Such group return may not be filed for a local organization which is a private foundation.

(2)(i) The filing of the group return shall be in lieu of the filing of a separate return by each of the local organizations included in the group return. The group return shall include only those local organizations which in writing have authorized the central organization to include them in the group return, and which have made and filed, with the central organization, their statements, specifically stating their items of gross income, receipts, and disbursements, and such other information relating to them as is required to be stated in the group return. Such an authorization and statement by a local organization shall be made under the penalties of perjury, shall be signed by a duly authorized officer of the local organization in his official capacity, and shall contain the following statement, or a statement of like import: "I hereby declare under the penalties of perjury that this authorization (including any accompanying schedules and statements) has been examined by me and to the best of my knowledge and belief is true, correct and complete and made in good faith." Such authorization and statement with respect to a local organization shall be retained by the central organization until the expiration of six years after the last taxable year for which a group return filed by such central organization includes such local organization.

(ii) There shall be attached to the group return and made a part thereof a schedule showing the name, address, and employer identification number of each of the local organizations and the total number thereof included in such return, and a schedule showing the name, address, and employer identification number of each of the local organizations and the total number thereof not included in the group return.

(3) The group return shall be on the basis of the established annual accounting period of the central organization. Where such central organization has no established annual accounting period, such return shall be on the basis of the calendar year. The same income, receipts, and disbursements of a local organization shall not be included in more than one group return.

(4) The group return shall be filed in accordance with these regulations and the instructions issued with respect to Form 990, and shall be considered the return of each local organization included therein. The tax exempt status of a local organization must be established under a group exemption letter issued to the central organization before a group return including the local organization will be considered as the return of the local organization. See § 1.501(a)-1 for requirements for establishing a tax-exempt status.

(5) In providing the information required by paragraph (a)(2)(ii)(f),(g), and (h) of this section, such information may be provided—

(i) with respect to the central or parent organization on its Form 990, and with respect to the local organizations on separate schedules attached to the group return for the year, or

(ii) on a consolidated basis for all the local organizations and the central or parent organization on the group return.

Such information need be provided only with respect to those local organizations which are not excepted from filing under the provisions of paragraph (g) of this section. A central or parent organization shall indicate whether it has provided such information in the manner described in subdivision (i) or in subdivision (ii) of this subparagraph, and may not change the manner in which it provides such information without the consent of the Commissioner.

(e) [Reserved]. For further guidance, see § 1.6033-2T(e).

(f) *Penalties and additions to tax.*—For penalties and additions to tax for failure to file a return and filing a false or fraudulent return, see sections 6652, 7203, 7206 and 7207.

(g) *Organizations not required to file annual returns.*—(1) Annual returns required by this sec-

tion are not required to be filed by an organization exempt from taxation under section 501(a) which is—

(i) A church, an interchurch organization of local units of a church, a convention or association of churches, or an integrated auxiliary of a church (as defined in paragraph (h) of this section);

(ii) An exclusively religious activity of any religious order;

(iii) An organization (other than a private foundation) described in section 6033(a)(3)(C), the gross receipts of which in each taxable year are normally not more than $5,000 (as described in paragraph (g)(3) of this section);

(iv) A mission society (other than an organization described in section 509(a)(3)) sponsored by or affiliated with one or more churches or church denominations, more than one-half of the activities of which society are conducted in, or directed at persons in foreign countries;

(v) A State institution, the income of which is excluded from gross income under section 115(a);

(vi) An organization described in section 501(c)(1), or

(vii) An educational organization (below college level) that is described in section 170(b)(1)(A)(ii), that has a program of a general academic nature, and that is affiliated (within the meaning of paragraph (h)(2) of this section) with a church or operated by a religious order.

(2) The provisions of section 6033(a) relieving certain specified types of organizations exempt from taxation under section 501(a) from filing annual returns do not abridge or impair in any way the powers and authority of district directors or directors of service centers provided for in other provisions of the Code and in regulations thereunder to require the filing of returns or notices by such organizations. See section 6001 and § 1.6001-1.

(3) For purposes of subparagraph (1)(iii) of this paragraph, the gross receipts (as defined in subparagraph (4) of this paragraph) of an organization are normally not more than $5,000 if—

(i) In the case of an organization which has been in existence for one year or less, the organization has received, or donors have pledged to give, gross receipts of $7,500 or less during the first taxable year of the organization;

(ii) In the case of an organization which has been in existence for more than one but less than 3 years, the average of the gross receipts received by the organization in its first 2 taxable years is $6,000 or less, and

(iii) In the case of an organization which has been in existence for 3 years or more, the average of the gross receipts received by the organization in the immediately preceding 3 taxable years, including the year for which the return would be required to be filed, is $5,000 or less.

(4) For purposes of this paragraph and paragraph (a)(2) of this section, "gross receipts" means the gross amount received by the organi-

zation during its annual accounting period from all sources without reduction for any costs or expenses including, for example, cost of goods or assets sold, cost of operations, or expenses of earning, raising, or collecting such amounts. Thus "gross receipts" includes, but is not limited to, (i) the gross amount received as contributions, gifts, grants, and similar amounts without reduction for the expenses of raising and collecting such amounts, (ii) the gross amount received as dues or assessments from members or affiliated organizations without reduction for expenses attributable to the receipt of such amounts, (iii) gross sales or receipts from business activities (including business activities unrelated to the purpose for which the organization qualifies for exemption, the net income or loss from which may be required to be reported on Form 990-T), (iv) the gross amount received from the sale of assets without reduction for cost or other basis and expenses of sale, and (v) the gross amount received as investment income, such as interest, dividends, rents, and royalties.

(5) [Reserved].

(6) The Commissioner may relieve any organization or class of organizations (other than an organization described in section 509(a)(3)) from filing, in whole or in part the annual return required by this section where he determines that such returns are not necessary for the efficient administration of the internal revenue laws.

(h) *Integrated auxiliary.*—(1) *In general.*—For purposes of this title, the term *integrated auxiliary of a church* means an organization that is—

　(i) Described both in sections 501(c)(3) and 509(a)(1), (2), or (3);

　(ii) Affiliated with a church or a convention or association of churches; and

　(iii) Internally supported.

(2) *Affiliation.*—An organization is affiliated with a church or a convention or association of churches, for purposes of paragraph (h)(1)(ii) of this section, if—

　(i) The organization is covered by a group exemption letter issued under applicable administrative procedures, (such as Rev. Proc. 80-27 (1980-1 C.B. 677); See § 601.601(a)(2)(ii)(*b*)), to a church or a convention or association of churches;

　(ii) The organization is operated, supervised, or controlled by or in connection with (as defined in § 1.509(a)-4) a church or a convention or association of churches; or

　(iii) Relevant facts and circumstances show that it is so affiliated.

(3) *Facts and circumstances.*—For purposes of paragraph (h)(2)(iii) of this section, relevant facts and circumstances that indicate an organization is affiliated with a church or a convention or association of churches include the following factors. However, the absence of one or more of the following factors does not necessarily preclude classification of an organization as being affiliated with a church or a convention or association of churches—

　(i) The organization's enabling instrument (corporate charter, trust instrument, articles of association, constitution or similar document) or by-laws affirm that the organization shares common religious doctrines, principles, disciplines, or practices with a church or a convention or association of churches;

　(ii) A church or a convention or association of churches has the authority to appoint or remove, or to control the appointment or removal of, at least one of the organization's officers or directors;

　(iii) The corporate name of the organization indicates an institutional relationship with a church or a convention or association of churches;

　(iv) The organization reports at least annually on its financial and general operations to a church or a convention or association of churches;

　(v) An institutional relationship between the organization and a church or a convention or association of churches is affirmed by the church, or convention or association of churches, or a designee thereof; and

　(vi) In the event of dissolution, the organization's assets are required to be distributed to a church or a convention or association of churches, or to an affiliate thereof within the meaning of this paragraph (h).

(4) *Internal support.*—An organization is internally supported, for purposes of paragraph (h)(1)(iii) of this section, unless it both—

　(i) Offers admissions, goods, services or facilities for sale, other than on an incidental basis, to the general public (except goods, services, or facilities sold at a nominal charge or for an insubstantial portion of the cost); and

　(ii) Normally receives more than 50 percent of its support from a combination of governmental sources, public solicitation of contributions, and receipts from the sale of admissions, goods, performance of services, or furnishing of facilities in activities that are not unrelated trades or businesses.

(5) *Special rule.*—Men's and women's organizations, seminaries, mission societies, and youth groups that satisfy paragraphs (h)(1)(i) and (ii) of this section are integrated auxiliaries of a church regardless of whether such an organization meets the internal support requirement under paragraph (h)(1)(iii) of this section.

(6) *Effective date.*—This paragraph (h) applies for returns filed for taxable years beginning after December 31, 1969. For returns filed for taxable years beginning after December 31, 1969 but beginning before December 20, 1995, the definition for the term *integrated auxiliary of a church* set forth in § 1.6033-2(g)(5) (as contained in the 26 CFR edition revised as of April 1, 1995) may be used as an alternative definition to such term set forth in this paragraph (h).

(7) *Examples of internal support.*—The internal support test of this paragraph (h) is illus-

trated by the following examples, in each of which it is assumed that the organization's provision of goods and services does not constitute an unrelated trade or business:

Example 1. Organization A is described in sections 501(c)(3) and 509(a)(2) and is affiliated (within the meaning of this paragraph (h)) with a church. Organization A publishes a weekly newspaper as its only activity. On an incidental basis, some copies of Organization A's publication are sold to nonmembers of the church with which it is affiliated. Organization A advertises for subscriptions at places of worship of the church. Organization A is internally supported, regardless of its sources of financial support, because it does not offer admissions, goods, services, or facilities for sale, other than on an incidental basis, to the general public. Organization A is an integrated auxiliary.

Example 2. Organization B is a retirement home described in sections 501(c)(3) and 509(a)(2). Organization B is affiliated (within the meaning of this paragraph (h)) with a church. Admission to Organization B is open to all members of the community for a fee. Organization B advertises in publications of general distribution appealing to the elderly and maintains its name on non-denominational listings of available retirement homes. Therefore, Organization B offers its services for sale to the general public on more than an incidental basis. Organization B receives a cash contribution of $50,000 annually from the church. Fees received by Organization B from its residents total $100,000 annually. Organization B does not receive any government support or contributions from the general public. Total support is $150,000 ($100,000 + $50,000), and $100,000 of that total is from receipts from the performance of services (66-2/3% of total support). Therefore, Organization B receives more than 50 percent of its support from receipts from the performance of services. Organization B is not internally supported and is not an integrated auxiliary.

Example 3. Organization C is a hospital that is described in sections 501(c)(3) and 509(a)(1). Organization C is affiliated (within the meaning of this paragraph (h)) with a church. Organization C is open to all persons in need of hospital care in the community, although most of Organization C's patients are members of the same denomination as the church with which Organization C is affiliated. Organization C maintains its name on hospital listings used by the general public, and participating doctors are allowed to admit all patients. Therefore, Organization C offers its services for sale to the general public on more than an incidental basis. Organization C annually receives $250,000 in support from the church, $1,000,000 in payments from patients and third party payors (including Medicare, Medicaid and other insurers) for patient care, $100,000 in contributions from the public, $100,000 in grants from the federal government (other than Medicare and Medicaid payments) and $50,000 in investment income. Total support is $1,500,000 ($250,000 + $1,000,000 + $100,000 +

$100,000 + $50,000), and $1,200,000 ($1,000,000 + $100,000 + $100,000) of that total is support from receipts from the performance of services, government sources, and public contributions (80% of total support). Therefore, Organization C receives more than 50 percent of its support from receipts from the performance of services, government sources, and public contributions. Organization C is not internally supported and is not an integrated auxiliary.

(i) *Records, statements, and other returns of tax-exempt organizations.*—(1) An organization that is exempt from taxation under section 501(a) and is not required to file annually an information return required by this section shall immediately notify in writing Exempt Organizations Determinations, at an address prescribed by publication (including publication on the Internal Revenue Service website), of any changes in its character, operations, or purpose for which it was originally created.

(2) Every organization which is exempt from tax, whether or not it is required to file an annual information return, shall submit such additional information as may be required by the Internal Revenue Service for the purpose of inquiring into its exempt status and administering the provisions of subchapter F (section 501 and following), chapter 1 of subtitle A of the Code, section 6033, and chapter 42 of subtitle D of the Code. See section 6001 and § 1.6001-1 with respect to the authority of the district directors or directors of service centers to require such additional information and with respect to the books of accounts or records to be kept by such organizations.

(3) An organization which has established its exemption from taxation under section 501(a), including an organization which is relieved under section 6033 and this section from filing annual returns of information, is not relieved of the duty of filing other returns of information. See, for example, sections 6041, 6043, 6051, 6057, 6058 and the regulations thereunder.

(j) *Unrelated business tax returns.*—In addition to the foregoing requirements of this section, certain organizations otherwise exempt from tax under section 501(a) which are subject to tax on unrelated business taxable income are also required to file returns on Form 990-T. See paragraph (e) of § 1.6012-2 and paragraph (a)(5) of § 1.6012-3 for requirements with respect to such returns.

(k) *Effective/applicability date.*—(1) *Generally.*— The provisions of this section shall apply with respect to returns filed for taxable years beginning after December 31, 1969.

(2) The applicability of paragraphs (g)(1)(iii), (g)(1)(iv), and (g)(6) of this section shall be limited to returns filed for taxable years ending after August 17, 2006. For returns filed for taxable years ending on or before August 17, 2006, § § 1.6033-(2)(g)(1)(iii), 1.6033-(2)(g)(1)(iv), and 1.6033-(2)(g)(6) (as contained in 26 CFR part 1 revised April 1, 2006) shall apply.

(3) The applicability of paragraphs (a)(2)(ii)(g) and (a)(2)(ii)(h) of this section shall be limited to returns filed on or after January 1, 2008. For returns filed before January 1, 2008, §§1.6033-(a)(2)(ii)(g) and 1.6033-2(a)(2)(ii)(h) (as contained in 26 CFR part 1 revised April 1, 2008) shall apply.

(4) The applicability of paragraph (a)(2)(ii)(l) of this section shall be limited to returns filed for taxable years ending after December 29, 2014. [Reg. §1.6033-2.]

☐ [T.D. 7122, 6-7-71. Amended by T.D. 7168, 3-8-72; T.D. 7223, 11-20-72; T.D. 7290, 11-16-73; T.D. 7454, 12-29-76; T.D. 7551, 7-3-78; T.D. 7785, 7-27-81; T.D. 7838, 10-5-82; T.D. 8026, 5-17-85; T.D. 8308, 8-30-90; T.D. 8640, 12-19-95; T.D. 9423, 9-8-2008; T.D. 9549, 9-7-2011, T.D. 9708, 12-29-2014 (corrected 5-1-2015) and T.D. 9821, 7-18-2017.]

[Reg. §1.6033-2T]

§1.6033-2T. Returns by exempt organizations (taxable years beginning after December 31, 1969) and returns by certain nonexempt organizations (taxable years beginning after December 31, 1980) (temporary).—(a) through (d) [Reserved]. For further guidance, see §1.6033-2(a) through (d).

(e) *Time and place for filing.*—The annual return required by this section shall be filed on or before the 15th day of the fifth calendar month following the close of the period for which the return is required to be filed. The annual return on Form 1065 required to be filed by a religious or apostolic association or corporation shall be filed on or before the date prescribed by section 6072(b). Each such return shall be filed in accordance with the instructions applicable thereto.

(f) through (j) [Reserved]. For further guidance, see §1.6033-2(f) through (j).

(k) *Applicability date.*—This section applies to returns filed on or after July 20, 2017. Section 1.6033-2 (as contained in 26 CFR part 1, revised April 2017) applies to returns filed before July 20, 2017.

(l) *Expiration date.*—The applicability of this section will expire on or before July 17, 2020. [Temporary Reg. §1.6033-2T.]

☐ T.D. 9821, 7-18-2017.]

[Reg. §1.6033-3]

§1.6033-3. Additional provisions relating to private foundations.—(a) *In general.*—The foundation managers (as defined in section 4946(b)) of every organization (including a trust described in section 4947(a)(1)) which is (or is treated as) a private foundation (as defined in section 509) the assets of which are at least $5,000 at any time during a taxable year shall include the following information on its annual return in addition to that information required under §1.6033-2(a):

(1) An itemized statement of its securities and all other assets at the close of the year, showing both book and market value,

(2) An itemized list of all grants and contributions made or approved for future payment during the year, showing the amount of each such grant or contribution, the name and address of the recipient (other than a recipient who is not a disqualified person and who receives, from the foundation, grants to indigent or needy persons that, in the aggregate, do not exceed $1,000 during the year), any relationship between any individual recipient and the foundation's managers or substantial contributors, and a concise statement of the purpose of each such grant or contribution,

(3) The address of the principal office of the foundation and (if different) of the place where its books and records are maintained,

(4) The names and addresses of its foundation managers (within the meaning of section 4946(b)), that are substantial contributors (within the meaning of section 507(d)(2)) or that own 10 percent or more of the stock of any corporation of which the foundation owns 10 percent or more of the stock, or corresponding interests in partnerships or other entities, in which the foundation has a 10 percent or greater interest.

For purposes of subparagraph (2) of this paragraph, the business address of an individual grant recipient or foundation manager may be used by the foundation in its annual return in lieu of the home address of such recipient or manager, and the term "relationship" shall include, but is not limited to, any case in which an individual recipient of a grant or contribution by a private foundation is (i) a member of the family (as defined in section 4946(d)) of a substantial contributor or foundation manager of such foundation, (ii) a partner of such substantial contributor or foundation manager, or (iii) an employee of such substantial contributor or foundation manager or of an organization which is effectively controlled (within the meaning of section 4946(a)(1)(H)(i) and the regulations thereunder), directly or indirectly, by one or more such substantial contributors or foundation managers.

(b) *Notice to public of availability of annual return.*—A copy of the notice required by section 6104(d) (relating to public inspection of private foundations' annual returns), and proof of publication thereof, shall be filed with the annual return required by §1.6033-2(a). A copy of such notice as published, and a statement signed by a foundation manager stating that such notice was published, setting forth the date of publication and the publication in which it appeared, shall be sufficient proof of publication for purposes of this paragraph.

(c) *Special rules.*—(1) *Furnishing of copies to State officers.*—The foundation managers of a private foundation shall furnish a copy of the annual return required by section 6033 and §1.6033-2 to the Attorney General of:

(i) each State which the foundation is required to list on its return pursuant to §1.6033-2(a)(2)(iv),

(ii) the State in which is located the principal office of the foundation, and

(iii) the State in which the foundation was incorporated or created.

The annual return shall be sent to each Attorney General described in paragraph (c)(1)(i), (ii), or (iii) of this section at the same time as it is sent to the Internal Revenue Service. Upon request the foundation managers shall also furnish a copy of the annual return to the Attorney General or other appropriate State officer (within the meaning of section 6104(c)(2)) of any state. The foundation managers shall attach to each copy of the annual return sent to State officers under this subparagraph a copy of the Form 4720, if any, filed by the foundation for the year.

(2) *Cross-reference.*—For additional rules with respect to private foundations' returns and the public inspection of such returns, see section 6104(d) and the regulations thereunder.

(d) *Special rules for certain foreign organizations.*—The provisions of paragraphs (b) and (c) of this section shall not apply with respect to an organization described in section 4948(b). The foundation managers of such organizations are not required to publish notice of availability of the annual return for inspection, to make the annual return available at the principal office of the foundation for public inspection under section 6104(d), or to send copies of the annual return to State officers.

(e) *Effective date.*—The provisions of this section shall apply with respect to returns filed for taxable years beginning after December 31, 1980. [Reg. §1.6033-3.]

☐ [*T.D.* 8026, 5-17-85.]

[Reg. §1.6033-4]

§1.6033-4. Required use of magnetic media for returns by organizations required to file returns under section 6033.—The return of an organization that is required to be filed on magnetic media under §301.6033-4 of this chapter must be filed in accordance with Internal Revenue Service revenue procedures, publications, forms, or instructions, including those posted electronically. (See §601.601(d)(2) of this chapter). [Reg. §1.6033-4.]

☐ [*T.D.* 9363, 11-9-2007.]

[Reg. §301.6033-4]

§301.6033-4. Required use of magnetic media for returns by organizations required to file returns under section 6033.—(a) *Returns by organizations required to file returns under section 6033 on magnetic media.*—An organization required to file a return under section 6033 on Form 990, "Return of Organization Exempt from Income Tax," or Form 990-PF, "Return of Private Foundation or Section 4947(a)(1) Trust Treated as a Private Foundation," must file its Form 990 or

990-PF on magnetic media if the organization is required by the Internal Revenue Code or regulations to file at least 250 returns during the calendar year ending with or within its taxable year. Returns filed on magnetic media must be made in accordance with applicable revenue procedures, publications, forms, or instructions. In prescribing revenue procedures, publications, forms, or instructions, the Commissioner may direct the type of magnetic media filing. (See §601.601(d)(2) of this chapter).

(b) *Waiver.*—The Commissioner may grant waivers of the requirements of this section in cases of undue hardship. A request for waiver must be made in accordance with applicable revenue procedures or publications. The waiver also will be subject to the terms and conditions regarding the method of filing as may be prescribed by the Commissioner.

(c) *Failure to file.*—If an organization required to file a return under section 6033 fails to file an information return on magnetic media when required to do so by this section, the organization is deemed to have failed to file the return. (See section 6652 for the addition to tax for failure to file a return.) In determining whether there is reasonable cause for failure to file the return, §301.6652-2(f) and rules similar to the rules in §301.6724-1(c)(3) (undue economic hardship related to filing information returns on magnetic media) will apply.

(d) *Meaning of terms.*—The following definitions apply for purposes of this section:

(1) *Magnetic media.*—The term *magnetic media* means any magnetic media permitted under applicable regulations, revenue procedures, or publications. These generally include magnetic tape, tape cartridge, and diskette, as well as other media, such as electronic filing, specifically permitted under the applicable regulations, procedures, publications, forms or instructions. (See §601.601(d)(2) of this chapter).

(2) *Return required under section 6033.*—The term *return required under section 6033* means a Form 990, "Return of Organization Exempt from Income Tax," and Form 990-PF, "Return of Private Foundation or Section 4947(a)(1) Trust Treated as a Private Foundation," along with all other related forms, schedules, and statements that are required to be attached to the Form 990 or Form 990-PF, and all members of the Form 990 series of returns, including amended and superseding returns.

(3) *Determination of 250 returns.*—For purposes of this section, an organization is required to file at least 250 returns if, during the calendar year ending with or within the taxable year of the organization, the organization is required to file at least 250 returns of any type, including information returns (for example, Forms W-2, Forms 1099), income tax returns, employment tax returns, and excise tax returns. In the case of a short year return, an organization is required to file at least 250 returns if, during the calendar

year which includes the short taxable year of the organization, the organization is required to file at least 250 returns of any type, including information returns (for example, Forms W-2, Forms 1099), income tax returns, employment tax returns, and excise tax returns.

(e) *Example.*—The following example illustrates the provisions of paragraph (d)(3) of this section. In the example, the organization is a calendar year taxpayer:

Example. In 2006, Organization T, with total assets in excess of $10 million, is required to file one Form 990, "Return of Organization Exempt from Income Tax," 200 Forms W-2, "Wage and Tax Statement," one Form 940, "Employer's Annual Federal Unemployment (FUTA) Tax Return," four Forms 941, "Employer's Quarterly Federal Tax Return," and 60 Forms 1099-MISC, "Miscellaneous Income." Because T is required to file 266 returns during the calendar year, T must file its 2006 Form 990 electronically.

(f) *Effective/applicability dates.*—This section applies to any organization required to file Form 990 for a taxable year ending on or after December 31, 2006, that has total assets as of the end of the taxable year of $10 million or more. This section applies to any organization required to file Form 990-PF for taxable years ending on or after December 31, 2006, except for the application of the short year rules in paragraph (d)(3) of this section, which is applicable for taxable years ending on or after November 13, 2007. [Reg. § 301.6033-4.]

☐ [*T.D.* 9363, 11-9-2007.]

[Reg. § 1.6033-5]

§ 1.6033-5. Disclosure by tax-exempt entities that are parties to certain reportable transactions.—(a) *In general.*—Every tax-exempt entity (as defined in section 4965(c)) shall file with the IRS on Form 8886-T, "Disclosure by Tax-Exempt Entity Regarding Prohibited Tax Shelter Transaction" (or a successor form), in accordance with this section and the instructions to the form, a disclosure of—

(1) Such entity's being a party (as defined in § 53.4965-4 of this chapter) to a prohibited tax shelter transaction (as defined in section 4965(e)); and

(2) The identity of any other party (whether taxable or tax-exempt) to such transaction that is known to the tax-exempt entity.

(b) *Frequency of disclosure.*—A single disclosure is required for each prohibited tax shelter transaction.

(c) *By whom disclosure is made.*—(1) *Tax-exempt entities referred to in section 4965(c)(1), (2) or (3).*—In the case of tax-exempt entities referred to in section 4965(c)(1), (2) or (3), the disclosure required by this section must be made by the entity.

(2) *Tax-exempt entities referred to in section 4965(c)(4), (5), (6) or (7).*—In the case of tax-exempt entities referred to in section 4965(c)(4),

(5), (6) or (7), including a fully self-directed qualified plan, IRA, or other savings arrangement, the disclosure required by this section must be made by the entity manager (as defined in section 4965(d)(2)) of the entity.

(d) *Time and place for filing.*—(1) *In general.*—The disclosure required by this section shall be filed on or before May 15 of the calendar year following the close of the calendar year during which the tax-exempt entity entered into the prohibited tax shelter transaction.

(2) *Subsequently listed transactions.*—In the case of subsequently listed transactions (as defined in section 4965(e)(2)), the disclosure required by this section shall be filed on or before May 15 of the calendar year following the close of the calendar year during which the transaction was identified by the Secretary as a listed transaction.

(3) *Transition rule.*—If a tax-exempt entity entered into a prohibited tax shelter transaction after May 17, 2006, and before January 1, 2007, the disclosure required by this section shall be filed on or before November 2, 2007.

(4) *No disclosure.*—Disclosure is not required with respect to any prohibited tax shelter transaction entered into by a tax-exempt entity on or before May 17, 2006.

(e) *Penalty for failure to provide disclosure statement.*—See section 6652(c)(3) for the penalty applicable to the failure to disclose a prohibited tax shelter transaction in accordance with this section.

(f) *Effective date/applicability date.*—This section applies with respect to transactions entered into by a tax-exempt entity after May 17, 2006. [Reg. § 1.6033-5.]

☐ [*T.D.* 9492, 7-2-2010.]

[Reg. § 301.6033-5]

§ 301.6033-5. Disclosure by tax-exempt entities that are parties to certain reportable transactions.—(a) *In general.*—For provisions relating to the requirement of the disclosure by a tax-exempt entity that it is a party to certain reportable transactions, see § 1.6033-5 of this chapter (Income Tax Regulations).

(b) *Effective date/applicability date.*—This section applies with respect to transactions entered into by a tax-exempt entity after May 17, 2006. [Reg. § 301.6033-5.]

☐ [*T.D.* 9492, 7-2-2010.]

[Reg. § 1.6033-6]

§ 1.6033-6. Notification requirement for entities not required to file an annual information return under section 6033(a)(1) (taxable years beginning after December 31, 2006).—(a) *In general.*—Except as otherwise provided in this paragraph, every organization exempt from taxation under section 501(a) that is not required to file a return described in § 1.6033-2(a)(2), other than an organization described in section 401(a) or 501(d), shall submit annually, in electronic form, a notification setting forth the items described in paragraph (c) of this section and such other information as may be prescribed in the instructions and publications issued with respect to the notification.

(b) *Organizations not required to submit annual electronic notification.*—(1) An organization exempt from taxation under section 501(a) that is required to file or files an annual information return under section 6033(a)(1) shall not submit an annual electronic notification under section 6033(i). This includes the following types of organizations:

(i) Any organization included in a group return for that year under § 1.6033-2(d).

(ii) All private foundations required to file under § 1.6033-2(a)(2)(i) Form 990-PF, "Return of Private Foundation or Section 4947(a)(1) Nonexempt Charitable Trust Treated as a Private Foundation."

(iii) Section 509(a)(3) supporting organizations required to file under § 1.6033-2(a)(2)(i) Form 990, "Return of Organization Exempt From Income Tax," or Form 990-EZ, "Short Form Return of Organization Exempt From Income Tax."

(iv) A section 501(c)(21) black lung trust required to file under § 1.6033-2(a)(2)(i) Form 990-BL, "Information and Initial Excise Tax Return for Black Lung Benefit Trusts and Certain Related Persons."

(v) Any organization that is required to file or files an annual information return under section 6033(a)(1) on any other form prescribed by the Internal Revenue Service for that purpose.

(2) An organization exempt from taxation under section 501(a) that is not required to file a return under section 6033(a)(1) is also not required to submit an annual electronic notification under section 6033(i). This includes the following types of organizations:

(i) A church, an interchurch organization of local units of a church, a convention or association of churches, or an integrated auxiliary of a church (as defined in § 1.6033-2(h)).

(ii) An exclusively religious activity of any religious order.

(iii) A mission society sponsored by or affiliated with one or more churches or church denominations, more than one-half of the activities of which society are conducted in, or directed at persons in, foreign countries.

(iv) An educational organization (below college level) described in section 170(b)(1)(A)(ii), that has a program of a general academic nature, and that is affiliated (within the meaning of § 1.6033-2(h)(2)) with a church or operated by a religious order.

(v) A State institution, the income of which is excluded from gross income under section 115(a).

(vi) An organization described in section 501(c)(1).

(vii) An organization that is a governmental unit or an affiliate of a governmental unit

exempt from Federal income tax under section 501(a).

(3) If an organization exempt from taxation under section 501(a) is not described in paragraph (b)(1) or (2) of this section, the organization must submit an annual electronic notification. Thus, a black lung trust that normally has gross receipts of $25,000 or less is not required to file Form 990-BL but is required to submit an annual electronic notification. A section 509(a)(3) supporting organization of a religious organization that normally has gross receipts of $5,000 or less is not required to file Form 990 or Form 990-EZ but is required to submit an annual electronic notification.

(c) *Additional notification requirements.*—(1) *In general.*—Any organization described in paragraph (a) of this section shall submit an annual electronic notification described in section 6033(i)(1). The annual electronic notification shall—

(i) Be in electronic form; and

(ii) Set forth—

(A) The legal name of the organization;

(B) Any name under which the organization operates or does business;

(C) The organization's mailing address and Internet Web site address (if any);

(D) The organization's taxpayer identification number;

(E) The name and address of a principal officer;

(F) Evidence of the continuing basis for the organization's exemption from the filing requirements under section 6033(a)(1); and

(G) Additional information necessary to process the notification.

(2) The mailing address required by section 6033(i)(1)(C) and submitted in the annual electronic notification shall be the organization's last known address as provided by § 301.6212-2(a) of this chapter. This last known address may be updated as provided under § 301.6212-2 of this chapter, or by clear and concise notification. The Internal Revenue Service will use this last known address as the organization's address of record and will direct all mailings to this address.

(3) By submitting the annual electronic notification described in paragraph (c)(1) of this section, an organization acknowledges that it is not required to file a return under section 6033(a) because its annual gross receipts are not normally in excess of $25,000. In order to make this determination, the organization must keep records that enable it to calculate its gross receipts. All organizations are required to maintain records under section 6001. These records will provide evidence of the continuing basis for the organization's exemption from the filing requirements under section 6033(a)(1).

(4) If an organization that is required to submit an annual electronic notification files a complete Form 990 or Form 990-EZ, the annual electronic notification requirement shall be deemed satisfied. The annual electronic notifica-

Reg. § 1.6033-6(c)(4)

tion requirement is not satisfied if the Form 990 or Form 990-EZ contains only those items of information that would have been required by submitting the notification in electronic form. Also, the filing of a complete Form 990 or Form 990-EZ, rather than the submission of an annual electronic notification, is the filing of a return that starts the period of limitations for assessment under section 6501(g)(2).

(d) *No effect on other filing requirements.*—An organization that is relieved from filing an information return under section 6033(a) is still subject to the requirements of §§1.6033-2(i) and (j), concerning: notice regarding changes in character, operations, or purpose; provision of additional information; duty to file other returns of information; and duty to file unrelated business tax returns. If an organization is required to file an unrelated business tax return, Form 990-T, "Exempt Organization Business Income Tax Return," the filing of that return does not relieve the organization from the requirement of submitting an annual electronic notification under section 6033(i).

(e) *Accounting period for submitting annual electronic notification.*—An annual electronic notification required by this section shall be on the basis of the established annual accounting period of the organization. If the organization has no established accounting period, the annual electronic notification shall be on the basis of the calendar year.

(f) *Time and place for submitting annual electronic notification.*—The annual electronic notification required by this section shall be submitted on or before the 15th day of the fifth calendar month following the close of the period for which the notification is required to be submitted. Thus, an organization with an accounting period ending December 31, 2007, is required to submit an annual electronic notification by May 15, 2008. The notification shall be submitted in accordance with instructions and publications, including those provided at the Internal Revenue Service Web site for exempt organizations.

(g) *Effective/applicability date.*—These regulations are applicable to annual periods beginning after 2006. [Reg. §1.6033-6.]

☐ [*T.D. 9454, 7-22-2009.*]

[Reg. §1.6034-1]

§1.6034-1. Information returns required of trusts described in section 4947(a) or claiming charitable or other deductions under section 642(c).—(a) *In general.*—Every trust (other than a trust described in paragraph (b) of this section) claiming a charitable or other deduction under section 642(c) for the taxable year shall file, with respect to such taxable year, a return of information on Form 1041-A. In addition, for taxable years beginning after December 31, 1969, every trust (other than a trust described in paragraph (b) of this section) described in section 4947(a)(2) (including trusts described in section 664) shall file such return for each taxable year, unless all

transfers in trust occurred before May 27, 1969. The return shall set forth the name and address of the trust and the following information concerning the trust in such detail as is prescribed by the form or in the instructions issued with respect to such form:

(1) The amount of the charitable or other deduction taken under section 642(c) for the taxable year (and, for taxable years beginning prior to January 1, 1970, showing separately for each class of activity for which disbursements were made (or amounts were permanently set aside) the amounts which, during such year, were paid out (or which were permanently set aside) for charitable or other purposes under section 642(c));

(2) The amount paid out during the taxable year which represents amounts permanently set aside in prior years for which charitable or other deductions have been taken under section 642(c), and separately listing for each class of activity, for which disbursements were made, the total amount paid out;

(3) The amount for which charitable or other deductions have been taken in prior years under section 642(c) and which had not been paid out at the beginning of the taxable year;

(4)(i) The amount paid out of principal in the taxable year for charitable, etc., purposes, and separately listing for each such class of activity, for which disbursements were made, the total amount paid out;

(ii) The total amount paid out of principal in prior years for charitable, etc., purposes;

(5) The gross income of the trust for the taxable year and the expenses attributable thereto, in sufficient detail to show the different categories of income and of expense; and

(6) A balance sheet showing the assets, liabilities, and net worth of the trust as of the beginning of the taxable year.

(b) *Exceptions.*—(1) *In general.*—A trust is not required to file a Form 1041-A for any taxable year with respect to which the trustee is required by the terms of the governing instrument and applicable local law to distribute currently all of the income of the trust. For this purpose, the income of the trust shall be determined in accordance with section 643(b) and §§1.643(b)-1 and 1.643(b)-2.

(2) *Trusts described in section 4947(a)(1).*—For taxable years beginning after December 31, 1980, a trust described in section 4947(a)(1) is not required to file a Form 1041-A.

(c) *Time and place for filing return.*—The return on Form 1041-A shall be filed on or before the 15th day of the 4th month following the close of the taxable year of the trust, with the internal revenue officer designated by the instructions applicable to such form. For extensions of time for filing returns under this section, see §1.6081-1.

(d) *Other provisions.*—For publicity of information on Form 1041-A, see section 6104 and the regulations thereunder in Part 301 of this chapter. For provisions relating to penalties for failure to file a return required by this section, see section 6652(d). For the criminal penalties for a willful failure to file a return and filing a false or fraudulent return, see sections 7203, 7206, and 7207. [Reg. § 1.6034-1.]

□ [*T.D. 6364, 2-13-59. Amended by T.D. 7012, 5-14-69; T.D. 7563, 9-8-78 and T.D. 8026, 5-17-85.*]

[Reg. § 301.6034-1]

§ 301.6034-1. Returns by trusts described in section 4947(a)(2) or claiming charitable or other deductions under section 642(c).—For provisions relating to the requirement of returns by trusts described in section 4947(a)(2) or claiming charitable or other deductions under section 642(c), see § 1.6034-1 of this chapter (Income Tax Regulations). [Reg. § 301.6034-1.]

□ [*T.D. 6498, 10-24-60. Amended by T.D. 7563, 9-8-78 and T.D. 8026, 5-17-85.*]

[Reg. § 1.6035-1]

§ 1.6035-1. Returns of U.S. officers, directors and 10-percent shareholders of foreign personal holding companies for taxable years beginning after September 3, 1982.—(a) *Requirement of returns.*—(1) *In general.*—For taxable years of a foreign personal holding company beginning after September 3, 1982, each United States citizen or resident who is an officer, director, or 10-percent shareholder of the foreign personal holding company (as defined in section 552) shall file with his income tax return, on or before the date that return is due, Form 5471 and the applicable schedules to be completed in accordance with the instructions setting forth corporate, shareholder, and income information for the foreign personal holding company's annual accounting period that ends with or within the officer's, director's, or shareholder's taxable year. In the case of a foreign personal holding company which is a specified foreign corporation (as defined in section 898), the taxable year of such corporation shall be treated as its annual accounting period.

(2) *General corporate information.*—The general foreign personal holding company information required by this section with respect to each taxable year is as follows:

(i) The name and address and employer identification number (if any) of the corporation;

(ii) The kind of business in which the corporation is engaged;

(iii) The date of its incorporation;

(iv) The country under the laws of which the corporation is incorporated;

(v) A description of each class of stock issued and outstanding by the corporation for the beginning and end of the annual accounting period;

(vi) The number of shares and par value of common stock of the corporation issued and outstanding as of the beginning and end of the taxable year;

(vii) The number of shares and par value of preferred stock of the corporation issued and outstanding as of the beginning and end of the taxable year, the rate of dividend on such stock and whether such dividend is cumulative or noncumulative; and

(viii) Any other information required by the appropriate form and its instructions.

For purposes of this paragraph, the term "share" includes any security convertible into a share in the corporation and any option granted by the corporation with respect to any share in the corporation.

(3) *Shareholder information.*—The shareholder information required by this section is as follows:

(i) The name, address and taxpayer identification number (if any) of each person, whether foreign or U.S., who was a shareholder during the taxable year and the class and number of shares held by each, together with an explanation of any changes in stock holdings during the taxable year;

(ii) The name and address of each holder during the taxable year of securities convertible into stock of the corporation and the class, number, and face value of the securities held by each, together with an explanation of any changes in the holdings of such securities during the taxable year;

(iii) The name and address of each holder during the taxable year of any option granted by the corporation with respect to any share in the corporation, and a full description of the options held by each, together with an explanation of any changes in the holdings of such options during the taxable year; and

(iv) Any other information required by the appropriate form and its instructions.

(4) *Income information.*—The income information required by this section is the gross income, deductions and credits, taxable income, foreign personal holding company income, and undistributed foreign personal holding company income for the taxable year and other information required by the appropriate form and its instructions.

(b) *Persons required to file return.*—(1) *In general.*—The determination of whether a United States citizen or resident is a person who is an officer, director, or 10-percent shareholder required to file a return with respect to any foreign corporation is made as of the date that Form 5471 is required to be filed. If there is no such person required to file on that date (because, for example, the corporation has been dissolved), then filing is required of the persons who were officers, directors or 10-percent shareholders on the last day of the most recent taxable year of the corporation for which there was such a person who was a United States citizen or resident.

(2) *10-percent shareholder.*—(i) The term "10-percent shareholder" means any individual who owns directly or indirectly (within the

meaning of section 554) 10 percent or more in value of the outstanding stock of a foreign corporation.

(ii) An individual who does not own 10 percent or more in value of the outstanding stock directly but is required to file solely by attribution of another United States person's stock ownership is excused from filing if the direct owner that is an individual furnishes all the information required.

(3) *Two or more persons required to submit the same information.*—If two or more persons are required to furnish the information for the same foreign personal holding company for the same period, one person may make one return on Form 5471. The single Form 5471 may be filed with the income tax return of any one of the persons and shall disclose the name, address, and identifying number of each other person or persons on whose behalf the return is filed. Each person on whose behalf the return if filed remains liable for any penalties imposed under sections 6679, 7203, 7206, and 7207.

(4) *Statement required.*—Any United States citizen or resident required to furnish information under this section with his return who does not do so by reason of the provisions of subparagraph (2)(ii) or (3) of this paragraph shall file a statement with his income tax return indicating that such requirement has been or will be satisfied and identifying the return with which the information was or will be filed and the place of filing.

(c) *Separate returns for each corporation.*—If a person is required to file returns under section 6035 and this section with respect to more than one foreign personal holding company, separate returns must be filed with respect to each company.

(d) *Corrective filing.*—If an information return with respect to a taxable year of a foreign personal holding company beginning after September 3, 1982, is filed before July 5, 1985, and that return does not contain all of the information required by this section, then the filer of the return shall file an amended information return containing all of such information within 90 days after June 4, 1985.

(e) *Penalties.*—(1) *Criminal penalties.*—For criminal penalties for failure to file a return and filing a false or fraudulent return, see sections 7203, 7206, and 7207.

(2) *Civil penalties.*—For civil penalties for failure to file a proper foreign personal holding company information return, see section 6679 and the regulations thereunder. [Reg. §1.6035-1.]

☐ *[T.D. 6364, 2-13-59. Amended by T.D. 7322, 8-23-74; T.D. 7517, 11-11-77; T.D. 7557, 8-4-78; T.D. 8028, 6-3-85 and T.D. 8573, 12-13-94.]*

[Reg. §301.6035-1]

§301.6035-1. Returns of officers, directors, and shareholders of foreign personal holding

companies.—For provisions relating to the requirement of returns by officers, directors, and shareholders of foreign personal holding companies, see §§1.6035-1 to 1.6035-3, inclusive, of this chapter (Income Tax Regulations). [Reg. §301.6035-1.]

☐ *[T.D. 6498, 10-24-60.]*

[Reg. §1.6035-2]

§1.6035-2. Transitional relief.—(a) *Statements due before June 30, 2016.*—Executors and other persons required to file or furnish a statement under section 6035(a)(1) or (2) after July 31, 2015 and before June 30, 2016, need not have done so until June 30, 2016.

(b) *Applicability Date.*—This section is applicable to executors and other persons who file a return required by section 6018(a) or (b) after July 31, 2015. [Reg. §1.6035-2.]

☐ *[T.D. 6364, 2-13-59. Amended by T.D. 7322, 8-23-74, T.D. 8028, 6-3-85 and T.D. 9797, 12-1-2016.]*

[Reg. §1.6035-3]

§1.6035-3. Returns of 50-percent U.S. shareholders of foreign personal holding companies for taxable years beginning before September 4, 1982.—For rules relating to information returns required to be filed by shareholders of foreign personal holding companies for taxable years beginning before September 4, 1982, see section 6035(b) (as in effect before the enactment of the Tax Equity and Fiscal Responsibility Act of 1982) and 26 CFR 1.6035-2 (Rev. as of April 1, 1981). [Reg. §1.6035-3.]

☐ *[T.D. 8028, 6-3-85.]*

[Reg. §1.6036-1]

§1.6036-1. Notice of qualification as executor or receiver.—For provisions relating to the notice required of fiduciaries, see the regulations under section 6036 contained in Part 301 of this chapter (Regulations on Procedure and Administration). [Reg. §1.6036-1.]

☐ *[T.D. 6455, 3-1-60.]*

[Reg. §20.6036-1]

§20.6036-1. Notice of qualification as executor.—(a) *Preliminary notice for estates of decedents dying before January 1, 1971.*—(1) A preliminary notice must be filed on Form 704 for the estate of every citizen or resident of the United States whose gross estate exceeded $60,000 in value on the date of his death.

(2) In the case of a nonresident not a citizen of the United States dying on or after November 14, 1966—

(i) Subject to the provisions of subdivisions (ii) and (iii) of this subparagraph, a preliminary notice must be filed on Form 705 if that part of the decedent's gross estate situated in the United States exceeded $30,000 in value on the date of his death (see §§20.2103-1 and 20.2104-1).

(ii) If the transfer of the estate is subject to the tax imposed by section 2107(a) (relating to expatriation to avoid tax), any amounts includible in the decedent's gross estate under section 2107(b) are to be added to the value on the date of his death of that part of his gross estate situated in the United States, for purposes of determining under subdivision (i) of this subparagraph whether his gross estate exceeded $30,000 in value on the date of his death.

(iii) If the transfer of the estate is subject to tax pursuant to a Presiden tial proclamation made under section 2108(a) (relating to Presidential proclamations of the application of pre-1967 estate tax provisions), a preliminary notice must be filed on Form 705 if the value on the date of the decedent's death of that part of his gross estate situated in the United States exceeded $2,000.

(3) A preliminary notice must be filed on Form 705 for the estate of every nonresident not a citizen of the United States dying before November 14, 1966, if the value on the date of his death of that part of his gross estate situated in the United States exceeded $2,000.

(4) The value of the gross estate on the date of death governs with respect to the requirement for filing the preliminary notice irrespective of whether the value of the gross estate is, at the executor's election, finally determined pursuant to the provisions of section 2032 as of a date subsequent to the date of death. If there is doubt as to whether the gross estate exceeds $60,000, $30,000, or $2,000, as the case may be, the notice shall be filed as a matter of precaution in order to avoid the possibility of penalties attaching.

(5) The primary purpose of the preliminary notice is to advise the Internal Revenue Service of the existence of taxable estates, and filing shall not be delayed beyond the period provided for in § 20.6071-1 merely because of uncertainty as to the exact value of the assets. The estimate of the gross estate called for by the notice shall be the best approximation of value which can be made within the time allowed. Duplicate copies of the preliminary notice are not required to be filed.

(6) For criminal penalties for failure to file a notice and filing a false or fraudulent notice, see sections 7203, 7207, and 7269. See § 20.6091-1 for the place for filing the notice. See § 20.6071-1 for the time for filing the notice.

(b) *Persons required to file.*—In the case of an estate of a citizen or resident of the United States described in paragraph (a) of this section, the preliminary notice must be filed by the duly qualified executor or administrator, or if none qualifies within 2 months after the decedent's death, by every person in actual or constructive possession of any property of the decedent at or after the time of the decedent's death. The signature of one executor or administrator on the preliminary notice is sufficient. In the case of a nonresident not a citizen, the notice must be filed by every duly qualified executor or administrator within the United States, or if none qualifies within 2 months after the decedent's death, by

every person in actual or constructive possession of any property of the decedent at or after the time of the decedent's death. [Reg. § 20.6036-1.]

☐ [*T.D. 6296, 6-23-58. Amended by T.D. 7238, 12-28-72 and T.D. 7296, 12-11-73.*]

[Reg. § 301.6036-1]

§ 301.6036-1. Notice required of executor or of receiver or other like fiduciary.— (a) *Receivers and other like fiduciaries.*—(1) *Exemption for bankruptcy proceedings.*—(i) A bankruptcy trustee, debtor in possession or other like fiduciary in a bankruptcy proceeding is not required by this section to give notice of appointment, qualification or authorization to act to the Secretary or his delegate. (However, see the notice requirements under the Bankruptcy Rules.)

(ii) Paragraph (a)(1)(i) of this section is effective for appointments, qualifications and authorizations to act made on or after January 29, 1988. For appointments, qualifications and authorizations to act made before the foregoing date, 26 CFR 301.6036-1(a)(1) and (4)(i) (revised as of April 1, 1986) apply.

(2) *Proceedings other than bankruptcy.*—A receiver in a receivership proceeding or a similar fiduciary in any proceeding (including a fiduciary in aid of foreclosure), designated by order of any court of the United States or of any State or Territory or of the District of Columbia as in control of all or substantially all the assets of a debtor or other party to such proceeding shall, on, or within 10 days of, the date of his appointment or authorization to act, give notice thereof in writing to the district director for the internal revenue district in which the debtor, or such other party, is or was required to make returns. Moreover, any fiduciary in aid of foreclosure not appointed by order of any such court, if he takes possession of all or substantially all the assets of the debtor, shall, on, or within 10 days of, the date of his taking possession, give notice thereof in writing to such district director.

(3) *Assignment for benefit of creditors.*—An assignee for the benefit of a creditor or creditors shall, on, or within 10 days of, the date of an assignment, give notice thereof in writing to the district director for the internal revenue district in which the debtor is or was required to make returns. For purposes of this subparagraph, an assignee for the benefit of creditors shall be any person who, by authority of law, by the order of any court, by oral or written agreement, or in any other manner acquires control or possession of or title to all or substantially all the assets of a debtor, and who under such acquisition is authorized to use, reassign, sell, or in any manner dispose of such assets so that the proceeds from the use, sale, or other disposition may be paid to or may inure directly or indirectly to the benefit of a creditor or creditors of such debtor.

(4) *Contents of notice.*—(i) *Proceedings other than bankruptcy.*—The written notice required under paragraph (a)(2) of this section shall contain—

Reg. § 301.6036-1(a)(4)(i)

(a) The name and address of the person making such notice and the date of his appointment or of his taking possession of the assets of the debtor or other person whose assets are controlled,

(b) The name, address, and, for notices filed after December 20, 1972, the taxpayer identification number of the debtor or other person whose assets are controlled, and

(c) In the case of a court proceeding—

(1) The name and location of the court in which the proceedings are pending,

(2) The date on which such proceedings were instituted,

(3) The number under which such proceedings are docketed, and

(4) When possible, the date, time, and place of any hearing, meeting of creditors, or other scheduled action with respect to such proceedings.

(ii) *Assignment for benefit of creditors.*—The written notice required under subparagraph (3) of this paragraph shall contain—

(a) The name and address of, and the date the asset or assets were assigned to, the assignee,

(b) The name, address, and, for notices filed after December 20, 1972, the taxpayer identification number of the debtor whose assets were assigned,

(c) A brief description of the assets assigned,

(d) An explanation of the action expected to be taken with respect to such assets, and

(e) When possible, the date, time, and place of any hearing, meeting of creditors, sale, or other scheduled action with respect to such assets.

(iii) The notice required by this section shall be sent to the attention of the Chief, Special Procedures Staff, of the District office to which it is required to be sent.

(b) *Executors, administrators, and persons in possession of property of decedent.*—For provisions relating to the requirement of filing, by an executor, administrator, or person in possession of property of a decedent, of a preliminary notice in the case of the estate of a decedent dying before January 1, 1971, see § 20.6036-1 of this chapter (Estate Tax Regulations).

(c) *Notice of fiduciary relationship.*—When a notice is required under § 301.6903-1 of a person acting in fiduciary capacity and is also required of such person under this section, notice given in accordance with the provisions of this section shall be considered as complying with both sections.

(d) *Suspension of period on assessment.*—For suspension of the running of the period of limitations on the making of assessments from the date a proceeding is instituted to a date 30 days after receipt of notice from a fiduciary in any proceeding under the Bankruptcy Act or from a receiver in any other court proceeding, see section 6872 and § 301.6872-1.

(e) *Applicability.*—Except as provided in paragraph (a)(1)(ii) of this section, the provisions of this section shall apply to those persons referred to in this section whose appointments, authorizations, or assignments occur on or after the date of the publication of these regulations in the Federal Register as a Treasury decision.

(f) *Cross references.*—(1) For criminal penalty for willful failure to supply information, see section 7203.

(2) For criminal penalties for willfully making false or fraudulent statements, see sections 7206 and 7207.

(3) For time for performance of acts where the last day falls on a Saturday, Sunday, or legal holiday, see section 7503 and § 301.7503-1 [Reg. § 301.6036-1.]

☐ [*T.D. 6517, 12-20-60. Amended by T.D. 7222, 11-20-72; T.D. 7238, 12-28-72 and T.D. 8172, 1-28-88.*]

[Reg. § 20.6036-2]

§ 20.6036-2. Notice of qualification as executor of estate of decedent dying after 1970.—In the case of the estate of a decedent dying after December 31, 1970, no special notice of qualification as executor of an estate is required to be filed. The requirement of section 6036 for notification of qualification as executor of an estate shall be satisfied by the filing of the estate tax return required by section 6018 and the regulations thereunder. [Reg. § 20.6036-2.]

☐ [*T.D. 7238, 12-28-72.*]

[Reg. § 1.6037-1]

§ 1.6037-1. Return of electing small business corporation.—(a) *In general.*—Every small business corporation (as defined in section 1371(a)) which has made an election under section 1372(a) not to be subject to the tax imposed by chapter 1 of the Code shall file, with respect to each taxable year for which the election is in effect, a return of income on Form 1120-S. The return shall set forth the items of gross income and the deductions allowable in computing taxable income as required by the return form or in the instructions issued with respect thereto and shall be signed in accordance with section 6062 by the person authorized to sign a return. The return shall also set forth the following information concerning the electing small business corporation:

(1) The names and addresses of all persons owning stock in the corporation at any time during the taxable year;

(2) The number of shares of stock owned by each shareholder at all times during the taxable year;

(3) The amount of money and other property distributed by the corporation during the taxable year to each shareholder;

(4) The date of each distribution of money and other property; and

(5) Such other information as is required by the form or by the instructions issued with respect to such form.

(b) *Time and place for filing return.*—The return shall be filed on or before the 15th day of the third month following the close of the taxable year with the internal revenue officer designated in the instructions applicable to Form 1120-S. (See section 6072.)

(c) *Other provisions.*—The return on Form 1120-S will be treated as a return filed by the corporation under section 6012, relating to persons required to make returns of income, for purposes of the provisions of chapter 66 of the Code, relating to limitations. Thus, for example, the period of limitation on assessment and collection of any corporate tax found to be due upon a subsequent determination that the corporation was not entitled to the benefits of subchapter S, chapter 1 of the Code, will run from the date of filing the return under section 6037, or from the date prescribed for filing such return, whichever is the later. For the rules requiring the disclosure of certain transactions, see § 1.6011-4T.

(d) *Penalties.*—For criminal penalties for failure to file a return, supply information, or pay tax, and for filing a false or fraudulent return, statement, or other document, see sections 7203, 7206, and 7207. [Reg. § 1.6037-1.]

☐ *[T.D. 6432, 12-18-59. Amended by T.D. 7012, 5-14-69 and T.D. 9000, 6-14-2002.]*

[Reg. § 301.6037-1]

§ 301.6037-1. Return of electing small business corporation.—For provisions relating to requirement of return of electing small business corporation, see § 1.6037-1 of this chapter (Income Tax Regulations). [Reg. § 301.6037-1.]

☐ *[T.D. 6498, 10-24-60.]*

[Reg. § 1.6037-2]

§ 1.6037-2. Required use of magnetic media for income tax returns of electing small business corporations.—The return of an electing small business corporation that is required to be filed on magnetic media under § 301.6037-2 of this chapter must be filed in accordance with Internal Revenue Service revenue procedures, publications, forms, or instructions, including those posted electronically. (See § 601.601(d)(2) of this chapter). [Reg. § 1.6037-2.]

☐ *[T.D. 9363, 11-9-2007.]*

[Reg. § 301.6037-2]

§ 301.6037-2. Required use of magnetic media for returns of electing small business corporation.—(a) *Returns of electing small business corporation required on magnetic media.*—An electing small business corporation required to file an electing small business return on Form 1120S, "U.S. Income Tax Return for an S Corporation," under § 1.6037-1 of this chapter must file its Form 1120S on magnetic media if the small business corporation is required by the Internal Rev-

enue Code and regulations to file at least 250 returns during the calendar year ending with or within its taxable year. Returns filed on magnetic media must be made in accordance with applicable revenue procedures, publications, forms, or instructions. In prescribing revenue procedures, publications, forms, or instructions, the Commissioner may direct the type of magnetic media filing. (See § 601.601(d)(2) of this chapter).

(b) *Waiver.*—The Commissioner may grant waivers of the requirements of this section in cases of undue hardship. A request for waiver must be made in accordance with applicable revenue procedures or publications. The waiver also will be subject to the terms and conditions regarding the method of filing as may be prescribed by the Commissioner.

(c) *Failure to file.*—If an electing small business corporation fails to file a return on magnetic media when required to do so by this section, the corporation is deemed to have failed to file the return. (See section 6651 for the addition to tax for failure to file a return.) In determining whether there is reasonable cause for failure to file the return, § 301.6651-1(c) and rules similar to the rules in § 301.6724-1(c)(3) (undue economic hardship related to filing information returns on magnetic media) will apply.

(d) *Meaning of terms.*—The following definitions apply for purposes of this section:

(1) *Magnetic media.*—The term *magnetic media* means any magnetic media permitted under applicable regulations, revenue procedures, or publications. These generally include magnetic tape, tape cartridge, and diskette, as well as other media, such as electronic filing, specifically permitted under the applicable regulations, procedures, publications, forms, or instructions. (See § 601.601(d)(2) of this chapter).

(2) *Corporation.*—The term *corporation* means a corporation as defined in section 7701(a)(3).

(3) *Electing small business corporation return.*—The term *electing small business corporation return* means a Form 1120S, "U.S. Income Tax Return for an S Corporation," along with all other related forms, schedules, and statements that are required to be attached to the Form 1120S, and all members of the Form 1120S series of returns, including amended and superseding returns.

(4) *Electing small business corporation.*—The term *electing small business corporation* means an S corporation as defined in section 1361(a)(1).

(5) *Determination of 250 returns.*—For purposes of this section, a corporation is required to file at least 250 returns if, during the calendar year ending with or within the taxable year of the corporation, the corporation is required to file at least 250 returns of any type, including information returns (for example, Forms W-2, Forms 1099), income tax returns, employment tax returns, and excise tax returns. In the case of

a short year return, a corporation is required to file at least 250 returns if, during the calendar year which includes the short taxable year of the corporation, the corporation is required to file at least 250 returns of any type, including information returns (for example, Forms W-2, Forms 1099), income tax returns, employment tax returns, and excise tax returns.

(e) *Example.*—The following example illustrates the provisions of paragraph (d)(5) of this section. In the example, the corporation is a calendar year taxpayer:

Example. In 2007, Corporation S, an electing small business corporation with assets in excess of $10 million, is required to file one Form 1120S, "U.S. Corporation Income Tax Return," 100 Forms W-2, "Wage and Tax Statement," 146 Forms 1099-DIV, "Dividends and Distributions," one Form 940, "Employer's Annual Federal Unemployment (FUTA) Tax Return," and four Forms 941, "Employer's Quarterly Federal Tax Return." Because S is required to file 252 returns during the calendar year, S is required to file its 2007 Form 1120S electronically.

(f) *Effective/applicability dates.*—This section applies to returns of electing small business corporations that report total assets at the end of the corporation's taxable year that equal or exceed $10 million on Schedule L of Form 1120S for taxable years ending on or after December 31, 2006, except for the application of the short year rules in paragraph (d)(5) of this section, which is applicable for taxable years ending on or after November 13, 2007. [Reg. § 301.6037-2.]

☐ [*T.D. 9363, 11-9-2007.*]

[Reg. § 301.6038-1]

§ 301.6038-1. Information returns required of United States persons with respect to certain foreign corporations.—For provisions relating to information returns required of United States persons with respect to certain foreign corporations, see § § 1.6038-1 and 1.6038-2 of this chapter (Income Tax Regulations). [Reg. § 301.6038-1.]

☐ [*T.D. 6555, 3-14-61. Amended by T.D. 6700,* 1-6-64.]

[Reg. § 1.6038-2]

§ 1.6038-2. Information returns required of United States persons with respect to annual accounting periods of certain foreign corporations.—(a) *Requirement of return.*—Every U.S. person shall make a separate annual information return with respect to each annual accounting period (described in paragraph (e) of this section) beginning after December 31, 1962, of each foreign corporation which that person controls (as defined in paragraph (b) of this section) for an uninterrupted period of 30 days or more during such annual accounting period. Such information shall not be required to be furnished, however, with respect to a corporation defined in section 1504(d) of the Code which makes a consolidated return for the taxable year. The return shall be made, with respect to annual ac-

counting periods ending with or within the United States person's taxable year, on—

(1) Form 2952, "Information Return with Respect to Controlled Foreign Corporations," if such taxable year ends before December 31, 1982;

(2) Form 5471, "Information Return of U.S. Persons with Respect to Certain Foreign Corporations," if such taxable year ends on or after December 31, 1983; or

(3) Either Form 5471 or Form 2952 if such taxable year ends on or after December 31, 1982 and before December 31, 1963.

(b) *Control.*—A person shall be deemed to be in control of a foreign corporation if at any time during that person's taxable year it owns stock possessing more than 50 percent of the total combined voting power of all classes of stock entitled to vote, or more than 50 percent of the total value of shares of all classes of stock of the foreign corporation. A person in control of a corporation which, in turn, owns more than 50 percent of the combined voting power, or of the value, of all classes of stock of another corporation is also treated as being in control of such other corporation. The provisions of this paragraph may be illustrated by the following example:

Example. Corporation A owns 51 percent of the voting stock in Corporation B. Corporation B owns 51 percent of the voting stock in Corporation C. Corporation C in turn owns 51 percent of the voting stock in Corporation D. Corporation D is controlled by Corporation A.

(c) *Attribution rules.*—For the purpose of determining control of domestic or foreign corporations the constructive ownership rules of section 318(a) shall apply except that:

(1) Stock owned by or for a partner or a beneficiary of an estate or trust shall not be considered owned by the partnership, estate, or trust when the effect is to consider a United States person as owning stock owned by a person who is not a United States person;

(2) A corporation will not be considered as owning stock owned by or for a 50 percent or more shareholder when the effect is to consider a United States person as owning stock owned by a person who is not a United States person; and

(3) If 10 percent or more in value of the stock in a corporation is owned, directly or indirectly, by or for any person, section 318(a)(2)(C) shall apply.

The constructive ownership rules of section 318(a) apply only for purposes of determining control as defined in paragraph (b) of this section.

(d) *U.S. person.*—(1) *In general.*—For purposes of section 6038 and this section, the term *United States person* has the meaning assigned to it by section 7701(a)(30), except as provided in paragraphs (d)(2) and (3) of this section.

(2) *Special rule for individuals residing in certain possessions.*—(i) With respect to an individual who is a bona fide resident of Puerto Rico,

the term United States person has the meaning assigned to it by §1.957-3 except that the rules of §1.937-2(g)(1) will apply.

(ii) With respect to an individual who is a bona fide resident of any section 931 possession, as defined in §1.931-1(c)(1), the term United States person has the meaning assigned to it by §1.957-3.

(3) *Special rule for certain nonresident aliens.*— An individual for whom an election under section 6013(g) or (h) is in effect will, subject to the exceptions contained in paragraph (d)(2) of this section, be considered a United States person for purposes of section 6038 and this section.

(e) *Period covered by return.*—The information required under paragraphs (f) and (g) of this section with respect to a foreign corporation shall be furnished for the annual accounting period of the foreign corporation ending with or within the United States person's taxable year. For purposes of this section, the annual accounting period of a foreign corporation is the annual period on the basis of which that corporation regularly computes its income in keeping its books. In the case of a specified foreign corporation (as defined in section 898), the taxable year of such corporation shall be treated as its annual accounting period. The term *annual accounting period* may refer to a period of less than one year, where, for example, the foreign income, war profits, and excess profits taxes are determined on the basis of an accounting period of less than one year as described in section 902(c)(5). If more than one annual accounting period ends with or within the United States person's taxable year, separate annual information returns shall be submitted for each annual accounting period.

(f) *Contents of return.*—The return on Form 5471 shall contain so much of the following information, and in such form or manner, as the form shall prescribe with respect to each foreign corporation:

(1) The name, address, and employer identification number, if any, of the corporation;

(2) The principal place of business of the corporation;

(3) The date of incorporation and the country under whose laws incorporated;

(4) The name and address of the foreign corporation's statutory or resident agent in the country of incorporation;

(5) The name, address, and identifying number of any branch office or agent of the foreign corporation located in the United States;

(6) The name and address of the person (or persons) having custody of the books of account and records of the foreign corporation, and the location of such books and records if different from such address;

(7) The nature of the corporation's business and the principal places where conducted;

(8) As regards the outstanding stock of the corporation—

(i) A description of each class of the corporation's stock, and

(ii) The number of shares of each class outstanding at the beginning and end of the annual accounting period;

(9) A list showing the name, address, and identifying number of, and the number of shares of each class of the corporation's stock held by, each United States person who is a shareholder owning at any time during the annual accounting period 5 percent or more in value of any class of the corporation's outstanding stock;

(10) For the annual accounting period, the amount of the corporation's:

(i) Current earnings and profits;

(ii) Foreign income, war profits, and excess profits taxes paid or accrued;

(iii) Distributions out of current earnings and profits for the period;

(iv) Distributions other than those described in paragraph (f)(10)(iii) of this section and the source thereof; and

(v) For Forms 5471 filed for taxable years ending after December 15, 1990, such earnings and profits information as the form shall prescribe, including post-1986 undistributed earnings described in section 902(c)(1), pre-1987 amounts, total earnings and profits, and previously taxed earnings and profits described in section 959(c); and

(11) *Transactions with certain related parties.*— (i) A summary showing the total amount of each of the following types of transactions of the corporation, which took place during the annual accounting period, with the person required to file this return, any other corporation or partnership controlled by that person, or any United States person owning at the time of the transaction 10 percent or more in value of any class of stock outstanding of the foreign corporation, or of any corporation controlling that foreign corporation—

(A) Sales and purchases of stock in trade;

(B) Sales and purchases of tangible property other than stock in trade;

(C) Sales and purchases of patents, inventions, models, or designs (whether or not patented), copyrights, trademarks, secret formulas or processes, or any other similar property rights;

(D) Compensation paid and compensation received for the rendition of technical, managerial, engineering, construction, scientific, or like services;

(E) Commissions paid and commissions received;

(F) Rents and royalties paid and rents and royalties received;

(G) Amounts loaned and amounts borrowed (except open accounts resulting from sales and purchases reported under other items listed in this paragraph (f)(11) that arise and are collected in full in the ordinary course of business);

Reg. §1.6038-2(f)(11)(i)(G)

(H) Dividends paid and dividends received;

(I) Interest paid and interest received; and

(J) Premiums paid and premiums received for insurance or reinsurance.

(ii) *Special rule for banks.*—For purposes of this paragraph (f)(11), if the United States person is a bank, as defined in section 581, or is controlled within the meaning of section 368(c) by a bank, the term transactions shall not, as to a corporation with respect to which a return is filed, include banking transactions entered into on behalf of customers; in any event, however, deposits in accounts between a foreign corporation, controlled (within the meaning of paragraph (b) of this section) by a United States person, and a person described in this paragraph (f)(11) and withdrawals from such accounts shall be summarized by reporting end-of-month balances.

(12) *Accrued payments and receipts.*—For purposes of the required summary under paragraph (f)(11) of this section, a corporation that uses an accrual method of accounting shall use accrued payments and accrued receipts for purposes of computing the total amount of each of the types of transactions listed.

(g) *Financial statements.*—The following information with respect to the foreign corporation shall be attached to and filed as part of the return required by this section. Forms 5471 filed after September 30, 1991, shall contain this information in such form or manner as the form shall prescribe with respect to each foreign corporation:

(1) A statement of the corporation's profit and loss for the annual accounting period;

(2) A balance sheet as of the end of the annual accounting period of the corporation showing—

(i) The corporation's assets;

(ii) The corporation's liabilities; and

(iii) The corporation's net worth; and

(3) An analysis of changes in the corporation's surplus accounts during the annual accounting period including both opening and closing balances.

The information listed in this paragraph (g) shall be prepared in conformity with generally accepted accounting principles, and in such detail as is customary for the corporation's accounting records.

(h) *Method of reporting.*—Except as provided in this paragraph (h), all amounts furnished under paragraphs (f) and (g) of this section shall be expressed in United States dollars with a statement of the exchange rates used. The following rules shall apply for taxable years ending after December 31, 1994, with respect to returns filed after December 31, 1995. All amounts furnished under paragraph (g) of this section shall be expressed in United States dollars computed and translated in conformity with United States gen-

erally accepted accounting principles. Amounts furnished under paragraph (g)(1) of this section shall also be furnished in the foreign corporation's functional currency as required on the form. Earnings and profits amounts furnished under paragraphs (f)(10)(i), (iii), (iv), and (v) of this section shall be expressed in the foreign corporation's functional currency except to the extent the form requires specific items to be translated into United States dollars. Tax amounts furnished under paragraph (f)(10)(ii) of this section shall be furnished in the foreign currency in which the taxes are payable and in United States dollars translated in accordance with section 986(a). All amounts furnished under paragraph (f)(11) of this section shall be expressed in U.S. dollars translated from functional currency at the weighted average exchange rate for the year as defined in § 1.989(b)-1. The foreign corporation's functional currency is determined under section 985. All statements submitted on or with the return required under this section shall be rendered in the English language.

(i) *Time and place for filing return.*—Returns on Form 5471 required under paragraph (a) of this section shall be filed with the United States person's income tax return on or before the date required by law for the filing of that person's income tax return. Directors of Field Operations and Field Directors are authorized to grant reasonable extensions of time for filing returns on Form 5471 in accordance with the applicable provisions of § 1.6081-1 of this chapter. An application for an extension of time for filing a return of income shall also be considered as an application for an extension of time for filing returns on Form 5471.

(j) *Two or more persons required to submit the same information.*—(1) *Return jointly made.*—If two or more persons are required to furnish information with respect to the same foreign corporation for the same period, such persons may, in lieu of making separate returns, jointly make one return. Such joint return shall be filed with the income tax return of any one of the persons making such joint return.

(2) *Persons excepted from furnishing information.*—(i) *Conditions.*—Any person required to furnish information under this section with respect to a foreign corporation need not furnish that information provided all of the following conditions are met:

(A) Such person does not directly own an interest in the foreign corporation;

(B) Such person is required to furnish the information solely by reason of attribution of stock ownership from a United States person under paragraph (c) of this section; and

(C) The person from whom the stock ownership is attributed furnishes all of the information required under this section of the person to whom the stock ownership is attributed. (For a rule regarding attribution from a nonresident alien, see paragraph (l) of this section).

(ii) If an individual who is a United States person required to furnish information with respect to a foreign corporation under section 6038 is entitled under a treaty to be treated as a nonresident of the United States, and if the individual claims this treaty benefit, and if there are no other United States persons that are required to furnish information under section 6038 with respect to the foreign corporation, then the individual may satisfy the requirements of paragraphs (f)(10), (f)(11), (g), and (h) of this section by filing the audited foreign financial statements of the foreign corporation with the individual's return required under section 6038.

(iii) *Illustrations.*—The rule of this paragraph (j)(2) is illustrated by the following examples:

Example (1). A, a U.S. person owns 100 percent of the stock of M, a domestic corporation. A also owns 100 percent of the stock of N, a foreign corporation organized under the laws of foreign country Y. A, in filing the information return required by this section with respect to N Corporation, in fact furnishes all of the information required of M Corporation with respect to N Corporation. M Corporation need not file the information.

Example (2). X, a domestic corporation owns 100 percent of the stock of Y, a domestic corporation, Y Corporation owns 100 percent of the stock of Z, a foreign corporation. X Corporation is not excused by this paragraph (j)(2) from filing information with respect to Z Corporation because X Corporation is deemed to control Z Corporation under the provisions of paragraph (b) of this section without recourse to the attribution rules in paragraph (c) of this section.

(3) *Statement required.*—Any United States person required to furnish information under this section with his return who does not do so by reason of the provisions of paragraph (j)(1) of this section shall file a statement with his income tax return indicating that such requirement has been (or will be) satisfied and identifying the return with which the information was or will be filed and the place of filing.

(k) *Failure to furnish information.*—(1) *Dollar amount penalty.*—(i) *In general.*—If any person required to file Form 5471 under section 6038 and this section fails to furnish any information described in paragraphs (f) and (g) of this section within the time prescribed by paragraph (i) of this section, such person shall pay a penalty of $10,000 for each annual accounting period of each foreign corporation with respect to which such failure occurs.

(ii) *Increase in penalty for continued failure after notification.*—If a failure described in paragraph (k)(1)(i) of this section continues for more than 90 days after the date on which the Director of Field Operations, Area Director, or Director of Compliance Campus Operations mails notice of such failure to the person required to file Form 5471, such person shall pay a penalty of $10,000, in addition to the penalty imposed by section

6038(b)(1) and paragraph (k)(1)(i) of this section, for each 30-day period (or a fraction of) during which such failure continues after such 90-day period has expired. The additional penalty imposed by section 6038(b)(2) and this paragraph (k)(1)(ii) shall be limited to a maximum of $50,000 for each failure.

(2) *Penalty of reducing foreign tax credit.*—(i) *Effect on foreign tax credit.*—Failure of a United States person to furnish, in accordance with the provisions of this section, any return of any information in any return, required to be filed for a taxable year under authority of section 6038 on or before the date prescribed in paragraph (i) of this section may affect the application of section 901 as provided in paragraph (k)(2)(ii) of this section and may affect the application of sections 902 and 960 as provided in paragraph (k)(2)(iii) of this section. Such failure may affect the application of sections 902 and 960 to any such United States person which is a corporation or to any person who acquires from any other person any portion (but only to the extent of such portion) of the interest of such other person in any such foreign corporation.

(ii) *Application of section 901.*—In the application of section 901 to a United States person referred to in paragraph (k)(2)(i) of this section, the amount of taxes paid or deemed paid by such person for any taxable year, with or within which the annual accounting period of a foreign corporation for which such person failed to furnish information required under this section ended, may be reduced by 10 percent. However, no tax reduced under paragraph (k)(2)(iii) of this section or deemed paid under section 904(c) shall be reduced under the provisions of this paragraph (k)(2)(ii).

(iii) *Application of sections 902 and 960.*—In the application of sections 902 and 960 to a United States person referred to in paragraph (k)(2)(i) of this section for any taxable year, the amount of taxes paid or deemed paid by each foreign corporation for the accounting period or periods for which such person was required for the taxable year of the failure to furnish information under this section may be reduced by 10 percent. The 10-percent reduction is not limited to the taxes paid or deemed paid by the foreign corporation with respect to which there is a failure to file information but may apply to the taxes paid or deemed paid by all foreign corporations controlled by that person. In applying subsections (a) and (b) of section 902, and in applying subsection (a) of section 960, the reduction provided by this paragraph (k)(2) shall not apply for purposes of determining the amount of accumulated profits in excess of income, war profits, and excess profits taxes.

(iv) *Reduction for continued failure after notice.*—(A) If the failure referred to in paragraph (k)(2)(i) of this section continues for more than 90 days after the date on which the Director of Field Operations mails notice of such failure to such United States person, then the amount of the reduction referred to in paragraph (k)(2)(ii) and (iii) of this section may be 10 percent plus an additional 5 percent for each 3-month period, or fraction thereof, during which such failure continues after the expiration of such 90-day period.

(B) No taxes shall be reduced under this paragraph (k)(2) more than once for the same failure. Taxes paid by a foreign corporation when once reduced for a failure shall not be reduced again for the same failure in their status as taxes deemed paid by a corporate shareholder. Where a failure continues, each additional periodic 5-percent reduction, referred to in paragraph (k)(2)(iv)(A) of this section, shall be considered as part of the one reduction.

(v) *Limitation on reduction of foreign tax credit.*—The amount of the reduction under this paragraph (k)(2) for each failure to furnish information with respect to a foreign corporation as required under this section shall not exceed the greater of:

(A) $10,000, or

(B) The income of the foreign corporation for its annual accounting period with respect to which the failure occurs. For purposes of this section if a person is required to furnish information with respect to more than one foreign corporation, controlled (within the meaning of paragraph (b) of this section) by that person, each failure to submit information for each such corporation constitutes a separate failure.

(vi) *Offset for dollar amount penalty imposed.*—The total amount of the reduction or reductions which, but for this paragraph (k)(2)(vi), may be made under this paragraph (k)(2) with respect to any separate failure, shall not exceed the maximum amount of such reductions which may be imposed, reduced (but not below zero) by the amount of the dollar amount penalty imposed by paragraph (k)(1) of this section with respect to such separate failure.

(3) *Reasonable cause.*—(i) For purposes of section 6038(b) and (c) and this section, the time prescribed for furnishing information under paragraph (i) of this section, and the beginning of the 90-day period after mailing of notice by the Director of Field Operations under paragraph (k)(1)(ii) and (k)(2)(iv)(A) of this section, shall be treated as being not earlier than the last day on which reasonable cause existed for failure to furnish the information.

(ii) To show that reasonable cause existed for failure to furnish information as required by

section 6038 and this section, the person required to report such information must make an affirmative showing of all facts alleged as reasonable cause for such failure in a written statement containing a declaration that it is made under the penalties of perjury. The statement must be filed with the district director for the district or the director of the service center where the return is required to be filed. The district director or the director of the service center shall determine whether the failure to furnish information was due to reasonable cause, and if so, the period of time for which such reasonable cause existed. In the case of a return that has been filed as required by this section except for an omission of, or error with respect to, some of the information required, if the person who filed the return establishes to the satisfaction of the district director or the director of the service center that the person has substantially complied with this section, then the omission or error shall not constitute a failure under this section.

(4) *Other penalties.*—The information required by section 6038 and this section must be furnished even though there are no foreign taxes which would be reduced under the provisions of this section, and even though the information required may not affect the amount of any tax due under the Internal Revenue Code. For criminal penalties for failure to file a return and filing a false or fraudulent return, see sections 7203, 7206, and 7207 of the Code.

(5) *Illustrations.*—The provisions of this paragraph may be illustrated by the following examples.

Example (1). M, a domestic corporation owns 100 percent of the stock of N, a foreign corporation. Both M and N use the calendar year as a taxable year and annual accounting period, and all of the following events occur in or with respect to the 1980 taxable year. The dividend from N is the only dividend from a foreign corporation received by M during the taxable year, and the foreign taxes listed are the only foreign taxes paid or deemed paid by M and N for the taxable year. On March 15, 1981, M filed its income tax return and paid its income tax, but M did not file Form 2952 with respect to N's 1980 accounting period. On June 1, 1961, the district director mailed notice to M of M's failure to file Form 2952 with respect to N. On November 30, 1981, M filed a complete Form 2952 with respect to N's 1980 annual accounting period.

(a)	Gains, profits, and income of N	$100,000
(b)	Foreign tax paid by N with respect to such gains, profits, and income . . .	40,000
(c)	Deduction of foreign tax paid by N (for purposes of M's section 902 deemed paid credit) resulting from M's failure to file information with respect to N as required under section 6038(a) and this section: failure to file within the time prescribed in paragraph (i) of this section, 10-percent reduction; continued failure for one additional 3-month period after 90-day period after notice mailed, 5-percent reduction; total reduction, 15 percent ($40,000 times 15 percent)	6,000
(d)	Foreign tax paid by N after section 6038(c)(1)(B) reduction	34,000
(e)	Dividend paid by N to M	45,000

(f)	Accumulated profits of N as defined in section 902(c)(1) (determined without regard to the section 6038(c)(1)(B) reduction)	100,000
(g)	Accumulated profits of N as described in section 902(a) (determined without regard to the section 6038(c)(1)(B) reduction)	60,000
(h)	For purposes of section 902 credit, M is deemed to have paid the same proportion of foreign taxes paid (reduced as provided under section 6038(c)) with respect to the accumulated profits described in section 902(a) (determined without regard to the reduction provided under section 6038(c)) as the amount of the dividend (determined without regard to section 78) bears to such amount of accumulated profits	25,500

$$(45,000 \div 60,000) \times 34,000 = 25,500$$

M must include $25,500 in gross income as a dividend under the provisions of section 78 of the Code. This example illustrates that the reductions in foreign taxes paid by the foreign corporation provided under section 8038(c) are taken into account in determining the amount included in gross income of the domestic corporation under section 78 of the Code as foreign taxes deemed paid, but such reductions are not taken into account in computing accumulated profits for purposes of determining the portion of foreign taxes deemed paid with respect to a particular dividend. The dollar amount penalty imposed by section 8038(b) and paragraph (k)(1) of this section does not apply with respect to information for annual accounting periods ending before September 4, 1982, and therefore does not apply to M with respect to M's failure to file Form 2952 in this example.

Example (2). The facts are the same as in example (1) except that all of the events occur in or with respect to the 1982 taxable year. On March 15, 1983, M filed its income tax return and paid its income tax, but M did not file Form 2952 or Form 5471 with respect to N's 1982 annual accounting period. On June 1, 1983, the district director mailed notice to M of M's failure to file Form 2952 or Form 5471 with respect to N. On November 30, 1983, M filed a complete Form 5471 with respect to N's 1982 annual accounting period. Under paragraph (k)(1)(i) of this section, M is subject to a penalty of $1,000. Under paragraph (k)(1)(ii) of this section, that penalty is increased by $4,000 because the failure continued for 92 days (three full 30-day periods and a fraction of a fourth 30-day period) after the end of the 90-day period following mailing of the notice by the district director, bringing M's dollar amount penalty under paragraph (k)(1) of this section to $5,000. For purpose of determining the foreign tax credit available to M, there may be imposed a reduction of foreign tax paid by N of $6,000, which would be the total of reductions under paragraph (k)(2) of this section with respect to M's failure to file under section 6038 for N's 1982 annual accounting period, before application of paragraph (k)(2)(vi) of this section. Under said paragraph (k)(2)(vi), the amount of the foreign tax reduction imposed is reduced by the amount of the dollar amount penalty, leaving a foreign tax reduction penalty of $1,000 which may be imposed in addition to the $5,000 dollar amount penalty. If imposed, the $1,000 tax reduction would then be applied in the calculation of taxes deemed paid by M under section 902 as in example (1), item (c), (d), and (h).

Example 3. A, a US person, owns 100 percent of the stock of FC. On April 15, 2008, A timely filed its 2007 income tax return but did not file Form 5471 with respect to FC's 2007 annual accounting period. On June 1, 2008, the Director of Field Operations mailed a notice to A of A's failure to file Form 5471 for 2007 with respect to FC. On August 1, 2008, A submits a written statement asserting facts for reasonable cause for failure to file the 2007 Form 5471 for FC. Based on A's statement and discussions with A, the Director of Field Operations agrees that A had reasonable cause for failure to file FC's 2007 Form 5471 and determined that it is reasonable for A to file FC's 2007 Form 5471 by September 15, 2008. The time prescribed for furnishing information under paragraph (i) of this section is September 15, 2008, and the 90-day period described under paragraphs (k)(1)(ii) and (k)(2)(iv)(A) of this section begins on that same date. Thus, if A files a completed Form 5471 by September 15, 2008, A is not subject to the penalties under paragraphs (k)(1) and (k)(2) of this section. If A does not file a completed Form 5471 by December 14, 2008, in addition to the penalties under paragraphs (k)(1) and (k)(2) of this section, A will also be subject to the penalties for continued failure under paragraphs (k)(1)(ii) and (k)(2)(iv)(A) of this section.

Example 4. The facts are the same as in Example 3 except A submits the written statement to the Director before a notice of failure to furnish information is mailed to A. The notice is mailed to A on September 7, 2008. Under these facts, the time prescribed for furnishing information under paragraph (i) of this section is September 15, 2008, and the 90-day period after mailing of notice of failure under paragraphs (k)(1)(ii) and (k)(2)(iv)(A) of this section begins on that same date.

(l) *Other persons excepted from filing.*—For tax years of foreign corporations ending on or after December 29, 1999, any person required to furnish information under this section with respect to a foreign corporation does not have to furnish that information if the following conditions are met—

(1) Such person does not own a direct or indirect interest in the foreign corporation; and

(2) Such person is required to furnish information solely by reason of attribution of stock ownership from a nonresident alien(s) under paragraph (c) of this section.

(m) *Applicability dates.*—Except as otherwise provided, this section applies with respect to information for annual accounting periods beginning on or after June 21, 2006. Paragraphs (k)(1) and (5) *Examples 3* and 4 of this section apply June 21, 2006. Paragraph (d) of this section applies to taxable years ending after April 9, 2008. Paragraph (j)(3) of this section applies to returns filed on or after December 31, 2013. [Reg. § 1.6038-2.]

☐ [*T.D.* 6621, 11-30-62. *Amended by T.D.* 6969, 8-22-68; *T.D.* 6997, 1-17-69; *T.D.* 8040, 7-23-85; *T.D.* 8573, 12-13-94; *T.D.* 8733, 10-6-97; *T.D.* 8850, 12-27-99; *T.D.* 9194, 4-6-2005; *T.D.* 9268, 6-20-2006; *T.D.* 9338, 7-12-2007; *T.D.* 9391, 4-4-2008, *T.D.* 9650, 12-30-2013 *and T.D.* 9806, 12-27-2016.]

[Reg. § 1.6038-3]

§ 1.6038-3. Information returns required of certain United States persons with respect to controlled foreign partnerships (CFPs).—(a) *Persons required to make return.*—(1) *Controlling fifty-percent partners.*—The term *controlling fifty-percent partner* means a United States person that controlled (as defined in paragraph (b)(1) of this section) the foreign partnership at any time during the partnership's tax year (as defined in paragraph (b)(8) of this section). Except as provided in paragraph (c), (d), or (e) of this section, for each tax year of a foreign partnership during which the partnership has one or more controlling fifty-percent partners, each controlling fifty-percent partner must complete and file Form 8865, "Return of U.S. Persons With Respect To Certain Foreign Partnerships," containing the information described in paragraph (g) of this section.

(2) *Controlling ten-percent partners.*—If at any point during a foreign partnership's tax year (as defined in paragraph (b)(8) of this section) a United States person owned a ten- percent or greater interest in the partnership while the partnership was controlled by United States persons owning ten-percent or greater interests, such United States person is a controlling ten-percent partner. See paragraph (b)(1) of this section for the definition of control. However, a United States person is not a controlling ten-percent partner with respect to a particular foreign partnership for a particular tax year of the foreign partnership if at any point during that year the partnership had a controlling fifty-percent partner, as defined in paragraph (a)(1) of this section. Except as provided in paragraph (c), (d), or (e) of this section, for each tax year of a partnership during which the partnership has controlling ten-percent partners, each controlling ten-percent partner must complete and file Form 8865 containing the information described in paragraph (g)(1) of this section.

(3) *Separate returns for each partnership.*—A United States person required to report under this paragraph (a) must file a separate Form 8865 for each foreign partnership with respect to which the person is a controlling fifty-percent partner or a controlling ten-percent partner.

(b) *Ownership determinations and definitions.*—(1) *Control.*—Control of a foreign partnership is ownership of more than a fifty-percent interest in the partnership.

(2) *Fifty-percent interest.*—A fifty-percent interest in a partnership is an interest equal to fifty percent of the capital interest in such partnership, an interest equal to fifty percent of the profits interest in such partnership, or an interest to which fifty percent of the deductions or losses of such partnership are allocated.

(3) *Ten-percent interest.*—A ten-percent interest in a partnership is an interest equal to ten percent of the capital interest in such partnership, an interest equal to ten percent of the profits interest in such partnership, or an interest to which ten percent of the deductions or losses of such partnership are allocated.

(4) *Constructive ownership rules.*—For purposes of determining an interest in a partnership, the constructive ownership rules of section 267(c) (other than section 267(c)(3)) apply, taking into account that such rules refer to corporations and not to partnerships. However, an interest will be attributed from a nonresident alien under the family attribution rules of section 267(c)(2) and (4) only if the person to whom the interest is attributed owns a direct or indirect (under the rules of 267(c)(1) or (5)) interest in the foreign partnership.

(5) *Determination of amount of interest.*—Whether a person owns a fifty-percent interest, or a ten-percent interest, as described in paragraphs (b)(2) and (3) of this section, is determined for each tax year of the foreign partnership by reference to the agreement of the partners relating to such interests during that tax year.

(6) *Definition of United States person.*—The term *United States person* is defined in section 7701(a)(30).

(7) *Definition of a foreign partnership.*—A foreign partnership is a partnership described in section 7701(a)(5).

(8) *Tax year of a foreign partnership.*—The tax year of a foreign partnership is determined under section 706.

(9) *Examples.*—The rules of paragraph (a) of this section and this paragraph (b) are illustrated by the following examples:

Example 1. Sole U.S. partner does not own more than a fifty-percent interest. No United States person owns any interest (directly or constructively) in *FPS*, a foreign partnership whose tax year under section 706 is the calendar year. On January 1, 2001, *US*, a United States person with the calendar year as its tax year, contributes property to FPS in exchange for a 40% interest in a section 721 transaction. No United States persons acquire directly or constructively any other interests in FPS during FPS's 2001 tax year. US is not a controlling fifty-percent partner during FPS's 2001 tax year. US did not own during that tax year, either directly or constructively, more than a 50% interest in the partnership under paragraphs (b)(2) and (4) of this section. Also, US is not a controlling ten-percent partner; although US owned a 10% or greater interest, US persons owning at least 10% interests did not control FPS. Therefore, US does not have to file with its 2001 income tax return a Form 8865 with respect to FPS under section 6038. (But see section 6038B for the reporting obligations of US with respect to its transfer of property to FPS and section 6046A for the reporting obligation of US with respect to its acquisition of an interest in FPS. See also § 1.6046A-1(f)(1) regarding the overlap between sections 6038B and 6046A).

Example 2. Controlling ten-percent partners. Assume the same facts as in *Example 1.* In addition, on January 1, 2002, US1, a United States person unrelated to US and a calendar year taxpayer, purchases a 15% interest in FPS from a foreign partner of FPS. Neither US nor US1 is a controlling fifty-percent partner during FPS's 2002 tax year because neither one owns more than a 50% percent interest in FPS during that year. However, US and US1 are controlling ten-percent partners for that year because each owns at least a 10% interest (US owns a 40% interest and US1 owns a 15% interest) and together they control FPS because collectively they own more than a 50% interest in FPS. As controlling ten-percent partners, under section 6038, each is required to file a Form 8865 with its 2002 income tax return. (US1 must also report its acquisition of the 15% interest in FPS under section 6046A on its Form 8865 filed with its 2002 income tax return.)

Example 3. Constructive ownership rules. Assume the same facts as in *Example 2.* In addition, on January 1, 2003, US2, a United States person and the brother of US, purchases 50% of the stock of FC, a foreign corporation. FC owns a 20% interest in FPS. Thus, under sections 6038(e)(3) and 267(c)(1), US2 indirectly owns a 10% interest in FPS (10% is US2's proportionate share of FC's 20% interest in FPS), and under sections 6038(e)(3) and 267(c)(2), US2 is attributed US's 40% interest. Additionally, US directly owns a 40% interest in FPS and is attributed US2's 10% interest pursuant to section 6038(e)(3) and section 267(c)(2). Therefore, US2 is considered to own a 50% interest (10% indirectly and 40% from US) in FPS, and US is considered to own a 50% interest in FPS (40% directly and 10% from US2). FPS has no controlling fifty-percent partners, because neither US, US1, nor US2, owns a greater than 50% interest. However, US, US1, and US2 are each controlling ten-percent partners and each must file Form 8865 pursuant to section 6038 for FPS's 2003 tax year ending December 31, 2003. Each must attach Form 8865 to its tax return for its 2003 tax year.

Example 4. Controlling fifty-percent partners. Assume the same facts as in *Example 3.* In addition, on June 1, 2004, US acquires an additional 1% direct interest in FPS. US is now a controlling fifty-percent partner of FPS, because US owns a 41% interest directly and a 10% interest constructively from US2. US2 is also a controlling fifty-percent partner, because US2 owns 10% indirectly and 41% constructively from US. Both US and US2 are required to file Form 8865 containing all the information required to be submitted by controlling fifty-percent partners. (But see paragraph (c)(1) of this section, which contains filing exceptions when there are multiple controlling fifty-percent partners). US1 is no longer a controlling ten-percent partner because FPS now has at least one controlling fifty-percent partner, and US1 does not qualify as a controlling fifty-percent partner. Therefore, US1 is not required to file Form 8865 under section 6038.

Example 5. Constructive ownership from a nonresident alien. US, a United States person, does not own directly or constructively an interest in FPS, a foreign partnership. The tax year of FPS is the calendar year. NRA, a nonresident alien, is the mother of US. In 2002, NRA acquires a 55% interest in FPS. Because US owns neither a direct nor a constructive interest in FPS under sections 6038(e)(3) and 267(c)(1) or (5), NRA's interest is not attributed to US under sections 6038(e)(3) and 267(c)(2). If in 2003 NRA becomes a United States person, NRA's interest will be attributed to US. However, US is excused from filing Form 8865 if US satisfies the requirements of the constructive owners exception in paragraph (c)(2) of this section. In 2003, NRA is a controlling fifty-percent partner and must file a Form 8865 under section 6038 for FPS's 2003 tax year.

(c) *Exceptions when more than one United States person is required to file Form 8865 pursuant to section 6038.*—(1) *Multiple controlling fifty-percent partners.*—(i) *In general.*—If, with respect to the same foreign partnership for the same tax year, more than one United States person is a controlling fifty-percent partner, then in lieu of each controlling fifty-percent partner filing a separate Form 8865, only one Form 8865 from one of the controlling fifty-percent partners is required, provided all of the requirements of paragraph (c)(1)(ii) of this section are satisfied. A person that is a controlling fifty-percent partner solely because of an interest to which deductions or losses are allocated may file the single return only if there is no United States person that is a controlling fifty-percent partner by reason of an interest in capital or profits.

(ii) *Requirements.*—(A) The person undertaking the filing obligation must file Form 8865 with that person's income tax return in the manner provided by Form 8865 and the accompanying instructions. The return must contain all of the information that would have been required to be reported by this section if each controlling fifty-percent partner had filed its own Form 8865.

(B) Any controlling fifty-percent partner not filing Form 8865 must file with its income tax return a statement titled "Controlled Foreign Partnership Reporting" containing the following information—

(1) A statement that the person qualified as a controlling fifty-percent partner, but is not submitting Form 8865 pursuant to the multiple controlling fifty-percent partners exception;

(2) The name, address, and taxpayer identification number (if any) of the foreign partnership of which the person qualified as a controlling fifty-percent partner;

(3) A representation that the filing requirement has been or will be satisfied;

(4) The name and address of the person filing the single return;

(5) The Internal Revenue Service Center where the single return is required to be filed; and

(6) Any additional information that Form 8865 and the accompanying instructions require.

(iii) *Penalties.*—If the requirements listed in paragraph (c)(1)(ii) of this section are not satisfied, a United States person that did not file a Form 8865 pursuant to this paragraph will be subject to the penalties in paragraph (k) of this section, unless the reasonable cause provision in paragraph (k)(4) of this section is satisfied.

(2) *Certain constructive owners excepted from furnishing information.*—(i) *In general.*—A United States person that does not own a direct interest in the foreign partnership and that is required to file Form 8865 under this section solely by reason of constructive ownership from a United States person(s) pursuant to paragraph (b)(4) of this section (an indirect partner) is not required to file Form 8865 if all of the requirements listed in paragraph (c)(2)(ii) of this section are met.

(ii) *Requirements.*—(A) The United States person(s) whose interest the indirect partner constructively owns reports all the information such person(s) is required to submit under this section, unless such person also is required to file solely by reason of constructive ownership from a United States person(s) pursuant to paragraph (b)(4) of this section, or another person reports the information pursuant to paragraph (c)(1) of this section.

(B) The indirect partner files with its income tax return a statement titled "Controlled Foreign Partnership Reporting" containing the following information—

(1) A representation that the indirect partner was required to file Form 8865, but is not doing so pursuant to the constructive owners exception;

(2) The names and addresses of the United States persons whose interests the indirect partner constructively owns;

(3) The name and address of the foreign partnership with respect to which the indirect partner would have had to have filed Form 8865 but for this exception; and

(4) Any additional information that Form 8865 and the accompanying instructions require.

(iii) *Penalties.*—A United States person that pursuant to this paragraph (c)(2) does not file a return will be subject to the penalties in paragraph (k) of this section if the requirements listed in paragraph (c)(2)(ii) of this section are not satisfied, unless such failure is due to reasonable cause, as defined in paragraph (k)(4) of this section.

(iv) *Overlap with multiple controlling fifty-percent partners exception.*—(A) If a United States person qualifies for both the exception in paragraph (c)(1) of this section and the exception in this paragraph (c)(2), such person may only utilize the multiple controlling fifty-percent partners exception in paragraph (c)(1) of this section to avoid filing Form 8865.

(B) *Example.*—The following example illustrates the operation of this paragraph (c)(2)(iv):

Example. US is a U.S. citizen. *US* owns 100% of the stock of *DC*, a domestic corporation. *DC* owns a 60% direct interest in *FPS*, a foreign partnership. *DC* and *US* are the only U.S. persons that own interests directly or constructively in *FPS*. *DC* owns directly a greater than 50% interest in *FPS*. *US* constructively owns *DC*'s interest pursuant to sections 6038(e)(3) and 267(c)(1). Therefore, both *DC* and *US* are controlling fifty-percent partners. *US* qualifies for both the exception in paragraph (c)(1) of this section (multiple controlling fifty-percent partners) and the exception in paragraph (c)(2) of this section (constructive owner exception). *US* may only utilize the paragraph (c)(1) exception to avoid its filing obligation. Accordingly, *DC* may file a single Form 8865 on behalf of *US* and itself. However, that form must contain all the information that would have been submitted had *DC* and *US* each submitted a separate Form 8865.

(3) *Members of an affiliated group of corporations filing a consolidated return.*—If one or more members of an affiliated group of corporations filing a consolidated return are required under section 6038 to file a Form 8865 for a particular foreign partnership, the common parent corporation may file one Form 8865 on behalf of all of the members of the group required to report under section 6038. Except with respect to group members who also qualify under the exception in paragraph (c)(2) of this section, the Form 8865 must contain all the information that would have been required to be submitted if each group member were required to file its own Form 8865.

(d) *Exception for certain trusts.*—Trusts relating to state and local government employee retirement plans are not required to report under this section, unless the instructions to Form 8865 provide otherwise.

(e) *Reporting under this section not required with respect to partnerships excluded from the application of subchapter K.*—The reporting requirements of this section will not apply to any United States person in respect of an eligible partnership as described in § 1.761-2(a) if such partnership has validly elected to be excluded from all of the provisions of subchapter K of chapter 1 of the Internal Revenue Code in the manner specified in § 1.761-2(b)(2)(i), or such partnership is deemed to have elected to be excluded from all of the provisions of subchapter K of chapter 1 of the Internal Revenue Code in accordance with the provisions of § 1.761-2(b)(2)(ii).

(f) *Period covered by return.*—The information required under this section must be furnished for the tax year of the foreign partnership ending with or within the United States person's tax year. See section 706 for rules regarding tax years of partnerships.

(g) *Contents of return.*—(1) *Information required to be submitted by controlling fifty-percent partners and controlling ten-percent partners.*—All controlling fifty-percent partners and all controlling ten-percent partners must submit the following information on Form 8865 in the form and manner and to the extent prescribed by Form 8865 and its instructions—

(i) The name, address, and taxpayer identification number (if any) of the foreign partnership of which the person qualified as a controlling fifty-percent partner or a controlling ten-percent partner;

(ii) A statement of the income, gain, losses, deductions and credits allocated to the direct interest in the partnership of the person reporting under section 6038;

(iii) A list of all partnerships (foreign or domestic) in which the foreign partnership owned a direct interest, or owned a constructive interest of ten percent of more under the rules of section 267(c)(1) or (5), during the partnership's tax year for which the Form 8865 is being filed;

(iv) Information about all foreign entities that were disregarded as entities separate from their owner under §§ 301.7701-2 and 301.7701-3 that were owned by the foreign partnership during the partnership's tax year for which the Form 8865 is being filed;

(v) A summary of the transactions that took place during the partnership's tax year between the partnership and the person filing the return, between the partnership and any other partnership of which the person filing the return is a controlling fifty-percent partner, and between the partnership and any corporation controlled (under section 6038(e)(2) and the regulations thereunder) by the person filing the return; and

(vi) Any other information that Form 8865 or its accompanying instructions require to be submitted.

(2) *Additional information required to be submitted by controlling fifty-percent partners.*—In addition to the information required pursuant to paragraph (g)(1) of this section, controlling fifty-percent partners must also submit the following

information in the form and manner and to the extent required by Form 8865 and its instructions—

(i) A list of the names, addresses and tax identification numbers (if any) of each United States person that owned a direct interest of ten percent or more in the partnership during the partnership's tax year, and of each United States and foreign person whose interests in the partnership the controlling fifty-percent partner constructively owned under paragraph (b)(4) of this section during the partnership's tax year;

(ii) A list of transactions between the partnership and any United States person owning at the time of the transaction at least a 10-percent direct interest (as defined in paragraph (b)(3) of this section) in the foreign partnership;

(iii) A statement of the aggregate of the partners' distributive shares of items of income, gain, losses, deductions and credits;

(iv) A statement of income, gain, losses, deductions and credits allocated to each United States person holding a direct interest in the foreign partnership of ten percent or more; and

(v) Any other information Form 8865 or its accompanying instructions require controlling fifty-percent partners to submit.

(h) *Method of reporting.*—Except as otherwise provided on Form 8865 or the accompanying instructions, all amounts required to be furnished on Form 8865 must be expressed in United States dollars. All statements required on or with Form 8865 pursuant to this section must be in English.

(i) *Time and place for filing return.*—(1) *In general.*—Form 8865 must be filed with the United States person's income tax return on or before the due date (including extensions) of that return. If the United States person is not required to file an income tax return for its tax year with which or within which the foreign partnership's tax year ends, but is required to file an information return for that year (for example, Form 1065, "U.S. Partnership Return of Income," or Form 990, "Return of Organization Exempt from Income Tax"), the Form 8865 must be filed with the United States person's information return filed on or before the due date (including extensions) of that return.

(2) *Duplicate return.*—If required by the instructions to Form 8865, a duplicate Form 8865 (including attachments and schedules) must also be filed.

(j) *Overlap with section 6031.*—A partner may be required to file Form 8865 under this section and the foreign partnership in which it is a partner may also be required to file a Form 1065 or Form 1065-B under section 6031(e) for the same

Reg. § 1.6038-3(j)

partnership tax year. For cases where a United States person is a controlling fifty-percent partner or a controlling ten-percent partner with respect to a foreign partnership, and that foreign partnership completes and files Form 1065 or Form 1065-B, the instructions for Form 8865 will specify the filing requirements that address this overlap in reporting obligations.

(k) *Failure to comply with reporting requirement.*—(1) *In general.*—Any United States person required to file Form 8865 under Section 6038 and this section that fails to comply (as defined in paragraph (k)(2) of this section) with the reporting requirements of this section, will be subject to the penalties described in paragraph (k)(3) of this section.

(2) *Failure to comply.*—A failure to comply is separately determined for each foreign partnership for which a United States person has a section 6038 reporting obligation. A failure to comply with the requirements of section 6038 includes the following—

(i) The failure to report at the proper time and in the proper manner any information required to be reported under the rules of this section; or

(ii) The provision of false or inaccurate information in purported compliance with the requirements of this section.

(3) *Penalties.*—A United States person that fails to comply (as defined in paragraph (k)(2) of this section) with the reporting requirements of this section must pay the following penalties, subject to the reasonable cause exception in paragraph (k)(4) of this section:

(i) *Dollar amount penalty.*—(A) *$10,000 penalty.*—A penalty of $10,000 shall be imposed for each tax year of each foreign partnership with respect to which a failure to comply occurs.

(B) *Increase in penalty.*—If a failure to comply with the applicable reporting requirements of section 6038 and this section continues for more than 90 days after the date on which the Commissioner or the Commissioner's delegate mails notice of the failure to the United States person required to file Form 8865, the person must pay an additional penalty of $10,000 for each 30-day period (or fraction thereof) during which the failure continues after the 90-day period has expired.

(C) *Limitation.*—The additional penalty imposed on any United States person by section 6038(b)(2) and paragraph (k)(3)(i)(B) of this section is limited to a maximum of $50,000 for each partnership for each tax year with respect to which the failure occurs.

(ii) *Penalty of reducing foreign tax credit.*—(A) *Effect on foreign tax credit.*—Failure to comply with the reporting requirements of section 6038 and this section may cause a reduction of foreign tax credits under section 901 (taxes of foreign countries and of possessions of the United States). In applying section 901 to a United States

person for any tax year with or within which its foreign partnership's tax year ended, the amount of taxes paid (and deemed paid under sections 902 and 960) by the United States person will be reduced by 10 percent if the person fails to comply. However, no tax deemed paid under section 904(c) will be reduced under the provisions of this paragraph (k)(3)(ii).

(B) *Reduction for continued failure.*—If a failure to comply with the reporting requirements of section 6038 and this section continues for more than 90 days after the date on which the Commissioner or the Commissioner's delegate mails notice of the failure to the person required to file Form 8865, then the amount of the reduction in paragraph (k)(3)(ii)(A) of this section will be 10 percent, plus an additional 5 percent for each 3-month period (or fraction thereof) during which the failure continues after the 90-day period has expired.

(C) *Limitation on reduction.*—The amount of the reduction under paragraphs (k)(3)(ii)(A) and (B) of this section for each failure to furnish information required under this section will not exceed the greater of $10,000, or the gross income of the foreign partnership for its tax year with respect to which the failure occurred.

(D) *Offset for dollar amount penalty imposed.*—The total amount of the reduction which, but for this paragraph (k)(3)(ii)(D), may be made under this paragraph (k)(3)(ii) with respect to any separate failure, may not exceed the maximum amount of the reductions that may be imposed, reduced (but not below zero) by the dollar amount penalty imposed by paragraph (k)(3)(i) of this section with respect to the failure.

(4) *Reasonable cause limitation.*—The time prescribed for filing a complete Form 8865, and the beginning of the 90-day period after the Commissioner or the Commissioner's delegate mails notice under paragraphs (k)(3)(i)(B) and (ii)(B) of this section, will be treated as being not earlier than the last day on which reasonable cause existed for failure to furnish the information. The United States person may show reasonable cause by providing a written statement to the Commissioner's delegate having jurisdiction over the person's return to which the Form 8865 should have been attached, setting forth the reasons for the failure to comply. Whether a failure to comply was due to reasonable cause will be determined by the Commissioner, or the Commissioner's delegate, under all the facts and circumstances.

(5) *Statute of limitations.*—For exceptions to the limitations on assessment in the event of a failure to provide information under section 6038, see section 6501(c)(8).

(l) *Effective date.*—Except as otherwise provided, this section shall apply for tax years of a foreign partnership ending on or after December 31, 2000. For tax years of a foreign partnership ending before December 23, 2002, see

§ 1.6038-3(j) in effect prior to the amendments made by T.D. 9033 (see 26 CFR part 1 revised April 1, 2002). [Reg. § 1.6038-3.]

☐ [*T.D. 8850, 12-27-99. Amended by T.D. 9033, 12-20-2002 and T.D. 9065, 6-30-2003.*]

[Reg. § 1.6038-4]

§ 1.6038-4. Information returns required of certain United States persons with respect to such person's U.S. multinational enterprise group.—(a) *Requirement of return.*—Except as provided in paragraph (h) of this section, every ultimate parent entity of a U.S. multinational enterprise (MNE) group must make an annual return on Form 8975, *Country-by-Country Report,* setting forth the information described in paragraph (d) of this section, and any other information required by Form 8975, with respect to the reporting period described in paragraph (c) of this section.

(b) *Definitions.*—(1) *Ultimate parent entity of a U.S. MNE group.*—An ultimate parent entity of a U.S. MNE group is a U.S. business entity that:

(i) Owns directly or indirectly a sufficient interest in one or more other business entities, at least one of which is organized or tax resident in a tax jurisdiction other than the United States, such that the U.S. business entity is required to consolidate the accounts of the other business entities with its own accounts under U.S. generally accepted accounting principles, or would be so required if equity interests in the U.S. business entity were publicly traded on a U.S. securities exchange; and

(ii) Is not owned directly or indirectly by another business entity that consolidates the accounts of such U.S. business entity with its own accounts under generally accepted accounting principles in the other business entity's tax jurisdiction of residence, or would be so required if equity interests in the other business entity were traded on a public securities exchange in its tax jurisdiction of residence.

(2) *Business entity.*—For purposes of this section, a business entity generally is any entity recognized for federal tax purposes that is not properly classified as a trust under § 301.7701-4 of this chapter. However, any grantor trust within the meaning of section 671, all or a portion of which is owned by a person other an individual, is a business entity for purposes of this section. Additionally, the term business entity includes any entity with a single owner that may be disregarded as an entity separate from its owner under § 301.7701-3 of this chapter and a permanent establishment, as defined in paragraph (b)(3) of this section, that prepares financial statements separate from those of its owner for financial reporting, regulatory, tax reporting, or internal management control purposes. A business entity does not include a decedent's estate or a bankruptcy estate described in section 1398.

(3) *Permanent establishment.*—For purposes of this section, the term permanent establishment includes:

(i) A branch or business establishment of a constituent entity in a tax jurisdiction that is treated as a permanent establishment under an income tax convention to which that tax jurisdiction is a party;

(ii) A branch or business establishment of a constituent entity that is liable to tax in the tax jurisdiction in which it is located pursuant to the domestic law of such tax jurisdiction; or

(iii) A branch or business establishment of a constituent entity that is treated in the same manner for tax purposes as an entity separate from its owner by the owner's tax jurisdiction of residence.

(4) *U.S. business entity.*—A U.S. business entity is a business entity that is organized or has its tax jurisdiction of residence in the United States. For purposes of this section, foreign insurance companies that elect to be treated as domestic corporations under section 953(d) are U.S. business entities that have their tax jurisdiction of residence in the United States.

(5) *U.S. MNE group.*—A U.S. MNE group comprises the ultimate parent entity of a U.S. MNE group as defined in paragraph (b)(1) of this section and all of the business entities required to consolidate their accounts with the ultimate parent entity's accounts under U.S. generally accepted accounting principles, or that would be so required if equity interests in the ultimate parent entity were publicly traded on a U.S. securities exchange, regardless of whether any such business entities could be excluded from consolidation solely on size or materiality grounds.

(6) *Constituent entity.*—With respect to a U.S. MNE group, a constituent entity is any separate business entity of such U.S. MNE group, except that the term constituent entity does not include a foreign corporation or foreign partnership for which the ultimate parent entity is not required to furnish information under section 6038(a) (determined without regard to §§ 1.6038-2(j) and 1.6038-3(c)) or any permanent establishment of such foreign corporation or foreign partnership.

(7) *Tax jurisdiction.*—For purposes of this section, a tax jurisdiction is a country or a jurisdiction that is not a country but that has fiscal autonomy. For purposes of this section, a U.S. territory or possession of the United States is considered to have fiscal autonomy.

(8) *Tax jurisdiction of residence.*—A business entity is considered a resident in a tax jurisdiction if, under the laws of that tax jurisdiction, the business entity is liable to tax therein based on place of management, place of organization, or another similar criterion. A business entity will not be considered a resident in a tax jurisdiction if the business entity is liable to tax in such tax jurisdiction only by reason of a tax imposed by

reference to gross amounts of income without any reduction for expenses, provided such tax applies only with respect to income from sources in such tax jurisdiction or capital situated in such tax jurisdiction. If a business entity is resident in more than one tax jurisdiction, then the applicable income tax convention rules, if any, should be applied to determine the business entity's tax jurisdiction of residence. If a business entity is resident in more than one tax jurisdiction and no applicable income tax convention exists between those tax jurisdictions, or if the applicable income tax convention provides that the determination of residence is based on a determination by the competent authorities of the relevant tax jurisdictions and no such determination has been made, the business entity's tax jurisdiction of residence is the tax jurisdiction of the business entity's place of effective management determined in accordance with Article 4 of the Organisation for Economic Co-operation and Development Model Tax Convention on Income and on Capital 2014, or as provided by Form 8975. A corporation that is organized or managed in a tax jurisdiction that does not impose an income tax on corporations will be treated as resident in that tax jurisdiction, unless such corporation is treated as resident in another tax jurisdiction under another provision of this section. The tax jurisdiction of residence of a permanent establishment is the jurisdiction in which the permanent establishment is located. If a business entity does not have a tax jurisdiction of residence, then solely for purposes of paragraph (b)(1) of this section, the tax jurisdiction of residence is the business entity's country of organization.

(9) *Applicable financial statements.*—An applicable financial statement is a certified audited financial statement that is accompanied by a report of an independent certified public accountant or similarly qualified independent professional that is used for purposes of reporting to shareholders, partners, or similar persons; for purposes of reporting to creditors in connection with securing or maintaining financing; or for any other substantial non-tax purpose.

(10) *U.S. territory or possession of the United States.*—The term U.S. territory or possession of the United States means American Samoa, Guam, the Northern Mariana Islands, Puerto Rico, or the U.S. Virgin Islands.

(11) *U.S. territory ultimate parent entity.*—A U.S. territory ultimate parent entity is a business entity organized in a U.S. territory or possession of the United States that controls (as defined in section 6038(e)) a U.S. business entity and that is not owned directly or indirectly by another business entity that consolidates the accounts of the U.S. territory ultimate parent entity with its accounts under generally accepted accounting principles in the other business entity's tax jurisdiction of residence, or would be so required if equity interests in the other business entity were

traded on a public securities exchange in its tax jurisdiction of residence.

(c) *Reporting period.*—The reporting period covered by Form 8975 is the period of the ultimate parent entity's applicable financial statement prepared for the 12-month period (or a 52-53 week period described in section 441(f)) that ends with or within the ultimate parent entity's taxable year. If the ultimate parent entity does not prepare an annual applicable financial statement, then the reporting period covered by Form 8975 is the 12-month period (or a 52-53 week period described in section 441(f)) that ends on the last day of the ultimate parent entity's taxable year.

(d) *Contents of return.*—(1) *Constituent entity information.*—The return on Form 8975 must contain so much of the following information with respect to each constituent entity of the U.S. MNE group, and in such form or manner, as Form 8975 prescribes:

(i) The complete legal name of the constituent entity;

(ii) The tax jurisdiction, if any, in which the constituent entity is resident for tax purposes;

(iii) The tax jurisdiction in which the constituent entity is organized or incorporated (if different from the tax jurisdiction of residence);

(iv) The tax identification number, if any, used for the constituent entity by the tax administration of the constituent entity's tax jurisdiction of residence; and

(v) The main business activity or activities of the constituent entity.

(2) *Tax jurisdiction of residence information.*—The return on Form 8975 must contain so much of the following information with respect to each tax jurisdiction in which one or more constituent entities of a U.S. MNE group is resident, presented as an aggregate of the information for the constituent entities resident in each tax jurisdiction, and in such form or manner, as Form 8975 prescribes:

(i) Revenues generated from transactions with other constituent entities;

(ii) Revenues not generated from transactions with other constituent entities;

(iii) Profit or loss before income tax;

(iv) Total income tax paid on a cash basis to all tax jurisdictions, and any taxes withheld on payments received by the constituent entities;

(v) Total accrued tax expense recorded on taxable profits or losses, reflecting only operations in the relevant annual period and excluding deferred taxes or provisions for uncertain tax liabilities;

(vi) Stated capital, except that the stated capital of a permanent establishment must be reported in the tax jurisdiction of residence of the legal entity of which it is a permanent establishment unless there is a defined capital requirement in the permanent establishment tax jurisdiction for regulatory purposes;

(vii) Total accumulated earnings, except that accumulated earnings of a permanent establishment must be reported by the legal entity of which it is a permanent establishment;

(viii) Total number of employees on a full-time equivalent basis; and

(ix) Net book value of tangible assets, which, for purposes of this section, does not include cash or cash equivalents, intangibles, or financial assets.

(3) *Special rules.*—(i) *Constituent entity with no tax jurisdiction of residence.*—The information listed in paragraph (d)(2) of this section also must be provided, in the aggregate, for any constituent entity or entities that have no tax jurisdiction of residence. In addition, if a constituent entity is an owner of a constituent entity that does not have a jurisdiction of tax residence, then the owner's share of such entity's revenues and profits will be aggregated with the information for the owner's tax jurisdiction of residence.

(ii) *Definition of revenue.*—For purposes of this section, the term revenue includes all amounts of revenue, including revenue from sales of inventory and property, services, royalties, interest, and premiums. The term revenue does not include payments received from other constituent entities that are treated as dividends in the payor's tax jurisdiction of residence. Distributions and remittances from partnerships and other fiscally transparent entities and permanent establishments that are constituent entities are not considered revenue of the recipient-owner. The term revenue also does not include imputed earnings or deemed dividends received from other constituent entities that are taken into account solely for tax purposes and that otherwise would be included as revenue by a constituent entity. With respect to a constituent entity that is an organization exempt from taxation under section 501(a) because it is an organization described in section 501(c), 501(d), or 401(a), a state college or university described in section 511(a)(2)(B), a plan described in section 403(b) or 457(b), an individual retirement plan or annuity as defined in section 7701(a)(37), a qualified tuition program described in section 529, a qualified ABLE program described in section 529A, or a Coverdell education savings account described in section 530, the term revenue includes only revenue that is reflected in unrelated business taxable income as defined in section 512.

(iii) *Number of employees.*—For purposes of this section, the number of employees on a full-time equivalent basis may be reported as of the end of the accounting period, on the basis of average employment levels for the annual accounting period, or on any other reasonable basis consistently applied across tax jurisdictions and from year to year. Independent contractors participating in the ordinary operating activities of a constituent entity may be reported as employees of such constituent entity. Reasonable rounding or approximation of the number of employees is permissible, provided that such rounding or approximation does not materially distort the relative distribution of employees across the various tax jurisdictions. Consistent approaches should be applied from year to year and across entities.

(iv) *Income tax paid and accrued tax expense of permanent establishment.*—In the case of a constituent entity that is a permanent establishment, the amount of income tax paid and the amount of accrued tax expense referred to in paragraphs (d)(2)(iv) and (v) of this section should not include the income tax paid or tax expense accrued by the business entity of which the permanent establishment would be a part, but for the third sentence of paragraph (b)(2) of this section, in that business entity's tax jurisdiction of residence on the income derived by the permanent establishment.

(v) *Certain transportation income.*—If a constituent entity of a U.S. MNE group derives income from international transportation or transportation in inland waterways that is covered by income tax convention provisions that are specific to such income and under which the taxing rights on such income are allocated exclusively to one tax jurisdiction, then the U.S. MNE group should report the information required under paragraph (d)(2) of this section with respect to such income for the tax jurisdiction to which the relevant income tax convention provisions allocate these taxing rights.

(e) *Reporting of financial amounts.*—(1) *Reporting in U.S. dollars required.*—All amounts furnished under paragraph (d)(2) of this section, other than paragraph (d)(2)(viii) of this section, must be expressed in U.S. dollars. If an exchange rate is used other than in accordance with U.S. generally accepted accounting principles for conversion to U.S. dollars, the exchange rate must be indicated.

(2) *Sources of financial amounts.*—All amounts furnished under paragraph (d)(2) of this section, other than paragraph (d)(2)(viii) of this section, should be based on applicable financial statements, books and records maintained with respect to the constituent entity, regulatory financial statements, or records used for tax reporting or internal management control purposes for an annual period of each constituent entity ending with or within the period described in paragraph (c) of this section.

(f) *Time and manner for filing.*—Returns on Form 8975 required under paragraph (a) of this section for a reporting period must be filed with the ultimate parent entity's income tax return for the taxable year, in or with which the reporting period ends, on or before the due date (including extensions) for filing that person's income tax return or as otherwise prescribed by Form 8975.

(g) *Maintenance of records.*—The U.S. person filing Form 8975 as an ultimate parent entity of a U.S. MNE group must maintain records to support the information provided on Form 8975. However, the U.S. person is not required to cre-

Reg. §1.6038-4(g)

ate and maintain records that reconcile the amounts provided on Form 8975 with the tax returns of any tax jurisdiction or applicable financial statements.

(h) *Exceptions to furnishing information.*—An ultimate parent entity of a U.S. MNE group is not required to report information under this section for the reporting period described in paragraph (c) of this section if the annual revenue of the U.S. MNE group for the immediately preceding reporting period was less than $850,000,000.

(i) [Reserved]

(j) *U.S. territories and possessions of the United States.*—A U.S. territory ultimate parent entity may designate a U.S. business entity that it controls (as defined in section 6038(e)) to file Form 8975 on the U.S. territory ultimate parent entity's behalf with respect to such U.S. territory ultimate parent entity and the business entities that would be required to consolidate their accounts with such U.S. territory ultimate parent entity under U.S. generally accepted accounting principles, or would be so required if equity interests in the U.S. territory ultimate parent entity were publicly traded on a U.S. securities exchange.

(k) *Applicability dates.*—The rules of this section apply to reporting periods of ultimate parent entities of U.S. MNE groups that begin on or after the first day of a taxable year of the ultimate parent entity that begins on or after June 30, 2016. [Reg. § 1.6038-4.]

☐ [T.D. 9773, 6-29-2016 (*corrected* 9-16-2016).]

[Reg. § 1.6038A-0]

§ 1.6038A-0. Table of contents.—This section lists the captions that appear in the regulations under section 6038A.

§ 1.6038A-1. General requirements and definitions.
(a) Purpose and scope.
(b) In general.
(c) Reporting corporation.
(1) In general.
(2) 25-percent foreign-owned.
(3) 25-percent foreign shareholder.
(i) In general.
(ii) Total voting power and value.
(iii) Direct 25-percent foreign shareholder.
(iv) Indirect 25-percent foreign shareholder.
(4) Application to prior open years.
(5) Exceptions.
(i) Treaty country residents having no permanent establishment.
(ii) Qualified exempt shipping income.
(iii) Status as a foreign related party.
(d) Related party.
(e) Attribution rules.
(1) Attribution under section 318.
(2) Attribution of transactions with related parties engaged in by a partnership.
(f) Foreign person.
(g) Foreign related party.

(h) Small corporation exception.
(i) Safe harbor for reporting corporations with related party transactions of *de minimis* value.
(1) In general.
(2) Aggregate value of gross payments made or received.
(j) Related reporting corporations.
(k) Consolidated return groups.
(1) Required information.
(2) Maintenance of records and authorization of agent.
(3) Monetary penalties.
(l) District Director.
(m) Examples.
(n) Effective dates.
(1) Section 1.6038A-1.
(2) Section 1.6038A-2.
(3) Section 1.6038A-3.
(4) Section 1.6038A-4.
(5) Section 1.6038A-5.
(6) Section 1.6038A-6.
(7) Section 1.6038A-7.

§ 1.6038A-2. Requirement of return.
(a) Form 5472 required.
(1) In general.
(2) Reportable transaction.
(b) Contents of return.
(1) Reporting corporation.
(2) Related party.
(3) Foreign related party transactions for which only monetary consideration is paid or received by the reporting corporation.
(4) Foreign related party transactions involving nonmonetary consideration or less than full consideration.
(5) Additional information.
(6) Reasonable estimate.
(i) Estimate within 25 percent of actual amount.
(ii) Other estimates.
(7) Small amounts.
(8) Accrued payments and receipts.
(9) Examples.
(c) Method of reporting.
(d) Time and place for filing returns.
(e) Untimely filed return.
(f) Exceptions.
(1) No reportable transactions.
(2) Transactions solely with a domestic reporting corporation.
(3) Transactions with a corporation subject to reporting under section 6038.
(4) Transactions with a foreign sales corporation.
(g) Filing Form 5472 when transactions with related parties engaged in by a partnership are attributed to a reporting corporation.
(h) Effective dates for certain reporting corporations.

§ 1.6038A-3. Record maintenance.
(a) General maintenance requirements.

(1) Section 6001 and section 6038A.

(2) Safe harbor.

(3) Examples.

(b) Other maintenance requirements.

(1) Indirectly related records.

(2) Foreign related party or third-party maintenance.

(3) Translation of records.

(4) Exception for foreign governments.

(c) Specific records to be maintained for safe harbor.

(1) In general.

(2) Descriptions of categories of documents to be maintained.

(i) Original entry books and transaction records.

(ii) Profit and loss statements.

(iii) Pricing documents.

(iv) Foreign country and third-party filings.

(v) Ownership and capital structure records.

(vi) Records of loans, services, and other non-sales transactions.

(3) Material profit and loss statements.

(4) Existing records test.

(5) Significant industry segment test.

(i) In general.

(ii) Form of the statements.

(iii) Special rule for component sales.

(iv) Level of specificity required.

(v) Examples.

(6) High profit test.

(i) In general.

(ii) Return on assets test.

(iii) Additional rules.

(7) Definitions.

(i) U.S.-connected products or services.

(ii) Industry segment.

(iii) Gross revenue of an industry segment.

(iv) Identifiable assets of an industry segment.

(v) Operating profit of an industry segment.

(vi) Product.

(vii) Related products or services.

(viii) Model.

(ix) Product line.

(8) Example.

(i) Facts.

(ii) Existing records test.

(iii) Significant industry segments.

(iv) High profit test.

(v) Material profit and loss statements.

(d) Liability for certain partnership record maintenance.

(e) Agreements with the District Director or the Assistant Commissioner (International).

(1) In general.

(2) Content of agreement.

(i) In general.

(ii) Significant industry segment test.

(iii) Example.

(3) Circumstances of agreement.

(4) Agreement as part of APA process.

(f) U.S. maintenance.

(1) General rule.

(2) Non-U.S. maintenance requirements.

(3) Prior taxable years.

(4) Scheduled production for high volume or other reasons.

(5) Required U.S. maintenance.

(g) Period of retention.

(h) Application of record maintenance rules to banks and other financial institutions. [Reserved]

(i) Effective dates.

§ 1.6038A-4. Monetary penalty.

(a) Imposition of monetary penalty.

(1) In general.

(2) Liability for certain partnership transactions.

(3) Calculation of monetary penalty.

(b) Reasonable cause.

(1) In general.

(2) Affirmative showing required.

(i) In general.

(ii) Small corporations.

(iii) Facts and circumstances taken into account.

(c) Failure to maintain records or to cause another to maintain records.

(d) Increase in penalty where failure continues after notification.

(1) In general.

(2) Additional penalty for another failure.

(3) Cessation of accrual.

(4) Continued failures.

(e) Other penalties.

(f) Examples.

Example (1)—Failure to file Form 5472.

Example (2)—Failure to maintain records.

(g) Effective dates.

§ 1.6038A-5. Authorization of agent.

(a) Failure to authorize.

(b) Authorization by related party.

(1) In general.

(2) Authorization for prior years.

(c) Foreign affiliated groups.

(1) In general.

(2) Application of noncompliance penalty adjustment.

(d) Legal effect of authorization of agent.

(1) Agent for purposes of commencing judicial proceedings.

(2) Foreign related party found where reporting corporation found.

(e) Successors in interest.

(f) Deemed compliance.

(1) In general.

(2) Reason to know.

(3) Effect of deemed compliance.

(g) Effective dates.

Reg. § 1.6038A-0

§ 1.6038A-6. *Failure to furnish information.*
  (a) In general.
  (b) Coordination with treaties.
  (c) Enforcement proceeding not required.
  (d) *De minimis* failure.
  (e) Suspension of statute of limitations.
  (f) Effective dates.

§ 1.6038A-7. *Noncompliance.*
  (a) In general.
  (b) Determination of the amount.
  (c) Separate application.
  (d) Effective dates. [Reg. § 1.6038A-0.]

☐ [*T.D.* 8353, 6-14-91. *Amended by T.D.* 9796, 12-12-2016.]

[Reg. § 1.6038A-1]

§ 1.6038A-1. General requirements and definitions.—(a) *Purpose and scope.*—This section and §§ 1.6038A-2 through 1.6038A-7 provide rules for certain foreign-owned U.S. corporations and foreign corporations engaged in trade or business within the United States (reporting corporations) relating to information that must be furnished, records that must be maintained, and the authorization of the reporting corporation to act as agent for related foreign persons for purposes of sections 7602, 7603, and 7604 that must be executed. Section 6038A(a) and this section require that a reporting corporation furnish certain information annually and maintain certain records relating to transactions between the reporting corporation and certain related parties. This section also provides definitions of terms used in section 6038A. Section 1.6038A-2 provides guidance concerning the information to be submitted and the filing of the required return. Section 1.6038A-3 provides guidance concerning the maintenance of records. Section 1.6038A-4 provides guidance concerning the application of the monetary penalty for the failure either to furnish information or to maintain records. Section 1.6038A-5 provides guidance concerning the authorization of an agent for purposes of sections 7602, 7603, and 7604. Section 1.6038A-6 provides guidance concerning the failure to furnish information requested by a summons. Finally, § 1.6038A-7 provides guidance concerning the application of the noncompliance penalty for failure by the related party to authorize an agent or by the reporting corporation to substantially comply with a summons.

  (b) *In general.*—A reporting corporation must furnish the information described in § 1.6038A-2 by filing an annual information return (Form 5472 or any successor), and must maintain records as described in § 1.6038A-3.

  (c) *Reporting corporation.*—(1) *In general.*—For purposes of section 6038A, a reporting corporation is either a domestic corporation that is 25-percent foreign-owned as defined in paragraph (c)(2) of this section, or a foreign corporation that is 25-percent foreign-owned and engaged in trade or business within the United States. After November 4, 1990, a foreign corporation engaged in a trade or business within the United States at any time during a taxable year is a reporting corporation. *See* section 6038C. A domestic business entity that is wholly owned by one foreign person and that is otherwise classified under § 301.7701-3(b)(1)(ii) of this chapter as disregarded as an entity separate from its owner is treated as an entity separate from its owner and classified as a domestic corporation for purposes of section 6038A. *See* § 301.7701-2(c)(2)(vi) of this chapter.

  (2) *25-percent foreign-owned.*—A corporation is 25-percent foreign-owned if it has at least one direct or indirect 25-percent foreign shareholder at any time during the taxable year.

  (3) *25-percent foreign shareholder.*—(i) *In general.*—A foreign person is a 25-percent foreign shareholder of a corporation if the person owns at least 25 percent of—
    (A) The total voting power of all classes of stock of the corporation entitled to vote, or
    (B) The total value of all classes of stock of the corporation.

    (ii) *Total voting power and value.*—In determining whether one foreign person owns 25 percent of the total voting power of all classes of stock of a corporation entitled to vote or 25 percent of the total value of all classes of stock of a corporation, consideration will be given to all the facts and circumstances of each case, under principles similar to § 1.957-1(b)(2) (consideration of arrangements to shift formal voting power away from a foreign person).

    (iii) *Direct 25-percent foreign shareholder.*—A foreign person is a direct 25-percent foreign shareholder if it owns directly at least 25 percent of the stock of the reporting corporation, either by vote or by value.

    (iv) *Indirect 25-percent foreign shareholder.*—A foreign person is an indirect 25-percent foreign shareholder if it owns indirectly (or under the attribution rules of section 318 is considered to own indirectly) at least 25 percent of the stock of the reporting corporation, either by vote or by value.

  (4) *Application to prior open years.*—For taxable years beginning before July 11, 1989, the definition of a reporting corporation under this paragraph applies in determining whether a foreign-owned corporation is a reporting corporation. An examination may be reopened if the statute of limitations period for that taxable year has not expired. A taxable year may not be reopened under section 6038A for examination purposes if the taxable year is open under section 6511 only for purposes of the carryback of net operating losses or net capital losses.

  (5) *Exceptions.*—(i) *Treaty country residents having no permanent establishment.*—A foreign corporation that has no permanent establishment in the United States under an applicable income tax convention is not a reporting corporation for purposes of section 6038A and this

section. Accordingly, such a foreign corporation is not subject to §§1.6038A-2, 1.6038A-3, and 1.6038A-5. It must timely and fully provide the required notice to the Commissioner under section 6114. See section 6114 and the regulations thereunder for the notice that such a corporation must file and the applicable penalties for failure to file such notice.

(ii) *Qualified exempt shipping income.*—A foreign corporation whose gross income is exempt from U.S. taxation under section 883 is not a reporting corporation provided that it timely and fully complies with the reporting requirements required to claim such exemption. In the event that such a corporation does not timely and fully comply with the reporting requirements under sections 887 and 883, it will be a reporting corporation subject to section 6038A, including the application of the monetary penalty for failure to file required information.

(iii) *Status as foreign related party.*—Nothing in this paragraph affects the determination of whether a person is a foreign related party as defined in paragraph (g) of this section.

(d) *Related party.*—The term "related party" means—

(1) Any direct or indirect 25-percent foreign shareholder of the reporting corporation,

(2) Any person who is related within the meaning of sections 267(b) or 707(b)(1) to the reporting corporation or to a 25-percent foreign shareholder of the reporting corporation, or

(3) Any other person who is related to the reporting corporation within the meaning of section 482 and the regulations thereunder.

However, the term "related party" does not include any corporation filing a consolidated federal income tax return with the reporting corporation.

(e) *Attribution rules.*—(1) *Attribution under section 318.*—For purposes of determining whether a corporation is 25-percent foreign-owned and whether a person is a related party under section 6038A, the constructive ownership rules of section 318 shall apply, and the attribution rules of section 267(c) also shall apply to the extent they attribute ownership to persons to whom section 318 does not attribute ownership. However, "10 percent" shall be substituted for "50 percent" in section 318(a)(2)(C), and section 318(a)(3)(A), (B), and (C) shall not be applied so as to consider a U.S. person as owning stock that is owned by a person who is not a U.S. person. Additionally, section 318(a)(3)(C) and §1.318-1(b) shall not be applied so as to consider a U.S. corporation as being a reporting corporation if, but for the application of such sections, the U.S. corporation would not be 25-percent foreign owned.

(2) *Attribution of transactions with related parties engaged in by a partnership.*—The transactions in which a domestic or foreign partnership engages shall be attributed to any reporting corporation whose interest in the capital or profits of the partnership, either directly or indirectly, combined with the interests of all related parties of the reporting corporation partner, equals 25 percent or more of the total partnership interests. Attribution of such transactions shall be made only to the extent of the partnership interest held by that reporting corporation partner. *See* sections 875 and 702(a) and the regulations thereunder. (Attribution shall not be made, however, of transactions directly between the partnership and a reporting corporation.) Accordingly, a reporting corporation partner that is deemed to engage in transactions with related parties under this rule is subject to the information reporting requirements of §1.6038A-2, to the record maintenance requirements of §1.6038A-3, to the monetary penalty under §1.6038A-4, to the requirement of authorization of agent under §1.6038A-5, to the rules of §1.6038A-6 relating to the requirement to produce records, and to the noncompliance penalty adjustment under §1.6038A-7.

(f) *Foreign person.*—For purposes of section 6038A, a foreign person is—

(1) Any individual who is not a citizen or resident of the United States, but not including any individual for whom an election under section 6013(g) or (h) (relating to an election to file a joint return) is in effect;

(2) Any individual who is a citizen of any possession of the United States and who is not otherwise a citizen or resident of the United States;

(3) Any partnership, association, company, or corporation that is not created or organized in the United States or under the law of the United States or any State thereof;

(4) Any foreign trust or foreign estate, as defined in section 7701(a)(31); or

(5) Any foreign government (or agency or instrumentality thereof). To the extent that a foreign government is engaged in the conduct of commercial activity as defined under section 892 and the regulations thereunder, it will be treated as a foreign person under section 6038A and this section only for purposes of the information reporting requirements of §1.6038A-2. A foreign government will not be treated as a foreign related party for purposes of §§1.6038A-3 and 1.6038A-5.

For purposes of section 6038A, a possession of the United States shall be considered to be a foreign country.

(g) *Foreign related party.*—A foreign related party is a foreign person as defined under paragraph (f) of this section that is also a related party as defined under paragraph (d) of this section.

(h) *Small corporation exception.*—A reporting corporation (other than an entity that is a reporting corporation as a result of being treated as a corporation under §301.7701-2(c)(2)(vi) of this chapter) that has less than $10,000,000 in U.S. gross receipts for a taxable year is not subject to §§1.6038A-3 and 1.6038A-5 for that taxable year. Such a corporation, however, remains subject to the information reporting requirements of §1.6038A-2 and the general record maintenance requirements of section 6001. For purposes of this paragraph, U.S. gross receipts includes all amounts received or accrued to the extent that such amounts are taken into account for the determination and computation of the gross income of the corporation. For purposes of this test, the U.S. gross receipts of all related reporting corporations shall be aggregated.

(i) *Safe harbor for reporting corporations with related party transactions of de minimis value.*—(1) *In general.*—A reporting corporation (other than an entity that is a reporting corporation as a result of being treated as a corporation under §301.7701-2(c)(2)(vi) of this chapter) is not subject to §§1.6038A-3 and 1.6038A-5 for any taxable year in which the aggregate value of all gross payments it makes to and receives from foreign related parties with respect to related party transactions (including monetary consideration, nonmonetary consideration, and the value of transactions involving less than full consideration) is not more than $5,000,000 and is less than 10 percent of its U.S. gross income. Such a corporation, however, remains subject to the information reporting requirements of §1.6038A-2 and the general record maintenance requirements of section 6001. For purposes of this paragraph, U.S. gross income means the gross income reportable by the reporting corporation (or the aggregate gross income reportable by all related reporting corporations) for U.S. income tax purposes. Gross payments made to or received from foreign related parties cannot be netted; rather, the gross payments made to and received from foreign related parties are to be aggregated. Thus, for example, if a reporting corporation receives $4,700,000 of gross payments from a related party and makes $500,000 of gross payments to the same related party, it has aggregate gross payments of $5,200,000, and, therefore, does not qualify for the safe harbor under this paragraph.

(2) *Aggregate value of gross payments made or received.*—The aggregate value of gross payments made to (or received from) a foreign related party with respect to foreign related party transactions is determined by totaling the dollar amounts of foreign related party transactions as described in §1.6038A-2(b)(3) and (4) on all Forms 5472 filed by the reporting corporation or related reporting corporations.

(j) *Related reporting corporations.*—A reporting corporation is related to another reporting corporation if it is related to that other reporting corporation under the principles described in paragraphs (d) and (e) of this section.

(k) *Consolidated return groups.*—(1) *Required information.*—If a reporting corporation is a member of an affiliated group for which a U.S. consolidated income tax return is filed, the return requirement of §1.6038A-2 may be satisfied by filing a consolidated Form 5472. The common parent, as identified on Form 851, must attach a schedule to the consolidated U.S. Form 5472 stating which members of the U.S. affiliated group are reporting corporations under section 6038A, and which of those are joining in the consolidated Form 5472. The schedule must provide the name, address, and taxpayer identification number of each member whose transactions are included on the consolidated Form 5472. A member is not required to join in filing a consolidated Form 5472 merely because other members of the group choose to file one or more Forms 5472 on a consolidated basis.

(2) *Maintenance of records and authorization of agent.*—Either the common parent or the principal operating company of an affiliated group filing a consolidated income tax return may be authorized under §1.6038A-5 to act as the agent for foreign related persons engaged in transactions with members of the group solely for purposes of section 7602, 7603, and 7604 under section 6038A(e)(1) and §1.6038A-5. Each member of the group, however, must maintain the records required under section 6038A(a) and §1.6038A-3 relating to its related party transactions.

(3) *Monetary penalties.*—The common parent (or principal operating company) and all reporting corporations that join in the filing of a consolidated Form 5472 are liable jointly and severally for penalties for failure to file Form 5472 and for failure to maintain records under section 6038A(d) and §1.6038A-4(e). *See* §1.1502-77(a) regarding the scope of agency of the common parent corporation.

(l) *District Director.*—For purposes of the regulations under section 6038A, the term "District Director" means any District Director, or the Assistant Commissioner (International) when performing duties similar to those of a District Director with respect to any person over which the Assistant Commissioner (International) has appropriate jurisdiction.

(m) *Examples.*—The following examples illustrate the rules of this section.

Example 1. P, a U.S. partnership that is engaged in a U.S. trade or business, is 75 percent owned by FC1, a foreign corporation that, in turn, is wholly owned by another foreign corporation, FC2. The remaining 25 percent of P is owned by Corp, a domestic corporation, that is wholly owned by FC3. P engages in transactions solely with FC2 and FC3. These transactions are attributed to FC1 and Corp. Under section 875, FC1 is considered as being engaged in a U.S. trade or business. For purposes of section 6038A and this section, FC1 and Corp are reporting corporations and must report their pro rata shares of the value of the transactions with FC2 and FC3. Thus, Corp must report 25 percent of P's transactions with FC3 and FC1 must report 75 percent of P's transactions with FC2.

Example 2. FC2 and FC3 are both foreign corporations that are wholly owned by FC1, also a foreign corporation. FC2 engages in a trade or business in the United States through a branch.

The branch engages in related party transactions with FC1. FC2 is a reporting corporation. FC3 is a foreign related party. FC1 is a direct 25-percent foreign shareholder of both FC2 and FC3. Neither FC1 nor FC3 is a reporting corporation.

Example 3. FC1 owns 25 percent of total voting power in each of FC2 and FC3. FC2 and FC3 each own 20 percent of the total voting power of Corp, a domestic corporation. The remaining stock of Corp is owned by an unrelated domestic corporation. Neither FC2 nor FC3 is engaged in a U.S. trade or business. Under section 318(a)(2)(C) and paragraph (e) of this section, FC1 constructively owns its proportionate share of the stock of Corp owned directly by FC2 and FC3. Thus, FC1 is treated as constructively owning five percent of Corp through each of FC2 and FC3 or a total of 10 percent of the Corp stock. Consequently, Corp is not a reporting corporation because no 25 percent shareholder exists.

Example 4. FP owns 100 percent of FC1 which, in turn, owns 100 percent of FC2. FC2 owns 100 percent of FC3 which owns 100 percent of RC. FP, FC1, and FC2 are indirect 25-percent foreign shareholders of RC, and FC3 is a direct 25-percent foreign shareholder.

Example 5. FP owns 100 percent of USS, a U.S. corporation, and 25 percent of FS, a foreign corporation. The remaining 75 percent of FS is publicly owned by numerous small shareholders. Sales transactions occur between USS and FS. Applying the rules of this section, USS is a reporting corporation. It is determined that USS and FS are each controlled by FP under section 482 and the regulations thereunder. Therefore, FS is related to USS within the meaning of section 482 and is a related party to USS. Accordingly, the sales transactions between USS and FS are subject to section 6038A.

Example 6. The facts are the same as in *Example 5,* except that the remaining 75 percent of FS is owned by one shareholder that is unrelated to the FP group and it is determined that FS is not controlled by FP for purposes of section 482. Under these facts, FS is not a related party of either FP or USS. Accordingly, section 6038A does not apply to the sales transactions between FS and USS.

Example 7. P, a U.S. multinational, is a holding company that wholly owns X, a U.S. operating company, which in turn wholly owns FS, a controlled foreign corporation. Applying the rule of section 318(a)(3)(C), FS is deemed to own the stock of X that is actually held by P. However, under the rules of paragraph (e) of this section, X will not be a reporting corporation by reason of section 318.

(n) *Effective dates.*—(1) *Section 1.6038A-1.*—Paragraphs (c) (relating to the definition of a reporting corporation), (d) (relating to the definition of a related party), (e)(1) (relating to the application of section 318), and (f) (relating to the definition of a foreign person) of this section are effective for taxable years beginning after July 10, 1989. The remaining paragraphs of this section are effective December 10, 1990, without regard to when the taxable year began. However, § 1.6038A-1 as it applies to entities that are reporting corporations as a result of being treated as a corporation under § 301.7701-2(c)(2)(vi) of this chapter applies to taxable years of such reporting corporations beginning after December 31, 2016, and ending on or after December 13, 2017.

(2) *Section 1.6038A-2.*—Section 1.6038A-2 (relating to the requirement to file Form 5472) generally applies for taxable years beginning after July 10, 1989. However, § 1.6038A-2 as it applies to reporting corporations whose sole trade or business in the United States is a banking, financing, or similar business as defined in § 1.864-4(c)(5)(i) applies for taxable years beginning after December 10, 1990. Section 1.6038A-2(d) applies for taxable years ending on or after June 10, 2011. For taxable years ending on or after June 10, 2011, but before December 24, 2014, see § 1.6038A-2(e) as contained in 26 CFR part 1 revised as of April 1, 2014. Section 1.6038A-2 as it applies to entities that are reporting corporations as a result of being treated as a corporation under § 301.7701-2(c)(2)(vi) of this chapter applies to taxable years of such reporting corporations beginning after December 31, 2016, and ending on or after December 13, 2017.

(3) *Section 1.6038A-4.*—Section 1.6038A-4 (relating to the monetary penalty) is generally effective for taxable years beginning after July 10, 1989, for the failure to file Form 5472. For the failure to maintain records or the failure to produce documents under § 1.6038A-4(f)(2), the section is effective December 10, 1990, without regard to when the taxable year to which the records relate began. For taxable years ending before December 24, 2014, see § 1.6038A-4(a)(1) as contained in 26 CFR part 1 revised as of April 1, 2014.

(4) *Section 1.6038A-5.*—Section 1.6038A-5 (relating to the authorization of agent requirement) is effective December 10, 1990, without regard to when the taxable year to which the records relate began.

(5) *Section 1.6038A-6.*—Section 1.6038A-6 (relating to the failure to furnish information under a summons) is effective November 6, 1990, without regard to when the taxable year to which the summons relates began.

(6) *Section 1.6038A-7.*—Section 1.6038A-7 (relating to the noncompliance penalty adjustment) is effective December 10, 1990, without regard to when the taxable year began. [Reg. § 1.6038A-1.]

☐ [*T.D. 8353,* 6-14-91. *Amended by T.D. 9161,* 9-14-2004; *T.D. 9456,* 7-31-2009; *T.D. 9529,* 6-9-2011; *T.D. 9667,* 6-5-2014, *T.D. 9707,* 12-23-2014 *and T.D. 9796,* 12-12-2016.]

[Reg. § 1.6038A-2]

§ 1.6038A-2. Requirement of return.—(a) *Form 5472 required.*—(1) *In general.*—Each reporting corporation as defined in § 1.6038A-1(c) (or members of an affiliated group filing together as described in §1.6038A-1(k)) shall make a separate annual information return on Form 5472 with respect to each related party as defined in §1.6038A-1(d) with which the reporting corporation(or any group member joining in a consolidated Form 5472) has had any reportable transaction during the taxable year. The information required by section 6038A and this section must be furnished even though it may not affect the amount of any tax due under the Code.

(2) *Reportable transaction.*—A reportable transaction is any transaction of the types listed in paragraphs (b)(3) and (4) of this section. However, if neither party to the transaction is a United States person as defined in section 7701(a)(30) (which, for purposes of section 6038A, includes an entity that is a reporting corporation as a result of being treated as a corporation under §301.7701-2(c)(2)(vi) of this chapter) and the transaction—

(i) Will not generate in any taxable year gross income from sources within the United States or income effectively connected, or treated as effectively connected, with the conduct of a trade or business within the United States, and

(ii) Will not generate in any taxable year any expense, loss, or other deduction that is allocable or apportionable to such income, the transaction is not a reportable transaction.

(b) *Contents of return.*—(1) *Reporting corporation.*—Form 5472 must provide the following information in the manner the form prescribes with respect to each reporting corporation:

(i) Its name, address (including mailing code), and U.S. taxpayer identification number; each country in which the reporting corporation files an income tax return as a resident under the tax laws of that country; its country or countries of organization, and incorporation; its total assets for U.S. reporting corporation; the places where it conducts its business; and its principal business activity.

(ii) The name, address, and U.S. taxpayer identification number, if applicable, of all its direct and indirect 25-percent foreign shareholders (for an indirect 25-percent foreign shareholder, explain the attribution of ownership); each country in which each 25-percent foreign shareholder files an income tax return as a resident under the tax laws of that country; the places where each 25-percent shareholder conducts its business; and the country or countries of organization, citizenship, and incorporation of each 25-percent foreign shareholder.

(iii) The number of Forms 5472 filed for the taxable year and the aggregate value in U.S. dollars of gross payments as defined in §1.6038A-1(h)(2) made with respect to all foreign related party transactions reported on all Forms 5472.

(2) *Related party.*—The reporting corporation must provide information on Form 5472, set forth in the manner the form prescribes, about each related party, whether foreign or domestic, with which the reporting corporation had a transaction of the types described in paragraphs (b) (3) and (4) of this section during its taxable year, including the following information:

(i) The name, U.S. taxpayer identification number, if applicable, and address of the related party.

(ii) The nature of the related party's business and the principal place or places where it conducts its business.

(iii) Each country in which the related party files an income tax return as a resident under the tax laws of that country.

(iv) The relationship of the reporting corporation to the related party.

(3) *Foreign related party transactions for which only monetary consideration is paid or received by the reporting corporation.*—If the related party is a foreign person, the reporting corporation must set forth on Form 5472 the dollar amounts of all reportable transactions for which monetary consideration (including U.S. and foreign currency) was the sole consideration paid or received during the taxable year of the reporting corporation. The total amount of such transactions, as well as the separate amounts for each type of transaction described below, must be reported on Form 5472, in the manner the form prescribes. Where actual amounts are not determinable, a reasonable estimate (as described in paragraph (b)(6) of this section) is permitted. The types of transactions described in this paragraph are:

(i) Sales and purchases of stock in trade (inventory);

(ii) Sales and purchases of tangible property other than stock in trade;

(iii) Rents and royalties paid and received (other than amounts reported under paragraph (b)(3)(iv) of this section);

(iv) Sales, purchases, and amounts paid and received as consideration for the use of all intangible property, including (but not limited to) copyrights, designs, formulas, inventions, models, patents, processes, trademarks, and other similar intangible property rights;

(v) Consideration paid and received for technical, managerial, engineering, construction, scientific, or other services;

(vi) Commissions paid and received;

(vii) Amounts loaned and borrowed (except open accounts resulting from sales and purchases reported under other items listed in this paragraph (b)(3) that arise and are collected in full in the ordinary course of business), to be reported as monthly averages or outstanding balances at the beginning and end of the taxable year, as the form shall prescribe;

(viii) Interest paid and received;

(ix) Premiums paid and received for insurance and reinsurance;

(x) Other amounts paid or received not specifically identified in this paragraph (b)(3) to the extent that such amounts are taken into account for the determination and computation of the taxable income of the reporting corporation; and

(xi) With respect to an entity that is a reporting corporation as a result of being treated as a corporation under § 301.7701-2(c)(2)(vi) of this chapter, any other transaction as defined by § 1.482-1(i)(7), such as amounts paid or received in connection with the formation, dissolution, acquisition and disposition of the entity, including contributions to and distributions from the entity.

(4) *Foreign related party transactions involving nonmonetary consideration or less than full consideration.*—If the related party is a foreign person, the reporting corporation must provide on Form 5472 a description of any reportable transaction, or group of reportable transactions, listed in paragraph (b)(3) of this section, for which any part of the consideration paid or received was not monetary consideration, or for which less than full consideration was paid or received. A description required under paragraph (b)(4) of this section shall include sufficient information from which to determine the nature and approximate monetary value of the transaction or group of transactions, and shall include:

(i) A description of all property (including monetary consideration), rights, or obligations transferred from the reporting corporation to the foreign related party and from the foreign related party to the reporting corporation;

(ii) A description of all services performed by the reporting corporation for the foreign related party and by the foreign related party for the reporting corporation; and

(iii) A reasonable estimate of the fair market value of all properties and services exchanged, if possible, or some other reasonable indicator of value.

If, for any transaction, the entire consideration received includes both tangible and intangible property and the consideration paid is solely monetary consideration, the transaction should be reported under paragraph (b)(3) of this section if the intangible property was related and incidental to the transfer of the tangible property (for example, a right to warranty services.)

(5) *Additional information.*—In addition to the information required under paragraphs (b)(3) and (4) of this section, a reporting corporation must provide on Form 5472, in the manner the form prescribes, the following information:

(i) If the reporting corporation imports goods from a foreign related party, whether the costs taken into account in computing the basis or inventory cost of such goods are greater than the costs taken into account in computing the valuation of the goods for customs purposes, adjusted pursuant to section 1059A and the regulations thereunder, and if so, the reasons for the difference.

(ii) If the costs taken into account in computing the basis or inventory cost of such goods are greater than the costs taken into account in computing the valuation of the goods for customs purposes, whether the documents support-

ing the reporting corporation's treatment of the items set forth in paragraph (b)(5)(i) of this section are in existence and available in the United States at the time Form 5472 is filed.

(6) *Reasonable estimate.*—(i) *Estimate within 25 percent of actual amount.*—Any amount reported under this section is considered to be a reasonable estimate if it is at least 75 percent and not more than 125 percent of the actual amount.

(ii) *Other estimates.*—If any amount reported under this paragraph (b) of this section fails to meet the reasonable estimate test of paragraph (b)(6)(i) of this section, the reporting corporation nevertheless may show that such amount is a reasonable estimate by making an affirmative showing of relevant facts and circumstances in a written statement containing a declaration that it is made under the penalties of perjury. The District Director shall determine whether the amount reported was a reasonable estimate.

(7) *Small amounts.*—If any actual amount required under this section does not exceed $50,000, the amount may be reported as "$50,000 or less."

(8) *Accrued payments and receipts.*—For purposes of this section, a reporting corporation that uses an accrual method of accounting shall use accrued payments and accrued receipts for purposes of computing the total amount of each of the types of transactions listed in this section.

(9) *Examples.*—The following examples illustrate the application of paragraph (b)(3) of this section:

Example 1. (i) In year 1, W, a foreign corporation, forms and contributes assets to X, a domestic limited liability company that does not elect to be treated as a corporation under § 301.7701-3(c) of this chapter. In year 2, W contributes funds to X. In year 3, X makes a payment to W. In year 4, X, in liquidation, distributes its assets to W.

(ii) In accordance with § 301.7701-3(b)(1)(ii) of this chapter, X is disregarded as an entity separate from W. In accordance with § 301.7701-2(c)(2)(vi) of this chapter, X is treated as an entity separate from W and classified as a domestic corporation for purposes of section 6038A. In accordance with paragraphs (a)(2) and (b)(3) of this section, each of the transactions in years 1 through 4 is a reportable transaction with respect to X. Therefore, X has a section 6038A reporting and record maintenance requirement for each of those years.

Example 2. (i) The facts are the same as in *Example 1* of this paragraph (b)(9) except that, in year 1, W also forms and contributes assets to Y, another domestic limited liability company that does not elect to be treated as a corporation under § 301.7701-3(c) of this chapter. In year 1, X and Y form and contribute assets to Z, another domestic limited liability company that does not elect to be treated as a corporation under

Reg. § 1.6038A-2(b)(9)

§ 301.7701-3(c) of this chapter. In year 2, X transfers funds to Z. In year 3, Z makes a payment to Y. In year 4, Z distributes its assets to X and Y in liquidation.

(ii) In accordance with § 301.7701-3(b)(1)(ii) of this chapter, Y and Z are disregarded as entities separate from each other, W, and X. In accordance with § 301.7701-2(c)(2)(vi) of this chapter, Y, Z and X are treated as entities separate from each other and W, and are classified as domestic corporations for purposes of section 6038A. In accordance with paragraph (b)(3) of this section, each of the transactions in years 1 through 4 involving Z is a reportable transaction with respect to Z. Similarly, W's contribution to Y and Y's contribution to Z in year 1, the payment to Y in year 3, and the distribution to Y in year 4 are reportable transactions with respect to Y. Moreover, X's contribution to Z in Year 1, X's funds transfer to Z in year 2, and the distribution to X in year 4 are reportable transactions with respect to X. Therefore, Z has a section 6038A reporting and record maintenance requirement for years 1 through 4; Y has a section 6038A reporting and record maintenance requirement for years 1, 3, and 4; and X has a section 6038A reporting and record maintenance requirement in years 1, 2, and 4 in addition to its section 6038A reporting and record maintenance described in *Example 1* of this paragraph (b)(9).

(c) *Method of reporting.*—All statements required on or with the Form 5472 under this section and § 1.6038A-5 shall be in the English language. All amounts required to be reported under paragraph (b) of this section shall be expressed in United States currency, with a statement of the exchange rates used.

(d) *Time for filing returns.*—A Form 5472 required under this section must be filed with the reporting corporation's income tax return for the taxable year by the due date (including extensions) of that return. In the case of an entity that is a reporting corporation as a result of being treated as a corporation under § 301.7701-2(c)(2)(vi) of this chapter, Form 5472 must be filed at such time and in such manner as the Commissioner may prescribe in forms or instructions.

(e) *Exceptions.*—(1) *No reportable transactions.*—A reporting corporation is not required to file Form 5472 if it has no transactions of the types listed in paragraphs (b)(3) and (4) of this section during the taxable year with any related party.

(2) *Transactions solely with a domestic reporting corporation.*—If all of a foreign reporting corporation's reportable transactions are with one or more related domestic reporting corporations that are not members of the same affiliated group, the foreign reporting corporation shall furnish on Form 5472 only the information required under paragraphs (b)(1) and (2) of this section, if the domestic reporting corporations provide the information required under paragraphs (b)(3) through (5) of this section.

Such a foreign reporting corporation nonetheless is subject to the record maintenance requirements of § 1.6038A-3 and the requirements of § § 1.6038A-5 and 1.6038A-6. The name, address, and taxpayer identification number of each domestic reporting corporation that provided such information must be indicated on Form 5472 in the space provided for the information under paragraphs (b)(1) and (2) of this section.

(3) *Transactions with a corporation subject to reporting under section 6038.*—A reporting corporation (other than an entity that is a reporting corporation as a result of being treated as a corporation under § 301.7701-2(c)(2)(vi) of this chapter) is not required to make a return of information on Form 5472 with respect to a related foreign corporation for a taxable year for which a U.S. person that controls the foreign related corporation makes a return of information on Form 5471 that is required under section 6038 and this section, if that return contains information required under § 1.6038-2(f)(11) with respect to the reportable transactions between the reporting corporation and the related corporation for that taxable year. Such a reporting corporation also is not subject to § § 1.6038A-3 and 1.6038A-5. It remains subject to the general record maintenance requirements of section 6001.

(4) *Transactions with a foreign sales corporation.*—A reporting corporation (other than an entity that is a reporting corporation as a result of being treated as a corporation under § 301.7701-2(c)(2)(vi) of this chapter) is not required to make a return of information on Form 5472 with respect to a related corporation that qualifies as a foreign sales corporation for a taxable year for which the foreign sales corporation files Form 1120-FSC.

(f) *Filing Form 5472 when transactions with related parties engaged in by a partnership are attributed to a reporting corporation.*—If transactions engaged in by a partnership are attributed under § 1.6038A-1(e)(2) to a reporting corporation, the reporting corporation need report on Form 5472 only the percentage of the value of the transaction or transactions equal to the percentage of its partnership interest. Thus, for example, if a partnership buys $1000 of widgets from the foreign parent of a reporting corporation whose partnership interest in the partnership equals 50 percent of the partnership interests (and the remaining 50 percent is held by unrelated parties), the reporting corporation must report $500 of purchases from a foreign related party on Form 5472.

(g) *Effective/applicability date.*—Except as otherwise provided, for applicability dates for this section for certain reporting corporations, see § 1.6038A-1(n). Paragraph (b)(8) of this section applies with respect to information for annual accounting periods beginning on or after June 21, 2006. [Reg. § 1.6038A-2.]

☐ [*T.D.* 8353, 6-14-91. *Amended by T.D.* 9113, 2-6-2004; *T.D.* 9161, 9-14-2004; *T.D.* 9268,

6-20-2006; *T.D. 9338,* 7-12-2007; *T.D. 9529,* 6-9-2011; *T.D. 9667,* 6-5-2014, *T.D. 9707,* 12-23-2014 *and T.D. 9796,* 12-12-2016.]

[Reg. §1.6038A-3]

§1.6038A-3. Record maintenance.— (a) *General maintenance requirements.*—(1) *Section 6001 and section 6038A.*—A reporting corporation must keep the permanent books of account or records as required by section 6001 that are sufficient to establish the correctness of the federal income tax return of the corporation, including information, documents, or records ("records") to the extent they may be relevant to determine the correct U.S. tax treatment of transactions with related parties. Under section 6001, the District Director may require any person to make such returns, render such statements, or keep such specific records as will enable the District Director to determine whether or not that person is liable for any of the taxes to which the regulations under Part I have application. *See* section 6001 and the regulations thereunder. Such records must be permanent, accurate, and complete, and must clearly establish income, deductions, and credits. Additionally, in appropriate cases, such records include sufficient relevant cost data from which a profit and loss statement may be prepared for products or services transferred between a reporting corporation and its foreign related parties. This requirement includes records of the reporting corporation itself, as well as to records of any foreign related party that may be relevant to determine the correct U.S. tax treatment of transactions between the reporting corporation and foreign related parties. The relevance of such records with respect to related party transactions shall be determined upon the basis of all the facts and circumstances. Section 6038A and this section provide detailed guidance regarding the required maintenance of records with respect to such transactions and specify penalties for noncompliance. Banks and other financial institutions shall follow the specific record maintenance rules described in paragraph (h) of this section.

(2) *Safe harbor.*—A safe harbor for record maintenance is provided under paragraph (c) of this section, which sets forth detailed guidance concerning the types of records to be maintained with respect to related party transactions. The safe harbor consists of an all-inclusive list of record types that could be relevant to different taxpayers under a variety of facts and circumstances. It does not constitute a checklist of records that every reporting corporation must maintain or that generally should be requested by the Service. A specific reporting corporation is required to maintain, and the Service will request, only those records enumerated in the safe harbor (including material profit and loss statements) that may be relevant to its business or industry and to the correct U.S. tax treatment of its transactions with its foreign related parties. Accordingly, not every item listed in the safe harbor must be maintained by every reporting

corporation. A corporation that maintains or causes another person to maintain the records listed in paragraph (c)(2) of this section that may be relevant to its foreign related party transactions and to its business or industry will be deemed to have met the record maintenance requirements of section 6038A.

(3) *Examples.*—The following examples illustrate the rules of this paragraph.

Example 1. RC, a U.S. reporting corporation, is owned by two shareholders, F and P. F is a foreign corporation that owns 30 percent of the stock of RC. P is a domestic corporation that owns the remaining 70 percent. RC purchases tangible property from F; however, the only potential audit issue with respect to these transactions is their treatment under section 482. It is determined that F does not in fact control RC and the two corporations do not constitute a group of "controlled taxpayers" for purposes of section 482 and the regulations thereunder. There are no other reportable transactions between RC and F. Under §1.6038A-1(g), F is a foreign related party with respect to RC. Accordingly, RC is required to report its purchases of property from F under the reporting requirements of §1.6038A-2. Nevertheless, because section 482 is not applicable to the transactions between RC and F, the records created by F with respect to its sales to RC are not relevant for purposes of determining the correct tax treatment of these transactions. RC is required to maintain its own records of these transactions under the requirements of section 6001, but the transactions are not subject to the record maintenance requirements of this section. If, however, on audit it is determined that F does control RC, all records relevant to determining the arm's length consideration for the tangible property under section 482 will be subject to these requirements.

Example 2. FP, a foreign person, owns 30 percent of the stock of RC, a reporting corporation. The remaining 70 percent of RC stock is held by persons that are not 25-percent foreign shareholders. It is determined that FP is related to RC within the meaning of section 482 and the regulations thereunder. The only transactions between FP and RC are FP's capital contributions, dividends paid from RC to FP, and loans from FP to RC. Under section 6001, RC is required to maintain all documentation necessary to establish the U.S. tax treatment of the capital contributions, dividends, and loans. RC is not required to maintain records in other categories listed in paragraph (c)(3) of this section because they are not relevant to the transactions between FP and RC. Records of FP not related to these transactions are not subject to the record maintenance requirements under section 6038A(a) and this section.

Example 3. G, a foreign multinational group, creates Sub, a wholly-owned U.S. subsidiary, in order to purchase tangible property from unrelated parties in the United States and resell such property to G. The property purchased by Sub is either used in G's business or resold to other unrelated parties by G. Sub's sole function is to act as a buyer for G and these purchases are the only transactions that G has with any U.S. affiliates. Under all the facts and circumstances of this case, it is determined that an analysis of the group's worldwide profit attributable to the property it purchases from Sub is not relevant for purposes of determining the tax treatment of the sales from Sub to G. Therefore, the records with respect to the profitability of G are not subject to the record maintenance requirements of this section. However, all records related to the appropriate method under section 482 for determining an arm's-length consideration for the property sold by Sub to G are subject to the record maintenance requirements of this section.

Example 4. S, a U.S. reporting corporation, provides computer consulting services for its foreign parent, X. Based on the application of section 482 and the regulations, it is determined that the cost of services plus method, as described in §1.482-9(e), will provide the most reliable measure of an arm's length result, based on the facts and circumstances of the controlled transaction between S and X. S is required to maintain records to permit verification upon audit of the comparable transactional costs (as described in §1.482-9(e)(2)(iii)) used to calculate the arm's length price. Based on the facts and circumstances, if it is determined that X's records are relevant to determine the correct U.S. tax treatment of the controlled transaction between S and X, the record maintenance requirements under section 6038A(a) and this section will be applicable to the records of X.

(b) *Other maintenance requirements.*—(1) *Indirectly related records.*—This section applies to records that are directly or indirectly related to transactions between the reporting corporation and any foreign related parties. An example of records that are indirectly related to such transactions is records possessed by a foreign subsidiary of a foreign related party that document the raw material or component costs of a product that is manufactured or assembled by the subsidiary and sold as a finished product by the foreign related party to the reporting corporation.

(2) *Foreign related party or third-party maintenance.*—If records that are required to be maintained under this section are in the control of a foreign related party, the records may be obtained or compiled (if not already in the possession of the foreign related party or already compiled) under the direction of the reporting corporation and then maintained by the reporting corporation, the foreign related party, or a third party. Thus, for example, a foreign related party may either itself maintain such records outside the United States or permit a third party to maintain such records outside the United States, provided that the conditions described in paragraph (f) of this section are met. Upon a request for such records by the Service, a foreign related party or third party may make arrange-

ments with the District Director to furnish the records directly, rather than through the reporting corporation.

(3) *Translation of records.*—When records are provided to the Service under a request for production, any portion of such records must be translated into the English language within 30 days of a request for translation of that portion by the District Director. To the extent that any requested documents are identical to documents that have already been translated, an explanation of how such documents are identical instead may be provided. An extension of this time period may be requested under paragraph (f)(4) of this section. Appropriate extensions will be liberally granted for translation requests where circumstances warrant. If a good faith effort is made to translate accurately the requested documents within the specified time period, the reporting corporation will not be subject to the penalties in §§1.6038A-4 and 1.6038A-7.

(4) *Exception for foreign governments.*—A foreign government is not subject to the obligation to maintain records under this section.

(5) *Records relating to conduit financing arrangements.*—See §1.881-4 relating to conduit financing arrangements.

(c) *Specific records to be maintained for safe harbor.*—(1) *In general.*—A reporting corporation that maintains or causes another person to maintain the records specified in this paragraph (c) that are relevant to its business or industry and to the correct U.S. tax treatment of its transactions with its foreign related parties will be deemed to have met the record maintenance requirements of this section. This paragraph provides general descriptions of the categories of records to be maintained; the particular title or label applied by a reporting corporation or related party does not control. Functional equivalents of the specified documents are acceptable. Record maintenance in accordance with this safe harbor, however, requires only the maintenance of types of documents described in paragraph (c)(2) of this section that are directly or indirectly related to transactions between the reporting corporation and any foreign related party. Additionally, to the extent the reporting corporation establishes that records in a particular category are not applicable to the industry or business of the reporting corporation and any foreign related party, maintenance of such records is not required under this paragraph. Record maintenance in accordance with this paragraph (c) generally does not require the original creation of records that are ordinarily not created by the reporting corporation or its related parties. (If, however, a document that is actually created is described in this paragraph (c), it is to be maintained even if the document is not of the type ordinarily created by the reporting corporation or its related parties.) There are two exceptions to the rule. First, basic accounting records that are sufficient to document the U.S. tax effects of transactions between related parties

Reg. §1.6038A-3(b)(1)

must be created and retained, if they do not otherwise exist. Second, records sufficient to produce material profit and loss statements as described in paragraphs (c)(2)(ii) and (3) of this section that are relevant for determining the U.S. tax treatment of transactions between the reporting corporation and foreign related parties must be created if such records are not ordinarily maintained. All internal records storage and retrieval systems used for each taxable year must be retained.

(2) *Descriptions of categories of documents to be maintained.*—The following records must be maintained in order to satisfy this paragraph (c) to the extent they may be relevant to determine the correct U.S. tax treatment of transactions between the reporting corporation and any foreign related party.

(i) *Original entry books and transaction records.*—This category includes books and records of original entry or their functional equivalents, however designated or labelled, that are relevant to transactions between any foreign related party and the reporting corporation. Examples include, but are not limited to, general ledgers, sales journals, purchase order books, cash receipts books, cash disbursement books, canceled checks and bank statements, workpapers, sales contracts, and purchase invoices. Descriptive material to explicate entries in the foregoing types of records, such as a chart of accounts or an accounting policy manual, is included in this category.

(ii) *Profit and loss statements.*—This category includes records from which the reporting corporation can compile and supply, within a reasonable time, material profit and loss statements of the reporting corporation and all related parties as defined in § 1.6038A-1(d) (the "related party group") that reflect profit or loss of the related party group attributable to U.S.-connected products or services as defined in paragraph (c)(7)(i) of this section. The determination of whether a profit and loss statement is material is made under the rules provided in paragraph (c)(3) of this section. The material profit and loss statements described in this paragraph (c)(2)(ii) must reflect the consolidated revenue and expenses of all members of the related party group. Thus, records in this category include the documentation of the cost of raw materials used by a related party to manufacture finished goods that are then sold by another related party to the reporting corporation. The records should be kept under U.S. generally accepted accounting principles if they are ordinarily maintained in such manner; if not, an explanation of the material differences between the accounting principles used and U.S. generally accepted accounting principles must be made available. The statements need not reflect tracing of the actual costs borne by the group with respect to its U.S.-connected products or services; rather, any reasonable method may be used to allocate the group's worldwide costs to the revenues generated by the sales of those products or services. An explanation of the methods used to allocate specific items to a particular profit and loss statement must be made available. The explanation of material differences between accounting principles and the explanation of allocation methods must be sufficient to permit a comparison of the profitability of the group to that of the reporting corporation attributable to the provision of U.S.-connected products or services.

(iii) *Pricing documents.*—This category includes all documents relevant to establishing the appropriate price or rate for transactions between the reporting corporation and any foreign related party. Examples include, but are not limited to, documents related to transactions involving the same or similar products or services entered into by the reporting corporation or a foreign related party with related and unrelated parties; shipping and export documents; commission agreements; documents relating to production or assembly facilities; third-party and intercompany purchase invoices; manuals, specifications, and similar documents relating to or describing the performance of functions conducted at particular locations; intercompany correspondence discussing any instructions or assistance relating to such transactions provided to the reporting corporations by the related foreign person (or vice versa); intercompany and intracompany correspondence concerning the price or the negotiation of the price used in such transactions; documents related to the value and ownership of intangibles used or developed by the reporting corporation or the foreign related party; documents related to cost of goods sold and other expenses; and documents related to direct and indirect selling, and general and administrative expenses (for example, relating to advertising, sales promotions, or warranties).

(iv) *Foreign country and third party filings.*—This category includes financial and other documents relevant to transactions between a reporting corporation and any foreign related party filed with or prepared for any foreign government entity, any independent commission, or any financial institution.

(v) *Ownership and capital structure records.*—This category includes records or charts showing the relationship between the reporting corporation and the foreign related party; the location, ownership, and status (for example, joint venture, partnership, branch, or division) of all entities and offices directly or indirectly involved in the transactions between the reporting corporation and any foreign related party; a worldwide organization chart; records showing the management structure of all foreign affiliates; and loan documents, agreements, and other documents relating to any transfer of the stock of the reporting corporation that results in the change of the status of a foreign person as a foreign related party.

Reg. § 1.6038A-3(c)(2)(v)

(vi) *Records of loans, services, and other non-sales transactions.*—This category includes relevant documents relating to loans (including all deposits by one foreign related party or reporting corporation with an unrelated party and a subsequent loan by that unrelated party to a foreign related party or reporting corporation that is in substance a direct loan between a reporting corporation and a foreign related party); guarantees of a foreign related party of debts of the reporting corporation, and vice versa; hedging arrangements or other risk shifting or currency risk shifting arrangements involving the reporting corporation and any foreign related party; security agreements between the reporting corporation and any foreign related party; research and development expense allocations between any foreign related party and the reporting corporation; service transactions between any foreign related party and the reporting corporation, including, for example, a description of the allocation of charges for management services, time or travel records, or allocation studies; import and export transactions between a reporting corporation and any foreign related party; the registration of patents and copyrights with respect to transactions between the reporting corporation and any foreign related party; and documents regarding lawsuits in foreign countries that relate to such transactions between a reporting corporation and any foreign related party (for example, product liability suits for U.S. products).

(vii) *Records relating to conduit financing arrangements.*—See § 1.881-4 relating to conduit financing arrangements.

(3) *Material profit and loss statements.*—For purposes of paragraph (c)(2)(ii) of this section, the determination of whether a profit and loss statement is material will be made according to the following rules. An agreement between the reporting corporation and the District Director as described in paragraph (e) of this section may identify material profit and loss statements of the related party group and describe the items to be included in any profit and loss statements for which records are to be maintained to satisfy the requirements of paragraph (c)(2)(ii) of this section. In the absence of such an agreement, a profit and loss statement will be material if it meets any of the following tests: the existing records test described in paragraph (c)(4) of this section, the significant industry segment test described in paragraph (c)(5) of this section, or the high profit test described in paragraph (c)(6) of this section.

(4) *Existing records test.*—A profit and loss statement is material under the existing records test described in this paragraph (c)(4) if any member of the related party group creates or compiles such statement in the course of its business operations and the statement reflects the profit or loss of the related party group attributable to the provision of U.S.-connected products or services (regardless of whether the profit and

loss attributable to U.S.-connected products or services is shown separately or included within the calculation of aggregate figures on the statement). For example, a profit and loss statement is described in this paragraph if it was produced for internal accounting or management purposes, or for disclosure to shareholders, financial institutions, government agencies, or any other persons. Such existing statements and the records from which they were compiled (to the extent such records relate to profit and loss attributable to U.S.-connected products or services) are subject to the record maintenance requirements described in paragraph (c)(2)(ii) of this section.

(5) *Significant industry segment test.*—(i) *In general.*—A profit and loss statement is material under the significant industry segment test described in this paragraph (c)(5) if—

(A) The statement reflects the profit or loss of the related party group attributable to the group's provision of U.S.-connected products or services within a single industry segment (as defined in paragraph (c)(7)(ii) of this section);

(B) The worldwide gross revenue attributable to such industry segment is 10 percent or more of the worldwide gross revenue attributable to the group's combined industry segments; and

(C) The amount of gross revenue earned by the group from the provision of U.S.-connected products or services within such industry segment is $25 million or more in the taxable year.

(ii) *Form of the statements.*—Profit and loss statements compiled for the group's provision of U.S.-connected products or services in each significant industry segment must reflect revenues and expenses attributable to the operations in such segment by all members of the related party group. Statements may show each related party's revenues and expenses separately, or may be prepared in a consolidated format. Any reasonable method may be used to allocate the group's worldwide costs within the industry segment to the U.S.-connected products or services within that segment. An explanation of the methods used to prepare consolidated statements and to allocate specific items to a particular profit and loss statement must be made available, and the records from which the consolidations and allocations were prepared must be maintained.

(iii) *Special rule for component sales.*—Where the U.S.-connected products or services consist of components that are incorporated into other products or services before sale to customers, the portion of the total gross revenue derived from sales of the finished products or services attributable to the components may be determined on the basis of relative costs of production. Thus, where relevant for determining whether the $25 million threshold in paragraph (c)(5)(i)(C) of this section has been met, the amount of gross revenue derived by the related party group from the provision of the finished products or services may be reduced by multiplying it by a fraction, the numerator of which is the costs of production of the related party group attributable to the component products or services that constitute U.S.-connected products or services and the denominator of which is the costs of production of the related party group attributable to the finished products in which such components are incorporated.

(iv) *Level of specificity required.*—In applying the significant industry segment test of this paragraph (c)(5), groups of related products and services must be chosen to provide a reasonable level of specificity that results in the greatest number of separate significant industry segments in comparison to other possible classifications. This determination must be made on the basis of the particular facts presented by the operations of the related party group. The following rules, however, provide general guidelines for making such classifications. First, the related party group's operations that involve the provision of U.S.-connected products should be grouped into product lines. The rules of this paragraph (c)(5) should then be applied to determine if any such product line would, standing alone, constitute a significant industry segment when compared to the related party group's operations as a whole. Any significant industry segments determined at the level of product lines should be further segregated, and tested for significant industry segments, at the level of separate products. Finally, any significant industry segments determined at the level of separate products should be segregated, and tested for significant industry segments, at the level of separate models. Similar principles should be applied in classifying and testing types of services. A profit and loss statement reflecting the related party group's provision of any product or service (or group of products or services as classified under these rules) that constitutes a significant industry segment will be considered material for purposes of this paragraph (c)(5). For definitions of the terms "product", "related products or services", "model", and "product line", see paragraph (c)(7) of this section.

(v) *Examples.*—The rules for determining reasonable levels of specificity for significant industry segments may be illustrated by the following examples.

Example 1. A related party group is engaged in the manufacture and worldwide sales of automobiles and aftermarket parts. The group's operations within the categories of "automobiles" and "aftermarket parts" are each sufficient to constitute significant industry segments for the group under the rules of this paragraph (c)(5). No narrower classification of aftermarket parts results in any significant industry segments. Automobiles produced by the group are generally classified for marketing purposes by trade names; aggregating groups of automobiles by these trade names results in three significant industry segments, those for

trade names A, B, and C. Finally, two car models sold under the trade name A ("A1" and "A2") and one car model sold under the trade name B ("B3"), produce sufficient revenue to constitute significant industry segments. Such classifications into trade names and car models are generally used in the related party group's industry; moreover, different types of classifications would produce fewer significant industry segments. Accordingly, a reasonable level of specificity for this related party group's industry segments would be eight categories of products consisting of "automobiles", "aftermarket parts", "A", "B", "C", "A1", "A2", and "B3".

Example 2. A related party group is engaged in manufacturing electronic goods that are distributed at retail in the United States by the reporting corporation. The group sells three types of products in the United States: televisions, radios, and video cassette recorders (VCRs). Each of these three broad product areas constitutes a significant industry segment for the group as a whole. VCRs can be further segregated by price into high-end and low-end models, and the provision of each constitutes a significant industry segment for the group. Revenues from only one VCR model, model number VCRX-10, are sufficiently large to make the provision of that model a significant industry segment. With respect to televisions, the group normally accounts for these products by size. Using this classification, portable televisions, medium-sized televisions, and consoles each constitute significant industry segments. Narrower classifications by television model numbers result in no additional significant industry segments. Finally, a single radio product line, those sold under the trade name R, produces sufficient revenue to constitute a significant industry segment, but no other radio models or product groups are large enough to constitute a significant industry segment. In each case, these classifications conform to normal business practices in the industry and result in the greatest possible number of significant industry segments for this related party group. Accordingly, a reasonable level of specificity for this related party group's industry segments would include the ten categories consisting of "VCRs", "high-end VCRs", "low-end VCRs", "model number VCRX-10", "televisions", "portable televisions", "medium-sized televisions", "console televisions", "radios", and "radio trade name R".

(6) *High profit test.*—(i) *In general.*—A profit and loss statement is material under the high profit test described in this paragraph (c)(6) if—

(A) The statement reflects the profit or loss of the related party group attributable to the group's provision of U.S.-connected products or services within a single industry segment (as defined in paragraph (c)(7)(ii) of this section);

(B) The amount of gross revenue earned by the group from the provision of U.S.-connected products or services within such industry segment is $100 million or more in the taxable year; and

Reg. § 1.6038A-3(c)(6)(i)(B)

(C) The return on assets test described in paragraph (c)(6)(ii) of this section is satisfied with respect to the products and services attributable to such segment.

Accordingly, a significant industry segment (as determined under paragraph (c)(5) of this section) must be divided into any narrower industry segments that meet the high profit test of this paragraph (c)(6), even if such narrower segments would not, standing alone, meet the significant industry segment test of paragraph (c)(5) of this section.

(ii) *Return on assets test.*—An industry segment meets the return on assets test if the rate of return on assets earned by the related party group on its worldwide operations within this industry segment exceeds 15 percent, and is at least 200 percent of the return on assets earned by the group in all industry segments combined. For purposes of this paragraph, the rate of return on assets earned by an industry segment is determined by dividing that segment's operating profit (as defined in paragraph (c)(7)(v) of this section) by its identifiable assets (as defined in paragraph (c)(7)(iv) of this section).

(iii) *Additional rules.*—The rules in paragraphs (c)(5)(ii) through (iv) of this section describing the application of the significant industry segment test shall apply in a similar manner for purposes of the high profit test.

(7) *Definitions.*—The following definitions apply for purposes of paragraphs (c)(2)(ii), (c)(5), and (c)(6) of this section.

(i) *U.S.-connected products or services.*—The term "U.S.-connected products or services" means products or services that are imported to or exported from the United States by transfers between the reporting corporation and any of its foreign related parties.

(ii) *Industry segment.*—An industry segment is a segment of the related party group's combined operations that is engaged in providing a product or service or a group of related products or services (as defined in paragraph (c)(7)(vii) of this section) primarily to customers that are not members of the related party group.

(iii) *Gross revenue of an industry segment.*— Gross revenue of an industry segment includes receipts (prior to reduction for cost of goods sold) both from sales to customers outside of the related party group and from sales or transfers to other industry segments within the related party group (but does not include sales or transfers between members of the related party group within the same industry segment). Interest from sources outside the related party group and interest earned on trade receivables between industry segments is included in gross revenue if the asset on which the interest is earned is included among the industry segment's identifiable assets, but interest earned on advances or loans to other industry segments is not included.

(iv) *Identifiable assets of an industry segment.*—The identifiable assets of an industry segment are those tangible and intangible assets of the related party group that are used by the industry segment, including assets that are used exclusively by that industry segment and an allocated portion of assets used jointly by two or more industry segments. The value of an identifiable asset may be determined using any reasonable method (such as book value or fair market value) applied consistently. Any allocation of assets among industry segments must be made on a reasonable basis, and a description of such basis must be provided. Assets of an industry segment that transfers products or services to another industry segment shall not be allocated to the receiving segment. Assets that represent part of the related party group's investment in an industry segment, such as goodwill, shall be included in the industry segment's identifiable assets. Assets maintained for general corporate purposes (that is, those not used in the operations of any industry segment) shall not be allocated to industry segments.

(v) *Operating profit of an industry segment.*—The operating profit of an industry segment is its gross revenue (as defined in paragraph (c)(7)(iii) of this section) minus all operating expenses. None of the following shall be added or deducted in computing the operating profit of an industry segment: revenue earned at the corporate level and not derived from the operations of any industry segment; general corporate expenses; interest expense; domestic and foreign income taxes; and other extraordinary items not reflecting the ongoing business operations of the industry segment.

(vi) *Product.*—The term "product" means an item of property (or combination of component parts) that is the result of a production process, is primarily sold to unrelated parties (or incorporated by the related party group into other products sold to unrelated parties), and performs a specific function.

(vii) *Related products or services.*—The term "related products or services" means groupings of products and types of services that reflect reasonable accounting, marketing, or other business practices within the industries in which the related party group operates.

(viii) *Model.*—The term "model" means a classification of products that incorporate particular components, options, styles, and any other unique features resulting in product differentiation. Examples of models are electronic products that are sold or accounted for under a single model number and automobiles sold under a single model name.

(ix) *Product line.*—The term "product line" means a group of products that are aggregated into a single classification for accounting, marketing, or other business purposes. Examples of product lines are groups of products that perform similar functions; products that are marketed under the same trade names, brand names, or trademarks; and products that are related economically (that is, having similar rates of profitability, similar degrees of risk, and similar opportunities for growth).

(8) *Example.*—The application of the rules for determining material profit and loss statements under paragraphs (c)(4) through (7) of this section is illustrated by the following example.

Example. (i) *Facts.* A multinational enterprise manufactures 50 different agricultural and chemical products that are sold through Sub1, its wholly owned U.S. subsidiary, and other subsidiaries located in foreign countries. The parent company of the enterprise, P, is a foreign corporation. The corporations participating in the enterprise form a related party group, and Sub1 is a reporting corporation for purposes of section 6038A. Under the facts and circumstances of this case, an analysis of the group's worldwide profit attributable to its products sold in the U.S. is relevant for determining an arm's length consideration under section 482 for the transfers of goods between Sub1 and its foreign affiliates.

(ii) *Existing records test.* For management purposes, the group prepares profit and loss statements that are segmented by sales in different geographic markets. One of these statements shows the combined worldwide profitability of the group. Another statement shows the profitability of the group attributable to its North American sales. Both of these profit and loss statements reflect aggregate figures that include sales to unrelated parties of products that have been transferred from P and other group members to Sub1 (that is, the group's "U.S.-connected products"). The two statements meet the existing records test described in paragraph (c)(4) of this section.

(iii) *Significant industry segments.* The group's worldwide gross revenue in all industry segments is $2 billion. An analysis of the group's 50 products demonstrates that they are reasonably grouped into eight industry segments (each of which earns roughly $250 million in worldwide gross revenue). Segments 1 through 6 relate to agricultural products and Segments 7 and 8 relate to other chemical products. More specific categories would result in groupings that generate less than 10 percent of the group's worldwide gross revenue (that is, less than $200 million each); these narrower categories would thus fail the gross revenue percentage test of paragraph (c)(5)(i)(B) of this section. The gross revenue in each of the eight segments from the sale to unrelated parties of U.S.-connected products is as follows: $180 million for Segment 1; $30 million for Segment 2; and less than $25 million for each of Segments 3 through 8. Under the $25 million threshold test of paragraph (c)(5)(i)(C) of this section, the group's significant industry segments are thus limited to Segments 1 and 2. In addition, the combined operations of the group related to agricultural products (encompassing Segments 1 through 6 on an aggregated basis), constitute a single significant industry segment.

(iv) *High profit test.* One highly profitable product line within Segment 1, HPPL, accounts for $120 million gross revenue from Sub1's domestic sales of U.S.-connected products (and thus exceeds the $100 million gross revenue threshold in paragraph (c)(6)(i)(B) of this section). The return on the identifiable assets attributable to the HPPL product line is 85 percent, which is more than 15 percent and more than twice the return on assets earned by the group from its worldwide operations in its combined industry segments. The group's industry segment for HPPL thus meets the high profit test described in paragraph (c)(6) of this section.

(v) *Material Profit and Loss Statements.* The group's material profit and loss statements consist of statements for combined worldwide sales and North American sales (under the existing records test); Segment 1, Segment 2, and aggregated Segments 1-6 (under the significant industry segment test); and HPPL (under the high profit test). Under paragraph (c) of this section, Sub1 is required to retain the combined worldwide sales and North American sales profit and loss statements and to maintain sufficient records so that it can compile and supply upon request statements of the group's profitability from sales of its U.S.-connected products within Segment 1, Segment 2, aggregated Segments 1-6, and HPPL. These records need not be in the possession of Sub1 and may be kept under the control of and produced by P or any third party. The statements for Segment 1, Segment 2, aggregated Segments 1-6, and HPPL do not require tracing of actual costs to the U.S.-connected products; rather, these statements may be prepared by using any reasonable method to allocate a portion of the industry segment's overall operating costs to the sales of U.S.-connected products within that segment.

(d) *Liability for certain partnership record maintenance.*—A reporting corporation to which transactions engaged in by a partnership are attributed under §1.6038A-1(e)(2) is subject to the record maintenance requirements of this section to the extent of the transactions so attributed.

(e) *Agreements with the District Director.*— (1) *In general.*—The District Director who has audit jurisdiction over the reporting corporation may negotiate and enter into an agreement with a reporting corporation that establishes the records the reporting corporation must maintain or cause another to maintain, how the records must be maintained, the period of retention for the records, and by whom the records must be maintained in order to satisfy the reporting corporation's obligations under this section.

(2) *Content of agreement.*—(i) *In general.*— The agreement may include provisions relating to the authorization of agent requirement, the record maintenance requirement, and the production and translation time periods that vary the rules contained in these regulations under section 6038A. The District Director will gener-

Reg. §1.6038A-3(e)(2)(i)

ally require a reporting corporation to maintain only those records specified under the safe harbor provisions of paragraph (c) of this section that permit an adequate audit of the income tax return of the reporting corporation and to provide such authorizations of agent that permit adequate access to such records. In most instances, required record maintenance for a particular reporting corporation under a negotiated agreement will be less than the broad range of records described under the safe harbor provisions. Additionally, a provision specifying the effective date and the expiration date of the agreement that may vary the effective date of the regulations may be included.

(ii) *Significant industry segment test.*—A District Director may determine which industry segment profit and loss statements are material for purposes of requiring the maintenance of records (under either paragraph (a)(1) of this section or the safe harbor described in paragraph (a)(2) of this section). The industry segments that the District Director determines are material need not be the industry segments that meet the significant industry segment test under paragraph (c)(5) of this section or the high profit test under paragraph (c)(6) of this section. For this purpose, a reporting corporation will be required to maintain only those records from which profit and loss statements for the related party group may be constructed with respect to industry segments identified by the District Director. To the extent that existing profit and loss statements are similar in scope and level of detail to statements for industry segments that would otherwise be described under the tests of paragraphs (c)(5) and (6) of this section, the District Director shall accept the existing statements instead of the statements that would otherwise be required under paragraphs (c)(5) and (6) of this section.

(iii) *Example.*—The following example illustrates the rules of paragraph (e)(2)(ii) of this section.

Example. The District Director determines that RC, a reporting corporation that is a manufacturer of related chemical products, has two industry segments, Segment 1 and Segment 2. While both industry segments meet the significant industry segment test of paragraph (c)(5) of this section, Segment 1 has a relatively low volume of sales to foreign related parties. Additionally, Segment 1 consists of products that produce only a small profit margin because the product is generic and other companies also sell the product. The District Director enters into an agreement with RC that requires only records from which a profit and loss statement for the related party group can be constructed for Segment 2. Therefore, RC is not required to maintain records for Segment 1 from which a profit and loss statement for the related party group can be constructed. The other record maintenance requirements under this section apply, however.

(3) *Circumstances of agreement.*—The District Director generally will enter into an agreement

under this paragraph (e) upon request by the reporting corporation when the District Director believes that the District has or can obtain sufficient knowledge of the business or industry of the reporting corporation to limit the record maintenance requirement to particular documents.

(4) *Agreement as part of APA process.*—An agreement with a reporting corporation under this paragraph (e) may be entered into as a part of the Advance Pricing Agreement (APA) process at any time during the APA process, insofar as the agreement relates to the subject matter of the APA.

(f) *U.S. maintenance.*—(1) *General rule.*— Records that must be maintained under this section must be maintained within the United States, unless the conditions described in paragraph (f)(2) of this section are met.

(2) *Non-U.S. maintenance requirements.*—A reporting corporation may maintain outside the United States records not ordinarily maintained in the United States but required to be maintained in the United States under this section. However, the reporting corporation must either:

(i) Deliver to the Service the original documents (or duplicates) requested within 60 days of the request by the Service for such records and provide translations of such documents within 30 days of a request for translations of specific documents; or

(ii) Move the original documents (or duplicates) requested to the United States within 60 days of the request of the Service for such records; provide the Service with an index to the requested records, the name and address of a custodian located within the United States having control over the records, and the address where the records are located within 60 days of the Service's request for the records; and continue to maintain the records within the United States throughout the period of retention described in paragraph (g) of this section. For summons procedures with respect to records that have been moved to the United States, see sections 6038A(e), 7602, 7603, and 7604.

With respect to any material profit and loss statements required to be created (either under paragraph (c) of this section or under an agreement with the District Director), unless otherwise specified, "120 days" shall be substituted for "60 days" in this paragraph (f)(2), and labels and text with respect to such statements must be in the English language.

(3) *Prior taxable years.*—The non-U.S. maintenance requirements described in paragraph (f)(2) of this section apply to records located outside the United States that were in existence on or after March 20, 1990, without regard to the taxable year to which such records relate.

(4) *Scheduled production for high volume or other reasons.*—Upon a written request, for good cause shown, the District Director may grant an extension of the time for the production or trans-

lation of the requested documents. Such requests should be made within 30 days of the request for records by the Service. If an extension is needed because of the volume of records requested or the amount of translation requested, the District Director may allow production or translation to be scheduled over a period of time so that not all records need be produced or translated at the same time.

(5) *Required U.S. maintenance.*—The District Director (with the concurrence of the Assistant Commissioner (International)), may require, for cause, the maintenance within the United States of any records specified in paragraph (f)(1) of this section. Such a requirement will be imposed only if there exists a clear pattern of failure to maintain or timely produce the required records. The assessment of a monetary penalty under section 6038A(d) and §1.6038A-4 for failure to maintain records is not necessarily sufficient to require the maintenance of records within the United States.

(g) *Period of retention.*—Records required to be maintained by section 6038A(a) and this section shall be kept as long as they may be relevant or material to determining the correct tax treatment of any transaction between the reporting corporation and a related party, but in no case less than the applicable statute of limitations on assessment and collection with respect to the taxable year in which the transaction or item to which the records relate affects the U.S. tax liability of the reporting corporation. *See* section 6001 and the regulations thereunder.

(h) *Application of record maintenance rules to banks and other financial institutions.*—[Reserved].

(i) *Effective/applicability date.*—(1) *In general.*—This section is generally applicable on December 10, 1990. However, records described in this section in existence on or after March 20, 1990, must be maintained, without regard to when the taxable year to which the records relate began. Paragraph (a)(3) *Example 4* of this section is generally applicable for taxable years beginning after July 31, 2009.

(2) *Election to apply regulation to earlier taxable years.*—A person may elect to apply the provisions of paragraph (a)(3) *Example 4* of this section to earlier taxable years in accordance with the rules set forth in §1.482-9(n)(2). [Reg. §1.6038A-3.]

☐ [*T.D. 8353, 6-14-91. Amended by T.D. 8611, 8-10-95; T.D. 9278, 7-31-2006 and T.D. 9456, 7-31-2009.*]

[Reg. §1.6038A-4]

§1.6038A-4. Monetary penalty.—(a) *Imposition of monetary penalty.*—(1) *In general.*—If a reporting corporation fails to furnish the information described in §1.6038A-2 within the time and manner prescribed in §1.6038A-2(d), fails to maintain or cause another to maintain records as required by §1.6038A-3, or (in the case of records maintained outside the

United States) fails to meet the non-U.S. record maintenance requirements within the applicable time prescribed in §1.6038A-3(f), a penalty of $10,000 shall be assessed for each taxable year with respect to which such failure occurs. The filing of a substantially incomplete Form 5472 constitutes a failure to file Form 5472. Where, however, the information described in §1.6038A-2(b)(3) through (5) is not required to be reported, a Form 5472 filed without such information is not a substantially incomplete Form 5472.

(2) *Liability for certain partnership transactions.*—A reporting corporation to which transactions engaged in by a partnership are attributed under §1.6038A-1(e)(2) is subject to the rules of this section to the extent failures occur with respect to the partnership transactions so attributed.

(3) *Calculation of monetary penalty.*—If a reporting corporation fails to maintain records as required by §1.6038A-3 of transactions with multiple related parties, the monetary penalty may be assessed for each failure to maintain records with respect to each related party. The monetary penalty, however, shall be imposed on a reporting corporation only once for a taxable year with respect to each related party for a failure to furnish the information required on Form 5472, for a failure to maintain or cause another to maintain records, or for a failure to comply with the non-U.S. maintenance requirements described in §1.6038A-3(f). An additional penalty for another failure may be imposed, however, under the rules of paragraph (d)(2) of this section. Thus, unless such failures continue after notification as described in paragraph (d) of this section, the maximum penalty under this paragraph with respect to each related party for all such failures in a taxable year is $10,000. The members of a group of corporations filing a consolidated return are jointly and severally liable for any monetary penalty that may be imposed under this section.

(b) *Reasonable cause.*—(1) *In general.*—Certain failures may be excused for reasonable cause, including not timely filing Form 5472, not maintaining or causing another to maintain records as required by §1.6038A-3, and not complying with the non-U.S. maintenance requirements described in §1.6038A-3(f). If an affirmative showing is made that the taxpayer acted in good faith and there is reasonable cause for a failure that results in the assessment of the monetary penalty, the period during which reasonable cause exists shall be treated as beginning on the day reasonable cause is established and ending not earlier than the last day on which reasonable cause existed for any such failure. Additionally, the beginning of the 90-day period after mailing of a notice by the District Director or the Director of an Internal Revenue Service Center of a failure described in paragraph (d) of this section shall be treated as not earlier than the last day on which reasonable cause existed.

(2) *Affirmative showing required.*—(i) *In general:*—To show that reasonable cause exists for purposes of paragraph (b)(1) of this section, the reporting corporation must make an affirmative showing of all the facts alleged as reasonable cause for the failure in a written statement containing a declaration that it is made under penalties of perjury. The statement must be filed with the District Director (in the case of failure to maintain or furnish requested information permitted to be maintained outside the United States within the time required under § 1.6038A-3(f) or a failure to file Form 5472) or the Director of the Internal Revenue Service Center where the Form 5472 is required to be filed (in the case of failure to file Form 5472). The District Director or the Director of the Internal Revenue Service Center where the Form 5472 is required to be filed, as appropriate, shall determine whether the failure was due to reasonable cause, and if so, the period of time for which reasonable cause existed. If a return has been filed as required by § 1.6038A-2 or records have been maintained as required by § 1.6038A-3, except for an omission of, or error with respect to, some of the information required or a record to be maintained, the omission or error shall not constitute a failure for purposes of section 6038A(d) if the reporting corporation that filed the return establishes to the satisfaction of the District Director or the Director of the Internal Revenue Service Center that it has substantially complied with the filing of Form 5472 or the requirement to maintain records.

(ii) *Small corporations.*—The District Director shall apply the reasonable cause exception liberally in the case of a small corporation that had no knowledge of the requirements imposed by section 6038A; has limited presence in and contact with the United States; and promptly and fully complies with all requests by the District Director to file Form 5472, and to furnish books, records, or other materials relevant to the reportable transaction. A small corporation is a corporation whose gross receipts for a taxable year are $20,000,000 or less.

(iii) *Facts and circumstances taken into account.*—The determination of whether a taxpayer acted with reasonable cause and in good faith is made on a case-by-case basis, taking into account all pertinent facts and circumstances. Circumstances that may indicate reasonable cause and good faith include an honest misunderstanding of fact or law that is reasonable in light of the experience and knowledge of the taxpayer. Isolated computational or transcriptional errors generally are not inconsistent with reasonable cause and good faith. Reliance upon an information return or on the advice of a professional (such as an attorney or accountant) does not necessarily demonstrate reasonable cause and good faith. Similarly, reasonable cause and good faith is not necessarily indicated by reliance on facts that, unknown to the taxpayer, are incorrect. Reliance on an information return, professional advice or other facts, however, constitutes reasonable cause and good faith if, under all the circumstances, the reliance was reasonable. A taxpayer, for example, may have reasonable cause for not filing a Form 5472 or for not maintaining records under section 6038A if the taxpayer has a reasonable belief that it is not owned by a 25-percent foreign shareholder. A reasonable belief means that the taxpayer does not know or has no reason to know that it is owned by a 25-percent foreign shareholder. For example, a reporting corporation would not know or have reason to know that it is owned by a 25-percent foreign shareholder if its belief that it is not so owned is consistent with other information reported or otherwise furnished to or known by the reporting corporation. A taxpayer may have reasonable cause for not treating a foreign corporation as a related party for purposes of section 6038A where the foreign corporation is a related party solely by reason of § 1.6038A-1(d)(3) (under the principles of section 482), and the taxpayer had a reasonable belief that its relationship with the foreign corporation did not meet the standards for related parties under section 482.

(c) *Failure to maintain records or to cause another to maintain records.*—A failure to maintain records or to cause another to maintain records is determined by the District Director upon the basis of the reporting corporation's overall compliance (including compliance with the non-U.S. maintenance requirements under § 1.6038A-3(f)(2)) with the record maintenance requirements. It is not an item-by-item determination. Thus, for example, a failure to maintain a single or small number of items may not constitute a failure for purposes of section 6038A(d), unless the item or items are essential to the correct determination of transactions between the reporting corporation and any foreign related parties. The District Director shall notify the reporting corporation in writing of any determination that it has failed to comply with the record maintenance requirement.

(d) *Increase in penalty where failure continues after notification.*—(1) *In general.*—If any failure described in this section continues for more than 90 days after the day on which the District Director or the Director of the Internal Revenue Service Center where the Form 5472 is required to be filed mails notice of the failure to the reporting corporation, the reporting corporation shall pay a penalty (in addition to the penalty described in paragraph (a) of this section) of $10,000 with respect to each related party for which a failure occurs for each 30-day period during which the failure continues after the expiration of the 90-day period. Any uncompleted fraction of a 30-day period shall count as a 30-day period for purposes of this paragraph (d).

(2) *Additional penalty for another failure.*—An additional penalty for a taxable year may be imposed, however, if at a time subsequent to the time of the imposition of the monetary penalty described in paragraph (a) of this section, a sec-

ond failure is determined and the second failure continues after notification under paragraph (d)(1) of this section. Thus, if a taxpayer fails to file Form 5472 and is assessed a monetary penalty and later, upon audit, is determined to have failed to maintain records, an additional penalty for the failure to maintain records may be assessed under the rules of this paragraph if the failure to maintain records continues after notification under this paragraph.

(3) *Cessation of accrual.*—The monetary penalty will cease to accrue if the reporting corporation either files Form 5472 (in the case of a failure to file Form 5472), furnishes information to substantially complete Form 5472, or demonstrates compliance with respect to the maintenance of records (in the case of a failure to maintain records) for the taxable year in which the examination occurs and subsequent years to the satisfaction of the District Director. The monetary penalty also will cease to accrue if requested information, documents, or records, kept outside the United States under the requirements of § 1.6038A-3(f) and not produced within the time specified are produced or moved to the United States under the rules of paragraph (f)(2)(ii) of this section.

(4) *Continued failures.*—If a failure under this section relating to a taxable year beginning before July 11, 1989 occurs, and if the failure continues following 90 days after the notice of failure under this paragraph is sent, the amount of the additional penalty to be assessed under this paragraph is $10,000 for each 30-day period beginning after November 5, 1990, during which the failure continues. There is no limitation on the amount of the monetary penalty that may be assessed after November 5, 1990.

(e) *Other penalties.*—For criminal penalties for failure to file a return and filing a false or fraudulent return, see sections 7203 and 7206 of the Code. For the penalty relating to an underpayment of tax, see section 6662.

(f) *Examples.*—The following examples illustrate the rules of this section.

Example 1—Failure to file Form 5472. Corp X, a U.S. reporting corporation, engages in related party transactions with FC. Corp X does not timely file a Form 5472 or maintain records relating to the transactions with FC for Year 1 or subsequent years. The Service Center with which Corp X files its income tax return imposes a $10,000 penalty for each of Years 1, 2, and 3 under section 6038A(d) and this section for failure to provide information as required on Form 5472 and mails a notice of failure to provide information. Corp X does not file Form 5472. Ninety days following the mailing of the notice of failure to Corp X an additional penalty of $10,000 is imposed. On the 135th day following the mailing of the notice of failure, Corp X files Form 5472 for Years 1, 2, and 3. The total penalty owed by Corp X for Year 1 is $30,000 ($10,000 for not timely filing Form 5472, $10,000 for the first 30-day period following the expiration of the

90-day period, and $10,000 for the fraction of the second 30-day period). The penalty for Years 2 and 3 for the failure to file Form 5472 is also $30,000 for each year, calculated in the same manner as for Year 1. The total penalty for failure to file Form 5472 for Years 1, 2, and 3 is $90,000.

Example 2—Failure to maintain records. Assume the same facts as in *Example 1.* In Year 5, Corp X is audited for Years 1 through 3. Corp X has not been maintaining records relating to the transactions with FC. The District Director issues a notice of failure to maintain records. Corp X has already been subject to the monetary penalty of $10,000 for each of Years 1, 2, and 3 for failure to file Form 5472 and, therefore, a monetary penalty under paragraph (a) of this section for failure to maintain records is not assessed. However, an additional penalty is assessed after the 90th day following the mailing of the notice of failure to maintain records. Corp X develops a record maintenance system as required by section 6038A and § 1.6038A-3. On the 180th day following the mailing of the notice of failure to maintain records, Corp X demonstrates to the satisfaction of the District Director that the newly developed record maintenance system will comply with the requirements of § 1.6038A-3 and the increase in the monetary penalty after notification ceases to accrue. The additional penalty for failure to maintain records is $30,000. An additional penalty of $30,000 per year is assessed for each of years 2 and 3 for the failure to maintain records for a total of $90,000.

(g) *Effective dates.*—For effective dates for this section, see § 1.6038A-1(n). [Reg. § 1.6038A-4.]

☐ [*T.D.* 8353, 6-14-91. *Amended by T.D. 9707,* 12-23-2014.]

[Reg. § 1.6038A-5]

§ 1.6038A-5. Authorization of agent.— (a) *Failure to authorize.*—The rules of § 1.6038A-7 shall apply to any transaction between a foreign related party and a reporting corporation (including any transaction engaged in by a partnership that is attributed to the reporting corporation under § 1.6038A-1(e)(2)), unless the foreign related party authorizes (in the manner described in paragraph (b) of this section) the reporting corporation to act as its limited agent solely for purposes of sections 7602, 7603, and 7604 with respect to any request by the Service to examine records or produce testimony that may be relevant to the tax treatment of such a transaction or with respect to any summons by the Service for such records or testimony. The fact that a reporting corporation is authorized to act as an agent for a foreign related party is to be disregarded for purposes of determining whether the foreign related party either has a trade or business in the United States for purposes of the Code or a permanent establishment or fixed base in the United States for purposes of an income tax treaty.

(b) *Authorization by related party.*—(1) *In general.*—Upon request by the Service, a foreign related party shall authorize as its agent (solely for purposes of sections 7602, 7603, and 7604) the reporting corporation with which it engages in transactions. The authorization must be signed by the foreign related party or an officer of the foreign related party possessing the authority to authorize an agent for purposes of Rule 4 of the Federal Rules of Civil Procedure. The reporting corporation will accept this appointment by providing a statement to that effect, signed by an officer of the reporting corporation possessing the authority to accept such an appointment. The agency shall be effective at all times. For taxable years beginning after July 10, 1989, the authorization and acceptance must be provided to the Service within 30 days of a request by the Service to the reporting corporation for such an authorization. The authorization must contain a heading and statement as set forth below. A foreign government is not subject to the authorization of agent requirement.

AUTHORIZATION OF AGENT

"[Name of foreign related party] hereby expressly authorizes [name of reporting corporation] to act as its agent solely for purposes of sections 7602, 7603, and 7604 of the Internal Revenue Code with respect to any request to examine records or produce testimony that may be relevant to the U.S. income tax treatment of any transaction between [name of the above-named foreign related party] and [name of reporting corporation] or with respect to any summons for such records or testimony.

_____   _____   _____
Signature of or for [name of foreign related party]   (Title)   (Date)
(If signed by a corporate officer, partner, or fiduciary on behalf of a foreign related party: I certify that I have the authority to execute this authorization of agent to act on behalf of [name of foreign related party]).

_____
Type or print your name below if signing for a foreign related party that is not an individual.

_____

[Name of reporting corporation] accepts this appointment to act as agent for [name of foreign related party] for the above purpose.

_____   _____   _____
Signature for [Name of Reporting Corporation]   (Title)   (Date)
I certify that I have the authority to accept this appointment to act as agent on behalf of [name of foreign related party] and agree to accept service of process for the above purposes. Type or print your name below.

(2) *Authorization for prior years.*—A foreign related party shall authorize a reporting corporation to act as its agent with respect to taxable years for which a Form 5472 is required to be filed prior to the date on which the final regulations under section 6038A are published by providing the above executed authorization of agent within 30 days of a request by the Service for such an authorization.

(c) *Foreign affiliated groups.*—(1) *In general.*—A foreign corporation that has effective legal authority to make the authorization of agent under paragraph (b) of this section on behalf of any group of foreign related parties may execute such an authorization for any members of the group. A single authorization may be made on a consolidated basis. In such a case, the common parent must attach a schedule to the authorization of agent stating which members of the group would otherwise be required to separately authorize the reporting corporation as agent. The schedule must provide the name, address, relationship to the reporting corporation, and U.S.

taxpayer identification number, if applicable, of each member.

(2) *Application of noncompliance penalty adjustment.*—In circumstances where a consolidated authorization of agent has been executed, if the agency authorization for any member of the group is not legally effective for purposes of sections 7602, 7603, and 7604, the noncompliance penalty adjustment under section 6038A(e) and §1.6038A-7 shall apply.

(d) *Legal effect of authorization of agent.*—The legal consequences of a foreign related party authorizing a reporting corporation to act as its agent for purposes of sections 7602, 7603, and 7604 of the Code are as follows.

(1) *Agent for purposes of commencing judicial proceedings.*—A reporting corporation that is authorized by a foreign related party to act as its agent for purposes of sections 7602, 7603, and 7604 (including service of process) is also the agent of the foreign related party for purposes of—

Reg. §1.6038A-5(b)(2)

(i) The filing of a petition to quash under section 6038A(e)(4)(A) or a petition to review an Internal Revenue Service determination of noncompliance under section 6038A(e)(4)(B), and

(ii) The commencement of a judicial proceeding to enforce a summons under section 7604, whether commenced in conjunction with a petition to quash under section 6038A(e)(4)(A) or commenced as a separate proceeding in the federal district court for the district in which the person to whom the summons is issued resides or is found.

(2) *Foreign related party found where reporting corporation found.*—For any purposes relating to sections 7602, 7603, or 7604 (including service of process), a foreign related party that authorizes a reporting corporation to act on its behalf under section 6038A(e)(1) and this section may be found anywhere where the reporting corporation has residence or is found.

(e) *Successors in interest.*—A successor in interest to a related party must execute the authorization of agent as described in paragraph (b) of this section.

(f) *Deemed compliance.*—(1) *In general.*—In exceptional circumstances, the District Director may treat a reporting corporation as authorized to act as agent for a related party for purposes of sections 7602, 7603, and 7604 in the absence of an actual agency appointment by the foreign related party, in circumstances where the actual absence of an appointment is reasonable. Factors to be considered include—

(i) If neither the reporting corporation nor the other party to the transaction knew or had reason to know that the two parties were related at the time of the transaction, and

(ii) The extent to which the taxpayer establishes to the satisfaction of the District Director that all transactions between the reporting corporation and the related party were on arm's length terms and did not involve the participation of any known related party.

(2) *Reason to know.*—Whether the reporting corporation or other party had reason to know that the two parties were related at the time of the transaction will be determined by all the facts and circumstances.

(3) *Effect of deemed compliance.*—If a reporting corporation is deemed under this paragraph (f) to have been authorized to act as an agent for a foreign related party for purposes of section 7602, 7603, and 7604, such deemed compliance is applicable only for that particular transaction and other reportable transactions entered into prior to the time when the reporting corporation knew or had reason to know that the related party, in fact, was related. The noncompliance rule of §1.6038A-7 shall apply to any transaction subsequent to that time with the same related party, unless the related party actually authorizes the reporting corporation to act as its agent under paragraph (a) of this section. In addition, the record maintenance requirements of

§1.6038A-3 will apply to all subsequent transactions and, with respect to prior transactions, will apply to relevant records in existence at the time the relationship was discovered.

(g) *Effective dates.*—For effective dates for this section, see §1.6038A-1(n). [Reg. §1.6038A-5.]

☐ [T.D. 8353, 6-14-91.]

[Reg. §1.6038A-6]

§1.6038A-6. Failure to furnish information.—(a) *In general.*—The rules of §1.6038A-7 may be applied with respect to a transaction between a foreign related party and the reporting corporation (including any transaction engaged in by a partnership that is attributed to the reporting corporation under §1.6038A-1(e)(2)) if a summons is issued to the reporting corporation to produce any records or testimony, either directly or as agent for such related party, to determine the correct treatment under Title 1 of the Code of such a transaction between the reporting corporation and the related party; and if—

(1)(i) The summons is not quashed in a proceeding, if any, begun under section 6038A(e)(4) and is not determined to be invalid in a proceeding, if any, begun under section 7604 to enforce such summons; and

(ii) The reporting corporation does not substantially and timely comply with the summons, and the District Director has sent by certified or registered mail a notice under section 6038A(e)(2)(C) to the reporting corporation that it has not so complied; or

(2) The reporting corporation fails to maintain or to cause another to maintain records as required by §1.6038A-3, and by reason of that failure, the summons is quashed in a proceeding under section 6038A(e)(4) or in a proceeding begun under section 7604 to enforce the summons, or the reporting corporation is not able to provide the records requested in the summons.

(b) *Coordination with treaties.*—Where records of a related party are obtainable on a timely and efficient basis under information exchange procedures provided under a tax treaty or tax information exchange agreement (TIEA), the Service generally will make use of such procedures before issuing a summons. The absence or pendency of a treaty or TIEA request may not be asserted as grounds for refusing to comply with a summons or as a defense against the assertion of the noncompliance penalty adjustment under §1.6038A-7. For purposes of this paragraph, information is available on a timely and efficient basis if it can be obtained within 180 days of the request.

(c) *Enforcement proceeding not required.*—The District Director is not required to begin an enforcement proceeding to enforce the summons in order to apply the rules of §1.6038A-7.

(d) *De minimis failure.*—Where a reporting corporation's failure to comply with the requirement to furnish information under this section is *de minimis*, the District Director, in the exercise of

Reg. §1.6038A-6(d)

discretion, may choose not to apply the noncompliance penalty. Thus, for example, in cases where a particular document or group of documents is not furnished upon request or summons, the District Director (in the District Director's sole discretion), may choose not to apply the noncompliance penalty if the District Director deems the document or documents not to have significant or sufficient value in the determination of the correctness of the tax treatment of the related party transaction.

(e) *Suspension of statute of limitations.*—If the reporting corporation brings an action under section 6038A(e)(4)(A) (proceeding to quash) or (e)(4)(B) (review of secretarial determination of noncompliance), the running of any period of limitation under section 6501 (relating to assessment and collection of tax) or under section 6531 (relating to criminal prosecutions) for the taxable year or years to which the summons that is the subject of such proceeding relates shall be suspended for the period during which such proceeding, and appeals therein, are pending. In no event shall any such period expire before the 90th day after the day on which there is a final determination in such proceeding.

(f) *Effective dates.*—For effective dates for this section, see § 1.6038A-1(n). [Reg. § 1.6038A-6.]

☐ [*T.D.* 8353, 6-14-91.]

[Reg. § 1.6038A-7]

§ 1.6038A-7. Noncompliance.—(a) *In general.*—In the case of any failure described in § 1.6038A-5 or § 1.6038A-6, the rules of this § 1.6038A-7 apply to the reporting corporation. In such a case—

(1) The amount of the deduction allowed under subtitle A for any amount paid or incurred by the reporting corporation to the related party in connection with such transaction, and

(2) The cost to the reporting corporation of any property acquired in such transaction from the related party or transferred by such corpora-

tion in such transaction to the related party, may be determined by the District Director.

(b) *Determination of the amount.*—The amount of the deduction or the cost to the reporting corporation shall be the amount determined by the District Director (in the District Director's sole discretion) from the District Director's own knowledge or from such information as the District Director may choose to obtain through testimony or otherwise. The District Director shall consider any information or materials that have been submitted by the reporting corporation or a foreign related party. The District Director, however, may disregard any information, documents, or records submitted by the reporting corporation or the related party if (in the District Director's sole discretion) the District Director deems that they are insufficiently probative of the relevant facts.

(c) *Separate application.*—If the noncompliance penalty of this section applies with respect to transactions with a related party of the reporting corporation, it will not be applied with respect to any other related parties of the reporting corporation solely upon the basis of that failure. Thus, for example, if a reporting corporation engages in transactions with related party A and related party B, and the reporting corporation does not respond to a summons for records related to the transactions between the reporting corporation and related party A, the noncompliance penalty imposed as a result of such failure will not apply to the transactions between the reporting corporation and related party B. If a separate summons is issued for records relating to the transactions between the reporting corporation and related party B and the reporting corporation does not produce such records, the noncompliance penalty may be applied to those transactions.

(d) *Effective dates.*—For effective dates for this section, see § 1.6038A-1(n). [Reg. § 1.6038A-7.]

☐ [*T.D.* 8353, 6-14-91.]

⧽⧽→ Caution: The Treasury Department has identified Reg. § 1.6038B-1, as amended by T.D. 9803, as a significant tax regulation that imposes an undue financial burden on U.S. taxpayers and/or adds undue complexity to the federal tax laws, pursuant to Executive Order 13789 (issued April 21, 2017) (Notice 2017-38, I.R.B. 2017-30). In a subsequent report, issued October 4, 2017, Treasury recommended planned actions that would reduce the burden of these regulations.

[Reg. § 1.6038B-1]

§ 1.6038B-1. Reporting of certain transfers to foreign corporations.—(a) *Purpose and scope.*—This section sets forth information reporting requirements under section 6038B concerning certain transfers of property to foreign corporations. Paragraph (b) of this section provides general rules explaining when and how to carry out the reporting required under section 6038B with respect to the transfers to foreign corporations. Paragraph (c) of this section and § 1.6038B-1T(d) specify the information that is required to be reported with respect to certain transfers of property that are described in section 6038B(a)(1)(A) and 367(d), respectively. Section

1.6038B-1(e) describes the filing requirements for property transfers described in section 367(e). Paragraph (f) of this section sets forth the consequences of a failure to comply with the requirements of section 6038B and this section. For effective dates, see paragraph (g) of this section. For rules regarding transfers to foreign partnerships, see section 6038B(a)(1)(B) and any regulations thereunder.

(b) *Time and manner of reporting.*—(1) *In general.*—(i) *Reporting procedure.*—Except for stock or securities qualifying under the special reporting rule of § 1.6038B-1(b)(2), and certain exchanges described in section 354 or 356 (listed below), any U.S. person that makes a transfer described in section 6038B(a)(1)(A), 367(d) or (e), is required to report pursuant to section 6038B and the rules of § 1.6038B-1 and must attach the required information to Form 926, "Return by a U.S. Transferor of Property to a Foreign Corporation." In addition, if the U.S. person files a statement under § 1.367(a)-3(d)(2)(vi)(C), a gain recognition agreement under § 1.367(a)-8, or a liquidation document under § 1.367(e)-2(b), such person must comply in all material respects with the requirements of such section pursuant to the terms of the statement, gain recognition agreement, or liquidation document, as applicable, in order to satisfy a reporting obligation under section 6038B. For special rules regarding cash transfers made in tax years beginning after February 5, 1999, see paragraphs (b)(3) and (g) of this section. For purposes of determining a U.S. transferor that is subject to section 6038B, the rules of § § 1.367(a)-1(c) and 1.367(a)-3(d) shall apply with respect to a transfer described in section 367(a), and the rules of § 1.367(a)-1(c) shall apply with respect to a transfer described in section 367(d). Additionally, if in an exchange described in section 354 or 356, a U.S. person exchanges stock or securities of a foreign corporation in a reorganization described in section 368(a)(1)(E), or a U.S. person exchanges stock or securities of a domestic or foreign corporation pursuant to an asset reorganization described in section 368(a)(1) (involving a transfer of assets under section 361) that is not treated as an indirect stock transfer under § 1.367(a)-3(d), then the U.S. person exchanging stock or securities is not required to report under section 6038B. Notwithstanding any statement to the contrary on Form 926, the form and attachments must be attached to, and filed by the due date (including extensions) of the transferor's income tax return for the taxable year that includes the date of the transfer (as defined in § 1.6038B-1T(b)(4)). For taxable years beginning before January 1, 2003, any attachment to Form 926 required under the rules of this section is filed subject to the transferor's declaration under penalties of perjury on Form 926 that the information submitted is true, correct and complete to the best of the transferor's knowledge and belief. For taxable years beginning after December 31, 2002, Form 926 and any attachments shall be verified by signing the income tax return with which the form and attachments are filed.

(ii) *Reporting by corporate transferor.*—For transfers by corporations in taxable years beginning before January 1, 2003, Form 926 must be signed by an authorized officer of the corporation if the transferor is not a member of an affiliated group under section 1504(a)(1) that files a consolidated Federal income tax return and by an authorized officer of the common parent corporation if the transferor is a member of such an affiliated group. For transfers by corporations in taxable years beginning after December 31, 2002, Form 926 shall be verified by signing the income tax return to which the form is attached.

(iii) *Transfers of jointly-owned property.*—If two or more persons transfer jointly-owned property to a foreign corporation in a transfer with respect to which a notice is required under this section, then each person must report with respect to the particular interest transferred, specifying the nature and extent of the interest. However, a husband and wife who jointly file a single Federal income tax return may file a single Form 926 with their tax return.

(2) *Exceptions and special rules for transfers of stock or securities under section 367(a).*— (i) *Transfers on or after July 20, 1998.*—A U.S. person that transfers stock or securities on or after July 20, 1998 in a transaction described in section 6038B(a)(1)(A) will be considered to have satisfied the reporting requirement under section 6038B and paragraph (b)(1) of this section if either—

(A) The U.S. transferor owned less than 5 percent of both the total voting power and the total value of the transferee foreign corporation immediately after the transfer (taking into account the attribution rules of section 318 as modified by section 958(b)), and either:

(1) The U.S. transferor qualified for nonrecognition treatment with respect to the transfer (i.e., the transfer was not taxable under § § 1.367(a)-3(b) or (c)); or

(2) The U.S. transferor is a tax-exempt entity and the income was not unrelated business income; or

(3) The transfer was taxable to the U.S. transferor under § 1.367(a)-3(c), and such person properly reported the income from the transfer on its timely-filed (including extensions) Federal income tax return for the taxable year that includes the date of the transfer; or

(4) The transfer is considered to be to a foreign corporation solely by reason of § 1.83-6(d)(1) and the fair market value of the property transferred did not exceed $100,000; or

(B) The U.S. transferor owned 5 percent or more of the total voting power or the total value of the transferee foreign corporation immediately after the transfer (taking into account the attribution rules of section 318 as modified by section 958(b)) and either:

(1) Except as provided in paragraph (b)(2)(iii) of this section, the U.S. transferor (or one or more successors) filed an initial gain recognition agreement under § 1.367(a)-8, and filed Form 926 in accordance with paragraph (b)(2)(iv) of this section; or

(2) The transferor is a tax-exempt entity and the income was not unrelated business income; or

(3) The transferor properly reported the income from the transfer on its timely-filed (including extensions) Federal income tax return for the taxable year that includes the date of the transfer; or

(4) The transfer is considered to be to a foreign corporation solely by reason of

Reg. § 1.6038B-1(b)(2)(i)(B)(4)

§ 1.83-6(d)(1) and the fair market value of the property transferred did not exceed $100,000.

(ii) *Transfers before July 20, 1998.*—With respect to transfers occurring after December 16, 1987, and prior to July 20, 1998, a U.S. transferor that transferred U.S. or foreign stock or securities in a transfer described in section 367(a) is not subject to section 6038B if such person is described in paragraph (b)(2)(i)(A) of this section.

(iii) *Timely filed initial gain recognition agreement.*—Paragraph (b)(2)(i)(B)(*1*) of this section will not apply unless the initial gain recognition agreement is timely filed as determined under § 1.367(a)-8(d)(1), but for purposes of this section, determined without regard to § 1.367(a)-8(p). However, see paragraph (f)(3) of this section for certain relief that may be available.

(iv) *Satisfaction of section 6038B reporting if a gain recognition agreement is timely filed.*—If the U.S. transferor is described in paragraph (b)(2)(i)(B)(*1*) of this section and is not otherwise required to file a Form 926 with respect to a transfer of assets other than the stock or securities to the transferee foreign corporation, the requirements of this section are satisfied with respect to the transfer of the stock or securities by completing Part I and Part II of Form 926, noting on the Form 926 that a gain recognition agreement is being filed pursuant to § 1.367(a)-8; reporting on the Form 926 the fair market value, adjusted tax basis, and gain recognized with respect to the transferred stock or securities; submitting on the Form 926 any other information that Form 926, its accompanying instructions, or other applicable guidance require to be submitted with respect to the transfer of the stock or securities; and attaching a signed copy of the Form 926 to its timely filed U.S. income tax return (including extensions) for the year of the transfer. If the U.S. transferor is required to file Form 926 with respect to a transfer of assets in addition to the stock or securities, the requirements of this section are satisfied with respect to the transfer of the stock or securities by noting on the Form 926 that a gain recognition agreement is being filed pursuant to § 1.367(a)-8; reporting on the Form 926 the fair market value, adjusted tax basis, and gain recognized with respect to the transferred stock or securities; and submitting on the Form 926 any other information that Form 926, its accompanying instructions, or other applicable guidance require to be submitted with respect to the transfer of the stock or securities.

(3) *Special rule for transfers of cash.*—A U.S. person that transfers cash to a foreign corporation in a transfer described in section 6038B(a)(1)(A) must report the transfer if—

(i) Immediately after the transfer such person holds directly, indirectly, or by attribution (determined under the rules of section 318(a), as modified by section 6038(e)(2)) at least 10 percent of the total voting power or the total value of the foreign corporation; or

(ii) The amount of cash transferred by such person or any related person (determined under section 267(b)(1) through (3) and (10) through (12)) to such foreign corporation during the 12-month period ending on the date of the transfer exceeds $100,000.

(4) [Reserved]. For further guidance, see § 1.6038B-1T(b)(4).

(c) *Information required with respect to transfers described in section 6038B(a)(1)(A).*—A United States person that transfers property to a foreign corporation in an exchange described in section 6038B(a)(1)(A) (including cash transferred in taxable years beginning after February 5, 1999, and other unappreciated property) must provide the following information, in paragraphs labeled to correspond with the number or letter set forth in this paragraph (c) and § 1.6038B-1T(c)(1) through (5). If a particular item is not applicable to the subject transfer, the taxpayer must list its heading and state that it is not applicable. For special rules applicable to transfers of stock or securities, see paragraph (b)(2)(ii) of this section.

(1) through (4) introductory text [Reserved]. For further guidance, see § 1.6038B-1T(c)(1) through (4) introductory text.

(i) *Active business property.*—Describe any transferred property that qualifies under § 1.367(a)-2(a)(2). Provide here a general description of the business conducted (or to be conducted) by the transferee, including the location of the business, the number of its employees, the nature of the business, and copies of the most recently prepared balance sheet and profit and loss statement. Property listed within this category may be identified by general type. For example, upon the transfer of the assets of a manufacturing operation, a reasonable description of the property to be used in the business might include the categories of office equipment and supplies, computers and related equipment, motor vehicles, and several major categories of manufacturing equipment. However, any property that is includible in both paragraphs (c)(4)(i) and (iii) of this section (property subject to depreciation recapture under § 1.367(a)-4(a)) must be identified in the manner required in paragraph (c)(4)(iii) of this section. If property is considered to be transferred for use in the active conduct of a trade or business under a special rule in paragraph (e), (f), or (g) of § 1.367(a)-2, specify the applicable rule and provide information supporting the application of the rule.

(ii) *Stock or securities.*—Describe any transferred stock or securities, including the class or type, amount, and characteristics of the transferred stock or securities, as well as the name, address, place of incorporation, and general description of the corporation issuing the stock or securities.

(iii) *Depreciated property.*—Describe any property that is subject to depreciation recapture under § 1.367(a)-4(a). Property within this category must be separately identified to the same extent as was required for purposes of the previously claimed depreciation deduction. Specify with respect to each such asset the relevant recapture provision, the number of months that such property was in use within the United States, the total number of months the property was in use, the fair market value of the property, a schedule of the depreciation deduction taken with respect to the property, and a calculation of the amount of depreciation required to be recaptured.

(iv) *Property not transferred for use in the active conduct of a trade or business.*—Describe any property that is eligible property, as defined in § 1.367(a)-2(b) taking into account the application of § 1.367(a)-2(c), that was transferred to the foreign corporation but not for use in the active conduct of a trade or business outside the United States (and was therefore not listed under paragraph (c)(4)(i) of this section).

(v) *Property transferred under compulsion.*— If property qualifies for the exception of § 1.367(a)-2(a)(2) under the rules of paragraph (h) of that section, provide information supporting the claimed application of such exception.

(vi) *Certain ineligible property.*—Describe any property that is described in § 1.367(a)-2(c) and that therefore cannot qualify under § 1.367(a)-2(a)(2) regardless of its use in the active conduct of a trade or business outside of the United States. The description must be divided into the relevant categories, as follows:

(A) *Inventory, etc.*—Property described in § 1.367(a)-2(c)(1);

(B) *Installment obligations, etc.*—Property described in § 1.367(a)-2(c)(2);

(C) *Foreign currency, etc.*—Property described in § 1.367(a)-2(c)(3); and

(D) *Leased property.*—Property described in § 1.367(a)-2(c)(4).

(vii) *Other property that is ineligible property.*—Describe any property, other than property described in § 1.367(a)-2(c), that cannot qualify under § 1.367(a)-2(a)(2) regardless of its use in the active conduct of a trade or business outside of the United States and that is not subject to the rules of section 367(d) under § 1.367(a)-1(b)(5) (treatment of certain property as subject to section 367(d)). Each item of property must be separately identified.

(viii) [Reserved]. For further guidance, see § 1.6038B-1T(c)(4)(viii).

(5) *Transfer of foreign branch with previously deducted losses.*—If the property transferred is property of a foreign branch with previously deducted losses subject to § § 1.367(a)-6 and -6T, provide the following information:

(i) through (iv) [Reserved]. For further information, see § 1.6038B-1T(c)(5)(i) through (iv).

(6) *Transfers subject to section 367(a)(5).*— (i) *In general.*—This paragraph (c)(6) applies to a domestic corporation (U.S. transferor) that transfers section 367(a) property (as defined in

§ 1.367(a)-7(f)(10)) to a foreign corporation in a section 361 exchange (as defined in § 1.367(a)-7(f)(8)) and to which the provisions of § 1.367(a)-7(c) apply. Paragraph (c)(6)(ii) of this section establishes the time and manner for the U.S. transferor to elect to apply the provisions of § 1.367(a)-7(c). Paragraph (c)(6)(iii) of this section establishes the manner for the U.S. transferor to satisfy the requirement of § 1.367(a)-7(c)(4).

(ii) *Election.*—The U.S. transferor elects to apply the provisions of § 1.367(a)-7(c) by including a statement entitled, "ELECTION TO APPLY EXCEPTION UNDER § 1.367(a)-7(c)," with its timely filed return (within the meaning of § 1.367(a)-7(f)(12)) for the taxable year during which the reorganization occurs and that includes the information described in paragraphs (c)(6)(ii)(A), (c)(6)(ii)(B), (c)(6)(ii)(C), (c)(6)(ii)(D), (c)(6)(ii)(E), (c)(6)(ii)(F), (c)(6)(ii)(G), and (c)(6)(ii)(H) of this section. See § 1.367(a)-7(c)(5)(ii) for the statement required to be filed by a control group member (as defined in § 1.367(a)-7(f)(1)) or final distributee (as defined in § 1.367(a)-7(d)).

(A) The name and taxpayer identification number (if any) of each control group member and final distributee (if any), the foreign acquiring corporation, and in the case of a triangular reorganization (within the meaning of § 1.358-6(b)(2)) the corporation that controls the foreign acquiring corporation, and the ownership interest percentage (as defined in § 1.367(a)-7(f)(7)) in the U.S. transferor of each control group member.

(B) A calculation of the gain recognized (if any) by the U.S. transferor under § 1.367(a)-7(c)(2)(i) and (c)(2)(ii), and the basis adjustments (if any) required to be made by each control group member under § 1.367(a)-7(c)(3).

(C) The date on which the U.S. transferor and each control group member or final distributee entered into the written agreement described in § 1.367(a)-7(c)(5)(iv).

(D) The amount of any deductible liability (as defined by § 1.367(a)-7(f)(2)).

(E) The fair market value (as defined by § 1.367(a)-7(f)(3)) of property transferred to the foreign acquiring corporation in the section 361 exchange.

(F) The inside basis (as defined by § 1.367(a)-7(f)(4)).

(G) The inside gain (as defined by § 1.367(a)-7(f)(5)).

(H) The section 367(a) percentage (as defined by § 1.367(a)-7(f)(9)).

(iii) *Agreement to amend U.S. transferor's tax return.*—The U.S. transferor complies with the requirement of § 1.367(a)-7(c)(4)(i) by attaching a statement to its timely filed return (within the meaning of § 1.367(a)-7(f)(12)) for the taxable year in which the reorganization occurs, entitled "STATEMENT UNDER § 1.367(a)-7(c)(4) FOR TRANSFERS OF ASSETS TO A FOREIGN CORPORATION IN A SECTION 361 EXCHANGE." The statement must certify that if a significant

Reg. § 1.6038B-1(c)(6)(iii)

amount of the section 367(a) property received by the foreign acquiring corporation from the U.S. transferor in the section 361 exchange is disposed of, directly or indirectly, in one or more related transactions described in paragraph (c)(6)(iii)(B) of this section occurring within the sixty (60) month period that begins on the date of distribution or transfer (within the meaning of § 1.381(b)-1(b)), then the exception provided in § 1.367(a)-7(c) will not apply to the section 361 exchange. Accordingly, the U.S. transferor will recognize the gain realized but not recognized in the section 361 exchange, computed as if the exception provided in § 1.367(a)-7(c) had never applied. A U.S. income tax return (or amended U.S. income tax return, as the case may be) for the year in which the reorganization occurred reporting the gain must be filed. If the section 361 exchange occurs in connection with a triangular reorganization (within the meaning of § 1.358-6(b)(2)) and the corporation that controls the foreign acquiring corporation is foreign, an indirect disposition of the section 367(a) property includes the disposition by such controlling foreign corporation of the stock of the foreign acquiring corporation.

(A) *Disposition of a significant amount.*— *(1) General rule.*—Except as provided in paragraphs (c)(6)(iii)(A)(2) and (c)(6)(iii)(A)(3) of this section, for purposes of this paragraph (c)(6)(iii), a disposition of a significant amount occurs if, in one or more related transactions, the foreign acquiring corporation disposes of an amount of the section 367(a) property received from the U.S. transferor in the section 361 exchange that is greater than 40 percent of the fair market value of all of the section 367(a) property transferred in the section 361 exchange.

(2) *Exception for certain nonrecognition exchanges.*—Section 367(a) property that is subsequently transferred (retransferred property) pursuant to a nonrecognition provision is not treated as disposed of for purposes of paragraph (c)(6)(iii)(A)(1) of this section, provided such transfer satisfies, and is treated in a manner consistent with the principles underlying § 1.367(a)-8(k). Thus, for example, if section 367(a) property is subsequently transferred to a foreign corporation in exchange solely for stock in a transaction described in section 351, such retransferred property is not treated as disposed of for purposes of paragraph (c)(6)(iii)(A)(1) of this section; in such a case, however, a subsequent disposition of either the retransferred property by the transferee foreign corporation, or of the stock of the transferee foreign corporation received in exchange for the retransferred property, is subject to the provisions of paragraph (c)(6)(iii)(A)(1) of this section.

(3) *Exception for dispositions occurring in the ordinary course of business.*—Dispositions of section 367(a) property described in section 1221(a)(2) occurring in the ordinary course of business of the foreign acquiring corporation are not treated as disposed of for purposes of paragraph (c)(6)(iii)(A)(1) of this section.

(B) *Gain recognition transaction.*— *(1) General rule.*—A transaction is described in this paragraph (c)(6)(iii)(B) if the transaction is entered into with a principal purpose of avoiding the U.S. tax that would have been imposed on the U.S. transferor on the disposition of the property transferred to the foreign acquiring corporation in the section 361 exchange. A disposition may have a principal purpose of tax avoidance even if the tax avoidance purpose is outweighed by other purposes when taken together.

(2) *Presumptive tax avoidance.*—For purposes of this paragraph (c)(6)(iii)(B), the principal purpose of the foreign acquiring corporation's disposition of a significant amount of the section 367(a) property within the two-year period that begins on the date of distribution or transfer (within the meaning of § 1.381(b)-1(b)) (whether in a recognition or nonrecognition transaction) will be presumed to be the avoidance of the U.S. tax that would have been imposed on the U.S. transferor on the disposition of the property transferred to the foreign acquiring corporation in the section 361 exchange. However, this presumption will not apply if it is demonstrated to the satisfaction of the Director of Field Operations, Large Business & International (or any successor to the roles and responsibilities of such person (Director) that the avoidance of U.S. tax was not a principal purpose of the disposition.

(3) *Interest.*—If additional tax is required to be paid as a result of a transaction described in paragraph (c)(6)(iii)(B) of this section, then interest must be paid on that amount at rates determined under section 6621 with respect to the period between the date prescribed for filing the U.S. transferor's income tax return for the year in which the reorganization occurs and the date on which the additional tax for that year is paid.

(d)(1) through (1)(iii) [Reserved]. For further guidance, see § 1.6038B-1T(d)(1) through (1)(iii).

(iv) *Intangible property transferred.*—Provide a description of the intangible property transferred, including its adjusted basis. Generally, each item of intangible property must be separately identified, including intangible property described in § 1.367(d)-1(g)(2)(i). Identify all property that is subject to the rules of section 367(d) under § 1.367(a)-1(b)(5) (treatment of certain property as subject to section 367(d)). Describe any property for which the income required to be taken into account under section 367(d) and the regulations thereunder will be recognized over a 20-year period pursuant to § 1.367(d)-1(c)(3)(ii). Estimate the anticipated income or cost reductions attributable to the intangible property's use beyond the 20-year period.

(v)–(vi) [Reserved]. For further guidance, see § 1.6038B-1T(d)(1)(v) through (1)(vi).

(vii) *Coordination with loss rules.*—List any intangible property subject to section 367(d) the transfer of which also gives rise to the recognition of gain under section 904(f)(3) or §§ 1.367(a)-6 or -6T. Provide a calculation of the gain required to be recognized with respect to such property, in accordance with the provisions of § 1.367(d)-1(g)(3).

(d)(1)(viii) through (d)(2) [Reserved]. For further guidance, see § 1.6038B-1T(d)(1)(viii) through (d)(2).

(e) *Transfers subject to section 367(e).*—(1) *In general.*—If a domestic corporation (distributing corporation) makes a distribution described in section 367(e)(1) or section 367(e)(2), the distributing corporation must comply with the reporting requirements of this paragraph (e). Unless otherwise provided in this section, a distributing corporation making a distribution described in sections 367(e)(1) or 367(e)(2) must file a Form 926, "Return by a U.S. Transferor of Property to a Foreign Corporation (under section 367)," as amended and modified by this section.

(2) *Reporting requirements for section 367(e)(1) distributions of domestic controlled corporations.*—A domestic distributing corporation making a distribution of the stock or securities of a domestic corporation under section 355 is not required to file a Form 926, as described in paragraph (e)(1) of this section, and shall have no other reporting requirements under section 6038B.

(3) *Reporting requirements for section 367(e)(1) distributions of foreign controlled corporations.*—If the distributing corporation makes a section 355 distribution of the stock or securities of a foreign controlled corporation to distributee shareholders who are not qualified U.S. persons, as defined in § 1.367(e)-1(b)(1), then the distributing corporation shall complete Part 1 of the Form 926 and attach a signed copy of such form to its U.S. income tax return for the year of the distribution. The distributing corporation shall also attach to its U.S. income tax return for the year of distribution a statement signed under the penalties of perjury entitled, "Addendum to Form 926." The addendum shall contain a brief description of the transaction, state the number of shares distributed to distributees who are not qualified U.S. persons (applying the rules contained in § 1.367(e)-1(d)), and state the basis and fair market value of the distributed stock or securities (including a list stating the amounts that were distributed to distributees who were not qualified U.S. persons and distributees who were qualified U.S. persons).

(4) *Reporting rules for section 367(e)(2) distributions by domestic liquidating corporations.*— (i) *General rule.*—Except as provided in paragraph (e)(4)(ii) of this section, if the distributing corporation makes a distribution of property in complete liquidation under section 332 to a foreign distributee corporation that meets the stock ownership requirements of section 332(b) with respect to the stock of the distributing corporation, then the distributing corporation must complete a Form 926 and attach a signed copy of such form to its timely filed U.S. income tax return (including extensions) for the taxable years that include one or more liquidating distributions. The property description contained in Part III of the Form 926 must contain a description, including the adjusted tax basis and fair market value, of all property distributed by the distributing corporation (regardless of whether the distribution of the property qualifies for nonrecognition treatment). The description must also identify the items of property for which nonrecognition treatment is claimed under § 1.367(e)-2(b)(2)(ii) or (iii), as applicable.

(ii) *Special rule.*—Except as provided in paragraph (e)(4)(iii) of this section, if the distributing corporation distributes items of property that will be used by the foreign distributee corporation in the conduct of a trade or business in the United States and the distributing corporation does not recognize gain or loss on such distribution under § 1.367(e)-2(b)(2)(i) with respect to such property, then the distributing corporation may satisfy the requirements of this section by completing Part I and Part II of Form 926, noting in Part III that the information required by Form 926 is contained in a statement required by § 1.367(e)-2(b)(2)(i)(C)(2), and attaching a signed copy of Form 926 to its timely filed U.S. income tax return (including extensions) for each taxable year that includes one or more distributions in liquidation. In addition, if the distributing corporation distributes stock of a domestic subsidiary corporation and does not recognize gain or loss on such distribution under § 1.367(e)-2(b)(2)(iii) with respect to such stock, then the distributing corporation may satisfy the requirements of this section by completing Part I and Part II of Form 926, noting in Part III that the information required by Form 926 is contained in a statement required by § 1.367(e)-2(b)(2)(iii)(D), and attaching a signed copy of Form 926 to its timely filed U.S. income tax return (including extensions) for the taxable years that include one or more distributions of domestic subsidiary stock.

(iii) *Properly filed statement.*—Paragraph (e)(4)(ii) will not apply if there is a failure to file an initial liquidation document as determined under § 1.367(e)-2(e)(3)(i), but for purposes of this section, determined without regard to § 1.367(e)-2(f). However, see paragraph (f)(3) of this section for certain relief that may be available.

(f) *Failure to comply with reporting requirements.*—(1) *Consequences of failure.*—If a U.S. person is required to file a notice (or otherwise comply) under paragraph (b) of this section and fails to comply with the applicable requirements of section 6038B and this section, then with respect to the particular property as to which there was a failure to comply—

(i) The U.S. person shall pay a penalty under section 6038B(b)(1) equal to 10 percent of the fair market value of the transferred property at the time of the exchange, but in no event shall the penalty exceed $100,000 unless the failure with respect to such exchange was due to intentional disregard (described under paragraph (g)(4) of this section); and

(ii) The period of limitations on assessment of tax upon the transfer of that property does not expire before the date which is 3 years after the date on which the Secretary is furnished the information required to be reported under this section. See section 6501(c)(8) and any regulations thereunder.

(2) *Failure to comply.*—A failure to comply with the requirements of section 6038B is—

(i) The failure to report at the proper time and in the proper manner any material information required to be reported under the rules of this section; or

(ii) The provision of false or inaccurate information in purported compliance with the requirements of this section. Thus, a transferor that timely files Form 926 with the attachments required under the rules of this section shall, nevertheless, have failed to comply if, for example, the transferor reports therein that property will be used in the active conduct of a trade or business outside of the United States, but in fact the property continues to be used in a trade or business within the United States.

(iii) With respect to an initial gain recognition agreement filed under § 1.367(a)-8, a failure to comply as determined under § 1.367(a)-8(j)(8), but for purposes of this section, determined without regard to the application of § 1.367(a)-8(p).

(iv) With respect to an initial liquidation document filed under § 1.367(e)-2(b)(2), a failure to comply as determined under § 1.367(e)-2(e)(4)(i), but for purposes of this section, determined without regard to the application of § 1.367(e)-2(f).

(3) *Reasonable cause for failure to comply.*— (i) *Request for relief.*—If the U.S. transferor fails to comply with any requirement of section 6038B and this section, the failure shall be deemed not to have occurred if the U.S. transferor is able to demonstrate that the failure was due to reasonable cause and not willful neglect using the procedure set forth in paragraph (f)(3)(ii) of this section. Whether the failure to timely comply was due to reasonable cause and not willful neglect will be determined by the Director of Field Operations, Cross Border Activities Practice Area of Large Business & International (Director) based on all the facts and circumstances.

(ii) *Procedures for establishing that a failure to timely comply was due to reasonable cause and not willful neglect.*—(A) *Time of submission.*—A U.S. transferor's statement that the failure to timely comply was due to reasonable cause and not willful neglect will be considered only if, promptly after the U.S. transferor becomes aware of the failure, an amended return is filed for the taxable year to which the failure relates that includes the information that should have been included with the original return for such taxable year or that otherwise complies with the rules of this section, and that includes a written statement explaining the reasons for the failure to timely comply.

(B) *Notice requirement.*—In addition to the requirements of paragraph (f)(3)(ii)(A) of this section, the U.S. transferor must comply with the notice requirements of this paragraph (f)(3)(ii)(B). If any taxable year of the U.S. transferor is under examination when the amended return is filed, a copy of the amended return and any information required to be included with such return must be delivered to the Internal Revenue Service personnel conducting the examination. If no taxable year of the U.S. transferor is under examination when the amended return is filed, a copy of the amended return and any information required to be included with such return must be delivered to the Director.

(4) *Definition of intentional disregard.*—If the transferor fails to qualify for the exception under paragraph (f)(3) of this section and if the taxpayer knew of the rule or regulation that was disregarded, the failure will be considered an intentional disregard of section 6038B, and the monetary penalty under paragraph (f)(1)(ii) of this section will not be limited to $100,000. See § 1.6662-3(b)(2).

(g) *Effective/applicability dates.*—(1) This section applies to transfers occurring on or after July 20, 1998, except as provided in paragraphs (g)(2) through (g)(7) of this section, and except for transfers of cash made in tax years beginning on or before February 5, 1999 (which are not required to be reported under section 6038B), and transfers described in paragraph (e) of this section (which applies to transfers that are subject to §§ 1.367(e)-1(f) and 1.367(e)-2(e)). See § 1.6038B-1T for transfers occurring prior to July 20, 1998. See also § 1.6038B-1T(e) in effect prior to August 9, 1999, (as contained in 26 CFR part 1 revised April 1, 1999) for transfers described in section 367(e) that are not subject to §§ 1.367(e)-1(f) and 1.367(e)-2(e).

(2) The rules of paragraph (b)(1)(i) of this section as they apply to section 368(a)(1)(A) reorganizations (including reorganizations described in section 368(a)(2)(D) or (E)) apply to transfers occurring on or after January 23, 2006.

(3) The rules of paragraph (b)(1)(i) of this section that provide an exception from reporting under section 6038B for transfers of stock or securities in a section 354 or 356 exchange, pursuant to a section 368(a)(1)(G) reorganization that is not treated as an indirect stock transfer under § 1.367(a)-3(d), apply to transfers occurring on or after January 23, 2006.

(4) The rules of paragraph (b)(1)(i) of this section that provide an exception from reporting under section 6038B for transfers of stock in a section 354 or 356 exchange, pursuant to a section 368(a)(1)(E) reorganization or an asset reorganization under section 368(a)(1) that is not treated as an indirect stock transfer under

§ 1.367(a)-3(d), apply to transfers occurring on or after January 23, 2006. The rules of paragraph (b)(1)(i) of this section that provide an exception from reporting under section 6038B for transfers of securities in a section 354 or 356 exchange, pursuant to a section 368(a)(1)(E) reorganization or an asset reorganization under section 368(a)(1) that is not treated as an indirect stock transfer under § 1.367(a)-3(d), apply only to transfers occurring after January 5, 2005 (although taxpayers may apply such provision to transfers of securities occurring on or after July 20, 1998 and on or before January 5, 2005 if done consistently to all transactions). See § 1.6038-1T(b)(i), as contained in 26 CFR Part 1 revised as of April 1, 2005, for transfers occurring prior to the effective dates described in paragraphs (g)(2) through (4) of this section.

(5) Paragraphs (c)(6) and (f)(3) of this section apply to transfers occurring on or after April 18, 2013. For guidance with respect to paragraphs (c)(6) and (f)(3) of this section before April 18, 2013, see 26 CFR part 1 revised as of April 1, 2012.

(6) The second sentence of paragraph (b)(1)(i) and paragraphs (b)(2)(i)(B)(1), (b)(2)(iii), (b)(2)(iv), (c), (e)(4), (f)(2)(iii), and (f)(2)(iv) of this section will apply to transfers for which documents are required to be filed on or after November 19, 2014, as well as to transfers that are the subject of requests for relief submitted on or after November 19, 2014. The second sentence of paragraph (b)(1)(i) and paragraphs (b)(2)(i)(B)(1), (b)(2)(iii), (b)(2)(iv), (c), and (f)(2)(iii) of this section will also apply to any transfer that is the subject of a request for relief submitted pursuant to § 1.367(a)-8(r)(3).

(7) Paragraphs (c)(4)(i) through (vii), (c)(5), and (d)(1)(iv) and (vii) of this section apply to transfers occurring on or after September 14, 2015, and to transfers occurring before September 14, 2015, resulting from entity classification elections made under § 301.7701-3 that are filed on or after September 14, 2015. For guidance with respect to paragraphs (c)(4), (c)(5), and (d)(1) of this section before this section is applicable, see §§ 1.6038B-1 and 1.6038B-1T as contained in 26 CFR part 1 revised as of April 1, 2016. [Reg. § 1.6038B-1.]

☐ [T.D. 8770, 6-18-98 (*corrected* 3-31-99). *Amended by T.D.* 8817, 2-4-99 (*corrected* 3-31-99); *T.D.* 8834, 8-6-99; *T.D.* 8850, 12-27-99; *T.D.* 9100, 12-18-2003; *T.D.* 9243, 1-23-2006; *T.D.* 9300, 12-7-2006; *T.D.* 9614, 3-18-2013; *T.D.* 9704, 11-18-2014 (*corrected* 1-2-2015), *T.D.* 9760, 3-18-2016 *and T.D.* 9803, 12-15-2016.]

⫸➔ *Caution: The Treasury Department has identified Temporary Reg. § 1.6038B-1T, as amended by T.D. 9803, as a significant tax regulation that imposes an undue financial burden on U.S. taxpayers and/or adds undue complexity to the federal tax laws, pursuant to Executive Order 13789 (issued April 21, 2017) (Notice 2017-38, I.R.B. 2017-30). In a subsequent report, issued October 4, 2017, Treasury recommended planned actions that would reduce the burden of these regulations.*

[Reg. § 1.6038B-1T]

§ 1.6038B-1T. Reporting of certain transactions to foreign corporations (temporary).—(a) through (b)(3) *[Reserved].*—For further guidance, see § 1.6038B-1(a) through (b)(3).

(4) *Date of transfer.*—(i) *In general.*—For purposes of this section, the date of a transfer described in section 367 is the first date on which title to, possession of, or rights to the use of stock, securities, or other property passes pursuant to the plan for purposes of subtitle A of the Internal Revenue Code. A transfer will not be considered to begin with a decision of a board of directors or similar action unless the transaction otherwise takes effect for purposes of subtitle A of the Internal Revenue Code on that date.

(ii) *Termination of section 1504(d) election.*— A transfer deemed to occur as a result of the termination of an election under section 1504(d) will be considered to occur on the date the contiguous country corporation first fails to continue to qualify for the election under section 1504(d). The rule of this paragraph (b)(3)(ii) is illustrated by the following example.

Example. Domestic corporation W previously made a valid election under section 1504(d) to have its Mexican subsidiary S treated as a domestic corporation. On August 1, 1986, W disposes of its right, title, and interest in 10 percent of the stock of S by selling such stock to an unrelated United States person who is not a director of S. S first fails to continue to qualify for the election under section 1504(d) on August 1, 1986, since on such date it ceases to be directly or indirectly wholly owned or controlled by W. The constructive transfer of assets from "domestic" corporation S to Mexican corporation S is considered to occur on that date.

(iii) *Change in classification.*—A transfer deemed to occur as a result of a change in classification of an entity caused by a change in the governing documents, articles, or agreements of the entity (as described in § 1.367(a)-1T(c)(6)) will be considered to occur on the date that such changes take effect for purposes of subtitle A of the Internal Revenue Code.

(iv) *U.S. resident under section 6013(g) or (h).*—A transfer made by an alien individual who is considered to be a U.S resident by reason of a timely election under section 6013(g) or (h) will be considered to occur, for purposes of this section (but not for purposes of section 367), on the later of—

(A) The date on which the election under section 6013(g) or (h) is made; or

(B) The date on which the transfer would otherwise be considered to occur under the rules of this paragraph (b)(3).

The rule of this paragraph (b)(3)(iv) is illustrated by the following example.

Example. D is a nonresident alien individual who is married to a United States citizen.

Reg. § 1.6038B-1T(b)(4)(iv)(B)

On March 1, 1986, D transfers property to a foreign corporation in an exchange described in section 351. On April 15, 1987, D and the spouse timely file with their tax return for the taxable year ended December 31, 1986, an election under section 6013(g) for D to be treated as a United States resident. The election is effective on January 1, 1986. For purposes of section 6038B, the transfer described in section 367(a) made by D in connection with the section 351 exchange is considered to occur on April 15, 1987, the date on which the timely election was made under section 6013(g).

(c) Introductory text [Reserved]. For further guidance, see § 1.6038B-1(c).

(1) *Transferor.*—Provide the name, U.S. taxpayer identification number, and address of the U.S. person making the transfer.

(2) *Transfer.*—Provide the following information concerning the transfer:

(i) Name, U.S. taxpayer identification number (if any), address, and country of incorporation of transferee foreign corporation;

(ii) A general description of the transfer, and any wider transaction of which it forms a part, including a chronology of the transfers involved and an identification of the other parties to the transaction to the extent known.

(3) *Consideration received.*—Provide a description of the consideration received by the U.S. person making the transfer, including its estimated fair market value and, in the case of stock or securities, the class or type, amount, and characteristics of the interest received.

(4) *Property transferred.*—Provide a description of the property transferred. The description must be divided into the following categories, and must include the estimated fair market value and adjusted basis of the property, as well as any additional information specified below.

(i) through (c)(5) introductory text [Reserved].

(i) *Branch operation.*—Describe the foreign branch the property of which is transferred, in accordance with the definition of § 1.367(a)-6T(g).

(ii) *Branch property.*—Describe the property of the foreign branch, including its adjusted basis and fair market value. For this purpose property must be identified with reasonable particularity, but may be identified by category rather than listing every asset separately. Substantially similar property may be listed together for this purpose, and property of minor value may be grouped into functional categories. For example, a reasonable description of the property of a business office might include the following categories: word processing or data processing equipment, other office equipment and furniture, and office supplies.

(iii) *Previously deducted losses.*—Set forth a detailed calculation of the sum of the losses incurred by the foreign branch before the transfer,

and a detailed calculation of any reduction of such losses, in accordance with § 1.367(a)-6T(d) and (e).

(iv) *Character of gain.*—Set forth a statement of the character of the gain required to be recognized, in accordance with § 1.367(a)-6T(c)(1).

(6) [Reserved]. For further guidance, see § 1.6038B-1(c)(6).

(d) *Transfers subject to section 367(d).*—(1) *Initial transfer.*—A U.S. person that transfers intangible property to a foreign corporation in an exchange described in section 351 or 361 must provide the following information in paragraphs labelled to correspond with the number or letter set forth below. If a particular item is not applicable to the subject transfer, list its heading and state that it is not applicable. The information required by subdivisions (i) through (iii) need only be provided if such information was not otherwise provided under paragraph (c) of this section. (Note that the U.S. transferor may subsequently be required to file another return under paragraph (d)(2) of this section.)

(i) *Transferor.*—Provide the name, U.S. taxpayer identification number, and address of the U.S. person making the transfer.

(ii) *Transfer.*—Provide information concerning the transfer, including:

(A) Name, U.S. taxpayer identification number (if any), address, and country of incorporation of the transferee foreign corporation;

(B) A general description of the transfer, and any wider transaction of which it forms a part, including a chronology of the transfers involved and an identification of the other parties to the transaction to the extent known.

(iii) *Consideration received.*—Provide a description of the consideration received by the U.S. person making the transfer, including its estimated fair market value and, in the case of stock or securities, the class or type, amount, and characteristics of the interest received.

(iv) [Reserved].

(v) *Annual payment.*—Provide and explain the calculation of the annual deemed payment for the use of the intangible property required to be recognized by the transferor under the rules of section 367(d).

(vi) *Election to treat as sale.*—List any intangible with respect to which an election is being made under § 1.367(d)-1T(g)(2) to treat the transfer as a sale. Include the fair market value of the intangible on the date of the transfer and a calculation of the gain required to be recognized in the year of the transfer by reason of the election.

(vii) [Reserved].

(viii) *Other intangibles.*—Describe any intangible property sold or licensed by the transferor to the transferee foreign corporation, and set forth the general terms of each sale or license.

(2) *Subsequent transfers.*—If a U.S. person transfers intangible property to a foreign corporation in an exchange described in section 351 or 361, and at any time thereafter (within the useful life of the intangible property) either that U.S. person disposes of the stock of the transferee foreign corporation or the transferee foreign corporation disposes of the transferred intangible, then the U.S. person must provide the following information in paragraphs labelled to correspond with the number or letter set forth below. The information required by subdivisions (i) and (ii) need only be provided if such information was not otherwise provided in the same return, pursuant to paragraph (c) or (d)(1) of this section. For purposes of determining the date on which a return under this subparagraph (2) is required to be filed, the date of transfer is the date of the subsequent transfer of stock or intangible property.

(i) *Transferor.*—Provide the name, U.S. taxpayer identification number, and address of the U.S. person making the transfer.

(ii) *Initial transfer.*—Provide the following information concerning the initial transfer:

(A) The date of the transfer;

(B) The name, U.S. taxpayer identification number (if any), address, and country of incorporation of the transferee foreign corporation; and

(C) A general description of the transfer and any wider transaction of which it formed a part.

(iii) *Subsequent transfer.*—Provide the following information concerning the subsequent transfer:

(A) A general description of the subsequent transfer and any wider transaction of which it forms a part;

(B) A calculation of any gain required to be recognized by the U.S. person under the rules of § 1.367(d)-1T(d) through (f); and

(C) The name, address, and identifying number of each person that under the rules of § 1.367(d)-1T(e) or (f) will be considered to receive contingent annual payments for the use of the intangible property.

(e) [Reserved]For further guidance, see § 1.6038B-1(e).

(f)(1) through (f)(2) [Reserved].—For further guidance, see § 1.6038B-1(f)(1) through (f)(2).

(3) [Reserved.]

(f)(4) [Reserved]. For further guidance, see § 1.6038B-1T(f)(4).

(g) *Effective date.*—This section applies to transfers occurring after December 31, 1984. See § 1.6038B-1T(a) through (b)(2), (c) introductory text, and (f) (26 CFR part 1, revised April 1, 1998) for transfers occurring prior to July 20, 1998. See § 1.6038B-1 for transfers occurring on or after July 20, 1998. [Temporary Reg. § 1.6038B-1T.]

☐ [T.D. 8087, 5-15-86. *Amended by* T.D. 8682, 8-9-96; T.D. 8770, 6-18-98; T.D. 8834, 8-6-99; T.D. 9100, 12-18-2003 (*corrected* 2-2-2004); T.D. 9243, 1-23-2006; T.D. 9300, 12-7-2006, T.D. 9615, 3-18-2013, T.D. 9760, 3-18-2016 *and* T.D. 9803, 12-15-2016.]

[Reg. § 1.6038B-2]

§ 1.6038B-2. Reporting of certain transfers to foreign partnerships.—(a) *Reporting requirements.*—(1) *Requirement to report transfers.*—A United States person that transfers property to a foreign partnership in a contribution described in section 721 (including section 721(b)) must report that transfer on Form 8865 "Information Return of U.S. Persons With Respect To Certain Foreign Partnerships" pursuant to section 6038B and the rules of this section, if—

(i) Immediately after the transfer, the United States person owns, directly, indirectly, or by attribution, at least a 10-percent interest in the partnership, as defined in section 6038(e)(3)(C) and the regulations thereunder;

(ii) The value of the property transferred, when added to the value of any other property transferred in a section 721 contribution by such person (or any related person) to the partnership during the 12-month period ending on the date of the transfer, exceeds $100,000; or

(iii) [Reserved]. For further guidance, see § 1.6038B-2T(a)(1)(iii).

(2) *Indirect transfer through a domestic partnership.*—For purposes of this section, if a domestic partnership transfers property to a foreign partnership in a section 721 transaction, the domestic partnership's partners shall be considered to have transferred a proportionate share of the property to the foreign partnership. However, if the domestic partnership properly reports all of the information required under this section with respect to the contribution, no partner of the transferor partnership, whether direct or indirect (through tiers of partnerships), is also required to report under this section. For illustrations of this rule, see *Examples 4* and 5 of paragraph (a)(7) of this section.

(3) [Reserved]. For further guidance see § 1.6038B-2T(a)(3).

(4) *Requirement to report dispositions.*—(i) *In general.*—If a United States person was required to report a transfer to a foreign partnership of appreciated property under paragraph (a)(1) or (2) of this section, and the foreign partnership disposes of the property while such United States person remains a direct or indirect partner, that United States person must report the disposition by filing Form 8865. The form must be attached to, and filed by the due date (including extensions) of, the United States person's income tax return for the year in which the disposition occurred.

(ii) *Disposition of contributed property in nonrecognition transaction.*—If a foreign partnership disposes of contributed appreciated property in a nonrecognition transaction and substituted basis property is received in exchange, and the substituted basis property has built-in gain under §1.704-3(a)(8), the original transferor is not required to report the disposition. However, the transferor must report the disposition of the substituted basis property in the same manner as provided for the contributed property.

(5) *Time for filing Form 8865.*—The Form 8865 on which a transfer is reported must be attached to the transferor's timely filed (including extensions) income tax return for the tax year that includes the date of the transfer. If the person required to report under this section is not required to file an income tax return for its tax year during which the transfer occurred, but is required to file an information return for that year (for example, Form 1065, "U.S. Partnership Return of Income," or Form 990, "Return of Organization Exempt from Income Tax"), the person should attach the Form 8865 to its information return.

(6) *Returns to be made.*—(i) *Separate returns for each partnership.*—If a United States person transfers property reportable under this section to more than one foreign partnership in a taxable year, the United States person must submit a separate Form 8865 for each partnership.

(ii) *Duplicate form to be filed.*—If required by the instructions accompanying Form 8865, a duplicate Form 8865 (including attachments and schedules) must also be filed by the due date for submitting the original Form 8865 under paragraph (a)(5)(i) or (ii) of this section, as applicable.

(7) *Examples.*—The application of this paragraph (a) may be illustrated by the following examples:

Example 1. On November 1, 2001, *US*, a United States person that uses the calendar year as its taxable year, contributes $200,000 to *FP*, a foreign partnership, in a transaction subject to section 721. After the contribution, *US* owns a 5% interest in *FP*. *US* must report the contribution by filing Form 8865 for its taxable year ending December 31, 2001. On March 1, 2002, *US* makes a $40,000 section 721 contribution to *FP*, after which *US* owns a 6% interest in *FP*. *US* must report the $40,000 contribution by filing Form 8865 for its taxable year ending December 31, 2002, because the contribution, when added to the value of the other property contributed by *US* to *FP* during the 12-month period ending on the date of the transfer, exceeds $100,000.

Example 2. *F*, a nonresident alien, is the brother of *US*, a United States person. *F* owns a 15% interest in *FP*, a foreign partnership. *US* contributes $99,000 to *FP*, in exchange for a 1-percent partnership interest. Under sections 6038(e)(3)(C) and 267(c)(2), *US* is considered to own at least a 10-percent interest in *FP* and, therefore, *US* must report the $99,000 contribution under this section.

Example 3. *US*, a United States person, owns 40 percent of *FC*, a foreign corporation. *FC* owns a 20-percent interest in *FP*, a foreign partnership. Under section 267(c)(1), *US* is considered to own

8 percent of *FP* due to its ownership of *FC*. *US* contributes $50,000 to *FP* in exchange for a 5-percent partnership interest. Immediately after the contribution, *US* is considered to own at least a 10-percent interest in *FP* and, therefore, must report the $50,000 contribution under this section.

Example 4. *US*, a United States person, owns a 60-percent interest in *USP*, a domestic partnership. On March 1, 2001, *USP* contributes $200,000 to *FP*, a foreign partnership, in exchange for a 5-percent partnership interest. Under paragraph (a)(2) of this section, *US* is considered as having contributed $120,000 to *FP* ($200,000 × 60%). However, under paragraph (a)(2), if *USP* properly reports the contribution to *FP*, *US* is not required to report its $120,000 contribution. If *US* directly contributes $5,000 to *FP* on June 10, 2001, *US* must report the $5,000 contribution because *US* is considered to have contributed more than $100,000 to *FP* in the 12-month period ending on the date of the $5,000 contribution.

Example 5. *US*, a United States person, owns an 80-percent interest in *USP*, a domestic partnership. *USP* owns an 80-percent interest in *USP1*, a domestic partnership. On March 1, 2001, *USP1* contributes $200,000 to *FP*, a foreign partnership, in exchange for a 3-percent partnership interest. Under paragraph (a)(2) of this section, *USP* is considered to have contributed $160,000 ($200,000 × 80%) to *FP*. *US* is considered to have contributed $128,000 to *FP* ($200,000 × 80% × 80%). However, if *USP1* reports the transfer of the $200,000 to *FP*, neither *US* nor *USP* are required to report under this section the amounts they are considered to have contributed. Additionally, regardless of whether *USP1* reports the $200,000 contribution, if *USP* reports the $160,000 contribution it is considered to have made, *US* does not have to report under this section the $128,000 contribution *US* is considered to have made.

(b) *Transfers by trusts relating to state and local government employee retirement plans.*—Trusts relating to state and local government employee retirement plans are not required to report transfers under this section, unless otherwise specified in the instructions to Form 8865.

(c) *Information required with respect to transfers of property.*—With respect to transfers required to be reported under paragraph (a)(1) or (2) of this section, the return must contain information in such form or manner as Form 8865 (and its accompanying instructions) prescribes with respect to reportable events, including—

(1) The name, address, and U.S. taxpayer identification number of the United States person making the transfer;

(2) The name, U.S. taxpayer identification number (if any), and address of the transferee foreign partnership, and the type of entity and country under whose laws the partnership was created or organized;

(3) A general description of the transfer, and of any wider transaction of which it forms a part, including the date of transfer;

(4) The names and addresses of the other partners in the foreign partnership, unless the transfer is solely of cash and the transferor holds less than a ten-percent interest in the transferee foreign partnership immediately after the transfer. However, for tax years of U.S. persons beginning on or after January 1, 2000, the person reporting pursuant to section 6038B (the transferor) must provide the names and addresses of each United States person that owned a ten-percent or greater direct interest in the foreign partnership during the transferor's tax year in which the transfer occurred, and the names and addresses of any other United States or foreign persons that were direct partners in the foreign partnership during that tax year and that were related to the transferor during that tax year. See paragraph (i)(4) of this section for the definition of a related person;

(5) A description of the partnership interest received by the United States person, including a change in partnership interest;

(6) A separate description of each item of contributed property that is appreciated property subject to the allocation rules of section 704(c) (except to the extent that the property is permitted to be aggregated in making allocations under section 704(c)), or is intangible property, including its estimated fair market value and adjusted basis;

(7) A description of other contributed property, not specified in paragraph (c)(6) of this section, aggregated by the following categories (with, in each case, a brief description of the property)—

    (i) Stock in trade of the transferor (inventory);

    (ii) Tangible property (other than stock in trade) used in a trade or business of the transferor;

    (iii) Cash;

    (iv) Stock, notes receivable and payable, and other securities; and

    (v) Other property;

(8) [Reserved]. For further guidance, see § 1.6038B-2T(c)(8); and

(9) [Reserved]. For further guidance, see § 1.6038B-2T(c)(9).

(d) *Information required with respect to dispositions of property.*—In respect of dispositions required to be reported under paragraph (a)(4) of this section, the return must contain information in such form or manner as Form 8865 (and its accompanying instructions) prescribes with respect to reportable events, including—

(1) The date and manner of disposition;

(2) The gain and depreciation recapture amounts, if any, realized by the partnership; and

(3) Any such amounts allocated to the United States person.

(e) *Method of reporting.*—Except as otherwise provided on Form 8865, or the accompanying instructions, all amounts reported as required under this section must be expressed in United States currency, with a statement of the exchange rates used. All statements required on or with Form 8865 pursuant to this section must be in the English language.

(f) *Reporting under this section not required of partnerships excluded from the application of subchapter K.*—(1) *Election to be wholly excluded.*—The reporting requirements of this section will not apply to any United States person in respect of an eligible partnership as described in § 1.761-2(a), if such partnership has validly elected to be excluded from all of the provisions of subchapter K of chapter 1 of the Internal Revenue Code in the manner specified in § 1.761-2(b)(2)(i).

(2) *Deemed excluded.*—The reporting requirements of this section will not apply to any United States person in respect of an eligible partnership as described in § 1.761-2(a), if such partnership is validly deemed to have elected to be excluded from all of the provisions of subchapter K of chapter 1 of the Internal Revenue Code in accordance with the provisions of § 1.761-2(b)(2)(ii).

(g) *Deemed contributions.*—Deemed contributions resulting from IRS-initiated section 482 adjustments are not required to be reported under section 6038B. However, taxpayers must report deemed contributions resulting from taxpayer-initiated adjustments. Such information will be furnished timely if filed by the due date, including extensions, for filing the taxpayer's income tax return for the year in which the adjustment is made.

(h) *Failure to comply with reporting requirements.*—(1) *Consequences of a failure.*—If a United States person is required to file a return under paragraph (a) of this section and fails to comply with the reporting requirements of section 6038B and this section, or § 1.721(c)-6T, then that person is subject to the following penalties:

    (i) The United States person is subject to a penalty equal to 10 percent of the fair market value of the property at the time of the contribution. Such penalty with respect to a particular transfer is limited to $100,000, unless the failure to comply with respect to such transfer was due to intentional disregard.

    (ii) The United States person must recognize gain (reduced by the amount of any gain recognized, with respect to that property, by the transferor after the transfer) as if the contributed property had been sold for fair market value at the time of the contribution. Adjustments to the basis of the partnership's assets and any relevant partner's interest as a result of gain being recognized under this provision will be made as though the gain was recognized in the year in which the failure to report was finally determined.

Reg. § 1.6038B-2(h)(1)(ii)

(2) *Failure to comply.*—A failure to comply with the requirements of section 6038B includes—

(i) The failure to report at the proper time and in the proper manner any information required to be reported under the rules of this section; and

(ii) The provision of false or inaccurate information in purported compliance with the requirements of this section.

(3) [Reserved]. For further guidance see § 1.6038B-2T(h)(3).

(4) *Statute of limitations.*—For exceptions to the limitations on assessment in the event of a failure to provide information under section 6038B, see section 6501(c)(8).

(i) *Definitions.*—(1) *Appreciated property.*—Appreciated property is property that has a fair market value in excess of basis.

(2) *Domestic partnership.*—A domestic partnership is a partnership described in section 7701(a)(4).

(3) *Foreign partnership.*—A foreign partnership is a partnership described in section 7701(a)(5).

(4) *Related person.*—Persons are related persons if they bear a relationship described in section 267(b)(1) through (3) or (10) through (12), after application of section 267(c) (except for (c)(3)), or in section 707(b)(1)(B).

(5) *Substituted basis property.*—Substituted basis property is property described in section 7701(a)(42).

(6) *Taxpayer-initiated adjustment.*—A taxpayer-initiated adjustment is a section 482 adjustment that is made by the taxpayer pursuant to § 1.482-1(a)(3).

(7) *United States person.*—A United States person is a person described in section 7701(a)(30).

(j) *Effective dates.*—(1) *In general.*—Except as otherwise provided in this section, this section applies to transfers made on or after January 1, 1998. However, for a transfer made on or after January 1, 1998, but before January 1, 1999, the filing requirements of this section may be satisfied by—

(i) Filing a Form 8865 with the taxpayer's income tax return (including a partnership return of income) for the first taxable year beginning on or after January 1, 1999; or

(ii) Filing a Form 926 (modified to reflect that the transferee is a partnership, not a corporation) with the taxpayer's income tax return (including a partnership return of income) for the taxable year in which the transfer occurred.

(2) *Transfers made between August 5, 1997 and January 1, 1998.*—A United States person that made a transfer of property between August 5, 1997, and January 1, 1998, that is required to be reported under section 6038B may satisfy its re-

porting requirement by reporting in accordance with the provisions of this section or in accordance with the provisions of Notice 98-17 (1998-11 IRB 6) (see § 601.601(d)(2) of this chapter).

(3) *Special rule for transfers made before January 1, 2000.*—Even if not reported in accordance with the rules provided in paragraph (a)(5) of this section, or paragraph (j)(1) or (2) of this section, a transfer that occurred before January 1, 2000 will nevertheless be considered timely reported if the transferor reports it on a Form 8865 attached to an amended tax return for the transferor's tax year in which the transfer occurred, provided such amended return is filed no later than September 15, 2000.

(4) through (5) [Reserved]. For further guidance, see § 1.6038B-2T(j)(4) through (5). [Reg. § 1.6038B-2.]

☐ [*T.D.* 8817, 2-4-99 (*corrected* 3-31-99). *Amended by T.D.* 8850, 12-27-99 *and T.D.* 9814, 1-18-2017.]

[Reg. § 1.6038B-2T]

§ 1.6038B-2T. Reporting of certain transfers to foreign partnerships (temporary).—(a) introductory text through (a)(1)(ii) [Reserved]. For further guidance, see § 1.6038B-2(a) introductory text through (a)(1)(ii).

(iii) The United States person is a U.S. transferor (as defined in § 1.721(c)-1T(b)(18)) that makes a gain deferral contribution and is required to report under § 1.721(c)-6T(b)(2). The reporting required under this paragraph (a) includes the annual reporting required by § 1.721(c)-6T(b)(3). For purposes of applying this paragraph (a)(1)(iii) to partnerships formed on or after January 18, 2017, a domestic partnership is treated as a foreign partnership pursuant to section 7701(a)(4).

(a)(2) [Reserved]. For further guidance, see § 1.6038B-2(a)(2).

(3) *Indirect transfer through a foreign partnership.*—Solely for purposes of this section, if a foreign partnership transfers section 721(c) property (as defined in § 1.721(c)-1T(b)(15)) to another foreign partnership in a transfer described in § 1.721(c)-3T(d) (tiered-partnership rules), then the transferor foreign partnership's partners will be considered to have transferred a proportionate share of the property to the foreign partnership.

(a)(4) through (c)(7) [Reserved]. For further guidance, see § 1.6038B-2(a)(4) through (c)(7).

(8) With respect to reporting required under § 1.721(c)-6T(b)(2) and paragraph (a)(1)(iii) of this section with regard to a gain deferral contribution, the information required by § 1.721(c)-6T(b)(2); and

(9) With respect to section 721(c) property for which a statement is required to be filed under § 1.721(c)-6T(b)(3) and paragraph (a)(1)(iii) of this section, the information required by § 1.721(c)-6T(b)(3).

(d) through (h)(2) [Reserved]. For further guidance, see § 1.6038B-2(d) through (h)(2).

(3) *Reasonable cause exception.*—Under section 6038B(c)(2) and this section, the provisions of paragraph (h)(1) of this section will not apply if the United States person shows, in a timely manner, that a failure to comply was due to reasonable cause and not willful neglect. A United States person's statement that the failure to comply was due to reasonable cause and not willful neglect will be considered timely only if, promptly after the United States person becomes aware of the failure, an amended return is filed for the taxable year to which the failure relates that includes the information that should have been included with the original return for such taxable year or that otherwise complies with the rules of this section, and that includes a written statement explaining the reasons for the failure to comply. If any taxable year of the United States person is under examination when the amended return is filed, a copy of the amended return must be delivered to the Internal Revenue Service personnel conducting the examination when the amended return is filed. If no taxable year of the United States person is under examination when the amended return is filed, a copy of the amended return must be delivered to the Director of Field Operations, Cross Border Activities Practice Area of Large Business & International (or any successor to the roles and responsibilities of such position, as appropriate) (Director). Whether a failure to comply was due to reasonable cause and not willful neglect will be determined by the Director under all the facts and circumstances.

(i) through (j)(3) [Reserved]. For further guidance, see § 1.6038B-2(i) through (j)(3).

(4) *Transfers of section 721(c) property.*—(i) *Applicability dates.*—Paragraph (c)(8) of this section applies to transfers occurring on or after August 6, 2015, and to transfers occurring before August 6, 2015, resulting from an entity classification election made under § 301.7701-3 of this chapter that is filed on or after August 6, 2015. Paragraphs (a)(1)(iii), (a)(3), and (c)(9) of this section apply to transfers occurring on or after January 18, 2017, and to transfers occurring before January 18, 2017, resulting from entity classification elections made under § 301.7701-3 of this chapter that are filed on or after January 18, 2017.

(ii) *Expiration date.*—The applicability of paragraphs (a)(1)(iii), (a)(3), and (c)(8) and (9) of this section expires on January 17, 2020.

(5) *Reasonable cause exception.*—(i) *Applicability date.*—Paragraph (h)(3) of this section applies to all requests for relief for transfers of property to partnerships filed on or after February 21, 2017.

(ii) *Expiration date.*—The applicability of paragraph (h)(3) of this section expires on January 17, 2020. [Temporary Reg. § 1.6038B-2T.]

☐ *T.D.* 9814, 1-18-2017.]

[Reg. § 1.6038D-0]

§ 1.6038D-0. Outline of regulation provisions.—This section lists the table of contents for §§ 1.6038D-1 through 1.6038D-8.

§ 1.6038D-1. Reporting with respect to specified foreign financial assets, definition of terms.

(a) In general.
(1) Specified person.
(2) Specified individual.
(3) Resident alien.
(4) Bona fide resident of a U.S. possession.
(5) U.S. possession.
(6) Specified foreign financial asset.
(7) Financial account.
(8) Financial institution.
(9) Foreign financial institution.
(10) Foreign entity.
(11) Annual return.
(12) Specified domestic entity.
(13) Model 1 IGA and Model 2 IGA.
(b) Effective/applicability dates.
(1) In general.
(2) Financial accounts.

§ 1.6038D-2. Requirement to report specified foreign financial assets.

(a) Reporting requirement.
(1) In general.
(2) Special rule for married specified individuals filing a joint annual return.
(3) Special rule for certain specified individuals living abroad.
(4) Special rule for married specified individuals filing a joint annual return and living abroad.
(5) Assets with no positive value.
(6) Aggregate value calculation in case of specified foreign financial asset excluded from reporting.
(i) Specified individual.
(ii) Specified domestic entity.
(7) Form 8938 filed with annual return.
(i) General rule.
(ii) Consolidated returns.
(8) Reporting required regardless of tax result.
(9) Reporting period.
(10) Successor forms.
(b) Interest in a specified foreign financial asset.
(1) In general.
(2) Property transferred in connection with the performance of services.
(3) Special rule for parent making an election under section 1(g)(7).
(4) Entities.
(i) In general.
(ii) Specified foreign financial assets held by certain trusts.
(iii) Specified foreign financial assets held by a disregarded entity.

Reg. § 1.6038D-0

(iv) Interest in a foreign trust or foreign estate.
(c) Special rules for joint interests.
(1) In general.
(i) Determining aggregate value of assets.
(ii) Reporting maximum value.
(2) Aggregate asset value for married specified individuals filing a joint annual return.
(3) Aggregate asset value for married specified individuals filing a separate annual return.
(i) Both spouses are specified individuals.
(ii) One spouse is not a specified individual.
(d) Annual return filed by a married specified individual.
(1) Joint annual return.
(2) Separate annual return.
(e) Special rules for dual resident taxpayers.
(1) In general.
(2) Dual resident taxpayer filing as a non-resident alien at end of taxable year.
(3) Dual resident taxpayer filing as a resident alien at end of taxable year.
(f) Example.
(1) Facts.
(2) Filing requirement.
(i) Married specified individuals filing separate annual returns.
(ii) Married specified individuals filing a joint annual return.
Effective/applicability dates.

§1.6038D-3. *Specified foreign financial assets.*
(a) Financial accounts.
(1) In general.
(2) Financial account in a U.S. possession.
(3) Excepted financial accounts.
(i) Accounts maintained by U.S. payors.
(ii) Mark-to-market election under section 475.
(b) Other specified foreign financial assets.
(1) In general.
(2) Mark-to-market election under section 475.
(3) Held for investment.
(4) Trade-or-business test.
(5) Direct relationship between holding an asset and a trade or business.
(i) In general.
(ii) Presumption of direct relationship.
(c) Special rule for interests in foreign trusts and foreign estates.
(d) Examples.
(e) Effective/applicability dates.

§1.6038D-4. *Information required to be reported.*
(a) Required information.
(b) Effective/applicability dates.

§1.6038D-5. *Valuation guidelines.*
(a) Fair market value.

(b) Valuation of assets.
(1) Maximum value.
(2) U.S. dollars.
(3) Asset with no positive value.
(c) Foreign currency conversion.
(1) In general.
(2) Other publicly available exchange rate.
(3) Currency exchange rate.
(4) Determination date.
(d) Financial accounts.
(e) Asset held in a financial account.
(f) Other specified foreign financial assets.
(1) General rule.
(2) Interests in trusts that are specified foreign financial assets.
(i) Maximum value.
(ii) Reporting threshold.
(3) Interests in estates, pension plans, and deferred compensation plans.
(i) Maximum value.
(ii) Reporting threshold.
(g) Effective/applicability dates.

§1.6038D-6. *Specified domestic entities.*
(a) Specified domestic entity.
(b) Corporations and partnerships.
(1) Formed or availed of.
(2) Closely held.
(i) Domestic corporation.
(ii) Domestic partnership.
(iii) Constructive ownership.
(3) Determination of passive income and assets.
(i) Definition of passive income.
(ii) Exception from passive income treatment for dealers.
(iii) Related entities.
(4) Examples.
(c) Domestic trusts.
(d) Excepted domestic entities.
(1) Certain persons described in section 1473(3).
(2) Certain domestic trusts.
(3) Domestic trusts owned by one or more specified persons.
(e) Effective/applicability dates.

§1.6038D-7. *Exceptions from the reporting of certain assets under section 6038D.*
(a) Elimination of duplicative reporting of assets.
(1) In general.
(2) Foreign grantor trusts.
(3) Joint Form 5471 or Form 8865 filing.
(b) Owner of certain trusts.
(c) Special rules for bona fide residents of a U.S. possession.
(d) Effective/applicability dates.

§1.6038D-8. *Penalties for failure to disclose.*
(a) In general.
(b) Married specified individuals filing a joint annual return.

Reg. §1.6038D-0

(c) Increase in penalty.

(d) Presumption of aggregate value.

(e) Reasonable cause exception.

    (1) In general.

    (2) Affirmative showing required.

    (3) Facts and circumstances taken into account.

(f) Penalties for underpayments attributable to undisclosed foreign financial assets.

    (1) Accuracy related penalty.

    (2) Criminal penalties.

(g) Effective/applicability dates.

[Reg. § 1.6038D-0.]

☐ [*T.D. 9706, 12-11-2014. Amended by T.D. 9752, 2-22-2016.*]

[Reg. § 1.6038D-1]

§ 1.6038D-1. Reporting with respect to specified foreign financial assets, definition of terms.—(a) *In general.*—The following definitions apply for purposes of section 6038D and the regulations—

(1) *Specified person.*—The term *specified person* means a specified individual or a specified domestic entity.

(2) *Specified individual.*—The term *specified individual* means an individual who is a—

    (i) U.S. citizen;

    (ii) Resident alien of the United States for any portion of the taxable year;

    (iii) Nonresident alien for whom an election under section 6013(g) or (h) is in effect; or

    (iv) Nonresident alien who is a bona fide resident of Puerto Rico or a section 931 possession (as defined in § 1.931-1(c)(1)).

(3) *Resident alien.*—The term *resident alien* has the meaning set forth in section 7701(b) and §§ 301.7701(b)-1 through 301.7701(b)-9 of this chapter.

(4) *Bona fide resident of a U.S. possession.*—The term *bona fide resident of a U.S. possession* means an individual who is a "bona fide resident" under section 937(a) and § 1.937-1.

(5) *U.S. possession.*—The term *U.S. possession* means American Samoa, Guam, the Northern Mariana Islands, Puerto Rico, or the U.S. Virgin Islands.

(6) *Specified foreign financial asset.*—The term *specified foreign financial asset* has the meaning set forth in § 1.6038D-3.

(7) *Financial account.*—The term *financial account* has the meaning set forth in § 1.1471-5(b), provided, however, that the exclusions of retirement and pension accounts and non-retirement savings accounts under § 1.1471-5(b)(2)(i) and retirement and pension accounts, non-retirement savings accounts, and accounts satisfying similar conditions in an applicable Model 1 IGA or Model 2 IGA under § 1.1471-5(b)(2)(vi) shall not apply (see the section 6038D coordination rule in § 1.1471-5(b)(2)(i)(D)). See § 1.6038D-3(a)(2) relat-

ing to financial accounts maintained by a financial institution that is organized under the laws of a U.S. possession.

(8) *Financial institution.*—The term *financial institution* has the meaning set forth in section 1471(d)(5) and the regulations thereunder.

(9) *Foreign financial institution.*—The term *foreign financial institution* has the meaning set forth in § 1.1471-5(d).

(10) *Foreign entity.*—The term *foreign entity* has the meaning set forth in § 1.1473-1(e).

(11) *Annual return.*—The term *annual return* means an annual federal income tax return of a specified individual or an annual federal income tax return or information return of a specified domestic entity filed with the Internal Revenue Service under section 876, 6011, 6012, 6013, 6031, or 6037, and the regulations.

(12) *Specified domestic entity.*—The term *specified domestic entity* has the meaning set forth in § 1.6038D-6.

(13) *Model 1 IGA and Model 2 IGA.*—The terms *Model 1 IGA* and *Model 2 IGA* have the meanings set forth in § 1.1471-1(b)(78) and (79), respectively.

(b) *Effective/applicability dates.*—(1) *In general.*—Except as otherwise provided in this paragraph (b), this section applies to taxable years ending after December 19, 2011. Taxpayers may elect to apply the rules of this section to taxable years ending prior to December 19, 2011.

(2) *Financial accounts.*—For purposes of applying the financial account definition in § 1.6038D-1(a)(7), the treatment under § 1.1471-5(b)(2)(vi) of retirement and pension accounts, non-retirement savings accounts, and accounts satisfying similar conditions in an applicable Model 1 IGA or Model 2 IGA (see § 1.1471-1(b)(78) and (79)) as financial accounts for purposes of the reporting required under section 6038D and § 1.6038D-2(a) shall apply to taxable years beginning after December 12, 2014. [Reg. § 1.6038D-1.]

☐ [*T.D. 9706, 12-11-2014. Amended by T.D. 9752, 2-22-2016.*]

[Reg. § 1.6038D-2]

§ 1.6038D-2. Requirement to report specified foreign financial assets.—(a) *Reporting requirement.*—(1) *In general.*—Except as otherwise provided, a specified person that has any interest in a specified foreign financial asset during the taxable year must attach Form 8938, "Statement of Specified Foreign Financial Assets," to that specified person's annual return for the taxable year to report the information required by section 6038D and § 1.6038D-4 if the aggregate value of all such assets exceeds—

    (i) $50,000 on the last day of the taxable year; or

    (ii) $75,000 at any time during the taxable year.

(2) *Special rule for married specified individuals filing a joint annual return.*—Except as provided in paragraph (a)(4) of this section, married specified individuals who file a joint annual return for the taxable year must attach a single Form 8938 to their joint annual return for the taxable year to report the information required by section 6038D and §1.6038D-4 if the aggregate value of all of the specified foreign financial assets in which either married specified individual has an interest exceeds—

(i) $100,000 on the last day of the taxable year; or

(ii) $150,000 at any time during the taxable year.

(3) *Special rule for certain specified individuals living abroad.*—Except as provided in paragraph (a)(4) of this section, a specified individual who is a qualified individual under section 911(d)(1) for the taxable year must attach a Form 8938 to his or her annual return for the taxable year to report the information required by section 6038D and §1.6038D-4 if the aggregate value of the specified foreign financial assets in which the specified individual has an interest exceeds—

(i) $200,000 on the last day of the taxable year; or

(ii) $300,000 at any time during the taxable year.

(4) *Special rule for married specified individuals filing a joint annual return and living abroad.*—A specified individual who is a qualified individual under section 911(d)(1) for the taxable year and the qualified individual's spouse who file a joint annual return for the taxable year must attach a single Form 8938 to their return for the taxable year to report the information required by section 6038D and §1.6038D-4 if the aggregate value of the all of the specified foreign financial assets in which either married individual has an interest exceeds—

(i) $400,000 on the last day of the taxable year; or

(ii) $600,000 at any time during the taxable year.

(5) *Assets with no positive value.*—A specified foreign financial asset is subject to reporting even if the specified foreign financial asset does not have a positive value. See §1.6038D-5(b)(3) to determine the maximum value of a specified foreign financial asset that does not have a positive value during the taxable year.

(6) *Aggregate value calculation in case of specified foreign financial asset excluded from reporting.*—(i) *Specified individual.*—The value of any specified foreign financial asset in which a specified individual has an interest and that is excluded from reporting on Form 8938 pursuant to §1.6038D-7(a) (concerning certain assets reported on another form) is included for purposes of determining the aggregate value of specified foreign financial assets. The value of any specified foreign financial asset in which a specified individual has an interest and that is excluded

from reporting under §1.6038D-7(b) (concerning assets held by certain domestic trusts) or §1.6038D-7(c) (concerning certain assets owned by a bona fide resident of a U.S. possession) is excluded for purposes of determining the aggregate value of specified foreign financial assets.

(ii) *Specified domestic entity.*—The value of any specified foreign financial asset in which a specified domestic entity has an interest and that is excluded from reporting on Form 8938 pursuant to §1.6038D-7(a) (concerning certain assets reported on another form) is excluded for purposes of determining the aggregate value of specified foreign financial assets. For purposes of determining the aggregate value of specified foreign financial assets, a specified domestic entity that is a corporation or partnership and that has an interest in any specified foreign financial asset is treated as owning all the specified foreign financial assets (excluding specified foreign financial assets excluded from reporting on Form 8938 pursuant to §1.6038D-7(a)) held by all domestic corporations and domestic partnerships that are closely held by the same specified individual as determined under §1.6038D-6(b)(2).

(7) *Form 8938 filed with annual return.*—(i) *General rule.*—A specified person, including a specified individual who is a bona fide resident of a U.S. possession, is not required to file Form 8938 with respect to a taxable year if the specified person is not required to file an annual return with the Internal Revenue Service with respect to such taxable year.

(ii) *Consolidated returns.*—If a specified domestic entity is a member of an affiliated group of corporations that files a consolidated income tax return, the Form 8938 of the specified domestic entity must be filed with the affiliated group's annual return.

(8) *Reporting required regardless of tax result.*—The Form 8938 required by section 6038D and this section must be furnished by a specified person even if none of the specified foreign financial assets that must be reported affect the specified person's tax liability under the Internal Revenue Code for the taxable year.

(9) *Reporting period.*—The reporting period covered by Form 8938 is the specified person's taxable year, except the reporting period for a specified person that is a specified individual for less than an entire taxable year is the portion of the taxable year that the specified person is a specified individual.

(10) *Successor forms.*—References to Form 8938 include any successor form.

(b) *Interest in a specified foreign financial asset.*—(1) *In general.*—A specified person has an interest in a specified foreign financial asset if any income, gains, losses, deductions, credits, gross proceeds, or distributions attributable to the holding or disposition of the specified foreign financial asset are or would be required to be reported, included, or otherwise reflected by the specified person on an annual return. A specified person has an interest in a specified foreign financial asset even if no income, gains, losses, deductions, credits, gross proceeds, or distributions are attributable to the holding or disposition of the specified foreign financial asset for the taxable year.

(2) *Property transferred in connection with the performance of services.*—A specified person that is transferred property in connection with the performance of personal services is first considered to have an interest in the property for purposes of section 6038D on the first date that the property is substantially vested (within the meaning of § 1.83-3(b)) or, in the case of property with respect to which a specified person makes a valid election under section 83(b), on the date of transfer of the property.

(3) *Special rule for parent making election under section 1(g)(7).*—A parent who makes an election under section 1(g)(7) to include certain unearned income of a child in the parent's gross income has an interest in any specified foreign financial asset held by the child for the purposes of section 6038D and the regulations.

(4) *Entities.*—(i) *In general.*—Except as provided in this paragraph (b)(4), a specified person is not treated as having an interest in any specified foreign financial assets held by a corporation, partnership, trust, or estate solely as a result of the specified person's status as a shareholder, partner, or beneficiary of such entity.

(ii) *Specified foreign financial assets held by certain trusts.*—A specified person that is treated as the owner of a trust or any portion of a trust under sections 671 through 679, other than a domestic liquidating trust under § 301.7701-4(d) of this chapter created pursuant to a court order issued in a bankruptcy under Chapter 7 (11 U.S.C. 701 *et seq.*) or a confirmed plan under Chapter 11 (11 U.S.C. 1101 *et seq.*) of the Bankruptcy Code, or a domestic widely held fixed investment trust under § 1.671-5, is treated as having an interest in any specified foreign financial assets held by the trust or the portion of the trust.

(iii) *Specified foreign financial assets held by a disregarded entity.*—A specified person that owns a foreign or domestic entity that is disregarded as an entity separate from its owner as described in § 301.7701-2 of this chapter (a disregarded entity) is treated as having an interest in any specified foreign financial assets held by the disregarded entity.

(iv) *Interest in a foreign trust or foreign estate.*—See § 1.6038D-3(c) to determine whether an interest in a foreign trust or foreign estate is a specified foreign financial asset. See § 1.6038D-5(f) to determine the maximum value of an interest in a foreign trust or foreign estate.

(c) *Special rules for joint interests.*—(1) *In general.*—(i) *Determining aggregate value of assets.*—Except as otherwise provided in this paragraph (c), each specified person that is a joint owner of a specified foreign financial asset (whether with a spouse or other person) must include the entire value of the specified foreign financial asset (and not the value of the specified person's interest) for purposes of determining whether the aggregate value of the specified person's specified foreign financial assets exceeds the reporting thresholds set forth in § 1.6038D-2(a).

(ii) *Reporting maximum value.*—Except as provided in paragraph (d) of this section, a specified person that is a joint owner of a specified foreign financial asset must report the entire value of each jointly owned specified foreign financial asset on Form 8938.

(2) *Aggregate asset value for married specified individuals filing a joint annual return.*—Married specified individuals who file a joint annual return must include the value of each specified foreign financial asset that they jointly own or in which both have an interest under paragraph (b)(1) of this section only once in determining whether the aggregate value of all of the specified foreign financial assets in which either married specified individual has an interest exceeds the reporting thresholds set forth in § 1.6038D-2(a).

(3) *Aggregate asset value for married specified individual filing a separate annual return.*—(i) *Both spouses are specified individuals.*—If a married specified individual files a separate annual return and his or her spouse is a specified individual, the married specified individual must include one-half of the value of a specified foreign financial asset that the married specified individual jointly owns with his or her spouse in determining whether the married specified individual has an interest in specified foreign financial assets the aggregate value of which exceeds the reporting thresholds set forth in § 1.6038D-2(a).

(ii) *One spouse is not a specified individual.*—If a married specified individual files a separate annual return and his or her spouse is not a specified individual, the married specified individual must include the entire value of a specified foreign financial asset that the married specified individual jointly owns with his or her spouse in determining whether the married specified individual has an interest in specified foreign financial assets the aggregate value of which exceeds the reporting thresholds set forth in § 1.6038D-2(a).

(d) *Annual return filed by a married specified individual.*—(1) *Joint annual return.*—Married specified individuals who file a joint annual return must file a single Form 8938 to fulfill their reporting requirements under section 6038D and § 1.6038D-2(a). The single Form 8938 must report all of the specified foreign financial assets in which either married specified individual has an interest. If both married specified individuals jointly own a specified foreign financial asset or if they have an interest in a specified foreign financial asset under paragraph (b)(1) of this section, the asset must be reported only once on the single Form 8938 filed for the taxable year.

(2) *Separate annual return.*—A married specified individual who files a separate annual return for the taxable year must fulfill the reporting requirements under section 6038D and § 1.6038D-2(a) by filing a separate Form 8938 with his or her return that reports all of the specified foreign financial assets in which the married specified individual has an interest, including each of the assets jointly owned with the married specified individual's spouse or with another person. If both of the spouses are specified individuals, each specified individual must report the entire value of each specified foreign financial asset that the spouses jointly own on Form 8938, not the value taken into account under paragraph (c)(3)(i) of this section for purposes of applying the applicable reporting thresholds.

(e) *Special rules for dual resident taxpayers.*—(1) *In general.*—Subject to the provisions of paragraphs (e)(2) and (3) of this section, a specified individual is not required to report specified foreign financial assets on Form 8938 for a taxable year or any portion of a taxable year that the individual is a dual resident taxpayer (within the meaning of § 301.7701(b)-7(a)(1) of this chapter) who is treated as a nonresident alien pursuant to § 301.7701(b)-7 of this chapter for purposes of computing his or her U.S. tax liability with respect to the portion of the taxable year the individual is considered a dual resident taxpayer.

(2) *Dual resident taxpayer filing as a nonresident alien at end of taxable year.*—If a specified individual to whom this paragraph (e) applies computes his or her U.S. income tax liability as a nonresident alien on the last day of the taxable year and complies with the filing requirements of § 301.7701(b)-7(b) and (c) of this chapter and, in particular, such individual timely files with the Internal Revenue Service Form 1040NR, "U.S. Nonresident Alien Income Tax Return," or Form 1040NR-EZ, "U.S. Income Tax Return for Certain Nonresident Aliens With No Dependents," as applicable, and attaches thereto Form 8833, "Treaty-Based Return Position Disclosure Under Section 6114 or 7701(b)," such individual will not be required to report specified foreign financial assets on Form 8938 with respect to the portion of the taxable year covered by Form 1040NR (or Form 1040NR-EZ).

(3) *Dual resident taxpayer filing as resident alien at end of taxable year.*—If a specified individual to whom this paragraph (e) applies computes his or her U.S. income tax liability as a resident alien on the last day of the taxable year and complies with the filing requirements of § 1.6012-1(b)(2)(ii)(a) and, in particular, such individual timely files with the Internal Revenue Service Form 1040, "U.S. Individual Income Tax Return," or Form 1040EZ, "Income Tax Return for Single and Joint Filers With No Dependents," as applicable, and attaches a properly completed

Form 8833 to the schedule required by § 1.6012-1(b)(2)(ii)(a), such individual will not be required to report specified foreign financial assets on Form 8938 with respect to the portion of the individual's taxable year reflected on the schedule to such Form 1040 or Form 1040EZ required by § 1.6012-1(b)(2)(ii)(a).

(f) *Example.*—The following example illustrates the application of paragraph (c) of this section:

Example. (1) *Facts.* Two married specified individuals, H and W, jointly own a specified foreign financial asset with a value of $90,000 at all times during the taxable year. H separately has an interest in a specified foreign financial asset with a value of $10,000 at all times during the taxable year. W separately has an interest in a specified foreign financial asset with a value of $1,000 at all times during the taxable year.

(2) *Filing requirement.*—(i) *Married specified individuals filing separate annual returns.* If H and W file separate annual returns, the aggregate value of the specified foreign financial assets in which H has an interest at the end of the taxable year is $55,000, comprising one-half of the value of the jointly owned asset, $45,000, and the value of H's separately owned specified foreign financial asset, $10,000. The aggregate value of the specified foreign financial assets in which W has an interest at the end of the taxable year is $46,000, comprising one-half of the value of the jointly owned asset, $45,000, and the value of W's separately owned specified foreign financial asset, $1,000. H must file Form 8938 with his annual return for the taxable year because the aggregate value of the specified foreign financial assets in which H has an interest exceeds the applicable reporting threshold ($50,000) set forth in § 1.6038D-2(a)(1). H must report the maximum value of the entire jointly owned asset, $90,000, and the maximum value of the separately owned asset, $10,000. See § 1.6038D-5(b) regarding the maximum value of a jointly owned specified foreign financial asset to be reported by a specified person, including a married specified individual, that is a joint owner of an asset. The aggregate value of the specified foreign financial assets in which W has an interest, $46,000, does not exceed the applicable reporting threshold set forth in § 1.6038D-2(a)(1). W is not required to file Form 8938 with her separate annual return.

(ii) *Married specified individuals filing a joint annual return.* If H and W file a joint annual return, they must file a single Form 8938 with their joint annual return for the taxable year because the aggregate value of all of the specified foreign financial assets in which either H or W have an interest ($90,000 (included only once), $10,000, and $1000, or $101,000) exceeds the applicable reporting threshold ($100,000) set forth in § 1.6038D-2(a)(2). The single Form 8938 must report the maximum value of the jointly owned specified foreign financial asset, $90,000, and the maximum value of the specified foreign financial assets separately owned by H and W, $10,000 and $1,000, respectively.

(g) *Effective/applicability dates.*—This section, with the exception of § 1.6038D-2(a)(6)(ii), applies to taxable years ending after December 19, 2011. Section 1.6038D-2(a)(6)(ii) applies to taxable years beginning after December 31, 2015. Taxpayers may elect to apply the rules of this section, with the exception of § 1.6038D-2(a)(6)(ii), to taxable years ending on or prior to December 19, 2011. [Reg. § 1.6038D-2.]

☐ [*T.D.* 9706, 12-11-2014. *Amended by T.D.* 9752, 2-22-2016.]

[Reg. § 1.6038D-3]

§ 1.6038D-3. Specified foreign financial assets.—(a) *Financial accounts.*—(1) *In general.*—Except as otherwise provided in this section, a specified foreign financial asset includes any financial account maintained by a foreign financial institution. An asset held in a financial account maintained by a foreign financial institution is not required to be separately reported on Form 8938, "Statement of Specified Foreign Financial Assets."

(2) *Financial account in a U.S. possession.*—A specified foreign financial asset includes a financial account maintained by a financial institution that is organized under the laws of a U.S. possession.

(3) *Excepted financial accounts.*—(i) *Accounts maintained by U.S. payors.*—A financial account maintained by a U.S. payor as defined in § 1.6049-5(c)(5)(i) (including assets held in such an account) is not a specified foreign financial asset for purposes of section 6038D and the regulations.

(ii) *Mark-to-market election under section 475.*—A financial account is not a specified foreign financial asset if the rules of section 475(a) apply to all of the holdings in the account or an election under section 475(e) or (f) is made with respect to all of the holdings in the account.

(b) *Other specified foreign financial assets.*—(1) *In general.*—Except as otherwise provided in this section, a specified foreign financial asset includes any of the following assets that are not financial accounts and that are held for investment and not held in an account maintained by a financial institution—

(i) Stock or securities issued by a person other than a United States person (including stock or securities issued by a person organized under the laws of a U.S. possession);

(ii) A financial instrument or contract that has an issuer or counterparty which is other than a United States person (including a financial instrument or contract issued by a person organized under the laws of a U.S. possession); and

(iii) An interest in a foreign entity.

(2) *Mark-to-market election under section 475.*—An asset is not a specified foreign financial asset if the rules of section 475(a) apply to the asset or an election under section 475(e) or (f) is made with respect to the asset.

(3) *Held for investment.*—An asset is held for investment for purposes of section 6038D and the regulations if that asset is not used in, or held for use in, the conduct of a trade or business of a specified person.

(4) *Trade-or-business test.*—For purposes of section 6038D and the regulations, an asset is used in, or held for use in, the conduct of a trade or business and not held for investment if the asset is—

(i) Held for the principal purpose of promoting the present conduct of the trade or business;

(ii) Acquired and held in the ordinary course of the trade or business, as, for example, in the case of an account or note receivable arising from that trade or business; or

(iii) Otherwise held in a direct relationship to the trade or business as determined under paragraph (b)(5) of this section.

(5) *Direct relationship between holding an asset and a trade or business.*—(i) *In general.*—In determining whether an asset is held in a direct relationship to the conduct of a trade or business by a specified person, principal consideration will be given to whether the asset is needed in the trade or business of the specified person. An asset shall be considered needed in the trade or business, for this purpose, only if the asset is held to meet the present needs of that trade or business and not its anticipated future needs. An asset shall be considered as needed in the trade or business if, for example, the asset is held to meet the operating expenses of the trade or business. Conversely, an asset shall be considered as not needed in the trade or business if, for example, the asset is held for the purpose of providing for future diversification into a new trade or business, future plant replacement, or future business contingencies. Stock is never considered used or held for use in a trade or business for purposes of applying this test.

(ii) *Presumption of direct relationship.*—An asset will be treated as held in a direct relationship to the conduct of a trade or business of a specified person if—

(A) The asset was acquired with funds generated by the trade or business of the specified person or the affiliated group of the specified person, if any;

(B) The income from the asset is retained or reinvested in the trade or business; and

(C) Personnel who are actively involved in the conduct of the trade or business exercise significant management and control over the investment of such asset.

(c) *Special rule for interests in foreign trusts and foreign estates.*—An interest in a foreign trust or a foreign estate is not a specified foreign financial asset of a specified person unless the person knows, or has reason to know based on readily accessible information, of the interest. Receipt of a distribution from the foreign trust or foreign estate constitutes actual knowledge for this purpose.

(d) *Examples.*—Examples of assets other than financial accounts that may be considered other specified foreign financial assets include, but are not limited to—

(1) Stock issued by a foreign corporation;

(2) A capital or profits interest in a foreign partnership;

(3) A note, bond, debenture, or other form of indebtedness issued by a foreign person;

(4) An interest in a foreign trust;

(5) An interest rate swap, currency swap, basis swap, interest rate cap, interest rate floor, commodity swap, equity swap, equity index swap, credit default swap, or similar agreement with a foreign counterparty; and

(6) Any option or other derivative instrument with respect to any of the items listed as examples in this paragraph or with respect to any currency or commodity that is entered into with a foreign counterparty or issuer.

(e) *Effective/applicability dates.*—This section applies to taxable years ending after December 19, 2011. Taxpayers may elect to apply the rules of this section to taxable years ending prior to December 19, 2011. [Reg. § 1.6038D-3.]

☐ *[T.D. 9706, 12-11-2014.]*

[Reg. § 1.6038D-4]

§ 1.6038D-4. Information required to be reported.—(a) *Required information.*—The following information must be reported on Form 8938, "Statement of Specified Foreign Financial Assets," with respect to each specified foreign financial asset:

(1) In the case of a financial account, the name and address of the foreign financial institution with which the account is maintained and the account number of the financial account;

(2) In the case of stock or securities, the name and address of the issuer, and information that identifies the class or issue of which the stock or security is a part;

(3) In the case of a financial instrument or contract, information that identifies the financial instrument or contract, including the names and addresses of all issuers and counterparties;

(4) In the case of an interest in a foreign entity, information that identifies the interest, including the name and address of the foreign entity in which the interest is held;

(5) The maximum value of the specified foreign financial asset during the portion of the taxable year in which the specified person has an interest in the asset;

(6) In the case of a financial account that is a depository account as defined in § 1.1471-5(b)(3)(i) or a custodial account as defined in § 1.1471-5(b)(3)(ii), whether the account was opened or closed during the taxable year;

(7) The date, if any, on which the specified foreign financial asset, other than a financial account that is a depository account as defined in § 1.1471-5(b)(3)(i) or a custodial account as de-

fined in § 1.1471-5(b)(3)(ii), was either acquired or disposed of (or both) during the taxable year;

(8) The amount of any income, gain, loss, deduction, or credit recognized for the taxable year with respect to the reported specified foreign financial asset, and the schedule, form, or return filed with the Internal Revenue Service on which the income, gain, loss, deduction, or credit, if any, is reported or included by the specified person;

(9) The foreign currency in which the account is maintained or the asset is denominated, the foreign currency exchange rate and, if the source of such rate is other than as described in § 1.6038D-5(c)(1), the source of the rate used to determine the specified foreign financial asset's U.S. dollar value, including maximum value;

(10) For any specified foreign financial asset excepted from reporting on Form 8938 under § 1.6038D-7(a), the specified person must report the number of Forms 3520, "Annual Return To Report Transactions With Foreign Trusts and Receipt of Certain Foreign Gifts," Forms 3520-A, "Annual Information Return of Foreign Trust With a U.S. Owner," Forms 5471, "Information Return of U.S. Persons With Respect To Certain Foreign Corporations," Forms 8621, "Return by a Shareholder of a Passive Foreign Investment Company or a Qualified Electing Fund," Forms 8865, "Return of U.S. Persons With Respect To Certain Foreign Partnerships," and, solely for taxable years beginning after March 18, 2010, and ending on or before December 31, 2013, Forms 8891, "U.S. Information Return for Beneficiaries of Certain Canadian Registered Retirement Plans," or such other form under Title 26 of the United States Code identified by the Secretary under § 1.6038D-7(a), timely filed with the Internal Revenue Service on which excepted foreign financial assets are reported or reflected for the taxable year; and

(11) Such other information as may be required by Form 8938 or its instructions or other guidance.

(b) *Effective/applicability dates.*—This section applies to taxable years ending after December 19, 2011. Taxpayers may elect to apply the rules of this section to taxable years ending prior to December 19, 2011. [Reg. § 1.6038D-4.]

☐ *[T.D. 9706, 12-11-2014.]*

[Reg. § 1.6038D-5]

§ 1.6038D-5. Valuation guidelines.—(a) *Fair market value.*—Except as provided in paragraphs (c) and (e) of this section, the value of a specified foreign financial asset for purposes of determining the aggregate value of specified foreign financial assets held by a specified person and the maximum value of a specified foreign financial asset required to be reported on Form 8938, "Statement of Specified Foreign Financial Assets," is the asset's fair market value.

(b) *Valuation of assets.*—(1) *Maximum value.*—Except as provided in this section, the maximum value of a specified foreign financial asset means a reasonable estimate of the asset's maximum fair market value during the taxable year.

(2) *U.S. dollars.*—For purposes of determining the aggregate value of specified foreign financial assets in which a specified person has an interest and determining the maximum value of a specified foreign financial asset, the value of a specified foreign financial asset denominated in a foreign currency during the taxable year must be determined in the foreign currency and then converted to U.S. dollars.

(3) *Asset with no positive value.*—If the maximum fair market value of a specified foreign financial asset is zero or less than zero, then the asset's value is treated as zero for purposes of determining the aggregate value of specified foreign financial assets in which a specified person has an interest, and the maximum value of the specified foreign financial asset is zero for purposes of reporting under § 1.6038D-4(a)(5).

(c) *Foreign currency conversion.*—(1) *In general.*—Except as provided in paragraphs (c)(2) and (d) of this section, the U.S. Treasury Department's Bureau of the Fiscal Service foreign currency exchange rate is to be used to convert the value of a specified foreign financial asset into U.S. dollars for purposes of determining the aggregate value of specified foreign financial assets in which a specified person has an interest and determining the maximum value of a specified foreign financial asset.

(2) *Other publicly available exchange rate.*—If no U.S. Treasury Department Bureau of the Fiscal Service foreign currency exchange rate is available for a particular currency, another publicly available foreign currency exchange rate may be used to convert the value of a specified foreign financial asset into U.S. dollars. In such case, the source of the foreign currency exchange rate must be disclosed on Form 8938.

(3) *Currency exchange rate.*—In converting the currency of a foreign country, the foreign currency exchange rate applicable for converting the currency into U.S. dollars (that is, to purchase U.S. dollars) must be used.

(4) *Determination date.*—In converting the currency of a foreign country into U.S. dollars for purposes of determining the maximum value of a specified foreign financial asset and determining the aggregate value of specified foreign financial assets in which a specified person has an interest, the applicable foreign currency exchange rate is the rate on the last day of the taxable year of the specified person, even if the specified person sold or otherwise disposed of a specified foreign financial asset prior to the last day of such year.

(d) *Financial accounts.*—A specified person may rely upon periodic account statements that are provided at least annually by or on behalf of a financial institution maintaining an account, including the foreign currency conversion re-

flected in those statements, to determine the financial account's maximum value unless the specified person has actual knowledge, or reason to know based on readily accessible information, that the statements do not reflect a reasonable estimate of the maximum account value during the taxable year.

(e) *Asset held in a financial account.*—The value of an asset held in a financial account maintained by a foreign financial institution is included in determining the value of that financial account for purposes of § 1.6038D-5(a).

(f) *Other specified foreign financial assets.*—(1) *General rule.*—Except as provided in paragraphs (f)(2) and (3) of this section, for specified foreign financial assets that are not financial accounts and that are held for investment and not held in an account maintained by a financial institution, a specified person may use the value of the asset as of the last day of the taxable year on which the specified person has an interest in the asset as the maximum value of that asset, unless the specified person has actual knowledge, or reason to know based on readily accessible information, that the value does not reflect a reasonable estimate of the maximum value of the asset during the taxable year.

(2) *Interests in trusts that are specified foreign financial assets.*—(i) *Maximum value.*—If a specified person is a beneficiary of a foreign trust, the maximum value of the specified person's interest in the trust is the sum of-

(A) The fair market value, determined as of the last day of the taxable year, of all of the currency or other property distributed from the foreign trust during the taxable year to the specified person as a beneficiary; and

(B) The value, determined as of the last day of the taxable year, of the specified person's right as a beneficiary to receive mandatory distributions from the foreign trust as determined under section 7520.

(ii) *Reporting threshold.*—For purposes of determining the aggregate value of specified foreign financial assets in which a specified person has an interest, if the specified person does not know, or have reason to know based on readily accessible information, the fair market value of the person's interest in a foreign trust during the taxable year, the value to be included in determining the aggregate value of the specified foreign financial assets is the maximum value of the specified person's interest in the foreign trust under paragraph (f)(2)(i) of this section.

(3) *Interests in estates, pension plans, and deferred compensation plans.*—(i) *Maximum value.*—The maximum value of a specified person's interest in a foreign estate, foreign pension plan, or foreign deferred compensation plan is the fair market value, determined as of the last day of the taxable year, of the specified person's beneficial interest in the assets of the foreign estate, foreign pension plan, or foreign deferred compensation plan. If the specified person does not

Reg. **§ 1.6038D-5(f)(3)(i)**

know, or have reason to know based on readily accessible information, such fair market value, the maximum value to be reported is the fair market value, determined as of the last day of the taxable year, of the currency and other property distributed during the taxable year to the specified person as a beneficiary or participant.

(ii) *Reporting threshold.*—For purposes of determining the aggregate value of specified foreign financial assets in which a specified person has an interest, if the specified person does not know, or have reason to know based on readily accessible information, the fair market value of the person's interest in a foreign estate, foreign pension plan, or foreign deferred compensation plan during the taxable year, the value to be included in determining the aggregate value of the specified foreign financial assets is the fair market value, determined as of the last day of the taxable year, of the currency and other property distributed during the taxable year to the specified person as a beneficiary or participant.

(g) *Effective/applicability dates.*—This section applies to taxable years ending after December 19, 2011. Taxpayers may elect to apply the rules of this section to taxable years ending prior to December 19, 2011. [Reg. § 1.6038D-5.]

☐ [*T.D.* 9706, 12-11-2014.]

[Reg. § 1.6038D-6]

§ 1.6038D-6. Specified domestic entities.— (a) *Specified domestic entity.*—A specified domestic entity is a domestic corporation, a domestic partnership, or a trust described in section 7701(a)(30)(E), if such corporation, partnership, or trust is formed or availed of for purposes of holding, directly or indirectly, specified foreign financial assets. Whether a domestic corporation, a domestic partnership, or a trust described in section 7701(a)(30)(E) is a specified domestic entity is determined annually.

(b) *Corporations and partnerships.*—(1) *Formed or availed of.*—Except as otherwise provided in paragraph (d) of this section, a domestic corporation or a domestic partnership is formed or availed of for purposes of holding, directly or indirectly, specified foreign financial assets if and only if—

(i) The corporation or partnership is closely held by a specified individual as determined under paragraph (b)(2) of this section; and

(ii) At least 50 percent of the corporation's or partnership's gross income for the taxable year is passive income or at least 50 percent of the assets held by the corporation or partnership for the taxable year are assets that produce or are held for the production of passive income as determined under paragraph (b)(3) of this section (passive assets). For purposes of this paragraph (b)(1)(ii), the percentage of passive assets held by a corporation or partnership for a taxable year is the weighted average percentage of passive assets (weighted by total assets and measured quarterly), and the value of assets of a corporation or partnership is the fair market value of the assets or the book value of the assets that is reflected on the corporation's or partnership's balance sheet (as determined under either a U.S. or an international financial accounting standard).

(2) *Closely held.*—(i) *Domestic corporation.*— A domestic corporation is closely held by a specified individual if at least 80 percent of the total combined voting power of all classes of stock of the corporation entitled to vote, or at least 80 percent of the total value of the stock of the corporation, is owned, directly, indirectly, or constructively, by a specified individual on the last day of the corporation's taxable year.

(ii) *Domestic partnership.*—A partnership is closely held by a specified individual if at least 80 percent of the capital or profits interest in the partnership is held, directly, indirectly, or constructively, by a specified individual on the last day of the partnership's taxable year.

(iii) *Constructive ownership.*—For purposes of this paragraph (b)(2), sections 267(c) and (e)(3) apply for the purpose of determining the constructive ownership of a specified individual in a corporation or partnership, except that section 267(c)(4) is applied as if the family of an individual includes the spouses of the individual's family members.

(3) *Determination of passive income and assets.*—(i) *Definition of passive income.*—Except as provided in paragraph (b)(3)(ii) of this section, for purposes of paragraph (b)(1)(ii) of this section, passive income means the portion of gross income that consists of—

(A) Dividends, including substitute dividends;

(B) Interest;

(C) Income equivalent to interest, including substitute interest;

(D) Rents and royalties, other than rents and royalties derived in the active conduct of a trade or business conducted, at least in part, by employees of the corporation or partnership;

(E) Annuities;

(F) The excess of gains over losses from the sale or exchange of property that gives rise to passive income described in paragraphs (b)(3)(i)(A) through (b)(3)(i)(E) of this section;

(G) The excess of gains over losses from transactions (including futures, forwards, and similar transactions) in any commodity, but not including—

(1) Any commodity hedging transaction described in section 954(c)(5)(A), determined by treating the corporation or partnership as a controlled foreign corporation; or

(2) Active business gains or losses from the sale of commodities, but only if substantially all the corporation or partnership's commodities are property described in paragraph (1), (2), or (8) of section 1221(a);

(H) The excess of foreign currency gains over foreign currency losses (as defined in section 988(b)) attributable to any section 988 transaction; and

(I) Net income from notional principal contracts as defined in § 1.446-3(c)(1).

(ii) *Exception from passive income treatment for dealers.*—Notwithstanding paragraph (b)(3)(i) of this section, in the case of a corporation or partnership that regularly acts as a dealer in property described in paragraph (b)(3)(i)(F) of this section (referring to the sale or exchange of property that gives rise to passive income), forward contracts, option contracts, or similar financial instruments (including notional principal contracts and all instruments referenced to commodities), the term passive income does not include—

(A) Any item of income or gain (other than any dividends or interest) from any transaction (including hedging transactions and transactions involving physical settlement) entered into in the ordinary course of such dealer's trade or business as such a dealer; and

(B) If such dealer is a dealer in securities (within the meaning of section 475(c)(2)), any income from any transaction entered into in the ordinary course of such trade or business as a dealer in securities.

(iii) *Related entities.*—For purposes of applying the passive income and asset thresholds of paragraph (b)(1)(ii) of this section, all domestic corporations and domestic partnerships that are closely held by the same specified individual as determined under paragraph (b)(2) of this section and that are connected through stock or partnership interest ownership with a common parent corporation or partnership are treated as owning the combined assets and receiving the combined income of all members of that group. For purposes of the preceding sentence, assets relating to any contract, equity, or debt existing between members of such a group, as well as any items of gross income arising under or from such contract, equity, or debt, are eliminated. A domestic corporation or a domestic partnership is considered connected through stock or partnership interest ownership with a common parent corporation or partnership if stock representing at least 80 percent of the total combined voting power of all classes of stock of the corporation entitled to vote or of the value of such corporation, or partnership interests representing at least 80 percent of the profits interests or capital interests of such partnership, in each case other than stock of or partnership interests in the common parent, is owned by one or more of the other connected corporations, connected partnerships, or the common parent.

(4) *Examples.*—The following examples illustrate the application of this section:

Example 1. Closely held and constructive ownership. (i) *Facts.* DC1 is a domestic corporation the total value of the stock of which is owned 60% by A, a specified individual, 30% by B, a member of A's family for purposes of section 267(c)(2) who is not a specified individual, and 10% by FC1, a foreign corporation. DC1 owns 90% of the total value of the stock of DC2, a domestic corporation. FC2, a foreign corporation, owns 10% of

DC2. Neither A nor B owns, directly, indirectly, or constructively, any stock in FC1 or FC2.

(ii) *Closely held ownership determination.* A is considered to own 90% and 81% of the total value of DC1 and DC2, respectively, by application of the rules of section 267(c) and this section. DC1 and DC2 are closely held by A within the meaning of paragraph (b)(2) of this section because A, a specified individual, is considered to own more than 80% of their total value.

Example 2. Application of aggregation rule and reporting threshold. (i) *Facts.* L is a specified individual. In Year X, L wholly owns DC1, a domestic corporation, and also owns a 90% capital interest in DP, a domestic partnership. DC1 owns 80% of the sole class of stock of DC2, a domestic corporation. DC1 has no assets other than its interest in DC2. DC2's only assets are assets that produce passive income, with a maximum value in Year X of $40,000 on October 12. DC2's assets are comprised in relevant part of specified foreign financial assets with a maximum value in Year X of $15,000 on October 12. DP's only assets are assets that produce passive income and that are specified foreign financial assets with a maximum value of $90,000 in Year X on October 12.

(ii) *Specified domestic entity status*—(A) *DC1 and DC2.* DC1 and DC2 are closely held by a specified individual for purposes of paragraph (b)(2) of this section. DC1 and DC2 are considered related entities that are connected through stock ownership with a common parent corporation under paragraph (b)(3)(iii) of this section, because DC1 and DC2 are closely held by L, and DC2 is connected with DC1 through DC1's ownership of stock of DC2 representing at least 80% of the voting power or value of DC2. As a result, for purposes of applying paragraph (b)(1)(ii) of this section, each of DC1 and DC2 is considered as owning the combined assets, and receiving the combined income, of both DC1 and DC2; however, DC1's equity interest in DC2 is disregarded for this purpose under paragraph (b)(3)(iii) of this section. Therefore, DC1 and DC2 each satisfies the passive asset threshold of paragraph (b)(1)(ii) of this section, because 100 percent of each company's assets is passive. DC1 and DC2 are specified domestic entities for Year X.

(B) *DP.* DP is closely held by a specified individual for purposes of paragraph (b)(2) of this section. DP is not considered a related entity with DC1 and DC2 under paragraph (b)(3)(iii) of this section, because DC1 and DP are not owned by a common parent corporation or partnership. As a result, whether the passive income or passive asset threshold of paragraph (b)(1)(ii) of this section is met with respect to DP is determined solely by reference to DP's separately earned passive income and separately held passive assets. DP holds only passive assets during Year X and therefore satisfies paragraph (b)(1)(ii) of this section. DP is a specified domestic entity for Year X.

(iii) *Reporting requirements*—(A) *DC1.* Under § 1.6038D-2(a)(6)(ii), DC1 is not treated as own-

Reg. § 1.6038D-6(b)(4)

ing the specified foreign financial assets held by DC2 and DP for purposes of applying the reporting threshold of §1.6038D-2(a)(1), because DC1 does not have an interest in any specified foreign financial assets. DC1 is not required to file Form 8938 because DC1 does not satisfy the reporting threshold of §1.6038D-2(a)(1).

(B) *DC2 and DP.* Under §1.6038D-3, DC2 and DP each has an interest in specified foreign financial assets. For purposes of applying the reporting threshold of §1.6038D-2(a)(1), §1.6038D-2(a)(6)(ii) provides that DC2 is treated as owning in addition to its own assets the assets of DP, and DP is treated as owning in addition to its own assets the assets of DC2. As a result, DC2 and DP each satisfies the reporting threshold of §1.6038D-2(a)(1), because the value of the specified foreign financial assets each is considered as owning for purposes of §1.6038D-2(a)(1) is $105,000 on October 12, Year X, which exceeds DC2's and DP's $75,000 reporting threshold. DC2 and DP must each file Form 8938 for Year X to report their respective specified foreign financial assets in which they have an interest and disclose their maximum values as provided in §1.6038D-4 ($15,000 in the case of DC2 and $90,000 in the case of DP).

Example 3. Application of aggregation rule and entity with an active trade or business. (i) *Facts.* The facts are the same as in *Example 2,* except that DC2 also owns an active business. The assets attributable to the business are not passive assets and constitute at least 60% of the value of DC2's assets at all times during Year X. The income from the business is not passive income and constitutes at least 60% of the gross income generated by DC2 in Year X.

(ii) *Specified domestic entity status*—(A) *DC1 and DC2.* DC1 and DC2 are considered related entities that are connected through stock ownership with a common parent corporation under paragraph (b)(3)(iii) of this section because DC1 and DC2 are closely held by L, and DC2 is connected with DC1 though DC1's ownership of stock of DC2 representing at least 80% of the voting power or value of DC2. As a result, for purposes of applying paragraph (b)(1)(ii) of this section, each of DC1 and DC2 is treated as owning the combined assets, and receiving the combined income, of both DC1 and DC2; however, DC1's equity interest in DC2 is disregarded for this purpose under paragraph (b)(3)(iii) of this section. As a result, no more than 40 percent of the value of DC1's and DC2's assets at all times during Year X are passive and no more than 40 percent of DC1's and DC2's gross income for Year X is passive. DC1 and DC2 do not satisfy the passive income or passive asset threshold in paragraph (b)(1)(ii) of this section for Year X. DC1 and DC2 are not specified domestic entities for Year X.

(B) *DP.* For the reasons described in paragraph (ii)(B) of *Example 2,* DP is a specified domestic entity for Year X.

(iii) *Reporting requirements*—(A) *DC1 and DC2.* DC1 and DC2 are not specified domestic entities for Year X, and are not required to file Form 8938.

(B) *DP.* Under §1.6038D-3, DP has an interest in specified foreign financial assets. Under §1.6038D-2(a)(6)(ii), DP is treated as owning in addition to its own assets the assets of DC2. As a result, DP satisfies the reporting threshold of §1.6038D-2(a)(1) because the value of the specified foreign financial assets it is considered to own for purposes of §1.6038D-2(a)(1) is $105,000 on October 12, Year X, which exceeds DP's $75,000 reporting threshold. DP must file Form 8938 for Year X to report the specified foreign financial assets in which it has an interest and disclose their maximum values as provided in §1.6038D-4, which is $90,000.

(c) *Domestic trusts.*—Except as otherwise provided in paragraph (d) of this section, a trust described in section 7701(a)(30)(E) is formed or availed of for purposes of holding, directly or indirectly, specified foreign financial assets if and only if the trust has one or more specified persons as a current beneficiary. The term current beneficiary means, with respect to the taxable year, any person who at any time during such taxable year is entitled to, or at the discretion of any person may receive, a distribution from the principal or income of the trust (determined without regard to any power of appointment to the extent that such power remains unexercised at the end of the taxable year). The term current beneficiary also includes any holder of a general power of appointment, whether or not exercised, that was exercisable at any time during the taxable year, but does not include any holder of a general power of appointment that is exercisable only on the death of the holder.

(d) *Excepted domestic entities.*—An entity is not considered to be a specified domestic entity if the entity is—

(1) *Certain persons described in section 1473(3).*—An entity, except for a trust that is exempt from tax under section 664(c), that is excepted from the definition of the term "specified United States person" under section 1473(3) and the regulations issued under that section;

(2) *Certain domestic trusts.*—A trust described in section 7701(a)(30)(E) provided that the trustee of the trust—

(i) Has supervisory authority over or fiduciary obligations with regard to the specified foreign financial assets held by the trust;

(ii) Timely files (including any applicable extensions) annual returns and information returns on behalf of the trust; and

(iii) Is —

(A) A bank that is examined by the Office of the Comptroller of the Currency, the Board of Governors of the Federal Reserve System, the Federal Deposit Insurance Corporation, or the National Credit Union Administration;

(B) A financial institution that is registered with and regulated or examined by the Securities and Exchange Commission; or

(C) A domestic corporation described in section 1473(3)(A) or (B), and the regulations issued with respect to those provisions.

(3) *Domestic trusts owned by one or more specified persons.*—A trust described in section 7701(a)(30)(E) to the extent such trust or any portion thereof is treated as owned by one or more specified persons under sections 671 through 678 and the regulations issued under those sections.

(e) *Effective/applicability dates.*—This section applies to taxable years beginning after December 31, 2015. [Reg. § 1.6038D-6.]

☐ *[T.D. 9706, 12-11-2014. Amended by T.D. 9752, 2-22-2016.]*

[Reg. § 1.6038D-7]

§ 1.6038D-7. Exceptions from the reporting of certain assets under Section 6038D.—
(a) *Elimination of duplicative reporting of assets.—*
(1) *In general.*—A specified person is not required to report a specified foreign financial asset on Form 8938, "Statement of Specified Foreign Financial Assets," if the specified person—

(i) Reports the asset on at least one of the following forms timely filed with the Internal Revenue Service for the taxable year—

(A) Form 3520, "Annual Return To Report Transactions With Foreign Trusts and Receipt of Certain Foreign Gifts" (in the case of a specified person that is the beneficiary of a foreign trust);

(B) Form 5471, "Information Return of U.S. Persons With Respect To Certain Foreign Corporations";

(C) Form 8621, "Return by a Shareholder of a Passive Foreign Investment Company or Qualified Electing Fund";

(D) Form 8865, "Return of U.S. Persons With Respect To Certain Foreign Partnerships";

(E) For taxable years beginning after March 18, 2010, and ending on or before December 31, 2013, Form 8891, "U.S. Information Return for Beneficiaries of Certain Canadian Registered Retirement Plans"; or

(F) Any other form under Title 26 of the United States Code timely filed with the Internal Revenue Service and identified for this purpose by the Secretary in regulations or other guidance; and

(ii) Reports on Form 8938 the filing of the form on which the asset is reported.

(2) *Foreign grantor trusts.*—A specified person that is treated as an owner of a foreign trust or any portion of a foreign trust under sections 671 through 679 is not required to report any specified foreign financial assets held by the foreign trust on Form 8938, provided—

(i) The specified person reports the trust on a Form 3520 timely filed with the Internal Revenue Service for the taxable year;

(ii) The trust timely files Form 3520-A, "Annual Information Return of Foreign Trust With a U.S. Owner," with the Internal Revenue Service for the taxable year; and

(iii) The Form 8938 filed by the specified person for the taxable year reports the filing of the Form 3520 and Form 3520-A.

(3) *Joint Form 5471 or Form 8865 filing.*—A specified person that is included as part of a joint Form 5471 filing pursuant to § 1.6038-2(j) or a joint Form 8865 filing pursuant to § 1.6038-3(c) and who notifies the Internal Revenue Service as required by § 1.6038-2(i) or § 1.6038D-(3)(c) will be considered to have filed a Form 5471 or Form 8865 for purposes of paragraph (a)(1) of this section.

(b) *Owner of certain trusts.*—A specified person that is treated as an owner of any portion of a domestic trust under sections 671 through 678 is not required to file Form 8938 to report any specified foreign financial asset held by the trust if the trust is—

(1) A widely-held fixed investment trust under § 1.671-5; or

(2) A liquidating trust within the meaning of § 301.7701-4(d) of this chapter that is created pursuant to a court order issued in a bankruptcy under Chapter 7 (11 U.S.C. 701 *et seq.*) or a confirmed plan under Chapter 11 (11 U.S.C. 1101 *et seq.*) of the Bankruptcy Code.

(c) *Special rules for bona fide residents of a U.S. possession.*—A specified individual who is a bona fide resident of a U.S. possession is not required to include the following specified foreign financial assets in the determination of the aggregate value of his or her specified foreign financial assets and, if required to file Form 8938 with the Internal Revenue Service, is not required to report the following specified foreign financial assets:

(1) A financial account maintained by a financial institution organized under the laws of the U.S. possession of which the specified individual is a bona fide resident;

(2) A financial account maintained by a branch of a financial institution not organized under the laws of the U.S. possession of which the specified individual is a bona fide resident, if the branch is subject to the same tax and information reporting requirements applicable to a financial institution organized under the laws of the U.S. possession;

(3) Stock or securities issued by an entity organized under the laws of the U.S. possession of which the specified individual is a bona fide resident;

(4) An interest in an entity organized under the laws of the U.S. possession of which the specified individual is a bona fide resident; and

(5) A financial instrument or contract held for investment, provided each issuer or counterparty that is not a United States person is—

(i) An entity organized under the laws of the U.S. possession of which the specified individual is a bona fide resident; or

(ii) A bona fide resident of the U.S. possession of which the specified individual is a bona fide resident.

(d) *Effective/applicability dates.*—This section applies to taxable years ending after December 19, 2011. Taxpayers may elect to apply the rules of this section to taxable years ending prior to December 19, 2011. [Reg. § 1.6038D-7.]

☐ [*T.D.* 9706, 12-11-2014.]

[Reg. § 1.6038D-8]

§ 1.6038D-8. Specified domestic entities.—(a) *In general.*—If a specified person fails to file a Form 8938, "Statement of Specified Foreign Financial Assets," that includes the information required by section 6038D(c) and § 1.6038D-4 with respect to any taxable year at the time and in the manner described in section 6038D(a) and § 1.6038D-2, a penalty of $10,000 will apply to that specified person.

(b) *Married specified individuals filing a joint annual return.*—Married specified individuals who file a joint annual return and fail to file a required Form 8938 that includes the information required by section 6038D(c) and § 1.6038D-4 with respect to any taxable year at the time and in the manner described in section 6038D(a) and § 1.6038D-2 are subject to penalties under this section as if the married specified individuals are a single specified individual. The liability of married specified individuals who file a joint annual return with respect to any penalties under this section is joint and several.

(c) *Increase in penalty.*—If any failure to comply with the applicable reporting requirement of section 6038D and the regulations continues for more than 90 days after the day on which the Commissioner or his delegate mails a notice of the failure to the specified person required to file the Form 8938, the specified person is required to pay an additional penalty of $10,000 for each 30-day period (or fraction thereof) during which the failure continues after the 90-day period has expired. The additional penalty imposed by section 6038D(d)(2) and this paragraph (c) is limited to a maximum of $50,000 for each such failure.

(d) *Presumption of aggregate value.*—For the purpose of assessing penalties imposed under section 6038D(d), if the Commissioner or his delegate determines that a specified person has an interest in one or more specified foreign financial assets and the specified person does not provide sufficient information to demonstrate the aggregate value of the assets upon request by the Commissioner or his delegate, then the aggregate value of the assets is treated as being in excess of the applicable reporting threshold set forth in § 1.6038D-2(a).

(e) *Reasonable cause exception.*—(1) *In general.*—If the failure to report the information required in section 6038D(c) and § 1.6038D-4 is shown to be due to reasonable cause and not due to willful neglect, no penalty will be imposed under section 6038D(d) or this section.

(2) *Affirmative showing required.*—In order to show that the failure to report the information required in section 6038D(c) and § 1.6038D-4 is due to reasonable cause and not due to willful neglect for purposes of section 6038D(g) and this section, the specified person must make an affirmative showing of all the facts alleged as reasonable cause for the failure to disclose.

(3) *Facts and circumstances taken into account.*—The determination of whether a failure to disclose a specified foreign financial asset on Form 8938 was due to reasonable cause and not due to willful neglect is made on a case-by-case basis, taking into account all pertinent facts and circumstances. The fact that a foreign jurisdiction would impose a civil or criminal penalty on the specified person (or any other person) for disclosing the required information is not reasonable cause.

(f) *Penalties for underpayments attributable to undisclosed foreign financial assets.*—(1) *Accuracy-related penalty.*—For application of the accuracy-related penalty in the case of any portion of an underpayment attributable to any undisclosed foreign financial asset understatement, see section 6662(j).

(2) *Criminal penalties.*—In addition to other penalties, failure to comply with the reporting requirements of section 6038D and the regulations, or any underpayment related to such failure, may result in criminal penalties under sections 7201, 7203, 7206, et seq., or other provisions of Federal law.

(g) *Effective/applicability dates.*—This section applies to taxable years ending after December 19, 2011. Taxpayers may elect to apply the rules of this section to taxable years ending prior to December 19, 2011. [Reg. § 1.6038D-8.]

☐ [*T.D.* 9706, 12-11-2014.]

[Reg. § 1.6039-1]

§ 1.6039-1. Returns required in connection with certain options.—(a) *Requirement of return with respect to incentive stock options under section 6039(a)(1).*—(1) Every corporation which in any calendar year transfers to any person a share of stock pursuant to such person's exercise of an incentive stock option shall, for such calendar year, file a return with respect to each transfer made during such year. This return must include the following information—

(i) The name, address, and employer identification number of the corporation transferring the stock;

(ii) If other than the corporation identified in paragraph (a)(1)(i) of this section, the name, address and employer identification number of the corporation whose stock is being transferred;

(iii) The name, address, and identifying number of the person to whom the share or shares of stock were transferred pursuant to the exercise of the option;

(iv) The date the option was granted to the person;

(v) The exercise price per share;

(vi) The date the option was exercised by the person;

(vii) The fair market value of a share of stock on the date the option was exercised by the person; and

(viii) The number of shares of stock transferred to the person pursuant to the exercise of the option.

(2) Each return required by this paragraph (a) shall be made on Form 3921, Exercise of an Incentive Stock Option Under Section 422(b) (or its designated successor) and shall be filed in such manner as provided in the instructions thereto.

(b) *Requirement of return with respect to stock purchased under an employee stock purchase plan under section 6039(a)(2).*—(1) Every corporation which in any calendar year records, or has by its agent recorded, a transfer of the legal title of a share of stock acquired by the transferor (person who acquires the shares pursuant to the exercise of the option) pursuant to the transferor's exercise of an option granted under an employee stock purchase plan as described in section 423(c) and where the exercise price is less than 100 percent of the value of the stock on date of grant or is not fixed or determinable on the date of the grant, shall, for such calendar year, file a return with respect each transfer made during such year. This return must include the following information—

(i) The name, address, and identifying number of the transferor;

(ii) The name, address and employer identification number of the corporation whose stock is being transferred;

(iii) The date the option was granted to the transferor;

(iv) The fair market value of the stock on the date the option was granted;

(v) The actual exercise price paid per share;

(vi) The exercise price per share determined as if the option were exercised on the date the option was granted to the transferor (to be provided only if the exercise price per share is not fixed or determinable on the date the option was granted);

(vii) The date the option was exercised by the transferor;

(viii) The fair market value of the stock on the date the option was exercised by the transferor;

(ix) The date the legal title of the shares was transferred by the transferor (see paragraph (b)(3) of this section); and

(x) The number of shares to which legal title was transferred by the transferor.

(2) Each return required by this paragraph (b) shall be made on Form 3922, Transfer of Stock Acquired Through an Employee Stock Purchase Plan Under Section 423(c) (or its designated successor) and shall be filed in such manner as provided in the instructions thereto.

(3) A return is required by reason of a transfer described in section 6039(a)(2) only with respect to the first transfer of legal title of the shares by the transferor, including the first transfer of legal title to a recognized broker or financial institution. If a contractual agreement exists or is entered into with a recognized broker or financial institution pursuant to which shares acquired upon exercise of the option will be immediately deposited into a brokerage account established on behalf of the transferor, then the deposit of shares by the transferor into the brokerage account following the exercise of the option is the first transfer of legal title of the shares acquired by the transferor, and the corporation is only required to file a return relating to such transfer of legal title.

(4) Every corporation that transfers any share of stock pursuant to the exercise of an option described in this paragraph shall identify such stock in a manner sufficient to enable the accurate reporting of the transfer of legal title to such shares. Such identification may be accomplished by assigning to the certificates of stock issued pursuant to the exercise of such options a special serial number or color.

(c) *Time for filing returns.*—Each return required by this section for a calendar year must be filed in accordance with the guidelines and procedures set forth in the instructions to Form 3921 and Form 3922.

(d) *Penalty.*—For provisions relating to the penalty applicable to the failure to file a return under this section, see section 6721.

(e) *Exception to return requirements of section 6039(a) for certain nonresident aliens.*—(1) *Return requirement under section 6039(a)(1).*—The return requirement of section 6039(a)(1) is not applicable to the exercise of an incentive stock option by an employee who is a nonresident alien (as defined in section 7701(b)) and to whom the corporation is not required to provide a Form W-2, Wage and Tax Statement (or its designated successor) for any calendar year within the time period beginning with the first day of the calendar year in which the option was granted to the employee and ending on the last day of the calendar year in which the employee exercised the option.

(2) *Return requirement under section 6039(a)(2).*—The return requirement of section 6039(a)(2) is not applicable to the first transfer of legal title of a share of stock by an employee who is a nonresident alien (as defined in section 7701(b)) and to whom the corporation is not required to provide a Form W-2 for any calendar year within the time period beginning with the

first day of the calendar year in which the option was granted to the employee and ending on the last day of the calendar year in which the employee first transferred legal title to shares acquired under the option as described in paragraph (b)(3) of this section.

(3) For purposes of this paragraph (e), the term *corporation* is defined in section 7701(a) and includes, but is not limited to, the corporation issuing the stock, a related corporation of the corporation, any agent of the corporation, any party distributing shares of stock or other payments in connection with the plan (for example, a brokerage firm), and any party in control of the payment of remuneration for employment to the employee.

(f) *Effective/applicability date.*—(1) *In general.*—This section is effective on November 17, 2009. This section will apply as of January 1, 2007.

(2) *Transition period.*—Taxpayers are not required to comply with the return requirements of paragraphs (a) and (b) of this section for stock transfers that occur during the 2007, 2008 and 2009 calendar years. [Reg. § 1.6039-1.]

[*T.D.* 9144, 8-2-2004 (*corrected* 10-15-2004). *Amended by T.D.* 9470, 11-16-2009.]

[Reg. § 301.6039-1]

§ 301.6039-1. Information returns and statements required in connection with certain options.—For provisions relating to information returns and statements required in connection with certain options, see § § 1.6039-1 and 1.6039-2 of this chapter (Income Tax Regulations). [Reg. § 301.6039-1.]

☐ [*T.D.* 7275, 5-4-73.]

[Reg. § 1.6039-2]

§ 1.6039-2. Statements to persons with respect to whom information is reported.—(a) *Requirement of statement with respect to incentive stock options under section 6039(b).*—(1) Every corporation filing a return under § 1.6039-1(a) shall furnish to each person whose name is set forth in such return a written statement with respect to the transfer or transfers made to such person during such year. This statement must include the information described in § 1.6039-1(a)(1).

(2) Each statement required by this paragraph (a) to be furnished to any person must be furnished to such person on Form 3921, Exercise of an Incentive Stock Option Under Section 422(b) (or its designated successor) and be delivered at such time and in such manner as provided in the instructions thereto.

(b) *Requirement of statement with respect to stock purchased under an employee stock purchase plan under section 6039(b).*—(1) Every corporation filing a return under § 1.6039-1(b) shall furnish to each person whose name is set forth in such return a written statement with respect to the transfer or transfers made by such person during such year. This statement must include the information described in § 1.6039-1(b)(1).

(2) Each statement required by this paragraph (b) to be furnished to any person must be furnished to such person on Form 3922, Transfer of Stock Acquired Through an Employee Stock Purchase Plan Under Section 423(c) (or its designated successor) and be delivered at such time and in such manner as provided in the instructions thereto.

(3) If the statement required by this paragraph is made by the authorized transfer agent of the corporation, it is deemed to have been made by the corporation. The term *transfer agent*, as used in this section, means any designee authorized to keep the stock ownership records of a corporation and to record a transfer of title of the stock of such corporation on behalf of such corporation.

(c) *Time for furnishing statements.*—(1) *In general.*—Each statement required by this section to be furnished to any person for a calendar year must be furnished to such person on or before January 31 of the year following the year for which the statement is required. However, for a statement required to be furnished after December 31, 2008, the February 15 due date under section 6045 applies to the statement if the statement is furnished in a consolidated reporting statement under section 6045. *See* § § 1.6045-1(k)(3), 1.6045-2(d)(2), 1.6045-3(e)(2), 1.6045-4(m)(3), and 1.6045-5(a)(3)(ii).

(2) *Extension of time.*—An extension of time to furnish statements required by this section may be granted in accordance with the guidelines and procedures set forth in the instructions to Form 3921 and Form 3922.

(d) *Penalty.*—For provisions relating to the penalty applicable to the failure to furnish a statement under this section, see section 6722.

(e) *Effective/applicability date.*—(1) *In general.*—This section is effective on November 17, 2009. This section will apply as of January 1, 2007.

(2) *Reliance and transition period.*—Notwithstanding § 1.6039-1(f), corporations must furnish information statements to employees in accordance with this section for stock transfers that are subject to § 1.6039-1(a) and (b), and occur during the 2007, 2008 and 2009 calendar years. For purposes of furnishing information statements for stock transfers that occur during the 2007 or 2008 calendar years, taxpayers may rely on § 1.6039-1 of the 2004 final regulations (69 FR 46401) or § 1.6039-2 of the 2008 proposed regulations (REG-103146-08) (73 FR 40999). For purposes of furnishing information statements for stock transfers that occur during the 2009 calendar year, taxpayers may rely on § 1.6039-1 of the 2004 final regulations (69 FR 46401), § 1.6039-2 of the 2008 proposed regulations (REG-103146-08) (73 FR 40999), or this section. [Reg. § 1.6039-2.]

[*T.D.* 9470, 11-16-2009 (*corrected* 12-22-2009). *Amended by T.D.* 9504, 10-12-2010.]

[Reg. §301.6039E-1]

§301.6039E-1. Information reporting by passport applicants.—(a) *In general.*—Every individual who applies for a U.S. passport or the renewal of a passport (passport applicant), other than a passport for use in diplomatic, military, or other official U.S. government business, shall include with his or her passport application the information described in paragraph (b)(1) of this section in the time and manner described in paragraph (b)(2) of this section.

(b) *Required information.*—(1) *In general.*—The information required under paragraph (a) of this section shall include the following information:

(i) The passport applicant's full name and, if applicable, previous name;

(ii) The passport applicant's permanent address and, if different, mailing address;

(iii) The passport applicant's taxpayer identifying number (TIN), if such a number has been issued to the passport applicant. A TIN means the individual's social security number (SSN) issued by the Social Security Administration. A passport applicant who does not have an SSN must enter zeros in the appropriate space on the passport application; and

(iv) The passport applicant's date of birth.

(2) *Time and manner for furnishing information.*—A passport applicant must provide the information required by this section with his or her passport application, whether by personal appearance or mail, to the Department of State (including United States Embassies and Consular posts abroad).

(c) *Penalties.*—(1) *In general.*—If the information required by paragraph (b)(1) of this section is incomplete or incorrect, or the information is not filed in the time and manner described in paragraph (b)(2) of this section, then the passport applicant may be subject to a penalty equal to $500 per application. Before assessing a penalty under this section, the IRS will provide to the passport applicant written notice of the potential assessment of the $500 penalty, requesting the information being sought, and offering the applicant an opportunity to explain why the information was not provided with the passport application. A passport applicant has 60 days from the date of the notice of the potential assessment of the penalty (90 days from such date if the notice is addressed to an applicant outside the United States) to respond to the notice. If the passport applicant demonstrates to the satisfaction of the Commissioner (or the Commissioner's delegate) that the failure is due to reasonable cause and not due to willful neglect, after considering all the surrounding circumstances, then the IRS will not assess the penalty.

(2) *Example.*—The following example illustrates the provisions of paragraph (c) of this section.

Example. C, a citizen of the United States, makes an error in supplying information on his passport application. Based on the nature of the error and C's timely response to correct the error after being contacted by the IRS, the Commissioner concludes that the mistake is due to reasonable cause and not due to willful neglect. Accordingly, no penalty is assessed.

(d) *Effective/applicability date.*—This section applies to passport applications submitted after July 18, 2014. [Reg. §301.6039E-1.]

☐ [T.D. 9679, 7-17-2014.]

[Reg. §1.6039I-1]

§1.6039I-1. Reporting of certain employer-owned life insurance contracts.—(a) *Requirement to report.*—Section 6039I requires every taxpayer that is an applicable policyholder owning one or more employer-owned life insurance contracts issued after August 17, 2006, to file a return showing the following information for each year the contracts are owned—

(1) The number of employees of the applicable policyholder at the end of the year;

(2) The number of such employees insured under such contracts at the end of the year;

(3) The total amount of insurance in force at the end of the year under such contracts;

(4) The name, address, and taxpayer identification number of the applicable policyholder and the type of business in which the policyholder is engaged; and

(5) That the applicable policyholder has a valid consent for each insured employee (or, if all such consents are not obtained, the number of insured employees for whom such consent was not obtained).

(b) *Time and manner of reporting.*—Applicable policyholders owning one or more employer-owned life insurance contracts issued after August 17, 2006, must provide the information required under §6039I by attaching Form 8925, "Report of Employer-Owned Life Insurance Contracts", to the policyholder's income tax return by the due date of that return, or by filing such other form at such time and in such manner as the Commissioner may in the future prescribe.

(c) *Effective/applicability date.*—These regulations are applicable for tax years ending after November 6, 2008. [Reg. §1.6039I-1.]

☐ [T.D. 9431, 11-5-2008.]

[Reg. §1.6041-1]

§1.6041-1. Return of information as to payments of $600 or more.—(a) *General rule.*—(1) *Information returns required.*—(i) *Payments required to be reported.*—Except as otherwise provided in §§1.6041-3 and 1.6041-4, every person engaged in a trade or business shall make an information return for each calendar year with respect to payments it makes during the calendar year in the course of its trade or business to another person of fixed or determinable income described in paragraph (a)(1)(i)(A) or (B) of this section. For purposes of the regulations under this section, the person described in this paragraph (a)(1)(i) is a payor.

(A) Salaries, wages, commissions, fees, and other forms of compensation for services rendered aggregating $600 or more.

(B) Interest (including original issue discount), rents, royalties, annuities, pensions, and other gains, profits, and income aggregating $600 or more.

(ii) *Information returns required under other provisions of the Internal Revenue Code.*—The payments described in paragraphs (a)(1)(i)(A) and (B) of this section shall not include any payments of amounts with respect to which an information return is required by, or may be required under authority of, section 6042(a) (relating to dividends), section 6043(a)(2) (relating to distributions in liquidation), section 6044(a) (relating to patronage dividends), section 6045 (relating to brokers' transactions with customers and certain other transactions), sections 6049(a)(1) and (2) (relating to interest), section 6050N(a) (relating to royalties), or section 6050P(a) or (b) (relating to cancellation of indebtedness). For information returns required under section 6045(f) (relating to payments to attorneys), see special rules in §§1.6041-1(a)(1)(iii) and 1.6045-5(c)(4). For payment card transactions (as described in §1.6050W-1(b)) and third party network transactions (as defined in §1.6050W-1(c)) required to be reported on information returns required under section 6050W (relating to payment card and third party network transactions), see special rules in §1.6041-1(a)(1)(iv).

(iii) *Information returns required under section 6045(f) on or after January 1, 2007.*—For payments made on or after January 1, 2007 to which section 6045(f) (relating to payments to attorneys) applies, the following rules apply. Not withstanding the provisions of paragraph (a)(1)(ii) of this section, payments to an attorney that are described in paragraph (a)(1)(i) of this section but which otherwise would be reportable under section 6045(f) are reported under section 6041 and this section and not section 6045(f). This exception applies only if the payments are reportable with respect to the same payee under both sections. Thus, a person who, in the course of a trade or business, pays $600 of taxable damages to a claimant by paying that amount to the claimant's attorney is required to file an information return under section 6041 with respect to the claimant, as well as another information return under section 6045(f) with respect to the claimant's attorney. For provisions relating to information reporting for payments to attorneys, see §1.6045-5.

(iv) *Information returns required under section 6050W for calendar years beginning after December 31, 2010.*—For payments made by payment card (as defined in §1.6050W-1(b)(3)) or through a third party payment network (as defined in §1.6050W-1(c)(3)) after December 31, 2010, that are required to be reported on an information return under section 6050W (relat-

ing to payment card and third party network transactions), the following rule applies. Transactions that are described in paragraph (a)(1)(ii) of this section that otherwise would be subject to reporting under both sections 6041 and 6050W are reported under section 6050W and not section 6041. For provisions relating to information reporting for payment card and third party network transactions, see §1.6050W-1. Solely for purposes of this paragraph, the de minimis threshold for third party network transactions in §1.6050W-1(c)(4) is disregarded in determining whether the transaction is subject to reporting under section 6050W.

(v) *Examples.*—The provisions of paragraph (a)(1)(iv) of this section are illustrated by the following examples:

Example 1. Restaurant owner A, in the course of business, pays $600 of fixed or determinable income to B, a repairman, by credit card. B is one of a network of unrelated persons that has agreed to accept A's credit card as payment under an agreement that provides standards and mechanisms for settling the transactions between a merchant acquiring bank and the persons who accept the cards. Merchant acquiring bank Y is responsible for making the payment to B. Under paragraph (a)(1)(iv) of this section, A, as payor, is not required to file an information return under section 6041 with respect to the transaction because Y, as the payment settlement entity for the payment card transaction, is required to file an information return under section 6050W.

Example 2. Restaurant owner A, in the course of business, pays $600 of fixed or determinable income to B, a repairman, through a third party payment network. B is one of a substantial number of persons who have established accounts with Y, a third party settlement organization that provides standards and mechanisms for settling the transactions and guarantees payments to those persons for goods or services purchased through the network. Y is responsible for making the payment to B. Under paragraph (a)(1)(iv) of this section, A, as payor, is not required to file an information return under section 6041 with respect to the transaction because the transaction is a third party network transaction that is subject to reporting under section 6050W. Solely for purposes of determining whether A is eligible for relief from reporting under section 6041, the de minimis threshold for third party network transactions in §1.6050W-1(c)(4) is disregarded.

(2) *Prescribed form.*—The return required by subparagraph (1) of this paragraph shall be made on Forms 1096 and 1099 except that (i) the return with respect to distributions to beneficiaries of a trust or of an estate shall be made on Form 1041, and (ii) the return with respect to certain payments of compensation to an employee by his employer shall be made on Forms W-3 and W-2 under the provisions of §1.6041-2 (relating to return of information as to payments to employees). Where Form 1099 is required to be filed under this section, a separate Form 1099

shall be furnished for each person to whom payments described in subdivision (i), (ii), or (iii) of subparagraph (1) of this paragraph are made. For time and place for filing Forms 1096 and 1099, see § 1.6041-6. For the requirement to submit the information required by Form 1099 on magnetic media for payments after December 31, 1983, see section 6011(e) and § 301.6011-2 of this chapter (Procedure and Administration Regulations).

(b) *Persons engaged in trade or business.*—(1) *In general.*—The term "all persons engaged in a trade or business", as used in section 6041(a), includes not only those so engaged for gain or profit, but also organizations the activities of which are not for the purpose of gain or profit. Thus, the term includes the organizations referred to in sections 401(a), 501(c), 501(d) and 521 and in paragraph (i) of this section. On the other hand, section 6041(a) applies only to payments in the course of trade or business; hence it does not apply to an amount paid by the proprietor of a business to a physician for medical services rendered by the physician to the proprietor's child.

(2) *Special rule for REMICs.*—For purposes of chapter 1 subtitle F, chapter 61A, part IIIB, the terms "all persons engaged in a trade or business" and "any service-recipient engaged in a trade or business" includes a real estate mortgage investment conduit or REMIC (as defined in section 860D).

(c) *Fixed or determinable income.*—Income is fixed when it is to be paid in amounts definitely predetermined. Income is determinable whenever there is a basis of calculation by which the amount to be paid may be ascertained. The income need not be paid annually or at regular intervals. The fact that the payments may be increased or decreased in accordance with the happening of an event does not for purposes of this section make the payments any the less determinable. A payment made jointly to two or more payees may be fixed and determinable income to one payee even though the payment is not fixed and determinable income to another payee. For example, property insurance proceeds paid jointly to the owner of damaged property and to a contractor that repairs the property may be fixed and determinable income to the contractor but not fixed and determinable income to the owner, and should be reported to the contractor. A salesman working by the month for a commission on sales which is paid or credited monthly receives determinable income.

(d) *Payments specifically included.*—(1) *In general.*—Amounts paid in respect of life insurance, endowment, or annuity contracts are required to be reported in returns of information under this section—

(i) Unless the payment is made in respect of a life insurance or endowment contract by reason of the death of the insured and is not required to be reported by paragraph (b) of § 1.6041-2,

(ii) Unless the payment is made by reason of the surrender prior to maturity or lapse of a policy, other than a policy which was purchased (*a*) by a trust described in section 401(a) which is exempt from tax under section 501(a), (*b*) as part of a plan described in section 403(a), or (*c*) by an employer described in section 403(b)(1)(A),

(iii) Unless the payment is interest as defined in § 1.6049-2 and is made after December 31, 1962,

(iv) Unless the payment is a payment with respect to which a return is required by § 1.6047-1, relating to employee retirement plans covering owner-employees,

(v) Unless the payment is payment with respect to which a return is required by § 1.6052-1, relating to payment of wages in the form of group-term life insurance.

(2) *Professional fees.*—Fees for professional services paid to attorneys, physicians, and members of other professions are required to be reported in returns of information if paid by persons engaged in a trade or business and paid in the course of such trade or business.

(3) *Prizes and awards.*—Amounts paid as prizes and awards that are required to be included in gross income under section 74 and § 1.74-1 when paid in the course of a trade or business are required to be reported in returns of information under this section.

(4) *Disability payments.*—Amounts paid as disability payments under section 105(d) are required to be reported in returns of information under this section.

(5) *Notional principal contracts.*—Except as provided in paragraphs (b)(5)(i) and (ii) of this section, amounts paid after December 31, 2000, with respect to notional principal contracts referred to in § 1.863-7 or 1.988-2(e) to persons who are not described in § 1.6049-4(c)(1)(ii) are required to be reported in returns of information under this section. The amount required to be reported under this paragraph (d)(5) is limited to the amount of cash paid from the notional principal contract as described in § 1.446-3(d). A nonperiodic payment is reportable for the year in which an actual payment is made. Any amount of interest determined under the provisions of § 1.446-3(g)(4) (dealing with interest in the case of a significant non-periodic payment) is reportable under this paragraph (d)(5) and not under section 6049 (see § 1.6049-5(b)(15)). See § 1.6041-4(a)(4) for reporting exceptions regarding payments to foreign persons. See, however, § 1.1461-1(c)(1) for reporting amounts described under this paragraph (d)(5) that are paid to foreign persons. The provisions of § 1.6049-5(d) shall apply for determining whether a payment with respect to a notional principal contract is made to a foreign person. See § 1.6049-4(a) for a definition of payor. For purposes of this paragraph (d)(5), a payor includes a middleman defined in § 1.6049-4(f)(4).

Reg. § 1.6041-1(d)(5)

(i) An amount paid with respect to a notional principal contract is not required to be reported if the amount is paid by a non-U.S. payor or a non-U.S. middleman and is paid and received outside the United States (as defined in § 1.6049-4(f)(16)).

(ii) An amount paid with respect to a notional principal contract is not required to be reported if the amount is paid by a payor that has no actual knowledge that the payee is a U.S. person and is paid and received outside the United States (as defined in § 1.6049-4(f)(16)), and the payor is—

(A) A U.S. payor or U.S. middleman that is not a U.S. person (such as a controlled foreign corporation defined in section 957(a) or certain foreign corporations or foreign partnerships engaged in a U.S. trade or business); or

(B) A foreign branch of a U.S. bank. See § 1.6049-5(c)(5) for a definition of a U.S. payor, a U.S. middleman, a non-U.S. payor, and a non-U.S. middleman.

(e) *Payment made on behalf of another person.*— (1) *In general.*—A person that makes a payment in the course of its trade or business on behalf of another person is the payor that must make a return of information under this section with respect to that payment if the payment is described in paragraph (a) of this section and, under all the facts and circumstances, that person—

(i) Performs management or oversight functions in connection with the payment (this would exclude, for example, a person who performs mere administrative or ministerial functions such as writing checks at another's direction); or

(ii) Has a significant economic interest in the payment (i.e., an economic interest that would be compromised if the payment were not made, such as by creation of a mechanic's lien on property to which the payment relates, or a loss of collateral).

(2) *Determination of payor obligated to report.*—If two or more persons meet the requirements for making a return of information with respect to a payment, as set forth in paragraph (e)(1) of this section, the person obligated to report the payment is the person closest in the chain to the payee, unless the parties agree in writing that one of the other parties meeting the requirements set forth in paragraph (e)(1) of this section will report the payment.

(3) *Special rule for payment by employee to employer.*—Notwithstanding the provisions of paragraph (e)(1) of this section, an employee acting in the course of his employment who makes a payment to his employer on behalf of another person is not required to make a return of information with respect to that payment.

(4) *Optional method to report.*—A person that makes a payment on behalf of another person but is not required to make an information return under paragraph (e)(1) of this section may

elect to do so pursuant to the procedures established by the Commissioner. See, e.g., Rev. Proc. 84-33 (1984-1 C.B. 502) (optional method for a paying agent to report and deposit amounts withheld for payors under the statutory provisions of backup withholding) (see § 601.601(d)(2) of this chapter).

(5) *Examples.*—The provisions of this paragraph (e) are illustrated by the following examples:

Example 1. Bank B provides financing to C, a real estate developer, for a construction project. B makes disbursements from the account for labor, materials, services, and other expenses related to the construction project. In connection with the payments, B performs the following functions: approves payments to the general contractor or subcontractors; ensures that loan proceeds are properly applied and that all approved bills are properly paid to avoid mechanics' or materialmen's liens; conducts site inspections to determine whether work has been completed (but does not check the quality of the work). B is performing management or oversight functions in connection with the payments and is subject to the information reporting requirements of section 6041 with respect to payments.

Example 2. Mortgage company D holds a mortgage on business property owned by E. When the property is damaged by a storm, E's insurance company issues a check payable to both D and E in settlement of E's claim. Pursuant to the contract between D and E, D holds the insurance proceeds in an escrow account and makes disbursements, according to E's instructions, to contractors and subcontractors performing repairs on the property. D is not performing management or oversight functions, but D has a significant economic interest in the payments because the purpose of the arrangement is to ensure that property on which D holds a mortgage is repaired or replaced. D is subject to the information reporting requirements of section 6041 with respect to the payments to contractors.

Example 3. Settlement agent F provides real estate closing services to real estate brokers and agents. F deposits money received from the buyer or lender in an escrow account and makes payments from the account to real estate agents or brokers, appraisers, land surveyors, building inspectors, or similar service providers according to the provisions of the real estate contract and written instructions from the lender. F may also make disbursements pursuant to oral instructions of the seller or purchaser at closing. F is not performing management or oversight functions and does not have a significant economic interest in the payments, and is not subject to the information reporting requirements of section 6041. For the rules relating to F's obligation to report the gross proceeds of the sale, see section 6045(e) and § 1.6045-4.

Example 4. Assume the same facts as in *Example 3.* In addition, the seller instructs F to hire a contractor to perform repairs on the property. F selects the contractor, negotiates the cost, monitors the progress of the project, and inspects the work to ensure it complies with the contract. With respect to the payments to the contractor, F is performing management or oversight functions and is subject to the information reporting requirements of section 6041.

Example 5. G is a rental agent who manages certain rental property on behalf of property owner H. G finds tenants, arranges leases, collects rent, responds to tenant inquiries regarding maintenance, and hires and makes payments to repairmen. G subtracts her commission and any maintenance payments from rental payments and remits the remainder to H. With respect to payments to repairmen, G is performing management or oversight functions and is subject to the information reporting requirements of section 6041. With respect to the payment of rent to H, G is subject to the information reporting requirements of section 6041 regardless of whether she performs management or oversight functions or has a significant economic interest in the payment. See § 1.6041-3(d) for rules relating to rental agents. See § 1.6041-1(f) to determine the amount that G should report to H as rent.

Example 6. Literary agent J receives a payment from publisher L of fees earned by J's client, author K. J deposits the payment into a bank account in J's name. From time to time and as directed by K, J makes payments from these funds to attorneys, managers, and other third parties for services rendered to K. After subtracting J's commission, J pays K the net amount. J does not order or direct the provision of services by the third parties to K, and J exercises no discretion in making the payments to the third parties or to K. J is not performing management or oversight functions and does not have a significant economic interest in the payments and is not subject to the information reporting requirements of section 6041 in connection with the payments to K or to the third parties. For the rules relating to L's obligation to report the payment of the fees to K, see paragraphs (a)(1)(i) and (f) of this section. For the rules relating to K's obligation to report the payment of the commission to J and the payments to the third parties for services, see paragraphs (a)(1)(i) and (d)(2) of this section.

Example 7. Attorney P deposits into a client trust fund a settlement payment from R, the defendant in a breach of contract action for lost profits in which P represented plaintiff Q. P makes payments from the client trust fund to service providers such as expert witnesses and private investigators for expenses incurred in the litigation. P decides whom to hire, negotiates the amount of payment, and determines that the services have been satisfactorily performed. In the event of a dispute with a service provider, P withholds payment until the dispute is settled. With respect to payments to the service providers, P is performing management or oversight functions and is subject to the information reporting requirements of section 6041.

Example 8. Assume the same facts as in *Example 7*. In addition, assume that after paying the service providers and deducting his legal fee, P pays Q the remaining funds that P had received from the settlement with R. With respect to the payment to Q, P is not performing management or oversight functions, does not have a significant economic interest in the payment, and is not subject to the information reporting requirements of section 6041. For the rules relating to R's obligation to report the payment of the settlement proceeds to P, see section 6045(f) and the regulations thereunder. For the rules relating to R's obligation to report the payment of the settlement proceeds to Q, see paragraphs (a)(1)(i) and (f) of this section. For the rules relating to Q's obligation to report the payment of attorney fees to P, see paragraphs (a)(1)(i) and (d)(2) of this section.

Example 9. Medical insurer S operates as the administrator of a health care program under a contract with a state. S makes payments of government funds to health care providers who provide care to eligible patients. S receives and reviews claims submitted by patients or health care providers, determines if the claims meet all the requirements of the program (e.g., that the care is authorized and that the patients are eligible beneficiaries), and determines the amount of payment. S is performing management or oversight functions and is subject to the information reporting requirements of section 6041 with respect to the payments.

Example 10. Race track employee T holds deposits made by horse owner U in a special escrow account in U's name. U enters into a contract with jockey V to ride U's horse in a race at the track. As directed by U, T pays V the fee for riding U's horse from U's escrow account. T is not performing management or oversight functions, does not have a significant economic interest in the payment, and is not subject to the information reporting requirements of section 6041. For the rules relating to U's obligation to report the payment of the fee to V, see paragraph (a)(1)(i) of this section.

Example 11. X is a certified public accountant employed by Firm Y, and is not a partner. Client Z pays X directly for accounting services. X remits the amount received to Y, as required by the terms of his employment. X does not have any reporting obligation with respect to the payment to Y. For the rules relating to Z's obligation to report the payment to Y for services, see paragraphs (a)(1)(i) and (d)(2) of this section.

Example 12. Bank contracts with Title Company with respect to the disbursement of funds on a construction loan. Pursuant to their arrangement, the contractor sends draw requests to Title Company, which inspects the work, verifies the amount requested, and then sends the draw request to Bank with supporting documents. Bank pays Title Company the amount of the draw request, and Title Company insures Bank against any loss if it cannot obtain the necessary lien waivers. Bank has a significant economic interest in the payment as a mortgagee, and Title Company exercises management or oversight over the payment. Since Title Com-

Reg. § 1.6041-1(e)(5)

pany is closest in the chain to the contractor, Title Company should report the payment, unless the parties agree in writing that Bank will report the payment.

(f) *Amount to be reported when fees, expenses or commissions are deducted.*—(1) *In general.*—The amount to be reported as paid to a payee is the amount includible in the gross income of the payee (which in many cases will be the gross amount of the payment or payments before fees, commissions, expenses, or other amounts owed by the payee to another person have been deducted), whether the payment is made jointly or separately to the payee and another person. The Commissioner may, by guidance published in the Internal Revenue Bulletin, illustrate the circumstances under which the gross amount or less than the gross amount may be reported.

(2) *Examples.*—The provisions of this paragraph (f) are illustrated by the following examples:

Example 1. Attorney P represents client Q in a breach of contract action for lost profits against defendant R. R settles the case for $100,000 damages and $40,000 for attorney fees. Under applicable law, the full $140,000 is includible in Q's gross taxable income. R issues a check payable to P and Q in the amount of $140,000. R is required to make an information return reporting a payment to Q in the amount of $140,000. For the rules with respect to R's obligation to report the payment to P, see section 6045(f) and the regulations thereunder.

Example 2. Assume the same facts as in *Example 1*, except that R issues a check to Q for $100,000 and a separate check to P for $40,000. R is required to make an information return reporting a payment to Q in the amount of $140,000. For the rules with respect to R's obligation to report the payment to P, see section 6045(f) and the regulations thereunder.

(g) *Payment made in medium other than cash.*—If any payment required to be reported on Form 1099 is made in property other than money, the fair market value of the property at the time of payment is the amount to be included on such form.

(h) *When payment deemed made.*—For purposes of a return of information, an amount is deemed to have been paid when it is credited or set apart to a person without any substantial limitation or restriction as to the time or manner of payment or condition upon which payment is to be made, and is made available to him so that it may be drawn at any time, and its receipt brought within his own control and disposition.

(i) *Payments made by United States or a State.*—Information returns on—

(1) Forms 1096 and 1099 and

(2) Forms W-3 and W-2 (when made under the provisions of § 1.6041-2)

of payments made by the United States or a State, or political subdivision thereof, or the District of Columbia, or any agency or instrumentality of any one or more of the foregoing, shall be

made by the officer or employee of the United States, or of such State, or political subdivision, or of the District of Columbia, or of such agency or instrumentality, as the case may be, having control of such payments or by the officer or employee appropriately designated to make such returns.

(j) *Effective/applicability date.*—This section applies to payments made on or after January 6, 2017. (For payments made after June 30, 2014, and before January 6, 2017, see this section as in effect and contained in 26 CFR part 1, as revised April 1, 2016. For payments made after December 31, 2010, and before July 1, 2014, see this section as in effect and contained in 26 CFR part 1, as revised April 1, 2013.) [Reg. § 1.6041-1.]

☐ [*T.D.* 6364, 2-13-59. *Amended by T.D.* 6628, 12-27-62; *T.D.* 6677, 9-16-63; *T.D.* 6888, 7-5-66; *T.D.* 7284, 8-2-73; *T.D.* 7580, 12-20-78; *T.D.* 7888, 4-22-83; *T.D.* 8458, 12-23-92; *T.D.* 8734, 10-6-97 (T.D. 8804 delayed the effective date of T.D. 8734 from January 1, 1999, to January 1, 2000; T.D. 8856 further delayed the effective date of T.D. 8734 until January 1, 2001); *T.D.* 8804, 12-30-98 (*corrected* 3-8-99); *T.D.* 8881, 5-15-2000; *T.D.* 9010, 7-25-2002; *T.D.* 9270, 7-12-2006 (*corrected* 8-15-2006); *T.D.* 9496, 8-13-2010, *T.D.* 9658, 2-28-2014 (*corrected* 6-30-2014 *and T.D.* 9808, 12-30-2016).]

[Reg. § 301.6041-1]

§ 301.6041-1. Returns of information regarding certain payments.—For provisions relating to the requirement of returns of information regarding certain payments see §§ 1.6041-1 to 1.6041-6, inclusive, of this chapter (Income Tax Regulations). [Reg. § 301.6041-1.]

☐ [*T.D.* 6498, 10-24-60.]

[Reg. § 1.6041-2]

§ 1.6041-2. Return of information as to payments to employees.—(a)(1) *In general.*—Wages, as defined in section 3401, paid to an employee are required to be reported on Form W-2. See section 6011 and the Employment Tax Regulations thereunder. All other payments of compensation, including the cash value of payments made in any medium other than cash, to an employee by his employer in the course of the trade or business of the employer must also be reported on Form W-2 if the total of such payments and the amount of the employee's wages (as defined in section 3401), if any, required to be reported on Form W-2 aggregates $600 or more in a calendar year. For example, if a payment of $700 was made to an employee and $400 thereof represents wages subject to withholding under section 3402 and the remaining $300 represents compensation not subject to withholding, such wages and compensation must both be reported on Form W-2. A separate Form W-2 shall be furnished for each employee for whom a return must be made. At the election of the employer, components of amounts required to be reported on Form W-2 pursuant to the provisions of this subparagraph may be reported on more than one Form W-2.

(2) *Transmittal form.*—The transmittal form for a return on Form W-2 made pursuant to the provisions of subparagraph (1) of this paragraph shall be Form W-3. In a case where an employer must file a Form W-3 under this paragraph and also under §31.6011(a)-4 or §31.6011(a)-5 of this chapter (Employment Tax Regulations), the Form W-3 filed under such §31.6011(a)-4 or §31.6011(a)-5 shall also be used as the transmittal form for a return on Form W-2 made pursuant to the provisions of this paragraph.

(3) *Time for filing.*—(i) *General rule.*—In a case where an employer must file Forms W-3 and W-2 under this paragraph and also under §31.6011(a)-4 or §31.6011(a)-5 of this chapter (Employment Tax Regulations), the time for filing such forms under this paragraph shall be the same as the time (including extensions thereof) for filing such forms under §31.6011(a)-4 or §31.6011(a)-5.

(ii) [Reserved]. For further guidance, see §1.6041-2T(a)(3)(ii).

(iii) *Cross reference.*—For extensions of time for filing returns, see section 6081 and the regulations thereunder.

(4) *Place for filing.*—The returns on Forms W-3 and W-2 required under this paragraph shall be filed pursuant to the rules contained in §31.6091-1 of this chapter (Employment Tax Regulations), relating to the place for filing certain returns.

(5) *Statement for employees.*—An employer required under this paragraph (a) to file Form W-2 with respect to an employee is also required under sections 6041(d) and 6051 to furnish a written statement to the employee. This written statement must be furnished on Form W-2 in accordance with section 6051 and the regulations.

(b) *Distributions under employees' trust or plan.*—(1) Amounts which are—

(i) Distributed or made available to a beneficiary, and to which section 402 (relating to employees' trusts) or section 403 (relating to employee annuity plans) applies, or

(ii) Described in section 72(m)(3)(B),

shall be reported on Forms 1096 and 1099 to the extent such amounts are includible in the gross income of such beneficiary if the amounts so includible aggregate $600 or more in any calendar year. In addition, every trust described in section 501(c)(17) which makes one or more payments (including separation and sick and accident benefits) totaling $600 or more in 1 year to an individual must file an annual information return on Form 1096, accompanied by a statement on Form 1099, for each such individual. Payments made by an employer or a person other than the trustee of the trust should not be considered in determining whether the $600 minimum has been paid by the trustee. The provisions of this subparagraph shall not be applicable to payments of supplemental unemployment compensation benefits made after December 31, 1970, which are treated as if they were wages for purposes of section 3401(a). Such amounts are required to be reported on Forms W-3 and W-2. See paragraph (b)(14) of §31.3401(a)-1 of this chapter (Employment Tax Regulations).

(2) Any amount with respect to which a statement is required by §1.6047-1, relating to employee retirement plans covering owner-employees, shall not be included in amounts required to be reported under section 6041.

(c) *Payments to foreign persons.*—See §1.6041-4 for reporting exemptions regarding payments to foreign persons. See §1.6049-5(d) for determining whether a payment is made to a foreign person. [Reg. §1.6041-2.]

☐ [*T.D.* 6364, 2-13-59. *Amended by T.D.* 6677, 9-16-63; *T.D.* 6972, 9-11-68; *T.D.* 7068, 11-10-70; *T.D.* 7284, 8-2-73; *T.D.* 7580, 12-20-78; *T.D.* 8734, 10-6-97 (*T.D.* 8804 delayed the effective date of *T.D.* 8734 from January 1, 1999, to January 1, 2000; *T.D.* 8856 further delayed the effective date of *T.D.* 8734 until January 1, 2001); *T.D.* 8895, 8-17-2000, *T.D.* 9114, 2-13-2004 *and T.D.* 9821, 7-18-2017.]

[Reg. §1.6041-2T]

§1.6041-2T. Return of information as to payments to employees (temporary).—(a)(1) through (2) [Reserved]. For further guidance, see §1.6041-2(a)(1) and (2).

(3)(i) [Reserved]. For further guidance, see §1.6041-2(a)(3)(i).

(ii) *Exception.*—In a case where an employer is not required to file Forms W-3 and W-2 under §31.6011(a)-4 or §31.6011(a)-5 of this chapter, returns on Forms W-3 and W-2 required under this paragraph (a) for any calendar year shall be filed on or before January 31 of the following year.

(b) through (c) [Reserved]. For further guidance, see §1.6041-2(b) through (c).

(d) *Applicability date.*—This section applies to returns filed on or after July 20, 2017. Section 1.6041-2 (as contained in 26 CFR part 1, revised April 2017) applies to returns filed before July 20, 2017.

(e) *Expiration date.*—The applicability of this section will expire on or before July 17, 2020. [Temporary Reg. §1.6041-2T.]

☐ *T.D.* 9821, 7-18-2017.]

[Reg. §1.6041-3]

§1.6041-3. Payments for which no return of information is required under section 6041.—Returns of information are not required under section 6041 and §§1.6041-1 and 1.6041-2 for payments described in paragraphs (a) through (q) of this section. See §1.6041-4 for reporting exemptions regarding payments to foreign persons.

(a) Payments of income required to be reported on Forms 1120-S, 941, W-2, and W-3, (however, see § 1.6041-2(a) with respect to Forms W-2 and W-3).

(b) Payments by a broker to his customer (but for reporting requirements as to certain of such payments, see sections 6042, 6045, and 6049 and the regulations thereunder in this part).

(c) Payments of bills for merchandise, telegrams, telephone, freight, storage, and similar charges.

(d) Payments of rent made to rental agents (but the agent is required to report payments of rent to the landlord in accordance with § 1.6041-1(a)(1)(i)(B) and (2)).

(e) Payments representing earned income for services rendered without the United States made to a citizen of the United States, if it is reasonable to believe that such amounts will be excluded from gross income under the provisions of section 911 and the regulations thereunder.

(f) Compensation and profits paid or distributed by a partnership to the individual partners (but for reporting requirements, see § 1.6031-1).

(g) Payments of commissions to general agents by fire insurance companies or other companies insuring property, except when specifically directed by the Commissioner to be filed.

(h)(1) *In general.*—Payments made under reimbursement or other expense allowance arrangements that meet the requirements of section 62(c) of the Code and § 1.62-2, that do not exceed the amount of the expenses substantiated (i.e., amounts which are treated as paid under an accountable plan), and that are received by an employee on or after January 1, 1989, with respect to expenses paid or incurred on or after January 1, 1989.

(2) *Transition rule.*—Payments made under reimbursement or other expense allowance arrangements that are received by an employee on or after January 1, 1989, but prior to July 1, 1990, to the extent that the employee is required to account (within the meaning of the term "account" as set forth in § 1.162-17(b)(4) or 1.274-5T(f)(4), whichever is applicable) and does so account to the payor for such expenses, provided the payor has made a reasonable, good faith effort to comply with the requirements of section 62(c). In general, compliance with the provisions of this section, as in effect for payments made under reimbursement or other expense allowance arrangements that were received by an employee before January 1, 1989, with respect to expenses paid or incurred before January 1, 1989, will constitute such reasonable good faith compliance. In no event, however, will reasonable good faith compliance exist if a payor fails to report payments made under an arrangement (other than a per diem or mileage allowance type arrangement) under which an employee is not required to substantiate expenses paid or incurred or is not required to

return amounts in excess of the substantiated expenses.

(i) Payments of interest on obligations of the United States, or a State, Territory, or political subdivision thereof, or the District of Columbia, or any agency or instrumentality of any one or more of the foregoing (but for requirements for reporting certain such payments by the United States or any agency or instrumentality thereof, see § § 1.1461-1 to 1.1461-3, inclusive).

(j) Payments of interest on corporate bonds (but for reporting requirements as to payments of interest on certain corporate bonds, see § 1.6049-5).

(k) Amounts paid as an allowance or reimbursement for traveling or other bona fide ordinary and necessary expenses, including an allowance for meals and lodging or a per diem allowance in lieu of subsistence, to persons in the service of an international organization (without regard to whether there is a requirement to account for such amounts) if—

(1) The organization is designated as an international organization by the President of the United States in Executive Orders issued pursuant to 22 U.S.C. 288, and

(2) The organization has immunity with respect to the inviolability of its archives pursuant to an international agreement having full force and effect in the United States;

(l) A payment to an informer as an award, fee, or reward for information relating to criminal activity, but only if such payment is made by the United States, a State, Territory, or political subdivision thereof, or the District of Columbia, or any agency or instrumentality of any one or more of the foregoing, or, with respect to payments made after December 31, 1987, by an organization that is described in section 501(c)(3) and that makes such payments in furtherance of a charitable purpose to lessen the burdens of government within the meaning of § 1.501(c)(3)-1(d)(2).

(m) On and after September 9, 1968, payments by a person carrying on the banking business of interest on a deposit evidenced by a negotiable time certificate of deposit (but for reporting requirements as to payments made after December 31, 1962, of interest on certain deposits, see section 6049 and the regulations thereunder in this part); and

(n) Payments to individuals as scholarships or fellowship grants within the meaning of section 117(b)(1), whether or not "qualified scholarships" as described in section 117(b). This exception does not apply to any amount of a scholarship or fellowship grant that represents payment for services within the meaning of section 117(c). Instead, these amounts are required to be reported as wages on Form W-2. See § 1.1461-1(c) for applicable reporting requirements for amounts paid to foreign persons.

(o) Per diem of certain alien trainees described under section 1441(c)(6).

(p) Payments made to the following persons:

(1) A corporation described in § 1.6049-4(c)(1)(ii)(A), except with respect to payments made to a corporation after December 31, 1997 for attorneys' fees, and except a corporation engaged in providing medical and health care services or engaged in the billing and collecting of payments in respect to the providing of medical and health care services. However, no reporting is required where payment is made to a hospital or extended care facility described in section 501(c)(3) which is exempt from taxation under section 501(a) or to a hospital or extended care facility owned and operated by the United States, a State, the District of Columbia, a possession of the United States, or a political subdivision, agency or instrumentality of any of the foregoing. For reporting requirements as to payments by cooperatives, and to certain other payments, see sections 6042, 6044, and 6049 and the regulations thereunder in this part.

(2) An organization exempt from taxation under section 501(a), as described in § 1.6049-4(c)(1)(ii)(B)(*1*), or an individual retirement plan, as described in § 1.6049-4(c)(1)(ii)(C).

(3) The United States, as described in § 1.6049-4(c)(1)(ii)(D).

(4) A State, the District of Columbia, a possession of the United States, or any political subdivision of any of the foregoing, as described in § 1.6049-4(c)(1)(ii)(E).

(5) A foreign government or political subdivision of a foreign government, as described in § 1.6049-4(c)(1)(ii)(F).

(6) An international organization, as described in § 1.6049-4(c)(1)(ii)(G).

(7) A foreign central bank of issue, as described in § 1.6049-4(c)(1)(ii)(H) and the Bank for International Settlements.

(8) Any wholly owned agency or instrumentality of any person described in paragraph (p)(2), (3), (4), (5), (6), or (7) of this section. [Reg. § 1.6041-3.]

□ [*T.D. 6364, 2-13-59. Amended by T.D. 6628, 12-27-62; T.D. 6966, 8-7-68; T.D. 7000, 1-17-69; T.D. 7119, 6-1-71; T.D. 7284, 8-2-73; T.D. 8151, 8-13-87; T.D. 8193, 4-12-88; T.D. 8276, 12-7-89; T.D. 8324, 12-14-90; T.D. 8734, 10-6-97 (T.D. 8804 delayed the effective date of T.D. 8734 from January 1, 1999, to January 1, 2000; T.D. 8856 further delayed the effective date of T.D. 8734 until January 1, 2001); T.D. 8804, 12-30-98; T.D. 9010, 7-25-2002 and T.D. 9270, 7-12-2006.*]

[Reg. § 1.6041-4]

§ 1.6041-4. Foreign-related items and other exceptions.—(a) *Exempted foreign-related items.*— (1) Returns of information are not required for payments that a payor can, prior to payment, reliably associate with documentation upon which it may rely to treat as made to a foreign beneficial owner in accordance with § 1.1441-1(e)(1)(ii) or as made to a foreign payee in accordance with § 1.6049-5(d)(1) or presumed to be made to a foreign payee under § 1.6049-5(d)(2), (3), (4), or (5). Returns of information are also not required for a payment that a payor or middleman can, prior to payment, reliably associate with documentation upon which it may rely to treat as made to a foreign intermediary or flow-through entity in accordance with § 1.1441-1(b) if it obtains from the intermediary or flow-through entity a withholding statement described in § 1.6049-5(b)(14) that allocates the payment to a chapter 4 withholding rate pool (as defined in § 1.6049-4(f)(5)) or specific payees to which withholding applies under chapter 4. Payments excepted from reporting under this paragraph (a)(1) may be reportable, for purposes of chapter 3 of the Internal Revenue Code (Code), under § 1.1461-1(b) and (c) and, for purposes of chapter 4 of the Code, under § 1.1474-1(d)(2). The provisions in § 1.6049-5(c) regarding documentation of foreign status shall apply for purposes of this paragraph (a)(1). The provisions in § 1.6049-5(c)(5) regarding the definitions of U.S. payor and non-U.S. payor shall also apply for purposes of this paragraph (a)(1). See § 1.1441-1(b)(3)(iii)(B) and (C) for special payee rules regarding scholarships, grants, pensions, annuities, etc. The provisions of § 1.1441-1 shall apply by substituting the term "payor" for the term "withholding agent" and without regard to the fact that the provisions apply only to amounts subject to withholding under chapter 3 of the Code and the regulations under that chapter.

(2) Returns of information are not required for payments of amounts from sources outside the United States (determined under the provisions of part I, subchapter N, chapter 1 of the Code and the regulations under those provisions) paid by a non-U.S. payor or non-U.S. middleman and that are paid and received outside the United States. For a definition of non-U.S. payor and non-U.S. middleman, see § 1.6049-5(c)(5). For circumstances in which an amount is considered to be paid and received outside the United States, see § 1.6049-4(f)(16).

(3) If a foreign intermediary, as described in § 1.1441-1(c)(13), or a U.S. branch that is not treated as a U.S. person receives a payment from a payor, which payment the payor can reliably associate with a valid withholding certificate described in § 1.1441-1(e)(3)(ii) or (iii), or § 1.1441-1(e)(3)(v), respectively, furnished by such intermediary or branch, then the intermediary or branch is not required to report such payment when it, in turn, pays the amount, unless, and to the extent, the intermediary or branch knows that the payment is required to be reported under this section and was not so reported. For example, if a U.S. branch described in § 1.1441-1(b)(2)(iv) fails to provide information regarding U.S. persons that are not exempt from reporting under § 1.6041-3(q) to the person from whom the U.S. branch receives the payment, the U.S. branch must report the payment on an information return. See, however, paragraph (a)(7) of this section for when reporting under section 6041is coordinated with reporting under chapter 4 of the Code or an applicable IGA (as defined in § 1.6049-4(f)(7)). The exception described in this paragraph (a)(3) for amounts paid by a foreign

intermediary shall not apply to a qualified intermediary that assumes reporting responsibility under chapter 61 of the Code with respect to amounts reportable under the agreement described in § 1.1441-1(e)(5)(iii).

(4) Returns of information are not required for amounts paid with respect to notional principal contracts referred to in § 1.863-7 or 1.988-2(e) which the payor may treat as effectively connected income of a foreign payee under the provisions of § 1.1441-4(a)(3) or if the payee provides a representation in a master agreement that governs the transactions in notional principal contracts between the parties (for example, an International Swap and Derivatives Association (ISDA) Agreement, including the Schedule thereto) or in the confirmation on the particular notional principal contract transaction that the counterparty is a foreign person. See, however, § 1.1461-1(c)(2)(i) for applicable reporting requirements.

(5) Returns of information are not required for the period that the amounts paid represent assets blocked as described in § 1.1441-2(e)(3). The exemption in this paragraph (a)(5) shall terminate when payment is deemed to occur in accordance with the provisions of § 1.1441-2(e)(3).

(6) For rules concerning direct sellers, see § 1.6041A-1(d)(3)(i)(C).

(7) Returns of information are not required for payments with respect to which a return is not required by applying the rules of § 1.6049-4(c)(4) (by substituting the term "a payment subject to reporting under section 6041" for the term "an interest payment").

(b) *Joint owners.*—Amounts paid to joint owners for which a certificate or documentation is required as a condition for being exempt from reporting under paragraph (a) of this section are presumed made to U.S. payees who are not exempt recipients if, prior to payment, the payor or middleman cannot reliably associate the payment either with a Form W-9 furnished by one of the joint owners in the manner required in §§ 31.3406(d)-1 through 31.3406(d)-5, or with documentation described in paragraph (a)(1) of this section furnished by each joint owner upon which the payor or middleman can rely to treat each joint owner as a foreign payee or foreign beneficial owner. However, in the case of a withholdable payment (as defined in § 1.6049-4(f)(15)) made to joint payees, if any joint payee does not appear to be an individual, the payment is presumed made to a foreign payee that is a nonparticipating FFI (as defined in § 1.1471-1(b)(82)). See § 1.1471-3(f)(7).

(c) *Conversion into United States dollars of amounts paid in foreign currency.*—For rules concerning foreign currency conversion, see § 1.6049-4(d)(3)(i).

(d) *Effective/applicability date.*—This section applies to payments made on or after January 6, 2017. (For payments made after June 30, 2014, and before January 6, 2017, see this section as in effect and contained in 26 CFR part 1, as revised April 1, 2016. For payments made after December 31, 2002, and before July 1, 2014, see this

section as in effect and contained in 26 CFR part 1, as revised April 1, 2013.) [Reg. § 1.6041-4.]

☐ [*T.D.* 6364, 2-13-59. *Amended by T.D.* 8734, 10-6-97; *T.D.* 8804, 12-30-98; *T.D.* 8856, 12-29-99; *T.D.* 8881, 5-15-2000, *T.D.* 9658, 2-28-2014 *and T.D.* 9808, 12-30-2016.]

[Reg. § 1.6041-5]

§1.6041-5. Information as to actual owner.—When a person receiving a payment described in section 6041 is not the actual owner of the income received, the name and address of the actual owner shall be furnished upon demand of the person paying the income, and in default of compliance with such demand the payee becomes liable for the penalties provided. See section 7203. [Reg. § 1.6041-5.]

☐ [*T.D.* 6364, 2-13-59.]

[Reg. § 1.6041-6]

§1.6041-6. Returns made on Forms 1096 and 1099 under section 6041; contents and time and place for filing.—[Reserved]. For further guidance, see § 1.6041-6T. [Reg. § 1.6041-6.]

☐ [*T.D.* 6364, 2-13-59. *Amended by T.D.* 6628, 12-27-62; *T.D.* 7284, 8-2-73, *T.D.* 8895, 8-17-2000 *and T.D.* 9821, 7-18-2017.]

[Reg. § 1.6041-6T]

§1.6041-6T. Returns made on Forms 1096 and 1099 under section 6041; contents and time and place for filing (temporary).—(a) *In general.*—Except as provided in paragraph (b) of this section, returns made under section 6041 on Forms 1096 and 1099 for any calendar year shall be filed on or before February 28 (March 31 if filed electronically) of the following year with any of the Internal Revenue Service Centers, the addresses of which are listed in the instructions for such forms. The name and address of the person making the payment and the name and address of the recipient of the payment shall be stated on Form 1099. If the present address of the recipient is not available, the last known post office address must be given. See section 6109 and the regulations thereunder for rules requiring the inclusion of identifying numbers in Form 1099.

(b) *Exception.*—Returns made on Form 1099 reporting nonemployee compensation shall be filed on or before January 31 of the year following the calendar year to which such returns relate.

(c) *Applicability date.*—This section applies to returns filed on or after July 20, 2017. Section 1.6041-6 (as contained in 26 CFR part 1, revised April 2017) applies to returns filed before July 20, 2017.

(d) *Expiration date.*—The applicability of this section will expire on or before July 17, 2020. [Temporary Reg. § 1.6041-6T.]

☐ *T.D.* 9821, 7-18-2017.]

[Reg. § 1.6041-7]

§1.6041-7. Magnetic media requirement.—(a) *General.*—For rules relating to permission to submit the information required by Form 1099 or W-2 on magnetic tape or other media, see § 1.9101-1. See also paragraph (b)(2) of

§ 31.6011(a)-7 of this chapter (Employment Tax Regulations) for additional rules relating to Form W-2. High-volume filers of information returns must file their returns on magnetic media. See section 6011(e) and § 301.6011-2 of this chapter (Procedure and Administration Regulations) for the requirements for filing on magnetic media.

(b) *Returns on magnetic tape by departments of health care carriers.*—(1) For calendar years beginning on or after January 1, 1971, a health care carrier, or an agent thereof, making payment of fees or other compensation to providers of medical and health care services, may make a separate return on magnetic tape for each separate department within a specific line of such carrier's business, so long as all of such returns taken together contain all of the information required by section 6041 with respect to each provider of medical and health care services to whom such health care carrier makes payments aggregating $600 or more during the calendar year. Examples of separate departments within a specific line of such carrier's business (such as health and accident insurance) include, but are not limited to, separate departments to process claims of individual and group policyholders; and separate departments established along geographic lines.

(2) For purposes of this paragraph, the term "health care carrier" means any person making health care payments: (i) In exchange for the payment of a premium, (ii) in accordance with an employee benefit program, or (iii) in connection with a government-sponsored health care program. [Reg. § 1.6041-7.]

☐ *[T.D. 6883, 5-2-66. Amended by T.D. 7106, 4-2-71 and T.D. 8734, 10-6-97 (T.D. 8804 delayed the effective date of T.D. 8734 from January 1, 1999, to January 1, 2000; T.D. 8856 further delayed the effective date of T.D. 8734 until January 1, 2001).]*

[Reg. § 1.6041-8]

§ 1.6041-8. Cross-reference to penalties.—For provisions relating to the penalty provided for failure to file timely a correct information return required under section 6041(a) or (b), see § 301.6721-1 of this chapter (Procedure and Administration Regulations). For provisions relating to the penalty provided for failure to furnish timely a correct payee statement required under section 6041(d), see § 301.6722-1 of this chapter. See § 301.6724-1 of this chapter for the waiver of a penalty if the failure is due to reasonable cause and is not due to willful neglect. [Reg. § 1.6041-8.]

☐ *[T.D. 8734, 10-6-97 (T.D. 8804 delayed the effective date of T.D. 8734 from January 1, 1999, to January 1, 2000; T.D. 8856 further delayed the effective date of T.D. 8734 until January 1, 2001).]*

[Reg. § 1.6041-9]

§ 1.6041-9. Coordination with reporting rules for widely held fixed investment trusts under § 1.671-5.—See § 1.671-5 for the reporting rules for widely held fixed investment trusts (WHFIT) (as defined under that section). For purposes of section 6041, middlemen and trustees of WHFITs are deemed to have management and oversight functions in connection with payments made by the WHFIT. [Reg. § 1.6041-9.]

☐ *[T.D. 9241, 1-23-2006.]*

[Reg. § 1.6041-10]

§ 1.6041-10. Return of information as to payments of winnings from bingo, keno, and slot machine play.—(a) *In general.*—Every person engaged in a trade or business (as defined in § 1.6041-1(b)) and who, in the course of such trade or business, makes a payment of reportable gambling winnings (defined in paragraph (b)(1) of this section) must make an information return with respect to such payment. Unless the provisions of paragraph (g) of this section (regarding aggregate reporting) apply, a separate information return is required with respect to each payment of reportable gambling winnings.

(b) *Definitions.*—(1) *Reportable gambling winnings.*—(i) For purposes of this section, the term reportable gambling winnings is defined as follows:

(A) For bingo, the term "reportable gambling winnings" means winnings of $1,200 or more from one bingo game, without reduction for the amount wagered. All winnings received from all wagers made during one bingo game are combined (for example, all winnings from all cards played during one bingo game are combined).

(B) For keno, the term "reportable gambling winnings" means winnings of $1,500 or more from one keno game reduced by the amount wagered on the same keno game. All winnings received from all wagers made during one keno game are combined (for example, all winnings from all "ways" on a multi-way keno ticket are combined).

(C) For slot machine play, the term "reportable gambling winnings" means winnings of $1,200 or more from one slot machine play, without reduction for the amount wagered.

(ii) Winnings and wagers from different types of games are not combined to determine if the reporting threshold is satisfied. Bingo, keno, and slot machine play are different types of games.

(iii) Winnings include the fair market value of a payment in any medium other than cash.

(iv) The amount wagered in the case of a free play is zero.

Reg. § 1.6041-10(b)(1)(iv)

(2) *Information reporting period.*—(i) *In general.*—For purposes of paragraph (g) of this section, the "information reporting period" begins when a patron places the first wager on a particular type of game at a gaming establishment, as defined in paragraph (b)(2)(iv) of this section, and ends when the patron places his or her last wager on the same type of game at the same gaming establishment before the end of the "information reporting period." An information reporting period is a 24-hour period. A payor may select a calendar day (as defined in paragraph (b)(2)(ii) of this section) or a gaming day (as defined in paragraph (b)(2)(iii) of this section) as the information reporting period for purposes of the aggregate reporting method in paragraph (g) of this section. For purposes of this paragraph (b)(2), time is determined by the time zone of the location where the patron places the wager. A payor must use the same information reporting period (a calendar day or gaming day) to report all "reportable gambling winnings" paid during the calendar year. Once selected, a payor may not change its information reporting period during a calendar year. Any changes to a payor's information reporting period from one calendar year to another must be implemented on January 1.

(ii) *Calendar day.*—A calendar day is determined with reference to a period beginning at 12 a.m. and ending no later than 11:59 p.m. of the same calendar day.

(iii) *Gaming day.*—(A) *In general.*—A gaming day is a 24-hour period other than a calendar day (as defined in paragraph (b)(2)(ii) of this section) selected by the payor, subject to the special rules for December 31 and January 1 in paragraphs (b)(2)(iii)(B) and (C) of this section.

(B) *Special rule for December 31.*—For purposes of paragraph (b)(2)(iii) of this section, the gaming day that begins on December 31 of any calendar year ends at 11:59 p.m. on December 31, regardless of the time on December 31 on which that gaming day began.

(C) *Special rule for January 1.*—For purposes of paragraph (b)(2)(iii) of this section, the gaming day of January 1 begins at 12:00 a.m. on January 1, regardless of the time and calendar day on which that gaming day ends, and may extend beyond 24 hours.

(iv) *Gaming establishment.*—For purposes of this section, a gaming establishment is a business entity of a payor of reportable gambling winnings with respect to bingo, keno, or slot machine play, and includes all gaming establishments owned by such payor using the same employer identification number (EIN) issued to such payor in accordance with section 6109.

(v) *Examples.*—The following examples illustrate the provisions of paragraph (b)(2) of this section.

Example 1. Casino R uses the aggregate reporting method under paragraph (g) of this section to report certain reportable gambling winnings. For other regulatory purposes, Casino R uses a gaming day that begins at 3 a.m. and ends at 2:59 a.m. the following calendar day. Casino R chooses to use its gaming day as its information reporting period for purposes of paragraph (b)(2) of this section during Year 1. Accordingly, the information reporting period for purposes of paragraph (g) of this section for each day during Year 1 begins at 3 a.m. and ends at 2:59 a.m. the following day. The information reporting period for December 31 of Year 1 begins at 3 a.m. on December 31 of Year 1 and ends at 11:59 p.m. on December 31 of Year 1. The information reporting period for January 1 of Year 2 begins at 12 a.m. on January 1 of Year 2 and ends at 2:59 a.m. on January 2 of Year 2.

Example 2. The facts are the same as Example 1, except Casino R uses a calendar day as its information reporting period for purposes of paragraph (b)(2) of this section during Year 1. Accordingly, the information reporting period for purpose of paragraph (g) of this section for each day during Year 1 begins at 12 a.m. and ends at 11:59 p.m. on the same day.

Example 3. Casino R uses the aggregate reporting method under paragraph (g) of this section to report certain reportable gambling winnings. For other regulatory purposes, Casino R uses a gaming day that begins at 9:00 p.m. and ends at 8:59 p.m. the following calendar day. Casino R chooses to use its gaming day as its information reporting period for purposes of paragraph (b)(2) of this section during Year 1. Accordingly, the information reporting period for purposes of paragraph (g) of this section for each day during Year 1 begins at 9:00 p.m. and ends at 8:59 p.m. the following day. The information reporting period for December 31 of Year 1 begins at 9:00 p.m. on December 30 and ends at 8:59 p.m. on December 31. A second information reporting period for December 31 then begins at 9:00 p.m. on December 31 and ends at 11:59 p.m. on December 31. The information reporting period for January 1 of Year 2 begins at 12:00 a.m. on January 1 and ends at 8:59 p.m. on January 1 of Year 2.

Example 4. Casino R uses the aggregate reporting method under paragraph (g) of this section to report certain reportable gambling winnings. In Year 1, Casino R chooses to use a "gaming day" that begins at 3 a.m. and ends at 2:59 a.m. the following day as its information reporting period. During the course of Year 1, Casino R decides that it would like to change its information reporting period to instead begin at 5 a.m. and end at 4:59 a.m. the following day. Casino R must wait until January 1 of Year 2 to implement such a change. On January 1 of Year 2, Casino R's information reporting period will begin at 12 a.m. and end at 4:59 a.m. on January 2. On December 31 of Year 2, Casino R's information reporting period will begin at 5 a.m. and end at 11:59 p.m.

(3) *Slot machine.*—The term "slot machine" means a device that, by application of the ele-

ment of chance, may deliver, or entitle the person playing or operating the device to receive cash, premiums, merchandise, or tokens whether or not the device is operated by insertion of a coin, token, or similar object.

(c) *Prescribed form; time and place for filing the return.*—The return described in paragraph (a) of this section is a Form W-2G, "Certain Gambling Winnings." The Form W-2G must be filed with the appropriate Internal Revenue Service location designated in the instructions to the form on or before February 28 (March 31, if filed electronically) of the year following the calendar year in which the reportable gambling winnings were paid. See section 6011 and §1.6011-2 for requirements to file electronically.

(d) *Information included on the return.*—(1) *In general.*—Each return required by paragraph (a) of this section must contain:

(i) The name, address, and taxpayer identification number of the payor;

(ii) The name, address, and taxpayer identification number of the payee;

(iii) A general description of the two types of identification (as described in paragraph (e) of this section), one of which must have the payee's photograph on it (except in the case of tribal member identification cards in certain circumstances as described in paragraph (d)(2) of this section) that the payor relied on to verify the payee's name, address, and taxpayer identification number;

(iv) The date and amount of payment;

(v) The type of wagering transaction (bingo, keno, or slot machine play);

(vi) In the case of a bingo or keno game, any number, color, or other designation assigned to the game for which the payment is made;

(vii) In the case of slot machine play, the identification number of the slot machine(s) (for example, location and asset number);

(viii) Any other information required by the forms, instructions, revenue procedures, or other applicable guidance published in the Internal Revenue Bulletin.

(2) *Special rule for tribal member identification cards.*—A tribal member identification card need not contain the payee's photograph to meet the identification requirement described in paragraph (d)(1)(iii) of this section if:

(i) The payee is a member of a federally recognized Indian tribe;

(ii) The payee presents the payor with a tribal member identification card issued by a federally recognized Indian tribe stating that the payee is a member of such tribe; and

(iii) The payor is a gaming establishment (as described in paragraph (b)(2)(iv) of this section) owned or licensed (in accordance with 25 U.S.C. 2710) by the tribal government that issued the tribal member identification card referred to in (d)(2)(ii).

(3) *Special rule for optional aggregate reporting method.*—In the case of aggregate reporting

under paragraph (g) of this section, the amount of the payment in paragraph (d)(1)(iv) of this section is the aggregate amount of payments of reportable gambling winnings from the same type of game (bingo, keno, or slot machine play) made to the same payee during the same information reporting period (as defined in paragraph (b)(2) of this section). Unless otherwise provided in forms, instructions, or other guidance, in the case of aggregate reporting under paragraph (g) of this section, the information required by paragraphs (d)(1)(v) through (viii) of this section must be maintained by the payor as described in paragraph (g)(3) of this section.

(e) *Identification.*—The following items are treated as identification for purposes of paragraph (d)(1)(iii) of this section—

(1) Government-issued identification (for example, a driver's license, passport, social security card, military identification card, tribal member identification card issued by a federally recognized Indian tribe, or voter registration card) in the name of the payee; and

(2) A Form W-9, "Request for Taxpayer Identification Number and Certification," signed by the payee, that includes the payee's name, address, taxpayer identification number, and other information required by the form. A Form W-9 is not acceptable for this purpose if the payee has modified the form (other than pursuant to instructions to the form) or if the payee has deleted the jurat or other similar provisions by which the payee certifies or affirms the correctness of the statements contained on the form.

(f) *Furnishing a statement to the payee.*—Every payor required to make a return under paragraph (a) of this section must also make and furnish to each payee, with respect to each payment of reportable gambling winnings, a written statement that contains the information that is required to be included on the return under paragraph (d) of this section. The payor must furnish the statement to the payee on or before January 31st of the year following the calendar year in which payment of the reportable gambling winnings is made. The statement will be considered furnished to the payee if it is provided to the payee at the time of payment or if it is mailed to the payee on or before January 31st of the year following the calendar year in which payment was made.

(g) *Aggregate reporting of bingo, keno, and slot machine winnings.*—(1) *In general.*—In lieu of filing a separate information return for each payment of reportable gambling winnings as required by paragraph (a) of this section, a payor may use the aggregate reporting method (defined in paragraph (g)(2) of this section) to report reportable gambling winnings from bingo, keno, or slot machine play. A payor using the aggregate reporting method to file information returns under paragraph (a) of this section must also furnish statements to the payee under paragraph (f) of this section using the aggregate reporting method.

Reg. §1.6041-10(g)(1)

(2) *Aggregate reporting method defined.*— (i) The aggregate reporting method is a method of reporting more than one payment of reportable gambling winnings from the same type of game (bingo, keno, or slot machine play) made to the same payee during the same information reporting period (as defined in this paragraph (b)(2) of this section) on one information return or statement.

(ii) A payor may use the aggregate reporting method for payments to some payees and not others, at its own discretion. In addition, with respect to a single payee, the payor may use the aggregate reporting method to report winnings from one type of game, but not for winnings from another type of game.

(iii) Failure to report some reportable gambling winnings from a particular type of game during one information reporting period to a particular payee under the aggregate reporting method (for whatever reason, including because the winnings are not permitted to be reported using the aggregate reporting method under paragraph (g)(4) of this section) will not disqualify the payor from using the aggregate reporting method to report other reportable gambling winnings from that type of game during that information reporting period to that payee. The payor may stop using the aggregate reporting method for a particular payee or for all payees before the end of the payor's information reporting period for any reason.

(3) *Recordkeeping under the aggregate reporting method.*—A payor using the aggregate reporting method must maintain a record of every payment of reportable gambling winnings from the same type of game made to the same payee during the information reporting period that will be reported using the aggregate reporting method. Every individual that the payor has determined is responsible for an entry in the record must confirm the information in the entry by signing the record in a manner that will enable the signature to be associated with the relevant entry. Each payment of a reportable gambling winning made to the same payee and reported under the aggregate reporting method must have its own entry in the record, however, the information required by paragraphs (d)(1)(i) through (iii) of this section is not required to be recorded more than one time per information reporting period. A payor that uses the aggregate reporting method must retain a copy of the record in its files. The record (which may be electronic provided the requirements set forth in forms, instructions, or guidance published in the Internal Revenue Bulletin are met) must include the following information about each payment:

(i) The payee's signature confirming the information in the record;

(ii) The information required under paragraph (d) of this section;

(iii) The time of the win resulting in the reportable gambling winnings;

(iv) The total amount of reportable gambling winnings with respect to all payments to the payee during the information reporting period;

(v) The amount of reportable gambling winnings with respect to each particular payment;

(vi) The method of payment to the payee (for example, cash, check, voucher, credit, token, or chips); and

(vii) The name and unique identification number of the individual who the payor has determined is responsible for ensuring that the entry with respect to the reportable gambling winnings (including the general description of two types of identification used to verify the payee's name, address, and taxpayer identification number) is complete and accurate and who is authorized to perform that function by the applicable gaming regulatory control authority. Such individual may or may not be the same individual who prepared the entry.

(4) *When the aggregate reporting method may not be used.*—A payor cannot use the aggregate reporting method if—

(i) The payment is to a foreign person, as described in section 1.6041-10(h);

(ii) The payor knows or has reason to know that the person making the wager is not the person entitled to the winnings or is not the only person entitled to the winnings (regardless of whether the person making the wager furnishes a Form 5754, "Statement by Person(s) Receiving Gambling Winnings"); or

(iii) Backup withholding under section 3406(a) applies to the payment.

(5) *Examples.*—The following examples illustrate the provisions of this section. For each example, assume that for purposes of the aggregate reporting method in paragraph (g) of this section, Casino R's "information reporting period" for all calendar years is a gaming day that begins at 3 a.m. and ends at 2:59 a.m. the following day (except for January 1 and December 31) and that individuals C, D, and E are U.S. persons.

Example 1. On Day 1, between 7 a.m. and 4 p.m., C places five wagers at casino R on five different slot machines. The first two wagers result in no win. The third wager results in a $1,500 win. The fourth wager results in a $2,500 win. The fifth wager results in an $800 win:

(i) Under paragraph (b)(1)(i)(C) of this section, there are reportable gambling winnings from the slot machine play of $4,000 ($1,500 + $2,500). The $800 win is not a reportable gambling winning from slot machine play because it does not equal or exceed the $1,200 threshold.

(ii) Because all of the amounts were won on the same type of game (even though each of the winnings occurred on different machines) during the same information reporting period, R is permitted to use the aggregate reporting method under this paragraph (g). If R decides not to use the aggregate reporting method, a separate Form W-2G would have to be filed and furnished for the payment of reportable gambling winnings of

$1,500 and for the payment of reportable gambling winnings of $2,500. However, if R decides to use the aggregate reporting method, R may report total reportable gambling winnings from slot machine play of $4,000 ($1,500 + $2,500) on one Form W-2G.

Example 2. Assume the same facts as *Example 1*, except that in addition to the winnings described in *Example 1*, at 5 a.m. on Day 2, C wins $3,250 from one slot machine play at casino R. Even though C played the same type of game (slot machine play) on Day 1 and Day 2, under paragraph (b)(2) of this section, the win at 5 a.m. on Day 2 is a win during a separate information reporting period. Under paragraph (g)(2)(i) of this section, the $3,250 of reportable gambling winnings on Day 2 cannot be aggregated with the reportable gambling winnings of $4,000 from Day 1 on a single Form W-2G. Accordingly, if R uses the aggregate reporting method, R must file two Forms W-2G with respect to C's reportable gambling winnings on Day 1 and Day 2. R must report $4,000 of reportable gambling winnings from slot machine play paid to C on Day 1 on the first Form W-2G, and $3,250 of reportable gambling winnings from slot machine play paid to C on Day 2 on the second Form W-2G.

Example 3. On December 31 of Year 1 at 4:00 p.m., C wins $10,000 from one slot machine play at casino R. At 12:30 a.m. on January 1 of Year 2, C wins $4,000 from one slot machine play at casino R. Under paragraphs (b)(2)(iii)(B) and (C) of this section, the win at 4 p.m. on December 31 of Year 1 and the win at 12:30 a.m. on January 1 of Year 2 are wins during different information reporting periods. Under paragraph (g)(2)(i) of this section, the $4,000 of reportable gambling winnings on January 1 cannot be aggregated with the reportable gambling winnings of $10,000 from December 31 on a single Form W-2G. Accordingly, if R uses the aggregate reporting method, R must file two Forms W-2G with respect to C's reportable gambling winnings on Day 1 and Day 2. R must report $10,000 of reportable gambling winnings from slot machine play paid to C on December 31 on the first Form W-2G and $4,000 of reportable gambling winnings from slot machine play paid to C on January 1 on the second Form W-2G.

Example 4. Assume the same facts as example 3, except that C also wins $5,000 from one slot machine play at 3:30 p.m. on January 1 and $7,000 from one slot machine play at 1:30 a.m. on January 2. Under the special rule of paragraph (b)(2)(iii) of this section, the "information reporting period" begins at 12:00 a.m. on January 1 and extends until the start of the next information reporting period, in this case 2:59 a.m. on January 2. Under paragraph (b)(1)(C) of this section, Casino R will pay C a total of $26,000 ($10,000 + $4,000 + $5,000 + $7,000) in reportable gambling winnings; however, $10,000 must be reported in Year 1, and $16,000 must be reported in Year 2. Because all of the amounts won in Year 2 were won on the same type of game and during the same information reporting period, R is permit-

ted to use the aggregate reporting method under this paragraph (g). If R decides to use the aggregate reporting method, R may report $10,000 of reportable gambling winnings from slot machine play paid to C on December 31 on the first Form W-2G and $16,000 of total reportable gambling winnings from slot machine play paid to C on January 1 on the second Form W-2G.

Example 5. At 2 p.m. on Day 1, D won $2,000 (after reducing the amount of the win by the amount wagered) playing one keno game at casino R. D provides R with his driver's license. The driver's license has D's photograph on it, as well as D's name and address. The driver's license does not include D's social security number. D cannot remember his social security number and has no other identification at the time with his social security number on it. D does not provide R with his social security number before R pays the winnings to D. Because D cannot remember his social security number, D cannot complete and sign a Form W-9. R deducts and withholds $560 (28 percent of $2,000) under the backup withholding provisions of section 3406(a) and pays the remaining $1,440 in winnings to D. D returns to casino R and at 6 p.m. on Day 1 wins $1,500 (after reducing the amount of the win by the amount wagered) in one keno game. D provides R with his driver's license as well as D's social security card. R generally uses the aggregate reporting method and in all cases where it is used, R complies with the requirements of this paragraph (g). At 8 p.m. and 10 p.m. on Day 1, D wins an additional $1,800 and $1,700 (after reducing the amount of the win by the amount wagered), respectively, from two different keno games. For each of these two wins, an employee of R obtains the information from D required by this paragraph (g):

(i) Under paragraph (b)(1)(i)(B) of this section, each of D's wins from the four games of keno on Day 1 ($2,000, $1,500, $1,800, and $1,700) are reportable gambling winnings. Because D's first win on Day 1 was at 2 p.m. and D's last win on Day 1 was at 10 p.m., all of D's reportable gambling winnings from keno are won during the same information reporting period. Because R satisfies the requirements of paragraph (g)(2)(i), R may use the aggregate reporting method to report D's reportable gambling winnings from keno. However, pursuant to paragraph (g)(4)(iii) of this section, the $2,000 payment made to D at 2 p.m. cannot be reported under the aggregate reporting method because that payment was subject to backup withholding. Accordingly, if R uses the aggregate reporting method under this paragraph (g), R will have to file two Forms W-2G with respect to D's reportable gambling winnings from keno on Day 1. On the first Form W-2G, R will report $2,000 of reportable gambling winnings and $560 of backup withholding with respect to the 2 p.m. win from keno, and, on the second Form W-2G, R will report $5,000 of reportable gambling winnings from keno (representing the three payments of $1,500, $1,800, and $1,700 that D won between 6 p.m. and 10 p.m. on Day 1).

Reg. §1.6041-10(g)(5)

Example 6. In one information reporting period on Day 1, E won five reportable gambling winnings from five different bingo games at a casino R. R generally uses the aggregate reporting method and in all cases where it is used, R complies with the requirements of this paragraph (g). Although E signed the entry in the record R maintains for payment of the first four reportable gambling winnings, E refuses to sign the entry in the record for the fifth payment of reportable gambling winnings. R may use the aggregate reporting method for the first four payments of reportable gambling winnings to E. However, because the entry in the record for the fifth payment of reportable gambling winnings does not include E's signature, as required by paragraph (g)(3)(i) of this section, that payment may not be reported under the aggregate reporting method. Accordingly, if R uses the aggregate reporting method under paragraph (g) of this section, R must prepare two Forms W-2G as follows: On the first Form W-2G, R must report the first four payments of reportable gambling winnings from bingo made to E on Day 1. On the second Form W-2G, R must report the fifth payment of reportable gambling winnings from bingo made to E on Day 1.

(h) *Payments to foreign persons.*—See § 1.6041-4 regarding payments to foreign persons. See § 1.6049-5(d) for determining whether the payee is a foreign person.

(i) *Effective/applicability date.*—Section 1.6041-10(b)(2), concerning payor-selected "information reporting periods," applies to payments of reportable gambling winnings from bingo, keno, or slot machine play made on or after January 1 of the year following the date these regulations are published in the **Federal Register**. All other sections contained herein apply to payments of reportable gambling winnings from bingo, keno, or slot machine play made on or after December 30, 2016.

(j) *Cross-references for certain gambling winnings.*—For provisions relating to backup withholding for winnings from bingo, keno, and slot machine play and other reportable gambling winnings, see § 31.3406(g)-2(d). For provisions relating to withholding and reporting for gambling winnings from lotteries, sweepstakes, wagering pools, and other wagering transactions, including a wagering transaction in a parimutuel pool with respect to horse races, dog races, or jai alai, see § 31.3402(q)-1. [Reg. § 1.6041-10.]

☐ [T.D. 9807, 12-29-2016.]

[Reg. § 1.6041A-1]

§ 1.6041A-1. Returns regarding payments of remuneration for services and certain direct sales.—(a) through (c) [Reserved].

(d) *Exceptions to return requirement.*—[Reserved].

(1) and (2) [Reserved].

(3) *Foreign transactions.*—(i) *In general.*—No return shall be required under section 6041A with respect to payments described in this paragraph (d)(3).

(A) Returns of information are not required for payments that a payor can, prior to payment, associate with documentation upon which it may rely to treat as made to a foreign beneficial owner in accordance with § 1.1441-1(e)(1)(ii) or as made to a foreign payee in accordance with § 1.6049-5(d)(1) or presumed to be made to a foreign payee under § 1.6049-5(d)(2), (3), (4), or (5). However, such payments may be reportable under § 1.1461-1(b) and (c). For purposes of this paragraph (d)(3)(i)(A), the provisions in § 1.6049-5(c) (regarding rules applicable to documentation of foreign status and definition of U.S. payor and non-U.S. payor) shall apply. The provisions of § 1.1441-1 shall apply by substituting the term *payor* for the term *withholding agent*.

(B) Returns of information are not required for payments of remuneration for services from sources outside the United States (determined under the provisions of part I, subchapter N, chapter 1 of the Internal Revenue Code and the regulations under those provisions) if payments are made outside the United States by a non-U.S. payor or non U.S. middleman. For a definition of non U.S. payor or non-U.S. middleman, see § 1.6049-5(c)(5). For circumstances in which a payment is considered to be made outside the United States, see § 1.6049-5(e).

(C) Returns of information are not required under sections 6041 or 6041A for amounts paid outside of the United States (within the meaning of § 1.6049-5(e)) as remuneration for services as a direct seller (within the meaning of section 3508) performed outside of the United States or for sales described in section 6041A(b) made outside of the United States of consumer products for resale outside of the United States.

(ii) *Payor.*—The term *payor* has the same meaning as described in § 1.6049-4(a)(2).

(iii) *Joint owners.*—Amounts paid to joint owners for which a certificate or documentation is required as a condition for being exempt from reporting under paragraph (d)(3)(i) of this section are presumed made to U.S. payees who are not exempt recipients if, prior to payment, the payor or middleman cannot reliably associate the payment either with a Form W-9 furnished by one of the joint owners in the manner required in §§ 31.3406(d)-1 through 31.3406(d)-5 of this chapter, or with documentation described in paragraph (d)(3)(i)(A) of this section furnished by each joint owner upon which it can rely to treat each joint owner as a foreign payee or foreign beneficial owner.

(iv) *Conversion into United States dollars of amounts paid in foreign currency.*—For rules concerning foreign currency conversion, see § 1.6049-4(d)(3)(i).

(v) *Effective date.*—The provisions of this paragraph (d)(3) apply to payments made after December 31, 2000.

(4) *Information returns required under section 6050W for calendar years beginning after December 31, 2010.*—(i) For payments made by payment card (as defined in § 1.6050W-1(b)(3)) or through a third party payment network (as defined in § 1.6050W-1(c)(3)) after December 31, 2010, that are required to be reported on an information return under section 6050W (relating to payment card and third party network transactions), the following rule applies. Transactions that otherwise would be reportable under both sections 6041A(a) and 6050W are reported under section 6050W and not section 6041A(a). For provisions relating to information reporting for payment card transactions and third party network transactions, see § 1.6050W-1. Solely for purposes of this paragraph, the de minimis threshold for third party network transactions in § 1.6050W-1(c)(4) is disregarded in determining whether the transaction is subject to reporting under section 6050W.

(ii) *Examples.*—The provisions of paragraph (d)(4) of this section are illustrated by the following examples:

Example 1. Service-recipient A, in the course of its business, pays remuneration of $600 to service provider B by credit card for services performed by B. B is one of a network of unrelated persons that has agreed to accept A's credit card as payment under an agreement that provides standards and mechanisms for settling the transactions between a merchant acquiring bank and the persons who accept the cards. Merchant acquiring bank Y is responsible for making the payment to B. Under paragraph (d)(4)(i) of this section, A is not required to file an information return under section 6041A(a) with respect to the transaction because Y, as the payment settlement entity for the payment card transaction, is required to file an information return under section 6050W.

Example 2. Service-recipient A, in the course of business, pays $600 of fixed or determinable income to B, a repairman, through a third party payment network. B is one of a substantial number of persons who have established accounts with Y, a third party settlement organization that provides standards and mechanisms for settling the transactions and guarantees payments to those persons for goods or services purchased through the network. Y is responsible for making the payment to B. Under paragraph (d)(4)(i) of this section, A is not required to file an information return under section 6041A(a) with respect to the transaction because the transaction is a third party network transaction that is subject to reporting under section 6050W. Solely for purposes of determining whether the transaction is subject to reporting under section 6050W, the de minimis threshold for third party network transactions in § 1.6050W-1(c)(4) is disregarded.

(iii) *Effective/applicability date.*—Paragraph (d)(4) of this section applies to payments made by payment card or through a third party payment network after December 31, 2010.

(e) [Reserved].

(f) *Statements to be furnished to persons with respect to whom information is required to be furnished.*—(1) [Reserved].

(2) *Time for furnishing statement.*—[Reserved].

(3) *Contents of statement.*—[Reserved].

(g) [Reserved].

(h) *Cross-reference to penalties.*—For provisions relating to the penalty provided for failure to file timely a correct information return required under section 6041A(a) or (b), see § 301.6721-1 of this chapter (Procedure and Administration Regulations). For provisions relating to the penalty provided for failure to furnish timely a correct payee statement required under section 6041A(e), see § 301.6722-1 of this chapter. See § 301.6724-1 of this chapter for the waiver of a penalty if the failure is due to reasonable cause and is not due to willful neglect. [Reg. § 1.6041A-1.]

☐ [*T.D.* 8734, 10-6-97. *Amended by T.D.* 8804, 12-30-98; *T.D.* 8856, 12-29-99; *T.D.* 8881, 5-15-2000 *and T.D.* 9496, 8-13-2010.]

[Reg. § 301.6042-1]

§ 301.6042-1. Returns of information regarding payments of dividends and corporate earnings and profits.—For provisions relating to the requirement of returns of information regarding payments of dividends and corporate earnings and profits, see § § 1.6042-1 to 1.6042-4, inclusive, of this chapter (Income Tax Regulations). [Reg. § 301.6042-1.]

☐ [*T.D.* 6498, 10-24-60. *Amended by T.D.* 6700, 1-6-64.]

[Reg. § 1.6042-2]

§ 1.6042-2. Returns of information as to dividends paid.—(a) *Requirement of reporting.*—(1) An information return on Form 1099 shall be made under section 6042(a) by—

(i) Every person who makes a payment of dividends (as defined in § 1.6042-3) to any other person during a calendar year. The information return shall show the aggregate amount of the dividends, the name, address, and taxpayer identifying number of the person to whom paid, the amount of tax deducted and withheld under section 3406 from the dividends, if any, and such other information as required by the forms. An information return is generally not required if the amount of dividends paid to the other person during the calendar year aggregates less than $10 or if the payment is made to a person who is an exempt recipient described in § 1.6049-4(c)(1)(ii) unless the payor backup withholds under section 3406 on such payment (because, for example, the payee has failed to furnish a Form W-9), in which case the payor must make a return under this section, unless the payor refunds the amount withheld pursuant to § 31.6413(a)-3 of this chapter. Further, a return of information is not required under this section for—

(A) Payments with respect to which a return is not required by applying the rules of

§ 1.6049-4(c)(4) (by substituting the term "dividend" for the term "interest"); or

    (B) Payments made by a paying agent on behalf of a corporation described in section 1297(a) with respect to a shareholder of the corporation if—

    (1) The paying agent obtains from the corporation a written certification signed by a person authorized to sign on behalf of the corporation, that states that the corporation is described in section 1297(a) for each calendar year during which the paying agent relies on the provisions of paragraph (a)(1)(i)(B) of this section, and the paying agent has no reason to know the written certification is unreliable or incorrect;

    (2) The paying agent identifies, prior to payment, the corporation as a participating FFI (including a reporting Model 2 FFI) (as defined in § 1.6049-4(f)(10) or (14), respectively), or reporting Model 1 FFI (as defined in § 1.6049-4(f)(13)), in accordance with the requirements of § 1.1471-3(d)(4) (substituting the terms "paying agent" and "corporation" for the terms "withholding agent" and "payee," respectively) and validates that status annually;

    (3) The paying agent obtains a written certification representing that the corporation shall report the payment as part of its reporting obligations under chapter 4 of the Code or an applicable IGA (as defined in § 1.6049-4(f)(7)) with respect to its U.S. accounts and provided the paying agent does not know that the corporation is not reporting the payment as required. The paying agent may rely on the written certification until there is a change in circumstances or the paying agent knows or has reason to know that the statement is unreliable or incorrect. A paying agent that knows that the corporation is not reporting the payment as required under chapter 4 of the Code or an applicable IGA (as defined in § 1.6049-4(f)(7)) must report all payments reportable under this section that it makes during the year in which it obtains such knowledge; and

    (4) The paying agent is not also acting in its capacity as a custodian, nominee, or other agent of the payee with respect to the payments.

    (ii) Every person, except to the extent that he acts as a nominee described in paragraph (a)(1)(iii) of this section, who receives payments of dividends as a nominee on behalf of another person shall make a return of information under this section for the calendar year of the payment. The information return shall show the aggregate amount of the dividends, the name, address, and taxpayer identification number of the person on whose behalf the dividends are received, the amount of tax deducted and withheld under section 3406 from the dividends, if any, and such other information as required by the forms. An information return is generally not required if the amount of the dividends received on behalf

of the other person during the calendar year aggregates less than $10. However, a return of information is not required under this section if—

    (A) The record owner is, pursuant to section 6012(a)(3) or (4) and § 1.6012-3, required to file a fiduciary return on Form 1041 that is filed for the estate or trust disclosing the name, address, and identifying number of both the record owner and actual owner and furnishes Form K-1 to each actual owner containing the information required to be shown on the form, including amounts withheld under section 3406;

    (B) The record owner is a nominee of a banking institution or trust company exercising trust powers, and such banking institution or trust company is, pursuant to section 6012(a)(3) or (4) and § 1.6012-3, required to file a fiduciary return on Form 1041 that is filed for the estate or trust disclosing the name, address, and identifying number of both the record owner and the actual owner and furnishes Form K-1 to each actual owner containing the information required to be shown on the form, including amounts withheld under section 3406; or

    (C) The record owner is a banking institution or trust company exercising trust powers, or a nominee thereof, and the actual owner is an organization exempt from taxation under section 501(a) for which such banking institution or trust company files an annual return but only if the name, address, and identifying number of the record owner are included on or with the annual return filed for the tax exempt organization).

    (iii) Every person who is a nominee acting as a custodian of a unit investment trust described in section 851(f)(1) and paragraph (d) of § 1.851-7 who, during a calendar year after 1968, receives payments of dividends in such capacity, shall make an information return on Forms 1096 and 1099, for such calendar year showing the information required by such forms and instructions thereto and the name, address, and identifying number of the nominee identified as such. This subdivision shall not apply if the regulated investment company agrees with the nominee to satisfy the requirements of section 6042 and the regulations thereunder with respect to each holder of an interest in the unit investment trust whose shares are being held by the nominee as custodian and within the time limit for furnishing statements prescribed by § 1.6042-4, files with the Internal Revenue Service office where such company's return is to be filed for the taxable year, a statement that the holders of the unit investment trust with whom the agreement was made have been directly notified by the regulated investment company. Such statement shall include the name, sponsor, and custodian of each unit investment trust whose holders have been directly notified. The nominee's requirements under this subdivision shall be deemed met if the regulated investment company transmits a copy of such statement to the nominee within such period; provided, however, if the regulated investment company fails or is unable to satisfy the requirements of section 6042 with respect to the holders of interest in the unit investment trust, it shall so notify the Internal Revenue Service within 45 days following the close of its taxable year. The custodian shall, upon notice by the Internal Revenue Service that the regulated investment company has failed to comply with the agreement, satisfy the requirements of this subdivision within 30 days of such notice.

(2) *Definitions.*—The term "person" when used in this section does not include the United States, a State, the District of Columbia, a foreign government, a political subdivision of a State or of a foreign government, or an international organization. Therefore, dividends paid by or to one of these entities need not be reported. For purposes of this section, a person who receives a dividend shall be considered to have received it as a nominee if he is not the actual owner of such dividend and if he was required under §1.6109-1 to furnish his identifying number to the payer of the dividend (or would have been so required if the total of such dividends for the year had been $10 or more), and such number was (or would have been) required to be included on an information return filed by the payer with respect to the dividend. However, a person shall not be considered to be a nominee as to any portion of a dividend which is actually owned by another person whose name is also shown on the information return filed by the payer or nominee with respect to such dividend. Thus, in the case of a stock jointly owned by a husband and wife, the husband will not be considered as receiving any portion of a dividend on that stock as a nominee for his wife if his wife's name is included on the information return filed by the payer with respect to the dividend.

(3) *Determination of person to whom a dividend is paid or for whom it is received.*—For purposes of applying the provisions of this section, the person whose identifying number is required to be included by the payer of a dividend on an information return with respect to such dividend shall be considered the person to whom the dividend is paid. In the case of a dividend received by a nominee on behalf of another person, the person whose identifying number is required to be included on an information return made by the nominee with respect to such dividend shall be considered the person on whose behalf such dividend is received by the nominee. Thus, in the case of a dividend made payable to a person other than the record owner of the stock with respect to which the dividend is paid, the record owner of the stock shall be considered the person to whom the dividend is paid for purposes of applying the reporting requirements in this section, since his identifying number is required to be included on the information return filed under this section by the payer of the dividend. Similarly, if a stockbroker receives a dividend on stock held in street name for the joint account of a husband and wife, the dividend is considered as received on behalf of the husband since his identifying number should be shown on the information return filed by the nominee under this section. Thus, if the wife has a separate account with the same stockbroker, any dividends received by the stockbroker for her separate account should not be aggregated with the dividends received for the joint account for purposes of information reporting. For regulations relating to the use of identifying numbers, see §1.6109-1.

(4) *Inclusion of other payments.*—The Form 1099 filed by any person with respect to payments of dividends to another person during a calendar year may, at the election of the maker, include other payments made by him to such other person during such year which are required to be reported on Form 1099. Similarly, the Form 1099 filed by a nominee with respect to payments of dividends received by him on behalf of any other person during a calendar year may include payments of interest received by him on behalf of such person during such year which are required to be reported on Form 1099.

(b) *When payment deemed made.*—For purposes of a return of information, an amount is deemed to have been paid when it is credited or set apart to a person without any substantial limitation or restriction as to the time or manner of payment or condition upon which payment is to be made, and is made available to him so that it may be drawn at any time, and its receipt brought within his own control and disposition.

(c) *Time and place for filing.*—The returns required under this section for any calendar year shall be filed after September 30 of such year, but not before the payer's final payment for the year, and on or before February 28 (March 31 if filed electronically) of the following year with any of the Internal Revenue Service Centers, the addresses of which are listed in the instructions for Form 1096. For extensions of time for filing returns under this section, see §1.6081-1.

(d) *Cross-reference to penalty.*—For provisions relating to the penalty provided for failure to file timely a correct information return required under section 6042(a), see §301.6721-1 of this chapter (Procedure and Administration Regulations). See §301.6724-1 of this chapter for the waiver of a penalty if the failure is due to reasonable cause and is not due to willful neglect.

(e) *Magnetic media requirement.*—For rules relating to permission to submit the information required by Form 1087 or 1099 on magnetic tape or other media, see §1.9101-1. For the requirement to submit the information required by Form 1099 on magnetic media for payments after December 31, 1983, see section 6011(e) and §301.6011-2 of this chapter (Procedure and Administration Regulations).

(f) *Effective/applicability date.*—This section applies to payments made on or after January 6, 2017. (For payments made after June 30, 2014, and before January 6, 2017, see this section as in effect and contained in 26 CFR part 1, as revised April 1, 2016. For payments made after December 31, 2000, and before July 1, 2014, see this section as in effect and contained in 26 CFR part 1, as revised April 1, 2013.) [Reg. §1.6042-2.]

☐ [T.D. 6628, 12-27-62. *Amended by T.D. 6677*, 9-16-63; *T.D. 6879*, 3-7-66; *T.D. 6883*, 5-2-66; *T.D. 6891*, 8-3-66; *T.D. 7000*, 1-17-69; *T.D. 7187*, 7-5-72; *T.D. 8734*, 10-6-97 (T.D. 8804 delayed the effective date of T.D. 8734 from January 1, 1999, to January 1, 2000; T.D. 8856 further delayed the effective date of T.D. 8734 until January 1, 2001); *T.D. 8804*, 12-30-98 (*corrected* 3-8-99); *T.D. 8895*, 8-17-2000, *T.D. 9658*, 2-28-2014 *and T.D. 9808*, 12-30-2016.]

[Reg. §1.6042-3]

§1.6042-3. Dividends subject to reporting.—
(a) *In general.*—Except as provided in paragraph (b) of this section, the term *dividend* for purposes of this section and §§1.6042-2 and 1.6042-4 means the amounts described in the following paragraphs (a)(1) through (3) of this section—

(1) Any distribution made by a corporation to its shareholders which is a dividend as defined in section 316; and

(2) Any payment made by a stockbroker to any person as a substitute for a dividend. Such a payment includes any payment made in lieu of a dividend to a person whose stock has been borrowed. See §1.6045-2(h) for coordination of the reporting requirements under sections 6042 and 6045(d) with respect to such payments; and

(3) A distribution from a regulated investment company (irrespective of the fact that any part of the distribution may not represent ordinary income (i.e., may, for example, represent a capital gain dividend as defined in section 852(b)(3)(C)).

(b) *Exceptions.*—(1) *In general.*—For purposes of §§1.6042-2 and 1.6042-4, the amounts described in paragraphs (b)(1)(i) through (vii) of this section are not dividends.

(i) Amounts paid by an insurance company to a policyholder, other than a dividend upon its capital stock.

(ii) Payments (however denominated) by a mutual savings bank, savings and loan association, or similar organization, in respect of deposits, investment certificates, or withdrawable or repurchasable shares. See, however, section 6049 and the regulations under that section for provisions requiring reporting of these payments.

(iii) Distributions or payments that a payor can, prior to payment, reliably associate with documentation upon which it may rely to treat as made to a foreign beneficial owner in accordance with §1.1441-1(e)(1)(ii) or as made to a foreign payee in accordance with §1.6049-5(d)(1) or presumed to be made to a foreign payee under §1.6049-5(d)(2), (3), (4), or (5). Returns of information are also not required for payments that a payor or middleman can, prior to payment, reliably associate with documentation upon which it may rely to treat as

made to a foreign intermediary in accordance with §1.1441-1(b) if it obtains from the intermediary entity a withholding statement (described in §1.6049-5(b)(14)) that allocates the payment to a chapter 4 withholding rate pool (as defined in §1.6049-4(f)(5)) or to specific payees to which withholding under chapter 4 applies. Payments excepted from reporting under this paragraph (b)(1)(iii) may be reportable, for purposes of chapter 3 of the Internal Revenue Code (Code), under §1.1461-1(b) and (c) or, for chapter 4 purposes, under §1.1474-1(d)(2). The provisions in §1.6049-5(c) regarding documentation of foreign status shall apply for purposes of this paragraph (b)(1)(iii). The provisions in §1.6049-5(c) regarding the definitions of U.S. payor and non-U.S. payor shall also apply for purposes of this paragraph (b)(1)(iii). The provisions of §1.1441-1 shall apply by substituting the term *payor* for the term *withholding agent* and without regard to the fact that the provisions apply only to amounts subject to withholding under chapter 3 of the Code.

(iv) Distributions or payments from sources outside the United States (as determined under the provisions of part I, subchapter N, chapter 1 of the Code and the regulations under those provisions) that are paid by a non-U.S. payor or non-U.S. middleman and that are paid and received outside the United States. For a definition of non-U.S. payor and non-U.S. middleman, see §1.6049-5(c)(5). For circumstances in which an amount is considered to be paid and received outside the United States, see §1.6049-4(f)(16).

(v) Distributions or payments for the period that the amounts represent assets blocked as described in §1.1441-2(e)(3). The exemption in this paragraph (b)(1)(v) shall terminate when payment is deemed to occur in accordance with the rules of §1.1441-2(e)(3).

(vi) If a foreign intermediary, as described in §1.1441-1(c)(13), or a U.S. branch that is not treated as a U.S. person receives a payment from a payor, which payment the payor can reliably associate with a valid withholding certificate described in §1.1441-1(e)(3)(ii) or (iii), or §1.1441-1(e)(3)(v), respectively, furnished by such intermediary or branch, then the intermediary or branch is not required to report such payment when it, in turn, pays the amount, unless, and to the extent, the intermediary or branch knows that the payment is required to be reported under this section and was not so reported. For example, if a U.S. branch described in §1.1441-1(b)(2)(iv) fails to provide information regarding U.S. persons that are not exempt from reporting under §1.6049-4(c)(1)(ii) to the person from whom the U.S. branch receives the payment, the amount paid by the U.S. branch to such person is a dividend. See, however, §1.6042-2(a)(1)(i)(A) for when reporting under section 6042 is coordinated with reporting under chapter 4 of the Code or an applicable IGA (as defined in §1.6049-4(f)(7)). The exception of this paragraph (b)(1)(vi) for amounts paid by a foreign intermediary shall not apply to a qualified intermediary that assumes reporting responsibility under chapter 61 of the Code with respect to amounts reportable under the agreement described in § 1.1441-1(e)(5)(iii).

(vii) With respect to amounts paid or credited after December 31, 1982, any amount paid or credited to any person described in § 1.6049-4(c)(1)(ii), unless a tax is withheld under section 3406 and is not refunded by the payor in accordance with § 31.6413(a)-3 of this chapter (Employment Tax Regulations).

(2) *Payor.*—The term *payor* has the same meaning as described in § 1.6049-4(a)(2).

(3) *Joint owners.*—Amounts paid to joint owners for which a certificate or documentation is required as a condition for being exempt from reporting under this paragraph (b) are presumed made to U.S. payees who are not exempt recipients if, prior to payment, the payor or middleman cannot reliably associate the payment either with a Form W-9 furnished by one of the joint owners in the manner required in § § 31.3406(d)-1 through 31.3406(d)-5 of this chapter, or with documentation described in paragraph (b)(1)(iii) of this section furnished by each joint owner upon which it can rely to treat each joint owner as a foreign payee or foreign beneficial owner. However in the case of a withholdable payment (as defined in § 1.6049-4(f)(15)) made to joint payees, if any such joint payee does not appear to be an individual, the payment is presumed made to a foreign payee that is a nonparticipating FFI (as defined in § 1.1471-1(b)(82)). See § 1.1471-3(f)(7). For purposes of applying this paragraph (b)(3), the grace period described in § 1.6049-5(d)(2)(ii) shall apply only if each payee qualifies for such grace period.

(4) *Conversion into United States dollars of amounts paid in foreign currency.*—For rules concerning foreign currency conversion, see § 1.6049-4(d)(3)(i).

(c) *Special rule.*—If a person makes a payment which may be a dividend, or if a nominee receives a payment which may be a dividend, but such person or nominee is unable to determine the portion of the payment which is a dividend (as defined in paragraphs (a) and (b) of this section) at the time he files his return under § 1.6042-2, he shall, for purposes of such section treat the entire amount of such payment as a dividend.

(d) *Effective/applicability date.*—This section applies on or after January 6, 2017. (For payments made after June 30, 2014, and before January 6, 2017, see this section as in effect and contained in 26 CFR part 1, as revised April 1, 2016. For payments made after December 31, 2000, and before July 1, 2014, see this section as in effect and contained in 26 CFR part 1, as revised April 1, 2013). [Reg. § 1.6042-3.]

☐ [T.D. 6628, 12-27-62. *Amended by* T.D. 6908, 12-30-66; T.D. 7987, 10-23-84; T.D. 8029, 6-4-85; T.D. 8734, 10-6-97; T.D. 8804, 12-30-98; T.D. 8856,

12-29-99; T.D. 8881, 5-15-2000, T.D. 9658, 2-28-2014 *and* T.D. 9808, 12-30-2016.]

[Reg. § 1.6042-4]

§ 1.6042-4. Statement to recipients of dividend payments.—(a) *Requirement.*—A person required to make an information return under section 6042(a)(1) and § 1.6042-2 must furnish a statement to each recipient whose identifying number is required to be shown on the related information return for dividend payments.

(b) *Form and content of the statement.*—The statement required by paragraph (a) of this section must be either the official Form 1099 prescribed by the Internal Revenue Service for the respective calendar year or an acceptable substitute statement that contains provisions that are substantially similar to those of the official Form 1099 for the respective calendar year. For further guidance on how to prepare an acceptable substitute statement, see Rev. Proc. 2012-38, 2012-48 IRB 575, also published as Publication 1179, "General Rules and Specifications for Substitute Forms 1096, 1098, 1099, 5498, and Certain Other Information Returns," or any successor guidance. An IRS truncated taxpayer identifying number (TTIN) may be used as the identifying number of the recipient. For provisions relating to the use of TTINs, see § 301.6109-4 of this chapter (Procedure and Administration Regulations).

(c) *Aggregation of payments.*—A payor may aggregate on one Form 1099 all payments made to a recipient with respect to each separate account during a calendar year.

(d) *Manner of providing statements to recipients.*—(1) *In general.*—The Form 1099, or acceptable substitute statement, must be provided to the recipient either in person or by first-class mail to the recipient's last known address in a statement mailing.

(2) *Statement mailing requirement.*—The mailing required under section 6042(c) of a Form 1099 to a payee-recipient must qualify as a statement mailing. A statement mailing must contain the required Form 1099 or acceptable substitute statement (written statement) and must comply with enclosure and envelope restrictions.

(i) *Enclosure restrictions.*—To qualify as a statement mailing, the mailing cannot contain any enclosures except those listed in this paragraph (d)(2)(i). Moreover, no promotional or advertising material is permitted in the mailing of the written statement. Even a *de minimis* amount of promotional or advertising material violates the statement mailing requirement. However, a logo on the envelope containing the written statement and on nontax enclosures described in paragraph (d)(2)(i)(A) through (D) of this section does not violate the written statement requirement. The written statement required under section 6042(c) and paragraph (a) of this section may be perforated to a check or to a statement of the recipient-payee's specific account with the payor described in paragraph (d)(2)(i)(A) or (C)

Reg. § 1.6042-4(d)(2)(i)

of this section. The enclosure to which the written statement is perforated must contain, in a bold and conspicuous type, the legend: "Important Tax Return Document Attached." The enclosures permitted in a mailing are limited to—

(A) A check with respect to the account reported on the written statement;

(B) A letter explaining why a check with respect to such account is not enclosed with the written statement (for example, because a dividend has not been declared payable);

(C) A statement of the taxpayer-recipient's specific account with the payor if payments on such account are reflected on the written statement;

(D) A letter limited to an explanation of the tax consequences of the information set forth on the enclosed written statement;

(E) Payee statements related to other Forms 1099, Form 1098, and Form 5498 (or the account balance on a Form 5498), Forms W-2 and W-2G; and

(F) Any document concerning the solicitation of the Form W-9, as described in § 31.3406(h)-3(a) of this chapter, or of the Form W-8 as described in § 1.1441-1(e)(1).

(ii) *Envelope and delivery restrictions.*— (A) *Envelope restrictions.*—The outside of the envelope in which the written statement is mailed and each nontax enclosure enclosed in the envelope must contain, in a bold and conspicuous type, the legend: "Important Tax Return Document Enclosed." For purposes of this paragraph (d)(2)(ii), a nontax enclosure is any item listed in paragraphs (d)(2)(i)(A) through (C) of this section. However, a payor is not required to include the legend on the outside of an envelope containing only the enclosures in paragraph (d)(2)(i)(D) through (F) of this section.

(B) *Delivery restrictions.*—The requirement to provide the written statement in person or by first-class mail may be satisfied by sending the written statement and any enclosures described in paragraph (d)(2)(i) of this section by intra-office mail, provided that intra-office mail is used by the payor in sending account activity, balance information, and other correspondence to the payee. If a payor does not personally deliver the written statement (i.e., the Form 1099 or its acceptable substitute) to the recipient or mail it to the recipient in a statement mailing as described in this paragraph (d), the payor is considered to have failed to mail the statement required under section 6042(c) and will be subject to the penalty under section 6722.

(e) *Time for furnishing statements.*—(1) *In general.*—Each statement required by section 6042(c) and this section to be furnished to any person for a calendar year must be furnished to such person after November 30 of the year and on or before January 31 (February 10 in the case of a nominee filing under § 1.6042-2(a)(1)(iii)) of the following year, but no statement may be furnished before the final dividend for the calendar year has been paid. However, the statement may be furnished at any time after April 30 if it is furnished with the final dividend for the calendar year. For a statement required to be furnished after December 31, 2008, the February 15 due date under section 6045 applies to the statement if the statement is furnished in a consolidated reporting statement under section 6045. *See* §§ 1.6045-1(k)(3), 1.6045-2(d)(2), 1.6045-3(e)(2), 1.6045-4(m)(3), and 1.6045-5(a)(3)(ii).

(2) *Extensions of time.*—For good cause upon written application of the person required to furnish statements under this section, the Director, Martinsburg Computing Center, may grant an extension of time not exceeding 30 days in which to furnish such statements. The application must be addressed to the Director, Martinsburg Computing Center, and must contain a full recital of the reasons for requesting the extension to aid the Director in determining the period of the extension, if any, that will be granted. Such a request in the form of a letter to the Director, Martinsburg Computing Center, signed by the applicant will suffice as an application. The application must be filed on or before the date prescribed in paragraph (e)(1) of this section.

(3) *Last day for furnishing statement.*—For provisions relating to the time for performance of an act when the last day prescribed for performance falls on Saturday, Sunday, or a legal holiday, see section 7503 and § 301.7503-1 of this chapter (Regulations on Procedure and Administration).

(f) *Cross-reference to penalty.*—For provisions relating to the penalty provided for failure to furnish timely a correct payee statement required under section 6042(c), see § 301.6722-1 of this chapter (Procedure and Administration Regulations). See § 301.6724-1 of this chapter for the waiver of a penalty if the failure is due to reasonable cause and is not due to willful neglect.

(g) *Effective/applicability date.*—This section is effective for payee statements due after December 31, 1995, without regard to extensions. The amendments to paragraph (b) are effective for payee statements due after December 31, 2014. For payee statements due before January 1, 2015, § 1.6042-4(b) (as contained in 26 CFR part 1, revised April 2013) shall apply. [Reg. § 1.6042-4.]

☐ [*T.D.* 6628, 12-27-62. *Amended by T.D.* 6879, 3-7-66; *T.D.* 7187, 7-5-72; *T.D.* 7624, 5-29-79; *T.D.* 8637, 12-20-95; *T.D.* 8734, 10-6-97 (*T.D.* 8804 delayed the effective date of *T.D.* 8734 from January 1, 1999, to January 1, 2000; *T.D.* 8856 further delayed the effective date of *T.D.* 8734 until January 1, 2001); *T.D.* 9504, 10-12-2010 *and T.D.* 9675, 7-14-2014.]

[Reg. § 1.6042-5]

§ 1.6042-5. Coordination with reporting rules for widely held fixed investment trusts under § 1.671-5.—See § 1.671-5 for the reporting rules for widely held fixed investment trusts (as defined under that section). [Reg. § 1.6042-5.]

☐ [*T.D.* 9241, 1-23-2006.]

[Reg. § 1.6043-1]

§ 1.6043-1. Return regarding corporate dissolution or liquidation.

—(a) *Requirement of returns.*—Within 30 days after the adoption of any resolution or plan for or in respect of the dissolution of a corporation or the liquidation of the whole or any part of its capital stock, the corporation shall file a return on Form 966, containing the information required by paragraph (b) of this section and by such form. Such return shall be filed with the district director for the district in which the income tax return of the corporation is filed. Further, if after the filing of a Form 966 there is an amendment of or supplement to the resolution or plan, an additional Form 966, based on the resolution or plan as amended or supplemented, must be filed within 30 days after the adoption of such amendment or supplement. A return must be filed under section 6043 and this section in respect of a liquidation whether or not any part of the gain or loss to the shareholders upon the liquidation is recognized under the provisions of section 1002.

(b) *Contents of return.*—(1) *In general.*—There shall be attached to and made a part of the return required by section 6043 and paragraph (a) of this section a certified copy of the resolution or plan, together with any amendments thereof or supplements thereto, and such return shall in addition contain the following information:

(i) The name and address of the corporation;

(ii) The place and date of incorporation;

(iii) The date of the adoption of the resolution or plan and the dates of any amendments thereof or supplements thereto; and

(iv) The internal revenue district in which the last income tax return of the corporation was filed and the taxable year covered thereby.

(2) *Returns in respect of amendments or supplements.*—If a return has been filed pursuant to section 6043 and this section, any additional return made necessary by an amendment of or a supplement to the resolution or plan will be deemed sufficient if it gives the date the prior return was filed and contains a duly certified copy of the amendment or supplement and all other information required by this section and by Form 966 which was not given in the prior return. [Reg. § 1.6043-1.]

☐ [*T.D. 6364, 2-13-59. Amended by T.D. 6949, 4-8-68 and T.D. 7926, 12-15-83.*]

[Reg. § 301.6043-1]

§ 301.6043-1. Returns regarding liquidation, dissolution, termination, or contraction.

—For provisions relating to the requirement of returns of information regarding liquidations, dissolutions, terminations, or contractions, see §§ 1.6043-1, 1.6043-2, and 1.6043-3 of this chapter (Income Tax Regulations). [Reg. § 301.6043-1.]

☐ [*T.D. 6498, 10-24-60. Amended by T.D. 7563, 9-8-73.*]

[Reg. § 1.6043-2]

§ 1.6043-2. Return of information respecting distributions in liquidation.

—(a) Unless the distribution is one in respect of which information is required to be filed pursuant to § 1.332-6(a), 1.368-3(a), or 1.1081-11, every corporation making any distribution of $600 or more during a calendar year to any shareholder in liquidation of the whole or any part of its capital stock shall file a return of information on Forms 1096 and 1099, giving all the information required by such form and by the regulations in this part. A separate Form 1099 must be prepared for each shareholder to whom such distribution was made, showing the name and address of such shareholder, the number and class of shares owned by him in liquidation of which such distribution was made, and the total amount distributed to him on each class of stock. If the amount distributed to such shareholder on any class of stock consisted in whole or in part of property other than money, the return on such form shall in addition show the amount of money distributed, if any, and shall list separately each class of property other than money distributed, giving a description of the property in each such class and a statement of its fair market value at the time of the distribution. Such forms, accompanied by transmittal Form 1096 showing the number of Forms 1099 filed therewith, shall be filed on or before February 28 (March 31 if filed electronically) of the year following the calendar year in which such distribution was made with any of the Internal Revenue Service Centers, the addresses of which are listed in the instructions for Form 1096.

(b) If the distribution is in complete liquidation of a domestic corporation pursuant to a plan of liquidation in accordance with which all the capital stock of the corporation is cancelled or redeemed, and the transfer of all property under the liquidation occurs within some one calendar month pursuant to section 333, and any shareholder claims the benefit of such section, the return on Form 1096 shall show:

(1) The amount of earnings and profits of the corporation accumulated after February 28, 1913, determined as of the close of such calendar month, without diminution by reason of distributions made during such calendar month, but including in such computation all items of income and expense accrued up to the date on which the transfer of all the property under the liquidation is completed;

(2) The ratable share of such earnings and profits of each share of stock canceled or redeemed in the liquidation;

(3) The date and circumstances of the acquisition by the corporation of any stock or securities distributed to shareholders in the liquidation;

(4) If the liquidation is pursuant to section 333(g), a schedule showing the amount of earnings and profits to which the corporation has succeeded after December 31, 1963, pursuant to any corporate reorganization or pursuant to a

liquidation to which section 332 applies, except earnings and profits which on December 31, 1963, constituted earnings and profits of a corporation referred to in section 333(g)(3), and except earnings and profits which were earned after such date by a corporation referred to in section 333(g)(3); and

(5) If the liquidation occurs after December 31, 1966, and is pursuant to section 333(g)(2), the amount of earnings and profits of the corporation accumulated after February 28, 1913, and before January 1, 1967, and the ratable share of such earnings and profits of each share of stock canceled or redeemed in the liquidation. [Reg. § 1.6043-2.]

☐ [T.D. 6464, 2-13-59. Amended by T.D. 6949, 4-8-68; T.D. 8734, 10-6-97 (T.D. 8804 and T.D. 8856 delayed the effective date of T.D. 8734); T.D. 8804, 12-30-98; T.D. 8895, 8-17-2000; T.D. 9264, 5-26-2006 and T.D. 9329, 6-13-2007.]

[Reg. § 1.6043-3]

§ 1.6043-3. Return regarding liquidation, dissolution, termination, or substantial contraction of organizations exempt from taxation under section 501(a).—(a) *In general.*—(1) *Requirement to provide information.*—Except as provided in paragraph (b) of this section, for taxable years beginning after December 31, 1969, every organization which for any of its last 5 taxable years preceding any liquidation, dissolution, termination, or substantial contraction of the organization was exempt from taxation under section 501(a) shall provide the information with respect to such liquidation, dissolution, termination, or substantial contraction required by the instructions accompanying the organization's annual return of information. The information required by this section shall be provided with, and at the time prescribed for filing, the organization's annual return of information for the period during which any liquidation, dissolution (or the adoption of a resolution or plan for the dissolution or liquidation in whole or part), termination or substantial contraction occurred with respect to the organization. An organization which is no longer exempt from taxation under section 501 (a) shall use the annual return of information it would have been required to file when the organization was exempt.

(2) *Transitional rule.*—In the case of an annual return of information of an organization which was filed before September 11, 1978, if the organization had failed to provide the information with such return in accordance with paragraph (a)(1) of this section, the organization may comply with this section by providing the information with the organization's first annual return of information filed after such date.

(b) *Exceptions.*—The following organizations are not required to provide the information under paragraph (a) of this section:

(1) Churches, their integrated auxiliaries, or conventions or associations of churches;

(2) Any organization which is not a private foundation (as defined in section 509(a)) and the gross receipts of which in each taxable year are normally not more than $5,000;

(3) Any organization which has terminated its private foundation status under section 507(b)(1)(B) with respect to a liquidation, dissolution, termination, or substantial contraction which is in connection with the termination under section 507(b)(1)(B);

(4) Any organization described in section 401(a) if the employer who established such organization files a return which provides the information under paragraph (a) of this section;

(5) Any organization described in section 501(c)(1) and any corporation described in section 501(c)(2) which holds title to property for such 501(c)(1) organizations;

(6) Any organization described in section 501(c)(14)(A) subject to a group exemption letter issued to a state regulatory body; and

(7) Any subordinate unit of a central organization (other than a private foundation) which established its exempt status under the group ruling procedure of regulations § 601.201(n)(7), if the central or parent organization files an annual information return for the group in accordance with § 1.6033-2(d); and

(8) Any organization no longer exempt from taxation under section 501(a) and that during the period of its exemption under such section was not an organization described in section 501(c)(3), a corporation described in section 501(c)(2) that held title to property for an organization described in section 501(c)(3), or an organization described in such other section as prescribed by publication, form, or instructions.

(9) The Commissioner may relieve any organization or class of organizations from filing the return required by section 6043(b) of this section, where it is determined that such information is not necessary for the efficient administration of the internal revenue laws.

(c) *Penalties.*—For provisions relating to the penalty provided for failure to furnish any information required by this section, see section 6652(d) and the regulations thereunder.

(d) *Definitions.*—(1) For the definition of the term "normally" as used in paragraph (b)(2) of this section, see § 1.6033-2(g)(3).

(2) For the definition of the term "integrated auxiliaries" as used in paragraph (b)(1) of this section, see § 1.6033-2(h).

(3) For returns filed for taxable years beginning before January 1, 2008, for purposes of this section the definition of the term "substantial contraction" set forth in § 1.6043-3(d)(1) (as contained in 26 CFR part 1 revised April 1, 2008) may be used.

(e) *Effective/applicability date.*—(1) *Generally.*— The provisions of this section shall apply with respect to returns filed for taxable years beginning after December 31, 1969.

(2) Paragraphs (b)(8) and (d) of this section shall apply for taxable years beginning on or after January 1, 2008. For taxable years beginning before January 1, 2008, §§1.6043-3(b)(8) and 1.6043-3(d) (as contained in 26 CFR part 1 revised April 1, 2008) shall apply. [Reg. §1.6043-3.]

☐ [*T.D. 7563, 9-8-78. Amended by T.D. 9423, 9-8-2008 and T.D. 9549, 9-7-2011.*]

[Reg. §1.6043-4]

§1.6043-4. Information returns relating to certain acquisitions of control and changes in capital structure.—(a) *Information returns for an acquisition of control or a substantial change in capital structure.*—(1) *General rule.*—If there is an acquisition of control (as defined in paragraph (c) of this section) or a substantial change in the capital structure (as defined in paragraph (d) of this section) of a domestic corporation (reporting corporation), the reporting corporation must file a completed Form 8806, "Information Return for Acquisition of Control or Substantial Change in Capital Structure," in accordance with the instructions to that form. The Form 8806 will request information with respect to the following and such other information specified in the instructions:

(i) *Reporting corporation.*—The name, address, and taxpayer identification number (TIN) of the reporting corporation

(ii) *Common parent, if any, of the reporting corporation.*—If the reporting corporation was a subsidiary member of an affiliated group filing a consolidated return immediately prior to the acquisition of control or the substantial change in capital structure, the name, address, and TIN of the common parent of that affiliated group.

(iii) *Acquiring corporation.*—The name, address and TIN of any corporation that acquired control of the reporting corporation within the meaning of paragraph (c) of this section or combined with or received assets from the reporting corporation pursuant to a substantial change in capital structure within the meaning of paragraph (d) of this section (acquiring corporation) and whether the acquiring corporation was newly formed prior to its involvement in the transaction.

(iv) *Information about acquisition of control or substantial change in capital structure.*

(A) A description of the transaction or transactions that gave rise to the acquisition of control or the substantial change in capital structure of the corporation;

(B) The date or dates of the transaction or transactions that gave rise to the acquisition of control or the substantial change in capital structure; and

(C) A description of and a statement of the fair market value of any stock and other property, if any, provided to the reporting corporation's shareholders in exchange for their stock.

(2) *Consent election.*—Form 8806 will provide the reporting corporation with the ability to elect to permit the Internal Revenue Service (IRS) to publish information that will inform brokers of the transaction and enable brokers to satisfy their reporting obligations under §1.6045-3. The information to be published, whether on the IRS website or in an IRS publication, would be limited to the name and address of the corporation, the date of the transaction, a description of the shares affected by the transaction, and the amount of cash and the fair market value of stock or other property provided to each class of shareholders in exchange for a share.

(3) *Time for making return.*—Form 8806 must be filed on or before the 45th day following the acquisition of control or substantial change in capital structure of the corporation, or, if earlier, on or before January 5th of the year following the calendar year in which the acquisition of control or substantial change in capital structure occurs.

(4) *Exception where transaction is reported under section 6043(a).*—No reporting is required under this paragraph (a) with respect to a transaction for which information is required to be reported pursuant to section 6043(a), provided the transaction is properly reported in accordance with that section.

(5) *Exception where shareholders are exempt recipients.*—No reporting is required under this paragraph (a) if the reporting corporation reasonably determines that all of its shareholders who receive cash, stock, or other property pursuant to the acquisition of control or substantial change in capital structure are exempt recipients under paragraph (b)(5) of this section.

(b) *Information returns regarding shareholders.*—(1) *General rule.*—A corporation that is required to file Form 8806 pursuant to paragraph (a)(1) of this section shall file a return of information on Forms 1096, "Annual Summary and Transmittal of U.S. Information Returns," and 1099-CAP, "Changes in Corporate Control and Capital Structure," with respect to each shareholder of record in the corporation (before or after the acquisition of control or the substantial change in capital structure) who receives cash, stock, or other property pursuant to the acquisition of control or the substantial change in capital structure and who is not an exempt recipient as defined in paragraph (b)(5) of this section. A corporation is not required to file a Form 1096 or 1099-CAP with respect to a clearing organization if the corporation makes the election described in paragraph (a)(2) of this section.

(2) *Time for making information returns.*—Forms 1096 and 1099-CAP must be filed on or before February 28 (March 31 if filed electronically) of the year following the calendar year in which the acquisition of control or the substantial change in capital structure occurs.

(3) *Contents of return.*—A separate Form 1099-CAP must be filed with respect to amounts received by each shareholder (who is not an exempt recipient as defined in paragraph (b)(5)

of this section). The Form 1099-CAP will request information with respect to the following and such other information as may be specified in the instructions:

(i) The name, address, telephone number and TIN of the reporting corporation;

(ii) The name, address and TIN of the shareholder;

(iii) The number and class of shares in the reporting corporation exchanged by the shareholder; and

(iv) The aggregate amount of cash and the fair market value of any stock or other property provided to the shareholder in exchange for its stock.

(4) *Furnishing of forms to shareholders.*—The Form 1099-CAP filed with respect to each shareholder must be furnished to such shareholder on or before January 31 of the year following the calendar year in which the shareholder receives cash, stock, or other property as part of the acquisition of control or the substantial change in capital structure. The Form 1099-CAP filed with respect to a clearing organization must be furnished to the clearing organization on or before January 5th of the year following the calendar year in which the acquisition of control or substantial change in capital structure occurred. A Form 1099-CAP is not required to be furnished to a clearing organization if the reporting corporation makes the election described in paragraph (a)(2) of this section. An IRS truncated taxpayer identifying number (TTIN) may be used as the identifying number of the shareholder in lieu of the identifying number appearing on the Form 1099-CAP filed with the Internal Revenue Service. For provisions relating to the use of TTINs, see § 301.6109-4 of this chapter (Procedure and Administration Regulations).

(5) *Exempt recipients.*—A corporation is not required to file a Form 1099-CAP pursuant to this paragraph (b) with respect to any of the following shareholders that is not a clearing organization:

(i) Any shareholder who receives stock in an exchange that is not subject to gain recognition under section 367(a) and the regulations.

(ii) Any shareholder if the corporation reasonably determines that the total amount of cash and the fair market value of stock and other property received by the shareholder does not exceed $1,000.

(iii) Any shareholder described in paragraphs (b)(5)(iii)(A) through (M) of this section if the corporation has actual knowledge that the shareholder is described in one of paragraphs (b)(5)(iii)(A) through (M) of this section or if the corporation has a properly completed exemption certificate from the shareholder (as provided in § 31.3406(h)-3 of this chapter). The corporation also may treat a shareholder as described in paragraphs (b)(5)(iii)(A) through (M) of this section based on the applicable indicators described in § 1.6049-4(c)(1)(ii).

(A) A corporation, as described in § 1.6049-4(c)(1)(ii)(A) (except for corporations for which an election under section 1362(a) is in effect).

(B) a tax-exempt organization, as described in § 1.6049-4(c)(1)(ii)(B)(*1*).

(C) An individual retirement plan, as described in § 1.6049-4(c)(1)(ii)(C).

(D) The United States, as described in § 1.6049-4(c)(1)(ii)(D).

(E) A state, as described in § 1.6049-4(c)(1)(ii)(E).

(F) A foreign government, as described in § 1.6049-4(c)(1)(ii)(F).

(G) An international organization, as described in § 1.6049-4(c)(1)(ii)(G).

(H) A foreign central bank of issue, as described in § 1.6049-4(c)(1)(ii)(H).

(I) A securities or commodities dealer, as described in § 1.6049-4(c)(1)(ii)(I).

(J) A real estate investment trust, as described in § 1.6049-4(c)(1)(ii)(J).

(K) An entity registered under the Investment Company Act of 1940 (15 U.S.C. 80a-1), as described in § 1.6049-4(c)(1)(ii)(K).

(L) A common trust fund, as described in § 1.6049-4(c)(1)(ii)(L).

(M) A financial institution such as a bank, mutual savings bank, savings and loan association, building and loan association, cooperative bank, homestead association, credit union, industrial loan association or bank, or other similar organization.

(iv) Any shareholder that the corporation, prior to the transaction, associates with documentation upon which the corporation may rely in order to treat payments to the shareholder as made to a foreign beneficial owner in accordance with § 1.1441-1(e)(1)(ii) or as made to a foreign payee in accordance with § 1.6049-5(d)(1) or presumed to be made to a foreign payee under § 1.6049-5(d)(2) or (3). For purposes of this paragraph (b)(5)(iv), the provisions in § 1.6049-5(c) (regarding rules applicable to documentation of foreign status and definition of U.S. payor and non-U.S. payor) shall apply. The provisions of § 1.1441-1 shall apply by using the terms "corporation" and "shareholder" in place of the terms "withholding agent" and "payee" and without regard to the fact that the provisions apply only to amounts subject to withholding under chapter 3 of the Internal Revenue Code. The provisions of § 1.6049-5(d) shall apply by using the terms "corporation" and "shareholder" in place of the terms "payor" and "payee". Nothing in this paragraph (b)(5)(iv) shall be construed to relieve a corporation of its withholding obligations under section 1441.

(v) Any shareholder if, on January 31 of the year following the calendar year in which the shareholder receives cash, stock, or other property, the corporation did not know and did not have reason to know that the shareholder received such cash, stock, or other property in a transaction or series of related transactions that would result in an acquisition of control or a substantial change in capital structure within the meaning of this section.

(6) *Coordination with other sections.*—In general, no reporting is required under this paragraph (b) with respect to amounts that are required to be reported under sections 6042 or 6045, unless the corporation knows or has reason to know that such amounts are not properly reported in accordance with those sections. A corporation must satisfy the requirements under this paragraph (b) with respect to any shareholder of record that is a clearing organization.

(c) *Acquisition of control of a corporation.*—(1) *In general.*—For purposes of this section, an acquisition of control of a corporation (first corporation) occurs if, in a transaction or series of related transactions —

(i) Before an acquisition of stock of the first corporation (directly or indirectly) by a second corporation, the second corporation does not have control of the first corporation;

(ii) After the acquisition, the second corporation has control of the first corporation;

(iii) The fair market value of the stock acquired in the transaction and in any related transactions as of the date or dates on which such stock was acquired is $100 million or more;

(iv) The shareholders of the first corporation receive stock or other property pursuant to the acquisition; and

(v) The first corporation or any shareholder of the first corporation is required to recognize gain (if any) under section 367(a) and the regulations, as a result of the transaction.

(2) *Control.*—For purposes of this section, control is determined in accordance with the first sentence of section 304(c)(1). For these purposes the rules of section 318 as modified by the rules of section 958(b) shall apply in determining the ownership of stock.

(d) *Substantial change in capital structure of a corporation.*—(1) *In general.*—A corporation has a substantial change in capital structure if it has a change in capital structure (as defined in paragraph (d)(2) of this section) and the amount of any cash and the fair market value of any property (including stock) provided to the shareholders of such corporation pursuant to the change in capital structure, as of the date or dates on which the cash or other property is provided, is $100 million or more.

(2) *Change in capital structure.*—For purposes of this section, a corporation has a change in capital structure if—

(i) The corporation in a transaction or series of transactions—

(A) Merges, consolidates or otherwise combines with another corporation or transfers all or substantially all of its assets to one or more corporations;

(B) Transfers all or part of its assets to another corporation in a title 11 or similar case and, in pursuance of the plan, distributes stock or securities of that corporation; or

(C) (C) Changes its identity, form or place of organization; and

(ii) The corporation or any shareholder is required to recognize gain (if any) under section 367(a) and the regulations, as a result of the transaction.

(e) *Reporting by successor entity.*—If a corporation (transferor) transfers all or substantially all of its assets to another entity (transferee) in a transaction that constitutes a substantial change in the capital structure of transferor, transferor must satisfy the reporting obligations in paragraph (a) and (b) of this section. If transferor does not satisfy one or both of those reporting obligations, then transferee must do so. If neither transferor nor transferee satisfies the reporting obligations in paragraphs (a) and (b) of this section, then transferor and transferee shall be jointly and severally liable for any applicable penalties (see paragraph (g) of this section).

(f) *Receipt of property.*—For purposes of this section, a shareholder is treated as receiving property (or as having property provided to it) pursuant to an acquisition of control or a substantial change in capital structure if a liability of the shareholder is assumed in the transaction and, as a result of the transaction, an amount is realized by the shareholder from the sale or exchange of stock.

(g) *Penalties for failure to file.*—For penalties for failure to file as required under this section, see section 6652(I). The information returns required to be filed under paragraphs (a) and (b) of this section shall be treated as one return for purposes of section 6652(I) and, accordingly, the penalty shall not exceed $500 for each day the failure continues (up to a maximum of $100,000) with respect to any acquisition of control or any substantial change in capital structure. Failure to file as required under this section also includes the failure to satisfy the requirement to file on magnetic media as required by section 6011(e) and §1.6011-2. In addition, criminal penalties under sections 7203, 7206 and 7207 may apply in appropriate cases.

(h) *Examples.*—The following examples illustrate the application of the rules of this section. For purposes of these examples, assume the transaction is not reported under sections 6042, 6043(a), or 6045, unless otherwise specified, and assume that the fair market value of the consideration provided to the shareholders exceeds $100 million. The examples are as follows:

Example 1. The shareholders of X, a domestic corporation and parent of an affiliated group, exchange their X stock for stock in Y, a foreign corporation, pursuant to sections 351 and 354. After the transaction, Y owns all the outstanding X stock. Assume that, under section 367(a) and the regulations, the X shareholders must recognize gain (if any) on the exchange of their stock. Because the transaction results in an acquisition of control of X, X must comply with the rules in paragraphs (a) and (b) of this section. X must file Form 8806 reporting the transaction. X must also

Reg. §1.6043-4(h)

file a Form 1099-CAP with respect to each shareholder who is not an exempt recipient showing the fair market value of the Y stock received by that shareholder, and X must furnish a copy of the Form 1099-CAP to that shareholder. If X elects on the Form 8806 to permit the IRS to publish information regarding the transaction, X is not required to file or furnish Forms 1099-CAP with respect to shareholders that are clearing organizations.

Example 2. The facts are the same as in *Example 1*, except X hires a transfer agent to effectuate the exchange. The transfer agent is treated as a broker under section 6045 and is required to report the fair market value of the Y stock received by X's shareholders under §1.6045-3. Under paragraph (b)(6) of this section, X is not required to file information returns under paragraph (b) of this section with respect to a shareholder of record, unless X knows or has reason to know that the transfer agent does not satisfy its information reporting obligation under §1.6045-3 with respect to that shareholder. Thus, if the transfer agent satisfies its information reporting require-

ments under §1.6045-3 with respect to shareholder I, an individual who receives X stock, X is not required to file a Form 1099-CAP with respect to I. Conversely, if the transfer agent does not have an information reporting obligation under §1.6045-3 with respect to one of X's shareholders of record (for example, a clearing organization that is an exempt recipient under §1.6045-3(b)(2)), or if X knows or has reason to know that the transfer agent has not satisfied its information reporting requirement with respect to a shareholder, then X must provide a Form 1099-CAP to that shareholder.

(i) *Effective/applicability date.*—This section applies to transactions occurring after December 5, 2005. The amendments to paragraph (b)(4) are effective for any Form 1099-CAP required to be furnished after December 31, 2014. For any Form 1099-CAP required to be furnished before January 1, 2015, §1.6043-4(b) (as contained in 26 CFR part 1, revised April 2013) shall apply. [Reg. §1.6043-4.]

☐ [*T.D. 9230, 12-2-2005. Amended by T.D. 9675, 7-14-2014.*]

»»→ Caution: *Temporary Reg. §1.6043-4T, below, was removed by T.D. 9230, but it remains outstanding with respect to transactions not covered by Reg. §1.6043-4 while the IRS considers additional information reporting requirements under Code Secs. 6043(c), 6043A and 6045.*

[Reg. §1.6043-4T]

§1.6043-4T. Information returns relating to certain acquisitions of control and changes in capital structure (temporary).—(a) *Information returns for an acquisition of control or a substantial change in capital structure.*—(1) *General rule.*—If there is an acquisition of control (as defined in paragraph (c) of this section) or a substantial change in the capital structure (as defined in paragraph (d) of this section) of a domestic corporation (reporting corporation), the reporting corporation must file a completed Form 8806, "Information Return for Acquisition of Control or Substantial Change in Capital Structure," in accordance with the instructions to that form. Form 8806 will request the information required in paragraphs (a)(1)(i) through (vi) of this section and any other information specified in the instructions.

(i) *Reporting corporation.*—Provide the name, address, and taxpayer identification number (TIN) of the reporting corporation.

(ii) *Common parent, if any, of the reporting corporation.*—If the reporting corporation was a subsidiary member of an affiliated group filing a consolidated return immediately prior to the acquisition of control or the substantial change in capital structure, provide the name, address, and TIN of the common parent of that affiliated group.

(iii) *Acquiring corporation.*—Provide the name, address and TIN of any corporation that acquired control of the reporting corporation within the meaning of paragraph (c) of this section or combined with or received assets from the reporting corporation pursuant to a substan-

tial change in capital structure within the meaning of paragraph (d) of this section (acquiring corporation). State whether the acquiring corporation is foreign (as defined in section 7701(a)(5)) or is a dual resident corporation (as defined in §1.1503-2(c)(2)). In either case, state whether the acquiring corporation was newly formed prior to its involvement in the transaction.

(iv) *Common parent, if any, of acquiring corporation.*—If the acquiring corporation named in paragraph (a)(1)(iii) of this section was a subsidiary member of an affiliated group filing a consolidated return immediately prior to the acquisition of control or the substantial change in capital structure, provide the name, address, and TIN of the common parent of that affiliated group.

(v) *Information about acquisition of control or substantial change in capital structure.*—Provide—

(A) A description of the transaction or transactions that gave rise to the acquisition of control or the substantial change in capital structure of the corporation;

(B) The date or dates of the transaction or transactions that gave rise to the acquisition of control or the substantial change in capital structure;

(C) A description of and a statement of the fair market value of any stock provided to the reporting corporation's shareholders in exchange for their stock if the reporting corporation reasonably determines that the shareholders are not required to recognize gain (if any) from the receipt of such stock for U.S. federal income tax purposes; and

⮞⮞⮞→ *Caution: Temporary Reg. §1.6043-4T, below, was removed by T.D. 9230, but it remains outstanding with respect to transactions not covered by Reg. §1.6043-4 while the IRS considers additional information reporting requirements under Code Secs. 6043(c), 6043A and 6045.*

(D) A statement of the amount of cash plus the fair market value of any property (including stock if the reporting corporation reasonably determines that its shareholders would be required to recognize gain (if any) on the receipt of such stock, but excluding stock described in paragraph (a)(1)(v)(C) of this section) provided to the reporting corporation's shareholders in exchange for each share of their stock.

(2) *Consent election.*—Form 8806 will provide the reporting corporation with the ability to elect to permit the IRS to publish information that will inform brokers of the transaction and enable brokers to satisfy their reporting obligations under § 1.6045-3T. The information to be published, on the IRS website and/or in an IRS publication, would be limited to the name and address of the corporation, the date of the transaction, a description of the shares affected by the transaction, and the amount of cash and the fair market value of any property (excluding stock described in paragraph (a)(1)(v)(C) of this section) provided to each class of shareholders in exchange for a share.

(3) *Time for making return.*—(i) *In general.*— Form 8806 must be filed on or before the 45Th day following the acquisition of control or substantial change in capital structure of the corporation, or, if earlier, on or before January 5th of the year following the calendar year in which the acquisition of control or substantial change in capital structure occurs.

(ii) *Transition rule.*—If an acquisition of control or a substantial change in capital structure of a corporation occurs after December 31, 2002, and before December 29, 2003, Form 8806 must be filed on or before January 5, 2004.

(4) *Exception where transaction is reported under section 6043(a).*—No reporting is required under paragraph (a) of this section with respect to a transaction for which information is required to be reported pursuant to section 6043(a), provided the transaction is properly reported in accordance with that section.

(5) *Exception where shareholders are exempt recipients.*—No reporting is required under paragraph (a) of this section if the reporting corporation reasonably determines that all of its shareholders who receive cash, stock or other property pursuant to the acquisition of control or substantial change in capital structure are exempt recipients under paragraph (b)(5) of this section.

(b) *Information returns regarding shareholders.*— (1) *General rule.*—A corporation that is required to file Form 8806 pursuant to paragraph (a)(1) of this section shall file a return of information on Forms 1096, "Annual Summary and Transmittal of U.S. Information Returns," and 1099-CAP, "Changes in Corporate Control and Capital Structure," with respect to each shareholder of

record in the corporation (before or after the acquisition of control or the substantial change in capital structure) who receives cash, stock, or other property pursuant to the acquisition of control or the substantial change in capital structure and who is not an exempt recipient as defined in paragraph (b)(5) of this section. A corporation is not required to file a Form 1096 or 1099-CAP with respect to a clearing organization if the corporation makes the election described in paragraph (a)(2) of this section.

(2) *Time for making information returns.*— Forms 1096 and 1099-CAP must be filed on or before February 28 (March 31 if filed electronically) of the year following the calendar year in which the acquisition of control or the substantial change in capital structure occurs.

(3) *Contents of return.*—A separate Form 1099-CAP must be filed with respect to amounts received by each shareholder (who is not an exempt recipient as defined in paragraph (b)(5) of this section) showing—

(i) The name, address, telephone number and TIN of the reporting corporation;

(ii) The name, address and TIN of the shareholder;

(iii) The number and class of shares in the reporting corporation exchanged by the shareholder;

(iv) The aggregate amount of cash and the fair market value of any stock (other than stock described in paragraph (a)(1)(v)(C) of this section) or other property provided to the shareholder in exchange for its stock; and

(v) Such other information as may be required by the instructions to Form 1099-CAP.

(4) *Furnishing of forms to shareholders.*—The Form 1099-CAP filed with respect to each shareholder must be furnished to such shareholder on or before January 31 of the year following the calendar year in which the shareholder receives cash, stock, or other property as part of the acquisition of control or the substantial change in capital structure. The Form 1099-CAP filed with respect to a clearing organization must be furnished to the clearing organization on or before January 5th of the year following the calendar year in which the acquisition of control or substantial change in capital structure occurred. A Form 1099-CAP is not required to be furnished to a clearing organization if the reporting corporation makes the election described in paragraph (a)(2) of this section.

(5) *Exempt recipients.*—A corporation is not required to file a Form 1099-CAP pursuant to this paragraph (b) of this section with respect to any of the following shareholders that is not a clearing organization:

(i) Any shareholder who receives solely stock described in paragraph (a)(1)(v)(C) of this section in exchange for its stock in the corporation.

>>>→ *Caution: Temporary Reg. §1.6043-4T, below, was removed by T.D. 9230, but it remains outstanding with respect to transactions not covered by Reg. §1.6043-4 while the IRS considers additional information reporting requirements under Code Secs. 6043(c), 6043A and 6045.*

(ii) Any shareholder who is required to recognize gain (if any) as a result of the receipt of cash, stock, or other property if the corporation reasonably determines that the amount of such cash plus the fair market value of such stock and other property does not exceed $1,000. Stock described in paragraph (a)(1)(v)(C) of this section is not taken into account for purposes of this paragraph (b)(5)(ii).

(iii) Any shareholder described in paragraphs (b)(5)(iii)(A) through (M) of this section if the corporation has actual knowledge that the shareholder is described in one of paragraphs (b)(5)(iii)(A) through (M) of this section or if the corporation has a properly completed exemption certificate from the shareholder (as provided in §31.3406(h)-3 of this chapter). The corporation also may treat a shareholder as described in paragraphs (b)(5)(iii)(A) through (M) of this section based on the applicable indicators described in §1.6049-4(c)(1)(ii).

(A) A corporation, as described in section §1.6049-4(c)(1)(ii)(A)(except for corporations for which an election under section 1362(a) is in effect).

(B) A tax-exempt organization, as described in §1.6049-4(c)(1)(ii)(B)(1).

(C) An individual retirement plan, as described in §1.6049-4(c)(1)(ii)(C).

(D) The United States, as described in §1.6049-4(c)(1)(ii)(D).

(E) A state, as described in §1.6049-4(c)(1)(ii)(E).

(F) A foreign government, as described in §1.6049-4(c)(1)(ii)(F).

(G) An international organization, as described in §1.6049-4(c)(1)(ii)(G).

(H) A foreign central bank of issue, as described in §1.6049-4(c)(1)(ii)(H).

(I) A securities or commodities dealer, as described in §1.6049-4(c)(1)(ii)(I).

(J) A real estate investment trust, as described in §1.6049-4(c)(1)(ii)(J).

(K) An entity registered under the Investment Company Act of 1940 (15 U.S.C. 80a-1), as described in §1.6049-4(c)(1)(ii)(K).

(L) A common trust fund, as described in §1.6049-4(c)(1)(ii)(L).

(M) A financial institution such as a bank, mutual savings bank, savings and loan association, building and loan association, cooperative bank, homestead association, credit union, industrial loan association or bank, or other similar organization.

(iv) Any shareholder that the corporation, prior to the transaction, associates with documentation upon which the corporation may rely in order to treat payments to the shareholder as made to a foreign beneficial owner in accordance with §1.1441-1(e)(1)(ii) or as made to a foreign payee in accordance with §1.6049-5(d)(1) or pre-

sumed to be made to a foreign payee under §1.6049-5(d)(2) or (3). For purposes of this paragraph (b)(5)(iv), the provisions in §1.6049-5(c) (regarding rules applicable to documentation of foreign status and definition of U.S. payor and non-U.S. payor) shall apply. The provisions of §1.1441-1 shall apply by using the terms *corporation* and *shareholder* in place of the terms *withholding agent* and *payee* and without regard to the fact that the provisions apply only to amounts subject to withholding under chapter 3 of the Internal Revenue Code. The provisions of §1.6049-5(d) shall apply by using the terms *corporation* and *shareholder* in place of the terms *payor* and *payee*. Nothing in this paragraph (b)(5)(iv) shall be construed to relieve a corporation of its withholding obligations under section 1441.

(v) Any shareholder if, on January 31 of the year following the calendar year in which the shareholder receives cash, stock, or other property, the corporation did not know and did not have reason to know that the shareholder received such cash, stock, or other property in a transaction or series of related transactions that would result in an acquisition of control or a substantial change in capital structure.

(6) *Coordination with other sections.*—In general, no reporting is required under paragraph (b) of this section with respect to amounts that are required to be reported under section 6042 or section 6045, unless the corporation knows or has reason to know that such amounts are not properly reported in accordance with those sections. A corporation must satisfy the requirements under paragraph (b) of this section with respect to any shareholder of record that is a clearing organization.

(c) *Acquisition of control of a corporation.*—(1) *In general.*—For purposes of this section, an acquisition of control of a corporation (first corporation) occurs if, in a transaction or series of related transactions, either—

(i) Stock representing control of the first corporation is distributed by a second corporation to shareholders of the second corporation and the fair market value of such stock on the date of distribution is $100,000,000 or more; or

(ii)(A) Before an acquisition of stock of the first corporation (directly or indirectly) by a second corporation, the second corporation does not have control of the first corporation;

(B) After the acquisition, the second corporation has control of the first corporation;

(C) The fair market value of the stock acquired in the transaction and in any related transactions as of the date or dates on which such stock was acquired is $100,000,000 or more; and

(D) The shareholders of the first corporation (determined without applying the con-

>>> *Caution: Temporary Reg. §1.6043-4T, below, was removed by T.D. 9230, but it remains outstanding with respect to transactions not covered by Reg. §1.6043-4 while the IRS considers additional information reporting requirements under Code Secs. 6043(c), 6043A and 6045.*

structive ownership rule of section 318(a)) receive cash, stock, or other property pursuant to the acquisition.

(2) *Control.*—For purposes of this section, control is determined in accordance with the first sentence of section 304(c)(1).

(3) *Constructive ownership.*—(i) Except as otherwise provided in this section, the constructive ownership rules of section 318(a) (except for section 318(a)(4), providing for constructive ownership through an option to acquire stock), modified as provided in section 304(c)(3)(B), shall apply for determining whether there has been an acquisition of control.

(ii) The determination of whether there has been an acquisition of control shall be made without regard to whether the person or persons from whom control was acquired retain indirect control of the first corporation under section 318(a).

(iii) For purposes of paragraph (c)(1)(ii) of this section, section 318(a) shall not apply to cause a second corporation to be treated as owning, before an acquisition of stock in a first corporation (directly or indirectly) by the second corporation, any stock that is acquired in the first corporation. For example, if the shareholders of a domestic corporation form a new holding company and then transfer their shares in the domestic corporation to the new holding company, the new holding company shall not be treated as having control of the domestic corporation before the acquisition. The new holding company acquires control of the domestic corporation as a result of the transfer. Similarly, if the shareholders of a domestic parent corporation transfer their shares in the parent corporation to a subsidiary of the parent in exchange for shares in the subsidiary, the subsidiary shall not be treated as having control of the parent before the transaction. The subsidiary acquires control of the parent as a result of the transfer.

(4) *Corporation includes group.*—For purposes of this paragraph (c), if two or more corporations act pursuant to a plan or arrangement with respect to acquisitions of stock, such corporations will be treated as one corporation for purposes of this section. Whether two or more corporations act pursuant to a plan or arrangement depends on the facts and circumstances.

(5) *Section 338 election.*—For purposes of this paragraph (c), an acquisition of stock of a corporation with respect to which an election under section 338 is made is treated as an acquisition of stock (and not as an acquisition of the assets of such corporation).

(d) *Substantial change in capital structure of a corporation.*—(1) *In general.*—A corporation has a substantial change in capital structure if it has a change in capital structure (as defined in paragraph (d)(2) of this section) and the amount of any cash and the fair market value of any property (including stock) provided to the shareholders of such corporation pursuant to the change in capital structure, as of the date or dates on which the cash or other property is provided, is $100,000,000 or more.

(2) *Change in capital structure.*—For purposes of this section, a corporation has a change in capital structure if the corporation in a transaction or series of transactions—

(i) Undergoes a recapitalization with respect to its stock;

(ii) Redeems its stock (including deemed redemptions);

(iii) Merges, consolidates or otherwise combines with another corporation or transfers all or substantially all of its assets to one or more corporations;

(iv) Transfers all or part of its assets to another corporation in a title 11 or similar case and, in pursuance of the plan, distributes stock or securities of that corporation; or

(v) Changes its identity, form or place of organization.

(e) *Reporting by successor entity.*—If a corporation (transferor) transfers all or substantially all of its assets to another entity (transferee) in a transaction that constitutes a substantial change in the capital structure of transferor, transferor must satisfy the reporting obligations in paragraph (a) or (b) of this section. If transferor does not satisfy the reporting obligations in paragraph (a) or (b) of this section, then transferee must satisfy those reporting obligations. If neither transferor nor transferee satisfies the reporting obligations in paragraphs (a) and (b) of this section, then transferor and transferee shall be jointly and severally liable for any applicable penalties (see paragraph (g) of this section).

(f) *Receipt of property.*—For purposes of this section, a shareholder is treated as receiving property (or as having property provided to it) pursuant to an acquisition of control or a substantial change in capital structure if a liability of the shareholder is assumed in the transaction and, as a result of the transaction, an amount is realized by the shareholder from the sale or exchange of stock.

(g) *Penalties for failure to file.*—For penalties for failure to file as required under this section, see section 6652(1). The information returns required to be filed under paragraphs (a) and (b) of this section shall be treated as one return for purposes of section 6652(1) and, accordingly, the penalty shall not exceed $500 for each day the failure continues (up to a maximum of $100,000) with respect to any acquisition of control or any substantial change in capital structure. Failure to file as required under this section also includes the requirement to file on magnetic media as required by section 6011(e) and §1.6011-2. In

Reg. §1.6043-4T(g)

»»→ Caution: *Temporary Reg. §1.6043-4T, below, was removed by T.D. 9230, but it remains outstanding with respect to transactions not covered by Reg. §1.6043-4 while the IRS considers additional information reporting requirements under Code Secs. 6043(c), 6043A and 6045.*

addition, criminal penalties under sections 7203, 7206 and 7207 may apply in appropriate cases.

(h) *Examples.*—The following examples illustrate the application of the rules of this section. For purposes of these examples, assume the transaction is not reported under sections 6042, 6043(a) or 6045, unless otherwise specified, and assume that the fair market value of the consideration provided to the shareholders exceeds $100,000,000. The examples are as follows:

Example 1. The shareholders of X, a domestic corporation and parent of an affiliated group, exchange their X stock for stock in Y, a newly-formed foreign holding corporation. After the transaction, Y owns all the outstanding X stock. The X shareholders must recognize gain (if any) on the exchange of their stock as a result of the application of section 367(a). Because the transaction results in an acquisition of control of X, X must comply with the rules in paragraphs (a) and (b) of this section. X must file Form 8806 reporting the transaction. X must also file a Form 1099-CAP with respect to each shareholder who is not an exempt recipient showing the fair market value of the Y stock received by that shareholder, and X must furnish a copy of the Form 1099-CAP to that shareholder. If X elects on the Form 8806 to permit the IRS to publish information regarding the transaction, X is not required to file or furnish Forms 1099-CAP with respect to shareholders that are clearing organizations.

Example 2. C, a domestic corporation, and parent of an affiliated group merges into D, an unrelated domestic corporation. Pursuant to the transaction, the C shareholders exchange their C stock for D stock or for a combination of short term notes and D stock. The transaction does not satisfy the requirements of section 368, and the C shareholders must recognize gain (if any) on the exchange. Because the transaction results in a substantial change in the capital structure of C, C (or D as the successor to C) must comply with the rules in paragraphs (a) and (b) of this section. C must file Form 8806. C (or D as the successor to C) also must file a Form 1099-CAP with respect to each shareholder who is not an exempt recipient showing the fair market value of the short term notes and the fair market value of the D stock provided to that shareholder. In addition, C (or D) must furnish a copy of the Form 1099-CAP to that shareholder.

Example 3. (i) The facts are the same as in *Example 2*, except that C reasonably determines that—

(A) The transaction satisfies the requirements of section 368;

(B) The C shareholders who exchange their C stock solely for D stock will not be required to recognize gain (if any) on the exchange; and

(C) The C shareholders who exchange their C stock for a combination of short term notes and D stock will be required to recognize gain (if

any) on the exchange solely with respect to the receipt of the short term notes.

(ii) C is required to file Form 8806 under paragraph (a) of this section. C (or D as the successor to C) must also comply with the rules in paragraph (b) of this section. With respect to each shareholder who receives a combination of short term notes and D stock, and who is not an exempt recipient, C (or D) must file a Form 1099-CAP showing the fair market value of the short term notes provided to the shareholder, and C (or D) must furnish a copy of the Form 1099-CAP to that shareholder. The Form 1099-CAP should not show the fair market value of the D stock provided to the shareholder. C and D are not required to file and furnish Forms 1099-CAP with respect to shareholders who receive only D stock in exchange for their C stock.

Example 4. The facts are the same as in *Example 3*, except C hires a transfer agent to effectuate the exchange. The transfer agent is treated as a broker under section 6045 and is required to report the fair market value of the short term notes provided to C's shareholders under §1.6045-3T. Under paragraph (b)(6) of this section, C and D are not required to file information returns under paragraph (b) of this section with respect to a shareholder of record, unless C or D knows or has reason to know that the transfer agent does not satisfy its information reporting obligation under §1.6045-3T with respect to that shareholder. Thus, if the transfer agent satisfies its information reporting requirements under §1.6045-3T with respect to shareholder I, an individual who receives both D stock and short term notes, C and D are not required to file a Form 1099-CAP with respect to I. Conversely, if the transfer agent does not have an information reporting obligation under §1.6045-3T with respect to one of C's shareholder's of record (for example, a clearing organization that is an exempt recipient under §1.6045-3T(b)(ii)), or if C or D knows or has reason to know that the transfer agent has not satisfied its information reporting requirement with respect to a shareholder, then C (or D) must provide a Form 1099-CAP to that shareholder.

(i) *Effective date.*—This section applies to any acquisition of control and any substantial change in capital structure occurring after December 31, 2001, if the reporting corporation or any shareholder is required to recognize gain (if any) as a result of the application of section 367(a) as a result of the transaction. However, paragraphs (a) through (h) of this section apply to acquisitions of control and substantial changes in capital structure occurring after December 31, 2002, if the reporting corporation or any shareholder is required to recognize gain (if any) as a result of the application of section 367(a) as a result of the transaction. For transactions prior to January 1, 2003, see §1.6043-4T as published in 26 CFR Part 1 (revised as of April 1, 2003). This section ex-

Reg. §1.6043-4T(h)

≫→ *Caution: Temporary Reg. §1.6043-4T, below, was removed by T.D. 9230, but it remains outstanding with respect to transactions not covered by Reg. §1.6043-4 while the IRS considers additional information reporting requirements under Code Secs. 6043(c), 6043A and 6045.*

pires on November 14, 2005. [Temporary Reg. §1.6043-4T.]

☐ [*T.D.* 9022, 11-13-2002 (*corrected* 2-5-2003). *Amended by T.D.* 9101, 12-29-2003. *Removed by T.D.* 9230, 12-2-2005.]

[Reg. §301.6044-1]

§301.6044-1. Returns of information regarding payments of patronage dividends.—For provisions relating to the requirement of returns of information regarding payments of patronage dividends, see §§1.6044-1 to 1.6044-5, inclusive, of this chapter (Income Tax Regulations). [Reg. §301.6044-1.]

☐ [*T.D.* 6498, 10-24-60. *Amended by T.D.* 6700, 1-6-64.]

[Reg. §1.6044-2]

§1.6044-2. Returns of information as to payments of patronage dividends.—(a) *Requirement of reporting.*—(1) *In general.*—Except as provided in §1.6044-4, every organization described in paragraph (b) of this section which makes payments with respect to patronage occurring on or after the first day of the first taxable year of the organization beginning after December 31, 1962, of amounts described in §1.6044-3 aggregating $10 or more to any person during any calendar year shall make an information return on Forms 1096 and 1099 for the calendar year showing the aggregate amount of such payments, the name and address of the person to whom paid, the total of such payments for all persons, and such other information as is required by the forms. The organization is required to make an information return regardless of the amount of the payment if the tax imposed by section 3406 is required to be withheld. Thus, in the case of any amount subject to backup withholding under section 3406 and not refunded by the payor before the due date of the information return in accordance with the regulations under section 3406, an information return shall be made even if the payment is not generally reportable because it is made to an exempt recipient described in §1.6049-4(c)(1)(ii) or the amount paid during the calendar year to the recipient aggregates less than $10.

(2) *Definitions.*—The term "person" when used in this section does not include the United States, a State, the District of Columbia, a foreign government, a political subdivision of a State or of a foreign government, or an international organization. Therefore, payment of amounts described in §1.6044-3 to one of these entities need not be reported.

(3) *Determination of person to whom a patronage dividend is paid.*—For purposes of applying the provisions of this section, the person whose identifying number is required to be included by the cooperative on an information return with respect to a patronage dividend shall

be considered the person to whom such dividend is paid. For regulations relating to the use of identifying numbers, see §1.6109-1.

(4) *Inclusion of other payments.*—The Form 1099 filed by an organization with respect to payments of patronage dividends made to any person during a calendar year may, at the election of the organization, include other payments made by it to such person during such year which are required to be reported on Form 1099.

(b) *Organizations subject to reporting requirement.*—The organizations subject to the reporting requirements of paragraph (a) of this section are—

(1) Any organization exempt from tax under section 521 (relating to exemption of farmers' cooperatives from tax), and

(2) Any corporation operating on a cooperative basis other than an organization—

(i) Which is exempt from tax under chapter 1 (other than section 521), or

(ii) Which is subject to the provisions of part II of subchapter H of chapter 1 (relating to mutual savings banks, etc.), or subchapter L of chapter 1 (relating to insurance companies), or

(iii) Which is engaged in furnishing electric energy, or providing telephone service, to persons in rural areas.

(c) *When payment deemed made.*—For purposes of this section, money or other property (except written notices of allocation) is deemed to have been paid when it is credited or set apart to a person without any substantial limitation or restriction as to the time or manner of payment or condition upon which payment is to be made, and is made available to him so that it may be drawn at any time, and its receipt brought within his own control and disposition. A written notice of allocation is considered to have been paid when it is issued by the organization to the distributee. Similarly, a qualified check (as defined in section 1388(d)(4)) is considered to have been paid when it is issued to the distributee.

(d) *Time and place for filing.*—The return required under this section on Forms 1096 and 1099 for any calendar year shall be filed after September 30 of such year, but not before the payer's final payment for the year, and on or before February 28 (March 31 if filed electronically) of the following year, with any of the Internal Revenue Service Centers, the addresses of which are listed in the instructions for such forms. For extensions of time for filing returns under this section, see §1.6081-1.

(e) *Cross-reference to penalty.*—For provisions relating to the penalty provided for failure to file timely a correct information return required under section 6044(a), see §301.6721-1 of this chapter (Procedure and Administration Regulations). See § 301.6724-1 of this chapter for the waiver of a penalty if the failure is due to reasonable cause and is not due to willful neglect.

(f) *Magnetic media requirement.*—For the requirement to submit the information required by Form 1099 on magnetic media for payments after December 31, 1983, see section 6011(e) and § 301.6011-2 of this chapter (Procedure and Administration Regulations). For rules relating to permission to submit the information required by Form 1099 on magnetic tape or other media, see § 1.9101-1. [Reg. § 1.6044-2.]

☐ [T.D. 6628, 12-27-62. *Amended by T.D. 6677,* 9-16-63; *T.D. 6879,* 3-7-66; *T.D. 6883,* 5-2-66; *T.D. 8734,* 10-6-97 (T.D. 8804 delayed the effective date of T.D. 8734 from January 1, 1999, to January 1, 2000; T.D. 8856 further delayed the effective date of T.D. 8734 until January 1, 2001) *and T.D. 8895,* 8-17-2000.]

[Reg. § 1.6044-3]

§ 1.6044-3. Amounts subject to reporting.—(a) *In general.*—Except as provided in paragraph (c) of this section, the amounts subject to reporting under § 1.6044-2 are—

(1) Payments by all organizations subject to such reporting requirements of—

(i) Patronage dividends (as defined in section 1388(a)) paid in money, qualified written notices of allocation (as defined in section 1388(c)), or other property (except nonqualified written notices of allocation as defined in section 1388(d)); and

(ii) Amounts described in section 1382(b)(2) (relating to redemption of nonqualified written notices of allocation previously paid as patronage dividends) paid in money or property (except written notices of allocation); and

(2) Payments by farmers' cooperatives exempt from tax under section 521 of—

(i) Amounts described in section 1382(c)(2)(A) (relating to distributions with respect to earnings derived from sources other than patronage) paid in money, qualified written notices of allocation, or other property (except nonqualified written notices of allocation); and

(ii) Amounts described in section 1382(c)(2)(B) (relating to redemption of nonqualified written notices of allocation previously paid as distributions with respect to earnings derived from sources other than patronage) paid in money or other property (except written notices of allocation).

(b) *Special rules.*—(1) If an organization makes a distribution consisting in whole or in part of a written notice of allocation and a qualified check and, at the time it files its return under § 1.6044-2, is unable to determine whether such written notice of allocation and such check constitute nonqualified written notices of allocation, such organization shall for purposes of such return treat such written notice of allocation as a qualified written notice of allocation and such qualified check as a payment in money.

(2) An amount described in paragraph (a) of this section is subject to reporting even though the organization paying such amount is allowed no deduction for it because it was not paid within the time prescribed in section 1382. Thus, a patronage dividend of $25 paid by a marketing cooperative must be reported even though it is paid after the end of the payment period (see section 1382(d)) for the organization's taxable year in which the patronage occurred.

(c) *Exceptions.*—An amount described in paragraph (a) of this section does not include—

(1) Any amount described in § 1.6042-3(b); or

(2) With respect to amounts paid or credited after December 31, 1982, any amount paid or credited to any person described in § 1.6049-4(c)(1)(ii).

(d) *Determination of amount paid.*—For purposes of § 1.6044-2 and this section, in determining the amount of any payment subject to reporting under paragraph (a) of this section—

(1) Property (other than a qualified written notice of allocation) shall be taken into account at its fair market value, and

(2) A qualified written notice of allocation shall be taken into account at its stated dollar amount. [Reg. § 1.6044-3.]

☐ [T.D. 6628, 12-27-62. *Amended by T.D. 8734,* 10-6-97 (T.D. 8804 delayed the effective date of T.D. 8734 from January 1, 1999, to January 1, 2000; T.D. 8856 further delayed the effective date of T.D. 8734 until January 1, 2001).]

[Reg. § 1.6044-4]

§ 1.6044-4. Exemption for certain consumer cooperatives.—(a) *In general.*—(1) *Determination of exemption.*—Exemption from the reporting requirements of § 1.6044-2 shall, upon application therefor, be granted by the district director to any cooperative which he determines is primarily engaged in selling at retail goods or services of a type which is generally for personal, living, or family use. A cooperative is not exempt from the reporting requirements merely because it is an organization of a type to which section 6044(c) and this section relate. In order for the exemption from reporting to apply, it is necessary that the cooperative file an application in accordance with this section and obtain a determination of exemption.

(2) *Basis of exemption.*—For a cooperative to qualify for the exemption from reporting provided by section 6044(c) and this section 85 percent of its gross receipts for the preceding taxable year, or 85 percent of its aggregate gross receipts for the preceding three taxable years, must have been derived from the sale at retail of goods or services of a type which is generally for personal, living, or family use. In determining whether an item is of a type that is generally for personal, living, or family use, an item which may be purchased either for such use or for business use and which when acquired for business purposes is generally purchased at whole-

sale will, when sold by a cooperative at retail, be treated as goods or services of a type generally for personal, living, or family use.

(3) *Period of exemption.*—A determination of exemption from reporting shall apply beginning with the payments made during the calendar year in which the determination is made and shall automatically cease to be effective beginning with payments made after the close of the first taxable year of the cooperative in which less than 70 percent of its gross receipts is derived from the sale at retail of goods or services of a type which is generally for personal, living, or family use.

(b) *Application for exemption.*—Application for exemption from the reporting requirements of section 6044 shall be made on Form 3491, and shall be filed with the district director for the internal revenue district in which the cooperative has its principal place of business. [Reg. § 1.6044-4.]

☐ [*T.D. 6628, 12-27-62.*]

[Reg. § 1.6044-5]

§ 1.6044-5. Statements to recipients of patronage dividends.—(a) *Requirement.*—A person required to make an information return under section 6044(a)(1) and § 1.6044-2 must furnish a statement to each recipient whose identifying number is required to be shown on the related information return for patronage dividends paid.

(b) *Form, manner, and time for providing statements to recipients.*—The statement required by paragraph (a) of this section must be either the official Form 1099 prescribed by the Internal Revenue Service for the respective calendar year or an acceptable substitute statement. The rules under § 1.6042-4 (relating to statements with respect to dividends) apply comparably in determining the form of an acceptable substitute statement permitted by this section. Those rules also apply for purposes of determining the manner of and time for providing the Form 1099 or its acceptable substitute to a recipient under this section. However, each Form 1099 or acceptable substitute statement required by this section must be furnished on or before January 31 of the following year, but no statement may be furnished before the final payment has been made for the calendar year. For a statement required to be furnished after December 31, 2008, the February 15 due date under section 6045 applies to the statement if the statement is furnished in a consolidated reporting statement under section 6045. *See* §§ 1.6045-1(k)(3), 1.6045-2(d)(2), 1.6045-3(e)(2), 1.6045-4(m)(3), and 1.6045-5(a)(3)(ii). An IRS truncated taxpayer identifying number (TTIN) may be used as the identifying number of the recipient in lieu of the identifying number appearing on the corresponding information return filed with the Internal Revenue Service. For provisions relating to the use of TTINs, see § 301.6109-4 of this chapter (Procedure and Administration Regulations).

(c) *Cross-reference to penalty.*—For provisions relating to the penalty provided for failure to furnish timely a correct payee statement required under section 6044(e), see § 301.6722-1 of this chapter (Procedure and Administration Regulations). See § 301.6724-1 of this chapter for the waiver of a penalty if the failure is due to reasonable cause and is not due to willful neglect.

(d) *Effective/applicability date.*—This section is effective for payee statements due after December 31, 1995, without regard to extensions. The amendments to paragraph (b) are effective for payee statements due after December 31, 2014. For payee statements due before January 1, 2015, § 1.6044-5(b) (as contained in 26 CFR part 1, revised April 2013) shall apply. [Reg. § 1.6044-5.]

☐ [*T.D. 6628, 12-27-62. Amended by T.D. 6879, 3-7-66; T.D. 7529, 12-27-77; T.D. 8637, 12-20-95; T.D. 8734, 10-6-97 (T.D. 8804 delayed the effective date of T.D. 8734 from January 1, 1999, to January 1, 2000; T.D. 8856 further delayed the effective date of T.D. 8734 until January 1, 2001); T.D. 9504, 10-12-2010 and T.D. 9675, 7-14-2014.*]

[Reg. § 1.6045-1]

§ 1.6045-1. Returns of information of brokers and barter exchanges.—(a) *Definitions.*—The following definitions apply for purposes of this section and § 1.6045-2:

(1) The term *broker* means any person (other than a person who is required to report a transaction under section 6043), U.S. or foreign, that, in the ordinary course of a trade or business during the calendar year, stands ready to effect sales to be made by others. A broker includes an obligor that regularly issues and retires its own debt obligations or a corporation that regularly redeems its own stock. However, with respect to a sale (including a redemption or retirement) effected at an office outside the United States, a broker includes only a person described as a U.S. payor or U.S. middleman in § 1.6049-5(c)(5). In addition, a broker does not include an international organization described in § 1.6049-4(c)(1)(ii)(G) that redeems or retires an obligation of which it is the issuer.

(2) The term "customer" means, with respect to a sale effected by a broker, the person (other than such broker) that makes the sale, if the broker acts as—

(i) An agent for such person in the sale;

(ii) A principal in the sale; or

(iii) The participant in the sale responsible for paying to such person or crediting to such person's account the gross proceeds on the sale.

(3) The term "security" means—

(i) A share of stock in a corporation (foreign or domestic);

(ii) An interest in a trust;

(iii) An interest in a partnership;

(iv) A debt obligation;

(v) An interest in or right to purchase any of the foregoing in connection with the issuance thereof from the issuer or an agent of the issuer

Reg. § 1.6045-1(a)(3)(v)

or from an underwriter that purchases any of the foregoing from the issuer;

(vi) An interest in a security described in paragraph (a)(3)(i) or (iv) of this section (but not including executory contracts that require delivery of such type of security);

(vii) An option described in paragraph (m)(2) of this section; or

(viii) A securities futures contract.

(4) The term "barter exchange" means any person with members or clients that contract either with each other or with such person to trade or barter property or services either directly or through such person. The term does not include arrangements that provide solely for the informal exchange of similar services on a non-commercial basis.

(5) The term "commodity" means—

(i) Any type of personal property or an interest therein (other than securities as defined in paragraph (a)(3)), the trading of regulated futures contracts in which has been approved by the Commodity Futures Trading Commission;

(ii) Lead, palm oil, rapeseed, tea, tin, or an interest in any of the foregoing; or

(iii) Any other personal property or an interest therein that is of a type the Secretary determines is to be treated as a "commodity" under this section, from and after the date specified in a notice of such determination published in the Federal Register.

(6) The term "regulated futures contract" means a regulated futures contract within the meaning of section 1256(b).

(7) The term "forward contract" means—

(i) An executory contract that requires delivery of a commodity in exchange for cash and which contract is not a regulated futures contract; or

(ii) An executory contract that requires delivery of personal property or an interest therein in exchange for cash, or a cash settlement contract, if such executory contract or cash settlement contract is of a type the Secretary determines is to be treated as a "forward contract" under this section, from and after the date specified in a notice of such determination published in the Federal Register.

(8) The term *closing transaction* means a lapse, expiration, settlement, abandonment, or other termination of a position. For purposes of the preceding sentence, a position includes a right or an obligation under a forward contract, a regulated futures contract, a securities futures contract, or an option.

(9) The term *sale* means any disposition of securities, commodities, options, regulated futures contracts, securities futures contracts, or forward contracts, and includes redemptions of stock, retirements of debt instruments (including a partial retirement attributable to a principal payment received on or after January 1, 2014), and enterings into short sales, but only to the extent any of these actions are conducted for cash. In the case of an option, a regulated futures contract, a securities futures contract, or a for-

ward contract, a sale includes any closing transaction. When a closing transaction for a contract described in section 1256(b)(1)(A) involves making or taking delivery, there are two sales, one resulting in profit or loss on the contract, and a separate sale on the delivery. When a closing transaction for a contract described in section 988(c)(5) involves making delivery, there are two sales, one resulting in profit or loss on the contract, and a separate sale on the delivery. For purposes of the preceding sentence, a broker may assume that any customer's functional currency is the U.S. dollar. When a closing transaction in a forward contract involves making or taking delivery, the broker may treat the delivery as a sale without separating the profit or loss on the contract from the profit or loss on the delivery, except that taking delivery for United States dollars is not a sale. The term *sale* does not include entering into a contract that requires delivery of personal property or an interest therein, the initial grant or purchase of an option, or the exercise of a purchased call option for physical delivery (except for a contract described in section 988(c)(5)). For purposes of this section only, a constructive sale under section 1259 and a mark to fair market value under section 475 or 1296 are not sales.

(10) The term "effect" means, with respect to a sale, to act as—

(i) An agent for a party in the sale wherein the nature of the agency is such that the agent ordinarily would know the gross proceeds from the sale; or

(ii) A principal in such sale.

Acting as an agent or principal with respect to grants or purchases of options, exercises of call options, or enterings into contracts that require delivery of personal property or an interest therein is not of itself effecting a sale. A broker that has on its books a forward contract under which delivery is made effects such delivery.

(11) The term "foreign currency" means currency of a foreign country.

(12) The term "cash" means United States dollars or any convertible foreign currency.

(13) The term *person* includes any governmental unit and any agency or instrumentality thereof.

(14) The term *specified security* means:

(i) Any share of stock (or any interest treated as stock, including, for example, an American Depositary Receipt) in an entity organized as, or treated for Federal tax purposes as, a corporation, either foreign or domestic (provided that, solely for purposes of this paragraph (a)(14)(i), a security classified as stock by the issuer is treated as stock, and if the issuer has not classified the security, the security is not treated as stock unless the broker knows that the security is reasonably classified as stock under general Federal tax principles);

(ii) Any debt instrument described in paragraph (a)(17) of this section, other than a debt instrument subject to section 1272(a)(6) (certain interests in or mortgages held by a REMIC, certain other debt instruments with payments subject to acceleration, and pools of debt instruments the yield on which may be affected by prepayments) or a short-term obligation described in section 1272(a)(2)(C);

(iii) Any option described in paragraph (m)(2) of this section; or

(iv) Any securities futures contract.

(15) The term *covered security* means a specified security described in this paragraph (a)(15).

(i) *In general.*—Except as provided in paragraph (a)(15)(iv) of this section, the following securities are covered securities:

(A) A specified security described in paragraph (a)(14)(i) of this section acquired for cash in an account on or after January 1, 2011, except stock for which the average basis method is available under § 1.1012-1(e).

(B) Stock for which the average basis method is available under § 1.1012-1(e) acquired for cash in an account on or after January 1, 2012.

(C) A specified security described in paragraphs (a)(14)(ii) and (n)(2)(i) of this section (not including the debt instruments described in paragraph (n)(2)(ii) of this section) acquired for cash in an account on or after January 1, 2014.

(D) A specified security described in paragraphs (a)(14)(ii) and (n)(3) of this section acquired for cash in an account on or after January 1, 2016.

(E) An option described in paragraph (a)(14)(iii) of this section granted or acquired for cash in an account on or after January 1, 2014.

(F) A securities futures contract described in paragraph (a)(14)(iv) of this section entered into in an account on or after January 1, 2014.

(G) A specified security transferred to an account if the broker or other custodian of the account receives a transfer statement (as described in § 1.6045A-1 reporting the security as a covered security.

(ii) *Acquired in an account.*—For purposes of this paragraph (a)(15), a security is considered acquired in a customer's account at a broker or custodian if the security is acquired by the customer's broker or custodian or acquired by another broker and delivered to the customer's broker or custodian. Acquiring a security in an account includes granting an option and entering into a short sale.

(iii) *Corporate actions and other events.*—For purposes of this paragraph (a)(15), a security acquired due to a stock dividend, stock split, reorganization, redemption, stock conversion, recapitalization, corporate division, or other similar action is considered acquired for cash in an account.

(iv) *Exceptions.*—Notwithstanding paragraph (a)(15)(i) of this section, the following securities are not covered securities:

(A) Stock acquired in 2011 that is transferred to a dividend reinvestment plan (as described in § 1.1012-1(e)(6) in 2011. However, a covered security acquired in 2011 that is transferred to a dividend reinvestment plan after 2011 remains a covered security.

(B) A security acquired through an event described in paragraph (a)(15)(iii) of this section if the basis of the acquired security is determined from the basis of a noncovered security.

(C) A security that is excepted at the time of its acquisition from reporting under paragraph (c)(3) or (g) of this section. However, a broker cannot treat a security as acquired by an exempt foreign person under paragraph (g)(1)(i) of this section at the time of acquisition if, at that time, the broker knows or should have known (including by reason of information that the broker is required to collect under section 1471 or 1472) that the customer is not a foreign person.

(D) A security for which reporting under this section is required by § 1.6049-5(d)(3)(ii) (certain securities owned by a foreign intermediary or flow-through entity).

(16) The term *noncovered security* means any security that is not a covered security.

(17) For purposes of this section, the terms *debt instrument, bond, debt obligation,* and *obligation* mean a debt instrument as defined in § 1.1275-1(d) and any instrument or position that is treated as a debt instrument under a specific provision of the Internal Revenue Code (for example, a regular interest in a REMIC as defined in section 860G(a)(1) and § 1.860G-1). Solely for purposes of this section, a security classified as debt by the issuer is treated as debt. If the issuer has not classified the security, the security is not treated as debt unless the broker knows that the security is reasonably classified as debt under general Federal tax principles or that the instrument or position is treated as a debt instrument under a specific provision of the Internal Revenue Code.

(18) For purposes of this section, the term *securities futures contract* means a contract described in section 1234B(c) whose underlying asset is described in paragraph (a)(14)(i) of this section and which is entered into on or after January 1, 2014.

(b) *Examples.*—The following examples illustrate the definitions in paragraph (a):

Example 1. The following persons generally are brokers within the meaning of paragraph (a)(1):

(i) A mutual fund, an underwriter of the mutual fund, or an agent for the mutual fund, any of which stands ready to redeem or repurchase shares in such mutual fund.

(ii) A professional custodian (such as a bank) that regularly arranges sales for custodial accounts pursuant to instructions from the owner of the property.

(iii) A depository trust or other person that regularly acts as an escrow agent in corporate acquisitions, if the nature of the activities of the agent is such that the agent ordinarily would know the gross proceeds from sales.

Reg. § 1.6045-1(b)

(iv) A stock transfer agent for a corporation, which agent records transfers of stock in such corporation, if the nature of the activities of the agent is such that the agent ordinarily would know the gross proceeds from sales.

(v) A dividend reinvestment agent for a corporation that stands ready to purchase or redeem shares.

Example 2. The following persons are not brokers within the meaning of paragraph (a)(1) in the absence of additional facts that indicate the person is a broker:

(i) A stock transfer agent for a corporation, which agent daily records transfers of stock in such corporation, if the nature of the activities of the agent is such that the agent ordinarily would not know the gross proceeds from sales.

(ii) A person (such as a stock exchange) that merely provides facilities in which others effect sales.

(iii) An escrow agent or nominee if such agency is not in the ordinary course of a trade or business.

(iv) An escrow agent, otherwise a broker, which agent effects no sales other than such transactions as are incidental to the purpose of the escrow (such as sales to collect on collateral).

(v) A floor broker on a commodities exchange, which broker maintains no records with respect to the terms of sales.

(vi) A corporation that issues and retires long-term debt on an irregular basis.

(vii) A clearing organization.

Example 3. A, B, and C belong to a carpool in which they commute to and from work. Every third day, each member of the carpool provides transportation for the other two members. Because the carpool arrangement provides solely for the informal exchange of similar services on a noncommercial basis, the carpool is not a barter exchange within the meaning of paragraph (a)(4).

Example 4. X is an organization whose members include retail merchants, wholesale merchants, and persons in the trade or business of performing services. X's members exchange property and services among themselves using credits on the books of X as a medium of exchange. Each exchange through X is reflected on the books of X by crediting the account of the member providing property or services and debiting the account of the member receiving such property or services. X also provides information to its members concerning property and services available for exchange through X. X charges its members a commission on each transaction in which credits on its books are used as a medium of exchange. X is a barter exchange within the meaning of paragraph (a)(4) of this section.

Example 5. A warehouse receipt is an interest in personal property for purposes of paragraph (a). Consequently, a warehouse receipt for a quantity of lead is a commodity under paragraph (a)(5)(ii). Similarly, an executory contract that requires delivery of a warehouse receipt for a quantity of lead is a forward contract under paragraph (a)(7)(ii).

Example 6. The only customers of a depositary trust acting as an escrow agent in corporate acquisitions, which trust is a broker, are shareholders to whom the trust makes payments or shareholders for whom the trust is acting as an agent.

Example 7. The only customers of a stock transfer agent, which agent is a broker, are shareholders to whom the agent makes payments or shareholders for whom the agent is acting as an agent.

Example 8. D, an individual not otherwise exempt from reporting, is the holder of an obligation issued by P, a corporation. R, a broker, acting as an agent for P, retires such obligation held by D. Such obligor payments from R represent obligor payments by P. (See paragraph (c)(3)(v)). D, the person to whom the gross proceeds are paid or credited by R, is the customer of R.

Example 9. E, an individual not otherwise exempt from reporting, maintains an account with S, a broker. On June 1, 2012, E instructs S to purchase stock that is a specified security for cash. S places an order to purchase the stock with T, another broker. E does not maintain an account with T. T executes the purchase. Custody of the purchased stock is transferred to E's account at S. Under paragraph (a)(15)(ii) of this section, the stock is considered acquired for cash in E's account at S. Because the stock is acquired on or after January 1, 2012, under paragraph (a)(15)(i) of this section, it is a covered security.

Example 10. F, an individual not otherwise exempt from reporting, is granted 100 shares of stock in F's employer by F's employer. Because F does not acquire the stock for cash or through a transfer to an account with a transfer statement (as described in §1.6045A-1, under paragraph (a)(15) of this section, the stock is not a covered security.

Example 11. G, an individual not otherwise exempt from reporting, owns 400 shares of stock in Q, a corporation, in an account with U, a broker. Of the 400 shares, 100 are covered securities and 300 are noncovered securities. Q takes a corporate action to split its stock in a 2-for-1 split. After the stock split, G owns 800 shares of stock. Because the adjusted basis of 600 of the 800 shares that G owns is determined from the basis of noncovered securities, under paragraphs (a)(15)(iii) and (a)(15)(iv)(B) of this section, these 600 shares are not covered securities and the remaining 200 shares are covered securities.

(c) *Reporting by brokers.*—(1) *Requirement of reporting.*—Any broker shall, except as otherwise provided, report in the manner prescribed in this section.1

(2) *Sales required to be reported.*—Except as provided in paragraphs (c)(3), (c)(5), and (g) of this section, a broker is required to make a return of information for each sale by a customer of the broker if, in the ordinary course of a trade or

business in which the broker stands ready to effect sales to be made by others, the broker effects the sale or closes the short position opened by the sale.

(3) *Exceptions.*—(i) *Sales effected for exempt recipients.*—(A) *In general.*—No return of information is required with respect to a sale effected for a customer that is an exempt recipient under paragraph (c)(3)(i)(B) of this section.

(B) *Exempt recipient defined.*—The term *exempt recipient* means—

(1) A corporation as defined in section 7701(a)(3), whether domestic or foreign, except that this exclusion does not apply to sales of covered securities acquired on or after January 1, 2012, by an S corporation as defined in section 1361(a);

(2) An organization exempt from taxation under section 501(a) or an individual retirement plan;

(3) The United States or a State, the District of Columbia, a possession of the United States, a political subdivision of any of the foregoing, a wholly owned agency or instrumentality of any one or more of the foregoing, or a pool or partnership composed exclusively of any of the foregoing;

(4) A foreign government, a political subdivision thereof, an international organization, or any wholly owned agency or instrumentality of the foregoing;

(5) A foreign central bank of issue as defined in § 1.895-1(b)(1) (i.e., a bank that is by law or government sanction the principal authority, other than the government itself, issuing instruments intended to circulate as currency);

(6) A dealer in securities or commodities registered as such under the laws of the United States or a State;

(7) A futures commission merchant registered as such with the Commodity Futures Trading Commission;

(8) A real estate investment trust (as defined in section 856);

(9) An entity registered at all times during the taxable year under the Investment Company Act of 1940 (15 U.S.C. 80a-1, et seq.);

(10) A common trust fund (as defined in section 584(a)); or

(11) A financial institution such as a bank, mutual savings bank, savings and loan association, building and loan association, cooperative bank, homestead association, credit union, industrial loan association or bank, or other similar organization.

(C) *Exemption certificate.*—(1) *In general.*—Except as provided in paragraph (c)(3)(i)(C)(2) of this section, a broker may treat a person described in paragraph (c)(3)(i)(B) of this section as an exempt recipient based on a properly completed exemption certificate (as provided in § 31.3406(h)-3 of this chapter); the broker's actual knowledge that the customer is a person described in paragraph (c)(3)(i)(B) of this section; or the applicable indicators described in

§ 1.6049-4(c)(1)(ii)(A) through (M). A broker may require an exempt recipient to file a properly completed exemption certificate and may treat an exempt recipient that fails to do so as a recipient that is not exempt.

(2) *Limitation for corporate customers.*—For sales of covered securities acquired on or after January 1, 2012, a broker may not treat a customer as an exempt recipient described in paragraph (c)(3)(i)(B)(1) of this section based on the indicators of corporate status described in § 1.6049-4(c)(1)(ii)(A). However, for sales of all securities, a broker may treat a customer as an exempt recipient if one of the following applies:

(i) The name of the customer contains the term "insurance company," "indemnity company," "reinsurance company," or "assurance company."

(ii) The name of the customer indicates that it is an entity listed as a per se corporation under § 301.7701-2(b)(8)(i) of this chapter.

(iii) The broker receives a properly completed exemption certificate (as provided in § 31.3406(h)-3 of this chapter) that asserts that the customer is not an S corporation as defined in section 1361(a).

(iv) The broker receives a withholding certificate described in § 1.1441-1(e)(2)(i) that includes a certification that the person whose name is on the certificate is a foreign corporation.

(ii) *Excepted sales.*—No return of information is required with respect to a sale effected by a broker for a customer if the sale is an excepted sale. For this purpose, a sale is an excepted sale if it is—

(A) So designated by the Internal Revenue Service in a revenue ruling or revenue procedure (see § 601.601(d)(2) of this chapter); or

(B) A sale with respect to which a return is not required by applying the rules of § 1.6049-4(c)(4) (by substituting the term "a sale subject to reporting under section 6045" for the term "an interest payment").

(iii) *Multiple brokers.*—If a broker is instructed to initiate a sale by a person that is an exempt recipient described in paragraph (c)(3)(i)(B)(6), (7), or (11) of this section, no return of information is required with respect to the sale by that broker. In a redemption of stock or retirement of securities, only the broker responsible for paying the holder redeemed or retired, or crediting the gross proceeds on the sale to that holder's account, is required to report the sale.

(iv) *Cash on delivery transactions.*—In the case of a sale of securities through a cash on delivery account, a delivery versus payment account, or other similar account or transaction, only the broker that receives the gross proceeds from the sale against delivery of the securities sold is required to report the sale. If, however, the broker's customer is another broker (second-party broker) that is an exempt recipient, then only the second-party broker is required to report the sale.

(v) *Fiduciaries and partnerships.*—No return of information is required with respect to a sale effected by a custodian or trustee in its capacity as such or a redemption of a partnership interest by a partnership, provided the sale is otherwise reported by the custodian or trustee on a properly filed Form 1041, or the redemption is otherwise reported by the partnership on a properly filed Form 1065, and all Schedule K-1 reporting requirements are satisfied.

(vi) *Money market funds.*—(A) *In general.*—No return of information is required with respect to a sale of shares in a regulated investment company that is permitted to hold itself out to investors as a money market fund under Rule 2a–7 under the Investment Company Act of 1940 (17 CFR 270.2a–7).

(B) *Effective/applicability date.*—Paragraph (c)(3)(vi)(A) of this section applies to sales of shares in calendar years beginning on or after July 8, 2016. Taxpayers and brokers (as defined in § 1.6045-1(a)(1)), however, may rely on paragraph (c)(3)(vi)(A) of this section for sales of shares in calendar years beginning before July 8, 2016.

(vii) *Obligor payments on certain obligations.*—No return of information is required with respect to payments representing obligor payments on—

(A) Nontransferable obligations (including savings bonds, savings accounts, checking accounts, and NOW accounts);

(B) Obligations as to which the entire gross proceeds are reported by the broker on Form 1099 under provisions of the Internal Revenue Code other than section 6045 (including stripped coupons issued prior to July 1, 1982); or

(C) Retirement of short-term obligations (i.e., obligations with a fixed maturity date not exceeding 1 year from the date of issue) that have original issue discount, as defined in section 1273(a)(1), with or without application of the de minimis rule. The preceding sentence does not apply to a debt instrument issued on or after January 1, 2014. For a short-term obligation issued on or after January 1, 2014, see paragraph (c)(3)(xiii) of this section.

(D) Demand obligations that also are callable by the obligor and that have no premium or discount. The preceding sentence does not apply to a debt instrument issued on or after January 1, 2014.

(viii) *Foreign currency.*—No return of information is required with respect to a sale of foreign currency other than a sale pursuant to a forward contract or regulated futures contract that requires delivery of foreign currency.

(ix) *Fractional share.*—No return of information is required with respect to a sale of a fractional share of stock if the gross proceeds on the sale of the fractional share are less than $20.

(x) *Certain retirements.*—No return of information is required from an issuer or its agent with respect to the retirement of book entry or registered form obligations as to which the relevant books and records indicate that no interim transfers have occurred. The preceding sentence does not apply to a debt instrument issued on or after January 1, 2014.

(xi) *Short sales.*—(A) *In general.*—A broker may not make a return of information under this section for a short sale of a security entered into on or after January 1, 2011, until the year a customer delivers a security to satisfy the short sale obligation. The return must be made without regard to the constructive sale rule in section 1259 or to section 1233(h). In general, the broker must report on a single return the information required by paragraph (d)(2)(i) of this section for the short sale except that the broker must report the date the short sale was closed in lieu of the sale date. In applying paragraph (d)(2)(i) of this section, the broker must report the relevant information regarding the security sold to open the short sale and the adjusted basis of the security delivered to close the short sale and whether any gain or loss on the closing of the short sale is long-term or short-term (within the meaning of section 1222).

(B) *Short sale closed by delivery of a noncovered security.*—A broker is not required to report adjusted basis and whether any gain or loss on the closing of the short sale is long-term or short-term if the short sale is closed by delivery of a noncovered security and the return so indicates. A broker that chooses to report this information is not subject to penalties under section 6721 or 6722 for failure to report this information correctly if the broker indicates on the return that the short sale was closed by delivery of a noncovered security.

(C) *Short sale obligation transferred to another account.*—If a short sale obligation is satisfied by delivery of a security transferred into a customer's account accompanied by a transfer statement (as described in § 1.6045A-1(b)(7)) indicating that the security was borrowed, the broker receiving custody of the security may not file a return of information under this section. The receiving broker must furnish a statement to the transferor that reports the amount of gross proceeds received from the short sale, the date of the sale, the quantity of shares, units, or amounts sold, and the Committee on Uniform Security Identification Procedures (CUSIP) number of the sold security (if applicable) or other security identifier number that the Secretary may designate by publication in the **Federal Register** or in the Internal Revenue Bulletin (see § 601.601(d)(2) of this chapter). The statement to the transferor also must include the transfer date, the name and contact information of the receiving broker, the name and contact information of the transferor, and sufficient information to identify the customer. If the customer subsequently closes the short sale obligation in the transferor's account with nonborrowed securities, the transferor must make the return of information required by this section. In that event, the transferor must take into account the information furnished under this paragraph (c)(3)(xi)(C) on the return unless the transferor knows that the information furnished under this paragraph is incorrect or incomplete. A failure to report correct information that arises solely from this reliance is deemed to be due to reasonable cause for purposes of penalties under sections 6721 and 6722. See § 301.6724-1(a)(1) of this chapter.

(xii) *Cross reference.*—For an exception for certain sales of agricultural commodities and certificates issued by the Commodity Credit Corporation after January 1, 1993, see paragraph (c)(7) of this section.

(xiii) *Short-term obligations issued on or after January 1, 2014.*—No return of information is required under this section with respect to a sale (including a retirement) of a short-term obligation, as described in section 1272(a)(2)(C), that is issued on or after January 1, 2014.

(xiv) *Certain redemptions.*—No return of information is required under this section for payments made by a stock transfer agent (as described in § 1.6045-1(b)(iv)) with respect to a redemption of stock of a corporation described in section 1297(a) with respect to a shareholder in the corporation if—

(A) The stock transfer agent obtains from the corporation a written certification signed by a person authorized to sign on behalf of the corporation, that states that the corporation is described in section 1297(a) for each calendar year during which the stock transfer agent relies on the provisions of paragraph (c)(3)(xiv) of this section, and the stock transfer agent has no reason to know that the written certification is unreliable or incorrect;

(B) The stock transfer agent identifies, prior to payment, the corporation as a participating FFI (including a reporting Model 2 FFI) (as defined in § 1.6049-4(f)(10) or (f)(14), respectively), or reporting Model 1 FFI (as defined in § 1.6049-4(f)(13)), in accordance with the requirements of § 1.1471-3(d)(4) (substituting the terms "stock transfer agent" and "corporation" for the terms "withholding agent" and "payee," respectively) and validates that status annually;

(C) The stock transfer agent obtains a written certification representing that the corporation shall report the payment as part of its account holder reporting obligations under chapter 4 of the Code or an applicable IGA (as defined in § 1.6049-4(f)(7)) and provided the stock transfer agent does not know that the corporation is not reporting the payment as required. The paying agent may rely on the written certification until there is a change in circumstances or the paying agent knows or has reason to know that the statement is unreliable or incorrect. A stock transfer agent that knows that the corporation is not reporting the payment as required under chapter 4 of the Code or an

applicable IGA must report all payments reportable under this section that it makes during the year in which it obtains such knowledge; and

(D) The stock transfer agent is not also acting in its capacity as a custodian, nominee, or other agent of the payee with respect to the payment.

(4) *Examples.*—The following examples illustrate the application of the rules in paragraph (c)(3) of this section:

Example 1. P, an individual who is not an exempt recipient, places an order with B, a person generally known in the investment community to be a federally registered broker/dealer, to effect a sale of P's stock in a publicly traded corporation. B, in turn, places an order to sell the stock with C, a second broker, who will execute the sale. B discloses to C the identity of the customer placing the order. C is not required to make a return of information with respect to the sale because C was instructed by B, an exempt recipient as defined in paragraph (c)(3)(i)(B)(6) of this section, to initiate the sale. B is required to make a return of information with respect to the sale because P is B's customer and is not an exempt recipient.

Example 2. Assume the same facts as in *Example 1* except that B has an omnibus account with C so that B does not disclose to C whether the transaction is for a customer of B or for B's own account. C is not required to make a return of information with respect to the sale because C was instructed by B, an exempt recipient as defined in paragraph (c)(3)(i)(B)(6) of this section, to initiate the sale. B is required to make a return of information with respect to the sale because P is B's customer and is not an exempt recipient.

Example 3. D, an individual who is not an exempt recipient, enters into a cash on delivery stock transaction by instructing K, a federally registered broker/dealer, to sell stock owned by D, and to deliver the proceeds to L, a custodian bank. Concurrently with the above instructions, D instructs L to deliver D's stock to K (or K's designee) against delivery of the proceeds from K. The records of both K and L with respect to this transaction show an account in the name of D. Pursuant to paragraph (h)(1) of this section, D is considered the customer of K and L. Under paragraph (c)(3)(iv) of this section, K is not required to make a return of information with respect to the sale because K will pay the gross proceeds to L against delivery of the securities sold. L is required to make a return of information with respect to the sale because D is L's customer and is not an exempt recipient.

Example 4. Assume the same facts as in *Example 3* except that E, a federally registered investment advisor, instructs K to sell stock owned by D and to deliver the proceeds to L. Concurrently with the above instructions, E instructs L to deliver D's stock to K (or K's designee) against delivery of the proceeds from K. The records of both K and L with respect to the transaction show an account in the name of D. Pursuant to paragraph (h)(1) of this section, D is considered the customer of K and L. Under paragraph (c)(3)(iv) of this section, K is not required to make a return of information with respect to the sale because K will pay the gross proceeds to L against delivery of the securities sold. L is required to make a return of information with respect to the sale because D is L's customer and is not an exempt recipient.

Example 5. Assume the same facts as in *Example 4* except that the records of both K and L with respect to the transaction show an account in the name of E. Pursuant to paragraph (h)(1) of this section, E is considered the customer of K and L. Under paragraph (c)(3)(iv) of this section, K is not required to make a return of information with respect to the sale because K will pay the gross proceeds to L against delivery of the securities sold. L is required to make a return of information with respect to the sale because E is L's customer and is not an exempt recipient. E is required to make a return of information with respect to the sale because D is E's customer and is not an exempt recipient.

Example 6. F, an individual who is not an exempt recipient, owns bonds that are held by G, a federally registered broker/dealer, in an account for F with G designated as nominee for F. Upon the retirement of the bonds, the gross proceeds are automatically credited to the account of F. G is required to make a return of information with respect to the retirement because G is the broker responsible for making payments of the gross proceeds to F.

Example 7. On June 24, 2010, H, an individual who is not an exempt recipient, opens a short sale of stock in an account with M, a broker. Because the short sale is entered into before January 1, 2011, paragraph (c)(3)(xi) of this section does not apply. Under paragraphs (c)(2) and (j) of this section, M must make a return of information for the year of the sale regardless of when the short sale is closed.

Example 8. (i) On August 25, 2011, H opens a short sale of stock in an account with M, a broker. H closes the short sale with M on January 25, 2012, by purchasing stock of the same corporation in the account in which H opened the short sale and delivering the stock to satisfy H's short sale obligation. The stock H purchased is a covered security.

(ii) Because the short sale is entered into on or after January 1, 2011, under paragraphs (c)(2) and (c)(3)(xi) of this section, the broker closing the short sale must make a return of information reporting the sale for the year in which the short sale is closed. Thus, M is required to report the sale for 2012. M must report on a single return the relevant information for the sold stock, the adjusted basis of the purchased stock, and whether any gain or loss on the closing of the short sale is long-term or short-term (within the meaning of section 1222). Thus, M must report the information about the short sale opening and closing transactions on a single return for taxable year 2012.

Example 9. (i) Assume the same facts as in *Example 8* except that H also has an account with N, a broker, and satisfies the short sale obligation with M by borrowing stock of the same corporation from N and transferring custody of the borrowed stock from N to M. N indicates on the transfer statement that the transferred stock was borrowed in accordance with §1.6045A-1(b)(7).

(ii) Under paragraph (c)(3)(xi)(C) of this section, M may not file the return of information required under this section. M must furnish a statement to N that reports the gross proceeds from the short sale on August 25, 2011, the date of the sale, the quantity of shares sold, the CUSIP number or other security identifier number of the sold stock, the transfer date, the name and contact information of M and N, and information identifying H such as H's name and the account number from which H transferred the borrowed stock.

(iii) N must report the gross proceeds from the short sale, the date the short sale was closed, the adjusted basis of the stock acquired to close the short sale, and whether any gain or loss on the closing of the short sale is long-term or short-term (within the meaning of section 1222) on the return of information N is required to file under paragraph (c)(2) of this section when H closes the short sale in the account with N.

(5) *Form of reporting for regulated futures contracts.*—(i) *In general.*—A broker effecting closing transactions in regulated futures contracts shall report information with respect to regulated futures contracts solely in the manner prescribed in this paragraph (c)(5). In the case of a sale that involves making a delivery pursuant to a regulated futures contract, only the profit or loss on the contract is reported as a transaction with respect to regulated futures contracts under this paragraph (c)(5); such sales are, however, subject to reporting under paragraph (d)(2). The information required under this paragraph (c)(5) must be reported on a calendar year basis, unless the broker is advised in writing by an account's owner that the owner's taxable year is other than a calendar year and the broker elects to report with respect to regulated futures contracts in such account on the basis of the owner's taxable year. The following information must be reported as required by Form 1099 with respect to regulated futures contracts held in a customer's account:

(A) The name, address, and taxpayer identification number of the customer.

(B) The net realized profit or loss from all regulated futures contracts closed during the calendar year.

(C) The net unrealized profit or loss in all open regulated futures contracts at the end of the preceding calendar year.

(D) The net unrealized profit or loss in all open regulated futures contracts at the end of the calendar year.

Reg. §1.6045-1(c)(5)

(E) The aggregate profit or loss from regulated futures contracts $((b) + (d) - (c))$ $[((B) + (D) - (C))]$.

(F) Any other information required by Form 1099.

See 17 CFR 1.33. For this purpose, the end of a year is the close of business of the last day of such year. In reporting under this paragraph (c)(5), the broker shall make such adjustments for commissions that have actually been paid and for option premiums as are consistent with the books of the broker. No additional returns of information with respect to regulated futures contracts so reported are required.

(ii) *Determination of profit or loss from foreign currency contracts.*—A broker effecting a closing transaction in foreign currency contracts (as defined in section 1256(g)) shall report information with respect to such contracts in the manner prescribed in paragraph (c)(5)(i) of this section. If a foreign currency contract is closed by making or taking delivery, the net realized profit or loss for purposes of paragraph (c)(5)(i)(B) of this section is determined by comparing the contract price to the spot price for the contract currency at the time and place specified in the contract. If a foreign currency contract is closed by entry into an offsetting contract, the net realized profit or loss for purposes of paragraph (c)(5)(i)(B) of this section is determined by comparing the contract price to the price of the offsetting contract. The net unrealized profit or loss in a foreign currency contract for purposes of paragraphs (c)(5)(i)(C) and (D) of this section is determined by comparing the contract price to the broker's price for similar contracts at the close of business of the relevant year.

(iii) *Examples.*—The following examples illustrate the application of the rules in this paragraph (c)(5):

Example 1. On October 30, 1984, A, an individual who is a calendar year taxpayer not otherwise exempt from reporting, buys one March 1985 put on Treasury Bond futures (i.e. A purchases an option to enter into a short regulated futures contract of $100,000 face value U.S. Treasury bonds). A pays $500 for the option. On December 19, 1984, A, through B, exercises the option and enters into the futures contract. On February 15, 1985, A, through B, enters into a closing transaction with respect to the futures contract. These are A's only transactions in the account. Since B's books list A's regulated futures contract on December 31, 1984, B must report for A, for 1984, the unrealized profit or loss in the contract as of December 31, 1984. For 1985, B will report the same amount for A as the unrealized profit or loss at the beginning of 1985. The return of information for 1985 will also include the gain or loss from the contract in the net realized profit or loss from all regulated futures contracts sales during 1985.

Example 2. The facts are the same as in Example (1) except that A does not enter into the closing transaction, but instead, on March 20,

1985, B informs A that A will make delivery under the contract. On March 22, 1985, A does so; consequently, A becomes entitled to the gross proceeds. B enters the closing transaction on its books on March 20, 1985. In addition to the return[s] of information required by paragraph (c)(5), as described in Example (1), B must report the March 22, 1985 delivery as a separate transaction. B may use as the sale date for the delivery either March 20, 1985, the date the transaction is entered on the books of B, or March 22, 1985, the date A becomes entitled to the gross proceeds. B may not deduct the $500 premium from the gross proceeds with respect to the March 22, 1985 delivery.

Example 3. The facts are the same as in Example (2) except that A buys a call on Treasury bond futures and takes delivery. B will supply the returns of information required by paragraph (c)(5), as described in Example (1). B is not required to make a return of information with respect to A's taking delivery.

Example 4. C, an individual who is a calendar year taxpayer not otherwise exempt from reporting, has an account with D, a broker. C trades both regulated futures contracts and forward contracts through C's account with D. D must report C's regulated futures contracts on an annual basis as required by paragraph (c)(5). With respect to C's forward contracts, D may elect to use the calendar month, quarter, or year as D's reporting period as provided in paragraph (c)(6).

(6) *Reporting periods and filing groups.*— (i) *Reporting period.*—(A) *In general.*—A broker may elect to use the calendar month, quarter, or year as the broker's reporting period. A broker may separately elect a reporting period for each filing group.

(B) *Election.*—For each calendar year, a broker shall elect a reporting period by filing Forms 1096 and 1099 in the manner elected. A different reporting period may be subsequently elected by filing in the manner subsequently elected, provided no duplication of reported transactions results.

(ii) *Filing group.*—(A) *In general.*—A broker may elect to group customers or customer accounts by office, branch, department or other method of operational classification and separately file Forms 1096 and 1099 for each filing group.

(B) *Election.*—For each calendar year, a broker shall elect filing groups by filing Forms 1096 and 1099 in the manner elected. Different filing groups may be subsequently elected by filing in the manner subsequently elected, provided no duplication of reported transactions results.

(iii) *Example.*—The following example illustrates the rules of this paragraph (c)(6):

Example. The A department of C, a broker, files a separate report for each month of 1984, whereas the B department of C files one report for all of 1984. C makes no other reports or returns of information under section 6045 for 1984. C has thereby elected two filing groups for 1984, the A department and the B department. The A department has the calendar month as its 1984 reporting period, whereas the B department has the calendar year as its 1984 reporting period. The same result would occur if A and B were offices or branches of C.

(7) *Exception for certain sales of agricultural commodities and commodity certificates.*— (i) *Agricultural commodities.*—No return of information is required under section 6045 for a spot or forward sale of an agricultural commodity. This paragraph (c)(7)(i) does not except from reporting sales of agricultural commodities pursuant to regulated futures contracts, sales of derivative interests in agricultural commodities, or sales described in paragraph (c)(7)(iii) of this section.

(ii) *Commodity Credit Corporation certificates.*—Except as otherwise provided in a revenue ruling or revenue procedure, no return of information is required under section 6045 with respect to a sale of a commodity certificate issued by the Commodity Credit Corporation under 7 CFR 1470.4 (1990).

(iii) *Sales involving designated warehouses.*—Paragraph (c)(7)(i) of this section does not apply to any sale involving a warehouse receipt for an agricultural commodity issued by a designated warehouse for an agricultural commodity of the type for which the warehouse is a designated warehouse.

(iv) *Definitions.*—For purposes of this paragraph (c)(7):

(A) *Agricultural commodity.*—An "agricultural commodity" includes, but is not limited to, a commodity within the meaning of paragraph (a)(5) of this section that is a grain, feed, livestock, meat, oil seed, timber, or fiber.

(B) *Spot sale.*—A spot sale is a sale that results in the substantially contemporaneous delivery of a commodity.

(C) *Forward sale.*—A forward sale is a sale pursuant to a forward contract within the meaning of paragraph (a)(7) of this section.

(D) *Designated warehouse.*—A designated warehouse is a warehouse, depository, or other similar entity, designated by a commodity exchange under 7 CFR 1.43 (1992), in which or out of which a particular type of agricultural commodity is deliverable in satisfaction of a regulated futures contract.

(d) *Information required.*—(1) *In general.*—A broker that is required to make a return of information under paragraph (c) of this section during a reporting period is required to report for each filing group on a separate Form 1096, "Annual Summary and Transmittal of U.S. Information Returns," or any successor form, the information required by the form in the manner and number of copies required by the form.

(2) *Transactional reporting.*—(i) *Required information.*—Except as provided in paragraph (c)(5) of this section, for each sale for which a broker is required to make a return of information under this section, the broker must report on Form 1099-B, "Proceeds From Broker and Barter Exchange Transactions," or any successor form the name, address, and taxpayer identification number of the customer, the property sold, the CUSIP number of the security sold (if applicable) or other security identifier number that the Secretary may designate by publication in the **Federal Register** or in the Internal Revenue Bulletin (*see* § 601.601(d)(2) of this chapter), the adjusted basis of the security sold, whether any gain or loss with respect to the security sold is long-term or short-term (within the meaning of section 1222), the gross proceeds of the sale, the sale date, and other information required by the form in the manner and number of copies required by the form. In addition, for a sale of a covered security on or after January 1, 2014, a broker must report on Form 1099-B whether any gain or loss is ordinary. See paragraph (m) of this section for additional rules related to options and paragraph (n) of this section for additional rules related to debt instruments.

(ii) *Specific identification of securities.*—Except as provided in § 1.1012-1(e)(7)(ii), for a specified security described in paragraph (a)(14)(i) of this section sold on or after January 1, 2011, or for a specified security described in paragraph (a)(14)(ii) of this section sold on or after January 1, 2014, a broker must report a sale of less than the entire position in an account of a specified security that was acquired on different dates or at different prices consistently with a customer's adequate and timely identification of the security to be sold. See § 1.1012-1(c). If the customer does not provide an adequate and timely identification for the sale, the broker must first report the sale of securities in the account for which the broker does not know the acquisition or purchase date followed by the earliest securities purchased or acquired, whether covered securities or noncovered securities.

(iii) *Sales of noncovered securities.*—A broker is not required to report adjusted basis and the character of any gain or loss for the sale of a noncovered security if the return identifies the sale as a sale of a noncovered security. A broker that chooses to report this information for a noncovered security is not subject to penalties under section 6721 or 6722 for failure to report this information correctly if the return identifies the sale as a sale of a noncovered security. For purposes of this paragraph (d)(2)(iii), a broker must treat a security for which a broker makes the singleaccount election described in § 1.1012-1(e)(11)(i) as a covered security.

(iv) *Information from other parties and other accounts.*—(A) *Transfer and issuer statements.*—When reporting a sale of a covered security, a broker must take into account all information, other than the classification of the security (such as stock), furnished on a transfer statement (as described in §1.6045A-1 and all information furnished or deemed furnished on an issuer statement (as described in §1.6045B-1, unless the statement is incomplete or the broker has actual knowledge that it is incorrect. A broker may treat a customer as a minority shareholder when taking the information on an issuer statement into account unless the broker knows that the customer is a majority shareholder and the issuer statement reports the action's effect on the basis of majority shareholders. A failure to report correct information that arises solely from reliance on information furnished on a transfer statement or issuer statement is deemed to be due to reasonable cause for purposes of penalties under sections 6721 and 6722. *See* §301.6724-1(a)(1) of this chapter.

(B) *Other information.*—A broker is permitted, but not required, to take into account information about a covered security other than what is furnished on a transfer statement or issuer statement, including any information the broker has about securities held by the same customer in other accounts with the broker. For purposes of penalties under sections 6721 and 6722, a broker that takes into account information received from a customer or third party other than information furnished on a transfer statement or issuer statement is deemed to have relied upon this information in good faith if the broker neither knows nor has reason to know that the information is incorrect. See §301.6724-1(c)(6) of this chapter.

(v) *Failure to receive a complete transfer statement.*—A broker that has not received a complete transfer statement as required under §1.6045A-1(a)(3) for a transfer of a specified security must request a complete statement from the applicable person effecting the transfer unless, under §1.6045A-1(a), the transferor has no duty to furnish a transfer statement for the transfer. The broker is only required to make this request once. If the broker does not receive a complete transfer statement after requesting it, the broker may treat the security as a noncovered security upon its subsequent sale or transfer. A transfer statement for a covered security is complete if, in the view of the receiving broker, it provides sufficient information to comply with this section when reporting the sale of the security. A transfer statement for a noncovered security is complete if it indicates that the security is a noncovered security.

(vi) *Reporting by other parties after a sale.*—(A) *Transfer statements.*—If a broker receives a transfer statement indicating that a security is a covered security after the broker reports the sale of the security, the broker must file a corrected return within thirty days of receiving the statement unless the broker reported the required information on the original return consistently with the transfer statement.

(B) *Issuer statements.*—If a broker receives or is deemed to receive an issuer statement after the broker reports the sale of a covered security, the broker must file a corrected return within thirty days of receiving the issuer statement unless the broker reported the required information on the original return consistently with the issuer statement.

(C) *Exception.*—A broker is not required to file a corrected return under this paragraph (d)(2)(vi) if the broker receives the transfer statement or issuer statement more than three years after the broker filed the return.

(vii) *Examples.*—The following examples illustrate the rules of this paragraph (d)(2):

Example 1. (i) On February 22, 2012, K sells 100 shares of stock of C, a corporation, at a loss in an account held with F, a broker. On March 15, 2012, K purchases 100 shares of C stock for cash in an account with G, a different broker. Because K acquires the stock purchased on March 15, 2012, for cash in an account after January 1, 2012, under paragraph (a)(15) of this section, the stock is a covered security. K asks G to increase K's adjusted basis in the stock to account for the application of the wash sale rules under section 1091 to the loss transaction in the account held with F.

(ii) Under paragraph (d)(2)(iv)(B) of this section, G is not required to take into account the information provided by K when subsequently reporting the adjusted basis and whether any gain or loss on the sale is long-term or short-term. If G chooses to take this information into account, under paragraph (d)(2)(iv)(B) of this section, G is deemed to have relied upon the information received from K in good faith for purposes of penalties under sections 6721 and 6722 if G neither knows nor has reason to know that the information provided by K is incorrect.

Example 2. (i) L purchases shares of stock of a single corporation in an account with F, a broker, on April 17, 1969, April 17, 2012, April 17, 2013, and April 17, 2014. In January 2015, L sells all the stock.

(ii) Under paragraph (d)(2)(i) of this section, F must separately report the gross proceeds and adjusted basis attributable to the stock purchased in 2014, for which the gain or loss on the sale is short-term, and the combined gross proceeds and adjusted basis attributable to the stock purchased in 2012 and 2013, for which the gain or loss on the sale is long-term. Under paragraph (d)(2)(iii) of this section, F must also separately report the gross proceeds attributable to the stock purchased in 1969 as the sale of noncovered securities in order to avoid treatment of this sale as the sale of covered securities.

(3) *Sales between interest payment dates.*—For each sale of a debt instrument prior to maturity with respect to which a broker is required to make a return of information under this section, a broker must show separately on Form 1099 the amount of accrued and unpaid qualified stated interest as of the sale date that must be reported

by the customer as interest income under § 1.61-7(d). *See* § 1.1273-1(c) for the definition of qualified stated interest. Such interest information must be shown in the manner and at the time required by Form 1099 and section 6049.

(4) *Sale date.*—With respect to sales of property that are reportable under this section, a broker must report a sale as occurring on the date the sale is entered on the books of the broker.

(5) *Gross proceeds.*—For purposes of this section, *gross proceeds* on a sale are the total amount paid to the customer or credited to the customer's account as a result of the sale reduced by the amount of any qualified stated interest reported under paragraph (d)(3) of this section and increased by any amount not paid or credited by reason of repayment of margin loans. In the case of a closing transaction (other than a closing transaction related to an option) that results in a loss, gross proceeds are the amount debited from the customer's account. For sales before January 1, 2014, a broker may, but is not required to, reduce gross proceeds by the amount of commissions and transfer taxes, provided the treatment chosen is consistent with the books of the broker. For sales on or after January 1, 2014, a broker must reduce gross proceeds by the amount of commissions and transfer taxes related to the sale of the security. For securities sold pursuant to the exercise of an option granted or acquired before January 1, 2014, a broker may, but is not required to, take the option premiums into account in determining the gross proceeds of the securities sold, provided the treatment chosen is consistent with the books of the broker. For securities sold pursuant to the exercise of an option granted or acquired on or after January 1, 2014, or for the treatment of an option granted or acquired on or after January 1, 2014, see paragraph (m) of this section. A broker must report the gross proceeds of identical stock (within the meaning of § 1.1012-1(e)(4) by averaging the proceeds of each share if the stock is sold at separate times on the same calendar day in executing a single trade order and the broker executing the trade provides a single confirmation to the customer that reports an aggregate total price or an average price per share. However, a broker may not average the proceeds if the customer notifies the broker in writing of an intent to determine the proceeds of the stock by the actual proceeds per share and the broker receives the notification by January 15 of the calendar year following the year of the sale. A broker may extend the January 15 deadline but not beyond the due date for filing the return required under this section.

(6) *Adjusted basis.*—(i) *In general.*—For purposes of this section, the adjusted basis of a security is determined from the initial basis under paragraph (d)(6)(ii) of this section as of the date the security is acquired in an account, increased by the commissions and transfer taxes related to its sale to the extent not accounted for in gross proceeds as described in paragraph (d)(5) of this section. A broker is not required to

consider transactions or events occurring outside the account except for an organizational action taken by an issuer during the period the broker holds custody of the security (beginning with the date that the broker receives a transferred security) reported on an issuer statement (as described in § 1.6045B-1) furnished or deemed furnished to the broker. Except as otherwise provided in paragraph (n) of this section, a broker is not required to consider customer elections. For rules related to the adjusted basis of a debt instrument, see paragraph (n) of this section.

(ii) *Initial basis.*—(A) *Cost basis.*—For a security acquired for cash, the initial basis generally is the total amount of cash paid by the customer or credited against the customer's account for the security, increased by the commissions and transfer taxes related to its acquisition. A broker may, but is not required to, take option premiums into account in determining the initial basis of securities purchased or acquired pursuant to the exercise of an option granted or acquired before January 1, 2014. For rules related to options granted or acquired on or after January 1, 2014, see paragraph (m) of this section. A broker may, but is not required to, increase initial basis for income recognized upon the exercise of a compensatory option or the vesting or exercise of other equity-based compensation arrangements, granted or acquired before January 1, 2014. A broker may not increase initial basis for income recognized upon the exercise of a compensatory option or the vesting or exercise of other equity-based compensation arrangements, granted or acquired on or after January 1, 2014. A broker must report the basis of identical stock (within the meaning of § 1.1012-1(e)(4) by averaging the basis of each share if the stock is purchased at separate times on the same calendar day in executing a single trade order and the broker executing the trade provides a single confirmation to the customer that reports an aggregate total price or an average price per share. However, a broker may not average the basis if the customer timely notifies the broker in writing of an intent to determine the basis of the stock by the actual cost per share in accordance with § 1.1012-1(c)(1)(ii).

(B) *Basis of transferred securities.*—(1) *In general.*—The initial basis of a security transferred to an account is generally the basis reported on the transfer statement (as described in § 1.6045A-1.

(2) *Securities acquired by gift.*—If a transfer statement indicates that the security is acquired as a gift, a broker must apply the relevant basis rules for property acquired by gift in determining the initial basis, but is not required to adjust basis for gift tax. A broker must treat the initial basis as equal to the gross proceeds from the sale determined under paragraph (d)(5) of this section if the relevant basis rules for property acquired by gift prevent recognizing both gain and loss, or if the relevant basis rules treat the initial basis of the security as its fair market

Reg. § 1.6045-1(d)(4)

value as of the date of the gift and the broker neither knows nor can readily ascertain this value. If the transfer statement did not report a date for the gift, the broker must treat the settlement date for the transfer as the date of the gift.

(iii) *Adjustments for wash sales.*—(A) *In general.*—A broker must apply the wash sale rules under section 1091 if both the sale and purchase transactions are of covered securities with the same CUSIP number or other security identifier number that the Secretary may designate by publication in the **Federal Register** or in the Internal Revenue Bulletin (*see* § 601.601(d)(2) of this chapter). When reporting the sale transaction that triggered the wash sale, the broker must report the amount of loss that is disallowed by section 1091 in addition to gross proceeds and adjusted basis. The broker must increase the basis of the purchased security by the amount of loss disallowed on the sale transaction.

(B) *Securities in different accounts.*—A broker is not required to apply paragraph (d)(6)(iii)(A) of this section if the securities are purchased and sold from different accounts, if the purchased security is transferred to another account before the wash sale, or if the securities are treated as held in separate accounts under § 1.1012-1(e). A security is not purchased in an account if it is purchased in another account and transferred into the account.

(C) *Effect of election under section 475(f)(1).*—A broker is not required to apply paragraph (d)(6)(iii)(A) of this section to securities in an account if a customer has in writing both informed the broker that the customer has made a valid and timely election under section 475(f)(1) and identified the account as solely containing securities subject to the election. For purposes of this paragraph (d)(6)(iii)(C), a writing may be in electronic format. If a customer subsequently informs a broker that the election no longer applies to the customer or the account, the broker must prospectively apply paragraph (d)(6)(iii)(A) of this section but is not required to apply paragraph (d)(6)(iii)(A) of this section for the period covered by the customer's prior instruction to the broker. A taxpayer that is not a trader in securities within the meaning of section 475(f)(1) does not become a trader in securities, or create an inference that it is a trader in securities, by notifying a broker that it has made a valid and timely election under section 475(f)(1).

(D) *Reporting at or near the time of sale.*—If a wash sale occurs after a broker has completed a return or statement reporting a sale of a covered security, the broker must redetermine adjusted basis under this paragraph (d)(6)(iii) and, if the return or statement included information inconsistent with this redetermination, correct the return or statement by the applicable original due date set forth in this section for the return or statement.

(iv) *Certain adjustments not taken into account.*—A broker is not required to apply section

1259 (regarding constructive sales), section 475 (regarding the mark-to-market method of accounting), section 1296 (regarding the mark-tomarket method of accounting for marketable stock in a passive foreign investment company), or section 1092 (regarding straddles) when reporting adjusted basis.

(v) *Average basis method adjustments.*—For a covered security for which basis may be determined by the average basis method, a broker must compute basis using the average basis method if a customer validly elects that method for the securities sold or, in the absence of any instruction from the customer, if the broker chooses that method as its default basis determination method. *See* § 1.1012-1(e).

(vi) *Regulated investment company and real estate investment trust adjustments.*—A broker must adjust the basis of a covered security issued by a regulated investment company or real estate investment trust for the effects of undistributed capital gains reported to or by the broker under section 852(b)(3)(D) or section 857(b)(3)(D).

(vii) *Examples.*—The following examples, in which all the securities are covered securities, illustrate the rules of this paragraph (d)(6):

Example 1. (i) On September 21, 2012, P purchases 100 shares of stock in an account with J, a broker. On December 14, 2012, P purchases 100 shares of stock with the same CUSIP number in the same account. On January 4, 2013, P sells the shares purchased on September 21, 2012, at a loss.

(ii) Because the sale of stock on January 4, 2013, and the purchase of stock on December 14, 2012, are of covered securities with the same CUSIP number, under paragraph (d)(6)(iii)(A) of this section, J must report the amount of loss disallowed by section 1091 in addition to the gross proceeds of the sale and the adjusted basis of the September 21, 2012, stock.

(iii) P later sells the stock acquired on December 14, 2012. When reporting the sale of the stock, under paragraph (d)(6)(iii)(A) of this section, J must increase the adjusted basis of the stock acquired on December 14, 2012, by the amount of loss disallowed on the January 4, 2013, sale.

Example 2. Assume the same facts as in *Example 1* except that the December 14, 2012, purchase occurs in another account P maintains with J. Because the December 14, 2012, purchase does not occur in the same account as the sale of the September 21, 2012, stock, under paragraph (d)(6)(iii)(B) of this section, J is not required to apply the wash sale rules in reporting the sale of stock acquired on September 21, 2012, or December 14, 2012. Under paragraphs (d)(2)(iii) and (d)(2)(iv)(B) of this section, J may choose to apply the wash sale rules as if the transactions occurred in the same account. The result is the same whether P keeps the stock purchased on December 14, 2012, in the other account or transfers the stock into the account from which P sells the stock sold on January 4, 2013.

Example 3. (i) K, a regulated investment company, offers two funds for sale, Fund D and Fund E. On April 22, 2012, Q purchases shares of Fund D and pays a separate load charge. By paying the load charge, Q acquires a reinvestment right in shares of Fund E. On April 23, 2012, at the request of Q, Fund D redeems the shares. Q uses the proceeds to purchase shares of Fund E in a separate account. As a result of the reinvestment right, Q pays no load charge in purchasing the Fund E shares.

(ii) Under paragraph (d)(6)(i) of this section, when reporting adjusted basis of the Fund D and Fund E shares at the time of their redemption, K is not required to adjust basis for any deferral of the load charge under section 852(f), because the transactions concerning Fund D and Fund E occur in separate accounts. Under paragraph (d)(2)(iv)(B) of this section, K may choose to apply the provisions of section 852(f).

Example 4. R, an employee of C, a corporation, participates in C's stock option plan. On April 2, 2014, C grants R a nonstatutory option under the plan to buy 100 shares of stock. The option becomes substantially vested on April 2, 2015. On October 2, 2015, R exercises the option and purchases 100 shares. On December 2, 2015, R sells the 100 shares. Under paragraph (d)(6)(ii)(A) of this section, C is required to determine adjusted basis from the amount R pays under the terms of the option. Under paragraph (d)(6)(ii)(A) of this section, C is not permitted to adjust basis for any amount R must include as wage income with respect to the October 2, 2015, stock purchase.

(7) *Long-term or short-term gain or loss.*— (i) *In general.*—In determining whether any gain or loss on the sale of a security is long-term or short-term within the meaning of section 1222 for purposes of this section, a broker must consider the information reported on a transfer statement (as described in § 1.6045A-1 and apply the relevant rules for property acquired from a decedent or by gift. A broker is not required to consider transactions, elections, or events occurring outside the account except for an organizational action taken by an issuer during the period the broker holds custody of the security (beginning with the date that the broker receives a transferred security) reported on an issuer statement (as described in § 1.6045B-1) furnished or deemed furnished to the broker.

(ii) *Adjustments for wash sales.*—(A) *In general.*—A broker must apply the wash sale rules under section 1091 if both the sale and purchase transactions are of covered securities with the same CUSIP number or other security identifier number that the Secretary may designate by publication in the **Federal Register** or in the Internal Revenue Bulletin (*see* § 601.601(d)(2) of this chapter).

(B) *Securities in different accounts.*—A broker is not required to apply paragraph (d)(7)(ii)(A) of this section if the securities are purchased and sold from different accounts, if

the purchased security is transferred to another account before the wash sale, or if the securities are treated as held in separate accounts under § 1.1012-1(e). A security is not purchased in an account if it is purchased in another account and transferred into the account.

(C) *Effect of election under section 475(f)(1).*—A broker is not required to apply paragraph (d)(7)(ii)(A) of this section to securities in an account if a customer has in writing both informed the broker that the customer has made a valid and timely election under section 475(f)(1) and identified the account as solely containing securities subject to the election. For purposes of this paragraph (d)(7)(ii)(C), a writing may be in electronic format. If a customer subsequently informs a broker that the election no longer applies to the customer or the account, the broker must prospectively apply paragraph (d)(7)(ii)(A) of this section but is not required to apply paragraph (d)(7)(ii)(A) of this section for the period covered by the customer's prior instruction to the broker. A taxpayer that is not a trader in securities within the meaning of section 475(f)(1) does not become a trader in securities, or create an inference that it is a trader in securities, by notifying a broker that it has made a valid and timely election under section 475(f)(1).

(D) *Reporting at or near the time of sale.*— If a wash sale occurs after a broker has completed a return or statement reporting a sale of a covered security, the broker must redetermine whether gain or loss on the sale is long-term or short-term under this paragraph (d)(7)(ii) and, if the return or statement included information inconsistent with this redetermination, correct the return or statement by the applicable original due date set forth in this section for the return or statement.

(iii) *Constructive sale and mark-to-market adjustments.*—A broker is not required to apply section 1259 (regarding constructive sales), section 475 (regarding the mark-to-market method of accounting), or section 1296 (regarding the mark-to-market method of accounting for marketable stock in a passive foreign investment company) when determining whether any gain or loss on the sale of a security is long-term or short-term.

(iv) *Regulated investment company and real estate investment trust adjustments.*—A broker is not required to apply sections 852(b)(4)(A) and 857(b)(8) (regarding effect of distributed and undistributed capital gain dividends on a loss on sale of regulated investment company or real estate investment trust shares held six months or less) or section 852(b)(4)(B) (regarding loss disallowance on sale of regulated investment company shares held six months or less due to receipt of tax-exempt dividends) when determining whether any gain or loss on the sale of a security is long-term or short-term.

(v) *No adjustments for hedging transactions or offsetting positions.*—A broker is not required to apply section 1092 (regarding straddles), section 1233(b)(2) (regarding effect of short sale on holding period of substantially identical property), or § 1.1221-2(b) (regarding hedging transactions) when determining whether any gain or loss on the sale of a security is long-term or short-term.

(8) *Conversion into United States dollars of amounts paid or received in foreign currency.*— (i) *Conversion rules.*—(A) When a payment other than a payment of interest is made in a foreign currency, a broker must determine the U.S. dollar amount of the payment by converting the foreign currency into U.S. dollars on the date it receives, credits, or makes the payment, as applicable, at the spot rate (as defined in § 1.988-1(d)(1)) or pursuant to a reasonable spot rate convention. (For interest payments, see paragraph (n)(4)(v) of this section concerning a customer's spot rate election.) When reporting the sale of a security traded on an established securities market, however, a broker must determine the U.S. dollar amounts at the spot rate or pursuant to a reasonable spot rate convention as of the settlement date of the purchase or sale, as applicable.

(B) A reasonable spot rate convention includes a month-end spot rate or a monthly average spot rate. A spot rate convention must be used consistently for all non-dollar amounts reported and from year to year. The convention may not be changed without the consent of the Commissioner or his or her delegate.

(ii) *Effect of identification under § 1.988-5(a), (b), or (c) when the taxpayer effects a sale and a hedge through the same broker.*—In lieu of the amounts reportable under paragraph (d)(8)(i) of this section, the gross proceeds and adjusted basis must each be the integrated amount computed under § 1.988-5(a), (b) or (c) if—

(A) A taxpayer effects through a broker a sale or exchange of nonfunctional currency (as defined in § 1.988-1(c) and hedges all or a part of the sale as provided in § 1.988-5(a), (b) or (c) with the same broker; and

(B) The taxpayer complies with the requirements of § 1.988-5(a), (b) or (c) and so notifies the broker prior to the end of the calendar year in which the sale occurs.

(iii) *Example.*—The following example illustrates the rules of this paragraph (d)(8):

Example. (i) Z, an individual, is a U.S. citizen. On July 4, 2012, Z purchases stock of C, SA, a French corporation traded on an established securities market, in an account with Q, a broker. Q uses a daily spot rate for converting euro and U.S. dollars. Z pays € 1,200 for the stock. On the settlement date for the purchase, the spot rate is € 1 = $1.30. On October 4, 2012, Z sells the stock for € 1,000. On the settlement date for the sale, the spot rate is € 1 = $1.35. On October 5, 2012, Z purchases additional shares of C, SA, that cause the € 200 loss on the stock sold on October 4, 2012, to be disallowed under section 1091.

(ii) Under paragraph (d)(8)(i)(A) of this section, Q must determine adjusted basis by converting the € 1,200 paid on behalf of Z into U.S. dollars using the € 1 = $1.30 spot rate on the settlement date of the purchase. Q must convert the € 1,000 gross proceeds into U.S. dollars using the € 1 = $1.35 spot rate on the settlement date for the sale. Thus, Q must report adjusted basis equal to $1,560, gross proceeds equal to $1,350, and $210 in loss disallowed by section 1091.

(9) *Coordination with the reporting rules for widely held fixed investment trusts under § 1.671-5.*—Information required to be reported under section 6045(a) for a sale of a security in a widely held fixed investment trust (WHFIT) (as defined under § 1.671-5 and the sale of an interest in a WHFIT must be reported as provided by this section unless the information is also required to be reported under § 1.671-5. To the extent that this section requires additional information under section 6045(g), those requirements are deemed to be met through compliance with the rules in § 1.671-5.

(e) *Reporting of barter exchanges.*—(1) *Requirement of reporting.*—A barter exchange shall, except as otherwise provided, report in the manner prescribed in this section.

(2) *Exchanges required to be reported.*—(i) *In general.*—Except as provided in paragraphs (e)(2)(ii) and (g) of this section, a barter exchange must make a return of information for exchanges of personal property or services through the barter exchange during the calendar year among its members or clients or between these persons and the barter exchange. For this purpose, property or services are exchanged through a barter exchange if payment for property or services is made by means of a credit on the books of the barter exchange or scrip issued by the barter exchange or if the barter exchange arranges a direct exchange of property or services among its members or clients or exchanges property or services with a member or client.

(ii) *Exemption.*—A barter exchange through which there are fewer than 100 exchanges during the calendar year is not required to report for, or make a return of information with respect to exchanges during, such calendar year. The Commissioner may require multiple barter exchanges to be combined for purposes of the preceding sentence upon a determination that a material purpose for the formation or continuation of one or more of the barter exchanges to be combined was to receive one or more exemptions pursuant to this subparagraph.

(f) *Information required.*—(1) *In general.*—A person that is a barter exchange during a calendar year shall report on Form 1096 showing the information required thereon for such year.

(2) *Transactional reporting.*—(i) *In general.*— As to each exchange for which a barter exchange is required to make a return of information under this section, the barter exchange must show on Form 1099-B, "Proceeds From Broker

Reg. § 1.6045-1(f)(2)(i)

and Barter Exchange Transactions," or any successor form the name, address, and taxpayer identification number of each member or client providing property or services in the exchange, the property or services provided, the amount received by the member or client for the property or services, the date on which the exchange occurred, and other information required by the form in the manner and number of copies required by the form.

(ii) *Exception for corporate member or client.*—As to each corporate member or client providing property or services in an exchange for which a return of information is required under this section, the barter exchange may report the name, address, and taxpayer identification number of the corporate member or client, the aggregate amount received by the corporate member or client during the reporting period for property or services provided by such corporate member or client in exchange for which a return of information is required, and such other information as may be required by Form 1099, in the form, manner, and number of copies required by Form 1099.

(iii) *Definition.*—For purposes of paragraph (f)(2)(ii) of this section, the term "corporate member or client" means a member or client of a barter exchange which is a corporation as defined in section 7701(a)(3) (including an insurance company). The term corporation includes a pool, syndicate, partnership, or unincorporated association composed exclusively of corporations. A barter exchange may treat a member or client as a corporation (and therefore as a corporate member or client) if such member or client provides an exemption certificate as described in § 31.3406(h)-3(a) of this chapter or provided that—

(A) The name of the member or client contains the term "insurance company," "indemnity company," "reinsurance company," or "assurance company";

(B) The name of the member or client contains one of the following unambiguous expressions of corporate status: Incorporated, Inc., Corporation, Corp., or P.C., but not Company or Co.; or

(C) The member or client is known to the barter exchange to be a corporation through a corporate resolution or similar document on file with the barter exchange clearly indicating corporate status.

(3) *Exchange date.*—For purposes of this section an exchange is considered to occur with respect to a member or client of a barter exchange on the date cash, property, a credit, or scrip is actually or constructively received by the member or client as a result of the exchange. (See § 1.451-2 for rules pertaining to constructive receipt.)

(4) *Amount received.*—The amount received by a member or client in an exchange includes cash received, the fair market value of any property or services received, and the fair market value of any credits to the account of the member or client on the books of the barter exchange or scrip issued to the member or client by the barter exchange, but does not include any amount received by the member or client in a subsequent exchange of credits or scrip. For purposes of this section, the fair market value of a credit or scrip is the value assigned to such credit or scrip by the issuing barter exchange for the purpose of exchanges unless the Commissioner requires the use of a different value that the Commissioner determines more accurately reflects fair market value.

(5) *Meaning of terms.*—For purposes of this paragraph (f)—

(i) A credit is an amount on the books of the barter exchange that is transferable from one member or client of the barter exchange to another such member or client, or to the barter exchange in payment for property or services;

(ii) Scrip is a token issued by the barter exchange that is transferable from one member or client of the barter exchange to another such member or client, or to the barter exchange, in payment for property or services; and

(iii) Property does not include a credit or scrip.

(6) *Reporting period.*—A barter exchange shall use the calendar year as the reporting period.

(g) *Exempt foreign persons.*—(1) *Brokers.*—No return of information is required to be made by a broker with respect to a customer who is considered to be an exempt foreign person under this paragraph (g)(1). A broker may treat a customer as an exempt foreign person under the circumstances described in paragraphs (g)(1)(i) through (iii) of this section.

(i) With respect to a sale effected at an office of a broker either inside or outside the United States, the broker may treat the customer as an exempt foreign person if the broker can, prior to the payment, reliably associate the payment with documentation upon which it can rely in order to treat the customer as a foreign beneficial owner in accordance with § 1.1441-1(e)(1)(ii), as made to a foreign payee in accordance with § 1.6049-5(d)(1), or presumed to be made to a foreign payee under § 1.6049-5(d)(2) or (3). For purposes of this paragraph (g)(1)(i), the provisions in § 1.6049-5(c) regarding rules applicable to documentation of foreign status shall apply with respect to a sale when the broker completes the acts necessary to effect the sale at an office outside the United States, as described in paragraph (g)(3)(iii)(A) of this section, and no office of the same broker within the United States negotiated the sale with the customer or received instructions with respect to the sale from the customer. The provisions in § 1.6049-5(c) regarding the definitions of U.S. payor, U.S. middleman, non-U.S. payor, and non-U.S. middleman shall also apply for purposes of this paragraph (g)(1)(i). The provisions of § 1.1441-1 shall apply by substituting the terms "broker" and "customer" for the terms "withholding agent" and "payee," respectively, and without regard for the fact that the provisions apply to amounts subject to withholding under chapter 3 of the Code. The provisions of § 1.6049-5(d) shall apply by substituting the terms "broker" and "customer" for the terms "payor" and "payee," respectively. For purposes of this paragraph (g)(1)(i), a broker that is required to obtain, or chooses to obtain, a beneficial owner withholding certificate described in § 1.1441-1(e)(2)(i) from an individual may rely on the withholding certificate only to the extent the certificate includes a certification that the beneficial owner has not been, and at the time the certificate is furnished, reasonably expects not to be present in the United States for a period aggregating 183 days or more during each calendar year to which the certificate pertains. The certification is not required if a broker receives documentary evidence under § 1.6049-5(c)(1) or (4).

(ii) With respect to a redemption or retirement of stock or an obligation (the interest or original issue discount on which is described in § 1.6049-5(b)(6), (7), (10), or (11) or the dividends on which are described in § 1.6042-3(b)(1)(iv)) that is effected at an office of a broker outside the United States by the issuer (or its paying or transfer agent), the broker may treat the customer as an exempt foreign person if the broker is not also acting in its capacity as a custodian, nominee, or other agent of the payee.

(iii) With respect to a sale effected by a broker at an office of the broker either inside or outside the United States, the broker may treat the customer as an exempt foreign person for the period that those proceeds are assets blocked as described in § 1.1441-2(e)(3). For purposes of this paragraph (g)(1)(iii) and section 3406, a sale is deemed to occur in accordance with paragraph (d)(4) of this section. The exemption in this paragraph (g)(1)(iii) shall terminate when payment of the proceeds is deemed to occur in accordance with the provisions of § 1.1441-2(e)(3).

(2) *Barter exchange.*—No return of information is required by a barter exchange with respect to a client or a member that the barter exchange may treat as a foreign person pursuant to the procedures described in paragraph (g)(1) of this section.

(3) *Applicable rules.*—(i) *Joint owners.*— Amounts paid to joint owners for which a certificate or documentation is required as a condition for being exempt from reporting under paragraph (g)(1)(i) or (2) of this section are presumed made to U.S. payees who are not exempt recipients if, prior to payment, the broker or barter exchange cannot reliably associate the payment either with a Form W-9 furnished by one of the joint owners in the manner required in § § 31.3406(d)-1 through 31.3406(d)-5 of this chapter, or with documentation described in paragraph (g)(1)(i) of this section furnished by each joint owner upon which it can rely to treat each joint owner as a foreign payee or foreign beneficial owner. For purposes of applying this

paragraph (g)(3)(i), the grace period described in § 1.6049-5(d)(2)(ii) shall apply only if each payee qualifies for such grace period.

(ii) *Special rules for determining who the customer is.*—For purposes of this paragraph (g), the determination of who the customer is shall be made on the basis of the provisions in § 1.6049-5(d) by substituting in that section the terms *payor* and *payee* with the terms *broker* and *customer.*

(iii) *Place of effecting sale.*—(A) *Sale outside the United States.*—For purposes of this paragraph (g), a sale is considered to be effected by a broker at an office outside the United States if, in accordance with instructions directly transmitted to such office from outside the United States by the broker's customer, the office completes the acts necessary to effect the sale outside the United States. The acts necessary to effect the sale may be considered to have been completed outside the United States without regard to whether—

(1) Pursuant to instructions from an office of the broker outside the United States, an office of the same broker within the United States undertakes one or more steps of the sale in the United States; or

(2) The gross proceeds of the sale are paid by a draft drawn on a United States bank account or by a wire or other electronic transfer from a United States account.

(B) *Sale inside the United States.*—For purposes of this paragraph (g), a sale that is considered to be effected by a broker at an office outside the United States under paragraph (g)(3)(iii)(A) of this section shall nevertheless be considered to be effected by a broker at an office inside the United States if either—

(1) The customer has opened an account with a United States office of that broker;

(2) The customer has transmitted instructions concerning this and other sales to the foreign office of the broker from within the United States by mail, telephone, electronic transmission or otherwise (unless the transmissions from the United States have taken place in isolated and infrequent circumstances);

(3) The gross proceeds of the sale are paid to the customer by a transfer of funds into an account (other than an international account as defined in § 1.6049-5(e)(4)) maintained by the customer in the United States or mailed to the customer at an address in the United States;

(4) The confirmation of the sale is mailed to a customer at an address in the United States; or

(5) An office of the same broker within the United States negotiates the sale with the customer or receives instructions with respect to the sale from the customer.

(iv) *Special rules where the customer is a foreign intermediary or certain U.S. branches.*—A foreign intermediary, as defined in § 1.1441-1(c)(13), is an exempt foreign person,

Reg. § 1.6045-1(g)(3)(iv)

except when the broker has actual knowledge (within the meaning of § 1.6049-5(c)(3)) that the person for whom the intermediary acts is a U.S. person that is not exempt from reporting under paragraph (c)(3) of this section or the broker is required to presume under § 1.6049-5(d)(3) that the payee is a U.S. person that is not an exempt recipient. If a foreign intermediary, as described in § 1.1441-1(c)(13), or a U.S. branch that is not treated as a U.S. person receives a payment from a payor or middleman, which payment the payor or middleman can reliably associate with a valid withholding certificate described in § 1.1441-1(e)(3)(ii) or (iii) or § 1.1441-1(e)(3)(v), respectively, furnished by such intermediary or branch, then the intermediary or branch is not required to report such payment when it, in turn, pays the amount, unless, and to the extent, the intermediary or branch knows that the payment is required to be reported under this section and was not so reported. For example, if a U.S. branch described in § 1.1441-1(b)(2)(iv) fails to provide information regarding U.S. persons that are not exempt from reporting under paragraph (c)(3) of this section to the person from whom the U.S. branch receives the payment, the U.S. branch must report the payment on an information return. See, however, paragraph (c)(3)(ii) of this section for when reporting under section 6045 is coordinated with reporting under chapter 4 of the Code or an applicable IGA (as defined in § 1.6049-4(f)(7)). The exception of this paragraph (g)(3)(iv) for amounts paid by a foreign intermediary shall not apply to a qualified intermediary that assumes reporting responsibility under chapter 61 of the Code except as provided under the agreement described in § 1.1441-1(e)(5)(iii).

(4) *Examples.*—The application of the provisions of this paragraph (g) may be illustrated by the following examples:

Example 1. FC is a foreign corporation that is not a U.S. payor or U.S. middleman described in § 1.6049-5(c)(5) that regularly issues and retires its own debt obligations. A is an individual whose residence address is inside the United States, who holds a bond issued by FC that is in registered form (within the meaning of section 163(f) and the regulations under that section). The bond is retired by FP, a foreign corporation that is a broker within the meaning of paragraph (a)(1) of this section and the designated paying agent of FC. FP mails the proceeds to A at A's U.S. address. The sale would be considered to be effected at an office outside the United States under paragraph (g)(3)(iii)(A) of this section except that the proceeds of the sale are mailed to a U.S. address. For that reason, the sale is considered to be effected at an office of the broker inside the United States under paragraph (g)(3)(iii)(B) of this section. Therefore, FC is a broker under paragraph (a)(1) of this section with respect to this transaction because, although it is not a U.S. payor or U.S. middleman, as described in § 1.6049-5(c)(5), it is deemed to effect the sale in the United States. FP is a broker for the same reasons. However, under the multi-

ple broker exception under paragraph (c)(3)(iii) of this section, FP, rather than FC, is required to report the payment because FP is responsible for paying the holder the proceeds from the retired obligations. Under paragraph (g)(1)(i) of this section, FP may not treat A as an exempt foreign person and must make an information return under section 6045 with respect to the retirement of the FC bond, unless FP obtains the certificate or documentation described in paragraph (g)(1)(i) of this section.

Example 2. The facts are the same as in *Example 1* except that FP mails the proceeds to A at an address outside the United States. Under paragraph (g)(3)(iii)(A) of this section, the sale is considered to be effected at an office of the broker outside the United States. Therefore, under paragraph (a)(1) of this section, neither FC nor FP is a broker with respect to the retirement of the FC bond. Accordingly, neither is required to make an information return under section 6045.

Example 3. The facts are the same as in *Example 2* except that FP is also the agent of A. The result is the same as in *Example 2.* Neither FP nor FC are brokers under paragraph (a)(1) of this section with respect to the sale since the sale is effected outside the United States and neither of them are U.S. payors (within the meaning of § 1.6049-5(c)(5)).

Example 4. The facts are the same as in *Example 1* except that the registered bond held by A was issued by DC, a domestic corporation that regularly issues and retires its own debt obligations. Also, FP mails the proceeds to A at an address outside the United States. Interest on the bond is not described in paragraph (g)(1)(ii) of this section. The sale is considered to be effected at an office outside the United States under paragraph (g)(3)(iii)(A) of this section. DC is a broker under paragraph (a)(1)(i)(B) of this section. DC is not required to report the payment under the multiple broker exception under paragraph (c)(3)(iii) of this section. FP is not required to make an information return under section 6045 because FP is not a U.S. payor described in § 1.6049-5(c)(5) and the sale is effected outside the United States. Accordingly, FP is not a broker under paragraph (a)(1) of this section.

Example 5. The facts are the same as in *Example 4* except that FP is also the agent of A. DC is a broker under paragraph (a)(1) of this section. DC is not required to report under the multiple broker exception under paragraph (c)(3)(iii) of this section. FP is not required to make an information return under section 6045 because FP is not a U.S. payor described in § 1.6049-5(c)(5) and the sale is effected outside the United States and therefore FP is not a broker under paragraph (a)(1) of this section.

Example 6. The facts are the same as in *Example 4* except that the bond is retired by DP, a broker within the meaning of paragraph (a)(1) of this section and the designated paying agent of DC. DP is a U.S. payor under § 1.6049-5(c)(5). DC is not required to report under the multiple broker exception under paragraph (c)(3)(iii) of this section. DP is required to make an information return under section 6045 because it is the person responsible for paying the proceeds from the retired obligations unless DP obtains the certificate or documentary evidence described in paragraph (g)(1)(i) of this section.

Example 7. Customer A owns U.S. corporate bonds issued in registered form after July 18, 1984, and carrying a stated rate of interest. The bonds are held through an account with foreign bank, X, and are held in street name. X is a wholly-owned subsidiary of a U.S. company and is not a qualified intermediary within the meaning of §1.1441-1(e)(5)(ii). X has no documentation regarding A. A instructs X to sell the bonds. In order to effect the sale, X acts through its agent in the United States, Y. Y sells the bonds and remits the sales proceeds to X. X credits A's account in the foreign country. X does not provide documentation to Y and has no actual knowledge that A is a foreign person but it does appear that A is an entity (rather than an individual).

(i) *Y's obligations to withhold and report.* Y treats X as the customer, and not A, because Y cannot treat X as an intermediary because it has received no documentation from X. Y is not required to report the sales proceeds under the multiple broker exception under paragraph (c)(3)(iii) of this section, because X is an exempt recipient. Further, Y is not required to report the amount of accrued interest paid to X on Form 1042-S under §1.1461-1(c)(2)(ii) because accrued interest is not an amount subject to reporting under chapter 3 unless the withholding agent knows that the obligation is being sold with a primary purpose of avoiding tax.

(ii) *X's obligations to withhold and report.* Although X has effected, within the meaning of paragraph (a)(1) of this section, the sale of a security at an office outside the United States under paragraph (g)(3)(iii) of this section, X is treated as a broker, under paragraph (a)(1) of this section, because as a wholly-owned subsidiary of a U.S. corporation, X is a controlled foreign corporation and therefore is a U.S. payor. See §1.6049-5(c)(5). Under the presumptions described in §1.6049-5(d)(2) (as applied to amounts not subject to withholding under chapter 3), X must apply the presumption rules of §1.1441-1(b)(3)(i) through (iii), with respect to the sales proceeds, to treat A as a partnership that is a U.S. non-exempt recipient because the presumption of foreign status for offshore obligations under §1.1441-1(b)(3)(iii)(D) does not apply. See paragraph (g)(1)(i) of this section. Therefore, unless X is an FFI (as defined in §1.1471-1(b)(47)) that is excepted from reporting the sales proceeds under paragraph (c)(3)(ii) of this section, the payment of proceeds to A by X is reportable on a Form 1099 under paragraph (c)(2) of this section. X has no obligation to backup withhold on the payment based on the exemption under §31.3406(g)-1(e) of this chapter, unless X has actual knowledge that A is a U.S. person that is not an exempt recipient. X is also required to separately report the accrued interest (see paragraph (d)(3) of this section) on Form 1099 under section 6049 because A is also presumed to be a U.S. person who is not an exempt recipient with respect to the payment because accrued interest is not an amount subject to withholding under chapter 3 and, therefore, the presumption of foreign status for offshore obligations under §1.1441-1(b)(3)(iii)(D) does not apply. See §1.6049-5(d)(2)(i).

Example 8. The facts are the same as in *Example 7*, except that X is a foreign corporation that is not a U.S. payor under §1.6049-5(c).

(i) *Y's obligations to withhold and report.* Y is not required to report the sales proceeds under the multiple broker exception under paragraph (c)(3)(iii) of this section, because X is the person responsible for paying the proceeds from the sale to A.

(ii) *X's obligations to withhold and report.* Although A is presumed to be a U.S. payee under the presumptions of §1.6049-5(d)(2), X is not considered to be a broker under paragraph (a)(1) of this section because it is a not a U.S. payor under §1.6049-5(c)(5). Therefore X is not required to report the sale under paragraph (c)(2) of this section.

(h) *Identity of customer.*—(1) *In general.*—For purposes of this section, a broker or barter exchange shall treat the person who appears on the books and records of the broker or barter exchange with respect to property or services as the principal with respect thereto.

(2) *Examples.*—The following examples illustrate the rule of this paragraph (h):

Example 1. The records of A, a broker, show an account in the name of "B". B is a nominee for C. All reporting with respect to such account shall treat B as the customer.

Example 2. J, an individual, places an order with H, a broker, to sell J's stock that is held by P, a broker/dealer, in an account for J with P designated as nominee for J, and to credit the gross proceeds from the sale to J's account with P. The account is in the name of P, so that H's customer is P.

(i) [Reserved.]

(j) *Time and place for filing; cross-reference to penalty.*—Forms 1096 and 1099 required under this section shall be filed after the last calendar day of the reporting period elected by the broker or barter exchange and on or before February 28 of the following calendar year with the appropriate Internal Revenue Service Center, the address of which is listed in the instructions for Form 1096. See paragraph (l) of this section for the requirement to file certain returns on magnetic media. For provisions relating to the penalty provided for the failure to file timely a correct information return under section 6045(a), see §301.6721-1 of this chapter. See §301.6724-1 of this chapter for the waiver of a penalty if the failure is due to reasonable cause and is not due to willful neglect.

Reg. §1.6045-1(j)

(k) *Requirement and time for furnishing state-ment; cross reference to penalty.*—(1) *General re-quirements.*—A broker or barter exchange making a return of information under this sec-tion must furnish to the person whose identify-ing number is (or is required to be) shown on the return a written statement showing the informa-tion required by paragraph (c)(5), (d), or (f) of this section and containing a legend stating that the information is being reported to the Internal Revenue Service. If the return of information is not made on magnetic media, this requirement may be satisfied by furnishing to the person a copy of all Forms 1099 or any successor form for the person filed with the Internal Revenue Ser-vice Center. A statement is considered to be furnished to a person to whom a statement is required to be made under this paragraph (k) if it is mailed to the person at the last address of the person known to the broker or barter exchange.

(2) *Time for furnishing statements.*—A broker or barter exchange may furnish the statements required under this paragraph (k) yearly, quar-terly, monthly, or on any other basis, without regard to the reporting period the broker or bar-ter exchange elects; however, all statements re-quired to be furnished under this paragraph (k) for a calendar year must be furnished on or before February 15 of the following calendar year.

(3) *Consolidated reporting.*—(i) The term *con-solidated reporting statement* means a grouping of statements the same broker or barter exchange furnishes to the same customer or group of cus-tomers on the same date for the same reporting year that includes a statement required under this section. A consolidated reporting statement is limited to statements based on the same rela-tionship of broker or barter exchange to cus-tomer as the statement required to be furnished under this section. For purposes of this para-graph (k)(3)(i), a broker may treat a shareholder of a broker as a customer of the broker and may treat a grouping of statements for a customer as including a statement required to be furnished under this section if the customer has an account with the broker for which a statement would be required to be furnished under this section if the customer purchased and sold stock in a corpora-tion in the account during the year.

(ii) A consolidated reporting statement must be furnished on or before February 15 of the year following the calendar year reported. Any statement that otherwise must be furnished on or before January 31 must be furnished on or before February 15 if it is furnished in the consol-idated reporting statement.

(iii) *Examples.*—The following examples illustrate the rules of this paragraph (k)(3):

Example 1. D has a taxable account with B, a broker, consisting solely of stock in a single corporation. In 2010, D receives reportable divi-dends from this stock and sells the stock. Under this section and §1.6042-4, B must furnish a Form 1099-B, "Proceeds From Broker and Barter Exchange Transactions," and Form 1099-DIV, "Dividends and Distributions," to D in 2011 for the sale and the dividends. Under paragraph (k)(2) of this section, B is required to furnish the required statement under this section to D by February 15, 2011. B must furnish the statement reporting the dividends by the January 31, 2011, due date provided in §1.6042-4. However, under paragraph (k)(3)(ii) of this section, B must fur-nish the statement reporting the dividends by February 15, 2011, if furnished in a consolidated reporting statement as defined in paragraph (k)(3)(i) of this section.

Example 2. Assume the same facts as in *Example 1* except that D has invested solely in a money market fund for which sales are excepted from the reporting required under this section. B therefore is not required to issue a statement under this section if D sells an interest in the money market fund. Under paragraph (k)(3)(i) of this section, B may treat a grouping of state-ments for D as including a required statement under this section because D has an account for which a statement would be required under this section if D purchased and sold stock in a corpo-ration in the account during the year. Therefore, under paragraph (k)(3)(ii) of this section, B must furnish the statement reporting the dividends by February 15, 2011.

Example 3. E has a nontaxable IRA account with B, a broker. This account is the only account E holds with B. E sells stock in 2010 in this account. E also receives a cash distribution from the account in 2010. The cash distribution from the IRA is reportable on Form 1099-R, "Distribu-tions From Pensions, Annuities, Retirement or Profit-Sharing Plans, IRAs, Insurance Contracts, etc.," under §1.408-7. Because the account is not taxable, sales in the account are not subject to reporting under this section. Therefore, because no statement is required under this section, under paragraph (k)(3) of this section, B may not furnish any statements to E in a consolidated reporting statement. B must furnish the Form 1099-R by the date required under §1.408-7.

Example 4. Assume the same facts as in *Example 3* except that E and F have a joint taxable account with B. Because sales in the joint taxable account are subject to reporting under this sec-tion, under paragraph (k)(3) of this section, B must furnish by February 15, 2011, all customer statements for 2010 that B otherwise must fur-nish jointly to E and F on or before January 31, 2011, if furnished on the same date in a consoli-dated reporting statement with the required statements under this section for any sales in the joint taxable account. However, B may not in-clude any statement for E's IRA account in the consolidated reporting statement furnished jointly to E and F because the statements are not furnished to the same customer or group of customers.

(4) *Cross-reference to penalty.*—For provisions for failure to furnish timely a correct payee state-ment, see §301.6724-1 of this chapter (Procedure

and Administration Regulations). See § 301.6724-1 of this chapter for the waiver of a penalty if the failure is due to reasonable cause and is not due to willful neglect.

(l) *Use of magnetic media.*—For information returns filed after December 31, 1996, see § 301.6011-2 of this chapter for rules relating to filing information returns on magnetic media and for rules relating to waivers granted for undue hardship. A broker or barter exchange that fails to file a Form 1099 on magnetic media, when required, may be subject to a penalty under section 6721 for each such failure. See paragraph (j) of this section.

(m) *Additional rules for option transactions.*— (1) *In general.*—This paragraph (m) provides rules for a broker to determine and report the information required under this section for an option that is a covered security under paragraph (a)(15)(i)(E) of this section.

(2) *Scope.*—(i) *In general.*—Paragraph (m) of this section applies to the following types of options granted or acquired on or after January 1, 2014:

(A) An option on one or more specified securities (which includes an index substantially all the components of which are specified securities);

(B) An option on financial attributes of specified securities, such as interest rates or dividend yields; or

(C) A warrant or a stock right.

(ii) *Delayed effective date for certain options.*—(A) Notwithstanding paragraph (m)(2)(i) of this section, if an option, stock right, or warrant is issued as part of an investment unit described in § 1.1273-2(h), paragraph (m) of this section applies to the option, stock right, or warrant if it is acquired on or after January 1, 2016.

(B) Notwithstanding paragraph (m)(2)(i) of this section, if the property referenced by an option (that is, the property underlying the option) is a debt instrument that is issued by a non-U.S. person or that provides for one or more payments denominated in, or determined by reference to, a currency other than the U.S. dollar, paragraph (m) of this section applies to the option if it is granted or acquired on or after January 1, 2016.

(iii) *Compensatory option.*—Notwithstanding paragraphs (m)(2)(i) and (m)(2)(ii) of this section, paragraph (m) of this section does not apply to compensatory options.

(3) *Option subject to section 1256.*—If an option described in paragraph (m)(2) of this section is also described in section 1256(b), a broker must apply the rules described in paragraph (c)(5) of this section by treating the option as if it were a regulated futures contract and must report the information required under paragraph (c)(5) of this section. A broker is permitted, but not required, to report the amounts for options and the amounts for regulated futures contracts

determined under paragraph (c)(5) of this section as a net amount for each reportable item.

(4) *Option not subject to section 1256.*—The following rules apply to an option that is described in paragraph (m)(2) of this section but is not also described in paragraph (m)(3) of this section:

(i) *Physical settlement.*—For purposes of paragraph (d) of this section, if a specified security (other than an option) is acquired or disposed of pursuant to the exercise of an option, the broker must adjust the basis of the acquired asset or the gross proceeds amount as appropriate to account for any payment related to the option, including the premium.

(ii) *Cash settlement.*—For purposes of paragraph (d) of this section, for an option that is settled for cash, a broker must reflect on Form 1099-B all payments made or received on the option. For a purchased option, a broker must report as basis the premium paid plus any costs (for example, commissions) related to the acquisition of the option and must report as proceeds the gross proceeds from settlement minus any costs related to the settlement of the option. For a written option, a broker must report as proceeds the premium received decreased by any amounts paid on the option and report $0 as the basis of the option.

(iii) *Rules for warrants and stock rights acquired in a section 305 distribution.*—For a right (including a warrant) to acquire stock received in the same account as the underlying security in a distribution that is described in section 305(a), a broker is permitted, but not required, to apply the rules described in sections 305 and 307 when reporting or accounting for the basis of the option and the underlying equity. If a stock right or warrant is acquired from the initial distributee, the buyer or transferee must treat it as an option covered by either paragraph (m)(4)(i) or (m)(4)(ii) of this section.

(iv) *Examples.*—The following examples illustrate the rules in this paragraph (m)(4):

Example 1. (i) On January 15, 2014, C, an individual who is neither a dealer nor a trader in securities, writes a 2-year exchange-traded option on 100 shares of Company X through Broker D. C receives a premium for the option of $100 and pays no commission. In C's hands, the option produces capital gain or loss and Company X stock is a capital asset. On December 16, 2014, C pays $110 to close out the option.

(ii) D is required to report information about the closing transaction because the option is a covered security as described in paragraph (a)(15)(i)(E) of this section and was part of a closing transaction described in paragraph (a)(8) of this section. Under paragraph (m)(4)(ii) of this section, D must report as gross proceeds on C's Form 1099-B -$10 (the $100 received as option premium minus the $110 C paid to close out the option) and report $0 in the basis box on the Form 1099-B. Under section 1234(b)(1) and para-

Reg. § 1.6045-1(m)(4)(iv)

graph (d)(2) of this section, D must also report the loss on the closing transaction as a short-term capital loss.

Example 2. (i) On January 15, 2014, E, an individual who is neither a dealer nor a trader in securities, buys a 2-year exchange-traded option on 100 shares of Company X through Broker F. E pays a premium of $100 for the option and pays no commission. In E's hands, both the option and Company X stock are capital assets. On December 16, 2014, E receives $110 to close out the option.

(ii) F is required to report information about the closing transaction because the option is a covered security as described in paragraph (a)(15)(i)(E) of this section and was part of a closing transaction described in paragraph (a)(8) of this section. Because the option is on the shares of a single company, it is an equity option described in section 1256(g)(6) and is not described in section 1256(b)(1)(C). Therefore, the rules of paragraph (m)(3) of this section do not apply, and F must report under paragraph (m)(4) of this section. Under paragraph (m)(4)(ii) of this section, F must report $110 as gross proceeds on the Form 1099-B for the gross proceeds E received and $100 in the basis box on the Form 1099-B to reflect the $100 option premium paid. Under section 1234(b)(1) and paragraph (d)(2) of this section, F must also report the gain on the closing transaction as a short-term capital gain.

(5) *Multiple options documented in a single contract.*—If more than one option described in paragraph (m)(2) of this section is documented in a single contract, a broker must separately report the required information for each option as that option is sold.

(6) *Determination of index status.*—Penalties will not be asserted under sections 6721 and 6722 if a broker in good faith determines that an index is, or is not, a narrow-based index described in section 1256(g)(6) and reports in a manner consistent with this determination.

(n) *Reporting for debt instrument transactions.*—(1) *In general.*—For purposes of this section, this paragraph (n) provides rules for a broker to determine and report information for a debt instrument that is a covered security under paragraph (a)(15)(i)(C) or (D) of this section. Neither a debt instrument subject to section 1272(a)(6) nor a short-term obligation described in section 1272(a)(2)(C) is subject to this paragraph (n) because neither is a specified security under paragraph (a)(14)(ii) of this section (a requirement for a debt instrument to be a covered security).

(2) *Debt instruments subject to January 1, 2014, reporting.*—(i) *In general.*—For purposes of paragraph (a)(15)(i)(C) of this section, except as provided in paragraph (n)(2)(ii) of this section, a debt instrument is described in this paragraph (n)(2)(i) if the debt instrument is one of the following:

(A) A debt instrument that provides for a single fixed payment schedule for which a yield and maturity can be determined for the instrument under § 1.1272-1(b);

(B) A debt instrument that provides for alternate payment schedules for which a yield and maturity can be determined for the instrument under § 1.1272-1(c); or

(C) A debt instrument for which the yield of the debt instrument can be determined under § 1.1272-1(d).

(ii) *Exceptions.*—A debt instrument is not described in paragraph (n)(2)(i) of this section if the debt instrument is one of the following:

(A) A debt instrument that provides for more than one rate of stated interest (including a debt instrument that provides for stepped interest rates);

(B) A convertible debt instrument described in § 1.1272-1(e);

(C) A stripped bond or stripped coupon subject to section 1286;

(D) A debt instrument that requires payment of either interest or principal in a currency other than the U.S. dollar;

(E) A debt instrument that, at one or more times in the future, entitles a holder to a tax credit;

(F) A debt instrument that provides for a payment-in-kind (PIK) feature (that is, under the terms of the debt instrument, a holder may receive one or more additional debt instruments of the issuer);

(G) A debt instrument issued by a non-U.S. issuer;

(H) A debt instrument for which the terms of the instrument are not reasonably available to the broker within 90 days of the date the debt instrument was acquired by the customer;

(I) A debt instrument that is issued as part of an investment unit described in § 1.1273-2(h); or

(J) A debt instrument evidenced by a physical certificate unless such certificate is held (whether directly or through a nominee, agent, or subsidiary) by a securities depository or by a clearing organization described in § 1.1471-1(b)(18).

(iii) *Remote or incidental.*—For purposes of paragraphs (n)(2)(i) and (n)(2)(ii) of this section, a remote or incidental contingency (as determined under § 1.1275-2(h)) is ignored.

(iv) *Penalty rate.*—For purposes of paragraph (n)(2)(ii)(A) of this section, a debt instrument does not provide for more than one rate of stated interest merely because the instrument provides for a penalty interest rate or an adjustment to the stated interest rate in the event of a default or similar event.

(3) *Debt instruments subject to January 1, 2016, reporting.*—For purposes of paragraph (a)(15)(i)(D) of this section, a debt instrument is described in this paragraph (n)(3) if it is described in paragraph (n)(2)(ii) of this section or it otherwise is not described in paragraph (n)(2)(i) of this section. For example, this paragraph

(n)(3) applies to variable rate debt instruments, inflation-indexed debt instruments, and contingent payment debt instruments because these instruments are not described in paragraph (n)(2)(i) of this section.

(4) *Holder elections.*—For purposes of this section, a broker is required to take into account an election described in this paragraph (n)(4), and the broker must take the election into account in accordance with the rules in paragraph (n)(5) of this section. A broker, however, may not take into account any other election. See paragraph (n)(11) of this section for the treatment of an election described in paragraph (n)(4)(iii) of this section (election to accrue market discount based on a constant yield) and an election described in paragraph (n)(4)(iv) of this section (election to treat all interest as OID).

(i) *Election to amortize bond premium.*—An election under section 171 and § 1.171-4 to amortize bond premium on a taxable debt instrument (this election applies to all taxable debt instruments held by a taxpayer during the taxable year the election is effective and thereafter; this election may be revoked with the consent of the Commissioner).

(ii) *Election to currently include accrued market discount.*—An election under section 1278(b) to include market discount in income as it accrues (this election applies to all debt instruments acquired by a taxpayer during the taxable year the election is effective and thereafter; this election may be revoked with the consent of the Commissioner).

(iii) *Election to accrue market discount based on a constant yield.*—An election under section 1276(b)(2) to compute accruals of market discount using a constant yield method (this election is generally made on an instrument-byinstrument basis and must be made for the earliest taxable year for which the taxpayer is required to determine accrued market discount on the debt instrument; this election may not be revoked).

(iv) *Election to treat all interest as OID.*—An election under § 1.1272-3 to treat all interest on a taxable debt instrument (adjusted for any acquisition premium or premium) as original issue discount (this election is generally made on an instrument-by-instrument basis and must be made for the taxable year the debt instrument is acquired by the taxpayer; this election may be revoked with the consent of the Commissioner). However, see paragraph (n)(11)(i)(A) of this section for a debt instrument acquired on or after January 1, 2014.

(v) *Election to translate interest income and expense at the spot rate.*—An election under § 1.988-2(b)(2)(iii)(B) to translate interest income and expense at the spot rate on the last day of the interest accrual period or, in the case of a partial accrual period, the last day of the taxable year (this election applies to all taxable debt instruments held by a taxpayer during the taxa-

ble year the election is effective and thereafter; this election may be revoked with the consent of the Commissioner).

(5) *Broker assumptions and customer notice to brokers.*—(i) *Broker assumptions if the customer does not notify the broker.*—Except as provided in paragraph (n)(5)(ii)(A) of this section, a broker must report the information required under paragraph (d) of this section by assuming that a customer has made the election to amortize bond premium described in paragraph (n)(4)(i) of this section. In addition, except as provided in paragraph (n)(5)(ii)(B) of this section, a broker must report the information required under paragraph (d) of this section by assuming that a customer has not made an election described in paragraph (n)(4)(ii), (n)(4)(iii), (n)(4)(iv), or (n)(4)(v) of this section. However, see paragraph (n)(11) of this section for the treatment of an election described in paragraph (n)(4)(iii) of this section (election to accrue market discount based on a constant yield) and an election described in paragraph (n)(4)(iv) of this section (election to treat all interest as OID).

(ii) *Effect of customer notification of an election or revocation.*—(A) *Election to amortize bond premium.*—If a customer notifies a broker in writing that the customer does not want the broker to take into account the election to amortize bond premium, the broker must report the information required under paragraph (d) of this section without taking into account the election to amortize bond premium. The customer must provide this notification to the broker by the end of the calendar year for which the customer does not want to amortize bond premium. If for a subsequent calendar year, the customer wants the broker to take into account the election to amortize bond premium, the customer must notify the broker in writing by the end of the calendar year that the customer wants to amortize bond premium. If the customer provides such notification, the broker must report the information required under paragraph (d) of this section as if the customer made the election to amortize bond premium for that year.

(B) *Other debt elections.*—If a customer notifies a broker in writing that the customer has made or will make an election described in paragraph (n)(4)(ii), (iii), (iv), or (v) of this section, the broker must report the information required under paragraph (d) of this section by taking into account the election. A customer must notify the broker in writing of the election by the end of the calendar year in which a debt instrument subject to the election is acquired in, or transferred into, an account with the broker or, if later, by the end of the calendar year for which the election is effective. If a customer has revoked or will revoke an election described in paragraph (n)(4)(ii), (n)(4)(iv), or (n)(4)(v) of this section for a calendar year, the customer must notify the broker of the revocation in writing by the end of the calendar year for which the revocation is effective. If the customer provides such notification, the broker must report the information required under paragraph (d) of this section by taking into account the revocation.

(iii) *Electronic notification.*—For purposes of paragraph (n)(5)(ii) of this section, the written notification to the broker includes a writing in electronic format.

(6) *Reporting of accrued market discount.*—In addition to the information required to be reported under paragraph (d) of this section, if a debt instrument is subject to the market discount rules in sections 1276 through 1278, a broker also must report the information described in paragraph (n)(6)(i) or (n)(6)(ii) of this section, whichever is applicable. Such information must be shown in the manner and at the time required by Form 1099 and section 6045.

(i) *Sale.*—A broker must report the amount of market discount that has accrued on a debt instrument as of the date of the instrument's sale, as defined in paragraph (a)(9) of this section. See paragraphs (n)(5) and (n)(11)(i)(B) of this section to determine whether the amount reported should take into account a customer election under section 1276(b)(2). See paragraph (n)(8) of this section to determine the accrual period to be used to compute the accruals of market discount. This paragraph (n)(6)(i) does not apply if the customer notifies the broker under the rules in paragraph (n)(5) of this section that the customer elects under section 1278(b) to include market discount in income as it accrues.

(ii) *Current inclusion election.*—If a customer notifies a broker under the rules in paragraph (n)(5) of this section that the customer elects under section 1278(b) to include market discount in income as it accrues, the broker is required to report to the customer the amount of market discount that accrued on a debt instrument during a taxable year while held by the customer in the account. The broker also must adjust basis in accordance with section 1278(b)(4). If a customer notifies a broker under the rules in paragraph (n)(5) of this section that the customer is revoking its election under section 1278(b), the broker will not report the market discount accrued during the taxable year of the revocation and thereafter and will cease to adjust basis in accordance with section 1278(b)(4). See paragraph (n)(8) of this section to determine the accrual period to be used to compute the accruals of market discount. See paragraphs (n)(5) and (n)(11)(i)(B) of this section to determine whether the amount reported should take into account a customer election under section 1276(b)(2).

(7) *Adjusted basis.*—For purposes of this section, a broker must use the rules in paragraph (n) of this section to determine the adjusted basis of a debt instrument.

(i) *Original issue discount.*—If a debt instrument is subject to the original issue discount rules in sections 1271 through 1275, section 1286, or section 1288, a broker must increase a cus-

tomer's basis in the debt instrument by the amount of original issue discount that accrued on the debt instrument while held by the customer in the account. See paragraph (n)(8) of this section to determine the accrual period to be used to compute the accruals of original issue discount.

(ii) *Amortizable bond premium.*—(A) *Taxable bond.*—A broker is required to adjust the customer's basis for any taxable bond acquired at a premium and held in the account in accordance with § 1.1016-5(b). If a customer, however, informs a broker under the rules in paragraph (n)(5)(ii)(A) of this section that the customer does not want to amortize bond premium, the broker must not adjust the customer's basis for any premium.

(B) *Tax-exempt bonds.*—A broker is required to adjust the customer's basis for any tax-exempt obligation acquired at a premium and held in the account in accordance with § 1.1016-5(b).

(iii) *Acquisition premium.*—If a debt instrument is acquired at an acquisition premium (as determined under § 1.1272-2(b)(3)), a broker must decrease the customer's basis in the debt instrument by the amount of acquisition premium that is taken into account each year to reduce the amount of the original issue discount that is otherwise includible in the customer's income for that year. See § 1.1272-2(b)(4) to determine the amount of the acquisition premium taken into account each year. However, if a broker took into account a customer election under § 1.1272-3 in 2014, the broker must decrease the customer's basis in the debt instrument by the amount of acquisition premium that is taken into account each year to reduce the amount of the original issue discount that is otherwise includible in the customer's income for that year in accordance with § § 1.1272-2(b)(5) and 1.1272-3.

(iv) *Market discount.*—See paragraph (n)(6) of this section for rules to determine the adjusted basis of a debt instrument with market discount.

(v) *Principal and certain other payments.*—A broker must decrease the customer's basis in a debt instrument by the amount of any payment made to the customer during the period the debt instrument is held in the account, other than a payment of qualified stated interest as defined in § 1.1273-1(c).

(8) *Accrual period.*—For purposes of this section, a broker generally must use the same accrual period that is used to report any original issue discount or stated interest to a customer under section 6049 for a debt instrument. In any other situation, a broker must use a semi-annual accrual period or, if a debt instrument provides for scheduled payments of principal or interest at regular intervals of less than six months over the entire term of the debt instrument, a broker must use an accrual period equal in length to this shorter interval. For example, if a debt in-

strument provides for monthly payments of interest over the entire term of the debt instrument, the broker must use a monthly accrual period. The rules in § 1.1272-1(b)(4)(iii) apply for purposes of an initial short accrual period. In computing the length of an accrual period, any reasonable counting convention may be used (for example, 30 days per month/360 days per year, or actual days per month/365 days per year).

(9) *Premium on convertible bond.*—If a customer acquires a convertible bond (as defined in § 1.171-1(e)(1)(iii)(C)) at a premium (as determined under § 1.171-1(d)), then, solely for purposes of this section and § 1.6049-9, a broker must assume that the premium is attributable to the conversion feature. Based on this assumption, no portion of the premium is amortizable for purposes of this section and § 1.6049-9.

(10) *Effect of broker assumptions on customer.*—The rules in this paragraph (n) only apply for purposes of a broker's reporting obligation under section 6045. A customer is not bound by the assumptions that the broker uses to satisfy the broker's reporting obligations under section 6045. In addition, a notification to the broker under paragraph (n)(5) of this section does not constitute an effective election or revocation under the applicable rules for the election.

(11) *Additional rules for certain holder elections.*—(i) *In general.*—For purposes of this section, the rules in this paragraph (n)(11) apply notwithstanding any other rule in paragraph (n) of this section.

(A) *Election to treat all interest as OID.*—A broker must report the information required under paragraph (d) of this section without taking into account any election described in paragraph (n)(4)(iv) of this section (the election to treat all interest as OID in § 1.1272-3). As a result, for example, a broker must determine the amount of any acquisition premium taken into account each year for purposes of this section in accordance with § 1.1272-2(b)(4). This paragraph (n)(11)(i)(A) applies to a debt instrument acquired on or after January 1, 2015. A broker, however, may rely on this paragraph (n)(11)(i)(A) for a debt instrument acquired on or after January 1, 2014, and before January 1, 2015.

(B) *Election to accrue market discount based on a constant yield.*—A broker must report the information required under paragraph (d) of this section by assuming that a customer has made the election described in paragraph (n)(4)(iii) of this section (the election to accrue market discount based on a constant yield). However, if a customer notifies a broker in writing that the customer does not want the broker to take into account this election, the broker must report the information required under paragraph (d) of this section without taking into account this election. The customer must provide this notification to the broker by the end of the calendar year in which the customer acquired the debt instrument in an account with the bro-

ker. This paragraph (n)(11)(i)(B) applies to a debt instrument acquired on or after January 1, 2015. A broker, however, may rely on this paragraph (n)(11)(i)(B) to report accrued market discount for a debt instrument that is a covered security acquired on or after January 1, 2014, and before January 1, 2015, if the customer had not informed the broker that the customer had made a section 1278(b) election and there were no principal payments on the debt instrument during this period.

(ii) [Reserved].

(12) *Certain debt instruments treated as noncovered securities.*—(i) *In general.*—Notwithstanding paragraph (a)(15) of this section, a debt instrument is treated as a noncovered security for purposes of this section if the terms of the debt instrument are not reasonably available to the broker within 90 days of the date the debt instrument was acquired by the customer and the debt instrument is either—

(A) A debt instrument issued by a non-U.S. issuer; or

(B) A tax-exempt obligation issued before January 1, 2014.

(ii) *Effective/applicability date.*—Paragraph (n)(12)(i) of this section applies to a debt instrument described in paragraph (n)(12)(i)(A) or (B) of this section that is acquired on or after February 18, 2016. However, a broker may rely on paragraph (n)(12)(i) of this section for a debt instrument described in paragraph (n)(12)(i)(A) or (B) of this section acquired before February 18, 2016.

(o) *Additional reporting by stock transfer agents.*—[Reserved]

(p) *Electronic filing.*—Notwithstanding the time prescribed for filing in paragraph (j) of this section, Forms 1096 and 1099 required under this section for reporting periods ending during a calendar year shall, if filed electronically, be filed after the last calendar day of the reporting period elected by the broker or barter exchange and on or before March 31 of the following calendar year.

(q) *Effective/applicability date.*—Except as otherwise provided in paragraphs (m)(2)(ii), and (n)(12)(ii) of this section, this section applies on or after January 6, 2017. (For rules that apply after June 30, 2014, and before January 6, 2017, see this section as in effect and contained in 26 CFR part 1, as revised April 1, 2016.) [Reg. § 1.6045-1.]

☐ [*T.D.* 7873, 3-3-83. *Amended by T.D.* 7880, 3-22-83; *T.D.* 7932, 12-28-83; *T.D.* 7960, 5-23-84; *T.D.* 8445, 11-5-92; *T.D.* 8452, 12-11-92; *T.D.* 8683, 10-9-96; *T.D.* 8734, 10-6-97; *T.D.* 8772, 6-29-98; *T.D.* 8804, 12-30-98; *T.D.* 8856, 12-29-99; *T.D.* 8881, 5-15-2000 (*corrected* 4-5-2001); *T.D.* 8895, 8-17-2000; *T.D.* 9010, 7-25-2002; *T.D.* 9241, 1-23-2006; *T.D.* 9504, 10-12-2010; *T.D.* 9616, 4-17-2013, *T.D.* 9658, 2-28-2014, *T.D.* 9713, 3-12-2015, *T.D.* 9750, 2-17-2016 (*corrected* 4-26-2016), *T.D.* 9774, 7-7-2016 *and T.D.* 9808, 12-30-2016 (*corrected* 6-29-2017).]

[Reg. § 1.6045-2]

§ 1.6045-2. Furnishing statement required with respect to certain substitute payments.— (a) *Requirement of furnishing statements.*—(1) *In general.*—Any broker (as defined in paragraph (a)(4)(ii) of this section) that transfers securities (as defined in § 1.6045-1(a)(3)) of a customer (as defined in paragraph (a)(4)(iii) of this section) for use in a short sale and receives on behalf of the customer a substitute payment (as defined in paragraph (a)(4)(i)) shall, except as otherwise provided, furnish a statement to the customer identifying such payment as being a substitute payment.

(2) *Special rule for transfers for broker's own use.*—Any broker that borrows securities of a customer for use in a short sale entered into for the broker's own account shall be deemed to have transferred the stock to itself and received on behalf of the customer any substitute payment made with respect to the transferred securities, and shall be required to furnish a statement with respect to such payment in accordance with paragraph (a)(1) of this section.

(3) *Special rule for furnishing statements to individual customers with respect to payments in lieu of dividends.*—(i) *In general.*—Except as otherwise provided in paragraph (a)(3)(ii) of this section, for taxable years beginning before January 1, 2003, a broker that receives a substitute payment in lieu of a dividend on behalf of a customer who is an individual ("individual customer") need not furnish a statement to the customer.

(ii) *Reporting for certain dividends.*—Any broker that receives on behalf of an individual customer a substitute payment in lieu of—

(A) An exempt-interest dividend (as defined in paragraph (a)(4)(vii) of this section);

(B) A capital gain dividend (as defined in paragraph (a)(4)(vi) of this section);

(C) A distribution treated as a return of capital under section 301(c)(2) or (c)(3); or

(D) An FTC dividend (as defined in paragraph (a)(4)(viii) of this section) shall furnish a statement to the individual customer identifying the payment as being a substitute payment as prescribed by this section, provided that the broker has reason to know not later than the record date of the dividend payment that the payment is a substitute payment in lieu of an exempt-interest dividend, a capital gain dividend, a distribution treated as a return of capital, or an FTC dividend.

(4) *Meaning of terms.*—The following definitions apply for purposes of this section.

(i) The term "substitute payment" means a payment in lieu of—

(A) Tax-exempt interest, to the extent that interest has accrued on the obligation for the period during which the short sale is open;

(B) A dividend, the ex-dividend date for which occurs during the period after the transfer of stock for use in a short sale, and prior to the closing of the short sale; or

(C) Any other item specified in a rule-related notice published in the *Federal Register* (provided that such items shall be subject to the rules of this section only subsequent to the time of such publication).

For purposes of this section original issue discount accruing on an obligation (the interest upon which is exempt from tax under section 103) for the period during which the short sale is open shall be deemed a payment in lieu of tax-exempt interest.

(ii) The term "broker" means both a person described in § 1.6045-1(a)(1) and a person that, in the ordinary course of a trade or business during the calendar year, loans securities owned by others.

(iii) The term "customer" means, with respect to a transfer of securities for use in a short sale, the person that is the record owner of the securities so transferred.

(iv) The term "dividend" means a dividend (as defined in section 316) or a distribution that is treated as a return of capital under section 301(c)(2) or (c)(3).

(v) The term "tax-exempt interest" means interest to which the exception in section 6049(b)(2)(B) applies.

(vi) The term "capital gain dividend" means a capital gain dividend as defined in section 852(b)(3)(C) or section 857(b)(3)(C).

(vii) The term "exempt-interest dividend" means an exempt-interest dividend as defined in section 852(b)(5)(A).

(viii) The term "FTC dividend" means a dividend with respect to which the recipient is entitled to claim a foreign tax credit under section 901 (but not by virtue of taxes deemed paid under sections 902 or 960).

(5) *Examples.*—The following examples illustrate the definition of a substitute payment in lieu of tax-exempt interest found in paragraph (a)(4)(i)(A) of this section.

Example (1). On September 1, 1984, L, a broker, borrows 200 State Q Bonds (the interest upon which is exempt from tax under section 103) held in street name for customer R and transfers the bonds to W for use in a short sale. The bonds each have a face value of $100 and bear 12% stated annual interest paid semiannually on January 1 and July 1 of each year. The bonds were not issued with original issue discount. On November 1, 1984, W closes the short sale and returns State Q Bonds to L. On January 1, 1985, L receives a $1200 interest payment (6% × $100 × 200 bonds = $1200) from State Q with respect to R's bonds. Four hundred dollars (2 months the bonds were on loan/6 months in the interest period = $1/3$ × $1200 = $400) of the interest payment represents accrued interest on the obligations for the period during which the short sale was open, and is a substitute payment in lieu of tax-exempt interest within the meaning of paragraph (a)(4)(i)(A) of this section. L must furnish a statement under paragraph (a) of this section to R for calendar year 1985 with respect to the $400 substitute payment.

Example (2). Assume the same facts as in Example (1), except that W closes the short sale on February 1, 1985. On January 1, 1985, L receives a $1200 payment from W with respect to R's bonds. Eight hundred dollars (4 months the bonds were on loan prior to January 1, 1985/6 months in the interest period = $2/3 \times $1200 = $800) of the payment represents accrued interest on the obligation for the period during which the short sale was open and is a substitute payment in lieu of tax-exempt interest. On July 1, 1985, L receives another $1200 payment from State Q. Two hundred dollars (1 month the bonds were on loan after December 31, 1984/6 months in the interest period = $1/6 \times $1200 = $200) of the payment represents accrued interest on the obligation for the period during which the short sale was open and is a substitute payment in lieu of the tax-exempt interest. Because both payments are received by L in 1985, L must furnish a statement under paragraph (a) of this section to R for that year with respect to both payments.

(b) *Exceptions.*—(1) *Minimal payments.*—No statement is required to be furnished under section 6045(d) or this section to any customer if the aggregate amount of the substitute payments received by a broker on behalf of the customer during a calendar year for which a statement must be furnished is less than $10.

(2) *Exempt recipients.*—(i) *In general.*—A statement shall not be required to be furnished with respect to substitute payments made to a broker on behalf of—

(A) An organization exempt from taxation under section 501(a);

(B) An individual retirement plan;

(C) The United States, a possession of the United States, or an instrumentality or a political subdivision or a wholly-owned agency of the foregoing;

(D) A State, the District of Columbia, or a political subdivision or a wholly-owned agency or instrumentality of either of the foregoing;

(E) A foreign government or a political subdivision thereof;

(F) An international organization, or

(G) A foreign central bank of issue, as defined in § 1.6049-4(c)(1)(ii)(H), or the Bank for International Settlements.

(ii) *Determination of whether a person is described in paragraph (b)(2)(i) of this section.*—The determination of whether a person is described in paragraph (b)(2)(i) of this section shall be made in the manner provided in § 1.6045-1(c)(3)(i)(B).

(3) *Exempt foreign persons.*—A statement shall not be required to be furnished with respect to substitute payments made to a broker on behalf of a person that is an exempt foreign person as described in § 1.6045-1(g).

(c) *Form of statement.*—A broker shall furnish the statement required by paragraph (a) of this section on Form 1099. The statement must show the aggregate dollar amount of all substitute payments received by the broker on behalf of a customer (for which the broker is required to furnish a statement) during a calendar year, and such other information as may be required by Form 1099. A statement shall be considered to be furnished to a customer if it is mailed to the customer at the last address of the customer known to the broker. An IRS truncated taxpayer identifying number (TTIN) may be used as the identifying number of the customer in lieu of the identifying number appearing on the information return filed with the Internal Revenue Service. For provisions relating to the use of TTINs, see § 301.6109-4 of this chapter (Procedure and Administration Regulations).

(d) *Time for furnishing statements.*—(1) *General requirements.*—A broker must furnish the statements required by paragraph (a) of this section for each calendar year. The statements must be furnished after April 30th of the calendar year but in no case before the final substitute payment for the calendar year is made, and on or before February 15 of the following calendar year.

(2) *Consolidated reporting.*—(i) The term *consolidated reporting statement* means a grouping of statements the same broker furnishes to the same customer or group of customers on the same date for the same reporting year that includes a statement required under this section. A consolidated reporting statement is limited to statements based on the same relationship of broker to customer as the statement required to be furnished under this section.

(ii) A consolidated reporting statement must be furnished on or before February 15 of the year following the calendar year reported. Any statement that otherwise must be furnished on or before January 31 must be furnished on or before February 15 if it is furnished in the consolidated reporting statement.

(e) *When substitute payment deemed received.*—A broker is deemed to have received a substitute payment on behalf of a customer when the amount is paid or deemed paid to the broker (or as it accrues in the case of original issue discount deemed a payment in lieu of tax-exempt interest).

(f) *Identification of customer and recordkeeping with respect to substitute payments.*—(1) *Payments in lieu of tax-exempt interest and exempt-interest dividends.*—A broker that receives substitute payments in lieu of tax-exempt interest, exempt-interest dividends, or other items (to the extent specified in a rule-related notice published pursuant to paragraph (a)(4)(i)(C) of this section) on behalf of a customer and is required to furnish a statement under paragraph (a) of this section must determine the identity of the customer whose security was transferred and on whose behalf the broker received such substitute payments by specific identification of the record owner of the security so transferred. A broker must keep adequate records of the determination so made.

(2) *Payments in lieu of dividends other than exempt-interest dividends.*—(i) *Requirements and methods.*—A broker that receives substitute payments in lieu of dividends other than exempt-interest dividends on behalf of a customer and is required to furnish a statement under paragraph (a) of this section must make a determination of the identity of the customer whose stock was transferred and on whose behalf such broker receives substitute payments. Such determination must be made as of the record date with respect to the dividend distribution, and must be made in a consistent manner by the broker in accordance with any of the following methods:

(A) Specific identification of the record owner of the transferred stock;

(B) The method of allocation and selection specified in paragraph (f)(2)(ii) of this section; or

(C) Any other method, with the prior approval of the Commissioner.

A broker must keep adequate records of the determination so made.

(ii) *Method of allocation and selection.*— (A) *Allocation to individual and nonindividual pools.*—With respect to each substitute payment in lieu of a dividend received by a broker, the broker must allocate the transferred shares (*i.e.,* the shares giving rise to the substitute payment) among all shares of stock of the same class and issue as the transferred shares which were (1) borrowed by the broker, and (2) which the broker holds (or has transferred in a transaction described in paragraph (a)(1) of this section) and is authorized by its customers to transfer (including shares of stock of the same class and issue held for the broker's own account) ("loanable shares"). The broker may first allocate the transferred shares to any borrowed shares. Then to the extent that the number of transferred shares exceeds the number of borrowed shares (or if the broker does not allocate to the borrowed shares first), the broker must allocate the transferred shares between two pools, one consisting of the loanable shares of all individual customers (the "individual pool") and the other consisting of the loanable shares of all nonindividual customers (the "nonindividual pool"). The transferred shares must be allocated to the individual pool in the same proportion that the number of loanable shares held by individual customers bears to the total number of loanable shares available to the broker. Similarly, the transferred shares must be allocated to the nonindividual pool in the same proportion that the number of loanable shares held by nonindividual customers bears to the total number of loanable shares available to the broker.

(B) *Selection of deemed transferred shares within the nonindividual pool.*—The broker must

select which shares within the nonindividual pool are deemed transferred for use in a short sale (the "deemed transferred shares"). Selection of deemed transferred shares may be made either by purely random lottery or on a first-in-first-out ("FIFO") basis.

(C) *Selection of deemed transferred shares within the individual pool.*—The broker must select which shares within the individual pool are deemed transferred shares (in the manner described in the preceding paragraph) only with respect to substitute payments as to which a statement is required to be furnished under paragraph (a)(2)(ii) of this section.

(3) *Examples.*—The following examples illustrate the identification of customer rules of paragraph (f)(2):

Example (1). A, a broker, holds X corporation common stock (of which there is only a single class) in street name for five customers: C, a corporation; D, a partnership; E, a corporation; F, an individual; and G, a corporation. C owns 100 shares of X stock, D owns 50 shares of X stock, E owns 100 shares of X stock, F owns 50 shares of X stock, and G owns 100 shares of X stock. A is authorized to loan all of the X stock of C, D, E, and F. G, however, has not authorized A to loan its X stocks. A transfers 150 shares of X stock to H for use in a short sale on July 1, 1985. A dividend of $2 per share is declared with respect to X stock on August 1, 1985, payable to the owners of record as of August 15, 1985 (the "record" date). A receives $2 per transferred share as a payment in lieu of a dividend with respect to X stock or a total of $300 on September 15, 1985. H closes the short sale and returns X stock to A on January 2, 1986. A's records specifically identify the owner of each loanable share of stock held in street name. From A's records it is determined that the shares transferred to H consisted of 100 shares owned by C, 25 shares owned by D, and 25 shares owned by F. The substitute payment in lieu of dividends with respect to X stock is therefore attributed to C, D and F based on the actual number of their shares that were transferred to H. Accordingly, C receives $200 (100 shares × $2 per share), and D and F each receive $50 (25 shares each × $2 per share). A must furnish statements identifying the payments as being in lieu of dividends to both C and D, unless they are exempt recipients as defined in paragraph (b)(2) of this section or as exempt foreign persons as defined in paragraph (b)(3) of this section. Assuming that A has no reason to know on the record date of the payment that the dividend paid by X is of a type described in paragraph (a)(3)(ii)(A)-(D) of this section, A need not furnish F with a statement under section 6045(d) because F is an individual. (However, A may be required to furnish F with a statement in accordance with section 6042 and the regulations thereunder. See paragraph (h) of this section.) By recording the ownership of each share transferred to H, A has complied with the identification requirement of paragraph (f)(2) of this section.

Example (2). Assume the same facts as in example (1), except that A's records do not specifically identify the record owner of each share of stock. Rather, all shares of X stock held in street name are pooled together. When A receives the $2 per share payment in lieu of a dividend, A determines the identity of the customers to which the payment relates by the method of allocation and selection prescribed in paragraph (f)(2)(ii) of this section. First, the transferred shares are allocated proportionately between the individual pool and the nonindividual pool. One-sixth of the transferred shares or 25 shares are allocated to the individual pool (50 loanable shares owned by individuals/300 total loanable shares = $^{1}/_{6}$; $^{1}/_{6}$ × 150 transferred shares = 25 shares). Assuming A has no reason to know by the record date of the payment that the payment is in lieu of a dividend of a type described in paragraph (a)(3)(ii)(A)-(D) of this section, no selection of deemed transferred shares within the individual customer pool is required. (However, A may be required to furnish F with a statement under section 6042 and the regulations thereunder. See paragraph (h) of this section.) Five-sixths of the transferred shares or 125 shares are allocated to the nonindividual pool (250 loanable shares owned by nonindividuals/300 total loanable shares = $^{5}/_{6}$; $^{5}/_{6}$ × 150 transferred shares = 125 shares). A must select which 125 shares within the nonindividual pool are deemed to have been transferred. Using a purely random lottery, A selects 100 shares identified as being owned by C, and 25 shares identified as being owned by D. Accordingly, A is deemed to have transferred 100 shares and 25 shares owned by C and D respectively, and received substitute payments in lieu of dividends of $200 (100 shares × $2 per share) and $50 (25 shares × $2 per share) on behalf of C and D respectively. A must furnish statements to both C and D identifying such payments as being in lieu of dividends unless they are exempt recipients as defined in paragraph (b)(2) of this section or exempt foreign persons as defined in paragraph (b)(3) of this section. A has complied with the identification requirement of paragraph (f)(2) of this section.

(g) *Reporting by brokers.*—(1) *Requirement of reporting.*—Any broker required to furnish a statement under paragraph (a) of this section shall report on Form 1096 showing such information as may be required by Form 1096, in the form, manner, and number of copies required by Form 1096. With respect to each customer for which a broker is required to furnish a statement, the broker shall make a return of information on Form 1099, in the form, manner and number of copies required by Form 1099.

(2) *Use of magnetic media.*—For information returns filed after December 31, 1996, see § 301.6011-2 of this chapter for rules relating to filing information returns on magnetic media and for rules relating to waivers granted for undue hardship. A broker or barter exchange

that fails to file a Form 1099 on magnetic media, when required, may be subject to a penalty under section 6721 for each such failure. See paragraph (g)(4) of this section.

(3) *Time and place of filing.*—The returns required under this paragraph (g) for any calendar year shall be filed after September 30 of such year, but not before the final substitute payment for the year is received by the broker, and on or before February 28 (March 31 if filed electronically) of the following year with any of the Internal Revenue Service Centers, the addresses of which are listed in the instructions for Form 1096.

(4) *Cross-reference to penalties.*—For provisions relating to the penalty provided for failure to file timely a correct information return required under section 6045(d) and § 1.6045-2(g)(1), including a failure to file on magnetic media, see § 301.6721-1 of this chapter. For provisions relating to the penalty provided for failure to furnish timely a correct payee statement required under section 6045(d) and § 1.6045-2(a), see § 301.6722-1 of this chapter. See § 301.6724-1 of this chapter for the waiver of a penalty if the failure is due to reasonable cause and is not due to willful neglect.

(h) *Coordination with section 6042.*—In cases in which reporting is required by both sections 6042 and 6045(d) with respect to the same substitute payment in lieu of a dividend, the provisions of section 6045(d) control, and no report or statement under section 6042 need be made. If reporting is not required under section 6045(d) with respect to a substitute payment in lieu of a dividend, a report under section 6042 must be made if required in accordance with the rules of section 6042 and the regulations thereunder. Thus, if a broker receives a substitute payment in lieu of a dividend on behalf of an individual customer and the broker does not have reason to know by the record date of the payment that the payment is in lieu of a dividend of a type described in paragraph (a)(3)(ii)(A)-(D) of this section, the broker must report with respect to the substitute payment if required in accordance with section 6042 and the regulations thereunder.

(i) *Effective/applicability date.*—These regulations apply to substitute payments received by a broker after December 31, 1984. The amendments to paragraph (c) apply to payee statements due after December 31, 2014. For payee statements due before January 1, 2015, § 1.6045-2(c) (as contained in 26 CFR part 1, revised April 2013) shall apply. With regard to paragraph (g)(2) of this section, see section 6011(e) of the Internal Revenue Code for information returns required to be filed after December 31, 1989, and before January 1, 1997; and see paragraph (g)(2) of this section for information returns required to be filed after December 31, 1996. [Reg. § 1.6045-2.]

□ [*T.D. 8029, 6-4-85. Amended by T.D. 8683,* 10-9-96; *T.D. 8734,* 10-6-97 (T.D. 8804 delayed the effective date of T.D. 8734 from January 1, 1999, to January 1, 2000; T.D. 8856 further delayed the effective date of T.D. 8734 until January 1, 2001); *T.D. 8772, 6-29-98; T.D. 8895, 8-17-2000; T.D. 9010, 7-25-2002; T.D. 9103, 12-24-2003; T.D. 9504, 10-12-2010 and T.D. 9675, 7-14-2014.*]

[Reg. § 1.6045-3]

§ 1.6045-3. Information reporting for an acquisition of control or a substantial change in capital structure.—(a) *In general.*—Any broker (as defined in § 1.6045-1 (a)(1)) that holds shares on behalf of a customer in a corporation that the broker knows or has reason to know based on readily available information (including, for example, information from a clearing organization or from information published by the Internal Revenue Service (IRS)) has engaged in a transaction described in § 1.6043-4(c) (acquisition of control) or § 1.6043-4(d) (substantial change in capital structure) shall file a return of information with respect to the customer, unless the customer is an exempt recipient as defined in paragraph (b) of this section.

(b) *Exempt recipients.*—A broker is not required to file a return of information under this section with respect to the following customers:

(1) Any customer who receives only cash in exchange for its stock in the corporation, which must be reported by the broker pursuant to § 1.6045-1.

(2) Any customer who is an exempt recipient as defined in § 1.6043-4(b)(5) or § 1.6045-1(c)(3)(i).

(c) *Form, manner and time for making information returns.*—The return required by paragraph (a) of this section must be on Forms 1096, "Annual Summary and Transmittal of U.S. Information Returns," and 1099-B, "Proceeds from Broker and Barter Exchange Transactions," or on an acceptable substitute statement. Such forms must be filed on or before February 28 (March 31 if filed electronically) of the year following the calendar year in which the acquisition of control or the substantial change in capital structure occurs.

(d) *Contents of return.*—A separate Form 1099-B must be prepared for each customer. The Form 1099-B will request information with respect to the following and such other information as may be specified in the instructions:

(1) The name, address and taxpayer identification number (TIN) of the customer;

(2) The name of the corporation which engaged in the transaction described in § 1.6043-4(c) or (d);

(3) The number and class of shares in the corporation exchanged by the customer; and

(4) The aggregate amount of cash and the fair market value of any stock or other property provided to the customer in exchange for its stock.

(e) *Furnishing of forms to customers.*—(1) *General requirements.*—A broker must furnish Form 1099-B to the customer on or before February 15 of the year following the calendar year in which the customer receives stock, cash or other property. An IRS truncated taxpayer identifying number (TTIN) may be used as the identifying number of the customer. For provisions relating to the use of TTINs, see § 301.6109-4 of this chapter (Procedure and Administration Regulations).

(2) *Consolidated reporting.*—(i) The term *consolidated reporting statement* means a grouping of statements the same broker furnishes to the same customer or group of customers on the same date for the same reporting year that includes a statement required under this section. A consolidated reporting statement is limited to statements based on the same relationship of broker to customer as the statement required to be furnished under this section.

(ii) A consolidated reporting statement must be furnished on or before February 15 of the year following the calendar year reported. Any statement that otherwise must be furnished on or before January 31 must be furnished on or before February 15 if it is furnished in the consolidated reporting statement.

(f) *Single Form 1099.*—If a broker is required to file a Form 1099-B with respect to a customer under § § 1.6045-3 and 1.6045-1(c) with respect to the same transaction, the broker may satisfy the requirements of both sections by filing and furnishing one Form 1099-B that contains all the relevant information, as provided in the instructions to Form 1099-B.

(g) *Effective/applicability date.*—This section applies with respect to any acquisition of control and any substantial change in capital structure occurring after December 5, 2005. The amendments to paragraph (e)(1) apply to payee statements due after December 31, 2014. For payee statements due before January 1, 2015, § 1.6045-3(e)(1) (as contained in 26 CFR part 1, revised April 2013) shall apply. [Reg. § 1.6045-3.]

□ [*T.D. 9230, 12-2-2005. Amended by T.D. 9504,* 10-12-2010 *and T.D. 9675, 7-14-2014.*]

⤞➜ *Caution: Temporary Reg. §1.6045-3T, below, was removed by T.D. 9230, but it remains outstanding with respect to transactions not covered by Reg. §1.6045-3 while the IRS considers additional information reporting requirements under Code Secs. 6043(c), 6043A and 6045.*

[Reg. § 1.6045-3T]

§ 1.6045-3T. Information reporting for an acquisition of control or a substantial change in capital structure (temporary).—(a) *In general.*—Any broker (as defined in § 1.6045-1(a)(1)) that

holds shares on behalf of a customer in a corporation that the broker knows or has reason to know based on readily available information (including, for example, information from a clearing organization or from information published

>>>→ *Caution: Temporary Reg. §1.6045-3T, below, was removed by T.D. 9230, but it remains outstanding with respect to transactions not covered by Reg. §1.6045-3 while the IRS considers additional information reporting requirements under Code Secs. 6043(c), 6043A and 6045.*

by the Internal Revenue Service (see §601.601(d)(2) of this chapter)) has engaged in a transaction described in §1.6043-4T(c) (acquisition of control) or §1.6043-4T(d) (substantial change in capital structure), shall file a return of information with respect to the customer, unless the customer is an exempt recipient as defined in paragraph (b) of this section.

(b) *Exempt recipients.*—A broker is not required to file a return of information under this section with respect to the following customers:

(1) Any customer who receives only cash in exchange for its stock in the corporation, which must be reported by the broker pursuant to §1.6045-1(a).

(2) Any customer who is an exempt recipient as defined in §1.6043-4T(b)(5) or §1.6045-1(c)(3)(i).

(c) *Form, manner and time for making information returns.*—The return required by paragraph (a) of this section must be on Forms 1096, "Annual Summary and Transmittal of U.S. Information Returns," and 1099-B, "Proceeds from Broker and Barter Exchange Transactions," or on an acceptable substitute statement. Such forms must be filed on or before February 28 (March 31 if filed electronically) of the year following the calendar year in which the acquisition of control or the substantial change in capital structure occurs.

(d) *Contents of return.*—A separate Form 1099-B must be prepared for each customer showing—

(1) The name, address and taxpayer identification number (TIN) of the customer;

(2) The name and address of the corporation which engaged in the transaction described in §1.6043-4T(c) or (d);

(3) The number and class of shares in the corporation exchanged by the customer;

(4) The aggregate amount of cash and the fair market value of any stock (other than stock described in 1.6043-4T(a)(1)(v)(C)) or other property provided to the customer in exchange for its stock; and

(5) Such other information as may be required by Form 1099-B.

(e) *Furnishing of forms to customers.*—The Form 1099-B prepared for each customer must be furnished to the customer on or before January 31 of the year following the calendar year in which the customer receives stock, cash or other property.

(f) *Single Form 1099.*—If a broker is required to file a Form 1099-B with respect to a customer under both this §1.6045-3T and §1.6045-1(b) with respect to the same transaction, the broker may satisfy the requirements of both sections by filing and furnishing one Form 1099-B that con-

tains all the relevant information, as provided in the instructions to Form 1099-B.

(g) *Effective date.*—(1) This section applies with respect to any acquisition of control and any substantial change in capital structure occurring after December 31, 2001, if the reporting corporation or any shareholder is required to recognize gain (if any) as a result of the application of section 367(a) as a result of the transaction. However, paragraphs (a) through (f) of this section apply to acquisitions of control and substantial changes in capital structure occurring after December 31, 2002, if the reporting corporation or any shareholder is required to recognize gain (if any) as a result of the application of section 367(a) as a result of the transaction. For transactions prior to that date, see §1.6045-3T as published in 26 CFR Part 1 (revised as of April 1, 2003). This section expires on November 14, 2005.

(2) For any acquisition of control or any substantial change in capital structure occurring during the 2003 calendar year, a broker may elect to satisfy the requirements of this section by using Form 1099-CAP in lieu of Form 1099-B. [Temporary Reg. §1.6045-3T.]

☐ [T.D. 9022, 11-13-2002 (corrected 2-5-2003). *Amended by T.D. 9101, 12-29-2003 (corrected 2-13-2004). Removed by T.D. 9230, 12-2-2005.]*

[Reg. §1.6045-4]

§1.6045-4. Information reporting on real estate transactions with dates of closing on or after January 1, 1991.—(a) *Requirement of reporting.*—Except as otherwise provided in paragraphs (c) and (d) of this section, a real estate reporting person ("reporting person") must make an information return with respect to a real estate transaction and, under paragraph (m) of this section, must furnish a statement to the transferor. A reporting person may also report with respect to transactions otherwise excepted in paragraphs (c) and (d) of this section. However, if the reporting person so elects, the return must be filed and the statement furnished in accordance with the provisions of this section. For the definition of a real estate transaction for purposes of these reporting requirements, see paragraph (b) of this section. For rules for determining the reporting person with respect to a real estate transaction, see paragraph (e) of this section.

(b) *Definition of real estate transaction.*—(1) *In general.*—A transaction is a "real estate transaction" under this section if the transaction consists in whole or in part of the sale or exchange of "reportable real estate" (as defined in paragraph (b)(2) of this section) for money, indebtedness, property other than money, or services. The term "sale or exchange" shall include any transaction properly treated as a sale or exchange for Federal income tax purposes,

Reg. §1.6045-4(b)(1)

whether or not the transaction is currently taxable. Thus, for example, a sale or exchange of a principal residence is a real estate transaction under this section even though the transferor is entitled to defer recognition under section 1034 (relating to rollover of gain on sale of principal residence), or the transferor is entitled to the special one-time exclusion of gain from the sale of a principal residence provided by section 121 to certain persons who have attained age 55.

(2) *Definition of reportable real estate.*— (i) Except as otherwise provided in paragraph (c)(2) of this section, the term "reportable real estate" means any present or future ownership interest in—

(A) Land (whether improved or unimproved), including air space;

(B) Any inherently permanent structure, including any residential, commercial or industrial building;

(C) Any condominium unit, including appurtenant fixtures and common elements (including land); or

(D) Any stock in a cooperative housing corporation (as defined in section 216).

(E) Any non-contingent interest in standing timber.

(ii) For purposes of this section, the term "ownership interest" includes fee simple interests, life estates, reversions, remainders, and perpetual easements. In addition, the term "ownership interest" includes any previously created rights to possession or use for all or a portion of any particular year (*i.e.*, a leasehold, easement, or "timeshare"), with a remaining term of at least 30 years, including any period for which such rights may be renewed at the option of the holder of the rights, as determined on the date of closing (as defined in paragraph (h)(2)(ii) of this section). Thus, for example, a pre-existing leasehold on a building with an original term of 99 years is an ownership interest in real estate for purposes of this section if it has a remaining term of 35 years as of the date of closing, but not if it has a remaining term of only 10 years as of the date of closing. However, the term "ownership interest" does not include an option to acquire otherwise reportable real estate. Further, the term "ownership interest" includes any contractual interest in a sale or exchange of standing timber for a lump-sum payment that is fixed and not contingent.

(c) *Exception for certain exempt transactions.*— (1) *Certain transfers.*—No return of information is required with respect to—

(i) A transaction that is not a sale or exchange (such as a gift (including a transaction treated as a gift under section 1041) or bequest, or a financing or refinancing that is not related to the acquisition of reportable real estate), even if the transaction involves reportable real estate, as defined in paragraph (b)(2) of this section;

(ii) A transfer in full or partial satisfaction of any indebtedness secured by the property so transferred including a foreclosure, a transfer in lieu of foreclosure or an abandonment; or

(iii) A transaction (a "de minimis transfer") in which it can be determined with certainty that the total consideration (in money, services and property), received or to be received in connection with the transaction is less than $600 in value (determined without regard to any allocation of gross proceeds among multiple transferors under paragraph (i)(5) of this section) as of the date of the closing (as defined in paragraph (h)(2)(ii) of this section), even if the transaction involves reportable real estate. Thus, for example, if a contract for sale of reportable real estate recites total consideration of "$1.00 plus other valuable consideration," the transfer is not a de minimis transfer unless the reporting person can determine that the "other valuable consideration" received or to be received is less than $599 in value as measured on the date of closing.

(2) *Certain property.*—Notwithstanding the provisions of paragraph (b)(2) of this section, no return of information is required with respect to a sale or exchange of an interest in any of the following property—provided the sale or exchange of such property is not related to the sale or exchange of reportable real estate—

(i) An interest in surface or subsurface natural resources (for example, water, ores, and other natural deposits) or crops, whether or not such natural resources or crops are severed from the land. For purposes of this section, the terms "natural resources" and "crops" do not include standing timber.

(ii) A burial plot or vault; or

(iii) A manufactured structure used as a dwelling that is manufactured and assembled at a location different from that where it is used, but only if such structure is not affixed, at the date of closing (as defined in paragraph (h)(2)(ii) of this section), to a foundation. Thus, a transfer of an unaffixed mobile home that is unrelated to the sale or exchange of reportable real estate is excepted from the reporting requirements of this section.

(d) *Exception for certain exempt transferors.*— (1) *General rule.*—No return of information is required with respect to a transferor that is a corporation under section 7701(a)(3) or section 7704(a) or is considered under paragraph (d)(2) of this section to be—

(i) A corporation;

(ii) A governmental unit; or

(iii) An exempt volume transferor.

In the case of a real estate transaction with respect to which there is one or more exempt transferor(s) and one or more non-exempt transferor(s), the reporting person is required to report with respect to any non-exempt transferor. The special rule for allocation of gross proceeds, as provided in paragraph (i)(5) of this section, applies to such a transaction.

(2) *Treatment as exempt transferor.*—Absent actual knowledge to the contrary, a reporting person may treat a transferor as—

(i) A corporation if—

(A) The name of the transferor contains an unambiguous expression of corporate status, such as Incorporated, Inc., Corporation, Corp., or P.C. (but not Company or Co.);

(B) The name of the transferor contains the term "insurance company," "reinsurance company," or "assurance company"; or

(C) The transfer or loan documents clearly indicate the corporate status of the transferor;

(ii) A governmental unit if the transferor is—

(A) The United States or a state, the District of Columbia, a possession of the United States, a political subdivision of any of the foregoing, or any wholly owned agency or instrumentality of any one or more of the foregoing; or

(B) A foreign government, a political subdivision thereof, an international organization, as defined in section 7701(a)(18), or any whollyowned agency or instrumentality of the foregoing; or

(iii) An exempt volume transferor if, and only if, the reporting person receives a certification of exempt status under paragraph (d)(3) of this section.

(3) *Certification of exempt status.*—(i) *In general.*—A certification of exempt status must contain—

(A) The name, address, and taxpayer identification number of the transferor (the address must be that of the permanent residence (in the case of an individual), that of the principal office (in the case of a corporation or partnership), or that of the permanent residence or principal office of any fiduciary (in the case of a trust or estate));

(B) Sufficient information to identify any otherwise reportable real estate not reported by virtue of the exempt status of the transferor; and

(C) A declaration that the transferor has sold or exchanged during either of the prior two calendar years, or previously sold or exchanged during the current calendar year, or, as of the date of closing (as defined in paragraph (h)(2)(ii) of this section); reasonably expects to sell or exchange during the current calendar year at least 25 separate items of reportable real estate (as defined in paragraph (b)(2) of this section) to at least 25 separate transferees, and that each such item, at the date of closing of the sale of such item was or will be held primarily for sale or resale to customers in the ordinary course of a trade or business. For example, the declaration may be worded as follows:

_____[INSERT NAME OF TRANSFEROR]

[check one or more]:

(1) _____has sold or exchanged during either of the prior two calendar years,

(2) _____previously sold or exchanged during the current calendar year,

(3) _____on the date of closing expects to sell or exchange during the current calendar year,

at least 25 separate items of reportable real estate to at least 25 separate transferees and each such item, at the date of closing of such item was or will be held primarily for sale or resale to customers in the ordinary course of a trade or business.

(ii) *Additional requirements.*—A certification of exempt status must be—

(A) Signed under penalties of perjury by the transferor or any person who is authorized to sign a declaration under penalties of perjury in behalf of the transferor as described in section 6061 and the regulations thereunder;

(B) Received by the reporting person no later than the time of closing; and

(C) Retained by the reporting person for four years following the close of the calendar year in which the date of closing (as determined under paragraph (h)(2)(ii) of this section) occurs.

(iii) *Reporting person may accept or disregard certification.*—A reporting person may solicit or merely accept a certification of exempt status. Moreover, notwithstanding a transferor's furnishing of such certification, a reporting person may disregard the certification and, instead, report with respect to the transaction. See paragraph (a) of this section for the requirement that such elective reporting must be in compliance with the provisions of this section.

(e) *Person required to report.*—(1) *In general.*—Although there may be other persons involved in a real estate transaction, only the reporting person is required to report with respect to any real estate transaction. Except as provided in a designation agreement under paragraph (e)(5) of this section, the reporting person with respect to a real estate transaction is—

(i) The person responsible for closing the transaction, as defined in paragraph (e)(3) of this section; or

(ii) If there is no person responsible for closing the transaction, the person determined to be the reporting person under paragraph (e)(4) of this section.

A person may be the reporting person with respect to a transaction whether or not such person performs or is licensed to perform real estate brokerage services for a commission or fee.

(2) *Employees, agents, and partners.*—For purposes of this paragraph (e), if an employee, agent, or partner (other than an employee, agent, or partner of the transferor or the transferee) acting within the scope of such person's employment, agency, or partnership participates in a real estate transaction—

(i) Such participation shall be attributed to such person's employer, principal, or partnership; and

(ii) Only the employer, principal, or partnership (and not such person) may be the reporting person with respect to such transaction as a result of such participation.

However, the participation of a person described in paragraph (e)(3)(i) of this section (*i.e.*, a person listed on the Uniform Settlement Statement as the settlement agent) acting as an agent of another is not attributed to the principal.

(3) *Person responsible for closing the transaction.*—(i) *Uniform Settlement Statement used.*—If a Uniform Settlement Statement prescribed under the Real Estate Settlement Procedures Act of 1974 (RESPA), 12 U.S.C. 2601 *et seq.* (a "Uniform Settlement Statement"), is used with respect to the real estate transaction and a person is listed as settlement agent on the statement, such person is the person responsible for closing the transaction. For purposes of this section, a Uniform Settlement Statement shall include any amendments or variations thereto, or substitutions therefor that may hereafter be prescribed under RESPA, provided that any such amended, varied, or substituted form requires disclosure of the parties to the transaction, the application of the proceeds of the transaction, and the identity of the settlement agent or other person responsible for preparing the form.

(ii) *Other closing statement used.*—If a Uniform Settlement Statement is not used, or if a Uniform Settlement Statement is used, but no person is listed as settlement agent, the person responsible for closing the transaction is the person who prepares a closing statement presented to the transferor and transferee at, or in connection with, the closing of the real estate transaction. For purposes of this section, a closing statement is any closing statement, settlement statement (including a Uniform Settlement Statement), or other written document that identifies the transferor and transferee, reasonably identifies the transferred real estate, and describes the manner in which the proceeds payable to the transferor are to be (or were) disbursed at, or in connection with, the closing.

(iii) *No closing statement used or multiple closing statements used.*—If no closing statement is used or multiple closing statements are used, the person responsible for closing the transaction is the first-listed of the persons that participate in the transaction as—

(A) The attorney for the transferee who is present at the occasion of the delivery of either the transferee's note or a significant portion of the cash proceeds to the transferor, or who prepares or reviews the preparation of the document(s) transferring legal or equitable ownership of the real estate;

(B) The attorney for the transferor who is present at the occasion of the delivery of either the transferee's note or a significant portion of the cash proceeds to the transferor, or who prepares or reviews the preparation of the document(s) transferring legal or equitable ownership of the real estate; or

(C) The disbursing title or escrow company that is most significant in terms of gross proceeds disbursed.

If more than one attorney would be the person responsible for closing the transaction under the preceding sentence, the person among such attorneys who is considered responsible for closing the transaction under this paragraph (e)(3)(iii) is the person whose involvement in the transaction is most significant.

(4) *Determination of the real estate reporting person in the absence of a person responsible for closing the transaction.*—If no person is responsible for closing the transaction (within the meaning of paragraph (e)(3) of this section), the reporting person with respect to the real estate transaction is the person first-listed below of the persons that participate in the transaction as—

(i) The mortgage lender (as defined in paragraph (e)(6)(i) of this section);

(ii) The transferor's broker (as defined in paragraph (e)(6)(ii) of this section);

(iii) The transferee's broker (as defined in paragraph (e)(6)(iii) of this section); or

(iv) The transferee (as defined in paragraph (e)(6)(iv) of this section).

(5) *Designation agreement.*—(i) *In general.*—If a written designation agreement executed at or prior to the time of closing designates one of the persons described in paragraph (e)(5)(ii) of this section as the reporting person with respect to the transaction and the designated person is a party to the agreement, the designated person is the reporting person with respect to the transaction. It is not necessary that all parties to the transaction (or that more than one party) be parties to the agreement.

(ii) *Persons eligible.*—A person may be designated as the reporting person under this paragraph (e)(5) only if the person is—

(A) The person responsible for closing the transaction (as defined in paragraph (e)(3) of this section);

(B) A person described in paragraph (e)(3)(iii)(A), (B) or (C) of this section (whether or not such person is responsible for closing the transaction); or

(C) The mortgage lender (as defined in paragraph (e)(6)(i) of this section).

(iii) *Form of designation agreement.*—A designation agreement may be in any form that is consistent with the requirements of this paragraph (e)(5), and may be included on a closing statement with respect to the transaction. The designation agreement must, however, include the name and address of the transferor and transferee and the address and any additional information necessary to identify the real estate transferred. The agreement must identify, by name and address, the person designated as the reporting person with respect to the transaction, and all other parties (if any) to the agreement. All parties to the agreement must date and sign the agreement and must retain the agreement for four years following the close of the calendar year in which the date of closing (as determined under paragraph (h)(2)(ii) of this section) occurs.

Reg. §1.6045-4(e)(3)

Upon request by the Internal Revenue Service, or any person involved in the transaction who did not participate in the designation agreement, the agreement must be made available for inspection.

(6) *Meaning of terms.*—(i) *Mortgage lender.*—For purposes of this paragraph (e), the term "mortgage lender" means the person who lends new funds in connection with the transaction, but only if the repayment of such funds is secured in whole or in part by the real estate transferred. If new funds are advanced by more than one person, the mortgage lender is the person who advances the largest amount of new funds. If two or more persons advance equal amounts of new funds and no other person advances a greater amount of new funds, the mortgage lender among the persons advancing such equal amounts is the person with the security interest that is most senior in terms of priority. For purposes of this paragraph (e)(6)(i), any amounts advanced by the transferor are not treated as new funds.

(ii) *Transferor's broker.*—For purposes of this paragraph (e), the term "transferor's broker" means only the broker that contracts with the transferor and is compensated in connection with the transaction.

(iii) *Transferee's broker.*—For purposes of this paragraph (e), the term "transferee's broker" means only the broker that participates to a significant extent in the preparation of the transferee's offer to acquire the real estate or that presents such offer to the transferor. If more than one person is so described, the transferee's broker is the person whose participation in the preparation of the transferee's offer to acquire the real estate is most significant or, in the event there is no such person, the person whose participation in the presentation of the offer is most significant.

(iv) *Transferee.*—For purposes of this paragraph (e), the term "transferee" means the person who acquires the greatest interest in the real estate. If there is no such person, the transferee is the person listed first on the document(s) transferring legal or equitable ownership of the real estate.

(f) *Multiple transferors.*—(1) *General rule.*—In the case of multiple transferors, each of which transfers an interest in the same reportable real estate, the reporting person shall make a separate information return with respect to each transferor. Paragraph (i)(5) of this section provides rules for the determination of gross proceeds to be reported in the case of multiple transferors.

(2) *Rules for spouses.*—Transferors who are husband and wife at the time of closing and hold the reportable real estate as tenants in common, joint tenants, tenants by the entirety, or community property are treated as a single transferor for purposes of paragraphs (f)(1), (h)(1)(i), (i)(5) and (l)(1)(i) of this section, unless the reporting person receives, at or prior to the time of closing, an uncontested allocation of gross proceeds between them. In the case of a husband and wife treated as a single transferor, the reporting person may treat either as the transferor for purposes of paragraphs (h)(1)(i) and (l)(1) of this section, relating to reporting and soliciting taxpayer identification numbers.

(g) *Prescribed form.*—Except as otherwise provided in paragraph (k) of this section, the information return required by paragraph (a) of this section shall be made on Form 1099.

(h) *Information required.*—(1) *In general.*—The following information must be set forth on the Form 1099 required by this section:

(i) The name, address, and taxpayer identification number (TIN) of the transferor (see also paragraph (f)(2) of this section);

(ii) A general description of the real estate transferred (in accordance with paragraph (h)(2)(i) of this section);

(iii) The date of closing (as defined in paragraph (h)(2)(ii) of this section);

(iv) To the extent required by the Form 1099 and its instructions, the entire gross proceeds with respect to the transaction (as determined under the rules of paragraph (i) of this section), and, in the case of multiple transferors, the gross proceeds allocated to the transferor (as determined under paragraph (i)(5) of this section);

(v) To the extent required by the Form 1099 and its instructions, an indication that the transferor—

(A) Received (or will, or may, receive) property (other than cash and consideration treated as cash in computing gross proceeds) or services as part of the consideration for the transaction,

(B) May receive property (other than cash) or services in satisfaction of an obligation having a stated principal amount, or

(C) May receive, in connection with a contingent payment transaction, an amount of gross proceeds that cannot be determined with certainty using the method described in paragraph (i)(3)(iii) of this section and is therefore not included in gross proceeds under paragraphs (i)(3)(i) and (i)(3)(iii) of this section;

(vi) The real estate reporting person's name, address, and TIN;

(vii) [Reserved]; and

(viii) Any other information required by the Form 1099 or its instructions.

(2) *Meaning of terms.*—(i) *General description of the real estate transferred.*—A general description of the real estate transferred includes the complete address of the property. If the address would not sufficiently identify the property, a general description of the real estate also includes a legal description (*e.g.*, section, lot, and block) of the property.

(ii) *Date of closing.*—In the case of a real estate transaction with respect to which a Uniform Settlement Statement is used, the date of closing shall be the date (if any) properly described as the "Settlement Date" on such statement. In all other cases, the date of closing shall be the earlier of the date on which title is transferred or the date on which the economic burdens and benefits of ownership of the real estate shift from the transferor to the transferee.

(i) *Gross proceeds.*—(1) *In general.*—Except as otherwise provided in this paragraph (i), the term "gross proceeds" means the total cash received or to be received by or on behalf of the transferor in connection with the real estate transaction. For purposes of this paragraph (i), the following amounts are treated as cash received or to be received by or on behalf of the transferor in connection with the real estate transaction:

(i) The stated principal amount of any obligation to pay cash to or for the benefit of the transferor in the future (including any obligation having a stated principal amount that may be satisfied by the delivery of property (other than cash) or services);

(ii) The amount of any liability of the transferor assumed by the transferee as part of the consideration for the transfer or of any liability to which the real estate acquired is subject (whether or not the transferor is personally liable for the debt); and

(iii) In the case of a contingent payment transaction, as defined in paragraph (i)(3)(ii) of this section, the maximum determinable proceeds, as defined in paragraph (i)(3)(iii) of this section.

Gross proceeds does not include the value of any property (other than cash and consideration treated as cash) or services received by, or on behalf of, the transferor in connection with the real estate transaction. See paragraph (h)(1)(v) of this section for the information that must be included on the Form 1099 required by this section in cases in which the transferor receives (or will, or may, receive) property (other than cash and consideration treated as cash) or services as part of the consideration for the transfer.

(2) *Treatment of sales commissions and similar expenses.*—In computing gross proceeds, the total cash received or to be received by or on behalf of the transferor shall not be reduced by expenses borne by the transferor (such as sales commissions, expenses of advertising the real estate, expenses of preparing the deed, and the cost of legal services in connection with the transfer).

(3) *Special rules for contingent payments.*—(i) *In general.*—If a real estate transaction is a contingent payment transaction, gross proceeds consist of the maximum determinable proceeds, if any.

(ii) *Contingent payment transaction.*—For purposes of this section, the term "contingent payment transaction" means a real estate transaction with respect to which the receipt, by or on behalf of the transferor, of cash or consideration

treated as cash under paragraph (i)(1)(i) of this section is subject to a contingency.

(iii) *Maximum determinable proceeds.*—For purposes of this section, the term "maximum determinable proceeds" means the gross proceeds determined by assuming that all of the contingencies contemplated by the documents available at closing are met or otherwise resolved in a manner that will maximize the gross proceeds. If the maximum amount of gross proceeds cannot be determined with certainty using this method, the maximum determinable proceeds are the greatest amount that can be determined with certainty using this method. See paragraph (h)(1)(v)(C) of this section for the information that must be included on the Form 1099 required by this section in cases in which the maximum amount of gross proceeds cannot, by using the method described in this paragraph (i)(3)(iii), be determined with certainty.

(4) *Uniform Settlement Statement used.*—If a Uniform Settlement Statement is used with respect to a real estate transaction involving a transfer of reportable real estate solely for cash and consideration treated as cash in computing gross proceeds, the gross proceeds generally will be the same amount as the contract sales price properly shown on that statement.

(5) *Special rules for multiple transferors.*—(i) *General rules.*—In the case of multiple transferors (within the meaning of paragraph (f) of this section) each of which transfers an interest in the same reportable real estate, the reporting person must request the transferors to provide an allocation of the gross proceeds among the transferors. The request must be made at or before the time of closing. Neither the request nor the response is required to be in writing. The reporting person must make a reasonable effort to contact all transferors of whom the reporting person has actual knowledge. The reporting person may, however, rely on the unchallenged response of any transferor and need not make additional efforts to contact other transferors after at least one complete allocation (whether or not contained in a single response) is received. Except as otherwise provided in this paragraph (i)(5), the reporting person shall report the gross proceeds in accordance with any allocation received at or before the time of closing. The reporting person may (but is not required to) report the gross proceeds in accordance with any allocation received after the time of closing and before the date (determined without regard to extensions) the Forms 1099 are required to be filed. The reporting person may not report the gross proceeds in accordance with any allocation received on or after the date (determined without regard to extensions) the Forms 1099 are required to be filed. If no gross proceeds are allocated to a transferor because no allocation or an incomplete allocation is received by the reporting person, the reporting person shall report the entire unallocated gross proceeds (if any) on the return of information made with respect to

Reg. § 1.6045-4(i)(1)

such transferor. If the reporting person receives conflicting allocations from the transferors, the reporting person shall report the entire gross proceeds on each return of information made with respect to the transaction.

(ii) *Rules for spouses.*—The reporting person need not request an allocation of gross proceeds if the only transferors are husband and wife at the time of closing. If there are other transferors, the reporting person need only make a reasonable effort to contact either the husband or wife in connection with the request for an allocation. See paragraph (f)(2) of this section for rules that treat a husband and wife as multiple transferors if an uncontested allocation of gross proceeds is received by the reporting person at or prior to the time of closing.

(6) *Multiple asset transactions.*—In the case of a real estate transaction reportable under this section that involves the transfer of reportable real estate and other assets, the amount attributable to both the real estate and other assets is treated as the gross proceeds with respect to that real estate transaction. No allocation of gross proceeds is made among the assets.

(j) *Time and place for filing.*—A reporting person shall file the information returns required by this section with respect to a real estate transaction after December 31 of the calendar year that includes the date of closing (as determined under paragraph (h)(2)(ii) of this section) and on or before February 28 (March 31 if filed electronically) of the following calendar year. The returns shall be filed with the appropriate Internal Revenue Service Center at the address listed in the Instructions to Form 1099.

(k) *Use of magnetic media and substitute forms.*—(1) *Magnetic media.*—(i) *General rule.*—A reporting person that is required to make a return of information under this section shall, except as otherwise provided in paragraph (k)(1)(ii) or (iii) of this section, submit the information required by this section on magnetic media (within the meaning of 26 CFR 301.6011-2). Returns on magnetic media shall be made in accordance with 26 CFR 301.6011-2 and applicable revenue procedures.

(ii) *Exception for low-volume filers.*—For rules allowing a reporting person to make the information returns required by this section on the prescribed paper Form 1099 if the reporting person is required by this section to file fewer than 250 returns during the calendar year, see section 6011(e) and guidance issued by the Internal Revenue Service thereunder.

(iii) *Undue hardship.*—The Commissioner may authorize a reporting person to file information returns on the prescribed paper Form 1099 instead of on magnetic media if undue hardship is shown either on Form 8508, Request for Waiver from Filing Information Returns on Magnetic Media, or on a written statement requesting a waiver for undue hardship filed with the Martinsburg Computing Center, Martinsburg, West

Virginia in accordance with applicable revenue procedures.

(2) *Substitute forms.*—A reporting person that is described in paragraph (k)(1)(ii) of this section or that receives permission to file returns on the prescribed paper Form 1099 under paragraph (k)(1)(iii) of this section may prepare and use a form that contains provisions identical with those of Form 1099 if the reporting person complies with all applicable revenue procedures relating to substitute Form 1099, including any requirement relating to the use of machine-readable paper forms.

(l) *Requesting taxpayer identification numbers (TINS).*—(1) *Solicitation.*—(i) *General requirements.*—A reporting person who is required to make an information return with respect to a real estate transaction under this section must solicit a TIN from the transferor at or before the time of closing. The solicitation may be made in person or in a mailing that includes other items. Any person whose TIN is solicited under this paragraph (l) must furnish such TIN to the reporting person and certify that the TIN is correct. See paragraph (f)(2) of this section for rules that treat a husband and wife as a single transferor (and provide for the TIN solicitation of either) in the absence of an allocation of gross proceeds under paragraph (i)(5) of this section.

(ii) *Content of solicitation.*—The solicitation shall be made by providing to the person from whom the TIN is solicited a written statement that the person is required by law to furnish a correct TIN to the reporting person, and that the person may be subject to civil or criminal penalties for failing to furnish a correct TIN. For example, the solicitation may be worded as follows:

You are required by law to provide [insert name of reporting person] with your correct taxpayer identification number. If you do not provide [insert name of reporting person] with your correct taxpayer identification number, you may be subject to civil or criminal penalties imposed by law.

The solicitation shall contain space for the name, address, and TIN of the person from whom the TIN is solicited and for the person to certify under penalties of perjury that the TIN furnished is that person's correct TIN. The wording of the certification must be substantially similar to the following: "Under penalties of perjury, I certify that the number shown on this statement is my correct taxpayer identification number." The requirements of this paragraph (l)(1)(ii) may be met by providing to the transferor a copy of Form W-9. In the case of a real estate transaction for which a Uniform Settlement Statement is used, the requirements of this paragraph (l)(1)(ii) may be met by providing to the transferor a copy of such statement that is modified to conform to the requirements of this paragraph (l)(1)(ii).

(iii) *Retention requirement.*—The solicitation shall be retained by the reporting person for four years following the close of the calendar year that includes the date of closing (as deter-

Reg. §1.6045-4(l)(1)(iii)

mined under paragraph (h)(2)(ii) of this section). Such solicitation must be made available for inspection upon request by the Internal Revenue Service.

(2) *No TIN provided.*—A reporting person that does not receive the transferor's TIN will not be subject to any penalty cross-referenced in paragraph (n) of this section by reason of failure to report such TIN if the reporting person has complied with the requirements of paragraph (l)(1) of this section in good faith (determined with proper regard for a course of conduct and the overall results achieved for the year).

(m) *Furnishing statements to transferors.*— (1)(i) *Requirement of furnishing statements.*—A reporting person who is required to make a return of information under paragraph (a) of this section shall furnish to the transferor whose TIN is required to be shown on the return a written statement of the information required to be shown on such return. The written statement must bear either the legend shown on the recipient copy of Form 1099 or the following: "This is important tax information and is being furnished to the Internal Revenue Service. If you are required to file a return, a negligence penalty or other sanction may be imposed on you if this item is required to be reported and the IRS determines that it has not been reported."

(ii) This requirement may be satisfied by furnishing to the transferor a copy of a completed Form 1099 (or substitute Form 1099 that complies with current revenue procedures). An IRS truncated taxpayer identifying number (TTIN) may be used as the identifying number of the transferor in lieu of the identifying number appearing on the information return filed with the Internal Revenue Service. For provisions relating to the use of TTINs, see § 301.6109-4 of this chapter (Procedure and Administration Regulations).

(iii) In the case of a real estate transaction for which a Uniform Settlement Statement is used, this requirement also may be satisfied by furnishing to the transferor a copy of a completed statement that is modified to comply with the requirements of this paragraph (m), and by designating on the Uniform Settlement Statement the items of information (such as gross proceeds or allocated gross proceeds) required to be set forth on the Form 1099. For purposes of this paragraph (m), a statement shall be considered furnished to a transferor if it is given to the transferor in person, either at the closing or thereafter, or is mailed to the transferor at the transferor's last known address.

(2) *Time for furnishing statement.*—The statement required under this paragraph (m) must be furnished to the transferor on or after the date of closing and on or before February 15 of the following calendar year.

(3) *Consolidated reporting.*—(i) The term *consolidated reporting statement* means a grouping of statements the same reporting person furnishes to the same transferor or group of transferors on

the same date for the same reporting year that includes a statement required under this section. A consolidated reporting statement is limited to statements based on the same relationship of reporting person to transferor as the statement required to be furnished under this section.

(ii) A consolidated reporting statement must be furnished on or before February 15 of the year following the calendar year reported. Any statement that otherwise must be furnished on or before January 31 must be furnished on or before February 15 if it is furnished in the consolidated reporting statement.

(n) *Cross-reference to penalties.*—See the following sections regarding penalties for failure to comply with the requirements of section 6045(e) and this section:

(1) Section 6721 for failure to file a correct information return;

(2) Section 6722 for failure to furnish a correct statement to the transferor;

(3) Section 6723 for failure to comply with other information reporting requirements (including the requirement to furnish a TIN);

(4) Section 6724 for definitions and rules relating to waiver and payment; and

(5) Section 7203 for willful failure to supply information (including a taxpayer identification number).

(o) *No separate charge.*—A reporting person may not separately charge any person involved in a real estate transaction for complying with any requirements of this section.

(p) *Backup withholding requirements.*— [Reserved.]

(q) *Federally-subsidized indebtedness.*— [Reserved.]

(r) *Examples.*—The following examples illustrate the application of this section:

Example (1)—Sale or exchange. (i) On June 1, 1991, A, an individual, buys a house from B, an individual, for $200,000. The entire $200,000 is financed by B under an "installment land contract," whereby A takes possession and assumes all significant economic benefits and burdens of ownership of the house, and B retains legal title to the property until A fully performs under the contract. On June 1, 1994, A refinances his purchase of the house with Z, a financial institution. The balance owed to B is repaid and B relinquishes title to the house. A retains possession and the benefits and burdens of ownership of the house.

(ii) For federal income tax purposes, the transaction occurring on June 1, 1991 is considered a sale of the house by B, notwithstanding his retention of legal title to the property. B's sale is subject to information reporting under this section. However, the transaction occurring on June 1, 1994 is not a sale or exchange for federal income tax purposes, and notwithstanding the change in legal title upon the deeding over of the property, that transaction is not subject to information reporting under this section.

Example (2)—Sale or exchange. On August 10, 1991, C, an individual, accepts an offer from Y, a corporation that acts on behalf of T (C's employer) to facilitate moves of T's transferred employees from one part of the country to another. Under the offer, C transfers his residence to Y for $250,000 by executing a deed to the property in blank and giving Y a power of attorney to dispose of the residence. C also immediately vacates the residence, whereupon Y begins paying all costs associated with the residence and is entitled to all income from the residence, including sales proceeds. On October 1, 1991, Y sells the residence to D and inserts C's name in the deed previously executed by C. Thus, neither Y nor T ever become record owners of the residence. C's transfer of the residence to Y on August 10, 1991 is a sale of reportable real estate and is subject to information reporting under this section; however, the sale on October 1, 1991 is not required to be reported because Y (the transferor in that sale) is a corporation. See paragraph (d) of this section.

Example (3)—Definition of ownership interest. E, an individual, owns a perpetual timeshare interest in a residential unit of real property at an oceanfront resort. For consideration, on November 15, 1991, E sells her rights in the property for the period January 1, 1992 through December 31, 1992 to F. The transfer of E's property interest is not the transfer of an ownership interest, as defined in paragraph (b)(2) of this section and therefore is not reportable real estate under paragraph (b)(2) of this section. Accordingly, the transfer is not a real estate transaction under section (b)(1) of this section, and no return of information is required with respect to E's property transfer.

Example (4)—Gross proceeds (exchange). (i) G, an individual, agrees to transfer Blackacre, which has a fair market value of $100,000, plus $10,000 cash to H, an individual, in exchange for Whiteacre, which has a fair market value of $120,000 and is encumbered by a $10,000 liability (which is assumed by G). No other liabilities are involved in the transaction.

(ii) With respect to the transfer of Blackacre by G to H, P must report gross proceeds of $ -0- (even though the exchange agreement may recite total exchange value of $120,000). See paragraph (i)(1) of this section. In addition (to the extent required by the Form 1099 and its instructions) P must indicate that G will receive property as part of the consideration for the transaction. See paragraph (h)(v)(A) of this section.

(iii) With respect to the transfer of Whiteacre by H to G, P must report gross proceeds of $20,000 (the amount received by H consisting of cash ($10,000) and consideration treated as cash ($10,000) under paragraph (i) of this section). No other amount is reported under paragraph (i)(1) of this section even though the exchange agreement may recite total exchange value of $120,000. In addition, to the extent required by the Form 1099 and its instructions, P must indicate that H will receive property as part of the

consideration for the transaction. See paragraph (h)(v)(A) of this section.

Example (5). Gross proceeds (deferred exchange). [Reserved]

Example (6). Gross proceeds (contingencies). K, an individual, sells an unencumbered apartment building to L for $500,000, payable at closing, plus an amount equal to 2% of gross rents from the apartment building for each of the next 5 years, the contingent payments to be made annually with adequate stated interest. The agreement provides that the maximum amount K may receive (including the downpayment but excluding the interest) is $600,000. Under paragraph (i)(3)(ii) of this section the real estate transaction is a "contingent payment transaction." Under paragraph (i) (3)(iii) of this section, the maximum amount of gross proceeds determined by assuming all contingencies are satisfied is $600,000. Thus, $600,000 is the "maximum determinable proceeds" and is the amount reported.

Example (7). Gross proceeds (contingencies). The facts are the same as in example (6), except that the agreement does not provide for adequate stated interest. The result is the same as in example (6).

Example (8). Gross proceeds (contingencies). The facts are [the] same as in example (6), except that no maximum amount is stated in the agreement (or any other document available at closing). Under paragraph (i)(3)(iii) of this section, assuming all contingencies are satisfied, the maximum amount of gross proceeds cannot be determined with certainty. The greatest amount that can be determined with certainty at the time of the closing, assuming all contingencies are satisfied, is $500,000, the cash downpayment. Therefore, $500,000 is the "maximum determinable proceeds" under paragraph (i)(3)(iii) of this section and is the amount reported. In addition, to the extent required by the Form 1099 and its instructions, the reporting person must indicate that the gross proceeds cannot be determined with certainty. See paragraph (h)(1)(iv)(C) of this section.

Example (9). Gross proceeds (contingencies). The facts are the same as in example (8), except that the agreement provides that the minimum amount K will receive (including the downpayment) is $570,000. Thus, under paragraph (i)(3)(iii) of this section, assuming all contingencies are satisfied, the maximum amount of gross proceeds cannot be determined with certainty. The greatest amount that can be determined with certainty at the time of the closing, assuming all contingencies are satisfied, is $570,000, the minimum amount stated in the agreement. Therefore, $570,000 is the "maximum determinable proceeds" under paragraph (i)(3)(iii) of this section and is the amount reported. In addition, to the extent required by the Form 1099 and its instructions, the reporting person must indicate that the gross proceeds cannot be determined with certainty. See paragraph (h)(1)(iv)(C) of this section.

(s) *Effective/applicability date.*—This section applies for real estate transactions with dates of closing (as determined under paragraph (h)(2)(ii) of this section) that occur on or after January 1, 1991. The amendments to paragraphs (b)(2)(i)(E), (b)(2)(ii) and (c)(2)(i) of this section shall apply to sales or exchanges of standing timber for lump-sum payments completed after May 28, 2009. The amendments to paragraph (m)(1) apply to payee statements due after December 31, 2014. For payee statements due before January 1, 2015, §1.6045-4(m)(1) (as contained in 26 CFR part 1, revised April 2013) shall apply. [Reg. §1.6045-4.]

☐ [*T.D.* 8323, 12-12-90. *Amended by T.D.* 8895, 8-17-2000; *T.D.* 9450, 5-27-2009; *T.D.* 9504, 10-12-2010 *and T.D.* 9675, 7-14-2014.]

[Reg. §1.6045-5]

§1.6045-5. Information reporting on payments to attorneys.—(a) *Requirement of reporting.*—(1) *In general.*—Except as provided in paragraph (c) of this section, every payor engaged in a trade or business who, in the course of that trade or business, makes payments aggregating $600 or more during a calendar year to an attorney in connection with legal services (whether or not the services are performed for the payor) must file an information return for such payments. The information return must be filed on the form and in the manner required by the Commissioner. For the time and place for filing the form, see §1.6041-6. For definitions of the terms under this section, see paragraph (d) of this section. The requirements of this paragraph (a)(1) apply whether or not—

(i) A portion of a payment is kept by the attorney as compensation for legal services rendered; or

(ii) Other information returns are required with respect to some or all of a payment under other provisions of the Internal Revenue Code and the regulations thereunder.

(2) *Information required.*—The information return required under paragraph (a)(1) of this section must include the following information:

(i) The name, address, and taxpayer identifying number (TIN) (as defined in section 7701(a)) of the payor;

(ii) The name, address, and TIN of the payee attorney;

(iii) The amount of the payment or payments (as defined in paragraph (d)(5) of this section); and

(iv) Any other information required by the Commissioner in forms, instructions or publications.

(3) *Requirement to furnish statement.*—(i) *General requirements.*—A person required to file an information return under paragraph (a)(1) of this section must furnish to the attorney a written statement of the information required to be shown on the return. This requirement may be met by furnishing a copy of the return to the attorney. An IRS truncated taxpayer identifying number (TTIN) may be used as the identifying number of the attorney in lieu of the identifying number appearing on the information return

filed with the Internal Revenue Service. For provisions relating to the use of TTINs, see §301.6109-4 of this chapter (Procedure and Administration Regulations). The written statement must be furnished to the attorney on or before February 15 of the year following the calendar year in which the payment was made.

(ii) *Consolidated reporting.*—(A) The term *consolidated reporting statement* means a grouping of statements the same payor furnishes to the same payee or group of payees on the same date for the same reporting year that includes a statement required under this section. A consolidated reporting statement is limited to statements based on the same relationship of payor to payee as the statement required to be furnished under this section.

(B) A consolidated reporting statement must be furnished on or before February 15 of the year following the calendar year reported. Any statement that otherwise must be furnished on or before January 31 must be furnished on or before February 15 if it is furnished in the consolidated reporting statement.

(b) *Special rules.*—(1) *Joint or multiple payees.*—(i) *Check delivered to one payee attorney.*—If more than one attorney is listed as a payee on a check, an information return must be filed under paragraph (a)(1) of this section with respect to the payee attorney to whom the check is delivered.

(ii) *Check delivered to payee nonattorney.*—If an attorney is listed as a payee on a check but the check is delivered to a nonattorney who is a payee on the check, an information return must be filed under paragraph (a)(1) of this section with respect to the payee attorney listed on the check. If more than one attorney is listed as a payee on a check but the check is delivered to a nonattorney who is a payee on the check, the information return must be filed with respect to the first-listed payee attorney on the check.

(iii) *Check delivered to nonpayee.*—If two or more attorneys are listed as payees on a check, but the check is delivered to a person who is not a payee on the check, an information return must be filed under paragraph (a)(1) of this section with respect to the first-listed payee attorney on the check.

(2) *Attorney required to report payments made to other attorneys.*—If an information return is required to be filed with respect to a payee attorney under paragraph (b)(1) of this section, the attorney with respect to whom the information return is required to be filed (tier-one attorney) must file an information return under this section for any payment that the tier-one attorney makes to other payee attorneys with respect to that check, regardless of whether the tier-one attorney is a payor under paragraph (d)(3) of this section.

(c) *Exceptions.*—Notwithstanding paragraphs (a) and (b) of this section, a return of information is not required under section 6045(f) with respect to the following payments:

(1) Payments of wages or other compensation paid to an attorney by the attorney's employer.

(2) Payments of compensation or profits paid or distributed to its partners by a partnership engaged in providing legal services.

(3) Payments of dividends or corporate earnings and profits paid to its shareholders by a corporation engaged in providing legal services.

(4) Payments made by a person to the extent that the person is required to report with respect to the same payee the payments or portions thereof under section 6041(a) and § 1.6041-1(a) (or would be required to so report the payments or portions thereof but for the dollar amount limitation contained in section 6041(a) and § 1.6041-1(a)).

(5) Payments made to a nonresident alien individual, foreign partnership, or foreign corporation that is not engaged in trade or business within the United States, and does not perform any labor or personal services in the United States, in the taxable year to which the payment relates. For how a payor determines whether a payment is subject to this exception, see § 1.6041-4(a)(1).

(6) Payments made to an attorney in the attorney's capacity as the person responsible for closing a transaction within the meaning of § 1.6045-4(e)(3) for the sale or exchange or financing of any present or future ownership interest in real estate described in § 1.6045-4(b)(2)(i) through (iv).

(7) Payments made to an attorney in the attorney's capacity as a trustee in bankruptcy under Title 11, United States Code.

(d) *Definitions.*—The following definitions apply for purposes of this section:

(1) *Attorney* means a person engaged in the practice of law, whether as a sole proprietorship, partnership, corporation, or joint venture.

(2) *Legal services* means all services related to, or in support of, the practice of law performed by, or under the supervision of, an attorney.

(3) *Payor* means a person who makes a payment if that person is an obligor on the payment, or the obligor's insurer or guarantor. For example, a payor includes—

(i) A person who pays a settlement amount to an attorney of a client who has asserted a tort, contract, violation of law, or workers' compensation claim against that person; and

(ii) The person's insurer if the insurer pays the settlement amount to the attorney.

(4) *Payments to an attorney* include payments by check or other method such as cash, wire or electronic transfer. Payment by check to an attorney means a check on which the attorney is named as a sole, joint, or alternative payee. The attorney is the payee on a check written to the attorney's client trust fund. However, the attorney is not a payee when the attorney's name is included on the payee line as "in care of," such as a check written to "client c/o attorney," or if

the attorney's name is included on the check in any other manner that does not give the attorney the right to negotiate the check.

(5) *Amount of the payment* means the amount tendered (e.g., the amount of a check) plus the amount required to be withheld from the payment under section 3406(a)(1), because a condition for withholding exists with respect to the attorney for whom an information return is required to be filed under paragraph (a)(1) of this section.

(e) *Attorney to furnish TIN.*—A payor that is required to file an information return under this section must solicit a TIN from the attorney at or before the time the payor makes a payment to the attorney. The attorney must furnish the correct TIN to the payor, but is not required to certify the TIN. A payment for which a return of information is required under this section is subject to backup withholding under section 3406 and the regulations thereunder.

(f) *Examples.*—The following examples illustrate the provisions of this section. The examples assume that P is not a payor with respect to A, the attorney, under section 6041. See section 6041 and the regulations thereunder for rules regarding whether P is required under section 6041 to file information returns with respect to C. The examples are as follows:

Example 1. One check—joint payees—taxable to claimant. Employee C, who sues employer P for back wages, is represented by attorney A. P settles the suit for $300,000. The $300,000 represents taxable wages to C under existing legal principles. P writes a settlement check payable jointly to C and A in the amount of $200,000, net of income and FICA tax withholding with respect to C. P delivers the check to A. A retains $100,000 of the payment as compensation for legal services and disburses the remaining $100,000 to C. P must file an information return with respect to A for $200,000 under paragraph (a)(1) of this section. P also must file an information return with respect to C under sections 6041 and 6051, in the amount of $300,000. See §§ 1.6041-1(f) and 1.6041-2.

Example 2. One check—joint payees—excludable to claimant. C, who sues corporation P for damages on account of personal physical injuries, is represented by attorney A. P settles the suit for a $300,000 damage payment that is excludable from C's gross income under section 104(a)(2). P writes a $300,000 settlement check payable jointly to C and A and delivers the check to A. A retains $120,000 of the payment as compensation for legal services and remits the remaining $180,000 to C. P must file an information return with respect to A for $300,000 under paragraph (a)(1) of this section. P does not file an information return with respect to tax-free damages paid to C.

Example 3. Separate checks—taxable to claimant. C, an individual plaintiff in a suit for lost profits against corporation P, is represented by attorney A. P settles the suit for $300,000, all of

Reg. § 1.6045-5(f)

which will be includible in C's gross income. A requests P to write two checks, one payable to A in the amount of $100,000 as compensation for legal services and the other payable to C in the amount of $200,000. P.writes the checks in accordance with A's instructions and delivers both checks to A. P must file an information return with respect to A for $100,000 under paragraph (a)(1) of this section. Pursuant to §1.6041-1(a) and (f), P must file an information return with respect to C for the $300,000.

Example 4. Check made payable to claimant, but delivered to nonpayee attorney. Corporation P is a defendant in a suit for damages in which C, the plaintiff, has been represented by attorney A throughout the proceeding. P settles the suit for $300,000. Pursuant to a request by A, P writes the $300,000 settlement check payable solely to C and delivers it to A at A's office. P is not required to file an information return under paragraph (a)(1) of this section with respect to A, because there is no payment to an attorney within the meaning of paragraph (d)(4) of this section.

Example 5. Multiple attorneys listed as payees. Corporation P, a defendant, settles a lost profits suit brought by C for $300,000 by issuing a check naming C's attorneys, Y, A, and Z, as payees in that order. Y, A, and Z do not belong to the same law firm. P delivers the payment to A's office. A deposits the check proceeds into a trust account and makes payments by separate checks to Y of $30,000 and to Z of $15,000, as compensation for legal services, pursuant to authorization from C to pay these amounts. A also makes a payment by check of $155,000 to C. A retains $100,000 as compensation for legal services. P must file an information return for $300,000 with respect to A under paragraphs (a)(1) and (b)(1)(i) of this section. A, in turn, must file information returns with respect to Y of $30,000 and to Z of $15,000 under paragraphs (a)(1) and (b)(2) of this section because A is not required to file information returns under section 6041 with respect to A's payments to Y and Z because A's role in making the payments to Y and Z is merely ministerial. See §1.6041-1(e)(1), (e)(2) and (e)(5) *Example 7* for information reporting requirements with respect to A's payments to Y and Z. As described in *Example 3,* P must also file an information return with respect to C, pursuant to §1.6041-1(a) and (f).

Example 6. Amount of the payment—attorney does not provide TIN. (i) Corporation P, a defendant, settles a suit brought by C for $300,000 of damages. P will pay the damages by a joint check to C and his attorney, A. A failed to furnish P with A's TIN. P is required to deduct and withhold 28 percent tax from the $300,000 under section 3406(a)(1)(A) and paragraph (e) of this section. P writes the check to C and A as joint payees, in the amount of $216,000. P also must file an information return with respect to A under paragraph (a)(1) of this section in the amount of $300,000, as prescribed in paragraph (d)(5) of this section. If the damages are reportable under section 6041 because they are not ex-

cludable from gross income under existing legal principles, and are not subject to any exception under section 6041, P must also file an information return with respect to C pursuant to §1.6041-1(a) and (f) in the amount of $300,000.

(ii) Rather than paying by joint check to C and A, P will pay the damages by a joint check to C and F, A's law firm. F failed to furnish its TIN to P. P is required to deduct and withhold 28 percent tax from the $300,000 under section 3406(a)(1)(A) and paragraph (e) of this section. P writes the check to C and F as joint payees, in the amount of $216,000. P also must file an information return with respect to F under paragraph (a)(1) of this section in the amount of $300,000, as prescribed in paragraph (d)(5) of this section. If the damages are reportable under section 6041 because they are not excludable from gross income under existing legal principles, and are not subject to any exception under section 6041, P must also file an information return with respect to C pursuant to §1.6041-1(a) and (f) in the amount of $300,000.

Example 7. Home mortgage lending transaction. (i) Individual P agrees to purchase a house that P will use solely as a residence. P obtains a loan from lender L to finance a portion of the cost of acquiring the house. L disburses loan proceeds of $300,000 to attorney A, who is the settlement agent, by a check naming A as the sole payee. A, in turn, writes checks from the loan proceeds and from other funds provided by P to the persons involved in the purchase of the house, including a check for $800 to attorney B, whom P hired to provide P with legal services relating to the closing.

(ii) P, not L, is the payor of the payment to A under paragraph (d)(3) of this section. P, however, is not required to file an information return with respect to A under paragraph (a)(1) of this section because the payment was not made in the course of P's trade or business. Even if P made the payment in the course of P's trade or business, P would not be required to file an information return under section 6045(f) with respect to A because P is excepted under paragraph (c)(6) of this section.

(iii) A is not required to file an information return under paragraph (a)(1) of this section with respect to the payment to B because A is not the payor as that term is defined under paragraph (d)(3) of this section. A is not required to file an information return under paragraph (b)(2) with respect to the payment to B because A was listed as sole payee on the check it received from P. See section 6041 and §1.6041-1(e) for whether A or L must file information returns under that section. See section 6045(e) and §1.6045-4 for whether A is required to file an information return under that section.

Example 8. Business mortgage lending transaction. The facts are the same as in *Example 7* except that P buys real property that P will use in a trade or business. P, not L, is the payor of the payment to A under paragraph (d)(3) of this section. P, however, is not required to file an information return under section 6045(f) with respect to A because P is excepted under paragraph (c)(6) of this section. A is not required to file an information return under paragraphs (a) or (b)(2) of this section with respect to the payment to B. See section 6041 and § 1.6041-1(e) to determine whether P or L must file an information return under that section with respect to the payment to A, and whether P or A must file a return with respect to the payment to B. See section 6045(e) for rules regarding whether A is required to file information returns under that section.

Example 9. Qualified settlement fund. Corporation P agrees to settle for $300,000 a class action lawsuit brought by attorney A on behalf of a claimant class. Pursuant to the settlement agreement and a preliminary order of approval by a court, A establishes a bank account in the name of Q Settlement Fund, which is a qualified settlement fund (QSF) under § 1.468B-1. A is also designated by the court as the administrator of the QSF. Corporation P transfers $300,000 by wire in Year 1 to A, who deposits the funds into the Q Settlement Fund. In Year 2, the court approves an award of attorney's fees of $105,000 for A. In Year 2, Q Settlement Fund delivers $105,000 to A. P is required to file an information return under paragraph (a) of this section with respect to A for Year 1 for the $300,000 payment it made to A. The Q Settlement Fund is required to file an information return under section 6041(a) and § 1.468B-2(1)(2) with respect to A for Year 2 for the $105,000 payment it made to A.

(g) *Cross reference to penalties.*—See the following sections regarding penalties for failure to comply with the requirements of section 6045(f) and this section:

(1) Section 6721 for failure to file a correct information return.

(2) Section 6722 for failure to furnish a correct payee statement.

(3) Section 6723 for failure to comply with other information reporting requirements (including the requirement to furnish a TIN).

(4) Section 7203 for willful failure to supply information (including a TIN).

(h) *Effective/applicability date.*—The rules in this section apply to payments made on or after January 1, 2007. The amendments to paragraph (a)(3)(i) apply to payee statements due after December 31, 2014. For payee statements due before January 1, 2015, § 1.6045-5(a)(3)(i) (as contained in 26 CFR part 1, revised April 2013) shall apply. [Reg. § 1.6045-5.]

☐ [T.D. 9270, 7-12-2006 (*corrected* 8-15-2006). *Amended by T.D. 9504, 10-12-2010 and T.D. 9675, 7-14-2014.]*

[Reg. § 1.6045A-1]

§ 1.6045A-1 Statements of information required in connection with transfers of securities.—(a) *Duty to furnish transfer statement.*— (1) *In general.*—(i) *Transfers between accounts.*— Except as provided in paragraphs (a)(1)(ii)

through (v) of this section, every applicable person (transferor) (as described in paragraph (a)(4) of this section) that transfers custody of a specified security to a broker (as described in paragraph (a)(5) of this section) must furnish to the receiving broker a transfer statement that includes the information described in paragraph (b) of this section with respect to the transferred security. Except as provided in paragraphs (b)(1)(vii) and (b)(3) of this section (relating to noncovered securities and certain securities for which basis is determined under an average basis method), a transferor must furnish a separate statement for each security and, if transferring custody of the same security acquired on different dates or at different prices, for each acquisition.

(ii) *Cash on delivery accounts and multiple broker arrangements.*—(A) *Sales.*—A custodian or other transferor that transfers custody of a security to a broker solely to effect a sale must furnish a transfer statement only to the broker that effects the sale. However, no transfer statement is required if the transferor itself either effects the sale or is required to report the sale of the security under § 1.6045-1.

(B) *Purchases.*—A broker that effects a purchase but does not receive custody of the security must furnish a transfer statement to the broker receiving custody. However, no transfer statement is required if the broker effects the purchase solely at the instruction of the broker receiving custody.

(iii) *Exempt recipients and exempt foreign payees.*—A transferor is not required to furnish a transfer statement for a security that, after the transfer, is held for a customer that is an exempt recipient under § 1.6045-1(c)(3)(i) or an exempt foreign person under § 1.6045-1(g)(1)(i).

(iv) *Securities lending transactions —transferor as principal.*—A transferor that lends or borrows securities as a principal is not required to furnish a transfer statement for a security that is transferred pursuant to such lending or borrowing arrangement (for example, when a customer opens or closes a short sale). This exception does not apply when a transferor transfers a security under a lending or borrowing arrangement of the customer. This exception also does not apply when a transferor transfers a previously borrowed security to another account of the same customer (for example, to satisfy an existing short sale obligation). *See* paragraph (b)(4) of this section.

(v) *Certain money market funds.*—A transferor of stock in a regulated investment company described in § 1.6045-1(c)(3)(vi) is not required to furnish a transfer statement.

(2) *Format of transfer statement.*—The transfer statement must be furnished in writing unless both the transferor and the receiving broker agree to a different format or method before the transfer. If a transfer occurs between accounts at the same or affiliated entities, a transfer state-

ment is deemed to have been furnished and received if the required information, including any required adjustments, is incorporated into the records for the recipient account.

(3) *Time for furnishing statement.*—A transferor must furnish a transfer statement within fifteen days after the date of settlement for the transfer.

(4) *Applicable person effecting transfer.*—Applicable person means any transferor who is a person described in § 1.6045-1(a)(1), a person that acts as a custodian of securities in the ordinary course of a trade or business, an issuer of securities, a trustee or custodian of an individual retirement plan, or any agent of these persons. Applicable person does not include the beneficial owner of a security or any agent substituted for an undisclosed beneficial owner, any governmental unit or agency or instrumentality of a governmental unit holding escheated securities, or any organization that holds and transfers obligations among members of the organization as a service to its members.

(5) *Broker receiving custody.*—Solely for purposes of this section, *broker* means any person described in § 1.6045-1(a)(1), any person that acts as a custodian of securities in the ordinary course of a trade or business, any issuer of securities, and any agent of these persons. Broker does not include the beneficial owner of a security or any agent substituted for an undisclosed beneficial owner, any governmental unit or agency or instrumentality of a governmental unit holding escheated securities, or any organization that holds and transfers obligations among members of the organization as a service to its members.

(6) *Other terms.*—For purposes of this section, the terms sale, specified security, covered security, noncovered security, and customer have the same meaning as in § 1.6045-1(a)(9), (a)(14), (a)(15), (a)(16), and (h)(1).

(7) *Examples.*—The following examples illustrate the rules of this paragraph (a). Unless otherwise stated, in each example the customer is not treated as an exempt recipient under § 1.6045-1(c)(3)(i) or an exempt foreign person under § 1.6045-1(g)(1)(i). The examples are as follows:

Example 1. V, an entity treated as an exempt recipient under § 1.6045-1(c)(3)(i), owns a security in an account with E, a broker. On February 1, 2012, V instructs E to transfer custody of the security to an account V maintains with F, another broker. Because E may treat V as an exempt recipient under § 1.6045-1(c)(3)(i), under paragraph (a)(1)(iii) of this section, E is not required to furnish a transfer statement.

Example 2. W maintains an account with G, a custodial broker. On August 1, 2012, W instructs G to purchase a security. G places an order to purchase the security with H, a broker with which G has a clearing agreement. W does not maintain a direct account with H. H executes the purchase and has the security delivered to G.

Under paragraph (a)(1)(ii)(B) of this section, H is not required to furnish a transfer statement because G received custody of the security and H purchased the security solely at the instruction of G.

Example 3. Assume the same facts as in *Example 2* except that W later instructs G to sell the security. G places an order with H to sell the security. H executes the sale. G delivers the security to settle the sale. G is required to report the sale of the security under § 1.6045-1. Therefore, under paragraph (a)(1)(ii)(A) of this section, G is not required to furnish a transfer statement.

Example 4. (i) X maintains an account with J, an introducing broker. J contracts with K, a clearing broker, to allow K to execute trades on J's behalf under a clearing agreement. K uses L, a custodian of securities in the ordinary course of a trade or business, to hold custody of the securities of K's customers. K maintains a separate disclosed account for X as a clearing broker with custody at L. On May 1, 2012, X instructs J to purchase a security for X as the beneficial owner. J instructs K to purchase the security. K effects the purchase and has the security delivered to L.

(ii) K is a broker and therefore is an applicable person that is a transferor within the meaning of paragraph (a)(4) of this section. L acts as a custodian of securities in the ordinary course of a trade or business and therefore is a broker within the meaning of paragraph (a)(5) of this section. Because K effects the purchase of the security but does not receive custody of the security, under paragraphs (a)(1)(i) and (a)(1)(ii)(B) of this section, K must furnish a transfer statement to L.

Example 5. (i) Assume the same facts as in *Example 4* except that X later instructs J to sell the security. J instructs K to sell the security. K sells the security. L transfers custody of the security to settle X's sale in accordance with its custody arrangement with K by delivering the security to the purchasing broker. K deposits the sale proceeds in X's account with K. K is required to report the sale of the security under § 1.6045-1.

(ii) L acts as a custodian of securities in the ordinary course of a trade or business and therefore is an applicable person that is a transferor within the meaning of paragraph (a)(4) of this section. Because L transfers custody of the security to the purchaser's broker solely to effect the sale, under paragraphs (a)(1)(i) and (a)(1)(ii)(A) of this section, L must furnish a transfer statement to K.

(iii) If the terms of their custody arrangement so provide, K may furnish the transfer statement as L's agent and satisfy L's duty to furnish the transfer statement under paragraphs (a)(1)(i) and (a)(1)(ii)(A) of this section. Under paragraph (a)(2) of this section, K may satisfy this duty by maintaining the information required on the transfer statement, including all required adjustments, in its records for X's account.

Example 6. (i) Y, an investment advisor, wants to purchase shares of stock in C, a corporation, for several of Y's customers. Y establishes a delivery-on-payment account with M, a broker, and provides M a standing instruction to deliver stock purchased in the account to Y's account at N, a custodian of securities in the ordinary course of a trade or business. On November 1, 2012, Y enters into a cash-on-delivery transaction by instructing M to purchase shares of C stock. M executes the purchase and effects delivery of the C stock to N.

(ii) M is a broker and therefore is an applicable person that is a transferor within the meaning of paragraph (a)(4) of this section. N acts as a custodian of securities in the ordinary course of a trade or business and therefore is a broker within the meaning of paragraph (a)(5) of this section. Because M effects the purchase of the stock and N receives custody of the stock, under paragraphs (a)(1)(i) and (a)(1)(ii)(B) of this section, M must furnish a transfer statement to N.

Example 7. (i) Z owns shares of stock in C, a corporation, in an account with O, a broker. On February 1, 2013, Z instructs O to transfer the C stock to C so that ownership is held on the books of the issuer. C has an arrangement with D, a transfer agent, to keep records of ownership of the company's stock, how that stock is held, and how many shares each investor owns. O transfers the stock to D.

(ii) O is a broker and therefore is an applicable person that is a transferor within the meaning of paragraph (a)(4) of this section. D is an agent of C, the issuer of the stock, and therefore is a broker within the meaning of paragraph (a)(5) of this section. Because O transfers custody of the stock to D, under paragraph (a)(1)(i) of this section, O must furnish a transfer statement to D.

Example 8. Assume the same facts as in *Example 7* except that Z later instructs D to transfer the stock to an account Z maintains with P, another broker. D transfers the stock to P. D is an agent of C, the issuer of the stock, and therefore is an applicable person that is a transferor within the meaning of paragraph (a)(4) of this section. Because P is a broker and D transfers custody of the stock to P, under paragraph (a)(1)(i) of this section, D must furnish a transfer statement to P.

(b) *Information required.*—(1) *In general.*—For all specified securities, each transfer statement must include the information described in this paragraph (b)(1).

(i) *Statement date.*—The date the statement is furnished.

(ii) *Applicable person effecting transfer.*— The name, address, and telephone number of the applicable person furnishing the statement.

(iii) *Broker receiving custody.*—The name, address, and telephone number of the broker receiving custody of the security.

(iv) *Customers.*—The name and account number of the customer or customers for the account from which the security is transferred and, if different, the name and account number

of the customer or customers for the account to which the security is transferred.

(v) *Security identifiers.*—The Committee on Uniform Security Identification Procedures (CUSIP) number of the security transferred (if applicable) or other security identifier number that the Secretary may designate by publication in the **Federal Register** or in the Internal Revenue Bulletin (*see* §601.601(d)(2) of this chapter), quantity of shares, units, or amounts, and classification of the security (such as stock or debt).

(vi) *Transfer dates.*—The date the transfer was initiated and the settlement date of the transfer (if known when furnishing the statement).

(vii) *Adjusted basis and acquisition date.*— The total adjusted basis of the security, the original acquisition date of the security, and, if applicable, the holding period adjustment required by section 1091. The transferor must determine this information as provided under §§1.6045-1(d), 1.6045-1(m), and 1.6045-1(n), including reporting the adjusted basis of the security in U.S. dollars. If the basis of the transferred security is determined using an average basis method (as described in §1.1012-1(e)), the transferor may report any securities acquired more than five years before the transfer on a single statement on which the original acquisition date is reported as "VARIOUS" if the other information reported on the statement applies to all of the securities.

(2) *Examples.*—The following examples illustrate the rules of paragraph (b)(1) of this section:

Example 1. (i) In a single account with P, a broker, Q purchases three lots of 100 shares of stock each in C, a corporation, at different prices on April 2, 2012, July 2, 2012, and October 2, 2012. Q instructs P to enroll the shares of the C stock in P's dividend reinvestment plan and to average the basis of the shares of the C stock. All of the C stock purchased by P has the same CUSIP number. On September 13, 2013, less than five years after the acquisition dates for all three lots, Q transfers all 300 shares of the C stock to an account with another broker.

(ii) Under paragraph (a)(1)(i) of this section, P must furnish three transfer statements. Under paragraph (b)(1) of this section, one statement must report the transfer of 100 shares with an original acquisition date of April 2, 2012, one statement must report the transfer of 100 shares with an original acquisition date of July 2, 2012, and one statement must report the transfer of 100 shares with an original acquisition date of October 2, 2012.

Example 2. Assume the same facts as in *Example 1* except that Q transfers the shares to the account with the other broker on September 13, 2017. For the 100 shares purchased on April 2, 2012, and the 100 shares purchased on July 2, 2012, under paragraph (b)(1)(vii) of this section, P may furnish a single transfer statement reporting the transfer of 200 shares with the original acquisition date as "VARIOUS" instead of furnishing two separate transfer statements.

Example 3. (i) Assume the same facts as in *Example 1* except that, on June 15, 2012, Q sells the 100 shares purchased on April 2, 2012, at a loss.

(ii) Under paragraph (a)(1)(i) of this section, P must furnish two transfer statements. Under paragraph (b)(1)(vii) of this section and § 1.6045-1(d)(6)(iii) and (d)(7)(ii), P must determine the average basis for the 200 transferred shares and the date for computing whether any gain or loss with respect to the stock purchased on July 2, 2012, is long-term or short-term by applying the rules for broker reporting of wash sales to the stock purchased on July 2, 2012. Therefore, on both transfer statements, P must increase the average basis of the stock by the amount of loss disallowed under section 1091 on the sale of the 100 shares purchased on April 2, 2012. On the transfer statement reporting the transfer of the 100 shares purchased on July 2, 2012, P must adjust the holding period of the July 2, 2012, shares in accordance with section 1091.

Example 4. (i) R, an employee of C, a corporation, participates in C's employee stock purchase program that satisfies the requirements of section 423. D administers the plan. R purchases stock in the plan at a 15 percent discount to the fair market value of the stock determined on the date of purchase. R purchases stock through the plan during 2012 until R terminates employment on October 15, 2012. R later instructs D to transfer the plan shares to S, a broker.

(ii) D is the agent of C, the issuer of the securities, and therefore is an applicable person within the meaning of paragraph (a)(4) of this section. Because S is a broker and D transfers custody of the stock to S, under paragraph (a)(1)(i) of this section, D must furnish a transfer statement to S.

(iii) Under paragraph (b)(1)(vii) of this section and § 1.6045-1(d)(6)(ii)(A), D must report adjusted basis on the transfer statement based on the amount paid by R. Under paragraph (b)(1)(vii) of this section and § 1.6045-1(d)(6)(ii)(A), D is permitted, but is not required, to increase the adjusted basis for the amount (if any) includible as wage income by R for R's purchases of the stock.

(3) *Additional information required for a transfer of a debt instrument.*—In addition to the information required in paragraph (b)(1) of this section, for a transfer of a debt instrument that is a covered security, the following additional information is required:

(i) A description of the payment terms used by the broker to compute any basis adjustments under § 1.6045-1(n);

(ii) The issue price of the debt instrument;

(iii) The issue date of the debt instrument (if different from the original acquisition date of the debt instrument);

(iv) The adjusted issue price of the debt instrument as of the transfer date;

(v) The customer's initial basis in the debt instrument;

(vi) Any market discount that has accrued as of the transfer date (as determined under § 1.6045-1(n));

(vii) Any bond premium that has been amortized as of the transfer date (as determined under § 1.6045-1(n));

(viii) Any acquisition premium that has been amortized as of the transfer date (as determined under § 1.6045-1(n));

(ix) Whether the transferring broker has computed any of the information described in this paragraph (b)(3) by taking into account one or more elections described in § 1.6045-1(n), and, if so, which election or elections were taken into account by the transferring broker; and

(x) For a transfer that occurs on or after January 1, 2016, the last date on or before the transfer date that the transferor made an adjustment for a particular item (for example, the last date on or before the transfer date that bond premium was amortized). A broker, however, may rely on this paragraph (b)(3)(x) for a transfer of a covered security that occurs on or after June 30, 2015, and before January 1, 2016.

(4) *Additional information required for option transfers.*—In addition to the information required in paragraph (b)(1) of this section, for a transfer of an option that is a covered security, the following additional information is required:

(i) The date of grant or acquisition of the option;

(ii) The amount of premium paid or received;

(iii) Any other information required to fully describe the option, which may include a security identifier used by option exchanges, or details about the underlying asset, quantity covered, exercise type, strike price, and maturity date; and

(iv) For a transfer of an option described in § 1.6045-1(m)(3) (section 1256 option) that occurs on or after January 1, 2016, the original basis of the option and the fair market value of the option as of the end of the prior calendar year.

(5) *Format of identification.*—An applicable person furnishing a transfer statement and a broker receiving the transfer statement may agree to combine the information required in paragraphs (b)(1), (b)(3), and (b)(4) of this section in any format or to use a code in place of one or more required items. For example, a transferor and a receiving broker may agree to use a single code to represent the broker instead of the broker's name, address, and telephone number, or may use a security symbol or other identification number or scheme instead of the security identifier required by paragraphs (b)(1), (b)(3), and (b)(4) of this section. As another example, a transferor and a receiving broker may agree to use a security identifier for an exchange-traded option if that information would be sufficient to inform the receiving broker of the terms for that option.

(6) *Transfers of noncovered securities.*—The information described in paragraphs (b)(1)(vii), (b)(3), (b)(4), (b)(8), and (b)(9) of this section is not required for a transfer of a noncovered security if the transfer statement identifies the security as a noncovered security. A transferor that chooses to report nonrequired information is not subject to penalties under section 6722 for failure to report this information correctly if the transfer statement identifies the security as a noncovered security. A single transfer statement may report the transfer of multiple noncovered securities if the transfer statement clearly conveys, either specifically or generally, the information described in paragraph (b)(1)(v) of this section to identify each security. For purposes of this paragraph (b)(6), a transferor must treat a security for which a broker makes a single-account election described in § 1.1012-1(e)(11)(i) as a covered security.

(7) *Transfers of borrowed securities.*—The transfer statement must indicate that a transferred security is borrowed if the transferor knows that the security is transferred pursuant to a lending or borrowing arrangement. The transfer statement must not report an adjusted basis If the transferor knows that the transferred security is lent or borrowed pursuant to a short sale. The receiving broker may be subject to special transfer reporting rules upon receipt of a borrowed security if the security is used to satisfy an existing short sale obligation. *See* § 1.6045-1(c)(3)(xi)(C).

(8) *Transfers pursuant to an inheritance.*—(i) *In general.*—A transfer statement for a transfer of a security from a decedent or decedent's estate must indicate that the security is inherited. The transfer statement must report the date of death as the original acquisition date and must report adjusted basis according to the instructions or valuations furnished by an authorized representative of the estate, including any required adjustments to basis for property acquired from a decedent. If a transferor has not received instructions or valuations from an authorized representative, the transferor must report basis as the fair market value of the security on the date of death. However, if the transferor neither knows nor can readily ascertain the fair market value of the security on the date of death at the time the transfer statement is prepared, the transfer statement must indicate that the transfer consists of an inherited security but may otherwise report the security as if it were a noncovered security. If the transferor cannot identify which securities in a joint account have been transferred from the decedent, the transferor must treat each security in the account as if it were a noncovered security but must not indicate that any security is an inherited security.

(ii) *Transfers of securities to satisfy a cash legacy.*—If a security is transferred from a decedent or a decedent's estate to satisfy a cash legacy, paragraphs (b)(1), (b)(3), and (b)(4) of this section apply and paragraph (b)(8)(i) of this section does not apply.

(iii) *Subsequent transfers of inherited securities.*—A transfer statement must indicate that the transfer consists of an inherited security if a prior transfer statement reported the security as inherited.

(9) *Gift or deemed gift transfers.*—(i) *In general.*—A transfer statement for a security transferred to a different owner (other than a transfer that the transferor knows is pursuant to a lending or borrowing arrangement or is from a decedent or decedent's estate) must indicate that the security is a gift and must report the date of the gift (if known when furnishing the statement) and the fair market value of the gift on that date (if known or readily ascertainable at the time the transfer statement is prepared). The transfer statement must report the adjusted basis and original acquisition date of the security in the hands of the donor. However, if the transfer is between persons for whom gift-related basis adjustments are inapplicable or between accounts that share at least one common customer, the transferor must apply paragraph (b)(1) of this section as if the security were not a gift or deemed gift.

(ii) *Subsequent transfers of gifts by the same customer.*—If a transferor transfers to a different account of the same customer a security that a prior transfer statement reported as a gifted security, the transferor must include on the transfer statement the information described in paragraph (b)(9)(i) of this section for the date of the gift to the customer. If the prior transfer statement did not report a date for the gift, the transferor must treat the settlement date for the prior transfer as the date of the gift.

(iii) *Examples.*—The following examples illustrate the rules of this paragraph (b)(9):

Example 1. X instructs S, a broker, to give to Y stock in a publicly traded company that X holds in an account with S. The stock is a covered security. On X's instruction, S transfers custody of the stock to T, Y's broker. The transfer settles on August 15, 2013. Under paragraph (b)(9)(i) of this section, S must provide a transfer statement to T that identifies the securities as gifted securities and indicates X's adjusted basis and original acquisition date. If S knows the settlement date, the transfer statement must also indicate that the date of the gift was August 15, 2013, and, because S can readily ascertain the fair market value of the stock on August 15, 2013, the fair market value of the stock on that date.

Example 2. Assume the same facts as in *Example 1* except that, one year later, Y transfers the stock to an account in his name with U, another broker. Under paragraph (b)(9)(ii) of this section, T must provide a transfer statement to U that identifies the securities as gifted securities and indicates X's adjusted basis and original acquisition date of the stock. The transfer statement must also indicate the date of the gift,

August 15, 2013, and the fair market value of the stock on that date either by reporting the value that S reported to T or, because T can readily ascertain the fair market value of the stock on August 15, 2013, by determining the fair market value of the stock on that date.

(10) *Specific identification of securities.*—Except as provided in § 1.1012-1(e)(7)(ii), a transfer statement must report a transfer of less than the entire position in an account of a security that was acquired on different dates or at different prices consistently with a customer's adequate and timely identification of the security to be transferred. *See* § 1.1012-1(c). If the customer does not provide an adequate and timely identification for the transfer, a transferor must first report the transfer of any securities in the account for which the transferor does not know the acquisition or purchase date followed by the earliest securities purchased or acquired, whether covered securities or noncovered securities.

(11) *Information from other parties and other accounts.*—(i) *Transfer and issuer statements and transfers pursuant to an inheritance.*—When reporting a transfer of a covered security, a transferor must take into account all information, other than the classification of the security (such as stock), furnished on a transfer statement, all information furnished or deemed furnished on an issuer statement (as described in § 1.6045B-1, and all instructions and valuations furnished by an authorized representative of the estate of a decedent, unless the statement or instructions are incomplete or the broker has actual knowledge that they are incorrect. A transferor may treat a customer as a minority shareholder when taking the information on an issuer statement into account unless the transferor knows that the customer is a majority shareholder and the issuer statement reports the action's effect on the basis of majority shareholders. Any failure to report correct information that arises solely from reliance on information furnished on a transfer statement or issuer statement or by an authorized representative of the estate is deemed to be due to reasonable cause for purposes of penalties under section 6722. *See* § 301.6724-1(a)(1) of this chapter.

(ii) *Other information.*—A transferor is permitted, but not required, to take into account information about a covered security other than what is furnished on a transfer statement or issuer statement or by an authorized representative of the estate of a decedent, including any information the transferor has about securities held by the same customer in other accounts with the transferor. For purposes of penalties under section 6722, a transferor that takes into account information received from a customer or third party other than information furnished on a transfer statement or issuer statement or by an authorized representative of the estate of a decedent is deemed to have relied upon this information in good faith if the transferor neither knows

nor has reason to know that the information is incorrect. *See* § 301.6724-1(c)(6) of this chapter.

(12) *Failure to receive a complete transfer statement.*—(i) *In general.*—A receiving broker that has not received a complete transfer statement as required under paragraph (a)(3) of this section for the transfer must request a complete statement from the transferor unless, under paragraph (a) of this section, the transferor has no duty to furnish a transfer statement for the transfer. The receiving broker is only required to make this request once. If the receiving broker does not receive a complete transfer statement after requesting it, the receiving broker may treat the security as a noncovered security upon its subsequent sale or transfer. A transfer statement for a covered security is complete if, in the view of the receiving broker, it provides sufficient information to comply with § 1.6045-1 when reporting the sale of the security. A transfer statement for a noncovered security is complete if it indicates that the security is a noncovered security.

(ii) *Transition rules for transfers of debt instruments, options, and securities futures contracts.*—If an option described in § 1.6045-1(a)(14)(iii), a securities futures contract described in § 1.6045-1(a)(14)(iv), or a debt instrument described in § 1.6045-1(a)(15)(i)(C) is transferred in 2014 and no transfer statement is received, the receiving broker is not required to request a transfer statement from the transferor and may treat the security as a noncovered security. If a debt instrument described in § 1.6045-1(a)(15)(i)(D) is transferred in 2016 and no transfer statement is received, the receiving broker is not required to request a transfer statement from the transferor and may treat the security as a noncovered security.

(c) *Reporting by other parties after a transfer.*—(1) *In general.*—A transferor that has furnished a transfer statement must furnish a corrected statement for a covered security within fifteen days of receiving a transfer statement, an issuer statement (as described in § 1.6045B-1, or instructions or valuations from an authorized representative of an estate, that provides information under paragraph (b) of this section that was not reported on the initial transfer statement.

(2) *Exception.*—A transferor is not required to furnish a corrected transfer statement for a covered security under this paragraph (c) if the transferor receives the transfer statement or issuer statement or receives the instructions or valuations from an authorized representative of an estate more than eighteen months after the transferor furnished the transfer statement.

(d) *Effective/applicability dates.*—This section applies to:

(1) A transfer on or after January 1, 2011, of stock other than stock in a regulated investment company within the meaning of § 1.1012-1(e)(5);

(2) A transfer on or after January 1, 2012, of stock in a regulated investment company;

(3) A transfer on or after January 1, 2015, of an option described in § 1.6045-1(a)(14)(iii), a securities futures contract described in § 1.6045-1(a)(14)(iv), or a debt instrument described in § 1.6045-1(a)(15)(i)(C); and

(4) A transfer on or after January 1, 2017, of a debt instrument described in § 1.6045-1(a)(15)(i)(D). [Reg. § 1.6045A-1.]

☐ [*T.D. 9504, 10-12-2010. Amended by T.D. 9616, 4-17-2013, T.D. 9713, 3-12-2015 and T.D. 9750, 2-17-2016 (corrected 4-26-2016).*]

[Reg. § 1.6045B-1]

§ 1.6045B-1 Returns relating to actions affecting basis of securities.—(a) *In general.*—(1) *Information required.*—An issuer of a specified security (within the meaning of § 1.6045-1(a)(14) that takes an organizational action that affects the basis of the security must file an issuer return setting forth the following information and any other information specified in the return form and instructions:

(i) *Reporting issuer.*—The name and taxpayer identification number of the reporting issuer.

(ii) *Security identifiers.*—The identifiers of each security involved in the organizational action including, as applicable, the Committee on Uniform Security Identification Procedures (CUSIP) number or other security identifier number that the Secretary may designate by publication in the **Federal Register** or in the Internal Revenue Bulletin (*see* § 601.601(d)(2) of this chapter), classification of the security (such as stock), account number, serial number, and ticker symbol, as well as any descriptions about the class of security affected.

(iii) *Contact at reporting issuer.*—The name, address, e-mail address, and telephone number of a contact person at the issuer.

(iv) *Information about action.*—The type or nature of the organizational action including, as applicable, the date of the action or the date against which shareholders' ownership is measured for the action.

(v) *Effect of the action.*—The quantitative effect of the organizational action on the basis of the security in the hands of a U.S. taxpayer as an adjustment per share or as a percentage of old basis, including a description of the calculation, the applicable Internal Revenue Code section and subsection upon which the tax treatment is based, the data supporting the calculation such as the market values of securities and valuation dates, any other information necessary to implement the adjustment including the reportable taxable year, and whether any resulting loss may be recognized.

(2) *Time for filing the return.*—(i) *In general.*—An issuer must file an issuer return with the IRS pursuant to the prescribed form and instructions on or before the 45th day following the organizational action, or, if earlier, January

15 of the year following the calendar year of the organizational action. For purposes of this paragraph (a)(2), a redemption occurs on the last day a holder may redeem a security. The issuer may file the return before the organizational action if the quantitative effect on basis is determinable beforehand.

(ii) *Reasonable assumptions.*—To report the quantitative effect on basis by the due date in paragraph (a)(2)(i) of this section, an issuer may make reasonable assumptions about facts that cannot be determined before the due date. An issuer must file a corrected return within forty-five days of determining facts that result in a different quantitative effect on basis from what the issuer previously reported. However, for purposes of this paragraph (a)(2)(ii), an issuer must treat a payment that may be a dividend consistently with its treatment of the payment under section 6042(b)(3) and § 1.6042-3(c).

(3) *Exception for public reporting.*—An issuer is not required to file a return with the IRS under this paragraph (a) if, by the due date described in paragraph (a)(2)(i) of this section, the issuer posts the return with the required information in a readily accessible format in an area of its primary public Web site dedicated to this purpose and keeps the return accessible for ten years to the public on its primary public Web site or the primary public Web site of any successor organization. An issuer may electronically sign a return that is publicly reported in accordance with this paragraph (a)(3). The electronic signature must identify the individual who attests to the declaration in the jurat.

(4) *Exception when holders are exempt recipients.*—No reporting is required under this paragraph (a) if the issuer reasonably determines that all of the holders of the security are exempt recipients under paragraph (b)(5) of this section.

(5) *Exception for certain money market funds.*—No reporting is required under this paragraph (a) by a regulated investment company described in § 1.6045-1(c)(3)(vi).

(b) *Statements to nominees and certificate holders.*—(1) *In general.*—An issuer required to file an information return under this section must furnish a written statement with the same information to each holder of record of the security or to the holder's nominee. This issuer statement must indicate that the information is being reported to the IRS. An issuer may satisfy this requirement by furnishing a copy of the information return.

(2) *Time for furnishing statements.*—An issuer must furnish each issuer statement on or before January 15 of the year following the calendar year of the organizational action. For purposes of this paragraph (b)(2), a redemption occurs on the last day a holder may redeem a security. An issuer may furnish the statement before the organizational action if the quantitative effect on basis is determinable beforehand. An issuer must furnish a statement that corresponds to a cor-

rected return described in paragraph (a)(2)(ii) of this section by the later of the due date described in this paragraph (b)(2) or forty-five days after determining the facts that result in a different quantitative effect on basis from what the issuer previously reported on the return.

(3) *Recipients of statements.*—An issuer must furnish a separate statement to each holder of record of the security as of the date of the organizational action and all subsequent holders of record up to the date the issuer furnishes the statement required under this section. If the issuer records the security on its books in the name of a nominee, the issuer must furnish the statement to the nominee in lieu of the holder. However, if the nominee is the issuer, an agent of the issuer, or a plan operated by the issuer, the issuer must furnish the statement to the holder.

(4) *Exception for public reporting.*—An issuer is deemed to furnish an issuer statement under this paragraph (b) to all holders and nominees if the issuer satisfies the public reporting requirements of paragraph (a)(3) of this section.

(5) *Exempt recipients.*—(i) *In general.*—An issuer is not required to furnish an issuer statement to a holder or its nominee if the holder is an exempt recipient under § 1.6045-1(c)(3)(i)(B), provided the issuer has actual knowledge that the holder is described in that section or has a properly completed exemption certificate from the holder asserting that the holder is an exempt recipient (as provided in § 31.3406(h)-3 of this chapter). An issuer may treat a holder as an exempt recipient based on the applicable indicators described in § 1.6049-4(c)(1)(ii)(A) through (M).

(ii) *Limitation for corporate holders.*—For an organizational action occurring on or after January 1, 2012, an issuer may treat a holder as an exempt recipient based on the indicator described in § 1.6049-4(c)(1)(ii)(A) only if one of the following applies:

(A) The name of the holder contains the term "insurance company," "indemnity company," "reinsurance company," or "assurance company."

(B) The name of the holder indicates that it is an entity listed as a per se corporation under § 301.7701-2(b)(8)(i) of this chapter.

(C) The issuer receives a properly completed exemption certificate (as provided in § 31.3406(h)-3 of this chapter) that asserts that the holder is not an S corporation as defined in section 1361(a).

(D) The issuer receives a withholding certificate described in § 1.1441-1(e)(2)(i) that includes a certification that the person whose name is on the certificate is a foreign corporation.

(iii) *Foreign holders.*—An issuer may treat a holder as an exempt recipient if the issuer, prior to the transaction, associates the holder with documentation upon which the issuer may rely in order to treat payments to the holder as

made to a foreign beneficial owner in accordance with § 1.1441-1(e)(1)(ii) or as made to a foreign payee in accordance with § 1.6049-5(d)(1) or presumed to be made to a foreign payee under § 1.6049-5(d)(2) or (3). For purposes of this paragraph (b)(5)(iii), the provisions in § 1.6049-5(c) (regarding rules applicable to documentation of foreign status and definition of U.S. payor and non-U.S. payor) apply. Rules similar to the rules of § 1.1441-1 apply by substituting the terms "issuer" and "holder" in place of the terms "withholding agent" and "payee" and without regard to the limitation to amounts subject to withholding under chapter 3 of the Internal Revenue Code. Rules similar to the rules of § 1.6049-5(d) apply by substituting the terms "issuer" and "holder" in place of the terms "payor" and "payee."

(c) *Special rule for S corporations.*—An S corporation (as defined in section 1361(a)) is deemed to satisfy the requirements of paragraphs (a) and (b) of this section for any organizational action affecting the basis of its stock if the corporation reports the effect of the organizational action on a timely filed Schedule K-1 (Form 1120S), "Shareholder's Share of Income, Deductions, Credits, etc.," for each shareholder and timely furnishes copies of these schedules to all proper parties.

(d) *Special rule for certain regulated investment companies and real estate investment trusts.*—A regulated investment company (RIC) that reports undistributed capital gains to shareholders under section 852(b)(3)(D) or a real estate investment trust (REIT) that reports undistributed capital gains to shareholders under section 857(b)(3)(D) is deemed to have satisfied the requirements of paragraphs (a) and (b) of this section for undistributed capital gains affecting the basis of its stock if the RIC or REIT timely files and furnishes the information returns required under section 852(b)(3)(D) or section 857(b)(3)(D) to all proper parties for the organizational action.

(e) *Acquiring and successor entities.*—An acquiring or successor entity of an issuer that fails to satisfy the reporting obligations of paragraphs (a) or (b) of this section must satisfy these reporting obligations. If neither the issuer nor the acquiring or successor entity satisfies these reporting obligations, both parties are jointly and severally liable for any applicable penalties.

(f) *Penalties.*—An issuer may use an agent to satisfy the requirements of this section for the issuer. Nonetheless, the issuer remains liable for penalty for any failure to comply unless it is shown that the failure is due to reasonable cause and not willful neglect. *See* sections 6721 through 6724.

(g) *Examples.*—The following examples illustrate the rules of this section:

Example 1. (i) C, a corporation, distributes stock to shareholders on March 31, 2013.

(ii) Under paragraph (a)(2)(i) of this section, C must file an issuer return with the IRS on or before May 15, 2013 (45 days after the distribution date), reporting the quantitative effect of this distribution on the basis of C's stock. Under paragraph (b)(2) of this section, C must furnish issuer statements to its nominees and certificate holders on or before January 15, 2014.

(iii) Alternatively, under paragraphs (a)(3) and (b)(4) of this section, C may post by May 15, 2013, and maintain for ten years, the return with the required information in a readily accessible format in an area of its primary public Web site dedicated to this purpose.

Example 2. (i) D, a corporation, makes a cash distribution to shareholders on December 10, 2013.

(ii) Under paragraphs (a)(2)(i) and (b)(2) of this section, D is required to file an issuer return with the IRS and furnish issuer statements to its nominees and certificate holders on or before January 15, 2014.

(iii) On January 15, 2014, D is unsure whether the distribution will exceed its earnings and profits for the fiscal year. For purposes of section 6042(b)(3) and §1.6042-3(c), D must treat the distribution as a dividend. Therefore, under paragraph (a)(2)(ii) of this section, D is not required to file an issuer return. If D later determines that dividend treatment was incorrect, D must file an issuer return reporting the correct quantitative effect on basis.

Example 3. E, a corporation, undertakes a stock split as of April 1, 2014. E furnishes issuer statements under paragraph (b) of this section on April 1, 2014, at which time the books and records of E show that 90 percent of its outstanding stock is owned by shareholders through a clearing organization as their nominee, 7 percent is owned by 5,000 individuals, and the remaining 3 percent is owned by a dividend reinvestment plan operated by E that has 1,000 members. Under paragraph (b)(3) of this section, E must furnish statements to the clearing organization, the 5,000 individuals, and the 1,000 members of the dividend reinvestment plan.

(h) *Rule for options.*—(1) *In general.*—For an option granted or acquired on or after January 1, 2014, if the original contract is replaced by a different number of option contracts, the following rules apply:

(i) If the option is an exchange-traded option, any clearinghouse or clearing facility that serves as a counterparty is treated as the issuer of the option for purposes of section 6045B.

(ii) If the option is not an exchange-traded option, the option writer is treated as the issuer of the option for purposes of section 6045B.

(2) *Examples.*—The following examples illustrate the rules of paragraph (h)(1) of this section:

Example 1. On January 15, 2014, F, an individual, purchases a one-year exchange-traded call option on 100 shares of Company X stock, with a strike price of $110. The call option is cleared through Clearinghouse G. Company X executes a 2-for-1 stock split as of April 1, 2014. Due to the stock split, the terms of F's option are altered, resulting in two option contracts, each on 100 shares of Company X stock with a strike price of $55. All other terms remain the same. Under paragraph (h)(1)(i) of this section, Clearinghouse G is required to prepare an issuer report for F.

Example 2. On January 31, 2014, J, an individual, purchases from K a non-exchange traded 7-month call option on 100 shares of Company X stock, with a strike price of $110. Company X executes a 2-for-1 stock split as of April 1, 2014. Due to the stock split, the terms of J's option are altered, resulting in one option contract on 200 shares of Company X stock with a strike price of $55. All other terms of the option remain the same. Under paragraph (h)(1) of this section, because the number of option contracts did not change, K is not required to prepare an issuer report for J.

(i) [Reserved]

(j) *Effective/applicability dates.*—This section applies to—

(1) Organizational actions occurring on or after January 1, 2011, that affect the basis of specified securities within the meaning of §1.6045-1(a)(14)(i) other than stock in a regulated investment company within the meaning of §1.1012-1(e)(5);

(2) Organizational actions occurring on or after January 1, 2012, that affect the basis of stock in a regulated investment company;

(3) Organizational actions occurring on or after January 1, 2014, that affect the basis of debt instruments described in §1.6045-1(n)(2)(i) (not including the debt instruments described in §1.6045-1(n)(2)(ii));

(4) Organizational actions occurring on or after January 1, 2016, that affect the basis of debt instruments described in §1.6045-1(n)(3);

(5) Organizational actions occurring on or after January 1, 2014, that affect the basis of options described in §1.6045-1(a)(14)(iii); and

(6) Organizational actions occurring on or after January 1, 2014, that affect the basis of securities futures contracts described in §1.6045-1(a)(14)(iv). [Reg. §1.6045B-1.]

☐ [*T.D.* 9504, 10-12-2010. *Amended by T.D.* 9616, 4-17-2013.]

[Reg. §1.6046-1]

§1.6046-1. Returns as to organization or reorganization of foreign corporations and as to acquisitions of their stock.—(a) *Officers or directors.*—(1) *When liability arises on January 1, 1963.*—Each United States citizen or resident who is on January 1, 1963, an officer or director of a foreign corporation shall make a return on Form 5471 (or subsequent form) showing the name, address, and identifying number of each United States person who, on January 1, 1963, owns 5 percent or more in value of the outstanding stock of such foreign corporation.

(2) *When liability arises after January 1, 1963.*—(i) *Requirement of return.*—Each United States citizen or resident who is at any time after January 1, 1963, an officer or director of a foreign corporation shall make a return on Form 5471 setting forth the information described in paragraph (a)(2)(ii) of this section with respect to each United States person who, during the time such citizen or resident is such an officer or director —

(a) Acquires (whether in one or more transactions) outstanding stock of such corporation which equals, or which when added to any such stock then owned by him equals, 10 percent or more of the total combined voting power of all classes of stock of the foreign corporation entitled to vote or the total value of the stock of the foreign corporation;

(b) Acquires (whether in one or more transactions) an additional 10 percent or more of the total combined voting power of all classes of stock of the foreign corporation entitled to vote or the total value of the stock of the foreign corporation; or

(c) Is not described in paragraph (a)(2)(i)(a) or (b) of this section, and who, at any time after January 1, 1987, is treated as a United States shareholder under section 953(c) with respect to such foreign corporation.

(ii) *Information required to be shown on return.*—The return required under subdivision (i) of this subparagraph shall contain the following information:

(a) Name, address, and identifying number of each shareholder with respect to whom the return is filed;

(b) A statement showing that the shareholder is either described in subdivision (i)(a) or (i)(b) of this subparagraph; and

(c) The date on which the shareholder became a person described in subdivision (i)(a) or (i)(b) of this subparagraph.

(3) *Application of rules.*—The provisions of this paragraph may be illustrated by the following examples:

Example (1). A, a United States citizen, is, on January 1, 1963, a director of M, a foreign corporation. X, on January 1, 1963, is a United States person owning 5 percent in value of the outstanding stock of M Corporation. A must file a return under the provisions of subparagraph (1) of this paragraph.

Example 2. (i) *Facts.* A, a United States citizen, is, on January 1, 2014, a director of M Corporation, a foreign corporation. X, on January 1, 2014, is a United States person owning 4% of the outstanding stock of M Corporation. On July 1, 2014, X acquires 4% of the outstanding stock of M Corporation and on September 1, 2014, he acquires an additional 4% of such stock.

(ii) *Results.* The July 1, 2014, transaction does not give rise to liability for A to file a return; however, A must file a return as a result of the September 1, 2014, transaction because X's holdings now exceed 10%.

Example 3. (i) *Facts.* The facts are the same as in *Example 2* and, on September 15, 2014, X acquires an additional 8% of the outstanding stock of M Corporation. (X's total holdings are now 20%.) On November 1, 2014, X acquires an additional 4% of the outstanding stock of M Corporation.

(ii) *Results.* The September 15, 2014, transaction does not give rise to liability to file a return since X has not acquired 10% of the outstanding stock of M Corporation since A last became liable to file a return. However, A must file a return as a result of the November 1, 2014, transaction because X has now acquired an additional 10% of the outstanding stock of M Corporation.

Example 4. (i) *Facts.* The facts are the same as in *Examples 2* and *3* and, in addition, B, a United States citizen, becomes an officer of M Corporation on September 10, 2014.

(ii) *Results.* B is not required to file a return either as a result of the facts set forth in *Example 2* or as a result of the September 15, 2014, transaction described in *Example 3*. However, B is required to file a return as a result of the November 1, 2014, transaction described in *Example 3* because X has acquired an additional 10% in value of the outstanding stock of M Corporation while B is an officer or director.

(b) *Returns required of United States persons when liability to file arises on January 1, 1963.*—Each United States person who, on January 1, 1963, owns 5 percent or more in value of the outstanding stock of a foreign corporation, shall make a return on Form 959 with respect to such foreign corporation setting forth the following information:

(1) The name, address, and identifying number of the shareholder (or shareholders) filing the return, and the internal revenue district in which such shareholder filed his most recent United States income tax return;

(2) The name, business address, and employer identification number, if any, of the foreign corporation, the name of the country under the laws of which it is incorporated, and the name of the country in which is located its principal place of business;

(3) The date of organization and, if any, of each reorganization of the foreign corporation if such reorganization occurred on or after January 1, 1960, while the shareholder owned 5 percent or more in value of the outstanding stock of such corporation;

(4) The name and address of the foreign corporation's statutory or resident agent in the country of incorporation;

(5) The name, address, and identifying number of any branch office or agent of the foreign corporation located in the United States;

(6) If the foreign corporation has filed a United States income tax return, or participated in the filing of a consolidated return, for any of its last three calendar or fiscal years immediately preceding January 1, 1963, state each year for which a return was filed (including, in the case of a consolidated return, the name of the corpo-

ration filing such return), the type of form used, the internal revenue office to which it was sent, and the amount of tax, if any, paid;

(7) The name and address of the person (or persons) having custody of the books of account and records of the foreign corporation, and the location of such books and records if different from such address;

(8) The names, addresses, and identifying numbers of all United States persons who are principal officers (for example, president, vice president, secretary, treasurer, and comptroller) or members of the board of directors of the foreign corporation as of January 1, 1963;

(9) A complete description of the principal business activities in which the foreign corporation is actually engaged and, if the foreign corporation is a member of a group constituting a chain of ownership with respect to each unit of which the shareholder owns 5 percent or more in value of the outstanding stock, a chart showing the foreign corporation's position in the chain of ownership and the percentages of ownership;

(10) The following information prepared in accordance with generally accepted accounting principles and in such detail as is customary for the corporation's accounting records:

(i) The corporation's profit and loss statement for the most recent complete annual accounting period; and

(ii) The corporation's balance sheet as of the end of the most recent complete annual accounting period;

(11) A statement showing as of January 1, 1963, the amount and type of any indebtedness of the foreign corporation—

(i) To any United States person owning 5 percent or more in value of its stock, or

(ii) To any other foreign corporation owning 5 percent or more in value of the outstanding stock of the foreign corporation with respect to which the return is filed provided that the shareholder filing the return owns 5 percent or more in value of the outstanding stock of such other foreign corporation,

together with the name, address, and identifying number, if any, of each such shareholder or entity;

(12) A statement, as of January 1, 1963, showing the name, address, and identifying number, if any, of each person who is, on January 1, 1963, a subscriber to the stock of the foreign corporation, and the number of shares subscribed to by each;

(13) A statement showing the number of shares of each class of stock of the foreign corporation owned by each shareholder filing the return and—

(i) If such stock was acquired after December 31, 1953, the dates of acquisition, the amounts paid or value given therefor, the method of acquisition, i.e., by original issue, purchase on open market, direct purchase, gift, inheritance, etc., and from whom acquired; or

(ii) If such stock was acquired before January 1, 1954, a statement that such stock was acquired before such date, and the value at which such stock is carried on the books of such shareholder;

(14) A statement showing as of January 1, 1963, the name, address, and identifying number of each United States person who owns 5 percent or more in value of the outstanding stock of the foreign corporation, the classes of stock held, the number of shares of each class held, including the name, address, and identifying number, if any, of each actual owner if such person is different from the shareholder of record and a statement of the nature and amount of the interests of each such actual owner; and

(15) The total number of shares of each class of outstanding stock of the foreign corporation (or other data indicating the shareholder's percentage of ownership).

(c) *Returns required of United States persons when liability to file arises after January 1, 1963.*— (1) *United States persons required to file.*—A return on Form 5471, containing the information required by paragraph (c)(4) of this section, shall be made by each United States person when at any time after January 1, 1963:

(i) Such person acquires (whether in one or more transactions) outstanding stock of such foreign corporation which equals, or which when added to any such stock then owned by him equals, 10 percent or more of the total combined voting power of all classes of stock of the foreign corporation entitled to vote or the total value of the stock of the foreign corporation;

(ii) Such person, having already acquired the interest referred to in paragraph (b) of this section or in paragraph (c)(1)(i) of this section —

(a) Acquires (whether in one or more transactions) an additional 10 percent or more of the total combined voting power of all classes of stock of the foreign corporation entitled to vote or the total value of the stock of the foreign corporation;

(b) Owns 10 percent or more of the total combined voting power of all classes of stock of the foreign corporation entitled to vote or the total value of the stock of the foreign corporation when such foreign corporation is reorganized (as defined in paragraph (f)); or

(c) Disposes of sufficient stock in such foreign corporation to reduce his interest to less than 10 percent of the total combined voting power of all classes of stock of the foreign corporation entitled to vote or the total value of the stock of the foreign corporation; or

(iii) Such person is, at any time after January 1, 1987, treated as a United States shareholder under *section 953(c)* with respect to a foreign corporation.

(2) *Examples.*—The provisions of paragraph (c)(1) of this section may be illustrated by the following examples:

Example 1. (i) *Facts.* On January 15, 2014, A, a United States person, acquires 10% of the outstanding stock of M, a foreign corporation.

Reg. § 1.6046-1(c)(2)

(ii) *Results.* A must file a return under the provisions of paragraph (c)(1) of this section.

Example 2. (i) *Facts.* On January 1, 2014, B, a United States person, owns 4% of the outstanding stock of M, a foreign corporation. On February 1, 2015, B acquires an additional 6% of the outstanding stock of M Corporation.

(ii) *Results.* B is not required to file a return for 2014 under the provisions of this section because he does not own 10% or more of the outstanding stock of M Corporation. B must file a return for 2015 under the provisions of paragraph (c)(1) of this section.

Example 3. (i) *Facts.* On January 1, 2014, C, a United States person, owns 12% of the outstanding stock of M Corporation, a foreign corporation. On February 1, 2014, C acquires an additional 4% of the outstanding stock of M Corporation in a transaction not involving a reorganization.

(ii) *Results.* C is not required to file a return under the provisions of paragraph (c)(1) of this section with respect to the acquisition of the additional 4% of M Corporation.

Example 4. (i) *Facts.* The facts are the same as in *Example 3* except that, in addition, on April 1, 2014, C acquires 4% of the outstanding stock of M Corporation in a transaction not involving a reorganization. (C's total holdings are now 20%.) On May 1, 2014, C acquires 2% of the outstanding stock of M Corporation.

(ii) *Results.* C is not required to file a return under the provisions of paragraph (c)(1) of this section as a result of the April 1, 2014, acquisition because he has not acquired 10% or more of the outstanding stock of M Corporation since he last became liable to file a return. C must file a return under the provisions of paragraph (c)(1) of this section as a result of the May 1, 2014, acquisition because C acquired 10% of the outstanding stock of M Corporation during 2014.

Example 5. (i) *Facts.* On June 1, 2014, D, a United States person, owns 24% of the outstanding stock of M Corporation, a foreign corporation. Also, on June 1, 2014, M Corporation is reorganized and, as a result of such reorganization, D owns only 12% of the outstanding stock of such foreign corporation.

(ii) *Results.* D must file a return under the provisions of paragraph (c)(1) of this section.

Example 6. (i) *Facts.* The facts are the same as in *Example 5* except that, in addition, on November 1, 2015, D donates 4% of the outstanding stock of M Corporation to a charity.

(ii) *Results.* Since D has disposed of sufficient stock to reduce his interest in M Corporation to less than 10% of the outstanding stock of such corporation, D must file a return under the provisions of paragraph (c)(1) of this section.

(3) *Shareholders who become United States persons.*—A return on Form 5471, containing the information required by paragraph (c)(4) of this section, shall be made by each person who at any time after January 1, 1963, becomes a United States person while owning 10 percent or more

of the total combined voting power of all classes of stock of the foreign corporation entitled to vote or the total value of the stock of the foreign corporation.

(4) *Information required to be shown on return.*—(i) *In general.*—The return on Form 5471, required to be filed by persons described in paragraph (c)(1) or (3) of this section, shall set forth the same information as is required by the provisions of paragraph (b) of this section except that where such provisions require information with respect to January 1, 1963, such information shall be furnished with respect to the date on which liability arises to file the return required under this paragraph.

(ii) *Additional information.*—In addition to the information required under paragraph (c)(4)(i) of this section, the following information shall also be furnished in the return required under this paragraph:

(*a*) The date on or after January 1, 1963, if any, on which such shareholder (or shareholders) last filed a return under this section with respect to the corporation;

(*b*) If a return is filed by reason of becoming a United States person, the date the shareholder became a United States person;

(*c*) If a return is filed by reason of the disposition of stock, the date and method of such disposition and the person to whom such disposition was made; and

(*d*) If a return is filed by reason of the organization or reorganization of the foreign corporation on or after January 1, 1963, the following information with respect to such organization or reorganization:

(*1*) A statement showing a detailed list of the classes and kinds of assets transferred to the foreign corporation including a description of the assets (such as a list of patents, copyrights, stock, securities, etc.), the fair market value of each asset transferred (and, if such asset is transferred by a United States person, its adjusted basis), the date of transfer, the name, address, and identifying number, if any, of the owner immediately prior to the transfer, and the consideration paid by the foreign corporation for such transfer;

(*2*) A statement showing the assets transferred and the notes or securities issued by the foreign corporation, the name, address, and identifying number, if any, of each person to whom such transfer or issue was made, and the consideration paid to the foreign corporation for such transfer or issue; and

(*3*) An analysis of the changes in the corporation's surplus accounts occurring on or after January 1, 1963.

(iii) *Exclusion of information previously furnished.*—In any case where any identical item of information required to be filed under this paragraph by a shareholder with respect to a foreign corporation has previously been furnished by such shareholder in any return made in accordance with the provisions of this section, such shareholder may satisfy the requirements of this paragraph by filing Form 5471, identifying such item of information, the date furnished, and stating that it is unchanged.

(d) *Associations, etc.*—Returns are required to be filed in accordance with the provisions of this section with respect to any foreign association, foreign joint-stock company, or foreign insurance company, etc., which would be considered to be a corporation under § 301.7701-2 of this chapter (Regulations on Procedure and Administration). Persons who would qualify by the nature of their functions and ownership in such associations, etc., as officers, directors, or shareholders thereof will be treated as such for purposes of this section without regard to their designations under local law.

(e) *Special provisions.*—(1) *Return jointly made.*—Any two or more persons required under paragraph (a) of this section to make a return with respect to one or more shareholders of the same corporation, or under paragraph (b) or (c) of this section to make a return with respect to the same corporation, may in lieu of making several returns, jointly make one return.

(2) *Separate return for each corporation.*—When returns are required with respect to more than one foreign corporation, a separate return must be made for each corporation.

(3) *Use of power of attorney by officers or directors.*—(i) *In general.*—Any two or more persons required under paragraph (a) of this section to make a return with respect to one or more shareholders of the same corporation may, by means of one or more duly executed powers of attorney, constitute one of their number as attorney in fact for the purpose of making such returns or for the purpose of making a joint return under subparagraph (1) of this paragraph.

(ii) *Nature of power of attorney.*—The power of attorney referred to in subdivision (i) of this subparagraph shall be limited to the making of returns required under paragraph (a) of this section and shall be limited to a single calendar year with respect to which such returns are required.

(iii) *Manner of execution of power of attorney.*—The use of technical language in the preparation of the power of attorney referred to in subdivision (i) of this subparagraph is not necessary. Such power of attorney shall be signed by the individual United States citizen or resident required to file a return or returns under paragraph (a) of this section. Such power of attorney must be acknowledged before a notary public or, in lieu thereof, witnessed by two disinterested persons. The notarial seal must be affixed unless such seal is not required under the laws of the state or country wherein such power of attorney is executed.

(iv) *Manner of execution of return under authority of power of attorney.*—A return made under authority of one or more powers of attorney

referred to in subdivision (i) of this subparagraph shall be signed by the attorney in fact for each principal for which such attorney in fact is acting. A copy of such one or more powers of attorney shall be kept at a convenient and safe location accessible to internal revenue officers, and shall at all times be available for inspection by such officers.

(v) *Effect on penalties.*—The fact that a return is made under authority of a power of attorney referred to in subdivision (i) of this subparagraph shall not affect the principal's liability for penalties provided for failure to file a return required under paragraph (a) of this section or for filing a false or fraudulent return.

(4) *Persons excepted from filing returns.*—(i) *Return required of officer or director under paragraph (a)(1).*—Notwithstanding paragraph (a)(1) of this section, any United States citizen or resident required to make a return under such paragraph with respect to shareholders of a foreign corporation, need not make such return if, on January 1, 1963, three or fewer United States persons own 95 percent or more in value of the outstanding stock of such foreign corporation and file a return or returns with respect to such corporation under paragraph (b) of this section.

(ii) *Return required of officer or director under paragraph (a)(2).*—Notwithstanding paragraph (a)(2) of this section, any United States citizen or resident required to make a return under such paragraph with respect to a person acquiring stock of a foreign corporation in an acquisition described in subdivision (i)(*a*) or (*b*) of such paragraph need not make such return, if—

(*a*) As a result of such acquisition of stock of such foreign corporation, a United States person files a return as a shareholder under paragraph (c)(1) of this section, and

(*b*) Immediately after such acquisition of stock, three or fewer United States persons own 95 percent or more in value of the outstanding stock of such foreign corporation.

(iii) *Return required by reason of attribution rules.*—Notwithstanding paragraph (b) or (c) of this section, any person required to make a return under such paragraph with respect to a foreign corporation need not make such return, if—

(*a*) Such person does not directly own an interest in the foreign corporation,

(*b*) Such person is required to furnish the information solely by reason of attribution of stock ownership from a United States person under paragraph (i) of this section, and

(*c*) The person from whom the stock ownership is attributed furnishes all of the information required under paragraph (b) or (c) of this section of the person to whom such stock ownership is attributed.

(iv) *Return required of officer or director with respect to person described in subdivision (iii).*—Notwithstanding paragraph (a) of this section, any

Reg. §1.6046-1(e)(4)(iv)

United States citizen or resident required to make a return under such paragraph with respect to a person exempted under subdivision (iii) of this subparagraph from making a return need not make a return with respect to such person.

(5) *Persons excepted from furnishing items of information.*—Any person required to furnish any item of information under paragraph (b) or (c) of this section with respect to a foreign corporation may, if such item of information is furnished by another person having an equal or greater stock interest (measured in terms of either the total combined voting power of all classes of stock of the foreign corporation entitled to vote or the total value of the stock of the foreign corporation) in such foreign corporation, satisfy such requirement by filing a statement with his return on Form 5471 indicating that such requirement has been satisfied and identifying the return in which such item of information was included. This paragraph (e)(5) does not apply to persons excepted from filing a return by reason of the provisions of paragraph (e)(4) of this section.

(f) *Meaning of terms.*—For purposes of this section—

(1) *Acquisition.*—Stock in a foreign corporation shall be considered acquired when a person has an unqualified right to receive such stock, even though such stock is not actually issued. For example, when under the law of a foreign country, all the necessary steps for incorporation are completed but stock in the corporation will not be issued within 30 days, every United States citizen or resident who is an officer or a director of such corporation, provided a United States person has an interest of 10 percent or more in such corporation, and every such United States person shall, within 90 days of the date of incorporation, file the returns required under section 6046 and this section. In the case of a reorganization, new stock may be acquired, depending on the type of reorganization, whether or not any stock certificates are surrendered or exchanged or the designation of such stock is altered.

(2) *Reorganization.*—With respect to a foreign corporation, the term "reorganization" shall mean not only a transaction described in section 368(a)(1) and the regulations thereunder but also any other transaction or series of transactions which has the same effect.

(3) *U.S. person.*—(i) *In general.*—For purposes of section 6046 and this section, the term *United States person* has the meaning assigned to it by section 7701(a)(30), except as provided in paragraphs (f)(3)(ii) and (iii) of this section.

(ii) *Special rule for individuals residing in certain possessions.*—(A) With respect to an individual who is a bona fide resident of Puerto Rico, the term United States person has the meaning assigned to it by § 1.957-3 except that the rules of § 1.937-2(g)(1) will apply.

(B) With respect to individuals who are bona fide residents of any section 931 possession,

as defined in § 1.931-1(c)(1), the term United States person has the meaning assigned to it by § 1.957-3.

(iii) *Special rule for certain nonresident aliens.*—An individual for whom an election under section 6013(g) or (h) is in effect will, subject to the exceptions contained in paragraph (f)(3)(ii) of this section, be considered a United States person for purposes of section 6046 and this section.

(4) [Reserved].

(5) *Accounting period and taxable year.*—In the case of a specified foreign corporation (as defined in section 898), the taxable year of such corporation shall be treated as its annual accounting period.

(g) *Method of reporting.*—All amounts furnished in returns prescribed under this section shall be expressed in United States currency with a statement of the exchange rates used. All statements required to be submitted on or with returns under this section shall be rendered in the English language. For taxable years ending after December 31, 1994, with respect to returns filed after December 31, 1995, all amounts furnished under paragraph (c) of this section shall be expressed in United States dollars computed and translated in conformity with United States generally accepted accounting principles. Amounts furnished under paragraph (c)(3)(i) of this section shall also be furnished in the foreign corporation's functional currency as required on the form. Information described in paragraphs (b)(10) and (c)(3) of this section shall be submitted in such form or manner as the form shall prescribe. If an individual who is a United States person required to make a return with respect to a foreign corporation under section 6046 is entitled under a treaty to be treated as a nonresident of the United States, and if the individual claims this treaty benefit, and if there are no other United States persons that are required to furnish information under section 6046 with respect to the foreign corporation, then the individual may satisfy the requirements of paragraphs (b)(10), (11) and (12), (c)(3)(ii)(d), and (g) of this section by filing the audited foreign financial statements of the foreign corporation with the individual's return required under section 6046.

(h) *Actual ownership of stock.*—If any shareholder, referred to in this section, is not the actual owner of the stock of the foreign corporation, the information required under this section shall be furnished in the name of and by such actual owner. For example, in the case of stock held by a nominee, the information required under this section shall be furnished by the actual owner of such stock.

(i) *Constructive ownership of stock.*—(1) *In general.*—Stock owned directly or indirectly by or for a foreign corporation or a foreign partnership shall be considered as being owned proportionately by its shareholders or partners. Thus, any United States person who is a member of a nonresident foreign partnership which becomes a shareholder in a foreign corporation shall be considered to be a shareholder in such foreign corporation to the extent of his proportionate share in such partnership.

(2) *Members of family.*—An individual shall be considered as owning the stock owned directly or indirectly by or for his brothers and sisters (whether by the whole or half blood), his spouse, his ancestors, and his lineal descendants. However, when stock is treated as owned by an individual under the rule provided in this subparagraph, it shall not be treated as owned by him for the purpose of again applying such rule in order to make another the constructive owner of such stock. The provisions of this subparagraph may be illustrated by the following example:

Example. H, W, and HF are United States citizens. W, wife of H, owns 20 percent of the value of the outstanding stock of X, a foreign corporation. X Corporation owns 90 percent of the value of the outstanding stock of Y Corporation, a foreign corporation. Y Corporation becomes the owner of 50 percent of the value of the outstanding stock of each of two newly organized foreign corporations, M and N. In applying the "members of family" rule, H is considered to own 20 percent of the value of the outstanding stock of X Corporation, and 18 percent of the value of the outstanding stock of Y Corporation, and 9 percent of M Corporation and N Corporation. However, HF, the father of H, is not considered to own stock of X, Y, M, or N since his son, H, is not treated as the owner of such stock for purposes of again applying the "members of family" rule.

(j) *Time and place for filing return.*—(1) *Time for filing.*—Any return required by section 6046 and this section shall be filed on or before the 90th day after the date on which a United States citizen, resident, or person becomes liable to file such return under any provision of section 6046(a) and of paragraph (a), (b), or (c) of this section. With respect to returns filed after September 3, 1982, such return shall be filed on or before such later date (if any) as may be authorized by the return form. The Director of the Internal Revenue Service Center where the return is required to be filed is authorized to grant reasonable extensions of time for filing returns under section 6046 and this section in accordance with the applicable provisions of section 6081(a) and § 1.6081-1.

(2) *Place for filing.*—Returns required by section 6046 and this section shall be filed with the Internal Revenue Service Center designated in the instructions of the applicable form.

(k) *Penalties.*—(1) For criminal penalties for failure to file a return and filing a false or fraudulent return, see sections 7203, 7206, and 7207.

(2) For civil penalty for failure to file return, or failure to show information required on a return, under this section, see section 6679.

(l) *Effective/applicability date.*—(1) Paragraph (f)(3) of this section applies to taxable years ending after April 9, 2008.

(2) Paragraph (c)(1)(iii) of this section applies to taxable years ending on or after December 31, 2013.

(3) Paragraph (e)(5) of this section applies to returns filed on or after December 31, 2013. See paragraph (e)(5) of § 1.6046-1, as contained in 26 CFR part 1 revised as of April 1, 2012, for returns filed before December 31, 2013. [Reg. § 1.6046-1.]

☐ [*T.D.* 6623, 11-30-62. *Amended by T.D.* 6997, 1-17-69; *T.D.* 7322, 8-23-74; *T.D.* 7925, 12-12-83; *T.D.* 8573, 12-13-94; *T.D.* 8733, 10-6-97; *T.D.* 9194, 4-6-2005; *T.D.* 9391, 4-4-2008, *T.D.* 9650, 12-30-2013 (*corrected* 5-9-2014) *and T.D.* 9806, 12-27-2016.]

[Reg. § 301.6046-1]

§ 301.6046-1. Returns as to organization or reorganization of foreign corporations and as to acquisitions of their stock.—For provisions relating to requirement of returns as to organization or reorganization of foreign corporations and as to acquisitions of their stock, see §§ 1.6046-1 to 1.6046-3, inclusive, of this chapter (Income Tax Regulations). [Reg. § 301.6046-1.]

☐ [*T.D.* 6498, 10-24-60. *Amended by T.D.* 6700, 1-6-64.]

[Reg. § 1.6046A-1]

§ 1.6046A-1. Return requirement for United States persons who acquire or dispose of an interest in a foreign partnership, or whose proportional interest in a foreign partnership changes substantially.—(a) *Return requirement.*—(1) *General rule.*—If a United States person has a reportable event (as defined in paragraph (b)(1) of this section) during the person's tax year, then, except as provided in paragraph (f) of this section, the United States person is required to complete and file Form 8865, "Return of U.S. Persons With Respect To Certain Foreign Partnerships," containing the information described in paragraph (c) of this section.

(2) *Separate return for each partnership.*—If a United States person has a reportable event with respect to an interest in more than one foreign partnership, the United States person must file a separate Form 8865 for each foreign partnership.

(b) *Definitions.*—(1) *Reportable event.*—There are three categories of reportable events under section 6046A: acquisitions, dispositions, and changes in proportional interests.

(i) *Acquisitions.*—A United States person that acquires a foreign partnership interest has a reportable event if—

(A) The person did not own a ten-percent or greater direct interest in the partnership and as a result of the acquisition the person owns a ten-percent or greater direct interest in the partnership. For purposes of this paragraph (b)(1)(i)(A), an acquisition includes an increase in a person's direct proportional interest; or

(B) Subject to paragraph (b)(2) of this section, compared to the person's direct interest when the person last had a reportable event, after the acquisition the person's direct interest has increased by at least a ten-percent interest.

(ii) *Dispositions.*—A United States person that disposes of a foreign partnership interest has a reportable event if—

(A) The person owned a ten-percent or greater direct interest in the partnership before the disposition and as a result of the disposition the person owns less than a ten-percent direct interest. For purposes of this paragraph (b)(1)(ii)(A), a disposition includes a decrease in a person's direct proportional interest; or

(B) Subject to paragraph (b)(2) of this section, compared to the person's direct interest when the person last had a reportable event, after the disposition the person's direct interest has decreased by at least a ten-percent interest.

(iii) *Changes in proportional interests not otherwise reportable as acquisitions or dispositions under paragraph (b)(1)(i)(A) or (b)(1)(ii)(A) of this section.*—A United States person has a reportable event if, subject to paragraph (b)(2) of this section, compared to the person's direct proportional interest the last time the person had a reportable event, the person's direct proportional interest has increased or decreased by at least the equivalent of a ten-percent interest.

(2) *Special rule for foreign partnership interests owned on December 31, 1999.*—If a United States person owned a ten-percent or greater direct interest in a foreign partnership on December 31, 1999, then to determine whether the person has a reportable event under paragraph (b)(1)(i)(B), (b)(1)(ii)(B), or (b)(1)(iii) of this section, the comparison should be made to the person's direct interest on December 31, 1999. Once the person has a reportable event after December 31, 1999, future comparisons should be made by reference to the last reportable event.

(3) *Change in a proportional interest.*—A partner's proportional interest in a foreign partnership may change for a number of reasons, for example, the change may be caused by changes in other partners' interests resulting from a partner withdrawing from the partnership. A proportional change may also occur by operation of the partnership agreement, for example, if the partnership agreement provides that a partner's interest in profits will change on a set date or when the partnership has earned a specified amount of profits and one of those events occurs.

(4) *Ten-percent interest.*—Under section 6046A(d) and this section, a *ten-percent interest* in a foreign partnership, as described in section 6038(e)(3)(C) and the regulations thereunder, means an interest equal to ten percent of the capital interest in such partnership, an interest equal to ten percent of the profits interest in such partnership, or an interest to which ten percent

of the deductions or losses of such partnership are allocated.

(5) *United States person.*—*United States person* means a person described in section 7701(a)(30).

(6) *Foreign partnership.*—*Foreign partnership* means any partnership that is a foreign partnership under sections 7701(a)(2) and (5).

(7) *Examples.*—The rules of paragraph (a) of this section and this paragraph (b) are illustrated by the following examples:

Example 1. Acquisition of an indirect interest. *FP*, a foreign partnership, has two partners, *FC1* and *FC2*, both foreign corporations. *FC1* owns a 40% interest in *FP*, and *FC2* owns a 60% interest in *FP*. No United States person owns an interest in *FP*, either directly, or constructively under section 6038(e)(3)(C) and section 267(c). On January 1, 2001, *US*, a United States person and calendar year taxpayer, acquires by purchase 100% of *FC2*'s stock. *US* has acquired an indirect interest of 60% in *FP*. See sections 6038(e)(3)(C) and 267(c)(1). However, *US* is not required to report the January 1, 2001 indirect acquisition under section 6046A. *US* did not own a 10% or greater direct interest in *FP* before the acquisition, and *US* does not own a 10% or greater direct interest as a result of the acquisition. (*US* must, however, comply with the reporting requirements under section 6038 (controlled foreign corporation and controlled foreign partnership reporting) with respect to *FC2* and *FP*.)

Example 2. Acquisition of direct interests. (i) Assume the same facts as *Example 1*. In addition, on June 1, 2001, *US* purchases a 5% direct interest in *FP* from *FC1*. *US* did not own a 10% or greater direct interest in *FP* before the acquisition. After the acquisition, *US* does not own a direct interest of 10% or more. *US* owns a 10% or greater total interest (direct and indirect), but only a 5% direct interest. Therefore, *US* is not required to report the June 1, 2001, acquisition under section 6046A.

(ii) On September 1, 2001, *US* purchases a 7% direct interest in *FP* from *FC1*. The September 1, 2001 acquisition constitutes a reportable event under paragraph (b)(1)(i)(A) of this section. Before the September 1 acquisition, *US* did not own a 10% or greater direct interest in *FP*. After the September 1 acquisition, *US* owns a 12% direct interest, and therefore, as a result of the September 1 acquisition, *US* now owns a 10% or greater direct interest in *FP*. Consequently, *US* must report its September 1 acquisition under section 6046A on Form 8865 filed with *US*'s 2001 income tax return.

(iii) On December 1, 2001, *US* acquires an additional 4% direct interest in *FP* from *FC1*, so that *US*'s total direct interest has increased from 12% to 16%. This acquisition does not constitute a reportable event. Compared to *US*'s direct interest when *US* last had a reportable event (12% on September 1, 2001), after acquiring the 4% interest *US*'s direct interest has not increased by at least a 10% direct interest (i.e., its direct inter-

Reg. §1.6046A-1(b)(1)(i)(B)

est increased by only 4%). Therefore, *US* does not have to report the December 1, 2001, acquisition under section 6046A. On April 1, 2002, *FC2* distributes a 6% direct interest in *FP* to *US*. *US* now owns a 22% direct interest in *FP*. Compared to *US*'s direct interest when *US* last had a reportable event (12% on September 1, 2001), after the April 1 acquisition *US*'s direct interest has increased by at least a 10% interest (12% to 22%). *US* must report the April 1, 2002 acquisition on a Form 8865 attached to *US*'s 2002 income tax return.

Example 3. Change in proportional interest resulting from withdrawal of a partner. Assume the same facts as *Example 3*. In addition, on January 5, 2003, *FC2* withdraws entirely from *FP*. As a result, the direct interests of *US* and *FC1* in *FP* each increase by at least the equivalent of 10% interests. Compared to *US*'s direct interest the last time *US* had a reportable event (22% on April 1, 2002), *US*'s direct interest has increased by at least the equivalent of a ten percent interest. Therefore, *US* has had a reportable event pursuant to paragraph (b)(1)(iii) of this section, and *US* must report the change in its interest resulting from *FC2*'s withdrawal from the partnership on *US*'s Form 8865 filed with *US*'s 2003 tax year income tax return.

Example 4. Change in proportional interest constituting an acquisition. FP is a foreign partnership that has no United States persons as direct or constructive partners. *US* is a United States person and a calendar year taxpayer. On January 1, 2001, *US* purchases an 8% direct interest in *FP*. *US* is not required to report this acquisition. *US* did not own a 10% or greater direct interest in *FP*, and *US* does not own a 10% or greater direct interest as a result of the acquisition. On March 1, 2001, *FC*, a foreign partner of *FP*, withdraws from *FP*, and as result, *US*'s direct interest in *FP* increases by a 7% interest. The increase in *US*'s direct interest is considered an acquisition of an interest under paragraph (b)(1)(i)(A) of this section. *US* did not own a 10% or greater direct interest in *FP* before *FC* withdrew, and as a result of the increase in *US*'s direct interest because of *FC*'s withdrawal from *FP*, *US* now owns a 10% or greater direct interest in *FP*. Therefore, *US* must report under section 6046A the increase in *US*'s direct interest resulting from the withdrawal of *FC* from *FP* on Form 8865 filed with *US*'s tax return for *US*'s 2001 tax year.

(c) *Content of return.*—The Form 8865 that must be filed under paragraph (a)(1) of this section must contain the following information in such form and manner and to the extent that Form 8865 and its instructions prescribe—

(1) The name, address, and taxpayer identification number of the United States person required to file the return;

(2) Information about other persons (foreign or domestic) whose interests in the foreign partnership the person reporting under section 6046A is considered to own under section 6038(e)(3)(C) and section 267(c);

(3) Information about all foreign entities that were disregarded as entities separate from their owners under "301.7701-2 and 301.7701-3 of this chapter that were owned by the foreign partnership during the partnership's tax year ending with or within the tax year of the person filing Form 8865 pursuant to section 6046A;

(4) For each reportable event, the date of the event, the type of event (acquisition, disposition, or change in proportional interest), and the United States person's direct percentage interest in the foreign partnership immediately before and immediately after the event;

(5) The fair market value of the interest acquired or disposed of;

(6) Information about partnerships (foreign and domestic) in which the foreign partnership owned a direct interest, or a constructive interest of ten percent or more under sections section 267(c)(1) and (5) and the regulations thereunder, during the partnership's tax year ending with or within the tax year of the person filing Form 8865 pursuant to section 6046A; and

(7) Any other information required to be submitted by Form 8865 and its instructions.

(d) *Time and manner for filing returns.*—The Form 8865 must be filed with the timely filed (including extensions) income tax return of the United States person for the tax year in which the reportable event occurs. If the United States person is not required to file an income tax return for its tax year in which the reportable event occurs, but is required to file an information return for that year (for example, Form 1065, "U.S. Partnership Return of Income," or Form 990, "Return of Organization Exempt from Income Tax"), the United States person should attach the Form 8865 to its information return filed for that tax year.

(e) *Duplicate returns.*—If required by the instructions to Form 8865, a duplicate Form 8865 (including attachments and schedules) must also be filed.

(f) *Persons excepted from filing return.*—(1) *Section 6038B overlap.*—If a United States person acquires an interest in a foreign partnership as a result of a section 721 contribution required to be reported under section 6038B, and the person properly reports the contribution under section 6038B, then the United States person is not required to report the acquisition of the partnership interest under section 6046A(a) should it constitute a reportable event under paragraph (b)(1) of this section. The acquisition will still constitute a reportable event for purposes of making future comparisons pursuant to paragraphs (b)(1)(i)(B), (b)(1)(ii)(B) and (b)(1)(iii) of this section. A person that fails to properly report the section 721 contribution under section 6038B and the regulations thereunder and that fails to properly report the acquisition of the partnership interest under section 6046A may be subject to the penalties applicable to a failure to comply with the requirements of section 6038B, as well as the penalties applicable for a failure to comply with the requirements of section 6046A. See paragraph (h) of this section for more information about the penalties for failure to comply with the requirements of section 6046A.

(2) *Trusts relating to state and local government employee retirement plans.*—The return requirement of section 6046A does not apply to trusts relating to state and local government employee retirement plans, unless the instructions to Form 8865 provide otherwise.

(3) *Reporting under this section not required of partnerships excluded from the application of subchapter K.*—The reporting requirements of this section will not apply to any United States person in respect of an eligible partnership as described in § 1.761-2(a) in which that United States person is a partner, if such partnership has validly elected to be excluded from all of the provisions of subchapter K of chapter 1 of the Internal Revenue Code in the manner specified in § 1.761-2(b)(2)(i), or is deemed to have elected to be excluded from all of the provisions of subchapter K of chapter 1 of the Internal Revenue Code in accordance with the provisions of § 1.761-2(b)(2)(ii).

(4) *Exclusion for satellite organizations.*—The return requirement of section 6046A does not apply to the International Telecommunications Satellite Organization (or a successor organization) or the International Maritime Satellite Organization (or a successor organization).

(g) *Method of reporting.*—Except as otherwise provided on Form 8865, or the accompanying instructions, any amounts required to be reported under section 6046A and this section must be expressed in United States dollars, with a statement of the exchange rates used. All statements required on or with Form 8865 pursuant to this section must be in English.

(h) *Penalties for violating section 6046A.*—For penalties for violating section 6046A, see sections 6679 and 7203.

(i) *Statute of limitations.*—For exceptions to the limitations on assessment in the event of a failure to provide information under section 6046A, see section 6501(c)(8).

(j) *Effective date.*—This section applies to reportable events occurring after December 31, 1999. No reporting under section 6046A is required for reportable events occurring on or before December 31, 1999. [Reg. § 1.6046A-1.]

☐ [T.D. 8851, 12-27-99.]

[Reg. § 1.6047-1]

§ 1.6047-1. Information to be furnished with regard to employee retirement plan covering an owner-employee.—(a) *Trustees and insurance companies.*—(1) *Requirement of return.*—(i) Every trustee of a trust described in section 401(a) and exempt from tax under section 501(a) which makes payments of amounts described in subparagraph (2) of this paragraph aggregating $10 or more during any calendar year to an individ-

ual(or his beneficiary) who was covered, within the meaning of paragraph (a)(2) of § 1.401-10, as an owner-employee under the plan of which such trust is a part shall make a return on Forms 1096 and 1099 for such year showing the name and address of the person to whom paid, the aggregate amount of such payments, specifically identified as an amount to which this paragraph applies, and such other information as is required by the forms. A separate Form 1099 shall be filed with respect to each payee. The term "owner-employee" means an owner-employee as defined in section 401(c)(3) and paragraph (d) of § 1.401-10. Any custodial account which satisfies the requirements of section 401(f) shall be treated as a qualified trust and the custodian of such a custodial account must comply with the requirements of this section as if he were the trustee.

(ii) Every issuer of a contract which is treated as an annuity contract under sections 401 through 404 purchased by a trust described in section 401(a) and exempt from tax under section 501(a) or under a plan described in section 403(a) which makes payments of amounts described in subparagraph (2) of this paragraph aggregating $10 or more during any calendar year to an individual (or his beneficiary) who was covered, within the meaning of paragraph (a)(2) of § 1.401-10, as an owner-employee under the plan of which such trust is a part or under which such contract was purchased shall make a return on Forms 1096 and 1099 for such year showing the name and address of the person to whom paid, the aggregate amount of such payments, specifically identified as an amount to which this paragraph applies, and such other information as is required by the form. A separate Form 1099 shall be filed with respect to each payee.

(2) *Amounts subject to this section.*—The amounts subject to reporting under subparagraph (1) of this paragraph include all amounts distributed or made available to which section 402(a) (relating to employees' trusts) or section 403(a) (relating to employee annuity plans) applies, whether or not such amounts are includible in gross income and whether or not attributable to contributions made while the individual to whom they relate was an owner-employee. However, amounts subject to reporting do not include any amounts distributed or made available by the trustee of any trust or the issuer of any contract under any plan with respect to which he has not received the notification provided in either subparagraph (3) of this paragraph or paragraph (b) of this section. Amounts distributed or made available under the plan include, for example, amounts received by the individual as loans on contracts purchased under the plan, and payments made to the individual by reason of the surrender of contracts purchased under the plan, whether or not prior to their maturity.

(3) *Notification by trustee.*—The trustee of any trust described in section 401(a) and exempt from tax under section 501(a) who receives noti-

fication from any owner-employee that contributions have been made to the trust on behalf of that owner-employee as an owner-employee shall notify in writing the issuer of any contract which is treated as an annuity contract under sections 401 through 404 purchased by the trust for the benefit of that owner-employee that such contributions have been made to such trust. Such notification shall be delivered to such issuer at the time such contract is purchased or within 90 days after the notification required by paragraph (b) of this section is received by the trustee, whichever is later. Only one such notification must be made with respect to any contract.

(4) *Record keeping.*—Any trustee, insurance company, or other person, which is referred to in subparagraph (1) of this paragraph and which is notified under section 6047(b) that contributions to the trust or under the plan have been made on behalf of an owner-employee shall maintain a record of such notification until all funds of the trust or under the plan on behalf of the owner-employee have been distributed.

(5) *Inclusion of other payments.*—The Form 1099 filed under this section by any person with respect to payments to another person during a calendar year may, at the election of the maker, include other payments made by him to such other person during such year which are required to be reported on Form 1099.

(6) *Time and place for filing.*—The return required under this section for any calendar year shall be filed after the close of that year and on or before February 28 (March 31 if filed electronically) of the following year with any of the Internal Revenue Service Centers, the addresses of which are listed in the instructions for Form 1096. For extensions of time for filing returns under this section, see § 1.6081-1.

(b) *Notification by owner-employee.*—Any owner-employee on behalf of whom contributions are made to a trust described in section 401(a) and exempt under section 501(a) or under a plan described in section 403(a) shall notify in writing—

(1) The trustee of such a trust, or

(2) The issuer of any contract which is treated as an annuity contract under sections 401 through 404 under such plan,

that such contributions have been made to such trust or plan. Such notification shall be delivered to such trustee or such issuer during the first calendar year in which such contributions are made or on or before February 28 of the year following such year. Only one such notification must be made with respect to any contract or any trust.

(c) *Penalties.*—For civil penalty for failure to file a return required by this section, and for criminal penalty for furnishing fraudulent information under this section, see §§ 301.6652-3 and 301.7207-1, respectively.

(d) *Permission to submit information required by Form 1099 on magnetic tape.*—For rules relating to

permission to submit the information required by Form 1099 on magnetic tape or other media, see § 1.9101-1. [Reg. § 1.6047-1.]

☐ [*T.D.* 6677, 9-16-63. *Amended by T.D.* 6883, 5-2-66; *T.D.* 7551, 7-3-78 *and T.D.* 8895, 8-17-2000.]

[Reg. § 301.6047-1]

§ 301.6047-1. Information relating to certain trusts and annuity and bond purchase plans.—For provisions relating to the requirement of returns of information regarding certain trusts and annuity and bond purchase plans, see § 1.6047-1 of this chapter (Income Tax Regulations). [Reg. § 301.6047-1.]

☐ [*T.D.* 6700, 1-6-64.]

[Reg. § 1.6047-2]

§ 1.6047-2. Information relating to qualifying longevity annuity contracts.—(a) *Requirement and form of report.*—(1) *In general.*—Any person issuing any contract that is intended to be a qualifying longevity annuity contract (QLAC), defined in A-17 of § 1.401(a)(9)-6, shall make the report required by this section. This requirement applies only to contracts purchased or held under any plan, annuity, or account described in section 401(a), 403(a), 403(b), or 408 (other than a Roth IRA) or eligible governmental plan under section 457(b).

(2) *Annual report.*—The issuer shall make annual calendar-year reports on the applicable form prescribed by the Commissioner for this purpose concerning the status of the contract. The report shall identify that the contract is intended to be a QLAC and shall contain the following information—

(i) The name, address, and identifying number of the issuer of the contract, along with information on how to contact the issuer for more information about the contract;

(ii) The name, address, and identifying number of the individual in whose name the contract has been purchased;

(iii) If the contract was purchased under a plan, the name of the plan, the plan number, and the Employer Identification Number (EIN) of the plan sponsor;

(iv) If payments have not yet commenced, the annuity starting date on which the annuity is scheduled to commence, the amount of the periodic annuity payable on that date, and whether that date may be accelerated;

(v) For the calendar year, the amount of each premium paid for the contract and the date of the premium payment;

(vi) The total amount of all premiums paid for the contract through the end of the calendar year;

(vii) The fair market value of the QLAC as of the close of the calendar year; and

(viii) Such other information as the Commissioner may require.

(b) *Manner and time for filing.*—(1) *Timing.*—The report required by paragraph (a)(2) of this section shall be filed in accordance with the forms and instructions prescribed by the Commissioner. Such a report must be filed for each calendar year beginning with the year in which premiums for a contract are first paid and ending with the earlier of the year in which the individual in whose name the contract has been purchased attains age 85 (as adjusted pursuant to A-17(d)(2)(ii) of § 1.401(a)(9)-6) or dies.

(2) *Surviving spouse.*—If the individual dies and the sole beneficiary under the contract is the individual's spouse (in which case the spouse's annuity would not be required to commence until the individual would have commenced benefits under the contract had the individual survived), the report must continue to be filed for each calendar year until the calendar year in which the distributions to the spouse commence or in which the spouse dies, if earlier.

(c) *Issuer statements.*—Each issuer required to file the annual report required by paragraph (a)(2) of this section shall furnish to the individual in whose name the contract has been purchased a statement containing the information required to be included in the report, except that such statement shall be furnished to a surviving spouse to the extent that the report is required to be filed under paragraph (b)(2) of this section. A copy of the required form may be used to satisfy the statement requirement of this paragraph (c). If a copy of the required form is not used to satisfy the statement requirement of this paragraph (c), the statement shall contain the following language: "This information is being furnished to the Internal Revenue Service." The statement required by this paragraph (c) shall be furnished on or before January 31 following the calendar year for which the report required by paragraph (a)(2) of this section is required.

(d) *Penalty for failure to file report.*—Section 6652(e) prescribes a penalty for failure to file the report required by paragraph (a)(2) of this section.

(e) *Effective/applicability date.*—This section applies to contracts purchased on or after July 2, 2014. [Reg. § 1.6047–2.]

□ [*T.D.* 9673, 7-1-2014.]

[Reg. § 16.3-1]

§ 16.3-1. **Returns as to the creation of or transfers to certain foreign trusts (Temporary).**—(a) *Requirement of return.*—Every United States person who, on or after October 16, 1962, either creates a foreign trust or transfers money or property to a foreign trust, directly or indirectly, shall file an information return on Form 3520, except as provided in subparagraph (4) of paragraph(d) of this section. The return must be filed by the grantor or the transferor, or the fiduciary of the estate in the case of a testamentary trust. The return must be filed whether or not any beneficiary is a United States person and whether or not the grantor or any other person may be treated as the substantial owner of any portion of the trust under sections 671-678.

(b) *Meaning of terms.*—For purposes of this section the following terms shall have the meaning assigned to them in this paragraph:

(1) *Foreign trust.*—See section 7701(a)(31) of the Code for the definition of foreign trust.

(2) *United States person.*—See section 7701(a)(30) of the Code for the definition of United States person.

(3) *Grantor.*—The term "grantor" refers to any United States person who by an inter vivos declaration or agreement creates a foreign trust.

(4) *Transferor.*—The term "transferor" refers to any United States person, other than a person who is the grantor or the fiduciary (as defined in subparagraph (5) of this paragraph), who transfers money or property to or for the benefit of a foreign trust. It does not refer to a person who transfers money or property to a foreign trust pursuant to a sale or an exchange which is made for full and adequate consideration.

(5) *Fiduciary of an estate.*—In the case of a testamentary trust expressed in the will of a decedent the term "fiduciary of an estate" refers to the executor or administrator who is responsible for establishing a foreign trust on behalf of the decedent.

(c) *Information required.*—The return required by section 6048 and this section shall be made on Form 3520 and shall set forth the following information:

(1) The name, address, and identifying number of the person (or persons) filing the return, a statement identifying each person named as either a grantor, fiduciary of an estate, or transferor, and the date of the transaction for which the return is being filed;

(2) In the case of a fiduciary of an estate, the name and identifying number of the decedent;

(3) The name of the trust and the name of the country under whose laws the foreign trust was created;

(4) The date the foreign trust was created and the name and address of the person (or persons) who created it;

(5) The date on which the trust is to terminate or a statement describing the conditions which will cause the trust to terminate;

(6) The name and business address of the foreign trustee (or trustees);

(7) A statement either that the trustee is required to distribute all of the trust's income currently (in which case the information required in subparagraph (9) of this paragraph need not be furnished) or a statement that the trust may accumulate some or all of its income;

(8) The name, address, and identifying number, if any, of each beneficiary who is either named in the instrument or whose identity is definitely ascertainable at the time the return required by this section is filed, and the date of birth for each beneficiary who is a United States person and whose rights under the trust are

determined, in whole or in part, by reference to the beneficiary's age;

(9) Except as provided in subparagraph (7) of this paragraph, a statement with respect to each beneficiary setting forth his right to receive income or corpus, or both, from the trust, his proportionate interest, if any, in the income or corpus, or both, of the trust, and any condition governing the time when a distribution to him may be made, such as a specific date or age (or in lieu of such statement a copy of the trust instrument which must be attached to the return);

(10) A detailed list of the property transferred to the foreign trust in the transaction for which the return is being filed, containing a complete description of each item transferred, its adjusted basis and its fair market value on the date transferred, and the consideration, if any, paid by the foreign trust for such transfer; and

(11) The name and address of the person (or persons) having custody of the books of account and records of the foreign trust, and the location of such books and records if different from such address.

(d) *Special provisions.*—(1) *Separate return for each foreign trust and each transfer.*—If a United States person creates more than one foreign trust or transfers money or property to more than one foreign trust, then separate returns must be filed with respect to each foreign trust where returns are required under section 6048 and this section. If a United States person transfers money or property to the same foreign trust at different times, then separate returns must be filed with respect to each transfer where returns are required under section 6048 and this section. However, where more than one transfer to the same foreign trust is made by a United States person during any 90-day period, such person may, at his election, file a single return, so long as the return includes the information required with respect to each transfer and is filed on or before the 90th day after the earliest transfer in any such period.

(2) *Joint returns.*—Where returns are required under section 6048 and this section by two or more persons who either jointly create a foreign trust or jointly transfer money or property to a foreign trust, they may jointly execute and file one return in lieu of filing several returns.

(3) *Actual ownership of money or property transferred.*—If any person referred to in this section is not the real party in interest as to the money or property transferred but is merely acting for a United States person, the information required under this section shall be furnished in the name of and by the actual owner of such money or property, except that a fiduciary of an estate shall file information relating to the decedent.

(4) *Payments to an employees' trust, etc.*—In the case of contributions made to a foreign trust

under a plan which provides pension, profit-sharing, stock bonus, sickness, accident, unemployment, welfare, or similar benefits or a combination of such benefits for employees, neither employers nor employees shall be required to file a return as set forth in this section.

(e) *Time and place for filing return.*—(1) *Time for filing.*—Any return required by section 6048 and this section shall be filed on or before the 90th day after either the creation of any foreign trust by a United States person or the transfer of any money or property to a foreign trust by a United States person. The Director of International Operations is authorized to grant reasonable extensions of time to file returns under section 6048 and this section in accordance with the applicable provisions of section 6081(a) and § 1.6081-1.

(2) *Place for filing.*—Returns required by section 6048 and this section shall be filed with the Director of International Operations, Internal Revenue Service, Washington 25, D.C.

(f) *Penalties.*—(1) *Criminal.*—For criminal penalties for failure to file a return see section 7203. For criminal penalties for filing a false or fraudulent return, see sections 7206 and 7207.

(2) *Civil.*—For civil penalty for failure to file a return or failure to show the information required on a return under this section, see section 6677. [Temporary Reg. § 16.3-1.]

☐ [T.D. 6632, 1-9-63.]

[Reg. § 301.6048-1]

§ 301.6048-1. Returns as to creation of or transfers to certain foreign trusts.—For provisions relating to the requirement of returns as to creation of or transfers to certain foreign trusts, see § 16.3-1 of this chapter (Temporary Regulations under the Revenue Act of 1962). [Reg. § 301.6048-1.]

☐ [T.D. 6700, 1-6-64.]

[Reg. § 404.6048-1]

§ 404.6048-1. Annual returns for foreign trusts with a United States beneficiary (Temporary).—(a) *Return required.*—(1) *In general.*—Each taxpayer subject to tax under section 679 with respect to a foreign trust having one or more United States beneficiaries must file Form 3520-A, Annual Return of Foreign Trust with U.S. Beneficiaries, together with any additional schedules or other information required by the form or the instructions to the form. Form 3520-A must be filed even if the taxpayer is treated as the owner of a foreign trust under both section 679 and some other provision of subpart E of Part I of Subchapter J.

(2) *Joint returns.*—If the taxpayer's spouse is also subject to tax under section 679 with respect to the same foreign trust for the same taxable year, and if both taxpayer and spouse file a joint return of income tax for that year, a single Form 3520-A may be filed jointly with respect to such trust for the year.

(b) *Period covered by return.*—The period covered by the return required by this section is the taxable year of the taxpayer required to file the return, regardless of the period used by the trust for accounting or any other purpose.

(c) *Time for filing.*—(1) *In general.*—The return required by this section must be filed no later than the 15th day of the fourth month following the end of the taxable period covered by the return.

(2) *Transitional rule.*—In the case of a return required by this section for a taxable period ending on or before June 30, 1977, the return must be filed no later than—

(i) October 15, 1977, in the case of a taxpayer treated as an owner with respect to the trust under both section 679 and a provision of sections 672 through 678, or

(ii) December 31, 1977, in all other cases.

(3) *Extensions of time for filing.*—For rules relating to extensions of time for filing, see section 6081 and the regulations thereunder.

(d) *Place for filing.*—The return required by this section must be filed with the Director, Internal Revenue Service Center, 11601 Roosevelt Boulevard, Philadelphia, Pennsylvania, 19155.

(e) *Effective date.*—This section is effective for taxable periods ending on or after December 31, 1976. [Temporary Reg. § 404.6048-1.]

☐ [*T.D.* 7502, 8-18-77.]

[Reg. § 1.6049-1]

§ 1.6049-1. Returns of information as to interest paid in calendar years before 1983 and original issue discount includible in gross income for calendar years before 1983.—(a) *Requirement of reporting.*—(1) *In general.*—(i) Every person who makes payments of interest (as defined in § 1.6049-2) aggregating $10 or more to any other person during a calendar year before 1983 shall make an information return on Forms 1096 and 1099 for such calendar year showing the aggregate amount of such payments, the name and address of the person to whom paid, the total of such payments for all persons, and such other information as is required by the forms. In the case of interest paid during calendar years beginning with 1963 and continuing until such time as the Commissioner determines that it is feasible to aggregate payments on two or more accounts, insurance contracts, or investment certificates, and this subdivision is amended accordingly to provide for reporting on an aggregate basis, the requirement of this subdivision for the filing of Form 1099 will be met if a person making payments of interest to another person on two or more such accounts, insurance contracts, or investment certificates files a separate Form 1099 with respect to each such account, contract, or certificate on which $10 or more of interest is paid to such other person during the calendar year. In the case of evidences of indebtedness described in section 6049(b)(1)(A), separate Forms 1099 may be filed as provided in the

preceding sentence with respect to holdings in different issues. Thus, if a bank pays to a person interest totaling $15 on one account and $20 on a second account, it may file separate Forms 1099 with respect to the payments of $15 and $20. If the interest on the second account totaled $5 instead of $20, no return would be required with respect to the $5.

(ii)(a) Every person which is a corporation that has outstanding any bond, debenture, note, or certificate or other evidence of indebtedness (referred to in this section and § 1.6049-2 as an obligation) in "registered form" (as defined in paragraph (d) of § 1.6049-2) issued after May 27, 1969 (other than an obligation issued by a corporation pursuant to a written commitment which was binding on May 27, 1969, and at all times thereafter) and on or before December 31, 1982, as to which there is during any calendar year before 1983 an amount of original issue discount (as defined in § 1.6049-2) aggregating $10 or more includible as interest in the gross income for such calendar year of any holder (determined, if semiannual record date reporting is being used under (b)(1) of this subdivision, by treating each holder as holding the obligation on every day it was outstanding during the calendar year), shall make an information return on Forms 1096 and 1099-OID for such calendar year showing the following:

(1) The name and address of each record holder for whom such aggregate amount of original issue discount is $10 or more and, for calendar years subsequent to 1972, the account, serial, or other identifying number of each obligation for which a return is being made.

(2) The aggregate amount of original issue discount includible by each such holder for the period during the calendar year for which the return is made (or, if the aggregation rules of (b)(2) of this subdivision are being used, that he held the obligations). If, however, the semiannual record date reporting rules are being used under (b)(1) of this subdivision, such aggregate amount shall be determined by treating each such record date holder as if he held each such obligation on every day it was outstanding during the calendar year. For purposes of this section, an obligation shall be considered to be outstanding from the date of original issue (as defined in paragraph (b)(3) of § 1.1232-3). In the case of a time deposit open account arrangement to which paragraph (e)(5) of § 1.1232-3A applies, for example, the amount to be shown under this subdivision (2) on the Forms 1096 and 1099-OID is the sum (computed under such paragraph (e)(5)) of the amounts separately computed for each deposit made pursuant to the arrangement.

(3) The issue price of the obligation (as defined in paragraph (b)(2) of § 1.1232-3).

(4) The stated redemption price of the obligation at maturity (as defined in paragraph (b)(1)(iii) of § 1.1232-3).

(5) The ratable monthly portion of original issue discount with respect to the obligation as defined in section 1232(a)(3)(A) (deter-

mined without regard to a reduction for a purchase allowance or whether the holder purchased at a premium).

(6) The name and address of the person filing the form.

(7) Such other information as is required by the form.
And

(8) The sum, for all such holders of the aggregate amounts of such original issue discount includible for such calendar year for each such holder.

(b) With respect to any obligation (other than an obligation to which paragraph (e) or (f) of §1.1232-3A applies (relating respectively to deposits in banks and similar financial institutions and to face-amount certificates), the issuing corporation (or an agent acting on its behalf):

(1) Shall be permitted (until this subdivision (1) is amended) to prepare a Form 1099-OID only for each person who is a holder of record of the obligation on the semiannual record date (if any) used by the corporation (or agent) for the payment of stated interest or, if there is no such date, the semiannual record dates shall be considered to be June 30, and December 31.

(2) Shall be permitted to aggregate all original issue discount with respect to 2 or more obligations of the same issue for which the amounts specified in (a) (2), (a)(3), (a)(4), and (a)(5) of this subdivision are proportional and, therefore, may file one Form 1099-OID for all such obligations being aggregated, except that for calendar year 1971 this aggregation rule shall apply only where such specified amounts are identical. For an illustration of proportional aggregation, see example (4) in (d) of this subdivision.

(c) In any case in which any one holder of a particular obligation for the calendar year held such obligation on more than one record date, only one Form 1099-OID shall be filed for that year with respect to that holder and that obligation. This provision applies only in the case in which any corporation prepares Forms 1099-OID in accordance with the record date reporting rule of (b)(1) of this subdivision.

(d) The requirements of (a)(3), (a)(4) and (a)(5) of this subdivision shall not apply to a time deposit open account arrangement to which paragraph (e)(5) of §1.1232-3A applies, or to a face-amount certificate to which paragraph (f) of §1.1232-3A applies.

(e) The provisions of this subdivision (ii) may be illustrated by the following examples:

Example (1). On January 1, 1971, a corporation issued a 10-year bond in registered form which pays stated interest to the holder of record on June 30 and December 31. The bond has an issue price (as defined in paragraph (b)(2) of §1.1232-3) of $7,600, a stated redemption price (as defined in paragraph (b)(1) of §1.1232-3) at maturity of $10,000, and a ratable monthly portion of original issue discount (as defined in section 1232(a)(3)(A)) of $20. The corporation's

books indicate that A was the holder of record on June 30, 1971, and B was the holder on December 31, 1971. Under (b)(1) of this subdivision, the corporation is permitted to file separate Forms 1099-OID for both A and B showing, on each form, all items required by (a) of this subdivision, including the total original issue discount of $240 for the entire calendar year (which includes original issue discount for all holders), the issue price of $7,600, the stated redemption price at maturity of $10,000, and the ratable monthly portion of original issue discount of $20.

Example (2). Assume the facts stated in Example (1), except that A is recorded on the books of the corporation as holding the bond on June 30 and December 31, 1971. The corporation shall complete and file only one Form 1099-OID for A.

Example (3). Assume the facts stated in Example (1), except that the books of the corporation show that A held 2 of the bonds at all times in 1971. The amounts of the items listed in (a)(2), (a)(3), (a)(4), and (a)(5) of this subdivision are identical for the 2 bonds. Under (b)(2) of this subdivision, the corporation is permitted to treat the 2 bonds as one for purposes of completing and filing a Form 1099-OID for 1971 and aggregate the amounts being reported.

Example (4). On January 1, 1972, a corporation issued to C 3 bonds in registered form of the same issue with stated redemption prices of $1,000, $5,000, and $10,000. The aggregate amounts of original issue discount for each year, the issue prices, the stated redemption prices, and the monthly portions of original issue discount are the same for each $1,000 of stated redemption price. Thus, all relevant amounts for any one bond are proportional to such amounts for any other bond. Therefore, so long as C holds the bonds the corporation shall be permitted to aggregate on one Form 1099-OID all original issue discount with respect to such obligations in accordance with (b)(2) of this subdivision.

Example (5). On June 1, 1971, a corporation issues a 10-year bond to D, for which the ratable monthly portion of original issue discount is $10. For 1971, the corporation uses the record date reporting system permitted by (b)(1) of this subdivision. The corporation's books show that E held the bond on June 30, 1971, and that F held the bond on December 31, 1971, the dates on which the corporation pays stated interest on the bond. The corporation shall file a Form 1099-OID for both E and F showing on each form the aggregate amount of original issue discount includible for 1971 of $70 since E and F are each treated as if each held the bond every day it was outstanding and it was outstanding 7 months in 1971. As to D, the corporation is not required to file a Form 1099-OID since D did not hold the bond on either of the 2 record dates.

(iii) Every person who during a calendar year before 1983 receives payments of interest as a nominee on behalf of another person aggregating $10 or more shall make an information return on Forms 1096 and 1087 for such calendar year showing the aggregate amount of such interest, the name and address of the person on whose behalf received, the total of such interest received on behalf of all persons, and such other information as is required by the forms.

(iv) Except with respect to an obligation to which paragraph (e) or (f) of §1.1232-3A applies (relating respectively to deposits in banks and similar financial institutions and to face-amount certificates), every person who is a nominee on behalf of the actual owner of an obligation as to which there is original issue discount aggregating $10 or more includible in the gross income of such owner during a calendar year after 1970, regardless of whether he receives a Form 1099-OID with respect to such discount, shall make an information return on Forms 1096 and 1087-OID for such calendar year showing in the manner prescribed on such forms the same information for the actual owner as is required or permitted in subdivision (ii) of this subparagraph for the record holder.

(v) Notwithstanding the provisions of subdivisions (iii) and (iv) of this subparagraph, the filing of Form 1087 or Form 1087-OID is not required if—

(a) The record owner is required to file a fiduciary return on Form 1041 disclosing the name, address, and identifying number of the actual owner;

(b) The record owner is a nominee of a banking institution or trust company exercising trust powers, and such banking institution or trust company is required to file a fiduciary return on Form 1041 disclosing the name, address, and identifying number of the actual owner; or

(c) The record owner is a banking institution or trust company exercising trust powers, or a nominee thereof, and the actual owner is an organization exempt from taxation under section 501(a) for which such banking institution or trust company files an annual return,

but only if the name, address, and identifying number of the record owner are included on or with the Form 1041 fiduciary return filed for the estate or trust or the annual return filed for the tax exempt organization.

(vi) Every person carrying on the banking business who makes payments of interest to another person (whether or not aggregating $10 or more) during a calendar year with respect to a certificate of deposit issued in bearer form (other than such a certificate issued in an amount of $100,000 or more) shall make an information return on Forms 1096 and 1099-BCD for such calendar year. The preceding sentence applies whether such payments are made during the term of the certificate or at its redemption. The information return required by this subdivision for the calendar year shall show the following:

(a) The name, address, and taxpayer identification number of the person to whom the interest is paid;

(b) The aggregate amount of interest paid to such person during the calendar year with respect to the certificate of deposit;

(c) The name, address, and taxpayer identification number of the person to whom the certificate was originally issued;

(d) The portion of the interest with respect to the certificate reported under (b) that is attributable to the current calendar year; and

(e) Such other information as is required by the form.

The application of this subdivision (vi) may be illustrated by the following examples:

Example (1). On June 1, 1978, X Bank issues a $1,000 bearer certificate of deposit to A. The certificate of deposit is not redeemable until May 31, 1979, and no interest is to be paid on the instrument until its redemption. On September 1, 1978, A transfers the bearer certificate to B and on May 31, 1979, B presents the certificate to X for payment and receives the $1,000 principal amount plus all the accrued interest. Under paragraph (a)(1)(vi) of this section, X is not required to make an information return for 1978 with respect to the bearer certificate of deposit because no interest is actually paid to a holder of the certificate during 1978. X is required to file an information return for 1979 with respect to the certificate, identifying B as the payee of the entire amount of the interest and A as the original purchaser of the certificate. (For rules relating to statements to be made to recipients of interest payments, see §1.6049-3.)

Example (2). On July 1, 1978, Y Bank issues a $5,000 bearer certificate of deposit to C. The certificate of deposit is not redeemable until June 30, 1981, and no interest is to be paid on the instrument until its redemption. C holds the certificate for the entire term and on June 30, 1981, presents it to Y for payment and receives the $5,000 principal amount plus the accrued interest. Under paragraph (a)(1)(vi) of this section, Y is not required to file an information return for calendar years 1978, 1979, or 1980 with respect to this bearer certificate of deposit because no interest is actually paid to C during those calendar years. Y is required to file an information return for 1981 with respect to the certificate identifying C as the payee of the entire amount of the interest and as the original purchaser. (Although Y is not required to file an information return for interest paid on the certificate until its redemption in 1981 C must report as income on his tax returns for 1978, 1979, 1980, and 1981 the ratable portion of such interest includible in income under section 1232.)

(2) *Definitions.*—(i) The term "person" when used in this section does not include the United States, a State, the District of Columbia, a foreign government, a political subdivision of a State or of a foreign government, or an international organization. Therefore interest paid by or to one of these entities need not be reported. Similarly, original issue discount in respect of an obligation issued by or to one of these entities need not be reported.

Reg. §1.6049-1(a)(1)(iv)

(ii) For purposes of this section, a person who receives interest shall be considered to have received it as a nominee if he is not the actual owner of such interest and if he was required under § 1.6109-1 to furnish his identifying number to the payer of the interest (or would have been so required if the total of such interest for the year had been $10 or more), and such number was (or would have been) required to be included on an information return filed by the payer with respect to the interest. However, a person shall not be considered to be a nominee as to any portion of an interest payment which is actually owned by another person whose name is also shown on the information return filed by the payer or nominee with respect to such interest payment. Thus, in the case of a savings account jointly owned by a husband and wife, the husband will not be considered as receiving any portion of the interest on that account as a nominee for his wife if his wife's name is included on the information return filed by the payer with respect to the interest.

(iii) For purposes of this section, in the case of a person who receives a Form 1099-OID, the determination of who is considered a nominee shall be made in a manner consistent with the principles of subdivision (ii) of this subparagraph.

(iv) For purposes of this section and § 1.6049-3, the term "Form 1099-OID" means the appropriate Form 1099 for original issue discount prescribed for the calendar year.

(3) *Determination of person to whom interest is paid or for whom it is received.*—For purposes of applying the provisions of this section, the person whose identifying number is required to be included by the payer of interest on an information return with respect to such interest shall be considered the person to whom the interest is paid. In the case of interest received by a nominee on behalf of another person, the person whose identifying number is required to be included on an information return made by the nominee with respect to such interest shall be considered the person on whose behalf such interest is received by the nominee. Thus, in the case of interest made payable to a person other than the record owner of the obligation with respect to which the interest is paid, the record owner of the obligation shall be considered the person to whom the interest is paid for purposes of applying the reporting requirements of this section, since his identifying number is required to be included on the information return filed under such section by the payer of the interest. Similarly, if a stockbroker receives interest on a bond held in street name for the joint account of a husband and wife, the interest is considered as received on behalf of the husband since his identifying number should be shown on the information return filed by the nominee under this section. Thus, if the wife has a separate account with the same stockbroker, any interest received by the stockbroker for her separate account should not be aggregated with the interest received for the joint account for purposes of information reporting. For regulations relating to the use of identifying numbers, see § 1.6109-1.

(4) *Determination of person by whom original issue discount is includible or for whom a Form 1099-OID showing original issue discount is received.*—For purposes of applying the provisions of this section, the determination of the person by whom original issue discount is includible or for whom a Form 1099-OID is received shall be made in a manner consistent with the principles of subparagraph (3) of this paragraph.

(5) *Inclusion of other payments.*—The Form 1099 filed by any person with respect to payments of interest to another person during a calendar year prior to 1972 may, at the election of the maker, include payments other than interest made by him to such other person during such year which are required to be reported on Form 1099. Similarly, the Form 1087 filed by a nominee with respect to payments of interest received by him on behalf of any other person during a calendar year prior to 1972 may include payments of dividends received by him on behalf of such person during such year which are required to be reported on Form 1087. However, except as provided in subparagraph (1)(ii)(*b*) of this paragraph, a separate Form 1087-OID or 1099-OID shall be filed for each obligation in respect of which original issue discount is required to be reported for any calendar year before 1983. In addition, any person required to report payments on both Forms 1087, 1087-OID, 1099, and 1099-OID, for any calendar year may use one Form 1096 to summarize and transmit such forms.

(b) *When payment deemed made.*—For purposes of section 6049, interest is deemed to have been paid when it is credited or set apart to a person without any substantial limitation or restriction as to the time or manner of payment or condition upon which payment is to be made, and is made available to him so that it may be drawn at any time, and its receipt brought within his own control and disposition.

(c) *Time and place for filing.*—(1) *Payment of interest.*—The returns required under this section for any calendar year for the payment of interest shall be filed after September 30 of such year, but not before the payer's first payment for the year, and on or before February 28 of the following year with any of the Internal Revenue Service Centers, the addresses of which are listed in the instructions for Form 1096. For extensions of time for filing returns under this section, see § 1.6081-1.

(2) *Original issue discount.*—(i) The returns required under this section for any calendar year for original issue discount shall be filed after December 31 of such year and on or before February 28 of the following year with any of the Internal Revenue Service Centers, the addresses of which are listed in the instructions for Form

Reg. § 1.6049-1(c)(2)(i)

1096. For extensions of time for filing returns under this section, see § 1.6081-1.

(ii) The time for filing returns for the calendar year 1971 required under this section for original issue discount in respect of obligations to which paragraph (e) of § 1.1232-3A applies (relating to deposits in banks and other similar financial institutions) is extended to April 15, 1972.

(d) *Penalty.*—For penalty for failure to file the statements required by this section, see § 301.6652-1 of this chapter (Regulations on Procedure and Administration).

(e) *Permission to submit information required by Form 1087 or 1099 on magnetic tape.*—For rules relating to permission to submit the information required by Form 1087 or 1099 on magnetic tape or other media, see § 1.9101-1. [Reg. § 1.6049-1.]

☐ [*T.D. 6628, 12-27-62. Amended by T.D. 6677, 9-16-63, T.D. 6879, 3-7-66, T.D. 6883, 5-2-66, T.D. 6891, 8-3-66, T.D. 7000, 1-17-69, T.D. 7154, 12-27-71, T.D. 7311, 3-29-74, T.D. 7584, 1-2-79, and T.D. 7881, 3-22-83.*]

[Reg. § 301.6049-1]

§ 301.6049-1. Returns regarding payments of interest.—For provisions relating to the requirement of returns regarding payments of interest, see §§ 1.6049-1 to 1.6049-3, inclusive, of this chapter (Income Tax Regulations). [Reg. § 301.6049-1.]

☐ [*T.D. 6700, 1-6-64.*]

[Reg. § 1.6049-2]

§ 1.6049-2. Interest and original issue discount subject to reporting in calendar years before 1983.—(a) *Interest in general.*—Except as provided in paragraph (b) of this section, the term "interest" when used in this section and §§ 1.6049-1 and 1.6049-3 means:

(1) Interest on evidences of indebtedness issued by a corporation in "registered form" (as defined in paragraph (d) of this section). The phrase "evidences of indebtedness" includes bonds, debentures, notes, certificates and other similar instruments regardless of how denominated. An evidence of indebtedness is in registered form if it is registered as to both principal and interest (or, for purposes of reporting with respect to original issue discount, if it is registered as to principal) and if its transfer must be effected by the surrender of the old instrument and either the reissuance by the corporation of the old instrument to the new holder or the issuance by the corporation of a new instrument to the new holder.

(2) Interest on deposits (except deposits evidenced by negotiable time certificates of deposit issued in an amount of $100,000 or more) paid (or credited) by persons carrying on the banking business. In the case of a certificate of deposit issued in bearer form, the term "interest", as used in the preceding sentence and in paragraph (a)(1)(vi) of § 1.6049-1, has the same meaning as

in § 1.61-7 (regardless of whether taxable to the payee in the year the information return is made).

(3) Amounts, whether or not designated as interest, paid (or credited) by mutual savings banks, savings and loan associations, building and loan associations, cooperative banks, homestead associations, credit unions, or similar organizations in respect of deposits, face amount certificates, investment certificates, or withdrawable or repurchasable shares. Thus, even though amounts paid or credited by such organizations with respect to deposits are designated as "dividends", such amounts are included in the definition of interest for purposes of section 6049.

(4) Interest on amounts held by insurance companies under agreements to pay interest thereon. This includes interest paid by insurance companies with respect to policy "dividend" accumulations (see sections 61 and 451 and the regulations thereunder for rules as to when such interest is considered paid), and interest paid with respect to the proceeds of insurance policies left with the insurer. The so-called "interest element" in the case of annuity or installment payments under life insurance or endowment contracts does not constitute interest for purposes of this section.

(5) Interest on deposits with stockbrokers, bondbrokers, and other persons engaged in the business of dealing in securities.

(b) *Exceptions.*—The term "interest" when used in section 6049 does not include—

(1) Interest on obligations described in section 103(a)(1) or (3), relating to certain governmental obligations.

(2) Any payment by—

(i) A foreign corporation,

(ii) A nonresident alien individual, or

(iii) A partnership composed in whole or in part of nonresident aliens,

if such corporation, individual, or partnership is not engaged in trade or business within the United States and does not have an office or place of business or a fiscal or paying agent in the United States.

(3) Any interest which is subject to withholding under section 1441 or 1442 (relating to withholding of tax on nonresident aliens and foreign corporations, respectively) by the person making the payment, or which would be so subject to withholding but for the provisions of a treaty, or for the fact that under section 861(a)(1) it is not from sources within the United States, or for the fact that withholding is not required by reason of paragraph (a) or (f) of § 1.1441-4.

(4) In the case of a nominee, any interest which he receives and with respect to which he is required to withhold under section 1441 or 1442 or would be so required to withhold but for the provisions of a treaty, or for the fact that under section 861(a)(1) it is not from sources within the United States, or for the fact that withholding is not required by reason of paragraph (a) or (f) of § 1.1441-4.

(5) Any amount on which the person making the payment is required to deduct and withhold a tax under section 1451 (relating to tax-free covenant bonds), or would be so required but for section 1451(d) (relating to benefit of personal exemptions).

(6) Any amount which is subject to reporting as original issue discount.

(c) *Original issue discount.*—(1) *In general.*— The term "original issue discount" when used in this section and §§1.6049-1 and 1.6049-3 means original issue discount subject to the ratable inclusion rules of paragraph (a) of §1.1232-3A, determined without regard to any reduction by reason of a purchase allowance under paragraph (a)(2)(ii) of §1.1232-3A or a purchase at a premium as defined in paragraph (d)(2) of §1.1232-3.

(2) *Coordination with interest reporting.*—In the case of an obligation issued after May 27, 1969 (other than an obligation issued pursuant to a written commitment which was binding on May 27, 1969, and at all times thereafter) and on or before December 31, 1982, original issue discount which is not subject to the reporting requirements of paragraph (a)(1)(ii) of §1.6049-1 is interest within the meaning of paragraph (a) of this section. Original issue discount which is subject to the reporting requirements of paragraph (a)(1)(ii) of §1.6049-1 is not interest within the meaning of paragraph (a) of this section.

(3) *Exceptions.*—Reporting of original issue discount is not required in respect of an obligation which paragraph (b)(2) of this section except from interest reporting.

(d) *Definition of "in registered form.".*—For purposes of §1.6049-1 and this section, an evidence of indebtedness is in registered form if it is registered as to both principal and interest (or, for purposes of reporting with respect to original issue discount, if it is registered as to principal) and if its transfer must be effected by the surrender of the old instrument and either the reissuance by the corporation of the old instrument to the new holder or the issuance by the corporation of a new instrument to the new holder. [Reg. §1.6049-2.]

☐ [*T.D. 6628, 12-27-62. Amended by T.D. 6908, 12-30-66, T.D. 6966, 8-7-68, T.D. 7154, 12-27-71, T.D. 7584, 1-2-79 and T.D. 7881, 3-22-83.*]

[Reg. §1.6049-3]

§1.6049-3. Statements to recipients of interest payments and holders of obligations to which there is attributed original issue discount in calendar years before 1983.— (a) *Requirement.*—Every person filing (1) a Form 1099 or 1087 under section 6049(a)(1) and §1.6049-1 with respect to payments of interest or (2) a Form 1099-OID or 1087-OID with respect to original issue discount includible in gross income, shall furnish to the person whose identifying number is (or should be) shown on the form a written statement showing the information re-

quired by paragraph (b) of this section. With respect to interest, no statement is required to be furnished under section 6049(c) and this section to any person if the aggregate of the payments to (or received on behalf of) such person shown on the form would be less than $10. With respect to original issue discount, no statement is required to be furnished under section 6049(c) and this section to any person if the aggregate amount of original issue discount on the statement to such person with respect to the obligation would be less than $10. References in this section to Form 1099 shall be construed to include Form 1099-BCD except that in applying paragraph (b)(2) of this section no information relating to the person to whom the certificate of deposit was originally issued shall be disclosed to another person to whom the payment of interest is made.

(b) *Form of statement.*—(1) *In general.*—The written statement required to be furnished to a person under paragraph (a) of this section shall show—

(i) With respect to payments of interest (as defined in §1.6049-2) aggregating $10 or more to any person during a calendar year before 1983—

(*a*) The aggregate amount of payments shown on the Form 1099 or 1087 as having been made to (or received on behalf of) such person and a legend stating that such amount is being reported to the Internal Revenue Service, and

(*b*) The name and address of the person filing the form, and

(ii) With respect to original issue discount (as defined in §1.6049-2) which would aggregate $10 or more on the statement to the holder during a calendar year after 1970 and prior to calendar year 1983—

(*a*) The aggregate amount of original issue discount includible by (or on behalf of) such person with respect to the obligation, as shown on Form 1099-OID or Form 1087-OID for such calendar year (determined by applying the rules of paragraph (a)(1)(ii) of §1.6049-1 for purposes of completing either form),

(*b*) All other items shown on such Form 1099-OID or Form 1087-OID for such calendar year (so determined), and

(*c*) A legend stating that such amount and such items are being reported to the Internal Revenue Service.

(2) *Special rule.*—The requirements of this section for the furnishing of a statement to any person, including the legend requirement of this paragraph, may be met by the furnishing to such person of a copy of the Form 1099, 1099-OID, 1087, or 1087-OID filed pursuant to §1.6049-1, or a reasonable facsimile thereof, in respect of such person. However, in the case of Form 1087-OID or 1099-OID, a copy of the instructions must also be sent to such person. A statement shall be considered to be furnished to a person within the meaning of this section if it is mailed to such person at his last known address.

(c) *Time for furnishing statements.*—(1) *In general.*—(i) *Payment of interest.*—Each statement required by this section to be furnished to any person for a calendar year for the payment of interest shall be furnished to such person after November 30 of the year and on or before January 31 of the following year, but no statement may be furnished before the final interest payment for the calendar year has been paid. However, the statement may be furnished at any time after April 30 if it is furnished with the final interest payment for the calendar year.

(ii) *Original issue discount.*—(a) Except as otherwise provided in this subdivision (ii), each statement required by this section to be furnished to any person for a calendar year for original issue discount shall be furnished to such person after December 31 of the year and on or before January 31 of the following year.

(b) The time for furnishing each statement required by this section to be furnished to any person for the calendar year 1971 for original issue discount in respect of obligations to which paragraph (e) of § 1.1232-3A applies (relating to deposits in banks and other similar financial institutions) is extended to March 15, 1972.

(c) The time for furnishing each statement required by this section to be furnished by a nominee to any person for the calendar year 1971 for original issue discount is extended to February 28, 1972.

(2) *Extensions of time.*—For good cause shown upon written application of the person required to furnish statements under this section, the district director may grant an extension of time not exceeding 30 days in which to furnish such statements. The application shall be addressed to the district director with whom the income tax returns of the applicant are filed and shall contain a full recital of the reasons for requesting the extension to aid the district director in determining the period of the extension, if any, which will be granted. Such a request in the form of a letter to the district director signed by the applicant will suffice as an application. The application shall be filed on or before the date prescribed in subparagraph (1) of this paragraph for furnishing the statements required by this section.

(3) *Last day for furnishing statement.*—For provisions relating to the time for performance of an act when the last day prescribed for performance falls on Saturday, Sunday, or a legal holiday, see § 301.7503-1 of this chapter (Regulations on Procedure and Administration).

(d) *Penalty.*—For provisions relating to the penalty provided for failure to furnish a statement under this section, see § 301.6678-1 of this chapter (Regulations on Procedure and Administration). [Reg. § 1.6049-3.]

☐ [*T.D.* 6628, 12-27-62. *Amended by T.D.* 6879, 3-7-66; *T.D.* 7154, 12-27-71; *T.D.* 7584, 1-2-79; *T.D.* 7624, 5-29-79 *and T.D.* 7881, 3-22-83.]

Reg. § 1.6049-3(c)(1)

[Reg. § 1.6049-4]

§ 1.6049-4. Return of information as to interest paid and original issue discount includible in gross income after December 31, 1982.—(a) *Requirement of reporting.*—(1) *In general.*—Except as provided in paragraph (c) of this section, an information return shall be made by a payor, as defined in paragraph (a)(2) of this section, of amounts of interest and original issue discount paid after December 31, 1982. Such return shall contain the information described in paragraph (b) of this section.

(2) *Payor.*—For payments made after December 31, 2002, a payor is a person described in paragraph (a)(2)(i) or (ii) of this section.

(i) Every person who makes a payment of the type and of the amount subject to reporting under this section (or under an applicable section under this chapter) to any other person during a calendar year.

(ii) Every person who collects on behalf of another person payments of the type and of the amount subject to reporting under this section (or under an applicable section under this chapter), or who otherwise acts as a middleman (as defined in paragraph (f)(4) of this section) with respect to such payment.

(b) *Information to be reported.*—(1) *Interest payments.*—Except as provided in paragraphs (b)(3) and (5) of this section, in the case of interest other than original issue discount treated as interest under § 1.6049-5(f), an information return on Form 1099 shall be made for the calendar year showing the aggregate amount of the payments, the name, address, and taxpayer identification number of the person to whom paid, the amount of tax deducted and withheld under section 3406 from the payments, if any, and such other information as required by the forms. An information return is generally not required if the amount of interest paid to a person aggregates less than $10 or if the payment is made to a person who is an exempt recipient described in paragraph (c)(1)(ii) of this section, unless the payor backup withholds under section 3406 on such payment (because, for example, the payee (*i.e.*, exempt recipient) has failed to furnish a Form W-9 on request), in which case the payor must make a return under this section, unless the payor refunds the amount withheld pursuant to § 31.6413(a)-3 (Employment Tax Regulations). For reporting interest paid to certain nonresident alien individuals, see § 1.6049-8.

(2) *Original issue discount.*—Except as provided in paragraph (b)(3) and (b)(5) of this section, in the case of original issue discount, an information return on Forms 1096 and 1099 shall be made for each calendar year of any holder of an obligation as to which there is original issue discount includible in gross income aggregating $10 or more. For calendar years before 1992, semiannual record date reporting under § 1.6049-1(a)(1)(ii)(b)(1) may be used, and if it is used, the original issue discount includible in gross income is determined by treating each

holder as holding the obligation on every day it was outstanding during the calendar year. An information return shall be made, however, in any case in which an amount of tax is required to be deducted and withheld under section 3406. In such case, the amount required to be reported is the amount subject to withholding even if the amount of original issue discount includible in gross income is less than $10. With respect to an obligation described in § 1.1232-3A(e) or (f) (relating respectively to deposits in banks and similar financial institutions and to face-amount certificates), § 1.6049-1(a)(1)(ii)(*d*) and the last sentence of § 1.6049-1(a)(1)(ii)(*a*)(2) shall apply. The information return shall show—

(i) The name, address, and taxpayer identification number of each record holder for whom an amount of original issue discount is includible in gross income;

(ii) The account, serial, or other identifying number of each obligation with respect to which a return is being made;

(iii) The aggregate amount of original issue discount includible in the gross income of each holder for the period during the calendar year for which the return is made (or, if the aggregation rules of § 1.6049-1(a)(1)(ii)(*b*)(2) are being used, the aggregate amount or original issue discount for the period such holder held the obligations). For calendar years before 1992, semiannual record date reporting under § 1.6049-1(a)(1)(ii)(*b*)(1) may be used, and if it is used, the original issue discount includible in gross income is determined by treating each holder as holding the obligation on every day it was outstanding during the calendar year. For purposes of this section, an obligation shall be considered to be outstanding from the date of original issue (as defined in § 1.1232-3(b)(3));

(iv) The amount of tax withheld under section 3406, if any;

(v) The name and address of the person filing the return; and

(vi) Such other information as is required by the forms. Section 1.6049-1(a)(1)(ii)(*b*)(2) and, for calendar years before 1992, § 1.6049-1(a)(1)(ii)(*b*)(1), and (c), apply for purposes of this paragraph.

(3) *Returns made by middleman.*—(i) *In general.*—Except as provided in paragraph (b)(5) of this section, every person acting as a middleman (as defined in paragraph (f)(4) of this section) shall make an information return for the calendar year. In the case of interest payments (other than original issue discount and other than interest described in § 1.6049-8), the information return shall be made on Form 1099 and shall show the aggregate amount of the interest, the name, address, and taxpayer identification number of the person on whose behalf received, the amount of tax withheld under section 3406, if any, and such other information as required by the forms. In the case of original issue discount, the information return shall show the information required to be shown for the person on whose behalf received, as described in paragraph (b)(2)

of this section. See § 1.6049-5(f) to determine whether a middleman is required to make an information return with respect to original issue discount. A middleman shall make an information return regardless of whether the middleman receives a Form 1099. A middleman shall not be required to make an information return if the payment of interest aggregates less than $10 or if the payment is made to an exempt recipient described in paragraph (c)(1)(ii) of this section, unless the payor backup withholds under section 3406 on such payment (because, for example, the payee has failed to furnish a Form W-9 on request), in which case the payor must make a return under this section, unless the payor refunds the amount withheld pursuant to § 31.6413(a)-3 of this chapter (Employment Tax Regulations).

(ii) *Forwarding of interest coupons and original issue discount obligations.*—In the case of a middleman who, from within the United States, forwards an interest coupon or discount obligation on behalf of a payee for presentation, collection or payment outside the United States, the middleman shall make an information return on Form 1099 for the calendar year showing, in the case of an interest coupon, the information required under paragraph (b)(3)(i) of this section and, in the case of a discount obligation, information required under paragraph (b)(2) of this section. For purposes of this paragraph (b)(3)(ii), a middleman is considered to forward an interest coupon or discount obligation on behalf of a payee for presentation, collection or payment outside the United States if the middleman forwards the coupon or obligations outside the United States on or after the date when the payee is entitled to be paid or at an earlier date that is within 90 days of such date or if the middleman has actual knowledge that the coupon or obligation is being forwarded outside the United States for presentation, collection, or payment outside the United States. However, the transfer, although subject to information reporting under this section, is not subject to backup withholding under section 3406.

(iii) *Example.*—The following example illustrates the provisions of paragraph (b)(3)(ii) of this section:

Example. Individual F, who is entitled to payment on an interest coupon, instructs an office of Bank M in the United States to forward the coupon to Bank N for collection by Bank N outside the United States. Bank M in the United States forwards the interest coupon to Bank N outside the United States. Bank M is required to make an information return for the calendar year under paragraph (b)(3)(ii) of this section showing the aggregate amount of the interest coupon forwarded, the name, address of the permanent residence, and the taxpayer identification number, if any, of Individual F and such other information as the form requires.

(4) *Returns made with respect to payments on certificates of deposit issued in bearer form.*—Except

as provided in paragraph (b)(5) of this section, every person carrying on the banking business who makes payments of interest to another person (whether or not aggregating $10 or more) during a calendar year with respect to a certificate of deposit issued in bearer form shall make an information return on Forms 1096 and 1099. The information return shall show the information required in § 1.6049-1(a)(1)(vi)(a) through (e) inclusive and a statement as to amount of tax withheld under section 3406, if any.

(5) *Interest payments to certain nonresident alien individuals.*—(i) *General rule.*—In the case of interest aggregating $10 or more paid to a nonresident alien individual (as defined in section 7701(b)(1)(B)) that is reportable under § 1.6049-8(a), the payor shall make an information return on Form 1042-S, "Foreign Person's U.S. Source Income Subject to Withholding," for the calendar year in which the interest is paid. The payor or middleman shall prepare and file Form 1042-S at the time and in the manner prescribed by section 1461 and the regulations under that section and by the form and its accompanying instructions. See §§ 1.1461-1(b) (rules regarding the preparation of a Form 1042) and §§ 1.6049-6(e)(4) (rules for furnishing a copy of the Form 1042-S to the recipient). To determine whether an information return is required for original issue discount, see §§ 1.6049-5(f) and §§ 1.6049-8(a).

(ii) *Effective/applicability date.*—Paragraph (b)(5)(i) of this section shall be applicable for payments made on or after January 1, 2013. (For interest paid to a Canadian nonresident alien individual on or before December 31, 2012, see paragraph (b)(5) of this section as in effect and contained in 26 CFR part 1 revised April 1, 2000,)

(c) *Information returns not required.*—(1) *Payment to exempt recipient.*—(i) *In general.*—No information return is required with respect to any payment made to an exempt recipient described in paragraph (c)(1)(ii) of this section, except to the extent otherwise provided in § 1.6049-5(d)(3)(ii) and (iii). However, if the payor backup withholds under section 3406 on such payment (because, for example, the payee has failed to furnish a Form W-9 on request), then the payor is required to make a return under this section, unless the payor refunds the amount withheld in accordance with § 31.6413(a)-3 of this chapter (Employment Tax Regulations).

(ii) *Exempt recipient defined.*—The term *exempt recipient* means any person described in paragraphs (c)(1)(ii)(A) through (Q) of this section. An exempt recipient is generally exempt from information reporting without filing a certificate claiming exempt status unless the provisions of this paragraph (c)(1)(ii) require a payee to file a certificate. A payor may, in any case, require a payee that is a U.S. person not otherwise required to file a certificate under this paragraph (c)(1)(ii) to file a certificate in order to qualify as an exempt recipient. See

§ 31.3406(h)-3(a)(1)(iii) and (c)(2) of this chapter for the certificate that a payee that is a U.S. person must provide when a payor requires the certificate to treat the payee as an exempt recipient under this paragraph (c)(1)(ii). A payor may treat a payee as an exempt recipient based upon a properly completed form as described in § 31.3406(h)-3(e)(2) of this chapter, its actual knowledge that the payee is a person described in this paragraph (c)(1)(ii), or the indicators described in this paragraph (c)(1)(ii).

(A) *Corporation.*—A corporation, as defined in section 7701(a)(3), whether domestic or foreign, is an exempt recipient. In addition, for purposes of this paragraph (c)(1), the term *corporation* includes a partnership all of whose members are corporations described in this paragraph (c)(1), but only if the partnership files with the payor a certificate stating that each member of the partnership meets one of the requirements of paragraphs (c)(1)(ii)(A)(1) through (4) of this section. Absent actual knowledge otherwise, a payor may treat a payee as a corporation (and, therefore, as an exempt recipient) if one of the requirements of paragraph (c)(1)(ii)(A)(1), (2), (3), or (4), of this section are met before a payment is made.

(1) The name of the payee contains an unambiguous expression of corporate status that is Incorporated, Inc., Corporation, Corp., P.C., (but not Company or Co.) or contains the term *insurance company, indemnity company, reinsurance company,* or *assurance company,* or its name indicates that it is an entity listed as a per se corporation under § 301.7701-2(b)(8)(i) of this chapter.

(2) The payor has on file a corporate resolution or similar document clearly indicating corporate status. For this purpose, a similar document includes a copy of Form 8832, filed by the entity to elect classification as an association under § 301.7701-3(b) of this chapter.

(3) The payor receives a Form W-9 which includes an EIN and a statement from the payee that it is a domestic corporation.

(4) The payor receives a withholding certificate described in § 1.1441-1(e)(2)(i), that includes a certification that the person whose name is on the certificate is a foreign corporation.

(B) *Tax exempt organization.*—(1) *In general.*—Any organization that is exempt from taxation under section 501(a) is an exempt recipient. A custodial account under section 403(b)(7) shall be considered an exempt recipient under this paragraph. A payor may treat an organization as an exempt recipient under this paragraph (c)(1)(ii)(B) without requiring a certificate if the organization's name is listed in the compilation by the Commissioner of organizations for which a deduction for charitable contributions is allowed, if the name of the organization contains an unambiguous indication that it is a tax-exempt organization, or if the organization is known to the payor to be a tax-exempt organization.

(2) Examples.—The application of the provisions of this paragraph (c)(1)(ii)(B) may be illustrated by the following examples:

Example 1. The following persons maintain accounts at M Bank: N College, O University, and P Church. M may treat N, O, and P as exempt recipients even though such persons have not filed an exemption certificate with M because the names of the organizations contain an unambiguous indication that they are tax exempt organizations.

Example 2. Q is listed in the current edition of Internal Revenue Service Publication 78 as an organization for which deductions are permitted for charitable contributions under section 170(c). Such listing has not been revoked by an announcement published in the Internal Revenue Bulletin (see § 601.601(d)(2) of this chapter). A payor may treat Q as an exempt recipient even though Q has not filed an exemption certificate with the payor.

Example 3. Employer R maintains a section 403(b)(7) custodial account with Regulated Investment Company S on behalf of R's employees. S may treat the account as an exempt recipient even though R or its employees have not filed an exemption certificate with S.

(C) *Individual retirement plan.*—An individual retirement plan as defined in section 7701(a)(37) is an exempt recipient. A payor may treat any such plan of which it is the trustee or custodian as an exempt recipient under this paragraph (c)(1) without requiring a certificate.

(D) *United States.*—The United States Government and any wholly-owned agency or instrumentality thereof are exempt recipients. A payor may treat a person as an exempt recipient under this paragraph (c)(1) without requiring a certificate if the name of such person reasonably indicates it is described in this paragraph (c)(1).

(E) *State.*—A State, the District of Columbia, a possession of the United States, a political subdivision of any of the foregoing, wholly-owned agency or instrumentality of any one or more of the foregoing, and a pool or partnership composed exclusively of any of the foregoing are exempt recipients. A payor may treat a person as an exempt recipient under this paragraph (c)(1) without requiring a certificate if the name of such person reasonably indicates it is described in this paragraph (c)(1) or if such person is known generally in the community to be a State, the District of Columbia, a possession of the United States or a political subdivision or a wholly-owned agency or instrumentality of any one or more of the foregoing (for example, an account held in the name of "Town of S" or "County of T" may be treated as held by an exempt recipient under this paragraph (c)(1)(ii)(E)).

(F) *Foreign government.*—A foreign government, a political subdivision of a foreign government, and any wholly-owned agency or

instrumentality of either of the foregoing are exempt recipients. A payor may treat a foreign government or a political subdivisions thereof as an exempt recipient under this paragraph (c)(1) without requiring a certificate provided that its name reasonably indicates that it is a foreign government or provided that it is known to the payor to be a foreign government or a political subdivision thereof (for example, an account held in the name of the "Government of V" may be treated as held by a foreign government).

(G) *International organization.*—An international organization and any wholly owned agency or instrumentality thereof are exempt recipients. The term *international organization* shall have the meaning ascribed to it in section 7701(a)(18). A payor may treat a payee as an international organization without requiring a certificate if the payee is designated as an international organization by executive order (pursuant to 22 U.S.C. 288 through 288(f)).

(H) *Foreign central bank of issue.*—A foreign central bank of issue is an exempt recipient. A foreign central bank of issue is a bank which is by law or government sanction the principal authority, other than the government itself, issuing instruments intended to circulate as currency. See § 1.895-1(b)(1). A payor may treat a person as a foreign central bank of issue (and, therefore, as an exempt recipient) without requiring a certificate provided that such person is known generally in the financial community as a foreign central bank of issue or if its name reasonably indicates that it is a foreign central bank of issue.

(I) *Securities or commodities dealer.*—A dealer in securities, commodities, or notional principal contracts, that is registered as such under the laws of the United States or a State or under the laws of a foreign country is an exempt recipient. A payor may treat a dealer as an exempt recipient under this paragraph (c)(1) without requiring a certificate if the person is known generally in the investment community to be a dealer meeting the requirements set forth in this paragraph (c)(1) (for example, a registered broker-dealer or a person listed as a member firm in the most recent publication of members of the National Association of Securities Dealers, Inc.).

(J) *Real estate investment trust.*—A real estate investment trust, as defined in section 856 and § 1.856-1, is an exempt recipient. A payor may treat a person as a real estate investment trust (and, therefore, as an exempt recipient) without requiring a certificate if the person is known generally in the investment community as a real estate investment trust.

(K) *Entity registered under the Investment Company Act of 1940.*—An entity registered at all times during the taxable year under the Investment Company Act of 1940, as amended (15 U.S.C. 80a-1), (or during such portion of the taxable year that it is in existence), is an exempt recipient. An entity that is created during the taxable year will be treated as meeting the registration requirement of the preceding sentence provided that such entity is so registered at all times during the taxable year for which such entity is in existence. A payor may treat such an entity as an exempt recipient under this paragraph (c)(1) without requiring a certificate if the entity is known generally in the investment community to meet the requirements of the preceding sentence.

(L) *Common trust fund.*—A common trust fund, as defined in section 584(a), is an exempt recipient. A payor may treat the fund as an exempt recipient without requiring a certificate provided that its name reasonably indicates that it is a common trust fund or provided that it is known to the payor to be a common trust fund.

(M) *Financial institution.*—A financial institution such as a bank, mutual savings bank, savings and loan association, building and loan association, cooperative bank, homestead association, credit union, industrial loan association or bank, or other similar organization, whether organized in the United States or under the laws of a foreign country is an exempt recipient. A financial institution also includes a clearing organization defined in § 1.163-5(c)(2)(i)(D)(8) and the Bank for International Settlements. A payor may treat any person described in the preceding sentence as an exempt recipient without requiring a certificate if the person's name (including a foreign name, such as "Banco" or "Banque") reasonably indicates the payee is a financial institution described in the preceding sentence. In the case of a foreign person, a payor may also treat a person on such list as the Internal Revenue Service may publish or approve (such as in the Thomson Bank Directory or a list approved by the Federal Reserve Board).

(N) *Trust.*—A trust which is exempt from tax under section 664(c) (i.e., a charitable remainder annuity trust or a charitable remainder unitrust) or is described in section 4947(a)(1) (relating to certain charitable trusts) is an exempt recipient. A payor which is a trustee of the trust may treat the trust as an exempt recipient without requiring a certificate.

(O) *Nominees or custodians.*—A nominee or custodian.

(P) *Brokers.*—A broker as defined in section 6045(c) and § 1.6045-1(a)(1).

(Q) *Swap dealers.*—A dealer in notional principal contracts as defined in § 1.446-3(c)(4)(iii).

(iii) *Exempt recipient no longer exempt.*— Any person who ceases to be an exempt recipient shall, no later than 10 days after such cessation, notify the payor in writing when it ceases to be an exempt recipient unless it reasonably appears that the person formerly qualifying as an exempt recipient will not thereafter receive a reportable payment from the payor. If a payor

treats a person as an exempt recipient by requiring the exempt recipient to file a certificate claiming exempt status, that person shall revoke the certificate as provided in the preceding sentence. If the exempt recipient terminates its relationship with the payor prior to the time that the notice of change in status is otherwise required, the exempt recipient is not required to notify the payor. If, however, the person who formerly qualified as an exempt recipient later reinstates the relationship with the payor, the person must, prior to receiving a reportable payment from such relationship, notify the payor that it no longer qualifies as an exempt recipient in case the payor relies upon the previous treatment.

(2) *Payments by certain middlemen.*—An information return shall not be required if—

(i) The record owner is required to file a fiduciary return on Form 1041 disclosing the name, address, and taxpayer identification number of the actual owner, and furnishes Form K-1 to each actual owner containing the information required to be shown on the form, including amounts withheld under section 3406;

(ii) The record owner is a nominee of a banking institution or trust company exercising trust powers, and such banking institution or trust company is required to file a fiduciary return on Form 1041 disclosing the name, address, and identifying number of the actual owner, and furnishes Form K-1 to each actual owner containing the information required to be shown on the form, including amounts withheld under section 3406;

(iii) The record owner is a banking institution or trust company exercising trust powers, or a nominee thereof, and the actual owner is an organization exempt from taxation under section 501(a) for which such banking institution or trust company files an annual return, but only if the name, address, and taxpayer identification number of the record owner is included on or with the Form 1041 fiduciary return filed for the estate or trust or the annual return filed for the tax exempt organization.

(3) *Coordination with reporting rules for widely held fixed investment trusts under § 1.671-5 of this chapter.*—See § 1.671-5 for the reporting rules for widely held fixed investment trusts (as defined under that section).

(4) *Coordination of reporting with chapter 4 reporting or an applicable IGA.*—(i) *U.S. accounts reported by FFIs that are non-U.S. payors.*—An information return shall not be required with respect to an interest payment made by a participating FFI (including a reporting Model 2 FFI), or registered deemed-compliant FFI (including a reporting Model 1 FFI), that is a non-U.S. payor (as defined in § 1.6049-5(c)(5)) to an account holder of an account maintained by the FFI, when the payment is not subject to withholding under chapter 4 or to backup withholding under section 3406, and the conditions of paragraphs (c)(4)(i)(A), (B), or (C) of this section, as applicable, are met. See paragraph (c)(4)(iii) of

this section for circumstances in which an FFI may allocate a payment described in this paragraph (c)(4)(i) to a chapter 4 withholding rate pool of U.S. payees.

(A) The FFI is a participating FFI (including a reporting Model 2 FFI) reporting the account holder of the U.S. account (as defined in § 1.1471-1(b)(133)) pursuant to either § 1.1471-4(d)(3) or (5) for the year in which the payment is made (including reporting of the account holder's TIN).

(B) The FFI is a registered deemed-compliant FFI (other than a reporting Model 1 FFI) reporting the account holder of the U.S. account pursuant to the conditions of its applicable deemed-compliant status under § 1.1471-5(f)(1) for the year in which the payment is made (including reporting of the account holder's TIN).

(C) The FFI is a reporting Model 1 FFI reporting the account holder of the reportable U.S. account pursuant to an applicable Model 1 IGA for the year in which the payment is made (including reporting of the account holder's TIN).

(ii) *Other accounts reported by FFIs under chapter 4.*—An information return shall not be required under this section with respect to a payment that is not subject to withholding under chapter 3 (as defined in § 1.1441-2(a)) or backup withholding under § 31.3406(g)-1(e) and that is made to a recalcitrant account holder of a participating FFI or registered deemed-compliant FFI (or non-consenting U.S. account of a reporting Model 2 FFI), provided that the FFI reports such account holder in accordance with the classes of account holders described in § 1.1471-4(d)(6) for the year in which the payment is made. See paragraph (c)(4)(iii) of this section for circumstances in which an FFI may allocate a payment described in this paragraph (c)(4)(ii) to a chapter 4 withholding rate pool of U.S. payees. In the case of a payment made by an FFI that is a reporting Model 1 FFI, an information return shall not be required with respect to a payment that is not subject to withholding under chapter 3 or backup withholding under § 31.3406(g)-1(e) and that is made to an account holder of the FFI if the account—

(A) Has U.S. indicia for which appropriate documentation sufficient to treat the account as held by other than a specified U.S. person has not been provided pursuant to the due diligence requirements described in an applicable Model 1 IGA, and

(B) Is therefore treated as a U.S. reportable account that the FFI is required to report pursuant to the applicable Model 1 IGA.

(iii) *Coordination of reporting exceptions with reporting of chapter 4 withholding rate pools.*— For purposes of paragraphs (c)(4)(i) and (ii) of this section, a participating FFI (including a reporting Model 2 FFI) or registered deemed-compliant FFI (including a reporting Model 1 FFI) receiving a payment from another payor may provide a withholding statement to the payor allocating the payment to a chapter 4 withholding rate of pool of U.S. payees only if the payment is excepted from reporting under paragraph (c)(4)(i) of this section or if the payment is both excepted from reporting under paragraph (c)(4)(ii) of this section and not subject to withholding under chapter 4. See § 1.6049-5(b)(14) (providing an exception from reporting under section 6049 to a payor that has been furnished a withholding statement from an participating FFI (including a reporting Model 2 FFI) or registered deemed-compliant FFI (including a reporting Model 1 FFI) and that allocates the payment to a chapter 4 withholding rate pool). Thus, for example, a U.S. payor that is a participating FFI may not allocate a payment to a chapter 4 withholding rate pool of U.S. payees on a withholding statement described in § 1.6049-5(b)(14) when the payment is made to a U.S. account maintained by the FFI, regardless of whether the FFI reports the account in accordance with § 1.1471-4(d)(3) because the U.S. payor is not excepted from reporting under this section pursuant to paragraph (c)(4)(i) of this section.

(iv) *Example.*—The application of the provisions of paragraphs (c)(4)(ii) and (iii) of this section may be illustrated by the following example:

Example. USP is a payor that makes an interest payment that is not a withholdable payment (as defined in paragraph (f)(15) of this section) to RM2, a U.S. payor and reporting Model 2 FFI. The payment is paid and received outside of the United States and is not an amount subject to withholding under chapter 3. RM2 receives the payment as an intermediary with respect to a preexisting account held by A. RM2 has account information with respect to A which includes U.S. indicia as described in § 1.1441-7(b)(5) or (8). A does not provide consent for RM2 to report A's account. Under the presumption rules described in § 1.6049-5(d)(2)(i), RM2 is required to treat A as a U.S. non-exempt recipient. Despite this presumption rule, and because backup withholding does not apply under § 31.3406(g)-1(e), no information return shall be required with respect to the payment under paragraph (c)(4)(ii) of this section if A is reported by RM2 consistent with § 1.1471-4(d)(6) as a non-consenting account holder. Additionally, RM2 may include A in the chapter 4 withholding rate pool of U.S. payees on the withholding statement provided to USP consistent with the requirements of paragraph (c)(4)(iii) of this section.

(d) *Special rules.*—(1) *Aggregation of payments.*—For purposes of paragraph (b) of this section, until such time as the Commissioner determines that it is feasible to require aggregation of payments on two or more accounts, insurance contracts, or investment certificates, and, until this section is amended accordingly to provide for reporting on an aggregate basis, the requirement for filing Form 1099 under this section will be met if a person making payments of interest subject to reporting files a separate Form 1099 with respect to each account, insurance contract, or investment certificate. In the case of obligations described in section 6049(b)(1)(A), separate Forms 1099 may be filed as provided in the preceding sentence with respect to holdings in different issues.

(2) *Treatment of original issue discount.*—The amount of original issue discount subject to reporting under section 6049 shall be the amount of original issue discount includible in the gross income of any holder that is treated as paid under § 1.6049-5(f).

(3) *Conversion into United States dollars of amounts paid in foreign currency.*—(i) *Conversion rules.*—When a payment is made in foreign currency, the U.S. dollar amount of the payment shall be determined by converting such foreign currency into U.S. dollars on the date of payment at the spot rate (as defined in § 1.988-1(d)(1)) or pursuant to a reasonable spot rate convention. For example, a withholding agent may use a month-end spot rate or a monthly average spot rate. A spot rate convention must be used consistently with respect to all non-dollar amounts withheld and from year to year. Such convention cannot be changed without the consent of the Commissioner or the Commissioner's delegate.

(ii) *Special rule for § 1.988-5(a) transactions where the payor on both components of a qualified hedging transaction is the same person.*—(A) *In general.*—Interest or original issue discount on a qualified debt instrument that is part of a qualified hedging transaction under § 1.988-5(a) shall be computed for section 6049 reporting purposes under the rules described in § 1.988-5(a)(9)(ii) if—

(1) The payor on the qualified debt instrument and the counterparty to the § 1.988-5(a) hedge are the same person; and

(2) The payee complies with the requirements of § 1.988-5(a) and so notifies its payor prior to the date required for filing Form 1099 as required by this section.

(B) *Effective date.*—The provisions of this paragraph (d)(3)(ii) apply to transactions entered into after December 31, 2000.

(4) *Determination of person to whom interest or original issue discount is paid or for whom it is received.*—Section 1.6049-1(a)(3) and (4) shall apply with respect to payments of interest and original issue discount after December 31, 1982.

(5) *Payments by governmental units.*—In the case of payments made by any governmental unit or any agency or instrumentality thereof, the officer or employee having control of the payment of interest or original issue discount (or the person appropriately designated for purposes of this section) shall make the returns and statements required under section 6049.

(6) *When payment deemed made.*—(i) *In general.*—Except as provided in paragraph (d)(6)(ii) of this section, for purposes of section 6049, interest is deemed to have been paid when it is credited or set apart to a person without any substantial limitation or restriction as to the time or manner of payment or condition upon which payment is to be made, and is made available to him so that it may be drawn at any time, and its receipt brought within his own control and disposition.

(ii) *Instruments paid on presentment or demand.*—In the case of a payment made on an obligation described in paragraph (e)(2) of this section (relating to transactional reporting), interest is deemed to have been paid at the time the obligation is presented for payment. For example, interest represented by a coupon detached from a bond is considered paid for purposes of section 6049 when the coupon is presented for payment.

(7) *Magnetic media requirement.*—For rules relating to permission to submit the information required by Form 1099 on magnetic tape or other media, see § 1.9101-1. For the requirement to submit the information required by Form 1099 on magnetic media for payments after December 31, 1983, see section 6011(e) and § 301.6011-2 of this chapter (Regulations on Procedure and Administration).

(8) *Obligations that are not exempt from taxation.*—When an issuer of an obligation that is not exempt from taxation receives an envelope or "shell", signed by the payee, stating that interest on the obligation is exempt from taxation under section 103(a) (as described in § 1.6049-5(b)(2)), the issuer shall make an information return under section 6049. The information return shall show the name, address, and taxpayer identification number of the person who signed the statement claiming that interest on the obligation is exempt from taxation, the amount of interest paid, and such other information as is required by the form. An information return is required regardless of the amount of interest. The issuer shall also furnish a written statement to such person showing the information required by § 1.6049-6(b).

(9) *Savings bonds.*—(i) *In general.*—A person who makes payment on a United States savings bond when the bond is presented for payment shall report the difference between the amount to be paid and the amount paid for the bond. The amount subject to reporting shall not be reduced to take into account—

(A) Amounts previously included in the income of a holder as a result of an election under 454 to include annually the increase in the redemption price of the bond; or

(B) Amounts accrued prior to transfer of the bond where the bond has been reissued in the name of the person presenting the bond for payment. With respect to a savings bond that is reissued in another person's name, the amount subject to reporting when the bond is reissued is the amount of interest that has accrued. With respect to a savings bond that is exchanged in a tax-deferred transaction (as described in section 1037), the amount subject o reporting is the amount of cash paid to the holder at the time of the transaction.

(ii) *Examples.*—The application of the provisions of paragraph (d)(9)(i) of this section may be illustrated by the following examples:

Example (1). On June 10, 1943, A purchases a $50 Series E savings bond. The amount paid for the savings bond is $37.50. A elects under section 454 to include the increase in the redemption price of the bond annually in income. A presents the bond to Bank M to be cashed on July 1, 1983. The amount to be paid on the bond on that date is $204.96. Bank M is required to make an information return under section 6049 showing that it paid $167.46 (the difference between $204.96 and $37.50) of interest, without regard to A's election to include annually the increase in the redemption price of the bond.

Example (2). On December 1, 1970, B purchases a $500 Series E savings bond. The amount paid for the bond is $375. On August 1, 1984, the bond is reissued by the Bureau of Public Debt by deleting B's name and inserting the name of B's child. At the time of reissue, the redemption value of the bond is $1,015.80. The accrued interest is $640.80 (the difference between $1,015.80 and $375). The reissue is a taxable transaction, and B must include in income the accrued interest at the time of reissue. The Bureau of Public Debt is required to make an information return under section 6049 showing that it paid $640.80 of interest to B.

Example (3). Assume the same facts as in example (2) except that B exchanges the bond for a Series HH savings bond in the amount of $1,000 issued in B's name. The exchange is tax-deferred under section 1037. The Bureau of Public Debt stamps a legend on the bond stating that interest of $625 has been deferred. The amount of $15.80 is paid to B. The Bureau of the Public Debt must make an information return showing that it paid $15.80 of interest to B.

Example (4). Assume the same facts as in example (3) except that the exchange is not a tax-deferred exchange. The Bureau of the Public Debt must make an information return showing that it paid $640.80 of interest to B.

(e) *Transactional reporting.*—(1) *In general.*—An information return required to be made under paragraph (b) of this section may be made on a transaction-by-transaction basis, rather than on an annual aggregation basis, if payment described in paragraph (e)(2) of this section is made by a person described in paragraph (e)(3) of this section.

(2) *Payments subject to transactional reporting.*—An information return may be made on a transactional basis if payment is made on—

(i) A United States savings bond,

(ii) An interest coupon (but see §1.6049-5(b) which provides that no information return is required to be made with respect to an interest coupon that is exempt from taxation),

(iii) A discount obligation having a maturity at issue of 1 year or less, including commercial paper and short-term government obligations defined in section 1232(a)(3), and

(iv) Any obligation similar to those described in subdivisions (i) through (iii). The information return with respect to payments on the types of obligations described in this paragraph shall be made on Form 1099-INT. A payor may include all interest paid in one transaction on one information return, irrespective of whether obligations of different issuers are paid as part of the transaction.

(3) *Persons subject to transactional reporting.*—A person may make a return on a transactional basis if the person is—

(i) A middleman (as defined in paragraph (f)(4) of this section) who is required to make an information return under paragraph (b)(3) of this section with respect to any payment described in paragraph (e)(2) of this section, or

(ii) A federal agency making payments on a United States savings bond.

(4) *Transaction defined.*—For purposes of this paragraph (e), a transaction means a payment at one time on one or more obligations. For example, if an individual who is exempt from withholding under section 3406 presents at one time five Series EE bonds on each of which $3 of interest has accrued, $15 of interest will be paid as part of the transaction. Accordingly, an information return is required under §1.6049-4(a)(2)(iii) because the interest paid in the transaction exceeds $10. If only three of the savings bonds were presented, however, no return would be required even if the remaining two bonds were redeemed the following day. See paragraph (a)(2)(i) of this section for the requirement that an information return be made if any amount of tax is withheld under section 3406.

(5) *Information required.*—The information return for any transaction under paragraph (e) of this section shall show the following:

(i) The name, address, and taxpayer identification number of the person to whom the interest is paid;

(ii) The name and address of the person filing the form;

(iii) The amount of interest paid;

(iv) The amount of tax withheld under section 3406 if any; and

(v) Such other information as is required by the form.

(f) *Definitions.*—For purposes of section 6049, this section, and §§1.6049-5 and 1.6049-6—

(1) *Person.*—The term "person" includes any governmental unit, international organization, and any agency or instrumentality thereof. Therefore, interest paid by one of these entities must be reported unless one of the exceptions under section 6049 applies.

Reg. §1.6049-4(f)(1)

(2) *Natural person.*—The term "natural person" means any individual, but shall not include a partnership (whether or not composed entirely of individuals), a trust, or an estate.

(3) *Obligation.*—The term *obligation* includes bonds, debentures, notes, certificates, and other evidences of indebtedness regardless of how denominated. For the definition of the term *offshore obligation*, see paragraph (f)(9) of this section.

(4) *Middleman.*—(i) *In general.*—The term "middleman" means any person, including a financial institution as described in paragraph (c)(1)(ii)(M) of this section, a broker as defined in section 6045(c), or a nominee, who makes payment of interest for, or collects interest on behalf of, another person, or otherwise acts in a capacity as intermediary between a payor and a payee. For example, a person (other than an issuer of an obligation) who makes payment on an interest coupon of the obligation to another person is a middleman, irrespective of whether such person purchases the coupon for his own account, accepts the coupon as agent for the payee, or otherwise deals with the coupon. The term "middleman" also includes a trustee, including a corporate trustee of a trust where the trust is the payee. See § 1.6049-4(c)(2) providing that the trustee does not have to make an information return on Form 1099 to a beneficiary if the trustee is required to file Form 1041 and furnishes Form K-1 to the beneficiary showing the information required to be shown on the form, including amounts withheld under section 3406. A person shall be considered to be a middleman as to any portion of an interest payment made to such person which portion is actually owned by another person, whether or not the other person's name is also shown on the information return filed with respect to such interest payment, except that a husband or wife will not be considered as acting in the capacity of a middleman with respect to his or her spouse. A person who, from within the United States, forwards an interest coupon or discount obligation on behalf of a payee for presentation, collection or payment outside the United States is also a middleman for purposes of this section (but the transfer, although subject to information reporting under this section, does not make the payment subject to backup withholding under section 3406).

(ii) *Example.*—The application of the provisions of paragraph (f)(4) of this section may be illustrated by the following example:

Example. In January 1984, Broker B, a U.S. payor, purchases on behalf of its customer, Individual A, an obligation issued by partnership in a public offering on that date. Broker B holds the obligation for A throughout 1984. Broker B is required to make an information return showing the amount of original issue discount treated as paid to A under § 1.6049-5(f).

(5) *Chapter 4 withholding rate pool.*—The term *chapter 4 withholding rate pool* has the meaning set forth in § 1.1471-1(b)(20). However, for

determining the U.S. payees included in a chapter 4 withholding rate pool for purposes of section 6049, see paragraph (c)(4)(iii) of this section.

(6) *Foreign financial institution (or FFI).*—The term *foreign financial institution* or *FFI* means an entity described in § 1.1471-1(b)(47),

(7) *Intergovernmental agreement (or IGA).*—The term *intergovernmental agreement* or *IGA* has the meaning set forth in § 1.1471-1(b)(67) (*i.e.,* either a *Model 1 IGA* described in § 1.1471-1(b)(78) or a *Model 2 IGA* described in § 1.1471-1(b)(79)).

(8) *Non-consenting U.S. accounts.*—The term *non-consenting U.S. accounts* has the meaning set forth in an applicable Model 2 IGA.

(9) *Offshore obligation.*—The term offshore obligation means an offshore obligation defined in § 1.6049-5(c)(1). For the definition of the term *obligation,* see paragraph (f)(3) of this section.

(10) *Participating FFI.*—The term *participating FFI* means an FFI that is described in § 1.1471-1(b)(91).

(11) *Recalcitrant account holder.*—The term *recalcitrant account holder* has the same meaning set forth in § 1.1471-1(b)(110).

(12) *Registered deemed-compliant FFI.*—The term *registered deemed-compliant FFI* means an FFI that is described in § 1.1471-1(b)(111).

(13) *Reporting Model 1 FFI.*—The term *reporting Model 1 FFI* means an FFI that is described in § 1.1471-1(b)(114).

(14) *Reporting Model 2 FFI.*—The term *reporting Model 2 FFI* means a participating FFI that is described in § 1.1471-1(b)(91).

(15) *Withholdable payment.*—The term *withholdable payment* means a payment described in § 1.1471-1(b)(145).

(16) *Paid and received outside the United States.*—(i) *In general.*—Except as otherwise provided in paragraphs (f)(16)(ii) and (iii) of this section, the term *paid and received outside the United States* means an amount that is paid by a payor or middleman outside the United States as described in § 1.6049-5(e).

(ii) *Transfers to the United States.*—Without regard to the location of the account from which the amount is drawn, an amount that is described in paragraph (f)(16)(ii)(A) or (B) of this section and paid by transfer to an account maintained by the payee in the United States or by mail to a United States address (including an amount paid with respect to a bond or a discount obligation described in § 1.6049-5(e)(4)) is not considered to be paid and received outside the United States.

(A) An amount is described in this paragraph (f)(16)(ii)(A) if it is paid by an issuer or the paying agent of the issuer with respect to an obligation that is—

(1) Issued by a U.S. payor, as defined in § 1.6049-5(c)(5);

(2) Registered under the Securities Act of 1933 (15 U.S.C. 77a); or

(3) Listed on an exchange that is registered as a national securities exchange in the United States or included in an interdealer quotation system in the United States.

(B) An amount is described in this paragraph (f)(16)(ii)(B) if it is paid by a U.S. middleman (as defined in §1.6049-5(c)(5)) that, as a custodian, nominee, or other agent of a payee, collects the amount for or on behalf of the payee.

(iii) *Deposits or accounts with banks and other financial institutions.*—In the case of an amount paid by a bank or other financial institution with respect to a deposit or an account that is considered paid at a branch or office outside the United States as described in §1.6049-5(e)(2), the amount is not considered paid and received outside the United States if the institution has knowledge that the customer has transmitted instructions to an agent, branch, or office of the institution from inside the United States by mail, telephone, electronic transmission, or otherwise concerning the deposit or account (unless the transmission from the United States has taken place in isolated and infrequent circumstances).

(iv) *Examples.*—The application of the provisions of paragraph (f)(16) of this section may be illustrated by the following examples:

Example 1. FC is a foreign corporation that is not a U.S. payor or U.S. middleman, as defined in §1.6049-5(c)(5). A holds FC coupon bonds that are not in registered form under section 163(f) and the regulations. FB, a foreign branch of DC, a domestic corporation, is the designated paying agent with respect to the bonds issued by FC. A does not have an account with FB. A presents a coupon to FB at its office outside the United States with instructions to transfer funds to a bank account maintained by A in the United States. FB transfers the funds in accordance with A's instructions. Even though the amount is credited to an account in the United States, the interest on the FC bonds is paid and received outside the United States under paragraph (f)(16)(ii) of this section and §1.6049-5(e)(3) because the coupon is presented for payment outside the United States; because FC is a foreign person that is not a U.S. payor or U.S. middleman, as defined in §1.6049-5(d)(1); because FB is not acting as A's agent; and because the obligation is not registered under the Securities Act of 1933 (15 U.S.C. 77a), listed on a securities exchange that is registered as a national securities exchange in the United States, or included in an interdealer quotation system.

Example 2. FC is a foreign corporation that is not a U.S. payor or U.S. middleman, as defined in §1.6049-5(d)(1). B, a United States citizen, holds a bond issued by FC in registered form under section 163(f) and the regulations thereunder and registered under the Securities Act of 1933 (15 U.S.C. 77a). The bond is not a foreign-targeted registered obligation as defined in §1.871-14(e)(2). DB, a United States branch of a foreign corporation engaged in the commercial banking business, is the registrar of the bonds issued by FC. DB supplies FC with a list of the holders of the FC bonds. Interest on the FC bonds is paid to B and other bondholders by checks prepared by FC at its principal office outside the United States, and B's check is mailed from there to his designated address in the United States. The bond is described in paragraph (f)(16)(ii)(A)(2) of this section. The interest on the FC bonds paid to B by FC is not paid and received outside the United States under paragraph (f)(16) of this section.

Example 3. The facts are the same as in *Example 2* except that the checks are prepared and mailed in the United States by DC, a U.S. corporation engaged in the commercial banking business that is the designated paying agent with respect to the bonds issued by FC, and B's check is mailed to his designated address outside the United States. For purposes of section 6049, the interest on the FC bonds paid by DC is not paid and received outside the United States under paragraph (f)(16)(i) of this section.

(g) *Time and place for filing a return for the payment of interest.*—(1) *Annual return.*—Except as provided in paragraph (g)(2) of this section, the returns required under this section for any calendar year for the payment of interest shall be filed after September 30 of such year, but not before the payor's final payment to the payee for the year, and on or before February 28 (March 31 if filed electronically) of the following year. Such returns shall be filed with the appropriate Internal Revenue Service Center, the address of which is listed in the instructions for Form 1096. For extensions of time for filing returns under this section, see §1.6081-1.

(2) *Transactional return.*—In the case of a return under paragraph (e) of this section, relating to returns on a transactional basis, such return shall be filed at any time but in no event later than February 28 (March 31 if filed electronically) of the year following the calendar year in which the interest was paid. The return shall be filed with the appropriate Internal Revenue Service Center, the address of which is listed in the instructions for Form 1096. For extensions of time for filing returns under this section, see §1.6081-1.

(3) *Cross-reference to penalty.*—For provisions relating to the penalty provided for failure to file timely a correct information return required under section 6049(a) and §1.6049-4(a)(1), see §301.6721-1 of this chapter (Procedure and Administration Regulations). See §301.6724-1 of this chapter for the waiver of a penalty if the failure is due to reasonable cause and is not due to willful neglect.

(h) *Effective/applicability dates.*—Except as otherwise provided in paragraphs (b)(5)(ii) and (d)(3)(ii)(B) of this section, this section applies to payments made on or after January 6, 2017. (For payments made after June 30, 2014, and before January 6, 2017, see this section as in effect and contained in 26 CFR part 1, as revised April 1, 2016.) [Reg. § 1.6049-4.]

☐ [*T.D. 7881*, 3-22-83. *Amended by T.D. 8366*, 9-27-91; *T.D. 8664*, 4-15-96; *T.D. 8734*, 10-6-97; *T.D. 8804*, 12-30-98; *T.D. 8856*, 12-29-99; *T.D. 8881*, 5-15-2000; *T.D. 8895*, 8-17-2000; *T.D. 9010*, 7-25-2002 *T.D. 9241*, 1-23-2006; *T.D. 9584*, 4-17-2012, *T.D. 9658*, 2-28-2014 *and T.D. 9808*, 12-30-2016.]

[Reg. § 1.6049-5]

§ 1.6049-5. Interest and original issue discount subject to reporting after December 31, 1982.—(a) *Interest subject to reporting requirement.*—For purposes of § § 1.6049-4, 1.6049-6 and this section, except as provided in paragraph (b) of this section, the term "interest" means—

(1) Interest on an obligation—

(i) In registered form (as defined in § 5f.103-1(c)), or

(ii) Of a type offered to the public. Principles consistent with § 5f.163-1 shall be applied to determine whether an obligation is of a type offered to the public.

(2) Interest on deposits with persons carrying on the banking business. Such term shall include deposits evidenced by time certificates of deposit issued in any amount whether negotiable or non-negotiable. The term "interest" includes payments to a mortgage escrow account and amounts paid with respect to repurchase agreements and banker's acceptances. Property which the payee receives from the payor as interest (or in lieu of a cash payment of interest) shall be interest for purposes of section 6049. The amount subject to reporting is the fair market value of such property.

(3) Amounts, whether or not designated as interest, paid or credited by mutual savings banks, savings and loan associations, building and loan associations, cooperative banks, homestead associations, credit unions, industrial loan associations or banks, or similar organizations, in respect of deposits, face amount certificates, investment certificates, or withdrawable or repurchasable shares. Thus, even though amounts paid or credited by such organizations with respect to deposits are designated as "dividends", such amounts are included in the definition of interest for purposes of section 6049. The term "interest" includes payments to a mortgage escrow account and amounts paid with respect to repurchase agreements. Property which the payee receives from the payor as interest (or in lieu of a cash payment of interest) is "interest" for purposes of section 6049. The fair market value of such property is the amount subject to reporting.

(4) Interest on amounts held by insurance companies under an agreement to pay interest thereon. Any increment in value of "advance premiums", "prepaid premiums", or "premium deposit funds" which is applied to the payment of premiums due on insurance policies, or made available for withdrawal by the policyholder, shall be considered interest subject to reporting.

Interest that an insurance company pays pursuant to an agreement with the policyholder to a beneficiary because the payment due has been delayed is interest subject to reporting. Interest subject to reporting also includes interest paid by insurance companies with respect to policy "dividend" accumulations (see sections 61 and 451 and the regulations thereunder for rules as to when such interest is considered paid), and interest paid with respect to the proceeds of insurance policies left with the insurer. The so-called "interest element" in the case of annuity or installment payments under life insurance or endowment contracts does not constitute interest for purposes of section 6049.

(5) Interest on deposits with brokers as defined in section 6045(c) and the regulations thereunder. Any payment made in lieu of interest to a person whose obligation has been borrowed in connection with a short sale or other similar transaction is subject to reporting under section 6049. See § 1.6045-2 for reporting requirements with respect to payments in lieu of tax-exempt interest.

(6) Interest paid on amounts held by investment companies as defined in section 3 of the Investment Company Act (15 U.S.C. section 80-a) and on amounts paid to pooled funds or trusts. The interest to be reported with respect to a widely held fixed investment trust, as defined in § 1.671-5(b)(22), shall be the interest earned on the assets held by the trust. See § 1.671-5 for reporting rules for widely held fixed investment trusts (as defined under that section).

(b) *Interest excluded from reporting requirement.*—The term *interest* or *original issue discount* (OID) does not include—

(1) Interest on any obligation issued by a natural person as defined in § 1.6049-4(f)(2), irrespective of whether such interest is collected on behalf of the holder of the obligation by a middleman.

(2) Interest on any obligation if such interest is exempt from taxation under section 103(a), relating to certain governmental obligations, or interest which is exempt from taxation under any other provision of law without regard to the identity of the holder. The holder of a tax exempt obligation that is not in registered form must provide written certification to the payor (other than the issuer of the obligation) that the obligation is exempt from taxation. A statement that interest coupons are tax exempt on the envelope or shell commonly used by financial institutions to process such coupons, signed by the payee, will be sufficient for this purpose if the envelope is properly completed (i.e., shows the name, address, and taxpayer identification number of the payee). A payor may rely on such written certification in treating such interest as tax exempt for purposes of section 6049. See § 1.6049-4(d)(8) with respect to the requirement that the issuer of a taxable obligation shall make an information return if such issuer receives an envelope which improperly claims that the interest coupons contained therein are tax exempt.

(3) Interest on amounts held in escrow to guarantee performance on a contract or to provide security. However, interest on amounts held in escrow with a person described in paragraph (a)(2) or (3) of this section is interest subject to reporting under section 6049.

(4) Interest that a governmental unit pays with respect to tax refunds.

(5) Interest on deposits for security, such as deposits posted with a public utility company. However, interest on deposits posted for security with a person described in paragraph (a)(2) or (3) of this section is interest subject to reporting under section 6049.

(6) Amounts from sources outside the United States (determined under the provisions of part I, subchapter N, chapter 1 of the Internal Revenue Code (Code) and the regulations under those provisions) paid by a non-U.S. payor or a non-U.S. middleman (as defined in paragraph (c)(5) of this section) and paid and received outside the United States. See § 1.6049-4(f)(16) for circumstances in which a payment is considered to be paid and received outside the United States.

(7) Portfolio interest, as defined in § 1.871-14(b)(1), paid with respect to obligations in bearer form described in section 871(h)(2)(A), as in effect prior to the amendment by section 502 of the Hiring Incentives to Restore Employment Act of 2010 (HIRE Act), Public Law 111-147, or section 881(c)(2)(A), as in effect prior to the amendment by section 502 of the HIRE Act, that were issued prior to March 19, 2012, or with respect to a foreign-targeted registered obligation described in § 1.871-14(e)(2) that was issued prior to January 1, 2016, and for which the documentation requirements described in § 1.871-14(e)(3) and (4) have been satisfied (other than by a U.S. middleman (as defined in paragraph (c)(5) of this section) that, as a custodian or nominee of the payee, collects the amount for, or on behalf of, the payee, regardless of whether the middleman is also acting as agent of the payor).

(8) Portfolio interest described in § 1.871-14(c)(1)(ii), paid with respect to obligations in registered form described in section 871(h)(2) or 881(c)(2) that is not described in paragraph (b)(7) of this section.

(9) Any amount paid by an international organization described in § 1.6049-4(c)(1)(ii)(G) (or its paying, transfer, or other agent that is not also a payee's agent) with respect to an obligation of which the international organization is the issuer.

(10)(i) Amounts paid and received outside the United States under § 1.6049-4(f)(16) (other than by a U.S. middleman (as defined in paragraph (c)(5) of this section) that are paid by a custodian or nominee or other agent of the payee, of amounts that that it receives for, or on behalf of, the payee, regardless of whether the middleman is also acting as agent of the payor) with respect to an obligation that: Has a face amount or principal amount of not less than $500,000 (as determined based on the spot rate on the date of issuance if in foreign currency); has a maturity (at issue) of 183 days or less; satisfies the requirements of sections 163(f)(2)(B)(i) and (ii)(I), as in effect prior to the amendment by section 502 of the HIRE Act, and the regulations thereunder (as if the obligation would otherwise be a registration-required obligation within the meaning of section 163(f)(2)(A)) (however, an original issue discount obligation with a maturity of 183 days or less from the date of issuance is not required to satisfy the certification requirement of § 1.163-5(c)(2)(i)(D)(3)) and is issued in accordance with the procedures of § 1.163-5(c)(2)(i)(D); and has on its face the following statement (or a similar statement having the same effect):

> By accepting this obligation, the holder represents and warrants that it is not a United States person (other than an exempt recipient described in section 6049(b)(4) of the Internal Revenue Code and regulations thereunder) and that it is not acting for or on behalf of a United States person (other than an exempt recipient described in section 6049(b)(4) of the Internal Revenue Code and the regulations thereunder).

(ii) If the obligation is in registered form, it must be registered in the name of an exempt recipient described in § 1.6049-4(c)(1)(ii). For purposes of this paragraph (b)(10), a middleman may treat an obligation as described in section 163(f)(2)(B)(i) and (f)(2)(B)(ii)(I), as in effect prior to the amendment by section 502 of the HIRE Act, and the regulations under that section if the obligation, or coupons detached therefrom, whichever is presented for payment, contains the statement described in this paragraph (b)(10). The exemption from reporting described in this paragraph (b)(10) shall not apply if the payor has actual knowledge that the payee is a U.S. person who is not an exempt recipient.

(11) Amounts paid with respect to an account or deposit with a U.S. or foreign branch of a domestic or foreign corporation or partnership that is paid with respect to an obligation described in either paragraph (b)(11)(i) or (ii) of this section, if the branch is engaged in the commercial banking business; and the interest or OID is paid and received outside the United States as defined in § 1.6049-4(f)(16) (other than by a U.S. middleman (as defined in paragraph (c)(5) of this section) that acts as a custodian, nominee, or other agent of the payee, and collects the amount for, or on behalf of, the payee, regardless of whether the middleman is also acting as agent of the payor). The exemption from reporting described in this paragraph (b)(11) shall not apply if the payor has actual knowledge that the payee is a U.S. person who is not an exempt recipient.

(i) An obligation is described in this paragraph (b)(11)(i) if it is not in registered form (within the meaning of section 163(f) and the regulations under that section), is described in section 163(f)(2)(B), as in effect prior to the amendment by section 502 of the HIRE Act, and issued in accordance with the procedures of § 1.163-5(c)(2)(i)(C) or (D), and, in the case of a U.S. branch, is part of a larger single public offering of securities. For purposes of this paragraph (b)(11)(i), a middleman may treat an obligation as described in section 163(f)(2)(B), as in effect prior to the amendment by section 502 of the HIRE Act, if the obligation, and any detachable coupons, contains the statement described in section 163(f)(2)(B)(ii)(II), as in effect prior to the amendment by section 502 of the HIRE Act, and the regulations under that section.

(ii)(A) An obligation is described in this paragraph (b)(11)(ii) if it produces income described in section 871(i)(2)(A); has a face amount or principal amount of not less than $500,000 (as determined based on the spot rate on the date of issuance if in foreign currency); satisfies the requirements of sections 163(f)(2)(B)(i) and (ii)(I), as in effect prior to the amendment by section 502 of the HIRE Act, and the regulations thereunder (as if the obligation would otherwise be a registration-required obligation within the meaning of section 163(f)(2)(A)) and is issued in accordance with the procedures of § 1.163-5(c)(2)(i)(C) or (D) (however, an original issue discount obligation with a maturity of 183 days or less from the date of issuance is not required to satisfy the certification requirement of § 1.163-5(c)(2)(i)(D)(3)). For purposes of this paragraph (b)(11)(ii), a middleman may treat an obligation as described in sections 163(f)(2)(B)(i) and (ii), as in effect prior to the amendment by section 502 of the HIRE Act, and the regulations under that section if the obligation, or any detachable coupon, contains the statement described in paragraph (b)(11)(ii)(B) of this section.

(B) The obligation must have on its face, and on any detachable coupons, the following statement (or a similar statement having the same effect):

> By accepting this obligation, the holder represents and warrants that it is not a United States person (other than an exempt recipient described in section 6049(b)(4) and regulations under that section) and that it is not acting for or on behalf of a United States person (other than an exempt recipient described in section 6049(b)(4) and the regulations under that section).

(C) If the obligation is in registered form, it must be registered in the name of an exempt recipient described in § 1.6049-4(c)(1)(ii).

(12) Payments that a payor can, prior to payment, reliably associate with documentation upon which it may rely to treat the payment as made to a foreign beneficial owner in accordance with § 1.1441-1(e)(1)(ii) or as made to a foreign payee in accordance with paragraph (d)(1) of this section or presumed to be made to a foreign payee under paragraph (d)(2) or (3) of this section. However, such payments may be reportable under § 1.1461-1(b) and (c) or under § 1.1474-1(d)(2) (for a chapter 4 reportable amount (as described in § 1.1471-1(b)(18)). The provisions of § 1.1441-1 shall apply by substituting the term "payor" for the term "withholding agent" and without regard to the fact that the provisions apply only to amounts subject to withholding under chapter 3 of the Code. In the event of a conflict between the provisions of § 1.1441-1 and paragraph (d) of this section in determining the foreign status of the payee, the provisions of § 1.1441-1 shall govern for payments of amounts subject to withholding under chapter 3 of the Code and the provisions of paragraph (d) of this section shall govern in other cases. This paragraph (b)(12) does not apply to interest paid on or after January 1, 2013, to a nonresident alien individual to the extent provided in § 1.6049-8.

(13) Amounts for the period that the debt obligation with respect to which the interest arises represents an asset blocked as described in § 1.1441-2(e)(3). Payment of such amounts, including interest that is past due and OID on obligations that mature on or before the date that the assets are no longer blocked, is deemed to occur in accordance with the rules of § 1.1441-2(e)(3).

(14) Payments that a payor or middleman can, prior to payment, reliably associate with documentation upon which it may rely to treat as made to a foreign intermediary or flow-through entity in accordance with § 1.1441-1(b) if it obtains from the foreign intermediary or flow-through entity a withholding statement under § 1.1471-3(c)(3)(iii)(B)(2) (describing an FFI withholding statement), § 1.1471-3(c)(3)(iii)(B)(3) (describing a chapter 4 withholding statement), § 1.1441-1(e)(3)(iv) (describing a withholding statement provided by a non-qualified intermediary), § 1.1441-1(e)(5)(v) (describing a withholding statement provided by a qualified intermediary), or under § 1.1441-5 (describing a withholding statement provided by a foreign partnership, foreign simple trust, or foreign grantor trust), that allocates the payment (or portion of a payment) to a chapter 4 withholding rate pool or specific payees to which withholding applies under chapter 4. The provisions of each of the foregoing sections shall apply by substituting the term "payor" for the term "withholding agent." A payor or middleman may rely on a withholding statement provided by a foreign intermediary or flow-through entity that identifies a chapter 4 withholding rate pool of U.S. payees (as described in § 1.6049-4(c)(4)) or, with respect to a withholdable payment, a chapter 4 withholding rate pool of recalcitrant account holders (as described in § 1.1471-4(d)(6)) provided that the payor or middleman identifies the foreign intermediary or flow-through entity that maintains the accounts (as described in § 1.1471-5(b)(5)) included in the chapter 4 with-

holding rate pool as a participating FFI (including a reporting Model 2 FFI) or registered deemed-compliant FFI (including a reporting Model 1 FFI) by applying the rules in § 1.1471-3(d)(4) or in § 1.1471-3(e)(4)(vi)(B), as applicable, for identifying the payee of a payment (by substituting the term "payor" for the term "withholding agent"). See, however, § 1.1441-1(e)(5)(v)(C)(2)(*i*) for when a qualified intermediary may provide a single pool of recalcitrant account holders (without the need to subdivide into the pools described in § 1.1471-4(d)(6)). Additionally, when a foreign intermediary or flow through entity provides to a payor or middleman a withholding statement that allocates the payment (or portion of a payment) to a chapter 4 withholding rate pool of U.S. payees, the payor or middleman may also rely on the withholding statement if the payor or middleman identifies the intermediary or flow-through entity as a qualified intermediary (as defined in § 1.1441-1(c)(15) by applying the rules described in § 1.1441-1(b)(2)(vii)) that provides the certification described in § 1.1441-1(e)(3)(ii)(D) with respect to U.S. payees that hold accounts with a foreign intermediary or flow-through entity other than the qualified intermediary providing the certification.

(15) If a foreign intermediary, as described in § 1.1441-1(c)(13), or a U.S. branch that is not treated as a U.S. person receives a payment from a payor, which payment the payor can reliably associate with a valid withholding certificate described in § 1.1441-1(e)(3)(ii) or (iii), or § 1.1441-1(e)(3)(v), respectively, furnished by such intermediary or branch, then the intermediary or branch is not required to report such payment when it, in turn, pays the amount, unless, and to the extent, the intermediary or branch knows that the payment is required to be reported under this section and was not so reported. For example, if a U.S. branch described in § 1.1441-1(b)(2)(iv) fails to provide information regarding U.S. persons that are not exempt from reporting under § 1.6049-4(c)(1)(ii) to the person from whom the U.S. branch receives the payment, the amount paid by the U.S. branch to such person is interest or original issue discount. See, however, § 1.6049-4(c)(4) for when reporting under section 6049 is coordinated with reporting under chapter 4 or an applicable IGA (as defined in § 1.6049-4(f)(7)). The exception for payments described in this paragraph (b)(15) shall not apply to a qualified intermediary that assumes reporting responsibility under chapter 61 of the Code for the payment under the agreement described in § 1.1441-1(e)(5)(iii).

(16) Amounts of interest as determined under the provisions of § 1.446-3(g)(4) (dealing with interest in the case of a significant nonperiodic payment with respect to a notional principal contract). Such amounts are governed by the provisions of section 6041. See § 1.6041-1(d)(5).

(c) *Applicable rules.*—(1) *Documentary evidence for offshore obligations and certain other obliga-*

tions.—(i) A payor may rely on documentary evidence described in § 1.1471-3(c)(5)(i) instead of a beneficial owner withholding certificate described in § 1.1441-1(e)(2)(i) in the case of an amount paid outside the United States (as described in paragraph (e) of this section) with respect to an offshore obligation, or, in the case of broker proceeds described in § 1.6045-1(c)(2), to the extent provided in § 1.6045-1(g)(1)(i). For purposes of this section, the term *offshore obligation* means—

(A) An account maintained at an office or branch of a bank or other financial institution located outside the United States; or

(B) An obligation as defined in § 1.6049-4(f)(3) (other than an account described in paragraph (c)(1)(i)(A) of this section), contract, or other instrument with respect to which the payor is either engaged in business as a broker or dealer in securities or a financial institution (as defined in § 1.1471-5(e)) that engages in significant activities at an office or branch located outside the United States. For purposes of the preceding sentence, an office or branch of such payor shall be considered to engage in significant activities with respect to an obligation when it participates materially and actively in negotiating the obligation under the principles described in § 1.864-4(c)(5)(iii) (substituting the term "obligation" for the term "stock or security").

(ii) A payor may rely on documentary evidence if the payor has established procedures to obtain, review, and maintain documentary evidence sufficient to establish the identity of the payee and the status of that person as a foreign person; and the payor obtains, reviews, and maintains such documentary evidence in accordance with those procedures. A payor maintains the documents reviewed for purposes of this paragraph (c)(1) by retaining an original, certified copy, or photocopy (including a microfiche, electronic scan, or similar means of electronic storage) of the documents reviewed for as long as it may be relevant to the determination of the payor's obligation to report under § 1.6049-4 and this section and noting in its records the date on which the document was received and reviewed. Documentary evidence furnished for a payment of an amount subject to withholding under chapter 3 of the Code or that is a chapter 4 reportable amount under § 1.1474-1(d)(2) must contain all of the information that is necessary to complete a Form 1042-S for that payment. See § § 1.1471-3(c) and 1.1471-4(c) for additional documentation requirements to identify a payee or account holder for chapter 4 purposes that may apply in addition to the requirements under paragraph (c) of this section.

(iii) Even if an account or obligation (as defined in § 1.6049-4(f)(3)) is not maintained outside the United States (maintained in the United States), a payor may rely on documentary evidence associated with a withholding certificate described in § 1.1441-1(e)(3)(iii) with respect to the persons for whom an entity acting as an intermediary collects the payment. A payor may also rely on documentary evidence associated with a flow-through withholding certificate for payments treated as made to foreign partners of a nonwithholding foreign partnership, as defined in § 1.1441-1(c)(28), the foreign beneficiaries of a foreign simple trust, as defined in § 1.1441-1(c)(24), or foreign owners of a foreign grantor trust, as defined in § 1.1441-1(c)(26), even though the partnership or trust account is an obligation maintained in the United States.

(iv) For accounts opened on or after July 1, 2014, and before January 1, 2015, and for obligations entered into on or after July 1, 2014, and before January 1, 2015, a payor may continue to apply the rules of § 1.6049-5(c)(1) and (c)(4) as in effect and contained in 26 CFR part 1 revised April 1, 2013, rather than this paragraph (c)(1) and paragraph (c)(4) of this section. A payor that applies the rules of § 1.6049-5(c)(1) and (c)(4) as in effect and contained in 26 CFR part 1 revised April 1, 2013, to an account or obligation must also apply § 1.1441-6(c)(2) (to the extent applicable) and § 1.6049-5(e) both as in effect and contained in 26 CFR part 1 revised April, 2013, with respect to the account or obligation.

(2) *Other applicable rules.*—The provisions of § 1.1441-1(e)(4)(i) through (xii) (regarding who may sign a certificate, validity period of certificates and documentary evidence, retention of certificates, reliance rules, etc.) shall apply (by substituting the term "payor" for the term "withholding agent" and disregarding the fact that the provisions under § 1.1441-1(e)(4) only apply to amounts subject to withholding under chapter 3 of the Code) to withholding certificates and documentary evidence furnished for purposes of this section. See § 1.1441-1(b)(2)(vii) for provisions dealing with reliable association of a payment with documentation.

(3) *Standards of knowledge.*—A payor may not rely on a withholding certificate or documentary evidence described in paragraph (c)(1) or (4) of this section if it has actual knowledge or reason to know that any information or certification stated in the certificate or documentary evidence is unreliable. A payor has reason to know that information or certifications are unreliable only if the payor would have reason to know under the provisions of § 1.1441-7(b)(2) and (3) that the information and certifications provided on the certificate or in the documentary evidence are unreliable or, in the case of a Form W-9 (or an acceptable substitute), it cannot reasonably rely on the documentation as set forth in § 31.3406(h)-3(e) of this chapter (see the information and certification described in § 31.3406(h)-3(e)(2)(i) through (iv) of this chapter that are required in order for a payor reasonably to rely on a Form W-9). The provisions of § 1.1441-7(b)(2) and (3) shall apply for purposes of this paragraph (c)(3) irrespective of the type of income to which § 1.1441-7(b)(2) is otherwise limited. The exemptions from reporting described in paragraphs (b)(10) and (11) of this section shall not apply if the payor has actual

knowledge that the payee is a U.S. person who is not an exempt recipient.

(4) *Special documentation rules for certain payments.*—This paragraph (c)(4) modifies the provisions of paragraph (c)(1) of this section for payments of amounts that are not subject to withholding under chapter 3 of the Code, other than amounts described in paragraph (d)(3)(iii) of this section (dealing with U.S. short-term OID and U.S. source deposit interest described in section 871(i)(2)(A) or 881(d)(3)). Amounts are not subject to withholding under chapter 3 of the Code if they are not included in the definition of amounts subject to withholding under § 1.1441-2(a) (*e.g.*, deposit interest with foreign branches of U.S. banks, foreign source income, or broker proceeds). A payor may rely upon documentation in lieu of documentary evidence (as described in paragraph (c)(1) of this section) or a written statement (as defined in § 1.1471-1(b)(150)) or another statement to the extent permitted in paragraphs (c)(4)(i) through (iii) of this section, until the payor knows or has reason to know of a change in circumstance that makes the documentation unreliable or incorrect (as defined in § 1.1441-1(e)) when the payor does not have customer information for the payee that includes any of the U.S. indicia described in § 1.1471-3(c)(6)(ii)(C)(1). Further, a payor may maintain such documentation or documentary evidence as required in paragraph (c)(4)(iv) of this section.

(i) *Statement in lieu of documentary evidence with respect to accounts.*—If under the local laws, regulations, or practices of a country in which an account is maintained, it is not customary to obtain documentary evidence described in paragraph (c)(1) of this section with respect to the type of account, the payor may, instead of obtaining a beneficial owner withholding certificate described in § 1.1441-1(e)(2)(i) or documentary evidence described in paragraph (c)(1) of this section, establish a payee's foreign status based on the statement described in this paragraph (c)(4)(i) (or such substitute statement as the Internal Revenue Service may prescribe) made on an account opening form. However, see, also § 1.1471-4(c) or an applicable IGA for additional documentation requirements that may apply to a participating FFI (including a reporting Model 2 FFI) for determining the status of its account holders for chapter 4 purposes. The statement referred to in this paragraph (c)(4)(i) must appear near the signature line and must state, "By opening this account and signing below, the account owner represents and warrants that he/she/it is not a U.S. person for purposes of U.S. Federal income tax and that he/she/it is not acting for, or on behalf of, a U.S. person. A false statement or misrepresentation of tax status by a U.S. person could lead to penalties under U.S. law. If your tax status changes and you become a U.S. citizen or a resident, you must notify us within 30 days." Additionally, a payor may, instead of obtaining a beneficial owner withholding certificate described in

§ 1.1441-1(e)(2)(i) or § 1.1471-3(c)(3)(ii) or documentary evidence described in paragraph (c)(1) of this section, establish a payee's foreign status based on a written statement described in paragraph § 1.1471-1(b)(150) to the extent a payor uses such written statement to establish a payee's chapter 4 status and is permitted to use the written statement under § 1.1471-3(d) (by substituting the term "payor" for the term "withholding agent") without any other documentary evidence.

(ii) *Documentation under IGA.*—A payor that is a reporting Model 1 FFI or reporting Model 2 FFI may rely upon documentation or information establishing a payee's status that is permitted under an applicable IGA for determining whether the account of the payee is other than a U.S. account and regardless of whether such documentation or certification is described in paragraph (c)(1) of this section or § 1.1441-1(e)(2).

(iii) *Maintenance of documentation and written statement.*—A payor maintains documentation if it either maintains the documentary evidence as described in paragraph (c)(1) of this section or retains a record of the documentary evidence reviewed if the payor is not required to retain copies of the documentation pursuant to the payor's AML due diligence (as defined in § 1.1471-1(b)(4)). A payor retains a record of documentary evidence reviewed by noting in its records the type of documentation reviewed, the date the document was reviewed, the document's identification number (if any), and whether such documentation contained any U.S. indicia described in § 1.1441-7(b)(8). Any statement described in paragraph (c)(4)(i) of this section, must be retained in accordance with § 1.1471-3(c)(6)(iii).

(5) *U.S. payor, U.S. middleman, non-U.S. payor, and non-U.S. middleman.*—The terms *payor* and *middleman* have the meanings ascribed to them under § 1.6049-4(a). A *non-U.S. payor* or *non-U.S. middleman* means a payor or middleman other than a U.S. payor or U.S. middleman. The term *U.S. payor* or *U.S. middleman* means—

(i) *Definition.*—(A) A person described in section 7701(a)(30) (including a foreign branch or office of such person);

(B) The government of the United States or the government of any State or political subdivision thereof (or any agency or instrumentality of any of the foregoing);

(C) A controlled foreign corporation within the meaning of section 957(a);

(D) A foreign partnership, if at any time during its tax year, one or more of its partners are U.S. persons (as defined in § 1.1441-1(c)(2)) who, in the aggregate hold more than 50 percent of the income or capital interest in the partnership or if, at any time during its tax year, it is engaged in the conduct of a trade or business in the United States;

(E) A foreign person 50 percent or more of the gross income of which, from all sources for the three-year period ending with the close of its taxable year preceding the collection or payment (or such part of such period as the person has been in existence), was effectively connected with the conduct of trade or business within the United States; or

(F) A U.S. branch or territory financial institution described in § 1.1441-1(b)(2)(iv) that is treated as a U.S. person.

(ii) *Reporting by U.S. payors in U.S. possessions.*—U.S. payors are not required to report on Form 1099 income that is from sources within a possession of the United States and that is exempt from taxation under section 931, 932, or 933, each of which sections exempts certain income from sources within a possession of the United States paid to a bona fide resident of that possession. For purposes of this paragraph (c)(5)(ii), a U.S. payor may treat the beneficial owner as a bona fide resident of the possession of the United States from which the income is sourced if, prior to payment of the income, the U.S. payor can reliably associate the payment with valid documentation that supports the claim of residence in the possession of the United States from which the income is sourced. This paragraph (c)(5)(ii) shall not apply if the U.S. payor has actual knowledge or reason to know that the documentation is unreliable or incorrect or that the income does not satisfy the requirements for exemption under section 931, 932, or 933. For the rules determining whether income is from sources within a possession of the United States, see section 937(b) and the regulations thereunder.

(6) *Examples.*—The following examples illustrate the provisions of paragraphs (b) and (c) of this section:

Example 1. FC is a foreign corporation that is not engaged in a trade or business in the United States during the current calendar year. D, an individual who is a resident and citizen of the United States, holds a registered obligation issued by FC in a public offering. Interest is paid on the obligation within the United States by DC, a U.S. corporation that is the designated paying agent of FC. D does not have an account with DC. Although interest paid on the obligation issued by FC is foreign source, the interest paid by DC to D is considered to be interest under paragraph (b)(6) of this section for purposes of information reporting under section 6049 because it is not paid and received outside the United States within the meaning of § 1.6049-4(f)(16).

Example 2. The facts are the same as in *Example 1* except that D is a nonresident alien individual who has furnished DC with a Form W-8 in accordance with the provisions of § 1.1441-1(e)(1)(ii). By reason of paragraph (b)(12) of this section, the payment of interest by DC to D is not considered to be a payment of interest for purposes of information reporting under section 6049. Therefore, DC is not required to make an information return under section 6049.

Reg. § 1.6049-5(c)(6)

Example 3. The facts are the same as in *Example 2* except that the obligation of FC is held in a custodial account for D by FB, a foreign branch of a U.S. financial institution. By reason of paragraph (c)(5) of this section, FB is considered to be a U.S. middleman. Therefore, FB is required to make an information return unless FB may treat D as a beneficial owner that is a foreign person in accordance with the provisions of §1.1441-1(e)(1)(ii).

Example 4. The facts are the same as in *Example 3* except that the FC obligation is held for D by NC, in a custodial account at NC's foreign branch. NC is a foreign corporation that is a non-U.S. middleman described in paragraph (c)(5) of this section. The payment by NC to D is paid and received outside of the United States under §1.6049-4(f)(16) and therefore is not considered to be a payment of interest for purposes of section 6049 pursuant to paragraph (b)(6) of this section. Therefore, NC is not required to make an information return under section 6049 with respect to the payment.

(d) *Determination of status as U.S. or foreign payee and applicable presumptions in the absence of documentation.*—(1) *Identifying the payee.*—The provisions of §§1.1441-1(b)(2), 1.1441-5(c)(1) and (e)(2) and (3) shall apply (by substituting the term "payor" for the term "withholding agent") to identify the payee (other than a payee included in a chapter 4 withholding rate pool described in paragraph (b)(14) of this section) for purposes of this section (and other sections of the regulations under this chapter to which this paragraph (d)(1) applies), except to the extent provided in this paragraph (d)(1) in the case of a payment of an amount that is not subject to withholding under chapter 3 of the Code and that is not a withholdable payment (as defined in §1.6049-4(f)(15)). Amounts are not subject to withholding under chapter 3 of the Code if they are not included in the definition of amounts subject to withholding under §1.1441-2(a) (*e.g.*, deposit interest with foreign branches of U.S. banks, foreign source income, or broker proceeds). The exceptions to the application of §1.1441-1(b)(2) to amounts that are not subject to withholding under chapter 3 of the Code and that are not withholdable payments are as follows:

(i) The provisions of §1.1441-1(b)(2)(ii), dealing with payments to a U.S. agent or intermediary of a foreign person, shall not apply. Thus, a payment to a U.S. agent or intermediary of a foreign person is treated as a payment to a U.S. payee.

(ii) Payments to U.S. branches or territory financial institution described in §1.1441-1(b)(2)(iv) shall be treated as payments to a foreign payee, irrespective of the fact that the U.S. branch or territory financial institution is otherwise treated as a U.S. person for payments of amounts subject to withholding under chapter 3 and withholdable payments, and irrespective of the fact that the branch or territory

financial institution is treated as a U.S. payor for purposes of paragraph (c)(5) of this section.

(2) *Presumptions of U.S. or foreign status in the absence of documentation.*—(i) *In general.*—Except as otherwise provided in this paragraph (d)(2)(i), for purposes of this section (and other sections of regulations under this chapter 61 to which this paragraph (d)(2) applies), the provisions of §1.1441-1(b)(3)(i) through (ix) and §1.1441-5(d) and (e)(6) shall apply (by substituting the term "payor" for the term "withholding agent") to determine the classification (*e.g.*, individual, corporation, partnership, trust), status (*i.e.*, a U.S. or a foreign person), and other relevant characteristics (*e.g.*, beneficial owner or intermediary) of a payee if a payment cannot be reliably associated with valid documentation under §1.1441-1(b)(2)(vii) irrespective of whether the payments are subject to withholding under chapter 3 of the Code or are withholdable payments. The provisions of §1.1441-1(b)(3)(iii)(D) and (vii)(B) (referencing presumption rules for payments with respect to offshore obligations) shall not apply to a payment of an amount not subject to withholding under chapter 3, unless it is an amount that is a withholdable payment made to a payee that is an entity. Thus, in the case of a withholdable payment made to an entity, the presumption rules of §1.1441-1(b)(3)(iii)(D) and (vii)(B) shall apply regardless of whether the payment is an amount subject to withholding under chapter 3. Additionally, in the case of an amount paid outside the United States with respect to an offshore obligation described in §1.1441-1(b)(3)(iii)(D) or (vii)(B) of an amount not subject to withholding under chapter 3 and that is treated as made to a payee that is an individual, the presumption rules of §1.1441-1(b)(3)(iii) shall not apply, and the payee shall be presumed a U.S. person only when the payee has any of the indicia of U.S. status that are described in §1.1441-7(b)(5) or (8). In a case in which a withholding agent makes a withholdable payment that cannot reliably be associated with documentation, see §1.1471-3(f)(4) and (5) for determining the status of the payee for chapter 4 purposes when the payment is treated as made to a foreign entity (by substituting the term "payor" for the term "withholding agent"). The rules of §1.1441-1(b)(2)(vii) shall apply for purposes of determining when a payment can reliably be associated with documentation, by substituting the term "payor" for the term "withholding agent." For this purpose, the information, documentary evidence, statement, or other documentation described in paragraph (c)(4) of this section can be treated as documentation with which a payment can be associated.

(ii) *Grace period in the case of indicia of a foreign payee.*—When the conditions of this paragraph (d)(2)(ii) are satisfied, the 30-day grace period provisions under section 3406(e) shall not apply and the provisions of this paragraph (d)(2)(ii) shall apply instead. A payor that, at any

Reg. §1.6049-5(d)

time during the grace period described in this paragraph (d)(2)(ii), credits an account with payments described in § 1.1441-6(c)(2) (or credits an account with broker proceeds from securities described in § 1.1441-6(c)(2)), that are reportable under section 6042, 6045, 6049, or 6050N may, instead of treating the account as owned by a U.S. person and applying backup withholding under section 3406, if applicable, choose to treat the account as owned by a foreign person (and apply the grace period described in § 1.1441-1(b)(3)(iv)) if, at the beginning of the grace period, the address that the payor has in its records for the account holder is in a foreign country, the payor has been furnished the information contained in a withholding certificate described in § 1.1441-1(e)(2), or the payor holds a withholding certificate that is no longer reliable other than because the validity period as described in § 1.1441-1(e)(4)(ii)(A) has expired. In the case of a newly opened account, the grace period begins on the date that the payor first credits the account. In the case of an existing account for which the payor holds a Form W-8 or documentary evidence of foreign status, the payor may apply the provisions of the grace period described in § 1.1441-1(b)(3)(iv), beginning on the date that the payor first credits the account after the existing documentation held with regard to the account can no longer be relied upon (other than because the validity period described in § 1.1441-1(e)(4)(ii)(A) has expired). A new account shall be treated as an existing account for purposes of this paragraph (d)(2)(ii) if the account holder already holds an account at the branch location at which the new account is opened, or if the account is treated as a consolidated obligation as defined in § 1.1471-1(1)(b)(23) for purpose of chapter 4 to the extent the account does not receive any amounts subject to withholding under chapter 3. A new account shall also be treated as an existing account for purposes of this paragraph (d)(2)(ii) if an account is held at another branch location if the institution maintains an account information system described in § 1.1441-1(e)(4)(ix). The grace period terminates on the earlier of the close of the 90th day from the date on which the grace period begins or the date that valid documentation is provided. The grace period also terminates when the remaining balance in the account (due to withdrawals or otherwise) is equal to or less than 28 percent (or other statutory tax rate that is applicable to backup withholding) of the total amounts credited since the beginning of the grace period that would be subject to backup withholding if the provisions of this paragraph (d)(2)(ii) did not apply. At the end of the grace period, the payor shall treat the amounts credited to the account, or paid with respect to an account, during the grace period as paid to a U.S. or foreign payee depending upon whether documentation has been furnished and the nature of any such documentation furnished upon which the payor may rely to treat the account as owned by a U.S. or foreign payee. If the documentation has not been received on or

before the date of expiration of the grace period, the payor may also apply the presumptions described in this paragraph (d) to amounts credited to the account after the date on which the grace period expires (until such time as the payor can reliably associate the documentation with amounts credited). See § 31.6413(a)-3(a)(1)(iv) of this chapter for treating backup withheld amounts under section 3406 as erroneously withheld when the documentation establishing foreign status is furnished prior to the end of the calendar year in which backup withholding occurs. If the provisions of this paragraph (d)(2)(ii) apply, the provisions of § 31.3406(d)-3 of this chapter shall not apply. For purposes of this paragraph (d)(2)(ii), an account holder's reinvestment of gross proceeds of a sale into other instruments constitutes a withdrawal and a nonqualified electronic transmission of information on a withholding certificate is a transmission that is not in accordance with the provisions of § 1.1441-1(e)(4)(iv). See § 1.1092(d)-1 for a definition of the term actively traded for purposes of this paragraph (d)(2)(ii).

(iii) *Joint owners.*—Amounts paid to accounts held jointly for which a certificate or documentation is required as a condition for being exempt from reporting under paragraph (b) of this section are presumed made to U.S. payees who are not exempt recipients if, prior to payment, the payor cannot reliably associate the payment either with a Form W-9 furnished by one of the joint owners in the manner required in §§ 31.3406(d)-1 through 31.3406(d)-5 of this chapter, or with documentation described in paragraph (b)(12) of this section furnished by each joint owner upon which it can rely to treat each joint owner as a foreign payee or foreign beneficial owner. In the case of an amount that is a withholdable payment made to a joint account, however, see § 1.1471-3(f)(7) for when the payment is treated as made to a foreign payee that is a nonparticipating FFI (as defined in § 1.1471-1(b)(82)). For purposes of applying this paragraph (d)(2)(iii), the grace period described in paragraph (d)(2)(ii) of this section shall apply only if each payee qualifies for such grace period.

(3) *Payments to foreign intermediaries or flow-through entities.*—(i) *Payments of amounts subject to withholding under chapter 3 of the Code or withholdable payments.*—In the case of payments of amounts that the payor may treat as made to a foreign intermediary or flow-through entity in accordance with §§ 1.1441-1(b)(3)(ii)(C) and (b)(3)(v)(A) and 1.1441-5(c) or (e) and that are subject to withholding under § 1.1441-2(a), the provisions of §§ 1.1441-1(b)(2)(v) and 1.1441-5(c)(1), (e)(2), and (3) shall apply (by substituting the term "payor" for the term "withholding agent") to identify the payee. If a payment of an amount subject to withholding cannot be reliably associated with valid documentation from a payee in accordance with § 1.1441-1(b)(2)(vii), the presumption rules of §§ 1.1441-1(b)(3)(v) and 1.1441-5(d) and (e)(6)

Reg. § 1.6049-5(d)(3)(i)

shall apply to determine the payee's status for purposes of this section (and other sections of regulations under this chapter to which this paragraph (d)(3) applies). In the case of an amount that is a withholdable payment, see § 1.1471-3(c)(3) for rules to identify the payee and see § 1.1471-3(f)(5) for the presumption rule that shall apply to amounts treated as made to a foreign intermediary or flow-through entity (by substituting the term "payor" for the term "withholding agent"). For example, where a withholdable payment is made to an intermediary under § 1.1471-3 that is treated as a nonparticipating FFI under § 1.1471-3(f)(5), the nonparticipating FFI shall be treated as the payee under § 1.1471-3(c)(3) and for purposes of this paragraph (d)(3)(i), therefore, no information return shall be required under this section.

(ii) *Payments of amounts not subject to withholding under chapter 3 of the Code and that are not withholdable payments.*—Except as provided in paragraph (d)(3)(iii) of this section, amounts that are not subject to withholding under chapter 3 of the Code and that are not withholdable payments that the payor may treat as paid to a foreign intermediary or flow-through entity shall be treated as made to an exempt recipient described in § 1.6049-4(c) except to the extent that the payor has actual knowledge that any person for whom the intermediary or flow-through entity is collecting the payment is a U.S. person who is not an exempt recipient. In the case of such actual knowledge, the payor shall treat the payment that it knows is allocable to such U.S. person as a payment to a U.S. payee who is not an exempt recipient and has actual knowledge of the amount allocable to such a person.

(iii) *Special rule for payments of certain short-term original issue discount.*—(A) *General rule.*—A payment of U.S. source bank deposit interest not subject to chapter 4 withholding or U.S. source interest or original issue discount on the redemption of an obligation with a maturity from the date of issue of 183 days or less (short-term OID) described in section 871(g)(1)(B) or 881(e) that the payor may treat as paid to a foreign intermediary or flow-through entity in accordance with the provisions of § § 1.1441-1(b)(3)(ii)(C), (b)(3)(v)(A), § 1.1441-5(d) or (e) (by substituting the term "payor" for the term "withholding agent"), shall be treated as paid to an undocumented U.S. payee that is not an exempt recipient under paragraph § 1.6049-4(c) unless the payor has documentation from the payees of the payment and the payment is allocated to foreign payees, as a group, and to each U.S. non-exempt recipient payee. See § 1.1441-1(e)(3)(iv)(C)(2). However, a payor may rely on a withholding statement provided by an intermediary described in § 1.1441-1(e)(3)(iv) (or similar withholding statement for a flow-through entity) that identifies a chapter 4 withholding rate pool of U.S. payees (as described in § 1.6049-4(c)(4)(iii)) only if it identifies the foreign intermediary or flow-through entity as a participating FFI (including a reporting Model 2

FFI) or registered deemed-compliant FFI (including a reporting Model 1 FFI) under § 1.1471-3(d)(4) (by substituting the term "payor" for the term "withholding agent"). See also § 1.6049-4(c)(4)(iii) for when an FFI may provide a chapter 4 withholding rate pool of U.S. payees on a withholding statement.

(B) *Payee may be an intermediary.*—If a payment is made to a person described in § 1.6049-4(c)(1)(ii) that has not provided an intermediary withholding certificate under § 1.1441-1(e)(3)(i) but the payor knows or has reason to know that the payee may be an intermediary, the payor must apply the rules of paragraph (d)(3)(iii)(A) of this section. A payor has reason to know that such a person may be an intermediary if that person has provided documentation as an intermediary for another account with the same payor.

(iv) *Short-term deposits and repurchase transactions.*—The provisions of paragraph (d)(3)(ii) of this section and not paragraph (d)(3)(iii) of this section shall apply to deposits with banks and other financial institutions that remain on deposit for a period of two weeks or less, to amounts of original issue discount arising from a sale and repurchase transaction that is completed within a period of two weeks or less, or to amounts described in paragraphs (b)(7), (10) and (11) of this section (relating to certain obligations issued in bearer form).

(4) *Examples.*—The rules of paragraphs (d)(1) through (3) of this section are illustrated by the examples in this paragraph (d)(4). Unless otherwise specified in an example, the following facts apply: all FFIs, such as a nonqualified intermediary that is an FFI, are treated as participating FFIs; all payees have been identified with chapter 4 statuses that do not require withholding under chapter 4; and none of the payments are withholdable payments.

Example 1. (i) *Facts.* USP is a U.S. payor as defined in paragraph (c)(5) of this section. USP pays interest from sources within the United States that is a withholdable payment to an account maintained in the United States by X. The interest is not deposit interest described in sections 871(i)(2)(A) or 881(d). USP does not have a Form W-9, or withholding certificate from X as defined in § 1.1441-1(c)(16). Moreover, USP cannot treat X as an exempt recipient, as defined in § 1.6049-4(c)(1)(ii), without documentation and there is no indication that X is an individual, trust, or estate.

(ii) *Analysis.* The U.S. source interest is an amount subject to withholding as defined in § 1.1441-2(a). Under paragraph (d)(1) of this section, USP must apply the provisions of § § 1.1441-1(b)(2) and 1.1441-5(c) and (e) to determine the payee of the interest. Under § 1.1441-1(b)(2)(i), X, the person to whom the payment is made, is considered to be the payee, unless X is determined to be a flow-through entity, in which case the rules of § 1.1441-5 apply to determine the payee. Under paragraph (d)(2)(i) of this section, the rules of § 1.1441-1(b)(3)(ii) apply to determine the classification of a payee as an individual, trust, estate, corporation, or partnership. Under § 1.1441-1(b)(3)(ii)(B), X is presumed to be a partnership, since X does not appear to be an individual, trust or estate, and X cannot be presumed to be an exempt recipient in the absence of documentation. Paragraph (d)(2)(i) of this section requires USP to apply the provisions of §§ 1.1441-1(b)(3)(iii) and 1.1441-5(d) to determine whether X is presumed to be a U.S. or foreign partnership. Under §§ 1.1441-1(b)(3)(iii) and 1.1441-5(d)(2), X is presumed to be a U.S. partnership in absence of any indicia of foreign partnership status. The presumption of U.S. status applies even though the payment is a withholdable payment (see paragraph (d)(2) of this section and § 1.1471-3(f)(2) cross referencing the presumption rules of § 1.1441-1(b)(3)). The U.S. source interest paid to X is reportable under section 6049 on Form 1099 and the interest is subject to backup withholding under section 3406 because X has not provided its TIN on a valid Form W-9. No withholding or reporting applies to the payment under chapter 3 or 4 of the Code.

Example 2. (i) *Facts.* The facts are the same as in *Example 1*, except that the interest paid by USP is from sources outside the United States.

(ii) *Analysis.* Interest from sources outside the United States is not an amount subject to withholding, as defined in § 1.1441-2(a) or a withholdable payment. Under paragraph (d)(1) of this section, USP must apply the provisions of §§ 1.1441-1(b)(2) and 1.1441-5(c) and (e) to determine the payee. Under § 1.1441-1(b)(2)(i), X, the person to whom the payment is made, is considered to be the payee, unless X is determined to be a flow-through entity, in which case the rules of § 1.1441-5(c) or (e) apply to determine the payee. Under paragraph (d)(2)(i) of this section, the rules of § 1.1441-1(b)(3)(ii) apply to determine the classification of a payee as an individual, trust, estate, corporation, or partnership. These rules apply irrespective of whether the payment is an amount subject to withholding. Under § 1.1441-1(b)(3)(ii)(B), X is presumed to be a partnership, since X does not appear to be an individual, trust or estate, and X cannot be presumed to be an exempt recipient in the absence of documentation. Paragraph (d)(2)(i) of this section requires USP to apply the provisions of §§ 1.1441-1(b)(3)(iii) and 1.1441-5(d) to determine whether X is presumed to be a U.S. or foreign partnership. Under §§ 1.1441-1(b)(3)(iii) and 1.1441-5(d)(2), X is presumed to be a U.S. partnership in absence of any indicia of foreign partnership status. The foreign source interest is a payment subject to reporting on Form 1099 under § 1.6049-5(a). Further, because X is a nonexempt recipient that has failed to provide its TIN on a valid Form W-9, the foreign source interest is subject to backup withholding under section 3406.

Example 3. (i) *Facts.* USP is a U.S. payor as defined in paragraph (c)(5) of this section. USP makes a payment of U.S. source interest outside the United States to an offshore account of X. See paragraphs (c)(1) for a definition of offshore account and (e) for a payment outside the United States. USP does not have a withholding certificate from X as defined in § 1.1441-1(c)(16) nor does it have documentary evidence as described in § 1.1441-1(e)(1)(ii)(A)(2) and § 1.6049-5(c)(1).

(ii) *Analysis.* The interest is an amount subject to withholding as defined in § 1.1441-2(a). Under paragraph (d)(1) of this section, USP must apply the provisions of § 1.1441-1(b)(2) and § 1.1441-5(c) and (e) to determine the payee. Under § 1.1441-1(b)(2)(i), X, the person to whom the payment is made, is considered to be the payee, unless X is determined to be a flow-through entity, in which case the rules of § 1.1441-5(c) or (e) apply to determine the payee. Under paragraph (d)(2)(i) of this section, the rules of § 1.1441-1(b)(3)(ii) apply to determine the classification of a payee as an individual, trust, estate, corporation, or partnership. Under § 1.1441-1(b)(3)(ii)(B), X is presumed to be a partnership, since X does not appear to be an individual, trust or estate, and X cannot be presumed to be an exempt recipient in the absence of documentation. Paragraph (d)(2)(i) of this section requires USP to apply the provisions of §§ 1.1441-1(b)(3)(iii) and 1.1441-5(d) to determine whether, X is presumed to be a U.S. or foreign partnership. Under §§ 1.1441-1(b)(3)(iii)(D) and 1.1441-5(d)(2), X is presumed to be a foreign partnership. Therefore, under paragraph (d)(1) of this section and § 1.1441-5(c)(1)(i)(E), the payees of the interest are presumed to be the partners of X. Under § 1.1441-5(d)(3), the partners are presumed to be undocumented foreign persons. Therefore, USP must withhold 30% of the interest payment under § 1.1441-1(b)(1) and report the payment on Form 1042-S in accordance with § 1.1461-1(c).

Example 4. (i) *Facts.* The facts are the same as in *Example 3*, except that the interest is paid by F, a non-U.S. payor.

(ii) *Analysis.* The analysis and result are the same as in *Example 3*. F is a withholding agent under § 1.1441-7 and its status as a non-U.S. payor under paragraph (c)(5) of this section is irrelevant.

Example 5. (i) *Facts.* USP is a U.S. payor as defined in paragraph (c)(5) of this section that is not an FFI. USP makes a payment outside the United States of interest from sources outside the United States with respect to an offshore obligation held by X. USP does not have a withholding certificate from X as defined in § 1.1441-1(c)(16) nor does it have documentary evidence as described in §§ 1.1471-3(c)(5)(i) and 1.6049-5(c)(1). USP does not have actual knowledge of an employer identification number for X. X does not appear to be an individual, trust, or estate and cannot be treated as an exempt recipient, as defined in § 1.6049-4(c)(1)(ii) in the absence of documentation.

(ii) *Analysis.* The interest is not an amount subject to withholding as defined in § 1.1441-2(a) and is not a withholdable payment. Under paragraph (d)(1) of this section, USP must apply the rules of §§ 1.1441-1(b)(2) and 1.1441-5(c) and (e) to determine the payee of the interest. Under § 1.1441-1(b)(2)(i), X, the person to whom the payment is made, is considered to be the payee, unless X is determined to be a flow-through entity, in which case the rules of § 1.1441-5(c) or (e) apply to determine the payee. Under paragraph (d)(2)(i) of this section, § 1.1441-1(b)(3)(ii) applies to determine X's classification as an individual, trust, estate, corporation or partnership. Under § 1.1441-1(b)(3)(ii)(B), X is treated as a partnership, since it does not appear to be an individual, trust, or estate and cannot be treated as an exempt recipient without documentation. Paragraph (d)(2)(i) of this section requires USP to apply the provisions of §§ 1.1441-1(b)(3)(iii) and 1.1441-5(d) to determine whether, X is presumed to be a U.S. or foreign partnership. Paragraph (d)(2)(i) of this section also states that the presumptions of foreign status for payments made with respect to offshore obligations contained in §§ 1.1441-1(b)(3)(iii)(D) and 1.1441-5(d)(2) do not apply to amounts that are not subject to withholding and that are not withholdable payments described in paragraph (d)(2)(i). Therefore, under §§ 1.1441-1(b)(3)(iii) and 1.1441-5(d)(2), X is presumed to be a U.S. partnership because it does not have actual knowledge that X's employer identification number begins with the digits "98." Therefore, USP must treat X as a U.S. person that is not an exempt recipient and report the payment on Form 1099 under section 6049. Under § 31.3406(g)-1(e) of this chapter, however, USP is not required to backup withhold on the payment unless it has actual knowledge that X is a U.S. person that is not an exempt recipient.

Example 6. (i) *Facts.* The facts are the same as in *Example 5*, except that the interest is paid by F, a non-U.S. payor, as defined under paragraph (c)(5) of this section.

(ii) *Analysis.* The analysis is the same as under *Example 5*. However, F is a non-U.S. payor paying foreign source interest outside the United States, and there is no indication that the amount is received in the United States under § 1.6049-4(f)(16). Thus, paragraph (b)(6) of this section exempts the payment from reporting under section 6049.

Example 7. (i) *Facts.* USP, a U.S. payor as defined in paragraph (c)(5) of this section that is not an FFI, makes a payment of U.S. source interest that is a withholdable payment to NQI, a nonqualified intermediary as defined in § 1.1441-1(c)(14), that is a certified deemed-compliant FFI under § 1.1471-5(f)(2). The interest is paid inside the United States to an account of a bank or other financial institution maintained in the United States. NQI has provided USP with a nonqualified intermediary withholding certificate, as described in § 1.1441-1(e)(3)(iii) that includes its chapter 4 status, but has not attached any documentation from the persons on whose behalf it acts or a withholding statement as described in § 1.1441-1(e)(3)(iv).

(ii) *Analysis.* U.S. source interest is an amount subject to withholding under § 1.1441-2(a). USP may treat the payment as made to a foreign intermediary under § 1.1441-1(b)(3)(v)(A) because USP has received a nonqualified intermediary withholding certificate from NQI and may except NQI from withholding under chapter 4 of the Code given NQI's status for chapter 4 purposes as a deemed-compliant FFI. Under paragraph (d)(3)(i) of this section, USP must then apply § 1.1471-3(c)(3) to treat the persons on whose behalf NQI is acting as the payees. Paragraph (d)(3)(i) of this section also requires USP to apply the presumption rules of § 1.1441-1(b)(3)(v) if it cannot reliably associate the payment with valid documentation from a payee. See § 1.1441-1(b)(2)(vii). As the payment is a withholdable payment, the interest is treated as paid to a nonparticipating FFI under § 1.1471-3(f)(4). Therefore, the payment is not subject to reporting on Form 1099 under paragraph (b)(12) of this section. See § 1.1471-2(a) for the withholding requirement with respect to the payment and § 1.1474-1(d)(2) for the requirement to report the payment on Form 1042-S.

Example 8. (i) *Facts.* The facts are the same as in *Example 7*, except that the interest is paid outside the United States, as defined in paragraph (e) of this section to an offshore account, as defined in paragraph (c)(1) of this section and is not a withholdable payment.

(ii) *Analysis.* Under § 1.1441-1(b)(3)(v)(B), the interest is treated as paid to an unknown foreign payee because it cannot be reliably associated with documentation under § 1.1441-1(b)(2)(vii). Therefore, the payment is not subject to reporting on Form 1099 under paragraph (b)(12) of this section because the payment is presumed made to a foreign person. The payment is subject to withholding, however, under § 1.1441-1(b) at a rate of 30% and is subject to reporting on Form 1042-S under § 1.1461-1(c).

Example 9. (i) *Facts.* The facts are the same as in *Example 8*, except that the interest is paid by F, a non-U.S. payor, as defined in paragraph (c)(5) of this section.

(ii) *Analysis.* The analysis and results are the same as in *Example 8*.

Example 10. (i) *Facts.* USP, a U.S. payor as defined in paragraph (c)(5) of this section, makes a payment of foreign source interest (other than deposit interest) to NQI, a foreign corporation and a nonqualified intermediary as defined in § 1.1441-1(c)(14). NQI has provided USP with a nonqualified intermediary withholding certificate, as described in § 1.1441-1(e)(3)(iii), but has not attached any documentation from the persons on whose behalf it acts or a withholding statement as described in § 1.1441-1(e)(3)(iv).

(ii) *Analysis.* Foreign source interest is not an amount subject to withholding under chapter 3 of the Code and is not a withholdable payment. See §§ 1.1441-2(a) and 1.1473-1(a). Under paragraph (d)(3)(ii) of this section, amounts that are not subject to withholding under chapter 3 of the Code and that are not withholdable payments described in paragraph (d)(2)(i) of this section that a payor may treat as paid to a foreign intermediary are treated as made to an exempt recipient described in §1.6049-4(c) absent actual knowledge that the payee is a U.S. person who is not an exempt recipient. Therefore, the foreign source interest is not subject to reporting on Form 1099.

Example 11. (i) *Facts.* USP is a U.S. payor as defined in paragraph (c)(5) of this section that is a bank. USP pays U.S. source original issue discount from the redemption of an obligation described in section 871(g)(1)(B) to NQI, a foreign corporation that is a nonqualified intermediary as defined in §1.1441-1(c)(14). The redemption proceeds are not paid outside of the United States as they are paid with respect to an account NQI has with a branch of a bank in the United States. See §1.6049-5(e)(2). NQI provides a nonqualified intermediary withholding certificate as described in §1.1441-1(e)(3)(iii) that includes a certification of its status as a registered deemed-compliant FFI but does not attach any payee documentation or a withholding statement described in §1.1441-1(e)(3)(iv).

(ii) *Analysis.* Under paragraph (d)(3)(ii)(A) of this section, USP must treat the payment as made to an undocumented U.S. payee that is not an exempt recipient and report the payment on Form 1099. Further, because the payment is made inside the United States, the exception to backup withholding with respect to offshore obligations contained in §31.3406(g)-1(e) of this chapter does not apply, and the payment is subject to backup withholding.

Example 12. (i) *Facts.* P, a payor, makes a payment to NQI of U.S. source interest on debt obligations issued prior to July 18, 1984, that mature 30 years from their issuance dates. Therefore, the interest does not qualify as portfolio interest under section 871(h) or 881(d). Additionally, the interest is not a withholdable payment under §1.1471-2(b) as the interest is a payment with respect of a grandfathered obligation for purposes of chapter 4 of the Code. NQI, a U.S. payor, is a nonqualified foreign intermediary, as defined in §1.1441-1(c)(14), and has furnished P a valid nonqualified intermediary withholding certificate described in §1.1441-1(e)(3)(iii) to which it has attached a valid Form W-9 for A, and two valid beneficial owner Forms W-8, one for B and one for C. A is not an exempt recipient under §1.6049-4(c). NQI furnishes a withholding statement, described in §1.1441-1(e)(3)(iv), in which it allocates 20% of the U.S. source interest to A, but does not allocate the remaining 80% of the interest between B and C. B's withholding certificate indicates that B is a foreign pension fund, exempt from U.S. tax under the U.S. income tax treaty with Country T. C's withholding certificate indicates that C is a foreign corporation not entitled to a reduced rate of withholding.

(ii) *Analysis.* As the interest is not a withholdable payment under paragraph (d)(3)(i) of this section, P applies the rules of §1.1441-1(b)(2)(v) to determine the payees of the

interest even though NQI has not certified its status for purposes of chapter 4 of the Code. Under that section, the payees are the persons on whose behalf NQI acts—A, B and C. Because P can reliably associate 20% of the payment with valid documentation provided by A, P must treat 20% of the interest as paid to A, a U.S. person not exempt from reporting, and report the payment on Form 1099. P cannot reliably associate the remaining 80% of the payment with valid documentation under §1.1441-1(b)(2)(vii) and, therefore, under paragraph (d)(3)(i) of this section must apply the presumption rules of §1.1441-1(b)(3)(v). Under that section, the interest is presumed paid to an unknown foreign payee. Under paragraph (b)(12) of this section, P is not required to report the interest presumed paid to a foreign person on Form 1099. Under §1.1441-1(b), 80% of the interest is subject to 30% withholding, however, and the interest is reportable on Form 1042-S under §1.1461-1(c).

Example 13. (i) *Facts.* The facts are the same as in *Example 12,* except that P can reliably associate 30% of the payment of interest to B, but cannot reliably associate the remaining 70 percent with A or C.

(ii) *Analysis.* Under paragraph (d)(3)(i) of this section, P applies the rules of §1.1441-1(b)(2)(v) to determine the payees of the interest. Under that section, the payees are the persons on whose behalf NQI acts—A, B and C. Because P can reliably associate 30% of the payment with B, a foreign pensions fund exempt from withholding under an income tax treaty, P may treat that payment as paid to B and not subject to reporting on Form 1099 under paragraph (b)(12) of this section. P cannot reliably associate the remaining 70% of the payment with valid documentation under §1.1441-1(b)(2)(vii) and, therefore, under paragraph (d)(3)(i) of this section must apply the presumption rules of §1.1441-1(b)(3)(v). Under that section, the interest is presumed paid to an unknown foreign payee. Under paragraph (b)(12) of this section, P is not required to report the interest presumed paid to a foreign person on Form 1099. Under §1.1441-1(b), 80% of the interest is subject to 30% withholding, however, and the interest is reportable on Form 1042-S under §1.1461-1(c).

Example 14. (i) *Facts.* The facts are the same as in *Example 12,* except that P also makes a payment of foreign source interest to NQI.

(ii) *Analysis.* Under paragraph (d)(3)(ii), P may treat the foreign source interest as paid to an exempt recipient as defined in §1.6049-4(c) and not subject to reporting on Form 1099 even though some or all of the foreign source interest may in fact be owned by A, the U.S. person that is not exempt from reporting.

Example 15. (i) *Facts.* The facts are the same as in *Example 12,* except that NQI is a non-U.S. payor.

(ii) *Analysis.* The analysis is the same as under *Example 12* with respect to B and C. However, because NQI is a non-U.S. payor, it may under §1.6049-4(c)(4)(iii) allocate the portion of the payment to A to a chapter 4 withholding rate pool of U.S. payees on a withholding statement provided to P in lieu of furnishing the Form W-9 to P when NQI reports the payments in accordance with § 1.6049-4(c)(4)(i). In such a case, provided that P obtains a certification form confirming NQI's status as a participating FFI, P is excepted from reporting the payment under paragraph (b)(14) of this section because P can reliably associate the payment with the documentation provided by NQI.

(e) *Determination of whether amounts are considered paid outside the United States.*—(1) *In general.*—For purposes of section 6049 and this section, an amount is considered to be paid by a payor or middleman outside the United States if the payor or middleman completes the acts necessary to effect payment outside the United States. See paragraphs (e)(2) through (5) of this section for further clarification of where amounts are considered paid. A payment shall not be considered to be made within the United States for purposes of section 6049 merely by reason of the fact that it is made on a draft drawn on a United States bank account or by a wire or other electronic transfer from a United States account.

(2) *Amounts paid with respect to deposits or accounts with banks and other financial institutions.*—Notwithstanding paragraph (e)(1) of this section, an amount paid by a bank or other financial institution with respect to a deposit or with respect to an account with the institution is considered paid at the branch or office at which the amount is credited unless the amount is collected by the financial institution as the agent of the payee. However, an amount will not be considered to be paid at the branch or office where the amount is considered to be credited unless the branch or office is a permanent place of business that is regularly maintained, occupied, and used to carry on a banking or similar financial business; the business is conducted by at least one employee of the branch or office who is regularly in attendance at such place of business during normal business hours; and the branch or office receives deposits and engages in one or more of the other activities described in § 1.864-4(c)(5)(i).

(3) *Coupon bonds and discount obligations in bearer form.*—Notwithstanding paragraph (e)(1) of this section, an amount paid with respect to a bond with coupons attached (including a certificate of deposit with detachable interest coupons) or a discount obligation that is not in registered form (within the meaning of section 163(f) and the regulations thereunder) is considered to be paid where the coupon or the discount obligation is presented to the payor or its paying agent for payment.

(4) *Foreign-targeted registered obligations.*—Notwithstanding paragraph (e)(1) of this section, where the payor is the issuer or the issuer's agent, an amount is considered paid outside the United States with respect to a foreign-targeted registered obligation issued before January 1,

2016, as described in § 1.871-14(e)(2), if either the amount is paid by transfer to an account maintained by the registered owner outside the United States, or by mail to an address of the registered owner outside the United States, or by credit to an international account. For purposes of this paragraph (e)(4), the term *international account* means the book-entry account of a financial institution (within the meaning of section 871(h)(4)(B)) or of an international financial organization with the Federal Reserve Bank of New York for which the Federal Reserve Bank of New York maintains records that specifically identify an international financial organization or a financial institution (within the meaning of section 871(h)(4)(B)) as either a non-United States person or a foreign branch of a United States person as registered owner. An international financial organization is a central bank or monetary authority of a foreign government or a public international organization of which the United States is a member to the extent that such central bank, authority, or organization holds obligations solely for its own account and is exempt from tax under section 892 or 895.

(5) *Examples.*—The application of the provisions of this paragraph (e) is illustrated by the following examples:

Example 1. FC is a foreign corporation that is not a U.S. payor or U.S. middleman, as defined in paragraph (c)(5) of this section. A holds FC coupon bonds that are not in registered form under section 163(f) and the regulations thereunder. FB, a foreign branch of DC, is the designated paying agent with respect to the bonds issued by FC. A does not have an account with FB. A presents a coupon from a FC bond for payment to FB at its office outside the United States. FB pays A with a check drawn against a bank account maintained in the United States. For purposes of section 6049, the place of payment of interest on the FC bond by FB to A is considered to be outside the United States under paragraph (e)(3) of this section.

Example 2. Individual C deposits funds in an account with FB, a foreign country X branch of DB, a U.S. corporation engaged in the commercial banking business. FB maintains an office and employees in foreign country X, accepts deposits, and conducts one or more of the other activities listed in § 1.864-4(c)(5)(i). The terms of C's deposit provide that it will be payable with accrued interest. Under paragraph (e)(2) of this section, FB is considered to pay the interest on C's deposit outside the United States.

Example 3. DC, a U.S. corporation engaged in the commercial banking business, maintains FB, a branch in foreign country X. FB has an office and employees in foreign country X, accepts deposits, and engages in one or more of the other activities listed in § 1.864-4(c)(5)(i). D, a United States citizen, purchases a certificate of deposit issued in 1980 by FB. The certificate of deposit has a maturity of 20 years and has detachable interest coupons payable at six-month intervals. D presents some of the coupons at the

U.S. office of DC and receives payment in cash. Because the coupon is presented to DC for payment within the United States, DC is considered to have made the payment within the United States under paragraph (e)(3) of this section.

Example 4. FB is recognized by both foreign country X and by the Federal Reserve Bank as a foreign country X branch of DC, a U.S. corporation engaged in the commercial banking business. A local foreign country X bank serves as FB's resident agent in Country X. FB maintains no physical office or employees in foreign country X. All the records, accounts, and transactions of FB are handled at the United States office of DC. E deposits funds in an amount maintained with FB. Interest earned on the deposit is periodically credited to E's account with FB by employees of DC. For purposes of section 6049, the place of payment of the interest on E's deposit with FB is considered to be within the United States by reason of paragraphs (e)(1) and (e)(2) of this section.

Example 5. DC is a U.S. corporation. A holds bonds that were issued by DC in registered form under section 163(f), as in effect prior to the amendment by section 502 of the HIRE Act of 2010, and the regulations thereunder and that are foreign-targeted registered obligations as defined in § 1.871-14(e)(2). DB, a commercial banking business, is the registrar of bonds issued by DC. Interest on the DC bonds is paid to A and other bondholders by check prepared by DB at its principal office inside the United States and mailed from there to A's address outside the United States. The check is drawn on a United States account maintained by DC with DB within the United States. The place of payment to A by DB of the interest on the DC bonds is considered to be outside the United States under paragraph (e)(4) of this section.

(f) *Original issue discount treated as payment of interest.*—In determining whether an obligation is one which was issued at a discount and the amount of discount which is includible in income of the holder, a payor (other than the issuer of the obligation) may rely on the Internal Revenue Service's publication of publicly traded original issue discount obligations. In the case of an obligation as to which there is during any calendar year an amount of original issue discount includible in the gross income of any holder (as determined under sections 1232 and 1232A and the regulations thereunder), the issuer of the obligation or a middleman (as defined in § 1.6049-4(f)(4)) shall be treated as having paid to such holder during such calendar year an amount of interest equal to the amount of original issue discount so includible without regard to any reduction by reason of a purchase allowance under section 1232(a)(2)(C)(ii), 1232A(a)(6) or (b)(4) or a purchase at a premium under 1232A(c)(4)(A) or paragraph (d)(2) of § 1.1232-3. Thus, the determination of the amount of original issue discount includible in the gross income of any holder with respect to any obligation shall be determined as if any holder of the obligation were the original holder.

However, see § 1.6049-9 for the reporting of premium for a debt instrument acquired on or after January 1, 2014. In the case of (1) an obligation to which section 1232A does not apply (for example, a short-term government obligation as defined in section 1232(a)(3)) and (2) and obligation issued on or before December 31, 1982, in bearer form, the amount of original issue discount includible in gross income shall be treated as if paid in the calendar year in which the date of maturity occurs or in which the date of redemption occurs if redemption occurs before maturity. The amount subject to reporting on an obligation issued in bearer form with a maturity at the date of issue of more than 1 year (a long term obligation) is the amount of original issue discount includible in the gross income of the holder during the calendar year of maturity or redemption if redemption occurs before maturity. The amount of original issue discount subject to reporting on a long term obligation shall not be reduced to reflect any purchase allowance. Discount on short term government obligations as defined in section 1232(a)(3), such as Treasury bills, and discount on other obligations with a maturity at the date of issue of not more than 1 year (a short term obligation), including commercial paper, when paid at maturity or redemption if redemption occurs before maturity, shall constitute a payment of interest for purposes of section 6049. In general, the amount subject to reporting on short term obligations is the difference between the stated redemption price at maturity and the original issue price. The procedure set forth in section 3455(b)(2)(B) and § 31.3455(b)-1(b)(3) for establishing the price at which a holder purchased an obligation subsequent to the date of original issue shall apply for purposes of section 6049. Original issue discount on an obligation (including an obligation with a maturity of not more than six months from the date of original issue) held by a nonresident alien individual or foreign corporation is interest described in paragraph (b)(1)(vi)(A) or (B) of this section and, therefore, is not interest subject to reporting under section 6049 unless it is described in § 1.6049-8(a) (relating to deposit interest paid on or after January 1, 2013, to certain nonresident alien individuals).

(g) *Effective/applicability date.*—This section applies to payments made on or after January 6, 2017. (For payments made after June 30, 2014, and before January 6, 2017, see this section as in effect and contained in 26 CFR part 1, as revised April 1, 2016. For payments made after December 31, 2000, and before July 1, 2014, see this section as in effect and contained in 26 CFR part 1, as revised April 1, 2013.) [Reg. § 1.6049-5.]

☐ [*T.D. 7881, 3-22-83. Amended by T.D. 7987, 10-23-84; T.D. 8029, 6-4-85; T.D. 8664, 4-15-96; T.D. 8734, 10-6-97; T.D. 8804, 12-30-98; T.D. 8856, 12-29-99; T.D. 8881, 5-15-2000 (corrected 4-5-2001); T.D. 9241, 1-23-2006 T.D. 9253, 3-13-2006; T.D. 9584, 4-17-2012, T.D. 9658, 2-28-2014, T.D. 9713, 3-12-2015 and T.D. 9808, 12-30-2016 (corrected 6-29-2017).*]

[Reg. §1.6049-6]

§1.6049-6. Statements to recipients of interest payments and holders of obligations for attributed original issue discount.— (a) *Requirement of furnishing statement to recipient.*—Every person filing a Form 1099 under section 6049(a) and §1.6049-4(e) shall furnish to the person whose identifying number is required to be shown on the form a written statement showing the information required by paragraph (b) of this section. With respect to interest other than interest reported on a transactional basis under §1.6049-4(e), no statement is required to be furnished under section 6049(c) and this section if the aggregate of the payments for the calendar year is less than $10, unless such payment is subject to the tax imposed under section 3406. In the case of any payment that is subject to withholding under section 3406, a statement shall be furnished irrespective of the amount of the payment. With respect to payments which are reported on a transactional basis, no statement is required to be furnished under section 6049(c) and this section to a person if the payment of interest to (or received on behalf of) such person for the transaction is less than $10 unless the payment is subject to withholding under section 3406. Again, in the case of any payment that is subject to withholding under section 3406, a statement shall be furnished irrespective of the amount of the payment.

(b) *Form of statement.*—The written statement required to be furnished to a person under paragraph (a) of this section shall show the following information:

(1) With respect to payments of interest (other than original issue discount) to any person during a calendar year, the statement shall show—

(i) The aggregate amount of payments shown on Form 1099 as having been made to (or received on behalf of) such person;

(ii) The amount of tax withheld under section 3406, if any;

(iii) The name and address of the person filing the form; and

(iv) A legend stating that such amount is being reported to the Internal Revenue Service.

(2) With respect to original issue discount includible in the gross income of a holder of an obligation during a calendar year, the statement shall show—

(i) The aggregate amount of original issue discount includible in the gross income by (or on behalf of) such person for the calendar year with respect to the obligation (determined by applying the rules of paragraph (b)(2) of §1.6049-4);

(ii) The amount of tax withheld under section 3406, if any;

(iii) The account, serial, or other identifying number of each obligation with respect to which a return is being made;

(iv) All other items shown on Form 1099 for such calendar year, and

(v) A legend stating that such amount and such items are being reported to the Internal Revenue Service.

(3) With respect to both statements to persons receiving payments of interest and persons holding obligations, the statement shall include the name, address, and taxpayer identifying number of such person. An IRS truncated taxpayer identifying number (TTIN) may be used as the identifying number for the person. For provisions relating to the use of TTINs, see §301.6109-4 of this chapter (Procedure and Administration Regulations).

(c) *Time for furnishing statements.*—Each statement required by this section to be furnished to any person for a calendar year with respect to a payment of interest (other than interest where a middleman or a Federal agency makes a return on a transactional basis (as described in paragraph (e) of §1.6049-4)) shall be furnished to such person after April 30 of the year of payment and on or before January 31 of the following year, but no statement may be furnished before the final interest payment for the calendar year. If a middleman or a Federal agency makes a return on a transactional basis, the statement shall be furnished at, or any time subsequent to, the time of payment, but in no event later than January 31 of the year following the calendar year of payment. However, for a statement required to be furnished after December 31, 2008, the February 15 due date under section 6045 applies to the statement if the statement is furnished in a consolidated reporting statement under section 6045. *See* §§1.6045-1(k)(3), 1.6045-2(d)(2), 1.6045-3(e)(2), 1.6045-4(m)(3), and 1.6045-5(a)(3)(ii).

(d) *Special rule.*—The requirements of this section for the furnishing of a statement to any person, including the legend requirement of paragraph (b)(1)(iv) and (2)(v) of this section, may be met by the furnishing to such person a copy of the Form 1099 filed pursuant to §1.6049-4, or an acceptable substitute, in respect of such person. However, in the case of Form 1099 with respect to original issue discount on obligations subject to section 1232A, a copy of the instructions must also be sent to such person. A statement shall be considered to be furnished to a person within the meaning of this section if it is mailed to such person at his last known address.

(e) *Statements to recipients.*—(1) *Requirement.*— A person required to make an information return under section 6049(a) and §1.6049-4 must furnish a statement to each recipient whose identifying number is required to be shown on the related information return for interest or original issue discount paid or accrued.

(2) *Form, manner, and time for providing statements to recipients.*—The statement required by paragraph (e)(1) of this section must be either the official Form 1099 prescribed by the Internal Revenue Service for the respective calendar year

or an acceptable substitute statement. The rules under §1.6042-4 (relating to statements with respect to dividends) apply comparably in determining the form of an acceptable substitute statement permitted by this paragraph (e). Those rules also apply for purposes of determining the manner of and time for providing the Form 1099 or its acceptable substitute to a recipient under paragraph (e)(1) of this section. However, with respect to original issue discount, the Form 1099 or acceptable substitute statement required by paragraph (e)(1) of this section must show the aggregate amount of original issue discount includible in the gross income by the recipient for the calendar year with respect to the obligation (determined by applying the rules of §1.6049-4(b)(2)), and the amount, serial number, or other identifying number of each obligation with respect to which a return is being made. With respect to interest or original issue discount, the Form 1099 or acceptable substitute statement required by paragraph (e)(1) of this section must be furnished to the recipient on or before January 31 of the year following the calendar year for which the return under section 6049(a)(1) was required to be made. However, for a statement required to be furnished after December 31, 2008, the February 15 due date under section 6045 applies to the statement if the statement is furnished in a consolidated reporting statement under section 6045. *See* §§1.6045-1(k)(3), 1.6045-2(d)(2), 1.6045-3(e)(2), 1.6045-4(m)(3), and 1.6045-5(a)(3)(ii).

(3) *Cross-reference to penalty.*—For provisions relating to the penalty provided for failure to furnish timely a correct payee statement required under section 6049(c) and §1.6049-6(a), see §301.6722-1 of this chapter (Procedure and Administration Regulations). See §301.6724-1 of this chapter for the waiver of a penalty if the failure is due to reasonable cause and is not due to willful neglect.

(4) *Special rule for amounts described in §1.6049-8(a).*—In the case of amounts described in §1.6049-8(a) (relating to payments of deposit interest to certain nonresident alien individuals) paid on or after January 1, 2013, any person who makes a Form 1042-S, "Foreign Person's U.S. Source Income Subject to Withholding," under section 6049(a) and §1.6049-4(b)(5) shall furnish a statement to the recipient either in person or by first class mail to the recipient's last known address. The statement shall include a copy of the Form 1042-S required to be prepared pursuant to §1.6049-4(b)(5) and a statement to the effect that the information on the form is being furnished to the United States Internal Revenue Service.

(5) *Effective/applicability date.*—Paragraph (b)(3) applies to payee statements due after December 31, 2014. Paragraph (e)(4) of this section applies to payee statements reporting payments of deposit interest to nonresident alien individuals paid on or after January 1, 2013. For the substantially similar statement mailing requirements that apply with respect to forms required

to be filed after October 22, 1986, and before January 1, 1996, see Rev. Proc. 84-70 (1984-2 C.B. 716)(or successor revenue procedures). See §601.601(d)(2) of this chapter. (For interest paid to a Canadian nonresident alien individual on or before December 31, 2012, see paragraph (e)(4) of this section as in effect and contained in 26 CFR part 1 revised April 1, 2000.) [Reg. §1.6049-6.]

☐ [T.D. 7881, 3-22-83. *Amended by T.D. 8637,* 12-20-95; *T.D. 8664,* 4-15-96; *T.D. 8734,* 10-6-97 (T.D. 8804 delayed the effective date of T.D. 8734 from January 1, 1999, to January 1, 2000; T.D. 8856 further delayed the effective date of T.D. 8734 until January 1, 2001) *T.D. 9504,* 10-12-2010; *T.D. 9584,* 4-17-2012 *and T.D. 9675,* 7-14-2014.]

[Reg. §1.6049-7]

§1.6049-7. Returns of information with respect to REMIC regular interests and collateralized debt instruments.—(a) *Definition of interest.*—(1) *In general.*—For purposes of section 6049(a), for taxable years beginning after December 31, 1986, the term "interest" includes:

(i) Interest actually paid with respect to a collateralized debt obligation (as defined in paragraph (d)(2) of this section),

(ii) Interest accrued with respect to a REMIC regular interest (as defined in section 860G(a)(1)), or

(iii) Original issue discount accrued with respect to a REMIC regular interest or a collateralized debt obligation.

(2) *Interest deemed paid.*—For purposes of this section and in determining who must make an information return under section 6049(a), interest as defined in paragraphs (a)(1)(ii) and (iii) of this section is deemed paid when includible in gross income under section 860B(b) or section 1272.

(b) *Information required to be reported to the Internal Revenue Service.*—(1) *Requirement of filing Form 8811 by REMICs and other issuers.*—(i) *In general.*—Except in the case of a REMIC all of whose regular interests are owned by one other REMIC, every REMIC and every issuer of a collateralized debt obligation (as defined in paragraph (d)(2) of this section) must make an information return on Form 8811, Information Return for Real Estate Mortgage Investment Conduits (REMICs) and Issuers of Collateralized Debt Obligations. Form 8811 must be filed in the time and manner prescribed in paragraph (b)(1)(iii) of this section. The submission of Form 8811 to the Internal Revenue Service does not satisfy the election requirement specified in §1.860D-1T(d) and does not require election of REMIC status.

(ii) *Information required to be reported.*—The following information must be reported to the Internal Revenue Service on Form 8811—

(A) The name, address, and employer identification number of the REMIC or the issuer of a collateralized debt obligation (as defined in paragraph (d)(2) of this section);

(B) The name, title, and either the address or the address and telephone number of the official or representative of the REMIC or the issuer of a collateralized debt obligation who will provide to any person specified in paragraph (e)(4) of this section the interest and original issue discount information specified in paragraph (e)(2) of this section;

(C) The startup day (as defined in section 860G(a)(9)) of the REMIC or the issue date (as defined in section 1275(a)(2)) of the collateralized debt obligation;

(D) The Committee on Uniform Security Identification Procedure (CUSIP) number, account number, serial number, or other identifying number or information, of each class of REMIC regular interest or collateralized debt obligation;

(E) The name, title, address, and telephone number of the official or representative of the REMIC or the issuer of a collateralized debt obligation whom the Internal Revenue Service may contact, and

(F) Any other information required by Form 8811.

(iii) *Time and manner of filing of information return.*—(A) *Manner of filing.*—Form 8811 must be filed with the Internal Revenue Service at the address specified on the form. The information specified in paragraph (b)(1)(ii) of this section must be provided on Form 8811 regardless of whether other information returns are filed by use of electronic media.

(B) *Time for filing.*—Form 8811 must be filed by each REMIC or issuer of a collateralized debt obligation on or before the later of July 31, 1989, or the 30th day after—

(1) the startup day (as defined in section 860G(a)(9)) in the case of a REMIC, or

(2) the issue date (as defined in section 1275(a)(2)) in the case of a collateralized debt obligation.

Further, each REMIC or issuer of a collateralized debt obligation must file a new Form 8811 on or before the 30th day after any change in the information previously provided on Form 8811.

(2) *Requirement of reporting by REMICs, issuers, and nominees.*—(i) *In general.*—Every person described in paragraph (b)(2)(ii) of this section who pays to another person $10 or more of interest (as defined in paragraph (a) of this section) during any calendar year must file an information return on Form 1099, unless the interest is paid to a person specified in paragraph (c) of this section.

(ii) *Person required to make reports.*—The persons required to make an information return under section 6049(a) and this section are—

(A) REMICs or issuers of collateralized debt obligations (as defined in paragraph (d)(2) of this section), and

(B) Any broker who holds as a nominee or middleman who holds as a nominee any REMIC regular interest or any collateralized debt obligation.

(iii) *Information to be reported.*—(A) *REMIC regular interests and collateralized debt obligations not issued with original issue discount.*—An information return on Form 1099 must be made for each holder of a REMIC regular interest or collateralized debt obligation not issued with original issue discount, but only if the holder has been paid interest (as defined in paragraph (a) of this section) of $10 or more for the calendar year. The information return must show—

(1) The name, address, and taxpayer identification number of the record holder,

(2) The CUSIP number, account number, serial number, or other identifying number or information, of each REMIC regular interest or collateralized debt obligation, with respect to which a return is being made,

(3) The aggregate amount of interest paid or deemed paid to the record holder for the period during the calendar year for which the return is made,

(4) The name, address, and taxpayer identification number of the person required to file this return, and

(5) Any other information required by the form.

(B) *REMIC regular interests and collateralized debt obligations issued with original issue discount.*—An information return on Form 1099 must be made for each holder of a REMIC regular interest or a collateralized debt obligation issued with original issue discount, but only if the holder has been paid interest (as defined in paragraph (a) of this section) of $10 or more for the calendar year. The information return must show—

(1) The name, address, and taxpayer identification number of the record holder,

(2) The CUSIP number, account number, serial number, or other identifying number or information, of each REMIC regular interest or collateralized debt obligation, with respect to which a return is being made,

(3) The aggregate amount of original issue discount deemed paid to the record holder for the period during the calendar year for which the return is made,

(4) The aggregate amount of interest, other than original issue discount, paid or deemed paid to the record holder for the period during the calendar year for which the return is made,

(5) The name, address, and taxpayer identification number of the person required to file this return, and

(6) Any other information required by the form.

(C) *Cross-reference.*—See § 1.67-3T(f)(3)(ii) for additional information required to be included on an information return on Form 1099 with respect to certain holders of regular interests in REMICs described in § 1.67-3T(a)(2)(ii).

(iv) *Time and place for filing a return with respect to amounts includible as interest.*—The returns required under this paragraph (b)(2) for any calendar year must be filed after September 30 of that year, but not before the payor's final payment to the payee for the year, and on or before February 28 (March 31 if filed electronically) of the following year. These returns must be filed with the appropriate Internal Revenue Service Center, the address of which is listed in the instructions for Form 1099. For extensions of time for filing returns under this section, see § 1.6081-1. For magnetic media filing requirements, see § 301.6011-2 of this chapter.

(c) *Information returns not required.*—An information return is not required under section 6049(a) and this section with respect to payments of interest on a REMIC regular interest or collateralized debt obligation, if the holder of the REMIC regular interest or the collateralized debt obligation is—

(1) An organization exempt from taxation under section 501(a) or an individual retirement plan;

(2) The United States or a State, the District of Columbia, a possession of the United States, or a political subdivision or a wholly-owned agency or instrumentality of any one or more of the foregoing;

(3) A foreign government, a political subdivision thereof, or an international organization;

(4) A foreign central bank of issue (as defined in § 1.895-1(b)(1)) or the Bank for International Settlements;

(5) A trust described in section 4947(a)(1) (relating to certain charitable trusts);

(6) For calendar quarters and calendar years after 1988, a broker (as defined in section 6045(c) and § 1.6045-1(a)(1));

(7) For calendar quarters and calendar years after 1988, a person who holds the REMIC regular interest or collateralized debt obligation as a middleman (as defined in § 1.6049-4(f)(4));

(8) For calendar quarters and calendar years after 1988, a corporation (as defined in section 7701(a)(3)), whether domestic or foreign;

(9) For calendar quarters and calendar years after 1988, a dealer in securities or commodities required to register as such under the laws of the United States or a State;

(10) For calendar quarters and calendar years after 1988, a real estate investment trust (as defined in section 856);

(11) For calendar quarters and calendar years after 1988, an entity registered at all times during the taxable year under the Investment Company Act of 1940;

(12) For calendar quarters and calendar years after 1988, a common trust fund (as defined in section 584(a));

(13) For calendar quarters and calendar years after 1988, a financial institution such as a mutual savings bank, savings and loan association, building and loan association, cooperative bank, homestead association, credit union, industrial loan association or bank, or other similar organization;

(14) For calendar quarters and calendar years after 1988, any trust which is exempt from tax under section 664(c) (*i.e.*, a charitable remainder annuity trust or a charitable remainder unitrust); and

(15) For calendar quarters and calendar years after 1988, a REMIC.

(d) *Special provisions and definitions.*—(1) *Incorporation of referenced rules.*—The special rules of § 1.6049-4(d) are incorporated in this section, as applicable, except that § 1.6049-4(d)(2) does not apply to any REMIC regular interest or any other debt instrument to which section 1272(a)(6) applies. Further, § 1.6049-5(c) does not apply to any REMIC regular interest or any other debt instrument to which section 1272(a)(6) applies.

(2) *Collateralized debt obligation.*—For purposes of this section, the term "collateralized debt obligation" means any debt instrument (except a tax-exempt obligation) described in section 1272(a)(6)(C)(ii) that is issued after December 31, 1986.

(e) *Requirement of furnishing information to certain nominees, corporations, and other specified persons.*—(1) *In general.*—For calendar quarters and calendar years after 1988, each REMIC or issuer of a collateralized debt obligation (as defined in paragraph (d)(2) of this section) must provide the information specified in paragraph (e)(2) of this section in the time and manner prescribed in paragraph (e)(3) of this section to any persons specified in paragraph (e)(4) of this section who request the information.

(2) *Information required to be reported.*—For each class of REMIC regular interest or collateralized debt obligation and for each calendar quarter specified by the person requesting the information, the REMIC or issuer of a collateralized debt obligation must provide the following information—

(i) The name, address and Employer Identification Number of the REMIC or issuer of a collateralized debt obligation;

(ii) The CUSIP number, account number, serial number, or other identifying number or information, of each specified class of REMIC regular interest or collateralized debt obligation and, for calendar quarters and calendar years after 1991, whether the information being reported is with respect to a REMIC regular interest or a collateralized debt obligation;

(iii) Interest paid on a collateralized debt obligation in the specified class for each calendar quarter, and the aggregate amount for the calendar year if the request is made for the last quarter of the calendar year;

(iv) Interest accrued on a REMIC regular interest in the specified class for each accrual period any day of which is in the specified calendar quarter, and the aggregate amount for the

Reg. § 1.6049-7(e)(2)(iv)

calendar year if the request is made for the last quarter of the calendar year;

(v) Original issue discount accrued on a collateralized debt obligation or REMIC regular interest in the specified class for each accrual period any day of which is in that calendar quarter, and the aggregate amount for the calendar year if the request is made for the last quarter of the calendar year;

(vi) The daily portion of original issue discount per $1,000 of original principal amount (or for calendar quarters prior to 1992, per other specified unit) as determined under section 1272(a)(6) and the regulations thereunder for each accrual period any day of which is in the specified calendar quarter;

(vii) The length of the accrual period;

(viii) The adjusted issue price (as defined in section 1275(a)(4)(B)(ii)) of the REMIC regular interest or the collateralized debt obligation at the beginning of each accrual period any day of which is in the specified calendar quarter;

(ix) The information required by paragraph (f)(3) of this section;

(x) Information required to compute the accrual of market discount including, for calendar years after 1989, the information required by paragraphs (f)(2)(i)(G) or (f)(2)(ii)(K) of this section; and

(xi) For calendar quarters and calendar years after 1991, if the REMIC is a single class REMIC (as described in §1.67-3T(a)(2)(ii)(B)), the information described in §1.67-3T(f)(1) and (f)(3)(ii)(A) and (B).

(3) *Time and manner for providing information.*—(i) *Manner of providing information.*—The information specified in paragraph (e)(2) of this section may be provided as follows—

(A) By telephone;

(B) By written statement sent by first class mail to the address provided by the requesting party;

(C) By causing it to be printed in a publication generally read by and available to persons specified in paragraph (e)(4) and by notifying the requesting persons in writing or by telephone of the publication in which it will appear, the date of its appearance, and, if possible, the page upon which it appears; or

(D) By any other method agreed to by the parties.
If the information is published, then the publication should also specify the date and, if possible, the page on which corrections, if any, will be printed.

(ii) *Time for furnishing the information.*—Each REMIC or issuer of a collateralized debt obligation must furnish the information specified in paragraph (e)(2) of this section on or before the later of—

(A) The 30th day after the close of the calendar quarter for which the information was requested, or

(B) The day that is two weeks after the receipt of the request.

(4) *Persons entitled to request information.*—The following persons may request the information specified in paragraph (e)(2) of this section with respect to a specified class of REMIC regular interests or collateralized debt obligations from a REMIC or issuer of a collateralized debt obligation in the manner prescribed in paragraph (e)(5) of this section—

(i) Any broker who holds on its own behalf or as a nominee any REMIC regular interest or collateralized debt obligation in the specified class,

(ii) Any middleman who is required to make an information return under section 6049(a) and paragraph (b)(2) of this section and who holds as a nominee any REMIC regular interest or collateralized debt obligation in the specified class,

(iii) Any corporation or non-calendar year taxpayer who holds a REMIC regular interest or collateralized debt obligation in the specified class directly, rather than through a nominee,

(iv) Any other person specified in paragraphs (c)(9) through (15) of this section who holds a REMIC regular interest or collateralized debt obligation in the specified class directly, rather than through a nominee, or

(v) A representative or agent for a person specified in paragraphs (e)(4)(i), (ii), (iii) or (iv) of this section.

(5) *Manner of requesting information from the REMIC.*—A requesting person specified in paragraph (e)(4) of this section should obtain Internal Revenue Service Publication 938, Real Estate Mortgage Investment Conduit (REMIC) and Collateralized Debt Obligation Reporting Information (or other guidance published by the Internal Revenue Service). This publication contains a directory of REMICs and issuers of collateralized debt obligations. The requesting person can locate the REMIC or issuer from whom information is needed and request the information from the official or representative of the REMIC or issuer in the manner specified in the publication. The publication will specify either an address or an address and telephone number. If the publication provides only an address, the request must be made in writing and mailed to the specified address. Further, the request must specify the calendar quarters (*e.g.*, all calendar quarters in 1989) and the classes of REMIC regular interests or collateralized debt obligations for which information is needed.

(f) *Requirement of furnishing statement to recipient.*—(1) *In general.*—Every person filing a Form 1099 under section 6049(a) and this section must furnish to the holder (the person whose identifying number is required to be shown on the form) a written statement showing the information required by paragraph (f)(2) of this section. The written statement provided by a REMIC must also contain the information specified in paragraph (f)(3) of this section.

(2) *Form of statement.*—(i) *REMIC regular interests and collateralized debt obligations not issued with original issue discount.*—For a REMIC regular interest or collateralized debt obligation issued without original issue discount, the written statement must specify for the calendar year the following information—

(A) The aggregate amount shown on Form 1099 to be included in income by that person for the calendar year;

(B) The name, address, and taxpayer identification number of the person required to furnish this statement;

(C) The name, address, and taxpayer identification number of the person who must include the amount of interest in gross income;

(D) A legend, including a statement that the amount is being reported to the Internal Revenue Service, that conforms to the legend on Form 1099, Copy B, For Recipient;

(E) The CUSIP number, account number, serial number, or other identifying number or information, of each REMIC regular interest or collateralized debt obligation, with respect to which a return is being made;

(F) All other items shown on Form 1099 for the calendar year; and

(G) Information necessary to compute accrual of market discount. For calendar years after 1989, this requirement is satisfied by furnishing to the holder for each accrual period during the year a fraction computed in the manner described in either paragraph (f)(2)(i)(G)(*1*) or (f)(2)(i)(G)(*2*) of this section. For calendar years after December 31, 1991, the REMIC or the issuer of the collateralized debt obligation must be consistent in the method used to compute this fraction.

(*1*) The numerator of the fraction equals the interest, other than original issue discount, allocable to the accrual period. The denominator of the fraction equals the interest, other than original issue discount, allocable to the accrual period plus the remaining interest, other than original issue discount, as of the end of that accrual period. The interest allocable to each accrual period and the remaining interest are calculated by taking into account events which have occurred before the close of the accrual period and the prepayment assumption, if any, determined as of the startup day (as defined in section 860G(a)(9)) of the REMIC or the issue date (as defined in section 1275(a)(2)) of the collateralized debt obligation that would be made in computing original issue discount if the debt instrument had been issued with original issue discount.

(*2*) If the REMIC regular interest or the collateralized debt obligation has de minimis original issue discount (as defined in section 1273(a)(3) and any regulations thereunder), then, at the option of the REMIC or the issuer of the collateralized debt obligation, the fraction may be computed in the manner specified in paragraph (f)(2)(ii)(K) of this section taking into account the de minimis original issue discount.

(ii) *REMIC regular interests and collateralized debt obligations issued with original issue discount.*—For a REMIC regular interest or collateralized debt obligation issued with original issue discount, the written statement must specify for the calendar year the following information—

(A) The aggregate amount of original issue discount includible in the gross income of the holder for the calendar year with respect to the REMIC regular interest or the collateralized debt obligation;

(B) The aggregate amount of interest, other than original issue discount, includible in the gross income of the holder for the calendar year with respect to the REMIC regular interest or the collateralized debt obligation;

(C) The name, address, and taxpayer identification number of the person required to file this form;

(D) The name, address, and taxpayer identification number of the person who must include the amount of interest specified in paragraphs (f)(2)(ii)(A) and (B) of this section in gross income;

(E) For calendar years after 1987, the daily portion of original issue discount per $1,000 of original principal amount (or for calendar years prior to 1992, per other specified unit) as determined under section 1272(a)(6) and the regulations thereunder for each accrual period any day of which is in that calendar year;

(F) For calendar years after 1987, the length of the accrual period;

(G) All other items shown on Form 1099 for the calendar year;

(H) A legend, including a statement that the information required under paragraphs (f)(2)(ii)(A), (B), (C), (D) and (G) of this section is being reported to the Internal Revenue Service, that conforms to the legend on Form 1099, Copy B, For Recipient;

(I) For calendar years after 1987, the adjusted issue price (as defined in section 1275(a)(4)(B)(ii)) of the REMIC regular interest or the collateralized debt obligation at the beginning of each accrual period with respect to which interest income is required to be reported on Form 1099 for the calendar year;

(J) The CUSIP number, account number, serial number, or other identifying number or information, of each class of REMIC regular interest or collateralized debt obligation, with respect to which a return is being made; and

(K) Information necessary to compute accrual of market discount. For calendar years after 1989, this information includes:

(*1*) For each accrual period in the calendar year, a fraction, the numerator of which equals the original issue discount allocable to that accrual period, and the denominator of which equals the original issue discount allocable to that accrual period plus the remaining original issue discount as of the end of that accrual period, and

(*2*) [Reserved]

Reg. § 1.6049-7(f)(2)(ii)(K)(2)

The original issue discount allocable to each accrual period and the remaining original issue discount are calculated by taking into account events which have occurred before the close of the accrual period and the prepayment assumption determined as of the startup day (as defined in section 860G(a)(9)) of the REMIC or the issue date (as defined in section 1275(a)(2)) of the collateralized debt obligation.

(3) *Information with respect to REMIC assets.*—(i) *95 percent asset test.*—For calendar years after 1988, the written statement provided by a REMIC must also contain the following information for each calendar quarter—

(A) The percentage of REMIC assets that are qualifying real property loans under section 593,

(B) The percentage of REMIC assets that are assets described in section 7701(a)(19), and

(C) The percentage of REMIC assets that are real estate assets defined in section 856(c)(6)(B),
computed by reference to the average adjusted basis (as defined in section 1011) of the REMIC assets during the calendar quarter (as described in § 1.860F-4(e)(1)(iii)). If for any calendar quarter the percentage of REMIC assets represented by a category is at least 95 percent, then the statement need only specify that the percentage for that category, for that calendar quarter, was at least 95 percent.

(ii) *Additional information required if the 95 percent test not met.*—If, for any calendar quarter after 1988, less than 95 percent of the assets of the REMIC are real estate assets defined in section 856(c)(6)(B), then, for that calendar quarter, the REMIC's written statement must also provide to any real estate investment trust (REIT) that holds a regular interest the following information—

(A) The percentage of REMIC assets described in section 856(c)(5)(A), computed by reference to the average adjusted basis of the REMIC assets during the calendar quarter (as described in § 1.860F-4(e)(1)(iii)),

(B) The percentage of REMIC gross income (other than gross income from prohibited transactions defined in section 860F(a)(2)) described in section 856(c)(3)(A) through (E), computed as of the close of the calendar quarter, and

(C) The percentage of REMIC gross income (other than gross income from prohibited transactions defined in section 860F(a)(2)) described in section 856(c)(3)(F), computed as of the close of the calendar quarter. For purposes of this paragraph (f)(3)(ii)(C), the term "foreclosure property" contained in section 856(c)(3)(F) shall have the meaning specified in section 860G(a)(8). In determining whether a REIT satisfies the limitations of section 856(c)(2), all REMIC gross income is deemed to be derived from a source specified in section 856(c)(2).

(iii) *Calendar years 1988 and 1989.*—For calendar years 1988 and 1989, the percentage of

assets required in paragraphs (f)(3)(i) and (ii) of this section may be computed by reference to the average fair market value of the assets of the REMIC during the calendar quarter (as described in § 1.860F-4(e)(1)(iii)), instead of by reference to the average adjusted basis of the assets of the REMIC during the calendar quarter.

(4) *Cross-reference.*—See § 1.67-3T(f)(2)(ii) for additional information that may be separately stated on the statement required by this paragraph (f) with respect to certain holders of regular interests in REMICs described in § 1.67-3T(a)(2)(ii).

(5) *Time for furnishing statements.*—(i) *For calendar quarters and calendar years after 1988.*— For calendar quarters and calendar years after 1988, each statement required under this paragraph (f) to be furnished to any person for a calendar year with respect to amounts includible as interest must be furnished to that person after April 30 of that year and on or before March 15 of the following year, but not before the final interest payment (if any) for the calendar year.

(ii) *For calendar quarters and calendar years prior to 1989.*—(A) *In general.*—For calendar quarters and calendar years prior to 1989, each statement required under this paragraph (f) to be furnished to any person for a calendar year with respect to amounts includible as interest must be furnished to that person after April 30 of that year and on or before January 31 of the following year, but not before the final interest payment (if any) for the calendar year.

(B) *Nominee reporting.*—For calendar quarters and calendar years prior to 1989, each statement required under this paragraph (f) to be furnished by a nominee must be furnished to the actual owner of a REMIC regular interest or a collateralized debt obligation to which section 1272(a)(6) applies on or before the later of—

(1) The 30th day after the nominee receives such information, or

(2) January 31 of the year following the calendar year to which the statement relates.

(6) *Special rules.*—(i) *Copy of Form 1099 permissible.*—The requirements of this paragraph (f) for the furnishing of a statement to any person, including the legend requirement of paragraphs (f)(2)(i)(D) and (f)(2)(ii)(H) of this section, may be met by furnishing to that person—

(A) A copy of the Form 1099 filed pursuant to paragraph (b)(2) of this section in respect of that person, plus a separate statement (mailed with the Form 1099) that contains the information described in paragraphs (f)(2)(i)(E) and (G), (f)(2)(ii)(E), (F), (I), and (K), (f)(3), and (f)(4) of this section, if applicable, or

(B) A substitute form that contains all the information required under this paragraph (f) and that complies with any current revenue procedure concerning the reproduction of paper substitutes of Forms 1099 and the furnishing of substitute statements to forms recipients. The inclusion on the substitute form of the information specified in this paragraph (f) that is not required by the official Forms 1099 will not cause the substitute form to fail to meet any requirements that limit the information that may be provided with a substitute form.

(ii) *Statement furnished by mail.*—A statement mailed to the last known address of any person shall be considered to be furnished to that person within the meaning of this section.

(7) *Requirement that nominees furnish information to corporations and certain other specified persons.*—(i) *In general.*—For calendar quarters and calendar years after 1988, every broker or middleman must provide in writing or by telephone the information specified in paragraph (e)(2) of this section to—

    (A) A corporation,

    (B) A non-calendar year taxpayer, or

    (C) Any other person specified in paragraphs (c)(9) through (15) of this section who requests the information and for whom the broker or middleman holds as a nominee a REMIC regular interest or a collateralized debt obligation. A corporation, non-calendar year taxpayer, or any other person specified in paragraphs (c)(9) through (15) of this section may request the information in writing or by telephone for any REMIC regular interest or collateralized debt obligation for calendar quarters any day of which the person held the interest or obligation.

(ii) *Time for furnishing information.*—The statement required in paragraph (f)(7)(i) of this section must be furnished on or before the later of—

    (A) The 45th day after receipt of the request,

    (B) The 45th day after the close of the calendar quarter for which the information was requested, or

    (C) If the request is made for the last calendar quarter in a year, March 15 of the year following the calendar quarter for which the information was requested. [Reg. §1.6049-7.]

☐ [*T.D.* 8366, 9-27-91. *Amended by T.D.* 8431, 9-2-92; *T.D.* 8734, 10-6-97 (T.D. 8804 delayed the effective date of T.D. 8734 from January 1, 1999, to January 1, 2000; T.D. 8856 further delayed the effective date of T.D. 8734 until January 1, 2001); *T.D.* 8888, 6-15-2000 *and T.D.* 8895, 8-17-2000.]

[Reg. §1.6049-8]

§1.6049-8. Interest and original issue discount paid to certain nonresident aliens.—(a) *Interest subject to reporting requirement.*—For purposes of §§1.6049-4, 1.6049-6, and this section, and except as provided in paragraph (b) of this section, the term *interest* means interest described in section 871(i)(2)(A) that relates to a deposit maintained at an office within the United States, and that is paid to a nonresident alien individual who is a resident of a country that is identified, in an applicable revenue procedure (see §601.601(d)(2) of this chapter) as of Decem-

ber 31 prior to the calendar year in which the interest is paid, as a country with which the United States has in effect an income tax or other convention or bilateral agreement relating to the exchange of tax information within the meaning of section 6103(k)(4), under which the competent authority is the Secretary of the Treasury or his delegate and the United States agrees to provide, as well as receive, information. Notwithstanding the foregoing, for purposes of §§1.6049-4, 1.6049-6, and this section, for any year for which the information return under §1.6049-4(b)(5) is required, a payor may elect to treat interest as including all interest described in section 871(i)(2)(A) that relates to a deposit maintained at an office within the United States and that is paid to any nonresident alien individual. A payor shall make this election by reporting all such interest. For purposes of the regulations under section 6049 (§§1.6049-1 through 1.6049-8), a nonresident alien individual is a person described in section 7701(b)(1)(B). A payor or middleman may rely upon the permanent residence address provided on a valid Form W-8BEN, "Beneficial Owners Certificate of Foreign Tax Status for U.S. Tax Withholding", to determine the country in which a nonresident alien individual is resident unless such payor or middleman knows or has reason to know that such documentation of the country of residence is unreliable or incorrect. Amounts described in this paragraph (a) are not subject to backup withholding under section 3406 if the payor may treat the payee as a foreign beneficial owner or foreign payee under the rules of §1.6049-5(b)(12). See §31.3406(g)-1(d) of this chapter. However, if the payor or middleman does not have either a valid Form W-8BEN or valid Form W-9, "Request for Taxpayer Identification Number and Certification", the payor or middleman must report the payment as made to a U.S. non-exempt recipient if it must so treat the payee under the presumption rules of §1.6049-5(d)(2) and §1.1441-1(b)(3)(iii), and the payor must also backup withhold under section 3406. (For interest paid to a Canadian nonresident alien individual on or before December 31, 2012, see paragraph (a) of this section as in effect and contained in 26 CFR part 1 revised April 1, 2000).

(b) *Interest excluded from reporting requirement.*—The term *interest* does not include an amount that is paid by the issuer or its agent outside the United States with respect to an obligation that is described in paragraph (b)(1) or (2) of this section.

(1)(i) The obligation is not in registered form (within the meaning of section 163(f) and the regulations thereunder); is part of a larger single public offering of securities; and is described in section 163(f)(2)(B).

(ii) Unless it has actual knowledge to the contrary, a middleman may treat an obligation as if it is described in section 163(f)(2)(B) if the obligation or coupon therefrom, whichever is presented for payment, contains the statement described in section 163(f)(2)(B)(ii)(II) and the regulations thereunder.

(2)(i) The obligation has a face or principal amount of not less than $500,000, and satisfies the requirements described in paragraphs (b)(2)(i)(A), (B), and (C) of this section.

(A) The obligation satisfies the requirements of sections 163(f)(2)(B)(i) and (ii)(I) and the regulations thereunder (as if it were a registration-required obligation within the meaning of section 163(f)(2)(A)) and is issued in accordance with the procedures of § 1.163-5(c)(2)(i)(D)).

(B) If the obligation is in registered form, it is registered in the name of an exempt recipient described in § 1.6049-4(c)(1)(ii).

(C) The obligation has on its face and on any detachable coupons the following statement (or a similar statement having the same effect):"By accepting this obligation or coupon, the holder represents and warrants that it is not a United States person (other than an exempt recipient described in the regulations under section 6049(b)(4) of the Internal Revenue Code and the regulations thereunder) and that it is not acting for or on behalf of a United States person (other than an exempt recipient described in the regulations under section 6049(b)(4) of the Internal Revenue Code and the regulations thereunder)."

(ii) Unless the middleman has actual knowledge to the contrary, it may treat an obligation as satisfying the requirements of sections 163(f)(2)(B)(i) and (ii)(I) and the regulations thereunder if the obligation or a coupon therefrom, whichever is presented for payment, contains the statement in paragraph (b)(2)(i)(C) of this section. [Reg. § 1.6049-8.]

☐ [*T.D.* 8664, 4-15-96. *Amended by T.D.* 8734, 10-6-97 (T.D. 8804 delayed the effective date of T.D. 8734 from January 1, 1999, to January 1, 2000; T.D. 8856 further delayed the effective date of T.D. 8734 until January 1, 2001) *and T.D.* 9584, 4-17-2012.]

[Reg. § 1.6049-9]

§ 1.6049-9. Premium subject to reporting for a debt instrument acquired on or after January 1, 2014.—(a) *General rule.*—Notwithstanding § 1.6049-5(f), for a debt instrument acquired on or after January 1, 2014, if a broker (as defined in § 1.6045-1(a)(1)) is required to file a statement for the debt instrument under § 1.6049-6, the broker generally must report any bond premium (as defined in § 1.171-1(d)) or acquisition premium (as defined in § 1.1272-2(b)(3)) for the calendar year. This section, however, only applies to a debt instrument that is a covered security as defined in § 1.6045-1(a)(15).

(b) *Reporting of bond premium amortization.*— Unless a broker has been notified in writing in accordance with § 1.6045-1(n)(5) that a customer does not want to amortize bond premium under section 171, the broker must report the amount of any amortizable bond premium allocable to a stated interest payment made to the customer

during the calendar year. See §§ 1.171-2 and 1.171-3 to determine the amount of amortizable bond premium allocable to a stated interest payment. Instead of reporting a gross amount for both stated interest and amortizable bond premium, a broker may report a net amount of stated interest that reflects the offset of the stated interest payment by the amount of amortizable bond premium allocable to the payment. In this case, the broker must not report the amortizable bond premium as a separate item. This paragraph (b) also applies to amortizable bond premium on a tax-exempt obligation, which is required to be amortized under section 171.

(c) *Reporting of acquisition premium amortization.*—A broker must report the amount of any acquisition premium amortization that reduces the amount of original issue discount includible in income by the customer during a calendar year. For a debt instrument acquired on or after January 1, 2015, a broker must use the rules in § 1.1272-2(b)(4) to determine the amount of acquisition premium amortization. However, for a debt instrument acquired on or after January 1, 2014, and before January 1, 2015, if a customer timely notifies the broker in accordance with § 1.6045-1(n)(5), a broker may use the rules in § 1.1272-3 to determine the amount of acquisition premium amortization. Instead of reporting a gross amount for both original issue discount and acquisition premium amortization, a broker may report a net amount of original issue discount that reflects the offset of the original issue discount includible in income by the customer for the calendar year by the amount of acquisition premium allocable to the original issue discount. In this case, the broker must not report the acquisition premium amortization as a separate item. See § 1.6049-10 for the reporting of acquisition premium on a tax-exempt obligation. [Reg. § 1.6049-9.]

☐ [*T.D.* 9713, 3-12-2015 (*corrected* 4-26-2016).]

[Reg. § 1.6049-10]

§ 1.6049-10. Reporting of original issue discount on a tax-exempt obligation.—(a) *In general.*—For purposes of section 6049, a payor (as defined in § 1.6049-4(a)(2)) of original issue discount (OID) on a tax-exempt obligation (as defined in section 1288(b)(2)) is required to report the daily portions of OID on the obligation as if the daily portions of OID that accrued during a calendar year were paid to the holder (or holders) of the obligation in the calendar year. The amount of the daily portions of OID that accrues during a calendar year is determined as if section 1272 and § 1.1272-1 applied to a tax-exempt obligation. Notwithstanding any other rule in section 6049 and the regulations thereunder, a payor must determine whether a tax-exempt obligation was issued with OID and the amount of OID that accrues for each relevant period. As prescribed by section 1288(b)(1), OID on a tax-exempt obligation is determined without regard to the de minimis rules in section 1273(a)(3) and § 1.1273-1(d).

(b) *Acquisition premium.*—A payor is required to report acquisition premium amortization on a tax-exempt obligation in accordance with the rules in § 1.6049-9(c) as if section 1272 applied to a tax-exempt obligation. See paragraph (a) of this section to determine the amount of OID allocable to an accrual period.

(c) *Effective/applicability date.*—This section applies to a tax-exempt obligation that is a covered security (within the meaning of § 1.6045-1(a)(15) and (n)(12)) acquired on or after January 1, 2017. For a taxable year beginning after December 31, 2016, a broker, however, may rely on this section to report OID and acquisition premium for a tax-exempt obligation that is a covered security acquired before January 1, 2017. [Reg. § 1.6049-10]

☐ [*T.D.* 9750, 2-17-2016.]

[Reg. § 1.6049(d)-5T]

§ 1.6049(d)-5T. Reporting by brokers of interest and original issue discount on and after January 1, 1986 (Temporary).—For purposes of § 1.6049-5(c), relating to original issue discount treated as interest subject to reporting, on and after January 1, 1986, a payor who is a broker or middleman holding as a nominee—

(a) A bank certificate of deposit (without regard to whether the broker or middleman sold the certificate of deposit to the owner), or

(b) Any other original issue discount debt instrument that is specified by the Commissioner,

must determine whether that obligation is one that was issued at a discount and the amount of discount that is includible in the income of the owner. However, before January 1, 1987, reporting is required only with respect to certificates of deposit (or any such other obligations) held by a broker or middleman as a nominee on or after June 1, 1986, that were sold by the broker or middleman (whether for the broker's account or as an agent of the issuer) to the owner. The preceding two sentences do not apply to certificates of deposit (or any such other obligations) held on or after January 1, 1986, but disposed of before June 1, 1986; reporting requirements with respect to such certificates of deposit (or any other such obligations) shall be determined under the provisions of § 1.6049-5(c) as in effect immediately prior to publication of this § 1.6049-5T. [Temporary Reg. § 1.6049(d)-5T.]

☐ [*T.D.* 8109, 12-12-86. *Redesignated by T.D.* 9658, 2-28-2014.]

[Reg. § 1.6050A-1]

§ 1.6050A-1. Reporting requirements of certain fishing boat operators.—(a) *Requirement of reporting.*—The operator of a boat on which one or more individuals during a calendar year performs services described in § 31.3121(b)(20)-1(a) shall make an information return on Form 1099-MISC for that calendar year. The return shall include the following information—

(1) The name and taxpayer identification number of each individual performing the services;

(2) The percentage of each individual's share of the catch of fish or other forms of aquatic life (hereinafter "fish");

(3) The percentage of the operator's share of the catch of fish;

(4) If the individual receives all or part of his share of the catch in kind, the type and weight of the share and, if it can be ascertained, the fair market value of his share;

(5) If the individual receives a share of the proceeds of the catch, the dollar amount received; and

(6) Any other information that is required by the form.

For purposes of this section, the term, "boat operator" means an employer (as defined in § 31.3121(d)-2) of an employee whose services are excepted from employment by section 3121(b)(20) and § 31.3121(b)(20)-1. The boat operator may make separate returns on Form 1099-MISC for each crew member for each voyage, or he may aggregate the information required by this paragraph for an individual for all or any part of a return period in which the type of catch (if required) and the percentage due the crew member remain the same.

(b) *Time and place for filing.*—Returns required to be made under this section on Form 1099-MISC shall be filed with the Internal Revenue Service Center, designated in the instructions for Form 1099-MISC, on or before February 28 (March 31 if filed electronically) of the year following the calendar year in which the relevant services were performed.

(c) *Requirement of and time for furnishing statements.*—(1) *Requirement of furnishing statement.*— Every person filing a Form 1099-MISC under this section shall furnish to the individual whose identifying number is (or should be) shown on the form a written statement showing the information required by paragraph (a) of this section. The requirement of the preceding sentence may be met by furnishing to the individual copy B of Form 1099-MISC or a reasonable facsimile of Form 1099-MISC that was filed pursuant to this section. An IRS truncated taxpayer identifying number (TTIN) may be used as the identifying number for the individual in lieu of the identifying number appearing on the information return filed with the Internal Revenue Service. For provisions relating to the use of TTINs, see § 301.6109-4 of this chapter (Procedure and Administration Regulations).

(2) *Time for furnishing statement.*—Each statement required by this paragraph to be furnished to any individual for a calendar year shall be furnished on or before January 31 of the year following the calendar year for which the return was made.

(d) *Cross-reference to penalties.*—For provisions relating to the penalty provided for failure to file timely a correct information return required under section 6050A(a) and § 1.6050A-1(a), see § 301.6721-1 of this chapter (Procedure and Administration Regulations). For provisions relating to the penalty provided for failure to furnish timely a correct payee statement required under section 6050A(b) and § 1.6050A-1(c), see § 301.6722-1 of this chapter. See § 301.6724-1 of this chapter for the waiver of a penalty if the failure is due to reasonable cause and is not due to willful neglect.

(e) *Effective/applicability date.*—The rules in this section apply to information returns and payee statements due after December 31, 2014. For rules applicable for information returns and payee statements due before January 1, 2015, § 1.6050A-1(c)(1) (as contained in 26 CFR part 1, revised April 2013) shall apply. [Reg. § 1.6050A-1.]

☐ [*T.D.* 7716, 8-26-80. *Amended by T.D.* 8734, 10-6-97 (T.D. 8804 delayed the effective date of T.D. 8734 from January 1, 1999, to January 1, 2000; T.D. 8856 further delayed the effective date of T.D. 8734 until January 1, 2001); *T.D.* 8895, 8-17-2000 *and T.D.* 9675, 7-14-2014.]

[Reg. § 301.6050A-1]

§ 301.6050A-1. Information returns regarding services performed by certain crewmen on fishing boats.—For provisions relating to the requirement of returns of information regarding services performed by certain crewmen on fishing boats, see § 1.6050A-1 of this chapter (Income Tax Regulations) and § 301.6652-1 of this chapter (Regulations on Procedure and Administration). [Reg. § 301.6050A-1.]

☐ [*T.D.* 7716, 8-26-80.]

[Reg. § 1.6050B-1]

§ 1.6050B-1. Information returns by person making unemployment compensation payments.—For taxable years beginning after December 31, 1978, every person who makes payments of unemployment compensation (as defined in section 85 (c)) aggregating $10 or more to any individual during any calendar year shall file a Form 1099UC in accordance with the instructions to such form. [Reg. § 1.6050B-1.]

☐ [*T.D.* 7705, 7-8-80.]

[§ 1.6050D-1]

§ 1.6050D-1. Information returns relating to energy grants and financing.—(a) *Requirement of reporting.*—Every person who administers a Federal, State, or local program a principal purpose of which is to provide subsidized energy financing (as defined in section 23(c)(10)(C) and the regulations thereunder) or grants for projects designed to conserve or produce energy shall make an information return for each calendar year beginning after December 31, 1983. However, the preceding sentence shall not apply if none of the financing and grants provided under such program during the calendar year relate either to expenditures described in section 23(c)(1) or (2), relating to the residential energy credit, made by a taxpayer before January 1,

1986, with respect to a dwelling unit or to section 38 property (as defined in section 48 and the regulations thereunder). That return shall be made on Form 6497 or, in the case of taxable grants, on Form 1099-G. (The latter form is prescribed pursuant to section 6041 as well as section 6050D.) The return shall include the following information:

(1) The name, address, and taxpayer identification number of each taxpayer receiving financing or a grant made under such program during the calendar year with respect to either section 38 property or, in the case of financing or a grant for energy conservation expenditures or renewable energy source expenditures made by the taxpayer before January 1, 1986, a dwelling unit that is located in the United States;

(2) The aggregate amount of financing and grants received by the taxpayer under the program during the calendar year;

(3) In the case of returns for financing or nontaxable grants, the name of the program under which the financing or grants are made; and

(4) Any other information that is required by the form.

For purposes of this section, the term "person" means the officer or employee having control of the program, or the person appropriately designated for purposes of section 6050D and this section.

(b) *Time and place for filing.*—Returns required to be made under this section shall be filed with the Internal Revenue Service Center designated in the instructions for Form 6497 or 1099-G on or before the last day of February (March 31 if filed electronically) of the year following the calendar year for which the return is made. [Reg. § 1.6050D-1.]

☐ [*T.D.* 8018, 3-28-85. *Amended by T.D.* 8146, 7-15-87 *and T.D.* 8895, 8-17-2000.]

[Reg. § 1.6050E-1]

§ 1.6050E-1. Reporting of State and local income tax refunds.—(a) *Applicability.*—Section 6050E and this section apply to any refund officer who, with respect to an individual, makes payments of refunds of State or local income taxes or allows credits or offsets with respect to such taxes aggregating $10 or more for such individual in any calendar year.

(b) *Definitions.*—For purposes of this section—

(1) The term "refund officer" means the officer or employee of a State or local taxing jurisdiction having control of payments of refunds or the allowance of credits or offsets, or the person appropriately designated for purposes of this section.

(2) The term "State" shall include the District of Columbia but shall not include the Commonwealth of Puerto Rico or any possession of the United States.

(3) The term "individual" shall not include an estate or trust.

(4) The term "credit or offset" means an overpayment of tax which, in lieu of being refunded to the taxpayer, is:

(i) Applied against an existing liability of the taxpayer,

(ii) Available for application against a future liability of the taxpayer, or

(iii) Otherwise used or available for use for the taxpayer's benefit.

(c) *Requirement of reporting.*—Every refund officer described in paragraph (a) of this section shall make an information return in accordance with this section for each calendar year. An information return must be made even if the refund officer is not required to furnish a statement to the applicable taxpayer under paragraph (k)(2) of this section.

(d) *Prescribed Form.*—Except as otherwise provided in paragraph (i) of this section, the information return required by paragraph (c) of this section shall be made on Forms 1096 and 1099.

(e) *Refunds involving different taxable years.*—In the case of refunds paid or credits or offsets allowed during a calendar year with respect to two or more taxable years of an individual, a separate Form 1099 shall be filed with respect to each taxable year of the individual. Thus, if during calendar year 1983 a refund officer pays to an individual a refund of $15 with respect to that individual's taxable year ending in 1982 and $20 with respect to that individual's taxable year ending in 1981, a separate Form 1099 shall be filed for each of the two payments. If, instead, the refund with respect to the individual's taxable year ending in 1982 were $5 instead of $15, no return would be required for the payment of $5.

(f) *Information required.*—The information required to be reported on Forms 1096 and 1099 includes the aggregate amount of refunds, credits, and offsets made or allowed during the calendar year with respect to the taxable year of the individual covered by the return; the name, address, and taxpayer identification number of the individual with respect to whom such payment, credit, or offset was made or allowed; the taxable year covered by the return; and such other information as may be required by the forms. In addition, the nature of the tax is required to be indicated on the Form 1099 in any case where the refund, credit or offset is made or allowed with respect to a payment attributable to an income tax that applies exclusively to income from a trade or business and is not a tax of general application.

(g) *When credit or offset deemed allowed.*—For purposes of a return of information under this section, a credit or offset is deemed to be allowed when the liability to pay or credit such amount is admitted by the State or local taxing jurisdiction. Thus, if an amount with respect to a taxpayer's 1982 taxable year is credited in 1983 to reduce the liability of the taxpayer to make estimated tax payments in 1983, it is reportable as a credit

allowed in 1983. It is not reportable in the taxable year that gives rise to the refund, credit or offset.

(h) *Time and place for filing.*—The returns required under this section for any calendar year shall be filed after September 30 of that calendar year, but not before the refund officer's final payment (or allowance of credit or offset) for the year, and on or before February 28 (March 31 if filed electronically) of the following year. Returns shall be filed with the appropriate Internal Revenue Service Center, the addresses of which are listed in the instructions for Forms 1099. For extensions of time for filing returns under this section, see § 1.6081-1.

(i) *Use of magnetic media and substitute forms.*—(1) *Magnetic media.*—A refund officer may be required to file the Forms 1099 required by this section on magnetic media or machine-readable paper forms. See section 6011(e) and applicable regulations and revenue procedures thereunder. If a refund officer is not required to file the Forms 1099 required by this section on magnetic media, the refund officer may request permission under applicable regulations and revenue procedures to submit the information required by this section on magnetic media.

(2) *Substitute forms.*—A refund officer may prepare and use a form which contains provisions identical with those of Form 1096 if the refund officer complies with all revenue procedures relating to substitute Form 1096 in effect at that time. In addition, if a refund officer is not required to file the Forms 1099 required by this section on magnetic media or machine-readable paper forms, the refund officer may prepare and use a form which contains provisions identical with those of Form 1099 if the refund officer complies with all revenue procedures relating to substitute Form 1099 in effect at that time.

(j) *Voluntary information exchange agreements.*—The requirements of reporting information to the Internal Revenue Service under this section may be satisfied for any calendar year by submission of the information required under paragraph (f) of this section in accordance with the terms of a voluntary information exchange agreement between the State and the United States in effect during such year.

(k) *Requirement of furnishing statements to recipients.*—(1) *In general.*—Except as provided in paragraph (k)(2) of this section, every refund officer required to make a return of information under this section shall furnish to the individual whose identifying number is required to be shown on the return a written statement showing the aggregate amount shown on the information return of refunds, credits and offsets made or allowed to such individual with respect to each taxable year of the individual, the name of the State or local taxing jurisdiction paying such refund or allowing such credits or offsets, the taxable year giving rise to the refund, credit or offset and a legend stating that such amount is being reported to the Internal Revenue Service.

The requirement of this paragraph may be met by furnishing to the individual a copy of the Form 1099 filed with respect to that individual provided that the form bears a legend stating that such amount is being reported to the Internal Revenue Service. For purposes of this paragraph, a statement shall be considered to be furnished to an individual if it is mailed to the individual at the individual's last known address. An IRS truncated taxpayer identifying number (TTIN) may be used as the identifying number of the individual in lieu of the identifying number appearing on the information return filed with the Internal Revenue Service. For provisions relating to the use of TTINs, see § 301.6109-4 of this chapter (Procedure and Administration Regulations).

(2) *Exception for nonitemizers.*—A refund officer need not furnish a statement to an individual under paragraph (k)(1) of this section if the refund officer verifies that the individual did not claim itemized deductions for Federal income tax purposes for the taxable year giving rise to the refund, credit, or offset. This exception shall not apply, however, if the refund, credit, or offset is made or allowed with respect to a payment attributable to an income tax that applies exclusively to income from a trade or business and is not a tax of general application. For purposes of this paragraph (k)(2), verification shall be made solely from—

(i) The State or local income tax return, or

(ii) Information obtained through a voluntary information exchange agreement with the United States for the applicable taxable year.

(3) *Verification from the State or local income tax return.*—A refund officer shall verify from the State or local income tax return that an individual did not claim itemized deductions for Federal income tax purposes for the applicable taxable year only if—

(i)(A) An individual who itemized deductions for Federal income tax purposes either must attach a copy of Schedule A of the individual's Federal income tax return to the State or local income tax return or must transcribe information from Schedule A of the individual's Federal income tax return on the State or local income tax return;

(B) The information contained on or transcribed from the Schedule A is required for the purpose of computing liability for the State or local income tax; and

(C) The omission of a copy of the Schedule A, or of the information required to be transcribed from the Schedule A, is consistent with the taxpayer's computation of tax on the State or local income tax return; or

(ii) Individuals are required to transcribe information from their Federal income tax return (other than from Schedule A) on the State or local income tax return for the purpose of computing liability for the State or local income tax and the information can be used to determine conclusively whether the taxpayer itemized deductions for Federal income tax purposes.

(4) *Example.*—The provisions of paragraph (k)(3)(ii) of this section may be illustrated by the following example:

Example. State X asks for transcription of the following information on its 1983 income tax return from the taxpayer's 1983 Federal income tax return: Adjusted gross income; taxable income; and number of exemptions claimed. The amount of adjusted gross income and the number of exemptions claimed on the Federal income tax return are taken into account in computing the liability for income tax under the laws of State X. The amount of taxable income transcribed from the Federal return, however, does not enter into the computatin of liability for income tax under the laws of State X. Thus, this amount may not be taken into account by the refund officer of State X for purposes of verifying whether a taxpayer itemized deductions for Federal income tax purposes. Since the refund officer of State X will not be able to determine conclusively from the amount of adjusted gross income and the number of exemptions transcribed from the Federal return whether a taxpayer itemized deductions for Federal income tax purposes, the transcribed information does not meet the requirements of paragraph (k)(3)(ii) of this section.

(l) *Time for furnishing statements.*—(1) *General rule.*—The statement required under paragraph (k) of this section shall be furnished after December 31 of the year in which the refund is paid or credit or offset is allowed, and on or before January 31 of the following year.

(2) *Extensions of time.*—For good cause shown upon written application of the refund officer, the service center director may grant an extension of time not exceeding 30 days in which to furnish statements under this paragraph. The application shall be addressed to the Service Center with which the Forms 1099 required under this section are required to be filed and shall contain a concise statement of the reasons for requesting the extension to aid the service center director in determining the period of the extension, if any, which will be granted. The application shall state at the top of the first page that it is made under this section and shall be signed by the refund officer. In general, the application shall be filed after September 30 of the year in which the refund is paid or credit or offset is allowed, and before January 15 of the following year.

(m) *Effective/applicability date.*—This section applies to payments of refunds and credits and offsets allowed after December 31, 1982. The amendments to paragraph (k)(1) apply to payee statements due after December 31, 2014. For payee statements due before January 1, 2015, § 1.6050E-5(k)(1) (as contained in 26 CFR part 1, revised April 2013) shall apply. [Reg. § 1.6050E-1.]

☐ [*T.D.* 8052, 9-12-85. *Amended by T.D.* 8895, 8-17-2000 *and T.D.* 9675, 7-14-2014.]

[Reg. §1.6050H-0]

§1.6050H-0. Table of contents.—This section lists the major captions that appear in §§1.6050H-1 and 1.6050H-2.

§1.6050H-1. Information reporting of mortgage interest received in a trade or business from an individual.

  (a) Information reporting requirement.
    (1) Overview.
    (2) Reporting requirement.
    (3) Optional reporting.
  (b) Qualified mortgage.
    (1) In general.
    (2) Mortgage.
      (i) In general.
      (ii) Transitional rule for certain obligations existing on December 31, 1984.
      (iii) Transitional rule for certain obligations existing on December 31, 1987.
    (3) Payor of record.
    (4) Lender of record.
  (c) Interest recipient.
    (1) Trade or business requirement.
    (2) Interest received or collected on behalf of another person.
      (i) General rule.
      (ii) Exception.
    (3) Interest received in the form of points.
      (i) In general.
      (ii) If designation agreement is in effect.
    (4) Governmental unit.
    (5) Examples.
  (d) Additional rules.
    (1) Reporting by foreign person.
    (2) Reporting with respect to nonresident alien individual.
      (i) In general.
      (ii) Nonresident alien individual status.
    (3) Reporting by cooperative housing corporations.
  (e) Amount of interest received on mortgage for calendar year.
    (1) In general.
    (2) Calendar year.
      (i) In general.
      (ii) De minimis rule.
      (iii) Applicability to points.
    (3) Certain interest not received on mortgage.
      (i) Interest received from seller on payor of record's mortgage.
      (ii) Interest received from governmental unit.
    (4) Interest calculated under Rule of 78s method of accounting.
  (f) Points treated as interest.
    (1) General rule.
    (2) Limitations.
    (3) Special rule.
      (i) Amounts paid directly by payor of record.
      (ii) Examples.
    (4) Construction loans.
      (i) In general.
      (ii) Limitation on refinancing of construction loans.
    (5) Amounts paid to mortgage brokers.
    (6) Effect on deduction of points.
  (g) Effective date.
    (1) In general.
    (2) Points.

§1.6050H-2. Time, form, and manner of reporting interest received on qualified mortgage.

  (a) Requirement to file return.
    (1) Form of return.
    (2) Information included on return.
    (3) Reimbursements of interest on a qualified mortgage.
    (4) Time and place for filing return.
    (5) Use of magnetic media.
  (b) Requirement to furnish statement.
    (1) In general.
    (2) Information included on statement.
    (3) Statement furnished pursuant to Federal mortgage program.
    (4) Copy of Form 1098 to payor of record.
    (5) Furnishing statement with other information reports.
    (6) Time and place for furnishing statement.
  (c) Notice requirement for use of Rule of 78s method of accounting.
    (1) In general.
    (2) Time and manner.
  (d) Reporting under designation agreement.
    (1) In general.
    (2) Qualified person.
    (3) Designation agreement.
    (4) Penalties.
  (e) Penalty provisions.
    (1) Returns and statements the due date for which (determined without regard for extensions) is after December 31, 1987, and before December 31, 1989.
      (i) Failure to file return or to furnish statement.
      (ii) Failure to furnish TIN.
      (iii) Failure to include correct information.
    (2) Returns and statements the due date for which (determined without regard for extensions) is after December 31, 1989.
      (i) Failure to file return or to furnish statement.
      (ii) Failure to furnish TIN.
      (iii) Failure to include correct information.
  (f) Requirement to request and to obtain TIN.
    (1) In general.
    (2) Manner of requesting TIN.
  (g) Effective date.

(1) In general.

(2) Points.

[Reg. § 1.6050H-0.]

☐ [*T.D.* 8191, 4-11-88. *Amended by T.D.* 8571, 12-7-94.]

[Reg § 1.6050H-1]

§ 1.6050H-1. Information reporting of mortgage interest received in a trade or business from an individual.—(a) *Information reporting requirement.*—(1) *Overview.*—The information reporting requirements of section 6050H, this section, and § 1.6050H-2 apply to an interest recipient who receives at least $600 of interest on a qualified mortgage for a calendar year or who makes a reimbursement of interest described in § 1.6050H-2(a)(2)(iv). Paragraph (b) of this section defines qualified mortgage. Paragraph (c) of this section defines interest recipient. Paragraph (d) of this section contains additional rules relating to the reporting requirement for foreign persons, cooperative housing corporations, and nonresident alien individuals. Paragraph (e) of this section contains rules for determining the amount of interest received on a mortgage for a calendar year. Paragraph (f) of this section provides rules for determining when prepaid interest in the form of points is taken into account as interest for purposes of section 6050H, and § 1.6050H-2.

(2) *Reporting requirement.*—Except as otherwise provided in this section and § 1.6050H-2, an interest recipient that either receives at least $600 of interest on a qualified mortgage for a calendar year or makes reimbursements of interest described in § 1.6050H-2(a)(2)(iv) must, with respect to that interest—

(i) File an information return with the Internal Revenue Service; and

(ii) Furnish a statement to the payor of record on the mortgage.

(3) *Optional reporting.*—An interest recipient may, but is not required to, report its receipt of less than $600 of interest on a qualified mortgage for a calendar year. Similarly, an interest recipient also may report reimbursements of interest on a qualified mortgage even if the reimbursements are not required to be reported by § 1.6050H-2(a)(2)(iv). An interest recipient that chooses, but is not required, to file a return as provided in this section and § 1.6050H-2(a) or to furnish a statement as provided in this section and § 1.6050H-2(b) is subject to the requirements of this section and § 1.6050H-2.

(b) *Qualified mortgage.*—(1) *In general.*—A mortgage is a qualified mortgage if the payor of record on the mortgage is an individual, including an individual acting in a capacity as a sole proprietor of a business. A mortgage is not a qualified mortgage if the payor of record on the mortgage is not an individual (such as a trust, estate, partnership, association, company, or corporation), even though an individual is a co-borrower on the mortgage and all the trustees, beneficiaries, partners, members, or shareholders of the payor of record are individuals.

(2) *Mortgage.*—(i) *In general.*—Except as otherwise provided in paragraphs (b)(2)(ii) and (b)(2)(iii) of this section, an obligation is a mortgage if real property (regardless of where located) secures all or part of the obligation. An interest recipient must determine whether real property secures an obligation at the time the obligation is created or, if security is added or removed at a later time, at that later time. Real property includes a manufactured home as defined in section 25(e)(10). An obligation includes a line of credit or a credit card obligation. For purposes of this section and § 1.6050H-2, a borrower incurs a line of credit or credit card obligation when the borrower first has the right to borrow against the line of credit or credit card, whether the borrower actually borrows an amount at that time. An obligation will not fail to be treated as a mortgage solely because, under an applicable State or local homestead law or other debtor protection law in effect on August 16, 1986, the security interest is ineffective or the enforceability of the security interest is restricted.

(ii) *Transitional rule for certain obligations existing on December 31, 1984.*—(A) *In general.*—An obligation that existed on December 31, 1984, is not a mortgage if, at the time the payor of record incurred the obligation, the interest recipient reasonably classified the obligation as other than a mortgage, real property loan, real estate loan, or other similar type of obligation. A reasonable classification of an obligation must be consistent with industry practices and determined according to the purpose of the obligation, the property securing the obligation, and any other reasonable factor. For purposes of this paragraph (b)(2)(ii)(A), an obligation was not reasonably classified as other than a mortgage, real property loan, real estate loan, or other similar type of obligation if, at the time the payor of record incurred the obligation, more than one-half of the obligations in the particular class in which the obligation was classified were secured primarily by real property.

(B) *Examples.*—The following examples illustrate the rules of paragraph (b)(2)(ii)(A) of this section:

Example (1). B offers an unsecured line of credit and a line of credit secured by real property. B separately markets the two credit lines, and they are governed by different terms and conditions. For accounting purposes, B classifies the two types of loans as a single class. For purposes of paragraph (b)(2)(ii)(A) of this section, the two types of loans are different classes of obligations.

Example (2). B operates a program to make loans to small businesses. Depending on the amount of the loan and the credit history of the borrower, B may or may not require security for the loan. If B requires security, it may consist of real or personal property. For accounting purposes, B classifies all of the loans within this program as a single class. For purposes of paragraph (b)(2)(ii)(A) of this section, all of the loans within this program may be classified as belonging to a single class.

(iii) *Transitional rule for certain obligations existing on December 31, 1987.*—An obligation that was incurred after December 31, 1984, and that existed on December 31, 1987, is not a mortgage if the obligation is not primarily secured by real property.

(3) *Payor of record.*—A payor of record on a mortgage is the person carried on the books and records of the interest recipient as the principal borrower on the mortgage. If the books and records of the interest recipient do not indicate which borrower is the principal borrower, the interest recipient must designate a borrower as the principal borrower.

(4) *Lender of record.*—The lender of record is the person who, at the time the loan is made, is named as the lender on the loan documents and whose right to receive payment from the payor of record is secured by the payor of record's principal residence. An intention by the lender of record to sell or otherwise transfer the loan to a third party subsequent to the close of the transaction will not affect the determination of who is the lender of record.

(c) *Interest recipient.*—(1) *Trade or business requirement.*—Except as provided in paragraph (c)(4) of this section, an interest recipient is a person that is engaged in a trade or business (whether or not the trade or business of lending money) and that, in the course of the trade or business, either receives interest on a mortgage or makes a reimbursement of interest on a qualified mortgage described in § 1.6050H-2(a)(3). For purposes of this paragraph (c)(1), if a person holds a mortgage which was originated or acquired in the course of a trade or business, the interest on the mortgage is considered to be received in the course of that trade or business. For example, if real estate developer A lends money to individual B to enable B to purchase a house in a subdivision owned and developed by A, and B gives a mortgage to A for the loan, A is an interest recipient for interest received on the mortgage. Alternatively, if C, a person engaged in the trade or business of being a physician, lends money to individual D to enable D to purchase C's home, and D gives a mortgage to C for the loan, C is not an interest recipient for interest received on the mortgage, because C will not receive the interest in the course of the trade or business of being a physician.

(2) *Interest received or collected on behalf of another person.*—(i) *General rule.*—Except as otherwise provided in paragraph (c)(2)(ii) or (3) of this section, a person that, in the course of its trade or business, receives or collects interest on a mortgage on behalf of another person (e.g., the lender of record) (the initial recipient) for the mortgage is the interest recipient. In this case, the reporting requirement of paragraph (a) of

this section does not apply to the transfer of interest from the initial recipient to the person for which the initial recipient receives or collects the interest. For example, if financial institution A collects interest on behalf of financial institution B, A is the initial recipient for the mortgage and is subject to the reporting requirements of section 6050H, and B is not required to report the interest received on the mortgage from A.

(ii) *Exception.*—(A) *Scope of exception.*—Paragraph (c)(2)(i) of this section does not apply for any period for which—

(1) An initial recipient does not possess the information needed to comply with the reporting requirement of paragraph (a) of this section; and

(2) The person for which the interest is received or collected would receive the interest in the course of its trade or business if the interest were paid directly to that person. For purposes of this paragraph (c)(2)(ii)(A)(2), if interest is received or collected on behalf of a person other than an individual, that person is presumed to receive interest in a trade or business.

(B) *Application of exception.*—If the exception provided by this paragraph (c)(2)(ii) applies, the person for which the interest is received or collected is the interest recipient with respect to interest received or collected on the mortgage during the period described in this paragraph (c)(2)(ii).

(3) *Interest received in the form of points.*—For purposes of this section and § 1.6050H-2, in the case of prepaid interest received in the form of points (as defined in paragraph (f) of this section):

(i) *In general.*—Except as provided in paragraph (c)(3)(ii) of this section, only the lender of record or a qualified person (as defined in § 1.6050H-2(d)(2)) is treated as receiving the points. The lender of record or qualified person is treated as receiving all points paid directly by the payor of record in connection with the purchase of the principal residence.

(ii) *If designation agreement is in effect.*—If a designation agreement is executed pursuant to § 1.6050H-2(d) with respect to points, only the designated party under the agreement is treated as receiving points with respect to any mortgage to which the agreement applies. The designated party is treated as receiving all points with respect to any mortgage to which the agreement applies.

(4) *Governmental unit.*—A governmental unit or an agency or instrumentality of a governmental unit that receives interest on a mortgage is an interest recipient without regard to the requirement of paragraph (c)(1) of this section that the interest be received in the course of a trade or business. A governmental unit or an agency or instrumentality of a governmental unit that is an interest recipient must designate an officer or employee to satisfy the reporting requirements of paragraph (a) of this section.

Reg. § 1.6050H-1(c)(4)

(5) *Examples.*—The following examples illustrate the rules of paragraph (c) of this section:

Example (1). Financial institution F collects mortgage interest on behalf of financial institution G and deposits the amount collected into G's account held with F. F possesses the information needed to comply with the reporting requirement of paragraph (a) of this section. F is the interest recipient for the mortgage. G is not required to report.

Example (2). The facts are the same as in example (1), except that F does not possess the information needed to comply with the reporting requirement. G, the person for which F collects the interest, is the interest recipient for the mortgage. F is not required to report.

Example (3). S, an individual, sells real property to another individual, P, and takes back a mortgage from P to finance the sale. S does not receive the interest in the course of a trade or business. B, a bank, collects P's payments of principal and interest on behalf of S and deposits that amount into an account held at the bank in S's name. B does not possess the information needed to comply with the reporting requirement of paragraph (a) of this section. B is the interest recipient for P's mortgage without regard to paragraph (c)(2)(ii) of this section, because S would not receive the interest in the course of a trade or business. S is not required to report.

Example (4). X collects mortgage interest on behalf of Y, who would receive the interest in the course of a trade or business. X possesses the information needed to comply with the reporting requirement of paragraph (a) of this section. On July 1, 1988, Z assumes X's interest collection responsibilities. Z does not possess the information needed to comply with the reporting requirement of paragraph (a) of this section. X is the interest recipient for interest received from January 1, 1988, through June 30, 1988. Because Z does not possess the requisite information and Y would receive the interest in the course of a trade or business, Y is the interest recipient for interest received from July 1, 1988, through December 31, 1988.

Example (5). On December 1, Borrower obtains from Lender funds with which to purchase an existing structure to be used as Borrower's principal residence. In connection with the mortgage, Lender charges Borrower $300 as points. Borrower pays this amount to Lender at closing using unborrowed funds. In addition, Lender receives from Borrower with respect to the mortgage $300 as interest (as determined under paragraph (e) of this section) other than points. Because Lender has received at least $600 in interest, including points, with respect to Borrower's mortgage during the calendar year, Lender must report the payments in accordance with paragraph (a) of this section and § 1.6050H-2. Under those sections, Lender must separately state on the information return and the statement to Borrower the $300 received as

interest (other than points) and the $300 received as points.

(d) *Additional rules.*—(1) *Reporting by foreign person.*—An interest recipient that is not a United States person (as defined in section 7701(a)(30)) must report interest received on a qualified mortgage only if it receives the interest—

(i) At a location in the United States, or

(ii) At a location outside the United States if the interest recipient is—

(A) A controlled foreign corporation (within the meaning of section 957(a)), or

(B) A person, 50 percent or more of the gross income of which, from all sources for the three-year period ending with the close of the taxable year preceding the receipt of interest (or for such part of the period as the person was in existence), was effectively connected with the conduct of a trade or business within the United States.

(2) *Reporting with respect to nonresident alien individual.*—(i) *In general.*—The reporting requirement of paragraph (a) of this section does not apply if—

(A) The payor of record is a nonresident alien individual, and

(B) Real property located in the United States does not secure the mortgage.

(ii) *Nonresident alien individual status.*—For purposes of paragraph (d)(2)(i)(A) of this section, an interest recipient must apply the following documentary evidence rules to determine whether a payor of record is a nonresident alien individual:

(A) If interest is paid outside the United States, the interest recipient must satisfy the documentary evidence standard provided in § 1.6049-5(c) with respect to the payor of record; and

(B) If interest is paid within the United States, the interest recipient must secure from the payor of record a Form W-8 or a substantially similar statement signed by the payor under penalty of perjury as described in § 1.1441-1(e)(1).

For purposes of this paragraph (d)(2)(ii), the place of payment is the place where the payor of record completes the acts necessary to effect payment. An amount paid by transfer to an account maintained by an interest recipient in the United States or by mail to a United States address is considered to be paid within the United States.

(3) *Reporting by cooperative housing corporations.*—For purposes of this section and § 1.6050H-2, an amount received by a cooperative housing corporation from an individual tenant-stockholder that represents the tenant-stockholder's proportionate share of interest described in section 216(a)(2) is interest received on a qualified mortgage in the course of the cooperative housing corporation's trade or business. A cooperative housing corporation is an interest recipient with respect to each tenant-stockholder's proportionate share of interest and must

report $600 or more of interest received from an individual tenant-stockholder. The terms "cooperative housing corporation," "tenant-stockholder," and "tenant-stockholder's proportionate share" are defined in section 216 and the regulations thereunder.

(e) *Amount of interest received on mortgage for calendar year.*—(1) *In general.*—For purposes of this section and § 1.6050H-2, interest includes mortgage prepayment penalties and late charges other than late charges for a specific mortgage service. Interest also includes prepaid interest in the form of points (as defined in paragraph (f) of this section). Whether an interest recipient receives $600 or more of interest on a mortgage for a calendar year is determined on a mortgage-by-mortgage basis. An interest recipient need not aggregate interest received on all of the mortgages of a payor of record held by the interest recipient to determine whether the $600 threshold is met. Therefore, an interest recipient need not report interest of less than $600 received on a mortgage, even though it receives a total of $600 or more of interest on all of the mortgages of the payor of record for a calendar year.

(2) *Calendar year.*—(i) *In general.*—Except as otherwise provided in paragraph (e)(2)(ii) or (iii) of this section, the calendar year for which interest is received is the later of the calendar year in which the interest is received or the calendar year in which the interest properly accrues.

(ii) *De minimis rule.*—An interest recipient may treat interest received during the current calendar year which properly accrues by January 15 of the subsequent calendar year as interest received for the current calendar year. For example, if an interest recipient receives a monthly interest payment on December 31, 1988, which includes interest accruing for the period December 5, 1988, to January 5, 1989, the interest recipient may treat the entire interest payment as received for 1988. If a portion of an interest payment received in a current calendar year accrues after January 15 of the subsequent calendar year, an interest recipient must report as interest received for the current calendar year only the portion that properly accrues by the end of the current calendar year. For example, if an interest recipient receives a monthly payment that includes interest accruing for the period December 20, 1988, through January 20, 1989, the interest recipient may not report as interest received for 1988 any interest accruing after December 31, 1988. The interest recipient must report the interest accruing after December 31, 1988, as received for calendar year 1989.

(iii) *Applicability to points.*—Paragraphs (e)(2)(i) and (ii) of this section do not apply to prepaid interest in the form of points (as defined in paragraph (f) of this section). Points (as defined in paragraph (f) of this section) must be reported in the calendar year in which they are received.

(3) *Certain interest not received on mortgage.*—(i) *Interest received from seller on payor of record's mortgage.*—Interest received from a seller or a person related to a seller within the meaning of section 267(b) or section 707(b)(1) on a payor of record's mortgage is not interest received on a mortgage. For example, interest is not received on a mortgage if a real estate developer deposits an amount in escrow with an interest recipient and advises it to draw on the account to pay interest on a payor of record's mortgage (e.g., a buy-down mortgage). Similarly, interest is not received on a mortgage if an interest recipient receives a lump sum from a real estate developer for interest on a payor of record's mortgage.

(ii) *Interest received from governmental unit.*—Interest received from a governmental unit or an agency or instrumentality of a governmental unit is not interest received on a mortgage. For example, interest is not received on a mortgage if received as a housing assistance payment from the Department of Housing and Urban Development on a mortgage insured under section 235 of the National Housing Act (12 U.S.C. 1701-1715z (1982 & Supp. 1983)). Except as otherwise provided in paragraph (e)(1) and (2) of this section, interest received on a mortgage is only the excess of interest received on the mortgage over interest received from a governmental unit or an agency or instrumentality of a governmental unit.

(4) *Interest calculated under Rule of 78s method of accounting.*—An interest recipient permitted by Revenue Procedure 83-40, 1983-1 C.B. 774, (or other revenue procedure) to use the Rule of 78s method of accounting to calculate interest earned on a transaction may report as interest received on a mortgage interest earned on the transaction as calculated under the Rule of 78s method of accounting only if the interest recipient satisifies the notice requirement of § 1.6050H-2(c).

(f) *Points treated as interest.*—(1) *General rule.*—Subject to the limitations of paragraph (f)(2) of this section, an amount is deemed to be points paid in respect of indebtedness incurred in connection with the purchase of the payor of record's principal residence (points) for purposes of this section and § 1.6050H-2 to the extent that the amount—

(i) Is clearly designated on the Uniform Settlement Statement prescribed under the Real Estate Settlement Procedures Act of 1974, 12 U.S.C. 2601 et seq., (e.g., the Form HUD-1) as points incurred in connection with the indebtedness, for example as *loan origination fees* (including amounts so designated on Veterans Affairs (VA) and Federal Housing Administration (FHA) loans), *loan discount*, *discount points*, or *points*;

(ii) Is computed as a percentage of the stated principal amount of the indebtedness incurred by the payor of record;

(iii) Conforms to an established practice of charging points in the area in which the loan is issued and does not exceed the amount generally charged in the area;

(iv) Is paid in connection with the acquisition by the payor of record of a residence that is the principal residence of the payor of record and that secures the loan. For this purpose, the lender of record may rely on a signed written statement of the payor of record that states whether the proceeds of the loan are for the purchase of the mortgagor's principal residence; and

(v) Is paid directly by the payor of record.

(2) *Limitations.*—An amount is not points for purposes of this section to the extent that the amount is—

(i) Paid in connection with indebtedness incurred for the improvement of a principal residence;

(ii) Paid in connection with indebtedness incurred to purchase or improve a residence that is not the payor of record's principal residence, such as a second home, vacation property, investment property, or trade or business property;

(iii) Paid in connection with a home equity loan or a line of credit, even though the loan is secured by the payor of record's principal residence;

(iv) Paid in connection with a refinancing loan (except as provided by paragraph (f)(4) of this section), including a loan incurred to refinance indebtedness owed by the borrower under the terms of a land contract, a contract for deed, or similar forms of seller financing;

(v) Paid in lieu of amounts that ordinarily are stated separately on the Form HUD-1, such as appraisal fees, inspection fees, title fees, attorney fees, and property taxes; or

(vi) Paid in connection with the acquisition of a principal residence, to the extent that the amount is allocable to indebtedness in excess of the aggregate amount that may be treated as acquisition indebtedness under section 163(h)(3)(B)(ii).

(3) *Special rule.*—(i) *Amounts paid directly by payor of record.*—For purposes of this section, an amount is considered *paid directly* by the payor of record if it is—

(A) Provided by the payor of record from funds that have not been borrowed from the lender of record for this purpose as part of the overall transaction. The amount provided may include amounts designated as down payments, escrow deposits, earnest money applied at the closing, and other funds actually paid over by the payor of record at or before the time of closing; or

(B) Paid as points (within the meaning of this paragraph (f)) on behalf of the payor of record by the seller. For this purpose, an amount paid as points to an interest recipient by the seller on behalf of the payor of record is treated as paid to the payor of record and then paid directly by the payor of record to the interest recipient.

(ii) *Examples.*—The provisions of this paragraph (f) are illustrated by the following examples:

Example 1. Financed payment of points. Buyer purchases a principal residence for $100,000. There is a total of $7,000 in closing costs (exclusive of down payment) charged in connection with the sale. Of this amount, $3,000 is charged as points (within the meaning of paragraph (f) of this section). At closing, Buyer makes a down payment of $20,000 and provides unborrowed funds in the amount of $4,000 for the payment of various closing costs other than points. Buyer finances payment of the points by increasing the principal amount of the loan by $3,000. Seller makes no payments on Buyer's behalf. Because Buyer has provided at closing funds that have not been borrowed from the lender of record for this purpose in an amount at least equal to the amount charged as points in the transaction, the lender of record (or a qualified person) must report $3,000 as points in accordance with this section and § 1.6050H-2.

Example 2. Seller-paid points. Buyer purchases a principal residence for $100,000. There is a total of $7,000 in closing costs (exclusive of down payment) charged in connection with the sale. Of this amount, $3,000 is charged as points (within the meaning of this paragraph (f)). Seller agrees to pay all closing costs on behalf of Buyer, including the amount charged as points. Accordingly, the amount paid by Seller as points is treated as paid directly by Buyer, and the lender of record (or a qualified person) must report the $3,000 as points in accordance with this section and § 1.6050H-2.

(4) *Construction loans.*—(i) *In general.*—An amount paid in connection with indebtedness incurred to construct a residence, or to refinance indebtedness incurred to construct a residence, is deemed to be points for purposes of this section to the extent the amount—

(A) Is clearly designated on the loan documents as points incurred in connection with the indebtedness, for example, as *loan origination fees, loan discount, discount points, or points;*

(B) Is computed as a percentage of the stated principal amount of the indebtedness incurred by the payor of record;

(C) Conforms to an established practice of charging points in the area in which the loan is issued and does not exceed the amount generally charged in the area;

(D) Is paid in connection with indebtedness incurred by the payor of record to construct (or to refinance construction of) a residence that is to be used, when completed, as the principal residence of the payor of record;

(E) Is paid directly by the payor of record; and

(F) Is not allocable to indebtedness in excess of the aggregate amount that may be treated as acquisition indebtedness under section 163(h)(3)(B)(ii).

(ii) *Limitation on refinancing of construction loans.*—Amounts paid in connection with refinancing indebtedness incurred to construct a residence are not treated as points to the extent they are allocable to indebtedness that exceeds the indebtedness incurred to construct the residence.

(5) *Amounts paid to mortgage brokers.*—Amounts received directly or indirectly by a mortgage broker are treated as points under this paragraph (f) to the same extent the amounts would be so treated if they were paid to and retained by the lender of record, and must be reported by the lender of record in accordance with this section and § 1.6050H-2.

(6) *Effect on deduction of points.*—This section and § 1.6050H-2 address only the information reporting requirements of section 6050H and do not affect a payor of record's deduction for any amount in accordance with applicable provisions of the Internal Revenue Code.

(g) *Effective date.*—(1) *In general.*—Except as provided in paragraph (g)(2) of this section, this section is effective for mortgage interest received after December 31, 1987. Section 1.6050H-1T contains rules for reporting mortgage interest received after December 31, 1984, and before January 1, 1988.

(2) *Points.*—The reporting requirements of this section do not apply to prepaid interest received in the form of points before January 1, 1995. In addition, the inclusion of points in the determination of interest under paragraph (e)(1) of this section applies only to transactions occurring after December 31, 1994. [Reg. § 1.6050H-1.]

□ *T.D. 8191, 4-11-88. Amended by T.D. 8571, 12-7-94 and T.D. 8734, 10-6-97 (T.D. 8804 delayed the effective date of T.D. 8734 from January 1, 1999, to January 1, 2000; T.D. 8856 further delayed the effective date of T.D. 8734 until January 1, 2001).]*

[Reg. § 1.6050H-1T]

§ 1.6050H-1T. Information reporting of mortgage interest received in a trade or business from individuals after 1985 and before 1988. (Temporary).—The following questions and answers relate to the requirement of reporting mortgage interest under section 6050H of the Internal Revenue Code of 1954, as added by section 145 of the Tax Reform Act of 1984 (Pub. L. 98-369, 98 Stat. 685):

Requirement of Reporting

In general

Q-1: What does section 6050H provide with respect to the reporting of mortgage interest?

A-1: In general, section 6050H provides that an information return must be made by any person who is engaged in a trade or business and who, in the course of such trade or business, receives from any individual $600 or more of interest on any mortgage in a calendar year. For purposes of this section—

(a) Any person who is engaged in a trade or business and who, in the course of such trade or business, receives interest on any mortgage is referred to as an "interest recipient"; and

(b) Any individual who pays interest on any mortgage is referred to as a "payor".

Interest subject to reporting

Q-2: Does the reporting requirement apply to all interest received by an interest recipient?

A-2: No. The reporting requirement applies only to interest received from a payor on a mortgage (as defined in A-4 and A-5 of this section). The reporting requirement does not apply to interest received from a trust, estate, partnership, association, company, or corporation.

Q-3: Does the reporting requirement apply to any amount of mortgage interest received from a payor?

A-3: No. The reporting requirement applies only if $600 or more of interest is received from a payor on any mortgage in a calendar year. The $600 threshold is determined on an obligation by obligation basis. Therefore, if the interest received from a payor on an obligation is less than $600, reporting with respect to that interest is not required even if the total interest received from the payor on all obligations held by the interest recipient exceeds $600 in a calendar year.

Q-4: What is a mortgage, for purposes of this section and section 6050H, with respect to obligations in existence on December 31, 1984?

A-4: An obligation in existence on December 31, 1984, that is secured primarily by real property (regardless of whether the property is located inside or outside the United States) is a mortgage unless, at the time the obligation was incurred, the interest recipient reasonably classified such obligation as other than a mortgage, real property loan, real estate loan, or other similar type of obligation. (See A-12 of this section for rules relating to interest received by foreign persons.) For example, if an obligation incurred in 1980 was secured primarily by real property, but the interest recipient reasonably classified the obligation as a commercial loan because the proceeds were used to finance the payor's trade or business, the obligation is not considered a mortgage for purposes of this section and section 6050H. If, however, a majority of the obligations in a particular class are primarily secured by real property, it is not reasonable to classify such obligations as other than mortgages, real property loans, real estate loans, or other similar types of obligations; such obligations are, therefore, mortgages for purposes of section 6050H and this section. For purposes of this definition, real property includes stock in a cooperative housing corporation. A mortgage does not include a credit card obligation that is secured primarily by real property or a line of credit that is secured primarily by real property.

Q-5: What is a mortgage, for purposes of this section and section 6050H, with respect to obligations incurred after December 31, 1984?

A-5: With respect to obligations incurred after December 31, 1984, a mortgage is any obligation that is secured primarily by real property, regardless of whether the property is located inside or outside the United States. (See A-12 of this section for rules relating to interest received by foreign persons.) For purposes of this definition, real property includes stock in a cooperative housing corporation. A mortgage does not include a credit card obligation that is secured primarily by real property or a line of credit that is secured primarily by real property. The determination of whether a particular obligation is a mortgage shall be made without regard to the interest recipient's classification of that obligation. For example, if an obligation is secured primarily by real property, but the interest recipient classifies the obligation as a commercial loan because the proceeds are to be used to finance the payor's trade or business, the obligation is nevertheless a mortgage for purposes of this section and section 6050H.

Q-6: If the amount of interest received on a mortgage in a calendar year is less than the amount of interest due on the mortgage, what amount of interest must be reported under this section?

A-6: The amount of interest received must be reported. For example, assume that $800 of interest is payable in a calendar year but only $600 of interest is received in the calendar year. The amount of interest received ($600) must be reported under this section. Similarly, assume that an interest recipient accrues $900 of interest on a mortgage in a calendar year but only $800 of interest is payable and is received in the calendar year (resulting in a $100 increase in the unpaid balance of the loan). The amount of interest received ($800) must be reported under this section.

Q-7: If a payor remits 13 payments of interest on any mortgage in a calendar year, but the interest recipient receives only 12 payments in the calendar year, what amount should the interest recipient report?

A-7: The interest recipient should report the interest actually received in the calendar year. For example, if a payor mails the 13th payment on December 31 of a calendar year, and the interest recipient does not receive it until the following calendar year, the interest recipient should report only the 12 payments received in the calendar year.

Trade or business requirement

Q-8: Must an interest recipient be engaged in the trade or business of lending money to be subject to the reporting requirement of this section?

A-8: No. An interest recipient (other than a governmental unit, or any agency or instrumentality thereof) is subject to this reporting requirement if the interest recipient is engaged in any trade or business and, in the course of such trade or business, receives from an individual $600 or more of interest on any mortgage in a calendar year. For example, if A, a real estate developer, provides financing to B, an individual, to enable B to purchase a house in a subdivision owned and developed by A, and that house is the primary security for the financing, A is subject to

this reporting requirement. Alternatively, if C, a physician, who is not engaged in any other trade or business, lends money to D to enable D to purchase C's home, C is not subject to the reporting requirement of this section because C will not receive the interest in the course of his sole trade or business of being a physician.

Q-9: How does the trade or business requirement apply to a governmental unit?

A-9: A governmental unit (or any agency or instrumentality thereof) which receives from a payor $600 or more of interest on any mortgage in a calendar year is subject to the reporting requirement without regard to the requirement that the money be received in the course of a trade or business. A governmental unit (or any agency or instrumentality thereof) that is subject to the reporting requirement must designate an officer or employee to make the return. The designated officer or employee must make the return in the form and manner prescribed by this section.

Treatment of cooperative housing corporations

Q-10: How does this reporting requirement apply in the case of cooperative housing corporations?

A-10: For purposes of section 6050H and this section, a cooperative housing corporation (as defined in section 216) is treated as a person who is engaged in a trade or business and who, in the course of such trade or business, receives interest from its tenant-stockholders on a mortgage. Therefore, a cooperative housing corporation is required to report under section 6050H and this section.

Interest received on behalf of another

Q-11: If, in the course of a trade or business, a person receives (collects) interest on behalf of another, who is required to report?

A-11: The person first receiving (collecting) the interest is required to report. For example, a servicing bank that receives $600 or more of mortgage interest in a calendar year from a payor on behalf of a lender is required to report the interest received under this section. No reporting is required under this section upon the transfer of the interest from the servicing bank to the lender for whom the interest was received.

Interest received by foreign persons

Q-12: Must an interest recipient that is a foreign person report under section 6050H and this section?

A-12: An interest recipient that is a foreign person must report with respect to mortgage interest that is recived at a location within the United States. In the case of interest received at locations outside the United States, an interest recipient that is a foreign person must report—

(a) If the foreign person is a controlled foreign corporation within the meaning of section 957 (a); or

(b) If the foreign person is a corporation any interest received from which would be considered to be from sources within the United States under section 861(a)(1)(C) (without regard to whether the interest is paid or credited by a domestic branch of a foreign corporation engaged in the commercial banking business).

Multiple borrowers

Q-13: When there is more than one borrower on a mortgage, must the interest recipient report with respect to each borrower?

A-13: No. The interest recipient must report only with respect to the payor of record (as defined in A-14 of this section) on the mortgage. The amount of interest subject to reporting is the full amount received by the interest recipient with respect to the mortgage during the calendar year.

Q-14: Who is a payor of record?

A-14: For purposes of this section, the payor of record is the individual carried on the books and records of the interest recipient as the principal borrower or the individual designated by the interest recipient as the payor of record.

Interest paid by third parties

Q-15: If an interest recipient receives interest on a mortgage from a person other than the borrower, must the interest recipient report this amount as received from the borrower?

A-15: In general, yes. Except as otherwise provided in this A-15 and A-15a of this section, an interest recipient must report all amounts received on a borrower's mortgage as received from the borrower under section 6050H and this section. For example, assume that N is the borrower on a mortgage and that interest is received on the mortgage from N's mother. The interest that is received from N's mother on N's mortgage is reportable under section 6050H and this section as received from N. However, interest that is paid by a seller on a purchaser's mortgage shall not be reported under section 6050H and this section as received from the purchaser. For example, if a real estate developer deposits an amount in escrow with the interest recipient and advises the interest recipient to draw on the account to pay interest on a purchaser's mortgage, this interest is not reportable under section 6050H and this section. Similarly, if a real estate developer pays a lump sum to the interest recipient for interest on a purchaser's mortgage, this interest is not reportable under section 6050H and this section. In addition, amounts received by the interest recipient as housing assistance payments from the Department of Housing and Urban Development ("HUD") on a borrower's mortgage that is insured under section 235 of the National Housing Act (12 U.S.C. § § 1701—1715z (1982 & Supp. 1983)) shall not be reported as interest received from the borrower. In such a case, therefore, only the amount of interest received on the mortgage that exceeds the amount of housing assistance payments received from HUD shall be reported.

Q-15a: If an interest recipient receives, with respect to a borrower's mortgage, an amount from a governmental unit, or any agency or instrumentality thereof (other than an amount received from HUD as described in A-15 of this

section), should the interest recipient report the amount as received from the borrower?

A-15a: If the interest is received after December 31, 1986, it must be reported in the same manner as interest on mortgages with respect to which housing assistance payments are received from HUD, as described in A-15 of this section. If the interest is received before January 1, 1987, it may, but need not, be reported.

Form and manner of return

Form of return

Q-16: What form must be used to make a return required by section 6050H and this section?

A-16: An interest recipient must make the return on Form 1098 (with Form 1096 as the transmittal form). The interest recipient may, however, prepare and use a form that contains provisions substantially similar to those of Forms 1096 and 1098 if that person complies with any revenue procedures relating to substitute Forms 1096 and 1098 in effect at that time. A separate return must be made for each mortgage with respect to which $600 or more of interest is received for a calendar year.

Information included on return

Q-17: What information must an interest recipient include on Form 1098?

A-17: An interest recipient must include the following information on the Form 1098:

(a) The name, address, and TIN (as defined in section 7701 (a)) of the payor or payor of record;

(b) The name and address of the interest recipient;

(c) The amount of interest (not including points and other prepaid interest) received on the mortgage in the calendar year; and

(d) Any other information as may be required by Form 1098 or its instructions.

Time for filing

Q-18: When must an interest recipient file the return or returns required by section 6050H and this section?

A-18: An interest recipient must file the return or returns on or before February 28 of the year following the calendar year in which the mortgage interest is received.

Place for filing

Q-19: Where must the return or returns required under section 6050H and this section be filed?

A-19: The return or returns must be filed with the same Internal Revenue Service Center where other returns of the interest recipient are filed.

Use of magnetic media

Q-20: What rules apply with respect to the use of magnetic media?

A-20: Any return required under section 6050H and this section must be filed on magnetic media to the extent required by section 6011(e) and the regulations thereunder. Any person not required by section 6011(e) to file returns on magnetic media may request permission to do so. See § 1.9101 for rules relating to permission to submit information on magnetic tape or other

Reg. § 1.6050H-1T

media. If a person required to file returns on magnetic media fails to do so, the penalty under section 6652 (failure to file an information return) applies.

Requirement of furnishing statements to payors
In general

Q-21: What statements are required to be furnished to payors under section 6050H and this section?

A-21: Any interest recipient required to make an information return under section 6050H must also furnish a statement to the payor or, if applicable, payor of record (see A-13 and A-14 of this section). For the date when the statement must be furnished, see A-26 of this section.

Q-22: Is the statement considered to be furnished to the payor or payor of record if it is mailed to him at his last known address?

A-22: Yes.

Q-23: If an interest recipient furnishes a statement required under a Federal mortgage program will the requirements of A-21 of this section be met?

A-23: Yes, if the statement furnished contains all the information required under A-24 of this section and is furnished to the payor or payor of record by the date required under A-26 of this section.

Information included on statement

Q-24: What information must be included on the statement required to be furnished to payors or payors of record under section 6050H and this section?

A-24: The statement must include the following information:

(a) The information required under A-17 of this section;

(b) A legend stating that the information is being reported to the Internal Revenue Service; and

(c) A legend stating that the amount reported on the statement is deductible by the payor for Federal income tax purposes only to the extent the payor actually paid the amount and was not reimbursed by another person.

Copy of Form 1098 to payors

Q-25: Can an interest recipient meet the requirement to furnish a statement to a payor or payor of record by furnishing a copy of the Form 1098 filed with respect to that payor or payor of record?

A-25: Yes. The requirement of furnishing a statement may be met by furnishing to the payor or payor of record a copy of the Form 1098 containing the same information filed with the Service with respect to such payor, or a form that contains provisions substantially similar to those of Form 1098, provided that the form bears the legends described in A-24 of this section.

Time for furnishing statement

Q-26: When is a statement required to be furnished by an interest recipient to the payor or payor of record?

A-26: A statement is required to be furnished by the interest recipient to the payor or payor of

record on or before January 31 of the year following the calendar year in which the mortgage interest is received.

Penalties
In general

Q-27: Are there any penalties for failing to comply with the requirements of section 6050H and this section?

A-27: Yes. The penalty for failing to make an information return with respect to a payor or payor of record is provided in section 6652. The penalty for failing to furnish a statement to a payor or payor of record is provided in section 6678.

Q-28: Are there any penalties for failing to furnish a TIN upon request?

A-28: Yes. Any payor or payor of record is subject to a $50 penalty by the Internal Revenue Service if such payor fails to furnish his TIN upon the request of an interest recipient. For rules relating to the requesting of TINs by interest recipients, see A-30 and A-31 of this section.

Q-29: Is an interest recipient subject to any penalties for failing to furnish the TIN of a payor or payor of record?

A-29: Yes. In general, the penalties provided under section 6676 will be assessed against interest recipients who fail to furnish to the Internal Revenue Service the TIN of a payor or payor of record. With respect to mortgages in existence on December 31, 1984, however, the interest recipient will not be subject to the section 6676 penalties if the interest recipient followed the rules of A-30 and A-31 of this section for requesting TINs and properly and promptly processed the responses.

Requesting TINs

Q-30: What rules apply with respect to the requesting of TINs by interest recipients?

A-30: With respect to obligations incurred after December 31, 1984, the interest recipient must take all reasonable steps to obtain the TIN of the payor or payor of record at the time the obligation is incurred. With respect to any mortgage for which the interest recipient does not have the TIN of the payor or payor of record in its accounting system, the interest recipient must request, at least once a year, the TIN of such payor.

The request for a TIN need not be in a separate mailing. The request may be included, for example, in the interest recipient's regular mailings of payment coupon booklets or annual statements. However, if the interest recipient makes no other mailings to the payor or payor of record during 1985 (or during the year in which the obligation is incurred for obligations incurred after 1985), then the interest recipient must request the TIN in a separate mailing.

Q-31: What form must the interest recipient use to request the TIN of a payor or a payor of record?

A-31: No particular form must be used to request the TIN. However, the request must be made on a separate piece of paper and the request must clearly notify the payor that the Internal Revenue Service requires the payor to furnish his TIN in order to verify any deduction for mortgage interest. The interest recipient must also notify such payor that he is subject to a $50 penalty, imposed by the Internal Revenue Service, if he fails to furnish his TIN.

Effective date

Q-32: When is this section effective?

A-32: This section generally is effective for mortgage interest received after December 31, 1984, and before January 1, 1988. However, Q/A-15a of this section is effective for mortgage interest received after December 31, 1986, and before January 1, 1988. [Temporary Reg. §1.6050H-1T.]

☐ [*T.D.* 8047, 8-16-65. *Amended by T.D.* 8191, 4-11-88.]

[Reg. §1.6050H-2]

§1.6050H-2. Time, form, and manner of reporting interest received on qualified mortgage.—(a) *Requirement to file return.*—(1) *Form of return.*—An interest recipient must file a return required by §1.6050H-1(a) on Form 1098 (with Form 1096 as the transmittal form). An interest recipient may use forms containing provisions substantially similar to those in Forms 1098 and 1096 if it complies with applicable revenue procedures relating to substitute Forms 1098 and 1096. An interest recipient must file a separate return for each qualified mortgage for which it receives $600 or more of interest for a calendar year.

(2) *Information included on return.*—An interest recipient must include on Form 1098:

(i) The name, address, and taxpayer identification number (TIN) (as defined in section 7701(a)(41)) of the payor of record;

(ii) The name, address, and TIN of the interest recipient;

(iii) The amount of interest (other than points) required to be reported with respect to the qualified mortgage for the calendar year;

(iv) With respect to reimbursements of interest on a qualified mortgage (as discussed in paragraph (a)(3) of this section) made to the payor of record in the calendar year—

(A) Reimbursements aggregating $600 or more; and

(B) Reimbursements aggregating less than $600, but only if $600 or more of interest on the qualified mortgage is received in the calendar year from the payor of record;

(v) The amount of points paid directly by the payor of record (within the meaning of §1.6050H-1(f)(3)) required to be reported with respect to the qualified mortgage for the calendar year; and

(vi) Any other information required by Form 1098 or its instructions.
Section 1.6050H-1(e) contains rules to determine the amount of interest received on a mortgage for a calendar year.

(3) *Reimbursements of interest on a qualified mortgage.*—For purposes of paragraph (a)(2)(iv) of this section, a reimbursement of interest on a

qualified mortgage is a reimbursement of an amount received in a prior year that was required to be reported for that prior year under paragraph (a)(2)(iii) of this section by any interest recipient. Only the interest recipient that makes the reimbursement is required to report the reimbursement under this section. Form 1098 and the statement furnished to the payor of record under paragraph (b) of this section must not include any amount that constitutes interest on the reimbursement paid to the payor of record. Rules relating to the requirement to report interest on a reimbursement are, in the case of a person carrying on the banking business (or a middleman, as defined in §1.6049-4(f)(4), of a person carrying on the banking business), provided in section 6049 and the regulations thereunder, and, for other persons, provided in section 6041 and the regulations thereunder. Reimbursements of interest on a qualified mortgage (as described in this section) made in 1993 and subsequent calendar years must be reported on Form 1098 and statements furnished to payors of record. Reimbursements made prior to 1993 are not required to be reported.

(4) *Time and place for filing return.*—An interest recipient must file a return required by this paragraph (a) on or before February 28 (March 31 if filed electronically) of the year following the calendar year for which it receives the mortgage interest. If no interest is required to be reported for the calendar year, but a reimbursement of interest on a qualified mortgage is required to be reported for the calendar year, then a return required by this paragraph (a) must be filed on or before February 28 (March 31 if filed electronically) of the year following the calendar year in which the reimbursement was made. An interest recipient must file the return required by paragraph (a) of this section with the IRS office designated in the instructions for Form 1098.

(5) *Use of magnetic media.*—An interest recipient must file the return required by paragraph (a) of this section on magnetic media only if required by section 6011(e) and the regulations thereunder. An interest recipient not required by section 6011(e) to file returns on magnetic media may request permission to do so. Section 301.6011-2 contains rules relating to the use of magnetic media. A failure to file on magnetic media when required constitutes a failure to file an information return under section 6721.

(b) *Requirement to furnish statement.*—(1) *In general.*—An interest recipient that must file a return under paragraph (a) of this section must furnish a statement to the payor of record.

(2) *Information included on statement.*—An interest recipient must include on the statement that it must furnish to a payor of record:

(i) The information required under paragraph (a)(2) of this section;

(ii) A legend that—

(A) Identifies the statement as important tax information that is being furnished to the IRS; and

(B) Notifies the payor of record that if the payor of record is required to file a return, a negligence penalty or other sanction may be imposed on the payor of record if the IRS determines that an underpayment of tax results because the payor of record overstated a deduction for this mortgage interest (if any) or understated income from this mortgage interest reimbursement (if any) on the payor of record's return;

(iii) A legend stating that the payor of record may be unable to deduct the full amount of mortgage interest reported on the statement; that limitations based on the cost and value of the property securing the mortgage may apply; and that the payor of record may only deduct mortgage interest to the extent it was incurred, actually paid by the payor of record, and not reimbursed by another person; and

(iv) With respect to any information required to be reported under paragraph (a)(2)(iv) of this section, an instruction providing that the amount of the reimbursement is not to be deducted and that the amount must be included in the gross income of the payor of record if the reimbursed interest was deducted by the payor of record in a prior year so as to reduce income tax.

(3) *Statement furnished pursuant to Federal mortgage program.*—An interest recipient that furnishes a statement to a payor of record under a Federal mortgage program will satisfy the requirement of paragraph (b)(1) of this section if the statement contains all the information and legends required by paragraph (b)(2) of this section and is furnished by the time and at the place required by paragraph (b)(6) of this section.

(4) *Copy of Form 1098 to payor of record.*—An interest recipient will satisfy the requirement of paragraph (b)(1) of this section by furnishing to a payor of record a copy of Form 1098 (or a substitute statement that complies with applicable revenue procedures) containing all the information filed with the Internal Revenue Service and all the legends required by paragraph (b)(2) of this section by the time and at the place required by paragraph (b)(6) of this section.

(5) *Furnishing statement with other information reports.*—An interest recipient may transmit the statement required by paragraph (b)(1) of this section to the payor of record with other information, including other information returns, as permitted by applicable revenue procedures.

(6) *Time and place for furnishing statement.*—An interest recipient must furnish a statement required by paragraph (b)(1) of this section to a payor of record on or before January 31 of the year following the calendar year for which it receives the mortgage interest. If no mortgage interest is required to be reported for the calendar year, but a reimbursement of interest on a qualified mortgage is required to be reported for the calendar year, then the statement required by

paragraph (b)(1) of this section must be furnished on or before January 31 of the year following the calendar year in which the reimbursement was made. The interest recipient will be considered to have furnished the statement to the payor of record if it mails the statement to the payor of record's last known address.

(c) *Notice requirement for use of Rule of 78's method of accounting.*—(1) *In general.*—An interest recipient seeking to report interest received on a mortgage under the Rule of 78s method of accounting as permitted under § 1.6050H-1(e)(4) must notify the payor of record that the Rule of 78s method of accounting was used to calculate interest received on the mortgage and that the payor of record may not deduct as interest the amount calculated under the Rule of 78s method of accounting unless the payor of record properly uses that method to determine interest deductions. The notice must state that the payor of record may use the Rule of 78s method of accounting to determine interest paid for Federal income tax purposes only for a self-amortizing consumer loan requiring level payments at regular intervals (at least annually) over no longer than a five-year period, with no balloon payment at the end of the loan term, and only when the loan agreement provides for use of the Rule of 78s method of accounting to determine interest earned. See Rev. Proc. 83-40, 1983-1 C.B. 774; Rev. Rul. 83-84, 1983-1 C.B. 97.

(2) *Time and manner.*—An interest recipient must provide notice required by paragraph (c)(1) of this section to a payor of record on or with the statement required by paragraph (b) of this section. An interest recipient may provide notice on a separate paper or on the statement required by paragraph (b) of this section.

(d) *Reporting under designation agreement.*—(1) *In general.*—An interest recipient that receives or collects interest (including points) on a mortgage may designate a qualified person to satisfy the reporting requirements of paragraphs (a), (b), and (c) of this section. If a designated qualified person reports as permitted under this paragraph (d), it will satisfy the requirement of paragraph (a)(2)(ii) of this section by including on Form 1098 (and Form 1096) the name, address, and TIN of the designated qualified person.

(2) *Qualified person.*—A qualified person is either—

(i) A trade or business with respect to which the interest recipient is under common control within the meaning of § 1.414(c)-2; or

(ii) A person who is named as the designee by the lender of record or by a qualified person (under paragraph (d)(2) of this section) in a designation agreement entered into in accordance with paragraph (d)(3) of this section, and who either was involved in the original loan transaction or is a subsequent purchaser of the loan.

(3) *Designation agreement.*—An interest recipient that designates a qualified person to satisfy the reporting requirements described in paragraphs (a), (b), and (c) of this section must make that designation in a written designation agreement. The designation agreement must identify the mortgage(s) and calendar years for which the designated qualified person must report, and must be signed by both the designator and designee. A designee may report an amount as having been paid directly by the payor of record (for purposes of paragraph (a)(2)(v) of this section) only if the designation agreement contains the designator's representation that it did not lend such amount to the payor of record as part of the overall transaction. The designator must retain a copy of the designation agreement for four years following the close of the calendar year in which the loan is made. The designation agreement need not be filed with the Internal Revenue Service.

(4) *Penalties.*—A designated qualified person is subject to any applicable penalties provided in part II of subchapter B of chapter 68 of the Internal Revenue Code as if it were an interest recipient. A designator is relieved from liability for applicable penalties by designating a qualified person under the provisions of paragraph (d)(3) of this section. Paragraph (e) of this section describes applicable penalties.

(e) *Penalty provisions.*—(1) *Returns and statements the due date for which (determined without regard for extensions) is after December 31, 1987, and before December 31, 1989.*—For purposes of this paragraph (e)(1) only, all references to sections of the Internal Revenue Code refer to sections of the Internal Revenue Code of 1986, as amended on or before December 31, 1987.

(i) *Failure to file return or to furnish statement.*—The section 6721 penalty applies to an interest recipient that fails to file a return required by paragraph (a) of this section with respect to a payor of record. The section 6722 penalty applies to an interest recipient that fails to furnish a statement required by paragraph (b) of this section to a payor of record.

(ii) *Failure to furnish TIN.*—The section 6676 penalty may apply to an interest recipient that fails to furnish the TIN of a payor of record on a return required by paragraph (a) of this section. The section 6676 penalty may apply to an interest recipient that fails to request and to obtain the TIN of a payor of record under paragraph (f) of this section.

(iii) *Failure to include correct information.*—The section 6723 penalty may apply to an interest recipient that fails to include correct information on a return required by paragraph (a) of this section or on a statement required by paragraph (b) of this section to be furnished to a payor of record.

(2) *Returns and statements the due date for which (determined without regard for extensions) is after December 31, 1989.*—(i) *Failure to file return or to furnish statement.*—The section 6721 penalty applies to an interest recipient that fails to file a return required by paragraph (a) of this section with respect to a payor of record. The section 6722 penalty applies to an interest recipient that fails to furnish a statement required by paragraph (b) of this section to a payor of record.

(ii) *Failure to furnish TIN.*—The section 6721 penalty may apply to an interest recipient that fails to furnish the TIN of a payor of record on a return required by paragraph (a) of this section. The section 6721 penalty may apply to an interest recipient that fails to request and to obtain the TIN of a payor of record under paragraph (f) of this section.

(iii) *Failure to include correct information.*—The section 6721 penalty may apply to an interest recipient that fails to include correct information on a return required by paragraph (a) of this section. The section 6722 penalty may apply to an interest recipient that fails to include correct information on a statement required by paragraph (b) of this section to be furnished to a payor record.

(f) *Requirement to request and to obtain TIN.*—(1) *In general.*—For obligations incurred after December 31, 1987, an interest recipient must make all reasonable efforts to obtain the TIN of a payor of record when the payor of record incurs the obligation. For example, an interest recipient may require a borrower to furnish a TIN during the mortgage approval or application process. If an interest recipient does not maintain the TIN of a payor of record on a mortgage, whenever incurred, it must request the TIN at least annually and must process responses properly and promptly.

(2) *Manner of requesting TIN.*—An interest recipient need not separately mail a request for a TIN. An interest recipient may include a request in its regular mailing of payment coupon booklets or annual statements. If an interest recipient makes no mailing to a payor of record during the year in which the payor of record incurs the obligation, it must request the TIN in a separate mailing. No particular form is required to request a TIN. Nevertheless, an interest recipient must make the request on a separate paper and must clearly notify a payor of record that the Internal Revenue Service requires the payor of record to furnish a TIN in order to verify any mortgage interest deduction. An interest recipient must notify a payor of record that failure to furnish a TIN subjects the payor of record to a $50 penalty imposed by the Internal Revenue Service. A request for a TIN made on Form W-9 satisfies the requirement of this paragraph (f)(2).

(g) *Effective date.*—(1) *In general.*—Except as provided in paragraph (g)(2) of this section, this section is effective for mortgage interest received after December 31, 1987. Section 1.6050H-1T contains rules for reporting mortgage interest received after December 31, 1984, and before January 1, 1988.

(2) *Points.*—The reporting requirement of this section does not apply to prepaid interest in the form of points received before January 1, 1995. [Reg. § 1.6050H-2.]

☐ [*T.D. 8191, 4-11-88. Amended by T.D. 8507, 12-28-93; T.D. 8571, 12-7-94 and T.D. 8895, 8-17-2000.*]

[Reg. § 1.6050H-3]

§ 1.6050H-3. Information reporting of mortgage insurance premiums.—(a) *Information reporting requirements.*—Any person who, in the course of a trade or business, receives premiums, including prepaid premiums, for mortgage insurance (as described in paragraph (b) of this section) from any individual aggregating $600 or more for any calendar year, must make an information return setting forth the total amount received from that individual during the calendar year.

(b) *Scope.*—Paragraph (a) of this section applies to mortgage insurance provided by the Federal Housing Administration, Department of Veterans Affairs, or the Rural Housing Service (or their successor organizations), or to private mortgage insurance (as defined by section 2 of the Homeowners Protection Act of 1998 (12 U.S.C. 4901) as in effect on December 20, 2006). The rule stated in paragraph (a) of this section applies to the receipt of all payments of mortgage insurance premiums, by cash or financing, without regard to source.

(c) *Aggregation.*—Whether a person receives $600 or more of mortgage insurance premiums is determined on a mortgage-by-mortgage basis. A recipient need not aggregate mortgage insurance premiums received on all of the mortgages of an individual to determine whether the $600 threshold is met. Therefore, a recipient need not report mortgage insurance premiums of less than $600 received on a mortgage, even though it receives a total of $600 or more of mortgage insurance premiums on all of the mortgages for an individual for a calendar year.

(d) *Time, form, and manner of reporting.*—Mortgage insurance premiums required to be reported under paragraph (a) of this section must be reported on the Form 1098 or successor form that is filed pursuant to § 1.6050H-2(a) with respect to the mortgage of the individual who paid the mortgage insurance premiums. For the requirements for furnishing statements with respect to Forms 1098 filed with the Internal Revenue Service, see § 1.6050H-2(b).

(e) *Cross reference.*—For rules concerning the allocation of certain prepaid qualified mortgage insurance premiums, see § 1.163-11 of this chapter.

(f) *Limitation on the reporting of mortgage insurance premiums.*—This section applies to mortgage insurance premiums described in paragraph (b) of this section that are paid or accrued on or after January 1, 2013, and during periods to which section 163(h)(3)(E) applies. This section does not apply to any amounts of mortgage insurance premiums that are allocable to any periods to which section 163(h)(3)(E) does not apply.

(g) *Effective/applicability date.*—This section applies to mortgage insurance premiums received on or after January 1, 2013. For regulations applicable before May 5, 2012, see § 1.6050H-3T as contained in 26 CFR part 1 (revised as of April 1, 2012). [Reg. § 1.6050H-3.]

☐ [*T.D. 9642, 11-26-2013.*]

[Reg. § 1.6050I-0]

§ 1.6050I-0. Table of contents.—This section lists the major captions that appear in §§ 1.6050I-1 and 1.6050I-2.

§ 1.6050I-1. Returns relating to cash in excess of $10,000 received in a trade or business.

(a) Reporting requirement.

  (1) Reportable transaction.

    (i) In general.

    (ii) Certain financial transactions.

  (2) Cash received for the account of another.

  (3) Cash received by agents.

    (i) General rule.

    (ii) Exception.

    (iii) Example.

(b) Multiple payments.

  (1) Initial payment in excess of $10,000.

  (2) Initial payment of $10,000 or less.

  (3) Subsequent payments.

  (4) Example.

(c) Meaning of terms.

  (1) Cash.

    (i) Amounts received prior to February 3, 1992.

    (ii) Amounts received on or after February 3, 1992.

    (iii) Designated reporting transaction.

    (iv) Exception for certain loans.

    (v) Exception for certain installment sales.

    (vi) Exception for certain down payment plans.

    (vii) Examples.

  (2) Consumer durable.

  (3) Collectible.

  (4) Travel or entertainment activity.

  (5) Retail sale.

  (6) Trade or business.

  (7) Transaction.

  (8) Recipient.

(d) Exceptions to the reporting requirements of section 6050I.

  (1) Receipt of cash by certain financial institutions.

  (2) Receipt of cash by certain casinos having gross annual gaming revenue in excess of $1,000,000.

    (i) In general.

    (ii) Casinos exempt under 31 CFR 103.45(c).

(iii) Reporting of cash received in a nongaming business.

(iv) Example.

(3) Receipt of cash not in the course of the recipient's trade or business.

(4) Receipt is made with respect to a foreign cash transaction.

(i) In general.

(ii) Example.

(e) Time, manner, and form of reporting.

(1) Time of reporting.

(2) Form of reporting.

(3) Manner of reporting.

(i) Where to file.

(ii) Verification.

(iii) Retention of returns.

(f) Requirement of furnishing statements.

(1) In general.

(2) Form of statement.

(3) When statement is to be furnished.

(g) Cross-reference to penalty provisions.

(1) Failure to file correct information return.

(2) Failure to furnish correct statement.

(3) Criminal penalties.

§ 1.6050I-2. Returns relating to cash in excess of $10,000 received as bail by court clerks.

(a) Reporting requirement.

(b) Meaning of terms.

(c) Time, form, and manner of reporting.

(1) Time of reporting.

(i) In general.

(ii) Multiple payments.

(2) Form of reporting.

(3) Manner of reporting.

(i) Where to file.

(ii) Verification of identity.

(d) Requirement to furnish statements.

(1) Information to Federal prosecutors.

(i) In general.

(ii) Form of statement.

(2) Information to payors of bail.

(i) In general.

(ii) Form of statement.

(iii) Aggregate amount.

(e) Cross-reference to penalty provisions.

(f) Effective date.

[Reg. § 1.6050I-0.]

☐ [*T.D.* 8652, 12-29-95. *Amended by T.D.* 8974, 12-28-2001.]

[Reg. § 1.6050I-1]

§ 1.6050I-1. Returns relating to cash in excess of $10,000 received in a trade or business.—(a) *Reporting requirement.*—(1) *Reportable transaction.*—(i) *In general.*—Any person(as defined in section 7701(a)(1)) who, in the course of a trade or business in which such person is engaged, receives cash in excess of $10,000 in 1 transaction (or 2 or more related transactions) shall, except as otherwise provided, make a return of information with respect to the receipt of cash.

(ii) *Certain financial transactions.*—Section 6050I of title 26 of the United States Code requires persons to report information about financial transactions to the Internal Revenue Service, and section 5331 of title 31 of the United States Code requires persons to report similar information about certain transactions to the Financial Crimes Enforcement Network. This information shall be reported on the same form as prescribed by the Secretary.

(2) *Cash received for the account of another.*—Cash in excess of $10,000 received by a person for the account of another must be reported under this section. Thus, for example, a person who collects delinquent accounts receivable for an automobile dealer must report with respect to the receipt of cash in excess of $10,000 from the collection of a particular account even though the proceeds of the collection are credited to the account of the automobile dealer (*i.e.*, where the rights to the proceeds from the account are retained by the automobile dealer and the collection is made on a fee-for-service basis).

(3) *Cash received by agents.*—(i) *General rule.*—Except as provided in paragraph (a)(3)(ii) of this section, a person who in the course of a trade or business acts as an agent (or in some other similar capacity) and receives cash in excess of $10,000 from a principal must report the receipt of cash under this section.

(ii) *Exception.*—An agent who receives cash from a principal and uses all of the cash within 15 days in a cash transaction (the "second cash transaction") which is reportable under section 6050 I or section 5312 of Title 31 of the United States Code and the regulations thereunder (31 CFR Part 103), and who discloses the name, address, and taxpayer identification number of the principal to the recipient in the second cash transaction need not report the initial receipt of cash under this section. An agent will be deemed to have met the disclosure requirements of this paragraph (a)(3)(ii) if the agent discloses only the name of the principal and the agent knows that the recipient has the principal's address and taxpayer identification number.

(iii) *Example.*—The following example illustrates the application of the rules in paragraphs (a)(3)(i) and (ii) of this section:

Example. B, the principal, gives D, an attorney, $75,000 in cash to purchase real property on behalf of B. Within 15 days D purchases real property for cash from E, a real estate developer, and discloses to E, B's name, address, and taxpayer identification number. Because the transaction qualifies for the exception provided in paragraph (a)(3)(ii) of this section, D need not report with respect to the initial receipt of cash under this section. The exception does not apply, however, if D pays E by means other than cash, or effects the purchase more than 15 days following receipt of the cash from B, or fails to disclose B's name, address, and taxpayer identification number (assuming D does not know that E already has B's address and taxpayer identification number), or purchases the property from a person whose sale of the property is not in the course of that person's trade or business. In any such case, D is required to report the receipt of cash from B under this section.

(b) *Multiple payments.*—The receipt of multiple cash deposits or cash installment payments (or other similar payments or prepayments) on or after January 1, 1990, relating to a single transaction (or two or more related transactions), is reported as set forth in paragraphs (b)(1) through (b)(3) of this section.

(1) *Initial payment in excess of $10,000.*—If the initial payment exceeds $10,000, the recipient must report the initial payment within 15 days of its receipt.

(2) *Initial payment of $10,000 or less.*—If the initial payment does not exceed $10,000, the recipient must aggregate the initial payment and subsequent payments made within one year of the initial payment until the aggregate amount exceeds $10,000, and report with respect to the aggregate amount within 15 days after receiving the payment that causes the aggregate amount to exceed $10,000.

(3) *Subsequent payments.*—In addition to any other required report, a report must be made each time that previously unreportable payments made within a 12-month period with respect to a single transaction (or two or more related transactions), individually or in the aggregate, exceed $10,000. The report must be made within 15 days after receiving the payment in excess of $10,000 or the payment that causes the aggregate amount received in the 12-month period to exceed $10,000. (If more than one report would otherwise be required for multiple cash payments within a 15-day period that relate to a single transaction (or two or more related transactions), the recipient may make a single combined report with respect to the payments. The combined report must be made no later than the date by which the first of the separate reports would otherwise be required to be made.) A report with respect to payments of $10,000 or less that are reportable under this paragraph (b)(3) and are received after December 31, 1989, but before July 10, 1990, is due July 24, 1990.

(4) *Example.*—The following example illustrates the application of the rules in paragraphs (b)(1) through (b)(3) of this section:

Example. On January 10, 1991, M receives an initial cash payment of $11,000 with respect to a transaction. M receives subsequent cash payments with respect to the same transaction of $4,000 on February 15, 1991, $6,000 on March 20, 1991, and $12,000 on May 15, 1991. M must make a report with respect to the payment received on January 10, 1991, by January 25, 1991. M must also make a report with respect to the payments totalling $22,000 received from February 15, 1991, through May 15, 1991. This report must be made by May 30, 1991, that is, within 15 days of the date that the subsequent payments, all of which were received within a 12-month period, exceeded $10,000.

(c) *Meaning of terms.*—The following definitions apply for purposes of this section—

(1) *Cash.*—(i) *Amounts received prior to February 3, 1992.*—For amounts received prior to February 3, 1992, the term "cash" means the coin and currency of the United States or of any other country, which circulate in and are customarily used and accepted as money in the country in which issued.

(ii) *Amounts received on or after February 3, 1992.*—For amounts received on or after February 3, 1992, the term "cash" means—

(A) The coin and currency of the United States or of any other country, which circulate in and are customarily used and accepted as money in the country in which issued; and

(B) A cashier's check (by whatever name called, including "treasurer's check" and "bank check"), bank draft, traveler's check, or money order having a face amount of not more than $10,000—

(1) Received in a designated reporting transaction as defined in paragraph (c)(1)(iii) of this section (except as provided in paragraphs (c)(1)(iv), (v), and (vi) of this section), or

(2) Received in any transaction in which the recipient knows that such instrument is being used in an attempt to avoid the reporting of the transaction under section 6050 I and this section.

(iii) *Designated reporting transaction.*—A designated reporting transaction is a retail sale (or the receipt of funds by a broker or other intermediary in connection with a retail sale) of—

(A) A consumer durable,

(B) A collectible, or

(C) A travel or entertainment activity.

(iv) *Exception for certain loans.*—A cashier's check, bank draft, traveler's check, or money order received in a designated reporting transaction is not treated as cash pursuant to paragraph (c)(1)(ii)(B)(1) of this section if the instrument constitutes the proceeds of a loan from a bank (as that term is defined in 31 CFR part 103). The recipient may rely on a copy of the loan document, a written statement from the bank, or similar documentation (such as a written lien instruction from the issuer of the instrument) to substantiate that the instrument constitutes loan proceeds.

(v) *Exception for certain installment sales.*—A cashier's check, bank draft, traveler's check, or money order received in a designated reporting transaction is not treated as cash pursuant to paragraph (c)(1)(ii)(B)(1) of this section if the instrument is received in payment on a promissory note or an installment sales contract (including a lease that is considered to be a sale for

Federal income tax purposes). However, the preceding sentence applies only if—

(A) Promissory notes or installment sales contracts with the same or substantially similar terms are used in the ordinary course of the recipient's trade or business in connection with sales to ultimate consumers; and

(B) The total amount of payments with respect to the sale that are received on or before the 60th day after the date of the sale does not exceed 50 percent of the purchase price of the sale.

(vi) *Exception for certain down payment plans.*—A cashier's check, bank draft, traveler's check, or money order received in a designated reporting transaction is not treated as cash pursuant to paragraph (c)(1)(ii)(B)(*1*) of this section if the instrument is received pursuant to a payment plan requiring one or more down payments and the payment of the balance of the purchase price by a date no later than the date of the sale (in the case of an item of travel or entertainment, a date no later than the earliest date that any item of travel or entertainment pertaining to the same trip or event is furnished). However, the preceding sentence applies only if—

(A) The recipient uses payment plans with the same or substantially similar terms in the ordinary course of its trade or business in connection with sales to ultimate consumers; and

(B) The instrument is received more than 60 days prior to the date of the sale (in the case of an item of travel or entertainment, the date on which the final payment is due).

(vii) *Examples.*—The following examples illustrate the definition of "cash" set forth in paragraphs (c)(1)(ii) through (vi) of this section.

Example 1. D, an individual, purchases gold coins from M, a coin dealer, for $13,200. D tenders to M in payment United States currency in the amount of $6,200 and a cashier's check in the face amount of $7,000 which D had purchased. Because the sale is a designated reporting transaction, the cashier's check is treated as cash for purposes of section 6050 I and this section. Therefore, because M has received more than $10,000 in cash with respect to the transaction, M must make the report required by section 6050 I and this section.

Example 2. E, an individual, purchases an automobile from Q, an automobile dealer, for $11,500. E tenders to Q in payment United States currency in the amount of $2,000 and a cashier's check payable to E and Q in the amount of $9,500. The cashier's check constitutes the proceeds of a loan from the bank issuing the check. The origin of the proceeds is evident from provisions inserted by the bank on the check that instruct the dealer to cause a lien to be placed on the vehicle as security for the loan. The sale of the automobile is a designated reporting transaction. However, under paragraph (c)(1)(iv) of this section, because E has furnished Q documentary information establishing that the cashier's check constitutes the proceeds of a loan from the bank issuing the check, the cashier's check is not treated as cash pursuant to paragraph (c)(1)(ii)(B)(*1*) of this section.

Example 3. F, an individual, purchases an item of jewelry from S, a retail jeweler, for $12,000. F gives S traveler's checks totalling $2,400 and pays the balance with a personal check payable to S in the amount of $9,600. Because the sale is a designated reporting transaction, the traveler's checks are treated as cash for purposes of section 6050 I and this section. However, because the personal check is not treated as cash for purposes of section 6050 I and this section, S has not received more than $10,000 in cash in the transaction and no report is required to be filed under section 6050 I and this section.

Example 4. G, an individual, purchases a boat from T, a boat dealer, for $16,500. G pays T with a cashier's check payable to T in the amount of $16,500. The cashier's check is not treated as cash because the face amount of the check is more than $10,000. Thus, no report is required to be made by T under section 6050 I and this section.

Example 5. H, an individual, arranges with W, a travel agent, for the chartering of a passenger aircraft to transport a group of individuals to a sports event in another city. H also arranges with W for hotel accommodations for the group and for admission tickets to the sports event. In payment, H tenders to W money orders which H had previously purchased. The total amount of the money orders, none of which individually exceeds $10,000 in face amount, exceeds $10,000. Because the transaction is a designated reporting transaction, the money orders are treated as cash for purposes of section 6050 I and this section. Therefore, because W has received more than $10,000 in cash with respect to the transaction, W must make the report required by section 6050 I and this section.

(2) *Consumer durable.*—The term "consumer durable" means an item of tangible personal property of a type that is suitable under ordinary usage for personal consumption or use, that can reasonably be expected to be useful for at least 1 year under ordinary usage, and that has a sales price of more than $10,000. Thus, for example, a $20,000 automobile is a consumer durable (whether or not it is sold for business use), but a $20,000 dump truck or a $20,000 factory machine is not.

(3) *Collectible.*—The term "collectible" means an item described in paragraphs (A) through (D) of section 408(m)(2) (determined without regard to section 408(m)(3)).

(4) *Travel or entertainment activity.*—The term "travel or entertainment activity" means an item of travel or entertainment (within the meaning of § 1.274-2(b)(1)) pertaining to a single trip or event where the aggregate sales price of the item and all other items pertaining to the same

trip or event that are sold in the same transaction (or related transactions) exceeds $10,000.

(5) *Retail sale.*—The term "retail sale" means any sale (whether for resale or for any other purpose) made in the course of a trade or business if that trade or business principally consists of making sales to ultimate consumers.

(6) *Trade or business.*—The term "trade or business" has the same meaning as under section 162 of the Internal Revenue Code of 1954.

(7) *Transaction.*—(i) The term "transaction" means the underlying event precipitating the payer's transfer of cash to the recipient. Transactions include (but are not limited to) a sale of goods or services; a sale of real property; a sale of intangible property; a rental of real or personal property; an exchange of cash for other cash; the establishment or maintenance of or contribution to a custodial, trust, or escrow arrangement; a payment of a preexisting debt; a conversion of cash to a negotiable instrument; a reimbursement for expenses paid; or the making or repayment of a loan. A transaction may not be divided into multiple transactions in order to avoid reporting under this section.

(ii) The term "related transactions" means any transaction conducted between a payer (or its agent) and a recipient of cash in a 24-hour period. Additionally, transactions conducted between a payer (or its agent) and a cash recipient during a period of more than 24 hours are related if the recipient knows or has reason to know that each transaction is one of a series of connected transactions.

(iii) The following examples illustrate the definition of paragraphs (c)(7)(i) and (ii).

Example (1). A person has a tacit agreement with a gold dealer to purchase $36,000 in gold bullion. The $36,000 purchase represents a single transaction under paragraph (c)(7)(i) of this section and the reporting requirements of this section cannot be avoided by recasting the single sales transaction into 4 separate $9,000 sales transactions.

Example (2). An attorney agrees to represent a client in a criminal case with the attorney's fee to be determined on an hourly basis. In the first month in which the attorney represents the client, the bill for the attorney's services comes to $8,000 which the client pays in cash. In the second month in which the attorney represents the client, the bill for the attorney's services comes to $4,000, which the client again pays in cash. The aggregate amount of cash paid ($12,000) relates to a single transaction as defined in paragraph (c)(7)(i) of this section, the sale of legal services relating to the criminal case, and the receipt of cash must be reported under this section.

Example (3). A person intends to contribute a total of $45,000 to a trust fund, and the trustee of the fund knows or has reason to know of that intention. The $45,000 contribution is a single transaction under paragraph (c)(7)(i) of this section and the reporting requirement of this section cannot be avoided by the grantor's making five separate $9,000 cash contributions to a single fund or by making five $9,000 cash contributions to five separate funds administered by a common trustee.

Example (4). K, an individual, attends a one day auction and purchases for cash two items, at a cost of $9,240 and $1,732.50 respectively (tax and buyer's premium included). Because the transactions are related transactions as defined in paragraph (c)(7)(ii) of this section, the auction house is required to report the aggregate amount of cash received from the related sales ($10,972.50), even though the auction house accounts separately on its books for each item sold and presents the purchaser with separate bills for each item purchased.

Example (5). F, a coin dealer, sells for cash $9,000 worth of gold coins to an individual on three successive days. Under paragraph (c)(7)(ii) of this section the three $9,000 transactions are related transactions aggregating $27,000 if F knows, or has reason to know, that each transaction is one of a series of connected transactions.

(8) *Recipient.*—(i) The term "recipient" means the person receiving the cash. Except as provided in paragraph (c)(8)(ii) of this section, each store, division, branch, department, headquarters, or office ("branch") (regardless of physical location) comprising a portion of a person's trade or business shall for purposes of this section be deemed a separate recipient.

(ii) A branch that receives cash payments will not be deemed a separate recipient if the branch (or a central unit linking such branch with other branches) would in the ordinary course of business have reason to know the identity of payers making cash payments to other branches of such person.

(iii) *Examples.*—The following examples illustrate the application of the rules in paragraphs (c)(8)(i) and (ii) of this section:

Example (1). N, an individual, purchases regulated futures contracts at a cost of $7,500 and $5,000, respectively, through two different branches of Commodities Broker X on the same day. N pays for each purchase with cash. Each branch of Commodities Broker X transmits the sales information regarding each of N's purchases to a central unit of Commodities Broker X (which settles the transactions against N's account). Under paragraph (c)(8)(ii) of this section the separate branches of Commodities Broker X are not deemed to be separate recipients; therefore, Commodities Broker X must report with respect to the two related regulated futures contracts sales in accordance with this section.

Example (2). P, a corporation, owns and operates a racetrack. P's racetrack contains 100 betting windows at which pari-mutuel wagers may be made. R, an individual, places cash wagers of $3,000 each at five separate betting windows. Assuming that in the ordinary course of business each betting window (or a central unit linking windows) does not have reason to know the identity of persons making wagers at other betting windows, each betting window would be deemed to be a separate cash recipient under paragraph (c)(8)(i) of this section. As no individual recipient received cash in excess of $10,000, no report need be made by P under this section.

(d) *Exceptions to the reporting requirements of section 6050I.*—(1) *Receipt of cash by certain financial institutions.*—A financial institution as defined in subparagraphs (A), (B), (C), (D), (E), (F), (G), (J), (K), (R), and (S) of section 5312(a)(2) of Title 31, United States Code is not required to report the receipt of cash exceeding $10,000 under section 6050 I.

(2) *Receipt of cash by certain casinos having gross annual gaming revenue in excess of $1,000,000.*—(i) *In general.*—If a casino receives cash in excess of $10,000 and is required to report the receipt of such cash directly to the Treasury Department under 31 CFR 103.22(a)(2) and 103.25 and is subject to the recordkeeping requirements of 31 CFR 103.36, then the casino is not required to make a return with respect to the receipt of such cash under section 6050 I and these regulations.

(ii) *Casinos exempt under 31 CFR 103.45(c).*—Under the authority of section 6050 I(c)(1)(A), the Secretary may exempt from the reporting requirements of section 6050 I casinos with gross annual gaming revenue in excess of $1,000,000 that are exempt under 31 CFR 103.45(c) from reporting certain cash transactions to the Treasury Department under 31 CFR 103.22(a)(2) and 103.25. The determination whether a casino which is granted an exemption under 31 CFR section 103.45(c) will be required to report under section 6050 I will be made on a case by case basis, concurrently with the granting of such an exemption.

(iii) *Reporting of cash received in a nongaming business.*—Nongaming businesses (such as shops, restaurants, entertainment, and hotels) at casino hotels and resorts are separate trades or businesses in which the receipt of cash in excess of $10,000 is reportable under section 6050 I and these regulations. Thus, a casino exempt under paragraph (d)(2)(i) or (ii) of this section must report with respect to cash in excess of $10,000 received in its nongaming businesses.

(iv) *Example.*—The following example illustrates the application of the rules in paragraphs (d)(2)(i) and (iii) of this section:

Example. A and B are casinos having gross annual gaming revenue in excess of $1,000,000. C is a casino with gross annual gaming revenue of less than $1,000,000. Casino A receives $15,000 in cash from a customer with respect to a gaming transaction which the casino reports to the Treasury Department under 31 CFR 103.22(a)(2) and 103.25. Casino B receives $15,000 in cash from a customer in payment for accommodations provided to that customer at Casino B's hotel. Casino C receives $15,000 in cash from a customer

with respect to a gaming transaction. Casino A is not required to report the transaction under section 6050 I or these regulations because the exception for certain casinos provided in paragraph (d)(2)(i) ("the casino exception") applies. Casino B is required to report under section 6050 I and these regulations because the casino exception does not apply to the receipt of cash from a nongaming activity. Casino C is required to report under section 6050 I and these regulations because the casino exception does not apply to casinos having gross annual gaming revenue of $1,000,000 or less which do not have to report to the Treasury Department under 31 CFR 103.22(a)(2) and 103.25.

(3) *Receipt of cash not in the course of the recipient's trade or business.*—The receipt of cash in excess of $10,000 by a person other than in the course of the person's trade or business is not reportable under section 6050 I. Thus, for example, F, an individual in the trade or business of selling real estate, sells a motorboat for $12,000, the purchase price of which is paid in cash. F did not use the motorboat in any trade or business in which F was engaged. F is not required to report under section 6050 I or these regulations because the exception provided in this paragraph (d)(3) applies.

(4) *Receipt is made with respect to a foreign cash transaction.*—(i) *In general.*—Generally, there is no requirement to report with respect to a cash transaction if the entire transaction occurs outside the United States (the fifty states and the District of Columbia). An entire transaction consists of both the transaction as defined in paragraph (c)(7)(i) of this section and the receipt of cash by the recipient. If, however, any part of an entire transaction occurs in the Commonwealth of Puerto Rico or a possession or territory of the United States and the recipient of cash in that transaction is subject to the general jurisdiction of the Internal Revenue Service under Title 26 of the United States Code, the recipient is required to report the transaction under this section.

(ii) *Example.*—The following example illustrates the application of the rules in paragraph (d)(4)(i) of this section:

Example. W, an individual engaged in the trade or business of selling aircraft, reaches an agreement to sell an airplane to a U.S. citizen living in Mexico. The agreement, no portion of which is formulated in the United States, calls for a purchase price of $125,000 and requires delivery of and payment for the airplane to be made in Mexico. Upon delivery of the airplane in Mexico, W receives $125,000 in cash. W is not required to report under section 6050 I or these regulations because the exception provided in paragraph (d)(4)(i) of this section ("foreign transaction exception") applies. If, however, any part of the agreement to sell has been formulated in the United States, the foreign transaction exception would not apply and W would be required to report the receipt of cash under section 6050 I and these regulations.

(e) *Time, manner, and form of reporting.*— (1) *Time of reporting.*—The reports required by this section must be filed with the Internal Revenue Service by the 15th day after the date the cash is received. However, in the case of multiple payments relating to a single transaction (or two or more related transactions), see paragraph (b) of this section.

(2) *Form of reporting.*—A report required by paragraph (a) of this section must be made on Form 8300. A return of information made in compliance with this paragraph must contain the name, address, and taxpayer identification number of the person from whom the cash was received; the name, address, and taxpayer identification number of the person on whose behalf the transaction was conducted (if the recipient knows or has reason to know that the person from whom the cash was received conducted the transaction as an agent for another person); the amount of cash received; the date and nature of the transaction; and any other information required by Form 8300. Form 8300 can be obtained from any Internal Revenue Service Forms Distribution Center.

(3) *Manner of reporting.*—(i) *Where to file.*—A person making a return of information under this section must file Form 8300 by mailing it to the address shown in the instructions to the form.

(ii) *Verification.*—A person making a return of information under this section must verify the identity of the person from whom the reportable cash is received. Verification of the identity of a person who purports to be an alien must be made by examination of such person's passport, alien identification card, or other official document evidencing nationality or residence. Verification of the identity of any other person may be made by examination of a document normally acceptable as a means of identification when cashing or accepting checks (for example, a driver's license or a credit card). In addition, a return will be considered incomplete if the person required to make a return knows (or has reason to know) that an agent is conducting the transaction for a principal, and the return does not identify both the principal and the agent.

(iii) *Retention of returns.*—A person required to make an information return under this section must keep a copy of each return filed for five years from the date of filing.

(f) *Requirement of furnishing statements.*—(1) *In general.*—Any person required to make an information return under this section must furnish a single, annual, written statement to each person whose name is set forth in a return ("identified person") filed with the Internal Revenue Service.

(2) *Form of statement.*—The statement required by the preceding paragraph need not follow any particular format, but it must contain the following information:

(i) The name and address of the person making the return;

(ii) The aggregate amount of reportable cash received by the person who made the information return required by this section during the calendar year in all cash transactions relating to the identified person; and

(iii) A legend stating that the information contained in the statement is being reported to the Internal Revenue Service.

(3) *When statement is to be furnished.*—Statements required under this paragraph (f) must be furnished to an identified person on or before January 31 of the year following the calendar year in which the cash is received. A statement shall be considered to be furnished to an identified person if it is mailed to the identified person at the identified person's last known address.

(g) *Cross-reference to penalty provisions.*— (1) *Failure to file correct information return.*—See section 6721 for civil penalties relating to the failure to file a correct return under section 6050 I(a) and paragraph (a) of this section.

(2) *Failure to furnish correct statement.*—See section 6722 for civil penalties relating to the failure to furnish a correct statement to identified persons under section 6050 I(e) and paragraph (f) of this section.

(3) *Criminal penalties.*—Any person who willfully fails to make a return or makes a false return under section 6050 I and this section may be subject to criminal prosecution. [Reg. § 1.6050I-1.]

☐ [*T.D.* 8098, 9-3-86. *Amended by T.D.* 8373, 11-14-91; *T.D.* 8479, 6-18-93 *and T.D.* 8974, 12-28-2001.]

[Reg. § 1.6050I-2]

§ 1.6050I-2. Returns relating to cash in excess of $10,000 received as bail by court clerks.— (a) *Reporting requirement.*—Any clerk of a Federal or State court who receives more than $10,000 in cash as bail for any individual charged with a specified criminal offense must make a return of information with respect to that cash receipt. For purposes of this section, a clerk is the clerk's office or the office, department, division, branch, or unit of the court that is authorized to receive bail. If someone other than a clerk receives bail on behalf of a clerk, the clerk is treated as receiving the bail for purposes of this paragraph (a).

(b) *Meaning of terms.*—The following definitions apply for purposes of this section—
Cash means—

(1) The coin and currency of the United States, or of any other country, that circulate in and are customarily used and accepted as money in the country in which issued; and

(2) A cashier's check (by whatever name called, including treasurer's check and bank check), bank draft, traveler's check, or money order having a face amount of not more than $10,000.

Specified criminal offense means—

(1) A Federal criminal offense involving a controlled substance (as defined in section 802 of title 21 of the United States Code), provided the offense is described in Part D of Subchapter I or Subchapter II of title 21 of the United States Code;

(2) Racketeering (as defined in section 1951, 1952, or 1955 of title 18 of the United States Code);

(3) Money laundering (as defined in section 1956 or 1957 of title 18 of the United States Code); and

(4) Any State criminal offense substantially similar to an offense described in this paragraph (b).

(c) *Time, form, and manner of reporting.*—(1) Time of reporting

(i) In general.—The information return required by this section must be filed with the Internal Revenue Service by the 15th day after the date the cash bail is received.

(ii) *Multiple payments.*—If multiple payments are made to satisfy bail reportable under this section and the initial payment does not exceed $10,000, the initial payment and subsequent payments must be aggregated and the information return required by this section must be filed with the Internal Revenue Service by the 15th day after receipt of the payment that causes the aggregate amount to exceed $10,000. However, if payments are made to satisfy separate bail requirements, no aggregation is required. Thus, if in Month 1 a clerk receives $6,000 in bail for an individual charged with a specified criminal offense and later, in Month 2, receives $7,000 in bail for that same individual charged with another specified criminal offense, no aggregation is required.

(2) *Form of reporting.*—The return of information required by paragraph (a) of this section must be made on Form 8300 and must contain the following information—

(i) The name, address, and taxpayer identification number (TIN) of the individual charged with the specified criminal offense;

(ii) The name, address, and TIN of each person posting the bail (payor of bail), other than a person posting bail who is licensed as a bail bondsman in the jurisdiction in which the bail is received;

(iii) The amount of cash received;

(iv) The date the cash was received; and

(v) Any other information required by Form 8300 or its instructions.

(3) *Manner of reporting.*—(i) Where to file.—Returns required by this section must be filed with the Internal Revenue Service office designated in the instructions for Form 8300. A copy of the information return required to be filed under this section must be retained for five years from the date of filing.

(ii) *Verification of identity.*—A clerk required to make an information return under this section must, in accordance with §1.6050I-1(e)(3)(ii), verify the identity of each payor of bail listed in the return.

(d) *Requirement to furnish statements.*—(1) Information to Federal prosecutors.—(i) In general.—A clerk required to make an information return under this section must furnish a written statement to the United States Attorney for the jurisdiction in which the individual charged with the specified crime resides and the United States Attorney for the jurisdiction in which the specified criminal offense occurred (applicable United States Attorney(s)). The written statement must be filed with the applicable United States Attorney(s) by the 15th day after the date the cash bail is received.

(ii) *Form of statement.*—The written statement must include the information required by paragraph (c)(2) of this section. The requirement of this paragraph (d)(1)(ii) will be satisfied if the clerk provides to the applicable United States Attorney(s) a copy of the Form 8300 that is filed with the Internal Revenue Service pursuant to this section.

(2) *Information to payors of bail.*—(i) In general.—A clerk required to make an information return under this section must furnish a written statement to each payor of bail whose name is set forth in a return required by this section. A statement required under this paragraph (d)(2) must be furnished to a payor of bail on or before January 31 of the year following the calendar year in which the cash is received. A statement will be considered furnished to a payor of bail if it is mailed to the payor's last known address.

(ii) *Form of statement.*—The statement required by this paragraph (d)(2) need not follow any particular format, but must contain the following information—

(A) The name and address of the clerk's office making the return;

(B) The aggregate amount of reportable cash received during the calendar year by the clerk who made the information return required by this section in all cash transactions relating to the payor of bail; and

(C) A legend stating that the information contained in the statement has been reported to the Internal Revenue Service and the applicable United States Attorney(s).

(iii) *Aggregate amount.*—The requirement of furnishing the aggregate amount in paragraph (d)(2)(ii)(B) of this section will be satisfied if the clerk provides to the payor of bail either a single written statement listing the aggregate amount, or a copy of each Form 8300 relating to that payor of bail.

(e) *Cross-reference to penalty provisions.*—See sections 6721 through 6724 for penalties relating to the failure to comply with the provisions of this section.

(f) *Effective date.*—This section applies to cash received by court clerks on or after February 13, 1995. [Reg. § 1.6050I-2.]

☐ [*T.D.* 8652, 12-29-95.]

[Reg. § 1.6050J-1T]

§ 1.6050J-1T. Questions and answers concerning information returns relating to foreclosures and abandonments of security (Temporary).—The following questions and answers relate to the requirement of reporting foreclosures and abandonments of security under section 6050J of the Internal Revenue Code of 1954, as added by section 148 of the Tax Reform Act of 1984 (98 Stat. 687).

Requirement of reporting

In general

Q-1. What does section 6050J provide with respect to the reporting of acquisitions and abandonments of property that secures indebtedness?

A-1. Section 6050J provides that an information return must be made by any person who, in connection with a trade or business conducted by the person (except as provided in A-13), lends money and, in full or partial satisfaction of the debt, acquires an interest in any property that is security for the debt, or has reason to know that the property has been abandoned. For purposes of these questions and answers, a person who lends money in connection with a trade or business is referred to as a "lender".

Trade or business requirement

Q-2. Must a person be in the trade or business of lending money in order to be subject to the reporting requirement of this section?

A-2. No. A person does not have to be in the trade or business of lending money to be subject to this reporting requirement. Thus, if L sells automobiles and lends money to B to enable B to purchase an automobile from L for use in B's trade or business, and that automobile is security for the loan, L would be subject to this reporting requirement. Similarly, if P promotes interests in an oil well, and lends money to I to enable I to invest in the oil well which is security for the loan, P would be subject to this reporting requirement.

Q-3. How does the reporting requirement apply in the case of pools, fixed investment trusts, or other similar arrangements through which undivided beneficial interests or participations in indebtedness are offered?

A-3. In these cases, the owners of the undivided beneficial interests or participations are not subject to this reporting requirement. Instead, the trustee, record owner, or person acting in a similar capacity is treated as the lender for purposes of this reporting requirement and is the party required to report. For purposes of both section 6050J and the applicable penalty provisions, only one return and one statement must be filed with respect to each loan or other evidence of indebtedness. For situations when more than one return or statement must be filed, see A-29, A-31, and A-41. The trustee, record owner, or person acting in a similar capacity, rather than

the owners of beneficial interests or participations, is subject to the applicable penalty provisions (see A-43).

Q-4. How does the reporting requirement apply in the case of corporate, tax-exempt, or other bond issues?

A-4. In these cases, the owners or holders of a bond issue are not required to report. Instead, the trustee or person acting in a similar capacity is treated as the lender for purposes of this reporting requirement and is the party required to report. For purposes of both section 6050J and the applicable penalty provisions, only one return and one statement must be filed with respect to a bond issue. For situations when more than one return or statement must be filed, see A-29, A-31, and A-41. The trustee or person acting in a similar capacity, rather than the owners or holders of a bond issue, is subject to the applicable penalty provisions (see A-43).

Property subject to reporting

Q-5. Does the reporting requirement apply to all types of property securing indebtedness?

A-5. No. The reporting requirement does not apply to any loan made to an individual and secured by an interest in tangible personal property which is neither held for investment nor used in a trade or business. For rules governing when the reporting requirement applies to tangible personal property of a type ordinarily used for personal purposes, see A-8.

Q-6. Does the reporting requirement apply when property securing indebtedness is held both for personal use and for use in a trade or business?

A-6. Yes. The reporting requirement applies when property securing indebtedness is held both for personal use and for use in a trade or business. Similarly, the reporting requirement applies when the borrower holds such property both for personal use and for investment purposes.

Q-7. Does the reporting requirement apply to indebtedness secured by a personal residence?

A-7. Yes. A lender is subject to the reporting requirement if the property that is security for the loan is real property, including a personal residence, whether or not held for investment or used in a trade or business.

Q-8. In the case of a loan made to an individual and secured by personal property of a type that is ordinarily used for personal purposes, how does a lender know whether such property is used in a trade or business or held for investment purposes?

A-8. In the case of a loan made to an individual and secured by personal property of a type that is ordinarily used for personal purposes, such as an automobile, computer, or boat, the lender is subject to the reporting requirement if the lender knows that the property will be used in a trade or business held for investment purposes. For this purpose, a lender knows information if the information is included on the books and records of the lender or its agents pertaining to the loan, or is known by the lender or agent's officers, partners, principals or employees, but only if such information was acquired in the course of their ordinary business activities on behalf of the lender. For example, if a borrower indicates on the loan agreement or disclosure statement that the borrower intends to use the property securing the loan in the borrower's trade or business, the lender is subject to this reporting requirement. Similarly, the borrower notifies the lender that the borrower intends to convert the property from personal use to use in a trade or business, the lender is subject to the reporting requirement.

Q-9. If a lender maintains a system under which the lender classifies loans according to the use of property that secures the loan (such as use in a trade or business or personal use), may the lender rely on this system in determining whether the reporting requirement applies?

A-9. Yes. A lender may rely on the classification system to determine whether the reporting requirement applies, provided that the classification system is designed and reasonably maintained to ensure accuracy in identifying the use of property.

Acquisition of an interest

Q-10. For purposes of the reporting requirement, when is a lender treated as acquiring an interest in property that is security for indebtedness?

A-10. In general, an interest in property is acquired on the earlier of the date title is transferred to the lender or the date possession and the burdens and benefits of ownership are transferred to the lender. If State or other applicable law provides for an objection period within which the borrower and other appropriate parties may object to the lender's proposal to retain the property in satisfaction of the indebtedness, a lender is treated as acquiring an interest in the property on the date this objection period expires. If the lender purchases the property at a sale held to satisfy the indebtedness, such as at a foreclosure or execution sale, the lender is treated as acquiring an interest in the property on the later of the date of the sale or the date the borrower's right of redemption, if any, expires. See A-15 for rules governing reporting when a party other than the lender acquires property securing indebtedness at a foreclosure, execution or similar sale.

Q-11. If a lender takes possession of property that is security for a loan for a limited purpose, such as completing construction on or improvement to the property, is the lender treated as having acquired an interest in the property at that point?

A-11. No. The lender in these circumstances is not treated as acquiring an interest in the property. However, the lender must report if he later acquires an interest in the property in full or partial satisfaction of the indebtedness (see A-10 or A-15).

Indirect Acquisition

Q-12. If a lender acquires an interest in a partnership, trust, or other entity in full or partial satisfaction of a loan that is secured by the assets or property owned by the partnership, trust, or other entity, is the lender treated as acquiring an interest in the property securing the loan?

A-12. Yes. A lender in this case acquires an interest in the underlying assets or property and the reporting requirements of this section apply to the acquisition of that interest in a partnership, trust, or other entity.

Treatment of governmental units

Q-13. How does the reporting requirement apply to a governmental unit?

A-13. A governmental unit (or any agency or instrumentality thereof) which lends money secured by property is subject to the reporting requirement without regard to the requirement that the money be lent in connection with a trade or business. A governmental unit (or any agency or instrumentality thereof) subject to the reporting requirement must designate an officer or employee to make the return. The officer or employee appropriately designated must make the return in the form and manner prescribed by this section.

Notification of sale under section 7425(b)

Q-14. Does a return filed as required under this section constitute a notification of sale under section 7425(b)?

A-14. No. A return filed under this section is not considered a notification of sale under section 7425(b).

Sale to third party

Q-15. If a party other than the lender purchases property securing a loan at a foreclosure, execution, or similar sale, must the lender report under this section?

A-15. Yes. The lender must report if a party other than the lender purchases property securing the lender's loan at a foreclosure, execution, or similar sale. If the proceeds of that sale are applied to satisfy all or any portion of the lender's loan, the lender must treat the property as having been abandoned. The lender will be treated as having reason to know that the property has been abandoned as of the date of the sale (see A-19). If no proceeds of such a sale are made available to satisfy any portion of the lender's loan but the lender's security interest foreclosed upon is terminated, reduced, or otherwise impaired by reason of the sale, the lender will be treated as having reason to know that the property has been abandoned as of the date of the sale (see A-19).

Treatment of foreign borrowers

Q-16. How does the reporting requirement apply in the case of foreign borrowers where the property securing the loan is located outside the United States?

A-16. No reporting is required where both of the following requirements are met: (a) the property securing the loan is located outside the United States, and (b) at any time before the lender is required to report, the borrower furnishes the lender with a statement, signed upon penalty of perjury, that he is an exempt foreign person (unless an employee or other agent of the lender who is responsible for receiving or reviewing these statements has actual knowledge that the statement is incorrect. For purposes of this section, the borrower is an exempt foreign person if he:

(1) Is not a citizen of the United States, a resident of the United States, a person treated as a resident of the United States by reason of an election under section 6013(g) or (h) or a United States corporation or other United States entity;

(2) Is not subject to the provisions of section 877; and

(3) At the time the statement is furnished, is not, or reasonably expects not to be, engaged in a trade or business in the United States during the current year in connection with the loan or property securing the loan.

If, after providing the statement, the borrower ceases to be an exempt foreign person, he must so notify the lender in writing within 30 days of this change in status. If the lender is so notified, this exemption from the reporting requirement no longer applies.

Abandonments

Q-17. For purposes of this reporting requirement, when has an abandonment occurred?

A-17. An abandonment has occurred when the objective facts and circumstances indicate that the borrower intended to and has permanently discarded the property from use.

Q-18. Does the fact that a lender knows or has reason to know of an abandonment of property securing a loan mean that the borrower is entitled to an abandonment loss?

A-18. No. The definition of an abandonment of property securing a loan in A-17 applies only for purposes of this reporting requirement and is not intended to apply for other purposes, such as determining whether a borrower would be entitled to an abandonment loss.

Q-19. Under what circumstances will a lender be considered to have reason to know that property which is security for a loan has been abandoned?

A-19. Whether a lender has reason to know that property which is security for a loan has been abandoned is to be determined with reference to all the facts and circumstances concerning the status of the property. When the lender in the ordinary course of business becomes aware or should become aware of circumstances indicating that the property has been abandoned, the lender will be deemed to know all the information that would have been discovered through a reasonable inquiry. For example, if a borrower has failed (without adequate explanation) to make payments on the loan for a substantial period, the lender must make a reasonable inquiry to determine whether there has been an abandonment. If a reasonable inquiry would reveal objective facts and circumstances indicating that the borrower intended to and has permanently discarded the property from use, then the lender has reason to know that the property has been abandoned. If a lender knows or has reason to know that the

property has been abandoned and reasonably expects to commence foreclosure, execution sale, or similar proceedings, see A-20.

Q-20. If a lender has reason to know that property that is security for a loan has been abandoned and reasonably expects to commence within three months foreclosure, execution sale, or similar proceedings, is reporting of the abandonment required?

A-20. In these circumstances, the lender need not report as of the date he knows or has reason to know that the property has been abandoned. Instead, the lender must report as of the date he acquires an interest in the property or a third party purchases the property at a foreclosure, execution or similar sale (see A-10 and A-15). In any other case, the lender must report as of the date the lender knows or has reason to know that the property has been abandoned (see A-18).

Q-21. If a lender has reason to know that property that is security for a loan has been abandoned and reasonably expects to commence within three months foreclosure, execution sale or similar proceedings but in fact does not commence such proceedings within the three month period, must the lender report?

A-21. Yes. In these circumstances, the lender's obligation to report the abandonment arises at the close of the three month period. For example, if on December 31, 1985, a lender first has reason to know that property securing his loan has been abandoned and reasonably expects to commence foreclosure proceedings within three months, the lender is not required to report as of December 31, 1985 (see A-20). However, if the lender does not in fact commence foreclosure proceedings by March 31, 1986, the lender's obligation to report arises on this date. The lender must provide information on the abandonment under A-27 as of the date the lender first had reason to know of the abandonment (December 31, 1985). The lender must file the return required under this section with the Internal Revenue Service on or before February 28, 1987, and furnish a statement to the borrower on or before January 31, 1987 (see A-33 and A-40).

Subsequent holder of a loan

Q-22. To whom does the reporting requirement apply when a person lends money secured by property and subsequently transfers his interest in the indebtedness to another person?

A-22. The subsequent holder of a loan is treated as the lender for purposes of this reporting requirement and is the party required to report with respect to events occurring after the date he acquires the loan. This rule applies to all subsequent holders of a secured loan, including governmental units or any agencies or instrumentalities thereof. For example, if the Federal National Mortgage Association purchases real property loans from a lender, it would be subject to the reporting requirement.

Multiple lenders

Q-23. If more than one person lends money secured by the same property, and one lender forecloses upon or otherwise acquires an interest in the property, must the other lenders report under this section?

A-23. Yes. In these circumstances, other lenders must report if they know or have reason to know that the property securing their loans is foreclosed upon or otherwise acquired by another lender and the sale or other acquisition terminates, reduces, or otherwise impairs their security interests in the property (see A-15). For example, if there is a first and second mortgage on a building, and the second mortgagee knows or has reason to know that the first mortgagee has foreclosed upon the building, the second mortgagee is subject to the reporting requirement even if no part of the indebtedness owed to him is satisfied by the proceeds of the foreclosure sale. For a description of the reporting requirement applicable to the first mortgagee, see A-10 and A-15.

Q-24. If more than one person lends money secured by property, and one lender knows or has reason to know that the property has been abandoned, must each lender report under this section?

A-24. No. Each lender is required to report only when he knows or has reason to know that property has been abandoned (see A-19).

Form and manner of return

Form of return

Q-25. What form shall be used to make a return required by section 6050J?

A-25. Except as provided in A-35, the return must be made on Forms 1096 and 1099. The person required to make the return, however, may prepare and use a form which contains provisions substantially similar with those of Forms 1096 and 1099 if the person complies with any revenue procedures relating to substitute Forms 1096 and 1099 in effect at that time.

Information included on return

Q-26. What information must be included on a return required by reason of an acquisition of an interest in property that is security for a loan?

A-26. The following information must be included on the return:

(a) The name and address of the borrower with respect to the secured indebtedness;

(b) The borrower's TIN, as defined in section 7701(a);

(c) A general description of the property in which an interest is acquired;

(d) Whether the borrower is personally liable for repayment of the indebtedness;

(e) The date on which the person acquired an interest in the property (see A-10 or A-15);

(f) The amount of the indebtedness outstanding at the time the interest in property is acquired;

(g) If the borrower is personally liable for repayment of the indebtedness, the fair market value of the property at the time the interest is acquired;

(h) The amount of the indebtedness satisfied by the acquisition; and

(i) Any other information as may be required by Forms 1096 and 1099.

Q-27. What information must be included on a return required because a person knows or has reason to know that property which is security for a loan has been abandoned?

A-27. The following information must be included on the return:

(a) The information required in A-26(a), (b), and (d);

(b) A general description of the property abandoned;

(c) The date on which the person first knows or has reason to know that the property has been abandoned;

(d) The amount of the indebtedness outstanding as of the date on which the person first knows or has reason to know that the property has been abandoned;

(e) If the borrower is personally liable for repayment of the indebtedness, the fair market value of the property at the time of abandonment; and

(f) Any other information as may be required by Forms 1096 and 1099.

Partnership borrower

Q-28. If a borrower is a partnership, must the TIN of each partner be reported?

A-28. No. If a borrower is a partnership, only the TIN of the partnership must be reported.

Multiple borrowers

Q-29. If there is more than one borrower on a single secured loan, must a person required to report under this section make a return with respect to each borrower on the loan?

A-29. Yes. Generally, a separate return must be made with respect to each borrower on a secured loan. However, only one report is required if the lender knows that the borrowers hold property as tenants by the entirety or that the property is held as community property.

General description of property

Q-30. What type of information constitutes a general description of the property?

A-30. A general description of the property consists of information that sufficiently identifies the property. In the case of real property, a general description consists of the property's address unless this information is not available or would not sufficiently identify the property, in which case a legal description (*i.e.,* section, lot, block) must be provided instead. A general description of personal property consists of the type, make and model (where applicable) of the property. For example, an automobile would be described as "Car—1983 Pontiac Firebird." However, in the case of a single loan secured by more than one piece of personal property, a general description consists of the type or category of the pieces acquired or abandoned. For example, if the security for a single loan is six desks and seven typewriters, a general description of the property would be "Office Equipment."

Reg. §1.6050J-1T

Multiple acquisitions and abandonments

Q-31. Must each acquisition and abandonment that occurs in a taxable year be reported on a separate return?

A-31. Generally, each acquisition and abandonment required to be reported by a person for a taxable year must be reported on a separate return. However, in the case of a single loan secured by more than one piece of property, separate returns will not be required when a person acquires an interest in, or knows or has reason to know of the abandonment of, more than one piece of property that is security for the single loan in a taxable year. Instead, the person shall make one return for all of the acquisitions and one return for all of the abandonments of property that are security for the loan for a taxable year.

Fair market value

Q-32. In the case of a foreclosure, execution, or similar sale, what is the fair market value of the property for purposes of the reporting requirement?

A-32. In general, in the absence of clear and convincing evidence to the contrary, the proceeds of the foreclosure, execution, or similar sale will be considered the fair market value of the property for purposes of this reporting requirement.

Time for filing

Q-33. When must a person file the return on returns required by section 6050J with the Internal Revenue Service?

A-33: The return or returns must be filed on or before February 28 (March 31 if filed electronically) of the year following the calendar year in which the acquisition of an interest in the property occurs or in which the lender knows or has reason to know of the abandonment of the property.

Place for filing

Q-34. Where must the return or returns be filed?

A-34. The return or returns must be filed with the appropriate Internal Revenue Service Center, the addresses of which are listed in the instructions for the Form 1099 series.

Use of magnetic media

Q-35. What rules apply with respect to the use of magnetic media?

A-35. Any return required under section 6050J must be filed on magnetic media to the extent required by section 6011(e). Any person not required by section 6011(e) to file returns under section 6050J on magnetic media may request permission to do so. See § 1.9101 for rules relating to permission to submit information on magnetic tape or other media. If a person required to file returns on magnetic media fails to do so, the penalty under section 6652 (failure to file an information return) applies.

Requirement of furnishing statements to borrowers
In general

Q-36. What statements must be furnished to borrowers?

A-36. Any person required to make an information return under section 6050J must furnish a statement to each borrower whose name is required to set forth in a return filed with the Internal Revenue Service. For the date when the statement must be furnished, see A-40.

Q-37. Is the statement considered to be furnished to the borrower if it is mailed to the borrower at the borrower's last known address?

A-37. Yes.

Information included on statement

Q-38. What information must be included on the statement?

A-38. The statement must include the following information:

(a) Except in the case where the return is made on behalf of a governmental unit (or any agency or instrumentality thereof), the name and address of the person required to make the information return;

(b) In the case where the return is made on behalf of a governmental unit or any agency or instrumentality thereof, the name and address of such unit, agency or instrumentality;

(c) The information required under A-26 or A-27, whichever is applicable; and

(d) A legend stating that the information is being reported to the Internal Revenue Service.

Copy of Form 1099 to borrowers

Q-39. May the requirement of furnishing a statement be met by furnishing a copy of the Form 1099 filed with respect to that borrower?

A-39. Yes. The requirement of furnishing a statement may be met by furnishing to the borrower a copy of the Form 1099 containing the same information filed with the Service with respect to that borrower, or a reasonable facsimile thereof, provided that the form or the reasonable facsimile bears a legend stating that the information is being reported to the Internal Revenue Service.

Time of furnishing statement

Q-40. When is a statement required to be furnished to the borrower?

A-40. A statement is required to be furnished to the borrower on or before January 31 of the year following the calendar year in which the acquisition or abandonment of property occurs.

Multiple borrowers

Q-41. If a person required to report under this section must make an information return with respect to more than one borrower on a single loan, of an interest in the property occurs or in which the lender knows or has reason to know of the abandonment of the property.

A-41. Yes. A separate statement must be furnished to each borrower with respect to which a separate return is required under section 6050J.

Extensions of time

Q-42. Are there any circumstances under which an extension of time may be granted with

Reg. § 1.6050J-1T

respect to the requirement of furnishing statements to borrowers?

A-42. Yes. Upon written application of the person required to report, the service center director may, for good cause shown, grant that person an additional period (not to exceed 30 days) in which to furnish statements under section 6050J with respect to any calendar year. The application for an extension must be addressed to the director of the service center with which the returns must be filed. The application must contain a concise statement of the reasons for requesting the extension in order to aid the service center director in determining the period of extension, if any, to be granted. The application must state at the top of the first page that it is made under section 1.6050J-1T and must be signed by the person required to report under section 6050J. In general, the application should be filed not earlier than September 30 of the year in which the acquisition of an interest in the property occurs or in which the lender knows or has reason to know of the abandonment of the property, and not later than January 15 of the following year.

Penalties

Q-43. Are there penalties for failing to comply with the requirements of section 6050J and the regulations thereunder?

A-43. Yes. The penalty for failing to make any information return with respect to any borrower under section 6050J is provided in section 6652. The penalty for failing to furnish a statement to any borrower is provided in section 6678.

Effective date

Q-44. When is section 6050J effective?

A-44. Section 6050J is effective for acquisitions and abandonments of property after December 31, 1984. [Temporary Reg. § 1.6050J-1T.]

☐ [*T.D. 7971, 8-30-84. Amended by T.D. 8895, 8-17-2000.*]

[Reg. § 1.6050K-1]

§ 1.6050K-1. Returns relating to sales or exchanges of certain partnership interests.—
(a) *Partnership return required.*—(1) *In general.*—Except as otherwise provided in this paragraph (a), a partnership shall make a separate return on Form 8308 with respect to each section 751(a) exchange (as defined in paragraph (a)(4)(i) of this section) of an interest in such partnership which occurs after December 31, 1984. A partnership that is in doubt as to whether partnership property constitutes section 751 property to any extent or as to whether a transfer of a partnership interest constitutes a section 751(a) exchange may file Form 8308 in order to avoid the risk of incurring a penalty under section 6721. The penalty under section 6721 will generally apply, however, to partnerships that do not file Form 8308 where in fact a section 751(a) exchange occurred, except as provided in paragraphs (a)(2) and (e) of this section.

(2) *Return required under section 6045.*—No return shall be required under section 6050K(a)

and paragraph (a)(1) of this section with respect to the sale or exchange of a partnership interest if a return is required to be filed under section 6045 with respect to such sale or exchange.

(3) *Single or composite documents.*—The Commissioner may authorize the use, at the option of the partnership, of a single document which includes all of the partnership's returns for a calendar year in the case of partnerships required under paragraph (a)(1) of this section to make 25 or more returns on Form 8308 for any calendar year. In addition, the Commissioner may authorize the use for this purpose, also at the option of such a partnership, of a composite document. These authorizations shall be subject to such conditions, limitations, and special rules governing the preparation, execution, filing, and correction thereof as the Commissioner may deem appropriate. Such composite document shall consist of a form prescribed by the Commissioner and an attachment or attachments of magnetic tape or other approved media. To the extent that the use of a single or composite document has been authorized by the Commissioner, references in this section to Form 8308 shall be deemed to refer also to returns included in a single or composite document under this paragraph (a)(3). Any single or composite document so authorized shall include the information required to be provided on Form 8308 under paragraph (b) of this section with respect to each section 751(a) exchange.

(4) *Definitions.*—For purposes of section 6050K of the Code and this section—

(i) *Section 751(a) exchange.*—The term "section 751(a) exchange" means any sale or exchange of a partnership interest (or portion thereof) in which any portion of any money or other property received by a transferor partner in exchange for all or a part of his or her interest in the partnership is attributable to section 751 property. The term does not include a distribution which is treated as a sale or exchange between the distributee and the partnership under section 751(b) of the Code.

(ii) *Section 751 property.*—The term "section 751 property" means unrealized receivables, as defined in section 751(c) of the Code, and inventory items which have appreciated substantially in value ("substantially appreciated inventory items"), as defined in section 751(d) of the Code.

(iii) *Transferor and transferee.*—The term "transferor" means the beneficial owner of a partnership interest immediately before the transfer of that interest. The term "transferee" means the beneficial owner of a partnership interest immediately after the transfer of that interest. However, if a partnership does not know the identity of the beneficial owner of an interest in the partnership, the record holder of such interest shall be treated as the transferor or transferee (as the case may be) for purposes of paragraphs (b) and (c) of this section.

(b) *Contents of return.*—The return on Form 8308 shall include the following information:

(1) The names, addresses, and taxpayer identification numbers of the transferee and transferor in the exchange and of the partnership filing the return;

(2) The date of the exchange; and

(3) Such other information as may be required by Form 8308 or its instructions.

(c) *Statement to be furnished to transferor and transferee.*—Every partnership required to file a return under paragraph (a) of this section must furnish to each person whose name is required to be set forth in such return a written statement on or before January 31 of the calendar year following the calendar year in which the section 751(a) exchange occurred to which the return under paragraph (a) relates (or, if later, 30 days after the partnership is notified of the exchange as defined in paragraph (e) of this section). The partnership shall use a copy of the completed Form 8308 as a statement unless the Form 8308 contains information with respect to more than one section 751(a) exchange (see paragraph (a)(3) of this section). If the partnership does not use a copy of Form 8308 as a statement, the statement shall include the information required to be shown on Form 8308 with respect to the section 751(a) exchange to which the person to whom the statement is furnished is a party. In addition, it shall state that—

(1) The information shown on the statement has been supplied to the Internal Revenue Service,

(2) A transferor of a partnership interest in a sale or exchange described in section 751(a) of the Internal Revenue Code is required to treat a portion of any gain or loss resulting from the sale or exchange as ordinary income or loss, and

(3) The transferor in a section 751(a) sale or exchange is required under paragraph (a)(3) of § 1.751-1 to attach a statement relating to the sale or exchange to his or her income tax return for the taxable year in which the sale or exchange occurred.

(d) *Requirement that transferor notify partnership.*—(1) *In general.*—The transferor of any partnership interest in a section 751(a) exchange shall notify the partnership of such exchange in writing within 30 days of the exchange (or, if earlier, January 15 of the calendar year following the calendar year in which the exchange occurred). The written notification from the transferor shall include the following information:

(i) The names and addresses of the transferor and transferee in the section 751(a) exchange;

(ii) The taxpayer identification numbers of the transferor and, if known, of the transferee; and

(iii) The date of the exchange.

Any transferor who notified a partnership under section 6050K(c)(1) prior to January 22, 1986 by a notification that does not meet the requirements of this paragraph (d) shall furnish such partnership with the written notification described in this paragraph (d) on or before February 21, 1986.

(2) *Return required under section 6045.*—No transferor shall be required to notify a partnership of the sale or exchange of a partnership interest under section 6050K(c)(1) or paragraph (d)(1) of this section if a return is required to be filed under section 6045 with respect to such sale or exchange.

(e) *Partnership not required to make a return or furnish statements under this section until it has notice of the exchange.*—A partnership shall not be required to make a return or furnish statements under section 6050K and this section with respect to any section 751(a) exchange until it has been notified of the exchange. For purposes of section 6050K(c)(2) and this section, a partnership is notified of a section 751(a) exchange when either:

(1) The partnership receives the written notification from the transferor required under paragraph (d) of this section; or

(2) The partnership has knowledge that there has been a transfer of a partnership interest or any portion thereof, and, at the time of the transfer, the partnership had any section 751 property. However, no return or statements are required under section 6050K if the transfer was not a section 751(a) exchange (*e.g.*, a transfer which in its entirety constitutes a gift for federal income tax purposes). For purposes of this paragraph (e)(2), the partnership may rely on a written statement from the transferor that the transfer was not a section 751(a) exchange in the absence of knowledge to the contrary. For rules applicable where the partnership is in doubt as to whether partnership property constitutes section 751 property to any extent or as to whether a transfer of a partnership interest constitutes a section 751(a) exchange, see paragraph (a)(1) of this section.

(f) *Partnership return is to be attached to Form 1065.*—(1) *In general.*—Any partnership return on Form 8308 required under this section shall be filed as an attachment to the partnership's Form 1065 for its taxable year in which the calendar year in which the section 751(a) exchange occurred ends and shall be filed at the time (determined with regard to any extension of time for filing) and place prescribed for filing of the partnership's Form 1065 for that taxable year (see paragraph (e) of § 1.6031-1 for the time and place for filing Form 1065).

(2) *Notification after Form 1065 is filed.*—If a partnership is notified of an exchange (as defined in paragraph (e) of this section) after the partnership has filed Form 1065 for the taxable year with respect to which the exchange should have been reported, Form 8308 shall be filed with the service center or other Internal Revenue office with which the partnership's Form 1065 was filed, on or before the thirtieth day after the partnership is notified of the exchange.

(g) *Penalties.*—For penalties for failure of:

(1) Transferors to furnish the notification required by paragraph (d) of this section see section 6722(b);

(2) Partnerships to furnish any statement required under paragraph (c) of this section see section 6722(a); and

(3) Partnerships to file the return on Form 8308 as required by paragraph (a) of this section see section 6721. [Reg. § 1.6050K-1.]

☐ [*T.D.* 8119, 12-31-86.]

[Reg. § 1.6050L-1]

§ 1.6050L-1. Information return by donees relating to certain dispositions of donated property.—(a) *Information returns.*—(1) *Disposition of charitable deduction property.*—If a donee of any charitable deduction property (as defined in paragraph (e) of this section) sells, exchanges, consumes, or otherwise disposes of (with or without consideration) such property (or any portion thereof) within 2 years after the date of the donor's contribution of such property, the donee shall make an information return on the form prescribed by the Internal Revenue Service. For special rules with respect to successor donees, see paragraph (c) of this section.

(2) *Disposition of items appraised for $500 or less.*—(i) *In general.*—Paragraph (a)(1) of this section shall not apply with respect to an item of charitable deduction property disposed of by sale if the Form 8283 appraisal summary (as described in § 1.170A-13(c)(4) for contributions made on or before July 30, 2018 and § 1.170A-16(d)(3) for contributions made after July 30, 2018), or a successor form, signed by the donee with respect to the item contains, at the time of the donee's signature, a statement signed by the donor that the appraised value of the item does not exceed $500. In the case of a Form 8283 appraisal summary that describes more than one item, this exception shall apply only with respect to an item clearly identified as having an appraised value of $500 or less. For purposes of this paragraph (a)(2)(i), items that form a set (such as, for example, a collection of books written by the same author, components of a stereo system, or a group of place settings of a pattern of silverware) are considered one item. In addition, all nonpublicly traded stock is considered one item as are all nonpublicly traded securities other than nonpublicly traded stock.

(ii) *Transitional rule.*—Paragraph (a)(2)(i) of this section is satisfied with respect to an appraisal summary submitted to the donee on or before January 31, 1986, if such donee obtained the required statement from the donor on or before March 31, 1986, on either an amended appraisal summary or an attachment to the original appraisal summary.

(3) *Consumption or distribution for exempt purpose.*—Paragraph (a)(1) of this section shall not apply with respect to an item of charitable deduction property consumed or distributed by a donee without consideration if the consumption or distribution is in furtherance of a purpose or function constituting a basis for such donee's exemption under section 501 of the Code. For example, no reporting is required with respect to medical supplies consumed or distributed by a tax-exempt relief organization in aiding disaster victims.

(b) *Information required to be provided on return.*—The information return required by paragraph (a)(1) of this section shall include the following:

(1) The name, address, and employer identification number of the donee making the information return;

(2) A description of the property (or portion disposed of) in sufficient detail to identify the charitable deduction property received by such donee;

(3) The name and taxpayer identification number of the donor (social security number if the donor is an individual or employer identification number if the donor is a corporation or partnership);

(4) The date of the contribution to such donee;

(5) Any amount received by such donee with respect to the disposition;

(6) The date of the disposition by such donee; and

(7) Such other information as may be specified by the form or its instructions.

(c) *Successor donees.*—(1) *In general.*—Section 6050L and this section shall apply to successor donees that receive charitable deduction property (as defined in paragraph (e) of this section) that was transferred by the original donee after July 5, 1988, (whether the successor donee received the property from the original donee or another successor donee). For definitions of the terms "donor," "donee," "original donee," and "successor donee," see § 1.170A-13(c)(7)(iv)-(vii).

(2) *Information required to be provided on return.*—With respect to charitable deduction property that is transferred to one or more successor donees to which this section applies, the information return required by paragraph (a)(1) of this section shall include, in addition to the information described in paragraph (b) of this section, the following:

(i) The name, address, and employer identification number of the immediately succeeding successor donee (if any) and the immediately preceding successor donee (if any);

(ii) The name, address, and employer identification number of the original donee if different from the information required by paragraph (b)(1) of this section;

(iii) The date of contribution to the original donee; and

(iv) Such other information as may be specified by the form or its instructions.

(3) *Information to be provided to transferor.*—Every successor donee to which this section applies that receives any charitable deduction

property within the 2-year period described in paragraph (a)(1) of this section shall provide its name, address, and employer identification number to that preceding donee on or before the 15th day the later of—

    (i) The date of transfer to such successor donee, or

    (ii) The date such successor donee receives a copy of the appraisal summary from the preceding donee.

(4) *Donees that transfer property to successor donees.*—In addition to complying with the requirements of paragraph (a)(1) of this section, every donee that transfers any charitable deduction property to a successor donee to which this section applies within the 2-year period described in paragraph (a)(1) of this section—

    (i) Shall provide its name, address, and employer identification number and a copy of the Form 8283 appraisal summary (as described in § 1.170A-13(c)(4) for contributions made on or before July 30, 2018 and § 1.170A-16(d)(3) for contributions made after July 30, 2018) relating to the transferred property to the successor donee on or before the 15th day after the latest of—

    (A) The date of such transfer, or

    (B) The date the original donee signs the appraisal summary, or

    (C) In a case in which the transferring donee is a successor donee, the date such donee receives a copy of the appraisal summary from such donee's transferor, and

    (ii) Shall provide a copy of its information return required by paragraph (a)(1) of this section to the successor donee on or before the 15th day after the transferring donee files the information return pursuant to paragraph (e)(2) of this section.

(5) *Donee.*—In the case of charitable deduction property that is transferred to a successor donee to which this section applies, the term "donee" as used in paragraph (a)(2) and (e) of this section means only the original donee.

(d) *Special rules.*—(1) *Statement to be furnished to donors.*—Every donee making a return under section 6050L and this section with respect to the disposition of charitable deduction property shall furnish a copy of the return to the donor of the property.

(2) *Retention of Form 8283 appraisal summary.*—Every donee shall retain the Form 8283 appraisal summary (as described in § 1.170A-13(c)(4) for contributions made on or before July 30, 2018 and § 1.170A-16(d)(3) for contributions made after July 30, 2018) in the donee's records for so long as it may be relevant in the administration of any internal revenue law.

(e) *Charitable deduction property.*—For purposes of this section, the term charitable deduction property means any property (other than money and publicly traded securities to which § 1.170A-13(c)(7)(xi)(B) does not apply) contributed after December 31, 1984, with respect to

which the donee signs (or is presented with for signature in cases described in § 1.170A-13(c)(4)(iv)(C)(2)) a Form 8283 appraisal summary (as described in § 1.170A-13(c)(4) for contributions made on or before July 30, 2018 and § 1.170A-16(d)(3) for contributions made after July 30, 2018). For purposes of this section, if such donee signs (or is presented with for signature in cases described in § 1.170A-13(c)(4)(iv)(C)(2)) the appraisal summary after the date of contribution of the property, the property is deemed to be charitable deduction property from the date of contribution.

(f) *Place and time for filing information returns.*— (1) *Place for filing.*—The donee information return required by section 6050L and this section shall be filed with the Internal Revenue Service center listed on the return form or its instructions.

(2) *Time for filing.*—(i) *In general.*—Except as provided in paragraph (f)(2)(ii) of this section, the donee information return shall be filed on or before the 125th day after a donee sells, exchanges, consumes or otherwise disposes of the charitable deduction property. A donee information return filed pursuant to this paragraph (f)(2)(i) does not have to include the information required by paragraphs (b)(3), (4), (5), or (6), or (c)(2)(i)-(iii) of this section if such information is not available to the donee by the due date of the return.

    (ii) *Exception.*—Notwithstanding paragraph (f)(2)(i) of this section, in the case of a donee who, on the date of receipt of the transferred property, had no reason to believe that the substantiation requirements of § 1.170A-13(c) or § 1.170A-16(d) apply with respect to the property, the donee information return is not required to be filed until the 60th day after the date on which such donee has reason to believe that the substantiation requirements of § 1.170A-13(c) or § 1.170A-16(d) apply with respect to the property. A donee information return filed pursuant to this paragraph (f)(2)(ii) does not have to include the information required by paragraphs (b)(3), (4), (5), or (6), or (c)(2)(i)-(iii) of this section if such information is not available to the donee by the due date of the return.

(g) *Penalties.*—For penalties for failure to comply with the requirements of this section, see sections 6676, 6721, and 6723.

(h) *Effective/applicability dates.*—The first two sentences of paragraph (a)(2)(i), paragraphs (c)(4)(i) and (d)(2), and the first sentences of paragraphs (e) and (f)(2)(ii) apply to contributions made after July 30, 2018. [Reg. § 1.6050L-1.]

    ☐ [*T.D.* 8199, 5-4-88. *Amended by T.D.* 9836, 7-27-2018.]

[Reg. § 1.6050L-2]

§ 1.6050L-2. **Information returns by donees relating to qualified intellectual property contributions.**—(a) *In general.*—Each donee organization described in section 170(c), except a private foundation (as defined in section 509(a)), other than a private foundation described in section 170(b)(1)(F), that receives or accrues net income during a taxable year from any qualified intellectual property contribution (as defined in section 170(m)(8)) must make an annual information return on the form prescribed by the IRS. The information return is required for any taxable year of the donee that includes any portion of the 10-year period beginning on the date of the contribution, but not for taxable years beginning after the expiration of the legal life of the qualified intellectual property.

(b) *Information required to be provided on return.*—The information return required by section 6050L and paragraph (a) of this section shall include the following—

(1) The name, address, taxable year, and employer identification number of the donee making the information return;

(2) The name, address, and taxpayer identification number of the donor;

(3) A description of the qualified intellectual property in sufficient detail to identify the qualified intellectual property received by such donee;

(4) The date of the contribution to the donee;

(5) The amount of net income of the donee for the taxable year that is properly allocable to the qualified intellectual property (determined without regard to paragraph (10)(B) of section 170(m) and with the modifications described in paragraphs (5) and (6) of such section); and

(6) Such other information as may be specified by the form or its instructions.

(c) *Special rule—statement to be furnished to donors.*—Every donee making an information return under section 6050L and this section with respect to a qualified intellectual property contribution shall furnish a copy of the information return to the donor of the property. The information return required by section 6050L and this section shall be furnished to the donor on or before the date the donee is required to file the return with the IRS.

(d) *Place and time for filing information return.*— (1) *Place for filing.*—The information return required by section 6050L and this section shall be filed with the IRS location listed on the prescribed form or in its instructions.

(2) *Time for filing.*—A donee is required to file the return required by section 6050L and this section on or before the last day of the first full month following the close of the donee's taxable year to which net income from the qualified intellectual property is properly allocable.

(e) *Penalties.*—For penalties for failure to comply with the requirements of this section, see sections 6721 through 6724.

(f) *Effective/applicability date.*—The rules of this section apply to qualified intellectual property

contributions made after June 3, 2004. [Reg. § 1.6050L-2.]

☐ [*T.D. 9392, 4-4-2008.*]

[Reg. § 1.6050M-1]

§ 1.6050M-1. Information returns relating to persons receiving contracts from certain Federal executive agencies.—(a) *General rule.*—Except as otherwise provided in paragraph (c) of this section, the head of every Federal executive agency or his or her delegate shall make an information return to the Internal Revenue Service reporting the following information with respect to each contract entered into by that Federal executive agency—

(1) Name and address of the contractor;

(2) Contractor's TIN and, if the contractor is a member of an affiliated group of corporations that files its Federal income tax returns on a consolidated basis, the name and TIN of the common parent of the affiliated group;

(3) The date of the contract action;

(4) The expected date of completion of the contract as determined under any reasonable method, such as the expected contract delivery date under the contract schedule;

(5) The total amount obligated under the contract action;

(6) Any other information required by Forms 8596 and 8596A and their instructions, or by any other administrative guidance issued by the Internal Revenue Service (such as a revenue procedure).

See paragraph (e) of this section relating to the manner in which to report increases in amounts obligated under existing contracts. See paragraph (d)(5) of this section for special rules for agencies that submit contract information to the Federal Procurement Data Center. For provisions concerning the requesting and furnishing of identifying numbers, see section 6109 and the regulations thereunder.

(b) *Definitions.*—The following definitions apply for purposes of this section—

(1) *Federal executive agency.*—The term "Federal executive agency" means—

(i) Any executive agency (as defined in 5 U.S.C. 105) other than the General Accounting Office;

(ii) Any military department (as defined in 5 U.S.C. 102); and

(iii) The United States Postal Service and the Postal Rate Commission.

(2) *Contract.*—(i) *General rule.*—The term "contract" means an obligation of a Federal executive agency to make payment of money (or other property) to a person in return for the sale of property, the rendering of services, or other consideration. The term "contract" includes, for example, such an obligation arising from a written agreement executed by the agency and the contractor, an award or notice of award, a job order or task letter issued under a basic ordering agreement, a letter contract, an order that be-

comes effective only upon written acceptance or performance, or an action described in paragraph (e) of this section.

(ii) *Exceptions.*—For purposes of this section, the term "contract" does not include—

(A) A license granted by a Federal executive agency;

(B) An obligation of a contractor (other than a Federal executive agency) to a subcontractor;

(C) A debt instrument of the United States Government or a Federal agency, such as a Treasury note, Treasury bond, Treasury bill, savings bond, or similar instrument; or

(D) An obligation of a Federal executive agency to lend money, lease property to a lessee, or sell property.

(iii) *Special rule for certain contracts of the Small Business Administration.*—Any subcontract entered into by the Small Business Administration (SBA) under a prime contract between the SBA and a procuring Federal executive agency pursuant to section 8(a) of the Small Business Act (15 U.S.C. 637(a)) shall not be treated as a contract of the SBA but shall be treated as a contract of the procuring agency for purposes of this section.

(iv) *Certain schedule contracts.*—For purposes of this section, any of the following contracts entered into on behalf of one or more Federal executive agencies is not a "contract" to be reported by the General Services Administration or the Department of Veteran's Affairs at the time of execution:

(A) A Federal Supply Schedule Contract entered into by the General Services Administration,

(B) An Automated Data Processing Schedule Contract entered into by the General Services Administration, or

(C) A schedule contract entered into by the Department of Veteran's Affairs.

Instead, an order placed by a Federal executive agency, including the General Services Administration or the Department of Veteran's Affairs, under such a schedule contract is a "contract" for purposes of this section.

(v) *Blanket purchase agreements.*—For purposes of this section, the term "contract" does not include a blanket purchase agreement between one or more Federal executive agencies and one or more contractors. Instead, an order placed by a Federal executive agency under the terms of a blanket purchase agreement is a "contract" for purposes of this section.

(vi) *Contracts entered into using non-appropriated funds.*—[Reserved]

(3) *Contractor.*—The term "contractor" means any person who enters into a contract with a Federal executive agency.

(4) *Person and TIN.*—The terms "person" and "TIN" are defined in sections 7701 (a)(1) and (41), respectively.

(c) *Exceptions to information reporting requirement.*—(1) *General exceptions.*—The following do not need to be reported pursuant to this section:

(i) Any contract or contract action for which the amount obligated is $25,000 or less;

(ii) Any contract with a contractor who, in making the agreement, is acting in his or her capacity as an employee of a Federal executive agency (*e.g.*, any contract of employment under which the employee is paid wages subject to the withholding provisions contained in chapter 24 of subtitle C);

(iii) Any contract between a Federal executive agency and another Federal governmental unit (or any agency or instrumentality thereof);

(iv) Any contract with a foreign government (or any agency or instrumentality thereof);

(v) Any contract with a state or local governmental unit (or any agency or instrumentality thereof);

(vi) Any contract with a person who is not required to have a TIN (see, for example, § 301.6109-1(g));

(vii) Any contract the terms of which provide that all amounts payable under the contract by any Federal executive agency will be paid on or before the 120th day following the date of the contract action, and for which it is reasonable to expect that all amounts will be so paid.

(viii) Any contract under which all money (or other property) that will be received by the contractor after the 120th day after the date of the contract action will come from persons other than a Federal executive agency or an agent of such an agency (*e.g.*, a contract under which the contractor will collect amounts owed to a Federal executive agency by the agency's debtor and will remit to the agency the money collected less an amount that serves as the contractor's consideration under the contract).

(ix) Any contract for which the Commissioner determines that the information described in paragraph (a) of this section will not facilitate the collection of Federal tax liabilities because of the manner, method, or timing of payment by the agency under that contract.

(2) *Special rule for certain classified or confidential contracts.*—Contracts described in section 6050M(e)(3), relating to certain classified or confidential contracts, are to be reported only in accordance with section 6050M(e)(2).

(d) *Filing requirements.*—(1) *Frequency and time for filing.*—The information returns required by this section with respect to contracts of a Federal executive agency entered into on or after January 1, 1989, must be filed on a quarterly basis for the calendar quarters ending on the last day of March, June, September, and December. Except as provided in paragraph (d)(5) of this section, the returns for contracts entered into during a calendar quarter must be filed on or before the last day of the month following that quarter. Notwithstanding the preceding sentence, returns filed before May 7, 1990 will be considered timely filed.

(2) *Form of reporting.*—(i) *General rule concerning magnetic media.*—The information returns required by this section with respect to contracts of a Federal executive agency for each calendar quarter shall be made in one submission (or in multiple submissions if permitted by paragraph (d)(4) of this section). Except as provided in paragraph (d)(2)(ii) of this section, the required returns shall be made on magnetic media (within the meaning of § 301.6011-2(a)(1)) in accordance with any applicable revenue procedure or other guidance promulgated by the Internal Revenue Service for the filing of such returns under section 6050M.

(ii) *Magnetic media exception for low-volume filers.*—Any Federal executive agency that on any October 1 has a reasonable expectation of entering into, during the one year period beginning on that date, fewer than 250 contracts that are subject to the reporting requirements under this section may make the information returns required by this section for each quarter of that one year period on the prescribed paper Form 8596 in accordance with the instructions accompanying such form.

(3) *Place of filing.*—(i) *Returns on magnetic media.*—Information returns made under this section on magnetic media shall be filed with the Internal Revenue Service at the Martinsburg Computing Center, Martinsburg, West Virginia 25401-1359, in accordance with any applicable revenue procedure or other guidance promulgated by the Internal Revenue Service relating to the filing of returns under section 6050M.

(ii) *Form 8596.*—Information returns made on Form 8596 shall be filed with the Internal Revenue Service at the location specified in the instructions for that form.

(4) *Special rule concerning multiple returns.*— To the extent permitted in any revenue procedure or other guidance relating to the filing of information returns under this section, a Federal executive agency which files information returns under this section on magnetic media may make more than one magnetic media submission for any quarter, if each submission for that quarter contains all of the information required by paragraph (a) of this section with respect to contracts entered into by one or more departments, branches, bureaus, agencies, or other readily identifiable operating functions (such as a geographic region) of the Federal executive agency.

(5) *Special rules for agencies reporting to the Federal Procurement Data Center.*—(i) *Election to have the Director of the Federal Procurement Data Center make returns on behalf of agency.*—If, in complying with the requirements of the Federal Procurement Data System (FPDS) (as established under the authority of the Office of Federal Procurement Policy Act, as amended, 41 U.S.C. 401 et. seq.), a Federal executive agency is required to submit to the Federal Procurement Data Center (FPDC) all the information with respect to one or more contracts required to be reported by paragraph (a) of this section, that Federal executive agency may, in lieu of making returns directly to the Internal Revenue Service with respect to those contracts, elect to have the Director of the FPDC (or his or her delegate) make the required returns with respect to all of those contracts on its behalf. In order to make this election for such contracts entered into during a calendar quarter, the head of a Federal executive agency (or his or her delegate) shall attach to its submission to the FPDC for that quarter a signed statement to the effect that:

(A) the Director of the FPDC (or his or her delegate) is authorized, in accordance with an election made under 26 CFR § 1.6050M-1(d)(5), to make, on the agency's behalf, the required returns for such contracts for that quarter, and

(B) under the penalties of perjury, such official has examined the information to be submitted by the agency to the FPDC for making those returns and certifies that information to be, to the best of such official's knowledge and belief, a compilation of agency records maintained in the normal course of business for the purpose of providing the information necessary for making true, correct, and complete returns as required by section 6050M.

If the election is made, the Director of the FPDC (or his or her delegate) shall, on the electing agency's behalf, make the returns required by paragraph (a) of this section with respect to the contracts to which the election applies.

(ii) *Time, manner, and place of filing.*—The Director of the FPDC (or his or her delegate) must—

(A) make the required returns for a quarter on or before the earlier of (1) 45 days following the date that the contract information is required to be submitted to the FPDC, or (2) 90 days following the end of the calendar quarter for which the election is made, except that, if that calendar quarter ends September 30, 105 days following the end of that quarter, and

(B) comply with paragraph (d)(2)(i) and (3)(i) of this section, relating to form and place of filing. Notwithstanding the preceding sentence, returns made before May 7, 1990 will be considered timely filed.

(iii) *Contracts reported directly to the Internal Revenue Service.*—Even if the election is made, all information with respect to any particular contract required to be reported under paragraph (a) of this section must be reported directly to the Internal Revenue Service by the electing agency if the FPDS does not require that information to be submitted to the FPDC. An electing agency shall not, however, make direct returns to the Internal Revenue Service of contract information that is subject to the election.

(6) *Certification of return.*—(i) *Returns made directly with the Internal Revenue Service.*—Each return made under this section by a Federal executive agency directly with the Internal Reve-

Reg. § 1.6050M-1(d)(6)(i)

nue Service on magnetic media or on Forms 8596 and 8596-A shall be signed by the head of the Federal executive agency (or his or her delegate) under the penalties of perjury, certifying that such official has examined the return, that it is prepared pursuant to the requirements of section 6050M and that, to the best of such official's knowledge and belief, it is compiled from agency records maintained in the normal course of business for the purpose of making a true, correct, and complete return as required by section 6050M.

(ii) *Returns made by Director of FPDC on agency's behalf.*—Each return made under this section by the Director of the FPDC on behalf of a Federal executive agency shall be signed by the Director of the FPDC (or his or her delegate) under the penalties of perjury, certifying that such official has examined the return, that it is prepared pursuant to the requirements of section 6050M and that, to the best of such official's knowledge and belief, it is compiled from information submitted by the Federal executive agency to the FPDC pursuant to § 1.6050M-1(d)(5)(i) for the purpose of making a true, correct, and complete return as required by section 6050M.

(e) *Special rules relating to increases in amount obligated.*—If, through the exercise of an option contained in a basic or initial contract or under any other rule of contract law, express or implied, the amount of money or other property obligated under the contract is increased by more than $25,000 in one contract action, then that action shall be treated as the entering into of a new contract with respect to which the information required by paragraph (a) of this section is to be reported to the Internal Revenue Service for the calendar quarter in which the increase occurs.

(f) *Effective date.*—(1) *Contracts required to be reported.*—Except as otherwise provided in this paragraph (f), this section applies to each Federal executive agency with respect to its contracts entered into on or after January 1, 1989 (including any increase in amount obligated on or after January 1, 1989, that is treated as a new contract under paragraph (e) of this section).

(2) *Contracts not required to be reported.*—A Federal executive agency is not required to report—

(i) any basic or initial contract entered into before January 1, 1989,

(ii) any increase contract action occurring before January 1, 1989, that is treated as a new contract under paragraph (e) of this section, or

(iii) any increase contract action that is treated as a new contract under paragraph (e) of this section if the basic or initial contract to which that contract action relates was entered into before January 1, 1989, and—

(A) the increase occurs before April 1, 1990, or

(B) the amount of the increase does not exceed $50,000.

(3) *Illustration.*—(i) If a Federal executive agency enters into an initial contract on December 1, 1988, and the amount of money obligated under the contract is increased by $55,000 on April 15, 1990, then (A) there is no reporting requirement with respect to the contract when entered into on December 1, 1988, and (B) the April 15, 1990, increase, which is treated as a new contract under paragraph (e) of this section, is subject to the reporting requirements of this section because it is considered to be a new contract entered into on April 15, 1990.

(ii) If the $55,000 increase had occurred before April 1, 1990, there would have been no reporting requirement with respect to that increase. [Reg. § 1.6050M-1.]

☐ [T.D. 8275, 12-5-89.]

[Reg. § 301.6050M-1]

§ 301.6050M-1. Information returns relating to persons receiving contracts from certain Federal executive agencies.—For provisions relating to the requirements of returns of information relating to persons receiving contracts from certain Federal executive agencies, see § 1.6050M-1 of this chapter (Income Tax Regulations). [Reg. § 301.6050M-1.]

☐ [T.D. 8275, 12-5-89.]

[Reg. § 1.6050N-1]

§ 1.6050N-1. Statements to recipients of royalties paid after December 31, 1986.—(a) *Requirement.*—A person required to make an information return under section 6050N(a) must furnish a statement to each recipient whose name is required to be shown on the related information return for royalties paid.

(b) *Form, manner, and time for providing statements to recipients.*—The statement required by paragraph (a) of this section must be either the official Form 1099 prescribed by the Internal Revenue Service for the respective calendar year or an acceptable substitute statement. The rules under § 1.6042-4 (relating to statements with respect to dividends) apply comparably in determining the form of the acceptable substitute statement permitted by this section. Those rules also apply for purposes of determining the manner of and time for providing the Form 1099 or its acceptable substitute statement to a recipient under this section. An IRS truncated taxpayer identifying number (TTIN) may be used as the identifying number of the recipient. For provisions relating to the use of TTINs, see § 301.6109-4 of this chapter (Procedure and Administration Regulations).

(c) *Exempted foreign-related items.*—(1) *In general.*—No return shall be required under paragraph (a) of this section for payments of the items described in paragraphs (c)(1)(i) through (iv) of this section.

(i) Returns of information are not required for payments of royalties that a payor can, prior to payment, associate with documentation upon which it may rely to treat as made to a foreign beneficial owner in accordance with §1.1441-1(e)(1)(ii) or as made to a foreign payee in accordance with §1.6049-5(d)(1) or presumed to be made to a foreign payee under §1.6049-5(d)(2), (3), (4), or (5). However, such payments may be reportable under §1.1461-1(b) and (c). For purposes of this paragraph (c)(1)(i), the provisions in §1.6049-5(c) (regarding rules applicable to documentation of foreign status and definition of U.S. payor and non-U.S. payor) shall apply. See §1.1441-1(b)(3)(iii)(B) and (C) for special payee rules regarding scholarships, grants, pensions, annuities, etc. The provisions of §1.1441-1 shall apply by substituting the term *payor* for the term *withholding agent* and without regard to the fact that the provisions apply only to amounts subject to withholding under chapter 3 of the Internal Revenue Code.

(ii) Returns of information are not required for payments of royalties from sources outside the United States paid by a non-U.S. payor or non-U.S. middleman and that are paid and received outside the United States. For a definition of non-U.S. payor or non-U.S. middleman, see §1.6049-5(c)(5). For circumstances in which a payment is considered to be paid and received outside the United States, see §1.6049-4(f)(16).

(iii) Returns of information are not required for payments made by a foreign intermediary described in §1.1441-1(e)(3)(i) that it has received in its capacity as an intermediary and that are associated with a valid withholding certificate described in §1.1441-1(e)(3)(ii) or (iii) and payments made by a U.S. branch of a foreign bank or of a foreign insurance company described in §1.1441-1(b)(2)(iv) that are associated with a valid withholding certificate described in §1.1441-1(e)(3)(v), which certificate the intermediary or branch has furnished to the payor or middleman from whom it has received the payment, unless, and to the extent, the intermediary or branch knows that the payments are required to be reported and were not so reported.

(2) *Definitions.*—(i) *Payor.*—For purposes of this section, the term *payor* shall have the meaning ascribed to it under §1.6049-4(a).

(ii) *Joint owners.*—Amounts paid to joint owners for which a certificate or documentation is required as a condition for being exempt from reporting under this paragraph (c) of this section are presumed made to U.S. payees who are not exempt recipients if, prior to payment, the payor cannot reliably associate the payment either with a Form W-9 furnished by one of the joint owners in the manner required in §§31.3406(d)-1 through 31.3406(d)-5 of this chapter, or with documentation described in paragraph (c)(1)(i) of this section furnished by each joint owner upon which it can rely to treat each joint owner as a foreign payee or foreign beneficial owner. For purposes of applying this paragraph (c)(2)(ii), the grace period described in §1.6049-5(d)(2)(ii)

shall apply only if each payee qualifies for such grace period.

(d) *Cross-reference to penalties.*—For provisions relating to the penalty provided for failure to file timely a correct information return required under section 6050N(a), see §301.6721-1 of this chapter (Procedure and Administration Regulations). For provisions relating to the penalty provided for failure to furnish timely a correct payee statement required under section 6050N(b) and §1.6050N-1(a), see §301.6722-1 of this chapter. See §301.6724-1 of this chapter for the waiver of a penalty if the failure is due to reasonable cause and is not due to willful neglect.

(e) *Effective/applicability date.*—This section applies to payee statements due after December 31, 2014, without regard to extensions. For payee statements due before January 1, 2015, §1.6050N-1 (as contained in 26 CFR part 1, revised April 2013) shall apply. [Reg. §1.6050N-1.]

☐ [*T.D. 8637, 12-20-95. Amended by T.D. 8734, 10-6-97; T.D. 8804, 12-30-98; T.D. 8856, 12-29-99, T.D. 9675, 7-14-2014 and T.D. 9808, 12-30-2016.*]

[Reg. §1.6050N-2]

§1.6050N-2. Coordination with reporting rules for widely held fixed investment trusts under §1.671-5.—See §1.671-5 for the reporting rules for widely held fixed investment trusts (as defined under that section). [Reg. §1.6050N-2.]

☐ [*T.D. 9241, 1-23-2006.*]

[Reg. §1.6050P-0]

§1.6050P-0. Table of contents.—This section lists the major captions that appear in §1.6050P-1 and §1.6050P-2.

§1.6050P-1 Information reporting for discharges of indebtedness by certain entities.

(a) Reporting requirement.
  (1) In general.
  (2) No aggregation.
  (3) Amounts not includible in income.
  (4) Time and place for reporting.
    (i) In general.
    (ii) Indebtedness discharged in bankruptcy.
(b) Date of discharge.
  (1) In general.
  (2) Identifiable events.
    (i) In general.
    (ii) Statute of limitations.
    (iii) Decision to discontinue collection activity; creditor's defined policy.
    (iv) Expiration of non-payment testing period.
    (v) Special rule for certain entities required to file in a year prior to 2008.
  (3) Permitted reporting.
(c) Indebtedness.
(d) Exceptions from reporting requirement.
  (1) Certain bankruptcy discharges.
    (i) In general.
    (ii) Business or investment debt.

(2) Interest.

(3) Non-principal amounts in lending transactions.

(4) Indebtedness of foreign persons held by foreign branches of U.S. financial institutions.

    (i) Reporting requirements.

    (ii) Definition.

(5) Acquisition of indebtedness by related party.

(6) Releases.

(7) Guarantors and sureties.

(e) Additional rules.

(1) Multiple debtors.

    (i) In general.

    (ii) Amount to be reported.

(2) Multiple creditors.

    (i) In general.

    (ii) Partnerships.

    (iii) Pass-through securitized indebtedness arrangement.

        (A) Reporting requirements.

        (B) Definition.

    (iv) REMICs.

    (v) No double reporting.

(3) Coordination with reporting under section 6050J.

(4) Direct or indirect subsidiary.

(5) Entity formed or availed of to hold indebtedness.

(6) Use of magnetic media.

(7) TIN solicitation requirement.

    (i) In general.

    (ii) Manner of soliciting TIN.

(8) Recordkeeping requirements.

(9) No multiple reporting.

(f) Requirement to furnish statement.

(1) In general.

(2) Furnishing copy of Form 1099-C.

(3) Time and place for furnishing statement.

(g) Penalties.

(h) Effective/applicability date.

§1.6050P-2 Organization a significant trade or business of which is the lending of money.

(a) In general.

(b) Safe harbors.

(1) Organizations not subject to section 6050P in the previous calendar year.

(2) Organizations that were subject to section 6050P in the previous calendar year.

(3) No test year.

(c) Seller financing.

(d) Gross income from lending of money.

(e) Acquisition of an indebtedness from a person other than the debtor included in lending money.

(f) Test year.

(g) Predecessor organization.

(h) Examples.

(i) Effective date.

[Reg. §1.6050P-0.]

[T.D. 8654, 1-3-96. *Amended by* T.D. 9160, 10-22-2004; T.D. 9430, 11-7-2008 *and* T.D. 9461, 9-16-2009.]

[Reg. §1.6050P-1]

§1.6050P-1. Information reporting for discharges of indebtedness by certain entities.—
(a) *Reporting requirement.*—(1) *In general.*—Except as provided in paragraph (d) of this section, any applicable entity (as defined in section 6050P(c)(1)) that discharges an indebtedness of any person (within the meaning of section 7701(a)(1)) of at least $600 during a calendar year must file an information return on Form 1099-C with the Internal Revenue Service. Solely for purposes of the reporting requirements of section 6050P and this section, a discharge of indebtedness is deemed to have occurred, except as provided in paragraph (b)(3) of this section, if and only if there has occurred an identifiable event described in paragraph (b)(2) of this section, whether or not an actual discharge of indebtedness has occurred on or before the date on which the identifiable event has occurred. The return must include the following information—

    (i) The name, address, and taxpayer identification number (TIN), as defined in section 7701(a)(41), of each person for which there was an identifiable event during the calendar year;

    (ii) The date on which the identifiable event occurred, as described in paragraph (b) of this section;

    (iii) The amount of indebtedness discharged, as described in paragraph (c) of this section;

    (iv) An indication whether the identifiable event was a discharge of indebtedness in a bankruptcy, if known; and

    (v) Any other information required by Form 1099-C or its instructions, or current revenue procedures.

(2) *No aggregation.*—For purposes of reporting under this section, multiple discharges of indebtedness of less than $600 are not required to be aggregated unless such separate discharges are pursuant to a plan to evade the reporting requirements of this section.

(3) *Amounts not includible in income.*—Except as otherwise provided in this section, discharged indebtedness must be reported regardless of whether the debtor is subject to tax on the discharged debt under sections 61 and 108 or otherwise by applicable law.

(4) *Time and place for reporting.*—(i) *In general.*—Except as provided in paragraph (a)(4)(ii) of this section, returns required by this section must be filed with the Internal Revenue Service office designated in the instructions for Form 1099-C on or before February 28 (March 31 if filed electronically) of the year following the calendar year in which the identifiable event occurs.

    (ii) *Indebtedness discharged in bankruptcy.*—Indebtedness discharged in bankruptcy that is required to be reported under this section must be reported for the later of the calendar year in which the amount of discharged indebtedness first becomes ascertainable, or the calendar year in which the identifiable event occurs.

(b) *Date of discharge.*—(1) *In general.*—Solely for purposes of this section, except as provided in paragraph (b)(3) of this section, indebtedness is discharged on the date of the occurrence of an identifiable event specified in paragraph (b)(2) of this section.

(2) *Identifiable events.*—(i) *In general.*—An identifiable event is—

(A) A discharge of indebtedness under title 11 of the United States Code (bankruptcy);

(B) A cancellation or extinguishment of an indebtedness that renders a debt unenforceable in a receivership, foreclosure, or similar proceeding in a federal or State court, as described in section 368(a)(3)(A)(ii) (other than a discharge described in paragraph (b)(2)(i)(A) of this section);

(C) A cancellation or extinguishment of an indebtedness upon the expiration of the statute of limitations for collection of an indebtedness, subject to the limitations described in paragraph (b)(2)(ii) of this section, or upon the expiration of a statutory period for filing a claim or commencing a deficiency judgment proceeding;

(D) A cancellation or extinguishment of an indebtedness pursuant to an election of foreclosure remedies by a creditor that statutorily extinguishes or bars the creditor's right to pursue collection of the indebtedness;

(E) A cancellation or extinguishment of an indebtedness that renders a debt unenforceable pursuant to a probate or similar proceeding;

(F) A discharge of indebtedness pursuant to an agreement between an applicable entity and a debtor to discharge indebtedness at less than full consideration; or

(G) A discharge of indebtedness pursuant to a decision by the creditor, or the application of a defined policy of the creditor, to discontinue collection activity and discharge debt.

(ii) *Statute of limitations.*—In the case of an expiration of the statute of limitations for collection of an indebtedness, an identifiable event occurs under paragraph (b)(2)(i)(C) of this section only if, and at such time as, a debtor's affirmative statute of limitations defense is upheld in a final judgment or decision of a judicial proceeding, and the period for appealing the judgment or decision has expired.

(iii) *Decision to discontinue collection activity; creditor's defined policy.*—For purposes of the identifiable event described in paragraph (b)(2)(i)(G) of this section, a creditor's defined policy includes both a written policy of the creditor and the creditor's established business practice. Thus, for example, a creditor's established

practice to discontinue collection activity and abandon debts upon expiration of a particular non-payment period is considered a defined policy for purposes of paragraph (b)(2)(i)(G) of this section.

(3) *Permitted reporting.*—If a discharge of indebtedness occurs before the date on which an identifiable event occurs, the discharge may, at the creditor's discretion, be reported under this section.

(c) *Indebtedness.*—For purposes of this section and § 1.6050P-2, indebtedness means any amount owed to an applicable entity, including stated principal, fees, stated interest, penalties, administrative costs and fines. The amount of indebtedness discharged may represent all, or only a part, of the total amount owed to the applicable entity.

(d) *Exceptions from reporting requirement.*—(1) *Certain bankruptcy discharges.*—(i) *In general.*—Reporting is required under this section in the case of a discharge of indebtedness in bankruptcy only if the creditor knows from information included in the reporting entity's books and records pertaining to the indebtedness that the debt was incurred for business or investment purposes as defined in paragraph (d)(1)(ii) of this section.

(ii) *Business or investment debt.*—Indebtedness is considered incurred for business purposes if it is incurred in connection with the conduct of any trade or business other than the trade or business of performing services as an employee. Indebtedness is considered incurred for investment purposes if it is incurred to purchase property held for investment, as defined in section 163(d)(5).

(2) *Interest.*—The discharge of an amount of indebtedness that is interest is not required to be reported under this section.

(3) *Non-principal amounts in lending transactions.*—In the case of a lending transaction, the discharge of an amount other than stated principal is not required to be reported under this section. For this purpose, a lending transaction is any transaction in which a lender loans money to, or makes advances on behalf of, a borrower (including revolving credits and lines of credit).

(4) *Indebtedness of foreign debtors held by foreign branches of U.S. financial institutions.*—(i) *Reporting requirements.*—[Reserved]

(ii) *Definition.*—An indebtedness held by a foreign branch of a U.S. financial institution is described in this paragraph (d)(4) only if—

(A) The financial institution is engaged through a branch or office in the active conduct of a banking or similar business outside the United States;

(B) The branch or office is a permanent place of business that is regularly maintained, occupied, and used to carry on a banking or similar financial business;

Reg. § 1.6050P-1(d)(4)(ii)(B)

(C) The business is conducted by at least one employee of the branch or office who is regularly in attendance at such place of business during normal working hours;

(D) The indebtedness is extended outside of the United States by the branch or office in connection with that trade or business; and

(E) The financial institution does not know or have reason to know that the debtor is a United States person.

(5) *Acquisition of indebtedness by related party.*—No reporting is required under this section in the case of a deemed discharge of indebtedness under section 108(e)(4) (relating to the acquisition of an indebtedness by a person related to the debtor), unless the disposition of the indebtedness by the creditor was made with a view to avoiding the reporting requirements of this section.

(6) *Releases.*—The release of a co-obligor is not required to be reported under this section if the remaining debtors remain liable for the full amount of any unpaid indebtedness.

(7) *Guarantors and sureties.*—Solely for purposes of the reporting requirements of this section, a guarantor is not a debtor. Thus, in the case of guaranteed indebtedness, reporting under this section is not required with respect to a guarantor, whether or not there has been a default and demand for payment made upon the guarantor.

(e) *Additional rules.*—(1) *Multiple debtors.*—(i) *In general.*—In the case of indebtedness of $10,000 or more incurred on or after January 1, 1995, that involves more than one debtor, a reporting entity is subject to the requirements of paragraph (a) of this section for each debtor discharged from such indebtedness. In the case of indebtedness incurred prior to January 1, 1995, and indebtedness of less than $10,000 incurred on or after January 1, 1995, involving multiple debtors, reporting under this section is required only with respect to the primary (or first-named) debtor. Additionally, only one return of information is required under this section if the reporting entity knows, or has reason to know, that co-obligors were husband and wife living at the same address when an indebtedness was incurred, and does not know or have reason to know that such circumstances have changed at the date of a discharge of the indebtedness. This paragraph (e)(1) applies to discharges of indebtedness after December 31, 1994.

(ii) *Amount to be reported.*—In the case of multiple debtors jointly and severally liable on an indebtedness, the amount of discharged indebtedness required to be reported under this section with respect to each debtor is the total amount of indebtedness discharged. For this purpose, multiple debtors are presumed to be jointly and severally liable on an indebtedness in the absence of clear and convincing evidence to the contrary.

(2) *Multiple creditors.*—(i) *In general.*—Except as otherwise provided in this paragraph (e)(2), if indebtedness is owned (or treated as owned for federal income tax purposes) by more than one creditor, each creditor that is an applicable entity must comply with the reporting requirements of this section with respect to any discharge of indebtedness of $600 or more allocable to such creditor. A creditor will be considered to have complied with the requirements of this section if a lead bank, fund administrator, or other designee of the creditor complies on its behalf in any reasonable manner, such as by filing a single return reporting the aggregate amount of indebtedness discharged, or by filing a return with respect to the portion of the discharged indebtedness allocable to the creditor. For purposes of this paragraph (e)(2)(i), any reasonable method may be used to determine the portion of discharged indebtedness allocable to each creditor.

(ii) *Partnerships.*—For purposes of paragraph (e)(2)(i) of this section, indebtedness owned by a partnership is treated as owned by the partners.

(iii) *Pass-through securitized indebtedness arrangement.*—(A) *Reporting requirements.*—[Reserved]

(B) *Definition.*—For purposes of this paragraph (e)(2)(iii), a pass-through securitized indebtedness arrangement is any arrangement whereby one or more debt obligations are pooled and held for twenty or more persons whose interests in the debt obligations are undivided co-ownership interests that are freely transferrable. Co-ownership interests that are actively traded personal property (as defined in §1.1092(d)-1) are presumed to be freely transferrable and held by twenty or more persons.

(iv) *REMICs.*—[Reserved]

(v) *No double reporting.*—If multiple creditors are considered to hold interests in an indebtedness for purposes of this paragraph (e)(2) by virtue of holding ownership interests in an entity, and the entity is required to report a discharge of that indebtedness under paragraph (e)(5) of this section, then the multiple creditors are not required to report the discharge of indebtedness.

(3) *Coordination with reporting under section 6050J.*—If, in the same calendar year, a discharge of indebtedness reportable under section 6050P occurs in connection with a transaction also reportable under section 6050J (relating to foreclosures and abandonments of secured property), an applicable entity need not file both a Form 1099-A and a Form 1099-C with respect to the same debtor. The filing requirements of section 6050J will be satisfied with respect to a borrower if, in lieu of filing Form 1099-A, a Form 1099-C is filed in accordance with the instructions for the filing of that form. This paragraph (e)(3) applies to discharges of indebtedness after December 31, 1994.

(4) *Direct or indirect subsidiary.*—For purposes of section 6050P(c)(2)(C), the term direct or indirect subsidiary means a corporation in a chain of corporations beginning with an entity described in section 6050P(c)(2)(A), if at least 50 percent of the total combined voting power of all classes of stock entitled to vote, or at least 50 percent of the total value of all classes of stock, of such corporation is directly owned by the entity described in section 6050P(c)(2)(A), or by one or more other corporations in the chain.

(5) *Entity formed or availed of to hold indebtedness.*—Notwithstanding § 1.6050P-2(b)(3), if an entity (the transferee entity) is formed or availed of by an applicable entity (within the meaning of section 6050P(c)(1)) for the principal purpose of holding indebtedness acquired (including originated) by the applicable entity, then, for purposes of section 6050P(c)(2)(D), the transferee entity has a significant trade or business of lending money.

(6) *Use of magnetic media.*—Any return required under this section must be filed on magnetic media to the extent required by section 6011(e) and the regulations thereunder. A failure to file on magnetic media when required constitutes a failure to file an information return under section 6721. Any person not required by section 6011(e) to file returns on magnetic media may request permission to do so under applicable regulations and revenue procedures.

(7) *TIN solicitation requirement.*—(i) *In general.*—For purposes of reporting under this section, a reasonable effort must be made to obtain the correct name/taxpayer identification number (TIN) combination of a person whose indebtedness is discharged. A TIN obtained at the time an indebtedness is incurred satisfies the requirement of this section, unless the entity required to file knows that such TIN is incorrect. If the TIN is not obtained prior to the occurrence of an identifiable event, it must be requested of the debtor for purposes of satisfying the requirement of this paragraph (e)(7).

(ii) *Manner of soliciting TIN.*—Solicitations made in the manner described in § 301.6724-1(e)(1)(i) and (2) of this chapter will be deemed to have satisfied the reasonable effort requirement set forth in paragraph (e)(7)(i) of this section. A TIN solicitation made after the occurrence of an identifiable event must clearly notify the debtor that the Internal Revenue Service requires the debtor to furnish its TIN, and that failure to furnish such TIN may subject the debtor to a $50 penalty imposed by the Internal Revenue Service. A TIN provided under this section is not required to be certified under penalties of perjury.

(8) *Recordkeeping requirements.*—Any applicable entity required to file a return with the Internal Revenue Service under this section must also retain a copy of the return, or have the ability to reconstruct the data required to be included on the return under paragraph (a)(1) of this section, for at least four years from the date such return is required to be filed under paragraph (a)(4) of this section.

(9) *No multiple reporting.*—If discharged indebtedness is reported under this section, no further reporting under this section is required for the amount so reported, notwithstanding that a subsequent identifiable event occurs with respect to the same amount. Further, no additional reporting or Form 1099-C correction is required if a creditor receives a payment of all or a portion of a discharged indebtedness reported under this section for a prior calendar year.

(f) *Requirement to furnish statement.*—(1) *In general.*—Any applicable entity required to file a return under this section must furnish to each person whose name is shown on such return a written statement that includes the following information—

(i) The information required by paragraph (a)(1) of this section. An IRS truncated taxpayer identifying number (TTIN) may be used as the TIN of the person for whom there was an identifiable event in lieu of the identifying number appearing on the information return filed with the Internal Revenue Service. For provisions relating to the use of TTINs, see § 301.6109-4 of this chapter (Procedure and Administration Regulations);

(ii) The name, address, and TIN of the applicable entity required to file a return under paragraph (a) of this section;

(iii) A legend identifying the statement as important tax information that is being furnished to the Internal Revenue Service; and

(iv) Any other information required by Form 1099-C or its instructions, or current revenue procedures.

(2) *Furnishing copy of Form 1099-C.*—The requirement to provide a statement to the debtor will be satisfied if the applicable entity furnishes copy B of the Form 1099-C or a substitute statement that complies with the requirements of the current revenue procedure for substitute Forms 1099.

(3) *Time and place for furnishing statement.*—The statement required by this paragraph (f) must be furnished to the debtor on or before January 31 of the year following the calendar year in which the identifiable event occurs. The statement will be considered furnished to the debtor if it is mailed to the debtor's last known address.

(g) *Penalties.*—For penalties for failure to comply with the requirements of this section, see sections 6721 through 6724.

(h) *Applicability dates.*—This section applies to information returns required to be filed, and payee statements required to be furnished, after December 31, 2016. Section 1.6050P-1 (as contained in 26 CFR part 1, revised April 2016) applies to information returns required to be filed, and payee statements required to be furnished, on or before December 31, 2016. [Reg. § 1.6050P-1.]

[*T.D. 8654, 1-3-96. Amended by T.D. 8895, 8-17-2000; T.D. 9160, 10-22-2004; T.D. 9430, 11-7-2008; T.D. 9461, 9-16-2009, T.D. 9675, 7-14-2014 and T.D. 9793, 11-9-2016.*]

[Reg. §1.6050P-2]

§1.6050P-2. **Organization a significant trade or business of which is the lending of money.**—(a) *In general.*—For purposes of section 6050P(c)(2)(D), the lending of money is a significant trade or business of an organization in a calendar year if the organization lends money on a regular and continuing basis during the calendar year.

(b) *Safe harbors.*—(1) *Organizations not subject to section 6050P in the previous calendar year.*—For an organization that was not required to report under section 6050P in the previous calendar year, the lending of money is not treated as a significant trade or business for the calendar year in which the lending occurs if gross income from lending money (as described in paragraph (d) of this section) in the organization's most recent test year (as defined in paragraph (f) of this section) is both less than $5 million and less than 15 percent of the organization's gross income for that test year.

(2) *Organizations that were subject to section 6050P in the previous calendar year.*—For an organization that was required to report under section 6050P for the previous calendar year, the lending of money is not treated as a significant trade or business for the calendar year in which the lending occurs if gross income from lending money (as described in paragraph (d) of this section) in each of the organization's three most recent test years is both less than $3 million and less than 10 percent of the organization's gross income for that test year.

(3) *No test year.*—The lending of money is not treated as a significant trade or business for an organization for the calendar year in which the lending occurs if the organization does not have a test year for that calendar year.

(c) *Seller financing.*—If the principal trade or business of an organization is selling nonfinancial goods or providing nonfinancial services and if the organization extends credit to the purchasers of those goods or services to finance the purchases, then, for purposes of section 6050P(c)(2)(D), these extensions of credit are not a significant trade or business of lending money.

(d) *Gross income from lending of money.*—For purposes of this section, gross income from lending of money includes—

(1) Income from interest, including qualified stated interest, original issue discount, and market discount;

(2) Gains arising from the sale or other disposition of indebtedness;

(3) Penalties with respect to indebtedness (whether or not the penalty is interest for Federal tax purposes); and

(4) Fees with respect to indebtedness, including merchant discount or interchange (whether or not the fee is interest for Federal tax purposes).

(e) *Acquisition of an indebtedness from a person other than the debtor included in lending money.*—For purposes of this section, lending money includes acquiring an indebtedness not only from the debtor at origination but also from a prior holder of the indebtedness. Gross income arising from indebtedness is gross income from the lending of money without regard to who originated the indebtedness. If an organization acquires an indebtedness, the organization is required to report any cancellation of the indebtedness if the organization is engaged in a significant trade or business of lending money.

(f) *Test year.*—For any calendar year, a *test year* is a taxable year of the organization that ends before July 1 of the previous calendar year.

(g) *Predecessor organization.*—If an organization acquires substantially all of the property that was used in a trade or business of some other organization (the predecessor) (including when two or more corporations are parties to a merger agreement under which the surviving corporation becomes the owner of the assets and assumes the liabilities of the absorbed corporation(s)) or was used in a separate unit of the predecessor, then whether the organization at issue qualifies for one of the safe harbors in paragraph (b) of this section is determined by also taking into account the test years, reporting obligations, and gross income of the predecessor.

(h) *Examples.*—The rules of this section are illustrated by the following examples:

Example 1. (i) *Facts.* Finance Company A, a calendar year taxpayer, was formed in Year 1 as a non-bank subsidiary of Manufacturing Company and has no predecessor. A lends money to purchasers of Manufacturing Company's products on a regular and continuing basis to finance the purchase of those products. A's gross income from stated interest in Year 1 is $4.7 million. In Year 1, A's gross income from fees and penalties with respect to the indebtedness is $0.5 million, and A has no other gross income from lending money within the meaning of paragraph (d) of this section.

(ii) *Results.* Section 6050P does not require A to report discharges of indebtedness occurring in Years 1 or 2, because A has no test year for those years. Notwithstanding that A lends money in those years on a regular and continuing basis, under paragraph (b)(3) of this section, A does not have a significant trade or business of lending money in those years for purposes of section 6050P(c)(2)(D). However, for Year 3, A's test year is Year 1. A's gross income from lending in Year 1 is not less than $5 million for purposes of the applicable safe harbor of paragraph (b)(1) of this section. Because A lends money on a regular and continuing basis and does not meet the applicable safe harbor, section 6050P requires A to report discharges of indebtedness occurring in Year 3.

Example 2. (i) *Facts.* The facts are the same as in Example 1, except that A is a division of Manufacturing Company, rather than a separate subsidiary. Manufacturing Company's principal activity is the manufacture and sale of non-financial products, and, other than financing the purchase of those products, Manufacturing Company does not extend credit or otherwise lend money.

(ii) *Results.* Under paragraph (c) of this section, that financing activity is not a significant trade or business of lending money for purposes of section 6050P(c)(2)(D), and section 6050P does not require Manufacturing Company to report discharges of indebtedness.

Example 3. (i) *Facts.* Company B, a calendar year taxpayer, is formed in Year 1. B has no predecessor and a part of its activities consists of the lending of money. B packages and sells part of the indebtedness it originates and holds the remainder. B is engaged in these activities on a regular and continuing basis. For Year 1, the sum of B's gross income from sales of the indebtedness, plus other income described in paragraph (d) of this section, is only $4.8 million, but it is 16% of B's gross income in Year 1.

(ii) *Results.* Because B lends money on a regular and continuing basis and does not meet the applicable safe harbor of paragraph (b)(1) of this section, section 6050P requires B to report discharges of indebtedness occurring in Year 3. B is not required to report discharges of indebtedness in Years 1 and 2 because B has no test year for Years 1 and 2.

Example 4. (i) *Facts.* The facts are the same as in *Example 3.* In addition, in each of Years 2, 3, and 4, the sum of B's gross income from sales of the indebtedness, plus other income described in paragraph (d) of this section, is less than both $3 million and 10% of B's gross income.

(ii) *Results.* (A) Because B was required to report under section 6050P for Year 3, the applicable safe harbor for Year 4 is paragraph (b)(2) of this section, which is satisfied only if B's gross income from lending activities for each of the three most recent test years is less than both $3 million and 10% of B's gross income. For Year 4, even though B has only two test years, B's gross income in one of those test years, Year 1, causes B to fail to meet this safe harbor. Accordingly, B is required to report discharges of indebtedness under section 6050P in Year 4. For Year 5, B's three most recent test years are Years 1, 2, and 3. However, B's gross income from lending activities in Year 1 is not less than $3 million and 10% of B's gross income. Accordingly, section 6050P requires B to report discharges of indebtedness in Year 5.

(B) For Year 6, B satisfies the applicable safe harbor requirements of paragraph (b)(2) of this section for each of the three most recent test years (Years 2, 3, and 4). Therefore, section 6050P

does not require B to report discharges of indebtedness in Year 6. Because B is not required to report for Year 6, the applicable safe harbor for Year 7 is the one contained in paragraph (b)(1) of this section, and thus the only relevant test year is Year 5.

Example 5. (i) *Facts.* (A) Company C, a calendar year taxpayer, was formed in Year 1 and, on a regular and continuing basis, enters into the following transactions with its clients, all of whom are unrelated parties to C. C does not have any other income.

(B) C's clients sell goods to customers, frequently accepting as payment accounts receivable that are due in 30 to 90 days. Under a contract with each client, C investigates the creditworthiness of the client's customers with respect to the prospective sales, and, for each customer, C determines whether, and to what extent, C is willing to assume the risk of loss on accounts receivable to be issued by the customer. C's decision whether to assume risk of loss may be based on an evaluation of the credit quality of particular customers or on the aggregate credit quality of all of the client's prospective customers. If C is unwilling to assume the risk, the client either may refuse to extend any credit to the customer or may accept the account receivable and bear the risk of loss.

(C) Pursuant to some contracts between C's clients and C, C's clients assign legal title to the accounts receivable to C when the accounts receivable are issued by the customers. For these accounts receivable, C agrees to undertake collections and to remit the amounts collected to the client, less a fee of 0.70 percent of the face value of the accounts receivable. Pursuant to other contracts between C's clients and C, C's clients retain legal title to the accounts receivable and retain the initial collection responsibility. For these accounts receivable, C's fee is reduced to 0.35 percent. Both groups of accounts receivable include accounts receivable for which C has assumed the risk of loss and accounts receivable for which C has not assumed the risk of loss.

(D) Based on all the facts and circumstances, C acquires ownership for Federal tax purposes of some, but not all, of the accounts receivable that it has agreed to collect and of some, but not all, of the accounts receivable for which the client has retained collection responsibility.

(E) In Year 1, C's total fee income with respect to accounts receivable of which it acquired tax ownership was $2 million. C's fee income in Year 1 from accounts receivable of which it did not acquire tax ownership was $700,000. C does not have any other income for Year 1.

(F) In Year 3, there were discharges of $950,000, representing $100,000 of customer defaults on those accounts receivable of which C was the owner for Federal tax purposes at the time of the identifiable event marking the discharge and $850,000 of customer defaults on the accounts receivable of which the clients, and not C, were the owner. Whenever C determined the uncollectibility of an account receivable for

Reg. §1.6050P-2(h)

which it had not assumed the risk of loss, C reassigned title to the account receivable to the appropriate client. Each defaulting customer defaulted on an account receivable with an outstanding balance of at least $600.

(ii) *Results.* (A) For Year 3, C's test year is Year 1. Under paragraph (e) of this section, C's $2 million fee income from the accounts receivable of which it acquired tax ownership is "gross income from lending money" for purposes of paragraph (b) of this section, because C was the owner of the accounts for Federal tax purposes. Under paragraph (e) of this section, C's $700,000 fee income from the accounts receivable of which it did not acquire tax ownership is not "gross income from lending money" for purposes of paragraph (b) of this section, because C was not the owner of the accounts receivable for Federal tax purposes. In Year 1, therefore, C's gross income from lending money is less than $5 million but is not less than 15% of C's gross income. Because C lends money on a regular and continuing basis and does not meet the applicable safe harbor, section 6050P requires C to report discharges of indebtedness occurring in Year 3.

(B) In Year 3, section 6050P requires C to report the $100,000 of discharges of the accounts receivable of which C was the owner for Federal tax purposes at the time of the identifiable event marking the discharge. Unless an exception to reporting under paragraph (b) or (c) of this section applies, section 6050P requires C's clients to report the $850,000 of discharges of the accounts receivable of which C did not become the owner.

(i) *Effective date.*—This section applies to discharges of indebtedness occurring on or after January 1, 2005. [Reg. § 1.6050P-2.]

☐ [*T.D.* 9160, 10-22-2004.]

[Reg. § 1.6050S-0]

§ 1.6050S-0. Table of contents.—This section lists captions contained in § § 1.6050S-1, 1.6050S-2T, 1.6050S-3, and 1.6050S-4T.

(2) Failure to furnish correct information statements.

(3) Waiver of penalties for failures to include a correct TIN.

(i) In general.

(ii) Acting in a responsible manner.

(iii) Manner of soliciting TIN.

(4) Failure to furnish TIN.

(f) Effective date.

§ 1.6050S-2T Electronic furnishing of information statements for qualified tuition and related expenses.

(a) Electronic furnishing of statements.

(1) In general.

(2) Consent.

(i) In general.

(ii) Change in hardware or software requirements.

(iii) Example.

(3) Required disclosures.

(i) In general.

(ii) Paper statement.

(iii) Scope and duration of consent.

(iv) Post-consent request for a paper statement.

(v) Withdrawal of consent.

(vi) Notice of termination.

(vii) Updating information.

(viii) Hardware and software requirements.

(4) Format.

(5) Posting.

(6) Notice.

(i) In general.

(ii) Undeliverable electronic address.

(iii) Corrected statements.

(7) Retention.

(b) Effective date.

§ 1.6050S-3 Information reporting for payments of interest on qualified education loans.

(a) Information reporting requirement in general.

(b) Definitions.

(1) Interest.

(2) Payor.

(c) Requirement to file return.

(1) Form of return.

(2) Information included on return.

(3) Time and place for filing return.

(i) In general.

(ii) Extensions of time.

(4) Use of magnetic media.

(d) Requirement to furnish statement.

(1) In general.

(2) Time and manner for furnishing statement.

(i) In general.

(ii) Extensions of time.

(3) Copy of Form 1098-E.

(e) Special rules.

(1) Transitional rule for reporting of loan origination fees and capitalized interest.

(2) Qualified education loan certification.

(3) Payments of interest received or collected by one or more persons.

(i) In general.

(ii) Exception.

(4) Reporting by foreign persons.

(5) Governmental units.

(f) Penalty provisions.

(1) Failure to file correct returns.

(2) Failure to furnish correct information statements.

(3) Waiver of penalties for failures to include a correct TIN.

(i) In general.

(ii) Acting in a responsible manner.

(iii) Manner of soliciting TIN.

(4) Failure to furnish TIN.

(g) Effective date.

§ 1.6050S-4T Electronic furnishing of information statements for payments of interest on qualified education loans.

(a) Electronic furnishing of statements.

(1) In general.

(2) Consent.

(i) In general.

(ii) Change in hardware or software requirements.

(iii) Example.

(3) Required disclosures.

(i) In general.

(ii) Paper statement.

(iii) Scope and duration of consent.

(iv) Post-consent request for a paper statement.

(v) Withdrawal of consent.

(vi) Notice of termination.

(vii) Updating information.

(viii) Hardware and software requirements.

(4) Format.

(5) Posting.

(6) Notice.

(i) In general.

(ii) Undeliverable electronic address.

(iii) Corrected statements.

(7) Retention.

(b) Effective date.

[Reg. § 1.6050S-0.]

□ [*T.D.* 8992, 4-26-2002. *Amended by T.D.* 9029, 12-18-2002.]

[Reg. § 1.6050S-1]

§ 1.6050S-1. Information reporting for qualified tuition and related expenses.— (a) *Information reporting requirement.*—(1) *In general.*—Except as provided in paragraph (a)(2) of this section, any eligible educational institution (as defined in section 25A(f)(2) and the regulations thereunder) (an institution) that enrolls (as determined under paragraph (d)(1) of this section) any individual for any academic period (as defined in the regulations under section 25A), and any person that is engaged in a trade or business of making payments under an insurance arrangement as reimbursements or refunds (or other similar amounts) of qualified tuition and related expenses (as defined in section 25A(f)(1) and the regulations thereunder) (an insurer) must—

(i) File an information return, as described in paragraph (b) of this section, with the Internal Revenue Service (IRS) with respect to each individual described in paragraph (b) of this section; and

(ii) Furnish a statement, as described in paragraph (c) of this section, to each individual described in paragraph (c) of this section.

(2) *Exceptions.*—(i) *No reporting by institution or insurer for nonresident alien individuals.*—The information reporting requirements of this section do not apply with respect to any individual who is a nonresident alien (as defined in section 7701(b) and § 301.7701(b)-3 of this chapter) during the calendar year, unless the individual requests the institution or insurer to report. If a nonresident alien individual requests an institution or insurer to report, the institution or insurer must comply with the requirements of this section for the calendar year with respect to which the request is made.

(ii) *No reporting by institutions for noncredit courses.*—(A) *In general.*—The information reporting requirements of this section do not apply with respect to any course for which no academic credit is offered by the institution.

(B) *Academic credit defined.*—*Academic credit* means credit offered by an institution for the completion of course work leading toward a post-secondary degree, certificate, or other recognized post-secondary educational credential.

(C) *Example.*—The following example illustrates the rules of this paragraph (a)(2)(ii):

Example. Student A, a medical doctor, takes a course at University X's medical school. Student A takes the course to fulfill State Y's licensing requirement that medical doctors attend continuing medical education courses each year. Student A is not enrolled in a degree program at University X and takes the medical course through University X's continuing professional education division. University X does not offer credit toward a post-secondary degree on an academic transcript for the completion of the course but gives Student A a certificate of attendance upon completion. Under this paragraph (a)(2)(ii), University X is not subject to the information reporting requirements of section 6050S and this section for the medical education course taken by Student A.

(iii) *No reporting by institutions for individuals whose qualified tuition and related expenses are waived or are paid with scholarships.*—The information reporting requirements of this section do not apply with respect to any individual whose qualified tuition and related expenses are waived in their entirety or are paid entirely with scholarships.

(iv) *No reporting by institutions for individuals whose qualified tuition and related expenses are covered by a formal billing arrangement.*—(A) *In general.*—The information reporting requirements of this section do not apply with respect to any individual whose qualified tuition and related expenses are covered by a formal billing arrangement as defined in paragraph (a)(2)(iv)(B) of this section.

(B) *Formal billing arrangement defined.*— A *formal billing arrangement* means—

(1) An arrangement in which the institution bills only an employer for education furnished by the institution to an individual who is the employer's employee and does not maintain a separate financial account for that individual;

(2) An arrangement in which the institution bills only a governmental entity for education furnished by the institution to an individual and does not maintain a separate financial account for that individual; or

(3) Any other similar arrangement in which the institution bills only an institutional third party for education furnished to an individual and does not maintain a separate financial account for that individual, but only if designated as a formal billing arrangement by the Commissioner in published guidance of general applicability or in guidance directed to participants in specific arrangements.

(b) *Requirement to file return.*—(1) *In general.*— Institutions may elect to report either the information described in paragraph (b)(2) of this section, or the information described in paragraph (b)(3) of this section. Once an institution elects to report under either paragraph (b)(2) or (3) of this section, the institution must use the same reporting method for all calendar years in which it is required to file returns, unless permission is granted to change reporting methods. Paragraph (b)(2) of this section requires institutions to report, among other information, the amount of payments received during the calendar year for qualified tuition and related expenses. Institutions must report separately adjustments made during the calendar year that relate to payments received for qualified tuition and related expenses that were reported for a prior calendar year. For purposes of paragraph (b)(2) of this section, an adjustment made to payments received means a reimbursement or refund. Paragraph (b)(3) requires institutions to report, among other information, the amounts billed during the calendar year for qualified tuition and related expenses. Institutions must report separately adjustments made during the calendar year that relate to amounts billed for qualified tuition and related expenses that were reported for a prior calendar year. For purposes of paragraph (b)(3) of this section, an adjustment made to amounts billed means a reduction in charges. Insurers must report the information described in paragraph (b)(4) of this section.

(2) *Information reporting requirements for institutions that elect to report payments received for qualified tuition and related expenses.*—(i) *In general.*—Except as provided in paragraph (a)(2) of this section, an institution reporting payments received for qualified tuition and related expenses must file an information return with the IRS on Form 1098-T, "Tuition Statement," with respect to each individual enrolled (as determined in paragraph (d)(1) of this section) for an academic period beginning during the calendar year or during a prior calendar year and for whom a transaction described in paragraphs (b)(2)(ii)(C), (E), (F) or (G) of this section is made during the calendar year. An institution may use a substitute Form 1098-T if the substitute form complies with applicable revenue procedures relating to substitute forms (see § 601.601(d)(2) of this chapter).

(ii) *Information included on return.*—An institution reporting payments received for qualified tuition and related expenses must include on Form 1098-T—

(A) The name, address, and taxpayer identification number (TIN) (as defined in section 7701(a)(41)) of the institution;

(B) The name, address, and TIN of the individual who is, or has been, enrolled by the institution;

(C) The amount of payments of qualified tuition and related expenses that the institution received from any source with respect to the individual during the calendar year;

(D) An indication by the institution whether any payments received for qualified tuition and related expenses reported for the calendar year relate to an academic period that begins during the first three months of the next calendar year;

(E) The amount of any scholarships or grants for the payment of the individual's costs of attendance that the institution administered and processed during the calendar year;

(F) The amount of any reimbursements or refunds of qualified tuition and related expenses made during the calendar year with respect to the individual that relate to payments of qualified tuition and related expenses that were reported by the institution for a prior calendar year;

(G) The amount of any reductions to the amount of scholarships or grants for the payment of the individual's costs of attendance that were reported by the institution with respect to the individual for a prior calendar year;

(H) A statement or other indication showing whether the individual was enrolled for at least half of the normal full-time work load for the course of study the individual is pursuing for at least one academic period that begins during the calendar year (see section 25A and the regulations thereunder);

(I) A statement or other indication showing whether the individual was enrolled in a program leading to a graduate-level degree, graduate-level certificate, or other recognized graduate-level educational credential; and

(J) Any other information required by Form 1098-T and its instructions.

(iii) *Reportable amount of payments received for qualified tuition and related expenses during calendar year determined.*—The amount of payments received for qualified tuition and related expenses with respect to an individual during the calendar year that is reportable on Form 1098-T is determined by netting the amount of payments received (as defined in paragraph (b)(2)(v) of this section) for qualified tuition and related expenses during the calendar year against any reimbursements or refunds (as defined in paragraph (b)(2)(vi) of this section) made during the calendar year that relate to payments received for qualified tuition and related expenses during the same calendar year.

(iv) *Separate reporting of reimbursements or refunds of payments of qualified tuition and related expenses that were reported for a prior calendar year.*—An institution must separately report on Form 1098-T any reimbursements or refunds (as defined in paragraph (b)(2)(vi) of this section) made during the current calendar year that relate to payments of qualified tuition and related expenses that were reported by the institution for a prior calendar year. Such reimbursements or refunds shall not be netted against the payments received for qualified tuition and related expenses during the current calendar year.

(v) *Payments received for qualified tuition and related expenses determined.*—For purposes of determining the amount of payments received for qualified tuition and related expenses during a calendar year, payments received with respect to an individual during the calendar year from any source (except for any scholarship or grant that, by its terms, must be applied to expenses other than qualified tuition and related expenses, such as room and board) are treated as payments of qualified tuition and related expenses up to the total amount billed by the institution for such expenses. For purposes of this section, a payment includes any positive account balance (such as any reimbursement or refund credited to an individual's account) that an institution applies toward current charges.

(vi) *Reimbursements or refunds of payments for qualified tuition and related expenses determined.*—For purposes of determining the amount of reimbursements or refunds made of payments received for qualified tuition and related expenses, any reimbursement or refund made with respect to an individual during a calendar year (except for any refund of a scholarship or grant that, by its terms, was required to be applied to expenses other than qualified tuition and related expenses, such as room and board) is treated as a reimbursement or refund of payments for qualified tuition and related expenses up to the amount of any reduction in charges for such expenses. For purposes of this section, a reimbursement or refund includes amounts that an institution credits to an individual's account, as well as amounts disbursed to, or on behalf of, the individual.

(vii) *Examples.*—The following examples illustrate the rules in this paragraph (b)(2):

Example 1. (i) In early August 2003, University X bills enrolled Student A $10,000 for qualified tuition and related expenses and $6,000 for room and board for the 2003 Fall semester. In late August 2003, Student A pays $11,000 to University X. In early September 2003, Student A drops to half-time enrollment for the 2003 Fall semester. In late September 2003, University X credits $5,000 to Student A's account, reflecting a $5,000 reduction in charges for qualified tuition and related expenses. In late September 2003, University X applies the $5,000 positive account balance toward current charges.

(ii) Under paragraph (b)(2)(v) of this section, the $11,000 payment is treated as a payment of qualified tuition and related expenses up to the $10,000 billed for qualified tuition and related expenses. Under paragraph (b)(2)(vi) of this section, the $5,000 credited to the student's account is treated as a reimbursement or refund of payments for qualified tuition and related expenses, because the current year charges for qualified tuition and related expenses were reduced by $5,000. Under paragraph (b)(2)(iii) of this section, University X is required to net the $10,000 payment received for qualified tuition and related expenses during 2003 against the $5,000 reimbursement or refund of payments received for qualified tuition and related expenses during 2003. Therefore, Institution X is required to report $5,000 of payments received for qualified tuition and related expenses during 2003.

Example 2. (i) The facts are the same as in *Example 1*, except that Student A pays the full $16,000 in late August 2003. In late September 2003, University X reduces the tuition charges by $5,000 and issues a $5,000 refund to Student A.

(ii) Under paragraph (b)(2)(v) of this section, the $16,000 payment is treated as a payment of qualified tuition and related expenses up to the $10,000 billed for qualified tuition and related expenses. Under paragraph (b)(2)(vi) of this section, the $5,000 refund is treated as reimbursement or refund of payments for qualified tuition and related expenses, because the current year charges for qualified tuition and related expenses were reduced by $5,000. Under paragraph (b)(2)(iii) of this section, University X is required to net the $10,000 payment received for qualified tuition and related expenses during 2003 against the $5,000 reimbursement or refund of payments received for qualified tuition and related expenses during 2003. Therefore, Institution X is required to report $5,000 of payments received for qualified tuition and related expenses during 2003.

Example 3. (i) The facts are the same as in *Example 1*, except that Student A is enrolled full-time, and, in early September 2003, Student A decides to live at home with her parents. In late September 2003, University X adjusts Student A's account to eliminate room and board charges and issues a $1,000 refund to Student A.

(ii) Under paragraph (b)(2)(v) of this section, the $11,000 payment is treated as a payment of qualified tuition and related expenses up to the $10,000 billed for qualified tuition and related expenses. Under paragraph (b)(2)(vi) of this section, the $1,000 refund is not treated as reimbursement or refund of payments for qualified tuition and related expenses, because there is no reduction in charges for qualified tuition and related expenses. Therefore, under paragraph (b)(2)(iii) of this section, University X is required to report $10,000 of payments received for qualified tuition and related expenses during 2003.

Example 4. (i) In early December 2003, College Y bills enrolled Student B $10,000 for qualified tuition and related expenses and $6,000 for room and board for the 2004 Spring semester. In late December 2003, Student B pays $16,000. In mid-January 2004, after the 2004 Spring semester classes begin, Student B drops to half-time enrollment. In mid-January 2004, College Y credits Student B's account with $5,000, reflecting a $5,000 reduction in charges for qualified tuition and related expenses, but does not issue a refund to Student B. In early August 2004, College Y bills Student B $10,000 for qualified tuition and related expenses and $6,000 for room and board for the 2004 Fall semester. In early September 2004, College Y applies the $5,000 positive account balance toward Student B's $16,000 bill for the 2004 Fall semester. In late September 2004, Student B pays $6,000 towards the charges.

(ii) In the reporting for calendar year 2003, under paragraph (b)(2)(v) of this section, the $16,000 payment in December 2003 is treated as a payment of qualified tuition and related expenses up to the $10,000 billed for qualified tuition and related expenses. Under paragraph (b)(2)(iii) of this section, College Y is required to report $10,000 of payments received for qualified tuition and related expenses during 2003. In addition, College Y is required to indicate that the payments reported for 2003 relate to an academic period that begins during the first three months of the next calendar year.

(iii) In the reporting for calendar year 2004, under paragraph (b)(2)(vi) of this section, the $5,000 credited to Student B's account is treated as a reimbursement or refund of qualified tuition and related expenses, because the charges for qualified tuition and related expenses were reduced by $5,000. Under paragraph (b)(2)(iv) of this section, the $5,000 reimbursement or refund of qualified tuition and related expenses must be separately reported on Form 1098-T because it relates to payments of qualified tuition and related expenses reported by College Y for 2003. Under paragraph (b)(2)(v) of this section, the $5,000 positive account balance that is applied toward charges for the 2004 Fall semester is treated as a payment. Therefore, College Y received total payments of $11,000 during 2004 (the $5,000 credit plus the $6,000 payment). Under paragraph (b)(2)(v) of this section, the $11,000 of total payments are treated as a payment of qualified tuition and related expenses up to the $10,000 billed for such expenses. Therefore, for 2004, College Y is required to report $10,000 of payments received for qualified tuition and related expenses during 2004 and a $5,000 refund of payments of qualified tuition and related expenses reported for 2003.

(3) *Information reporting requirements for institutions that elect to report amounts billed for qualified tuition and related expenses.*—(i) *In general.*— Except as provided in paragraph (a)(2) of this section, an institution reporting amounts billed for qualified tuition and related expenses must file an information return on Form 1098-T with respect to each individual enrolled (as determined in paragraph (d)(1) of this section) for an academic period beginning during the calendar year or during a prior calendar year and for whom a transaction described in paragraphs (b)(3)(ii)(C), (E), (F) or (G) of this section is made during the calendar year. An institution may use a substitute Form 1098-T if the substitute form complies with applicable revenue procedures relating to substitute forms (see § 601.601(d)(2) of this chapter).

(ii) *Information included on return.*—An institution reporting amounts billed for qualified tuition and related expenses must include on Form 1098-T—

(A) The name, address, and taxpayer identification number (TIN) (as defined in section 7701(a)(41)) of the institution;

(B) The name, address, and TIN of the individual who is, or has been, enrolled by the institution;

(C) The amount billed for qualified tuition and related expenses with respect to the individual during the calendar year;

(D) An indication by the institution whether any amounts billed for qualified tuition and related expenses reported for the calendar year relate to an academic period that begins during the first three months of the next calendar year;

(E) The amount of any scholarships or grants for the payment of the individual's costs of attendance that the institution administered and processed during the calendar year;

(F) The amount of any reductions in charges made during the calendar year with respect to the individual that relate to amounts billed for qualified tuition and related expenses that were reported by the institution for a prior calendar year;

(G) The amount of any reductions to the amount of scholarships or grants for the payment of the individual's costs of attendance that were reported by the institution with respect to the individual for a prior calendar year;

(H) A statement or other indication showing whether the individual was enrolled for at least half of the normal full-time work load for the course of study the individual is pursuing for at least one academic period that begins during the calendar year (see section 25A and the regulations thereunder);

(I) A statement or other indication showing whether the individual was enrolled in a program leading to a graduate-level degree, graduate-level certificate, or other recognized graduate-level educational credential; and

(J) Any other information required by Form 1098-T and its instructions.

(iii) *Reportable amounts billed for qualified tuition and related expenses during calendar year determined.*—The amount billed for qualified tuition and related expenses with respect to an individual during the calendar year that is reportable on Form 1098-T is determined by netting the amounts billed for qualified tuition and related expenses during the calendar year against any reductions in charges for qualified tuition and related expenses made during the calendar year that relate to amounts billed for qualified tuition and related expenses during the same calendar year.

(iv) *Separate reporting of reductions made to amounts billed for qualified tuition and related expenses that were reported for a prior calendar year.*— An institution must separately report on Form 1098-T any reductions in charges made during the current calendar year that relate to amounts billed for qualified tuition and related expenses that were reported by the institution for a prior calendar year. Such reductions shall not be netted against amounts billed for qualified tuition and related expenses during the current calendar year.

(v) *Examples.*—The following examples illustrate the rules in this paragraph (b)(3):

Example 1. (i) In early August 2003, University X bills enrolled Student A $10,000 for qualified tuition and related expenses and $6,000 for room and board for the 2003 Fall semester. In late August 2003, Student A pays $11,000 to University X. In early September 2003, Student A drops to half-time enrollment for the 2003 Fall semester. In late September 2003, University X adjusts Student A's account and reduces the charges for qualified tuition and related expenses by $5,000 to reflect half-time enrollment. In late September 2003, University X applies the $5,000 account balance toward current charges.

(ii) Under paragraph (b)(3)(iii) of this section, University X is required to net the $10,000 amount of qualified tuition and related expenses billed during 2003 against the $5,000 reduction in charges for qualified tuition and related expenses during 2003. Therefore, Institution X is required to report $5,000 in amounts billed for qualified tuition and related expenses during 2003.

Example 2. (i) The facts are the same as in *Example 1,* except that, in addition, in early December 2003, College X bills Student A $10,000 for qualified tuition and related expenses and $6,000 for room and board for the 2004 Spring semester. In early January 2004, Student A pays $16,000. In mid-January 2004, after the 2004

Spring semester classes begin, Student A drops to half-time enrollment. In mid-January 2004, College X credits $5,000 to Student A's account, reflecting a $5,000 reduction in charges for qualified tuition and related expenses, but does not issue a refund check to Student A. In early August 2004, College X bills Student A $10,000 for qualified tuition and related expenses and $6,000 for room and board for the 2004 Fall semester. In early September 2004, College X applies the $5,000 positive account balance toward Student A's $16,000 bill for the 2004 Fall semester. In late September 2004, Student A pays $6,000 toward the charges.

(ii) In the reporting for calendar year 2003, under paragraph (b)(3)(iii) of this section, College X is required to report $15,000 amounts billed for qualified tuition and related expenses during 2003 ($5,000 for the 2003 Fall semester and $10,000 for the 2004 Spring semester). In addition, College X is required to indicate that some of the amounts billed for qualified tuition and related expenses reported for 2003 relate to an academic period that begins during the first three months of the next calendar year.

(iii) In the reporting for calendar year 2004, under paragraph (b)(3)(iv) of this section, the $5,000 reduction in charges for qualified tuition and related expenses must be separately reported on Form 1098-T because it relates to amounts billed for qualified tuition and related expenses that were reported by College X for 2003. Under paragraph (b)(3)(iii) of this section, College X is required to report $10,000 in amounts billed for qualified tuition and related expenses during 2004.

(4) *Requirements for insurers.*—(i) *In general.*—Except as otherwise provided in this section, an insurer must file an information return for each individual with respect to whom reimbursements or refunds of qualified tuition and related expenses are made during the calendar year on Form 1098-T. An insurer may use a substitute Form 1098-T if the substitute form complies with applicable revenue procedures relating to substitute forms (see §601.601(d)(2) of this chapter).

(ii) *Information included on return.*—An insurer must include on Form 1098-T—

(A) The name, address, and taxpayer identification number (TIN) (as defined in section 7701(a)(41)) of the insurer;

(B) The name, address, and TIN of the individual with respect to whom reimbursements or refunds of qualified tuition and related expenses were made;

(C) The aggregate amount of reimbursements or refunds of qualified tuition and related expenses that the insurer made with respect to the individual during the calendar year; and

(D) Any other information required by Form 1098-T and its instructions.

(5) *Time and place for filing return.*—(i) *In general.*—Except as provided in paragraphs (b)(5)(ii) and (iii) of this section, Form 1098-T must be filed on or before February 28 (March 31 if filed electronically) of the year following the calendar year in which payments were received, or amounts were billed, for qualified tuition or related expenses, or reimbursements, refunds, or reductions of such amounts were made. An institution or insurer must file Form 1098-T with the IRS according to the instructions to Form 1098-T.

(ii) *Return for nonresident alien individual.*—In general, an institution or insurer is not required to file a return on behalf of a nonresident alien individual. However, if a nonresident alien individual requests an institution or insurer to report, the institution or insurer must file a return described in paragraph (b) of this section with the IRS on or before the date prescribed in paragraph (b)(5)(i) of this section, or on or before the thirtieth day after the request, whichever is later.

(iii) *Extensions of time.*—The IRS may grant an institution or insurer an extension of time to file returns required in this section upon a showing of good cause. See General Instructions for Forms 1099 series, 1098 series, 5498 series, and W-2G, "Certain Gambling Winnings," and applicable revenue procedures for rules relating to extensions of time to file (see §601.601(d)(2) of this chapter).

(6) *Use of magnetic media.*—See section 6011(e) and §301.6011-2 of this chapter for rules relating to the requirement to file Forms 1098-T on magnetic media.

(c) *Requirement to furnish statement.*—(1) *In general.*—An institution or insurer must furnish a statement to each individual for whom it is required to file a Form 1098-T. The statement must include—

(i) The information required under paragraph (b) of this section. An IRS truncated taxpayer identifying number (TTIN) may be used as the TIN of the individual in lieu of the identifying number appearing on the information return filed with the Internal Revenue Service. For provisions relating to the use of TTINs, see §301.6109-4 of this chapter (Procedure and Administration Regulations);

(ii) A legend that identifies the statement as important tax information that is being furnished to the IRS;

(iii) Instructions that—

(A) State that the statement reports either total payments received by the institution for qualified tuition and related expenses during the calendar year, or total amounts billed by the institution for qualified tuition and related expenses during the calendar year, or the total reimbursements or refunds made by the insurer;

(B) State that, under section 25A and the regulations thereunder, the taxpayer may claim an education tax credit only with respect to qualified tuition and related expenses actually paid during the calendar year; and that the taxpayer may not be able to claim an education tax credit with respect to the entire amount of payments received, or amounts billed, for qualified tuition and related expenses reported for the calendar year;

(C) State that the amount of any scholarships or grants reported for the calendar year and other similar amounts not reported (because they are not administered and processed by the institution) may reduce the amount of any allowable education tax credit for the taxable year;

(D) State that the amount of any reimbursements or refunds of payments received, or reductions in charges, for qualified tuition and related expenses, or any reductions to the amount of scholarships or grants, reported by the institution with respect to the individual for a prior calendar year may affect the amount of any allowable education tax credit for the prior calendar year (and may result in an increase in tax liability for the year of the refund);

(E) State that the amount of any reimbursements or refunds of qualified tuition and related expenses reported by an insurer may reduce the amount of an allowable education tax credit for a taxable year (and may result in an increase in tax liability for the year of the refund);

(F) State that the taxpayer should refer to relevant IRS forms and publications, and should not refer to the institution or the insurer, for explanations relating to the eligibility requirements for, and calculation of, any allowable education tax credit; and

(G) Include the name, address, and phone number of the information contact of the institution or insurer that filed the Form 1098-T.

(2) *Time and manner for furnishing statement.*—(i) *In general.*—Except as provided in paragraphs (c)(2)(ii) and (iii) of this section, an institution or insurer must furnish the statement described in paragraph (c)(1) of this section to each individual for whom it is required to file a return, on or before January 31 of the year following the calendar year in which payments were received, or amounts were billed, for qualified tuition and related expenses, or reimbursements, refunds, or reductions of such amounts were made. If mailed, the statement must be sent to the individual's permanent address, or the individual's temporary address if the institution or insurer does not know the individual's permanent address. If furnished electronically, the statement must be furnished in accordance with the applicable regulations.

(ii) *Statement to nonresident alien individual.*—If an information return is filed for a nonresident alien individual, the institution or insurer must furnish a statement described in paragraph (c)(1) of this section to the individual in the manner prescribed in paragraph (c)(2)(i) of this section. The statement must be furnished on or before the later of the date prescribed in paragraph (c)(2)(i) of this section or the thirtieth day after the nonresident alien's request to report.

(iii) *Extensions of time.*—The IRS may grant an institution or insurer an extension of time to furnish the statements required in this section upon a showing of good cause. See General Instructions for Forms 1099 series, 1098 series, 5498 series, and W-2G, "Certain Gambling Winnings," and applicable revenue procedures for rules relating to extensions of time to furnish statements (see § 601.601(d)(2) of this chapter).

(3) *Copy of Form 1098-T.*—An institution or insurer may satisfy the requirement of this paragraph (c) by furnishing either a copy of Form 1098-T and its instructions or another document that contains all of the information filed with the IRS and the information required by paragraph (c)(1) of this section if the document complies with applicable revenue procedures relating to substitute statements (see § 601.601(d)(2) of this chapter).

(d) *Special rules.*—(1) *Enrollment determined.*—An institution may determine its enrollment for each academic period under its own rules and policies for determining enrollment or as of any of the following dates—

(i) 30 days after the first day of the academic period;

(ii) A date during the academic period on which enrollment data must be collected for purposes of the Integrated Post Secondary Education Data System administered by the Department of Education; or

(iii) A date during the academic period on which the institution must report enrollment data to the State, the institution's governing body, or some other external governing body.

(2) *Payments of qualified tuition and related expenses received or collected by one or more persons.*—(i) *In general.*—Except as otherwise provided in paragraph (d)(2)(ii) of this section, if a person collects or receives payments of qualified tuition and related expenses on behalf of another person (e.g., an institution), the person collecting or receiving payments must satisfy the requirements of paragraphs (b) and (c) of this section. In this case, those requirements do not apply to the transfer of the payments to the institution.

(ii) *Exception.*—If the person collecting or receiving payments of qualified tuition and related expenses on behalf of another person (e.g., an institution) does not possess the information needed to comply with the requirements of paragraphs (b) and (c) of this section, the other person must satisfy those requirements.

(3) *Governmental units.*—An institution or insurer that is a governmental unit, or an agency or instrumentality of a governmental unit, is subject to the requirements of paragraphs (b) and (c) of this section and an appropriately designated officer or employee of the governmental entity must satisfy those requirements.

(e) *Penalty provisions.*—(1) *Failure to file correct returns.*—The section 6721 penalty may apply to an institution or insurer that fails to file information returns required by section 6050S and this section on or before the required filing date; that fails to include all of the required information on the return; or that includes incorrect information on the return. See section 6721, and the regulations thereunder, for rules relating to penalties for failure to file correct returns. See section 6724, and the regulations thereunder, for rules relating to waivers of penalties for certain failures due to reasonable cause.

(2) *Failure to furnish correct information statements.*—The section 6722 penalty may apply to an institution or insurer that fails to furnish statements required by section 6050S and this section on or before the prescribed date; that fails to include all the required information on the statement; or that includes incorrect information on the statement. See section 6722, and the regulations thereunder, for rules relating to penalties for failure to furnish correct statements. See section 6724, and the regulations thereunder, for rules relating to waivers of penalties for certain failures due to reasonable cause.

(3) *Waiver of penalties for failures to include a correct TIN.*—(i) *In general.*—In the case of a failure to include a correct TIN on Form 1098-T or a related information statement, penalties may be waived if the failure is due to reasonable cause. Reasonable cause may be established if the failure arose from events beyond the institution's or insurer's control, such as a failure of the individual to furnish a correct TIN. However, the institution or insurer must establish that it acted in a responsible manner both before and after the failure.

(ii) *Acting in a responsible manner.*—An institution or insurer must request the TIN of each individual for whom it is required to file a return if it does not already have a record of the individual's correct TIN. If the institution or insurer does not have a record of the individual's correct TIN, then it must solicit the TIN in the manner described in paragraph (e)(3)(iii) of this section on or before December 31 of each year during which it receives payments, or bills amounts, for qualified tuition and related expenses or makes reimbursements, refunds, or reductions of such amounts with respect to the individual. If an individual refuses to provide his or her TIN upon request, the institution or insurer must file the return and furnish the statement required by this section without the individual's TIN, but with all other required information. The specific solicitation requirements of paragraph (e)(3)(iii) of this section apply in lieu of the solicitation requirements of §301.6724-1(e) and (f) of this chapter for the purpose of determining whether an institution or insurer acted in a responsible manner in attempting to obtain a correct TIN. An institution or insurer that complies with the requirements of this paragraph (e)(3) will be considered to have acted in a responsible manner within the meaning of §301.6724-1(d) of this chapter with respect to any failure to include the correct TIN of an individual on a return or statement required by section 6050S and this section.

(iii) *Manner of soliciting TIN.*—An institution or insurer must request the individual's TIN in writing and must clearly notify the individual that the law requires the individual to furnish a TIN so that it may be included on an information return filed by the institution or insurer. A request for a TIN made on Form W-9S, "Request for Student's or Borrower's Taxpayer Identification Number and Certification," satisfies the requirements of this paragraph (e)(3)(iii). An institution or insurer may establish a system for individuals to submit Forms W-9S electronically as described in applicable forms and instructions. An institution or insurer may also develop a separate form to request the individual's TIN or incorporate the request into other forms customarily used by the institution or insurer, such as admission or enrollment forms or financial aid applications.

(4) *Failure to furnish TIN.*—The section 6723 penalty may apply to any individual who is required (but fails) to furnish his or her TIN to an institution or insurer. See section 6723, and the regulations thereunder, for rules relating to the penalty for failure to furnish a TIN.

(f) *Effective/applicability date.*—The rules in this section apply to information returns required to be filed, and information statements required to be furnished, after December 31, 2003. Paragraph (c)(1)(i) applies to payee statements due after December 31, 2014. For payee statements due before January 1, 2015, §1.6050S-1 (as contained in 26 CFR part 1, revised April 2013) shall apply. [Reg. §1.6050S-1.]

☐ [*T.D.* 9029, 12-18-2002 (*corrected* 2-6-2003). *Amended by T.D.* 9675, 7-14-2014.]

[Reg. §1.6050S-2]

§1.6050S-2. Information reporting for payments and reimbursements or refunds of qualified tuition and related expenses.— (a) *Electronic furnishing of statements.*—(1) *In general.*—A person required by section 6050S(d) to furnish a written statement regarding payments and reimbursements or refunds of qualified tuition and related expenses (furnisher) to the individual to whom it is required to be furnished (recipient) may furnish the statement in an electronic format in lieu of a paper format. A furnisher who meets the requirements of paragraphs (a)(2) through (6) of this section is treated as furnishing the required statement.

(2) *Consent.*—(i) *In general.*—The recipient must have affirmatively consented to receive the statement in an electronic format. The consent may be made electronically in any manner that reasonably demonstrates that the recipient can access the statement in the electronic format in which it will be furnished to the recipient. Alternatively, the consent may be made in a paper document if it is confirmed electronically.

(ii) *Withdrawal of consent.*—The consent requirement of this paragraph (a)(2) is not satisfied if the recipient withdraws the consent and the withdrawal takes effect before the statement is furnished. The furnisher may provide that a withdrawal of consent takes effect either on the date it is received by the furnisher or on a subsequent date. The furnisher may also provide that a request for a paper statement will be treated as a withdrawal of consent.

(iii) *Change in hardware or software requirements.*—If a change in the hardware or software required to access the statement creates a material risk that the recipient will not be able to access the statement, the furnisher must, prior to changing the hardware or software, provide the recipient with a notice. The notice must describe the revised hardware and software required to access the statement and inform the recipient that a new consent to receive the statement in the revised electronic format must be provided to the furnisher. After implementing the revised hardware and software, the furnisher must obtain from the recipient, in the manner described in paragraph (a)(2)(i) of this section, a new consent or confirmation of consent to receive the statement electronically.

(iv) *Examples.*—The following examples illustrate the rules of this paragraph (a)(2):

Example 1. Furnisher F sends Recipient R a letter stating that R may consent to receive statements required by section 6050S(d) electronically on a website instead of in a paper format. The letter contains instructions explaining how to consent to receive the statements electronically by accessing the website, downloading the consent document, completing the consent document and emailing the completed consent back to F. The consent document posted on the website uses the same electronic format that F will use for the electronically furnished statements. R reads the instructions and submits the consent in the manner provided in the instructions. R has consented to receive the statements electronically in the manner described in paragraph (a)(2)(i) of this section.

Example 2. Furnisher F sends Recipient R an e-mail stating that R may consent to receive statements required by section 6050S(d) electronically instead of in a paper format. The e-mail contains an attachment instructing R how to consent to receive the statements electronically. The e-mail attachment uses the same electronic format that F will use for the electronically furnished statements. R opens the attachment, reads the instructions, and submits the consent in the manner provided in the instructions. R has consented to receive the statements electronically in the manner described in paragraph (a)(2)(i) of this section.

Example 3. Furnisher F posts a notice on its website stating that Recipient R may receive statements required by section 6050S(d) electronically instead of in a paper format. The website contains instructions on how R may access a secure webpage and consent to receive the statements electronically. By accessing the secure webpage and giving consent, R has consented to receive the statements electronically in the man-

ner described in paragraph (a)(2)(i) of this section.

(3) *Required disclosures.*—(i) *In general.*—Prior to, or at the time of, a recipient's consent, the furnisher must provide to the recipient a clear and conspicuous disclosure statement containing each of the disclosures described in paragraphs (a)(3)(ii) through (viii) of this section.

(ii) *Paper statement.*—The recipient must be informed that the statement will be furnished on paper if the recipient does not consent to receive it electronically. ·

(iii) *Scope and duration of consent.*—The recipient must be informed of the scope and duration of the consent. For example, the recipient must be informed whether the consent applies to statements furnished every year after the consent is given until it is withdrawn in the manner described in paragraph (a)(3)(v)(A) of this section or only to the statement required to be furnished on or before the January 31 immediately following the date on which the consent is given.

(iv) *Post-consent request for a paper statement.*—The recipient must be informed of any procedure for obtaining a paper copy of the recipient's statement after giving the consent described in paragraph (a)(2)(i) of this section and whether a request for a paper statement will be treated as a withdrawal of consent.

(v) *Withdrawal of consent.*—The recipient must be informed that—

(A) The recipient may withdraw a consent by writing (electronically or on paper) to the person or department whose name, mailing address, telephone number, and e-mail address is provided in the disclosure statement;

(B) The furnisher will confirm the withdrawal and the date on which it takes effect in writing (either electronically or on paper); and

(C) A withdrawal of consent does not apply to a statement that was furnished electronically in the manner described in this paragraph (a) before the date on which the withdrawal of consent takes effect.

(vi) *Notice of termination.*—The recipient must be informed of the conditions under which a furnisher will cease furnishing statements electronically to the recipient.

(vii) *Updating information.*—The recipient must be informed of the procedures for updating the information needed by the furnisher to contact the recipient. The furnisher must inform the recipient of any change in the furnisher's contact information.

(viii) *Hardware and software requirements.*—The recipient must be provided with a description of the hardware and software required to access, print, and retain the statement, and the date when the statement will no longer be available on the website.

(4) *Format.*—The electronic version of the statement must contain all required information

and comply with applicable revenue procedures relating to substitute statements to recipients.

(5) *Notice.*—(i) *In general.*—If the statement is furnished on a website, the furnisher must notify the recipient that the statement is posted on a website. The notice may be delivered by mail, electronic mail, or in person. The notice must provide instructions on how to access and print the statement. The notice must include the following statement in capital letters, "IMPORTANT TAX RETURN DOCUMENT AVAILABLE." If the notice is provided by electronic mail, the foregoing statement must be on the subject line of the electronic mail.

(ii) *Undeliverable electronic address.*—If an electronic notice described in paragraph (a)(5)(i) of this section is returned as undeliverable, and the correct electronic address cannot be obtained from the furnisher's records or from the recipient, then the furnisher must furnish the notice by mail or in person within 30 days after the electronic notice is returned.

(iii) *Corrected statements.*—If the furnisher has corrected a recipient's statement that was furnished electronically, the furnisher must furnish the corrected statement to the recipient electronically. If the recipient's statement was furnished through a website posting and the furnisher has corrected the statement, the furnisher must notify the recipient that it has posted the corrected statement on the website within 30 days of such posting in the manner described in paragraph (a)(5)(i) of this section. The corrected statement or the notice must be furnished by mail or in person if—

(A) An electronic notice of the website posting of an original statement was returned as undeliverable; and

(B) The recipient has not provided a new e-mail address.

(6) *Access Period.*—Statements furnished on a website must be retained on the website through October 15 of the year following the calendar year to which the statements relate (or the first business day after such October 15, if October 15 falls on a Saturday, Sunday, or legal holiday). The furnisher must maintain access to corrected statements that are posted on the website through October 15 of the year following the calendar year to which the statements relate (or the first business day after such October 15, if October 15 falls on a Saturday, Sunday, or legal holiday) or the date 90 days after the corrected statements are posted, whichever is later.

(b) *Paper statements after withdrawal of consent.*—If a recipient withdraws consent to receive a statement electronically and the withdrawal takes effect before the statement is furnished electronically, a paper statement must be furnished. A paper statement furnished after the statement due date under this paragraph (b) will be considered timely if furnished within 30 days after the date the withdrawal of consent is received by the furnisher.

(c) *Effective date.*—This section applies to statements required to be furnished after February 13, 2004. Paragraph (a)(6) of this section also applies to statements required to be furnished after December 31, 2003. [Reg. § 1.6050S-2.]

☐ [T.D. 9114, 2-13-2004.]

[Reg. § 1.6050S-3]

§ 1.6050S-3. Information reporting for payments of interest on qualified education loans.—(a) *Information reporting requirement in general.*—Except as otherwise provided in this section, any person engaged in a trade or business that, in the course of that trade or business, receives from any payor (as defined in paragraph (b)(2) of this section) interest payments that aggregate $600 or more for any calendar year on one or more qualified education loans (as defined in section 221(e)(1) and the regulations thereunder)(a payee) must—

(1) File an information return, as described in paragraph (c) of this section, with the Internal Revenue Service with respect to the payor; and

(2) Furnish a statement, as described in paragraph (d) of this section, to the payor.

(b) *Definitions.*—The following definitions apply for purposes of this section:

(1) *Interest.*—Interest includes stated interest, loan origination fees (other than fees for services), and capitalized interest as described in the regulations under section 221. See paragraph (e)(1) of this section for a special transitional rule relating to reporting of loan origination fees and capitalized interest.

(2) *Payor.*—Payor means the individual who is carried on the books and records of the payee as the borrower on a qualified education loan. If there are multiple borrowers, the principal borrower on the payee's books and records is treated as the payor for purposes of section 6050S and this section.

(c) *Requirement to file return.*—(1) *Form of return.*—A payee must file an information return for the payor on Form 1098-E, "Student Loan Interest Statement." A payee may use a substitute for Form 1098-E if the substitute form complies with the applicable revenue procedures relating to substitute forms.

(2) *Information included on return.*—A payee must include on Form 1098-E—

(i) The name, address, and taxpayer identification number (TIN)(as defined in section 7701(a)(41)) of the payee;

(ii) The name, address, and TIN of the payor;

(iii) The aggregate amount of interest payments received during the calendar year from the payor; and

(iv) Any other information required by Form 1098-E and its instructions.

(3) *Time and place for filing return.*—(i) *In general.*—Except as provided in paragraph (c)(3)(ii) of this section, the Form 1098-E must be

filed on or before February 28 (March 31 if filed electronically) of the year following the calendar year in which interest payments were received. A payee must file Form 1098-E with the Internal Revenue Service according to the instructions to Form 1098-E.

(ii) *Extensions of time.*—The Internal Revenue Service may grant a payee an extension of time to file returns required in this section upon a showing of good cause. See the instructions to Form 1098-E and applicable revenue procedures for rules relating to extensions of time to file.

(4) *Use of magnetic media.*—See section 6011(e) and §301.6011-2 of this chapter for rules relating to the requirement to file Forms 1098-E on magnetic media.

(d) *Requirement to furnish statement.*—(1) *In general.*—A payee must furnish a statement to each payor for whom it is required to file a Form 1098-E. The statement must include—

(i) The information required under paragraph (c)(2) of this section. An IRS truncated taxpayer identifying number (TTIN) may be used as the TIN of the payor in lieu of the identifying number appearing on the information return filed with the Internal Revenue Service. For provisions relating to the use of TTINs, see §301.6109-4 of this chapter (Procedure and Administration Regulations).

(ii) A legend that identifies the statement as important tax information that is being furnished to the Internal Revenue Service;

(iii) Instructions that—

(A) State that, under section 221 and the regulations thereunder, the payor may not be able to deduct the full amount of interest reported on the statement;

(B) In the case of qualified education loans made before September 1, 2004, for which the payee does not report payments of interest other than stated interest, state that the payor may be able to deduct additional amounts (such as certain loan origination fees and capitalized interest) not reported on the statement;

(C) State that the payor should refer to relevant Internal Revenue Service forms and publications, and should not refer to the payee, for explanations relating to the eligibility requirements for, and calculation of, any allowable deduction for interest paid on a qualified education loan; and

(D) Include the name, address, and phone number of the office or department of the payee that is the information contact for the payee that filed the Form 1098-E.

(2) *Time and manner for furnishing statement.*—(i) *In general.*—Except as provided in paragraph (d)(2)(ii) of this section, a payee must furnish the statement described in paragraph (d)(1) of this section to the payor on or before January 31 of the year following the calendar year in which payments of interest on a qualified education loan were received. If mailed, the statement must be sent to the payor's last known

address. If furnished electronically, the statement must be furnished in accordance with the applicable regulations.

(ii) *Extensions of time.*—The Internal Revenue Service may grant a payee an extension of time to furnish statements required in this section upon a showing of good cause. See the instructions to Form 1098-E and applicable revenue procedures for rules relating to extensions of time to furnish statements.

(3) *Copy of Form 1098-E.*—A payee may satisfy the requirement of this paragraph (d) by furnishing either a copy of Form 1098-E and its instructions or another document that contains all the information filed with the Internal Revenue Service and the information required by paragraph (d)(1) of this section if the document complies with applicable revenue procedures relating to substitute statements.

(e) *Special rules.*—(1) *Transitional rule for reporting of loan origination fees and capitalized interest.*—(i) *Loans made before September 1, 2004.*—For qualified education loans made before September 1, 2004, a payee is not required to report payments of loan origination fees or capitalized interest or to take such payments into account in determining the $600 amount for purposes of paragraph (a)(1) of this section.

(ii) *Loans made on or after September 1, 2004.*—For qualified education loans made on or after September 1, 2004, a payee is required to report payments of interest as described in §1.221-1(f). Under §1.221-1(f), interest includes loan origination fees that represent charges for the use or forbearance of money and capitalized interest. Under this paragraph (e)(1)(ii), a payee shall take such payments of interest into account in determining the $600 amount for purposes of paragraph (a)(1) of this section. For purposes of this section and section 6050S, interest (including capitalized interest and loan origination fees) is treated as received, and is reportable, in the year the interest is treated as paid under the allocation rules in §1.221-1(f)(3). See §1.221-1(f) for rules relating to capitalized interest, and §1.221-1(f)(2)(ii) for rules relating to loan origination fees, on qualified education loans.

(2) *Qualified education loan certification.*—If a loan is not subsidized, guaranteed, financed, or is not otherwise treated as a student loan under a program of the Federal, state, or local government or an eligible educational institution, a payee must request a certification from the payor that the loan will be used solely to pay for qualified higher education expenses. A payee may use Form W-9S, "Request for Student's or Borrower's Social Security Number and Certification," to obtain the certification. A payee may establish an electronic system for payors to submit Forms W-9S electronically as described in applicable forms and instructions. A payee may also develop a separate form to obtain the payor certification or may incorporate the certification into other forms customarily used by the payee,

such as loan applications, provided the certification is clearly set forth. If the certification is not received, the loan is not a qualified education loan for purposes of section 6050S and this section.

(3) *Payments of interest received or collected by one or more persons.*—(i) *In general.*—Except as otherwise provided in paragraph (e)(3)(ii) of this section, if a person collects or receives payments of interest on a qualified education loan on behalf of another person (e.g., a lender), the person collecting or receiving the interest must satisfy the information reporting requirements of this section. In this case, the reporting requirements do not apply to the transfer of interest to the other person.

(ii) *Exception.*—If the person collecting or receiving payments of interest on a qualified education loan on behalf of another person (e.g., a lender) does not possess the information needed to comply with the information reporting requirements of this section, the other person must satisfy the information reporting requirements of this section.

(4) *Reporting by foreign persons.*—A payee that is not a United States person (as defined in section 7701(a)(30)) must report payments of interest it receives on a qualified education loan only if it receives the payment—

(i) At a location in the United States; or

(ii) At a location outside the United States if the payee is—

(A) A controlled foreign corporation (within the meaning of section 957(a)); or

(B) A person 50 percent or more of the gross income of which, from all sources for the three-year period ending with the close of the taxable year preceding the taxable year in which interest payments were received (or for such part of the period as the person was in existence), was effectively connected with the conduct of a trade or business within the United States.

(5) *Governmental units.*—A governmental unit, or an agency or instrumentality of a governmental unit, that receives from any payor interest payments that aggregate $600 or more for any calendar year on one or more qualified education loans is a payee, without regard to the requirement of paragraph (a) of this section that the interest be received in the course of a trade or business.

(f) *Penalty provisions.*—(1) *Failure to file correct returns.*—The section 6721 penalty may apply to a payee that fails to file information returns required by section 6050S and this section on or before the required filing date; that fails to include all of the required information on the return; or that includes incorrect information on the return. See section 6721, and the regulations thereunder, for rules relating to penalties for failure to file correct returns. See section 6724, and the regulations thereunder, for rules relating to waivers of penalties for certain failures due to reasonable cause.

(2) *Failure to furnish correct information statements.*—The section 6722 penalty may apply to a payee that fails to furnish statements required by section 6050S and this section on or before the prescribed date; that fails to include all the required information on the statement; or that includes incorrect information on the statement. See section 6722, and the regulations thereunder, for rules relating to penalties for failure to furnish correct statements. See section 6724, and the regulations thereunder, for rules relating to waivers of penalties for certain failures due to reasonable cause.

(3) *Waiver of penalties for failures to include a correct TIN.*—(i) *In general.*—In the case of a failure to include a correct TIN on Form 1098-E or a related information statement, penalties may be waived if the failure is due to reasonable cause. Reasonable cause may be established if the failure arose from events beyond the payee's control, such as a failure of the payor to furnish a correct TIN. However, the payee must establish that it acted in a responsible manner both before and after the failure.

(ii) *Acting in a responsible manner.*—A payee must request the TIN of each payor if it does not already have a record of the payor's correct TIN. If the payee does not have a record of the payor's correct TIN, then it must solicit the TIN in the manner described in paragraph (f)(3)(iii) of this section on or before December 31 of each year during which it receives payments of interest. If a payor refuses to provide his or her TIN upon request, the payee must file the return and furnish the statement required by this section without the payor's TIN, but with all other required information. The specific solicitation requirements of paragraph (f)(3)(iii) of this section apply in lieu of the solicitation requirements of § 301.6724-1(e) and (f) of this chapter for the purpose of determining whether a payee acted in a responsible manner in attempting to obtain a correct TIN. A payee that complies with the requirements of this paragraph (f)(3) will be considered to have acted in a responsible manner within the meaning of § 301.6724-1(d) of this chapter with respect to any failure to include the correct TIN of a payor on a return or statement required by section 6050S and this section.

(iii) *Manner of soliciting TIN.*—A payee must request the payor's TIN in writing and must clearly notify the payor that the law requires the payor to furnish a TIN so that it may be included on an information return filed by the payee. A request for a TIN made on Form W-9S, "Request for Student's or Borrower's Social Security Number and Certification," satisfies the requirements of this paragraph (f)(3)(iii). A payee may establish a system for payors to submit Forms W-9S electronically as described in applicable forms and instructions. A payee may also develop a separate form to request the payor's TIN or incorporate the request into other forms customarily used by the payee, such as loan applications.

(4) *Failure to furnish TIN.*—The section 6723 penalty may apply to any payor who is required (but fails) to furnish his or her TIN to a payee. See section 6723, and the regulations thereunder, for rules relating to the penalty for failure to furnish a TIN.

(g) *Effective/applicability date.*—The rules of this section apply to information returns required to be filed, and payee statements required to be furnished after December 31, 2014. For information returns required to be filed, and payee statements required to be furnished before January 1, 2015, § 1.6050S-3 (as contained in 26 CFR part 1, revised April 2013) shall apply. [Reg. § 1.6050S-3.]

☐ [*T.D.* 8992, 4-26-2002. *Amended by T.D.* 9125, 5-6-2004 *and T.D.* 9675, 7-14-2014.]

[Reg. § 1.6050S-4]

§ 1.6050S-4. Information reporting for payments of interest on qualified education loans.—(a) *Electronic furnishing of statements.*—(1) *In general.*—A person required by section 6050S(d) to furnish a written statement regarding payments of interest on qualified education loans (furnisher) to the individual to whom it is required to be furnished (recipient) may furnish the statement in an electronic format in lieu of a paper format. A furnisher who meets the requirements of paragraphs (a)(2) through (6) of this section is treated as furnishing the required statement.

(2) *Consent.*—(i) *In general.*—The recipient must have affirmatively consented to receive the statement in an electronic format. The consent may be made electronically in any manner that reasonably demonstrates that the recipient can access the statement in the electronic format in which it will be furnished to the recipient. Alternatively, the consent may be made in a paper document if it is confirmed electronically.

(ii) *Withdrawal of consent.*—The consent requirement of this paragraph (a)(2) is not satisfied if the recipient withdraws the consent and the withdrawal takes effect before the statement is furnished. The furnisher may provide that a withdrawal of consent takes effect either on the date it is received by the furnisher or on a subsequent date. The furnisher may also provide that a request for a paper statement will be treated as a withdrawal of consent.

(iii) *Change in hardware or software requirements.*—If a change in the hardware or software required to access the statement creates a material risk that the recipient will not be able to access the statement, the furnisher must, prior to changing the hardware or software, provide the recipient with a notice. The notice must describe the revised hardware and software required to access the statement and inform the recipient that a new consent to receive the statement in the revised electronic format must be provided to the furnisher. After implementing the revised hardware and software, the furnisher must obtain from the recipient, in the manner described

in paragraph (a)(2)(i) of this section, a new consent or confirmation of consent to receive the statement electronically.

(iv) *Examples.*—The following examples illustrate the rules of this paragraph (a)(2):

Example 1. Furnisher F sends Recipient R a letter stating that R may consent to receive statements required by section 6050S(d) electronically on a website instead of in a paper format. The letter contains instructions explaining how to consent to receive the statements electronically by accessing the website, downloading the consent document, completing the consent document and e-mailing the completed consent back to F. The consent document posted on the website uses the same electronic format that F will use for the electronically furnished statements. R reads the instructions and submits the consent in the manner provided in the instructions. R has consented to receive the statements electronically in the manner described in paragraph (a)(2)(i) of this section.

Example 2. Furnisher F sends Recipient R an e-mail stating that R may consent to receive statements required by section 6050S(d) electronically instead of in a paper format. The e-mail contains an attachment instructing R how to consent to receive the statements electronically. The e-mail attachment uses the same electronic format that F will use for the electronically furnished statements. R opens the attachment, reads the instructions, and submits the consent in the manner provided in the instructions. R has consented to receive the statements electronically in the manner described in paragraph (a)(2)(i) of this section.

Example 3. Furnisher F posts a notice on its website stating that Recipient R may receive statements required by section 6050S(d) electronically instead of in a paper format. The website contains instructions on how R may access a secure webpage and consent to receive the statements electronically. By accessing the secure webpage and giving consent, R has consented to receive the statements electronically in the manner described in paragraph (a)(2)(i) of this section.

(3) *Required disclosures.*—(i) *In general.*—Prior to, or at the time of, a recipient's consent, the furnisher must provide to the recipient a clear and conspicuous disclosure statement containing each of the disclosures described in paragraphs (a)(3)(ii) through (viii) of this section.

(ii) *Paper statement.*—The recipient must be informed that the statement will be furnished on paper if the recipient does not consent to receive it electronically.

(iii) *Scope and duration of consent.*—The recipient must be informed of the scope and duration of the consent. For example, the recipient must be informed whether the consent applies to statements furnished every year after the consent is given until it is withdrawn in the manner described in paragraph (a)(3)(v)(A) of this section or only to the statement required to be furnished on or before the January 31 immediately following the date on which the consent is given.

(iv) *Post-consent request for a paper statement.*—The recipient must be informed of any procedure for obtaining a paper copy of the recipient's statement after giving the consent described in paragraph (a)(2)(i) of this section and whether a request for a paper statement will be treated as a withdrawal of consent.

(v) *Withdrawal of consent.*—The recipient must be informed that—

(A) The recipient may withdraw a consent by writing (electronically or on paper) to the person or department whose name, mailing address, telephone number, and e-mail address is provided in the disclosure statement;

(B) The furnisher will confirm the withdrawal and the date on which it takes effect in writing (either electronically or on paper); and

(C) A withdrawal of consent does not apply to a statement that was furnished electronically in the manner described in this paragraph (a) before the date on which the withdrawal of consent takes effect.

(vi) *Notice of termination.*—The recipient must be informed of the conditions under which a furnisher will cease furnishing statements electronically to the recipient.

(vii) *Updating information.*—The recipient must be informed of the procedures for updating the information needed by the furnisher to contact the recipient. The furnisher must inform the recipient of any change in the furnisher's contact information.

(viii) *Hardware and software requirements.*—The recipient must be provided with a description of the hardware and software required to access, print, and retain the statement, and the date when the statement will no longer be available on the website.

(4) *Format.*—The electronic version of the statement must contain all required information and comply with applicable revenue procedures relating to substitute statements to recipients.

(5) *Notice.*—(i) *In general.*—If the statement is furnished on a website, the furnisher must notify the recipient that the statement is posted on a website. The notice may be delivered by mail, electronic mail, or in person. The notice must provide instructions on how to access and print the statement. The notice must include the following statement in capital letters, "IMPORTANT TAX RETURN DOCUMENT AVAILABLE." If the notice is provided by electronic mail, the foregoing statement must be on the subject line of the electronic mail.

(ii) *Undeliverable electronic address.*—If an electronic notice described in paragraph (a)(5)(i) of this section is returned as undeliverable, and the correct electronic address cannot be obtained from the furnisher's records or from the recipient, then the furnisher must furnish the notice by mail or in person within 30 days after the electronic notice is returned.

(iii) *Corrected statements.*—If the furnisher has corrected a recipient's statement that was furnished electronically, the furnisher must furnish the corrected statement to the recipient electronically. If the recipient's statement was furnished though a website posting and the furnisher has corrected the statement, the furnisher must notify the recipient that it has posted the corrected statement on the website within 30 days of such posting in the manner described in paragraph (a)(5)(i) of this section. The corrected statement or the notice must be furnished by mail or in person if—

(A) An electronic notice of the website posting of an original statement or the corrected statement was returned as undeliverable; and

(B) The recipient has not provided a new e-mail address.

(6) *Access Period.*—Statements furnished on a website must be retained on the website through October 15 of the year following the calendar year to which the statements relate (or the first business day after such October 15, if October 15 falls on a Saturday, Sunday, or legal holiday). The furnisher must maintain access to corrected statements that are posted on the website through October 15 of the year following the calendar year to which the statements relate (or the first business day after such October 15, if October 15 falls on a Saturday, Sunday, or legal holiday) or the date 90 days after the corrected statements are posted, whichever is later.

(b) *Effective date.*—This section applies to statements required to be furnished after February 13, 2004. Paragraph (a)(6) of this section also applies to statements required to be furnished after December 31, 2003. [Reg. § 1.6050S-4.]

☐ [*T.D.* 9114, 2-13-2004.]

⟫→ *Caution: Reg. Sec. 1.6050W-1, below, applies to returns for calendar years beginning after December 31, 2010.*

[Reg. § 1.6050W-1]

§ 1.6050W-1. Information reporting for payments made in settlement of payment card and third party network transactions.—(a) *In general.*—(1) *General rule.*—Every payment settlement entity, as defined in paragraph (a)(4) of this section, must file an information return for each calendar year with respect to payments made in settlement of reportable payment transactions, as defined in paragraph (a)(3) of this section, setting forth the following information:

(i) The name, address, and taxpayer identification number (TIN) of each participating payee, as defined in paragraph (a)(5) of this section, to whom one or more payments in settlement of reportable payment transactions are made.

⋙→ Caution: *Reg. Sec. 1.6050W-1, below, applies to returns for calendar years beginning after December 31, 2010.*

(ii) With respect to each participating payee, the gross amount, as defined in paragraph (a)(6) of this section, of—

(A) The aggregate reportable payment transactions for the calendar year; and

(B) The aggregate reportable payment transactions for each month of the calendar year.

(iii) Any other information required by the form, instructions or current revenue procedures.

(2) *Payments in settlement of reportable payment transactions.*—A payment settlement entity, as defined in paragraph (a)(4) of this section (or an electronic payment facilitator, as defined in paragraph (d)(2) of this section), makes a payment in settlement of a reportable payment transaction if the payment settlement entity (or electronic payment facilitator) submits the instruction to transfer funds to the account of the participating payee for purposes of settling the reportable payment transaction.

(3) *Reportable payment transaction.*—The term *reportable payment transaction* means any payment card transaction (as defined in paragraph (b)(1) of this section) and any third party network transaction (as defined in paragraph (c)(1) of this section).

(4) *Payment settlement entity.*— (i) *Definition.*—The term *payment settlement entity* means a domestic or foreign entity that is—

(A) In the case of a payment card transaction, a merchant acquiring entity (as defined in paragraph (b)(2) of this section); and

(B) In the case of a third party network transaction, a third party settlement organization (as defined in paragraph (c)(2) of this section).

(ii) *Multiple payment settlement entities.*—If two or more persons qualify as payment settlement entities (as defined in paragraph (a)(4)(i) of this section) with respect to a reportable payment transaction, then only the payment settlement entity that in fact makes payment in settlement of the reportable payment transaction must file the information return required by paragraph (a)(1) of this section.

(5) *Participating payee.*—(i) *Definition.*—In general, the term *participating payee* means any person, including any governmental unit (and any agency or instrumentality thereof), who:

(A) In the case of a payment card transaction, accepts a payment card (as defined in paragraph (b)(3) of this section) as payment; and

(B) In the case of a third party network transaction, accepts payment from a third party settlement organization (as defined in paragraph (c)(2) of this section) in settlement of such transaction.

(ii) *Foreign payees.*—(A) *In general.*—For payments pursuant to contractual obligations entered into after December 31, 2010, a payment settlement entity that is a person described as a U.S. payor or U.S. middleman in § 1.6049-5(c)(5) is not required to make a return of information for payments to a participating payee with a foreign address as long as, prior to payment, the payment settlement entity has in its files documentation upon which the payment settlement entity may rely to treat the payment as made to a foreign person in accordance with § 1.1441-1(e)(1)(ii). For purposes of this paragraph (a)(5)(ii), the provisions of § 1.1441-1 shall apply by substituting the term payor for the term withholding agent and without regard to the limitation to amounts subject to withholding under chapter 3 of the Internal Revenue Code and the regulations under that chapter. Such a payment settlement entity need not make a return of information for payments made outside the United States (within the meaning of § 1.6049-5(e)) to an offshore account (as defined in § 1.6049-5(c)(1)) to a participating payee with only a foreign address if the name of the participating payee indicates that it is an entity listed as a per se corporation under § 301.7701-2(b)(8)(i) and the payment settlement entity does not know or have reason to know that the participating payee is a United States person. A payment settlement entity may apply the grace period rules of § 1.6049-5(d)(2)(ii) of the regulations for payments to a participating payee with only a foreign address, without regard to whether the amounts paid are described in § 1.1441-6(c)(2) or are reportable under section 6042, 6045, 6049, or 6050N. For payments pursuant to contractual obligations entered into before January 1, 2011, a payment settlement entity that is a person described as a U.S. payor or U.S. middleman in § 1.6049-5(c)(5) is not required to make a return of information for payments to a participating payee with a foreign address as long as the payment settlement entity neither knows nor has reason to know that the participating payee is a United States person. For this purpose, a renewal of such a contractual obligation will not result in a new contractual obligation unless there is a material modification to the contractual obligation.

(B) *Non-U.S. payor or middleman.*—A payment settlement entity that is not a person described as a U.S. payor or U.S middleman in § 1.6049-5(c)(5) is not required to make a return of information for a payment to a participating payee that does not have a United States address as long as the payment settlement entity neither knows nor has reason to know that the participating payee is a United States person. If the participating payee has any United States address, the payment settlement entity may treat the participating payee as a foreign person only if the payment settlement entity has in its files documentation upon which the payment settlement entity may rely to treat the payment as made to a foreign person in accordance with § 1.1441-1(e)(1)(ii).

>>>→ *Caution: Reg. Sec. 1.6050W-1, below, applies to returns for calendar years beginning after December 31, 2010.*

(C) *Foreign address; United States address.*—For purposes of this section, *foreign address* means any address that is not within the United States, as defined in section 7701(a)(9) of the Internal Revenue Code (the States and the District of Columbia). *United States address* means any address that is within the United States.

(6) *Gross amount.*—For purposes of this section, *gross amount* means the total dollar amount of aggregate reportable payment transactions for each participating payee without regard to any adjustments for credits, cash equivalents, discount amounts, fees, refunded amounts or any other amounts. The dollar amount of each transaction is determined on the date of the transaction.

(b) *Payment card transactions.*—(1) *Definition.*—The term *payment card transaction* means any transaction in which a payment card, or any account number or other indicia associated with a payment card, is accepted as payment.

(2) *Merchant acquiring entity.*—The term *merchant acquiring entity* means the bank or other organization that has the contractual obligation to make payment to participating payees (as defined in paragraph (a)(5)(i)(A) of this section) in settlement of payment card transactions.

(3) *Payment card.*—(i) The term *payment card* means any card, including any stored-value card as defined in paragraph (b)(4) of this section, issued pursuant to an agreement or arrangement that provides for—

(A) One or more issuers of such cards;

(B) A network of persons unrelated to each other, and to the issuer, who agree to accept such cards as payment; and

(C) Standards and mechanisms for settling the transactions between the merchant acquiring entities and the persons who agree to accept the cards as payment.

(ii) Persons who agree to accept such cards as payment as described in this paragraph (b)(3) are participating payees within the meaning of paragraph (a)(5)(i)(A) of this section.

(4) *Stored-value cards.*—The term *stored-value card* means any card with a prepaid value, including any gift card.

(5) *Transactions for which no return of information is required under section 6050W.*—(i) *Withdrawals and cash advances.*—The use of a "payment card" as defined in paragraph (b)(3) of this section by a cardholder to withdraw funds at an automated teller machine, or to obtain a cash advance or loan against the cardholder's account, is not a payment card transaction under paragraph (b)(1) of this section because the card is not being accepted as payment by a merchant or other payee.

(ii) *Convenience checks.*—The acceptance of a check issued in connection with a payment card account by a merchant or other payee is not

a payment card transaction under paragraph (b)(1) of this section because the check is accepted and processed through the banking system in the same manner as a traditional check, not as a payment card.

(iii) *Payee related to issuer.*—No return of information is required under this section for any transaction in which a payment card within the meaning of paragraph (b)(3) is accepted as payment by a merchant or other payee who is related to the issuer of the payment card.

(c) *Third party network transactions.*—(1) *Definition.*—The term *third party network transaction* means any transaction that is settled through a third party payment network.

(2) *Third party settlement organization.*—The term *third party settlement organization* means the central organization that has the contractual obligation to make payments to participating payees (as defined in paragraph (a)(5)(i)(B) of this section) of third party network transactions. A central organization is a third party settlement organization if it provides a third party payment network (as defined in paragraph (c)(3)(i) of this section) that enables purchasers to transfer funds to providers of goods and services.

(3) *Third party payment network.*—(i) The term *third party payment network* means any agreement or arrangement that—

(A) Involves the establishment of accounts with a central organization by a substantial number of providers of goods or services who are unrelated to the organization and who have agreed to settle transactions for the provision of the goods or services to purchasers according to the terms of the agreement or arrangement;

(B) Provides standards and mechanisms for settling the transactions; and

(C) Guarantees payment to the persons providing goods or services in settlement of transactions with purchasers pursuant to the agreement or arrangement.

(ii) A third party payment network does not include any agreement or arrangement that provides for the issuance of payment cards.

(iii) Persons who are providers of goods and services as described in this paragraph (c)(3) are participating payees within the meaning of paragraph (a)(5)(i)(B) of this section.

(4) *Exception for de minimis payments.*—A third party settlement organization is required to report any information under paragraph (a)(1) of this section with respect to third party network transactions of any participating payee only if—

(i) The amount that would otherwise be reported under paragraph (a)(1)(ii) of this section with respect to such transactions exceeds $20,000; and

(ii) The aggregate number of such transactions exceeds 200.

⫸→ *Caution: Reg. Sec. 1.6050W-1, below, applies to returns for calendar years beginning after December 31, 2010.*

(d) *Special rules.*—(1) *Aggregated payees.*—If a person receives payments from a payment settlement entity (as defined in paragraph (a)(4) of this section) on behalf of one or more participating payees and distributes such payments to one or more participating payees (as defined in paragraph (a)(5) of this section), the person is treated as:

(i) The participating payee with respect to the payment settlement entity; and

(ii) The payment settlement entity with respect to the participating payees to whom the person distributes payments.

(2) *Electronic payment facilitator.*—If a payment settlement entity (as defined in paragraph (a)(4) of this section) contracts with an electronic payment facilitator or other third party to make payments in settlement of reportable payment transactions on behalf of the payment settlement entity, the facilitator must file the annual information return under this section in lieu of the payment settlement entity. The facilitator need not have any agreement or arrangement with the participating payee. Also, the payment need not come from the facilitator's account. The facilitator need only submit instructions to transfer funds to the account of the participating payee in settlement of the reportable payment transaction. The facilitator is liable for any applicable penalties for failure to comply with the information reporting requirements of section 6050W.

(3) *Designations.*—The party with the obligation to file the annual information return under this section may designate by written agreement any other person to satisfy the requirements of this section. Thus, notwithstanding the rule in paragraph (d)(2) of this section imposing the obligation to file the annual information return on the electronic payment facilitator in lieu of the payment settlement entity, the payment settlement entity may file the information return by designation if the parties agree in writing. However, a designation does not relieve the party with the reporting obligation from liability for any reporting failures. The party with the obligation to file the annual information return under this section remains liable for any applicable penalties under sections 6721 and 6722 if the requirements of this section are not satisfied.

(4) *Conversion into United States dollars of amounts paid in foreign currency.*—When a payment is made or received in a foreign currency, the U.S. dollar amount shall be determined by converting such foreign currency into U.S. dollars on the date of the transaction at the spot rate (as defined in §1.988-1(d)(1)) or pursuant to a reasonable spot rate convention. For example, a payor may use a month-end spot rate or a monthly average spot rate. A spot rate convention must be used consistently with respect to all non-dollar amounts reported and from year to year. Such convention cannot be changed without the consent of the Commissioner or his or her delegate.

(5) *Unrelated persons.*—For purposes of this section, *unrelated* means any person who is not related to another person within the meaning of section 267(b) (providing a list of relationships), including the application of section 267(c) and (e)(3) (providing rules relating to constructive ownership), and section 707(b)(1) (relationships with partnerships).

(e) *Examples.*—The following examples illustrate the provisions of this section:

Example 1. Merchant acquiring entity. Customer A purchases goods from merchant B using a credit card issued by Bank X. B is one of a network of unrelated persons that has agreed to accept credit cards issued by X as payment under an agreement that provides standards and mechanisms for settling the transaction between a merchant acquiring bank and the persons who accept the cards. Bank Z is the merchant acquiring bank with the contractual obligation to make payment to B for goods provided to A in this transaction. As defined in paragraph (b)(2) of this section, Z is the merchant acquiring entity that must file the annual information return required under paragraph (a)(1) of this section to report the payment made to settle the transaction for the sale of goods from B to A.

Example 2. Third party settlement organization. (i) Merchant B is one of a substantial number of persons selling goods or services over the Internet that have an account with X, an Internet payment service provider. None of these persons, including B, are related to X, and all have agreed to settle transactions for the sale of goods or services to customers according to the terms of their contracts with X. X has guaranteed payment to all of these persons, including B, for the sale of goods or services to customers. Customer A purchases goods from B. A pays X for the goods purchased from B. X, in turn, makes payment to B in settlement of the transaction for the sale of goods from B to A.

(ii) X's arrangement constitutes a third party payment network as defined in paragraph (c)(3) of this section because a substantial number of persons that are unrelated to X, including B, have established accounts with X, and X is contractually obligated to settle transactions for the provision of goods or services by these persons to purchasers. Thus, under paragraph (c)(2) of this section, X is a third party settlement organization and the transaction discussed in this *Example* is a third party network transaction under paragraph (c)(1) of this section. Therefore, X must file the annual information return required under paragraph (a)(1) of this section to report the payment made to B in settlement of the transaction with A provided that X's aggregate payments to B from third party network transactions exceed $20,000 and the aggregate number of X's transactions with B exceeds 200 (as provided in paragraph (c)(4) of this section).

Reg. §1.6050W-1(e)

>>> *Caution: Reg. Sec. 1.6050W-1, below, applies to returns for calendar years beginning after December 31, 2010.*

Example 3. Automated clearinghouse network. A operates an automated clearinghouse ("ACH") network that merely processes electronic payments (such as wire transfers, electronic checks, and direct deposit payments) between buyers and sellers. There are no contractual agreements between A and the sellers for the purpose of permitting the sellers to use the ACH network. Thus, A is not a third party settlement organization under paragraph (c)(2) of this section, the ACH network is not a third party payment network under paragraph (c)(3) of this section, and the electronic payment transactions are not third party network transactions under paragraph (c)(1) of this section. A is not required to file the annual information return required under paragraph (a)(1) of this section.

Example 4. ACH processor. B provides a variety of ACH payment processing services to a large number of merchants, such as converting checks received in payment of bills into ACH transactions. B groups payment transactions into an ACH file and transmits the ACH file into the ACH network on behalf of merchants in order to initiate payment to merchants through the ACH network. B makes payments to the merchants after the ACH network verifies that the customers' accounts have sufficient funds. Because the ACH network is not a third party payment network under paragraph (c)(3) of this section, B cannot be a third party settlement organization with respect to the ACH network. Similarly, because the ACH itself is not a third party settlement organization under paragraph (c)(2) of this section, B cannot be an electronic payment facilitator because B is not acting on behalf of a payment settlement entity. However, B may itself be operating third party payment network under paragraph (c)(3) of this section if B has a separate agreement or arrangement that: involves the establishment of accounts with B by a substantial number of unrelated merchants who provide goods or services and have agreed to settle transactions for the provision of the goods or services pursuant to the agreement or arrangement; provides for standards and mechanisms for settling the transactions; and guarantees persons providing goods or services pursuant to such agreement or arrangement that these persons will be paid for providing such goods or services.

Example 5. Gross amount. On Day 1, Customer A uses a payment card to purchase $100 worth of goods from merchant B. Bank X, the merchant acquiring entity for B, is the party with the contractual obligation to make payment to B in settlement of the transaction. On Day 2, X, after deducting fees of $2, makes payment of $98 to settle the transaction for the sale of goods from B to A. Under paragraph (a)(6) of this section, X must report the amount of $100, the amount of the transaction on Day 1, without any reduction for fees or any other amount, as the gross amount of this reportable payment transaction on the annual information return filed under paragraph (a)(1) of this section.

Example 6. Gift card. (i) Customer A purchases a gift card from Merchant X that may be used only at X and its related network of stores. A purchases the gift card using cash. A gives the gift card to B. B uses the gift card to purchase goods at one of X's stores. The purchase of the gift card by A using cash is not a payment card transaction described in paragraph (b)(1) of this section and, thus, is not required to be reported in a return of information required under paragraph (a)(1) of this section. Under paragraph (b)(3) of this section, the gift card is not a payment card because the gift card is only accepted as payment by persons who are related to the issuer of the gift card and to each other. Therefore, the use of the gift card by B is not required to be reported in a return of information required under paragraph (a)(1) of this section.

(ii) The facts are the same as in paragraph (i), except that B adds value to the gift card using a credit card. The use of the credit card to add value to the gift card is a reportable payment transaction (as defined in paragraph (a)(3) of this section) and must be reported in a return of information under this section by the bank or other organization that has the contractual obligation to make payment to X in settlement of the transaction.

Example 7. Private label card. Bank B issues a card imprinted with Retailer C's logo to cardholder A. The "C-card" is accepted as payment only at C or at stores related (within the meaning of section 267(b), (c) and (e)(3) and, section 707(b)(1)) to C. A uses the card at C to purchase electronics equipment. Under paragraph (b)(3) of this section, the C-card is not a payment card because the card is accepted as payment only within a network of persons who are related to each other. Therefore, the use of the card by A at C is not required to be reported in a return of information required under paragraph (a)(1) of this section.

Example 8. Quasi-private label card. Bank B issues a card to cardholder A. The card, known as an "E-card," is issued by B pursuant to an agreement that provides that the E-card is accepted as payment only within a limited network of merchants that carry electronics equipment. The agreement provides for standards and mechanisms for settling the transactions between the merchants and the merchant acquiring entities. The merchants accepting the E-card as payment are not related (within the meaning of section 267(b), (c) and (e)(3) and section 707(b)(1)) to each other or to B. A uses the card to purchase electronics equipment at F Store, one of the stores within the network of merchants accepting the E-card. Under paragraph (b)(3) of this section, the E-card is a payment card because the card is issued pursuant to an agree-

⋙→ *Caution: Reg. Sec. 1.6050W-1, below, applies to returns for calendar years beginning after December 31, 2010.*

ment that provides for a network of persons unrelated to each other, and to the issuer, who agree to accept the card as payment. Therefore, the use of the E-card by A to purchase electronics equipment at F Store must be reported in a return of information required under paragraph (a)(1) of this section.

Example 9. Campus card. (i) University Y issues Student A a card that may be used on campus at various university-owned merchants and at various local merchants unrelated to Y. A uses the card in the university-owned cafeteria to purchase lunch. Under paragraph (b)(5)(iii) of this section, no return of information is required because the card is being accepted as payment by a person who is related to the issuer of the card.

(ii) The facts are the same as in paragraph (i), except that A uses the campus card to purchase lunch at a local restaurant, unrelated to Y, that has agreed to accept the campus card as payment. Under paragraph (b)(3) of this section, the campus card is a payment card in this transaction because the card is accepted as payment by a person that is unrelated to this issuer of the card pursuant to an agreement. Therefore, the use of the card by A in the local restaurant for the purchase of lunch must be reported in a return of information required under paragraph (a)(1) of this section by the bank or other organization that has the contractual obligation to make payment to the restaurant in settlement of the transaction.

Example 10. Mall card. Customer B purchases a card that is issued by shopping mall A. Pursuant to an agreement or arrangement, the card is accepted as payment by various merchants located within the mall, who are unrelated to the issuer of the card and to each other. B uses the card in the mall to purchase goods from merchant C. Under paragraph (b)(3) of this section, the mall card is a payment card because the card is accepted as payment by a network of persons who are unrelated to the issuer of the card and to the other merchants who have agreed to accept the card as payment. Therefore, the use of the mall card by B to purchase goods from merchant C is required to be reported in a return of information required under paragraph (a)(1) of this section.

Example 11. Electronic benefit transactions card. Government Agency A issues benefits electronically to recipients by loading these benefits onto a payment card. Pursuant to an agreement, a network of merchants unrelated to A, and to each other, has agreed to accept the benefits card as payment. A issues a card to B, who uses the card to purchase goods from Merchant C. The card issued by A is a payment card (as defined in paragraph (b)(3) of this section) because the card is accepted as payment by a network of persons that are unrelated to the issuer of the card, and to each other. The use of the card by B to purchase goods from C must be reported in a return of

information required under paragraph (a)(1) of this section.

Example 12. Prepaid telephone card. A purchases a prepaid telephone card from Company X that may be used to make telephone calls using various long-distance providers unrelated to X that have agreed to accept the card as payment. A places a telephone call using the prepaid card as payment for the telephone call. Under paragraph (b)(3) of this section, the prepaid telephone card is a payment card because the card is accepted as payment by a person that is unrelated to the issuer of the card pursuant to an agreement. Therefore, the use of the prepaid card to make payment for the telephone call must be reported in a return of information required under paragraph (a)(1) of this section by the bank or other organization that has the contractual obligation to make payment to the long distance provider in settlement of the transaction.

Example 13. Transit card. City Z accepts a transit card as payment for use of its mass transit system. The transit card is issued by B, an organization unrelated to Z. A network of persons, including Z, who are unrelated to each other and to B, have agreed to accept the transit card issued by B as payment for transit and for other goods and services. Transit rider X purchases a transit card and uses the card to pay for travel on Z's mass transit system. Under paragraph (b)(3) of this section, the transit card is a payment card because the card is accepted as payment by a person who is one of a network of persons that are unrelated to the issuer of the card, and to each other, and that have agreed to accept the card as payment. Therefore, the use of the transit card by X to pay for transit on Z's mass transit system is a payment card transaction described in paragraph (b)(1) of this section that must be reported in a return of information required under paragraph (a)(1) of this section by the bank or other organization that has the contractual obligation to make payment to Z. Z is the participating payee, described in paragraph (a)(5)(i)(A) of this section, of the payment card transaction.

Example 14. Cash advance. Bank A issues Cardholder B a credit card that is a payment card under paragraph (b)(3) of this section. B uses the card at a local bank to obtain a cash advance. Under paragraph (b)(5)(i) of this section, B's use of the payment card to obtain a cash advance is not a payment card transaction (as defined in paragraph (b)(1) of this section) because the card is not being accepted as payment by a merchant.

Example 15. Withdrawals from automated teller machines. Bank A issues Cardholder B a credit card that is a payment card under paragraph (b)(3) of this section. B uses the card at an automated teller machine to obtain cash. Under paragraph (b)(5)(i) of this section, B's use of the payment card to obtain cash is not a payment card transaction (as defined in paragraph (b)(1)

Reg. §1.6050W-1(e)

>>>→ *Caution: Reg. Sec. 1.6050W-1, below, applies to returns for calendar years beginning after December 31, 2010.*

of this section) because the card is not being accepted as payment by a merchant.

Example 16. Convenience checks. Bank A issues Cardholder B a credit card that is a payment card under paragraph (b)(3) of this section. A sends B paper checks imprinted with the account number associated with the credit card. B uses one of the checks to purchase goods from Merchant S. The check is accepted by S and processed through the bank system in the same manner as a traditional check. Under paragraph (b)(5)(ii) of this section, B's use of the convenience check to purchase goods is not a payment card transaction (as defined in paragraph (b)(1) of this section) because the check is accepted and processed as a traditional check, not as a payment card.

Example 17. Healthcare network. Health carrier A operates healthcare network Y. A collects premiums from covered persons pursuant to a plan agreement between A and the covered persons for the cost of membership in Y. Separately, A pays healthcare providers pursuant to provider agreements to compensate these providers for services rendered to covered persons who are members of Y. A is not a third party settlement organization under paragraph (c)(2) of this section because A does not operate a third party payment network that enables purchasers to transfer funds to providers of goods and services. Therefore, A is not required to file the annual information return required under paragraph (a)(1) of this section.

Example 18. Third party accounts payable. X is a "shared-service" organization that performs accounts payable services for numerous purchasers that are unrelated to X. A substantial number of providers of goods and services have established accounts with X and have agreed to accept payment from X in settlement of their transactions with purchasers. The provider agreement with X includes standards and mechanisms for settling the transactions and guarantees payment to the providers, and the arrangement enables purchasers to transfer funds to providers. Under paragraph (c)(3) of this section, X's accounts payable services constitute a third party payment network, of which X is the third party settlement organization (as defined in paragraph (c)(2) of this section). For each payee, X must file the annual information return required under paragraph (a)(1) of this section to report payments made by X in settlement of accounts payable to that payee if X's aggregate payments to that payee exceed $20,000 and the aggregate number of transactions with that payee exceeds 200 (as provided in paragraph (c)(4) of this section).

Example 19. Toll collection network. State A charges a toll to vehicles that travel its state highways. The tolling agency for A contracted with organization X to perform its toll collection. X provides an electronic toll collection system that allows the toll facility to record the passage of a vehicle with a transponder affixed to the vehicle. The customer account associated with the transponder is automatically debited for the amount of the toll. The customer funds a balance in the account, which is then depleted as the toll transactions occur. X periodically bills the customer to replenish the account. X then makes payment to A to settle the toll transactions that are recorded by the transponder. X also contracts with a substantial number of other entities unrelated to X that have established accounts with X and have agreed to accept payment using the electronic toll collection system provided by X. X guarantees payment to the entities for all toll transactions that are recorded by the transponders, and the arrangement enables customers to transfer funds to State A and other entities that charge tolls. Under paragraph (c)(3) of this section, X's electronic toll collection system constitutes a third party payment network, of which X is the third party settlement organization (as defined in paragraph (c)(2) of this section). For each payee, including A, X must file the annual information return required under paragraph (a)(1) of this section to report payments made by X in settlement of toll transactions if X's aggregate payments to that payee exceed $20,000 and the aggregate number of transactions with that payee exceeds 200 (as provided in paragraph (c)(4) of this section).

Example 20. Hotel kiosk. Under a "hotel kiosk" arrangement, Hotel B permits its customers to charge, to their room account, transactions for goods and services at a substantial number of sellers unrelated to B that operate on B's premises, or on the premises of hotels related to B, and that have established accounts in B's hotel kiosk system. Customers settle their room account with B when they check out, and B in turn settles the hotel kiosk transactions with the unrelated sellers. B guarantees payment to the sellers for these transactions and the arrangement enables customers to transfer funds to the sellers by means of one payment made to the hotel. Under paragraph (c)(3) of this section, B's hotel kiosk system constitutes a third party payment network, of which B is the third party settlement organization (as defined in paragraph (c)(2) of this section). For each payee, B must file the annual information return required under paragraph (a)(1) of this section to report payments made by B in settlement of the hotel kiosk transactions if B's aggregate payments to that payee exceed $20,000 and the aggregate number of transactions with that payee exceeds 200 (as provided in paragraph (c)(4) of this section).

Example 21. Aggregated payee. Corporation A, acting on behalf of A's independently-owned franchise stores, receives payment from Bank X for credit card sales effectuated at these franchise stores. X, the payment settlement entity (as defined in paragraph (a)(4)(i) of this section), is required under paragraph (d)(1)(i) of this section to report the gross amount of the reportable payment transactions distributed to A (notwith-

>>> *Caution: Reg. Sec. 1.6050W-1, below, applies to returns for calendar years beginning after December 31, 2010.*

standing the fact that A does not accept payment cards and would not otherwise be treated as a participating payee). In turn, under paragraph (d)(1)(ii) of this section, A is required to report the gross amount of the reportable payment transactions allocable to each franchise store. X has no reporting obligation under this section with respect to payments made by A to its franchise stores.

Example 22. Electronic payment facilitator. (i) Bank A is a merchant acquiring entity (as defined in paragraph (b)(2) of this section) with the contractual obligation to make payments to participating merchants to settle certain credit card transactions. A enters into a contract with Processor X. Pursuant to this contract, X prepares and submits instructions to move funds from A's account to the accounts of participating merchants to settle credit card transactions. X is making payment on A's behalf in settlement of payment card transactions pursuant to a contract between X and A. Therefore, under paragraph (d)(2) of this section, X is an electronic payment facilitator and must file the information return required under paragraph (a)(1) of this section with respect to credit card transactions settled by X. A has no reporting obligation with respect to payments made by X on A's behalf.

(ii) The facts are the same as in paragraph (i) except that A and X state in their contract that A will file the information return required under paragraph (a)(1) of this section. A may file the information return pursuant to this designation. However, X is liable for any applicable penalties under sections 6721 and 6722 if the reporting requirements of this section are not satisfied.

(iii) The facts are the same as in paragraph (i) except that X merely prepares the instructions to move the funds to the accounts of participating merchants, and the instructions are actually submitted by A. A, not X, is making payment in settlement of payment card transactions. Therefore, A retains the obligation to file the information return required under paragraph (a)(1) of this section with respect to credit card transactions settled by A.

(f) *Prescribed form.*—The return required by paragraph (a)(1) of this section must be made according to the forms and instructions published by the Internal Revenue Service.

(g) *Time and place for filing.*—Returns made under this section for any calendar year must be filed on or before February 28th (March 31st if filing electronically) of the following year at the Internal Revenue Service Center location designated in the instructions to the relevant form.

(h) *Time and place for furnishing statement.*—(1) *In general.*—Every payment settlement entity required to file a return under this section must also furnish to each participating payee a written statement with the same information (as described in paragraph (h)(2) of this section). The statement must be furnished to the payee on or before January 31st of the year following the calendar year in which the reportable payment is made. If the return of information is not made on magnetic media, this requirement may be satisfied by furnishing to such person a copy of all Forms 1099-K, "Merchant card and third-party payments," or any successor form with respect to such person filed with the Internal Revenue Service Center. The statement will be considered furnished to the payee if it is mailed to the payee's last known address. The payment settlement entity may furnish the statement electronically in accordance with the rules provided in § 1.6050W-2.

(2) *Information to be shown on statement furnished to payee.*—Each written statement furnished under paragraph (h)(1) of this section must include the following information—

(i) The name, address, and phone number (or email address if the statement is furnished electronically) of the information contact of the payment settlement entity.

(ii) With respect to the participating payee, the gross amount of—

(A) The aggregate reportable payment transactions for the calendar year; and

(B) The aggregate reportable payment transactions for each month of the calendar year.

(iii) Any other information required by the form, instructions, or current revenue procedures.

(i) *Cross-reference to penalties.*—For provisions relating to the penalty for failure to file timely a correct information return required under section 6050W, see section 6721 and the associated regulations. For provisions relating to the penalty for failure to furnish timely a correct payee statement required under section 6050W(f), see section 6722 and the associated regulations. See section 6724 and the associated regulations for the waiver of a penalty if failure is due to reasonable cause and is not due to willful neglect.

(j) *Effective/applicability date.*—The rules in this section apply to returns for calendar years beginning after December 31, 2010. [Reg. § 1.6050W-1.]

☐ [*T.D.* 9496, 8-13-2010.]

>>> *Caution: Reg. Sec. 1.6050W-2, below, applies to returns for calendar years beginning after December 31, 2010.*

[Reg. § 1.6050W-2]

§ 1.6050W-2. Electronic furnishing of information statements for payments made in settlement of payment card and third party network

transactions.—(a) *Electronic furnishing of statements.*—(1) *In general.*—A person required by section 6050W to furnish a written statement (furnisher) regarding payments made in settle-

⋙→ *Caution: Reg. Sec. 1.6050W-2, below, applies to returns for calendar years beginning after December 31, 2010.*

ment of payment card and third party network transactions to the person to whom it is required to be furnished (recipient) may furnish the statement in an electronic format in lieu of a paper format. A furnisher who meets the requirements of paragraphs (a)(2) through (a)(5) of this section is treated as furnishing the required statement.

(2) *Consent.*—(i) *In general.*—The recipient must have affirmatively consented to receive the statement required under section 6050W in an electronic format or, in the alternative, have previously consented to receive other federal tax statements in an electronic format from the furnisher. The consent may be made electronically in any manner that reasonably demonstrates that the recipient can access the statement in the electronic format in which it will be furnished to the recipient. Alternatively, the consent may be made in a paper document if it is confirmed electronically. Consents must be kept at all times available for inspection by the Internal Revenue Service. Recipients currently receiving electronic communications from the furnisher may elect to receive the statement required under section 6050W in a paper document in lieu of an electronic format. The election to receive a paper document may be made by notifying the furnisher electronically or in a paper document.

(ii) *Withdrawal of consent.*—The consent requirement of paragraph (a)(2)(i) of this section is not satisfied if the recipient withdraws the consent to receive electronic statements and the withdrawal takes effect before the statement is furnished. The furnisher may provide that a withdrawal of consent takes effect either on the date it is received by the furnisher or on a subsequent date. The furnisher may also provide that a request for a paper statement will be treated as a withdrawal of consent.

(iii) *Change in hardware or software requirements.*—If a change in the hardware or software required to access the statement creates a material risk that the recipient will not be able to access the statement, the furnisher must, prior to changing the hardware or software, provide notice to the recipient. The notice must describe the revised hardware and software required to access the statement and inform the recipient that a new consent to receive the statement in the revised electronic format must be provided to the furnisher. After implementing the revised hardware and software, the furnisher must obtain from the recipient, in the manner described in paragraph (a)(2)(i) of this section, a new consent or confirmation of consent to receive the statement electronically.

(iv) *Examples.*—The following examples illustrate the rules of this paragraph (a)(2):

Example 1. Recipient R has consented to receive the statements required under section 6041 in electronic format from Furnisher F. F has retained R's consent and keeps it available for inspection by the IRS. F may furnish to R the statement required under section 6050W in electronic format without securing an affirmative consent from R with respect to the statements required under section 6050W.

Example 2. Recipient R has not consented to receive any electronic federal income tax statements from Furnisher F. F may not furnish to R the statements required under section 6050W unless F first secures from R a consent to receive those statements in electronic format in accordance with the requirements of paragraphs (a)(2) through (a)(5) of this section.

Example 3. Furnisher F sends Recipient R a letter stating that R may consent to receive statements required by section 6050W(f) electronically on a website instead of in a paper format. The letter contains instructions explaining how to consent to receive the statements electronically by accessing the website, downloading the consent document, completing the consent document, and e-mailing the completed consent back to F. The consent document posted on the website uses the same electronic format that F uses to furnish statements electronically. R reads the instructions and submits the consent in the manner provided in the instructions. R has consented to receive the statements electronically in the manner described in paragraph (a)(2)(i) of this section.

Example 4. Furnisher F sends Recipient R an e-mail stating that R may consent to receive statements required by section 6050W(f) electronically instead of in a paper format. The e-mail contains an attachment instructing R how to consent to receive the statements electronically. The e-mail attachment uses the same electronic format that F uses to furnish statements electronically. R opens the attachment, reads the instructions, and submits the consent in the manner provided in the instructions. R has consented to receive the statements electronically in the manner described in paragraph (a)(2)(i) of this section.

Example 5. Furnisher F posts a notice on its website stating that Recipient R may receive statements required by section 6050W(f) electronically instead of in a paper format. The website contains instructions on how R may access a secure web page and consent to receive the statements electronically. By accessing the secure web page and giving consent, R has consented to receive the statements electronically in the manner described in paragraph (a)(2)(i) of this section.

(3) *Required disclosures.*—(i) *In general.*—Prior to, or at the time of, a recipient's consent, the furnisher must provide to the recipient a clear and conspicuous disclosure statement containing each of the disclosures described in paragraphs (a)(3)(ii) through (a)(3)(viii) of this section.

⫸→ *Caution: Reg. Sec. 1.6050W-2, below, applies to returns for calendar years beginning after December 31, 2010.*

(ii) *Paper statement.*—The recipient must be informed that the statement will be furnished on paper if the recipient does not consent to receive it electronically.

(iii) *Scope and duration of consent.*—The recipient must be informed of the scope and duration of the consent. For example, the recipient must be informed whether the consent applies to statements furnished every year after the consent is given until it is withdrawn in the manner described in paragraph (a)(3)(v)(A) of this section or only to the statement required to be furnished on or before the January 31st immediately following the date on which the consent is given.

(iv) *Post-consent request for a paper statement.*—The recipient must be informed of any procedure for obtaining a paper copy of the recipient's statement after giving the consent described in paragraph (a)(2)(i) of this section and whether a request for a paper statement will be treated as a withdrawal of consent.

(v) *Withdrawal of consent.*—The recipient must be informed that—

(A) The recipient may withdraw a consent by writing (electronically or on paper) to the person or department whose name, mailing address, telephone number, and e-mail address is provided in the disclosure statement;

(B) The furnisher will confirm the withdrawal and the date on which it takes effect in writing (either electronically or on paper); and

(C) A withdrawal of consent does not apply to a statement that was furnished electronically in the manner described in this paragraph (a) before the date on which the withdrawal of consent takes effect.

(vi) *Notice of termination.*—The recipient must be informed of the conditions under which a furnisher will cease furnishing statements electronically to the recipient.

(vii) *Updating information.*—The recipient must be informed of the procedures for updating the information needed by the furnisher to contact the recipient. The furnisher must inform the recipient of any change in the furnisher's contact information.

(viii) *Hardware and software requirements.*—The recipient must be provided with a description of the hardware and software required to access, print, and retain the statement, and the date when the statement will no longer be available on the website.

(4) *Format.*—The electronic version of the statement must contain all required information and comply with applicable revenue procedures relating to substitute statements to recipients.

(5) *Notice.*—(i) *In general.*—If the statement is furnished on a website, the furnisher must notify the recipient that the statement is posted on a website. The notice may be delivered by mail, electronic mail, or in person. The notice must provide instructions on how to access and print the statement. The notice must include the following statement in capital letters, "IMPORTANT TAX RETURN DOCUMENT AVAILABLE." If the notice is provided by electronic mail, the foregoing statement must be on the subject line of the electronic mail.

(ii) *Undeliverable electronic address.*—If an electronic notice described in paragraph (a)(5)(i) of this section is returned as undeliverable, and the correct electronic address cannot be obtained from the furnisher's records or from the recipient, then the furnisher must furnish the notice by mail or in person within 30 days after the electronic notice is returned.

(b) *Effective/applicability date.*—The rules in this section apply to returns for calendar years beginning after December 31, 2010. [Reg. § 1.6050W-2.]

□ [*T.D.* 9496, 8-13-2010.]

[Reg. § 31.6051-1]

§ 31.6051-1. Statement for employees.—(a) *Requirement if wages are subject to withholding of income tax.*—(1) *General rule.*—(i) Every employer, as defined in section 3401(d), required to deduct and withhold from an employee a tax under section 3402, or who would have been required to deduct and withhold a tax under section 3402 (determined without regard to section 3402(n)) if the employee had claimed no more than one withholding exemption, shall furnish to each such employee, in respect of the remuneration paid by such employer to such employee during the calendar year, the tax return copy and the employee's copy of a statement on Form W-2. For example, if the wage bracket method of withholding provided in section 3402(c)(1) is used, a statement on Form W-2 must be furnished to each employee whose wages during any payroll period are equal to or in excess of the smallest wage from which tax must be withheld in the case of an employee claiming one exemption. If the percentage method is used, a statement on Form W-2 must be furnished to each employee whose wages during any payroll period, reduced by the amount of one withholding exemption, are equal to or in excess of the smallest amount of wages from which tax must be withheld. See section 3402(a) and (b) and the regulations thereunder. Each statement on Form W-2 shall show the following:

(a) The name, address, and identification number of the employer,

(b) The name and address of the employee, and his social security account number if wages as defined in section 3121(a) have been paid or if Form W-2 is required to be furnished to the employee for a period commencing after December 31, 1962,

(c) The total amount of wages as defined in section 3401(a),

(d) The total amount deducted and withheld as tax under section 3402,

(e) The total amount of wages as defined in section 3121(a),

(f) The total amount of employee tax under section 3101 deducted and withheld (increased by any adjustment in the calendar year for overcollection, or decreased by any adjustment in such year for undercollection, of such tax during any prior year) and the proportion thereof (expressed either as a dollar amount, as a percentage of the total amount of wages as defined in section 3121(a), or as a percentage of the total amount of employee tax under section 3101) withheld as tax under section 3101(b) for financing the cost of hospital insurance benefits,

(g) Such information relating to coverage the employee has earned under the Federal Insurance Contributions Act, as may be required by Form W-2 or its instructions, and

(h) The total amount paid to the employee under section 3507 (relating to advance payment of earned income credit).

See paragraph (d) of this section for provisions relating to the time for furnishing the statement required by this subparagraph. See paragraph (f) of this section for an exception for employers filing composite returns from the requirement that statements for employees be on Form W-2. For the requirements relating to Form W-2 with respect to qualified State individual income taxes, see paragraph (d)(3)(ii) of §301.6361-1 of this chapter (Regulations on Procedure and Administration).

(ii) Payments made in 1955 under a wage continuation plan shall be reported on Form W-2 to the extent, and in the manner, provided in paragraph (b)(8)(i) of §31.3401(a)-1 of Subpart E of the regulations in this part.

(iii) In the case of statements furnished by the employer for whom services are performed, with respect to wages paid after December 31, 1955, "the total amount of wages as defined in section 3401(a)", as used in section 6051(a)(3), shall include all payments made directly by such employer under a wage continuation plan which constitute wages in accordance with §31.3401(a)-1(b)(8)(ii)(a), without regard to whether tax has been withheld on such amounts.

(iv) Form W-2 is not required in respect of any wage continuation payment made to an employee by or on behalf of a person who is not the employer for whom the employee performs services but who is regarded as an employer under section 3401(d)(1). See paragraph (b)(8) of §31.3401(a)-1 of Subpart E of the regulations in this part.

(v) In the case of remuneration paid for service described in section 3121(m), relating to service in the uniformed services, performed after 1956, "wages as defined in section 3121(a)", as used in section 6051(a)(2) and (5), shall be determined in accordance with section 3121(i)(2) and section 3122.

(vi) In the case of remuneration in the form of tips received by an employee in the course of his employment, the amounts required to be shown by paragraphs (3) and (5) of section 6051(a) (see subdivision (i)(c) and (e) of this subparagraph) shall include only such tips as are reported by the employee to the employer in a written statement furnished to the employer pursuant to section 6053(a).

(2) *Statements for members of the Armed Forces of the United States.*—Section 6051(b) contains certain special provisions which are applicable in the case of members of the Armed Forces of the United States in active service. In such case, Form W-2 shall be furnished to each such member of the Armed Forces if any tax has been withheld under section 3402 during the calendar year from the remuneration of such member or if any of the remuneration paid during the calendar year for such active service is includible under chapter 1 in the gross income of such member. Form W-2, in the case of such member, shall show, as "the total amount of wages as defined in section 3401(a)", as used in section 6051(a)(3), the amount of the remuneration paid during the calendar year which is not excluded under chapter 1 of the Internal Revenue Code of 1954 from the gross income of such member, whether or not such remuneration constitutes wages as defined in section 3401(a) and whether or not paid for such active service.

(3) *Undelivered statements for employees.*—The Internal Revenue Service copy and the employee's copy of each withholding statement for the calendar year which the employer is required to furnish to the employee and which after reasonable effort he is unable to deliver to the employee shall be retained by the employer for the 4-year period prescribed in paragraph (e)(2) of §31.6001-1.

(b) *Requirement if wages are not subject to withholding of income tax.*—(1) *General rule.*—If during the calendar year an employer pays to an employee wages subject to the employee tax imposed by section 3101, but not subject to income tax withholding under section 3402, the employer shall furnish to such employee the tax return copy and the employee's copy of a statement on Form W-2 for such calendar year. Such statement shall show the following:

(i) The name and address of the employer,

(ii) The name, address, and social security account number of the employee,

(iii) The total amount of wages as defined in section 3121(a),

(iv) The total amount of employee tax deducted and withheld from such wages (increased by any adjustment in such year for overcollection, or decreased by any adjustment in such year for undercollection, of employee tax during any prior year) and the proportion thereof (expressed either as a dollar amount, as a percentage of the total amount of wages as defined in section 3121(a), or as a percentage of the total amount of employee tax under section

3101) withheld as tax under section 3101(b) for financing the cost of hospital insurance benefits,

(v) Such information relating to coverage the employee has earned under the Federal Insurance Contributions Act, as may be required by Form W-2 or its instructions, and

(vi) The total amount paid to the employee under section 3507 (relating to advance payment of earned income credit).

See paragraph (d) of this section for provisions relating to the time for furnishing the statement required by this paragraph.

(2) *Uniformed services.*—In the case of remuneration paid for service described in section 3121(m), relating to service in the uniformed services, performed after 1956, "wages as defined in section 3121(a)", as used in section 6051(a)(5), shall be determined in accordance with section 3121(i)(2) and section 3122.

(c) *Correction of statements.*—(1) *Federal Insurance Contributions Act.*—If (i) the amount of employee tax under section 3101 deducted and withheld in the calendar year from the wages, as defined in section 3121(a), paid during such year was less or greater than the tax imposed by section 3101 on such wages by reason of the adjustment in such year of an overcollection or undercollection of the tax in any prior year, or (ii) regardless of the reason for the error or the method of its correction, the amount of wages as defined in section 3121(a), or tax under section 3101, entered on a statement furnished pursuant to this section to an employee for a prior year was incorrect, a corrected statement for such prior year reflecting the adjustment or the correct data shall be furnished to the employee. Such statement shall be marked "Corrected by Employer."

(2) *Income tax withholding.*—A corrected statement shall be furnished to the employee with respect to a prior calendar year (i) to show the correct amount of wages, as defined in section 3401(a), paid during the prior calendar year if the amount of such wages entered on a statement furnished to the employee for such prior year is incorrect, or (ii) to show the amount actually deducted and withheld as tax under section 3402 if such amount is less or greater than the amount entered as tax withheld on the statement furnished the employee for such prior year. Such statement shall be indicated as corrected.

(3) *Cross reference.*—For provisions relating to the disposition of the Internal Revenue Service copy of a corrected statement, see paragraph (b)(2) of §31.6011(a)-4 and paragraph (b) of §31.6051-2.

(d) *Time for furnishing statements.*—(1) *In general.*—(i) Each statement required by this section for a calendar year and each corrected statement required for the year shall be furnished to the employee on or before January 31 of the year

succeeding such calendar year. If an employee's employment is terminated before the close of such calendar year, the employer, at his option, shall furnish the statement to the employee at any time after the termination but no later than January 31 of the year succeeding such calendar year. However, if an employee whose employment is terminated before the close of such calendar year requests the employer to furnish him the statement at an earlier time, and if there is no reasonable expectation on the part of both employer and employee of further employment during the calendar year, then the employer shall furnish the statement to the employee on or before the later of the 30th day after the day of the request or the 30th day after the day on which the last payment of wages is made. For provisions relating to the filing of the Internal Revenue Service copies of the statement, see §31.6051-2.

(ii) *Expedited furnishing.*—(A) *General rule.*—If an employer is required to make a final return under §31.6011(a)-6(a)(1) (relating to the final return for Federal Insurance Contributions Act taxes and income tax withholding from wages) on Form 941, or a variation thereof, the employer must furnish the statement required by this section on or before the date required for filing the final return. See §31.6071(a)-1(a)(1). However, if the final return under §31.6011(a)-6(a)(1) is a monthly return, as described in §31.6011(a)-5, the employer must furnish the statement required by this section on or before the last day of the month in which the final return is required to be filed. See §31.6071(a)-1(a)(2). Except as provided in paragraph (d)(2)(i) of this section, in no event may an employer furnish the statement required by this section later than January 31 of the year succeeding the calendar year to which it relates. The requirements set forth in this paragraph (d)(1)(ii) do not apply to employers with respect to employees whose wages are for domestic service in the private home of the employer. See §31.6011(a)-1(a)(3).

(B) *Requests by employees.*—An employer is not permitted to furnish a statement pursuant to the provisions of the third sentence of paragraph (d)(1)(i) of this section (relating to written requests by terminated employees for Form W-2) at a time later than that required by the provisions of paragraph (d)(1)(ii)(A) of this section.

(C) *Effective date.*—This paragraph (d)(1)(ii) is effective January 1, 1997.

(2) *Extensions of time.*—(i) *In general.*— (a) The Director, Martinsburg Computing Center, may grant an extension of time in which to furnish to employees the statements required by this section. A request may be made by a letter to the Director, Martinsburg Computing Center. The request must contain:

(1) *The employer's name and address;*

(2) *The employer's taxpayer identification numbers;*

(3) *The type of return (i.e., Form W-2);.*—and

(4) *A concise statement of the reasons for requesting the extension.*

(b) The application must be mailed or delivered on or before the applicable due date prescribed in paragraph (d)(1) of this section for furnishing the statements required by this section.

(c) In any case in which an employer is unable, by reason of illness, absence, or other good cause, to sign a request for an extension, any person standing in close personal or business relationship to the employer may sign the request on his behalf, and shall be considered as a duly authorized agent for this purpose, provided the request sets forth a reason for a signature other than the employer's and the relationship existing between the employer and the signer. For provisions relating to extensions of time for filing the Social Security Administration copies of the statement, see § 31.6081(a)-1(a)(2).

(ii) *Automatic extension of time.*—The Commissioner may, in appropriate cases, publish procedures for automatic extensions of time to furnish Forms W-2 where the employer is required to furnish the Form W-2 on an expedited basis.

(3) *Cross references.*—For provisions relating to the penalties provided for the willful furnishing of a false or fraudulent statement, or for the willful failure to furnish a statement, see § 31.6674-1 and section 7204.

(e) *Reporting of reimbursements of or payments of expenses of moving from one residence to another residence after July 23, 1971.*—Every employer who after July 23, 1971, makes reimbursement to, or payment to (other than direct cash reimbursement), an employee for his expenses of moving from one residence to another residence which is includible in gross income under section 82 shall furnish to the best of his ability to such employee information sufficient to assist the employee in the computation of any deduction allowable under section 217 with respect to such reimbursement or payment. The information required under this paragraph may be furnished on Form 4782 provided by the Internal Revenue Service or may be furnished on forms provided by the employer so long as the employee receives the same information he would have received had he been furnished with a completed Form 4782. The information shall include the amount of the reimbursement or payment and whether the reimbursement or payment was made directly to a third party for the benefit of an employee or furnished in kind to the employee. In addition, information shall be furnished as to whether the reimbursement or payment represents an expense described in sub-

paragraphs (A) through (E) of section 217(b)(1), and if so, the amount and nature of the expenses described in each such subparagraph. The information described in this paragraph shall be furnished at the same time or before the written statement required by section 6051(a) is furnished in respect of the calendar year for which the information provided under this paragraph is required. The information required under this paragraph shall be provided for the taxable year in which the payment or reimbursement is received by the employee. For determining the taxable year in which a payment or reimbursement is received, see section 82 and § 1.82-1.

(f) *Statements with respect to compensation, as defined in the Railroad Retirement Tax Act, paid after December 31, 1967.*—(1) *Required information relating to excess medicare tax on compensation paid after December 31, 1971.*—(i) *Notification of possible credit or refund.*—With respect to compensation (as defined in section 3231(e)) paid after December 31, 1971, every employer (as defined in section 3231(a)) who is required to deduct and withhold from an employee (as defined in section 3231(b)) a tax under section 3201, shall include on or with the statement required to be furnished such employee under section 6051(a), a notice concerning the provisions of this title with respect to the allowance of a credit or refund of the tax on wages imposed by section 3101(b) and the tax on compensation imposed by section 3201 or 3211 which is treated as a tax on wages imposed by section 3101(b). Such notice shall inform such employee of the eligibility of persons having a second employment, in addition to railroad employment, for a credit or refund of any excess hospital insurance tax which such persons have paid because of employment under both social security (includingemployee and self-employment coverage) and railroad retirement. See section 6413(c)(3) and paragraph (c) of § 31.6413(c)-1, relating to special refunds with respect to compensation as defined in the Railroad Retirement Tax Act.

(ii) *Information to be supplied to employees upon request.*—With respect to compensation (as defined in section 3231(e)) paid after December 31, 1971, every employer (as defined in section 3231(a)) who is required to deduct and withhold tax under section 3201 from an employee (as defined in section 3231(b)) who has also received wages during such year subject to the tax imposed by section 3101(b), shall upon request of such employee furnish to him a written statement showing—

(a) The total amount of compensation with respect to which the tax imposed by section 3101(b) was deducted.

(b) The total amount of employee tax under section 3201 deducted and withheld (increased by any adjustment in the calendar year for overcollection, or decreased by any adjustment in such year for undercollection, of such tax during any prior year), and

(c) The proportion thereof (expressed either as a dollar amount, or a percentage of the total amount of compensation as defined in section 3231(e), or as a percentage of the total amount of employee tax under section 3201) withheld as tax under section 3201 for financing the cost of hospital insurance benefits.

(2) *Statements on Form W-2 (RR).*— (i) *Compensation paid during 1970 or 1971.*—With respect to compensation (as defined in section 3231(e)) paid during 1970 or 1971, every employer (as defined in section 3231(a)) who is required to deduct and withhold from an employee (as defined in section 3231(b)) a tax under section 3402 with respect to compensation, or who would have been required to deduct and withhold a tax under section 3402 (determined without regard to section 3402(n)) if the employee had claimed no more than one withholding exemption, shall furnish to each such employee in respect of such compensation the tax return copy and the employee's copy of a statement on Form W-2 (RR) instead of Form W-2, unless such employers are permitted by the Internal Revenue Service to continue to use Form W-2 in lieu of Form W-2 (RR). If the wage bracket method of withholding provided in section 3402(c)(1) is used in respect of such compensation, a statement on Form W-2 (RR) must be furnished to each employee whose wages during any payroll period are equal to or in excess of the smallest wages from which tax must be withheld in the case of an employee claiming one exemption. If the percentage method is used, a statement on Form W-2 (RR) must be furnished to each employee whose wages during any payroll period are in excess of one withholding exemption for such payroll period as shown in the percentage method withholding table contained in section 3402(b)(1). Each statement on Form W-2 (RR) shall show the following:

(*a*) The name, address, and identification number of the employer,

(*b*) The name and address of the employee and his social security account number,

(*c*) The total amount of wages as defined in section 3401(a),

(*d*) The total amount deducted and withheld as tax under section 3402,

(*e*) The total amount of compensation as defined in section 3231(e), and

(*f*) The total amount of employee tax under section 3201 deducted and withheld (increased by any adjustment in the calendar year for overcollection, or decreased by any adjustment in such year for undercollection, of such tax during any prior year) and the proportion thereof (expressed either as a dollar amount, as a percentage of the total amount of compensation as defined in section 3231(e), or as a percentage of the total amount of employee tax under section 3201) withheld as tax under section 3201 for financing the cost of hospital insurance benefits.

The provisions of this chapter applicable to Form W-2, other than those relating solely to the Federal Insurance Contributions Act, are hereby made applicable to Form W-2 (RR). See paragraph (d) of this section for provisions relating to

the time and place for furnishing the statement required by this subparagraph.

(ii) *Compensation paid during 1968 or 1969.*—At the option of the employer, the provisions of subdivision (i) of this subparagraph may apply with respect to compensation paid during 1968 or 1969.

(iii) Every employer who, pursuant to subdivision (i) or (ii) of this subparagraph, does not provide Form W-2 (RR) with respect to compensation must furnish the additional information required by Form W-2 (RR) upon request by the employee.

(g) *Employers filing composite returns.*—Every employer who files a composite return pursuant to §31.6011(a)-8 shall furnish to his employees the statements required under this section, except that in lieu of Form W-2 the statements may be in any form which is suitable for retention by the employee and which contains all information required to be shown on Form W-2.

(h) *Statements with respect to the refundable earned income credit.*—(1) *In general.*—In respect of remuneration paid in any calendar year beginning after December 31, 1986, for services performed after December 31, 1986, every employer shall furnish Notice 797 (You May Be Eligible for a Refund on Your Federal Income Tax Return Because of the Earned Income Credit (EIC)), or a written statement that contains an exact reproduction of the wording contained in Notice 797, to each employee with respect to whom the employer paid wages (within the meaning of section 3401(a)) during the calendar year and who did not have any income tax withheld by the employer during the calendar year. Notwithstanding the preceding sentence, no such statement need be furnished to an employee who claimed exemption from withholding pursuant to section 3402(n) for the calendar year.

(2) *Time for furnishing statement.*—(i) *General rule.*—Except as otherwise provided in paragraph (h)(2)(ii) of this section, the statement required by this paragraph (h) for a calendar year shall be furnished—

(A) In the case of an employee who is required to be furnished a Form W-2, Wage and Tax Statement, for the calendar year, within one week of (before or after) the date that the employee is furnished a timely Form W-2 for the calendar year (or, if a Form W-2 is not so furnished, on or before the date by which it is required to be furnished), and

(B) In the case of an employee who is not required to be furnished a Form W-2 for the calendar year, on or before February 7 of the year succeeding the calendar year.

(ii) *Special rule with respect to certain Forms W-2 for 1987 and 1988.*—With respect to an employee who is not furnished a Form W-2 for calendar year 1987 before October 24, 1988, or who was furnished such form on or before June 11, 1987, the statement required by this paragraph (h) shall be furnished on or before October

24, 1988. With respect to an employee who is furnished a Form W-2 after June 11, 1987, and before October 24, 1988, the statement required by this paragraph (h) shall be furnished within one week of (before or after) the date the employee is furnished the Form W-2. With respect to an employee who is required to be furnished a Form W-2 for calendar year 1988 before October 24, 1988, but is not so furnished, the statement required by this paragraph (h) shall be furnished on or before that date.

(3) *Manner of furnishing statement.*—If an employee is furnished a Form W-2 in a timely manner, the statement required by this paragraph (h) may be furnished with the employee's Form W-2. Any statement not so furnished shall be furnished by direct, personal delivery to the employee or by first class mail addressed to the employee at his or her current or last known address. For purposes of the preceding sentence, direct, personal delivery means hand delivery to the employee. Thus, for example, an employer does not meet the requirements of this paragraph (h) if the statement is sent through inter-office mail or is posted on a bulletin board.

(i) *Cross references.*—For provisions relating to the penalties provided for the willful furnishing of a false or fraudulent statement, or for the willful failure to furnish a statement, see §31.6674-1 and section 7204. For additional provisions relating to the inclusion of identification numbers and account numbers in statements on Form W-2, see §31.6109-1. For provisions relating to the penalty for failure to report an identification number or an account number, as required by §31.6109-1, see §301.6676-1 of this chapter (Regulations on Procedure and Administration). For the penalties applicable to information returns and payee statements the due date for which (determined without regard to extensions) is after December 31, 1989, see sections 6721-6724 as amended by section 7711 of the Omnibus Budget Reconciliation Act of 1989. See section 6723 (prior to its amendment by section 7711 of the Omnibus Budget Reconciliation Act of 1989 (Pub. L. 101-239, 103 Stat. 2106 (1989)) and §301.6723-1A of this Chapter (as issued thereunder) for provisions relating to the penalty for failure to include correct information on an information return or a payee statement and for the exceptions to the penalty, particularly the exception for timely correction, with respect to information returns and payee statements the due date for which, determined without regard to extensions, is after December 31, 1986, and before January 1, 1990.

(j) *Electronic furnishing of statements.*—(1) *In general.*—A person required by section 6051 to furnish a written statement on Form W-2 (furnisher) to the individual to whom it is required to be furnished (recipient) may furnish the Form W-2 in an electronic format in lieu of a paper format. A furnisher who meets the requirements of paragraphs (j)(2) through (6) of this section is treated as furnishing the Form W-2 in a timely manner.

(2) *Consent.*—(i) *In general.*—The recipient must have affirmatively consented to receive the Form W-2 in an electronic format. The consent may be made electronically in any manner that reasonably demonstrates that the recipient can access the Form W-2 in the electronic format in which it will be furnished to the recipient. Alternatively, the consent may be made in a paper document if it is confirmed electronically.

(ii) *Withdrawal of consent.*—The consent requirement of this paragraph (j)(2) is not satisfied if the recipient withdraws the consent and the withdrawal takes effect before the statement is furnished. The furnisher may provide that a withdrawal of consent takes effect either on the date it is received by the furnisher or on a subsequent date. The furnisher may also provide that a request for a paper statement will be treated as a withdrawal of consent.

(iii) *Change in hardware or software requirements.*—If a change in hardware or software required to access the Form W-2 creates a material risk that the recipient will not be able to access the Form W-2, the furnisher must, prior to changing the hardware or software, provide the recipient with a notice. The notice must describe the revised hardware and software required to access the Form W-2 and inform the recipient that a new consent to receive the Form W-2 in the revised electronic format must be provided to the furnisher. After implementing the revised hardware and software, the furnisher must obtain from the recipient, in the manner described in paragraph (j)(2)(i) of this section, a new consent or confirmation of consent to receive the Form W-2 electronically.

(iv) *Examples.*—The following examples illustrate the rules of this paragraph (j)(2):

Example 1. Furnisher F sends Recipient R a letter stating that R may consent to receive Form W-2 electronically on a website instead of in a paper format. The letter contains instructions explaining how to consent to receive Form W-2 electronically by accessing the website, downloading the consent document, completing the consent document and e-mailing the completed consent back to F. The consent document posted on the website uses the same electronic format that F will use for the electronically furnished Form W-2. R reads the instructions and submits the consent in the manner provided in the instructions. R has consented to receive the statements electronically in the manner described in paragraph (j)(2)(i) of this section.

Example 2. Furnisher F sends Recipient R an e-mail stating that R may consent to receive Form W-2 electronically instead of in a paper format. The e-mail contains an attachment instructing R how to consent to receive Form W-2 electronically. The e-mail attachment uses the same electronic format that F will use for the electronically furnished Form W-2. R opens the attachment, reads the instructions, and submits the consent in the manner provided in the instructions. R has consented to receive Form W-2 electronically in the manner described in paragraph (j)(2)(i) of this section.

Example 3. Furnisher F posts a notice on its website stating that Recipient R may receive Form W-2 electronically instead of in a paper format. The website contains instructions on how R may access a secure webpage and consent to receive the statements electronically. By accessing the secure webpage and giving consent, R has consented to receive Form W-2 electronically in the manner described in paragraph (j)(2)(i) of this section.

(3) *Required disclosures.*—(i) *In general.*— Prior to, or at the time of, a recipient's consent, the furnisher must provide to the recipient a clear and conspicuous disclosure statement containing each of the disclosures described in paragraphs (j)(3)(ii) through (viii) of this section.

(ii) *Paper statement.*—The recipient must be informed that the Form W-2 will be furnished on paper if the recipient does not consent to receive it electronically.

(iii) *Scope and duration of consent.*—The recipient must be informed of the scope and duration of the consent. For example, the recipient must be informed whether the consent applies to each Form W-2 required to be furnished after the consent is given until it is withdrawn in the manner described in paragraph (j)(3)(v)(A) of this section or only to the first Form W-2 required to be furnished following the date on which the consent is given.

(iv) *Post-consent request for a paper statement.*—The recipient must be informed of any procedure for obtaining a paper copy of the recipient's statement after giving the consent described in paragraph (j)(2)(i) of this section and whether a request for a paper statement will be treated as a withdrawal of consent.

(v) *Withdrawal of consent.*—The recipient must be informed that—

(A) The recipient may withdraw a consent by writing (electronically or on paper) to the person or department whose name, mailing address, telephone number, and e-mail address is provided in the disclosure statement;

(B) The furnisher will confirm the withdrawal and the date on which it takes effect in writing (either electronically or on paper); and

(C) A withdrawal of consent does not apply to a statement that was furnished electronically in the manner described in this paragraph (j) before the date on which the withdrawal of consent takes effect.

(vi) *Notice of termination.*—The recipient must be informed of the conditions under which a furnisher will cease furnishing statements electronically to the recipient (for example, termination of the recipient's employment with furnisher-employer).

(vii) *Updating information.*—The recipient must be informed of the procedures for updating the information needed by the furnisher to contact the recipient. The furnisher must inform the recipient of any change in the furnisher's contact information.

(viii) *Hardware and software requirements.*—The recipient must be provided with a description of the hardware and software required to access, print, and retain the Form W-2, and the date when the Form W-2 will no longer be available on the website. The recipient must be informed that the Form W-2 may be required to be printed and attached to a Federal, State, or local income tax return.

(4) *Format.*—The electronic version of the Form W-2 must contain all required information and comply with applicable revenue procedures relating to substitute statements to recipients.

(5) *Notice.*—(i) *In general.*—If the statement is furnished on a website, the furnisher must notify the recipient that the statement is posted on a website. The notice may be delivered by mail, electronic mail, or in person. The notice must provide instructions on how to access and print the statement. The notice must include the following statement in capital letters, "IMPORTANT TAX RETURN DOCUMENT AVAILABLE." If the notice is provided by electronic mail, the foregoing statement must be on the subject line of the electronic mail.

(ii) *Undeliverable electronic address.*—If an electronic notice described in paragraph (j)(5)(i) of this section is returned as undeliverable, and the correct electronic address cannot be obtained from the furnisher's records or from the recipient, then the furnisher must furnish the notice by mail or in person within 30 days after the electronic notice is returned.

(iii) *Corrected Form W-2.*—If the furnisher has corrected a recipient's Form W-2 that was furnished electronically, the furnisher must furnish the corrected Form W-2 to the recipient electronically. If the recipient's Form W-2 was furnished though a website posting and the furnisher has corrected the Form W-2, the furnisher must notify the recipient that it has posted the corrected Form W-2 on the website within 30 days of such posting in the manner described in paragraph (j)(5)(i) of this section. The corrected Form W-2 or the notice must be furnished by mail or in person if—

(A) An electronic notice of the website posting of an original Form W-2 or the corrected Form W-2 was returned as undeliverable; and

(B) The recipient has not provided a new e-mail address.

(6) *Access period.*—Forms W-2 furnished on a website must be retained on the website through October 15 of the year following the calendar year to which the Forms W-2 relate (or the first business day after October 15, if October 15 falls on a Saturday, Sunday, or legal holiday). The furnisher must maintain access to corrected

Forms W-2 that are posted on the website through October 15 of the year following the calendar year to which the Forms W-2 relate (or the first business day after such October 15, if October 15 falls on a Saturday, Sunday, or legal holiday) or the date 90 days after the corrected forms are posted, whichever is later.

(7) *Paper statements after withdrawal of consent.*—If a recipient withdraws consent to receive a statement electronically and the withdrawal takes effect before the statement is furnished electronically, a paper statement must be furnished. A paper statement furnished after the statement due date under this paragraph (j)(7) will be considered timely if furnished within 30 days after the date the withdrawal of consent is received by the furnisher.

(8) *Effective date.*—This paragraph (j) applies to Forms W-2 required to be furnished after February 13, 2004. Paragraph (j)(6) of this section also applies to Forms W-2 required to be furnished after December 31, 2003. [Reg. §31.6051-1.]

☐ [*T.D.* 6155, 12-29-55. *Amended by T.D.* 6472, 6-22-60; *T.D.* 6606, 8-24-62; *T.D.* 6983, 12-3-68; *T.D.* 7001, 1-17-69; *T.D.* 7048, 6-23-70; *T.D.* 7115, 5-20-71; *T.D.* 7195, 7-10-72; *T.D.* 7351, 4-16-75; *T.D.* 7374, 7-23-75; *T.D.* 7577, 12-19-78; *T.D.* 7580, 12-20-78; *T.D.* 7656, 11-28-79; *T.D.* 7683, 3-12-80; *T.D.* 8155, 9-9-87; *T.D.* 8222, 8-23-88; *T.D.* 8344, 4-12-91; *T.D.* 8636, 12-20-95; *T.D.* 9061, 6-10-2003 and T.D. 9114, 2-13-2004.]

[Reg. §301.6051-1]

§301.6051-1. Receipts for employees.—For provisions relating to statements for employees regarding remuneration paid during calendar year, see §31.6051-1 of this chapter (Employment Tax Regulations). [Reg. §301.6051-1.]

☐ [*T.D.* 6498, 10-24-60.]

[Reg. §31.6051-2]

§31.6051-2. Information returns on Form W-3 and Social Security Administration copies of Forms W-2.—(a) *In general.*—Every employer who is required to make a return of tax under §31.6011(a)-1 (relating to returns under the Federal Insurance Contributions Act), §31.6011(a)-4 (relating to returns of income tax withheld from wages), or §31.6011(a)-5 (relating to monthly returns) for a calendar year or any period therein shall file the Social Security Administration copy of each Form W-2 required under §31.6051-1 to be furnished by the employer with respect to wages paid during the calendar year. Each Form W-2 and the transmittal Form W-3 shall together constitute an information return to be filed with the Social Security Administration office indicated on the instructions to such forms. However, in the case of an employer who elects to file a composite return pursuant to §31.6011(a)-8, the information return required by this section shall consist of magnetic tape (or other approved media) containing all information required to be

on the employee statement, together with transmittal Form 4804.

(b) *Corrected returns.*—The Social Security Administration copies of corrected Forms W-2 (or magnetic tape or other approved media) for employees for the calendar year shall be submitted with Form W-3 (or Form 4804), on or before the date on which information returns for the period in which the correction is made would be due under paragraph (a)(3)(ii) of §31.6071(a)-1, to the Social Security Administration office with which Forms W-2 are required to be filed.

(c) *Cross references.*—For provisions relating to the time for filing the information returns required by this section and to extensions of the time for filing, see §§31.6071(a)-1(a)(3) and 31.6081(a)-1(a)(2), respectively. For the penalty provided in case of each failure to file, see paragraph (a) of §301.6652-1 of this chapter (Regulations on Procedure and Administration). For the penalties applicable to information returns and payee statements the due date for which (determined without regard to extensions) is after December 31, 1989, see sections 6721-6724 as amended by section 7711 of the Omnibus Budget Reconciliation Act of 1989 (Pub. L. 101-239, 103 Stat. 2106 (1989)). See section 6723 (prior to its amendment by section 7711 of the Omnibus Reconciliation Act of 1989) and §301.6723-1A of this Chapter for provisions relating to the penalty for failure to include correct information on an information return or a payee statement and for the exceptions to the penalty, particularly the exception for timely correction, with respect to information returns and payee statements the due date for which, determined without regard to extensions, is after December 31, 1986, and before January 1, 1990. [Reg. §31.6051-2.]

☐ [*T.D.* 7351, 4-16-75. *Amended by T.D.* 7580, 12-28-78; *T.D.* 8155, 9-9-87; *T.D.* 8344, 4-12-91; *T.D.* 8636, 12-20-95 *and T.D.* 9061, 6-10-2003.]

[Reg. §31.6051-3]

§31.6051-3. Statements required in case of sick pay paid by third parties.—(a) *Statements required from payor.*—(1) Every payor of sick pay shall furnish to the employer of the payee of the sick pay a written statement. The written statement must contain the following information:

(i) The name and, if there is withholding from sick pay under section 3402(o) and the regulations thereunder, the social security account number of the payee.

(ii) The total amount of sick pay paid to the payee during the calendar year, and

(iii) The total amount (if any) deducted and withheld from sick pay under section 3402(o) and the regulations thereunder. The statement must be furnished to the employer on or before January 15 of the year following the calendar year in which any sick pay was paid.

(2) These reporting requirements are in lieu of the requirements of sections 6051(a) (relating to written statements for employees) and 6041

(relating to information returns). Statements required to be furnished by this paragraph shall be treated as statements required under section 6051 to be furnished to employees for purposes of sections 6674 (relating to fraudulent statement or failure to furnish statement to employee) and 7204 (relating to fraudulent statement or failure to make statement to employees).

(3) A multiemployer plan paying sick pay pursuant to a collectively bargained agreement may furnish the statement required to be furnished by this paragraph, which shall include the total amount of sick pay paid to the employee under the plan regardless of the identity or number of employers for whom the employee worked during the calendar year under the plan, to one of the following:

(i) The employer for whom the employee worked the most hours during the calendar year for which the statement is to be furnished,

(ii) The employer for whom the employee first worked during such year,

(iii) The employer for whom the employee last worked during such year,

(iv) The employer for whom the employee worked immediately preceding his absence for which sick pay was paid,

(v) The employer for whom the employee worked immediately following his absence for which sick pay was paid,

(vi) The employer designated through the operation of a specific clause of the collective bargaining agreement, or

(vii) The employer designated through the operation of a specific system of designation chosen by the payor.

(b) *Information required to be furnished by employer.*—Every employer of a payee of sick pay who receives a statement under paragraph (a) from a payor of sick pay shall furnish to each payee of sick pay a written statement, which must be furnished on Form W-2. The written statement must contain the following information:

(1) All of the information required to be furnished under paragraph (a),

(2) The name, the address, and the Employer Identification Number (EIN) of the employer,

(3) The words "sick pay", which shall be written in the box labelled "Employer's use", and

(4) If any portion of the sick pay is excludable from gross income under section 104(a)(3), the amount of the portion which is not so excludable and of the portion which is so excludable. Only sick pay payments includable in gross income shall be reported in the box labelled "Wages, tips, other compensation" on Form W-2. Any amount excludable from gross income under section 104(a)(3) shall be reported in the box labelled "Employer's use" on Form W-2 and any amount so reported shall be described as "Nontaxable". The information required to be furnished by this paragraph may be furnished either on the same Form W-2 that is required to be furnished under section 6051(a) or on a separate Form W-2. To the extent practicable, this statement should be furnished to the payee along with the statement (if any) required under section 6051(a) (relating to written statements for employees). The statement must be furnished to the payee on or before January 31 of the year following the calendar year in which any sick pay was paid. The employer shall file copy A of Form W-2 and Form W-3 with the Social Security Administration in accordance with section 6051(d) (relating to statements to constitute information returns) and the regulations thereunder.

(c) *Optional rule.*—The payor and the employer may at their option enter into an agency agreement valid under local law whereby the employer designates the payor to be the employer's agent for purposes of fulfilling the requirements of this section. This agreement must specify what portion, if any, of the sick pay is excludable from gross income under section 104(a)(3). If they enter into such an agreement, the payor shall not provide the statement required by paragraph (a) but shall instead furnish statements that meet all of the requirements of paragraph (b), except that the agreement must provide that the payor will furnish the statements with the payor's, rather than the employer's, name, address, and Employer Identification Number (EIN) if "Sick Pay Statement Furnished under an Agency Agreement with Your Employer" appears in the box labelled "Employer's Use" on Form W-2. Subparagraph (a)(2) remains applicable to statements furnished under this paragraph. In the case of sick pay paid under a multiemployer plan pursuant to a collectively bargained agreement, an amendment to either the multiemployer plan or the collectively bargained agreement designating the payor to be the employers' agent for purposes of fulfilling the requirements of this section shall be deemed an agency agreement that fulfills the requirements of the first sentence of this paragraph.

(d) *Definitions.*—For purposes of this section, the terms "payor", "payee", and "sick pay" shall have the same meaning as ascribed thereto in section 3402(o) and the regulations thereunder. For purposes of this section, the term "employer" shall have the same meaning as ascribed thereto in section 3401(d) and the regulations thereunder, except that the term "employer" shall not include the payor for purposes of this section.

(e) *Additional requirements.*—(1) Statements furnished to payees under this section must also comply with all requirements of section 6051(c) and (d) and the regulations thereunder.

(2) The provisions of §1.9101-1 (relating to permission to submit information required by certain returns and statements on magnetic tape) shall be applicable to the information required by this section to be furnished on Form W-2 if the employer properly complies with those provisions.

Reg. §31.6051-3(e)(2)

(3) The provisions of section 6109 (relating to identifying numbers) and the regulations thereunder shall be applicable to Form W-2 and to any payee of sick pay to whom a statement on Form W-2 is required by this section to be furnished. Thus the employer must include the social security account number of the payee on all Forms W-2.

(f) *Effective date.*—The provisions of this section shall apply to payments of sick pay made on or after May 1, 1981.

(g) *Transitional rule.*—Payors may report all sick pay paid to a payee after December 31, 1980, and before May 1, 1981, on the same statement required to be furnished under paragraph (a) as is used to report sick pay paid to a payee on or after May 1, 1981. If the payor reports on the statement required to be furnished under paragraph (a), he shall not report sick pay paid after December 31, 1980, and before May 1, 1981, on Form 1099, if otherwise required to do so. If no sick pay is paid on or after May 1, 1981, the payor may report all sick pay paid to a payee after December 31, 1980, and before May 1, 1981, on the statement required to be furnished under paragraph (a). If he reports on the statement required to be furnished under paragraph (a), he shall not report sick pay paid on Form 1099, if otherwise required to do so. [Reg. §31.6051-3.]

☐ [*T.D.* 7813, 3-15-82.]

[Reg. §31.6051-4]

§31.6051-4. Statement required in case of backup Withholding.—(a) *Statements required from payor.*—Every payor of any reportable payment(as defined in section 3406(b)(1)) who is required to deduct and withhold tax under section 3406 must furnish to the payee a written statement containing the information required by paragraph(c) of this section.

(b) *Prescribed form.*—The prescribed form for the statement required by this section is Form 1099. In the case of any reportable interest or dividend payment as defined in section 3406(b)(2), the prescribed form is the Form 1099 required in §1.6042-4 of this chapter (relating to payments of dividends), §1.6044-5 of this chapter (relating to payments of patronage dividends), or §1.6049-6(e) of this chapter (relating to payments of interest or original issue discount). Statements required to be furnished by this section will be treated as statements required by the respective sections with respect to any reportable payment, except that the statement required under this section must include the amount of tax withheld under section 3406. In no event will a statement be required under this section if a statement with the same information is required to be furnished to the recipient under another section.

(c) *Information required.*—Each statement on Form 1099 must show the following:

(1) The name, address, and taxpayer identification number of the person receiving any reportable payment;

(2) Except as provided in the prescribed form or instructions, the amount subject to reporting under section 6041, 6041A(a), 6042, 6044, 6045, 6049, 6050A, 6050N, or 6050W whether or not the amount of the reportable payment is less than the amount for which an information return is required or, if tax is withheld under section 3406, the amount of the payment withheld upon;

(3) The amount of tax deducted and withheld under section 3406;

(4) The name and address of the person filing the form;

(5) A legend stating that such amount is being reported to the Internal Revenue Service; and

(6) Such other information as is required by the form.

(d) *Time for furnishing statements.*—The statement must be furnished to the payee no later than January 31 of the year following the calendar year in which the payment was made. However, for a statement required to be furnished after December 31, 2008, the February 15 due date under section 6045 applies to the statement if the statement reports tax withheld from a payment reportable under section 6045 or is furnished in a consolidated reporting statement under section 6045. See §§1.6045-1(k)(3), 1.6045-2(d)(2), 1.6045-3(e)(2), 1.6045-4(m)(3), and 1.6045-5(a)(3)(ii) of this chapter.

(e) *Aggregation.*—The payor or broker may combine the information required to be shown under this section with information required to be shown under another section even if they do not relate to the same type of reportable payment. [Reg. §31.6051-4.]

☐ [*T.D.* 8637, 12-20-95. *Amended by T.D.* 9496, 8-13-2010; *T.D.* 9504, 10-12-2010.]

[Reg. §1.6052-1]

§1.6052-1. Information returns regarding payment of wages in the form of group-term life insurance.—(a) *Requirement of reporting.*—(1) *In general.*—Every employer, who during any calendar year provides any one of his employees remuneration for services in the form of group-term life insurance on the life of such employee any part of the cost of which is to be included in such employee's gross income as provided in section 79(a), shall make a separate return on Form W-2 with respect to each such employee for such year which includes the following information:

(i) Name, address, and identifying number of the employer;

(ii) Name, address, and social security number of the employee; and

(iii) Total amount includible in the employee's gross income by reason of the provisions of section 79(a), computed as if each employee reported his income on the basis of a calendar year (determined as if the employer making such return is the only employer paying the employee remuneration in the form of group-term life insurance on his life which is includible in his gross income under section 79(a)).

Returns on Form W-2 required to be filed pursuant to the provisions of this section shall be transmitted by Form W-3. In a case where, with respect to the same employee, an employer must make a return on Form W-2 under this section and also under § 31.6011(a)-4 or § 31.6011(a)-5 of this chapter (Employment Tax Regulations), or under § 1.6041-2 (relating to return of information as to payments to employees), such employer may make such returns on the same Form W-2 or on separate Forms W-2. In a case where an employer must file a Form W-3 under this section and also under § 31.6011(a)-4 or § 31.6011(a)-5 of this chapter (Employment Tax Regulations), the Form W-3 filed under such § 31.6011(a)-4 or § 31.6011(a)-5 shall also be used as the transmittal form for a return on Form W-2 made pursuant to the provisions of this section.

(2) *Definitions.*—Terms used in paragraph (a)(1) of this section and in section 79 and the regulations thereunder have the meaning ascribed to them in section 79 and the regulations thereunder.

(b) *Time and place for filing.*—(1) *Time for filing.*—(i) *General rule.*—In a case where an employer must file Forms W-3 and W-2 under this section and also under § 31.6011(a)-4 or § 31.6011(a)-5 of this chapter (Employment Tax Regulations), the time for filing such forms under this section shall be the same as the time (including extensions thereof) for filing such forms under § 31.6011(a)-4 or § 31.6011(a)-5.

(ii) *Exception.*—In a case where an employer is not required to file Forms W-3 and W-2 under § 31.6011(a)-4 or § 31.6011(a)-5 of this chapter, returns on Forms W-3 and W-2 required under paragraph (a) of this section for any calendar year shall be filed on or before February 28 (March 31 if filed electronically) of the following year.

(iii) *Cross reference.*—For extensions of time for filing returns, see section 6081 and the regulations thereunder.

(2) *Place for filing.*—The returns on Forms W-3 and W-2 required under paragraph (a) of this section shall be filed pursuant to the rules contained in § 31.6091-1 of this chapter (Employment Tax Regulations), relating to the place for filing certain returns.

(c) *Special rule for calendar years before 1972.*—For calendar years before 1972, the provisions of this section will be deemed to have been complied with if the returns for such years were filed in accordance with the provisions of this section in effect prior to [insert date on which final regulations under this section are published in the Federal Register] or with the instructions applicable to the appropriate forms.

(d) *Last day for filing return.*—For provisions relating to the time for performance of an act when the last day prescribed for performance falls on Saturday, Sunday, or a legal holiday, see § 301.7503-1 of this chapter (Regulations on Procedure and Administration).

(e) *Penalty.*—For provisions relating to the penalty provided for failure to file the information returns required by this section, see section 6652 and the regulations thereunder. [Reg. § 1.6052-1.]

☐ [*T.D. 6888, 7-5-66. Amended by T.D. 7284, 8-2-73, T.D. 7580, 12-20-78; T.D. 7623, 5-14-79 and T.D. 8895, 8-17-2000.*]

[Reg. § 301.6052-1]

§ 301.6052-1. Information returns and statements regarding payment of wages in the form of group-term life insurance.—For provisions relating to information returns and statements required in connection with the payment of wages in the form of group-term life insurance, see § § 1.6052-1 and 1.6052-2 of this chapter (Income Tax Regulations). [Reg. § 301.6052-1.]

☐ [*T.D. 7275, 5-4-73.*]

[Reg. § 1.6052-2]

§ 1.6052-2. Statements to be furnished employees with respect to wages paid in the form of group-term life insurance.—(a) *Requirement.*—Every employer filing a return under section 6052(a) and § 1.6052-1 with respect to group-term life insurance on the life of an employee shall furnish to the employee whose name is set forth in such return a written statement showing the information required by paragraph (b) of this section.

(b) *Form of statement.*—The written statement required to be furnished to an employee under paragraph (a) of this section shall show—

(1) The total amount includible in the employee's gross income by reason of the provisions of section 79(a), but determined as if the employer furnishing such statement is the only employer paying the employee remuneration in the form of group-term life insurance on his life which is includible in his gross income under section 79(a).

(2) The name, address, and identifying number of the employer filing the statement.

The requirement of this section for the furnishing of a statement to an employee may be satisfied by the furnishing to such employee of a copy of the return filed pursuant to § 1.6052-1 in respect of such employee. A statement shall be considered to be furnished to a person within the meaning of this section if it is mailed to such person at his last known address.

(c) *Time for furnishing statements.*—(1) *In general.*—Each statement required by this section to be furnished to any employee for a calendar year shall be furnished to such person after the close of that year and on or before January 31 of the following year.

Reg. § 1.6052-2(c)(1)

(2) *Extensions of time.*—For good cause shown upon written application of the employer required to furnish statements under this section, the district director may grant an extension of time not exceeding 30 days in which to furnish such statements. The application shall be addressed to the district director with whom the income tax returns of the applicant are filed and shall contain a full recital of the reasons for requesting the extension to aid the district director in determining the period of the extension, if any, which will be granted. Such a request in the form of a letter to the district director signed by the applicant will suffice as an application. The application shall be filed on or before the date prescribed in subparagraph (1) of this paragraph for furnishing the statements required by this section.

(3) *Last day for furnishing statement.*—For provisions relating to the time for performance of an act when the last day prescribed for performance falls on Saturday, Sunday, or a legal holiday, see § 301.7503-1 of this chapter (Regulations on Procedure and Administration).

(d) *Special rule where Form W-2 is used.*—The provisions of this paragraph shall apply notwithstanding anything to the contrary in paragraph (b) or (c) of this section. The requirement of this section for the furnishing of a statement to an employee may be satisfied by furnishing to such employee the employee's copy of Form W-2 filed pursuant to § 1.6052-1 in respect of such employee. In a case where the statement furnished by an employer to an employee for purposes of complying with this section is the employee's copy of a Form W-2, then the rules in § 31.6051-1 of this chapter (Employment Tax Regulations) shall apply with respect to the means and time (including extensions thereof) for furnishing such statements to the employee and making corrections on such form.

(e) *Definitions.*—Terms used in this section and in section 79 and the regulations thereunder have the meaning ascribed to them in section 79 and the regulations thereunder.

(f) *Penalty.*—For provisions relating to the penalty provided for failure to furnish a statement under this section, see section 6678 and the regulations thereunder.

(g) *Special rule for calendar years before 1972.*—For calendar years before 1972, the provisions of this section will be deemed to have been complied with if the statements for such years were furnished in accordance with the provisions of this section in effect prior to [insert date on which final regulations under this section are published in the Federal Register] or with the instructions applicable to the appropriate forms. [Reg. § 1.6052-2.]

☐ [*T.D.* 6888, 7-5-66. *Amended by T.D.* 7284, 8-2-73, *T.D.* 7580, 12-20-78 *and T.D.* 7623, 5-14-79.]

Reg. § 1.6052-2(c)(2)

[Reg. §31.6053-1]

§31.6053-1. Report of tips by employee to employer.—(a) *Requirement that tips be reported.*—(1) *In general.*—An employee who receives, in the course of employment by an employer, tips that constitute wages as defined in section 3121(a) or section 3401, or compensation as defined in section 3231(e), must furnish to the employer a statement, or statements, disclosing the total amount of the tips received by the employee in the course of employment by the employer. Tips received by an employee in a calendar month in the course of employment by an employer that are required to be reported to the employer must be reported on or before the 10th day of the following month. For example, tips received by an employee in January 2000 are required to be reported by the employee to the employer on or before February 10, 2000.

(2) *Cross references.*—For provisions relating to the treatment of tips as wages for purposes of the Federal Insurance Contributions Act (FICA) tax under sections 3101 and 3111, see sections 3102(c), 3121(a)(12), and 3121(q) and §§ 31.3102-3 and 31.3121(a)(12)-1. For provisions relating to the treatment of tips as wages for purposes of the tax under section 3402 (income tax withholding), see sections 3401(a)(16), 3401(f), and 3402(k) and §§ 31.3401(a)(16)-1, 31.3401(f)-1, and 31.3402(k)-1. For provisions relating to the treatment of tips as compensation for purposes of the Railroad Retirement Tax Act (RRTA) tax under sections 3201 and 3221, see section 3231(e) and § 31.3231(e)-1(a).

(b) *Statement for use in reporting tips.*—(1) *In general.*—The statement described in paragraph (a) of this section can be provided on paper or transmitted electronically. The statement must be signed by the employee and must disclose:

(i) The name, address, and social security number of the employee.

(ii) The name and address of the employer.

(iii) The period for which, and the date on which, the statement is furnished. If the statement is for a calendar month, the month and year should be specified. If the statement is for a period of less than 1 calendar month, the beginning and ending dates of the period must be included (for example, January 1 through January 8, 1998).

(iv) The total amount of tips received by the employee during the period covered by the statement which are required to be reported to the employer (see paragraph (a) of this section).

(2) *Form of statement.*—(i) *In general.*—No particular form is prescribed for use in furnishing the statement required by this section. The statement may be furnished on paper or transmitted electronically. An electronic system and all tip statements generated by that system must meet the requirements of paragraph (d) of this section. If the employer does not provide any other means for the employee to report tips, the employee may use Form 4070, "Employee's Report of Tips to Employer."

(ii) *Single-purpose forms.*—A statement may be furnished on an employer-provided form. The form may be on paper or in electronic form. An employer that provides a paper form must make blank copies of the form readily available to all tipped employees. Any form, whether paper or electronic, provided by an employer for use by its tipped employees solely to report tips must meet all the requirements of paragraph (b)(1) of this section.

(iii) *Regularly used forms.*—Instead of requiring that tips be reported as described in paragraph (b)(2)(ii) of this section on a special form used solely for tip reporting, an employer may prescribe regularly used forms for use by employees in reporting tips. A regularly used form may be on paper or in electronic form (such as a time card or report), must meet the requirements of paragraph (b)(1)(iii) and (iv) of this section, must contain identifying information that will ensure accurate identification of the employee by the employer, and is permitted to be used only if the employer furnishes the employee a statement suitable for retention showing the amount of tips reported by the employee for the period. The employer statement may be furnished when the employee reports the tips, when wages are first paid following the reporting of tips by the employee, or within a short time after the wages are paid. The employer may meet this requirement, for example, through the use of a payroll check stub or other payroll document regularly furnished (if not less frequent than monthly) by the employer to the employee showing gross pay and deductions.

(c) *Period covered by, and due date of, tip statement.*—(1) *In general.*—A tip statement furnished by an employee to an employer may not cover a period greater than 1 calendar month. An employer may, however, require the submission of a statement in respect of a specified period of time, for example, on a weekly or biweekly basis, regular payroll period, etc. An employer may specify, subject to the limitation in paragraph (a) of this section, the time within which, or the date on which, the statement for a specified period of time should be submitted by the employee. For example, a statement covering a payroll period may be required to be submitted on the first (or second) day following the close of the payroll period. A statement submitted by an employee after the date specified by the employer for its submission nevertheless is a statement furnished pursuant to section 6053(a) and this section if it is submitted to the employer on or before the 10th day following the month in which the tips were received.

(2) *Termination of employment.*—If an employee's employment terminates, the employee must furnish a tip statement to the employer when the employee ceases to perform services for the employer. A statement submitted by an employee after the date on which the employee ceases to perform services for the employer is a

statement furnished pursuant to section 6053(a) and this section if the statement is submitted to the employer on or before the earlier of the day on which the final wage payment is made by the employer to the employee or the 10th day following the month in which the tips were received.

(d) *Requirements for electronic systems.*—(1) *In general.*—The electronic system must ensure that the information received is the information transmitted by the employee and must document all occasions of access that result in the transmission of a tip statement. In addition, the design and operation of the electronic system, including access procedures, must make it reasonably certain that the person accessing the system and transmitting the statement is the employee identified in the statement transmitted.

(2) *Same information as on paper statement.*—The electronic tip statement must provide the employer with all the information required by paragraph (b)(1) of this section.

(3) *Signature.*—The electronic tip statement must be signed by the employee. The electronic signature must identify the employee transmitting the electronic tip statement and must authenticate and verify the transmission. For this purpose, the terms *authenticate* and *verify* have the same meanings as they do when applied to a written signature on a paper tip statement. Any form of electronic signature that satisfies the foregoing requirements is permissible.

(4) *Copies of electronic tip statements.*—Upon request by the Internal Revenue Service (IRS), the employer must supply the IRS with a hard copy of the electronic tip statement and a statement that, to the best of the employer's knowledge, the electronic tip statement was filed by the named employee. The hard copy of the electronic tip statement must provide the information required by paragraph (b)(1) of this section, but need not be a facsimile of Form 4070 or any employer-designed form.

(5) *Record retention.*—The record retention requirements applicable to automatic data processing systems also apply to electronic tip reporting systems.

(6) *Effective date.*—The provisions pertaining to electronic systems and electronic tip reports are applicable as of December 13, 2000. However, employers may apply these provisions to earlier periods. [Reg. § 31.6053-1.]

☐ [*T.D.* 7001, 1-17-69. *Amended by T.D.* 8910, 12-12-2000.]

[Reg. § 31.6053-2]

§ 31.6053-2. Employer statement of uncollected employee tax.—(a) *Requirement that statement be furnished.*—If—

(1) The amount of the employee tax imposed by section 3101 in respect of tips reported

by an employee to his employer pursuant to section 6053(a) (see § 31.6053-1) exceeds

(2) The amount of employee tax imposed by section 3101 in respect of such tips which can be collected by the employer from wages (exclusive of tips) of such employee or from funds furnished to the employer by the employee,

the employer shall furnish to the employee a statement showing the amount of the excess. For provisions relating to the collection of, and liability for, employee tax on tips, see § 31.3102-3.

(b) *Form of statement.*—Form W-2 is the form prescribed for use in furnishing the statement required by paragraph (a) of this section, except that if an employer files a composite return pursuant to § 31.6011(a)-8 he may furnish to the employee, in lieu of Form W-2, a statement containing the required information in a form suitable for retention by the employee. A statement is required under this section in respect of an excess referred to in paragraph (a) of this section, even though the employer may not be required to furnish a statement to the employee under § 31.6051. Provisions applicable to the furnishing of a statement under § 31.6051 shall be applicable to statements under this section.

(c) *Excess to be shown on statement.*—If there is an excess in respect of the tips reported by an employee in two or more statements furnished pursuant to section 6053(a), only the total excess for the period covered by the employer statement shall be shown on such statement. [Reg. § 31.6053-2.]

☐ [*T.D. 7001, 1-17-69. Amended by T.D. 7351, 4-16-75.*]

[Reg. § 31.6053-3]

§ 31.6053-3. Reporting by certain large food or beverage establishments with respect to tips.—(a) *Information return by an employer with respect to tips.*—(1) *In general.*—An employer shall file a separate information return for each calendar year (as defined in paragraph (j)(14) of this section) with respect to each large food or beverage establishment (as defined in paragraph (j)(7) of this section) in which such employer has employees. The information return shall contain the following:

(i) The employer's name, address, and employer identification number;

(ii) The establishment's name, address, and identification number (see paragraph (a)(5) of this section);

(iii) The aggregate gross receipts (other than nonallocable receipts) of the establishment from the provision of food or beverages;

(iv) The aggregate amount of charge receipts (other than nonallocable receipts) on which there were charged tips;

(v) The aggregate amount of charged tips shown on such charge receipts;

(vi) The aggregate amount of tips actually received by food or beverage employees of the establishment during the calendar year and reported to the employer under section 6053(a) (see paragraph (j)(15) of this section);

(vii) The aggregate amount the employer is required to report under section 6051 and the regulations thereunder with respect to service charges of less than 10 percent.

(viii) The name and social security number of each employee of the establishment during the calendar year to whom an allocation was made under section 6053(c)(3) and paragraph (d) of this section and the amount of such allocation.

(2) *Calendar year 1983 information return.*—In the case of the 1983 calendar year information return, the information required by paragraph (a)(1)(iii)-(viii) of this section shall be reported for the period beginning with the first payroll period ending on or after April 1, 1983, and ending with the end of the 1983 calendar year. See paragraph (c) of this section relating to information required for the first quarter of 1983.

(3) *Prescribed form.*—The return required by this paragraph shall be made on Form 8027 with the transmittal form being Form 8027T. The information required by paragraph (a)(1)(viii) of this section may be provided by attaching to Form 8027 photocopies of each employee's W-2 for whom an allocation was made. A copy of any written good faith agreements applicable to a given calendar year (see paragraph (e) of this section) shall be attached to Form 8027 for such calendar year.

(4) *Time and place for filing.*—The information return required by this paragraph (a) shall be filed on or before the last day of February (March 31 if filed electronically) of the year following the calendar year for which the return is made with the Internal Revenue Service Center specified by the Form 8027 or its instructions. See section 6652(a) relating to the penalty for failure to file this information return.

(5) *Large food or beverage establishment identification number.*—Each large food or beverage establishment shall have a unique identification number to be included on Form 8027 and any employer's application pursuant to paragraph (h) of this section. If an identification number is changed for any reason, for example if the establishment becomes a different "type" of establishment as described in paragraph (a)(5)(ii) of this section, or if the employer identification number changes, the employer shall notify the Service by including both the old and new identification numbers on the Form 8027 filed for the year in which the identification number was changed. An establishment identification number shall be determined as follows:

(i) The first nine digits shall be the employer's identification number (EIN).

(ii) The next digit shall identify the type of large food or beverage establishment, with the categories as follows:

(A) The number "1" signifies an establishment that serves evening meals only (with or without alcoholic beverages).

(B) The number "2" signifies an establishment that serves evening meals and other meals (with or without alcoholic beverages).

(C) The number "3" signifies an establishment that serves only meals other than evening meals (with or without alcoholic beverages).

(D) The number "4" signifies an establishment that serves food, if at all, as only an incidental part of the business of serving alcoholic beverages.

(iii) The last five digits are to differentiate between multiple establishments reporting under the same EIN number. For this purpose, the employer shall assign each establishment reporting under such employer's EIN number a unique five digit number. For example, each establishment could be assigned a unique number by beginning with "00001" and progressing in numerical sequence (i.e., "00002", "00003", "00004", "00005") until each establishment has been assigned a number.

(6) *Definitions.*—See paragraph (j) of this section for definitions of various terms used in this section.

(b) *Employer statement to employees.*—(1) *In general.*—The employer shall furnish to each employee to whom an amount is allocated under section 6053(c)(3) and paragraph (d) of this section a written statement for each calendar year containing the following information:

(i) The employer's name and address;

(ii) The name of the employee;

(iii) The aggregate amount allocated to the employee for the calendar year.

(2) *Prescribed form.*—The written statement required by this paragraph shall be made on Form W-2.

(3) *Time and manner for furnishing the statement.*—The written statement required by this paragraph shall be due at the same time and shall be furnished in the same manner as the statement required to be furnished under section 6051. See section 6678 relating to the penalty for failure to file this statement.

(4) *Employee's request for an early W-2.*—If an employee's employment is terminated prior to the end of a calendar year and the employee requests an early W-2 under section 6051 and § 31.6051(d), a tip allocation under section 6053(c) is not required to be shown on such early W-2. However, the employer may include on such early W-2 the employee's actual tip allocation under section 6053(c), if known, or a good faith estimate of such allocation. A good faith estimate of an allocation shall be signified by placing the word "estimate" next to the allocation on the employee's copy of the early W-2. An amended W-2 must be furnished to each employee to whom an amount is allocated under section 6053(c), during January of the calendar year following the calendar year for which the statement is made, if there is no tip allocation on the early W-2 or if the estimated allocation is

found to vary from the actual allocation by more than 5 percent of the amount of the actual allocation.

(5) *Employee reporting of tip income.*—Regardless of whether an employee receives an allocation under section 6053(c) and § 31.6053-3, the employee is required to report as income on his or her Federal income tax return all tips received. For tips received before October 1, 1985, an employee must be able to substantiate the amount of reported tip income as provided in section 6001 and the regulations thereunder. For tips received on or after October 1, 1985, an employee must be able to substantiate the amount of reported tip income as provided in § 31.6053-4. The Internal Revenue Service may determine that a tipped employee received a larger amount of tip income than is reflected by the employee's allocation.

(c) *First quarter report of 1983.*—(1) *In general.*—For the period beginning with the first day of calendar year 1983, and ending on the last day of the last payroll period ending before April 1, 1983, an employer must file an information return for each large food or beverage establishment that was a large food or beverage establishment on January 1, 1983, that contains the information required by paragraph (a)(1)(i)-(vii) of this section for such period.

(2) *Prescribed form.*—The information return required by this paragraph shall be made on Form 8027. The returns for the first calendar quarter of 1983 and for calendar year 1983 may be incorporated onto a single Form 8027 but must separately set forth the required information for each of the two return periods.

(3) *Time and place for filing.*—The time and place for filing the information return required by this paragraph shall be the same as the calendar year 1983 information return. See paragraph (a)(4) of this section.

(d) *Allocation of excess of 8 percent of gross receipts over the aggregate amounts of reported tips.*—(1) *In general.*—An employer that operates a large food or beverage establishment shall allocate (as tips for purposes of the requirements of section 6053(c)) among tipped employees at such establishment performing services during any payroll period an amount equal to the excess of:

(i) Eight percent of the gross receipts (other than nonallocable receipts) of such establishment for the payroll period, over

(ii) The aggregate amount of tips reported by employees at such establishment to the employer under section 6053(a) for such period. For this purpose, if an employee reports under section 6053(a) on the basis of a period other than a payroll period such employee may specify what portion of his or her reported tips are attributable to a given payroll period when reporting tips to the employer under section 6053(a). In the absence of any specification by the employee, the employer shall allocate the amount of tips reported by an employee to a given payroll period either:

Reg. § 31.6053-3(d)(1)(ii)

(A) By multiplying the aggregate amount of those reported tips by a fraction, the numerator of which is the gross receipts attributable to the tipped employee for the payroll period and the denominator of which is the gross receipts attributable by the employee for the entire tip reporting period; or

(B) By multiplying the aggregate amount of those reported tips by a fraction, the numerator of which is the hours worked by the employee during the payroll period and the denominator of which is the total hours worked by the employee during the entire tip reporting period.

With respect to each establishment, the employer shall choose the method described in either paragraph (d)(1)(ii)(A) or paragraph (d)(1)(ii)(B) of this section for a calendar year and apply such method consistently in making all allocations required by the preceding sentence. If an employee is employed in more than one of an employer's food or beverage operations, such employee may specify what portion of his or her reported tips are attributable to a given operation when reporting tips to the employer under section 6053(a). In the absence of any specification by the employee, the employer shall allocate the amount of tips reported by the employee to a given food or beverage operation in a manner similar to that provided above for allocation of tips among payroll periods. The employer shall choose the method described in either paragraph (d)(1)(ii)(A) or paragraph (d)(1)(ii)(B) of this section for a calendar year and apply such method consistently in making all allocations required by the preceding sentence.

(2) *Employer not liable to employees for allocations.*—An employer who makes allocations (as tips for purposes of the requirements of section 6053(c) and this section) among such employer's employees in accordance with paragraph (d) and either paragraph (e) or (f) of this section shall not be liable to any employee if any amount is improperly allocated. However, if an employee's total tip allocations for a calendar year as reported on Form W-2 varies from the correct allocation amount by more than 5 percent of the correct allocation amount, the employer shall adjust such employee's allocation. If such an adjustment of an employee's allocation is required, the employer shall also review all tips allocations made to other employees in the same establishment to assure that the error did not distort other allocated amounts by more than 5 percent. Any adjustments made for variances of more than 5 percent shall be reflected in amended W-2's issued to the affected employees. Tip allocations made under this section shall have no effect on the withholding responsibilities of the employer under subtitle C of the Code Withholding on tips is authorized only with respect to amounts of tips reported to employers by employees under section 6053(a).

(e) *Allocation pursuant to a good faith agreement.*—The amount determined under paragraph (d)(2) of this section for each payroll period must be allocated among tipped employees providing services during such payroll period either on the basis of a good faith agreement described in this paragraph, or, if there is no good faith agreement applicable with respect to the payroll period on the basis of the allocation method provided in paragraph (f) of this section. A good faith agreement is a written agreement consented to by the employer and at least two-thirds of the members of each occupational category of tipped employees (*e.g.*, waiters, busboys, maitre d's) employed in the large food or beverage establishment at the time the agreement is adopted which:

(1) Provides for the allocation of the amount described in paragraph (d)(1) among tipped employees in a manner that, in combination with the tips reported by such employees under section 6053(a), will reflect a good faith approximation of the actual distribution of tip income among such tipped employees;

(2) Is effective prospectively beginning with the first day of a payroll period that begins after the date of adoption, but in no event later than the first day of the succeeding calendar year. However, a good faith agreement may be effective for calendar year 1983 if adopted on or before December 31, 1983.

(3) Is adopted at a time when there are tipped employees employed by the employer in each occupational category of tipped employees (*e.g.*, waiters, busboys, maitre d's) which would be affected by the agreement; and

(4) May be revoked prospectively by a written instrument adopted by at least two-thirds of the tipped employees who are employed in the establishment in occupational categories affected by the agreement at the time of the revocation. A revocation of an agreement shall be effective only at the beginning of a payroll period.

(f) *Allocation method to be used in the absence of a good faith agreement.*—(1) In a case in which there is no good faith agreement in effect and the aggregate amount of tips reported pursuant to section 6053(a) with respect to a payroll period is less than 8 percent of the establishment's gross receipt's for the payroll period, the employer shall allocate the difference as tips for purposes of section 6053(c) as provided in this paragraph. No allocations shall be made to indirectly tipped employees. An allocation shall be made to each directly tipped employee performing services for the establishment who has a reporting shortfall (as determined under paragraph (f)(1)(v) of this section) for the payroll period. The amount of each allocation shall be determined in the following manner:

(i) Multiply the amount of the establishment's gross receipts for the payroll period by 8 percent (0.08).

(ii) Determine the aggregate amount of tips reported for the payroll period by indirectly tipped employees.

(iii) Subtract from the amount determined under paragraph (f)(1)(i) the aggregate amount of tips reported by indirectly tipped employees as determined under paragraph (f)(1)(ii). The excess is the directly tipped employees' aggregate share of 8 percent of the gross receipts of the establishment for the payroll period.

(iv) For each directly tipped employee, multiply the amount determined under paragraph (f)(1)(iii) by a fraction, the numerator of which is the amount of gross receipts of the establishment for the payroll period that is attributable to the employee and the denominator of which is the aggregate amount of gross receipts for the payroll period that is attributable to all directly tipped employees. The product is each directly tipped employee's share of 8 percent of the gross receipts of the establishment for the payroll period. The employer may determine the fraction described in the first sentence of this subparagraph by substituting for the numerator the number of hours worked by the directly tipped employee during the payroll period and by substituting for the denominator the number of hours worked by all directly tipped employees during the payroll period. For payroll periods beginning after December 31, 1986, the method of allocation described in the preceding sentence may be used only by an employer that employs less than the equivalent of 25 full-time employees (as defined in paragraph (j)(19) of this section) at the establishment during the payroll period.

(v) For each directly tipped employee, determine the excess, if any, of the amount determined under paragraph (f)(1)(iv) over the amount reported as tips by the employee for the payroll period pursuant to section 6053(a). Such excess, if any, is the employee's shortfall for the payroll period.

(vi) Subtract from the amount determined under paragraph (f)(1)(i) the aggregate amount of tips reported pursuant to section

6053(a) by all directly and indirectly tipped employees for the payroll period. The excess is the amount to be allocated as tips among directly tipped employees who had a shortfall for the payroll period as determined under paragraph (f)(1)(v).

(vii) For each directly tipped employee who had a shortfall for the payroll period, multiply the amount determined under paragraph (f)(1)(vi) by a fraction, the numerator of which is the amount of such employee's shortfall (determined under paragraph (f)(1)(v) and the denominator of which is the aggregate of all shortfalls for the payroll period for all directly tipped employees. The product is the employee's allocation for the payroll period.

(2) The provisions of this paragraph may be illustrated by the following examples:

Example (1). X is a large food or beverage establishment that has chosen to make tip allocations using its actual payroll period and gross receipts attributable to employees. X had gross receipts for a payroll period of $100,000 and tips reported for the payroll period of $6,200. Directly tipped employees reported $5,700 while indirectly tipped employees reported $500.

Directly tipped employees	Gross receipts for payroll period	Tips reported
A	$18,000	$1,080
B	16,000	880
C	23,000	1,810
D	17,000	800
E	12,000	450
F	14,000	680
Total	$100,000	$5,700

The allocation computations would be as follows:

(1) $100,000 (gross receipts) × 0.08 = $8,000.

(2) Tips reported by indirectly tipped employees = $500.

(3) $8,000 − $500 (indirect employees' tips) = $7,500.

(4)

Directly tipped employees	Directly tipped share of 8% gross		Gross receipts ratio		Employee share of 8% gross
A	$7,500	×	18,000/100,000 =		$1,350
B	7,500	×	16,000/100,000 =		1,200
C	7,500	×	23,000/100,000 =		1,725
D	7,500	×	17,000/100,000 =		1,275
E	7,500	×	12,000/100,000 =		900
F	7,500	×	14,000/100,000 =		1,050
Total					$7,500

(5)

Directly tipped employees	Employee share of 8% gross		Tips reported		Employee shortfall
A	$1,350	−	$1,080	=	$270
B	1,200	−	880	=	320
C	1,725	−	1,810	=	. . .
D	1,275	−	800	=	475
E	900	−	450	=	450
F	1,050	−	680	=	370
Total shortfall					$1,885

Reg. §31.6053-3(f)(2)

Since employee C has no reporting shortfall there is no allocation to C.

(6) $8,000 − 6,200 (total tips reported) = $1,800 (amount allocable among shortfall employees).

(7)

Shortfall employees	Allocable amount		Shortfall ratio		Amount of allocation
A	$1,800	×	270/1885	=	$258
B	1,800	×	320/1885	=	306
D	1,800	×	475/1885	=	454
E	1,800	×	450/1885	=	430
F	1,800	×	370/1885	=	353

Example (2). Assume the same facts as in example (1) except that the employer uses employee hours worked to calculate tip allocations.

Directly tipped employees	Hours worked in payroll period	Tips reported
A	40	$1,080
B	35	880
C	45	1,810
D	40	800
E	15	450
F	25	680
Total	200	$5,700

The allocation computations would be as follows:

(1) $100,000 (gross receipts) × 0.08 = $8,000.

(2) Tips reported by indirectly tipped employees = $500.

(3) $8,000 − $500 (indirect employees' tips) = $7,500.

(4)

Directly tipped employees	Directly tipped share of 8% gross		Hours worked ratio		Employee share of 8% gross
A	$7,500	×	40/200	=	$1,500
B	7,500	×	35/200	=	1,313
C	7,500	×	45/200	=	1,688
D	7,500	×	40/200	=	1,500
E	7,500	×	15/200	=	563
F	7,500	×	25/200	=	938

(5)

Directly tipped employees	Employee share of 8% gross	Tips reported	Employee shortfall
A	$1,500	$1,080	$420
B	1,313	880	433
C	1,688	1,810	...
D	1,500	800	700
E	563	450	113
F	938	680	258
Total shortfall			$1,924

Since employee C has no reporting shortfall there is no allocation to C.

(6) $8,000 − 6,200 (total tips reported) = $1,800 (amount allocable among shortfall employees).

(7)

Shortfall employees	Allocable amount	×	Shortfall ratio	=	Amount of allocation
A	$1,800		420/1,924		$393
B	1,800		433/1,924		405
D	1,800		700/1,924		655
E	1,800		113/1,924		106
F	1,800		258/1,924		241

Example (3). X is a large food or beverage establishment that has chosen to make tip allocations using a calendar year period. X had gross receipts for a calendar year of $2,000,000 and tips reported for the calendar year of $176,000. The amount to be allocated as tips is equal to the excess of 8 percent of the gross receipts of the establishment for the calendar year over the aggregate amount of tips reported by the employees of the establishment to the employer under section 6053(a) for the calendar year. Because the reported tips for the year ($176,000) are in excess of 8 percent of the gross receipts ($2,000,000 × .08 = $160,000), no tip allocations are made to the employees of this establishment for the calendar year.

Example (4). X is a large food or beverage establishment that has chosen to make tip allocations using a calendar year period and gross receipts attributable to employees. X had gross receipts for a calendar year of $1,500,000 and tips reported for the calendar year of $110,000. Directly tipped employees reported $94,000 while indirectly tipped employees reported $16,000.

Directly tipped employees	Gross receipts for calendar year	Tips reported
A.........	$260,000	$18,600
B.........	240,000	14,600
C.........	380,000	31,200
D.........	260,000	13,000
E.........	160,000	6,000

Directly tipped employees	Gross receipts for calendar year	Tips reported
F..........	200,000	10,600
Total	$1,500,000	$94,000

The allocation computations are as follows:

(1) $1,500,000 (gross receipts) × 0.08 = $120,000.

(2) Tips reported by indirectly tipped employees = $16,000.

(3) $120,000 − 16,000 (indirect employees tips) = $104,000.

(4)

Directly tipped employees	Directly tipped share × of 8% gross	Gross receipts ratio	= Employee share of 8% gross
A	$104,000	260,000/1,500,000	$18,027
B	104,000	240,000/1,500,000	16,640
C	104,000	380,000/1,500,000	26,347
D	104,000	260,000/1,500,000	18,027
E	104,000	160,000/1,500,000	11,093
F	104,000	200,000/1,500,000	13,867

(5)

Directly tipped employees	Employee share of 8% gross −	Tips reported =	Employee shortfall
A	$18,027	$18,600	. . .
B	16,640	14,600	$2,040
C	26,347	31,200	. . .
D	18,027	13,000	5,027
E	11,093	6,000	5,093
F	13,867	10,600	3,267
Total shortfall			$15,427

Since employees A and C do not have a reporting shortfall there are no allocations to them.

(6) $120,000 − 110,000 (total tips reported) = $10,000 (amount allocable among shortfall employees).

(7)

Shortfall employees	Allocable amount ×	Shortfall ratio =	Amount of allocation
B	$10,000	2,040/15,427	$1,322
D	10,000	5,027/15,427	3,259
E	10,000	5,093/15,427	3,301
F	10,000	3,267/15,427	2,118
Total			$10,000

Example (5). Assume the same facts as in example (4) except that the employer has chosen the employee hours worked method of computing tip allocations, the calendar year gross receipts were $1,000,000, and the tips reported for the calendar year were $74,000. Directly tipped employees reported $70,000 while indirectly tipped employees reported $4,000.

Directly tipped employees	Hours worked in the calendar year	Tips reported
A	2,000	$11,800
B	1,750	9,800
C	2,250	15,100
D	2,000	9,000
E	750	4,500
F	1,250	7,800

Directly tipped employees	Hours worked in the calendar year	Tips reported
G	490	3,200
H	510	2,800
I	200	800
J	1,000	5,200
Total	12,200	$70,000

The allocation computations would be as follows:

(1) $1,000,000 (gross receipts) × 0.08 = $80,000.

(2) Tips reported by indirectly tipped employees = $4,000.

(3) $80,000 − $4,000 (indirect employee tips) = $76,000.

Reg. §31.6053-3(f)(2)

(4)

Directly tipped employees	Directly tipped share × of 8% gross	Hours worked ratio	=	Employee share of 8% gross
A	$76,000	2,000/12,200		$12,459
B	76,000	1,750/12,200		10,902
C	76,000	2,250/12,200		14,016
D	76,000	2,000/12,200		12,459
E	76,000	750/12,200		4,672
F	76,000	1,250/12,200		7,787
G	76,000	490/12,200		3,052
H	76,000	510/12,200		3,177
I	76,000	200/12,200		1,246
J	76,000	1,000/12,200		6,230
Total				$76,000

(5)

Directly tipped employees	Employee share of 8% gross	−	Tips reported	=	Employee shortfall
A	$12,459		$11,800		$659
B	10,902		9,800		1,102
C	14,016		15,100		. . .
D	12,459		9,000		3,459
E	4,672		4,500		172
F	7,787		7,800		. . .
G	3,052		3,200		. . .
H	3,177		2,800		377
I	1,246		800		446
J	6,230		5,200		1,030
Total shortfall					$7,245

Since employees C, F, and G have no reporting shortfalls, there are no allocations made to them.

(6) $80,000 − 74,000 (total tips reported) = $6,000.

(7)

Shortfall employees	Allocable amount ×	Shortfall ratio	=	Amount of allocation
A	$6,000	659/7,245		$546
B	6,000	1,102/7,245		913
D	6,000	3,459/7,245		2,865
E	6,000	172/7,245		142
H	6,000	377/7,245		312
I	6,000	446/7,245		369
J	6,000	1,030/7,245		853
Total				$6,000

(g) *Period of allocation.*—In applying paragraphs (d), (e), (f), and (h)(3) of this section an employer may substitute the calendar year or any period that results from a reasonable division of a calendar year for the term "payroll period" each place it appears in such paragraphs. If an employer makes such a substitution with respect to a large food or beverage establishment the substituted period shall be stated on Form 8027 for such large food or beverage establishment and shall be effective for such employer's large food or beverage establishment for the entire calendar year.

(h) *Lowering the percentage to be used.*—(1) *In general.*—On and after July 18, 1984, an employer or a majority of the employees (as defined in paragraph (h)(2)(iii) of this section) of an employer may petition the district director for the internal revenue district in which the employer's establishment is located to have the percentage of gross receipts that is used to determine the amount to be allocated under section 6053(c)(3)(A) and paragraph (d) of §31.6053-3 reduced from 8 percent to the percentage that the petitioning employer or employees believe to be the actual percentage of the amount of the establishment's gross receipts that reflects the amount of tips. The district director may thereafter reduce the percentage of gross receipts used to determine the amount to be so allocated to the percentage that the district director determines to be the proper estimate of the actual percentage of gross receipts constituting tips. The district director, however, may not reduce the percentage below 2 percent. For the rules in effect prior to July 18, 1984, see 26 CFR §31.6053-3(h) Rev. as of April 1, 1984).

(2) *Time and manner for petition to have percentage reduced.*—(i) *In general.*—The petition shall be in writing and shall include sufficient information to allow the district director to estimate with reasonable accuracy the actual tip rate of the establishment. For example, such information might include the charged tip rate, the type

Reg. §31.6053-3(g)

of establishment, menu prices, the location of the establishment, the amount of "self-service" required, the days and hours open for business, and whether the customer receives the check from or pays the server for the meal.

(ii) *Employer petitions.*—In the case of employer-originated petitions, the employer has the burden of supplying sufficient information to allow the district director to estimate with reasonable accuracy the actual tip rate of the establishment. The employer also shall attach to the petition copies of Form 8027 (if any) filed for the establishment for the 3 immediately preceding calendar years.

(iii) *Employee petitions.*—(A) In the case of employee-originated petitions, a majority of the employees of an establishment must consent to the petition. A majority for purposes of this paragraph is more than one-half of all the directly tipped employees (within the meaning of paragraph (j)(12) of this section) employed by the establishment at the time the petition is filed. In the case of a single petition for certain multi-establishment employers (see paragraph (h)(4) of this section), more than one-half of the aggregate directly tipped employees (at the time the petition is filed) of the establishments covered by the petition must consent. The petition filed with the district director must state the total number of directly tipped employees employed by the establishment (or establishments) and the number of the directly tipped employees consenting to the petition.

(B) The petitioning employees have the burden of supplying sufficient information to allow the district director to estimate with reasonable accuracy the actual tip rate of the establishment to the extent they possess such information. If the employer possesses relevant information, the employer must provide such information to the district director upon the request of the petitioning employees or district director. Employees who file a petition under this paragraph must promptly notify their employer of the petition. Promptly upon receipt of such notification, their employer must submit to the district director copies of the Form 8027 (if any) filed for the establishment for the 3 immediately preceding calendar years. Any information supplied by the employer during the petitioning process constitutes return information (as defined in section 6103(b)(2)) which shall not be disclosed by the Internal Revenue Service (except as provided in section 6103) to any employees of the employer or to representatives of such employees.

(3) *Effective date for reduced percentage.*—The district director shall determine the term for which the reduced percentage is to be effective. At the end of such term, the reduced percentage shall cease to apply unless previously extended by the district director for the district in which the large food or beverage establishment is located. In no event shall the reduced percentage be applied to payroll periods before the date the petition described in paragraph (h)(2) of this section is filed unless the establishment is a new business (as described in paragraph (i) of § 31.6053-3). In the case of a new business or a petition for reduction filed prior to September 30, 1983, the district director may allow the approved reduced percentage to be applied retroactively to the first day of the calendar year of the petition. Until such time as the employer is notified in writing by the district director of approval of a reduction, the employer must continue to use 8 percent of gross receipts for purposes of complying with section 6053(c) and this section.

(4) *Single petition for certain multi-establishment employers.*—An employer (including a single employer as defined in section 52(a) or (b)) or a majority of the employees of such employer may use a single petition for two or more of the employer's establishments if such establishments are essentially the same type of business, the petitioning employer or employees have made a good faith determination that the tip rates at such establishments are essentially the same, and the establishments are located in the same internal revenue region. Single petitions shall include the names and locations of the establishments for which a reduction is requested and the information required by paragraph (h)(2) of this section for a typical establishment. A single petition for multi-establishments located within an internal revenue region shall be filed with the district director for the internal revenue district in which the greatest number of the establishments included in the petition are located. If there is an equal number of establishments located in two or more internal revenue districts the employer or employees petitioning may choose the district to which the petition is sent.

(i) *Application of reporting requirements to new businesses.*—(1) *In general.*—A food or beverage operation is a new business if the employer of the operation did not operate any food or beverage operations during the preceding calendar year. An employer will not be considered to have operated a food or beverage operation during a calendar year if each food or beverage operation of the employer was operated for less than one calendar month during such year. In a calendar year in which a food or beverage operation is a new business, the determination of whether the operation is a large food or beverage establishment shall be made as provided in paragraph (i)(2) of this section and the employer shall comply with section 6053(c) and this section as provided in paragraph (i)(3) of this section.

(2) *Determination of status as a large food or beverage establishment.*—A food or beverage operation shall be considered a large food or beverage establishment during the calendar year in which it is a new business if the average number of hours worked per business day by all employees of the employer at the new business during each of any two consecutive calendar months of the calendar year, computed in the manner pro-

Reg. § 31.6053-3(i)(2)

vided in the second sentence of paragraph (j)(9) of this section, is greater than 80 hours.

(3) *New business compliance under section 6053(c).*—A new business that is determined to be a large food or beverage establishment under paragraph (i)(2) of this section shall comply with section 6053(c) and this section beginning with the first payroll period that begins after the first period of two consecutive calendar months described in paragraph (i)(2) of this section.

(j) *Definitions.*—For purposes of section 6053(c) and this section:

(1) *Gross receipts.*—Gross receipts shall include all receipts (other than nonallocable receipts), from the provision of food or beverages by a large food or beverage establishment from cash sales, charge receipts (including charged tips only to the extent the cash sales amount has been reduced due to the employer paying cash to tipped employees for charged tips due them), charges to a hotel room (excluding tips charged to a hotel room only to the extent that the employer's accounting procedures allow such tips to be segregated out and excluding charges that are otherwise included in charge receipts), and the retail value of complimentary food or beverages (as defined in paragraph (j)(16) of this section) served to customers. Gross receipts shall not include state or local taxes. In the case of a trade or business that does not charge separately for the provision of food or beverages (*i.e.,* a trade or business that provides other goods or services along with food or beverages for a combined price, such as a "package deal" for food and lodging), the employer shall make a good faith estimate of the gross receipts attributable to the provision of the food or beverages that reflects the cost to the employer of providing the food or beverages plus a reasonable profit factor.

(2) *Gross receipts attributable to a directly tipped employee.*—Gross receipts attributable to a directly tipped employee are those gross receipts (as defined in paragraph (j)(1) of this section) from the provision of food or beverages to customers with respect to which the employee provided services. For example, if a directly tipped employee's name is on every check given to customers for whom the employee has provided services, the gross receipts attributable to such employee could be determined by aggregating the amounts of all checks bearing that employee's name (other than amounts from nonallocable receipts).

(3) *Nonallocable receipts.*—Nonallocable receipts are receipts which are attributable to carryout sales or to services with respect to which a service charge of 10 percent or more is added. Carryout sales are sales of food or beverages for consumption off the premises of the establishment. Room service is not a carryout sale. If an establishment's accounting system does not segregate receipts from carryout sales from the establishment's other receipts, receipts from carryout sales may be determined as an esti-

mated percentage of total receipts. The applicable percentage shall be determined in good faith by the employer on the basis of generally accepted accounting practices, including but not limited to, surveys of carryout sales as a percentage of gross sales. An employer may rely upon estimates as to carryout sales which are established in good faith between the employer and state or local governments for purposes of state or local taxation.

(4) *Charge receipts.*—Charge receipts shall include credit card charges and charges under any other credit arrangement (e.g., house charges, city ledger, and charge arrangements to country club members. Charges to a hotel room may be excluded from charge receipts if such exclusion is consistent with the employer's normal accounting practices and the employer applies such exclusion consistently for a given large food or beverage establishment. Otherwise, charges to a hotel room shall be included in charge receipts.

(5) *Charged tips.*—A tip included on a charge receipt is a charged tip.

(6) *Food or beverage operation.*—A "food or beverage operation" is any business activity which provides food or beverages for consumption on the premises (other than "fast food" operations). If an employer conducts activities that provide food or beverages at more than one location, the activity at each separate location shall be considered to be a separate food or beverage operation. Each activity conducted within a single building shall be considered to be conducted at a separate location if the customers of the activity while being provided with food or beverages, occupy an area separate from that occupied by customers of other activities and the gross receipts of the activity are recorded separately from the gross receipts of other activities. For example, a gourmet restaurant, a coffee shop, and a cocktail lounge in a hotel would each be treated as a separate food or beverage operation if gross receipts from each activity are recorded separately. In addition, an employer may treat different activities conducted in the identical place at different times as separate food or beverage operations if the gross receipts of the activities at each time are recorded separately. For example, a restaurant may record the gross receipts from its cafeteria style lunch operation separately from the gross receipts of its full service food or beverage operations.

(7) *Large food or beverage establishment.*—A food or beverage operation is a "large food or beverage establishment" if:

(i) The employer at the food or beverage operation normally employed more than 10 employees on a typical business day during the preceding calendar year, and

(ii) The tipping of food or beverage employees of the food or beverage operation is customary. Generally, tipping would not be considered customary for a cafeteria style operation (as defined in paragraph (j)(18) of this section) or for a food or beverage operation where at least 95 percent of its total sales are nonallocable receipts, within the meaning of paragraph (j)(3) of this section, by reason of the addition of a service charge of 10 percent or more. Total sales shall include only gross receipts (as defined in paragraph (j)(1) of this section) and nonallocable receipts (other than carryout receipts) from the provision of food or beverages. In the case of an operation such as a restaurant that is cafeteria style operation at lunch and that has full service with tipping customary at dinner, the entire operation is generally a large food or beverage establishment if the employer meets the 10-employee test. However, if the gross receipts of the cafeteria style operation at lunch are recorded separately from the dinner operation gross receipts the employer may treat the dinner operation as a large food or beverage establishment and the lunch operation as a separate food or beverage operation that is not a large food or beverage establishment due to the fact that tipping is not considered customary for cafeteria style operations.

(8) *Employee.*—The term "employee" has the same meaning as in section 3401(c) and § 31.3401(c)-1.

(9) *More than 10 employees on a typical business day.*—An employer shall be considered to have normally employed more than 10 employees on a typical business day during a calendar year if one-half of the sum of the average number of employee hours worked per business day during the calendar month in which the aggregate gross receipts from food or beverage operations were the greatest plus the average number of employee hours worked per business day during the calendar month in which the aggregate gross receipts from food or beverage operations were the least, is greater than 80 hours. The average number of employee hours worked per business day during a month shall be computed by dividing the total number of hours worked during the month by all employees of the employer who are employed in a food or beverage operation by the average of the number of days during the month that each food or beverage operation at which such employees worked was open for business. If an employer operates both a food or beverage operation and a nonfood or beverage operation, and one or more of his or her employees work for both operations, the employer may make a good faith estimate of the number of hours such employees worked for each operation in a given month. Similarly, in cases where one or more of an employer's employees work for more than one of such employer's food or beverage operations, a good faith estimate may be made of the number of hours such employees worked for each operation in a given month. For purposes of this subparagraph, employees who are employed in a food or beverage operation include all employees of the operation, not just food or beverage employees. The employees of an employer shall include all employees at all food or beverage

operations who, along with the employees of such employer, would be treated as employees of a single employer under section 52(a) or (b) (as in effect on September 3, 1982) and the regulations thereunder. For example, if an employer at a food or beverage operation is a member of a controlled group of corporations, then all employees of all corporations which are members of such controlled group of corporations shall be treated as employed by each such employer for purposes of this paragraph. However, an individual who owns 50 percent or more in value of the stock of a corporation operating an establishment shall not be treated as an employee of any establishment owned by the corporation.

(10) *Food or beverage employee.*—A "food or beverage employee" is an employee who provides services in connection with the provision of food or beverages. Such employees include, but are not limited to, waiters, waitresses, busboys, bartenders, persons in charge of seating (such as a hostess, maitre d' or dining room captain), wine stewards, cooks, and kitchen help. Examples of employees who are not food or beverage employees include, but are not limited to, coat check persons, bellhops, and doormen.

(11) *Tipped employee.*—A "tipped employee" of a food or beverage operation is an employee who is a food or beverage employee that customarily receives tip income from employment at that operation. An employee who occasionally receives small amounts of tip income is not a tipped employee. Generally, an employee who receives less than $20 per month in tip income would not be considered as customarily receiving tip income.

(12) *Directly tipped employee.*—A "directly tipped employee" is any tipped employee who receives tips directly from customers, including an employee who after receiving tips directly from customers turns all the tips over to a tip pool. Examples of directly tipped employees are waiters, waitresses, and bartenders.

(13) *Indirectly tipped employee.*—An "indirectly tipped employee" is a tipped employee who does not normally receive tips directly from customers. Examples of indirectly tipped employees are busboys, service bartenders and cooks. An employee, such as a maitre d', who receives tips both directly from customers and indirectly through tip splitting or tip pooling shall be treated as a directly tipped employee.

(14) *Calendar year.*—The term "calendar year" shall mean either the period from January 1 through December 31 or the period that begins with the first day of the first payroll period ending on or after January 1 and ends with the last day of the last payroll period ending in December of the same year. With respect to any establishment, the employer shall choose one of these two descriptions and apply it consistently.

(15) *Tips reported for a specified period.*—Tips reported to an employer for a specified period under section 6053(a) are those tips actually re-

ceived by an employee during such period without regard to the time when the tips are reported to the employer. Thus, if an employee reports to the employer in calendar year 1984 tips the employee actually received in calendar year 1983, the amount of tips actually received in calendar year 1983 must be included by the employer when making such information returns, statements and allocations required under section 6053(c) and this section for calendar year 1983.

(16) *Complimentary food or beverages.*—Food or beverages served to customers without charge are complimentary if:

(i) Tipping for the provision of such food or beverages is customary at the establishment, and

(ii) Such food or beverages are provided in connection with an activity that is engaged in for profit and whose receipts would not be included in gross receipts as defined in paragraph (j)(1) of this section but for this subparagraph and are not nonallocable receipts which are attributable to services with respect to which a service charge of 10 percent or more is added.

For example, the retail values of complimentary hors d'oeuvres served at a bar or a complimentary dessert served to a regular patron of a restaurant would not be included in gross receipts because the receipts of the bar or restaurant would be included in gross receipts as defined in paragraph (j)(1) of this section. The retail value of a complimentary fruit basket placed in a hotel room generally would not be included in gross receipts because tipping for the provision of such items is not customary. The retail value of complimentary drinks served to customers in a gambling casino would be included in gross receipts because tipping for the provision of such items is customary, the gambling casino is an activity engaged in for profit, and the gambling receipts of the casino would not be included in gross receipts as defined in paragraph (j)(1) of this section except for this subparagraph.

(17) *Fast food operation.*—An operation is a "fast food" operation only if its customers order, pick up, and pay for food or beverages at a counter, window, etc., and then carry the food or beverages to another location (either on or off the premises of such activities).

(18) *Cafeteria style operation.*—The term "cafeteria style" operation means a food or beverage operation which is primarily self-service and in which the total cost of food or beverages selected by a customer is paid prior to the customers' being seated or is stated on a check provided to the customer prior to the customers' being seated and is paid by the customer to a cashier. Generally, operations are primarily self-service if food or beverages are ordered or selected by a customer at one location and carried by the customer from such location to the customer's seat. For example, cafeteria lines, buffets, and smorgasbords are primarily self-service. If, after a customer is seated, a food or beverage employee delivers items such as an item that required additional preparation after being selected by the customer, condiments, beverages, or refills at no additional cost to the customer, a food or beverage operation's status as primarily self-service would not be affected.

(19) *Less than the equivalent of 25 full-time employees.*—For purposes of paragraph (f)(1)(iv) of this section, an employer shall be considered to employ less than the equivalent of 25 full-time employees at an establishment during a payroll period (as defined in section 3401(b) and the regulations thereunder) if the average number of employee hours worked per business day during a payroll period is less than 200 hours. The average number of employee hours worked per business day during a payroll period shall be computed by dividing the total number of hours worked during the period by all employees of the employer who are employed in a food or beverage operation by the average of the number of days during the period that each food or beverage operation at which such employees worked was open for business. If an employer operates both a food or beverage operation and a nonfood or beverage operation, and one or more of his employees work for both operations, the employer may make a good faith estimate of the number of hours such employees worked for each operation in a given payroll period. Similarly, in cases where one or more of an employer's employees work for more than one of such employer's food or beverage operations, a good faith estimate may be made of the number of hours such employees worked for each operation in a given payroll period. If there is more than one payroll period for the establishment, the payroll period which is used for the greatest number of employees shall be the payroll period for purposes of this paragraph (j)(19). For purposes of this paragraph (j)(19), employees who are employed in a food or beverage operation include all employees of the operation, not just food or beverage employees. The employees of an employer shall include all employees at all food or beverage operations who, along with the employees of such employer, would be treated as employees of a single employer under section 52(a) or (b) (as in effect on September 3, 1982) and the regulations thereunder. For example, if an employer at a food or beverage operation is a member of a controlled group of corporations, then all employees of all corporations which are members of such controlled group of corporations shall be treated as employed by each such employer for purposes of this paragraph.

(k) *Permission to submit information on magnetic tape.*—For rules relating to permission to submit the information required by section 6053(c) and this section on magnetic tape of other media, see §31.6011(a)-8.

(l) *Recordkeeping requirements.*—An employer shall keep records sufficient to substantiate any information returns, employer statements to employees, applications, or tip allocations made pursuant to section 6053(c) and this section. The records required by this paragraph shall be retained for 3 years after the due date of the return or statement to which they pertain.

(m) *Food or beverage operations outside the United States.*—Employers at food or beverage operations outside the United States (as defined in section 7701(a)(9)) are not subject to the reporting requirements under section 6053(c) and this section.

(n) *Effective date.*—This section is effective for calendar year 1983 and thereafter. [Reg. § 31.6053-3.]

☐ [*T.D.* 7906, 8-10-83. *Amended by T.D.* 8039, 7-18-85; *T.D.* 8141, 6-5-87 *and T.D.* 8895, 8-17-2000.]

[Reg. § 31.6053-4]

§ 31.6053-4. Substantiation requirements for tipped employees.—(a) *Substantiation of tip income.*—(1) *In general.*—An employee shall maintain sufficient evidence to establish the amount of tip income received by the employee during a taxable year. A daily record maintained by the employee (as described in paragraph (a)(2) of this section) shall constitute sufficient evidence. If the employee does not maintain a daily record, other evidence of the amount of tip income received during the year, such as documentary evidence (as described in paragraph (a)(3) of this section), shall constitute sufficient evidence, but only if such other evidence is as credible and as reliable as a daily record. The Commissioner may by revenue ruling, procedure or other guidance of general applicability provide for other methods of demonstrating evidence of tip income. However, notwithstanding any other provision of this paragraph (a)(1), a daily record or other evidence that is as credible and as reliable as a daily record may not be sufficient evidence if there are facts or circumstances which indicate that the employee received a larger amount of tip income. Moreover, oral statements of the employee, without corroboration, cannot constitute sufficient evidence.

(2) *Daily record.*—The daily record shall state the employee's name and address, the employer's name, and the establishment's name. The daily record shall show for each work day the amount of cash tips and charge tips received directly from customers or from other employees, and the amount of tips, if any, paid out to other employees through tip sharing, tip pooling or other arrangements and the names of such employees. The record shall also show the date that each entry is made. Form 4070A, *Employee's Daily Record of Tips,* may be used to maintain such daily record. In addition, an electronic system maintained by the employer that collects substantially similar information as Form 4070A may be used to maintain such daily record, provided the employee receives and maintains a paper copy of the daily record. The daily record of tips received by an employee shall be prepared and maintained in such manner that each entry is made on or near the date the tip income is received. A daily record made on or near the date the tip income is received has a high degree of credibility not present with respect to a record prepared subsequent thereto when generally there is a lack of accurate recall. An entry is made "near the date the tip income is received" if the required information with respect to tips received and paid out by the employee for the day is recorded at a time when the employee has full present knowledge of those receipts and payments.

(3) *Documentary evidence.*—Documentary evidence consists of copies of any documents that contain (i) amounts that were added to a check by customers as a tip and paid over to the employee or (ii) amounts that were paid by a customer for food or beverages with respect to which tips generally would be received by the employee. Examples of documentary evidence are copies of restaurant bills, credit card charges, or charges under any other arrangement (see § 31.6053-3(j)(4)) containing amounts added by the customer as a tip.

(b) *Retention of records.*—Records maintained under this section shall be kept at all times available for inspection by authorized internal revenue officers or employees, and shall be retained so long as the contents thereof may become material in the administration of any internal revenue law.

(c) *Effective date.*—The substantiation requirements of this § 31.6053-4 shall be effective for tips received on or after October 1, 1985. For the rules in effect prior to October 1, 1985, see section 6001 and the regulations thereunder. Substantiation considered sufficient as provided in this § 31.6053-4 will also be considered sufficient for tips received before October 1, 1985. [Reg. § 31.6053-4.]

☐ [*T.D.* 8141, 6-5-87. *Amended by T.D.* 8910, 12-12-2000.]

[Reg. § 1.6055-1]

§ 1.6055-1. Information reporting for minimum essential coverage.—(a) *Information reporting requirement.*—Every person that provides minimum essential coverage to an individual during a calendar year must file an information return and transmittal and furnish statements to responsible individuals on forms prescribed by the Internal Revenue Service.

(b) *Definitions.*—(1) *In general.*—The definitions in this paragraph (b) apply for purposes of this section.

(2) *Affordable Care Act.*—The term *Affordable Care Act* refers to the Patient Protection and Affordable Care Act, Public Law 111-148 (124 Stat. 119 (2010)), and the Health Care and Education Reconciliation Act of 2010, Public Law 111-152 (124 Stat. 1029 (2010)), and amendments to those acts.

(3) *ERISA.*—The term *ERISA* means the Employee Retirement Income Security Act of 1974, as amended (29 U.S.C. 1001 et seq.).

(4) *Exchange.*—*Exchange* has the same meaning as in 45 CFR 155.20.

(5) *Government employer.*—The term *government employer* means an employer that is a governmental unit or an agency or instrumentality of a governmental unit.

(6) *Governmental unit.*—The term *governmental unit* refers to the government of the United States, any State or political subdivision of a State, or any Indian tribal government (as defined in section 7701(a)(40)) or subdivision of an Indian tribal government (as defined in section 7871(d)).

(7) *Agency or instrumentality of a governmental unit.*—[Reserved]

(8) *Minimum essential coverage.*—*Minimum essential coverage* is defined in section 5000A(f) and regulations issued under that section.

(9) *Qualified health plan.*—The term *qualified health plan* has the same meaning as in section 1301(a) of the Affordable Care Act (42 U.S.C. 18021(a)).

(10) *Reporting entity.*—A *reporting entity* is any person that must report, under section 6055 and this section, minimum essential coverage provided to an individual.

(11) *Responsible individual.*—The term *responsible individual* includes a primary insured, employee, former employee, uniformed services sponsor, parent, or other related person named on an application who enrolls one or more individuals, including him or herself, in minimum essential coverage.

(12) *Taxpayer identification number.*—The term *taxpayer identification number* (TIN) has the same meaning as in section 7701(a)(41).

(c) *Persons required to report.*—(1) *In general.*—The following persons must file the information return and transmittal form required under paragraph (a) of this section to report minimum essential coverage—

(i) Health insurance issuers, or carriers (as used in 5 U.S.C. 8901), for all insured coverage, except as provided in paragraph (c)(3)(ii) of this section;

(ii) Plan sponsors of self-insured group health plan coverage;

(iii) The executive department or agency of a governmental unit that provides coverage under a government-sponsored program (within the meaning of section 5000A(f)(1)(A)); and

(iv) Any other person that provides minimum essential coverage to an individual.

(2) *Plan sponsors of self-insured group health plan coverage.*—(i) *In general.*—For purposes of this section, a plan sponsor of self-insured group health plan coverage is—

(A) The employer for a self-insured group health plan or arrangement established or maintained by a single employer (determined without application of section 414(b), (c), (m) or (o) in the case of an employer described in paragraph (f)(2)(i) of this section), including each participating employer with respect to a self-insured group health plan or arrangement established or maintained by more than one employer (and not including a multiemployer plan as defined in section 3(37) of ERISA or a Multiple Employer Welfare Arrangement as defined in section 3(40) of ERISA);

(B) The association, committee, joint board of trustees, or other similar group of representatives of the parties who establish or maintain the plan for a self-insured group health plan or arrangement that is a multiemployer plan (as defined in section 3(37) of ERISA).

(C) The employee organization for a self-insured group health plan or arrangement maintained solely by an employee organization;

(D) Each participating employer for a self-insured group health plan or arrangement maintained by a Multiple Employer Welfare Arrangement (as defined in section 3(40) of ERISA) with respect to the participating employer's own employees; and

(E) For a self-insured group health plan or arrangement for which a plan sponsor is not otherwise identified in paragraphs (c)(2)(i)(A) through (c)(2)(i)(D) of this section, the person designated by plan terms as the plan sponsor or plan administrator or, if no person is designated as the administrator and a plan sponsor cannot be identified, each entity that maintains the plan or arrangement.

(ii) *Government employers.*—Unless otherwise provided by statute or regulation, a government employer that maintains a self-insured group health plan or arrangement may enter into a written agreement with another governmental unit, or an agency or instrumentality of a governmental unit, that designates the other governmental unit, agency, or instrumentality as the person required to file the returns and to furnish the statements required by this section for some or all of the individuals receiving minimum essential coverage under that plan or arrangement. The designated governmental unit, agency, or instrumentality must be part of or related to the same governmental unit as the government employer (for example, a political subdivision of a State may designate the State or another political subdivision of the state) and agree to the designation. The government employer must make or revoke the designation before the earlier of the deadline for filing the returns or furnishing the statements required by this section and must retain a copy of the designation in its books and records. If the requirements of this paragraph (c)(2)(ii) are met, the designated governmental unit, agency, or instrumentality is the sponsor under paragraph (c)(2)(i) of this section. If no entity is designated, the government employer that maintains the self-insured group health plan or arrangement is the sponsor under paragraph (c)(2)(i) of this section.

(3) *Special rules for government-sponsored programs.*—(i) *Medicaid and Children's Health Insurance Program (CHIP) coverage.*—The State agency that administers the Medicaid program under title XIX of the Social Security Act (42 U.S.C. 1396 and following sections) or the CHIP program under title XXI of the Social Security Act (42 U.S.C. 1396 and following sections) must file the returns and furnish the statements required by this section for those programs.

(ii) *Government-sponsored coverage provided through health insurance issuers.*—An executive department or agency of a governmental unit that provides coverage under a government-sponsored program through a health insurance issuer (such as Medicaid, CHIP, or Medicare, including Medicare Advantage) must file the returns and furnish the statements required by this section.

(iii) *Nonappropriated Fund Health Benefits Program.*—The Secretary of Defense may designate the Department of Defense components (as used in DoD Directive 5100.01, Functions of the Department of Defense and Its Major Components (December 21, 2010)) that must file the returns and furnish the statements required by this section for the Nonappropriated Fund Health Benefits Program.

(4) *Other arrangements recognized as minimum essential coverage.*—The Commissioner may designate in published guidance, see § 601.601(d) of this chapter, the reporting entity for arrangements the Secretary of Health and Human Services, in coordination with the Secretary of the Treasury, recognizes under section 5000A(f)(1)(E) as minimum essential coverage.

(d) *Reporting not required.*—(1) *Qualified health plans.*—A health insurance issuer is not required to file a return or furnish a report under this section for coverage in a qualified health plan in the individual market enrolled in through an Exchange.

(2) *Additional health benefits.*—No reporting is required under paragraph (a) of this section for minimum essential coverage that provides benefits in addition or as a supplement to a health plan or arrangement that constitutes minimum essential coverage if—

(i) The primary and supplemental coverages have the same plan sponsor; or

(ii) The coverage supplements government-sponsored coverage (as defined in section 5000A(f)(1)(A) and the regulations under that section) such as Medicare.

(3) *Individuals not enrolled in coverage.*—No reporting is required under this section for coverage offered to individuals who do not enroll.

(e) *Information required to be reported to the Internal Revenue Service.*—(1) *In general.*—All information returns required by this section must report the following information for the calendar year of coverage—

(i) The name, address, and employer identification number (EIN) of the reporting entity required to file the return;

(ii) The name, address, and TIN, or date of birth if a TIN is not available, of the responsible individual, except that reporting entities may but are not required to report the TIN of a responsible individual not enrolled in the coverage;

(iii) The name and TIN, or date of birth if a TIN is not available, of each individual who is covered under the policy or program;

(iv) For each covered individual, the months for which, for at least one day, the individual was enrolled in coverage and entitled to receive benefits; and

(v) Any other information specified in forms, instructions, or published guidance, see § § 601.601(d) and 601.602 of this chapter.

(2) *Information relating to employer-provided coverage.*—In addition to the information described in paragraph (e)(1) of this section, information returns reporting minimum essential coverage provided to an individual that is coverage provided by a health insurance issuer through a group health plan must report—

(i) The name, address, and EIN of the employer sponsoring the plan;

(ii) Whether the coverage is a qualified health plan enrolled in through the Small Business Health Options Program (SHOP) and the SHOP's unique identifier; and

(iii) Other information specified in forms, instructions, or published guidance, see § § 601.601(d) and 601.602 of this chapter.

(f) *Time and manner for filing return.*—(1) *In general.*—A reporting entity must file the return and transmittal form required under paragraph (a) of this section on or before February 28 (March 31 if filed electronically) of the year following the calendar year in which it provided minimum essential coverage to an individual. A reporting entity must file the return and transmittal form as specified in forms or instructions. For extensions of time for filing returns under this section see § § 1.6081-1 and 1.6081-8. See § 301.6011-2 of this chapter for rules relating to electronic filing.

(2) *Form of return.*—(i) *Applicable large employer members.*—A reporting entity that is reporting under section 6055 as an applicable large employer member (as defined in § 54.4980H-1(a)(5) of this chapter) makes the return required under this paragraph (f) on Form 1094-C and Form 1095-C or other form designated by the Internal Revenue Service.

(ii) *Reporting entities not reporting as applicable large employer members.*—Entities reporting as health insurance issuers or carriers, sponsors of self-insured group health plans that are not reporting as applicable large employer members, sponsors of multiemployer plans, and providers

Reg. § 1.6055-1(f)(2)(ii)

of government-sponsored coverage, will report under section 6055 on Form 1094-B and Form 1095-B or other form designated by the Internal Revenue Service.

(iii) *Substitute forms.*—Reporting entities may make the return required under this paragraph (f) on a substitute form. A substitute form must comply with revenue procedures or other published guidance (see § 601.601(d)(2) of this chapter) that apply to substitute forms.

(g) *Statements to be furnished to responsible individuals.*—(1) *In general.*—Every person required to file a return under this section must furnish to the responsible individual identified on the return a written statement. For purposes of the penalty under section 6722, furnishing a statement to the responsible individual is treated as furnishing a statement to the payee. The statement must show—

(i) The phone number for a person designated as the reporting entity's contact person and policy number, if any; and

(ii) Information described in paragraph (e) of this section required to be shown on the section 6055 return for the responsible individual and each covered individual listed on the return.

(2) *Statements for individuals other than the responsible individual.*—A reporting entity is not required to provide a statement described in paragraph (g)(1) of this section to an individual who is not the responsible individual.

(3) *Form of the statement.*—A statement required under this paragraph (g) may be made either by furnishing to the responsible individual a copy of the return filed with the Internal Revenue Service or on a substitute statement. A substitute statement must include the information required to be shown on the return filed with the Internal Revenue Service and must comply with requirements in published guidance (see § 601.601(d)(2) of this chapter) relating to substitute statements. An Internal Revenue Service truncated taxpayer identification number may be used as the identification number for an individual in lieu of the identification number appearing on the corresponding information return filed with the Internal Revenue Service.

(4) *Time and manner for furnishing statements.*—(i) *Time for furnishing.*—(A) *In general.*— A reporting entity must furnish the statements required under this paragraph (g) on or before January 31 of the year following the calendar year in which minimum essential coverage is provided.

(B) *Extensions of time.*—(1) *In general.*— For good cause upon written application of the person required to furnish statements under this section, the Internal Revenue Service may grant an extension of time not exceeding 30 days in which to furnish these statements. The application must be addressed to the Internal Revenue Service, and must contain a full recital of the reasons for requesting the extension to aid the Internal Revenue Service in determining the period of the extension, if any, that will be granted. A request in the form of a letter to the Internal Revenue Service, signed by the applicant, suffices as an application. The application must be filed on or before the date prescribed in paragraph (g)(4)(i)(A) of this section.

(2) *Automatic extension of time.*—The Commissioner may, in appropriate cases, prescribe additional guidance or procedures, published in the Internal Revenue Bulletin (see § 601.601(d)(2) of this chapter), for automatic extensions of time to furnish to one or more individuals the statement required under section 6055.

(ii) *Manner of furnishing.*—If mailed, the statement must be sent to the responsible individual's last known permanent address or, if no permanent address is known, to the individual's temporary address. For purposes of this paragraph (g)(4), a reporting entity's first class mailing to the last known permanent address, or if no permanent address is known, the temporary address, discharges the requirement to furnish the statement. A reporting entity may furnish the statement electronically if the requirements of § 1.6055-2 are satisfied.

(h) *Penalties.*—(1) *In general.*—For provisions relating to the penalty for failure to file timely a correct information return required under section 6055, see section 6721 and the regulations under that section. For provisions relating to the penalty for failure to furnish timely a correct statement to responsible individuals required under section 6055, see section 6722 and the regulations under that section. See section 6724 and the regulations under that section for rules relating to the waiver of penalties if a failure to file timely or accurately is due to reasonable cause and is not due to willful neglect.

(2) *Application of section 6721 and 6722 penalties to section 6055 reporting.*—For purposes of section 6055 reporting, if the information reported on a return (including a transmittal) or a statement required by this section is incomplete or incorrect as a result of a change in circumstances (such as a retroactive change in coverage), a failure to timely file or furnish a corrected document is a failure to file or furnish a correct return or statement under sections 6721 and 6722.

(i) [Reserved.]

(j) *Effective/applicability date.*—This section applies for calendar years beginning after December 31, 2014. Reporting entities will not be subject to penalties under section 6721 or 6722 for failure to comply with the section 6055 reporting requirements for coverage in 2014 (for information returns filed and statements furnished in 2015). [Reg. § 1.6055-1.]

☐ [T.D. 9660, 3-5-2014 (*corrected* 4-29-2014).]

[Reg. § 1.6055-2]

§ 1.6055-2. Electronic furnishing of statements.—(a) *Electronic furnishing of statements.*— (1) *In general.*—A person required by section 6055 to furnish a statement (furnisher) to a responsible individual (a recipient) may furnish the statement in an electronic format in lieu of a paper format. A furnisher who meets the requirements of paragraphs (a)(2) through (a)(6) of this section is treated as furnishing the statement in a timely manner.

(2) *Consent.*—(i) *In general.*—The recipient must have affirmatively consented to receive the statement in an electronic format. The consent may be made electronically in any manner that reasonably demonstrates that the recipient can access the statement in the electronic format in which it will be furnished. Alternatively, the consent may be made in a paper document that is confirmed electronically.

(ii) *Withdrawal of consent.*—The consent requirement of this paragraph (a)(2) is not satisfied if the recipient withdraws the consent and the withdrawal takes effect before the statement is furnished. The furnisher may provide that a withdrawal of consent takes effect either on the date the furnisher receives it or on another date no more than 60 days later. The furnisher also may provide that a recipient's request for a paper statement will be treated as a withdrawal of the recipient's consent.

(iii) *Change in hardware or software requirements.*—If a change in the hardware or software required to access the statement creates a material risk that the recipient will not be able to access a statement, a furnisher must, prior to changing the hardware or software, notify the recipient. The notice must describe the revised hardware and software required to access the statement and inform the recipient that a new consent to receive the statement in the revised electronic format must be provided to the furnisher. After implementing the revised hardware or software, the furnisher must obtain from the recipient, in the manner described in paragraph (a)(2)(ii) of this section, a new consent or confirmation of consent to receive the statement electronically.

(iv) *Examples.*—The following examples illustrate the rules of this paragraph (a)(2):

Example 1. Furnisher F sends Recipient R a letter stating that R may consent to receive the statement required under section 6055 electronically on a web site instead of in a paper format. The letter contains instructions explaining how to consent to receive the statement electronically by accessing the web site, downloading and completing the consent document, and e-mailing the completed consent back to F. The consent document posted on the web site uses the same electronic format that F will use for the electronically furnished statement. R reads the instructions and submits the consent in the manner provided in the instructions. R has consented to receive the statement required under section 6055 electronically in the manner described in paragraph (a)(2)(i) of this section.

Example 2. Furnisher F sends Recipient R an e-mail stating that R may consent to receive the statement required under section 6055 electronically instead of in a paper format. The e-

mail contains an attachment instructing R how to consent to receive the statement electronically. The e-mail attachment uses the same electronic format that F will use for the electronically furnished statement. R opens the attachment, reads the instructions, and submits the consent in the manner provided in the instructions. R has consented to receive the statement required under section 6055 electronically in the manner described in paragraph (a)(2)(i) of this section.

Example 3. Furnisher F posts a notice on its web site stating that Recipient R may receive the statement required under section 6055 electronically instead of in a paper format. The web site contains instructions on how R may access a secure web page and consent to receive the statement electronically. The consent via the secure web page uses the same electronic format that F will use for electronically furnishing the statement. R accesses the secure web page and follows the instructions for giving consent. R has consented to receive the statement required under section 6055 electronically in the manner described in paragraph (a)(2)(i) of this section.

(3) *Required disclosures.*—(i) *In general.*—Prior to, or at the time of, a recipient's consent, a furnisher must provide to the recipient a clear and conspicuous disclosure statement containing each of the disclosures described in this paragraph (a)(3).

(ii) *Paper statement.*—The furnisher must inform the recipient that the statement will be furnished on paper if the recipient does not consent to receive it electronically.

(iii) *Scope and duration of consent.*—The furnisher must inform the recipient of the scope and duration of the consent. For example, the recipient must be informed whether the consent applies to each statement required to be furnished after the consent is given until it is withdrawn or only to the first statement required to be furnished following the date of the consent.

(iv) *Post-consent request for a paper statement.*—The furnisher must inform the recipient of any procedure for obtaining a paper copy of the recipient's statement after giving the consent described in paragraph (a)(2)(i) of this section and whether a request for a paper statement will be treated as a withdrawal of consent.

(v) *Withdrawal of consent.*—The furnisher must inform the recipient that—

(A) The recipient may withdraw a consent by writing (electronically or on paper) to the person or department whose name, mailing address, telephone number, and e-mail address is provided in the disclosure statement;

(B) The furnisher will confirm the withdrawal and the date on which it takes effect in writing (either electronically or on paper); and

Reg. §1.6055-2(a)(3)(v)(B)

(C) A withdrawal of consent does not apply to a statement that was furnished electronically in the manner described in this paragraph (a) before the date on which the withdrawal of consent takes effect.

(vi) *Notice of termination.*—The furnisher must inform the recipient of the conditions under which the furnisher will cease furnishing statements electronically to the recipient (for example, termination of the recipient's employment with a furnisher who is the recipient's employer).

(vii) *Updating information.*—The furnisher must inform the recipient of the procedures for updating the information needed to contact the recipient. The furnisher must inform the recipient of any change in the furnisher's contact information.

(viii) *Hardware and software requirements.*—The furnisher must provide the recipient with a description of the hardware and software required to access, print, and retain the statement, and the date when the statement will no longer be available on the web site. The furnisher must advise the recipient that the statement may be required to be printed and attached to a Federal, State, or local income tax return.

(4) *Format.*—The electronic version of the statement must contain all required information and comply with applicable published guidance (see § 601.601(d) of this chapter) relating to substitute statements to recipients.

(5) *Notice.*—(i) *In general.*—If a statement is furnished on a web site, the furnisher must notify the recipient. The notice may be delivered by mail, electronic mail, or in person. The notice must provide instructions on how to access and print the statement and include the following statement in capital letters, "IMPORTANT TAX RETURN DOCUMENT AVAILABLE." If the notice is provided by electronic mail, this statement must be on the subject line of the electronic mail.

(ii) *Undeliverable electronic address.*—If an electronic notice described in paragraph (a)(5)(i) of this section is returned as undeliverable, and the furnisher cannot obtain the correct electronic address from the furnisher's records or from the recipient, the furnisher must furnish the notice by mail or in person within 30 days after the electronic notice is returned.

(iii) *Corrected statement.*—If the furnisher has corrected a recipient's statement and the original statement was furnished electronically, the furnisher must furnish a corrected statement to the recipient electronically. If the original statement was furnished through a web site posting, the furnisher must notify the recipient that it has posted the corrected statement on the web site in the manner described in paragraph (a)(5)(i) of this section within 30 days of the posting. The corrected statement or the notice must be furnished by mail or in person if—

(A) An electronic notice of the web site posting of an original statement or the corrected statement was returned as undeliverable; and

(B) The recipient has not provided a new e-mail address.

(6) *Access period.*—Statements furnished on a web site must be retained on the web site through October 15 of the year following the calendar year to which the statements relate (or the first business day after October 15, if October 15 falls on a Saturday, Sunday, or legal holiday). The furnisher must maintain access to corrected statements that are posted on the web site through October 15 of the year following the calendar year to which the statements relate (or the first business day after such October 15, if October 15 falls on a Saturday, Sunday, or legal holiday) or the date 90 days after the corrected forms are posted, whichever is later.

(7) *Paper statements after withdrawal of consent.*—A furnisher must furnish a paper statement if a recipient withdraws consent to receive a statement electronically and the withdrawal takes effect before the statement is furnished. A paper statement furnished after the statement due date under this paragraph (a)(7) is timely if furnished within 30 days after the date the furnisher receives the withdrawal of consent.

(b) *Effective/applicability date.*—This section applies for calendar years beginning after December 31, 2014. Reporting entities will not be subject to penalties under section 6722 with respect to the reporting requirements for 2014 (for statements furnished in 2015). [Reg. § 1.6055-2.]

☐ [*T.D.* 9660, 3-5-2014.]

[Reg. § 301.6056-1]

§ 301.6056-1. Rules relating to reporting by applicable large employers on health insurance coverage offered under employer-sponsored plans.—(a) *In general.*—Section 6056 requires an applicable large employer subject to the requirements of section 4980H to report certain health insurance coverage information to the Internal Revenue Service, and to furnish certain related employee statements to its full-time employees. Paragraph (b) of this section contains definitions for purposes of this section. Paragraph (c) of this section prescribes general rules for filing the required information with the IRS and furnishing the required employee statements to employees. Paragraphs (d) and (e) of this section describe the information required to be reported on a section 6056 information return and the time and manner for filing. Paragraph (f) of this section provides information about the statement required to be furnished to a full-time employee. Paragraph (g) of this section prescribes the time and manner of furnishing the statement, including extensions of time to furnish, to a full-time employee. Paragraph (h) addresses corrections of returns. Paragraph (i) of this section describes the information return penalties applicable to section 6056 returns. Paragraph (j) of this section describes alternative reporting methods available to certain applicable large employers with certain employees. Paragraph (k) of this section describes certain special rules applicable to applicable large employers that are governmental units.

(b) *Definitions.*—(1) *In general.*—The definitions in this paragraph (b) apply for purposes of this section.

(2) *Applicable large employer.*—The term *applicable large employer* has the same meaning as in section 4980H(c)(2) and § 54.4980H-1(a)(4) of this chapter.

(3) *Applicable large employer member.*—The term *applicable large employer member* has the same meaning as in § 54.4980H-1(a)(5) of this chapter.

(4) *Dependent.*—The term *dependent* has the same meaning as in § 54.4980H-1(a)(11) of this chapter.

(5) *Eligible employer-sponsored plan.*—The term *eligible employer-sponsored plan* has the same meaning as in section 5000A(f)(2) and § 1.5000A-2(c)(1) of this chapter.

(6) *Full-time employee.*—The term *full-time employee* has the same meaning as in section 4980H and § 54.5980H-1(a)(21) [§ 54.4980H-1(a)(21)]of this chapter, as applied to the determination and calculation of liability under section 4980H(a) and (b) with respect to any individual employee, and not as applied to the determination of status as an applicable large employer, if different.

(7) *Governmental unit.*—The term *governmental unit* refers to the government of the United States, any State or political subdivision thereof, or any Indian tribal government (as defined in section 7701(a)(40)) or subdivision of an Indian tribal government (as defined in section 7871(d)).

(8) *Agency or instrumentality of a governmental unit.*—[Reserved]

(9) *Minimum essential coverage.*—The term *minimum essential coverage* has the same meaning as in section 5000A(f) and the regulations issued under that section.

(10) *Minimum value.*—The term *minimum value* has the same meaning as in section 36B and any applicable regulations.

(11) *Person.*—The term *person* has the same meaning as in section 7701(a)(1) and applicable regulations.

(c) *Content and timing of reporting by applicable large employer members.*—(1) *In general.*—Each applicable large employer member required to make a return and furnish a related statement to its full-time employees under section 6056 for a calendar year must make a return and furnish the related statement using such form(s) as may be prescribed by the Internal Revenue Service. An applicable large employer member will satisfy its reporting requirements under section 6056 if it files with the Internal Revenue Service a return for each full-time employee using Form 1095-C or another form the IRS designates, and a transmittal form using Form 1094-C or another form the IRS designates, as prescribed in this section and in the instructions to the forms. Each Form 1095-C and the transmittal Form 1094-C will together constitute an information return to be filed with the Internal Revenue Service.

(2) *Reporting facilitated by third parties.*—A separate section 6056 information return must be filed for each applicable large employer member. If more than one section 6056 information return is being filed for an applicable large employer member, there must be one authoritative section 6056 transmittal (Form 1094-C) reporting aggregate employer-level data for all full-time employees of the applicable large employer member, in accordance with forms and instructions. Additionally, there must be only one section 6056 employee statement (Form 1095-C) for each full-time employee with respect to that full-time employee's employment with the applicable large employer member, so that all required information for a particular full-time employee of the applicable large employer member is reflected on a single Form 1095-C.

(d) *Information required to be reported to the Internal Revenue Service.*—(1) *In general.*—Except as provided in paragraph (j) of this section (relating to alternative reporting methods for eligible applicable large employer members), every applicable large employer member must make a section 6056 information return with respect to each full-time employee. Each section 6056 information return must show—

(i) The name, address, and employer identification number of the applicable large employer member,

(ii) The name and telephone number of the applicable large employer member's contact person,

(iii) The calendar year for which the information is reported,

(iv) A certification as to whether the applicable large employer member offered to its full-time employees (and their dependents) the opportunity to enroll in minimum essential coverage under an eligible employer-sponsored plan, by calendar month,

(v) The months during the calendar year for which minimum essential coverage under the plan was available,

(vi) Each full-time employee's share of the lowest cost monthly premium (self-only) for coverage providing minimum value offered to that full-time employee under an eligible employer-sponsored plan, by calendar month;

(vii) The number of full-time employees for each month during the calendar year,

(viii) The name, address, and taxpayer identification number of each full-time employee during the calendar year and the months, if any, during which the employee was covered under the plan, and

Reg. § 301.6056-1(d)(1)(viii)

(ix) Any other information specified in forms, instructions, or published guidance, see §§ 601.601(d) and 601.602 of this chapter.

(2) *Form of the return.*—A return required under this paragraph (d) may be made on Forms 1094-C and 1095-C or other form(s) designated by the Internal Revenue Service, or a substitute form. A substitute form must include the information required to be reported on Forms 1094-C and 1095-C and must comply with applicable revenue procedures or other published guidance relating to substitute statements. See § 601.601(d)(2) of this chapter.

(e) *Time and manner for filing return.*—An applicable large employer member must file the return and transmittal form required under paragraph (d)(2) of this section on or before February 28 (March 31 if filed electronically) of the year succeeding the calendar year to which it relates in accordance with any applicable guidance and the instructions to the form. An applicable large employer member must file the return and transmittal form at the address specified on the return form or its instructions. For extensions of time for filing returns under this section, see §§ 1.6081-1 and 1.6081-8 of this chapter. See § 301.6011-2 for rules relating to electronic filing.

(f) *Statements required to be furnished to full-time employees.*—(1) *In general.*—Except as provided in paragraph (j) of this section, every applicable large employer member required to file a return under section 6056 must furnish to each of its full-time employees identified on the return a written statement showing—

(i) The name, address and employer identification number of the applicable large employer member, and

(ii) The information required to be shown on the section 6056 return with respect to the full-time employee.

(2) *Form of the statement.*—A statement required under this paragraph (f) may be made either by furnishing to the full-time employee a copy of Form 1095-C or another form the IRS designates as prescribed in this section and in the instructions to such forms, or a substitute statement. A substitute statement must include the information required to be shown on the return filed with the IRS and must comply with requirements in published guidance (see § 601.601(d)(2) of this chapter) relating to substitute statements. An IRS truncated taxpayer identification number may be used as the identifying number for an individual in lieu of the identifying number appearing on the corresponding information return filed with the IRS.

(g) *Time and manner for furnishing statements.*—(1) *Time for furnishing.*—(i) *In general.*—Each statement required by this section for a calendar year must be furnished to a full-time employee on or before January 31 of the year succeeding that calendar year in accordance with applicable Internal Revenue Service procedures and instructions

(ii) *Extensions of time.*—(A) *In general.*—For good cause upon written application of the person required to furnish statements under this section, the Internal Revenue Service may grant an extension of time not exceeding 30 days in which to furnish such statements. The application must be addressed to the Internal Revenue Service, and must contain a full recital of the reasons for requesting the extension to aid the Internal Revenue Service in determining the period of the extension, if any, that will be granted. A request in the form of a letter to the Internal Revenue Service, signed by the applicant, suffices as an application. The application must be filed on or before the date prescribed in paragraph (g)(1) of this section.

(B) *Automatic extension of time.*—The Commissioner may, in appropriate cases, prescribe additional guidance or procedures, published in the Internal Revenue Bulletin (see § 601.601(d)(2) of this chapter), for automatic extensions of time to furnish to one or more full-time employees the statement required under section 6056.

(2) *Manner of furnishing.*—If mailed, the statement must be sent to the full-time employee's last known permanent address or, if no permanent address is known, to the employee's temporary address. For purposes of this paragraph (g), an applicable large employer member's first class mailing to the last known permanent address, or if no permanent address is known, the temporary address, discharges the requirement to furnish the statement. An applicable large employer member may furnish the statement electronically in accordance with § 301.6056-2.

(h) *Correction of returns.*—See § 301.6056-1(i)(2).

(i) *Penalties.*—(1) *In general.*—For provisions relating to the penalty for failure to file timely a correct information return required under section 6056, see section 6721 and the regulations under that section. For provisions relating to the penalty for failure to furnish timely a correct statement to full-time employees required under section 6056, see section 6722 and the regulations under that section. See section 6724 and the regulations under that section for rules relating to the waiver of penalties if a failure to file timely or accurately is due to reasonable cause and is not due to willful neglect.

(2) *Application of section 6721 and 6722 penalties to section 6056 reporting.*—For purposes of section 6056 reporting, if the information reported on a return (including a transmittal) or a statement required by this section is incomplete or incorrect as a result of a change in circumstances (such as a retroactive change in coverage), a failure to timely file or furnish a corrected document is a failure to file or furnish a correct return or statement under sections 6721 and 6722.

(j) *Alternative reporting methods for eligible applicable large employer members.*—In lieu of the general reporting method described in paragraph (d) of this section, eligible applicable large employer members may use the following alternative reporting methods described in this paragraph (j).

(1) *Certification of qualifying offer.*—An applicable large employer member is an eligible applicable large employer member and is treated as meeting its reporting obligation under section 6056 if:

(i) The applicable large employer member certifies on the section 6056 transmittal form, in accordance with the form and the instructions to the form, that it made a qualifying offer. A qualifying offer is an offer to one or more of its full-time employees for all months during the year for which the employee was a full-time employee and which are not within a limited nonassessment period (as defined in § 54.4980H-1(a)(26) of this chapter), of minimum essential coverage providing minimum value at an employee cost for employee-only coverage not exceeding 9.5 percent of the mainland single federal poverty line, and that includes an offer of minimum essential coverage to the employees' spouses and dependents. For this purpose, the applicable federal poverty line is the federal poverty line as defined in § 54.4980H-1(a)(19) of this chapter, as calculated and applied to the 48 contiguous states and the District of Columbia;

(ii) The applicable large employer member provides on the Form 1095-C or other form as designated by the IRS, in accordance with the form and the instructions to the form, the information with respect to each full-time employee to whom a qualifying offer, as defined in paragraph (j)(1)(i) of this section, is made for all twelve months of the applicable calendar year;

(iii) The applicable large employer member provides a statement to each full-time employee to whom a qualifying offer (as defined in paragraph (j)(1)(i) of this section) was made for all twelve months of the applicable calendar year, in such form and manner as prescribed by the Secretary, or a copy of the Form 1095-C filed with the IRS with respect to that full-time employee; and

(D) The applicable large employer member files section 6056 returns and furnishes section 6056 employee statements with respect to all other full-time employees under the general reporting method described in paragraph (d) of this section, in accordance with forms and instructions.

(2) *Option to report without separate identification of full-time employees if certain conditions related to offers of coverage are satisfied (98 percent offers).*—An applicable large employer member that otherwise meets its reporting obligation under section 6056 is not required to identify on its section 6056 return whether a particular employee is a full-time employee for one or more calendar months of the reporting year or report the total number of its full-time employees for the reporting year, if it certifies that it offered minimum essential coverage providing minimum value that was affordable under section 4980H to at least 98 percent of the employees (and their dependents) with respect to whom it reports for purposes of section 6056 in accordance with paragraph (d) of this section (regardless of whether the employee is a full-time employee for purposes of section 4980H for a calendar month during the year).

(k) *Special rules for governmental units.*— (1) *Person appropriately designated.*—In the case of any applicable large employer member that is a governmental unit or any agency or instrumentality thereof, the person or persons appropriately designated under section 6056(e) for purposes of the filing and furnishing requirements of section 6056 must be part of or related to the same governmental unit as the applicable large employer member. The applicable large employer member must make (or revoke) the designation before the earlier of the deadline for filing the returns or furnishing the statements required by this section. A person that has been appropriately designated under section 6056(e) must file a separate section 6056 return and transmittal for each applicable large employer member for which the person is reporting. The person appropriately designated under section 6056(e) assumes responsibility for the section 6056 requirements on behalf of the applicable large employer member for which the person is designated. Notwithstanding the designation, a separate section 6056 information return must be filed for each applicable large employer member that is a governmental unit. If more than one section 6056 information return is being filed for an applicable large employer member, there must be one authoritative section 6056 transmittal (Form 1094-C) reporting aggregate employer-level data for all full-time employees of the applicable large employer member, in accordance with forms and instructions. In addition, notwithstanding the designation, there must be only one section 6056 employee statement (Form 1095-C) for each full-time employee with respect to that full-time employee's employment with the applicable large employer member, so that all required information for a particular full-time employee of the applicable large employer member is reflected on a single Form 1095-C.

(2) *Written designation.*—The designation under section 6056(e) must be made in writing, must be signed by both the applicable large employer member and the designated person, and must be effective under all applicable laws. The designation must set forth the name, address, and employer identification number of the designated person, and appoint such person as the person responsible for reporting under section 6056 on behalf of the applicable large employer member. The designation must contain information identifying the category of full-time employees (which may be full-time employees eligible for a specified health plan, or in a particular job

Reg. § 301.6056-1(k)(2)

category, as long as the specific employees covered by the designation can be identified) for which the designated person is responsible for reporting under section 6056 on behalf of the applicable large employer member. If the designated person is responsible for reporting under section 6056 for all full-time employees of an applicable large employer member, the designation must so indicate. The designation must contain language that the designated person agrees and certifies that it is the appropriately designated person under section 6056(e), and an acknowledgement that the designated person is responsible for reporting under section 6056 on behalf of the applicable large employer member and subject to the requirements of section 6056, including for purposes of information reporting requirements under sections 6721, 6722, and 6724. The designation must also set forth the name and employer identification number of the applicable large employer member, identifying the applicable large employer member as the person subject to the requirements of section 4980H. An equivalent applicable statutory or regulatory designation containing the language described in this paragraph (k)(2) will be treated as a written designation for purposes of section 6056(e) and this section. The designation will not be submitted to the IRS and should be maintained under the normal record-retention rules under section 6103.

(3) *Application to alternative reporting methods.*—A person designated under this paragraph (k) may use the alternative reporting method identified in paragraph (j)(1) of this section for the full-time employees for which it is reporting with respect to a particular governmental unit if that particular governmental unit meets the eligibility requirements with respect to those employees, but may use the alternative reporting method identified in paragraph (j)(2) of this section only if the governmental unit on whose behalf it is reporting would itself be eligible to use that alternative reporting method.

(l) *Additional guidance.*—The Commissioner may prescribe additional guidance of general applicability, published in the Internal Revenue Bulletin (see §601.601(d)(2) of this chapter) to provide additional rules under section 6056, including rules permitting use of alternative optional methods to meet reporting requirements.

(m) *Effective/applicability date.*—This section applies for calendar years beginning after December 31, 2014. Reporting entities will not be subject to penalties under sections 6721 or 6722 for failure to comply with the section 6056 reporting requirements for 2014 (for information returns filed and for statements furnished to employees in 2015). [Reg. §301.6056-1.]

☐ [*T.D.* 9661, 3-5-2014.]

[Reg. §301.6056-2]

§301.6056-2. Electronic furnishing of statements.—(a) *Electronic furnishing of statements.*—(1) *In general.*—An applicable large employer

member required by §301.6056-1 to furnish a statement (furnisher) to a full-time employee (a recipient) as required by section 6056 may furnish the section 6056 employee statement (the statement) in an electronic format in lieu of a paper format, provided that the furnisher meets the requirements of paragraphs (a)(2) through (a)(6) of this section. An applicable large employer member who meets the requirements of paragraphs (a)(2) through (6) of this section is treated as furnishing the statement in a timely manner.

(2) *Consent.*—(i) *In general.*—The recipient must have affirmatively consented to receive the statement in an electronic format. The recipient may make the consent electronically in any manner that reasonably demonstrates that the recipient can access the statement in the electronic format in which it will be furnished to the recipient. Alternatively, the recipient may make the consent in a paper document if the recipient confirms the consent electronically.

(ii) *Withdrawal of consent.*—The consent requirement of this paragraph (a)(2) is not satisfied if the recipient withdraws the consent and the withdrawal takes effect before the statement is furnished. The furnisher may provide that a withdrawal of consent takes effect either on the date it is received by the furnisher or on a subsequent date. The furnisher may also provide that a recipient's request for a paper statement will be treated as a withdrawal of the recipient's consent.

(iii) *Change in hardware or software requirements.*—If a change in the hardware or software required to access the statement creates a material risk that the recipient will not be able to access the statement, the furnisher must, prior to changing the hardware or software, provide the recipient with a notice. The notice must describe the revised hardware and software required to access the statement and inform the recipient that a new consent to receive the statement in the revised electronic format must be provided to the furnisher. After implementing the revised hardware and software, the furnisher must obtain from the recipient, in the manner described in paragraph (a)(2)(i) of this section, a new consent or confirmation of consent to receive the statement electronically.

(iv) *Examples.*—The following examples illustrate the rules of this paragraph (a)(2):

Example 1. Furnisher F sends Recipient R a letter stating that R may consent to receive the statement required under section 6056 electronically on a web site instead of in a paper format. The letter contains instructions explaining how to consent to receive the statement electronically by accessing the web site, downloading the consent document, completing the consent document and e-mailing the completed consent back to F. The consent document posted on the web site uses the same electronic format that F will use for the electronically furnished statement. R reads the instructions and accesses the web site, downloads and completes the consent document, and emails the completed consent back to F. R has consented to receive the statement required under section 6056 electronically in the manner described in paragraph (a)(2)(i) of this section.

Example 2. Furnisher F sends Recipient R an e-mail stating that R may consent to receive the statement required under section 6056 electronically instead of in a paper format. The e-mail contains an attachment instructing R how to consent to receive the statement electronically. The e-mail attachment uses the same electronic format that F will use for the electronically furnished statement. R opens the attachment, reads the instructions, and submits the consent in the manner provided in the instructions. R has consented to receive the statement required under section 6056 electronically in the manner described in paragraph (a)(2)(i) of this section.

Example 3. Furnisher F posts a notice on its web site stating that Recipient R may receive the statement required under section 6056 electronically instead of in a paper format. The web site contains instructions on how R may access a secure web page and consent to receive the statement electronically. The consent via the secure web page uses the same electronic format that F will use for the electronically furnished statement. R accesses the web site and follows the instructions for giving consent. R has consented to receive section 6056 statements electronically in the manner described in paragraph (a)(2)(i) of this section.

(3) *Required disclosures.*—(i) *In general.*—Prior to, or at the time of, a recipient's consent, a furnisher must provide to the recipient a clear and conspicuous disclosure statement containing each of the disclosures described in paragraphs (a)(3)(ii) through (viii) of this section.

(ii) *Paper statement.*—The furnisher must inform the recipient that the statement will be furnished on paper if the recipient does not consent to receive it electronically.

(iii) *Scope and duration of consent.*—The furnisher must inform the recipient of the scope and duration of the consent. For example, the recipient must be informed whether the consent applies to each statement required to be furnished after the consent is given until it is withdrawn in the manner described in paragraph (a)(3)(v)(A) of this section or only to the first statement required to be furnished following the date of the consent.

(iv) *Post-consent request for a paper statement.*—The furnisher must inform the recipient of any procedure for obtaining a paper copy of the recipient's statement after giving the consent described in paragraph (a)(2)(i) of this section and whether a request for a paper statement will be treated as a withdrawal of consent.

(v) *Withdrawal of consent.*—The furnisher must inform the recipient that—

(A) The recipient may withdraw a consent by writing (electronically or on paper) to the person or department whose name, mailing address, telephone number, and email address is provided in the disclosure statement;

(B) The furnisher will confirm the withdrawal and the date on which it takes effect in writing (either electronically or on paper), and

(C) A withdrawal of consent does not apply to a statement that was furnished electronically in the manner described in this paragraph (a) before the date on which the withdrawal of consent takes effect.

(vi) *Notice of termination.*—The furnisher must inform the recipient of the conditions under which a furnisher will cease furnishing statements electronically to the recipient (for example, termination of the recipient's employment with furnisher-employer).

(vii) *Updating information.*—The furnisher must inform the recipient of the procedures for updating the information needed to contact the recipient. The furnisher must inform the recipient of any change in the furnisher's contact information.

(viii) *Hardware and software requirements.*—The furnisher must provide the recipient with a description of the hardware and software required to access, print, and retain the statement, and the date when the statement will no longer be available on the Web site. The furnisher must advise the recipient that the statement may be required to be printed and attached to a Federal, State, or local income tax return.

(4) *Format.*—The electronic version of the statement must contain all required information and comply with applicable revenue procedures relating to substitute statements to recipients.

(5) *Notice.*—(i) *In general.*—If the statement is furnished on a Web site, the furnisher must notify the recipient that the statement is posted on a Web site. The notice may be delivered by mail, electronic mail, or in person. The notice must provide instructions on how to access and print the statement. The notice must include the following statement in capital letters, "IMPORTANT TAX RETURN DOCUMENT AVAILABLE." If the notice is provided by electronic mail, the foregoing statement must be on the subject line of the electronic mail.

(ii) *Undeliverable electronic address.*—If an electronic notice described in paragraph (a)(5)(i) of this section is returned as undeliverable, and the correct electronic address cannot be obtained from the furnisher's records or from the recipient, then the furnisher must furnish the notice by mail or in person within 30 days after the electronic notice is returned.

(iii) *Corrected statement.*—If the furnisher has corrected a recipient's statement as directed in § 301.6056-1(k) and the original statement was furnished electronically, the furnisher must furnish the corrected statement to the recipient electronically. If the original statement was furnished through a Web site posting and the furnisher has corrected the statement, the furnisher must notify the recipient that it has posted the corrected statement on the web site within 30 days of such posting in the manner described in paragraph (a)(5)(i) of this section. The corrected statement or the notice must be furnished by mail or in person if-

(A) An electronic notice of the web site posting of an original statement or the corrected statement was returned as undeliverable, and

(B) The recipient has not provided a new e-mail address.

(6) *Access period.*—Statements furnished on a web site must be retained on the web site through October 15 of the year following the calendar year to which the statements relate (or the first business day after October 15, if October 15 falls on a Saturday, Sunday, or legal holiday). The furnisher must maintain access to corrected statements that are posted on the web site through October 15 of the year following the calendar year to which the statements relate (or the first business day after such October 15, if October 15 falls on a Saturday, Sunday, or legal holiday) or the date 90 days after the corrected forms are posted, whichever is later.

(7) *Paper statements after withdrawal of consent.*—A furnisher must furnish a paper statement if a recipient withdraws consent to receive a statement electronically and the withdrawal takes effect before the statement is furnished. A paper statement furnished after the statement due date under this paragraph (a)(7) is timely if furnished within 30 days after the date the furnisher receives the withdrawal of consent.

(b) *Effective/applicability date.*—This section applies for calendar years beginning after December 31, 2014. Reporting entities will not be subject to penalties under section 6722 with respect to the reporting requirements for 2014 (for statements furnished in 2015). [Reg. § 301.6056-2.]

☐ [*T.D.* 9661, 3-5-2014.]

[Reg. § 301.6057-1]

§ 301.6057-1. Employee retirement benefit plans; identification of participant with deferred vested retirement benefit.—(a) *Annual registration statement.*—(1) *In general.*—Under section 6057(a), the plan administrator (within the meaning of section 414(g)) of an employee retirement benefit plan must file with the Internal Revenue Service information relating to each plan participant who separates from service covered by the plan and is entitled to a deferred vested retirement benefit under the plan, but is not paid this retirement benefit. Plans subject to this filing requirement are described in subparagraph(3) of this paragraph. Subparagraph (4) describes how the information is to be filed with the Internal Revenue Service. In the case of a plan to which only one employer contributes, the time for filing the information with respect to

each separated participant is described in subparagraph(5). In the case of a plan to which more than one employer contributes the time for filing the information with respect to a participant is described in paragraph (b)(2). Paragraph (b) also provides other rules applicable only to plans to which more than one employer contributes.

(2) *Deferred vested retirement benefit.*—For purposes of this section, a plan participant's deferred retirement benefit is considered a vested benefit if it is vested under the terms of the plan at the close of the plan year described in paragraph (a)(5) or (b)(4) (whichever is applicable) for which information relating to any deferred vested retirement benefit of the participant must be filed. A participant's deferred retirement benefit need not be a nonforfeitable benefit within the meaning of section 411(a) for the filing requirements described in this section to apply. Accordingly, information relating to a participant's deferred vested retirement benefit must be filed as required by this section notwithstanding that the benefit is subject to forfeiture by reason of an event or condition occurring subsequent to the close of the plan year described in paragraph (a)(5) or (b)(4) (whichever is applicable) for which information relating to any deferred vested retirement benefit of the participant must be filed.

(3) *Plans subject to filing requirement.*—The term "employee retirement benefit plan" means a plan to which the vesting standards of section 203 of part 2 of subtitle B of Title I of the Employee Retirement Income Security Act of 1974 (88 Stat. 854) apply for any day in the plan year. (For purposes of this section, "plan year" means the plan year as determined for purposes of the annual return required by section 6058(a). Accordingly, a plan need not be a qualified plan within the meaning of section 401(a) to be subject to these filing requirements. A plan to which more than one employer contributes must file the report of deferred vested retirement benefits described in this section, but see paragraph (b) for special rules applicable to such a plan. The filing requirements described in this section and § 301.6057-2 (relating to notification of change in plan status) do not apply to a governmental or church plan described in section 414(d) or (e).

(4) *Filing requirements.*—Information relating to the deferred vested retirement benefit of a plan participant must be filed on Schedule SSA as an attachment to the Annual Return/Report of Employee Benefit Plan (Form 5500 series). Schedule SSA shall be filed on behalf of an employee retirement benefit plan for each plan year for which information relating to the deferred vested retirement benefit of a plan participant is filed under paragraph (a)(5) or (b)(2) of this section. There shall be filed on Schedule SSA the name and Social Security number of the participant, a description of the nature, form and amount of the deferred vested retirement benefit to which the participant is entitled, and such other information as is required by section

6057(a) or Schedule SSA and the accompanying instructions. The form of the benefit reported on Schedule SSA shall be the normal form of benefit under the plan, or, if the plan administrator (within the meaning of section 414(g)) considers it more appropriate, any other form of benefit.

(5) *Time for reporting deferred vested retirement benefit.*—(i) *In general.*—In the case of a plan to which only one employer contributes, information relating to the deferred vested retirement benefit of a plan participant must be filed no later than on the Schedule SSA filed for the plan year following the plan year within which the participant separates from service covered by the plan. Information relating to a separated participant may, at the option of the plan administrator, be reported earlier (that is, on the Schedule SSA filed for the plan year in which the participant separates from service covered by the plan). For purposes of this paragraph a participant is not considered to separate from service covered by the plan solely because the participant incurs a break in service under the plan. In addition, for purposes of this paragraph, in the case of a plan which uses the elapsed time method described in Department of Labor regulations for crediting service for benefit accrual purposes, a participant is considered to separate from service covered by the plan on the date the participant severs from service covered by the plan.

(ii) *Exception.*—Notwithstanding subdivision (i), no information relating to the deferred vested retirement benefit of a separated participant is required to be filed on Schedule SSA if, before the date such Schedule SSA is required to be filed (including any extension of time for filing granted pursuant to section 6081), the participant (A) is paid some or all of the deferred vested retirement benefit under the plan, (B) returns to service covered by the plan, or (C) forfeits all of the deferred vested retirement benefit under the plan.

(b) *Plans to which more than one employer contributes.*—(1) *Application.*—Section 6057 and this section apply to a plan to which more than one employer contributes with the modifications set forth in this paragraph. For purposes of section 6057 and this section, whether or not more than one employer contributes to a plan shall be determined by the number of employers who are required to contribute to the plan. Thus, for example, this paragraph applies to plans maintained by more than one employer which are collectively bargained as described in section 413(a), multiple-employer plans described in section 413(c) and the regulations thereunder, multiemployer plans described in section 414(f), and plans adopted by more than one employer of certain controlled and common control groups described in section 414(b) and (c).

(2) *Time for reporting deferred vested retirement benefit.*—(i) *In general.*—In the case of a plan to which more than one employer contributes, information relating to the deferred vested retirement benefit of a plan participant must be filed no later than on the Schedule SSA filed for the plan year within which the participant completes the second of two consecutive one-year breaks in service (as defined in the plan for vesting percentage purposes) in service computation periods (as defined in the plan for vesting percentage purposes) which begin after December 31, 1974. At the option of the plan administrator, information relating to a participant's deferred vested retirement benefit may be filed earlier (that is, on the Schedule SSA filed for the plan year in which the participant incurs the first one-year break in service or, in the case of a separated participant, on the Schedule SSA filed for the plan year in which the participant separates from service).

(ii) *Special rules.*—For purposes of this subparagraph (1)—

(A) For the definition of the term "one-year break in service" in the case of a plan which uses the elapsed time method described in Department of Labor Regulations for crediting service for vesting percentage purposes, see § 1.411(a)-6(c)(2).

(B) In the case of a plan which does not define the term "one-year break in service" for vesting percentage purposes, a plan participant shall be deemed to incur a one-year break in service under the plan in any plan year within which the participant does not complete more than 500 hours of service covered by the plan.

(iii) *Transitional rule.*—Notwithstanding subdivision (i), if the second consecutive one-year break in service described in subdivision (i) is incurred in a plan year beginning before January 1, 1978, information relating to the participant's deferred vested retirement benefit is not required to be filed earlier than on the Schedule SSA filed for the first plan year beginning after December 31, 1977.

(iv) *Exception.*—Notwithstanding subdivision (i) or (iii) of this subparagraph, no information relating to a participant's deferred vested retirement benefit is required to be filed on Schedule SSA if, before the date such Schedule SSA is required to be filed (including any extension of time for filing granted pursuant to section 6081), the participant (A) is paid some or all of the deferred vested retirement benefit under the plan, (B) accrues additional retirement benefits under the plan, or (C) forfeits all of the deferred vested retirement benefit under the plan.

(3) *Information relating to deferred vested retirement benefit.*—(i) *Incomplete records.*—Section 6057(a) and paragraph (a)(4) of this section require the filing on Schedule SSA of a description of the deferred vested retirement benefit to which the participant is entitled. If the plan administrator of a plan to which more than one employer contributes maintains records of a participant's service covered by the plan which are incomplete as of the close of the plan year with respect to which the plan administrator files information relating to the participant on Schedule

SSA, the plan administrator may elect to file the information required by Schedule SSA based only upon these incomplete records. The plan administrator is not required, for purposes of completing Schedule SSA, to compile from sources other than such records a complete record of a participant's years of service covered by the plan. Similarly, if retirement benefits under the plan are determined by taking into account a participant's service with an employer which is not service covered by the plan, but the plan administrator maintains records only with respect to periods of service covered by the plan, the plan administrator may complete Schedule SSA taking into account only the participant's period of service covered by the plan.

(ii) *Inability to determine correct amount of participant's deferred vested retirement benefit.*—If the amount of a participant's deferred vested retirement benefit which is filed on Schedule SSA is computed on the basis of plan records maintained by the plan administrator which—

(A) Are incomplete with respect to the participant's service covered by the plan (as described in subdivision (i)), or

(B) Fail to account for the participant's service not covered by the plan which is relevant to a determination of the participant's deferred vested retirement benefit under the plan (as described in subdivision (i)),

then the plan administrator must indicate on Schedule SSA that the amount of the deferred vested retirement benefit shown therein may be other than that to which the participant is actually entitled because the amount is based upon incomplete records.

(iii) *Inability to determine whether participant vested in deferred retirement benefit.*—Where, as described in subdivision (i), information to be reported on Schedule SSA is to be based upon records which are incomplete with respect to a participant's service covered by the plan or which fail to take into account relevant service not covered by the plan, the plan administrator may be unable to determine whether or not the participant is vested in any deferred retirement benefit. If, in view of information provided either by the incomplete records or the plan participant, there is a significant likelihood that the plan participant is vested in a deferred retirement benefit under the plan, information relating to the participant must be filed on Schedule SSA with the notation that the participant may be entitled to a deferred vested retirement benefit under the plan, but information relating to the amount of the benefit may be omitted. This subdivision (iii) does not apply in a case in which it can be determined from plan records maintained by the plan administrator that the participant is vested in a deferred retirement benefit. Subdivision (ii), however, may apply in such a case.

(c) *Voluntary filing.*—(1) *In general.*—The plan administrator of an employee retirement benefit plan described in paragraph (a)(3) of this section, or any other employee retirement benefit plan

(including a governmental or church plan), may at its option, file on Schedule SSA information relating to the deferred vested retirement benefit of any plan participant who separates at any time from service covered by the plan, including plan participants who separate from service in plan years beginning before 1976.

(2) *Deleting previously filed information.*—If, after information relating to the deferred vested retirement benefit of a plan participant is filed on Schedule SSA, the plan participant—

(i) Is paid some or all of the deferred vested retirement benefit under the plan, or

(ii) Forfeits all of the deferred vested retirement benefit under the plan, the plan administrator may, at its option, file on Schedule SSA (or such other form as may be provided for this purpose) the name and social security number of the participant with the notation that information previously filed relating to the participant's deferred vested retirement benefit should be deleted.

(d) *Filing incident to cessation of payment of benefits.*—(1) *In general.*—As described in this section, no information relating to the deferred vested retirement benefit of a plan participant is required to be filed on Schedule SSA if before the date such Schedule SSA is required to be filed, some of the deferred vested retirement benefit is paid to the participant, and information relating to a participant's deferred vested retirement benefit which was previously filed on Schedule SSA may be deleted if the participant is paid some of the deferred vested retirement benefit. If payment of the deferred vested retirement benefit ceases before all of the benefit to which the participant is entitled is paid to the participant, information relating to the deferred vested retirement benefit to which the participant remains entitled shall be filed on the Schedule SSA filed for the plan year following the last plan year within which a portion of the benefit is paid to the participant.

(2) *Exception.*—Notwithstanding subparagraph (1) of this paragraph, no information relating to the deferred vested retirement benefit to which the participant remains entitled is required to be filed on Schedule SSA if, before the date such Schedule SSA is required to be filed (including any extension of time for filing granted pursuant to section 6081), the participant (i) returns to service covered by the plan, (ii) accrues additional retirement benefits under the plan, or (iii) forfeits the benefit under the plan.

(e) *Individual statement to participant.*—The plan administrator of an employee retirement benefit plan defined in paragraph (a)(3) of this section must provide each participant with respect to whom information is required to be filed on Schedule SSA a statement describing the deferred vested retirement benefit to which the participant is entitled. The description provided the participant must include the information filed with respect to the participant on Schedule

SSA. The statement is to be delivered to the participant or forwarded to the participant's last known address no later than the date on which any Schedule SSA reporting information with respect to the participant is required to be filed (including any extension of time for filing granted pursuant to section 6081).

(f) *Penalties.*—For amounts imposed in the case of failure to file the report of deferred vested retirement benefits required by section 6057(a) and paragraph (a) or (b) of this section, see section 6652(e)(1). For the penalty relating to a failure to provide the participant the individual statement of deferred vested retirement benefit required by section 6057(e) and paragraph (e) of this section, see section 6690.

(g) *Effective dates.*—(1) *Plans to which only one employer contributes.*—In the case of a plan to which only one employer contributes, this section is effective for plan years beginning after December 31, 1975, and with respect to a participant who separates from service covered by the plan in plan years beginning after that date.

(2) *Plans to which more than one employer contributes.*—In the case of a plan to which more than one employer contributes, this section is effective for plan years beginning after December 31, 1977, and with respect to a participant who completes two consecutive one-year breaks in service under the plan in service computation periods beginning after December 31, 1974. [Reg. § 301.6057-1.]

☐ [*T.D.* 7561, 8-24-78.]

[Reg. § 301.6057-2]

§ 301.6057-2. Employee retirement benefit plans; notification of change in plan status.—(a) *Change in plan status.*—The plan administrator (within the meaning of section 414(g)) of an employee retirement benefit plan defined in § 301.6057-1(a)(3) (including a plan to which more than one employer contributes, as described in § 301.6057-1(b)(1)) must notify the Internal Revenue Service of the following changes in plan status—

(1) A change in the name of the plan,

(2) A change in the name or address of the plan administrator,

(3) The termination of the plan, or

(4) The merger or consolidation of the plan with another plan or the division of the plan into two or more plans.

(b) *Notification.*—A notification of a change in status described in paragraph (a) must be filed on the Annual Return/Report of Employee Benefit Plan (Form 5500 series) for the plan year in which the change in status occurred. The notification must be filed at the time and place and in the manner prescribed in the form and any accompanying instructions.

(c) *Penalty.*—For amounts imposed in the case of failure to file a notification of a change in plan status required by section 6057(b) and this section, see section 6652(e)(2).

(d) *Effective date.*—This section is effective for changes in plan status occurring within plan years beginning after December 31, 1975. [Reg. § 301.6057-2.]

☐ [*T.D.* 7561, 8-24-78.]

[Reg. § 301.6057-3]

§ 301.6057-3. Required use of magnetic media for filing requirements relating to deferred vested retirement benefit.—(a) *Magnetic media filing requirements under section 6057.*—A registration statement required under section 6057(a) or a notification required under section 6057(b) with respect to an employee benefit plan must be filed on magnetic media if the filer is required by the Internal Revenue Code or regulations to file at least 250 returns during the calendar year that includes the first day of the plan year. Returns filed on magnetic media must be made in accordance with applicable revenue procedures, publications, forms, instructions, or other guidance on the IRS.gov Internet website. In prescribing revenue procedures, publications, forms, instructions, or other guidance on the IRS.gov Internet website, the Commissioner may direct the type of magnetic media filing. See § 601.601(d)(2)(ii)(*b*) of this chapter.

(b) *Economic hardship waiver.*—The Commissioner may waive the requirements of this section in cases of undue economic hardship. The principal factor in determining hardship will be the amount, if any, by which the cost of filing the registration statements or notifications on magnetic media in accordance with this section exceeds the cost of filing the registration statements or notifications on other media. A request for a waiver must be made in accordance with applicable published guidance, publications, forms, instructions, or other guidance on the IRS.gov Internet website. See § 601.601(d)(2)(ii)(*b*) of this chapter. The waiver will specify the type of filing (that is, a registration statement or notification under section 6057) and the period to which it applies. In addition, the waiver will be subject to such terms and conditions regarding the method of filing as may be prescribed by the Commissioner.

(c) *Failure to file.*—If a filer required to file a registration statement or other notification under section 6057 fails to file the statement or other notification on magnetic media when required to do so by this section, the filer is deemed to have failed to file the statement or other notification. See section 6652(d) for the amount imposed for the failure to file a registration statement or other notification required under section 6057. In determining whether there is reasonable cause for the failure to file the registration statement or notification under section 6057, § 301.6652-3(b) and rules similar to the rules in § 301.6724-1(c)(3)(ii) (regarding undue economic hardship related to filing information returns on magnetic media) will apply.

(d) *Meaning of terms.*—The following definitions apply for purposes of this section.

(1) *Magnetic media.*—The term *magnetic media* means electronic filing, as well as other media specifically permitted under applicable regulations, revenue procedures, or publications, forms, instructions, or other guidance on the IRS.gov Internet website. See § 601.601(d)(2)(ii)(*b*) of this chapter.

(2) *Registration statement required under section 6057(a).*—The term *registration statement required under section 6057(a)* means a Form 8955-SSA (or its successor).

(3) *Notification required under section 6057(b).*—The term *notification required under section 6057(b)* means either a Form 8955-SSA (or its successor) or a return in the Form 5500 series (or its successor).

(4) *Determination of 250 returns.*—(i) *In general.*—For purposes of this section, a filer is required to file at least 250 returns if, during the calendar year that includes the first day of the plan year, the filer is required to file at least 250 returns of any type, including information returns (for example, Forms W-2 and Forms 1099), income tax returns, employment tax returns, and excise tax returns.

(ii) *Definition of filer.*—For purposes of this section, the term *filer* means the plan administrator within the meaning of section 414(g). If the plan administrator within the meaning of section 414(g) is the employer, the special rules in § 1.6058-2(d)(3)(iii) will apply.

(e) *Example.*—The following example illustrates the provisions of paragraph (d)(4) of this section:

Example. In 2015, P, the plan administrator of Plan B, is required to file 252 returns (including Forms 1099-R, "Distributions From Pensions, Annuities, Retirement or Profit-Sharing Plans, IRAs, Insurance Contracts, etc.;" Form 8955-SSA, "Annual Registration Statement Identifying Separated Participants with Deferred Vested Benefits;" Form 5500, "Annual Return/Report of Employee Benefit Plan;" and Form 945, "Annual Return of Withheld Federal Income Tax"). Plan B's plan year is the calendar year. Because P is required to file at least 250 returns during the 2015 calendar year, P must file the 2015 Form 8955-SSA for Plan B electronically.

(f) *Effective/applicability date.*—This section is applicable for registration statements and other notifications required to be filed under section 6057 for plan years that begin on or after January 1, 2014, but only for filings with a filing deadline (not taking into account extensions) on or after July 31, 2015. [Reg. § 301.6057-3.]

☐ [*T.D.* 9695, 9-26-2014.]

[Reg. § 301.6058-1]

§ 301.6058-1. Information required in connection with certain plans of deferred compensation.—(a) *Reporting of information.*—(1) *Annual return.*—For each funded plan of deferred compensation an annual return must be filed with the Internal Revenue Service. The annual return of the plan is the appropriate Annual Return/Report of Employee Benefit Plan (Form 5500 series) as determined under these forms. The annual period for the annual return of the plan shall be either the plan year or the taxable year of the employer maintaining the plan as determined under these forms. These forms are hereinafter referred to as the "forms prescribed by section 6058(a)."

(2) *Plans subject to requirements.*—For purposes of this section, the term "funded plan of deferred compensation" means each pension, annuity, stock bonus, profit-sharing, or other funded plan of deferred compensation described in part 1 of subchapter D of chapter 1. Accordingly, the term includes qualified plans under sections 401(a), 403(a), and 405(a); individual retirement accounts and annuities described in sections 408(a) and 408(b); and custodial accounts under section 403(b)(7). The term also includes: funded plans of deferred compensation which are not qualified plans; funded governmental plans and church plans, whether or not qualified (See sections 414(d) and 414(e).); and plans maintained outside the United States primarily for nonresident aliens (as described in subsection (b)(4) of section 4 of Subtitle A of Title I of the Employee Retirement Income Security Act of 1974 (88 Stat. 840)). The term does not include annuity contracts described in section 403(b)(1) or individual retirement accounts (an individual participant or surviving beneficiary in such account must file under paragraph (d)(2) of this section) and bonds described in sections 408(c) and 409.

(3) *Required information.*—The information required to be furnished on the forms prescribed by section 6058(a) shall include such information concerning the qualification of the plan, the financial condition of the trust, fund, or custodial or fiduciary account which is a part of the plan, and the operation of the plan as shall be required by the forms, applicable accompanying schedules and related instructions applicable to the annual period.

(4) *Time of filing.*—The forms prescribed by section 6058(a) shall be filed in the manner and at the time as required by the forms and related instructions applicable to the annual period.

(b) *Who must file.*—(1) *In general.*—The annual return required to be filed under section 6058(a) and paragraph (a) of this section for the annual period shall be filed by either the employer maintaining the plan or the plan administrator (as defined in section 414(g)) of the plan for that annual period. Whether the employer or plan administrator files shall be determined under the forms prescribed by section 6058(a) and related instructions applicable to the annual period. Nothing in these forms shall preclude an employer from filing the return on behalf of the plan administrator, or the plan administrator from filing on behalf of the employer.

(2) *Definition of employer.*—For purposes of subparagraph (1) of this paragraph, the term "employer" includes a sole proprietor and a partnership.

(c) *Other rules applicable to annual returns.*— (1) *Extensions of time for filing.*—For rules relating to the extension of time for filing, see section 6081 and the regulations thereunder and the instructions on the forms prescribed by section 6058(a).

(2) *Amended filing.*—Any form prescribed by this section may be filed as an amendment to a form previously filed under this section with respect to the same annual period pursuant to the instructions for such forms.

(3) *Additional information.*—In addition to the information otherwise required to be furnished by this section, the district director may require any further information that is considered necessary to determine allowable deductions under section 404, qualification under section 401, or the financial condition and operation of the plan.

(4) *Records.*—Records substantiating all data and information required by this section to be filed must be kept at all times available for inspection by internal revenue officers at the principal office or place of business of the employer or plan administrator.

(5) *Relief from filing.*—Notwithstanding paragraph (a) of this section, the Commissioner may, in his discretion, relieve an employer, or plan administrator, from reporting information on the forms prescribed by section 6058(a). This discretion includes the ability to relieve an employer, or plan administrator, from filing the applicable form.

(d) *Special rules for individual retirement arrangements.*—(1) *Application.*—This paragraph, in lieu of paragraph (a) of this section, applies to an individual retirement account described in section 408(a) and an individual retirement annuity described in section 408(b), including such accounts and annuities for which a deduction is allowable under section 220 (spousal individual retirement arrangements).

(2) *General rule.*—For each taxable year beginning after December 31, 1974, every individual who during such taxable year—

(i) Establishes or maintains an individual retirement account described in section 408(a) (including an individual who is a participant in an individual retirement account described in section 408(c)),

(ii) Purchases or maintains an individual retirement annuity described in section 408(b), or

(iii) Is a surviving beneficiary with respect to an account or annuity referred to in this subparagraph which is in existence during such taxable year, shall file Form 5329 (or any other form designated by the Commissioner for this purpose), as an attachment to or part of the Form 1040 filed by such individual for such taxable

year, setting forth in full the information required by that form and the accompanying instructions.

(3) *Special information returns.*—If an individual described in subparagraph (2) of this paragraph is not required to file a Form 1040 for such taxable year, such individual shall file a Form 5329 (or any other designated form) with the Internal Revenue Service by the 15th day of the 4th month following the close of such individual's taxable year setting forth in full information required by that form and the accompanying instructions.

(4) *Relief from filing.*—The Commissioner may, in his discretion, relieve an individual from filing the form prescribed by this paragraph.

(5) *Retirement bonds.*—An individual who purchases, holds, or maintains a retirement bond described in section 409 may be required to file a return under other provisions of the Code.

(e) *Actuarial statement in case of mergers, etc.*—For requirements with respect to the filing of actuarial statements in the case of a merger, consolidation, or transfer of assets or liabilities, see section 6058(b) and section 414(1) and the regulations thereunder.

(f) *Effective dates.*—(1) *Section 6058(a) requirements.*—The rules with respect to annual returns required under section 6058(a) (the rules in this section, other than paragraph (e) thereof) are effective for plan years beginning after September 2, 1974.

(2) *Section 6058(b) requirements.*—The requirements of section 6058(b) relating to mergers, etc., and paragraph (e) of this section are effective on September 2, 1974, with respect to events described in section 6058(b) occurring on or after such date. [Reg. § 301.6058-1.]

☐ [*T.D.* 7551, 7-3-78.]

[Reg. § 301.6058-2]

§ 301.6058-2. Required use of magnetic media for filing requirements relating to information required in connection with certain plans of deferred compensation.—(a) *Magnetic media filing requirements under section 6058.*—A return required under section 6058 with respect to an employee benefit plan must be filed on magnetic media if the filer is required by the Internal Revenue Code or regulations to file at least 250 returns during the calendar year that includes the first day of the plan year. Returns filed on magnetic media must be made in accordance with applicable revenue procedures, publications, forms, instructions, or other guidance on the IRS.gov Internet website. In prescribing revenue procedures, publications, forms, and instructions, or other guidance on the IRS.gov Internet site, the Commissioner may direct the type of magnetic media filing. See § 601.601(d)(2)(ii)(*b*) of this chapter.

(b) *Economic hardship waiver.*—The Commissioner may waive the requirements of this section in cases of undue economic hardship. The principal factor in determining hardship will be the amount, if any, by which the cost of filing the return on magnetic media in accordance with this section exceeds the cost of filing the returns on other media. A request for a waiver must be made in accordance with applicable published guidance, publications, forms, instructions, or other guidance on the IRS.gov Internet website. See § 601.601(d)(2)(ii)(*b*) of this chapter. The waiver will specify the type of filing (that is, a return required under section 6058) and the period to which it applies. In addition, the waiver will be subject to such terms and conditions regarding the method of filing as may be prescribed by the Commissioner.

(c) *Failure to file.*—If a filer required to file a return under section 6058 fails to file the return on magnetic media when required to do so by this section, the filer is deemed to have failed to file the return. See section 6652(e) for the amount imposed for the failure to file a return required under section 6058. In determining whether there is reasonable cause for failure to file the return, § 301.6652-3(b) and rules similar to the rules in § 301.6724-1(c)(3)(ii) (regarding undue economic hardship related to filing information returns on magnetic media) will apply.

(d) *Meaning of terms.*—The following definitions apply for purposes of this section.

(1) *Magnetic media.*—The term *magnetic media* means electronic filing, as well as other media specifically permitted under applicable regulations, revenue procedures, or publications, forms, instructions, or other guidance on the IRS.gov Internet website. See § 601.601(d)(2)(ii)(*b*) of this chapter.

(2) *Return required under section 6058.*—The term *return required under section 6058* means a return in the Form 5500 series (or its successor).

(3) *Determination of 250 returns.*—(i) *In general.*—For purposes of this section, a filer is required to file at least 250 returns if, during the calendar year that includes the first day of the plan year, the filer is required to file at least 250 returns of any type, including information returns (for example, Forms W-2 and Forms 1099), income tax returns, employment tax returns, and excise tax returns.

(ii) *Definition of filer.*—For purposes of this section, the term *filer* means the employer or employers maintaining the plan and the plan administrator within the meaning of section 414(g).

(iii) *Special rules relating to determining 250 returns.*—For purposes of applying paragraph (d)(3)(ii) of this section, the aggregation rules of section 414(b), (c), (m), and (o) will apply to a filer that is or includes an employer. Thus, for example, a filer that is a member of a controlled group of corporations within the meaning of section 414(b) must file the Form 5500 series on magnetic media if the aggregate number of re-

turns required to be filed by all members of the controlled group of corporations is at least 250.

(e) *Example.*—The following example illustrates the provisions of paragraph (d)(3) of this section:

Example. In 2016 Employer X (the plan sponsor of Plan A) and P (the plan administrator of Plan A) are required to file 267 returns. Employer X is required to file the following: one Form 1120, "U.S. Corporation Income Tax Return;" 195 Forms W-2, "Wage and Tax Statement;" 25 Forms 1099-DIV, "Dividends and Distributions;" one Form 940, "Employer's Annual Federal Unemployment (FUTA) Tax Return;" and four Forms 941, "Employer's Quarterly Federal Tax Return." P is required to file 40 Forms 1099-R, "Distributions From Pensions, Annuities, Retirement, Profit-Sharing Plans, IRAs, Insurance Contracts, etc." P and Employer X are jointly required to file one Form 5500 series return. Plan A's plan year is the calendar year. Because P and Employer X, in the aggregate, are required to file at least 250 returns during the calendar year, the 2016 Form 5500 for Plan A must be filed electronically.

(f) *Effective/applicability date.*—This section is applicable for returns required to be filed under section 6058 for plan years that begin on or after January 1, 2015, but only for filings with a filing deadline (not taking into account extensions) after December 31, 2015. [Reg. § 301.6058-2.]

☐ [T.D. 9695, 9-26-2014.]

[Reg. § 301.6059-1]

§ 301.6059-1. Periodic report of actuary.—(a) *In general.*—The actuarial report described in this section must be filed on behalf of a defined benefit plan to which the minimum funding standards of section 412 apply. The actuarial report must be filed by the plan administrator (within the meaning of section 414(g)) on Schedule B as an attachment to the annual Return/Report of Employee Benefit Plan (Form 5500 series). The instructions accompanying the Form 5500 series prescribe the place and date for filing Schedule B.

(b) *Plan years for which report required.*—In the case of a plan in existence on January 1, 1974, Schedule B must be filed for the first plan year beginning after December 31, 1975, for which the minimum funding standards apply to the plan, and for each plan year thereafter for which the Schedule must be filed under the instructions accompanying the Schedule and the Form 5500 series. In the case of a plan not in existence on January 1, 1974, Schedule B must be filed for the first plan year beginning after September 2, 1974, for which the minimum funding standards apply to the plan, and for each plan year thereafter for which the Schedule must be filed under the instructions accompanying the Schedule and the Form 5500 series. For rules relating to when a plan is considered to be in existence, see § 1.410(a)-2(c). For purposes of this section, "plan year" means the plan year as determined for purposes of the minimum funding standards.

(c) *Contents of report.*—The actuarial report of a plan filed on Schedule B must contain—

(1) The date of the actuarial valuation applicable to the plan year for which the report is filed (see section 412(c)(9) for rules relating to the frequency with which an actuarial valuation of the plan is required to be made),

(2) A description of the funding method and actuarial assumptions used to determine costs under the plan,

(3) A certification of the contribution necessary to reduce the accumulated funding deficiency (as defined in section 412(a)) to zero,

(4) A statement by the enrolled actuary signing the report that to the best of the actuary's knowledge the report is complete and accurate,

(5) A statement by the enrolled actuary signing the report that in the actuary's opinion, the actuarial assumptions used are in the aggregate (i) reasonably related to the experience under the plan and to reasonable expectations, and (ii) represent the actuary's best estimate of anticipated experience under the plan,

(6) Such other information as may be necessary to fully and fairly disclose the actuarial position of the plan, and

(7) Such other information as may be required by Schedule B or the instructions accompanying the Schedule and the Form 5500 series.

(d) *Certification by enrolled actuary.*—The actuarial report filed on Schedule B must be signed by an enrolled actuary (within the meaning of section 7701(a)(35)) or there may be attached to the report a statement signed by the actuary that contains the statements described in paragraph (d)(1)(v) and paragraph (c)(4) and (5) of this section.

An actuarial report filed for a plan year ending after January 25, 1982, does not satisfy the requirements of this section if the actuary seeks to materially qualify such statements. For this purpose, the following are not considered to materially qualify a statement required by paragraph (c)(4) or (5) of this section:

(1) A statement that the report is based in part on information provided to the actuary by another person, that such information would customarily not be verified by the actuary, and that the actuary has no reason to doubt the substantial accuracy of the information (taking into account the facts and circumstances that are known or reasonably should be known to the actuary, including the contents of any other actuarial report prepared by the actuary for the plan),

(2) A statement that the report is based in part on information provided by another person, that the actuary believes such information is or may be inaccurate or incomplete, but that the inaccuracies or omissions are not material, the inaccuracies or omissions are not so numerous or flagrant as to suggest that there may be material inaccuracies, and that therefore the actuarial re-

port is substantially accurate and complete and fairly discloses the actuarial position of the plan,

(3) A statement that the report reflects the requirement of a regulation or ruling, and that any statement regarding the actuarial position of the plan is made only in light of such requirement,

(4) A statement that the report reflects an interpretation of a statute, regulation or ruling, that the actuary has no reason to doubt the validity of that interpretation, and that any statement regarding the actuarial position of the plan is made only in light of such interpretation,

(5) A statement that in the opinion of the actuary the report fully reflects the requirements of an applicable statute, but does not conform to the requirements of a regulation or ruling promulgated under the statute that the actuary believes is contrary to the statute, or

(6) A statement reflecting the requirements of paragraph (c)(6) of this section.

A statement otherwise described in a subparagraph of this paragraph (d) shall not be considered to satisfy the requirements of such subparagraph unless the statement identifies, with particularity, that matter to which the statement relates and the facts and circumstances surrounding the statement. In addition, a statement otherwise described in subparagraph (5) of this paragraph (d) shall not be considered to satisfy the requirements of that subparagraph unless the statement indicates whether an accumulated funding deficiency or a contribution that is not wholly deductible may result if the actuary's belief is determined to be incorrect.

(e) *Relief from filing.*—Notwithstanding paragraph (a) of this section, the Commissioner may, in the Commissioner's discretion, relieve a plan administrator from filing Schedule B or from reporting information required by Schedule B or paragraph (c) of this section.

(f) *Penalty.*—For the penalty imposed in the case of a failure to file the actuarial report required by this section, see section 6692 and § 301.6692-1. [Reg. § 301.6059-1.]

☐ [T.D. 7798, 11-23-81.]

[Reg. § 301.6059-2]

§ 301.6059-2. Required use of magnetic media for filing requirements relating to periodic report of actuary.—(a) *Magnetic media filing requirements under section 6059.*—An actuarial report required under section 6059 with respect to an employee benefit plan must be filed on magnetic media if the filer is required by the Internal Revenue Code or regulations to file at least 250 returns during the calendar year that includes the first day of the plan year. Actuarial reports filed on magnetic media must be made in accordance with applicable revenue procedures, publications, forms, instructions, or other guidance on the IRS.gov Internet website. In prescribing revenue procedures, publications, forms, instructions, or other guidance on the IRS.gov Internet website, the Commissioner may direct the type of magnetic media filing. See § 601.601(d)(2)(ii)(*b*) of this chapter.

(b) *Economic hardship waiver.*—The Commissioner may waive the requirements of this section in cases of undue economic hardship. The principal factor in determining hardship will be the amount, if any, by which the cost of filing the reports on magnetic media in accordance with this section exceeds the cost of filing the reports on other media. A request for a waiver must be made in accordance with applicable published guidance, publications, forms, instructions, or other guidance on the IRS.gov Internet website. See § 601.601(d)(2)(ii)(*b*) of this chapter. The waiver will specify the type of filing (that is, an actuarial report required under section 6059) and the period to which it applies. In addition, the waiver will be subject to such terms and conditions regarding the method of filing as may be prescribed by the Commissioner.

(c) *Failure to file.*—If a filer required to file an actuarial report under section 6059 fails to file the report on magnetic media when required to do so by this section, the filer is deemed to have failed to file the report. See section 6692 for the penalty for the failure to file an actuarial report. In determining whether there is reasonable cause for failure to file the report, § 301.6692-1(c) and rules similar to the rules in § 301.6724-1(c)(3)(ii) (regarding undue economic hardship related to filing information returns on magnetic media) will apply.

(d) *Meaning of terms.*—The following definitions apply for purposes of this section.

(1) *Magnetic media.*—The term *magnetic media* means electronic filing, as well as other media specifically permitted under applicable regulations, revenue procedures, or publications, forms, instructions, or other guidance on the IRS.gov Internet website. See § 601.601(d)(2)(ii)(*b*) of this chapter.

(2) *Actuarial report required under section 6059.*—(i) *Single employer plans.*—For a single employer plan, the term *actuarial report required under section 6059* means the Schedule SB, "Single-Employer Defined Benefit Plan Actuarial Information," of the Form 5500 series (or its successor).

(ii) *Multiemployer and certain money purchase plans.*—For multiemployer and certain money purchase plans, the term *actuarial report required under section 6059* means the Schedule MB, "Multiemployer Defined Benefit Plan and Certain Money Purchase Plan Actuarial Information," of the Form 5500 series (or its successor).

(3) *Determination of 250 returns.*—(i) *In general.*—For purposes of this section, a filer is required to file at least 250 returns if, during the calendar year that includes the first day of the plan year, the filer is required to file at least 250 returns of any type, including information returns (for example, Forms W-2 and Forms 1099),

income tax returns, employment tax returns, and excise tax returns.

(ii) *Definition of filer.*—For purposes of this section, the term *filer* means the plan administrator within the meaning of section 414(g). If the plan administrator within the meaning of section 414(g) is the employer, the special rules in § 1.6058-2(d)(3)(iii) will apply.

(e) *Example.*—The following example illustrates the provisions of paragraph (d)(3) of this section:

Example. In 2016, P, the plan administrator of Plan B (a single employer defined benefit plan), is required to file 266 returns (including Forms 1099-R "Distributions From Pensions, Annuities, Retirement, Profit-Sharing Plans, IRAs, Insurance Contracts, etc." and one Form 5500 series). Plan B's plan year is the calendar year. Because P is required to file at least 250 returns during the calendar year, P must file the 2016 Schedule SB of the Form 5500 series return for Plan B electronically.

(f) *Effective/ applicability date.*—This section is applicable for actuarial reports required to be filed under section 6059 for plan years that begin on or after January 1, 2015, but only for filings with a filing deadline (not taking into account extensions) after December 31, 2015. [Reg. § 301.6059-2.]

☐ [*T.D.* 9695, 9-26-2014.]

[Reg. § 1.6060-1]

§ 1.6060-1. Reporting requirements for tax return preparers.—(a) *In general.*—(1) Each person who employs one or more signing tax return preparers to prepare any return of tax or claim for refund of tax, other than for the person, at any time during a return period shall satisfy the requirements of section 6060 of the Internal Revenue Code by—

(i) Retaining a record of the name, taxpayer identification number, and principal place of work during the return period of each tax return preparer employed by the person at any time during that period; and

(ii) Making that record available for inspection upon request by the Commissioner.

(2) The record described in this paragraph (a) must be retained and kept available for inspection for the 3-year period following the close of the return period to which that record relates.

(3) The person may choose any form of documentation to be used under this section as a record of the signing tax return preparers employed during a return period. The record, however, must disclose on its face which individuals were employed as tax return preparers during that period.

(4) For the definition of the term "signing tax return preparer", see § 301.7701-15(b)(1) of this chapter. For the definition of the term "return period", see paragraph (b) of this section.

(5)(i) For purposes of this section, any individual who, in acting as a signing tax return preparer, is not employed by another tax return preparer shall be treated as his or her own employer. Thus, a sole proprietor shall retain and make available a record with respect to himself (or herself) as provided in this section.

(ii) A partnership shall, for purposes of this section, be treated as the employer of the partners of the partnership and shall retain and make available a record with respect to the partners and others employed by the partnership as provided in this section.

(b) *Return period defined.*—For purposes of this section, the term "return period" means the 12-month period beginning on July 1 of each year.

(c) *Penalty.*—For the civil penalty for failure to retain and make available a record of the tax return preparers employed during a return period as required under this section, or for failure to include an item in the record required to be retained and made available under this section, see § 1.6695-1(e).

(d) *Effective/applicability date.*—This section is applicable to returns and claims for refund filed after December 31, 2008. [Reg. § 1.6060-1.]

□ [*T.D.* 7519, 11-17-77. *Amended by T.D.* 7640, 8-22-79 *and T.D.* 9436, 12-15-2008.]

[Reg. § 20.6060-1]

§ 20.6060-1. Reporting requirements for tax return preparers.—(a) *In general.*—A person that employs one or more tax return preparers to prepare a return or claim for refund of estate tax under chapter 11 of subtitle B of the Internal Revenue Code, other than for the person, at any time during a return period, shall satisfy the recordkeeping and inspection requirements in the manner stated in § 1.6060-1 of this chapter.

(b) *Effective/applicability date.*—This section is applicable to returns and claims for refund filed after December 31, 2008. [Reg. § 20.6060-1.]

□ [*T.D.* 9436, 12-15-2008.]

[Reg. § 25.6060-1]

§ 25.6060-1. Reporting requirements for tax return preparers.—(a) *In general.*—A person that employs one or more tax return preparers to prepare a return or claim for refund of gift tax under chapter 12 of subtitle B of the Internal Revenue Code, other than for the person, at any time during a return period, shall satisfy the record keeping and inspection requirements in the manner stated in § 1.6060-1 of this chapter.

(b) *Effective/applicability date.*—This section is applicable to returns and claims for refund filed after December 31, 2008. [Reg. § 25.6060-1.]

□ [*T.D.* 9436, 12-15-2008.]

[Reg. § 26.6060-1]

§ 26.6060-1. Reporting requirements for tax return preparers.—(a) *In general.*—A person that employs one or more tax return preparers to prepare a return or claim for refund of generation-skipping transfer tax under chapter 13 of subtitle B of the Internal Revenue Code, other than for the person, at any time during a return period, shall satisfy the record keeping and inspection requirements in the manner stated in § 1.6060-1 of this chapter.

(b) *Effective/applicability date.*—This section is applicable to returns and claims for refund filed after December 31, 2008. [Reg. § 26.6060-1.]

□ [*T.D.* 9436, 12-15-2008.]

[Reg. § 31.6060-1]

§ 31.6060-1. Reporting requirements for tax return preparers.—(a) *In general.*—A person that employs one or more tax return preparers to prepare a return or claim for refund of employment tax under chapters 21 through 25 of subtitle C of the Internal Revenue Code, other than for the person, at any time during a return period, shall satisfy the record keeping and inspection requirements in the manner stated in § 1.6060-1 of this chapter.

(b) *Effective/applicability date.*—This section is applicable to returns and claims for refund filed after December 31, 2008. [Reg. § 31.6060-1.]

□ [*T.D.* 9436, 12-15-2008.]

[Reg. § 40.6060-1]

§ 40.6060-1. Reporting requirements for tax return preparers.—(a) *In general.*—A person that employs one or more tax return preparers to prepare a return or claim for refund of any tax to which this part 40 applies other than for the person, at any time during a return period, shall satisfy the recordkeeping and inspection requirements in the manner stated in § 1.6060-1 of this chapter.

(b) *Effective/applicability date.*—This section is applicable to returns and claims for refund filed after December 31, 2008. [Reg. § 40.6060-1.]

□ [*T.D.* 9436, 12-15-2008 (*corrected* 1-28-2009).]

[Reg. § 41.6060-1]

§ 41.6060-1. Reporting requirements for tax return preparers.—(a) *In general.*—A person that employs one or more tax return preparers to prepare a return or claim for refund of excise tax under section 4481, other than for the person, at any time during a return period, shall satisfy the record keeping and inspection requirements in the manner stated in § 1.6060-1 of this chapter.

(b) *Effective/applicability date.*—This section is applicable for returns and claims for refund filed after December 31, 2008. [Reg. § 41.6060-1.]

□ [*T.D.* 9436, 12-15-2008.]

[Reg. § 44.6060-1]

§ 44.6060-1. Reporting requirements for tax return preparers.—(a) *In general.*—A person that employs one or more tax return preparers to prepare a return or claim for refund of tax on wagers under sections 4401 or 4411, other than for the person, at any time during a return period, shall satisfy the record keeping and inspection requirements in the manner stated in § 1.6060-1 of this chapter.

(b) *Effective/applicability date.*—This section is applicable to returns and claims for refund filed after December 31, 2008. [Reg. § 44.6060-1.]

☐ [*T.D.* 9436, 12-15-2008.]

[Reg. § 53.6060-1]

§ 53.6060-1. Reporting requirements for tax return preparers.—(a) *In general.*—A person that employs one or more tax return preparers to prepare a return or claim for refund of tax under Chapter 42 of the Internal Revenue Code, other than for the person, at any time during a return period, shall satisfy the record keeping and inspection requirements in the manner stated in § 1.6060-1 of this chapter.

(b) *Effective/applicability date.*—This section is applicable to returns and claims for refund filed after December 31, 2008. [Reg. § 53.6060-1.]

☐ [*T.D.* 9436, 12-15-2008.]

[Reg. § 54.6060-1]

§ 54.6060-1. Reporting requirements for tax return preparers.—(a) *In general.*—A person that employs one or more tax return preparers to prepare a return or claim for refund under Chapter 43 of subtitle D of the Internal Revenue Code, other than for the person, at any time during a return period, shall satisfy the record keeping and inspection requirements in the manner stated in § 1.6060-1 of this chapter.

(b) *Effective/applicability date.*—This section is applicable to returns and claims for refund filed after December 31, 2008. [Reg. § 54.6060-1.]

☐ [*T.D.* 9436, 12-15-2008.]

[Reg. § 55.6060-1]

§ 55.6060-1. Reporting requirements for tax return preparers.—(a) *In general.*—A person that employs one or more tax return preparers to prepare a return or claim for refund under chapter 44 of subtitle D of the Internal Revenue Code, other than for the person, at any time during a return period, shall satisfy the record keeping and inspection requirements in the manner stated in § 1.6060-1 of this chapter.

(b) *Effective/applicability date.*—This section is applicable to returns and claims for refund filed after December 31, 2008. [Reg. § 55.6060-1.]

☐ [*T.D.* 9436, 12-15-2008.]

[Reg. § 56.6060-1]

§ 56.6060-1. Reporting requirements for tax return preparers.—(a) *In general.*—A person that employs one or more tax return preparers to prepare a return or claim for refund of tax under chapter 41 of subtitle D of the Internal Revenue Code, other than for the person, at any time during a return period, shall satisfy the record keeping and inspection requirements in the manner stated in § 1.6060-1 of this chapter.

(b) *Effective/applicability date.*—This section is applicable to returns and claims for refund filed after December 31, 2008. [Reg. § 56.6060-1.]

☐ [*T.D.* 9436, 12-15-2008.]

[Reg. § 156.6060-1]

§ 156.6060-1. Reporting requirements for tax return preparers.—(a) *In general.*—A person that employs one or more tax return preparers to prepare a return or claim for refund under section 5881 of the Internal Revenue Code, other than for the person, at any time during a return period, shall satisfy the record keeping and inspection requirements in the manner stated in § 1.6060-1 of this chapter.

(b) *Effective/applicability date.*—This section is applicable to returns and claims for refund filed after December 31, 2008. [Reg. § 156.6060-1.]

☐ [*T.D.* 9436, 12-15-2008.]

[Reg. § 157.6060-1]

§ 157.6060-1. Reporting requirements for tax return preparers.—(a) *In general.*—A person that employs one or more tax return preparers to prepare a return or claim for refund for tax under section 5891 of the Internal Revenue Code, other than for the person, at any time during a return period, shall satisfy the record keeping and inspection requirements in the manner stated in § 1.6060-1 of this chapter.

(b) *Effective/applicability date.*—This section is applicable to returns and claims for refund filed after December 31, 2008. [Reg. § 157.6060-1.]

☐ [*T.D.* 9436, 12-15-2008.]

Signing and Verifying of Returns and Other Documents

[Reg. § 1.6061-1]

§ 1.6061-1. Signing of returns and other documents by individuals.—(a) *Requirement.*—Each individual (including a fiduciary) shall sign the income tax return required to be made by him, except that the return may be signed for the taxpayer by an agent who is duly authorized in accordance with paragraph (a)(5) or (b) of § 1.6012-1 to make such return. Other returns, statements, or documents required under the provisions of subtitle A or F of the Code or of the regulations thereunder to be made by any person with respect to any tax imposed by subtitle A of the Code shall be signed in accordance with any regulations contained in this chapter, or any instructions, issued with respect to such returns, statements, or other documents.

(b) *Cross references.*—For provisions relating to the signing of returns, statements, or other documents required to be made by corporations and partnerships with respect to any tax imposed by subtitle A of the Code, see §§ 1.6062-1 and

1.6063-1, respectively. For provisions relating to the making of returns by agents, see paragraphs (a)(5) and (b) of §1.6012-1; and to the making of returns for minors and persons under a disability, see paragraph (a)(4) of §1.6012-1 and paragraph (b) of §1.6012-3. [Reg. §1.6061-1.]

☐ [*T.D. 6364, 2-13-59. Amended by T.D. 7332,* 12-20-74.]

[Reg. §20.6061-1]

§20.6061-1. Signing of returns and other documents.—Any return, statement, or other document required to be made under any provision of chapter 11 of subtitle F of the Code or regulations prescribed thereunder with respect to any tax imposed by chapter 11 of the Code shall be signed by the executor, administrator or other person required or duly authorized to sign in accordance with the regulations, forms or instructions prescribed with respect to such return, statement, or other document. See §20.2203 for definition of executor, administrator, etc. The person required or duly authorized to make the return may incur liability for the penalties provided for erroneous, false, or fraudulent returns. For criminal penalties see sections 7201, 7203, 7206, 7207, and 7269. [Reg. §20.6061-1.]

☐ [*T.D. 6600, 5-28-62.*]

[Reg. §25.6061-1]

§25.6061-1. Signing of returns and other documents.—Any return, statement, or other document required to be made under any provision of chapter 12 or subtitle F of the Code or regulations prescribed thereunder with respect to any tax imposed by chapter 12 of the Code shall be signed by the donor or other person required or duly authorized to sign in accordance with the regulations, forms or instructions prescribed with respect to such return, statement, or other document. The person required or duly authorized to make the return may incur liability for the penalties provided for erroneous, false, or fraudulent returns. For criminal penalties see sections 7201, 7203, 7206, 7207, and 7269. [Reg. §25.6061-1.]

☐ [*T.D. 6600, 5-28-62.*]

[Reg. §31.6061-1]

§31.6061-1. Signing of returns.—Each return required under the regulations in this subpart shall, if signature is called for by the form or instructions relating to the return, be signed by (a) the individual, if the person required to make the return is an individual; (b) the president, vice president, or other principal officer, if the person required to make the return is a corporation; (c) a responsible and duly authorized member or officer having knowledge of its affairs, if the person required to make the return is a partnership or other unincorporated organization; or (d) the fiduciary, if the person required to make the return is a trust or estate. The return may be signed for the taxpayer by an agent who is duly

authorized in accordance with §31.6011(a)-7 to make such return. [Reg. §31.6061-1.]

☐ [*T.D. 6472, 6-22-60.*]

[Reg. §53.6061-1]

§53.6061-1. Signing of returns and other documents.—Any return, statement, or other document required to be made with respect to a tax imposed by chapter 42 or the regulations thereunder shall be signed by the person required to file such return, statement or document, or by such other persons required or duly authorized to sign in accordance with the regulations, forms or instructions prescribed with respect to such return, statement or other document. The person required or duly authorized to make the return may incur liability for penalties provided for erroneous, false or fraudulent returns. For criminal penalties see sections 7201, 7203, 7206, and 7207. [Reg. §53.6061-1.]

☐ [*T.D. 7368, 7-15-75.*]

[Reg. §54.6061-1]

§54.6061-1. Signing of returns and other documents.—Effective for any Form 8928 that is due on or after January 1, 2010, any return, statement, or other document required to be made with respect to a tax imposed by section 4980B, 4980D, 4980E, or 4980G of the Code or the regulations under section 4980B, 4980D, 4980E, or 4980G must be signed by the person required to file the return, statement, or other document, or by the persons required or duly authorized to sign in accordance with the regulations, forms, or instructions prescribed with respect to such return, statement, or document. An individual's signature on such return, statement, or other document shall be prima facie evidence that the individual is authorized to sign the return, statement, or other document. [Reg. §54.6061-1.]

☐ [*T.D. 9457, 9-4-2009.*]

[Reg. §55.6061-1]

§55.6061-1. Signing of returns and other documents.—Any return required to be made by a real estate investment trust or a regulated investment company with respect to the tax imposed by chapter 44 shall be signed by a person authorized by section 6062 of the Code to sign the income tax return of the real estate investment trust or the regulated investment company. Any statement or other document required to be made with respect to the tax imposed by chapter 44 shall be signed by the person required or duly authorized to sign in accordance with the regulations, forms, or instructions prescribed with respect to such statement or document. An individual's signature on a return, statement, or other document made by or for the real estate investment trust or the regulated investment company shall be prima facie evidence that the individual is authorized to sign the return, statement, or other document. [Reg. §55.6061-1.]

☐ [*T.D. 7767, 2-3-81. Amended by T.D. 8180,* 2-29-88.]

[Reg. § 156.6061-1]

§ 156.6061-1. Signing of returns and other documents.—Any return, statement, or other document required to be made with respect to a tax imposed by chapter 54 (Greenmail) of the Code or the regulations thereunder shall be signed by the person required to file the return, statement, or other document, or by the persons required or duly authorized to sign in accordance with the regulations, forms, or instructions prescribed with respect to such return, statement, or document. An individual's signature on such a return, statement, or other document shall be prima facie evidence that the individual is authorized to sign the return, statement, or other document. [Reg. § 156.6061-1.]

☐ [*T.D.* 8379, 12-17-91.]

[Reg. § 157.6061-1]

§ 157.6061-1. Signing of returns and other documents.—Any return, statement, or other document required to be made with respect to a tax imposed by chapter 55 (Structured Settlement Factoring Transactions) of the Internal Revenue Code or the regulations under chapter 55 must be signed by the person required to file the return, statement, or other document, or by the persons required or duly authorized to sign in accordance with the regulations, forms, or instructions prescribed with respect to such return, statement, or document. An individual's signature on such return, statement, or other document shall be prima facie evidence that the individual is authorized to sign the return, statement, or other document. [Reg. § 157.6061-1.]

☐ [*T.D.* 9134, 7-7-2004.]

[Reg. § 301.6061-1]

§ 301.6061-1. Signing of returns and other documents.—(a) *In general.*—For provisions concerning the signing of returns and other documents, see the regulations relating to the particular tax.

(b) *Method of signing.*—The Secretary may prescribe in forms, instructions, or other appropriate guidance the method of signing any return, statement, or other document required to be made under any provision of the internal revenue laws or regulations.

(c) *Effective dates.*—The rule in paragraph (a) is effective December 12, 1996. The rule in paragraph (b) is effective on July 21, 1995. [Reg. § 301.6061-1.]

☐ [*T.D.* 6498, 10-24-60. *Amended by T.D.* 8689, 12-11-96.]

[Reg. § 1.6062-1]

§ 1.6062-1. Signing of returns, statements, and other documents made by corporations.—(a) *Returns.*—(1) *In general.*—Returns required to be made by corporations under the provisions of subtitle A or F of the Code, or the regulations thereunder, with respect to any tax imposed by subtitle A of the Code, shall be signed for the

corporation by the president, vice-president, treasurer, assistant treasurer, chief accounting officer, or any other officer duly authorized to sign such returns. It is not necessary that the corporate seal be affixed to the return. Spaces provided on return forms for affixing the corporate seal are for the convenience of corporations required by charter, or by the law of the jurisdiction in which they are incorporated, to affix their corporate seals in the execution of instruments.

(2) *By fiduciaries.*—A return with respect to income required to be made for a corporation by a fiduciary, pursuant to the provisions of section 6012(b)(3), shall be signed by such fiduciary. See paragraph (b)(4) of § 1.6012-3.

(3) *By agents.*—A return with respect to income required to be made by an agent for a foreign corporation shall be signed by such agent. See paragraph (g) of § 1.6012-2.

(b) *Statements and other documents.*—Statements and other documents required to be made by or for corporations under the provisions of subtitle A or F of the Code, or the regulations thereunder, with respect to any tax imposed by subtitle A, shall be signed in accordance with the regulations contained in this chapter, or the forms and instructions, issued with respect to such statements or other documents.

(c) *Evidence of authority to sign.*—An individual's signature on a return, statement, or other document made by or for a corporation shall be prima facie evidence that such individual is authorized to sign such return, statement, or other document.

(d) *Related provisions.*—For the rules relating to the verification of returns, see § 1.6065-1. [Reg. § 1.6062-1.]

☐ [*T.D.* 6364, 2-13-59. *Amended by T.D.* 6455, 3-1-60 and *T.D.* 7293, 11-27-73.]

[Reg. § 301.6062-1]

§ 301.6062-1. Signing of corporation returns.—For provisions relating to the signing of corporation income tax returns, see § 1.6062-1 of this chapter (Income Tax Regulations). [Reg. § 301.6062-1.]

☐ [*T.D.* 6498, 10-24-60.]

[Reg. § 1.6063-1]

§ 1.6063-1. Signing of returns, statements, and other documents made by partnerships.—(a) *In general.*—Returns, statements, and other documents required to be made by partnerships under the provisions of subtitle A or F of the Code, or the regulations thereunder, with respect to any tax imposed by subtitle A of the Code shall be signed by any one of the partners. However, with respect to the signing of powers of attorney, see paragraph (a)(2) of § 601.504 of this chapter (Statement of Procedural Rules).

(b) *Evidence of authority to sign.*—A partner's signature on a return, statement, or other document made by or for a partnership of which he is a member shall be prima facie evidence that such partner is authorized to sign such return, statement, or other document.

(c) *Certain partnership elections.*—(1) *In general.*—For rules regarding the authority of a partner to sign a partnership return filed solely for the purpose of making certain partnership-level elections, see § 1.6031(a)-1(b)(5)(ii).

(2) *Effective date.*—Paragraph (c) of this section applies to taxable years of a partnership beginning after December 31, 1999. [Reg. § 1.6063-1.]

☐ [*T.D.* 6498, 10-24-60. *Amended by T.D.* 8841, 11-10-99.]

[Reg. § 301.6063-1]

§ 301.6063-1. Signing of partnership returns.—For provisions relating to the signing of returns of partnership income, see § 1.6063-1 of this chapter (Income Tax Regulations). [Reg. § 301.6063-1.]

☐ [*T.D.* 6498, 10-24-60.]

[Reg. § 301.6064-1]

§ 301.6064-1. Signature presumed authentic.—An individual's name signed to a return, statement, or other document shall be prima facie evidence for all purposes that the return, statement, or other document was actually signed by him. [Reg. § 301.6064-1.]

☐ [*T.D.* 6498, 10-24-60.]

[Reg. § 1.6065-1]

§ 1.6065-1. Verification of returns.—(a) *Persons signing returns.*—If a return, declaration, statement, or other document made under the provisions of subtitle A or F of the Code, or the regulation thereunder, with respect to any tax imposed by subtitle A of the Code is required by the regulations contained in this chapter, or the form and instructions, issued with respect to such return, declaration, statement, or other document, to contain or be verified by a written declaration that it is made under the penalties of perjury, such return, declaration, statement, or other document shall be so verified by the person signing it.

(b) *Persons preparing returns.*—(1) *In general.*—Except as provided in subparagraph (2) of this paragraph, if a return, declaration, statement, or other document is prepared for a taxpayer by another person for compensation or as an incident to the performance of other services for which such person receives compensation, and the return, declaration, statement, or other document requires that it shall contain or be verified by a written declaration that it is prepared under the penalties of perjury, the preparer must so verify the return, declaration, statement, or other document. A person who renders mere mechanical assistance in the preparation of a return, declaration, statement, or other document as, for example, a stenographer or typist, is not considered as preparing the return, declaration, statement, or other document.

(2) *Exception.*—The verification required by subparagraph (1) of this paragraph is not required on returns, declarations, statements, or other documents which are prepared—

(i) For an employee either by his employer or by an employee designated for such purpose by the employer, or

(ii) For an employer as a usual incident of the employment of one regularly or continuously employed by such employer. [Reg. § 1.6065-1.]

☐ [*T.D.* 6364, 2-13-59.]

[Reg. § 20.6065-1]

§ 20.6065-1. Verification of returns.—(a) *Penalties of perjury.*—If a return, statement, or other document made under the provisions of chapter 11 or subtitle F of the Code or the regulations thereunder with respect to any tax imposed by chapter 11 of the Code, or the form and instructions issued with respect to such return, statement, or other document, requires that it shall contain or be verified by a written declaration that it is made under the penalties of perjury, it must be so verified by the person or persons required to sign such return, statement or other document. In addition, any other statement or document submitted under any provision of chapter 11 or subtitle F of the Code or regulations thereunder with respect to any tax imposed by chapter 11 of the Code may be required to contain or be verified by a written declaration that it is made under the penalties of perjury.

(b) *Oath.*—Any return, statement, or other document required to be submitted under chapter 11 or subtitle F of the Code or regulations prescribed thereunder with respect to any tax imposed by chapter 11 of the Code may be required to be verified by an oath. [Reg. § 20.6065-1.]

☐ [*T.D.* 6600, 5-28-62.]

[Reg. § 25.6065-1]

§ 25.6065-1. Verification of returns.—(a) *Penalties of perjury.*—If a return, statement, or other document made under the provisions of chapter 12 or subtitle F of the Code or the regulations thereunder with respect to any tax imposed by chapter 12 of the Code, or the form and instructions issued with respect to such return, statement, or other document, requires that it shall contain or be verified by a written declaration that it is made under the penalties of perjury, it must be so verified by the person or persons required to sign such return, statement, or other document. In addition, any other statement or document submitted under any provision of chapter 12 or subtitle F of the Code or regulations thereunder with respect to any tax imposed by chapter 12 of the Code may be required to contain or be verified by a written declaration that it is made under the penalties of perjury.

(b) *Oath.*—Any return, statement, or other document required to be submitted under chapter 12 or subtitle F of the Code or regulations prescribed thereunder with respect to any tax imposed by chapter 12 of the Code may be required to be verified by an oath. [Reg. §25.6065-1.]

☐ [*T.D.* 6600, 5-28-62.]

[Reg. §53.6065-1]

§53.6065-1. Verification of returns.— (a) *Penalties of perjury.*—If a return, statement, or other document made under the provisions of chapter 42 or subtitle F of the Code or the regulations thereunder with respect to any tax imposed by chapter 42 of the Code, or the form and instructions issued with respect to such return, statement, or other document, requires that it shall contain or be verified by a written declaration that it is made under the penalties of perjury, it must be so verified by the person or persons required to sign such return, statement, or other document. In addition, any other statement or document submitted under any provision of chapter 42 or subtitle F of the Code or regulations thereunder with respect to any tax imposed by chapter 42 of the Code may be required to contain or be verified by a written declaration that it is made under the penalties of perjury.

(b) *Oath.*—Any return, statement, or other document required to be submitted under chapter 42 or subtitle F of the Code or regulations prescribed thereunder with respect to any tax imposed by chapter 42 of the Code may be required to be verified by an oath. [Reg. §53.6065-1.]

☐ [*T.D.* 7368, 7-15-75.]

[Reg. §55.6065-1]

§55.6065-1. Verification of returns.—If a return, statement, or other document made under the provisions of chapter 44 or subtitle F of the Code or the regulations thereunder with respect to any tax imposed by chapter 44 of the Code, or the form and instructions issued with respect to such return, statement, or other document, requires that it shall contain or be verified by a written declaration that it is made under the penalties of perjury, it must be so verified by the person or persons required to sign such return, statement, or other document. In addition, any other statement or document submitted under any provision of chapter 44 of subtitle F of the Code or regulations thereunder with respect to any tax imposed by chapter 44 of the Code may be required to contain or be verified by a written declaration that it is made under the penalties of perjury. [Reg. §55.6065-1.]

☐ [*T.D.* 7767, 2-3-81.]

[Reg. §156.6065-1]

§156.6065-1. Verification of returns.—If a return, statement, or other document made under the provisions of chapter 54 (Greenmail) or of subtitle F of the Code, or the regulations thereunder with respect to any tax imposed by chapter 54, or the form and instructions issued with

respect to such return, statement, or other document, requires that it shall contain or be verified by a written declaration that it is made under the penalties of perjury, it must be so verified by the person or persons required to sign such return, statement, or other document. In addition, any other statement or document submitted under any provision of chapter 54 or of subtitle F of the Code, or the regulations thereunder with respect to any tax imposed by chapter 54 may be required to contain or be verified by a written declaration that is made under the penalties of perjury. [Reg. §156.6065-1.]

☐ [*T.D.* 8379, 12-17-91.]

[Reg. §157.6065-1]

§157.6065-1. Verification of returns.—If a return, statement, or other document made under the provisions of chapter 55 (Structured Settlement Factoring Transactions) or of subtitle F of the Internal Revenue Code, or the regulations under those provisions with respect to any tax imposed by chapter 55, or the form and instructions issued with respect to such return, statement, or other document, requires that it shall contain or be verified by a written declaration that it is made under the penalties of perjury, it must be so verified by the person or persons required to sign such return, statement, or other document. In addition, any other statement or document submitted under any provision of chapter 55 or subtitle F, or the regulations under those provisions, with respect to any tax imposed by chapter 55 may be required to contain or be verified by written declaration that it is made under the penalties of perjury. [Reg. §157.6065-1.]

☐ [*T.D.* 9134, 7-7-2004.]

[Reg. §301.6065-1]

§301.6065-1. Verification of returns.—For provisions concerning the verification of returns and other documents, see the regulations relating to the particular tax. [Reg. §301.6065-1.]

☐ [*T.D.* 6498, 10-24-60.]

[Reg. §31.6065(a)-1]

§31.6065(a)-1. Verification of returns or other documents.—If a return, statement, or other document made under the regulations in this part is required by the regulations contained in this part, or the form and instructions issued with respect to such return, statement, or other document, to contain or be verified by a written declaration that it is made under the penalties of perjury, such return, statement, or other document shall be so verified by the person signing it. [Reg. §31.6065(a)-1.]

☐ [*T.D.* 6472, 6-22-60.]

[Reg. §1.6071-1]

§1.6071-1. Time for filing returns and other documents.—(a) *In general.*—Whenever a return, statement, or other document is required to be made under the provisions of subtitle A or F of the Code, or the regulations thereunder, with respect to any tax imposed by subtitle A of the Code, and the time for filing such return, statement, or other document is not provided for by the Code, it shall be filed at the time prescribed by the regulations contained in this chapter with respect to such return, statement, or other document.

(b) *Return for a short period.*—In the case of a return with respect to tax under subtitle A of the Code for a short period (as defined in section 443), the district director or director of the Internal Revenue Service Center may, upon a showing by the taxpayer of unusual circumstances, prescribe a time for filing the return for such period later than the time when such return would otherwise be due. However, the district director or director of the Internal Revenue Service Center may not extend the time when the return for a DISC (as defined in Section 992(a)(1)) must be filed, as specified in section 6072(b).

(c) *Time for filing certain information returns.*— (1) For provisions relating to the time for filing returns of partnership income, see paragraph (e)(2) of § 1.6031-1.

(2) For provisions relating to the time for filing information returns by banks with respect to common trust funds, see § 1.6032-1.

(3) For provisions relating to the time for filing information returns by certain organizations exempt from taxation under section 501(a), see paragraph (e) of § 1.6033-1.

(4) For provisions relating to the time for filing returns by trusts claiming charitable deductions under section 642(c), see paragraph (c) of § 1.6034-1.

(5) For provisions relating to the time for filing information returns by officers, directors, and shareholders of foreign personal holding companies, see § § 1.6035-1 and 1.6035-2.

(6) For provisions relating to the time for filing information returns with respect to certain stock option transactions, see paragraph (c) of § 1.6039-1.

(7) For provisions relating to the time for filing information returns by persons making certain payments, see § 1.6041-2(a)(3) and § 1.6041-6.

(8) For provisions relating to the time for filing information returns regarding payments of dividends, see § 1.6042-2(c).

(9) For provisions relating to the time for filing information returns by corporations with respect to contemplated dissolution or liquidations, see paragraph (a) of § 1.6043-1.

(10) For provisions relating to the time for filing information returns by corporations with respect to distributions in liquidation, see paragraph (a) of § 1.6043-2.

(11) For provisions relating to the time for filing information returns with respect to payments of patronage dividends, see § 1.6044-2(d).

(12) For provisions relating to the time for filing information returns with respect to formation or reorganization of foreign corporations, see § 1.6046-1.

(13) For provisions relating to the time for filing information returns regarding certain payments of interest, see § 1.6049-4(g).

(14) For provisions relating to the time for filing information returns with respect to payment of wages in the form of group-term life insurance, see paragraph (b) of § 1.6052-1.

(15) For provisions relating to the time for filing an annual information return on Form 1042-S, "Foreign Person's U.S. Source Income subject to Withholding," or Form 8805, "Foreign Partner's Information Statement of Section 1446 Withholding Tax," for any tax withheld under chapter 3 of the Internal Revenue Code (relating to withholding of tax on nonresident aliens and foreign corporations and tax-free covenant bonds), see § 1.1461-1(c) and § 1.1446-3(d).

(16) for provisions relating to the time for filing annual information returns on Form 1042S of the tax withheld under chapter 3 of the Code (relating to withholding of tax on nonresident aliens and foreign corporations and tax-free covenant bonds), see paragraph (c) of § 1.1461-2.

(d) *Effective/Applicability date.*—The references to Form 8805 and § 1.1446-3(d) in paragraph (c)(15) of this section shall apply to partnership taxable years beginning after April 29, 2008. [Reg. § 1.6071-1.]

☐ [*T.D. 6364, 2-13-59. Amended by T.D. 6628,* 12-27-62; *T.D. 6887, 6-23-66; T.D. 6908, 12-30-66; T.D. 7284, 8-2-73; T.D. 7533, 2-14-78; T.D. 8734,* 10-6-97 (T.D. 8804 delayed the effective date of T.D. 8734 from January 1, 1999, to January 1, 2000; T.D. 8856 further delayed the effective date of T.D. 8734 until January 1, 2001) *and T.D. 9394,* 4-28-2008.]

[Reg. § 20.6071-1]

§ 20.6071-1. Time for filing preliminary notice required by § 20.6036-1.—In the case of the estate of a decedent dying before January 1, 1971, if a duly qualified executor or administrator of the estate of such a decedent who was a resident or a citizen of the United States qualifies within 2 months after a decedent's death, or if a duly qualified executor or administrator of the estate of such a decedent who was a nonresident not a citizen qualifies within the United States within 2 months after the decedent's death, the preliminary notice required by § 20.6036-1 must be filed within 2 months after his qualification. If no such executor or administrator qualifies within that period, the preliminary notice must be filed within 2 months of the decedent's death. [Reg. § 20.6071-1.]

☐ [*T.D. 7238, 12-28-72.*]

[Reg. § 44.6071-1]

§ 44.6071-1. Time for filing return.—
(a) *Return on Form 730.*—Each return required to
be made on Form 730 pursuant to § 44.6011(a)-1
shall be filed on or before the last day of the first
calendar month following the period for which it
is made. For provisions relating to the time for
filing a return when the prescribed due date falls
on Saturday, Sunday, or a legal holiday, see the
provisions of the Regulations on Procedure and
Administration(Part 301 of this chapter) under
section 7503.

(b) *Return on Form 11-C.*—(1) The first return
required to be made on Form 11-C shall be filed
to cover the period beginning with the first day
of the calendar month in which a person engages
(or expects to engage) in activities which make
him liable for the special tax imposed by section
4411 and ending with the following June 30.
Thereafter, each return required to be made on
Form 11-C shall be filed on or before July 1 to
cover a 1-year period (beginning July 1 and ending June 30 of the following calendar year) during which taxable activity continues.

(2) For additional provisions relating to the
return on Form 11-C, see § 44.4412-1 and
§ § 44.4901 to 44.4905-3, inclusive. [Reg.
§ 44.6071-1.]

☐ [T.D. 6370, 4-4-59.]

[Reg. § 53.6071-1]

§ 53.6071-1. Time for filing returns.—
(a) *General rule.*—Except as otherwise provided
in this section, a return required by § 53.6011-1
shall be filed at the time the private foundation
or trust described in section 4947(a)(2) is required to file its annual information or tax return
under section 6033 or 6012 (as may be
applicable).

(b) *Exception.*—The Form 4720 of a person
whose taxable year ends on a date other than
that on which the taxable year of the foundation
or trust ends shall be filed on or before the 15th
day of the fifth month following the close of such
person's taxable year.

(c) *Form 5227.*—A Form 5227 required to be
filed by paragraph (d) of § 53.6011-1 for a trust
described in section 4947(a) shall be filed on or
before the 15th day of the fourth month following the close of the trust's taxable year.

(d) *Taxes related to black lung benefit trusts.*—
Forms 990-BL and 6069 shall be filed on or
before the 15th day of the fifth month following
the close of the filer's taxable year.

(e) *Taxes related to political expenditures of organizations described in section 501(c)(3) of the Internal Revenue Code.*—A Form 4720 required to be
filed by § 53.6011-1(b) for an organization liable
for tax imposed by section 4955(a) must be filed
by the unextended due date for filing its annual
information return under section 6033 or, if the
organization is exempt from filing, the date the
organization would be required to file an annual

information return if it was not exempt from
filing. The Form 4720 of a person whose taxable
year ends on a date other than that on which the
taxable year of the organization described in section 501(c)(3) ends must be filed on or before the
15th day of the fifth month following the close of
the person's taxable year.

(f) *Taxes imposed on excess benefit transactions
engaged in by organizations described in sections
501(c)(3) (except private foundations) and
501(c)(4).*—(1) *General rule.*—A Form 4720 required by § 53.6011-1(b) for a disqualified person
or organization manager liable for tax imposed
by section 4958(a) shall be filed by that person on
or before the 15th day of the fifth month following the close of such person's taxable year.

(2) *Special rule for taxable years ending after
September 13, 1995, and on or before July 30,
1996.*—A Form 4720 required by § 53.6011-1(b)
for a disqualified person or organization manager liable for tax imposed by section 4958(a) on
an excess benefit transaction occurring in such
person's taxable year ending after September 13,
1995, and on or before July 30, 1996, is due on or
before December 15, 1996.

(g) *Taxes imposed with respect to prohibited tax
shelter transactions to which tax-exempt entities are
parties.*—(1) *Returns by certain tax-exempt entities.*—A Form 4720, "Return of Certain Excise
Taxes Under Chapters 41 and 42 of the Internal
Revenue Code," required by § 53.6071-1(b) for a
tax-exempt entity described in section 4965(c)(1),
(c)(2) or (c)(3) that is a party to a prohibited tax
shelter transaction and is liable for tax imposed
by section 4965(a)(1) shall be filed on or before
the due date (not including extensions) for filing
the tax-exempt entity's annual information return under section 6033(a)(1). If the tax-exempt
entity is not required to file an annual information return under section 6033(a)(1), the Form
4720 shall be filed on or before the 15th day of
the fifth month after the end of the tax-exempt
entity's taxable year or, if the entity has not
established a taxable year for Federal income tax
purposes, the entity's annual accounting period.

(2) *Returns by entity managers of tax-exempt
entities described in section 4965(c)(1), (c)(2) or
(c)(3).*—A Form 4720, required by § 53.6011-1(b)
for an entity manager of a tax-exempt entity
described in section 4965(c)(1), (c)(2) or (c)(3)
who is liable for tax imposed by section
4965(a)(2) shall be filed on or before the 15th day
of the fifth month following the close of the
entity manager's taxable year during which the
entity entered into the prohibited tax shelter
transaction.

(3) *Transition rule.*—A Form 4720, for a section 4965 tax that was due on or before October
4, 2007, will be deemed to have been filed on the
due date if it was filed by October 4, 2007, and if
all section 4965 taxes required to be reported on
that Form 4720 were paid by October 4, 2007.

(h) *Taxes on failures by charitable hospital organizations to satisfy the community health needs assess-*

ment requirements of section 501(r)(3).—A hospital organization (as defined in § 1.501(r)-1(b)(18)) liable for tax imposed by section 4959 must file a Form 4720 as required by § 53.6011-1(b), on or before the 15th day of the fifth month after the end of the hospital organization's taxable year for which it failed to meet the requirements of section 501(r)(3).

(i) *Effective/applicability date.*—(1) Paragraph (g) of this section applies on and after July 6, 2007.

(2) Paragraph (h) of this section applies on and after August 15, 2013. [Reg. § 53.6071-1.]

☐ [*T.D.* 7368, 7-15-75. *Amended by T.D.* 7407, 3-3-76; *T.D.* 7838, 10-5-82; *T.D.* 8628, 12-4-95; *T.D.* 8736, 10-6-97; *T.D.* 9334, 7-5-2007; *T.D.* 9492, 7-2-2010 (*corrected* 8-3-2010); *T.D.* 9629, 8-14-2013 *and T.D.* 9708, 12-29-2014.]

[Reg. § 54.6071-1]

§ 54.6071-1. Time for filing returns.— (a) *Returns under section 4980B.*—(1) *Due date for filing of return by employers or other persons responsible for benefits under a group health plan.*—If the person liable for the excise tax is an employer or other person responsible for providing or administering benefits under a group health plan (such as an insurer or a third party administrator), the return required by § 54.6011-2 must be filed on or before the due date for filing the person's income tax return and must reflect the portion of the noncompliance period for each failure under section 4980B that falls during the person's taxable year. An extension to file the person's income tax return does not extend the date for filing Form 8928.

(2) *Due date for filing of return by multiemployer plans.*—If the person liable for the excise tax is a multiemployer plan, the return required by § 54.6011-2 must be filed on or before the last day of the seventh month following the end of the plan's plan year. The filing of Form 8928 by a plan must reflect the portion of the noncompliance period for each failure under section 4980B that falls during the plan's plan year.

(b) *Returns under section 4980D.*—(1) *Due date for filing of return by employers.*—If the person liable for the excise tax is an employer, the return required by § 54.6011-2 must be filed on or before the due date for filing the employer's income tax return and must reflect the portion of the noncompliance period for each failure under chapter 100 that falls during the employer's taxable year. An extension to file the employer's income tax return does not extend the date for filing Form 8928.

(2) *Due date for filing of return by multiemployer plans or multiple employer health plans.*—If the person liable for the excise tax is a multiemployer plan or a specified multiple employer health plan, the return required by § 54.6011-2 must be filed on or before the last day of the seventh month following the end of the plan's plan year. The filing of Form 8928 by a plan must

reflect the portion of the noncompliance period for each failure under chapter 100 that falls during the plan's plan year.

(c) *Returns under section 4980E.*—Any employer who is liable for the excise tax under section 4980E must report this tax by filing the return required by § 54.6011-2 on or before the 15th day of the fourth month following the calendar year in which the noncomparable contributions were made.

(d) *Returns under section 4980G.*—Any employer who is liable for the excise tax under section 4980E must report this tax by filing the return required by § 54.6011-2 on or before the 15th day of the fourth month following the calendar year in which the noncomparable contributions were made. See Q & A-4 of § 54.4980G-1 for the rules on computation of the excise tax under section 4980G.

(e) *Effective/applicability date.*—The rules in this section are effective for any Form 8928 that is due on or after January 1, 2010. [Reg. § 54.6071-1.]

☐ [*T.D.* 9457, 9-4-2009.]

[Reg. § 55.6071-1]

§ 55.6071-1. Time for filing returns.— (a) *Returns for calendar years beginning after December 31, 1986.*—A return required by § 55.6011-1 for any calendar year beginning after December 31, 1986, shall be filed on or before March 15 of the following calendar year. See § 55.6081-1 for rules relating to extensions of time for filing a return required by § 55.6011-1.

(b) *Returns for excise tax under section 4981 as in effect before amendment by the Tax Reform Act of 1986.*—A return required by § 55.6011-1 for any excise tax under section 4981, as in effect before amendment by the Tax Reform Act of 1986, shall be filed at the time (including any extension of time granted or allowed under section 6081) that the real estate investment trust is required to file its income tax return under section 6012 for the taxable year for which the tax under section 4981, as in effect before amendment by the Tax Reform Act of 1986, is imposed. [Reg. § 55.6071-1.]

☐ [*T.D.* 7767, 2-3-81. *Amended by T.D.* 8180, 2-29-88.]

[Reg. § 156.6071-1]

§ 156.6071-1. Time for filing returns relating to greenmail.—(a) *In general.*—Returns required by § 156.6011-1 (relating to liability for tax on greenmail under section 5881) shall be filed on or before the ninetieth day following receipt of any portion of the greenmail. Greenmail is considered to be received when gain or other income is realized, as determined according to the taxpayer's method of accounting, without regard to any provision of the Code providing for deferral of recognition.

(b) *Returns relating to greenmail received before the date these regulations become final.*—Returns required by §156.6011-1 that relate to greenmail received on or before December 18, 1991, shall be filed on or before March 18, 1991. [Reg. §156.6071-1.]

☐ [*T.D.* 8379, 12-17-91.]

[Reg. §157.6071-1]

§157.6071-1. Time for filing returns.—(a) *In general.*—Except as provided in paragraph (b) of this section, returns required by §157.6011-1 (relating to returns of tax with respect to structured settlement factoring transactions) must be filed on or before the ninetieth day following the receipt of structured settlement payment rights in a structured settlement factoring transaction.

(b) *Returns relating to structured settlement payment rights received before February 19, 2003.*—Returns required by §157.6011-1 that relate to structured settlement payment rights received on or before February 19, 2003, must be filed on or before May 20, 2003. [Reg. §157.6071-1.]

☐ [*T.D.* 9134, 7-7-2004.]

[Reg. §301.6071-1]

§301.6071-1. Time for filing returns and other documents.—For provisions concerning the time for filing returns and other documents, see the regulations relating to the particular tax. [Reg. §301.6071-1.]

☐ [*T.D.* 6498, 10-24-60.]

[Reg. §31.6071(a)-1]

§31.6071(a)-1. Time for filing returns and other documents.—(a) *Federal Insurance Contributions Act and income tax withheld from wages and from nonpayroll payments.*—(1) *Quarterly or annual returns.*—Except as provided in paragraph (a)(4) of this section, each return required to be made under §31.6011(a)-1, in respect of the taxes imposed by the Federal Insurance Contributions Act (26 U.S.C. 3101-3128), or required to be made under §31.6011(a)-4, in respect of income tax withheld, shall be filed on or before the last day of the first calendar month following the period for which it is made. A return may be filed on or before the 10th day of the second calendar month following such period if timely deposits under section 6302(c) of the Code and the regulations have been made in full payment of such taxes due for the period.

(2) *Monthly tax returns.*—Each return in respect of the taxes imposed by the Federal Insurance Contributions Act or of income tax withheld which is required to be made under paragraph (a) of §31.6011(a)-5 shall be filed on or before the fifteenth day of the first calendar month following the period for which it is made.

(3) [Reserved]. For further guidance, see §31.6071(a)-1T(a)(3).

(4) *Employee returns under Federal Insurance Contributions Act.*—A return of employee tax under section 3101 required under paragraph (d) of §31.6011(a)-1 to be made by an individual for a calendar year on Form 1040 shall be filed on or before the due date of such individual's return of income (see §1.6012-1 of this chapter (Income Tax Regulations)) for the calendar year, or, if the individual makes his return of income on a fiscal year basis, on or before the due date of his return of income for the fiscal year beginning in the calendar year for which a return of employee tax is required. A return of employee tax under section 3101 required under paragraph (d) of §31.6011(a)-1 to be made for a calendar year—

(i) On Form 1040SS or Form 1040PR, or

(ii) On Form 1040 by an individual who is not required to make a return of income for the calendar year or for a fiscal year beginning in such calendar year,

shall be filed on or before the 15th day of the fourth month following the close of the calendar year.

(b) *Railroad Retirement Tax Act.*—Each return of the taxes imposed by the Railroad Retirement Tax Act required to be made under §31.6011(a)-2 shall be filed on or before the last day of the second calendar month following the period for which it is made.

(c) *Federal Unemployment Tax Act.*—Each return of the tax imposed by the Federal Unemployment Tax Act required to be made under §31.6011(a)-3 shall be filed on or before the last day of the first calendar month following the period for which it is made. However, a return may be filed on or before the 10th day of the second calendar month following such period if timely deposits under section 6302(c) of the Code and the regulations thereunder have been made in full payment of such taxes due for the period.

(d) *Last day for filing.*—For provisions relating to the time for filing a return when the prescribed due date falls on Saturday, Sunday, or a legal holiday, see the provisions of §301.7503-1 of this chapter (Regulations on Procedure and Administration).

(e) *Late filing.*—For additions to the tax in case of failure to file a return within the prescribed time, see the provisions of §301.6651-1 of this chapter (Regulations on Procedure and Administration).

(f) *Cross reference.*—For extensions of time for filing returns and other documents, see §31.6081(a)-1. [Reg. §31.6071(a)-1.]

☐ [*T.D.* 6354, 1-13-59. *Amended by T.D.* 6893, 8-29-66; *T.D.* 6941, 12-15-67; *T.D.* 7001, 1-17-69; *T.D.* 7078, 12-5-70; *T.D.* 7351, 4-16-75; *T.D.* 7953, 5-8-84; *T.D.* 8504, 12-22-93; *T.D.* 8636, 12-20-95; *T.D.* 8895, 8-17-2000; *T.D.* 8952, 6-25-2001; *T.D.* 9239, 12-30-2005; *T.D.* 9507, 12-2-2010; *T.D.* 9524, 5-6-2011, *T.D.* 9566, 12-9-2011, *T.D.* 9586, 4-24-2012 *and T.D.* 9821, 7-18-2017.]

[Reg. §31.6071(a)-1T]

§31.6071(a)-1T. Time for filing returns and other documents (temporary).—(a) *Federal Insurance Contributions Act and income tax withheld from wages and from nonpayroll payments.*—(1) through (2) [Reserved]. For further guidance, see §31.6071(a)-1(a)(1) and (2).

(3) *Information returns.*—(i) *General rule.*—Each information return in respect of wages as defined in Federal Insurance Contributions Act or of income tax withheld from wages as required under §31.6051-2 must be filed on or before January 31 of the year following the calendar year for which it is made, except that, if a tax return under §31.6011(a)-5(a) is filed as a final return for a period ending prior to December 31, the information return must be filed on or before the last day of the first calendar month following the period for which the tax return is filed.

(ii) *Expedited filing.*—If an employer who is required to make a return pursuant to §31.6011(a)-1 or §31.6011(a)-4 is required to make a final return on Form 941, or a variation thereof, under §31.6011(a)-6(a)(1) (relating to the final return for Federal Insurance Contributions Act taxes and income tax withholding from wages), the return which is required to be made under §31.6051-2 must be filed on or before the last day of the first calendar month following the period for which the final return is filed. The requirements set forth in this paragraph (a)(3)(ii) do not apply to employers with respect to employees whose wages are for domestic service in the private home of the employer. See §31.6011(a)-1(a)(3).

(b) through (f) [Reserved]. For further guidance, see §31.6071(a)-1(b) through (f).

(g) *Applicability date.*—This section applies to returns filed after July 20, 2017. Section 31.6071(a)-1 (as contained in 26 CFR part 31, revised April 2017) applies to returns filed before July 20, 2017.

(h) *Expiration date.*—The applicability of this section will expire on or before July 17, 2020. [Temporary Reg. §31.6071(a)-1T.]

☐ *T.D. 9821, 7-18-2017.]*

[Reg. §40.6071(a)-1]

§40.6071(a)-1. Time for filing returns.—(a) *Quarterly returns.*—Each quarterly return required under §40.6011(a)-1 (a)(2) must be filed by the last day of the first calendar month following the quarter for which it is made.

(b) *Monthly and semimonthly returns.*—(1) *Monthly returns.*—Each monthly return required under §40.6011(a)-1(b) must be filed by the fifteenth day of the month following the month for which it is made.

(2) *Semimonthly returns.*—Each semimonthly return required under §40.6011(a)-1(b) must be filed by the last day of the semimonthly period (as defined in §40.0-1(c)) following the semimonthly period for which it is made.

(c) *Fees on health insurance policies and self-insured health plans.*—(1) *Specified health insurance policies.*—A return that reports liability for the fee imposed by section 4375 must be filed by July 31 of the calendar year immediately following the last day of the policy year. For issuers that determine the average number of lives covered under the policy for section 4375 using the member months method under §46.4375-1(c)(2)(v) or the state form method under §46.4375-1(c)(2)(vi), the return must be filed by July 31 of the immediately following calendar year. Thus, for example, a return that reports liability for the fee imposed by section 4375 for the year ending on December 31, 2012, must be filed by July 31, 2013.

(2) *Applicable self-insured health plans.*—A return that reports liability for the fee imposed by section 4376 for a plan year must be filed by July 31 of the calendar year immediately following the last day of the plan year. Thus, for example, a return that reports liability for the fee imposed by section 4376 for the plan year ending on January 31, 2013, must be filed by July 31, 2014.

(d) *Effective/Applicability date.*—Paragraphs (a) and (b) of this section apply to returns for calendar quarters beginning on or after October 1, 2001, and paragraph (c) of this section applies to returns that report liability imposed by section 4375 or 4376. [Reg. §40.6071(a)-1.]

☐ *[T.D. 8442, 10-21-92. Amended by T.D. 8963, 8-8-2001 and T.D. 9602, 12-5-2012.]*

[Reg. §41.6071(a)-1]

§41.6071(a)-1. Time for filing returns.—(a) *In general.*—Except as provided in paragraph (b) of this section, a return described in §41.6011(a)-1 must be filed by the last day of the month following the month in which—

(1) A person becomes liable for tax under §41.4481-2(a)(1)(i)(A), (B), or (C);

(2) A person that is liable for tax under §41.4481-2(a)(1)(i)(D) is notified by the Commissioner that the tax has not been paid in full; or

(3) A transferee described in §41.4483-3(f) acquires the vehicle.

(b) *Certain transit-type buses.*—In the case of any bus of the transit type, the first taxable use of which in any taxable period occurs prior to the close of the test period (see paragraph (c) of §41.4483-2) with reference to which liability for the tax on the use of such transit-type bus for such taxable period is determined, the person in whose name the bus is registered at the time of such use shall, after such test period and on or before the last day of the following month make a return of such tax for such taxable period on the use of such transit-type bus.

(c) *Effect of sale during taxable period.*—A person that is liable for tax under §41.4481-2(a)(1)(i)(A), (B), (C), or (D) after taking into account the modification required under §41.4481-2(a)(2) is treated as liable for tax under the same provision of §41.4481-2(a)(1)(i) for purposes of this section.

(d) *Effective/applicability date.*—Paragraph (c) of this section applies on and after July 1, 2015. For rules applicable before that date, see 26 CFR 41.6071(a)-1 (revised as of April 1, 2014). [Reg. §41.6071(a)-1.]

☐ [*T.D. 6216, 12-6-56. Amended by T.D. 6743, 6-22-64; T.D. 8879, 3-30-2000; T.D. 9537, 7-15-2011 and T.D. 9698, 10-28-2014.*]

[Reg. § 40.6071(a)-3]

§ 40.6071(a)-3. Time for an eligible air carrier to file a return for the third calendar quarter of 2001.—(a) *In general.*—If, in the case of an eligible air carrier, the quarterly return required under § 40.6011(a)-1(a) for the third calendar quarter of 2001 includes tax imposed by subchapter C of chapter 33—

(1) The requirements of § 40.6071(a)-2 as in effect on August 7, 2001, do not apply to the return; and

(2) The return must be filed by January 15, 2002.

(b) *Definition of eligible air carrier.*—Eligible air carrier has the same meaning as provided in section 301(a)(2) of the Air Transportation Safety and System Stabilization Act; that is, any domestic corporation engaged in the trade or business of transporting (for hire) persons by air if such transportation is available to the general public.

(c) *Effective date.*—This section is applicable with respect to returns that relate to the third calendar quarter of 2001. [Reg. § 40.6071(a)-3.]

☐ [*T.D. 8983, 2-5-2002.*]

[Reg. § 1.6072-1]

§ 1.6072-1. Time for filing returns of individuals, estates, and trusts.—(a) *In general.*—(1) *Returns of income for individuals, estates and trusts.*—Except as provided in paragraphs (b) and (c) of this section, returns of income required under sections 6012, 6013, 6014, and 6017 of individuals, estates, domestic trusts, and foreign trusts having an office or place of business in the United States (including unrelated business tax returns of such trusts referred to in section 511(b)(2)) shall be filed on or before the fifteenth day of the fourth month following the close of the taxable year.

(2) *Return of trust, or portion of a trust, treated as owned by a decedent.*—(i) *In general.*—In the case of a return of a trust, or portion of a trust, that was treated as owned by a decedent under subpart E (section 671 and following), part I, subchapter J, chapter 1 of the Internal Revenue Code as of the date of the decedent's death that is filed in accordance with § 1.671-4(a) for the fractional part of the year ending with the date of the decedent's death, the due date of such return shall be the fifteenth day of the fourth month following the close of the 12-month period which began with the first day of the decedent's taxable year.

(ii) *Effective date.*—This paragraph (a)(2) applies to taxable years ending on or after December 24, 2002.

(b) *Decedents.*—In the case of a final return of a decedent for a fractional part of a year, the due date of such return shall be the fifteenth day of the fourth month following the close of the 12-month period which began with the first day of such fractional part of the year.

(c) *Nonresident alien individuals and foreign trusts.*—The income tax return of a nonresident alien individual (other than one treated as a resident under section 6013(g) or (h)) and of a foreign trust which does not have an office or place of business in the United States (including unrelated business tax returns of such trusts referred to in section 511(b)(2)) shall be filed on or before the fifteenth day of the sixth month following the close of the taxable year. However, a nonresident alien individual who for the taxable year has wages subject to withholding under chapter 24 of the Code shall file his income tax return on or before the fifteenth day of the fourth month following the close of the taxable year.

(d) *Last day for filing return.*—For provisions relating to the time for filing a return where the last day for filing falls on Saturday, Sunday, or a legal holiday, see section 7503 and § 301.7503-1 of this chapter (Regulations on Procedure and Administration). [Reg. § 1.6072-1.]

☐ [*T.D. 6364, 2-13-59. Amended by T.D. 7426, 8-6-76; T.D. 7670, 1-30-80 and T.D. 9032, 12-23-2002.*]

[Reg. § 301.6072-1]

§ 301.6072-1. Time for filing income tax returns.—For provisions relating to time for filing income tax returns, see § § 1.6072-1 to 1.6072-4, inclusive, of this chapter (Income Tax Regulations). [Reg. § 301.6072-1.]

☐ [*T.D. 6498, 10-24-60.*]

[Reg. § 1.6072-2]

§ 1.6072-2. Time for filing returns of corporations.—(a) [Reserved]. For further guidance, see § 1.6072-2T(a).

(b) *Foreign corporations not having an office or place of business in the United States.*—The income tax return of a foreign corporation which does not have an office or place of business in the United States shall be filed on or before the fifteenth day of the sixth month following the close of the taxable year.

(c) *Exempt organizations.*—For taxable years beginning after November 10, 1978, the income tax return required under section 6012 and § 1.6012-2(e) of an organization exempt from taxation under section 501(a) (other than an employee's trust under section 401(a)) shall be filed on or before the fifteenth day of the fifth month following the close of the organization's taxable year.

(d) *Cooperative organizations.*—The income tax return of the following cooperative organizations shall be filed on or before the fifteenth day of the ninth month following the close of the taxable year:

(1) [Reserved]. For further guidance, see § 1.6072-2T(d)(1); and

(2) [Reserved]. For further guidance, see § 1.6072-2T(d)(2).

(e) *DISC's and former DISC's.*—The return required under section 6011(c)(2) of a corporation which is a DISC (as defined in section 992(a)) shall be filed on or before the 15th day of the 9th month following the close of the taxable year. For the rule that a DISC may not have an extension of time in which to file such return, see §§ 1.6071-1(b), 1.6081-1(a), and 1.6081-3(e). The return required under § 1.6011-2(b)(1) by a former DISC shall be filed at the time it is required to file its income tax return.

(f) *Cross references.*—For provisions relating to the time for filing a return where the last day for filing falls on Saturday, Sunday, or a legal holiday, see section 7503 and § 301.7503-1 of this chapter (Regulations on Procedure and Administration). For provisions relating to the fixing of a later time for filing in the case of a return for a short period, see paragraph (b) of § 1.6071-1. For provisions relating to time for filing consolidated returns and separate returns for short periods not included in consolidated returns, see §§ 1.1502-75 and 1.1502-76. [Reg. § 1.6072-2.]

☐ [*T.D. 6364, 2-13-59. Amended by T.D. 6643, 4-1-63; T.D. 7244, 12-29-72; T.D. 7533, 2-14-78, T.D. 7896, 5-26-83 and T.D. 9821, 7-18-2017.*]

[Reg. § 1.6072-2T]

§ 1.6072-2T. Time for filing returns of corporations (temporary).—(a) *Domestic and certain foreign corporations.*—(1) *In general.*—(i) *C corporations.*—Except as provided in paragraph (a)(2) of this section, the income tax return required under section 6012 of a domestic C corporation (as defined in section 1361(a)(2)) or of a foreign C corporation having an office or place of business in the United States shall be filed on or before the fifteenth day of the fourth month following the close of the taxable year.

(ii) *S corporations.*—The income tax return required under section 6012 and 6037 of an S corporation (as defined in section 1361(a)(1)) shall be filed on or before the fifteenth day of the third month following the close of the taxable year.

(2) *Exception.*—For taxable years beginning before January 1, 2026, the income tax return of a C corporation described in paragraph (a)(1)(i) of this section that has a taxable year that ends on June 30 shall be filed on or before the fifteenth day of the third month following the close of the taxable year. For purposes of this paragraph (a)(2), the return for a short period (within the meaning of section 443) that ends on any day in June shall be treated as the return for a taxable year that ends on June 30.

(b) through (c) [Reserved]. For further guidance, see § 1.6072-2(b) and (c).

(d) introductory text [Reserved]. For further guidance, see § 1.6072-2(d) introductory text.

(1) *Section 521 associations.*—A farmers', fruit growers', or like association, organized and operated in compliance with the requirements of section 521 and § 1.521-1; and

(2) *Section 1381 corporations.*—For a taxable year beginning after December 31, 1962, a corporation described in section 1381(a)(2), which is under a valid enforceable written obligation to pay patronage dividends (as defined in section 1388(a) and paragraph (a) of § 1.1388-1) in an amount equal to at least 50 percent of its net earnings from business done with or for its patrons, or which paid patronage dividends in such an amount out of the net earnings from business done with or for patrons during the most recent taxable year for which it had such net earnings. Net earnings for this purpose shall not be reduced by any taxes imposed by Subtitle A of the Code and shall not be reduced by dividends paid on capital stock or other proprietary interest.

(e) through (f) [Reserved]. For further guidance, see § 1.6072-2(e) and (f).

(g) *Applicability date.*—This section applies to returns filed on or after July 20, 2017. Section 1.6072-2 (as contained in 26 CFR part 1, revised April 2017) applies to returns before July 20, 2017.

(h) *Expiration date.*—The applicability of this section will expire on or before July 17, 2020. [Temporary Reg. § 1.6072-2T.]

☐ *T.D. 9821, 7-18-2017.*]

[Reg. § 1.6072-3]

§ 1.6072-3. Income tax due dates postponed in case of China Trade Act corporations.—(a) With respect to a taxable year beginning after December 31, 1948, and ending before October 1, 1956, the income tax return of any corporation organized under the China Trade Act of 1922 (15 U.S.C.c. 4), as amended, shall not become due until December 31, 1956, provided that during any such taxable year conditions in China have been generally so unsettled as to militate against the normal commercial operations and corporate activities of such corporation. However, the postponement of the due date shall not apply to an income tax return for any such taxable year if—

(1) The books of account and business records are available so as to permit the filing of a proper return, and the corporation has otherwise been in a position to carry on its commercial operations and corporate activities and to make a proper distribution of its earnings or profits, if any, so as to permit the certification required by section 941(b); or

(2) All the commercial operations and corporate activities of such corporation have been carried on in Hong Kong, Macao, or Taiwan (Formosa).

(b) Notwithstanding the provisions of paragraph (a)(1) or (2) of this section, the postponed due date referred to in this section will apply if a corporation satisfies the Commissioner that special circumstances exist, related to the unsettled conditions in China, which warrant such postponement.

Reg. § 1.6072-3(b)

(c) The postponed due date provided for in this section is expressly subject to the power of the Commissioner to extend, as in other cases, the time for filing the income tax return. See section 6081 and the regulations thereunder. [Reg. § 1.6072-3.]

☐ [T.D. 6364, 2-13-59.]

[Reg. § 1.6072-4]

§ 1.6072-4. Time for filing other returns of income.—(a) *Reports for recovery of excessive profits on Government contracts.*—For the time for filing annual reports by persons completing Government contracts, see 26 CFR (1939) 17.16 (Treasury Decision 4906, approved June 23, 1939), and 26 CFR (1939) 16.15 (Treasury Decision 4909, approved June 28, 1939), as made applicable to section 1471 of the Internal Revenue Code of 1954 by Treasury Decision 6091, approved August 16, 1954 (19 F.R. 5167, C.B. 1954-2, 47).

(b) *Returns of tax on transfers to avoid income tax.*—For the time for filing returns of tax under chapter 5 of the Code, see § 1.1494-1. [Reg. § 1.6072-4.]

☐ [T.D. 6364, 2-13-59. *Amended by T.D.* 6908, 12-30-66.]

[Reg. § 20.6075-1]

§ 20.6075-1. Returns; time for filing estate tax return.—The estate tax return required by section 6018 must be filed on or before the due date. The due date is the date on or before which the return is required to be filed in accordance with the provisions of section 6075(a) or the last day of the period covered by an extension of time as provided in § 20.6081-1. The due date, for a decedent dying after December 31, 1970, is, unless an extension of time for filing has been obtained, the day of the ninth calendar month after the decedent's death numerically corresponding to the day of the calendar month on which death occurred. However, if there is no numerically corresponding day in the ninth month, the last day of the ninth month is the due date. For example, if the decedent dies on July 31, 2000, the estate tax return and tax payment must be made on or before April 30, 2001. When the due date falls on Saturday, Sunday, or a legal holiday, the due date for filing the return is the next succeeding day that is not Saturday, Sunday, or a legal holiday. For the definition of a legal holiday, see section 7503 and § 301.7503-1 of this chapter. As to additions to the tax in the case of failure to file the return or pay the tax within the prescribed time, see section 6651 and § 301.6651-1 of this chapter. For rules with respect to the right to elect to have the property valued as of a date or dates subsequent to the decedent's death, see section 2032 and § 20.2032-1, and section 7502 and § 301.7502-1 of this chapter. This section applies to estates of decedents dying after August 16, 1954. [Reg. § 20.6075-1.]

☐ [T.D. 7238, 12-28-72. *Amended by T.D.* 8957, 7-24-2001.]

[Reg. § 25.6075-1]

§ 25.6075-1. Returns, time for filing gift tax returns for gifts made after December 31, 1981.—(a) *In general.*—Except as provided in paragraphs (b)(1) and (2) of this section, a return required to be filed under section 6019 for gifts made after December 31, 1981, must be filed on or before the 15th day of April following the close of the calendar year in which the gift was made.

(b) *Special rules.*—(1) *Extensions.*—Except as provided in paragraph (b)(2) of this section, if a taxpayer files an income tax return on the calendar year basis and the taxpayer is granted an extension of time for filing the return of income tax imposed by Subtitle A of the Internal Revenue Code, then such taxpayer shall also be deemed to have been granted an extension of time for filing the gift tax return under section 6019 for such calendar year equal to the extension of time granted for filing the income tax return. See section 6081 and the regulations thereunder for rules relating to extension of time for filing returns.

(2) *Death of donor.*—Where a gift is made during the calendar year in which the donor dies, the time for filing the return made under section 6019 shall not be later than the time (including extensions) for filing the return made under section 6018 (relating to estate tax returns) with respect to such donor. In addition, should the time for filing the estate tax return fall later than the 15th day of April following the close of the calendar year, the time for filing the gift tax return shall be on or before the 15th day of April following the close of the calendar year, unless an extension (not extending beyond the time for filing the estate tax return) was granted for filing the gift tax return. If no estate tax return is required to be filed, the time for filing the gift tax return shall be on or before the 15th day of April following the close of the calendar year, unless an extension was granted for filing the gift tax return.

(c) Paragraphs (a) and (b) may be illustrated by the following examples.

Example (1). Donor makes a taxable gift on April 1, 1982, for which a return must be made under section 6019. Donor files the income tax return on the calendar year basis. The donor was granted a 4-month extension from April 15, 1983 to August 15, 1983, in which to file the 1982 income tax return. Under these circumstances, the donor is not required to file the gift tax return prior to August 15, 1983. See paragraph (b)(1) of this section.

Example (2). Donor makes a taxable gift on April 1, 1982, for which a return must be made under section 6019. The donor dies on May 1, 1982. Under these circumstances, since the due date for filing the estate tax return, February 1, 1983 (assuming an estate tax return under 6018 was required to be filed), falls prior to the due date for the gift tax return (as specified in section 6075(b)(1)), the last day for filing the gift tax return is February 1, 1983. See paragraph (b)(2) of this section.

Example (3). The facts are the same as in example (2), except the donor dies on November 30, 1982. Although the estate tax return if [is] due on or before August 30, 1983, the last day for filing the gift tax return is April 15, 1983. See paragraph (b) of this section.

Example (4). The facts are the same as in example (3), except that the executor receives a 4-month extension for filing the decedent's income tax return. Under these circumstances, the last day for filing the gift tax return is August 15, 1983. See paragraphs (b)(1) and (2) of this section.

Example (5). The facts are the same as in example (3), except that the donor-decedent receives an extension of 6 months for filing the gift tax return. See section 6081 and §25.6081-1. Since section 6075(b)(3) and §25.6075-2(b) provide that the time for filing the gift tax return made under section 6019 shall not be later than the time (including extensions) for filing the estate tax return made under section 6018, the last day for filing the gift tax return is August 30, 1983.

(d) See section 7503 and §301.7503-1 concerning the timely filing of a return that falls due on a Saturday, Sunday or [or] legal holiday. As to additions to the tax for failure to file the return within the prescribed time, see section 6651 and §301.6651-1. [Reg. §25.6075-1.]

☐ [T.D. 7910, 9-6-83.]

[Reg. §25.6075-2]

§25.6075-2. Returns, time for filing gift tax returns for gifts made after December 31, 1976, and before January 1, 1982.—(a) *Due date for filing quarterly gift tax returns.*—(1) Except as provided in paragraph (b) of this section, a return required to be filed under section 6019 for the first, second, or third calendar quarter of any calendar year must be filed on or before the 15th day of the second month following the close of the calendar quarter in which the taxable gift was made.

(2) If a return is required to be filed under section 6019 for the fourth calendar quarter, then—

(i) For gifts made after December 31, 1976 and before January 1, 1979, the return must be filed on or before February 15th following the close of the fourth calendar quarter, or

(ii) For gifts made after December 31, 1978, and before January 1, 1982, the return must be filed on or before April 15th following the close of the fourth calendar quarter.

(b) *Special rule.*—(1) If the total amount of taxable gifts (determined after the application of paragraph (c)(1) of this section, relating to split gifts) made by a person during a calendar quarter is $25,000 or less, the return required under section 6019 for that quarter must be filed on or before the date prescribed in paragraph (a)(1) of this section for filing the return for gifts made in the first subsequent calendar quarter (unless the first subsequent calendar quarter is the fourth calendar quarter in which case see paragraph (b)(2) of this section) in the calendar year in which the sum of—

(i) The taxable gifts made during such subsequent calendar quarter, plus

(ii) All other taxable gifts made in prior quarters of the calendar year for which no return has yet been required to be filed, exceeds $25,000.

The return must include transfers by gift (as required by section 6019 and the regulations under that section) made during such subsequent and prior quarters of the calendar year for which no return has yet been required to be filed and identify in which quarter such transfers were made. The return must meet all the requirements for a separate return as if a separate return had been made for each quarter in which a transfer by gift was made. This return will be treated as a separate return for each of the quarters identified on the return.

(2) If a return is not required to be filed under paragraph (b)(1) of this section, then—

(i) For gifts made after December 31, 1976 and before January 1, 1979, the return must be filed on or before February 15th following the close of the fourth calendar quarter, or

(ii) For gifts made after December 31, 1978, and before January 1, 1982, the return must be filed on or before April 15th following the close of the fourth calendar quarter.

The return must include all transfers by gift (as required under section 6019 and the regulations under that section) made during the calendar year for which no return has yet been required to be filed and identify in which quarter such transfers were made. The return must meet all the requirements for a separate return as if a separate return had been made for each quarter in which a transfer by gift was made. This return will be treated as a separate return for each of the quarters identified on the return.

(3) Under section 6075(b)(3), any extension of time granted a taxpayer for filing the return of income taxes imposed by subtitle A for any taxable year which is a calendar year shall be treated as an extension of time granted the taxpayer for filing any return under section 6019 which is due (under paragraphs (a)(2)(ii) and (b)(2)(ii) of this section) on or before April 15th following the close of the fourth calendar quarter. See also section 6081 and §25.6081-1 for other rules relating to extensions of time for filing returns.

(4) See section 7503 and §301.7503-1 for the due date of a return that falls on a Saturday, Sunday, or a legal holiday. As to additions to the tax for failure to file the return within the prescribed time, see section 6651 and §301.6651-1.

(c) *Effect of section 2513.*—(1) In determining whether taxable gifts made during any calendar quarter exceed $25,000, and in determining whether taxable gifts made in the current calendar quarter and the preceding calendar quarters of the calendar year for which no return has yet been required to be filed exceed $25,000, the effect of section 2513 is not taken into account for any gifts made in the current or previous quarters for which a return is now being filed unless an irrevocable consent was made by either spouse on a return that was required to be filed prior to the due date of the current return. See § 25.2513-3 for the rules relating to when a consent becomes irrevocable.

(2) Paragraph (c)(1) of this section may be illustrated by the following examples:

Example (1). During the first quarter of 1980 A made taxable gifts of $17,000 ($20,000—$3,000 annual exclusion under section 2503(b)) to D. During the second quarter A made another taxable gift of $10,000 to D. A's taxable gifts for the first two quarters are $27,000. Therefore, A is required to file a return for the first and second quarters on or before August 15, 1980. On that return A's wife, B, consented to the application of section 2513 (relating to split gifts) for the second quarter. Even though A split the second quarter gift with his wife, A's return is nevertheless required to be filed on or before August 15, 1980 because in determining whether taxable gifts exceed $25,000, the effect of section 2513 is only taken into account for the quarter in which an irrevocable consent was made on a return required to be filed before August 15, 1980.

Example (2). Assume the same facts as in Example (1). In addition, during the third quarter A made another taxable gift of $20,000 to D, and B made a taxable gift of $24,000 to D. B is required to file a return reporting the taxable gifts made during the second and third quarters on or before November 15, 1980 because B's total taxable gifts exceed $25,000 (second quarter gifts after taking section 2513 into account = $^1/_2$ ($10,000) − $3,000 (annual exclusion under section 2503(b)) = $2,000 plus a $24,000 gift in the third quarter). Even if A and B had consented to the application of section 2513 for the third quarter, B's return would nevertheless be due on or before November 15, 1980, because an irrevocable consent was not made on a return that was required to be filed prior to November 15, 1980. However, the effect of section 2513 is taken into account for the second quarter because an irrevocable consent was made on a return that was required to be filed prior to November 15, 1980.

Example (3). During the first quarter of 1980 A made taxable gifts of $27,000 to F ($30,000 − $3,000 annual exclusion under section 2503(b)). A is required to file a return on or before May 15, 1980. A fails to file a return until August 1, 1980. On that return B, A's spouse, consented to the application of section 2513. The consent on that return is irrevocable under § 25.2513-3. During the second quarter B made taxable gifts of $14,000 to F. A and B made no other gifts during 1980. B has made total taxable gifts of $26,000 ($12,000 for the first quarter and $14,000 for the second quarter). Therefore, B is required to file a return on or before August 15, 1980. Even if A and B had consented to the application of section 2513 for the second quarter, B's return is nevertheless due on or before August 15, 1980. Assuming no other gifts were made during the year, A's return reporting the second quarter split gift would be due on or before April 15, 1981.

Example (4). During the first quarter of 1980 A made taxable gifts of $20,000 to G. B, A's spouse, files a gift tax return on June 15, 1980 reporting that gift and both A and B signify their consent to the application of section 2513 on that return. In determining whether either spouse has exceeded the $25,000 amount for the remainder of 1980, the effect of section 2513 will be taken into account for the transfer by gift made in the first quarter.

(d) *Nonresident not citizens of the United States.*—In the case of a donor who is a nonresident not a citizen of the United States, paragraphs (a) and (b) of this section shall be applied by substituting "$12,500" for "$25,000" each place it appears. For rules relating to whether certain residents of possessions are considered nonresidents not citizens of the United States, see section 2501(c) and § 25.2501-1(d).

(e) *Effective date.*—This section is effective for gifts made after December 31, 1976, and before January 1, 1982. [Reg. § 25.6075-2.]

☐ [*Amended by T.D. 7012, 5-14-69, T.D. 7238, 12-28-72 and T.D. 7757, 1-16-81. Redesignated and amended by T.D. 7910, 9-6-83.*]

Extension of Time for Filing Returns

[Reg. § 1.6081-1]

§ 1.6081-1. Extension of time for filing returns.—(a) [Reserved]. For further guidance, see § 1.6081-1T(a).

(b) *Application for extension of time.*—(1) *In general.*—Under other sections in this chapter, certain taxpayers may request an automatic extension of time to file certain returns. Except in undue hardship cases, no extension of time to file a return will be allowed under this section until an automatic extension of time to file the return has been allowed under the applicable section. No extension of time to file a return will

be granted under this section for a period of time greater than that provided for by automatic extension. A taxpayer desiring an extension of the time for filing a return, statement, or other document shall submit an application for extension on or before the due date of such return, statement, or other document. If a form exists for the application for an extension, the taxpayer should use the form; however, taxpayers may apply for an extension in a letter that includes the information required by this paragraph. Except as provided in § 301.6091-1(b) of this chapter (relating to hand-carried documents), the taxpayer should make the application for extension to the Internal Revenue Service office where such return, statement, or other document is required to be filed. Except for requests for automatic extensions of time to file certain returns provided for elsewhere in this chapter, the application must be in writing, signed by the taxpayer or his duly authorized agent, and must clearly set forth—

(i) The particular tax return, information return, statement, or other document, including the taxable year or period thereof, for which the taxpayer requests an extension; and

(ii) An explanation of the reasons for requesting the extension to aid the internal revenue officer in determining whether to grant the request.

(2) *Taxpayer unable to sign.*—In any case in which a taxpayer is unable, by reason of illness, absence, or other good cause, to sign a request for an extension, any person standing in close personal or business relationship to the taxpayer may sign the request on his behalf, and shall be considered as a duly authorized agent for this purpose, provided the request sets forth the reasons for a signature other than the taxpayer's and the relationship existing between the taxpayer and the signer.

(c) *Effective/applicability dates.*—This section applies to requests for extension of time filed after July 1, 2008. [Reg. § 1.6081-1.]

☐ [*T.D.* 6364, 2-13-59. *Amended by T.D.* 6371, 4-6-59; *T.D.* 6436, 12-30-59; *T.D.* 6581, 12-5-61; *T.D.* 6950, 4-3-68; *T.D.* 7133, 7-21-71; *T.D.* 7160, 2-1-72; *T.D.* 7260, 2-9-73; *T.D.* 7533, 2-14-78; *T.D.* 7651, 10-25-79; *T.D.* 8241, 2-22-89; *T.D.* 9163, 12-6-2004, *T.D.* 9407, 6-30-2008 *and T.D.* 9821, 7-18-2017.]

[Reg. § 1.6081-1T]

§ 1.6081-1T. Extension of time for filing returns (temporary).—(a) *In general.*—The Commissioner is authorized to grant a reasonable extension of time for filing any return, declaration, statement, or other document that relates to any tax imposed by subtitle A of the Code and that is required under the provisions of subtitle A or F of the Code or the regulations thereunder. However, other than in the case of taxpayers who are abroad or as specified in section 6081(b), such extensions of time shall not be granted for more than six months, and the extension of time for filing the return of a DISC (as defined in section 992(a)), as specified in section 6072(b), shall not be granted. Except in the case of an extension of time pursuant to § 1.6081-5, an extension of time for filing an income tax return shall not operate to extend the time for the payment of the tax unless specified to the contrary in the extension. For rules relating to extensions of time for paying tax, see § 1.6161-1.

(b) [Reserved]. For further guidance, see § 1.6081-1(b).

(c) *Applicability date.*—This section applies to requests for extension of time to file returns on or after July 20, 2017. Section 1.6081-1 (as con-

tained in 26 CFR part 1, revised April 2017) applies to requests for extension of time to file returns before July 20, 2017.

(d) *Expiration date.*—The applicability of this section will expire on or before July 17, 2020. [Temporary Reg. § 1.6081-1T.]

☐ *T.D.* 9821, 7-18-2017.]

[Reg. § 20.6081-1]

§ 20.6081-1. Extension of time for filing the return.—(a) *Procedures for requesting an extension of time for filing the return.*—A request for an extension of time to file the return required by section 6018 must be made by filing Form 4768, "Application for Extension of Time To File a Return and/or Pay U. S. Estate (and Generation-Skipping Transfer) Taxes." Form 4768 must be filed with the Internal Revenue Service office designated in the application's instructions (except as provided in § 301.6091-1(b) of this chapter for hand-carried documents). Form 4768 must include an estimate of the amounts of estate and generation-skipping transfer tax liabilities with respect to the estate.

(b) *Automatic extension.*—An estate will be allowed an automatic 6-month extension of time beyond the date prescribed in section 6075(a) to file Form 706, "United States Estate (and Generation-Skipping Transfer) Tax Return," if Form 4768 is filed on or before the due date for filing Form 706 and in accordance with the procedures under paragraph (a) of this section.

(c) *Extension for good cause shown.*—In its discretion, the Internal Revenue Service may, upon the showing of good and sufficient cause, grant an extension of time to file the return required by section 6018 in certain situations. Such an extension may be granted to an estate that did not request an automatic extension of time to file Form 706 prior to the due date under paragraph (b) of this section, to an estate or person that is required to file forms other than Form 706, or to an executor who is abroad and is requesting an additional extension of time to file Form 706 beyond the 6-month automatic extension. Unless the executor is abroad, the extension of time may not be for more than 6 months beyond the filing date prescribed in section 6075(a). To obtain such an extension, Form 4768 must be filed in accordance with the procedures under paragraph (a) of this section and must contain a detailed explanation of why it is impossible or impractical to file a reasonably complete return by the due date. Form 4768 should be filed sufficiently early to permit the Internal Revenue Service time to consider the matter and reply before what otherwise would be the due date of the return. Failure to file Form 4768 before that due date may indicate negligence and constitute sufficient cause for denial of the extension. If an estate did not request an automatic extension of time to file Form 706 under paragraph (b) of this section, Form 4768 must also contain an explanation showing good cause for not requesting the automatic extension.

(d) *Filing the return.*—A return as complete as possible must be filed before the expiration of the extension period. The return thus filed will be the return required by section 6018(a), and any tax shown on the return will be the amount determined by the executor as the tax referred to in section 6161(a)(2), or the amount shown as the tax by the taxpayer upon the taxpayer's return referred to in section 6211(a)(1)(A). The return cannot be amended after the expiration of the extension period although supplemental information may subsequently be filed that may result in a finally determined tax different from the amount shown as the tax on the return.

(e) *Payment of the tax.*—An extension of time for filing a return does not operate to extend the time for payment of the tax. See § 20.6151-1 for the time for payment of the tax, and §§ 20.6161-1 and 20.6163-1 for extensions of time for payment of the tax. If an extension of time to file a return is obtained, but no extension of time for payment of the tax is granted, interest will be due on the tax not paid by the due date and the estate will be subject to all applicable late payment penalties.

(f) *Effective date.*—This section applies to estates of decedents dying after August 16, 1954, except for paragraph (b) of this section which applies to estate tax returns due after July 25, 2001. [Reg. § 20.6081-1.]

☐ [*T.D. 6296, 6-23-58. Amended by T.D. 6711, 3-23-64; T.D. 7238, 12-28-72; T.D. 7710, 7-28-80 and T.D. 8957, 7-24-2001.*]

[Reg. § 25.6081-1]

§ 25.6081-1. Automatic extension of time for filing gift tax returns.—(a) *In general.*—Under section 6075(b)(2), an automatic six-month extension of time granted to a donor to file the donor's return of income under § 1.6081-4 of this chapter shall be deemed also to be a six-month extension of time granted to file a return on Form 709, "United States Gift (and Generation-Skipping Transfer) Tax Return." If a donor does not obtain an extension of time to file the donor's return of income under § 1.6081-4 of this chapter, the donor will be allowed an automatic 6-month extension of time to file Form 709 after the date prescribed for filing if the donor files an application under this section in accordance with paragraph (b) of this section. In the case of an individual described in § 1.6081-5(a)(5) or (6) of this chapter, the automatic 6-month extension of time to file Form 709 will run concurrently with the extension of time to file granted pursuant to § 1.6081-5 of this chapter.

(b) *Requirements.*—To satisfy this paragraph (b), a donor must—

(1) Submit a complete application on Form 8892, "Payment of Gift/GST Tax and/or Application for Extension of Time To File Form 709," or in any other manner prescribed by the Commissioner;

(2) File the application on or before the later of—

(i) The date prescribed for filing the return; or

(ii) The expiration of any extension of time to file granted pursuant to § 1.6081-5 of this chapter; and

(3) File the application with the Internal Revenue Service office designated in the application's instructions.

(c) *No extension of time for the payment of tax.*—An automatic extension of time for filing a return granted under paragraph (a) of this section will not extend the time for payment of any tax due on such return.

(d) *Termination of automatic extension.*—The Commissioner may terminate an extension at any time by mailing to the donor a notice of termination at least 10 days prior to the termination date designated in such notice. The Commissioner must mail the notice of termination to the address shown on the Form 8892, or to the donor's last known address. For further guidance regarding the definition of last known address, see § 301.6212-2 of this chapter.

(e) *Penalties.*—See section 6651 for failure to file a gift tax return or failure to pay the amount shown as tax on the return.

(f) *Effective/applicability dates.*—This section is applicable for applications for an extension of time to file Form 709 filed after July 1, 2008. [Reg. § 25.6081-1.]

☐ [*T.D. 9407, 6-30-2008.*]

[Reg. § 26.6081-1]

§ 26.6081-1. Automatic extension of time for filing generation-skipping transfer tax returns.—(a) *In general.*—A skip person distributee required to file a return on Form 706-GS(D), "Generation-Skipping Transfer Tax Return for Distributions," or a trustee required to file a return on Form 706-GS(T), "Generation-Skipping Transfer Tax Return for Terminations," will be allowed an automatic 6-month extension of time to file the return after the date prescribed for filing if the skip person distributee or trustee files an application under this section in accordance with paragraph (b) of this section.

(b) *Requirements.*—To satisfy this paragraph (b), a skip person distributee or trustee must—

(1) Submit a complete application on Form 7004, "Application for Automatic Extension of Time to File Certain Business Income Tax, Information, and Other Returns," or in any other manner prescribed by the Commissioner;

(2) File the application on or before the date prescribed for filing the return with the Internal Revenue Service office designated in the application's instructions; and

(3) Remit the amount of the properly estimated unpaid tax liability on or before the date prescribed for payment.

(c) *No extension of time for the payment of tax.*—An automatic extension of time for filing a return granted under paragraph (a) of this section will not extend the time for payment of any tax due on such return.

(d) *Termination of automatic extension.*—The Commissioner may terminate an automatic extension at any time by mailing to the skip person distributee or trustee a notice of termination at least 10 days prior to the termination date designated in such notice. The Commissioner must mail the notice of termination to the address shown on the Form 7004 or to the skip person distributee or trustee's last known address. For further guidance regarding the definition of last known address, see § 301.6212-2 of this chapter.

(e) *Penalties.*—See section 6651 for failure to file a generation-skipping transfer tax return or failure to pay the amount shown as tax on the return.

(f) *Effective/applicability dates.*—This section is applicable for applications for an automatic extension of time to file a generation-skipping transfer tax return filed after July 1, 2008. [Reg. § 26.6081-1.]

☐ [*T.D.* 9407, 6-30-2008.]

[Reg. § 53.6081-1]

§ 53.6081-1. Automatic extension of time for filing the return to report taxes due under section 4951 for self-dealing with a nuclear decommissioning fund.—(a) *In general.*—A "disqualified person" for purposes of section 4951(e)(4) who engaged in self-dealing with a Nuclear Decommissioning Fund, and must report tax due under section 4951 on Form 1120-ND, "Return for Nuclear Decommissioning Funds and Certain Related Persons," will be allowed an automatic 6-month extension of time to file the return after the date prescribed for filing the return if the disqualified person files an application under this section in accordance with paragraph (b) of this section. For guidance on requesting an extension of time to file Form 1120-ND for purposes of reporting contributions received, income earned, administrative expenses of operating the fund, and the tax on modified gross income, see § 1.6081-3 of this chapter.

(b) *Requirements.*—To satisfy this paragraph (b), a disqualified person must—

(1) Submit a complete application on Form 7004, "Application for Automatic Extension of Time to File Certain Business Income Tax, Information, and Other Returns," or in any other manner prescribed by the Commissioner;

(2) File the application on or before the date prescribed for filing the return with the Internal Revenue Service office designated in the application's instructions; and

(3) Remit the amount of the properly estimated unpaid tax liability on or before the date prescribed for payment.

(c) *No extension of time for the payment of tax.*— An automatic extension of time for filing a return granted under paragraph (a) of this section will not extend the time for payment of any tax due on such return.

(d) *Termination of automatic extension.*—The Commissioner may terminate an automatic extension at any time by mailing to the disqualified person a notice of termination at least 10 days prior to the termination date designated in such notice. The Commissioner must mail the notice of termination to the address shown on the Form 7004 or to the disqualified person's last known address. For further guidance regarding the definition of last known address, see § 301.6212-2 of this chapter.

(e) *Penalties.*—See section 6651 for failure to file or failure to pay the amount shown as tax on the return.

(f) *Effective/applicability dates.*—This section is applicable for applications for an automatic extension of time to file a return to report taxes due under section 4951 for self-dealing with a Nuclear Decommissioning Fund filed after July 1, 2008. [Reg. § 53.6081-1.]

☐ [*T.D.* 9407, 6-30-2008.]

[Reg. § 54.6081-1]

§ 54.6081-1. Automatic extension of time for filing returns for certain excise taxes under Chapter 43.—(a) *In general.*—An employer, other person or health plan that is required to file a return on Form 8928, "Return of Certain Excise Taxes Under Chapter 43 of the Internal Revenue Code," will be allowed an automatic 6-month extension of time to file the return after the date prescribed for filing the return if the employer, other person or health plan files an application under this section in accordance with paragraph (b) of this section.

(b) *Requirements.*—To satisfy this paragraph (b), an employer, other person or health plan must—

(1) Submit a complete application on Form 7004, "Application for Automatic Extension of Time To File Certain Business Income Tax, Information, and Other Returns," or in any other manner prescribed by the Commissioner;

(2) File the application on or before the date prescribed for filing the return with the Internal Revenue Service office designated in the application's instructions; and

(3) Remit the amount of the properly estimated unpaid tax liability on or before the date prescribed for payment.

(c) *No extension of time for the payment of tax.*— An automatic extension of time for filing a return granted under paragraph (a) of this section will not extend the time for payment of any tax due on such return.

(d) *Termination of automatic extension.*—The Commissioner may terminate an automatic extension at any time by mailing to the employer, other person, or health plan a notice of termination at least 10 days prior to the termination date designated in such notice. The Commissioner must mail the notice of termination to the address shown on the Form 7004 or to the estate or trust's last known address. For further guidance regarding the definition of last known address, see § 301.6212-2 of this chapter.

(e) *Penalties.—See* section 6651 for failure to file a pension excise tax return or failure to pay the amount shown as tax on the return.

(f) *Effective/applicability date.—*This section is applicable for applications for an automatic extension of time to file a return due under chapter 43, filed on or after June 24, 2011. [Reg. § 54.6081-1.]

☐ [*T.D.* 9531, 6-23-2011.]

[Reg. § 55.6081-1]

§ 55.6081-1. Automatic extension of time for filing a return due under Chapter 44.—(a) *In general.—*A Real Estate Investment Trust (REIT) required to file a return on Form 8612, "Return of Excise Tax on Undistributed Income of Real Estate Investment Trusts," or a Regulated Investment Company (RIC) required to file a return on Form 8613, "Return of Excise Tax on Undistributed Income of Regulated Investment Companies," will be allowed an automatic 6-month extension of time to file the return after the date prescribed for filing the return if the REIT or RIC files an application under this section in accordance with paragraph (b) of this section.

(b) *Requirements.—*To satisfy this paragraph (b), a REIT or RIC must—

(1) Submit a complete application on Form 7004, "Application for Automatic Extension of Time to File Certain Business Income Tax, Information, and Other Returns," or in any other manner prescribed by the Commissioner;

(2) File the application on or before the date prescribed for filing the return with the Internal Revenue Service office designated in the application's instructions; and

(3) Remit the amount of the properly estimated unpaid tax liability on or before the date prescribed for payment.

(c) *No extension of time for the payment of tax.—* An automatic extension of time for filing a return granted under paragraph (a) of this section will not extend the time for payment of any tax due on such return.

(d) *Termination of automatic extension.—*The Commissioner may terminate an automatic extension at any time by mailing to the REIT or RIC a notice of termination at least 10 days prior to the termination date designated in such notice. The Commissioner must mail the notice of termination to the address shown on the Form 7004 or to the REIT or RIC's last known address. For further guidance regarding the definition of last known address, see § 301.6212-2 of this chapter.

(e) *Penalties.—*See section 6651 for failure to file or failure to pay the amount shown as tax on the return.

(f) *Effective/applicable dates.—*This section is applicable for applications for an automatic extension of time to file a return due under chapter 44, filed after July 1, 2008. [Reg. § 55.6081-1.]

☐ [*T.D.* 9407, 6-30-2008.]

[Reg. § 156.6081-1]

§ 156.6081-1. Automatic extension of time for filing a return due under chapter 54.—(a) *In general.—*A taxpayer required to file a return on Form 8725, "Excise Tax on Greenmail," will be allowed an automatic 6-month extension of time to file the return after the date prescribed for filing the return if the taxpayer files an application under this section in accordance with paragraph (b) of this section.

(b) *Requirements.—*To satisfy this paragraph (b), a taxpayer must—

(1) Submit a complete application on Form 7004, "Application for Automatic Extension of Time to File Certain Business Income Tax, Information, and Other Returns," or in any other manner prescribed by the Commissioner;

(2) File the application on or before the date prescribed for filing the return with the Internal Revenue Service office designated in the application's instructions; and

(3) Remit the amount of the properly estimated unpaid tax liability on or before the date prescribed for payment.

(c) *No extension of time for the payment of tax.—* An automatic extension of time for filing a return granted under paragraph (a) of this section will not extend the time for payment of any tax due on such return.

(d) *Termination of automatic extension.—*The Commissioner may terminate an automatic extension at any time by mailing to the taxpayer a notice of termination at least 10 days prior to the termination date designated in such notice. The Commissioner must mail the notice of termination to the address shown on the Form 7004 or to the taxpayer's last known address. For further guidance regarding the definition of last known address, see § 301.6212-2 of this chapter.

(e) *Penalties.—*See section 6651 for failure to file or failure to pay the amount shown as tax on the return.

(f) *Effective/applicable dates.—*This section is applicable for applications for an automatic extension of time to file a return due under chapter 54, filed after July 1, 2008. [Reg. § 156.6081-1.]

☐ [*T.D.* 9407, 6-30-2008.]

[Reg. § 157.6081-1]

§ 157.6081-1. Automatic extension of time for filing a return due under chapter 55.—(a) *In general.—*A taxpayer required to file a return on Form 8876, "Excise Tax on Structured Settlement Factoring Transactions," will be allowed an automatic 6-month extension of time to file the return after the date prescribed for filing the return if the taxpayer files an application under this section in accordance with paragraph (b) of this section.

(b) *Requirements.*—To satisfy this paragraph (b), the taxpayer must—

(1) Submit a complete application on Form 7004, "Application for Automatic Extension of Time to File Certain Business Income Tax, Information, and Other Returns," or in any other manner prescribed by the Commissioner;

(2) File the application on or before the date prescribed for filing the return with the Internal Revenue Service office designated in the application's instructions; and

(3) Remit the amount of the properly estimated unpaid tax liability on or before the date prescribed for payment.

(c) *No extension of time for the payment of tax.*— An automatic extension of time for filing a return granted under paragraph (a) of this section will not extend the time for payment of any tax due on such return.

(d) *Termination of automatic extension.*—The Commissioner may terminate an automatic extension at any time by mailing to the taxpayer a notice of termination at least 10 days prior to the termination date designated in such notice. The Commissioner must mail the notice of termination to the address shown on the Form 7004 or to the taxpayer's last known address. For further guidance regarding the definition of last known address, see § 301.6212-2 of this chapter.

(e) *Penalties.*—See section 6651 for failure to file or failure to pay the amount shown as tax on the return.

(f) *Effective/applicability dates.*—This section is applicable for applications for an automatic extension of time to file a return due under chapter 55, filed after July 1, 2008. [Reg. § 157.6081-1.]

☐ [*T.D. 9407, 6-30-2008.*]

[Reg. § 301.6081-1]

§ 301.6081-1. Extension of time for filing returns.—For provisions concerning extensions of time for filing returns or other documents, see the regulations relating to the particular tax. [Reg. § 301.6081-1.]

☐ [*T.D. 6498, 10-24-60.*]

[Reg. § 1.6081-2]

§ 1.6081-2. Automatic extension of time to file certain returns filed by partnerships.— (a) *In general.*—(1) [Reserved]. For further guidance, see § 1.6081-2T(a)(1).

(2) An electing large partnership (ELP) required to file Form 1065-B, "U.S. Return of Income for Electing Large Partnerships," for any taxable year will be allowed an automatic 6-month extension of time to file the return after the date prescribed for filing the return if the partnership files an application under this section in accordance with paragraph (b) of this section.

(b) *Requirements.*—To satisfy this paragraph (b), the partnership must—

(1) Submit a complete application on Form 7004, "Application for Automatic Extension of Time to File Certain Business Income Tax, Information, and Other Returns," or in any other manner prescribed by the Commissioner;

(2) File the application on or before the later of—

(i) The date prescribed for filing the return of the partnership; or

(ii) The expiration of any extension of time to file granted under § 1.6081-5(a); and

(3) File the application with the Internal Revenue Service office designated in the application's instructions.

(c) *Payment of section 7519 amount.*—An automatic extension of time for filing a partnership return of income granted under paragraph (a) of this section does not extend the time for payment of any amount due under section 7519, relating to required payments for entities electing not to have a required taxable year.

(d) *Section 444 election.*—An automatic extension of time for filing a partnership return of income will run concurrently with any extension of time for filing a return allowed because of section 444, relating to the election of a taxable year other than a required taxable year.

(e) *Effect of extension on partner.*—An automatic extension of time for filing a partnership return of income under this section does not extend the time for filing a partner's income tax return or the time for the payment of any tax due on a partner's income tax return.

(f) *Termination of automatic extension.*—The Commissioner may terminate an automatic extension at any time by mailing to the partnership a notice of termination at least 10 days prior to the termination date designated in such notice. The Commissioner must mail the notice of termination to the address shown on the Form 7004 or to the partnership's last known address. For further guidance regarding the definition of last known address, see § 301.6212-2 of this chapter.

(g) *Penalties.*—See section 6698 for failure to file a partnership return.

(h) *Effective/applicability dates.*—This section applies to applications for an automatic extension of time to file the partnership returns listed in paragraph (a) of this section filed on or after June 24, 2011. [Reg. § 1.6081-2.]

☐ [*T.D. 9531, 6-23-2011. Amended by T.D. 9821, 7-18-2017.*]

[Reg. § 1.6081-2T]

§ 1.6081-2T. Automatic extension of time to file certain returns filed by partnerships (temporary).—(a) *In general.*—(1) A partnership required to file Form 1065, "U.S. Partnership Return of Income," or Form 8804, "Annual Return for Partnership Withholding Tax," for any taxable year will be allowed an automatic six-month extension of time to file the return after the date prescribed for filing the return if the partnership files an application under this section in accordance with paragraph (b) of this section. No additional extension will be allowed pursuant to § 1.6081-1(b) beyond the automatic six-month extension provided by this section. In the case of a partnership described in § 1.6081-5(a)(1), the automatic extension of time to file allowed under this section runs concurrently with an extension of time to file granted pursuant to § 1.6081-5.

(2) [Reserved]. For further guidance, see § 1.6081-2(a)(2).

(b) through (g) [Reserved]. For further guidance, see § 1.6081-2(b) through (g).

(h) *Applicability date.*—This section applies to applications for an automatic extension of time to file the partnership returns listed in paragraph (a) of this section on or after July 20, 2017. Section 1.6081-2 (as contained in 26 CFR part 1, revised April 2017) applies to applications for an automatic extension of time to file before July 20, 2017.

(i) *Expiration date.*—The applicability of this section will expire on or before July 17, 2020. [Temporary Reg. § 1.6081-2T.]

□ *T.D. 9821, 7-18-2017.*]

[Reg. § 301.6081-2]

§ 301.6081-2. Automatic extension of time for filing an information return with respect to certain foreign trusts.—(a) *In general.*—A trust required to file a return on Form 3520-A, "Annual Information Return of Foreign Trust with a U.S. Owner," will be allowed an automatic 6-month extension of time to file the return after the date prescribed for filing the return if the trust files an application under this section in accordance with paragraph (b) of this section.

(b) *Requirements.*—To satisfy this paragraph (b), a trust must—

(1) Submit a complete application on Form 7004, "Application for Automatic Extension of Time to File Certain Business Income Tax, Information, and Other Returns," or in any other manner prescribed by the Commissioner; and

(2) File the application on or before the date prescribed for filing the return with the Internal Revenue Service office designated in the application's instructions.

(c) *Termination of automatic extension.*—The Commissioner may terminate an automatic extension at any time by mailing to the trust a notice of termination at least 10 days prior to the termination date designated in such notice. The Commissioner must mail the notice of termination to the address shown on the Form 7004 or to the trust's last known address. For further guidance regarding the definition of last known address, see § 301.6212-2 of this chapter.

(d) *Penalties.*—See section 6677 for failure to file information returns with respect to certain foreign trusts.

(e) *Effective/applicability dates.*—This section is applicable for applications for an automatic extension of time to file an information return with respect to certain foreign trusts listed in paragraph (a) of this section filed after July 1, 2008. [Reg. § 301.6081-2.]

□ [T.D. 9407, 6-30-2008.]

[Reg. § 1.6081-3]

§ 1.6081-3. Automatic extension of time for filing corporation income tax returns.—(a) introductory text [Reserved]. For further guidance, see § 1.6081-3T(a) introductory text.

(1) An application must be submitted on Form 7004, "Application for Automatic Extension of Time to File Certain Business Income Tax, Information, and Other Returns," or in any other manner prescribed by the Commissioner.

(2) The application must be filed on or before the date prescribed for the filing of the return of the corporation (or the consolidated return of the affiliated group of corporations) with the Internal Revenue Service office designated in the application's instructions.

(3) The corporation (or affiliated group of corporations filing a consolidated return) must remit the amount of the properly estimated unpaid tax liability on or before the date prescribed for payment.

(4) The application must include a statement listing the name and address of each member of the affiliated group if the affiliated group will file a consolidated return. Upon the timely filing of Form 7004, the 6-month extension of time to file shall be considered as granted to the affiliated group for the filing of its consolidated return or for the filing of each member's separate return.

(b) *No extension of time for the payment of tax.*—Any automatic extension of time for filing a corporation income tax return granted under paragraph (a) of this section shall not operate to extend the time for payment of any tax due on such return.

(c) *Termination of automatic extension.*—The Commissioner may terminate an automatic extension at any time by mailing a notice of termination to the corporation (parent corporation in the case of an affiliated group of corporations filing a consolidated return). The notice shall be mailed at least 10 days prior to the termination date designated in such notice. The notice of termination shall be sufficient for all purposes when mailed to the corporation at the address shown on Form 7004 or to the corporation's last known address. For further guidance regarding the definition of last known address, see § 301.6212-2 of this chapter.

(d) *No extension for DISCs.*—Paragraphs (a) through (c) of this section shall not apply to returns filed by a DISC pursuant to section 6011(c)(2).

(e) [Reserved]. For further guidance, see § 1.6081-3T(e).

(f) [Reserved]. For further guidance, see § 1.6081-3T(f).

(g) *Applicability dates.*—This section applies to requests for extension of time to file corporation income tax returns filed after July 1, 2008. [Reg. § 1.6081-3.]

☐ [*T.D. 6364, 2-13-59. Amended by T.D. 6914, 3-7-67; T.D. 6950, 4-3-68; T.D. 7138, 8-10-71; T.D. 7260, 2-9-73; T.D. 7533, 2-14-78; T.D. 7567, 10-2-78, T.D. 7885, 4-13-83; T.D. 8939, 1-11-2001; T.D. 9163, 12-6-2004; T.D. 9229, 11-4-2005, T.D. 9407, 6-30-2008 and T.D. 9821, 7-18-2017.*]

[Reg. § 1.6081-3T]

§ 1.6081-3T. Automatic extension of time for filing corporation income tax returns (temporary).—(a) *In general.*—Except as provided in paragraphs (e) and (f) of this section, a corporation or an affiliated group of corporations filing a consolidated return will be allowed an automatic 6-month extension of time to file its income tax return after the date prescribed for filing the return if the following requirements are met.

(1) through (4) [Reserved]. For further guidance, see § 1.6081-3(a)(1) through (4).

(b) through (d) [Reserved]. For further guidance, see § 1.6081-3(b) through (d).

(e) *Exception.*—In the case of any return for a taxable year of a C corporation that ends on June 30 and begins before January 1, 2026, the first sentence of paragraph (a) of this section shall be applied by substituting "7-month" for "6-month." For purposes of this paragraph (e), the return for a short period (within the meaning of section 443) that ends on any day in June shall be treated as the return for a taxable year that ends on June 30.

(f) *Cross reference.*—For provisions relating to extensions of time to file Form 1120-POL, "U.S. Income Tax Return for Certain Political Organizations," see § 1.6081-9.

(g) *Applicability date.*—This section applies to requests for extension of time to file corporation income tax returns on or after July 20, 2017. Section 1.6081-3 (as contained in 26 CFR part 1, revised April 2017) applies to applications for an automatic extension of time to file before July 20, 2017.

(h) *Expiration date.*—The applicability of this section will expire on or before July 17, 2020. [Temporary Reg. § 1.6081-3T.]

☐ *T.D. 9821, 7-18-2017.*]

[Reg. § 1.6081-4]

§ 1.6081-4. Automatic extension of time for filing individual income tax return.—(a) *In general.*—An individual who is required to file an individual income tax return will be allowed an automatic 6-month extension of time to file the return after the date prescribed for filing the return if the individual files an application under this section in accordance with paragraph (b) of this section. In the case of an individual described in § 1.6081-5(a)(5) or (6), the automatic 6-month extension will run concurrently with the extension of time to file granted pursuant to § 1.6081-5.

(b) *Requirements.*—To satisfy this paragraph (b), an individual must—

(1) Submit a complete application on Form 4868, "Application for Automatic Extension of Time To File U.S Individual Income Tax Return," or in any other manner prescribed by the Commissioner;

(2) File the application on or before the later of—

(i) The date prescribed for filing the return; or

(ii) The expiration of any extension of time to file granted pursuant to § 1.6081-5;

(3) File the application with the Internal Revenue Service office designated in the application's instructions; and

(4) Show the full amount properly estimated as tax for the taxable year.

(c) *No extension of time for the payment of tax.*—An automatic extension of time for filing a return granted under paragraph (a) of this section will not extend the time for payment of any tax due on such return.

(d) *Termination of automatic extension.*—The Commissioner may terminate an automatic extension at any time by mailing to the individual a notice of termination at least 10 days prior to the termination date designated in such notice. The Commissioner must mail the notice of termination to the address shown on the Form 4868 or to the individual's last known address. For further guidance regarding the definition of last known address, see § 301.6212-2 of this chapter.

(e) *Penalties.*—See section 6651 for failure to file an individual income tax return or failure to pay the amount shown as tax on the return. In particular, see § 301.6651-1(c)(3) of this chapter (relating to a presumption of reasonable cause in certain circumstances involving an automatic extension of time for filing an individual income tax return).

(f) *Effective/applicability dates.*—This section is applicable for applications for an automatic extension of time to file an individual income tax return filed after July 1, 2008. [Reg. § 1.6081-4.]

☐ [*T.D. 9407, 6-30-2008.*]

[Reg. § 1.6081-5]

§ 1.6081-5. Extensions of time in the case of certain partnerships, corporations and U.S. citizens and residents.—(a) An extension of time for filing returns of income and for paying any tax shown on the return is hereby granted to and including the fifteenth day of the sixth month following the close of the taxable year in the case of—

(1) [Reserved]. For further guidance, see § 1.6081-5T(a)(1);

(2) Domestic corporations which transact their business and keep their records and books of account outside the United States and Puerto Rico;

(3) Foreign corporations which maintain an office or place of business within the United States;

Reg. § 1.6081-5(a)(3)

(4) Domestic corporations whose principal income is from sources within the possessions of the United States;

(5) United States citizens or residents whose tax homes and abodes, in a real and substantial sense, are outside the United States and Puerto Rico; and

(6) United States citizens and residents in military or naval service on duty, including non-permanent or short term duty, outside the United States and Puerto Rico.

(b) In order to qualify for the extension under this section—

(1) A statement must be attached to the return showing that the person for whom the return is made is a person described in paragraph (a) of this section; or

(2) If a person described in paragraph (a) of this section requests additional time to file, the person must request the extension on or before the fifteenth day of the sixth month following the close of the taxable year and check the appropriate box on Form 4868, "Application for Automatic Extension of Time To File a U.S. Individual Income Tax Return," or Form 7004, "Application for Automatic Extension of Time to File Certain Business Income Tax, Information, and Other Returns," whichever is applicable, or in any other manner prescribed by the Commissioner.

(c) For purposes of paragraph (a)(5) of this section, whether a person is a United States resident will be determined in accordance with section 7701(b) of the Code. The term "tax home," as used in paragraph (a)(5), will have the same meaning which it has for purposes of section 162(a)(2) (relating to travel expenses away from home). If a person does not have a regular or principal place of business, that person's tax home will be considered to be his regular place of abode in a real and substantial sense.

(d) In order to qualify for the extension under paragraph (a)(6), the assigned tour of duty outside the United States and Puerto Rico must be for a period that includes the entire due date of the return.

(e) A person otherwise qualifying for the extension under paragraph (a)(5) or paragraph (a)(6) shall not be disqualified because he is physically present in the United States or Puerto Rico at any time, including the due date of the return.

(f) *Effective/applicability date.*—This section is applicable for returns of income due after July 1, 2008. [Reg. § 1.6081-5.]

□ [*T.D.* 8312, 9-7-90. *Amended by T.D.* 9163, 12-6-2004; *T.D.* 9229, 11-4-2005, *T.D.* 9407, 6-30-2008 *and T.D.* 9821, 7-18-2017.]

[Reg. § 1.6081-5T]

§ 1.6081-5T. Extensions of time in the case of certain partnerships, corporations and U.S. citi-zens and residents (temporary).—
(a) introductory text [Reserved]. For further guidance, see § 1.6081-5(a) introductory text.

(1) Partnerships, which are required under section 6072(b) to file returns on the fifteenth day of the third month following the close of the taxable year of the partnership, that keep their records and books of account outside the United States and Puerto Rico;

(2) through (6) [Reserved]. For further guidance, see § 1.6081-5(a)(2) through (6).

(b) through (e) [Reserved]. For further guidance, see § 1.6081-5(b) through (e).

(f) This section applies to returns filed on or after July 20, 2017. Section 1.6081-5 (as contained in 26 CFR part 1, revised April 2017) applies to applications for an automatic extension of time to file returns before July 20, 2017.

(g) The applicability of this section will expire on or before July 17, 2020. [Temporary Reg. § 1.6081-5T.]

□ *T.D.* 9821, 7-18-2017.]

[Reg. § 1.6081-6]

§ 1.6081-6. Automatic extension of time to file estate or trust income tax return.—(a) *In general.*—(1) [Reserved]. For further guidance, see § 1.6081-6T(a)(1).

(2) A bankruptcy estate that is created when an individual debtor files a petition under either chapter 7 or chapter 11 of Title 11 of the U.S. Code that is required to file an income tax return on Form 1041, "U.S. Income Tax Return for Estates and Trusts," and an estate or trust required to file an income tax return on Form 1041-N, "U.S. Income Tax Return for Electing Alaska Native Settlement," or Form 1041-QFT, "U.S. Income Tax Return for Qualified Funeral Trusts" for any taxable year will be allowed an automatic 6-month extension of time to file the return after the date prescribed for filing the return if the estate files an application under this section in accordance with paragraph (b) of this section.

(b) *Requirements.*—To satisfy this paragraph (b), an estate or trust must—

(1) Submit a complete application on Form 7004, "Application for Automatic Extension of Time to File Certain Business Income Tax, Information, and Other Returns," or in any other manner prescribed by the Commissioner;

(2) File the application on or before the date prescribed for filing the return with the Internal Revenue Service office designated in the application's instructions; and

(3) Show the amount properly estimated as tax for the estate or trust for the taxable year.

(c) *No extension of time for the payment of tax.*—An automatic extension of time for filing a return granted under paragraph (a) of this section will not extend the time for payment of any tax due on such return.

(d) *Effect of extension on beneficiary.*—An automatic extension of time to file an estate or trust income tax return under this section will not extend the time for filing the income tax return of a beneficiary of the estate or trust or the time for the payment of any tax due on the beneficiary's income tax return.

(e) *Termination of automatic extension.*—The Commissioner may terminate an automatic extension at any time by mailing to the estate or trust a notice of termination at least 10 days prior to the termination date designated in such notice. The Commissioner must mail the notice of termination to the address shown on the Form 7004 or to the estate or trust's last known address. For further guidance regarding the definition of last known address, see § 301.6212-2 of this chapter.

(f) *Penalties.*—*See* section 6651 for failure to file an estate or trust income tax return or failure to pay the amount shown as tax on the return.

(g) *Effective/applicability dates.*—This section applies to applications for an automatic extension of time to file an estate or trust income tax return filed on or after June 24, 2011. [Reg. § 1.6081-6.]

☐ [*T.D. 9531, 6-23-2011. Amended by T.D. 9821, 7-18-2017.*]

[Reg. § 1.6081-6T]

§ 1.6081-6T. Automatic extension of time to file estate or trust income tax return (temporary).—(a) *In general.*—(1) Except as provided in paragraph (a)(2) of this section, any estate, including but not limited to an estate defined in section 2031, or trust required to file an income tax return on Form 1041, "U.S. Income Tax Return for Estates and Trusts," will be allowed an automatic five and one-half month extension of time to file the return after the date prescribed for filing the return if the estate or trust files an application under this section in accordance with paragraph (b) of this section. No additional extension will be allowed pursuant to § 1.6081-1(b) beyond the automatic five and one-half month extension provided by this section.

(2) [Reserved]. For further guidance, see § 1.6081-6(a)(2).

(b) through (f) [Reserved]. For further guidance, see § 1.6081-6(b) through (f).

(g) *Applicability date.*—This section applies to applications for an automatic extension of time to file an estate or trust income tax return on or after July 20, 2017. Section 1.6081-6 (as contained in 26 CFR part 1, revised April 2017) applies to applications for an automatic extension of time to file a return before July 20, 2017.

(h) *Expiration date.*—The applicability of this section will expire on or before July 17, 2020. [Temporary Reg. § 1.6081-6T.]

☐ *T.D. 9821, 7-18-2017.]*

[Reg. § 1.6081-7]

§ 1.6081-7. Automatic extension of time to file Real Estate Mortgage Investment Conduit (REMIC) income tax return.—(a) *In general.*—A Real Estate Mortgage Investment Conduit (REMIC) required to file an income tax return on Form 1066, "U.S. Real Estate Mortgage Investment Conduit Income Tax Return," or Form 8831, "Excise Tax on Excess Inclusions of REMIC Residual Interests," for any taxable year will be allowed an automatic 6-month extension of time to file the return after the date prescribed for filing the return if the REMIC files an application under this section in accordance with paragraph (b) of this section.

(b) *Requirements.*—To satisfy this paragraph (b), a REMIC must—

(1) Submit a complete application on Form 7004, "Application for Automatic Extension of Time to File Certain Business Income Tax, Information, and Other Returns," or in any other manner prescribed by the Commissioner;

(2) File the application on or before the date prescribed for filing the return with the Internal Revenue Service office designated in the application's instructions; and

(3) Show the full amount properly estimated as tax for the REMIC for the taxable year.

(c) *No extension of time for the payment of tax.*—An automatic extension of time for filing a return granted under paragraph (a) of this section will not extend the time for payment of any tax due on such return.

(d) *Effect of extension on residual or regular interest holders.*—An automatic extension of time to file a REMIC income tax return under this section will not extend the time for filing the income tax return of a residual or regular interest holder of the REMIC or the time for the payment of any tax due on the residual or regular interest holder's income tax return. An automatic extension will also not extend the time for payment of any excise tax on excess inclusions of REMIC residual interests.

(e) *Termination of automatic extension.*—The Commissioner may terminate an automatic extension at any time by mailing to the REMIC a notice of termination at least 10 days prior to the termination date designated in such notice. The Commissioner must mail the notice of termination to the address shown on the Form 7004 or to the REMIC's last known address. For further guidance regarding the definition of last known address, see § 301.6212-2 of this chapter.

(f) *Penalties.*—See sections 6698 and 6651 for failure to file a REMIC income tax return or failure to pay an amount shown as tax on the return.

(g) *Effective/applicability dates.*—This section applies to applications for an automatic extension of time to file REMIC income and excise tax returns listed in paragraph (a) of this section filed after July 1, 2008. [Reg. § 1.6081-7.]

☐ [*T.D. 9407, 6-30-2008.]*

≫→ *Caution: Reg. §1.6081-8, below, as amended by T.D. 9838, applies to requests for extensions of time to file information returns required to be filed after December 31, 2018.*

[Reg. §1.6081-8]

§1.6081-8. Extension of time to file certain information returns.—(a) *Certain information returns eligible for an automatic extension of time to file.*—(1) *Automatic extension of time to file.*—A person required to file an information return (the filer) on the forms or form series listed in Table 1 will be allowed one automatic 30-day extension of time to file the information return beyond the due date for filing, if the filer or the person transmitting the information return for the filer (the transmitter) files an application in accordance with paragraph (c)(1) of this section.

Table 1 to paragraph (a)(1)

Form or Form Series	Name of Form
Form W-2G	"Certain Gambling Winnings"
Form 1042-S	"Foreign Person's U.S. Source Income Subject to Withholding"
Form 1094-C	"Transmittal of Employer-Provided Health Insurance Offer and Coverage Information Returns"
Form 1095-B	"Health Coverage"
Form 1095-C	"Employer-Provided Health Insurance Offer and Coverage"
Form 3921	"Exercise of an Incentive Stock Option Under Section 422(b)"
Form 3922	"Transfer of Stock Acquired Through an Employee Stock Purchase Plan Under Section 423(c)"
Form 8027	"Employer's Annual Information Return of Tip Income and Allocated Tips"
Form 1097 series	
Form 1098 series	
Form 1099 series (except forms reporting nonemployee compensation)	
Form 5498 series	

(2) *Non-automatic extension of time to file.*—One additional 30-day extension of time to file an information return on a form listed in paragraph (a)(1) of this section may be allowed if the filer or transmitter submits a request for the additional extension of time to file before the expiration of the automatic 30-day extension of time to file. No extension of time to file will be granted under this paragraph (a)(2) unless the filer or transmitter has first obtained an automatic extension of time to file under paragraph (a)(1) of this section. To request the additional 30-day extension of time to file, the filer or transmitter must satisfy the requirements of paragraph (c)(2) of this section. No additional extension of time to file will be allowed for an information return on a form listed in paragraph (a)(1) of this section under §1.6081-1 beyond the extensions of time to file provided by paragraph (a)(1) of this section and this paragraph (a)(2).

(b) *The Form W-2 series (except Form W-2G) or forms reporting nonemployee compensation.*—Except as provided in paragraph (f) of this section, the filer or transmitter of an information return on the Form W-2 series (except Form W-2G) or a form reporting nonemployee compensation may only request one non-automatic 30-day extension of time to file the information return beyond the due date for filing it. To make such a request, the filer or transmitter must submit an application for an extension of time to file in accordance with paragraph (c)(2) of this section. No additional extension of time to file will be allowed for an information return on a form listed in this paragraph (b) under §1.6081-1 beyond the 30-day extension of time to file provided by this paragraph (b).

(c) *Requirements.*—(1) *Automatic extension of time to file.*—To satisfy this paragraph (c)(1), an application must—

(i) Be submitted on Form 8809, "Request for Extension of Time to File Information Returns," or in any other manner as may be prescribed by the Commissioner; and

(ii) Be filed with the Internal Revenue Service office designated in the application's instructions on or before the due date for filing the information return.

(2) *Non-automatic extension of time to file.*—To satisfy this paragraph (c)(2), a filer or transmitter must—

(i) Submit a complete application on Form 8809, or in any other manner prescribed by the Commissioner, indicating that at least one of the criteria set forth in the forms, instructions, or other guidance for granting an extension applies;

≫→ *Caution: Reg. §1.6081-8, below, as amended by T.D. 9838, applies to requests for extensions of time to file information returns required to be filed after December 31, 2018.*

(ii) File the application with the Internal Revenue Service in accordance with forms, instructions, or other appropriate guidance on or before the due date for filing the information return (for purposes of paragraph (a)(2) of this section, determined with regard to the extension of time to file under paragraph (a)(1) of this section); and

(iii) Sign the application under penalties of perjury.

(d) *Penalties.*—See sections 6652, 6693, and 6721 through 6724 of the Code for failure to comply with information reporting requirements on information returns described in this section.

(e) *No effect on time to furnish statements.*—An extension of time to file an information return under this section does not extend the time for furnishing a statement to the person with respect to whom the information is required to be reported.

(f) *Form W-2 filed on expedited basis.*—This section does not apply to an information return on a form in the W–2 series if the procedures authorized in Rev. Proc. 96-57 (1996-2 CB 389) (or a successor revenue procedure) allow an automatic extension of time to file the information return. See § 601.601(d)(2)(ii)(*b*) of this chapter.

(g) *Applicability date.*—This section applies to requests for extensions of time to file information returns required to be filed after December 31, 2018. Section 1.6081-8T (as contained in 26 CFR part 1, revised April 1, 2018) applies to extensions of time to file information returns required to be filed before January 1, 2019. [Reg. § 1.6081-8.]

☐ [*T.D.* 9163, 12-6-2004. *Amended by T.D.* 9660, 3-5-2014, *T.D.* 9730, 8-12-2015 *and T.D.* 9838, 8-1-2018.]

≫→ *Caution: Temporary Reg. §1.6081-8T, below, was removed by T.D. 9838, but applies to extensions of time to file information returns required to be filed before January 1, 2019.*

[Reg. § 1.6081-8T]

§ 1.6081-8T. Extension of time to file certain information returns (temporary).— (a) *Information returns on Form W-2G, 1042-S, 1094-C, 1095-B, 1095-C, 1097 series, 1098 series, 1099 series, 3921, 3922, 5498 series, or 8027*

(1) *Automatic extension of time to file.*—A person required to file an information return (the filer) on Form W-2G, 1042-S, 1094-C, 1095-B, 1095-C, 1097 series, 1098 series, 1099 series, 3921, 3922, 5498 series, or 8027 will be allowed one automatic 30-day extension of time to file the information return beyond the due date for filing it if the filer or the person transmitting the information return for the filer (the transmitter) files an application in accordance with paragraph (c)(1) of this section.

(2) *Non-automatic extension of time to file.*— One additional 30-day extension of time to file an information return on a form listed in paragraph (a)(1) of this section may be allowed if the filer or transmitter submits a request for the additional extension of time to file before the expiration of the automatic 30-day extension of time to file. No extension of time to file will be granted under this paragraph (a)(2) unless the filer or transmitter has first obtained an automatic extension of time to file under paragraph (a)(1) of this section. To request the additional 30-day extension of time to file, the filer or transmitter must satisfy the requirements of paragraph (c)(2) of this section. No additional extension of time to file will be allowed for an information return on a form listed in paragraph (a)(1) of this section pursuant to § 1.6081-1 beyond the extensions of time to file provided by paragraph (a)(1) of this section and this paragraph (a)(2).

(b) *Information returns on forms in the W-2 series (except Form W-2G).*—Except as provided in paragraph (f) of this section, the filer or transmitter of an information return on forms in the W-2 series (except Form W-2G) may only request one non-automatic 30-day extension of time to file the information return beyond the due date for filing it. To make such a request, the filer or transmitter must submit an application for an extension of time to file in accordance with paragraph (c)(2) of this section. No additional extension of time to file will be allowed for information returns on forms in the W-2 series pursuant to § 1.6081-1 beyond the 30-day extension of time to file provided by this paragraph (b).

(c) *Requirements.*—(1) *Automatic extension of time to file.*—To satisfy this paragraph (c)(1), an application must—

(i) Be submitted on Form 8809, "Request for Extension of Time to File Information Returns," or in any other manner as may be prescribed by the Commissioner; and

(ii) Be filed with the Internal Revenue Service office designated in the application's instructions on or before the due date for filing the information return.

(2) *Non-automatic extension of time to file.*—To satisfy this paragraph (c)(2), a filer or transmitter must—

(i) Submit a complete application on Form 8809, or in any other manner prescribed by the Commissioner, including a detailed explanation of why additional time is needed;

(ii) File the application with the Internal Revenue Service in accordance with forms, instructions, or other appropriate guidance on or before the due date for filing the information return (for purposes of paragraph (a)(2) of this

>>>→ *Caution: Temporary Reg. §1.6081-8T, below, was removed by T.D. 9838, but applies to extensions of time to file information returns required to be filed before January 1, 2019.*

section, determined with regard to the extension of time to file under paragraph (a)(1) of this section); and

(iii) Sign the application under penalties of perjury.

(d) *Penalties.*—See sections 6652, 6693, and 6721 through 6724 for failure to comply with information reporting requirements on information returns described in this section.

(e) *No effect on time to furnish statements.*—An extension of time to file an information return under this section does not extend the time for furnishing a statement to the person with respect to whom the information is required to be reported.

(f) *Form W-2 filed on expedited basis.*—This section does not apply to an information return on a form in the W–2 series if the procedures authorized in Rev. Proc. 96-57 (1996-2 CB 389) (or a successor revenue procedure) allow an automatic extension of time to file the information return. See §601.601(d)(2)(ii)(b) of this chapter.

(g) *Effective/applicability date.*—This section applies to requests for extensions of time to file information returns due after December 31, 2016.

(h) *Expiration date.*—The applicability of this section expires on August 10, 2018. [Temporary Reg. §1.6081-8T.]

☐ [*T.D. 9730, 8-12-2015. Removed by T.D. 9838, 8-1-2018.*]

[Reg. §1.6081-9]

§1.6081-9. Automatic extension of time to file exempt organization returns.— (a) [Reserved]. For further guidance, see §1.6081-9T(a).

(b) *Requirements.*—To satisfy this paragraph (b), an application for an automatic extension under this section must—

(1) [Reserved]. For further guidance, see §1.6081-9T(b)(1);

(2) Be filed with the Internal Revenue Service office designated in the application's instructions on or before the date prescribed for filing the return;

(3) [Reserved]. For further guidance, see §1.6081-9T(b)(3); and

(4) Be accompanied by the full remittance of the amount properly estimated as tentative tax which is unpaid as of the date prescribed for the filing of the return.

(c) [Reserved]. For further guidance, see §1.6081-9T(c).

(d) [Reserved]. For further guidance, see §1.6081-9T(d).

(e) [Reserved]. For further guidance, see §1.6081-9T(e).

(f) *Effective date.*—This section applies to requests for extensions of time to file an exempt

organization return due after December 7, 2004. [Reg. §1.6081-9.]

☐ [*T.D. 9163, 12-6-2004. Amended by T.D. 9821, 7-18-2017.*]

[Reg. §1.6081-9T]

§1.6081-9T. Automatic extension of time to file exempt or political organization returns (temporary).—(a) *In general.*—An entity required to file a return on a form in the Form 990 series (Form 990, "Return of Organization Exempt From Income Tax," Form 990-BL, "Information and Initial Excise Tax Return for Black Lung Benefit Trusts and Certain Related Persons," Form 990-EZ, "Short Form Return of Organization Exempt From Income Tax," Form 990-PF, "Return of Private Foundation," and Form 990-T, "Exempt Organization Business Tax Return"), Form 1041-A, "U.S. Information Return-Trust Accumulation of Charitable Amounts," Form 1120-POL, "U.S. Income Tax Return for Certain Political Organizations," Form 4720, "Return of Certain Excise Taxes Under Chapters 41 and 42 of the Internal Revenue Code," Form 5227, "Split-Interest Trust Information Return," Form 6069, "Return of Excise Tax on Excess Contributions to Black Lung Benefit Trust Under Section 4953 and Computation of Section 192 Deduction," and Form 8870, "Information Return for Transfers Associated With Certain Personal Benefit Contracts," will be allowed an automatic six-month extension of time to file the return after the date prescribed for filing if the entity files an application in accordance with paragraph (b) of this section.

(b) introductory text [Reserved]. For further guidance, see §1.6081-9(b) introductory text.

(1) Be submitted on Form 7004, "Application for Automatic Extension of Time to File Certain Business Income Tax, Information, and Other Returns" (in the case of an extension of time to file Form 1120-POL), Form 8868, "Application for Automatic Extension of Time to File an Exempt Organization Return" (in the case of an extension of time to file any other return listed in paragraph (a) of this section), or in any other manner as may be prescribed by the Commissioner;

(2) [Reserved]. For further guidance, see §1.6081-9(b)(2);

(3) Show the full amount properly estimated as tentative tax for the entity for the taxable year; and

(4) [Reserved]. For further guidance, see §1.6081-9(b)(4).

(c) *Termination of automatic extension.*—The Commissioner may terminate an automatic extension at any time by mailing to the entity a notice of termination. The notice must be mailed at least 10 days prior to the termination date designated in such notice. The notice of termination must be mailed to the address shown on the application for extension or to the entity's last known address. For further guidance regarding the definition of last known address, see §301.6212-2 of this chapter.

(d) *Penalties.*—See sections 6651 and 6652(c) for failure to file a return or failure to pay the amount shown as tax on the return.

(e) *Coordination with §1.6081-1.*—No extension of time will be granted under §1.6081-1 for filing a return listed in paragraph (a) of this section until an automatic extension has been allowed pursuant to this section.

(f) *Applicability date.*—This section applies to requests for extensions of time to file returns listed in paragraph (a) of this section on or after July 20, 2017. Sections 1.6081-3 and 1.6081-9 (as contained in 26 CFR part 1, revised April 2017) apply to requests for extensions before July 20, 2017.

(g) *Expiration date.*—The applicability of this section will expire on or before July 17, 2020. [Temporary Reg. §1.6081-9T.]

☐ *T.D. 9821, 7-18-2017.]*

[Reg. §1.6081-10]

§1.6081-10. Automatic extension of time to file withholding tax return for U.S. source income of foreign persons.—(a) *In general.*—A withholding agent or intermediary required to file a return on Form 1042, "Annual Withholding Tax Return for U.S. Source Income of Foreign Persons," for any taxable year will be allowed an automatic 6-month extension of time to file the return after the date prescribed for filing the return if the withholding agent or intermediary files an application under this section in accordance with paragraph (b) of this section.

(b) *Requirements.*—To satisfy this paragraph (b), a withholding agent or intermediary must—

(1) Submit a complete application on Form 7004, "Application for Automatic Extension of Time to File Certain Business Income Tax, Information, and Other Returns," or in any other manner as may be prescribed by the Commissioner;

(2) File the application on or before the date prescribed for filing the return with the Internal Revenue Service office designated in the application's instructions; and

(3) Remit the amount of the properly estimated unpaid tax liability on or before the date prescribed for payment.

(c) *No extension of time for the payment of tax.*—An automatic extension of time for filing a return granted under paragraph (a) of this section will not extend the time for payment of any tax due on such return.

(d) *Termination of automatic extension.*—The Commissioner may terminate an automatic extension at any time by mailing to the withholding agent or intermediary a notice of termination at least 10 days prior to the termination date designated in such notice. The Commissioner must mail the notice of termination to the address shown on the Form 7004 or to the with-

holding agent or intermediary's last known address. For further guidance regarding the definition of last known address, see §301.6212-2 of this chapter.

(e) *Penalties.*—See section 6651 for failure to file a return or failure to pay an amount shown as tax on the return.

(f) *Effective/applicability dates.*—This section is applicable for applications for an automatic extension of time to file the withholding tax return for U.S. source income of foreign persons return filed after July 1, 2008. [Reg. §1.6081-10.]

☐ [*T.D. 9407, 6-30-2008.]*

[Reg. §1.6081-11]

§1.6081-11. Automatic extension of time for filing certain employee plan returns.—(a) *In general.*—An administrator or sponsor of an employee benefit plan required to file a return under the provisions of chapter 61 or the regulations under that chapter on Form 5500 (series), "Annual Return/Report of Employee Benefit Plan," will be allowed an automatic extension of time to file the return until the 15th day of the third month following the date prescribed for filing the return if the administrator or sponsor files an application under this section in accordance with paragraph (b) of this section.

(b) *Requirements.*—To satisfy this paragraph (b), an administrator or sponsor must—

(1) Submit a complete application on Form 5558, "Application for Extension of Time To File Certain Employee Plan Returns," or in any other manner as may be prescribed by the Commissioner; and

(2) File the application with the Internal Revenue Service office designated in the application's instructions on or before the date prescribed for filing the information return.

(c) *Termination of automatic extension.*—The Commissioner may terminate an automatic extension at any time by mailing to the administrator or sponsor a notice of termination at least 10 days prior to the termination date designated in such notice. The Commissioner must mail the notice of termination to the address shown on the Form 5558 or to the administrator or sponsor's last known address. For further guidance regarding the definition of last known address, see §301.6212-2 of this chapter.

(d) *Penalties.*—See sections 6652, 6692, and the Employee Retirement Income Security Act of 1974 for penalties for failure to file a timely and complete Form 5500.

(e) *Effective/applicability dates.*—This section is applicable for applications for an automatic extension of time to file Forms 5500 for plan years ending after July 1, 2008. [Reg. §1.6081-11.]

☐ [*T.D. 9407, 6-30-2008.]*

[Reg. §31.6081(a)-1]

§31.6081(a)-1. Extensions of time for filing returns and other documents.—(a) *Federal In-*

surance Contributions Act; income tax withheld from wages; and Railroad Retirement Tax Act.—(1) In general.—Except as otherwise provided in subparagraphs (2) and (3) of this paragraph, no extension of time for filing any return or other document required in respect of the Federal Insurance Contributions Act, income tax withheld from wages, or the Railroad Retirement Tax Act will be granted.

(2) Information returns of employers on Forms W-2 and W-3.—(i) In general.—The Commissioner may grant an extension of time in which to file the Social Security Administration copy of Forms W-2 and the accompanying transmittal form which constitutes an information return under § 31.6051-2(a). For further guidance regarding extensions of time to file the Social Security Administration copy of Forms W-2 and W-3, see § 1.6081-8 of this chapter.

(ii) Automatic extension of time.—The Commissioner may, in appropriate cases, publish procedures for automatic extensions of time to file Forms W-2 where the employer is required to file the Form W-2 on an expedited basis.

(b) Federal Unemployment Tax Act.—[Not reproduced herein.—CCH.]

(c) Duly authorized agent.—In any case in which an employer is unable, by reason of illness, absence, or other good cause, to sign a request for an extension, any person standing in close personal or business relationship to the employer may sign the request on his behalf, and shall be considered as a duly authorized agent for this purpose, provided the request sets forth the reasons for a signature other than the employer's and the relationship existing between the employer and the signer.

(d) Effective date.—Paragraph (a)(2)(i) of this section applies to requests for extensions of time to file the Social Security Administration copy of Forms W-2 and W-3 due after December 7, 2004. [Reg. § 31.6081(a)-1.]

☐ [T.D. 6354, 1-13-59. Amended by T.D. 6950, 4-3-68; T.D. 7351, 4-16-75; T.D. 8636, 12-20-95; T.D. 9061, 6-10-2003 and T.D. 9163, 12-6-2004.]

Place for Filing Returns or Other Documents

[Reg. § 1.6091-1]

§ 1.6091-1. Place for filing returns or other documents.—(a) In general.—Except as provided in § 1.6091-4, whenever a return, statement, or other document is required to be made under the provisions of subtitle A or F of the Code, or the regulations thereunder, with respect to any tax imposed by subtitle A of the Code, and the place for filing such return, statement, or other document is not provided for by the Code, it shall be filed at the place prescribed by the regulations contained in this chapter.

(b) Place for filing certain information returns.—(1) For the place for filing returns of partnership income, see paragraph (e)(1) of § 1.6031(a)-1.

(2) For the place for filing information returns by banks with respect to common trust funds, see § 1.6032-1.

(3) For the place for filing information returns by certain organizations exempt from taxation under section 501(a), see paragraph (e) of § 1.6033-1.

(4) For the place for filing information returns by trusts claiming charitable deductions under section 642(c), see paragraph (c) of § 1.6034-1.

(5) For the place for filing information returns by officers, directors, and shareholders of foreign personal holding companies, see § 1.6035-1.

(6) For the place for filing information returns relating to certain stock option transactions, see paragraph (c) of § 1.6039-1.

(7) For the place for filing returns of information reporting certain payments, see paragraph (a)(5) of § 1.6041-2 and § 1.6041-6.

(8) For the place for filing returns of information regarding payments of dividends, see paragraph (c) of § 1.6042-2 (relating to returns for calendar years after 1962).

(9) For the place for filing information returns by corporations relating to contemplated dissolution or liquidation, see paragraph (a) of § 1.6043-1.

(10) For the place for filing information returns by corporations relating to distributions in liquidation, see paragraph (a) of § 1.6043-2.

(11) For the place for filing returns of information regarding payments of patronage dividends, see paragraph (d) of § 1.6044-2.

(12) For the place for filing information returns relating to formation or reorganization of foreign corporations, see paragraph (j)(2) of § 1.6046-1.

(13) For the place for filing information returns regarding certain payments of interest, see paragraph (c) of § 1.6049-1.

(14) For the place for filing information returns with respect to payment of wages in the form of group-term life insurance, see paragraph (b) of § 1.6052-1.

(15) For the place for filing information returns on Forms 1042-S with respect to certain amounts paid to foreign persons, see instructions to the form.

(16) For the place for filing information returns on Form 5074 with respect to the allocation of individual income tax to Guam, see paragraph (b)(3) of § 1.935-1 and paragraph (d) of § 301.7654-1 of this chapter (Regulations on Procedure and Administration).

(17) For the place for filing information returns on Form 8805, "Foreign Partner's Information Statement of Section 1446 Withholding Tax,"

with respect to certain amounts paid on behalf of foreign partners, see the instructions to the form.

(c) *Effective/Applicability date.*—Paragraph (b)(17) of this section shall apply to partnership taxable years beginning after April 29, 2008. [Reg. § 1.6091-1.]

☐ [*T.D. 6364, 2-13-59. Amended by T.D. 6628,* 12-27-62; *T.D. 6887,* 6-23-66; *T.D. 6922,* 6-16-67; *T.D. 7284,* 8-2-73; *T.D. 7385,* 10-28-75; *T.D. 8734,* 10-6-97 (T.D. 8804 delayed the effective date of T.D. 8734 from January 1, 1999, to January 1, 2000; T.D. 8856 further delayed the effective date of T.D. 8734 until January 1, 2001); *T.D. 9156,* 9-15-2004 *and T.D. 9394, 4-28-2008.*]

[Reg. § 20.6091-1]

§ 20.6091-1. Place for filing returns or other documents.—(a) *General rule.*—If the decedent was domiciled in the United States at the time of his death, the preliminary notice required by § 20.6036-1 in the case of the estate of a decedent dying before January 1, 1971, and the estate tax return required by § 20.6018-1 shall be filed with:

(1) The service center serving the location in which the decedent was domiciled at the time of his death, if the instructions applicable to the estate tax return provide that the return shall be filed with a service center, or

(2) Any person assigned the responsibility to receive returns in the local Internal Revenue Service office serving the location in which the decedent was domiciled at the time of his death, if paragraph (1) does not apply.

(b) *Non-U.S. domiciliaries.*—If the decedent was not domiciled in the United States at the time of his death, the preliminary notice required by § 20.6036-1 in the case of the estate of a decedent dying before January 1, 1971, and the estate tax return required by § 20.6018-1 shall be filed with the Internal Revenue Service Center, Philadelphia, Pennsylvania, or as designated on the return form or in the instructions issued with respect to such form. This paragraph applies whether or not the decedent was a citizen of the United States and whether or not the return is made by hand-carrying. [Reg. § 20.6091-1.]

☐ [*T.D. 6600, 5-28-62; T.D. 7238, 12-28-72; T.D. 7302, 1-24-74; T.D. 7495, 6-29-77 and T.D. 9156, 9-15-2004.*]

[Reg. § 25.6091-1]

§ 25.6091-1. Place for filing returns and other documents.—(a) *In general.*—If the donor is a resident of the United States, the gift tax return required by section 6019 shall be filed with any person assigned the responsibility to receive returns in the local Internal Revenue Service office that serves the legal residence or principal place of business of the donor. If the donor is a nonresident (whether or not a citizen), and his principal place of business is served by a local Internal Revenue Service office, the gift tax return shall be filed with any person assigned the responsibility to receive returns in that office.

(b) *Returns filed with service centers.*—Notwithstanding paragraph (a) of this section, unless a return is filed by hand-carrying, whenever instructions applicable to gift tax returns provide that the returns be filed with a service center, the returns must be so filed in accordance with the instructions. Returns which are filed by hand carrying shall be filed with any person assigned the responsibility to receive hand-carried returns in the local Internal Revenue Service office in accordance with paragraph (a) of this section.

(c) *Returns of certain nonresidents.*—If the donor is a nonresident (whether or not a citizen), and he does not have a principal place of business in the United States, the gift tax return required by section 6019, whether or not such return is made by hand carrying, shall be filed with the Internal Revenue Service Center, Philadelphia, Pennsylvania, or as designated on the return form or in the instructions issued with respect to such form. [Reg. § 25.6091-1.]

☐ [*Amended by T.D. 7012, 5-14-69; T.D. 7238, 12-28-72; T.D. 7302, 1-2-74; T.D. 7495, 6-29-77 and T.D. 9156, 9-15-2004.*]

[Reg. § 31.6091-1]

§ 31.6091-1. Place for filing returns.— (a) *Persons other than corporations.*—Except as provided in paragraph (c) of this section, the return of a person other than a corporation shall be filed with any person assigned the responsibility to receive returns in the local Internal Revenue Service office that serves the principal place of business or legal residence of such person.

(b) *Corporations.*—The return of a corporation shall be filed with any person assigned the responsibility to receive returns in the local Internal Revenue Service office that serves the principal place of business or principal office or agency of the corporation, except as provided in paragraph (c) of this section.

(c) *Returns of taxpayers outside the United States.*—The return of a person (other than a corporation) outside the United States having no legal residence or principal place of business in the United States, or the return of a corporation having no principal place of business or principal office or agency in the United States, shall be filed with the Internal Revenue Service, Philadelphia, Pennsylvania 19255, or as otherwise directed in the applicable forms and instructions.

(d) *Returns filed with internal revenue service centers or Social Security Administration offices.*— Notwithstanding paragraphs (a), (b), and (c) of this section, whenever instructions applicable to such returns provide that the returns shall be filed with an internal revenue service center or an office of the Social Security Administration, such returns shall be filed in accordance with such instructions.

(e) *Hand-carried returns.*—Except as provided in subparagraph (3) of this paragraph, and notwithstanding paragraphs (1) and (2) of section 6091 (b) and paragraph (d) of this section—

(1) *Persons other than corporations.*—Returns of persons other than corporations which are filed by hand carrying shall be filed with any person assigned the responsibility to receive hand-carried returns in the local Internal Revenue Service office as provided in paragraph (a) of this section.

(2) *Corporations.*—Returns of corporations which are filed by hand carrying shall be filed with any person assigned the responsibility to receive hand-carried returns in the local Internal Revenue Service office as provided in paragraph (b) of this section.

(3) *Exceptions.*—This paragraph shall not apply to returns of—

(i) Persons who have no legal residence, no principal place of business, nor principal office or agency served by a local Internal Revenue Service office,

(ii) Citizens of the United States whose principal place of abode for the period with respect to which the return is filed is outside the United States,

(iii) Persons who claim the benefits of section 911 (relating to earned income from sources without the United States), section 922 (relating to special deduction for Western Hemisphere trade corporations), section 931 (relating to income from sources within possessions of the United States), section 933 (relating to income from sources within Puerto Rico), or section 941 (relating to the special deduction for China Trade Act corporations), and

(iv) Nonresident alien persons and foreign corporations.

(f) *Permission to file in office other than required office.*—The Commissioner may permit the filing of any return required to be made under the regulations in this subpart in any local Internal Revenue Service office, notwithstanding the provisions of paragraphs (1), (2), and (4) of section 6091 (b) and paragraphs (a), (b), (c), (d) and (e) of this section.

(g) *Returns of officers and employees of the Internal Revenue Service.*—The Commissioner may require any officer or employee of the Internal Revenue Service to file any return required of him under the regulations in this subpart in any local Internal Revenue Service office selected by the Commissioner, notwithstanding the provisions of paragraphs (1), (2), and (4) of section 6091(b) and paragraphs (a), (b), (c), (d), and (e) of this section. [Reg. § 31.6091-1.]

☐ [*T.D. 6472, 6-22-60. Amended by T.D. 6915, 3-28-67; T.D. 7495, 6-29-77; T.D. 7580, 12-20-78 and T.D. 9156, 9-15-2004.*]

[Reg. § 40.6091-1]

§ 40.6091-1. Place for filing returns.—(a) *Quarterly returns.*—Except as provided in paragraphs (b) and (c) of this section, returns must be filed in accordance with the instructions applicable to the form on which the return is made.

(b) *Hand-carried returns.*—(1) *Persons other than corporations.*—Returns of persons other than corporations that are filed by hand carrying must be filed with any person assigned the responsibility to receive hand-carried returns in the local Internal Revenue Service office that serves the principal place of business or legal residence of the person.

(2) *Corporations.*—Returns of corporations that are filed by hand carrying must be filed with any person assigned the responsibility to receive hand-carried returns in the local Internal Revenue Service office that serves the principal place of business or principal office or agency of the corporation.

(c) *Monthly and semimonthly returns.*—Monthly and semimonthly returns required under § 40.6011(a)-1(b) must be filed in accordance with the forms and instructions, or other published guidance. [Reg. § 40.6091-1.]

☐ [*T.D. 8442, 10-21-92. Amended by T.D. 8963, 8-8-2001; T.D. 9156, 9-15-2004 and T.D. 9602, 12-5-2012.*]

[Reg. § 41.6091-1]

§ 41.6091-1. Place for filing returns.—(a) *In general.*—Except as provided in paragraph (b) of this section, returns must be filed in accordance with the instructions applicable to the form on which the return is made.

(b) *Hand-carried returns.*—(1) *Persons other than corporations.*—Returns of persons other than corporations that are filed by hand carrying must be filed with any person assigned the responsibility to receive hand-carried returns in the local Internal Revenue Service office that serves the principal place of business or legal residence of the person.

(2) *Corporations.*—Returns of corporations that are filed by hand carrying must be filed with any person assigned the responsibility to receive hand-carried returns in the local Internal Revenue Service office that serves the principal place of business or principal office or agency of the corporation. [Reg. § 41.6091-1.]

☐ [*T.D. 6216. Amended by T.D. 6743, 6-22-64; T.D. 8159, 9-3-87; T.D. 8879, 3-30-2000 and T.D. 9156, 9-15-2004.*]

[Reg. § 44.6091-1]

§ 44.6091-1. Place for filing returns.—(a) *In general.*—Except as provided in paragraph (b) of this section, a return on Form 730 or Form 11-C shall be filed with any person assigned the responsibility to receive returns in the local Internal Revenue Service office that serves the legal residence or principal place of business of the person making the return.

(b) *Returns of individuals outside the United States.*—The returns on Form 730 and Form 11-C individuals (whether citizens of the United States, citizens of possessions of the United States, or aliens) outside the United States having no legal residence or principal place of business in the United States shall be filed with the Internal Revenue Service Center, Cincinnati, Ohio 45999, or as otherwise directed in the applicable forms and instructions.

(c) *Returns filed with service centers.*—Notwithstanding paragraphs (a) and (b) of this section, whenever instructions applicable to returns filed on Form 730 or Form 11-C provide that the returns be filed with a service center, the returns shall be so filed in accordance with the instructions.

(d) *Hand-carried returns.*—Returns which are filed by hand carrying shall be filed with any person assigned the responsibility to receive hand-carried returns in the local Internal Revenue Service office as provided in paragraph (a) of this section. See § 301.6091-1(c) of this chapter (Regulations on Procedure and Administration) for provisions relating to the definition of hand carried. [Reg. § 44.6091-1.]

☐ [Subsections (a) and (b) adopted by T.D. 6370. Subsections (c) and (d) adopted by T.D. 7630. *Amended by T.D. 9156, 9-15-2004.*]

[Reg. § 53.6091-1]

§ 53.6091-1. Place for filing chapter 42 tax returns.—Except as provided in § 53.6091-2 (relating to exceptional cases)—

(a) *Persons other than corporations.*—Chapter 42 tax returns of persons other than corporations shall be filed with any person assigned the responsibility to receive returns in the local Internal Revenue Service office that serves the legal residence or principal place of business of the person required to make the return.

(b) *Corporations.*—Chapter 42 tax returns of corporations shall be filed with any person assigned the responsibility to receive returns in the local Internal Revenue Service office that serves the principal place of business or principal office or agency of the corporation.

(c) *Returns filed with service centers.*—Notwithstanding paragraphs (a) and (b) of this section, unless a return is filed by hand carrying, whenever instructions applicable to chapter 42 tax returns provide that the returns be filed with a service center, the returns must be so filed in accordance with the instructions. Returns which are filed by hand carrying shall be filed with any person assigned the responsibility to receive hand-carried returns in the local Internal Revenue Service office in accordance with paragraph (a) or (b) of this section, whichever is applicable.

(d) *Returns of persons subject to a termination assessment.*—Notwithstanding paragraph (c) of this section, income tax returns of persons with respect to whom a chapter 42 tax assessment was made under section 6852(a) with respect to the taxable year must be filed with any person assigned the responsibility to receive returns in the local Internal Revenue Service office as provided in paragraphs (a) and (b) of this section. [Reg. § 53.6091-1.]

☐ [T.D. 7368, 7-15-75. *Amended by T.D. 7495, 6-29-77; T.D. 8628, 12-4-95 and T.D. 9156, 9-15-2004.*]

[Reg. § 54.6091-1]

§ 54.6091-1. Place for filing excise tax returns under section 4980B, 4980D, 4980E, or 4980G.—Effective for any Form 8928 that is due on or after January 1, 2010, the return required by § 54.6011-2 must be filed at the place specified in the forms and instructions provided by the Internal Revenue Service. [Reg. § 54.6091-1.]

☐ [T.D. 9457, 9-4-2009.]

[Reg. § 55.6091-1]

§ 55.6091-1. Place for filing chapter 44 tax returns.—Except as provided in § 55.6091-2 (relating to exceptional cases)—

(a) *In general.*—Chapter 44 tax returns shall be filed with any person assigned the responsibility to receive returns in the local Internal Revenue Service office serving the principal place of business or principal office or agency of the real estate investment trust or regulated investment company.

(b) *Returns filed with service centers or by hand carrying.*—Notwithstanding paragraph (a) of this section, unless a return is filed by hand carrying, whenever instructions applicable to chapter 44 tax returns provide that the returns be filed with a service center, the returns must be so filed in accordance with the instructions. Returns which are filed by hand carrying shall be filed with any person assigned the responsibility to receive hand-carried returns in the local Internal Revenue Service office in accordance with paragraph (a) of this section. [Reg. § 55.6091-1.]

☐ [T.D. 7767, 2-3-81. *Amended by T.D. 8180, 2-29-88 and T.D. 9156, 9-15-2004.*]

[Reg. § 156.6091-1]

§ 156.6091-1. Place for filing chapter 54 (Greenmail) tax returns.—Except as provided in § 156.6091-2 (relating to exceptional cases):

(a) *Individuals, estates, and trusts.*—In general, tax returns under chapter 54 of the Code of individuals, estates, and trusts shall be filed with any person assigned the responsibility to receive returns in the local Internal Revenue Service office that serves the legal residence or the principal place of business of the person required to make the return.

(b) *Corporations.*—In general, tax returns under chapter 54 of the Code of corporations shall be filed with any person assigned the responsibility to receive returns in the local Internal Revenue Service office that serves the principal place of business or the principal office or agency of the corporation.

(c) *Partnerships.*—In general, tax returns under chapter 54 of the Code of partnerships shall be filed with any person assigned the responsibility to receive returns in the local Internal Revenue Service office that serves the principal place of business or the principal office or agency of the partnership.

(d) *Returns of taxpayers outside the United States.*—The return of a person (other than a partnership or a corporation) outside the United States having no legal residence or principal place of business or agency in the United States, or the return of a partnership or a corporation having no principal place of business or principal office or agency in the United States, shall be filed with the Internal Revenue Service, Philadelphia, PA 19255, or as otherwise directed in the applicable forms and instructions.

(e) *Returns filed with service centers or by hand carrying.*—Notwithstanding paragraph (a), (b), (c), or (d) of this section, unless a return is filed by hand carrying, whenever instructions applicable to tax returns under chapter 54 of the Code provide that the returns be filed with a service center, the returns must be so filed in accordance with the instructions. Returns that are filed by hand carrying shall be filed with any person assigned the responsibility to receive hand-carried returns in the local Internal Revenue Service office in accordance with paragraphs (a), (b), (c), or (d) of this section. [Reg. § 156.6091-1.]

☐ [*T.D. 8379, 12-17-91. Amended by T.D. 9156, 9-15-2004.*]

[Reg. § 157.6091-1]

§ 157.6091-1. Place for filing returns.—The return required by § 157.6011-1 (relating to returns of tax with respect to structured settlement factoring transactions) must be filed at the place specified in the forms and instructions provided by the Internal Revenue Service. [Reg. § 157.6091-1.]

☐ [*T.D. 9134, 7-7-2004.*]

[Reg. § 301.6091-1]

§ 301.6091-1. Place for filing returns of other documents.—(a) *General rule.*—For provisions concerning the place for filing returns, including hand-carried returns, see the regulations relating to the particular tax. Except as provided in paragraph(b) of this section, for provisions concerning the place for filing documents other than returns, see the regulations relating to the particular tax.

(b) *Exception for hand-carried documents other than returns.*—Notwithstanding any other provisions of this chapter—

(1) *Persons other than corporations.*—If a document, other than a return, of a person (other than a corporation) is hand carried, and if the document is otherwise required to be filed with a service center, such document may be filed with any person assigned the responsibility to receive hand-carried returns in the local Internal Revenue Service office that serves the legal residence or principal place of business of such person, or, in the case of an estate, the local Internal Revenue Service office serving the domicile of the decedent at the time of his death. A document may also be filed by hand carrying such

document to the appropriate service center, or, in the case of a document required to be filed with an office of the Alcohol and Tobacco Tax and Trade Bureau, by hand carrying as specified in regulations of the Alcohol and Tobacco Tax and Trade Bureau, see, 27 CFR chapter I, subchapter F.

(2) *Corporations.*—If a document, other than a return, of a corporation is hand carried, and if the document is otherwise required to be filed with a service center, such document may be filed with any person assigned the responsibility to receive hand-carried returns in the local Internal Revenue Service office that serves the principal place of business or principal office or agency of the corporation. A document may also be filed by hand carrying such document to the appropriate service center, or, in the case of a document required to be filed with an office of the Alcohol and Tobacco Tax and Trade Bureau, by hand carrying as specified in regulations of the Alcohol and Tobacco Tax and Trade Bureau, see, 27 CFR chapter I, subchapter F.

(c) *Definition of hand carried.*—For purposes of this section and section 6091(b)(4) and the regulations issued thereunder, a return or document will be considered to be hand carried if it is brought to any person assigned the responsibility to receive hand-carried returns in the local Internal Revenue Service office by the person required to file the return or other document, or by his agent. Examples of persons who will be considered to be agents, for purposes of the preceding sentence, are: Members of the taxpayer's family, an employee of the taxpayer, the taxpayer's attorney, accountant, or tax advisor, and messengers employed by the taxpayer. A return or document will not be considered to be hand carried if it is sent to the Internal Revenue Service through the U.S. Mail. [Reg. § 301.6091-1.]

☐ [*T.D. 6498, 10-24-60. Amended by T.D. 6950, 4-3-68; T.D. 7008, 2-28-69; T.D. 7012, 5-14-69; T.D. 7188, 6-28-72; T.D. 7238, 12-28-72; T.D. 7495, 6-29-77 and T.D. 9156, 9-15-2004.*]

[Reg. § 1.6091-2]

§ 1.6091-2. Place for filing income tax returns.—Except as provided in § 1.6091-3 (relating to certain international income tax returns) and § 1.6091-4 (relating to exceptional cases)—

(a) *Individuals, estates, and trusts.*—(1) Except as provided in paragraph (c) of this section, income tax returns of individuals, estates, and trusts shall be filed with any person assigned the responsibility to receive returns at the local Internal Revenue Service office that serves the legal residence or principal place of business of the person required to make the return.

(2) An individual employed on a salary or commission basis who is not also engaged in conducting a commercial or professional enterprise for profit on his own account does not have a "principal place of business" within the meaning of this section.

(b) *Corporations.*—Except as provided in paragraph (c) of this section, income tax returns of corporations shall be filed with any person assigned the responsibility to receive returns in the local Internal Revenue Service office that serves the principal place of business or principal office or agency of the corporation.

(c) *Returns filed with service centers.*—Notwithstanding paragraphs (a) and (b) of this section, whenever instructions applicable to income tax returns provide that the returns be filed with a service center, the returns must be so filed in accordance with the instructions.

(d) *Hand-carried returns.*—Notwithstanding paragraphs (1) and (2) of section 6091(b) and paragraph (c) of this section—

(1) *Persons other than corporations.*—Returns of persons other than corporations which are filed by hand carrying shall be filed with any person assigned the responsibility to receive hand-carried returns in the local Internal Revenue Service office as provided in paragraph (a) of this section.

(2) *Corporations.*—Returns of corporations which are filed by hand carrying shall be filed with any person assigned the responsibility to receive hand-carried returns in the local Internal Revenue Service office as provided in paragraph (b) of this section.

See § 301.6091-1 of this chapter (Regulations on Procedure and Administration) for provisions relating to the definition of hand carried.

(e) *Amended returns.*—In the case of amended returns filed after April 14, 1968, except as provided in paragraph (d) of this section—

(1) *Persons other than corporations.*—Amended returns of persons other than corporations shall be filed with the service center serving the legal residence or principal place of business of the person required to make the return.

(2) *Corporations.*—Amended returns of corporations shall be filed with the service center serving the principal place of business or principal office or agency of the corporation.

(f) *Returns of persons subject to a termination assessment.*—Notwithstanding paragraph (c) of this section—

(1) *Persons other than corporations.*—Returns of persons other than corporations with respect to whom an assessment was made under section 6851(a) with respect to the taxable year shall be filed with any person assigned the responsibility to receive returns in the local Internal Revenue Service office as provided in paragraph (a) of this section.

(2) *Corporations.*—Returns of corporations with respect to whom an assessment was made under section 6851(a) with respect to the taxable year shall be filed with any person assigned the responsibility to receive returns in the local Inter-

nal Revenue Service office as provided in paragraph (b) of this section.

(g) *Returns of persons subject to a termination assessment.*—Notwithstanding paragraph (c) of this section, income tax returns of persons with respect to whom an income tax assessment was made under section 6852(a) with respect to the taxable year must be filed with any person assigned the responsibility to receive returns in the local Internal Revenue Service office as provided in paragraphs (a) and (b) of this section. [Reg. § 1.6091-2.]

☐ [*T.D.* 6364, 2-13-59. *Amended by T.D.* 6950, 4-3-68; *T.D.* 7012, 5-14-69; *T.D.* 7495, 6-2-77; *T.D.* 7575, 12-15-78; *T.D.* 8628, 12-4-95 *and T.D.* 9156, 9-15-2004.]

[Reg. § 20.6091-2]

§ 20.6091-2. Exceptional cases.—Notwithstanding the provisions of § 20.6091-1 the Commissioner may permit the filing of the preliminary notice required by § 20.6036-1 and the estate tax return required by § 20.6018-1 in any local Internal Revenue Service office. [Reg. § 20.6091-2.]

☐ [*T.D.* 6600, 5-28-62. *Amended by T.D.* 9156, 9-15-2004.]

[Reg. § 25.6091-2]

§ 25.6091-2. Exceptional cases.—Notwithstanding the provisions of § 25.6091-1 the Commissioner may permit the filing of the gift tax return required by section 6019 in any local Internal Revenue Service office. [Reg. § 25.6091-2.]

☐ [*T.D.* 6600, 5-28-62. *Amended by T.D.* 9156, 9-15-2004.]

[Reg. § 53.6091-2]

§ 53.6091-2. Exceptional cases.—Notwithstanding the provisions of § 53.6091-1, the Commissioner may permit the filing of any chapter 42 tax return in any local Internal Revenue Service office. [Reg. § 53.6091-2.]

☐ [*T.D.* 7368, 7-15-75. *Amended by T.D.* 9156, 9-15-2004.]

[Reg. § 55.6091-2]

§ 55.6091-2. Exceptional cases.—Notwithstanding the provisions of § 55.6091-1, the Commissioner may permit the filing of any chapter 44 tax return in any local Internal Revenue Service office. [Reg. § 55.6091-2.]

☐ [*T.D.* 7767, 2-3-81. *Amended by T.D.* 9156, 9-15-2004.]

[Reg. § 156.6091-2]

§ 156.6091-2. Exceptional cases.—Notwithstanding the provisions of § 156.6091-1, the Commissioner may permit the filing of any tax return under chapter 54 (Greenmail) of the Code in any local Internal Revenue Service office. [Reg. § 156.6091-2.]

☐ [*T.D.* 8379, 12-17-91. *Amended by T.D.* 9156, 9-15-2004.]

[Reg. §1.6091-3]

§1.6091-3. Filing certain international income tax returns.—The following income tax returns shall be filed as directed in the applicable forms and instructions:

(a) Income tax returns on which all, or a portion, of the tax is to be paid in foreign currency. See §§301.6316-1 to 301.6316-6 inclusive, and §§301.6316-8 and 301.6316-9 of this chapter (Regulations on Procedure and Administration).

(b) Income tax returns of an individual citizen of the United States whose principal place of abode for the period with respect to which the return is filed is outside the United States. A taxpayer's principal place of abode will be considered to be outside the United States if his legal residence is outside the United States or if his return bears a foreign address.

(c) Income tax returns of an individual citizen of a possession of the United States (whether or not a citizen of the United States) who has no legal residence or principal place of business in any internal revenue district in the United States.

(d) Except in the case of any departing alien return under section 6851 and §1.6851-2, the income tax return of any nonresident alien (other than one treated as a resident under section (g) or (h)).

(e) The income tax return of an estate or trust the fiduciary of which is outside the United States and has no legal residence or principal place of business in any internal revenue district in the United States.

(f) Income tax returns of foreign corporations.

(g) The return by a withholding agent of the income tax required to be withheld at source under chapter 3 of the Code on nonresident aliens and foreign corporations and tax-free covenant bonds, as provided in §1.1461-2.

(h) Income tax returns of persons who claim the benefits of section 911 (relating to earned income from sources without the United States).

(i) Income tax returns of corporations which claim the benefits of section 922 (relating to special deduction for Western Hemisphere trade corporations) except in the case of consolidated returns filed pursuant to the regulations under section 1502.

(j) Income tax returns of persons who claim the benefits of section 931 (relating to income from sources within possessions of the United States).

(k) Income tax returns of persons who claim the benefits of section 933 (relating to income from sources within Puerto Rico).

(l) Income tax returns of corporations which claim the benefits of section 941 (relating to the special deduction for China Trade Act corporations). [Reg. §1.6091-3.]

☐ [T.D. 6364, 2-13-59. *Amended by T.D. 6872*, 1-5-66; *T.D. 6922, 6-16-67; T.D. 6950, 4-3-68; T.D. 7012, 5-14-69; T.D. 7670, 1-30-80 and T.D. 9156, 9-15-2004.*]

[Reg. §1.6091-4]

§1.6091-4. Exceptional cases.—(a) *Permission to file in office other than required office.*—(1) The Commissioner may permit the filing of any income tax return required to be made under the provisions of subtitle A or F of the Code, or the regulations in this part, in any Internal Revenue Service office, notwithstanding the provisions of paragraphs (1) and (2) of section 6091(b) and §§1.6091-1 to 1.6091-3, inclusive.

(2) In cases where the Commissioner authorizes (for all purposes except venue) an internal revenue service center to receive returns, such returns pursuant to instructions issued with respect thereto, may be sent directly to that service center and are thereby filed there for all purposes except as a factor in determining venue. However, after initial processing all such returns shall be forwarded by the service center to the office with which such returns are, without regard to this subparagraph, required to be filed. For the sole purpose of determining venue, such returns are filed only with such office.

(3) Notwithstanding the provisions of other sections of this chapter or any rule issued under this chapter—

(i) In cases where, in accordance with subparagraph (2) of this paragraph, a return is filed with a service center, the authority of the members of the office with whom such return would, without regard to such subparagraph, be required to be filed shall remain the same as if the return had been so filed,

(ii) Unless a return or other document is a proper attachment to, or is, a return which the service center is expressly authorized to receive, such return or other document shall be filed as if all returns sent directly to the service centers, in accordance with subparagraph (2) of this paragraph, were filed in the office where such returns are, without regard to such subparagraph, required to be filed; and

(iii) Unless the performance of an act is directly related to the sending of a return directly to the service center, such act shall be performed as if all returns sent directly to the service centers, in accordance with subparagraph (2) of this paragraph, were filed in the office where such returns are, without regard to such subparagraph, required to be filed.

(4) The application of paragraphs (a)(2) and (3) of this section may be illustrated by the following example:

Example. The Commissioner has authorized the Internal Revenue Service Center, Philadelphia, Pennsylvania (for all purposes except venue), to receive Form 1120. Except for that authorization, A, a corporation with its principal place of business in Greensboro, North Carolina, is required to file its Form 1120 for Year X with the Internal Revenue Service Center, Atlanta, Georgia. In addition, A may file an election to defer development expenditures paid or incurred in Year X. Under §1.616-2(e)(2) and applicable published guidance (in this case Notice 2003-19 (2003-1 C.B. 703)) that statement of election must be filed with the service center that serves A's principal place of business where A filed its income tax return. A may make that election on its income tax return or by filing it separately. Under paragraph (a)(2) of this section, A may send its Form 1120 to either the Internal Revenue Service Center, Philadelphia, Pennsylvania, or to the Internal Revenue Service Center, Atlanta, Georgia. If A files its statement of election separately from its income tax return for Year X, then the statement of election is not a proper attachment to A's income tax return and A should send the statement of election to the Internal Revenue Service Center, Atlanta, Georgia (with which A must, without regard to paragraph (a)(2) of this section, file its income tax return), no later than the time prescribed for filing Form 1120 for Year X (including extensions).

(b) *Returns of officers and employees of the Internal Revenue Service.*—The Commissioner may require any officer or employee of the Internal Revenue Service to file his income tax return in any Internal Revenue Service office selected by the Commissioner.

(c) *Residents of Guam.*—Income tax returns of an individual citizen of the United States who is a resident of Guam shall be filed with Guam, as provided in paragraph (b)(1) of §1.935-1. [Reg. §1.6091-4.]

☐ [*T.D. 6364, 2-13-59. Amended by T.D. 6793, 1-20-65; T.D. 7385, 10-28-75 and T.D. 9156, 9-15-2004.*]

Presidential Election Campaign Fund

[Reg. §301.6096-1]

§301.6096-1. Designation by individuals for taxable years beginning after December 31, 1972.—(a) *In general.*—Every individual (other than a nonresident alien) whose income tax liability, as defined in paragraph (b) of this section, is one dollar or more may, at his option, designate that one dollar shall be paid over to the Presidential Election Campaign Fund, in accordance with the provisions of section 9006. In the case of a joint return of a husband and wife, each spouse may designate that one dollar be paid to the fund as provided in this paragraph only if the joint income tax liability of the husband and wife is two dollars or more.

(b) *Income tax liability.*—For purposes of paragraph (a) of this section, the income tax liability of an individual for any taxable year is the amount of the tax imposed by chapter 1 on such individual for the taxable year (as shown on his or her return) reduced by the sum of the credits (as shown on his or her return) allowable under sections 33, 37, 38, 40, 41, 42, 44, and 44A.

(c) *Manner and time of designation.*—(1) A designation under paragraph (a) of this section may be made with respect to any taxable year at the time of the filing of the return of the tax imposed by chapter 1 for such taxable year, and shall be made either on the first page of the return or on the page bearing the taxpayer's signature, in accordance with the instructions applicable thereto.

(2) With respect to any taxable year beginning after December 31, 1972, for which no designation was made under paragraph (c)(1) of this section, a designation may be made on the form furnished by the Internal Revenue Service for such purpose, filed within 20 and one half months after the due date for the original return for such taxable year. In the case of a joint return where neither spouse made a designation or where only one spouse made a designation, a designation may be made, as provided in this subparagraph, by the spouse or spouses who had not previously made a designation.

(3) A designation once made, whether by an original return or otherwise, may not be revoked.

(d) *Effective date.*—This section shall apply to taxable years beginning after December 31, 1972. [Reg. §301.6096-1.]

☐ [*T.D. 7304, 2-1-74. Amended by T.D. 7391, 12-1-75 and T.D. 7643, 8-27-79.*]

[Reg. §301.6096-2]

§301.6096-2. Designation by individuals for taxable years ending on or after December 31, 1972 and beginning before January 1, 1973.—(a) *In general.*—(1) For taxable years ending on or after December 31, 1972 and beginning before January 1, 1973, every individual (other than a nonresident alien) whose income tax liability, as defined in paragraph (b) of this section, is one dollar or more, may, at his option, designate that one dollar shall be paid over to the Presidential Election Campaign Fund, referred to in §301.6096-1(a). Where in accordance with prior law, such a designation was made for the account of any candidate of any specified political party, or for a general account for all candidates for election to the offices of President and Vice President of the United States, such a designation shall be treated solely as a designation to such fund.

(2) In the case of a joint return of a husband and wife, each spouse may designate that one dollar be paid to the fund as provided in paragraph (a)(1) of this section only if the joint income tax liability of the husband and wife is two dollars or more.

(b) *Income tax liability.*—For purposes of paragraph (a) of this section, the income tax liability of an individual for any taxable year is the amount of the tax imposed by chapter 1 on such individual for such taxable year (as shown on his return), reduced by the sum of the credits (as shown on his return).

(c) *Manner and time of designation.*—(1) A designation under paragraph (a) of this section may be made with respect to any such taxable year at the time of the filing of the return of the tax imposed by chapter 1 for such taxable year. If such designation is made at the time of filing the original return for such year, it shall be made by the individual on the form furnished by the Internal Revenue Service for such purpose in accordance with the instructions applicable thereto.

(2) With respect to any taxable year ending on or after December 31, 1972 and beginning before January 1, 1973, for which no designation was made under paragraph (c)(1) of this section, a designation may be made on the form furnished by the Internal Revenue Service for such purpose, filed within 20 and one half months after the due date for the original return for such taxable year. In the case of a joint return where neither spouse made a designation or where only one spouse made a designation, a designation may be made, as provided in this subparagraph, by the spouse or spouses who had not previously made a designation.

(3) A designation once made, whether by an original return or otherwise, may not be revoked. [Reg. §301.6096-2.]

□ [*T.D.* 7304, 2-1-74.]

Miscellaneous Provisions

[Reg. §31.6101-1]

§31.6101-1. Period covered by returns.—The period covered by any return required under the regulations in this subpart shall be as provided in those provisions of the regulations under which the return is required to be made. See §31.6011(a)-1, relating to returns of taxes under the Federal Insurance Contributions Act; §31.6011(a)-2, relating to returns of taxes under the Railroad Retirement Tax Act; §31.6011(a)-3, relating to returns of tax under the Federal Unemployment Tax Act; §31.6011(a)-4, relating to returns of income tax withheld under section 3402; and §31.6011(a)-5, relating to monthly returns of taxes under the Federal Insurance Contributions Act and of income tax withheld under section 3402. [Reg. §31.6101-1.]

□ [*T.D.* 6472, 6-22-60.]

[Reg. §40.6101-1]

§40.6101-1. Period covered by returns.—See §40.6011(a)-1(a)(2) for the rules relating to the period covered by the return. [Reg. §40.6101-1.]

□ [*T.D.* 8442, 10-21-92. *Amended by T.D.* 8963, 8-8-2001.]

[Reg. §41.6101-1]

§41.6101-1. Period covered by returns.—Each return is for a taxable period as defined in section 4482. [Reg. §41.6101-1.]

□ [*T.D.* 6216. *Amended by T.D.* 6743, 6-22-64 *and T.D.* 8879, 3-30-2000.]

[Reg. §301.6101-1]

§301.6101-1. Period covered by returns or other documents.—For provisions concerning the period covered by returns or other documents, see the regulations relating to the particular tax. [Reg. §301.6101-1.]

□ [*T.D.* 6498, 10-24-60.]

[Reg. §1.6102-1]

§1.6102-1. Computations on returns or other documents.—For provisions with respect to the rounding off to whole-dollar amounts of money items on returns and accompanying schedules, see §301.6102-1 of this chapter (Regulations on Procedure and Administration). [Reg. §1.6102-1.]

□ [*T.D.* 6364, 2-13-59.]

[Reg. §301.6102-1]

§301.6102-1. Computations on returns or other documents.—(a) *Amounts shown on forms.*—To the extent permitted by any internal revenue form or instructions prescribed for use with respect to any internal revenue return, declaration, statement, other document, or supporting schedules, any amount required to be reported on such form shall be entered at the nearest whole dollar amount. The extent to which, and the conditions under which, such whole dollar amounts shall be entered on any form will be set forth in the instructions issued with respect to such form. For the purpose of the computation to the nearest dollar, a fractional part of a dollar shall be disregarded unless it amounts to one-half dollar or more, in which case the amount (determined without regard to the fractional part of a dollar) shall be increased by $1. The following illustrates the application of this paragraph:

Exact amount	*To be reported as—*
$18.49	$18
18.50	19
18.51	19

(b) *Election not to use whole dollar amounts.*—(1) *Method of election.*—Where any internal revenue form, or the instructions issued with respect to such form, provide that whole dollar amounts shall be reported, any person making a return, declaration, statement, or other document on such form may elect not to use whole dollar amounts by reporting thereon all amounts in full, including cents.

(2) *Time of election.*—The election not to use whole dollar amounts must be made at the time of filing the return, declaration, statement, or other document. Such election may not be revoked after the time prescribed for filing such return, declaration, statement, or other document, including extensions of time granted for such filing. Such election may be made on any return, declaration, statement, or other document which is filed after the time prescribed for filing (including extensions of time), and such an election is irrevocable.

(3) *Effect of election.*—The taxpayer's election shall be binding only on the return, declaration, statement, or other document filed for a taxable year or period, and a new election may be made on the return, declaration, statement, or other document filed for a subsequent taxable year or period. An election by either a husband or a wife not to report whole dollar amounts on a separate income tax return shall be binding on any subsequent joint return filed under the provisions of section 6013(b).

(4) *Fractional part of a cent.*—For treatment of the fractional part of a cent in the payment of taxes, see section 6313 and §301.6313-1.

(c) *Inapplicability to computation of amount.*—The provisions of paragraph (a) of this section apply only to amounts required to be reported on a return, declaration, statement, or other document. They do not apply to items which must be taken into account in making the computations necessary to determine such amounts. For example, each item of receipt must be taken into account at its exact amount, including cents, in computing the amount of total receipts required to be reported on an income tax return or supporting schedule. It is the amount of total receipts, so computed, which is to be reported at the nearest whole dollar on the return or supporting schedule.

(d) *Effect on accounting method.*—Section 6102 and this section have no effect on any authorized accounting method. [Reg. §301.6102-1.]

☐ [*T.D. 6142, 9-2-55. Amended by T.D. 6498, 10-24-60.*]

[Reg. §301.6103(a)-1]

§301.6103(a)-1. Disclosures after December 31, 1976 by officers and employees of Federal agencies of returns and return information (including taxpayer return information) disclosed to such officers and employees by the Internal Revenue Service before January 1, 1977 for a purpose not involving tax administration.—(a) *General rule.*—Except as provided by paragraph (b) of this section, a return or return information (including taxpayer return information), as defined in section 6103(b)(1), (2), and (3) of the Internal Revenue Code, disclosed by the Internal Revenue Service before January 1, 1977, to an officer or employee of a Federal agency (as defined in section 6103(b)(9)) for a purpose not involving tax administration (as defined in section 6103(b)(4)) pursuant to the authority of section 6103 (or any order of the President under section 6103 or rules and regulations thereunder prescribed by the Secretary or his delegate and approved by the President) before amendment of such section by section 1202 of the Tax Reform Act of 1976 (Pub. L. 94-455, 90 Stat. 1667) may be disclosed by, or on behalf of, such officer, employee, or agency after December 31, 1976, for any purpose authorized by such section (or such order or rules and regulations) before such amendment.

(b) *Exception.*—Notwithstanding the provisions of paragraph (a) of this section, a return or return information (including taxpayer return information) disclosed before January 1, 1977, by the Service to an officer or employee of a Federal agency for a purpose unrelated to tax administration as described in paragraph (a) may, after December 31, 1976, be disclosed by, or on behalf of, such agency, officer, or employee in an administrative or judicial proceeding only if such proceeding is one described in section 6103(i)(4) of the Code and if the requirements of section 6103(i)(4) have first been met. [Reg. §301.6103(a)-1.]

☐ [*T.D. 7723, 9-30-80.*]

[Reg. §301.6103(a)-2]

§301.6103(a)-2. Disclosures after December 31, 1976 by attorneys of the Department of Justice and officers and employees of the Office of the Chief Counsel for the Internal Revenue Service of returns and return information (including taxpayer return information) disclosed to such attorneys, officers, and employees by the Service before January 1, 1977 for a purpose involving tax administration.—(a) *General rule.*—Except as provided by paragraph (b) of this section and subject to the requirements of this paragraph, a return or return information (including taxpayer return information), as defined in section 6103(b)(1), (2), and (3) of the Internal Revenue Code disclosed by the Internal Revenue Service before January 1, 1977, to an attorney of the Department of Justice (including a United States attorney) or to an officer or employee of the Office of the Chief Counsel for the Service for a purpose involving tax administration(as defined in section 6103(b)(4)) pursuant to the authority of section 6103 (or any order of the President under section 6103 or rules and regulations thereunder prescribed by the Secretary or his delegate and approved by the President) before amendment of such section by section 1202 of the Tax Reform Act of 1976 (Pub. L. 94-455, 90 Stat. 1667) may be disclosed by, or on behalf of, such attorney, officer, or employee after December 31, 1976, for any purpose authorized by such section (or such order or rules and regulations) before such amendment.

(b) *Exception.*—Notwithstanding the provisions of paragraph (a) of this section, a return or return information (including taxpayer return information) disclosed before January 1, 1977, by the Service to an attorney of the Department of Justice or to an officer or employee of the Office of the Chief Counsel for the Service for a purpose related to tax administration as described in paragraph (a) may, after December 31, 1976, be disclosed by, or on behalf of, such attorney, officer, or employee in an administrative or judicial proceeding only if such proceeding is one described in section 6103(h)(4) of the Code and if the requirements of section 6103(h)(4) have first been met. [Reg. §301.6103(a)-2.]

☐ [*T.D. 7723, 9-30-80.*]

[Reg. § 301.6103(c)-1]

§ 301.6103(c)-1. Disclosure of returns and return information to designee of taxpayer.—
(a) *Overview.*—Subject to such requirements and conditions as the Secretary may prescribe by regulation, section 6103(c) of the Internal Revenue Code authorizes the Internal Revenue Service to disclose a taxpayer's return or return information to such person or persons as the taxpayer may designate in a request for or consent to such disclosure, or to any other person at the taxpayer's request to the extent necessary to comply with the taxpayer's request to such other person for information or assistance. This regulation contains the requirements that must be met before, and the conditions under which, the Internal Revenue Service may make such disclosures. Paragraph (b) of this section provides the requirements that are generally applicable to designate a third party to receive the taxpayer's returns and return information. Paragraph (c) of this section provides requirements under which the Internal Revenue Service may disclose information in connection with a taxpayer's written or nonwritten request for a third party to provide information or assistance with regard to a tax matter, for example, a Congressional inquiry. Paragraph (d) of this section provides the parameters for disclosure consents connected with electronic return filing programs and combined Federal-State filing. Finally, paragraph (e) of this section provides definitions and general rules related to requests for or consents to disclosure.

(b) *Disclosure of returns and return information to person or persons designated in a written request or consent.*—(1) *General requirements.*—Pursuant to section 6103(c) of the Internal Revenue Code, the Internal Revenue Service (or an agent or contractor of the Internal Revenue Service) may disclose a taxpayer's return or return information (in written or nonwritten form) to such person or persons as the taxpayer may designate in a request for or consent to such disclosure. A request for or consent to disclosure under this paragraph (b) must be in the form of a separate written document pertaining solely to the authorized disclosure. (For the meaning of separate written document, see paragraph (e)(1) of this section.) The separate written document must be signed (see paragraph (e)(2) of this section) and dated by the taxpayer who filed the return or to whom the return information relates. At the time it is signed and dated by the taxpayer, the written document must also indicate—

(i) The taxpayer's taxpayer identity information described in section 6103(b)(6);

(ii) The identity of the person or persons to whom the disclosure is to be made;

(iii) The type of return (or specified portion of the return) or return information (and the particular data) that is to be disclosed; and

(iv) The taxable year or years covered by the return or return information.

(2) *Requirement that request or consent be received within one hundred twenty days of when signed and dated.*—The disclosure of a return or return information authorized by a written request for or written consent to the disclosure shall not be made unless the request or consent is received by the Internal Revenue Service (or an agent or contractor of the Internal Revenue Service) within 120 days following the date upon which the request or consent was signed and dated by the taxpayer.

(c) *Disclosure of returns and return information to designee of taxpayer to comply with taxpayer's request for information or assistance.*—If a taxpayer makes a written or nonwritten request, directly to another person or to the Internal Revenue Service, that such other person (for example, a member of Congress, friend, or relative of the taxpayer) provide information or assistance relating to the taxpayer's return or to a transaction or other contact between the taxpayer and the Internal Revenue Service, the Internal Revenue Service (or an agent or contractor of the Internal Revenue Service or a Federal government agency performing a Federal tax administration function) may disclose returns or return information (in written or nonwritten form) to such other person under the circumstances set forth in paragraphs (c)(1) through (3) of this section.

(1) *Written request for information or assistance.*—(i) The taxpayer's request for information or assistance may be in the form of a letter or other written document, which must be signed (see paragraph (e)(2) of this section) and dated by the taxpayer. The taxpayer must also indicate in the written request—

(A) The taxpayer's taxpayer identity information described in section 6103(b)(6);

(B) The identity of the person or persons to whom disclosure is to be made; and

(C) Sufficient facts underlying the request for information or assistance to enable the Internal Revenue Service to determine the nature and extent of the information or assistance requested and the returns or return information to be disclosed in order to comply with the taxpayer's request.

(ii) A person who receives a copy of a taxpayer's written request for information or assistance but who is not the addressee of the request, such as a member of Congress who is provided with a courtesy copy of a taxpayer's letter to another member of Congress or to the Internal Revenue Service, cannot receive returns or return information under paragraph (c)(1) of this section.

(2) *Nonwritten request or consent.*—(i) A request for information or assistance may also be nonwritten. Disclosure of returns and return information to a designee pursuant to a taxpayer's nonwritten request will be made only after the Internal Revenue Service has—

(A) Obtained from the taxpayer sufficient facts underlying the request for information or assistance to enable the Internal Revenue Service to determine the nature and extent of the information or assistance requested and the return or return information to be disclosed in order to comply with the taxpayer's request;

   (B) Confirmed the identity of the taxpayer and the designee; and

   (C) Confirmed the date, the nature, and the extent of the information or assistance requested.

  (ii) Examples of disclosures pursuant to nonwritten requests for information or assistance under this paragraph (c)(2) include, but are not limited to, disclosures to a friend, relative, or other person whom the taxpayer brings to an interview or meeting with Internal Revenue Service officials, and disclosures to a person whom the taxpayer wishes to involve in a telephone conversation with Internal Revenue Service officials.

  (iii) As long as the requirements of this paragraph (c)(2) are met, the taxpayer does not need to be present, either in person or as part of a telephone conversation, for disclosures of returns and return information to be made to the other person.

  (3) *Rules applicable to written and nonwritten requests for information or assistance.*—A return or return information will be disclosed to the taxpayer's designee as provided by this paragraph only to the extent considered necessary by the Internal Revenue Service to comply with the taxpayer's request or consent. Such disclosures shall not be made unless the request or consent is received by the Internal Revenue Service, its agent or contractor, or a Federal government agency performing a Federal tax administration function in connection with a request for advice or assistance relating to such function. This paragraph (c) does not apply to disclosures to a taxpayer's representative in connection with practice before the Internal Revenue Service (as defined in Treasury Department Circular No. 230, 31 CFR Part 10). For disclosures in these cases, see section 6103(e)(6) and §§ 601.501 through 601.508 of this chapter.

 (d) *Acknowledgments of electronically filed returns and other documents; combined filing programs with State tax agencies.*—The requirements of paragraphs (b) and (c) of this section do not apply to this paragraph (d).

  (1) *Acknowledgment of, and notices regarding, electronically filed returns and other documents.*—When a taxpayer files returns or other documents or information with the Internal Revenue Service electronically, the taxpayer may consent to the disclosure of return information to the transmitter or other third party, such as the taxpayer's financial institution, necessary to acknowledge that the electronic transmission was received and either accepted or rejected by the Internal Revenue Service, the reason for any rejection, and such other information as the Internal Revenue Service determines is necessary to the operation of the electronic filing program. The consent must inform the taxpayer of the return information that will be transmitted and to whom disclosure will be made.

  (2) *Combined return filing programs with State tax agencies.*—(i) A taxpayer's participation in a combined return filing program between the Internal Revenue Service and a State agency, body, or commission (State agency) described in section 6103(d)(1) constitutes a consent to the disclosure by the Internal Revenue Service, to the State agency, of taxpayer identity information, signature, and items of common data contained on the return. For purposes of this paragraph, common data means information reflected on the Federal return required by State law to be attached to or included on the State return. Instructions accompanying the forms or published procedures involved in such program must indicate that by participating in the program, the taxpayer is consenting to the Internal Revenue Service's disclosure to the State agency of the taxpayer identity information, signature, and items of common data, and that such information will be treated by the State agency as if it had been directly filed with the State agency. Such instructions or procedures must also describe any verification that takes place before the taxpayer identity information, signature and common data is transmitted by the Internal Revenue Service to the State agency.

  (ii) No disclosures may be made under this paragraph (d)(2) unless there are provisions of State law protecting the confidentiality of such items of common data.

 (e) *Definitions and rules applicable to this section.*—(1) *Separate written document.*—(i) For the purposes of paragraph (b) of this section, *separate written document* means—

  (A) Text appearing on one or more sheets of $8^1/2$-inch by 11-inch or larger paper, each of which pertains solely to the authorized disclosure, so long as such sheet or sheets, taken together, contain all the elements described in paragraph (b)(1) of this section;

  (B) Text appearing on one or more computer screens, each of which pertains solely to the authorized disclosure, so long as such screen or, taken together, such screens—

   (1) contain all the elements described in paragraph (b)(1) of this section,

   (2) can be signed (see paragraph (e)(2) of this section) and dated by the taxpayer, and

   (3) can be reproduced, if necessary; or

  (C) A consent on the record in an administrative or judicial proceeding, or a transcript of such proceeding recording such consent, containing the information required under paragraph (b)(1) of this section.

  (ii) A provision included in a taxpayer's application for a loan or other benefit authorizing the grantor of the loan or other benefit to obtain any financial information, including returns or return information, from any source as the grantor may request for purposes of verifying information supplied on the application, does not meet the requirements of paragraph (b)(1) of this section because the provision is not a separate written document relating solely to the disclosure of returns and return information. In addition, the provision does not contain the other information specified in paragraph (b)(1) of this section.

(2) *Method of signing.*—A request for or consent to disclosure may be signed by any method of signing the Secretary has prescribed pursuant to § 301.6061-1(b) in forms, instructions, or other appropriate guidance.

(3) *Permissible designees and public forums.*— Permissible designees under this section include individuals; trusts; estates; corporations; partnerships; Federal, State, local and foreign government agencies or subunits of such agencies; or the general public. When disclosures are to be made in a public forum, such as in a courtroom or congressional hearing, the request for or consent to disclosure must describe the circumstances surrounding the public disclosure, *e.g.*, congressional hearing, judicial proceeding, media, and the date or dates of the disclosure. When a designee is an individual, this section does not authorize disclosures to other individuals associated with such individual, such as employees of such individual or members of such individual's staff.

(4) *Authority to execute a request for or consent to disclosure.*—Any person who may obtain returns under section 6103(e)(1) through (5), except section 6103(e)(1)(D)(iii), may execute a request for or consent to disclose a return or return information to third parties. For taxpayers that are legal entities, such as corporations and municipal bond issuers, any officer of the entity with authority under applicable State law to legally bind the entity may execute a request for or consent to disclosure. A person described in section 6103(e)(6) (a taxpayer's representative or individual holding a power of attorney) may not execute a request for or consent to disclosure unless the designation of representation or power of attorney specifically delegates such authority. A designee pursuant to this section does not have authority to execute a request for or consent to disclosure permitting the Internal Revenue Service to disclose returns or return information to another person.

(5) *No disclosure of return information if impairment.*—A disclosure of return information shall not be made under this section if the Internal Revenue Service determines that the disclosure would seriously impair Federal tax administration (as defined in section 6103(b)(4) of the Internal Revenue Code).

(f) *Applicability date.*—This section is applicable on April 29, 2003, except that paragraph (b)(2) is applicable to section 6103(c) authorizations signed on or after October 19, 2009.

(g) *Effective date.*—This section is effective on April 29, 2003, except that paragraphs (b)(2) and (f) are effective on May 7, 2013. [Reg. § 301.6103(c)-1.]

□ [*T.D.* 9054, 4-28-2003. *Amended by T.D. 9618*, 5-6-2013.]

[Reg. § 301.6103(h)(2)-1]

§ 301.6103(h)(2)-1. **Disclosure of returns and return information (including taxpayer return information) to and by officers and employees of the Department of Justice for use in Federal grand jury proceeding, or in preparation for proceeding or investigation, involving tax administration.**—(a) *Disclosure of returns and return information (including taxpayer return information) to and by officers and employees of the Department of Justice.*—(1) Returns and return information (including taxpayer return information), as defined in section 6103(b)(1), (2), and (3) of the Internal Revenue Code, shall, to the extent provided by section 6103(h)(2)(A), (B), and (C) and subject to the requirements of section 6103(h)(3), be open to inspection by or disclosure to officers and employees of the Department of Justice (including United States attorneys) personally and directly engaged in, and for their necessary use in, any Federal grand jury proceeding, or preparation for any proceeding (or for their necessary use in an investigation which may result in such a proceeding) before a Federal grand jury or any Federal or State court, in a matter involving tax administration (as defined in section 6103(b)(4)), including any such proceeding (or any such investigation) also involving the enforcement of a related Federal criminal statute which has been referred by the Secretary to the Department of Justice.

(2) Returns and return information (including taxpayer return information) inspected by or disclosed to officers and employees of the Department of Justice as provided in paragraph (a)(1) of this section may also be used by such officers and employees or disclosed by them to other officers and employees (including United States attorneys and supervisory personnel, such as Section Chiefs, Deputy Assistant Attorneys General, Assistant Attorneys General, the Deputy Attorney General, and the Attorney General), of the Department of Justice where necessary—

(i) In connection with any Federal grand jury proceeding, or preparation for any proceeding (or with an investigation which may result in such a proceeding), described in paragraph (a)(1), or

(ii) In connection with any Federal grand jury proceeding, or preparation for any proceeding (or with an investigation which may result in such a proceeding), described in paragraph (a)(1) which also involves enforcement of a specific Federal criminal statute other than one described in paragraph (a)(1) to which the United States is or may be a party, provided such matter involves or arises out of the particular facts and circumstances giving rise to the proceeding (or investigation) described in paragraph (a)(1) and further provided the tax portion of such proceeding (or investigation) has been duly authorized by or on behalf of the Assistant Attorney General for the Tax Division of the Department of Justice, pursuant to the request of the Secretary, as a proceeding (or investigation) described in paragraph (a)(1). If, in the course of a Federal grand jury proceeding, or preparation for a proceeding (or the conduct of an investigation which may result in such a proceeding), described in subdivision (ii) of this subparagraph, the tax administration portion thereof is terminated for any reason, any further use or disclosure of such returns or taxpayer return information in such Federal grand jury proceeding, or preparation or investigation, with respect to the remaining portion may be made only pursuant to, and upon the grant of, a court order as provided by section 6103(i)(1)(A), provided, however, that the returns and taxpayer return information may in any event be used for purposes of obtaining the necessary court order.

(b) *Disclosure of returns and return information (including taxpayer return information) by officers and employees of the Department of Justice.*—(1) Returns and return information (including taxpayer return information), as defined in section 6103(b)(1), (2), and (3) of the Code, inspected by or disclosed to officers and employees of the Department of Justice as provided by paragraph (a) of this section may be disclosed by such officers and employees to other persons, including, but not limited to, persons described in paragraph (b)(2), but only to the extent necessary in connection with a Federal grand jury proceeding, or the proper preparation for a proceeding (or in connection with an investigation which may result in such a proceeding), described in paragraph (a). Such disclosures may include, but are not limited to, disclosures—

(i) To properly accomplish any purpose or activity of the nature described in section 6103(k)(6) and the regulations thereunder which is essential to such Federal grand jury proceeding, or to such proper preparation (or to such investigation);

(ii) To properly interview, consult, depose, or interrogate or otherwise obtain relevant information from, the taxpayer to whom such return or return information relates (or such taxpayer's legal representative) or from any witness who may be called to give evidence in the proceeding; or

(iii) To properly conduct negotiations concerning, or obtain authorization for, settlement or disposition of the proceeding, in whole or in part, or stipulations of fact in connection with the proceeding.
Disclosure of a return or return information to a person other than the taxpayer to whom such return or return information relates or such taxpayer's legal representative to properly accomplish any purpose or activity described in this paragraph should be made, however, only if such purpose or activity cannot otherwise properly be accomplished without making such disclosure.

(2) Among those persons to whom returns and return information may be disclosed by officers and employees of the Department of Jus-

tice as provided by paragraph (a)(1) of this section are—

(i) Other officers and employees of the Department of Justice, such as personnel of an office, board, division, or bureau of such department (for example, the Federal Bureau of Investigation or the Drug Enforcement Administration), clerical personnel (for example secretaries, stenographers, docket and file room clerks, and mail room employees) and supervisory personnel (such as supervisory personnel of the Federal Bureau of Investigation or the Drug Enforcement Administration);

(ii) Officers and employees of another Federal agency (as defined in section 6103(b)(9)) working under the direction and control of any such officers and employees of the Department of Justice; and

(iii) Court reporters. [Reg. § 301.6103(h)(2)-1.]

☐ [*T.D. 7573, 11-28-78. Amended by T.D. 7723,* 9-30-80.]

[Reg. § 301.6103(h)(4)-1]

§ 301.6103(h)(4)-1. Disclosure of returns and return information in whistleblower administrative proceedings.—(a) *In general.*—A whistleblower administrative proceeding (as described in § 301.7623-3) is an administrative proceeding pertaining to tax administration within the meaning of section 6103(h)(4).

(b) *Disclosures in whistleblower administrative proceedings.*—Pursuant to section 6103(h)(4) and paragraph (a) of this section, the Director, officers, and employees of the Whistleblower Office may disclose returns and return information (as defined by section 6103(b)) to a whistleblower (or the whistleblower's legal representative, if any) to the extent necessary to conduct a whistleblower administrative proceeding (as described in § 301.7623-3), including but not limited to—

(1) By communicating a preliminary award recommendation or preliminary denial letter to the whistleblower;

(2) By providing the whistleblower with an award report package;

(3) By conducting a meeting with the whistleblower to review documents supporting the preliminary award recommendation; and

(4) By sending an award decision letter, award determination letter, or award denial letter to the whistleblower.

(c) *Effective/applicability date.*—This rule is effective on August 12, 2014. This rule applies to information submitted on or after August 12, 2014, and to claims for award under sections 7623(a) and 7623(b) that are open as of August 12, 2014. [Reg. § 301.6103(h)(4)-1.]

☐ [*T.D. 9687, 8-7-2014.*]

[Reg. § 301.6103(i)-1]

§ 301.6103(i)-1. Disclosure of returns and return information (including taxpayer return information) to and by officers and employees of the Department of Justice or another Federal agency for use in Federal grand jury proceeding, or preparation for proceeding or investigation, involving enforcement of Federal criminal statute not involving tax administration.— (a) *Disclosure of returns and return information (including taxpayer return information) to officers and employees of the Department of Justice or another Federal agency.*—Returns and return information (including taxpayer return information), as defined in section 6103(b)(1), (2), and (3) of the Internal Revenue Code, shall, to the extent provided by section 6103(i)(1), (2), and (3) and subject to the requirements of section 6103(i)(1) and (2), be open to inspection by or disclosure to officers and employees of the Department of Justice (including United States attorneys) or of another Federal agency (as defined in section 6103(b)(9)) personally and directly engaged in, and for their necessary use in, any Federal grand jury proceeding, or preparation for any administration or judicial proceeding (or their necessary use in an investigation which may result in such a proceeding), pertaining to enforcement of a specifically designated Federal criminal statute not involving or related to tax administration to which the United States or such agency is or may be a party.

(b) *Disclosure of returns and return information (including taxpayer return information) by officers and employees of the Department of Justice or another Federal agency.*—(1) Returns and return information (including taxpayer return information), as defined in section 6103(b)(1), (2), and (3) of the Code, disclosed to officers and employees of the Department of Justice or other Federal agency (as defined in section 6103(b)(9)) as provided by paragraph (a) of this section may be disclosed by such officers and employees to other persons, including, but not limited to, persons described in subparagraph (2) of this paragraph, but only to the extent necessary in connection with a Federal grand jury proceeding, or the proper preparation for a proceeding (or in connection with an investigation which may result in such a proceeding), described in paragraph (a). Such disclosures may include, but are not limited to, disclosures where necessary—

(i) To properly obtain the services of persons having special knowledge or technical skills (such as, but not limited to, handwriting analysis, photographic development, sound recording enhancement, or voice identification);

(ii) To properly interview, consult, depose, or interrogate or otherwise obtain relevant information from, the taxpayer to whom such return or return information relates (or such taxpayer's legal representative) or any witness who may be called to give evidence in the proceeding; or

(iii) To properly conduct negotiations concerning, or obtain authorization for, disposition of the proceeding, in whole or in part, or stipulations of fact in connection with the proceeding.

Disclosure of a return or return information to a person other than the taxpayer to whom such return or return information relates or such taxpayer's legal representative to properly accomplish any purpose or activity described in this subparagraph should be made, however, only if such purpose or activity cannot otherwise properly be accomplished without making such disclosures.

(2) Among those persons to whom returns and return information may be disclosed by officers and employees of the Department of Justice or other Federal agency as provided by subparagraph (1) of this paragraph are—

(i) Other officers and employees of the Department of Justice (including an office, board, division, or bureau of such department, such as the Federal Bureau of Investigation or the Drug Enforcement Administration) or other Federal agency described in subparagraph (1), such as clerical personnel (for example, secretaries, stenographers, docket and file room clerks, and mail room employees) and supervisory personnel (for example, in the case of the Department of Justice, Section Chiefs, Deputy Assistant Attorneys General, Assistant Attorneys General, the Deputy Attorney General, the Attorney General, and supervisory personnel of the Federal Bureau of Investigation or the Drug Enforcement Administration);

(ii) Officers and employees of another Federal agency (as defined in section 6103(b)(9)) working under the direction and control of such officers and employees of the Department of Justice or other Federal agency described in subparagraph (1); and

(iii) Court reporters. [Reg. § 301.6103(i)-1.]

☐ [T.D. 7723, 9-30-80.]

[Reg. § 301.6103(j)(1)-1]

§ 301.6103(j)(1)-1. **Disclosures of return information reflected on returns to officers and employees of the Department of Commerce for certain statistical purposes and related activities.**—(a) *General rule.*—Pursuant to the provisions of section 6103(j)(1) of the Internal Revenue Code and subject to the requirements of paragraph (d) of this section, officers or employees of the Internal Revenue Service will disclose return information (as defined by section 6103(b)(2) but not including return information described in section 6103(o)(2)) reflected on returns to officers and employees of the Department of Commerce to the extent, and for such purposes as may be, provided by paragraphs (b) and (c) of this section. Further, in the case of any disclosure of return information reflected on returns so provided by paragraphs (b) and (c) of this section, the tax period or accounting period to which such information relates will also be disclosed. "Return information reflected on returns" includes, but is not limited to, information on returns, information derived from processing such returns, and information derived from the Social Security Administration and other sources for the purposes of establishing and maintaining taxpayer information relating to returns.

(b) *Disclosure of return information reflected on returns to officers and employees of the Bureau of the*

Census.—(1) Officers or employees of the Internal Revenue Service will disclose the following return information reflected on returns of individual taxpayers to officers and employees of the Bureau of the Census for purposes of, but only to the extent necessary in, conducting and preparing, as authorized by chapter 5 of title 13, United States Code, intercensal estimates of population and income for all geographic areas included in the population estimates program and demographic statistics programs, censuses, and related program evaluation:

(i) Taxpayer identity information (as defined in section 6103(b)(6) of the Internal Revenue Code), validity code with respect to the taxpayer identifying number (as described in section 6109), and taxpayer identity information of spouse and dependents, if reported.

(ii) Location codes (including area/district office and campus/service center codes).

(iii) Marital status.

(iv) Number and classification of reported exemptions.

(v) Wage and salary income.

(vi) Dividend income.

(vii) Interest income.

(viii) Gross rent and royalty income.

(ix) Total of—

(A) Wages, salaries, tips, etc.;

(B) Interest income;

(C) Dividend income;

(D) Alimony received;

(E) Business income;

(F) Pensions and annuities;

(G) Income from rents, royalties, partnerships, estates, trusts, etc.;

(H) Farm income;

(I) Unemployment compensation; and

(J) Total Social Security benefits.

(x) Adjusted gross income.

(xi) Type of tax return filed.

(xii) Entity code.

(xiii) Code indicators for Form 1040, Form 1040 (Schedules A, C, D, E, F, and SE), and Form 8814.

(xiv) Posting cycle date relative to filing.

(xv) Social Security benefits.

(xvi) Earned Income (as defined in section 32(c)(2).

(xvii) Number of Earned Income Tax Credit-eligible qualifying children.

(xviii) Electronic Filing System Indicator.

(xix) Return Processing Indicator.

(xx) Paid Preparer Code.

(2) Officers or employees of the Internal Revenue Service will disclose to officers and employees of the Bureau of the Census for purposes of, but only to the extent necessary in, conducting, as authorized by chapter 5 of title 13, United States Code, demographic, economic, and agricultural statistics programs and censuses and related program evaluation—

(i) From the business master files of the Internal Revenue Service—the taxpayer name directory and entity records consisting of taxpayer identity information (as defined in section 6103(b)(6)) with respect to taxpayers engaged in a trade or business, the principal industrial activity code, the filing requirement code, the employment code, the physical location, the location codes (including area/district office and campus/service center codes), and monthly corrections of, and additions to, such entity records;

(ii) From Form SS-4—all information reflected on such form;

(iii) From an employment tax return—

(A) Taxpayer identifying number (as described in section 6109) of the employer;

(B) Total compensation reported;

(C) Master file tax account code (MFT);

(D) Taxable period covered by such return;

(E) Employer code;

(F) Document locator number;

(G) Record code;

(H) Total number of individuals employed in the taxable period covered by the return;

(I) Total taxable wages paid for purposes of chapter 21; and

(J) Total taxable tip income reported for purposes of chapter 21;

(iv) From Form 1040 (Schedule SE)—

(A) Taxpayer identifying number of self-employed individual;

(B) Business activities subject to the tax imposed by chapter 21;

(C) Net earnings from farming;

(D) Net earnings from nonfarming activities;

(E) Total net earnings from self-employment; and

(F) Taxable self-employment income for purposes of chapter 2;

(v) Total Social Security taxable earnings; and

(vi) Quarters of Social Security coverage.

(3) Officers or employees of the Internal Revenue Service will disclose the following business-related return information reflected on returns of taxpayers to officers and employees of the Bureau of the Census for purposes of, but only to the extent necessary in, conducting and preparing, as authorized by chapter 5 of title 13, United States Code, demographic and economic statistics programs, censuses, and surveys. (The "returns of taxpayers" include, but are not limited to: Form 941; Form 990 series; Form 1040 series and Schedules C and SE; Form 1065 and all attending schedules and Form 8825; Form 1120 series and all attending schedules and Form 8825; Form 851; Form 1096; and other business returns, schedules and forms that the Internal Revenue Service may issue.):

(i) Taxpayer identity information (as defined in section 6103(b)(6)) including parent corporation, shareholder, partner, and employer identity information.

(ii) Gross income, profits, or receipts.

(iii) Returns and allowances.

(iv) Cost of labor, salaries, and wages.

(v) Total expenses or deductions.

(vi) Total assets.

(vii) Beginning-and end-of-year inventory.

(viii) Royalty income.

(ix) Interest income, including portfolio interest.

(x) Rental income, including gross rents.

(xi) Tax-exempt interest income.

(xii) Net gain from sales of business property.

(xiii) Other income.

(xiv) Total income.

(xv) Percentage of stock owned by each shareholder.

(xvi) Percentage of capital ownership of each partner.

(xvii) Principal industrial activity code, including the business description.

(xviii) Consolidated return indicator.

(xix) Wages, tips, and other compensation.

(xx) Social Security wages.

(xxi) Deferred wages.

(xxii) Social Security tip income.

(xxiii) Total Social Security taxable earnings.

(xxiv) Gross distributions from employer-sponsored and individual retirement plans from Form 1099-R.

(xxv) From Form 6765 (when filed with corporation income tax returns)—total qualified research expenses.

(xxvi) Social Security tip income.

(xxvii) Total Social Security taxable earnings.

(xxviii) Gross distributions from employer-sponsored and individual retirement plans from Form 1099-R.

(xxix) Total number of documents reported on Form 1096 transmitting Forms 1099-MISC.

(xxx) Total amount reported on Form 1096 transmitting Forms 1099-MISC.

(4) Officers or employees of the Internal Revenue Service will disclose return information reflected on returns of taxpayers contained in the exempt organization master files of the Internal Revenue Service to officers and employees of the Bureau of the Census for purposes of, but only to the extent necessary in, conducting and preparing, as authorized by chapter 5 of title 13, United States Code, economic censuses. This return information reflected on returns of taxpayers consists of taxpayer identity information (as defined in section 6103(b)(6)), activity codes, and filing requirement code, and monthly corrections of, and additions to, such information.

(5) Subject to the requirements of paragraph (d) of this section and §301.6103(p)(2)(B)-1, officers or employees of the Social Security Administration to whom the following return information reflected on returns has been disclosed as provided by section 6103(l)(1)(A) or (l)(5) may disclose such information to officers and employees of the Bureau of the Census for necessary purposes described in paragraph (b)(2) or (3) of this section:

(i) From Form SS-4—all information reflected on such form.

(ii) From Form 1040 (Schedule SE)—

(A) Taxpayer identifying number of self-employed individual;

(B) Business activities subject to the tax imposed by chapter 21;

(C) Net earnings from farming;

(D) Net earnings from nonfarming activities;

(E) Total net earnings from self-employment; and

(F) Taxable self-employment income for purposes of chapter 2.

(iii) From Form W-2, and related forms and schedules—

(A) Social Security number;

(B) Employer identification number;

(C) Wages, tips, and other compensation;

(D) Social Security wages; and

(E) Deferred wages.

(iv) Total Social Security taxable earnings.

(v) Quarters of Social Security coverage.

(6)(i) Officers or employees of the Internal Revenue Service will disclose the following return information (but not including return information described in section 6103(o)(2)) reflected on returns of corporations with respect to the tax imposed by chapter 1 to officers and employees of the Bureau of the Census for purposes of, but only to the extent necessary in, developing and preparing, as authorized by law, the Quarterly Financial Report:

(A) From the business master files of the Internal Revenue Service—

(1) Taxpayer identity information (as defined in section 6103(b)(6)), including parent corporation identity information;

(2) Document code;

(3) Location codes (including area/district office and campus/service center codes);

(4) Consolidated return and final return indicators;

(5) Principal industrial activity code;

(6) Partial year indicator,

(7) Annual accounting period;

(8) Gross receipts less returns and allowances; and

(9) Total assets.

(B) From Form SS-4—

(1) Month and year in which such form was executed;

(2) Taxpayer identity information; and

(3) Principal industrial activity, geographic, firm size, and reason for application codes.

(ii) Subject to the requirements of paragraph (d) of this section and § 301.6103(p)(2)(B)-1, officers or employees of the Social Security Administration to whom return information reflected on returns of corporations described in paragraph (b)(6)(i)(B) of this section has been disclosed as provided by section 6103(1)(1)(A) or (1)(5) may disclose such information to officers and employees of the Bureau of the Census for a purpose described in this paragraph (b)(6).

(iii) Return information reflected on employment tax returns disclosed pursuant to paragraphs (b)(2)(iii) (A), (B), (D), (I) and (J) of this section may be used by officers and employees of the Bureau of the Census for the purpose described in and subject to the limitations of this paragraph (b)(6).

(7) Officers or employees of the Internal Revenue Service will disclose the following return information reflected on Form 1098 "Mortgage Interest Statement" to officers and employees of the Bureau of the Census for purposes of, but only to the extent necessary in, conducting and preparing, as authorized by chapter 5 of title 13, United States Code, demographic statistics programs, censuses, and surveys—

(i) Payee/Payer/Employee Taxpayer Identification Number;

(ii) Payee/Payer/Employee Name (First, Middle, Last, Suffix);

(iii) Street Address;

(iv) City;

(v) State;

(vi) ZIP Code (9 digit);

(vii) Posting Cycle Week;

(viii) Posting Cycle Year; and

(ix) Document Code.

(c) *Disclosure of return information reflected on returns of corporations to officers and employees of the Bureau of Economic Analysis.*—(1) As authorized by law for purposes of, but only to the extent necessary in, conducting and preparing statistical analyses, the Internal Revenue Service will disclose to officers and employees of the Bureau of Economic Analysis all return information, regardless of format or medium and including edited information from the Statistics of Income sample, of designated classes or categories of corporations with respect to the tax imposed by chapter 1 of the Internal Revenue Code.

(2) [Reserved].

(3) The Internal Revenue Service will disclose the following return information reflected on returns filed by corporations to officers and employees of the Bureau of Economic Analysis:

(i) From the business master files of the Internal Revenue Service—

(A) Taxpayer identity information (as defined in section 6103(b)(6)) with respect to corporate taxpayers;

(B) Business or industry activity codes;

(C) Filing requirement code; and

(D) Physical location.

(ii) From Form SS-4, "Application for Employer Identification Number," filed by an entity identifying itself on the form as a corporation or a private services corporation—

(A) Taxpayer identity information (as defined in section 6103(b)(6), including legal, trade, and business name);

(B) Physical location;

(C) State or country of incorporation;

(D) Entity type (corporate only);

(E) Estimated highest number of employees expected in the next 12 months;

(F) Principal activity of the business;

(G) Principal line of merchandise;

(H) Posting cycle date relative to filing; and

(I) Document code.

(iii) From an employment tax return filed by a corporation—

(A) Taxpayer identity information (as defined in section 6103(b)(6));

(B) Total compensation reported;

(C) Taxable wages paid for purposes of Chapter 21 to each employee;

(D) Master file tax account code (MFT);

(E) Total number of individuals employed in the taxable period covered by the return;

(F) Posting cycle date relative to filing;

(G) Accounting period covered; and

(H) Document code.

(iv) From returns of corporate taxpayers, including Form 1120, "U.S. Corporation Income Tax Return," Form 851, "Affiliations Schedule," and other business returns, schedules and forms that the Internal Revenue Service may issue—

(A) Taxpayer identity information (as defined in section 6103(b)(6)), including that of a parent corporation, affiliate, or subsidiary; a shareholder; a foreign corporation of which one or more U.S. shareholders (as defined in section 951(b)) own at least 10% of the voting stock; a foreign trust; and a U.S. agent of a foreign trust;

(B) Gross sales and receipts;

(C) Gross income, including life insurance company gross income;

(D) Gross income from sources outside the U.S.;

(E) Gross rents from real property;

(F) Other Gross Rents;

(G) Total Gross Rents;

(H) Returns and allowances;

(I) Percentage of foreign ownership of corporations and trusts;

(J) Fact of ownership of foreign partnerships;

(K) Fact of ownership of foreign entity disregarded as a foreign entity;

(L) Country of the foreign owner;

(M) Gross value of the portion of the foreign trust owned by filer;

(N) Country of incorporation;

(O) Cost of labor, salaries, and wages;

(P) Total assets;

(Q) The quantity of certain forms attached that are returns of U.S. persons with respect to foreign disregarded entities, partnerships, and corporations.

(R) Posting cycle date relative to filing;

(S) Accounting period covered;

(T) Master file tax account code (MFT);

(U) Document code; and

(V) Principal industrial activity code.

(d) *Procedures and restrictions.*—Disclosure of return information reflected on returns by officers or employees of the Internal Revenue Service or the Social Security Administration as provided by paragraphs (b) and (c) of this section will be made only upon written request to the Commissioner of Internal Revenue by the Secretary of Commerce describing—

(1) The particular return information reflected on returns to be disclosed;

(2) The taxable period or date to which such return information reflected on returns relates; and

(3)(i) The particular purpose for which the return information reflected on returns is to be used, and designating by name and title the officers and employees of the Bureau of the Census or the Bureau of Economic Analysis to whom such disclosure is authorized.

(ii) No such officer or employee to whom return information reflected on returns is disclosed pursuant to the provisions of paragraph (b) or (c) of this section shall disclose such information to any person, other than the taxpayer to whom such return information reflected on returns relates or other officers or employees of such bureau whose duties or responsibilities require such disclosure for a purpose described in paragraph (b) or (c) of this section, except in a form which cannot be associated with, or otherwise identify, directly or indirectly, a particular taxpayer. If the Internal Revenue Service determines that the Bureau of the Census or the Bureau of Economic Analysis, or any officer or employee thereof, has failed to, or does not, satisfy the requirements of section 6103(p)(4) of the Internal Revenue Code or regulations or published procedures thereunder (see § 601.601(d)(2) of this chapter), the Internal Revenue Service may take such actions as are deemed necessary to ensure that such requirements are or will be satisfied, including suspension of disclosures of return information reflected on returns otherwise authorized by section 6103(j)(1) and paragraph (b) or (c) of this section, until the Internal Revenue Service determines that such requirements have been or will be satisfied.

(e) *Effective/applicability date.*—Paragraphs (b)(1)(xviii) through (xx) and (b)(7) of this section

apply to disclosures to the Bureau of the Census made on or after July 15, 2014. For rules that apply to disclosures to the Bureau of the Census before that date, see 26 CFR 301.6103(j)(1)-1 (revised as of April 1, 2014). [Reg. § 301.6103(j)(1)-1.]

☐ [*T.D.* 7724, 10-2-80. *Amended by T.D.* 7824, 7-30-82; *T.D.* 8118, 1-29-86; *T.D.* 8296, 3-27-90; *T.D.* 8377, 12-13-91; *T.D.* 8811, 1-22-99; *T.D.* 8908, 11-29-2000); *T.D.* 9037, 1-17-2003; *T.D.* 9188, 3-10-2005; *T.D.* 9267, 7-6-2006; *T.D.* 9372, 12-26-2007; *T.D.* 9439, 12-24-2008; *T.D.* 9500, 8-25-2010, *T.D.* 9631, 8-26-2013 *and T.D.* 9754, 2-24-2016.]

[Reg. § 301.6103(j)(1)-1T]

§ 301.6103(j)(1)-1T. Disclosures of return information reflected on returns to officers and employees of the Department of Commerce, for certain statistical purposes and related activities (Temporary).—(a) through (b)(2)(iii)(H) [Reserved]. For further guidance see § 301.6103(j)(1)-1(a) through (b)(2)(iii)(H).

(I) Total taxable wages paid for purposes of chapter 21;

(J) [Reserved]. For further guidance see § 301.6103(j)(1)-1(b)(2)(iii)(J).

(K) If a business has closed or stopped paying wages;

(L) Final date a business paid wages; and

(M) If a business is a seasonal employer and does not have to file a return for every quarter of the year;

(b)(2)(iv) through (b)(3)(iv) [Reserved]. For further guidance see § 301.6103(j)(1)-1(b)(2)(iv) through (b)(3)(iv).

(v) Total expenses or deductions, including totals of the following components thereof:

(A) Repairs (and maintenance) expense;

(B) Rents (or lease) expense;

(C) Taxes and licenses expense;

(D) Interest expense, including mortgage or other interest;

(E) Depreciation expense;

(F) Depletion expense;

(G) Advertising expense;

(H) Pension and profit-sharing plans (retirement plans) expense;

(I) Employee benefit programs expense;

(J) Utilities expense;

(K) Supplies expense;

(L) Contract labor expense; and

(M) Management (and investment advisory) fees.

(b)(3)(vi) through (b)(3)(xxiv) [Reserved]. For further guidance see § 301.6103(j)(1)-1(b)(3)(vi) through (b)(3)(xxiv).

(xxv) From Form 6765 (when filed with corporation income tax returns)—

(A) Indicator that total qualified research expenses is greater than zero, but less than $1 million; greater than or equal to $1 million, but less than $3 million; or, greater than or equal to $3 million;

(B) Cycle posted; and

(C) Research tax credit amount to be carried over to a business return, schedule, or form.

(xxvi) Total number of documents reported on Form 1096 transmitting Forms 1099-MISC.

(xxvii) Total amount reported on Form 1096 transmitting Forms 1099-MISC.

(xxviii) Type of REIT.

(xxix) From Form 1125-A—purchases.

(xxx) From Form 1040, Schedule C—

(A) Purchases less cost of items withdrawn for personal use; and

(B) Materials and supplies.

(xxxi) Electronic filing system indicator.

(xxxii) Posting cycle date relative to filing.

(xxxiii) Dividends, including ordinary or qualified.

(xxxiv) From Form 1120S, Schedule K-1—ordinary business income (loss).

(xxxv) From Form 1065, Schedule K-1—

(A) Publicly-traded partnership indicator;

(B) Partner's share of nonrecourse, qualified nonrecourse, and recourse liabilities; and

(C) Ordinary business income (loss).

(b)(4) through (b)(6)(i)(B) [Reserved]. For further guidance see § 301.6103(j)(1)-1(b)(4) through (b)(6)(i)(B).

(C) From Form 1120-REIT—

(1) Type of REIT; and

(2) Gross rents from real property;

(D) From Form 1120F—corporation's method of accounting.

(E) From Form 1096—total amount reported.

(b)(6)(ii) through (d)(3)(ii) [Reserved]. For further guidance see § 301.6103(j)(1)-1(b)(6)(ii) through (d)(3)(ii).

(e) *Applicability date.*—This section applies to disclosures to the Bureau of the Census made on or after December 9, 2016.

(f) *Expiration date.*—The applicability of this section expires on or before December 9, 2019. [Temporary Reg. § 301.6103(j)(1)-1T.]

☐ [*T.D.* 9802, 12-8-2016.]

[Reg. § 301.6103(j)(5)-1]

§ 301.6103(j)(5)-1. Disclosures of return information reflected on returns to officers and employees of the Department of Agriculture for conducting the census of agriculture.— (a) *General rule.*—Pursuant to the provisions of section 6103(j)(5) of the Internal Revenue Code and subject to the requirements of paragraph (c) of this section, officers or employees of the Internal Revenue Service will disclose return information reflected on returns to officers and employees of the Department of Agriculture to the extent, and for such purposes, as may be provided by paragraph (b) of this section. "Return information reflected on returns" includes, but is not limited to, information on returns, information derived from processing such returns, and information derived from other sources for the purposes of establishing and maintaining taxpayer information relating to returns.

(b) *Disclosure of return information reflected on returns to officers and employees of the Department of Agriculture.*—(1) Officers or employees of the Internal Revenue Service will disclose the following return information reflected on returns described in this paragraph (b) for individuals, partnerships and corporations with agricultural activity, as determined generally by industry code classification or the filing of returns for such activity, to officers and employees of the Department of Agriculture for purposes of, but only to the extent necessary in, structuring, preparing, and conducting, as authorized by chapter 55 of title 7, United States Code, the census of agriculture.

(2) From Form 1040 "U.S. Individual Income Tax Return", Form 1041 "U.S. Income Tax Return for Estates and Trusts", Form 1065 "U.S. Return of Partnership Income" and Form 1065-B "U.S. Return of Income for Electing Large Partnerships" (Schedule F)—

(i) Taxpayer identity information (as defined in section 6103(b)(6) of the Internal Revenue Code);

(ii) Spouse's Social Security Number;

(iii) Annual accounting period;

(iv) Principal Business Activity (PBA) code;

(v) Taxable cooperative distributions;

(vi) Income from custom hire and machine work;

(vii) Gross income;

(viii) Master File Tax (MFT) code;

(ix) Document Locator Number (DLN);

(x) Cycle posted;

(xi) Final return indicator;

(xii) Part year return indicator; and

(xiii) Taxpayer telephone number.

(3) From Form 943, "Employer's Annual Tax Return for Agricultural Employees"—

(i) Taxpayer identity information;

(ii) Annual accounting period;

(iii) Total wages subject to Medicare taxes;

(iv) MFT code;

(v) DLN;

(vi) Cycle posted;

(vii) Final return indicator; and

(viii) Part year return indicator.

(4) From Form 1120 series, "U.S. Corporation Income Tax Return"—

(i) Taxpayer identity information;

(ii) Annual accounting period;

(iii) Gross receipts less returns and allowances;

(iv) PBA code;

(v) MFT Code;

(vi) DLN;

(vii) Cycle posted;

(viii) Final return indicator;

(ix) Part year return indicator; and

(x) Consolidated return indicator.

(5) From Form 1065 series, "U.S. Return of Partnership Income" —

(i) Taxpayer identity information;

(ii) Annual accounting period;

(iii) PBA code;

(iv) Gross receipts less returns and allowances;

(v) Net farm profit (loss);

(vi) MFT code;

(vii) DLN;

(viii) Cycle posted;

(ix) Final return indicator; and

(x) Part year return indicator.

(c) *Procedures and Restrictions.*—(1) Disclosure of return information reflected on returns by officers or employees of the Internal Revenue Service as provided by paragraph (b) of this section will be made only upon written request designating, by name and title, the officers and employees of the Department of Agriculture to whom such disclosure is authorized, to the Commissioner of Internal Revenue by the Secretary of Agriculture and describing—

(i) The particular return information reflected on returns for disclosure;

(ii) The taxable period or date to which such return information reflected on returns relates; and

(iii) The particular purpose for the requested return information reflected on returns.

(2)(i) No such officer or employee to whom the Internal Revenue Service discloses return information reflected on returns pursuant to the provisions of paragraph (b) of this section shall disclose such information to any person, other than the taxpayer to whom such return information reflected on returns relates or other officers or employees of the Department of Agriculture whose duties or responsibilities require such disclosure for a purpose described in paragraph (b)(1) of this section, except in a form that cannot be associated with, or otherwise identify, directly or indirectly, a particular taxpayer.

(ii) If the Internal Revenue Service determines that the Department of Agriculture, or any officer or employee thereof, has failed to, or does not, satisfy the requirements of section 6103(p)(4) of the Internal Revenue Code or regulations or published procedures, the Internal Revenue Service may take such actions as are deemed necessary to ensure that such requirements are or will be satisfied, including suspension of disclosures of return information reflected on returns otherwise authorized by section 6103(j)(5) and paragraph (b) of this section, until the Internal Revenue Service determines that such requirements have been or will be satisfied.

(d) *Effective date.*—This section is applicable on February 22, 2006. [Reg. § 301.6103(j)(5)-1.]

☐ [*T.D.* 9245, 2-21-2006.]

[Reg. § 301.6103(k)(6)-1]

§ 301.6103(k)(6)-1. Disclosure of return information by certain officers and employees for investigative purposes.—(a) *General rule.*—(1) Pursuant to the provisions of section 6103(k)(6) and subject to the conditions of this section, an internal revenue employee or an Office of Treasury Inspector General for Tax Administration (TIGTA) employee, in connection with official duties relating to any examination, administrative appeal, collection activity, administrative, civil or criminal investigation, enforcement activity, ruling, negotiated agreement, prefiling activity, or other proceeding or offense under the internal revenue laws or related statutes, or in preparation for any proceeding described in section 6103(h)(2) (or investigation which may result in such a proceeding), may disclose return information, of any taxpayer, to the extent necessary to obtain information relating to such official duties or to accomplish properly any activity connected with such official duties, including, but not limited to—

(i) Establishing or verifying the correctness or completeness of any return or return information;

(ii) Determining the responsibility for filing a return, for making a return if none has been made, or for performing such acts as may be required by law concerning such matters;

(iii) Establishing or verifying the liability (or possible liability) of any person, or the liability (or possible liability) at law or in equity of any transferee or fiduciary of any person, for any tax, penalty, interest, fine, forfeiture, or other imposition or offense under the internal revenue laws or related statutes or the amount thereof for collection;

(iv) Establishing or verifying misconduct (or possible misconduct) or other activity proscribed by the internal revenue laws or related statutes;

(v) Obtaining the services of persons having special knowledge or technical skills (such as, but not limited to, knowledge of particular facts and circumstances relevant to a correct determination of a liability described in paragraph (a)(1)(iii) of this section or skills relating to handwriting analysis, photographic development, sound recording enhancement, or voice identification) or having recognized expertise in matters involving the valuation of property if relevant to proper performance of official duties described in this paragraph;

(vi) Establishing or verifying the financial status or condition and location of the taxpayer against whom collection activity is or may be directed, to locate assets in which the taxpayer has an interest, to ascertain the amount of any liability described in paragraph (a)(1)(iii) of this section for collection, or otherwise to apply the provisions of the Internal Revenue Code relating to establishment of liens against such assets, or levy, seizure, or sale on or of the assets to satisfy any such liability;

(vii) Preparing for any proceeding described in section 6103(h)(2) or conducting an investigation which may result in such a proceeding; or

(viii) Obtaining, verifying, or establishing information concerned with making determinations regarding a taxpayer's liability under the Internal Revenue Code, including, but not limited to, the administrative appeals process and any ruling, negotiated agreement, or prefiling process.

(2) Disclosure of return information for the purpose of obtaining information to carry out properly the official duties described by this paragraph, or any activity connected with the official duties, is authorized only if the internal revenue or TIGTA employee reasonably believes, under the facts and circumstances, at the time of a disclosure, the information is not otherwise reasonably available, or if the activity connected with the official duties cannot occur properly without the disclosure.

(3) Internal revenue and TIGTA employees may identify themselves, their organizational affiliation (e.g., Internal Revenue Service (IRS), Criminal Investigation (CI) or TIGTA, Office of Investigations (OI)), and the nature of their investigation, when making an oral, written, or electronic contact with a third party witness. Permitted disclosures include, but are not limited to, the use and presentation of any identification media (such as a Federal agency badge, credential, or business card) or the use of an information document request, summons, or correspondence on Federal agency letterhead or which bears a return address or signature block that reveals affiliation with the Federal agency.

(4) This section does not address or affect the requirements under section 7602(c) (relating to contact of third parties).

(b) *Disclosure of return information in connection with certain personnel or claimant representative matters.*—In connection with official duties relating to any investigation concerned with enforcement of any provision of the Internal Revenue Code, including enforcement of any rule or directive prescribed by the Secretary or the Commissioner of Internal Revenue under any provision of the Internal Revenue Code, or the enforcement of any provision related to tax administration, that affects or may affect the personnel or employment rights or status, or civil or criminal liability, of any former, current, or prospective employee of the Treasury Department, Bureau of Alcohol, Tobacco, Firearms, and Explosives, United States Customs Service, United States Secret Service, or any successor agency, or the rights of any person who is, or may be, a party to an administrative action or proceeding pursuant to 31 U.S.C. 330 (relating to practice before the Treasury Department), an internal revenue, TIGTA, or other Federal officer or employee who is responsible for investigating such employees and persons and is properly in possession of relevant return information is authorized to disclose such return information to the extent necessary for the purpose of obtaining, verifying, or establishing other information which is or may be relevant and material to the investigation.

(c) *Definitions.*—The following definitions apply to this section—

(1) *Disclosure of return information to the extent necessary* means a disclosure of return information which an internal revenue or TIGTA employee, based on the facts and circumstances, at the time of the disclosure, reasonably believes is necessary to obtain information to perform properly the official duties described by this section, or to accomplish properly the activities connected with carrying out those official duties. The term *necessary* in this context does not mean essential or indispensable, but rather appropriate and helpful in obtaining the information sought. Nor does *necessary* in this context refer to the necessity of conducting an investigation or the appropriateness of the means or methods chosen to conduct the investigation. Section 6103(k)(6) does not limit or restrict internal revenue or TIGTA employees with respect to the decision to initiate or the conduct of an investigation. Disclosures under this paragraph (c)(1), however, may not be made indiscriminately or solely for the benefit of the recipient or as part of a negotiated quid pro quo arrangement. This paragraph (c)(1) is illustrated by the following examples:

Example 1. A revenue agent contacts a taxpayer's customer regarding the customer's purchases made from the taxpayer during the year under investigation. The revenue agent is able to obtain the purchase information only by disclosing the taxpayer's identity and the fact of the investigation. Depending on the facts and circumstances known to the revenue agent at the time of the disclosure, such as the way the customer maintains his records, it also may be necessary for the revenue agent to inform the customer of the date of the purchases and the types of merchandise involved for the customer to find the purchase information.

Example 2. A revenue agent contacts a third party witness to obtain copies of invoices of sales made to a taxpayer under examination. The third party witness provides copies of the sales invoices in question and then asks the revenue agent for the current address of the taxpayer because the taxpayer still owes money to the third party witness. The revenue agent may not disclose that current address because this disclosure would be only for the benefit of the third party witness and not necessary to obtain information for the examination.

Example 3. A revenue agent contacts a third party witness to obtain copies of invoices of sales made to a taxpayer under examination. The third party witness agrees to provide copies of the sales invoices in question only if the revenue agent provides him with the current address of the taxpayer because the taxpayer still owes money to the third party witness. The revenue agent may not disclose that current address because this disclosure would be a negotiated quid pro quo arrangement.

(2) *Disclosure of return information to accomplish properly an activity connected with official duties* means a disclosure of return information to carry out a function associated with official duties generally consistent with established practices and procedures. This paragraph (c)(2) is illustrated by the following example:

Example. A taxpayer failed to file an income tax return and pay the taxes owed. After the taxes were assessed and the taxpayer was notified of the balance due, a revenue officer filed a notice of federal tax lien and then served a notice of levy on the taxpayer's bank. The notices of lien and levy contained the taxpayer's name, social security number, amount of outstanding liability, and the tax period and type of tax involved. The taxpayer's assets were levied to satisfy the tax debt, but it was determined that, prior to the levy, the revenue officer failed to issue the taxpayer a notice of intent to levy, as required by section 6331, and a notice of right to hearing before the levy, as required by section 6330. The disclosure of the taxpayer's return information in the notice of levy is authorized by section 6103(k)(6) despite the revenue officer's failure to issue the notice of intent to levy or the notice of right to hearing. The ultimate validity of the underlying levy is irrelevant to the issue of whether the disclosure was authorized by section 6103(k)(6).

(3) *Information not otherwise reasonably available* means information that an internal revenue or TIGTA employee reasonably believes, under the facts and circumstances, at the time of a disclosure, cannot be obtained in a sufficiently accurate or probative form, or in a timely manner, and without impairing the proper performance of the official duties described by this section, without making the disclosure. This definition does not require or create the presumption or expectation that an internal revenue or TIGTA employee must seek information from a taxpayer or authorized representative prior to contacting a third party witness in an investigation. Neither the Internal Revenue Code, IRS procedures, nor these regulations require repeated contacting of an uncooperative taxpayer. Moreover, an internal revenue or TIGTA employee may make a disclosure to a third party witness to corroborate information provided by a taxpayer. This paragraph (c)(3) is illustrated by the following examples:

Example 1. A revenue agent is conducting an examination of a taxpayer. The taxpayer refuses to cooperate or provide any information to the revenue agent. Information relating to the taxpayer's examination would be information not otherwise reasonably available because of the taxpayer's refusal to cooperate and supply any information to the revenue agent. The revenue agent may seek information from a third party witness.

Example 2. A special agent is conducting a criminal investigation of a taxpayer. The special agent has acquired certain information from the

taxpayer. Although the special agent has no specific reason to disbelieve the taxpayer's information, the special agent contacts several third party witnesses to confirm the information. The special agent may contact third party witnesses to verify the correctness of the information provided by the taxpayer because the IRS is not required to rely solely on information provided by a taxpayer, and a special agent may take appropriate steps, including disclosures to third party witnesses under section 6103(k)(6), to verify independently or corroborate information obtained from a taxpayer.

(4) *Internal revenue employee* means, for purposes of this section, an officer or employee of the IRS or Office of Chief Counsel for the IRS, or an officer or employee of a Federal agency responsible for administering and enforcing taxes under Chapters 32 (Part III of Subchapter D), 51, 52, or 53 of the Internal Revenue Code, or investigating tax refund check fraud under 18 U.S.C. 510.

(5) *TIGTA employee* means an officer or employee of the Office of Treasury Inspector General for Tax Administration.

(d) *Examples.*—The following examples illustrate the application of this section:

Example 1. A revenue agent is conducting an examination of a taxpayer. The taxpayer has been very cooperative and has supplied copies of invoices as requested. Some of the taxpayer's invoices show purchases that seem excessive in comparison to the size of the taxpayer's business. The revenue agent contacts the taxpayer's suppliers for the purpose of corroborating the invoices the taxpayer provided. In contacting the suppliers, the revenue agent discloses the taxpayer's name, the dates of purchase, and the type of merchandise at issue. These disclosures are permissible under section 6103(k)(6) because, under the facts and circumstances known to the revenue agent at the time of the disclosures, the disclosures were necessary to obtain information (corroboration of invoices) not otherwise reasonably available because suppliers would be the only source available for corroboration of this information.

Example 2. A revenue agent is conducting an examination of a taxpayer. The revenue agent asks the taxpayer for business records to document the deduction of the cost of goods sold shown on Schedule C of the taxpayer's return. The taxpayer will not provide the business records to the revenue agent, who contacts a third party witness for verification of the amount on the Schedule C. In the course of the contact, the revenue agent shows the Schedule C to the third party witness. This disclosure is not authorized under section 6103(k)(6). Section 6103(k)(6) permits disclosure only of return information, not the return (including schedules and attachments) itself. If necessary, a revenue agent may disclose return information extracted from a return when questioning a third party witness. Thus, the revenue agent could have extracted the amount of cost of goods sold from the Schedule C and disclosed that amount to the third party witness.

Example 3. A special agent is conducting a criminal investigation of a taxpayer, a doctor, for tax evasion. Notwithstanding the records provided by the taxpayer and the taxpayer's bank, the special agent decided to obtain information from the taxpayer's patients to verify amounts paid to the taxpayer for his services. Accordingly, the special agent sent letters to the taxpayer's patients to verify these amounts. In the letters, the agent disclosed that he was a special agent with IRS-CI and that he was conducting a criminal investigation of the taxpayer. Section 6103(k)(6) permits these disclosures (including the special agent disclosing his affiliation with CI and the nature of the investigation) to confirm the taxpayer's income. The decision whether to verify information already obtained is a matter of investigative judgment and is not limited by section 6103(k)(6).

Example 4. Corporation A requests a private letter ruling (PLR) as to the tax consequences of a planned transaction. Corporation A has represented that it is in compliance with laws administered by Agency B that may relate to the tax consequences of the proposed transaction. Further information is needed from Agency B relating to possible tax consequences. Under section 6103(k)(6), the IRS may disclose Corporation A's return information to Agency B to the extent necessary to obtain information from Agency B for the purpose of properly considering the tax consequences of the proposed transaction that is the subject of the PLR.

(e) *Effective date.*—This section is applicable on July 6, 2006. [Reg. § 301.6103(k)(6)-1.]

☐ [*T.D.* 9274, 7-6-2006 (*corrected* 10-16-2006).]

[Reg. § 301.6103(k)(9)-1]

§ 301.6103(k)(9)-1. Disclosure of returns and return information relating to payment of tax by credit card and debit card.—Officers and employees of the Internal Revenue Service may disclose to card issuers, financial institutions, or other persons such return information as the Commissioner deems necessary in connection with processing credit card and debit card transactions to effectuate payment of tax as authorized by § 301.6311-2. Officers and employees of the Internal Revenue Service may disclose such return information to such persons as the Commissioner deems necessary in connection with billing or collection of the amounts charged or debited, including resolution of errors relating to the credit card or debit card account as described in § 301.6311-2(d). [Reg. § 301.6103(k)(9)-1.]

☐ [*T.D.* 8969, 12-13-2001.]

[Reg. § 301.6103(l)-1]

§ 301.6103(l)-1. Disclosure of returns and return information for purposes other than tax administration.—(a) *Definition.*—For purposes of applying the provisions of section 6103(l) of the Internal Revenue Code, the term *agent* includes a contractor.

(b) *Effective date.*—This section is applicable January 6, 2004. [Reg. § 301.6103(l)-1.]

☐ [*T.D.* 9111, 12-31-2003.]

[Reg. § 301.6103(l)(2)-1]

§ 301.6103(l)(2)-1. Disclosure of returns and return information to Pension Benefit Guaranty Corporation for purposes of research and studies.—(a) *General rule.*—Pursuant to the provisions of section 6103(l)(2) of the Internal Revenue Code and subject to the requirements of paragraph (b) of this section, officers and employees of the Internal Revenue Service may disclose returns and return information (as defined by section 6103(b)) to officers and employees of the Pension Benefit Guaranty Corporation for purposes of, but only to the extent necessary in, conducting research and studies authorized by title IV of the Employee Retirement Income Security Act of 1974.

(b) *Procedures and restrictions.*—Disclosure of returns or return information by officers or employees of the Service as provided by paragraph (a) of this section will be made only upon written request to the Commissioner of Internal Revenue by the Executive Director of the Pension Benefit Guaranty Corporation describing the returns or return information to be disclosed, the taxable period or date to which such returns or return information relates, and the purpose for which the returns or return information is needed in the administration of title IV of the Employee Retirement Income Security Act of 1974, and designating by title the officers and employees of such corporation to whom such disclosure is authorized. No such officer or employee to whom returns or return information is disclosed pursuant to the provisions of paragraph (a) shall disclose such returns or return information to any person, other than the taxpayer by whom the return was made or to whom the return information relates or other officers or employees of such corporation whose duties or responsibilities require such disclosure for a purpose described in paragraph (a), except in a form which cannot be associated with, or otherwise identify, directly or indirectly, a particular taxpayer. [Reg. § 301.6103(l)(2)-1.]

☐ [*T.D.* 7723, 9-30-80.]

[Reg. § 301.6103(l)(2)-2]

§ 301.6103(l)(2)-2. Disclosure of returns and return information to Department of Labor for purposes of research and studies.—(a) *General rule.*—Pursuant to the provisions of section 6103(l)(2) of the Internal Revenue Code and subject to the requirements of paragraph (b) of this section, officers or employees of the Internal Revenue Service may disclose returns and return information (as defined by section 6103(b)) to officers and employees of the Department of Labor for purposes of, but only to the extent necessary in, conducting research and studies authorized by section 513 of the Employee Retirement Income Security Act of 1974.

(b) *Procedures and restrictions.*—Disclosure of returns or return information by officers or employees of the Service as provided by paragraph (a) of this section will be made only upon written request to the Commissioner of Internal Revenue by the Administrator of the Pension and Welfare Benefit Programs of the Department of Labor describing the returns or return information to be disclosed, the taxable period or date to which such returns or return information relates, and the purpose for which the returns or return information is needed in the administration of title I of the Employee Retirement Income Security Act of 1974, and designating by title the officers and employees of such department to whom such disclosure is authorized. No such officer or employee to whom returns or return information is disclosed pursuant to the provisions of paragraph (a) shall disclose such returns or return information to any person, other than the taxpayer by whom the return was made or to whom the return information relates or other officers or employees of such department whose duties or responsibilities require such disclosure for a purpose described in paragraph (a), except in a form which cannot be associated with, or otherwise identify, directly or indirectly, a particular taxpayer. [Reg. § 301.6103(l)(2)-2.]

☐ [*T.D.* 7723, 9-30-80.]

[Reg. § 301.6103(l)(2)-3]

§ 301.6103(l)(2)-3. Disclosure to Department of Labor and Pension Benefit Guaranty Corporation of certain returns and return information.—(a) *Disclosures following general requests.*—Pursuant to the provisions of section 6103(l)(2) of the Internal Revenue Code and subject to the requirements of this paragraph, officers or employees of the Internal Revenue Service may disclose the following returns and return information(as defined by section 6103(b)) to officers and employees of the Department of Labor or the Pension Benefit Guaranty Corporation for purposes of, but only to the extent necessary in, the administration of title I or IV of the Employee Retirement Income Security Act of 1974 (hereinafter referred to in this section as the Act)—

(1) Notification of receipt by the Service of an application by a particular taxpayer for a determination of whether a pension, profit-sharing, or stock bonus plan, a trust which is a part of such a plan, or an annuity or bond purchase plan meets the applicable requirements of part I of subchapter D of chapter 1 of the Code;

(2) Notification that a particular application described in subparagraph (1) of this paragraph alleges that certain employees may be excluded from participation by reason of section 410(b)(2)(A) and (B) for the purpose of obtaining the finding necessary for the application of such section;

(3) An application by a particular taxpayer for a determination of whether a pension, profit-sharing, or stock bonus plan, or an annuity or

bond purchase plan, meets the applicable requirements of part I of subchapter D of chapter 1 of the Code with respect to a termination or proposed termination of the plan or to a partial termination or proposed partial termination of the plan, and any statement filed as provided by section 6058(b);

(4) Notification that the Service has determined that a plan or trust described in subparagraph (1) or (3) of this paragraph meets or does not meet the applicable requirements of part I of subchapter D of chapter 1 of the Code and has issued a determination letter to such effect to a particular taxpayer or that an application for such a determination has been withdrawn by the taxpayer;

(5) If the Department of Labor or the Pension Benefit Guaranty Corporation has commented on an application upon which a determination letter described in subparagraph (4) of this paragraph has been issued, a copy of the letter or document issued to the applicant;

(6) Notification to a particular taxpayer that the Service intends to disqualify a pension, profit-sharing, or stock bonus plan, a trust which is a part of such plan, or an annuity or bond purchase plan because such plan or trust does not meet the requirements of section 410(a) or 411 as of the date that such notification is issued;

(7) Notification required by section 3002(a) of the Act of the commencement of any proceeding to determine whether a particular pension, profit-sharing, or stock bonus plan, a trust which is a part of such plan, or an annuity or bond purchase plan meets the requirements of section 410(a) or 411;

(8) Prior to issuance of a notice of deficiency to a particular taxpayer under section 6212, notification that the Service has determined that a deficiency exists under section 6211 with respect to the tax imposed by section 4971(a) or (b) on such taxpayer, except that if the Service determines that the collection of such tax is in jeopardy within the meaning of section 6861(a), such notification may be disclosed after issuance of the notice of deficiency or jeopardy assessment;

(9) Notification of receipt by the Service of, and action taken with respect to, an application by or on behalf of a particular taxpayer for a waiver of the tax imposed by section 4971(b);

(10) Prior to issuance of a notice of deficiency to a particular taxpayer under section 6212, notification that a deficiency exists under section 6211 with respect to the tax imposed by section 4975(a) or (b) on such taxpayer, except that if the Service determines that the collection of such tax is in jeopardy within the meaning of section 6861(a), such notification may be disclosed after issuance of the notice of deficiency or jeopardy assessment;

(11) Notification that the Service has waived the tax imposed by section 4975(b) on a particular taxpayer;

(12) Notification of applicability of section 4975 to a particular pension, profit-sharing, or

stock bonus plan, a trust which is a part of such plan, or an annuity or stock purchase plan engaged in prohibited transactions within the meaning of section 4975(c);

(13) Notification to a plan administrator that the Service has determined that a pension, profit-sharing, stock bonus, annuity, or stock purchase plan no longer meets the requirements of section 401(a) or 404(a)(2);

(14) Notification that the Service has determined that there has been a termination or partial termination of a particular pension, profit-sharing, stock bonus, annuity, or stock purchase plan within the meaning of section 411(d)(3);

(15) Notification of the occurrence of an event (other than an event described in subparagraph (13), (14), or (18) of this paragraph) which the Service has determined to indicate that a particular pension, profit-sharing, stock bonus, annuity, or stock purchase plan may not be sound under section 4043(c)(2) of the Act;

(16) Notification that the Service has received and responded to a request on behalf of a particular pension, profit-sharing, or stock bonus plan, a trust which is a part of such plan, or an annuity or stock purchase plan for an extension of time for filing an annual return by such plan or trust;

(17) Notification that the Service has received and responded to a request on behalf of a particular pension, profit-sharing, or stock bonus plan, a trust which is a part of such plan, or an annuity or stock purchase plan to change the annual accounting period of such plan or trust;

(18) Notification that the Service has determined that a particular plan does not meet the requirements of section 412 without regard to whether such plan is one described in section 4021(a)(2) of the Act;

(19) Notification of the results of an investigation by the Service requested by the Department of Labor or the Pension Benefit Guaranty Corporation, or both, with respect to whether the tax described in section 4971 should be imposed on any employer named in such request or whether the tax imposed by section 4975 should be paid by any person named in the request;

(20) Notification of receipt by the Service of an application by a particular taxpayer for exemption under section 4975(c)(2) or of initiation by the Service of an administrative proceeding for such exemption;

(21) Notification of receipt by the Service of, and action taken with respect to, an application by or on behalf of a particular taxpayer for a waiver or variance of the minimum funding standard under section 303 of the Act or section 412(d);

(22) Notification that the Service intends to undertake, is undertaking, or has completed an examination to determine whether—

(i) A particular pension, profit-sharing, or stock bonus plan, a trust which is a part of such plan, or an annuity or stock purchase plan meets the applicable requirements of part 1 of subchapter D of chapter 1 of the Code;

(ii) Any particular person is or may be liable for any tax imposed by section 4971 or 4975; or

(iii) A particular employee welfare benefit plan, as defined in section 3(1) of the Act, meets the applicable requirements of section 501(c) or 120,

together with any completed Department of Labor or Pension Benefit Guaranty Corporation form (and supplemental schedules) relating to such examination;

(23) Copies of initial pleadings indicating that the Service intends to intervene in a civil action under section 502(h) of the Act. Return information disclosed under this paragraph includes the taxpayer identity information (as defined in section 6103(b)(6)) of the plan or trust, the name and address of the sponsor and administrator of the plan or trustee of the trust, and the name and address of the person authorized to represent the plan or trust before the Service. Disclosure of returns or return information as provided by this paragraph will be made only following receipt by the Commissioner of Internal Revenue of an annual written request for such disclosure by the Administrator of Pension and Benefit Welfare Programs of the Department of Labor or the Executive Director of the Pension Benefit Guaranty Corporation describing the categories of returns or return information to be disclosed by the Service and the particular purpose for which the returns or return information is needed in the administration of title I or IV of the Act, and designating by title the officers and employees of the Department of Labor or such corporation to whom such disclosure is authorized; and

(24) Notification of receipt by the Service of a request for technical advice as to whether a particular pension, profit-sharing, or stock bonus plan, a trust which is a part of such plan, or an annuity or bond purchase plan should be disqualified because of fiduciary actions subject to part 4 of subtitle B of title I of the Act which may violate the exclusive benefit rule of section 401(a);

(25) Notification of receipt by the National Office of the Service of a request by or on behalf of a particular taxpayer for a ruling, opinion, variance, or waiver under any provision of title I of the Act and a copy of any such ruling, opinion, variance or waiver;

(26) Notification that the Service proposes to take substantive action which would significantly impact on or substantially affect collectively bargained plans and a description of such proposed substantive action; and

(27) Notification of receipt by the Service of, and action taken with respect to, a request by a particular taxpayer for a ruling under section 412(c)(8), 412(e), or 412(f).

Disclosure of returns or return information as provided by this paragraph will be made only following receipt by the Commissioner of Internal Revenue or his delegate of an annual written request for such disclosure by the Secretary of

Labor or his delegate or the Executive Director of the Pension Benefit Guaranty Corporation or his delegate describing the categories of returns or return information to be disclosed by the Service and the particular purpose for which the returns or return information is needed in the administration of title I or IV of the Act, and designating by title the officers and employees of the Department of Labor or such corporation to whom such disclosure is authorized.

(b) *Additional returns and return information subject to disclosure.*—(1) *Returns and return information relating to automatic notification.*—(i) Subject to the requirements of subparagraph (3)(i) of this paragraph, officers or employees of the Service may disclose to officers and employees of the Department of Labor or the Pension Benefit Guaranty Corporation for purposes of, but only to the extent necessary in, the administration of title I or IV of the Act additional returns and return information relating to any item described in paragraph (a) of this section.

(ii) Subject to the requirements of subparagraph (3)(ii) of this paragraph, in connection with the disclosure of any item as provided by paragraph (a) of this section, officers and employees of the Service may disclose to officers and employees of the Department of Labor or the Pension Benefit Guaranty Corporation such additional returns and return information relating to such item as the Service determines are or may be necessary in the administration of title I or IV of the Act.

(2) *Other returns and return information.*—Subject to the requirements of subparagraph (3)(i) of this paragraph, officers or employees of the Service may disclose to officers and employees of the Department of Labor or the Pension Benefit Guaranty Corporation returns and return information (other than returns and return information disclosed as provided by paragraph (a) of this section or § 301.6103(l)(2)-1 or § 301.6103(l)(2)-2 for purposes of, but only to the extent necessary in, administration of title I or IV of the Act.

(3) *Procedures.*—(i) Disclosure of returns or return information by officers or employees of the Service as provided by subparagraph (1)(i) or (2) of this paragraph will be made only following receipt by the Commissioner of Internal Revenue or his delegate of a written request for such disclosure by the Secretary of Labor or his delegate or the Executive Director of the Pension Benefit Guaranty Corporation or his delegate identifying the particular taxpayer by whom such return was made or to whom such return information relates, describing the particular returns or return information to be disclosed, stating the purpose for which the returns or return information is needed in the administration of title I or IV of the Act, and designating by title the officers and employees of such department or corporation to whom such disclosure is authorized.

(ii) Disclosure of returns or return information by officers or employees of the Service as provided by subparagraph (1)(ii) of this paragraph will be made only following receipt by the Commissioner of Internal Revenue or his delegate of an annual written request for such disclosure by the Secretary of Labor or his delegate or the Executive Director of the Pension Benefit Guaranty Corporation or his delegate stating the purpose for which the returns or return information is needed in the administration of title I or IV of the Act, and designating by title the officers and employees of such department or corporation to whom such disclosure is authorized.

(c) *Disclosure and use of returns and return information by officers and employees of Department of Labor, Pension Benefit Guaranty Corporation, and Department of Justice.*—(1) *Use by officers and employees of Department of Labor and Pension Benefit Guaranty Corporation.*—Returns and return information disclosed to officers and employees of the Department of Labor and the Pension Benefit Guaranty Corporation as provided by this section may be used by such officers and employees for purposes of, but only to the extent necessary in, administration of any provision of title I or IV of the Act, including any preparation for any administrative or judicial proceeding (or investigation which may result in such a proceeding) authorized by, or described in, title I or IV of the Act.

(2) *Disclosure by officers and employees of Department of Labor and Pension Benefit Guaranty Corporation to, and use by, other persons, including officers and employees of the Department of Justice.*—(i) Returns and return information disclosed to officers and employees of the Department of Labor or the Pension Benefit Guaranty Corporation as provided by this section may be disclosed by such officers and employees to officers and employees of the Department of Justice (including United States attorneys) personally and directly engaged in, and for their necessary use in, any Federal grand jury proceeding, or preparation for any civil or criminal judicial proceeding (or for their necessary use in an investigation which may result in such a proceeding), authorized by, or described in, title I or IV of the Act.

(ii) Returns and return information disclosed to officers and employees of the Department of Labor, the Pension Benefit Guaranty Corporation, and the Department of Justice as provided by this section may be disclosed by such officers and employees to other persons, including, but not limited to, persons described in subparagraph (2)(iii) of this paragraph, but only to the extent necessary in connection with administration of the provisions of title I or IV of the Act, including a Federal grand jury proceeding, and proper preparation for a proceeding (or investigation), described in subparagraph (1) or (2)(i). Such disclosures may include, but are not limited to, disclosures where necessary—

(A) To properly obtain the services of persons having special knowledge or technical skills;

(B) To properly interview, consult, depose, or interrogate or otherwise obtain relevant information from, the taxpayer to whom such return or return information relates (or the legal representative of such taxpayer) or any witness who may be called to give evidence in the proceeding; or

(C) To properly conduct negotiations concerning, or obtain authorization for, settlement or disposition of the proceeding, in whole or in part, or stipulations of fact in connection with the proceeding.

Disclosure of a return or return information to a person other than the taxpayer to whom such return or return information relates (or the legal representative of such taxpayer) to properly accomplish any purpose or activity described in this subparagraph should be made, however, only if such purpose or activity cannot otherwise properly be accomplished without making such disclosure.

(iii) Among those persons to whom returns and return information may be disclosed by officers and employees of the Department of Labor, the Pension Benefit Guaranty Corporation, and the Department of Justice as provided by subparagraph (2)(ii) of this paragraph are:

(A) Other officers and employees of the Department of Labor, the Pension Benefit Guaranty Corporation, and the Department of Justice;

(B) Officers and employees of another Federal agency (as defined in section 6103(b)(9)) working under the direction and control of such officers and employees of the Department of Labor, the Pension Benefit Guaranty Corporation, or the Department of Justice; and

(C) Court reporters.

Disclosure of returns or return information to other persons by officers and employees of the Department of Labor or the Pension Benefit Guaranty Corporation as provided by subparagraph (2)(ii) of this paragraph for purposes of conducting research, surveys, studies, and publications referred to in section 513(a), or authorized by title IV, of the Act shall be restricted, however, to disclosure to other officers and employees of such department or corporation to whom such disclosure is necessary in connection with such conduct or to the taxpayer by whom such return was made or to whom such return information relates if the return or return information can be associated with, or otherwise identify, directly or indirectly, a particular taxpayer.

(3) *Disclosure in judicial proceedings.*—A return or return information disclosed to officers and employees of the Department of Labor, the Pension Benefit Guaranty Corporation, or the Department of Justice as provided by this section may be entered into evidence by such officers or employees in a civil or criminal judicial proceeding authorized by, or described in, title I or IV of the Act, provide that, in the case of a judicial proceeding described in section 6103(i)(4), the requirements of section 6103(i)(4) have first been met.

(d) *Disclosure of returns and return information in connection with certain consultations between Departments of the Treasury and Labor.*—Upon general written request to the Commissioner of Internal Revenue by the Secretary of Labor, officers and employees of the Service may disclose to officers and employees of the Department of Labor such returns and return information as may be necessary to properly carry out any consultation required by section 3002, 3003, or 3004 of the Act.

(e) *Return information open to public inspection under section 6104.*—Nothing in these regulations shall be construed to deny officers and employees of the Department of Labor and the Pension Benefit Guaranty Corporation the right to inspect return information available to the public under section 6104 of the Code. [Reg. § 301.6103(l)(2)-3.]

☐ [T.D. 7723, 9-30-80. *Amended by T.D. 7757,* 1-16-81 *and T.D. 7911, 9-6-83.*]

[Reg. § 301.6103(l)(14)-1]

§ 301.6103(l)(14)-1. **Disclosure of return information to United States Customs Service.**— (a) *General rule.*—Pursuant to the provisions of section 6103(l)(14) of the Internal Revenue Code, officers and employees of the Internal Revenue Service may disclose to officers and employees of the United States Customs Service return information (as defined by section 6103(b)) with respect to taxes imposed by chapters 1 and 6 of the Internal Revenue Code solely for purposes of, and only to the extent necessary in—

(1) Ascertaining the correctness of any entry in audits as provided for in section 509 of the Tariff Act of 1930 or;

(2) Other actions to recover any loss of revenue, or to collect duties, taxes, and fees, determined to be due and owing pursuant to such audits.

(b) *Procedures.*—Disclosure of return information by officers or employees of the Internal Revenue Service as provided by paragraph (a) of this section will be made only following receipt by the Internal Revenue Service of a written request for the disclosure by the Commissioner of the U.S. Customs Service identifying—

(1) The particular items of return information to be disclosed;

(2) The particular taxpayer to whom the return information relates;

(3) The taxable period or date to which the return information relates;

(4) The particular purpose for which each item of return information is needed, including an explanation as to how the requested information is necessary to accomplish that purpose. In addition, the request must designate by title the officers and employees of the Customs Service to whom the disclosure is authorized and certify that the Customs Service has initiated or intends to initiate, under section 509 of the Tariff Act of 1930, an audit of each taxpayer for whom return information is requested or that the taxpayer has a transactional or ownership relationship with the subject of such an audit.

(c) *Return information subject to disclosure.*—Any return information requested must be necessary to a Customs determination of the correctness of any entry in audits conducted under section 509 of the Tariff Act of 1930. Taxpayers as to whom return information is requested must either be the subject of a Customs audit (or intended audit) or have a transactional or ownership relationship with the subject of a Customs audit. Requested information must relate to the declared value, classification or rate of duty applicable to entered merchandise. Requested information may also include any adjustment by the IRS to the items of return information described by this paragraph.

(d) *Return information not subject to disclosure.*—The following return information may not be requested or disclosed pursuant to section 6103(l)(14) of the Internal Revenue Code: any Advance Pricing Agreement or information submitted to or generated by the IRS as part of the negotiation process for an Advance Pricing Agreement, or any information to the extent its disclosure would be inconsistent with a tax treaty or executive agreement with respect to which the United States is a party.

(e) *Impairment of tax administration.*—Return information with respect to a taxpayer may not be disclosed pursuant to this section if the IRS determines that the disclosure would identify a confidential informant or seriously impair any civil or criminal tax investigation or proceeding.

(f) *Use by Customs Service.*—Return information disclosed under this section may be used by the U.S. Customs Service to the extent necessary to ascertain or to document the correctness of any entry in audits as provided for in section 509 of the Tariff Act of 1930 and in any related administrative proceedings to recover any loss of revenue, or to collect duties, taxes or fees, determined to be due and owing pursuant to these audits. Uses may include, to the extent necessary, disclosure to the importer (or the legal representative of such importer) subject to the audit with respect to which the information was requested.

(g) *Disclosure to, and use by, the Department of Justice.*—Return information disclosed to officers and employees of the U.S. Customs Service as provided by this section may be disclosed by these officers and employees to officers and employees of the Department of Justice (including United States attorneys) personally and directly engaged in, and solely for their necessary use in, advocating or defending the correctness of Customs determinations with respect to any entry, in any civil judicial proceeding, or any preparations therefor (or for their necessary use in an investigation which may result in such a proceeding), to recover any loss of revenue, or to collect duties, taxes or fees, determined to be due and owing as a consequence of an audit provided for in section 509 of the Tariff Act of 1930.

(h) *Disclosure by officers and employees of the Department of Justice.*—Return information disclosed to officers and employees of the Department of Justice (including United States Attorneys) as provided by this section may be disclosed by these officers and employees to other persons as is necessary to properly accomplish the purposes or activities described in paragraph (g). Disclosure of return information to a person, other than the importer (or the legal representative of the importer) subject to the audit with respect to which the information was originally requested, to properly accomplish any purpose or activity described in paragraph (g) may be made, however, only if the purpose or activity cannot otherwise properly be accomplished without making the disclosure. Disclosures may include, but are not limited to, disclosures where necessary—

(1) To properly obtain the services of persons having special knowledge or technical skills;

(2) To properly interview, consult, depose, or interrogate or otherwise obtain relevant information from, the taxpayer (or the legal representative of the taxpayer) to whom the return information relates or any witness who may be called to give evidence in the proceeding; or

(3) To properly conduct negotiations concerning, or obtain authorization for, settlement or disposition of the proceeding, in whole or in part, or stipulations of fact in connection with the proceeding.

(i) *Use in criminal judicial proceedings.*—Return information disclosed pursuant to this section may not be used in any criminal judicial proceeding, or any preparations therefor (or in a criminal investigation which may result in such a proceeding), involving the enforcement of a criminal statute, without compliance with the requirements of section 6103(i)(1) or (2) as appropriate. However, the return information may in any event be used for purposes of complying with the requirements of section 6103(i).

(j) *Restrictions.*—Return information disclosed to officers and employees of the U.S. Customs Service or to the Department of Justice as provided by this section may not be used or disclosed for any purpose other than to ascertain, advocate or defend the correctness of, Customs determinations with respect to, any entry in the audits for which the information was requested or in certain actions resulting from the audits as described above. Return information disclosed to officers and employees of the U.S. Customs Service or to the Department of Justice as provided by this section may not be disclosed to any person, including any contractor of the U.S. Customs Service, except as provided by this section, or as otherwise provided by section 6103 of the Internal Revenue Code. [Reg. § 301.6103(l)(14)-1.]

☐ [*T.D.* 8527, 3-8-94. *Amended by T.D.* 8694, 12-16-96.]

[Reg. § 301.6103(l)(21)-1]

§ 301.6103(l)(21)-1. Disclosure of return information to the Department of Health and Human Services to carry out eligibility requirements for health insurance affordability programs.—(a) *General rule.*—Pursuant to the provisions of section 6103(l)(21)(A) of the Internal Revenue Code, officers and employees of the Internal Revenue Service will disclose, upon written request, for each relevant taxpayer on a single application those items of return information that are described under section 6103(l)(21)(A) and paragraphs (a)(1) through (7) of this section, for the reference tax year, as applicable, to officers, employees, and contractors of the Department of Health and Human Services. Such information shall be provided solely for purposes of, and to the extent necessary in, establishing an individual's eligibility for participation in an Exchange established under the Patient Protection and Affordable Care Act, verifying the appropriate amount of any premium tax credit under section 36B or cost-sharing reduction under section 1402 of the Patient Protection and Affordable Care Act, or determining eligibility for the State programs described in section 6103(l)(21)(A).

(1) With respect to each relevant taxpayer for the reference tax year where the amount of social security benefits not included in gross income under section 86 of the Internal Revenue Code of that relevant taxpayer is unavailable:

(i) The aggregate amount of the following items of return information —

(A) Adjusted gross income, as defined by section 62 of the Internal Revenue Code;

(B) Any amount excluded from gross income under section 911 of the Internal Revenue Code; and

(C) Any amount of interest received or accrued by the taxpayer during the taxable year that is exempt from tax.

(ii) Information indicating that the amount of social security benefits not included in gross income under section 86 of the Internal Revenue Code is unavailable.

(2) Adjusted gross income, as defined by section 62 of the Internal Revenue Code, of a relevant taxpayer for the reference tax year, in circumstances where the modified adjusted gross income (MAGI), as defined by section 36B(d)(2)(B) of the Internal Revenue Code, of that relevant taxpayer is unavailable, as well as information indicating that the components of MAGI other than adjusted gross income must be taken into account to determine MAGI;

(3) The amount of social security benefits of the relevant taxpayer that is included in gross income under section 86 of the Internal Revenue Code for the reference tax year;

(4) Information indicating that certain return information of a relevant taxpayer is unavailable for the reference tax year because the relevant taxpayer jointly filed a U.S. Individual Income Tax Return for that year with a spouse who is not a relevant taxpayer listed on the same application;

(5) Information indicating that, although a return for an individual identified on the application as a relevant taxpayer for the reference tax year is available, return information is not being provided because of possible authentication issues with respect to the identity of the relevant taxpayer;

(6) Information indicating that a relevant taxpayer who is identified as a dependent for the tax year in which the premium tax credit under section 36B of the Internal Revenue Code would be claimed, did not have a filing requirement for the reference tax year based upon the U.S. Individual Income Tax Return the relevant taxpayer filed for the reference tax year; and

(7) Information indicating that a relevant taxpayer who received advance payments of the premium tax credit in the reference tax year did not file a tax return for the reference tax year reconciling the advance payments of the premium tax credit with any premium tax credit under section 36B of the Internal Revenue Code available for that year.

(b) *Relevant taxpayer defined.*—For purposes of paragraph (a) of this section, a relevant taxpayer is defined to be any individual listed, by name and social security number, on an application submitted pursuant to Title I, Subtitle E, of the Patient Protection and Affordable Care Act, whose income may bear upon a determination of any advance payment of any premium tax credit under section 36B of the Internal Revenue Code, cost-sharing reduction under section 1402 of the Patient Protection and Affordable Care Act, or eligibility for any program described in section 6103(l)(21)(A) of the Internal Revenue Code.

(c) *Reference tax year defined.*—For purposes of section 6103(l)(21)(A) of the Internal Revenue Code and this section, the reference tax year is the first calendar year or, where no return information is available in that year, the second calendar year, prior to the submission of an application pursuant to Title I, Subtitle E, of the Patient Protection and Affordable Care Act.

(d) *Effective/applicability date.*—This section applies to disclosures to the Department of Health and Human Services on or after August 14, 2013. [Reg. § 301.6103(l)(21)-1.]

☐ {*T.D.* 9628, 8-13-2013.}

[Reg. § 301.6103(m)-1]

§ 301.6103(m)-1. Disclosure of taxpayer identity information.—(a) *Definition.*—For purposes of applying the provisions of section 6103(m) of the Internal Revenue Code, the term *agent* includes a contractor.

(b) *Effective date.*—This section is applicable January 6, 2004. [Reg. § 301.6103(m)-1.]

☐ [*T.D.* 9111, 12-31-2003.]

[Reg. § 301.6103(n)-1]

§ 301.6103(n)-1. **Disclosure of returns and return information in connection with written contracts or agreements for the acquisition of property or services for tax administration purposes.**—(a) *General rule.*—(1) Pursuant to the provisions of section 6103(n) of the Internal Revenue Code and subject to the conditions of this section, officers and employees of the Treasury Department, a State tax agency, the Social Security Administration, or the Department of Justice, are authorized to disclose returns and return information (as defined in section 6103(b)) to any person (including, in the case of the Treasury Department, any person described in section 7513(a)), or to an officer or employee of the person, for purposes of tax administration (as defined in section 6103(b)(4)), to the extent necessary in connection with a written contract or agreement for the acquisition of—

(i) Equipment or other property; or

(ii) Services relating to the processing, storage, transmission, or reproduction of returns or return information, the programming, maintenance, repair, or testing of equipment or other property, or the providing of other services.

(2) Any person, or officer or employee of the person, who receives returns or return information under paragraph (a)(1) of this section, may—

(i) Further disclose the returns or return information to another officer or employee of the person whose duties or responsibilities require the returns or return information for a purpose described in this paragraph (a); or

(ii) Further disclose the returns or return information, when authorized in writing by the Internal Revenue Service (IRS), to the extent necessary to carry out the purposes described in this paragraph (a). Disclosures may include disclosures to an agent or subcontractor of the person, or officer or employee of the agent or subcontractor.

(3) An agent or subcontractor, or officer or employee of the agent or subcontractor, who receives returns or return information under paragraph (a)(2)(ii) of this section, may further disclose the returns or return information to another officer or employee of the agent or subcontractor whose duties or responsibilities require the returns or return information for a purpose described in this paragraph (a).

(4) Any person, or officer, employee, agent or subcontractor of the person, or officer or employee of the agent or subcontractor, who receives returns or return information under this paragraph (a), may, subject to the provisions of § 301.6103(p)(2)(B)-1 (concerning disclosures by a Federal, State, or local agency, or its agents or contractors), further disclose the returns or return information for a purpose authorized, and subject to all applicable conditions imposed, by section 6103.

(b) *Limitations.*—(1) Disclosure of returns or return information in connection with a written contract or agreement for the acquisition of property or services described in paragraph (a) of this section will be treated as necessary only if the performance of the contract or agreement cannot otherwise be reasonably, properly, or economically carried out without the disclosure.

(2) Disclosure of returns or return information in connection with a written contract or agreement for the acquisition of property or services described in paragraph (a) of this section shall be made only to the extent necessary to reasonably, properly, or economically perform the contract. For example, disclosure of returns or return information to employees of a contractor for purposes of programming, maintaining, repairing, or testing computer equipment used by the IRS or a State tax agency shall be made only if the services cannot be reasonably, properly, or economically performed without the disclosure. If it is determined that disclosure of returns or return information is necessary, and if the services can be reasonably, properly, or economically performed by disclosure of only parts or portions of a return or if deletion of taxpayer identity information (as defined in section 6103(b)(6)) reflected on a return would not seriously impair the ability of the employees to perform the services, then only the parts or portions of the return, or only the return with taxpayer identity information deleted, may be disclosed.

(c) *Penalties.*—Any person, or officer, employee, agent or subcontractor of the person, or officer or employee of the agent or subcontractor, who receives returns or return information under paragraph (a) of this section, is subject to the civil and criminal penalty provisions of sections 7431, 7213, and 7213A for the unauthorized inspection or disclosure of the returns or return information.

(d) *Notification requirements.*—Any person, or agent or subcontractor of the person, who receives returns or return information under paragraph (a) of this section shall provide written notice to his, her, or its officers and employees receiving the returns or return information that—

(1) Returns or return information disclosed to the officer or employee may be used only for a purpose and to the extent authorized by paragraph (a) of this section and that the officer or employee is subject to the civil and criminal penalty provisions of sections 7431, 7213, and 7213A for the unauthorized inspection or disclosure of the returns or return information;

(2) Further inspection of any returns or return information for a purpose or to an extent not authorized by paragraph (a) of this section constitutes a misdemeanor, punishable upon conviction by a fine of as much as $1,000, or imprisonment for as long as 1 year, or both, together with costs of prosecution;

(3) Further disclosure of any returns or return information for a purpose or to an extent not authorized by paragraph (a) of this section constitutes a felony, punishable upon conviction

by a fine of as much as $5,000, or imprisonment for as long as 5 years, or both, together with the costs of prosecution;

(4) Further inspection or disclosure of returns or return information by any person who is not an officer or employee of the United States for a purpose or to an extent not authorized by paragraph (a) of this section may result also in an award of civil damages against that person in an amount not less than $1,000 for each act of unauthorized inspection or disclosure; or the sum of actual damages sustained by the plaintiff as a result of the unauthorized inspection or disclosure plus, in the case of a willful inspection or disclosure or an inspection or disclosure that is the result of gross negligence, punitive damages. In addition, costs and reasonable attorneys fees may be awarded; and

(5) A conviction for an offense referenced in paragraph (d)(2) or (3) of this section shall, in addition to any other punishment, result in dismissal from office or discharge from employment if the person convicted is an officer or employee of the United States.

(e) *Safeguards.*—(1) Any person, or agent or subcontractor of the person, who may receive returns or return information under paragraph (a) of this section, shall agree, before disclosure of any returns or return information to the person, agent, or subcontractor, to permit an inspection by the IRS of his, her, or its site or facilities.

(2) Any person, or officer, employee, agent or subcontractor of the person, or officer or employee of the agent or subcontractor, who receives returns or return information under paragraph (a) of this section, shall comply with all applicable conditions and requirements as the IRS may prescribe from time to time (prescribed requirements) for the purposes of protecting the confidentiality of returns and return information and preventing any disclosure or inspection of returns or return information in a manner not authorized by this section.

(3) The terms of any written contract or agreement for the acquisition of property or services as described in paragraph (a) of this section shall provide, or shall be amended to provide, that any person, or officer, employee, agent or subcontractor of the person, or officer or employee of the agent or subcontractor, who receives returns or return information under paragraph (a) of this section, shall comply with the prescribed requirements. Any contract or agreement shall be made available to the IRS before execution of the contract or agreement. For purposes of this paragraph (e)(3), a written contract or agreement shall include any contract or agreement between a person and an agent or subcontractor of the person to provide the property or services described in paragraph (a) of this section.

(4) If the IRS determines that any person, or officer, employee, agent or subcontractor of the person, or officer or employee of the agent or subcontractor, who receives returns or return information under paragraph (a) of this section,

has failed to, or does not, satisfy the prescribed requirements, the IRS, consistent with the regulations under section 6103(p)(7), may take any actions it deems necessary to ensure that the prescribed requirements are or will be satisfied, including—

(i) Suspension of further disclosures of returns or return information by the IRS to the State tax agency, the Social Security Administration, or the Department of Justice, until the IRS determines that the conditions and requirements have been or will be satisfied;

(ii) Suspension of further disclosures by the Treasury Department otherwise authorized by paragraph (a) of this section; and

(iii) Suspension or termination of any duty or obligation arising under a contract or agreement with the Treasury Department.

(f) *Definitions.*—For purposes of this section—

(1) The term *Treasury Department* includes the IRS, the Office of the Chief Counsel for the IRS, and the Office of the Treasury Inspector General for Tax Administration;

(2) The term *State tax agency* means an agency, body, or commission described in section 6103(d); and

(3) The term *Department of Justice* includes offices of the United States Attorneys.

(g) *Effective date.*—This section is applicable on June 5, 2007. [Reg. § 1.6103(n)-1.]

☐ [*T.D.* 7723, 9-30-80. *Amended by T.D.* 8271, 11-2-89; *T.D.* 8695, 12-16-96; *T.D.* 9044, 3-11-2003 and *T.D.* 9327, 6-4-2007.]

[Reg. § 301.6103(n)-2]

§ 301.6103(n)-2. Disclosure of return information in connection with written contracts among the IRS, whistleblowers, and legal representatives of whistleblowers.—(a) *General rule.*—(1) Pursuant to the provisions of sections 6103(n) and 7623 of the Internal Revenue Code and subject to the conditions of this section, an officer or employee of the Treasury Department is authorized to disclose return information (as defined in section 6103(b)(2)) to a whistleblower and, if applicable, the legal representative of the whistleblower, to the extent necessary in connection with a written contract among the Internal Revenue Service (IRS), the whistleblower and, if applicable, the legal representative of the whistleblower, for services relating to the detection of violations of the internal revenue laws or related statutes.

(2) The IRS shall have the discretion to determine whether to enter into a written contract pursuant to section 7623 with the whistleblower and, if applicable, the legal representative of the whistleblower, for services described in paragraph (a)(1) of this section.

(b) *Limitations.*—(1) Disclosure of return information in connection with a written contract for services described in paragraph (a)(1) of this section shall be made only to the extent the IRS deems it necessary in connection with the reasonable or proper performance of the contract. Disclosures may include, but are not limited to, disclosures to accomplish properly any purpose or activity of the nature described in section 6103(k)(6) and the regulations thereunder.

(2) If the IRS determines that the services of a whistleblower and, if applicable, the legal representative of the whistleblower, as described in paragraph (a)(1) of this section, can be performed reasonably or properly by disclosure of only parts or portions of return information, then only the parts or portions of the return information shall be disclosed.

(3) Upon written request by a whistleblower, or a legal representative of a whistleblower, with whom the IRS has entered into a written contract for services as described in paragraph (a)(1) of this section, the Director of the Whistleblower Office, or designee of the Director, may inform the whistleblower and, if applicable, the legal representative of the whistleblower, of the status of the whistleblower's claim for award under section 7623, including whether the claim is being evaluated for potential investigative action, or is pending due to an ongoing examination, appeal, collection action, or litigation. The information may be disclosed only if the IRS determines that the disclosure would not seriously impair Federal tax administration.

(4) Return information disclosed to a whistleblower and, if applicable, a legal representative of a whistleblower, under this section, shall not be further disclosed or otherwise used by the whistleblower or a legal representative of a whistleblower, except as expressly authorized in writing by the IRS.

(c) *Penalties.*—Any whistleblower, or legal representative of a whistleblower, who receives return information under this section, is subject to the civil and criminal penalty provisions of sections 7431, 7213, and 7213A for the unauthorized inspection or disclosure of the return information.

(d) *Safeguards.*—(1) Any whistleblower, or the legal representative of a whistleblower, who receives return information under this section, shall comply with all applicable conditions and requirements as the IRS may prescribe from time to time for the purposes of protecting the confidentiality of the return information and preventing any disclosure or inspection of the return information in a manner not authorized by this section (prescribed requirements).

(2) Any written contract for services as described in paragraph (a)(1) of this section shall provide that any whistleblower and, if applicable, the legal representative of a whistleblower, who has access to return information under this section, shall comply with the prescribed requirements.

(3) Any whistleblower, or the legal representative of a whistleblower, who may receive return information under this section, shall agree in writing, before any disclosure of return infor-

mation is made, to permit an inspection of the whistleblower's or the legal representative's premises by the IRS relative to the maintenance of the return information disclosed under these regulations and, upon completion of services as described in the written contract with the IRS, to dispose of all return information by returning the return information, including any and all copies or notes made, to the IRS, or to the extent that it cannot be returned, by destroying the information in a manner consistent with prescribed requirements.

(4) If the IRS determines that any whistleblower, or the legal representative of a whistleblower, who has access to return information under this section, has failed to, or does not, satisfy the prescribed requirements, the IRS, using the procedures described in the regulations under section 6103(p)(7), may take any action it deems necessary to ensure that the prescribed requirements are or will be satisfied, including—

(i) Suspension of further disclosures of return information by the IRS to the whistleblower and, if applicable, the legal representative of the whistleblower, until the IRS determines that the conditions and requirements have been or will be satisfied; and

(ii) Suspension or termination of any duty or obligation arising under the contract with the IRS.

(e) *Definitions.*—For purposes of this section—

(1) The term *Treasury Department* includes the IRS and the Office of the Chief Counsel for the IRS.

(2) The term *whistleblower* means an individual who provides information to the IRS regarding violations of the tax laws or related statutes and submits a claim for an award under section 7623 with respect to the information.

(3) The term *legal representative* means any individual who is a member in good standing in the bar of the highest court of any state, possession, territory, commonwealth, or the District of Columbia, and who has a written power of attorney executed by the whistleblower.

(f) *Effective/applicability date.*—This section is applicable on March 15, 2011. [Reg. § 301.6103(n)-2.]

☐ [T.D. 9516, 3-14-2011.]

[Reg. § 301.6103(p)(2)(B)-1]

§ 301.6103(p)(2)(B)-1. Disclosure of returns and return information by other agencies.— (a) *General rule.*—Subject to the requirements of paragraphs (b), (c), and (d) of this section, returns or return information that have been obtained by a Federal, state or local agency, or its agents or contractors, in accordance with section 6103 (the first recipient) may be disclosed by the first recipient to another recipient authorized to receive such returns or return information under section 6103 (the second recipient).

(b) *Approval by Commissioner.*—A disclosure described in paragraph (a) of this section may be made if the Commissioner of Internal Revenue (the Commissioner) determines, after receiving a written request under this section, that such returns or return information are more readily available from the first recipient than from the Internal Revenue Service (IRS). The disclosure authorization by the Commissioner shall be directed to the head of the first recipient and may contain such conditions or restrictions as the Commissioner may prescribe. The disclosure authorization may be revoked by the Commissioner at any time.

(c) *Requirements and restrictions.*—The second recipient may receive only returns or return information as authorized by the provision of section 6103 applicable to such second recipient. Any returns or return information disclosed may be used by the second recipient only for a purpose authorized by and subject to any conditions imposed by section 6103 and the regulations thereunder, including, if applicable, safeguards imposed by section 6103(p)(4).

(d) *Records and reports of disclosure.*—The first recipient shall maintain to the satisfaction of the IRS a permanent system of standardized records regarding such disclosure authorization described in paragraph (a) of this section and any disclosure of returns and return information made pursuant to such authorization, and shall provide such information as prescribed by the Commissioner in order to enable the IRS to comply with its obligations under section 6103(p)(3) to keep accountings for disclosures and to make annual reports of disclosures to the Joint Committee on Taxation. The information required for reports to the Joint Committee on Taxation must be provided within 30 days after the close of each calendar year. The requirements of this paragraph do not apply to the disclosure of returns and return information as provided by paragraph (a) of this section which, had such disclosures been made directly by the IRS, would not have been subject to the recordkeeping requirements imposed by section 6103(p)(3)(A).

(e) *Effective date.*—This section is applicable on January 21, 2003. [Reg. § 301.6103(p)(2)(B)-1.]

☐ [*T.D.* 9036, 1-17-2003.]

[Reg. § 301.6103(p)(4)-1]

§ 301.6103(p)(4)-1. Procedures relating to safeguards for returns or return information.— For security guidelines and other safeguards for protecting returns and return information, see guidance published by the Internal Revenue Service. For procedures for administrative review of a determination that an authorized recipient has failed to safeguard returns or return information, see § 301.6103(p)(7)-1. [Reg. § 301.6103(p)(4)-1.]

☐ [*T.D.* 9445, 2-10-2009.]

[Reg. § 301.6103(p)(7)-1]

§ 301.6103(p)(7)-1. Procedures for administrative review of a determination that an authorized recipient has failed to safeguard returns or return information.—(a) *In general.*—Notwith-

standing any section of the Internal Revenue Code (Code), the Internal Revenue Service (IRS) may terminate or suspend disclosure of returns and return information to any authorized recipient specified in section (p)(4) of section 6103, if the IRS determines that:

(1) The authorized recipient has allowed an unauthorized inspection or disclosure of returns or return information and that the authorized recipient has not taken adequate corrective action to prevent the recurrence of an unauthorized inspection or disclosure; or

(2) The authorized recipient does not satisfactorily maintain the safeguards prescribed by section 6103(p)(4), and has made no adequate plan to improve its system to maintain the safeguards satisfactorily.

(b) *Notice of IRS's intention to terminate or suspend disclosure.*—Prior to terminating or suspending authorized disclosures, the IRS will notify the authorized recipient in writing of the IRS's preliminary determination and of the IRS's intention to discontinue disclosure of returns and return information to the authorized recipient. Upon so notifying the authorized recipient, the IRS, if it determines that tax administration otherwise would be seriously impaired, may suspend further disclosures of returns and return information to the authorized recipient pending a final determination by the Commissioner or a Deputy Commissioner described in paragraph (d)(2) of this section.

(c) *Authorized recipient's right to appeal.*—An authorized recipient shall have 30 days from the date of receipt of a notice described in paragraph (b) of this section to appeal the preliminary determination described in paragraph (b) of this section. The appeal shall be made directly to the Commissioner.

(d) *Procedures for administrative review.*—(1) To appeal a preliminary determination described in paragraph (b) of this section, the authorized recipient shall send a written request for a conference to: Commissioner of Internal Revenue (Attention: SE:S:CLD:GLD), 1111 Constitution Avenue, NW., Washington, DC 20224. The request must include a complete description of the authorized recipient's present system of safeguarding returns or return information received by the authorized recipient (and its authorized contractors or agents, if any). The request must state the reason or reasons the authorized recipient believes that such system or practice (including improvements, if any, to such system or practice expected to be made in the near future) is or will be adequate to safeguard returns or return information.

(2) Within 45 days of the receipt of the request made in accordance with the provisions of paragraph (d)(1) of this section, the Commissioner or Deputy Commissioner personally shall hold a conference with representatives of the authorized recipient, after which the Commissioner or Deputy Commissioner shall make a final determination with respect to the appeal.

(e) *Effective/applicability date.*—This section applies to all authorized recipients of returns and return information that are subject to the safeguard requirements set forth in section 6103(p)(4) on or after February 11, 2009. [Reg. § 301.6103(p)(7)-1.]

☐ [*T.D.* 9445, 2-10-2009.]

[Reg. § 301.6104(a)-1]

§ 301.6104(a)-1. Public inspection of material relating to tax-exempt organizations.—
(a) *Applications for exemption from Federal income tax, applications for a group exemption letter, and supporting documents.*—If the Internal Revenue Service determines that an organization described in section 501(c) or section 501(d) is exempt from Federal income tax for any taxable year, the application upon which the determination is based, together with any supporting documents, shall be open to public inspection. Such applications and supporting documents shall be open for public inspection even after any revocation of the Internal Revenue Service's determination that the organization is exempt from Federal income tax. In the past, some applications were destroyed and therefore are not available for inspection. For purposes of determining the availability for public inspection, a claim for exemption from Federal income tax filed to re-establish exempt status after denial thereof under the provisions of section 503 or 504 (as in effect on December 31, 1969), or under the corresponding provisions of any prior revenue law, is considered an application for exemption from Federal income tax.

(b) *Notices of status filed by political organizations.*—If, in accordance with section 527(i), an organization notifies the Internal Revenue Service that it is a political organization as described in section 527, exempt from Federal income tax for any taxable year, the notice of status filed by the political organization shall be open to public inspection.

(c) *Letters or documents issued by the Internal Revenue Service with respect to an application for exemption from Federal income tax.*—If an application for exemption from Federal income tax is filed with the Internal Revenue Service after October 31, 1976, and is open to public inspection under paragraph (a) of this section, then any letter or document issued to the applicant by the Internal Revenue Service that relates to the application is also open to public inspection. For rules relating to when a letter or document is issued, see § 301.6110-2(h). Letters or documents to which this paragraph (c) applies include, but are not limited to—

(1) Favorable rulings and determination letters, including group exemption letters, issued in response to applications for exemption from Federal income tax;

(2) Technical advice memoranda issued with respect to the approval, or subsequent approval, of an application for exemption from Federal income tax;

(3) Letters issued in response to an application for exemption from Federal income tax (including applications for a group exemption letter) that propose a finding that the applicant is not entitled to be exempt from Federal income tax, if the applicant is subsequently determined, on the basis of that application, to be exempt from Federal income tax; and

(4) Any letter or document issued by the Internal Revenue Service relating to an organization's status as an organization described in section 509(a), 4940(d)(2), 4942(j)(3), or 4943(f), including a determination letter that the organization is or is not a private foundation.

(d) *Requirement of exempt status.*—An application for exemption from Federal income tax (including applications for a group exemption letter), supporting documents, and letters or documents issued by the Internal Revenue Service that relate to the application shall not be open to public inspection before the organization is determined, on the basis of that application, to be exempt from Federal income tax for any taxable year. If an organization is determined to be exempt from Federal income tax for any taxable year, these materials shall not be withheld from public inspection on the basis that the organization is subsequently determined not to be exempt for any other taxable year.

(e) *Documents included in the term "application for exemption from Federal income tax".*—For purposes of this section—

(1) *Prescribed application form.*—If a form is prescribed for an organization's application for exemption from Federal income tax, the application includes the form and all documents and statements that the Internal Revenue Service requires to be filed with the form, any amendments or revisions to the original application, or any resubmitted applications where the original application was submitted in draft form or was withdrawn. An application includes an application for reinstatement of tax-exempt status after an organization's tax exempt status has been revoked pursuant to section 6033(j). An application submitted in draft form or an application submitted and later withdrawn is not considered an application.

(2) *No prescribed application form.*—If no form is prescribed for an organization's application for exemption from Federal income tax, the application includes the submission by letter requesting recognition of tax exemption and any statements or documents as prescribed by Revenue Procedure 2011-9, IRB 2011-2 (January 10, 2011), or any successor guidance describing procedures for application for exempt status pursuant to section 501 and section 521 of the Internal Revenue Code. See § 601.601(d)(2)(ii)(*b*).

(3) *Application for a Group Exemption Letter.*—The application for a group exemption letter includes the letter submitted by or on behalf of subordinate organizations that seek exempt status pursuant to a group exemption letter and

any statements or documents as prescribed by Revenue Procedure 80-27, 1980-1 CB 677 (June 20, 1980), and any successor guidance. See § 601.601(d)(2)(ii)(*b*).

(4) *Notice of status filed under section 527(i)*.— For purposes of this section, documents included in the term "notice of status filed under section 527(i)" include—

(i) Form 8871, "Political Organization Notice of Section 527 Status";

(ii) Form 8453-X, "Declaration of Electronic Filing of Notice of Section 527 Status"; and

(iii) Any other additional forms or documents that the Internal Revenue Service may prescribe.

(f) *Material open to public inspection under section 6110*.—Under section 6110, certain written determinations, including negative determinations issued to organizations that applied for an exemption from Federal income tax, issued by the Internal Revenue Service are made available for public inspection. Section 6110 does not apply, however, to material that is open to public inspection under section 6104. See sections 6104(a)(1) and 6110(l)(1).

(g) *Supporting documents defined*.—For purposes of this section, "supporting documents," with respect to an application for exemption from Federal income tax, means any statement or document not described in paragraph (e) of this section that is submitted by the organization or group in support of its application prior to a determination described in paragraph (a) of this section. Items submitted in connection with an application in draft form, or with an application submitted and later withdrawn, are not supporting documents. There are no supporting documents with respect to Notices of Status filed by political organizations.

(h) *Statement of exempt status*.—For efficient tax administration, the Internal Revenue Service may publish, in paper or electronic format, the names of organizations currently recognized as exempt from Federal income tax, including organizations recognized as exempt from Federal income tax under particular paragraphs of section 501(c) or section 501(d). In addition to having the opportunity to inspect material relating to an organization exempt from Federal income tax, a person may request a statement, or the Internal Revenue Service may disclose, in response to or in anticipation of a request, the following information—

(1) The subsection and paragraph of section 501 (or the corresponding provision of any prior revenue law) under which the organization or group has been determined, on the basis of an application open to public inspection, to qualify for exemption from Federal income tax; and

(2) Whether an organization or group is currently recognized as exempt from Federal income tax.

(i) *Publication of non-exempt status*.—(1) For publication of the notice of the revocation of a determination that an organization is described in section 501(c)(3), see section 7428(c).

(2) For publication of a list including any organization the tax exemption of which is revoked for failure to file required returns or notices for three consecutive years, see section 6033(j).

(3) For publication of notice of suspension of tax exemption of terrorist organizations, see section 501(p).

(j) *Withholding of certain information from public inspection*.—For rules relating to certain information contained in an application for exemption from Federal income tax and supporting documents that will be withheld from public inspection, see § 301.6104(a)-5(a).

(k) *Procedures for inspection*.—For rules relating to procedures for public inspection of applications for exemption from Federal income tax and supporting documents, see § 301.6104(a)-6.

(l) *Effective/applicability date*.—The rules of this section apply February 29, 2012. [Reg. § 301.6104(a)-1.]

☐ [*T.D.* 7845, 11-5-82. *Amended by T.D.* 9581, 2-28-2012.]

[Reg. § 301.6104(a)-2]

§ 301.6104(a)-2. Public inspection of material relating to pension and other plans.— (a) *Material open to inspection*.—Except as provided in § 301.6104(a)-4 with respect to plans having fewer than 26 participants, an application for a determination letter which is filed with the Internal Revenue Service after September 2, 1974, together with supporting documents filed by the applicant in support of the application, will be open to public inspection under section 6104(a)(1)(B)(i) and (ii). An application for a determination letter and supporting documents will be open to public inspection whether or not the application is withdrawn by the applicant, and whether or not the Internal Revenue Service determines that the plan, account, or annuity to which the application relates is qualified or that any related trust or custodial account is exempt from tax.

(b) *Documents included in the term "application for a determination letter"*.—(1) *Employees' plans and individual retirement plans*.—For purposes of this section, the term "application for a determination letter" includes the documents that an applicant files with respect to a request that the Internal Revenue Service determine the qualification of—

(i) A pension, profit-sharing, or stock bonus plan under section 401(a),

(ii) An annuity plan under section 403(a),

(iii) A bond purchase plan under section 405(a), or

(iv) An individual retirement account or annuity described in section 408(a), (b), or (c).

(2) *Tax exempt trusts or custodial accounts*.— The term "application for a determination letter"

also includes the documents an applicant files with respect to a request that the Internal Revenue Service determine the exemption from tax under section 501(a) of an organization forming part of a plan or account described in subparagraph (1) of this paragraph, or a custodial account described in section 401(f).

(3) *Master, prototype and pattern plans.*—The term "application for a determination letter" also includes documents which an applicant files with respect to a request for approval of a master, prototype, pattern or other such plan or account.

(4) *Prescribed forms and application letters.*—With respect to an application for a determination letter described in this paragraph (b) for which an application form is prescribed, the application for a determination letter includes the form and all documents and statements required to be filed in connection with the form. With respect to an application for a determination letter for which no application form is prescribed, the application for a determination letter includes the application letter and all documents and statements the Internal Revenue Service requires to be submitted with the application letter.

(c) *Documents not constituting an "application for a determination letter.".*—The following are not applications for a determination letter for purposes of this section:

(1) An incomplete application that is returned without action for proper completion,

(2) An application that is returned without action to the applicant for failure to notify all interested parties in accordance with the regulations under section 7476 (relating to declaratory judgments), and

(3) A request for a ruling as to whether a proposed transaction is a prohibited transaction under section 4975.

(d) *Supporting documents.*—"Supporting documents", as used with respect to an application for a determination letter which is open to public inspection under this section, means any statement or document submitted in support of the application which is not specifically required by the application form or the Internal Revenue Service. For example, a legal brief submitted in support of an application for a determination letter is a supporting document.

(e) *Applicant.*—For purposes of this section, §301.6104(a)-3 (relating to Internal Revenue Service letters and documents open to public inspection) and §301.6104(a)-5 (relating to the withholding of certain information from public inspection), an "applicant" includes, but is not limited to, an employer, plan administrator (as defined in section 414(g)), labor union, bank, or insurance company that files an application for a determination letter. [Reg. §301.6104(a)-2.]

☐ [*T.D.* 7845, 11-5-82.]

[Reg. §301.6104(a)-3]

§301.6104(a)-3. Public inspection of Internal Revenue Service letters and documents relating to pension and other plans.—(a) *In general.*—Except as provided in §301.6104(a)-4 with respect to plans having fewer than 26 participants, a letter or other document issued by the Internal Revenue Service after September 2, 1974, is open to public inspection under section 6104(a)(1)(B)(iv) and this section, if it is issued with respect to—

(1) The qualification of a pension, profit-sharing or stock bonus plan under section 401(a), an annuity plan under section 403(a), a bond purchase plan under section 405(a), or an individual retirement account or annuity described in section 408(a), (b) or (c),

(2) The exemption from tax under section 501(a) of an organization forming part of such a plan or account, or a custodial account described in section 401(f), or

(3) The approval of a master, prototype, pattern or other such plan or account.

(b) *Scope.*—Internal Revenue Service letters and documents open to public inspection under section 6104(a)(1)(B)(iv) and this section are not limited to those issued in response to an application for a determination letter described in §301.6104(a)-2. They are, however, limited to those issued by the Internal Revenue Service to the person or organization which either did or could file an application for a determination letter for the plan, account or annuity to which the letter or document relates. If such a person or organization designates a representative having a power of attorney, however, then the letter or document will be open to inspection if issued to the representative. For rules relating to when a letter or document is issued, see §301.6110-2(h). Internal Revenue Service letters and documents are open to public inspection under section 6104(a)(1)(B)(iv) and this section whether or not the Internal Revenue Service determines that the plan, account or annuity to which the letter or document relates is qualified or that any related trust or custodial account is exempt from tax.

(c) *Letters and documents open to public inspection.*—Internal Revenue Service letters and documents open to public inspection under section 6104(a)(1)(B)(iv) and this section include, but are not limited to:

(1) Determination letters relating to the qualification of a plan, account or annuity described in paragraph (a)(1) of this section (see §601.201(o)),

(2) Technical advice memoranda (see §601.201(n)(9)) relating to the issuance of such determination letters,

(3) Technical advice memoranda relating to the continuing qualification of a plan, account or annuity previously determined to be qualified, or to the qualification of a plan, account or annuity for which no determination letter has been issued,

(4) Letters or documents revoking or modifying any prior favorable determination letter or denying the qualification of a plan, account or annuity for which no determination letter has been issued,

(5) Determination letters relating to the exemption from tax of a trust or custodial account described in paragraph (a)(2) of this section (see § 601.201(o)(2)(i)(*b*)), or

(6) Opinion letters relating to the acceptability of the form of any master, prototype or other such plan or account (see § 601.201(p) and (q)) or notification letters issued with respect to pattern plans.

(d) *Extent letter or document open to public inspection.*—A letter or document issued by the Internal Revenue Service is open to public inspection under section 6104(a)(1)(B)(iv) and this section only to the extent it relates directly to the qualification of a plan, account or annuity, the exemption from tax of a related organization or custodial account, or the approval of a master, prototype, pattern or other such plan. Any part of the letter or document which does not directly relate to such a qualification, exemption or approval is not open to public inspection. For example, a letter to an employer which concludes that an employees' plan is not qualified and the related trust is not tax exempt will be open to public inspection. However, that same letter may also assert an income tax deficiency because employer contributions to the trust are, therefore, not deductible. In such a case, that part of the letter relating to the tax deficiency will be deleted before the letter is opened to public inspection.

(e) *Letters or documents issued with respect to tax return examination.*—In the case of an examination of a taxpayer's return or consideration of a taxpayer's claim for credit or refund, no letter or document issued to the taxpayer before the preliminary or "30-day" letter described in § 601.105(d)(1) is issued to the taxpayer will be open to public inspection under section 6104(a)(1)(B)(iv) and this section. The "30-day" letter and any statutory notice of deficiency subsequently issued to the taxpayer under section 6212 will be open to public inspection to the extent provided in paragraph (d) of this section. If any letter or document other than a statutory notice of deficiency is issued to the taxpayer after the "30-day" letter is issued, such letter or document will be open to inspection to the extent provided in paragraph (d) of this section only if it finally resolves or otherwise disposes of a plan qualification or tax exemption issue raised in the "30-day" letter.

(f) *Letters or documents issued after September 2, 1974.*—Section 6104(a)(1)(B)(iv) and this section apply to letters or documents issued by the Internal Revenue Service after September 2, 1974, even though the relevant application for a determination letter or other initiating correspondence from the applicant was filed with the Internal Revenue Service before September 2, 1974. [Reg. § 301.6104(a)-3.]

□ [*T.D.* 7845, 11-5-82.]

[Reg. § 301.6104(a)-4]

§ 301.6104(a)-4. Requirement for 26 or more plan participants.—(a) *Inspection by plan participants.*—In the case of a plan, annuity or account described in § 301.6104(a)-2(b) and § 301.6104(a)-3(a) that has fewer than 26 participants, material described in §§ 301.6104(a)-2 and 301.6104(a)-3 as open to public inspection is only open to inspection by a plan participant or the participant's authorized representative. This limitation does not apply, however, with respect to documents which an applicant files with respect to a request for approval of a master, prototype, pattern or other such plan (see § 301.6104(a)-2(b)(3)) or to opinion, notification or other such letters issued by the Internal Revenue Service with respect to such plans (see § 301.6104(a)-3(a)(3)).

(b) *Determining number of plan participants.*—(1) *In general.*—For purposes of determining whether a plan has fewer than 26 participants, the number of plan participants will be the number indicated on the most recent annual return filed for the plan under section 6058. Where an annual return indicates the number of participants both at the beginning and end of the plan year, the number indicated on the return means the number at the end of the plan year. If no annual return has been filed for the plan, then the number of plan participants will be the number indicated on the most recent application for a determination letter filed for the plan. If, however, the number of plan participants is increased prior to final Internal Revenue Service action on the application, the number of plan participants will be that increased number.

(2) *Decreasing number of plan participants.*—If a plan having 26 or more participants, as indicated on an annual return or application for a determination letter, subsequently files an annual return indicating fewer than 26 plan participants, then material relating to the plan which is issued or received by the Internal Revenue Service after the date the annual return is filed will be open to inspection only by plan participants or their authorized representatives. Similarly, if a plan having 26 or more participants as indicated on an annual return or an application for a determination letter, subsequently files an application for a determination letter which indicates fewer than 26 plan participants, then that application and related material, as well as any other material relating to the plan which is received or issued by the Internal Revenue Service after the date of receipt of that application, will be open to inspection only by plan participants or their authorized representatives. In either case, material open to public inspection pursuant to the number of plan participants indicated on previous annual returns or applications for a determination letter will remain open to public inspection.

(3) *Increasing number of plan participants.*—If a plan having fewer than 26 plan participants, as indicated on an annual return or application for a determination letter, files a subsequent return or application indicating 26 or more plan participants, all the plan's prior applications and other material received or issued by the Internal Revenue Service after September 2, 1974, will be open to public inspection regardless of the number of plan participants indicated on any prior return or application.

(c) *Plan participant.*—Solely for purposes of determining who is a plan participant permitted to inspect material relating to a plan having fewer than 26 participants, the term "plan participant" includes, but is not limited to, former employees (such as certain retired and terminated employees) who have a nonforfeitable right to benefits under the plan. An individual who is merely a beneficiary of an employee or former employee is not a plan participant, unless the individual is a beneficiary of a deceased former employee and is receiving benefits or entitled to receive future benefits under the plan. The term "plan participant" also includes the administrator, executor, or trustee of the estate of a deceased plan participant if such administrator, executor, or trustee is receiving benefits or entitled to receive future benefits under the plan in his or her official capacity. That material may be available for inspection to an individual under this paragraph does not constitute a determination by the Internal Revenue Service that the individual is a plan participant for any purpose other than inspection under section 6104(a)(1)(B).

(d) *Authorized representative.*—"Authorized representative" means the representative of a plan participant designated by the participant in writing to inspect material described in §§ 301.6104(a)-2 and 301.6104(a)-3. The document designating the authorized representative must be signed by the plan participant and must specify that the representative is authorized to inspect the material. The document, or a copy, must be filed with the office of the Internal Revenue Service in which the authorized representative is to inspect the material. A copy which is reproduced by a photographic process need not be certified as a true and correct copy of the original. [Reg. § 301.6104(a)-4.]

☐ [T.D. 7845, 11-5-82.]

[Reg. § 301.6104(a)-5]

§ 301.6104(a)-5. Withholding of certain information from public inspection.—(a) *Tax exempt organizations.*—(1) *Trade secrets, patents, processes, styles of work, or apparatus.*—An organization whose application for tax exemption is open to public inspection under section 6104(a)(1)(A) and § 301.6104(a)-1 may in writing request the withholding of information contained in the application or supporting documents which relates to any trade secret, patent, process, style of work, or apparatus of the organization. The information will be withheld from the public inspection

if the Commissioner determines that the disclosure of such information would adversely affect the organization. Requests for withholding information from public inspection should be filed with the office with which the organization files the documents containing the information. The request must clearly identify the material desired to be withheld (the document, page, paragraph, and line) and must state why the information should not be open to public inspection. The organization will be notified of the Commissioner's determination as to whether the information will be withheld from public inspection. If the Commissioner determines that the information will be disclosed, the organization will be given 15 days after notification of the Commissioner's decision to contest that decision before the document is disclosed.

(2) *National defense material.*—The Internal Revenue Service will withhold from public inspection any information which is submitted by an organization whose application for tax exemption is open to inspection under section 6104(a)(1)(A) and § 301.6104(a)-1, if the Commissioner determines that public disclosure would adversely affect the national defense.

(b) *Pension and other plans.*—(1) *Applicant's exclusion of certain information.*—Except as provided in subparagraph (2) of this paragraph, information that, in the opinion of the applicant, is of the type described in section 6104(a)(1)(C) or (D) should not be included in an application for a determination letter, supporting documents, or any other document open to inspection under section 6104(a)(1)(B). Accordingly, an applicant should not include in an application for a determination letter or supporting documents confidential compensation information as described in subparagraph (4) of this paragraph. Neither should an applicant include information relating to any trade secret, patent, process, style of work or apparatus, the disclosure of which would be adverse to the applicant.

(2) *Exception for separate document.*—The rule that an applicant should exclude from an application for a determination letter or other documents information of the type in section 6104(a)(1)(C) or (D) does not apply—

(i) In the case of the separate schedule to certain applications for a determination letter which is provided for the purpose of setting forth confidential compensation information (as described in subparagraph (4) of this paragraph) which must be submitted by the applicant,

(ii) If the applicant determines that it is impossible to provide the Internal Revenue Service with sufficient information to support an application for a determination letter without submitting what is believed to be information of the type described in section 6104(a)(1)(C) or (D), or

(iii) If the Internal Revenue Service requests that the applicant submit information of the type described in section 6104(a)(1)(C) and (D).

In a case described in subdivision (ii) or (iii) of this subparagraph, the applicant is to set forth the information in a document separate from the remainder of the application for a determination letter or other documents. The separate document is to state why the information is to be withheld from public inspection under section 6104(a)(1)(C) or (D). If the Internal Revenue Service has not requested the information, the separate document is to also state why it is impossible to provide the Internal Revenue Service sufficient information to support the application for a determination letter without including information which is to be withheld. The separate document should clearly identify the relevant portion of the application for a determination letter or other document (the document, page, paragraph, and line) to which the information set forth in the separate document relates. The Internal Revenue Service will withhold from public inspection (including inspection by a plan participant or authorized representative) information contained in the separate document if the Commissioner determines that the information is in fact information of the type described in section 6104(a)(1)(C) or (D), and, in the case of information relating to any trade secret, patent, process, style of work or apparatus, the Commissioner further determines that disclosure would be adverse to the applicant. If the Commissioner determines that the information will be disclosed, the organization will be given 15 days after notification of the Commissioner's decision to contest the decision before the document is disclosed.

(3) *National defense material.*—The Internal Revenue Service will withhold from public inspection (including inspection by a plan participant or authorized representative) any information which is included in an application for a determination letter or supporting documents if the Commissioner determines that public disclosure would adversely affect the national defense. The information will be withheld whether or not submitted on a separate document pursuant to subparagraph (2) of this paragraph.

(4) *Confidential compensation information.*—If an application for a determination letter, supporting document, or related letter or document referred to in section 6104(a)(1)(B) and §§ 301.6104(a)-2 and 301.6104(a)-3 contains information (including aggregate figures) from which an individual's compensation (including deferred compensation) may be ascertained, that information is not open to public inspection (including inspection by a plan participant or authorized representative). Confidential compensation information includes the amount of benefit a specific plan participant may expect to receive at normal or early retirement age and the amount of the employer's contributions under the plan that may be allocated to a specific plan participant. However, so long as a plan has more than one participant, the amount of benefit provided under the plan to plan participants, in general, at normal or early retirement age, or the amount of the employer's contributions under the plan that are allocable to plan participants, in general, does not constitute confidential compensation information. Further, a description of the numbers of individuals covered and not covered by a plan, listed by compensation range, does not constitute confidential compensation information. [Reg. § 301.6104(a)-5.]

☐ [*T.D.* 7845, 11-5-82.]

[Reg. § 301.6104(a)-6]

§ 301.6104(a)-6. Procedural rules for inspection.—(a) *Place of inspection; tax exempt organizations and pension and other plans.*—Material relating either to tax exempt organizations or to pension and other plans that is open to public inspection under section 6104(a)(1) and § 301.6104(a)-1 through § 301.6104(a)-3 will be made available for inspection at the Freedom of Information Reading Room, National Office, Internal Revenue Service, 1111 Constitution Avenue, N.W., Washington, D.C. 20224, and in the office of any district director of internal revenue.

(b) *Request for inspection.*—(1) *Tax exempt organizations and pension and other plans; public inspection.*—Material relating to either tax exempt organizations or pension and other plans that is open to public inspection under section 6104(a)(1) and §§ 301.6104(a)-1 through 301.6104(a)-3 will be available for inspection only upon request. If inspection at the National Office is desired, a request should be made in writing to the Commissioner of Internal Revenue, Attention: Freedom of Information Reading Room, 1111 Constitution Avenue, N.W., Washington, D.C. 20224. Requests for inspection in the office of a district director should be made in writing to the district director's office. The request must describe the material to be inspected in reasonably sufficient detail so that Internal Revenue Service personnel can locate the material. If a tax exempt organization has more than one application for tax exemption open to public inspection, or if a pension or other plan has more than one application for a determination letter open to public inspection, only the most recent application and related material will be made available for inspection unless the request states otherwise. Further, in the case of a pension or other plan, only Internal Revenue Service documents issued or delivered after the date of the filing of the most recent application for a determination letter will be made available for inspection, unless the request states otherwise.

(2) *Pension and other plans; inspection by plan participant or authorized representative.*—As described in § 301.6104(a)-4, material relating to plans having fewer than 26 participants is only open to inspection by a plan participant or authorized representative. In the case of such a plan, the rules described in subparagraph (1) of this paragraph apply. The request for inspection must include satisfactory evidence that the person requesting inspection is a plan participant (see § 301.6104(a)-4(c)) or an authorized representative of such a plan participant within the meaning of § 301.6104(a)-4(d).

(c) *Time and extent of inspection.*—A person requesting inspection will be notified when the material will be made available for inspection. The material will be made available for inspection at times that will not interfere with its use by the Internal Revenue Service or exclude other persons from inspecting it. In addition, the Commissioner or district director may limit the number of applications for tax exemption, applications for a determination letter, supporting documents, or letters and documents issued by the Internal Revenue Service that will be made available to any person for inspection on a given date. Inspection will be allowed only in the presence of an Internal Revenue Service employee and only during regular business hours.

(d) *Copies.*—Notes may be taken of the material open for inspection. Copies may be made manually or, if a person provides the equipment, photographically at the place of inspection. Photographic copying is subject to reasonable supervision with regard to the facilities and equipment used. Any fees the Internal Revenue Service may charge for furnishing copies under this section shall be no more than under the fee schedule promulgated pursuant to section (a)(4)(A)(i) of the Freedom of Information Act, 5 U.S.C. 552, by the Commissioner from time to time. Copies will be certified upon request. [Reg. §301.6104(a)-6.]

☐ [T.D. 7845, 11-5-82. Amended by T.D. 9070, 7-8-2003 and T.D. 9173, 1-4-2005.]

[Reg. §301.6104(b)-1]

§301.6104(b)-1. Publicity of information on certain information returns.—(a) *In general.*—The following information, together with the name and address of the organization or trust furnishing such information, shall be a matter of public record:

(1) Except as otherwise provided in section 6104 and the regulations thereunder, the information required by section 6033.

(2) The information furnished pursuant to section 6034 (relating to returns by certain trusts) on Form 1041-A.

(3) The information required to be furnished by section 6058.

(b) *Nondisclosure of certain information.*—(1) *Names and addresses of contributors.*—The names and addresses of contributors to an organization other than a private foundation shall not be made available for public inspection under section 6104(b).

(2) *Amounts of contributions.*—The amounts of contributions and bequests to an organization shall be available for public inspection unless the disclosure of such information can reasonably be expected to identify any contributor. Notwithstanding the preceding sentence, the amounts of contributions and bequests to a private foundation shall be available for public inspection.

(3) *Foreign organizations.*—The names, addresses, and amounts of contributions or bequests of persons who are not citizens of the United States to a foreign organization described in section 4948(b) shall not be made available for public inspection under section 6104(b).

(4) *Confidential business information.*—Confidential business information of contributors to any trust described in section 501(c)(21) (black lung trusts) shall not be available for public inspection under section 6104(b) provided:

(i) A request is filed with the office with which the trustee filed the documents in which the information to be withheld is contained,

(ii) Such request clearly specifies the information to be withheld and the reasons supporting the request for withholding, and

(iii) The Commissioner determines that such information is confidential business information.

Information such as the contributor's estimated total liability for black lung benefits, the contributor's coal pricing policies, or any background information necessary to establish estimated total liability or coal pricing policies are examples of confidential business information that shall not be disclosed to the public under this subparagraph.

(c) *Place of inspection.*—Information furnished on the public portion of returns (as described in paragraph (a) of this section) shall be made available for public inspection at the Freedom of Information Reading Room, Internal Revenue Service, 1111 Constitution Avenue, N.W., Washington, D.C. 20224, and at the office of any district director.

(d) *Procedure for public inspection.*—(1) *Requests for inspection.*—Information furnished on the public portion of returns (as described in paragraph (a) of this section) shall be available for public inspection only upon request. Requests for public inspection must be in writing to or at any of the offices mentioned in paragraph (c) of this section. Persons submitting requests for inspection must provide the name and address of the organization that filed the return, the type of return, and the year for which the organization filed.

(2) *Time and extent of inspection.*—A person requesting public inspection in the manner specified in subparagraph (1) of this paragraph shall be notified by the Internal Revenue Service when the material he desires to inspect will be made available for his inspection. Information on returns required by sections 6033, 6034, and 6058 will be made available for public inspection at such reasonable and proper times, and under such conditions, that will not interfere with their use by the Internal Revenue Service and will not exclude other persons from inspecting them. In addition, the Commissioner, Director of the Service Center, or district director may limit the number of returns to be made available to any person for inspection on a given date. Inspection

will be allowed only in the presence of an internal revenue officer or employee and only during the regular hours of business of the Internal Revenue Service office.

(3) *Returns available.*—Returns filed before January 1, 1970, shall be available for public inspection only pursuant to the provisions of section 6104 in effect for such years. The information furnished on all returns filed after December 31, 1969, pursuant to the requirements of section 6033, 6034, or 6058, shall be available for public inspection in accordance with the provisions of section 6104.

(4) *Copies.*—Notes may be taken of material opened for inspection under this section. Copies may be made manually or, if a person provides the equipment, photographically at the place of inspection, subject to reasonable supervision with regard to the facilities and equipment to be employed. Copies of the material opened for inspection will be furnished by the Internal Revenue Service to any person making request therefor. Request for such copies shall be made in the same manner as requests for inspection (see subparagraph (1) of this paragraph) to the office of the Internal Revenue Service in which such material is available for inspection as provided in paragraph (c) of this section. Copies may also be obtained by written request to the director of any service center. If made at the time of inspection, the request for copies need not be in writing. Any copies furnished will be certified upon request. Any fees the Internal Revenue Service may charge for furnishing copies under this section shall be no more than under the fee schedule promulgated pursuant to section (a)(4)(A)(i) of the Freedom of Information Act, 5 U.S.C. 552, by the Commissioner from time to time. [Reg. § 301.6104(b)-1.]

□ [*T.D.* 6331, 10-31-58. *Amended by T.D.* 6565, 8-2-61; *T.D.* 6645, 4-1-63; *T.D.* 7122, 6-7-71; *T.D.* 7173, 3-16-72; *T.D.* 7290, 11-16-73; *T.D.* 7350, 4-3-75; *T.D.* 7785, 7-27-81. *Redesignated by T.D.* 7845, 11-5-82. *Amended by T.D.* 8019, 4-11-85; *T.D.* 9070, 7-8-2003 *and T.D.* 9173, 1-4-2005.]

[Reg. § 301.6104(c)-1]

§ 301.6104(c)-1. Disclosure of certain information to State officers.—(a) *Notification of determinations.*—(1) *Automatic notification.*—Upon making a determination described in paragraph(c) of this section, the Internal Revenue Service will notify the Attorney General and the principal tax officer of each of the following States of such determination without application or request by such State officer—

(i) In the case of any organization described in section 501(c)(3), the State in which the principal office of the organization is located (as shown on the last-filed return required by section 6033, or on the application for exemption if no return has been filed), and the State in which the organization was incorporated, or if a trust, in which it was created, and

(ii) In the case of a private foundation, each State which the organization was required to list as an attachment to its last-filed return pursuant to § 1.6033-2(a)(2)(iv).

(2) *Applications for notification by other State officers.*—Other officers of States described in subparagraph (1) of this paragraph, and officers of States not described in such subparagraph, may request that they be notified (either generally or with respect to a particular organization or type of organization) of determinations described in paragraph (c) of this section. In such cases, these State officers must show that they are appropriate State officers within the meaning of section 6104(c)(2). The required showing may be made by presenting a letter from the Attorney General of the State setting forth (i) the functions and authority of the State officer under State law, and (ii) sufficient facts for the Internal Revenue Service to determine that such officer is an appropriate State officer within the meaning of section 6104(c)(2).

(3) *Manner of notification.*—A State officer who is entitled to be notified of a determination under this paragraph will be notified by sending him a copy of the communication from the Internal Revenue Service to the organization which informs such organization of the determination.

(b) *Inspection by State officers.*—(1) *In general.*—After a determination described in paragraph (c) of this section has been made, appropriate State officers within the meaning of section 6104(c)(2) may inspect the material described in subparagraph (3) of this paragraph. Such material may be inspected at an office of the Internal Revenue Service which will be designated upon receipt of a request for inspection; the location of such office will be determined with due consideration of the needs of the Internal Revenue Service and the needs of the State officer entitled to inspect.

(2) *State officers who may inspect material.*—Any State officer entitled to be notified of a determination without application (under paragraph (a)(1) of this section) may inspect the material described in subparagraph (3) of this paragraph upon demonstrating that he is so entitled. Any State officer who has in fact been notified by the Internal Revenue Service of a determination may inspect such material without further demonstration, unless it shall be determined by the Internal Revenue Service that such officer was not entitled to be so notified. Other State officers must demonstrate to the satisfaction of the Internal Revenue Service that they are entitled to be notified under paragraph (a)(2) of this section before they may inspect such material.

(3) *Material which may be inspected.*—(i) Except as provided in subdivision (ii) of this subparagraph, a State officer who is so entitled under subparagraphs (1) and (2) of this paragraph will be permitted to inspect and copy all returns, filed statements, records, reports, and

other information relating to a determination described in paragraph (c) of this section which is relevant to a determination under State law, and which is in the hands of the Internal Revenue Service.

(ii) The following material will not be made available for inspection by State officers under section 6104(c) and this section—

(a) Interpretations by the Internal Revenue Service or other federal agency of federal laws (including the Internal Revenue Code of 1954 and its predecessors) which would not otherwise be made available to State officers under section 6103(d),

(b) Reports of informers, or any other material which would disclose the identity, or threaten the safety or anonymity, of an informer,

(c) Returns of persons (other than those exempt from taxation) which would not be available under section 6103(d) to the State officer requesting inspection, or

(d) Other material the disclosure of which the Commissioner has determined would prejudice the proper administration of the internal revenue laws.

(4) *Statement by State officer.*—Before any State officer will be permitted to inspect material described in this paragraph, he must submit a statement to the Internal Revenue Service that he intends to use such material solely in fulfilling his functions under State law relating to organizations of the type described in section 501(c)(3); material is made available to State officers under this section in reliance on such statements. For provisions relating to penalties for misuse of information which is made available under section 6104(c) and this section, see 18 U.S.C. 1001.

(c) *Determinations defined.*—For purposes of this section, a determination means a final determination by the Internal Revenue Service that—

(1) An organization is refused recognition as an organization described in section 501(c)(3), or has been operated in such a manner that it will not, or will no longer, be recognized as meeting the requirements for exemption under that section, or

(2) A deficiency of tax exists under section 507 or chapter 41 or 42.

For purposes of this paragraph, a determination by the Internal Revenue Service is not final until all administrative review with respect to such determination has been completed. For purposes of this section, a waiver of restrictions on assessment and collection of deficiency in tax is treated as a final determination that a deficiency of tax exists when such waiver has been finally accepted by the Internal Revenue Service. For example, a final determination that a deficiency of tax exists under section 507 or chapter 41 or 42 is made when the organization is sent a notice of deficiency with respect to such tax.

(d) *Effective date.*—The provisions of this section apply with respect to all determinations made after December 31, 1969. [Reg. § 301.6104(c)-1.]

☐ [*T.D.* 7122, 6-7-71. *Amended by T.D.* 7290, 11-16-73 *and T.D.* 7785, 7-27-81, *Redesignated by T.D.* 7845, 11-5-82.]

[Reg. § 301.6104(d)-0]

§ 301.6104(d)-0. Table of contents.—This section lists the major captions contained in §§ 301.6104(d)-1 through 301.6104(d)-3 as follows:

(2) Annual information returns.

(3) Failure to comply.

(g) Failure to comply with public inspection or copying requirements.

(h) Effective date.

(1) In general.

(2) Private foundation annual information returns.

§ *301.6104(d)-2 Making applications and returns widely available.*

(a) In general.

(b) Widely available.

(1) In general.

(2) Internet posting.

(i) In general.

(ii) Transition rule.

(iii) Reliability and accuracy.

(c) Discretion to prescribe other methods for making documents widely available.

(d) Notice requirement.

(e) Effective date.

§ *301.6104(d)-3 Tax-exempt organization subject to harassment campaign.*

(a) In general.

(b) Harassment.

(c) Special rule for multiple requests from a single individual or address.

(d) Harassment determination procedure.

(e) Effect of a harassment determination.

(f) Examples.

(g) Effective date.

[Reg. § 301.6104(d)-0.]

☐ [*T.D.* 8818, 4-8-99. *Redesignated and amended by T.D.* 8861, 1-12-2000.]

[Reg. § 301.6104(d)-1]

§ 301.6104(d)-1. Public inspection and distribution of applications for tax exemption and annual information returns of tax-exempt organizations.—(a) *In general.*—Except as otherwise provided in this section, if a tax-exempt organization (as defined in paragraph (b)(1) of this section) filed an application for recognition of exemption under section 501, it shall make its application for tax exemption (as defined in paragraph(b)(3) of this section) available for public inspection without charge at its principal, regional and district offices during regular business hours. Except as otherwise provided in this section, a tax-exempt organization shall make its annual information returns (as defined in paragraph(b)(4) of this section) available for public inspection without charge in the same offices during regular business hours. Each annual information return shall be made available for a period of three years beginning on the date the return is required to be filed (determined with regard to any extension of time for filing) or is actually filed, whichever is later. In addition, except as provided in § § 301.6104(d)-2 and 301.6104(d)-3, an organization shall provide a copy without charge, other than a reasonable fee for reproduction and actual postage costs, of all

or any part of any application or return required to be made available for public inspection under this paragraph to any individual who makes a request for such copy in person or in writing. See paragraph (d)(3) of this section for rules relating to fees for copies.

(b) *Definitions.*—For purposes of applying the provisions of section 6104(d), this section and § § 301.6104(d)-2 and 301.6104(d)-3, the following definitions apply:

(1) *Tax-exempt organization.*—The term *tax-exempt organization* means any organization that is described in section 501(c) or section 501(d) and is exempt from taxation under section 501(a). The term tax-exempt organization also includes any nonexempt charitable trust described in section 4947(a)(1) or nonexempt private foundation that is subject to the reporting requirements of section 6033 pursuant to section 6033(d).

(2) *Private foundation.*—The term *private foundation* means a private foundation as defined in section 509(a) or a nonexempt charitable trust described in section 4947(a)(1) or a nonexempt private foundation subject to the information reporting requirements of section 6033 pursuant to section 6033(d).

(3) *Application for tax exemption.*—(i) *In general.*—Except as described in paragraph (b)(3)(iii) of this section, the term *application for tax exemption* includes any prescribed application form (such as Form 1023 or Form 1024), all documents and statements the Internal Revenue Service requires an applicant to file with the form, any statement or other supporting document submitted by an organization in support of its application, and any letter or other document issued by the Internal Revenue Service concerning the application (such as a favorable determination letter or a list of questions from the Internal Revenue Service about the application). For example, a legal brief submitted in support of an application, or a response to questions from the Internal Revenue Service during the application process, is part of an application for tax exemption.

(ii) *No prescribed application form.*—If no form is prescribed for an organization's application for tax exemption, the application for tax exemption includes—

(A) The application letter and copy of the articles of incorporation, declaration of trust, or other similar instrument that sets forth the permitted powers or activities of the organization;

(B) The organization's bylaws or other code of regulations;

(C) The organization's latest financial statements showing assets, liabilities, receipts and disbursements;

(D) Statements describing the character of the organization, the purpose for which it was organized, and its actual activities;

(E) Statements showing the sources of the organization's income and receipts and their disposition; and

(F) Any other statements or documents the Internal Revenue Service required the organization to file with, or that the organization submitted in support of, the application letter.

(iii) *Exceptions.*—The term *application for tax exemption* does not include—

(A) Any application for tax exemption filed by an organization that the Internal Revenue Service has not yet recognized, on the basis of the application, as exempt from taxation under section 501 for any taxable year;

(B) Any application for tax exemption filed before July 15, 1987, unless the organization filing the application had a copy of the application on July 15, 1987;

(C) In the case of a tax-exempt organization other than a private foundation, the name and address of any contributor to the organization; or

(D) Any material, including the material listed in § 301.6104(a)-1(i) and information that the Secretary would be required to withhold from public inspection, that is not available for public inspection under section 6104.

(iv) *Local or subordinate organizations.*—For rules relating to applications for tax exemption of local or subordinate organizations, see paragraph (f)(1) of this section.

(4) *Annual information return.*—(i) *In general.*—Except as described in paragraph (b)(4)(ii) of this section, the term *annual information return* includes an exact copy of any return filed by a tax-exempt organization pursuant to section 6033. It also includes any amended return the organization files with the Internal Revenue Service after the date the original return is filed. Returns filed pursuant to section 6033 include Form 990, Return of Organization Exempt From Income Tax, Form 990-PF, Return of Private Foundation, or any other version of Form 990 (such as Forms 990-EZ or 990-BL, except Form 990-T) and Form 1065. Each copy of a return must include all information furnished to the Internal Revenue Service on the return, as well as all schedules, attachments and supporting documents. For example, in the case of a Form 990, the copy must include Schedule A of Form 990 (containing supplementary information on section 501(c)(3) organizations), and those parts of the return that show compensation paid to specific persons (currently, Part V of Form 990 and Parts I and II of Schedule A of Form 990).

(ii) *Exceptions.*—The term *annual information return* does not include Schedule A of Form 990-BL, Form 990-T, Exempt Organization Business Income Tax Return, Schedule K-1 of Form 1065 or Form 1120-POL, U.S. Income Tax Return For Certain Political Organizations. In the case of a tax-exempt organization other than a private foundation, the term *annual information return*

does not include the name and address of any contributor to the organization.

(iii) *Returns more than 3 years old.*—The term *annual information return* does not include any return after the expiration of 3 years from the date the return is required to be filed (including any extension of time that has been granted for filing such return) or is actually filed, whichever is later. If an organization files an amended return, however, the amended return must be made available for a period of 3 years beginning on the date it is filed with the Internal Revenue Service.

(iv) *Local or subordinate organizations.*—For rules relating to annual information returns of local or subordinate organizations, see paragraph (f)(2) of this section.

(5) *Regional or district offices.*—(i) *In general.*—A regional or district office is any office of a tax-exempt organization, other than its principal office, that has paid employees, whether part-time or full-time, whose aggregate number of paid hours a week are normally at least 120.

(ii) *Site not considered a regional or district office.*—A site is not considered a regional or district office, however, if—

(A) The only services provided at the site further exempt purposes (such as day care, health care or scientific or medical research); and

(B) The site does not serve as an office for management staff, other than managers who are involved solely in managing the exempt function activities at the site.

(c) *Special rules relating to public inspection.*— (1) *Permissible conditions on public inspection.*—A tax-exempt organization may have an employee present in the room during an inspection. The organization, however, must allow the individual conducting the inspection to take notes freely during the inspection. If the individual provides photocopying equipment at the place of inspection, the organization must allow the individual to photocopy the document at no charge.

(2) *Organizations that do not maintain permanent offices.*—If a tax-exempt organization does not maintain a permanent office, the organization shall comply with the public inspection requirements of paragraph (a) of this section by making its application for tax exemption and its annual information returns, as applicable, available for inspection at a reasonable location of its choice. Such an organization shall permit public inspection within a reasonable amount of time after receiving a request for inspection (normally not more than 2 weeks) and at a reasonable time of day. At the organization's option, it may mail, within 2 weeks of receiving the request, a copy of its application for tax exemption and annual information returns to the requester in lieu of allowing an inspection. The organization may charge the requester for copying and actual postage costs only if the requester consents to the charge. An organization that has a permanent office, but has no office hours or very limited

hours during certain times of the year, shall make its documents available during those periods when office hours are limited or not available as though it were an organization without a permanent office.

(d) *Special rules relating to copies.*—(1) *Time and place for providing copies in response to requests made in-person.*—(i) *In general.*—Except as provided in paragraph (d)(1)(iii) of this section, a tax-exempt organization shall provide copies of the documents it is required to provide under section 6104(d) in response to a request made in person at its principal, regional and district offices during regular business hours. Except as provided in paragraph (d)(1)(ii) of this section, an organization shall provide such copies to a requester on the day the request is made.

(ii) *Unusual circumstances.*—In the case of an in-person request, where unusual circumstances exist such that fulfilling the request on the same business day places an unreasonable burden on the tax-exempt organization, the organization must provide the copies no later than the next business day following the day that the unusual circumstances cease to exist or the fifth business day after the date of the request, whichever occurs first. Unusual circumstances include, but are not limited to, receipt of a volume of requests that exceeds the organization's daily capacity to make copies; requests received shortly before the end of regular business hours that require an extensive amount of copying; or requests received on a day when the organization's managerial staff capable of fulfilling the request is conducting special duties, such as student registration or attending an off-site meeting or convention, rather than its regular administrative duties.

(iii) *Agents for providing copies.*—A principal, regional or district office of a tax-exempt organization subject to the requirements of this section may retain a local agent to process requests made in person for copies of its documents. A local agent must be located within reasonable proximity of the applicable office. A local agent that receives a request made in person for copies must provide the copies within the time limits and under the conditions that apply to the organization itself. For example, a local agent generally must provide a copy to a requester on the day the agent receives the request. When a principal, regional or district office of a tax-exempt organization using a local agent receives a request made in person for a copy, it must immediately provide the name, address and telephone number of the local agent to the requester. An organization that provides this information is not required to respond further to the requester. However, the penalty provisions of sections 6652(c)(1)(C), 6652(c)(1)(D), and 6685 continue to apply to the tax-exempt organization if the organization's local agent fails to provide the documents as required under section 6104(d).

(2) *Request for copies in writing.*—(i) *In general.*—A tax-exempt organization must honor a written request for a copy of documents (or the requested part) that the organization is required to provide under section 6104(d) if the request—

(A) Is addressed to, and delivered by mail, electronic mail, facsimile, or a private delivery service as defined in section 7502(f) to a principal, regional or district office of the organization; and

(B) Sets forth the address to which the copy of the documents should be sent.

(ii) *Time and manner of fulfilling written requests.*—(A) *In general.*—A tax-exempt organization receiving a written request for a copy shall mail the copy of the requested documents (or the requested parts of documents) within 30 days from the date it receives the request. However, if a tax-exempt organization requires payment in advance, it is only required to provide the copies within 30 days from the date it receives payment. For rules relating to payment, see paragraph (d)(3) of this section. In the absence of evidence to the contrary, a request or payment that is mailed shall be deemed to be received by an organization 7 days after the date of the postmark. A request that is transmitted to the organization by electronic mail or facsimile shall be deemed received the day the request is transmitted successfully. If an organization requiring payment in advance receives a written request without payment or with an insufficient payment, the organization must, within 7 days from the date it receives the request, notify the requester of its prepayment policy and the amount due. A copy is deemed provided on the date of the postmark or private delivery mark (or if sent by certified or registered mail, the date of registration or the date of the postmark on the sender's receipt). If an individual making a request consents, a tax-exempt organization may provide a copy of the requested document exclusively by electronic mail. In such case, the material is provided on the date the organization successfully transmits the electronic mail.

(B) *Request for a copy of parts of document.*—A tax-exempt organization must fulfill a request for a copy of the organization's entire application for tax exemption or annual information return or any specific part or schedule of its application or return. A request for a copy of less than the entire application or less than the entire return must specifically identify the requested part or schedule.

(C) *Agents for providing copies.*—A tax-exempt organization subject to the requirements of this section may retain an agent to process written requests for copies of its documents. The agent shall provide the copies within the time limits and under the conditions that apply to the organization itself. For example, if the organization received the request first (e.g., before the agent), the deadline for providing a copy in response to a request shall be determined by reference to when the organization received the request, not when the agent received the request. An organization that transfers a request for a copy to such an agent is not required to respond further to the request. If the organization's agent fails to provide the documents as required under section 6104(d), however, the penalty provisions of sections 6652(c)(1)(C), 6652(c)(1)(D), and 6685 continue to apply to the tax-exempt organization.

(3) *Fees for copies.*—(i) *In general.*—A tax-exempt organization may charge a reasonable fee for providing copies. A fee is reasonable only if it is no more than the total of the applicable perpage copying charge prescribed by the fee schedule promulgated pursuant to section (a)(4)(A)(i) of the Freedom of Information Act, 5 U.S.C. 552, by the Commissioner from time to time, and the actual postage costs incurred by the organization to send the copies. The applicable per-page copying charge shall be determined without regard to any applicable fee exclusion provided in the fee schedule for an initial or de minimis number of pages (e.g. the first 100 pages). Before the organization provides the documents, it may require that the individual requesting copies of the documents pay the fee. If the organization has provided an individual making a request with notice of the fee, and the individual does not pay the fee within 30 days, or if the individual pays the fee by check and the check does not clear upon deposit, the organization may disregard the request.

(ii) *Form of payment.*—(A) *Request made in person.*—If a tax-exempt organization charges a fee for copying (as permitted under paragraph (d)(3)(i) of this section), it shall accept payment by cash and money order for requests made in person. The organization may accept other forms of payment, such as credit cards and personal checks.

(B) *Request made in writing.*—If a tax-exempt organization charges a fee for copying and postage (as permitted under paragraph (d)(3)(i) of this section), it shall accept payment by certified check, money order, and either personal check or credit card for requests made in writing. The organization may accept other forms of payment.

(iii) *Avoidance of unexpected fees.*—Where a tax-exempt organization does not require prepayment and a requester does not enclose payment with a request, an organization must receive consent from a requester before providing copies for which the fee charged for copying and postage exceeds $20.

(iv) *Responding to inquiries of fees charged.*—In order to facilitate a requester's ability to receive copies promptly, a tax-exempt organization shall respond to any questions from potential requesters concerning its fees for copying and postage. For example, the organization shall inform the requester of its charge for copying and mailing its application for exemption and each annual information return, with and without attachments, so that a requester may include payment with the request for copies.

(e) *Documents to be provided by regional and district offices.*—Except as otherwise provided, a regional or district office of a tax-exempt organization must satisfy the same rules as the principal office with respect to allowing public inspection and providing copies of its application for tax exemption and annual information returns. A regional or district office is not required, however, to make its annual information return available for inspection or to provide copies until 30 days after the date the return is required to be filed (including any extension of time that is granted for filing such return) or is actually filed, whichever is later.

(f) *Documents to be provided by local and subordinate organizations.*—(1) *Applications for tax exemption.*—Except as otherwise provided, a tax-exempt organization that did not file its own application for tax exemption (because it is a local or subordinate organization covered by a group exemption letter referred to in § 1.508-1 of this chapter) must, upon request, make available for public inspection, or provide copies of, the application submitted to the Internal Revenue Service by the central or parent organization to obtain the group exemption letter and those documents which were submitted by the central or parent organization to include the local or subordinate organization in the group exemption letter. However, if the central or parent organization submits to the Internal Revenue Service a list or directory of local or subordinate organizations covered by the group exemption letter, the local or subordinate organization is required to provide only the application for the group exemption ruling and the pages of the list or directory that specifically refer to it. The local or subordinate organization shall permit public inspection, or comply with a request for copies made in person, within a reasonable amount of time (normally not more than 2 weeks) after receiving a request made in person for public inspection or copies and at a reasonable time of day. In a case where the requester seeks inspection, the local or subordinate organization may mail a copy of the applicable documents to the requester within the same time period in lieu of allowing an inspection. In such a case, the organization may charge the requester for copying and actual postage costs only if the requester consents to the charge. If the local or subordinate organization receives a written request for a copy of its application for tax exemption, it must fulfill the request in the time and manner specified in paragraph (d)(2) of this section. The requester has the option of requesting from the central or parent organization, at its principal office, inspection or copies of the application for group exemption and the material submitted by the central or parent organization to include a local or subordinate organization in the group ruling. If the central or parent organization submits to the Internal Revenue Service a list or directory of local or subordinate organizations covered by the group exemption letter, it must make such list or directory available for public inspection, but it is required to provide copies only of those pages of the list or directory that refer to particular local or subordinate organizations specified by the requester. The central or parent organization must fulfill such requests in the time and manner specified in paragraphs (c) and (d) of this section.

(2) *Annual information returns.*—A local or subordinate organization that does not file its own annual information return (because it is affiliated with a central or parent organization that files a group return pursuant to § 1.6033-2(d) of this chapter) must, upon request, make available for public inspection, or provide copies of, the group returns filed by the central or parent organization. However, if the group return includes separate schedules with respect to each local or subordinate organization included in the group return, the local or subordinate organization receiving the request may omit any schedules relating only to other organizations included in the group return. The local or subordinate organization shall permit public inspection, or comply with a request for copies made in person, within a reasonable amount of time (normally not more than 2 weeks) after receiving a request made in person for public inspection or copies and at a reasonable time of day. In a case where the requester seeks inspection, the local or subordinate organization may mail a copy of the applicable documents to the requester within the same time period in lieu of allowing an inspection. In such a case, the organization may charge the requester for copying and actual postage costs only if the requester consents to the charge. If the local or subordinate organization receives a written request for a copy of its annual information return, it must fulfill the request by providing a copy of the group return in the time and manner specified in paragraph (d)(2) of this section. The requester has the option of requesting from the central or parent organization, at its principal office, inspection or copies of group returns filed by the central or parent organization. The central or parent organization must fulfill such requests in the time and manner specified in paragraphs (c) and (d) of this section.

(3) *Failure to comply.*—If an organization fails to comply with the requirements specified in this paragraph, the penalty provisions of sections 6652(c)(1)(C), 6652(c)(1)(D), and 6685 apply.

(g) *Failure to comply with public inspection or copying requirements.*—If a tax-exempt organization denies an individual's request for inspection or a copy of an application for tax exemption or an annual information return as required under this section, and the individual wants to alert the Internal Revenue Service to the possible need for enforcement action, the individual may provide a statement to the district director for the key district in which the applicable tax-exempt or-

ganization's principal office is located (or such other person as the Commissioner may designate) that describes the reason why the individual believes the denial was in violation of the requirements of section 6104(d).

(h) *Effective date.*—(1) *In general.*—For a tax-exempt organization, other than a private foundation, this section is applicable June 8, 1999. For a private foundation, this section is applicable (except as provided in paragraph (h)(2) of this section) beginning March 13, 2000.

(2) *Private foundation annual information returns.*—This section does not apply to any private foundation return the due date for which (determined with regard to any extension of time for filing) is before the applicable date for private foundations specified in paragraph (h)(1) of this section. [Reg. § 301.6104(d)-1.]

☐ [*T.D. 8818, 4-8-99. Redesignated and amended by T.D. 8861, 1-12-2000. Amended by T.D. 9070, 7-8-2003 and T.D. 9173, 1-4-2005.*]

[Reg. § 301.6104(d)-2]

§ 301.6104(d)-2. Making applications and returns widely available.—(a) *In general.*—A tax-exempt organization is not required to comply with a request for a copy of its application for tax exemption or an annual information return pursuant to § 301.6104(d)-1(a) if the organization has made the requested document widely available in accordance with paragraph (b) of this section. An organization that makes its application for tax exemption and/or annual information return widely available must nevertheless make the document available for public inspection as required under § 301.6104(d)-1(a), as applicable.

(b) *Widely available.*—(1) *In general.*—A tax-exempt organization makes its application for tax exemption and/or an annual information return widely available if the organization complies with the requirements specified in paragraph (b)(2) of this section, and if the organization satisfies the requirements of paragraph (d) of this section.

(2) *Internet posting.*—(i) *In general.*—A tax-exempt organization can make its application for tax exemption and/or an annual information return widely available by posting the document on a World Wide Web page that the tax-exempt organization establishes and maintains or by having the document posted, as part of a database of similar documents of other tax-exempt organizations, on a World Wide Web page established and maintained by another entity. The document will be considered widely available only if—

(A) the World Wide Web page through which it is available clearly informs readers that the document is available and provides instructions for downloading it;

(B) the document is posted in a format that, when accessed, downloaded, viewed and printed in hard copy, exactly reproduces the image of the application for tax exemption or annual information return as it was originally filed with the Internal Revenue Service, except for any information permitted by statute to be withheld from public disclosure. (See section 6104(d)(3) and § 301.6104(d)-3(b)(3) and (4)); and

(C) any individual with access to the Internet can access, download, view and print the document without special computer hardware or software required for that format (other than software that is readily available to members of the public without payment of any fee) and without payment of a fee to the tax-exempt organization or to another entity maintaining the World Wide Web page.

(ii) *Transition rule.*—A tax-exempt organization that posted its application for tax exemption or its annual information returns on a World Wide Web page on or before April 9, 1999 in a manner consistent with regulation project REG-246250-96 (1997 C.B. 627) (See § 601.601(d)(2) of this chapter.) will be treated as satisfying the requirements of paragraphs (b)(2)(i)(B) & (C) of this section until June 8, 2000 provided that an individual can access, download, view and print the document without payment of a fee to the tax-exempt organization or to another entity maintaining the World Wide Web page.

(iii) *Reliability and accuracy.*—In order for the document to be widely available through an Internet posting, the entity maintaining the World Wide Web page must have procedures for ensuring the reliability and accuracy of the document that it posts on the page and must take reasonable precautions to prevent alteration, destruction or accidental loss of the document when posted on its page. In the event that a posted document is altered, destroyed or lost, the entity must correct or replace the document.

(c) *Discretion to prescribe other methods for making documents widely available.*—The Commissioner, from time to time, may prescribe additional methods, other than an Internet posting meeting the requirements of paragraph (b)(2) of this section, that a tax-exempt organization may use to make its documents widely available.

(d) *Notice requirement.*—If a tax-exempt organization has made its application for tax exemption and/or an annual information return widely available it must notify any individual requesting a copy where the documents are available (including the address on the World Wide Web, if applicable). If the request is made in person, the organization shall provide such notice to the individual immediately. If the request is made in writing, the notice shall be provided within 7 days of receiving the request.

(e) *Effective date.*—For a tax-exempt organization, other than a private foundation, this section is applicable June 8, 1999. For a private foundation, this section is applicable beginning March 13, 2000. [Reg. § 301.6104(d)-2.]

☐ [*T.D.* 8818, 4-8-99. *Redesignated and amended by T.D.* 8861, 1-12-2000.]

[Reg. § 301.6104(d)-3]

§ 301.6104(d)-3. Tax-exempt organization subject to harassment campaign.—(a) *In general.*—If the district director for the key district in which the organization's principal office is located (or such other person as the Commissioner may designate) determines that the organization is the subject of a harassment campaign and compliance with the requests that are part of the harassment campaign would not be in the public interest, a tax-exempt organization is not required to fulfill a request for a copy (as otherwise required by § 301.6104(d)-1(a)) that it reasonably believes is part of the campaign.

(b) *Harassment.*—A group of requests for an organization's application for tax exemption or annual information returns is indicative of a harassment campaign if the requests are part of a single coordinated effort to disrupt the operations of a tax-exempt organization, rather than to collect information about the organization. Whether a group of requests constitutes such a harassment campaign depends on the relevant facts and circumstances. Facts and circumstances that indicate the organization is the subject of a harassment campaign include: a sudden increase in the number of requests; an extraordinary number of requests made through form letters or similarly worded correspondence; evidence of a purpose to deter significantly the organization's employees or volunteers from pursuing the organization's exempt purpose; requests that contain language hostile to the organization; direct evidence of bad faith by organizers of the purported harassment campaign; evidence that the organization has already provided the requested documents to a member of the purported harassing group; and a demonstration by the tax-exempt organization that it routinely provides copies of its documents upon request.

(c) *Special rule for multiple requests from a single individual or address.*—A tax-exempt organization may disregard any request for copies of all or part of any document beyond the first two received within any 30-day-period or the first four received within any one-year-period from the same individual or the same address, regardless of whether the district director for the applicable key district (or such other person as the Commissioner may designate) has determined that the organization is subject to a harassment campaign.

(d) *Harassment determination procedure.*—A tax-exempt organization may apply for a determination that it is the subject of a harassment campaign and that compliance with requests that are part of the campaign would not be in the public interest by submitting a signed application to the district director for the key district where the organization's principal office is located (or such other person as the Commissioner may designate). The application shall consist of a written statement giving the organization's name, address, employer identification number, and the name, address and telephone number of the person to contact regarding the application. The application must describe in detail the facts and circumstances that the organization believes support a determination that the organization is subject to a harassment campaign. The organization may suspend compliance with respect to any request for a copy of its documents based on its reasonable belief that such request is part of a harassment campaign, provided that the organization files an application for a determination within 10 business days from the day the organization first suspends compliance with respect to a request that is part of the alleged campaign. In addition, the organization may suspend compliance with any request it reasonably believes to be part of the harassment campaign until it receives a response to its application for a harassment campaign determination.

(e) *Effect of a harassment determination.*—If the appropriate district director (or such other person as the Commissioner may designate) determines that a tax-exempt organization is the subject of a harassment campaign and it is not in the public interest to comply with requests that are part of the campaign, such organization is not required to comply with any request for copies that it reasonably believes is part of the campaign. This determination may be subject to other terms and conditions set forth by the district director (or such other person as the Commissioner may designate). A person (as defined in section 6652(c)(4)(C)) shall not be liable for any penalty under sections 6652(c)(1)(C), 6652(c)(1)(D) or 6685 for failing to timely provide a copy of documents in response to a request covered in a request for a harassment determination if the organization fulfills the request within 30 days of receiving a determination from the district director (or such other person as the Commissioner may designate) that the organization is not subject to a harassment campaign. Notwithstanding the preceding sentence, if the district director (or such other person as the Commissioner may designate) further determines that the organization did not have a reasonable basis for requesting a determination that it was subject to a harassment campaign or reasonable belief that a request was part of the campaign, the person (as defined in section 6652(c)(4)(C)) remains liable for any penalties that result from not providing the copies in a timely fashion.

(f) *Examples.*—The provisions of this section are illustrated by the following examples:

Example 1. V, a tax-exempt organization, receives an average of 25 requests per month for copies of its three most recent information returns. In the last week of May, V is mentioned in a national news magazine story that discusses information contained in V's 1996 information return. From June 1 through June 30, 1997 V receives 200 requests for a copy of its documents. Other than the sudden increase in the number of requests for copies, there is no other evidence to suggest that the requests are part of an organized campaign to disrupt V's operations. Although

fulfilling the requests will place a burden on V, the facts and circumstances do not show that V is subject to a harassment campaign. Therefore, V must respond timely to each of the 200 requests it receives in June.

Example 2. Y is a tax-exempt organization that receives an average of 10 requests a month for copies of its annual information returns. From March 1, 1997 to March 31, 1997, Y receives 25 requests for copies of its documents. Fifteen of the requests come from individuals Y knows to be active members of the board of organization X. In the past X has opposed most of the positions and policies that Y advocates. None of the requesters have asked for copies of documents from Y during the past year. Y has no other information about the requesters. Although the facts and circumstances show that some of the individuals making requests are hostile to Y, they do not show that the individuals have organized a campaign that will place enough of a burden on Y to disrupt its activities. Therefore, Y must respond to each of the 25 requests it receives in March.

Example 3. The facts are the same as in *Example 2,* except that during March 1997, Y receives 100 requests. In addition to the fifteen requests from members of organization X's board, 75 of the requests are similarly worded form letters. Y discovers that several individuals associated with X have urged the X's members and supporters, via the Internet, to submit as many requests for a copy of Y's annual information returns as they can. The message circulated on the Internet provides a form letter that can be used to make the request. Both the appeal via the Internet and the requests for copies received by Y contain hostile language. During the same year but before the 100 requests were received, Y provided copies of its annual information returns to the headquarters of X. The facts and circumstances show that the 75 form letter requests are coordinated for the purpose of disrupting Y's operations, and not to collect information that has already been provided to an association representing the requesters' interests. Thus, the fact and circumstances show that Y is the subject of an organized harassment campaign. To confirm that it may disregard the 90 requests that constitute the harassment campaign, Y must apply to the applicable district director (or such other person as the Commissioner may designate) for a determination. Y may disregard the 90 requests while the application is pending and after the determination is received. However, it must respond within the applicable time limits to the 10 requests it received in March that were not part of the harassment campaign.

Example 4. The facts are the same as in *Example 3,* except that Y receives 5 additional requests from 5 different representatives of the news media who in the past have published articles about Y. Some of these articles were hostile to Y. Normally, the Internal Revenue Service will not consider a tax-exempt organization to have a reasonable belief that a request from a member of the news media is part of a harassment campaign absent additional facts that demonstrate that the organization could reasonably believe the particular requests from the news media to be part of a harassment campaign. Thus, absent such additional facts, Y must respond within the applicable time limits to the 5 requests that it received from representatives of the news media.

(g) *Effective date.*—For a tax-exempt organization, other than a private foundation, this section is applicable June 8, 1999. For a private foundation, this section is applicable beginning March 13, 2000. [Reg. § 301.6104(d)-3.]

☐ [*T.D.* 8818, 4-8-99. *Redesignated and amended by T.D.* 8861, 1-12-2000.]

[Reg. § 1.6107-1]

§ 1.6107-1. Tax return preparer must furnish copy of return or claim for refund to taxpayer and must retain a copy or record.— (a) *Furnishing copy to taxpayer.*—(1) A person who is a signing tax return preparer of any return of tax or claim for refund of tax under the Internal Revenue Code shall furnish a completed copy of the return or claim for refund to the taxpayer (or nontaxable entity) not later than the time the return or claim for refund is presented for the signature of the taxpayer (or nontaxable entity). The signing tax return preparer may, at its option, request a receipt or other evidence from the taxpayer (or nontaxable entity) sufficient to show satisfaction of the requirement of this paragraph (a).

(2) The tax return preparer must provide a complete copy of the return or claim for refund filed with the IRS to the taxpayer in any media, including electronic media, that is acceptable to both the taxpayer and the tax return preparer. In the case of an electronically filed return, a complete copy of a taxpayer's return or claim for refund consists of the electronic portion of the return or claim for refund, including all schedules, forms, pdf attachments, and jurats, that was filed with the IRS. The copy provided to the taxpayer must include all information submitted to the IRS to enable the taxpayer to determine what schedules, forms, electronic files, and other supporting materials have been filed with the return. The copy, however, need not contain the identification number of the paid tax return preparer. The electronic portion of the return or claim for refund may be contained on a replica of an official form or on an unofficial form. On an unofficial form, however, data entries must reference the line numbers or descriptions on an official form.

(3) For electronically filed Forms 1040EZ, "Income Tax Return for Single Filers and Joint Filers With No Dependents," and Form 1040A, "U.S. Individual Income Tax Return," filed for the 2009, 2010 and 2011 taxable years, the information may be provided on a replica of a Form 1040, "U.S. Individual Income Tax Return", that provides all of the information. For other electronically filed returns, the information may be provided on a replica of an official form that provides all of the information.

(b) *Copy or record to be retained.*—(1) A person who is a signing tax return preparer of any return or claim for refund shall—

(i)(A) Retain a completed copy of the return or claim for refund; or

(B) Retain a record, by list, card file, or otherwise of the name, taxpayer identification number, and taxable year of the taxpayer (or nontaxable entity) for whom the return or claim for refund was prepared, and the type of return or claim for refund prepared;

(ii) Retain a record, by retention of a copy of the return or claim for refund, maintenance of a list, card file, or otherwise, for each return or claim for refund presented to the taxpayer (or nontaxable entity), of the name of the individual tax return preparer required to sign the return or claim for refund pursuant to § 1.6695-1(b); and

(iii) Make the copy or record of returns and claims for refund and record of the individuals required to sign available for inspection upon request by the Commissioner.

(2) The material described in this paragraph (b) shall be retained and kept available for inspection for the 3-year period following the close of the return period during which the return or claim for refund was presented for signature to the taxpayer (or nontaxable entity). In the case of a return that becomes due (with extensions, if any) during a return period following the return period during which the return was presented for signature, the material shall be retained and kept available for inspection for the 3-year period following the close of the later return period in which the return became due. For the definition of "return period," see section 6060(c). If the person subject to the record retention requirement of this paragraph (b) is a corporation or a partnership that is dissolved before completion of the 3-year period, then all persons who are responsible for the winding up of the affairs of the corporation or partnership under state law shall be subject, on behalf of the corporation or partnership, to these record retention requirements until completion of the 3-year period. If state law does not specify any person or persons as responsible for winding up, then, collectively, the directors or general partners shall be subject, on behalf of the corporation or partnership, to the record retention requirements of this paragraph (b). For purposes of the penalty imposed by section 6695(d), such designated persons shall be deemed to be the tax return preparer and will be jointly and severally liable for each failure.

(c) *Tax return preparer.*—For the definition of "signing tax return preparer," see § 301.7701-15(b)(1) of this chapter. For purposes of applying this section, a corporation, partnership or other organization that employs a signing tax return preparer to prepare for compensation (or in which a signing tax return preparer is compensated as a partner or member to prepare) a return of tax or claim for refund shall be treated as the sole signing tax return preparer.

(d) *Penalties.*—(1) For the civil penalty for failure to furnish a copy of the return or claim for refund to the taxpayers (or nontaxable entity) as required under paragraph (a) of this section, see section 6695(a) and § 1.6695-1(a).

(2) For the civil penalty for failure to retain a copy of the return or claim for refund, or to retain a record as required under paragraph (b) of this section, see section 6695(d) and § 1.6695-1(d).

(e) *Effective/applicability date.*—This section is applicable to returns and claims for refund filed after December 31, 2008. [Reg. § 1.6107-1.]

☐ [*T.D.* 7519, 11-17-77. *Amended by T.D.* 7640, 8-22-79; *T.D.* 7948, 3-7-84 *and T.D.* 9436, 12-15-2008 (*corrected* 1-28-2009).]

[Reg. § 20.6107-1]

§ 20.6107-1. Tax return preparer must furnish copy of return to taxpayer and must retain a copy or record.—(a) *In general.*—A person who is a signing tax return preparer of any return or claim for refund of estate tax under chapter 11 of subtitle B of the Internal Revenue Code shall furnish a completed copy of the return or claim for refund to the taxpayer and retain a completed copy or record in the manner stated in § 1.6107-1 of this chapter.

(b) *Effective/applicability date.*—This section is applicable to returns and claims for refund filed after December 31, 2008. [Reg. § 20.6107-1.]

☐ [*T.D.* 9436, 12-15-2008.]

[Reg. § 25.6107-1]

§ 25.6107-1. Tax return preparer must furnish copy of return to taxpayer and must retain a copy or record.—(a) *In general.*—A person who is a signing tax return preparer of any return or claim for refund of gift tax under chapter 12 of subtitle B of the Internal Revenue Code shall furnish a completed copy of the return or claim for refund to the taxpayer, and retain a completed copy or record in the manner stated in § 1.6107-1 of this chapter.

(b) *Effective/applicability date.*—This section is applicable to returns and claims for refund filed after December 31, 2008. [Reg. § 25.6107-1.]

☐ [*T.D.* 9436, 12-15-2008.]

[Reg. § 26.6107-1]

§ 26.6107-1. Tax return preparer must furnish copy of return to taxpayer and must retain a copy or record.—(a) *In general.*—A person who is a signing tax return preparer of any return or claim for refund of generation-skipping transfer tax under chapter 13 of subtitle B of the Internal Revenue Code shall furnish a completed copy of the return or claim for refund to the taxpayer, and retain a completed copy or record in the manner stated in § 1.6107-1 of this chapter.

(b) *Effective/applicability date.*—This section is applicable to returns and claims for refund filed after December 31, 2008. [Reg. § 26.6107-1.]

☐ [*T.D.* 9436, 12-15-2008.]

[Reg. § 31.6107-1]

§ 31.6107-1. Tax return preparer must furnish copy of return to taxpayer and must retain a copy or record.—(a) *In general.*—A person who is a signing tax return preparer of any return or claim for refund of employment tax under chapters 21 through 25 of subtitle C of the Internal Revenue Code shall furnish a completed copy of the return or claim for refund to the taxpayer and retain a completed copy or record in the manner stated in § 1.6107-1 of this chapter.

(b) *Effective/applicability date.*—This section is applicable to returns and claims for refund filed after December 31, 2008. [Reg. § 31.6107-1.]

☐ [*T.D.* 9436, 12-15-2008.]

[Reg. § 40.6107-1]

§ 40.6107-1. Tax return preparer must furnish copy of return to taxpayer and must retain a copy or record.—(a) *In general.*—A person who is a signing tax return preparer of any return or claim for refund of any tax to which this part 40 applies shall furnish a completed copy of the return or claim for refund to the taxpayer and retain a completed copy or record in the manner stated in § 1.6107-1 of this chapter.

(b) *Effective/applicability date.*—This section is applicable for returns and claims for refund filed after December 31, 2008. [Reg. § 40.6107-1.]

☐ [*T.D.* 9436, 12-15-2008 (*corrected* 1-28-2009).]

[Reg. § 41.6107-1]

§ 41.6107-1. Tax return preparer must furnish copy of return to taxpayer and must retain a copy or record.—(a) *In general.*—A person who is a signing tax return preparer of any return or claim for refund of excise tax under section 4481 shall furnish a completed copy of the return or claim for refund to the taxpayer and retain a completed copy or record in the manner stated in § 1.6107-1 of this chapter.

(b) *Effective/applicability date.*—This section is applicable for returns and claims for refund filed after December 31, 2008. [Reg. § 41.6107-1.]

☐ [*T.D.* 9436, 12-15-2008.]

[Reg. § 44.6107-1]

§ 44.6107-1. Tax return preparer must furnish copy of return to taxpayer and must retain a copy or record.—(a) *In general.*—A person who is a signing tax return preparer of any return or claim for refund of tax on wagers under sections 4401 or 4411 shall furnish a completed copy of the return or claim for refund to the taxpayer, and retain a completed copy or record in the manner stated in § 1.6107-1 of this chapter.

(b) *Effective/applicability date.*—This section is applicable for returns and claims for refund filed after December 31, 2008. [Reg. § 44.6107-1.]

☐ [*T.D.* 9436, 12-15-2008.]

[Reg. § 53.6107-1]

§ 53.6107-1. Tax return preparer must furnish copy of return or claim for refund to taxpayer and must retain a copy or record.—(a) *In general.*—A person who is a signing tax return preparer of any return or claim for refund of tax under Chapter 42 of the Internal Revenue Code shall furnish a completed copy of the return or claim for refund to the taxpayer and retain a completed copy or record in the manner stated in § 1.6107-1 of this chapter.

(b) *Effective/applicability date.*—This section is applicable to returns and claims for refund filed after December 31, 2008. [Reg. § 53.6107-1.]

☐ [*T.D.* 9436, 12-15-2008.]

[Reg. § 54.6107-1]

§ 54.6107-1. Tax return preparer must furnish copy of return or claims for refund to taxpayer and must retain a copy or record.—(a) *In general.*—A person who is a signing tax return preparer of any return or claim for refund of tax under Chapter 43 of subtitle D of the Internal Revenue Code, shall furnish a completed copy of the return or claim for refund to the taxpayer, and retain a completed copy or record in the manner stated in § 1.6107-1 of this chapter.

(b) *Effective/applicability date.*—This section is applicable to returns and claims for refund filed after December 31, 2008. [Reg. § 54.6107-1.]

☐ [*T.D.* 9436, 12-15-2008.]

[Reg. § 55.6107-1]

§ 55.6107-1. Tax return preparer must furnish copy of return or claim for refund to taxpayer and must retain a copy or record.—(a) *In general.*—A person who is a signing tax return preparer of any return or claim for refund of tax under Chapter 44 of subtitle D of the Internal Revenue Code shall furnish a completed copy of the return or claim for refund to the taxpayer, and retain a completed copy or record in the manner stated in § 1.6107-1 of this chapter.

(b) *Effective/applicability date.*—This section is applicable to returns and claims for refund filed after December 31, 2008. [Reg. § 55.6107-1.]

☐ [*T.D.* 9436, 12-15-2008.]

[Reg. § 56.6107-1]

§ 56.6107-1. Tax return preparer must furnish copy of return and claim for refund to taxpayer and must retain a copy or record.—(a) *In general.*—A person who is a signing tax return preparer of any return or claim for refund of tax under Chapter 41 of subtitle D of the Internal Revenue Code shall furnish a completed copy of the return or claim for refund to the public charity and retain a completed copy or record in the manner stated in § 1.6107-1 of this chapter.

(b) *Effective/applicability date.*—This section is applicable to returns and claims for refund filed after December 31, 2008. [Reg. § 56.6107-1.]

☐ [*T.D.* 9436, 12-15-2008.]

[Reg. § 156.6107-1]

§ 156.6107-1. Tax return preparer must furnish copy of return and claim for refund to taxpayer and must retain a copy or record.—(a) *In general.*—A person who is a signing tax return preparer of any return or claim for refund of tax under section 5881 of the Internal Revenue Code shall furnish a completed copy of the return or claim for refund to the taxpayer and retain a completed copy or record in the manner stated in § 1.6107-1 of this chapter.

(b) *Effective/applicability date.*—This section is applicable to returns and claims for refund filed after December 31, 2008. [Reg. § 156.6107-1.]

☐ [*T.D.* 9436, 12-15-2008.]

[Reg. § 157.6107-1]

§ 157.6107-1. Tax return preparer must furnish copy of return or claim for refund to taxpayer and must retain a copy or record.—(a) *In general.*—A person who is a signing tax return preparer of any return or claim for refund of tax under section 5891 of the Internal Revenue Code shall furnish a completed copy of the return or claim for refund to the taxpayer and retain a completed copy or record in the manner stated in § 1.6107-1 of this chapter.

(b) *Effective/applicability date.*—This section is applicable to returns and claims for refund filed after December 31, 2008. [Reg. § 157.6107-1.]

☐ [*T.D.* 9436, 12-15-2008.]

[Reg. § 1.6107-2]

§ 1.6107-2. Form and manner of furnishing copy of return and retaining copy or record.—(a) *In general.*—The Commissioner may prescribe the form and manner of satisfying the requirements imposed by section 6107(a) and (b) and § 1.6107-1(a) and (b) in forms, instructions, or other appropriate guidance (see § 601.601(d)(2) of this chapter).

(b) *Effective date.*—To the extent this section relates to section 6107(a) and § 1.6107-1(a), it applies to income tax returns and claims for refund presented to a taxpayer for signature after December 31, 2002. To the extent this section relates to section 6107(b) and § 1.6107-1(b), it applies after December 31, 2002, to returns and claims for refund for which the 3-year period described in section 6107(b) expires after December 31, 2002. [Reg. § 1.6107-2.]

☐ [*T.D.* 9119, 3-24-2004.]

[Reg. § 301.6108-1]

§ 301.6108-1. Publication of statistics of income.—Pursuant to and in accordance with the provisions of section 6108, statistics reasonably available with respect to the operation of the income tax laws shall be prepared and published annually by the Commissioner. [Reg. § 301.6108-1.]

☐ [*T.D.* 6546, 1-18-61.]

[Reg. § 1.6109-1]

§ 1.6109-1. Identifying numbers.—(a) *Information to be furnished after April 15, 1974.*—For provisions concerning the requesting and furnishing of identifying numbers with respect to returns, statements, and other documents which must be filed after April 15, 1974, see § 301.6109-1 of this chapter (Regulations on Procedure and Administration).

(b) *Information to be furnished before April 16, 1974.*—For provisions concerning the requesting and furnishing of identifying numbers with respect to returns, statements, and other documents which must be filed before April 16, 1974, see 26 CFR § 1.6109-1 (revised as of April 1, 1973). [Reg. § 1.6109-1.]

☐ [*T.D.* 6606, 8-24-62. *Amended by T.D.* 7012, 5-14-69 *and T.D.* 7306, 3-14-74.]

[Reg. § 20.6109-1]

§ 20.6109-1. Tax return preparers furnishing identifying numbers for returns or claims for refund.—(a) *In general.*—Each estate tax return or claim for refund prepared by one or more signing tax return preparers must include the identifying number of the preparer required by § 1.6695-1(b) of this chapter to sign the return or claim for refund in the manner stated in § 1.6109-2 of this chapter.

(b) *Effective/applicability date.*—Paragraph (a) of this section is applicable to returns and claims for refund filed after December 31, 2008. [Reg. § 20.6109-1.]

☐ [*T.D.* 9436, 12-15-2008.]

[Reg. § 25.6109-1]

§ 25.6109-1. Tax return preparers furnishing identifying numbers for returns or claims for refund.—(a) *In general.*—Each gift tax return or claim for refund prepared by one or more signing tax return preparers must include the identifying number of the preparer required by § 1.6695-1(b) of this chapter to sign the return or claim for refund in the manner stated in § 1.6109-2 of this chapter.

(b) *Effective/applicability date.*—Paragraph (a) of this section is applicable to returns and claims for refund filed after December 31, 2008. [Reg. § 25.6109-1.]

☐ [*T.D.* 9436, 12-15-2008.]

[Reg. § 26.6109-1]

§ 26.6109-1. Tax return preparers furnishing identifying numbers for returns or claims for refund.—(a) *In general.*—Each generation-skipping transfer tax return or claim for refund prepared by one or more signing tax return preparers must include the identifying number of the preparer required by § 1.6695-1(b) of this chapter to sign the return or claim for refund in the manner stated in § 1.6109-2 of this chapter.

(b) *Effective/applicability date.*—Paragraph (a) of this section is applicable to returns and claims for refund filed after December 31, 2008. [Reg. § 26.6109-1.]

☐ [*T.D.* 9436, 12-15-2008.]

[Reg. § 31.6109-1]

§ 31.6109-1. Supplying of identifying numbers.—(a) *In general.*—The returns, statements, and other documents required to be filed under this subchapter shall reflect such identifying numbers as are required by each return, statement, or document and its related instructions. See § 301.6109-1 of this chapter (Regulations on Procedure and Administration).

(b) *Effective date.*—The provisions of this section are effective for information which must be furnished after April 15, 1974. See 26 CFR § 31.6109-1 (revised as of April 1, 1973) for provisions with respect to information which must be furnished before April 16, 1974. [Reg. § 31.6109-1.]

☐ [*T.D.* 6606, 8-24-62. *Amended by T.D.* 7306, 3-14-74.]

[Reg. § 40.6109-1]

§ 40.6109-1. Tax return preparers furnishing identifying numbers for returns or claims for refund.—(a) *In general.*—Each return or claim for refund of any tax to which this part 40 applies prepared by one or more signing tax return preparers must include the identifying number of the preparer required by § 1.6695-1(b) of this chapter to sign the return or claim for refund in the manner stated in § 1.6109-2 of this chapter.

(b) *Effective/applicability date.*—This section is applicable to returns and claims for refund filed after December 31, 2008. [Reg. § 40.6109-1.]

☐ [*T.D.* 9436, 12-15-2008 (*corrected* 1-28-2009).]

[Reg. § 41.6109-1]

§ 41.6109-1. Identifying numbers.—Every person required under § 41.6011(a)-1 to make a return must provide the identifying number required by the instructions to the form on which the return is made. [Reg. § 41.6109-1.]

☐ [*T.D.* 6606, 8-24-62. *Amended by T.D.* 7012, 5-14-69 *and T.D.* 8879, 3-30-2000.]

[Reg. § 44.6109-1]

§ 44.6109-1. Tax return preparers furnishing identifying numbers for returns or claims for refund.—(a) *In general.*—Each tax return or claim for refund of tax under sections 4401 or 4411 prepared by one or more signing tax return preparers must include the identifying number of the preparer required by § 1.6695-1(b) of this chapter to sign the return or claim for refund in the manner stated in § 1.6109-2 of this chapter.

(b) *Effective/applicability date.*—This section is applicable for returns and claims for refund filed after December 31, 2008. [Reg. § 44.6109-1.]

☐ [*T.D.* 9436, 12-15-2008.]

[Reg. §53.6109-1]

§53.6109-1. Tax return preparers furnishing identifying numbers for returns or claims for refund filed.—(a) *In general.*—Each tax return or claim for refund under Chapter 42 of the Internal Revenue Code prepared by one or more signing tax return preparers must include the identifying number of the preparer required by §1.6695-1(b) of this chapter to sign the return or claim for refund in the manner stated in §1.6109-2 of this chapter.

(b) *Effective/applicability date.*—Paragraph (a) of this section is applicable to returns and claims for refund filed after December 31, 2008. [Reg. §53.6109-1.]

□ [*T.D.* 9436, 12-15-2008.]

[Reg. §54.6109-1]

§54.6109-1. Tax return preparers furnishing identifying numbers for returns or claims for refund filed.—(a) *In general.*—Each tax return or claim for refund of tax under Chapter 43 of subtitle D prepared by one or more signing tax return preparers must include the identifying number of the preparer required by §1.6695-1(b) of this chapter to sign the return or claim for refund in the manner stated in §1.6109-2 of this chapter. [Reg. §54.6109-1.]

(b) *Effective/applicability date.*—Paragraph (a) of this section is applicable to returns and claims for refund filed after December 31, 2008. [Reg. §54.6109-1.]

□ [*T.D.* 9436, 12-15-2008.]

[Reg. §55.6109-1]

§55.6109-1. Tax return preparers furnishing identifying numbers for returns or claims for refund.—(a) *In general.*—Each tax return or claim for refund of tax under chapter 44 of Subtitle D prepared by one or more signing tax return preparers must include the identifying number of the preparer required by §1.6695-1(b) of this chapter to sign the return or claim for refund in the manner stated in §1.6109-2 of this chapter.

(b) *Effective/applicability date.*—Paragraph (a) of this section is applicable to returns and claims for refund filed after December 31, 2008. [Reg. §55.6109-1.]

□ [*T.D.* 9436, 12-15-2008.]

[Reg. §56.6109-1]

§56.6109-1. Tax return preparers furnishing identifying numbers for returns or claims for refund.—(a) *In general.*—Each tax return or claim for refund for tax under chapter 41 of subtitle D prepared by one or more signing tax return preparers must include the identifying number of the preparer required by §1.6695-1(b) of this chapter to sign the return or claim for refund in the manner stated in §1.6109-2 of this chapter.

(b) *Effective/applicability date.*—Paragraph (a) of this section is applicable to returns and claims for refund filed after December 31, 2008. [Reg. §56.6109-1.]

□ [*T.D.* 9436, 12-15-2008.]

[Reg. §156.6109-1]

§156.6109-1. Tax return preparers furnishing identifying numbers for returns or claims for refund.—(a) *In general.*—Each tax return or claim for refund for tax under section 5881 of the Internal Revenue Code prepared by one or more signing tax return preparers must include the identifying number of the preparer required by §1.6695-1(b) of this chapter to sign the return or claim for refund in the manner stated in §1.6109-2 of this chapter.

(b) *Effective/applicability date.*—Paragraph (a) of this section is applicable to returns and claims for refund filed after December 31, 2008. [Reg. §156.6109-1.]

□ [*T.D.* 9436, 12-15-2008.]

[Reg. §157.6109-1]

§157.6109-1. Tax return preparers furnishing identifying numbers for returns or claims for refund.—(a) *In general.*—Each tax return or claim for refund for tax under section 5891 of the Internal Revenue Code prepared by one or more signing tax return preparers must include the identifying number of the preparer required by §1.6695-1(b) of this chapter to sign the return or claim for refund in the manner stated in §1.6109-2 of this chapter.

(b) *Effective/applicability date.*—Paragraph (a) of this section is applicable to returns and claims for refund filed after December 31, 2008. [Reg. §157.6109-1.]

□ [*T.D.* 9436, 12-15-2008.]

[Reg. §301.6109-1]

§301.6109-1. Identifying numbers.—(a) *In general.*—(1) *Taxpayer identifying numbers.*—(i) *Principal types.*—There are several types of taxpayer identifying numbers that include the following: social security numbers, Internal Revenue Service (IRS) individual taxpayer identification numbers, IRS adoption taxpayer identification numbers, and employer identification numbers. Social security numbers take the form 000-00-0000. IRS individual taxpayer identification numbers and IRS adoption taxpayer identification numbers also take the form 000-00-0000 but include a specific number or numbers designated by the IRS. Employer identification numbers take the form 00-0000000.

(ii) *Uses.*—Social security numbers, IRS individual taxpayer identification numbers, and IRS adoption taxpayer identification numbers are used to identify individual persons. Employer identification numbers are used to identify employers. For the definition of social security number and employer identification number, see §§301.7701-11 and 301.7701-12, respectively. For the definition of IRS individual taxpayer identification number, see paragraph (d)(3) of this section. For the definition of IRS adoption taxpayer identification number, see § 301.6109-3(a). Except as otherwise provided in applicable regulations under this chapter or on a return, statement, or other document, and related instructions, taxpayer identifying numbers must be used as follows:

(A) Except as otherwise provided in paragraph (a)(1)(ii)(B) and (D) of this section, and § 301.6109-3, an individual required to furnish a taxpayer identifying number must use a social security number.

(B) Except as otherwise provided in paragraph (a)(1)(ii)(D) of this section and § 301.6109-3, an individual required to furnish a taxpayer identifying number but who is not eligible to obtain a social security number must use an IRS individual taxpayer identification number.

(C) Any person other than an individual (such as corporations, partnerships, non-profit associations, trusts, estates, and similar nonindividual persons) that is required to furnish a taxpayer identifying number must use an employer identification number.

(D) An individual, whether U.S. or foreign, who is an employer or who is engaged in a trade or business as a sole proprietor should use an employer identification number as required by returns, statements, or other documents and their related instructions.

(2) *A trust that is treated as owned by one or more persons pursuant to sections 671 through 678.*—(i) *Obtaining a taxpayer identification number.*—(A) *General rule.*—Unless the exception in paragraph (a)(2)(i)(B) of this section applies, a trust that is treated as owned by one or more persons under sections 671 through 678 must obtain a taxpayer identification number as provided in paragraph (d)(2) of this section.

(B) *Exception for a trust all of which is treated as owned by one grantor or one other person and that reports under § 1.671-4(b)(2)(i)(A) of this chapter.*—A trust that is treated as owned by one grantor or one other person under sections 671 through 678 need not obtain a taxpayer identification number, provided the trust reports pursuant to § 1.671-4(b)(2)(i)(A) of this chapter. The trustee must obtain a taxpayer identification number as provided in paragraph (d)(2) of this section for the first taxable year that the trust is no longer owned by one grantor or one other person or for the first taxable year that the trust does not report pursuant to § 1.671-4(b)(2)(i)(A) of this chapter.

(ii) *Obligations of persons who make payments to certain trusts.*—Any payor that is required to file an information return with respect to payments of income or proceeds to a trust must show the name and taxpayer identification number that the trustee has furnished to the payor on the return. Regardless of whether the trustee furnishes to the payor the name and taxpayer identification number of the grantor or other person treated as an owner of the trust, or the name and taxpayer identification number of the trust, the payor must furnish a statement to recipients to the trustee of the trust, rather than to the grantor or other person treated as the owner of the trust. Under these circumstances, the payor satisfies the obligation to show the name and taxpayer identification number of the payee on the information return and to furnish a statement to recipients to the person whose taxpayer identification number is required to be shown on the form.

(3) *Obtaining a taxpayer identification number for a trust, or portion of a trust, following the death of the individual treated as the owner.*—(i) *In general.*—(A) *A trust all of which was treated as owned by a decedent.*—In general, a trust all of which is treated as owned by a decedent under subpart E (section 671 and following), part I, subchapter J, chapter 1 of the Internal Revenue Code as of the date of the decedent's death must obtain a new taxpayer identification number following the death of the decedent if the trust will continue after the death of the decedent.

(B) *Taxpayer identification number of trust with multiple owners.*—With respect to a portion of a trust treated as owned under subpart E (section 671 and following), part I, subchapter J, chapter 1 (subpart E) of the Internal Revenue Code by a decedent as of the date of the decedent's death, if, following the death of the decedent, the portion treated as owned by the decedent remains part of the original trust and the other portion (or portions) of the trust continues to be treated as owned under subpart E by a grantor(s) or other person(s), the trust reports under the taxpayer identification number assigned to the trust prior to the decedent's death and the portion of the trust treated as owned by the decedent prior to the decedent's death (assuming the decedent's portion of the trust is not treated as terminating upon the decedent's death) continues to report under the taxpayer identification number used for reporting by the other portion (or portions) of the trust. For example, if a trust, reporting under § 1.671-4(a) of this chapter, is treated as owned by three persons and one of them dies, the trust, including the portion of the trust no longer treated as owned by a grantor or other person, continues to report under the tax identification number assigned to the trust prior to the death of that person. See § 1.671-4(a) of this chapter regarding rules for filing the Form 1041, "U.S. Income Tax Return for Estates and Trusts," where only a portion of the trust is treated as owned by one or more persons under subpart E.

(ii) *Furnishing correct taxpayer identification number to payors following the death of the decedent.*—If the trust continues after the death of the decedent and is required to obtain a new taxpayer identification number under paragraph (a)(3)(i)(A) of this section, the trustee must furnish payors with a new Form W-9, "Request for Taxpayer Identification Number and Certification," or an acceptable substitute Form W-9, containing the new taxpayer identification number required under paragraph (a)(3)(i)(A) of this section, the name of the trust, and the address of the trustee.

(4) *Taxpayer identification number to be used by a trust upon termination of a section 645 election.*— (i) *If there is an executor.*—Upon the termination of the section 645 election period, if there is an executor, the trustee of the former electing trust may need to obtain a taxpayer identification number. If §1.645-1(g) of this chapter regarding the appointment of an executor after a section 645 election is made applies to the electing trust, the electing trust must obtain a new TIN upon termination of the election period. See the instructions to the Form 1041 for whether a new taxpayer identification number is required for other former electing trusts.

(ii) *If there is no executor.*—Upon termination of the section 645 election period, if there is no executor, the trustee of the former electing trust must obtain a new taxpayer identification number.

(iii) *Requirement to provide taxpayer identification number to payors.*—If the trustee is required to obtain a new taxpayer identification number for a former electing trust pursuant to this paragraph (a)(4), or pursuant to the instructions to the Form 1041, the trustee must furnish all payors of the trust with a completed Form W-9 or acceptable substitute Form W-9 signed under penalties of perjury by the trustee providing each payor with the name of the trust, the new taxpayer identification number, and the address of the trustee.

(5) *Persons treated as payors.*—For purposes of paragraphs (a)(2), (3), and (4) of this section, a *payor* is a person described in §§1.671-4(b)(4) of this chapter.

(6) *Effective date.*—Paragraphs (a)(3), (4), and (5) of this section apply to trusts of decedents dying on or after December 24, 2002.

(b) *Requirement to furnish one's own number.*— (1) *U.S. persons.*—Every U.S. person who makes under this title a return, statement, or other document must furnish its own taxpayer identifying number as required by the forms and the accompanying instructions. A U.S. person whose number must be included on a document filed by another person must give the taxpayer identifying number so required to the other person on request. For penalties for failure to supply taxpayer identifying numbers, see sections 6721 through 6724. For provisions dealing specifically with the duty of employees with respect to their social security numbers, see §31.6011(b)-2(a) and (b) of this chapter (Employment Tax Regulations). For provisions dealing specifically with the duty of employers with respect to employer identification numbers, see §31.6011(b)-1 of this chapter (Employment Tax Regulations).

(2) *Foreign persons.*—The provisions of paragraph (b)(1) of this section regarding the furnishing of one's own number shall apply to the following foreign persons—

(i) A foreign person that has income effectively connected with the conduct of a U.S. trade or business at any time during the taxable year;

(ii) A foreign person that has a U.S. office or place of business or a U.S. fiscal or paying agent at any time during the taxable year;

(iii) A nonresident alien treated as a resident under section 6013(g) or (h);

(iv) A foreign person that makes a return of tax (including income, estate, and gift tax returns), an amended return, or a refund claim under this title but excluding information returns, statements, or documents;

(v) A foreign person that makes an election under §301.7701-3(c);

(vi) A foreign person that furnishes a withholding certificate described in §1.1441-1(e)(2) or (3) of this chapter or §1.1441-5(c)(2)(iv) or (3)(iii) of this chapter to the extent required under §1.1441-1(e)(4)(vii) of this chapter;

(vii) A foreign person whose taxpayer identifying number is required to be furnished on any return, statement, or other document as required by the income tax regulations under section 897 or 1445. This paragraph (b)(2)(vii) applies as of November 3, 2003; and

(viii) A foreign person that furnishes a withholding certificate described in §1.1446-1(c)(2) or (3) of this chapter or whose taxpayer identification number is required to be furnished on any return, statement, or other document as required by the income tax regulations under section 1446. This paragraph (b)(2)(viii) shall apply to partnership taxable years beginning after May 18, 2005, or such earlier time as the regulations under §§1.1446-1 through 1.1446-5 of this chapter apply by reason of an election under §1.1446-7 of this chapter.

(c) *Requirement to furnish another's number.*— Every person required under this title to make a return, statement, or other document must furnish such taxpayer identifying numbers of other U.S. persons and foreign persons that are described in paragraph (b)(2)(i), (ii), (iii), (vi), (vii), or (viii) of this section as required by the forms and the accompanying instructions. The taxpayer identifying number of any person furnishing a withholding certificate referred to in paragraph (b)(2)(vi) or (viii) of this section shall also be furnished if it is actually known to the person making a return, statement, or other document described in this paragraph (c). If the person making the return, statement, or other document does not know the taxpayer identifying number of the other person, and such other person is one that is described in paragraph (b)(2)(i), (ii), (iii), (vi), (vii), or (viii) of this section, such person must request the other person's number. The request should state that the identifying number is required to be furnished under authority of law. When the person making the return, statement, or other document does not know the number of the other person, and has complied with the request provision of this paragraph (c), such person must sign an affidavit on the transmittal document forwarding such returns, statements, or other documents to the Internal Revenue Service, so stating. A person required to file a taxpayer identifying number shall correct any errors in such filing when such person's attention has been drawn to them. References in this paragraph (c) to paragraph (b)(2)(viii) of this section shall apply to partnership taxable years beginning after May 18, 2005, or such earlier time as the regulations under §§ 1.1446-1 through 1.1446-5 of this chapter apply by reason of an election under § 1.1446-7 of this chapter.

(d) *Obtaining a taxpayer identifying number.*—(1) *Social security number.*—Any individual required to furnish a social security number pursuant to paragraph (b) of this section shall apply for one, if he has not done so previously, on Form SS-5, which may be obtained from any Social Security Administration or Internal Revenue Service office. He shall make such application far enough in advance of the first required use of such number to permit issuance of the number in time for compliance with such requirement. The form, together with any supplementary statement, shall be prepared and filed in accordance with the form, instructions, and regulations applicable thereto, and shall set forth fully and clearly the data therein called for. Individuals who are ineligible for or do not wish to participate in the benefits of the social security program shall nevertheless obtain a social security number if they are required to furnish such a number pursuant to paragraph (b) of this section.

(2) *Employer identification number.*—(i) *In general.*—Any person required to furnish an employer identification number must apply for one, if not done so previously, on Form SS-4. A Form SS-4 may be obtained from any office of the Internal Revenue Service, U.S. consular office abroad, or from an acceptance agent described in paragraph (d)(3)(iv) of this section. The person must make such application far enough in advance of the first required use of the employer identification number to permit issuance of the number in time for compliance with such requirement. The form, together with any supplementary statement, must be prepared and filed in accordance with the form, accompanying instructions, and relevant regulations, and must set forth fully and clearly the requested data.

(ii) *Updating of application information.*—(A) *Requirements.*—Persons issued employer identification numbers in accordance with the application process set forth in paragraph (d)(2)(i) of this section must provide to the Internal Revenue Service any updated application information in the manner and frequency required by forms, instructions, or other appropriate guidance.

(B) *Effective/applicability date.*—Paragraph (d)(2)(ii)(A) of this section applies to all persons possessing an employer identification number on or after January 1, 2014.

(iii) *Special rule for Section 708(b)(1)(B) terminations.*—A new partnership that is formed as a result of the termination of a partnership under section 708(b)(1)(B) will retain the employer identification number of the terminated partnership. This paragraph (d)(2)(iii) applies to terminations of partnerships under section 708(b)(1)(B) occurring on or after May 9, 1997; however, this paragraph (d)(2)(iii) may be applied to terminations occurring on or after May 9, 1996, provided that the partnership and its partners apply this paragraph (d)(2)(iii) to the termination in a consistent manner.

(3) *IRS individual taxpayer identification number.*—(i) *Definition.*—The term *IRS individual taxpayer identification number* means a taxpayer identifying number issued to an alien individual by the Internal Revenue Service, upon application, for use in connection with filing requirements under this title. The term *IRS individual taxpayer identification number* does not refer to a social security number or an account number for use in employment for wages. For purposes of this section, the term *alien individual* means an individual who is not a citizen or national of the United States.

(ii) *General rule for obtaining number.*—Any individual who is not eligible to obtain a social security number and is required to furnish a taxpayer identifying number must apply for an IRS individual taxpayer identification number on Form W-7, Application for IRS Individual Taxpayer Identification Number, or such other form as may be prescribed by the Internal Revenue Service. Form W-7 may be obtained from any office of the Internal Revenue Service, U.S. consular office abroad, or any acceptance agent described in paragraph (d)(3)(iv) of this section. The individual shall furnish the information required by the form and accompanying instructions, including the individual's name, address, foreign tax identification number (if any), and specific reason for obtaining an IRS individual taxpayer identification number. The individual must make such application far enough in advance of the first required use of the IRS individual taxpayer identification number to permit issuance of the number in time for compliance with such requirement. The application form, together with any supplementary statement and documentation, must be prepared and filed in accordance with the form, accompanying instructions, and relevant regulations, and must set forth fully and clearly the requested data.

(iii) *General rule for assigning number.*—Under procedures issued by the Internal Revenue Service, an IRS individual taxpayer identification number will be assigned to an individual upon the basis of information reported on Form W-7 (or such other form as may be prescribed by the Internal Revenue Service) and any such accompanying documentation that may be required by the Internal Revenue Service. An applicant for an IRS individual taxpayer identification number must submit such documentary evidence as the Internal Revenue Service may prescribe in order to establish alien status and identity. Examples of acceptable documentary evidence for this purpose may include items such as an original (or a certified copy of the original) passport, driver's license, birth certificate, identity card, or immigration documentation.

(iv) *Acceptance agents.*—(A) *Agreements with acceptance agents.*—A person described in paragraph (d)(3)(iv)(B) of this section will be accepted by the Internal Revenue Service to act as an acceptance agent for purposes of the regulations under this section upon entering into an agreement with the Internal Revenue Service, under which the acceptance agent will be authorized to act on behalf of taxpayers seeking to obtain a taxpayer identifying number from the Internal Revenue Service. The agreement must contain such terms and conditions as are necessary to insure proper administration of the process by which the Internal Revenue Service issues taxpayer identifying numbers to foreign persons, including proof of their identity and foreign status. In particular, the agreement may contain—

(1) Procedures for providing Form SS-4 and Form W-7, or such other necessary form to applicants for obtaining a taxpayer identifying number;

(2) Procedures for providing assistance to applicants in completing the application form or completing it for them;

(3) Procedures for collecting, reviewing, and maintaining, in the normal course of business, a record of the required documentation for assignment of a taxpayer identifying number;

(4) Procedures for submitting the application form and required documentation to the Internal Revenue Service, or if permitted under the agreement, submitting the application form together with a certification that the acceptance agent has reviewed the required documentation and that it has no actual knowledge or reason to know that the documentation is not complete or accurate;

(5) Procedures for assisting taxpayers with notification procedures described in paragraph (g)(2) of this section in the event of change of foreign status;

(6) Procedures for making all documentation or other records furnished by persons applying for a taxpayer identifying number promptly available for review by the Internal Revenue Service, upon request; and

(7) Provisions that the agreement may be terminated in the event of a material failure to comply with the agreement, including failure to exercise due diligence under the agreement.

(B) *Persons who may be acceptance agents.*—An acceptance agent may include any financial institution as defined in section 265(b)(5) or §1.165-12(c)(1)(v) of this chapter, any college or university that is an educational organization as defined in §1.501(c)(3)-1(d)(3)(i) of this chapter, any federal agency as defined in section 6402(f) or any other person or categories of persons that may be authorized by regulations or Internal Revenue Service procedures. A person described in this paragraph (d)(3)(iv)(B) that seeks to qualify as an acceptance agent must have an employer identification number for use in any communication with the Internal Revenue Service. In addition, it must establish to the satisfaction of the Internal Revenue Service that it has adequate resources and procedures in place to comply with the terms of the agreement described in paragraph (d)(3)(iv)(A) of this section.

(4) *Coordination of taxpayer identifying numbers.*—(i) *Social security number.*—Any individual who is duly assigned a social security number or who is entitled to a social security number will not be issued an IRS individual taxpayer identification number. The individual can use the social security number for all tax purposes under this title, even though the individual is, or later becomes, a nonresident alien individual. Further, any individual who has an application pending with the Social Security Administration will be issued an IRS individual taxpayer identification number only after the Social Security Administration has notified the individual that a social security number cannot be issued. Any alien individual duly issued an IRS individual taxpayer identification number who later becomes a U.S. citizen, or an alien lawfully permitted to enter the United States either for permanent residence or under authority of law permitting U.S. employment, will be required to obtain a social security number. Any individual who has an IRS individual taxpayer identification number and a social security number, due to the circumstances described in the preceding sentence, must notify the Internal Revenue Service of the acquisition of the social security number and must use the newly-issued social security number as the taxpayer identifying number on all future returns, statements, or other documents filed under this title.

(ii) *Employer identification number.*—Any individual with both a social security number (or an IRS individual taxpayer identification number) and an employer identification number may use the social security number (or the IRS individual taxpayer identification number) for individual taxes, and the employer identification number for business taxes as required by returns, statements, and other documents and their related instructions. Any alien individual duly assigned an IRS individual taxpayer identification number who also is required to obtain an employer identification number must furnish the previously-assigned IRS individual taxpayer identification number to the Internal Revenue Service on Form SS-4 at the time of application for the employer identification number. Similarly, where an alien individual has an employer identification number and is required to obtain an IRS individual taxpayer identification number, the Individual must furnish the previously-assigned employer identification number to the Internal Revenue Service on Form W-7, or such other form as may be prescribed by the Internal Revenue Service, at the time of application for the IRS individual taxpayer identification number.

(e) *Banks, and brokers and dealers in securities.*— For additional requirements relating to deposits, share accounts, and brokerage accounts, see 31 CFR 103.34 and 103.35.

(f) *Penalty.*—For penalties for failure to supply taxpayer identifying numbers, see sections 6721 through 6724.

(g) *Special rules for taxpayer identifying numbers issued to foreign persons.*—(1) *General rule.*— (i) *Social security number.*—A social security number is generally identified in the records and database of the Internal Revenue Service as a number belonging to a U.S. citizen or resident alien individual. A person may establish a different status for the number by providing proof of foreign status with the Internal Revenue Service under such procedures as the Internal Revenue Service shall prescribe, including the use of a form as the Internal Revenue Service may specify. Upon accepting an individual as a nonresident alien individual, the Internal Revenue Service will assign this status to the individuals social security number.

(ii) *Employer identification number.*—An employer identification number is generally identified in the records and database of the Internal Revenue Service as a number belonging to a U.S. person. However, the Internal Revenue Service may establish a separate class of employer identification numbers solely dedicated to foreign persons which will be identified as such in the records and database of the Internal Revenue Service. A person may establish a different status for the number either at the time of application or subsequently by providing proof of U.S. or foreign status with the Internal Revenue Service under such procedures as the Internal Revenue Service shall prescribe, including the use of a form as the Internal Revenue Service may specify. The Internal Revenue Service may require a person to apply for the type of employer identification number that reflects the status of that person as a U.S. or foreign person.

(iii) *IRS individual taxpayer identification number.*—An IRS individual taxpayer identification number is generally identified in the records and database of the Internal Revenue Service as a number belonging to a nonresident alien individual. If the Internal Revenue Service determines at the time of application or subsequently, that an individual is not a nonresident alien individual, the Internal Revenue Service may require that the individual apply for a social security number. If a social security number is not available, the Internal Revenue Service may accept that the individual use an IRS individual taxpayer identification number, which the Internal Revenue Service will identify as a number belonging to a U.S. resident alien.

(2) *Change of foreign status.*—Once a taxpayer identifying number is identified in the records and database of the Internal Revenue Service as a number belonging to a U.S. or foreign person, the status of the number is permanent until the circumstances of the taxpayer change. A taxpayer whose status changes (for example, a nonresident alien individual with a social security number becomes a U.S. resident alien) must notify the Internal Revenue Service of the change of status under such procedures as the Internal Revenue Service shall prescribe, including the use of a form as the Internal Revenue Service may specify.

(3) *Waiver of prohibition to disclose taxpayer information when acceptance agent acts.*—As part of its request for an IRS individual taxpayer identification number or submission of proof of foreign status with respect to any taxpayer identifying number, where the foreign person acts through an acceptance agent, the foreign person will agree to waive the limitations in section 6103 regarding the disclosure of certain taxpayer information. However, the waiver will apply only for purposes of permitting the Internal Revenue Service and the acceptance agent to communicate with each other regarding matters related to the assignment of a taxpayer identifying number, including disclosure of any taxpayer identifying number previously issued to the foreign person, and change of foreign status. This paragraph (g)(3) applies to payments made after December 31, 2001.

(h) *Special rules for certain entities under § 301.7701-3.*—(1) *General rule.*—Any entity that has an employer identification number (EIN) will retain that EIN if its federal tax classification changes under § 301.7701-3.

(2) *Special rules for entities that are disregarded as entities separate from their owners.*—(i) *When an entity becomes disregarded as an entity separate from its owner.*—Except as otherwise provided in regulations or other guidance, a single owner entity that is disregarded as an entity separate from its owner under § 301.7701-3, must use its owner's taxpayer identifying number (TIN) for federal tax purposes.

(ii) *When an entity that was disregarded as an entity separate from its owner becomes recognized as a separate entity.*—If a single owner entity's classification changes so that it is recognized as a separate entity for federal tax purposes, and that entity had an EIN, then the entity must use that EIN and not the TIN of the single owner. If the entity did not already have its own EIN, then the entity must acquire an EIN and not use the TIN of the single owner.

Reg. § 301.6109-1(h)(2)(ii)

(3) *Effective date.*—The rules of this paragraph (h) are applicable as of January 1, 1997.

(i) *Special rule for qualified subchapter S subsidiaries (Qsubs).*—(1) *General rule.*—Any entity that has an employer identification number (EIN) will retain that EIN if a QSub election is made for the entity under § 1.1361-3 or if a QSub election that was in effect for the entity terminates under § 1.1361-5.

(2) *EIN while QSub election in effect.*—Except as otherwise provided in regulations or other published guidance, a QSub must use the parent S corporation's EIN for Federal tax purposes.

(3) *EIN when QSub election terminates.*—If an entity's QSub election terminates, it may not use the EIN of the parent S corporation after the termination. If the entity had an EIN prior to becoming a QSub or obtained an EIN while it was a QSub in accordance with regulations or other published guidance, the entity must use that EIN. If the entity had no EIN, it must obtain an EIN upon termination of the QSub election.

(4) *Effective date.*—The rules of this paragraph (i) apply on January 20, 2000.

(j) *Effective date.*—(1) *General rule.*—Except as otherwise provided in this paragraph (j), the provisions of this section are generally effective for information that must be furnished after April 15, 1974. However, the provisions relating to IRS individual taxpayer identification numbers apply on and after May 29, 1996. An application for an IRS individual taxpayer identification number (Form W-7) may be filed at any time on or after July 1, 1996.

(2) *Special rules.*—(i) *Employer identification number of an estate.*—The requirement under paragraph (a)(1)(ii)(C) of this section that an estate obtain an employer identification number applies on and after January 1, 1984.

(ii) *Taxpayer identifying numbers of certain foreign persons.*—The requirement under paragraph (b)(2)(iv) of this section that certain foreign persons furnish a TIN on a return of tax is effective for tax returns filed after December 31, 1996.

(iii) Paragraphs (a)(1)(i), (a)(1)(ii) introductory text, (a)(1)(ii)(A), and (a)(1)(ii)(B) of this section apply to income tax returns due (without regard to extensions) on or after April 15, 1998. [Reg. § 301.6109-1.]

☐ [*T.D. 6606, 8-24-62. Amended by T.D. 7306, 3-14-74; T.D. 7670, 1-30-80; T.D. 7796, 11-23-81; T.D. 8633, 12-20-95; T.D. 8637, 12-20-95; T.D. 8671, 5-23-96; T.D. 8697, 12-17-96; T.D. 8717, 5-8-97; T.D. 8734, 10-6-97 (T.D. 8804 delayed the effective date of T.D. 8734 from January 1, 1999, to January 1, 2000; T.D. 8856 further delayed the effective date of T.D. 8734 until January 1, 2001); T.D. 8739, 11-21-97; T.D. 8839, 9-21-99; T.D. 8844, 11-26-99; T.D. 8869, 1-20-2000; T.D. 8977, 1-16-2002; T.D. 9023, 11-21-2002; T.D. 9032, 12-23-2002; T.D. 9082, 8-4-2003; T.D. 9200,* 5-13-2005; *T.D. 9241, 1-23-2006 and T.D. 9617, 5-3-2013.*]

[Reg. § 40.6109(a)-1]

§ 40.6109(a)-1. Identifying numbers.—Every person required under § 40.6011(a)-1 to make a return must provide the identifying number required by the instructions applicable to the form on which the return is made. [Reg. § 40.6109(a)-1.]

☐ [*T.D. 8442, 10-21-92. Amended by T.D. 8963, 8-8-2001.*]

[Reg. § 1.6109-2]

§ 1.6109-2. Tax return preparers furnishing identifying numbers for returns or claims for refund and related requirements.— (a) *Furnishing identifying number.*—(1) Each filed return of tax or claim for refund of tax under the Internal Revenue Code prepared by one or more tax return preparers must include the identifying number of the tax return preparer required by § 1.6695-1(b) to sign the return or claim for refund. In addition, if there is an employment arrangement or association between the individual tax return preparer and another person (except to the extent the return prepared is for the person), the identifying number of the other person must also appear on the filed return or claim for refund. For the definition of the term "tax return preparer," see section 7701(a)(36) and § 301.7701-15 of this chapter.

(2)(i) For tax returns or claims for refund filed on or before December 31, 2010, the identifying number of an individual tax return preparer is that individual's social security number or such alternative number as may be prescribed by the Internal Revenue Service in forms, instructions, or other appropriate guidance.

(ii) For tax returns or claims for refund filed after December 31, 2010, the identifying number of a tax return preparer is the individual's preparer tax identification number or such other number prescribed by the Internal Revenue Service in forms, instructions, or other appropriate guidance.

(3) The identifying number of a person (whether an individual or entity) who employs or associates with an individual tax return preparer described in paragraph (a)(2) of this section to prepare the return or claim for refund (other than a return prepared for the person) is the person's employer identification number.

(b) and (c) [Reserved]. For further guidance, see § 1.6109-2A(b) and (c).

(d) Beginning after December 31, 2010, all tax return preparers must have a preparer tax identification number or other prescribed identifying number that was applied for and received at the time and in the manner, including the payment of a user fee, as may be prescribed by the Internal Revenue Service in forms, instructions, or other appropriate guidance. Except as provided in paragraph (h) of this section, beginning after December 31, 2010, to obtain a preparer tax identification number or other prescribed identifying number, a tax return preparer must be an attorney, certified public accountant, enrolled agent, or registered tax return preparer authorized to practice before the Internal Revenue Service under 31 U.S.C. 330 and the regulations thereunder.

(e) The Internal Revenue Service may designate an expiration date for any preparer tax identification number or other prescribed identifying number and may further prescribe the time and manner for renewing a preparer tax identification number or other prescribed identifying number, including the payment of a user fee, as set forth in forms, instructions, or other appropriate guidance. The Internal Revenue Service may provide that any identifying number issued by the Internal Revenue Service prior to the effective date of this regulation will expire on December 31, 2010, unless properly renewed as set forth in forms, instructions, or other appropriate guidance, including these regulations.

(f) As may be prescribed in forms, instructions, or other appropriate guidance, the IRS may conduct a Federal tax compliance check on a tax return preparer who applies for or renews a preparer tax identification number or other prescribed identifying number.

(g) Only for purposes of paragraphs (d), (e), and (f) of this section, the term *tax return preparer* means any individual who is compensated for preparing, or assisting in the preparation of, all or substantially all of a tax return or claim for refund of tax. Factors to consider in determining whether an individual is a tax return preparer under this paragraph (g) include, but are not limited to, the complexity of the work performed by the individual relative to the overall complexity of the tax return or claim for refund of tax; the amount of the items of income, deductions, or losses attributable to the work performed by the individual relative to the total amount of income, deductions, or losses required to be correctly reported on the tax return or claim for refund of tax; and the amount of tax or credit attributable to the work performed by the individual relative to the total tax liability required to be correctly reported on the tax return or claim for refund of tax. The preparation of a form, statement, or schedule, such as Schedule EIC (Form 1040), "Earned Income Credit," may constitute the preparation of all or substantially all of a tax return or claim for refund based on the application of the foregoing factors. A tax return preparer does not include an individual who is not otherwise a tax return preparer as that term is defined in § 301.7701-15(b)(2), or who is an individual described in § 301.7701-15(f). The provisions of this paragraph (g) are illustrated by the following examples:

Example 1. Employee A, an individual employed by Tax Return Preparer B, assists Tax Return Preparer B in answering telephone calls, making copies, inputting client tax information gathered by B into the data fields of tax preparation software on a computer, and using the computer to file electronic returns of tax prepared by B. Although Employee A must exercise judg-

ment regarding which data fields in the tax preparation software to use, A does not exercise any discretion or independent judgment as to the clients' underlying tax positions. Employee A, therefore, merely provides clerical assistance or incidental services and is not a tax return preparer required to apply for a PTIN or other identifying number as the Internal Revenue Service may prescribe in forms, instructions, or other appropriate guidance.

Example 2. The facts are the same as in *Example 1,* except that Employee A also interviews B's clients and obtains from them information needed for the preparation of tax returns. Employee A determines the amount and character of entries on the returns and whether the information provided is sufficient for purposes of preparing the returns. For at least some of B's clients, A obtains information and makes determinations that constitute all or substantially all of the tax return. Employee A is a tax return preparer required to apply for a PTIN or other identifying number as the Internal Revenue Service may prescribe in forms, instructions, or other appropriate guidance. Employee A is a tax return preparer even if Employee A relies on tax preparation software to prepare the return.

Example 3. C is an employee of a firm that prepares tax returns and claims for refund of tax for compensation. C is responsible for preparing a Form 1040, "U.S. Individual Income Tax Return," for a client. C obtains the information necessary for the preparation of the tax return during a meeting with the client, and makes determinations with respect to the proper application of the tax laws to the information in order to determine the client's tax liability. C completes the tax return and sends the completed return to employee D, who reviews the return for accuracy before signing it. Both C and D are tax return preparers required to apply for a PTIN or other identifying number as the Internal Revenue Service may prescribe in forms, instructions, or other appropriate guidance.

Example 4. E is an employee at a firm which prepares tax returns and claims for refund of tax for compensation. The firm is engaged by a corporation to prepare its Federal income tax return on Form 1120, "U.S. Corporation Income Tax Return." Among the documentation that the corporation provides to E in connection with the preparation of the tax return is documentation relating to the corporation's potential eligibility to claim a recently enacted tax credit for the taxable year. In preparing the return, and specifically for purposes of the new tax credit, E (with the corporation's consent) obtains advice from F, a subject matter expert on this and similar credits. F advises E as to the corporation's entitlement to the credit and provides his calculation of the amount of the credit. Based on this advice from F, E prepares the corporation's Form 1120 claiming the tax credit in the amount recommended by F. The additional credit is one of many tax credits and deductions claimed on the tax return, and determining the credit amount does not constitute preparation of all or substan-

Reg. § 1.6109-2(g)

tially all of the corporation's tax return under this paragraph (g). F will not be considered to have prepared all or substantially all of the corporation's tax return, and F is not a tax return preparer required to apply for a PTIN or other identifying number as the Internal Revenue Service may prescribe in forms, instructions, or other appropriate guidance. The analysis is the same whether or not the tax credit is a substantial portion of the return under § 301.7701-15 of this chapter (as opposed to substantially all of the return), and whether or not F is in the same firm with E. E is a tax return preparer required to apply for a PTIN or other identifying number as the Internal Revenue Service may prescribe in forms, instructions, or other appropriate guidance.

(h) The Internal Revenue Service, through forms, instructions, or other appropriate guidance, may prescribe exceptions to the requirements of this section, including the requirement that an individual be authorized to practice before the Internal Revenue Service before receiving a preparer tax identification number or other prescribed identifying number, as necessary in the interest of effective tax administration. The Internal Revenue Service, through other appropriate guidance, may also specify specific returns, schedules, and other forms that qualify as tax returns or claims for refund for purposes of these regulations.

(i) *Effective/applicability date.*—Paragraph (a)(1) of this section is applicable to tax returns and claims for refund filed after December 31, 2008. Paragraph (a)(2)(i) of this section is applicable to tax returns and claims for refund filed on or before December 31, 2010. Paragraph (a)(2)(ii) of this section is applicable to tax returns and claims for refund filed after December 31, 2010. Paragraph (d) of this section is applicable to tax return preparers after December 31, 2010. Paragraphs (e) through (h) of this section are effective after September 30, 2010. [Reg. § 1.6109-2.]

☐ *[T.D. 9014, 8-12-2002. Amended by T.D. 9436, 12-15-2008 and T.D. 9501, 9-28-2010.]*

[Reg. § 1.6109-2A]

§ 1.6109-2A. Furnishing identifying number of income tax return preparer.—(a) *Furnishing identifying number.*—For returns or claims for refund filed prior to January 1, 2000, each return of tax under subtitle A of the Internal Revenue Code or claim for refund of tax under subtitle A of the Internal Revenue Code prepared by one or more income tax return preparers must bear the identifying number of the preparer required by § 1.6695-1(b) to sign the return or claim for refund. In addition, if there is a partnership or employment arrangement between two or more preparers, the identifying number of the partnership or the person who employs (or engages) one or more other persons to prepare for compensation the return or claim for refund shall also appear on the return or claim for refund. If the preparer is—

(1) An individual (not described in subparagraph (2) of this paragraph (a)) who is a citizen or resident of the United States, such preparer's social security account number shall be affixed; and

(2) A person (whether an individual, corporation, or partnership) who employs (or engages) one or more persons to prepare the return or claim for refund (other than for the person), or who is not a citizen or resident of the United States and also is not employed or engaged by another preparer, such preparer's employer identification number shall be affixed.

For the definition of the term "income tax return preparer" (or "preparer") see section 7701(a)(36) and § 301.7701-15.

(b) *Furnishing address.*—(1) Each return or claim for refund which is prepared by one or more income tax return preparers shall bear the street address, city, State, and postal ZIP code of that preparer's place of business where the preparation of the return or claim for refund was completed. However, if this place of business is not maintained on a year-round basis, the return or claim for refund shall bear the street address, city, State, and postal ZIP code of such preparer's principal office or business location which is maintained on a year-round basis, or, if none, that preparer's residence.

(2) For purposes of satisfying the requirement of the first sentence of paragraph (b)(1) of this section, an income tax return preparer may, on returns and claims for refund, disclose only the postal ZIP code of the described place of business as a satisfactory address, but only if the preparer first by written notice advises each affected Internal Revenue Service Center that he intends to follow this practice.

(c) *Penalty.*—For the civil penalty for failure to furnish an identifying number as required under paragraph (a) of this section, see section 6695(c) and § 1.6695-1(c).

(d) *Effective date.*—Paragraph (a) of this section and this paragraph (d) apply to returns or claims for refund filed prior to January 1, 2000. For returns or claims for refund filed after December 31, 1999, see § 1.6109-2(a). [Reg. § 1.6109-2A.]

☐ *[T.D. 7519, 11-17-77. Amended by T.D. 8835, 8-11-99. Redesignated and amended by T.D. 9014, 8-12-2002.]*

[Reg. § 31.6109-2]

§ 31.6109-2. Tax return preparers furnishing identifying numbers for returns or claims for refund.—(a) *In general.*—Each employment tax return or claim for refund of employment tax under chapters 21 through 25 of subtitle C of the Internal Revenue Code prepared by one or more signing tax return preparers must include the identifying number of the preparer required by § 1.6695-1(b) of this chapter to sign the return or claim for refund in the manner stated in § 1.6109-2 of this chapter.

(b) *Effective/applicability date.*—Paragraph (a) of this section is applicable to returns and claims for refund filed after December 31, 2008. [Reg. §31.6109-2.]

☐ [*T.D.* 9436, 12-15-2008.]

[Reg. §41.6109-2]

§41.6109-2. Tax return preparers furnishing identifying numbers for returns or claims for refund filed after December 31, 2008.—(a) *In general.*—Each excise tax return or claim for refund under section 4481 prepared by one or more signing tax return preparers must include the identifying number of the preparer required by §1.6695-1(b) of this chapter to sign the return or claim for refund in the manner stated in §1.6109-2 of this chapter.

(b) *Effective/applicability date.*—This section is applicable for returns and claims for refund filed after December 31, 2008. [Reg. §41.6109-2.]

☐ [*T.D.* 9436, 12-15-2008.]

[Reg. §301.6109-2]

§301.6109-2. Authority of the Secretary of Agriculture to collect employer identification numbers for purposes of the Food Stamp Act of 1977.—(a) *In general.*—The Secretary of Agriculture may require each applicant retail food store or wholesale food concern to furnish its employer identification number in connection with the administration of section 9 of the Food Stamp Act of 1977 (7 U.S.C. 2018) (relating to the determination of the qualifications of applicants under the Food Stamp Act).

(b) *Limited purpose.*—The Secretary of Agriculture may have access to the employer identification numbers obtained pursuant to paragraph (a) of this section, but only for the purpose of establishing and maintaining a list of the names and employer identification numbers of the stores and concerns for use in determining those applicants who have been previously sanctioned or convicted under section 12 or 15 of the Food Stamp Act of 1977 (7 U.S.C. 2021 or 2024). The Secretary of Agriculture may use this determination of sanctions and convictions in administering section 9 of the Food Stamp Act of 1977.

(c) *Sharing of information.*—(1) *Sharing permitted with certain United States agencies and instrumentalities.*—The Secretary of Agriculture may share the information contained in the list described in paragraph (b) of this section with any other agency or instrumentality of the United States that otherwise has access to employer identification numbers, but only to the extent the Secretary of Agriculture determines sharing such information will assist in verifying and matching that information against information maintained by the other agency or instrumentality.

(2) *Restrictions on the use of shared information.*—The information shared by the Secretary of Agriculture pursuant to this section may be used by any other agency or instrumentality of the United States only for the purpose of effective administration and enforcement of the Food Stamp Act of 1977 or for the purpose of investigation of violations of other Federal laws or enforcement of those laws.

(d) *Safeguards.*—(1) *Restrictions on access to employer identification numbers by individuals.*—(i) *Numbers maintained by the Secretary of Agriculture.*—The individuals who are permitted access to employer identification numbers obtained pursuant to paragraph (a) of this section and maintained by the Secretary of Agriculture are officers and employees of the United States whose duties or responsibilities require access to such employer identification numbers for the purpose of effective administration or enforcement of the Food Stamp Act of 1977 or for the purpose of sharing the information in accordance with paragraph (c) of this section.

(ii) *Numbers maintained by any other agency or instrumentality.*—The individuals who are permitted access to employer identification numbers obtained pursuant to paragraph (c) of this section and maintained by any agency or instrumentality of the United States other than the Department of Agriculture are officers and employees of the United States whose duties or responsibilities require access to such employer identification numbers for the purpose of effective administration and enforcement of the Food Stamp Act of 1977 or for the purpose of investigation of violations of other Federal laws or enforcement of those laws.

(2) *Other safeguards.*—The Secretary of Agriculture, and the head of any other agency or instrumentality referred to in paragraph (c) of this section, must provide for any additional safeguards that the Secretary of the Treasury determines to be necessary or appropriate to protect the confidentiality of the employer identification numbers. The Secretary of Agriculture, and the head of any other agency or instrumentality referred to in paragraph (c) of this section, may also provide for any additional safeguards to protect the confidentiality of employer identification numbers, provided these safeguards are consistent with safeguards determined by the Secretary of the Treasury to be necessary or appropriate.

(e) *Confidentiality and disclosure of employer identification numbers.*—Employer identification numbers obtained pursuant to paragraph (a) or (c) of this section are confidential. No officer or employee of the United States who has or had access to any such employer identification number may disclose that number in any manner to an individual not described in paragraph (d) of this section. For purposes of this paragraph (e), *officer or employee* includes a former officer or employee.

(f) *Sanctions.*—(1) *Unauthorized, willful disclosure of employer identification numbers.*—Sections 7213(a)(1), (2), and (3) apply with respect to the unauthorized, willful disclosure to any person of employer identification numbers that are maintained pursuant to this section by the Secretary of Agriculture, or any other agency or instrumentality with which information is shared pursuant to paragraph (c) of this section, in the same manner and to the same extent as sections 7213(a)(1), (2), and (3) apply with respect to unauthorized disclosures of returns and return information described in those sections.

(2) *Willful solicitation of employer identification numbers.*—Section 7213(a)(4) applies with respect to the willful offer of any item of material value in exchange for any employer identification number maintained pursuant to this section by the Secretary of Agriculture, or any other agency or instrumentality with which information is shared pursuant to paragraph (c) of this section, in the same manner and to the same extent as section 7213(a)(4) applies with respect to offers (in exchange for any return or return information) described in that section.

(g) *Delegation.*—All references in this section to the Secretary of Agriculture are references to the Secretary of Agriculture or his or her delegate.

(h) *Effective date.*—Except as provided in the following sentence, this section is effective on February 1, 1992. Any provisions relating to the sharing of information by the Secretary of Agriculture with any other agency or instrumentality of the United States are effective on August 15, 1994. [Reg. § 301.6109-2.]

☐ [*T.D. 8369, 9-30-91. Amended by T.D. 8621, 10-2-95.*]

[Reg. § 301.6109-3]

§ 301.6109-3. IRS adoption taxpayer identification numbers.—(a) *In general.*—(1) *Definition.*—An *IRS adoption taxpayer identification number*(ATIN) is a temporary taxpayer identifying number assigned by the Internal Revenue Service (IRS) to a child (other than an alien individual as defined in § 301.6109-1(d)(3)(i)) who has been placed, by an authorized placement agency, in the household of a prospective adoptive parent for legal adoption. An ATIN is assigned to the child upon application for use in connection with filing requirements under the Internal Revenue Code and the regulations thereunder. When an adoption becomes final, the adoptive parent must apply for a social security number for the child. After the social security number is assigned, that number, rather than the ATIN, must be used as the child's taxpayer identification number on all returns, statements, or other documents required under the Internal Revenue Code and the regulations thereunder.

(2) *Expiration and extension.*—An ATIN automatically expires two years after the number is assigned. However, upon request, the IRS may grant an extension if the IRS determines the extension is warranted.

(b) *Definitions.*—For purposes of this section—

(1) *Authorized placement agency.*—has the same meaning as in § 1.152-2(c) of this chapter;

(2) *Prospective adoptive child.*—or *child* means a child who has not been adopted, but who has been placed in the household of a prospective adoptive parent for legal adoption by an authorized placement agency; and

(3) *Prospective adoptive parent.*—or *parent* means an individual in whose household a prospective adoptive child is placed by an authorized placement agency for legal adoption.

(c) *General rule for obtaining a number.*— (1) *Who may apply.*—A prospective adoptive parent may apply for an ATIN for a child if—

(i) The prospective adoptive parent is eligible to claim a personal exemption under section 151 with respect to the child;

(ii) An authorized placement agency places the child with the prospective adoptive parent for legal adoption;

(iii) The Social Security Administration will not process an application for an SSN by the prospective adoptive parent on behalf of the child (for example, because the adoption is not final); and

(iv) The prospective adoptive parent has used all reasonable means to obtain the child's assigned social security number, if any, but has been unsuccessful in obtaining this number (for example, because the biological parent who obtained the number is not legally required to disclose the number to the prospective adoptive parent).

(2) *Procedure for obtaining an ATIN.*—If the requirements of paragraph (c)(1) of this section are satisfied, the prospective adoptive parent may apply for an ATIN for a child on Form W-7A, *Application for Taxpayer Identification Number for Pending Adoptions* (or such other form as may be prescribed by the IRS). An application for an ATIN should be made far enough in advance of the first intended use of the ATIN to permit issuance of the ATIN in time for such use. An application for an ATIN must include the information required by the form and accompanying instructions, including the name and address of each prospective adoptive parent and the child's name and date of birth. In addition, the application must include such documentary evidence as the IRS may prescribe to establish that a child was placed in the prospective adoptive parent's household by an authorized placement agency for legal adoption. Examples of acceptable documentary evidence establishing placement for legal adoption by an authorized placement agency may include—

(i) A copy of a placement agreement entered into between the prospective adoptive parent and an authorized placement agency;

(ii) An affidavit or letter signed by the adoption attorney or government official who placed the child for legal adoption pursuant to state law;

(iii) A document authorizing the release of a newborn child from a hospital to a prospective adoptive parent for adoption; and

(iv) A court document ordering or approving the placement of a child for adoption.

(d) *Effective date.*—The provisions of this section apply to income tax returns due (without regard to extension) on or after April 15, 1998. [Reg. § 301.6109-3.]

☐ [*T.D.* 8839, 9-21-99.]

[Reg. § 301.6109-4]

§ 301.6109-4. IRS truncated taxpayer identification numbers.—(a) *In general*—*Definition.*— An IRS truncated taxpayer identification number (TTIN) is an individual's social security number (SSN), IRS individual taxpayer identification number (ITIN), IRS adoption taxpayer identification number (ATIN), or IRS employer identification number (EIN) in which the first five digits of the nine-digit number are replaced with Xs or asterisks. The TTIN takes the same format of the identifying number it replaces, for example XXX-XX-1234 when replacing an SSN, or XX-XXX1234 when replacing an EIN.

(b) *Use of a TTIN.*—(1) *In general.*—Except as provided in paragraph (b)(2) of this section, a TTIN may be used to identify any person on any statement or other document that the internal revenue laws require to be furnished to another person. Use of a TTIN is permissive and not mandatory. Use of a TTIN as permitted by this section will not result in application of any penalty for failure to include a correct taxpayer identifying number on any payee statement or other document. For example, the section 6722 penalty for failure to timely furnish a correct statement would not apply solely because the payor used a TTIN as permitted by this section.

(2) *TTIN not permitted.*—Use of a TTIN is not permitted in the following circumstances:

(i) A TTIN may not be used on a statement or other document if such use is prohibited by statute, regulation, other guidance published in the Internal Revenue Bulletin, form, or instructions.

(ii) A TTIN may not be used on a statement or document if a statute, regulation, other guidance published in the Internal Revenue Bulletin, form, or instructions, specifically requires use of a SSN, ITIN, ATIN, or EIN. For example, a TTIN may not be used on a Form W-8ECI or Form W-8IMY because the forms and/or form instructions specifically prescribe use of an SSN, EIN, or ITIN for the U.S. taxpayer identification number.

(iii) A TTIN may not be used on any return, statement, or other document that is required to be filed with or furnished to the Internal Revenue Service.

(iv) A person may not truncate its own taxpayer identifying number on any statement or other document that it furnishes to another person. For example, an employer may not truncate its EIN on a Form W-2, Wage and Tax Statement, that the employer furnishes to an employee; and a person may not truncate its TIN on a Form W-9, Request for Taxpayer Identification Number and Certification.

(3) *Example.*—The provisions of paragraph (a) are illustrated by the following example:

Example. On April 5, year 1, Donor contributes a used car with a blue book value of $1100 to Charitable Organization. On April 20, year 1, Charitable Organization sends Donor copies B and C of the Form 1098-C as a contemporaneous written acknowledgement of the $1100 contribution as required by section 170(f)(12). In late-February, year 2, Charitable Organization prepares and files copy A of Form 1098-C with the IRS, reporting Donor's donation of a qualified vehicle in year 1. The Charitable Organization may use a TTIN in lieu of Donor's complete SSN in the Donor's Identification Number box on copies B and C of the Form 1098-C because copies B and C of the Form 1098-C are documents required by the Internal Revenue Code and regulations to be furnished to another person, there are no applicable statutes, regulations, other published guidance, forms or instructions, that prohibit the use of a TTIN on those copies, and, there are no applicable statutes, regulations, other published guidance, forms, or instructions that specifically require use of an SSN or other identifying number on those copies. A TTIN cannot be used on copy A of the Form 1098-C, however, because copy A is required to be filed with the IRS.

(c) *Effective/applicability date.*—This section applies on and after July 15, 2014. [Reg. § 301.6109-4.]

☐ [*T.D.* 9675, 7-14-2014.]

[Reg. § 301.6110-1]

§ 301.6110-1. Public inspection of written determinations and background file documents.—(a) *General rule.*—Except as provided in § 301.6110-3, relating to deletion of certain information, § 301.6110-5(b), relating to actions to restrain disclosure, paragraph (b)(2) of this section, relating to technical advice memoranda involving civil fraud and criminal investigations, and jeopardy and termination assessments, and paragraph (b)(3) of this section, relating to general written determinations relating to accounting or funding periods and methods, the text of any written determination (as defined in § 301.6110-2(a)) issued pursuant to a request postmarked or hand delivered after October 31, 1976, shall be open to public inspection in the places provided in paragraph (c)(1) of this section. The text of any written determination issued pursuant to a request postmarked or hand delivered before November 1, 1976, shall be open to public inspection pursuant to section 6110(h) and § 301.6110-6, when funds are appropriated by Congress for such purpose. The procedures and rules set forth in § § 301.6110-1 through 301.6110-5 and § 301.6110-7 do not apply to written determinations issued pursuant to requests postmarked or hand delivered before November 1, 1976, unless § 301.6110-6 states otherwise. There shall also be open to public inspection in each place of public inspection an index to the written determinations subject to inspection at such place. Each such index shall be arranged by section of the Internal Revenue Code, related statute or tax treaty and by subject matter description within such section in such manner as the Commissioner may from time to time provide. The Commissioner shall not be required to make any written determination or background file document open to public inspection pursuant to section 6110 or refrain from disclosure of any such documents or any information therein, except as provided by section 6110 or with respect to a discovery order made in connection with a judicial proceeding. The provisions of section 6110 shall not apply to material that is open to public inspection under section 6104. See section 6110(l)(1).

(b) *Items that may be inspected only under certain circumstances.*—(1) *Background file documents.*—A background file document (as such term is defined in § 301.6110-2(g)) relating to a particular written determination issued pursuant to a request postmarked or hand delivered after October 31, 1976, shall not be subject to inspection until such written determination is open to public inspection or available for inspection pursuant to paragraph (b)(2) or (3) of this section, and then only if a written request pursuant to paragraph (c)(4) of this section is made for inspection of such background file document. Background file documents relating to written determinations issued pursuant to requests postmarked or hand delivered before November 1, 1976, shall be subject to inspection pursuant to section 6110(h) and § 301.6110-6, when funds are appropriated by Congress for such purpose. The version of the background file document which is available for inspection shall be the version originally made available for inspection, as modified by any additional disclosure pursuant to section 6110(d)(3) and (f)(4).

(2) *Technical advice memoranda involving civil fraud and criminal investigations, jeopardy and termination assessments.*—Any technical advice memorandum (as such term is defined in § 301.6110-2(f)) involving any matter that is the subject of a civil fraud or criminal investigation, a jeopardy assessment (as such term is defined in section 6861), or a termination assessment (as such term is defined in section 6851) shall not be subject to inspection until all actions relating to such investigation or assessment are completed and then only if a written request pursuant to paragraph (c)(4) of this section is made for inspection of such technical advice memorandum. A "civil fraud investigation" is any administrative step or judicial proceeding in which an issue for determination is whether the Commissioner should impose additional tax pursuant to section 6653(b). A "criminal investigation" is any administrative step or judicial proceeding in which an issue for determination is whether a taxpayer

should be charged with or is guilty of criminal conduct. An action relating to a civil fraud or criminal investigation includes any such administrative step or judicial proceeding, the review of subsequent related activities and related returns of the taxpayer or related taxpayers, and any other administrative step or judicial procedure or proceeding or appellate process that is initiated as a consequence of the facts and circumstances disclosed by such investigation. An action relating to a jeopardy or termination assessment includes any administrative step or judicial proceeding that is initiated to determine whether to make such assessment, that is brought pursuant to section 7429 to determine the appropriateness or reasonableness of such assessment, or that is brought to resolve the legal consequences of the tax status or liability issue underlying the making of such assessment. Any action relating to a civil fraud or criminal investigation, a jeopardy assessment, or a termination assessment is not completed until all available administrative steps and judicial proceedings and remedies, including appeals, have been completed.

(3) *Written determinations with respect to adoption of or change in certain accounting or funding periods and methods.*—Any general written determination (as defined in § 301.6110-2(c)) that relates solely to approval of any adoption of or change in:

(i) The funding method or plan year of a plan under section 412,

(ii) A taxpayer's annual accounting period under section 442,

(iii) A taxpayer's method of accounting under section 446(e), or

(iv) A partnership's or partner's taxable year under section 706

shall not be subject to inspection until such written determination would, but for this paragraph (b)(3), be open to public inspection pursuant to § 301.6110-5(c) and then only if a written request pursuant to paragraph (c)(4) of this section is made for inspection of such written determination.

(c) *Procedure for public inspection.*—(1) *Place of public inspection.*—The text of any ruling (as such term is defined in § 301.6110-2(d)) or technical advice memorandum that is open to public inspection pursuant to section 6110 shall be located in the National Office Reading Room. The text of any determination letter (as such term is defined in § 301.6110-2(e)) that is open to public inspection pursuant to section 6110 shall be located in the Reading Room of the Regional Office in which is located the district office that issued such determination letter. Inspection of any written determination subject to inspection only upon written request shall be requested from the National Office Reading Room. Inspection of any background file document shall be requested only from the reading room in which the related written determination is either open to public inspection or subject to inspection upon written request. The locations and mailing addresses of the reading rooms are set forth in § 601.702(b)(3)(ii) of this chapter.

(2) *Time and manner of public inspection.*— The inspection authorized by section 6110 will be allowed only in the place provided for such inspection in the presence of an Internal Revenue officer or employee and only during the regular hours of business of the Internal Revenue Service office in which the reading room is located. The public will not be allowed to remove any record from a reading room. A person who wishes to inspect reading room material without visiting a reading room may submit a written request pursuant to paragraph (c)(4) of this section for copies of any such material to the Internal Revenue Service reading room in which is located such material.

(3) *Copies.*—Notes may be taken of any material open to public inspection under section 6110, and copies may be made manually. Copies of any material open to public inspection or subject to inspection upon written request will be furnished by the Internal Revenue Service to any person making requests therefor pursuant to paragraph (c)(4) of this section. If made at the time of inspection, the request for copies need not be in writing, unless the material is not immediately available for copying. The Commissioner may prescribe fees pursuant to section 6110(j) for furnishing copies of material open or subject to inspection.

(4) *Requests.*—Any request for copies of written determinations, for inspection of general written determinations relating to accounting or funding periods and methods or technical advice memoranda involving civil fraud and criminal investigations, and jeopardy and termination assessments, for inspection or copies of background file documents, and for copies of the index shall be submitted to the reading room in which is located the requested material. If made in person, the request may be submitted to the Internal Revenue employee supervising the reading room. The request shall contain:

(i) Authorization for the Internal Revenue Service to charge the person making such request for making copies, searching for material, and making deletions therefrom;

(ii) The maximum amount of charges which the Internal Revenue Service may incur without further authorization from the person making such request;

(iii) With respect to requests for inspection and copies of background file documents, the file number of the written determination to which such background file document relates and a specific identification of the nature or type of the background file document requested;

(iv) With respect to requests for inspection of general written determinations relating to accounting or funding periods and methods, the day, week, or month of issuance of such written determination, and the applicable category as

selected from a special summary listing of categories prepared by the Internal Revenue Service;

(v) With respect to requests for copies of written determinations, the file number of the written determination to be copied, which can be ascertained in the reading room or from the index;

(vi) With respect to requests for copies of portions of the index, the section of the Internal Revenue Code, related statute or tax treaty in which the person making such request is interested;

(vii) With respect to material which is to be mailed, the name, address, and telephone number of the person making such request and the address to which copies of the requested material should be sent; and

(viii) Such other information as the Internal Revenue Service may from time to time require in its operation of reading rooms.

(d) *Effective/applicability date.*—The rules of paragraph (a) apply February 29, 2012. [Reg. § 301.6110-1.]

☐ [*T.D.* 7524, 12-15-77. *Amended by T.D.* 9581, 2-28-2012.]

[Reg. § 301.6110-2]

§ 301.6110-2. **Meanings of terms.**—(a) *Written determination.*—A "written determination" is a ruling, a determination letter, or a technical advice memorandum, as such terms are defined in paragraphs (d), (e), and (f) of this section, respectively. Notwithstanding paragraphs (d) through (f) of this section, a written determination does not include, for example, opinion letters (as defined in § 601.201(a)(4) of this chapter), information letters (as defined in § 601.201(a)(5) of this chapter), technical information responses, technical assistance memoranda, notices of deficiency, reports on claims for refund, Internal Revenue Service decisions to accept taxpayers' offers in compromise, earnings and profits determinations, or documents issued by the Internal Revenue Service in the course of tax administration that are not disclosed to the persons to whose tax returns or tax liability the documents relate.

(b) *Reference written determination.*—A "reference written determination" is any written determination that the Commissioner determines to have significant reference value. Any written determination that the Commissioner determines to be the basis for a published Revenue Ruling is a reference written determination until such Revenue Ruling is obsoleted, revoked, superseded or otherwise held to have no effect.

(c) *General written determination.*—A "general written determination" is any written determination that is not a reference written determination.

(d) *Ruling.*—A "ruling" is a written statement issued by the National Office to a taxpayer or to the taxpayer's authorized representative (as such term is defined in § 601.201(e)(7) of this chapter) on behalf of the taxpayer, that interprets and applies tax laws to a specific set of facts. A ruling generally recites the relevant facts, sets forth the applicable provisions of law, and shows the application of the law to the facts.

(e) *Determination letter.*—A "determination letter" is a written statement issued by a district director in response to a written inquiry by an individual or an organization that applies principles and precedents previously announced by the National Office to the particular facts involved.

(f) *Technical advice memorandum.*—A "technical advice memorandum" is a written statement issued by the National Office to, and adopted by, a district director in connection with the examination of a taxpayer's return or consideration of a taxpayer's claim for refund or credit. A technical advice memorandum generally recites the relevant facts, sets forth the applicable law, and states a legal conclusion.

(g) *Background file document.*—(1) *General rule.*—A "background file document" is:

(i) The request for a written determination.

(ii) Any written material submitted in support of such request by the person by whom or on whose behalf the request for a written determination was made.

(iii) Any written communication, or memorandum of a meeting, telephone communication, or other contact, between employees of the Internal Revenue Service or Office of its Chief Counsel and persons outside the Internal Revenue Service in connection with such request or written determination which is received prior to the issuance (as such term is defined in paragraph (h) of this section) of the written determination, but not including communications described in paragraph (g)(2) of this section, and

(iv) Any subsequent communication between the National Office and a district director concerning the factual circumstances underlying the request for a technical advice memorandum, or concerning a request by the district director for reconsideration by the National Office of a proposed technical advice memorandum.

(2) *Limitations.*—Notwithstanding paragraph (g)(1) of this section, a "background file document" shall not include any:

(i) Communication between the Department of Justice and the Internal Revenue Service or the Office of its Chief Counsel relating to any pending civil or criminal case or investigation,

(ii) Communication between Internal Revenue Service employees and employees of the Office of its Chief Counsel,

(iii) Internal memorandum or attorney work product prepared by the Internal Revenue Service or Office of its Chief Counsel which relates to the development of the conclusion of the Internal Revenue Service in a written determination, including, with respect to a technical advice memorandum, the Transmittal Memorandum, as defined in §601.105(b)(5)(vi)(*c*) of this chapter,

(iv) Correspondence or any portion of correspondence between the Internal Revenue Service and any person relating solely to the making of or extent of deletions pursuant to section 6110(c), or a request pursuant to section 6110(g)(3) and (4) for postponement of the time at which a written determination is made open or subject to inspection,

(v) Material relating to (A) a request for a ruling or determination letter that is withdrawn prior to issuance thereof or that the Internal Revenue Service declines to answer, (B) a request for technical advice that the National Office declines to answer, or (C) the appeal of a taxpayer from the decision of a district director not to seek technical advice, or

(vi) Response to a request for technical advice which the district director declines to adopt, and the district director's request for reconsideration thereof.

(h) *Issuance.*—"Issuance" of a written determination occurs, with respect to rulings and determination letters, upon the mailing of the ruling or determination letter to the person to whom it pertains. Issuance of a technical advice memorandum occurs upon the adoption of the technical advice memorandum by the district director.

(i) *Person to whom written determination pertains.*—A "person to whom a written determination pertains" is the person by whom a ruling or determination letter is requested, but if requested by an authorized representative, the person on whose behalf the request is made. With respect to a technical advice memorandum, a "person to whom a written determination pertains" is the taxpayer whose return is being examined or whose claim for refund or credit is being considered.

(j) *Person to whom a background file document relates.*—A "person to whom a background file document relates" is the person to whom the related written determination pertains, as such term is defined in paragraph (i) of this section.

(k) *Person who has a direct interest in maintaining confidentiality.*—A "person who has direct interest in maintaining the confidentiality of a written determination" is any person whose name and address is listed in the request for such written determination, as required by §601.201(e)(2) of this chapter. A "person who has a direct interest in maintaining the confidentiality of a background file document" is any person whose name and address is in such background file document, or who has a direct interest in maintaining the confidentiality of the written determination to which such background file document relates.

(l) *Successor in interest.*—A "successor in interest" to any person to whom a written determination pertains or background file document relates is any person who acquires the rights and assumes the liabilities of such person with respect to the transaction which was the subject matter of the written determination, provided that the successor in interest notifies the Commissioner with respect to the succession in interest. [Reg. § 301.6110-2.]

☐ [T.D. 7524, 12-15-77.]

[Reg. § 301.6110-3]

§ 301.6110-3. Deletion of certain information in written determinations open to public inspection.—(a) *Information subject to deletion.*—There shall be deleted from the text of any written determination open to public inspection or subject to inspection upon written request and background file document subject to inspection upon written request pursuant to section 6110 the following types of information:

(1) *Identifying details.*—(i) The names, addresses, and identifying numbers (including telephone, license, social security, employer identification, credit card, and selective service numbers) of any person, other than the identifying details of a person who makes a third-party communication described in § 301.6110-4(a), and

(ii) Any other information that would permit a person generally knowledgeable with respect to the appropriate community to identify any person. The determination of whether information would permit identification of a particular person will be made in view of information available to the public at the time the written determination or background file document is made open or subject to inspection and in view of information that will subsequently become available, provided the Internal Revenue Service is made aware of such information and the potential that such information may identify any person. The "appropriate community" is that group of persons who would be able to associate a particular person with a category of transactions one of which is described in the written determination or background file document. The appropriate community may vary according to the nature of the transaction which is the subject of the written determination. For example, if a steel company proposes to enter a transaction involving the purchase and installation of blast furnaces, the "appropriate community" may include all steel producers and blast furnace manufacturers, but if the installation process is a unique process of which everyone in national industry is aware, the "appropriate community" might also include the national industrial community. On the other hand, if the steel company proposes to enter a transaction involving the purchase of land on which to construct a building to house the blast furnaces, the "appropriate community" may also include those residing or doing business within the geographical locale of the land to be purchased.

(2) *Information concerning national defense and foreign policy.*—Information specifically authorized under criteria established by an Executive order to be kept secret in the interest of national defense or foreign policy and which is in fact properly classified pursuant to such order.

(3) *Information exempted by other statutes and agency rules.*—Information specifically exempted from disclosure by any statute other than the Internal Revenue Code of 1954 and 5 U.S.C. 552 which is applicable to the Internal Revenue Service, and any information obtained by the Internal Revenue Service solely and directly from another Federal agency subject to a nondisclosure rule of such agency. Deletion of information shall not be made solely because the same information was submitted to another Federal agency subject to a nondisclosure rule applicable only to such agency.

(4) *Trade secrets and privileged or confidential commercial or financial information.*—(i) *Deletions to be made.*—Any—

(A) Trade secrets, and

(B) Commercial or financial information obtained from any person which, despite the fact that identifying details are deleted pursuant to paragraph (a)(1) of this section, nonetheless remains privileged or confidential.

(ii) *Trade secret.*—For purposes of paragraph (a)(4)(i)(A) of this section, a trade secret may consist of any formula, pattern, device or compilation of information that is used in one's business, and that gives one an opportunity to obtain an advantage over competitors who do not know or use it. It may be a formula for a chemical compound, a process of manufacturing, treating or preserving materials, a pattern for a machine or other device, or a list of customers. The subject of a trade secret must be secret, that is, it must not be of public knowledge or of a general knowledge in the trade or business. Novelty, in the patent law sense, is not required for a trade secret.

(iii) *Privileged or confidential.*—For purposes of paragraph (a)(4)(i)(B) of this section, information is privileged or confidential if from examination of the request and supporting documents relating to a written determination, and in consideration of the fact that identifying details are deleted pursuant to paragraph (a)(1) of this section, it is determined that disclosure of such information would cause substantial harm to the competitive position of any person. For example, while determining whether disclosure of certain information would cause substantial harm to X's competitive position, the Internal Revenue Service becomes aware that this information has previously been disclosed to the public. In this situation, the Internal Revenue Service will not agree with X's argument that disclosure of the information would cause substantial harm to X's competitive position. An example of information previously disclosed to the public is financial information contained in the published annual reports of widely held public corporations.

(5) *Information within the ambit of personal privacy.*—Information the disclosure of which would constitute a clearly unwarranted invasion of personal privacy, despite the fact that identifying details are deleted pursuant to paragraph (a)(1) of this section. Personal privacy informa-

tion encompasses embarrassing or sensitive information that a reasonable person would not reveal to the public under ordinary circumstances. Matters of personal privacy include, but are not limited to, details not yet public of a pending divorce, medical treatment for physical or mental disease or injury, adoption of a child, the amount of a gift, and political preferences. A clearly unwarranted invasion of personal privacy exists if from analysis of information submitted in support of the request for a written determination it is determined that the public interest purpose for requiring disclosure is outweighed by the potential harm attributable to such invasion of personal privacy.

(6) *Information concerning agency regulation of financial institutions.*—Information contained in or related to reports prepared by, on behalf of, or for the use of an agency responsible for the regulation or supervision of financial institutions concerning examination, operation or condition of a financial institution, disclosure of which would damage the standing of such financial institution.

(7) *Information concerning wells.*—Geological or geophysical information and data, including maps, concerning wells.

(b) *Manner of deletions.*—Whenever information, which is not to be disclosed pursuant to section 6110(c), is deleted from the text of a written determination or background file document, substitutions therefore shall be made to the extent feasible if necessary for an understanding of the legal analysis developed in such written determination or to make the disclosed text of a background file document comprehensible. Wherever any material is deleted, an indication of such deletion, and of any substitution therefor, shall be made in such manner as the Commissioner deems appropriate.

(c) *Limitations on the making of deletions.*—Any portion of a written determination or background file document that has been deleted will be restored to the text thereof—

(1) If pursuant to section 6110(d)(3) or (f)(4)(A) a court orders disclosure of such portion, or

(2) If pursuant to § 301.6110-5(d)(1) an agreement is reached to disclose information. [Reg. § 301.6110-3.]

☐ [T.D. 7524, 12-15-77.]

[Reg. § 301.6110-4]

§ 301.6110-4. Communications from third parties.—(a) *General rule.*—Except as provided in paragraph (b) of this section, a record will be made of any communication, whether written, by telephone, at a meeting, or otherwise, received by the Internal Revenue Service or Office of its Chief Counsel prior to the issuance of a written determination from any person other than a person to whom the written determination pertains or the authorized respresentative of such person. This rule applies to any communi-

cation concerning such written determination, any communication concerning the request for such written determination, or any communication concerning other matters involving such written determination. A notation that such communication has been made shall be placed on such written determination when it is made open to public inspection or available for inspection upon written request pursuant to § 301.6110-5. The notation to be placed on a written determination shall consist of the date on which the communication was received and the category of the person making such communication, for example, Congressional, Department of Commerce, Treasury, trade association, White House, educational institution. Any person may request the Internal Revenue Service to disclose the name of any person about whom a notation has been made pursuant to this paragraph.

(b) *Limitations.*—The provisions of paragraph (a) of this section shall not apply to communications received by the Internal Revenue Service from employees of the Internal Revenue Service or Office of its Chief Counsel, from the Chief of Staff of the Joint Committee on Internal Revenue Taxation, from the Department of Justice with respect to any pending civil or criminal case or investigation, or from another government agency in response to a request made by the Internal Revenue Service to such agency for assistance involving the expertise of such agency.

(c) *Action to obtain disclosure of identity of person to whom written determination pertains.*—(1) *Creation of remedy.*—With respect to any written determination on which a notation has been placed pursuant to paragraph (a) of this section, any person may file a petition in the United States Tax Court or file a complaint in the United States District Court for the District of Columbia for an order requiring that the identity of any person to whom such written determination pertains be disclosed, but such petition or complaint must be filed within 36 months of the date such written determination is made open or subject to inspection.

(2) *Necessary disclosure.*—Whenever an action is brought pursuant to section 6110(d)(3), the court may order that the identity of any person to whom the written determination pertains be disclosed. Such disclosure may be ordered if the court determines that there is evidence in the record from which it could reasonably be concluded that an impropriety occurred or undue influence was exercised with respect to such written determination by or on behalf of the person to whom the written determination pertains. The court may, pursuant to section 6110(d)(3), also order the disclosure of any material deleted pursuant to section 6110(c) if such disclosure is in the public interest. The written determination or background file document with respect to which the disclosure was sought shall be revised to disclose the information which the court orders to be disclosed.

(3) *Required notice.*—If a proceeding is commenced pursuant to section 6110(d)(3) and paragraph (c)(1) of this section with respect to any written determination, the Secretary shall send notice of the commencement of such proceeding to any person whose identity is subject to being disclosed and to the person about whom a third-party communication notation has been made pursuant to section 6110(d)(1). Such notice shall be sent, by registered or certified mail, to the last known address of the persons described in this paragraph (c)(3) within 15 days after notice of the petition or complaint filed pursuant to section 6110(d)(3) is served on the Secretary. For further guidance regarding the definition of last known address, see § 301.6212-2.

(4) *Intervention.*—Any person who is entitled to receive notice pursuant to paragraph (c)(3) of this section shall have the right to intervene in any action brought pursuant to section 6110(d)(3). If appropriate such person shall be permitted to intervene anonymously. [Reg. § 301.6110-4.]

☐ [*T.D. 7524, 12-15-77. Amended by T.D. 8939,* 1-11-2001.]

[Reg. § 301.6110-5]

§ 301.6110-5. Notice and time requirements; actions to restrain disclosure; actions to obtain additional disclosure.—(a) *Notice.*—(1) *General rule.*—Before a written determination is made open to public inspection or subject to inspection upon written request, or before a background file document is subject to inspection upon written request, the person to whom the written determination pertains or background file document relates shall be notified by the Commissioner of intention to disclose such written determination or background file document. The notice with respect to a written determination, other than a written determination described in § 301.6110-1(b)(2) or (3) shall be mailed when such written determination is issued. The notice with respect to any written determination relating to accounting or funding periods and methods, any technical advice memoranda involving civil fraud and criminal investigations, and jeopardy and termination assessments, and any background file document shall be mailed within a reasonable time after the receipt of the first written request for inspection thereof.

(2) *Contents of notice.*—The notice required by paragraph (a)(1) of this section shall—

(i) Include a copy of the text of the written determination or background file document, which the Commissioner proposes to make open to public inspection or subject to inspection pursuant to a written request, on which is indicated (A) the material that the Commissioner proposes to delete pursuant to section 6110(c), (B) any substitutions proposed to be made therefor, and (C) any third-party communication notations required to be placed pursuant to § 301.6110-4(a) on the face of the written determination,

(ii) State that the written determination or background file document is to be open to public inspection or subject to inspection pursuant to a written request pursuant to section 6110,

(iii) State that the recipient of the notice has the right to seek administrative remedies pursuant to paragraph (b)(1) of this section and to commence judicial proceedings pursuant to section 6110(f)(3) within indicated time periods, and

(iv) Prominently indicate the date on which the notice is mailed.

(b) *Actions to restrain disclosure.*—(1) *Administrative remedies.*—Any person to whom a written determination pertains or background file document relates, and any successor in interest, executor or authorized representative of such person may pursue the administrative remedies described in § 601.105(b)(5)(iii)(*i*) and (vi)(*f*) and § 601.201(e)(11) and (16) of this chapter. Any person who has a direct interest in maintaining the confidentiality of any written determination or background file document or portion thereof may pursue the administrative remedies described in § 601.105(b)(5)(vi)(*f*) and § 601.201(e)(16) of this chapter. No person about whom a third-party communication notation has been made pursuant to § 301.6110-4(a) may pursue any administrative remedy for the purpose of restraining disclosure of the identity of such person where such identity appears with respect to the making of such third-party communication.

(2) *Judicial remedy.*—Except as provided in paragraph (b)(3) of this section, any person permitted to resort to administrative remedies pursuant to paragraph (b)(1) of this section may, if such person proposes any deletion not made pursuant to § 301.6110-3 by the Commissioner, file a petition in the United States Tax Court pursuant to section 6110(f)(3) for a determination with respect to such proposed deletion. If appropriate, such petition may be filed anonymously. Any petition filed pursuant to section 6110(f)(3) must be filed within 60 days after the date on which the Commissioner mails the notice of intention to disclose required by section 6110(f)(1).

(3) *Limitations on right to bring judicial actions.*—No petition shall be filed pursuant to section 6110(f)(3) unless the administrative remedies provided by paragraph (b)(1) of this section have been exhausted. However, if the petitioner has responded within the prescribed time period to the notice pursuant to section 6110(f)(1) of intention to disclose, but has not received the final administrative conclusion of the Internal Revenue Service within 50 days after the date on which the Commissioner mails the notice of intention to disclose required by section 6110(f)(1), the petitioner may file a petition pursuant to section 6110(f)(3). No judicial action with respect to any written determination or background file document shall be commenced pursuant to section 6110(f)(3) by any person who has received a notice with respect to such written

determination or background file document pursuant to paragraph (b)(4) of this section.

(4) *Required notice.*—If a proceeding is commenced pursuant to section 6110(f)(3) with respect to any written determination or background file document, the Secretary shall send notice of the commencement of such proceeding to any person to whom such written determination pertains or to whom such background file document relates. No notice is required to be sent to persons who have filed the petition that commenced the proceeding pursuant to section 6110(f)(3) with respect to such written determination or background file document. The notice shall be sent, by registered or certified mail, to the last known address of the persons described in this paragraph (b)(4) within 15 days after notice of the petition filed pursuant to section 6110(f)(3) is served on the Secretary. For further guidance regarding the definition of last known address, see § 301.6212-2.

(5) *Intervention.*—Any person who is entitled to receive notice pursuant to paragraph (b)(4) of this section shall have the right to intervene in any action brought pursuant to this section. If appropriate, such person shall be permitted to intervene anonymously.

(c) *Time at which open to public inspection.*— (1) *General rule.*—Except as otherwise provided in paragraph (c)(2) of this section, the text of any written determination or background file document open to public inspection or available for inspection upon written request pursuant to section 6110 shall be made open to or available for inspection no earlier than 75 days and no later than 90 days after the date on which the Commissioner mails the notice required by paragraph (a)(1) of this section. However, if an action is brought pursuant to section 6110(f)(3) to restrain disclosure of any portion of such written determination or background file document the disputed portion of such written determination or background file document shall be made open to or available for inspection pursuant to paragraph (c)(2)(i) of this section.

(2) *Limitations.*—(i) *Court order.*—The portion of the text of any written determination or background file document that was subject to an action pursuant to section 6110(f)(3) to restrain disclosure in which the court determined that such disclosure should not be restrained shall be made open to or available for inspection within 30 days of the date that the court order becomes final. However, in no event shall such portion of the text of such written determination or background file document be made open to or available for inspection earlier than 75 days after the date on which the Commissioner mails the notice of intention to disclose required by section 6110(f)(1) and paragraph (a)(1) of this section. Such 30-day period may be extended for such time as the court finds necessary to allow the Commissioner to comply with its decision. Any portion of a written determination or background file document which a court orders open

to public inspection or subject to inspection upon written request pursuant to section 6110(f)(4) or disclosed pursuant to section 6110(d)(3) shall be made open or subject to inspection or disclosed within such time as the court provides.

(ii) *Postponement based on incomplete status of underlying transaction.*—(A) *Initial period not to exceed 90 days.*—The time period set forth in paragraph (c)(1) of this section within which a written determination shall be made open to public inspection or available for inspection upon written request shall be extended, upon the written request of the person to whom such written determination pertains or the authorized representative of such person, until 15 days after the date on which the transaction set forth in the written determination is scheduled to be completed, but such day shall be no later than 180 days after the date on which the Commissioner mails the notice of intention to disclose.

(B) *Additional period.*—The time period determined pursuant to paragraph (c)(2)(ii)(A) of this section shall be further extended upon an additional written request, if the Commissioner determines from the information contained in such request that good cause exists to warrant such extension. This further extension shall be until 15 days after the date on which the transaction set forth in the written determination is expected to be completed, but such day shall be no later than 360 days after the date on which the Commissioner mails the notice of intention to disclose. The good cause required by this (B) exists if the person requesting the delay in inspection demonstrates to the satisfaction of the Commissioner that it is likely that the lack of such extension will cause interference with consummation of the pending transaction.

(C) *Written request for extension.*—The written request for extension of the time when a written determination is to be made open to public inspection or available for inspection upon written request shall set forth the date on which it is expected that the underlying transaction will be completed, and, with respect to the additional extension described in paragraph (c)(2)(ii)(B) of this section, set forth the reason for requesting such extension. A request for extension of time may not be submitted until the notice of intention to disclose is mailed and must be received by the Internal Revenue Service office which issued such written determination no later than—

(1) In the case of the initial extension, 60 days after the date on which the Commissioner mails the notice of intention to disclose, or

(2) In the case of the additional extension, 15 days before the day on which, for purposes of paragraph (c)(2)(ii)(A) of this section, the transaction set forth in the written determination was expected to have been completed.

(D) *Notice and determination of actual completion.*—If an extension of time for inspection has been granted, and the transaction is completed prior to the day on which it was expected to have been completed, the Internal Revenue Service office which issued such written determination shall be so notified by the person who requested such extension. In such event, the written determination shall be made open to public inspection or available for inspection upon written request on the earlier of (1) 30 days after the day on which the Commissioner is notified that the transaction is completed, or (2) the day on which the written determination was scheduled to be made open to public inspection or available for inspection upon written request pursuant to paragraph (c)(2)(ii) of this section. Similarly, if the Commissioner determines that the transaction was completed prior to the day on which it was expected to have been completed, even if the person requesting such extension has not so notified the Internal Revenue Service, the written determination shall be made open to public inspection or available for inspection upon written request on the earlier of (1) the day which is 30 days after the Commissioner ascertains that the transaction is completed sooner than has been expected, or (2) the day on which the written determination was scheduled to be made open to public inspection or available for inspection upon written request pursuant to paragraph (c)(2)(ii) of this section.

(d) *Actions to obtain additional disclosure.*— (1) *Administrative remedies.*—Under section 6110(f)(4) any person may seek to obtain additional disclosure of information contained in any written determination or background file document that has been made open or subject to inspection. A request for such additional disclosure shall be submitted to the Internal Revenue Service office which issued such written determination, or to which the request for inspection of such background file document has been submitted pursuant to § 301.6110-1(c)(4), and must contain the file number of the written determination or a description of the background file document (including the file number of the related written determination), the deleted information which in the opinion of such person should be open or subject to inspection, and the basis for such opinion. If the Internal Revenue Service determines that the request constitutes a request for disclosure of the name, address, or the identifying numbers described in § 301.6110-3(a)(1)(i) of any person, it shall within a reasonable time notify the person requesting such disclosure that disclosure will not be made. If the Internal Revenue Service determines that the request or any portion thereof constitutes a request for disclosure of information other than the name, address, or the identifying numbers described in § 301.6110-3(a)(1)(i) of any person, it shall send a notice that such additional disclosure has been requested to any person to whom the written determination pertains or background file document relates, and to all persons who are identified by name and address in the written determination or background file document. Notice that such persons have been contacted shall

be sent to the person requesting the additional disclosure. The notice that additional disclosure has been requested shall state that the Internal Revenue Service has determined that additional disclosure of information other than the name, address, or the identifying numbers described in § 301.6110-3(a)(1)(i) of any person has been requested, inform the recipient of the notice that the person seeking the additional disclosure has the right under section 6110(f)(4) to bring a judicial action to attempt to compel such disclosure, and request the recipient of the notice to reply within 20 days by submitting a statement of whether or not the recipient of the notice agrees to the requested disclosure or portion thereof. If all persons to whom a notice is sent pursuant to this (1) agree to disclose the requested information or any portion thereof, the person seeking such disclosure will be so informed; the written determination or background file document shall be accordingly revised to disclose the information with respect to which an agreement to disclose has been reached. If any of the persons to whom a notice is sent pursuant to this (1) do not agree to the additional disclosure or do not respond to such notice, the Internal Revenue Service shall within a reasonable time so notify the person requesting such disclosure, and deny the request for additional disclosure.

(2) *Judicial remedy.*—Except as provided in paragraph (d)(3) of this section, any person who seeks to obtain additional disclosure of information contained in any written determination or background file document may file a petition pursuant to section 6110(f)(4) in the United States Tax Court or a complaint in the United States District Court for the District of Columbia for an order requiring that such information be made open or subject to inspection. Nothing in this paragraph shall prevent the Commissioner from disposing of written determinations and related background file documents pursuant to § 301.6110-7(a).

(3) *Limitations on right to bring judicial action.*—(i) *Exhaustion of administrative remedies.*— No petition or complaint shall be filed pursuant to section 6110(f)(4) unless the administrative remedies provided by paragraph (d)(1) of this section have been exhausted. However, if the Internal Revenue Service does not approve or deny the request for additional disclosure within 180 days after the request is submitted, the person making the request may file a petition pursuant to section 6110(f)(4).

(ii) *Actions to obtain identity.*—No petition or complaint shall be filed pursuant to section 6110(f)(4) to obtain disclosure of the identity of any person to whom a written determination on which a third-party communication notation has been placed pursuant to § 301.6110-4(a) pertains. Such actions shall be brought pursuant to section 6110(d)(3).

(4) *Required notice.*—If a proceeding is commenced pursuant to section 6110(f)(4) with respect to any written determination or

background file document, the Secretary shall send notice of the commencement of such proceeding to any person to whom the written determination pertains or background file document relates, and to all persons who are identified by name and address in the written determination or background file document. The notice shall be sent, by registered or certified mail, to the last known address of the persons described in this paragraph (d)(4) within 15 days after notice of the petition or complaint filed pursuant to section 6110(f)(4) is served on the Secretary.

(5) *Intervention.*—Any person who is entitled to receive notice pursuant to paragraph (d)(4) of this section shall have the right to intervene in any action brought pursuant to this section. If appropriate, such person shall be permitted to intervene anonymously. [Reg. §301.6110-5.]

☐ [*T.D. 7524, 12-15-77. Amended by T.D. 8939, 1-11-2001.*]

[Reg. §301.6110-6]

§301.6110-6. Written determinations issued in response to requests submitted before November 1, 1976.—(a) *Inspection of written determinations and background file documents.*—(1) *General rule.*—Except as provided in this section, the text of any written determination issued in response to a request postmarked or hand delivered before November 1, 1976 and any related background file document shall be open or subject to inspection in accordance with the rules in §§301.6110-1 through 301.6110-5 and 301.6110-7. However, the rules in §301.6110-4 do not apply to inspection under this section. The rules in §301.6110-5(a), (b) and (c) also do not apply, except with respect to background file documents.

(2) *Exclusions.*—The following written determinations are not open or subject to inspection:

(i) Written determinations with respect to matters for which the determination of whether public inspection should occur is made under section 6104. Some of these matters are listed in §301.6110-1(a).

(ii) Written determinations issued before September 2, 1974, dealing with the qualification of a plan described in section 6104(a)(1)(B)(i) or the exemption from tax under section 501(a) of an organization forming part of such a plan.

(iii) General written determinations that related solely to accounting or funding periods and methods, as defined in §301.6110-1(b)(3).

(iv) Determination letters.

(v) Written determinations issued pursuant to requests submitted before November 1, 1976 with respect to the exempt status under section 501(a) of organizations described in section 501(c) or (d), the status of organizations as private foundations under section 509(a), or the status of organizations as operating foundations under section 4942(j)(3).

(3) *Items that may be inspected only under certain circumstances.*—(i) *Background file documents.*—A background file document relating to a particular written determination issued in response to a request submitted before November 1, 1976 shall not be subject to inspection until the related written determination is open to public inspection or available for inspection, and then only if a written request pursuant to §301.6110-1(c)(4) is made for inspection of the background file document. However, the following background file documents are not open or subject to inspection:

(A) Background file documents relating to general written determinations issued before July 5, 1967.

(B) Background file documents relating to written determinations described in paragraph (a)(2) of this section.

(ii) *General written determinations issued before July 5, 1967.*—General written determinations issued before July 5, 1967 shall not be subject to inspection until all other written determinations issued in response to requests postmarked or hand delivered before November 1, 1976 that are open to inspection under this section have been made open to public inspection, and then only if a written request pursuant to §301.6110-1(c)(4) is made for inspection of the written determination. In this regard, the request for inspection must also contain the section of the Internal Revenue Code in which the requester is interested and the dates of issuance of the written determinations.

(b) *Notice and time requirements, and actions to restrain disclosure.*—(1) *Notice.*—(i) *General rule.*—Before a written determination is made open to public inspection and before a particular written determination is subject to inspection in response to the first written request therefor, the Commissioner shall publish in the Federal Register a notice that the written determination is to be made open or subject to inspection. Notices with respect to written determinations, other than those described in paragraph (a)(3)(ii) of this section, shall be published at the earliest practicable time after this regulation is adopted as a Treasury decision. Notices with respect to written determinations subject to inspection upon written request shall be published within a reasonable time after the receipt of the first written request for inspection thereof, but no sooner than the day as of which all other written determinations open to public inspection under this section have been made open to public inspection. Notices with respect to background file documents shall be sent in accordance with the rules in §301.6110-5(a) and will be mailed by the Internal Revenue Service to the most recent addresses of the persons to whom the background file document relates that are in the written determination file.

(ii) *Sequence of notices.*—Notices with respect to written determinations, other than general written determinations issued before July 5,

1967, shall be published in the following order. The first category is notices with respect to reference written determinations issued under the Internal Revenue Code of 1954. The second category is notices with respect to general written determinations issued after July 4, 1967. The third category is notices with respect to reference written determinations issued under the Internal Revenue Code of 1939 or corresponding provisions of prior law. Within a category, the Commissioner may publish notices individually or for groups of written determinations arranged according to the jurisdictions of the ruling branches in the Offices of the Assistant Commissioner (Technical) and the Assistant Commissioner (Employee Plans and Exempt Organizations), as the Commissioner may find reasonable. To the extent practicable, notices published individually shall be published in the reverse order of the issuance of the written determinations for which they are published, starting with the most recent written determination issued. To the extent practicable, each group shall consist of consecutively issued written determinations. Notices for groups shall be published, to the extent practicable, in the reverse order of the time period of issuance of the written determinations in each group, starting with the most recent time period.

(iii) *Contents of notice.*—The notice required by paragraph (b)(1)(i) of this section shall—

(A) Identify by subject matter description and dates of issuance the written determinations that the Commissioner proposes to make open or subject to inspection,

(B) State that the written determinations will be made open or subject to inspection pursuant to section 6110(h),

(C) State that the persons to whom the written determinations pertain have the right to seek administrative remedies under paragraph (b)(2)(ii) of this section and to commence judicial proceedings under section 6110(h)(4) within indicated time periods,

(D) State that there exist the possibilities that someone might request additional disclosure under section 6110(f)(4) and that someone might request inspection of a related background file document, and

(E) State that any notice that must be mailed by the Internal Revenue Service will be sent to the most recent address of the person to whom the notice must be sent that is in the relevant written determination file.

(2) *Actions to restrain disclosure.*—(i) *Information on written determinations described by notice.*—Any person may, within 15 days after the Commissioner publishes in the Federal Register a notice of intention to disclose a written determination under section 6110(h), request the Internal Revenue Service to provide certain information. This information includes whether any of the written determinations described by

the notice is one that was issued to the person requesting this information. The Internal Revenue Service will also inform the person whether any of the written determinations described by the notice is one that was issued to a person with respect to whom the person requesting this information is a successor in interest, executor or authorized representative. However, in order to do so, the Internal Revenue Service must be given the name and taxpayer identifying number of this other person and documentation of the relationship between that person and the person requesting the information. If the person requesting this information is a person to whom a written determination described by the notice pertains, or a successor in interest, executor, or authorized representative of that person, the Internal Revenue Service will also provide the person with a copy of the written determination on which is indicated the material that the Commissioner proposes to delete under section 6110(c) and any substitution proposed to be made therefor.

(ii) *Administrative remedies.*—Any person to whom a written determination described by the notice in the Federal Register pertains, and any successor in interest, executor or authorized representative of that person may pursue the administrative remedies described in this paragraph (b)(2)(ii). If, after receiving the information described in paragraph (b)(2)(i) of this section, the person pursuing these administrative remedies desires to protest the disclosure of certain information in the written determination, that person must within 35 days after the notice is published submit a written statement identifying those deletions not made by the Internal Revenue Service which the person believes should have been made. The person pursuing these administrative remedies must also submit a copy of the version of the written determination proposed to be open or subject to inspection on which that person indicates, by the use of brackets, the deletions which the person believes should have been made. The Internal Revenue Service shall, within 20 days after receipt of the response by the person pursuing these administrative remedies, mail to that person its final administrative conclusion with respect to the deletions to be made.

(iii) *Judicial remedy.*—Except as provided in paragraph (b)(2)(iv) of this section, any person permitted to resort to administrative remedies under paragraph (b)(2)(ii) of this section may, if that person proposed any deletion not made under section 6110(c) by the Commissioner, file a petition in the United States Tax Court under section 6110(h)(4) for a determination with respect to the proposed deletion. If appropriate, the petition may be filed anonymously. Any petition filed under section 6110(h)(4) must be filed within 75 days after the date on which the Commissioner publishes in the Federal Register the notice of intention to disclose required under section 6110(h)(4).

Reg. § 301.6110-6(b)(2)(iii)

(iv) *Limitations on right to bring judicial actions.*—No petition shall be filed under section 6110(h)(4) unless the administrative remedies provided by paragraph (b)(2)(ii) of this section have been exhausted. However, under two circumstances the petition may be filed even though the administrative remedies have not been exhausted. The first circumstance is if the petitioner requests the information described in paragraph (b)(2)(i) of this section within 15 days after the notice of intention to disclose is published in the Federal Register, but does not receive it within 30 days after the notice is published. The other circumstance is if the petitioner submits the statement of deletions within 35 days after the notice is published, but does not receive the final administrative conclusion of the Internal Revenue Service within 65 days after the notice is published. No judicial action with respect to any written determination shall be commenced under section 6110(h)(4) by any person who has received a notice with respect to the written determination under paragraph (b)(2)(v) of this section.

(v) *Required notice.*—If a proceeding is commenced under section 6110(h)(4) with respect to any written determination, the Secretary shall send notice of the commencement of the proceeding to any person to whom the written determination pertains. No notice is required to be sent to persons who have filed the petition that commenced the proceeding under section 6110(h)(4) with respect to the written determination. The notice shall be sent, by registered or certified mail, to the last known address of the persons described in this paragraph (b)(2)(v) within 15 days after notice of the petition filed under section 6110(h)(4) is served on the Secretary. For further guidance regarding the definition of last known address, see §301.6212-2.

(vi) *Intervention.*—Any person who is entitled to receive notice under paragraph (b)(2)(v) of this section has the right to intervene in any action brought under this paragraph (b)(2). If appropriate, this person shall be permitted to intervene anonymously.

(vii) *Background file documents.*—The following qualifications of the rules in §301.6110-5(b) apply with respect to the restraint of disclosure of background file documents related to written determinations to which this section applies. First, the administrative remedies described in §§601.105(b)(5)(iii) (*i*) and 601.201(e)(11) of this chapter do not apply. Second, the rule in those sections that the Internal Revenue Service will not consider the deletion of material not proposed for deletion prior to the issuance of the written determination does not apply.

(3) *Time at which open to public inspection.*—(i) *General rule.*—Except as otherwise provided in paragraph (b)(3)(ii) of this section, the text of any written determination open to public inspection or available for inspection upon written request under section 6110 shall be made open to

or available for inspection no earlier than 90 days and no later than 120 days after the date on which the Commissioner publishes in the Federal Register the notice of intention to disclose required under section 6110(h)(4). However, if an action is brought under section 6110(h)(4) to restrain disclosure of any portion of a written determination, the disputed portion of that written determination shall be made open to or available for inspection under paragraph (b)(3)(ii) of this section.

(ii) *Limitation on account of court order.*—The portion of the text of any written determination that was subject to an action under section 6110(h)(4) to restrain disclosure in which the court determined that the disclosure should be restrained shall be made open to or available for inspection within 30 days of the date that the court order becomes final. However, in no event shall that portion of the text of that written determination be made open to or available for inspection earlier than 90 days after the date on which the Commissioner publishes in the Federal Register the notice of intention to disclose required by section 6110(h)(4) and paragraph (b)(1) of this section. This 30-day period may be extended for such time as the court finds necessary to allow the Commissioner to comply with its decision. Any portion of a written determination which a court orders open to public inspection or subject to inspection upon written request under section 6110(f)(4) shall be open or subject to inspection within such time as the court provides.

(iii) *Background file documents.*—The rules in §301.6110-5(c)(2)(ii) do not apply with respect to the time at which background file documents related to written determinations to which this section applies are subject to inspection. [Reg. §301.6110-6.]

☐ [*T.D.* 7548, 5-12-78. *Amended by T.D.* 8939, 1-11-2001.]

[Reg. §301.6110-7]

§301.6110-7. Miscellaneous provisions.—(a) *Disposition of written determinations and background file documents.*—(1) *Reference written determinations.*—The Internal Revenue Service shall not dispose of any reference written determinations or related background file documents. The Commissioner may reclassify reference written determinations as general written determinations if the classification as reference was erroneous or if the Commissioner determined that such written determination no longer has any significant reference value. Notwithstanding the preceding sentence, the Commissioner shall not classify as a general written determination any written determination which is determined to be the basis for a published Revenue Ruling unless such Revenue Ruling is obsolete, revoked, superseded or otherwise held to have no effect.

(2) *General written determinations.*—The Internal Revenue Service may dispose of general written determinations and any background file

document relating to such written determination pursuant to its established records disposition procedures. Disposition of a written determination shall not occur earlier than 3 years after the date on which such written determination is made open to public inspection or available for inspection upon written request. Disposition of a background file document shall not occur earlier than 3 years after the date on which the related written determination is made open to public inspection or available for inspection upon written request.

(b) *Precedential status of written determinations open to public inspection.*—A written determination may not be used or cited as precedent, but the rule set forth in this paragraph shall not apply to change the precedential status, if any, of written determinations issued with respect to taxes imposed by subtitle D of the Internal Revenue Code of 1954.

(c) *Civil remedies.*—(1) *Liability for failure to make deletions or to conform to time limitations.*—(i) *Creation of remedy.*—An exclusive remedy against the Commissioner shall exist in the Court of Claims for—

(A) The person to whom the written determination pertains whenever the Commissioner fails to act in accordance with the time requirements of section 6110(g), and

(B) The person to whom the written determination pertains and any person identified in such written determination whenever the Commissioner fails to make deletions required by section 6110(c) if as a consequence of such failure there is disclosed the identity of such person or other information with respect to such person that is required to be deleted pursuant to section 6110(c).

(ii) *Limitations.*—The remedy provided in paragraph (c)(1)(i) of this section for failure to make deletions shall be available only if—

(A) The failure of the Commissioner to make the deletions required by section 6110(c) is intentional or willful.

(B) The Commissioner fails to make any deletion required by section 6110(c) which the Commissioner has agreed to make, or

(C) The Commissioner fails to make any deletion which a court has ordered to be made pursuant to section 6110(f)(3).

(iii) *Damages.*—In any suit brought pursuant to paragraph (c)(1)(i) of this section in which the court determines that an employee of the Internal Revenue Service intentionally or willfully failed to make a deletion required by section 6110(c), or intentionally or willfully failed to act in accordance with the time requirements of section 6110(g), the United States shall be liable, to the person described in paragraph (c)(1)(i) of this section who brought the action, in an amount equal to the sum of—

(A) Actual damages sustained by such person but in no case shall such person be entitled to receive less than the sum of $1,000,

(B) The costs of the action, and

(C) Reasonable attorney's fees as determined by the court.

(2) *Liability for making additional disclosure of information.*—The Commissioner shall not be liable for making any additional disclosure ordered pursuant to an action described in § 301.6110-5(d)(2) if the notice required by § 301.6110-5(d)(4) is sent.

(3) *Obligation to defend action for additional disclosure.*—The Commissioner shall not be required to defend any action brought to obtain additional disclosure pursuant to section 6110(f)(4) if the notice required by § 301.6110-5(d)(4) is sent.

(4) *Obligation to make deletions.*—The Commissioner shall be obligated to make only those deletions required by section 6110(c) which he has agreed to make, those which a court has ordered to be made pursuant to § 301.6110-5(b)(2) and those the omission of which would be intentional or willful.

(d) *Fees.*—(1) *General rule.*—(i) *Copies.*—The Commissioner may prescribe fees pursuant to § 601.702(f)(4) of this chapter for the costs of furnishing copies of material open to public inspection or subject to inspection upon written request pursuant to section 6110.

(ii) *Preparation of information available upon request.*—The Commissioner may prescribe fees pursuant to § 601.702(f) of this chapter for the costs of searching for and making deletions from any written determinations and background file documents that are subject to inspection only upon written request pursuant to § 301.6110-1(b).

(2) *Reduction or waiver of fees.*—(i) *Public interest.*—The Commissioner shall reduce or waive the fees described in paragraph (d)(1) of this section if the Commissioner determines that furnishing copies of, searching for, or making deletions from any written determination or background file document primarily benefits the general public, as described in § 601.702(f)(2)(ii)(B) of this chapter.

(ii) *Previous requests.*—The Commissioner may waive the fees described in paragraph (d)(1) of this section for searching for any written determination or background file document if the search for such written determination or background file document was made pursuant to a previous request for inspection thereof. The Commissioner shall waive the fees described in paragraph (d)(1) of this section for making deletions from any written determination or background file document if the making of such deletions from such written determination or background file document was made pursuant to a previous request to inspection thereof. Nothing in this (d)(2)(ii) shall prevent the Commissioner from prescribing fees for making additional deletions from such written determination or background file document pursuant to § 301.6110-5(b). [Reg. § 301.6110-7.]

☐ [*T.D.* 7524, 12-15-77.]

[Reg. § 301.6111-1T]

§ 301.6111-1T. Questions and answers relating to tax shelter registration (Temporary).— The following questions and answers relate to the tax shelter registration requirements of section 6111 of the Internal Revenue Code of 1954, as added by section 14-1(a) of the Tax Reform Act of 1984 (Pub. L. 98-369, 98 Stat. 678).

Table of Contents

The following table of contents is provided as part of these temporary regulations to help the reader locate relevant provisions. The headings are to be used only as a matter of convenience and have no substantive effect.

In general

Q-1. What is tax shelter registration?

A-1. Tax shelter registration is a new provision of the Internal Revenue Code that affects organizers, sellers, investors and certain other persons associated with investments that are considered tax shelters. The new provision imposes the following three requirements. First, a tax shelter must be registered by the tax shelter organizer. (See A-4 of this section for the definition of a tax shelter. See A-25 through A-39 of this section for rules relating to tax shelter organizers. See A-26 of this section for rules regarding when the seller of an interest in a tax shelter is treated as the tax shelter organizer.) Registration is accomplished by filing a properly completed Form 8264 with the Internal Revenue Service. The Internal Revenue Service will assign a registration number to each tax shelter that is registered. Second, any person who sells or otherwise transfers an interest in a tax shelter must furnish the registration number of the tax shelter to the purchaser or transferee of the interest. (See A-51 through A-54 of this section for the time and manner in which the number must be furnished.) Third, any person who claims a deduction, loss, credit, or other tax benefit or reports any income from the tax shelter must report the registration number of the tax shelter on any return on which the deduction, loss, credit, benefit, or income is included. (See A-55 through A-57 of this section for rules relating to the reporting of tax shelter registration numbers.)

Q-2. Are penalties provided for failure to comply with the requirements of tax shelter registration?

A-2. Yes. Separate penalties are provided for failure to satisfy any of the requirements set forth in A-1 of this section. See A-1 of § 301.6707-1T for the penalty for failure to register a tax shelter and A-8 of § 301.6707-1T for the penalty for filing false or incomplete information with respect to the registration of a tax shelter. See A-12 of § 301.6707-1T for the penalty for failure to furnish the tax shelter registration number to purchasers or transferees. See A-13 of § 301.6707-1T for the penalty for failure to report the tax shelter registration number on a tax return on which a deduction, loss, credit, income, or other tax benefit is included. In addition, criminal penalties may be imposed for willful noncompliance with the requirements of tax shelter registration. See, for example, section 7203, relating to willful failure to supply information, and section 7206, relating to fraudulent and false statements.

Q-3. Does registration of a tax shelter with the Internal Revenue Service indicate that the Internal Revenue Service has reviewed, examined, or approved the tax shelter or the claimed tax benefits?

A-3. No. Moreover, any representation to prospective investors that states that a tax shelter is registered with the Internal Revenue Service (or that registration is being sought) must include a legend stating that registration does not indicate that the Internal Revenue Service has reviewed, examined or approved the tax shelter or any of the claimed tax benefits. (See A-50 of this section for the form and content of the legend.)

Tax shelter defined

Q-4. What investments are tax shelters that are required to be registered with the Internal Revenue Service?

A-4. A tax shelter is any investment that meets the following two requirements:

(I) The investment must be one with respect to which a person could reasonably infer, from the representations made or to be made in connection with any offer for sale of any interest in the investment, that the tax shelter ratio for any investor may be greater than 2 to 1 as of the close of any of the first 5 years ending after the date on which the investment is offered for sale.

(II) The investment must be (i) required to be registered under a federal or state law regulating securities, (ii) sold pursuant to an exemption from registration requiring the filing of a notice with a federal or state agency regulating the offering or sale of securities, or (iii) a substantial investment. An investment that satisfies these two requirements is considered a tax shelter for registration purposes regardless of whether it is marketed or customarily designated as a tax shelter. See A-5 of this section for the definition of tax shelter ratio. See A-17 and A-18 of this section for the definition of an investment required to be registered under a federal or state law regulating securities. See A-19 and A-20 of this section for the definition of an investment sold pursuant to an exemption from registration requiring the filing of a notice. See A-21 of this section for the definition of a substantial investment.

Tax shelter ratio

Q-5. What does the term "tax shelter ratio" mean?

A-5. The term "tax shelter ratio" means, with respect to any year, the ratio that the aggregate amount of deductions and 200 percent of the credits that are or will be represented as potentially allowable to an investor under subtitle A of the Internal Revenue Code for all periods up to (and including) the close of such year, bears to the investment base for such investor as of the close of such year.

Deductions and credits represented as potentially allowable

Q-6. What do the terms "amount of deductions" and "credits" mean?

A-6. The term "amount of deductions" means the amount of gross deductions and other similar tax benefits potentially allowable with respect to the investment. The gross deductions are not to be offset by any gross income to be derived or potentially derived from the investment. Thus, the term "amount of deductions" is not equivalent to the net loss, if any, attributable to the investment. The term "credits" means the gross amount of credits potentially allowable with respect to the investment without regard to any possible tax liability resulting from the investment or any potential recapture of the credits.

Q-7. What does the term "year" mean for purposes of determining the tax shelter ratio?

A-7. The term "year" means the taxable year of a tax shelter, or if the tax shelter has no taxable year, the calendar year.

Q-8. Under what circumstances is a deduction or credit considered to be represented as being potentially allowable to an investor?

A-8. A deduction or credit is considered to be represented as being potentially allowable to an investor if any statement is made (or will be made) in connection with the offering for sale of an interest in an investment indicating that a tax deduction or credit is available or may be used to reduce federal income tax or federal taxable income. Representations of tax benefits may be oral or written and include those made at the time of the initial offering for sale of interests in the investment, such as advertisements, written offering materials, prospectuses, or tax opinions, and those that are expected to be made subsequent to the initial offering. Representations are not confined solely to statements regarding actual dollar amounts of tax benefits, but also include general representations that tax benefits are available with respect to an investment. Thus, for example, an advertisement stating that "purchase of restaurant includes trade fixtures (5-year write-off and investment tax credit)" constitutes an explicit representation of tax benefits.

Q-9. If a deduction or credit is not explicitly represented as being potentially allowable to an investor may it be inferred as a represented tax benefit that is includible in the tax shelter ratio?

A-9. Yes. Although some explicit representation concerning tax benefits is necessary before an investment may be considered a tax shelter, once an explicit representation is made (or will be made) regarding any tax benefit, all deductions or credits typically associated with the investment will be inferred to have been represented as potentially allowable. Thus, the tax shelter ratio will be determined with reference to those tax benefits that are explicitly represented as being potentially allowable as well as all other tax benefits that are typically associated with the investment. The amount of each deduction or credit that is includible in the tax shelter ratio, if not specifically represented as to amount, should be reasonably estimated based on representations of economic value or economic projections, if any, or on any other information available to the tax shelter organizer. Reasonable estimates of deductions or credits may take into account past experience with similar investments. Reasonable estimates must assume use of the most accelerated allowable basis for cost recovery deductions.

As an example of the application of this A-9, assume that an advertisement explicitly states that a building is eligible for the investment tax credit for rehabilitation of a certified historic structure, but makes no mention of cost recovery deductions, amortization deductions for construction period interest and taxes, real estate taxes after construction, ongoing maintenance expenses, or other deductions or credits typically associated with a building. Reasonable estimates of all such deductions and credits must be included with the investment tax credit explicitly represented in determining the tax shelter ratio associated with any investor's acquisition of an interest in the building.

Q-10. Does the fact that representations are made (or to be made) indicating that a deduction may be offset by income from the investment or that a deduction or credit may be subject to recapture or may be disallowed on audit affect the computation of the tax shelter ratio?

A-10. No. Deductions and credits represented as being potentially allowable are taken into account in computing the tax shelter ratio regardless of whether any qualifying statements are made.

Q-11. Is interest to be paid by an investor with respect to a debt obligation incurred in connection with the acquisition of an interest in the tax shelter included in the aggregate amount of deductions?

A-11. If a deduction for such interest is explicitly represented (or will be represented) as being potentially allowable, the interest is includible in the aggregate amount of the deductions. In addition, any interest to be paid with respect to a debt obligation the proceeds of which reduce the investment base (see A-14 of this section), regardless of whether a deduction for such interest is explicitly represented as being allowable, will be considered a deduction typically associated with the investment (see A-9 of this section). Accordingly, such interest will be considered to be represented as being potentially allowable and must be taken into account in computing the tax shelter ratio. If interest to be paid with respect to a debt obligation the proceeds of which do not reduce the investment base (see A-14 of this section) is not explicitly represented as being potentially allowable, however, such interest will not be considered typically associated with the investment and will not be taken into account in computing the tax shelter ratio.

Q-12. If representations are made that part or all of an amount invested in a tax shelter will be deductible upon the occurrence of an unintended event, will the deduction be included in the aggregate amount of deductions?

A-12. No. Thus, for example, if representations are made that a person's investment in a tax shelter may give rise to a loss deduction if the investment becomes worthless, the amount of the loss deduction will not be included in the aggregate amount of deductions and will not be taken into account in computing the tax shelter ratio. Similarly, if representations are made that the costs of acquiring oil and gas lease interests may be deductible if the lease is proved worthless by abandonment, the amount of any loss deduction will not be included in the aggregate amount of deductions.

Investment base

Q-13. What does the term "investment base" mean?

A-13. The term "investment base" means, with respect to any year (as defined in A-7 of this section), the cumulative amount of money and the adjusted basis of other property (reduced by any liability to which such other property is subject) that is unconditionally required to be contributed or paid directly to the tax shelter on or before the close of such year by an investor.

Q-14. What amounts must be eliminated from the investment base?

A-14. The investment base must be reduced by the following amounts:

(1) Any amount borrowed by the investor, even if borrowed on a recourse basis, from any person who participated in the organization, sale, or management of the investment or who has an interest (other than an interest as a creditor) in the investment ("a participating person") or from any person who is related (as defined in section 168(e)(4)) to a participating person, unless the amount is unconditionally required to be repaid by the investor before the close of the year for which the determination is being made. An amount will be considered unconditionally required to be repaid by the investor only if any offering material in which the borrowed amount is described and any agreement to be entered into between a participating (or related) person and the investor provide that the amount must be repaid (without exception) by the end of the year for which the determination is being made. An amount that is to be repaid only from earnings of the investment is not an amount that is unconditionally required to be repaid and is thus excluded from the investment base. In addition, an amount is not unconditionally required to be repaid if the amount will be (or is expected to be) reloaned to the investor during the 5-year period ending after the date the investment is offered for sale.

(2) Any amount borrowed by the investor, even if borrowed on a recourse basis, from any person, if the loan is arranged by a participating (or related) person, unless the amount is unconditionally required to be repaid by the investor before the close of the year for which the determination is being made. Any borrowing that is represented (orally or in writing) as being available from a specific source will be treated as arranged by a participating (or related) person, if the participating (or related) person provides a list of investors, or information relating to the investment, to the lender or otherwise informs the lender about the investment. However, in the case of an amount borrowed on a recourse basis, the mere fact that a lender who is actively and regularly engaged in the business of lending money obtained information relating to the investment, from a participating (or related) person, solely in response to a lender's request made in connection with such borrowing or a prior loan to the investment, a participating (or related) person, or an investor, will not, by itself, result in a determination that the loans are arranged by a participating (or related) person. Financing may be treated as arranged by a participating (or related) person regardless of whether a commitment to provide the financing is made by the lender to the participating or related person.

For example, assume that a tax shelter organizer represents that the purchase of an interest in a tax shelter may be financed with the proceeds of a revolving loan, and the tax shelter organizer provides investors with the names of several banks or other lending institutions to which the tax shelter organizer has provided information about the investment. Assume further that the information was not provided in response to requests from such lending institutions made in connection with prior loans. The proceeds of the revolving loan will be excluded from the investment base because the loan is not unconditionally required to be repaid and it is treated as having been arranged by the tax shelter organizer.

(3) Any amount borrowed, directly or indirectly, from a lender located outside the United States ("foreign-connected financing"), of which a participating (or related) person knows or has reason to know.

(4) Any amounts to be held for the benefit of investors in cash, cash equivalents, or marketable securities. An amount is to be held in cash equivalents if the amount is to be held in a checking account, savings account, mutual fund, certificate of deposit, book entry government obligation, or any other similar account or arrangement. Marketable securities are any securities that are part of an issue any portion of which is traded on an established securities market and any securities that are regularly quoted by brokers or dealers making a market.

(5) Any distributions (whether of cash or property) that will be made without regard to the income of the tax shelter, but only to the extent such distributions exceed the amount to be held as of the close of the year in cash, cash equivalents, or marketable securities.

Tax shelter ratio—Miscellaneous

Q-15. Does an investment satisfy the requirement in A-4(I) of this section ("the tax shelter ratio requirement") if it may be inferred from the representations made or to be made to investors that the tax shelter ratio for some, but not all, of the investors may be greater than 2 to 1 as of the close of any one of the first five years?

A-15. Yes. If the tax shelter ratio for any one investor may be greater than 2 to 1, the investment satisfies the tax shelter ratio requirement and is a tax shelter if it also meets the requirement in A-4 (II) of this section. Moreover, an investment will satisfy the tax shelter ratio requirement even if the tax shelter ratio for a single investor exceeds 2 to 1 as of the close of only one of the first five years.

For purposes of computing the tax shelter ratio for a year, all persons with interests in the investment are considered investors, except that general partners in a limited partnership will not be treated as investors in the partnership if the general partners' aggregate interest in each item of partnership income, gain, loss, deduction, and credit for such year is not expected to exceed 2 percent. In determining the general partners' interest in such items, limited partnership interests owned by general partners shall not be taken into account. For purposes other than the computation of the tax shelter ratio, however, all general partners will be treated as investors. Thus, for example, a general partner with a 1 percent interest in a limited partnership will be treated as an investor for the purpose of determining whether the partnership is a substantial investment.

Q-16. If a person could reasonably infer from the representations made or to be made about an investment that the tax shelter ratio for the investment may be greater than 2 to 1 under one arrangement for financing the purchase of an interest by an investor, but would be 2 to 1 or less under an alternative financing arrangement, does the investment satisfy the tax shelter ratio requirement of A-4(I) of this section?

A-16. Yes. An investment satisfies the tax shelter ratio requirement of A-4(I) of this section if a person could reasonably infer from the representations made or to be made that the tax shelter ratio for any person may be greater than 2 to 1 as of the close of any one of the first five years. The tax shelter ratio requirement is met if the tax shelter ratio may exceed 2 to 1 under any type of financing arrangement that is or will be represented as being available to investors.

Investments subject to securities regulation

Q-17. What is an investment that is required to be registered under a federal law regulating securities?

A-17. An investment required to be registered under a federal law regulating securities is any public offering of an investment that is required to be registered under the Securities Act of 1933 (1933 Act), the Investment Company Act of 1940, or any other federal law regulating securities. An investment is required to be registered under the 1933 Act, the Investment Company Act, or any other federal law regulating securities, if failure to register the investment would result in a violation of the applicable federal law, whether or not the investment has in fact been registered and, if proper notice has not been filed, whether or not the investment could have been sold pursuant to an exemption listed in A-19 of this section if such notice had been filed.

Q-18. What is an investment required to be registered under a state law regulating securities?

A-18. An investment required to be registered under a state law regulating securities is any investment required to be registered under a blue sky law or other similar state statute regulating securities. The term "state" includes the 50 states, the District of Columbia, and possessions of the United States.

Q-19. What is an investment sold pursuant to an exemption from registration requiring the filing of a notice with a federal agency regulating the offering or sale of securities?

A-19. An investment sold pursuant to an exemption from registration requiring the filing of a notice with such a federal agency is any investment that is sold pursuant to an exemption from registration requiring the filing or submission of a notice or other document with the Securities and Exchange Commission or any other federal agency regulating the offering or sale of securities, including the following exemptions (and applicable filing):

(1) Regulation A, as promulgated under section (3)(b) of the 1933 Act (Form 1(A)),

(2) Regulation B, as promulgated under section 3(b) of the 1933 Act (Schedules A through F),

(3) Regulation D, as promulgated under sections (3)(b) and 4(2) of the 1933 Act (Form D), and

(4) Any other statutory or regulatory exemption from registration requiring the filing or submission of a notice or other document.

Q-20. What is an investment sold pursuant to an exemption from registration requiring the filing of a notice with a state agency regulating the offering or sale of securities?

A-20. An investment sold pursuant to an exemption from registration requiring the filing of a notice with such a state agency is any investment sold pursuant to an exemption under a blue sky law or other similar state statutory or regulatory scheme that requires the filing or submission of a notice or other document with such a state agency. See A-18 of this section for the definition of state.

Substantial investments

Q-21. What is a substantial investment?

A-21. An investment is a substantial investment if the aggregate amount that may be offered for sale to all investors exceeds $250,000 and 5 or more investors are expected. The aggregate amount offered for sale is the aggregate amount to be received from the sale of interests in the investment and includes all cash, the fair market value of all property contributed, and the principal amount of all indebtedness received in exchange for interests in the investment, regardless of whether the proceeds of the indebtedness are included in the investment base under A-14 of this section.

For purposes of determining whether 5 or more investors are expected in an investment involving real property (and related personal property) that is used as a farm (as defined in section 2032A(e)(4)) for farming purposes (as defined in section 2032A(e)(5)), interests in the investment expected to be held by a husband and wife, their children and parents, and the spouses of their children (or any of them) will be treated as if the interests were to be held by one investor. Thus, for example, interests in a farm that are offered to two brothers and their wives would be treated as interests offered to one investor. Such an investment could be a substantial investment only if four or more persons who were not members of the family were expected to be investors in the farm.

Q-22. Will an investment be considered a substantial investment if the investment involves a number of parts each including fewer than 5 investors or an aggregate amount of $250,000 or less?

A-22. Yes, under the circumstances described in this A-22. For purposes of determining whether investments are parts of a substantial investment, similar investments offered by the same person or related persons (as defined in section 168(e)(4)) are aggregated together. Investments are considered similar if they involve similar principal business assets and similar plans or arrangements. Investments that include no business assets will be considered similar if they involve similar plans or arrangements.

Similar investments are aggregated solely for the purpose of determining whether investments involving fewer than 5 investors or an aggregate amount of $250,000 or less are substantial investments. For this purpose, similar investments are aggregated even though some, but not all, of the investments are (i) required to be registered under a federal or state law regulating securities or are sold pursuant to an exemption from securities registration requiring the filing of a notice with a federal or state agency regulating the offering or sale of securities (*i.e.*, required to be registered as tax shelters whether or not a substantial investment) or (ii) substantial investments without regard to aggregation.

Assume, for example, that a person develops similar arrangements involving 8 different partnerships, each investing in a separate but similar asset (such as a separate master recording or separate piece of similar real estate), each with a different general partner and each with 3 different limited partners. Assume further that the arrangements of all of the partnerships are similar. These partnerships involving similar arrangements and similar assets would be aggregated together. Thus, if each partner is expected to invest $11,000, there will be 32 investors (1 general partner plus 3 limited partners times 8 partnerships) and an aggregate investment of $352,000 (32 partners times $11,000). Accordingly, each partnership will constitute part of a substantial investment. If representations are made that $1,000 in tax credits and $3,000 in deductions are available to each limited partner in the first year and $10,000 of the cash invested was expected to be the proceeds of a loan arranged by the organizer, the tax shelter

ratio as of the close of the first year (assuming there are no deductions or credits typically associated with such investment, as described in A-9 of this section) would be 5 to 1 ($5,000 in total tax benefits and $1,000 investment base). Accordingly, the organizer would be required to register the partnerships with the Internal Revenue Service.

Q-23. If an investment involving fewer than 5 investors or an aggregate amount of $250,000 or less is offered for sale and, at the time of the offering, it is not known (and there is no reason to know) that subsequent similar investments will be offered by the person who made the first offering (or a related person), will subsequent similar investments offered by that person (or a related person) be aggregated with the first investment for purposes of determining whether the investments constitute a substantial investment?

A-23. No. However, a tax shelter organizer will be presumed to have known of any similar investments (as defined in A-22 of this section) offered during the 12 months following the first offering of an investment.

Exceptions from tax shelter registration

Q-24. Are there any investments that will not be subject to tax shelter registration even if they satisfy the requirements of a tax shelter (as defined in A-4 of this section)?

A-24. Yes. The following investments are not subject to tax shelter registration:

(1) Sales of residences primarily to persons who are expected to use the residences as their principal place of residence,

(2) Sales or leases of tangible personal property (other than master sound recordings, motion picture or television films, videotapes, lithograph plates, or other property relating to a literary, musical, or artistic composition) by the manufacturer (or a member of an affiliated group, within the meaning of section 1502, including the manufacturer) of the property primarily to persons who are expected to use the property in their principal active trade or business (see, however, A-32 and A-46 of this section for the additional rules applicable to a purchaser of property described in this A-24 who organizes an investment involving the property),

(3) Any other investment as specified by the Secretary in a rule-related notice published in the Federal Register.

Q-24A. Under what other circumstances are particular sales or leases of tangible personal property to certain persons or the performance of particular services for certain persons exempt from tax shelter registration?

A-24A. A person who, in the ordinary course of a trade or business, sells or leases tangible personal property (other than collectibles (as defined in section 408(m)(2)), master sound recordings, motion picture or television films, videotapes, lithograph plates, or other property that includes or relates to a literary, musical or artistic composition) to a purchaser or lessee who is reasonably expected to use the property either for a personal use or in the purchaser's or lessee's principal active trade or business is not required for any purpose to treat such a purchaser or lessee as an investor in a tax shelter. Property may be reasonably expected to be used by a purchaser or lessee for personal use only if sold or leased to the purchaser or lessee in a quantity that is customary for such use. Similarly, a person who performs services for another person in connection with the principal active trade or business of the recipient of the services or for the recipient's personal use is not required to treat the recipient as an investor in a tax shelter. Persons who are not reasonably expected to use property or services either in their principal active trade or business or for personal use must be treated as tax shelter investors in the event the sales, leases, or performance of services otherwise constitute a tax shelter.

Assume, for example, that an organizer forms Z corporation to feed cattle and to provide services in connection with the cattle feeding operations. Z will agree to serve customers with a minimum of 200 head of cattle. The fee for the services is $20 per head. Feed for the cattle will cost $280 per head. Z represents that the service fee and the cost of the feed may be financed by $5,000 of cash and $55,000 of proceeds of a revolving recourse note that Z has arranged to be available. Z provides its services to 100 customers. Ninety-five of the customers are persons whose principal active trade or business is reasonably expected to be farming (as defined in section 464(e)(1)). Five of the customers are not reasonably expected to engage in farming as their principal active trade or business. Although all the individual investments involve similar principal business assets and similar plans or arrangements, only the 5 customers who are not reasonably expected to be in the principal active trade or business of farming will be treated as investors in a tax shelter and aggregated to determine whether a substantial investment exists. Thus, there will be 5 investors and an aggregate investment of $300,000. If representations are made that the service fee and the cost of the feed are tax deductible, the tax shelter ratio (assuming there are no deductions or credits typically associated with such an investment, as described in A-9 of this section) would be 12 to 1 ($60,000 in total tax benefits and $5,000 investment base) and the organizer would be required to register the five aggregated feeding arrangements as a tax shelter. The registration number of the tax shelter must be provided to the five customers treated as investors in the tax shelter, but would not be required to be furnished to the customers whose principal active trade or business is reasonably expected to be farming.

Persons required to register a tax shelter.

Q-25. Who has the legal obligation to register a tax shelter?

A-25. A tax shelter organizer is obligated to register the tax shelter.

Q-26. What is the definition of tax shelter organizer?

A-26. Several categories of persons may be tax shelter organizers. In general, the term tax shelter organizer means a person principally responsible for organizing a tax shelter. If a person principally responsible for organizing a tax shelter has not registered the tax shelter by the day on which interests in the shelter are first offered for sale, any other person who participated in the organization of the tax shelter will be treated as a tax shelter organizer. If neither a person principally responsible for organizing the tax shelter nor any other person who participated in the organization of tax shelter has registered the tax shelter by the day on which interests in the tax shelter are first offered for sale, then any person who participates in the management of the tax shelter at a time when the tax shelter is not registered will be treated as a tax shelter organizer. Finally, if a person participates in the sale of a tax shelter at a time when the person knows or has reason to know that a tax shelter has not been registered, that person will be treated as a tax shelter organizer. See A-38 of this section for rules relating to the execution of an agreement among persons who may be treated as tax shelter organizers to designate one person to register a tax shelter.

Q-27. Who is a person principally responsible for organizing a tax shelter?

A-27. A person principally responsible for organizing a tax shelter ("principal organizer") is any person who discovers, creates, investigates, or initiates the investment, devises the business or financial plans for the investment, or carries out those plans through negotiations or transactions with others.

Q-28. What constitutes participation in the organization of a tax shelter?

A-28. Participation in the organization of a tax shelter includes the performance of any act (directly or through an agent) related to the establishment of the tax shelter, including the following:

(1) Preparation of any document establishing the tax shelter (for example, articles of incorporation, a trust instrument, or a partnership agreement);

(2) Preparation of any document in connection with the registration (or exemption from registration) of the tax shelter with any federal, state, or local government body;

(3) Preparation of a prospectus, offering memorandum, financial statement, or other statement describing the tax shelter;

(4) Preparation of a tax or other legal opinion relating to the tax shelter;

(5) Preparation of an appraisal relating to the tax shelter;

(6) Negotiation or other participation on behalf of the tax shelter in the purchase of any property relating to the tax shelter.

Q-29. What constitutes participation in the management of a tax shelter?

A-29. Participation in the management of a tax shelter includes managing the assets of the tax shelter, directing the business activity of the tax shelter, or, depending on the form of the tax shelter, acting as a general partner who actively participates in the management of a partnership, a trustee of a trust, a director or an officer of a corporation (including a corporate general partner of a partnership), or performing activities similar to those performed by such a general partner, a trustee, a director, or an officer.

Q-30. Will the performance of any act described in A-27 through A-29 of this section constitute participation in the organization or management of a tax shelter if the person performing the act is unrelated to the tax shelter (or any principal organizer of the tax shelter) and does not participate in the entrepreneurial risks or benefits of the tax shelter?

A-30. No. The performance of an act described in A-27 through A-29 of this section will not constitute participation in the organization or management of a tax shelter unless the person performing the act is related to the tax shelter (or any principal organizer of the tax shelter) or the person participates in the entrepreneurial risks or benefits of the tax shelter. A person will be considered related to a tax shelter if the person is related to the tax shelter or a principal organizer of the tax shelter within the meaning of section 168(e)(4) or is employed by the tax shelter or a principal organizer of the tax shelter or has an interest (other than an interest as a creditor) in the tax shelter. A person will be considered a participant in the entrepreneurial risks or benefits of a tax shelter if the person's compensation for performing an act described in A-27 through A-29 of this section is contingent on any matter relating to the tax shelter (*e.g.*, the compensation is based in whole or in part upon (i) whether interests in the tax shelter are actually sold or (ii) the number or value of the units in the tax shelter that are sold), or if the person will receive an interest in the tax shelter as part or all of the person's compensation.

For example, assume that A forms Z partnership, a tax shelter for which registration is required. Z hires the X law firm, none of the partners of which is related to the tax shelter, to prepare the documents necessary to register the offering of Z securities with the Securities and Exchange Commission. X charges $100 an hour for its services in connection with the preparation of the necessary documents, and payment of the fee is not contingent. X will not be treated as a participant in the organization of the tax shelter. If, however, X were to charge a fee equal to 1 percent of the value of the units in the tax shelter that are sold, X would be considered a participant in the organization of the shelter.

As another example, assume that individual C is an attorney employed by W corporation, the corporate general partner and principal organizer of Z, and that C prepares the documents necessary to register the tax shelter with the Securities and Exchange Commission. C will be treated as having participated in the organization of the tax shelter regardless of the way in which C's compensation is structured, because C, as an employee, is related to the principal organizer of the tax shelter.

Q-31. What constitutes participation in the sale of a tax shelter?

A-31. Participation in the sale of a tax shelter includes any marketing activities (directly or through an agent) with respect to an investment, including the following:

(1) Direct contact with a prospective purchaser of an interest, or with a representative or agent of a prospective purchaser, but only if the contact relates to the possible purchase of an interest in the tax shelter;

(2) Solicitation of investors using the mail, telephone, or other means, or by placing an advertisement for the tax shelter in a newspaper, magazine, or other publication or medium;

(3) Instructing or advising salespersons regarding the tax shelter or sales presentations.

Q-32. May persons be treated as tax shelter organizers if such persons do not make any representations of tax benefits to investors?

A-32. Yes. If a person described in A-26 of this section knows or has reason to know that representations of tax benefits have been made, that person may be treated as a tax shelter organizer. For example, a participant in the sale of a tax shelter may know or have reason to know that representations of tax benefits have been made by the principal organizer or others who participate in the organization of the tax shelter. In addition, a person who acquires property from a manufacturer in a transaction exempt from tax shelter registration under A-24 of this section and who organizes an investment involving the property may know or have reason to know of any representation of tax benefits made by the manufacturer.

Q-33. If a person performs support services such as typing, photocopying, or printing for a tax shelter (or a tax shelter organizer) or performs other ministerial functions for the tax shelter (or a tax shelter organizer), may the person be considered to have participated in the organization, management, or sale of the tax shelter?

A-33. No. Merely performing support services or ministerial functions will not be considered participation in the organization, management, or sale of a tax shelter.

Circumstances under which tax shelter organizers are required to register a tax shelter

Q-34. When is a principal organizer or a person who participates in the organization of a tax shelter required to register a tax shelter?

A-34. A principal organizer or a person who participates in the organization of a tax shelter (*i.e.*, a person who could be treated as a tax shelter organizer within the meaning of A-26 of this section) is required to register the tax shelter by the day on which the first offering for sale of interests in the tax shelter occurs, unless the

Reg. §301.6111-1T

person has signed a designation agreement pursuant to A-38 of this section. If a group of persons who could be treated as tax shelter organizers has signed a designation agreement pursuant to A-38 of this section, the designated organizer is required to register the tax shelter by the day on which the first offering for sale of interests in the tax shelter occurs. See A-39 of this section for additional rules applicable to tax shelter organizers (other than a designated organizer) who have signed a designation agreement.

Q-35. When is a person who participates in the management of a tax shelter ("manager") required to register a tax shelter?

A-35. A manager who has not signed a designation agreement pursuant to A-38 of this section must register the tax shelter if the manager participates in the management of the tax shelter on or after the first offering for sale of interests in the tax shelter at a time when the tax shelter has not been properly registered (*i.e.*, the manager is treated as a tax shelter organizer within the meaning of A-26 of this section). Such a manager must register the tax shelter by the day on which the first offering for sale of interests in the tax shelter occurs, or by the day on which the manager's participation in the management of the tax shelter commences, whichever is later. See A-39 of this section for rules applicable to a manager who has signed a designation agreement.

Q-36. When is a person who participates in the sale of a tax shelter ("seller") required to register the tax shelter?

A-36. A seller who has not signed a designation agreement pursuant to A-38 of this section must register the tax shelter if the seller participates in the sale of the tax shelter at a time when the seller knows or has reason to know that the tax shelter has not been properly registered (*i.e.*, the seller is treated as a tax shelter organizer within the meaning of A-26 of this section). A seller who has not signed a designation agreement will be deemed to have reason to know that the tax shelter has not been properly registered if the seller does not receive a copy of the Internal Revenue Service tax shelter registration notice containing the registration number within the 30-day period after the seller first offers interests in the tax shelter for sale. A seller must register the tax shelter as soon as practicable after the seller first knows or has reason to know that the tax shelter has not been properly registered. See A-39 of this section for rules applicable to a seller who has signed a designation agreement.

Q-37. When is a person who acts in more than one capacity with respect to a tax shelter required to register the shelter?

A-37. A person who acts in more than one capacity with respect to a tax shelter (*i.e.*, as two or more of the following: principal organizer, participant in the organization, manager, or seller) must register the tax shelter by the earliest day on which a tax shelter organizer acting in any of the person's several capacities would be required to register the tax shelter.

Q-38. May a group of persons who could be treated as tax shelter organizers under A-26 of this section designate one person to register the tax shelter?

A-38. Yes. A group of persons who could be treated as tax shelter organizers under A-26 of this section may enter into a written agreement designating one person as the tax shelter organizer responsible for registering the tax shelter ("designated organizer"). The designated organizer should ordinarily be a person principally responsible for organizing the tax shelter, but may be any person who participates in the organization of the tax shelter. Although persons who participate only in the sale or management of a tax shelter may sign a designation agreement, they may not be the designated organizer. In addition, the designated organizer may not be a person who is resident in a country other than the United States. Any person who signs a designation agreement, other than the designated organizer, will not be liable for failing to register the tax shelter and will not be subject to a penalty, even if the designated organizer fails to register the tax shelter, unless the person fails to register the tax shelter when such registration is required under A-39 of this section. See A-7 of § 301.6707-1T for additional rules relating to the reasonable cause exception applicable to persons who sign a designation agreement.

Q-39. Is a tax shelter organizer who has signed a designation agreement and who is not the designated organizer required to register the tax shelter under any circumstances?

A-39. Yes. If a tax shelter organizer who has signed a designation agreement pursuant to A-38 of this section knows or has reason to know on or after the day on which the first offering for sale of interests in a tax shelter occurs that the designated organizer failed to register the tax shelter, such tax shelter organizer must register the tax shelter as soon as practicable after he first knows or has reason to know of the failure. A tax shelter organizer who has signed a designation agreement is deemed to have reason to know that the designated organizer has failed to register the tax shelter if the tax shelter organizer does not receive a copy of the Internal Revenue Service registration notice containing the registration number from the designated organizer within the 60-day period after the day on which the first offering for sale of interests in the tax shelter occurs (or the person signs the designation agreement, if later). See A-41 of this section for the requirement that the designated organizer provide a copy of the registration notice and number to persons who have signed the designation agreement.

Registration—General Rules

Q-40. By what date must a tax shelter be registered?

A-40. A tax shelter must be registered not later than the day on which the first offering for sale of an interest in the tax shelter occurs.

Q-41. Is a tax shelter organizer (including a designated organizer) who registers a tax shelter

Reg. § 301.6111-1T

responsible for performing any act with respect to tax shelter registration other than registering the tax shelter?

A-41. Yes. A tax shelter organizer (including a designated organizer) who registers a tax shelter must provide a copy of the Internal Revenue Service registration notice, containing the registration number within 7 days after the notice is received from the Internal Revenue Service to the principal organizer (if a different person) and to any persons who the tax shelter organizer knows or has reason to know are participating in the sale of interests in the tax shelter (if such persons begin to participate after the registration number is received, they must be provided the notice within 7 days after they commence their participation). In addition, a designated organizer must provide a copy of the notice within 7 days after it is received to all persons who have signed the designation agreement.

Q-42. What is the sale of an interest in a tax shelter?

A-42. The sale of an interest in a tax shelter includes the sale of property, or any interest in property, the entry into a leasing arrangement, a consulting, management or other agreement for the performance of services, or the sale or entry into any other plan, investment, or arrangement.

Q-43. What does the term "offering for sale" mean?

A-43. The term "offering for sale" means making any representation, whether oral or written, relating to participation in a tax shelter as an investor. The term includes any advertisement relating to the tax shelter and any mail, telephonic, or other contact with prospective investors. A representation relating to participation in a tax shelter will be considered an offering for sale of an interest in the tax shelter even though there is included in the representation an explicit statement that the representation does not constitute an offer to sell or a solicitation of an offer to buy an interest in the tax shelter. In determining whether an offering for sale of an interest has occurred, federal and state laws regulating securities are not controlling.

Q-44. After a tax shelter has been registered, must it be registered again each year that it continues to be offered for sale?

A-44. No. Registration is effective for the year in which first accomplished and all subsequent years.

Q-45. If the facts relating to a tax shelter change after the tax shelter has been registered, must the tax shelter be registered again or must an amended application for registration be filed by the tax shelter organizer?

A-45. No. The tax shelter organizer, however, is permitted to file an amended application if a material change in facts occurs after the initial registration. A material change in facts is—

(1) A change in the identifying information relating to the tax shelter or tax shelter organizer,

(2) The acquisition or construction of a principal asset not reported on the initial application for registration,

(3) A change in the method of financing a minimum investment unit, or

(4) A change in the principal business activity.

In addition, a change in any tax shelter ratio reported on the initial application for registration that increases or decreases the reciprocal of the tax shelter ratio (i.e., the fraction in which the amount of the applicable investment base is the numerator and the amount of the applicable deductions and credits is the denominator) by 50 percent or more is a material change in facts. For example, if the tax shelter ratio increases from 2 to 1 to 4 to 1, the reciprocal of the tax shelter ratio decreases from $1/2$ to $1/4$, a 50-percent decrease. Similarly, if the tax shelter ratio decreases from 6 to 1 to 4 to 1, the reciprocal of the tax shelter ratio increases from $1/6$ to $1/4$, a 50-percent increase. In either case, there is a material change in facts and an amended application could be filed.

Q-45A. What information should be included on an amended application for registration?

A-45A. The tax shelter organizer must include the identifying information requested on Form 8264, Application for Registration of a Tax Shelter, and the tax shelter registration number that has been assigned to the tax shelter. In addition, the tax shelter organizer should include any other information requested on Form 8264 (1) that has changed since the tax shelter was registered, or (2) that the tax shelter organizer did not know at the time the tax shelter was registered but has learned of since the registration.

For example, assume that A organizes partnership L, a blind pool that will invest in real estate. Before the real estate is identified or acquired, interests in L will be offered to the public in an offering that must be registered with the Securities and Exchange Commission. Although A does not know what real estate L will acquire and therefore is unable to calculate the tax shelter ratio with certainty, A concludes (based on representations made or to be made) that the tax shelter ratio will exceed 2 to 1 as to some of the investors. Accordingly, A registers L as a tax shelter. A attaches a statement to the application for registration, explaining that L is a blind pool organized to invest in real estate, but that L has not yet acquired any real estate. In addition, A attaches a statement explaining that although the tax shelter ratio is expected to exceed 2 to 1, A cannot compute the tax shelter ratio with certainty because L has not yet acquired any real estate. Several months after L is registered, L acquires a shopping center. A may file an amended application for registration. In addition to reporting the identifying information and the tax shelter registration number on the amended application, A should report the shopping center as the principal asset and the recomputed tax shelter ratio.

As another example, assume that C organizes a limited partnership that is a tax shelter. On the application for registration, C reports that the tax shelter ratio is 2.2 to 1. After the partnership has been registered, C finds that the partnership is unable to attract sufficient investors. To make

Reg. §301.6111-1T

investing in the partnership more attractive, C decides to offer financing for the purchase of interests in the partnership. As a result of the change in financing, the tax shelter ratio will be 5 to 1. Because there is a change in financing and a change in the tax shelter ratio that decreases the reciprocal of the tax shelter ratio by 50 percent or more, C may file an amended application for registration. In addition to reporting the identifying information and the tax shelter registration number on the amended application, C should report the recomputed tax shelter ratio and information relating to the change in financing.

Q-46. If assets constituting a tax shelter are sold ("original sale") and, subsequently, either the assets or interests in the assets are offered for sale by the purchaser ("resale"), must the purchaser file a new application for registration if the resale is an offering or sale of interests in a tax shelter?

A-46. If the resale constitutes a tax shelter, the purchaser must file a new application for registration, unless the tax shelter organizer with respect to the original sale is also the tax shelter organizer with respect to the resale and the facts pertaining to the resale were reflected in the application for registration filed with respect to the original sale. For example, assume that A intends to sell a building with an estimated fair market value of $2.5 million to a group of 5 investors (*i.e.,* a substantial investment, as defined in A-21 of this section). A also intends to make representations of tax benefits attributable to an investment in the building. Based on these representations and the investment base, the tax shelter ratio attributable to an investment in the building may be greater than 2 to 1. A therefore files an application for registration relating to the building with the Internal Revenue Service. The Internal Revenue Service issues a registration number for the investment, and A furnishes the registration number to each of the 5 investors in accordance with A-53 of this section. In an unrelated transaction, the 5 investors decide to syndicate the building and to offer interests in the syndicate to approximately 500 investors. In connection with this offer, the investors expect to make representations concerning tax benefits with respect to the syndication. If based on these representations and the investment base, the tax shelter ratio may be greater than 2 to 1 for an investor in the syndicate, the 5 investors must file an application for registration for the syndicate before interests in the syndicate may be offered for sale. The investors in the syndicate must be furnished with the new registration number and not the registration number issued with respect to A. On the other hand, if the original sale and the syndication were part of A's plan to sell interests in the building, A is a tax shelter organizer with respect to the syndication. If the facts pertaining to the syndication were reflected on A's application for registration with respect to the original sale, a second application for registration would not be required with respect to the syndication. However, the investors

in the syndicate would have to be furnished with the tax shelter registration number issued to A.

Q-47. When is a tax shelter considered registered?

A-47. A tax shelter is considered registered when a properly completed Form 8264, Application for Registration of a Tax Shelter, is filed with the appropriate Internal Revenue Service Center. See A-7 of §301.6111-2T for rules relating to the information required to be included on the form, and A-8 of §301.6707-1T for rules relating to the penalty for filing incomplete information.

Q-48. Must a person registering a tax shelter that is a substantial investment only by reason of an aggregation of multiple investments under A-22 of this section complete a separate Form 8264 for each investment constituting part of the substantial investment?

A-48. A separate Form 8264 must be completed for each investment that differs from the other investments in a substantial investment with respect to any of the following:

(1) Principal asset,

(2) Accounting methods,

(3) Federal or state agencies with which the investment is registered or with which an exemption notice is filed,

(4) Methods of financing the purchase of an interest in the investment,

(5) Tax shelter ratio.

Such aggregated investments, however, are part of a single tax shelter.

Q-49. Do the rules of section 7502 of the Internal Revenue Code, regarding timely mailing, apply to the filing of registration forms?

A-49. Yes.

Q-50. After a tax shelter has been registered, may representations that the investment has been registered with the Internal Revenue Service be made to potential investors?

A-50. Investors may be informed that the investment has been registered with the Internal Revenue Service. Investors also must be informed, however, that registration does not imply that the Internal Revenue Service has reviewed, examined, or approved the investment or the claimed tax benefits. The disclaimer must be substantially in the form provided below:

Issuance of a registration number does not indicate that this investment or the claimed tax benefits have been reviewed, examined, or approved by the Internal Revenue Service.

See A-53 of this section for rules relating to the legend that must be included on any statement on which the tax shelter registration number is furnished to investors.

Furnishing tax shelter registration numbers

Q-51. Who must furnish investors in a tax shelter with the registration number of the tax shelter?

A-51. Any person who sells (or otherwise transfers) an interest in a tax shelter is required to furnish the registration number assigned to that tax shelter to each person who purchases (or otherwise acquires) an interest in that tax shelter from the seller or transferor. For example, X, a tax shelter organizer, sells an interest in a tax shelter to A. One year later A sells A's interest in the shelter to B. X must furnish the tax shelter registration number to A, and A must furnish the number to B. If B sells or otherwise transfers the interest (by gift, for example), B must furnish the number to the purchaser or transferee of B's interest in the tax shelter.

Q-52. When must the registration number be furnished to purchasers of interests in the tax shelter?

A-52. The person who sells (or otherwise transfers) an interest in a tax shelter must furnish the registration number to the purchaser (or transferee) at the time of sale (or transfer) of the interest (or, if later, within 20 days after the seller or transferor receives the registration number). If the registration number is not furnished at the time of the sale (or other transfer), the seller (or transferor) must furnish the statement described in A-54 to the purchaser (or transferee) at the time of the sale (or other transfer). If interests in a tax shelter were sold before September 1, 1984, all investors who acquired their interests in the tax shelter before September 1, 1984, must be furnished with the registration number of the tax shelter by December 31, 1984. The registration number will be considered furnished to the investor if it is mailed to the investor at the last address of the investor known to the person required to furnish the number.

Q-53. How is a seller or transferor of an interest in a tax shelter required to furnish the registration number to investors?

A-53. The person who sells (or otherwise transfers) an interest in a tax shelter must furnish the registration number of the tax shelter to the purchaser (or transferee) on a written statement. The written statement shall show the name, registration number, and taxpayer identification number of the tax shelter, and include a prominent legend in bold and conspicuous type stating that the registration number must be included on any return on which the investor claims any deduction, loss, credit, or other tax benefit, or reports any income, by reason of the tax shelter. The statement must also include a prominent legend in bold and conspicuous type stating that the issuance of the registration number does not indicate that the Internal Revenue Service has reviewed, examined, or approved the investment or the claimed tax benefits. The statement shall be substantially in the form provided below:

You have acquired an interest in [name and address of tax shelter]whose taxpayer identification number is [if any]. The Internal Revenue Service has issued [name of tax shelter] the following tax shelter registration number: [Number]

You must report this registration number to the Internal Revenue Service, if you claim any deduction, loss, credit, or other tax benefit or report any income by reason of your investment in [name of tax shelter].

You must report the registration number (as well as the name, and taxpayer identification number of [name of tax shelter]) on Form 8271.

Form 8271 must be attached to the return on which you claim the deduction, loss, credit, or other tax benefit or report any income.

Issuance of a registration number does not indicate that this investment or the claimed tax benefits have been reviewed, examined, or approved by the Internal Revenue Service.

This statement may be modified as necessary if the tax shelter is not a separate entity (e.g., certain Schedule F or Schedule C activities) or has no name or taxpayer identification number.

Q-54. If a registration number has not been received by a seller (or transferor) from the person who registered the tax shelter by the time interests in the tax shelter are sold (or otherwise transferred), must the seller (or transferor) of the interests furnish the purchaser (or transferee) with any information regarding the registration?

A-54. Yes. At the time of the sale (or other transfer) the seller (or other transferor) must furnish the purchaser (or transferee) with a written statement in substantially the form prescribed in A-53 of this section, except that the second sentence of the form prescribed in A-53 shall be replaced by a statement in the form provided below:

On behalf of [name of tax shelter], [name of tax shelter organizer who has applied for registration] has applied to the Internal Revenue Service for a tax shelter registration number. The number will be furnished to you when it is received.

Including the registration number on tax returns

Q-55. Is an investor required to report the registration number of a tax shelter in which the investor has acquired an interest to the Internal Revenue Service?

A-55. Yes. Any person claiming any deduction, loss, credit, or other tax benefit by reason of a tax shelter must report the registration number of the tax shelter on Form 8271, Investor Reporting of Tax Shelter Registration Number, which must be attached to the return on which any deduction, loss, credit, or other tax benefit attributable to the tax shelter is claimed. For purposes of determining whether the tax shelter registration number must be reported by an investor, income attributable to an investment, such as a partner's distributive share of income, constitutes a deduction or tax benefit that is claimed, because gross deductions and other tax benefits are included in the net income reported by the investor. Thus, the registration number also must be reported on any return on which an investor reports any income attributable to a tax shelter.

Q-56. What should the investor do if the investor has received a notice that a registration number for the tax shelter has been applied for, but the investor has not received the registration number by the time the investor files a return on which a deduction, loss, credit, other tax benefit, or income attributable to the tax shelter is included?

A-56. The investor must attach to the return a Form 8271 with the words "Applied For" written in the space for the registration number and must include on the Form 8271 the name and taxpayer identification number (if any) of the tax

Reg. §301.6111-1T

shelter and the name of the person who has applied for registration of the tax shelter.

Q-57. Does the requirement to include the tax shelter registration number on a return apply to applications for tentative refund (Form 1045 and Form 1139) and amended returns (Form 1040X, Form 1120X)?

A-57. Yes. A completed Form 8271 must be attached to any such return on which any deduction, loss, credit, other tax benefit, or income relating to a tax shelter is included.

Projected income investments

Q-57A. Are the registration requirements suspended with respect to any tax shelters?

A-57A. Yes. If a tax shelter is a projected income investment, it is not required to be registered before the first offering for sale of an interest in the tax shelter occurs, but is subject only to the registration requirements set forth in A-57H through A-57J of this section. A tax shelter is a projected income investment if—

(a) The tax shelter is not expected to reduce the cumulative tax liability of any investor for any year during the 5-year period described in A-4(I) of this section; and

(b) The assets of the tax shelter do not include or relate to any property described in A-57E of this section.

Q-57B. Under what circumstances does a tax shelter satisfy the requirement of paragraph (a) of A-57A of this section?

A-57B. A tax shelter is not expected to reduce the cumulative tax liability of an investor for any year during the 5-year period described in A-4(I) of this section only if—

(a) A written financial projection or other written representation that is provided to investors before the sale of interests in the investment states (or leads a reasonable investor to believe) that the investment will not reduce the cumulative tax liability of any investor with respect to any year (within the meaning of A-7 of this section) in such 5-year period; and

(b) No written or oral projections or representations, other than those related to circumstances that are highly unlikely to occur, state (or lead a reasonable investor to believe) that the investment may reduce the cumulative tax liability of any investor with respect to any such year.

Thus, a tax shelter for which there are multiple written or oral financial projections or other representations is not a projected income investment if any such projection or representation that relates to circumstances that are not highly unlikely to occur states (or leads a reasonable investor to believe) that the investment may reduce the cumulative tax liability of any investor. See A-57D and A-57F of this section for rules relating to financial projections or other representations that are not made in good faith, that are not based on reasonable economic and business assumptions, or that relate to circumstances that are highly unlikely.

Q-57C. When does an investment reduce the cumulative tax liability of an investor?

A-57C. (a) An investment reduces the cumulative tax liability of an investor with respect to a year during the 5-year period described in A-4(I) of this section if, as of the close of such year, (i) cumulative projected deductions for the investor exceed cumulative projected income for the investor, or (ii) cumulative projected credits for the investor exceed cumulative projected tax liability (without regard to credits) for the investor.

(b) The cumulative projected deductions for an investor as of the close of a year are the gross deductions of the investor with respect to the investment, for all periods up to (and including) the end of such year, that are included in the financial projection or upon which the representation is based. The deductions with respect to an investment include all deductions explicitly represented as being allowable and all deductions typically associated (within the meaning of A-9 of this section) with the investment. Therefore, interest to be paid by the investor that is taken into account in determining the tax shelter ratio of the investment (see A-11 of this section) is treated as a deduction with respect to the investment.

(c) The cumulative projected income for an investor as of the close of a year is the gross income of the investor with respect to the investment, for all periods up to (and including) the end of such year, that is included in the financial projection or upon which the representation is based. For this purpose, income attributable to cash, cash equivalents, or marketable securities (within the meaning of A-14(4) of this section) may not be treated as income from the investment.

(d) The cumulative projected credits for an investor as of the close of a year are the gross credits of the investor with respect to the investment, for all periods up to (and including) the close of such year, that are included in the financial projection or upon which the representation is based. The credits with respect to an investment include all credits explicitly represented as being allowable and all credits typically associated (within the meaning of A-9 of this section) with the investment.

(e) The cumulative projected tax liability (without regard to credits) for an investor as of the close of a year is 50 percent of the excess of cumulative projected income for the investor over cumulative projected deductions for the investor with respect to the investment as of the close of such year.

(f) The following examples illustrate the application of the principles of this A-57C:

Example (1). The promotional material with respect to a tax shelter includes a written financial projection indicating that the expected income of the investment in each of its first 5 years

Reg. §301.6111-1T

is $800,000. In subsequent oral discussions, investors are advised that, in certain circumstances that are not highly unlikely, the income expected from the investment may be as little as $500,000 per year. The subsequent oral discussions are taken into account in determining whether any projections or representations state or lead a reasonable investor to believe that the investment may reduce the cumulative tax liability of any investor. Thus, if the written financial projections indicate that the gross deductions attributable to the investment in each of its first 5 years are expected to be $600,000 and the subsequent oral discussions do not indicate that the amount of those deductions will change under the circumstances in which the income expected may be as little as $500,000, the subsequent oral discussions taken together with the written financial projections state (or lead a reasonable investor to believe) that the cumulative tax liability of an investor may be reduced (*i.e.,* the subsequent oral discussions (taken together with the projections) state or lead a reasonable investor to believe that cumulative projected deductions may exceed cumulative projected income under circumstances that are not highly unlikely). Accordingly, under paragraph (b) of A-57B of this section, the tax shelter would not qualify as a projected income investment.

Example (2). The written promotional material with respect to a tax shelter states that certain deductions are allowable to an investor (without specifying their amount), but there is no written statement relating to the amount of income expected from the investment. Because there is no written financial projection or other written representation that states or leads a reasonable investor to believe that the investment will not reduce the investor's cumulative tax liability (*i.e.,* the cumulative projected deductions, although not specified in the projections, may exceed the cumulative projected income (0)), the requirement of paragraph (a) of A-57B of this section would not be satisfied. The result in this example would be the same if there were only oral representations that the income to be derived from the investment would exceed the deductions with respect to the investment, because there would be no written statement as required by paragraph (a) of A-57B of this section. The tax shelter in this case would qualify as a projected income investment, however, if the written promotional material contains good-faith representations based on reasonable economic and business assumptions that state or lead reasonable investors to believe that the cumulative projected income from the investment will exceed the cumulative projected deductions allowable with respect to the investment for each year in the 5-year period, even though the amounts of income and deductions are not specified.

Example (3). The written promotional material with respect to a tax shelter includes a good-faith financial projection for the first 5 years of the investment. Based on reasonable economic and business assumptions, the projection indicates that the expected net income of the investment in

each of its first 4 years is $100,000 ($500,000 of gross income and $400,000 of gross deductions), but as a result of the anticipated acquisition of new business assets a loss of $20,000 is expected in the fifth year of the investment ($500,000 of gross income and $520,000 of gross deductions). The projection also indicates that a credit of $50,000 is expected in the fifth year of the investment. Such a written financial projection would be considered to state that the investment will not reduce the cumulative tax liability of any investor with respect to any year in the 5-year period described in A-4(I) of this section. Although a loss and a credit are projected in the fifth year of the investment, as of the close of such year, cumulative projected income ($2,500,000) exceeds cumulative projected deductions ($2,120,000), and cumulative projected tax liability (without regard to credits) ($380,000 × 50 percent = $190,000) exceeds cumulative projected credits ($50,000). Assuming no contrary oral or written projections or representations are made, the tax shelter would thus be a projected income investment.

Example (4). The written promotional material with respect to a tax shelter states that an investor will be entitled to a "1.5 to 1 write-off" in the year of investment. This statement is a representation that the investment will reduce the cumulative tax liability of an investor with respect to the first year of the investment and, accordingly, the investment is not a projected income investment. The result in this example would be the same if any "write-off" were represented, even if the write-off were less than 1.5 to 1.

Q-57D. Are all financial projections and representations relating to the cumulative tax liability of an investor taken into account for purposes of A-57B of this section?

A-57D. (a) No. A financial projection or other representation relating to the cumulative tax liability of an investor is not taken into account for purposes of A-57B of this section unless it is made in good faith and is based on reasonable economic and business assumptions. In addition, a financial projection or other representation is not taken into account if it relates to circumstances that are highly unlikely. Moreover, a general statement or disclaimer indicating that projected income is not guaranteed or otherwise assured, standing alone, is not a projection or representation for purposes of paragraph (b) of A-57B of this section.

(b) The following example illustrates the application of the principles of this A-57D:

Example. The written promotional material with respect to a tax shelter contains a representation stating that the investment is projected to produce net income for all investors in each of its first five years and there are no credits potentially allowable with respect to the investment. This statement is based on reasonable economic and business assumptions. Such a written representation, if made in good faith, would be considered under paragraph (a) of A-57B of this section to state that the investment will not reduce the cumulative tax liability of any investor with respect to any year in the 5-year period described in A-4(I) of this section. In addition, no oral or written statements or representations are communicated to investors that would indicate under paragraph (b) of A-57B of this section that the investment might reduce the cumulative tax liability of any investor with respect to any year in the 5-year period.

Assume the tax shelter organizer has knowledge of certain other facts that lead the tax shelter organizer to believe that it is more likely than not that the investment will produce a net loss in the first year. The representation projecting net income is thus contrary to the tax shelter organizer's belief that it is more likely than not that the investment will produce a net loss in the first year. Therefore, the representation is not made in good faith. Since representations are not made in good faith are ignored under A-57D, the tax shelter would not be a projected income investment. If, on the other hand, the tax shelter organizer did not know of the other facts so that the tax shelter organizer did not believe that the investment would produce a net loss in the first year, the representation projecting income is made in good faith. In that case, the tax shelter would be a projected income investment.

Q-57E. What assets may not be held by a projected income investment?

A-57E. A tax shelter is not a projected income investment if more than an incidental amount of its assets include or relate to any interest in a collectible (as defined in section 408(m)(2)), a master sound recording, motion picture or television film, videotape, lithograph plate, copyright, or a literary, musical, or artistic composition.

Q-57F. What are the consequences if financial projections or other representations are not made in good faith or are not based on reasonable economic and business assumptions?

A-57F. If a tax shelter is not a projected income investment because the financial projections or other representations are not made in good faith or are not based on reasonable economic and business assumptions, it must be registered not later than the day on which the first offering for sale of an interest in the tax shelter occurs. If the tax shelter is not registered timely, the tax shelter organizer may be subject to a penalty. (See A-1 of § 301.6707-1T.)

Q-57G. When does a tax shelter cease to be a projected income investment?

A-57G. A tax shelter ceases to be a projected income investment on the last day of the first year (as defined in A-7 of this section) in the 5-year period described in A-4(I) of this section for which, for any investor, (i) the gross deductions allocable to the investor for that year and prior years exceed the gross income allocable to the investor for such years, or (ii) the credits allocable to the investor for that year and prior years exceed 50 percent of the amount by which gross income allocable to the investor exceeds gross deductions allocable to the investor for

such years. For purposes of determining when a tax shelter ceases to be a projected income investment, the tax shelter organizer is not required to take into account interest that may be incurred by an investor with respect to debt described in A-14(2) or (3) of this section, but is required to take into account interest incurred by an investor with respect to debt described in A-14(1) of this section. In addition, the tax shelter organizer may not take into account income attributable to cash, cash equivalents, or marketable securities (within the meaning of A-14(4) of this section).

Q-57H. How does the requirement to register apply with respect to a tax shelter that is a projected income investment?

A-57H. In the case of a tax shelter that is a projected income investment, registration is not required unless the tax shelter ceases to be a projected income investment under A-57G of this section. If the tax shelter ceases to be a projected income investment, the tax shelter organizer must register the tax shelter in accordance with the rules set forth in A-1 through A-39 and A-41 through A-50 of this section. The tax shelter must be registered—

(a) Within 30 days after the date on which the tax shelter ceases to be a projected income investment, and

(b) Before the date on which the tax shelter or a tax shelter organizer sends the investor any schedule of profit or loss, or income, deduction, or credit that may be used in preparing the investor's income tax return for the taxable year that includes the date on which the tax shelter ceases to be a projected income investment. If a tax shelter organizer fails to register timely as required by this A-57H, the tax shelter organizer may be subject to a penalty. (See A-1 of § 301.6707-1T.) For example, assume that C is the principal organizer and general partner of a limited partnership. Interests in the partnership will be offered for sale in a public offering required to be registered with the Securities and Exchange Commission. C knows that the tax shelter ratio (as defined in A-5 of this section) for the limited partners will be 5 to 1. Although C knows the partnership is a tax shelter, C does not register the partnership by the day on which the first offering for sale of an interest occurs because C believes the partnership is a projected income investment. In the second year of the partnership, the gross deductions allocable to each of the limited partners for the first two years of the partnership exceed the gross income allocable to the limited partners in such years. Thus, the partnership ceases to be a projected income investment under A-57G of this section. Assuming further that C continues as the general partner and knowingly fails to register the partnership as a tax shelter within the time prescribed in this A-57H, C will be subject to a penalty of 1 percent of the aggregate amount invested in the partnership. Because there is an intentional disregard of the registration requirements, the $10,000 limitation will not apply.

Q-57I. How does the requirement to furnish registration numbers (A-51 through A-54 of this section) apply in the case of a tax shelter that is a projected income investment?

A-57I. In the case of a tax shelter that is a projected income investment, a person who sells or transfers an interest in the tax shelter is not required to furnish a registration number under A-51 of this section or a notice under A-54 of this section unless the tax shelter ceases to be a projected income investment. If the tax shelter ceases to be a projected income investment, the tax shelter organizer who registers the tax shelter is required to furnish the registration number to all persons who the tax shelter organizer knows or has reason to know are participating in the sale of interests in the tax shelter and to all persons who the tax shelter organizer knows or has reason to know have acquired interests in the tax shelter. A person who sold (or otherwise transferred) an interest in the tax shelter before the date on which the tax shelter ceased to be a projected income investment is required to furnish the registration number to the purchaser or transferee as provided in A-51 of this section only if the seller or transferor knows or has reason to know that the tax shelter has ceased to be a projected income investment and that the tax shelter organizer who registered the tax shelter has not provided a registration number to such purchaser or transferee. In the case of persons who acquired interests in the tax shelter before the date on which the tax shelter ceased to be a projected income investment, the registration number must be provided not later than the date described in paragraph (b) of A-57H of this section or, if the tax shelter does not provide any schedule described in paragraph (b) of A-57H of this section, within 60 days after the date on which the tax shelter ceases to be a projected income investment. Thus, for example, if a tax shelter that ceases to be a projected income investment is a partnership, the tax shelter organizer would be required to provide the registration number to each partner not later than the date the Schedule K-1 for the year in which the tax shelter ceases to be a projected income investment is provided to each partner.

The registration number must be provided in accordance with A-51 and A-52 of this section and must be accompanied by a statement explaining that the tax shelter has ceased to be a projected income investment and instructing the recipient to furnish the registration number to any persons to whom the recipient has sold or otherwise transferred interests in the tax shelter. A tax shelter organizer who fails to provide the registration number as provided in this A-57I may be subject to penalties. (See A-12 of §301.6707-1T.)

Q-57J. How does the requirement to include the registration number on tax returns (A-55 through A-57 of this section) apply in the case of a tax shelter that is a projected income investment?

A-57J. In the case of a tax shelter that is a projected income investment, an investor is not required to report a registration number on the investor's tax return unless the tax shelter ceases to be a projected income investment. If the tax shelter ceases to be a projected income investment, the requirements of A-55 through A-57 apply with respect to returns for taxable years ending on or after the date on which the tax shelter ceases to be a projected income investment.

Effective dates

Q-58. On what date does the requirement to register a tax shelter become effective?

A-58. In general, a tax shelter must be registered if any interest in the tax shelter (other than an interest previously sold to an investor) is sold on or after September 1, 1984 (whether or not interests in the tax shelter were sold or offered for sale before September 1, 1984). The tax shelter must be registered with the Internal Revenue Service not later than the first day after August 31, 1984 on which an interest in the tax shelter is offered for sale.

Q-59. By what date must the tax shelter registration number be furnished to investors who acquired interests before September 1, 1984 in a tax shelter that is required to be registered.

A-59. All investors who acquired their interests in a tax shelter before September 1, 1984 must be supplied with the tax shelter registration number by December 31, 1984. See A-52 of this section for the date by which registration numbers must be furnished to investors who acquire their interests on or after September 1, 1984.

Q-60. What interests will be taken into account in determining whether an investment in which interests were sold before September 1, 1984, is a substantial investment?

A-60. The determination of whether an investment is a substantial investment will be made by taking into account only the interests that are offered for sale on or after September 1, 1984. An investment will be considered a substantial investment if there are expected to be 5 or more investors on or after September 1, 1984, and the aggregate amount offered for sale on or after September 1, 1984 is expected to exceed $250,000. Amounts received from the sale of interests before September 1, 1984, however, are taken into account in computing the amount of the penalty for failure to register. [Temporary Reg. §301.6111-1T.]

☐ [T.D. 7964, 8-13-84 (*corrected* 12-1-2008). *Amended by T.D. 7990, 10-26-84 and T.D. 8078, 3-3-86.*]

[Reg. §301.6111-2]

§301.6111-2. Confidential corporate tax shelters.—(a) *In general.*—(1) Under section 6111(d) and this section, a confidential corporate tax shelter is treated as a tax shelter subject to the requirements of sections 6111(a) and (b).

(2) A confidential corporate tax shelter is any transaction—

(i) A significant purpose of the structure of which is the avoidance or evasion of Federal income tax, as described in paragraph (b) of this section, for a direct or indirect corporate participant;

(ii) That is offered to any potential participant under conditions of confidentiality, as described in paragraph (c) of this section; and

(iii) For which the tax shelter promoters may receive fees in excess of $100,000 in the aggregate, as described in paragraph (d) of this section.

(3) For purposes of this section, references to the term *transaction* include all of the factual elements relevant to the expected tax treatment of any investment, entity, plan, or arrangement, and include any series of steps carried out as part of a plan. For purposes of this section, the term *substantially similar* includes any transaction that is expected to obtain the same or similar types of tax consequences and that is either factually similar or based on the same or similar tax strategy. Receipt of an opinion regarding the tax consequences of the transaction is not relevant to the determination of whether the transaction is the same as or substantially similar to another transaction. Further, the term *substantially similar* must be broadly construed in favor of registration. For examples, see § 1.6011-4(c)(4) of this chapter.

(4) A transaction described in paragraph (b) of this section is for a direct or an indirect corporate participant if it is expected to provide Federal income tax benefits to any corporation (U.S. or foreign) whether or not that corporation participates directly in the transaction.

(b) *Transactions structured for avoidance or evasion of Federal income tax.*—(1) *In general.*—The avoidance or evasion of Federal income tax will be considered a significant purpose of the structure of a transaction if the transaction is described in paragraph (b)(2) or (3) of this section. However, a transaction described in paragraph (b)(3) of this section need not be registered if the transaction is described in paragraph (b)(4) of this section. For purposes of this section, Federal income tax benefits include deductions, exclusions from gross income, nonrecognition of gain, tax credits, adjustments (or the absence of adjustments) to the basis of property, status as an entity exempt from Federal income taxation, and any other tax consequences that may reduce a taxpayer's Federal income tax liability by affecting the amount, timing, character, or source of any item of income, gain, expense, loss, or credit.

(2) *Listed transactions.*—A transaction is described in this paragraph (b)(2) if the transaction is the same as or substantially similar to one of the types of transactions that the Internal Revenue Service (IRS) has determined to be a tax avoidance transaction and identified by notice, regulation, or other form of published guidance as a listed transaction. If a transaction becomes a listed transaction after the date on which registration would otherwise be required under this section, and if the transaction otherwise satisfies the confidentiality and fee requirements of paragraphs (a)(2)(ii) and (iii) of this section, registration shall in all events be required with

respect to any interests in the transaction that are offered for sale after the transaction becomes a listed transaction. However, because a transaction identified as a listed transaction is generally considered to have been structured for a significant tax avoidance purpose, such a transaction ordinarily will have been subject to registration under this section before becoming a listed transaction if the transaction previously satisfied the confidentiality and fee requirements of paragraphs (a)(2)(ii) and (iii) of this section.

(3) *Other tax-structured transactions.*—A transaction is described in this paragraph (b)(3) if it has been structured to produce Federal income tax benefits that constitute an important part of the intended results of the transaction and the tax shelter promoter (or other person who would be responsible for registration under this section) reasonably expects the transaction to be presented in the same or substantially similar form to more than one potential participant, unless the promoter reasonably determines that—

(i) The potential participant is expected to participate in the transaction in the ordinary course of its business in a form consistent with customary commercial practice (a transaction involving the acquisition, disposition, or restructuring of a business, including the acquisition, disposition, or other change in the ownership or control of an entity that is engaged in a business, or a transaction involving a recapitalization or an acquisition of capital for use in the taxpayer's business, shall be considered a transaction carried out in the ordinary course of a taxpayer's business); and

(ii) There is a generally accepted understanding that the expected Federal income tax benefits from the transaction (taking into account any combination of intended tax consequences) are properly allowable under the Internal Revenue Code for substantially similar transactions. There is no minimum period of time for which such a generally accepted understanding must exist. In general, however, a tax shelter promoter (or other person who would be responsible for registration under this section) cannot reasonably determine whether the intended tax treatment of a transaction has become generally accepted unless information relating to the tax treatment and tax structure of such transactions has been in the public domain (e.g., rulings, published articles, etc.) and widely known for a sufficient period of time (ordinarily a period of years) to provide knowledgeable tax practitioners and the IRS reasonable opportunity to evaluate the intended tax treatment. The mere fact that one or more knowledgeable tax practitioners have provided an opinion or advice to the effect that the intended tax treatment of the transaction should or will be sustained, if challenged by the IRS, is not sufficient to satisfy the requirements of this paragraph (b)(3)(ii).

(4) *Excepted transactions.*—The avoidance or evasion of Federal income tax will not be consid-

ered a significant purpose of the structure of a transaction if the transaction is described in either paragraph (b)(4)(i), (ii), or (iii) of this section.

(i) In the case of a transaction other than a transaction described in paragraph (b)(2) of this section, the tax shelter promoter (or other person who would be responsible for registration under this section) reasonably determines that there is no reasonable basis under Federal tax law for denial of any significant portion of the expected Federal income tax benefits from the transaction. This paragraph (b)(4)(i) applies only if the tax shelter promoter (or other person who would be responsible for registration under this section) reasonably determines that there is no basis that would meet the standard applicable to taxpayers under § 1.6662-3(b)(3) of this chapter under which the IRS could disallow any significant portion of the expected Federal income tax benefits of the transaction. Thus, the reasonable basis standard is not satisfied by an IRS position that would be merely arguable or that would constitute merely a colorable claim. However, the determination of whether the IRS would or would not have a reasonable basis for such a position must take into account the entirety of the transaction and any combination of tax consequences that are expected to result from any component steps of the transaction, must not be based on any unreasonable or unrealistic factual assumptions, and must take into account all relevant aspects of Federal tax law, including the statute and legislative history, treaties, administrative guidance, and judicial decisions that establish principles of general application in the tax law (e.g., *Gregory v. Helvering*, 293 U.S. 465 (1935)). The determination of whether the IRS would or would not have such a reasonable basis is qualitative in nature and does not depend on any percentage or other quantitative assessment of the likelihood that the taxpayer would ultimately prevail if a significant portion of the expected tax benefits were disallowed by the IRS.

(ii) The IRS makes a determination by published guidance that the transaction is not subject to the registration requirements of this section.

(iii) The IRS makes a determination by individual ruling under paragraph (b)(5) of this section that a specific transaction is not subject to the registration requirements of this section for the taxpayer requesting the ruling.

(5) *Requests for ruling.*—If a tax shelter promoter (or other person who would be responsible for registration under this section) is uncertain whether a transaction is properly classified as a confidential corporate tax shelter or is otherwise uncertain whether registration is required under this section, that person may, on or before the date that registration would otherwise be required under this section, submit a request to the IRS for a ruling as to whether the transaction is subject to the registration requirements of this section. If the request fully discloses all relevant facts relating to the transaction, that person's potential obligation to register the transaction will be suspended during the period that the ruling request is pending and, if the IRS subsequently concludes that the transaction is a confidential corporate tax shelter subject to registration under this section, until the sixtieth day after the issuance of the ruling (or, if the request is withdrawn, sixty days from the date that the request is withdrawn). In the alternative, that person may register the transaction in accordance with the requirements of this section and append a statement to the Form 8264, "Application for Registration of a Tax Shelter," which states that the person is uncertain whether the transaction is required to be registered as a confidential corporate tax shelter, and that the Form 8264 is being filed on a protective basis.

(6) *Example.*—The following example illustrates the application of paragraphs (b)(1) through (4) of this section. Assume, for purposes of the example, that the transaction is not the same as or substantially similar to any of the types of transactions that the IRS has identified as listed transactions under section 6111 and, thus, is not described in paragraph (b)(2) of this section. The example is as follows:

Example. (i) *Facts.* Y has designed a combination of financial instruments to be issued as a package by corporations. The financial instruments are expected to be treated as equity for financial accounting purposes and as debt giving rise to allowable interest deductions for Federal income tax purposes. Y reasonably expects to present this method of raising capital to more than one potential corporate participant. Assume that, because of the unusual nature of the combination of financial instruments, Y cannot conclude either that the transaction represented by the financial instruments is in customary commercial form or that there is a generally accepted understanding that interest deductions are available to issuers of substantially similar combinations of financial instruments. Further, assume that Y cannot reasonably determine that the IRS would have no reasonable basis to deny the deductions.

(ii) *Analysis.* The transaction represented by this combination of financial instruments is a transaction described in paragraph (b)(3) of this section. However, if Y is uncertain whether this transaction is described in paragraph (b)(3) of this section, or is otherwise uncertain whether registration is required, Y may apply for a ruling under paragraph (b)(5) of this section, and Y will not be required to register the transaction while the ruling is pending or for sixty days thereafter.

(c) *Conditions of confidentiality.*—(1) *In general.*—All the facts and circumstances relating to the transaction will be considered when determining whether an offer is made under conditions of confidentiality as described in section 6111(d)(2), including prior conduct of the parties. Pursuant to section 6111(d)(2)(A), if an offeree's disclosure of the tax treatment or tax structure of the transaction is limited in any manner by an express or implied understanding or agreement with or for the benefit of any tax shelter promoter, an offer is considered made under conditions of confidentiality, whether or not such understanding or agreement is legally binding. The tax treatment of a transaction is the purported or claimed Federal income tax treatment of the transaction. The tax structure of a transaction is any fact that may be relevant to understanding the purported or claimed Federal income tax treatment of the transaction. Pursuant to section 6111(d)(2)(B), an offer will also be considered made under conditions of confidentiality in the absence of any such understanding or agreement if any tax shelter promoter knows or has reason to know that the offeree's use or disclosure of information relating to the tax treatment or tax structure of the transaction is limited for the benefit of any person other than the offeree in any other manner, such as where the transaction is claimed to be proprietary or exclusive to the tax shelter promoter or any party other than the offeree.

(2) *Exceptions.*—(i) *Securities law.*—An offer is not considered made under conditions of confidentiality if disclosure of the tax treatment or tax structure of the transaction is subject to restrictions reasonably necessary to comply with securities laws and such disclosure is not otherwise limited.

(ii) *Mergers and acquisitions.*—In the case of a proposed taxable or tax-free acquisition of historic assets of a corporation (other than an investment company, as defined in section 351(e), that is not publicly traded) that constitute an active trade or business the acquirer intends to continue, or a proposed taxable or tax-free acquisition of more than 50 percent of the stock of a corporation (other than an investment company, as defined in section 351(e), that is not publicly traded) that owns historic assets used in an active trade or business the acquirer intends to continue, the transaction is not considered offered under conditions of confidentiality under paragraph (c)(1) of this section if the offeree is permitted to disclose the tax treatment and tax structure of the transaction no later than the earlier of the date of the public announcement of discussions relating to the transaction, the date of the public announcement of the transaction, or the date of the execution of an agreement (with or without conditions) to enter into the transaction. However, this exception is not available where the offeree's ability to consult any tax advisor (including a tax advisor independent from all other entities involved in the transaction) regarding the tax treatment or tax structure of the transaction is limited in any way.

(3) *Presumption.*—Unless facts and circumstances indicate otherwise, an offer is not considered made under conditions of confidentiality if the tax shelter promoter provides express written authorization to each offeree permitting the offeree (and each employee, representative, or other agent of such offeree) to disclose to any and all persons, without limitation of any kind, the tax treatment and tax structure of the transaction, and all materials of any kind (including opinions or other tax analyses) that are provided to the offeree related to such tax treatment and tax structure. Except as provided in paragraph (c)(2) of this section, this presumption is available only in cases in which each written authorization permits the offeree to disclose the tax treatment and tax structure of the transaction immediately upon commencement of discussions with the tax shelter promoter providing the authorization and each written authorization is given no later than 30 days from the day the tax shelter promoter commenced discussions with the offeree. A transaction that is exclusive or proprietary to any party other than the offeree will not be considered offered under conditions of confidentiality if written authorization to disclose is provided to the offeree in accordance with this paragraph (c)(3) and the transaction is not otherwise confidential.

(d) *Determination of fees.*—All the facts and circumstances relating to the transaction will be considered when determining the amount of fees, in the aggregate, that the tax shelter promoters may receive. For purposes of this paragraph (d), all consideration that tax shelter promoters may receive is taken into account, including contingent fees, fees in the form of equity interests, and fees the promoters may receive for other transactions as consideration for promoting the tax shelter. For example, if a tax shelter promoter may receive a fee for arranging a transaction that is a confidential corporate tax shelter and a separate fee for another transaction that is not a confidential corporate tax shelter, part or all of the fee paid with respect to the other transaction may be treated as a fee paid with respect to the confidential corporate tax shelter if the facts and circumstances indicate that the fee paid for the other transaction is in consideration for the confidential corporate tax shelter. For purposes of determining whether the tax shelter promoters may receive fees in excess of $100,000, the fees from all substantially similar transactions are considered part of the same tax shelter and must be aggregated.

(e) *Registration.*—(1) *Time for registering.*—(i) *In general.*—A tax shelter must be registered not later than the day on which the first offering for sale of interests in the shelter occurs. An offer to participate in a confidential corporate tax shelter shall be treated as an offer for sale. If interests in a confidential corporate tax shelter were first offered for sale on or before February 28, 2000, the first offer for sale of interests in the shelter that occurs after February 28, 2000 shall be considered the first offer for sale under this section.

(ii) *Special rule.*—If a transaction becomes a confidential corporate tax shelter (e.g., because of a change in the law or factual circumstances, or because the transaction becomes a listed transaction) subsequent to the first offering for sale after February 28, 2000, and the transaction was not previously required to be registered as a confidential corporate tax shelter under this section, the transaction must be registered under this section if interests are offered for sale after the transaction becomes a confidential corporate tax shelter. The transaction must be registered by the next offering for sale of interests in the shelter. If, subsequent to the first offering for sale, a transaction becomes a confidential corporate tax shelter because the transaction becomes a listed transaction on or after February 28, 2003, and the transaction was not previously required to be registered as a confidential corporate tax shelter under this section, the transaction must be registered under this section within 60 days after the transaction becomes a listed transaction/confidential corporate tax shelter if any interests were offered for sale within the previous six years.

(2) *Procedures for registering.*—To register a confidential corporate tax shelter, the person responsible for registering the tax shelter must file Form 8264, "Application for Registration of a Tax Shelter." (Form 8264 is also used to register tax shelters defined in section 6111(c).) Similar to the treatment provided under Q&A-22 and Q&A-48 of § 301.6111-1T, transactions involving similar business assets and similar plans or arrangements that are offered to corporate taxpayers by the same person or related persons are aggregated and considered part of a single tax shelter. However, in contrast with the requirement of Q&A-48 of § 301.6111-1T, the tax shelter promoter may file a single Form 8264 with respect to any such aggregated tax shelter, provided an amended Form 8264 is filed to reflect any material changes and to include any additional or revised written materials presented in connection with an offer to participate in the shelter. Furthermore, all transactions that are part of the same tax shelter and that are to be carried out by the same corporate participant (or one or more other members of the same affiliated group within the meaning of section 1504) must be registered on the same Form 8264.

(f) *Definition of tax shelter promoter.*—For purposes of section 6111(d)(2) and this section, the term *tax shelter promoter* includes a tax shelter organizer and any other person who participates in the organization, management or sale of a tax shelter (as those persons are described in section 6111(e)(1) and § 301.6111-1T (Q&A-26 through Q&A-33) or any person related (within the meaning of section 267 or 707) to such tax shelter organizer or such other person.

(g) *Person required to register.*—(1) *Tax shelter promoters.*—The rules in section 6111(a) and (e) and § 301.6111-1T (Q&A-34 through Q&A-39) determine who is required to register a confidential corporate tax shelter. A promoter of a confidential corporate tax shelter must register the tax shelter only if it is a person required to register under the rules in section 6111(a) and (e) and § 301.6111-1T (Q&A-34 through Q&A-39).

(2) *Persons who discuss the transaction; all promoters are foreign persons.*—(i) *In general.*—If all of the tax shelter promoters of a confidential corporate tax shelter are foreign persons, any person who discusses participation in the transaction must register the shelter under this section within 90 days after beginning such discussions.

(ii) *Exceptions.*—Registration by a person discussing participation in a transaction is not required if either—

(A) The person does not participate, directly or indirectly, in the shelter and notifies the tax shelter promoter in writing, within 90 days of beginning such discussions, that the person will not participate; or

(B) Within 90 days after beginning such discussions, the person obtains and reasonably relies on both—

(1) A written statement from one of the tax shelter promoters that such promoter has registered the tax shelter under this section; and

(2) A copy of the registration.

(iii) *Determination of foreign status.*—For purposes of this paragraph (g)(2), a person must presume that all tax shelter promoters are foreign persons unless the person either—

(A) Discusses participation in the tax shelter with a promoter that is a United States person; or

(B) Obtains and reasonably relies on a written statement from one of the promoters that at least one of the promoters is a United States person.

(iv) *Discussion.*—Discussing participation in a transaction includes discussing such participation with any person that conveys the tax shelter promoter's proposal. For purposes of this paragraph (g)(2), any person that participates directly or indirectly in a transaction will be treated as having discussed participation in the transaction not later than the date of the agreement to participate. Thus, a tax shelter participant will be treated as having discussed participation in the transaction even if all discussions were conducted by an intermediary and the agreement to participate was made indirectly through another person acting on the participant's behalf (for example, through an intermediary empowered to commit the participant to participate in the shelter).

(v) *Special rule for controlled entities.*—A person (first person) will be treated as participating indirectly in a confidential corporate tax shelter if a foreign person controlled by the first person participates in the shelter, and a significant purpose of the shelter is the avoidance or evasion of the first person's Federal income tax. For purposes of this paragraph (g)(2)(v), control of a foreign corporation or partnership will be determined under the rules of section 6038(e)(2) and (3), except that such section shall be applied by substituting "10" for "50" each place it appears and "at least" for "more than" each place it appears. In addition, section 6038(e)(2) shall be applied for these purposes without regard to the constructive ownership rules of section 318 and by treating stock as owned if it is owned directly or indirectly. Section 6038(e)(3) shall be applied for these purposes without regard to the last sentence of section 6038(e)(3)(B). Any beneficiary with a 10 percent or more interest in a foreign trust or estate shall be treated as controlling that trust or estate for purposes of this paragraph (g)(2)(v).

(vi) *Other rules.*—(A) For purposes of the registration requirements under section 6111(d)(3), it is presumed that the tax shelter promoters will receive fees in excess of $100,000 in the aggregate unless the person responsible for registering the tax shelter can show otherwise.

(B) Any person treated as a tax shelter promoter under section 6111(d) solely by reason of being related (within the meaning of section 267 or 707) to a foreign promoter will be treated as a foreign promoter for purposes of this paragraph (g)(2).

(h) *Effective dates.*—This section applies to confidential corporate tax shelters in which any interests are offered for sale after February 28, 2000. If an interest is sold after February 28, 2000, it is treated as offered for sale after February 28, 2000, unless the sale was pursuant to a written binding contract entered into on or before February 28, 2000. However, paragraphs (a) through (g) of this section apply to confidential corporate tax shelters in which any interests are offered for sale on or after February 28, 2003, and to transactions described in paragraph (e)(1)(ii) of this section. The rules that apply to confidential corporate tax shelters in which any interests are offered for sale after February 28, 2000, and before February 28, 2003, are contained in §301.6111-2T in effect prior to February 28, 2003 (see 26 CFR part 301 revised as of April 1, 2002, 2002-28 I.R.B. 91, and 2002-45 I.R.B. 823 (see §601.601(d)(2) of this chapter)). [Reg. §301.6111-2.]

☐ [*T.D. 9046*, 2-28-2003.]

[Reg. §301.6111-3]

§301.6111-3. Disclosure of reportable transactions.—(a) *In general.*—Each material advisor, as defined in paragraph (b) of this section, with respect to any reportable transaction, as defined in §1.6011-4(b) of this chapter, must file a return as described in paragraph (d) of this section by the date described in paragraph (e) of this section.

(b) *Material advisor.*—(1) *In general.*—A person is a material advisor with respect to a transaction if the person provides any material aid, assistance, or advice with respect to organizing, managing, promoting, selling, implementing, insuring, or carrying out any reportable transaction, and directly or indirectly derives gross income in excess of the threshold amount as defined in paragraph (b)(3) of this section for the material aid, assistance, or advice. The term transaction includes all of the factual elements relevant to the expected tax treatment of any

investment, entity, plan or arrangement, and includes any series of steps carried out as part of a plan.

(2) *Material aid, assistance, or advice.*—(i) *In general.*—Except as provided in paragraph (b)(5) of this section, a person provides material aid, assistance, or advice with respect to organizing, managing, promoting, selling, implementing, insuring, or carrying out any transaction if the person makes or provides a tax statement to or for the benefit of—

(A) A taxpayer who either is required to disclose the transaction under §§1.6011-4, 20.6011-4, 25.6011-4, 26.6011-4, 31.6011-4, 53.6011-4, 54.6011-4, or 56.6011-4 of this chapter because the transaction is a listed transaction or a transaction of interest, or would have been required to disclose the transaction under §§1.6011-4, 20.6011-4, 25.6011-4, 26.6011-4, 31.6011-4, 53.6011-4, 54.6011-4, or 56.6011-4 of this chapter if the transaction had become a listed transaction or a transaction of interest within the period of limitations in §1.6011-4(e) of this chapter;

(B) A taxpayer who the potential material advisor knows is or reasonably expects to be required to disclose the transaction under §1.6011-4 of this chapter because the transaction is or is reasonably expected to become a transaction described in §1.6011-4(b)(3) through (5) or (7) of this chapter;

(C) A material advisor who is required to disclose the transaction under this section because it is a listed transaction or a transaction of interest; or

(D) A material advisor who the potential material advisor knows is or reasonably expects to be required to disclose the transaction under this section because the transaction is or is reasonably expected to become a transaction described in §1.6011-4(b)(3) through (5) or (7) of this chapter.

(ii) *Tax statement.*—(A) *In general.*—A tax statement is any statement (including another person's statement), oral or written, that relates to a tax aspect of a transaction that causes the transaction to be a reportable transaction as defined in §1.6011-4(b)(2) through (7) of this chapter. A tax statement under this section includes tax result protection that insures some or all of the tax benefits of a reportable transaction.

(B) *Confidential transactions.*—A statement relates to a tax aspect of a transaction that causes it to be a confidential transaction if the statement concerns a tax benefit related to the transaction and either the taxpayer's disclosure of the tax treatment or tax structure of the transaction is limited in the manner described in §1.6011-4(b)(3) of this chapter by or for the benefit of the person making the statement, or the person making the statement knows the taxpayer's disclosure of the tax structure or tax aspects of the transaction is limited in the manner described in §1.6011-4(b)(3) of this chapter.

(C) *Transactions with contractual protection.*—A statement relates to a tax aspect of a transaction that causes it to be a transaction with contractual protection if the statement concerns a tax benefit related to the transaction and either—

(1) The taxpayer has the right to a full or partial refund of fees paid to the person making the statement or the fees are contingent in the manner described in § 1.6011-4(b)(4) of this chapter; or

(2) The person making the statement knows or has reason to know that the taxpayer has the right to a full or partial refund of fees (described in § 1.6011-4(b)(4)(ii) of this chapter) paid to another if all or part of the intended tax consequences from the transaction are not sustained or that fees (as described in § 1.6011-4(b)(4)(ii) of this chapter) paid by the taxpayer to another are contingent on the taxpayer's realization of tax benefits from the transaction in the manner described in § 1.6011-4(b)(4) of this chapter.

(D) *Loss transactions.*—A statement relates to a tax aspect of a transaction that causes it to be a loss transaction if the statement concerns an item that gives rise to a loss described in § 1.6011-4(b)(5) of this chapter.

(E) *[Reserved].*

(iii) *Special rules.*—(A) *Capacity as an employee.*—A material advisor generally does not include a person who makes a tax statement solely in the person's capacity as an employee, shareholder, partner or agent of another person. Any tax statement made by that person will be attributed to that person's employer, corporation, partnership or principal. However, a person shall be treated as a material advisor if that person forms or avails of an entity with the purpose of avoiding the rules of section 6111 or 6112 or the penalties under section 6707 or 6708.

(B) *Post-filing advice.*—A person will not be considered to be a material advisor with respect to a transaction if that person does not make or provide a tax statement regarding the transaction until after the first tax return reflecting tax benefit(s) of the transaction is filed with the IRS. However, this exception does not apply to a person who makes a tax statement with respect to the transaction if it is expected that the taxpayer will file a supplemental or amended return reflecting additional tax benefits from the transaction.

(C) *Publicly filed statements.*—A tax statement with respect to a transaction that includes only information about the transaction contained in publicly available documents filed with the Securities and Exchange Commission no later than the close of the transaction will not be considered a tax statement to or for the benefit of a person described in paragraph (b)(2) of this section.

(3) *Gross income derived for material aid, assistance, or advice.*—(i) *Threshold amount.*—(A) *In general.*—The threshold amount of gross income

is $50,000 in the case of a reportable transaction substantially all of the tax benefits from which are provided to natural persons (looking through any partnerships, S corporations, or trusts). For all other transactions, the threshold amount is $250,000.

(B) *Listed transactions and transactions of interest.*—For listed transactions described in §§ 1.6011-4, 20.6011-4, 25.6011-4, 26.6011-4, 31.6011-4, 53.6011-4, 54.6011-4, or 56.6011-4 of this chapter, the threshold amounts in paragraph (b)(3)(i)(A) of this section are reduced from $50,000 to $10,000 and from $250,000 to $25,000. For transactions of interest described in §§ 1.6011-4, 20.6011-4, 25.6011-4, 26.6011-4, 31.6011-4, 53.6011-4, 54.6011-4, or 56.6011-4 of this chapter, the threshold amounts in paragraph (b)(3)(i)(A) of this section may be reduced as identified in the published guidance describing the transaction.

(C) *[Reserved].*

(D) *Substantially all of the tax benefits.*— For purposes of this section, the determination of whether substantially all of the tax benefits from a reportable transaction are provided to natural persons is made based on all the facts and circumstances. Generally, unless the facts and circumstances prove otherwise, if 70 percent or more of the tax benefits from a reportable transaction are provided to natural persons (looking through any partnerships, S corporations, or trusts) then substantially all of the tax benefits will be considered to be provided to natural persons.

(ii) *Gross income derived directly or indirectly for the material aid, assistance, or advice.*—In determining the amount of gross income a person derives directly or indirectly for material aid, assistance, or advice, all fees for a tax strategy or for services for advice (whether or not tax advice) or for the implementation of a reportable transaction are taken into account. Fees include consideration in whatever form paid, whether in cash or in kind, for services to analyze the transaction (whether or not related to the tax consequences of the transaction), for services to implement the transaction, for services to document the transaction, and for services to prepare tax returns to the extent return preparation fees are unreasonable in light of all of the facts and circumstances. A fee does not include amounts paid to a person, including an advisor, in that person's capacity as a party to the transaction. For example, a fee does not include reasonable charges for the use of capital or the sale or use of property. The IRS will scrutinize carefully all of the facts and circumstances in determining whether consideration received in connection with a reportable transaction constitutes gross income derived directly or indirectly for aid, assistance, or advice. For purposes of this section, the threshold amount must be met independently for each transaction that is a reportable transaction and aggregation of fees among transactions is not required.

(4) *Date a person becomes a material advisor.*—(i) *In general.*—A person will be treated as becoming a material advisor when all of the following events have occurred (in no particular order)—

    (A) The person provides material aid, assistance or advice as described in paragraph (b)(2) of this section;

    (B) The person directly or indirectly derives gross income in excess of the threshold amount as described in paragraph (b)(3) of this section; and

    (C) The transaction is entered into by the taxpayer to whom or for whose benefit the person provided the tax statement, or in the case of a tax statement provided to another material advisor, when the transaction is entered into by a taxpayer to whom or for whose benefit that material advisor provided a tax statement.

    (ii) *Determining if the taxpayer entered into the transaction.*—Material advisors, including those who cease providing services before the time the transaction is entered into, must make reasonable and good faith efforts to determine whether the event described in paragraph (b)(4)(i)(C) of this section has occurred.

    (iii) *Listed transactions and transactions of interest.*—If a transaction that was not a reportable transaction is identified as a listed transaction or a transaction of interest in published guidance after the occurrence of the events described in paragraph (b)(4)(i) of this section, the person will be treated as becoming a material advisor on the date the transaction is identified as a listed transaction or a transaction of interest.

(5) *Other persons designated as material advisors.*—Published guidance may identify other types or classes of persons as material advisors.

(c) *Definitions.*—For purposes of this section, the following definitions apply:

(1) *Reportable transaction.*—The term *reportable transaction* is defined in § 1.6011-4(b)(1) of this chapter.

(2) *Listed transaction.*—The term *listed transaction* is defined in § 1.6011-4(b)(2) of this chapter. See also § § 20.6011-4(a), 25.6011-4(a), 26.6011-4, 31.6011-4(a), 53.6011-4(a), 54.6011-4(a), or 56.6011-4(a) of this chapter.

(3) *Derive.*—The term *derive* means receive or expect to receive.

(4) *Person.*—The term *person* means any person described in section 7701(a)(1), including an affiliated group of corporations that join in the filing of a consolidated return under section 1501.

(5) *Substantially similar.*—The term *substantially similar* is defined in § 1.6011-4(c)(4) of this chapter.

(6) *Tax.*—The term *tax* means Federal tax.

(7) *Tax benefit.*—A tax benefit includes deductions, exclusions from gross income, nonrecognition of gain, tax credits, adjustments (or the absence of adjustments) to the basis of property, status as an entity exempt from Federal income taxation, and any other tax consequences that may reduce a taxpayer's Federal tax liability by affecting the amount, timing, character, or source of any item of income, gain, expense, loss, or credit.

(8) *Tax return.*—The term *tax return* means a Federal tax return and a Federal information return.

(9) *Tax structure.*—The tax structure of a transaction is any fact that may be relevant to understanding the purported or claimed Federal tax treatment of the transaction.

(10) *Tax treatment.*—The tax treatment of a transaction is the purported or claimed Federal tax treatment of the transaction.

(11) *Taxpayer.*—The term *taxpayer* is defined in § 1.6011-4(c)(1) of this chapter.

(12) *Tax result protection.*—The term *tax result protection* includes insurance company and other third party products commonly described as tax result insurance.

(13) *Transaction of interest.*—The term *transaction of interest* is defined in § 1.6011-4(b)(6) of this chapter. See also § § 20.6011-4(a), 25.6011-4(a), 26.6011-4, 31.6011-4(a), 53.6011-4(a), 54.6011-4(a), or 56.6011-4(a) of this chapter.

(d) *Form and content of material advisor's disclosure statement.*—(1) *In general.*—A material advisor required to file a disclosure statement under this section must file a completed Form 8918, "Material Advisor Disclosure Statement" (or successor form) in accordance with this paragraph (d) and the instructions to the form. To be considered complete, the information provided on the form must describe the expected tax treatment and all potential tax benefits expected to result from the transaction, describe any tax result protection with respect to the transaction, and identify and describe the transaction in sufficient detail for the IRS to be able to understand the tax structure of the reportable transaction and the identity of any material advisor(s) whom the material advisor knows or has reason to know acted as a material advisor as defined in paragraph (b) of this section with respect to the transaction. An incomplete form containing a statement that information will be provided upon request is not considered a complete disclosure statement. A material advisor may file a single form for substantially similar transactions. An amended form must be filed if information previously provided is no longer accurate, if additional information that was not disclosed becomes available, or if there are material changes to the transaction. A material advisor is not required to file an additional form for each additional taxpayer that enters into the same or substantially similar transaction. If the form is not completed in accordance with the provisions in this paragraph (d) and the instructions to the form, the material advisor will not be considered to have complied with the disclosure requirements of this section.

(2) *Reportable transaction number.*—The IRS will issue to a material advisor a reportable transaction number with respect to the disclosed reportable transaction. Receipt of a reportable transaction number does not indicate that the disclosure statement is complete, nor does it indicate that the transaction has been reviewed, examined, or approved by the IRS. Material advisors must provide the reportable transaction number to all taxpayers and material advisors for whom the material advisor acts as a material advisor as defined in paragraph (b) of this section. The reportable transaction number must be provided at the time the transaction is entered into, or, if the transaction is entered into prior to the material advisor receiving the reportable transaction number, within 60 calendar days from the date the reportable transaction number is mailed to the material advisor.

(e) *Time of providing disclosure.*—The material advisor's disclosure statement for a reportable transaction must be filed with the Office of Tax Shelter Analysis (OTSA) by the last day of the month that follows the end of the calendar quarter in which the advisor became a material advisor with respect to the reportable transaction or in which the circumstances necessitating an amended disclosure statement occur. The disclosure statement must be sent to OTSA at the address provided in the instructions for Form 8918 (or a successor form).

(f) *Designation agreements.*—If more than one material advisor is required to disclose a reportable transaction under this section, the material advisors may designate by written agreement a single material advisor to disclose the transaction. The transaction must be disclosed by the last day of the month following the end of the calendar quarter that includes the earliest date on which a material advisor who is a party to the agreement became a material advisor with respect to the transaction as described in paragraph (b)(4) of this section. The designation of one material advisor to disclose the transaction does not relieve the other material advisors of their obligation to disclose the transaction to the IRS in accordance with this section, if the designated material advisor fails to disclose the transaction to the IRS in a timely manner.

(g) *Protective disclosures.*—If a potential material advisor is uncertain whether a transaction must be disclosed under this section, the advisor may disclose the transaction in accordance with the requirements of this section and comply with all the provisions of this section, and indicate on the disclosure statement that the disclosure statement is being filed on a protective basis. The IRS will not treat disclosure statements filed on a protective basis any differently than other disclosure statements filed under this section. For a protective disclosure to be effective, the advisor must comply with the regulations under this section and §301.6112-1 by providing to the IRS all information requested by the IRS under these sections.

(h) *Rulings.*—If a potential material advisor requests a ruling as to whether a specific transaction is a reportable transaction on or before the date that disclosure would otherwise be required under this section, the Commissioner in his discretion may determine that the submission satisfies the disclosure rules under this section for that transaction if the request fully discloses all relevant facts relating to the transaction which would otherwise be required to be disclosed under this section. The potential obligation of the person to disclose the transaction under this section (or to maintain or furnish the list under §301.6112-1) will not be suspended during the period that the ruling request is pending.

(i) *Effective/applicability date.*—(1) *In general.*—This section applies to transactions with respect to which a material advisor makes a tax statement on or after August 3, 2007. However, this section applies to transactions of interest entered into on or after November 2, 2006, with respect to which a material advisor makes a tax statement under this section on or after November 2, 2006. Paragraphs (b)(2)(i)(A), (b)(3)(i)(B), (c)(2), and (c)(13) of this section apply to transactions with respect to which a material advisor makes a tax statement under this section after November 14, 2011. Paragraph (h) of this section applies to ruling requests received on or after November 2, 2006. Otherwise, the rules that apply on or before November 14, 2011 are contained in this section in effect prior to November 14, 2011 (see 26 CFR part 301 revised as of April 1, 2011).

(2) *[Reserved].*

[Reg. §301.6111-3.]

☐ [*T.D. 9351, 7-31-2007. Amended by T.D. 9556, 11-10-2011.*]

[Reg. §301.6112-1]

§301.6112-1. Material advisors of reportable transactions must keep lists of advisees, etc.—(a) *In general.*—Each material advisor, as defined in §301.6111-3(b), with respect to any reportable transaction, as defined in §1.6011-4(b) of this chapter, shall prepare and maintain a list in accordance with paragraph (b) of this section and shall furnish such list to the Internal Revenue Service (IRS) in accordance with paragraph (e) of this section.

(b) *Preparation and maintenance of lists.*—(1) *In general.*—A separate list must be prepared and maintained for each reportable transaction. However, one list must be maintained for substantially similar transactions. A material advisor will have 30 calendar days from the date the list maintenance requirement first arises (see §301.6111-3(b)(4) and paragraph (a) of this section) with respect to a reportable transaction to prepare the list that must be maintained under this section with respect to that transaction. The Commissioner in his discretion also may provide in published guidance designating a transaction as a reportable transaction a list preparation time period greater than 30 calendar days. If a list is requested under this section during the list preparation time period, the request for the list will be treated as having been made on the day after the list preparation time period ends. A list must be maintained in a form that enables the IRS to determine without undue delay or difficulty the information required in paragraph (b)(3) of this section. The Commissioner in his discretion may provide in published guidance a form or method for maintaining or furnishing the list.

(2) *Persons required to be included on lists.*—A material advisor is required to maintain a list identifying each person with respect to whom the advisor acted as a material advisor with respect to the reportable transaction. However, a material advisor is not required to identify a person on the list if the person entered into a listed transaction or a transaction of interest more than 6 years before the transaction was identified in published guidance as a listed transaction or a transaction of interest.

(3) *Contents.*—Each list must include the three components described in paragraph (b)(3)(i), (ii), and (iii) of this section.

(i) *Statement.*—An itemized statement containing the following information—

(A) The name of each reportable transaction, the citation to the published guidance number identifying the transaction if the transaction is a listed transaction or a transaction of interest, and the reportable transaction number obtained under section 6111;

(B) The name, address, and TIN of each person required to be included on the list;

(C) The date on which each person required to be included on the list entered into each reportable transaction, if known by the material advisor;

(D) The amount invested in each reportable transaction by each person required to be included on the list, if known by the material advisor;

(E) A summary or schedule of the tax treatment that each person is intended or expected to derive from participation in each reportable transaction; and

(F) The name of each other material advisor to the transaction, if known by the material advisor.

(ii) *Description of the transaction.*—A detailed description of each reportable transaction that describes both the tax structure of the transaction and the purported tax treatment of the transaction.

(iii) *Documents.*—The following documents—

(A) A copy of any designation agreement (as described in paragraph (f) of this section) to which the material advisor is a party; and

(B) Copies of any additional written materials, including tax analyses or opinions, relating to each reportable transaction that are material to an understanding of the purported tax treatment or tax structure of the transaction that have been shown or provided to any person who acquired or may acquire an interest in the transactions, or to their representatives, tax advisors, or agents, by the material advisor or any related party or agent of the material advisor. However, a material advisor is not required to retain earlier drafts of a document provided the material advisor retains a copy of the final document (or, if there is no final document, the most recent draft of the document) and the final document (or most recent draft) contains all the information in the earlier drafts of such document that is material to an understanding of the purported tax treatment or the tax structure of the transaction.

(c) *Definitions.*—For purposes of this section, the following terms are defined as:

(1) *Material advisor.*—The term *material advisor* is defined in § 301.6111-3(b).

(2) *Reportable transaction.*—The term *reportable transaction* is defined in § 1.6011-4(b)(1) of this chapter.

(3) *Listed transaction.*—The term *listed transaction* is defined in § 1.6011-4(b)(2) of this chapter. See also § § 20.6011-4(a), 25.6011-4(a), 26.6011-4, 31.6011-4(a), 53.6011-4(a), 54.6011-4(a), or 56.6011-4(a) of this chapter.

(4) *Substantially similar.*—The term *substantially similar* is defined in § 1.6011-4(c)(4) of this chapter.

(5) *Person.*—The term *person* is defined in § 301.6111-3(c)(4).

(6) *Related party.*—A person is a related party with respect to another person if such person bears a relationship to such other person described in section 267(b) or 707(b).

(7) *Tax.*—The term *tax* is defined in § 301.6111-3(c)(6).

(8) *Tax benefit.*—The term *tax benefit* is defined in § 301.6111-3(c)(7).

(9) *Tax return.*—The term *tax return* is defined in § 301.6111-3(c)(8).

(10) *Tax structure.*—The term *tax structure* is defined in § 301.6111-3(c)(9).

(11) *Tax treatment.*—The term *tax treatment* is defined in § 301.6111-3(c)(10).

(12) *Transaction of interest.*—The term *transaction of interest* is defined in § 1.6011-4(b)(6) of this chapter. See also § § 20.6011-4(a), 25.6011-4(a), 26.6011-4, 31.6011-4(a), 53.6011-4(a), 54.6011-4(a), or 56.6011-4(a) of this chapter.

(d) *Retention of lists.*—Each material advisor must maintain each component of the list described in paragraph (b)(3) of this section in a readily accessible form for seven years following the earlier of the date on which the material advisor last made a tax statement relating to the transaction, or the date the transaction was last entered into, if known. If the material advisor required to prepare, maintain, and furnish the list is a corporation, partnership, or other entity (entity) that has dissolved or liquidated before completion of the seven-year period, the person responsible under state law for winding up the affairs of the entity must prepare, maintain and furnish each component of the list on behalf of the entity, unless the entity submits the list to the Office of Tax Shelter Analysis (OTSA) within 60 days after the dissolution or liquidation. If state law does not specify any person as responsible for winding up the affairs, then each of the directors of the corporation, the general partners of the partnership, or the trustees, owners, or members of the entity are responsible for preparing, maintaining and furnishing each component of the list on behalf of the entity, unless the entity submits the list to the OTSA within 60 days after the dissolution or liquidation. The responsible person must also provide notice to OTSA of such dissolution or liquidation within 60 days after the dissolution or liquidation. The list and the notice provided to OTSA must be sent to: Internal Revenue Service, OTSA Mail Stop 4915, 1973 North Rulon White Blvd., Ogden, Utah 84404, or to such other address as provided by the Commissioner.

(e) *Furnishing of lists.*—(1) *In general.*—Each material advisor responsible for maintaining a list must, upon written request by the IRS, make each component of the list described in paragraph (b)(3) of this section available to the IRS. Each component of the list must be furnished to the IRS in a form that enables the IRS to determine without undue delay or difficulty the information required in paragraph (b)(3) of this section. If any component of the list is not in a form that enables the IRS to determine without undue delay or difficulty the information required in paragraph (b)(3) of this section, the material advisor will not be considered to have complied with the list maintenance provisions in section 6112 and this section. A material advisor must make the list or each component of the list available to the IRS within the period prescribed in section 6708 or published guidance relating to section 6708.

(2) *Claims of privilege.*—Each material advisor who is required to maintain a list with respect to a reportable transaction, must still maintain the list pursuant to the requirements of this section even if a person asserts a claim of privilege with respect to the information specified in paragraph (b)(3)(iii)(B) of this section.

(f) *Designation agreements.*—If more than one material advisor is required to maintain a list of persons for a reportable transaction, in accordance with paragraph (b) of this section, the material advisors may designate by written agreement a single material advisor (the designated material advisor) to maintain the list or a portion of the list. A designation agreement does not relieve material advisors from their obligation to maintain a list in accordance with paragraph (b) of this section or to furnish their list to the IRS in accordance with paragraph (e)(1) of this section, but a designation agreement may allow one material advisor to maintain a list on behalf of the other material advisors who are a party to the designation agreement. A material advisor is not relieved from the requirement of this section because a material advisor is unable to obtain the list from any designated material advisor, any designated material advisor did not maintain a list, or the list maintained by any designated material advisor is not complete. The existence of a designation agreement does not affect the ability of the IRS to request a list from any party to the designation agreement. The IRS may request a list from any party to the designation agreement, and the party receiving the request must furnish their list to the IRS in accordance with paragraph (e)(1) of this section, regardless of whether their list was maintained by another party pursuant to the terms of a designation agreement.

(g) *Effective/applicability date.*—In general, this section applies to transactions with respect to which a material advisor makes a tax statement under §301.6111-3 on or after August 3, 2007. However, this section applies to transactions of interest entered into on or after November 2, 2006, with respect to which a material advisor makes a tax statement under §301.6111-3 on or after November 2, 2006. Paragraphs (b)(1), (c)(3), (c)(12), and (f) of this section apply to transactions with respect to which a material advisor makes a tax statement under §301.6111-3 after November 14, 2011. Otherwise, the rules that apply on or before November 14, 2011 are contained in this section in effect prior to November 14, 2011 (see 26 CFR part 301 revised as of April 1, 2011). [Reg. §301.6112-1.]

☐ [*T.D. 9046*, 2-28-2003. *Amended by T.D. 9108*, 12-29-2003 *T.D. 9295*, 11-1-2006; *T.D. 9352*, 7-31-2007 *and T.D. 9556*, 11-10-2011.]

[Reg. §301.6114-1]

§301.6114-1. Treaty-based return positions.—(a) *Reporting requirement.*—(1) *General rule.*—(i) Except as provided in paragraph (c) of this section, if a taxpayer takes a return position that any treaty of the United States (including, but not limited to, an income tax treaty, estate and gift tax treaty, or friendship, commerce and navigation treaty) overrules or modifies any provision of the Internal Revenue Code and thereby effects (or potentially effects) a reduction of any tax incurred at any time, the taxpayer shall disclose such return position on a statement (in the form required in paragraph (d) of this section) attached to such return.

(ii) If a return of tax would not otherwise be required to be filed, a return must nevertheless be filed for purposes of making the disclosure required by this section. For this purpose, such return need include only the taxpayer's name, address, taxpayer identifying number, and be signed under penalties of perjury (as well as the subject disclosure). Also, the taxpayer's taxable year shall be deemed to be the calendar year (unless the taxpayer has previously established, or timely chooses for this purpose to establish, a different taxable year). In the case of a disclosable return position relating solely to income subject to withholding (as defined in §1.1441-2(a) of this chapter), however, the statement required to be filed in paragraph (d) of this section must instead be filed at times and in accordance with procedures published by the Internal Revenue Service.

(2) *Application.*—(i) A taxpayer is considered to adopt a return position when the taxpayer determines its tax liability with respect to a particular item of income, deduction or credit. A taxpayer may be considered to adopt a return position whether or not a return is actually filed. To determine whether a return position is a "treaty-based return position" so that reporting is required under this paragraph (a), the taxpayer must compare:

(A) The tax liability (including credits, carrybacks, carryovers, and other tax consequences or attributes for the current year as well as for any other affected tax years) to be reported on a return of the taxpayer, and

(B) The tax liability (including such credits, carrybacks, carryovers, and other tax consequences or attributes) that would be reported if the relevant treaty provision did not exist.

If there is a difference (or potential difference) in these two amounts, the position taken on a return is a treaty-based return position that must be reported.

(ii) In the event a taxpayer's return position is based on a conclusion that a treaty provision is consistent with a Code provision, but the effect of the treaty provision is to alter the scope of the Code provision from the scope that it would have in the absence of the treaty, then the return position is a treaty-based return position that must be reported.

(iii) A return position is a treaty-based return position unless the taxpayer's conclusion that no reporting is required under paragraphs (a)(2)(i) and (ii) of this section has a substantial probability of successful defense if challenged.

(3) *Examples.*—The application of section 6114 and paragraph (a)(2) of this section may be illustrated by the following examples:

Example (1). X, a Country A corporation, claims the benefit of a provision of the income tax treaty between the United States and Country A that modifies a provision of the Code. This position does not result in a change of X's U.S. tax liability for the current tax year but does give rise to, or increases, a net operating loss which may be carried back (or forward) such that X's tax liability in the carryback (or forward) year may be affected by the position taken by X in the

current year. X must disclose this treaty-based return position with its tax return for the current tax year.

Example (2). Z, a domestic corporation, is engaged in a trade or business in Country B. Country B imposes a tax on the income from certain of Z's petroleum activities at a rate significantly greater than the rate applicable to income from other activities. Z claims a foreign tax credit for this tax on its tax return. The tax imposed on Z is specifically listed as a creditable tax in the income tax treaty between the United States and Country B; however, there is no specific authority that such tax would otherwise be a creditable tax for U.S. purposes under sections 901 or 903 of the Code. Therefore, in the absence of the treaty, the creditability of this petroleum tax would lack a substantial probability of successful defense if challenged, and Z must disclose this treaty-based return position (see also paragraph (b)(7) of this section).

(b) *Reporting specifically required.*—Reporting is required under this section except as expressly waived under paragraph (c) of this section. The following list is not a list of all positions for which reporting is required under this section but is a list of particular positions for which reporting is specifically required. These positions are as follows:

(1) That a nondiscrimination provision of a treaty precludes the application of any otherwise applicable Code provision, other than with respect to the making of or the effect of an election under section 897(i);

(2) That a treaty reduces or modifies the taxation of gain or loss from the disposition of a United States real property interest;

(3) That a treaty exempts a foreign corporation from (or reduces the amount of tax with respect to) the branch profits tax (section 884(a)) or the tax on excess interest (section 884(f)(1)(B));

(4) That, notwithstanding paragraph (c)(1)(i) of this section,

(i) A treaty exempts from tax, or reduces the rate of tax on, interest or dividends paid by a foreign corporation that are from sources within the United States by reason of section 861(a)(2)(B) or section 884(f)(1)(A); or

(ii) A treaty exempts from tax, or reduces the rate of tax on, fixed or determinable annual or periodical income subject to withholding under section 1441 or 1442 that a foreign person receives from a U.S. person, but only if described in paragraphs (b)(4)(ii)(A) and (B) of this section, or in paragraph (b)(4)(ii)(C) or (D) of this section as follows—

(A) The payment is not properly reported to the Service on a Form 1042S; and

(B) The foreign person is any of the following:

(1) A controlled foreign corporation (as defined in section 957) in which the U.S. person is a U.S. shareholder within the meaning of section 951(b);

(2) A foreign corporation that is controlled within the meaning of section 6038 by the U.S. person;

(3) A foreign shareholder of the U.S. person that, in the case of tax years beginning on or before July 10, 1989, is controlled within the meaning of section 6038A by the foreign shareholder, or, in the case of tax years beginning after July 10, 1989, is 25-percent owned within the meaning of section 6038A by the foreign shareholder; or

(4) With respect to payments made after October 10, 1990, a foreign related party, as defined in section 6038A(c)(2)(B), to the U.S. person; or

(C) For payments made after December 31, 2000, with respect to a treaty that contains a limitation on benefits article, that—

(1) The treaty exempts from tax, or reduces the rate of tax on income subject to withholding (as defined in § 1.1441-2(a) of this chapter) that is received by a foreign person (other than a State, including a political subdivision or local authority) that is the beneficial owner of the income and the beneficial owner is related to the person obligated to pay the income within the meaning of sections 267(b) and 707(b), and the income exceeds $500,000; and

(2) A foreign person (other than an individual or a State, including a political subdivision or local authority) meets the requirements of the limitation on benefits article of the treaty; or

(D) For payments made after December 31, 2000, with respect to a treaty that imposes any other conditions for the entitlement of treaty benefits, for example as a part of the interest, dividends, or royalty article, that such conditions are met;

(5) That, notwithstanding paragraph (c)(1)(i) of this section, under a treaty—

(i) Income that is effectively connected with a U.S. trade or business of a foreign corporation or a nonresident alien is not attributable to a permanent establishment or a fixed base of operations in the United States and, thus, is not subject to taxation on a net basis, or that

(ii) Expenses are allowable in determining net business income so attributable, notwithstanding an inconsistent provision of the Code;

(6) Except as provided in paragraph (c)(1)(iv) of this section, that a treaty alters the source of any item of income or deduction;

(7) That a treaty grants a credit for a specific foreign tax for which a foreign tax credit would not be allowed by the Code; or

(8) For returns relating to taxable years for which the due date for filing returns (without extensions) is after December 15, 1997, that residency of an individual is determined under a treaty and apart from the Internal Revenue Code.

(c) *Reporting requirement waived.*—(1) Pursuant to the authority contained in section 6114(b), reporting is waived under this section with respect to any of the following return positions taken by the taxpayer:

(i) For amounts received on or after January 1, 2001, reporting under paragraph (b)(4)(ii) is waived, unless reporting is specifically required under paragraphs (b)(4)(ii)(A) and (B) of this section, paragraph (b)(4)(ii)(C) of this section, or paragraph (b)(4)(ii)(D) of this section;

(ii) Notwithstanding paragraph (b)(4) or (5) of this section, that a treaty has reduced the rate of withholding tax otherwise applicable to a particular type of fixed or determinable annual or periodical income subject to withholding under section 1441 or 1442, such as dividends, interest, rents, or royalties to the extent such income is beneficially owned by an individual or a State (including a political subdivision or local authority);

(iii) For returns relating to taxable years for which the due date for filing returns (without extensions) is on or before December 15, 1997, that residency of an individual is determined under a treaty and apart from the Internal Revenue Code.

(iv) That a treaty reduces or modifies the taxation of income derived from dependent personal services, pensions, annuities, social security and other public pensions, or income derived by artistes, athletes, students, trainees or teachers;

(v) That income of an individual is resourced (for purposes of applying the foreign tax credit limitation) under a treaty provision relating to elimination of double taxation;

(vi) That a nondiscrimination provision of a treaty allows the making of an election under section 897(i);

(vii) That a Social Security Totalization Agreement or a Diplomatic or Consular Agreement reduces or modifies the taxation of income derived by the taxpayer; or

(viii) That a treaty exempts the taxpayer from the excise tax imposed by section 4371, but only if:

(A) The person claiming such treaty-based return position is an insured, as defined in section 4372(d) (without the limitation therein referring to section 4371(1)), or a U.S. or foreign broker of insurance risks,

(B) Reporting under this section that would otherwise be required to be made by foreign insurers or reinsurers on a Form 720 on a quarterly basis is made on an annual basis on a Form 720 by a date no later than the date on which the return is due for the first quarter after the end of the calendar year, or

(C) A closing agreement relating to entitlement to the exemption from the excise tax has been entered into with the Service by the foreign insurance company that is the beneficial recipient of the premium that is subject to the excise tax.

(ix) Notwithstanding paragraph (b)(1) of this section, that a nondiscrimination provision of a qualified income tax treaty, as defined in Treas. Reg. § 1.5000C-1(c)(13), exempts a payment from tax under section 5000C, but only if the foreign person claiming such relief has provided a Section 5000C Certificate (such as Form W-14, "Certificate of Foreign Contracting Party Receiving Federal Procurement Payments") to the acquiring agency in accordance with section 5000C and the regulations thereunder.

(2) Reporting is waived for an individual if payments or income items otherwise reportable under this section (other than by reason of paragraph (b)(8) of this section), received by the individual during the course of the taxable year do not exceed $10,000 in the aggregate or, in the case of payments or income items reportable only by reason of paragraph (b)(8) of this section, do not exceed $100,000 in the aggregate.

(3) Reporting with respect to payments or income items the treatment of which is mandated by the terms of a closing agreement with the Internal Revenue Service, and that would otherwise be subject to the reporting requirements of this section, is also waived.

(4) If a partnership, trust, or estate that has the taxpayer as a partner or beneficiary discloses on its information return a position for which reporting is otherwise required by the taxpayer, the taxpayer (partner or beneficiary) is then excused from disclosing that position on a return.

(5) This section does not apply to a withholding agent with respect to the performance of its withholding functions.

(6)(i) For taxable years ending after December 31, 2004, except as provided in paragraph (c)(6)(ii) of this section, reporting under paragraph (b)(4)(ii) of this section is waived for amounts received by a related party, within the meaning of section 6038A(c)(2), from a withholding agent that is a reporting corporation, within the meaning of section 6038A(a), and that are properly reported on Form 1042-S.

(ii) Paragraph (c)(6)(i) of this section does not apply to any amounts for which reporting is specifically required under the instructions to Form 8833.

(7)(i) For taxable years ending after December 31, 2004, except as provided in paragraph (c)(7)(iv) of this section, reporting under paragraph (b)(4)(ii) of this section is waived for amounts properly reported on Form 1042-S (on either a specific payee or pooled basis) by a withholding agent described in paragraph (c)(7)(ii) of this section if the beneficial owner is described in paragraph (c)(7)(iii) of this section.

(ii) A withholding agent described in this paragraph (c)(7)(ii) is a U.S. financial institution, as defined in §1.1441-1(c)(5) of this chapter, a qualified intermediary, as defined in §1.1441-1(e)(5)(ii) of this chapter, a withholding foreign partnership, as defined §1.1441-5(c)(2)(i) of this chapter, or a withholding foreign trust, as defined in §1.1441-5(e)(5)(v) of this chapter.

(iii) A beneficial owner described in this paragraph (c)(7)(iii) of this section is a direct account holder of a U.S. financial institution or qualified intermediary, a direct partner of a withholding foreign partnership, or a direct beneficiary or owner of a simple or grantor trust that is a withholding foreign trust. A beneficial owner described in this paragraph (c)(7)(iii) also includes an account holder to which a qualified intermediary has applied section 4A.01 or 4A.02 of the qualified intermediary agreement, contained in Revenue Procedure 2000-12 (2000-1 C.B. 387), (as amended by Revenue Procedure 2003-64, (2003-2 C.B. 306); Revenue Procedure 2004-21 (2004-1 C.B. 702); Revenue Procedure 2005-77 (2005-51 I.R.B. 1176) (see §601.601(b)(2) of this chapter) a partner to which a withholding foreign partnership has applied section 10.01 or 10.02 of the withholding foreign partnership agreement, and a beneficiary or owner to which a withholding foreign trust has applied section 10.01 or 10.02 of the withholding foreign trust agreement, contained in Revenue Procedure 2003-64, (2003-2 C.B. 306), (as amended by Revenue Procedure 2004-21 (2004-1 C.B. 702); Revenue Procedure 2005-77 (2005-51 I.R.B. 1176); (see §601.601(b)(2) of this chapter).

(iv) Paragraph (c)(7)(i) of this section does not apply to any amounts for which reporting is specifically required under the instructions to Form 8833.

(8)(i) For taxable years ending after December 31, 2004, except as provided in paragraph (c)(8)(ii) of this section, reporting under paragraph (b)(4)(ii) of this section is waived for taxpayers that are not individuals or States and that receive amounts of income that have been properly reported on Form 1042-S, that do not exceed $500,000 in the aggregate for the taxable year and that are not received through an account with an intermediary, as defined in §1.1441-1(c)(13), or with respect to interest in a flow-through entity, as defined in §1.1441-1(c)(23),

(ii) The exception contained in paragraph (c)(8)(i) of this section does not apply to any amounts for which reporting is specifically required under the instructions to Form 8833.

(d) *Information to be reported.*—(1) *Returns due after December 15, 1997.*—When reporting is required under this section for a return relating to a taxable year for which the due date (without extensions) is after December 15, 1997, the taxpayer must furnish, in accordance with paragraph (a) of this section, as an attachment to the return, a fully completed Form 8833 (Treaty-Based Return Position Disclosure Under Section 6114 or 7701(b)) or appropriate successor form.

(2) *Earlier returns.*—For returns relating to taxable years for which the due date for filing returns (without extensions) is on or before December 15, 1997, the taxpayer must furnish information in accordance with paragraph (d) of this section in effect prior to December 15, 1997 (see §301.6114-1(d) as contained in 26 CFR part 301, revised April 1, 1997).

(3) *In general.*—(i) *Permanent establishment.*—For purposes of determining the nature and amount (or reasonable estimate thereof) of gross receipts, if a taxpayer takes a position that

it does not have a permanent establishment or a fixed base in the United States and properly discloses that position, it need not separately report its payment of actual or deemed dividends or interest exempt from tax by reason of a treaty (or any liability for tax imposed by reason of section 884).

(ii) *Single income item.*—For purposes of the statement of facts relied upon to support each separate Treaty-Based Return Position taken, a taxpayer may treat payments or income items of the same type (e.g., interest items) received from the same ultimate payor (e.g., the obligor on a note) as a single separate payment or income item.

(iii) *Foreign source effectively connected income.*—If a taxpayer takes the return position that, under the treaty, income that would be income effectively connected with a U.S. trade or business is not subject to U.S. taxation because it is income treated as derived from sources outside the United States, the taxpayer may treat payments or income items of the same type (e.g., interest items) as a single separate payment or income item.

(iv) *Sales or services income.*—Income from separate sales or services, whether or not made or preformed by an agent (independent or dependent), to different U.S. customers on behalf of a foreign corporation not having a permanent establishment in the United States may be treated as a single payment or income item.

(v) *Foreign insurers or reinsurers.*—For purposes of reporting by foreign insurers or reinsurers, as described in paragraph (c)(1)(vii)(B) of this section, such reporting must separately set forth premiums paid with respect to casualty insurance and indemnity bonds (subject to section 4371(1)); life insurance, sickness and accident policies, and annuity contracts (subject to section 4371(2)); and reinsurance (subject to section 4371(3)). All premiums paid with respect to each of these three categories may be treated as a single payment or income item within that category. For reports first due before May 1, 1991, the report may disclose, for each of the three categories, the total amount of premiums derived by the foreign insurer or reinsurer in U.S. dollars (even if a portion of these premiums relate to risks that are not U.S. situs). Reasonable estimates of the amounts required to be disclosed will satisfy these reporting requirements.

(e) *Effective/applicability date.*—(1) *In general.*—This section is effective for taxable years of the taxpayer for which the due date for filing returns (without extensions) occurs after December 31, 1988. However, if—

(i) A taxpayer has filed a return for such a taxable year, without complying with the reporting requirement of this section, before November 13, 1989, or

(ii) A taxpayer is not otherwise than by paragraph (a) of this section required to file a return for a taxable year before November 13,

1989, such taxpayer must file (apart from any earlier filed return) the statement required by paragraph (d) of this section before June 12, 1990, by mailing the required statement to the Internal Revenue Service, P.O. Box 21086, Philadelphia, PA 19114. Any such statement filed apart from a return must be dated, signed and sworn to by the taxpayer under the penalties of perjury. In addition, with respect to any return due (without extensions) on or before March 10, 1990, the reporting required by paragraph (a) of this section must be made no later than June 12, 1990. If a taxpayer files or has filed a return on or before November 13, 1989, that provides substantially the same information required by paragraph (d) of this section, no additional submission will be required. Foreign insurers and reinsurers subject to reporting described in paragraph (c)(7)(ii) of this section must so report for calendar years 1988 and 1989 no later than August 15, 1990.

(2) *Section 5000C.*—Paragraph (c)(1)(ix) of this section applies to payments made on and after November 16, 2016 pursuant to contracts entered into on and after January 2, 2011. However, a taxpayer that receives payments exempt from tax under section 5000C by reason of a qualified income tax treaty before November 16, 2016 is not required to disclose this position on Form 8833, provided it has properly relied on Notice 2015-35, I.R.B. 2016-14, 533, in claiming the exemption.

(f) *Cross reference.*—For the provisions concerning penalties for failure to disclose a treaty-based return position, see section 6712 and §301.6712-1. [Reg. §301.6114-1.]

☐ [*T.D.* 8292, 3-13-90. *Amended by T.D.* 8305, 7-11-90; *T.D.* 8733, 10-6-97; *T.D.* 8734, 10-6-97; *T.D.* 8804, 12-30-98; *T.D.* 8856, 12-29-99, *T.D.* 9253, 3-13-2006 *and T.D.* 9782, 8-17-2016.]

[Reg. §1.6115-1]

§1.6115-1. Disclosure requirements for quid pro quo contributions.—(a) *Good faith estimate defined.*—(1) *In general.*—A good faith estimate of the value of goods or services provided by an organization described in section 170(c) in consideration for a taxpayer's payment to that organization is an estimate of the fair market value, within the meaning of §1.170A-1(c)(2), of the goods or services. The organization may use any reasonable methodology in making a good faith estimate, provided it applies the methodology in good faith. If the organization fails to apply the methodology in good faith, the organization will be treated as not having met the requirements of section 6115. See section 6714 for the penalties that apply for failure to meet the requirements of section 6115.

(2) *Good faith estimate for goods or services that are not commercially available.*—A good faith estimate of the value of goods or services that are not generally available in a commercial transaction may be determined by reference to the fair market value of similar or comparable goods or

services. Goods or services may be similar or comparable even though they do not have the unique qualities of the goods or services that are being valued.

(3) *Examples.*—The following examples illustrate the rules of this paragraph (a).

Example 1. Facility not available on a commercial basis. Museum *M*, an organization described in section 170(c), is located in Community *N*. In return for a payment of $50,000 or more, *M* allows a donor to hold a private event in a room located in *M*. Private events other than those held by such donors are not permitted to be held in *M*. In Community *N*, there are four hotels, *O*, *P*, *Q*, and *R*, that have ballrooms with the same capacity as the room in *M*. Of these hotels, only *O* and *P* have ballrooms that offer amenities and atmosphere that are similar to the amenities and atmosphere of the room in *M* (although *O* and *P* lack the unique collection of art that is displayed in the room in *M*). Because the capacity, amenities, and atmosphere of ballrooms in *O* and *P* are comparable to the capacity, amenities, and atmosphere of the room in *M*, a good faith estimate of the benefits received from *M* may be determined by reference to the cost of renting either the ballroom in *O* or the ballroom in *P*. The cost of renting the ballroom in *O* is $2500 and, therefore, a good faith estimate of the fair market value of the right to host a private event in the room at *M* is $2500. In this example, the ballrooms in *O* and *P* are considered similar and comparable facilities to the room in *M* for valuation purposes, notwithstanding the fact that the room in *M* displays a unique collection of art.

Example 2. Services available on a commercial basis. Charity *S* is an organization described in section 170(c). *S* offers to provide a one-hour tennis lesson with Tennis Professional *T* in return for the first payment of $500 or more that it receives. *T* provides one-hour tennis lessons on a commercial basis for $100. Taxpayer pays $500 to *S* and in return receives the tennis lesson with *T*. A good faith estimate of the fair market value of the lesson provided in exchange for Taxpayer's payment is $100.

Example 3. Celebrity presence. Charity *U* is an organization described in section 170(c). In return for the first payment of $1000 or more that it receives, *U* will provide a dinner for two followed by an evening tour of Museum *V* conducted by Artist *W*, whose most recent works are on display at *V*. *W* does not provide tours of *V* on a commercial basis. Typically, tours of *V* are free to the public. Taxpayer pays $1000 to *U* and

in return receives a dinner valued at $100 and an evening tour of *V* conducted by *W*. Because tours of *V* are typically free to the public, a good faith estimate of the value of the evening tour conducted by *W* is $0. In this example, the fact that Taxpayer's tour of *V* is conducted by *W* rather than *V*'s regular tour guides does not render the tours dissimilar or incomparable for valuation purposes.

(b) *Certain goods or services disregarded.*—For purposes of section 6115, an organization described in section 170(c) may disregard goods or services described in § 1.170A-13(f)(8)(i).

(c) *Value of the right to purchase tickets to college or university athletic events.*—For purposes of section 6115, the right to purchase tickets for seating at an athletic event in exchange for a payment described in section 170(l) is treated as having a value equal to twenty percent of such payment.

(d) *Goods or services provided to employees or partners of donors.*—(1) *Certain goods or services disregarded.*—For purposes of section 6115, goods or services provided by an organization described in section 170(c) to employees of a donor or to partners of a partnership that is a donor in return for a payment to the donee organization may be disregarded to the extent that the goods or services provided to each employee or partner are the same as those described in § 1.170A-13(f)(8)(i).

(2) *Description permitted in lieu of good faith estimate for other goods or services.*—The written disclosure statement required by section 6115 may include a description of goods or services, in lieu of a good faith estimate of their value, if the donor is—

(i) An employer and, in return for the donor's quid pro quo contribution, an organization described in section 170(c) provides the donor's employees with goods or services other than those described in paragraph (d)(1) of this section; or

(ii) A partnership and, in return for its quid pro quo contribution, the organization provides partners in the partnership with goods or services other than those described in paragraph (d)(1) of this section.

(e) *Effective date.*—This section applies to contributions made on or after December 16, 1996. However, taxpayers may rely on the rules of this section for contributions made on or after January 1, 1994. [Reg. § 1.6115-1.]

☐ [*T.D.* 8690, 12-13-96.]

[The next page is 66,801.]

Time and Place for Paying Tax
PLACE AND DUE DATE FOR PAYMENT OF TAX

See p. 20,601 for regulations not amended to reflect law changes

[Reg. § 1.6151-1]

§ 1.6151-1. Time and place for paying tax shown on returns.—(a) *In general.*—Except as provided in section 6152 and paragraph (b) of this section, the tax shown on any income tax return shall, without assessment or notice and demand, be paid to the internal revenue officer with whom the return is filed at the time fixed for filing the return (determined without regard to any extension of time for filing the return). For provisions relating to the time for filing income tax returns, see section 6072 and §§ 1.6072-1 to 1.6072-4, inclusive. For provisions relating to the place for filing income tax returns, see section 6091 and §§ 1.6091-1 to 1.6091-4, inclusive.

(b) *Returns on which tax is not shown.*—If a taxpayer files a return and, in accordance with section 6014 and the regulations thereunder, elects not to show the tax on the return, the amount of tax determined to be due shall be paid within 30 days after the date of mailing to the taxpayer a notice stating the amount payable and making demand upon the taxpayer therefor. However, if the notice is mailed to the taxpayer more than 30 days before the due date of the return, payment of the tax shall not be required prior to such due date.

(c) *Date fixed for payment of tax.*—In any case in which a tax imposed by subtitle A of the Code is required to be paid on or before a certain date, or within a certain period, any reference in subtitle A or F of the Code to the date fixed for payment of such tax shall be deemed a reference to the last day fixed for such payment (determined without regard to any extension of time for paying the tax).

(d) *Use of Government depositaries.*—(1) For provisions relating to the use of authorized financial institutions in depositing income and estimated income taxes of certain corporations, see § 1.6302-1.

(2) For provisions relating to the use of such financial institutions for the deposit of taxes required to be withheld under chapter 3 of the Code on nonresident aliens and foreign corporations and tax-free covenant bonds, see § 1.6302-2. With respect to section 1446, the previous sentence shall apply only to a publicly traded partnership described in § 1.1446-4.

(e) *Effective/Applicability date.*—Paragraph (d)(2) of this section shall apply to publicly traded partnerships described in § 1.1446-4 for partnership taxable years beginning after April 29, 2008. [Reg. § 1.6151-1.]

☐ [*T.D. 6364, 2-13-59. Amended by T.D. 6914, 3-7-67; T.D. 6922, 6-16-67; T.D. 6950, 4-3-68; T.D. 7102, 3-23-71; T.D. 7953, 5-8-84; T.D. 8952, 6-25-2001 and T.D. 9394, 4-28-2008 (corrected 4-1-2009).*]

[Reg. § 20.6151-1]

§ 20.6151-1. Time and place for paying tax shown on the return.—(a) *General rule.*—The tax shown on the estate tax return is to be paid at the time and place fixed for filing the return (determined without regard to any extension of time for filing the return). For provisions relating to the time and place for filing the return, see §§ 20.6075-1 and 20.6091-1. For the duty of the executor to pay the tax, see § 20.2002-1.

(b) *Extension of time for paying.*—(1) *In general.*—For general provisions relating to extension of time for paying the tax, see § 20.6161-1.

(2) *Reversionary or remainder interests.*—For provisions relating to extension of time for payment of estate tax on the value of a reversionary or remainder interest in property, see § 20.6163-1.

(c) *Payment with obligations of the United States.*—Treasury bonds of certain issues which were owned by the decedent at the time of his death or which were treated as part of his gross estate under the rules contained in § 306.28 of Treasury Department Circular No. 300, Revised (31 CFR Part 306), may be redeemed at par plus accrued interest for the purpose of payment of the estate tax, as provided in said section. Whether bonds of particular issues may be redeemed for this purpose will depend on the terms of the offering circulars cited on the face of the bonds. A current list of eligible issues may be obtained from any Federal reserve bank or branch, or from the Bureau of Public Debt, Washington, D.C. See section 6312 and §§ 301.6312-1 and 301.6312-2 of this chapter (Regulations on Procedure and Administration) for provisions relating to the payment of taxes with United States Treasury obligations.

(d) *Receipt for payment.*—For provisions relating to duplicate receipts for payment of the tax, see § 20.6314-1. [Reg. § 20.6151-1.]

☐ [*T.D. 6296, 6-23-58.*]

[Reg. § 25.6151-1]

§ 25.6151-1. Time and place for paying tax shown on return.—The tax shown on the gift tax return is to be paid by the donor at the time and place fixed for filing the return (determined without regard to any extension of time for filing the return), unless the time for paying the tax is extended in accordance with the provisions of section 6161. However, for provisions relating to certain cases in which the time for paying the gift tax is postponed by reason of an individual serving in, or in support of, the Armed Forces of the United States in a combat zone, see section 7508. For provisions relating to the time and place for filing the return, see §§ 25.6075-1 and 25.6091-1. [Reg. § 25.6151-1.]

☐ [*T.D. 6334, 11-14-58.*]

[Reg. § 31.6151-1]

§ 31.6151-1. Time for paying tax.—(a) *In general.*—The tax required to be reported on each tax return required under this subpart is due and payable to the internal revenue officer with whom the return is filed at the time prescribed in § 31.6071(a)-1 for filing such return. See the applicable sections in Part 301 of this chapter (Regulations on Procedure and Administration), for provisions relating to interest on underpayments, additions to tax, and penalties.

(b) *Cross references.*—For provisions relating to the use of authorized financial institutions in depositing the taxes, see §§ 31.6302(c)-1, 31.6302(c)-2, and 31.6302(c)-3. For rules relating to the payment of taxes in nonconvertible foreign currency, see § 301.6316-7 of this chapter (Regulations on Procedure and Administration). [Reg. § 31.6151-1.]

☐ [*T.D.* 6354, 1-13-59. *Amended by T.D.* 6872, 1-5-66; *T.D.* 6915, 3-28-67; *T.D.* 7037, 4-27-70; *T.D.* 7953, 5-8-84 *and T.D.* 8952, 6-25-2001.]

[Reg. § 40.6151(a)-1]

§ 40.6151(a)-1. Time and place for paying tax shown on return.—Except as provided by statute, the tax must be paid at the time prescribed in § 40.6071(a)-1 for filing the return, and at the place prescribed in § 40.6091-1 for filing the return. [Reg. § 40.6151(a)-1.]

☐ [*T.D.* 8442, 10-21-92. *Amended by T.D.* 8963, 8-8-2001.]

[Reg. § 41.6151(a)-1]

§ 41.6151(a)-1. Time and place for paying tax.—(a) *In general.*—The tax must be paid at the time prescribed in § 41.6071(a)-1 for filing the return and at the place prescribed in § 41.6091-1 for filing the return.

(b) *Effective/applicability date.*—This section applies on and after July 1, 2015. For rules applicable before that date, see 26 CFR 41.6151(a)-1 and 41.6151(a)-1T (revised as of April 1, 2014). [Reg. § 41.6151(a)-1.]

☐ [*T.D.* 6216. *Amended by T.D.* 6743, 6-22-64; *T.D.* 8879, 3-30-2000; *T.D.* 9537, 7-15-2011 *and T.D.* 9698, 10-28-2014.]

[Reg. § 44.6151-1]

§ 44.6151-1. Time and place for paying taxes.—The taxes imposed by sections 4401 and 4411 shall, without assessment or notice and demand, be paid to the internal revenue officer with whom the returns are required to be filed at the time fixed for filing the returns. For provisions relating to the time for filing returns, see §§ 44.6071 and 44.6071-1. For provisions relating to the place for filing returns, see §§ 44.6091 and 44.6091-1. [Reg. § 44.6151-1.]

☐ [*T.D.* 6370.]

[Reg. § 53.6151-1]

§ 53.6151-1. Time and place for paying tax shown on returns.—The chapter 42 tax shown on any return shall, without assessment or notice and demand, be paid to the internal revenue officer with whom the return is filed at the time

and place for filing such return (determined without regard to any extension of time for filing the return). For provisions relating to the time and place for filing such return, see §§ 53.6071-1 and 53.6091-1. For provisions relating to the extension of time for paying the tax, see § 53.6161-1. [Reg. § 53.6151-1.]

☐ [*T.D.* 7368, 7-15-75.]

[Reg. § 54.6151-1]

§ 54.6151-1. Time and place for paying of tax shown on returns.—Effective for any Form 8928 that is due on or after January 1, 2010, the tax shown on any return which is imposed under section 4980B, 4980D, 4980E or 4980G shall, without assessment or notice and demand, be paid to the internal revenue officer with whom the return is filed at the time and place for filing such return (determined without regard to any extension of time for filing the return). For provisions relating to the time and place for fling such return, see §§ 54.6071-1 and 54.6091-1. [Reg. § 54.6151-1.]

☐ [*T.D.* 9457, 9-4-2009.]

[Reg. § 55.6151-1]

§ 55.6151-1. Time and place for paying of tax shown on returns.—The tax shown on any return which is imposed by Chapter 44 shall, without notice or assessment and demand, be paid to the internal revenue officer with whom the return is filed at the time and place for filing such return (determined without regard to any extension of time for filing the return). For provisions relating to the time and place for filing such return, see §§ 55.6071-1 and 55.6091-1. For provisions relating to the extension of time for paying the tax, see § 55.6161-1. [Reg. § 55.6151-1.]

☐ [*T.D.* 8180, 2-28-88.]

[Reg. § 156.6151-1]

§ 156.6151-1. Time and place for paying of tax shown on returns.—The tax under chapter 54 (Greenmail) of the Code shown on any return shall, without notice of assessment and demand, be paid to the internal revenue officer with whom the return is filed at the time and place for filing such return (determined without regard to any extension of time for filing the return). For provisions relating to the time and place for filing such return, see §§ 156.6071-1 and 156.6091-1. For provisions relating to the extension of time for paying the tax, see § 156.6161-1. [Reg. § 156.6151-1.]

☐ [*T.D.* 8379, 12-17-91.]

[Reg. § 157.6151-1]

§ 157.6151-1. Time and place for paying of tax shown on returns.—The tax under chapter 55

(Structured Settlement Factoring Transactions) of the Internal Revenue Code shown on any return must, without assessment or notice and demand, be paid at the time and place specified in the forms and instructions provided by the Internal Revenue Service. For provisions relating to the time and place for filing such return, see §157.6071-1 and §157.6091-1. For provisions relating to the extension of time for paying the tax, see §157.6161-1. [Reg. §157.6151-1.]

→ *Caution: Former Code Sec. 6153 was repealed and reenacted in part in Code Sec. 6654.*

→ *Caution: Former Code Sec. 6154 was repealed and reenacted in part in Code Sec. 6655.*

[Reg. §301.6155-1]

§301.6155-1. Payment on notice and demand.—Upon receipt of notice and demand from the district director (including the Director of International Operations) or the director of the regional service center, there shall be paid at the place and time stated in such notice and amount of any tax (including any interest, additional amounts, additions to the tax, and assessable penalties) stated in such notice and demand. [Reg. §301.6155-1.]

☐ [*T.D.* 6498, 10-24-60. *Amended by T.D.* 6585, 12-27-61.]

[Reg. §6.3]

§6.3. Election by a qualified bank holding corporation to pay in installments the tax attributable to sales under the Bank Holding Company Act (Temporary).—[Reg. §6.3 was redesignated as Reg. §301.9100-11T by T.D. 8435, 9-18-92.—CCH.]

[Reg. §300.0]

§300.0. User fees; in general.—(a) *In general.*—The regulations in this part 300 are designated the User Fee Regulations and provide rules relating to user fees under 31 U.S.C. 9701.

(b) *Applicability.*—User fees are imposed on the following services:

(1) Entering into an installment agreement.

(2) Restructuring or reinstating an installment agreement.

(3) Processing an offer to compromise.

(4) Taking the special enrollment examination to become an enrolled agent.

(5) Enrolling an enrolled agent.

(6) Renewing the enrollment of an enrolled agent.

(7) Enrolling an enrolled actuary.

(8) Renewing the enrollment of an enrolled actuary.

(9) Taking the special enrollment examination to become an enrolled retirement plan agent.

(10) Enrolling an enrolled retirement plan agent.

(11) Renewing the enrollment of an enrolled retirement plan agent.

(12) Taking the registered tax return preparer competency examination.

☐ [*T.D.* 9134, 7-7-2004.]

[Reg. §301.6151-1]

§301.6151-1. Time and place for paying tax shown on returns.—For provisions concerning the time and place for paying tax shown on returns with respect to a particular tax, see regulations relating to such tax. [Reg. §301.6151-1.]

☐ [*T.D.* 6498, 10-24-60.]

(13) Applying for a preparer tax identification number. [Reg. § 300.0.]

☐ [*T.D.* 8589, 2-10-95. *Amended by T.D.* 9086, 8-14-2003; *T.D.* 9288, 10-3-2006; *T.D.* 9306, 12-27-2006; *T.D.* 9370, 12-18-2007; *T.D.* 9503, 9-28-2010; *T.D.* 9523, 4-14-2011 *and T.D.* 9559, 11-22-2011.]

[Reg. §300.1]

§300.1. Installment agreement fee.—(a) *Applicability.*—This section applies to installment agreements under section 6159 of the Internal Revenue Code.

(b) *Fee.*—The fee for entering into an installment agreement before January 1, 2017, is $120. The fee for entering into an installment agreement on or after January 1, 2017, is $225. A reduced fee applies in the following situations:

(1) For installment agreements entered into before January 1, 2017, the fee is $52 when the taxpayer pays by way of a direct debit from the taxpayer's bank account. The fee is $107 when the taxpayer pays by way of a direct debit from the taxpayer's bank account for installment agreements entered into on or after January 1, 2017;

(2) For online payment agreements entered into before January 1, 2017, the fee is $120, except that the fee is $52 when the taxpayer pays by way of a direct debit from the taxpayer's bank account. The fee is $149 for entering into online payment agreements on or after January 1, 2017, except that the fee is $31 when the taxpayer pays by way of a direct debit from the taxpayer's bank account; and

(3) Notwithstanding the type of installment agreement and method of payment, the fee is $43 if the taxpayer is a low-income taxpayer, that is, an individual who falls at or below 250 percent of the dollar criteria established by the poverty guidelines updated annually in the **Federal Register** by the U.S. Department of Health and Human Services under authority of section 673(2) of the Omnibus Budget Reconciliation Act of 1981 (95 Stat. 357, 511), or such other measure that is adopted by the Secretary, except that the fee is $31 when the taxpayer pays by way of a direct debit from the taxpayer's bank account with respect to online payment agreements entered into on or after January 1, 2017;

Reg. §300.1(b)(3)

(c) *Person liable for fee.*—The person liable for the installment agreement fee is the taxpayer entering into an installment agreement.

(d) *Applicability date.*—This section is applicable beginning January 1, 2017. [Reg. § 300.1.]

□ [T.D. 8589, 2-10-95. *Amended by T.D. 9306*, 12-27-2006; *T.D. 9503*, 9-28-2010, *T.D. 9647*, 11-29-2013 *and T.D. 9798*, 11-29-2016.]

[Reg. § 300.2]

§ 300.2. Restructuring or reinstatement of installment agreement fee.—(a) *Applicability.*—This section applies to installment agreements under section 6159 of the Internal Revenue Code that are in default. An installment agreement is deemed to be in default when a taxpayer fails to meet any of the conditions of the installment agreement.

(b) *Fee.*—The fee for restructuring or reinstating an installment agreement before January 1, 2017, is $50. The fee for restructuring or reinstating an installment agreement on or after January 1, 2017, is $89. If the taxpayer is a low-income taxpayer, that is, an individual who falls at or below 250 percent of the dollar criteria established by the poverty guidelines updated annually in the **Federal Register** by the U.S. Department of Health and Human Services under authority of section 673(2) of the Omnibus Budget Reconciliation Act of 1981 (95 Stat. 357, 511), or such other measure that is adopted by the Secretary, then the fee for restructuring or reinstating an installment agreement on or after January 1, 2017 is $43.

(c) *Person liable for fee.*—The person liable for the restructuring or reinstatement fee is the taxpayer that has an installment agreement restructured or reinstated.

(d) *Applicability date.*—This section is applicable beginning January 1, 2017. [Reg. § 300.2.]

□ [T.D. 8589, 2-10-95. *Amended by T.D. 9306*, 12-27-2006; *T.D. 9503*, 9-28-2010, *T.D. 9647*, 11-29-2013 *and T.D. 9798*, 11-29-2016.]

[Reg. § 300.3]

§ 300.3. Offer to compromise fee.—(a) *Applicability.*—This section applies to the processing of offers to compromise tax liabilities pursuant to § 301.7122-1 of this chapter. Except as provided in this section, this fee applies to all offers to compromise accepted for processing.

(b) *Fee.*—(1) The fee for processing an offer to compromise before January 1, 2014, is $150. The fee for processing an offer to compromise on or after January 1, 2014, is $186. No fee will be charged if an offer is—

(i) Based solely on doubt as to liability as defined in § 301.7122-1(b)(1) of this chapter; or

(ii) Made by a low income taxpayer, that is, an individual who falls at or below the dollar criteria established by the poverty guidelines updated annually in the Federal Register by the U.S. Department of Health and Human Services under authority of section 673(2) of the Omnibus Budget Reconciliation Act of 1981 (95 Stat. 357, 511) or such other measure that is adopted by the Secretary.

(2) The fee will be applied against the amount of the offer, unless the taxpayer requests that it be refunded, if the offer is—

(i) Accepted to promote effective tax administration pursuant to § 301.7122-1(b)(3) of this chapter; or

(ii) Accepted based on doubt as to collectibility and a determination that collection of an amount greater than the amount offered would create economic hardship within the meaning of § 301.6343-1 of this chapter.

(3) Except as otherwise provided in this paragraph (b), the fee will not be refunded to the taxpayer if the offer is accepted, rejected, withdrawn, or returned as nonprocessable after acceptance for processing.

(4) No additional fee will be charged if a taxpayer resubmits an offer the Secretary determines to have been rejected in error or returned in error after acceptance for processing.

(c) *Person liable for the fee.*—The person liable for the processing fee is the taxpayer whose tax liabilities are the subject of the offer.

(d) *Effective/applicability date.*—This section is applicable beginning January 1, 2014. [Reg. § 300.3.]

□ [T.D. 9086, 8-14-2003. *Amended by T.D. 9503*, 9-28-2010 *and T.D. 9647*, 11-29-2013.]

[Reg. § 300.4]

§ 300.4. Enrolled agent special enrollment examination fee.—(a) *Applicability.*—This section applies to the special enrollment examination to become an enrolled agent pursuant to 31 CFR 10.4(a).

(b) *Fee.*—The fee for taking the enrolled agent special enrollment examination is $81 per part, which is the cost to the government for overseeing the development and administration of the examination and does not include any fees charged by the administrator of the examination.

(c) *Person liable for the fee.*—The person liable for the special enrollment examination fee is the applicant taking the examination.

(d) *Applicability date.*—This section applies to registrations that occur on or after March 1, 2018, for the enrolled agent special enrollment examination. Section 300.4 (as contained in 26 CFR part 300, revised April 2017) applies to registrations that occur before March 1, 2018. [Reg. § 300.4.]

□ [T.D. 9288, 10-3-2006. *Amended by T.D. 9503*, 9-28-2010, *T.D. 9523*, 4-14-2011 *and T.D. 9820*, 7-18-2017.]

[Reg. § 300.5]

§ 300.5. Enrollment of enrolled agent fee.— (a) *Applicability.*—This section applies to the initial enrollment of enrolled agents with the IRS Office of Professional Responsibility pursuant to 31 CFR 10.5(b).

(b) *Fee.*—The fee for initially enrolling as an enrolled agent with the IRS is $30.

(c) *Person liable for the fee.*—The person liable for the enrollment fee is the applicant filing for enrollment as an enrolled agent with the IRS Office of Professional Responsibility.

(d) *Effective/applicability date.*—This section is applicable beginning April 19, 2011. [Reg. § 300.5.]

☐ [*T.D. 9288, 10-3-2006. Amended by T.D. 9503, 9-28-2010 and T.D. 9523, 4-14-2011.*]

[Reg. § 300.6]

§ 300.6. Renewal of enrollment of enrolled agent fee.—(a) *Applicability.*—This section applies to the renewal of enrollment of enrolled agents with the IRS Office of Professional Responsibility pursuant to 31 CFR 10.6(d)(6).

(b) *Fee.*—The fee for renewal of enrollment as an enrolled agent with the IRS is $30.

(c) *Person liable for the fee.*—The person liable for the renewal of enrollment fee is the person renewing their enrollment as an enrolled agent with the IRS Office of. Professional Responsibility.

(d) *Effective/applicability date.*—This section is applicable beginning April 19, 2011. [Reg. § 300.6.]

☐ [*T.D. 9288, 10-3-2006. Amended by T.D. 9503, 9-28-2010; and T.D. 9523, 4-14-2011.*]

[Reg. § 300.7]

§ 300.7. Enrollment of enrolled actuary fee.— (a) *Applicability.*—This section applies to the initial enrollment of enrolled actuaries with the Joint Board for the Enrollment of Actuaries pursuant to 20 CFR Part 901.

(b) *Fee.*—The fee for initially enrolling as an enrolled actuary with the Joint Board for the Enrollment of Actuaries is $250.00.

(c) *Person liable for the fee.*—The person liable for the enrollment fee is the applicant filing for enrollment as an enrolled actuary with the Joint Board for the Enrollment of Actuaries.

(d) *Effective/applicability date.*—This section is applicable beginning January 22, 2008. [Reg. § 300.7.]

☐ [*T.D. 9370, 12-18-2007. Amended by T.D. 9503, 9-28-2010.*]

[Reg. § 300.8]

§ 300.8. Renewal of enrollment of enrolled actuary fee.—(a) *Applicability.*—This section applies to the renewal of enrollment of enrolled actuaries with the Joint Board for the Enrollment of Actuaries pursuant to 20 CFR Part 901.

(b) *Fee.*—The fee for renewal of enrollment as an enrolled actuary with the Joint Board for the Enrollment of Actuaries is $250.00.

(c) *Person liable for the fee.*—The person liable for the renewal of enrollment fee is the person renewing their enrollment as an enrolled actuary with the Joint Board for the Enrollment of Actuaries.

(d) *Effective/applicability date.*—This section is applicable beginning January 22, 2008. [Reg. § 300.8.]

☐ [*T.D. 9370, 12-18-2007. Amended by T.D. 9503, 9-28-2010.*]

[Reg. § 300.9]

§ 300.9. Enrolled retirement plan agent special enrollment examination fee.— (a) *Applicability.*—This section applies to the special enrollment examination to become an enrolled retirement plan agent pursuant to 31 CFR 10.4(b).

(b) *Fee.*—The fee for taking the enrolled retirement plan agent special enrollment examination is $11 per part, which is the cost to the government for overseeing the examination and does not include any fees charged by the administrator of the examination.

(c) *Person liable for the fee.*—The person liable for the enrolled retirement plan agent special enrollment examination fee is the applicant taking the examination.

(d) *Effective/applicability date.*—This section is applicable beginning April 19, 2011. [Reg. § 300.9.]

☐ [*T.D. 9523, 4-14-2011.*]

[Reg. § 300.10]

§ 300.10. Enrolled retirement plan agent special enrollment examination fee.— (a) *Applicability.*—This section applies to the initial enrollment of enrolled retirement plan agents with the IRS pursuant to 31 CFR 10.5(b).

(b) *Fee.*—The fee for initially enrolling as an enrolled retirement plan agent with the IRS is $30.

(c) *Person liable for the fee.*—The person liable for the enrollment fee is the applicant filing for enrollment as an enrolled retirement plan agent with the IRS.

(d) *Effective/applicability date.*—This section is applicable beginning April 19, 2011. [Reg. § 300.10.]

☐ [*T.D. 9523, 4-14-2011.*]

[Reg. § 300.11]

§ 300.11. Renewal of enrollment of enrolled retirement plan agent fee.—(a) *Applicability.*— This section applies to the renewal of enrollment of enrolled retirement plan agents with the IRS pursuant to 31 CFR 10.5(b).

(b) *Fee.*—The fee for renewal of enrollment as an enrolled retirement plan agent with the IRS is $30.

(c) *Person liable for the fee.*—The person liable for the renewal of enrollment fee is the person renewing enrollment as an enrolled retirement plan agent with the IRS.

(d) *Effective/applicability date.*—This section is applicable beginning April 19, 2011. [Reg. §300.11.]

☐ [*T.D.* 9523, 4-14-2011.]

[Reg. §300.12]

§300.12. Registered tax return preparer competency examination fee.—(a) *Applicability.*—This section applies to the competency examination to become a registered tax return preparer pursuant to 31 CFR 10.4(c).

(b) *Fee.*—The fee for taking the registered tax return preparer competency examination is $27, which is the government cost for overseeing the examination and does not include any fees charged by the administrator of the examination.

(c) *Person liable for the fee.*—The person liable for the competency examination fee is the applicant taking the examination.

(d) *Effective/applicability date.*—This section is applicable beginning November 25, 2011. [Reg. §300.12.]

☐ [*T.D.* 9559, 11-22-2011.]

[Reg. §300.13]

§300.13. Fee for obtaining a preparer tax identification number.—(a) *Applicability.*—This section applies to the application for and renewal of a preparer tax identification number pursuant to 26 CFR 1.6109-2(d).

(b) *Fee.*—The fee to apply for or renew a preparer tax identification number is $33 per year, which is the cost to the government for processing the application for a preparer tax identification number and does not include any fees charged by the vendor.

(c) *Person liable for the fee.*—The individual liable for the application or renewal fee is the individual applying for and renewing a preparer tax identification number from the IRS.

(d) *Applicability date.*—This section will be applicable for applications for and renewal of a preparer tax identification number filed on or after September 9, 2016. [Reg. §300.13.]

☐ [*T.D.* 9503, 9-28-2010. *Redesignated by T.D.* 9523, 4-14-2011, T.D. 9559, 11-22-2011, *T.D. 9742,* 10-29-2015 *and T.D. 9781,* 8-9-2016.]

[Reg. §301.6159-0]

§301.6159-0. Table of contents.— (a) Authority.

(b) Procedures for submission and consideration of proposed installment agreements.

(c) Acceptance, form, and terms of installment agreements.

(d) Rejection of a proposed installment agreement.

(e) Modification or termination of installment agreements by the Internal Revenue Service.

(f) Effect of installment agreement or pending installment agreement on collection activity.

(g) Suspension of the statute of limitations on collection.

(h) Annual statement.

(i) Biennial review of partial payment installment agreements.

(j) Cross reference.

(k) Effective/applicability date. [Reg. §301.6159-0.]

☐ [*T.D.* 9473, 11-24-2009.]

[Reg. §301.6159-1]

§301.6159-1. Agreements for payment of tax liability in installments.—(a) *Authority.*—The Commissioner may enter into a written agreement with a taxpayer that allows the taxpayer to make scheduled periodic payments of any tax liability if the Commissioner determines that such agreement will facilitate full or partial collection of the tax liability.

(b) *Procedures for submission and consideration of proposed installment agreements.*—(1) *In general.*— A proposed installment agreement must be submitted according to the procedures, and in the form and manner, prescribed by the Commissioner.

(2) *When a proposed installment agreement becomes pending.*—A proposed installment agreement becomes pending when it is accepted for processing. The Internal Revenue Service (IRS) may not accept a proposed installment agreement for processing following reference of a case involving the liability that is the subject of the proposed installment agreement to the Department of Justice for prosecution or defense. The proposed installment agreement remains pending until the IRS accepts the proposal, the IRS notifies the taxpayer that the proposal has been rejected, or the proposal is withdrawn by the taxpayer. If a proposed installment agreement that has been accepted for processing does not contain sufficient information to permit the IRS to evaluate whether the proposal should be accepted, the IRS will request the taxpayer to provide the needed additional information. If the taxpayer does not submit the additional information that the IRS has requested within a reasonable time period after such a request, the IRS may reject the proposed installment agreement.

(3) *Revised proposals of installment agreements submitted following rejection.*—If, following the rejection of a proposed installment agreement, the IRS determines that the taxpayer made a good faith revision of the proposal and submitted the revision within 30 days of the date of rejection, the provisions of this section shall apply to that revised proposal. If, however, the IRS determines that a revision was not made in good faith, the provisions of this section do not apply to the revision and the appeal period in paragraph (d)(3) of this section continues to run from the date of the original rejection.

(c) *Acceptance, form, and terms of installment agreements.*—(1) *Acceptance of an installment agreement.*—(i) *In general.*—A proposed installment agreement has not been accepted until the IRS notifies the taxpayer or the taxpayer's representative of the acceptance. Except as provided in paragraph (c)(1)(iii) of this section, the Commissioner has the discretion to accept or reject any proposed installment agreement.

(ii) *Acceptance does not reduce liabilities.*—The acceptance of an installment agreement by the IRS does not reduce the amount of taxes, interest, or penalties owed. (However, penalties may continue to accrue at a reduced rate pursuant to section 6651(h).)

(iii) *Guaranteed installment agreements.*—In the case of a liability of an individual for income tax, the Commissioner shall accept a proposed installment agreement if, as of the date the individual proposes the installment agreement—

(A) The aggregate amount of the liability (not including interest, penalties, additions to tax, and additional amounts) does not exceed $10,000;

(B) The taxpayer (and, if the liability relates to a joint return, the taxpayer's spouse) has not, during any of the preceding five taxable years—

(1) Failed to file any income tax return;

(2) Failed to pay any required income tax; or

(3) Entered into an installment agreement for the payment of any income tax;

(C) The Commissioner determines that the taxpayer is financially unable to pay the liability in full when due (and the taxpayer submits any information the Commissioner requires to make that determination);

(D) The installment agreement requires full payment of the liability within three years; and

(E) The taxpayer agrees to comply with the provisions of the Internal Revenue Code for the period the agreement is in effect.

(2) *Form of installment agreements.*—An installment agreement must be in writing. A written installment agreement may take the form of a document signed by the taxpayer and the Commissioner or a written confirmation of an agreement entered into by the taxpayer and the Commissioner that is mailed or personally delivered to the taxpayer.

(3) *Terms of installment agreements.*—(i) Except as otherwise provided in this section, an installment agreement is effective from the date the IRS notifies the taxpayer or the taxpayer's representative of its acceptance until the date the agreement ends by its terms or until it is superseded by a new installment agreement.

(ii) By its terms, an installment agreement may end upon the expiration of the period of limitations on collection in section 6502 and § 301.6502-1, or at some prior date.

(iii) As a condition to entering into an installment agreement with a taxpayer, the Commissioner may require that—

(A) The taxpayer agree to a reasonable extension of the period of limitations on collection; and

(B) The agreement contain terms that protect the interests of the Government.

(iv) Except as otherwise provided in an installment agreement, all payments made under the installment agreement will be applied in the best interests of the Government.

(v) While an installment agreement is in effect, the Commissioner may request, and the taxpayer must provide, a financial condition update at any time.

(vi) At any time after entering into an installment agreement, the Commissioner and the taxpayer may agree to modify or terminate an installment agreement or may agree to a new installment agreement that supersedes the existing agreement.

(d) *Rejection of a proposed installment agreement.*—(1) *When a proposed installment agreement becomes rejected.*—A proposed installment agreement has not been rejected until the IRS notifies the taxpayer or the taxpayer's representative of the rejection, the reason(s) for rejection, and the right to an appeal.

(2) *Independent administrative review.*—The IRS may not notify a taxpayer or taxpayer's representative of the rejection of an installment agreement until an independent administrative review of the proposed rejection is completed.

(3) *Appeal of rejection of a proposed installment agreement.*—The taxpayer may administratively appeal a rejection of a proposed installment agreement to the IRS Office of Appeals (Appeals) if, within the 30-day period commencing the day after the taxpayer is notified of the rejection, the taxpayer requests an appeal in the manner provided by the Commissioner.

(e) *Modification or termination of installment agreements by the Internal Revenue Service.*—(1) *Inadequate information or jeopardy.*—The Commissioner may terminate an installment agreement if the Commissioner determines that—

(i) Information which was provided to the IRS by the taxpayer or the taxpayer's representative in connection with either the granting of the installment agreement or a request for a financial update was inaccurate or incomplete in any material respect; or

(ii) Collection of any liability to which the installment agreement applies is in jeopardy.

(2) *Change in financial condition, failure to timely pay an installment or another Federal tax liability, or failure to provide requested financial information.*—The Commissioner may modify or terminate an installment agreement if—

(i) The Commissioner determines that the financial condition of a taxpayer that is party to the agreement has significantly changed; or

(ii) A taxpayer that is party to the installment agreement fails to—

(A) Timely pay an installment in accordance with the terms of the installment agreement;

(B) Pay any other Federal tax liability when the liability becomes due; or

(C) Provide a financial condition update requested by the Commissioner.

(3) *Request by taxpayer.*—Upon request by a taxpayer that is a party to the installment agreement, the Commissioner may terminate or modify the terms of an installment agreement if the Commissioner determines that the financial condition of the taxpayer has significantly changed. The taxpayer's request will not suspend the statute of limitations under section 6502 for collection of any liability. While the Commissioner is considering the request, the taxpayer shall comply with the terms of the existing installment agreement.

(4) *Notice.*—Unless the Commissioner determines that collection of the tax is in jeopardy, the Commissioner will notify the taxpayer in writing at least 30 days prior to modifying or terminating an installment agreement pursuant to paragraph (e)(1) or (2) of this section. The notice provided pursuant to this section must briefly describe the reason for the intended modification or termination. Upon receiving notice, the taxpayer may provide information showing that the reason for the proposed modification or termination is incorrect.

(5) *Appeal of modification or termination of an installment agreement.*—The taxpayer may administratively appeal the modification or termination of an installment agreement to Appeals if, following issuance of the notice required by paragraph (e)(4) of this section and prior to the expiration of the 30-day period commencing the day after the modification or termination is to take effect, the taxpayer requests an appeal in the manner provided by the Commissioner.

(f) *Effect of installment agreement or pending installment agreement on collection activity.*—(1) *In general.*—No levy may be made to collect a tax liability that is the subject of an installment agreement during the period that a proposed installment agreement is pending with the IRS, for 30 days immediately following the rejection of a proposed installment agreement, during the period that an installment agreement is in effect, and for 30 days immediately following the termination of an installment agreement. If, prior to the expiration of the 30-day period following the rejection or termination of an installment agreement, the taxpayer appeals the rejection or termination decision, no levy may be made while the rejection or termination is being considered by Appeals. This section will not prohibit levy to collect the liability of any person other than the person or persons named in the installment agreement.

(2) *Exceptions.*—Paragraph (f)(1) of this section shall not prohibit levy if the taxpayer files a written notice with the IRS that waives the restriction on levy imposed by this section, the IRS determines that the proposed installment agreement was submitted solely to delay collection, or the IRS determines that collection of the tax to which the installment agreement or proposed installment agreement relates is in jeopardy.

(3) *Other actions by the IRS while levy is prohibited.*—(i) *In general.*—The IRS may take actions other than levy to protect the interests of the Government with regard to the liability identified in an installment agreement or proposed installment agreement. Those actions include, for example—

(A) Crediting an overpayment against the liability pursuant to section 6402;

(B) Filing or refiling notices of Federal tax lien; and

(C) Taking action to collect from any person who is not named in the installment agreement or proposed installment agreement but who is liable for the tax to which the installment agreement relates.

(ii) *Proceedings in court.*—Except as otherwise provided in this paragraph (f)(3)(ii), the IRS will not refer a case to the Department of Justice for the commencement of a proceeding in court, against a person named in an installment agreement or proposed installment agreement, if levy to collect the liability is prohibited by paragraph (f)(1) of this section. Without regard to whether a person is named in an installment agreement or proposed installment agreement, however, the IRS may authorize the Department of Justice to file a counterclaim or third-party complaint in a refund action or to join that person in any other proceeding in which liability for the tax that is the subject of the installment agreement or proposed installment agreement may be established or disputed, including a suit against the United States under 28 U.S.C. 2410. In addition, the United States may file a claim in any bankruptcy proceeding or insolvency action brought by or against such person. If a person named in an installment agreement is joined in a proceeding, the United States obtains a judgment against that person, and the case is referred back to the IRS for collection, collection will continue to occur pursuant to the terms of the installment agreement. Notwithstanding the installment agreement, any claim or suit permitted will be for the full amount of the liabilities owed.

(g) *Suspension of the statute of limitations on collection.*—The statute of limitations under section 6502 for collection of any liability shall be suspended during the period that a proposed installment agreement relating to that liability is pending with the IRS, for 30 days immediately following the rejection of a proposed installment agreement, and for 30 days immediately following the termination of an installment agreement. If, within the 30 days following the rejection or termination of an installment agreement, the taxpayer files an appeal with Appeals, the statute of limitations for collection shall be suspended while the rejection or termination is being considered by Appeals. The statute of limitations for collection shall continue to run if an exception under paragraph (f)(2) of this section applies and levy is not prohibited with respect to the taxpayer.

(h) *Annual statement.*—The Commissioner shall provide each taxpayer who is party to an installment agreement under this section with an annual statement setting forth the initial balance owed at the beginning of the year, the payments made during the year, and the remaining balance as of the end of the year.

(i) *Biennial review of partial payment installment agreements.*—The Commissioner shall perform a review of the taxpayer's financial condition in the case of a partial payment installment agreement at least once every two years. The purpose of this review is to determine whether the taxpayer's financial condition has significantly changed so as to warrant an increase in the value of the payments being made or termination of the agreement.

(j) *Cross reference.*—Pursuant to section 6601(b)(1), the last day prescribed for payment is determined without regard to any installment agreement, including for purposes of computing penalties and interest provided by the Internal Revenue Code. For special rules regarding the computation of the failure to pay penalty while certain installment agreements are in effect, see section 6651(h) and § 301.6651-1(a)(4).

(k) *Effective/applicability date.*—This section is applicable on November 25, 2009. [Reg. § 301.6159-1.]

☐ [*T.D.* 8583, 12-22-94. *Amended by T.D.* 9473, 11-24-2009.]

[Reg. § 1.6161-1]

§ 1.6161-1. Extension of time for paying tax or deficiency.—(a) *In general.*—(1) *Tax shown or required to be shown on return.*—A reasonable extension of the time for payment of the amount of any tax imposed by subtitle A of the Code and shown or required to be shown on any return, or for payment of the amount of any installment of such tax, may be granted by the district directors (including the Director of International Operations) at the request of the taxpayer. The period of such extension shall not be in excess of six months from the date fixed for payment of such tax or installment, except that if the taxpayer is abroad the period of the extension may be in excess of six months.

(2) *Deficiency.*—The time for payment of any amount determined as a deficiency in respect of tax imposed by chapter 1 of the Code, or for the payment of any part thereof, may, at the request of the taxpayer, be extended by the internal revenue officer to whom the tax is required to be paid for a period not to exceed 18 months from the date fixed for payment of the defi-

ciency, as shown on the notice and demand, and, in exceptional cases, for a further period not in excess of 12 months. No extension of the time for payment of a deficiency shall be granted if the deficiency is due to negligence, to intentional disregard of rules and regulations, or to fraud with intent to evade tax.

(b) *Undue hardship required for extension.*—An extension of the time for payment shall be granted only upon a satisfactory showing that payment on the due date of the amount with respect to which the extension is desired will result in an undue hardship. The extension will not be granted upon a general statement of hardship. The term "undue hardship" means more than an inconvenience to the taxpayer. It must appear that substantial financial loss, for example, loss due to the sale of property at a sacrifice price, will result to the taxpayer from making payment on the due date of the amount with respect to which the extension is desired. If a market exists, the sale of property at the current market price is not ordinarily considered as resulting in an undue hardship.

(c) *Application for extension.*—An application for an extension of the time for payment of the tax shown or required to be shown on any return, or for the payment of any installment thereof, or for the payment of any amount determined as a deficiency shall be made on Form 1127 and shall be accompanied by evidence showing the undue hardship that would result to the taxpayer if the extension were refused. Such application shall also be accompanied by a statement of the assets and liabilities of the taxpayer and an itemized statement showing all receipts and disbursements for each of the three months immediately preceding the due date of the amount to which the application relates. The application, with supporting documents, must be filed on or before the date prescribed for payment of the amount with respect to which the extension is desired. If the tax is required to be paid to the Director of International Operations, such application must be filed with him, otherwise, the application must be filed with the applicable district director referred to in paragraph (a) or (b) of § 1.6091-2, regardless of whether the return is to be filed with, or tax is to be paid to, such district director. The application will be examined, and within 30 days, if possible, will be denied, granted, or tentatively granted subject to certain conditions of which the taxpayer will be notified. If an additional extension is desired, the request therefor must be made on or before the expiration of the period for which the prior extension is granted.

(d) *Payment pursuant to extension.*—If an extension of time for payment is granted, the amount the time for payment of which is so extended shall be paid on or before the expiration of the period of the extension without the necessity of notice and demand. The granting of an extension of the time for payment of the tax or deficiency does not relieve the taxpayer from liability for the payment of interest thereon during the period of the extension. See section 6601 and § 301.6601-1 of this chapter (Regulations on Procedure and Administration). Further, the granting of an extension of the time for payment of one installment of the tax does not extend the time for payment of subsequent installments.

(e) *Cross reference.*—For extensions of time for payment of estimated tax, see §§ 1.6073-4 and 1.6074-3. [Reg. § 1.6161-1.]

☐ [*T.D. 6364, 2-13-59. Amended by T.D. 6950, 4-3-68, T.D. 7133, 7-21-71, and T.D. 7260, 2-9-73.*]

[Reg. § 20.6161-1]

§ 20.6161-1. Extension of time for paying tax shown on the return.—(a) *Basis for granting an extension of time.*—(1) *Reasonable cause.*—With respect to the estate of a decedent dying after December 31, 1970, an extension of time beyond the due date to pay any part of the tax shown on the estate tax return may be granted for a reasonable period of time, not to exceed 12 months, by the district director or the director of a service center, at the request of the executor, if an examination of all the facts and circumstances discloses that such request is based upon reasonable cause. (See paragraph (b) of this section for rules relating to application for extension.) The following examples illustrate cases involving reasonable cause for granting an extension of time pursuant to this paragraph:

Example (1). An estate includes sufficient liquid assets to pay the estate tax when otherwise due. The liquid assets, however, are located in several jurisdictions and are not immediately subject to the control of the executor. Consequently, such assets cannot readily be marshalled by the executor, even with the exercise of due diligence.

Example (2). An estate is comprised in substantial part of assets consisting of rights to receive payments in the future (i.e., annuities, copyright royalties, contingent fees, or accounts receivable). These assets provide insufficient present cash with which to pay the estate tax when otherwise due and the estate cannot borrow against these assets except upon terms which would inflict loss upon the estate.

Example (3). An estate includes a claim to substantial assets which cannot be collected without litigation. Consequently, the size of the gross estate is unascertainable as of the time the tax is otherwise due.

Example (4). An estate does not have sufficient funds (without borrowing at a rate of interest higher than that generally available) with which to pay the entire estate tax when otherwise due, to provide a reasonable allowance during the remaining period of administration of the estate for the decedent's widow and dependent children, and to satisfy claims against the estate that are due and payable. Furthermore, the executor has made a reasonable effort to convert assets in his possession (other than an interest in a closely held business to which § 6166 applies) into cash.

(2) *Undue hardship.*—(i) *General rule.*—In any case where the district director finds that payment on the due date of any part of the tax shown on the return, or payment of any part of an installment under section 6166 (including any part of a deficiency prorated to an installment the date for payment of which had not arrived) on the date fixed for payment thereof, would impose undue hardship upon the estate, he may extend the time for payment for a period or periods not to exceed one year for any one period and for all periods not to exceed 10 years from the date prescribed in section 6151(a) for payment of the tax. See paragraph (a) of § 20.6151-1. In addition, if the district director finds that payment upon notice and demand of any part of a deficiency prorated under the provisions of section 6166 to installments the date for payment of which had arrived would impose undue hardship upon the estate, he may extend the time for payment for a similar period or periods.

(ii) *Definition of "undue hardship".*—The extension provided under this subparagraph on the basis of undue hardship to the estate will not be granted upon a general statement of hardship or merely upon a showing of reasonable cause. The term "undue hardship" means more than an inconvenience to the estate. A sale of property at a price equal to its current fair market value, where a market exists, is not ordinarily considered as resulting in an undue hardship to the estate. The following examples illustrate cases in which an extension of time will be granted based on undue hardship pursuant to this paragraph:

Example (1). A farm (or other closely held business) comprises a significant portion of an estate, but the percentage requirements of section 6166(a) (relating to an extension where the estate includes a closely held business) are not satisfied and, therefore, that section does not apply. Sufficient funds for the payment of the estate tax when otherwise due are not readily available. The farm (or closely held business) could be sold to unrelated persons at a price equal to its fair market value, but the executor seeks an extension of time to facilitate the raising of funds from other sources for the payment of the estate tax.

Example (2). The assets in the gross estate which must be liquidated to pay the estate tax can only be sold at a sacrifice price or in a depressed market if the tax is to be paid when otherwise due.

(b) *Application for extension.*—An application containing a request for an extension of time for paying the tax shown on the return shall be in writing, shall state the period of the extension requested, and shall include a declaration that it is made under penalties of perjury. If the application is based upon reasonable cause (see paragraph (a)(1) of this section), a statement of such reasonable cause shall be included in the application. If the application is based upon undue hardship to the estate (see paragraph (a)(2) of this section), the application shall include a statement explaining in detail the undue hardship to the estate that would result if the requested extension were refused. At the option of the executor, an application for an extension of time based upon undue hardship may contain an alternative request for an extension based upon reasonable cause if the application for an extension based upon undue hardship is denied. However, an application for an extension of time based solely upon reasonable cause will be treated as such even though an examination of all the facts and circumstances discloses that an application for an extension of time based upon undue hardship might have been granted had such an application therefor been made. If the application is based solely on reasonable cause, it shall be filed with the internal revenue officer with whom the estate tax return is required to be filed under the provisions of § 20.6091-1(a). If the application is based on undue hardship (including an application in which the executor makes an alternative request for an extension based on reasonable cause), it shall be filed with the appropriate district director referred to in paragraph (a)(2) of § 20.6091-1 whether or not the return is to be filed with, or the tax is to be paid to, such district director. An application for an extension of time relating to the estate of a decedent who was not domiciled in the United States at the time of death shall be filed with the Director of International Operations, Internal Revenue Service, Washington, D. C. 20225. When received, the application will be examined, and, if possible, within 30 days will be denied, granted, or tentatively granted subject to certain conditions of which the executor will be notified. An application for an extension of time for payment of the tax, or of an installment under section 6166 (including any part of a deficiency prorated to an installment the date for payment of which had not arrived), will not be considered unless the extension is applied for on or before the date fixed for payment of the tax or installment. Similarly, an application for such extension of time for payment of any part of a deficiency prorated under the provisions of section 6166 to installments the date for payment of which had arrived, will not be considered unless the extension is applied for on or before the date prescribed for payment of the deficiency as shown by the notice and demand from the district director. If the executor desires to obtain an additional extension of time for payment of any part of the tax shown on the return, or any part of an installment under section 6166 (including any part of a deficiency prorated to installment), it must be applied for on or before the date of the expiration of the previous extension. The granting of the extension of time for paying the tax is discretionary with the appropriate internal revenue officer and his authority will be exercised under such conditions as he may deem advisable. However, if a request for an extension of time for payment of estate tax under this section is denied by a district director or a director of a

service center, a written appeal may be made, by registered or certified mail or hand delivery, to the regional commissioner with authority over such district director or service center director within 10 days after the denial is mailed to the executor. The provisions of sections 7502 (relating to timely mailing treated as timely filing) and 7503 (relating to time for performance of acts where the last day falls on Saturday, Sunday, or a legal holiday) apply in the case of appeals filed under this paragraph. When received, the appeal will be examined, and if possible, within 30 days will be denied, granted, or tentatively granted subject to certain conditions of which the executor will be notified. If in the mistaken belief that an estate satisfies the requirements of section 6166 the executor, within the time prescribed in paragraph (e) of § 20.6166-1, files a notification of election to pay estate tax in installments, the notification of election to pay tax in installments will be treated as a timely filed application for an extension, under section 6161, of time for payment of the tax if the executor so requests, in writing, within a reasonable time after being notified by the district director that the estate does not satisfy the requirements of section 6166. A request that the election under section 6166 be treated as a timely filed application for an extension under section 6161 must contain, or be supported by the same information required by this paragraph with respect to an application for such an extension.

(c) *Special rules.*—(1) *Payment pursuant to extension.*—The amount of the tax for which an extension is granted, with the additions thereto, shall be paid on or before the expiration of the period of extension without the necessity of notice and demand from the district director.

(2) *Interest.*—The granting of an extension of the time for payment of the tax will not relieve the estate from liability for the payment of interest thereon during the period of the extension. See section 6601.

(3) *Duty to file timely return.*—The granting of an extension of time for paying the tax will not relieve the executor from the duty of filing the return on or before the date provided for in § 20.6075-1.

(4) *Credit for taxes.*—An extension of time to pay the tax may extend the period within which State and foreign death taxes allowed as a credit under sections 2011 and 2014 are required to be paid and the credit therefor claimed. See paragraph (c) of § § 20.2011-1 and 20.2014-6.

(d) *Cross references.*—For provisions requiring the furnishing of security for the payment of the tax for which an extension is granted, see paragraph (a) of § 20.6165-1. For provisions relating to extensions of time for payment of tax on the value of a reversionary or remainder interest in property, see § 20.6163-1. [Reg. § 20.6161-1.]

☐ [*Amended by T.D. 6711, 3-23-64, T.D. 7238, 12-28-72 and T.D. 7384, 10-21-75.*]

Reg. § 20.6161-1(d)

[Reg. § 25.6161-1]

§ 25.6161-1. Extension of time for paying tax or deficiency.—(a) *In general.*—(1) *Tax shown on return.*—A reasonable extension of time to pay the amount of tax shown on the return may be granted by the district director at the request of the donor. The period of such extension shall not be in excess of six months from the date fixed for the payment of the tax, except that if the taxpayer is abroad the period of extension may be in excess of six months.

(2) *Deficiency.*—The time for payment of any amount determined as a deficiency in respect of tax imposed by chapter 12 of the Code, or for payment of any part thereof may be extended by the district director at the request of the donor for a period not to exceed 18 months from the date fixed for the payment of the deficiency, as shown on the notice and demand from the district director, and, in exceptional cases, for a further period not in excess of 12 months. No extension of time for the payment of a deficiency shall be granted if the deficiency is due to negligence, to intentional disregard of rules and regulations, or to fraud with intent to evade tax.

(3) *Extension of time for filing distinguished.*—The granting of an extension of time for filing a return does not operate to extend the time for the payment of the tax or any part thereof, unless so specified in the extension.

(b) *Undue hardship required for extension.*—An extension of the time for payment shall be granted only upon a satisfactory showing that payment on the due date of the amount with respect to which the extension is desired will result in an undue hardship. The extension will not be granted upon a general statement of hardship. The term "undue hardship" means more than an inconvenience to the taxpayer. It must appear that substantial financial loss, for example, loss due to the sale of property at a sacrifice price, will result to the donor from making payment on the due date of the amount with respect to which the extension is desired. If a market exists, the sale of the property at the current market price is not ordinarily considered as resulting in an undue hardship.

(c) *Application for extension.*—An application for an extension of the time for payment of the tax shown on the return, or for the payment of any amount determined as a deficiency, shall be in writing and shall be accompanied by evidence showing the undue hardship that would result to the donor if the extension were refused. The application shall also be accompanied by a statement of the assets and liabilities of the donor and an itemized statement showing all receipts and disbursements for each of the three months immediately preceding the due date of the amount to which the application relates. The application, with supporting documents, must be filed with the applicable district director referred to in paragraph (a) of § 25.6091-1 regardless of whether the return is to be filed with, or the tax is to be paid to, such district director on or before the date prescribed for payment of the amount with respect to which the extension is desired. The application will be examined by the district director, and within 30 days, if possible, will be denied, granted, or tentatively granted subject to certain conditions of which the donor will be notified. If an additional extension is desired, the request therefor must be made to the district director on or before the expiration of the period for which the prior extension is granted.

(d) *Payment pursuant to extension.*—If an extension of time for payment is granted, the amount the time for payment of which is so extended shall be paid on or before the expiration of the period of the extension without the necessity of notice and demand from the district director. The granting of an extension of the time for payment of the tax or deficiency does not relieve the donor from liability for the payment of interest thereon during the period of the extension. See section 6601 and § 301.6601-1 of this chapter (Regulations on Procedure and Administration). [Reg. § 25.6161-1.]

☐ [*T.D. 6334, 11-14-58. Amended by T.D. 7012, 5-14-69.*]

[Reg. § 53.6161-1]

§ 53.6161-1. Extension of time for paying tax or deficiency.—(a) *In general.*—(1) *Tax shown or required to be shown on return.*—A reasonable extension of the time for payment of the amount of any tax imposed by chapter 42 and shown or required to be shown on any return, may be granted by the district directors and directors of the service centers at the request of the taxpayer. The period of such extension shall not be in excess of 6 months from the date fixed for payment of such tax, except that if the taxpayer is abroad the period of the extension may be in excess of 6 months.

(2) *Deficiency.*—The time for payment of any amount determined as a deficiency in respect of tax imposed by chapter 42 may, at the request of the taxpayer, be extended by the internal revenue officer to whom the tax is required to be paid for a period not to exceed 18 months from the date fixed for payment of the deficiency, as shown on the notice and demand, and, in exceptional cases for a further period not in excess of 12 months. No extension of the time for payment of a deficiency shall be granted if the deficiency is due to negligence, to intentional disregard of rules and regulations, or to fraud with intent to evade tax.

(3) *Extension of time for filing distinguished.*—The granting of an extension of time for filing a return does not operate to extend the time for the payment of the tax or any part thereof unless so specified in the extension.

(b) *Undue hardship required for extension.*—An extension of the time for payment shall be granted only upon a satisfactory showing that payment on the due date of the amount with respect to which the extension is desired will result in an undue hardship. The extension will not be granted upon a general statement of hardship. The term "undue hardship" means more than an inconvenience to the taxpayer. It must appear that substantial financial loss, for example, loss due to the sale of property at a sacrifice price, will result to the taxpayer from making payment on the due date of the amount with respect to which the extension is desired. If a market exists, the sale of the property at the current market price is not ordinarily considered as resulting in an undue hardship.

(c) *Application for extension.*—An application for an extension of the time for payment of the tax shown or required to be shown on any return, or for the payment of any amount determined as a deficiency shall be made on Form 1127 and shall be accompanied by evidence showing the undue hardship that would result to the taxpayer if the extension were refused. Such application shall also be accompanied by a statement of the assets and liabilities of the taxpayer and an itemized statement showing all receipts and disbursements for each of the three months immediately preceding the due date of the amount to which the application relates. The application, with supporting documents, must be filed on or before the date prescribed for payment of the amount with respect to which the extension is desired with the internal revenue officer to whom the tax is to be paid. The application will be examined, and within 30 days, if possible, will be denied, granted, or tentatively granted subject to certain conditions of which the taxpayer will be notified. If an additional extension is desired, the request therefor must be made on or before the expiration of the period for which the prior extension is granted.

(d) *Payment pursuant to extension.*—If an extension of time for payment is granted, the amount the time for payment of which is so extended shall be paid on or before the expiration of the period of the extension without the necessity of notice and demand. The granting of an extension of the time for payment of the tax or deficiency does not relieve the taxpayer from liability for the payment of interest thereon during the period of the extension. See section 6601 and § 301.6601-1 of this chapter (Regulations on Procedure and Administration). [Reg. § 53.6161-1.]

☐ [*T.D. 7368, 7-15-75.*]

[Reg. § 55.6161-1]

§ 55.6161-1. Extension of time for paying tax or deficiency.—(a) *In general.*—(1) *Tax shown or required to be shown on return.*—A reasonable extension of the time for payment of the amount of any tax imposed by chapter 44 and shown or required to be shown on any return, may be granted by the district directors at the request of the taxpayer. The period of such extension shall not be in excess of 6 months from the date fixed for payment of such tax.

(2) *Deficiency.*—The time for payment of any amount determined as a deficiency in re-

spect of tax imposed by Chapter 44 may, at the request of the taxpayer, be extended by the internal revenue officer to whom the tax is required to be paid. The extension may be for a period not to exceed 18 months from the date fixed for payment of the deficiency, as shown on the notice and demand. In exceptional cases, a further extension for a period not in excess of 12 months may be granted. No extension of time for payment of a deficiency shall be granted if the deficiency is due to negligence, to intentional disregard of rules and regulations, or to fraud with intent to evade tax.

(3) *Extension of time for filing distinguished.*—The granting of an extension of time for filing a return does not operate to extend the time for the payment of the tax or any part thereof unless so specified in the extension.

(b) *Certain rules relating to extension of time for paying income tax to apply.*—The provisions of § 1.6161-1 (b), and (c), and (d) of this chapter (relating to a requirement for undue hardship, the application for extension, and payment pursuant to an extension) shall apply to extensions of time for payment of the tax imposed by Chapter 44. [Reg. § 55.6161-1.]

☐ [*T.D. 7767, 2-3-81.*]

[Reg. § 156.6161-1]

§ 156.6161-1. Extension of time for paying tax or deficiency.—(a) *In general.*—(1) *Tax shown or required to be shown on return.*—A reasonable extension of the time for payment of the amount of any tax imposed by chapter 54 (Greenmail) of the Code and shown or required to be shown on any return may be granted by the appropriate district director at the request of the taxpayer. The period of such extension shall not exceed 6 months from the date fixed for payment of such tax.

(2) *Deficiency.*—The time for payment of any amount determined as a deficiency in respect of tax imposed by chapter 54 of the Code may, at the request of the taxpayer, be extended by the internal revenue officer to whom the tax is required to be paid. The extension may be for a period not to exceed 18 months from the date fixed for payment of the deficiency, as shown on the notice and demand. In exceptional cases, a further extension for a period not in excess of 12 months may be granted. No extension of time for payment of a deficiency shall be granted if the deficiency is due to negligence, to intentional disregard of rules and regulations, or to fraud with intent to evade tax.

(3) *Extension of time for filing distinguished.*—The granting of an extension of time for filing a return does not operate to extend the time for the payment of the tax or any part thereof unless so specified in the extension.

(b) *Certain rules relating to extensions of time for paying income tax to apply.*—The provisions of § 1.6161-1(b), (c), and (d) of this chapter (relating to a requirement for undue hardship, to the application for extension, and to payment pursuant to an extension) shall apply to extensions of time for payment of the tax imposed by chapter 54 of the Code. [Reg. § 156.6161-1.]

☐ [*T.D.* 8379, 12-17-91.]

[Reg. § 157.6161-1]

§ 157.6161-1. Extension of time for paying tax.—(a) *In general.*—(1) *Tax shown or required to be shown on return.*—The Internal Revenue Service may, at the request of the taxpayer, grant a reasonable extension of time for payment of the amount of any tax imposed by chapter 55 (Structured Settlement Factoring Transactions) of the Internal Revenue Code and shown or required to be shown on any return. The period of such extension shall not exceed 6 months from the date fixed for payment of such tax, except that in the case of a taxpayer that is abroad, such extension may exceed 6 months.

(2) *Extension of time for filing distinguished.*— The granting of an extension of time for filing a return does not extend the time for the payment of the tax or any part thereof unless so specified in the extension.

(b) *Certain rules relating to extension of time for paying income tax to apply.*—The provisions of § 1.6161-1(b), (c), and (d) of this chapter (relating to a requirement for undue hardship, to the application for extension, and to payment pursuant to an extension) shall apply to extensions of time for payment of the tax imposed by chapter 55 of the Code. [Reg. § 157.6161-1.]

☐ [*T.D.* 9134, 7-7-2004.]

[Reg. § 301.6161-1]

§ 301.6161-1. Extension of time for paying tax.—For provisions concerning the extension of time for paying a particular tax or for paying an amount determined as a deficiency, see the regulations relating to such tax. [Reg. § 301.6161-1.]

☐ [*T.D.* 6498, 10-24-60.]

[Reg. § 31.6161(a)(1)-1]

§ 31.6161(a)(1)-1. Extensions of time for paying tax.—No extension of time will be granted for payment of any of the taxes to which the regulations in this part have application. [Reg. § 31.6161(a)(1)-1.]

☐ [*T.D.* 6472, 6-22-60.]

[Reg. § 20.6161-2]

§ 20.6161-2. Extension of time for paying deficiency in tax.—(a) In any case in which the district director finds that payment, on the date prescribed therefor, of any part of a deficiency would impose undue hardship upon the estate, he may extend the time for payment for a period or periods not to exceed one year for any one period and for all periods not to exceed four years from the date prescribed for payment thereof. However, see § 20.6161-1 for extensions of time for payment of the part of a deficiency which is prorated to installments under the provisions of section 6166.

(b) The extension will not be granted upon a general statement of hardship. The term "undue hardship" means more than an inconvenience to the estate. It must appear that a substantial financial loss, for example, due to the sale of property at a sacrifice price, will result to the estate from making payment of the deficiency at the date prescribed therefor. If a market exists, a sale of property at the current market price is not ordinarily considered as resulting in an undue hardship. No extension will be granted if the deficiency is due to negligence or intentional disregard of rules and regulations or to fraud with intent to evade the tax.

(c) An application for such an extension must be in writing and must contain, or be supported by, information in a written statement declaring that it is made under penalties of perjury showing the undue hardship that would result to the estate if the extension were refused. The application, with the supporting information, must be filed with the district director. When received, it will be examined, and, if possible, within thirty days will be denied, granted, or tentatively granted subject to certain conditions of which the executor will be notified. The district director will not consider an application for such an extension unless it is applied for on or before the date prescribed for payment of the deficiency, as shown by the notice and demand from the district director. If the executor desires to obtain an additional extension, it must be applied for on or before the date of the expiration of the previous extension. The granting of the extension of time for paying the deficiency is discretionary with the district director.

(d) The amount of the deficiency for which an extension is granted, with the additions thereto, shall be paid on or before the expiration of the period of extension without the necessity of notice and demand from the district director.

(e) The granting of an extension of time for paying the deficiency will not operate to prevent the running of interest. See section 6601. An extension of time to pay the deficiency may extend the period within which State and foreign death taxes allowed as a credit under sections 2011 and 2014 are required to be paid and the credit therefor claimed. See paragraph (c) of § 20.2011-1 and § 20.2014-6.

(f) For provisions requiring the furnishing of security for the payment of the deficiency for which an extension is granted, see § 20.6165-1. [Reg. § 20.6161-2.]

☐ [*T.D.* 6296, 6-23-58. *Amended by T.D.* 6522, 12-28-60.]

[Reg. § 20.6163-1]

§ 20.6163-1. Extension of time for payment of estate tax on value of reversionary or remainder interest in property.—(a)(1) In case there is included in the gross estate a reversionary or remainder interest in property, the payment of the part of the tax attributable to that interest may, at the election of the executor, be postponed until six months after the termination of the precedent interest or interests in the property. The provisions of this section are limited to cases in which the reversionary or remainder interest is included in the decedent's gross estate as such and do not extend to cases in which the decedent creates future interests by his own testamentary act.

(2) If the district director finds that the payment of the tax at the expiration of the period of postponement described in subparagraph (1) of this paragraph would result in undue hardship to the estate, he may—

(i) After September 2, 1958, and before February 27, 1964, extend the time for payment for a reasonable period or periods not to exceed in all 2 years from the expiration of the period of postponement, but only if the precedent interest or interests in the property terminated after March 2, 1958, or

(ii) After February 26, 1964, extend the time for payment for a reasonable period or periods not to exceed in all 3 years from the expiration of the period of postponement, but only if the time for payment of the tax, including any extensions thereof, did not expire before February 26, 1964.

See paragraph (a)(2)(ii) of §20.6161-1 for the meaning of the term "undue hardship". An example of undue hardship is a case where, by reason of the time required to settle the complex issues involved in a trust, the decedent's heirs or beneficiaries cannot reasonably expect to receive the decedent's remainder interest in the trust before the expiration of the period of postponement. The extension will be granted only in the manner provided in paragraph (b) of §20.6161-1, and the amount of the tax for which the extension is granted, with the additions thereto, shall be paid on or before the expiration of the period of extension without the necessity of notice and demand from the district director.

(b) Notice of the exercise of the election to postpone the payment of the tax attributable to a reversionary or remainder interest should be filed with the district director before the date prescribed for payment of the tax. The notice of election may be made in the form of a letter addressed to the district director. There shall be filed with the notice of election a certified copy of the will or other instrument under which the reversionary or remainder interest was created, or a copy verified by the executor if the instrument is not filed of record. The district director may require the submission of such additional proof as he deems necessary to disclose the complete facts. If the duration of the precedent interest is dependent upon the life of any person, the notice of election must show the date of birth of that person.

(c) If the decedent's gross estate consists of both a reversionary or remainder interest in property and other property, the tax attributable to the reversionary or remainder interest, within the meaning of this section, is an amount which bears the same ratio to the total tax as the value of the reversionary or remainder interest (re-

duced as provided in the following sentence) bears to the entire gross estate (reduced as provided in the last sentence of this paragraph). In applying this ratio, the value of the reversionary or remainder interest is reduced by (1) the amount of claims, mortgages, and indebtedness which is a lien upon such interest; (2) losses in respect of such interest during the settlement of the estate which are deductible under the provisions of section 2054 or section 2106(a)(1); (3) any amount deductible in respect of such interest under section 2055 or 2106(a)(2) for charitable, etc., transfers; and (4) the portion of the marital deduction allowed under the provisions of section 2056 on account of bequests, etc., of such interests to the decedent's surviving spouse. Likewise, in applying the ratio, the value of the gross estate is reduced by such deductions having similar relationship to the items comprising the gross estate.

(d) For provisions requiring the payment of interest during the period of the extension occurring before July 1, 1975, see section 6601(b) prior to its amendment by section 7(d)(1) of the Act of Jan. 3, 1975 (Pub. L. 93-625, 88 Stat. 2115). For provisions requiring the furnishing of security for the payment of the tax for which the extension is granted, see paragraph (b) of §20.6165-1. For provisions concerning the time within which credit for State and foreign death taxes on such a reversionary or remainder interest may be taken, see section 2015 and the regulations thereunder. [Reg. §20.6163-1.]

☐ [T.D. 6296, 6-23-58. Amended by T.D. 6526, 1-18-61, T.D. 6716, 3-25-64, T.D. 6736, 5-27-64, T.D. 7238, 12-28-72, and T.D. 7384, 10-21-75.]

[Reg. §1.6164-1]

§1.6164-1. Extensions of time for payment of taxes by corporations expecting carrybacks.— (a) *In general.*—If a corporation in any taxable year files a statement with respect to an expected net operating loss carryback from such taxable year, such corporation may extend the time for the payment of all or part of any tax imposed by subtitle A of the Code for the taxable year immediately preceding such taxable year to the extent and subject to the limitations provided in section 6164. A corporation may extend the time for payment with respect to only such taxes as meet the following requirements:

(1) The tax must be one imposed by subtitle A of the Code;

(2) The tax must be for the taxable year immediately preceding the taxable year of the expected net operating loss;

(3) The tax must be shown on the return or must be assessed within the taxable year of the expected net operating loss; and

(4) The tax must not have been paid or required to have been paid prior to the filing of the statement.

(b) *Statement for purpose of extending time for payment.*—(1) The time for payment of the tax is automatically extended upon the filing of a statement on Form 1138 by the corporation with the district director for the district where the tax is payable. The statement on Form 1138 must be filled out in accordance with the instructions accompanying the form, and all information required by the form and the instructions must be furnished by the taxpayer. The district director, upon request, will furnish a receipt for any statement filed. Such receipt will show the date the statement was filed.

(2) The period of extension is that provided in section 6164(d) and §1.6164-5 unless sooner terminated by action of either the district director or the corporation. [Reg. §1.6164-1.]

☐ [*T.D.* 6364, 2-13-59.]

[Reg. §301.6164-1]

§301.6164-1. Extension of time for payment of taxes by corporations expecting carrybacks.—For provisions relating to the extension of time for payment of taxes by corporations expecting carrybacks, see §§1.6164-1 to 1.6164-9, inclusive, of this chapter (Income Tax Regulations). [Reg. §301.6164-1.]

☐ [*T.D.* 6498, 10-24-60.]

[Reg. §1.6164-2]

§1.6164-2. Amount of tax the time for payment of which may be extended.—(a) *Total amount to which extension may relate.*—The total amount of tax the time for payment of which may be extended under section 6164 may not exceed the amount of the reduction of the taxes previously determined attributable to the expected carryback.

(b) *Amount of tax to which extension may relate.*—(1) The taxpayer shall specify on Form 1138 the kind of tax and the amount thereof the time for payment of which is to be extended. The amount of tax to which an extension may relate shall not exceed the amount of such tax shown on the return as filed, increased by any amount assessed as a deficiency (or as interest or addition to the tax) prior to the date of filing the statement and decreased by any amount paid or required to be paid prior to such date. In determining the amount of tax required to be paid prior to the date of filing the statement, only the following amounts shall be taken into consideration:

(i) The amount of the tax shown on the return as filed; and

(ii) Any amount assessed as a deficiency (or as interest or addition to the tax) if the tenth day after notice and demand for its payment occurs prior to the date of the filing of the statement.

(2) Delinquent installments are to be considered amounts required to be paid prior to the date of filing the statement. In the case of any authorized extension of time under sections 6161 and 6162, the amount of tax the time for payment of which is so extended is not to be considered required to be paid prior to the end of such extension. Similarly, any amount assessed as a deficiency (or as interest or addition to the tax) is

not to be considered required to be paid prior to the date of the filing of the statement unless the tenth day after notice and demand for its payment falls prior to the date of the filing of the statement.

(3) The taxpayer may choose to extend the time for payment of all of one or more taxes, or it may choose to extend the time for payment of portions of several taxes. The taxes chosen by the taxpayer need not be those taxes which are affected by the carryback. [Reg. §1.6164-2.]

☐ [*T.D.* 6364, 2-13-59.]

[Reg. §1.6164-3]

§1.6164-3. Computation of the amount of reduction of the tax previously determined.—(a) *Tax previously determined.*—The taxpayer is to determine the amount of the reduction, attributable to the expected carryback, in the aggregate of the taxes previously determined for taxable years prior to the taxable year of the expected net operating loss. The tax previously determined is to be ascertained in accordance with the method prescribed in section 1314(a). Thus, the tax previously determined will be the tax shown on the return as filed, increased by any amounts assessed (or collected without assessment) as deficiencies prior to the date of the filing of the statement, and decreased by any amounts abated, credited, refunded, or otherwise repaid prior to such date. Any items as to which the Internal Revenue Service and the taxpayer are in disagreement at the time of the filing of the statement shall be taken into account in ascertaining the tax previously determined only if, and to the extent that, they were reported in the return, or were reflected in any amounts assessed (or collected without assessment) as deficiencies, or in any amounts abated, credited, refunded, or otherwise repaid, prior to the date of the filing of the statement. The tax previously determined will reflect the foreign tax credit and the credit for tax withheld at source provided in section 32.

(b) *Reduction attributable to the expected carryback.*—The reduction, attributable to the expected carryback or related adjustments, in any tax previously determined is to be ascertained by applying the expected carryback as if it were a determined net operating loss carryback, in accordance with the provisions of section 172 and the regulations thereunder. Items must be taken into account only to the extent that such items were included in the return, or were reflected in amounts assessed (or collected without assessment) as deficiencies, or in amounts abated, credited, refunded, or otherwise repaid, prior to the date of the filing of the statement. Thus, for example, if the taxpayer claims a deduction for depreciation of $10,000 in its return and the Internal Revenue Service asserts that only $4,000 is properly deductible, no change is to be made in the $10,000 depreciation deduction as shown by the taxpayer on his return unless a deficiency has been assessed, or an amount collected without assessment, prior to the date of filing of the statement as a result of a change in the depreciation deduction, or unless such change in the depreciation deduction was reflected in an amount abated, credited, refunded, or otherwise repaid prior to such date. [Reg. § 1.6164-3.]

☐ [*T.D. 6364, 2-13-59. Amended by T.D. 6862, 11-17-65.*]

[Reg. § 1.6164-4]

§ 1.6164-4. Payment of remainder of tax where extension relates to only part of the tax.—(a) *Time for payment.*—If an extension of time relates to only part of the tax, the time for payment of the remainder of the tax shall be considered to be the dates on which payments would have been required if such remainder had been the tax and the taxpayer had elected to pay the tax in installments as provided in section 6152(a).

(b) *Example.*—The provisions of this section may be illustrated by the following example:

Example. Corporation X, which keeps its books and makes its tax returns on the calendar year basis, filed its income tax return for 1956 on March 15, 1957. The corporation showed a tax of $1,000 on its return and paid 50 percent of such tax, or $500 on March 15, 1957. On June 3, 1957, corporation X, pursuant to the provisions of section 6164, extended the time for payment of $400 of such tax. The remainder of the tax the time for payment of which was not so extended, i.e., $600, is to be considered the tax for purposes of determining when it is to be paid. The remainder is considered to be due on the dates on which payment would have been required if such remainder had been the tax. Since the taxable year ended on December 31, 1956, the tax is payable in two equal installments of $300 each on March 15, 1957, and June 17, 1957. The taxpayer, having paid $500 on March 15, 1957, will have $100 to pay on June 17, 1957. [Reg. § 1.6164-4.]

☐ [*T.D. 6364, 2-13-59.*]

[Reg. § 1.6164-5]

§ 1.6164-5. Period of extension.—If the time for the payment of any tax has been extended pursuant to section 6164, such extension shall expire:

(a) On the last day of the month in which falls the last date prescribed by law (including any extension of time granted the taxpayer) for the filing of the return for the taxable year of the expected net operating loss; or

(b) If an application for a tentative carryback adjustment provided in section 6411 with respect to such loss is filed before the expiration of the period specified in paragraph (a) of this section, on the date on which notice is mailed by registered mail prior to September 3, 1958, and by either registered or certified mail on and after September 3, 1958, to the taxpayer that such application is allowed or disallowed in whole or in part. [Reg. § 1.6164-5.]

☐ [*T.D. 6364, 2-13-59.*]

[Reg. § 1.6164-6]

§ 1.6164-6. Revised statements.—(a) *Requirements and effect.*—A corporation may file more than one statement under section 6164 with respect to any one taxable year. Each statement is to be considered a new statement and not an amendment of any prior statement. Each such new statement is to be in lieu of the last statement previously filed with respect to the taxable year. The new statement may extend the time for payment of a greater or lesser amount of tax than was extended under the prior statement or may charge the kind of tax the time for payment of which is to be extended. The extension may not relate to any amount of tax which was paid or required to be paid prior to the date of filing the new statement. Any amount of tax the time for payment of which was extended under a prior statement, however, may continue to be extended under the new statement. If the amount the time for payment of which is extended under the new statement is less than the amount so extended under the last statement previously filed, the extension of time shall be terminated on the date the new statement is filed as to the difference between the two amounts. See § 1.6164-8 for the dates on which such difference must be paid. If a corporation pays any amount of tax, the time for payment of which was extended, prior to the date the extension would otherwise terminate, the extension with respect to such amount shall be deemed terminated, without regard to whether a new statement is filed, on the date such amount is paid. The corporation shall indicate on each new statement filed that it has already filed one or more prior statements with respect to the taxable year. The corporation shall likewise indicate the date each prior statement was filed and the amount of each tax the time for payment of which was extended under each prior statement.

(b) *Example.*—The provisions of this section may be illustrated by the following example:

Example. Corporation Y, which keeps its books and makes its tax returns on the calendar year basis, filed its income tax return for 1956 on March 15, 1957, showing a tax of $100,000. At the same time it filed a statement under section 6164 in which it stated that it expected to have a net operating loss of $75,000 in 1957 and that the reduction in the tax previously determined for 1955 (the second taxable year preceding the year of the expected net operating loss) attributable to the expected net operating loss carryback resulting from such expected loss, would be $39,000. The corporation accordingly extended the time for payment of $39,000 of its income tax for 1956, and paid $30,500 (50 percent of the excess of $100,000 over $39,000) of such tax on March 15, 1957 (see section 6164(c) and § 1.6164-4). As a result of its operations during the next several months, the corporation filed a second statement on June 3, 1957, in which it stated that its expected net operating loss for 1957 would amount to $150,000 and that the corresponding reduction in the tax for 1955 would amount to $78,000.

Reg. § 1.6164-6(b)

Corporation Y under the new statement may extend the time for payment of $30,500, the installment due on June 17, 1957, and the time for payment of the $39,000 extended under the first statement filed on March 15, 1957, may continue to be extended under the second statement. The $30,500 which was paid on March 15, 1957, will not be affected by the second statement filed on June 3, 1957. [Reg. § 1.6164-6.]

☐ [*T.D. 6364, 2-13-59.*]

[Reg. § 1.6164-7]

§ 1.6164-7. Termination by district director.— (a) *After an examination of the statement filed by the corporation is made.*—The district director is authorized to make such examination of the statements filed as he deems necessary and practicable. If, upon such examination as he may make, the district director believes that, as of the time he makes the examination, all or any part of the statement is in a material respect erroneous or unreasonable, he will terminate the extension as to any part of the amount to which such extension relates which he deems should be terminated.

(b) *Jeopardy.*—If the district director believes that the collection of any amount to which an extension under section 6164 relates is in jeopardy, he will immediately terminate the extension. In the case of such a termination, notice and demand shall be made by the district director for payment of such amount, and there may be no further extension of time under section 6164 with respect to such amount. [Reg. § 1.6164-7.]

☐ [*T.D. 6364, 2-13-59.*]

[Reg. § 1.6164-8]

§ 1.6164-8. Payments on termination.—(a) *In general.*—If an extension of time under section 6164 is terminated with respect to any amount either (1) by the filing of a new statement by the taxpayer under section 6164(e) extending the time for payment of a lesser amount than was extended in a prior statement, or (2) by action of the district director under section 6164(f) after making an examination of the statement filed by the corporation, no further extension of time may be made under section 6164 with respect to such amount. The time for payment of such amount shall be the dates on which payments would have been required if there had been no extension with respect to such amount and the taxpayer had elected under section 6152(a) to pay the tax in installments.

(b) *Example.*—The provisions of this section may be illustrated by the following example:

Example. Corporation Z, which keeps its books and makes its tax returns on the calendar year basis, filed its income tax return for 1956 on March 15, 1957, showing a tax of $100,000. At the same time it filed a statement under section 6164 extending the time for payment of the entire $100,000 on the basis of an expected net operating loss carryback from 1957. On April 10, 1957, the corporation filed a new statement indicating

that the reduction, attributable to the carryback from 1957, in its income tax for 1956, would only be $80,000, and thus terminated the above extension of $20,000. The time for payment of such $20,000 may not be extended again, and such $20,000 is payable as if it were the tax for 1956 and corporation Z had elected to pay such tax in installments. That is, $10,000 is payable on March 15, 1957, and $10,000 payable on June 17, 1957. Inasmuch as the March 15 date had already passed when the corporation Z terminated the extension with respect to the $20,000, $10,000 is payable immediately upon such termination, and the other installment of $10,000 is payable on June 17, 1957. This example would also apply if the extension of time for payment of the $20,000 were terminated instead by the district director on April 10, 1957. [Reg. § 1.6164-8.]

☐ [*T.D. 6364, 2-13-59.*]

[Reg. § 1.6164-9]

§ 1.6164-9. Cross references.—For provisions with respect to interest due on amounts the payment of which is extended under section 6164, see section 6601 and paragraph (e) of § 301.6601-1 of this chapter (Regulations on Procedure and Administration). For extensions of time under section 6164 in the case of corporations making or required to make consolidated returns, see § 1.1502-77(a). [Reg. § 1.6164-9.]

☐ [*T.D. 6364, 2-13-59. Amended by T.D. 7244, 12-29-72.*]

[Reg. § 1.6165-1]

§ 1.6165-1. Bonds where time to pay the tax or deficiency has been extended.—The district director, including the Director of International Operations, may, as a condition to the granting of an extension of time within which to pay any tax or any deficiency therein, require the taxpayer to furnish a bond in an amount not exceeding double the amount of the tax with respect to which the extension is granted. Such bond shall be furnished in accordance with the provisions contained in section 7101 and the regulations in Part 30 of this Chapter (Regulations on Procedure and Administration). [Reg. § 1.6165-1.]

☐ [*T.D. 6455, 3-1-60.*]

[Reg. § 20.6165-1]

§ 20.6165-1. Bonds where time to pay tax or deficiency has been extended.—(a) *Extensions under sections 6161 and 6163(b) of time to pay tax or deficiency.*—If an extension of time for payment of tax or deficiency is granted under section 6161 or 6163(b), the district director may, if he deems it necessary, require the executor to furnish a bond for the payment of the amount in respect of which the extension is granted in accordance with the terms of the extension. However, such bond shall not exceed double the amount with respect to which the extension is granted. For other provisions relating to bonds required where extensions of time to pay estate taxes or deficiencies are granted under sections 6161 and

6163(b), see the regulations under section 7101 contained in Part 301 of this chapter (Regulations on Procedure and Administration).

(b) *Extensions under section 6163 of time to pay estate tax attributable to reversionary or remainder interests.*—As a prerequisite to the postponement of the payment of the tax attributable to a reversionary or remainder interest as provided in §20.6163-1, a bond equal to double the amount of the tax and interest for the estimated duration of the precedent interest must be furnished conditioned upon the payment of the tax and interest accrued thereon within six months after the termination of the precedent interest. If after the acceptance of a bond it is determined that the amount of the tax attributable to the reversionary or remainder interest was understated in the bond, a new bond or a supplemental bond may be required, or the tax, to the extent of the understatement, may be collected. The bond must be conditioned upon the principal or surety promptly notifying the district director when the precedent interest terminates and upon the principal or surety notifying the district director during the month of September of each year as to the continuance of the precedent interest, if the duration of the precedent interest is dependent upon the life or lives of any person or persons, or is otherwise indefinite. For other provisions relating to bonds where an extension of time has been granted for paying the tax, see the regulations under section 7101 contained in Part 301 of this chapter (Regulations on Procedure and Administration). [Reg. §20.6165-1.]

☐ [*T.D.* 6296, 6-23-58. *Amended by T.D.* 6526, 1-18-61, *T.D.* 6600, 5-28-62.]

[Reg. §25.6165-1]

§25.6165-1. Bonds where time to pay tax or deficiency has been extended.—If an extension of time for payment of tax or deficiency is granted under section 6161, the district director may, if he deems it necessary, require a bond for the payment of the amount in respect of which the extension is granted in accordance with the terms of the extension. However, such bond shall not exceed double the amount with respect to which the extension is granted. For provisions relating to form of bonds, see the regulations under section 7101 contained in Part 301 of this chapter (Regulations on Procedure and Administration). [Reg. §25.6165-1.]

☐ [*T.D.* 6334, 11-14-58. *Amended by T.D.* 6600, 5-28-62.]

[Reg. §53.6165-1]

§53.6165-1. Bonds where time to pay tax or deficiency has been extended.—If an extension of time for payment of tax or deficiency is granted under section 6161, the district director or the director of the service center may, if he deems it necessary, require a bond for the payment of the amount in respect of which the extension is granted in accordance with the terms of the extension. However, such bond shall not exceed double the amount with respect to which the extension is granted. For provisions relating to form of bonds, see the regulations under section 7101 contained in Part 301 of this chapter (Regulations on Procedure and Administration). [Reg. §53.6165-1.]

☐ [*T.D.* 7368, 7-15-75.]

[Reg. §55.6165-1]

§55.6165-1. Bonds where time to pay tax or deficiency has been extended.—If an extension of time for payment of tax or deficiency is granted under section 6161, the district director or the director of the service center may, if he deems it necessary, require a bond for the payment of the amount in respect of which the extension is granted in accordance with the terms of the extension. However, the bond shall not exceed double the amount with respect to which the extension is granted. For provisions relating to form of bonds, see the regulations under section 7101 contained in Part 301 of this chapter (Regulations on Procedure and Administration). [Reg. §55.6165-1.]

☐ [*T.D.* 7767, 2-3-81.]

[Reg. §156.6165-1]

§156.6165-1. Bonds where time to pay tax or deficiency has been extended.—If an extension of time for payment is granted under section 6161 of the Code, the district director or the director of the service center may, if he deems it necessary, require a bond for the payment of the amount in respect to which the extension is granted in accordance with the terms of the extension. However, the bond shall not exceed double the amount with respect to which the extension is granted. For provisions relating to form of bonds, see the regulations under section 7101 of the Code contained in Part 301 of title 26 (Regulations on Procedure and Administration). [Reg. §156.6165-1.]

☐ [*T.D.* 8379, 12-17-91.]

[Reg. §157.6165-1]

§157.6165-1. Bonds where time to pay tax has been extended.—If an extension of time for payment is granted under section 6161, the Internal Revenue Service may, if it deems necessary, require a bond for the payment, in accordance with the terms of the extension, of the amount with respect to which the extension is granted. However, the bond shall not exceed double the amount with respect to which the extension is granted. For provisions relating to the form of bonds, see the regulations under section 7101 contained in part 301 (Regulations on Procedure and Administration) of this chapter. [Reg. §157.6165-1.]

☐ [*T.D.* 9134, 7-7-2004.]

[Reg. §301.6165-1]

§301.6165-1. Bonds where time to pay the tax or deficiency has been extended.—For provisions concerning bonds where time to pay a tax or deficiency has been extended, see the regulations relating to the particular tax. [Reg. §301.6165-1.]

☐ [*T.D.* 6498, 10-24-60.]

[Reg. §20.6166-1]

§20.6166-1. Election of alternate extension of time for payment of estate tax where estate consists largely of interest in closely held business.—(a) *In general.*—Section 6166 allows an executor to elect to extend payment of part or all of the portion of the estate tax which is attributable to a closely held business interest (as defined in section 6166(b)(1)). If it is made at the time the estate tax return is filed, the election is applicable both to the tax originally determined to be due and to certain deficiencies. If no election is made when the estate tax return is filed, up to the full amount of certain later deficiencies (but not any tax originally determined to be due) may be paid in installments.

(b) *Time and manner of election.*—The election provided under section 6166(a) is made by attaching to a timely filed estate tax return a notice of election containing the following information:

(1) The decedent's name and taxpayer identification number as they appear on the estate tax return;

(2) The amount of tax which is to be paid in installments;

(3) The date selected for payment of the first installment;

(4) The number of annual installments, including the first installment, in which the tax is to be paid;

(5) The properties shown on the estate tax return which constitute the closely held business interest (identified by schedule and item number); and

(6) The facts which formed the basis for the executor's conclusion that the estate qualifies for payment of the estate tax in installments. In the absence of a statement in the notice of election as to the amount of tax to be paid in installments, the date selected for payment of the first installment, or the number of installments, the election is presumed to be for the maximum amount so payable and for payment thereof in 10 equal installments, the first of which is due on the date which is 5 years after the date prescribed in section 6151(a) for payment of estate tax.

(c) *Treatment of certain deficiencies.*—(1) *No election before assessment of deficiency.*—Where a deficiency is assessed and no election, including a protective election, has been made under section 6166(a) to pay any tax in installments, the executor may elect under section 6166(h) to pay the portion of the deficiency attributable to the closely held business interest in installments. However, this is true only if the estate qualifies under section 6166 based upon values as finally determined (or agreed to following examination of a return). Such an election is exercised by filing a notice of election with the Internal Revenue Service office where the estate tax return was filed. The notice of election must be filed within 60 days after issuance of notice and demand for payment of the deficiency, and it must

contain the same information as is required under paragraph (b) of this section. The notice of election is to be accompanied by payment of the amount of tax and interest, the date for payment of which has arrived as determined under paragraphs (e) and (f) of this section, plus any amount of unpaid tax and interest which is not attributable to the closely held business interest and which is not eligible for further extension (or currently extended) under another section (other than section 6166A).

(2) *Election made with estate tax return.*—If the executor makes an election under section 6166(a) (other than a protective election) at the time the estate tax return is filed and a deficiency is later assessed, the portion of the deficiency which is attributable to the closely held business interest (but not any accrued interest thereon) will be prorated to the installments payable pursuant to the original section 6166(a) election. Any part of the deficiency prorated to an installment, the date for payment of which has arrived, is due upon notice and demand. Interest for any such period, including the deferral period, is payable upon notice and demand.

(3) *Portion of deficiency attributable to closely held business interest.*—Only that portion of any deficiency which is attributable to a closely held business interest may be paid in installments under section 6166. The amount of any deficiency which is so attributable is the difference between the amount of tax which the executor has previously elected to pay in installments under section 6166 and the maximum amount of tax which the executor could have elected to pay in installments on the basis of a return which reflects the adjustments that resulted in the deficiency.

(d) *Protective election.*—A protective election may be made to defer payment of any portion of tax remaining unpaid at the time values are finally determined (or agreed to following examination of a return) and any deficiencies attributable to the closely held business interest (within the meaning of paragraph (c)(3) of this section). Extension of tax payments pursuant to this election is contingent upon final values meeting the requirements of section 6166. A protective election does not, however, extend the time for payment of any amount of tax. Rules for such extensions are contained in sections 6161, 6163, and 6166A. A protective election is made by filing a notice of election with a timely filed estate tax return stating that the election is being made. Within 60 days after values are finally determined (or agreed to following examination of a return), a final notice of election which sets forth the information required under paragraph (b) of this section must be filed with the Internal Revenue Service office where the original estate tax return was filed. That notice of final election is to be accompanied by payment of any amount of previously unpaid tax and interest, the date for payment of which has arrived as determined under paragraphs (e) and (f) of this section, plus any amount of unpaid tax and interest which is not attributable to the closely held business interest and which is not eligible for further extension (or currently extended) under another section (other than section 6166A).

(e) *Special rules.*—(1) *Effect of deficiencies and protective elections upon payment.*—Upon election to extend the time for payment of a deficiency or upon final determination of values following a protective election, the executor must prorate the tax or deficiency attributable to the closely held business interest among all installments. All amounts attributed to installments which would have been due had the election been made at the time the tax was due to be paid under section 6151(a) and all accrued interest must be paid at the time the election is made.

(2) *Determination of date for payment of first installment.*—The executor may defer payment of tax (but not interest) for any period up to 5 years from the date determined under section 6151(a) for payment of the estate tax. The date chosen for payment of the first installment of tax is not required to be on an annual anniversary of the original due date of the tax; however, it must be the date within any month which corresponds to the day of the month determined under section 6151(a).

(f) *Rule for computing interest.*—Section 6601(j) provides a special 4 percent interest rate for the amount of tax (including deficiencies) which is to be paid in installments under section 6166. This special interest rate applies only to that amount of tax which is to be paid in installments and which does not exceed the limitation of section 6601(j)(2). Where payment of a greater amount of tax than is subject to section 6601(j)(2) is extended under section 6166, each installment is deemed to be comprised of both tax subject to the 4 percent interest rate and tax subject to the rate otherwise prescribed by section 6621. The percentage of any installment subject to the special 4 percent rate is equal to the percentage of the total tax payable in installments which is subject to the 4 percent rate. Where an election is made under the provisions of paragraphs (b) or (c)(1) of this section, the 4 percent rate applies from the date on which the estate tax was originally due to be paid. If only a protective election is made, section 6601(j) applies to the amount which is to be paid in installments, limited to the amount of any deficiency, from the due date for payment of estate tax. After the date upon which the section 6166 election is made final, section 6601(j) applies to the entire amount to be paid in installments.

(g) *Relation of section 6166 and 6166A.*—No election may be made under section 6166 if an election under section 6166A applies with respect to an estate. For example, no election can be made under section 6166(h) where an executor has made an election under section 6166A. If an election is timely made under either section

6166 or section 6166A, however, a protective election can be made under the other section at the same time. If the executor then files a timely notice of final election under the section protectively elected and pays any amounts determined to be due currently following final determination of (or agreement as to) estate tax values, the original election under the other provision will be deemed never to have applied to the estate.

(h) *Special rule for estates for which elections under section 6166 are made on or before August 30, 1980.*—An election to extend payment of estate tax under section 6166 that is made on or before August 30, 1980 may be revoked. To revoke an election, the executor must file a notice of revocation with the Internal Revenue Service office where the original estate tax return was filed on or before January 31, 1981 (or if earlier, the date on which the period of limitation on assessment expires). This notice of revocation must contain the decedent's name, date of death, and taxpayer identification number, and is to be accompanied by remittance of any additional amount of estate tax and interest determined to be due.

(i) *Examples.*—The provisions of this section may be illustrated by the following examples:

Example (1)—(i). Based upon values shown on decedent A's timely filed estate tax return, 60 percent of the value of A's adjusted gross estate consisted of a farm which was a closely held business within the meaning of section 6166. A's executor, B, made a protective election under section 6166 when he filed A's estate tax return. B also applied for an extension of time under section 6161 to pay $15,000 of the $30,000 of estate tax shown due on the return. The requested extension was granted and was renewed at the end of 1 year. Eighteen months after the return was filed and after examination of A's estate tax return, the value of the farm was found to constitute 67 percent of the adjusted gross estate. B entered into an agreement consenting to the values as established on examination and to a deficiency of $5,000. B then filed a final notice of election under section 6166, choosing a 5-year deferral followed by 10 annual installment payments and thereby terminated his extension under section 6161 because that amount of tax was then included under the section 6166 election. B could have extended payment of 67 percent of the total estate tax, or $23,450. $23,450 is eligible for installment payments under section 6166 and the section 6166 election is considered to be for that amount. B is considered to have prepaid $3,450 of tax since only $20,000 of tax remained unpaid. The $3,450 is attributed to the first installment of $2,345 and to $1,105 of the second installment which would have been payable under the section 6166 election.

(ii) Had B been granted an extension of time under section 6161 to pay $20,000 of tax, $25,000 would remain unpaid when the final section 6166 election is made. Payment of the full $23,450 (67 percent) of tax which is attributable to the closely held business interest is included under the section 6166 election. The balance of unpaid tax ($1,550) is due upon expiration of the estate's section 6161 extension.

(iii) Assume the facts under example (1)(i). B must pay all unpaid accrued interest with his notice of final election. Since only 18 months have passed, no installments of tax are due. Interest on the $5,000 deficiency is computed at 4 percent per annum for the entire 18 months, and interest for 12 months of that period is currently due to be paid. Interest for the remaining 6 months is due at the next succeeding date for payment of interest. Interest on the $15,000 of tax extended under section 6161 is computed at the rate determined under section 6621 until the date of the final section 6166 election and is due upon termination of the section 6161 extension. After that date, the interest on the $15,000 will also accrue at 4 percent per annum.

Example (2). Assume the facts as in example (1), except B initially made an election under section 6166A and made no protective election under section 6166. Following final determination of values, B is not permitted to make any election under section 6166; however, had B protectively elected section 6166 at the time he made the section 6166A election, he could have terminated the section 6166A election and finally elected under section 6166. In such a case, the full $23,450 of tax attributable to the farm would have been eligible for extension under section 6166. The 4 percent interest rate would apply to the $5,000 deficiency from the original due date of the tax, and, as with the extension under section 6161, it would apply to the amounts extended under section 6166A only from the date on which the election under section 6166 was finalized.

Example (3). C died in 1977. His estate owes Federal estate taxes of $750,000, $500,000 of which is attributable to a closely held business interest. Payment of the $500,000 was extended under section 6166. A 5-year deferral followed by 10 annual installment payments was chosen by C's executor. Under paragraph (f) of this section, only 63.16 percent of each installment will be subject to the special 4 percent interest rate and the remainder will be subject to the rate determined under section 6621. The same rule applies in computing interest for the 5 years during which payment of tax is deferred. (This is so because the 4 percent interest rate applies only to a maximum of $345,800 of tax less the $30,000 of credit allowable under section 2010(a) rather than to the entire $500,000 extended amount.) [Reg. § 20.6166-1.]

☑ [T.D. 7710, 7-28-80.]

[Reg. § 20.6166A-1]

§ 20.6166A-1. Extension of time for payment of estate tax where estate consists largely of interest in closely held business.—(a) *In general.*—Section 6166 provides that where the value of an interest in a closely held business, which is included in the gross estate of a decedent who was a citizen or resident of the United States at the time of his death, exceeds either (1) 35 percent of the value of the gross estate, or (2) 50 percent of the taxable estate, the executor may elect to pay part or all of the Federal estate tax in installments. The election to pay the tax in installments applies to deficiencies in tax as well as to the tax shown on the return, unless the deficiency is due to negligence, to intentional disregard of rules and regulations, or to fraud with intent to evade tax. Except as otherwise provided in section 6166(i) and § 20.6166-4, the provisions of section 6166 and this section apply only if the due date of the return is after September 2, 1958. See § 20.6166-4 for special rules applicable where the decedent died after August 16, 1954, and the due date of the return was on or before September 2, 1958. See also § 20.6075-1 for the due date of the return, and § 20.6166-2 for definition of the term "interest in a closely held business." Since the election must be made on or before the due date of the return, the provisions of section 6166 will not apply to a deficiency in a case where, for whatever reason, no election was made to pay in installments the tax shown on the return. However, see paragraph (e)(3) of this section concerning a protective election. The general administrative provisions of subtitle F of the Code are applicable in connection with an election by the executor to pay the estate tax in installments in the same manner in which they are applied in a case where an extension of time under section 6161 is granted for payment of the tax. See paragraph(a) of § 20.6165-1 for provisions requiring the furnishing of security for the payment of the tax in cases where an extension is granted under section 6161.

(b) *Limitation on amount of tax payable in installments.*—The amount of estate tax which the executor may elect to pay in installments is limited to an amount A, which bears the same ratio to B (the gross Federal estate tax, reduced by the credits authorized by sections 2011 through 2014 and any death tax convention) as C (the value of the interest in a closely held business which is included in the gross estate) bears to D (the value of the gross estate). Stated algebraically, the limitation (A) equals

$$\frac{\text{value of interest in a closely held business}}{\text{value of gross estate (D)}} \times \text{gross Federal estate tax, reduced by the credits authorized by sections 2011 through 2014 and any death tax convention (B).}$$

The executor may elect to pay in installments an amount less than the amount computed under the limitation in this paragraph. For example, if the total estate tax payable is $100,000 and the amount computed under the limitation in this paragraph is $60,000, the executor may elect to pay in installments some lesser sum such as $30,000, in which event the executor must pay

$73,000 to the district director on or before the date prescribed by section 6151(a) for payment of the tax. Of such payment, $70,000 represents tax which the executor either could not elect to pay in installments or did not choose to so elect, and $3,000 represents a payment of the first installment of the tax which the executor elected to pay in installments.

(c) *Number of installments and dates for payment.*—The executor may elect to pay part or all of the tax (determined after application of the limitation contained in paragraph (b) of this section) in two or more, but not exceeding 10, equal annual installments. The first installment shall be paid on or before the date prescribed by section 6151(a) for payment of the tax (see paragraph (a) of § 20.6151-1), and each succeeding installment shall be paid on or before the date which is one year after the date prescribed for the payment of the preceding installment. See § 20.6166-3 for the circumstances under which the privilege of paying the tax in installments will terminate.

(d) *Deficiencies.*—The amount of a deficiency which may be paid in installments shall not exceed the difference between the amount of tax which the executor elected to pay in installments and the maximum amount of tax (determined under paragraph (b) of this section) which the executor could have elected to pay in installments on the basis of a return which reflects the adjustments which resulted in the deficiency. This amount is then prorated to the installments in which the executor elected to pay the tax. The part of the deficiency prorated to installments not yet due shall be paid at the same time as, and as a part of, such installments. The part of the deficiency prorated to installments already paid or due shall be paid upon notice and demand from the district director. At the time the executor receives such notice and demand he may, of course, prepay the portions of the deficiency which have been prorated to installments not yet due. See paragraph (h) of this section.

(e) *Notice of election.*—(1) *Filing of notice.*—The notice of election to pay the estate tax in installments shall be filed with the district director on or before the due date of the return. However, if the due date of the return is after September 2, 1958, but before November 3, 1958, the election will be considered as timely made if the notice is filed with the district director on or before November 3, 1958. See § 20.6075-1 for the due date of the return.

(2) *Form of notice.*—The notice of election to pay the estate tax in installments may be in the form of a letter addressed to the district director. The executor shall state in the notice the amount of tax which he elects to pay in installments, and the total number of installments (including the installment due 9 months (15 months, in the case of a decedent dying before January 1, 1971) after the date of the decedent's death) in which he elects to pay the tax. The properties in the gross estate which constitute the decedent's interest in a closely held business should be listed in the notice, and identified by the schedule and item number at which they appear on the estate tax return. The notice should set forth the facts which formed the basis for the executor's conclusion that the estate qualifies for the payment of the estate tax in installments.

(3) *Protective election.*—In a case where the estate does not qualify under section 6166(a) on the basis of the values as returned, or where the return shows no tax as due, an election may be made, contingent upon the values as finally determined meeting the percentage requirements set forth in section 6166(a), to pay in installments any portion of the estate tax, including a deficiency, which may be unpaid at the time of such final determination and which does not exceed the limitation provided in section 6166(b). The protective election must be made on or before the due date of the return and should state that it is a protective election. In the absence of a statement in the protective election as to the amount of tax to be paid in installments and the number of installments, the election will be presumed to be made for the maximum amount so payable and for the payment thereof in 10 equal annual installments, the first of which would have been due on the date prescribed in section 6151(a) for payment of the tax. The unpaid portion of the tax which may be paid in installments is prorated to the installments which would have been due if the provisions of section 6166(a) had applied to the tax, if any, shown on the return. The part of the unpaid portion of the tax so prorated to installments the date for payment of which would not have arrived before the deficiency is assessed shall be paid at the time such installments would have been due. The part of the unpaid portion of the tax so prorated to any installment the date for payment of which would have arrived before the deficiency is assessed shall be paid upon receipt of notice and demand from the district director. At the time the executor receives such notice and demand he may, of course, prepay the unpaid portions of the tax which have been prorated to installments not yet due. See paragraph (h) of this section.

(f) *Time for paying interest.*—Under the provisions of section 6601, interest at the annual rate referred to in the regulations under section 6621 shall be paid on the unpaid balance of the estate tax which the executor has elected to pay in installments, and on the unpaid balance of any deficiency prorated to the installments. Interest on such unpaid balance of estate tax shall be paid annually at the same time as, and as a part of, each installment of the tax. Accordingly, interest is computed on the entire unpaid balance for the period from the preceding installment date to the current installment date, and is paid with the current installment. In making such a computation, proper adjustment shall be made for any advance payments made during the period, whether the advance payments are voluntary or are brought about by the operation of section 6166(h)(2). In computing the annual interest payment, the portion of any deficiency

Reg. § 20.6166A-1(f)

66,824
Place and Due Date for Payment of Tax
See p. 20,601 for regulations not amended to reflect law changes

which is prorated to installments the date for payment of which has not arrived shall be added to the unpaid balance at the beginning of the annual period during which the assessment of the deficiency occurs. Interest on such portion of the deficiency for the period from the original due date of the tax to the date fixed for payment of the last installment preceding the date of assessment of a deficiency shall be paid upon notice and demand from the district director. Any extension of time under section 6161(a)(2) (on account of undue hardship to the estate) for payment of an installment will not extend the time for payment of the interest which is due on the installment date.

(g) *Extensions of time for payment in hardship cases.*—The provisions of section 6161, under which extensions of time may be granted for payment of estate tax in cases involving undue hardship, apply to both the portion of the tax which may be paid in installments under section 6166 and the portion of the tax which is not so payable. Therefore, in a case involving undue hardship, the executor may elect under section 6166 to pay in installments the portion of the tax which is attributable to the interest in the closely held business and, in addition, may file an application under section 6161 for an extension of time to pay both the portion of the tax which is not attributable to the interest in the closely held business and such of the installments as are payable within the period of the requested extension. If an executor files a notice of election to pay the tax in installments and thereafter it is determined that the estate does not qualify for the privilege of paying the tax in installments, the executor is not deprived of the right to request an extension under section 6161 of time for payment of the tax to which the purported election applied. See § 20.6161-1 for the circumstances under which a timely filed election to pay the tax in installments will be treated as a timely filed application for an extension of time to pay the tax on account of undue hardship to the estate.

(h) *Prepayments.*—Voluntary prepayment may be made at any time of all, or of any part, of the unpaid portion of the tax (including deficiencies) payable in installments. Voluntary prepayments shall be applied in payment of such installments, installment, or part of an installment as the person making the prepayment shall designate. For purposes of this paragraph, a payment described in paragraph (d)(2) of § 20.6166-3 of tax in an amount not less than the amount of money or other property distributed in a section 303 redemption is considered to be a voluntary prepayment to the extent paid before the date prescribed for payment of the first installment after the redemption or, if paid on the date prescribed for payment of such installment, to the extent it exceeds the amount due on the installment. See paragraph (b)(3) of § 20.6166-3 for the application to be made of the prepayment required by section 6166(h)(2). [Reg. § 20.6166A-1.]

[T.D. 6522, 12-28-60. *Amended by T.D. 7238, 12-28-72 and T.D. 7384, 10-21-75. Redesignated by T.D. 7710, 7-28-80.*]

[Reg. § 20.6166A-2]

§ 20.6166A-2. Definition of an interest in a closely held business.—(a) *In general.*—For purposes of §§ 20.6166-1, 20.6166-3, and 20.6166-4, the term "interest in a closely held business" means

(1) An interest as a proprietor in a trade or business carried on as a proprietorship.

(2) An interest as a partner in a partnership carrying on a trade or business if 20 percent or more of the total capital interest in the partnership is included in determining the decedent's gross estate or if the partnership had 10 or less partners.

(3) Stock in a corporation carrying on a trade or business if 20 percent or more in value of the voting stock of the corporation is included in determining the decedent's gross estate or if the corporation had 10 or less shareholders.

(b) *Number of partners or shareholders.*—The number of partners of the partnership or shareholders of the corporation is determined as of the time immediately before the decedent's death. Where an interest in a partnership, or stock in a corporation, is the community property of husband and wife, both the husband and the wife are counted as partners or shareholders in arriving at the number of partners or shareholders. Similarly, if stock is held by co-owners, tenants in common, tenants by the entirety, or joint tenants, each co-owner, tenant in common, tenant by the entirety, or joint tenant is counted as a shareholder.

(c) *Carrying on a trade or business.*—(1) In order for the interest in a partnership or the stock of a corporation to qualify as an interest in a closely held business it is necessary that the partnership or the corporation be engaged in carrying on a trade or business at the time of the decedent's death. However, it is not necessary that all the assets of the partnership or the corporation be utilized in the carrying on of the trade or business.

(2) In the case of a trade or business carried on as a proprietorship, the interest in the closely held business includes only those assets of the decedent which were actually utilized by him in the trade or business. Thus, if a building was used by the decedent in part as a personal residence and in part for the carrying on of a mercantile business, the part of the building used as a residence does not form any part of the interest in the closely held business. Whether an asset will be considered as used in the trade or business will depend on the facts and circumstances of the particular case. For example, if a bank account was held by the decedent in his individual name (as distinguished from the trade or business name) and it can be clearly shown that the amount on deposit represents working capital of the business as well as nonbusiness funds

(e.g., receipts from investments, such as dividends and interest), then that part of the amount on deposit which represents working capital of the business will constitute a part of the interest in the closely held business. On the other hand, if a bank account is held by the decedent in the trade or business name and it can be shown that the amount represents nonbusiness funds as well as working capital, then only that part of the amount on deposit which represents working capital of the business will constitute a part of the interest in the closely held business. In a case where an interest in a partnership or stock of a corporation qualifies as an interest in a closely held business, the decedent's entire interest in the partnership, or the decedent's entire holding of stock in the corporation, constitutes an interest in a closely held business even though a portion of the partnership or corporate assets is used for a purpose other than the carrying on of a trade or business.

(d) *Interests in two or more closely held businesses.*—For purposes of paragraphs (a) and (b) of §20.6166-1 and paragraphs (d) and (e) of §20.6166-3, interests in two or more closely held businesses shall be treated as an interest in a single closely held business if more than 50 percent of the total value of each such business is included in determining the value of the decedent's gross estate. For the purpose of the 50 percent requirement set forth in the preceding sentence, an interest in a closely held business which represents the surviving spouse's interest in community property shall be considered as having been included in determining the value of the decedent's gross estate. [Reg. §20.6166A-2.]

☐ [*T.D. 6522, 12-28-60. Redesignated by T.D. 7710, 7-28-80.*]

[Reg. §20.6166A-3]

§20.6166A-3. Acceleration of payment.— (a) *In general.*—Under the circumstances described in this section all or a part of the tax which the executor has elected to pay in installments shall be paid before the dates fixed for payment of the installments. Upon an estate's having undistributed net income described in paragraph (b) of this section for any taxable year after its fourth taxable year, the executor shall pay an amount equal to such undistributed net income in liquidation of the unpaid portion of the tax payable in installments. Upon the happening of any of the events described in paragraphs (c), (d), and (e) of this section, any unpaid portion of the tax payable in installments shall be paid upon notice and demand from the district director.

(b) *Undistributed net income of estate.*—(1) If an estate has undistributed net income for any taxable year after its fourth taxable year, the executor shall pay an amount equal to such undistributed net income in liquidation of the unpaid portion of the tax payable in installments. The amount shall be paid to the district director on or before the time prescribed for the filing of the estate's income tax return for such taxable year. For this purpose extensions of time granted for the filing of the income tax return are taken into consideration in determining the time prescribed for filing the return and making such payment. In determining the number of taxable years, a short taxable year is counted as if it were a full taxable year.

(2) The term "undistributed net income" of the estate for any taxable year for purposes of this section is the amount by which the distributable net income of the estate, as defined in section 643, exceeds the sum of—

(i) The amount for such year specified in section 661(a)(1) and (2),

(ii) The amount of the Federal income tax imposed on the estate for such taxable year under chapter 1 of the Code, and

(iii) The amount of the Federal estate tax, including interest thereon, paid for the estate during such taxable year (other than any amount paid by reason of the application of this acceleration rule).

(3) The payment described in subparagraph (1) of this paragraph shall be applied against the total unpaid portion of the tax which the executor elected to pay in installments, and shall be divided equally among the installments due after the date of such payment. The application of this subparagraph may be illustrated by the following example:

Example. The decedent died on January 1, 1959. The executor elects under section 6166 to pay tax in the amount of $100,000 in 10 installments of $10,000. The first installment is due on April 1, 1960. The estate files its income tax returns on a calendar year basis. For its fifth taxable year (calendar year 1963) it has undistributed net income of $6,000. If the prepayment of $6,000 required by section 6166(h)(2)(A), and due on or before April 15, 1964, is paid before the fifth installment (due April 1, 1964), the $6,000 is apportioned equally among installments 5 through 10, leaving $9,000 as the amount due on each of such installments. However, if the prepayment of $6,000 is paid after the fifth installment, it is apportioned equally among installments 6 through 10, leaving $8,800 as the amount due on each of such installments.

(c) *Failure to pay installment on or before due date.*—If any installment of tax is not paid on or before the date fixed for its payment (including any extension of time for the payment thereof), the whole of the unpaid portion of the tax which is payable in installments becomes due and shall be paid upon notice and demand from the district director. See paragraph (c) of §20.6166-1 for the dates fixed for the payment of installments. See also §20.6161-1 for the circumstances under which an extension of time for the payment of an installment will be granted.

(d) *Withdrawal of funds from business.*—(1) In any case where money or other property is withdrawn from the trade or business and the aggregate withdrawals of money or other property

Reg. §20.6166A-3(d)(1)

equal or exceed 50 percent of the value of the trade or business, the privilege of paying the tax in installments terminates and the whole of the unpaid portion of the tax which is payable in installments becomes due and shall be paid upon notice and demand from the district director. The withdrawals of money or other property from the trade or business must be in connection with the interest therein included in the gross estate, and must equal or exceed 50 percent of the value of the entire trade or business (and not just 50 percent of the value of the interest therein included in the gross estate). The withdrawal must be a withdrawal of money or other property which constitutes "included property" within the meaning of that term as used in paragraph (d) of § 20.2032-1. The provisions of this section do not apply to the withdrawal of money or other property which constitutes "excluded property" within the meaning of that term as used in such subparagraph (d).

(2) If a distribution in redemption of stock is (by reason of the provisions of section 303 or so much of section 304 as relates to section 303) treated for income tax purposes as a distribution in full payment in exchange for the stock so redeemed, the amount of such distribution is not counted as a withdrawal of money or other property made with respect to the decedent's interest in the trade or business for purposes of determining whether the withdrawals of money or other property made with respect to the decedent's interest in the trade or business for purposes of determining whether the withdrawals of money or other property made with respect to the decedent's interest in the trade or business equal or exceed 50 percent of the value of the trade or business. However, in the case described in the preceding sentence the value of the trade or business for purposes of applying the rule set forth in subparagraph (1) of this paragraph is the value thereof reduced by the proportionate part thereof which such distribution represents. The proportionate part of the value of the trade or business which the distribution represents is determined at the time of the distribution, but the reduction in the value of the trade or business represented by it relates back to the time of the decedent's death, or the alternate valuation date if an election is made under section 2032, for purposes of determining whether other withdrawals with respect to the decedent's interest in the trade or business constitute withdrawals equaling or exceeding 50 percent of the value of the trade or business. See example (3) of paragraph (e)(6) of this section for illustration of this principle. The rule stated in the first sentence of this subparagraph does not apply unless after the redemption, but on or before the date prescribed for payment of the first installment which becomes due after the redemption, there is paid an amount of estate tax not less than the amount of money or other property distributed. Where there are a series of section 303 redemptions, each redemption is treated separately and the failure of one redemption to qualify under the rule stated in the first sentence of this subparagraph does not necessarily mean that another redemption will not qualify.

(3) The application of this paragraph may be illustrated by the following examples, in each of which the executor elected to pay the estate tax in installments:

Example (1). A, who died on July 1, 1957, owned an 80 percent interest in a partnership which qualified as an interest in a closely held business. B owned the other 20 percent interest in the partnership. On the date of A's death the value of the business was $200,000 and the value of A's interest therein was included in his gross estate at $160,000. On October 1, 1958, when the value of the business was the same as at A's death, the executor withdrew $80,000 from the business. On December 1, 1958, when the value of the remaining portion of the business was $160,000, the executor withdrew $20,000 from the business and B withdrew $10,000. On February 1, 1959, when the value of the then remaining portion of the business was $150,000 the executor withdrew $15,000. The withdrawals of money or other property from the trade or business with respect to the interest therein included in the gross estate are considered as not having equaled or exceeded 50 percent of the value of the trade or business until February 1, 1959. The executor is considered as having withdrawn 40 percent of the value of the trade or business on October 1, 1958, computed as follows:

$$\frac{\$80,000 \text{ (withdrawal)}}{\$200,000 \text{ (value of trade or business at time of withdrawal)}} \times 100 \text{ percent} = 40 \text{ percent}$$

Immediately following the October withdrawal the remaining portion of the business represents 60 percent of the value of the trade or business in existence at the time of A's death (100 percent less 40 percent withdrawn). The executor is considered as having withdrawn 7.5 percent of the value of the trade or business on December 1, 1958, and B as having withdrawn 3.75 percent of the value thereof at that time, computed as follows:

Executor's withdrawal—

$$\frac{\$20,000 \text{ (withdrawal)}}{\$160,000 \text{ (value of trade or business at time of withdrawal)}} \times 60 \text{ percent} = 7.5 \text{ percent}$$

Reg. § 20.6166A-3(d)(2)

B's withdrawal—

$$\frac{\$10,000 \text{ (withdrawal)}}{\$160,000 \text{ (value of trade or business at time of withdrawal)}} \times 60 \text{ percent} = 3.75 \text{ percent}$$

Immediately following the December withdrawal the then remaining portion of the business represented 48.75 percent of the value of the trade or business in existence at the time of A's death (100 percent less 40 percent withdrawn by executor in October, 7.5 percent withdrawn by executor in December, and 3.75 percent withdrawn by B in December). It should be noted that while at this point the total withdrawals by the executor and B from the trade or business exceed 50 percent of the value thereof, the aggregate of the withdrawals by the executor were less than 50 percent of the value of the trade or business. Also it should be noted that while the total withdrawals by the executor exceeded 50 percent of the value of A's interest in the trade or business, they did not exceed 50 percent of the value of the entire trade or business. The executor is considered as having withdrawn 4.875 percent of the value of the trade or business on February 1, 1959, computed as follows:

$$\frac{\$15,000 \text{ (withdrawal)}}{\$150,000 \text{ (value of trade or business at time of withdrawal)}} \times 48.75 \text{ percent} = 4.875 \text{ percent}$$

As of February 1, 1959, the total withdrawals from the trade or business made with respect to A's interest therein was 52.375 percent of the value of the trade or business.

Example (2). The decedent's 40 percent interest in the XYZ partnership constituted an interest in a closely held business. Since the decedent's interest in the closely held business amounted to less than 50 percent of the value of the business, money or other property equaling or exceeding 50 percent of the value of the business could not be withdrawn from the decedent's interest in the business. Therefore, withdrawals of money or other property from this trade or business never would accelerate the payment of the tax under the provisions of this paragraph.

Example (3). The decedent died on September 1, 1957. He owned 100 shares of B Corporation (the total number of shares outstanding at the time of his death) and a 75 percent interest in a partnership of which C was the other partner. The B Corporation stock and the interest in the partnership together make up the interest in the closely held business which was included in the decedent's gross estate. The B Corporation stock was included in the gross estate at a value of $400,000 and the interest in the partnership was included at a value of $300,000. On November 1, 1957, at which time the value of the corporation's assets had not changed, in a section 303 redemption the executor surrendered 26 shares of B Corporation stock for $104,000. On December 1, 1957, at which time the value of the partnership's assets had not changed, the partners withdrew 90 percent of the assets of the partnership, with the executor receiving $270,000 and C receiving $90,000. The estate tax amounts to $240,000, of which the executor elected under section 6166 to pay $140,000 in 10 installments of $14,000 each. On December 1, 1958, the due date for paying the estate tax which was not payable in installments and for paying the first installment under section 6166, the executor paid estate tax of $114,000, of which $100,000 represented the tax not payable in installments and $14,000 represented the first installment. Inasmuch as after the section 303 distribution and on or before the due date of the first installment (December 1, 1958) after the section 303 distribution the executor paid as estate tax an amount not less than the amount of the distribution, the section 303 distribution does not constitute a withdrawal of money or other property from the business for purposes of section 6166(h)(1). Therefore, the value of the trade or business is reduced by the amount of the section 303 distribution. Accordingly, the value of the entire trade or business is $696,000, of which $400,000 represents the value of the partnership and $296,000 represents the value of the B Corporation stock. Since the executor is considered as having withdrawn only $270,000 (the withdrawal from the partnership) from the trade or business, the withdrawal of money or other property from the trade or business made with respect to the decedent's interest therein was 270,000/696,000 of the value of the entire trade or business, or less than 50 percent thereof.

(e) *Disposition of interest in business.*—(1) In any case where in the aggregate 50 percent or more of the decedent's interest in a closely held business has been distributed, sold, exchanged, or otherwise disposed of, the privilege of paying the tax in installments terminates and the whole of the unpaid portion of the tax which is payable in installments becomes due and shall be paid upon notice and demand from the district director. A transfer by the executor of an interest in a closely held business to a beneficiary or trustee named in the decedent's will or to an heir who is entitled to receive it under the applicable intestacy law does not constitute a distribution thereof for purposes of determining whether 50 percent or more of an interest in a closely held business has been distributed, sold, exchanged, or otherwise disposed of. However, a subsequent transfer of the interest by the beneficiary,

Reg. § 20.6166A-3(e)(1)

trustee, or heir will constitute a distribution, sale, exchange, or other disposition thereof for such purposes. The disposition must be a disposition of an interest which constitutes "included property" within the meaning of that term as used in paragraph (d) of § 20.2032-1. The provisions of this section do not apply to the disposition of an interest which constitutes "excluded property" within the meaning of that term as used in such paragraph (d).

(2) The phrase "distributed, sold, exchanged, or otherwise disposed of" comprehends all possible ways by which an interest in a closely held business ceases to form a part of the gross estate. The term includes the surrender of a stock certificate for corporate assets in complete or partial liquidation of a corporation pursuant to section 331. The term also includes the surrender of stock for stock pursuant to a transaction described in subparagraphs (A), (B), or (C) of section 368(a)(1). In general the term does not, however, extend to transactions which are mere changes in form. It does not include a transfer of assets to a corporation in exchange for its stock in a transaction with respect to which no gain or loss would be recognizable for income tax purposes under section 351. It does not include an exchange of stock in a corporation for stock in the same corporation or another corporation pursuant to a plan of reorganization described in subparagraphs (D), (E), or (F) of section 368(a)(1), nor to an exchange to which section 355 (or so much of section 356 as relates to section 355) applies. However, any stock received in an exchange to which the two preceding sentences apply shall for purposes of this paragraph be treated as an interest in a closely held business.

(3) An interest in a closely held business may be "distributed" by either a trustee who received it from the executor, or a trustee of an interest which is included in the gross estate under sections 2035 through 2038, or section 2041. See subparagraph (1) of this paragraph relative to the distribution of an interest by the executor to the person entitled to receive it under the decedent's will or an intestacy law.

(4) An interest in a closely held business may be "sold, exchanged, or otherwise disposed of" by (i) the executor; (ii) a trustee or other donee to whom the decedent in his lifetime transferred the interest included in his gross estate under sections 2035 through 2038, or section 2041; (iii) a beneficiary, trustee, or heir entitled to receive the property from the executor under the decedent's will or under the applicable law of descent and distribution, or to whom title to the interest passed directly under local law; (iv) a surviving joint tenant or tenant by the entirety; or (v) any other person.

(5) If a ·distribution in redemption of stock is (by reason of the provisions of section 303 or so much of section 304 as relates to section 303) treated for income tax purposes as a distribution in full payment in exchange for the stock redeemed, the stock so redeemed is not counted as distributed, sold, exchanged, or otherwise disposed of for purposes of determining whether 50 percent or more of the decedent's interest in a closely held business has been distributed, sold, exchanged, or otherwise disposed of. However, in the case described in the preceding sentence the interest in the closely held business for purposes of applying the rule set forth in subparagraph (1) of this paragraph is such interest reduced by the proportionate part thereof which the redeemed stock represents. The proportionate part of the interest which the redeemed stock represents is determined at the time of the redemption, but the reduction in the interest represented by it relates back to the time of the decedent's death, or the alternate valuation date if an election is made under section 2032, for purposes of determining whether other distributions, sales, exchanges, and dispositions of the decedent's interest in the closely held business equal or exceed in the aggregate 50 percent of such interest. See example (3) of subparagraph (6) of this paragraph for illustration of this principle. The rule stated in the first sentence of this subparagraph does not apply unless after the redemption, but on or before the date prescribed for payment of the first installment which becomes due after the redemption, there is paid an amount of estate tax not less than the amount of money or other property distributed. Where there are a series of section 303 redemptions, each redemption is treated separately and the failure of one redemption to qualify under the rule stated in the first sentence of this subparagraph does not necessarily mean that another redemption will not qualify.

(6) The application of this paragraph may be illustrated by the following examples, in each of which the executor elected to pay the tax in installments:

Example (1). The decedent died on October 1, 1957. He owned 8,000 of the 12,000 shares of D Corporation outstanding at the time of his death and 3,000 of the 5,000 shares of E Corporation outstanding at that time. The D Corporation stock was included in the gross estate at $50 per share, or a total of $400,000. The E Corporation stock was included in the gross estate at $100 per share, or a total of $300,000. On November 1, 1958, the executor sold the 3,000 shares of E Corporation and on February 1, 1959, he sold 1,000 shares of D Corporation. Since the decedent's shares of D Corporation and E Corporation together constituted the interest in a closely held business, the value of such interest was $700,000 ($400,000 plus $300,000) and the D Corporation stock represented 400,000/700,000 thereof and the E Corporation stock represented 300,000/700,000 thereof. While the sale of 3,000 shares of E Corporation on November 1, 1958, was a sale of the decedent's entire interest in E Corporation and a sale of more than 50 percent of the outstanding stock of E Corporation, nevertheless it constituted a sale of only 300,000/700,000 of the interest in the closely held business. The sale of 1,000 shares of D Corporation stock on February 1, 1959, represented a sale of 50,000/700,000 of the interest in the closely held business. The numerator of $50,000 is determined as follows:

$$\frac{1,000 \text{ (shares sold)}}{8,000 \text{ (shares owned)}} \times \$400,000 \quad \text{(value of shares owned, as included in gross estate)}$$

Taken together the two sales represented a sale of 50 percent (350,000/700,000) of the interest in the closely held business. Therefore, as of February 1, 1959 (the date of the sale of 1,000 shares of E Corporation), 50 percent or more in value of the interest in the closely held business is considered as distributed, sold, exchanged, or otherwise disposed of.

Example (2). The decedent died on September 1, 1958. The interest owned by him in a closely held business consisted of 100 shares of the M Corporation. On February 1, 1959, in a section 303 redemption, 20 shares were redeemed for cash and an amount equivalent to the proceeds was paid on the Federal estate tax before the date of the next installment. On July 1, 1959, the executor sold 40 of the remaining shares of the stock. The section 303 redemption is not considered to be a distribution, sale, exchange, or other disposition of the portion of the interest represented by the 20 shares redeemed. As a result of the section 303 redemption the remaining 80 shares represent the decedent's entire interest in the closely held business for purposes of determining whether in the aggregate 50 percent or more of the interest in the closely held business has been distributed, sold, exchanged, or otherwise disposed of. The sale on July 1, 1959, of the 40 shares represents a sale of 50 percent of the interest in the closely held business.

Example (3). The facts are the same as in example (2) except that the 40 shares were sold on December 1, 1958 (before the section 303 redemption was made) instead of on July 1, 1959 (after the section 303 redemption was made). The sale of the 40 shares in December represents, as of that date, a sale of 40 percent of the interest in the closely held business. However, the section 303 redemption of 20 shares does not count as a distribution, sale, exchange, or other disposition of the interest, but it does reduce the interest to 80 shares (100 shares less 20 shares redeemed) for purposes of determining whether other distributions, sales, exchanges, and dispositions in the aggregate equal or exceed 50 percent of the interest in the closely held business. Since the reduction of the interest to 80 shares relates back to the time of the decedent's death, or the alternate valuation date if an election is made under section 2032, the sale of the 40 shares, as recomputed represents a sale of 50 percent of the interest. However, since the sale of the 40 shares did not represent a sale of 50 percent of the interest until the section 303 distribution was made, February 1, 1959 (the date of the section 303 distribution) is considered the date on which 50 percent of the interest was distributed, sold, exchanged, or otherwise disposed of.

(f) *Information to be furnished by executor.*— (1) If the executor acquires knowledge of the happening of any transaction described in paragraph (d) or (e) of this section which, in his opinion, standing alone or when taken together with other transactions of which he has knowledge, would result in

(i) Aggregate withdrawals of money or other property from the trade or business equal to or exceeding 50 percent of the value of the entire trade or business, or

(ii) Aggregate distributions, sales, exchanges, and other dispositions equal to or exceeding 50 percent of the interest in the closely held business which was included in the gross estate,

the executor shall so notify the district director, in writing, within 30 days of acquiring such knowledge.

(2) On the date fixed for payment of each installment of tax (determined without regard to any extension of time for the payment thereof), other than the final installment, the executor shall furnish the district director, in writing, with either

(i) A complete disclosure of all transactions described in paragraphs (d) and (e) of this section of which he has knowledge and which have not previously been made known by him to the district director, or

(ii) A statement that to the best knowledge of the executor all transactions described in paragraphs (d) and (e) of this section which have occurred have not produced a result described in subparagraph (1)(i) or (ii) of this paragraph.

(3) The district director may require the submission of such additional information as is deemed necessary to establish the estate's right to continue payment of the tax in installments. [Reg. § 20.6166A-3.]

☐ [*T.D.* 6522, 12-28-60. *Redesignated by T.D.* 7710, 7-28-80.]

[Reg. § 20.6166A-4]

§ 20.6166A-4. Special rules applicable where due date of return was before September 3, 1958.—(a) *In general.*—Section 206(f) of the Small Business Tax Revision Act of 1958 (72 Stat. 1685) provides that section 6166(i) of the Code shall apply in cases where the decedent died after August 16, 1954, but only if the date for filing the estate tax return (including extensions thereof) expired before September 3, 1958. Therefore, the privilege of paying the estate tax in installments as described in §§ 20.6166-1 through 20.6166-3 is available also in cases where the due date of the return is before September 3, 1958, but under somewhat different circumstances. These differences are explained in paragraphs (b) through (e) of this section. Therefore, except as otherwise provided in paragraphs (b) through (e) of this section, the regulations contained in §§ 20.6166-1 through 20.6166-3 apply also in cases where the due date of the return is before September 3, 1958. See § 20.6075-1 for the due date of the return. The value of the gross estate as determined for purposes of a deficiency in tax assessed after September 2, 1958, and the value at which the interest in the closely held business, to which the election applies, is included in such value of the gross estate are used in ascertaining whether an estate coming within the purview of section 6166(i) and this section satisfies the percentage requirements as to qualification set forth in section 6166(a).

(b) *Tax to which election applies.*—In a case where the due date of the return was before September 3, 1958, an election to pay estate tax in installments does not apply to the tax shown on the return nor to a deficiency in tax assessed before that date. It does apply to a deficiency in tax assessed after September 2, 1958, unless the deficiency is due to negligence, to intentional disregard of rules and regulations, or to fraud with intent to evade tax. The amount of the deficiency which may be paid in installments shall not exceed that proportion of the total tax (including the deficiency) which is determined by applying thereto the ratio set forth in paragraph (b) of § 20.6166-1. See paragraph (c) of this section for the method of prorating the deficiency to the installments.

(c) *Proration of deficiency to installments.*—The deficiency in tax which may be paid in installments is prorated to the installments which would have been due if the provisions of section 6166(a) had applied to the tax shown on the return and if an election had been timely made at the time the estate tax return was filed. The part of the deficiency so prorated to any installment the date for payment of which would have arrived before the election is made shall be paid at the time the election is made. The portion of the deficiency so prorated to installments the date for payment of which would not have arrived before the election is made shall be paid at the time such installments would have been due if such an election had been made.

(d) *Notice of election.*—The notice of election to pay the deficiency in installments shall be filed with the district director not later than 60 days after issuance of notice and demand by the district director for payment of the deficiency. The number of installments in which the executor elects to pay the deficiency includes those installments the dates for payment of which would have arrived within the meaning of paragraph (c) of this section. See paragraph (c)(2) of § 20.6166-1 for further information relative to the notice of election.

(e) *Undistributed income of estate.*—In any case where the due date of the estate tax return was before September 3, 1958, the provisions of paragraph (b) of § 20.6166-3 (providing for acceleration of payment of estate tax by amount of estate's undistribtuted net income for any taxable year after its fourth taxable year) shall not apply with respect to the estate's undistributed net income for any taxable year ending before January 1, 1960. [Reg. § 20.6166A-4.]

☐ [*T.D.* 6522, *12-28-60. Redesignated by T.D.* 7710, *7-28-80.*]

Assessment

IN GENERAL

See p. 20,601 for regulations not amended to reflect law changes

[Reg. § 301.6201-1]

§ 301.6201-1. Assessment authority.—(a) *In general.*—The district director is authorized and required to make all inquiries necessary to the determination and assessment of all taxes imposed by the Internal Revenue Code of 1954 or any prior internal revenue law. The district director is further authorized and required, and the director of the regional service center is authorized, to make the determinations and the assessments of such taxes. However, certain inquiries and determinations are, by direction of the Commissioner, made by other officials, such as assistant regional commissioners. The term "taxes" includes interest, additional amounts, additions to the taxes, and assessable penalties. The authority of the district director and the director of the regional service center to make assessments includes the following:

(1) *Taxes shown on return.*—The district director or the director of the regional service center shall assess all taxes determined by the taxpayer or by the district director or the director of the regional service center and disclosed on a return or list.

(2) *Unpaid taxes payable by stamp.*—(i) If without the use of the proper stamp:

(a) Any article upon which a tax is required to be paid by means of a stamp is sold or removed for sale or use by the manufacturer thereof, or

(b) Any transaction or act upon which a tax is required to be paid by means of a stamp occurs;

the district director, upon such information as he can obtain, must estimate the amount of the tax which has not been paid and the district director or the director of the regional service center must make assessment therefor upon the person the district director determines to be liable for the tax. However, the district director or the director of the regional service center may not assess any tax which is payable by stamp unless the taxpayer fails to pay such tax at the time and in the manner provided by law or regulations.

(ii) If a taxpayer gives a check or money order as a payment for stamps but the check or money order is not paid upon presentment, then the district director or the director of the regional service center shall assess the amount of the check or money order against the taxpayer as if it were a tax due at the time the check or money order was received by the district director.

(3) *Erroneous income tax prepayment credits.*— If the amount of income tax withheld or the amount of estimated income tax paid is overstated by a taxpayer on a return or on a claim for refund, the amount so overstated which is allowed against the tax shown on the return or which is allowed as a credit or refund shall be assessed by the district director or the director of the regional service center in the same manner as in the case of a mathematical error on the return. See section 6213(b)(1), relating to exceptions to restrictions on assessment.

(b) *Estimated income tax.*—Neither the district director nor the director of the regional service center shall assess any amount of estimated income tax required to be paid under section 6153 or 6154 which is unpaid.

(c) *Compensation of child.*—Any income tax assessed against a child, to the extent of the amount attributable to income included in the gross income of the child solely by reason of section 73(a) or the corresponding provision of prior law, if not paid by the child, shall, for the purposes of the income tax imposed by chapter 1 (or the corresponding provisions of prior law), be considered as having also been properly assessed against the parent. In any case in which the earnings of the child are included in the gross income of the child solely by reason of section 73(a) or the corresponding provision of prior law, the parent's liability is an amount equal to the amount by which the tax assessed against the child (and not paid by him) has been increased by reason of the inclusion of such earnings in the gross income of the child. Thus, if for the calendar year 1954 the child has income of $1,000 from investments and of $3,000 for services rendered, and the latter amount is includible in the gross income of the child under section 73(a) and the child has no wife or dependents, the tax liability determined under section 3 is $625. If the child had only the investment income of $1,000, his tax liability would be $62. If the tax of $625 is assessed against the child, the difference between $625 and $62, or $563, is the amount of such tax which is considered to have been properly assessed against the parent, if not paid by the child. [Reg. § 301.6201-1.]

☐ [*T.D.* 6119, 12-31-54. *Amended by T.D.* 6498, 10-24-60 *and T.D.* 6885, 12-27-61.]

[Reg. § 301.6203-1]

§ 301.6203-1. Method of assessment.—The district director and the director of the regional

service center shall appoint one or more assessment officers. The district director shall also appoint assessment officers in a Service Center servicing his district. The assessment shall be made by an assessment officer signing the summary record of assessment. The summary record, through supporting records, shall provide identification of the taxpayer, the character of the liability assessed, the taxable period, if applicable, and the amount of the assessment. The amount of the assessment shall, in the case of tax shown on a return by the taxpayer, be the amount so shown, and in all other cases the amount of the assessment shall be the amount shown on the supporting list or record. The date of the assessment is the date the summary record is signed by an assessment officer. If the taxpayer requests a copy of the record of assessment, he shall be furnished a copy of the pertinent parts of the assessment which set forth the name of the taxpayer, the date of assessment, the character of the liability assessed, the taxable period, if applicable, and the amounts assessed. [Reg. § 301.6203-1.]

☐ [*T.D.* 6119, 12-31-54. *Amended by T.D.* 6585, 12-27-61 *and T.D.* 7838, 10-5-82.]

[Reg. § 301.6204-1]

§ 301.6204-1. Supplemental assessments.—If any assessment is incomplete or incorrect in any material respect, the district director or the director of the regional service center, subject to the restrictions with respect to the assessment of deficiencies in income, estate, gift, chapter 41, 42, 43, and 44 taxes, and subject to the applicable period of limitation, may make a supplemental assessment for the purpose of correcting or completing the original assessment. [Reg. § 301.6204-1.]

☐ [*T.D.* 6119, 12-31-54. *Amended by T.D.* 6585, 12-27-61 *and T.D.* 7838, 10-5-82.]

[Reg. § 31.6205-1]

§ 31.6205-1. Adjustments of underpayments.—(a) *In general.*—(1) An employer who has underreported and underpaid employee Federal Insurance Contributions Act (FICA) tax under section 3101 or employer FICA tax under section 3111, employee Railroad Retirement Tax Act (RRTA) tax under section 3201 or employer RRTA tax under section 3221, or income tax required under section 3402 to be withheld, with respect to any payment of wages or compensation, shall correct such error as provided in this section. Such correction may constitute an interest-free adjustment as provided in paragraph (b) or (c) of this section.

(2) No correction will be eligible for interest-free adjustment treatment if the failure to report relates to an issue that was raised in an examination of a prior return period or if the employer knowingly underreported its employment tax liability.

(3) Every correction under this section of an underpayment of tax with respect to a payment of wages or compensation shall be made on the

form prescribed by the IRS that corresponds to the return being corrected. The form, filed in accordance with this section and the instructions, will constitute an adjusted return for the return period being corrected.

(4) Every adjusted return on which an underpayment is corrected pursuant to this section shall designate the return period in which the error was ascertained and the return period being corrected, explain in detail the grounds and facts relied upon to support the correction, and set forth such other information as may be required by the regulations in this section and by the instructions relating to the adjusted return.

(5) For purposes of this section, an error is ascertained when the employer has sufficient knowledge of the error to be able to correct it.

(6) No correction will be eligible for interest-free adjustment treatment pursuant to this section after the earlier of the following:

    (i) Receipt from the IRS of notice and demand for payment thereof based upon an assessment.

    (ii) Receipt from the IRS of a Notice of Determination of Worker Classification (Notice of Determination) in connection with such underpayment. Prior to receipt of a Notice of Determination, the taxpayer may, in lieu of making a payment, make a cash bond deposit that would have the effect of stopping the accrual of any interest, but would not deprive the taxpayer of its right to receive a Notice of Determination and to petition the Tax Court under section 7436.

(7) Subject to the exceptions specified in paragraphs (a)(2) and (a)(6) of this section, Form 2504, "Agreement and Collection of Additional Tax and Acceptance of Overassessment (Excise or Employment Tax)," Form 2504-WC, "Agreement to Assessment and Collection of Additional Tax and Acceptance of Overassessment in Worker Classification Cases (Employment Tax)," and such other forms as may be prescribed by the IRS, constitute adjusted returns for purposes of this section.

(8) For provisions related to furnishing employee statements and corrected employee statements reporting wages and withheld taxes, see sections 6041 and 6051 and §§ 1.6041-2 and 31.6051-1. For provisions relating to filing information returns and corrected information returns reporting wages and withheld taxes, see sections 6041 and 6051 and §§ 1.6041-2 and 31.6051-2.

(9) For the period of limitations upon assessment and collection of taxes, see § 301.6501(a)-1.

(b) *Federal Insurance Contributions Act and Railroad Retirement Tax Act.*—(1) *Undercollection ascertained before return is filed.*—If an employer collects less than the correct amount of employee FICA or RRTA tax from an employee with respect to a payment of wages or compensation, and if the employer ascertains the error before filing the return on which the employee tax with respect to such wages or compensation is required to be reported, the employer shall never-

theless report on the return and pay to the IRS the correct amount of employee tax. If the employer does not report the correct amount of tax in these circumstances, the employer may not later correct the error through an interest-free adjustment.

(2) *Error ascertained after return is filed.*— (i) If an employer files a return on which FICA tax or RRTA tax is required to be reported, and reports on the return less than the correct amount of employee or employer FICA or RRTA tax with respect to a payment of wages or compensation, and if the employer ascertains the error after filing the return, the employer shall correct the error through an interest-free adjustment as provided in this section, except as provided in paragraph (b)(4) of this section for Additional Medicare Tax. The employer shall adjust the underpayment of tax by reporting the additional amount due on an adjusted return for the return period in which the wages or compensation was paid, accompanied by a detailed explanation of the amount being reported on the adjusted return and any other information as may be required by this section and by the instructions relating to the adjusted return. The reporting of the underpayment on an adjusted return constitutes an adjustment within the meaning of this section only if the adjusted return is filed within the period of limitations for assessment for the return period being corrected, and by the due date for filing the return for the return period in which the error is ascertained. For purposes of the preceding sentence, the due date for filing the adjusted return is determined by reference to the return being corrected, without regard to the employer's current filing requirements. For example, an employer with a current annual filing requirement who is correcting an error on a previously filed quarterly return must file the adjusted return by the due date for filing a quarterly return for the quarter in which the error is ascertained. The amount of the underpayment adjusted in accordance with this section must be paid to the IRS by the time the adjusted return is filed. If an adjustment is reported pursuant to this section, but the amount of the adjustment is not paid when due, interest accrues from that date (see section 6601).

    (ii) If an employer files a return reporting FICA tax for a return period although the employer was required to file a return reporting RRTA tax, and if the employer ascertains the error after filing the return, the employer shall correct the error through an interest-free adjustment as provided in this section. However, if the employer also reported less than the correct amount of Additional Medicare Tax, the employer shall correct the underwithheld and underpaid Additional Medicare Tax in accordance with paragraph (b)(4) of this section. The employer shall adjust the underpayment of RRTA tax by reporting the correct amount of RRTA tax on an original return for reporting RRTA tax for the return period for which the incorrect return was filed, accompanied by an adjusted return corresponding to the incorrect return that was filed to correct the erroneously reported and paid FICA tax. The adjusted return must include a detailed explanation of the amounts being reported on the original return and the adjusted return and any other information as may be required by the regulations in this section and by the instructions relating to the adjusted return. The reporting of the correct amounts for the period constitutes an adjustment within the meaning of this section only if the returns are filed by the due date of the return for reporting the RRTA tax for the return period in which the error is ascertained. Pursuant to §31.3503-1, the amount of erroneously paid FICA tax will be credited against the underpaid RRTA tax. Any remaining underpayment of RRTA tax adjusted in accordance with this section must be paid to the IRS by the time the returns are filed in accordance with this paragraph. If an adjustment is reported pursuant to this section, but the amount of the remaining underpayment is not paid when due, interest accrues from that date (see section 6601).

(iii) If an employer files a return reporting RRTA tax for a return period although the employer was required to file a return reporting FICA tax, and if the employer ascertains the error after filing the return, the employer shall correct the error through an interest-free adjustment as provided in this section. However, if the employer also reported less than the correct amount of Additional Medicare Tax, the employer shall correct the underwithheld and underpaid Additional Medicare Tax in accordance with paragraph (b)(4) of this section. The employer shall adjust the underpayment of FICA tax by reporting the correct amount of FICA tax on an original return for reporting FICA tax for the return period for which the incorrect return was filed (or an adjusted return for reporting the FICA tax if an original return was already filed for such return period to report the income tax required to be withheld under section 3402), accompanied by an adjusted return corresponding to the incorrect return that was filed to correct the erroneously reported and paid RRTA tax. The adjusted return(s) must include a detailed explanation of the amount being reported on the original return and/or the adjusted return(s) and any other information as may be required by the regulations in this section and by the instructions relating to the form. The reporting of the correct amounts for the period constitutes an adjustment within the meaning of this section only if the returns are filed by the due date of the return for reporting the FICA tax for the return period in which the error is ascertained. Pursuant to §31.3503-1, the amount of erroneously paid RRTA tax will be credited against the underpaid FICA tax. Any remaining underpayment of FICA tax adjusted in accordance with this section must be paid to the IRS by the time the returns are filed in accordance with this paragraph (b)(2)(iii). If an adjustment is reported pursuant to this section, but the amount of the

remaining underpayment is not paid when due, interest accrues from that date (see section 6601).

(3) *Return not filed because of failure to treat individual as employee.*—If an employer fails to file a return for a return period solely because the employer failed to treat any individuals properly as employees for the return period (and, therefore, failed to withhold and pay any employer or employee FICA or RRTA tax with respect to wages or compensation paid to the employees) and if the employer ascertains the error after the due date of the return, the employer shall correct the error through an interest-free adjustment as provided in this section. The employer shall report the amount due by filing an original return required to be filed to report the tax for the return period for which the employer failed to file a return, accompanied by an adjusted return as provided in the instructions to the adjusted return. The adjusted return must include a detailed explanation of the amount being reported on the original return and adjusted return and any other information as may be required by this section and by the instructions relating to the adjusted return. The reporting of the correct amount of tax for the return period constitutes an adjustment within the meaning of this section only if the original and adjusted returns are filed by the due date of the return for reporting such tax for the return period in which the error is ascertained. For purposes of the preceding sentence, the due date for filing the adjusted return is determined by reference to the return being corrected, without regard to the employer's current filing requirements. For example, an employer with a current annual filing requirement who is correcting an error on a previously filed quarterly return must file the adjusted return by the due date for filing a quarterly return for the quarter in which the error is ascertained. However, an adjustment of Additional Medicare Tax required to be withheld under section 3101(b)(2) or section 3201(a) may only be reported pursuant to this section if the error is ascertained within the same calendar year that the wages or compensation were paid to the employee, or if section 3509 applies to determine the amount of the underpayment, or if the adjustment is reported on a Form 2504 or Form 2504-WC. See paragraph (b)(4) of this section. The amount of the underpayment adjusted in accordance with this section must be paid to the IRS by the time the returns are filed in accordance with this paragraph. If an adjustment is reported pursuant to this section, but the amount of the adjustment is not paid when due, interest accrues from that date (see section 6601).

(4) *Additional Medicare Tax.*—If an employer files a return on which FICA tax or RRTA tax is required to be reported, and reports on the return less than the correct amount of Additional Medicare Tax required to be withheld with respect to a payment of wages or compensation, and if the employer ascertains the error after filing the return, the employer shall correct the

error through an interest-free adjustment as provided in this section. An adjustment of Additional Medicare Tax may only be reported pursuant to this paragraph (b)(4) if the error is ascertained within the same calendar year that the wages or compensation were paid to the employee, unless the underpayment is attributable to an administrative error (that is, an error involving the inaccurate reporting of the amount actually withheld), section 3509 applies to determine the amount of the underpayment, or the adjustment is reported on a Form 2504 or Form 2504-WC. The employer shall adjust the underpayment of Additional Medicare Tax by reporting the additional amount due on an adjusted return for the return period in which the wages or compensation were paid, accompanied by a detailed explanation of the amount being reported on the adjusted return and any other information as may be required by this section and by the instructions relating to the adjusted return. The reporting of the underpayment on an adjusted return constitutes an adjustment within the meaning of this section only if the adjusted return is filed within the period of limitations for assessment for the return period being corrected, and by the due date for filing the return for the return period in which the error is ascertained. For purposes of the preceding sentence, the due date for filing the adjusted return is determined by reference to the return being corrected, without regard to the employer's current filing requirements. For example, an employer with a current annual filing requirement who is correcting an error on a previously filed quarterly return must file the adjusted return by the due date for filing a quarterly return for the quarter in which the error is ascertained. The amount of the underpayment adjusted in accordance with this section must be paid to the IRS by the time the adjusted return is filed. If an adjustment is reported pursuant to this section, but the amount of the adjustment is not paid when due, interest accrues from that date (see section 6601).

(c) *Income tax required to be withheld from wages.*—(1) *Undercollection ascertained before return is filed.*—If an employer collects less than the correct amount of income tax required to be withheld from wages under section 3402, and if the employer ascertains the error before filing the return on which the withheld tax is required to be reported, the employer shall nevertheless report on the return and pay to the IRS the correct amount of tax required to be withheld. If the employer does not report the correct amount of tax in these circumstances, the employer may not correct the error through an interest-free adjustment.

(2) *Error ascertained after return is filed.*—If an employer files a return on which income tax required to be withheld from wages is required to be reported and reports on the return less than the correct amount of income tax required to be withheld, and if the employer ascertains the error after filing the return, the employer shall

correct the error through an interest-free adjustment as provided in this section. The employer shall adjust the underpayment of tax by reporting the additional amount due on an adjusted return for the return period in which the wages were paid, accompanied by a detailed explanation of the amount being reported on the adjusted return and any other information as may be required by this section and by the instructions relating to the adjusted return. The reporting of the underpayment on an adjusted return constitutes an adjustment within the meaning of this section only if the adjusted return is filed by the due date for filing the return for the return period in which the error is ascertained. For purposes of the preceding sentence, the due date for filing the adjusted return is determined by reference to the return being corrected, without regard to the employer's current filing requirements. For example, an employer with a current annual filing requirement who is correcting an error on a previously filed quarterly return must file the adjusted return by the due date for filing a quarterly return for the quarter in which the error is ascertained. However, an adjustment may only be reported pursuant to this section if the error is ascertained within the same calendar year that the wages to the employee were paid, unless the underpayment is attributable to an administrative error (that is, an error involving the inaccurate reporting of the amount actually withheld), section 3509 applies to determine the amount of the underpayment, or the adjustment is reported on a Form 2504 or Form 2504-WC. The amount of the underpayment adjusted in accordance with this section must be paid to the IRS by the time the adjusted return is filed. If an adjustment is reported pursuant to this section, but the amount of the adjustment is not paid when due, interest accrues from that date (see section 6601).

(3) *Return not filed because of failure to treat individual as employee.*—If an employer fails to file a return for a return period solely because the employer failed to treat any individuals properly as employees for the return period (and, therefore, failed to withhold and pay any income tax required to be withheld from wages), the employer shall correct the error through an interest-free adjustment as provided in this section. The employer shall report the amount due by filing an original return for the return period for which the employer failed to file a return, accompanied by an adjusted return as provided in the instructions to the adjusted return. The adjusted return must include a detailed explanation of the amount being reported on the original and adjusted returns and any other information as may be required by this section and by the instructions relating to the adjusted return. The reporting of the correct amount of tax for the return period constitutes an adjustment within the meaning of this section only if the original and adjusted returns are filed by the due date of the return for reporting such tax for the return period in which the error is ascertained. For

purposes of the preceding sentence, the due date for filing the adjusted return is determined by reference to the return being corrected, without regard to the employer's current filing requirements. For example, an employer with a current annual filing requirement who is correcting an error on a previously filed quarterly return must file the adjusted return by the due date for filing a quarterly return for the quarter in which the error is ascertained. However, an adjustment may only be reported pursuant to this section if the error is ascertained within the same calendar year that the wages to the employee were paid, or if section 3509 applies to determine the amount of the underpayment, or if the adjustment is reported on a Form 2504 or Form 2504-WC. The amount of the underpayment adjusted in accordance with this section must be paid to the IRS by the time the returns are filed in accordance with this paragraph. If an adjustment is reported pursuant to this section, but the amount of the adjustment is not paid when due, interest accrues from that date (see section 6601).

(d) *Deductions from employee.*—(1) *Federal Insurance Contributions Tax Act and Railroad Retirement Tax Act.*—If an employer collects less than the correct amount of employee FICA or RRTA tax from an employee with respect to a payment of wages or compensation, the employer must collect the amount of the undercollection by deducting the amount from remuneration of the employee, if any, paid after the employer ascertains the error. If an employer collects less than the correct amount of Additional Medicare Tax required to be withheld under section 3101(b)(2) or section 3201(a), the employer must collect the amount of the undercollection on or before the last day of the calendar year by deducting the amount from remuneration of the employee, if any, paid after the employer ascertains the error. Such deductions may be made even though the remuneration, for any reason, does not constitute wages or compensation. The correct amount of employee tax must be reported and paid, as provided in paragraph (b) of this section, whether or not the undercollection is corrected by a deduction made as prescribed in this paragraph (d)(1), and even if the deduction is made after the return on which the employee tax must be reported is due. If such a deduction is not made, the obligation of the employee to the employer with respect to the undercollection is a matter for settlement between the employee and the employer. If an employer makes an erroneous collection of employee tax from two or more of its employees, a separate settlement must be made with respect to each employee. An overcollection of employee tax from one employee may not be used to offset an undercollection of such tax from another employee. For

provisions relating to the employer's liability for the tax, whether or not it collects the tax from the employee, see §§ 31.3102-1(d), 31.3102-4(c), and 31.3202-1. This paragraph (d)(1) does not apply if section 3509 applies to determine the employer's liability.

(2) *Income tax required to be withheld from wages.*—If an employer collects less than the correct amount of income tax required to be withheld from wages during a calendar year, the employer must collect the amount of the undercollection on or before the last day of the year by deducting the amount from remuneration of the employee, if any, paid after the employer ascertains the error. Such deductions may be made even though the remuneration, for any reason, does not constitute wages. The correct amount of of income tax must be reported and paid, as provided in paragraph (c) of this section, whether or not the undercollection is corrected by a deduction made as prescribed in this paragraph (d)(2), and even if the deduction is made after the return on which the tax must be reported is due. If such a deduction is not made, the obligation of the employee to the employer with respect to the undercollection is a matter for settlement between the employee and the employer within the calendar year. If an employer makes an erroneous collection of income tax from two or more of its employees, a separate settlement must be made with respect to each employee. An overcollection of income tax from one employee may not be used to offset an undercollection of such tax from another employee. For provisions relating to the employer's liability for the tax, whether or not it collects the tax from the employee, see § 31.3403-1. For provisions relating to the employer's liability for an underpayment of tax unless the employer can show that the income tax against which the tax under section 3402 may be credited has been paid, see § 31.3402(d)-1. This paragraph (d)(2) does not apply if section 3509 applies to determine the employer's liability.

(e) *Effective/applicability date.*—Paragraphs (b) and (d) of this section apply to adjusted returns filed on or after November 29, 2013. [Reg. § 31.6205-1.]

☐ [*T.D. 6472, 6-22-60. Amended by T.D. 7783, 7-22-81; T.D. 8959, 7-31-2001; T.D. 9405, 6-30-2008 and T.D. 9645, 11-26-2013.*]

[Reg. § 301.6205-1]

§ 301.6205-1. Special rules applicable to certain employment taxes.—For regulations under section 6205, see Reg. § 31.6205-1 of this chapter (Employment Tax Regulations). [Reg. § 301.6205-1.]

☐ [*T.D. 6119, 12-31-54. Amended by T.D. 6498, 10-24-60.*]

DEFICIENCY PROCEDURES

[Reg. § 301.6211-1]

§ 301.6211-1. Deficiency defined.—(a) In the case of the income tax imposed by subtitle A of the Code, the estate tax imposed by chapter 11,

subtitle B, of the Code, the gift tax imposed by chapter 12, subtitle B, of the Code, and any excise tax imposed by chapter 41, 42, 43, or 44 of the Code, the term "deficiency" means the excess of the tax (income, estate, gift, or excise tax as the case may be) over the sum of the amount shown as such tax by the taxpayer upon his return and the amounts previously assessed (or collected without assessment) as a deficiency; but such sum shall first be reduced by the amount of rebates made. If no return is made, or if the return (except a return of income tax pursuant to sec. 6014) does not show any tax, for the purpose of the definition "the amount shown as the tax by the taxpayer upon his return" shall be considered as zero. Accordingly, in any such case, if no deficiencies with respect to the tax have been assessed, or collected without assessment, and no rebates with respect to the tax have been made, the deficiency is the amount of the income tax imposed by subtitle A, the estate tax imposed by chapter 11, the gift tax imposed by chapter 12, or any excise tax imposed by chapter 41, 42, 43, or 44. Any amount shown as additional tax on an "amended return," so-called (other than amounts of additional tax which such return clearly indicates the taxpayer is protesting rather than admitting) filed after the due date of the return, shall be treated as an amount shown by the taxpayer "upon his return" for purposes of computing the amount of a deficiency.

(b) For purposes of the definition, the income tax imposed by subtitle A and the income tax shown on the return shall both be determined without regard to the credit provided in section 31 for income tax withheld at the source and without regard to so much of the credit provided in section 32 for income taxes withheld at the source as exceeds 2 percent of the interest on tax-free covenant bonds described in section 1451. Payments on account of estimated income tax, like other payments of tax by the taxpayer, shall likewise be disregarded in the determination of a deficiency. Any credit resulting from the collection of amounts assessed under section 6851 or 6852 as the result of a termination assessment shall not be taken into account in determining a deficiency.

(c) The computation by the Internal Revenue Service, pursuant to section 6014, of the income tax imposed by subtitle A shall be considered as having been made by the taxpayer and the tax so computed shall be considered as the tax shown by the taxpayer upon his return.

(d) If so much of the credit claimed on the return for income taxes withheld at the source as exceeds 2 percent of the interest on tax-free covenant bonds is greater than the amount of such credit allowable, the unpaid portion of the tax attributable to such difference will be collected not as a deficiency but as an underpayment of the tax shown on the return.

(e) This section may be illustrated by the following examples:

Example (1). The amount of income tax shown by the taxpayer upon his return for the calendar year 1954 was $1,600. The taxpayer had no amounts previously assessed (or collected without assessment) as a deficiency. He claimed a credit in the amount of $2,050 for tax withheld at source on wages under section 3402, and a refund of $450 (not a rebate under section 6211) was made to him as an overpayment of tax for the taxable year. It is later determined that the correct tax for the taxable year is $1,850. A deficiency of $250 is determined as follows:

Tax imposed by subtitle A	$1,850
Tax shown on return	$1,600
Tax previously assessed (or collected without assessment) as a deficiency	None
Total	$1,600
Amount of rebates made	None
Balance	$1,600
Deficiency	250

Example (2). The taxpayer made a return for the calendar year 1954 showing a tax of $1,250 before any credits for tax withheld at the source. He claimed a credit in the amount of $800 for tax withheld at source on wages under section 3402 and $60 for tax paid at source under section 1451 upon interest on bonds containing a tax-free covenant. The taxpayer had no amounts previously assessed (or collected without assessment) as a deficiency. The district director determines that the 2 percent tax paid at the source on tax-free covenant bonds is $40 instead of $60 as claimed by the taxpayer and that the tax imposed by subtitle A is $1,360 (total tax $1,400 less $40 paid at source on tax-free covenant bonds). A deficiency in the amount of $170 is determined as follows:

Tax imposed by subtitle A ($1,400 minus $40)	$1,360
Tax shown on return ($1,250 minus $60)	$1,190
Tax previously assessed (or collected without assessment) as a deficiency	None
Total	$1,190
Amount of rebates made	None
Balance	$1,190
Deficiency	170

(f) As used in section 6211, the term "rebate" means so much of an abatement, credit, refund, or other repayment as is made on the ground that the income tax imposed by subtitle A, the estate tax imposed by chapter 11, the gift tax imposed by chapter 12, or the excise tax imposed by chapter 41, 42, 43, or 44, is less than the excess of (1) the amount shown as the tax by the taxpayer upon the return increased by the amount previously assessed (or collected without assessment) as a deficiency over (2) the amount of rebates previously made. For example, assume that the amount of income tax shown by the taxpayer upon his return for the taxable year is $600 and the amount claimed as a credit under section 31 for income tax withheld at the source is $900. If the district director determines that the tax imposed by subtitle A is $600 and makes a refund of $300, no part of such refund constitutes a "rebate" since the refund is not made on the ground that the tax imposed by subtitle A is less than the tax shown on the return. If, however, the district director determines that the tax imposed by subtitle A is $500 and refunds $400, the amount of $100 of such refund would constitute a rebate since it is made on the ground that the tax imposed by subtitle A ($500) is less than the tax shown on the return ($600). The amount of such rebate ($100) would be taken into account in arriving at the amount of any deficiency subsequently determined. [Reg. § 301.6211-1.]

☐ [*T.D.* 6119, 12-31-54. *Amended by T.D.* 6498, 10-24-60; *T.D.* 7102, 3-23-71; *T.D.* 7498, 7-12-77; *T.D.* 7575, 12-15-78; *T.D.* 7838, 10-5-82 *and T.D.* 8628, 12-4-95.]

[Reg. § 301.6212-1]

§ 301.6212-1. Notice of deficiency.— (a) *General rule.—*If a district director or director of a service center (or regional director of appeals), determines that there is a deficiency in respect of income, estate, or gift tax imposed by subtitle A or B, or excise tax imposed by chapter 41, 42, 43, or 44, of the Code, such official is authorized to notify the taxpayer of the deficiency by either registered or certified mail.

(b) *Address for notice of deficiency.—*(1) *Income, gift, and chapter 41, 42, 43, and 44 taxes.—*Unless the district director for the district in which the return in question was filed has been notified under the provisions of section 6903 as to the existence of a fiduciary relationship, notice of a deficiency in respect of income tax, gift tax, or tax imposed by chapter 41, 42, 43, or 44 shall be sufficient if mailed to the taxpayer at his last known address, even though such taxpayer is deceased, or is under a legal disability, or, in the case of a corporation, has terminated its existence.

(2) *Joint income tax returns.—*If a joint income tax return has been filed by husband and wife, the district director (or assistant regional commissioner, appellate) may, unless the district director for the district in which such joint return was filed has been notified by either spouse that a separate residence has been established, send either a joint or separate notice of deficiency to the taxpayers at their last known address. If, however, the proper district director has been so notified, a separate notice of deficiency, that is, a duplicate original of the joint notice, must be sent by registered mail prior to September 3, 1958, and by either registered or certified mail on and after September 3, 1958, to each spouse at his or her last known address. The notice of separate residences should be addressed to the district director for the district in which the joint return was filed.

(3) *Estate tax.—*In the absence of notice, under the provisions of section 6903 as to the existence of a fiduciary relationship, to the dis-

trict director for the district in which the estate tax return was filed, notice of a deficiency in respect of the estate tax imposed by chapter 11 of subtitle B shall be sufficient if addressed in the name of the decedent or other person subject to liability and mailed to his last known address.

(c) *Further deficiency letters restricted.—*If the district director or director of a service center (or regional director of appeals) mails to the taxpayer notice of a deficiency, and the taxpayer files a petition with the Tax Court within the prescribed period, no additional deficiency may be determined with respect to income tax for the same taxable year, gift tax for the same "calendar period" (as defined in § 25.2502-1(c)(1)), estate tax with respect to the taxable estate of the same decedent, chapter 41, 43, or 44 tax of the taxpayer for the same taxable year, section 4940 tax for the same taxable year, or chapter 42 tax of the taxpayer (other than under section 4940) with respect to the same act (or failure to act) to which such petition relates. This restriction shall not apply in the case of fraud, assertion of deficiencies with respect to any qualified tax (as defined in paragraph (b) of § 301.6361-4) in respect of which no deficiency was asserted for the taxable year in the notice, assertion of deficiencies with respect to the Federal tax when deficiencies with respect to only a qualified tax (and not the Federal tax) were asserted for the taxable year in the notice, assertion of greater deficiencies before the Tax Court as provided in section 6214(a), mathematical errors as provided in section 6213(b)(1), termination assessments in section 6851 or 6852, or jeopardy assessments as provided in section 6961(c). Solely for purposes of applying the restriction of section 6212(c), a notice of deficiency with respect to second tier tax under chapter 43 shall be deemed to be a notice of deficiency for the taxable year in which the taxable event occurs. See § 53.4963-1(e)(7)(iii) or (iv) for the date on which the taxable event occurs. [Reg. § 301.6212-1.]

☐ [*T.D.* 6119, 12-31-54. *Amended by T.D.* 6425, 11-10-59; *T.D.* 6498, 10-24-60; *T.D.* 7238, 12-28-72; *T.D.* 7577, 12-19-78; *T.D.* 7838, 10-5-82; *T.D.* 7910, 9-6-83; *T.D.* 8084, 5-1-86 *and T.D.* 8628, 12-4-95.]

[Reg. § 301.6212-2]

§ 301.6212-2. Definition of last known address.—(a) *General rule.—*Except as provided in paragraph (b)(2) of this section, a taxpayer's last known address is the address that appears on the taxpayer's most recently filed and properly processed Federal tax return, unless the Internal Revenue Service (IRS) is given clear and concise notification of a different address. Further information on what constitutes clear and concise notification of a different address and a properly processed Federal tax return can be found in Rev. Proc. 90-18 (1990-1 C.B. 491) or in procedures subsequently prescribed by the Commissioner.

(b) *Address obtained from third party.—*(1) *In general.—*Except as provided in paragraph (b)(2) of this section, change of address information that a taxpayer provides to a third party, such as a payor or another government agency, is not clear and concise notification of a different address for purposes of determining a last known address under this section.

(2) *Exception for address obtained from the United States Postal Service.*—(i) *Updating taxpayer addresses.*—The IRS will update taxpayer addresses maintained in IRS records by referring to data accumulated and maintained in the United States Postal Service (USPS) National Change of Address database that retains change of address information for thirty-six months (NCOA database). Except as provided in paragraph (b)(2)(ii) of this section, if the taxpayer's name and last known address in IRS records match the taxpayer's name and old mailing address contained in the NCOA database, the new address in the NCOA database is the taxpayer's last known address, unless the IRS is given clear and concise notification of a different address.

(ii) *Duration of address obtained from NCOA database.*—The address obtained from the NCOA database under paragraph (b)(2)(i) of this section is the taxpayer's last known address until one of the following events occurs—

(A) The taxpayer files and the IRS properly processes a Federal tax return with an address different from the address obtained from the NCOA database; or

(B) The taxpayer provides the Internal Revenue Service with clear and concise notification of a change of address, as defined in procedures prescribed by the Commissioner, that is different from the address obtained from the NCOA database.

(3) *Examples.*—The following examples illustrate the rules of paragraph (b)(2) of this section:

Example 1. (i) A is an unmarried taxpayer. The address on A's 1999 Form 1040, U.S. Individual Income Tax Return, filed on April 14, 2000, and 2000 Form 1040 filed on April 13, 2001, is 1234 Anyplace Street, Anytown, USA 43210. On May 15, 2001, A informs the USPS of a new permanent address (9876 Newplace Street, Newtown, USA 12345) using the USPS Form 3575, "Official Mail Forwarding Change of Address Form." The change of address is included in the weekly update of the USPS NCOA database. On May 29, 2001, A's address maintained in IRS records is changed to 9876 Newplace Street, Newtown, USA 12345.

(ii) In June 2001 the IRS determines a deficiency for A's 1999 tax year and prepares to issue a notice of deficiency. The IRS obtains A's address for the notice of deficiency from IRS records. On June 15, 2001, the Internal Revenue Service mails the notice of deficiency to A at 9876 Newplace Street, Newtown, USA 12345. For purposes of section 6212(b), the notice of deficiency mailed on June 15, 2001, is mailed to A's last known address.

Example 2. (i) The facts are the same as in *Example 1*, except that instead of determining a deficiency for A's 1999 tax year in June 2001, the IRS determines a deficiency for A's 1999 tax year in May 2001.

(ii) On May 21, 2001, the IRS prepares a notice of deficiency for A and obtains A's address from IRS records. Because A did not inform the USPS of the change of address in sufficient time for the IRS to process and post the new address in Internal Revenue Service's records by May 21, 2001, the notice of deficiency is mailed to 1234 Anyplace Street, Anytown, USA 43210. For purposes of section 6212(b), the notice of deficiency mailed on May 21, 2001, is mailed to A's last known address.

Example 3. (i) C and D are married taxpayers. The address on C and D's 2000 Form 1040, U.S. Individual Income Tax Return, filed on April 13, 2001, and 2001 Form 1040 filed on April 15, 2002, is 2468 Spring Street, Little City, USA 97531. On August 15, 2002, D informs the USPS of a new permanent address (8642 Peachtree Street, Big City, USA 13579) using the USPS Form 3575, "Official Mail Forwarding Change of Address Form." The change of address is included in the weekly update of the USPS NCOA database. On August 29, 2002, D's address maintained in IRS records is changed to 8642 Peachtree Street, Big City, USA 13579.

(ii) In October 2002 the IRS determines a deficiency for C and D's 2000 tax year and prepares to issue a notice of deficiency. The Internal Revenue Service obtains C's address and D's address for the notice of deficiency from IRS records. On October 15, 2002, the IRS mails a copy of the notice of deficiency to C at 2468 Spring Street, Little City, USA 97531, and to D at 8642 Peachtree Street, Big City, USA 13579. For purposes of section 6212(b), the notices of deficiency mailed on October 15, 2002, are mailed to C and D's respective last known addresses.

(c) *Last known address for all notices, statements, and documents.*—The rules in paragraphs (a) and (b) of this section apply for purposes of determining whether all notices, statements, or other documents are mailed to a taxpayer's last known address whenever the term *last known address* is used in the Internal Revenue Code or the regulations thereunder.

(d) *Effective Date.*—(1) *In general.*—Except as provided in paragraph (d)(2) of this section, this section is effective on January 29, 2001.

(2) *Individual moves in the case of joint filers.*—In the case of taxpayers who file joint returns under section 6013, if the NCOA database contains change of address information for only one spouse, paragraphs (b)(2) and (3) of this section will not apply to notices, statements, and other documents mailed before the processing of the taxpayers' 2000 joint return. [Reg. § 301.6212-2.]

☐ [*T.D.* 8939, 1-11-2001.]

[Reg. § 301.6213-1]

§ 301.6213-1. Restrictions applicable to deficiencies; petition to Tax Court.—(a) *Time for filing petition and restrictions on assessment.*—

(1) *Time for filing petition.*—Within 90 days after notice of the deficiency is mailed (or within 150 days after mailing in the case of such notice addressed to a person outside the States of the Union and the District of Columbia), as provided in section 6212, a petition may be filed with the Tax Court of the United States for a redetermination of the deficiency. In determining such 90-day or 150-day period, Saturday, Sunday, or a legal holiday in the District of Columbia is not counted as the 90th or 150th day. In determining the time for filing a petition with the Tax Court in the case of a notice of deficiency mailed to a resident of Alaska prior to 12:01 p.m., e.s.t., January 3, 1959, and in the case of a notice of deficiency mailed to a resident of Hawaii prior to 4:00 p.m. e.d.s.t., August 21, 1959, the term "States of the Union" does not include Alaska or Hawaii, respectively, and the 150-day period applies. In determining the time within which a petition to the Tax Court may be filed in the case of a notice of deficiency mailed to a resident of Alaska after 12:01 p.m., e.s.t., January 3, 1959, and in the case of a notice of deficiency mailed to a resident of Hawaii after 4:00 p.m., e.d.s.t., August 21, 1959, the term "States of the Union" includes Alaska and Hawaii, respectively, and the 90-day period applies.

(2) *Restrictions on assessment.*—Except as otherwise provided by this section, by sections 6851, 6852, and 6861(a) (relating to termination and jeopardy assessments), by section 6871(a) (relating to immediate assessment of claims for income, estate, and gift taxes in bankruptcy and receivership cases), or by section 7485 (in case taxpayer petitions for a review of a Tax Court decision without filing bond), no assessment of a deficiency in respect to a tax imposed by subtitle A or B or chapter 41, 42, 43, or 44 of the Code and no levy or proceeding in court for its collection shall be made until notice of deficiency has been mailed to the taxpayer, nor until the expiration of the 90-day or 150-day period within which a petition may be filed with the Tax Court, nor, if a petition has been filed with the Tax Court, until the decision of the Tax Court has become final. As to the date on which a decision of the Tax Court becomes final, see section 7481. Notwithstanding the provisions of section 7421(a), the making of an assessment or the beginning of a proceeding or levy which is forbidden by this paragraph may be enjoined by a proceeding in the proper court. In any case where the running of the time prescribed for filing a petition in the Tax Court with respect to a tax imposed by chapter 42 or 43 is suspended under section 6213(e), no assessment of a deficiency in respect of such tax shall be made until expiration of the entire period for filing the petition.

(b) *Exceptions to restrictions on assessment of deficiencies.*—(1) *Mathematical errors.*—If a taxpayer is notified of an additional amount of tax due on account of a mathematical error appearing upon the return, such notice is not deemed a notice of deficiency, and the taxpayer has no right to file a petition with the Tax Court upon the basis of such notice, nor is the assessment of such additional amount prohibited by section 6213(a).

(2) *Tentative carryback adjustments.*—(i) If the district director or the director of the regional service center determines that any amount applied, credited, or refunded under section 6411(b) with respect to an application for a tentative carryback adjustment is in excess of the overassessment properly attributable to the carryback upon which such application was based, the district director or the director of the regional service center may assess the amount of the excess as a deficiency as if such deficiency were due to a mathematical error appearing on the return. That is, the district director or the director of the regional service center may assess an amount equal to the excess, and such amount may be collected, without regard to the restrictions on assessment and collection imposed by section 6213(a). Thus, the district director or the director of the regional service center may assess such amount without regard to whether the taxpayer has been mailed a prior notice of deficiency. Either before or after assessing such an amount, the district director or the director of the regional service center will notify the taxpayer that such assessment has been or will be made. Such notice will not constitute a notice of deficiency, and the taxpayer may not file a petition with the Tax Court of the United States based on such notice. However, the taxpayer within the applicable period of limitation, may file a regular claim for credit or refund based on the carryback, if he has not already filed such a claim, and may maintain a suit based on such claim if it is disallowed or if it is not acted upon by the Internal Revenue Service within 6 months from the date the claim was filed.

(ii) The method provided in subdivision (i) of this subparagraph to recover any amount applied, credited, or refunded in respect of an application for a tentative carryback adjustment which should not have been so applied, credited, or refunded is not an exclusive method. Two other methods are available to recover such amount: (*a*) By way of a deficiency notice under section 6212; or (*b*) by a suit to recover an erroneous refund under section 7405. Any one or more of the three available methods may be used to recover any amount which was improperly applied, credited, or refunded in respect of an application for a tentative carryback adjustment.

(3) *Assessment of amount paid.*—Any payment made after the mailing of a notice of deficiency which is made by the taxpayer as a payment with respect to the proposed deficiency may be assessed without regard to the restrictions on assessment and collection imposed by section 6213(a) even though the taxpayer has not filed a waiver of restrictions on assessment as provided in section 6213(d). A payment of all or part of the deficiency asserted in the notice together with the assessment of the amount so paid will not affect the jurisdiction of the Tax Court. If any payment is made before the mail-

ing of a notice of deficiency, the district director or the director of the regional service center is not prohibited by section 6213(a) from assessing such amount, and such amount may be assessed if such action is deemed to be proper. If such amount is assessed, the assessment is taken into account in determining whether or not there is a deficiency for which a notice of deficiency must be issued. Thus, if such a payment satisfies the taxpayer's tax liability, no notice of deficiency will be mailed and the Tax Court will have no jurisdiction over the matter. In any case in which there is a controversy as to the correct amount of the tax liability, the assessment of any amount pursuant to the provisions of section 6213(b)(3) shall in no way be considered to be the acceptance of an offer by the taxpayer to settle such controversy.

(4) *Jeopardy.*—If the district director believes that the assessment or collection of a deficiency will be jeopardized by delay, such deficiency shall be assessed immediately, as provided in section 6861(a).

(c) *Failure to file petition.*—If no petition is filed with the Tax Court within the period prescribed in section 6213(a), the district director or the director of the regional service center shall assess the amount determined as the deficiency and of which the taxpayer was notified by registered or certified mail and the taxpayer shall pay the same upon notice and demand therefor. In such case the district director will not be precluded from determining a further deficiency and notifying the taxpayer thereof by registered or certified mail. If a petition is filed with the Tax Court the taxpayer should notify the district director who issued the notice of deficiency that the petition has been filed in order to prevent an assessment of the amount determined to be the deficiency.

(d) *Waiver of restrictions.*—The taxpayer may at any time by a signed notice in writing filed with the district director waive the restrictions on the assessment and collection of the whole or any part of the deficiency. The notice must in all cases be filed with the district director or other authorized official under whose jurisdiction the audit or other consideration of the return in question is being conducted. The filing of such notice with the Tax Court does not constitute filing with the district director within the meaning of the Internal Revenue Code. After such waiver has been acted upon by the district director and the assessment has been made in accordance with its terms, the waiver cannot be withdrawn.

(e) *Suspension of filing period for certain chapter 42 and chapter 43 taxes.*—The period prescribed by section 6213(a) for filing a petition in the Tax Court with respect to the taxes imposed by section 4941, 4942, 4943, 4944, 4945, 4951, 4952, 4955, 4958, 4971, or 4975, shall be suspended for any other period which the Commissioner has allowed for making correction under § 53.4963-1(e)(3). Where the time for filing a petition with the Tax Court has been suspended under the authority of this paragraph (e), the extension shall not be reduced as a result of the correction being made prior to expiration of the period allowed for making correction. [Reg. § 301.6213-1.]

☐ [T.D. 6119, 12-31-54. *Amended by* T.D. 6425, 11-10-59; T.D. 6498, 10-24-60; T.D. 6585, 12-27-61; T.D. 7838, 10-5-82; T.D. 8084, 5-1-86; T.D. 8628, 12-4-95 *and* T.D. 8920, 1-9-2001.]

[Reg. § 301.6215-1]

§ 301.6215-1. Assessment of deficiency found by Tax Court.—Where a petition has been filed with the Tax Court, the entire amount redetermined as the deficiency by the decision of the Tax Court which has become final shall be assessed by the district director or the director of the regional service center and the unpaid portion of the amount so assessed shall be paid by the taxpayer upon notice and demand therefor. [Reg. § 301.6215-1.]

☐ [T.D. 6119, 12-13-54. *Amended by* T.D. 6585, 12-27-61.]

TAX TREATMENT OF PARTNERSHIP ITEMS

[Reg. § 301.6221-1]

§ 301.6221-1. Tax treatment determined at partnership level.—(a) *In general.*—A partner's treatment of partnership items on the partner's return may not be changed except as provided in sections 6222 through 6231 and the regulations thereunder. Thus, for example, if a partner treats an item on the partner's return consistently with the treatment of the item on the partnership return, the IRS generally cannot adjust the treatment of that item on the partner's return except through a partnership-level proceeding. Similarly, the taxpayer may not put partnership items in issue in a proceeding relating to nonpartnership items. For example, the taxpayer may not offset a potential increase in taxable income based on changes to nonpartnership items by a potential decrease based on partnership items.

(b) *Restrictions inapplicable after items become nonpartnership items.*—Section 6221 and paragraph (a) of this section cease to apply to items arising from a partnership with respect to a partner when those items cease to be partnership items with respect to that partner under section 6231(b).

(c) *Penalties determined at partnership level.*—Any penalty, addition to tax, or additional amount that relates to an adjustment to a partnership item shall be determined at the partnership level. Partner-level defenses to such items can only be asserted through refund actions following assessment and payment. Assessment of any penalty, addition to tax, or additional amount that relates to an adjustment to a partnership item shall be made based on partnership-level determinations. Partnership-level determinations include all the legal and factual determinations that underlie the determination of any penalty, addition to tax, or additional amount, other than partner-level defenses specified in paragraph (d) of this section.

(d) *Partner-level defenses.*—Partner-level defenses to any penalty, addition to tax, or additional amount that relates to an adjustment to a partnership item may not be asserted in the partnership-level proceeding, but may be asserted through separate refund actions following assessment and payment. See section 6230(c)(4). Partner-level defenses are limited to those that are personal to the partner or are dependent upon the partner's separate return and cannot be determined at the partnership level. Examples of these determinations are whether any applicable threshold underpayment of tax has been met with respect to the partner or whether the partner has met the criteria of section 6664(b) (penalties applicable only where return is filed), or section 6664(c)(1) (reasonable cause exception) subject to partnership-level determinations as to the applicability of section 6664(c)(2).

(e) *Cross-references.*—See §§301.6231(c)-1 and 301.6231(c)-2 for special rules relating to certain applications and claims for refund based on losses, deductions, or credits from abusive tax shelter partnerships.

(f) *Effective date.*—This section is applicable to partnership taxable years beginning on or after October 4, 2001. For years beginning prior to October 4, 2001, see §301.6221-1T contained in 26 CFR part 1, revised April 1, 2001. [Reg. §301.6221-1.]

  □ [*T.D.* 8965, 10-3-2001.]

[Reg. §301.6221(b)-1]

§301.6221(b)-1. **Election out for certain partnerships with 100 or fewer partners.**—(a) *In general.*—The provisions of subchapter C of chapter 63 of the Internal Revenue Code (subchapter C of chapter 63) do not apply for any partnership taxable year for which an eligible partnership under paragraph (b) of this section makes a valid election in accordance with paragraph (c) of this section. For rules regarding deficiency procedures, see subchapter B of chapter 63 of the Internal Revenue Code and §§301.6211-1 through 301.6215-1.

(b) *Eligible partnership.*—(1) *In general.*—Only an eligible partnership may make an election under this section. A partnership is an eligible partnership for purposes of this section if—

(i) The partnership has 100 or fewer partners as determined in accordance with paragraph (b)(2) of this section, and

(ii) Each statement the partnership is required to furnish under section 6031(b) for the partnership taxable year is furnished to a partner

that was an eligible partner (as defined in paragraph (b)(3) of this section) for the partnership's entire taxable year.

(2) *100 or fewer partners.*—(i) *In general.*—Except as provided in paragraph (b)(2)(ii) of this section, a partnership has 100 or fewer partners if the partnership is required to furnish 100 or fewer statements under section 6031(b) for the taxable year.

(ii) *Special rule for S corporations.*—For purposes of this paragraph (b)(2), a partnership with a partner that is an S corporation (as defined in section 1361(a)(1)) must take into account each statement required to be furnished by the S corporation to its shareholders under section 6037(b) for the taxable year of the S corporation ending with or within the partnership's taxable year.

(iii) *Examples.*—The following examples illustrate the provisions of this paragraph (b)(2). For purposes of these examples, each partnership is required to file a return under section 6031(a):

Example 1. During its 2020 partnership taxable year, Partnership has four partners each owning an interest in Partnership. Two of the partners are Spouse 1 and Spouse 2 who are married to each other during all of 2020. Spouse 1 and Spouse 2 each own a separate interest in Partnership. The two other partners are unmarried individuals. Under section 6031(b), Partnership is required to furnish a separate statement (that is, Schedule K-1 (Form 1065), *Partner's Share of Income, Deductions, Credits, etc.*) to each individual partner, including separate statements to Spouse 1 and Spouse 2. Therefore, for purposes of this paragraph (b)(2), Partnership has four partners during its 2020 taxable year.

Example 2. The facts are the same as in *Example 1* of this paragraph (b)(2)(iii), except Spouse 2 does not separately own an interest in Partnership during 2020 and Spouse 1 and Spouse 2 live in a community property state, State A. Spouse 1 acquired the partnership interest in such a manner that by operation of State A law, Spouse 2 has a community property interest in Spouse 1's partnership interest. Because Spouse 2's community property interest in Spouse 1's partnership interest is not taken into account for purposes of determining the number of statements Partnership is required to furnish under section 6031(b), Partnership is required to furnish a statement to Spouse 1, but not to Spouse 2. Therefore, for purposes of this paragraph (b)(2), Partnership has three partners during its 2020 taxable year.

Example 3. At the beginning of 2020, Partnership, which has a taxable year ending December 31, 2020, has three partners - individuals A, B, and C. Each individual owns an interest in Partnership. On June 30, 2020, Individual A dies, and A's interest in Partnership becomes an asset of A's estate. A's estate owns the interest for the remainder of 2020. On September 1, 2020, B sells his interest in Partnership to Individual D, who holds the interest for the remainder of the year. Under section 6031(b), Partnership is required to furnish five statements for its 2020 taxable year – one each to Individual A, the estate of Individual A, Individual B, Individual C, and Individual D. Therefore, for purposes of this paragraph (b)(2), Partnership has five partners during its 2020 taxable year.

Example 4. During its 2020 taxable year, Partnership has 51 partners - 50 partners who are individuals and S, an S corporation. S and Partnership are both calendar year taxpayers. S has 50 shareholders during the 2020 taxable year. Under section 6031(b), Partnership is required to furnish 51 statements for the 2020 taxable year – one to S and one to each of Partnership's 50 partners who are individuals. Under section 6037(b), S is required to furnish a statement (that is, Schedule K-1 (Form 1120-S), *Shareholder's Share of Income, Deductions, Credits, etc.*) to each of its 50 shareholders. Under paragraph (b)(2)(ii) of this section, the number of statements required to be furnished by S under section 6037(b), which is 50, is taken into account to determine whether partnership has 100 or fewer partners. Accordingly, for purposes of this paragraph (b)(2), Partnership has a total of 101 partners (51 statements furnished by Partnership to its partners plus 50 statements furnished by S to its shareholders) and is therefore not an eligible partnership under paragraph (b)(1) of this section. Because Partnership is not an eligible partnership, it cannot make the election under paragraph (a) of this section.

Example 5. During its 2020 taxable year, Partnership has two partners, A, an individual, and E, an estate of a deceased partner. E has 10 beneficiaries. Under section 6031(b), Partnership is required to furnish two statements, one to A and one to E. Any statements that E may be required to furnish to its beneficiaries are not taken into account for purposes of this paragraph (b)(2). Therefore, for purposes of this paragraph (b)(2), Partnership has two partners.

(3) *Eligible Partners.*—(i) *In general.*—For purposes of paragraph (b)(1)(ii) of this section, the term *eligible partner* means a partner that is an individual, a C corporation (as defined by section 1361(a)(2)), an eligible foreign entity described in paragraph (b)(3)(iii) of this section, an S corporation, or an estate of a deceased partner. An S corporation is an eligible partner regardless of whether one or more shareholders of the S corporation are not an eligible partner.

(ii) *Partners that are not eligible partners.*— A partner is not an eligible partner under paragraph (b)(3)(i) of this section if the partner is —

(A) A partnership,

(B) A trust,

(C) A foreign entity that is not an eligible foreign entity described in paragraph (b)(3)(iii) of this section,

(D) A disregarded entity described in § 301.7701-2(c)(2)(i),

(E) An estate of an individual other than a deceased partner, or

(F) Any person that holds an interest in the partnership on behalf of another person.

(iii) *Eligible foreign entity.*—For purposes of this paragraph (b)(3), a foreign entity is an eligible partner if the foreign entity would be treated as a C corporation if it were a domestic entity. For purposes of the preceding sentence, a foreign entity would be treated as a C corporation if it were a domestic entity if the entity is classified as a per se corporation under § 301.7701-2(b)(1), (3), (4), (5), (6), (7), or (8), is classified by default as an association taxable as a corporation under § 301.7701-3(b)(2)(i)(B), or is classified as an association taxable as a corporation in accordance with an election under § 301.7701-3(c).

(iv) *Examples.*—The following examples illustrate the rules of this paragraph (b)(3). For purposes of these examples, each partnership is required to file a return under section 6031(a):

Example 1. During the 2020 taxable year, Partnership has four equal partners. Two partners are individuals. One partner is a C corporation. The fourth partner, D, is a partnership. Because D is a partnership, D is not an eligible partner under paragraph (b)(3)(i) of this section. Accordingly, Partnership is not an eligible partnership under paragraph (b)(1) of this section and, therefore, cannot make the election under paragraph (a) of this section for its 2020 taxable year.

Example 2. During its 2020 taxable year, Partnership has four equal partners. Two partners are individuals. One partner is a C corporation. The fourth partner, S, is an S corporation. S has ten shareholders. One of S's shareholders is a disregarded entity, and one is a qualified small business trust. S is an eligible partner under paragraph (b)(3)(i) of this section even though S's shareholders would not be considered eligible partners if those shareholders held direct interests in Partnership. See paragraph (b)(3)(i) of this section. Accordingly, Partnership meets the requirements under this paragraph (b)(3) for its 2020 taxable year.

Example 3. During its 2020 taxable year, Partnership has two equal partners, A, an individual, and C, a disregarded entity, wholly owned by B, an individual. C is not an eligible partner under paragraph (b)(3)(i) of this section. Accordingly, Partnership is not an eligible partnership under paragraph (b)(1) of this section and, therefore, is ineligible to make the election under paragraph (a) of this section for its 2020 taxable year.

(c) *Election.*—(1) *In general.*—An election under this section must be made on the eligible partnership's timely filed return, including extensions, for the taxable year to which the election applies and include all information required by the Internal Revenue Service (IRS) in forms, instructions, or other guidance. An election is not valid unless the partnership discloses to the

IRS all of the information required under paragraph (c)(2) of this section and, in the case of a partner that is an S corporation, the shareholders of such S corporation. An election once made may not be revoked without the consent of the IRS.

(2) *Disclosure of partner information to the IRS.*—A partnership making an election under this section must disclose to the IRS information about each person that was a partner at any time during the taxable year of the partnership to which the election applies, including each partner's name and correct U.S. taxpayer identification number (TIN) (or alternative form of identification required by forms, instructions, or other guidance), each partner's Federal tax classification, an affirmative statement that the partner is an eligible partner under paragraph (b)(3)(i) of this section, and any other information required by the IRS in forms, instructions, or other guidance. If a partner is an S corporation, the partnership must also disclose to the IRS information about each shareholder of the S corporation that was a shareholder at any time during the taxable year of the S corporation ending with or within the partnership's taxable year, including each shareholder's name and correct TIN (or alternative form of identification as prescribed by forms, instructions, or other guidance), each shareholder's Federal tax classification, and any other information required by the IRS in forms, instructions, or other guidance.

(3) *Partner notification.*—A partnership that makes an election under this section must notify each of its partners of the election within 30 days of making the election in the form and manner determined by the partnership.

(d) *Election made by a partnership that is a partner.*—(1) *In general.*—The fact that a partnership has made an election under this section does not affect whether the provisions of subchapter C of chapter 63 apply to any other partnership, including a partnership in which the partnership making the election is a partner. Accordingly, the provisions of subchapter C of chapter 63 that apply to partners in a partnership that has not made an election under this section apply, to the extent provided in the regulations under subchapter C of chapter 63, to partners (that are themselves partnerships that have made an election under this section) in their capacity as partners in the other partnership.

(2) *Examples.*—The following examples illustrate the rules of paragraph (d)(1) of this section. For purposes of these examples, each partnership is required to file a return under section 6031(a):

Example 1. During its 2020 taxable year, Partnership, a calendar year taxpayer, has two partners. One partner, A, is also a calendar year partnership. A files a valid election under this section with its timely filed partnership return for its 2020 taxable year. Partnership does not file an election under this section. Notwithstanding A's valid election under this section, with respect to A's interest in Partnership, A is subject to the rules applicable to partners in a partnership subject to the rules under subchapter C of chapter 63, including the consistency requirements of section 6222 and the regulations thereunder.

Example 2. The facts are the same as *Example 1* of this paragraph (d)(2). The IRS mails to Partnership a notice of final partnership adjustment under section 6231 with respect to Partnership's 2020 taxable year. Partnership timely elects the alternative to payment of imputed underpayment under section 6226 and the regulations thereunder. Partnership must provide A with a statement under section 6226 reflecting A's share of the adjustments for Partnership's 2020 taxable year. A is subject to the rules applicable to partners in a partnership subject to the rules under subchapter C of chapter 63 with respect to A's interest in Partnership.

(e) *Effect of an election.*—(1) *In general.*—An election made under this section is an action taken under subchapter C of chapter 63 by the partnership for purposes of section 6223. Accordingly, the partnership and all partners are bound by an election of the partnership under this section unless the IRS determines that the election is invalid. See § 301.6223-2 for the binding nature of actions taken by a partnership under subchapter C of chapter 63.

(2) *IRS determination that election is invalid.*—If the IRS determines that an election under this section for a partnership taxable year is invalid, the IRS will notify the partnership in writing and the provisions of subchapter C of chapter 63 will apply to that partnership taxable year.

(f) *Applicability date.*—These regulations are applicable to partnership taxable years beginning after December 31, 2017. [Reg. § 301.6221(b)-1.]

☐ [*T.D. 9829, 12-29-2017.*]

[Reg. § 301.6222(a)-1]

§ 301.6222(a)-1. Consistent treatment of partnership items.—(a) *In general.*—The treatment of a partnership item on the partner's return must be consistent with the treatment of that item by the partnership on the partnership return in all respects including the amount, timing, and characterization of the item.

(b) *Treatment must be consistent with partnership return.*—The treatment of a partnership item on the partner's return must be consistent with the treatment of that item on the partnership return. Thus, a partner who treats an item consistently with a schedule or other information furnished to the partner by the partnership has not satisfied the requirement of paragraph (a) of this section if the treatment of that item is inconsistent with the treatment of the item on the partnership return actually filed. For rules relating to the election to be treated as having reported the inconsistency where the partner treats an item consistently with an incorrect schedule, see § 301.6222(b)-3.

(c) *Examples.*—The following examples illustrate the principles of this section:

Example 1. B is a partner of Partnership P. Both B and P use the calendar year as the taxable year. In December 2001, P receives an advance payment for services to be performed in 2002 and reports this amount as income for calendar year 2001. However, B reports B's distributive share of this amount on B's income tax return for 2002 and not on B's return for 2001. B's treatment of this partnership item is inconsistent with the treatment of the item by P.

Example 2. Partnership P incurred certain start-up costs before P was actively engaged in its business. P capitalized these costs. C, a partner in P, deducted C's proportionate share of these start-up costs. C's treatment of the partnership expenditure is inconsistent with the treatment of that item by P.

Example 3. D is a partner in partnership P. P reports a loss of $100,000 on its return, $5,000 of which it reports on the Schedule K-1 attached to its return as D's distributive share. However, P reports $15,000 as D's distributive share of P's loss on the Schedule K-1 furnished to D. D reports the $15,000 loss on D's income tax return. D has not satisfied the consistent reporting requirement. See, however, § 301.6222(b)-3 for an election to be treated as having reported the inconsistency.

(d) *Effective date.*—This section is applicable to partnership taxable years beginning on or after October 4, 2001. For years beginning prior to October 4, 2001, see § 301.6222(a)-1T contained in 26 CFR part 1, revised April 1, 2001. [Reg. § 301.6222(a)-1.]

☐ [*T.D.* 8965, 10-3-2001.]

[Reg. § 301.6222(a)-2]

§ 301.6222(a)-2. Application of consistent reporting and notification rules to indirect partners.—(a) *In general.*—The consistent reporting requirement of § 301.6222(a)-1 is generally applied with respect to the *source partnership.* For purposes of this section, the term source partnership means the partnership (within the meaning of section 6231(a)(1)) from which the partnership item originates.

(b) *Indirect partner files consistently with source partnership.*—An indirect partner who treats an item from a source partnership in a manner consistent with the treatment of that item on the source partnership's return satisfies the consistency requirement of section 6222(a) regardless of whether the indirect partner treats that item in a manner consistent with the treatment of that item by the pass-thru partner through which the indirect partner holds the interest in the source partnership. Under these circumstances, therefore, the Internal Revenue Service shall not send to the indirect partner the notice described in section 6231(b)(1)(A).

(c) *Indirect partner files inconsistently with source partnership.*—(1) *Indirect partner notifies the Internal Revenue Service of inconsistency.*—An indirect partner who—

(i) Treats an item from a source partnership in a manner inconsistent with the treatment of that item on the source partnership's return; and

(ii) Files a statement identifying the inconsistency with the source partnership in accordance with § 301.6222(b)-1, shall not be subject to a computational adjustment to conform the treatment of that item to the treatment of that item on the return of the source partnership.

(2) *Indirect partner does not notify the Internal Revenue Service of inconsistency.*—Except as provided in paragraph (c)(3) of this section, an indirect partner who—

(i) Treats an item from a source partnership in a manner inconsistent with the treatment of that item on the source partnership's return; and

(ii) Fails to file a statement identifying the inconsistency with the source partnership in accordance with § 301.6222(b)-1, is subject to a computational adjustment to conform the treatment of that item to the treatment of that item on the return of the source partnership.

(3) *Indirect partner files consistently with a pass-thru partner that notifies the Internal Revenue Service of the inconsistency.*—If an indirect partner treats an item from a source partnership in a manner consistent with the treatment of that item by a pass-thru partner through which the indirect partner holds the interest in the source partnership and that pass-thru partner—

(i) Treats that item in a manner inconsistent with the treatment of that item on the source partnership's return; and

(ii) Files a statement identifying the inconsistency with the source partnership in accordance with § 301.6222(b)-1, the indirect partner is not subject to a computational adjustment to conform to the treatment of that item on the return of the source partnership.

(d) *Examples.*—The following examples illustrate the principles of this section:

Example 1. One of the partners in Partnership A is Partnership B, which has four equal partners C, D, E, and F. Both A and B are partnerships within the meaning of section 6231(a)(1). On its return, A reports $100,000 as B's distributive share of A's ordinary income. B, however, reports only $80,000 as its distributive share of the income and does not notify the Internal Revenue Service of this inconsistent treatment with respect to A. C reports $20,000 as its distributive share of the item. Although C reports the item consistently with B, C is subject to a computational adjustment to conform the treatment of that item on C's return to the treatment of that item on A's return.

Example 2. Assume the same facts as in *Example 1,* except that B notified the Internal Revenue Service of its inconsistent treatment with respect to source partnership A. C is not subject to a computational adjustment.

Example 3. Assume the same facts as in *Example 1.* D reports only $15,000 as D's distributive share of the income and does not report the inconsistency. F reports only $9,000 as its distributive share of the item but reports this inconsistency with respect to source partnership A. D is subject to a computational adjustment to conform the treatment of that item on D's return to the treatment of that item on A's return. F is not subject to a computational adjustment.

Example 4. Assume the same facts as in *Example 3,* except that F reported the inconsistency with respect to B and did not report the inconsistency with respect to source partnership A. F is subject to a computational adjustment to conform the treatment of that item on F's return to the treatment of that item on A's return.

Example 5. Assume the same facts as in *Example 1.* E reports $25,000 as its distributive share of the item. Regardless of whether E reports the inconsistency between its treatment of the item and that by B, E is neither subject to a computational adjustment to conform E's treatment of that item to that of B nor subject to the notice described in section 6231(b)(1)(A) with respect to any such notification of inconsistent treatment.

(e) *Effective date.*—This section is applicable to partnership taxable years beginning on or after October 4, 2001. For years beginning prior to October 4, 2001, see § 301.6222(a)-2T contained in 26 CFR part 1, revised April 1, 2001. [Reg. § 301.6222(a)-2.]

☐ [*T.D.* 8965, 10-3-2001.]

[Reg. § 301.6222(b)-1]

§ 301.6222(b)-1. Notification to the Internal Revenue Service when partnership items are treated inconsistently.—(a) *In general.*—The statement identifying an inconsistency described in section 6222(b)(1)(B) shall be filed by filing the form prescribed for that purpose in accordance with the instructions accompanying that form.

(b) *Effective date.*—This section is applicable to partnership taxable years beginning on or after October 4, 2001. For years beginning prior to October 4, 2001, see § 301.6222(b)-1T contained in 26 CFR part 1, revised April 1, 2001. [Reg. § 301.6222(b)-1.]

☐ [*T.D.* 8965, 10-3-2001.]

[Reg. § 301.6222(b)-2]

§ 301.6222(b)-2. Effect of notification of inconsistent treatment.—(a) *In general.*—Generally, if a partner treats a partnership item on the partner's return in a manner inconsistent with the treatment of that item on the partnership return, the Internal Revenue Service may make a computational adjustment to conform the treatment of the item by the partner with the treatment of that item on the partnership return. Any additional tax resulting from that computational adjustment may be assessed without either the commencement of a partnership proceeding or

notification to the partner that all partnership items arising from that partnership will be treated as nonpartnership items. However, if a partner notifies the Internal Revenue Service of the inconsistent treatment of a partnership item in the manner prescribed in § 301.6222(b)-1, the Internal Revenue Service generally may not make an adjustment with respect to that partnership item unless the Internal Revenue Service—

(1) Conducts a partnership-level proceeding; or

(2) Notifies the partner under section 6231(b)(1)(A) that all partnership items arising from that partnership will be treated as nonpartnership items. See, however, § § 301.6231(c)-1 and 301.6231(c)-2 for special rules relating to certain applications and claims for refund based on losses, deductions, or credits from abusive tax shelter partnerships.

(b) *Partner protected only to extent of notification.*—(1) A partner who reports the inconsistent treatment of partnership items on the partner's return is protected from computational adjustments under section 6222(c) only with respect to those partnership items the inconsistent treatment of which is reported. Thus, if a partner notifying the Internal Revenue Service with respect to one item fails to report the inconsistent treatment of another item, the partner is subject to a computational adjustment with respect to that other item.

(2) The following example illustrates the principles of this paragraph (b):

Example. Partner A of Partnership P treats a deduction and a capital gain arising from P on A's return in a manner that is inconsistent with the treatment of those items by P. A reports the inconsistent treatment of the deduction but not of the gain. A is subject to a computational adjustment under section 6222(c) with respect to the gain.

(c) *Adjustments in a separate proceeding not limited to conforming adjustments.*—(1) If the Internal Revenue Service conducts a separate proceeding with a partner whose partnership items are treated as nonpartnership items under section 6231(b), the Internal Revenue Service is not limited to making adjustments that merely conform the partner's return to the partnership return.

(2) *Example.*—The following example illustrates the principles of this paragraph (c):

Example. Partnership P allocates to E, one of its partners, a loss of $8,000. E, however, claims a loss of $9,000 and reports the inconsistent treatment. The Internal Revenue Service notifies E that it will treat all of E's partnership items arising from P as nonpartnership items. As a result of a separate proceeding with E, the Internal Revenue Service may issue a deficiency notice which could include reducing the loss to $3,000.

(d) *Effective date.*—This section is applicable to partnership taxable years beginning on or after October 4, 2001. For years beginning prior to October 4, 2001, see § 301.6222(b)-2T contained in

26 CFR part 1, revised April 1, 2001. [Reg. § 301.6222(b)-2.]

☐ [*T.D.* 8965, 10-3-2001.]

[Reg. § 301.6222(b)-3]

§ 301.6222(b)-3. Partner receiving incorrect schedule.—(a) *In general.*—A partner shall be treated as having complied with section 6222(b)(1)(B) and § 301.6222(b)-1 with respect to a partnership item if the partner—

(1) Demonstrates that the treatment of the partnership item on the partner's return is consistent with the treatment of that item on the schedule prescribed by the Internal Revenue Service and furnished to the partner by the partnership showing the partner's share of income, credits, deductions, etc.; and

(2) Elects in accordance with the rules prescribed in paragraph (b) of this section to have this section apply with respect to that item.

(b) *Election provisions.*—(1) *Time and manner of making election.*—The election described in paragraph (a) of this section shall be made by filing a statement with the Internal Revenue Service office issuing the notice of computational adjustment within 30 days after the notice is mailed to the partner.

(2) *Contents of statement.*—The statement described in paragraph (b)(1) of this section shall be—

(i) Clearly identified as an election under section 6222(b)(2);

(ii) Signed by the partner making the election; and

(iii) Accompanied by copies of the schedule furnished to the partner by the partnership and of the notice of computational adjustment. The partner need not enclose a copy of the notice of computational adjustment, however, if the partner clearly identifies the notice of computational adjustment. Generally, the requirement described in paragraph (a)(1) of this section will be satisfied by attaching to the statement a copy of the schedule furnished to the partner by the partnership. However, if it is not clear from the information contained on the schedule that the treatment of the partnership item on the schedule is consistent with the partner's treatment of such item on the partner's return the statement shall also include an explanation of how the treatment of such item on the schedule is consistent with the treatment on the partner's return with respect to the characterization, timing, and amount of such item.

(c) *Effective date.*—This section is applicable to partnership taxable years beginning on or after October 4, 2001. For years beginning prior to October 4, 2001, see § 301.6222(b)-3T contained in 26 CFR part 1, revised April 1, 2001. [Reg. § 301.6222(b)-3.]

☐ [*T.D.* 8965, 10-3-2001.]

[Reg. § 301.6223-1]

§ 301.6223-1. Partnership representative.—(a) *Each partnership must have a partnership representative.*—A partnership subject to subchapter C of chapter 63 of the Internal Revenue Code (subchapter C of chapter 63) for a partnership taxable year must designate a partnership representative for the partnership taxable year in accordance with this section. There may be only one designated partnership representative for a partnership taxable year at any time. The designation of a partnership representative for a partnership taxable year under this section remains in effect until the date on which the designation of the partnership representative is terminated by valid resignation (as described in paragraph (d) of this section), valid revocation (as described in paragraph (e) of this section), or a determination by the Internal Revenue Service (IRS) that the designation is not in effect (as described in paragraph (f) of this section). A designation of a partnership representative for a partnership taxable year under paragraphs (e) or (f) of this section supersedes all prior designations of a partnership representative for that year. If required by forms, instructions, and other guidance prescribed by the IRS, a partnership representative must update the partnership representative's contact information when such information changes. Only a person designated as a partnership representative in accordance with this section will be recognized as the partnership representative under section 6223. A power of attorney (including a Form 2848, Power of Attorney) may not be used to designate a partnership representative. See § 301.6223-2(a), (b), and (c) with regard to the binding effect of actions taken by the partnership representative. See § 301.6223-2(d) with regard to the sole authority of the partnership representative to act on behalf of the partnership. See paragraph (f) of this section for rules regarding designation of a partnership representative by the IRS.

(b) *Eligibility to serve as a partnership representative.*—(1) *In general.*—Any person (as defined in section 7701(a)(1)) that meets the requirements of paragraphs (b)(2) and (3) of this section, as applicable, is eligible to serve as a partnership representative, including a wholly owned entity disregarded as separate from its owner for federal tax purposes. A person designated under this section as partnership representative is deemed to be eligible to serve as the partnership representative unless and until the IRS determines that the person is ineligible. A partnership can designate itself as its own partnership representative provided it meets the requirements of paragraphs (b)(2) and (3) of this section.

(2) *Substantial presence in the United States.*—A person must have substantial presence in the United States to be the partnership representative. A person has substantial presence in the United States for the purposes of this section if—

(i) The person makes themselves available to meet in person with the IRS in the United

States at a reasonable time and place as determined by the IRS in accordance with § 301.7605-1; and

(ii) The person has a United States taxpayer identification number, a street address that is in the United States and a telephone number with a United States area code.

(3) *Eligibility of an entity to be a partnership representative.*—(i) *In general.*—A person who is not an individual may be a partnership representative only if an individual who meets the requirements of paragraph (b)(2) of this section is appointed by the partnership as the sole individual through whom the partnership representative will act for all purposes under subchapter C of chapter 63. A partnership representative meeting the requirements of this paragraph (b)(3) is an *entity partnership representative*, and the individual through whom such entity partnership representative acts is the *designated individual*. Designated individual status automatically terminates on the date that the designation of the entity partnership representative for which the designated individual was appointed is no longer in effect in accordance with paragraph (d), (e), or (f) of this section.

(ii) *Appointment of a designated individual.*—A designated individual must be appointed by the partnership at the time of the designation of the entity partnership representative in the manner prescribed by the IRS in forms, instructions, and other guidance. Accordingly, if the entity partnership representative is designated on the partnership return for the taxable year in accordance with paragraph (c)(2) of this section, the designated individual must be appointed by the partnership at that time. Similarly, if the entity partnership representative is designated under paragraph (e) of this section (regarding revocation and subsequent designation after revocation of a partnership representative), the designated individual must be appointed at that time. If the partnership fails to appoint a designated individual at the time and in the manner set forth in this paragraph (b)(3)(ii), the IRS may determine that the entity partnership representative designation is not in effect under paragraph (f) of this section.

(4) *Examples.*—The following examples illustrate the rules of this paragraph (b).

Example 1. Partnership designates PR as its partnership representative for its 2018 tax year on its timely filed 2018 partnership return. The IRS initiates an administrative proceeding with respect to Partnership's 2018 tax year. PR has a United States taxpayer identification number, a United States street address, and a phone number with a United States area code. The IRS contacts PR and requests an in-person meeting with respect to the administrative proceeding. PR works with the IRS and agrees to meet. PR has substantial presence in the United States because she meets all the requirements under paragraph (b)(2) of this section.

Example 2. The facts are the same as in *Example 1* of this paragraph (b)(4), except that PR is an entity and Partnership appointed DI, a designated individual to act on behalf of PR for its 2018 tax year on its timely filed 2018 partnership return. DI has a United States taxpayer identification number and a phone number with a United States area code. However, the address provided for DI is not a United States address. Accordingly, PR is not an eligible partnership representative because PR is an entity and DI does not satisfy the requirements of paragraph (b)(3)(i) of this section. Although DI does not have substantial presence in the United States under paragraph (b)(2) of this section and therefore PR is not an eligible partnership representative, until there is a resignation or revocation under paragraph (d) or (e) of this section or until the IRS determines the partnership representative designation is no longer in effect under paragraph (f) of this section, the designation of PR as the partnership representative remains in effect in accordance with paragraph (a) of this section, and Partnership and all its partners are bound by the actions of PR as the partnership representative.

Example 3. The facts are the same as in *Example 1* of this paragraph (b)(4), except PR works in a foreign country and spends the majority of her time there. Unless PR otherwise fails to meet one of the requirements under paragraph (b)(2) of this section, PR has substantial presence in the United States. However, even if PR fails to meet one of the requirements under paragraph (b)(2) of this section, until there is a resignation or revocation under paragraph (d) or (e) of this section or until the IRS determines the partnership representative designation is no longer in effect under paragraph (f) of this section, the designation of PR as the partnership representative remains in effect in accordance with paragraph (a) of this section, and Partnership and all its partners are bound by the actions of PR as the partnership representative.

(c) *Designation of partnership representative by the partnership.*—(1) *In general.*—The partnership must designate a partnership representative separately for each taxable year. The designation of a partnership representative for one taxable year is effective only for the taxable year for which it is made.

(2) *Designation.*—Except in the case of a designation of a partnership representative (and the appointment of the designated individual, if applicable) after an event described in paragraph (d) of this section (regarding resignation), paragraph (e) of this section (regarding revocation by the partnership), or paragraph (f) of this section (regarding designation made by the IRS), or except as prescribed in forms, instructions, and other guidance, designation of a partnership representative (and the appointment of the designated individual, if applicable) must be made on the partnership return for the partnership taxable year to which the designation relates and must include all of the information required by

forms, instructions, and other guidance, including information about the designated individual if paragraph (b)(3) of this section applies. The designation of the partnership representative (and the appointment of the designated individual, if applicable) is effective on the date that the partnership return is filed.

(3) *Example.*—The following example illustrates the rules of this paragraph (c).

Example. Partnership properly designates PR1 as its partnership representative for taxable year 2018 on its 2018 partnership return. Partnership designates PR2 as its partnership representative for taxable year 2021 on its 2021 partnership return. In 2022, the IRS mails Partnership a notice of administrative proceeding under section 6231(a)(1) with respect to Partnership's 2018 taxable year. PR1 is the partnership representative for the 2018 partnership taxable year, notwithstanding the designation of PR2 as partnership representative for the 2021 partnership taxable year.

(d) *Resignations.*—(1) *In general.*—A partnership representative or designated individual may resign as partnership representative or designated individual, as applicable, for a partnership taxable year for any reason by notifying the IRS in writing of the resignation in accordance with forms, instructions, and other guidance prescribed by the IRS. A resigning partnership representative may not designate a successor partnership representative. A resigning designated individual may not designate a successor designated individual or partnership representative. No later than 30 days after the IRS receives a written notification of resignation, the IRS will send written confirmation of receipt of the written notification to the partnership and the resigning partnership representative (to the attention of the designated individual if appropriate). A failure by the IRS to send any notification under this paragraph (d) does not invalidate a valid resignation made pursuant to this paragraph (d). A failure by the partnership representative (or designated individual, if the designated individual is the person resigning) to satisfy the requirements of this paragraph (d) is treated as if there were no resignation, and the partnership representative designation (and designated individual appointment, if applicable) remains in effect until the designation (or appointment) is terminated by valid resignation (as described in this paragraph (d)), valid revocation by the partnership (as described in paragraph (e) of this section), or a determination by the IRS that the designation is not in effect (as described in paragraph (f) of this section). See § 301.6223-2 for binding nature of actions taken by the partnership representative or designated individual on behalf of a partnership representative, if applicable, prior to resignation.

(2) *Time for resignation.*—A partnership representative or designated individual may submit the written notification of resignation described in paragraph (d)(1) of this section to the IRS only after the IRS issues a notice of administrative proceeding (NAP) under section 6231(a)(1) for the partnership taxable year for which the partnership representative designation is in effect or at such other time as prescribed by the IRS in forms, instructions, or other guidance. If the IRS withdraws the NAP pursuant to § 301.6231-1(f), any valid resignation by the partnership representative or designated individual under this paragraph (d) prior to the withdrawal of the NAP remains in effect.

(3) *Effective date of resignation.*—A valid resignation is immediately effective upon the IRS's receipt of the written notification described in paragraph (d)(1) of this section. As of the effective date of the resignation—

(i) The resigning partnership representative (and designated individual, if applicable) may not take any action on behalf of the partnership with respect to the partnership taxable year affected by the resignation;

(ii) The partnership representative designation is no longer in effect with respect to the partnership taxable year affected by the resignation;

(iii) In the case of a resigning entity partnership representative, the appointment of the designated individual is no longer in effect with respect to the partnership taxable year affected by the resignation; and

(iv) In the case of a resigning designated individual, the designation of the entity partnership representative is no longer in effect with respect to the partnership taxable year affected by the resignation.

(e) *Revocations.*—(1) *In general.*—A partnership may revoke a designation of a partnership representative or appointment of a designated individual for a partnership taxable year for any reason by notifying the IRS in writing of the revocation in accordance with forms, instructions, and other guidance prescribed by the IRS. The partnership may make such revocation regardless of when and how the designation or appointment was made, except as provided in paragraph (e)(6) of this section (regarding designation by the IRS). The revocation must include the designation of a successor partnership representative (and the appointment of a designated individual, if applicable). In the case of a revocation of only the designated individual appointment, the partnership must designate a successor designated individual. No later than 30 days after the IRS receives a written notification of revocation submitted at the time described in paragraph (e)(2) of this section, the IRS will send written confirmation of receipt of the written notification to the partnership, the revoked partnership representative or, in the case of a revocation of only the appointment of a designated individual, to the revoked designated individual, and to the newly designated partnership representative. In the case of a revocation of an entity partnership representative, the notification will be sent to the entity partnership representative, to the attention of the designated individual. A failure by the IRS to send any notification under this paragraph (e) does not invalidate a valid revocation made pursuant to this paragraph (e). A failure by the partnership to satisfy the requirements of this paragraph (e), including failure to designate a successor, is treated as if no revocation has occurred and the partnership representative designation (and designated individual appointment, if applicable) remains in effect until the designation (or appointment) is terminated either by valid resignation (as described in paragraph (d) of this section), valid revocation by the partnership (as described in this paragraph (e)), or determination by the IRS that the designation is not in effect (as described in paragraph (f) of this section). See § 301.6223-2 for binding nature of actions taken by the partnership representative or designated individual on behalf of a partnership representative, if applicable, prior to revocation.

(2) *Time for revocation.*—(i) *Revocation during an administrative proceeding.*—Except as provided in paragraph (e)(2)(ii) of this section or in forms, instructions, or other guidance prescribed by the IRS, a partnership may revoke a designation of a partnership representative or appointment of a designated individual only after the IRS issues a notice of selection for examination or a NAP under section 6231(a)(1) for the partnership taxable year for which the designation or appointment is in effect. If the IRS withdraws the NAP pursuant to § 301.6231-1(f), any valid revocation of a partnership representative designation or designated individual appointment under this paragraph (e) prior to the withdrawal of the NAP remains in effect.

(ii) *Revocation with an AAR.*—The partnership may revoke a designation of a partnership representative or appointment of a designated individual for the taxable year prior to receiving a notice of selection for examination or a NAP by filing a valid administrative adjustment request (AAR) in accordance with section 6227 for a partnership taxable year. A partnership may not use the form prescribed by the IRS for filing an AAR solely for the purpose of revoking a designation of a partnership representative or appointment of a designated individual. See § 301.6227-1 for the rules regarding the time and manner of filing an AAR.

(3) *Effective date of revocation.*—Except as described in paragraph (e)(6)(ii) of this section (regarding the effective date of a revocation of a partnership representative designated by the IRS under paragraph (f)(5) of this section), a valid revocation is immediately effective upon the IRS's receipt of the written notification described in paragraph (e)(1) of this section. A revocation of a partnership representative designation and a designation of a new partnership representative (and appointment of a new designated individual, if applicable) is effective on the date the partnership files a valid AAR. Similarly, a revocation of a designated individual appointment

and appointment of a new designated individual is effective on the date the partnership files a valid AAR. As of the effective date of the revocation—

(i) The revoked partnership representative (and designated individual, if applicable) may not take any action on behalf of the partnership with respect to the partnership taxable year affected by the revocation;

(ii) The designation of the revoked partnership representative is no longer in effect, and the successor partnership representative designation (and designated individual appointment, if applicable) is in effect with respect to the partnership taxable year affected by the revocation;

(iii) In the case of a revoked entity partnership representative, the appointment of the designated individual is no longer in effect with respect to the partnership taxable year affected by the revocation; and

(iv) In the case of a revoked designated individual where the designation of the entity partnership representative has not been revoked, the revoked designated individual may not take any action on behalf of the partnership with respect to the partnership taxable year affected by the revocation, the appointment of the revoked designated individual is no longer in effect, and the appointment of the successor designated individual is in effect.

(4) *Partners who may sign revocation.*—A revocation under this paragraph (e) must be signed by a person who was a partner at any time during the partnership taxable year to which the revocation relates or as provided in forms, instructions, and other guidance prescribed by the IRS.

(5) *Form of the revocation.*—The written notification of revocation described in paragraph (e)(1) of this section must include the items described in this paragraph (e)(5). A notification of revocation described in paragraph (e)(1) of this section that does not include each of the following items is not a valid revocation:

(i) A certification under penalties of perjury that the person signing the notification is a partner described in paragraph (e)(4) of this section authorized by the partnership to revoke the designation of the partnership representative (or appointment of the designated individual, if applicable).

(ii) A statement that the person signing the notification is revoking the designation of the partnership representative (or appointment of the designated individual, if applicable);

(iii) A designation of a successor partnership representative (and appointment of a designated individual, if applicable) in accordance with this section and forms, instructions, and other guidance prescribed by the IRS; and

(iv) In the case of a revocation of an appointment of a designated individual, appointment of a successor designated individual in accordance with this section and forms, instructions, and other guidance prescribed by the IRS.

Reg. § 301.6223-1(e)(5)(iv)

(6) *Partnership representative designated by the IRS.*—(i) *In general.*—If a partnership representative is designated (and a designated individual is appointed, if applicable) by the IRS pursuant to paragraph (f)(5) of this section, the partnership may only revoke that designation (or the appointment of the designated individual, if applicable) with the permission of the IRS, which the IRS will not unreasonably withhold.

(ii) *Effective date of revocation.*—The effective date of any revocation submitted in accordance with paragraph (e)(6)(i) of this section is the date on which the IRS sends notification that the revocation is valid.

(7) *Multiple revocations.*—(i) *In general.*—The IRS may determine that a designation is not in effect under paragraph (f) of this section if:

(A) The IRS receives a revocation of a designation of a partnership representative or appointment of a designated individual, and

(B) Within the 90-day period prior to the date the revocation described in paragraph (e)(7)(i)(A) of this section was received, the IRS received another revocation for the same partnership taxable year.

(ii) *Time limitation.*—The IRS may not determine that a designation is not in effect in accordance with paragraph (e)(7)(i) of this section later than 90 days after the IRS's receipt of the revocation described in paragraph (e)(7)(i)(A) of this section.

(8) *Examples.*—The following examples illustrate the rules of this paragraph (e).

Example 1. Partnership properly designates PR, an individual, as partnership representative for its 2018 taxable year on its timely filed 2018 partnership return. In 2020, Partnership mails written notification to the IRS to revoke designation of PR as its partnership representative for Partnership's 2018 taxable year. The revocation is not made in connection with an AAR for Partnership's 2018 taxable year, and the IRS has not mailed Partnership a notice of selection for examination or a NAP under section 6231(a)(1) with respect to Partnership's 2018 taxable year. Because the revocation was not made when permitted under paragraph (e)(2) of this section, the revocation is not effective and B remains the partnership representative for Partnership's 2018 taxable year unless and until B's status as partnership representative is properly revoked under paragraph (e) of this section or terminated in accordance with paragraph (d) (regarding resignation) or (f) (regarding IRS designation) of this section.

Example 2. During an administrative proceeding with respect to Partnership's 2018 taxable year, Partnership provides the IRS with written notification to revoke its designation of PR, an individual, as its partnership representative for the 2018 taxable year. The written notification does not include a designation of a new partnership representative for Partnership's 2018 taxable year. Because the revocation does not include a designation of a new partnership representative as required under paragraph (e)(1) of this section, the revocation is not effective and PR remains the partnership representative for Partnership's 2018 taxable year unless and until B's status as partnership representative is properly revoked under paragraph (e) of this section or terminated in accordance with paragraph (d) (regarding resignation) or (f) (regarding IRS designation) of this section.

(f) *Designation of the partnership representative by the IRS.*—(1) *In general.*—If the IRS determines that a designation of a partnership representative is not in effect for a partnership taxable year in accordance with paragraph (f)(2) of this section, the IRS will notify the partnership that a partnership representative designation is not in effect. The IRS will also notify the most recent partnership representative for the partnership taxable year, except as described in paragraph (f)(2)(iii) of this section. In the case of an entity partnership representative, the notification will be sent to the entity partnership representative, to the attention of the designated individual. The determination that a designation is not in effect is effective on the date the IRS mails the notification. Except as described in paragraph (f)(4) of this section, the partnership may designate, in accordance with paragraph (f)(3) of this section, a successor partnership representative (and designated individual, if applicable) eligible under paragraph (b) of this section within 30 days of the date the IRS mails the notification. In the case of a resignation of a partnership representative, this notification may include the written confirmation of receipt described in paragraph (d)(1) of this section. See paragraph (f)(2)(iv) of this section. If the partnership does not designate a successor within 30 days from the date of IRS notification, the IRS will designate a partnership representative in accordance with paragraph (f)(5) of this section. A partnership representative designation made in accordance with paragraphs (c), (e), or (f) of this section remains in effect until the IRS determines the designation is not in effect. See § 301.6223-2 for binding nature of actions taken by the partnership representative or designated individual on behalf of a partnership representative, if applicable, prior to a determination by the IRS that the designation is not in effect.

(2) *IRS determination that partnership representative designation not in effect.*—The IRS may, but is not required to, determine that a partnership representative designation is not in effect. The IRS is not obligated to search for or otherwise seek out information related to the circumstances in which the IRS may determine a partnership representative designation is not in effect, and the fact that the IRS is aware of any such circumstances does not obligate the IRS to determine that a partnership representative designation is not in effect. The IRS may determine that the partnership representative designation is not in effect if the IRS determines that—

(i) The partnership representative or the designated individual does not have substantial presence as described in paragraph (b)(2) of this section;

(ii) The partnership failed to appoint a designated individual as described in paragraph (b)(3) of this section, as applicable;

(iii) The partnership failed to make a valid designation as described in paragraph (c) of this section;

(iv) The partnership representative or designated individual resigns as described in paragraph (d) of this section;

(v) The partnership has made multiple revocations as described in paragraph (e)(7) of this section; or

(vi) The partnership representative designation is no longer in effect as described in other published guidance.

(3) *Designation by the partnership during the 30-day period.*—Designation of a partnership representative (and appointment of a designated individual, if applicable) by the partnership during the 30-day period described in paragraph (f)(1) of this section must be made in accordance with forms, instructions, and other guidance prescribed by the IRS. If the partnership fails to provide all information required by forms, instructions, and other guidance, the partnership will have failed to make a designation (and appointment, if applicable). If the partnership does not fully comply with the requirement of this paragraph (f)(3) within the 30-day period described in paragraph (f)(1) of this section, the IRS will designate a partnership representative (and appoint a designated individual, if applicable).

(4) *No opportunity for designation by the partnership in the case of multiple revocations.*—In the event that the IRS determines a partnership representative designation is not in effect due to multiple revocations as described in paragraph (e)(7) of this section, the partnership will not be given an opportunity to designate the successor partnership representative prior to the designation by the IRS as described in paragraph (f)(5) of this section. However, see paragraph (e)(6) of this section regarding revocation of a partnership representative designated by the IRS.

(5) *Designation by the IRS.*—(i) *In general.*—The IRS designates a partnership representative under this paragraph (f)(5) by notifying the partnership of the name, address, and telephone number of the new partnership representative. If the IRS designates an entity partnership representative, the IRS will also appoint a designated individual to act on behalf of the entity partnership representative. The designation of a partnership representative (and appointment of a designated individual, if applicable) by the IRS is effective on the date on which the IRS mails the notification of the designation (and appointment, if applicable) to the partnership. The IRS will also mail a copy of the notification of the designation (and appointment, if applicable) to the new partnership representative (through the new designated individual, if applicable) that has been designated (and appointed, if applicable) by the IRS under this section.

(ii) *Factors considered when partnership representative designated by the IRS.*—The IRS will ordinarily consider one or more of the factors set forth in this paragraph (f)(5)(ii) when determining whom to designate as partnership representative. No single factor is determinative, and other than as described in paragraph (f)(5)(iii) of this section, the IRS may exercise its discretion to designate a person as partnership representative even if none of the factors are applicable to such person. The factors are not requirements for eligibility to be designated by the IRS as partnership representative; the only requirements for eligibility are described under paragraph (b) of this section. The IRS is not obligated to search for or otherwise seek out information related to the factors, and the fact that the IRS is aware of any information related to such factors does not obligate the IRS to designate a particular person. Although the IRS may designate any person to be the partnership representative, a principal consideration in determining whom to designate as a partnership representative is whether there is a reviewed year partner that is eligible to serve as the partnership representative in accordance with paragraph (b)(1) of this section or whether there is a partner at the time the partnership representative designation is made that is eligible to serve as the partnership representative. Other factors that will ordinarily be considered by the IRS in determining whom to designate as a partnership representative include, but are not limited to:

(A) The views of the partners having a majority interest in the partnership regarding the designation;

(B) The general knowledge of the person in tax matters and the administrative operation of the partnership;

(C) The person's access to the books and records of the partnership;

(D) Whether the person is a United States person (within the meaning of section 7701(a)(30)); and

(E) The profits interest of the partner in the case of a partner.

(iii) *IRS employees.*—The IRS will not designate a current employee, agent, or contractor of the IRS as the partnership representative unless that employee, agent, or contractor was a reviewed year partner or is currently a partner in the partnership.

(6) *Examples.*—The following examples illustrate the rules of this paragraph (f).

Example 1. The IRS determines that Partnership has designated a partnership representative that does not have substantial presence in the United States as defined in paragraph (b)(2) of

Reg. §301.6223-1(f)(6)

this section. The IRS may, but is not required to, determine that the designation is not in effect and designate a new partnership representative after following the procedures in this paragraph (f).

Example 2. Partnership designates as its partnership representative a corporation but fails to appoint a designated individual to act on behalf of the corporation as required under paragraph (b)(3) of this section. The IRS may, but is not required to, determine that the partnership representative designation is not in effect and may designate a new partnership representative after following the procedures in this paragraph (f).

Example 3. The partnership representative resigns pursuant to paragraph (d) of this section. The IRS mails Partnership a notification informing Partnership that no designation is in effect and that the IRS plans to designate a new partnership representative. Partnership fails to respond within 30 days of the date the IRS mails the notification. The IRS must designate a partnership representative pursuant to this paragraph (f).

Example 4. Partnership designated on its partnership return a partnership representative, PR1. After Partnership received a NAP, Partnership submits to the IRS the form described in paragraph (e)(4) of this section requesting the revocation of PR1's designation as partnership representative and designating PR2 as the partnership representative. Sixty days later, Partnership signs and submits a form described in paragraph (e)(4) of this section requesting the revocation of PR2's designation as partnership representative and designating PR3 as the partnership representative. The IRS accepts the revocation of PR2 and designation of PR3 as valid and effective upon receipt pursuant to paragraph (e)(3) of this section. However, because PR2's revocation was within 90 days of PR1's revocation, the IRS may determine within 90 days of IRS's receipt of PR2's revocation, pursuant to paragraphs (e)(7) and (f)(2) of this section, that there is no designation in effect due to multiple revocations. The IRS may then designate a new partnership representative pursuant to this paragraph (f) without allowing Partnership an opportunity to designate a partnership representative within the 30-day period described in paragraph (f)(1) of this section.

(g) *Reliance on forms required by this section.*— The IRS may rely on any form or other document filed or submitted under this section as evidence of the designation, resignation, or revocation on such form and as evidence of the date on which such form was filed or submitted relating to a designation, resignation, or revocation.

(h) *Applicability date.*—(1) *In general.*—Except as provided in paragraph (h)(2) of this section, this section applies to partnership taxable years beginning after December 31, 2017.

(2) *Election under §301.9100-22 in effect.*— This section applies to any partnership taxable years beginning after November 2, 2015 and before January 1, 2018 for which a valid election

under §301.9100-22 is in effect. [Reg. §301.6223-1.]

☐ [*T.D.* 9839, 8-6-2018.]

[Reg. §301.6223-2]

§301.6223-2. Binding effect of actions of the partnership and partnership representative.— (a) *Binding nature of actions by partnership and final decision in a partnership proceeding.*—The actions of the partnership and the partnership representative taken under subchapter C of chapter 63 of the Internal Revenue Code (subchapter C of chapter 63) and any final decision in a proceeding brought under subchapter C of chapter 63 with respect to the partnership bind the partnership, all partners of the partnership (including partnership-partners as defined in §301.6241-1(a)(7) that have a valid election under section 6221(b) in effect for any taxable year that ends with or within the taxable year of the partnership), and any other person whose tax liability is determined in whole or in part by taking into account directly or indirectly adjustments determined under subchapter C of chapter 63 (for example, indirect partners as defined in §301.6241-1(a)(4)). For instance, a settlement agreement entered into by the partnership representative on behalf of the partnership, a notice of final partnership adjustment (FPA) with respect to the partnership that is not contested by the partnership, or the final decision of a court with respect to the partnership if the FPA is contested, binds all persons described in the preceding sentence.

(b) *Actions by the partnership representative before termination of designation.*—A termination of the designation of a partnership representative because of a resignation under §301.6223-1(d) or a revocation under §301.6223-1(e), or as a result of a determination by the Internal Revenue Service (IRS) under §301.6223-1(f) that the designation is not in effect, does not affect the validity of any action taken by that partnership representative during the period prior to such termination. For example, if a partnership representative properly designated under §301.6223-1 consented to an extension of the period of limitations on making adjustments under section 6235(b) in accordance with §301.6235-1(d), that extension remains valid even after termination of the designation of that partnership representative.

(c) *Actions by the partnership representative upon withdrawal of notice of administrative proceeding.*— If the IRS issues a notice of administrative proceeding (NAP) under section 6231(a)(1) and subsequently withdraws such NAP pursuant to §301.6231-1(f), any actions taken by a partnership representative (or successor partnership representative after a change to the partnership representative that occurred after the issuance of the NAP and before the NAP was withdrawn) are binding as described in paragraph (a) of this section even though the NAP has been withdrawn and has no effect for purposes of subchapter C of chapter 63.

(d) *Partnership representative has the sole authority to act on behalf of the partnership.*—(1) *In general.*—The partnership representative has the sole authority to act on behalf of the partnership for all purposes under subchapter C of chapter 63. In the case of an entity partnership representative, the designated individual has the sole authority to act on behalf of the partnership representative and the partnership. Except for a partner that is the partnership representative or the designated individual, no partner, or any other person, may participate in an administrative proceeding without the permission of the IRS. The failure of the partnership representative to follow any state law, partnership agreement, or other document or agreement has no effect on the authority of the partnership representative or the designated individual as described in section 6223, § 301.6223-1, and this section. Nothing in this section affects, or otherwise restricts, the ability of a partnership representative to authorize a person to represent the partnership representative, in the partnership representative's capacity as the partnership representative, before the IRS under a valid power of attorney in a proceeding involving the partnership under subchapter C of chapter 63.

(2) *Designation provides authority to bind the partnership.*—(i) *Partnership representative.*—A partnership representative, by virtue of being designated under section 6223 and § 301.6223-1, has the authority to bind the partnership for all purposes under subchapter C of chapter 63.

(ii) *Designated individual.*—A partnership that is required to appoint a designated individual described under § 301.6223-1(b)(3)(i) acts through such designated individual. By virtue of being appointed as part of the designation of the partnership representative under § 301.6223-1, the designated individual has the sole authority to bind the partnership representative and therefore the partnership, its partners, and any other person as described in paragraph (a) of this section for all purposes under subchapter C of chapter 63 so long as the partnership representative designation and designated individual appointment are in effect.

(e) *Examples.*—The following examples illustrate the rules of this section.

Example 1. Partnership designates a partnership representative, PR, on its timely filed partnership return for 2020. PR is a partner in Partnership. The partnership agreement for Partnership includes a clause that requires PR to consult with an identified management group of partners in Partnership before taking any action with respect to an administrative proceeding before the IRS. The IRS initiates an administrative proceeding with respect to Partnership's 2020 taxable year. During the course of the administrative proceeding, PR consents to an extension of the period of limitations on making adjustments under section 6235(b) allowing additional time for the IRS to mail an FPA. PR failed to consult with the management group of partners prior to agreeing to this extension of time. PR's consent provided to the IRS to extend the time period is valid and binding on Partnership because, pursuant to section 6223, PR, as the designated partnership representative, has authority to bind Partnership and all its partners.

Example 2. Partnership designates a partnership representative, PR, on its timely filed partnership return for 2020. PR is not a partner in Partnership. During an administrative proceeding with respect to Partnership's 2020 taxable year, PR agrees to certain partnership adjustments and within 45 days after the issuance of the FPA elects the alternative to payment of the imputed underpayment under section 6226. Certain partners in Partnership challenge the actions taken by PR during the administrative proceeding and the validity of the section 6226 statements furnished to those partners, alleging that PR was never authorized to act on behalf of Partnership under state law or the partnership agreement. Because PR was designated by Partnership as the partnership representative under section 6223 and this section, PR was authorized to act on behalf of Partnership for all purposes under subchapter C of chapter 63, and the IRS may rely on that designation as conclusive evidence of PR's authority to act on behalf of Partnership.

Example 3. Partnership designates an entity partnership representative, EPR, and appoints an individual, A, as the designated individual on its timely filed partnership return for 2020. EPR is a C corporation. A is unaffiliated with EPR and is not an officer, director, or employee of EPR. During an administrative proceeding with respect to Partnership's 2020 taxable year, A, acting for EPR, agrees to an extension of the period of limitations on making adjustments under section 6235(b) from March 15, 2024 to December 31, 2024. The IRS mails an FPA with respect to the 2020 partnership taxable year on December 13, 2024, before expiration of the extended period of limitations on making adjustments as agreed to by EPR, but after the expiration of the unextended period of limitations on making adjustments. Partnership challenges the FPA as untimely, alleging that A was not authorized under state law to act on behalf of EPR and thus the extension agreement was invalid. Because A was appointed by the partnership as the designated individual to act on behalf of EPR, A was authorized to act on behalf of EPR for all purposes under subchapter C of chapter 63, and the IRS may rely on that appointment as conclusive evidence of A's authority to act on behalf of EPR and Partnership.

Example 4. The partnership representative, PR, consents to an extension of the period of limitations on making adjustments under section 6235(b) and § 301.6235-1(d) for Partnership for the partnership taxable year. After signing the consent, PR resigns as partnership representative in accordance with § 301.6223-1(d). The consent to extend the period of limitations on making adjustments under section 6235(b) remains valid even after PR resigns.

Example 5. Partnership designates a partnership representative who does not make themselves available to meet with the IRS in person in the United States as required by §301.6223-1(b). Although the partnership representative does not have substantial presence in the United States within the meaning of §301.6223-1(b)(2), until a termination occurs under §301.6223-1(d) or (e) or the IRS determines the partnership representative designation is no longer in effect under §301.6223-1(f), the partnership representative designation remains in effect, and Partnership and all its partners are bound by the actions of the partnership representative.

Example 6. Partnership designates PR1 as the partnership representative on its timely filed partnership return for 2020. On September 1, 2022, the IRS sends a NAP for the 2020 taxable year to Partnership and PR, and Partnership revokes PR1's designation and designates PR2 as the partnership representative in accordance with §301.6223-1(e). On November 1, 2023, PR2 consents to an extension of the period of limitations on making adjustments under section 6235(b) and §301.6235(d) for Partnership's 2020 taxable year. On December 1, 2023, the IRS then withdraws the NAP. PR2 remains the partnership representative, and the consent to extend the period of limitations on making adjustments under section 6235(b) remains valid even after the NAP is withdrawn.

(f) *Applicability date.*—(1) *In general.*—Except as provided in paragraph (f)(2) of this section, this section applies to partnership taxable years beginning after December 31, 2017.

(2) *Election under §301.9100-22 in effect.*—This section applies to any partnership taxable years beginning after November 2, 2015 and before January 1, 2018 for which a valid election under §301.9100-22 is in effect. [Reg. §301.6223-2.]

☐ [*T.D.* 9839, 8-6-2018.]

[Reg. §301.6223(a)-1]

§301.6223(a)-1. Notice sent to tax matters partner.—(a) *In general.*—For purposes of subchapter C of chapter 63 of the Internal Revenue Code, a notice is treated as mailed to the tax matters partner on the earlier of—

(1) The date on which the notice is mailed to "THE TAX MATTERS PARTNER" at the address of the partnership (as provided on the partnership return, except as updated under §301.6223(c)-1); or

(2) The date on which the notice is mailed to the person who is the tax matters partner at the address of that person (as provided on the partner's return, except as updated under §301.6223(c)-1) or the partnership. See §301.6223(c)-1 for rules relating to the information used by the Internal Revenue Service in providing notices, etc.

(b) *Example.*—The provisions of this section may be illustrated by the following example:

Example. Partnership P designates B as its tax matters partner in accordance with §301.6231(a)(7)-1(b). On December 1 a notice of the beginning of an administrative proceeding is mailed to "THE TAX MATTERS PARTNER" at the address of P. On January 10, a copy of the notice is mailed to B at B's address. December 1 is treated as the date that the notice was mailed to the tax matters partner.

(c) *Effective date.*—This section is applicable to partnership taxable years beginning on or after October 4, 2001. For years beginning prior to October 4, 2001, see §301.6223(a)-2T contained in 26 CFR part 1, revised April 1, 2001. [Reg. §301.6223(a)-1.]

☐ [*T.D.* 8965, 10-3-2001.]

[Reg. §301.6223(a)-2]

§301.6223(a)-2. Withdrawal of notice of the beginning of an administrative proceeding.—(a) *In general.*—If the Internal Revenue Service, within 45 days after the day on which the notice specified in section 6223(a)(1) is mailed to the tax matters partner, decides not to propose any adjustments to the partnership return as filed, the Internal Revenue Service may withdraw the notice specified in section 6223(a)(1) by mailing a letter to that effect to the tax matters partner within that 45-day period. Even if the Internal Revenue Service does not withdraw the notice specified in section 6223(a)(1), the Internal Revenue Service is not required to issue a notice of final partnership administrative adjustment. If the Internal Revenue Service withdraws the notice specified in section 6223(a)(1), neither the Internal Revenue Service nor the tax matters partner is required to furnish any notice with respect to that proceeding to any other partner. Except as provided in paragraph (b) of this section, a notice specified in section 6223(a)(1) which has been withdrawn shall be treated for purposes of subchapter C of chapter 63 of the Internal Revenue Code as if that notice had never been mailed to the tax matters partner.

(b) *Internal Revenue Service may not reissue notice except under certain circumstances.*—If the notice specified in section 6223(a)(1) was mailed to the tax matters partner with respect to a partnership taxable year and that notice was later withdrawn as provided in paragraph (a) of this section, the Internal Revenue Service shall not mail a second notice specified in section 6223(a)(1) with respect to that taxable year unless—

(1) There is evidence of fraud, malfeasance, collusion, concealment, or misrepresentation of a material fact;

(2) The prior proceeding involved the misapplication or erroneous interpretation of an established Internal Revenue Service position existing at the time of the previous examination, or the failure to make an adjustment based on such a position; or

(3) Other circumstances exist which indicate that failure to reissue the notice would be a serious administrative omission.

(c) *Effective date.*—This section is applicable to partnership taxable years beginning on or after October 4, 2001. For years beginning prior to October 4, 2001, see § 301.6223(a)-2T contained in 26 CFR part 1, revised April 1, 2001. [Reg. § 301.6223(a)-2.]

☐ [*T.D. 8965, 10-3-2001.*]

[Reg. § 301.6223(b)-1]

§ 301.6223(b)-1. Notice group.—(a) *In general.*—If a group of partners having in the aggregate a 5 percent or more interest in the profits of a partnership requests and designates one of their members to receive the notices described in section 6223(a)(1) and (2), the member so designated shall be treated as a partner to whom section 6223(a) applies. Thus, the designated representative is entitled to receive any notice described in section 6223(a) that is mailed to the tax matters partner 30 days or more after the day on which the Internal Revenue Service receives the request from the group.

(b) *Request for notice.*—(1) *In general.*—The Internal Revenue Service shall mail to the member of the notice group designated to receive such notice any notice described in section 6223(a) that is mailed to the tax matters partner 30 days or more after the day on which the Internal Revenue Service receives the request for notice from the group if such request for notice is made in accordance with the rules prescribed in this paragraph (b).

(2) *Content of request.*—The request for notice from a notice group shall—

(i) Identify the partnership by name, address, and taxpayer identification number;

(ii) Specify the taxable year or years for which the notice group is formed;

(iii) Designate the member of the group to receive the notices;

(iv) Set out the name, address, taxpayer identification number, and profits interest of each member of the group; and

(v) Be signed by all partners comprising the notice group.

(3) *Place for filing.*—The request for notice from a notice group generally must be filed with the service center where the partnership return is filed. However, if the notice group representative knows that the notice described in section 6223(a)(1) (beginning of an administrative proceeding) has already been mailed to the tax matters partner, the statement should be filed with the Internal Revenue Service office that mailed that notice.

(4) *Copy to be sent to the tax matters partner.*—A copy of the request for notice from a notice group shall be provided to the tax matters partner by the notice group representative within 30

days after the request is filed with the Internal Revenue Service.

(5) *Years covered by request.*—A request for notice by a notice group may relate only to partnership taxable years that have ended before the request is filed. A request, however, may relate to more than one partnership taxable year if the 5 percent or more profits interest requirement of section 6223(b)(2) is satisfied for each year to which the request relates.

(c) *Composition of notice group.*—(1) *In general.*—A notice group shall be comprised only of persons who were partners at some time during the partnership taxable year for which the group is formed. If a notice group is formed for more than one taxable year, each member of the group must have been a partner at some time during at least one of the taxable years for which the group is formed. A notice group may include a partner entitled to separate notice. See section 6231(d) and § 301.6231(d)-1 for rules relating to determining the interest of a partner in the profits of a partnership for a partnership taxable year for purposes of section 6223(b). See paragraph (c)(6) of this section for rules relating to indirect and pass-thru partners.

(2) *Partner may be a member of only one group.*—A partner cannot be a member of more than one notice group with respect to the same partnership for the same partnership taxable year. See paragraph (c)(6) of this section for rules relating to indirect and pass-thru partners.

(3) *Partner may join group after formation.*—A partner may join a notice group at any time after the formation of that group by filing with the Internal Revenue Service office where the notice group filed its request a statement that it is joining the notice group. The statement shall identify the partner joining the notice group, the partnership, and the members of the notice group by name, address, and taxpayer identification number and shall be signed by the joining partner. A copy of the statement shall be provided by the joining partner to both the tax matters partner and the notice group representative within 30 days after the request is filed with the Internal Revenue Service. The partner shall become a member of the notice group for each partnership taxable year for which the group was formed and for which the partner was a partner at any time during such partnership taxable year.

(4) *Date on which a partner becomes a member of notice group.*—A partner shall become a member of a notice group on the 30th day after the day on which the Internal Revenue Service receives—

(i) A request for notice from a notice group that identifies that partner as a member of that notice group; or

(ii) A statement filed in accordance with paragraph (c)(3) of this section that states that the partner is joining the notice group.

(5) *No withdrawal from notice group.*—A partner who has signed a notice group request filed

with the Internal Revenue Service remains a member of that notice group until the group terminates. A partner cannot withdraw from the notice group.

(6) *Indirect and pass-thru partners.*—(i) *Pass-thru partners and unidentified indirect partners.*—A pass-thru partner may become a member of a notice group as provided in this section. For purposes of applying the aggregate interest requirement specified in paragraph (a) of this section to a pass-thru partner, the partnership interest held by the pass-thru partner shall not include any interest held through the pass-thru partner by an indirect partner that has been identified as provided in section 6223(c)(3) and § 301.6223(c)-1 before the date on which the pass-thru partner becomes a member of the notice group.

(ii) *Indirect partners identified before the pass-thru partner joins a notice group.*—An indirect partner may become a member of a notice group with respect to a partnership taxable year only if—

(A) The indirect partner held an interest in the partnership (either directly or through one or more pass-thru partners) at some time during that taxable year; and

(B) The indirect partner was identified as provided in section 6223(c)(3) and § 301.6223(c)-1 on or before the date on which the pass-thru partner became a member of a notice group.

(d) *Termination of notice group.*—Unless the original request for notice from the notice group or a subsequent statement filed by the representative (in accordance with paragraphs (b)(3) and (4) of this section) designates a successor to the designated group representative, the group terminates if the representative dies (or, in the case of an entity, if the entity is dissolved), resigns, or is adjudicated incompetent.

(e) *Notice group is not a 5-percent group.*—The forming of a notice group under this section does not constitute the forming of a 5-percent group for purposes of litigation. A notice group is formed solely for the purpose of receiving notices. A 5-percent group is formed solely for the purpose of filing a petition for judicial review or appealing a judicial determination. See § 301.6226(b)-1. Thus, a member of a notice group may choose not to join a 5-percent group formed by other members of the notice group.

(f) *Effective date.*—This section is applicable to partnership taxable years beginning on or after October 4, 2001. For years beginning prior to October 4, 2001, see § 301.6223(b)-1T contained in 26 CFR part 1, revised April 1, 2001. [Reg. § 301.6223(b)-1.]

☐ [*T.D. 8965, 10-3-2001.*]

[Reg. § 301.6223(c)-1]

§ 301.6223(c)-1. Additional information regarding partners furnished to the Internal Revenue Service.—(a) *In general.*—In addition to the names, addresses, and profits interests as shown on the partnership return, the Internal Revenue Service will use additional information as provided in this section for purposes of administering subchapter C of chapter 63 of the Internal Revenue Code.

(b) *Procedure for furnishing additional information.*—(1) *In general.*—Any person may furnish additional information at any time by filing a written statement with the Internal Revenue Service. However, the information contained in the statement will be considered for purposes of determining whether a partner is entitled to a notice described in section 6223(a) only if the Internal Revenue Service receives the statement at least 30 days before the date on which the Internal Revenue Service mails the notice to the tax matters partner. Similarly, information contained in the statement generally will not be taken into account for other purposes by the Internal Revenue Service until 30 days after the statement is received.

(2) *Where statement must be filed.*—A statement furnished under this section generally must be filed with the service center where the partnership return is filed. However, if the person filing the statement knows that the notice described in section 6223(a)(1) (beginning of an administrative proceeding) has already been mailed to the tax matters partner, the statement should be filed with the Internal Revenue Service office that mailed such notice.

(3) *Contents of statement.*—The statement shall—

(i) Identify the partnership, each partner for whom information is supplied, and the person supplying the information by name, address, and taxpayer identification number;

(ii) Explain that the statement is furnished to correct or supplement earlier information with respect to the partners in the partnership;

(iii) Specify the taxable year to which the information relates;

(iv) Set out the corrected or additional information; and

(v) Be signed by the person supplying the information.

(c) *No incorporation by reference to previously furnished documents.*—Incorporation by reference of information contained in another document previously furnished to the Internal Revenue Service will not be given effect for purposes of section 6223(c) or 6229(e). For example, reference to a return filed by a pass-thru partner which contains identifying information with respect to the indirect partners of that pass-thru partner is not sufficient to identify the indirect partners unless a copy of the document referred to is attached to the statement. Furthermore, reference to a prior general notification to the Internal Revenue Service that a partner who would otherwise be the tax matters partner is a debtor in a bankruptcy proceeding or has had a receiver appointed for the partner in a receivership proceeding is not sufficient unless a copy of the notification document referred to is attached to the statement.

(d) *Information supplied by a person other than the tax matters partner.*—The Internal Revenue Service may require appropriate verification in the case of information furnished by a person other than the tax matters partner. The 30-day period referred to in paragraph (b)(1) of this section shall not begin until that verification is supplied.

(e) *Power of attorney.*—(1) *In general.*—This paragraph (e) applies to powers of attorney with respect to proceedings under subchapter C of chapter 63 of the Internal Revenue Code (chapter 63C) that begin on or after January 2, 2002.

(2) *Specifically for purposes of subchapter C of chapter 63 of the Internal Revenue Code.*—A power of attorney specifically for purposes of subchapter C of chapter 63 of the Internal Revenue Code shall be furnished in accordance with paragraph (b)(2) of this section.

(3) *Existing power of attorney.*—A power of attorney granted to another person by a partner for other tax purposes shall not be given effect for purposes of subchapter C of chapter 63 unless the partner specifically requests that the power be given such effect in a statement furnished to the Internal Revenue Service in accordance with paragraph (b) of this section.

(f) *Internal Revenue Service may use other information.*—In addition to the information on the partnership return and that supplied on statements filed under this section, the Internal Revenue Service may use other information in its possession (for example, a change in address reflected on a partner's return) in administering subchapter C of chapter 63 of the Internal Revenue Code. However, the Internal Revenue Service is not obligated to search its records for information not expressly furnished under this section.

(g) *Effective date.*—Except as provided in paragraph (e)(1) of this section, this section is applicable to partnership taxable years beginning on or after October 4, 2001. For years beginning prior to October 4, 2001, see § 301.6223(c)-1T contained in 26 CFR part 1, revised April 1, 2001. [Reg. § 301.6223(c)-1.]

□ [*T.D.* 8965, 10-3-2001.]

[Reg. § 301.6223(e)-1]

§ 301.6223(e)-1. Effect of Internal Revenue Service's failure to provide notice.—(a) *Notice group.*—Section 6223(e)(1)(B)(ii) applies with respect to a notice group only if the request for notice described in § 301.6223(b)-1 is received by the Internal Revenue Service at least 30 days before the notice is mailed to the tax matters partner.

(b) *Indirect partners.*—(1) *In general.*—For purposes of section 6223(e), the Internal Revenue Service's failure to provide notice to a pass-thru partner entitled to notice under section 6223(b) is deemed a failure to provide notice to indirect partners holding an interest in the partnership through the pass-thru partner. However, this rule does not apply if the indirect partner—

(i) Receives notice from the Internal Revenue Service;

(ii) Is identified as provided in section 6223(c)(3) and § 301.6223(c)-1 at least 30 days before the notice is mailed to the tax matters partner; or

(iii) Is a member of a notice group entitled to notice under paragraph (a) of this section.

(2) *Examples.*—The provisions of paragraph (b)(1) of this section may be illustrated by the following examples:

Example 1. Partnership ABC has as one of its partners, A, a partnership with three partners, X, Y, and Z. ABC does not have more than 100 partners, and partnership A is entitled to notice under section 6223(a). In addition, Z was identified as provided in section 6223(c)(3) and § 301.6223(c)-1 on May 1, 2002. The Internal Revenue Service mailed a notice to the tax matters partner of ABC on July 1, 2002, but failed to provide notice to partnership A. Notwithstanding the Internal Revenue Service's notice to the tax matters partner, the Internal Revenue Service is deemed to have failed to provide notice to X and Y. The Internal Revenue Service's failure to provide notice to A, however, has no effect on Z; whether notice was provided to Z is determined independently.

Example 2. Assume the same facts as in *Example 1,* except that the Internal Revenue Service provided notice to partnership A but did not provide separate notice to Z. Notwithstanding the Internal Revenue Service's notice to partnership A, the Internal Revenue Service is deemed to have failed to provide notice to Z.

Example 3. Assume the same facts as in *Example 1,* except that partnership ABC has more than 100 partners and partnership A is entitled to notice under section 6223(b) because it had at least a 1 percent profits interest in partnership ABC. In addition, X became a member of a notice group on June 1, 2002, and the Internal Revenue Service mailed a notice to the designated member of that notice group. The Internal Revenue Service also mailed a separate notice to Z. The Internal Revenue Service's failure to provide notice to partnership A only affects Y, who is deemed not to have been provided notice by the Internal Revenue Service.

(c) *Effective date.*—This section is applicable to partnership taxable years beginning on or after October 4, 2001. For years beginning prior to October 4, 2001, see § 301.6223(e)-1T contained in 26 CFR part 1, revised April 1, 2001. [Reg. § 301.6223(e)-1.]

□ [*T.D.* 8965, 10-3-2001.]

[Reg. § 301.6223(e)-2]

§ 301.6223(e)-2. Elections if Internal Revenue Service fails to provide timely notice.—(a) *In general.*—This section applies in any case in which the Internal Revenue Service fails to timely mail any notice described in section 6223(a) of the Internal Revenue Code to a partner entitled to such notice within the period specified in section 6223(d). The failure to issue any notice within the period specified in section 6223(d) does not invalidate the notice of the beginning of an administrative proceeding or final partnership administrative adjustment (FPAA). An untimely FPAA enables the recipient of the untimely notice to make the elections described in paragraphs (b), (c), and (d) of this section. The period within which to make the elections described in paragraphs (b), (c), and (d) of this section commences with the mailing of an FPAA to the partner. In the absence of an election, paragraphs (b) and (c) of this section provide for the treatment of a partner's partnership items.

(b) *Proceeding finished.*—If at the time the Internal Revenue Service mails the partner an FPAA—

(1) The period within which a petition for review of the FPAA under section 6226 may be filed has expired and no petition has been filed; or

(2) The decision of a court in an action begun by such a petition has become final, the partner may elect in accordance with paragraph (d) of this section to have that adjustment, that decision, or a settlement agreement described in section 6224(c)(2) with respect to the partnership taxable year to which the adjustment relates apply to that partner. If the partner does not make an election in accordance with paragraph (d) of this section, the partnership items of the partner for the partnership taxable year to which the proceeding relates shall be treated as having become nonpartnership items as of the day on which the Internal Revenue Service mails the partner the FPAA.

(c) *Proceeding still going on.*—If at the time the Internal Revenue Service mails the partner an FPAA, paragraphs (b)(1) and (2) of this section do not apply, the partner shall be a party to the proceeding unless the partner elects, in accordance with paragraph (d) of this section, to have—

(1) A settlement agreement described in section 6224(c)(2) with respect to the partnership taxable year to which the proceeding relates apply to the partner; or

(2) The partnership items of the partner for the partnership taxable year to which the proceeding relates treated as having become nonpartnership items as of the day on which the Internal Revenue Service mails the partner the FPAA.

(d) *Election.*—(1) *In general.*—The election described in paragraph (b) or (c) of this section shall be made in the manner prescribed in this paragraph (d). The election shall apply to all partnership items for the partnership taxable year to which the election relates.

(2) *Time and manner of making election.*—The election shall be made by filing a statement with the Internal Revenue Service office mailing the FPAA within 45 days after the date on which the FPAA was mailed to the partner making the election.

(3) *Contents of statement.*—The statement shall—

(i) Be clearly identified as an election under section 6223(e)(2) or (3);

(ii) Specify the election being made (that is, application of final partnership administrative adjustment, court decision, consistent settlement agreement, or nonpartnership item treatment);

(iii) Identify the partner making the election and the partnership by name, address, and taxpayer identification number;

(iv) Specify the partnership taxable year to which the election relates; and

(v) Be signed by the partner making the election.

(e) *Effective date.*—This section is applicable to partnership taxable years beginning on or after October 4, 2001. For years beginning prior to October 4, 2001, see § 301.6223(e)-2T contained in 26 CFR part 1, revised April 1, 2001. [Reg. § 301.6223(e)-2.]

☐ [*T.D.* 8965, 10-3-2001.]

[Reg. § 301.6223(f)-1]

§ 301.6223(f)-1. Duplicate copy of final partnership administrative adjustment.—(a) *In general.*—Section 6223(f) does not prohibit the Internal Revenue Service from issuing a duplicate copy of the notice of final partnership administrative adjustment (for example, in the event the original notice is lost).

(b) *Effective date.*—This section is applicable to partnership taxable years beginning on or after October 4, 2001. For years beginning prior to October 4, 2001, see § 301.6223(f)-1T contained in 26 CFR part 1, revised April 1, 2001. [Reg. § 301.6223(f)-1.]

☐ [*T.D.* 8965, 10-3-2001.]

[Reg. § 301.6223(g)-1]

§ 301.6223(g)-1. Responsibilities of the tax matters partner.—(a) *Notices described in section 6223(a).*—(1) *Notice of beginning of proceeding.*—Except as otherwise provided in § 301.6223(a)-2, the tax matters partner shall, within 75 days after the Internal Revenue Service mails the notice specified in section 6223(a)(1), forward a copy of that notice to each partner not entitled to notice from the Internal Revenue Service under section 6223. See § 301.6230(e)-1 for information to be furnished to the Internal Revenue Service.

(2) *Notice of final partnership administrative adjustment.*—The tax matters partner shall, within 60 days after the Internal Revenue Service mails the notice specified in section 6223(a)(2), forward a copy of that notice to each partner not entitled to notice from the Internal Revenue Service under section 6223.

(3) *Requirement inapplicable in certain cases.*— The tax matters partner is not required to send notice to a partner if—

(i) Before the expiration of the applicable 75-day or 60-day period the partnership items of that partner have become nonpartnership items (for example, by settlement);

(ii) That partner is an indirect partner and has not been identified to the tax matters partner at least 30 days before the tax matters partner is required to send such notice;

(iii) That partner is treated as a partner solely by virtue of §301.6231(a)(2)-1;

(iv) That partner was a member of a notice group as of the date on which the notice was mailed to the tax matters partner (see §301.6223(b)-1(c)(4) for the date on which a partner becomes a member of a notice group);

(v) The notice has already been provided to that partner by another person; or

(vi) The notice is withdrawn by the Internal Revenue Service under §301.6223(a)-2.

(b) *Other notices or information.*—(1) *In general.*—The tax matters partner shall furnish to the partners specified in paragraph (b)(2) of this section information with respect to the following—

(i) Closing conference with the examining agent;

(ii) Proposed adjustments, rights of appeal, and requirements for filing of a protest;

(iii) Time and place of any Appeals conference;

(iv) Acceptance by the Internal Revenue Service of any settlement offer;

(v) Consent to the extension of the period of limitations with respect to all partners;

(vi) Filing of a request for administrative adjustment (including a request for substituted return treatment under §301.6227(c)-1) on behalf of the partnership;

(vii) Filing by the tax matters partner or any other partner of any petition for judicial review under sections 6226 or 6228(a);

(viii) Filing of any appeal with respect to any judicial determination provided for in sections 6226 or 6228(a); and

(ix) Final judicial redetermination.

(2) *Partners to be notified.*—The tax matters partner shall provide information with respect to any action or other matter specified in paragraph (b)(1) of this section to all notice group representatives and all other partners except partners—

(i) Whose partnership items become nonpartnership items before the expiration of the period specified in paragraph (b)(3) of this section for furnishing that information;

(ii) Who are indirect partners and who are not identified to the tax matters partner at least 30 days before the tax matters partner is required to provide the information;

(iii) Who are treated as partners solely by virtue of §301.6231(a)(2)-1;

(iv) Who are members of a notice group as of the date on which the tax matters partner takes that action or receives information with respect to that matter (see §301.6223(b)-1(c)(4) for the date on which a partner becomes a member of a notice group); or

(v) Who have already received information with respect to the action or matter from any other person.

(3) *Time for furnishing information.*—The tax matters partner shall furnish information with respect to an action or other matter described in paragraph (b)(1) of this section within 30 days of taking the action or receiving information with respect to that matter.

(c) *Effective date.*—This section is applicable to partnership taxable years beginning on or after October 4, 2001. For years beginning prior to October 4, 2001, see §301.6223(g)-1T contained in 26 CFR part 1, revised April 1, 2001. [Reg. §301.6223(g)-1.]

☐ [*T.D.* 8965, 10-3-2001.]

[Reg. §301.6223(h)-1]

§301.6223(h)-1. Responsibilities of pass-thru partner.—(a) *In general.*—The pass-thru partner shall, within 30 days of receiving notice or any other information regarding a partnership proceeding from the Internal Revenue Service, the tax matters partner, or another pass-thru partner, forward a copy of that notice or information to the person or persons holding an interest through the pass-thru partner in the profits or losses of the partnership for the partnership taxable year to which the notice or information relates. In the case of a pass-thru partner that is a partnership within the meaning of section 6231(a)(1), the tax matters partner of such partnership shall forward copies of the notice or information to the partners of such partnership.

(b) *Effective date.*—This section is applicable to partnership taxable years beginning on or after October 4, 2001. For years beginning prior to October 4, 2001, see §301.6223(h)-1T contained in 26 CFR part 1, revised April 1, 2001. [Reg. §301.6223(h)-1.]

☐ [*T.D.* 8965, 10-3-2001.]

[Reg. §301.6224(a)-1]

§301.6224(a)-1. Participation in administrative proceedings.—(a) *In general.*—Every partner in the partnership, including an indirect partner, has the right to participate in any phase of administrative proceedings. However, except as provided in section 6223 and the regulations thereunder, neither the Internal Revenue Service nor the tax matters partner is required to provide notice of any proceeding to the partners. Consequently, a partner who wishes, for example, to be present during a preliminary discussion between an examining agent and the tax matters partner should make special arrangements with the tax matters partner to obtain information as to the time and place of the discussion. The Internal Revenue Service and the tax matters partner will determine the time and place for all administrative proceedings. Arrangements will

Reg. §301.6224(a)-1(a)

generally not be changed merely for the convenience of another partner.

(b) *Effective date.*—This section is applicable to partnership taxable years beginning on or after October 4, 2001. For years beginning prior to October 4, 2001, see § 301.6224(a)-1T contained in 26 CFR part 1, revised April 1, 2001. [Reg. § 301.6224(a)-1.]

☐ [T.D. 8965, 10-3-2001.]

[Reg. § 301.6224(b)-1]

§ 301.6224(b)-1. Partner may waive rights.—(a) *In general.*—A partner may at any time waive any right that the partner has or any restriction on action by the Internal Revenue Service under subchapter C of chapter 63 of the Internal Revenue Code.

(b) *Form and manner of making waiver.*—The waiver described in paragraph (a) of this section shall be made by a written statement. If the Internal Revenue Service furnishes a form to be used for this purpose, the partner may make the waiver by completing the form in accordance with the form's instructions. If such a form is not furnished, the statement shall—

(1) Be clearly identified as a waiver under section 6224(b);

(2) Identify the partner and the partnership by name, address, and taxpayer identification number;

(3) Specify the right or restriction being waived and the taxable year(s) to which the waiver applies;

(4) Be signed by the partner making the waiver; and

(5) Be filed with the service center where the partnership return is filed. However, if the person filing the statement knows that the notice described in section 6223(a)(1) (beginning of an administrative proceeding) has already been mailed to the tax matters partner, the statement shall be filed with the Internal Revenue Service office that mailed such notice.

(c) *Effective date.*—This section is applicable to partnership taxable years beginning on or after October 4, 2001. For years beginning prior to October 4, 2001, see § 301.6224(b)-1T contained in 26 CFR part 1, revised April 1, 2001. [Reg. § 301.6224(b)-1.]

☐ [T.D. 8965, 10-3-2001.]

[Reg. § 301.6224(c)-1]

§ 301.6224(c)-1. Tax matters partner may bind nonnotice partners.—(a) *In general.*—In the absence of a showing of fraud, malfeasance, or misrepresentation of fact, if the tax matters partner enters into a settlement agreement with the Internal Revenue Service with respect to partnership items, including partnership-level determinations relating to any penalty, addition to tax, or additional amounts that relate to adjustments to partnership items, and expressly states that the agreement shall be binding on the other part-

ners, then that agreement shall be binding on all partners except those who—

(1) Are, as of the day on which the agreement is entered into, either notice partners or members of a notice group (see § 301.6223(b)-1(c)(4) for the date on which a partner becomes a member of a notice group); or

(2) Have, at least 30 days before the day on which the agreement is entered into, filed with the Internal Revenue Service the statement described in paragraph (c) of this section.

(b) *Indirect partners.*—(1) *In general.*—If, under paragraph (a) of this section, a pass-thru partner is not bound by an agreement entered into by the tax matters partner, all indirect partners holding an interest in the partnership through that pass-thru partner shall not be bound by that agreement. If, however, the pass-thru partner is bound by an agreement entered into by the tax matters partner, paragraph (a) of this section shall be applied separately to each indirect partner holding an interest in the partnership through the pass-thru partner to determine whether the indirect partner is also bound by the agreement.

(2) *Example.*—The following example illustrates the principles of this section:

Example. Partnership P has over 100 partners. Partnership J is a partner in partnership P with a profits interest of less than 1 percent. Partnership J has three partners, A, B, and C. A is a member of a notice group with respect to partnership P, but B and C are not. On July 1, 2002, B filed the statement described in paragraph (c) of this section not to be bound by any settlement agreement entered into by the tax matters partner of partnership P. On August 1, 2002, the tax matters partner of partnership P enters into a settlement agreement with the Internal Revenue Service and states that the agreement is binding on other partners as provided in section 6224(c)(3). Because partnership J is bound by the settlement agreement, paragraph (a) of this section is applied separately to each of the indirect partners to determine whether they are bound. A is not bound by the agreement because A was a member of a notice group on the day the agreement was entered into and B is not bound because B filed the statement not to be bound at least 30 days before the agreement was entered into. C is bound by the settlement agreement.

(c) *Statement not to be bound.*—(1) *Contents of statement.*—The statement referred to in paragraph (a)(2) of this section shall—

(i) Be clearly identified as a statement to deny settlement authority to the tax matters partner under section 6224(c)(3)(B);

(ii) Identify the partner and partnership by name, address, and taxpayer identification number;

(iii) Specify the taxable year or years to which the statement applies; and

(iv) Be signed by the partner filing the statement.

(2) *Place where statement is to be filed.*—The statement described in paragraph (c)(1) of this section generally shall be filed with the Internal Revenue Service service center where the partnership return is filed. However, if the partner knows that the notice described in section 6223(a)(1) (beginning of an administrative proceeding) has already been mailed to the tax matters partner, the statement shall be filed with the Internal Revenue Service office that mailed that notice.

(3) *Consolidated statements.*—The statement described in paragraph (c)(1) of this section may be filed with respect to more than one partner if the requirements of that paragraph (c)(1) (including signatures) are satisfied with respect to each partner.

(d) *Effective date.*—This section is applicable to partnership taxable years beginning on or after October 4, 2001. For years beginning prior to October 4, 2001, see § 301.6224(c)-1T contained in 26 CFR part 1, revised April 1, 2001. [Reg. § 301.6224(c)-1.]

☐ [*T.D.* 8965, 10-3-2001.]

[Reg. § 301.6224(c)-2]

§ 301.6224(c)-2. Pass-thru partner binds indirect partners.—(a) *Pass-thru partner binds unidentified indirect partners.*—(1) *In general.*—If a pass-thru partner enters into a settlement agreement with the Internal Revenue Service with respect to partnership items, that agreement binds all indirect partners holding an interest in that partnership through the pass-thru partner except those indirect partners who have been identified as provided in section 6223(c)(3) and § 301.6223(c)-1 at least 30 days before the date on which the agreement is entered into. A settlement with respect to partnership items includes partnership-level determinations relating to any penalty, addition to tax, and additional amounts that relate to adjustments to partnership items. However, if, in addition to the interest in the partnership held through the pass-thru partner entering into a settlement agreement, an indirect partner holds a separate interest in that partnership, either directly or indirectly through a different pass-thru partner, then the indirect partner shall not be bound by that settlement agreement with respect to the interests held directly or indirectly through a pass-thru partner other than the pass-thru partner entering into the settlement agreement.

(2) *Example.*—The provisions of paragraph (a)(1) of this section may be illustrated by the following example:

Example. Partnership J is a partner in partnership P. C is a partner in J but has not been identified as provided in section 6223(c)(3) and § 301,6223(c)-1. The only interest that C holds in P is through J. The tax matters partner of J enters into a settlement agreement with the Internal Revenue Service with respect to partnership items arising from P. C is bound by the settle-

ment agreement entered into by the tax matters partner of J.

(b) *Person in pass-thru partner authorized to enter into settlement agreement that binds indirect partners.*—In the case of a pass-thru partner that is—

(1) A partnership within the meaning of section 6231(a)(1), the tax matters partner of that partnership;

(2) A partnership other than a partnership described in paragraph (b)(1) of this section, any general partner of that partnership;

(3) An S corporation, any officer of that S corporation; or

(4) A trust, estate, or nominee, any person authorized in writing to act on behalf of that trust, estate, or nominee, may enter into a settlement agreement with the Internal Revenue Service on behalf of its respective entity that would bind the unidentified indirect partners that hold a partnership interest through the pass-thru partner.

(c) *Effective date.*—This section is applicable to partnership taxable years beginning on or after October 4, 2001. For years beginning prior to October 4, 2001, see § 301.6224(c)-2T contained in 26 CFR part 1, revised April 1, 2001. [Reg. § 301.6224(c)-2.]

☐ [*T.D.* 8965, 10-3-2001.]

[Reg. § 301.6224(c)-3]

§ 301.6224(c)-3. Consistent settlements.—(a) *In general.*—If the Internal Revenue Service enters into a settlement agreement with any partner with respect to partnership items, whether comprehensive or partial, the Internal Revenue Service shall offer to any other partner who so requests in accordance with paragraph (c) of this section, settlement terms consistent with those contained in the settlement agreement entered into.

(b) *Requirements for consistent settlement terms.*—(1) *In general.*—Consistent settlement terms are those based on the same determinations with respect to partnership items. However, consistent settlement terms also may include partnership-level determinations of any penalty, addition to tax, or additional amount that relates to partnership items. Settlements with respect to partnership items shall be self-contained; thus, a concession by one party with respect to a partnership item may not be based upon a concession by another party with respect to any item that is not a partnership item other than a partnership-level determination of any penalty, addition to tax, or additional amount that relates to an adjustment to a partnership item. Consistent agreements must be identical to the original settlement (that is, the settlement upon which the offered settlement terms are based). A consistent agreement must mirror the original settlement and may not be limited to selected items from the original settlement. Once a partner has settled a partnership item, or a partnership-level determination of any penalty, addition to tax, or additional amount that relates to an adjustment to a partnership item, that partner may not subsequently request settlement terms consistent with a settlement that contains the previously settled item. The requirement for consistent settlement terms applies only if—

(i) The items were partnership items (or a partnership-level determination of any related penalty, addition to tax, or additional amount) for the partner entering into the original settlement immediately before the original settlement; and

(ii) The items are partnership items (or a partnership-level determination of any related penalty, addition to tax, or additional amount) for the partner requesting the consistent settlement at the time the partner files the request.

(2) *Effect of consistent agreement.*—Consistent settlement terms are reflected in a consistent agreement. A consistent agreement is not a settlement agreement that gives rise to further consistent settlement rights because it is required to be given without volitional agreement of the Secretary. Therefore, a consistent agreement required to be offered to a requesting taxpayer is not a settlement agreement under section 6224(c)(2) or paragraph (c)(3) of this section which starts a new period for requesting consistent settlement terms. For all other purposes of the Internal Revenue Code, however, (e.g., binding effect under section 6224(c)(1) and conversion to nonpartnership items under section 6231(b)(1)(C)), a consistent agreement is treated as a settlement agreement.

(c) *Time and manner of requesting consistent settlements.*—(1) *In general.*—A partner desiring settlement terms consistent with the terms of any settlement agreement entered into between any other partner and the Internal Revenue Service shall submit a written statement to the Internal Revenue Service office that entered into the settlement.

(2) *Contents of statement.*—Except as otherwise provided in instructions to the taxpayer from the Internal Revenue Service, the written statement described in paragraph (c)(1) of this section shall—

(i) Identify the statement as a request for consistent settlement terms under section 6224(c)(2);

(ii) Contain the name, address, and taxpayer identification number of the partnership and of the partner requesting the settlement offer (and, in the case of an indirect partner, of the pass-thru partner through which the indirect partner holds an interest);

(iii) Identify the earlier agreement to which the request refers; and

(iv) Be signed by the partner making the request.

(3) *Time for filing request.*—The statement shall be filed not later than the later of—

(i) The 150th day after the day on which the notice of final partnership administrative adjustment is mailed to the tax matters partner; or

(ii) The 60th day after the day on which the settlement agreement was entered into.

(d) *Examples.*—The following examples illustrate the principles of this section:

Example 1. The Internal Revenue Service seeks to disallow a $100,000 loss reported by Partnership P $20,000 of which was allocated to partner X, and $10,000 of which was allocated to partner Y. The Internal Revenue Service agrees to a settlement with X in which the Internal Revenue Service allows $12,000 of the loss, accepts the treatment of all other partnership items on the partnership return, and imposes a penalty for negligence related to the $8,000 loss disallowance. Partner Y requests settlement terms consistent with the settlement made between X and the Internal Revenue Service. The items are partnership items (or a related penalty) for X immediately before X enters into the settlement agreement and are partnership items (or a related penalty) for Y at the time of the request. The Internal Revenue Service must offer Y settlement terms allowing a $6,000 loss, a negligence penalty on the $4,000 disallowance, and otherwise reflecting the treatment of partnership items on the partnership return.

Example 2. F files inconsistently with Partnership P and reports the inconsistency. The Internal Revenue Service notifies F that it will treat all partnership items arising from P as nonpartnership items with respect to F. Later, the Internal Revenue Service enters into a settlement with F on these items. The Internal Revenue Service is not required to offer the other partners of P settlement terms consistent with the settlement reached between F and the Internal Revenue Service because the items arising from P are not partnership items with respect to F.

Example 3. G, a partner in Partnership P, filed suit under section 6228(b) after the Internal Revenue Service failed to allow an administrative adjustment request with respect to a partnership item arising from P for a taxable year. Under section 6231(b)(1)(B), the partnership items of G for the partnership taxable year became nonpartnership items as of the date G filed suit. After G filed suit, another partner and the Internal Revenue Service entered into a settlement agreement with respect to items arising from P in that year. G is not entitled to consistent settlement terms because, at the time of the settlement, the items arising from P are no longer partnership items with respect to G.

(e) *Effective date.*—This section is applicable to partnership taxable years beginning on or after October 4, 2001. For years beginning prior to October 4, 2001, see § 301.6224(c)-3T contained in 26 CFR part 1, revised April 1, 2001. [Reg. § 301.6224(c)-3.]

☐ [T.D. 8965, 10-3-2001.]

[Reg. § 301.6226(a)-1]

§ 301.6226(a)-1. Principal place of business of partnership.—(a) *In general.*—The principal place of a partnership's business for purposes of determining the appropriate district court in which a petition for a readjustment of partnership items may be filed is its principal place of business as of the date the petition is filed.

(b) *Example.*—The provisions of paragraph (a) of this section may be illustrated by the following example:

Example. The principal place of Partnership A's business on the day that the notice of the final partnership administrative adjustment was mailed to A's tax matters partner was Cincinnati, Ohio. However, by the day on which a petition seeking judicial review of that adjustment was filed, A had moved its principal place of business to Louisville, Kentucky. For purposes of section 6226(a)(2), A's principal place of business is Louisville.

(c) *Effective date.*—This section is applicable to partnership taxable years beginning on or after October 4, 2001. For years beginning prior to October 4, 2001, see § 301.6226(a)-1T contained in 26 CFR part 1, revised April 1, 2001. [Reg. § 301.6226(a)-1.]

☐ *[T.D. 8965, 10-3-2001.]*

[Reg. § 301.6226(b)-1]

§ 301.6226(b)-1. 5-percent group.—(a) *In general.*—All members of a 5-percent group shall join in filing any petition for judicial review. The designation of a partner as a representative of a notice group does not authorize that partner to file a petition for a readjustment of partnership items on behalf of the notice group.

(b) *Effective date.*—This section is applicable to partnership taxable years beginning on or after October 4, 2001. For years beginning prior to October 4, 2001, see § 301.6226(b)-1T contained in 26 CFR part 1, revised April 1, 2001. [Reg. § 301.6226(b)-1.]

☐ *[T.D. 8965, 10-3-2001.]*

[Reg. § 301.6226(e)-1]

§ 301.6226(e)-1. Jurisdictional requirement for bringing an action in District Court or United States Court of Federal Claims.—(a) *Amount to be deposited.*—(1) *In general.*—The jurisdictional amount that the filing partner (or, in the case of a petition filed by a 5-percent group, each member of the group, or, for civil actions beginning on or after April 2, 2002, in the case of a petition filed by a pass-thru partner, each indirect partner holding an interest through the pass-thru partner) shall deposit is the amount by which the tax liability of the partner would be increased if the treatment of the partnership items on the partner's return were made consistent with the treatment of partnership items on the partnership return, as adjusted by the notice of final partnership administrative adjustment. The partner is not required to pay

other outstanding liabilities in order to deposit a jurisdictional amount.

(2) *Example.*—The provisions of paragraph (a)(1) of this section may be illustrated by the following example:

Example. A files a petition for readjustment of partnership items in the United States Court of Federal Claims. A's tax liability would be increased by $4,000 if partnership items on A's return were conformed to the partnership return, as adjusted by the notice of final partnership administrative adjustment. A has an unpaid liability of $10,000 attributable to nonpartnership items. A is required to deposit $4,000 in order to satisfy the jurisdictional requirement.

(b) *Deposit taken into account in computing interest.*—The amount deposited is treated as a payment of tax for purposes of chapter 67 of the Internal Revenue Code (relating to interest).

(c) *Deposit generally not treated as payment of tax.*—Except as provided in paragraph (b) of this section, an amount deposited under section 6226(e) shall not be treated as a payment of tax. Thus, the Internal Revenue Service may proceed against the depositor for a deficiency based on nonpartnership items without regard to this deposit.

(d) *Amount deposited may be applied against assessment.*—If the restriction on assessment provided under section 6225(a) lapses with respect to a deficiency attributable to partnership items for a partnership taxable year while an amount is on deposit under section 6226(e) in connection with a petition relating to those items, the Internal Revenue Service may apply the amount deposited against any such deficiency that is assessed.

(e) *Effective date.*—Except as otherwise provided in paragraph (a)(1) of this section, this section is applicable to civil actions beginning on or after October 4, 2001. For civil actions beginning prior to October 4, 2001, see § 301.6226(e)-1T contained in 26 CFR part 1, revised April 1, 2001. [Reg. § 301.6226(e)-1.]

☐ *[T.D. 8965, 10-3-2001.]*

[Reg. § 301.6226(f)-1]

§ 301.6226(f)-1. Scope of judicial review.—(a) *In general.*—A court reviewing a notice of final partnership administrative adjustment has jurisdiction to determine all partnership items for the taxable year to which the notice relates and the proper allocation of such items among the partners. Thus, the review is not limited to the items adjusted in the notice. In addition, the court has jurisdiction in the partnership-level proceeding to determine any penalty, addition to tax, or additional amount that relates to an adjustment to a partnership item. However, the court does not have jurisdiction in the partnership-level proceeding to consider any partner-level defenses to any penalty, addition to tax, or additional amount that relates to an adjustment to a partnership item. See section 6230(c)(4) and § 301.6221-1(c) and (d).

(b) *Example.*—The provisions of paragraph (a) of this section may be illustrated by the following example:

Example. The Internal Revenue Service issues a notice of final partnership administrative adjustment with respect to Partnership ABC in which the only item adjusted is depreciation. A petition for judicial review of that notice is filed. During the judicial proceeding, a partner of ABC, in accordance with the applicable court rules, raises an issue relating to the treatment of intangible drilling costs. The court reviewing the notice has jurisdiction to determine the intangible drilling cost issue in addition to the depreciation issue.

(c) *Effective date.*—This section is applicable to partnership taxable years beginning on or after October 4, 2001. For years beginning prior to October 4, 2001, see § 301.6226(f)-1T contained in 26 CFR part 1, revised April 1, 2001. [Reg. § 301.6226(f)-1.]

☐ [*T.D.* 8965, 10-3-2001.]

[Reg. § 301.6227(c)-1]

§ 301.6227(c)-1. Administrative adjustment request by the tax matters partner on behalf of the partnership.—(a) *In general.*—A request for an administrative adjustment filed by the tax matters partner on behalf of the partnership shall be filed on the form prescribed by the Internal Revenue Service for that purpose in accordance with that form's instructions. Except as otherwise provided in that form's instructions, the request shall be—

(1) Filed with the service center where the original partnership return was filed (but, if the notice described in section 6223(a)(1) (beginning of an administrative proceeding) has already been mailed to the tax matters partner, the statement should be filed with the Internal Revenue Service office that mailed such notice);

(2) Signed by the tax matters partner; and

(3) Accompanied by revised schedules showing the effects of the proposed changes on each partner and an explanation of the changes.

(b) *Denied request for treatment as a substituted return remains administrative adjustment request.*—An administrative adjustment request filed by the tax matters partner on behalf of the partnership for which substituted return treatment is requested but not granted remains an administrative adjustment request. Thus, for example, the tax matters partner may file suit under section 6228(a) if the Internal Revenue Service fails to take timely action on the request.

(c) *Effective date.*—This section is applicable to partnership taxable years beginning on or after October 4, 2001. For years beginning prior to October 4, 2001, see § 301.6227(b)-1T contained in 26 CFR part 1, revised April 1, 2001. [Reg. § 301.6227(c)-1.]

☐ [*T.D.* 8965, 10-3-2001.]

[Reg. § 301.6227(d)-1]

§ 301.6227(d)-1. Administrative adjustment request filed on behalf of a partner.—(a) *In general.*—A request for an administrative adjustment on behalf of a partner shall be filed on the form prescribed by the Internal Revenue Service for that purpose in accordance with that form's instructions. Except as otherwise provided in that form's instructions, the request shall—

(1) Be filed in duplicate, the original copy filed with the partner's amended income tax return (on which the partner computes the amount by which the partner's tax liability should be adjusted if the request is granted) and the other copy filed with the service center where the partnership return is filed (but, if the notice described in section 6223(a)(1) (beginning of an administrative proceeding) has already been mailed to the tax matters partner, the statement should be filed with the Internal Revenue Service office that mailed such notice);

(2) Identify the partner and the partnership by name, address, and taxpayer identification number;

(3) Specify the partnership taxable year to which the administrative adjustment request applies;

(4) Relate only to partnership items; and

(5) Relate only to one partnership and one partnership taxable year.

(b) *Effective date.*—This section is applicable to partnership taxable years beginning on or after October 4, 2001. For years beginning prior to October 4, 2001, see § 301.6227(c)-1T contained in 26 CFR part 1, revised April 1, 2001. [Reg. § 301.6227(d)-1.]

☐ [*T.D.* 8965, 10-3-2001.]

[Reg. § 301.6229(b)-1]

§ 301.6229(b)-1. Extension by agreement.—(a) *In general.*—Any partnership may authorize any person to extend the period described in section 6229(a) with respect to all partners by filing a statement to that effect with the service center where the partnership return is filed (but, if the notice described in section 6223(a)(1) (beginning of an administrative proceeding) has already been mailed to the tax matters partner, the statement should be filed with the Internal Revenue Service office that mailed such notice). The statement shall—

(1) Provide that it is an authorization for a person other than the tax matters partner to extend the assessment period with respect to all partners;

(2) Identify the partnership and the person being authorized by name, address, and taxpayer identification number;

(3) Specify the partnership taxable year or years for which the authorization is effective; and

(4) Be signed by all persons who were general partners (or, in the case of an LLC, member-managers, as those terms are defined in

§ 301.623(a)(7)-2(b)) at any time during the year or years for which the authorization is effective.

(b) *Effective date.*—This section is applicable to partnership taxable years beginning on or after October 4, 2001. For years beginning prior to October 4, 2001, see § 301.6229(b)-1T contained in 26 CFR part 1, revised April 1, 2001. [Reg. § 301.6229(b)-1.]

☐ [*T.D.* 8965, 10-3-2001.]

[Reg. § 301.6229(b)-2]

§ 301.6229(b)-2. Special rule with respect to debtors in Title 11 cases.—(a) *In general.*—Notwithstanding any other law or rule of law, if an agreement is entered into under section 6229(b)(1)(B), and the agreement is signed by a person who would be the tax matters partner but for the fact that, at the time that the agreement is executed, the person is a debtor in a bankruptcy proceeding under Title 11 of the United States Code, such agreement shall be binding on all partners in the partnership unless the Internal Revenue Service has been notified of the bankruptcy proceeding in accordance with paragraph (b) of this section.

(b) *Procedures for notifying the Internal Revenue Service of a partner's bankruptcy proceeding.*— (1) The Internal Revenue Service shall be notified of the bankruptcy proceeding of the tax matters partner in accordance with the procedures set forth in § 301.6223(c)-1.

(2) In addition to the information specified in § 301.6223(c)-1, notification that a person is (or was) a debtor in a bankruptcy proceeding shall include the date the bankruptcy proceeding was filed, the name and address of the court in which the bankruptcy proceeding exists (or took place), the caption of the bankruptcy proceeding (including the docket number or other identification number used by the court), and the status of the proceeding as of the date of notification.

(c) *Effective date.*—This section is applicable to partnership taxable years beginning on or after October 4, 2001. For years beginning prior to October 4, 2001, see § 301.6229(b)-2T contained in 26 CFR part 1, revised April 1, 2001. [Reg. § 301.6229(b)-2.]

☐ [*T.D.* 8965, 10-3-2001.]

[Reg. § 301.6229(c)(2)-1]

§ 301.6229(c)(2)-1. Substantial omission of income.—(a) *Partnership return.*—(1) *General rule.*—(i) If any partnership omits from the gross income stated in its return an amount properly includible therein and that amount is described in clause (i) of section 6501(e)(1)(A), subsection (a) of section 6229 shall be applied by substituting "6 years" for "3 years."

(ii) For purposes of paragraph (a)(1)(i) of this section, the term *gross income*, as it relates to a trade or business, means the total of the amounts received or accrued from the sale of goods or services, to the extent required to be shown on the return, without reduction for the cost of those goods or services.

(iii) For purposes of paragraph (a)(1)(i) of this section, the term *gross income*, as it relates to any income other than from the sale of goods or services in a trade or business, has the same meaning as provided under section 61(a), and includes the total of the amounts received or accrued, to the extent required to be shown on the return. In the case of amounts received or accrued that relate to the disposition of property, and except as provided in paragraph (a)(1)(ii) of this section, gross income means the excess of the amount realized from the disposition of the property over the unrecovered cost or other basis of the property. Consequently, except as provided in paragraph (a)(1)(ii) of this section, an understated amount of gross income resulting from an overstatement of unrecovered cost or other basis constitutes an omission from gross income for purposes of section 6229(c)(2).

(iv) An amount shall not be considered as omitted from gross income if information sufficient to apprise the Commissioner of the nature and amount of the item is disclosed in the return, including any schedule or statement attached to the return.

(b) *Effective/applicability date.*—This section applies to taxable years with respect to which the period for assessing tax was open on or after September 24, 2009. [Reg. § 301.6229(c)(2)-1.]

☐ [*T.D.* 9511, 12-14-2010.]

[Reg. § 301.6229(e)-1]

§ 301.6229(e)-1. Information with respect to unidentified partner.—(a) *In general.*—A partner who is not properly identified on the partnership return (including an indirect partner) remains an unidentified partner for purposes of section 6229(e) until identifying information is furnished as provided in § 301.6223(c)-1.

(b) *Effective date.*—This section is applicable to partnership taxable years beginning on or after October 4, 2001. For years beginning prior to October 4, 2001, see § 301.6229(e)-1T contained in 26 CFR part 1, revised April 1, 2001. [Reg. § 301.6229(e)-1.]

☐ [*T.D.* 8965, 10-3-2001.]

[Reg. § 301.6229(f)-1]

§ 301.6229(f)-1. Special rule for partial settlement agreements.—(a) *In general.*—If a partner enters into a settlement agreement with the Internal Revenue Service with respect to the treatment of some of the partnership items or partnership-level determinations of any penalty, addition to tax, or additional amount in dispute for a partnership taxable year, but one or more other partnership items or determinations remain in dispute, the period of limitations for assessing any tax attributable to the settled items shall be determined as if such agreement had not been entered into.

(b) *Other items remaining in dispute.*—Pursuant to section 6226(c), a partner is a party to a partnership-level judicial proceeding with respect to partnership items and partnership-level determinations of penalties, additions to tax or additional amounts. When a partner settles partnership items, the settled partnership items convert to nonpartnership items under section 6231(b)(1)(C) and will not be subject to any future or pending partnership-level proceeding pursuant to section 6226(d)(1). The remaining unsettled partnership items, as well as any unsettled penalty, addition to tax, or additional amount that relates to an adjustment to a partnership item (regardless of whether the partnership item to which it relates has been settled), however, will remain subject to determination under partnership-level administrative and judicial procedures. Consequently, any remaining unsettled items, including any unsettled penalty, addition to tax, or additional amount that relates to an adjustment to a partnership item, will be deemed to remain in dispute. Thus, the period for assessing any tax attributable to the settled items will be governed by the period for assessing any tax attributable to the remaining unsettled items.

(c) *Effective date.*—This section is applicable to partnership taxable years beginning on or after October 4, 2001. For years beginning prior to October 4, 2001, see §301.6229(f)-1T contained in 26 CFR part 1, revised April 1, 2001. [Reg. §301.6229(f)-1.]

☐ [*T.D.* 8965, 10-3-2001.]

[Reg. §301.6230(b)-1]

§301.6230(b)-1. Request that correction not be made.—(a) *In general.*—The request that a correction not be made under section 6230(b)(2) shall be in writing and shall—

(1) State that it is a request that a correction not be made under section 6230(b);

(2) Identify the partnership and the partner filing the request by name, address, and taxpayer identification number;

(3) Be signed by the partner filing the request; and

(4) Be filed with the Internal Revenue Service office that provided the notice of the correction of the error.

(b) *Effective date.*—This section is applicable to partnership taxable years beginning on or after October 4, 2001. For years beginning prior to October 4, 2001, see §301.6230(b)-1T contained in 26 CFR part 1, revised April 1, 2001. [Reg. §301.6230(b)-1.]

☐ [*T.D.* 8965, 10-3-2001.]

[Reg. §301.6230(c)-1]

§301.6230(c)-1. Claim arising out of erroneous computation, etc.—(a) *In general.*—A claim for refund under section 6230(c) shall state the grounds for the claim and shall be filed with the service center where the partner's return is filed.

(b) *Effective date.*—This section is applicable to partnership taxable years beginning on or after October 4, 2001. For years beginning prior to October 4, 2001, see §301.6230(c)-1T contained in

26 CFR part 1, revised April 1, 2001. [Reg. §301.6230(c)-1.]

☐ [*T.D.* 8965, 10-3-2001.]

[Reg. §301.6230(e)-1]

§301.6230(e)-1. Tax matters partner required to furnish names.—(a) *In general.*—If a notice of the beginning of an administrative proceeding is mailed to the tax matters partner with respect to any partnership taxable year, the tax matters partner shall furnish to the Internal Revenue Service office that issued the notice the name, address, profits interest, and taxpayer identification number of each person who was a partner in the partnership at any time during that taxable year if that information was not provided on the partnership return filed for that year.

(b) *Revised or additional information.*—If the tax matters partner discovers that any information furnished to the Internal Revenue Service on the partnership return or under paragraph (a) of this section was incorrect or incomplete, the tax matters partner shall furnish revised or additional information to the Internal Revenue Service within 15 days of discovering that the information furnished to the Internal Revenue Service was incorrect or incomplete.

(c) *Information required with respect to indirect partners.*—The requirements of this section for identifying information apply with respect to indirect partners to the extent that the tax matters partner has such information.

(d) *Effective date.*—This section is applicable to partnership taxable years beginning on or after October 4, 2001. For years beginning prior to October 4, 2001, see §301.6230(e)-1T contained in 26 CFR part 1, revised April 1, 2001. [Reg. §301.6230(e)-1.]

☐ [*T.D.* 8965, 10-3-2001.]

[Reg. §301.6231(a)(1)-1]

§301.6231(a)(1)-1. Exception for small partnerships.—(a) *In general.*—For purposes of the exception for small partnerships under section 6231(a)(1)(B), the rules contained in this section shall apply.

(1) *10 or fewer.*—The 10 or fewer limitation described in section 6231(a)(1)(B)(i) is applied to the number of natural persons, C corporations, and estates of deceased partners that were partners at any one time during the partnership taxable year. Thus, for example, a partnership that at no time during the taxable year had more than 10 partners may be treated as a small partnership even if, because of transfers of interests in the partnership, 11 or more natural persons, C corporations, or estates of deceased partners owned interests in the partnership for some portion of the taxable year. See section 1361(a)(2) for the definition of a C corporation. For purposes of section 6231(a)(1)(B) and this section, a husband and wife (and their estates) are treated as one person.

(2) *Pass-thru partner.*—The exception provided in section 6231(a)(1)(B) does not apply to a partnership for a taxable year if any partner in the partnership during that taxable year is a pass-thru partner as defined in section 6231(a)(9). For purposes of this paragraph (a)(2), an estate shall not be treated as a pass-thru partner.

(3) *Determination made annually.*—The determination of whether a partnership meets the requirements for the exception for small partnerships under section 6231(a)(1)(B) and this paragraph (a) shall be made with respect to each partnership taxable year. Thus, a partnership that does not qualify as a small partnership in one taxable year may qualify as a small partnership in another taxable year if the requirements for the exception under section 6231(a)(1)(B) and this paragraph (a) are met with respect to that other taxable year.

(b) *Election to have subchapter C of chapter 63 apply.*—(1) *In general.*—Any partnership that meets the requirements set forth in section 6231(a)(1)(B) and paragraph (a) of this section (relating to the exception for small partnerships) may elect under paragraph (b)(2) of this section to have the provisions of subchapter C of chapter 63 of the Internal Revenue Code apply with respect to that partnership.

(2) *Method of election.*—A partnership shall make the election described in paragraph (b)(1) of this section by attaching a statement to the partnership return for the first taxable year for which the election is to be effective. The statement shall be identified as an election under section 6231(a)(1)(B)(ii), shall be signed by all persons who were partners of that partnership at any time during the partnership taxable year to which the return relates, and shall be filed at the time (determined with regard to any extension of time for filing) and place prescribed for filing the partnership return. However, for any partnership taxable year for which the due date of the return (determined without regard to extensions) is before January 2, 2002, the partnership may file the statement described in the preceding sentence on or before the date which is one year before the date specified in section 6229(a) for the expiration of the period of limitations with respect to that partnership (determined with regard to extensions of that period under section 6229(b)).

(3) *Years covered by election.*—The election shall be effective for the partnership taxable year to which the return relates and all subsequent partnership taxable years unless revoked with the consent of the Commissioner.

(c) *Effective date.*—This section is applicable to partnership taxable years beginning on or after October 4, 2001. For years beginning prior to October 4, 2001, see §301.6231(a)(1)-1T contained in 26 CFR part 1, revised April 1, 2001. [Reg. §301.6231(a)(1)-1.]

☐ [*T.D.* 8965, 10-3-2001.]

[Reg. §301.6231(a)(2)-1]

§301.6231(a)(2)-1. **Persons whose tax liability is determined indirectly by partnership items.**—(a) *Spouse filing joint return with individual holding a separate interest.*—(1) *In general.*—Except as otherwise provided in this paragraph (a), a spouse who files a joint return with an individual holding a separate interest in the partnership shall be treated as a partner for purposes of subchapter C of chapter 63 of the Internal Revenue Code. Thus, the spouse who files a joint return with a partner will be permitted to participate in administrative and judicial proceedings.

(2) *Counting rules.*—A spouse who files a joint return with an individual holding a separate interest in the partnership shall not be counted as a partner for purposes of applying section 6223(b) (relating to special rules for partnerships with more than 100 partners) and section 6231(a)(1)(B) (relating to the exception for small partnerships).

(3) *Notice rules.*—(i) *In general.*—Except as provided in paragraph (a)(3)(ii) of this section, for purposes of subchapter C of chapter 63 of the Internal Revenue Code, a spouse who files a joint return with an individual holding a separate interest in the partnership shall be treated as receiving any notice received by the individual holding the separate interest.

(ii) *Spouse identified on partnership return or by statement.*—Paragraph (a)(3)(i) of this section shall not apply to a spouse who files a joint return with an individual holding a separate interest in the partnership if that spouse—

    (A) Is identified on the partnership return; or

    (B) Is identified as a partner entitled to notice as provided in §301.6223(c)-1(b).

(4) Conversion of partnership items

    (i) Individual holding a separate interest. A spouse who files a joint return with an individual holding a separate interest in the partnership shall cease to be treated as a partner in the partnership under paragraph (a)(1) of this section upon the conversion of the partnership items of the individual holding the separate interest in the partnership to nonpartnership items pursuant to section 6231(b). If each spouse holds a separate interest in the partnership, the previous sentence shall be applied separately with respect to each partnership interest.

    (ii) *Spouse who files a joint return with an individual holding a separate interest in the partnership.*—A spouse who files a joint return with an individual holding a separate interest in the partnership shall cease to be treated as a partner in the partnership under paragraph (a)(1) of this section upon the occurrence of an event that would convert the partnership items of the spouse to nonpartnership items if the spouse were the owner of a separate interest.

(iii) *Examples.*—The following examples illustrate the application of paragraph (a)(4) of this section:

Example 1. Husband owns a separate interest in ABC partnership and files a joint return with Wife. Husband files for bankruptcy. Pursuant to §301.6231(c)-7, upon filing for bankruptcy, the partnership items of the debtor convert to nonpartnership items. Thus, Husband's partnership items converted to nonpartnership items upon the filing of Husband's bankruptcy petition. Pursuant to paragraph (a)(4)(i) of this section, Wife is no longer treated as a partner of ABC partnership as of the date the partnership items of Husband converted to nonpartnership items.

Example 2. Wife owns a separate interest in XYZ partnership and files a joint return with Husband. Husband files for bankruptcy. Because the filing of the bankruptcy petition by Husband is an event that would convert Husband's partnership items to nonpartnership items if Husband were the owner of a separate interest, Husband shall no longer be treated as a partner as of the filing of the bankruptcy petition. Pursuant to paragraph (a)(4)(ii) of this section, the partnership items of Wife are not affected by Husband's bankruptcy.

(5) *Cross-reference.*—See §301.6231(a)(12)-1 for special rules relating to spouses holding a joint interest in a partnership.

(b) *Shareholder of C corporation.*—A shareholder of a C corporation (as defined in section 1361(a)(2)) is not a partner in a partnership merely because the C corporation is a partner in that partnership.

(c) *Effective date.*—This section is applicable to partnership taxable years beginning on or after October 4, 2001. For years beginning prior to October 4, 2001, see §301.6231(a)(2)-1T contained in 26 CFR part 1, revised April 1, 2001. [Reg. §301.6231(a)(2)-1.]

☐ [T.D. 8965, 10-3-2001.]

[Reg. §301.6231(a)(3)-1]

§301.6231(a)(3)-1. Partnership items.—(a) *In general.*—For purposes of subtitle F of the Internal Revenue Code of 1954, the following items which are required to be taken into account for the taxable year of a partnership under subtitle A of the Code are more appropriately determined at the partnership level than at the partner level and, therefore, are partnership items:

(1) The partnership aggregate and each partner's share of each of the following:

(i) Items of income, gain, loss, deduction, [   ] of the partnership;

[   ]nditures by the partnership not [   ]ting its taxable income (for [   ]ributions);

[   ] partnership which may [   ]s under section 57(a) for

(iv) Income of the partnership exempt from tax;

(v) Partnership liabilities (including determinations with respect to the amount of the liabilities, whether the liabilities are nonrecourse, and changes from the preceding taxable year); and

(vi) Other amounts determinable at the partnership level with respect to partnership assets, investments, transactions and operations necessary to enable the partnership or the partners to determine—

(A) The investment credit determined under section 46(a);

(B) Recapture under section 47 of the investment credit;

(C) Amounts at risk in any activity to which section 465 applies;

(D) The depletion allowance under section 613A with respect to oil and gas wells; and

(E) The application of section 751(a) and (b);

(2) Guaranteed payments;

(3) Optional adjustments to the basis of partnership property pursuant to an election under section 754 (including necessary preliminary determinations, such as the determination of a transferee partner's basis in a partnership interest); and

(4) Items relating to the following transactions, to the extent that a determination of such items can be made from determinations that the partnership is required to make with respect to an amount, the character of an amount, or the percentage interest of a partner in the partnership, for purposes of the partnership books and records or for purposes of furnishing information to a partner:

(i) Contributions to the partnership;

(ii) Distributions from the partnership; and

(iii) Transactions to which section 707(a) applies (including the application of section 707(b)).

(b) *Factors that affect the determination of partnership items.*—The term "partnership item" includes the accounting practices and the legal and factual determinations that underlie the determination of the amount, timing, and characterization of items of income, credit, gain, loss, deduction, etc. Examples of these determinations are: The partnership's method of accounting, taxable year, and inventory method; whether an election was made by the partnership; whether partnership property is a capital asset, section 1231 property, or inventory; whether an item is currently deductible or must be capitalized; whether partnership activities have been engaged in with the intent to make a profit for purposes of section 183; and whether the partnership qualifies for the research and development credit under section 30.

(c) *Illustrations.*—(1) *In general.*—This paragraph (c) illustrates the provisions of paragraph (a)(4) of this section. The determinations illustrated in this paragraph (c) that the partnership is required to make are not exhaustive; there may be additional determinations that the partnership is required to make which relate to a transaction listed in paragraph (a)(4) of this section. The critical element is that the partnership needs to make a determination with respect to a matter for the purposes stated; failure by the partnership actually to make a determination (for example, because it does not maintain proper books and records) does not prevent an item from being a partnership item.

(2) *Contributions.*—For purposes of its books and records, or for purposes of furnishing information to a partner, the partnership needs to determine:

(i) The character of the amount received from a partner (for example, whether it is a contribution, a loan, or a repayment of a loan);

(ii) The amount of money contributed by a partner;

(iii) The applicability of the investment company rules of section 721(b) with respect to a contribution; and

(iv) The basis to the partnership of contributed property (including necessary preliminary determinations, such as the partner's basis in the contributed property).

To the extent that a determination of an item relating to a contribution can be made from these and similar determinations that the partnership is required to make, therefore, that item is a partnership item. To the extent that the determination requires other information, however, that item is not a partnership item. For example, it may be necessary to determine whether contribution of the property causes recapture by the contributing partner of the investment credit under section 47 in certain circumstances in which that determination is irrelevant to the partnership.

(3) *Distributions.*—For purposes of its books and records, or for purposes of furnishing information to a partner, the partnership needs to determine:

(i) The character of the amount transferred to a partner (for example, whether it is a distribution, a loan, or a repayment of a loan);

(ii) The amount of money distributed to a partner;

(iii) The adjusted basis to the partnership of distributed property; and

(iv) The character of partnership property (for example, whether an item is inventory or a capital asset).

To the extent that a determination of an item relating to a distribution can be made from these and similar determinations that the partnership is required to make, therefore, that item is a partnership item. To the extent that that determination requires other information, however, that item is not a partnership item. Such other information would include those factors used in determining the partner's basis for the partnership interest that are not themselves partnership

items, such as the amount that the partner paid to acquire the partnership interest from a transferor partner if that transfer was not covered by an election under section 754.

(4) *Transactions to which section 707(a) applies.*—For purposes of its books and records, the partnership needs to determine:

(i) The amount transferred from the partnership to a partner or from a partner to the partnership in any transaction to which section 707(a) applies;

(ii) The character of such an amount (for example, whether or not it is a loan; in the case of amounts paid over time for the purchase of an asset, what portion is interest); and

(iii) The percentage of the capital interests and profits interests in the partnership owned by each partner.

To the extent that a determination of an item relating to a transaction to which section 707(a) applies can be made from these and similar determinations that the partnership is required to make, therefore, that item is a partnership item. To the extent that that determination requires other information, however, that item is not a partnership item. An example of such other information is the cost to the partner of goods sold to the partnership.

(d) *Effective date.*—This section shall apply with respect to partnership taxable years beginning after September 3, 1982. This section shall also apply with respect to any partnership taxable year ending after September 3, 1982, if with respect to that year there is an agreement entered into pursuant to section 407(a)(3) of the Tax Equity and Fiscal Responsibility Act of 1982. [Reg. § 301.6231(a)(3)-1.]

☐ [T.D. 8082, 4-15-86.]

[Reg. § 301.6231(a)(5)-1]

§ 301.6231(a)(5)-1. Definition of affected item.—(a) *In general.*—The term *affected item* means any item to the extent such item is affected by a partnership item. It includes items unrelated to the items reflected on the partnership return (for example, an item, such as the threshold for the medical expense deduction under section 213, that varies if there is a change in an individual partner's adjusted gross income).

(b) *Basis in a partner's partnership interest.*—The basis of a partner's partnership interest is an affected item to the extent it is not a partnership item.

(c) *At-risk limitation.*—The application of the at-risk limitation under section 465 to a partner with respect to a loss incurred by a partnership is an affected item to the extent it is not a partnership item.

(d) *Passive losses.*—The application of the passive loss rules under section 469 to a partner with respect to a loss incurred by a partnership is an affected item to the extent it is not a partnership item.

(e) *Penalty, addition to tax, or additional amount.*—(1) *In general.*—The term *affected item* includes any penalty, addition to tax, or additional amount provided by subchapter A of chapter 68 of the Internal Revenue Code of 1986 to the extent provided in this paragraph (e).

(2) *Penalty, addition to tax, or additional amount without floor.*—If a penalty, addition to tax, or additional amount that does not contain a floor (that is, a threshold amount of underpayment or understatement necessary before the imposition of the penalty, addition to tax, or additional amount) is imposed on a partner as the result of an adjustment to a partnership item, the term *affected item* shall include the penalty, addition to tax, or additional amount computed with reference to the portion of the underpayment that is attributable to the partnership item adjustment(s) to which the penalty, addition to tax, or additional amount applies.

(3) *Penalty, addition to tax, or additional amount containing floor.*—(i) *Floor exceeded prior to adjustment.*—If a partner would have been subject to a penalty, addition to tax, or additional amount that contains a floor in the absence of an adjustment to a partnership item (that is, the partner's understatement or underpayment exceeded the floor even without an adjustment to a partnership item) the term *affected item* shall include only the portion of the penalty, addition to tax, or additional amount computed with reference to the partnership item (or affected item) adjustments.

(ii) *Floor not exceeded prior to adjustment.*—In the case of a penalty, addition to tax, or additional amount that contains a floor, if the taxpayer's understatement or underpayment does not exceed the floor prior to an adjustment to a partnership item but does so after such adjustment, the term *affected item* shall include the penalty, addition to tax, or additional amount computed with reference to the entire underpayment or understatement to which the penalty, addition to tax, or additional amount applies.

(4) *Examples.*—The provisions of this paragraph (e) may be illustrated by the following examples:

Example 1. A, a partner of P, had an aggregate underpayment of $1,000 of which $100 is attributable to an adjustment to partnership items. A is negligent in reporting the partnership items. The accuracy-related penalty under section 6662 for negligence computed with reference to the $100 underpayment attributable to the partnership item adjustments is an affected item.

Example 2. B, a partner of P, understated B's ~~tax liability attributable to nonpartner-~~ ~~by $6,000.~~ An adjustment to a partner- ~~ulting from a partnership~~ ~~B's income tax by an addi-~~ ~~e adjustment, B would~~ ~~accuracy-related penalty~~ ~~a substantial understate-~~ ~~with respect to the $6,000~~

understatement attributable to nonpartnership items. The portion of the accuracy-related penalty under section 6662 computed with reference to the $2,000 understatement attributable to partnership items to which the accuracy-related penalty applies is an affected item. The portion of the accuracy-related penalty under section 6662 computed with reference to the $6,000 pre-existing understatement is not an affected item.

Example 3. C, a partner in partnership P, understated C's income tax liability attributable to nonpartnership items by $4,000. As a result of an adjustment to partnership items, that understatement is increased to $10,000. Prior to the adjustment, C would not have been subject to the accuracy-related penalty under section 6662 for a substantial understatement of income tax. The accuracy-related penalty under section 6662 computed with reference to the entire $10,000 understatement to which the accuracy-related penalty applies is an affected item.

(f) *Effective date.*—This section is applicable to partnership taxable years beginning on or after October 4, 2001. For years beginning prior to October 4, 2001, see § 301.6231(a)(5)-1T contained in 26 CFR part 1, revised April 1, 2001. [Reg. § 301.6231(a)(5)-1.]

☐ [*T.D.* 8965, 10-3-2001.]

[Reg. § 301.6231(a)(6)-1]

§ 301.6231(a)(6)-1. Computational adjustments.—(a) *Changes in a partner's tax liability.*—(1) *In general.*—A change in the tax liability of a partner to properly reflect the treatment of a partnership item under subchapter C of chapter 63 of the Internal Revenue Code is made through a computational adjustment. A computational adjustment includes a change in tax liability that reflects a change in an affected item where that change is necessary to properly reflect the treatment of a partnership item, or any penalty, addition to tax, or additional amount that relates to an adjustment to a partnership item. However, if a change in a partner's tax liability cannot be made without making one or more partner-level determinations, that portion of the change in tax liability attributable to the partner-level determinations shall be made under the deficiency procedures(as described in subchapter B of chapter 63 of the Internal Revenue Code), except for any penalty, addition to tax, or additional amount that relates to an adjustment to a partnership item.

(2) *Affected items that do not require partner-level determinations.*—Changes in a partner's tax liability with respect to affected items that do not require partner-level determinations (such as the threshold amount of medical deductions under section 213 that changes as the result of determinations made at the partnership level) are computational adjustments that are directly assessed. When making computational adjustments, the Internal Revenue Service may assume that amounts the partner reported on the partner's individual return include all amounts reported

to the partner by the partnership (on the Schedule K-1s attached to the partnership's original return), absent contrary notice to the Internal Revenue Service (for example, a "Notice of Inconsistent Treatment" pursuant to § 301.6222(a)-2(c)). Such an assumption by the Internal Revenue Service does not constitute a partner-level determination. Moreover, substituting redetermined partnership items for the partner's previously reported partnership items (including partnership items included in carryover amounts) does not constitute a partner-level determination where the Internal Revenue Service otherwise accepts, for the sole purpose of determining the computational adjustment, all nonpartnership items (including, for example, nonpartnership item components of carryover amounts) as reported.

(3) *Affected items that require partner-level determinations.*—Changes in a partner's tax liability with respect to affected items that require partner-level determinations (such as a partner's at-risk amount to the extent it depends upon the source from which the partner obtained the funds that the partner contributed to the partnership) are computational adjustments that are subject to the deficiency procedures. Notwithstanding the preceding sentence, any penalty, addition to tax, or additional amount that relates to an adjustment to a partnership item is not subject to the deficiency procedures, but rather may be directly assessed as part of the computational adjustment that is made following the partnership proceeding, based on determinations in that proceeding, regardless of whether any partner-level determinations may be required.

(b) *Interest.*—A computational adjustment includes any interest due with respect to any underpayment or overpayment of tax attributable to adjustments to reflect properly the treatment of partnership items.

(c) *Effective date.*—This section is applicable to partnership taxable years beginning on or after October 4, 2001. For years beginning prior to October 4, 2001, see § 301.6231(a)(6)-1T contained in 26 CFR part 1, revised April 1, 2001. [Reg. § 301.6231(a)(6)-1.]

☐ [*T.D.* 8965, 10-3-2001.]

[Reg. § 301.6231(a)(7)-1]

§ 301.6231(a)(7)-1. Designation or selection of tax matters partner.—(a) *In general.*—A partnership may designate a partner as its tax matters partner for a specific taxable year only as provided in this section. Similarly, the designation of a partner as the tax matters partner for a specific taxable year may be terminated only as provided in this section. If a partnership does not designate a general partner as the tax matters partner for a specific taxable year, or if the designation is terminated without the partnership designating another general partner as the tax matters partner, the tax matters partner is the partner determined under this section.

(b) *Person who may be designated tax matters partner.*—(1) *General requirement.*—A person may be designated as the tax matters partner of a partnership for a taxable year only if that person—

(i) Was a general partner in the partnership at some time during the taxable year for which the designation is made; or

(ii) Is a general partner in the partnership as of the time the designation is made.

(2) *Limitation on designation of tax matters partner who is not a United States person.*—If any United States person would be eligible under paragraph (a) of this section to be designated as the tax matters partner of a partnership for a taxable year, no person who is not a United States person may be designated as the tax matters partner of the partnership for that year without the consent of the Commissioner. For the definition of *United States person*, see section 7701(a)(30).

(c) *Designation of tax matters partner at time partnership return is filed.*—The partnership may designate a tax matters partner for a partnership taxable year on the partnership return for that taxable year in accordance with the instructions for that form.

(d) *Certification by current tax matters partner of selection of successor.*—If a partner properly designated as the tax matters partner of a partnership for a partnership taxable year under this section certifies that another partner has been selected as the tax matters partner of the partnership for that taxable year, that other partner is thereby designated as the tax matters partner for that year. The current tax matters partner shall make the certification by filing with the service center with which the partnership return is filed a statement that—

(1) Identifies the partnership, the partner filing the statement, and the successor tax matters partner by name, address, and taxpayer identification number;

(2) Specifies the partnership taxable year to which the designation relates;

(3) Declares that the partner filing the statement has been properly designated as the tax matters partner of the partnership for the partnership taxable year and that that designation is in effect immediately before the filing of the statement;

(4) Certifies that the other named partner has been selected as the tax matters partner of the partnership for that taxable year in accordance with the partnership's procedure for making that selection; and

(5) Is signed by the partner filing the statement.

(e) *Designation by general partners with majority interest.*—The partnership may designate a tax matters partner for a partnership taxable yea[r] any time after the filing of a partnership r[eturn] for that taxable year by filing a stateme[nt] the service center with which the partnership return was filed. The statement shall—

(1) Identify the partnership and the designated partner by name, address, and taxpayer identification number;

(2) Specify the partnership taxable year to which the designation relates;

(3) Declare that it is a designation of a tax matters partner for the taxable year specified; and

(4) Be signed by persons who were general partners at the close of the year and were shown on the return for that year to hold more than 50 percent of the aggregate interest in partnership profits held by all general partners as of the close of that taxable year. For purposes of this paragraph (e)(4), all limited partnership interests held by general partners shall be included in determining the aggregate interest in partnership profits held by such general partners.

(f) *Designation by partners with majority interest under certain circumstances.*—(1) *In general.*—A tax matters partner may be designated for a partnership taxable year under this paragraph (f) only if, at the time the designation is made, each partner who was a general partner at the close of such partnership taxable year is described in one or more of paragraphs (f)(1)(i) through (iv) of this section as follows:

(i) The general partner is dead, or, if the general partner is an entity, has been liquidated or dissolved;

(ii) The general partner has been adjudicated by a court of competent jurisdiction to be no longer capable of managing his or her person or estate;

(iii) The general partner's partnership items have become nonpartnership items under section 6231(b); or

(iv) The general partner is no longer a partner in the partnership.

(2) *Method of making designation.*—A tax matters partner for a partnership taxable year may be designated under this paragraph (f) at any time after the filing of the partnership return for such taxable year by filing a written statement with the service center with which the partnership return was filed. The statement shall—

(i) Identify the partnership and the designated tax matters partner by name, address, and taxpayer identification number;

(ii) Specify the partnership taxable year to which the designation relates;

(iii) Declare that it is a designation of a [m]atters partner for the partnership taxable [spec]ified; and

[s]igned by persons who were part[ners] [such] taxable year and were [shown on] that year to hold more [than 50 percent of the ag]gregate interest in part[nership profits held by a]ll partners as of the close

(g) *Designation of alternate tax matters partner.*—If an individual is designated as the tax matters partner of a partnership under paragraph (c), (d), (e), or (f) of this section, the document by which that individual is designated may also designate an alternate tax matters partner who will become tax matters partner upon the occurrence of one or more of the events described in paragraph (l)(1)(i) or (ii) of this section. The person designated as the alternate tax matters partner becomes the tax matters partner as of the time the designation of the tax matters partner is terminated under paragraph (l)(1)(i) or (ii) of this section. The designation of a person as the alternate tax matters partner shall have no effect in any other case.

(h) *Prior designations superseded.*—A designation of a tax matters partner for a partnership taxable year under paragraphs (d), (e), or (f) of this section shall supersede all prior designations of a tax matters partner for that year, including a prior designation of an alternate tax matters partner under paragraph (g) of this section.

(i) *Resignation of designated tax matters partner.*—A person designated as the tax matters partner of a partnership under this section may resign at any time by a written statement to that effect. The statement shall specify the partnership taxable year to which the resignation relates and shall identify the partnership and the tax matters partner by name, address, and taxpayer identification number. The statement shall also be signed by the resigning tax matters partner and shall be filed with the service center with which the partnership return was filed.

(j) *Revocation of designation.*—The partnership may revoke the designation of the tax matters partner for a partnership taxable year at any time after the filing of a partnership return for that taxable year by filing a statement with the service center with which the partnership return was filed. The statement shall—

(1) Identify by name, address, and taxpayer identification number the partnership and the general partner whose designation as tax matters partner is being revoked;

(2) Specify the partnership taxable year to which the revocation relates;

(3) Declare that it is a revocation of a designation of the tax matters partner for the taxable year specified; and

(4) Be signed by the persons described in paragraph (e)(4) of this section, or, if at the time that the revocation is made, each partner who was a general partner at the close of the partnership taxable year to which the revocation relates is described in one or more of paragraphs (f)(1)(i) through (iv) of this section, by the persons described in paragraph (f)(2)(iv) of this section.

(k) *When designation, etc., becomes effective.*—(1) *In general.*—Except as otherwise provided in paragraph (k)(2) of this section, a designation, resignation, or revocation provided for in this section becomes effective on the day that the statement required by the applicable paragraph of this section is filed.

(2) *Notice of proceeding mailed.*—If a notice of beginning of an administrative proceeding with respect to a partnership taxable year is mailed before the date on which a statement of designation, resignation, or revocation provided for in this section with respect to that taxable year is filed, the Service is not required to give effect to such designation, resignation, or revocation until 30 days after the statement is filed.

(l) *Termination of designation.*—(1) *In general.*— A designation of a tax matters partner for a taxable year under this section shall remain in effect until—

(i) The death of the designated tax matters partner;

(ii) An adjudication by a court of competent jurisdiction that the individual designated as the tax matters partner is no longer capable of managing the individual's person or estate;

(iii) The liquidation or dissolution of the tax matters partner, if the tax matters partner is an entity;

(iv) The partnership items of the tax matters partner become nonpartnership items under section 6231(c) (relating to special enforcement areas); or

(v) The day on which—

(A) The resignation of the tax matters partner under paragraph (i) of this section;

(B) A subsequent designation under paragraph (d), (e), or (f) of this section; or

(C) A revocation of the designation under paragraph (j) of this section becomes effective.

(2) *Actions by the tax matters partner before termination of designation.*—The termination of the designation of a partner as the tax matters partner under paragraph (l)(1) of this section does not affect the validity of any action taken by that partner as tax matters partner before the designation is terminated. For example, if that tax matters partner had previously consented to an extension of the period for assessments under section 6229(b)(1)(B), that extension remains valid even after termination of the designation.

(m) *Tax matters partner where no partnership designation made.*—(1) *In general.*—The tax matters partner for a partnership taxable year shall be determined under this paragraph (m) if—

(i) The partnership has not designated a tax matters partner under this section for that taxable year; or

(ii) The partnership has designated a tax matters partner under this section for that taxable year, that designation has been terminated under paragraph (l)(1) of this section, and the partnership has not made a subsequent designation under this section for that taxable year.

(2) *General partner having the largest profits interest is the tax matters partner.*—The tax matters

partner for any partnership taxable year to which this paragraph (m) applies is the general partner having the largest profits interest in the partnership at the close of that taxable year (or where there is more than one such partner, the one of such partners whose name would appear first in an alphabetical listing). For purposes of this paragraph (m)(2), all limited partnership interests held by a general partner shall be included in determining that general partner's profits interest in the partnership. For purposes of this paragraph (m)(2), the general partner with the largest profits interest is determined based on the year-end profits interests reported on the Schedules K-1 filed with the partnership income tax return for the taxable year for which the determination is being made.

(3) *Termination of designation.*—A designation of a tax matters partner for a partnership taxable year under this paragraph (m) shall remain in effect until the earlier of the occurrence of one or more of the events described in paragraphs (l)(1)(i) through (iv) of this section or the day on which a designation under paragraph (d), (e), or (f) of this section becomes effective. If a designation of a tax matters partner for a partnership taxable year is terminated under this paragraph (m)(3) and the partnership has not subsequently designated a tax matters partner for that taxable year under paragraph (d), (e), or (f) of this section, the tax matters partner for that taxable year shall be determined under paragraph (m)(2) of this section, and, for purposes of applying paragraph (m)(2) of this section, the general partner whose designation was so terminated shall be treated as having no profits interest in the partnership for that taxable year.

(n) *Selection of tax matters partner by Commissioner when impracticable to apply the largest-profits-interest rule.*—If the partnership has not designated a tax matters partner under this section for the taxable year and it is impracticable (as determined under paragraph (o) of this section) to apply the largest-profits-interest rule of paragraph (m)(2) of this section, the Commissioner will select a tax matters partner as described in paragraph (p) of this section.

(o) *Impracticability of largest-profits-interest rule.*—It is impracticable to apply the largest-profits-interest rule of paragraph (m)(2) of this section if, on the date the rule is applied, any one of the following three conditions is met:

(1) *General partner with the largest profits interest is not apparent.*—The general partner with the largest profits interest is not apparent from the Schedules K-1 and is not otherwise readily determinable.

(2) *Each general partner is deemed to have no profits interest in the partnership.*—Each general partner is deemed to have no profits interest in the partnership under paragraph (m)(3) of this section (concerning termination of a designation under the largest-profits-interest rule) because the occurrence of one or more of the

described in paragraphs (l)(1)(i) through (iv) of this section (involving death, adjudication of incompetency, liquidation, and conversion of partnership items to nonpartnership items).

(3) *General partner with the largest profits interest is disqualified.*—The general partner with the largest profits interest determined under paragraph (m)(2) of this section—

(i) Has been notified of suspension from practice before the Internal Revenue Service;

(ii) Is incarcerated;

(iii) Is residing outside the United States, its possessions, or territories; or

(iv) Cannot be located or cannot perform the functions of a tax matters partner for any reason, except that lack of cooperation with the Internal Revenue Service by the general partner with the largest profits interest is not a basis for finding that the partner cannot perform the functions of a tax matters partner.

(p) *Commissioner's selection of the tax matters partner.*—(1) *When the general partner with the largest profits interest is not apparent.*—If it is impracticable under paragraph (o)(1) of this section to apply the largest-profits-interest rule of paragraph (m)(2) of this section, the Commissioner will select (in accordance with the notification procedures set forth in paragraph (r) of this section) as the tax matters partner any person who was a general partner at any time during the taxable year under examination.

(2) *When each general partner is deemed to have no profits interest in the partnership.*—If it is impracticable under paragraph (o)(2) of this section to apply the largest-profits-interest rule of paragraph (m)(2) of this section, the Commissioner will select a partner (including a general or limited partner) as the tax matters partner in accordance with the criteria set forth in paragraph (q) of this section. The Commissioner will notify, within 30 days of the selection, the partner selected, the partnership, and all partners required to receive notice under section 6223(a) of the selection of the tax matters partner, effective as of the date specified in the notice.

(3) *When the general partner with the largest profits interest is disqualified.*—(i) *In general.*—Except as otherwise provided in paragraph (p)(3)(ii) of this section, if it is impracticable under paragraph (o)(3) of this section to apply the largest-profits-interest rule of paragraph (m)(2) of this section, the Commissioner will treat each general partner who fits the criteria contained in paragraph (o)(3) of this section as having no profits interest in the partnership for the taxable year and will select (in accordance with the notification procedures set forth in paragraph (r) of this section) a tax matters partner ... remaining persons who were general ... during the taxable year.

... if no general partner may ... al partners during the ... eated as having no prof- ... ership for the taxable year

under paragraph (m)(3) of this section (concerning termination of a designation under the largest-profits-interest rule) or are described in paragraph (o)(3) of this section (general partner with the largest profits interest is disqualified), the Commissioner will select a partner (including a general or limited partner) as the tax matters partner in accordance with the criteria set forth in paragraph (q) of this section. The Commissioner will notify both the partner selected and the partnership of the selection, effective as of the date specified in the notice.

(q) *Criteria for selecting a partner as tax matters partner.*—(1) *In general.*—The Commissioner will select a partner as the tax matters partner under paragraph (p)(2) or (3)(ii) of this section only if the partner was a partner in the partnership at the close of the taxable year under examination.

(2) *Criteria to be considered.*—The Commissioner may consider the following criteria in selecting a partner as the tax matters partner:

(i) The general knowledge of the partner in tax matters and the administrative operation of the partnership.

(ii) The partner's access to the books and records of the partnership.

(iii) The profits interest held by the partner.

(iv) The views of the partners having a majority interest in the partnership regarding the selection.

(v) Whether the partner is a partner of the partnership at the time the tax-matters-partner selection is made.

(vi) Whether the partner is a United States person (within the meaning of section 7701(a)(30)).

(3) *Limited restriction on subsequent designation of a tax matters partner by the partnership.*—For purposes of paragraphs (p)(2) and (3)(ii) of this section, the partnership cannot designate a partner who is not a general partner to serve as tax matters partner in lieu of a partner selected by the Commissioner.

(r) *Notification of partnership.*—(1) *In general.*—If the Commissioner selects a tax matters partner under the provisions of paragraph (p)(1) or (p)(3)(i) of this section, the Commissioner will notify, within 30 days of the selection, the partner selected, the partnership, and all partners required to receive notice under section 6223(a) of the selection of the tax matters partner, effective as of the date specified in the notice.

(2) *Limited opportunity for partnership to designate the tax matters partner.*—(i) Before the Commissioner selects a tax matters partner under paragraphs (p)(1) and (3)(i) of this section, the Commissioner will notify the partnership by mail that, after 30 days from the date of the notice, the Commissioner will make a determination that it is impracticable to apply the largest-profits-interest rule of paragraph (m)(2) of this section and will select the tax matters partner unless a prior designation is made by the

partnership. This delay in making the determination will permit the partnership to designate a tax matters partner under paragraph (e) of this section (designation by general partners with a majority interest) or paragraph (f) of this section (designation by partners with a majority interest under certain circumstances), thereby avoiding a selection made by the Commissioner.

(ii) During the 30-day period and prior to a tax-matters-partner designation by the partnership, the Commissioner will communicate with the partnership by sending all correspondence or notices to "The Tax Matters Partner" in care of the partnership at the partnership's address.

(iii) Any subsequent designation of a tax matters partner by the partnership after the 30-day period will become effective as provided under paragraph (k)(2) of this section (concerning designations made after a notice of beginning of administrative proceeding is mailed).

(s) *Effective date.*—This section applies to all designations, selections, and terminations of a tax matters partner occurring on or after December 23, 1996, except for paragraphs (p)(2) and (r)(1), that are applicable on or after October 4, 2001. [Reg. § 301.6231(a)(7)-1.]

☐ [*T.D.* 8698, 12-20-96. *Amended by T.D.* 8808, 1-25-99 *and T.D.* 8965, 10-3-2001.]

[Reg. § 301.6231(a)(7)-2]

§ 301.6231(a)(7)-2. Designation or selection of tax matters partner for a limited liability company (LLC).—(a) *In general.*—Solely for purposes of applying section 6231(a)(7) and § 301.6231(a)(7)-1 to an LLC, only a member-manager of an LLC is treated as a general partner, and a member of an LLC who is not a member-manager is treated as a partner other than a general partner.

(b) *Definitions.*—(1) *LLC.*—Solely for purposes of this section, *LLC* means an organization—

(i) Formed under a law that allows the limitation of the liability of all members for the organization's debts and other obligations within the meaning of § 301.7701-3(b)(2)(ii); and

(ii) Classified as a partnership for Federal tax purposes.

(2) *Member.*—Solely for purposes of this section, *member* means any person who owns an interest in an LLC.

(3) *Member-manager.*—Solely for purposes of this section, *member-manager* means a member of an LLC who, alone or together with others, is vested with the continuing exclusive authority to make the management decisions necessary to conduct the business for which the organization was formed. Generally, an LLC statute may permit the LLC to choose management by one or more managers (whether or not members) or by all of the members. If there are no elected or designated member-managers (as so defined in this paragraph (b)(3)) of the LLC, each member

will be treated as a member-manager for purposes of this section.

(c) *Effective date.*—This section applies to all designations, selections, and terminations of a tax matters partner of an LLC occurring on or after December 23, 1996. Any other reasonable designation or selection of a tax matters partner of an LLC is binding for periods prior to December 23, 1996. [Reg. § 301.6231(a)(7)-2.]

☐ [*T.D.* 8698, 12-20-96.]

[Reg. § 301.6231(a)(12)-1]

§ 301.6231(a)(12)-1. Special rules relating to spouses.—(a) *Spouses holding a joint interest.*—(1) *In general.*—Except as otherwise provided in this section, spouses holding a joint interest in a partnership shall be treated as separate partners for purposes of subchapter C of chapter 63 of the Internal Revenue Code. Thus, both spouses may participate in administrative and judicial proceedings. The term *joint interest* includes tenancies in common, joint tenancies, tenancies by the entirety, and community property.

(2) *Identification of joint interest.*—For purposes of this section, an interest shall be treated as a joint interest in a partnership only if both spouses are identified on the partnership return or are identified as partners entitled to notice as provided in § 301.6223(c)-1(b).

(3) *Failure to identify both spouses as partners.*—If both spouses are not identified as set forth in paragraph (a)(2) of this section, then the partnership interest shall be treated as separately owned by the identified spouse.

(4) *Example.*—The following example illustrates the application of paragraph (a)(3) of this section:

Example. Wife owns an interest in ABC Partnership and is identified on the Schedule K-1 of the partnership return. Wife and Husband live in a community property state. The partnership return of ABC partnership does not identify Husband, and Husband is not identified as a partner entitled to notice as provided in § 301.6223(c)-1(b). Pursuant to paragraph (a)(3) of this section, the partnership interest of Wife shall be treated as separately owned by Wife.

(b) *Notice and counting rules.*—(1) *In general.*—Except as provided in paragraph (b)(2) of this section, for purposes of applying section 6223 (relating to notice to partners of proceedings) and section 6231(a)(1)(B) (relating to the exception for small partnerships), spouses holding a joint interest in a partnership shall be treated as one partner. Except as provided in paragraph (b)(2) of this section, the Internal Revenue Service or the tax matters partner may send any required notice to either spouse.

(2) *Identified spouse entitled to notice.*—For purposes of applying section 6223 (relating notice to partners of proceeding) for a partnership taxable year, an individual who holds joint interest in a partnership with a spouse

is entitled to notice under section 6223 shall be entitled to receive separate notice under section 6223 if such individual—

(i) Is identified as a partner on the partnership return for that taxable year; or

(ii) Is identified as a partner entitled to notice as provided in § 301.6223(c)-1(b).

(c) *Conversion of partnership items.*—(1) *In general.*—If spouses holding a joint interest in a partnership are treated as separate partners under this section, then section 6231(b) (relating to the conversion of partnership items) shall be applied separately to each spouse.

(2) *Example.*—The following example illustrates the application of paragraph (c) of this section:

Example. Husband and Wife own a joint interest in XYZ Partnership. The partnership return identifies both spouses on the Schedule K-1. Under this section, each spouse is treated as a separate partner. If Wife enters into a settlement agreement, Wife's partnership items convert to nonpartnership items pursuant to section 6231(b)(1)(C). Accordingly, Wife no longer has the right to participate in the partnership proceeding subsequent to entering into the settlement agreement. Pursuant to paragraph (c) of this section, however, the partnership items of Husband are not affected by the conversion of the partnership items of Wife, and Husband continues to have the right to participate in the partnership proceeding. This result is the same regardless of whether the partnership items are reported on a joint return or on separate returns.

(d) *Cross-reference.*—See § 301.6231(a)(2)-1(a) for special rules relating to spouses who file joint returns with individuals holding a separate interest in a partnership.

(e) *Effective date.*—This section is applicable to partnership taxable years beginning on or after October 4, 2001. For years beginning prior to October 4, 2001, see § 301.6231(a)(12)-1T contained in 26 CFR part 1, revised April 1, 2001. [Reg. § 301.6231(a)(12)-1.]

☐ [T.D. 8965, 10-3-2001.]

[Reg. § 301.6231(c)-1]

§ 301.6231(c)-1. Special rules for certain applications for tentative carryback and refund adjustments based on partnership losses, deductions, or credits.—(a) *Application subject to this section.*—This section applies in the case of an application under section 6411 (relating to tentative carryback and refund adjustments) based on losses, deductions, or credits of a partnership if the Commissioner, or the Commissioner's delegate, determines, after review of the relevant information, that it is highly ~~a person described in section~~ with respect to the partner-

of holding an interest in the partnership that would be subject to a penalty under section 6700 (relating to penalty for promoting abusive tax shelters, etc.). This section applies only with respect to an application based upon the original reporting on the partner's income tax return of partnership losses, deductions, or credits. Thus, this section does not apply to a request for administrative adjustment under section 6227 through which a partner seeks to change the partner's reporting of partnership items on the partner's income tax return (or on an earlier request for administrative adjustment).

(b) *Determination of special enforcement area.*— In the case of an application under section 6411 described in paragraph (a) of this section, precluding an assessment under section 6225 that would be permitted under section 6213(b)(3) (relating to assessments arising out of tentative carryback or refund adjustments) with respect to any amount applied, credited, or refunded as a result of the application may encourage the proliferation of abusive tax shelter partnerships and make the eventual collection of taxes due more difficult. Consequently, the Secretary hereby determines that such applications present special enforcement considerations within the meaning of section 6231(c)(1)(E).

(c) *Assessment permitted under section 6213(b)(3).*—Notwithstanding section 6225 (relating to restrictions on assessment with respect to partnership items), an assessment that would be permitted under section 6213(b)(3) with respect to any amount applied, credited, or refunded as a result of an application described in paragraph (a) of this section may be made before there is a final partnership-level determination with respect to the losses, deductions, or credits on which the application is based. As provided in section 6213(b)(1), the Internal Revenue Service shall mail notice of any such assessment to the partner filing the application. The notice shall also inform the partner of the partner's limited right to elect to treat items as nonpartnership items as provided in paragraph (d) of this section.

(d) *Limited right to elect to treat items as nonpartnership items.*—(1) *In general.*—A partner to whom the Internal Revenue Service mails a notice of suspension of action on a refund claim under paragraph (c) of this section may elect in accordance with this paragraph (d) to have all partnership items for the partnership taxable year in which the losses, deductions, or credits at issue arose treated as nonpartnership items.

(2) *Time and place of making election.*—The election shall be made by filing a statement with the Internal Revenue Service office that mailed the notice of suspension. The statement may be filed at any time—

(i) After the date which is one year after the date on which the partnership return was filed for the partnership taxable year in which the items at issue arose; and

(ii) Before the date on which the Internal Revenue Service mails to the tax matters partner the notice of final partnership administrative adjustment for the partnership taxable year in which the items at issue arose. For purposes of this paragraph (d)(2), a partnership return filed before the last day prescribed by law for its filing (determined without regard to extensions) shall be treated as filed on the last day.

(3) *Contents of the statement.*—The statement shall—

(i) Be clearly identified as an election to have partnership items treated as nonpartnership items because of notification of an assessment under section 6213(b)(3);

(ii) Identify the partnership by name, address, and taxpayer identification number;

(iii) Identify the partner making the election by name, address, and taxpayer identification number;

(iv) Specify the partnership taxable year to which the election applies; and

(v) Be signed by the partner making the election.

(e) *Effective date.*—This section is applicable to partnership taxable years beginning on or after October 4, 2001. For years beginning prior to October 4, 2001, see § 301.6231(c)-1T contained in 26 CFR part 1, revised April 1, 2001. [Reg. § 301.6231(c)-1.]

☐ [*T.D.* 8965, 10-3-2001.]

[Reg. § 301.6231(c)-2]

§ 301.6231(c)-2. Special rules for certain refund claims based on losses, deductions, or credits from abusive tax shelter partnerships.— (a) *Claims subject to this section.*—This section applies in the case of a claim for credit or refund based on losses, deductions or credits of a partnership if the Commissioner, or the Commissioner's delegate, determines, after review of available relevant information, that it is highly likely that a person described in section 6700(a)(1) made, with respect to the partnership—

(1) A gross valuation overstatement; or

(2) A false or fraudulent statement with respect to the tax benefits to be secured by reason of holding an interest in the partnership that would be subject to a penalty under section 6700 (relating to penalty for promoting abusive tax shelters, etc.). This section applies only with respect to a claim that is based upon the partner's original reporting on the partner's income tax return of partnership losses, deductions, or credits. Thus, this section does not apply to a request for administrative adjustment under section 6227 through which a partner seeks to change the partner's reporting of partnership items on the partner's income tax return (or on an earlier request for administrative adjustment). For purposes of this section, any income tax return requesting a credit or refund shall be treated as a claim for a credit or refund.

(b) *Determination of special enforcement area.*— Granting a claim for credit or refund described in paragraph (a) of this section may encourage the proliferation of abusive tax shelter partnerships and make the eventual collection of taxes more difficult. Consequently, the Secretary hereby determines that such claims present special enforcement considerations within the meaning of section 6231(c)(1)(E).

(c) *Action on refund claims suspended.*—In the case of a claim described in paragraph (a) of this section, the Internal Revenue Service may mail to the partner filing the claim a notice stating that no action will be taken on the partner's claim until the completion of the partnership-level proceedings. The notice shall also inform the partner of the partner's limited right to elect to treat items as nonpartnership items as provided in paragraph (d) of this section.

(d) *Limited right to elect to treat items as nonpartnership items.*—(1) *In general.*—A partner to whom the Internal Revenue Service mails a notice of suspension under paragraph (c) of this section may elect in accordance with this paragraph (d) to have all partnership items for the partnership taxable year in which the losses, deductions, or credits at issue arose treated as nonpartnership items.

(2) *Time and place of making election.*—The election shall be made by filing a statement with the Internal Revenue Service office that mailed the notice of suspension. The statement may be filed at any time—

(i) After the date which is one year after the date on which the partnership return was filed for the partnership taxable year in which the items at issue arose; and

(ii) Before the date on which the Internal Revenue Service mails to the tax matters partner the notice of final partnership administrative adjustment for the partnership taxable year in which the items at issue arose. For purposes of this paragraph (d)(2), a partnership return filed before the last day prescribed by law for its filing (determined without regard to extensions) shall be treated as filed on the last day.

(3) *Contents of the statement.*—The statement shall—

(i) Be clearly identified as an election to have partnership items treated as nonpartnership items because of notification of suspension of action on a refund claim;

(ii) Identify the partnership by name, address, and taxpayer identification number;

(iii) Identify the partner making the election by name, address, and taxpayer identification number;

(iv) Specify the partnership taxable year to which the election applies; and

(v) Be signed by the partner making the election.

(e) *Effective date.*—This section applies with respect to any claim described in paragraph this section that is filed on or after Oct

2001. For claims filed prior to October 4, 2001, see §301.6231(c)-2T contained in 26 CFR part 1, revised April 1, 2001. [Reg. §301.6231(c)-2.]

☐ [*T.D.* 8965, 10-3-2001.]

[Reg. §301.6231(c)-3]

§301.6231(c)-3. Limitation on applicability of §§301.6231(c)-4 through 301.6231(c)-8.—(a) *In general.*—A provision of §§301.6231(c)-4 through 301.6231(c)-8 shall not apply with respect to partnership items arising in a partnership taxable year if, as of the date on which those items would otherwise begin to be treated as nonpartnership items under that provision—

(1) A notice of final partnership administrative adjustment with respect to those items has been mailed to the tax matters partner; and

(2) Either—

(i) The period during which an action with respect to that final partnership administrative adjustment may be brought under section 6226 has expired and no such action has been brought; or

(ii) The decision of the court in an action brought under section 6226 with respect to that final partnership administrative adjustment has become final.

(b) *Effective date.*—This section is applicable to partnership taxable years beginning on or after October 4, 2001. For years beginning prior to October 4, 2001, see §301.6231(c)-3T contained in 26 CFR part 1, revised April 1, 2001. [Reg. §301.6231(c)-3.]

☐ [*T.D.* 8965, 10-3-2001.]

[Reg. §301.6231(c)-4]

§301.6231(c)-4. Termination and jeopardy assessment.—(a) *In general.*—The treatment of items as partnership items with respect to a partner against whom an assessment of income tax under section 6851 (termination assessment) or section 6861 (jeopardy assessment) is made will interfere with the effective and efficient enforcement of the internal revenue laws. Accordingly, partnership items of such a partner arising in any partnership taxable year ending with or within the partner's taxable year for which an assessment of income tax under section 6851 or 6861 is made shall be treated as nonpartnership items as of the moment before such assessment is made.

(b) *Effective date.*—This section is applicable to partnership taxable years beginning on or after October 4, 2001. For years beginning prior to October 4, 2001, see §301.6231(c)-4T contained in 26 CFR part 1, revised April 1, 2001. [Reg. §301.6231(c)-4.]

☐ [*T.D.* 8965, 10-3-2001.]

[Reg. §301.6231(c)-5]

§301.6231(c)-5. Criminal investigations.—(a) *In general.*—The treatment of items as partnership items with respect to a partner under investigation for ... or violation of the internal ... ng to income tax will in-terfere with the effective and efficient enforcement of the internal revenue laws. Accordingly, partnership items of such a partner arising in any partnership taxable year ending on or before the last day of the latest taxable year of the partner to which the criminal investigation relates shall be treated as nonpartnership items as of the date on which the partner is notified that the partner is the subject of a criminal investigation and written notification is sent by the Internal Revenue Service that the partner's partnership items shall be treated as nonpartnership items. The partnership items of a partner who is notified that the partner is the subject of a criminal investigation shall not be treated as nonpartnership items under this section unless and until such partner is sent written notification from the Internal Revenue Service of such treatment.

(b) *Effective date.*—This section is applicable to partnership taxable years beginning on or after October 4, 2001. For years beginning prior to October 4, 2001, see §301.6231(c)-5T contained in 26 CFR part 1, revised April 1, 2001. [Reg. §301.6231(c)-5.]

☐ [*T.D.* 8965, 10-3-2001.]

[Reg. §301.6231(c)-6]

§301.6231(c)-6. Indirect method of proof of income.—(a) *In general.*—The treatment of items as partnership items with respect to a partner whose taxable income is determined by use of an indirect method of proof of income will interfere with the effective and efficient enforcement of the internal revenue laws. Accordingly, partnership items of such a partner arising in any partnership taxable year ending on or before the last day of the taxable year of the partner for which a deficiency notice based upon an indirect method of proof of income is mailed to the partner shall be treated as nonpartnership items as of the date on which that deficiency notice is mailed to the partner.

(b) *Effective date.*—This section is applicable to partnership taxable years beginning on or after October 4, 2001. For years beginning prior to October 4, 2001, see §301.6231(c)-6T contained in 26 CFR part 1, revised April 1, 2001. [Reg. §301.6231(c)-6.]

☐ [*T.D.* 8965, 10-3-2001.]

[Reg. §301.6231(c)-7]

§301.6231(c)-7. Bankruptcy and receivership.—(a) *Bankruptcy.*—The treatment of items as partnership items with respect to a partner named as a debtor in a bankruptcy proceeding will interfere with the effective and efficient enforcement of the internal revenue laws. Accordingly, partnership items of such a partner arising in any partnership taxable year ending on or before the last day of the latest taxable year of the partner with respect to which the United States could file a claim for income tax due in the bankruptcy proceeding shall be treated as nonpartnership items as of the date the petition naming the partner as debtor is filed in bankruptcy.

(b) *Receivership.*—The treatment of items as partnership items with respect to a partner for whom a receiver has been appointed in any receivership proceeding before any court of the United States or of any State or the District of Columbia will interfere with the effective and efficient enforcement of the internal revenue laws. Accordingly, partnership items of such a partner arising in any partnership taxable year ending on or before the last day of the latest taxable year of the partner with respect to which the United States could file a claim for income tax due in the receivership proceeding shall be treated as nonpartnership items as of the date a receiver is appointed in any receivership proceeding before any court of the United States or of any State or the District of Columbia.

(c) *Effective date.*—This section is applicable to partnership taxable years beginning on or after October 4, 2001. For years beginning prior to October 4, 2001, see § 301.6231(c)-7T contained in 26 CFR part 1, revised April 1, 2001. [Reg. § 301.6231(c)-7.]

□ [*T.D.* 8965, 10-3-2001.]

[Reg. § 301.6231(c)-8]

§ 301.6231(c)-8. Prompt assessment.—(a) *In general.*—The treatment of items as partnership items with respect to a partner on whose behalf a request for a prompt assessment of tax under section 6501(d) is filed will interfere with the effective and efficient enforcement of the internal revenue laws. Accordingly, partnership items of such a partner arising in any partnership taxable year ending with or within any taxable year of the partner with respect to which a request for a prompt assessment of tax is filed shall be treated as nonpartnership items as of the date that the request is filed.

(b) *Effective date.*—This section is applicable to partnership taxable years beginning on or after October 4, 2001. For years beginning prior to October 4, 2001, see § 301.6231(c)-8T contained in 26 CFR part 1, revised April 1, 2001. [Reg. § 301.6231(c)-8.]

□ [*T.D.* 8965, 10-3-2001.]

[Reg. § 301.6231(d)-1]

§ 301.6231(d)-1. Time for determining profits interest of partners for purposes of sections 6223(b) and 6231(a)(11).—(a) *Partner owns interest at close of year.*—For purposes of section 6223(b) (relating to special rules for partnerships with more than 100 partners) and section 6231(a)(11) (relating to 5-percent groups), except as otherwise provided in this section, the profits interest held by a partner, directly or indirectly through one or more pass-thru partners, in a partnership (the source partnership) to which subchapter C of chapter 63 of the Internal Revenue Code applies shall be determined at the close of the source partnership's taxable year.

(b) *Partner does not own interest at close of year.*—If the entire direct and indirect interest of

a partner in a source partnership is terminated by virtue of a disposition by such partner of such interest (or by virtue of the disposition of an interest held by one or more pass-thru partners through which the partner holds an interest), then the profits interest of such partner in the source partnership shall be measured as of the moment before the disposition causing such termination. The preceding sentence shall not apply with respect to a termination if subsequent to such termination and before the close of the source partnership's taxable year the partner acquires a direct or indirect interest in the source partnership.

(c) *Disposition of last remaining portion of interest is disposition of entire interest.*—If a partner (or a pass-thru partner through which a partner holds an interest) makes several partial dispositions of an interest in a source partnership during a taxable year of the source partnership, paragraph (b) of this section will apply with respect to the disposition which causes a termination of the partner's entire direct and indirect interest in the source partnership.

(d) *No profits interest in certain cases.*—If—

(1) The interest of a partner in a partnership is entirely disposed of before the close of the taxable year of the partnership; and

(2) No items of the partnership for that taxable year are required to be taken into account by the partner, then that partner has no profits interest in the partnership for that taxable year.

(e) *Examples.*—The provisions of this section may be illustrated by the following examples. Assume in all examples that there have been no reacquisitions prior to the close of the source partnership's taxable year. The examples are as follows:

Example 1. B holds an interest in partnership P through T, a pass-thru partner. P uses a fiscal year ending June 30 as P's taxable year; B and T use the calendar year as the taxable year. As of the close of P's taxable year ending June 30, 2002, T holds an interest in P and B holds an interest in P through T. The profits interest held by B in P through T for that year is determined as of June 30, 2002.

Example 2. Assume the same facts as in *Example 1*, except that B sold the entire interest that B held in P through T on November 5, 2001. The profits interest held by B in P through T for P's taxable year ending June 30, 2002, is determined as of the moment before the sale on November 5, 2001.

Example 3. C holds an interest in partnership P through T, a pass-thru partner. C, P, and T all use the calendar year as the taxable year. T disposes of T's interest in P on June 5, 2002. The profits interest held by C in P through T for 200⊘ is determined as of the moment before the disⓐⓢition on June 5, 2002.

Example 4. Assume the same facts as in ⓘⓔple 3, except that C sold C's entire inter⊘

(and, therefore, C's entire interest that C held in P through T) on March 15, 2002. The profits interest held by C in P through T for 2002 is determined as of the moment before the sale on March 15, 2002.

Example 5. On January 1, 2002, D held a 2 percent profits interest in partnership P. Both D and P use the calendar year as the taxable year. On August 1, 2002, D transfers three-fourths of D's profits interest in P to E. On September 1, 2002, D sells D's remaining .5 percent profits interest in P to F. For purposes of sections 6223(b) and 6231(a)(11), D had a .5 percent profits interest in P for 2002.

Example 6. Assume the same facts as in *Example 5*, except that on January 1, 2002, D also held a 1 percent profits interest in partnership P through T, a pass-thru partner which also uses the calendar year as the taxable year. In addition to the sale to E on August 1, 2002, D sold a portion of D's interest in T on December 1, 2002, such that after the sale, D held a .2 percent profits interest in P through T. D made no other transfers of interests in either P or T. For purposes of sections 6223(b) and 6231(a)(11), D had a .7 percent profits interest in P for 2002.

(f) *Effective date.*—This section is applicable to partnership taxable years beginning on or after October 4, 2001. For years beginning prior to October 4, 2001, see § 301.6231(d)-1T contained in 26 CFR part 1, revised April 1, 2001. [Reg. § 301.6231(d)-1.]

☐ [*T.D.* 8965, 10-3-2001.]

[Reg. § 301.6231(e)-1]

§ 301.6231(e)-1. Effect of a determination with respect to a nonpartnership item on the determination of a partnership item.—(a) *In general.*—The determination of an item after it has become a nonpartnership item with respect to a partner is not controlling in the determination of that item with respect to other partners. Thus, for example, the determination by a court in a separate proceeding relating to a partner that a certain partnership expenditure was deductible does not bind either the Internal Revenue Service or the other partners in a later partnership or other proceeding.

(b) *Effective date.*—This section is applicable to partnership taxable years beginning on or after October 4, 2001. For years beginning prior to October 4, 2001, see § 301.6231(e)-1T contained in 26 CFR part 1, revised April 1, 2001. [Reg. § 301.6231(e)-1.]

☐ [*T.D.* 8965, 10-3-2001.]

[Reg. § 301.6231(e)-2]

§ 231(e)-2. Judicial decision not a bar to ~~~tments.—(a) *In general.*—A court ~~~~pect to a partner's income tax ~~~~to nonpartnership items ~~~~her proceedings with ~~~~income tax liability if ~~~~hip items become non~~~~ the appropriate time to

~~~~.(f)

include such nonpartnership items in the earlier court proceeding has passed. Thus, the Internal Revenue Service could issue a later deficiency notice for the same taxable year with respect to that partner or that partner could bring a refund suit with respect to those items that have become nonpartnership items.

(b) *Effective date.*—This section is applicable to partnership taxable years beginning on or after October 4, 2001. For years beginning prior to October 4, 2001, see § 301.6231(e)-2T contained in 26 CFR part 1, revised April 1, 2001. [Reg. § 301.6231(e)-2.]

☐ [*T.D.* 8965, 10-3-2001.]

[Reg. § 301.6231(f)-1]

§ 301.6231(f)-1. Disallowance of losses and credits in certain cases.—(a) *Application of section.*—This section applies if—

(1) A partnership, whether domestic or foreign, that is required to file a return under section 6031 for a taxable year fails to file the return within the time prescribed; and

(2) At any time after the close of that taxable year, either—

(i) The tax matters partner of that partnership resides outside the United States; or

(ii) The books and records of that partnership are maintained outside the United States.

(b) *Computational adjustment permitted if return is not filed after mailing of notice.*—Except as otherwise provided in paragraph (c) of this section, if—

(1) This section applies with respect to a partnership for a partnership taxable year;

(2) The Internal Revenue Service mails notice to a partner that the losses and credits arising from that partnership for that year will be disallowed to that partner unless the partnership files a return for that year within 60 days after the date on which the notice is mailed; and

(3) The partnership fails to file a return for that year within that 60-day period, the Internal Revenue Service may, without conducting a partnership-level proceeding, mail a notice of computational adjustment to that partner to reflect the disallowance of any loss (including a capital loss) or credit arising from that partnership for that year.

(c) *Restriction on notices under paragraph (b) of this section.*—Neither the notice referred to in paragraph (b)(2) of this section nor the notice of computational adjustment referred to in paragraph (b) of this section may be mailed on a day on which—

(1) The tax matters partner of the partnership resides within the United States; and

(2) The books and records of the partnership are maintained within the United States. Thus, if this section applies with respect to a partnership for a taxable year solely because the tax matters partner of that partnership resided outside the. United States for a period after the close of that taxable year and the tax matters

partner later takes up residence within the United States, no notice may be mailed under paragraph (b) of this section while the tax matters partner resides within the United States.

(d) *No disallowance in certain circumstances.*—If the person to whom the notice referred to in paragraph (b)(2) of this section is mailed establishes to the satisfaction of the Internal Revenue Service—

(1) That the losses and credits arising from the partnership for the year are proper; and

(2) That the partner has made a good faith effort to have the partnership file the required return; the Internal Revenue Service may allow the losses and credits in whole or in part.

(e) *Effective date.*—This section is applicable to partnership taxable years beginning on or after October 4, 2001. For years beginning prior to October 4, 2001, see §301.6231(f)-1T contained in 26 CFR part 1, revised April 1, 2001. [Reg. §301.6231(f)-1.]

☐ [*T.D.* 8965, 10-3-2001.]

[Reg. §301.6233-1]

§301.6233-1. Extension to entities filing partnership returns.—(a) *Entities filing a partnership return.*—Except as provided in paragraph (c)(1) of this section, the provisions of subchapter C of chapter 63 of the Internal Revenue Code (subchapter C) and the regulations thereunder shall apply with respect to any taxable year of an entity for which such entity files a partnership return as well as to such entity's items for that taxable year and to any person holding an interest in such entity at any time during that taxable year. Any final partnership administrative adjustment or judicial determination resulting from a proceeding under subchapter C with respect to such taxable year may include a determination that the entity is not a partnership for such taxable year as well as determinations with respect to all items of the entity that would be partnership items, as defined in section 6231(a)(3) and the regulations thereunder, if such entity had been a

partnership in such taxable year (including, for example, any amounts taxable to an entity determined to be an association taxable as a corporation). For example, a final determination under subchapter C that an entity that filed a partnership return is an association taxable as a corporation will serve as a basis for a computational adjustment reflecting the disallowance of any loss or credit claimed by a purported partner with respect to thai entity.

(b) *Partnership return filed but no entity found to exist.*—Paragraph (a) of this section shall apply where a partnership return is filed for a taxable year but it is determined that there is no entity for such taxable year. For purposes of applying paragraph (a) of this section, the partnership return shall be treated as if it were filed by an entity. However, any final partnership administrative adjustment or judicial determination resulting from a proceeding under subchapter C with respect to such taxable year may also include a determination that there is no entity for such taxable year.

(c) *Exceptions.*—Paragraph (a) of this section shall not apply to—

(1) Entities for any taxable year in which such entity would be excepted from the provisions of subchapter C of the Internal Revenue Code under section 6231(a)(1)(B) and the regulations thereunder (relating to the exception for small partnerships) if such entity were a partnership for such taxable year; and

(2) Entities for any taxable year for which a partnership return was filed for the sole purpose of making the election described in section 761(a).

(d) *Effective dates.*—This section is applicable to partnership taxable years beginning on or after October 4, 2001. For years beginning prior to October 4, 2001, see §301.6233-1T contained in 26 CFR part 1, revised April 1, 2001. [Reg. §301.6233-1.]

☐ [*T.D.* 8965, 10-3-2001.]

TAX TREATMENT OF SUBCHAPTER S ITEMS

⟫→ *Caution: Temporary Reg. §301.6241-1T, below, was issued under former Code Sec. 6241, which was repealed by P.L. 104-188, effective for tax years beginning after December 31, 1996.*

[Reg. §301.6241-1T]

§301.6241-1T. Tax treatment determined at corporate level (Temporary).—(a) *In general.*—For a taxable year of an S corporation beginning after December 31, 1982, a shareholder's treatment of a subchapter S item (as defined in §301.6245-1T) on the shareholder's return may not be changed except as provided in sections 6241-6245 of the Code and the regulations thereunder. Thus, for example if a shareholder treats an item on the shareholder's return consistently with the treatment of that item on the S corporation return, the Internal Revenue Service generally cannot adjust the treatment of that item on the shareholder's return except through a corporate-level proceeding. Similarly, the shareholder

may not put a subchapter S item in issue in a proceeding relating to nonsubchapter S items. For example, the shareholder may not offset a potential increase in taxable income based on changes in nonsubchapter S items by a potential decrease based on subchapter S items.

(b) *Restrictions inapplicable after items become nonsubchapter S items.*—Section 6241 and paragraph (a) of this section cease to apply to items arising from an S corporation with respect to a shareholder when those items cease to be subchapter S items with respect to that shareholder under section 6231(b)(1) (as extended to made applicable to subchapter S items section 6244).

»»→ *Caution: Temporary Reg. §301.6241-1T, below, was issued under former Code Sec. 6241, which was repealed by P.L. 104-188, effective for tax years beginning after December 31, 1996.*

(c) *S corporation.*—(1) *In general.*—For purposes of subchapter D of chapter 63 of the Code, except as provided in paragraph (c)(2) of this section, the term "S corporation" means any corporation required to file a return under section 6037(a).

(2) *Exception for small S corporations.*—(i) *Effective date.*—This paragraph (c)(2) shall apply to any taxable year of an S corporation the due date of the return for which (determined without regard to extensions) is on or after January 30, 1987.

(ii) *Five or fewer shareholders.*—For purposes of this paragraph (c), an S corporation shall not include a small S corporation. A small S corporation is defined as an S corporation with 5 or fewer shareholders, each of whom is a natural person or an estate. For purposes of this paragraph (c)(2), a husband and wife (and their estates) are treated as one shareholder. If stock (owned other than by a husband and wife) is owned by tenants in common or joint tenants, each tenant in common or joint tenant is considered to be a shareholder of the corporation. The limitation is applied to the number of natural persons and estates that were shareholders at any one time during the taxable year of the corporation. Thus, for example, an S corporation that at no time during the taxable year had more than 5 shareholders may be treated as a small S corporation even if, because of transfers of interests in the corporation, 6 or more natural persons or estates owned stock in the corporation for some portion of the taxable year.

(iii) *Special rule.*—The exception provided in paragraph (c)(2)(ii) of this section does not apply to an S corporation for a taxable year if any shareholder in the corporation during that taxable year is a pass-through shareholder. For purposes of this paragraph (c)(2)(iii), a pass-through shareholder is—

(A) A trust;

(B) A nominee; or

(C) Other similar pass-through persons through whom other persons have an ownership interest in the stock of the S corporation.
For purposes of the preceding sentence, a shareholder's estate shall not be treated as a pass-through shareholder.

(iv) *Determination made annually.*—The determination of whether an S corporation meets the requirements for the exception under paragraph (c)(2)(ii) of this section shall be made for each taxable year of the corporation. Thus, an S corporation which does not qualify as a small S corporation in one taxable year may qualify as a small S corporation in another taxable year if the requirements for the exception under paragraph (c)(2)(ii) of this section are met with respect to that other taxable year.

(v) *Election to have subchapter D of chapter 63 apply.*—(A) *In general.*—Notwithstanding paragraph (c)(2)(ii) of this section, a small S corporation may elect to have the provisions of subchapter D of chapter 63 of the Code apply with respect to that corporation.

(B) *Method of election.*—A small S corporation shall make the election described in paragraph (c)(2)(v)(A) of this section for a taxable year of the corporation by attaching a statement to the corporate return for the first taxable year for which the election is to be effective. The statement shall be identified as an election under §301.6241-1T(c)(2)(v)(A), shall be signed by all persons who were shareholders of that corporation at any time during the corporate taxable year to which the return relates, and shall be filed at the time (determined with regard to any extensions of time for filing) and place prescribed for filing the corporate return.

(C) *Years covered by election.*—The election shall be effective for the taxable year of the corporation to which the return relates and all subsequent taxable years of the corporation unless revoked with the consent of the Commissioner. [Temporary Reg. §301.6241-1T.]

☐ [*T.D.* 8122, 1-27-87.]

»»→ *Caution: Temporary Reg. §301.6245-1T, below, was issued under former Code Sec. 6245, which was repealed by P.L. 104-188, effective for tax years beginning after December 31, 1996.*

[Reg. §301.6245-1T]

§301.6245-1T. Subchapter S items (Temporary).—(a) *In general.*—For purposes of subtitle F of the Internal Revenue Code of 1986, the following items which are required to be taken into account for the taxable year of an S corporation ~~nder~~ subtitle A of the Code are more appropri~~ately~~ ~~determined~~ at the corporate level than at ~~sharehol~~der level and, therefore, are sub-

~~corpor~~ation aggregate and each ~~shareholder~~ and any factor necessary ~~to~~ ~~determine the~~ following:

~~(i) incom~~e, gain, loss, deduction, ~~credit,~~ ~~deduc~~tion;

(ii) Expenditures by the corporation not deductible in computing its taxable income (for example, charitable contributions);

(iii) Items of the corporation that may be tax preference items under section 57(a) for any shareholder;

(iv) Items of income of the corporation that are exempt from tax;

(v) Corporate liabilities (including determinations of the amount of the liability, whether the corporate liability is to a shareholder of the corporation, and changes from the preceding year); and

(vi) Other amounts determinable at the corporate level with respect to corporate assets,

~~...der~~
~~...and~~
~~...under~~
~~...41-1T(b)~~

~~...c)(1)~~

>>>→ *Caution: Temporary Reg. §301.6245-1T, below, was issued under former Code Sec. 6245, which was repealed by P.L. 104-188, effective for tax years beginning after December 31, 1996.*

investments, transactions, and operations necessary to enable the S corporation or the shareholders to determine—

(A) The general business credit provided by section 38;

(B) Recapture under section 47 of the credit provided by section 38;

(C) Amounts at risk in any activity to which section 465 applies;

(D) The depletion allowance under section 613A with respect to oil and gas wells;

(E) Amortization of reforestation expenses under section 194;

(F) The credit provided by section 34 for certain uses of gasoline and special fuels; and

(G) The taxes imposed at the corporate level, such as the taxes imposed under section 56, 1374, or 1375;

(2) Any factor necessary to determine whether the entity is an S corporation under section 1361, such as the number, eligibility, and consent of shareholders and the classes of stock;

(3) Any factor necessary to determine whether the entity has properly elected to be an S corporation under section 1362 for the taxable year;

(4) Any factor necessary to determine whether and when the S corporation election of the entity has been revoked or terminated under section 1362 for the taxable year (for example, the existence and amount of subchapter C earnings and profits, and passive investment income); and

(5) Items relating to the following transactions, to the extent that a determination of such items can be made from determinations that the corporation is required to make with respect to an amount, the character of an amount, or the percentage of stock ownership of a shareholder in the corporation, for purposes of the corporation's books and records or for purposes of furnishing information to a shareholder:

(i) Contributions to the corporation; and

(ii) Distributions from the corporation.

(b) *Factors that affect the determination of subchapter S items.*—The term "subchapter S item" includes the accounting practices and the legal and factual determinations that underlie the determination of the existence, amount, timing, and characterization of items of income, credit, gain, loss, deduction, etc. Examples of these determinations are: The S corporation's method of accounting, taxable year, and inventory method; whether an election was made by the corporation; whether corporate property is a capital asset, section 1231 property, or inventory; whether an item is currently deductible or must be capitalized; whether corporate activities had been engaged in with the intent to make a profit for purposes of section 183; whether the corporation qualified for the credit for increasing research activities under section 41; and whether the corporation qualified for the credit for clinical testing expenses for a rare disease or condition under section 28.

(c) *Illustrations.*—(1) *In general.*—This paragraph (c) illustrates the provisions of paragraph (a)(5) of this section. The determinations illustrated in this paragraph (c) that the corporation is required to make are not exhaustive; there may be additional determinations that the corporation is required to make which relate to a determination listed in paragraph (a)(5) of this section. The critical element is that the corporation is required to make a determination with respect to a matter for the purposes stated; failure by the corporation actually to make a determination (for example, because it does not maintain proper books and records) does not prevent an item from being a subchapter S item.

(2) *Contributions.*—For purposes of its books and records, or for purposes of furnishing information to a shareholder, the S corporation must determine:

(i) The character of the amount received by the corporation (for example, whether it is a contribution, loan, or repayment of a loan);

(ii) The amount of money received by the corporation; and

(iii) The basis to the corporation of contributed property (including necessary preliminary determinations, such as the shareholder's basis in the contributed property).

To the extent that a determination of an item relating to a contribution can be made from these and similar determinations that the corporation is required to make, that item is a subchapter S item. To the extent that the determination requires other information, however, that item is not a subchapter S item. Such other information would include those factors used in determining whether there is recapture under section 47 by the contributing shareholder of the general business credit because of the contribution of property in circumstances in which that determination is irrelevant to the corporation.

(3) *Distributions.*—For purposes of its books and records, or for purposes of furnishing information to a shareholder, the S corporation must determine:

(i) The character of the amount transferred to a shareholder (for example, whether it is a dividend, compensation, loan, or repayment of a loan);

(ii) The amount of money distributed to a shareholder;

(iii) The fair market value of property distributed to a shareholder;

(iv) The adjusted basis to the corporation of distributed property; and

(v) The character of corporation property (for example, whether an item is inventory or capital asset).

To the extent that a determination of an relating to a distribution can be made fro

>>>→ *Caution: Temporary Reg. §301.6245-1T, below, was issued under former Code Sec. 6245, which was repealed by P.L. 104-188, effective for tax years beginning after December 31, 1996.*

and similar determinations that the corporation is required to make, that item is a subchapter S item. To the extent that the determination requires other information, however, that item is not a subchapter S item. Such other information would include the determination of a shareholder's basis in the shareholder's stock or in the indebtedness of the S corporation to the shareholder.

(d) *Cross reference.*—For the definition of subchapter S item for purposes of the windfall profit tax, see §51.6245-1T.

(e) *Effective date.*—This section shall apply to taxable years beginning after December 31, 1982. [Temporary Reg. §301.6245-1T.]

☐ [*T.D.* 8122, 1-27-87.]

Collection

GENERAL PROVISIONS

See p. 20,601 for regulations not amended to reflect law changes

[Reg. §301.6301-1]

§301.6301-1. Collection authority.—The taxes imposed by the internal revenue laes shall be collected by district directors of internal revenue. See, however, section 6304, relating to the collection of certain taxes under the provisions of the Tariff Act of 1930. [Reg. §301.6301-1.]

☐ [*T.D.* 6119, 12-31-54. *Amended by T.D.* 6498, 10-24-60.]

[Reg. §31.6302-0]

§31.6302-0. Table of contents.—This section lists the table of contents for §§31.6302-1 through 31.6302-4.

§31.6302-1. Deposit rules for taxes under the Federal Insurance Contributions Act (FICA) and withheld income taxes.

  (i) Electroni transfer.

  (ii) Taxpaye

  (5) Exemption

  (6) Separation sits.

  (7) Payment of due.

  (8) Time deem sited.

  (9) Time deeme

(i) Time and man eposit.

  (1) General rule

  (2) Payment of due.

  (3) Time deeme

  (4) Procuremen coupons.

  (5) Time deeme ted.

  (6) Time deeme

(j) Voluntary payn electronic funds transfer.

(k) Special rules.

  (1) Notice except

  (2) Wages paid i nvertible foreign currency.

(l) [Reserved].

(m) Cross references

  (1) Failure to dep alty.

  (2) Saturday, Sun egal holiday.

(n) Effective/applica ates.

(o) Effective/Applica ate.

§ 31.6302-2. Deposit rules s under the Railroad Retirement Tax Act A.).

(a) General rule.

(b) Separate applicatio posit rules.

(c) Modification onthly rule determination.

  (1) General rule.

  (2) Exception.

(d) Effective/applicabi e.

§ 31.6302-3. Federal tax dep s for amounts withheld under the backup with requirements of Section 3406 for payments m December 31, 1992.

(a) General Rule.

(b) Treatment of bac ithholding amounts separately.

(c) Example.

§ 31.6302-4. Deposit rules for income taxes attributable to nonpayroll ta [Reg. § 31.6302-0.]

☐ [T.D. 8436, 9-22-92. Amen T.D. 9239, 12-30-2005; T.D. 9405, 6-30- T.D. 9440, 12-24-2008; T.D. 9507, 12-2-201 T.D. 9566, 12-9-2011.]

[Reg. § 1.6302-1

§ 1.6302-1. Deposit rules for ration income and estimated income ta d certain taxes of tax-exempt or ations.—
(a) Requirement.—A corporation organization subject to the tax imposed tion 511, and any private foundation si je the tax imposed by section 4940, shall dep ll payments of tax imposed by chapte 1 of ternal Revenue Code (or treated as so mp v section 6154(h)), including any pyme esti-

mated tax, on or before the date otherwise prescribed for paying such tax. This paragraph (a) does not apply to a foreign corporation or entity that has no office or place of business in the United States.

(b) Deposits by electronic funds transfer.—For the requirement to deposit corporation income and estimated income taxes and certain taxes of tax-exempt organizations by electronic funds transfer, see § 31.6302-1(h) of this chapter. A tax-payer not required to deposit by electronic funds transfer pursuant to § 31.6302-1(h) of this chapter remains subject to the rules of paragraph (b)(1) of this section.

(c) Failure to deposit.—For provisions relating to the penalty for failure to make a deposit within the prescribed time, see section 6656.

(d) Effective/applicability date.—This section applies to deposits and payments made after December 31, 2010. [Reg. § 1.6302-1.]

☐ [T.D. 6914, 3-7-67. Amended by T.D. 6941, 12-15-67; T.D. 7293, 11-27-73; T.D. 7953, 5-8-84; T.D. 8157, 9-4-87; T.D. 8723, 7-11-97; T.D. 8947, 6-14-2001; T.D. 8952, 6-25-2001; T.D. 9239, 12-30-2005 and T.D. 9507, 12-2-2010.]

[Reg. § 20.6302-1]

§ 20.6302-1. Voluntary payments of estate taxes by electronic funds transfer.—Any person may voluntarily remit by electronic funds transfer any payment of tax to which this part 20 applies. Such payment must be made in accordance with procedures prescribed by the Commissioner. [Reg. § 20.6302-1.]

☐ [T.D. 8828, 7-12-99.]

[Reg. § 25.6302-1]

§ 25.6302-1. Voluntary payments of gift taxes by electronic funds transfer.—Any person may voluntarily remit by electronic funds transfer any payment of tax to which this part 25 applies. Such payment must be made in accordance with procedures prescribed by the Commissioner. [Reg. § 25.6302-1.]

☐ [T.D. 8828, 7-12-99.]

[Reg. § 31.6302-1]

§ 31.6302-1. Deposit rules for taxes under the Federal Insurance Contributions Act (FICA) and withheld income taxes.—(a) Introduction.—With respect to employment taxes attributable to payments made after December 31, 1992, an employer is either a monthly depositor or a semi-weekly depositor based on an annual determination. An employer must generally deposit employment taxes under one of two rules: the Monthly rule in paragraph (c)(1) of this section, or the Semi-Weekly rule in paragraph (c)(2) of this section. Various exceptions and safe harbors are provided. Paragraph (f) of this section provides certain safe harbors for employers who inadvertently fail to deposit the full amount of taxes. Paragraph (c)(3) of this section provides an overriding exception to the Monthly and Semi-

Weekly rules where an employer has accumulated $100,000 or more of employment taxes. Paragraph (e) of this section provides the definition of employment taxes.

(b) *Determination of status.*—(1) *In general.*— The determination of whether an employer is a monthly or semi-weekly depositor for a calendar year is based on an annual determination and generally depends upon the aggregate amount of employment taxes reported by the employer for the lookback period as defined in paragraph (b)(4) of this section.

(2) *Monthly depositor.*—(i) *In general.*—An employer is a monthly depositor for the entire calendar year if the aggregate amount of employment taxes reported for the lookback period is $50,000 or less.

(ii) *Special rule.*—An employer ceases to be a monthly depositor on the first day after the employer is subject to the One-Day ($100,000) rule in paragraph (c)(3) of this section. At that time, the employer immediately becomes a semi-weekly depositor for the remainder of the calendar year and for the following calendar year.

(3) *Semi-weekly depositor.*—An employer is a semi-weekly depositor for the entire calendar year if the aggregate amount of employment taxes reported for the lookback period exceeds $50,000.

(4) *Lookback period.*—(i) *In general.*—For employers who file Form 941, "Employer's QUARTERLY Federal Tax Return," (or any related Spanishlanguage returns or returns for U.S. possessions) the lookback period for each calendar year is the twelve month period ended the preceding June 30. For example, the lookback period for calendar year 2006 is the period July 1, 2004, to June 30, 2005. The lookback period for employers who file Form 944, "Employer's ANNUAL Federal Tax Return," or filed Form 944 (or any related Spanish-language returns or returns for U.S. possessions) for either of the two previous calendar years, is the second calendar year preceding the current calendar year. For example, the lookback period for calendar year 2006 is calendar year 2004. In ... ning status as either a monthly or semi-depositor, an employer should determin aggregate amount of employment tax lia reported on its return(s) (Forms 941 or F) for the lookback period. The amount of ment tax liabilities reported for the lookb iod is the amount the employer reported her Forms 941 or Form 944 even if the e r is required to file the other form for t ent calendar year. New employers shall ted as having employment tax liabilitie for any part of the lookback period befo date the employer started or acquired its ss.

(ii) *Adjustment* ims for refund.—The employment tax liabi rted on the original return for the return is the amount taken into account in deter whether the aggregate amount of emp t taxes reported for the lookback peri eeds $50,000. Any amounts reported o ed returns or claims for refund pursuant ons 6205, 6402, 6413, and 6414 filed after e date of the original return are not take account when determining the aggreg ount of employment taxes reported for t back period. Prior period adjustments re on Forms 941 or Form 944 for 2008 and years are taken into account in determi e employment tax liability for the retur d in which the adjustments are reported

(c) *Deposit rules* Monthly rule.—An employer that is a m depositor must deposit employment taxe aulated with respect to payments made a calendar month by electronic funds t by the 15th day of the following month. 5th day of the following month is a Satur nday, or legal holiday in the District of ia under section 7503, taxes will be tre timely deposited if deposited on the n ceeding day which is not a Saturday, Sun egal holiday.

(2) *Semi-W* ule.—(i) *In general.*—An employer that ni-weekly depositor for a calendar year m osit employment taxes by electronic fund fer by the dates set forth below:

Payment dates/semi-weekly periods	osit date
(A) Wednesday, Thursday and/or Friday	On or before the ing Wednesday.
(B) Saturday, Sunday, Monday and/or Tuesday	On or before th ving Friday.

(ii) *Semi-weekly period spanning two return periods.*—If the return period ends during a semi-weekly period in which an employer has two or more payment dates, two deposit obligations may exist. For example, if one quarterly return period ends on Thursday and a new quarterly return period begins on Friday, employment taxes from payments on Wednesday and Thursday are subject to one deposit obligation, and employment taxes from payments on Friday are subject to a separate deposit obligation. Two separate federal tax deposits are required.

(iii) *Sp* le for computing days.—Semi-weekly depo ave at least three business days followi close of the semi-weekly period by whi eposit employment taxes accumulated the semi-weekly period. Business da de every calendar day other than Satur ndays, or legal holidays in the District of ia under section 7503. If any of the three v s following the close of a semi-weekly p i a legal holiday, the employer has an ac a day for each day that is a legal holiday li to make the required deposit. For exa if e Monday following the close of a Wednesday to Friday semi-weekly period is Memorial Day, a legal holiday, the required deposit for the semi-weekly period is not due until the following Thursday rather than the following Wednesday.

(3) *Exception—One-Day rule.*—Notwithstanding paragraphs (c)(1) and (c)(2) of this section, if on any day within a deposit period (monthly or semi-weekly) an employer has accumulated $100,000 or more of employment taxes, those taxes must be deposited by electronic funds transfer in time to satisfy the tax obligation by the close of the next day. If the next day is a Saturday, Sunday, or legal holiday in the District of Columbia under section 7503, the taxes will be treated as timely deposited if deposited on the next succeeding day which is not a Saturday, Sunday, or legal holiday. For purposes of determining whether the $100,000 threshold is met—

(i) A monthly depositor takes into account only those employment taxes accumulated in the calendar month in which the day occurs; and

(ii) A semi-weekly depositor takes into account only those employment taxes accumulated in the Wednesday-Friday or Saturday-Tuesday semi-weekly period in which the day occurs.

(4) *Deposits required only on business days.*—No taxes are required to be deposited under this section on any day that is a Saturday, Sunday, or legal holiday. Deposits are required only on business days. Business days include every calendar day other than Saturdays, Sundays, or legal holidays. For purposes of this paragraph (c), legal holidays shall have the same meaning provided in section 7503. Pursuant to section 7503, the term *legal holiday* means a legal holiday in the District of Columbia. For purposes of this paragraph (c), the term "legal holiday" does not include other Statewide legal holidays.

(5) *Exception to the monthly and semi-weekly deposit rules for employers in the Employers' Annual Federal Tax Program (Form 944).*—Generally, an employer who files Form 944 for a taxable year may remit its accumulated employment taxes with its timely filed return for that taxable year and is not required to deposit under either the monthly or semi-weekly rules set forth in paragraphs (c)(1) and (c)(2) of this section during that taxable year. An employer who files Form 944 whose actual employment tax liability exceeds the eligibility threshold, as set forth in §§ 31.6011(a)-1(a)(5) and 31.6011(a)-4(a)(4), will not qualify for this exception and should follow the deposit rules set forth in this section.

(6) *Extension of time to deposit for employers in the Employers' Annual Federal Tax Program (Form 944) during the preceding year.*—An employer who filed Form 944 for the preceding year but will file Forms 941 instead for the current year will be deemed to have timely deposited its current year's January deposit obligation(s) under paragraphs (c)(1) through (c)(4) of this section if the employer deposits the amount of such deposit obligation(s) by March 15 of that year.

(7) *Exception to the monthly and semi-weekly deposit rules for employers making interest-free adjustments.*—An employer filing an adjusted return under § 31.6205-1 to report taxes that were accumulated in a prior return period shall pay the amount of the adjustment by the time it files the adjusted return, and the amount timely paid will be deemed to have been timely deposited by the employer. The payment may be made by a check or money order with the adjusted return, by electronic funds transfer, or by other methods of payment as provided by the instructions relating to the adjusted return.

(d) *Examples.*—The provisions of paragraphs (a), (b) and (c) of this section are illustrated by the following examples:

Example 1. Monthly depositor. (i) *Determination of status.* For calendar year 2011, Employer A determines its depositor status using the look-back period July 1, 2009 to June 30, 2010. For the four calendar quarters within this period, A reported aggregate employment tax liabilities of $42,000 on its quarterly Forms 941. Because the aggregate amount did not exceed $50,000, A is a monthly depositor for the entire calendar year 2011.

(ii) *Monthly rule.* During December 2011, A (a monthly depositor) accumulates $3,500 in employment taxes. A has a $3,500 deposit obligation that must be satisfied by the 15th day of the following month. Since January 15, 2012, is a Sunday, and January 16, 2012, Dr. Martin Luther King, Jr.'s Birthday, is a legal holiday, A's deposit obligation will be satisfied if the deposit is made by electronic funds transfer by the next business day, January 17, 2012.

Example 2. Semi-weekly depositor. (i) *Determination of status.* For the calendar year 2011, Employer B determines its depositor status using the lookback period July 1, 2009 to June 30, 2010. For the four calendar quarters within this period, B reported aggregate employment tax liabilities of $88,000 on its quarterly Forms 941. Because that amount exceeds $50,000, B is a semi-weekly depositor for the entire calendar year 2011.

(ii) *Semi-weekly rule.* On Friday, January 7, 2011, B (a semi-weekly depositor) has a pay day on which it accumulates $4,000 in employment taxes. B has a $4,000 deposit obligation that must be satisfied by the following Wednesday, January 12, 2011.

(iii) *Deposit made within three business days.* On Friday, January 14, 2011, B (a semi-weekly depositor) has a pay day on which it accumulates $4,200 in employment taxes. Generally, B would have a required deposit obligation of employment taxes that must be satisfied by the following Wednesday, January 19, 2011. Because Monday, January 17, 2011, is Dr. Martin Luther King, Jr.'s Birthday, a legal holiday, B has an additional day to make the required deposit. B has a $4,200 deposit obligation that must be satisfied by the following Thursday, January 20, 2011.

Example 3. One-Day rule. On Monday, January 10, 2011, Employer C accumulates $110,000 in employment taxes with respect to wages paid on that date. C has a deposit obligation of $110,000 that must be satisfied by the next business day. If C was not subject to the semi-weekly rule on January 10, 2011, C becomes subject to that rule as of January 11, 2011. See paragraph (b)(2)(ii) of this section.

Example 4. One-Day rule in combination with subsequent deposit obligation. Employer D is subject to the semiweekly rule for calendar year 2011. On Monday, January 10, 2011, D accumulates $115,000 in employment taxes. D has a deposit obligation that must be satisfied by the next business day. On Tuesday, January 11, D accumulates an additional $30,000 in employment taxes. Although D has a $115,000 deposit obligation incurred earlier in the semiweekly period, D has an additional and separate deposit obligation of $30,000 on Tuesday that must be satisfied by the following Friday.

Example 5. Legal Holidays. Employer E conducts business in State X. Wednesday, August 31, 2011, is a statewide legal holiday in State X which is not a legal holiday in the District of Columbia. On Friday, August 26, 2011, E (a semi-weekly depositor) has a pay day on which it accumulates $4,000 in employment taxes. E has a $4,000 deposit obligation that must be satisfied on or before the following Wednesday, August 31, 2011, notwithstanding that the day is a statewide legal holiday in State X.

Example 6. Extension of time to deposit for employers who filed Form 944 for the preceding year satisfied. F (a monthly depositor) was notified to file Form 944 to report its employment tax liabilities for the 2006 calendar year. F filed Form 944 on January 31, 2007, reporting a total employment tax liability for 2006 of $3,000. Because F's annual employment tax liability for the 2006 taxable year exceeded $1,000 (the applicable eligibility threshold for that taxable year), the IRS notified F to file Forms 941 for calendar year 2007 and thereafter. Based on F's liability during the lookback period (calendar year 2005, pursuant to paragraph (b)(4)(i) of this section), F is a monthly depositor for 2007. F accumulates $1,000 in employment taxes during January 2007. Because F is a monthly depositor, F's January deposit obligation is due February 15, 2007. F does not deposit these accumulated employment taxes on February 15, 2007. F accumulates $1,500 in employment taxes during February 2007. F's February deposit is due March 15, 2007. F deposits the $2,500 of employment taxes accumulated during January and February on March 15, 2007. Pursuant to paragraph (c)(6) of this section, F will be deemed to have timely deposited the employment taxes due for January 2007, and, thus, the IRS will not impose a failure-to-deposit penalty under section 6656 for that month.

(e) *Employment taxes defined.*—(1) For purposes of this section, the term "employment taxes" means—

(i) The employee portion of the tax withheld under section 3102;

(ii) The employer tax under section 3111;

(iii) The income tax withheld under sections 3402 and 3405, except income tax withheld with respect to payments made after December 31, 1993, on the following—

(A) Certain gambling winnings under section 3402(q);

(B) Retirement pay for services in the Armed Forces of the United States under section 3402;

(C) Certain annuities described in section 3402(o)(1)(B); and

(D) Pensions, annuities, IRAs, and certain other deferred income under section 3405; and

(iv) The income tax withheld under section 3406, relating to backup withholding with respect to reportable payments made before January 1, 1994.

(2) The term *employment taxes* does not include taxes with respect to wages for domestic service in a private home of the employer, unless the employer is otherwise required to file a Form 941 or Form 944 under §31.6011(a)-4 or §31.6011(a)-5. In the case of employers paying advance earned income credit amounts for periods ending before January 1, 2011, the amount of taxes required to be deposited shall be reduced by advance amounts paid to employees. Also, see §31.6302-3 concerning a taxpayer's option with respect to payments made before January 1, 1994, to treat backup withholding amounts under section 3406 separately.

(f) *Save harbor/De minimis rules.*—(1) *Single deposit safe harbor.*—An employer will be considered to have satisfied its deposit obligation imposed by this section if—

(i) The amount of any shortfall does not exceed the greater of $100 or 2 percent of the amount of employment taxes required to be deposited; and

(ii) The employer deposits the shortfall on or before the shortfall make-up date.

(2) *Shortfall defined.*—For purposes of this paragraph (f), the term "shortfall" means the excess of the amount of employment taxes required to be deposited for the period over the amount deposited for the period. For this purpose, a period is either a monthly, semi-weekly or daily period.

(3) *Shortfall make-up date.*—(i) *Monthly rule.*—A shortfall with respect to a deposit required under the Monthly rule must be deposited or remitted no later than the due date for the quarterly return, in accordance with the applicable form and instructions.

(ii) *Semi-Weekly rule and One-Day rule.*—A shortfall with respect to a deposit required under the Semi-Weekly rule or the One-Day rule must be deposited on or before the first Wednesday or Friday (whichever is earlier), falling on or after the 15th day of the month following the month in which the deposit was required to be made, or, if earlier, the return due date for the return period.

(4) *De minimis rule.*—(i) *De minimis deposit rules for quarterly and annual return periods beginning on or after January 1, 2001.*—If the total amount of accumulated employment taxes for the return period is de minimis and the amount is fully deposited or remitted with a timely filed return for the return period, the amount deposited or remitted will be deemed to have been timely deposited. The total amount of accumulated employment taxes is de minimis if it is less than $2,500 for the return period or if it is de minimis pursuant to paragraph (f)(4)(ii) of this section.

(ii) *De minimis deposit rule for quarterly return periods beginning on or after January 1, 2010.*— For purposes of paragraph (f)(4)(i) of this section, if the total amount of accumulated employment taxes for the immediately preceding quarter was less than $2,500, unless § 31.6302-1(c)(3) applies to require a deposit at the close of the next day, then the employer will be deemed to have timely deposited the employer's employment taxes for the current quarter if the employer complies with the time and method payment requirements contained in paragraph (f)(4)(i) of this section.

(iii) *De minimis deposit rule for employers who file Form 944.*—An employer who files Form 944 whose employment tax liability for the year equals or exceeds $2,500 but whose employment tax liability for a quarter of the year is de minimis pursuant to paragraph (f)(4)(i) of this section will be deemed to have timely deposited the employment taxes due for that quarter if the employer fully deposits the employment taxes accumulated during the quarter by the last day of the month following the close of that quarter. Employment taxes accumulated during the fourth quarter can be either deposited by January 31 or remitted with a timely filed return for the return period.

(5) *Examples.*—The provisions of this paragraph (f) may be illustrated by the following examples:

Example 1. Safe-harbor rule satisfied. On Monday, January 4, 1993, J (a semi-weekly depositor), pays wages and accumulates employment taxes. As required under this section, J makes a deposit on or before the following Friday, January 8, 1993, in the amount of $4,000. Subsequently, J determines that it was actually required to deposit $4,090 by Friday. J has a shortfall of $90. The $90 shortfall does not exceed the greater of $100 or 2% of the amount required to be deposited (2% of $4,090 = $81.80). Therefore, J satisfies the safe harbor of paragraph (f)(1) of this section as long as the $90 shortfall is deposited by the first deposit date (Wednesday or Friday) on or

after the 15th day of the next month (in this case Wednesday, February 17, 1993).

Example 2. Safe-harbor rule not satisfied. The facts are the same as in *Example 1* except that on Friday, January 8, 1993, J makes a deposit of $25,000, and later determines that it was actually required to deposit $26,000. Since the $1,000 shortfall ($26,000 less $25,000) exceeds $520 (the greater of $100 or 2% of the amount required to be deposited (2% of $26,000 = $520)), the safe harbor of paragraph (f)(1) of this section is not satisfied, and absent reasonable cause, J will be subject to a failure-to-deposit penalty under section 6656.

Example 3. De minimis deposit rule for employers who file Form 944 satisfied. K (a monthly depositor) was notified to file Form 944 to report its employment tax liabilities for the 2006 calendar year. In the first quarter of 2006, K accumulates employment taxes in the amount of $1,000. On April 28, 2006, K deposits the $1,000 of employment taxes accumulated in the first quarter. K accumulates another $1,000 of employment taxes during the second quarter of 2006. On July 31, 2006, K deposits the $1,000 of employment taxes accumulated in the second quarter. K's business grows and accumulates $1,500 in employment taxes during the third quarter of 2006. On October 31, 2006, K deposits the $1,500 of employment taxes accumulated in the third quarter. K accumulates another $2,000 in employment taxes during the fourth quarter. K files Form 944 on January 31, 2007, reporting a total employment tax liability for 2006 of $5,500 and submits a check for the remaining $2,000 of employment taxes with the return. K will be deemed to have timely deposited the employment taxes due for all of 2006 because K complied with the de minimis deposit rule provided in paragraph (f)(4)(iii) of this section. Therefore, the IRS will not impose a failure-to-deposit penalty under section 6656 for any month of the year. Under this de minimis deposit rule, because K was required to file Form 944 for calendar year 2006, if K's employment tax liability for a quarter is de minimis, then K may deposit that quarter's liability by the last day of the month following the close of the quarter. This de minimis rule allows K to have the benefit of the same quarterly de minimis amount K would have received if K filed Form 941 each quarter instead of Form 944 annually. Thus, because K's employment tax liability for each quarter was de minimis, K could deposit quarterly.

(g) *Agricultural employers—special rules.*— (1) *In general.*—An agricultural employer reports wages paid to farm workers annually on Form 943 (Employer's Annual Tax Return for Agricultural Employees) and reports wages paid to nonfarm workers quarterly on Form 941 or annually on Form 944. Accordingly, an agricultural employer must treat employment taxes reportable on Form 943 ("Form 943 taxes") separately from employment taxes reportable on Form 941 or Form 944 ("Form 941 or Form 944 taxes"). Form 943 taxes and Form 941 or Form 944 taxes are not combined for purposes of determining whether a deposit of either is due, whether the One-Day rule of paragraph (c)(3) of this section applies, or whether any safe harbor is applicable. In addition, Form 943 taxes and Form 941 or Form 944 taxes must be deposited separately. (See paragraph (b) of this section for rules for determining an agricultural employer's deposit status for Form 941 taxes). Whether an agricultural employer is a monthly or semi-weekly depositor of Form 943 taxes is determined according to the rules of this paragraph (g).

(2) *Monthly depositor.*—An agricultural employer is a monthly depositor of Form 943 taxes for a calendar year if the amount of Form 943 taxes accumulated in the lookback period (as defined in paragraph (g)(4) of this section) is $50,000 or less. An agricultural employer ceases to be a monthly depositor of Form 943 taxes on the first day after the employer is subject to the One-Day rule in paragraph (c)(3) of this section. At that time, the agricultural employer immediately becomes a semi-weekly depositor of Form 943 taxes for the remainder of the calendar year and the succeeding calendar year.

(3) *Semi-weekly depositor.*—An agricultural employer is a semi-weekly depositor of Form 943 taxes for a calendar year if the amount of Form 943 taxes accumulated in the lookback period (as defined in paragraph (g)(4) of this section) exceeds $50,000.

(4) *Lookback period.*—(i) *In general.*—For purposes of this paragraph (g), the lookback period for Form 943 taxes is the second calendar year preceding the current calendar year. For example, the lookback period for calendar year 1993 is calendar year 1991. New employers shall be treated as having employment tax liabilities of zero for any lookback period before the date the employer started or acquired its business.

(ii) *Adjustments and Claims for Refund.*— The employment tax liability reported on the original return for the return period is the amount taken into account in determining whether the amount of Form 943 taxes accumulated in the lookback period exceeds $50,000. Any amounts reported on adjusted returns or claims for refund pursuant to sections 6205, 6402, 6413 and 6414 filed after the due date of the original return are not taken into account when determining the amount of Form 943 taxes accumulated in the lookback period. However, prior period adjustments reported on Form 943 for 2008 and earlier years are taken into account in determining the employment tax liability for the return period in which the adjustments are reported.

(5) The following example illustrates the provisions of this section.

Example. A, an agricultural employer, employs both farm workers and nonfarm workers (employees in its administrative offices). *A*'s depositor status for calendar year 1993 for Form 941 taxes will be based upon its employment tax liabilities reported on Forms 941 for the third and fourth quarters of 1991 and the first and second quarters of 1992 (the period July 1 to June 30). *A*'s depositor status for Form 943 taxes will be based upon its employment tax liability reported on its annual Form 943 for calendar year 1991.

(h) *Time and manner of deposit—deposits required to be made by electronic funds transfer.*—(1) *In general.*—Section 6302(h) requires the Secretary to prescribe such regulations as may be necessary for the development and implementation of an electronic funds transfer system to be used for the collection of the depository taxes as described in paragraph (h)(3) of this section. Section 6302(h)(2) provides a phase-in schedule that sets forth escalating minimum percentages of those depository taxes to be deposited by electronic funds transfer. This paragraph (h) prescribes the rules necessary for implementing an electronic funds transfer system for collection of depository taxes and for effecting an orderly and expeditious phase-in of that system.

(2) *Applicability of requirement.*—(i) *Deposits for return periods beginning before January 1, 2000.*—(A) Taxpayers whose aggregate deposits of the taxes imposed by Chapters 21 (Federal Insurance Contributions Act), 22 (Railroad Retirement Tax Act), and 24 (Collection of Income Tax at Source on Wages) of the Internal Revenue Code during a 12-month determination period exceed the applicable threshold amount are required to deposit all depository taxes described in paragraph (h)(3) of this section by electronic funds transfer (as defined in paragraph (h)(4) of this section) unless exempted under paragraph (h)(5) of this section. If the applicable effective date is January 1, 1995, or January 1, 1996, the requirement to deposit by electronic funds transfer applies to all deposits required to be made on or after the applicable effective date. If the applicable effective date is July 1, 1997, the requirement to deposit by electronic funds transfer applies to all deposits required to be made on or after July 1, 1997 with respect to deposit obligations incurred for return periods beginning on or after January 1, 1997. If the applicable effective date is January 1, 1998, or thereafter, the requirement to deposit by electronic funds transfer applies to all deposits required to be made with respect to deposit obligations incurred for return periods beginning on or after the applicable effective date. In general, each applicable effective date has one 12-month determination period. However, for the applicable effective date January 1, 1996, there are two determination periods. If the applicable threshold amount is exceeded in either of those determination periods, the taxpayer becomes subject to the requirement to deposit by electronic funds transfer, effective January 1, 1996. The threshold amounts, determination periods and applicable effective dates for purposes of this paragraph (h)(2)(i)(A) are as follows:

Threshold Amount	Determination Period	Applicable Effective Date
$78 million	1–1–93 to 12–31–93	January 1, 1995
$47 million	1–1–93 to 12–31–93	January 1, 1996
$47 million	1–1–94 to 12–31–94	January 1, 1996
$50 thousand	1–1–95 to 12–31–95	July 1, 1997
$50 thousand	1–1–96 to 12–31–96	January 1, 1998
$50 thousand	1–1–97 to 12–31–97	January 1, 1999

(B) Unless exempted under paragraph (h)(5) of this section, a taxpayer that does not deposit any of the taxes imposed by chapters 21, 22, and 24 during the applicable determination periods set forth in paragraph (h)(2)(i)(A) of this section, but that does make deposits of other depository taxes (as described in paragraph (h)(3) of this section), is nevertheless subject to the requirement to deposit by electronic funds transfer if the taxpayer's aggregate deposits of all depository taxes exceed the threshold amount set forth in this paragraph (h)(2)(i)(B) during an applicable 12-month determination period. This requirement to deposit by electronic funds transfer applies to all depository taxes due with respect to deposit obligations incurred for return periods beginning on or after the applicable effective date. The threshold amount, determination periods, and applicable effective dates for purposes of this paragraph (h)(2)(i)(B) are as follows:

Threshold Amount	Determination Period	Applicable Effective Date
$50 thousand	1–1–95 to 12–31–95	January 1, 1998
$50 thousand	1–1–96 to 12–31–96	January 1, 1998
$50 thousand	1–1–97 to 12–31–97	January 1, 1999

(C) This paragraph (h)(2)(i) applies only to deposits required to be made for return periods beginning before January 1, 2000. Thus, a taxpayer, including a taxpayer that is required under this paragraph (h)(2)(i) to make deposits by electronic funds transfer beginning in 1999 or an earlier year, is not required to use electronic funds transfer to make deposits for return periods beginning after December 31, 1999, unless deposits by electronic funds transfer are required under paragraph (h)(2)(ii) of this section.

(ii) *Deposits for return periods beginning after December 31, 1999, and made before January 1, 2011.*—Unless exempted under paragraph (h)(5) of this section, for deposits for return periods beginning after December 31, 1999, and made before January 1, 2011, a taxpayer that deposits more than $200,000 of taxes described in paragraph (h)(3) of this section during a calendar year beginning after December 31, 1997, must use electronic funds transfer (as defined in paragraph (h)(4) of this section) to make all deposits of those taxes that are required to be made for return periods beginning after December 31 of the following year and must continue to deposit by electronic funds transfer in all succeeding years. As an example, a taxpayer that exceeds the $200,000 deposit threshold during calendar year 1998 is required to make deposits for return periods beginning in or after calendar year 2000 by electronic funds transfer.

(iii) *Deposits made after December 31, 2010.*—Unless exempted under paragraph (h)(5) of this section, a taxpayer that has a required tax deposit obligation described in paragraph (h)(3) of this section must use electronic funds transfer (as defined in paragraph (h)(4) of this section) to make all deposits of those taxes made after December 31, 2010.

(iv) *Voluntary deposits.*—A taxpayer that is authorized to make payment of taxes with a return under regulations may voluntarily make a deposit by electronic funds transfer.

(3) *Taxes required to be deposited by electronic funds transfer.*—The requirement to deposit by electronic funds transfer under paragraph (h)(2) of this section applies to all the taxes required to be deposited under §§1.6302-1, 1.6302-2, and 1.6302-3 of this chapter; §§31.6302-1, 31.6302-2, 31.6302-3, 31.6302-4, and 31.6302(c)-3; and §40.6302(c)-1 of this chapter.

(4) *Definitions.*—(i) *Electronic funds transfer.*—An *electronic funds transfer* is any transfer of depository taxes made in accordance with Revenue Procedure 97-33, (1997-30 I.R.B.), (see §601.601(d)(2) of this chapter), or in accordance with procedures subsequently prescribed by the Commissioner.

(ii) *Taxpayer.*—For purposes of this section, a *taxpayer* is any person required to deposit federal taxes, including not only individuals, but also any trust, estate, partnership, association, company or corporation.

(5) *Exemptions.*—If any categories of taxpayers are to be exempted from the requirement to deposit by electronic funds transfer, the Commissioner will identify those taxpayers by guidance published in the Internal Revenue Bulletin. (See §601.601(d)(2)(ii)(*b*) of this chapter.)

(6) *Separation of deposits.*—A deposit for one return period must be made separately from a deposit for another return period.

(7) *Payment of balance due.*—If the aggregate amount of taxes reportable on the applicable tax return for the return period exceeds the total amount deposited by the taxpayer with regard to the return period, then the balance due must be

remitted in accordance with the applicable form and instructions.

(8) *Time deemed deposited.*—A deposit of taxes by electronic funds transfer will be deemed made when the amount is withdrawn from the taxpayer's account, provided the U.S. Government is the payee and the amount is not returned or reversed.

(9) *Time deemed paid.*—In general, an amount deposited under this paragraph (h) will be considered to be a payment of tax on the last day prescribed for filing the applicable return for the return period (determined without regard to any extension of time for filing the return) or, if later, at the time deemed deposited under paragraph (h)(8) of this section. In the case of the taxes imposed by chapters 21 and 24 of the Internal Revenue Code, solely for purposes of section 6511 and the regulations thereunder (relating to the period of limitation on credit or refund), if an amount is deposited prior to April 15th of the calendar year immediately succeeding the calendar year that includes the period for which the amount was deposited, the amount will be considered paid on April 15th.

(i) *Time and manner of remittance with a return.*—(1) *General rules.*—A remittance required to be made by this section that is authorized to be made with a return under regulations and is made with a return must be made separately from a remittance required by any other section. Further, a remittance for a deposit period in one return period must be made separately from a remittance for a deposit period in another return period.

(2) *Payment of balance due.*—If the aggregate amount of taxes reportable on the return for the return period exceeds the total amount deposited by the employer with regard to the return period pursuant to this section, the balance due must be remitted in accordance with the applicable form and instructions.

(3) *Time deemed paid.*—In general, amounts remitted with a return under this section will be considered as paid on the date payment is received by the Internal Revenue Service at the place prescribed for filing by regulations or forms and instructions (or if section 7502(a) applies, by the date the payment is treated as received under section 7502(a)), or on the last day prescribed for filing the return (determined without regard to any extension of time for filing the return), whichever is later. In the case of the taxes imposed by chapter 21 and 24 of the Internal Revenue Code, solely for purposes of section 6511 and the regulations thereunder (relating to the period of limitation on credit or refund), if an amount is remitted with a return under this section prior to April 15th of the calendar year immediately succeeding the calendar year that contains the period for which the amount was remitted, the amount will be considered paid on April 15th of the succeeding calendar year.

(j) *Voluntary payments by electronic funds transfer.*—Any person may voluntarily remit by electronic funds transfer any payment of tax imposed by subtitle C of the Internal Revenue Code. Such payment must be made in accordance with procedures prescribed by the Commissioner.

(k) *Special rules.*—(1) *Notice exception.*—The provisions of this section are not applicable with respect to employment taxes for any month in which the employer receives notice that a return is required under §31.6011(a)-5 (or for any subsequent month for which such a return is required), if those taxes are also required to be deposited under the separate accounting procedures provided in §301.7512-1 of the Regulations on Procedure and Administration (which procedures are applicable if notification is given by the Commissioner of failure to comply with certain employment tax requirements). In cases in which a monthly return is required under §31.6011(a)-5 but the taxes are not required to be deposited under the separate accounting procedures provided in §301.7512-1, the provisions of this section shall apply except those provisions shall not authorize the deferral of any deposit to a date after the date on which the return is required to be filed.

(2) *Wages paid in nonconvertible foreign currency.*—The provisions of this section are not applicable with respect to wages paid in nonconvertible foreign currency pursuant to §301.6316-7.

(l) [Reserved].

(m) *Cross references.*—(1) *Failure to deposit penalty.*—For provisions relating to the penalty for failure to make a deposit within the prescribed time, see section 6656.

(2) *Saturday, Sunday, or legal holiday.*—For provisions relating to the time for performance of acts where the last day falls on Saturday, Sunday, or a legal holiday, see the provisions of §301.7503-1.

(n) *Effective/applicability dates.*—Sections 31.6302-1 through 31.6302-3 apply with respect to the deposit of employment taxes attributable to payments made after December 31, 1992. To the extent that the provisions of §§31.6302-1 through 31.6302-3 are inconsistent with the provisions of §§31.6302(c)-1 and 31.6302(c)-2, a taxpayer will be considered to be in compliance with §§31.6302-1 through 31.6302-3 if the taxpayer makes timely deposits during 1993 in accordance with §§31.6302(c)-1 and 31.6302(c)-2. Paragraphs (b)(4), (c)(5), (c)(6), (d) *Example 6*, (e)(2), (f)(4)(i), (f)(4)(iii), (f)(5) *Example 3*, and (g)(1) of this section apply to taxable years beginning on or after December 30, 2008. Paragraph (f)(4)(ii) of this section applies to taxable years beginning on or after January 1, 2010. The rules of paragraphs (e)(2) and (g)(1) of this section that apply to taxable years beginning before December 30, 2008, are contained in §31.6302-1 as in effect prior to December 30, 2008. The rules of paragraphs (b)(4), (c)(5), (c)(6), (d) *Example 6*, (f)(4)(i), (f)(4)(iii), and (f)(5) *Example 3* of this section that apply to taxable years beginning on or after January 1, 2006, and before December 30, 2008, are contained in §31.6302-1T as in effect prior to December 30, 2008. The rules of paragraphs (b)(4) and (f)(4) of this section that apply to taxable years beginning before January 1, 2006, are contained in §31.6302-1 as in effect prior to January 1, 2006. The rules of paragraph (g) of this section eliminating use of Federal tax deposit coupons apply to deposits and payments made after December 31, 2010.

(o) *Effective/applicability date.*—Paragraphs (c), (d) *Examples 1 through 5*, (h)(2)(ii), (h)(2)(iii), (h)(2)(iv),(i)(1) and (i)(3) of this section apply to deposits and payments made after December 31, 2010. [Reg. §31.6302-1.]

☐ [T.D. 8436, 9-22-92 (*corrected 10-27-92 and 2-9-94*). *Amended by* T.D. 8504, 12-22-93; T.D. 8723, 7-11-97; T.D. 8771, 6-15-98; T.D. 8822, 6-16-99; T.D. 8828, 7-12-99; T.D. 8909, 12-5-2000; T.D. 8946, 5-22-2001; T.D. 8947, 6-14-2001; T.D. 8952, 6-25-2001; T.D. 9239, 12-30-2005; T.D. 9405, 6-30-2008; T.D. 9440, 12-24-2008 T.D. 9507, 12-2-2010; T.D. 9524, 5-6-2011; T.D. 9566, 12-9-2011 *and* T.D. 9586, 4-24-2012.]

[Reg. §51.6302-1]

§51.6302-1. Method of paying the branded prescription drug fee.—(a) *Fee to be paid by electronic funds transfer.*—Under the authority of section 6302(a), the fee imposed on branded prescription drug sales by section 9008 and §51.5 must be paid by electronic funds transfer as defined in §31.6302-1(h)(4)(i) of this title, as if the fee were a depository tax. For the time for paying the fee, see §51.8.

(b) *Effective/applicability date.*—This section applies on and after July 28, 2014. [Reg. §51.6302-1.]

☐ [T.D. 9684, 7-24-2014.]

[Reg. §57.6302-1]

§57.6302-1. Method of paying the health insurance providers fee.—(a) *Fee to be paid by electronic funds transfer.*—Under the authority of section 6302(a), the fee imposed on covered entities engaged in the business of providing health insurance for United States health risks under section 9010 and §57.4 must be paid by electronic funds transfer as defined in §31.6302-1(h)(4)(i) of this chapter, as if the fee were a depository tax. For the time for paying the fee, see §57.7.

(b) *Effective/Applicability date.*—This section applies with respect to any fee that is due on or after September 30, 2014. [Reg. §57.6302-1.]

☐ [T.D. 9643, 11-26-2013.]

[Reg. §301.6302-1]

§301.6302-1. Manner or time of collection of taxes.—(a) *Employment and excise taxes.*—For provisions relating to the manner or time of collection of certain employment and excise taxes and deposits in connection with the payment thereof, see the regulations relating to the particular tax.

(b) *Income taxes.*—(1) For provisions relating to the deposits of income and estimated income taxes of certain corporations, see §1.6302-1 of this chapter (Income Tax Regulations).

(2) For provisions relating to the deposits of tax required to be withheld under chapter 3 of the Code on nonresident aliens and foreign corporations and tax-free covenant bonds, see §1.6302-2 of this chapter.

(c) *Effective/applicability date.*—This section applies to deposits and payments made after December 31, 2010. [Reg. §301.6302-1.]

☐ [T.D. 6498, 10-24-60. *Amended by* T.D. 6922, 6-16-67; T.D. 8952, 6-25-2001 *and* T.D. 9507, 12-2-2010.]

[Reg. §1.6302-2]

§1.6302-2. Deposit rules for tax withheld on nonresident aliens and foreign corporations.— (a) *Time for making deposits.*—(1) *Deposits.*— (i) *Monthly deposits.*—Except as provided in paragraphs (a)(1)(ii) and (iv) of this section, every withholding agent that, pursuant to chapter 3 of the Internal Revenue Code, has accumulated at the close of any calendar month an aggregate amount of undeposited taxes of $200 or more shall deposit such aggregate amount by the 15th day of the following month. However, the preceding sentence shall not apply if the withholding agent has made a deposit of taxes pursuant to paragraph (a)(1)(ii) of this section to a quarter-monthly period that occurred during such month. If the 15th day of the following month is a Saturday, Sunday, or legal holiday in the District of Columbia under section 7503, taxes will be treated as timely deposited if deposited on the next succeeding day which is not a Saturday, Sunday, or legal holiday. With respect to section 1446, this section applies only to a publicly traded partnership described in §1.1446-4.

(ii) *Quarter-monthly deposits.*—If at the close of any quarter-monthly period within a calendar month, the aggregate amount of undeposited taxes required to be withheld pursuant to chapter 3 of the Internal Revenue Code is $2,000 or more, the withholding agent shall deposit such aggregate amount within 3 business days after the close of such quarter-monthly period. Business days include every calendar day other than Saturdays, Sundays, or legal holidays in the District of Columbia under section 7503. If any of the three weekdays following the close of a quarter-monthly period is a legal holiday under section 7503, the withholding agent has an additional day for each day that is a legal holiday by which to make the required deposit. For example, if the Monday following the close of a quarter-monthly period is New Year's Day, a legal holiday, the required deposit for the quarter-monthly period is not due until the following Thursday rather than the following Wednesday.

(iii) *Excess deposits.*—The excess (if any) of a deposit over the actual taxes for a monthly or quarter-monthly deposit period shall be applied in order of time to each of the withholding agent's succeeding deposits with respect to the same calendar year, until exhausted, to the extent that the amount by which the taxes for a subsequent deposit period exceed the deposit for such subsequent deposit period.

(iv) *Annual deposits.*—If at the close of December of each calendar year, the aggregate amount of undeposited taxes required to be withheld pursuant to chapter 3 of the Internal Revenue Code is less than $200, the withholding agent may deposit such aggregate amount by March 15 of the following calendar year. If such aggregate amount is not so deposited, it shall be remitted in accordance with paragraph (a)(1) of § 1.1461-1.

(2) *Cross reference.*—For rules relating to the adjustment of deposits, see § § 1.1461-2(b) and 1.6414-1. For rules requiring payment of any undeposited tax, see § 1.1461-1.

(b) *Manner of payment.*—(1) *Payments not required by electronic funds transfer.*—A payment that is not required to be deposited by this section shall be made separately from a payment required by any other section. The payment may be submitted with the filed return. The timeliness of the payment will be determined by the date payment is received by the Internal Revenue Service at the place prescribed for filing by regulations or forms and instructions, or if section 7502(a) applies, by the date the payment is treated as received under section 7502(a), or on the last day prescribed for filing the return (determined without regard to any extension of time for filing the return), whichever is later. Each withholding agent making payments under this section shall report on the return, for the period to which such payments are made, information regarding such payments according to the instructions that apply to such return.

(2) *Voluntary deposits.*—An amount of tax which is not required to be deposited may nevertheless be deposited if the withholding agent so desires.

(3) *Separation of deposits.*—A deposit required by paragraph (a) of this section for any period occurring in one calendar year shall be made separately from any deposit for any period occurring in another calendar year. In addition, a deposit required to be made by paragraph (a) of this section shall be made separately from a deposit required by any other section.

(4) *Multiple remittances.*—A withholding agent may make one, or more than one, remittance of the amount required to be deposited if each remittance is accompanied by the applicable deposit form.

(5) *Time deemed paid.*—In general, amounts deposited under this section shall be considered as paid on the last day prescribed for filing the return (Form 1042) in respect of such tax (determined without regard to any extension of time for filing such return), or at the time deposited, whichever is later. For purposes of section 6511 and the regulations thereunder, relating to period of limitation on credit or refund, if an amount is so deposited prior to April 15th of a calendar year immediately succeeding the calendar year in which occurs the period for which such amount was so deposited, such amount shall be considered as paid on such April 15th.

(c) *Deposits by electronic funds transfer.*—For the requirement to deposit taxes withheld on nonresident aliens and foreign corporations by electronic funds transfer, see § 31.6302-1(h) of this chapter. A taxpayer not required to deposit by electronic funds transfer pursuant to § 31.6302-1(h) of this chapter remains subject to the rules of paragraph (b) of this section.

(d) *Penalties for failure to make deposits.*—For provisions relating to the penalty for failure to make a deposit within the prescribed time, see section 6656.

(e) *Saturday, Sunday, or legal holidays.*—For provisions relating to the time for performance of acts where the last day falls on Saturday, Sunday, or a legal holiday, see § 301.7503-1 of this chapter (Procedure and Administration Regulations).

(f) *Employer identification number.*—For the definition of the term "employer identification number," see § 301.7701-12 of this chapter (Procedure and Administration Regulations). For provisions relating to the penalty for failure to include the employer identification number in a return, statement, or other document, see § 301.6676-1 of such chapter.

(g) *Effective/Applicability date.*—Except as otherwise provided, this section shall apply to tax required to be withheld under chapter 3 of the Internal Revenue Code after 1966. The last sentence of paragraph (a)(1)(i) of this section shall apply to partnership taxable years beginning after April 29, 2008. Paragraph (b)(1) of this section applies to deposits and payments made after December 31, 2010. [Reg. § 1.6302-2.]

☐ [*T.D.* 6922, 6-16-67. *Amended by T.D.* 6941, 12-15-67; *T.D.* 6957, 6-3-68; *T.D.* 7243, 1-2-73; *T.D.* 7953, 5-8-84; *T.D.* 8723, 7-11-97; *T.D.* 8947, 6-14-2001; *T.D.* 8952, 6-25-2001; *T.D.* 9239, 12-30-2005; *T.D.* 9394, 4-28-2008 *and T.D.* 9507, 12-2-2010.]

[Reg. § 31.6302-2]

§ 31.6302-2. Deposit rules for taxes under the Railroad Retirement Tax Act (RRTA).—(a) *General rule.*—Except as otherwise provided in this section, the rules of § 31.6302-1 determine the time and manner of making deposits of employee tax withheld under section 3202 and employer tax imposed under sections 3221(a) and

(b) attributable to payments made after December 31, 1992. Railroad retirement taxes described in section 3221(c) arising during the month must be deposited on or before the first date after the 15th day of the following month on which taxes are otherwise required to be deposited under §31.6302-1.

(b) *Separate application of deposit rules.*—A person who accumulates tax under sections 3202 or 3221 shall not take that tax into account for purposes of determining when taxes described in paragraph (e) of §31.6302-1 must otherwise be deposited.

(c) *Modification of Monthly rule determination.*—(1) *General rule.*—Except as otherwise provided in this section, any person is allowed to use the Monthly rule of §31.6302-1(c)(1) for an entire calendar year unless the amount of R.R.T.A. taxes required to be deposited under this section during the lookback period was more than $50,000. The lookback period is defined as the calendar year preceding the calendar year just ended. Thus, for purposes of determining if an R.R.T.A. employer qualifies to use the Monthly rule for calendar year 1993, a lookback must be made to calendar year 1991. New employers shall be treated as having employment tax liabilities of zero for any calendar year during which the employer did not exist.

(2) *Exception.*—An employer shall immediately cease to be allowed to use the Monthly rule after any day on which that employer is subject to the One-Day rule set forth in §31.6302-1(c)(3). Such employer immediately becomes subject to the Semi-Weekly rule of §31.6302-1(c)(2) for the remainder of the calendar year and the following calendar year.

(d) *Effective/applicability date.*—This section applies to deposits and payments made after December 31, 2010. [Reg. §31.6302-2.]

☐ [*T.D.* 8436, 9-22-92. *Amended by T.D.* 9507, 12-2-2010.]

[Reg. §1.6302-3]

§1.6302-3. Deposit rules for estimated taxes of certain trusts.—(a) *Requirement.*—A bank or other financial institution described in paragraph (b) of this section shall deposit all payments of estimated tax under section 6654(l) with respect to trusts for which such institution acts as a fiduciary by the date otherwise prescribed for paying such tax in the manner set forth in published guidance, publications, forms and instructions.

(b) *Banks and financial institutions subject to this requirement.*—The requirement of paragraph (a) of this section applies to banks and other financial institutions described in sections 581 and 591 that have been designated as authorized Federal tax depositaries described in section 6302(c) and that act as fiduciaries for at least 200 trusts to which section 6654(l) applies that during the calendar year are required to make installment payments of estimated tax with respect to such

trusts. For purposes of this section, a fiduciary is the person responsible for filing the tax returns and paying the taxes with respect to a trust.

(c) *Cross-references.*—For the requirement to deposit estimated tax payments of taxable trusts by electronic funds transfer, see §31.6302-1(h) of this chapter.

(d) *Effective/applicability date.*—This section applies to deposits and payments made after December 31, 2010. [Reg. §1.6302-3.]

☐ [*T.D.* 8192, 4-8-88. *Amended by T.D.* 8723, 7-11-97; *T.D.* 8952, 6-25-2001 *and T.D.* 9507, 12-2-2010.]

[Reg. §31.6302-3]

§31.6302-3. Federal tax deposit rules for amounts withheld under the backup withholding requirements of section 3406 for payments made after December 31, 1992.—(a) *General rule.*—The rules of §31.6302-1 shall apply to determine the time and manner of making deposits of amounts withheld under the backup withholding requirements of section 3406.

(b) *Treatment of backup withholding amounts separately.*—A taxpayer that withholds income tax under section 3406 with respect to reportable payments made after December 31, 1992, and before January 1, 1994, may, in accordance with the instructions provided with Form 941, deposit such tax under the rules of §31.6302-1 without taking into account the other taxes described in paragraph (e) of §31.6302-1 for purposes of determining when tax withheld under section 3406 must be deposited. A taxpayer that treats backup withholding amounts separately with respect to reportable payments made after December 31, 1992, and before January 1, 1994, shall not take tax withheld under section 3406 into account for purposes of determining when the other taxes described in paragraph (e) of §31.6302-1 must otherwise be deposited under that section. See §31.6302-4 for rules regarding the deposit of income tax withheld under section 3406 with respect to reportable payments made after December 31, 1993.

(c) *Example.*—The following example illustrates the provisions of this section.

Example. For the last two calendar quarters of 1991 and the first two calendar quarters of 1992, Bank *A* reports employment taxes with respect to wages paid totalling in excess of $50,000. For the same four quarters, pursuant to section 3406, *A* withholds income tax with respect to dividend payments in an amount aggregating less than $50,000. For deposit and reporting purposes, *A* treated the backup withholding amounts separately from the employment taxes with respect to wages paid. Accordingly, for calendar year 1993, if *A* chooses to treat the items separately, *A* must use the Semi-Weekly rule of §31.6302-1(c)(2) to deposit taxes with respect to wages paid but may use the Monthly rule of §31.6302-1(c)(1) for the deposit of backup withholding amounts. If *A* chooses not to treat the items separately, the

Reg. §31.6302-3(c)

Semi-Weekly rule would apply to the combined amount of both the taxes with respect to wages paid and the backup withholding amounts. [Reg. §31.6302-3.]

☐ [*T.D. 8436, 9-22-92. Amended by T.D. 8504, 12-22-93.*]

[Reg. §1.6302-4]

§1.6302-4. Voluntary payments by electronic funds transfer.—(a) *Electronic funds transfer.*— Any person may voluntarily remit any payment of tax imposed by subtitle A of the Internal Revenue Code, including any payment of estimated tax. Such payment must be made in the manner set forth in published guidance, publications, forms and instructions.

(b) *Effective/applicability date.*—This section applies to deposits and payments made after December 31, 2010. [Reg. §1.6302-4.]

☐ [*T.D. 8723, 7-11-97. Amended by T.D. 8828, 7-12-99 and T.D. 9507, 12-2-2010.*]

[Reg. §31.6302-4]

§31.6302-4. Deposit rules for withheld income taxes attributable to nonpayroll payments.—(a) *General rule.*—With respect to nonpayroll withheld taxes attributable to nonpayroll payments made after December 31, 1993, a taxpayer is either a monthly or a semi-weekly depositor based on an annual determination. Except as provided in this section, the rules of §31.6302-1 shall apply to determine the time and manner of making deposits of nonpayroll withheld taxes as though they were employment taxes. Paragraph (b) of this section defines nonpayroll withheld taxes. Paragraph (c) of this section provides rules for determining whether a taxpayer is a monthly or a semi-weekly depositor.

(b) *Nonpayroll withheld taxes defined.*—For purposes of this section, effective with respect to payments made after December 31, 1993, *nonpayroll withheld taxes* means—

(1) Amounts withheld under section 3402(q), relating to withholding on certain gambling winnings;

(2) Amounts withheld under section 3402 with respect to amounts paid as retirement pay for service in the Armed Forces of the United States;

(3) Amounts withheld under section 3402(o)(1)(B), relating to certain annuities;

(4) Annuities withheld under section 3405, relating to withholding on pensions, annuities, IRAs, and certain other deferred income; and

(5) Amounts withheld under section 3406, relating to backup withholding with respect to reportable payments.

(c) *Determination of deposit status.*—(1) *Rules for calendar years 1994 and 1995.*—On January 1, 1994, a taxpayer's depositor status for nonpayroll withheld taxes is the same as the taxpayer's status on January 1, 1994, for taxes

reported on Form 941 under §31.6302-1. A taxpayer generally retains that depositor status for nonpayroll withheld taxes for all of calendar years 1994 and 1995. However, a taxpayer that under this paragraph (c) is a monthly depositor for 1994 and 1995 will immediately lose that status and become a semi-weekly depositor of nonpayroll withheld taxes if the One-Day rule of §31.6302-1(c)(3) is triggered with respect to nonpayroll withheld taxes. See paragraph (d) of this section for a special rule regarding the application of the One-Day rule of §31.6302-1(c)(3) to nonpayroll withheld taxes.

(2) *Rules for calendar years after 1995.*—(i) *In general.*—For calendar years after 1995, the determination of whether a taxpayer is a monthly or a semi-weekly depositor for a calendar year is based on an annual determination and generally depends on the aggregate amount of nonpayroll withheld taxes reported by the taxpayer for the lookback period as defined in paragraph (c)(2)(iv) of this section.

(ii) *Monthly depositor.*—A taxpayer is a monthly depositor of nonpayroll withheld taxes for a calendar year if the amount of nonpayroll withheld taxes accumulated in the lookback period (as defined in paragraph (c)(2)(iv) of this section) is $50,000 or less. A taxpayer ceases to be a monthly depositor of nonpayroll withheld taxes on the first day after the taxpayer is subject to the One-Day rule in §31.6302-1(c)(3) with respect to nonpayroll withheld taxes. At that time, the taxpayer immediately becomes a semi-weekly depositor of nonpayroll withheld taxes for the remainder of the calendar year and the succeeding calendar year. See paragraph (d) of this section for a special rule regarding the application of the One-Day rule of §31.6302-1(c)(3) to nonpayroll withheld taxes.

(iii) *Semi-weekly depositor.*—A taxpayer is a semi-weekly depositor of nonpayroll withheld taxes for a calendar year if the amount of nonpayroll withheld taxes accumulated in the lookback period (as defined in paragraph (c)(2)(iv) of this section) exceeds $50,000.

(iv) *Lookback period.*—For purposes of this section, the lookback period for nonpayroll withheld taxes is the second calendar year preceding the current calendar year. For example, the lookback period for calendar year 1996 is calendar year 1994. A new taxpayer is treated as having nonpayroll withheld taxes of zero for any calendar year in which the taxpayer did not exist.

(d) *Special rules.*—A taxpayer must treat nonpayroll withheld taxes, which are reported on Form 945, "Annual Return of Withheld Federal Income Tax," separately from taxes reportable on Form 941, "Employer's QUARTERLY Federal Tax Return" (or any other return, for example, Form 943, "Employer's Annual Federal Tax Return for Agricultural Employees"). Taxes reported on Form 945 and taxes reported on Form 941 are not combined for purposes of determining whether a deposit of either is due, whether the One-Day rule of §31.6302-1(c)(3) applies, or whether any safe harbor is applicable. In addition, taxes reported on Form 945 and taxes reported on Form 941 must be deposited separately. (See paragraph (b) of §31.6302-1 for rules for determining an employer's deposit status for taxes reported on Form 941.) Taxes reported on Form 945 for one calendar year must be deposited separately from taxes reported on Form 945 for another calendar year.

(e) *Effective/applicability date.*—Section 31.6302-4(d) applies to deposits and payments made after December 31, 2010. [Reg. §31.6302-4.]

☐ [T.D. 8504, 12-22-93. *Amended by T.D. 9507,* 12-2-2010; *T.D. 9524, 5-6-2011 and T.D. 9586,* 4-24-2012.]

[Reg. §40.6302(a)-1]

§40.6302(a)-1. Voluntary payments of excise taxes by electronic funds transfer.—Any person may voluntarily remit by electronic funds transfer any payment of tax to which this part 40 applies. Such payment must be made in accordance with procedures prescribed by the Commissioner. [Reg. §40.6302(a)-1.]

☐ [T.D. 8828, 7-12-99.]

[Reg. §31.6302(b)-1]

§31.6302(b)-1. Method of collection.—For provisions relating to collection by means of returns of the taxes imposed by chapter 21 (Federal Insurance Contributions Act), see §§31.6011(a)-1 and 31.6011(a)-5. [Reg. §31.6302(b)-1.]

☐ [T.D. 6516, 12-20-60.]

[Reg. §31.6302(c)-1]

§31.6302(c)-1. Use of Government depositaries in connection with taxes under Federal Insurance Contributions Act and income tax withheld for amounts attributable to payments made before January 1, 1993.—(a) *Requirement for calendar months beginning after December 31, 1980, but before January 1, 1993.*—(1) *In general.*— (i) In the case of a calendar month which begins after December 31, 1980, but before April 1, 1991—

(a) Except as provided in paragraph (b) of this section and hereinafter in this subdivision (i), if at the close of any calendar month the aggregate amount of undeposited taxes (as defined in paragraph (a)(1)(iii) of this section) is $500 or more, the employer shall deposit the undeposited taxes in a Federal Reserve bank or authorized financial institution (see subparagraph (3)(iii) of this paragraph) within 15 calendar days after the close of such calendar month. However, this (a) of subdivision (i) shall not apply if the employer was required to make a deposit of taxes pursuant to (b) of this subdivision (i) with respect to an eighth-monthly period which occurred during the calendar month.

(b) Except as provided in paragraph (b) of this section and except in the case of first-time 3-banking-day depositors, if at the close of any

eighth-monthly period the aggregate amount of undeposited taxes is $3,000 or more, the employer shall deposit the undeposited taxes in a Federal Reserve bank or authorized financial institution within 3 banking days after the close of such eighth-monthly period. For purposes of determining the amount of undeposited taxes at the close of an eighth-monthly period, undeposited taxes with respect to wages paid during a prior eighth-monthly period shall not be taken into account if the employer has made a deposit with respect to such prior eighth-monthly period. An employer will be considered to have complied with the requirements of this subdivision (i)(b) for a deposit with respect to the close of an eighth-monthly period if—

(1) His deposit is not less than 95 percent (90 percent before January 1, 1982) of the aggregate amount of the taxes with respect to wages paid during the period for which the deposit is made, and

(2) If such eighth-monthly period occurs in a month other than the last month of a period for which a return is required to be filed (hereinafter in this subparagraph referred to as a return period), he deposits any underpayment with his first deposit which is otherwise required by this subdivision (i)(b) to be made after the 15th day of the following month. For purposes of this subdivision (i)(b), a "first-time 3-banking-day depositor" is an employer who establishes to the satisfaction of the Commissioner that he was not required (but for this exception) to make a deposit pursuant to this subdivision (i)(b) (or pursuant to subdivision (ii)(b) of this subparagraph) with respect to each period in any preceding month of the current calendar quarter and with respect to each period in the 4 calendar quarters preceding the current calendar quarter. An employer may in no event qualify as a "first-time 3-banking-day depositor" with respect to any eighth-monthly period if the undeposited taxes at the close of that period are $10,000 or more.

The excess (if any) of a deposit over the actual taxes for a deposit period shall be applied in order of time to each of the employer's succeeding deposits with respect to the same return period, until exhausted, to the extent that the amount by which the taxes for a subsequent deposit period exceed the deposit for such subsequent deposit period. For purposes of this subdivision (i), "eight-monthly period" means the first 3 days of a calendar month, the 4th day through the 7th day of a calendar month, the 8th day through the 11th day of a calendar month, the 12th day through the 15th day of a calendar month, the 16th day through the 19th day of a calendar month, the 20th day through the 22nd day of a calendar month, the 23rd day through the 25th day of a calendar month, or the portion of a calendar month following the 25th day of such month.

(c) The periods within which taxes must be deposited under this section are determined, in the case of employers paying advance earned income credit amounts, by reference to the amount of taxes required to be deposited after reduction for advance amounts paid to employees.

(ii) In the case of a calendar month which begins after March 31, 1991, but before January 1, 1993—

(a) Except as provided in § 31.6302(c)-1(a)(1)(ii)(b) or (c), or § 31.6302(c)-1(b), if with respect to any calendar month the aggregate amount of taxes (as defined in § 31.6302(c)-1(a)(1)(iii)) accumulated with respect to wages paid is $500 or more, but less than $3,000, then the employer shall deposit that aggregate amount in a Federal Reserve bank or authorized financial institution within 15 calendar days after the close of that calendar month. Taxes accumulated with respect to wages paid in a prior calendar month within the same return period shall not be taken into account in determining the aggregate amount of taxes accumulated if a deposit was required to be made under this section with respect to such tax amounts. Deposits made during the calendar month of taxes with respect to wages paid during that month do not reduce the aggregate amount of taxes accumulated for purposes of determining the deposit requirement (if any) for that month. However, this paragraph (a)(1)(ii)(a) shall not apply if the employer was required to make a deposit of taxes pursuant to paragraph (a)(1)(ii)(b) of this section with respect to an eighth-month period which occurred during the calendar month.

Example 1: Employer A's aggregate amount of taxes accumulated with respect to wages paid in April 1991 is $800. Since that amount is in excess of $500, but less than $3,000, A must deposit the $800 in a Federal Reserve bank or authorized financial institution by May 15, 1991.

Example 2: Employer B's aggregate amount of taxes accumulated with respect to wages paid in April 1991 is $400. Since that amount is less than $500, B has no deposit obligation for the month of April. In May 1991 B's aggregate amount of taxes accumulated with respect to wages paid during the month is $450. Since the $400 in taxes in April was not required to be deposited, that amount is taken into account in determining if a deposit is required for May. The aggregate amount of taxes accumulated with respect to wages paid for the two months is in excess of $500, thus requiring a deposit. Since June 15, 1991, is a Saturday, B must deposit the $850 in a Federal Reserve bank or authorized financial institution by Monday, June 17, 1991, pursuant to section 7503 of the Code.

Example 3: The facts are the same as in *Example 2* except that B deposits the $400 in taxes from April on May 15, 1991. Because the $400 was not required to be deposited, that amount is taken into account in determining if a deposit obligation exists for May. Since the aggregate amount of taxes accumulated with respect to wages paid for the two months, $850, is in excess

of $500, a deposit in the aggregate amount of $850 is required by Monday, June 17, 1991. Since $400 was previously deposited, B must deposit an additional $450 by June 17, 1991.

Example 4: On Friday, April 5, 1991, a payroll date, Employer C accumulates $450 in taxes with respect to wages paid on that date. Although not required to do so, C deposits the $450 in an authorized depository. On Friday, April 19, 1991, C accumulates an additional $450 in taxes with respect to wages paid. The aggregate amount of taxes accumulated with respect to wages paid during the calendar month is $900. C has a deposit obligation of $900 for the calendar month and must deposit an additional $450 in an authorized depository by May 15, 1991.

(b) Except as provided in § 31.6302(c)-1(a)(1)(ii)(c) or § 31.6302(c)-1(b), and except in the case of first-time 3-banking-day depositors (as defined in § 31.6302(c)-1(a)(1)(i)(b)(2)), if with respect to any eighth-monthly period (as defined in § 31.6302(c)-1(a)(1)(i)(b)) the aggregate amount of taxes accumulated with respect to wages paid is $3,000 or more, but less than $100,000, the employer shall deposit that aggregate amount in a Federal Reserve bank or authorized financial institution within 3 banking days after the close of that eighth-monthly period. Taxes accumulated with respect to wages paid during a prior eighth-monthly period shall not be taken into account if a deposit was required to be made under this section with respect to such tax amounts. Deposits made during the eighth-monthly period of taxes with respect to wages paid during that eighth-monthly period do not reduce the aggregate amount of taxes accumulated for purposes of determining the deposit requirement (if any) for that eighth-monthly period. Solely for purposes of the examples in this paragraph (a)(1)(ii)(b) and paragraphs (a)(1)(ii)(c), (d), and (f) of this section, "banking days" are assumed to include all calendar days except Saturdays, Sundays, and Federal holidays.

Example 1: For the eighth-monthly period April 1-3, 1991, Employer D's aggregate amount of taxes accumulated with respect to wages paid is $3,500. Since that amount is in excess of $3,000, but less than $100,000, D has a deposit obligation of $3,500 that must be satisfied by April 8, 1991, the third banking day after the close of the eighth-monthly period.

Example 2: For the eighth-monthly period April 1-3, 1991, Employer E's aggregate amount of taxes accumulated with respect to wages paid is $3,500. E has a deposit obligation of $3,500 that must be satisfied by April 8, 1991, three banking days after the close of the April 1-3 eighth-monthly period. For the eighth-monthly period April 4-7, 1991, E's aggregate amount of taxes accumulated with respect to wages paid is $2,800. Since E was required to make a deposit for the April 1-3 eighth-monthly period, that $3,500 amount is not taken into account in determining any obligations that arise in subsequent eighth-monthly periods. E does not have an eighth-monthly deposit obligation with respect to the April 4-7 period.

Example 3: For the eighth-monthly period April 1-3, 1991, Employer F's aggregate amount of taxes accumulated with respect to wages paid is $2,800. Since that amount is less than $3,000, no deposit is required with respect to that eighth-monthly period. For the eighth-monthly period April 4-7, 1991, F's aggregate amount of taxes accumulated with respect to wages paid is $2,500. Since F was not required to deposit the $2,800 in taxes from the April 1-3 eighth-monthly period, that amount is taken into account in determining F's deposit obligation for the April 4-7 eighth-monthly period. The aggregate amount of taxes accumulated for the two eighth-monthly periods is $5,300. F has a deposit obligation of $5,300 that must be satisfied by April 10, 1991, three banking days after the close of the April 4-7 eighth-monthly period.

Example 4: The facts are the same as in *Example 3* except that F deposits the $2,800 from the April 1-3 eighth-monthly period on April 4, 1991. Because the $2,800 was not required to be deposited, that amount is taken into account in determining F's deposit obligation for the April 4-7 eighth-monthly period. The aggregate amount of taxes accumulated for the two eighth-monthly periods is $5,300. Since that amount is in excess of $3,000, a deposit obligation exists after the close of the April 4-7 eighth-monthly period. As $2,800 of that amount was previously deposited, F has a deposit obligation of $2,500 that must be satisfied by April 10, 1991, three banking days after the close of the April 4-7 eighth-monthly period.

Example 5: On Friday, April 12, 1991, the beginning of an eighth-monthly period (April 12-15), G accumulates $3,500 in taxes with respect to wages paid and deposits the $3,500 in an authorized depository on that date although a deposit of the $3,500 was not required to be made on that date. On Monday, April 15, 1991, the end of the April 12-15 eighth-monthly period, G accumulates an additional $2,000 in taxes with respect to wages paid. The aggregate amount of taxes accumulated with respect to wages paid during the April 12-15 eighth-monthly period is $5,500. G has a deposit obligation for the eighth-monthly period of $5,500. Since $3,500 of that amount was previously deposited, G has a remaining deposit obligation of $2,000 that must be satisfied by Thursday, April 18, 1991, three banking days after the close of the eighth-monthly period.

(c) If on any day within an eighth-monthly period the aggregate amount of taxes accumulated with respect to wages paid is $100,000 or more, the employer shall deposit that aggregate amount in a Federal Reserve bank or authorized financial institution on the first banking day after that day. Taxes accumulated with respect to wages paid prior to that day shall not be taken into account if a deposit was required under this section with respect to such tax amounts. Taxes deposited on any given day with respect to wages paid on that day do not reduce

the aggregate amount of taxes accumulated on that day for purposes of determining the deposit requirement (if any) for that day.

Example 1: On Thursday, April 4, 1991, the beginning of the April 4-7 eighth-monthly period, Employer H accumulates $55,000 in taxes with respect to wages paid on that date. On Saturday, April 6, 1991, H accumulates an additional $50,000 in taxes with respect to wages paid. H has a deposit obligation of $105,000 that must be satisfied by Monday, April 8, the next banking day after Saturday, April 6.

Example 2: On Friday, April 12, 1991, the beginning of the April 12-15 eighth-monthly period, J accumulates $60,000 in taxes with respect to wages paid and deposits the $60,000 in an authorized depository on that date although a deposit of the $60,000 was not required to be made on that date. On Monday, April 15, 1991, the last day in the April 12-15 eighth-monthly period, J accumulates an additional $50,000 in taxes with respect to wages paid. On Monday, April 15, the aggregate amount of taxes accumulated with respect to wages paid during the eighth-monthly period to date totals $110,000. J has a $110,000 deposit obligation that must be satisfied by the next banking day after the $100,000 threshold is reached. Since $60,000 of the $110,000 was already deposited, J has a remaining deposit obligation of $50,000 that must be satisfied by Tuesday, April 16, 1991, the next banking day following April 15th.

Example 3: On Monday, April 1, 1991, Employer K accumulates $105,000 in taxes with respect to wages paid on that date. On that same day, K deposits in an authorized depository $10,000 of the $105,000 accumulated. K has a $105,000 deposit obligation that must be satisfied by the next banking day, April 2, 1991. The $10,000 deposited on April 1 cannot be used to reduce the aggregate amount of accumulated taxes with respect to that date. K has a remaining deposit obligation of $95,000 that must be satisfied by April 2, 1991.

(d) If, with respect to any eighth-monthly period, an employer incurs an obligation to deposit in accordance with §31.6302(c)-1(a)(1)(ii)(c), and later, within the same eighth-monthly period, accumulates with respect to wages paid taxes of $3,000 or more, but less than $100,000, an additional deposit is required in accordance with §31.6302(c)-1(a)(1)(ii)(b). However, if the amount of taxes is $100,000 or more, an additional deposit is required in accordance with §31.6302(c)-1(a)(1)(ii)(c).

Example: On Tuesday, April 2, 1991, Employer L accumulates $110,000 in aggregate taxes with respect to wages paid. In accordance with paragraph (a)(1)(ii)(c) of this section, L has a $110,000 deposit obligation that must be satisfied by Wednesday, April 3, 1991, the next banking day following April 2. On Wednesday, April 3, 1991, L accumulates an additional $10,000 in taxes with respect to wages paid that date. In accordance with paragraph (a)(1)(ii)(b), L now has an additional deposit obligation of $10,000 that must be satisfied by Monday, April 8, 1991, the 3rd banking day following the close of the April 1-3 eighth-monthly period. The obligation to deposit the $10,000 is separate and distinct from the obligation to deposit the $110,000.

(e) An employer will be considered to have satisfied the deposit obligation imposed by paragraphs (a)(1)(ii)(b), (c) and (d) of this section if—

(1) The deposit that is made is not less than 95 percent of the aggregate amount of taxes accumulated with respect to wages paid during the period for which the deposit is made, and

(2) If the eighth-monthly period (or, in the case of a deposit required under paragraph (a)(1)(ii)(c) of this section, the day on which the obligation arose) is in a month other than the last month of the return period, the employer deposits any remaining amount due with the first deposit otherwise required to be made after the fifteenth day of the following month. In the case of the last month of the return period, see § 31.6302(c)-1(a)(1)(iv).

(f) Any excess of a deposit over the actual taxes required to be deposited to date (overdeposit) during the return period shall be applied in order of time to each of the employer's succeeding deposit obligations within the same return period. In the determination of the aggregate amount of taxes accumulated with respect to wages paid in succeeding deposit periods, the overdeposit does not reduce the aggregate amount accumulated although the overdeposit is credited to the depositor's account.

Example: Employer M's deposit obligation for the eighth-monthly period April 1-3, 1991, is $3,200. On April 8, 1991, three banking days after the close of the eighth-monthly period, M deposits $4,000 in an authorized depository, $800 in excess of the amount required to be deposited. During the eighth-monthly period April 4-7, 1991, M accumulates $3,750 in taxes with respect to wages paid during such period. Although the $800 overdeposit for the April 1-3 eighth-monthly period is credited to M's account, it may not be used to determine whether a deposit obligation exists for the April 4-7 eighth-monthly period. The two deposit obligations are separate and distinct. Since the amount of taxes accumulated with respect to the April 4-7 eighth-monthly period is an amount greater than $3,000, a deposit is required under paragraph (a)(1)(ii)(b) of this section within three banking days after the close of the period. M has a remaining deposit obligation of $2,950 ($3,750 accumulated less $800 overdeposit) that must be satisfied by April 10, 1991, three banking days after the close of the period.

(g) The periods within which taxes must be deposited under this section are determined, in the case of employers paying advance earned income credit amounts, by reference to the amount of taxes required to be deposited

after reduction for advance amounts paid to employees.

(h) For purposes of this paragraph (a)(1)(ii), the term "wages paid" includes all amounts included in wages, e.g., under section 3121(v) of the Code, regardless of whether they have actually been paid.

(iii) As used in subdivisions (i) and (ii) of this subparagraph, the term "taxes" means—

(a) The employee tax withheld under section 3102,

(b) The employer tax under section 3111, and

(c) The income tax withheld under section 3402, including amounts withheld with respect to qualified State individual income taxes, exclusive of taxes with respect to wages for domestic service in a private home of the employer or, if paid before April 1, 1971, wages for agricultural labor. In addition, with respect to wages paid after December 31, 1970, and before April 1, 1971, for agricultural labor, any taxes described in subparagraph (2)(ii) of this paragraph which are not required under such subparagraph to be deposited, and any income tax (including qualified State individual income tax) withheld under section 3402 with respect to such wages, shall be deemed to be "taxes" on and after April 1, 1971. For the requirements relating to the deposit and payment of withheld tax with respect to qualified State individual income taxes, see paragraph (d)(3)(iii) of § 301.6361-1 of this chapter (Regulations on Procedure and Administration).

(iv) If the aggregate amount of taxes reportable on a return (other than a return on Form 942) for a return period exceeds the total amount deposited by the employer pursuant to subdivision (i) or (ii) of this subparagraph for such return period (a) by $500 or more in the case of a return period which ends after December 31, 1980, or (b) by more than $200 in the case of a return period which ends after December 31, 1970, and before January 1, 1981, the employer shall, on or before the last day of the first calendar month following the return period, deposit with a Federal Reserve bank or authorized financial institution an amount equal to the amount by which the taxes reportable on the return exceed the total deposits (if any) made pursuant to subdivision (i) or (ii) of this subparagraph for such period. As used in this subdivision, the term "taxes" shall have the meaning assigned to such term in subdivision (iii) of this subparagraph, except that the term shall include the taxes referred to in (a), (b), and (c) of such subdivision (iii) of this subparagraph with respect to any wages for domestic service in a private home of the employer which the employer elects to report on a quarterly return other than a quarterly return made on Form 942.

(v) If the aggregate amount of taxes reportable on Form CT-1, the return relating to an employer's railroad retirement tax payments, for a return period exceeds the total amount deposited by the employer pursuant to paragraph (a)(1)(i) of this section for such return period by

$100 or more, the employer shall, on or before the last day of the second calendar month following the return period, deposit with a Federal Reserve bank or authorized financial institution an amount equal to the amount by which the taxes reportable on Form CT-1 exceed the total deposits (if any) of such taxes made pursuant to subdivision (i) of this subparagraph for such period.

(2) *Depositary forms.*—(i) *In general.*—A deposit required to be made by this section shall be made separately from a deposit required by any other section. An employer may make one, or more than one, remittance of the amount required to be deposited. However, a deposit for a period in one calendar quarter shall be made separately from any deposit for a period in another calendar quarter. An amount of tax which is not required to be deposited may nevertheless be deposited if the employer so desires.

(ii) *Deposits.*—Each remittance of amounts required to be deposited under paragraph (a)(1) of this section shall be accompanied by a Federal Tax Deposit form. Such form shall be prepared in accordance with the instructions applicable thereto. The remittance, together with the Federal Tax Deposit form, shall be forwarded to a financial institution authorized as a depositary for Federal taxes in accordance with 31 CFR Part 214 or, at the election of the employer, to a Federal Reserve bank. For procedures governing the deposit of Federal taxes at a Federal Reserve bank, see 31 CFR Part 214.7. The timeliness of the deposit will be determined by the date stamped on the Federal Tax Deposit form by the Federal Reserve bank or the authorized financial institution or, if section 7502(e) applies, by the date the deposit is treated as received under section 7502(e). Each employer making deposits under this section shall report on the return, for the period with respect to which such deposits are made, information regarding such deposits according to the instructions that apply to such return and pay at that time (or deposit by the due date of such return) the balance, if any, of the taxes due for such period.

(iii) *Time deemed paid.*—In general, amounts deposited under subdivision (ii) of this subparagraph shall be considered as paid on the last day prescribed for filing the return in respect of such tax (determined without regard to any extension of time for filing such return), or at the time deposited, whichever is later. For purposes of section 6511 and the regulations thereunder, relating to period of limitation on credit or refund, if an amount is so deposited prior to April 15th of a calendar year immediately succeeding the calendar year which contains the period for which such amount was so deposited, such amount shall be considered as paid on such April 15th.

(3) *Procurement of prescribed form.*—Copies of the Federal Tax Deposit form will so far as possible be furnished employers. An employer will not be excused from making a deposit, however, by the fact that no form has been furnished to it. An employer not supplied with the Federal Tax Deposit form should make application therefor in ample time to make the required deposits within the time prescribed. The employer may secure the form or additional forms by application therefor; such application shall supply the employer's name, identification number, address, and the taxable period to which the deposits will relate.

(b) *Exceptions.*—(1) *Monthly returns.*—The provisions of this section are not applicable with respect to taxes for the month in which the employer receives notice that returns are required under § 31.6011(a)-5 (or for any subsequent month for which such a return is required), if those taxes are also required to be deposited under the separate accounting procedures provided in § 301.7512-1 of this chapter (Regulations on Procedure and Administration) (which procedures are applicable if notification is given of failure to comply with certain employment tax requirements). In cases in which a monthly return is required under § 31.6011(a)-5 but the taxes are not required to be deposited under the separate accounting procedures provided in § 301.7512-1, the provisions of this section shall apply except that paragraph (a)(1)(iv) shall not authorize the deferral of any deposit to a date after the date on which the return is required to be filed.

(2) *Wages paid in nonconvertible foreign currency.*—The provisions of this section are not applicable with respect to taxes paid in nonconvertible foreign currency pursuant to § 301.6316-7 of this chapter (Regulations on Procedure and Administration). [Reg. § 31.6302(c)-1.]

□ [*T.D.* 6354, 1-13-59. *Amended by T.D.* 6872, 1-5-66; *T.D.* 6884, 5-16-66; *T.D.* 6903, 12-19-66; *T.D.* 6915, 3-28-67; *T.D.* 6941, 12-15-67; *T.D.* 6957, 6-3-68; *T.D.* 7078, 12-4-70; *T.D.* 7096, 3-17-71; *T.D.* 7574, 11-30-78; *T.D.* 7577, 12-19-78; *T.D.* 7701, 6-9-80; *T.D.* 7766, 1-28-81; *T.D.* 7931, 12-23-83; *T.D.* 7953, 5-8-84; *T.D.* 8341, 3-27-91; *T.D.* 8436, 9-22-92 and T.D. 9239, 12-30-2005.]*

[Reg. § 40.6302(c)-1]

§ 40.6302(c)-1. Deposits.—(a) *In general.*—(1) *Semimonthly deposits required.*—Except as provided by statute or by paragraph (e) of this section, each person required under § 40.6011(a)-1(a)(2) to file a quarterly return must make a deposit of tax for each semimonthly period (as defined in § 40.0-1(c)) in which tax liability is incurred.

(2) *Treatment of taxes imposed by chapter 33.*—For purposes of this part 40, tax imposed by chapter 33 (relating to communications and air transportation) is treated as a tax liability incurred during the semimonthly period—

(i) In which that tax is collected; or

(ii) In the case of the alternative method, in which that tax is considered as collected.

(3) *Definition of net tax liability.*—Net tax liability means the tax liability for the specified period plus or minus any adjustments allowable in accordance with the instructions applicable to the form on which the return is made.

(4) *Computation of net tax liability for a semimonthly period.*—The net tax liability for a semimonthly period may be computed by—

(i) Determining the net tax liability incurred during the semimonthly period; or

(ii) Dividing by two the net tax liability incurred during the calendar month that includes that semimonthly period, provided that this method of computation is used for all semimonthly periods in the calendar quarter.

(b) *Amount of deposit.*—(1) *In general.*—The deposit of tax for each semimonthly period must be not less than 95 percent of the amount of net tax liability incurred during the semimonthly period.

(2) *Safe harbor rules.*—(i) *Applicability.*—The safe harbor rules of this paragraph (b)(2) are applied separately to taxes deposited under the alternative method provided in § 40.6302(c)-3 (alternative method taxes) and to the other taxes for which deposits are required under this section (regular method taxes).

(ii) *Regular method taxes.*—Any person that made a return of tax reporting regular method taxes for the second preceding calendar quarter (the look-back quarter) is considered to have complied with the requirement of this part 40 for deposit of regular method taxes for the current calendar quarter if—

(A) The deposit of regular method taxes for each semimonthly period in the current calendar quarter is not less than 1/6 of the net tax liability for regular method taxes reported for the look-back quarter;

(B) Each deposit is made on time;

(C) The amount of any underpayment of regular method taxes is paid by the due date of the return; and

(D) The person's liability does not include any regular method tax that was not imposed at all times during the look-back quarter or a tax on a chemical not subject to tax at all times during the look-back quarter.

(iii) *Alternative method taxes.*—Any person that made a return of tax reporting alternative method taxes for the look-back quarter is considered to have complied with the requirement of this part 40 for deposit of alternative method taxes for the current calendar quarter if—

(A) The deposit of alternative method taxes for each semimonthly period in the current calendar quarter is not less than 1/6 of the net tax liability for alternative method taxes reported for the look-back quarter;

(B) Each deposit is made on time;

(C) The amount of any underpayment of alternative method taxes is paid by the due date of the return; and

(D) The person's liability does not include any alternative method tax that was not imposed at all times during the look-back quarter and the month preceding the look-back quarter.

(iv) *Modification for tax rate increase.*—The safe harbor rules of this paragraph (b)(2) do not apply to regular method taxes or alternative method taxes for the first and second calendar quarters beginning on or after the effective date of an increase in the rate of any tax to which this part 40 applies unless the deposit of those taxes for each semimonthly period in the calendar quarter is not less than 1/6 of the tax liability the person would have had with respect to those taxes for the look-back quarter if the increased rate of tax had been in effect for the look-back quarter.

(v) *Failure to comply with deposit requirements.*—If a person fails to make deposits as required under this part 40, the IRS may withdraw the person's right to use the safe harbor rules of this paragraph (b)(2).

(c) *Time to deposit.*—(1) *In general.*—The deposit of tax for any semimonthly period must be made by the 14th day of the following semimonthly period unless such day is a Saturday, Sunday, or legal holiday in the District of Columbia in which case the immediately preceding day which is not a Saturday, Sunday, or legal holiday in the District of Columbia is treated as the 14th day. Thus, generally, the deposit of tax for the first semimonthly period in a month is due by the 29th day of that month and the deposit of tax for the second semimonthly period in a month is due by the 14th day of the following month.

(2) *Exceptions.*—See § 40.6302(c)-2 for the special rules for September. See § 40.6302(c)-3 for the special rules for deposits under the alternative method.

(d) *Deposits required by electronic funds transfer.*—All deposits required by this part must be made by *electronic funds transfer*, as that term is defined in § 31.6302-1(h)(4) of this chapter.

(e) *Exceptions.*—(1) *Taxes excluded.*—No deposit is required in the case of the taxes imposed by—

(i) Section 4042 (relating to fuel used on inland waterways);

(ii) Section 4161 (relating to sport fishing equipment and bows and arrow components);

(iii) Section 4682(h) (relating to floor stocks tax on ozone-depleting chemicals);

(iv) Sections 4375 and 4376 (relating to fees on health insurance policies and self-insured health plans); and

(v) Section 5000B (relating to indoor tanning services).

(2) *One-time filings.*—No deposit is required in the case of any taxes reportable on a one-time filing (as defined in § 40.6011(a)-2(b)).

(3) *De minimis exception.*—For any calendar quarter, no deposit is required if the net tax liability for the quarter does not exceed $2,500.

(f) *Effective/applicability date.*—This section applies to deposits and payments made after March 31, 2013. For rules that apply before that date, see 26 CFR part 40 (revised as of April 1, 2013). [Reg. § 40.6302(c)-1.]

☐ [T.D. 8442, 10-21-92. *Amended by T.D.* 8609, 8-4-95; *T.D.* 8685, 11-8-96; *T.D.* 8723, 7-11-97; *T.D.* 8887, 6-7-2000; *T.D.* 8952, 6-25-2001; *T.D.* 8963, 8-8-2001; *T.D.* 9486, 6-11-2010; *T.D.* 9507, 12-2-2010; *T.D.* 9602, 12-5-2012 *and T.D.* 9621, 6-10-2013.]

[Reg. § 46.6302(c)-1]

§ 46.6302(c)-1. Use of Government depositaries.—(a) *Requirements.*—(1) *In general.*—(i) Except as provided in subdivision (ii) of this subparagraph, if for any calendar month, other than the last month of a calendar quarter, any person required to file a quarterly excise tax return on Form 720 has a total liability of more than $100 for all excise taxes reportable on such form, the amount of such liability for taxes (to which this part relates) shall be deposited by him with a Federal Reserve bank on or before the last day of the month following such month.

(ii) This subdivision shall apply to excise taxes (to which this part relates) which are reportable on Form 720 by any person for February and March 1967, or for a calendar quarter thereafter, if such person's total liability for all excise taxes reportable on such form for any calendar month in the preceding calendar quarter exceeded $2,000. In any case to which this subdivision applies, the excise tax for a semimonthly period (as defined in paragraph (b)(1) of this section) shall be deposited by such person in a Federal Reserve Bank on or before the depositary receipt date (as defined in paragraph (b)(2) of this section). A person will be considered to have complied with the requirements of this subdivision for a semimonthly period if—

(a)(1) His deposit for such semimonthly period is not less than 90 percent of the total amount of the excise taxes (to which this part and Part 48 relate) reportable by him on Form 720 for such period, and (2) if such period occurs in a month other than the last month in a calendar quarter, he deposits any underpayment for such month by the first day of the second month following such month; or

(b)(1) His deposit for each semimonthly period in the month is not less than 45 percent of the total amount of the excise taxes (to which this part and Part 48 relate) reportable by him on Form 720 for the month, and (2) if such month is other than the last month in a calendar quarter, he deposits any underpayment for such month by the first day of the second month following such month; or

(c)(1) His deposit for each semimonthly period in the month is not less than 50 percent of the total amount of the excise taxes (to which this part and Part 118 relate) reportable by him on Form 720 for the preceding calendar month, and (2) if such month is other than the last month in a calendar quarter, he deposits any underpayment for such month by the first day of the second month following such month.

Accordingly, a person who makes his deposits in accordance with the provisions of (b) or (c) of this subdivision will not find it necessary to keep his books and records on a semimonthly basis. However, (b) and (c) of this subdivision shall not apply to any such person who normally incurs in the first semimonthly period in each month more than 75 percent of his total excise tax liability (to which this part and Part 48 relate) for the month.

(iii) The provisions of this section shall not apply with respect to taxes for the month or the semimonthly period in which the taxpayer receives notice from the district director that returns are required under paragraph (b) of § 46.6011(a)-1, or for any subsequent month or semimonthly period for which such a return is required.

(2) *Special requirement.*—The provisions of this subparagraph shall apply to every person (whether or not required by subparagraph (1) of this paragraph to make a deposit of taxes) required to file a quarterly excise tax return on Form 720 for a calendar quarter which begins after March 31, 1968, who has a total liability for all excise taxes (to which this part and Part 48 of this chapter relate) reportable on such form which exceeds by more than $100 the total amount of taxes deposited by him pursuant to subparagraph (1) of this paragraph for such quarter. Such person shall, on or before the last day of the month following the calendar quarter for which the return is required to be filed, deposit with a Federal Reserve bank or authorized financial institution the full amount by which his liability for all excise taxes reportable on such form for that calendar quarter exceeds the amount of excise taxes previously deposited by him for that calendar quarter.

(b) *Definitions.*—For purposes of this part—

(1) *Semimonthly period.*—A "semimonthly period" means the first 15 days of a calendar month or the portion of a calendar month following the 15th day of such month.

(2) *Depositary receipt date.*—With respect to the first semimonthly period of a month, the "depositary receipt date" is the first day of the month following such month. With respect to the second semimonthly period of a month, the "depositary receipt date" is the 15th day of the month following such month.

(c) *Depositary forms.*—(1) *In general.*—A person required to make deposits by paragraph (a) of this section may make one, or more than one, remittance of the amount required to be deposited. An amount of such tax which is not required to be deposited may nevertheless be deposited if the person liable for the tax so desires.

(2) *Deposits.*—Each remittance of amounts required to be deposited shall be accompanied by a Federal Tax Deposit form which shall be prepared in accordance with the instructions applicable thereto. The remittance, together with a Federal Tax Deposit form, shall be forwarded to a financial institution authorized as a depositary for Federal taxes in accordance with 31 CFR Part 214 or, at the election of the person making the remittance, to a Federal Reserve bank. For procedures covering the deposit of Federal taxes at a Federal Reserve bank, see 31 CFR part 214.7. The timeliness of the deposit is determined by the date stamped on the Federal Tax Deposit form by the Federal Reserve bank or the authorized financial institution or, if section 7502(e) applies, by the date the deposit is treated as received under section 7502(e). Each person making deposits under this section shall report on the return, for the period with respect to which such deposits are made, information regarding such deposits according to the instructions that apply to such return and pay at that time (or deposit by the due date of such return) the balance, if any, of the taxes due for such period.

(3) *Time deemed paid.*—Amounts deposited under subparagraph (2) of this paragraph shall be considered as paid on the last day prescribed for filing the return in respect of such tax (determined without regard to any extension of time for filing such return), or at the time deposited, whichever is later.

(d) *Procurement of prescribed form.*—Copies of the Federal Tax Deposit form will so far as possible be furnished persons required to deposit. Such a person will not be excused from making a deposit, however, by the fact that no form has been furnished to it. A person not supplied with the proper form should make application therefor in ample time to make the required deposits within the time prescribed. The person may secure the Federal Tax Deposit form or additional forms by applying therefor and supplying its name, identification number, address, and the taxable period to which the deposits will relate. Copies of the Federal Tax Deposit form may be secured by application therefor to the district director or director of a service center. [Reg. § 46.6302(c)-1.]

☐ [*T.D.* 6498. *Amended by T.D.* 6910, 1-27-67; *T.D.* 6915, 3-28-67; *T.D.* 6941, 12-15-67; *T.D.* 6957, 6-3-68 *and T.D.* 7953, 5-9-84.]

[Reg. § 49.6302(c)-1]

§ 49.6302(c)-1. Use of Government depositaries.—(a) *Requirement.*—(1) *In general.*—(i) If for any calendar month, other than the last month of a calendar quarter, any person required to file a quarterly excise tax return on Form 720 has a total liability of more than $100 for all excise taxes collected (see subdivision (iii) of this subparagraph for amounts which are considered as collected) during such month and reportable on such form, the amount of such total liability shall be deposited by him with a Federal Reserve

bank on or before the last day of the month following such month.

(ii) This subdivision shall apply to excise taxes (to which this part relates) which are collected (see subdivision (iii) of this subparagraph for amounts which are considered as collected), by any person required to pay over such taxes, if such person's total liability for all excise taxes reportable on Form 720 for any calendar month in the preceding calendar quarter exceeded $2,000. A person shall deposit the excise taxes to which this subdivision applies in a Federal Reserve bank within 3 banking days after the close of the semimonthly period (as defined in paragraph (b) of this section) during which such taxes were collected. A person will be considered to have complied with the requirements of this subdivision for a semimonthly period if—

(a)(1) His deposit for such semimonthly period is not less than 90 percent of the total amount of the excise taxes (to which this part relates) collected by him during such period, and (2) if such period occurs in a month other than the last month in a calendar quarter, he deposits any underpayment for such month by the last day of the following month; or

(b)(1) His deposit for each semimonthly period in the month is not less than 45 percent of the total amount of the excise taxes (to which this part relates) collected by him during the month, and (2) if such month is other than the last month in a calendar quarter, he deposits any underpayment for such month by the last day of the following month; or

(c)(1) His deposit for each semimonthly period in the month is not less than 50 percent of the total amount of the excise taxes (to which this part relates) collected by him during the preceding calendar month, and (2) if such month is other than the last month in a calendar quarter, he deposits any underpayment for such month by the last day of the following month.

Accordingly, a person who makes his deposits in accordance with the provisions of (b) or (c) of this subdivision will not find it necessary to keep his books and records on a semimonthly basis. However, (b) and (c) of this subdivision shall not apply to any such person who normally collects in the first semimonthly period in each month more than 75 percent of his total excise taxes (to which this part relates) collected during the month.

(iii) For purposes of applying this subparagraph to a person who computes amounts of tax required to be paid over on the basis of amounts billed (in the case of the tax imposed by section 4251) or tickets sold (in the case of the tax imposed by section 4261), the tax so computed for a monthly period ended after March 31, 1967, shall be considered as collected during the succeeding monthly period and the tax so computed for a semimonthly period shall be considered as collected during the second succeeding semimonthly period. A person must notify the Commissioner before changing from one method of computing the tax to another, so that proper adjustments may be made in order to properly reflect the person's excise tax liability.

(iv) The provisions of this section shall not apply with respect to taxes for the month or the semimonthly period in which the person receives notice from the district director that returns are required under paragraph (b) of §49.6011(a)-1, or for any subsequent month or semimonthly period for which such a return is required.

(v) See paragraph (e) of this section for special rule in case of continuation of certain excise tax rates.

(2) *Special requirement.*—The provisions of this subparagraph shall apply to every person (whether or not required by subparagraph (1) of this paragraph to make a deposit of taxes) required to file a quarterly excise tax return on Form 720 for a calendar quarter which begins after March 31, 1968, who has a total liability for all excise taxes (to which this part relates) reportable on such form which exceeds by more than $100 the total amount of taxes deposited by him pursuant to subparagraph (1) of this paragraph for such quarter. Such person shall, on or before the last day of the second month following the calendar quarter for which the return is required to be filed, deposit with a Federal Reserve bank or authorized financial institution the full amount by which liability for all excise taxes reportable on such form for that calendar quarter exceeds the amount of excise taxes previously deposited by him for that calendar quarter.

(b) *Definition of semimonthly period.*—A "semimonthly period" means the first 15 days of a calendar month or the portion of a calendar month following the 15th day of such month.

(c) *Depositary forms.*—(1) *In general.*—A person required to make deposits by paragraph (a) of this section may make one, or more than one, remittance of the amount required to be deposited. An amount of such tax which is not required to be deposited may nevertheless be deposited if the person liable for the tax so desires.

(2) *Deposits.*—Each remittance of amounts required to be deposited shall be accompanied by a Federal Tax Deposit form which shall be prepared in accordance with the instructions applicable thereto. The remittance, together with a Federal Tax Deposit form, shall be forwarded to a financial institution authorized as a depositary for Federal taxes in accordance with 31 CFR Part 214 or, at the election of the person making the remittance, to a Federal Reserve bank. For procedures governing the deposit of Federal taxes at a Federal Reserve bank, see 31 CFR Part 214.7. The timeliness of the deposit is determined by the date stamped on the Federal Tax Deposit form by the Federal Reserve bank or the authorized financial institution or, if section 7502(e) applies, by the date the deposit is treated as received under section 7502(e). Each person making deposits under this section shall report on the return, for the period with respect to which such deposits are made, information regarding such deposits according to the instructions that apply to such return and pay at that time (or deposit by the due date of such return) the balance, if any, of the taxes due for such period.

(3) *Times deemed paid.*—Amounts deposited under subparagraph (2) of this paragraph shall be considered as paid on the last day prescribed for filing the return in respect of such tax (determined without regard to any extension of time for filing such return), or at the time deposited, whichever is later.

(4) *Procurement of prescribed form.*—Copies of the Federal Tax Deposit form will so far as possible be furnished persons required to deposit. Such a person will not be excused from making a deposit, however, by the fact that no form has been furnished to it. A person not supplied with the form should make application therefor in ample time to make the required deposits within the time prescribed. The person may secure the form or additional forms by applying therefor and supplying its name, identification number, address, and the taxable period to which the deposits will relate. Copies of the Federal Tax Deposit form may be secured by application therefor to the district director or director of a service center.

(d) *Special rule in case of certain continuation of tax rates.*—(1) *Application of paragraph.*—This paragraph shall apply to amounts, due under section 4251 with respect to amounts paid pursuant to bills first rendered after April 30, 1968, and collected (see paragraph (a)(1)(iii) of this section for amounts considered as collected) during any monthly or semimonthly period ending before the date of enactment of legislation, enacted subsequent to April 30, 1968, which increases the rate of tax applicable under section 4251 to such amounts.

(2) *Amount to be deposited under this paragraph.*—The amount to be deposited under this paragraph is an amount equal to the difference between—

(i) The amount required to be deposited, with respect to amounts paid pursuant to bills first rendered during the period described in subparagraph (1) of this paragraph, determined by reference to a sale of tax of one percent, and

(ii) The amount required to be deposited, with respect to amounts paid pursuant to bills first rendered during such period, determined by reference to a rate of tax of 10 percent.

(3) *Time for making deposits.*—The amount described in subparagraph (2) of this paragraph shall be deposited on or before the later of—

(i) The third banking day following the enactment of the legislation described in subparagraph (1) of this paragraph,

(ii) July 3, 1968, or

(iii) The date prescribed by paragraph (a) of this section. [Reg. § 49.6302(c)-1.]

Reg. § 49.6302(c)-1(d)(3)(iii)

☐ [*T.D. 6910, 1-27-67. Amended by T.D. 6915, 3-28-67; T.D. 6941, 12-15-67; T.D. 6957, 6-3-68; T.D. 6959, 6-18-68 and T.D. 7953, 5-9-84.*]

[Reg. §31.6302(c)-2]

§31.6302(c)-2. Use of Government depositaries in connection with employee and employer taxes under Railroad Retirement Tax Act for amounts attributable to payments made before January 1, 1993.—(a) *Requirement.*—(1) *In general: after 1983 and before April 1, 1991.*—In the case of a calendar month which begins after December 31, 1983, and before April 1, 1991, if, at a time prescribed under §31.6302(c)-1(a)(1) (i) or (v) for the deposit of undeposited taxes, the aggregate amount of undeposited employee tax withheld after December 31, 1983, and before April 1, 1991, under section 3202 and employer tax imposed after December 31, 1983, and before April 1, 1991, under section 3221(a) and (b) equals an amount required to be deposited under §31.6302(c)-1(a)(1) (i) or (v) the employer shall deposit the undeposited railroad retirement taxes described in sections 3202 and 3221 at such time in the manner prescribed in §31.6302(c)-1(a)(1) (i) or (v) (except that undeposited railroad retirement taxes described in section 3221 (c) shall in no case be required to be deposited earlier than the first day on which a deposit is otherwise required by §31.6302(c)-1(a)(1)(i) to be made after the 15th day of the month following the month in which the section 3221 (c) tax arises).

Notwithstanding the preceding sentence, and notwithstanding subdivision (v) of §31.6302 (c)-1 (a) (1), if, for the calendar year prior to the current calendar year, the aggregate amount of taxes imposed under sections 3202 and 3221 with respect to an employer equalled or exceeded $1 million, such employer shall deposit his undeposited railroad retirement taxes required to be deposited for the current calendar year in accordance with Revenue Procedure 83-90, 1983-52 I.R.B. 18, (relating to transfers by wire to the Treasury).

(2) *In general: After March 31, 1991 and before January 1, 1993.*—In the case of a calendar month which begins after March 31, 1991, if, at a time prescribed under §31.6302(c)-1(a)(1)(ii) or (v) for the deposit of accumulated taxes, the aggregate amount of accumulated employee tax withheld after March 31, 1991, under section 3202 and employer tax imposed after March 31, 1991, under section 3221(a) and (b) equals an amount required to be deposited under §31.6302(c)-1(a)(1)(ii) or (v), the employer shall deposit the accumulated railroad retirement taxes described in sections 3202 and 3221 at the time and in the manner prescribed in §31.6302(c)-1(a)(1)(ii) or (v) (except that accumulated railroad retirement taxes described in section 3221(c) shall in no case be required to be deposited earlier than the first day on which a deposit is otherwise required by §31.6302(c)-1(a)(1)(ii) to be made after the 15th day of the month following the month in which

the section 3221(c) tax arises). Notwithstanding the preceding sentence, and notwithstanding §31.6302(c)-1(a)(1)(v), if, for the calendar year prior to the calendar year preceding the current calendar year, the aggregate amount of taxes imposed under sections 3202 and 3221 with respect to an employer equalled or exceeded $1 million, such employer shall deposit the aggregate amount of railroad retirement taxes required to be deposited for the current calendar year in accordance with Revenue Procedure 83-90, 1983-2 C.B. 615 (relating to transfers by wire to the Treasury).

(3) *Special requirement.*—If an employer files a return on Form CT-1 for a return period beginning before January 1, 1984, and the taxes shown thereon exceed by more than $100 the total amount deposited by him pursuant to paragraph (a)(1) of this section for such return period the employer shall, on or before the last day of the second calendar month following the period for which the return is filed, deposit with a Federal Reserve bank or authorized financial institution an amount equal to the amount by which the taxes shown on the return exceed the total deposits (if any) made pursuant to paragraph (a)(1) of this section for such return period.

(b) *Depositary forms.*—(1) *In general.*—A deposit required to be made by this section shall be made separately from a deposit required by any other section. An employer may make one, or more than one remittance of the amount required to be deposited. An amount of tax which is not required to be deposited may nevertheless be deposited if the employer so desires. If the aggregate amount of the taxes deposited is in excess of the taxes shown on the return, a credit or refund may be obtained; and in the event the excess is applied as a credit against such taxes for a subsequent return period, the employer shall reduce the amount of one or more of the deposits otherwise required for such subsequent return period by the amount of such credit.

(2) *Deposits.*—Each remittance of amounts required to be deposited shall be accompanied by a Federal Tax Deposit form which shall be prepared in accordance with the instructions applicable thereto. Except as provided in paragraph (a)(1) or (a)(2) of this section, the remittance, together with the form, shall be forwarded to a financial institution authorized as a depositary for Federal taxes in accordance with 31 CFR part 214 or, at the election of the employer, to a Federal Reserve bank. For procedures governing the deposit of Federal taxes at a Federal Reserve bank, see 31 CFR part 214.7. The timeliness of the deposit will be determined by the date stamped on the Federal Tax Deposit form by the Federal Reserve bank or the authorized financial institution or, if section 7502(e) applies, by the date the deposit is treated as received under section 7502(e). Each employer making deposits under this section shall report on the return, for the period with respect to which such deposits are made, information re-

garding such deposits according to the instructions that apply to such return and pay at that time (or deposit by the due date of such return) the balance, if any, of the taxes due for such period.

(3) *Time deemed paid.*—In general, amounts deposited under subparagraph (2) of this paragraph shall be considered as paid on the last day prescribed for filing the return in respect of such tax (determined without regard to any extension of time for filing such return), or at the time deposited, whichever is later. For purposes of section 6511 and the regulations thereunder, relating to period of limitation on credit or refund, if an amount is so deposited prior to April 15th of a calendar year immediately succeeding the calendar year in which occurs the period for which such amount was so deposited, such amount shall be considered as paid on such April 15th.

(c) *Procurement of prescribed form.*—Copies of the Federal Tax Deposit form will so far as possible be furnished employers. An employer will not be excused from making a deposit, however, by the fact that no form has been furnished to it. An employer not supplied with the form should make application therefor in ample time to make the required deposits within the time prescribed. The employer may secure the form or additional forms by applying therefor and supplying its name, identification number, address, and the taxable period to which the deposits will relate. Copies of the Federal Tax Deposit form may be secured by application therefor. [Reg. § 31.6302(c)-2.]

☐ [T.D. 6516, 12-20-60. *Amended by T.D.* 6941, 12-16-67; *T.D.* 6957, 6-3-68; *T.D.* 7419, 5-12-76; *T.D.* 7931, 12-23-83; *T.D.* 7953, 5-8-84; *T.D.* 8341, 3-27-91; *T.D.* 8436, 9-22-92 *and T.D.* 9239, 12-30-2005.]

[Reg. § 40.6302(c)-2]

§ 40.6302(c)-2. Special rules for September.— (a) *In general.*—(1) *Separate deposits required for the second semimonthly period.*—In the case of deposits of taxes not deposited under the alternative method (regular method taxes) for the second semimonthly period in September, separate deposits are required for the period September 16th through 26th and for the period September 27th through 30th.

(2) *Amount of deposit.*—(i) *In general.*—The deposits of regular method taxes for the period September 16th through 26th and the period September 27th through 30th must be not less than 95 percent of the net tax liability for regular method taxes incurred during the respective periods. The net tax liability for regular method taxes incurred during these periods may be computed by—

(A) Determining the amount of net tax liability for regular method taxes reasonably expected to be incurred during the second semimonthly period in September;

(B) Treating 11/15 of the amount determined under paragraph (a)(2)(i)(A) of this section as the net tax liability for regular method taxes incurred during the period September 16th through 26th; and

(C) Treating the remainder of the amount determined under paragraph (a)(2)(i)(A) of this section (adjusted to reflect the amount of net tax liability for regular method taxes actually incurred through the end of September) as the net tax liability for regular method taxes incurred during the period September 27th through 30th.

(ii) *Safe harbor rules.*—The safe harbor rules in § 40.6302(c)-1(b)(2) do not apply for the third calendar quarter unless—

(A) The deposit of taxes for the period September 16th through 26th is not less than 11/90 of the net tax liability for regular method taxes reported for the look-back quarter; and

(B) The total deposit of taxes for the second semimonthly period in September is not less than 1/6 of the net tax liability for regular method taxes reported for the look-back quarter.

(3) *Time to deposit.*—(i) The deposit required for the period beginning September 16th must be made by September 29th unless—

(A) September 29th is a Saturday, in which case the deposit must be made by September 28th; or

(B) September 29th is a Sunday, in which case the deposit must be made by September 30th.

(ii) The deposit required for the period ending September 30th must be made at the time prescribed in § 40.6302(c)-1(c).

(b) *Persons not required to use electronic funds transfer.*—The rules of this section are applied with the following modifications in the case of a person not required to deposit taxes by electronic funds transfer.

(1) *Periods.*—The deposit periods for the separate deposits required under paragraph (a) of this section are September 16th through 25th and September 26th through 30th.

(2) *Amount of deposit.*—In computing the amount of deposit required under paragraph (a)(2)(i)(B) of this section, the applicable fraction is 10/15. In computing the amount of deposit required under paragraph (a)(2)(ii)(A) of this section, the applicable fraction is 10/90.

(3) *Time to deposit.*—In the case of the deposit required under paragraph (a) of this section for the period beginning September 16th, the deposit must be made by September 28th unless—

(i) September 28th is a Saturday, in which case the deposit must be made by September 27th; or

(ii) September 28th is a Sunday, in which case the deposit must be made by September 29th.

(c) *Effective date.*—This section is applicable with respect to deposits that relate to calendar quarters beginning on or after October 1, 2001, except that paragraph (b) of this section does not apply after December 31, 2010. [Reg. §40.6302(c)-2.]

☐ [T.D. 8442, 10-21-92. *Amended by T.D. 8685*, 11-8-96; *T.D. 8887, 6-7-2000; T.D. 8963, 8-8-2001 and T.D. 9507, 12-2-2010.*]

[Reg. §31.6302(c)-3]

§31.6302(c)-3. Deposit rules for taxes under the Federal Unemployment Tax Act.— (a) *Requirement.*—(1) *In general.*—Except as provided in paragraph (a)(2) of this section, every person that, by reason of the provisions of section 6157, computes the tax imposed by section 3301 on a quarterly or other time period basis shall—

(i) If the person is described in section (a)(1) of section 6157, deposit the amount of such tax by the last day of the first calendar month following the close of each of the first three calendar quarters in the calendar year; or

(ii) If the person is other than a person described in section (a)(1) of section 6157, deposit the amount of such tax by the last day of the first calendar month following the close of—

(*a*) The period beginning with the first day of the calendar year and ending with the last day of the calendar quarter (excluding the last calendar quarter) in which such person becomes an employer (as defined in section 3306(a)), and

(*b*) The third calendar quarter of such year, if the period specified in (*a*) of this subdivision includes only the first two calendar quarters of the calendar year.

(2) *Special rule where accumulated amount does not exceed $500.*—The provisions of paragraph (a)(1) of this section shall not apply with respect to any period described therein if the amount of the tax imposed by section 3301 for such period (as computed under section 6157) plus amounts not deposited for prior periods does not exceed $500 ($100 in the case of periods ending on or before December 31, 2004). Thus, an employer shall not be required to make a deposit for a period unless his tax for such period plus tax not deposited for prior periods exceeds $500.

(b) *Manner of deposit.*—(1) *In general.*—A deposit required to be made by an employer under this section shall be made separately from a deposit required by any other section. An employer may make one, or more than one, remittance of the amount required to be deposited. An employer that is not required to deposit an amount of tax by this section may nevertheless voluntarily make that deposit. For the requirement to deposit tax under the Federal Unemployment Tax Act by electronic funds transfer, see §31.6302-1(h).

(2) *Time deemed paid.*—For the time an amount deposited by electronic funds transfer is deemed paid, see §31.6302-1(h)(9). For the time an amount remitted with a return is deemed paid, see §31.6302-1(i)(3).

(c) *Effective/applicability date.*—This section applies to deposits and payments made after December 31, 2010. [Reg. §31.6302(c)-3.]

☐ [T.D. 7037, 4-27-70. *Amended by T.D. 7062*, 9-23-70; *T.D. 7953, 5-8-84; T.D. 8723, 7-11-97; T.D. 8952, 6-25-2001; T.D. 9162, 11-30-2004; T.D. 9239, 12-30-2005 and T.D. 9507, 12-2-2010.*]

[Reg. §40.6302(c)-3]

§40.6302(c)-3. Deposits under chapter 33.— (a) *Overview.*—This section sets forth an alternative method for computing the amount of deposits of taxes imposed by chapter 33, and provides rules relating to the time for making a deposit and the amount of tax to be reported on the return of tax for each quarter by persons using the alternative method. The safe harbor rules for computing deposits of tax using the alternative method and the general rules relating to deposits are set forth in §40.6302(c)-1 and apply unless inconsistent with the rules set forth below.

(b) *Alternative method for computing deposits.*— (1) *In general.*—(i) *Alternative method.*—Any person required to collect and pay over any tax imposed by chapter 33 may compute the amount of that tax to be deposited on the basis of amounts considered as collected (the "alternative method") instead of on the basis of actual collections of tax.

(ii) *Using more than one method to compute deposits.*—A person may compute deposits of tax imposed by one or more sections of chapter 33 using the alternative method provided by this section and compute deposits of taxes imposed by other sections of chapter 33 on the basis of amounts actually collected using the rule of §40.6302(c)-1(c)(1). For purposes of this paragraph (b)(1)(ii), the taxes imposed by section 4261(a) and (b) are treated as taxes imposed by the same section.

(2) *Applicability.*—(i) *In general.*—A person may use the alternative method with respect to a tax only if the person—

(A) Separately accounts for the tax in accordance with paragraph (b)(2)(ii) of this section; and

(B) Makes a return of the tax on the basis of the amount of the tax that is considered as collected.

(ii) *Separate account.*—The account required under paragraph (b)(2)(i)(A) of this section (the separate account)—

(A) Must reflect for each month all items of tax that are included in amounts billed or tickets sold to customers during the month;

(B) May not reflect an item of adjustment for any month during a quarter if the adjustment results from a refusal to pay or inability to collect the tax and the uncollected tax has not been reported under §49.4291-1 of this chapter on or before the due date of the return for that quarter; and

(C) Must reflect for each month items of adjustment (including bad debts and errors) relating to the tax for prior months within the period of limitations on credits or refunds.

(iii) *Change of method.*—The method of computing deposits of tax imposed by a section of chapter 33 (as described in paragraph (b)(1)(ii) of this section) may be changed only at the beginning of a calendar quarter. Before a person changes the method used to compute the amount of tax to be deposited and reported for a calendar quarter, the person must notify the Commissioner so that proper adjustments may be made in order to properly reflect that person's collections of excise tax.

(3) *Period during which tax is considered as collected.*—For purposes of this section, the tax included in amounts billed or tickets sold during a semimonthly period (as defined in § 40.0-1(c)) is considered as collected during the first seven days of the second following semimonthly period. Thus, the tax included in amounts billed or tickets sold during the first semimonthly period of a calendar month is considered as collected during the period of the 1st day through the 7th day of the following month; the tax included in amounts billed or tickets sold during the second semimonthly period of a calendar month is considered as collected during the period of the 16th day through the 22nd day of the following month.

(4) *When amounts are billed.*—For purposes of this section, an amount is billed on the earlier of the date the amount is received or the date a bill for the amount is rendered.

(c) *Time to deposit.*—Under the alternative method, the deposit of tax for any semimonthly period must be made by the third business day after the seventh day of that semimonthly period. For purposes of this paragraph (c), a "business day" is any calendar day other than a Saturday, Sunday, or legal holiday. The term *legal holiday* means a legal holiday in the District of Columbia as defined in section 7503. Thus, for example, the deposit for the semimonthly period beginning on January 1, 2011 (relating to amounts billed between December 1st and December 15, 2010) is due by January 12, 2011, three business days after January 7, the seventh day of the semimonthly period. The deposit for the semimonthly period beginning on October 1, 2011 (relating to amounts billed between September 1st and September 15, 2011), is due by October 13, 2011, due to the October 10, 2011, Columbus Day holiday.

(d) *Computation of net amount of tax that is considered as collected during a semimonthly period.*—The net amount of tax that is considered as collected during the semimonthly period must be either the net amount of tax reflected in the separate account for the corresponding semimonthly period of the preceding month or one-half the net amount of tax reflected in the separate account for the preceding month.

(e) *Reporting of tax.*—If a tax is deposited under the alternative method for a calendar quarter, the return of tax for the quarter must report the net amount of the tax that is considered as collected during the quarter and not the amount of the tax that is actually collected during the quarter. The amount to be reported for each month is the net amount of tax reflected in the separate account for the preceding month. For example, amounts billed in December, January, and February are considered as collected during January, February, and March, and are reported as the collections of tax for January, February, and March (the first calendar quarter). Thus, the net amount of tax reflected in the separate accounts for December, January, and February is the amount reported as collections for the first quarter.

(f) *Special rules for September.*—(1) *Deposits required.*—In the case of alternative method taxes charged (that is, included in amounts billed or tickets sold) during the first semimonthly period in September, separate deposits are required for the taxes charged during the period September 1st-11th and the period September 12th-15th.

(2) *Time to deposit.*—(i) *In general.*—The deposit required for alternative method taxes charged during the period beginning September 1st must be made by September 29. The deposit required for alternative method taxes charged during the period ending September 15th must be made at the time prescribed in paragraph (c) of this section for making deposits for the first semimonthly period in October.

(ii) *Due date on Saturday or Sunday.*—A deposit that would otherwise be due on September 29 must be made by September 28 if September 29 is a Saturday and by September 30 if September 29 is a Sunday.

(3) *Amount of deposit.*—The deposits of alternative method taxes required for the period September 1st-11th and the period September 12th-15th must be not less than the amount of alternative method taxes charged during the respective periods. The amount of alternative method taxes charged during these periods may be computed by—

(i) Determining the net amount of alternative method taxes reflected in the separate account for the first semimonthly period in September (or one-half of the net amount of alternative method taxes reasonably expected to be reflected in the separate account for the month of September);

(ii) Treating $^{11}/_{15}$ of that amount as the amount of taxes charged during the period September 1st-11th; and

(iii) Treating the remainder of the amount determined under paragraph (f)(3)(i) of this section (adjusted, if that amount is based on reasonable expectations, to reflect actual taxes charged through the end of September) as the amount charged during the period September 12th-15th.

Reg. § 40.6302(c)-3(f)(3)(iii)

(4) *Safe harbor rule based on look-back quarter liability.*—The safe harbor rule of §40.6302(c)-1(b)(2) does not apply for the fourth calendar quarter unless—

(i) The deposit for alternative method taxes charged during the period September 1st-11th is not less than $11/90$ of the net tax liability reported for alternative method taxes for the look-back quarter; and

(ii) The total deposit for alternative method taxes charged during the first semi-monthly period in September is not less than $1/6$ of the net tax liability reported for alternative method taxes for the look-back quarter.

(5) *Persons not required to use electronic funds transfer.*—In the case of a person that is not required to deposit excise taxes by electronic funds transfer (a non-EFT depositor), the rules of this paragraph (f) apply with the following modifications:

(i) The taxes for which separate deposits must be made are the taxes charged during the periods September 1st-10th and September 11th-15th.

(ii) The deposit required for taxes charged during the period beginning September 1st must be made by September 28. A deposit that would otherwise be due on September 28 must be made by September 27 if September 28 is a Saturday and by September 29 if September 28 is a Sunday.

(iii) The generally applicable fractions and percentage are modified to reflect the different deposit periods in accordance with the following table:

Generally applicable fractions and percentage	Modifications for non-EFT depositors
$15/11$	$15/10$
$90/11$	$90/10$
69.67 percent	63.33 percent

(g) *Effective date.*—This section is applicable with respect to deposits and returns that relate to taxes that are considered as collected in calendar quarters beginning on or after October 1, 2001, except that paragraph (b)(2)(ii)(B) of this section is applicable October 1, 2004, and except that paragraph (f)(5) of this section does not apply after December 31, 2010. [Reg. §40.6302(c)-3.]

☐ [T.D. 8442, 10-21-92. *Amended by T.D.* 8685, 11-8-96 *(technical amendments,* 3-30-98); *T.D.* 8963, 8-8-2001; *T.D.* 9051, 4-1-2003; *T.D.* 9149, 8-9-2004; *T.D.* 9221, 8-24-2005 *and T.D.* 9507, 12-2-2010 *(corrected* 1-5-2011).]

[Reg. §31.6302(c)-4]

§31.6302(c)-4. Cross references.—(a) *Failure to deposit.*—For provisions relating to the penalty for failure to make a deposit within the prescribed time, see section 6656.

(b) *Saturday, Sunday, or legal holiday.*—For provisions relating to the time for performance of acts where the last day falls on Saturday, Sunday, or a legal holiday, see the provisions of the Regulations on Procedure and Administration (Part 301 of this chapter) under section 7503. [Reg. §31.6302(c)-4.]

☐ [T.D. 6354, 1-13-59. *Amended by T.D.* 7037, 4-27-70 *and T.D.* 8947, 6-14-2001.]

PAYMENT OF FEDERAL TAXES AND THE TREASURY TAX AND LOAN PROGRAM—31 CFR, Part 203

Subpart A—General Information

[Reg. §203.1]

§203.1. Scope.—The regulations in this part govern the processing of Federal tax payments by financial institutions and the Federal Reserve Banks (FRB) using electronic payment or paper methods; the designation of Treasury Tax and Loan (TT&L) depositaries; and the operation of the Department of the Treasury's (Treasury) investment program. [Reg. §203.1.]

☐ [*Final Rule,* 2-2-98.]

[Reg. §203.2]

§203.2. Definitions.—As used in this part:

(a) *Advice of credit.*—means the Treasury form used in the Federal Tax Deposit system that is supplied to depositaries to summarize and report Federal tax deposits. The current form is Treasury Form 2284. Advice of credit information also may be delivered electronically.

(b) *Automated Clearing House (ACH) credit entry.*—means a transaction originated by a financial institution in accordance with applicable ACH formats and applicable laws, regulations, and procedural instructions.

(c) *Automated Clearing House (ACH) debit entry.*—means a transaction originated by a Treasury Financial Agent (TFA), in accordance with applicable ACH formats and applicable laws, regulations, and instructions.

(d) *Business day.*—means any day on which the FRB of the district is open.

(e) *Direct Access transaction.*—means same-day Federal tax payment information transmitted by a financial institution directly to the Electronic Tax Application at an FRB using the Fedline Taxpayer Deposit Application.

(f) *Direct investment.*—means placement of Treasury funds with a depositary and a corresponding increase in a depositary's note balance.

(g) *Direct investment.*—means placement of Treasury funds with a depositary and a corresponding increase in a depositary's main note balance.

(h) *Electronic Tax Application (ETA).*—means a sub-system of EFTPS that receives, processes, and transmits same-day Federal tax payment information for taxpayers. ETA activity is comprised of Fedwire value transfers, Fedwire non-value transactions, and Direct Access transactions.

(i) *Electronic Tax Application (ETA) reference number.*—means the unique number assigned to each ETA transaction by an FRB.

(j) *Federal funds rate.*—means the Federal funds rate published weekly by the Board of Governors of the Federal Reserve System.

(k) *Federal Reserve account.*—means an account with reserve or clearing balances held by a financial institution at an FRB.

(l) *Federal Reserve Bank of the district.*—means the FRB that services the geographical area in which the financial institution is located, or such other FRB that may be designated in an FRB operating circular.

(m) *Federal Tax Deposit (FTD).*—means a tax deposit or payment made using an FTD coupon.

(n) *Federal Tax Deposit coupon (FTD coupon).*—means a paper form supplied to a taxpayer by the Treasury for use in the FTD system to accompany deposits of Federal taxes. The current paper form is Form 8109.

(o) *Federal Tax Deposit system (FTD system).*—means the paper-based system through which taxpayers remit Federal tax payments by presenting an FTD coupon and payment to a depositary or an FRB. The depositary prepares an advice of credit summarizing all FTDs.

(p) *Federal taxes.*—means those Federal taxes or other payments specified by the Secretary of the Treasury as eligible for payment through the procedures prescribed in this part.

(q) *Fedwire.*—means the funds transfer system owned and operated by the FRBs.

(r) *Fedwire non-value transaction.*—means the same-day Federal tax payment information transmitted by a financial institution to an FRB using a Fedwire type 1090 message to authorize a payment.

(s) *Fedwire value transfer.*—means a Federal tax payment made by a financial institution using a Fedwire type 1000 message.

(t) *Financial institution.*—means any bank, savings bank, savings and loan association, credit union, or similar institution.

(u) *Fiscal Agent.*—means the Federal Reserve acting as agent for the Treasury.

(v) *Input Message Accountability Data (IMAD).*—means a unique number assigned to each Fedwire transaction by the financial institution sending the transaction to an FRB.

(w) *Main note balance.*—means an open-ended interest-bearing note balance maintained at the FRB of the district.

(x) *Note option.*—means that program available to a TT & L depositary under which Treasury invests in obligations of the depositary. The amount of such investments will be evidenced by interest-bearing note balances maintained at the FRB of the district.

(y) *Procedural instructions.*—means the procedures contained in the Treasury Financial Manual, Volume IV (IV TFM), other Treasury instructions issued through the TFAs, and FRB operating circulars issued consistent with this part.

(z) *Recognized insurance coverage.*—means the insurance provided by the Federal Deposit Insurance Corporation, the National Credit Union Administration, and by insurance organizations specifically qualified by the Secretary.

(aa) *Remittance option.*—means that program available to a depositary that processes FTD payments, under which the amount of deposits credited by the depositary to the TT&L account will be withdrawn by the FRB for deposit to the Treasury General Account on the day that the FRB receives the advices of credit supporting such deposits.

(bb) *Same-day payment.*—means the following ETA payment options:

    (1) Direct Access transaction;

    (2) Fedwire non-value transaction; and

    (3) Fedwire value transfer.

(cc) *Secretary.*—means the Secretary of the Treasury, or the Secretary's delegate.

(dd) *Special direct investment.*—means the placement of Treasury funds with a depositary and a corresponding increase in a depositary's main note balance, where the investment specifically is identified as a "special direct investment" and may be secured by collateral retained in the possession of the depositary pursuant to the terms of § 203.24(c)(2)(i).

(ee) *Tax due date.*—means the day on which a tax payment is due to Treasury, as determined by statute and Internal Revenue Service (IRS) regulations.

(ff) *Term investment option.*—means the program available to financial institutions that offers the ability to borrow excess Treasury operating funds for a predetermined period of time.

(gg) *Term note balance.*—means an interest-bearing note balance maintained at the FRB of the district for a predetermined period of time.

(hh) *Transaction trace number.*—means an identifying number assigned by the taxpayer's financial institution to each ACH credit transaction.

(ii) *Treasury Financial Agent (TFA).*—means a financial institution designated as an agent of Treasury for processing EFTPS enrollments, receiving EFTPS tax payment information, and originating ACH debit entries on behalf of Treasury as authorized by the taxpayer.

(jj) *Treasury General Account (TGA).*—means an account maintained in the name of the United States Treasury at an FRB.

(kk) *Treasury Tax and Loan (TT&L) account.*— means the Treasury account maintained by a depositary in which funds are credited by the depositary after receiving and collateralizing FTDs.

(ll) *Treasury Tax and Loan depositary (depositary).*—means a financial institution designated as a depositary by the FRB of the district for the purpose of maintaining a TT&L account and/or note balance.

(mm) *Treasury Tax and Loan (TT&L) Program.*— means the program for collecting Federal taxes and investing the Government's excess operating funds.

(nn) *Treasury Tax and Loan (TT & L) rate of interest.*—means the interest charged on the main note balance. The TT & L rate of interest is the rate prescribed by the Secretary taking into consideration prevailing market interest rates. The rate and any rate changes will be announced through a *TT & L Special Notice to Depositaries* and will be published in the Federal Register and on a web site maintained by Treasury's Financial Management Service at http://www.fms.treas.gov. [Reg. § 203.2.]

☐ *[Final Rule, 2-2-98. Amended by Final Rule, 3-14-2002.]*

[Reg. § 203.3]

§ 203.3. Financial institution eligibility for designation as a Treasury Tax and Loan depositary.—(a) To be designated as a TT&L depositary, a financial institution shall be insured as a national banking association, state bank, savings bank, savings and loan, building and loan, homestead association, Federal home loan bank, credit union, trust company, or a U.S. branch of a foreign banking corporation, the establishment of which has been approved by the Comptroller of the Currency.

(b) A financial institution shall possess the authority to pledge collateral to secure TT&L account balances and/or a note balance.

(c) In order to be designated as a TT & L depositary for the purposes of processing tax deposits in the FTD system, a financial institution shall possess under its charter either general or specific authority permitting the maintenance of the TT & L account, the balance of which is payable on demand without previous notice of intended withdrawal. In addition, note option depositaries shall possess either general or specific authority permitting the maintenance of a note balance. In the case of note option depositaries maintaining main note balances, the authority shall permit the maintenance of a main note balance which is payable on demand without previous notice of intended withdrawal. [Reg. § 203.3.]

☐ *[Final Rule, 2-2-98. Amended by Final Rule, 3-14-2002.]*

[Reg. § 203.4]

§ 203.4. Designation of financial institutions as Treasury Tax and Loan depositaries.— (a) *Parties to the agreement.*—To be designated as a TT&L depositary, a financial institution shall enter into a depositary agreement with Treasury's fiscal agent, the FRB. By entering into this agreement, the financial institution agrees to be bound by this part, and procedural instructions issued pursuant to this part.

(b)(1) *Application procedures.*—An eligible financial institution seeking designation as a depositary and, thereby, the authority to maintain a TT&L account and/or a note balance shall file with the FRB, Financial Management Service Form 458, "Financial Institution Agreement and Application for Designation as a TT&L Depositary," and Financial Management Service Form 459, "Resolution Authorizing the Financial Institution Agreement and Application for Designation as a TT&L Depositary," certified by its board of directors. Financial Management Service Forms 458 and 459 are available upon request from the FRB of the district.

(2) Depositaries processing tax payments in the FTD system are required to elect either the remittance or the note option.

(c) *Designation.*—Each financial institution satisfying the eligibility requirements and the application procedures will receive from the FRB notification of its specific designation as a TT&L depositary. A financial institution is not authorized to maintain a TT&L account or note balance until it has been designated as a TT&L depositary by the FRB. [Reg. § 203.4.]

☐ *[Final Rule, 2-2-98.]*

[Reg. § 203.5]

§ 203.5. Obligations of the depositary.—A depositary shall:

(a) Administer a note balance, if not participating in the FTD System.

(b) Administer a TT&L account and, if applicable, a note balance, if participating in the FTD System.

(c) Comply with the requirements of Section 202 of Executive Order 11246, entitled "Equal Employment Opportunity" (3 CFR, 1964-1965 Comp. p. 339) as amended by Executive Orders 11375 and 12086 (3 CFR, 1966-1970 Comp., p. 684; 3 CFR, 1978 Comp. p. 230), and the regulations issued thereunder at 41 CFR Chapter 60.

(d) Comply with the requirements of Section 503 of the Rehabilitation Act of 1973, as amended, and the regulations issued thereunder at 41 CFR part 60-741, requiring Federal contractors to take affirmative action to employ and advance in employment qualified individuals with disabilities.

(e) Comply with the requirements of Section 503 of the Vietnam Era Veterans' Readjustment Assistance Act of 1972, as amended, 38 U.S.C. 4212, Executive Order 11701 (3 CFR 1971-1975 Comp. p. 752), and the regulations issued thereunder at 41 CFR parts 60-250 and 61-250, requiring Federal contractors to take affirmative action to employ and advance in employment qualified special disabled veterans and Vietnam-era veterans. [Reg. §203.5.]

☐ [*Final Rule*, 2-2-98.]

[Reg. §203.6]

§203.6. Compensation for services.—Except as provided in the procedural instructions, Treasury will not compensate financial institutions for servicing and maintaining the TT&L account, or for processing tax payments through the EFTPS or the FTD system. [Reg. §203.6.]

☐ [*Final Rule*, 2-2-98.]

[Reg. §203.7]

§203.7. Termination of agreement or change of election or option.—(a) *Termination by Treasury.*—The Secretary may terminate the agreement of a depositary at any time upon notice to that effect to that depositary, effective on the date set forth in the notice.

(b) *Termination or change of election or option by the depositary.*—A depositary may terminate its depositary agreement, or change its option or election, consistent with this part and the procedural instructions, by submitting notice to that effect in writing to the FRB effective at a prospective date set forth in the notice. [Reg. §203.7.]

☒ [*Final Rule*, 2-2-98.]

[Reg. §203.8]

§203.8. Application of part and procedural instructions.—The terms of this part and procedural instructions issued pursuant to this part shall be binding on financial institutions that process tax payments and/or maintain a note balance under this part. By accepting or originating Federal tax payments, the financial institution agrees to be bound by this part and by procedural instructions issued pursuant to this part. [Reg. §203.8.]

☐ [*Final Rule*, 2-2-98.]

Subpart B—Electronic Federal Tax Payments

[Reg. §203.9]

§203.9. Scope of the subpart.—This subpart prescribes the rules by which financial institutions shall process Federal tax payment transactions electronically. A financial institution does not need to be designated as a TT&L depositary in order to process electronic Federal tax payments. In addition, a financial institution that does process electronic Federal tax payments under this subpart does not thereby become a Federal Government depositary and shall not advertise itself as one because of that fact. [Reg. §203.9.]

☐ [*Final Rule*, 2-2-98.]

[Reg. §203.10]

§203.10. Enrollment.—(a) *General.*—Taxpayers shall complete an enrollment process with the TFA prior to making their first electronic Federal tax payment.

(b) *Enrollment forms.*—The TFA shall provide financial institutions and taxpayers with enrollment forms upon request. The taxpayer is responsible for completing the enrollment form, obtaining the verifications required on the form, and returning the enrollment form to the TFA.

(c) *Verification.*—If the taxpayer elects the ACH debit entry method of paying taxes, an authorized representative of the financial institution shall verify the accuracy of the financial institution routing number, taxpayer account number, and taxpayer account type at the request of the taxpayer. [Reg. §203.10.]

☐ [*Final Rule*, 2-2-98.]

[Reg. §203.11]

§203.11. Electronic payment methods.—(a) *General.*—Electronic payment methods for Federal tax payments available under this subpart include ACH debit entries, ACH credit entries, and same-day payments. Any financial institution that is capable of originating and/or receiving transactions for these payment methods, by itself or through a correspondent financial institution, may do so on behalf of a taxpayer.

(b) *Conditions to making an electronic payment.*—Nothing contained in this part shall affect the authority of financial institutions to enter into contracts with their customers regarding the terms and conditions for processing payments, provided that such terms and conditions are not inconsistent with this subpart and applicable law governing the particular transaction type.

(c) *Payment of interest for time value of funds held.*—Treasury will not pay interest on any payments erroneously paid to Treasury and subsequently refunded to the financial institution. [Reg. §203.11.]

☒ [*Final Rule*, 2-2-98.]

[Reg. §203.12]

§203.12. Future-day reporting and payment mechanisms.—(a) *General.*—A financial institution may receive an ACH debit entry, originated by the TFA at the direction of the taxpayer; or, a financial institution may originate an ACH credit entry, at the direction of the taxpayer. Taxpayers will be credited for the actual amount received by Treasury.

(b) *ACH debit.*—A financial institution receiving an ACH debit entry originated by the TFA shall, as applicable:

(1) Timely verify the account number and account type contained in an ACH prenotification entry;

(2) Timely and properly return a prenotification entry that contains an invalid account

number or account type, or otherwise is erroneous or unprocessable;

(3) Timely and accurately notify the TFA of incorrect information on entries received, using a Notification of Change entry; and

(4) Timely and accurately return an entry not posted, including but not limited to, a return or a contested dishonored return for acceptable return reasons, as set forth in the procedural instructions.

(c) *ACH credit.*—A financial institution originating an ACH credit entry at the direction of a taxpayer shall:

(1) At the request of the taxpayer, originate either an ACH prenotification containing the taxpayer's identification number or a zero dollar ACH entry with the appropriate addenda record. Additional format information is contained in the procedural instructions;

(2) Format the ACH credit entry in the ACH format approved by Treasury for Federal tax payments;

(3) Originate an ACH credit entry by the appropriate deadline, as specified by the FRB or Treasury, whichever is earlier, in order to meet the tax due date specified by the taxpayer; and

(4) Provide the taxpayer, upon request, a transaction trace number, or some other method to trace the tax payment.

(d) *ACH credit reversals.*—Reversals may be initiated for a duplicate or erroneous file or entry. No advance approval from, or notification to, the IRS is required when originating an ACH credit reversal. Documentation of reversals shall be made available as set forth in the procedural instructions. [Reg. § 203.12.]

☐ [*Final Rule,* 2-2-98.]

[Reg. § 203.13]

§ 203.13. Same-day reporting and payment mechanisms.—(a) *General.*—A financial institution or its authorized correspondent may initiate same-day reporting and payment transactions on behalf of taxpayers. A same-day payment must be received by the FRB of the district by the deadline established by the Treasury in the procedural instructions. Taxpayers will be credited for the actual amount received by Treasury.

(b) *Fedwire value transfer.*—To initiate a Fedwire value tax payment, the financial institution shall be a Fedwire participant and shall comply with the FRB's Fedwire format for tax payments. The taxpayer's financial institution shall provide the taxpayer, upon request, the IMAD and the ETA reference numbers for a Fedwire value transfer. The financial institution may obtain the ETA reference number for Fedwire value transfers from its FRB by supplying the related IMAD number. Fedwire value transfers settle immediately to the TGA and thus are not credited to a depositary's main note balance.

(c) *Fedwire non-value transaction.*—By initiating a Fedwire non-value transaction, a financial institution authorizes the FRB of the district to debit its Federal Reserve account or, for a TT&L depositary, to debit the Federal Reserve account of the depositary or its designated correspondent financial institution, for the amount of the tax payment specified in the transaction. To initiate a Fedwire non-value transaction, the financial institution shall be a Fedwire participant and shall comply with the FRB's Fedwire format for tax payments. The taxpayer's financial institution shall provide the taxpayer, upon request, the IMAD and ETA reference numbers for the Fedwire non-value transaction. The financial institution may obtain the ETA reference number for Fedwire non-value transactions from its FRB by supplying the related IMAD number.

(1) For a note option depositary using a Fedwire non-value transaction, the tax payment amount will be credited to the depositary's main note balance on the day of the transaction.

(2) For a remittance option depositary using a Fedwire non-value transaction, the tax payment amount will be debited from the Federal Reserve account of the depositary or the depositary's designated correspondent and credited to the TGA on the day of the transaction.

(3) For a non-TT&L depositary financial institution using a Fedwire non-value transaction, the tax payment amount will be debited from the financial institution's Federal Reserve account and credited to the TGA on the day of the transaction.

(d) *Direct Access Transaction.*—By initiating a Direct Access transaction, a financial institution authorizes the FRB of the district to debit its Federal Reserve account or, for a TT&L depositary, to debit the Federal Reserve account of the depositary or its designated correspondent financial institution for the amount of the tax payment specified in the transaction. The taxpayer's financial institution shall provide the taxpayer, upon request, the ETA reference number for the Direct Access transaction.

(1) For a note option depositary using a Direct Access transaction, the tax payment amount will be credited to the depositary's main note balance on the day of the transaction.

(2) For a remittance option depositary or a non-TT&L depositary financial institution using a Direct Access transaction, the tax payment amount will be debited from the Federal Reserve account of the financial institution or its designated correspondent financial institution, and credited to the TGA on the day of the transaction.

(e) *Cancellations and reversals.*—In addition to cancellations due to insufficient funds in the financial institution's Federal Reserve account, the FRB may reverse a same-day transaction:

(1) If the transaction:

(i) Is originated by a financial institution after the deadline established by the Treasury in the procedural instructions;

(ii) Has an unenrolled taxpayer identification number; or

(iii) Does not meet the edit and format requirements set forth in the procedural instructions; or,

(2) At the direction of the IRS, for the following reasons:

(i) Incorrect taxpayer name;

(ii) Overpayment; or

(iii) Unidentified payment; or,

(3) At the request of the financial institution that sent the same-day transaction, if the request is made prior to the deadline established by Treasury in the procedural instructions on the day the payment was made.

(f) Other than as stated in paragraph (e) of this section, Treasury is not obligated to reverse all or any part of a payment. [Reg. § 203.13.]

☐ [*Final Rule*, 2-2-98. *Amended by Final Rule*, 3-14-2002.]

[Reg. § 203.14]

§ 203.14. Electronic Federal Tax Payment System interest assessments.—(a) *Circumstances subject to interest assessments.*—Treasury may assess interest on a financial institution in instances where a taxpayer that failed to meet a tax due date proves to the IRS that the delivery of tax payment instructions to the financial institution was timely and that the taxpayer satisfied the conditions imposed by the financial institution pursuant to § 203.11(b). Treasury also may assess interest where a financial institution failed to respond to an ACH prenotification entry on an ACH debit as required in § 203.12(b) or failed to originate an ACH prenotification or zero dollar entry on an ACH credit as described in § 203.12(c) which then resulted in a late payment.

(b) *Calculation of interest assessment.*—Any interest assessed under this section will be at the TT&L rate. The interest will be assessed from the day the taxpayer specified that its payment should settle to the Treasury until the receipt of the payment by Treasury, subject to the following limitations: for ACH debit transactions, interest will be limited to no more than seven calendar days; for ACH credit and same-day transactions, interest will be limited to no more than 45 calendar days. The limitation of liability in this paragraph does not apply to any interest assessment in which there is an indication of fraud, the presentation of a false claim, or misrepresentation or embezzlement on the part of the financial institution or any employee or agent of the financial institution.

(c) *Authorization to assess interest.*—A financial institution that processes Federal tax payments made by electronic payment methods under this subpart is deemed to authorize the FRB to debit its Federal Reserve account or the account of its designated correspondent financial institution for any interest assessed under this section. Upon the direction of Treasury, the FRB shall debit the Federal Reserve account of the financial institution or the account of its designated correspondent financial institution for the amount of the assessed interest.

(d)(1) *Circumstances not subject to the assessment of interest.*—Treasury will not assess interest on a taxpayer's financial institution if a taxpayer fails to meet a tax due date because the taxpayer has not satisfied conditions imposed by the financial institution pursuant to § 203-11(b) and the financial institution has not contributed to the delay. The burden is on the financial institution to establish, pursuant to the procedures in § 203.16, that the taxpayer has not satisfied the conditions and that the financial institution has not contributed to the delay.

(2) Treasury will not assess interest on a financial institution if the delay causing the interest assessment is due to the FRB or the TFA and the financial institution did not contribute to the delay. The burden is on the financial institution to establish, pursuant to the procedures in § 203.16, that it did not cause or contribute to the delay. [Reg. § 203.14.]

☐ [*Final Rule*, 2-2-98.]

[Reg. § 203.15]

§ 203.15. Prohibited debits through the Automated Clearing House.—(a) *General.*—The Treasury has instituted operational safeguards to scrutinize all entries that remove funds from the TGA. In the event funds are removed from the TGA without authority, this section sets forth the liability of financial institutions originating such entries. Accordingly, a financial institution shall not originate an ACH transaction to debit the TGA without the prior written permission of Treasury. Unauthorized entries under this section do not include reversal entries of previously initiated ACH credits authorized in § 203.12(d).

(b) *Liability.*—A financial institution that originates an unauthorized ACH entry that debits the TGA shall be liable to Treasury for the amount of the transaction and shall be liable for interest charges as specified in paragraph (d) of this section.

(c) *Authorization to recover principal and assess interest charge.*—By initiating unauthorized debits to the TGA through the ACH, a financial institution is deemed to authorize the FRB to debit its Federal Reserve account or the account of its designated correspondent-financial institution for any principal and, if applicable, an interest charge assessed by Treasury under this section.

(d) *Interest charge calculation.*—The interest charge shall be at a rate equal to the Federal funds rate plus two percent. The interest charge shall be assessed for each calendar day from the day the TGA was debited to the day the TGA is recredited with the full amount of principal due. [Reg. § 203.15.]

☐ [*Final Rule*, 2-2-98.]

[Reg. § 203.16]

§ 203.16. Appeal and dispute resolution.—(a) *Contest.*—A financial institution may contest any interest assessed under § 203.14, any principal or interest assessed under § 203.15, or any late fees assessed under §203.20. The financial institution shall submit information supporting its position and the relief sought. The information must be received, in writing, by the Treasury officer or fiscal agent identified in the procedural instructions, no later than 90 calendar days after the date the FRB debits the reserve account of the financial institution under §§203.14, 203.15, or 203.20. The Treasury officer or fiscal agent will: uphold the assessment, or reverse the assessment, or modify the assessment, or mandate other action.

(b) *Appeal.*—The financial institution may appeal the decision to Treasury as set forth in the procedural instructions. No further administrative review of the Treasury's decision is available under this Part.

(c) *Recoveries.*—In the event of an over or under recovery of either interest, principal, or late fees, Treasury will instruct the FRB to credit or debit the Federal Reserve account of the financial institution or its designated correspondent financial institution, as appropriate. [Reg. §203.16.]

☐ [*Final Rule,* 2-2-98.]

Subpart C—Federal Tax Deposits

[Reg. §203.17]

§203.17. Scope of the subpart.—This subpart applies to all depositaries that accept FTD coupons and governs the acceptance and processing of those coupons. [Reg. §203.17.]

☐ [*Final Rule,* 2-2-98.]

[Reg. §203.18]

§203.18. Tax deposits using Federal Tax Deposit coupons.—(a) *FTD coupons.*—A depositary that accepts FTD coupons, through any of its offices that accept demand and/or savings deposits, shall:

(1) Accept from a taxpayer, cash, a postal money order drawn to the order of the depositary, or a check or draft drawn on and to the order of the depositary, covering an amount to be deposited as Federal taxes when accompanied by an FTD coupon on which the amount of the deposit has been properly entered in the space provided. A depositary may accept, at its discretion, a check drawn on another financial institution, but it does so at its option and absorbs for its own account any float and other costs involved.

(2) Issue a counter receipt when requested to do so by a taxpayer that makes an FTD deposit over the counter.

(3) Place a stamp impression on the face of each FTD coupon in the space provided. The stamp shall reflect the date on which the tax deposit was received and the name and location of the depositary. The timeliness of the tax payment will be determined by reference to the date stamped by the depositary on the FTD coupon.

(4) Credit, on the date of receipt, all FTD deposits to the TT&L account and administer that account pursuant to the provisions of this part.

(5) Forward, each day, to the IRS Center servicing the geographical area in which the depositary is located, the FTD coupons for all FTD deposits received that day. The FTD coupons shall be accompanied by an advice of credit reflecting the total amount of all FTD coupons.

(6) Establish an adequate record of all FTD deposits prior to transmittal to the IRS Center so that the depositary will be able to identify deposits in the event tax deposit coupons are lost in shipment. For tracking purposes, a record shall be made of each FTD deposit showing, at a minimum, the date of deposit, the taxpayer identification number, and the amount of the deposit. The depositary's copy of the advice of credit may be used to provide the necessary information if individual deposits are listed separately, showing date, taxpayer identification number, and amount.

(7) Deliver its advices of credit to the FRB by the cutoff hour designated by the FRB for receipt of advices.

(8) Not accept compensation from taxpayers for accepting FTDs and handling them as required by this section.

(b) *FTD deposits with Federal Reserve Banks.*—An FRB shall:

(1) Accept an FTD directly from a taxpayer when such tax deposit is:

(i) Mailed or delivered by a taxpayer; and

(ii) Provided in the form of cash or a check or postal money order payable to the order of that FRB; and,

(iii) Accompanied by an FTD coupon on which the amount of the tax deposit has been properly entered in the space provided.

(2) Issue a counter receipt, when requested to do so by a taxpayer that makes an FTD over the counter; and,

(3) Place, in the space provided on the face of each FTD coupon accepted directly from a taxpayer, a stamp impression reflecting the name of the FRB and the date on which the tax deposit will be credited to the TGA. Timeliness of the Federal tax payment will be determined by this date. However, if a deposit is mailed to an FRB, it shall be subject to the "Timely mailing treated as timely filing and paying" clause of the Internal Revenue Code, 26 U.S.C. §7502; and,

(4) Credit the TGA with the amount of the tax payment;

(i) On the date the payment is received, if payment is made in cash; or,

(ii) On the date the proceeds of the tax payment are collected, if payment is made by postal money order or check. [Reg. §203.18.]

☐ [*Final Rule,* 2-2-98.]

[Reg. §203.19]

§203.19. Note option.—(a) *Late delivery of advices of credit.*—If an advice of credit does not arrive at the FRB before the designated cutoff hour for receipt of such advices, the FRB will post the funds to the main note balance as of the next business day after the date on the advice of credit. This is the date on which funds will begin to earn interest for Treasury.

(b) *Transfer of funds from TT & L account to the main note balance.*—For a depositary selecting the note option, funds equivalent to the amount of deposits credited by a depositary to the TT & L account shall be withdrawn by the depositary and credited to the main note balance on the business day following the receipt of the tax payment. [Reg. § 203.19.]

☐ [*Final Rule, 2-2-98. Amended by Final Rule,* 3-14-2002.]

[Reg. § 203.20]

§ 203.20. Remittance option.—(a) *FTD late fee.*—If an advice of credit does not arrive at the FRB before the designated cutoff hour for receipt of such advices, an FTD late fee in the form of interest at the TT&L rate will be assessed for each day's delay in receipt of such advice. Upon the direction of Treasury, the FRB shall debit the Federal Reserve account of the financial institution or the account of its designated correspondent financial institution for the amount of the late fee.

(b) *Withdrawals.*—For a depositary selecting the Remittance Option, the amount of deposits credited by a depositary to the TT&L account will be withdrawn upon receipt by the FRB of the advices of credit. The FRB will charge the depositary's Federal Reserve account or the account of the depositary's designated correspondent financial institution. [Reg. § 203.20.]

☐ [*Final Rule, 2-2-98.*]

Subpart D—Investment Program and Collateral Security Requirements for Treasury Tax and Loan Depositaries

[Reg. § 203.21]

§ 203.21. Scope of the subpart.—This subpart provides rules for TT & L depositaries on crediting main note balances under the various payment methods; debiting main note balances; maintaining term note balances; and pledging collateral security. [Reg. § 203.21.]

☐ [*Final Rule, 2-2-98. Amended by Final Rule,* 3-14-2002.]

[Reg. § 203.22]

§ 203.22. Sources of balances.—Depositaries electing to participate in the investment program can receive Treasury's investments in obligations of the depositary from the following sources:

(a) FTDs that have been credited to the TT&L account pursuant to subpart C of this part;

(b) EFTPS ACH credit and debit transactions, Fedwire non-value transactions, and Direct Ac-

cess transactions pursuant to subpart B of this part;

(c) Direct investments and special direct investments pursuant to subpart D of this part; and

(d) Other excess Treasury operating funds. [Reg. § 203.22.]

☐ [*Final Rule, 2-2-98. Amended by Final Rule,* 3-14-2002.]

[Reg. § 203.23]

§ 203.23. Note balance.—(a) *Additions.*—Treasury will invest funds in obligations of depositaries selecting the note option. Such obligations shall be in the form of open-ended, interest-bearing notes; and additions and reductions will be reflected on the books of the FRB of the district.

(1) *FTD system.*—A depositary processing tax deposits using the FTD system and electing the note option shall debit the TT & L account and credit its main note balance as stated in § 203.19(b).

(2) *EFTPS.*—(i) *ACH debit and ACH credit.*—A note option depositary processing EFTPS ACH debit entries and/or ACH credit entries shall credit its main note balance for the value of the transactions on the date that an exchange of funds is reflected on the books of the Federal Reserve Bank of the district. Financial institutions may refer to the procedural instructions for information on how to ascertain the amount of the credit to the main note balance.

(ii) *Fedwire non-value and Direct Access.*—A note option depositary processing Fedwire non-value and/or Direct Access transactions pursuant to subpart B of this part shall credit its main note balance and debit its customer's account for the value of the transactions on the date ETA receives and processes the transactions.

(b) *Other additions.*—Other funds from Treasury may be offered from time to time to certain note option depositaries through direct investments, special direct investments, or other investment programs.

(c) *Main note balance withdrawals.*—The amount of the main note balance shall be payable on demand without prior notice. Calls for payment on the note will be by direction of the Secretary through the FRBs. On behalf of Treasury, the FRB shall charge the reserve account of the depositary or the depositary's designated correspondent on the day specified in the call for payment.

(d) *Interest.*—A main note balance shall bear interest at the TT & L rate. Such interest is payable by a charge to the Federal Reserve account of the depositary or its designated correspondent in the manner prescribed in the procedural instructions.

(e) *Maximum balance.*—(1) *Note option depositaries.*—A depositary selecting the note option shall establish a maximum for its main note balance by providing notice to that effect in writing to the FRB of the district. The maximum balance is the amount of funds for which a main note option depositary is willing to provide collateral in accordance with § 203.24(c)(1). The depositary shall provide the advance notice required in the procedural instructions before reducing the established maximum balance unless it is a reduction resulting from a collateral re-evaluation as determined by the depositary's FRB. That portion of any advice of credit or EFTPS tax payment, which, when posted at the FRB, would cause the main note balance to exceed the maximum balance amount specified by the depositary, will be withdrawn by the FRB that day.

(2) *Direct investment depositaries.*—A main note option depositary that participates in direct investment shall set a maximum for its main note balance for direct investment purposes which is higher than its peak balance normally generated by the depositary's advices of credit and EFTPS tax payment inflow. The direct investment note option depositary shall provide the advance notice required in the procedural instructions before reducing the established maximum balance.

(3) *Special direct investment depositaries.*—Special direct investments, when credited to the main note balance, shall not be considered in setting the amount of the maximum balance or in determining the amounts to be withdrawn where a depositary's maximum balance is exceeded.

(f) *Term investment option.*—Treasury may, from time to time, invest excess operating funds in obligations of depositaries selecting the term investment option. Such obligations shall be in the form of interest-bearing notes payable upon a predetermined period of time not to exceed 90 days. Such notes shall bear interest at a rate prescribed by the Secretary by auction or otherwise taking into consideration prevailing market interest rates. [Reg. § 203.23.]

☐ *[Final Rule, 2-2-98. Amended by Final Rule, 3-14-2002.]*

[Reg. § 203.24]

§ 203.24. Collateral security requirements.—Financial institutions that process EFTPS tax payments, but are not TT&L depositaries, have no collateral requirements under this part. Financial institutions that are note option depositaries or remittance option depositaries have collateral security requirements, as follows:

(a) *Note option—main note balance.*—(1) *FTD deposits and EFTPS tax payments.*—A depositary shall pledge collateral security in accordance with the requirements of paragraphs (d)(1), (e), and (f) of this section in an amount that is sufficient to cover the pre-established maximum balance for the main note balance, and, if applicable, the closing balance in the TT & L account which exceeds recognized insurance coverage. Depositaries shall pledge collateral for the full amount of the maximum balance at the

time the maximum balance is established. If the depositary maintains a TT & L account, the depositary shall pledge collateral security before crediting deposits to the TT & L account.

(2) *Direct investments.*—A note option depositary that participates in direct investment is not required to pledge collateral continuously in the amount of the pre-established maximum balance. However, each note option depositary participating in direct investment shall pledge, no later than the day the direct investment is placed, the additional collateral in accordance with paragraphs (d)(1), (e), and (f) of this section to cover the total main note balance including those funds received through direct investment. If a direct investment depositary has a history of frequent collateral deficiencies, it shall fully collateralize its maximum balance at all times.

(3) *Special direct investments.*—Before special direct investments are credited to a depositary's main note balance, the note option depositary shall pledge collateral security, in accordance with the requirements of paragraphs (d)(2) and (f) of this section, to cover 100 percent of the amount of the special direct investments to be received.

(b) *Note option—term note balance.*—Each note option depositary participating in the term investment program shall pledge, prior to the time the term investment is placed, collateral in accordance with paragraphs (d)(1), (e), and (f) of this section sufficient to cover the total term note balance.

(c) *Remittance option.*—Prior to crediting FTD deposits to the TT&L account, a remittance option depositary shall pledge collateral security in accordance with the requirements of paragraph (c)(1), (d), and (e) of this section in an amount which is sufficient to cover the balance in the TT&L account at the close of business each day, less recognized insurance coverage.

(d) *Deposits of securities.*—(1) Collateral security required under paragraphs (a)(1), (2), (b), and (c) of this section shall be deposited with the FRB of the district, or, where appropriate, with a custodian or custodians within the United States designated by the FRB, under terms and conditions prescribed by the FRB.

(2)(i) Collateral security required under paragraph (a)(3) of this section shall be pledged under a written security agreement on a form provided by the FRB of the district. The collateral security pledged to satisfy the requirements of paragraph (a)(3) of this section may remain in the pledging depositary's possession and the fact that it has been pledged shall be evidenced by advices of custody to be incorporated by reference in the written security agreement. The written security agreement and all advices of custody covering collateral security pledged under that agreement shall be provided by the depositary to the FRB of the district. Collateral security pledged under the agreement shall not be substituted for or released without the advance approval of the FRB of the district, and any collateral security subject to the security agreement shall remain so subject until an approved substitution is made. No substitution or release shall be approved until an advice of custody containing the description required by the written security agreement is received by the FRB of the district.

(ii) Treasury's security interest in collateral security pledged by a depositary in accordance with paragraph (c)(2)(i) of this section to secure special direct investments is perfected without Treasury taking possession of the collateral security for a period not to exceed 21 calendar days from the day of the depositary's receipt of the special direct investment.

(e) *Acceptable securities.*—Types and valuations of acceptable collateral security are addressed in 31 CFR Part 380. For a current list of acceptable classes of securities and instruments described in 31 CFR Part 380 and their valuations, see the Bureau of the Public Debt's web site at www.publicdebt.treas.gov.

(f) *Assignment of securities.*—A TT&L depositary that pledges acceptable securities which are not negotiable without its endorsement or assignment may furnish, in lieu of placing its unqualified endorsement on each security, an appropriate resolution and irrevocable power of attorney authorizing the FRB to assign the securities. The resolution and power of attorney shall conform to such terms and conditions as the FRB shall prescribe.

(g) *Effecting payments of principal and interest on securities pledged as collateral.*—(1) *General.*—If the depositary fails to pay, when due, the whole or any part of the funds received by it for credit to the TT&L account, and/or if applicable, its note balance; or otherwise violates or fails to perform any of the terms of this part, or fails to pay when due amounts owed to the United States or the United States Treasury; or if the depositary is closed for business by regulatory action or by proper corporate action, or in the event that a receiver, conservator, liquidator or any other officer is appointed; then the Treasury, without notice or demand, may sell, or otherwise collect the proceeds of all or part of the collateral, including additions and substitutions; and apply the proceeds, to satisfy any claims of the United States against the depositary. All principal and interest payments on any security pledged to protect the note balance (if applicable) and/or the TT&L account (if applicable), due as of the date of the insolvency or closure, or thereafter becoming due, shall be held separate and apart from any other assets and shall constitute a part of the pledged security available to satisfy any claim of the United States.

(2) *Payment procedures.*—(i) Subject to the waiver in paragraph (f)(2)(iii) of this section, each depositary (including, with respect to such depositary, an assignee for the benefit of creditors, a trustee in bankruptcy, or a receiver in equity) shall immediately remit each payment of principal and/or interest received by it with respect to collateral pledged pursuant to this section to the FRB of the district, as fiscal agent of the United States, and in any event shall so remit no later than 10 days after receipt of such a payment.

(ii) Subject to the waiver in paragraph (f)(2)(iii) of this section, each obligor on a security pledged by a depositary pursuant to this section, upon notification that the Treasury is entitled to any payment associated with that pledged security, shall make each payment of principal and/or interest due with respect to such security directly to the FRB of the district, as fiscal agent of the United States.

(iii) The requirements of paragraphs (f)(2)(i) and (ii) of this section are hereby waived for only so long as a pledging depositary avoids both termination from the program under § 203.7; and also, those circumstances identified in paragraph (f)(1) which may lead to the collection of the proceeds of collateral or the waiver is otherwise terminated by Treasury. [Reg. § 203.24.]

☐ [*Final Rule*, 2-2-98. *Amended by Final Rule*, 9-12-2000 *and Final Rule*, 3-14-2002.]

[Reg. § 301.6303-1]

§ 301.6303-1. Notice and demand for tax.—(a) *General rule.*—Where it is not otherwise provided by the Code, the district director or the director of the regional service center shall, after the making of an assessment of a tax pursuant to section 6203, give notice to each person liable for the unpaid tax, stating the amount and demanding payment thereof. Such notice shall be given as soon as possible and within 60 days. However, the failure to give notice within 60 days does not invalidate the notice. Such notice shall be left at the dwelling or usual place of business of such person, or shall be sent by mail to such person's last known address. For further guidance regarding the definition of last known address, see § 301.6212-2.

(b) *Assessment prior to last date for payment.*—If any tax is assessed prior to the last date prescribed for payment of such tax, demand that such tax be paid will not be made before such last date, except where it is believed collection would be jeopardized by delay. [Reg. § 301.6303-1.]

☐ [*T.D.* 6119, 12-31-54. *Amended by T.D.* 6585, 12-27-61 *and T.D.* 8939, 1-11-2001.]

[Reg. § 301.6305-1]

§ 301.6305-1. Assessment and collection of certain liability.—(a) *Scope.*—Section 6305(a) requires the Secretary of the Treasury or his delegate to assess and collect amounts which have been certified by the Secretary of Health and Human Services as the amount of a delinquency determined under a court order, or an order of an administrative process established under State law, for support and maintenance of a child or of a child and the parent with whom the child is living. These amounts, referred to as "child and spousal support", are to be collected in the same manner and with the same powers exercised by the Secretary of the Treasury or his delegate in the collection of an employment tax which would be jeopardized by delay. However, where the assessment is the first assessment against an individual for a delinquency described in this paragraph for a particular individual or individuals, the collection is to be stayed for a period of 60 days following notice and demand. In addition, no interest or penalties (with the exception of the penalties imposed by sections 6332(c)(2) and 6657) shall be assessed or collected on the amounts, paragraphs (4), (6) and (8) of section 6334(a) (relating to property exempt from levy) shall not apply; and, there shall be exempt from levy so much of the salary, wages, or other income of the individual which is subject to garnishment pursuant to a judgment entered by a court for the support of his or her minor children. Section 6305(b) provides that sole jurisdiction for any action brought to restrain or review assessment and collection of the certified amounts shall be in a State court or a State administrative agency.

(b) *Assessment and collection.*—(1) *General rule.*—Upon receipt of a certification or recertification from the Secretary of Health and Human Services or his delegate under section 452(b) of Title IV of the Social Security Act as amended (relating to collection of child and spousal support obligations with respect to an individual), the district director or his delegate shall assess and collect the certified amount (or recertified amount). Except as provided in paragraph (c) of this section, the amount so certified shall be assessed and collected in the same manner, with the same powers, and subject to the same limitations as if the amount were an employment tax the collection of which would be jeopardized by delay. However, the provisions of subtitle F with respect to assessment and collection of taxes shall not apply with respect to assessment and collection of a certified amount where such provisions are clearly inappropriate to, and incompatible with, the collection of certified amounts generally. For example, section 6861(g) which allows the Secretary or his delegate to abate a jeopardy assessment if he finds a jeopardy does not exist will not apply.

(2) *Method of assessment.*—An assessment officer appointed by the district director pursuant to §301.6203-1 to make assessments of tax shall also make assessments of certified amounts. The assessment of a certified amount shall be made by the assessment officer signing the summary record of assessment. The date of assessment is the date the summary record is signed by the assessment officer. The summary record, through supporting records as necessary, shall provide—

(i) The assessed amount;

(ii) The name, social security number, and last known address of the individual owing the assessed amount. For further guidance regarding the definition of last known address, see §301.6212-2;

(iii) A designation of the assessed amount as a certified amount, together with the date on which the amount was certified and the name, position, and governmental address of the officer of the Department of Health and Human Services who certified the amount;

(iv) The period to which the child and spousal support obligation represented by the certified amount relates;

(v) The State in which was entered the court or administrative order giving rise to the child and spousal support obligation represented by the certified amount;

(vi) The name of the person or persons to whom the child and spousal support obligation represented by the certified amount is owed; and

(vii) The name of the child or children or the parent of the child or children for whose benefit the child and spousal support obligation exists.

Upon request, the individual assessed shall be furnished a copy of pertinent parts of this assessment which set forth the information listed in subdivision (i) through (vii) of this paragraph (b)(2).

(3) *Supplemental assessments and abatements.*—If any assessment is incomplete or incorrect in any material respect, the district director or his delegate may make a supplemental assessment or abatement but only for the purpose of completing or correcting the original assessment. A supplemental assessment will not be used as a substitute for an additional assessment against an individual.

(4) *Method of collection.*—(i) The district director or his delegate shall make notice and demand for immediate payment of certified amounts. Upon failure or refusal to pay such amounts, collection by levy shall be lawful without regard to the 10-day waiting period provided in section 6331(a). However, in the case of certain first assessments, paragraph (c)(4) of this section provides a rule for a stay of collection for 60 days. For purposes of collection, refunds of any internal revenue tax owed to the individual may be offset against a certified amount.

(ii) The district director or his delegate shall make diligent and reasonable efforts to collect certified amounts as if such amounts were taxes. He shall have no authority to compromise a proceeding by collection of only part of a certified amount in satisfaction of the full certified amount owing. However, he may arrange for payment of a certified amount by installments where advisable.

(iii) The district director or his delegate may offset the amount of any overpayment of any internal revenue tax (as described in section 301.6401-1) to be refunded to the person making the overpayment by the amount of any past-due support (as defined in the regulations under section 6402) owed by the person making the overpayment. The amounts offset under section

6402(c) may be amounts of child and spousal support certified (or recertified) for collection under section 6305 and this section or they may be amounts of past-due support of which the Secretary of the Treasury has been notified under section 6402(c) and the regulations under that section.

(5) *Credits or refunds.*—In the case of any overpayment of a certified amount, the Secretary of the Treasury or his delegate, within the period of limitations for credit or refund of employment taxes, may credit the amount of the overpayment against any liability in respect of an internal revenue tax on the part of the individual who made the overpayment and shall refund any balance to the individual. However, the full amount of any overpayment collected by levy upon property described in paragraph (c)(2) (i), (ii), or (iii) of this section shall be refunded to the individual. For purposes of applying this subparagraph, the rules of § 301.6402-2 apply where appropriate.

(6) *Disposition of certified amounts collected.*— Any certified amount collected shall be deposited in the general fund of the United States, and the officer of the Department of Health and Human Services who certified the amount shall be promptly notified of its collection. There shall be established in the Treasury, pursuant to section 452 of Title IV of the Social Security Act as amended, a revolving fund which shall be available to the Secretary of Health and Human Services or his delegate, without fiscal year limitation, for distribution to the States in accordance with the provisions of section 457 of the Act. Section 452(c)(2) of the Act appropriates to this revolving fund out of any monies not otherwise appropriated, amounts equal to the certified amounts collected under this paragraph reduced by the amounts credited or refunded as overpayments of the certified amounts so collected. The certified amounts deposited shall be transferred at least quarterly from the general fund of the Treasury to the revolving fund on the basis of estimates made by the Secretary of the Treasury or his delegate. Proper adjustments shall be made in the amounts subsequently transferred to the extent prior estimates were in excess of or less than the amounts required to be transferred. See, however, paragraph (c)(1) of this section for the special rule requiring retention in the general fund of certain penalties which may be collected.

(c) *Additional limitations and conditions.*— (1) *Interest and penalties.*—No interest, penalties or additional amounts, other than normal and reasonable collection costs, may be assessed or collected in addition to the certified amount, other than the penalty imposed by section 6332(c)(2) for failure to surrender property subject to levy and the penalty imposed by section 6657 for the tender of bad checks. Any such penalties and collection costs, if collected, will not be treated as part of the certified amount and will be retained by the United States as a part of

its general fund. No interest shall be allowed or paid on any overpayment of a certified amount.

(2) *Property not exempt from levy.*—In addition to property not exempt from levy under section 6334(c) and the regulations thereunder, the following property shall not be exempt from a levy to collect a certified amount:

(i) Unemployment benefits described in section 6334(a)(4);

(ii) Certain annuities and pension payments described in section 6334(a)(6); or

(iii) Salary, wages, or other income described in section 6334(a)(8).

(3) *Property exempt from levy.*—In addition to property exempt from levy under section 6334(a) and the regulations thereunder, other than property described in paragraph (c)(2)(i), (ii), or (iii) of this section, there shall be exempt from levy to collect a certified amount so much of the salary, wages, or other income of an individual as is withheld therefrom in garnishment pursuant to judgment entered by a court of competent jurisdiction for the support of minor children of the individual.

(4) *First assessment.*—In the case of a first assessment against an individual for a certified amount in whole or part for the benefit of a particular child or children or the child or children and their parent, the collection of the certified amount shall be stayed for the period of 60 days immediately following notice and demand as described in section 6303. However, no other stay of the collection of a certified amount may be granted. Thus, the provisions of section 6863(a), relating to bonds to stay collection of jeopardy assessments, shall not apply to the collection of certified amounts.

(5) *Priority of liens.*—A lien for a certified amount shall be valid as against a lien for taxes imposed by section 6321 only if the date of assessment of the certified amount precedes the date of assessment of the taxes. However, no amount collected by levy upon property described in paragraph (c)(2)(i), (ii), or (iii) of this section may be applied other than in whole or partial satisfaction of certified amounts. In the case of two liens for certified amounts, the lien for the certified amount which is first assessed shall be valid as against the lien for the certified amount which is later assessed.

(6) *Statute of limitations on collections.*—The periods of limitation on collection of taxes after assessment prescribed by section 6502 shall apply to the collection of certified (or recertified) amounts. Such periods of limitation with respect to a certified amount shall terminate upon recertification of the amount, and the period of limitation prescribed by section 6502 shall then apply and commence to run with respect to the recertified amount.

(d) *Review of assessments and collections.*— (1) *Federal courts.*—No court of the United States established under article I or article III of the Constitution has jurisdiction of any legal or equitable action to restrain or review the assessment or collection of certified amounts by the district director or his delegate. See, however, paragraph (d)(3) of this section for the rule that the prohibition of this paragraph (d)(1) does not preclude courts established for the District of Columbia from exercising jurisdiction over certain actions.

(2) *Secretary of the Treasury.*—Neither the Secretary of the Treasury nor his delegate may subject to review the assessment or collection of certified amounts in any legal, equitable, or administrative proceeding.

(3) *State courts.*—This paragraph (d) does not preclude a State court or appropriate State agency, as the case may be, from exercising juris-diction over a legal, equitable, or administrative action against the State by an individual to determine his liability for any certified amount assessed against him and collected, or to recover any such certified amount collected, under section 6305 and this section. For purposes of the preceding sentence, the term "State" includes the District of Columbia.

(e) *Internal Revenue regional service centers.*— For purposes of this section, the terms "district director or his delegate" and "district director" include the director of the Internal Revenue service center or his delegate, as the case may be. [Reg. § 301.6305-1.]

☐ [*T.D.* 7576, 12-20-78. *Amended by T.D.* 7808, 2-3-82 *and T.D.* 8939, 1-11-2001.]

RECEIPT OF PAYMENT

[Reg. § 301.6311-1]

§301.6311-1. Payment by check or money order.—(a) *Authority to receive.*—(1) *In general.*— (i) District directors, Service Center directors, and Compliance Center directors (director) may accept checks or drafts drawn on any financial institution incorporated under the laws of the United States or under the laws of any State, the District of Columbia, or any possession of the United States, or money orders in payment for internal revenue taxes, provided the checks, drafts, or money orders are collectible in United States currency at par, and subject to the further provisions contained in this section. The director may accept the checks, drafts, or money orders in payment for internal revenue stamps to the extent and under the conditions prescribed in paragraph (a)(2) of this section. A check or money order in payment for internal revenue taxes or internal revenue stamps should be made payable to the United States Treasury. A check or money order is payable at par only if the full amount thereof is payable without any deduction for exchange or other charges. As used in this section, the term "money order" means: (*a*) United States postal, bank, express, or telegraph money order; (*b*) money order issued by a domestic building and loan association (as defined in section 7701(a)(19)) or by a similar association incorporated under the laws of a possession of the United States; (*c*) a money order issued by such other organization as the Commissioner may designate; and (*d*) a money order described in subdivision (ii) of this paragraph in cases therein described. However, the director may refuse to accept any personal check whenever he or she has good reason to believe that such check will not be honored upon presentment.

(ii) An American citizen residing in a country with which the United States maintains direct exchange of money orders on a domestic basis may pay his tax by postal money order of such country. For a list of such countries, see section 171.27 of the Postal Manual of the United States.

(iii) If one check or money order is remitted to cover two or more persons' taxes, the remittance should be accompanied by a letter of transmittal clearly identifying—

(*a*) Each person whose tax is to be paid by the remittance;

(*b*) The amount of the payment on account of each such person; and

(*c*) The kind of tax paid.

(2) *Payment for internal revenue stamps.*—The director may accept checks, drafts, and money orders described in paragraph (a)(1) of this section in payment for internal revenue stamps. However, the director may refuse to accept any personal check whenever he or she has good reason to believe that such check will not be honored upon presentment.

(b) *Checks or money orders not paid.*—(1) *Ultimate liability.*—The person who tenders any check (whether certified or uncertified, cashier's, treasurer's, or other form of check or draft) or money order in payment for taxes or stamps is not released from his or her liability until the check, draft, or money order is paid; and, if the check, draft, or money order is not duly paid, the person shall also be liable for all legal penalties and additions, to the same extent as if such check, draft, or money order had not been tendered.

(2) *Liability of financial institutions and others.*—If any certified, treasurer's, or cashier's check, or other guaranteed draft, or money order is not duly paid, the United States shall have a lien for the amount of such check or draft upon all assets of the financial institution on which drawn, or for the amount of such money order upon the assets of the issuer thereof. The unpaid amount shall be paid out of such assets in preference to any other claims against such financial institution or issuer except the necessary costs and expenses of administration and the reimbursement of the United States for the amount expended in the redemption of the circulating notes of such financial institution. In addition,

the Government has the right to exact payment from the person required to make the payment.

(c) *Payment in nonconvertible foreign currency.*— For rules relating to payment of income taxes and taxes under the Federal Insurance Contributions Act in nonconvertible foreign currency, see section 6316 and the regulations thereunder.

(d) *Financial institution.*—For purposes of section 6311 and this section, *financial institution* includes but is not limited to—

(1) A bank or trust company (as defined in section 581);

(2) A domestic building and loan association (as defined in section 7701(a)(19));

(3) A mutual savings bank (including but not limited to a mutual savings bank as defined in section 591(b));

(4) A credit union (including both state and federal credit unions, and including but not limited to a credit union as defined in section 501(c)(14)); and,

(5) A regulated investment company (as defined in section 851(a)). [Reg. § 301.6311–1.]

☐ [*T.D.* 6119, 12-31-54. *Amended by T.D.* 6498, 10-24-60; *T.D.* 6872, 1-5-66; *T.D.* 6890, 7-18-66; *T.D.* 7188, 6-28-72; *T.D.* 8595, 4-27-95 *and T.D.* 8969, 12-13-2001.]

[Reg. § 301.6311-2]

§ 301.6311-2. Payment by credit card and debit card.—(a) *Authority to receive.*—(1) *Payments by credit card and debit card.*—Internal revenue taxes may be paid by credit card or debit card as authorized by this section. Payment of taxes by credit card or debit card is voluntary on the part of the taxpayer. Only credit cards or debit cards approved by the Commissioner may be used for this purpose, only the types of tax liabilities specified by the Commissioner may be paid by credit card or debit card, and all such payments must be made in the manner and in accordance with the forms, instructions and procedures prescribed by the Commissioner. All references in this section to *tax* also include interest, penalties, additional amounts, and additions to tax.

(2) *Payments by electronic funds transfer other than payments by credit card and debit card.*—Provisions relating to payments by electronic funds transfer other than payments by credit card and debit card are contained in section 6302 and the Treasury Regulations promulgated pursuant to section 6302.

(3) *Definitions.*—(i) *Credit card.*—means any credit card as defined in section 103(k) of the Truth in Lending Act (15 U.S.C. 1602(k)), including any credit card, charge card, or other credit device issued for the purpose of obtaining money, property, labor, or services on credit.

(ii) *Debit card.*—means any accepted card or other means of access as defined in section 903(1) of the Electronic Fund Transfer Act (15 U.S.C. 1693a(1)), including any debit card or similar device or means of access to an account issued for the purpose of initiating electronic fund transfers to obtain money, property, labor, or services.

(b) *When payment is deemed made.*—A payment of tax by credit card or debit card shall be deemed made when the issuer of the credit card or debit card properly authorizes the transaction, provided that the payment is actually received by the United States in the ordinary course of business and is not returned pursuant to paragraph (d)(3) of this section.

(c) *Payment not made.*—(1) *Continuing liability of taxpayer.*—A taxpayer who tenders payment of taxes by credit card or debit card is not relieved of liability for such taxes until the payment is actually received by the United States and is not required to be returned pursuant to paragraph (d)(3) of this section. This continuing liability of the taxpayer is in addition to, and not in lieu of, any liability of the issuer of the credit card or debit card or financial institution pursuant to paragraph (c)(2) of this section.

(2) *Liability of financial institutions.*—If a taxpayer has tendered a payment of internal revenue taxes by credit card or debit card, the credit card or debit card transaction has been guaranteed expressly by a financial institution, and the United States is not duly paid, then the United States shall have a lien for the guaranteed amount of the transaction upon all the assets of the institution making such guarantee. The unpaid amount shall be paid out of such assets in preference to any other claims whatsoever against such guaranteeing institution, except the necessary costs and expenses of administration and the reimbursement of the United States for the amount expended in the redemption of the circulating notes of such institution.

(d) *Resolution of errors relating to the credit card or debit card account.*—(1) *In general.*—Payments of taxes by credit card or debit card shall be subject to the applicable error resolution procedures of section 161 of the Truth in Lending Act (15 U.S.C. 1666), section 908 of the Electronic Fund Transfer Act (15 U.S.C. 1693f), or any similar provisions of state or local law, for the purpose of resolving errors relating to the credit card or debit card account, but not for the purpose of resolving any errors, disputes or adjustments relating to the underlying tax liability.

(2) *Matters covered by error resolution procedures.*—(i) The error resolution procedures of paragraph (d)(1) of this section apply to the following types of errors—

(A) An incorrect amount posted to the taxpayer's account as a result of a computational error, numerical transposition, or similar mistake;

(B) An amount posted to the wrong taxpayer's account;

(C) A transaction posted to the taxpayer's account without the taxpayer's authorization; and

(D) Other similar types of errors that would be subject to resolution under section 161 of the Truth in Lending Act (15 U.S.C. 1666), section 908 of the Electronic Fund Transfer Act (15 U.S.C. 1693f), or similar provisions of state or local law.

(ii) An error described in paragraph (d)(2)(i) of this section may be resolved only through the procedures referred to in paragraph (d)(1) of this section and cannot be a basis for any claim or defense in any administrative or court proceeding involving the Commissioner or the United States.

(3) *Return of funds pursuant to error resolution procedures.*—Notwithstanding section 6402, if a taxpayer is entitled to a return of funds pursuant to the error resolution procedures of paragraph (d)(1) of this section, the Commissioner may, in the Commissioner's sole discretion, effect such return by arranging for a credit to the taxpayer's account with the issuer of the credit card or debit card or any other financial institution or person that participated in the transaction in which the error occurred.

(4) *Matters not subject to error resolution procedures.*—The error resolution procedures of paragraph (d)(1) of this section do not apply to any error, question, or dispute concerning the amount of tax owed by any person for any year. For example, these error resolution procedures do not apply to determine a taxpayer's entitlement to a refund of tax for any year for any reason, nor may they be used to pay a refund. All such matters shall be resolved through administrative and judicial procedures established pursuant to the Internal Revenue Code and the rules and regulations thereunder.

(5) *Section 170 of the Truth in Lending Act not applicable.*—Payments of taxes by credit card or debit card are not subject to section 170 of the Truth in Lending Act (15 U.S.C. 1666i) or to any similar provision of state or local law.

(e) *Fees or charges.*—The Internal Revenue Service may not impose any fee or charge on persons making payment of taxes by credit card or debit card. This section does not prohibit the imposition of fees or charges by issuers of credit cards or debit cards or by any other financial institution or person participating in the credit card or debit card transaction. The Internal Revenue Service may not receive any part of any fees that may be charged.

(f) *Authority to enter into contracts.*—The Commissioner may enter into contracts related to receiving payments of tax by credit card or debit card if such contracts are cost beneficial to the Government. The determination of whether the contract is cost beneficial shall be based on an analysis appropriate for the contract at issue and at a level of detail appropriate to the size of the Government's investment or interest. The Commissioner may not pay any fee or charge or provide any other monetary consideration under such contracts for such payments.

(g) *Use and disclosure of information relating to payment of taxes by credit card and debit card.*—Any information or data obtained directly or indirectly by any person other than the taxpayer in connection with payment of taxes by a credit card or debit card shall be treated as confidential, whether such information is received from the Internal Revenue Service or from any other person (including the taxpayer).

(1) No person other than the taxpayer shall use or disclose such information except as follows—

(i) Card issuers, financial institutions, or other persons participating in the credit card or debit card transaction may use or disclose such information for the purpose and in direct furtherance of servicing cardholder accounts, including the resolution of errors in accordance with paragraph (d) of this section. This authority includes the following—

(A) Processing the credit card or debit card transaction, in all of its stages through and including the crediting of the amount charged on account of tax to the United States Treasury;

(B) Billing the taxpayer for the amount charged or debited with respect to payment of the tax liability;

(C) Collecting the amount charged or debited with respect to payment of the tax liability;

(D) Returning funds to the taxpayer in accordance with paragraph (d)(3) of this section;

(E) Sending receipts or confirmation of a transaction to the taxpayer, including secured electronic transmissions and facsimiles; and

(F) Providing information necessary to make a payment to state or local government agencies, as explicitly authorized by the taxpayer (e.g., name, address, taxpayer identification number).

(ii) Card issuers, financial institutions or other persons participating in the credit card or debit card transaction may use and disclose such information for the purpose and in direct furtherance of any of the following activities—

(A) Assessment of statistical risk and profitability;

(B) Transfer of receivables or accounts or any interest therein;

(C) Audit of account information;

(D) Compliance with federal, state, or local law; and

(E) Cooperation in properly authorized civil, criminal, or regulatory investigations by federal, state, or local authorities.

(2) Notwithstanding the provisions of paragraph (g)(1) of this section, use or disclosure of information relating to credit card and debit card transactions for purposes related to any of the following is not authorized—

(i) Sale of such information (or transfer of such information for consideration) separate from a sale of the underlying account or receivable (or transfer of the underlying account or receivable for consideration);

(ii) Marketing for any purpose, such as, marketing tax-related products or services, or marketing any product or service that targets those who have used a credit card or debit card to pay taxes; and

(iii) Furnishing such information to any credit reporting agency or credit bureau, except with respect to the aggregate amount of a cardholder's account, with the amount attributable to payment of taxes not separately identified.

(3) Use and disclosure of information other than as authorized by this paragraph (g) may result in civil liability under sections 7431(a)(2) and (h).

(h) *Effective date*.—This section applies to payments of taxes made on and after December 14, 2001. [Reg. § 301.6311-2.]

☐ [*T.D.* 8969, 12-13-2001 (*corrected* 1-10-2002).]

[Reg. § 301.6313-1]

§ 301.6313-1. Fractional parts of a cent.—In the payment of any tax not payable by stamp, a fractional part of a cent shall be disregarded unless it amounts to one-half cent or more, in which case it shall be increased to one cent. Fractional parts of a cent shall not be disregarded in the computation of taxes. [Reg. § 301.6313-1.]

☐ [*T.D.* 6119, 12-31-54.]

[Reg. § 20.6314-1]

§ 20.6314-1. Duplicate receipts for payments of estate taxes.—The internal revenue officer with whom the estate tax return is filed will, upon request, give to the person paying the tax duplicate receipts, either of which will be sufficient evidence of such payment and entitle the executor to be credited with the amount by any court having jurisdiction to audit or settle his accounts. [Reg. § 20.6314-1.]

☐ [*T.D.* 6296, 6-23-58. *Amended by T.D.* 7238, 12-28-72.]

[Reg. § 301.6314-1]

§ 301.6314-1. Receipt for taxes.—(a) *In general*.—The district director or the director of a service center shall, upon request, issue a receipt for each tax payment made (other than a payment for stamps sold and delivered). In addition, the district director or the director of a service center shall issue a receipt for each payment of one dollar or more made in cash, whether or not requested. In the case of payments made by check, the cancelled check is usually a sufficient receipt. No receipt shall be issued in lieu of a stamp representing a tax, whether the payment is in cash or otherwise.

(b) *Duplicate receipt for payment of estate taxes*.—Upon request, the district director or the director of a service center will issue duplicate receipts to the person paying the estate tax, either of which will be sufficient evidence of such payment and entitle the executor to be credited with the amount by any court having jurisdiction to audit or settle his accounts. For definition of the term "executor", see section 2203. [Reg. § 301.6314-1.]

☐ [*T.D.* 6119, 12-31-54. *Amended by T.D.* 7214, 10-30-72.]

[Reg. § 301.6315-1]

§ 301.6315-1. Payments of estimated income tax.—The payment of any installment of the estimate income tax (see sections 6015 and 6016) shall be considered payment on account of the income tax for the taxable year for which the estimate is made. The aggregate amount of the payments of estimated tax should be entered upon the income tax return for such taxable year as payments to be applied against the tax shown on such return. [Reg. § 301.6315-1.]

☐ [*T.D.* 6119, 12-31-54.]

[Reg. § 301.6316-1]

§ 301.6316-1. Payment of income tax in foreign currency.—Subject to the provisions of §§ 301.6316-3 to 301.6316-5, inclusive, that portion of the income tax which is attributable to amounts received by a citizen of the United States in nonconvertible foreign currency may be paid in such currency—

(a) For any taxable year beginning on or after January 1, 1955, and before January 1, 1964, if such amounts—

(1) Are disbursed from funds made available to a foundation or commission established in a foreign country pursuant to an agreement made under the authority of section 32(b) of the Surplus Property Act of 1944, as amended (50 U.S.C. App. 1641(b)(2)), or re-established under the authority of the Mutual Educational and Cultural Exchange Act of 1961, as amended (22 U.S.C. 2451);

(2) Constitute either a grant made for authorized purposes of the agreement or compensation for personal services performed in the employ of the foundation or commission;

(3) Are at least 75 percent of the entire amount of the grant or compensation; and

(4) Are treated as income from sources without the United States under the provisions of sections 861 to 864, inclusive, and §§ 1.861-1 to 1.864, inclusive, of this chapter (Income Tax Regulations); and

(b) For any taxable year beginning on or after January 1, 1964, if such amounts—

(1) Are disbursed from funds made available either to a foundation or commission, established pursuant to an agreement made under the authority of section 32(b) of the Surplus Property Act of 1944, as amended, or to a foundation or commission established or continued pursuant to an agreement made under the authority of the Mutual Educational and Cultural Exchange Act of 1961, as amended; or are paid from grants made to such citizen, or to a foundation or an educational or other institution, under the authority of the Mutual Educational and Cultural Exchange Act of 1961, as amended, or section 104(h), (j), (k), (o), or (p) of the Agricultural

Trade Development and Assistance Act of 1954, as amended (7 U.S.C. 1704(h), (j), (k), (o), (p));

(2) Constitute either a grant made for a purpose authorized under any such agreement or law, or compensation for personal services performed in the employ of any organization engaged in administering any program or activity pursuant to any such agreement or law;

(3) Are at least 70 percent of the entire amount of the grant or compensation; and

(4) Are treated as income from sources without the United States under the provisions of sections 861 to 864, inclusive, and §§ 1.861-1 to 1.864, inclusive, of this chapter (Income Tax Regulations). [Reg. § 301.6316-1.]

☐ [*T.D.* 6191, 7-18-56. *Amended by T.D.* 6498, 10-24-60 *and T.D.* 6872, 1-5-66.]

[Reg. § 301.6316-2]

§ 301.6316-2. Definitions.—For purposes of §§ 301.6316-1 to 301.6316-9, inclusive:

(a) The term "tax", as used in §§ 301.6316-1, 301.6316-3, 301.6316-4, 301.6316-5, and 301.6316-6 means the income tax imposed for the taxable year by chapter 1 of the Internal Revenue Code of 1954, and as used in § 301.6316-7 means the Federal Insurance Contributions Act taxes imposed by chapter 21 of the Code (or by the corresponding provisions of the Internal Revenue Code of 1939). The term "tax", as used in §§ 301.6316-8 and 301.6316-9 shall relate to either of such taxes, whichever is appropriate.

(b) The term "nonconvertible foreign currency" means currency of the government of a foreign country which, owing to (1) monetary, exchange, or other restrictions imposed by the foreign country, (2) an agreement entered into with the United States of America, or (3) the terms and conditions of the United States Government grant, is not convertible into United States dollars or into other money which is convertible into United States dollars. The term shall not, however, include currency which, notwithstanding such restrictions, agreement, terms, or conditions, is in fact converted into United States dollars or into property which is readily disposable for United States dollars.

(c) If the taxpayer computes taxable income under the accrual method, then the term "received" shall be construed to mean "accrued". [Reg. § 301.6316-2.]

☐ [*T.D.* 6191, 7-18-56. *Amended by T.D.* 6498, 10-24-60 *and T.D.* 6872, 1-5-66.]

[Reg. § 301.6316-3]

§ 301.6316-3. Allocation of tax attributable to foreign currency.—(a) *Adjusted gross income ratio.*—The portion of the tax which is attributable to amounts received in nonconvertible foreign currency shall, for purposes of applying § 301.6316-1 to the currency of each foreign country, be the amount by which:

(1) The amount which bears the same ratio to the entire tax for the taxable year as (i) the taxpayer's adjusted gross income received in that

currency bears to (ii) the adjusted gross income determined under section 62 by taking into account the entire gross income and all deductions allowable under that section without distinction as to amounts received in foreign currency, exceeds

(2) The total of the allowable credits against tax, and payments on account of tax, which are properly allocable to the amount of that currency included in gross income.

(b) *Example.*—(1) For the calendar year 1955 Mr. Jones and his wife filed a joint return on which the adjusted gross income is as follows, after amounts received in foreign currency had been properly translated into United States dollars for tax computation purposes:

Fulbright grant received by Mr. Jones in nonconvertible foreign currency	$8,000
Dividends received by Mr. Jones entitled to dividends-received credit	500
Compensation for personal services of Mrs. Jones	3,000
Net profit from business carried on by Mrs. Jones	2,500
Total adjusted gross income	$14,000

(2) The following amounts are allowable as properly deductible from adjusted gross income, no determination being made as to whether or not any part of them is properly allocable to the Fulbright grant:

Deduction for personal exemptions	$3,000
Charitable contributions	500
Interest expense	400
Taxes	300
Total allowable deductions	$4,200

(3) For the taxable year the following amounts are allowable as credits against the tax, or as payments on account of the tax:

Foreign tax credit for foreign taxes paid on Fulbright grant		$300.00
Dividends-received credit		20.00
Credit for income tax withheld upon compensation of Mrs. Jones		304.80
Payments of estimated tax (see § 301.6316-6(b)(2) for determination of amounts):		
United States dollars	$426.32	
Foreign currency	893.88	1,320.20
Total allowable credits and payments		$1,945.00

(4) The portion of the tax which is attributable to amounts received in nonconvertible foreign currency is $33.49, determined as follows:

Adjusted gross income	$14,000.00
Less: Allowable deductions	4,200.00
Taxable income	9,800.00
Tax computed under section 2	2,148.00
Ratio of adjusted gross income received in nonconvertible foreign currency to entire adjusted gross income ($8,000 ÷ $14,000) (percent)	57.14
Portion of tax attributable to nonconvertible foreign currency ($2,148 × 57.14) (percent)	$1,227.37

Less: Credit for foreign taxes paid on Fulbright grant	$300.00	
Payment in foreign currency of estimated tax . . .	893.88	$1,193.88

Portion of tax attributable to amounts received in nonconvertible foreign currency $33.49

[Reg. § 301.6316-3.]

☐ [T.D. 6191, 7-18-56.]

[Reg. § 301.6316-4]

§ 301.6316-4. Return requirements.—(a) *Place for filing.*—A return of income which includes amounts received in foreign currency on which the tax is paid in accordance with § 301.6316-1 shall be filed with the Director of International Operations, Internal Revenue Service, Washington, D.C. 20225. For the time for filing income tax returns, see sections 6072 and 6081 and §§ 1.6072-1, 1.6081-1, and 1.6081-2 of this chapter(Income Tax Regulations).

(b) *Statements required.*—(1) A statement, prepared by the taxpayer, and certified by the foundation, commission, or other person having control of the payments made to the taxpayer in nonconvertible foreign currency, shall be attached to the return showing that for the taxable year involved the taxpayer is entitled to pay tax in foreign currency in accordance with section 6316 and the regulations thereunder. This statement shall disclose the total amount of grants or compensation received by the taxpayer during the taxable year under the authority of section 32(b) of the Surplus Property Act of 1944, as amended (50 U.S.C. App. 1641(b)(2)), or of the Mutual Educational and Cultural Exchange Act of 1961, as amended (22 U.S.C. 2451), or section 104(h), (j), (k), (o), or (p) of the Agricultural Trade Development and Assistance Act of 1954, as amended (7 U.S.C. 1704(h), (j), (k), (o), (p)), and the amount thereof paid in nonconvertible foreign currency. It shall also state that with respect to the grant or compensation the applicable percentage requirement of § 301.6316-1 is satisfied.

(2) The taxpayer shall also attach to the return a detailed statement showing (i) the computation, in the manner prescribed by § 301.6316-3, of the portion of the tax attributable to amounts received in nonconvertible foreign currency and (ii) the rates of exchange used in determining the tax liability in United States dollars. See paragraph (c) of § 301.6316-5. [Reg. § 301.6316-4.]

☐ [T.D. 6191, 7-18-56. Amended by T.D. 6498, 10-24-60 and T.D. 6872, 1-5-66.]

[Reg. § 301.6316-5]

§ 301.6316-5. Manner of paying tax by foreign currency.—(a) *Time and place to pay.*—The unpaid tax required to be shown on a return filed in accordance with § 301.6316-4, whether payable in whole or in part in foreign currency, is due and payable to the Director of Interna-

tional Operations, Internal Revenue Service, Washington, D.C. 20225, at the time the return is filed. However, see paragraph (d) of this section with respect to the depositing of the foreign currency with the disbursing officer of the Department of State.

(b) *Certified statement.*—Every taxpayer who desires to pay tax in foreign currency under the provisions of § 301.6316-1 shall first obtain the certified statement referred to in paragraph (b)(1) of § 301.6316-4.

(c) *Determination of the tax.*—In determining the tax payable for the taxable year in United States dollars, the taxpayer, with respect to amounts described in paragraph (a) of § 301.6316-1, or amounts described in paragraph (b) of § 301.6316-1 received before November 1, 1965, shall use the rates of exchange which most clearly reflect the correct tax liability in dollars, whether it be the official rate, the open market rate, or any other appropriate rate. With respect to amounts described in paragraph (b) of § 301.6316-1 received on or after November 1, 1965, the taxpayer shall use the official rate of exchange in determining the tax payable for the taxable year in United States dollars. After determining the correct tax liability in United States dollars the taxpayer shall then ascertain, in accordance with the principles of § 301.6316-3, the portion of the tax which is attributable to amounts received in nonconvertible foreign currency.

(d) *Deposit of foreign currency with disbursing officer.*—(1) After the portion of the tax which is attributable to amounts received in nonconvertible foreign currency is determined in United States dollars, the amount so determined shall be deposited in the same nonconvertible foreign currency with the disbursing officer of the Department of State for the foreign country where the fund is located from which the payments in nonconvertible foreign currency are made to the taxpayer. The amount of foreign currency to be deposited shall be that amount which, when converted at the rate of exchange used on the date of deposit by that disbursing officer for the acquisition of such currency for his official disbursements, equals the portion of the tax so determined in United States dollars.

(2) The disbursing officer may rely upon the taxpayer for the determination of the amount of tax payable in foreign currency but may not accept any such currency for deposit until the taxpayer has presented for inspection the certified statement referred to in paragraph (b)(1) of § 301.6316-4. Upon acceptance of foreign currency for deposit the disbursing officer shall give the taxpayer a receipt in duplicate showing the name and address of the depositor, the date of deposit, the amount of foreign currency deposited, and its equivalent in United States dollars on the date of deposit.

(3) Every taxpayer making a deposit of foreign currency in accordance with this paragraph shall attach to the return required to be filed in

accordance with § 301.6316-4, in part or full payment of the taxes shown thereon, the original of the receipt given by the disbursing officer and shall pay to the Director of International Operations in United States dollars the balance, if any, of the tax shown to be due. Tender of such receipt to the Director of International Operations shall be considered as payment of tax in an amount equal to the United States dollars represented by the receipt.

(4) A taxpayer shall make the deposit required by this paragraph in ample time to permit him to attach the receipt to his return for filing within the time prescribed by section 6072 or 6081 and the regulations thereunder. [Reg. § 301.6316-5.]

☐ [T.D. 6191, 7-18-56. *Amended by T.D. 6498, 10-24-60 and T.D. 6872, 1-5-66.*]

[Reg. § 301.6316-6]

§ 301.6316-6. Declarations of estimated tax.—
(a) *Filing of declaration.*—A declaration of estimated tax in respect of amounts on which the tax is to be paid in foreign currency under the provisions of § 301.6316-1 shall be filed with the Director of International Operations, Internal Revenue Service, Washington, D.C. 20225, and shall have attached thereto the statements required by paragraph (b)(1) and (2)(i) of § 301.6316-4 in respect of the tax return except that the statement certified by the foundation, commission, or other person having control of the payments to the taxpayer in nonconvertible foreign currency may be based upon amounts expected to be received by the taxpayer during the taxable year if they are not in fact known at the time of certification. A copy of this certified statement shall be retained by the taxpayer for the purpose of exhibiting it to the disbursing officer when making installment deposits of foreign currency under the provisions of paragraph (c) of this section. For the time for filing declarations of estimated tax, see sections 6073 and 6081 and §§ 1.6073-1 to 1.6073-4, inclusive, and §§ 1.6081-1 and 1.6081-2 of this chapter (Income Tax Regulations).

(b) *Determination of estimated tax.*—(1) *Allocation of tax attributable to foreign currency.*—In determining the amount of estimated tax for purposes of this section, all items of income, deduction, and credit, whether or not attributable to amounts received in nonconvertible foreign currency, shall be taken into account. The portion of the estimated tax which is attributable to amounts to be received during the taxable year in nonconvertible foreign currency shall be determined consistently with the manner prescribed by § 301.6316-3.

(2) *Example.*—(i) For the calendar year 1955 Mr. Jones and his wife filed a joint declaration of estimated tax in the determination of which the adjusted gross income was estimated to be as follows, after amounts received in foreign currency had been properly translated into United States dollars for tax computation purposes:

Fulbright grant to be received by Mr. Jones in nonconvertible foreign currency	$8,000
Dividends to be received by Mr. Jones entitled to dividends-received credit	375
Compensation to be received by Mrs. Jones for personal services	3,000
Net profit to be derived from business carried on by Mrs. Jones	1,625
Total estimated adjusted gross income	$13,000

(ii) The following amounts were determined to be allowable as properly deductible from estimated adjusted gross income, no determination being made as to whether or not any part of them was properly allocable to the Fulbright grant:

Deduction for personal exemptions	$3,000
Charitable contributions	300
Interest expense	400
Taxes	300
Total allowable deductions	$4,000

(iii) The following estimated amounts were determined to be allowable as credits against the tax for the taxable year:

Foreign tax credit for foreign taxes to be paid on Fulbright grant	$300.00
Credit for income tax expected to be withheld upon compensation of Mrs. Jones	304.80
Dividends-received credit	15.00
Total allowable estimated credits	$619.80

(iv) The portion of the estimated tax which is attributable to amounts to be received during the taxable year in nonconvertible foreign currency is $893.88, determined as follows:

Estimated adjusted gross income	$13,000.00
Less: Allowable deductions	4,000.00
Estimated taxable income	9,000.00
Tax computed under section 2	1,940.00
Ratio of estimated adjusted gross income to be received in nonconvertible foreign currency to entire estimated adjusted gross income ($8,000 ÷ $13,000) (percent)	61.54
Portion of above tax attributable to nonconvertible foreign currency ($1,940 × 61.54) (percent)	1,193.88
Less: Credit for foreign taxes expected to be paid on Fulbright grant	300.00
Portion of estimated tax which is attributable to amounts to be received during the taxable year in nonconvertible foreign currency	$893.88

(v) The portion of the estimated tax which is payable in United States dollars is $426.32, determined as follows:

Tax computed under section 2	$1,940.00
Less: Total allowable estimated credits	619.80
Total estimated tax	$1,320.20
Less: Portion of estimated tax payable in foreign currency	893.88
Portion of estimated tax payable in United States dollars	$426.32

(c) *Payment of estimated tax.*—(1) The provisions of § 301.6316-5 relating to the certified statement, determination of the tax, and the depositing of the foreign currency shall apply for purposes of this section. The full amount of estimated tax payable in foreign currency, as determined under paragraph (b) of this section, may be deposited before the date prescribed for the payment thereof.

(2) Every taxpayer making a deposit of foreign currency in accordance with this paragraph shall tender to the Director of International Operations, Internal Revenue Service, Washington, D.C. 20225, the original of the receipt from the disbursing officer as payment, to the extent of the amount represented thereby in United States dollars, of the estimated tax. For the dates prescribed for the payment of estimated tax, see sections 6153 and 6161 and §§1.6153-1 to 1.6153-4, inclusive, and §1.6161-1 of this chapter (Income Tax Regulations). A taxpayer should make the deposit required by this paragraph in ample time to permit him to tender such receipt by the date prescribed for payment of the estimated tax.

(d) *Credit on return for the taxable year.*—The receipt given by the disbursing officer of the Department of State and tendered in payment of estimated tax under this section shall, for purposes of paragraph (a)(2) of §301.6316-3, be considered as payment on account of the tax for the taxable year. The amount so considered to be paid shall be the amount in United States dollars represented by the receipt. [Reg. §301.6316-6.]

☐ [T.D. 6191, 7-18-56. *Amended by T.D.* 6498, 10-24-60 *and T.D.* 6872, 1-5-66.]

[Reg. §301.6316-7]

§301.6316-7. Payment of Federal Insurance Contributions Act taxes in foreign currency.—
(a) *In general.*—The taxes imposed on employees and employers by sections 3101 and 3111, respectively, of chapter 21 of the Code (Federal Insurance Contributions Act) or the corresponding sections of the Internal Revenue Code of 1939 may, with respect to wages (as defined in section 3121(a) of chapter 21 of the Code or the corresponding section of the Internal Revenue Code of 1939) paid in nonconvertible foreign currency(as defined in paragraph (b) of §301.6316-2) for services performed on or after January 1, 1951, be paid in that currency if all such wages—

(1) Are paid from funds made available to a foundation or commission established in a foreign country pursuant to an agreement made under the authority of section 32(b) of the Surplus Property Act of 1944, as amended (50 U.S.C. App. 1641(b)(2)), or established or continued pursuant to an agreement made under authority of the Mutual Educational and Cultural Exchange Act of 1961, as amended (22 U.S.C. 2451); and

(2) Are paid to a United States citizen for services performed in the employ of such foundation or commission.

(b) *Return requirements.*—(1) *Statements required.*—(i) A return on which payment of Federal Insurance Contributions Act taxes is made in accordance with this section shall have attached thereto a statement, certified by the foundation or commission filing the return, stating that the foundation or commission is an organization established pursuant to an agreement made under authority of section 32(b) of the Surplus Property Act of 1944, as amended, or established or continued pursuant to an agreement made under authority of the Mutual Educational and Cultural Exchange Act of 1961, as amended.

(ii) The taxpayer shall also attach to the return a statement showing the rates of exchange used in determining in United States dollars the wages reported on the return and the taxes due with respect thereto. See paragraph (c)(1) of this section.

(2) *Cross references.*—For the place for filing returns of the Federal Insurance Contributions Act taxes, see §31.6091-1(c) of this chapter (Employment Tax Regulations). For the time for filing returns of the Federal Insurance Contributions Act taxes, see §31.6071(a)-1 of this chapter (Employment Tax Regulations).

(c) *Payment of tax.*—(1) *Determination of the tax.*—In determining in United States dollars the wages required to be reported on the return and the taxes due with respect thereto, the taxpayer shall use the rate of exchange which most clearly reflects the correct equivalent in dollars, whether it be the official rate, the open market rate, or any other appropriate rate.

(2) *Deposit of foreign currency with disbursing officer.*—(i) After determination is made in United States dollars of the Federal Insurance Contributions Act taxes with respect to wages paid in nonconvertible foreign currency, the amount so determined shall be deposited in the same nonconvertible foreign currency with the disbursing officer of the Department of State for the foreign country where the fund is located from which such wages were paid. The amount of the foreign currency to be deposited shall be that amount which, when converted at the rate of exchange used on the date of deposit by the disbursing officer for the acquisition of such currency for his official disbursement, equals the taxes determined in United States dollars.

(ii) The disbursing officer may rely upon the taxpayer for the determination of the amount of tax payable in foreign currency but may not accept any such currency for deposit until the taxpayer has presented for inspection the certified statement referred to in paragraph (b)(1) of this section. Upon acceptance of foreign currency for deposit the disbursing officer shall give the taxpayer a receipt in duplicate showing the name and address of the depositor, the date of the deposit, the amount of foreign currency deposited and its equivalent in United States dollars on the date of deposit, and the kind of tax for which the deposit is made.

(iii) Every taxpayer making a deposit of foreign currency in accordance with this paragraph shall attach to the return required to be filed in accordance with paragraph (b) of this section the original of the receipt given by the disbursing officer. Tender of such receipt to the Director of International Operations shall be considered as payment of tax in an amount equal to the United States dollars represented by the receipt.

(iv) A taxpayer shall make the deposit required by this paragraph in ample time to permit it to attach the receipt to its return for filing within the time prescribed by § 31.6071(a)-1 of this chapter (Employment Tax Regulations). [Reg. § 301.6316-7.]

☐ [*T.D.* 6872, 1-5-66.]

[Reg. § 301.6316-8]

§ 301.6316-8. Refunds and credits in foreign currency.—(a) *Refunds.*—The refund of any overpayment of tax which has been paid under section 6316 in foreign currency may, in the discretion of the Commissioner, be made in the same foreign currency by which the tax was paid. The amount of any such refund made in foreign currency shall be the amount of the overpayment in United States dollars converted, on the date of the refund check, at the rate of exchange then used for his official disbursements by the disbursing officer of the Department of State in the country where the foreign currency was originally deposited.

(b) *Credits.*—Unless otherwise in the best interest of the Internal Revenue Service, no credit of any overpayment of tax which has been paid under section 6316 in foreign currency shall be allowed against any outstanding liability of the person making the overpayment except in respect of that portion of the liability which, in accordance with § 301.6316-1 or § 301.6316-7, would otherwise be permitted to be paid in the same foreign currency. [Reg. § 301.6316-8.]

☐ [*T.D.* 6191, 7-18-56. *Amended by T.D.* 6872, 1-5-66.]

[Reg. § 301.6316-9]

§ 301.6316-9. Interest, additions to tax, etc.—Any reference in § § 301.6316-1 to 301.6316-8, inclusive, to "tax" shall be deemed also to refer to the interest, additions to the tax, additional amounts, and penalties attributable to the tax. [Reg. § 301.6316-9.]

☐ [*T.D.* 6191, 7-18-56. *Amended by T.D.* 6872, 1-5-66.]

LIEN FOR TAXES

[Reg. § 301.6320-1]

§ 301.6320-1. Notice and opportunity for hearing upon filing of notice of federal tax lien.—(a) *Notification.*—(1) *In general.*—For a notice of Federal tax lien (NFTL) filed on or after January 19, 1999, the Commissioner, or his or her delegate (the Commissioner), will prescribe procedures to notify the person described in section 6321 of the filing of a NFTL not more than five business days after the date of any such filing. The Collection Due Process Hearing Notice (CDP Notice) and other notices given under section 6320 must be given in person, left at the dwelling or usual place of business of such person, or sent by certified or registered mail to such person's last known address, not more than five business days after the day the NFTL was filed. For further guidance regarding the definition of last known address, see § 301.6212-2.

(2) *Questions and answers.*—The questions and answers illustrate the provisions of this paragraph (a) as follows:

Q-A1. Who is the person entitled to notice under section 6320?

A-A1. Under section 6320(a)(1), notification of the filing of a NFTL on or after January 19, 1999, is required to be given only to the person described in section 6321 who is named on the NFTL that is filed. The person described in section 6321 is the person liable to pay the tax due after notice and demand who refuses or neglects to pay the tax due (hereinafter, referred to as the taxpayer).

Q-A2. When will the Internal Revenue Service (IRS) provide the notice required under section 6320?

A-A2. The IRS will provide this notice within five business days after the filing of the NFTL.

Q-A3. Will the IRS give notification to the taxpayer for each tax period listed in a NFTL filed on or after January 19, 1999?

A-A3. Yes. A NFTL can be filed for more than one tax period. The notification of the filing of a NFTL will specify each unpaid tax and tax period listed in the NFTL.

Q-A4. Will the IRS give notification to the taxpayer of any filing of a NFTL for the same tax period or periods at another place of filing?

A-A4. Yes. The IRS will notify a taxpayer when a NFTL is filed on or after January 19, 1999, for a tax period or periods at any recording office.

Q-A5. Will the IRS give notification to the taxpayer if a NFTL is filed on or after January 19, 1999, for a tax period or periods for which a NFTL was filed in another recording office prior to that date?

A-A5. Yes. The IRS will notify a taxpayer when each NFTL is filed on or after January 19, 1999, for a tax period or periods at any recording office.

Q-A6. Will the IRS give notification to the taxpayer when a NFTL is refiled on or after January 19, 1999?

A-A6. No. Section 6320(a)(1) does not require the IRS to notify the taxpayer of the refiling of a NFTL. A taxpayer may, however, seek reconsideration by the IRS office that is collecting the tax or refiling the NFTL, an administrative hearing before the IRS Office of Appeals (Appeals), or assistance from the National Taxpayer Advocate.

Q-A7. Will the IRS give notification to a known nominee of, or a person holding property of, the taxpayer of the filing of the NFTL?

A-A7. No. Such person is not the person described in section 6321 and, therefore, is not entitled to notice, but such persons have other remedies. See A-B5 of paragraph (b)(2) of this section.

Q-A8. Will the IRS give notification to the taxpayer when a subsequent NFTL is filed for the same period or periods?

A-A8. Yes. If the IRS files an additional NFTL with respect to the same tax period or periods for which an original NFTL was filed, the IRS will notify the taxpayer when the subsequent NFTL is filed. Not all such notices will, however, give rise to a right to a CDP hearing (see paragraph (b) of this section).

Q-A9. How will notification under section 6320 be accomplished?

A-A9. The IRS will notify the taxpayer by letter. Included with this letter will be the additional information the IRS is required to provide taxpayers as well as, when appropriate, a Form 12153, Request for a Due Process Hearing. The IRS may effect delivery of the letter (and accompanying materials) in one of three ways: by delivering the notice personally to the taxpayer; by leaving the notice at the taxpayer's dwelling or usual place of business; or by mailing the notice to the taxpayer at his last known address by certified or registered mail.

Q-A10. What must a CDP Notice given under section 6320 include?

A-A10. These notices must include, in simple and nontechnical terms:

(i) The amount of the unpaid tax.

(ii) A statement concerning the taxpayer's right to request a CDP hearing during the 30-day period that commences the day after the end of the five business day period within which the IRS is required to provide the taxpayer with notice of the filing of the NFTL.

(iii) The administrative appeals available to the taxpayer with respect to the NFTL and the procedures relating to such appeals.

(iv) The statutory provisions and the procedures relating to the release of liens on property.

Q-A11. What are the consequences if the taxpayer does not receive or accept a CDP Notice that is properly left at the taxpayer's dwelling or usual place of business, or sent by certified or registered mail to the taxpayer's last known address?

A-A11. A CDP Notice properly sent by certified or registered mail to the taxpayer's last known address or left at the taxpayer's dwelling or usual place of business is sufficient to start the 30-day period, commencing the day after the end of the five business day notification period,

within which the taxpayer may request a CDP hearing. Actual receipt is not a prerequisite to the validity of the CDP Notice.

Q-A12. What if the taxpayer does not receive the CDP Notice because the IRS did not send that notice by certified or registered mail to the taxpayer's last known address, or failed to leave it at the dwelling or usual place of business of the taxpayer, and the taxpayer fails to request a CDP hearing with Appeals within the 30-day period commencing the day after the end of the five business day notification period?

A-A12. A NFTL becomes effective upon filing. The validity and priority of a NFTL is not conditioned on notification to the taxpayer pursuant to section 6320. Therefore, the failure to notify the taxpayer concerning the filing of a NFTL does not affect the validity or priority of the NFTL. When the IRS determines that it failed properly to provide a taxpayer with a CDP Notice, it will promptly provide the taxpayer with a substitute CDP Notice and provide the taxpayer with an opportunity to request a CDP hearing. Substitute CDP Notices are discussed in Q & A-B3 of paragraph (b)(2) and Q & A-C8 of paragraph (c)(2) of this section.

(3) *Examples.*—The following examples illustrate the principles of this paragraph (a):

Example 1. H and W are jointly and severally liable with respect to a jointly filed income tax return for 1996. IRS files a NFTL with respect to H and W in County X on January 26, 1999. This is the first NFTL filed on or after January 19, 1999, for their 1996 liability. H and W will each be notified of the filing of the NFTL.

Example 2. Employment taxes for 1997 are assessed against ABC Corporation. A NFTL is filed against ABC Corporation for the 1997 liability in County X on June 5, 1998. A NFTL is filed against ABC Corporation for the 1997 liability in County Y on June 17, 1999. The IRS will notify the ABC Corporation with respect to the filing of the NFTL in County Y.

Example 3. Federal income tax liability for 1997 is assessed against individual D. D buys an asset and puts it in individual E's name. A NFTL is filed against D in County X on June 5, 1999, for D's federal income tax liability for 1997. On June 17, 1999, a NFTL for the same tax liability is filed in County Y against E, as nominee of D. The IRS will notify D of the filing of the NFTL in both County X and County Y. The IRS will not notify E of the NFTL filed in County X. The IRS is not required to notify E of the NFTL filed in County Y. Although E is named on the NFTL filed in County Y, E is not the person described in section 6321 (the taxpayer) who is named on the NFTL.

(b) *Entitlement to a CDP hearing.*—(1) *In general.*—A taxpayer is entitled to one CDP hearing with respect to the first filing of a NFTL (on or after January 19, 1999) for a given tax period or periods with respect to the unpaid tax shown on the NFTL if the taxpayer timely requests such a hearing. The taxpayer must request such a hearing during the 30-day period that commences the day after the end of the five business day period within which the IRS is required to provide the taxpayer with notice of the filing of the NFTL.

(2) *Questions and answers.*—The questions and answers illustrate the provisions of this paragraph (b) as follows:

Q-B1. Is a taxpayer entitled to a CDP hearing with respect to the filing of a NFTL for a type of tax and tax periods previously subject to a CDP Notice with respect to a NFTL filed in a different location on or after January 19, 1999?

A-B1. No. Although the taxpayer will receive notice of each filing of a NFTL, under section 6320(b)(2), the taxpayer is entitled to only one CDP hearing under section 6320 for the type of tax and tax periods with respect to the first filing of a NFTL that occurs on or after January 19, 1999, with respect to that unpaid tax. Accordingly, if the taxpayer does not timely request a CDP hearing with respect to the first filing of a NFTL on or after January 19, 1999, for a given tax period or periods with respect to an unpaid tax, the taxpayer foregoes the right to a CDP hearing with Appeals and judicial review of the Appeals determination with respect to the NFTL. Under such circumstances, the taxpayer may request an equivalent hearing as described in paragraph (i) of this section.

Q-B2. Is the taxpayer entitled to a CDP hearing when a NFTL for an unpaid tax is filed on or after January 19, 1999, in one recording office and a NFTL was previously filed for the same unpaid tax in another recording office prior to that date?

A-B2. Yes. Under section 6320(b)(2), the taxpayer is entitled to a CDP hearing under section 6320 for each tax period with respect to the first filing of a NFTL on or after January 19, 1999, with respect to an unpaid tax, whether or not a NFTL was filed prior to January 19, 1999, for the same unpaid tax and tax period or periods.

Q-B3. When the IRS provides the taxpayer with a substitute CDP Notice and the taxpayer timely requests a CDP hearing, is the taxpayer entitled to a CDP hearing before Appeals?

A-B3. Yes. Unless the taxpayer provides the IRS a written withdrawal of the request that Appeals conduct a CDP hearing, the taxpayer is entitled to a CDP hearing before Appeals. Following the hearing, Appeals will issue a Notice of Determination, and the taxpayer is entitled to seek judicial review of that Notice of Determination.

Q-B4. If the IRS sends a second CDP Notice under section 6320 (other than a substitute CDP Notice) for a tax period and with respect to an unpaid tax for which a section 6320 CDP Notice was previously sent, is the taxpayer entitled to a section 6320 CDP hearing based on the second CDP Notice?

A-B4. No. The taxpayer is entitled to a CDP hearing under section 6320 for each tax period

only with respect to the first filing of a NFTL on or after January 19, 1999, with respect to an unpaid tax.

Q-B5. Is a nominee of, or a person holding property of, the taxpayer entitled to a CDP hearing or an equivalent hearing?

A-B5. No. Such person is not the person described in section 6321 and is, therefore, not entitled to a CDP hearing or an equivalent hearing (as discussed in paragraph (i) of this section). Such person, however, may seek reconsideration by the IRS office collecting the tax or filing the NFTL, an administrative hearing before Appeals under its Collection Appeals Program, or assistance from the National Taxpayer Advocate. However, any such administrative hearing would not be a CDP hearing under section 6320 and any determination or decision resulting from the hearing would not be subject to judicial review under section 6320. Such person also may avail himself of the administrative procedure included in section 6325(b)(4) or of any other procedures to which he is entitled.

(3) *Examples.*—The following examples illustrate the principles of this paragraph (b):

Example 1. H and W are jointly and severally liable with respect to a jointly filed income tax return for 1996. The IRS files a NFTL with respect to H and W in County X on January 26, 1999. This is the first NFTL filed on or after January 19, 1999, for their 1996 liability. H and W are each entitled to a CDP hearing with respect to the NFTL filed in County X. On June 17, 1999, a NFTL for the same tax liability is filed against H and W in County Y. The IRS will give H and W notification of the NFTL filed in County Y. H and W, however, are not entitled to a CDP hearing or an equivalent hearing with respect to the NFTL filed in County Y.

Example 2. Federal income tax liability for 1997 is assessed against individual D. D buys an asset and puts it in individual E's name. A NFTL is filed against E, as nominee of D in County X on June 5, 1999, for D's federal income tax liability for 1997. The IRS will give D a CDP Notice with respect to the NFTL filed in County X. The IRS will not notify E of the NFTL filed in County X. The IRS is not required to notify E of the filing of the NFTL in County X. Although E is named on the NFTL filed in County X, E is not the person described in section 6321 (the taxpayer) who is named on the NFTL.

(c) *Requesting a CDP hearing.*—(1) *In general.*—When a taxpayer is entitled to a CDP hearing under section 6320, the CDP hearing must be requested during the 30-day period that commences the day after the end of the five business day period within which the IRS is required to provide the taxpayer with a CDP Notice with respect to the filing of the NFTL.

(2) *Questions and answers.*—The questions and answers illustrate the provisions of this paragraph (c) as follows:

Reg. § 301.6320-1(b)(2)

Q-C1. What must a taxpayer do to obtain a CDP hearing?

A-C1. (i) The taxpayer must make a request in writing for a CDP hearing. The request for a CDP hearing shall include the information and signature specified in A-C1(ii) of this paragraph (c)(2). See A-D7 and A-D8 of paragraph (d)(2).

(ii) The written request for a CDP hearing must be dated and must include the following:

(A) The taxpayer's name, address, daytime telephone number (if any), and taxpayer identification number (e.g., SSN, ITIN or EIN).

(B) The type of tax involved.

(C) The tax period at issue.

(D) A statement that the taxpayer requests a hearing with Appeals concerning the filing of the NFTL.

(E) The reason or reasons why the taxpayer disagrees with the filing of the NFTL.

(F) The signature of the taxpayer or the taxpayer's authorized representative.

(iii) If the IRS receives a timely written request for CDP hearing that does not satisfy the requirements set forth in A-C1(ii) of this paragraph (c)(2), the IRS will make a reasonable attempt to contact the taxpayer and request that the taxpayer comply with the unsatisfied requirements. The taxpayer must perfect any timely written request for a CDP hearing that does not satisfy the requirements set forth in A-C1(ii) of this paragraph (c)(2) within a reasonable period of time after a request from the IRS.

(iv) Taxpayers are encouraged to use Form 12153, "Request for a Collection Due Process Hearing," in requesting a CDP hearing so that the request can be readily identified and forwarded to Appeals. Taxpayers may obtain a copy of Form 12153 by contacting the IRS office that issued the CDP Notice, by downloading a copy from the IRS Internet site, *www.irs.gov/pub/irs-pdf/f12153.pdf*, or by calling, toll-free, 1-800-829-3676.

(v) The taxpayer must affirm any timely written request for a CDP hearing which is signed or alleged to have been signed on the taxpayer's behalf by the taxpayer's spouse or other unauthorized representative by filing, within a reasonable period of time after a request from the IRS, a signed, written affirmation that the request was originally submitted on the taxpayer's behalf. If the affirmation is filed within a reasonable period of time after a request, the timely CDP hearing request will be considered timely with respect to the non-signing taxpayer. If the affirmation is not filed within a reasonable period of time after a request, the CDP hearing request will be denied with respect to the non-signing taxpayer.

Q-C2. Must the request for the CDP hearing be in writing?

A-C2. Yes. There are several reasons why the request for a CDP hearing must be in writing. The filing of a timely request for a CDP hearing is the first step in what may result in a court proceeding. A written request will provide proof that the CDP hearing was requested and thus permit the court to verify that it has jurisdiction over any subsequent appeal of the Notice of Determination issued by Appeals. In addition, the receipt of the written request will establish the date on which the periods of limitation under section 6502 (relating to collection after assessment), section 6531 (relating to criminal prosecutions), and section 6532 (relating to suits) are suspended as a result of the CDP hearing and any judicial appeal. Moreover, because the IRS anticipates that taxpayers will contact the IRS office that issued the CDP Notice for further information or assistance in filling out Form 12153, or to attempt to resolve their liabilities prior to going through the CDP hearing process, the requirement of a written request should help prevent any misunderstanding as to whether a CDP hearing has been requested. If the information requested on Form 12153 is furnished by the taxpayer, the written request also will help to establish the issues for which the taxpayer seeks a determination by Appeals.

Q-C3. When must a taxpayer request a CDP hearing with respect to a CDP Notice issued under section 6320?

A-C3. A taxpayer must submit a written request for a CDP hearing within the 30-day period that commences the day after the end of the five business day period following the filing of the NFTL. Any request filed during the five business day period (before the beginning of the 30-day period) will be deemed to be filed on the first day of the 30-day period. The period for submitting a written request for a CDP hearing with respect to a CDP Notice issued under section 6320 is slightly different from the period for submitting a written request for a CDP hearing with respect to a CDP Notice issued under section 6330. For a CDP Notice issued under section 6330, the taxpayer must submit a written request for a CDP hearing within the 30-day period commencing the day after the date of the CDP Notice.

Q-C4. How will the timeliness of a taxpayer's written request for a CDP hearing be determined?

A-C4. The rules and regulations under section 7502 and section 7503 will apply to determine the timeliness of the taxpayer's request for a CDP hearing, if properly transmitted and addressed as provided in A-C6 of this paragraph (c)(2).

Q-C5. Is the 30-day period within which a taxpayer must make a request for a CDP hearing extended because the taxpayer resides outside the United States?

A-C5. No. Section 6320 does not make provision for such a circumstance. Accordingly, all taxpayers who want a CDP hearing under section 6320 must request such a hearing within the 30-day period that commences the day after the end of the five business day notification period.

Q-C6. Where must the written request for a CDP hearing be sent?

A-C6. The written request for a CDP hearing must be sent, or hand delivered (if permitted), to the IRS office and address as directed on the CDP Notice. If the address of that office does not appear on the CDP Notice, the taxpayer should obtain the address of the office to which the written request should be sent or hand delivered by calling, toll-free, 1-800-829-1040 and providing the taxpayer's identification number (e.g., SSN, ITIN or EIN).

Q-C7. What will happen if the taxpayer does not request a CDP hearing in writing within the 30-day period that commences the day after the end of the five business day notification period?

A-C7. If the taxpayer does not request a CDP hearing in writing within the 30-day period that commences on the day after the end of the five-business-day notification period, the taxpayer foregoes the right to a CDP hearing under section 6320 with respect to the unpaid tax and tax periods shown on the CDP Notice. A written request submitted within the 30-day period that does not satisfy the requirements set forth in A-C1(ii)(A), (B), (C), (D) or (F) of this paragraph (c)(2) is considered timely if the request is perfected within a reasonable period of time pursuant to A-C1(iii) of this paragraph (c)(2). If the request for CDP hearing is untimely, either because the request was not submitted within the 30-day period or not perfected within the reasonable period provided, the taxpayer will be notified of the untimeliness of the request and offered an equivalent hearing. In such cases, the taxpayer may obtain an equivalent hearing without submitting an additional request. See paragraph (i) of this section.

Q-C8. When must a taxpayer request a CDP hearing with respect to a substitute CDP Notice?

A-C8. A CDP hearing with respect to a substitute CDP Notice must be requested in writing by the taxpayer prior to the end of the 30-day period commencing the day after the date of the substitute CDP Notice.

Q-C9. Can taxpayers attempt to resolve the matter of the NFTL with an officer or employee of the IRS office collecting the tax or filing the NFTL either before or after requesting a CDP hearing?

A-C9. Yes. Taxpayers are encouraged to discuss their concerns with the IRS office collecting the tax or filing the NFTL, either before or after they request a CDP hearing. If such a discussion occurs before a request is made for a CDP hearing, the matter may be resolved without the need for Appeals consideration. However, these discussions do not suspend the running of the 30-day period, commencing the day after the end of the five business day notification period, within which the taxpayer is required to request a CDP hearing, nor do they extend that 30-day period. If discussions occur after the request for a CDP hearing is filed and the taxpayer resolves the matter with the IRS office collecting the tax or filing the NFTL, the taxpayer may withdraw in writing the request that a CDP hearing be conducted by Appeals. The taxpayer can also waive in writing some or all of the requirements

regarding the contents of the Notice of Determination.

(3) *Examples.*—The following examples illustrate the principles of this paragraph (c):

Example 1. A NFTL for a 1997 income tax liability assessed against individual A is filed in County X on June 17, 1999. The IRS mails a CDP Notice to individual A's last known address on June 18, 1999. Individual A has until July 26, 1999, a Monday, to request a CDP hearing. The five business day period within which the IRS is required to notify individual A of the filing of the NFTL in County X expires on June 24, 1999. The 30-day period within which individual A may request a CDP hearing begins on June 25, 1999. Because the 30-day period expires on July 24, 1999, a Saturday, individual A's written request for a CDP hearing will be considered timely if it is properly transmitted and addressed to the IRS in accordance with section 7502 and the regulations thereunder no later than July 26, 1999.

Example 2. Same facts as in *Example 1*, except that individual A is on vacation, outside the United States, or otherwise does not receive or read the CDP Notice until July 19, 1999. As in *Example 1*, individual A has until July 26, 1999, to request a CDP hearing. If individual A does not request a CDP hearing, individual A may request an equivalent hearing as to the NFTL at a later time. The taxpayer should make a request for an equivalent hearing at the earliest possible time.

Example 3. Same facts as in *Example 2*, except that individual A does not receive or read the CDP Notice until after July 26, 1999, and does not request a hearing by July 26, 1999. Individual A is not entitled to a CDP hearing. Individual A may request an equivalent hearing as to the NFTL at a later time. The taxpayer should make a request for an equivalent hearing at the earliest possible time.

Example 4. Same facts as in *Example 1*, except the IRS determines that the CDP Notice mailed on June 18, 1999, was not mailed to individual A's last known address. As soon as practicable after making this determination, the IRS will mail a substitute CDP Notice to individual A at individual A's last known address, hand deliver the substitute CDP Notice to individual A, or leave the substitute CDP Notice at individual A's dwelling or usual place of business. Individual A will have 30 days commencing on the day after the date of the substitute CDP Notice within which to request a CDP hearing.

(d) *Conduct of CDP hearing.*—(1) *In general.*—If a taxpayer requests a CDP hearing under section 6320(a)(3)(B) (and does not withdraw that request), the CDP hearing will be held with Appeals. The taxpayer is entitled under section 6320 to a CDP hearing for the unpaid tax and tax periods set forth in a NFTL only with respect to the first filing of a NFTL on or after January 19, 1999. To the extent practicable, the CDP hearing requested under section 6320 will be held in conjunction with any CDP hearing the taxpayer requests under section 6330. A CDP hearing will be conducted by an employee or officer of Appeals who, prior to the first CDP hearing under section 6320 or section 6330, has had no involvement with respect to the unpaid tax for the tax periods to be covered by the hearing, unless the taxpayer waives this requirement.

(2) *Questions and answers.*—The questions and answers illustrate the provisions of this paragraph (d) as follows:

Q-D1. Under what circumstances can a taxpayer receive more than one CDP hearing under section 6320 with respect to a tax period?

A-D1. The taxpayer may receive more than one CDP hearing under section 6320 with respect to a tax period where the tax involved is a different type of tax (for example, an employment tax liability, where the original CDP hearing for the tax period involved an income tax liability), or where the same type of tax for the same period is involved, but where the amount of the unpaid tax has changed as a result of an additional assessment of tax (not including interest or penalties) for that period or an additional accuracy-related or filing-delinquency penalty has been assessed. The taxpayer is not entitled to another CDP hearing under section 6320 if the additional assessment represents accruals of interest, accruals of penalties, or both.

Q-D2. Will a CDP hearing with respect to one tax period be combined with a CDP hearing with respect to another tax period?

A-D2. To the extent practicable, a CDP hearing with respect to one tax period shown on the NFTL will be combined with any and all other CDP hearings which the taxpayer has requested.

Q-D3. Will a CDP hearing under section 6320 be combined with a CDP hearing under section 6330?

A-D3. To the extent practicable, a CDP hearing under section 6320 will be held in conjunction with a CDP hearing under section 6330.

Q-D4. What is considered to be prior involvement by an employee or officer of Appeals with respect to the unpaid tax and tax period involved in the hearing?

A-D4. Prior involvement by an Appeals officer or employee includes participation or involvement in a matter (other than a CDP hearing held under either section 6320 or section 6330) that the taxpayer may have had with respect to the tax and tax period shown on the CDP Notice. Prior involvement exists only when the taxpayer, the tax and the tax period at issue in the CDP hearing also were at issue in the prior non-CDP matter, and the Appeals officer or employee actually participated in the prior matter.

Q-D5. How can a taxpayer waive the requirement that the officer or employee of Appeals have no prior involvement with respect to the tax and tax periods involved in the CDP hearing?

A-D5. The taxpayer must sign a written waiver.

Q-D6. How are CDP hearings conducted?

A-D6. The formal hearing procedures required under the Administrative Procedure Act, 5 U.S.C. 551 *et seq.*, do not apply to CDP hearings. CDP hearings are much like Collection Appeal Program (CAP) hearings in that they are informal in nature and do not require the Appeals officer or employee and the taxpayer, or the taxpayer's representative, to hold a face-to-face meeting. A CDP hearing may, but is not required to, consist of a face-to-face meeting, one or more written or oral communications between an Appeals officer or employee and the taxpayer or the taxpayer's representative, or some combination thereof. A transcript or recording of any face-to-face meeting or conversation between an Appeals officer or employee and the taxpayer or the taxpayer's representative is not required. The taxpayer or the taxpayer's representative does not have the right to subpoena and examine witnesses at a CDP hearing.

Q-D7. If a taxpayer wants a face-to-face CDP hearing, where will it be held?

A-D7. Except as provided in A-D8 of this paragraph (d)(2), a taxpayer who presents in the CDP hearing request relevant, non-frivolous reasons for disagreement with the NFTL filing will ordinarily be offered an opportunity for a face-to-face conference at the Appeals office closest to taxpayer's residence. A business taxpayer will ordinarily be offered an opportunity for a face-to-face conference at the Appeals office closest to the taxpayer's principal place of business. If that is not satisfactory to the taxpayer, the taxpayer will be given an opportunity for a hearing by telephone or by correspondence. In all cases, the Appeals officer or employee will review the case file, as described in A-F4 of paragraph (f)(2). If no face-to-face or telephonic conference is held, or other oral communication takes place, review of the documents in the case file, as described in A-F4 of paragraph (f)(2), will constitute the CDP hearing for purposes of section 6320(b).

Q-D8. In what circumstances will a face-to-face CDP conference not be granted?

A-D8. A taxpayer is not entitled to a face-to-face CDP conference at a location other than as provided in A-D7 of this paragraph (d)(2) and this A-D8. If all Appeals officers or employees at the location provided for in A-D7 of this paragraph (d)(2) have had prior involvement with the taxpayer as provided in A-D4 of this paragraph (d)(2), the taxpayer will not be offered a face-to-face conference at that location, unless the taxpayer elects to waive the requirement of section 6320(b)(3). The taxpayer will be offered a face-to-face conference at another Appeals office if Appeals would have offered the taxpayer a face-to-face conference at the location provided in A-D7 of this paragraph (d)(2), but for the disqualification of all Appeals officers or employees at that location. A face-to-face CDP conference concerning a taxpayer's underlying liability will not be granted if the request for a hearing or other taxpayer communication indicates that the taxpayer wishes only to raise irrelevant or frivolous issues concerning that liability. A face-to-face CDP conference concerning a collection alternative, such as an installment agreement or an offer to compromise liability, will not be granted unless other taxpayers would be eligible for the alternative in similar circumstances. For example, because the IRS does not consider offers to compromise from taxpayers who have not filed required returns or have not made certain required deposits of tax, as set forth in Form 656, "Offer in Compromise," no face-to-face conference will be granted to a taxpayer who wishes to make an offer to compromise but has not fulfilled those obligations. Appeals in its discretion, however, may grant a face-to-face conference if Appeals determines that a face-to-face conference is appropriate to explain to the taxpayer the requirements for becoming eligible for a collection alternative. In all cases, a taxpayer will be given an opportunity to demonstrate eligibility for a collection alternative and to become eligible for a collection alternative, in order to obtain a face-to-face conference. For purposes of determining whether a face-to-face conference will be granted, the determination of a taxpayer's eligibility for a collection alternative is made without regard to the taxpayer's ability to pay the unpaid tax. A face-to-face conference need not be granted if the taxpayer does not provide the required information set forth in A-C1(ii)(E) of paragraph (c)(2). See also A-C1(iii) of paragraph (c)(2).

(3) *Examples.*—The following examples illustrate the principles of this paragraph (d):

Example 1. Individual A timely requests a CDP hearing concerning a NFTL filed with respect to the 1998 income tax liability assessed against individual A. Appeals employee B previously conducted a CDP hearing regarding a proposed levy for individual A's 1998 income tax liability. Because employee B's only prior involvement with individual A's 1998 income tax liability was in connection with a section 6330 CDP hearing, employee B may conduct the CDP hearing under section 6320 involving the NFTL filed for the 1998 income tax liability.

Example 2. Individual C timely requests a CDP hearing concerning a NFTL filed with respect to the 1998 income tax liability assessed against individual C. Appeals employee D previously conducted a Collection Appeals Program (CAP) hearing regarding a NFTL filed with respect to individual C's 1998 income tax liability. Because employee D(s prior involvement with individual C's 1998 income tax liability was in connection with a non-CDP hearing, employee D may not conduct the CDP hearing under section 6320 unless individual C waives the requirement that the hearing will be conducted by an Appeals officer or employee who has had no prior involvement with respect to individual C's 1998 income tax liability.

Example 3. Same facts as in *Example 2*, except that the prior CAP hearing only involved individual C's 1997 income tax liability and employ-

ment tax liabilities for 1998 reported on Form 941, "Employer's Quarterly Federal Tax Return." Employee D would not be considered to have prior involvement because the prior CAP hearing in which she participated did not involve individual C's 1998 income tax liability.

Example 4. Appeals employee F is assigned to a CDP hearing concerning a NFTL filed with respect to a trust fund recovery penalty (TFRP) assessed pursuant to section 6672 against individual E. Appeals employee F participated in a prior CAP hearing involving individual E's 1999 income tax liability, and participated in a CAP hearing involving the employment taxes of business entity X, which incurred the employment tax liability to which the TFRP assessed against individual E relates. Appeals employee F would not be considered to have prior involvement because the prior CAP hearings in which he participated did not directly involve the TFRP assessed against individual E.

Example 5. Appeals employee G is assigned to a CDP hearing concerning a NFTL filed with respect to a TFRP assessed pursuant to section 6672 against individual H. In preparing for the CDP hearing, Appeals employee G reviews the Appeals case file concerning the prior CAP hearing involving the TFRP assessed pursuant to section 6672 against individual H. Appeals employee G is not deemed to have participated in the previous CAP hearing involving the TFRP assessed against individual H by such review.

(e) *Matters considered at CDP hearing.*—(1) *In general.*—Appeals will determine the timeliness of any request for a CDP hearing that is made by a taxpayer. Appeals has the authority to determine the validity, sufficiency, and timeliness of any CDP Notice given by the IRS and of any request for a CDP hearing that is made by a taxpayer. Prior to issuance of a determination, Appeals is required to obtain verification from the IRS office collecting the tax that the requirements of any applicable law or administrative procedure with respect to the filing of the NFTL have been met. The taxpayer may raise any relevant issue relating to the unpaid tax at the hearing, including appropriate spousal defenses, challenges to the appropriateness of the NFTL filing, and offers of collection alternatives. The taxpayer also may raise challenges to the existence or amount of the underlying liability, including a liability reported on a self-filed return, for any tax period specified on the CDP Notice if the taxpayer did not receive a statutory notice of deficiency for that tax liability or did not otherwise have an opportunity to dispute the tax liability. Finally, the taxpayer may not raise an issue that was raised and considered at a previous CDP hearing under section 6330 or in any other previous administrative or judicial proceeding if the taxpayer participated meaningfully in such hearing or proceeding. Taxpayers will be expected to provide all relevant information requested by Appeals, including financial statements, for its consideration of the facts and issues involved in the hearing.

(2) *Spousal defenses.*—A taxpayer may raise any appropriate spousal defenses at a CDP hearing unless the Commissioner has already made a final determination as to spousal defenses in a statutory notice of deficiency or final determination letter. To claim a spousal defense under section 66 or section 6015, the taxpayer must do so in writing according to rules prescribed by the Commissioner or the Secretary. Spousal defenses raised under sections 66 and 6015 in a CDP hearing are governed in all respects by the provisions of sections 66 and section 6015 and the regulations and procedures thereunder.

(3) *Questions and answers.*—The questions and answers illustrate the provisions of this paragraph (e) as follows:

Q-E1. What factors will Appeals consider in making its determination?

A-E1. Appeals will consider the following matters in making its determination:

(i) Whether the IRS met the requirements of any applicable law or administrative procedure.

(ii) Any issues appropriately raised by the taxpayer relating to the unpaid tax.

(iii) Any appropriate spousal defenses raised by the taxpayer.

(iv) Any challenges made by the taxpayer to the appropriateness of the NFTL filing.

(v) Any offers by the taxpayer for collection alternatives.

(vi) Whether the continued existence of the filed NFTL represents a balance between the need for the efficient collection of taxes and the legitimate concern of the taxpayer that any collection action be no more intrusive than necessary.

Q-E2. When is a taxpayer entitled to challenge the existence or amount of the tax liability specified in the CDP Notice?

A-E2. A taxpayer is entitled to challenge the existence or amount of the underlying liability for any tax period specified on the CDP Notice if the taxpayer did not receive a statutory notice of deficiency for such liability or did not otherwise have an opportunity to dispute such liability. Receipt of a statutory notice of deficiency for this purpose means receipt in time to petition the Tax Court for a redetermination of the deficiency determined in the notice of deficiency. An opportunity to dispute the underlying liability includes a prior opportunity for a conference with Appeals that was offered either before or after the assessment of the liability. An opportunity for a conference with Appeals prior to the assessment of a tax subject to deficiency procedures is not a prior opportunity for this purpose.

Q-E3. Are spousal defenses subject to the limitations imposed under section 6330(c)(2)(B) on a taxpayer's right to challenge the tax liability specified in the CDP Notice at a CDP hearing?

A-E3. The limitations imposed under section 6330(c)(2)(B) do not apply to spousal defenses. When a taxpayer asserts a spousal defense, the taxpayer is not disputing the amount or existence of the liability itself, but asserting a defense to the liability which may or may not be disputed. A spousal defense raised under section 66 or section 6015 is governed by section 66 or section 6015 and the regulations and procedures thereunder. Any limitation under those sections, regulations, and procedures therefore will apply.

Q-E4. May a taxpayer raise at a CDP hearing a spousal defense under section 66 or section 6015 if that defense was raised and considered administratively and the Commissioner has issued a statutory notice of deficiency or final determination letter addressing the spousal defense?

A-E4. No. A taxpayer is precluded from raising a spousal defense at a CDP hearing when the Commissioner has made a final determination under section 66 or section 6015 in a final determination letter or statutory notice of deficiency. However, a taxpayer may raise spousal defenses in a CDP hearing when the taxpayer has previously raised spousal defenses, but the Commissioner has not yet made a final determination regarding this issue.

Q-E5. May a taxpayer raise at a CDP hearing a spousal defense under section 66 or section 6015 if that defense was raised and considered in a prior judicial proceeding that has become final?

A-E5. No. A taxpayer is precluded by the doctrine of res judicata and by the specific limitations under section 66 or section 6015 from raising a spousal defense in a CDP hearing under these circumstances.

Q-E6. What collection alternatives are available to the taxpayer?

A-E6. Collection alternatives include, for example, a proposal to withdraw the NFTL in circumstances that will facilitate the collection of the tax liability, subordination of the NFTL, discharge of the NFTL from specific property, an installment agreement, an offer to compromise, the posting of a bond, or the substitution of other assets. A collection alternative is not available unless the alternative would be available to other taxpayers in similar circumstances. See A-D8 of paragraph (d)(2).

Q-E7. What issues may a taxpayer raise in a CDP hearing under section 6320 if the taxpayer previously received a notice under section 6330 with respect to the same tax and tax period and did not request a CDP hearing with respect to that notice?

A-E7. The taxpayer may raise appropriate spousal defenses, challenges to the appropriateness of the NFTL filing, and offers of collection alternatives. The existence or amount of the underlying liability for any tax period specified in the CDP Notice may be challenged only if the taxpayer did not have a prior opportunity to dispute the tax liability. If the taxpayer previously received a CDP Notice under section 6330 with respect to the same tax and tax period and did not request a CDP hearing with respect to that earlier CDP Notice, the taxpayer had a prior opportunity to dispute the existence or amount of the underlying tax liability.

Q-E8. How will Appeals issue its determination?

A-E8. (i) Taxpayers will be sent a dated Notice of Determination by certified or registered mail. The Notice of Determination will set forth Appeals' findings and decisions. It will state whether the IRS met the requirements of any applicable law or administrative procedure; it will resolve any issues appropriately raised by the taxpayer relating to the unpaid tax; it will include a decision on any appropriate spousal defenses raised by the taxpayer; it will include a decision on any challenges made by the taxpayer to the appropriateness of the NFTL filing; it will respond to any offers by the taxpayer for collection alternatives; and it will address whether the continued existence of the filed NFTL represents a balance between the need for the efficient collection of taxes and the legitimate concern of the taxpayer that any collection action be no more intrusive than necessary. The Notice of Determination will also set forth any agreements that Appeals reached with the taxpayer, any relief given the taxpayer, and any actions the taxpayer or the IRS are required to take. Lastly, the Notice of Determination will advise the taxpayer of the taxpayer's right to seek judicial review within 30 days of the date of the Notice of Determination.

(ii) Because taxpayers are encouraged to discuss their concerns with the IRS office collecting the tax or filing the NFTL, certain matters that might have been raised at a CDP hearing may be resolved without the need for Appeals consideration. Unless, as a result of these discussions, the taxpayer agrees in writing to withdraw the request that Appeals conduct a CDP hearing, Appeals will still issue a Notice of Determination. The taxpayer can, however, waive in writing Appeals' consideration of some or all of the matters it would otherwise consider in making its determination.

Q-E9. Is there a period of time within which Appeals must conduct a CDP hearing or issue a Notice of Determination?

A-E9. No. Appeals will, however, attempt to conduct a CDP hearing and issue a Notice of Determination as expeditiously as possible under the circumstances.

Q-E10. Why is the Notice of Determination and its date important?

A-E10. The Notice of Determination will set forth Appeals' findings and decisions with respect to the matters set forth in A-E1 of this paragraph (e)(3). The 30-day period within which the taxpayer is permitted to seek judicial review of Appeals' determination commences the day after the date of the Notice of Determination.

Q-E11. If an Appeals officer considers the merits of a taxpayer's liability in a CDP hearing when the taxpayer had previously received a statutory notice of deficiency or otherwise had an opportunity to dispute the liability prior to the NFTL, will the Appeals officer's determina-

tion regarding those liability issues be considered part of the Notice of Determination?

A-E11. No. An Appeals officer may consider the existence and amount of the underlying tax liability as a part of the CDP hearing only if the taxpayer did not receive a statutory notice of deficiency for the tax liability in question or otherwise have a prior opportunity to dispute the tax liability. Similarly, an Appeals officer may not consider any other issue if the issue was raised and considered at a previous hearing under section 6330 or in any other previous administrative or judicial proceeding in which the person seeking to raise the issue meaningfully participated. In the Appeals officer's sole discretion, however, the Appeals officer may consider the existence or amount of the underlying tax liability, or such other precluded issues, at the same time as the CDP hearing. Any determination, however, made by the Appeals officer with respect to such a precluded issue shall not be treated as part of the Notice of Determination issued by the Appeals officer and will not be subject to any judicial review. Because any decisions made by the Appeals officer on such precluded issues are not properly a part of the CDP hearing, such decisions are not required to appear in the Notice of Determination issued following the hearing. Even if a decision concerning such precluded issues is referred to in the Notice of Determination, it is not reviewable by the Tax Court because the precluded issue is not properly part of the CDP hearing.

(4) *Examples.*—The following examples illustrate the principles of this paragraph (e):

Example 1. The IRS sends a statutory notice of deficiency to the taxpayer at his last known address asserting a deficiency for the tax year 1995. The taxpayer receives the notice of deficiency in time to petition the Tax Court for a redetermination of the asserted deficiency. The taxpayer does not timely file a petition with the Tax Court. The taxpayer is precluded from challenging the existence or amount of the tax liability in a subsequent CDP hearing.

Example 2. Same facts as in *Example 1*, except the taxpayer does not receive the notice of deficiency in time to petition the Tax Court and did not have another prior opportunity to dispute the tax liability. The taxpayer is not precluded from challenging the existence or amount of the tax liability in a subsequent CDP hearing.

Example 3. The IRS properly assesses a trust fund recovery penalty against the taxpayer. The IRS offers the taxpayer the opportunity for a conference with Appeals at which the taxpayer would have the opportunity to dispute the assessed liability. The taxpayer declines the opportunity to participate in such a conference. The taxpayer is precluded from challenging the existence or amount of the tax liability in a subsequent CDP hearing.

(f) *Judicial review of Notice of Determination.*—(1) *In general.*—Unless the taxpayer provides the IRS a written withdrawal of the request that

Appeals conduct a CDP hearing, Appeals is required to issue a Notice of Determination in all cases where a taxpayer has timely requested a CDP hearing. The taxpayer may appeal such determinations made by Appeals within the 30-day period commencing the day after the date of the Notice of Determination to the Tax Court.

(2) *Questions and answers.*—The questions and answers illustrate the provisions of this paragraph (f) as follows:

Q-F1. What must a taxpayer do to obtain judicial review of a Notice of Determination?

A-F1. Subject to the jurisdictional limitations described in A-F2 of this paragraph (f)(2), the taxpayer must, within the 30-day period commencing the day after the date of the Notice of Determination, appeal the determination by Appeals to the Tax Court.

Q-F2. With respect to the relief available to the taxpayer under section 6015, what is the time frame within which a taxpayer may seek Tax Court review of Appeals' determination following a CDP hearing?

A-F2. If the taxpayer seeks Tax Court review not only of Appeals' denial of relief under section 6015, but also of relief requested with respect to other issues raised in the CDP hearing, the taxpayer should request Tax Court review within the 30-day period commencing the day after the date of the Notice of Determination. If the taxpayer only seeks Tax Court review of Appeals' denial of relief under section 6015, then the taxpayer should request Tax Court review, as provided by section 6015(e), within 90 days of Appeals' determination. If a request for Tax Court review is filed after the 30-day period for seeking judicial review under section 6320, then only the taxpayer's section 6015 claims may be reviewable by the Tax Court.

Q-F3. What issue or issues may the taxpayer raise before the Tax Court if the taxpayer disagrees with the Notice of Determination?

A-F3. In seeking Tax Court review of a Notice of Determination, the taxpayer can only ask the court to consider an issue, including a challenge to the underlying tax liability, that was properly raised in the taxpayer's CDP hearing. An issue is not properly raised if the taxpayer fails to request consideration of the issue by Appeals, or if consideration is requested but the taxpayer fails to present to Appeals any evidence with respect to that issue after being given a reasonable opportunity to present such evidence.

Q-F4. What is the administrative record for purposes of Tax Court review?

A-F4. The case file, including the taxpayer's request for hearing, any other written communications and information from the taxpayer or the taxpayer's authorized representative submitted in connection with the CDP hearing, notes made by an Appeals officer or employee of any oral communications with the taxpayer or the taxpayer's authorized representative, memoranda created by the Appeals officer or employee in connection with the CDP hearing, and any other documents or materials relied upon by the Appeals officer or employee in making the determination under section 6330(c)(3), will constitute the record in the Tax Court review of the Notice of Determination issued by Appeals.

(g) *Effect of request for CDP hearing and judicial review on periods of limitation and collection activity.*—(1) *In general.*—The periods of limitation under section 6502 (relating to collection after assessment), section 6531 (relating to criminal prosecutions), and section 6532 (relating to suits) are suspended until the date the IRS receives the taxpayer's written withdrawal of the request for a CDP hearing by Appeals or the determination resulting from the CDP hearing becomes final by expiration of the time for seeking judicial review or the exhaustion of any rights to appeals following judicial review. In no event shall any of these periods of limitation expire before the 90th day after the date on which the IRS receives the taxpayer's written withdrawal of the request that Appeals conduct a CDP hearing or the determination with respect to such hearing becomes final upon either the expiration of the time for seeking judicial review or upon exhaustion of any rights to appeals following judicial review.

(2) *Questions and answers.*—The questions and answers illustrate the provisions of this paragraph (g) as follows:

Q-G1. For what period of time will the periods of limitation under sections 6502, 6531, and 6532 remain suspended if the taxpayer timely requests a CDP hearing concerning the filing of a NFTL?

A-G1. The suspension period commences on the date the IRS receives the taxpayer's written request for a CDP hearing. The suspension period continues until the IRS receives a written withdrawal by the taxpayer of the request for a CDP hearing or the Notice of Determination resulting from the CDP hearing becomes final. In no event shall any of these periods of limitation expire before the 90th day after the day on which the IRS receives the taxpayer's written withdrawal of the request that Appeals conduct a CDP hearing or there is a final determination with respect to such hearing. The periods of limitation that are suspended under section 6320 are those which apply to the taxes and the tax period or periods to which the CDP Notice relates.

Q-G2. For what period of time will the periods of limitation under sections 6502, 6531, and 6532 be suspended if the taxpayer does not request a CDP hearing concerning the filing of a NFTL, or the taxpayer requests a CDP hearing, but his request is not timely?

A-G2. Under either of these circumstances, section 6320 does not provide for a suspension of the periods of limitation.

Q-G3. What, if any, enforcement actions can the IRS take during the suspension period?

A-G3. Section 6330(e), made applicable to section 6320 CDP hearings by section 6320(c), provides for the suspension of the periods of limitation discussed in paragraph (g)(1) of these regulations. Section 6330(e) also provides that levy actions that are the subject of the requested CDP hearing under that section shall be suspended during the same period. Levy actions, however, are not the subject of a CDP hearing under section 6320. The IRS may levy for tax periods and taxes covered by the CDP Notice under section 6320 and for other taxes and periods if the CDP requirements under section 6330 for those taxes and periods have been satisfied. The IRS also may file NFTLs for tax periods or taxes not covered by the CDP Notice, may file a NFTL for the same tax and tax period stated on the CDP Notice at another recording office, and may take other non-levy collection actions such as initiating judicial proceedings to collect the tax shown on the CDP Notice or offsetting overpayments from other periods, or of other taxes, against the tax shown on the CDP Notice. Moreover, the provisions in section 6330 do not apply when the IRS levies for the tax and tax period shown on the CDP Notice to collect a state tax refund due the taxpayer, or determines that collection of the tax is in jeopardy. Finally, section 6330 does not prohibit the IRS from accepting any voluntary payments made for the tax and tax period stated on the CDP Notice.

(3) *Examples.*—The following examples illustrate the principles of this paragraph (g):

Example 1. The period of limitation under section 6502 with respect to the taxpayer's tax period listed in the NFTL will expire on August 1, 1999. The IRS sent a CDP Notice to the taxpayer on April 30, 1999. The taxpayer timely requested a CDP hearing. The IRS received this request on May 15, 1999. Appeals sends the taxpayer its determination on June 15, 1999. The taxpayer timely seeks judicial review of that determination. The period of limitation under section 6502 would be suspended from May 15, 1999, until the determination resulting from that hearing becomes final by expiration of the time for seeking review or reconsideration before the Tax Court, plus 90 days.

Example 2. Same facts as in *Example 1*, except the taxpayer does not seek judicial review of Appeals' determination. Because the taxpayer requested the CDP hearing when fewer than 90 days remained on the period of limitation, the period of limitation will be extended to October 13, 1999 (90 days from July 15, 1999).

(h) *Retained jurisdiction of Appeals.*—(1) *In general.*—The Appeals office that makes a determination under section 6320 retains jurisdiction over that determination, including any subsequent administrative hearings that may be requested by the taxpayer regarding the NFTL and any collection actions taken or proposed with respect to Appeals' determination. Once a taxpayer has exhausted his other remedies, Appeals' retained jurisdiction permits it to consider whether a change in the taxpayer's circumstances affects its original determination. Where a taxpayer alleges a change in circumstances that affects Appeals' original determination, Appeals

may consider whether changed circumstances warrant a change in its earlier determination.

(2) *Questions and answers.*—The questions and answers illustrate the provisions of this paragraph (h) as follows:

Q-H1. Are the periods of limitation suspended during the course of any subsequent Appeals consideration of the matters raised by a taxpayer when the taxpayer invokes the retained jurisdiction of Appeals under section 6330(d)(2)(A) or (d)(2)(B)?

A-H1. No. Under section 6320(b)(2), a taxpayer is entitled to only one CDP hearing under section 6320 with respect to the tax and tax period or periods specified in the CDP Notice. Any subsequent consideration by Appeals pursuant to its retained jurisdiction is not a continuation of the original CDP hearing and does not suspend the periods of limitation.

Q-H2. Is a decision of Appeals resulting from a retained jurisdiction hearing appealable to the Tax Court?

A-H2. No. As discussed in A-H1, a taxpayer is entitled to only one CDP hearing under section 6320 with respect to the tax and tax period or periods specified in the CDP Notice. Only determinations resulting from CDP hearings are appealable to the Tax Court.

(i) *Equivalent hearing.*—(1) *In general.*—A taxpayer who fails to make a timely request for a CDP hearing is not entitled to a CDP hearing. Such a taxpayer may nevertheless request an administrative hearing with Appeals, which is referred to herein as an "equivalent hearing." The equivalent hearing will be held by Appeals and generally will follow Appeals' procedures for a CDP hearing. Appeals will not, however, issue a Notice of Determination. Under such circumstances, Appeals will issue a Decision Letter.

(2) *Questions and answers.*—The questions and answers illustrate the provisions of this paragraph (i) as follows:

Q-I1. What must a taxpayer do to obtain an equivalent hearing?

A-I1. (i) A request for an equivalent hearing must be made in writing. A written request in any form that requests an equivalent hearing will be acceptable if it includes the information and signature required in A-I1(ii) of this paragraph (i)(2).

(ii) The request must be dated and must include the following:

(A) The taxpayer's name, address, daytime telephone number (if any), and taxpayer identification number (e.g., SSN, ITIN or EIN).

(B) The type of tax involved.

(C) The tax period at issue.

(D) A statement that the taxpayer is requesting an equivalent hearing with Appeals concerning the filing of the NFTL.

(E) The reason or reasons why the taxpayer disagrees with the filing of the NFTL.

(F) The signature of the taxpayer or the taxpayer's authorized representative.

(iii) The taxpayer must perfect any timely written request for an equivalent hearing that does not satisfy the requirements set forth in A-I1(ii) of this paragraph (i)(2) within a reasonable period of time after a request from the IRS. If the requirements are not satisfied within a reasonable period of time, the taxpayer's equivalent hearing request will be denied.

(iv) The taxpayer must affirm any timely written request for an equivalent hearing that is signed or alleged to have been signed on the taxpayer's behalf by the taxpayer's spouse or other unauthorized representative, and that otherwise meets the requirements set forth in A-I1(ii) of this paragraph (i)(2), by filing, within a reasonable period of time after a request from the IRS, a signed written affirmation that the request was originally submitted on the taxpayer's behalf. If the affirmation is filed within a reasonable period of time after a request, the timely equivalent hearing request will be considered timely with respect to the non-signing taxpayer. If the affirmation is not filed within a reasonable period of time, the equivalent hearing request will be denied with respect to the non-signing taxpayer.

Q-I2. What issues will Appeals consider at an equivalent hearing?

A-I2. In an equivalent hearing, Appeals will consider the same issues that it would have considered at a CDP hearing on the same matter.

Q-I3. Are the periods of limitation under sections 6502, 6531, and 6532 suspended if the taxpayer does not timely request a CDP hearing and is subsequently given an equivalent hearing?

A-I3. No. The suspension period provided for in section 6330(e) relates only to hearings requested within the 30-day period that commences on the day after the end of the five business day period following the filing of the NFTL, that is, CDP hearings.

Q-I4. Will collection action, including the filing of additional NFTLs, be suspended if a taxpayer requests and receives an equivalent hearing?

A-I4. Collection action is not required to be suspended. Accordingly, the decision to take collection action during the pendency of an equivalent hearing will be determined on a case-by-case basis. Appeals may request the IRS office with responsibility for collecting the taxes to suspend all or some collection action or to take other appropriate action if it determines that such action is appropriate or necessary under the circumstances.

Q-I5. What will the Decision Letter state?

A-I5. The Decision Letter will generally contain the same information as a Notice of Determination.

Q-I6. Will a taxpayer be able to obtain Tax Court review of a decision made by Appeals with respect to an equivalent hearing?

A-I6. Section 6320 does not authorize a taxpayer to appeal the decision of Appeals with respect to an equivalent hearing. A taxpayer may

under certain circumstances be able to seek Tax Court review of Appeals' denial of relief under section 6015. Such review must be sought within 90 days of the issuance of Appeals' determination on those issues, as provided by section 6015(e).

Q-I7. When must a taxpayer request an equivalent hearing with respect to a CDP Notice issued under section 6320?

A-I7. A taxpayer must submit a written request for an equivalent hearing within the one-year period commencing the day after the end of the five-business-day period following the filing of the NFTL. This period is slightly different from the period for submitting a written request for an equivalent hearing with respect to a CDP Notice issued under section 6330. For a CDP Notice issued under section 6330, a taxpayer must submit a written request for an equivalent hearing within the one-year period commencing the day after the date of the CDP Notice issued under section 6330.

Q-I8. How will the timeliness of a taxpayer's written request for an equivalent hearing be determined?

A-I8. The rules and regulations under section 7502 and section 7503 will apply to determine the timeliness of the taxpayer's request for an equivalent hearing, if properly transmitted and addressed as provided in A-I10 of this paragraph (i)(2).

Q-I9. Is the one-year period within which a taxpayer must make a request for an equivalent hearing extended because the taxpayer resides outside the United States?

A-I9. No. All taxpayers who want an equivalent hearing concerning the filing of the NFTL must request the hearing within the one-year period commencing the day after the end of the five-business-day period following the filing of the NFTL.

Q-I10. Where must the written request for an equivalent hearing be sent?

A-I10. The written request for an equivalent hearing must be sent, or hand delivered (if permitted), to the IRS office and address as directed on the CDP Notice. If the address of the issuing office does not appear on the CDP Notice, the taxpayer should obtain the address of the office to which the written request should be sent or hand delivered by calling, toll-free, 1-800-829-1040 and providing the taxpayer's identification number (e.g., SSN, ITIN or EIN).

Q-I11. What will happen if the taxpayer does not request an equivalent hearing in writing within the one-year period commencing the day after the end of the five-business-day period following the filing of the NFTL?

A-I11. If the taxpayer does not request an equivalent hearing with Appeals within the one-year period commencing the day after the end of the five-business-day period following the filing of the NFTL, the taxpayer foregoes the right to an equivalent hearing with respect to the unpaid tax and tax periods shown on the CDP Notice. A written request submitted within the one-year period that does not satisfy the requirements set forth in A-I1(ii) of this paragraph (i)(2) is considered timely if the request is perfected within a reasonable period of time pursuant to A-I1(iii) of this paragraph (i)(2). If a request for equivalent hearing is untimely, either because the request was not submitted within the one-year period or not perfected within the reasonable period provided, the equivalent hearing request will be denied. The taxpayer, however, may seek reconsideration by the IRS office collecting the tax, assistance from the National Taxpayer Advocate, or an administrative hearing before Appeals under its Collection Appeals Program or any successor program.

(j) *Effective date.*—This section is applicable on or after November 16, 2006 with respect to requests made for CDP hearings or equivalent hearings on or after November 16, 2006. [Reg. §301.6320-1.]

☐ [*T.D. 8979, 1-17-2002. Amended by T.D. 9290, 10-16-2006.*]

[Reg. §20.6321-1]

§20.6321-1. Lien for taxes.—For regulations concerning the lien for taxes, see §301.6321-1 of this chapter (Regulations on Procedure and Administration). [Reg. §20.6321-1.]

☐ [*T.D. 6296, 6-23-58.*]

[Reg. §25.6321-1]

§25.6321-1. Lien for taxes.—For regulations concerning the lien for taxes, see §301.6321-1 of this chapter (Regulations on Procedure and Administration). [Reg. §25.6321-1.]

☐ [*T.D. 6334, 10-14-58.*]

[Reg. §301.6321-1]

§301.6321-1. Lien for taxes.—If any person liable to pay any tax neglects or refuses to pay the same after demand, the amount (including any interest, additional amount, addition to tax, or assessable penalty, together with any costs that may accrue in addition thereto) shall be a lien in favor of the United States upon all property and rights to property, whether real or personal, tangible or intangible, belonging to such person. For purposes of section 6321 and this section, the term "any tax" shall include a State individual income tax which is a "qualified tax", as defined in paragraph(b) of §301.6361-4. The lien attaches to all property and rights to property belonging to such person at any time during the period of the lien, including any property or rights to property acquired by such person after the lien arises. Solely for purposes of sections 6321 and 6331, any interest in restricted land held in trust by the United States for an individual noncompetent Indian (and not for a tribe) shall not be deemed to be property, or a right to property, belonging to such Indian. For the method of allocating amounts collected pursuant to a lien between the Federal Government and a State or States imposing a qualified tax with respect to which the lien attached, see paragraph (f) of

§301.6361-1. For the special lien for estate and gift taxes, see section 6324 and §301.6324-1. [Reg. §301.6321-1.]

☐ [*T.D. 6119, 12-31-54. Amended by T.D. 7139, 8-11-71 and T.D. 7577, 12-19-78.*]

[Reg. §20.6323-1]

§20.6323-1. Validity and priority against certain persons.—For regulations concerning the validity of the lien imposed by section 6321 against certain persons, see §§301.6323(a)-1 through 301.6323(i)-1 of this chapter (Regulations on Procedure and Administration). [Reg. §20.6323-1.]

☐ [*T.D. 6296, 6-23-58. Amended by T.D. 7429, 8-20-76.*]

[Reg. §25.6323-1]

§25.6323-1. Validity and priority against certain persons.—For regulations concerning the validity of the lien imposed by section 6321 against certain persons, see §§301.6323(a)-1 through 301.6323(i)-1 of this chapter (Regulations on Procedure and Administration). [Reg. §25.6323-1.]

☐ [*T.D. 6334, 10-14-58. Amended by T.D. 7429, 8-20-76.*]

[Reg. §301.6323(a)-1]

§301.6323(a)-1. Purchasers, holders of security interests, mechanic's lienors, and judgment lien creditors.—(a) *Invalidity of lien without notice.*—The lien imposed by section 6321 is not valid against any purchaser (as defined in paragraph (f) of §301.6323(h)-1), holder of a security interest (as defined in paragraph (a) of §301.6323(h)-1), mechanic's lienor (as defined in paragraph (b) of §301.6323(h)-1), or judgment lien creditor (as defined in paragraph (g) of §301.6323(h)-1) until a notice of lien is filed in accordance with §301.6323(f)-1. Except as provided by section 6323, if a person becomes a purchaser, holder of a security interest, mechanic's lienor, or judgment lien creditor after a notice of lien is filed in accordance with §301.6323(f)-1, the interest acquired by such person is subject to the lien imposed by section 6321.

(b) *Cross references.*—For provisions relating to the protection afforded a security interest arising after tax lien filing, which interest is covered by a commercial transactions financing agreement, real property construction or improvement financing agreement, or an obligatory disbursement agreement, see §§301.6323(c)-1, 301.6323(c)-2, and 301.6323(c)-3, respectively. For provisions relating to the protection afforded to a security interest coming into existence by virtue of disbursements made before the 46th day after the date of tax lien filing, see §301.6323(d)-1. For provisions relating to priority afforded to interest and certain other expenses with respect to a lien or security interest having priority over the lien imposed by section 6321, see §301.6323(e)-1. For provisions relating to certain other interests arising after tax lien filing, see §301.6323(b)-1. [Reg. §301.6323(a)-1.]

☐ [*T. D.* 7429, 8-20-76.]

[Reg. §301.6323(b)-1]

§301.6323(b)-1. Protection for certain interests even though notice filed.—(a) *Securities.*— (1) *In general.*—Even though a notice of a lien imposed by section 6321 is filed in accordance with §301.6323(f)-1, the lien is not valid with respect to a security (as defined in paragraph (d) of §301.6323(h)-1) against—

(i) A purchaser (as defined in paragraph (f) of §301.6323(h)-1) of the security who at the time of purchase did not have actual notice or knowledge (as defined in paragraph (a) of §301.6323(i)-1) of the existence of the lien;

(ii) A holder of a security interest (as defined in paragraph (a) of §301.6323(h)-1) in the security who did not have actual notice or knowledge (as defined in paragraph (a) of §301.6323(i)-1) of the existence of the lien at the time the security interest came into existence or at the time such security interest was acquired from a previous holder for a consideration in money or money's worth; or

(iii) A transferee of an interest protected under subdivision (i) or (ii) of this subparagraph to the same extent the lien is invalid against his transferor.

For purposes of subdivision (iii) of this subparagraph, no person can improve his position with respect to the lien by reacquiring the interest from an intervening purchaser or holder of a security interest against whom the lien is invalid.

(2) *Examples.*—The application of this paragraph may be illustrated by the following examples:

Example (1). On May 1, 1969, in accordance with §301.6323(f)-1, a notice of lien is filed with respect to A's delinquent tax liability. On May 20, 1969, A sells 100 shares of common stock in X corporation to B, who, on the date of the sale, does not have actual notice or knowledge of the existence of the lien. Because B purchased the stock without actual notice or knowledge of the lien, under subdivision (i) of subparagraph (1) of this paragraph, the stock purchased by B is not subject to the lien.

Example (2). Assume the same facts as in example (1) except that on May 30, 1969, B sells the 100 shares of common stock in X corporation to C who on May 5, 1969, had actual notice of the existence of the tax lien against A. Because the X stock when purchased by B was not subject to the lien, under subdivision (iii) of subparagraph (1) of this paragraph, the stock purchased by C is not subject to the lien. C succeeds to B's rights, even though C had actual notice of the lien before B's purchase.

Example (3). On June 1, 1970, in accordance with §301.6323(f)-1, a notice of lien is filed with respect to D's delinquent tax liability. D owns 20 $1,000 bonds issued by the Y company. On June 10, 1970, D obtains a loan from M bank for $5,000 using the Y company bonds as collateral. At the time the loan is made M bank does not have actual notice or knowledge of the existence of the tax lien. Because M bank did not have actual notice or knowledge of the lien when the security interest came into existence, under subdivision (ii) of subparagraph (1) of this paragraph, the tax lien is not valid against M bank to the extent of its security interest.

Example (4). Assume the same facts as in example (3) except that on June 19, 1970, M bank assigns the chose in action and its security interest to N, who had actual notice or knowledge of the existence of the lien on June 1, 1970. Because the security interest was not subject to the lien to the extent of M bank's security interest, the security interest held by N is to the same extent entitled to priority over the tax lien because N succeeds to M bank's rights. See subdivision (iii) of subparagrah (1) of this paragraph.

Example (5). On July 1, 1970, in accordance with §301.6323(f)-1, a notice of lien is filed with respect to E's delinquent tax liability. E owns ten $1,000 bonds issued by the Y company. On July 5, 1970, E borrows $4,000 from F and delivers the bonds to F as collateral for the loan. At the time the loan is made, F has actual knowledge of the existence of the tax lien and, therefore, holds the security interest subject to the lien on the bonds. On July 10, 1970, F sells the security interest to G for $4,000 and delivers the Y company bonds pledged as collateral. G does not have actual notice or knowledge of the existence of the lien on July 10, 1970. Because G did not have actual notice or knowledge of the lien at the time he purchased the security interest, under subdivision (ii) of subparagraph (1) of this paragraph, the tax lien is not valid against G to the extent of his security interest.

Example (6). Assume the same facts as in example (5) except that, instead of purchasing the security interest from F on July 10, 1970, G lends $4,000 to F and takes a security interest in F's security interest in the bonds on that date. Because G became the holder of a security interest in a security interest after notice of lien was filed and does not directly have a security interest in a security, the security interest held by G is not entitled to a priority over the tax lien under the provisions of subparagraph (1) of this paragraph.

(b) *Motor vehicles.*—(1) *In general.*—Even though a notice of a lien imposed by section 6321 is filed in accordance with §301.6323(f)-1, the lien is not valid against a purchaser (as defined in paragraph (f) of §301.6323(h)-1) of a motor vehicle (as defined in paragraph (c) of §301.6323(h)-1) if—

(i) At the time of the purchase, the purchaser did not have actual notice or knowledge (as defined in paragraph (a) of §301.6323(i)-1) of the existence of the lien, and

(ii) Before the purchaser obtains such notice or knowledge, he has acquired actual possession of the motor vehicle and has not thereafter relinquished actual possession to the seller or his agent.

(2) *Examples.*—The application of this paragraph may be illustrated by the following examples:

Example (1). A, a delinquent taxpayer against whom a notice of tax lien has been filed in accordance with § 301.6323(f)-1, sells his automobile (which qualifies as a motor vehicle under paragraph (c) of § 301.6323(h)-1) to B, an automobile dealer. B takes actual possession of the automobile and does not thereafter relinquish actual possession to the seller or his agent. Subsequent to his purchase, B learns of the existence of the tax lien against A. Even though notice of lien was filed before the purchase, the lien is not valid against B, because B did not know of the existence of the lien before the purchase and before acquiring actual possession of the vehicle.

Example (2). C is a wholesaler of used automobiles. A notice of lien has been filed with respect to C's delinquent tax liability in accordance with § 301.6323(f)-1. Subsequent to such filing, D, a used automobile dealer, purchases and takes actual possession of 20 automobiles (which qualify as motor vehicles under the provisions of paragraph (c) of § 301.6323(h)-1) from C at an auction and places them on his lot for sale. C does not reacquire possession of any of the automobiles. At the time of his purchase, D does not have actual notice or knowledge of the existence of the lien against C. Even though notice of lien was filed before D's purchase, the lien was not valid against D because D did not know of the existence of the lien before the purchase and before acquiring actual possession of the vehicles.

(3) *Cross reference.*—For provisions relating to additional circumstances in which the lien imposed by section 6321 may not be valid against the purchaser of tangible personal property (including a motor vehicle) purchased at retail, see paragraph (c) of this section.

(c) *Personal property purchased at retail.*—(1) *In general.*—Even though a notice of a lien imposed by section 6321 is filed in accordance with § 301.6323(f)-1, the lien is not valid against a purchaser (as defined in paragraph (f) of § 301.6323(h)-1) of tangible personal property purchased at a retail sale (as defined in subparagraph (2) of this paragraph) unless at the time of purchase the purchaser intends the purchase to (or knows that the purchase will) hinder, evade, or defeat the collection of any tax imposed by the Internal Revenue Code of 1954.

(2) *Definition of retail sale.*—For purposes of this paragraph, the term "retail sale" means a sale, made in the ordinary course of the seller's trade or business, of tangible personal property of which the seller is the owner. Such term includes a sale in customary retail quantities by a seller who is going out of business, but does not include a bulk sale or an auction sale in which goods are offered in quantities substantially

greater than are customary in the ordinary course of the seller's trade or business or an auction sale of goods the owner of which is not in the business of selling such goods.

(3) *Example.*—The application of this paragraph may be illustrated by the following example:

Example. A purchases a refrigerator from the M company, a retail appliance dealer. Prior to such purchase, a notice of lien was filed with respect to M's delinquent tax liability in accordance with § 301.6323(f)-1. At the time of the purchase A knows of the existence of the lien. However, A does not intend the purchase to hinder, evade, or defeat the collection of any internal revenue tax, and A does not have any reason to believe that the purchase will affect the collection of any internal revenue tax. Even though notice of lien was filed before the purchase, the lien is not valid against A because A in good faith purchased the refrigerator at retail in the ordinary course of the M company's business.

(d) *Personal property purchased in casual sale.*— (1) *In general.*—Even though a notice of a lien imposed by section 6321 is filed in accordance with § 301.6323(f)-1, the lien is not valid against a purchaser (as defined in § 301.6323(h)-1(f)) of household goods, personal effects, or other tangible personal property of a type described in § 301.6334-1 (which includes wearing apparel; school books; fuel; provisions; furniture; arms for personal use, livestock, and poultry (whether or not the seller is the head of a family); and books and tools of a trade, business, or profession (whether or not the trade, business, or profession of the seller)), purchased, other than for resale, in a casual sale for less than $1,380, effective for 2010 and adjusted each year based on the rate of inflation (excluding interest and expenses described in § 301.6323(e)-1).

(2) *Limitation.*—This paragraph applies only if the purchaser does not have actual notice or knowledge (as defined in paragraph (a) of § 301.6323(i)-1)—

(i) Of the existence of the tax lien, or

(ii) That the sale is one of a series of sales. For purposes of subdivision (ii) of this subparagraph, a sale is one of a series of sales if the seller plans to dispose of, in separate transactions, substantially all of his household goods, personal effects, and other tangible personal property described in § 301.6334-1.

(3) *Examples.*—The application of this paragraph may be illustrated by the following examples:

Example (1). A, an attorney's widow, sells a set of law books for $200 to B, for B's own use. Prior to the sale a notice of lien was filed with respect to A's delinquent tax liability in accordance with § 301.6323(f)-1. B has no actual notice or knowledge of the tax lien. In addition, B does not know that the sale is one of a series of sales. Because the sale is a casual sale for less than $1,380 and involves books of a profession (tangible personal property of a type described in §301.6334-1, irrespective of the fact that A has never engaged in the legal profession), the tax lien is not valid against B even though a notice of lien was filed prior to the time of B's purchase.

Example (2). Assume the same facts as in example (1) except that B purchases the books for resale in his second-hand bookstore. Because B purchased the books for resale, he purchased the books subject to the lien.

Example (3). In an advertisement appearing in a local newspaper, G indicates that he is offering for sale a lawn mower, a used television set, a desk, a refrigerator, and certain used dining room furniture. In response to the advertisement, H purchases the dining room furniture for $200. H does not receive any information which would impart notice of a lien, or that the sale is one of a series of sales, beyond the information contained in the advertisement. Prior to the sale a notice of lien was filed with respect to G's delinquent tax liability in accordance with §301.6323(f)-1. Because H had no actual notice or knowledge that substantially all of G's household goods were being sold or that the sale is one of a series of sales, and because the sale is a casual sale for less than $1,380, H does not purchase the dining room furniture subject to the lien. The household goods are of a type described in §301.6334-1(a)(2) irrespective of whether G is the head of a family or whether all such household goods offered for sale exceed $8,250 in value.

(e) *Personal property subject to possessory liens.*—Even though a notice of a lien imposed by section 6321 is filed in accordance with §301.6323(f)-1, the lien is not valid against a holder of a lien on tangible personal property which under local law secures the reasonable price of the repair or improvement of the property if the property is, and has been, continuously in the possession of the holder of the lien from the time the possessory lien arose. For example, if local law gives an automobile repairman the right to retain possession of an automobile he has repaired as security for payment of the repair bill and the repairman retains continuous possession of the automobile until his lien is satisfied, a tax lien filed in accordance with §301.6323(f)(1) which has attached to the automobile will not be valid to the extent of the reasonable price of the repairs. It is immaterial that the notice of tax lien was filed before the repairman undertook his work or that he knew of the lien before undertaking the work.

(f) *Real property tax and special assessment liens.*—(1) *In general.*—Even though a notice of a lien imposed by section 6321 is filed in accordance with §301.6323(f)-1, the lien is not valid against the holder of another lien upon the real property (regardless of when such other lien arises), if such other lien is entitled under local law to priority over security interests in real property which are prior in time and if such other lien on real property secures payment of—

(i) A tax of general application levied by any taxing authority based upon the value of the property;

(ii) A special assessment imposed directly upon the property by any taxing authority, if the assessment is imposed for the purpose of defraying the cost of any public improvement; or

(iii) Charges for utilities or public services furnished to the property by the United States, a State or political subdivision thereof, or an instrumentality of any one or more of the foregoing.

(2) *Examples.*—The application of this paragraph may be illustrated by the following examples:

Example (1). A owns Blackacre in the city of M. A notice of lien affecting Blackacre is filed in accordance with §301.6323(f)-1. Subsequent to the filing of the notice of lien, the city of M acquires a lien against Blackacre to secure payment of real estate taxes. Such taxes are levied against all property in the city in proportion to the value of the property. Under local law, the holder of a lien for real property taxes is entitled to priority over a security interest in real property even though the security interest is prior in time. Because the real property tax lien held by the city of M secures payment of a tax of general application and is entitled to priority over security interests which are prior in time, the lien held by the city of M is entitled to priority over the Federal tax lien with respect to Blackacre.

Example (2). B owns Whiteacre in N county. A notice of lien affecting Whiteacre is filed in accordance with §301.6323(f)-1. Subsequent to the filing of the notice of lien, N county constructs a sidewalk, paves the street, and installs water and sewer lines adjacent to Whiteacre. In order to defray the cost of these improvements, N county imposes upon Whiteacre a special assessment which under local law results in a lien upon Whiteacre that is entitled to priority over security interests that are prior in time. Because the special assessment lien is (i) entitled under local law to priority over security interests which are prior in time, and (ii) imposed directly upon real property to defray the cost of a public improvement, the special assessment lien has priority over the Federal tax lien with respect to Whiteacre.

Example (3). C owns Greenacre in town O. A notice of lien affecting Greenacre is filed in accordance with §301.6323(f)-1. Town O furnishes water and electricity to Greenacre and periodically collects a fee for these services. Subsequent to the filing of the notice of lien, town O supplies water and electricity to Greenacre, and C fails to pay the charges for these services. Under local law, town O acquires a lien to secure charges for the services, and this lien has priority over security interests which are prior in time. Because the lien of town O (i) is for services furnished to the real property and (ii) has priority over earlier security interests, town O's lien has priority over the Federal tax lien with respect to Greenacre.

Reg. § 301.6323(b)-1(f)(2)

(g) *Residential property subject to a mechanic's lien for certain repairs and improvements.*—(1) *In general.*—Even though a notice of a lien imposed by section 6321 is filed in accordance with § 301.6323(f)-1, the lien is not valid against a mechanic's lienor (as defined in § 301.6323(h)-1(b)) who holds a lien for the repair or improvement of a personal residence if—

(i) The residence is occupied by the owner and contains no more than four dwelling units, and

(ii) The contract price on the prime contract with the owner for the repair or improvement (excluding interest and expenses described in § 301.6323(e)-1) is not more than $6,890, effective for 2010 and adjusted each year based on the rate of inflation.

(iii) For purposes of paragraph (g)(1)(ii) of this section, the amounts of subcontracts under the prime contract with the owner are not to be taken into consideration for purposes of computing the $6,890 prime contract price. It is immaterial that the notice of tax lien was filed before the contractor undertakes his work or that he knew of the lien before undertaking his work.

(2) *Examples.*—The application of this paragraph may be illustrated by the following examples:

Example (1). A owns a building containing four apartments, one of which he occupies as his personal residence. A notice of lien which affects the building is filed in accordance with § 301.6323(f)-1. Thereafter, A enters into a contract with B in the amount of $800, which includes labor and materials, to repair the roof of the building. B purchases roofing shingles from C for $300. B completes the work and A fails to pay B the agreed amount. In turn, B fails to pay C for the shingles. Under local law, B and C acquire mechanic's liens on A's building. Because the contract price on the prime contract with A is not more than $6,890 and under local law B and C acquire mechanic's liens on A's building, the liens of B and C have priority over the Federal tax lien.

Example (2). Assume the same facts as in *Example 1*, except that the amount of the prime contract between A and B is $7,100. Because the amount of the prime contract with the owner, A, is in excess of $6,890, the tax lien has priority over the entire amount of each of the mechanic's liens of B and C, even though the amount of the contract between B and C is $300.

Example (3). Assume the same facts as in *Example 1*, except that A and B do not agree in advance upon the amount due under the prime contract but agree that B will perform the work for the cost of materials and labor plus 10 percent of such cost. When the work is completed, it is determined that the total amount due is $850. Because the prime contract price is not more than $6,890 and under local law B and C acquire mechanic's liens on A's residence, the liens of B and C have priority over the Federal tax lien.

(h) *Attorney's liens.*—(1) *In general.*—Even though notice of a lien imposed by section 6321 is filed in accordance with § 301.6323(f)-1, the lien is not valid against an attorney who, under local law, holds a lien upon, or a contract enforceable against, a judgment or other amount in settlement of a claim or of a cause of action. The priority afforded an attorney's lien under this paragraph shall not exceed the amount of the attorney's reasonable compensation for obtaining the judgment or procuring the settlement. For purposes of this paragraph, reasonable compensation means the amount customarily allowed under local law for an attorney's services for litigating or settling a similar case or administrative claim. However, reasonable compensation shall be determined on the basis of the facts and circumstances of each individual case. It is immaterial that the notice of tax lien is filed before the attorney undertakes his work or that the attorney knows of the tax lien before undertaking his work. This paragraph does not apply to an attorney's lien which may arise from the defense of a claim or cause of action against a taxpayer except to the extent such lien is held upon a judgment or other amount arising from the adjudication or settlement of a counterclaim in favor of the taxpayer. In the case of suits against the taxpayer, see § 301.6325-1(d)(2) for rules relating to the subordination of the tax lien to facilitate tax collection.

(2) *Claim or cause of action against the United States.*—Paragraph (h)(1) of this section does not apply to an attorney's lien with respect to—

(i) Any judgment or other fund resulting from the successful litigation or settlement of an administrative claim or cause of action against the United States to the extent that the United States, under any legal or equitable right, offsets its liability under the judgment or settlement against any liability of the taxpayer to the United States, or

(ii) Any amount credited against any liability of the taxpayer in accordance with section 6402.

(3) *Examples.*—The provisions of this paragraph may be illustrated by the following examples:

Example (1). A notice of lien is filed against A in accordance with § 301.6323(f)-1. Subsequently, A is struck by an automobile and retains B, an attorney to institute suit on A's behalf against the operator of the automobile. B knows of the tax lien before he begins his work. Under local law, B is entitled to a lien upon any recovery in order to secure payment of his fee. A is awarded damages of $10,000. B charges a fee of $3,000 which is the fee customarily allowed under local law in similar cases and which is found to be reasonable under the circumstances of this particular case. Because, under local law, B holds a lien for the amount of his reasonable compensation for obtaining the judgment, B's lien has priority over the Federal tax lien.

Example (2). Assume the same facts as in example (1), except that before suit is instituted A and the owner of the automobile settle out of court for $7,500. B charges a reasonable and customary fee of $1,800 for procuring the settlement and under local law holds a lien upon the settlement in order to secure payment of the fee. Because, under local law, B holds a lien for the amount of his reasonable compensation for obtaining the settlement, B has priority over the Federal tax lien.

Example (3). In accordance with § 301.6323(f)-1, a notice of lien in the amount of $8,000 is filed against C, a contractor. Subsequently C retains D, an attorney, to initiate legal proceedings to recover the amount allegedly due him for construction work he has performed for the United States. C and D enter into an agreement which provides that D will receive a reasonable and customary fee of $2,500 as compensation for his services. Under local law, the agreement will give rise to a lien which is enforceable by D against any amount recovered in the suit. C is successful in the suit and is awarded $10,000. D claims $2,500 of the proceeds as his fee. The United States, however, exercises its right to set-off and applies $8,000 of the $10,000 award to satisfy C's tax liability. Because the $10,000 award resulted from the successful litigation of a cause of action against the United States, B's contract for attorney's fees is not enforceable against the amount recovered to the extent the United States offsets its liability under the judgment against C's tax liability. It is immaterial that D had no notice or knowledge of the tax lien at the time he began work on the case.

(i) *Certain insurance contracts.*—(1) *In general.*—Even though a notice of a lien imposed by section 6321 is filed in accordance with § 301.6323(f)-1, the lien is not valid with respect to a life insurance, endowment, or annuity contract, against an organization which is the insurer under the contract, at any time—

(i) Before the insuring organization has actual notice or knowledge (as defined in paragraph (a) of § 301.6323(i)-1) of the existence of the tax lien,

(ii) After the insuring organization has actual notice or knowledge of the lien (as defined in paragraph (a) of § 301.6323(i)-1), with respect to advances (including contractual interest thereon as provided in paragraph (a) of § 301.6323(e)-1) required to be made automatically to maintain the contract in force under an agreement entered into before the insuring organization had such actual notice or knowledge, or

(iii) After the satisfaction of a levy pursuant to section 6332(b), unless and until the Internal Revenue Service delivers to the insuring organization a notice (for example, another notice of levy, a letter, etc.) executed after the date of such satisfaction, that the lien exists.

Delivery of the notice described in subdivision (iii) of this subparagraph may be made by any means, including regular mail, and delivery of the notice shall be effective only from the time of actual receipt of the notification by the insuring organization. The provisions of this paragraph are applicable to matured as well as unmatured insurance contracts.

(2) *Examples.*—The provisions of this paragraph may be illustrated by the following examples:

Example (1). On May 1, 1964, the X insurance company issues a life insurance policy to A. On June 1, 1970, a tax assessment is made against A, and on June 2, 1970, a notice of lien with respect to the assessment is filed in accordance with § 301.6323(f)-1. On July 1, 1970, without actual notice or knowledge of the tax lien, the X company makes a "policy loan" to A. Under subparagraph (1)(i) of this paragraph, the loan, including interest (in accordance with the provisions of paragraph (a) of § 301.6323(e)-1), will have priority over the tax lien because X company did not have actual notice or knowledge of the tax lien at the time the policy loan was made.

Example (2). On May 1, 1964, B enters into a life insurance contract with the Y insurance company. Under one of the provisions of the contract, in the event a premium is not paid, Y is to advance out of the cash loan value of the policy the amount of an unpaid premium in order to maintain the contract in force. The contract also provides for interest on any advances so made. On June 1, 1971, a tax assessment is made against B, and on June 2, 1971, in accordance with section 6323(f)-1, a notice of lien is filed. On July 1, 1971, B fails to pay the premium due on that date, and Y makes an automatic premium loan to keep the policy in force. At the time the automatic premium loan is made, Y had actual knowledge of the tax lien. Under subparagraph (1)(ii) of this paragraph, the lien is not valid against Y with respect to the advance (and the contractual interest thereon), because the advance was required to be made automatically under an agreement entered into before Y had actual notice or knowledge of the tax lien.

Example (3). On May 1, 1964, C enters into a life insurance contract with the Z insurance company. On January 4, 1971, an assessment is made against C for $5,000 unpaid income taxes, and on January 11, 1971, in accordance with § 301.6323(f)-1, a notice of lien is filed. On January 29, 1971, a notice of levy with respect to C's delinquent tax is served on Z company. The amount which C could have had advanced to him from Z company under the contract on the 90th day after service of the notice of levy on Z company is $2,000. The Z company pays $2,000 pursuant to the notice of levy, thereby satisfying the levy upon the contract in accordance with section 6332(b). On February 1, 1973, Z company advances $500 to C, which is the increment in policy loan value since satisfaction of the levy of January 29, 1971. On February 5, 1973, a new notice of levy for the unpaid balance of the delinquent taxes, executed after the first levy was satisfied, is served upon Z company. Because the new notification was not received by Z company until after the policy loan was made, under paragraph (1)(iii) of this paragraph, the tax lien is not valid against Z company with respect to the policy loan (including interest thereon in accordance with paragraph (a) of § 301.6323(e)-1).

Example (4). On June 1, 1973, a tax assessment is made against D and on June 2, 1973, in accordance with § 301.6323(f)-1, a notice of lien with respect to the assessment is filed. On July 2, 1973, D executes an assignment of his rights, as the insured, under an insurance contract to M bank as security for a loan. M bank holds its security interest subject to the lien because it is not an insurer entitled to protection under section 6323(b)(9) and did not become a holder of the security interest prior to the filing of the notice of lien for purposes of section 6323(a). It is immaterial that a notice of levy had not been served upon the insurer before the assignment to M bank was made.

(j) *Effective/applicability date.*—(1) *In general.*—This section applies to any notice of Federal tax lien filed on or after April 4, 2011. [Reg. § 301.6323(b)-1.]

☐ [*T.D.* 7429, 8-20-76. *Amended by T.D.* 9520, 4-1-2011.]

[Reg. § 301.6323(c)-1]

§ 301.6323(c)-1. **Protection for commercial transactions financing agreements.**—(a) *In general.*—Even though a notice of a lien imposed by section 6321 is filed in accordance with § 301.6323(f)-1, the lien is not valid with respect to a security interest which:

(1) Comes into existence after the tax lien filing,

(2) Is in qualified property covered by the terms of a commercial transactions financing agreement entered into before the tax lien filing, and

(3) Is protected under local law against a judgment lien arising, as of the time of the tax lien filing, out of an unsecured obligation.

See paragraphs (a) and (e) of § 301.6323(h)-1 for definitions of the terms "security interest" and "tax lien filing," respectively. For purposes of this section, a judgment lien is a lien held by a judgment lien creditor as defined in paragraph (g) of § 301.6323(h)-1.

(b) *Commercial transactions financing agreement.*—For purposes of this section, the term "commercial transactions financing agreement" means a written agreement entered into by a person in the course of his trade or business—

(1) To make loans to the taxpayer (whether or not at the option of the person agreeing to make such loans) to be secured by commercial financing security acquired by the taxpayer in the ordinary course of his trade or business, or

(2) To purchase commercial financing security, other than inventory, acquired by the taxpayer in the ordinary course of his trade or business.

Such an agreement qualifies as a commercial transactions financing agreement only with re-spect to loans or purchases made under the agreement before (i) the 46th day after the date of tax lien filing or, (ii) the time when the lender or purchaser has actual notice or knowledge (as defined in paragraph (a) of § 301.6323(i)-1) of the tax lien filing, if earlier. For purposes of this paragraph, a loan or purchase is considered to have been made in the course of the lender's or purchaser's trade or business if such person is in the business of financing commercial transactions (such as a bank or commercial factor) or if the agreement is incidental to the conduct of such person's trade or business. For example, if a manufacturer finances the accounts receivable of one of his customers, he is considered to engage in such financing in the course of his trade or business. The extent of the priority of the lender or purchaser over the tax lien is the amount of his disbursements made before the 46th day after the date the notice of tax lien is filed, or made before the day (before such 46th day) on which the lender or purchaser has actual notice or knowledge of the filing of the notice of the tax lien.

(c) *Commercial financing security.*—(1) *In general.*—The term "commercial financing security" means—

(i) Paper of a kind ordinarily arising in commercial transactions,

(ii) Accounts receivable (as defined in subparagraph (2) of this paragraph),

(iii) Mortgages on real property, and

(iv) Inventory.

For purposes of this subparagraph, the term "paper of a kind ordinarily arising in commercial transactions" in general includes any written document customarily used in commercial transactions. For example, such written documents include paper giving contract rights (as defined in subparagraph (2) of this paragraph), chattel paper, documents of title to personal property, and negotiable instruments or securities. The term "commercial financing security" does not include general intangibles such as patents or copyrights. A mortgage on real estate (including a deed of trust, contract for sale, and similar instrument) may be commercial financing security if the taxpayer has an interest in the mortgage as a mortgagee or assignee. The term "commercial financing security" does not include a mortgage where the taxpayer is the mortgagor of realty owned by him. For purposes of this subparagraph, the term "inventory" includes raw materials and goods in process as well as property held by the taxpayer primarily for sale to customers in the ordinary course of his trade or business.

(2) *Definitions.*—For purposes of §§ 301.6323(d)-1, 301.6323(h)-1 and this section—

(i) A contract right is any right to payment under a contract not yet earned by performance and not evidenced by an instrument or chattel paper, and

(ii) An account receivable is any right to payment for goods sold or leased or for services rendered which is not evidenced by an instrument or chattel paper.

(d) *Qualified property.*—For purposes of paragraph (a) of this section, qualified property consists solely of commercial financing security acquired by the taxpayer-debtor before the 46th day after the date of tax lien filing. Commercial financing security acquired before such day may be qualified property even though it is acquired by the taxpayer after the lender received actual notice or knowledge of the filing of the notice of the tax lien. For example, although the receipt of actual notice or knowledge of the filing of the tax lien has the effect of ending the period within which protected disbursements may be made to the taxpayer, property which is acquired by the taxpayer after the lender receives actual notice or knowledge of such filing and before such 46th day, which otherwise qualifies as a commercial financing security, becomes commercial financing security to which the priority of the lender extends for loans made before he received the actual notice or knowledge. An account receivable (as defined in paragraph (c)(2)(ii) of this section) is acquired by a taxpayer at the time, and to the extent, a right to payment is earned by performance. Chattel paper, documents of title, negotiable instruments, securities, and mortgages on real estate are acquired by a taxpayer when he obtains rights in the paper or mortgage. Inventory is acquired by the taxpayer when title passes to him. A contract right (as defined in paragraph (c)(2)(i) of this section) is acquired by a taxpayer when the contract is made. Identifiable proceeds, which arise from the collection or disposition of qualified property by the taxpayer, are considered to be acquired at the time such qualified property is acquired if the secured party has a continuously perfected security interest in the proceeds under local law. The term "proceeds" includes whatever is received when collateral is sold, exchanged, or collected. For purposes of this paragraph, the term "identifiable proceeds" does not include money, checks and the like which have been commingled with other cash proceeds. Property acquired by the taxpayer after the 45th day following tax lien filing, by the expenditure of proceeds, is not qualified property.

(e) *Purchaser treated as acquiring security interest.*—A person who purchases commercial financing security, other than inventory, pursuant to a commercial transactions financing agreement is treated, for purposes of this section, as having acquired a security interest in the commercial financing security. In the case of a bona fide purchase at a discount, a purchaser of commercial financing security who satisfies the requirements of this section has priority over the tax lien to the full extent of the security.

(f) *Examples.*—The provisions of this section may be illustrated by the following examples:

Example (1). (i) On June 1, 1970, a tax is assessed against M, a tool manufacturer, with respect to his delinquent tax liability. On June 15, 1970, M enters into a written financing agreement with X, a bank. The agreement provides that, in consideration of such sums as X may advance to M, X is to have a security interest in all of M's presently owned and subsequently acquired commercial paper, accounts receivable, and inventory (including inventory in the manufacturing stages and raw materials). On July 6, 1970, notice of the tax lien is filed in accordance with § 301.6323(f)-1. On August 3, 1970, without actual notice or knowledge of the tax lien filing, X advances $10,000 to M. On August 5, 1970, M acquires additional inventory through the purchase of raw materials. On August 20, 1970, M has accounts receivable, arising from the sale of tools, amounting to $5,000. Under local law X's security interest arising by reason of the $10,000 advance on August 3, 1970, has priority, with respect to the raw materials and accounts receivable, over a judgment lien against M arising July 6, 1970 (the date of the tax lien filing) out of an unsecured obligation.

(ii) Because the $10,000 advance was made before the 46th day after the tax lien filing, and the accounts receivable in the amount of $5,000 and the raw materials were acquired by M before such 46th day, X's $10,000 security interest in the accounts receivable and the inventory has priority over the tax lien. The priority of X's security interest also extends to the proceeds, received on or after the 46th day after the tax lien filing, from the liquidation of the accounts receivable and inventory held by M on August 20, 1970, if X has a continuously perfected security interest in identifiable proceeds under local law. However, the priority of X's security interest will not extend to other property acquired with such proceeds.

Example (2). Assume the same facts as in example (1) except that on July 15, 1970, X has actual knowledge of the tax lien filing. Because an agreement does not qualify as a commercial transactions financing agreement when a disbursement is made after tax lien filing with actual knowledge of the filing, X's security interest will not have priority over the tax lien with respect to the $10,000 advance made on August 3, 1970.

Example (3). Assume the same facts as in example (1) except that, instead of additional inventory, on August 5, 1970, M acquires an account receivable as the result of the sale of machinery which M no longer needs in his business. Even though the account receivable was acquired by taxpayer M before the 46th day after tax lien filing, the tax lien will have priority over X's security interest arising in the account receivable pursuant to the earlier written agreement because the account receivable was not acquired by the taxpayer in the ordinary course of his trade or business.

Example (4). Pursuant to a written agreement with the N Manufacturing Company entered into on January 4, 1971, Y, a commercial factor, purchases the accounts receivable arising out of N's regular sales to its customers. On November 1, 1971, in accordance with § 301.6323(f)-1, a notice of lien is filed with respect to N's delinquent tax liability. On December 6, 1971, Y, without actual notice or knowledge of the tax lien filing, purchases all of the accounts receivable resulting from N's November 1971 sales. Y has taken appropriate steps under local law so that the December 6, 1971, purchase is protected against a judgment lien arising November 1, 1971 (the date of tax lien filing) out of an unsecured obligation. Because the purchaser of commercial financing security, other than inventory, is treated as having acquired a security interest in commercial financing security, and because Y otherwise meets the requirements of this section, the tax lien is not valid with respect to Y's December 6, 1971, purchase of N's accounts receivable. [Reg. § 301.6323(c)-1.]

☐ [T.D. 7429, 8-20-76.]

[Reg. § 301.6323(c)-2]

§ 301.6323(c)-2. Protection for real property construction or improvement financing agreements.—(a) *In general.*—Even though a notice of a lien imposed by section 6321 is filed in accordance with § 301.6323(f)-1, the lien is not valid with respect to a security interest which:

(1) Comes into existence after the tax lien filing,

(2) Is in qualified property covered by the terms of real property construction or improvement financing agreement entered into before the tax lien filing, and

(3) Is protected under local law against a judgment lien arising, as of the time of tax lien filing, out of an unsecured obligation.

For purposes of this section, it is immaterial that the holder of the security interest had actual notice or knowledge of the lien at the time disbursements were made pursuant to such an agreement. See paragraphs (a) and (e) of § 301.6323(h)-1 for general definitions of the terms "security interest" and "tax lien filing." For purposes of this section, a judgment lien is a lien held by a judgment lien creditor as defined in paragraph (g) of § 301.6323(h)-1.

(b) *Real property construction or improvement financing agreement.*—For purposes of this section, the term "real property construction or improvement financing agreement" means any written agreement to make cash disbursements (whether or not at the option of the party agreeing to make such disbursements):

(1) To finance the construction, improvement, or demolition of real property if the agreement provides for a security interest in the real property with respect to which the construction, improvement, or demolition has been or is to be made;

(2) To finance a contract to construct or improve, or demolish real property if the agreement provides for a security interest in the proceeds of the contract; or

(3) To finance the raising or harvesting of a farm crop or the raising of livestock or other animals if the agreement provides for a security

interest in any property subject to the lien imposed by section 6321 at the time of tax lien filing, in the crop raised or harvested, or in the livestock or other animals raised.

For purposes of subparagraphs (1) and (2) of this paragraph, construction or improvement may include demolition. For purposes of any agreement described in subparagraph (3) of this paragraph, the furnishing of goods and services is treated as the disbursement of cash.

(c) *Qualified property.*—For purposes of this section, the term "qualified property" includes only—

(1) In the case of an agreement described in paragraph (b)(1) of this section, the real property with respect to which the construction or improvement has been or is to be made;

(2) In the case of an agreement described in paragraph (b)(2) of this section, the proceeds of the contract to construct or improve real property; or

(3) In the case of an agreement described in paragraph (b)(3) of this section, property subject to the lien imposed by section 6321 at the time of tax lien filing, the farm crop raised or harvested, or the livestock or other animals raised.

(d) *Examples.*— The provisions of this paragraph may be illustrated by the following examples:

Example (1). A, in order to finance the construction of a dwelling on a lot owned by him, mortgages the property to B. The mortgage, executed January 4, 2006, includes an agreement that B will make cash disbursements to A as the construction progresses. On February 1, 2006, in accordance with § 301.6323(f)-1-1, a notice of lien is filed and recorded in the public index with respect to A's delinquent tax liability. A continues the construction, and B makes cash disbursements on June 15, 2006, and December 15, 2006. Under local law B's security interest arising by virtue of the disbursements is protected against a judgment lien arising February 1, 2006 (the date of tax lien filing) out of an unsecured obligation. Because B is the holder of a security interest coming into existence by reason of cash disbursements made pursuant to a written agreement, entered into before tax lien filing, to make cash disbursements to finance the construction of real property, and because B's security interest is protected, under local law, against a judgment lien arising as of the time of tax lien filing out of an unsecured obligation, B's security interest has priority over the tax lien.

Example (2). (i) C is awarded a contract for the demolition of several buildings. On March 3, 2004, C enters into a written agreement with D which provides that D will make cash disbursements to finance the demolition and also provides that repayment of the disbursements is secured by any sums due C under the contract. On April 1, 2004, in accordance with § 301.6323(f)-1, a notice of lien is filed with respect to C's delinquent tax liability. With actual notice of the tax lien, D makes cash disbursements to C on August 13, September 13, and October 13, 2004. Under local law D's security interest in the proceeds of the contract with respect to the disbursements is entitled to priority over a judgment lien arising on April 1, 2004 (the date of tax lien filing) out of an unsecured obligation.

(ii) Because D's security interest arose by reason of disbursements made pursuant to a written agreement, entered into before tax lien filing, to make cash disbursements to finance a contract to demolish real property, and because D's security interest is valid under local law against a judgment lien arising as of the time of tax lien filed out of an unsecured obligation, the tax lien is not valid with respect to D's security interest in the proceeds of the demolition contract.

Example (3). Assume the same facts as in *Example 2* and, in addition, assume that, as further security for the cash disbursements, the March 3, 2004, agreement also provides for a security interest in all of C's demolition equipment. Because the protection of the security interest arising from the disbursements made after tax lien filing under the agreement is limited under section 6323(c)(3) to the proceeds of the demolition contract and because, under the circumstances, the security interest in the equipment is not otherwise protected under section 6323, the tax lien will have priority over D's security interest in the equipment.

Example (4). (i) On January 3, 2006, F and G enter into a written agreement, whereby F agrees to provide G with cash disbursements, seed, fertilizer, and insecticides as needed by G, in order to finance the raising and harvesting of a crop on a farm owned by G. Under the terms of the agreement F is to have a security interest in the crop, the farm, and all other property then owned or thereafter acquired by G. In accordance with § 301.6323(f)-1, on January 10, 2006, a notice of lien is filed and recorded in the public index with respect to G's delinquent tax liability. On March 3, 2006, with actual notice of the tax lien, F makes a cash disbursement of $5,000 to G and furnishes him seed, fertilizer, and insecticides having a value of $10,000. Under local law F's security interest, coming into existence by reason of the cash disbursement and the furnishing of goods, has priority over a judgment lien arising January 10, 2006 (the date of tax lien filing and recording in the public index) out of an unsecured obligation.

(ii) Because F's security interest arose by reason of a disbursement (including the furnishing of goods) made under a written agreement which was entered into before tax lien filing and which constitutes an agreement to finance the raising or harvesting of a farm crop, and because F's security interest is valid under local law against a judgment lien arising as of the time of tax lien filing out of an unsecured obligation, the tax lien is not valid with respect to F's security interest in the crop even though a notice of lien was filed before the security interest arose. Furthermore, because the farm is property subject to the tax lien at the time of tax lien filing, F's

security interest with respect to the farm also has priority over the tax lien.

Example (5). Assume the same facts as in *Example 4* and in addition that on October 2, 2006, G acquires several tractors to which F's security interest attaches under the terms of the agreement. Because the tractors are not property subject to the tax lien at the time of tax lien filing, the tax lien has priority over F's security interest in the tractors.

(e) *Effective/applicability date.*—This section applies with respect to any notice of Federal tax lien filed on or after April 4, 2011. [Reg. § 301.6323(c)-2.]

☐ [*T.D.* 7429, 8-20-76. *Amended by T.D.* 9520, 4-1-2011.]

[Reg. § 301.6323(c)-3]

§ 301.6323(c)-3. Protection for obligatory disbursement agreements.—(a) *In general.*—Even though a notice of a lien imposed by section 6321 is filed in accordance with § 301.6323(f)-1, the lien is not valid with respect to a security interest which:

   (1) Comes into existence after the tax lien filing,

   (2) Is in qualified property covered by the terms of an obligatory disbursement agreement entered into before the tax lien filing, and

   (3) Is protected under local law against a judgment lien arising, as of the time of tax lien filing, out of an unsecured obligation.

See paragraphs (a) and (e) of § 301.6323(h)-1 for definitions of the terms "security interest" and "tax lien filing." For purposes of this section, a judgment lien is a lien held by a judgment lien creditor as defined in paragraph (g) of § 301.6323(h)-1.

(b) *Obligatory disbursement agreement.*—For purposes of this section the term "obligatory disbursement agreement" means a written agreement, entered into by a person in the course of his trade or business, to make disbursements. An agreement is treated as an obligatory disbursement agreement only with respect to disbursements which are required to be made by reason of the intervention of the rights of a person other than the taxpayer. The obligation to pay must be conditioned upon an event beyond the control of the obligor. For example, the provisions of this section are applicable where an issuing bank obligates itself to honor drafts or other demands for payment on a letter of credit and a bank, in good faith, relies upon that letter of credit in making advances. The provisions of this section are also applicable, for example, where a bonding company obligates itself to make payments to indemnify against loss or liability and, under the terms of the bond, makes a payment with respect to a loss. The priority described in this section is not applicable, for example, in the case of an accommodation endorsement by an endorser who assumes his obligation other than in the course of his trade or business.

Reg. § 301.6323(c)-3(b)

(c) *Qualified property.*—Except as provided under paragraph (d) of this section, the term "qualified property," for purposes of this section, means property subject to the lien imposed by section 6321 at the time of tax lien filing and, to the extent that the acquisition is directly traceable to the obligatory disbursement, property acquired by the taxpayer after tax lien filing.

(d) *Special rule for surety agreements.*—Where the obligatory disbursement agreement is an agreement insuring the performance of a contract of the taxpayer and another person, the term "qualified property" shall be treated as also including—

(1) The proceeds of the contract the performance of which was insured, and

(2) If the contract the performance of which was insured is a contract to construct or improve real property, to produce goods, or to furnish services, any tangible personal property used by the taxpayer in the performance of the insured contract.

For example, a surety company which holds a security interest, arising from cash disbursements made after tax lien filing under a payment or performance bond on a real estate construction project, has priority over the tax lien with respect to the proceeds of the construction contract and, in addition, with respect to any tangible personal property used by the taxpayer in the construction project if its security interest in the tangible personal property is protected under local law against a judgment lien arising, as of the time the tax lien was filed, out of an unsecured obligation.

(e) *Examples.*—This section may be illustrated by the following examples:

Example (1). (i) On January 2, 1969, H, an appliance dealer, in order to finance the acquisition from O of a large inventory of appliances, enters into a written agreement with Z, a bank. Under the terms of the agreement, in return for a security interest in all of H's inventory, presently owned and subsequently acquired, Z issues an irrevocable letter of credit to allow H to make the purchase. On December 31, 1968 and January 10, 1969, in accordance with §301.6323(f)-1, separate notices of lien are filed with respect to H's delinquent tax liabilities. On March 31, 1969, Z honors the letter of credit. Under local law, Z's security interest in both existing and after-acquired inventory is protected against a judgment lien arising on or after January 10, 1969, out of an unsecured obligation. Under local law, Z's security interest in the inventory purchased under the letter of credit qualifies as a purchase money security interest and is valid against persons acquiring security interests in or liens upon such inventory at any time.

(ii) Because Z's security interest in H's inventory did not arise under a written agreement entered into before the filing of notice of the first tax lien on December 31, 1968, that lien is superior to Z's security interest except to the extent of Z's purchase money security interest. Because

Z's interest qualifies as a purchase money security interest with respect to the inventory purchased under the letter of credit, the tax liens attach under section 6321 only to the equity acquired by H, and the rights of Z in the inventory so purchased are superior even to the lien filed on December 31, 1968, without regard to this section.

(iii) Because Z's security interest arose by reason of disbursements made under a written agreement which was entered into before the filing of notice of the second tax lien on January 10, 1969, and which constitutes an agreement to make disbursements required to be made by reason of the intervention of the rights of O, a person other than the taxpayer, and because Z's security interest is valid under local law against a judgment lien arising as of the time of such tax lien filing on January 10, 1969, out of an unsecured obligation, the second tax lien is, under this section, not valid with respect to Z's security interest in inventory owned by H on January 10, 1969, as well as any after-acquired inventory directly traceable to Z's disbursements (apart from such greater protection as Z enjoys, with respect to the latter, under its purchase money security interest). No protection against the second tax lien is provided under this section with respect to a security interest in any other inventory acquired by H after January 10, 1969, because such other inventory is neither subject to the tax lien at the time of tax lien filing nor directly traceable to Z's disbursements.

Example (2). On June 1, 1971, K is awarded a contract to construct an office building. At the same time, S, a surety company, agrees in writing to insure the performance of the contract. The agreement provides that in the event S must complete the job as the result of a default by K, S will be entitled to the proceeds of the contract. In addition, the agreement provides that S is to have a security interest in all property belonging to K. On December 1, 1971, prior to the completion of the building, K defaults. On the same date, under §301.6323(f)-1, a notice of lien is filed with repect to K's delinquent tax liability. S completes the building on June 1, 1972. Under local law S's security interest in the proceeds of the contract and S's security interest in the property of K are entitled to priority over a judgment lien arising December 1, 1971 (the date of tax lien filing) out of an unsecured obligation. Because, for purposes of an obligatory disbursement agreement which is a surety agreement, the security interest may be in the proceeds of the insured contract, S's security interest in the proceeds of the contract has priority over the tax lien even though a notice of lien was filed before S's security interest arose. Furthermore, because the insured contract was a contract to construct real property, S's security interest in any of K's tangible personal property used in the performance of the contract also has priority over the tax lien.

Example (3). (i) On February 2, 1970, L enters into an agreement with M, a contractor, to construct an apartment building on land owned by

L. Under a separate agreement, N bank agrees to furnish funds on a short-term basis to L for the payment of amounts due to M during the course of construction. Simultaneously, X, a financial institution, makes a binding commitment to N bank and L to provide long-term financing for the project after its completion. Under its commitment, X is obligated to pay off the balance of the construction loan held by N bank upon the execution by L of a new promissory note secured by a mortgage deed of trust upon the improved property. On September 4, 1970, in accordance with § 301.6323(f)-1, notice of lien is properly filed with respect to L's delinquent tax liability. On September 8, 1970, X obtains actual notice of the tax lien filing. On September 14, 1970, the documents creating X's security interest are executed and recorded, N bank's lien for its construction loan is released, and X makes the required disbursements to N bank. Under local law, X's security interest is protected against a judgment lien arising on September 4, 1970 (the time of tax lien filing) out of an unsecured obligation.

(ii) Because X's security interest arose by reason of a disbursement made under a written agreement entered into before tax lien filing, which constitutes an agreement to make disbursements required to be made by reason of the intervention of the rights of N bank, a person other than the taxpayer, and because X's security interest is valid under local law against a judgment lien arising as of the time of the tax lien filing out of an unsecured obligation, the tax lien is not valid with respect to X's security interest to the extent of the disbursement to N bank. The obligatory disbursement is protected under section 6323(c)(4) even if X is not subrogated to N bank's rights or X's agreement is not itself a real property construction financing agreement. [Reg. § 301.6323(c)-3].

☐ [*T.D.* 7429, 8-20-76.]

[Reg. § 301.6323(d)-1]

§ 301.6323(d)-1. 45-day period for making disbursements.—(a) *In general.*—Even though a notice of a lien imposed by section 6321 is filed in accordance with § 301.6323(f)-1, the lien is not valid with respect to a security interest which comes into existence, after tax lien filing, by reason of disbursements made before the 46th day after the date of tax lien filing, or if earlier, before the person making the disbursements has actual notice or knowledge of the tax lien filing, but only if the security interest is—

(1) In property which is subject, at the time of tax lien filing, to the lien imposed by section 6321 and which is covered by the terms of a written agreement entered into before tax lien filing, and

(2) Protected under local law against a judgment lien arising, as of the time of tax lien filing, out of an unsecured obligation.

For purposes of subparagraph (1) of this paragraph, a contract right (as defined in paragraph (c)(2)(i) of § 301.6323(c)-1) is subject, at the time

of tax lien filing, to the lien imposed by section 6321 if the contract has been made by such time. An account receivable (as defined in paragraph (c)(2)(ii) of § 301.6323(c)-1) is subject, at the time of tax lien filing, to the lien imposed by section 6321 if, and to the extent, a right to payment has been earned by performance at such time. For purposes of subparagraph (2) of this paragraph, a judgment lien is a lien held by a judgment lien creditor as defined in paragraph (g) of § 301.6323(h)-1. For purposes of this section, it is immaterial that the written agreement provides that the disbursements are to be made at the option of the person making the disbursements. See paragraphs (a) and (e) of § 301.6323(h)-1 for definitions of the terms "security interest" and "tax lien filing," respectively. See paragraph (a) of § 301.6323(i)-1 for certain circumstances under which a person is deemed to have actual notice or knowledge of a fact.

(b) *Examples.*—The application of this section may be illustrated by the following examples:

Example (1). On December 1, 1967, an assessment is made against A with respect to his delinquent tax liability. On January 2, 1968, A enters into a written agreement with B whereby B agrees to lend A $10,000 in return for a security interest in certain property owned by A. On January 10, 1968, in accordance with § 301.6323(f)-1 notice of the tax lien affecting the property is filed. On February 1, 1968, B, without actual notice or knowledge of the tax lien filing, disburses the loan to A. Under local law, the security interest arising by reason of the disbursement is entitled to priority over a judgment lien arising January 10, 1968 (the date of tax lien filing) out of an unsecured obligation. Because the disbursement was made before the 46th day after tax lien filing, because the disbursement was made pursuant to a written agreement entered into before tax lien filing, and because the resulting security interest is protected under local law against a judgment lien arising as of the date of tax lien filing out of an unsecured obligation, B's $10,000 security interest has priority over the tax lien.

Example (2). Assume the same facts as in example (1) except that when B disburses the $10,000 to A on February 10, 1968, B has actual knowledge of the tax lien filing. Because the disbursement was made with actual knowledge of tax lien filing, B's security interest does not have priority over the tax lien even though the disbursement was made before the 46th day after the tax lien filing. Furthermore, B is not protected under § 301.6323(a)-1(a) as a holder of a security interest because he had not parted with money or money's worth prior to the time the notice of tax lien was filed (Jan. 10, 1968) even though he had made a firm commitment to A before that time. [Reg. § 301.6323(d)-1.]

☐ [*T.D.* 7429, 8-20-76.]

[Reg. § 301.6323(e)-1]

§ 301.6323(e)-1. Priority of interest and expenses.—(a) *In general.*—If the lien imposed by section 6321 is not valid as against another lien or security interest, the priority of the other lien or security interest also extends to each of the following items to the extent that under local law the item has the same priority as the lien or security interest to which it relates:

(1) Any interest or carrying charges (including finance, service, and similar charges) upon the obligation secured,

(2) The reasonable charges and expenses of an indenture trustee (including, for example, the trustee under a deed of trust) or agent holding the security interest for the benefit of the holder of the security interest,

(3) The reasonable expenses, including reasonable compensation for attorneys, actually incurred in collecting or enforcing the obligation secured,

(4) The reasonable costs of insuring, preserving, or repairing the property to which the lien or security interest relates,

(5) The reasonable costs of insuring payment of the obligation secured (including amounts paid by the holder of the security interest for mortgage insurance, such as that issued by the Federal Housing Administration), and

(6) Amounts paid to satisfy any lien on the property to which the lien or security interest relates, but only if the lien so satisfied is entitled to priority over the lien imposed by section 6321.

(b) *Collection expenses.*—The reasonable expenses described in paragraph (a)(3) of this section include expenditures incurred by the protected holder of the lien or security interest to establish the priority of his interest or to collect, by foreclosure or otherwise, the amount due him from the property subject to his lien. Accordingly, the amount of the encumbrance which is protected is increased by the amounts so expended by the holder of the security interest.

(c) *Costs of insuring, preserving, etc.*—The reasonable costs of insuring, preserving, or repairing described in paragraph (a)(4) of this section include expenditures by the holder of a security interest for fire and casualty insurance on the property subject to the security interest and amounts paid by the holder of the lien or security interest to repair the property. Such reasonable costs also include the amounts paid by the holder of the lien or security interest in a leasehold to the lessor of the leasehold to preserve the leasehold subject to the lien or security interest. Accordingly, the amount of the lien or security interest which is protected is increased by the amounts so expended by the holder of the lien or security interest.

(d) *Satisfaction of liens.*—The amounts described in paragraph (a)(6) of this section include expenditures incurred by the protected holder of a lien or security interest to discharge a statutory lien for State sales taxes on the property subject to his lien or security interest if both his lien or security interest and the sales tax lien have priority over a Federal tax lien. Accordingly, the amount of the lien or security interest is in-

creased by the amounts so expended by the holder of the lien or security interest even though under local law the holder of the lien or security interest is not subrogated to the rights of the holder of the State sales tax lien. However, if the holder of the lien or security interest is subrogated, within the meaning of paragraph (b) of § 301.6323(i)-1, to the rights of the holder of the sales tax lien, he will also be entitled to any additional protection afforded by section 6323(i)(2). [Reg. § 301.6323(e)-1.]

☐ [*T.D.* 7429, 8-20-76.]

[Reg. § 301.6323(f)-1]

§ 301.6323(f)-1. Place for filing notice; form.—(a) *Place for filing.*—The notice of lien referred to in § 301.6323(a)-1 shall be filed as follows:

(1) *Under State laws.*—(i) *Real property.*—In the case of real property, notice shall be filed in one office within the State (or the county or other governmental subdivision), as designated by the laws of the State, in which the property subject to the lien is deemed situated under the provisions of paragraph (b)(1) of this section.

(ii) *Personal property.*—In the case of personal property, whether tangible or intangible, the notice shall be filed in one office within the State (or the county or other governmental subdivision), as designated by the laws of the State, in which the property subject to the lien is deemed situated under the provisions of paragraph (b)(2) of this section.

(2) *With the clerk of the U.S. district court.*—Whenever a State has not by law designated one office which meets the requirements of subparagraph (1)(i) or (1)(ii) of this paragraph, the notice shall be filed in the office of the clerk of the U.S. district court for the judicial district in which the property subject to the lien is deemed situated under the provisions of paragraph (b) of this section. For example, a State has not by law designated one office meeting the requirements of subparagraph (1)(i) of this paragraph if more than one office is designated within the State, county, or other governmental subdivision for filing notices with respect to all real property located in such State, county, or other governmental subdivision. A State has not by law designated one office meeting the requirements of subparagraph (1)(ii) of this paragraph if more than one office is designated in the State, county, or other governmental subdivision for filing notices with respect to all of the personal property of a particular taxpayer. A state law that conforms to or reenacts a federal law establishing a national filing system does not constitute a designation by state law of an office for filing liens against personal property. Thus, if state law provides that a notice of lien affecting personal property must be filed in the office of the county clerk for the county in which the taxpayer resides and also adopts a federal law that requires a notice of lien to be filed in another location in order to attach to a specific type of property, the

state is considered to have designated only one office for the filing of the notice of lien, and to protect its lien the Internal Revenue Service need only file its notice in the office of the county clerk for the county in which the taxpayer resides.

(3) *With the Recorder of Deeds of the District of Columbia.*—If the property subject to the lien imposed by section 6321 is deemed situated, under the provisions of paragraph (b) of this section, in the District of Columbia, the notice shall be filed in the office of the Recorder of Deeds of the District of Columbia.

(b) *Situs of property subject to lien.*—For purposes of paragraph (a) of this section, property is deemed situated as follows:

(1) *Real property.*—Real property is deemed situated at its physical location.

(2) *Personal property.*—Personal property, whether tangible or intangible, is deemed situated at the residence of the taxpayer at the time the notice of lien is filed.
For purposes of subparagraph (2) of this paragraph the residence of a corporation or partnership is deemed to be the place at which the principal executive office of the business is located, and the residence of a taxpayer whose residence is not within the United States is deemed to be in the District of Columbia.

(c) *National filing system.*—The filing of federal tax liens is to be governed solely by the Internal Revenue Code and is not subject to any other federal law that may establish a national system for filing liens and encumbrances against a particular type of personal property. Thus, for example, the Service is not subject to the requirements established by the Federal Aviation Agency for filing liens against civil aircraft in Oklahoma City, Oklahoma.

(d) *Form.*—(1) *In general.*—The notice referred to in § 301.6323 (a)-1 shall be filed on Form 668, "Notice of Federal Tax Lien under Internal Revenue Laws". Such notice is valid notwithstanding any other provision of law regarding the form or content of a notice of lien. For example, omission from the notice of lien of a description of the property subject to the lien does not affect the validity thereof even though State law may require that the notice contain a description of the property subject to the lien.

(2) *Form 668 defined.*—The term *Form 668* means either a paper form or a form transmitted electronically, including a form transmitted by facsimile (fax) or electronic mail (e-mail). A Form 668 must identify the taxpayer, the tax liability giving rise to the lien, and the date the assessment arose regardless of the method used to file the notice of Federal tax lien.

(e) *Examples.*—The provisions of this section may be illustrated by the following examples:

Example (1). The law of State X provides that notices of Federal tax lien affecting personal property are to be filed in the Office of the Recorder of Deeds of the county where the tax-

payer resides. The laws of State X also provide that notices of lien affecting real property are to be filed with the recorder of deeds of the county where the real property is located. On June 1, 1970, in accordance with § 301.6323(f)-1, a notice of lien is filed in county M with respect to the delinquent tax liability of A. At the time the notice is filed, A is a resident of county M and owns real property in that county. One year later A moves to county N and one year after that A moves to county O. Because the situs of personal property is deemed to be at the residence of the taxpayer at the time the notice of lien is filed, the notice continues to be effectively filed with respect to A's personal property even though A no longer resides in county M. Furthermore, because the situs of real property is deemed to be at its physical location, the notice of lien also continues to be effectively filed with respect to A's real property.

Example (2). B is a resident of Canada but owns personal property in the United States. On January 4, 1971, in accordance with § 301.6323(f)-1, a notice of lien is filed with the Office of the Recorder of Deeds of the District of Columbia. On January 2, 1973, B changes his residence to State Y in the United States. Because the residence of a taxpayer who is not a resident of the United States is deemed to be in the District of Columbia and the situs of personal property is deemed to be at the residence of the taxpayer at the time of filing, the lien continues to be effectively filed with respect to the personal property of B located in the United States even though B has returned to the United States and taken up residence in State Y and even though B has at no time been in the District of Columbia.

Example (3). The law of State Z in effect before July 1, 1967, provides that notices of lien affecting real property are to be filed in the office of the recorder of deeds of the county in which the real property is located, but that if the real property is registered under the Torrens system of title registration the notice is to be filed with the registrar of titles rather than the recorder of deeds. The law of State Z in effect after June 30, 1967, provides that all notices of lien affecting real property are to be filed with the recorder of deeds of the county in which the real property is located. Accordingly, where the Torrens system is adopted by a county in State Z, there were before July 1, 1967, two offices designated for filing notices of Federal tax lien affecting real property in the county because one office was designated for Torrens real property and another office was designated for non-Torrens real property. Because State Z had not designated one office within the State, county, or other governmental subdivision for filing notices before July 1, 1967, with respect to all real property located in the State, county, or governmental subdivision, before July 1, 1967, the place for filing notices of lien under this section, affecting property located in counties adopting the Torrens system, was with the clerk of the U.S. district court for the judicial district in which the real property is located. However, after June 30, 1967, the place for filing notices of lien under this section, affecting both Torrens and non-Torrens real property in counties adopting the Torrens system is with the recorder of deeds for each such county. Notices of lien filed under this section with the clerk of the U.S. district court before July 1, 1967, remain validly filed whether or not refiled with the recorder of deeds after the change in State law or upon refiling during the required refiling period.

Example (4). The law of State W provides that notices of lien affecting personal property of corporations and partnerships are to be filed in the office of the Secretary of State. Notices of lien affecting personal property of any other person are to be filed in the office of the clerk of court for the county where the person resides. Because the State law designates only one filing office within State W with respect to personal property of any particular taxpayer, notices of lien filed under this section, affecting personal property, shall be filed in the office designated under State law.

Example 5. The law of State F provides that notices of lien affecting personal property are to be filed with the clerk of the circuit court in the county in which the personal property is located. State F has conformed state law to federal law to provide that all instruments affecting title to an interest in any civil aircraft of the United States must be recorded in the Office of the Federal Aviation Administrator (FAA) in Oklahoma City, Oklahoma. On July 1, 1990, a tax lien arises against ABC airline, which owns aircraft situated in State F. The Internal Revenue Service files a Notice of Federal Tax Lien with the clerk of the circuit court in the county in which the aircraft is located but does not file the notice with the FAA in Oklahoma City, Oklahoma. Because the FAA system adopted by State F does not constitute a second place of filing pursuant to section 6323(f), the federal tax lien is validly filed.

Example 6. Assume the same facts as *Example 5* except that State F did not reenact or conform state law to the FAA requirements. The result is the same because the filing of federal tax liens is governed solely by the Internal Revenue Code, and is not subject to any other national filing system.

(f) *Effective/applicability date.* This section applies with respect to any notice of Federal tax lien filed on or after April 4, 2011. [Reg. §301.6323(f)-1.]

☐ [*T.D. 7429, 8-20-76. Amended by T.D. 8234, 11-23-88; T.D. 8557, 7-26-94; and T.D. 9520, 4-1-2011.*]

[Reg. §301.6323(g)-1]

§301.6323(g)-1. Refiling of notice of tax lien.—(a) *In general.*—(1) *Requirement to refile.*— In order to continue the effect of a notice of lien, the notice must be refiled in the place described in paragraph (b) of this section during the required refiling period (described in paragraph (c) of this section). If two or more notices of lien are filed with respect to a particular tax assess-

ment, and each notice of lien contains a certificate of release that releases the lien when the required refiling period ends, the failure to comply with the provisions of paragraphs (b)(1)(i) and (c) of this section in respect to one of the notices of lien releases the lien and renders ineffective the refiling of any other notice of lien.

(2) *Effect of refiling.*—A timely refiled notice of lien is effective as of the date on which the notice of lien to which it relates was effective.

(3) *Effect of failure to refile.*—If the Internal Revenue Service fails to refile a notice of lien in the manner described in paragraphs (b) and (c) of this section, the notice is not effective, after the expiration of the required refiling period, as against any person described in section 6323(a),without regard to when the interest of the person in the property subject to the lien was acquired. If a notice of lien contains a certificate of release that provides that the lien is released at the end of the required refiling period unless the notice of lien is refiled, and the notice of lien is not refiled, then the lien is extinguished and the notice of lien is ineffective.

(i) However, neither the failure to refile before the expiration of the refiling period, nor the release of the lien, shall alter or impair any right of the United States to property or its proceeds that is the subject of a levy or judicial proceeding commenced prior to the end of the refiling period or the release of the lien, except to the extent that a person acquires an interest in the property for adequate consideration after the commencement of the proceeding and does not have notice of, and is not bound by, the outcome of the proceeding.

(ii) If a suit or levy referred to in the preceding sentence is dismissed or released and the property is subject to the lien at such time, a notice of lien with respect to the property is not effective after the suit or levy is dismissed or released unless refiled during the required refiling period.

(4) *Filing of new notice.*—If a notice of lien is not refiled, and the notice of lien contains a certificate of release that automatically releases the lien when the required refiling period ends, the lien is released as of that date and is no longer in existence. The Internal Revenue Service must revoke the release before it can file a new notice of lien. This new filing must meet the requirements of section 6323(f) and §301.6323(f)-1 and is effective from the date on which such filing is made.

(b) *Place for refiling notice of lien.*—(1) *In general.*—A notice of lien refiled during the required refiling period (described in paragraph (c) of this section) shall be effective only—

(i) If the notice of lien is refiled in the office in which the prior notice of lien (including a refiled notice) was filed under the provisions of section 6323; and

(ii) In any case in which 90 days or more prior to the date the refiling of the notice of lien under subdivision (i) is completed, the Internal Revenue Service receives written information (in the manner described in subparagraph (2) of this paragraph) concerning a change in the taxpayer's residence, if a notice of such lien is also filed in accordance with section 6323(f)(1)(A)(ii) in the State in which such new residence is located (or, if such new residence is located without the United States, in the District of Columbia).

A notice of lien is considered as refiled in the office in which the prior notice or refiled notice was filed under the provisions of section 6323 if it is refiled in the office which, pursuant to a change in the applicable local law, assumed the functions of the office in which the prior notice or refiled notice was filed. If on or before the 90th day referred to in subdivision (ii) more than one written notice is received concerning a change in the taxpayer's residence, a notice of lien is required by this subdivision to be filed only with respect to the residence shown on the written notice received on the most recent date. Subdivision (ii) is applicable regardless of whether the taxpayer resides at the new residence on the date the refiling of notice of lien under subdivision (i) of this subparagraph is completed.

(2) *Notice of change of taxpayer's residence.*— (i) *In general.*—Except as provided in subdivision (ii) or (iii) of this subparagraph, for purposes of this section, a notice of change of a taxpayer's residence will be effective only if it (A) is received, in writing, from the taxpayer or his representative by the district director or the service center director having jurisdiction where the original notice of lien was filed, (B) relates to an unpaid tax liability of the taxpayer, and (C) states the taxpayer's name and the address of his new residence. Although it is not necessary that a written notice contain the taxpayer's identifying number authorized by section 6109, it is preferable that it include such number. For purposes of this subdivision, a notice of change of a taxpayer's residence shown on a return or an amended return (including a return of the same tax) will not be effective to notify the Internal Revenue Service.

(ii) *Notice received before August 23, 1976.*— For purposes of this section, a notice of a change of a taxpayer's residence will also be effective if it (A) is received, in writing, by any office of the Internal Revenue Service before August 23, 1976, from the taxpayer or his representative, (B) relates to an unpaid tax liability of the taxpayer, and (C) states the taxpayer's name and the address of his new residence.

(iii) *By return or amended return.*—For purposes of this section, in the case of a notice of lien which relates to an assessment of tax made after December 31, 1966, a notice of change of a taxpayer's residence will also be effective if it is contained in a return or amended return of the same type of tax filed with the Internal Revenue Service by the taxpayer or his representative

which on its face indicates that there is a change in the taxpayer's address and correctly states the taxpayer's name, the address of his new residence, and his identifying number required by section 6109.

(iv) *Other rules applicable.*—Except as provided in subdivisions (i), (ii), and (iii) of this subparagraph, no communication (either written or oral) to the Internal Revenue Service will be considered effective as notice of a change of a taxpayer's residence under this section, whether or not the Service has actual notice or knowledge of the taxpayer's new residence. For the purpose of determining the date on which a notice of change of a taxpayer's residence is received under this section, the notice shall be treated as received on the date it is actually received by the Internal Revenue Service without reference to the provisions of section 7502.

(3) *Examples.*—The following examples illustrate the provisions of this section:

Example 1. A, a delinquent taxpayer, is a resident of State M and owns real property in State N. In accordance with § 301.6323(f)-1, notices of lien are filed in States M and N. The notices of lien contain certificates of release that release the lien at the end of the required refiling period. In order to continue the effect of the notice of lien filed in either M or N, the Internal Revenue Service must refile, during the required refiling period, the notice of lien with the appropriate office in M as well as with the appropriate office in N.

Example (2). B, a delinquent taxpayer, is a resident of State M. In accordance with § 301.6323(f)-1, notice of lien is properly filed in that State. One year before the beginning of the required refiling period, B establishes his residence in State N, and B immediately notifies the Internal Revenue Service of his change in residence in accordance with the provisions of paragraph (b)(2) of this section. In order to continue the effect of the notice of lien filed in M, the Internal Revenue Service must refile, during the required refiling period, notices of lien with (i) the appropriate office in M, and (ii) the appropriate office in N, because B properly notified the Internal Revenue Service of his change in residence to N more than 89 days prior to the date refiling of the notice of lien in M is completed. Even if the Internal Revenue Service had acquired actual notice or knowledge of B's change in residence by other means, if B had not properly notified the Internal Revenue Service of his change in residence, the effect of the notice of lien in State M could have been continued without any refiling in State N.

Example (3). C, a delinquent taxpayer, is a resident of State O. In accordance with § 301.6323(f)-1, notice of lien is properly filed in that State. Four years before the required refiling period, C establishes his residence in State P, and C immediately notifies the Internal Revenue Service of his change in residence in accordance with the provisions of paragraph (b)(2) of this section. Three years before the required refiling period, C establishes his residence in State R, and again C immediately notifies the Internal Revenue Service of his change in residence in accordance with the provisions of paragraph (2) of this section. In order to continue the effect of the notice of lien filed in O, the Internal Revenue Service must refile, during the required refiling period, notices of lien with (i) the appropriate office in O, and (ii) the appropriate office in R. Refiling in R is required because the notice received by the Service of C's change in residence to R was the most recent notice received more than 89 days prior to the date refiling in O is completed. The notice of lien is not required to be filed in P, even though C properly notified the Internal Revenue Service of his change in residence to P, because such notice is not the most recent one received.

Example (4). Assume the same facts as in example (3), except that C does not notify the Internal Revenue Service of his change in residence to R in accordance with the provisions of paragraph (b)(2) of this section. In order to continue the effect of the notice of lien filed in O, the Internal Revenue Service must refile, during the required refiling period, the notice of lien with (i) the appropriate office in O, and (ii) the appropriate office in P. Refiling in P is required because C properly notified the Internal Revenue Service of his change in residence to P, even though C is not a resident of P on the date refiling of the notice of lien in O is completed. The Internal Revenue Service is not required to file a notice of lien in R because C did not properly notify the Service of his change in residence to R.

Example 5. D, a delinquent taxpayer, is a resident of State M and owns real property in States N and O. In accordance with § 301.6323(f)-1, the Internal Revenue Service files notices of lien in M, N, and O States. Nine years and 6 months after the date of the assessment shown on the notice of lien, D establishes his residence in P, and at that time the Internal Revenue Service receives from D a notification of his change in residence in accordance with the provisions of paragraph (b)(2) of this section. On a date which is 9 years and 7 months after the date of the assessment shown on the notice of lien, the Internal Revenue Service properly refiles notices of lien in M, N, and O which refilings are sufficient to continue the effect of each of the notices of lien. The Internal Revenue Service is not required to file a notice of lien in P because D did not notify the Internal Revenue Service of his change of residence to P more than 89 days prior to the date each of the refilings in M, N, and O was completed.

Example (6). Assume the same facts as in example (5) except that the refiling of the notice of lien in O occurs 100 days after D notifies the Internal Revenue Service of his change in residence to P in accordance with the provisions of paragraph (b)(2) of this section. In order to continue the effect of the notice of lien filed in O, in addition to refiling the notice of lien in O, the Internal Revenue Service must also refile, during the required refiling period, a notice of lien in P because D properly notified the Internal Revenue Service of his change of residence to P more than 89 days prior to the date the refiling in O was completed. However, the Internal Revenue Service is not required to refile the notice of lien in P to maintain the effect of the notices of lien in M and N because D did not notify the Internal Revenue Service of his change in residence to P more than 89 days prior to the date the refilings in M and N were completed.

Example (7). E, a delinquent taxpayer, is a resident of State T. Because T has not designated one office in the case of personal property for filing notices of lien in accordance with the provisions of section 6323(f)(1)(A)(ii), the Internal Revenue Service properly files a notice of lien with the clerk of the appropriate United States district court. However, solely as a matter of convenience for those who may have occasion to search for notices of lien, and not as a matter of legal effectiveness, the Internal Revenue Service also files notice of lien with the recorder of deeds of the county in T where E resides. In addition, the Internal Revenue Service sends a copy of the notice of lien to the X life insurance company to give the company actual notice of the notice of lien. In order to continue the effect of the notice of lien, the Internal Revenue Service must refile the notice of lien with the clerk of the appropriate United States district court during the required refiling period. In order to continue the effect of the notice of the lien, it is not necessary to refile the notice of lien with the recorder of deeds of the county where E resides, because the refiling of the notice of lien with the recorder of deeds does not constitute a proper filing for the purposes of section 6323(f). In addition, to continue the effect of the notice of lien under this section it is not necessary to send a copy of the notice of lien to the X life insurance company, because the sending of a notice of lien to an insurance company does not constitute a proper filing for the purposes of section 6323(f).

(c) *Required refiling period.*—(1) *In general.*—For the purpose of this section, except as provided in paragraph (c)(2) of this section, the term *required refiling period* means—

(i) The 1-year period ending 30 days after the expiration of 10 years after the date of the assessment of the tax; and

(ii) The 1-year period ending with the expiration of 10 years after the close of the preceding required refiling period for such notice of lien.

(2) *Examples.*—The following examples illustrate the provisions of this paragraph:

Example 1. On March 10, 1998, an assessment of tax is made against B, a delinquent taxpayer, and a lien for the amount of the assessment arises on that date. On July 10, 1998, in accordance with § 301.6323(f)-1, a notice of lien is filed. The notice of lien filed on July 10, 1998, is effective through April 9, 2008. The first required refiling period for the notice of lien begins on April 10, 2007, and ends on April 9, 2008. A refiling of the notice of lien during that period will extend the effectiveness of the notice of lien filed on July 10, 1998, through April 9, 2018. The second required refiling period for the notice of lien begins on April 10, 2017, and ends on April 9, 2018.

Example 2. Assume the same facts as in *Example 1*, except that the Internal Revenue Service fails to refile a notice of lien during the first required refiling period (April 10, 2007, through April 9, 2008). A notice of lien is filed on June 9, 2009, in accordance with § 301.6323(f)-1. This notice is ineffective if the original notice contained a certificate of release, as the certificate of release would have had the effect of extinguishing the lien as of April 10, 2008. The Internal Revenue Service could revoke the release and file a new notice of lien, which would be effective as of the date it was filed.

(d) *Effective/applicability date.*—This section applies with respect to any notice of Federal tax lien filed on or after April 4, 2011. [Reg. § 301.6323(g)-1.]

☐ [*T.D.* 7429, 8-20-76. *Amended by T.D.* 9520, 4-1-2011.]

[Reg. § 301.6323(h)-0]

§ 301.6323(h)-0. Scope of definitions.—Except as otherwise provided by § 301.6323(h)-1, the definitions provided by § 301.6323(h)-1 apply for purposes of §§ 301.6323(a)-1 through 301.6324-1. [Reg. § 301.6323(h)-0.]

☐ [*T.D.* 7429, 8-20-76.]

[Reg. § 301.6323(h)-1]

§ 301.6323(h)-1. Definitions.—(a) *Security interest.*—(1) *In general.*—The term "security interest" means any interest in property acquired by contract for the purpose of securing payment or performance of an obligation or indemnifying against loss or liability. A security interest exists at any time—

(i) If, at such time, the property is in existence and the interest has become protected under local law against a subsequent judgment lien (as provided in subparagraph (2) of this paragraph) arising out of an unsecured obligation; and

(ii) To the extent that, at such time, the holder has parted with money or money's worth (as defined in subparagraph (3) of this paragraph).

For purposes of this subparagraph, a contract right (as defined in paragraph (c)(2)(i) of § 301.6323(c)-1) is in existence when the contract is made. An account receivable (as defined in paragraph (c)(2)(ii) of § 301.6323(c)-1) is in existence when, and to the extent, a right to payment is earned by performance.

A security interest must be in existence, within the meaning of this paragraph, at the time as of which its priority against a tax lien is determined. For example, to be afforded priority under the provisions of paragraph (a) of § 301.6323(a)-1 a security interest must be in existence

tence within the meaning of this paragraph before a notice of lien is filed.

(2) *Protection against a subsequent judgment lien.*—(i) For purposes of this paragraph, a security interest is deemed to be protected against a subsequent judgment lien on—

(A) The date on which all actions required under local law to establish the priority of a security interest against a judgment lien have been taken, or

(B) If later, the date on which all required actions are deemed effective under local law, to establish the priority of the security interest against a judgment lien.

For purposes of this subdivision, the dates described in (A) and (B) of this subdivision (i) shall be determined without regard to any rule or principle of local law which permits the relation back of any requisite action to a date earlier than the date on which the action is actually performed. For purposes of this paragraph, a judgment lien is a lien held by a judgment lien creditor as defined in paragraph (g) of this section.

(ii) The following example illustrates the application of paragraph (a)(2):

Example. (i) Under the law of State X, a security interest in certificated securities, negotiable documents, or instruments may be perfected, and hence protected against a judgment lien, by filing or by the secured party taking possession of the collateral. However, a security interest in such intangible personal property is considered to be temporarily perfected for a period of 20 days from the time the security interest attaches, to the extent that it arises for new value given under an authenticated security agreement. Under the law of X, a security interest attaches to such collateral when there is an agreement between the creditor and debtor that the interest attaches, the debtor has rights in the property, and consideration is given by the creditor. Under the law of X, in the case of temporary perfection, the security interest in such property is protected during the 20-day period against a judgment lien arising, after the security interest attaches, out of an unsecured obligation. Upon expiration of the 20-day period, the holder of the security interest must perfect its security interest under local law.

(ii) Because the security interest is perfected during the 20-day period against a subsequent judgment lien arising out of an unsecured obligation, and because filing or the taking of possession before the conclusion of the period of temporary perfection is not considered, for purposes of paragraph (a)(2)(i) of this section, to be a requisite action which relates back to the beginning of such period, the requirements of this paragraph are satisfied. Because filing or taking possession is a condition precedent to continued perfection, filing or taking possession of the collateral is a requisite action to establish such priority after expiration of the period of temporary perfection. If there is a lapse of perfection for failure to file or take possession, the determination of when the security interest exists (for purposes of protection against the tax lien) is made without regard to the period of temporary perfection.

(3) *Money or money's worth.*—For purposes of this paragraph, the term *money or money's worth* includes money, a security (as defined in paragraph (d) of this section), tangible or intangible property, services, and other consideration reducible to a money value. Money or money's worth also includes any consideration which otherwise would constitute money or money's worth under the preceding sentence which was parted with before the security interest would otherwise exist if, under local law, past consideration is sufficient to support an agreement giving rise to a security interest, and provided that the grant of the security interest is not a fraudulent transfer under local law or 28 U.S.C. § 3304(a)(2). A firm commitment to part with money, a security, tangible or intangible property, services, or other consideration reducible to a money value does not, in itself, constitute a consideration in money or money's worth. A relinquishing or promised relinquishment of dower, curtesy, or of a statutory estate created in lieu of dower or curtesy, or of other marital rights is not a consideration in money or money's worth. Nor is love and affection, promise of marriage, or any other consideration not reducible to a money value a consideration in money or money's worth.

(4) *Holder of a security interest.*—For purposes of this paragraph, the holder of a security interest is the person in whose favor there is a security interest. For provisions relating to the treatment of a purchaser of commercial financing security as a holder of a security interest, see § 301.6323(c)-1(e).

(b) *Mechanic's lienor.*—(1) *In general.*—The term "mechanic's lienor" means any person who under local law has a lien on real property (or on the proceeds of a contract relating to real property) for services, labor, or materials furnished in connection with the construction or improvement (including demolition) of the property. A mechanic's lienor is treated as having a lien on the later of—

(i) The date on which the mechanic's lien first becomes valid under local law against subsequent purchasers of the real property without actual notice, or

(ii) The date on which the mechanic's lienor begins to furnish the services, labor, or materials.

(2) *Examples.*—The provisions of this paragraph may be illustrated by the following example:

Example (1). On February 1, 1968, A lets a contract for the construction of an office building on property owned by him. On March 1, 1968, in accordance with § 301.6323(f)-1, a notice of lien for delinquent Federal taxes owed by A is filed. On April 1, 1968, B, a lumber dealer, delivers lumber to A's property. On May 1, 1968, B

records a mechanic's lien against the property to secure payment of the price of the lumber. Under local law, B's mechanic's lien is valid against subsequent purchasers of real property without notice from February 1, 1968, which is the date the construction contract was entered into. Because the date on which B's mechanic's lien is valid under local law against subsequent purchasers is February 1, and the date on which B begins to furnish the materials is April 1, the date on which B becomes a mechanic's lienor within the meaning of this paragraph is April 1, the later of these two dates. Under paragraph (a) of § 301.6323(a)-1, B's mechanic's lien will not have priority over the Federal tax lien, even though under local law the mechanic's lien relates back to the date of the contract.

(c) *Motor vehicle.*—(1) The term "motor vehicle" means a self-propelled vehicle which is registered for highway use under the laws of any State, the District of Columbia, or a foreign country.

(2) A motor vehicle is "registered for highway use" at the time of a sale if immediately prior to the sale it is so registered under the laws of any State, the District of Columbia, or a foreign country. Where immediately prior to the sale of a motor vehicle by a dealer, the dealer is permitted under local law to operate it under a dealer's tag, license, or permit issued to him, the motor vehicle is considered to be registered for highway use in the name of the dealer at the time of the sale.

(d) *Security.*—The term "security" means any bond, debenture, note, or certificate or other evidence of indebtedness, issued by a corporation or a government or political subdivision thereof, with interest coupons or in registered form, share of stock, voting trust certificate, or any certificate of interest or participation in, certificate of deposit or receipt for, temporary or interim certificate for, or warrant or right to subscribe to or purchase, any of the foregoing; negotiable instrument; or money.

(e) *Tax lien filing.*—The term "tax lien filing" means the filing of notice of the lien imposed by section 6321 in accordance with § 301.6323(f)-1.

(f) *Purchaser.*—(1) *In general.*—The term "purchaser" means a person who, for adequate and full consideration in money or money's worth (as defined in subparagraph (3) of this paragraph), acquires an interest (other than a lien or security interest) in property which is valid under local law against subsequent purchasers without actual notice.

(2) *Interest in property.*—For purposes of this paragraph, each of the following interests is treated as an interest in property, if it is not a lien or security interest:

(i) A lease of property,

(ii) A written executory contract to purchase or lease property,

(iii) An option to purchase or lease property and any interest therein, or

(iv) An option to renew or extend a lease of property.

(3) *Adequate and full consideration in money or money's worth.*—For purposes of this paragraph, the term "adequate and full consideration in money or money's worth" means a consideration in money or money's worth having a reasonable relationship to the true value of the interest in property acquired. See paragraph (a)(3) of this section for definition of the term "money or money's worth." Adequate and full consideration in money or money's worth may include the consideration in a bona fide bargain purchase. The term also includes the consideration in a transaction in which the purchaser has not completed performance of his obligation, such as the consideration in an installment purchase contract, even though the purchaser has not completed the installment payments.

(4) *Examples.*—The provisions of this paragraph may be illustrated by the following examples:

Example (1). A enters into a contract for the purchase of a house and lot from B. Under the terms of the contract A makes a down payment and is to pay the balance of the purchase price in 120 monthly installments. After payment of the last installment, A is to receive a deed to the property. A enters into possession, which under local law protects his interest in the property against subsequent purchasers without actual notice. After A has paid five monthly installments, a notice of lien for Federal taxes is filed against B in accordance with § 301.6323(f)-1. Because the contract is an executory contract to purchase property and is valid under local law against subsequent purchasers without actual notice, A qualifies as a purchaser under this paragraph.

Example (2). C owns a residence which he leases to his son-in-law, D, for a period of 5 years commencing January 1, 1968. The lease provides for payment of $100 a year, although the fair rental value of the residence is $2,500 a year. The lease is recorded on December 31, 1967. On March 1, 1968, a notice of tax lien for unpaid Federal taxes of C is filed in accordance with § 301.6323(f)-1. Under local law, D's interest is protected against subsequent purchasers without actual notice. However, because the rental paid by D has no reasonable relationship to the value of the interest in property acquired, D does not qualify as a purchaser under this paragraph.

(g) *Judgment lien creditor.*—The term "judgment lien creditor" means a person who has obtained a valid judgment, in a court of record and of competent jurisdiction, for the recovery of specifically designated property or for a certain sum of money. In the case of a judgment for the recovery of a certain sum of money, a judgment lien creditor is a person who has perfected a lien under the judgment on the property involved. A judgment lien is not perfected until the identity of the lienor, the property subject to the lien, and the amount of the lien are established. Accord-

ingly, a judgment lien does not include an attachment or garnishment lien until the lien has ripened into judgment, even though under local law the lien of the judgment relates back to an earlier date. If recording or docketing is necessary under local law before a judgment becomes effective against third parties acquiring liens on real property, a judgment lien under such local law is not perfected with respect to real property until the time of such recordation or docketing. If under local law levy or seizure is necessary before a judgment lien becomes effective against third parties acquiring liens on personal property, then a judgment lien under such local law is not perfected until levy or seizure of the personal property involved. The term "judgment" does not include the determination of a quasi-judicial body or of an individual acting in a quasi-judicial capacity such as the action of State taxing authorities.

(h) *Effective/applicability date.*—This section applies with respect to any notice of Federal tax lien filed on or after April 4, 2011. [Reg. § 301.6323(h)-1.]

☐ [*T.D. 7429, 8-20-76. Amended by T.D. 9520, 4-1-2011.*]

[Reg. § 301.6323(i)-1]

§ 301.6323(i)-1. Special rules.—(a) *Actual notice or knowledge.*—For purposes of subchapter C (section 6321 and following), chapter 64 of the Code, an organization is deemed, in any transaction, to have actual notice or knowledge of any fact from the time the fact is brought to the attention of the individual conducting the transaction, and in any event from the time the fact would have been brought to the individual's attention if the organization had exercised due diligence. An organization exercises due diligence if it maintains reasonable routines for communicating significant information to the person conducting the transaction and there is reasonable compliance with the routines. Due diligence does not require an individual acting for the organization to communicate information unless such communication is part of his regular duties or unless he has reason to know of the transaction and that the transaction would be materially affected by the information.

(b) *Subrogation.*—(1) *In general.*—Where, under local law, one person is subrogated to the rights of another with respect to a lien or interest, such person shall be subrogated to such rights for purposes of any lien imposed by section 6321 or 6324. Thus, if a tax lien imposed by section 6321 or 6324 is not valid with respect to a particular interest as against the holder of that interest, then the tax lien also is not valid with respect to that interest as against any person who, under local law, is a successor in interest to the holder of that interest.

(2) *Example.*—The application of this paragraph may be illustrated by the following example:

Example. On February 1, 1968, an assessment is made and a tax lien arises with respect to A's delinquent tax liability. On February 25, 1968, in accordance with §301.6323(f)-1, a notice of lien is properly filed. On March 1, 1968, A negotiates a loan from B, the security for which is a second mortgage on property owned by A. The first mortgage on the property is held by C and has priority over the tax lien. Upon default by A, C begins proceedings to foreclose upon the first mortgage. On September 1, 1968, B pays the amount of principal and interest in default to C in order to protect the second mortgage against the pending foreclosure of C's senior mortgage. Under local law, B is subrogated to C's rights to the extent of the payment to C. Therefore, the tax lien is invalid against B to the extent he became subrogated to C's rights even though the tax lien is valid against B's second mortgage on the property.

(c) *Disclosure of amount of outstanding lien.*—If a notice of lien has been filed (see §301.6323(f)-1), the amount of the outstanding obligation secured by the lien is authorized to be disclosed as a matter of public record on Form 668 "Notice of Federal Tax Lien Under Internal Revenue Laws." The amount of the outstanding obligation secured by the lien remaining unpaid at the time of an inquiry is authorized to be disclosed to any person who has a proper interest in determining this amount. Any person who has a right in the property or intends to obtain a right in the property by purchase or otherwise will, upon presentation by him of satisfactory evidence, be considered to have a proper interest. Any person desiring this information may make his request to the office of the Internal Revenue Service named on the notice of lien with respect to which the request is made. The request should clearly describe the property subject to the lien, identify the applicable lien, and give the reasons for requesting the information. [Reg. §301.6323(i)-1.]

☐ [*T.D.* 7429, 8-20-76.]

[Reg. §301.6323(j)-1]

§301.6323(j)-1. Withdrawal of notice of federal tax lien in certain circumstances.—(a) *In general.*—The Commissioner or his delegate (Commissioner) may withdraw a notice of federal tax lien filed under this section, if the Commissioner determines that any of the conditions in paragraph(b) of this section exist. A notice of federal tax lien is withdrawn by the filing by the Commissioner of a notice of withdrawal in the office in which the notice of federal tax lien is filed. If a notice of withdrawal is filed, chapter 64 of subtitle F, relating to collection, will be applied as if the withdrawn notice had never been filed. A copy of the notice of withdrawal will be provided to the taxpayer. Upon written request by a taxpayer with respect to whom a notice of federal tax lien has been or will be withdrawn, the Commissioner will promptly make reasonable efforts to notify any credit reporting agency and any financial institution or creditor identi-

fied by the taxpayer of the withdrawal of such notice. The withdrawal of a notice of federal tax lien will not affect the underlying federal tax lien.

(b) *Conditions authorizing withdrawal.*—The Commissioner may authorize the withdrawal of a notice of federal tax lien upon determining that one of the following conditions exists:

(1) *Premature or not in accordance with administrative procedures.*—The filing of the notice of federal tax lien was premature or otherwise not in accordance with the administrative procedures of the Secretary.

(2) *Installment agreement.*—The taxpayer has entered into an agreement under section 6159 to satisfy the liability for which the lien was imposed by means of installment payments. Entry into an installment agreement may not, however, be the basis for withdrawal of a notice of lien if the installment agreement specifically provides that a notice of federal tax lien will not be withdrawn.

(3) *Facilitate collection.*—The withdrawal of the notice of federal tax lien will facilitate the collection of the tax liability for which the lien was imposed.

(4) *Best interests of the United States and the taxpayer.*—(i) *In general.*—The taxpayer or the National Taxpayer Advocate (or his delegate) has consented to the withdrawal of the notice of federal tax lien, and withdrawal of the notice would be in the best interest of the taxpayer, as determined by the taxpayer or the National Taxpayer Advocate (or his delegate), and in the best interest of the United States, as determined by the Commissioner.

(ii) *Best interest of the taxpayer.*—When a taxpayer requests the withdrawal of notice of federal tax lien based on the best interests of the United States and the taxpayer, the National Taxpayer Advocate (or his delegate) generally will determine whether the withdrawal of the notice of federal tax lien is in the best interest of the taxpayer. If, however, a taxpayer requests the Commissioner to withdraw a notice and has not specifically requested the National Taxpayer Advocate (or his delegate) to determine the taxpayer's best interest, a finding by the Commissioner that the withdrawal of notice is in the best interest of the taxpayer will be sufficient to support withdrawal. If the Commissioner decides independently of a request by the taxpayer to withdraw a notice of federal tax lien, the taxpayer or the National Taxpayer Advocate (or his delegate) must consent to the withdrawal.

(5) *Examples.*—The following examples illustrate the provisions of this paragraph (b):

Example 1. A owes $1,000 in Federal income taxes. The IRS files a notice of federal tax lien to secure A's tax liability. However, the IRS failed to follow procedure provided by the Internal Revenue Manual (but not required by statute) with regard to managerial approval prior to the filing of a notice of federal tax lien. The Commissioner may withdraw the notice of federal tax lien because the filing of the notice was not in accordance with the Secretary's administrative procedures.

Example 2. A owes $1,000 in federal income taxes. A enters into an agreement to pay the outstanding federal income tax liability in installments. The agreement provides that a notice of federal tax lien may be filed if the taxpayer defaults. A timely pays the installments each month and has not defaulted in any way. Eleven months after entering into the installment agreement, the Internal Revenue Service files a notice of federal tax lien. Noting that there has been no default, the taxpayer asks the Internal Revenue Service to withdraw the notice of federal tax lien. In this situation, the Commissioner may withdraw the notice of federal tax lien because the taxpayer has entered into an installment agreement.

Example 3. A is an employee of X Corporation. A notice of federal tax lien has been filed to secure an outstanding tax liability against A. A, who has no assets and no other secured creditors, has agreed to pay the balance of tax due through payroll deductions at a rate higher than the Internal Revenue Service could obtain through a wage levy in order to get the notice of federal tax lien withdrawn. X Corporation has agreed to allow A to enter into a payroll deduction agreement. In this situation, the Commissioner may withdraw the notice of federal tax lien to facilitate collection.

Example 4. A is owner of a farm machinery dealership against whom a notice of federal tax lien has been filed to secure an outstanding tax liability. A currently is paying the tax liability by an installment agreement. X Corporation has agreed to provide A with 100 tractors to increase A's inventory if the notice of federal tax lien is withdrawn. A asks the Internal Revenue Service to withdraw the notice of federal tax lien. The Commissioner determines that the larger inventory would enable A to generate additional tractor sales. Increased sales would enable A to increase the amount of installment payments and, consequently, reduce the amount of time needed to satisfy the liability. A, who has no other assets or secured creditors, has agreed to modify the installment agreement. The Commissioner may withdraw the notice of federal tax lien because the withdrawal is in the best interest of the taxpayer and the United States.

(c) *Determinations by the Commissioner.*—The Commissioner must determine whether any of the conditions authorizing the withdrawal of a notice of federal tax lien exist if a taxpayer submits a request for withdrawal in accordance with paragraph (d) of this section. The Commissioner may also make this determination independent of a request from the taxpayer based on information received from a source other than the taxpayer. If the Commissioner determines that conditions authorizing the withdrawal are not present, the Commissioner may not authorize the withdrawal. If the Commissioner determines conditions for withdrawal are present, the Commissioner may (but is not required to) authorize the withdrawal.

(d) *Procedures for request for withdrawal.*— (1) *Manner.*—A request for the withdrawal of a notice of federal tax lien must be made in writing in accordance with procedures prescribed by the Commissioner.

(2) *Form.*—The written request will include the following information and documents—

(i) Name, current address, and taxpayer identification number of the person requesting the withdrawal of notice of federal tax lien;

(ii) A copy of the notice of federal tax lien affecting the taxpayer's property, if available;

(iii) The grounds upon which the withdrawal of notice of federal tax lien is being requested;

(iv) A list of the names and addresses of any credit reporting agency and any financial institution or creditor that the taxpayer wishes the Commissioner to notify of the withdrawal of notice of federal tax lien; and

(v) A request to disclose the withdrawal of notice of federal tax lien to the persons listed in paragraph (d)(2)(iv) of this section.

(e) *Supplemental list of credit agencies, financial institutions, and creditors.*—(1) *In general.*—If the Commissioner grants a withdrawal of notice of federal tax lien, the taxpayer may supplement the list in paragraph (d)(2)(iv) of this section. If no list was provided in the request to withdraw the notice of federal tax lien, the list in paragraph (d)(2)(iv) of this section and the request for notification in paragraph (d)(2)(v) of this section may be submitted after the notice is withdrawn.

(2) *Manner.*—A request to supplement the list of any credit agencies and any financial institutions or creditors that the taxpayer wishes the Commissioner to notify of the withdrawal of notice of federal tax lien must be made in writing in accordance with procedures prescribed by the Commissioner.

(3) *Form.*—The request must include the following information and documents—

(i) Name, current address, and taxpayer identification number of the taxpayer requesting the notification of any credit agency or any financial institution or creditor of the withdrawal of notice of federal tax lien;

(ii) A copy of the notice of withdrawal, if available;

(iii) A supplemental list, identified as such, of the names and addresses of any credit reporting agency and any financial institution or creditor that the taxpayer wishes the Commissioner to notify of the withdrawal of notice of federal tax lien; and

(iv) A request to disclose the withdrawal of notice of federal tax lien to the persons listed in paragraph (e)(3)(iii) of this section.

(f) *Effective date.*—This section applies on or after June 22, 2001, with respect to a withdrawal of any notice of federal tax lien. [Reg. §301.6323(j)-1.]

☐ [*T.D.* 8951, 6-21-2001.]

[Reg. §20.6324-1]

§20.6324-1. Special lien for estate tax.—For regulations concerning the special lien for the estate tax, see §301.6324-1 of this chapter (Regulations on Procedure and Administration). [Reg. §20.6324-1.]

☐ [*T.D.* 6296, 6-23-58.]

[Reg. §25.6324-1]

§25.6324-1. Special lien for gift tax.—For regulations concerning the special lien for the gift tax, see §301.6324-1 of this chapter (Regulations on Procedure and Administration). [Reg. §25.6324-1.]

☐ [*T.D.* 6334, 10-14-58.]

[Reg. §301.6324-1]

§301.6324-1. Special liens for estate and gift taxes; personal liability of transferees and others.—(a) *Estate tax.*—(1) The lien imposed by section 6324(a) attaches at the date of the decedent's death to every part of the gross estate, whether or not the property comes into the possession of the duly qualified executor or administrator. The lien attaches to the extent of the tax shown to be due by the return and of any deficiency in tax found to be due upon review and audit. If the estate tax is not paid when due, then the spouse, transferee, trustee (except the trustee of an employee's trust which meets the requirements of section 401(a)), surviving tenant, person in possession of the property by reason of the exercise, nonexercise, or release of a power of appointment, or beneficiary, who receives, or has on the date of the decedent's death, property included in the gross estate under sections 2034 to 2042, inclusive, shall be personally liable for the tax to the extent of the value, at the time of the decedent's death, of the property.

(2) Unless the tax is paid in full or becomes unenforceable by reason of lapse of time, and except as otherwise provided in paragraph (c) of this section, the lien upon the entire property constituting the gross estate continues for a period of 10 years after the decedent's death, except that the lien shall be divested with respect to—

(i) The portion of the gross estate used for the payment of charges against the estate and expenses of its administration allowed by any court having jurisdiction thereof;

(ii) Property included in the gross estate under sections 2034 to 2042, inclusive, which is transferred by (or transferred by the transferee of) the spouse, transferee, trustee, surviving tenant, person in possession of the property by reason of the exercise, nonexercise, or release of a power of appointment, or beneficiary to a purchaser or holder of a security interest. In such case a like lien attaches to all the property of the spouse, transferee, trustee, surviving tenant, person in possession, beneficiary, or transferee of any such person, except the part which is transferred to a purchaser or a holder of a security interest. See section 6323(h)(1) and (6) and the regulations thereunder, respectively, for the definitions of "security interest" and "purchaser";

(iii) The portion of the gross estate (or any interest therein) which has been transferred to a purchaser or holder of a security interest if payment is made of the full amount of tax determined by the district director pursuant to a request of the fiduciary (executor, in the case of the estate of a decedent dying before January 1, 1971) for discharge from personal liability as authorized by section 2204 (relating to discharge of fiduciary from personal liability) but there is substituted a like lien upon the consideration received from the purchaser or holder of a security interest; and

(iv) Property as to which the district director has issued a certificate releasing a lien under section 6325(a) and the regulations thereunder.

(b) *Lien for gift tax.*—Except as provided in paragraph (c) of this section, a lien attaches upon all gifts made during the period for which the return was filed (see §25.6019-1 of this chapter) for the amount of tax imposed upon the gifts made during such period. The lien extends for a period of 10 years from the time the gifts are made, unless the tax is sooner paid in full or becomes unenforceable by reason of lapse of time. If the tax is not paid when due, the donee of any gift becomes personally liable for the tax to the extent of the value of his gift. Any part of the property comprised in the gift transferred by the donee (or by a transferee of the donee) to a purchaser or holder of a security interest is divested of the lien, but a like lien, to the extent of the value of the gift, attaches to all the property (including after-acquired property) of the donee (or the transferee) except any part transferred to a purchaser or holder of a security interest. See section 6323(h)(1) and (6) and the regulations thereunder, respectively, for the definitions of "security interest" and "purchaser."

(c) *Exceptions.*—(1) A lien described in either paragraph (a) or paragraph (b) of this section is not valid against a mechanic's lienor (as defined in section 6323(h)(2) and the regulations thereunder) and, subject to the conditions set forth under section 6323(b) (relating to protection for certain interests even though notice filed), is not valid with respect to any lien or interest described in section 6323(b) and the regulations thereunder.

(2) If a lien described in either paragraph (a) or paragraph (b) of this section is not valid against a lien or security interest (as defined in section 6323(h)(1) and the regulations thereunder), the priority of the lien or security interest extends to any item described in section 6323(e) (relating to priority of interest and expenses) to the extent that, under local law, the item has the

same priority as the lien or security interest to which it relates.

(d) *Application of lien imposed by section 6321.*— The general lien under section 6321 and the special lien under subsection (a) or (b) of section 6324 for the estate or gift tax are not exclusive of each other, but are cumulative. Each lien will arise when the conditions precedent to the creation of such lien are met and will continue in accordance with the provisions applicable to the particular lien. Thus, the special lien may exist without the general lien being in force, or the general lien may exist without the special lien being in force, or the general lien and the special lien may exist simultaneously, depending upon the facts and pertinent statutory provisions applicable to the respective liens. [Reg. § 301.6324-1.]

☐ [*T.D.* 6119, 12-31-54. *Amended by T.D.* 6498, 10-24-60 *and T.D.* 7238, 12-28-72.]

[Reg. § 20.6324A-1]

§ 20.6324A-1. Special lien for estate tax deferred under section 6166 or 6166A.—(a) *In general.*—If the executor of an estate of a decedent dying after December 31, 1976, makes an election under section 6166 or 6166A (as in effect prior to its repeal by the Economic Recovery Tax Act of 1981) to defer the payment of estate tax, the executor may make an election under section 6324A. An election under section 6324A will cause a lien in favor of the United States to attach to the estate's section 6166 lien property, as defined in paragraph (b)(1) of this section. This lien is in lieu of the bonds required by sections 2204 and 6165 and in lieu of any lien under section 6324 on the same property with respect to the same estate. The value of the property which the district director may require under section 6324A as section 6166 lien property may not exceed the sum of the deferred amount (as defined in paragraph (e)(1) of this section) and the required interest amount (as defined in paragraph (e)(2) of this section). The unpaid portion of the deferred amount (plus any unpaid interest, additional amount, addition to tax, assessable penalty, and cost attributable to the deferred amount) shall be a lien in favor of the United States on the section 6166 lien property. See § 301.6324A-1 of this chapter (Regulations on Procedure and Administration) for provisions relating to the election of and agreement to the special lien for estate tax deferred under section 6166 or 6166A (as in effect prior to its repeal by the Economic Recovery Tax Act of 1981).

(b) *Section 6166 lien property.*—(1) *In general.*— Section 6166 lien property consists of those interests in real and personal property designated in the agreement referred to in section 6324A(c) (see paragraph (b) of § 301.6324A-1 of this chapter). An interest in property may be designated as section 6166 lien property only to the extent such interest can be expected to survive the deferral period (as defined in paragraph (e)(3) of this section). Property designated, however,

need not be property included in the decedent's estate.

(2) *Maximum value of required property.*—The fair market value of the property required by the district director to be designated as section 6166 lien property with respect to any estate shall not be greater than the sum of the deferred amount and the required interest amount, as these terms are defined in paragraphs (e)(1) and (2) of this section. However, the parties to the agreement referred to in section 6324A(c) may voluntarily designate property having a fair market value in excess of that sum. The fair market value of the section 6166 lien property shall be determined as of the date prescribed in section 6151(a) (without regard to any extension) for payment of the estate tax. Such value must take into account any encumbrance on the property (such as a mortgage or a lien under section 6324B).

(3) *Additional lien property may be required.*— If, at any time, the unpaid portion of the deferred amount and the required interest amount exceeds the fair market value of the section 6166 lien property, the district director may require the addition of property to the agreement in an amount up to such excess. When additional property is required, the district director shall make notice and demand upon the agent designated in the agreement setting forth the amount of additional property required. Property having the required value (or other security equal to the required value) must be added to the agreement within 90 days after notice and demand from the district director. Failure to comply with the demand within the 90-day period shall be treated as an act accelerating payment of installments under section 6166(g) or 6166A(h) (as in effect prior to its repeal by the Economic Recovery Tax Act of 1981).

(4) *Partial substitution of bond.*—See paragraph (c) of § 301.6324A-1 of this chapter for rules relating to the partial substitution of a bond for the lien where the value of property designated as section 6166 lien property is less than the amount of unpaid estate tax plus interest.

(c) *Special rules.*—(1) *Period of lien.*—The lien under section 6324A arises at the earlier of the date—

(i) The executor is discharged from liability under section 2204; or

(ii) Notice of lien is filed in accordance with § 301.6323(f)-1 of this chapter.
The section 6324A lien continues until the liability for the deferred amount is satisfied or becomes unenforceable by reason of lapse of time. The provisions of § 301.6325-1(c), relating to release of lien or discharge of property, shall apply to this paragraph (c)(1).

(2) *Requirement that lien be filed.*—The lien imposed by section 6324A is not valid against a purchaser (as defined in paragraph (f) of § 301.6323(h)-1), holder of a security interest (as defined in paragraph (a) of § 301.6323(h)-1), mechanic's lienor (as defined in paragraph (b) of

§ 301.6323(h)-1), or judgment lien creditor (as defined in paragraph (g) of § 301.6323(h)-1) until notice of the lien is filed. Once filed, the notice of lien remains effective without being refiled.

(3) *Priorities.*—Although a notice of lien under section 6324A has been properly filed, that lien is not valid—

(i) To the extent provided in section 6323(b)(6), relating to real property tax and special assessment liens, regardless of whether such liens came into existence before or after the filing of the notice of Federal tax lien;

(ii) In the case of any real property subject to a lien for repair or improvement, as against a mechanic's lienor, whether or not such lien came into existence before or after the notice of tax lien was filed; and

(iii) As against any security interest set forth in section 6323(c)(3), relating to real property construction or improvement financing agreements, regardless whether such security interest came into existence before or after the filing of the notice of tax lien.

However, paragraphs (c)(3)(ii) and (iii) of this section shall not apply to any security interest that came into existence after the date of filing of notice (in a manner similar to a notice filed under section 6323(f)) that payment of the deferred amount has been accelerated under section 6166(g) or 6166A(h) (as in effect prior to its repeal by the Economic Recovery Tax Act of 1981).

(d) *Release or discharge of lien.*—For rules relating to release of the lien imposed by section 6324A or discharge of the section 6166 lien property, see section 6325 and § 301.6325-1 of this chapter.

(e) *Definitions.*—For purposes of section 6324A of this section—

(1) *Deferred amount.*—The deferred amount is the aggregate amount of estate tax deferred under section 6166 or 6166A (as in effect prior to its repeal by the Economic Recovery Tax Act of 1981) determined as of the date prescribed by section 6151(a) for payment of the estate tax.

(2) *Required interest amount.*—The required interest amount is the aggregate amount of interest payable over the first four years of the deferral period. For purposes of computing the required interest amount, the interest rate prescribed by section 6621 in effect on the date prescribed by section 6151(a) for payment of the estate tax shall be used for computing the interest for the first four years of the deferral period. The 4-percent interest rate prescribed by section 6601(j) shall apply to the extent provided in that section. For purposes of computing interest during deferral periods beginning after December 31, 1982, interest shall be compounded daily.

(3) *Deferral period.*—The deferral period is the period for which the payment of tax is deferred pursuant to the election under section 6166 or 6166A (as in effect prior to its repeal by the Economic Recovery Tax Act of 1981).

(4) *Application of definitions.*—In the case of a deficiency, a separate deferred amount, required interest amount, and deferral period shall be determined as of the due date of the first installment after the deficiency is prorated to installments under section 6166 or 6166A (as in effect prior to its repeal by the Economic Recovery Tax Act of 1981). [Reg. § 20.6324A-1.]

☐ [*T.D. 7710, 7-28-80. Amended by T.D. 7941, 2-6-84.*]

[Reg. § 301.6324A-1]

§ 301.6324A-1. Election of and agreement to special lien for estate tax deferred under section 6166 or 6166A.—(a) *Election of lien.*—If payment of a portion of the estate tax is deferred under section 6166 or 6166A (as in effect prior to its repeal by [the] Economic Recovery Tax Act of 1981), an executor of a decedent's estate who seeks to be discharged from personal liability may elect a lien in favor of the United States in lieu of the bonds required by sections 2204 and 6165. This election is made by applying to the Internal Revenue Service office where the estate tax return is filed at any time prior to payment of the full amount of estate tax and interest due. The application is to be a notice of election requesting the special lien provided by section 6324A and is to be accompanied by the agreement described in paragraph (b)(1) of this section.

(b) *Agreement to lien.*—(1) *In general.*—A lien under this section will not arise unless all parties having any interest in all property designated in the notice of election as property to which the lien is to attach sign an agreement in which they consent to the creation of the lien. (Property so designated need not be property included in the decedent's estate.) The agreement is to be attached to the notice in which the lien under section 6324A is elected. It must be in a form that is binding on all parties having any interest on the property and must contain the following:

(i) The decedent's name and taxpayer identification number as they appear on the estate tax return;

(ii) The amount of the lien;

(iii) The fair market value of the property to be subject to the lien as of the date of the decedent's death and the date of the election under this section;

(iv) The amount, as of the date of the decedent's death and the date of the election, of all encumbrances on the property, including mortgages and any lien under section 6324B;

(v) A clear description of the property which is to be subject to the lien, and in the case of property other than land, a statement of its estimated remaining useful life; and

(vi) Designation of an agent (including the agent's address) for the beneficiaries of the estate and the consenting parties to the lien for all dealings with the Internal Revenue Service on matters arising under section 6166 or 6166A (as in effect prior to its repeal by [the] Economic Recovery Tax Act of 1981), or under section 6324A.

(2) *Persons having an interest in designated property.*—An interest in property is any interest which as of the date of the election can be asserted under applicable local law so as to affect the disposition of any property designated in the agreement required under this section. Any person in being at the date of the election who has any such interest in the property, whether present or future, or vested or contingent, must enter into the agreement. Included among such persons are owners of remainder and executory interests, the holders of general or special powers of appointment, beneficiaries of a gift over in default of exercise of any such power, co-tenants, joint tenants, and holders of other undivided interests when the decedent held a joint or undivided interest in the property, and trustees of trusts holding any interest in the property. An heir who has the power under local law to caveat (challenge) a will and thereby affect disposition of the property is not, however, considered to be a person with an interest in property under section 6324A solely by reason of that right. Likewise, creditors of an estate are not such persons solely by reason of their status as creditors.

(3) *Consent on behalf of interested party.*—If any person required to enter into the agreement provided for by this paragraph either desires that an agent act for him or her or cannot legally bind himself or herself due to infancy or other incompetency, a representative authorized under local law to bind the interested party in an agreement of this nature is permitted to sign the agreement on his or her behalf.

(4) *Duties of agent designated in agreement.*— The Internal Revenue Service will contact the agent designated in the agreement under paragraph (b)(1) on all matters relating to continued qualification of the estate under section 6166 or 6166A (as in effect prior to its repeal by [the] Economic Recovery Tax Act of 1981) and on all matters relating to the special lien arising under section 6324A. It is the duty of the agent as attorney-in-fact for the parties with interests in the property subject to the lien under section 6324A to furnish the Service with any requested information and to notify the Service of any event giving rise to acceleration of the deferred amount of tax.

(c) *Partial substitution of bond for lien.*—If the amount of unpaid estate tax plus interest exceeds the value (determined for purposes of section 6324A(b)(2)) of property listed in the agreement under paragraph (b) of this section, the Internal Revenue Service may condition the release from personal liability upon the executor's submitting an agreement listing additional property or furnishing an acceptable bond in the amount of such excess.

(d) *Relation of sections 6324A and 2204.*—The lien under section 6324A is deemed to be a bond under section 2204 for purposes of determining an executor's release from personal liability. If an election has been made under section 6324A, the executor may not substitute a bond pursuant to section 2204 in lieu of that lien. If a bond has been supplied under section 2204, however, the executor may, by filing a proper notice of election and agreement, substitute a lien under section 6324A for any part or all of such bond.

(e) *Relation of sections 6324A and 6324.*—If there is a lien under this section on any property with respect to an estate, that lien is in lieu of the lien provided by section 6324 on such property with respect to the same estate.

(f) *Section 6324A lien to be in lieu of bond under section 6165.*—The lien under section 6324A is in lieu of any bond otherwise required under section 6165 with respect to tax to be paid in installments under section 6166 or section 6166A (as in effect prior to its repeal by [the] Economic Recovery Tax Act of 1981).

(g) *Special rule for estates for which elections under section 6324A are made on or before August 30, 1980.*—If a lien is elected under section 6324A on or before August 30, 1980, the original election may be revoked. To revoke an election, the executor must file a notice of revocation containing the decedent's name, date of death, and taxpayer identification number with the Internal Revenue Service office where the original estate tax return for the decedent was filed. The notice must be filed on or before January 31, 1981 (or if earlier, the date on which the period of limitation for assessment expires). [Reg. §301.6324A-1.]

☐ [*T.D.* 7710, 7-28-80. *Amended by T.D.* 7941, 2-6-84.]

[Reg. §20.6324B-1]

§20.6324B-1. Special lien for additional estate tax attributable to farm, etc., valuation.— (a) *General rule.*—In the case of an estate of a decedent dying after December 31, 1976, which includes any interest in qualified real property, if the executor elects to value part or all of such property pursuant to section 2032A, a lien arises in favor of the United States on the property to which the election applies. The lien is in the amount equal to the adjusted tax difference attributable to such interest (as defined by section 2032A(c)(2)(B)). The term "qualified real property" means qualified real property as defined in section 2032A(b), qualified replacement property within the meaning of section 2032A(h)(3)(B), and qualified exchange property within the meaning of section 2032A(i)(3). The rules set forth in the regulations under section 2032A shall apply in determining whether this section is applicable to otherwise qualified real property held by a partnership, corporation or trust.

(b) *Period of lien.*—The lien shall arise at the time the executor files an election under section

2032A. It shall remain in effect until one of the following occurs:

(1) The liability for the additional estate tax under section 2032A(c) with respect to such interest has been satisfied; or

(2) Such liability has become unenforceable by reason of lapse of time; or

(3) The district director is satisfied that no further liability for additional estate tax with respect to such interest may arise under section 2032A(c), i.e., the required time period has elapsed since the decedent's death without the occurrence of an event described in section 2032A(c)(1), or the qualified heir (as defined in section 2032A(e)(1)) has died.

For procedures regarding the release or subordination of liens or discharge of property from liens, see § 301.6325-1 of this chapter (Regulations on Procedure and Administration).

(c) *Substitution of security for lien.*—The district director may, upon written application of the qualified heir (as defined in section 2032A(e)(1)) acquiring any interest in qualified real property to which a lien imposed by section 6324B attaches, issue a certificate of discharge of any or all property subject to such lien, after receiving a bond or other security in an amount or value determined by the district director as sufficient security for the maximum potential liability for additional estate tax with respect to such interest. Any bond shall be in the form and with the security prescribed in § 301.7101-1 of this chapter.

(d) *Special rules.*—The rules set forth in section 6324A(d)(1), (3), and (4), and the regulations thereunder, shall apply with respect to a lien imposed by section 6324B as if it were a lien imposed by section 6324A. [Reg. § 20.6324B-1.]

□ [*T.D.* 7847, 11-9-82.]

[Reg. § 20.6325-1]

§ 20.6325-1. Release of lien or partial discharge of property; transfer certificates in nonresident estates.—(a) A transfer certificate is a certificate permitting the transfer of property of a nonresident decedent without liability. Except as provided in paragraph (b) of this section, no domestic corporation or its transfer agent should transfer stock registered in the name of a nonresident decedent (regardless of citizenship) except such shares which have been submitted for transfer by a duly qualified executor or administrator who has been appointed and is acting in the United States, without first requiring a transfer certificate covering all of the decedent's stock of the corporation and showing that the transfer may be made without liability. Corporations, transfer agents of domestic corporations, transfer agents of foreign corporations (except as to shares held in the name of a nonresident decedent not a citizen of the United States), banks, trust companies, or other custodians in actual or constructive possession of property, of such a decedent can insure avoidance of liability for taxes and penalties only by demanding and re-

ceiving transfer certificates before transfer of property of nonresident decedents.

(b)(1) Subject to the provisions of paragraph (b)(2) of this section—

(i) In the case of a nonresident not a citizen of the United States dying on or after January 1, 1977, a transfer certificate is not required with respect to the transfer of any property of the decedent if the value on the date of death of that part of the decedent's gross estate situated in the United States did not exceed the lesser of $60,000 or $60,000 reduced by the adjustments, if any, required by section 6018(a)(4) for certain taxable gifts made by the decedent and for the aggregate amount of certain specific exemptions.

(ii) In the case of a nonresident not a citizen of the United States dying on or after November 14, 1966, a transfer certificate is not required with respect to the transfer before June 24, 1981, of any property of the decedent if the value on the date of death of that part of the decedent's gross estate situated in the United States did not exceed $30,000.

(2)(i) If the transfer of the estate is subject to the tax imposed by section 2107(a) (relating to expatriation to avoid tax), any amounts which are includible in the decedent's gross estate under section 2107(b) must be added to the date of death value of the decedent's gross estate situated in the United States to determine the value on the date of death of the decedent's gross estate for purposes of paragraph (b)(1) of this section.

(ii) If the transfer of the estate is subject to tax pursuant to a Presidential proclamation made under section 2108(a) (relating to Presidential proclamations of the application of pre-1967 estate tax provisions), a transfer certificate is not required with respect to the transfer of any property of the decedent if the value on the date of death of that part of the decedent's gross estate situated in the United States did not exceed $2,000.

(3) A corporation, transfer agent, bank, trust company, or other custodian will not incur liability for a transfer of the decedent's property without a transfer certificate if the corporation or other person, having no information to the contrary, first receives from the executor or other responsible person, who may be reasonably regarded as in possession of the pertinent facts, a statement of the facts relating to the estate showing that the sum of the value on the date of the decedent's death of that part of his gross estate situated in the United States, and, if applicable, any amounts includible in his gross estate under section 2107(b), is such an amount that, pursuant to the provisions of paragraph (b)(1) or (b)(2) of this section, a transfer certificate is not required.

(4) For the determination of the gross estate situated in the United States, see §§ 20.2103-1 and 20.2104-1.

(c) A transfer certificate will be issued by the service center director or the district director when he is satisfied that the tax imposed upon the estate, if any, has been fully discharged or provided for. The tax will be considered fully discharged for purposes of the issuance of a transfer certificate only when investigation has been completed and payment of the tax, including any deficiency finally determined, has been made. If the tax liability has not been fully discharged, transfer certificates may be issued permitting the transfer of particular items of property without liability upon the filing with the district director of such security as he may require. No transfer certificate is required in an estate of a resident decedent. Further, in the case of an estate of a nonresident decedent (regardless of citizenship) a transfer certificate is not required with respect to property which is being administered by an executor or administrator appointed, qualified, and acting within the United States. For additional regulations under section 6325, see §301.6325-1 of this chapter (Regulations on Procedure and Administration). [Reg. §20.6325-1.]

☐ [*T.D.* 6296, 6-23-58. *Amended by T.D.* 7296, 12-11-73, *T.D.* 7302, 1-2-74 *and T.D.* 7825, 8-12-82.]

[Reg. §301.6325-1]

§301.6325-1. Release of lien or discharge of property.—(a) *Release of lien.*—(1) *Liability satisfied or unenforceable.*—The appropriate official shall issue a certificate of release for a filed notice of Federal tax lien, no later than 30 days after the date on which he finds that the entire tax liability listed in such notice of Federal tax lien either has been fully satisfied (as defined in paragraph (a)(4) of this section) or has become legally unenforceable. In all cases, the liability for the payment of the tax continues until satisfaction of the tax in full or until the expiration of the statutory period for collection, including such extension of the period for collection as is agreed to.

(2) *Bond accepted.*—The appropriate official shall issue a certificate of release of any tax lien if he is furnished and accepts a bond that is conditioned upon the payment of the amount assessed (together with all interest in respect thereof), within the time agreed upon in the bond, but not later than 6 months before the expiration of the statutory period for collection, including any agreed upon extensions. For provisions relating to bonds, see sections 7101 and 7102 and §§301.7101-1 and 301.7102-1.

(3) *Certificate of release for a lien which has become legally unenforceable.*—The appropriate official shall have the authority to file a notice of Federal tax lien which also contains a certificate of release pertaining to those liens which become legally unenforceable. Such release will become effective as a release as of a date prescribed in the document containing the notice of Federal tax lien and certificate of release.

(4) *Satisfaction of tax liability.*—For purposes of paragraph (a)(1) of this section, satisfaction of the tax liability occurs when—

(i) The appropriate official determines that the entire tax liability listed in a notice of

Federal tax lien has been fully satisfied. Such determination will be made as soon as practicable after tender of payment; or

(ii) The taxpayer provides the appropriate official with proof of full payment (as defined in paragraph (a)(5) of this section) with respect to the entire tax liability listed in a notice of Federal tax lien together with the information and documents set forth in paragraph (a)(7) of this section. See paragraph (a)(6) of this section if more than one tax liability is listed in a notice of Federal tax lien.

(5) *Proof of full payment.*—As used in paragraph (a)(4)(ii) of this section, the term *proof of full payment* means—

(i) An internal revenue cashier's receipt reflecting full payment of the tax liability in question;

(ii) A canceled check in an amount sufficient to satisfy the tax liability for which the release is being sought;

(iii) A record, made in accordance with procedures prescribed by the Commissioner, of proper payment of the tax liability by credit or debit card or by electronic funds transfer; or

(iv) Any other manner of proof acceptable to the appropriate official.

(6) *Notice of a Federal tax lien which lists multiple liabilities.*—When a notice of Federal tax lien lists multiple tax liabilities, the appropriate official shall issue a certificate of release when all of the tax liabilities listed in the notice of Federal tax lien have been fully satisfied or have become legally unenforceable. In addition, if the taxpayer requests that a certificate of release be issued with respect to one or more tax liabilities listed in the notice of Federal tax lien and such liability has been fully satisfied or has become legally unenforceable, the appropriate official shall issue a certificate of release. For example, if a notice of Federal tax lien lists two separate liabilities and one of the liabilities is satisfied, the taxpayer may request the issuance of a certificate of release with respect to the satisfied tax liability and the appropriate official shall issue a release.

(7) *Taxpayer requests.*—A request for a certificate of release with respect to a notice of Federal tax lien shall be submitted in writing to the appropriate official. The request shall contain the information required in the appropriate IRS Publication.

(b) *Discharge of specific property from the lien.*— (1) *Property double the amount of the liability.*— (i) The appropriate official may, in his discretion, issue a certificate of discharge of any part of the property subject to a Federal tax lien imposed under chapter 64 of the Internal Revenue Code if he determines that the fair market value of that part of the property remaining subject to the Federal tax lien is at least double the sum of the amount of the unsatisfied liability secured by the Federal tax lien and of the amount of all other liens upon the property which have priority over the Federal tax lien. In general, fair market value is that amount which one ready and willing but not compelled to buy would pay to another ready and willing but not compelled to sell the property.

(ii) The following example illustrates a case in which a certificate of discharge may not be given under this subparagraph:

Example. The Federal tax liability secured by a lien is $1,000. The fair market value of all property which after the discharge will continue to be subject to the Federal tax lien is $10,000. There is a prior mortgage on the property of $5,000, including interest, and the property is subject to a prior lien of $100 for real estate taxes. Accordingly, the taxpayer's equity in the property over and above the amount of the mortgage and real estate taxes is $4,900, or nearly five times the amount required to pay the assessed tax on which the Federal tax lien is based. Nevertheless, a discharge under this subparagraph is not permissible. In the illustration, the sum of the amount of the Federal tax liability ($1,000) and of the amount of the prior mortgage and the lien for real estate taxes ($5,000 + $100 = $5,100) is $6,100. Double the sum is $12,200, but the fair market value of the remaining property is only $10,000. Hence, a discharge of the property is not permissible under this subparagraph, since the Code requires that the fair market value of the remaining property be at least double the sum of two amounts, one amount being the outstanding Federal tax liability and the other amount being all prior liens upon such property. In order that the discharge may be issued, it would be necessary that the remaining property be worth not less than $12,200.

(2) *Part payment; interest of United States valueless.*—(i) *Part payment.*—The appropriate official may, in his discretion, issue a certificate of discharge of any part of the property subject to a Federal tax lien imposed under chapter 64 of the Internal Revenue Code if there is paid over to him in partial satisfaction of the liability secured by the Federal tax lien an amount determined by him to be not less than the value of the interest of the United States in the property to be so discharged. In determining the amount to be paid, the appropriate official will take into consideration all the facts and circumstances of the case, including the expenses to which the government has been put in the matter. In no case shall the amount to be paid be less than the value of the interest of the United States in the property with respect to which the certificate of discharge is to be issued.

(ii) *Interest of the United States valueless.*—The appropriate official may, in his discretion, issue a certificate of discharge of any part of the property subject to the Federal tax lien if he determines that the interest of the United States in the property to be so discharged has no value.

(3) *Discharge of property by substitution of proceeds of sale.*—The appropriate official may, in his discretion, issue a certificate of discharge of any part of the property subject to a Federal tax lien imposed under chapter 64 of the Internal Revenue Code if such part of the property is sold and, pursuant to a written agreement with the appropriate official, the proceeds of the sale are held, as a fund subject to the Federal tax liens and claims of the United States, in the same manner and with the same priority as the Federal tax liens or claims had with respect to the discharged property. This paragraph does not apply unless the sale divests the taxpayer of all right, title, and interest in the property sought to be discharged. Any reasonable and necessary expenses incurred in connection with the sale of the property and the administration of the sale proceeds shall be paid by the applicant or from the proceeds of the sale before satisfaction of any Federal tax liens or claims of the United States.

(4) *Right of substitution of value.*—(i) *Issuance of certificate of discharge to property owner who is not the taxpayer.*—If an owner of property subject to a Federal tax lien imposed under chapter 64 of the Internal Revenue Code submits an application for a certificate of discharge pursuant to paragraph (b)(5) of this section, the appropriate official shall issue a certificate of discharge of such property after the owner either deposits with the appropriate official an amount equal to the value of the interest of the United States in the property, as determined by the appropriate official pursuant to paragraph (b)(6) of this section, or furnishes an acceptable bond in a like amount. This paragraph does not apply if the person seeking the discharge is the person whose unsatisfied liability gave rise to the Federal tax lien. Thus, if the property is owned by both the taxpayer and another person, the other person may obtain a certificate of discharge of the property under this paragraph, but the taxpayer may not.

(ii) *Refund of deposit and release of bond.*—The appropriate official may, in his discretion, determine that either the entire unsatisfied tax liability listed on the notice of Federal tax lien can be satisfied from a source other than the property sought to be discharged, or the value of the interest of the United States is less than the prior determination of such value. The appropriate official shall refund the amount deposited with interest at the overpayment rate determined under section 6621 or release the bond furnished to the extent that he makes this determination.

(iii) *Refund request.*—If a property owner desires an administrative refund of his deposit or release of the bond, the owner shall file a request in writing with the appropriate official. The request shall contain such information as the appropriate IRS Publication may require. The request must be filed within 120 days after the date the certificate of discharge is issued. A refund request made under this paragraph neither is required nor is effective to extend the period for filing an action in court under section 7426(a)(4).

Reg. §301.6325-1(b)(1)(ii)

(iv) *Internal Revenue Service's use of deposit if court action not filed.*—If no action is filed under section 7426(a)(4) for refund of the deposit or release of the bond within the 120-day period specified therein, the appropriate official shall, within 60 days after the expiration of the 120-day period, apply the amount deposited or collect on such bond to the extent necessary to satisfy the liability listed on the notice of Federal tax lien, and shall refund, with interest at the overpayment rate determined under section 6621, any portion of the amount deposited that is not used to satisfy the liability. If the appropriate official has not completed the application of the deposit to the unsatisfied liability before the end of the 60-day period, the deposit will be deemed to have been applied to the unsatisfied liability as of the 60th day.

(5) *Application for certificate of discharge.*— Any person desiring a certificate of discharge under this paragraph (b) shall submit an application in writing to the appropriate official. The application shall contain the information required by the appropriate IRS Publication. For purposes of this paragraph (b), any application for certificate of discharge made by a property owner who is not the taxpayer, and any amount submitted pursuant to the application, will be treated as an application for discharge and a deposit under section 6325(b)(4) unless the owner of the property submits a statement, in writing, that the application is being submitted under another paragraph of section 6325 and not under section 6325(b)(4), and the owner in writing waives the rights afforded under paragraph (b)(4), including the right to seek judicial review.

(6) *Valuation of interest of United States.*—For purposes of paragraphs (b)(2) and (b)(4) of this section, in determining the value of the interest of the United States in the property, or any part thereof, with respect to which the certificate of discharge is to be issued, the appropriate official shall give consideration to the value of the property and the amount of all liens and encumbrances thereon having priority over the Federal tax lien. In determining the value of the property, the appropriate official may, in his discretion, give consideration to the forced sale value of the property in appropriate cases.

(c) *Estate or gift tax liability fully satisfied or provided for.*—(1) *Certificate of discharge.*—If the appropriate official determines that the tax liability for estate or gift tax has been fully satisfied, he may issue a certificate of discharge of any or all property from the lien imposed thereon. If the appropriate official determines that the tax liability for estate or gift tax has been adequately provided for, he may issue a certificate discharging particular items of property from the lien. If a lien has arisen under section 6324B (relating to special lien for additional estate tax attributable to farm, etc., valuation) and the appropriate official determines that the liability for additional estate tax has been fully secured in accordance with § 20.6324B-1(c) of this chapter, the appropri-

ate official may issue a certificate of discharge of the real property from the section 6324B lien. The issuance of such a certificate is a matter resting within the discretion of the appropriate official, and a certificate will be issued only in case there is actual need therefor. The primary purpose of such discharge is not to evidence payment or satisfaction of the tax, but to permit the transfer of property free from the lien in case it is necessary to clear title. The tax will be considered fully satisfied only when investigation has been completed and payment of the tax, including any deficiency determined, has been made.

(2) *Application for certificate of discharge.*—An application for a certificate of discharge of property from the lien for estate or gift tax should be filed with the appropriate official responsible for the collection of the tax. It should be made in writing under penalties of perjury and should explain the circumstances that require the discharge, and should fully describe the particular items for which the discharge is desired. Where realty is involved each parcel sought to be discharged from the lien should be described on a separate page and each such description submitted in duplicate. In the case of an estate tax lien, the application should show the applicant's relationship to the estate, such as executor, heir, devisee, legatee, beneficiary, transferee, or purchaser. If the estate or gift tax return has not been filed, a statement under penalties of perjury may be required showing (i) the value of the property to be discharged, (ii) the basis for such valuation, (iii) in the case of the estate tax, the approximate value of the gross estate and the approximate value of the total real property included in the gross estate, (iv) in the case of the gift tax, the total amount of gifts made during the calendar year and the prior calendar years subsequent to the enactment of the Revenue Act of 1932 and the approximate value of all real estate subject to the gift tax lien, and (v) if the property is to be sold or otherwise transferred, the name and address of the purchaser or transferee and the consideration, if any, paid or to be paid by him.

(d) *Subordination of lien.*—(1) *By payment of the amount subordinated.*—The appropriate official may, in his discretion, issue a certificate of subordination of a lien imposed under chapter 64 of the Internal Revenue Code upon any part of the property subject to the lien if there is paid over to the appropriate official an amount equal to the amount of the lien or interest to which the certificate subordinates the lien of the United States. For this purpose, the tax lien may be subordinated to another lien or interest on a dollar-for-dollar basis. For example, if a notice of a Federal tax lien is filed and a delinquent taxpayer secures a mortgage loan on a part of the property subject to the tax lien and pays over the proceeds of the loan to the appropriate official after an application for a certificate of subordination is approved, the appropriate official will issue a certificate of subordination. This certificate will have the effect of subordinating the tax lien to the mortgage.

(2) *To facilitate tax collection.*—(i) *In general.*—The appropriate official may, in his discretion, issue a certificate of subordination of a lien imposed under chapter 64 of the Internal Revenue Code upon any part of the property subject to the lien if the appropriate official believes that the subordination of the lien will ultimately result in an increase in the amount realized by the United States from the property subject to the lien and will facilitate the ultimate collection of the tax liability.

(ii) *Examples.*—The provisions of this subparagraph may be illustrated by the following examples:

Example (1). A, a farmer, needs money in order to harvest his crop. A Federal tax lien, notice of which has been filed, is outstanding with respect to A's property. B, a lending institution, is willing to make the necessary loan if the loan is secured by a first mortgage on the farm which is prior to the Federal tax lien. Upon examination, the appropriate official believes that ultimately the amount realizable from A's property will be increased and the collection of the tax liability will be facilitated by the availability of cash when the crop is harvested and sold. In this case, the appropriate official may, in his discretion, subordinate the tax lien on the farm to the mortgage securing the crop harvesting loan.

Example (2). C owns a commercial building which is deteriorating and in unsalable condition. Because of outstanding Federal tax liens, notices of which have been filed, C is unable to finance the repair and rehabilitation of the building. D, a contractor, is willing to do the work if his mechanic's lien on the property is superior to the Federal tax liens. Upon examination, the appropriate official believes that ultimately the amount realizable from C's property will be increased and the collection of the tax liability will be facilitated by arresting deterioration of the property and restoring it to salable condition. In this case, the appropriate official may, in his discretion, subordinate the tax lien on the building to the mechanic's lien.

Example (3). E, a manufacturer of electronic equipment, obtains financing from F, a lending institution, pursuant to a security agreement, with respect to which a financing statement was duly filed under the Uniform Commercial Code on June 1, 1970. On April 15, 1971, F gains actual notice or knowledge that notice of a Federal tax lien had been filed against E on March 31, 1971, and F refuses to make further advances unless its security interest is assured of priority over the Federal tax lien. Upon examination, the appropriate official believes that ultimately the amount realizable from E's property will be increased and the collection of the tax liability will be facilitated if the work in process can be completed and the equipment sold. In this case, the appropriate official may, in his discretion, subordinate the tax lien to F's

security interest for the further advances required to complete the work.

Example (4). Suit is brought against G by H, who claims ownership of property the legal title to which is held by G. A Federal tax lien against G, notice of which has previously been filed, will be enforceable against the property if G's title is confirmed. Because section 6323(b)(8) is inapplicable, J, an attorney, is unwilling to defend the case for G unless he is granted a contractual lien on the property, superior to the Federal tax lien. Upon examination, the appropriate official believes that the successful defense of the case by G will increase the amount ultimately realizable from G's property and will facilitate collection of the tax liability. In this case, the appropriate official may, in his discretion, subordinate the tax lien to J's contractual lien on the disputed property to secure J's reasonable fees and expenses.

(3) *Subordination of section 6324B lien.*—The appropriate official may issue a certificate of subordination with respect to a lien imposed by section 6324B if the appropriate official determines that the interests of the United States will be adequately secured after such subordination. For example, A, a qualified heir of qualified real property, needs to borrow money for farming purposes. If the current fair market value of the real property is $150,000, the amount of the claim to which the special lien is to be subordinated is $40,000, the potential liability for additional tax (as defined in section 2032A(c)) is less than $55,000, and there are no other facts to indicate that the interest of the United States will not be adequately secured, the appropriate official may issue a certificate of subordination. The result would be the same if the loan were for bona fide purposes other than farming.

(4) *Application for certificate of subordination.*—Any person desiring a certificate of subordination under this paragraph shall submit an application therefor in writing to the appropriate official responsible for the collection of the tax. The application shall contain such information as the appropriate official may require.

(e) *Nonattachment of lien.*—If the appropriate official determines that, because of confusion of names or otherwise, any person (other than the person against whom the tax was assessed) is or may be injured by the appearance that a notice of lien filed in accordance with §301.6323(f)-1 refers to such person, the appropriate official may issue a certificate of nonattachment. Such certificate shall state that the lien, notice of which has been filed, does not attach to the property of such person. Any person desiring a certificate of nonattachment under this paragraph shall submit an application therefor in writing to the appropriate official responsible for the collection of the tax. The application shall c ontain such information as the appropriate official may require.

(f) *Effect of certificate.*—(1) *Conclusiveness.*—Except as provided in subparagraphs (2) and (3) of this paragraph, if a certificate is issued under section 6325 by the appropriate official and the certificate is filed in the same office as the notice of lien to which it relates (if the notice of lien has been filed), the certificate shall have the following effect—

(i) In the case of a certificate of release issued under paragraph (a) of this section, the certificate shall be conclusive that the tax lien referred to in the certificate is extinguished;

(ii) In the case of a certificate of discharge issued under paragraph (b) or (c) of this section, the certificate shall be conclusive that the property covered by the certificate is discharged from the tax lien;

(iii) In the case of a certificate of subordination issued under paragraph (d) of this section, the certificate shall be conclusive that the lien or interest to which the Federal tax lien is subordinated is superior to the tax lien; and

(iv) In the case of a certificate of nonattachment issued under paragraph (e), the certificate shall be conclusive that the lien of the United States does not attach to the property of the person referred to in the certificate.

(2) *Revocation of certificate of release or nonattachment.*—(i) *In general.*—If the appropriate official determines that either—

(a) A certificate of release or a certificate of nonattachment of the general tax lien imposed by section 6321 was issued erroneously or improvidently, or

(b) A certificate of release of such lien was issued in connection with a compromise agreement under section 7122 which has been breached,

and if the period of limitation on collection after assessment of the tax liability has not expired, the appropriate official may revoke the certificate and reinstate the tax lien. The provisions of this subparagraph do not apply in the case of the lien imposed by section 6324 relating to estate and gift taxes.

(ii) *Method of revocation and reinstatement.*—The revocation and reinstatement described in subdivision (i) of this subparagraph is accomplished by—

(a) Mailing notice of the revocation to the taxpayer at his last known address (see § 301.6212-2 for further guidance regarding the definition of last known address); and

(b) Filing notice of the revocation of the certificate in the same office in which the notice of lien to which it relates was filed (if the notice of lien has been filed).

(iii) *Effect of reinstatement.*—(a) *Effective date.*—A tax lien reinstated in accordance with the provisions of this subparagraph is effective on and after the date the notice of revocation is mailed to the taxpayer in accordance with the provisions of subdivision (ii)(a) of this subparagraph, but the reinstated lien is not effective before the filing of notice of revocation, in accordance with the provisions of subdivision (ii)(b) of this subparagraph, if the filing is required by

reason of the fact that a notice of the lien had been filed.

(b) *Treatment of reinstated lien.*—As of the effective date of reinstatement, a reinstated lien has the same force and effect as a general tax lien imposed by section 6321 which arises upon assessment of a tax liability. The reinstated lien continues in existence until the expiration of the period of limitation on collection after assessment of the tax liability to which it relates. The reinstatement of the lien does not retroactively reinstate a previously filed notice of lien. The reinstated lien is not valid against any holder of a lien or interest described in § 301.6323(a)-1 until notice of the reinstated lien has been filed in accordance with the provisions of § 301.6323(f)-1 subsequent to or concurrent with the time the reinstated lien became effective.

(iv) *Example.*—The provisions of this subparagraph may be illustrated by the following example:

Example. On March 1, 1967, an assessment of an unpaid Federal tax liability is made against A. On March 1, 1968, notice of the Federal tax lien, which arose at the time of assessment, is filed. On April 1, 1968, A executes a bona fide mortgage on property belonging to him to B. On May 1, 1968, a certificate of release of the tax lien is erroneously issued and is filed by A in the same office in which the notice of lien was filed. On June 3, 1968, the lien is reinstated in accordance with the provisions of this subparagraph. On July 1, 1968, A executes a bona fide mortgage on property belonging to him to C. On August 1, 1968, a notice of the lien which was reinstated is properly filed in accordance with the provisions of § 301.6323(f)-1. The mortgages of both B and C will have priority over the rights of the United States with respect to the tax liability in question. Because a reinstated lien continues in existence only until the expiration of the period of limitation on collection after assessment of the tax liability to which the lien relates, in the absence of any extension or suspension of the period of limitation on collection after assessment, the reinstated lien will become unenforceable by reason of lapse of time after February 28, 1973.

(3) *Certificates void under certain conditions.*—Notwithstanding any other provisions of subtitle F of the Internal Revenue Code, any lien for Federal taxes attaches to any property with respect to which a certificate of discharge has been issued if the person liable for the tax reacquires the property after the certificate has been issued. Thus, if property subject to a Federal tax lien is discharged therefrom and is later reacquired by the delinquent taxpayer at a time when the lien is still in existence, the tax lien attaches to the reacquired property and is enforceable against it as in the case of after-acquired property generally.

(g) *Filing of certificates and notices.*—If a certificate or notice described in this section may not be filed in the office designated by State law in which the notice of lien imposed by section 6321 (to which the certificate or notice relates) is filed, the certificate or notice is effective if filed in the office of the clerk of the United States district court for the judicial district in which the State office where the notice of lien is filed is situated.

(h) As used in this section, the term *appropriate official* means either the official or office identified in the relevant IRS Publication or, if such official or office is not so identified, the Secretary or his delegate.

(i) *Effective/applicability date.*—This section applies to any release of lien or discharge of property that is requested after January 31, 2008. [Reg. § 301.6325-1.]

☐ [*T.D.* 6119, 12-31-54. *Amended by T.D.* 6425, 11-10-59; *T.D.* 6498, 10-24-60; *T.D.* 6700, 1-6-64; *T.D.* 7429, 8-20-76; *T.D.* 7847, 11-9-82; *T.D.* 8939, 1-11-2001 *and T.D.* 9378, 1-30-2008 (*corrected* 2-21-2008).]

[Reg. § 301.6326-1]

§ 301.6326-1. Administrative appeal of the erroneous filing of notice of federal tax lien.—(a) *In general.*—Any person may appeal to the district director of the district in which a notice of federal tax lien was filed on the property or rights to property of such person for a release of lien alleging an error in the filing of notice of lien. Such appeal may be used only for the purpose of correcting the erroneous filing of a notice of lien, not to challenge the underlying deficiency that led to the impositon of a lien. If the district director determines that the Internal Revenue Service has erroneously filed the notice of any federal tax lien, the district director shall expeditiously, and, to the extent practicable, within 14 days after such determination, issue a certificate of release of lien. The certificate of release of such lien shall include a statement that the filing of notice of lien was erroneous.

(b) *Appeal alleging an error in the filing of notice of lien.*—For purposes of paragraph (a) of this section, an appeal of the filing of notice of federal tax lien must be based on any one of the following allegations:

(1) The tax liability that gave rise to the lien, plus any interest and additions to tax associated with said liability, was satisfied prior to the filing of notice of lien;

(2) The tax liability that gave rise to the lien was assessed in violation of the deficiency procedures set forth in section 6213 of the Internal Revenue Code;

(3) The tax liability that gave rise to the lien was assessed in violation of Title 11 of the United States Code (the Bankrupty Code); or

(4) The statutory period for collection of the tax liability that gave rise to the lien expired prior to the filing of notice of federal tax lien.

(c) *Notice of federal tax lien that lists multiple liabilities.*—When a notice of federal tax lien lists multiple liabilities, a person may appeal the filing of notice of lien with respect to one or more of the liabilities listed in the notice, if the notice was erroneously filed with respect to such liabili-

ties. If a notice of federal tax lien was erroneously filed with respect to one or more liabilities listed in the notice, the district director shall issue a certificate of release with respect to such liabilities. For example, if a notice of federal tax lien lists tax liabilities for years 1980, 1981 and 1982, and the entire liabilities for 1981 and 1982 were paid prior to the filing of notice of lien, the taxpayer may appeal the filing of notice of lien with respect to the 1981 and 1982 liabilities and the district director must issue a certificate of release with respect to the 1981 and 1982 liabilities.

(d) *Procedures for appeal.*—(1) *Manner.*—An appeal of the filing of notice of federal tax lien shall be made in writing to the district director (marked for the attention of the Chief, Special Procedures Function) of the district in which the notice of federal tax lien was filed.

(2) *Form.*—The appeal shall include the following information and documents:

(i) Name, current address, and taxpayer identification number of the person appealing the filing of notice of federal tax lien;

(ii) A copy of the notice of federal tax lien affecting the property, if available; and

(iii) The grounds upon which the filing of notice of federal tax lien is being appealed.

(A) If the ground upon which the filing of notice is being appealed is that the tax liability in question was satisfied prior to the filing, proof of full payment as defined in paragraph (e) of this section must be provided.

(B) If the ground upon which the filing of notice is being appealed is that the tax liability that gave rise to lien was assessed in violation of the deficiency procedures set forth in section 6213 of the Internal Revenue Code, the appealing party must explain how the assessment was erroneous.

(C) If the ground upon which the filing of notice is being appealed is that the tax liability that gave rise to the lien was assessed in violation of Title 11 of the United States Code (the Bankruptcy Code), the appealing party must provide the following:

(*1*) The identity of the court and the district in which the bankruptcy petition was filed; and

(*2*) The docket number and the date of filing of the bankruptcy petition.

(3) *Time.*—An administrative appeal of the erroneous filing of notice of federal tax lien shall be made within 1 year after the taxpayer becomes aware of the erroneously filed tax lien.

(e) *Proof of full payment.*—As used in paragraph (d)(2)(iii) of this section, the term "proof of full payment" means:

(1) An internal revenue cashier's receipt reflecting full payment of the tax liability in question prior to the date the federal tax lien at issue was filed;

(2) A canceled check to the Internal Revenue Service in an amount which was sufficient to

satisfy the tax liability for which release is being sought; or

(3) Any other manner of proof acceptable to the district director.

(f) *Exclusive remedy.*—The appeal established by section 6326 of the Internal Revenue Code and by this section shall be the exclusive admin-istrative remedy with respect to the erroneous filing of a notice of federal tax lien.

(g) *Effective date.*—The provisions of this section are effective July 7, 1989. [Reg. § 301.6326-1.]

☐ [*T.D. 8250, 5-5-89. Amended by T.D. 8347, 4-30-91.*]

SEIZURE OF PROPERTY FOR COLLECTION OF TAXES

[Reg. § 301.6330-1]

§ 301.6330-1. Notice and opportunity for hearing prior to levy.—(a) *Notification.*—(1) *In general.*—Except as specified in paragraph (a)(2) of this section, the Commissioner, or his or her delegate(the Commissioner), will prescribe procedures to provide persons upon whose property or rights to property the IRS intends to levy (hereinafter referred to as the taxpayer) on or after January 19, 1999, notice of that intention and to give them the right to, and the opportunity for, a pre-levy Collection Due Process (CDP) hearing with the Internal Revenue Service (IRS) Office of Appeals (Appeals). This pre-levy Collection Due Process Hearing Notice (CDP Notice) must be given in person, left at the dwelling or usual place of business of the taxpayer, or sent by certified or registered mail, return receipt requested, to the taxpayer's last known address. For further guidance regarding the definition of last known address, see § 301.6212-2.

(2) *Exceptions.*—(i) *state tax refunds.*—Section 6330(f) does not require the Commissioner to provide the taxpayer with notification of the taxpayer's right to a CDP hearing prior to issuing a levy to collect state tax refunds owing to the taxpayer. However, the Commissioner will prescribe procedures to give the taxpayer notice of the right to, and the opportunity for, a CDP hearing with Appeals with respect to any such levy issued on or after January 19, 1999, within a reasonable time after the levy has occurred. The notification required to be given following a levy on a state tax refund is referred to as a post-levy CDP Notice.

(ii) *Jeopardy.*—Section 6330(f) does not require the Commissioner to provide the taxpayer with notification of the taxpayer's right to a CDP hearing prior to a levy when there has been a determination that collection of the tax is in jeopardy. However, the Commissioner will prescribe procedures to provide notice of the right to, and the opportunity for, a CDP hearing with Appeals to the taxpayer with respect to any such levy issued on or after January 19, 1999, within a reasonable time after the levy has occurred. The notification required to be given following a jeopardy levy also is referred to as post-levy CDP Notice.

(3) *Questions and answers.*—The questions and answers illustrate the provisions of this paragraph (a) as follows:

Q-A1. Who is the person to be notified under section 6330?

A-A1. Under section 6330(a)(1), a pre-levy or post-levy CDP Notice is required to be given only to the person whose property or right to property is intended to be levied upon, or, in the case of a levy made on a state tax refund or a jeopardy levy, the person whose property or right to property was levied upon. The person described in section 6330(a)(1) is the same person described in section 6331(a)—i.e., the person liable to pay the tax due after notice and demand who refuses or neglects to pay (referred to here as the taxpayer). A pre-levy or post-levy CDP Notice therefore will be given only to the taxpayer.

Q-A2. Will the IRS give notification to a known nominee of, a person holding property of, or a person who holds property subject to a lien with respect to, the taxpayer of the IRS' intention to issue a levy?

A-A2. No. Such a person is not the person described in section 6331(a)(1), but such persons have other remedies. See A-B5 of paragraph (b)(2) of this section.

Q-A3. Will the IRS give notification for each tax and tax period it intends to include or has included in a levy issued on or after January 19, 1999?

A-A3. Yes. The notification of an intent to levy or of the issuance of a jeopardy or state tax refund levy will specify each tax and tax period that will be or was included in the levy.

Q-A4. Will the IRS give notification to a taxpayer with respect to levies for a tax and tax period issued on or after January 19, 1999, even though the IRS had issued a levy prior to January 19, 1999, with respect to the same tax and tax period?

A-A4. Yes. The IRS will provide appropriate pre-levy or post-levy notification to a taxpayer regarding the first levy it intends to issue or has issued on or after January 19, 1999, with respect to a tax and tax period, even though it had issued a levy with respect to that same tax and tax period prior to January 19, 1999.

Q-A5. When will the IRS provide this notice?

A-A5. Beginning on January 19, 1999, the IRS will give a pre-levy CDP Notice to the taxpayer of the IRS' intent to levy on property or rights to property, other than in state tax refund and jeopardy levy situations, at least 30 days prior to the first such levy with respect to a tax and tax period. If the taxpayer has not received a

Reg. § 301.6330-1(a)(3)

pre-levy CDP Notice and the IRS levies on a state tax refund or issues a jeopardy levy on or after January 19, 1999, the IRS will provide a post-levy CDP Notice to the taxpayer within a reasonable time after that levy.

Q-A6. What must a pre-levy CDP Notice include?

A-A6. Pursuant to section 6330(a)(3), a pre-levy CDP Notice must include, in simple and nontechnical terms:

(i) The amount of the unpaid tax.

(ii) Notification of the right to request a CDP hearing.

(iii) A statement that the IRS intends to levy.

(iv) The taxpayer's rights with respect to the levy action, including a brief statement that sets forth—

(A) The statutory provisions relating to the levy and sale of property;

(B) The procedures applicable to the levy and sale of property;

(C) The administrative appeals available to the taxpayer with respect to the levy and sale and the procedures relating to those appeals;

(D) The alternatives available to taxpayers that could prevent levy on the property (including installment agreements); and

(E) The statutory provisions and the procedures relating to the redemption of property and the release of liens on property.

Q-A7. What must a post-levy CDP Notice include?

A-A7. A post-levy CDP Notice must include, in simple and nontechnical terms:

(i) The amount of the unpaid tax.

(ii) Notification of the right to request a CDP hearing.

(iii) A statement that the IRS has levied upon the taxpayer's state tax refund or has made a jeopardy levy on property or rights to property of the taxpayer, as appropriate.

(iv) The taxpayer's rights with respect to the levy action, including a brief statement that sets forth—

(A) The statutory provisions relating to the levy and sale of property;

(B) The procedures applicable to the levy and sale of property;

(C) The administrative appeals available to the taxpayer with respect to the levy and sale and the procedures relating to those appeals;

(D) The alternatives available to taxpayers that could prevent any further levies on the taxpayer's property (including installment agreements); and

(E) The statutory provisions and the procedures relating to the redemption of property and the release of liens on property.

Q-A8. How will this pre-levy or post-levy notification under section 6330 be accomplished?

A-A8. The IRS will notify the taxpayer by means of a pre-levy CDP Notice or a post-levy CDP Notice, as appropriate. The additional information the IRS is required to provide, to-

gether with Form 12153, Request for a Collection Due Process Hearing, will be included with the CDP Notice.

(i) The IRS may effect delivery of a pre-levy CDP Notice (and accompanying materials) in one of three ways:

(A) By delivering the notice personally to the taxpayer.

(B) By leaving the notice at the taxpayer's dwelling or usual place of business.

(C) By mailing the notice to the taxpayer at the taxpayer's last known address by certified or registered mail, return receipt requested.

(ii) The IRS may effect delivery of a post-levy CDP Notice (and accompanying materials) in one of three ways:

(A) By delivering the notice personally to the taxpayer.

(B) By leaving the notice at the taxpayer's dwelling or usual place of business.

(C) By mailing the notice to the taxpayer at the taxpayer's last known address by certified or registered mail.

Q-A9. What are the consequences if the taxpayer does not receive or accept the notification which was properly left at the taxpayer's dwelling or usual place of business, or properly sent by certified or registered mail, return receipt requested, to the taxpayer's last known address?

A-A9. Notification properly sent to the taxpayer's last known address or left at the taxpayer's dwelling or usual place of business is sufficient to start the 30-day period within which the taxpayer may request a CDP hearing. See paragraph (c) of this section for when a request for a CDP hearing must be filed. Actual receipt is not a prerequisite to the validity of the CDP Notice.

Q-A10. What if the taxpayer does not receive the CDP Notice because the IRS did not send that notice by certified or registered mail to the taxpayer's last known address, or failed to leave it at the dwelling or usual place of business of the taxpayer, and the taxpayer fails to request a CDP hearing with Appeals within the 30-day period commencing the day after the date of the CDP Notice?

A-A10. When the IRS determines that it failed properly to provide a taxpayer with a CDP Notice, it will promptly provide the taxpayer with a substitute CDP Notice and provide the taxpayer with an opportunity to request a CDP hearing. Substitute CDP Notices are discussed in Q&A-B3 of paragraph (b) (2) and Q&A-C8 of paragraph (c) (2) of this section.

(4) *Examples.*—The following examples illustrate the principles of this paragraph (a):

Example 1. Prior to January 19, 1999, the IRS issues a continuous levy on a taxpayer's wages and a levy on that taxpayer's fixed right to future payments. The IRS is not required to release either levy on or after January 19, 1999, until the requirements of section 6343(a)(1) are met. The taxpayer is not entitled to a CDP Notice or a CDP hearing under section 6330 with respect to either levy because both levy actions were initiated prior to January 19, 1999.

Example 2. The same facts as in *Example 1*, except the IRS intends to levy upon a taxpayer's bank account on or after January 19, 1999. The taxpayer is entitled to a pre-levy CDP Notice with respect to this proposed new levy.

(b) *Entitlement to a CDP hearing.*—(1) *In general.*—A taxpayer is entitled to one CDP hearing with respect to the unpaid tax and tax periods covered by the pre-levy or post-levy CDP Notice provided to the taxpayer. The taxpayer must request the CDP hearing within the 30-day period commencing on the day after the date of the CDP Notice.

(2) *Questions and answers.*—The questions and answers illustrate the provisions of this paragraph (b) as follows:

Q-B1. Is the taxpayer entitled to a CDP hearing where a levy for state tax refunds is issued on or after January 19, 1999, even though the IRS had previously issued other levies prior to January 19, 1999, seeking to collect the taxes owed for the same period?

A-B1. Yes. The taxpayer is entitled to a CDP hearing under section 6330 for the type of tax and tax periods set forth in the state tax refund levy issued on or after January 19, 1999.

Q-B2. Is the taxpayer entitled to a CDP hearing when the IRS, more than 30 days after issuance of a CDP Notice under section 6330 with respect to the unpaid tax and periods, provides subsequent notice to that taxpayer that the IRS intends to levy on property or rights to property of the taxpayer for the same tax and tax periods shown on the CDP Notice?

A-B2. No. Under section 6330, only the first pre-levy or post-levy CDP Notice with respect to the unpaid tax and tax periods entitles the taxpayer to request a CDP hearing. If the taxpayer does not timely request a CDP hearing with Appeals following that first notification, the taxpayer foregoes the right to a CDP hearing with Appeals and judicial review of Appeals' determination with respect to levies relating to that tax and tax period. The IRS generally provides additional notices or reminders (reminder notifications) to the taxpayer of its intent to levy when no collection action has occurred within 180 days of a proposed levy. Under such circumstances, a taxpayer may request an equivalent hearing as described in paragraph (i) of this section.

Q-B3. When the IRS provides a taxpayer with a substitute CDP Notice and the taxpayer timely requests a CDP hearing, is the taxpayer entitled to a CDP Hearing before Appeals?

A-B3. Yes. Unless the taxpayer provides the IRS a written withdrawal of the request that Appeals conduct a CDP hearing, the taxpayer is entitled to a CDP hearing before Appeals. Following the hearing, Appeals will issue a Notice of Determination, and the taxpayer is entitled to seek judicial review of that Notice of Determination.

Q-B4. If the IRS sends a second CDP Notice under section 6330 (other than a substitute CDP Notice) for a tax period and with respect to an unpaid tax for which a CDP Notice under section 6330 was previously sent, is the taxpayer entitled to a section 6330 CDP hearing based on the second CDP Notice?

A-B4. No. The taxpayer is entitled to only one CDP hearing under section 6330 with respect to the tax and tax period. The taxpayer must request the CDP hearing within 30 days of the date of the first CDP Notice provided for that tax and tax period.

Q-B5. Will the IRS give pre-levy or post-levy CDP Notices to known nominees of, persons holding property of, or persons holding property subject to a lien with respect to the taxpayer?

A-B5. No. Such person is not the person described in section 6331(a) and is, therefore, not entitled to a CDP hearing or an equivalent hearing (as discussed in paragraph (i) of this section). Such person, however, may seek reconsideration by the IRS office collecting the tax, assistance from the National Taxpayer Advocate, or an administrative hearing before Appeals under its Collection Appeals Program. However, any such administrative hearing would not be a CDP hearing under section 6330 and any determination or decision resulting from the hearing would not be subject to judicial review.

(3) *Example.*—The following example illustrates the principles of this paragraph (b):

Example. Federal income tax liability for 1997 is assessed against individual D. D buys an asset and puts it in individual E's name. The IRS gives D a CDP Notice of intent to levy with respect to the 1997 tax liability. The IRS will not notify E of its intent to levy. The IRS is not required to notify E of its intent to levy although E holds property of individual D. E is not the taxpayer.

(c) *Requesting a CDP hearing.*—(1) *In general.*— When a taxpayer is entitled to a CDP hearing under section 6330, the CDP hearing must be requested during the 30-day period that commences the day after the date of the CDP Notice.

(2) *Questions and answers.*—The questions and answers illustrate the provisions of this paragraph (c) as follows:

Q-C1. What must a taxpayer do to obtain a CDP hearing?

A-C1. (i) The taxpayer must make a request in writing for a CDP hearing. The request for a CDP hearing shall include the information and signature specified in A-C1(ii) of this paragraph (c)(2). See A-D7 and A-D8 of paragraph (d)(2).

(ii) The written request for a CDP hearing must be dated and must include the following:

(A) The taxpayer's name, address, daytime telephone number (if any), and taxpayer identification number (e.g., SSN, ITIN or EIN).

(B) The type of tax involved.

(C) The tax period at issue.

Reg. §301.6330-1(c)(2)

(D) A statement that the taxpayer requests a hearing with Appeals concerning the proposed levy.

(E) The reason or reasons why the taxpayer disagrees with the proposed levy.

(F) The signature of the taxpayer or the taxpayer's authorized representative.

(iii) If the IRS receives a timely written request for CDP hearing that does not satisfy the requirements set forth in A-C1(ii) of this paragraph (c)(2), the IRS will make a reasonable attempt to contact the taxpayer and request that the taxpayer comply with the unsatisfied requirements. The taxpayer must perfect any timely written request for a CDP hearing that does not satisfy the requirements set forth in A-C1(ii) of this paragraph (c)(2) within a reasonable period of time after a request from the IRS.

(iv) Taxpayers are encouraged to use Form 12153, "Request for a Collection Due Process Hearing," in requesting a CDP hearing so that the request can be readily identified and forwarded to Appeals. Taxpayers may obtain a copy of Form 12153 by contacting the IRS office that issued the CDP Notice, by downloading a copy from the IRS Internet site, *www.irs.gov/pub/irs-pdf/f12153.pdf*, or by calling, toll-free, 1-800-829-3676.

(v) The taxpayer must affirm any timely written request for a CDP hearing which is signed or alleged to have been signed on the taxpayer's behalf by the taxpayer's spouse or other unauthorized representative by filing, within a reasonable period of time after a request from the IRS, a signed, written affirmation that the request was originally submitted on the taxpayer's behalf. If the affirmation is filed within a reasonable period of time after a request, the timely CDP hearing request will be considered timely with respect to the non-signing taxpayer. If the affirmation is not filed within a reasonable period of time after a request, the CDP hearing request will be denied with respect to the non-signing taxpayer.

Q-C2. Must the request for the CDP hearing be in writing?

A-C2. Yes. There are several reasons why the request for a CDP hearing must be in writing. The filing of a timely request for a CDP hearing is the first step in what may result in a court proceeding. A written request will provide proof that the CDP hearing was requested and thus permit the court to verify that it has jurisdiction over any subsequent appeal of the Notice of Determination issued by Appeals. In addition, the receipt of the written request will establish the date on which the periods of limitation under section 6502 (relating to collection after assessment), section 6531 (relating to criminal prosecutions), and section 6532 (relating to suits) are suspended as a result of the CDP hearing and any judicial appeal. Moreover, because the IRS anticipates that taxpayers will contact the IRS office that issued the CDP Notice for further information or assistance in filling out Form 12153, or to attempt to resolve their liabilities prior to going through the CDP hearing process, the requirement of a written request should help prevent any misunderstanding as to whether a CDP hearing has been requested. If the information requested on Form 12153 is furnished by the taxpayer, the written request also will help to establish the issues for which the taxpayer seeks a determination by Appeals.

Q-C3. When must a taxpayer request a CDP hearing with respect to a CDP Notice issued under section 6330?

A-C3. A taxpayer must submit a written request for a CDP hearing within the 30-day period commencing the day after the date of the CDP Notice issued under section 6330. This period is slightly different from the period for submitting a written request for a CDP hearing with respect to a CDP Notice issued under section 6320. For a CDP Notice issued under section 6320, a taxpayer must submit a written request for a CDP hearing within the 30-day period commencing the day after the end of the five business day period following the filing of the notice of federal tax lien (NFTL).

Q-C4. How will the timeliness of a taxpayer's written request for a CDP hearing be determined?

A-C4. The rules and regulations under section 7502 and section 7503 will apply to determine the timeliness of the taxpayer's request for a CDP hearing, if properly transmitted and addressed as provided in A-C6 of this paragraph (c)(2).

Q-C5. Is the 30-day period within which a taxpayer must make a request for a CDP hearing extended because the taxpayer resides outside the United States?

A-C5. No. Section 6330 does not make provision for such a circumstance. Accordingly, all taxpayers who want a CDP hearing under section 6330 must request such a hearing within the 30-day period commencing the day after the date of the CDP Notice.

Q-C6. Where must the written request for a CDP hearing be sent?

A-C6. The written request for a CDP hearing must be sent, or hand delivered (if permitted), to the IRS office and address as directed on the CDP Notice. If the address of that office does not appear on the CDP Notice, the taxpayer should obtain the address of the office to which the written request should be sent or hand delivered by calling, toll-free, 1-800-829-1040 and providing the taxpayer's identification number (e.g., SSN, ITIN or EIN).

Q-C7. What will happen if the taxpayer does not request a CDP hearing in writing within the 30-day period commencing on the day after the date of the CDP Notice issued under section 6330?

A-C7. If the taxpayer does not request a CDP hearing in writing within the 30-day period that commences on the day after the date of the CDP Notice, the taxpayer foregoes the right to a CDP hearing under section 6330 with respect to the unpaid tax and tax periods shown on the

CDP Notice. A written request submitted within the 30-day period that does not satisfy the requirements set forth in A-C1(ii)(A), (B), (C), (D) or (F) of this paragraph (c)(2) is considered timely if the request is perfected within a reasonable period of time pursuant to A-C1(iii) of this paragraph (c)(2). If the request for CDP hearing is untimely, either because the request was not submitted within the 30-day period or not perfected within the reasonable period provided, the taxpayer will be notified of the untimeliness of the request and offered an equivalent hearing. In such cases, the taxpayer may obtain an equivalent hearing without submitting an additional request. See paragraph (i) of this section.

Q-C8. When must a taxpayer request a CDP hearing with respect to a substitute CDP Notice?

A-C8. A CDP hearing with respect to a substitute CDP Notice must be requested in writing by the taxpayer prior to the end of the 30-day period commencing the day after the date of the substitute CDP Notice.

Q-C9. Can taxpayers attempt to resolve the matter of the proposed levy with an officer or employee of the IRS office collecting the tax liability stated on the CDP Notice either before or after requesting a CDP hearing?

A-C9. Yes. Taxpayers are encouraged to discuss their concerns with the IRS office collecting the tax, either before or after they request a CDP hearing. If such a discussion occurs before a request is made for a CDP hearing, the matter may be resolved without the need for Appeals consideration. However, these discussions do not suspend the running of the 30-day period within which the taxpayer is required to request a CDP hearing, nor do they extend that 30-day period. If discussions occur after the request for a CDP hearing is filed and the taxpayer resolves the matter with the IRS office collecting the tax, the taxpayer may withdraw in writing the request that a CDP hearing be conducted by Appeals. The taxpayer can also waive in writing some or all of the requirements regarding the contents of the Notice of Determination.

(3) *Examples.*—The following examples illustrate the principles of this paragraph (c):

Example 1. The IRS mails a CDP Notice of intent to levy to individual A's last known address on June 24, 1999. Individual A has until July 26, 1999, a Monday, to request a CDP hearing. The 30-day period within which individual A may request a CDP hearing begins on June 25, 1999. Because the 30-day period expires on July 24, 1999, a Saturday, individual A's written request for a CDP hearing will be considered timely if it is properly transmitted and addressed to the IRS in accordance with section 7502 and the regulations thereunder no later than July 26, 1999.

Example 2. Same facts as in *Example 1,* except that individual A is on vacation, outside the United States, or otherwise does not receive or read the CDP Notice until July 19, 1999. As in *Example 1,* individual A has until July 26, 1999, to request a CDP hearing. If individual A does not request a CDP hearing, individual A may request an equivalent hearing as to the levy at a later time. The taxpayer should make a request for an equivalent hearing at the earliest possible time.

Example 3. Same facts as in *Example 2,* except that individual A does not receive or read the CDP Notice until after July 26, 1999, and does not request a hearing by July 26, 1999. Individual A is not entitled to a CDP hearing. Individual A may request an equivalent hearing as to the levy at a later time. The taxpayer should make a request for an equivalent hearing at the earliest possible time.

Example 4. Same facts as in *Example 1,* except the IRS determines that the CDP Notice mailed on June 24, 1999, was not mailed to individual A's last known address. As soon as practicable after making this determination, the IRS will mail a substitute CDP Notice to individual A at individual A's last known address, hand deliver the substitute CDP Notice to individual A, or leave the substitute CDP Notice at individual A's dwelling or usual place of business. Individual A will have 30 days commencing on the day after the date of the substitute CDP Notice within which to request a CDP hearing.

(d) *Conduct of CDP hearing.*—(1) *In general.*—If a taxpayer requests a CDP hearing under section 6330(a)(3)(B) (and does not withdraw that request), the CDP hearing will be held with Appeals. The taxpayer is entitled to only one CDP hearing under section 6330 with respect to the unpaid tax and tax periods shown on the CDP Notice. To the extent practicable, the CDP hearing requested under section 6330 will be held in conjunction with any CDP hearing the taxpayer requests under section 6320. A CDP hearing will be conducted by an employee or officer of Appeals who, prior to the first CDP hearing under section 6320 or section 6330, has had no involvement with respect to the tax for the tax periods to be covered by the hearing, unless the taxpayer waives this requirement.

(2) *Questions and answers.*—The questions and answers illustrate the provisions of this paragraph (d) as follows:

Q-D1. Under what circumstances can a taxpayer receive more than one pre-levy CDP hearing under section 6330 with respect to a tax period?

A-D1. The taxpayer may receive more than one CDP pre-levy hearing under section 6330 with respect to a tax period where the tax involved is a different type of tax (for example, an employment tax liability, where the original CDP hearing for the tax period involved an income tax liability), or where the same type of tax for the same period is involved, but where the amount of the unpaid tax has changed as a result of an additional assessment of tax (not including interest or penalties) for that period or an additional accuracy-related or filing-delinquency penalty has been assessed. The taxpayer is not entitled to another CDP hearing under section

Reg. § 301.6330-1(d)(2)

6330 if the additional assessment represents accruals of interest, accruals of penalties, or both.

Q-D2. Will a CDP hearing with respect to one tax period be combined with a CDP hearing with respect to another tax period?

A-D2. To the extent practicable, a CDP hearing with respect to one tax period shown on a CDP Notice will be combined with any and all other CDP hearings which the taxpayer has requested.

Q-D3. Will a CDP hearing under section 6330 be combined with a CDP hearing under section 6320?

A-D3. To the extent it is practicable, a CDP hearing under section 6330 will be held in conjunction with a CDP hearing under section 6320.

Q-D4. What is considered to be prior involvement by an employee or officer of Appeals with respect to the tax and tax period or periods involved in the hearing?

A-D4. Prior involvement by an Appeals officer or employee includes participation or involvement in a matter (other than a CDP hearing held under either section 6320 or section 6330) that the taxpayer may have had with respect to the tax and tax period shown on the CDP Notice. Prior involvement exists only when the taxpayer, the tax and the tax period at issue in the CDP hearing also were at issue in the prior non-CDP matter, and the Appeals officer or employee actually participated in the prior matter.

Q-D5. How can a taxpayer waive the requirement that the officer or employee of Appeals have no prior involvement with respect to the tax and tax period or periods involved in the CDP hearing?

A-D5. The taxpayer must sign a written waiver.

Q-D6. How are CDP hearings conducted?

A-D6. The formal hearing procedures required under the Administrative Procedure Act, 5 U.S.C. 551 *et seq.*, do not apply to CDP hearings. CDP hearings are much like Collection Appeal Program (CAP) hearings in that they are informal in nature and do not require the Appeals officer or employee and the taxpayer, or the taxpayer's representative, to hold a face-to-face meeting. A CDP hearing may, but is not required to, consist of a face-to-face meeting, one or more written or oral communications between an Appeals officer or employee and the taxpayer or the taxpayer's representative, or some combination thereof. A transcript or recording of any face-to-face meeting or conversation between an Appeals officer or employee and the taxpayer or the taxpayer's representative is not required. The taxpayer or the taxpayer's representative does not have the right to subpoena and examine witnesses at a CDP hearing.

Q-D7. If a taxpayer wants a face-to-face CDP hearing, where will it be held?

A-D7. Except as provided in A-D8 of this paragraph (d)(2), a taxpayer who presents in the CDP hearing request relevant, non-frivolous reasons for disagreement with the proposed levy will ordinarily be offered an opportunity for a face-to-face conference at the Appeals office closest to taxpayer's residence. A business taxpayer will ordinarily be offered an opportunity for a face-to-face conference at the Appeals office closest to the taxpayer's principal place of business. If that is not satisfactory to the taxpayer, the taxpayer will be given an opportunity for a hearing by telephone or by correspondence. In all cases, the Appeals officer or employee will review the case file, as described in A-F4 of paragraph (f)(2). If no face-to-face or telephonic conference is held, or other oral communication takes place, review of the documents in the case file, as described in A-F4 of paragraph (f)(2), will constitute the CDP hearing for purposes of section 6330(b).

Q-D8. In what circumstances will a face-to-face CDP conference not be granted?

A-D8. A taxpayer is not entitled to a face-to-face CDP conference at a location other than as provided in A-D7 of this paragraph (d)(2) and this A-D8. If all Appeals officers or employees at the location provided for in A-D7 of this paragraph (d)(2) have had prior involvement with the taxpayer as provided in A-D4 of this paragraph (d)(2), the taxpayer will not be offered a face-to-face conference at that location, unless the taxpayer elects to waive the requirement of section 6330(b)(3). The taxpayer will be offered a face-to-face conference at another Appeals office if Appeals would have offered the taxpayer a face-to-face conference at the location provided in A-D7 of this paragraph (d)(2), but for the disqualification of all Appeals officers or employees at that location. A face-to-face CDP conference concerning a taxpayer's underlying liability will not be granted if the request for a hearing or other taxpayer communication indicates that the taxpayer wishes only to raise irrelevant or frivolous issues concerning that liability. A face-to-face CDP conference concerning a collection alternative, such as an installment agreement or an offer to compromise liability, will not be granted unless other taxpayers would be eligible for the alternative in similar circumstances. For example, because the IRS does not consider offers to compromise from taxpayers who have not filed required returns or have not made certain required deposits of tax, as set forth in Form 656, "Offer in Compromise," no face-to-face conference will be granted to a taxpayer who wishes to make an offer to compromise but has not fulfilled those obligations. Appeals in its discretion, however, may grant a face-to-face conference if Appeals determines that a face-to-face conference is appropriate to explain to the taxpayer the requirements for becoming eligible for a collection alternative. In all cases, a taxpayer will be given an opportunity to demonstrate eligibility for a collection alternative and to become eligible for a collection alternative, in order to obtain a face-to-face conference. For purposes of determining whether a face-to-face conference will be granted, the determination of a taxpayer's eligibility for a collection alternative is made without regard to the taxpayer's ability to pay the unpaid tax. A face-to-face conference need not be granted if the taxpayer does not provide the required information set forth in A-C1(ii)(E) of paragraph (c)(2). See also A-C1(iii) of paragraph (c)(2).

(3) *Examples.*—The following examples illustrate the principles of this paragraph (d):

Example 1. Individual A timely requests a CDP hearing concerning a proposed levy for the 1998 income tax liability assessed against individual A. Appeals employee B previously conducted a CDP hearing regarding a NFTL filed with respect to individual A's 1998 income tax liability. Because employee B's only prior involvement with individual A's 1998 income tax liability was in connection with a section 6320 CDP hearing, employee B may conduct the CDP hearing under section 6330 involving the proposed levy for the 1998 income tax liability.

Example 2. Individual C timely requests a CDP hearing concerning a proposed levy for the 1998 income tax liability assessed against individual C. Appeals employee D previously conducted a Collection Appeals Program (CAP) hearing regarding a NFTL filed with respect to individual C's 1998 income tax liability. Because employee D's prior involvement with individual C's 1998 income tax liability was in connection with a non-CDP hearing, employee D may not conduct the CDP hearing under section 6330 unless individual C waives the requirement that the hearing will be conducted by an Appeals officer or employee who has had no prior involvement with respect to individual C's 1998 income tax liability.

Example 3. Same facts as in *Example 2,* except that the prior CAP hearing only involved individual C's 1997 income tax liability and employment tax liabilities for 1998 reported on Form 941, "Employer's Quarterly Federal Tax Return." Employee D would not be considered to have prior involvement because the prior CAP hearing in which she participated did not involve individual C's 1998 income tax liability.

Example 4. Appeals employee F is assigned to a CDP hearing concerning a proposed levy for a trust fund recovery penalty (TFRP) assessed pursuant to section 6672 against individual E. Appeals employee F participated in a prior CAP hearing involving individual E's 1999 income tax liability, and participated in a CAP hearing involving the employment taxes of business entity X, which incurred the employment tax liability to which the TFRP assessed against individual E relates. Appeals employee F would not be considered to have prior involvement because the prior CAP hearings in which he participated did not directly involve the TFRP assessed against individual E.

Example 5. Appeals employee G is assigned to a CDP hearing concerning a proposed levy for a TFRP assessed pursuant to section 6672 against individual H. In preparing for the CDP hearing, Appeals employee G reviews the Appeals case file concerning the prior CAP hearing involving the TFRP assessed pursuant to section 6672 against individual H. Appeals employee G is not deemed to have participated in the previous CAP hearing involving the TFRP assessed against individual H by such review.

(e) *Matters considered at CDP hearing.*—(1) *In general.*—Appeals will determine the timeliness of any request for a CDP hearing that is made by a taxpayer. Appeals has the authority to determine the validity, sufficiency, and timeliness of any CDP Notice given by the IRS and of any request for a CDP hearing that is made by a taxpayer. Prior to issuance of a determination, Appeals is required to obtain verification from the IRS office collecting the tax that the requirements of any applicable law or administrative procedure with respect to the proposed levy have been met. The taxpayer may raise any relevant issue relating to the unpaid tax at the hearing, including appropriate spousal defenses, challenges to the appropriateness of the proposed levy, and offers of collection alternatives. The taxpayer also may raise challenges to the existence or amount of the underlying liability, including a liability reported on a self-filed return, for any tax period specified on the CDP Notice if the taxpayer did not receive a statutory notice of deficiency for that tax liability or did not otherwise have an opportunity to dispute the tax liability. Finally, the taxpayer may not raise an issue that was raised and considered at a previous CDP hearing under section 6320 or in any other previous administrative or judicial proceeding if the taxpayer participated meaningfully in such hearing or proceeding. Taxpayers will be expected to provide all relevant information requested by Appeals, including financial statements, for its consideration of the facts and issues involved in the hearing.

(2) *Spousal defenses.*—A taxpayer may raise any appropriate spousal defenses at a CDP hearing unless the Commissioner has already made a final determination as to spousal defenses in a statutory notice of deficiency or final determination letter. To claim a spousal defense under section 66 or section 6015, the taxpayer must do so in writing according to rules prescribed by the Commissioner or the Secretary. Spousal defenses raised under sections 66 and 6015 in a CDP hearing are governed in all respects by the provisions of sections 66 and section 6015 and the regulations and procedures thereunder.

(3) *Questions and answers.*—The questions and answers illustrate the provisions of this paragraph (e) as follows:

Q-E1. What factors will Appeals consider in making its determination?

A-E1. Appeals will consider the following matters in making its determination:

(i) Whether the IRS met the requirements of any applicable law or administrative procedure.

(ii) Any issues appropriately raised by the taxpayer relating to the unpaid tax.

(iii) Any appropriate spousal defenses raised by the taxpayer.

(iv) Any challenges made by the taxpayer to the appropriateness of the proposed collection action.

(v) Any offers by the taxpayer for collection alternatives.

(vi) Whether the proposed collection action balances the need for the efficient collection of taxes and the legitimate concern of the taxpayer that any collection action be no more intrusive than necessary.

Q-E2. When is a taxpayer entitled to challenge the existence or amount of the tax liability specified in the CDP Notice?

A-E2. A taxpayer is entitled to challenge the existence or amount of the underlying liability for any tax period specified on the CDP Notice if the taxpayer did not receive a statutory notice of deficiency for such liability or did not otherwise have an opportunity to dispute such liability. Receipt of a statutory notice of deficiency for this purpose means receipt in time to petition the Tax Court for a redetermination of the deficiency determined in the notice of deficiency. An opportunity to dispute the underlying liability includes a prior opportunity for a conference with Appeals that was offered either before or after the assessment of the liability. An opportunity for a conference with Appeals prior to the assessment of a tax subject to deficiency procedures is not a prior opportunity for this purpose.

Q-E3. Are spousal defenses subject to the limitations imposed under section 6330(c)(2)(B) on a taxpayer's right to challenge the tax liability specified in the CDP Notice at a CDP hearing?

A-E3. The limitations imposed under section 6330(c)(2)(B) do not apply to spousal defenses. When a taxpayer asserts a spousal defense, the taxpayer is not disputing the amount or existence of the liability itself, but asserting a defense to the liability which may or may not be disputed. A spousal defense raised under section 66 or section 6015 is governed by section 66 or section 6015 and the regulations and procedures thereunder. Any limitation under those sections, regulations, and procedures therefore will apply.

Q-E4. May a taxpayer raise at a CDP hearing a spousal defense under section 66 or section 6015 if that defense was raised and considered administratively and the Commissioner has issued a statutory notice of deficiency or final determination letter addressing the spousal defense?

A-E4. No. A taxpayer is precluded from raising a spousal defense at a CDP hearing when the Commissioner has made a final determination (under section 66 or section 6015) as to spousal defenses in a final determination letter or statutory notice of deficiency. However, a taxpayer may raise spousal defenses in a CDP hearing when the taxpayer has previously raised spousal defenses, but the Commissioner has not yet made a final determination regarding this issue.

Q-E5. May a taxpayer raise at a CDP hearing a spousal defense under section 66 or section 6015 if that defense was raised and considered in

a prior judicial proceeding that has become final?

A-E5. No. A taxpayer is precluded by the doctrine of res judicata and by the specific limitations under section 66 or section 6015 from raising a spousal defense in a CDP hearing under these circumstances.

Q-E6. What collection alternatives are available to the taxpayer?

A-E6. Collection alternatives include, for example, a proposal to withhold the proposed levy or future collection action in circumstances that will facilitate the collection of the tax liability, an installment agreement, an offer to compromise, the posting of a bond, or the substitution of other assets. A collection alternative is not available unless the alternative would be available to other taxpayers in similar circumstances. See A-D8 of paragraph (d)(2).

Q-E7. What issues may a taxpayer raise in a CDP hearing under section 6330 if the taxpayer previously received a notice under section 6320 with respect to the same tax and tax period and did not request a CDP hearing with respect to that notice?

A-E7. The taxpayer may raise appropriate spousal defenses, challenges to the appropriateness of the proposed collection action, and offers of collection alternatives. The existence or amount of the underlying liability for any tax period specified in the CDP Notice may be challenged only if the taxpayer did not have a prior opportunity to dispute the tax liability. If the taxpayer previously received a CDP Notice under section 6320 with respect to the same tax and tax period and did not request a CDP hearing with respect to that earlier CDP Notice, the taxpayer had a prior opportunity to dispute the existence or amount of the underlying tax liability.

Q-E8. How will Appeals issue its determination?

A-E8. (i) Taxpayers will be sent a dated Notice of Determination by certified or registered mail. The Notice of Determination will set forth Appeals' findings and decisions. It will state whether the IRS met the requirements of any applicable law or administrative procedure; it will resolve any issues appropriately raised by the taxpayer relating to the unpaid tax; it will include a decision on any appropriate spousal defenses raised by the taxpayer; it will include a decision on any challenges made by the taxpayer to the appropriateness of the collection action; it will respond to any offers by the taxpayer for collection alternatives; and it will address whether the proposed collection action represents a balance between the need for the efficient collection of taxes and the legitimate concern of the taxpayer that any collection action be no more intrusive than necessary. The Notice of Determination will also set forth any agreements that Appeals reached with the taxpayer, any relief given the taxpayer, and any actions the taxpayer or the IRS are required to take. Lastly, the Notice of Determination will advise the taxpayer of the taxpayer's right to seek judicial review within 30 days of the date of the Notice of Determination.

(ii) Because taxpayers are encouraged to discuss their concerns with the IRS office collecting the tax, certain matters that might have been raised at a CDP hearing may be resolved without the need for Appeals consideration. Unless, as a result of these discussions, the taxpayer agrees in writing to withdraw the request that Appeals conduct a CDP hearing, Appeals will still issue a Notice of Determination, but the taxpayer can waive in writing Appeals' consideration of some or all of the matters it would otherwise consider in making its determination.

Q-E9. Is there a period of time within which Appeals must conduct a CDP hearing or issue a Notice of Determination?

A-E9. No. Appeals will, however, attempt to conduct a CDP hearing and issue a Notice of Determination as expeditiously as possible under the circumstances.

Q-E10. Why is the Notice of Determination and its date important?

A-E10. The Notice of Determination will set forth Appeals' findings and decisions with respect to the matters set forth in A-E1 of this paragraph (e)(3). The 30-day period within which the taxpayer is permitted to seek judicial review of Appeals' determination commences the day after the date of the Notice of Determination.

Q-E11. If an Appeals officer considers the merits of a taxpayer's liability in a CDP hearing when the taxpayer had previously received a statutory notice of deficiency or otherwise had an opportunity to dispute the liability prior to the issuance of a notice of intention to levy, will the Appeals officer's determination regarding those liability issues be considered part of the Notice of Determination?

A-E11. No. An Appeals officer may consider the existence and amount of the underlying tax liability as a part of the CDP hearing only if the taxpayer did not receive a statutory notice of deficiency for the tax liability in question or otherwise have a prior opportunity to dispute the tax liability. Similarly, an Appeals officer may not consider any other issue if the issue was raised and considered at a previous hearing under section 6320 or in any other previous administrative or judicial proceeding in which the person seeking to raise the issue meaningfully participated. In the Appeals officer's sole discretion, however, the Appeals officer may consider the existence or amount of the underlying tax liability, or such other precluded issues, at the same time as the CDP hearing. Any determination, however, made by the Appeals officer with respect to such a precluded issue shall not be treated as part of the Notice of Determination issued by the Appeals officer and will not be subject to any judicial review. Because any decisions made by the Appeals officer on such precluded issues are not properly a part of the CDP hearing, such decisions are not required to appear in the Notice of Determination issued following the hearing. Even if a decision concerning such precluded issues is referred to in the Notice of Determination, it is not reviewable by the Tax Court because the precluded issue is not properly part of the CDP hearing.

(4) *Examples.*—The following examples illustrate the principles of this paragraph (e):

Example 1. The IRS sends a statutory notice of deficiency to the taxpayer at his last known address asserting a deficiency for the tax year 1995. The taxpayer receives the notice of deficiency in time to petition the Tax Court for a redetermination of the asserted deficiency. The taxpayer does not timely file a petition with the Tax Court. The taxpayer is precluded from challenging the existence or amount of the tax liability in a subsequent CDP hearing.

Example 2. Same facts as in *Example 1*, except the taxpayer does not receive the notice of deficiency in time to petition the Tax Court and did not have another prior opportunity to dispute the tax liability. The taxpayer is not precluded from challenging the existence or amount of the tax liability in a subsequent CDP hearing.

Example 3. The IRS properly assesses a trust fund recovery penalty against the taxpayer. The IRS offers the taxpayer the opportunity for a conference with Appeals at which the taxpayer would have the opportunity to dispute the assessed liability. The taxpayer declines the opportunity to participate in such a conference. The taxpayer is precluded from challenging the existence or amount of the tax liability in a subsequent CDP hearing.

(f) *Judicial review of Notice of Determination.*—(1) *In general.*—Unless the taxpayer provides the IRS a written withdrawal of the request that Appeals conduct a CDP hearing, Appeals is required to issue a Notice of Determination in all cases where a taxpayer has timely requested a CDP hearing. The taxpayer may appeal such determinations made by Appeals within the 30-day period commencing the day after the date of the Notice of Determination to the Tax Court.

(2) *Questions and answers.*—The questions and answers illustrate the provisions of this paragraph (f) as follows:

Q-F1. What must a taxpayer do to obtain judicial review of a Notice of Determination?

A-F1. Subject to the jurisdictional limitations described in A-F2 of this paragraph (f)(2), the taxpayer must, within the 30-day period commencing the day after the date of the Notice of Determination, appeal the determination by Appeals to the Tax Court.

Q-F2. With respect to the relief available to the taxpayer under section 6015, what is the time frame within which a taxpayer may seek Tax Court review of Appeals' determination following a CDP hearing?

A-F2. If the taxpayer seeks Tax Court review not only of Appeals' denial of relief under section 6015, but also of relief with respect to other issues raised in the CDP hearing, the taxpayer should request Tax Court review within the 30-day period commencing the day after the date of the Notice of Determination. If the taxpayer only seeks Tax Court review of Appeals' denial of relief under section 6015, the taxpayer should request review by the Tax Court, as provided by section 6015(e), within 90 days of Appeals' determination. If a request for Tax Court review is filed after the 30-day period for seeking judicial review under section 6330, then only the taxpayer's section 6015 claims may be reviewable by the Tax Court.

Q-F3. What issue or issues may the taxpayer raise before the Tax Court if the taxpayer disagrees with the Notice of Determination?

A-F3. In seeking Tax Court review of a Notice of Determination, the taxpayer can only ask the court to consider an issue, including a challenge to the underlying tax liability, that was properly raised in the taxpayer's CDP hearing. An issue is not properly raised if the taxpayer fails to request consideration of the issue by Appeals, or if consideration is requested but the taxpayer fails to present to Appeals any evidence with respect to that issue after being given a reasonable opportunity to present such evidence.

Q-F4. What is the administrative record for purposes of Tax Court review?

A-F4. The case file, including the taxpayer's request for hearing, any other written communications and information from the taxpayer or the taxpayer's authorized representative submitted in connection with the CDP hearing, notes made by an Appeals officer or employee of any oral communications with the taxpayer or the taxpayer's authorized representative, memoranda created by the Appeals officer or employee in connection with the CDP hearing, and any other documents or materials relied upon by the Appeals officer or employee in making the determination under section 6330(c)(3), will constitute the record in the Tax Court review of the Notice of Determination issued by Appeals.

(g) *Effect of request for CDP hearing and judicial review on periods of limitation and collection activity.*—(1) *In general.*—The periods of limitation under section 6502 (relating to collection after assessment), section 6531 (relating to criminal prosecutions), and section 6532 (relating to suits) are suspended until the date the IRS receives the taxpayer's written withdrawal of the request for a CDP hearing by Appeals or the determination resulting from the CDP hearing becomes final by expiration of the time for seeking judicial review or the exhaustion of any rights to appeals following judicial review. In no event shall any of these periods of limitation expire before the 90th day after the date on which the IRS receives the taxpayer's written withdrawal of the request that Appeals conduct a CDP hearing or the Notice of Determination with respect to such hearing becomes final upon either the expiration of the time for seeking judicial review or upon exhaustion of any rights to appeals following judicial review.

(2) *Questions and answers.*—The questions and answers illustrate the provisions of this paragraph (g) as follows:

Q-G1. For what period of time will the periods of limitation under section 6502, section 6531, and section 6532 remain suspended if the taxpayer timely requests a CDP hearing concerning a pre-levy or post-levy CDP Notice?

A-G1. The suspension period commences on the date the IRS receives the taxpayer's written request for a CDP hearing. The suspension period continues until the IRS receives a written withdrawal by the taxpayer of the request for a CDP hearing or the Notice of Determination resulting from the CDP hearing becomes final upon either the expiration of the time for seeking judicial review or upon exhaustion of any rights to appeals following judicial review. In no event shall any of these periods of limitation expire before the 90th day after the day on which there is a final determination with respect to such hearing. The periods of limitation that are suspended under section 6330 are those which apply to the taxes and the tax period or periods to which the CDP Notice relates.

Q-G2. For what period of time will the periods of limitation under section 6502, section 6531, and section 6532 be suspended if the taxpayer does not request a CDP hearing concerning the CDP Notice, or the taxpayer requests a CDP hearing, but his request is not timely?

A-G2. Under either of these circumstances, section 6330 does not provide for a suspension of the periods of limitation.

Q-G3. What, if any, enforcement actions can the IRS take during the suspension period?

A-G3. Section 6330(e) provides for the suspension of the periods of limitation discussed in paragraph (g)(1) of these regulations. Section 6330(e) also provides that levy actions that are the subject of the requested CDP hearing under that section shall be suspended during the same period. The IRS, however, may levy for other taxes and periods not covered by the CDP Notice if the CDP requirements under section 6330 for those taxes and periods have been satisfied. The IRS also may file NFTLs for tax periods and taxes, whether or not covered by the CDP Notice issued under section 6330, and may take other non-levy collection actions such as initiating judicial proceedings to collect the tax shown on the CDP Notice or offsetting overpayments from other periods, or of other taxes, against the tax shown on the CDP Notice. Moreover, the provisions in section 6330 do not apply when the IRS levies for the tax and tax period shown on the CDP Notice to collect a state tax refund due the taxpayer, or determines that collection of the tax is in jeopardy. Finally, section 6330 does not prohibit the IRS from accepting any voluntary payments made for the tax and tax period stated on the CDP Notice.

(3) *Examples.*—The following examples illustrate the principles of this paragraph (g):

Example 1. The period of limitation under section 6502 with respect to the taxpayer's tax period listed in the CDP Notice will expire on August 1, 1999. The IRS sent a CDP Notice to the taxpayer on April 30, 1999. The taxpayer timely requested a CDP hearing. The IRS received this request on May 15, 1999. Appeals sends the taxpayer its determination on June 15, 1999. The taxpayer timely seeks judicial review of that determination. The period of limitation under section 6502 would be suspended from May 15, 1999, until the determination resulting from that hearing becomes final by expiration of the time for seeking review or reconsideration before the Tax Court, plus 90 days.

Example 2. Same facts as in *Example 1*, except the taxpayer does not seek judicial review of Appeals' determination. Because the taxpayer requested the CDP hearing when fewer than 90 days remained on the period of limitation, the period of limitation will be extended to October 13, 1999 (90 days from July 15, 1999).

(h) *Retained jurisdiction of Appeals.*—(1) *In general.*—The Appeals office that makes a determination under section 6330 retains jurisdiction over that determination, including any subsequent administrative hearings that may be requested by the taxpayer regarding levies and any collection actions taken or proposed with respect to Appeals' determination. Once a taxpayer has exhausted his other remedies, Appeals' retained jurisdiction permits it to consider whether a change in the taxpayer's circumstances affects its original determination. Where a taxpayer alleges a change in circumstances that affects Appeals' original determination, Appeals may consider whether changed circumstances warrant a change in its earlier determination.

(2) *Questions and answers.*—The questions and answers illustrate the provisions of this paragraph (h) as follows:

Q-H1. Are the periods of limitation suspended during the course of any subsequent Appeals consideration of the matters raised by a taxpayer when the taxpayer invokes the retained jurisdiction of Appeals under section 6330(d)(2)(A) or (B)?

A-H1. No. Under section 6330(b)(2), a taxpayer is entitled to only one CDP hearing under section 6330 with respect to the tax and tax periods specified in the CDP Notice. Any subsequent consideration by Appeals pursuant to its retained jurisdiction is not a continuation of the original CDP hearing and does not suspend the periods of limitation.

Q-H2. Is a decision of Appeals resulting from a retained jurisdiction hearing appealable to the Tax Court?

A-H2. No. As discussed in A-H1, a taxpayer is entitled to only one CDP hearing under section 6330 with respect to the tax and tax period or periods specified in the CDP Notice. Only determinations resulting from CDP hearings are appealable to the Tax Court.

(i) *Equivalent hearing.*—(1) *In general.*—A taxpayer who fails to make a timely request for a CDP hearing is not entitled to a CDP hearing. Such a taxpayer may nevertheless request an administrative hearing with Appeals, which is referred to herein as an "equivalent hearing." The equivalent hearing will be held by Appeals and generally will follow Appeals procedures for a CDP hearing. Appeals will not, however, issue a Notice of Determination. Under such circumstances, Appeals will issue a Decision Letter.

(2) *Questions and answers.*—The questions and answers illustrate the provisions of this paragraph (i) as follows:

Q-I1. What must a taxpayer do to obtain an equivalent hearing?

A-I1. (i) A request for an equivalent hearing must be made in writing. A written request in any form that requests an equivalent hearing will be acceptable if it includes the information and signature required in A-I1(ii) of this paragraph (i)(2).

(ii) The request must be dated and must include the following:

(A) The taxpayer's name, address, daytime telephone number (if any), and taxpayer identification number (e.g., SSN, ITIN or EIN).

(B) The type of tax involved.

(C) The tax period at issue.

(D) A statement that the taxpayer is requesting an equivalent hearing with Appeals concerning the levy.

(E) The reason or reasons why the taxpayer disagrees with the proposed levy.

(F) The signature of the taxpayer or the taxpayer's authorized representative.

(iii) The taxpayer must perfect any timely written request for an equivalent hearing that does not satisfy the requirements set forth in A-I1(ii) of this paragraph (i)(2) within a reasonable period of time after a request from the IRS. If the requirements are not satisfied within a reasonable period of time, the taxpayer's equivalent hearing request will be denied.

(iv) The taxpayer must affirm any timely written request for an equivalent hearing that is signed or alleged to have been signed on the taxpayer's behalf by the taxpayer's spouse or other unauthorized representative, and that otherwise meets the requirements set forth in A-I1(ii) of this paragraph (i)(2), by filing, within a reasonable period of time after a request from the IRS, a signed written affirmation that the request was originally submitted on the taxpayer's behalf. If the affirmation is filed within a reasonable period of time after a request, the timely equivalent hearing request will be considered timely with respect to the non-signing taxpayer. If the affirmation is not filed within a reasonable period of time, the equivalent hearing request will be denied with respect to the non-signing taxpayer.

Q-I2. What issues will Appeals consider at an equivalent hearing?

A-I2. In an equivalent hearing, Appeals will consider the same issues that it would have considered at a CDP hearing on the same matter.

Q-I3. Are the periods of limitation under sections 6502, 6531, and 6532 suspended if the taxpayer does not timely request a CDP hearing and is subsequently given an equivalent hearing?

A-I3. No. The suspension period provided for in section 6330(e) relates only to hearings requested within the 30-day period that commences the day following the date of the pre-levy or post-levy CDP Notice, that is, CDP hearings.

Q-I4. Will collection action be suspended if a taxpayer requests and receives an equivalent hearing?

A-I4. Collection action is not required to be suspended. Accordingly, the decision to take collection action during the pendency of an equivalent hearing will be determined on a case-by-case basis. Appeals may request the IRS office with responsibility for collecting the taxes to suspend all or some collection action or to take other appropriate action if it determines that such action is appropriate or necessary under the circumstances.

Q-I5. What will the Decision Letter state?

A-I5. The Decision Letter will generally contain the same information as a Notice of Determination.

Q-I6. Will a taxpayer be able to obtain Tax Court review of a decision made by Appeals with respect to an equivalent hearing?

A-I6. Section 6330 does not authorize a taxpayer to appeal the decision of Appeals with respect to an equivalent hearing. A taxpayer may under certain circumstances be able to seek Tax Court review of Appeals' denial of relief under section 6015. Such review must be sought within 90 days of the issuance of Appeals' determination on those issues, as provided by section 6015(e).

Q-I7. When must a taxpayer request an equivalent hearing with respect to a CDP Notice issued under section 6330?

A-I7. A taxpayer must submit a written request for an equivalent hearing within the one-year period commencing the day after the date of the CDP Notice issued under section 6330. This period is slightly different from the period for submitting a written request for an equivalent hearing with respect to a CDP Notice issued under section 6320. For a CDP Notice issued under section 6320, a taxpayer must submit a written request for an equivalent hearing within the one-year period commencing the day after the end of the five-business-day period following the filing of the NFTL.

Q-I8. How will the timeliness of a taxpayer's written request for an equivalent hearing be determined?

A-I8. The rules and regulations under section 7502 and section 7503 will apply to determine the timeliness of the taxpayer's request for an equivalent hearing, if properly transmitted and addressed as provided in A-I10 of this paragraph (i)(2).

Q-I9. Is the one-year period within which a taxpayer must make a request for an equivalent hearing extended because the taxpayer resides outside the United States?

A-I9. No. All taxpayers who want an equivalent hearing must request the hearing within the one-year period commencing the day after the date of the CDP Notice issued under section 6330.

Q-I10. Where must the written request for an equivalent hearing be sent?

A-I10. The written request for an equivalent hearing must be sent, or hand delivered (if permitted), to the IRS office and address as directed on the CDP Notice. If the address of the issuing office does not appear on the CDP Notice, the taxpayer should obtain the address of the office to which the written request should be sent or hand delivered by calling, toll-free, 1-800-829-1040 and providing the taxpayer's identification number (e.g., SSN, ITIN or EIN).

Q-I11. What will happen if the taxpayer does not request an equivalent hearing in writing within the one-year period commencing the day after the date of the CDP Notice issued under section 6330?

A-I11. If the taxpayer does not request an equivalent hearing with Appeals within the one-year period commencing the day after the date of the CDP Notice issued under section 6330, the taxpayer foregoes the right to an equivalent hearing with respect to the unpaid tax and tax periods shown on the CDP Notice. A written request submitted within the one-year period that does not satisfy the requirements set forth in A-I1(ii) of this paragraph (i)(2) is considered timely if the request is perfected within a reasonable period of time pursuant to A-I1(iii) of this paragraph (i)(2). If a request for equivalent hearing is untimely, either because the request was not submitted within the one-year period or not perfected within the reasonable period provided, the equivalent hearing request will be denied. The taxpayer, however, may seek reconsideration by the IRS office collecting the tax, assistance from the National Taxpayer Advocate, or an administrative hearing before Appeals under its Collection Appeals Program or any successor program.

(j) *Effective date.*—This section is applicable on or after November 16, 2006 with respect to requests made for CDP hearings or equivalent hearings on or after November 16, 2006. [Reg. § 301.6330-1.]

☐ [*T.D.* 8980, 1-17-2002. *Amended by T.D.* 9291, 10-16-2006.]

[Reg. § 301.6331-1]

§ 301.6331-1. Levy and distraint.— (a) *Authority to levy.*—(1) *In general.*—If any person liable to pay any tax neglects or refuses to pay the tax within 10 days after notice and demand, the district director to whom the assessment is charged (or, upon his request, any other district director) may proceed to collect the tax by levy. The district director may levy upon any property, or rights to property, whether real or personal, tangible or intangible, belonging to the taxpayer. The district director may also levy upon property with respect to which there is a lien provided by section 6321 or 6324 for the payment of the tax. For exemption of certain property from levy, see section 6334 and the regulations thereunder. As used in section 6331 and this section, the term "tax" includes any interest, additional amount, addition to tax, or assessable penalty, together with costs and expenses. Property subject to a Federal tax lien which has been sold or otherwise transferred by the taxpayer may be seized while in the hands of the transferee or any subsequent transferee. However, see provisions under sections 6323 and 6324(a)(2) and (b) for protection of certain transferees against a Federal tax lien. Levy may be made by serving a notice of levy on any person in possession of, or obligated with respect to, property or rights to property subject to levy, including receivables, bank accounts, evidences of debt, securities, and salaries, wages, commissions, or other compensation. A levy on a bank reaches any interest that accrues on the taxpayer's balance under the terms of the bank's agreement with the depositor during the 21-day holding period provided for in section 6332(c). Except as provided in § 301.6331-1(b)(1) with regard to a levy on salary or wages, a levy extends only to property possessed and obligations which exist at the time of the levy. Obligations exist when the liability of the obligor is fixed and determinable although the right to receive payment thereof may be deferred until a later date. For example, if on the first day of the month a delinquent taxpayer sold personal property subject to an agreement that the buyer remit the purchase price on the last day of the month, a levy made on the buyer on the 10th day of the month would reach the amount due on the sale, although the buyer need not satisfy the levy by paying over the amount to the district director until the last day of the month. Similarly, a levy only reaches property in the possession of the person levied upon at the time the levy is made together with interest that accrues during the 21-day holding period provided for in section 6332(c). For example, a levy made on a bank with respect to the account of a delinquent taxpayer is satisfied if the bank surrenders the amount of the taxpayer's balance at the time the levy is made. The levy has no effect upon any subsequent deposit made in the bank by the taxpayer. Subsequent deposits may be reached only by a subsequent levy on the bank.

(2) *Jeopardy cases.*—If the district director finds that the collection of any tax is in jeopardy, he or she may make notice and demand for immediate payment of such tax and, upon failure or refusal to pay such tax, collection thereof by levy shall be lawful without regard to the 10-day period provided in section 6331(a), the 30-day period provided in section 6331(d), or the limitation on levy provided in section 6331(g)(1).

(3) *Bankruptcy or receivership cases.*—During a bankruptcy proceeding or a receivership proceeding in either a Federal or a State court, the assets of the taxpayer are in general under the control of the court in which such proceeding is pending. Taxes cannot be collected by levy upon assets in the custody of a court, whether or not such custody is incident to a bankruptcy or receivership proceeding, except where the proceeding has progressed to such a point that the levy would not interfere with the work of the court or where the court grants permission to levy. Any assets which under applicable provisions of law are not under the control of the court may be levied upon, for example, property exempt from court custody under State law or the bankrupt's earnings and property acquired after the date of bankruptcy. However, levy upon such property is not mandatory and the Government may rely upon payment of taxes in the proceeding.

(4) *Certain types of compensation.*—(i) *Federal employees.*—Levy may be made upon the salary or wages of any officer or employee (including members of the Armed Forces), or elected or appointed official, of the United States, the District of Columbia, or any agency or instrumentality of either, by serving a notice of levy on the employer of the delinquent taxpayer. As used in this subdivision, the term "employer" means (*a*) the officer or employee of the United States, the District of Columbia, or of the agency or instrumentality of the United States or the District of Columbia, who has control of the payment of the wages, or (*b*) any other officer or employee designated by the head of the branch, department, agency, or instrumentality of the United States or of the District of Columbia as the party upon whom service of the notice of levy may be made. If the head of such branch, department, agency, or instrumentality designates an officer or employee other than one who has control of the payment of the wages, as the party upon whom service of the notice of levy may be made, such head shall promptly notify the Commissioner of the name and address of each officer or employee so designated and the scope or extent of his authority as such designee.

(ii) *State and municipal employees.*—Salaries, wages, or other compensation of any officer, employee, or elected or appointed official of a State or Territory, or of any agency, instrumentality, or political subdivision thereof, are also subject to levy to enforce collection of any Federal tax.

(iii) *Seamen.*—Notwithstanding the provisions of section 12 of the Seamen's Act of 1915 (38 Stat. 1169; 46 U.S.C. 601), wages of seamen, apprentice seamen, or fishermen employed on fishing vessels are subject to levy. See section 6334(c).

(5) *Noncompetent Indians.*—Solely for purposes of sections 6321 and 6331, any interest in restricted land held in trust by the United States for an individual noncompetent Indian (and not

for a tribe) shall not be deemed to be property, or a right to property, belonging to such Indian.

(b) *Continuing levies and successive seizures.*—(1) *Continuing effect of levy on salary and wages.*—A levy on salary or wages has continuous effect from the time the levy originally is made until the levy is released pursuant to section 6343. For this purpose, the term *salary or wages* includes compensation for services paid in the form of fees, commissions, bonuses, and similar items. The levy attaches to both salary or wages earned but not yet paid at the time of the levy, advances on salary or wages made subsequent to the date of the levy, and salary or wages earned and becoming payable subsequent to the date of levy, until the levy is released pursuant to section 6343. In general, salaries or wages that are the subject of a continuing levy and are not exempt from levy under section 6334(a)(8) or (9), are to be paid to the district director, the service center director, or the compliance center director (director) on the same date the payor would otherwise pay over the money to the taxpayer. For example, if an individual normally is paid on the Wednesday following the close of each work week, a levy made upon his or her employer on any Monday would apply to both wages due for the prior work week and wages for succeeding work weeks as such wages become payable. In such a case, the levy would be satisfied if, on the first Wednesday after the levy and on each Wednesday thereafter until the employer receives a notice of release from levy described in section 6343, the employer pays over to the director wages that would otherwise be paid to the employee on such Wednesday (less any exempt amount pursuant to section 6334).

(2) *Successive seizures.*—Whenever any property or rights to property upon which a levy has been made are not sufficient to satisfy the claim of the United States for which the levy is made, the district director may thereafter, and as often as may be necessary, proceed to levy in like manner upon any other property or rights to property subject to levy of the person against whom such claim exists or on which there is a lien imposed by section 6321 or 6324 (or the corresponding provision of prior law) for the payment of such claim until the amount due from such person, together with all costs and expenses, is fully paid.

(c) *Service of notice of levy by mail.*—A notice of levy may be served by mailing the notice to the person upon whom the service of a notice of levy is authorized under paragraph (a)(1) of this section. In such a case the date and time the notice is delivered to the person to be served is the date and time the levy is made. If the notice is sent by certified mail, return receipt requested, the date of delivery on the receipt is treated as the date the levy is made. If, after receipt of a notice of levy, an officer or other person authorized to act on behalf of the person served signs and notes the date and time of receipt on the notice of levy, the date and time so noted will be presumed to

be, in the absence of proof to the contrary, the date and time of delivery. Any person may, upon written notice to the district director having audit jurisdiction over such person, have all notices of levy by mail sent to one designated office. After such a notice is received by the district director, notices of levy by mail will be sent to the designated office until a written notice withdrawing the request or a written notice designating a different office is received by the district director.

(d) *Effective date.*—These regulations are effective December 10, 1992. [Reg. § 301.6331-1.]

☐ [*T.D.* 6119, 12-31-54. *Amended by T.D.* 6498, 10-24-60; *T.D.* 7139, 8-11-71; *T.D.* 7180, 4-12-72; *T.D.* 7253, 2-23-73; *T.D.* 7620, 5-11-79; *T.D.* 7874, 3-8-83 *and T.D.* 8558, 7-29-94.]

[Reg. § 301.6331-2]

§ 301.6331-2. Procedures and restrictions on levies.—(a) *Notice of intent to levy.*—(1) *In general.*—Levy may be made upon the salary, wages, or other property of a taxpayer for any unpaid tax no less than 30 days after the district director, the service center director, or the compliance center director (director) has notified the taxpayer in writing of the intent to levy. The notice must be given in person, be left at the dwelling or usual place of business of the taxpayer, or be sent by registered or certified mail to the taxpayer's last known address. For further guidance regarding the definition of last known address, see § 301.6212-2. The notice of intent to levy is separate from, but may be given at the same time as, the notice and demand described in § 301.6331-1.

(2) *Content of Notice.*—The notice of intent to levy is to contain a brief statement in nontechnical terms including the following information—

(i) The Internal Revenue Code provisions and the procedures relating to levy and sale of property;

(ii) The administrative appeals available with respect to the levy and sale of property and the procedures relating to such appeals;

(iii) The alternatives available that could prevent levy on the property (including the use of an installment agreement under section 6159); and

(iv) The Internal Revenue Code provisions and the procedures relating to redemption of property and release of liens on property.

(b) *Uneconomical levy.*—(1) *In general.*—No levy may be made on property if the director estimates that the anticipated expenses with respect to the levy and sale will exceed the fair market value of the property. The estimate is to be made on an aggregate basis for all of the items that are anticipated to be seized pursuant to the levy. Generally, no levy should be made on individual items of insignificant monetary value. For the definition of fair market value, see § 301.6325-1(b)(1)(i). See § 301.6341-1 concerning the expenses of levy and sale.

(2) *Time of estimate.*—The estimate, which may be formal or informal, is to be made at the time of the seizure or within a reasonable period of time prior to a seizure. The estimate may be based on earlier estimates of fair market value and anticipated expenses of the same or similar property.

(3) *Examples.*—The following examples illustrate the application of this paragraph (b):

Example 1. A director anticipates that the taxpayer has only one item of property that can be seized and sold. This item is estimated to have a fair market value of $250.00. The director also estimates that the costs of seizure and sale will total $300.00 if this item is seized. The director is prohibited from levying on this one item of the taxpayer's property because the costs of seizure and sale are estimated to exceed the property's fair market value.

Example 2. The facts are the same as in *Example 1* except that the director anticipates that the taxpayer has 10 items of property that can be seized and sold. Each of those items is estimated to have a fair market value of $250.00. The director also estimates that the costs of seizure and sale will total $300.00 regardless of how many of those items are seized. The director is prohibited from levying on only one item of the taxpayer's property because the costs of seizure and sale are estimated to exceed the fair market value of the single item of property. The director, however, would not be prohibited from levying on two or more items of the taxpayer's property because the aggregate fair market value of the seized property would exceed the estimated costs of seizure and sale.

Example 3. The taxpayer has three items of property, A, B, and C. The director anticipates that the value of items A, B, and C depends on their being sold as a unit. The director estimates that due to high anticipated costs of storing or maintaining item B prior to the sale, the aggregate fair market value of items A, B, and C will not exceed the anticipated expenses of seizure and sale if all three items are seized. Accordingly, the director is prohibited from levying on items A, B, and C.

Example 4. The facts are the same as in *Example 3* except that the director does not anticipate that the value of items A, B, and C depends on those items being sold as a unit. If the director estimates that the aggregate fair market value of items A and C exceeds the aggregate anticipated costs of the seizure and sale of those two items, items A and C can be seized and sold. The director is prohibited from levying on item B because the high cost of storing or maintaining item B is estimated to exceed the fair market value of item B.

(c) *Restriction on levy on date of appearance.*—Except for continuing levies on salaries or wages described in § 301.6331-1(b)(1), no levy may be made on any property of a person on the day that person, or an officer or employee of that person, is required to appear in response to a summons served for the purpose of collecting any underpayment of tax from that person. For purposes of this paragraph (c), the date on which an appearance is required is the date fixed by an officer or employee of the Internal Revenue Service pursuant to section 7605 or the date (if any) fixed as the result of a judicial proceeding instituted under sections 7604 and 7402(b) seeking the enforcement of the summons.

(d) *Jeopardy.*—Paragraphs (a) and (c) of this section do not apply to a levy if the director finds, for purposes of § 301.6331-1(a)(2), that the collection of tax is in jeopardy.

(e) *Effective date.*—These regulations are effective December 10, 1992. [Reg. § 301.6331-2.]

☐ [*T.D. 7620, 5-11-79. Amended by T.D. 8558, 7-29-94 and T.D. 8939, 1-11-2001.*]

[Reg. § 301.6331-3]

§ 301.6331-3. Restrictions on levy while offers to compromise are pending.—*Cross-reference.* For provisions relating to the making of levies while an offer to compromise is pending, see § 301.7122-1.

☐ [*T.D. 9027, 12-17-2002.*]

[Reg. § 301.6331-4]

§ 301.6331-4. Restrictions on levy while installment agreements are pending or in effect.—(a) *Prohibition on levy.*—(1) *In general.*—No levy may be made to collect a tax liability that is the subject of an installment agreement during the period that a proposed installment agreement is pending with the Internal Revenue Service (IRS), for 30 days immediately following the rejection of a proposed installment agreement, during the period that an installment agreement is in effect, and for 30 days immediately following the termination of an installment agreement. If, within the 30 days following the rejection or termination of an installment agreement, the taxpayer files an appeal with the IRS Office of Appeals, no levy may be made while the rejection or termination is being considered by Appeals. This section will not prohibit levy to collect the liability of any person other than the person or persons named in the installment agreement.

(2) *When a proposed installment agreement becomes pending.*—A proposed installment agreement becomes pending when it is accepted for processing. The IRS may not accept a proposed installment agreement for processing following reference of a case involving the liability that is the subject of the proposed installment agreement to the Department of Justice for prosecution or defense. The proposed installment agreement remains pending until the IRS accepts the proposal, the IRS notifies the taxpayer that the proposal has been rejected, or the proposal is withdrawn by the taxpayer. If a proposed installment agreement that has been accepted for processing does not contain sufficient information to permit the IRS to evaluate whether the proposal should be accepted, the IRS will request

the taxpayer to provide the needed additional information. If the taxpayer does not submit the additional information that the IRS has requested within a reasonable time period after such a request, the IRS may reject the proposed installment agreement.

(3) *Revised proposals of installment agreements submitted following rejection.*—If, following the rejection of a proposed installment agreement, the taxpayer makes a good faith revision of the proposal and submits the revision within 30 days of the date of rejection, the provisions of this section shall apply to that revised proposal.

(4) *Exceptions.*—Paragraph (a)(1) of this section shall not prohibit levy if the taxpayer files a written notice with the IRS that waives the restriction on levy imposed by this section, the IRS determines that the proposed installment agreement was submitted solely to delay collection, or the IRS determines that collection of the tax to which the installment agreement or proposed installment agreement relates is in jeopardy.

(b) *Other actions by the IRS while levy is prohibited.*—(1) *In general.*—The IRS may take actions other than levy to protect the interests of the Government with regard to the liability identified in an installment agreement or proposed installment agreement. Those actions include, for example—

(i) Crediting an overpayment against the liability pursuant to section 6402;

(ii) Filing or refiling notices of Federal tax lien; and

(iii) Taking action to collect from any person who is not named in the installment agreement or proposed installment agreement but who is liable for the tax to which the installment agreement relates.

(2) *Proceedings in court.*—Except as otherwise provided in this paragraph (b)(2), the IRS will not refer a case to the Department of Justice for the commencement of a proceeding in court, against a person named in an installment agreement or proposed installment agreement, if levy to collect the liability is prohibited by paragraph (a)(1) of this section. Without regard to whether a person is named in an installment agreement or proposed installment agreement, however, the IRS may authorize the Department of Justice to file a counterclaim or third-party complaint in a refund action or to join that person in any other proceeding in which liability for the tax that is the subject of the installment agreement or proposed installment agreement may be established or disputed, including a suit against the United States under 28 U.S.C. 2410. In addition, the United States may file a claim in any bankruptcy proceeding or insolvency action brought by or against such person. If a person named in an installment agreement is joined in a proceeding, the United States obtains a judgment against that person, and the case is referred back to the IRS for collection, collection will continue to occur pursuant to the terms of the installment agreement.

(c) *Statute of limitations.*—(1) *Suspension of the statute of limitations on collection.*—The statute of limitations under section 6502 for collection of any liability shall be suspended during the period that a proposed installment agreement relating to that liability is pending with the IRS, for 30 days immediately following the rejection of a proposed installment agreement, and for 30 days immediately following the termination of an installment agreement. If, within the 30 days following the rejection or termination of an installment agreement, the taxpayer files an appeal with the IRS Office of Appeals, the statute of limitations for collection shall be suspended while the rejection or termination is being considered by Appeals. The statute of limitations for collection shall continue to run if an exception under paragraph (a)(4) of this section applies and levy is not prohibited with respect to the taxpayer.

(2) *Waivers of the statute of limitations on collection.*—The IRS may continue to request, to the extent permissible under section 6502 and § 301.6159-1, that the taxpayer agree to a reasonable extension of the statute of limitations for collection.

(d) *Cross-reference.*—For provisions relating to the making of levies while an installment agreement is pending or in effect, see § 301.6159-1.

(e) *Effective /applicability date.*—Paragraphs (a), (b), and (c) are applicable beginning December 18, 2002. Paragraph (d) is applicable beginning November 25, 2009. [Reg. § 301.6331-4.]

☐ [*T.D. 9027, 12-17-2002. Amended by T.D. 9473, 11-24-2009.*]

[Reg. § 301.6332-1]

§ 301.6332-1. Surrender of property subject to levy.—(a) *Requirement.*—(1) *In general.*—Except as otherwise provided in § 301.6332-2, relating to levy in the case of life insurance and endowment contracts, and in § 301.6332-3, relating to property held by banks, any person in possession of (or obligated with respect to) property or rights to property subject to levy and upon which a levy has been made shall, upon demand of the district director, surrender the property or rights (or discharge the obligation) to the district director, except that part of the property or rights (or obligation) which, at the time of the demand, is actually or constructively under the jurisdiction of a court because of an attachment or execution under any judicial process.

(2) *Levy on bank deposits held in offices outside the United States.*—Notwithstanding subparagraph (1) of this paragraph, if a levy has been made upon property or rights to property subject to levy which a bank engaged in the banking business in the United States or a possession of the United States is in possession of (or obligated with respect to), the Commissioner shall not enforce the levy with respect to any deposits held in an office of the bank outside the United States or a possession of the United States, unless the notice of levy specifies that the district director

intends to reach such deposits. The notice of levy shall not specify that the district director intends to reach such deposits unless the district director believes—

(i) That the taxpayer is within the jurisdiction of a United States court at the time the levy is made and that the bank is in possession of (or obligated with respect to) deposits of the taxpayer in an office of the bank outside the United States or a possession of the United States; or

(ii) That the taxpayer is not within the jurisdiction of a United States court at the time the levy is made, that the bank is in possession of (or obligated with respect to) deposits of the taxpayer in an office outside the United States or a possession of the United States, and that such deposits consist, in whole or in part, of funds transferred from the United States or a possession of the United States in order to hinder or delay the collection of a tax imposed by the Code.

For purposes of this subparagraph, the term "possession of the United States" includes Guam, the Midway Islands, the Panama Canal Zone, the Commonwealth of Puerto Rico, American Samoa, the Virgin Islands, and Wake Island.

(b) *Enforcement of levy.*—(1) *Extent of personal liability.*—Any person who, upon demand of the district director, fails or refuses to surrender any property or rights to property subject to levy is liable in his own person and estate in a sum equal to the value of the property or rights not so surrendered, together with costs and interest. The liability, however, may not exceed the amount of the taxes for the collection of which the levy was made. Interest is to be computed at the annual rate referred to in regulations under section 6621 from the date of the levy, or, in the case of a continuing levy on salary or wages (see section 6331(d)(3)), from the date the person would otherwise have been obligated to pay over the wages or salary to the taxpayer. Any amount recovered, other than costs, will be credited against the tax liability for the collection of which the levy was made.

(2) *Penalty for violation.*—In addition to the personal liability described in subparagraph (1) of this paragraph, any person who is required to surrender property or rights to property and who fails or refuses to surrender them without reasonable cause is liable for a penalty equal to 50 percent of the amount recoverable under section 6332(d)(1). No part of the penalty described in this subparagraph shall be credited against the tax liability for the collection of which the levy was made. The penalty described in this subparagraph is not applicable in cases where bona fide dispute exists concerning the amount of the property to be surrendered pursuant to a levy or concerning the legal effectiveness of the levy. However, if a court in a later enforcement suit sustains the levy, then reasonable cause would usually not exist to refuse to honor a later levy made under similar circumstances.

(c) *Effect of honoring levy.*—(1) *In general.*—Any person in possession of, or obligated with respect to, property or rights to property subject to levy and upon which a levy has been made who, upon demand by the district director, surrenders the property or rights to property, or discharges the obligation, to the district director, or who pays a liability described in paragraph (b)(1) of this section, is discharged from any obligation or liability to the delinquent taxpayer and any other person with respect to the property or rights to property arising from the surrender or payment.

(2) *Exception for certain incorrectly surrendered property.*—Any person who surrenders to the Internal Revenue Service property or rights to property not properly subject to levy in which the delinquent taxpayer has no apparent interest is not relieved of liability to a third party who has an interest in the property. However, if the delinquent taxpayer has an apparent interest in property or rights to property, a person who makes a good faith determination that such property or rights to property in his or her possession has been levied upon by the Internal Revenue Service and who surrenders the property to the United States in response to the levy is relieved of liability to a third party who has an interest in the property or rights to property, even if it is subsequently determined that the property was not properly subject to levy.

(3) *Remedy.*—In situations described in paragraphs (c)(1) and (c)(2) of this section, taxpayers and third parties who have an interest in property surrendered in response to a levy may secure from the Internal Revenue Service the administrative relief provided for in section 6343(b) or may bring suit to recover the property under section 7426.

(4) *Examples.*—The provisions of this paragraph (c) may be illustrated by the following examples:

Example 1. M Bank is served with a notice of levy for an unpaid tax liability due from A in the amount of $2,000. M Bank holds $2,000 in a checking account in the names of A or B or C. Although all of the deposits into the account were made by B and C, A has an unrestricted right to withdraw the funds from the account. M Bank surrenders the entire account to the district director at the end of the holding period provided in section 6332(c). Under paragraph (c)(1) of this section, M Bank is not liable to B or C for any amount, even if B or C prove that the funds in the account did not belong to A, because A's unrestricted right to withdraw the funds is an interest which is subject to levy. B or C may, however, seek the return of the funds from the United States as provided in sections 6343(b) and 7426 of the Internal Revenue Code.

Example 2. A is indebted to B for $400. Unbeknownst to A, B has assigned his right to receive payment to C. A is served with a notice of levy for an unpaid tax liability due from B for $400. A, acting with no knowledge of the assignment

Reg. §301.6332-1(c)(4)

to C, surrenders $400 to the district director. A is discharged from his obligation to pay B, the taxpayer. Under paragraph (c)(2) of this section, because B had an apparent interest in the funds that A owed to B, and because A determined in good faith that those funds had been levied upon, A is also discharged from any liability to C, even though the money is not properly subject to levy. C may, however, seek return of the payment from the United States as provided in sections 6343(b) and 7426 of the Internal Revenue Code.

Example 3. M Bank is served with a notice of levy for an unpaid tax liability due from "John H. Smith, Sr." in the amount of $5,000. M Bank fails to read the notice of levy carefully. When searching its records, M Bank finds the name of "John H. Smith, Jr." and looks no further. M Bank surrenders $5,000 from John H. Smith, Jr.'s checking account to the district director. M Bank is not discharged from liability under section 6332(e) of the Internal Revenue Code because the delinquent taxpayer (John H. Smith, Sr.) had no apparent interest in the account of John H. Smith, Jr. (Generally, John H. Smith Jr. may seek return of the payment from the United States as provided in sections 6343 and 7426 of the Internal Revenue Code.)

Example 4. M Bank is served with a notice of levy for an unpaid tax liability due from "Robert A. Jones" in the amount of $5,000. M Bank searches its records and identifies four separate accounts of $1,000 each in the name of "Robert A. Jones." All four accounts list different addresses and social security identification numbers. M Bank surrenders all four accounts totalling $4,000 in response to the levy. M Bank could not in good faith have determined that all four accounts were levied upon. Therefore, M Bank is not discharged from liability to any person other than the taxpayer whose account was levied upon.

(5) *Effective date.*—Paragraph (c) of this section is effective [January 11, 1993]. However, persons surrendering property to the Internal Revenue Service may rely on the regulations with respect to levies issued after November 10, 1988.

(d) *Person defined.*—The term "person," as used in section 6332(a) and this section, includes an officer or employee of a corporation or a member or employee of a partnership, who is under a duty to surrender the property or rights to property or to discharge the obligation. In the case of a levy upon the salary or wages of an officer, employee, or elected or appointed official of the United States, the District of Columbia, or any agency or instrumentality of either, the term "person" includes the officer or employee of the United States, of the District of Columbia, or of such agency or instrumentality who is under a duty to discharge the obligation. As to the officer or employee who is under such duty, see paragraph (a)(4)(i) of § 301.6331-1. [Reg. § 301.6332-1.]

☐ [*T.D.* 6119, 12-31-54. *Amended by T.D.* 6498, 10-24-60; *T.D.* 6746, 7-20-64; *T.D.* 7180, 4-12-72; *T.D.* 7384, 10-21-75; *T.D.* 7620, 5-11-79; *T.D.* 8466, 12-31-92 *and T.D.* 8467, 1-11-93.]

[Reg. § 301.6332-2]

§ 301.6332-2. Surrender of property subject to levy in the case of life insurance and endowment contracts.—(a) *In general.*—This section provides special rules relating to the surrender of property subject to levy in the case of life insurance and endowment contracts. The provisions of § 301.6332-1 which relate generally to the surrender of property subject to levy apply, to the extent not inconsistent with the special rules set forth in this section, to a levy in the case of life insurance and endowment contracts.

(b) *Effect of service of notice of levy.*—(1) *In general.*—(i) A notice of levy served by a district director on an insuring organization with respect to a life insurance or endowment contract issued by the organization shall constitute—

(A) A demand by the district director for the payment of the cash loan value of the contract adjusted in accordance with paragraph (c) of this section, and

(B) The exercise of the right of the person against whom the tax is assessed to the advance of such cash loan value.

(ii) It is unnecessary for the district director to surrender the contract document to the insuring organization upon which the levy is made. However, the notice of levy will include a certification by the district director that a copy of the notice of levy has been mailed to the person against whom the tax is assessed at his last known address. For further guidance regarding the definition of last known address, see § 301.6212-2. At the time of service of the notice of levy, the levy is effective with respect to the cash loan value of the insurance contract, subject to the condition that if the levy is not satisfied or released before the 90th day after the date of service, the levy can be satisfied only by payment of the amount described in paragraph (c) of this section. Other than satisfaction or release of the levy, no event during the 90-day period subsequent to the date of service of the notice of levy shall release the cash loan value from the effect of the levy. For example, the termination of the policy by the taxpayer or by the death of the insured during such 90-day period shall not release the levy. For the rules relating to the time when the insuring organization is to pay over the required amount, see paragraph (c) of this section.

(2) *Notification of amount subject to levy.*—(i) *Full payment before the 90th day.*—In the event that the unpaid liability to which the levy relates is satisfied at any time during the 90-day period subsequent to the date of service of the notice of levy, the district director will promptly give the insuring organization written notification that the levy is released.

(ii) *Notification after the 90th day.*—In the event that notification is not given under subdivision (i) of this subparagraph, the district director will, promptly following the 90th day after service of the notice of levy, give the insuring organization written notification of the current status of all accounts listed on the notice of levy, and of the total payments received since service of the notice of levy. This notification will be given to the insuring organization whether or not there has been any change in the status of the accounts.

(c) *Satisfaction of levy.*—(1) *In general.*—The levy described in paragraph (b) of this section with respect to a life insurance or endowment contract shall be deemed to be satisfied if the insuring organization pays over to the district director the amount which the person against whom the tax is assessed could have had advanced to him by the organization on the 90th day after service of the notice of levy on the organization. However, this amount is increased by the amount of any advance (including contractual interest thereon), generally called a policy loan, made to the person on or after the date the organization has actual notice or knowledge, within the meaning of section 6323 (i)(1), of the existence of the tax lien with respect to which the levy is made. The insuring organization may, nevertheless, make an advance (including contractual interest thereon), generally called an automatic premium loan, made automatically to maintain the contract in force under an agreement entered into before the organization has such actual notice or knowledge. In any event, the amount paid to the district director by the insuring organization is not to exceed the amount of the unpaid liability shown on the notification described in paragraph (b)(2) of this section. The amount, determined in accordance with the provisions of this section, subject to the levy shall be paid to the district director by the insuring organization promptly after receipt of the notification described in paragraph (b)(2). The satisfaction of a levy with respect to a life insurance or endowment contract will not discharge the contract from the tax lien. However, see section 6323(b)(9)(C) and the regulations thereunder concerning the liability of an insurance company after satisfaction of a levy with respect to a life insurance or endowment contract. If the person against whom the tax is assessed so directs, the insuring organization, on a date before the 90th day after service of the notice of levy, may satisfy the levy by paying over an amount computed in accordance with the provisions of this subparagraph substituting such date for the 90th day. In the event of termination of the policy by the taxpayer or by the death of the insured on a date before the 90th day after service of the notice of levy, the amount to be paid over to the district director by the insuring organization in satisfaction of the levy shall be an amount computed in accordance with the provisions of this subparagraph substituting the date of termination of the policy or the date of death for the 90th day.

(2) *Examples.*—The provisions of this section may be illustrated by the following examples:

Example (1). On March 5, 1968, a notice of levy for an unpaid income tax assessment due from A in the amount of $3,000 is served on the X Insurance Company with respect to A's life insurance policy. On March 5, 1968, the cash loan value of the policy is $1,500. On April 9, 1968, A does not pay a premium due on the policy in the amount of $200. Under an automatic premium advance provision contained in the policy originally issued in 1960, X advances the premium out of the cash value of the policy. As of June 3, 1968 (the 90th day after service of the notice of levy), pursuant to the provisions of the policy, the amount of accrued charges upon the automatic premium advance in the amount of $200 for the period April 9, 1968, through June 3, 1968, is $2. On June 5, 1968, the district director gives written notification to X indicating that A's unpaid tax assessment is $2,500. Under this section, X is required to pay to the district director, promptly after receipt of the June 5, 1968, notification, the sum of $1,298 ($1,500 less $200 less $2), which is the amount A could have had advanced to him by X on June 3, 1968.

Example (2). Assume the same facts as in example (1) except that on May 10, 1968, A requests and X grants an advance in the amount of $1,000. X has actual notice of the existence of the lien by reason of the service of the notice of levy on March 5, 1968. This advance is not required to be made automatically under the policy and reduces the amount of the cash value of the policy. For the use of the $1,000 advance during the period May 10, 1968, through June 3, 1968, X charges A the sum of $3. Under this section, X is required to pay to the district director, promptly after receipt of the June 5, 1968, notification, the sum of $1,298. This $1,298 amount is composed of the $295 amount ($1,500 less $200 less $2 less $1,000 less $3) A could have had advanced to him by X on June 3, 1968, plus the $1,000 advance plus the charges in the amount of $3 with respect thereto.

Example (3). Assume the same facts as in example (1) except that the insurance contract does not contain an automatic premium advance provision. The contract does provide that, upon default in the payment of premiums, the policy shall automatically be converted to paid-up term insurance with no cash or loan value. A fails to make the premium payment of $200 due on April 9, 1968. After expiration of a grace period to make the premium payment, the X Insurance Company applies the cash loan value of $1,500 to effect the conversion. Since the service of the notice of levy constitutes the exercise of A's right to receive the cash loan value and the amount applied to effect the conversion is not an automatic advance to A to maintain the policy in force, the conversion of the policy is not an event which will release the cash loan value from the effect of the levy. Therefore, X Insurance Company is required to pay to the district director, promptly after receipt of the June 5, 1968 notification, the sum of $1,500.

(d) *Other enforcement proceedings.*—The satisfaction of the levy described in paragraph (b) of this section by an insuring organization shall be without prejudice to any civil action for the enforcement of any Federal tax lien with respect to a life insurance or endowment contract. Thus, this levy procedure is not the exclusive means of subjecting the life insurance and endowment contracts of the person against whom a tax is assessed to the collection of his unpaid assessment. The United States may choose to foreclose the tax lien in any case where it is appropriate, as, for example, to reach the cash surrender value (as distinguished from cash loan value) of a life insurance or endowment contract.

(e) *Cross references.*—(1) For provisions relating to priority of certain advances with respect to a life insurance or endowment contract after satisfaction of a levy pursuant to section 6332(b), see section 6323(b)(9) and the regulations thereunder.

(2) For provisions relating to the issuance of a certificate of discharge of a life insurance or endowment contract subject to a tax lien, see section 6325(b) and the regulations thereunder. [Reg. § 301.6332-2.]

☐ [*T.D.* 7180, 4-12-72. *Amended by T.D.* 8939, 1-11-2001.]

[Reg. § 301.6332-3]

§ 301.6332-3. The 21-day holding period applicable to property held by banks.—(a) *In general.*—This section provides special rules relating to the surrender, after 21 days, of deposits subject to levy which are held by banks. The provisions of § 301.6332-1 which relate generally to the surrender of property subject to levy apply, to the extent not inconsistent with the special rules set forth in this section, to a levy on property held by banks.

(b) *Definition of bank.*—For purposes of this section, the term "bank" means—

(1) A bank or trust company or domestic building and loan association incorporated and doing business under the laws of the United States (including laws relating to the District of Columbia) or of any State, a substantial part of the business of which consists of receiving deposits and making loans and discounts, or of exercising fiduciary powers similar to those permitted to national banks under authority of the Comptroller of the Currency, and which is subject by law to supervision and examination by State or Federal authority having supervision over banking institutions;

(2) Any credit union the member accounts of which are insured in accordance with the provisions of title II of the Federal Credit Union Act, 12 U.S.C. 1781 et seq.; and

(3) A corporation which, under the laws of the State of its incorporation, is subject to super-

vision and examination by the Commissioner of Banking or other officer of such State in charge of the administration of the banking laws of such State.

(c) *21-day holding period.*—(1) *In general.*—When a levy is made on deposits held by a bank, the bank shall surrender such deposits (not otherwise subject to an attachment or execution under judicial process) only after 21 calendar days after the date the levy is made. The district director may request an extension of the 21-day holding period pursuant to paragraph (d)(2) of this section. During the prescribed holding period, or any extension thereof, the levy shall be released only upon notification to the bank by the district director of a decision by the Internal Revenue Service to release the levy. If the bank does not receive such notification from the district director within the prescribed holding period, or any extension thereof, the bank must surrender the deposits, including any interest thereon as determined in accordance with paragraph (c)(2) of this section (up to the amount of the levy), on the first business day after the holding period, or any extension thereof, expires. See § 301.6331-1(c) to determine when a levy served by mail is made.

(2) *Payment of interest on deposits.*—When a bank surrenders levied deposits at the end of the 21-day holding period (or at the end of any longer period that has been requested by the district director), the bank must include any interest that has accrued on the deposits prior to and during the holding period, and any extension thereof, under the terms of the bank's agreement with its depositor, but the bank must not surrender an amount greater than the amount of the levy. If the deposits are held in a non-interest bearing account at the time the levy is made, the bank need not include any interest on the deposits at the end of the holding period, or any extension thereof, under this paragraph. Interest that accrues on deposits and is surrendered to the district director at the end of the holding period, or any extension thereof, is treated as a payment to the bank's customer.

(3) *Transactions affecting accounts.*—A levy on deposits held by a bank applies to those funds on deposit at the time the levy is made, up to the amount of the levy, and is effective as of the time the levy is made. No withdrawals may be made on levied upon deposits during the 21-day holding period, or any extension thereof.

(4) *Waiver of 21-day holding period.*—A depositor may waive the 21-day holding period by notifying the bank of the depositor's intention to do so. Where more than one depositor is listed as the owner of a levied account, all depositors listed as owners of the account must agree to a waiver of the 21-day holding period. If the 21-day holding period is waived, the bank must include with the surrendered deposits a notification to the district director of the waiver.

(5) *Examples.*—The provisions of this paragraph (c) may be illustrated by the following examples:

Example 1. On April 2, 1992, a notice of levy for an unpaid income tax assessment due from A in the amount of $10,000 is served on X Bank with respect to A's savings account. At the time the notice of levy is served, X Bank holds $5,000 in A's interest-bearing savings account. On April 24, 1992, (the first business day after the 21-day holding period) X Bank must surrender $5,000 plus any interest that accrued on the account under the terms of A's contract with X Bank up through April 23, 1992 (the last day of the holding period).

Example 2. The facts are the same as in *Example 1* except that on April 3, 1992, A deposits an additional $5,000 into the account. On April 24, 1992, X Bank must still surrender only $5,000 plus the interest which accrued thereon until the end of the holding period, because the notice of levy served on April 2, 1992, attached only to those funds on deposit at the time the notice was served and not to any subsequent deposits.

Example 3. The facts are the same as in *Example 1* except that at the time the notice of levy is served on X Bank, A's savings account contains $50,000. On April 24, 1992, X Bank must surrender $10,000, which is the amount of the levy. The levy will not apply to any interest that accrues on the deposit during the 21-day holding period, because the entire amount of the levy is satisfied by the deposits existing at the time the levy is served.

Example 4. The facts are the same as in *Example 1* except that the amount of the levy is $5,002. Under the terms of A's contract with the bank, the account will earn more than $2 of interest during the 21-day holding period. On April 24, 1992, X Bank must surrender $5,002 to the district director. The remaining interest which accrued during the 21-day holding period is not subject to the levy.

Example 5. On September 3, 1992, A opens a $5,000 six-month certificate of deposit account with X Bank. Under the terms of the account, the depositor must forfeit up to 30 days of interest on the account in the event of early withdrawal. On January 4, 1993, a notice of levy for an unpaid income tax assessment due from A in the amount of $10,000 is served with respect to A's certificate of deposit account. On January 26, 1993, the bank must surrender $5,000 plus the interest which accrued on the account through January 25, 1993, minus the penalty of 30 days of interest as provided in the deposit agreement.

Example 6. Same facts as in *Example 5* except that the notice of levy is served on X Bank on February 15, 1993. The certificate matures on March 2, 1993. On March 8, X Bank must surrender $5,000 plus the interest that accrued on the certificate without any reduction for penalties.

(d) *Notification to the district director of errors with respect to levied upon bank accounts.*—(1) *In general.*—If a depositor believes that there is an error with respect to the levied upon account which the depositor wishes to have corrected, the depositor shall notify the district director to whom the assessment is charged by telephone to the telephone number listed on the face of the notice of levy in order to enable the district director to conduct an expeditious review of the alleged error. The district director may require any supporting documentation necessary to the review of the alleged error. The notification by telephone provided for in this section does not constitute or substitute for the filing by a third party of a written request under §301.6343-1(b)(2) for the return of property wrongfully levied upon.

(2) *Disputes regarding the merits of the underlying assessment.*—This section does not constitute an additional procedure for an appeal regarding the merits of an underlying assessment. However, if in the judgment of the district director a genuine dispute regarding the merits of an underlying assessment appears to exist, the district director may request an extension of the 21-day holding period.

(3) *Notification of errors from sources other than the depositor.*—The district director may take action to release the levy on the bank account based on information obtained from a source other than the depositor, including the bank in which the account is maintained.

(e) *Effective date.*—These provisions are effective with respect to levies issued on or after January 4, 1993. [Reg. §301.6332-3.]

☐ [*T.D.* 8466, 12-31-92.]

[Reg. §301.6333-1]

§301.6333-1. Production of books.—If a levy has been made or is about to be made on any property or rights to property, any person, having custody or control of any books or records containing evidence or statements relating to the property or rights to property subject to levy, shall, upon demand of the internal revenue officer who has made or is about to make the levy, exhibit such books or records to such officer. [Reg. §301.6333-1.

☐ [*T.D.* 6119, 12-31-54.]

[Reg. §301.6334-1]

§301.6334-1. Property exempt from levy.—(a) *Enumeration.*—In addition to exemptions allowed as a matter of Internal Revenue Service policy, there shall be exempt from levy—

(1) *Wearing apparel and school books.*—Such items of wearing apparel and such school books as are necessary for the taxpayer or for members of his family. Expensive items of wearing apparel, such as furs, which are luxuries and are not necessary for the taxpayer or for members of his family, are not exempt from levy.

(2) *Fuel, provisions, furniture, and personal effects.*—So much of the fuel, provisions, furniture, and personal effects in the taxpayer's household, and of the arms for personal use, livestock, and

poultry of the taxpayer, that does not exceed $6,250 in value.

(3) *Books and tools of a trade, business or profession.*—So many of the books and tools necessary for the trade, business, or profession of an individual taxpayer as do not exceed in the aggregate $3,125 in value.

(4) *Unemployment benefits.*—Any amount payable to an individual with respect to his unemployment (including any portion thereof payable with respect to dependents) under an unemployment compensation law of the United States, of any State, or of the District of Columbia or of the Commonwealth of Puerto Rico.

(5) *Undelivered mail.*—Mail, addressed to any person, which has not been delivered to the addressee.

(6) *Certain annuity and pension payments.*—Annuity or pension payments under the Railroad Retirement Act (45 U.S.C. ch. 9), benefits under the Railroad Unemployment Insurance Act (45 U.S.C. ch. 11), special pension payments received by a person whose name has been entered on the Army, Navy, Air Force, and Coast Guard Medal of Honor roll (38 U.S.C. 562), and annuities based on retired or retainer pay under chapter 73 of title 10 of the United States Code.

(7) *Workmen's compensation.*—Any amount payable to an individual as workmen's compensation (including any portion thereof payable with respect to dependents) under a workmen's compensation law of the United States, any State, the District of Columbia, or the Commonwealth of Puerto Rico.

(8) *Judgments for support of minor children.*—If the taxpayer is required under any type of order or decree (including an interlocutory decree or a decree of support pendente lite) of a court of competent jurisdiction, entered prior to the date of levy, to contribute to the support of that taxpayer's minor children, so much of that taxpayer's salary, wages, or other income as is necessary to comply with such order or decree. The taxpayer must establish the amount necessary to comply with the order or decree. The Service is not required to release a levy until such time as it is established that the amount to be released from levy actually will be applied in satisfaction of the support obligation. The Service may make arrangements with a delinquent taxpayer to establish a specific amount of such taxpayer's salary, wage, or other income for each pay period that shall be exempt from levy, for purposes of complying with a support obligation. If the taxpayer has more than one source of income sufficient to satisfy the support obligation imposed by the order or decree, the amount exempt from levy, at the discretion of the Service, may be allocated entirely to one salary, wage or source of other income or be apportioned between the several salaries, wages, or other sources of income.

(9) *Minimum exemption for wages, salary, and other income.*—Amounts payable to or received by the taxpayer as wages or salary for personal services, or as other income, to the extent provided in § 301.6334-2 through § 301.6334-4.

(10) *Certain service-connected disability payments.*—Any amount payable to an individual as a service-connected (within the meaning of section 101(16) of title 38, United States Code (U.S.C.)) disability benefit under—

(i) Subchapters II (wartime disability compensation), III (wartime death compensation), IV (peacetime disability compensation), V (peacetime death compensation), or VI (general compensation provisions) of chapter 11 of title 38, U.S.C.; or

(ii) Chapters 13 (dependency and indemnity compensation for service commenced deaths), 21 (specially adapted housing for disabled veterans), 23 (burial benefits), 31 (vocational rehabilitation), 32 (post-Vietnam era veterans' educational assistance), 34 (veterans' educational assistance), 35 (survivors' and dependents' educational assistance), 37 (home, condominium, and mobile home loans), or 39 (automobiles and adaptive equipment for certain disabled veterans and members of the armed forces) of title 38, U.S.C.

(11) *Certain public assistance payments.*—Any amount payable to an individual as a recipient of public assistance under—

(i) Title IV or title XVI (relating to supplemental security income for the aged, blind, and disabled) of the Social Security Act, (42 U.S.C. 301 et seq.); or

(ii) State or local government public assistance or public welfare programs for which eligibility is determined by a needs or income test.

(12) *Assistance under Job Training Partnership Act.*—Any amount payable to a participant under the Job Training Partnership Act (29 U.S.C. 1501 et seq.) from funds appropriated pursuant to such Act.

(13) *Residences exempt in small deficiency cases and principal residences and certain business assets exempt in absence of certain approval or jeopardy.*—(i) *Residences in small deficiency cases.* If the amount of the levy does not exceed $5,000, any real property used as a residence of the taxpayer or any real property of the taxpayer (other than real property which is rented) used by any other individual as a residence.

(ii) *Principal residences and certain business assets.* Except to the extent provided in section 6334(e), the principal residence (within the meaning of section 121) of the taxpayer and tangible personal property or real property (other than real property which is rented) used in the trade or business of an individual taxpayer.

(b) *Appraisal.*—The internal revenue officer seizing property of the type described in section 6334(a) shall appraise and set aside to the owner the amount of such property declared to be exempt. If the taxpayer objects at the time of the

Seizure of Property For Collection of Taxes
66,997
See p. 20,601 for regulations not amended to reflect law changes

seizure to the valuation fixed by the officer making the seizure, such officer shall summon three disinterested individuals who shall make the valuation.

(c) *Other property.*—No other property or rights to property are exempt from levy except the property specifically exempted by section 6334(a). No provision of a State law may exempt property or rights to property from levy for the collection of any Federal tax. Thus, property exempt from execution under State personal or homestead exemption laws is, nevertheless, subject to levy by the United States for collection of its taxes.

(d) *Levy allowed on principal residence.*—The Service will seek approval, in writing, by a judge or magistrate of a district court of the United States prior to levy of property that is owned by the taxpayer and used as the principal residence of the taxpayer, the taxpayer's spouse, the taxpayer's former spouse, or the taxpayer's minor child.

(1) *Nature of judicial proceeding.*—The Government will initiate a proceeding for judicial approval of levy on a principal residence by filing a petition with the appropriate United States District Court demonstrating that the underlying liability has not been satisfied, the requirements of any applicable law or administrative procedure relevant to the levy have been met, and no reasonable alternative for collection of the taxpayer's debt exists. The petition will ask the court to issue to the taxpayer an order to show cause why the principal residence property should not be levied and will also ask the court to issue a notice of hearing.

(2) The taxpayer will be granted a hearing to rebut the Government's prima facie case if the taxpayer files an objection within the time period required by the court raising a genuine issue of material fact demonstrating that the underlying tax liability has been satisfied, that the taxpayer has other assets from which the liability can be satisfied, or that the Service did not follow the applicable laws or procedures pertaining to the levy. The taxpayer is not permitted to challenge the merits underlying the tax liability in the proceeding. Unless the taxpayer files a timely and appropriate objection, the court would be expected to enter an order approving the levy of the principal residence property.

(3) *Notice letter to be issued to certain family members.*—If the property to be levied is owned by the taxpayer but is used as the principal residence of the taxpayer's spouse, the taxpayer's former spouse, or the taxpayer's minor child, the Government will send a letter to each such person providing notice of the commencement of the proceeding. The letter will be addressed in the name of the taxpayer's spouse or exspouse, individually or on behalf of any minor children. If it is unclear who is living in the principal residence property and/or what such person's relationship is to the taxpayer, a letter will be addressed to "Occupant". The purpose of the letter is to provide notice to the family members that the property may be levied. The family members may not be joined as parties to the judicial proceeding because the levy attaches only to the taxpayer's legal interest in the subject property and the family members have no legal standing to contest the proposed levy.

(e) *Levy allowed on certain business assets.*—The property described in section 6334(a)(13)(B)(ii) shall not be exempt from levy if—

(1) An Area Director of the Service personally approves (in writing) the levy of such property; or

(2) The Secretary finds that the collection of tax is in jeopardy. An Area Director may not approve a levy under paragraph (e)(1) unless the Area Director determines that the taxpayer's other assets subject to collection are insufficient to pay the amount due, together with expenses of the proceeding. When other assets of an individual taxpayer include permits issued by a State and required under State law for the harvest of fish or wildlife in the taxpayer's trade or business, the taxpayer's other assets also include future income that may be derived by such taxpayer from the commercial sale of fish or wildlife under such permit.

(f) *Levy allowed on certain specified payments.*—Any payment described in section 6331(h)(2)(B) or (C) shall not be exempt from levy if the Secretary approves the levy thereon under section 6331(h).

(g) *Inflation adjustment.*—For any calendar year beginning after 1999, each dollar amount referred to in paragraphs (a)(2) and (3) of this section will be increased by an amount equal to the dollar amount multiplied by the cost-of-living adjustment determined under section 1(f)(3) for the calendar year (using the language "calendar year 1998" instead of "calendar year 1992" in section 1(f)(3)(B)). If any dollar amount as adjusted is not a multiple of $10, the dollar amount will be rounded to the nearest multiple of $10 (rounding up if the amount is a multiple of $5).

(h) *Effective date.*—This section is generally effective with respect to levies made on or after July 1, 1989. However, any reasonable attempt by a taxpayer to comply with the statutory amendments addressed by the regulations in this section prior to February 21, 1995, will be considered as meeting the requirements of the regulations in this section. In addition, paragraph (a)(11)(i) of this section is applicable with respect to levies issued after December 31, 1996. Paragraphs (a)(2), (a)(3), (a)(8), (a)(13), (d), (e), (f), (g) and (h) of this section apply as of March 7, 2005. [Reg. § 301.6334-1.]

☐ [T.D. 6119, 12-31-54. *Amended by* T.D. 6292, 4-18-58; T.D. 6425, 11-10-59; T.D. 6498, 10-24-60; T.D. 6870, 12-30-65; T.D. 7180, 4-12-72; T.D. 7182, 4-20-72; T.D 7620, 5-11-79; T.D. 8568, 10-20-94; T.D. 8725, 7-21-97 and T.D. 9189, 3-4-2005.]

[Reg. §301.6334-2]

§301.6334-2. Wages, salary and other income.—(a) *In general.*—Under section 6334(a)(9) and (d) certain amounts payable to or received by a taxpayer as wages, salary, or other income are exempt from levy. This section describes the income of a taxpayer that is eligible for the exemption from levy (paragraph (b) of this section) and how exempt amounts are to be paid to the taxpayer(paragraph (c) of this section). Section 301.6334-3 describes that sum that will be exempt from levy for each of the taxpayer's pay periods. Pay periods are described in §301.6334-3. For the amounts exempt from levy, see §301.6334-3.

(b) *Eligible taxpayer income.*—Only wages, salary, or other income payable to the taxpayer after the levy is made on the payor may be exempt from levy under section 6334(a)(9). No amount of wages, salary, or other income that is paid to the taxpayer before levy is made on the payor will be so exempt from levy under section 6334(a)(9). The provisions of this paragraph (b) may be illustrated by the following example:

Example. Delinquent taxpayer A, an individual, is employed by the M Corporation and is paid wages on Friday of each week. Accordingly, A is paid wages on Friday, February 16, 1990. On Saturday, February 17, A deposits these wages into his personal checking account at Bank N. On Tuesday, February 20, a notice of levy is served on the M Corporation and also on Bank N. Amounts payable to A as wages on Friday, February 23, 1990, and any payday thereafter may be exempt from levy under section 6334(a)(9). No amount of wages A deposited in his account at Bank N on February 17, 1990, is exempt from levy under section 6334(a)(9).

(c) *Payment of exempt amounts to taxpayer.*—(1) *From wages, salary, or income from other sources where levy on all sources not made.*—In the case of a taxpayer who has more than one source of wages, salary, or other income, the district director may elect to levy on only one or more sources while leaving other sources of income free from levy. If the wages, salary, or other income that the district director leaves free from levy equal or exceed the amount to which the taxpayer is entitled as an exemption from levy under section 6334(a)(9), computed in accordance with §301.6334-3 (and are not otherwise exempt), the district director may treat no amount of the taxpayer's wages, salary, or other income on which the district director elects to levy as exempt from levy. In such a case, the district director must notify the employer or other person upon whom the levy is served that no amount of the taxpayer's wages, salary, or other income is exempt from levy. The employer or other person upon whom the levy is served may rely on such notification in paying over amounts pursuant to the levy. In the absence of such notification from the district director, however, the employer or other person upon whom the levy is served must determine the amount exempt from levy pursuant

to §301.6334-3 as if that employer or other person upon whom the levy is served is the only source of wages, salary, or other income. Amounts not exempt from levy are to be paid to the district director in accordance with the terms of the levy. The provisions of this paragraph (c)(1) may be illustrated by the following example:

Example. Delinquent taxpayer C is an employee of O Corporation and is paid wages totalling $450 on Friday of each week. C also performs services for P Corporation and is paid a salary of $250 on Friday of each week. On Tuesday, February 20, 1990, a levy is served on O Corporation with respect to the wages payable to C. A levy is not served on P Corporation. C's filing status is single and C is entitled to 1 personal exemption. Under §301.6334-3, C is entitled to an exemption from levy under 6334(a)(9) totalling $101.92 for each weekly pay period. However, because levy has not been made on C's salary paid by the P Corporation ($250 per week) and that salary exceeds the weekly amount ($101.92) to which C is entitled as exempt from levy, the district director may treat no amount of C's wages paid by the O Corporation as exempt from levy. If the district director requires such treatment, the district director must notify O Corporation that no amount of C's wages is exempt from levy and O Corporation may rely on such notification; in the absence of such notification O Corporation must treat $101.92 as exempt from levy.

(2) *Where sources not levied upon are less than exempt amount.*—If the taxpayer's income upon which the district director does not levy is less than the amount to which the taxpayer is entitled as exempt from levy, then an additional amount, determined to be exempt from levy pursuant to §301.6334-3, may be paid to the taxpayer from the sources of wages, salary, or other income upon which levy has been made. In such a case, the district director must designate those wages, salary, or other income from which the exempt amount is to be paid to the taxpayer, and must notify the employer or other person upon whom the levy is served of the amount of the taxpayer's wages, salary, or other income that is exempt from levy. The employer or other person may rely on such notification in paying over amounts pursuant to the levy. In the absence of such notification from the district director, the employer or other person upon whom the levy is served must determine the amount exempt from levy pursuant to §301.6334-3 as if that employer or other person upon whom the levy is served is the only source of wages, salary, or other income. Amounts not exempt from levy are to be paid to the district director in accordance with the terms of the levy. The provisions of this paragraph (c)(2) may be illustrated by the following example:

Example. Delinquent taxpayer C is an employee of O Corporation and is paid wages totalling $50 on Friday of each week. C also performs services for P Corporation and is paid a salary of

$75 on Friday of each week. On Tuesday, February 20, 1990, a levy is served on P Corporation with respect to the wages and salary of C. C's filing status is single and C is entitled to 1 personal exemption. Under § 301.6334-3, C is entitled to an exemption from levy under section 6334(a)(9) totalling $101.92 for each weekly pay period. The district director may notify P Corporation that only $51.92 of C's wages is exempt from levy and P Corporation may rely on such notification; in the absence of such notification, P Corporation must treat the entire $75 salary as exempt from levy.

(d) *Effective date.*—These provisions are effective with respect to levies made on or after July 1, 1989. However, any reasonable attempt by a taxpayer to comply with the statutory amendments addressed by these regulations prior to February 21, 1995 will be considered as meeting the requirements of these regulations. [Reg. § 301.6334-2.]

□ [*T.D.* 7620, *5-11-79. Amended by T.D.* 8568, 10-20-94.]

[Reg. § 301.6334-3]

§ 301.6334-3. Determination of exempt amount.—(a) *Individuals paid on weekly basis.*—In the case of any individual who is paid or receives all of his or her wages, salary, and other income on a weekly basis, the amount of wages, salary, and other income payable to or received by him or her during any week that is exempt from levy under section 6334(a)(9) is the exempt amount.

(b) *Term defined.*—The term *exempt amount* means an amount equal to—

(1) The sum of—

(i) The standard deduction (including additional standard deductions on account of age or blindness); and

(ii) The aggregate amount of the deductions for personal exemptions allowed the taxpayer under section 151 in the taxable year in which such levy occurs;

(2) Divided by 52.

(c) *Written and properly verified statement.*—Unless the taxpayer submits to the employer for forwarding to the district director a written and properly verified statement (as described in § 301.6334-4) specifying the facts necessary to determine the proper amount under paragraphs (b)(1)(i) and (ii) of this section, paragraphs (b)(1)(i) and (ii) of this section must be applied as if the taxpayer were a married individual filing a separate return with only 1 personal exemption.

(d) *Individuals paid on basis other than weekly.*—(1) *In general.*—In the case of an individual who is paid or receives wages, salary, and other income other than on a weekly basis, the amount payable to that individual during any applicable pay period that is exempt from levy under section 6334(a)(9) is the amount that as nearly as possible will result in the same total exemption from levy for such individual over that period of time other than weekly as that to which the individual would have been entitled under paragraph (b) of this section if, during such period of time, the individual were paid or received such wages, salary, and other income on a regular weekly basis.

(2) *Specific pay periods other than weekly.*—In the case of wages, salary, or other income paid to an individual on the basis of an established calendar period regularly used by the employer or other person levied upon for payroll or payment purposes, the exempt amount of wages, salary, and other income payable to or received by an individual during an applicable pay period other than weekly equals—

(i) The sum of—

(A) The standard deduction (including additional standard deductions on account of age or blindness); and

(B) The aggregate amount of the deductions for personal exemptions allowed the taxpayer under section 151 in the taxable year in which such levy occurs;

(ii) Divided by—

(A) 260 in the case of a daily pay period;

(B) 26 in the case of a bi-weekly pay period;

(C) 24 in the case of a semi-monthly pay period; and

(D) 12 in the case of a monthly pay period.

(3) *Nonspecific pay periods.*—In the case of wages, salary, or other income paid to an individual on a one-time or a recurrent but irregular basis and which is not paid on the basis of an established calendar period regularly used by the employer or other person levied upon for payroll or payment purposes, the exempt amount of wages, salary, and other income payable to or received by an individual equals the exempt amount defined in paragraph (b) of this section multiplied by the number (but not more than 52) of full weeks (consisting of seven calendar days) to which such payment is attributable. The provisions of this paragraph (d)(3) may be illustrated by the following example:

Example. Taxpayer A's exempt amount per week (as determined under paragraph (b) of this section) is $100. Taxpayer A is hired by Corporation X to perform a specific task for Corporation X at a flat fee of $1,500 which is to be paid at the completion of the task. Taxpayer A completes the task in 10 weeks. The total exempt amount is $1,000 and $500 is subject to levy.

(e) *Levies continuing into following years.*—The exempt amount is computed on the basis of the standard deduction (including additional standard deductions on account of age or blindness) for the taxpayer's filing status and the amount of the deduction for a personal exemption in effect in the taxable year in which the original notice of levy is served. Unless the taxpayer submits a new verified statement in accordance with § 301.6334-4, the exempt amount remains the same for pay periods following the pay period in which the notice of levy is served even if there is a change in the taxpayer's factual situation or a change by operation of law (such as by indexing or otherwise) to the standard deduction or personal exemption amounts.

(f) *Effective date.*—These provisions are effective with respect to levies made on or after July 1, 1989. However, any reasonable attempt by a taxpayer to comply with the statutory amendments addressed by these regulations prior to February 21, 1995 will be considered as meeting the requirements of these regulations. [Reg. § 301.6334-3.]

☐ [T.D. 7620, 5-11-79. *Amended by T.D. 8568,* 10-20-94.]

[Reg. § 301.6334-4]

§ 301.6334-4. Verified statements.—(a) *In general.*—For purposes of § § 301.6334-2 and 301.6334-3, the amount of wages, salary, or other income that is exempt from levy must be determined on the basis of a written and properly verified statement submitted by the taxpayer to his or her employer for submission to the district director specifying the facts necessary to determine the standard deduction and the aggregate amount of the deductions for personal exemptions allowed the taxpayer under section 151 in the taxable year in which the levy is served. In the absence of submission of such statement, the amount that is exempt from levy must be determined as if the taxpayer were a married individual filing a separate return with only 1 personal exemption.

(b) *Content of statement.*—The statement in paragraph (a) of this section must be a written statement signed under penalty of perjury, and dated, containing the following information—

(1) The filing status of the taxpayer as either:

(i) Single;

(ii) Married filing a joint return;

(iii) Married filing a separate return;

(iv) Head of household; or

(v) Qualifying widow or widower with dependent child;

(2) The name, relationship, and Social Security Number of each individual whom the taxpayer can claim as a personal exemption on the taxpayer's income tax return; and

(3) Any additional standard deductions that the taxpayer can claim on account of age (65 or older) or blindness on the taxpayer's income tax return.

(c) *Submission of verified statement.*—(1) *Obligation of employer.*—An employer upon whom a notice of levy for wages, salary, or other income of a taxpayer is served must promptly notify the taxpayer of the fact that a notice of levy has been served. Unless otherwise indicated on the face of the notice of levy, the employer must request the taxpayer to provide the employer with a written statement signed under penalty of perjury, and

dated, containing the information set forth in paragraph (b) of this section, and this statement must be submitted by the employer to the district director. The employer must submit this statement to the district director at the time employer first responds to the notice of levy.

(2) *Submission by taxpayer.*—The taxpayer must provide the employer upon whom the notice of levy has been served with a verified statement complying with paragraph (b) of this section. Unless the taxpayer provides a verified statement, the amount that is exempt from levy must be determined as if the taxpayer were a married individual filing a separate return with only 1 personal exemption.

(3) *Additional statements.*—A taxpayer may submit a verified statement to his or her employer at any time. Except as otherwise provided in paragraph (d) of this section, such verified statement will be effective for any payment of wages, salary, or other income made after the date of submission and will replace any previously submitted verified statement. The employer must provide the district director with the statement on the next occasion on which the employer responds to the notice of levy.

(d) *Effect of verified statement.*—(1) A verified statement submitted by an employee is effective upon receipt by the employer, and the employer is required to compute the exempt amount on the basis of the information contained in the verified statement unless notified to the contrary by the Internal Revenue Service.

(2) The Internal Revenue Service may find that a verified statement submitted by an employee contains a materially incorrect statement, or it may determine, after written request to the employee for verification of information contained in the verified statement, that it lacks sufficient information to determine whether the verified statement is correct. If the Internal Revenue Service so finds or determines, and notifies the employer in writing that the verified statement is defective, upon receipt of such notice the employer shall consider the verified statement to be defective for purposes of computing the exempt amount.

(3) If the Internal Revenue Service notifies the employer that the verified statement is defective, the Internal Revenue Service will, based upon its finding, advise the employer that the employer is to compute the exempt amount as if no verified statement had been submitted by the employee or will describe upon what basis the exempt amount is to be computed. The Internal Revenue Service will also specify which Internal Revenue Service office to contact for further information.

(4) In addition to any notice furnished to the employer for the employer's use, the Internal Revenue Service will provide the employer with a copy for the employee of each notice it furnishes the employer.

(5) The employer must promptly furnish the employee with a copy of any Internal Reve-

nue Service notice with respect to a verified statement submitted by the employee.

(6) Once paragraph (d)(3) of this section applies, the employer must continue to compute the exempt amount on the basis of the written notice from the Internal Revenue Service until the Internal Revenue Service by written notice advises the employer to compute the exempt amount on the basis of a new verified statement (as described in paragraph (d)(7) of this section) and revokes its earlier written notice.

(7) Once paragraph (d)(3) of this section applies, the employee may submit a new verified statement together with a written explanation of any circumstances of the employee which have changed since the Internal Revenue Service's earlier written notice, or any other circumstances or reasons as justification or support for the claims made by the employee on the new verified statement. The employee may submit the new verified statement and written explanation either—

(i) To the Internal Revenue Service office specified in the notice furnished to the employer under paragraph (d)(3) of this section; or

(ii) To the employer, who must forward the new verified statement and written explanation to the Internal Revenue Service office specified in the notice earlier furnished to the employer on the next occasion on which the employer responds to the notice of levy.

(e) *Effective date.*—These provisions are effective with respect to levies made on or after July 1, 1989. However, any reasonable attempt by a taxpayer to comply with the statutory amendments addressed by these regulations prior to February 21, 1995 will be considered as meeting the requirements of these regulations. [Reg. § 301.6334-4.]

☐ [*T.D. 7620, 5-11-79. Amended by T.D. 8568, 10-20-94.*]

[Reg. § 301.6335-1]

§ 301.6335-1. Sale of seized property.— (a) *Notice of seizure.*—As soon as practicable after seizure of property, the internal revenue officer seizing the property shall give notice in writing to the owner of the property (or, in the case of personal property, to the possessor thereof). The written notice shall be delivered to the owner (or to the possessor, in the case of personal property) or left at his usual place of abode or business if he has such within the internal revenue district where the seizure is made. If the owner cannot be readily located, or has no dwelling or place of business within such district, the notice may be mailed to his last known address. Such notice shall specify the sum demanded and shall contain, in the case of personal property, a list sufficient to identify the property seized and, in the case of real property, a description with reasonable certainty of the property seized.

(b) *Notice of sale.*—(1) As soon as practicable after seizure of the property, the district director shall give notice of sale in writing to the owner.

Such notice shall be delivered to the owner or left at his usual place of abode or business if located within the internal revenue district where the seizure is made. If the owner cannot be readily located, or has no dwelling or place of business within such district, the notice may be mailed to his last known address. For further guidance regarding the definition of last known address, see § 301.6212-2. The notice shall specify the property to be sold, and the time, place, manner, and conditions of the sale thereof, and shall expressly state that only the right, title, and interest of the delinquent taxpayer in and to such property is to be offered for sale. The notice shall also be published in some newspaper published in the county wherein the seizure is made or in a newspaper generally circulated in that county. For example, if a newspaper of general circulation in a county but not published in that county will reach more potential bidders for the property to be sold than a newspaper published within the county, or if there is a newspaper of general circulation within the county but no newspaper published within the county, the district director may cause public notice of the sale to be given in the newspaper of general circulation within the county. If there is no newspaper published or generally circulated in the county, the notice shall be posted at the post office nearest the place where the seizure is made, and in not less than two other public places.

(2) The district director may use other methods of giving notice of sale and of advertising seized property in addition to those referred to in subparagraph (1) when he believes that the nature of the property to be sold is such that a wider or more specialized advertising coverage will enhance the possibility of obtaining a higher price for the property.

(3) Whenever levy is made without regard to the 10-day period provided in section 6331(a) (relating to cases in which collection is in jeopardy), a public notice of sale of the property seized shall not be made within such 10-day period unless section 6336 (relating to perishable goods) is applicable.

(c) *Time, place, manner, and conditions of sale.*— The time, place, manner, and conditions of the sale of property seized by levy shall be as follows:

(1) *Time and place of sale.*—The time of sale shall not be less than 10 days nor more than 40 days from the time of giving public notice under section 6335(b) (see paragraph (b) of this section). The place of sale shall be within the county in which the property is seized, except that if it appears to the district director under whose supervision the seizure was made that substantially higher bids may be obtained for the property if the sale is held at a place outside such county, he may order that the sale be held in such other place. The sale shall be held at the time and place stated in the notice of sale.

(2) *Adjournment of sale.*—When it appears to the district director that an adjournment of the

sale will best serve the interest of the United States or that of the taxpayer, the district director may adjourn, or cause the internal revenue officer conducting the sale to adjourn, the sale from time to time, but the date of the sale shall not be later than one month after the date fixed in the original notice of sale.

(3) *Determinations relating to minimum price.*—(i) *Minimum price.*—Before the sale of property seized by levy, the district director shall determine a minimum price, taking into account the expenses of levy and sale, for which the property shall be sold. The internal revenue officer conducting the sale may either announce the minimum price before the sale begins, or defer announcement of the minimum price until after the receipt of the highest bid, in which case, if the highest bid is greater than the minimum price, no announcement of the minimum price shall be made.

(ii) *Purchase by the United States.*—Before the sale of property seized by levy, the district director shall determine whether the purchase of property by the United States at the minimum price would be in the best interest of the United States. In determining whether the purchase of property would be in the best interest of the United States, the district director may consider all relevant facts and circumstances including for example—

(a) Marketability of the property;

(b) Cost of maintaining the property;

(c) Cost of repairing or restoring the property;

(d) Cost of transporting the property;

(e) Cost of safeguarding the property;

(f) Cost of potential toxic waste cleanup; and

(g) Other factors pertinent to the type of property.

(iii) *Effective date.*—This paragraph (c)(3) applies to determinations relating to minimum price made on or after December 17, 1996.

(4) *Disposition of property at sale.*—(i) *Sale to highest bidder at or above minimum price.*—If one or more persons offer to buy the property for at least the amount of the minimum price, the property shall be sold to the highest bidder.

(ii) *Property deemed sold to United States at minimum price.*—If no one offers at least the amount of the minimum price for the property and the Secretary has determined that it would be in the best interest of the United States to purchase the property for the minimum price, the property shall be declared to be sold to the United States for the minimum price.

(iii) *Release to owner.*—If the property is not declared to be sold under paragraph (c)(4)(i) or (ii) of this section, the property shall be released to the owner of the property and the expense of the levy and sale shall be added to the amount of tax for the collection of which the

United States made the levy. Any property released under this paragraph (c)(4)(iii) shall remain subject to any lien imposed by subchapter C of chapter 64 of subtitle F of the Internal Revenue Code.

(iv) *Effective date.*—This paragraph (c)(4) applies to dispositions of property at sale made on or after December 17, 1996.

(5) *Offering of property.*—(i) *Sale of indivisible property.*—If any property levied upon is not divisible, so as to enable the district director by sale of a part thereof to raise the whole amount of the tax and expenses of levy and sale, the whole of such property shall be sold. For application of surplus proceeds of sale, see section 6342(b).

(ii) *Separately, in groups, or in the aggregate.*—The seized property may be offered for sale—

(a) As separate items, or

(b) As groups of items, or

(c) In the aggregate, or

(d) Both as separate items (or in groups) and in the aggregate. In such cases, the property shall be sold under the method which produces the highest aggregate amount.

The district director shall select whichever of the foregoing methods of offering the property for sale as, in his opinion, is most feasible under all the facts and circumstances of the case, except that if the property to be sold includes both real and personal property, only the personal property may be grouped for the purpose of offering such property for sale. However, real and personal property may be offered for sale in the aggregate, provided the real property, as separate items, and the personal property as a group, or as groups, or as separate items, are first offered separately.

(iii) *Condition of title and of property.*—Only the right, title, and interest of the delinquent taxpayer in and to the property seized shall be offered for sale, and such interest shall be offered subject to any prior outstanding mortgages, encumbrances, or other liens in favor of third parties which are valid as against the delinquent taxpayer and are superior to the lien of the United States. All seized property shall be offered for sale "as is" and "where is" and without recourse against the United States. No guaranty or warranty, express or implied, shall be made by the internal revenue officer offering the property for sale, as to the validity of the title, quality, quantity, weight, size, or condition of any of the property, or its fitness for any use or purpose. No claim shall be considered for allowance or adjustment or for rescission of the sale based upon failure of the property to conform with any representation, express or implied.

(iv) *Terms of payment.*—The property shall be offered for sale upon whichever of the following terms is fixed by the district director in the public notice of sale:

Reg. § 301.6335-1(c)(3)

(a) Payment in full upon acceptance of the highest bid, without regard to the amount of such bid, or

(b) If the aggregate price of all property purchased by a successful bidder at the sale is more than $200, an initial payment of $200 or 20 percent of the purchase price, whichever is the greater, and payment of the balance (including all costs incurred for the protection or preservation of the property subsequent to the sale and prior to final payment) within a specified period, not to exceed one month from the date of the sale.

(6) *Method of sale.*—The district director shall sell the property either—

(i) At public auction, at which open competitive bids shall be received, or

(ii) At public sale under sealed bids. The following rules, in addition to the other rules provided in this paragraph, shall be applicable to public sale under sealed bids:

(a) Invitation to bidders.—Bids shall be solicited through a public notice of sale.

(b) Form for use by bidders.—A bid shall be submitted on a form which will be furnished by the district director upon request. The form shall be completed in accordance with the instructions thereon.

(c) Remittance with bid.—If the total bid is $200 or less, the full amount of the bid shall be submitted therewith. If the total bid is more than $200, 20 percent of such bid or $200, whichever is greater, shall be submitted therewith. (In the case of alternative bids submitted by the same bidder for items of property offered separately, or in groups, or in the aggregate, the bidder shall remit the full amount of the highest alternative bid submitted, if that bid is $200 or less. If the highest alternative bid submitted is more than $200, the bidder shall remit 20 percent of the highest alternative bid or $200, whichever is greater.) Such remittance shall be by a certified, cashier's, or treasurer's check drawn on any bank or trust company incorporated under the laws of the United States or under the laws of any State, Territory, or possession of the United States, or by a United States postal, bank, express, or telegraph money order.

(d) Time for receiving and opening bids.— Each bid shall be submitted in a securely sealed envelope. The bidder shall indicate in the upper left hand corner of the envelope his name and address and the time and place of sale as announced in the public notice of sale. A bid will not be considered unless it is received by the internal revenue officer conducting the sale prior to the opening of the bids. The bids will be opened at the time and place stated in the notice of sale, or at the time fixed in the announcement of the adjournment of the sale.

(e) Consideration of bids.—The public notice of sale shall specify whether the property is to be sold separately, by groups, or in the aggregate or by a combination of these methods, as provided in subparagraph (4)(ii) of this paragraph. If the notice specifies an alternative method, bidders may submit bids under one or more of the alternatives. In case of error in the extension of prices in any bid, the unit price will govern. The internal revenue officer conducting the sale shall have the right to waive any technical defects in a bid. In the event two or more highest bids are equal in amount, the internal revenue officer conducting the sale shall determine the successful bidder by drawing lots. After the opening, examination, and consideration of all bids, the internal revenue officer conducting the sale shall announce the amount of the highest bid or bids and the name of the successful bidder or bidders. Any remittance submitted in connection with an unsuccessful bid shall be returned at the conclusion of the sale.

(f) Withdrawal of bids.—A bid may be withdrawn on written or telegraphic request received from the bidder prior to the time fixed for opening the bids. A technical defect in a bid confers no right on the bidder for the withdrawal of his bid after it has been opened.

(7) *Payment of bid price.*—All payments for property sold under this section shall be made by cash or by a certified, cashier's, or treasurer's check drawn on any bank or trust company incorporated under the laws of the United States or under the laws of any State, Territory, or possession of the United States, or by a United States postal, bank, express, or telegraph money order. If payment in full is required upon acceptance of the highest bid, the payment shall be made at such time. If deferred payment is permitted, the initial payment shall be made upon acceptance of the bid, and the balance shall be paid on or before the date fixed for payment thereof. Any remittance submitted with a successful sealed bid shall be applied toward the purchase price.

(8) *Delivery and removal of personal property.*—Responsibility of the United States for the protection or preservation of seized personal property shall cease immediately upon acceptance of the highest bid. The risk of loss is on the purchaser of personal property upon acceptance of his bid. Possession of any personal property shall not be delivered to the purchaser until the purchase price has been paid in full. If payment of part of the purchase price for personal property is deferred, the United States will retain possession of such property as security for the payment of the balance of the purchase price and, as agent for the purchaser, will cause the property to be cared for until the purchase price has been paid in full or the sale is declared null and void for failure to make full payment of the purchase price. In such case, all charges and expenses incurred in caring for the property after the acceptance of the bid shall be borne by the purchaser.

(9) *Default in payment.*—If payment in full is required upon acceptance of the bid and is not

then and there paid, the internal revenue officer conducting the sale shall forthwith proceed again to sell the property in the manner provided in section 6335(e) and the regulations thereunder. If the conditions of the sale permit part of the payment to be deferred, and if such part is not paid within the prescribed period, suit may be instituted against the purchaser for the purchase price or such part thereof as has not been paid, together with interest at the rate of 6 percent per annum from the date of the sale; or, in the discretion of the district director, the sale may be declared by the district director to be null and void for failure to make full payment of the purchase price and the property may again be advertised and sold as provided in subsections (b), (c), and (e) of section 6335 and the regulations thereunder. In the event of such readvertisement and sale, any new purchaser shall receive such property or rights to property free and clear of any claim or right of the former defaulting purchaser, of any nature whatsoever, and the amount paid upon the bid price by such defaulting purchaser shall be forfeited to the United States.

(10) *Stay of sale of seized property pending Tax Court decision.*—For restrictions on sale of seized property pending Tax Court decision, see section 6863(b)(3) and the regulations thereunder.

(d) *Right to request the sale of seized property.*— (1) *In general.*—The owner of any property seized by levy may request that the district director sell such property within 60 days after such request, or within any longer period specified by the owner. The district director must comply with such a request unless the district director determines that compliance with the request is not in the best interests of the Internal Revenue Service and notifies the owner of such determination within the 60 day period, or any longer period specified by the owner.

(2) *Procedures to request the sale of seized property.*—(i) *Manner.*—A request for the sale of seized property shall be made in writing to the group manager of the revenue officer whose signature is on Levy Form 668-B. If the owner does not know the group manager's name or address, the owner may send the request to the revenue officer, marked for the attention of his or her group manager.

(ii) *Form.*—The request for sale of seized property within 60 days, or such longer period specified by the owner, shall include:

(A) The name, current address, current home and work telephone numbers and any convenient times to be contacted, and taxpayer identification number of the owner making the request;

(B) A description of the seized property that is the subject of the request;

(C) A copy of the notice of seizure, if available;

(D) The period within which the owner is requesting that the property be sold; and

(E) The signature of the owner or duly authorized representative. For purposes of these regulations, a duly authorized representative is any attorney, certified public accountant, enrolled actuary, or any other person permitted to represent the owner before the Internal Revenue Service who is not disbarred or suspended from practice before the Internal Revenue Service and who has a written power of attorney executed by the owner.

(3) *Notification to owner.*—The group manager shall respond in writing to a request for sale of seized property as soon as practicable after receipt of such request and in no event later than 60 days after receipt of the request, or, if later, the date specified by the owner for the sale. [Reg. § 301.6335-1.]

☐ [*T.D.* 6119, 12-31-54. *Amended by T.D.* 6498, 10-24-60; *T.D.* 7180, 4-12-72; *T.D.* 8398, 3-2-92; *T.D.* 8691, 12-16-96 *and T.D.* 8939, 1-11-2001.]

[Reg. § 301.6336-1]

§ 301.6336-1. Sale of perishable goods.— (a) *Appraisal of certain seized property.*—If the district director determines that any property seized by levy is liable to perish or become greatly reduced in price or value by keeping, or that such property cannot be kept without great expense, he shall appraise the value of such property and return it to the owner if the owner complies with the conditions prescribed in paragraph (b) of this section or, if the owner does not comply with such conditions, dispose of the property in accordance with paragraph (c) of this section.

(b) *Return to owner.*—If the owner of the property can be readily found, the district director shall give him written notice of his determination of the appraised value of the property. However, if the district director determines that the circumstances require immediate action, he may give the owner an oral notice of his determination of the appraised value of the property, which notice shall be confirmed in writing prior to sale. The property shall be returned to the owner if, within the time specified in the notice, the owner—

(1) Pays to the district director an amount equal to the appraised value, or

(2) Gives an acceptable bond as prescribed by section 7101 and the regulations thereunder. Such bond shall be in an amount not less than the appraised value of the property and shall be conditioned upon the payment of such amount at such time as the district director determines to be appropriate in the circumstances.

(c) *Immediate sale.*—If the owner does not pay the amount of the appraised value of the seized property within the time specified in the notice, or furnish bond as provided in paragraph (b) within such time, the district director shall as soon as practicable make public sale of the property in accordance with the following terms and conditions—

(1) *Notice of sale.*—If the owner can readily be found, a notice shall be given to him. A notice of sale also shall be posted in two public places in the county in which the property is to be sold. The notice shall specify the time and place of sale, the property to be sold, and the manner and conditions of sale. The district director may give such other notice and in such other manner as he deems advisable under the circumstances.

(2) *Sale.*—The property shall be sold at public auction to the highest bidder.

(3) *Terms.*—The purchase price shall be paid in full upon acceptance of the highest bid. The payment shall be made in cash, or by a certified, cashier's, or treasurer's check drawn on any bank or trust company incorporated under the laws of the United States or under the laws of any State, Territory, or possession of the United States, or by a United States postal, bank express, or telegraph money order. [Reg. § 301.6336-1.]

☐ [*T.D.* 6119, 12-31-54. *Amended by T.D.* 6498, 10-24-60.]

[Reg. § 301.6337-1]

§ 301.6337-1. Redemption of property.—(a) *Before sale.*—Any person whose property has been levied upon shall have the right to pay the amount due, together with costs and expenses of the proceeding, if any, to the district director at any time prior to the sale of the property. Upon such payment the district director shall restore such property to the owner and all further proceedings in connection with the levy on such property shall cease from the time of such payment.

(b) *Redemption of real estate after sale.*—(1) *Period.*—The owner of any real estate sold as provided in section 6335, his heirs, executors, or administrators, or any person having any interest therein, or a lien thereon, or any person in their behalf, shall be permitted to redeem the property sold, or any particular tract of such property, at any time within 120 days after the sale thereof.

(2) *Price.*—Such property or tract of property may be redeemed upon payment to the purchaser, or in case he cannot be found in the county in which the property to be redeemed is situated, then to the district director for the internal revenue district in which the property is situated, for the use of the purchaser, his heirs, or assigns, the annum. In case real and personal property (or several tracts of real property) are purchased in the aggregate, the redemption price of the real property (or of each of the several tracts) shall be determined on the basis of the ratio, as of the time of sale, of the value of the real property (or tract) to the value of the total property purchased. For this purpose the minimum price or the highest bid price, whichever is higher, offered for the property separately or in groups shall be treated as the value.

(c) *Record.*—When any real property is redeemed, the district director shall cause entry of the fact to be made upon the record of sale kept in accordance with section 6340, and such entry shall be evidence of such redemption. The party who redeems the property shall notify the district director of the internal revenue district in which the property is situated of the date of such redemption and of the transfer of the certificate of sale, the amount of the redemption price, and the name of the party to whom such redemption price was paid. [Reg. § 301.6337-1.]

☐ [*T.D.* 6119, 12-31-54. *Amended by T.D.* 7180, 4-12-72.]

[Reg. § 301.6338-1]

§ 301.6338-1. Certificate of sale; deed of real property.—(a) *Certificate of sale.*—In the case of property sold as provided in section 6335 (relating to sale of seized property), the district director shall give to the purchaser a certificate of sale upon payment in full of the purchase price. A certificate of sale of real property shall set forth the real property purchased, for whose taxes the same was sold, the name of the purchaser, and the price paid therefor.

(b) *Deed to real property.*—In the case of any real property sold as provided in section 6335 and not redeemed in the manner and within the time prescribed in section 6337, the district director shall execute (in accordance with the laws of the State in which the real property is situated pertaining to sales of real property under execution) to the purchaser of such real property at the sale or his assigns, upon surrender of the certificate of sale, a deed of the real property so purchased, reciting the facts set forth in the certificate.

(c) *Deed to real property purchased by the United States.*—If real property is declared purchased by the United States at a sale pursuant to section 6335, the district director shall at the proper time execute a deed therefor and shall, without delay, cause the deed to be duly recorded in the proper registry of deeds. [Reg. § 301.6338-1.]

☐ [*T.D.* 6119, 12-31-54. *Amended by T.D.* 6425, 11-10-59 *and T.D.* 7180, 4-12-72.]

[Reg. § 301.6339-1]

§ 301.6339-1. Legal effect of certificate of sale of personal property and deed of real property.—(a) *Certificate of sale of property other than real property.*—In all cases of sale pursuant to section 6335 of property (other than real property), the certificate of such sale—

(1) *As evidence.*—Shall be prima facie evidence of the right of the officer to make such sale, and conclusive evidence of the regularity of his proceedings in making the sale; and

(2) *As conveyance.*—Shall transfer to the purchaser all right, title, and interest of the party delinquent in and to the property sold; and

(3) *As authority for transfer of corporate stock.*—If such property consists of corporate stocks, shall be notice, when received, to any corporation, company, or association of such

transfer, and shall be authority to such corporation, company, or association to record the transfer on its books and records in the same manner as if the stocks were transferred or assigned by the party holding the stock certificate, in lieu of any original or prior certificate, which shall be void, whether canceled or not; and

(4) *As receipts.*—If the subject of sale is securities or other evidences of debt, shall be a good and valid receipt to the person holding the certificate of sale as against any person holding or claiming to hold possession of such securities or other evidences of debt; and

(5) *As authority for transfer of title to motor vehicle.*—If such property consists of a motor vehicle, shall be notice, when received, to any public official charged with the registration of title to motor vehicles, of such transfer and shall be authority to such official to record the transfer on his books and records in the same manner as if the certificate of title to such motor vehicle were transferred or assigned by the party holding the certificate of title, in lieu of any original or prior certificate, which shall be null and void, whether canceled or not.

(b) *Deed to real property.*—In the case of the sale of real property pursuant to section 6335—

(1) *Deed as evidence.*—The deed of sale given pursuant to section 6338 shall be prima facie evidence of the facts therein stated; and

(2) *Deed as conveyance of title.*—If the proceedings of the district director as set forth have been substantially in accordance with the provisions of law, such deed shall be considered and operate as a conveyance of all the right, title, and interest the party delinquent had in and to the real property thus sold at the time the lien of the United States attached thereto.

(c) *Effect of junior encumbrances.*—A certificate of sale of personal property given or a deed to real property executed pursuant to section 6338 discharges the property from all liens, encumbrances, and titles over which the lien of the United States, with respect to which the levy was made, has priority. For example, a mortgage on real property executed after a notice of a federal tax lien has been filed is extinguished when the district director executes a deed to the real property to a purchaser thereof at a sale pursuant to section 6335 following the seizure of the property by the United States. The proceeds of such a sale are distributed in accordance with priority of the liens, encumbrances, or titles. See section 6342(b) and the regulations thereunder for provisions relating to the distribution of surplus proceeds. See section 7426(a)(2) and the regulations thereunder for judicial procedures with respect to surplus proceeds. [Reg. § 301.6339-1.]

□ [*T.D.* 6119, 12-31-54. *Amended by T.D.* 7180, 4-12-72.]

[Reg. § 301.6340-1]

§ 301.6340-1. Records of sale.—(a) *Requirement.*—Each district director shall keep a record of all sales under section 6335 of real property situated within his district and of redemptions of such property. The records shall set forth (1) the tax for which any such sale was made, the dates of seizure and sale, the name of the party assessed and all proceedings in making such sale, the amount of expenses, the names of the purchasers, the date of the deed, and, in the case of redemption of the property, (2) the date of such redemption and of the transfer of the certificate of sale, the amount of the redemption price, and the name of the party to whom such redemption price was paid.

(b) *Copy as evidence.*—A copy of such record, or any part thereof, certified by the district director shall be evidence in any court of the truth of the facts therein stated. [Reg. § 301.6340-1.]

□ [*T.D.* 6119, 12-31-54.]

[Reg. § 301.6341-1]

§ 301.6341-1. Expense of levy and sale.—The district director shall determine the expenses to be allowed in all cases of levy and sale. Such expenses shall include the expenses of protection and preservation of the property during the period subsequent to the levy, as well as the actual expenses incurred in connection with the sale thereof. In case real and personal property (or several tracts of real property) are sold in the aggregate, the district director shall properly apportion the expenses to the real property (or to each tract). [Reg. § 301.6341-1.]

□ [*T.D.* 6119, 12-31-54.]

[Reg. § 301.6342-1]

§ 301.6342-1. Application of proceeds of levy.—(a) *Collection of liability.*—Any money realized by proceedings under subchapter D, chapter 64, of the Code or by sale of property redeemed by the United States (if the interest of the United States in the property was a lien arising under the provisions of the Internal Revenue Code) is applied in the manner specified in subparagraphs (1), (2), and (3) of this paragraph. Money realized by proceedings under subchapter D, chapter 64, of the Code includes money realized by seizure, by sale of seized property, or by surrender under section 6332 (except money realized by the imposition of a 50% penalty pursuant to section 6332(c)(2)).

(1) *Expense of levy and sale.*—First, against the expenses of the proceedings or sale, including expenses allowable under section 6341 and amounts paid by the United States to redeem property.

(2) *Specific tax liability on seized property.*—If the property seized and sold is subject to a tax imposed by any internal revenue law which has not been paid, the amount remaining after applying subparagraph (1) shall then be applied

against such tax liability (and, if such tax was not previously assessed, it shall then be assessed).

(3) *Liability of delinquent taxpayer.*—The amount, if any, remaining after applying subparagraphs (1) and (2) of this paragraph shall then be applied against the liability in respect of which the levy was made or the sale of redeemed property was conducted.

(b) *Surplus proceeds.*—Any surplus proceeds remaining after the application of paragraph (a) of this section shall, upon application and satisfactory proof in support thereof, be credited or refunded by the district director to the person or persons legally entitled thereto. The delinquent taxpayer is the person entitled to the surplus proceeds unless another person establishes a superior claim thereto. [Reg. § 301.6342-1.]

□ *[T.D. 6119, 12-31-54. Amended by T.D. 6498, 10-24-60 and T.D. 7180, 4-12-72.]*

[Reg. § 301.6343-1]

§ 301.6343-1. Requirement to release levy and notice of release.—(a) *In general.*—A district director, service center director, or compliance center director (*director*) must promptly release a levy upon all, or part of, property or rights to property levied upon and must promptly notify the person upon whom the levy was made of such a release, if the director determines that any of the conditions in paragraph (b) of this section (conditions requiring release) exist. The director must make a determination whether any of the conditions requiring release exist if a taxpayer submits a request for release of levy in accordance with paragraph (c) or (d) of this section; however, the director may make this determination based upon information received from a source other than the taxpayer. The director may require any supporting documentation as is reasonably necessary to determine whether a condition requiring release exists.

(b) *Conditions requiring release.*—The director must release the levy upon all or a part of the property or rights to property levied upon if he or she determines that one of the following conditions exists—

(1) *Liability satisfied or unenforceable.*—(i) *General rule.*—The liability for which the levy was made is satisfied or the period of limitations provided in section 6502 (and any period during which the period of limitations is suspended as provided by law) has lapsed. A levy is considered made on the date on which the notice of seizure provided in section 6335(a) is given. A levy that is made within the period of limitations provided in section 6502 does not become unenforceable simply because the person who receives the levy does not surrender the subject property within the period of limitations. In this case, the liability remains enforceable to the extent of the value of the levied upon property. However, a levy made outside the period of limitations (normally ten years without suspensions) must be released unless—

(A) The taxpayer agreed in writing to extend the period of limitations as provided in section 6502(a)(2) and § 301.6502-1; or

(B) A proceeding in court to collect the liability has begun within the period of limitations.

(ii) *Special situations.*—A continuing levy on salary or wages made under section 6331(e) must be released at the end of the period of limitations in section 6502. However, a levy on a fixed and determinable right to payment which right includes payments to be made after the period of limitations expires does not become unenforceable upon the expiration of the period of limitations and will not be released under this condition unless the liability is satisfied.

(2) *Release will facilitate collection.*—The release of the levy will facilitate collection of the liability. A director has the discretion to release the levy in all situations, including those where the proceeds from the sale will not fully satisfy the tax liabilities of the taxpayer, under terms and conditions as he or she determines are warranted.

(i) *Example.*—The following example illustrates the provisions of this paragraph (b)(2):

Example. A and B each own machines which, when used together, produce widgets. A owes delinquent federal taxes. A notice of federal tax lien is properly filed against all property or rights to property belonging to A. A's machine is seized to satisfy A's delinquent tax liability. The fair market value of A's property is greater than the expenses of seizure and sale, but less than the amount of A's tax liability. A and B find a buyer who wants to buy both machines together. The buyer will only buy the machines together. A's property has a greater value as part of the package than it does by itself. The larger value, as shown in the sale contract, is enough to pay A's tax liability in full. In this situation a release of the levy will facilitate collection because the sale of both machines can be completed and A's liability will be paid in full at the settlement.

(ii) *Compliance with other conditions.*—The director may find that collection will be facilitated by the taxpayer's compliance with conditions other than immediate payment, such as:

(A) The delinquent taxpayer delivers a satisfactory arrangement, which is accepted by the director, for placing property in escrow to secure the payment of the liability (including the expenses of the levy) which is the basis of the levy.

(B) The delinquent taxpayer delivers an acceptable bond to the director conditioned upon the payment of the liability (including the expenses of levy) which is the basis of the levy. This bond shall be in the form provided in section 7101 and § 301.7101-1.

(C) There is paid to the director an amount determined by the director to be equal to the interest of the United States in the seized property or the part of the seized property to be released.

(D) The delinquent taxpayer executes an agreement to extend the statute of limitations in accordance with section 6502(a)(2) and § 301.6502-1.

(iii) *Expenses of sale exceed the government's interest.*—If the director determines that the value of the United States' interest in the seized property does not exceed the expenses of sale of the property, a release of the levy will be deemed to facilitate collection of the liability even though the fair market value of property which has been seized exceeds the expenses of seizure and sale.

(3) *Installment agreement.*—The taxpayer has entered into an agreement under section 6159 to satisfy the liability by means of installment payments, unless the agreement provides otherwise. However, the director is not required to release the levy under this condition if a release of the levy will jeopardize the secured creditor status of the United States, e.g., where there is an intervening judgment lien creditor and a notice of tax lien has not been filed.

(4) *Economic hardship.*—(i) *General rule.*—The levy is creating an economic hardship due to the financial condition of an individual taxpayer. This condition applies if satisfaction of the levy in whole or in part will cause an individual taxpayer to be unable to pay his or her reasonable basic living expenses. The determination of a reasonable amount for basic living expenses will be made by the director and will vary according to the unique circumstances of the individual taxpayer. Unique circumstances, however, do not include the maintenance of an affluent or luxurious standard of living.

(ii) *Information from taxpayer.*—In determining a reasonable amount for basic living expenses the director will consider any information provided by the taxpayer including—

(A) The taxpayer's age, employment status and history, ability to earn, number of dependents, and status as a dependent of someone else;

(B) The amount reasonably necessary for food, clothing, housing (including utilities, home-owner insurance, home-owner dues, and the like), medical expenses (including health insurance), transportation, current tax payments (including federal, state, and local), alimony, child support, or other court-ordered payments, and expenses necessary to the taxpayer's production of income (such as dues for a trade union or professional organization, or child care payments which allow the taxpayer to be gainfully employed);

(C) The cost of living in the geographic area in which the taxpayer resides;

(D) The amount of property exempt from levy which is available to pay the taxpayer's expenses;

(E) Any extraordinary circumstances such as special education expenses, a medical catastrophe, or natural disaster; and

(F) Any other factor that the taxpayer claims bears on economic hardship and brings to the attention of the director.

(iii) *Good faith requirement.*—In addition, in order to obtain a release of a levy under this subparagraph, the taxpayer must act in good faith. Examples of failure to act in good faith include, but are not limited to, falsifying financial information, inflating actual expenses or costs, or failing to make full disclosure of assets.

(5) *Fair market value exceeds liability.*—The fair market value of the property exceeds the liability for which the levy was made and release of the levy on a part of the property can be made without hindering the collection of the liability. The following example illustrates the provisions of this paragraph (b)(5):

Example. The Internal Revenue Service levies upon ten widgets which belong to the taxpayer to satisfy the taxpayer's outstanding tax liabilities. Subsequent to the levy, the taxpayer establishes that market conditions have increased the aggregate fair market value of widgets so that the value of seven widgets equals the aggregate anticipated expenses of sale and seizure and the tax liabilities for which the levy was made. The director must release three widgets from the levy and return them to the taxpayer.

(c) *Request for release of levy.*—(1) *Information to be submitted by taxpayer.*—A taxpayer who wishes to obtain a release of a levy must submit a request for release in writing or by telephone to the district director for the Internal Revenue district in which the levy was made. The taxpayer making the request must provide the following information—

(i) The name, address, and taxpayer identification number of the taxpayer;

(ii) A description of the property levied upon;

(iii) The type of tax and the period for which the tax is due;

(iv) The date of the levy and the originating Internal Revenue district, if known; and

(v) A statement of the grounds upon which the request for release of the levy is based.

(2) *Time for submission.*—Except in extraordinary circumstances, a request for release of a levy must be made more than five days prior to a scheduled sale of the property to which the levy relates.

(3) *Determination by director.*—(i) *When required.*—The director must promptly make a determination concerning release prior to sale in all cases where a request for release of a levy is made except those where the request for release is made five or fewer days prior to a scheduled sale of the property to which the levy relates.

(ii) *Time for making required determination.*—The determination will be made, generally, within 30 days of a request for release made 30 or more days prior to a scheduled sale of the property to which the levy relates. If a request for release is made less than 30 days prior to the scheduled sale but more than 5 days before the scheduled sale, a determination must be made prior to the scheduled sale. If necessary the director may postpone the scheduled sale in order to make this determination.

(iii) *Discretionary determination.*—The director has the discretion, but is not required, to make a determination concerning release prior to sale in cases where a request for release of a levy is made five or fewer days prior to a scheduled sale of the property to which the levy relates.

(4) *Notification to taxpayer of determination.*— The director must promptly notify the taxpayer if the levy is released. If the director determines that none of the conditions requiring release of the levy exist, the director must promptly notify the taxpayer of the decision not to release the levy and the reason why the levy is not being released.

(d) *Expedited determination with respect to certain business property.*—(1) *General procedure.*— (i) *Submission by taxpayer.*—If a levy is made on essential business property as is described in paragraph (d)(2) of this section, the taxpayer may obtain an expedited determination of whether any of the conditions requiring release of the levy exist. In order to obtain an expedited determination, the taxpayer must submit, within the time frame specified in paragraph (c)(2) of this section, the information required in paragraph (c)(1) of this section and include with the information an explanation of why the property levied upon qualifies for an expedited determination of whether a condition requiring release of the levy exists.

(ii) *Time for making required determination.*—The director must make such a determination by the later of 10 business days from the time the director receives the request for release, or 10 business days from the time the director receives any necessary supporting documentation, if 10 or more business days remain before a scheduled sale of the property to which the levy relates. An expedited determination concerning release must be made prior to sale in all cases where a request for release of a levy is made within the time frame specified in paragraph (c)(2) of this section. If necessary the director may postpone the scheduled sale in order to make this determination.

(iii) *Discretionary determination.*—The director has the discretion, but is not required, to make an expedited determination concerning release in cases where the taxpayer does not submit, within the time frame specified in paragraph (c)(2) of this section, the information required in paragraph (c)(1) of this section and include with the information an explanation of why the property levied upon qualifies for an

expedited determination of whether a condition requiring release of the levy exists.

(2) *Essential business property defined.*—For purposes of this section, *essential business property* means tangible personal property used in carrying on the trade or business of the taxpayer which when levied upon prevents the taxpayer from continuing to carry on the trade or business.

(3) *Seizure of perishable goods.*—The provisions of this paragraph do not apply in the case of a seizure of perishable goods. Those seizures are governed by the provisions of section 6336 and § 301.6336-1.

(e) *Effect of a release of levy.*—If property has not yet been surrendered to the director in response to a levy, a release of the levy under section 6343(a) will relieve the possessor of any obligation to surrender the property. Otherwise, a release of a levy under section 6343(a) will cause the property to be returned to the custody of the person or persons legally entitled thereto. The release of a levy on any property under this section does not prevent any subsequent levy on the property. Section 301.6343-2, dealing with return of wrongfully levied upon property, is subject to section 6402 which prohibits the Internal Revenue Service from refunding a payment of money that has been deposited in the Treasury and credited to the taxpayer's liability unless there is an overpayment.

(f) *Effective date.*—This section is effective as of December 30, 1994. [Reg. § 301.6343-1.]

☐ [*T.D.* 6119, 12-31-54. *Amended by T.D.* 6425, 11-10-59; *T.D.* 6498, 10-24-60; *T.D.* 7180, 4-12-72 *and T.D.* 8587, 12-30-94.]

[Reg. § 301.6343-2]

§ 301.6343-2. Return of wrongfully levied upon property.—(a) *Return of property.*— (1) *General rule.*—If the Internal Revenue Service (IRS) determines that property has been wrongfully levied upon, the IRS may return—

(i) The specific property levied upon;

(ii) An amount of money equal to the amount of money levied upon; or

(iii) An amount of money equal to the amount of money received by the United States from a sale of the property.

(2) *Time of return.*—If the United States is in possession of specific property, the property may be returned at any time. An amount equal to the amount of money levied upon or received from a sale of the property may be returned at any time before the expiration of 9 months from the date of the levy. When a request described in paragraph (b) of this section is filed for the return of property before the expiration of 9 months from the date of levy, an amount of money may be returned after a reasonable period of time subsequent to the expiration of the 9-month period if necessary for the investigation and processing of such request.

(3) *Specific property.*—In general the specific property levied upon will be returned whenever possible. For this purpose, money that is specifically identifiable, as in the case of a coin collection which may be worth substantially more than its face value, is treated as specific property.

(4) *Purchase by United States.*—For purposes of paragraph (a)(1)(iii) of this section, if property is declared purchased by the United States at a sale pursuant to section 6335(e), the United States is treated as having received an amount of money equal to the minimum price determined by the IRS before the sale or, if larger, the amount received by the United States from the resale of the property.

(b) *Request for return of property.*—A written request for the return of property wrongfully levied upon must be given to the IRS official, office and address specified in IRS Publication 4528, "Making an Administrative Wrongful Levy Claim Under Internal Revenue Code (IRC) Section 6343(b)," or any successor publication. The relevant IRS publications may be downloaded from the IRS internet site at *www.irs.gov*. Under this section, a request for the return of property wrongfully levied upon is not effective if it is given to an office other than the office listed in the relevant publication. The written request must contain the following information—

(1) The name and address of the person submitting the request;

(2) A detailed description of the property levied upon;

(3) A description of the claimant's basis for claiming an interest in the property levied upon; and

(4) The name and address of the taxpayer, the originating IRS office, and the date of the levy as shown on the notice of levy form, or levy form, or, in lieu thereof, a statement of the reasons why such information cannot be furnished.

(c) *Inadequate request.*—A request for the return of property wrongfully levied upon will not be considered adequate unless it is a written request containing the information required by paragraph (b) of this section. However, unless a notification is mailed by the IRS to the claimant within 30 days of receipt of the request to inform the claimant of the inadequacies, any written request will be considered adequate. If the IRS timely notifies the claimant of the inadequacies of his request, the claimant has 30 days from the receipt of the notification of inadequacy to supply in writing any omitted information. Where the omitted information is so supplied within the 30-day period, the request will be considered to be adequate from the time the original request was made for purposes of determining the applicable period of limitation upon suit under section 6532(c).

(d) *Payment of interest.*—Interest is paid at the overpayment rate established under section 6621—

(1) In the case of money returned under paragraph (a)(1)(ii) of this section, from the date the IRS received the money to a date (to be determined by the director) preceding the date of return by not more than 30 days; or

(2) In the case of money returned under paragraph (a)(1)(iii) of this section, from the date of the sale of the property to a date (to be determined by the IRS) preceding the date of return by not more than 30 days.

(e) *Effective/applicability date.*—These regulations are effective on July 8, 2008. [Reg. § 301.6343-2.]

☐ *T.D.* 8587, 12-30-94. *Amended by T.D.* 9344, 7-19-2007 *and T.D.* 9410, 7-7-2008.]

[Reg. § 301.6343-3]

§ 301.6343-3. Return of property in certain cases.—(a) *In general.*—If money has been levied upon and applied toward the taxpayer's liability, or property has been levied upon and sold, and the receipts have been applied toward the taxpayer's liability, or property has been levied upon and purchased by the United States and the United States still possesses the property, and the Commissioner determines that any of the conditions in paragraph (c) of this section exist, the Commissioner may return—

(1) An amount of money equal to the amount of money levied upon;

(2) An amount of money equal to the amount of money received by the United States from a sale of the property; or

(3) The specific property levied upon and purchased by the United States.

(b) *Return of levied upon property in possession of the Internal Revenue Service (IRS) pending sale under section 6335.*—Other than as provided in § 301.6343-1(b) or in paragraph (d) of this section, the Commissioner, in his or her discretion, may return levied upon property that is in the possession of the United States pending sale under section 6335.

(c) *Conditions authorizing the return of property.*—The Commissioner may return property upon determining that one of the following conditions exist:

(1) *Premature or not in accordance with administrative procedures.*—The levy was premature or otherwise not in accordance with the administrative procedures of the Secretary.

(2) *Installment agreement.*—Subsequent to the levy, the taxpayer enters into an agreement under section 6159 to satisfy the liability for which the levy was made by means of installment payments. If, however, the agreement specifically provides that already levied upon property will not be returned under section 6343(d), the Commissioner may not grant a request for return of property under this paragraph (c)(2).

(3) *Facilitate collection.*—The return of property will facilitate the collection of the tax liability for which the levy was made.

(4) *Best interests of the United States and the taxpayer.*—(i) *In general.*—The taxpayer or the National Taxpayer Advocate (or his or her delegate) has consented to the return of property, and the return of property would be in the best interest of the taxpayer, as determined by the National Taxpayer Advocate (or his or her delegate), and in the best interest of the United States, as determined by the Commissioner.

(ii) *Best interest of the taxpayer.*—The National Taxpayer Advocate (or his or her delegate) generally will determine whether the return of property is in the best interest of the taxpayer. If, however, a taxpayer requests the Commissioner to return property and has not specifically requested the National Taxpayer Advocate (or his or her delegate) to determine the taxpayer's best interest, a finding by the Commissioner that the return of property is in the best interest of the taxpayer will be sufficient to support the return of property. Only the National Taxpayer Advocate (or his or her delegate) may determine that a return of property is not in the best interest of the taxpayer.

(5) *Examples.*—The following examples illustrate the provisions of this paragraph (c):

Example 1. A owes $1,000 in Federal income taxes. The IRS levies on a broker with respect to a money market account belonging to the taxpayer and receives payment from the broker which it applies to the taxpayer's outstanding liability. However, the IRS failed to follow procedure provided by the Internal Revenue Manual (but not required by statute) with regard to managerial approval prior to the making of the levy. The Commissioner may return an amount of money equal to the amount of money the IRS levied upon and applied toward the taxpayer's tax liability.

Example 2. B owes $1,000 in Federal income taxes. The IRS levies on a bank with respect to a savings account belonging to the taxpayer and receives funds from the bank, which it applies to the taxpayer's liability. Subsequent to the levy, B enters into an installment agreement, under which B will pay timely installments to satisfy the entire liability. The installment agreement does not by its terms preclude the return of levied upon property. The revenue officer verifies that B is financially capable of paying the entire liability, including accruals, in the agreed-upon installment payments. The Commissioner may return an amount of money equal to the amount of money levied upon and applied toward the taxpayer's liability.

Example 3. C owns a house that is deteriorating and in unsalable condition. C is in the process of renovating the house for sale when the IRS levies upon C's bank account for the payment of a $20,000 outstanding Federal tax liability and receives funds in the amount of $3,000, which it applies toward C's liability. A notice of federal tax lien is the only lien encumbrancing the house. C requests that an amount of money equal to the amount seized from the bank account be returned so that C can complete the renovations on the house. Without the funds, C will be unable to complete the renovations and sell the house. Upon examination, the Commissioner determines that the IRS will be able to collect the entire tax liability if C's house is restored to salable condition. If the National Taxpayer Advocate, or the Commissioner in lieu of the National Taxpayer Advocate, determines that the return of the seized money is in the taxpayer's best interest, the Commissioner may return an amount of money equal to the amount seized from the bank account, in the best interest of the taxpayer and the United States.

(d) *Best interests of the United States and the taxpayer to release levy and return of property where levy made in violation of law.*—(1) *In general.*—If the IRS makes a levy in violation of the law, it is in the best interests of the United States and the taxpayer to release the levy and the IRS will return to the taxpayer any property obtained pursuant to the levy. For example, the IRS will release the levy and return the taxpayer's property if the levy was made—

(i) Without giving the requisite thirty-day notice of the right to a hearing under section 6330;

(ii) During the pendency of a proceeding for refund of divisible tax in violation of section 6331(i);

(iii) Before investigation of the status of levied upon property in violation of section 6331(j);

(iv) During the pendency of an offer-in-compromise in violation of section 6331(k)(1); or

(v) During the period an offer to enter into an installment agreement is pending (or for 30 days following the rejection of an offer, or, if the rejection is timely appealed, during the period that the appeal is pending) or during the period an installment agreement is in effect (or during the 30 days following a termination or, if a timely appeal of termination is filed, during the period the appeal is pending) in violation of section 6331(k)(2).

(2) *Property may not be credited to outstanding liability without the taxpayer's permission.*—When the release of a levy and the return of property are required under this paragraph (d), the property or the proceeds from the sale of the property received by the IRS pursuant to the levy must be returned to the taxpayer unless the taxpayer requests otherwise. The property or proceeds of sale may not be credited to any outstanding tax liability of the taxpayer, including the one with respect to which the IRS made the levy, without the written permission of the taxpayer.

(e) *Time of return.*—Levied upon property in possession of the IRS (other than money) may be returned under paragraphs (c) and (d) of this section at any time. An amount of money equal to the amount of money levied upon or received from a sale of property may be returned at any time before the expiration of 9 months from the date of the levy. When a request for the return of money filed in accordance with paragraph (h) of this section is filed before the expiration of the 9-month period, or a determination to return an amount of money is made before the expiration of the 9-month period, the money may be returned within a reasonable period of time after the expiration of the 9-month period if additional time is necessary for investigation or processing.

(f) *Purchase by the United States.*—For purposes of paragraph (a)(2) of this section, if property is declared purchased by the United States at a sale pursuant to section 6335(e)(1)(C), the United States will be treated as having received an amount of money equal to the minimum price determined by the Commissioner before the sale.

(g) *Determinations by the Commissioner.*—The Commissioner must determine whether any of the conditions authorizing the return of property exists if a taxpayer submits a request for the return of property in accordance with paragraph (h) of this section. The Commissioner also may make this determination independently. If the Commissioner determines that conditions authorizing the return of property are not present, the Commissioner may not authorize the return of property. If the Commissioner determines that conditions authorizing the return of property are present, the Commissioner may (but is not required to, unless the reason for the return of property is that the levy was made in violation of law and is governed by paragraph (d) of this section) authorize the return of property. If the Commissioner decides independently to return

property under paragraph (c)(4) of this section based on the best interests of the taxpayer and the United States, the taxpayer or the National Taxpayer Advocate (or his or her delegate) must consent to the return of property.

(h) *Procedures for request for the return of property.*—(1) *Manner.*—A request for the return of property must be made in writing to the address on the levy form.

(2) *Form.*—The written request must include the following information—

(i) The name, current address, and taxpayer identification number of the person requesting the return of money (or property purchased by the United States);

(ii) A description of the property levied upon;

(iii) The date of the levy; and

(iv) A statement of the grounds upon which the return of money is being requested (or property purchased by the United States).

(i) *No interest.*—No interest will be paid on any money returned under this section.

(j) *Administrative collection upon default.*—If the Commissioner returns property under this section, and the taxpayer fails to pay the previously assessed liability for which the levy was made on the returned property, the Commissioner may administratively collect the liability. Collection may include levying again on the returned property as long as statutory and administrative requirements are followed.

(k) *Effective date.*—This section is applicable on July 14, 2005. [Reg. §301.6343-3.]

☐ *T.D.* 9213, 7-13-2005.]

COLLECTION OF STATE INDIVIDUAL INCOME TAXES

[Reg. §1.6361-1]

§1.6361-1. Collection and administration of qualified State individual income taxes.—Except as otherwise provided in §§301.6361-1 to 301.6365-2, inclusive, of this chapter (Regulations on Procedure and Administration), the provisions of this part under subtitle F of the Internal Revenue Code of 1954 relating to the collection and administration of the taxes imposed by chapter 1 of such Code on the incomes of individuals (or relating to civil or criminal sanctions with respect to such collection and administration) shall apply to the collection and administration of qualified State individual income taxes (as defined in section 6362 of such Code and the regulations thereunder) as if such taxes were imposed by chapter 1. [Reg. §1.6361-1.]

☐ [*T.D.* 7577, 12-19-78.]

[Reg. §31.6361-1]

§31.6361-1. Collection and administration of qualified State individual income taxes.—Except as otherwise provided in §§301.6361-1 to 301.6365-2, inclusive, of this chapter (Regulations on Procedure and Administration), the provi-

sions of this part under subtitle F or chapter 24 of the Internal Revenue Code of 1954 relating to the collection and administration of the taxes imposed by chapter 1 of such Code on the incomes of individuals (or relating to civil or criminal sanctions with respect to such collection and administration) shall apply to the collection and administration of qualified State individual income taxes (as defined in section 6362 of such Code and the regulations thereunder) as if such taxes were imposed by chapter 1 or chapter 24. [Reg. §31.6361-1.]

☐ [*T.D.* 7577, 12-19-78.]

[Reg. §301.6361-1]

§301.6361-1. Collection and administration of qualified taxes.—(a) *In general.*—In the case of any State which has in effect a State agreement (as defined in paragraph (a) of §301.6361-4), the Commissioner of Internal Revenue shall collect and administer each qualified tax (as defined in paragraph (b) of §301.6361-4) of such State. No fee or other charge shall be imposed upon any State for the collection or administration of any qualified tax of such State or any other State. In any such case of collection and administration of qualified taxes, the provisions of subtitle F (relating to procedure and administration), subtitle G (relating to the Joint Committee on Taxation), and chapter 24 (relating to the collection of income tax at source on wages), and the provisions of regulations thereunder, insofar as such provisions relate to the collection and administration of the taxes imposed on the income of individuals by chapter 1 (and the civil and criminal sanctions provided by subtitle F, or by title 18 of the United States Code (relating to crimes and criminal procedure), with respect to such collection and administration) shall apply to the collection and administration of qualified taxes as if such taxes were imposed by chapter 1, except to the extent that the application of such provisions (and sanctions) are modified by regulations issued under subchapter E (as defined in paragraph (d) of §301.6361-4). Any extension of time which is granted for the making of a payment, or for the filing of any return, which relates to any Federal tax imposed by subtitle A (or by subtitle C with respect to filing a return) shall constitute automatically an extension of the same amount of time for the making of the corresponding payment or for the filing of the corresponding return relating to any qualified tax.

(b) *Returns of qualified taxes.*—Every individual, estate, or trust which has liability for one or more qualified taxes for a taxable year—

(1) Shall file a Federal income tax return at the time prescribed pursuant to section 6072(a) (whether or not such return is required by section 6012), and shall file therewith on the prescribed form a return under penalties of perjury for each tax which is—

(i) A qualified resident tax imposed by a State of which the taxpayer was a resident, as defined in §301.6362-6, for any part of the taxable year;

(ii) A qualified nonresident tax imposed by a State within which was located the source or sources from which the taxpayer derived, while not a resident of such State and while not exempt from liability for the tax by reason of a reciprocal agreement between such State and the State of which he is a resident, 25 percent or more of his aggregate wage and other business income, as defined in paragraph (c) of §301.6362-5, for the taxable year; or

(iii) A qualified resident or nonresident tax with respect to which any amount was currently collected from the taxpayer's income (including collection by withholding on wages or by payment of estimated income tax), as provided in paragraph (f) of §301.6362-6, for any part of the taxable year; and

(2) Shall declare (in addition to the declaration required with respect to the return of the Federal income tax and in the place and manner prescribed by form or instructions thereto) under penalties of perjury that, to the best of the knowledge and belief of the taxpayer (or, in the case of an estate or trust, of the fiduciary who executes the Federal income tax return), he has no liability for any qualified tax for the taxable year other than any such liabilities returned with the Federal income tax return (pursuant to subparagraph (1) of this paragraph). Such declaration shall constitute a return indicating no liability with respect to each qualified tax other than any such tax for which liability is so returned. A Federal income tax return form which is filed but which does not contain such declaration shall constitute a Federal income tax return only if the taxpayer in fact has no liability for any qualified State tax for the taxable year.

(c) *Credits.*—(1) *Credit for tax of another State or political subdivision.*—(i) *In general.*—A credit allowable under a qualified tax law against the tax imposed by such law for a taxpayer's tax liability to another State or a political subdivision of another State shall be allowed if the requirements of subdivision (ii) of this subparagraph are met, and if the credit meets the requirements of paragraph (c) of §301.6362-4. Such credit shall be allowed without regard to whether the tax imposed by the other State or subdivision thereof is a qualified tax, and without regard to whether such tax has been paid.

(ii) *Substantiation of tax liability for which a credit is allowed.*—If the liability which gives rise to a credit of the type described in subdivision (i) of this subparagraph is with respect to a qualified tax, then the fact of such liability shall be substantiated by filing the return on which such liability is reported. If such liability is not with respect to a qualified tax, then the Commissioner may require a taxpayer who claims entitlement to such a credit to complete a form to be submitted with his return of the qualified tax against which the credit is claimed. On such form the taxpayer shall identify each of the other States (the liabilities to which were not substantiated as provided in the first sentence of this subdivision) or political subdivisions to which the taxpayer reported a liability for a tax giving rise to the credit, furnish the name or description of each such tax, state the amount of the liability so reported with respect to each such tax and the beginning and ending dates of the taxable period for which such liability was reported, and provide such other information as is requested in the form or in the instructions thereto. In addition, the taxpayer shall agree on such form to notify the Commissioner in the event that the amount of any tax liability (or portion thereof) which is claimed as giving rise to a credit of the type described in subdivision (i) of this subparagraph is changed or adjusted, whether as a result of an amended return filed by the taxpayer, a determination by the jurisdiction imposing the tax, or in any other manner.

(2) *Credit or withheld qualified tax.*—An individual from whose wages an amount is withheld on account of a qualified tax shall receive a credit for such amount against his aggregate liability for all such qualified taxes and the Federal income tax for the taxable year, whether or not such tax has been paid over to the Federal Gov-

ernment by the employer. The credit shall operate in the manner provided by section 31(a) of the Code and the regulations thereunder with respect to Federal income tax withholding.

(d) *Collection of qualified taxes at source on wages.*—(1) *In general.*—Except as otherwise provided in subparagraph (2) of this paragraph, every employer making payment of wages to an employee described in such subparagraph shall deduct and withhold upon such wages the amount prescribed with respect to the qualified tax designated in such subparagraph. The amounts prescribed for withholding with respect to each such qualified tax shall be published in Circular E (Employer's Tax Guide) or other appropriate Internal Revenue Service publications. See paragraph (f)(1) of §301.6362-7 with respect to civil and criminal penalties to which an employer shall be subject with respect to his responsibilities relating to qualified taxes.

(2) *Specific withholding requirements.*—An employer shall deduct and withhold upon an employee's wages the amount prescribed with respect to a qualified tax with respect to which such employee is subject to the current collection provisions pursuant to paragraph (f) of §301.6362-6, unless:

(i) In the case of a qualified resident tax, the employee's services giving rise to the wages are performed in another State, and such other State or a political subdivision thereof imposes a nonresident tax on such employee with respect to which the withholding amount exceeds the prescribed withholding amount with respect to such qualified resident tax, and the State imposing such qualified resident tax grants a credit against it for such nonresident tax.

(ii) In the case of a qualified nonresident tax, either:

(A) Residents of the State in which the employee resides are exempt from liability for the qualified nonresident tax imposed by the State from sources within which his wage income is derived, by reason of an interstate compact or agreement to which the two States are parties, or

(B) The State in which the employee resides imposes a qualified resident tax on such employee with respect to which the prescribed withholding amounts exceed the prescribed withholding amounts with respect to the qualified nonresident tax imposed by the State from sources within which his wage income is derived, and the State in which he resides grants a credit against its qualified resident tax for such qualified nonresident tax.

If the nonresident tax described in subdivision (i) of this subparagraph is a qualified nonresident tax imposed by a State, then the reference in such subdivision to the State in which the services are performed shall be construed as a reference to the State from sources within which the wage income is derived, within the meaning of paragraph (d)(1) of §301.6362-5.

(3) *Forms, procedures, and returns relating to withholding with respect to qualified taxes.*—(i) *Forms W-4 and W-4P.*—Forms W-4 (Employee's Withholding Allowance Certificate) and W-4P (Annuitant's Request for Income Tax Withholding) shall include information as to the State in which the employee resides, and shall be used for purposes of withholding with respect to both Federal and qualified taxes. An employee shall show on his Form W-4 the State in which he resides for purposes of this paragraph, and shall file a new Form W-4 within 10 days after he changes his State of residence. An employee who fails to meet either of the requirements set forth in the preceding sentence, with the intent to evade the withholding tax imposed with respect to a qualified tax, shall be subject to the penalty provided in section 7205 of the Code. An employer shall be responsible for determining the State within which are located the sources from which the employee's wage income is derived for purposes of this paragraph; and, if the employee does not file a Form W-4, the employer shall assume for such purposes that the employee resides in that State. When an employer and an employee enter into a voluntary withholding agreement pursuant to §31.3402(p)-1, the employer shall withhold the amount prescribed with respect to the qualified resident tax imposed by the State in which the employee resides, as indicated on Form W-4. Similarly, if an annuitant requests withholding with respect to his annuity payments pursuant to section 3402(o)(1)(B) of the Code, the payer shall withhold the whole dollar amount specified by the annuitant with respect to a qualified resident tax, provided that the combined withholding with respect to Federal and qualified taxes on each annuity payment shall be a whole dollar amount not less than $5, and that the net amount of any annuity payment received by the payee shall not be reduced to less than $10.

(ii) *Forms W-2 and W-2P.*—Forms W-2 (Wage and Tax Statement) and W-2P (the corresponding form for annuities) shall show:

(A) The total amount withheld with respect to the Federal income tax;

(B) The total amount withheld with respect to qualified taxes;

(C) The name of each State imposing a qualified tax in which the employee (or annuitant) resided during the taxable year, as shown on Form W-4 (or W-4P);

(D) The name of each State imposing a qualified nonresident tax within which were located sources from which the employee's wage income was derived during a period of the taxable year in which he was not shown as a resident of such State on Form W-4, and the amount of the employee's wage income so derived; and

(E) The name of each State or locality that imposes an income tax which is not a qualified tax and with respect to which the employer withheld on the employee's wage income for the taxable year, and the amount of wage income with respect to which the employer so withheld.

(iii) Requirements relating to deposit and payment of withheld tax.—Rules relating to the deposit and remittance of withheld Federal income and FICA taxes, including those prescribed in section 6302 of the Code and the regulations thereunder, shall apply also to amounts withheld with respect to qualified taxes. Thus, an employer's liability with respect to the deposit and payment of withheld taxes shall be for the combined amount of withholding with respect to Federal and qualified taxes. The Federal Tax Deposit form shall separately indicate:

    (A) The combined total amount of Federal income, FICA, and qualified taxes withheld;

    (B) The combined total amount of qualified taxes withheld; and

    (C) The total amount of qualified taxes withheld with respect to each electing State.

Data indicating the total amount of tax deposits processed by the Internal Revenue Service with respect to the qualified taxes of an electing State will be available to that State upon request on as frequent as a weekly basis. These data will be available no later than 10 working days after the end of the calendar week in which the deposits were processed by the Service.

    (iv) Employment tax returns.—Forms 941 (Employer's Quarterly Federal Tax Return), 941-E (Quarterly Return of Withheld Income Tax), 941-M (Employer's Monthly Federal Tax Return), 942 (Employer's Quarterly Tax Return for Household Employees), and 943 (Employer's Annual Tax Return for Agricultural Employees) shall indicate the total amount withheld with respect to each qualified tax, as directed by such forms or their instructions.

(e) Criminal penalties.—A criminal offense committed with respect to a qualified tax shall be treated as a separate offense from a similar offense committed with respect to the Federal tax. Thus, for example, if a taxpayer willfully attempts to evade both the Federal tax and a qualified tax by failing to report a portion of his income, he shall be considered as having committed two criminal offenses, each subject to a separate penalty under section 7201. See also § 301.6362-7(f) with respect to criminal penalties.

(f) Allocation of amounts collected with respect to tax and criminal fines.—(1) *In general.*—The aggregate amount that has been collected from a taxpayer (including amounts collected by withholding) in respect of liability for both one or more qualified taxes and the Federal income tax for a taxable year shall be allocated among the Federal Government and the States imposing qualified taxes for which the taxpayer is liable in the proportion which the taxpayer's liability for each such tax bears to his aggregate liability for such year to all of such taxing jurisdictions with respect to such taxes. A reallocation shall be made either when an amount is collected from the taxpayer or his employer or is credited or refunded to the taxpayer, subsequent to the making of the initial allocation, or when a determination is made by the Commissioner that an

error was made with respect to a previous allocation. However, any such allocation or reallocation shall not affect the amount of a taxpayer's or employer's liability to either jurisdiction, or the amount of the assessment and collection which may be made with respect to a taxpayer or employer. Accordingly, such allocations and reallocations shall not be taken into consideration for purposes of the application of statutes of limitation or provisions relating to interest, additions to tax, penalties, and criminal sanctions. See example (4) in subparagraph (4) of this paragraph. In addition, any such allocation or reallocation shall not affect the amount of the deduction to which a taxpayer is entitled under section 164 for a year in which he made payment (including payments made by withholding) of an amount which was designated as being in respect of his liability for a qualified tax. However, to the extent that an amount which was paid by a taxpayer and designated as being in respect of his liability for a qualified tax is allocated or reallocated in such a manner as to apply it toward the taxpayer's liability for the Federal income tax, such allocation or reallocation shall be treated as a refund to the taxpayer of an amount paid in respect of a State income tax, and shall be included in the gross income of the taxpayer to the extent appropriate under section 111 and the regulations thereunder in the year in which the allocation or reallocation is made. See section 451 and the regulations thereunder. Similarly, to the extent that an amount which was paid by a taxpayer and designated as being in respect of his Federal income tax liability is allocated or reallocated in such a manner as to apply it toward his liability for a qualified tax, such allocation or reallocation shall be treated as a payment made by the taxpayer in respect of a State income tax, and shall be deductible under section 164 in the year in which the allocation or reallocation is made. The Internal Revenue Service shall notify the taxpayer in writing of any allocation or reallocation of tax liabilities in a proportion other than that of the respective tax liabilities shown on the taxpayer's returns.

(2) *Amounts of collections and liabilities.*—For purposes of this paragraph the aggregate amount that has been collected from a taxpayer or his employer in respect of tax liability shall include the amounts of interest provided in chapter 67, and additions to tax and assessable penalties provided in chapter 68, which are collected with respect to such tax; but shall not include criminal fines provided in chapter 75, or in title 18 of the United States Code, which are collected with respect to offenses relating to such tax. (See subparagraph (3) of this paragraph with respect to the treatment of such criminal fines.) However, for purposes of this paragraph, the amount of the taxpayer's liability for each tax shall exclude his liability for such interest, additions to tax, and assessable penalties with respect to such tax, and his liability for criminal fines imposed with respect to offenses relating to such tax. For purposes of this paragraph, the amount

of the taxpayer's liability for each tax shall be computed by taking credits into account, except that there shall be no reduction for any amounts paid on account of such liability, whether by means of withholding, estimated tax payment, or otherwise.

(3) *Special rules relating to criminal fines.*— (i) Except as otherwise provided in subdivision (ii) of this subparagraph, when a criminal charge is brought against a taxpayer with respect to a taxable year pursuant to chapter 75, or to title 18 of the United States Code, or to a corresponding provision of a qualified tax law, alleging that an offense was committed against the United States with respect to the Federal income tax or against a State with respect to a qualified tax, and an amount of money is collected by the Federal Government as a fine as a result of such charge, then the Federal Government shall remit an amount to each State, if any, which is an affected jurisdiction. The amount remitted to each such State shall bear the same proportion to the total amount collected as a fine as the taxpayer's liability with respect to the qualified taxes of that State bears to the aggregate of the taxpayer's income tax liabilities to all affected jurisdictions for the taxable year, as determined under subparagraphs (1) and (2) of this paragraph. For purposes of this subparagraph, an affected jurisdiction is (A) a jurisdiction with respect to the tax of which a criminal charge described in the preceding sentence was brought for the taxable year, or (B) a jurisdiction with respect to the Federal income tax or the qualified tax of which the acts or omissions alleged in such a criminal charge would constitute the basis for the bringing of a criminal charge for the same taxable year. However, in no case shall the amount received by an affected State, or the amount of the excess of the amount received by the Federal Government over the amount of its remissions to the States, with respect to a fine exceed the maximum fine prescribed by statute for the offense against that jurisdiction with respect to which a criminal charge was brought, or with respect to which the bringing of a criminal charge could have been supported on the basis of the acts or omissions alleged in a criminal charge brought. For purposes of this subparagraph, the amount collected as a fine as a result of a criminal charge shall include amounts paid in settlement of an actual or potential liability for a fine, amounts paid pursuant to a conviction and amounts paid pursuant to a plea of guilty or *nolo contendere.*

(ii) If a criminal charge described in the first sentence of subdivision (i) of this subparagraph is actually brought with respect to the income tax of every affected jurisdiction with respect to the taxable year, and if a Court adjudicates on the merits the taxpayer's liability for a fine to each such jurisdiction, and includes in its decree a direction of the amount, if any, to be paid as a fine to each such jurisdiction, then that decree shall govern the allocation of the amount of money collected by the Federal Government as a fine with respect to the taxable year.

(4) *Examples.*—The application of this paragraph may be illustrated by the following examples:

Example (1). The total combined amount of State X qualified tax and Federal income tax collected from A, a resident of State X, for the taxable year is $5,100. The amounts of A's liabilities for such taxes for that year are $800 to State X and $4,000 to the Federal Government. Since A's tax liability to State X is one-sixth of the combined tax liability ($4,800), one-sixth ($50) of the amount to be refunded to A ($300) is chargeable against State X's account, and five-sixths ($250) is chargeable against the Federal Government's account.

Example (2). Assume the same facts as in example (1) except that the total amount collected from A is $4,500. Since A's liabilities for the State X tax and the Federal tax are one-sixth and five-sixths, respectively, of the combined tax liability, the Federal Government shall pay over to State X one-sixth ($750) of the amount actually collected from A, and the Federal Government shall retain five-sixths ($3,750).

Example (3). The total amount of State X qualified tax, State Y qualified tax, and Federal income tax collected from B, a resident of State X who is employed in State Y, for the taxable year is $5,500. The amounts of B's liabilities for such taxes for that year are: $250 for the State X tax (after allowance of a credit for State Y's qualified tax), $750 for the State Y tax, and $4,000 for the Federal tax. Since B's liability for the State X tax ($250) is 5 percent of the combined tax liability ($5,000), his liability for the State Y tax ($750) is 15 percent of such combined liability, and his liability for the Federal tax ($4,000) is 80 percent of such combined liability, the total amount to be refunded to B ($500) shall be chargeable in the following manner: 5 percent ($25) against State X's account, 15 percent ($75) against State Y's account, and 80 percent ($400) against the Federal Government's account.

Example (4). C is liable for $2,000 in Federal income tax and $500 in State X qualified tax (a resident tax) for the taxable year. However, on his Federal income tax return for such year, C erroneously described himself as a resident of State Y (which does not have a qualified tax), and he filed with such return his declaration to the effect that he had no qualified tax liability for the year. Accordingly, C paid only $2,000 for his Federal tax liability, and such amount was retained in the account of the Federal Government. Subsequently, C's error is discovered. The amount collected by the Federal Government from C for such year must be allocated between the Federal Government and State X in proportion to C's tax liability to both. Accordingly, the Federal Government must pay over to State X the amount of $400 (which is $1/5$ ($500/$2,500) of the $2,000 collected). If the Federal Government collects from C the additional $500 owed, it will retain $400 of such amount and pay the remaining $100 to State X. Similarly, if the Federal Government collects from C any interest, or any additions to tax or assessable penalties under chapter 68, $^4/_5$ of the amount of such collections shall be retained by the Federal Government, and $^1/_5$ of such amount shall be paid over to State X. However, notwithstanding the allocation of the funds between the taxing jurisdictions, C's liability for the $500 retains its character as a liability for State X tax. Therefore, any interest, additions to tax, or assessable penalties imposed with respect to the State X tax shall be imposed with respect to C's full $500 liability for such tax, notwithstanding the fact that amounts collected with respect to such items shall be allocated $^4/_5$ to the Federal Government.

Example (5). A criminal charge is brought against D pursuant to chapter 75, alleging that he willfully evaded the payment of Federal income tax by failing to report interest income derived from obligations of the United States. D enters a plea of *non contendere* to the charge and pays $2,500 as a fine to the Federal Government. The act alleged in the criminal charge would not support the bringing of a criminal charge under a State law corresponding to chapter 75, or to title 18 of the United States Code, with respect to the qualified tax of any State; accordingly, the United States is the only affected jurisdiction, and no remittances shall be made to any State with respect to the amount collected by the Federal Government as a fine.

Example (6). A criminal charge is brought against E pursuant to chapter 75, alleging that he willfully attempted to evade the assessment of liability for both Federal income tax and the qualified tax of State X by filing false and fraudulent income tax returns. E's case is settled upon the condition that he pay a fine in the amount of $5,000. As determined pursuant to subparagraph (2) of this paragraph, E's liabilities for the taxable year are in the amounts of $7,200 to the Federal Government and $800 to State X. Accordingly, after the Federal Government collects the fine, $500 ($5,000 × $800/$8,000) is remitted to State X.

Example (7). Assume the same facts as in example (6), except that E is tried and convicted on both charges, and pursuant to court decree he pays to the United States a fine of $6,000 with respect to each charge, or a total of $12,000. Because a criminal charge was brought with respect to each affected jurisdiction, and the allocation of the total amount paid as a fine was specifically imposed by a court decree, the direction of the Court shall govern the allocation. Accordingly, after the Federal Government collects the fine it pays over $6,000 to the account of State X. [Reg. § 301.6361-1.]

☐ [*T.D.* 7577, 12-19-78.]

[Reg. § 301.6361-2]

§ 301.6361-2. Judicial and administrative proceedings; Federal representation of State interests.—(a) *Civil proceedings.*—(1) *General rule.*— Any person shall have the same right to bring or contest a civil action, and to obtain a review thereof, with respect to a qualified tax (including the current collection thereof) in the same court or courts which would be available to him, and pursuant to the same requirements and procedures to which he would be subject, under chapter 76 (relating to judicial proceedings), and under title 28 of the United States Code (relating to the judiciary and judicial procedure), if the tax were imposed by section 1 or chapter 24 of the Internal Revenue Code. For purposes of this section, the term "person" includes the Federal Government. Except as provided in subparagraph (2) of this paragraph, to the extent that the preceding sentence provides judicial procedures (including review procedures) with respect to any matter, such procedures shall replace civil judicial procedures under State law.

(2) *Exception.*—The right or power of the courts of any State to pass on matters involving the constitution of such State is unaffected by any provision of this paragraph; however, the jurisdiction of a State court in such matters shall not extend beyond the issue of constitutionality. Thus, if in a case involving the validity of a qualified tax statute under the State constitution, the State court holds such statute constitutional, such court shall not proceed to decide the amount of the tax liability.

(b) *Criminal proceedings.*—Only the Federal Government shall have the right to bring a criminal action with respect to a qualified tax (including the current collection thereof). Such an action shall be brought in the same court or courts which would be available to the Federal Government, and pursuant to the same requirements and procedures to which the Federal Government would be subject, if the tax were imposed by section 1 or chapter 24 of the Internal Revenue Code.

(c) *Administrative proceedings.*—Any person shall have the same rights in administrative proceedings of the Internal Revenue Service with respect to a qualified tax (including the current collection thereof) which would be available to him, and shall be subject to the same administrative requirements and procedures to which he would be subject, if the tax were imposed by section 1 or chapter 24 of the Internal Revenue Code.

(d) *United States representation of State interests.*—(1) *General rule.*—Except as provided in subparagraphs (2) and (3) of this paragraph, the Federal Government shall appear on behalf of any State the qualified tax of which it collects (or did collect for the year in issue), and shall represent such State's interests in any administrative or judicial proceeding, either civil or criminal in nature, which relates to the administration and collection of such qualified tax, in the same manner as it represents the interests of the United States in corresponding proceedings involving Federal income tax matters.

(2) *Exceptions.*—The Federal Government shall not so represent a State's interests either—

(i) In proceedings in a State court involving the constitution of such State, to the extent of such constitutional issue, or

(ii) In proceedings in any court involving the relationship between the United States and the State, to the extent of the issue pertaining to such relationship, if either:

(A) The proceeding is one which is initiated by the United States against the State, or by the State against the United States, and no individual (except in his official capacity as a governmental official) is an original party to the proceeding, or

(B) The proceeding is not one described in (A), but the State elects to represent its own interests to the extent permissible under this subdivision.

(3) *Finality of Federal administrative determinations.*—State and local government officials and employees may not review Federal administrative determinations concerning tax liabilities of, refunds owed to, or criminal prosecutions of, individuals with respect to qualified taxes. See, however, § 301.6363-3 relating to State administration of a qualified tax with respect to transition years. If requested by an electing State, the Commissioner or his delegate may, under terms and conditions set forth in an agreement with such State, permit such State to carry on operations supplementary to the Federal administration of the State's qualified tax (including supplemental audits or examinations of tax returns by State audit personnel), but all administrative determinations shall be made by the Federal Government without review by the State. An agreement which permits supplemental audits or examinations of tax returns by State audit personnel shall provide that the audits and examinations shall be conducted under the supervision and control of the Commissioner or his delegate, who shall have the authority to determine which returns shall be audited and when the audits shall occur. Also, such agreements shall provide that the results of any such supplemental audit shall be referred to the Commissioner or his delegate for final administrative determination. The Commissioner or his delegate shall, to the extent permitted by law, allow an electing State reasonable access to tax returns and other appropriate records and information relating to its qualified tax for the purpose of conducting any such supplemental operations. In addition, the Secretary or his delegate shall permit an electing State to inspect the workpapers which are compiled in the course of verification by the Treasury Department of the correctness of the accounting by which the amounts of the actual net collections attributable to the electing State's qualified taxes are determined. [Reg. § 301.6361-2.]

☐ [T.D. 7577, 12-19-78.]

[Reg. § 301.6361-3]

§ 301.6361-3. Transfers to States.—(a) *Periodic transfers.*—In general, amounts collected by the Federal Government which are allocable to qualified taxes (including criminal fines which are required to be paid to a State, as determined under paragraph (f)(3) of § 301.6361-1) shall be promptly transferred to each State imposing such a tax. Transfers of such amounts, based on percentages of estimated Federal collections, shall be made not less frequently than every third business day unless the State agrees to accept transfers at less frequent intervals.

(b) *Determination of amounts of transfers.*—The amounts allocable to the qualified taxes of each State for purposes of periodic transfer shall be determined as a percentage of the estimated aggregate net individual income tax collections made by the Federal Government. For purposes of this paragraph, the "aggregate net individual income tax collections" shall include amounts collected on account of the Federal individual income tax and all qualified taxes by all means (including withholding, tax returns, and declarations of estimated tax), and shall be reduced to the extent of any liability to taxpayers for credits or refunds by reason of overpayments of such taxes. The percentage of the estimated amount of such collections which is allocated to each State shall be based on an estimate which is to be made by the Office of Tax Analysis prior to the beginning of each calendar year as to what portion of the estimated aggregate net individual income tax collections for the forthcoming year will be attributable to the qualified taxes of that State. Each State will be notified prior to the beginning of each calendar year of the amount which it is estimated that the State will receive by application of that percentage for the year. However, the Office of Tax Analysis shall, from time to time throughout the calendar year, revise the percentage estimates when such a revision is, in the opinion of that office necessary to conform such estimates to the actual receipts. When such a revision is made, the payments to the State will be adjusted accordingly.

(c) *Adjustment of difference between actual collections and periodic transfers.*—At least once annually the Secretary or his delegate shall determine the difference between the aggregate amount of the actual net collections made (taking into account credits, refunds, and amounts received by withholding with respect to which a tax return is not filed) which is attributable to each State's qualified taxes during the preceding year and the aggregate amount actually transferred to such State based on estimates during such year. The amount of such difference, as so determined, shall be a charge against, or an addition to, the amounts otherwise determined to be payable to the State.

(d) *Recipient of transferred funds.*—All funds transferred pursuant to section 6361(c) and paragraph (a) of this section shall be transferred by the Federal Government to the State official designated by the Governor to receive such funds in the State agreement pursuant to paragraph (d)(5) of § 301.6363-1, unless the Governor notifies the Secretary or his delegate in writing of the designation of a different State official to receive the funds. [Reg. § 301.6361-3.]

☐ [*T.D.* 7577, 12-19-78.]

[Reg. § 301.6361-4]

§ 301.6361-4. Definitions.—For purposes of the regulations in this part under subchapter E of chapter 64 of the Internal Revenue Code of 1954, relating to collection and administration of State individual income taxes—

(a) *State agreement.*—The term "State agreement" means an agreement between a State and the Federal Government which was entered into pursuant to section 6363 and the regulations thereunder, and which provides for the Federal collection and administration of the qualified tax or taxes of that State.

(b) *Qualified tax.*—The term "qualified tax" means a tax which is a "qualified State individual income tax," as defined in section 6362 (including subsection (f)(1) thereof, which requires that a State agreement be in effect) and the regulations thereunder.

(c) *Chapters and subtitles.*—References in regulations in this part under subchapter E to chapters and subtitles are to chapters and subtitles of the Internal Revenue Code of 1954, unless otherwise indicated.

(d) *Subchapter E.*—The term "subchapter E" means subchapter E of chapter 64 of the Internal Revenue Code of 1954, relating to collection and administration of State individual income taxes, as amended from time to time. [Reg. § 301.6361-4.]

☐ [*T.D.* 7577, 12-19-78.]

[Reg. § 301.6361-5]

§ 301.6361-5. Effective date of section 6361.— Section 6361 shall take effect on the first January 1 which is more than 1 year after the first date on which at least one State has filed a notice of election with the Secretary or his delegate to enter into a State agreement. For purposes of this section, a notice of election shall be deemed to have been filed by a State only if there is no defect in either the State's notice of election or the State's tax law of which the Secretary notified the Governor pursuant to paragraph (c) of § 301.6363-1, and which has not been retroactively cured under the provisions of such paragraph. [Reg. § 301.6361-5.]

☐ [*T.D.* 7577, 12-19-78.]

[Reg. § 301.6362-1]

§ 301.6362-1. Types of qualified tax.—(a) *In general.*—A qualified tax may be either a "qualified resident tax" within the meaning of paragraph (b) of this section, or a "qualified nonresident tax" within the meaning of paragraph (c) of this section.

(b) *Qualified resident tax.*—A tax imposed by a State on the income of individuals, estates, and trusts which are residents of such State within

the meaning of section 6362(e) and § 301.6362-6 shall be a "qualified resident tax" if it is either:

(1) A tax based on Federal taxable income which meets the requirements of section 6362(b), (e), and (f), and of § § 301.6362-2, 301.6362-6, and 301.6362-7; or

(2) A tax which is a percentage of the Federal tax and which meets the requirements of section 6362(c), (e), and (f), and of § § 301.6362-3, 301.6362-6, and 301.6362-7.

(c) *Qualified nonresident tax.*—A tax imposed by a State on the wage and other business income of individuals who are not residents of such State within the meaning of section 6362(e)(1) and paragraph (b) of § 301.6362-6 shall be a "qualified nonresident tax" if it meets the requirements of section 6362(d), (e), and (f), and of § § 301.6362-5, 301.6362-6, and 301.6362-7. [Reg. § 301.6362-1.]

☐ [*T.D.* 7577, 12-19-78.]

[Reg. § 301.6362-2]

§ 301.6362-2. Qualified resident tax based on taxable income.—(a) *In general.*—A tax meets the requirements of section 6362(b) and this section only if it is imposed on the amount of the taxable income, as defined in section 63, of the individual, estate, or trust, adjusted—

(1) By subtracting an amount equal to the amount of the taxpayer's interest on obligations of the United States which was included in his gross income for the taxable year;

(2) By adding an amount equal to the amount of the taxpayer's net State income tax deduction, as defined in paragraph (a) of § 301.6362-4, for the taxable year;

(3) By adding an amount equal to the amount of the taxpayer's net tax-exempt income, as defined in paragraph (b) of § 301.6362-4, for the taxable year; and

(4) If a credit is allowed against the tax in accordance with paragraph (b)(3) of this section for sales tax imposed by the State or a political subdivision thereof, by adding an amount equal to the amount of the taxpayer's deduction under section 164(a)(4) for such sales tax.

The tax may provide for either a single rate or multiple rates which vary with the amount of taxable income, as adjusted.

(b) *Permitted adjustments.*—A tax which otherwise meets the requirements of paragraph (a) of this section shall not be deemed to fail to meet such requirements solely because it provides for one or more of the following adjustments:

(1) A credit meeting the requirements of paragraph (c) of § 301.6362-4 is allowed against the tax for taxpayer's income tax liability to another State or a political subdivision thereof.

(2) A tax is imposed on the amount taxed under section 56 (relating to the minimum tax for tax preferences).

(3) A credit is allowed against the tax for all or a portion of any general sales tax imposed by the State or a political subdivision thereof with

respect to sales either to the taxpayer or to one or more of his dependents.

(c) *Method of making mandatory adjustments.*— The mandatory adjustments provided in paragraph (a) of this section shall be made directly to taxable income. Except as provided in paragraph (c)(2) of § 301.6362-4, no account shall be taken of any reduction or increase in the Federal adjusted gross income which would result from the exclusion from, or inclusion in, gross income of the items which are the subject of the adjustments. Thus, for example, when for purposes of the calculation the taxpayer's Federal taxable income is adjusted to reflect the exclusion from gross income of interest on obligations of the United States, no change shall be made in the amount of the taxpayer's deduction for medical expenses, or in the amount of his charitable contribution base, even though such amounts would ordinarily depend upon the amount of adjusted gross income. [Reg. § 301.6362-2.]

☐ [*T.D.* 7577, 12-19-78.]

[Reg. § 301.6362-3]

§ 301.6362-3. Qualified resident tax which is a percentage of Federal tax.—(a) *In general.*—A tax meets the requirements of section 6362(c) and this section only if:

(1) The tax is imposed as a single specified percentage of the excess of the taxes imposed by chapter 1 over the sum of the credits allowable under part IV of subchapter A of chapter 1 (other than the credits allowable under sections 31 and 39), and

(2) The amount of the tax is decreased by the amount of the decrease in such liability which would result from excluding from the taxpayer's gross income an amount equal to the amount of interest on obligations of the United States which was included in his gross income for the taxable year.

(b) *Permitted adjustments.*—A tax which otherwise meets the requirements of paragraph (a) of this section shall not be deemed to fail to meet such requirements solely because it provides for one or more of the following three adjustments:

(1) The amount of a taxpayer's liability for tax is increased by the amount of the increase in such liability which would result from including in such taxpayer's gross income all of the following:

(i) An amount equal to the amount of his net State income tax deduction, as defined in paragraph (a) of § 301.6362-4, for the taxable year,

(ii) An amount equal to the amount of his net tax-exempt income, as defined in paragraph (b) of § 301.6362-4, for the taxable year, and

(iii) If a credit is allowed against the tax under paragraph (b)(3) of this section for sales tax imposed by the State or a political subdivision thereof, an amount equal to the amount of his deduction under section 164(a)(4) for such sales tax.

(2) A credit meeting the requirements of paragraph (c) of § 301.6362-4 is allowed against the tax for the income tax of another State or a political subdivision thereof.

(3) A credit is allowed against the tax for all or a portion of any general sales tax imposed by the State or a political subdivision thereof with respect to sales either to the taxpayer or to one or more of his dependents.

(c) *Method of making adjustments.*—Except as specifically provided in paragraphs (a)(2) and (b)(1) of this section and in paragraphs (c)(2) of § 301.6362-4, no account shall be taken of any reduction or increase in the Federal adjusted gross income which would result from the exclusion from, or inclusion in, gross income of the items which are the subject of the adjustments provided in those paragraphs. Thus, for example, when for purposes of the calculation the taxpayer's Federal income tax liability is adjusted to reflect the exclusion from gross income of interest on obligations of the United States, no change shall be made in the amount of the taxpayer's deduction for medical expenses, or in the amount of his charitable contribution base, even though such amounts would ordinarily depend upon the amount of adjusted gross income. Also, when calculating the adjusted Federal tax liability to which the rate of the State tax is to be applied, no adjustment shall be made in the amount of any credit against Federal tax to which a taxpayer is entitled. [Reg. § 301.6362-3.]

☐ [*T.D.* 7577, 12-19-78.]

[Reg. § 301.6362-4]

§ 301.6362-4. Rules for adjustments relating to qualified resident taxes.—(a) *Net State income tax deduction.*—For purposes of section 6362(b)(1)(B) and (c)(3)(B), and § § 301.6362-2 and 301.6362-3, the "net State income tax deduction" shall be the excess (if any) of (1) the amount deducted from income under section 164(a)(3) as taxes paid to a State or to a political subdivision thereof, over (2) the amounts included in income as recoveries of prior income taxes which were paid to a State or to a political subdivision thereof and which had been deducted under section 164(a)(3).

(b) *Net tax-exempt income.*—For purposes of section 6362(b)(1)(C) and (c)(3)(A) and § § 301.6362-2 and 301.6362-3, the "net tax-exempt income" shall be the excess (if any) of:

(1) The sum of (i) the interest on obligations described in section 103(a)(1) other than obligations of the State imposing the tax and the political subdivisions thereof, and (ii) the interest on obligations described in such section of such State and the political subdivisions thereof which under the law of the State is subject to the tax; over

(2) The sum of (i) the amount of deductions allocable to the interest described in subparagraph (1)(i) or (ii) of this paragraph which is disallowed pursuant to section 265 and the regulations thereunder, and (ii) the amount of the

adjustment to basis allocable to such obligations which is required to be made for the taxable year under section 1016(a)(5) or (6).

For purposes of subparagraph (1)(ii) of this paragraph, a State may, at its option, subject to the tax the interest from all, none, or some of its section 103(a)(1) obligations and those of its political subdivisions. For example, a State may subject to tax all of such obligations other than those which it or its political subdivisions issued prior to a specified date, which may be the date that subchapter E became applicable to the State.

(c) *Credits for taxes of other jurisdictions.*—(1) *In general.*—A State tax law that provides for a credit, pursuant to section 6362(b)(2)(B) or (C) or section 6362(c)(4), and paragraph (b)(1) of §301.6362-2 or paragraph (b)(2) of §301.6362-3, for income tax of another State or a political subdivision thereof shall provide that, in the case of each taxpayer, the amount of the credit shall equal the amount of his liability with respect to such other jurisdiction's tax for the taxable year which runs concurrently with, or which ends in, the taxable year used by the taxpayer for purposes of the State tax which provides for the credit. Such a credit may be allowed with respect to every income tax (whether or not qualified) imposed on the taxpayer by another State or a political subdivision thereof, or only with respect to certain of such taxes. However, for purposes of this paragraph, the amount which is treated as being the amount of the taxpayer's liability with respect to any such tax imposed by another jurisdiction shall not exceed the amount of liability for such tax which is both—

(A) Reported to the taxing authorities responsible for collecting such other jurisdiction's tax, and

(B) Substantiated pursuant to the requirements of paragraph (c)(1)(ii) of §301.6361-1.

(2) *Limitation.*—The amount of any credit allowed for the taxable year pursuant to this paragraph shall not exceed the product of the amount of the resident tax against which the credit is allowed, as computed without subtracting any such credit, multiplied by a fraction the numerator of which is the amount of income subject to tax by both the State imposing the resident tax against which the credit is allowed and the other jurisdiction whose tax is being credited, and the denominator of which is the amount of income subject to tax by the State imposing the resident tax against which the credit is allowed. For purposes of the preceding sentence, "income subject to tax" means the amount of the taxpayer's adjusted gross income which is taken into account for purposes of computing tax liability; in the case of a qualified resident tax, an appropriate modification shall be made to take into account any adjustments which are made pursuant to paragraph (a)(1) and (3) of §301.6362-2, or pursuant to paragraph (a)(2) or (b)(1)(ii) of §301.6362-3.

(3) *Examples.*—The application of this paragraph may be illustrated by the following examples:

Example (1). (i) A, a calendar-year, cash-basis taxpayer, is a resident of State X throughout the taxable year. For such year, his adjusted gross income for Federal income tax purposes consists of $24,000, consisting of $3,000 derived from employment in State X, $5,000 derived from employment in State Y, $15,000 derived from employment in State Z, and $1,000 in interest income from United States savings bonds. In addition, he received net tax-exempt income in the amount of $2,000. For the taxable year, he incurs liabilities of $200 for the State Y nonresident income tax, and $1,400 for the State Z nonresident income tax. State X, which has in effect a State agreement for the taxable year, imposes a resident tax against which credits are allowed for the nonresident taxes imposed by States Y and Z. Without taking any such credits into account, however, the amount of A's liability for such resident tax would be $1,500. A properly reports his nonresident income tax liabilities to States Y and Z at the same time that he files his return with respect to the State X tax, and he substantiates on such return his liabilities to States Y and Z.

(ii) The amount of A's income subject to tax in State X is $25,000 (his adjusted gross income of $24,000, minus the United States savings bond income of $1,000, plus the net tax-exempt income of $2,000). The amount of the credit allowable against the State X resident tax for the amount of A's liability with respect to the State Y nonresident tax is calculated as follows: The maximum amount of credit is the actual amount of his liability to Y, or $200. Under subparagraph (2) of this paragraph, the amount of the credit is limited to $300 ($1,500 × $5,000/$25,000). Thus, such limit has no effect, and the full $200 is allowable as a credit against A's liability for the resident tax of State X. The amount of the credit allowable against the State X resident tax for the amount of A's liability with respect to the State Z nonresident tax is calculated as follows: The maximum amount of the credit is the actual amount of his liability to Z, or $1,400. Under subparagraph (2) of this paragraph, the amount of the credit is limited to $900 ($1,500 × $15,000/$25,000). Thus, such limit has the effect of reducing to $900 the amount of the credit allowable for tax of State Z against A's liability for the resident tax of State X.

Example (2). (i) (B), a calendar-year, cash-basis taxpayer, is a resident of State X employed in State Y through March 14, 1977. On March 15, 1977, B becomes a resident of State Z and remains a resident of such State through the remainder of 1977. For 1977, the amount of B's adjusted gross income for Federal income tax purposes is $20,000, consisting of $6,000 derived from employment in State Y which B held during the period of his residence in State X, $12,000 derived from employment in State Z which B held during the period of his residence in State Z, and $2,000 in interest income from various bank accounts. During 1977, B has no interest income from United States obligations, and no tax-exempt income. For 1977, B incurs a liability of $200 to State Y on account of its nonresident income tax imposed with respect to his $6,000 of income derived from sources within that State. State Z, which has in effect a State agreement for 1977, imposes a resident income tax on B which, if B had been a resident of State Z for all 1977, would amount to $1,200 prior to the allowance of any credits under this paragraph. However, by reason of paragraph (e)(1) of § 301.6362-6, B's liability for the resident tax of State Z, before taking into account credits allowed under this paragraph, is reduced to $960 ($1,200 × 292/365, or ⁴/₅). Furthermore, State Z allows a credit for the nonresident tax imposed by State Y.

(ii) The amount of the credit allowable against the State Z resident tax for the amount of B's liability with respect to the State Y nonresident tax is calculated as follows: The maximum amount of the credit is the amount of his actual liability to State Y, or $200. Under subparagraph (2) of this paragraph, the amount of the credit is limited to $288 ($960 × $6,000/$20,000). Thus, such limit has no effect, and the full $200 is allowable as a credit for tax of State Y against B's liability for the resident tax of State Z. [Reg. § 301.6362-4.]

☐ [T.D. 7577, 12-19-78.]

[Reg. § 301.6362-5]

§ 301.6362-5. Qualified nonresident tax.—
(a) *In general.*—A tax meets the requirements of section 6362(d) and this section only if:

(1) The tax is imposed by a State which simultaneously imposes a resident tax meeting the requirements of section 6362(b) and § 301.6362-2 or of section 6362(c) and § 301.6362-3;

(2) The tax is required to be computed in accordance with either the method prescribed in paragraph (b) of this section or another method of which the Secretary or his delegate approves upon submission by the State of the laws pertaining to the tax;

(3) The tax is imposed only on the wage and other business income derived from sources within such State (as defined in paragraph (d) of this section), of all individuals each of whom derives 25 percent or more of his aggregate wage and other business income for the taxable year from sources within such State while he is neither (i) a resident of such State within the meaning of section 6362(e) and § 301.6362-6, nor (ii) exempt from liability for the tax by reason of a reciprocal agreement between such State and the State of which he is a resident within the meaning of those provisions;

(4) The amount of the tax imposed with respect to any individual does not exceed the amount of tax for which such individual would be liable under the qualified resident tax imposed by such State if he were a resident of the State for the period during which he earned wage or other business income from sources

within the State, and if his taxable income for such period were an amount equal to the sum of the zero bracket amount (within the meaning of section 63(d) and determined as if he had been a resident of the State for such period) and the excess of:

(i) The amount of his wage and other business income derived from sources within the State, over

(ii) That portion of the sum of the zero bracket amount and the nonbusiness deductions (*i.e.,* all deductions from adjusted gross income allowable in computing taxable income) taken into account for purposes of the State's qualified resident tax which bears the same ratio to such sum as the amount described in subdivision (i) of this subparagraph bears to his total adjusted gross income for the year; and

(5) For purposes of the tax, wage or other business income is considered as being the income of the individual whose income it is for purposes of section 61.

(b) *Approved method of computing liability for qualified nonresident tax.*—A tax satisfies the requirement of paragraph (a)(2) of this section if the amount of the tax is computed either as a percentage of the excess of the amount described in paragraph (a)(4)(i) of this section over the amount described in paragraph (a)(4)(ii) of this section, or by application of progressive rates to such excess.

(c) *Definition of wage and other business income.*—For purposes of section 6362(d) and this section, the term "wage and other business income" means the following types of income:

(1) Wages, as defined in section 3401(a) and the regulations thereunder, but for these purposes:

(i) The amount of wages shall exclude amounts which are treated as wages under section 3402(o) or (p) (relating to supplemental unemployment compensation benefits, annuity payments, and voluntary withholding agreements), and amounts which are treated as disability payments to the extent that they are excluded from gross income for Federal income tax purposes, pursuant to section 105(d), and

(ii) The amount of wages shall be reduced by those expenses which are directly related to the earning of such wages and with respect to which deductions are properly claimed from gross income in computing adjusted gross income;

(2) Net earnings from self-employment, as defined in section 1402(a); and

(3) The distributive share of income of any trade or business carried on by a trust, estate, or electing small business corporation (as defined in section 1371(a) and the regulations thereunder), to the extent that such share:

(i) Is includible in the gross income of the taxpayer for the taxable year, and

(ii) Would constitute net earnings from self-employment if the trade or business were carried on by a partnership.

For purposes of this subparagraph, "distributive share" includes the income of a trust or estate which is taxable to the taxpayer as a beneficiary under applicable Federal income tax rules, and the undistributed taxable income of an electing small business corporation which is taxable to the taxpayer as a shareholder under section 1373.

(d) *Income derived from sources within a State.*—(1) *Income attributable primarily to services.*—Except as otherwise provided by Federal statute (see paragraphs (h), (i), and (j) of § 301.6362-7), wage income and other business income (net earnings from self-employment or distributive shares) which is attributable more to services performed by the taxpayer than to a capital investment of the taxpayer shall be considered to have been derived from sources within a State only if the services of the taxpayer which give rise to the income are performed in such State. If for a taxable year only a portion of the taxpayer's services giving rise to the income from one employment, trade, or business is performed within a State, then it shall be presumed that the amount of income from such employment, trade, or business which is derived from sources within that State equals that portion of the total income derived from such employment, trade, or business for the year which the amount of time spent by the taxpayer for such year performing services with respect to that employment, trade, or business in that State bears to the aggregate amount of time spent by the taxpayer for such year performing all of such services. However, the presumption stated in the preceding sentence may be rebutted in the event that the taxpayer proves, by use of detailed records, that the correct allocation of his income is otherwise.

(2) *Income attributable primarily to investment.*—Except as otherwise provided by Federal statute (see paragraph (j) of § 301.6362-7), business income (net earnings from self-employment or distributive shares) which is attributable more to a capital investment of the taxpayer than to services performed by the taxpayer shall be considered to have been derived from sources within the State, if any, in which the significant activities of the trade or business are conducted. If for the taxable year only a portion of the significant activities conducted with respect to one trade or business is conducted within a certain State, then the portion of the taxpayer's total income for the year from such trade or business which is considered to be derived from sources within that State shall be computed as follows:

(i) *Allocation by records.*—The portion of the taxpayer's total income from the trade or business which is considered to be derived from sources within the State shall be the portion which is allocable to such sources according to the records of the taxpayer or of the partnership, trust, estate, or electing small business corporation from which his income is derived, provided that the taxpayer establishes to the satisfaction of the district director, when requested to do so, that those records fairly and equitably reflect the income which is allocable to sources within the State. An allocation made pursuant to this subdivision shall be based on the location of the significant activities of the trade or business, and not on the location at which the taxpayer's personal services are performed.

(ii) *Allocation by formula.*—If the taxpayer (or the trade or business) does not keep records meeting the requirements of subdivision (i) of this subparagraph, or if the taxpayer fails to meet the burden of proof set forth therein, then the amount of the taxpayer's income from the trade or business which is considered to be derived from sources within the State shall be determined by multiplying the total of his income (as defined in paragraphs (c)(2) and (3) of this section) from the trade or business for the taxable year by the percentage which is the average of these three percentages:

(A) *Property percentage.*—The percentage computed by dividing the average of the value, at the beginning and end of the taxable year, of real and tangible personal property connected with the taxpayer's trade or business and located within the State, by the average of the value, at the beginning and end of the taxable year, of all such property located both within and without the State. For this purpose, real property shall include real property rented to the taxpayer in connection with the trade or business, or rented to the trade or business.

(B) *Payroll percentage.*—The percentage computed by dividing the total wages, salaries, and other compensation for personal services which is paid or incurred during the taxable year to employees in connection with the taxpayer's trade or business, and which would be treated as derived by such employees from sources within the State pursuant to subparagraph (1) of this paragraph, by the total of all such wages, salaries, and other compensation for personal services which is so paid or incurred without regard to whether such payments would be treated as derived by the employees from sources within the State. For purposes of this subdivision (ii), no amount paid as deferred compensation pursuant to a retirement plan to a former employee shall be taken into consideration.

(C) *Gross income percentage.*—The percentage computed by dividing the gross sales or charges for services performed by or through an agency located within the State by the total of all gross sales or charges for services performed both within and without the State. The sales or charges to be allocated to the State shall include all sales which are negotiated, and charges which are for services performed, by an employee, agent, agency, or independent contractor chiefly situated at, or working principally out of an office located within, the State.

(3) *Income attributable to real estate investment.*—Notwithstanding subparagraph (2) of this paragraph, income and deductions from the rental of real property, and gain and loss from

Reg. § 301.6362-5(d)(3)

the sale, exchange, or other disposition of real property, shall not be subject to allocation under subparagraph (2), but shall be considered as entirely derived from sources located within the State in which such property is located.

(4) *Treatment of losses.*—A loss attributable to the taxpayer's employment, or to his conduct of, participation in, or investment in a trade or business, shall be allocated in the same manner as the income attributable to such employment or trade or business would be allocated pursuant to this paragraph.

(5) *Examples.*—The application of this paragraph may be illustrated by the following examples:

Example (1). A, an employee who earns $10,000 in wage income attributable to services, and who has no other wage or other business income, spends 60 percent of his working time performing services for his employer in State X, 30 percent in State Y, and 10 percent in State Z. In the absence of the requisite proof to the contrary, A's wage income is considered to have been derived 60 percent from sources located within State X, 30 percent within State Y, and 10 percent within State Z. Assuming that A is a nonresident with respect to all three States, and that they all impose qualified nonresident taxes, then the qualified nonresident tax of State X is imposed on $6,000, the qualified nonresident tax of State Y is imposed on $3,000, and the qualified nonresident tax of State Z is not imposed on any of the income because A did not derive at least 25 percent of his wage and other business income from sources located within State Z.

Example (2). B, who earns no wage income but who has a total of $10,000 of other business income for the taxable year, all of which is net income from self-employment attributable primarily to services, spends 45 percent of his working time performing services in State X, 30 percent in State Y, and 25 percent in State Z. However, the rates that B is able to charge for his services and the business expenses which he incurs vary in the different States, and he is able to prove by detailed records that his net income from self-employment was in fact derived 50 percent from sources located within State X, 35 percent from sources within State Y, and 15 percent from sources located within State Z. Assuming that B is a nonresident with respect to all three States, and that they all impose qualified nonresident taxes, then the qualified nonresident tax of State X is imposed on $5,000, the qualified nonresident tax of State Y is imposed on $3,500, and the qualified nonresident tax of State Z is not imposed on any of the income because B did not derive at least 25 percent of his wage and other business income from sources located within State Z.

Example (3). C is a partner in a profitable business concern, in which he has a substantial capital investment. His net earnings from self-employment attributable to his partnership interest are $75,000 for the taxable year. The fair market value of the services which C performs for the partnership during the taxable year is $30,000. C's income is therefore attributable primarily to his capital investment. The partnership business is carried on partially within and partially without State X. Neither C nor the partnership maintains records from which the portion of C's $75,000 income which is considered to be derived from sources within State X can be satisfactorily proven. As determined under subparagraph (2) of this paragraph, the partnership's "property percentage" in State X is 70, its "payroll percentage" therein is 60, and its "gross income percentage" therein is 56. The amount of C's partnership income considered to be derived from sources within State X is $46,500 ($75,000 × 62 percent). This result would obtain even if C's services for the partnership are performed entirely within State X.

Example (4). Assume the same facts as in (3), except that the records of the partnership of which C is a member indicate that the net profits of the partnership are derived 40 percent from business activities conducted in State X, and 60 percent from business activities conducted in State Y. C is requested to prove that those records fairly and equitably reflect the income which is allocable to sources within State X. The documentary evidence which he adduces in support of the allocation made by the records shows how such allocation results from a careful step-by-step tracing of the profitability of each phase and aspect of the partnership's operations, and shows the State in which each such phase and aspect of the operations is conducted. C's proof is satisfactory to show that the percentage allocation, and the amount of his partnership income considered to be derived from sources within State X is $30,000, or $75,000 multiplied by 40 percent. This result would obtain even if B's services for the partnership are performed entirely within State X. [Reg. § 301.6362-5.]

☐ [*T.D. 7577, 12-19-78.*]

[Reg. § 301.6362-6]

§ 301.6362-6. **Requirements relating to residence.**—(a) *In general.*—A tax imposed by a State meets the requirements of section 6362(e) and this section if in effect it provides that:

(1) The State of residence of an individual, estate, or trust is determined according to paragraph (1), (2), or (3), respectively, of section 6362(e), and according to paragraph (b), (c), or (d), respectively, of this section.

(2) The liability for a resident tax imposed by such State upon an individual or trust which changes residence to another State in the taxable year is determined according to section 6362(e)(4) and paragraph (e) of this section.

(3) The rules relating to current collection of tax apply as provided in section 6362(e)(5) and paragraph (f) of this section.

(b) *Residence of an individual.*—(1) *In general.*— Except as otherwise provided in subparagraph (5) of this paragraph, an individual is treated as a resident of a State with respect to a taxable year only if:

(i) His principal place of residence (as defined in subparagraph (2) of this paragraph) is within such State for a period of at least 135 consecutive days, at least 30 days of which are in such taxable year; or

(ii) In the case of a citizen or resident of the United States who is not a resident of any State (determined as provided in subdivision (i) of this subparagraph) with respect to such taxable year, his domicile (as defined in subparagraph (3) of this paragraph) is in such State for at least 30 days during such taxable year.

With respect to an individual who is a resident (determined as provided in subdivision (i) of this subparagraph) of more than one State during a taxable year, see paragraph (e) of this section.

(2) *Principal place of residence.*— (i) *Definition.*—For purposes of subparagraph (1)(i) of this paragraph and paragraph (d)(4) of this section, the term "principal place of residence" shall mean the place which is an individual's primary home. An individual's temporary absence from his primary home shall not effect a change with respect thereto. On the other hand, if an individual moves to another State, other than as a mere transient or sojourner, he shall be treated as having changed the location of his primary home.

(ii) *Examples.*—The application of this subparagraph may be illustrated by the following examples:

Example (1). A has a city home and a country home. He resides in the city home for 7 months of the year and uses the address of that home as his legal residence for purposes of driver's license, automobile registration, and voter registration. He resides in the country home 5 months of the year. His city home is considered his principal place of residence.

Example (2). During the taxable year, B, a construction worker, is employed at several different locations in different States. The duration of each job on which he is employed ranges from a few weeks to several months, and he knows when he accepts a job what its approximate duration will be. He owns a house in State X which he uses as his legal residence for purposes of driver's license, automobile registration, and voter registration. In addition, his family lives there during the entire year, and B lives there during periods between jobs. However, the duration of the jobs and the distance between the job-sites and his house require him to live in the localities of the respective job-sites during the period of his employment, although occasionally he returns to his house in State X on weekends. B's house in State X is his principal place of residence during all of the taxable year.

Example (3). C, a dependent of his parents who are residents of State X, is a full-time student in a 4-year degree program at a college in State Y. During the 9-month academic year, C lives on the college campus, but he returns to his parents' home in State X for the summer recess. C gives the State Y as his residence for purposes

of his driver's license and voter registration, but lists the address of his parents' home in State X as his "permanent address" on the records of the college which he attends. Although C's domicile remains at his parents' home in State X, his presence in State Y cannot be regarded as that of a mere transient or sojourner; accordingly, C's principal place of residence is in State Y for that portion of the taxable year during which he attends college.

Example (4). D loses his job in State X, where he lived and worked for many years. After a series of unsuccessful attempts to find other employment in State X, he accepts a job in State Y. D gives up his apartment in State X and moves to State Y upon commencing his new job; however, he intends to continue to explore available employment opportunities in State X so that he may return there as soon as an opportunity to do so arises. D changes his principal place of residence when he moves to State Y.

(3) *Domicile defined.*—For purposes of subparagraph (1)(ii) of this paragraph and paragraph (d)(4) of this section, the term "domicile" shall mean an individual's fixed or permanent home. An individual acquires a domicile in a place by living there; even for a brief period of time, with no definite present intention of later removing therefrom. Residence without the requisite intention to remain indefinitely will not suffice to change domicile, nor will intention to change domicile effect such a change until accompanied by actual removal. A domicile, once acquired, is maintained until a new domicile is acquired.

(4) *Period of residence.*—(i) *General rule.*—An individual who becomes a resident of a State pursuant to subparagraph (1) of this paragraph, or who is at the beginning of a taxable year a resident of a State pursuant to such provision, shall be treated as continuing to be a resident of such State through the end of the taxable year, unless, prior thereto, such individual becomes a resident, under the principles of subparagraph (1), of another State or a possession or foreign country. In the event that the individual becomes a resident of such another jurisdiction prior to the end of the taxable year, his residence in such State shall be treated as ending on the day prior to the day on which he becomes a resident of such other jurisdiction pursuant to subparagraph (1).

(ii) *Examples.*—The application of this subparagraph may be illustrated by the following examples:

Example (1). A, a calendar-year taxpayer, has his principal place of residence in State X from the beginning of 1976 through August 1, 1976, when he gives up permanently such principal place of residence. He spends the remainder of 1976 traveling outside of the United States, but does not become a resident of any other country. A is considered to be a resident of State X for the entire year 1976.

Example (2). Assume the same facts as in example (1), except that A ceases his traveling and establishes his principal place of residence in State Y on November 15, 1976. Assume, also, that A maintains that principal place of residence for more than 135 consecutive days. Under these circumstances, for his taxable year 1976, A is considered to be a resident of State X from January 1 through November 14, and a resident of State Y from November 15 through December 31.

(5) *Special rules.*—(i) No provision of subchapter E or the regulations thereunder shall be construed to require or authorize the treatment of a Senator, Representative, Delegate, or Resident Commissioner as a resident of a State other than the State which he represents in Congress.

(ii) For special rules relating to members of the Armed Forces, see paragraph (h) of § 301.6362-7.

(6) *Examples.*—The application of this paragraph may be illustrated by the following examples:

Example (1). A, a calendar-year taxpayer, maintains his principal place of residence in State X from December 1, 1976, through April 15, 1977. Assuming that A was not a resident of any other jurisdiction at any time during 1976, A is treated as a resident of State X for the entire year 1976. Such result would obtain even if A was absent from State X on vacation for some portion of December 1976. Moreover, such result would obtain even if it is assumed that A was a domiciliary of State Y from January 1, 1976, through April 15, 1977, because an individual's domicile does not determine his residence so long as residence in one State for the taxable year can be determined from the general rule stated in the first sentence of paragraph (b)(1) of this section.

Example (2). Assume the same facts as in example (1) (including the fact of A's domicile in State Y), except that A maintained his principal place of residence in State Z from September 15, 1975, through January 31, 1976, inclusive. With respect to the year 1976, A is treated as a resident of State Z from January 1 through November 30, and as a resident of State X from December 1 through December 31. A's liability for the qualified taxes of the respective States for 1976 shall be determined pursuant to the provisions in paragraph (e) of this section.

(c) *Residence of an estate.*—An estate of an individual is treated as a resident of the last State of which such individual was a resident, as determined under the rules of paragraph (b) of this section, prior to his death. However, the estate of an individual who was not a resident of any State (as determined without regard to the 30-day requirement in paragraph (b)(1) of this section) immediately prior to his death, and who was not a resident of any State at any time during the 3-year period ending on the date of his death, is not treated as a resident of any State. For purposes of determining the decedent's last State of residence, the rules of paragraph (b)

shall be applied irrespective of whether subchapter E was in effect at the time the period of 135 consecutive days of residence began, or whether the decedent's last State of residence is a State electing to enter into an agreement pursuant to subchapter E. The determination of the State of residence of an estate pursuant to this paragraph shall not be governed by any determination under State law as to which State is treated as the residence or domicile of the decedent for purposes other than its individual income tax (such as liability for State inheritance tax or jurisdiction of probate proceedings).

(d) *Residence of a trust.*—(1) *In general.*—(i) The State of residence of a trust shall be determined by reference to the circumstances of the individual who, by either an inter-vivos transfer or a testamentary transfer, is deemed to be the "principal contributor" to the trust under the provisions of subdivision (ii) of this subparagraph.

(ii) If only one individual has ever contributed assets to the trust, including the assets which were transferred to the trust at its inception, then such individual is the principal contributor to the trust. However, if on any day subsequent to the initial creation of the trust, such trust receives assets having a value greater than the aggregate value of all assets theretofore contributed to it, then the trust shall be deemed (for the limited purpose of determining the State of residence) to have been "created" anew, and the individual who on the day of such creation contributed more (in value) than any other individual contributed on that day shall become the principal contributor to the trust. When a trust is created anew, all references in this paragraph to the creation of the trust shall be construed as referring to the most recent creation. For purposes of this paragraph, the value of any asset shall be its fair market value on the day that it was contributed to the trust; any subsequent appreciation or depreciation in the value of the asset shall be disregarded.

(2) *Testamentary trust.*—A trust with respect to which a deceased individual is the principal contributor by reason of property passing on his death is treated as a resident of the last State of which such individual was a resident, as determined under the rules of paragraph (b) of this section, before his death. However, if such deceased individual was not a resident of any State (as determined without regard to the 30-day requirement in paragraph (b)(1) of this section) immediately prior to his death, and was not a resident of any State at any time during the 3-year period ending on the date of his death, then a testamentary trust of which he is the principal contributor by reason of property passing on his death is not treated as a resident of any State. All property passing on the transferor's death is treated for this purpose as a contribution made to the trust on the date of death, regardless of when the property is actually paid over to the trust.

(3) *Nontestamentary trust.*—A trust which is not a trust described in subparagraph (2) of this paragraph is treated as a resident of the State in which the principal contributor to the trust, during the 3-year period ending on the date of the creation of the trust, had his principal place of residence for an aggregate number of days longer than the aggregate number of days he had his principal place of residence in any other State. However, if the principal contributor to such a trust was not a resident of any State at any time during such 3-year period, then the trust is not treated as a resident of any State.

(4) *Special rules.*—If the application of the provisions of the foregoing subparagraphs of this paragraph results in a determination of more than one State of residence for a trust, or does not provide a rule by which the residence or nonresidence of the trust can be determined, then the determination of the State of residence of such trust shall be made according to the rules of the applicable subdivision of this subparagraph.

(i) If, at the time of creation of the trust, 50 percent or more in value of the trust corpus consists of real property, then the trust shall be treated as a resident of the State in which more of the real property (in value) which was in the trust at such time was located than any other State.

(ii) If, at the time of creation of the trust, less than 50 percent in value of the trust corpus consists of real property, then the trust shall be treated as a resident of the State in which, at such time, the trustee, if an individual, had his principal place of residence, or, if a corporation, had its principal place of business. If there were two or more trustees, then the foregoing sentence shall be applied by reference to the principal places of residence, or of business, of the majority of trustees who had authority to make investment and other management decisions for the trust.

(iii) If, after application of the provisions of subdivisions (i) and (ii) of this subparagraph, the State of residence of the trust still cannot be ascertained, then the Commissioner of Internal Revenue shall determine the State of residence of such trust for purposes of qualified taxes. Such determination shall be made by reference to the number of significant contacts each State had with the trust at the time of its creation. Significant contacts shall include the principal place of residence of the principal contributor or contributors to the trust, the principal place of residence or business of the trustee (or trustees), the situs of the assets of which the trust corpus was composed, and the location from which management decisions emanated with respect to the business and investment interests of the trusts.

(5) *Examples.*—The application of this paragraph may be illustrated by the following examples:

Example (1). A created a trust in 1950 by transferring to it certain stock in a corporation. At the time of such transfer, the stock had a fair market value of $1,000. A at all relevant times had his principal place of residence in State X, and accordingly the trust is treated as a resident of such State for qualified tax purposes. As of January 1, 1977, the stock originally contributed by A, which was at all times the only property in the trust, has a fair market value of $3,000. On such date, B, who has had his principal place of residence in State Y for more than 3 years, contributes to the trust property having a fair market value of $1,200. For purposes of determining the identity of the principal contributor to the trust and the State of residence of the trust, the stock contributed by A in 1950 continues to be valued for such purposes at $1,000. Thus, the trust is treated as being created anew on January 1, 1977, with B as the principal contributor, and with State Y as its State of residence.

Example (2). C has his principal place of residence in State X continuously for many years, until August 1, 1978, when he establishes his principal place of residence in State Y. The change of residence is intended to be permanent, and C has no further contact with State X after such change. On January 1, 1980, C creates a nontestamentary trust. During the 3-year period ending on such date C had his principal place of residence in State X for 576 days, and in State Y for 519 days. Therefore, the trust is treated as a resident of State X.

(e) *Liability for tax on change of residence during taxable year.*—(1) *In general.*—If, under the principles contained in paragraph (b) or (d) of this section, an individual or trust becomes a resident, or ceases to be a resident, of a State, and is also a resident of another jurisdiction outside of such State during the same taxable year, the liability of such individual or trust for the resident tax of such State shall be determined by multiplying the amount which would be his or its liability for tax (computed after allowing the nonrefundable credits (i.e., credits not corresponding to the credits referred to in section 6401(b) available against the tax)) if he or it had been a resident of such State for the entire taxable year by a fraction, the numerator of which is the number of days he or it was a resident of such State during the taxable year, and the denominator of which is the total number of days in the taxable year. The preceding sentence shall not apply by reason of the fact that an individual is born or dies during the taxable year, or by reason of the fact that a trust comes into existence or ceases to exist during the taxable year.

(2) *Residence determined by domicile.*—When an individual is treated as a resident of a State by reason of being domiciled in such State, pursuant to paragraph (b)(1)(ii) of this section, then the numerator of the fraction provided in subparagraph (1) of this paragraph shall be the number of days the individual was domiciled in the State during the taxable year.

(3) *Example.*—The application of this paragraph may be illustrated by the following example:

Example. A, a calendar-year taxpayer, is a resident of State X continuously for many years prior to March 15, 1977. On such date, A retires and establishes a new principal place of residence in State Y. A earns $6,000 in 1977 prior to March 15, but receives no taxable income for the remainder of such year. If A had been a resident of State X for the entire taxable year 1977, his liability with respect to the qualified tax of such State (computed after allowing the nonrefundable credits available against the tax) would be $600. If he had been a resident of State Y for the entire taxable year 1977, his liability with respect to the qualified tax on that State (computed similarly) would be $400. Pursuant to the provisions in paragraph (e) of this section, A's liabilities for State qualified taxes for 1977 are as follows:

$$\text{Liability for State } X \text{ tax} = \$600 \times \frac{73}{365} = \$120$$

$$\text{Liability for State } Y \text{ tax} = \$400 \times \frac{292}{365} = \$320.$$

(f) *Current collection of tax.*—The State tax laws shall contain provisions for methods of current collection with respect to individuals which correspond to the provisions of the Internal Revenue Code of 1954 with respect to such current collection, including chapter 24 (relating to the collection of income tax at source on wages) and sections 6015, 6073, 6153, and other provisions of the Code relating to declarations (and amendments thereto) and payments of estimated income tax. Except as otherwise provided by Federal statute (see paragraphs (h), (i), and (j) of §301.6362-7), in applying such provisions of the State tax laws:

(1) In the case of a resident tax, an individual shall be subject to the current collection provisions if either—

(i) He is a resident of the State within the meaning of paragraph (b) of this section, or

(ii) He has his principal place of residence (as defined in paragraph (b)(2) of this section) within the State,

and it is reasonable to expect him to have it within the State for 30 days or more during the taxable year.

(2) In the case of a nonresident tax, an individual shall be subject to the current collection provisions if he does not meet either description relating to an individual in subparagraph (1) of this paragraph, if he is not exempt from liability for the tax by reason of a reciprocal agreement between the State of which he is a resident and the State imposing the tax, and if it is reasonable to expect him to receive wage or other business income derived from sources within the State imposing the tax (as defined in paragraph (d) of §301.6362-5) for services performed on 30 days or more of the taxable year.

For additional rules relating to withholding see paragraph (d) of §301.6361-1. [Reg. §301.6362-6.]

☐ [*T.D.* 7577, 12-19-78.]

[Reg. §301.6362-7]

§301.6362-7. Additional requirements.—A State tax meets the additional requirements of section 6362(f) and this section only if:

(a) *State agreement must be in effect for period concerned.*—A State agreement, as defined in paragraph (a) of §301.6361-4, is in effect with respect to such tax for the taxable period in question.

(b) *State laws contain certain provisions.*—Under the laws of such State, the provisions of subchapter E and the regulations thereunder, as in effect from time to time, are applicable for the entire period for which the State agreement is in effect. Any change made by the State in such tax (other than an adjustment in the State law which is made solely in order to comply with a change in the Federal law or regulations) shall not apply to taxable years beginning in any calendar year for which the State agreement is in effect unless the change is enacted before November 1 of such year.

(c) *State individual income tax laws can be only of certain kinds.*—Such State does not impose any tax on the income of individuals other than (1) a qualified resident tax, and (2) either or both a qualified nonresident tax and a separate tax on income which is not wage and other business income as defined in paragraph (c) of §301.6362-5 and which is received or accrued by individuals who are domiciled in the State, but who are not residents of the State (as defined in paragraph (b) of §301.6362-6). For purposes of this paragraph, a tax imposed on the amount taxed under section 56 (as permitted under §301.6362-2(b)(2)) shall be treated as an adjustment to and a part of the qualified resident tax. Also, tax laws which were in effect prior to the effective date of a State agreement and which are not repealed, but which are made inapplicable for the period during which the State agreement is in effect, shall be disregarded.

(d) *Taxable years must coincide.*—The taxable years of all individuals, estates, and trusts under such tax are required to coincide with their taxable years used for purposes of the taxes imposed by chapter 1. Accordingly, when subchapter E begins to apply to a State, a taxpayer whose taxable year for purposes of the Federal income tax is different from his taxable year for purposes of the State income tax which precedes the qualified tax may have one short taxable year for purposes of such State income tax, so that thereafter his taxable years for purposes of the qualified tax will coincide with the Federal taxable year.

(e) *Married individuals.*—Individuals who are married within the meaning of section 143 of the Code are prohibited from filing (1) a joint return for purposes of such State tax if they file separate Federal income tax returns, or (2) separate returns for purposes of such State tax if they file a joint Federal income tax return.

(f) *Penalties; no double jeopardy.*—Under the laws of such State:

(1) Civil and criminal sanctions identical to those provided by subtitle F, and by title 18 of the United States Code (relating to crimes and criminal procedures), with respect to the taxes imposed on the income of individuals by chapter 1 and on the wages of individuals by chapter 24, apply to individuals and their employers who are subject to such State tax (and the collection and administration thereof, including the corresponding withholding tax imposed to implement the current collection of such State tax) as if such tax were imposed by chapter 1 (or chapter 24, in the case of the withholding tax), except to the extent that the application of such sanctions is modified by regulations issued under subchapter E; and

(2) No other sanctions or penalties apply with respect to any act or omission to act in respect of such State tax.
See also paragraph (e) of § 301.6361-1 with respect to criminal penalties.

(g) *Partnerships, trusts, subchapter S corporations, and other conduit entities.*—Under the laws of such State, the State tax treatment of—

(1) Partnerships and partners,

(2) Trusts and their beneficiaries,

(3) Estates and their beneficiaries,

(4) Electing small business corporations (within the meaning of section 1371(a)) and their shareholders, and

(5) Any other entity and the individuals having beneficial interests therein (such as a co-operative corporation and its shareholders), to the extent that such entity is treated as a conduit for purposes of the taxes imposed by chapter 1,
corresponds to the tax treatment provided therefor with respect to the taxes imposed by chapter 1. For example, a subchapter S corporation shall not be subject to the State's corporate income tax on amounts which are includible in shareholders' incomes which are subject to that State's individual income tax, except to the extent that the subchapter S corporation is subject to tax under Federal law. Similarly, a partnership shall not be subject to the State's unincorporated business income tax on amounts which are includible in partners' incomes which are subject to that State's individual income tax. However, the laws of the State which set forth the provisions of such State individual income tax shall authorize the Commissioner of Internal Revenue to require that the conduit entities described in this paragraph (or some of them) supply information to the Federal Government with respect to the source of income, the State of residence, or the amount of income of a particular type, of an individual, estate, or trust holding a beneficial interest in such conduit entity.

(h) *Members of armed forces.*—The relief provided to any member of the Armed Forces by section 514 of the Soldiers' and Sailors' Civil Relief Act (50 U.S.C. App. sec. 574) is in no way diminished. Accordingly, for purposes of such State tax, an individual shall not be considered to have become a resident of a State solely because of his absence from his original State of residence under military order. Moreover, compensation for military service shall not be considered as income derived from a source within a State of which the individual earning such compensation is not a resident, within the meaning of paragraph (d) of § 301.6362-5. The preceding sentence shall not apply to nonmilitary compensation. Thus, for example, if an individual who is serving in State X as a member of the Armed Forces, and who is regarded as a resident of State Y under the Soldiers' and Sailors' Civil Relief Act, earns nonmilitary income in State X from a part-time job, such nonmilitary income may be subject to a qualified nonresident tax imposed by State X.

(i) *Withholding on compensation of employees of railroads, motor carriers, airlines, and water carriers.*—There is no contravention of the provisions of section 26, 226A, or 324 of the Interstate Commerce Act, or of section 1112 of the Federal Aviation Act of 1958, with respect to the withholding of compensation to which such sections apply for purposes of the nonresident tax.

(j) *Income derived from interstate commerce.*—There is no contravention of the provisions of the Act of September 14, 1959 (73 Stat. 555), with respect to the taxation of income derived from interstate commerce to which such statute applies. [Reg. § 301.6362-7.]

☐ [T.D. 7577, 12-19-78.]

[Reg. § 301.6363-1]

§ 301.6363-1. State agreements.—(a) *Notice of election.*—If a State elects to enter into a State agreement it shall file notice of such election with the Secretary or his delegate. The notice of election shall include the following:

(1) *Statement by the Governor.*—A written statement by the Governor of the electing State:

(i) Requesting that the Secretary enter into a State agreement, and

(ii) Binding the Governor and his successors in office to notify the Secretary or his delegate immediately of the enactment, between the time of the filing of the notice of election and the time of the execution of the State agreement, of any law of that State which meets the description given in any of the subdivisions of subparagraph (2) of this paragraph, whether or not such law is intended to be administered by the United States pursuant to subchapter E.

(2) *Copy of State laws.*—Certified copies of all laws of that State described in any of the following subdivisions of this subparagraph, and a specification of laws described in subdivision (i) of this subparagraph as "subchapter E laws", of laws described in subdivision (ii) as "other tax laws", of laws described in subdivision (iii) as "non-tax laws", and of laws described in subdivision (iv) as "interstate cooperation laws":

(i) All of the State individual income tax laws (including laws relating to the collection or administration of such taxes or to the prosecution of alleged civil or criminal violations with respect to such taxes) which the State would expect the United States to administer pursuant to subchapter E if the State agreement is executed as requested. In order to have a valid notice, the State must have a tax which would meet the requirements for qualification specified in section 6362 and the regulations thereunder if a State agreement were in effect with respect thereto, with no conditions attached to the effectiveness of such tax other than the execution of a State agreement. Such tax must be effective no later than the January 1 specified in the State's notice of election as the date as of which subchapter E is desired to become applicable to the electing State, except that such effective date shall be deferred to the date provided in the State agreement for the beginning of applicability of subchapter E to the State, if the latter date is different from the date specified in the notice of election.

(ii) All of the State income tax laws applicable to individuals (including laws relating to the collection or administration of such taxes or to the prosecution of alleged civil or criminal violations with respect to such taxes) which the State would not expect the United States to administer but which may be in effect simultaneously (for any period of time) with the State agreement.

(iii) All of the State laws other than individual income tax laws which provide for the making of any payments by the State based on one or more criteria which the State may desire to verify by reference to information contained in returns of qualified taxes.

(iv) All of the State laws which may be in effect simultaneously (for any period of time) with the State agreement and which provide for cooperation or reciprocal agreement between the electing State and another State with respect to income taxes applicable to individuals.

(3) *Approval by legislature or authorization by constitutional amendment.*—A certified copy of an Act or Resolution of the legislature of the electing State in which the legislature affirmatively expresses its approval of the State's entry into a State agreement, or a certified copy of an amendment to the constitution of such State by which the voters of the State affirmatively authorize such entry.

(4) *Opinion by State Attorney General or judgment of highest court.*—A written statement by the State Attorney General to the effect that, in his opinion, no provision of the State's Constitution would be violated by the State law's incorporation by reference of the Federal individual income tax laws and regulations, as amended from time to time, by the Federal prosecution and trial of individuals who are alleged to have committed crimes with respect to the State's qualified tax (when it goes into effect as such), or by any other provision relating to such tax, considered as of the time it is being collected and administered by the Federal Government pursuant to subchapter E. However, if such a statement is not included in the notice of election, a judgment of the highest court of the State to the same effect may be submitted in its place.

(5) *Effective date.*—A written specification of the January as of which subchapter E is desired to become applicable to the electing State.

(b) *Rules relating to time for filing notice of election.*—An electing State must file its notice of election more than 6 months prior to the January 1 as of which the notice specifies that the provisions of subchapter E are desired to become applicable to such State. Thus, for example, if the date specified in the notice is January 1, 1979, the notice must be filed no later than June 30, 1978. However, because under the provisions of section 204(b) of the Federal-State Tax Collection Act of 1972 (86 Stat. 945), as amended by section 2116(a) of the Tax Reform Act of 1976 (90 Stat. 1910), the provisions of subchapter E will initially take effect on the first January 1 which is more than 1 year after the first date on which at least one State has filed a notice of its election (see § 301.6361-5), the notice of an election which causes subchapter E to initially take effect must be filed with the Secretary or his delegate more than 1 year prior to the January 1 as of which such notice specifies that the provisions of subchapter E are desired to become applicable to such State. Thus, for example, if such an initially electing State desires to elect subchapter E as of January 1, 1979, its notice must be filed no later than December 31, 1977. For purposes of this section, if the notice of election is sent by either registered or certified mail to the Secretary of the Treasury, Washington, D.C. 20220, then it shall be deemed to be filed on the date of mailing; otherwise, the notice of election shall be deemed to be filed when it is received by the Secretary or his delegate.

(c) *Procedures relating to defects in notice or tax laws.*—If a State has filed a notice of election, then the Secretary shall, within 90 days after the notice is filed, notify the Governor of such State in writing of any defect in the notice of election which prevents it from being valid, and of any defect in the State's tax laws which causes the tax submitted to fail to meet the requirements for qualification specified in section 6362 and the regulations thereunder, other than the fact that no State agreement is in effect with respect thereto. Any such defect of which the Secretary does not notify the Governor within such 90-day period is waived. The Secretary or his delegate may, in his discretion, permit any of such defects of which the Governor is timely notified to be cured retroactively to the date of the filing of the notice of election, by amendment of the notice or the State law. Judicial review of the Secretary's determination that the notice of election or the tax laws, or both, contain defects, may be obtained as set forth in section 6363(d) and § 301.6363-4.

(d) *Execution and contents of State agreement.*—If the Secretary does not timely notify the Governor of a defect in the notice of election or in the State's tax laws, as provided in paragraph (c) of this section, or if, as provided in such paragraph, all such defects have been cured retroactively, then the Secretary shall enter into a State agreement. The agreement shall include the following elements:

(1) *Effective date.*—The agreement shall specify the January 1 as of which subchapter E will commence to be applicable to the State. Such date shall be the same as that specified in the notice of election pursuant to paragraph (a)(5) of this section, unless the parties agree to a different January 1, except that in no event shall a State agreement executed after November 1 specify the next January 1.

(2) *Obligation of Governor to notify the United States of changes in pertinent State laws.*—The agreement shall require the Governor of the State, and his successors in office, to notify the Secretary or his delegate within 30 days of the enactment of any law of the State, after the execution of the agreement, of a type described in paragraph (a)(2) of this section.

(3) *Obligation of Governor to furnish to the United States information needed to administer State tax laws.*—The agreement shall require the Governor and his successors to furnish to the Secretary or his delegate any information needed by the Federal Government to administer the State tax laws. Such information shall include, for example, a list (which shall be maintained on a current basis) of those obligations of the State or its political subdivisions described in section 103(a)(1) from which the interest is not subject to the qualified taxes of the State.

(4) *Identification of State official to act as liaison with Federal Government.*—The agreement shall include a designation by the Governor of the State official or officials with whom the Secretary or his delegate should coordinate in connection with any questions or problems which may arise during the period for which the State agreement is effective, including those which may result from changes or contemplated changes in pertinent State laws.

(5) *Identification of State official to receive transferred funds.*—The agreement shall include a designation by the Governor of the State official who shall initially receive the funds on behalf of the State when they are transferred pursuant to section 6361(c) and § 301.6361-3.

(6) *Other obligations.*—If the Secretary and the Governor both so agree, the agreement shall provide for additional obligations.

(e) *State agreement superseding certain other agreements.*—For the period of its effectiveness, a State agreement shall supersede an otherwise effective agreement entered into by the State and the Secretary for the withholding of State income taxes from the compensation of Federal employees pursuant to 5 U.S.C. 5517 (or pursuant to 5 U.S.C. 5516, in the case of the District of Columbia). [Reg. § 301.6363-1.]

☐ [*T.D.* 7577, 12-19-78.]

[Reg. § 301.6363-2]

§ 301.6363-2. Withdrawal from State agreements.—(a) *By notification.*—If a State which has entered into a State agreement desires to withdraw from the agreement, its Governor shall file a notice of withdrawal with the Secretary or his delegate. A notice of withdrawal shall include the following documents:

(1) *Request by the Governor.*—A request by the Governor of the State that the State agreement cease to be effective with respect to taxable years beginning on or after a specified January 1, except as provided in paragraph (b)(2) of § 301.6365-2 with respect to withholding in the case of fiscal-year taxpayers.

(2) *Legislative approval of withdrawal.*—A certified copy of an act or Resolution of the legislature of the State in which the legislature affirmatively expresses its approval of the State's withdrawal from the State agreement.

(3) *Identification of State official.*—A written identification of the State official or officials with whom the Secretary or his delegate should coordinate in connection with the State's withdrawal from the State agreement.

(b) *By change in State law.*—If any law of a State which has entered into a State agreement is enacted pertaining to individual income taxes (including the collection or administration of such taxes, and the prosecution of alleged civil or criminal violations with respect to such taxes), and if the Secretary or his delegate determines that as a result of such law the State no longer has a qualified tax, then such change in the State law shall be treated as a notification of withdrawal from the agreement. The Secretary shall notify the Governor in writing when a change is to be so treated. Such notification shall have the same effect as if, on the effective date of the disqualifying change in the law, the Governor had filed with the Secretary or his delegate a valid and sufficient notice of withdrawal requesting that the State agreement cease to be effective with respect to taxable years beginning on or after the first January 1 which is more than 6 months thereafter, subject to the exception with respect to withholding in the case of fiscal-year taxpayers. However, the cessation of effectiveness may be deferred to a subsequent January 1 if the Governor so requests and if the Secretary or his delegate in his discretion determines that the date of cessation provided in the preceding sentence would subject the State or its taxpayers to undue hardship. In addition, the Governor may request the Secretary or his delegate to permit the State's early withdrawal from the agreement, pursuant to paragraph (c)(2) of this section. Until the date of cessation of effectiveness of the State agreement, the change in State law which was treated as a notification of withdrawal, and any other such subsequent change that would be similarly treated, shall not be given effect for purposes of the Federal collection and administration of the State taxes. Similarly, such changes shall not be given effect for such purposes during the period of litigation if the State seeks judicial review of the action of the Secretary or his delegate pursuant to section 6363(d) or § 301.6363-4, even if such changes are ultimately found by the court not to disqualify the State's qualified tax. However, a change in State law which would be treated as a notice of withdrawal in the absence of this sentence shall not be so treated if, prior to the last November 1 preceding the January 1 on which the cessation of effectiveness of the State agreement is to occur, either such change in State law is retroactively repealed, or the State law is retroactively modified and the Secretary or his delegate determines that with such modification the State has a qualified tax.

(c) *Rules relating to time of withdrawal.*— (1) *General rule.*—Except as provided in subparagraph (2) of this paragraph, a notice of withdrawal shall not be valid unless the January 1 specified therein is not earlier than the first January 1 which is more than 6 months subsequent to the date on which the notice is received by the Secretary of his delegate. Thus, for example, if the notice specifies January 1, 1980, for withdrawal, the notice must be received no later than June 30, 1979.

(2) *Early withdrawal.*—The Secretary or his delegate may, in his discretion and upon written request by a Governor of a State who has filed a notice of withdrawal, waive the 6-months requirement of section 6363(b)(1) and subparagraph (1) of this paragraph if the Secretary determines that:

(i) The State will suffer a hardship if required to meet such requirement, and

(ii) The early withdrawal requested by the Governor would be practicable from the standpoint of orderly collection of the qualified tax and administration of the State law by the Federal Government. [Reg. § 301.6363-2.]

☐ [*T.D.* 7577, 12-19-78.]

[Reg. § 301.6363-3]

§ 301.6363-3. Transition years.—The State may by law provide for the transition to or from a qualified tax to the extent necessary to prevent double taxation or other unintended hardships, or to prevent unintended benefits, under State law. Generally, such provisions shall be administered by the State; but, if requested to do so by the Governor of the State, the Secretary or his delegate may, in his discretion, agree to administer such provisions either solely or jointly with the State. [Reg. § 301.6363-3.]

☐ [*T.D.* 7577, 12-19-78.]

[Reg. § 301.6363-4]

§ 301.6363-4. Judicial review.—(a) *General rule.*—If the Secretary or his delegate determines

pursuant to paragraph (c) of § 301.6363-1 that a State did not file a valid notice of election or does not have a tax which would meet the requirements for qualification specified in section 6362 and the regulations thereunder if a State agreement were in effect with respect thereto, or if he determines pursuant to paragraph (b) of § 301.6363-2 that a participating State has enacted a law as a result of which the State no longer has a qualified tax, such State may, within 60 days after its Governor has received notification of such determination, file a petition for the review of such determination with either the United States Court of Appeals for the circuit in which the State is located or the United States Court of Appeals for the District of Columbia. If a State files such a petition, the clerk of the court shall forthwith transmit a copy of the petition to the Secretary or his delegate, who in turn shall thereupon file in the court the record of proceedings on which the determination adverse to the States was based, as provided in section 2112 of title 28, United States Code.

(b) *Court of Appeals' jurisdiction.*—The Court of Appeals may affirm or set aside, in whole or in part, the action of the Secretary or his delegate; and (subject to the rules delaying the effectiveness of the change in State law provided in paragraph (b) of § 301.6363-2) the court may issue such other orders as may be appropriate with respect to taxable years which include any part of the period of litigation.

(c) *Review of Court of Appeals' judgment.*—The judgment of the Court of Appeals shall be subject to review by the Supreme Court of the United States upon certiorari or certification sought by either party as provided in section 1254 of title 28, United States Code.

(d) *Effect of final judgment.*—If a final judgment, rendered with respect to litigation involving a State's petition to review a determination of the Secretary or his delegate to the effect that the State's individual income tax laws included in its notice of election would not meet the requirements for qualification specified in section 6362 and the regulations thereunder if a State agreement were in effect with respect thereto, includes a determination that the State's tax would in fact meet such requirements, then the provisions of subchapter E shall apply to the State with respect to taxable years beginning on or after the first January 1 which is more than 6 months after the date of such final judgment. If a final judgment, rendered with respect to litigation involving a State's petition to review a determination of the Secretary or his delegate to the effect that the State's previously-qualified tax ceases to qualify because of a change in the State's law, includes a determination that the State's tax does in fact cease to qualify, then the provisions of subchapter E (other than section 6363) shall cease to apply to the State with respect to taxable years beginning on or after the first January 1 which is more than 6 months after the date of such final judgment. See paragraph

(b) of §301.6365-2 for special rules with respect to withholding in the case of fiscal-year taxpayers.

(e) *Expeditious treatment of judicial proceedings.*—Under section 6363(d)(4), any judicial proceedings to which a State and the United States are parties, and which are brought pursuant to section 6363, are entitled to receive a preference, and to be heard and determined as expeditiously as possible, upon request of the Secretary or the State. [Reg. §301.6363-4.]

☐ [*T.D.* 7577, 12-19-78.]

[Reg. §301.6365-1]

§301.6365-1. Definitions.—(a) *State.*—For purposes of subchapter E and the regulations thereunder, the term "State" shall include the District of Columbia, but shall not include the Commonwealth of Puerto Rico or any possession of the United States.

(b) *Governor.*—For purposes of subchapter E and the regulations thereunder, the term "Governor" shall include the Mayor of the District of Columbia. [Reg. §301.6365-1.]

☐ [*T.D.* 7577, 12-19-78.]

[Reg. §301.6365-2]

§301.6365-2. Commencement and cessation of applicability of subchapter E to individual taxpayers.—(a) *General rule.*—Except for purposes of chapter 24 (relating to the collection of income tax at source on wages), whenever subchapter E begins or ceases to apply to any State (i.e., a State agreement begins or ceases to be effective) as of any January 1, such commencement or cessation of applicability shall apply to taxable years of individuals beginning on or after such date. For example, if subchapter E begins to apply to a particular State on January 1, 1980, it would become applicable for calendar year 1980 for calendar-year taxpayers in that

State; but if a taxpayer in the State is using a fiscal year running from July 1 to June 30, the subchapter would begin to apply (except for purposes of chapter 24) to that taxpayer on July 1, 1980, for his taxable year ending June 30, 1981. Similarly, if the subchapter ceases to apply to such State on January 1, 1982, it would cease to apply to calendar-year taxpayers after the end of calendar year 1981; but it would cease to apply (except for purposes of chapter 24) to fiscal-year taxpayers at the end of their fiscal years which are in progress on January 1, 1982. The cessation of applicability of subchapter E to a State does not affect rights, duties, and liabilities with respect to any taxable year for which subchapter E does apply with respect to any taxpayer (or his employer).

(b) *Special rules pertaining to withholding.*—(1) *Subchapter E beginning to apply.*—The Federal withholding system provided in chapter 24 shall go into effect for State individual income tax purposes with respect to wages paid on or after January 1 as of which subchapter E begins to apply to a State. If an employee is subject to a qualified tax imposed by the State, such withholding system shall apply to his wages paid on or after that January 1, without regard to whether he is a calendar-year or fiscal-year taxpayer. See §301.6363-3 with respect to transition-year rules.

(2) *Subchapter E ceasing to apply.*—The Federal withholding system provided in chapter 24 shall cease to be effective for State tax purposes with respect to wages paid on or after the January 1 as of which subchapter E ceases to apply to the State, although fiscal-year taxpayers of that State continue to be subject to the other provisions of subchapter E for the remainder of their fiscal years then in progress. See §301.6363-3 with respect to transition-year rules. [Reg. §301.6365-2.]

☐ [*T.D.* 7577, 12-19-78.]

Abatements, Credits and Refunds

PROCEDURE IN GENERAL

See p. 20,601 for regulations not amended to reflect law changes

[Reg. §301.6401-1]

§301.6401-1. Amounts treated as overpayments.—(a) The term "overpayment" includes:

(1) Any payment of any internal revenue tax which is assessed or collected after the expiration of the period of limitation applicable thereto.

(2) Any amount allowable for a taxable year as credits under sections 31 (relating to tax withheld on wages), 39 (relating to certain uses of gasoline, special fuels, and lubricating oil), 43 (relating to earned income credit), and 667(b) (relating to taxes paid by certain trusts) which exceeds the tax imposed by subtitle A of the Code (reduced by the credits allowable under subpart A of part IV of subchapter A of chapter 1

of the Code, other than the credits allowable under sections 31, 39 and 43) for such year.

(b) An amount paid as tax shall not be considered not to constitute an overpayment solely by reason of the fact that there was no tax liability in respect of which such amount was paid. [Reg. §301.6401-1.]

☐ [*T.D.* 6119, 12-31-54. *Amended by T.D.* 6498, 10-24-60; *T.D.* 7204, 8-24-72 *and T.D.* 7537, 3-31-78.]

[Reg. §301.6402-1]

§301.6402-1. Authority to make credits or refunds.—The Commissioner, within the applicable period of limitations, may credit any overpayment of tax, including interest thereon, against any outstanding liability for any tax (or for any interest, additional amount, addition to the tax, or assessable penalty) owed by the person making the overpayment and the balance, if any, shall be refunded, subject to section 6402(c) and (d) and the regulations thereunder, to that person by the Commissioner. [Reg. §301.6402-1.]

☐ [*T.D. 6119, 12-31-54. Amended by T.D. 7808, 2-3-82 and T.D. 8053, 9-27-85.*]

[Reg. §301.6402-2]

§301.6402-2. Claims for credit or refund.—
(a) *Requirement that claim be filed.*—(1) Credits or refunds of overpayments may not be allowed or made after the expiration of the statutory period of limitation properly applicable unless, before the expiration of such period, a claim therefor has been filed by the taxpayer. Furthermore, under section 7422, a civil action for refund may not be instituted unless a claim has been filed within the properly applicable period of limitation.

(2) Except as provided in paragraph (b) of §301.6091-1 (relating to hand-carried documents), if a taxpayer is required to file a claim for credit or refund using a particular form, then the claim, together with appropriate supporting evidence, shall be filed in a manner consistent with such form, form instructions, publications, or other guidance found on the IRS.gov website. If a taxpayer is filing a claim in response to an IRS notice or correspondence, then the claim must be filed in accordance with the specific instructions contained in the notice or correspondence regarding the manner of filing. Any other claim not described in the preceding sentences generally must be filed with the service center at which the taxpayer currently would be required to file a tax return for the type of tax to which the claim relates or via the appropriate electronic portal. For rules relating to interest in the case of credits or refunds, see section 6611. For rules treating timely mailing as timely filing, see section 7502. For rules relating to the time for filing a claim when the last day falls on Saturday, Sunday, or a legal holiday, see section 7503.

(b) *Grounds set forth in claim.*—(1) No refund or credit will be allowed after the expiration of the statutory period of limitation applicable to the filing of a claim therefor except upon one or more of the grounds set forth in a claim filed before the expiration of such period. The claim must set forth in detail each ground upon which a credit or refund is claimed and facts sufficient to apprise the Commissioner of the exact basis thereof. The statement of the grounds and facts must be verified by a written declaration that it is made under the penalties of perjury. A claim which does not comply with this paragraph will not be considered for any purpose as a claim for refund or credit.

(2) The IRS does not have the authority to refund on equitable grounds penalties or other amounts legally collected.

(c) *Form for filing claim.*—If a particular form is prescribed on which the claim must be made, then the claim must be made on the form so prescribed. For special rules applicable to refunds of income taxes, see §301.6402-3. For provisions relating to credits and refunds of taxes other than income tax, see the regulations relating to the particular tax. All claims by taxpayers for the refund of taxes, interest, penalties, and additions to tax that are not otherwise provided for must be made on Form 843, "Claim for Refund and Request for Abatement."

(d) *Separate claims for separate taxable periods.*—In the case of income and gift taxes, income tax withheld, taxes under the Federal Insurance Contributions Act, taxes under the Railroad Retirement Tax Act, and taxes under the Federal Unemployment Tax Act, a separate claim must be made for each return for each taxable period.

(e) *Proof of representative capacity.*—If a return is filed by an individual and, after his death, a refund claim is filed by his legal representative, certified copies of the letters testamentary, letters of administration, or other similar evidence must be annexed to the claim, to show the authority of the legal representative to file the claim. If an executor, administrator, guardian, trustee, receiver, or other fiduciary files a return and thereafter a refund claim is filed by the same fiduciary, documentary evidence to establish the legal authority of the fiduciary need not accompany the claim, provided a statement is made in the claim showing that the return was filed by the fiduciary and that the latter is still acting. In such cases, if a refund is to be paid, letters testamentary, letters of administration, or other evidence may be required, but should be submitted only upon the receipt of a specific request therefor. If a claim is filed by a fiduciary other than the one by whom the return was filed, the necessary documentary evidence should accompany the claim. A claim may be executed by an agent of the person assessed, but in such case a power of attorney must accompany the claim.

(f) *Mailing of refund check.*—(1) Checks in payment of claims allowed will be drawn in the names of the persons entitled to the money and, except as provided in subparagraph (2) of this paragraph, the checks may be sent direct to the claimant or to such person in care of an attorney or agent who has filed a power of attorney specifically authorizing him to receive such checks.

(2) Checks in payment of claims which have either been reduced to judgment or settled in the course or as a result of litigation will be drawn in the name of the person or persons entitled to the money and will be sent to the Assistant Attorney General, Tax Division, Department of Justice, for delivery to the taxpayer or the counsel of record in the court proceeding.

(3) For restrictions on the assignment of claims, see sections 3477 of the Revised Statutes (31 U.S.C. 203).

(g) *Effective/applicability date.*—Paragraphs (a)(2), (b)(2), (c), and (d) of this section apply to claims for credit or refund filed on or after July 24, 2015. Paragraphs (a)(1), (b)(1), (e), and (f) of this section apply to claims for credit or refund filed before, on or after July 24, 2015. [Reg. §301.6402-2.]

☐ [*T.D.* 6119, 12-31-54. *Amended by T.D.* 6292, 4-18-58; *T.D.* 6498, 10-24-60; *T.D.* 6585, 12-27-61; *T.D.* 6950, 4-3-68; *T.D.* 7008, 2-28-69; *T.D.* 7188, 6-28-72; *T.D.* 7410, 3-15-76, *T.D.* 7484, 4-29-77 *and T.D.* 9727, 7-23-2015.]

[Reg. §301.6402-3]

§301.6402-3. Special rules applicable to income tax.—(a) The following rules apply to a claim for credit or refund of income tax:—

(1) In general, in the case of an overpayment of income taxes, a claim for credit or refund of such overpayment shall be made on the appropriate income tax return.

(2) In the case of an overpayment of income taxes for a taxable year of an individual for which a Form 1040 or 1040A has been filed, a claim for refund shall be made on Form 1040X ("Amended U.S. Individual Income Tax Return").

(3) In the case of an overpayment of income taxes for a taxable year of a corporation for which a Form 1120 has been filed, a claim for refund shall be made on Form 1120X ("Amended U.S. Corporation Income Tax Return").

(4) In the case of an overpayment of income taxes for a taxable year for which a form other than Form 1040, 1040A, or 1120 was filed (such as Form 1041 (U.S. Fiduciary Income Tax Return) or Form 990T (Exempt Organization Business Income Tax Return)), a claim for credit or refund shall be made on the appropriate amended income tax return.

(5) A properly executed individual, fiduciary, or corporation original income tax return or an amended return (on 1040X or 1120X if applicable) shall constitute a claim for refund or credit within the meaning of section 6402 and section 6511 for the amount of the overpayment disclosed by such return (or amended return). For purposes of section 6511, such claim shall be considered as filed on the date on which such return (or amended return) is considered as filed, except that if the requirements of §301.7502-1, relating to timely mailing treated as timely filing are met, the claim shall be considered to be filed on the date of the postmark stamped on the cover in which the return (or amended return) was mailed. A return or amended return shall constitute a claim for refund or credit if it contains a statement setting forth the amount determined as an overpayment and advising whether such amount shall be refunded to the taxpayer or shall be applied as a credit against the taxpayer's estimated income tax for the taxable year immediately succeeding the taxable year for which such return (or amended return) is filed. If the taxpayer indicates on its return (or amended return) that all or part of the overpayment shown by its return (or

amended return) is to be applied to its estimated income tax for its succeeding taxable year, such indication shall constitute an election to so apply such overpayment, and no interest shall be allowed on such portion of the overpayment credited and such amount shall be applied as a payment on account of the estimated income tax for such year or the installments thereof.

(6) Notwithstanding paragraph (a)(5) of this section, the Internal Revenue Service, within the applicable period of limitations, may credit any overpayment of individual, fiduciary, or corporation income tax, including interest thereon, against—

(i) First, any outstanding liability for any tax (or for any interest, additional amount, additions to the tax, or assessable penalty) owed by the taxpayer making the overpayment;

(ii) Second, in the case of an individual taxpayer, amounts of past-due support assigned to a State under section 402(a)(26) or 471(a)(17) of the Social Security Act under procedures set forth in the regulations under section 6402(c);

(iii) Third, past-due and legally enforceable debt under procedures set forth in the regulations under section 6402(d); and

(iv) Fourth, qualifying amounts of past-due support not assigned to a State under procedures set forth in the regulations under section 6402(c).

Only the balance, if any, of the overpayment remaining after credits described in this paragraph (a)(6) shall be treated in the manner so elected.

(b) [Reserved]

(c) If the taxpayer is not required to show the tax on the form (see section 6014 and the accompanying regulations), the IRS will treat a properly filed income tax return as a claim for refund and such return will constitute a claim for refund within the meaning of section 6402 and section 6511 for the amount of the overpayment shown by the computation of the tax made by the IRS on the basis of the return. For purposes of the limitations period of section 6511, such claim will be treated as filed on the date the return is treated as filed.

(d) In any case in which a taxpayer elects to have an overpayment refunded to him he may not thereafter change his election to have the overpayment applied as a payment on account of his estimated income tax.

(e) In the case of a nonresident alien individual or foreign corporation, the appropriate income tax return on which the claim for refund or credit is made must contain the tax identification number of the taxpayer required pursuant to section 6109 and the entire amount of income of the taxpayer subject to tax, even if the tax liability for that income was fully satisfied at source through withholding under chapters 3 or 4 of the Internal Revenue Code (Code). Also, if the overpayment of tax resulted from the withholding of tax at source under chapter 3 or 4 of the Code, a copy of the Form 1042-S, "Foreign Person's U.S. Source Income subject to Withholding," Form

8805, "Foreign Partner's Information Statement of Section 1446 Withholding Tax," or other statement (required under § 1.1446-3(d)(2) of this chapter) required to be provided to the beneficial owner or partner pursuant to § 1.1461-1(c)(1)(i), § 1.1474-1(d)(1)(i), or § 1.1446-3(d) of this chapter must be attached to the return. For purposes of claiming a refund, the Form 8805 or other statement must include the taxpayer identification number of the beneficial owner or partner even if not otherwise required. No claim for refund or credit under chapter 65 of the Code may be made by the taxpayer for any amount that the payor has repaid to the taxpayer pursuant to reimbursement or set-off procedures (described in § 1.1461-2(a)(2), (3) or § 1.1474-2(a)(3), (4) of this chapter). In addition, no claim for refund or credit may be made by a taxpayer for any amount that has been repaid to a qualified intermediary (as described in § 1.1441-1(e)(5)(ii) or a participating FFI (as described in § 1.1471-1b)(91)) pursuant to a collective refund filed by such entity on behalf of the taxpayer. See § 1.1441-1(e)(5)(iii) (describing a qualified intermediary agreement) and § 1.1471-4(h) (describing a collective refund). Upon request, a taxpayer must also submit such documentation as the IRS, may require establishing that the taxpayer is the beneficial owner of the income for which a claim for refund or credit is being made and verifying the grounds and facts set forth in taxpayer's claim as required by § 301.6402-2(b)(1). See § 1.1474-5 for additional requirements that may apply in the case of a refund of tax withheld under chapter 4.

(f) *Effective/applicability date.*—(1) Except as provided in paragraph (f)(2) of this section, this section applies on or after January 6, 2017. (For payments made after June 30, 2014, and before January 6, 2017, see this section as in effect and contained in 26 CFR part 1, revised April 1, 2016.)

(2) References in paragraph (e) of this section to Form 8805 or other statements required under § 1.1446-3(d)(2) shall apply to partnership taxable years beginning after April 29, 2008. References in paragraph (e) of this section to amounts withheld under chapter 4 of the Code and claims made with respect to amounts withheld under chapter 4 of the Code shall apply to withholdable payments made after June 30, 2014. [Reg. § 301.6402-3.]

☐ [*T.D.* 6119, 12-31-54. *Amended by T.D.* 6292, 4-18-58; *T.D.* 6425, 11-10-59; *T.D.* 6498, 10-24-60; *T.D.* 6585, 12-27-61; *T.D.* 7057, 9-2-70; *T.D.* 7102, 3-23-71; *T.D.* 7234, 12-20-72; *T.D.* 7269, 4-12-73; *T.D.* 7293, 11-27-73; *T.D.* 7298, 12-21-73; *T.D.* 7410, 3-15-76; *T.D.* 7808, 2-3-82; *T.D.* 8053, 9-27-85; *T.D.* 8734, 10-6-97 (T.D. 8804 delayed the effective date of T.D. 8734 from January 1, 1999, to January 1, 2000; T.D. 8856 further delayed the effective date of T.D. 8734 until January 1, 2001); *T.D.* 9394, 4-28-2008, *T.D.* 9658, 2-28-2014, *T.D.* 9727, 7-23-2015 *and T.D.* 9808, 12-30-2016.]

[Reg. § 301.6402-4]

§ 301.6402-4. Payments in excess of amounts shown on return.—(a) If the IRS determines that the payments by the taxpayer that are made within the period prescribed for payment and before the filing of the return exceed the amount of tax shown on the return (for example, excessive estimated income tax payments or excessive withholding), the IRS may credit or refund such overpayment without awaiting examination of the completed return and without awaiting the filing of a claim for refund. The provisions of §§ 301.6402-2 and 301.6402-3 are applicable to such overpayment, and taxpayers should submit claims for refund (if the income tax return is not itself a claim for refund, as provided in § 301.6402-3) to protect themselves in the event the IRS fails to make such determination and credit or refund. The provisions of section 6405 (relating to reports of refunds in excess of the statutorily prescribed threshold referral amount to the Joint Committee on Taxation) do not apply to the overpayments described in this section.

(b) *Effective/applicability date.*—The rules of this section apply to payments made on or after July 24, 2015. [Reg. § 301.6402-4.]

☐ [*T.D.* 6119, 12-31-54. *Amended by T.D.* 6585, 12-27-61 *and T.D.* 9727, 7-23-2015.]

[Reg. § 301.6402-5]

§ 301.6402-5. Offset of past-due support against overpayments.—(a) *Introduction.*—(1) *Scope.*—Section 6402(c) requires the Secretary of the Treasury or his delegate to reduce the amount of any overpayment to be refunded to a person making an overpayment by the amount of past-due support owed by that person of which the Secretary has been notified in accordance with section 464 of the Social Security Act. Past-due support shall be collected by offset under section 6402(c) and this section in the same manner as if it were a liability for tax imposed by the Internal Revenue Code of 1954 (except that a liability for tax shall be given priority with respect to offset arising under section 6402(a)). Collection by offset under section 6402(c) of this section is a collection procedure separate from the collection procedures provided by section 6305 and § 301.6305-1, relating to assessment and collection of certain child and spousal support liabilities. The sole collection procedure provided by section 6402(c) and this section is that of offset against overpayment. Section 6305 and § 301.6305-1, by contrast, provide for other collection procedures in addition to collection by offset against overpayment. Sections 6305 and 6402(c) have differing procedural requirements and may be used separately or in conjunction with each other.

(2) *General rule.*—An amount of past-due support qualifies for offset under this section if it satisfies the requirements of paragraph (b) of this section. A State shall submit to the Department of Health and Human Services a notification of liability for qualifying past-due support contain-

ing the information described in paragraph (c) of this section. A qualifying amount of past-due support owed by a taxpayer who has made an overpayment shall be collected in accordance with the procedures set forth in paragraph (d) of this section. Under paragraph (d), the balance of any overpayment remaining after crediting of the overpayment under section 6402(a) to any liability for an internal revenue tax on the part of the taxpayer shall be offset by the amount of past-due support of which the Internal Revenue Service has been notified. The amount of the overpayment not subject to offset for any liability for an internal revenue tax or for past-due support shall be promptly refunded to the taxpayer. Paragraph (e) of this section requires that the Internal Revenue Service notify the taxpayer of the amount of the offset and of the State to which it has been paid. Under procedures set forth in paragraph (f) of this section, amounts collected by offset shall be transferred to a special account maintained by the Bureau of Government Financial Operations for distribution to the States. The Internal Revenue Service shall make monthly collection reports to the Secretary of Health and Human Services or his delegate. The States shall reimburse the Secretary of the Treasury for the full cost of the refund offset under paragraph (g) of this section.

(b) *Past-due support.*—(1) *Definition.*—For purposes of this section, the term "past-due support" means the amount of a delinquent obligation, which amount was determined under a court order, or an order pursuant to an administrative process established under State law, for support and maintenance of a child or of a child and the parent with whom the child is living.

(2) *Past-due support qualifying for offset.*—Past-due support qualifies for offset under section 6402(c) and this section if—

(i) There has been an assignment of the support obligation to a State pursuant to section 402(a)(26) of the Social Security Act (relating to aid and service to needy families with children) and that State has made reasonable efforts to collect the amount of the obligation;

(ii) The amount of past-due support is not less than $150.00;

(iii) The past-due support has been delinquent for three months or longer; and

(iv) A notification of liability for past-due support has been received by the Secretary of the Treasury as prescribed by paragraph (c) of this section.

(c) *Notification of liability for past-due support.*—(1) *Form.*—A State shall, by October 1 of each year, submit a notification (or notifications) of liability for past-due support on magnetic tape to the Special Collection Activities Unit, Office of Child Support Enforcement, Department of Health and Human Services, 6110 Executive Boulevard, Suite 900, Rockville, Maryland 20852, Attention: Tax Refund Offset—Tape Processing.

(2) *Content.*—The notification of liability for past-due support shall contain with respect to each taxpayer—

(i) The name of the taxpayer who owes the past-due support;

(ii) The social security number of that taxpayer;

(iii) The amount of past-due support owed; and

(iv) The alphabetical designation of the State submitting the notification of liability for past-due support.
The Secretary of Health and Human Services may also require such other information from the State submitting the notification as is necessary for his orderly consolidation of data for transmittal to the Internal Revenue Service.

(3) *Transmittal of notification to Internal Revenue Service.*—The Secretary of Health and Human Services shall, by December 1 of each year, consolidate and transmit to the Internal Revenue Service on magnetic tape the data contained in the notifications of liability for past-due support submitted by the participating States.

(4) *Correction of notification.*—If, after submitting a notification of liability for past-due support, a State determines that an error has been made with respect to the information contained in the notification, or if a State receives a payment or credits a payment to the account of a taxpayer named in this notification, the State shall promptly notify the Office of Child Support Enforcement of the Department of Health and Human Services of these corrections in accordance with any time limitations specified by the Office of Child Support Enforcement. That Office shall promptly transmit these corrections to the Internal Revenue Service and the Internal Revenue Service shall make the appropriate correction of the notification of liability for past-due support. However, in no case shall a State notify the Office of Child Support Enforcement under this paragraph (c)(4) of an increased amount of past-due support owed by a taxpayer named in its notification of liability for past-due support. The correction of notification described in this paragraph (c)(4) is to be submitted only for the purpose of completing or correcting the information contained in the notification of liability for past-due support.

(d) *Collection.*—(1) *Priority of offset for outstanding tax liability.*—Under section 6402(a) and § 301.6402-1, the Commissioner may credit any overpayment of tax against any outstanding liability for any tax owed by the person making the overpayment. Only the balance remaining after such crediting is available for offset under section 6402(c) of this section. Thus, if a taxpayer making an overpayment has both an outstanding tax liability and a liability for past-due support subject to this section, then the entire amount of the overpayment shall be credited first against the outstanding tax liability under section 6402(a) and § 301.6402-1 and only the remainder, if any, of the overpayment will be offset by the amount of past-due support. However, an overpayment shall be offset by an amount of past-due support under section 6402(c) before any crediting of the overpayment to any future liability for an internal revenue tax. Thus, for example, if no outstanding tax liability is owed and the amount of an overpayment is equal to or less than the amount of past-due support, the Internal Revenue Service shall offset the overpayment by the amount of past-due support before crediting the overpayment against the taxpayer's estimated income tax for the succeeding taxable year under section 6402(b).

(2) *Amounts subject to offset.*—The balance of any overpayment remaining after a crediting of the overpayment under section 6402(a) to any outstanding liability for tax on the part of the taxpayer shall be offset by the amount of past-due support of which the Internal Revenue Service has been notified under this section.

(3) *Amounts not subject to offset.*—The amount of an overpayment not subject to offset for any liability for tax or for past-due support shall be promptly refunded to the taxpayer.

(e) *Notice of offset.*—The Internal Revenue Service shall notify the taxpayer in writing of the amount and date of the offset for past-due support and of the State to which this amount of past-due support has been paid.

(f) *Disposition of amounts collected.*—Amounts collected under this section shall be transferred to a special account maintained by the Bureau of Government Financial Operations. The Internal Revenue Service shall advise the Secretary of Health and Human Services or his delegate on a monthly basis of the names and social security numbers of the taxpayers from whom the amounts of past-due support were collected, of the amounts collected from each taxpayer, and of the State on whose behalf each collection was made. After authorization by the Division of Finance of the Social Security Administration, the Bureau of Government Financial Operations of the Department of the Treasury shall pay to the participating States amounts equal to the amounts collected under this section.

(g) *Fee.*—A refund offset fee in the amount of $17.00 per offset for taxable year 1981, or such greater or smaller amount as the Secretary of the Treasury and the Secretary of Health and Human Services have agreed to be sufficient to reimburse the Internal Revenue Service for the full cost of the offset procedure, shall be billed and collected from the participating States by the Secretary of Health and Human Services or his delegate and deposited in the United States Treasury and credited to the appropriation accounts of the Internal Revenue Service which bore all or part of the costs involved in making the collection.

(h) *Effective dates.*—This section applies to refunds payable on or before January 1, 1999. For the rules applicable after January 1, 1999, see 31 CFR part 285. [Reg. § 301.6402-5.]

□ [*T.D.* 7895, 5-19-83. *Amended by T.D.* 8837, 9-3-99.]

[Reg. § 301.6402-6]

§ 301.6402-6. Offset of past-due, legally enforceable debt against overpayment.—(a) *General rule.*—(1) A Federal agency (as defined in section 6402(f)) that has entered into an agreement with the Internal Revenue Service with regard to its participation in the tax refund offset program and that is owed a past-due, legally enforceable debt may refer the past-due, legally enforceable debt to the Internal Revenue Service to be collected by Federal tax refund offset. The Service shall, after making appropriate credits as provided by § 301.6402-3(a)(6)(i) and (ii), reduce the amount of any overpayment payable to a taxpayer by the amount of any past-due, legally enforceable debt owed to the agency and properly referred to the Service. This section does not apply to any debt subject to section 464 of the Social Security Act (past-due support).

(2)(i) This section applies to OASDI overpayments provided the requirements of 31 U.S.C. 3720A(f)(1) and (2) are met with respect to such overpayments.

(ii) For purposes of this section, "OASDI overpayment" means any overpayment of benefits made to an individual under title II of the Social Security Act.

(b) *Eligible Federal agencies.*—(1) A Federal agency is eligible to participate in the tax refund offset program if the agency—

(i) Has promulgated temporary or final regulations under 31 U.S.C. 3720A, governing the operation of the Federal tax refund offset program in the agency;

(ii) Has promulgated temporary or final regulations under 31 U.S.C. 3716, governing the operation of the administrative offset program in the agency; and

(iii) Has promulgated temporary or final regulations under 5 U.S.C. 5514(a), governing the operation of the salary offset program in the agency (unless the agency has certified that, relying on the most current information reasonably available, it will not refer to the Service any names of present or former Federal employees or other persons whose debts are subject to offset under the provisions of 5 U.S.C. 5514(a)(1)).

(2) An agency prohibited by Federal law from meeting any of the requirements of paragraph (b)(1) or (c) of this section shall notify the Service in writing of the specific legal impediment to meeting these requirements. This notification shall be made prior to entering into an agreement with the Service to participate in the tax refund offset program. The Service will determine in writing whether the agency is prohibited by Federal law from meeting any of the requirements of paragraph (b)(1) or (c) of this section. The Service will waive in writing any requirement that it determines the agency is prohibited by Federal law from meeting.

(c) *Past-due, legally enforceable debt eligible for refund offset.*—For purposes of this section, a Federal agency may refer a past-due, legally enforceable debt to the Service for offset if—

(1) Except in the case of a judgment debt or any debts specifically exempt from this requirement (for example, debts referred by the Department of Education that were pending on or after April 9, 1991, and referred to the Service for offset before November 15, 1992), the debt is referred for offset within ten years after the agency's right of action accrues;

(2) The debt cannot be currently collected pursuant to the salary offset provisions of 5 U.S.C. 5514(a)(1);

(3) The debt is ineligible for administrative offset under 31 U.S.C. 3716(a) by reason of 31 U.S.C. 3716(c)(2), or cannot be currently collected by administrative offset under 31 U.S.C. 3716(a) by the referring agency against amounts payable to the taxpayer by the referring agency;

(4) The agency has notified, or has made a reasonable attempt to notify, the taxpayer that the debt is past-due, and unless repaid within 60 days thereafter, will be referred to the Service for offset against an overpayment of tax;

(5) The agency has given the taxpayer at least 60 days to present evidence that all or part of the debt is not past-due or legally enforceable, has considered any evidence presented by the taxpayer, and has determined that the debt is past-due and legally enforceable;

(6) The debt has been disclosed by the agency to a consumer reporting agency as authorized by 31 U.S.C. 3711(f), unless the consumer reporting agency would be prohibited from reporting information concerning the debt by reason of 15 U.S.C. 1681c, or unless the amount of the debt does not exceed $100;

(7) The debt is at least $25; and

(8) In the case of an OASDI overpayment—

(i) The individual is not currently entitled to monthly insurance benefits under title II of the Social Security Act;

(ii) The notice describes conditions under which the Department of Health and Human Services is required to waive recovery of the overpayment, as provided under section 204(b) of the Social Security Act; and

(iii) If the taxpayer files for a waiver under section 204(b) of the Social Security Act within the 60-day notice period, the agency has considered the taxpayer's request.

(d) *Pre-offset notice and consideration of evidence.*—(1) For purposes of paragraph (c)(4) of this section, an agency has made a reasonable attempt to notify the taxpayer if the agency uses the most recent address information obtained from the Service pursuant to section 6103(m)(2), (4), or (5) of the Code, unless the agency receives clear and concise notification from the taxpayer that notices from the agency are to be sent to an address different from the address obtained from the Service. Clear and concise notification means that the taxpayer has provided the agency with

written notification including the taxpayer's name and identifying number (as defined in section 6109), the taxpayer's new address, and the taxpayer's intent to have agency notices sent to the new address.

(2) For purposes of paragraph (c)(5) of this section, if the evidence presented by the taxpayer is considered by an agent of the agency, or other entities or persons acting on the agency's behalf, the taxpayer must be accorded at least 30 days from the date the agent or other entity or person determines that all or part of the debt is past-due and legally enforceable to request review by an officer or employee of the agency of any unresolved dispute. The agency must then notify the taxpayer of its decision.

(e) *Referral of past-due, legally enforceable debt.*—A Federal agency must refer a past-due, legally enforceable debt to the Service in the time and manner prescribed by the Service. The referral must contain—

(1) The name and identifying number (as defined in section 6109) of the taxpayer who is responsible for the debt;

(2) The amount of such past-due and legally enforceable debt;

(3) The date on which the debt became past-due;

(4) The designation of the Federal agency or subagency referring the debt; and

(5) In the case of an OASDI overpayment, a certification by the Secretary of Health and Human Services designating whether the amount payable to the agency is to be deposited in either the Federal Old-Age and Survivors Insurance Trust Fund or the Federal Disability Insurance Trust Fund, but not both.

(f) *Correction of referral.*—If, after referring a past-due, legally enforceable debt to the Service as provided by paragraph (e) of this section, an agency determines that an error has been made with respect to the information transmitted to the Service, or if an agency receives a payment or credits a payment to the account of a taxpayer referred to the Service for offset, the agency shall promptly notify the Service. The Service shall make the appropriate correction of its records. However, this paragraph (f) does not permit an agency to increase the amount of a past-due, legally enforceable debt or refer additional debtors to the Service for offset after an agency makes its original referral of debts for tax refund offset. The agency may refer additional debts to the Service for refund offset in subsequent tax refund offset years.

(g) *Priorities for offset.*—(1) An overpayment shall be reduced first by the amount of an outstanding liability for any tax under section 6402(a); second, by the amount of any past-due support assigned to a State under section 402(a)(26) or section 471(a)(17) of the Social Security Act which is to be offset under section 6402(c) and the regulations thereunder; third, by the amount of any past-due, legally enforceable debt owed to a Federal agency under section

Reg. §301.6402-6(g)(1)

6402(d) and this section; and fourth, by the amount of any qualifying past-due support not assigned to a State which is to be offset under section 6402(c) and the regulations thereunder.

(2) If a taxpayer owes more than one past-due, legally enforceable debt to a Federal agency or agencies, the overpayment shall be credited against the debts in the order in which the debts accrued. A debt shall be considered to have accrued at the time at which the agency determines that the debt became past due.

(3) Reduction of the overpayment pursuant to section 6402(a), (c), and (d) shall occur prior to crediting the overpayment to any future liability for an internal revenue tax. Any amount remaining after offset under section 6402(a), (c), and (d) shall be refunded to the taxpayer, or applied to estimated tax, if elected by the taxpayer.

(h) *Post-offset notice to the taxpayer and the agency.*—(1) The Service shall notify the taxpayer in writing of the amount and date of the offset for a past-due, legally enforceable debt and of the Federal agency to which this amount has been paid or credited. For joint returns, see paragraph (i) of this section.

(2) The Service shall advise each agency of the names, mailing addresses, and identifying numbers of the taxpayers from whom amounts of past-due, legally enforceable debt were collected and of the amounts collected from each taxpayer. If the refund from which an amount of past-due, legally enforceable debt is to be withheld is based upon a joint return, the Service shall notify the agency and furnish the names and addresses of each taxpayer filing the joint return.

(i) *Offset made with regard to refund based upon joint return.*—(1) In the case of an offset from a refund based on a joint return, the Service shall issue a notice in writing to any person who may have filed a joint return with the taxpayer, including the amount and date of any offset and the steps which the non-debtor spouse may take in order to secure his or her proper share of the refund (unless the non-debtor spouse has already taken these steps prior to offset).

(2) If the person filing the joint return with the taxpayer owing the past-due, legally enforceable debt takes appropriate action to secure his or her proper share of a refund from which an offset was made, the Service shall pay the person his or her share of the refund and shall deduct that amount from amounts payable to the agency.

(j) *Disposition of amounts collected.*—Amounts collected under this section shall be transferred to a special account maintained by the Financial Management Service (FMS) for each Federal agency. If an erroneous payment is made to any agency, the Service shall deduct the amount of such payment from amounts payable to the agency.

(k) *Fees.*—The agency shall enter into a separate agreement with the Service and FMS to reimburse the Service and FMS for the full cost of administering the tax refund offset program. The fees shall be deducted from amounts collected prior to disposition. The fees shall be deposited in the United States Treasury and credited to the appropriation accounts which bore all or part of the costs involved in administering the refund offset procedures.

(l) *Review of offset of refunds.*—Any reduction of a taxpayer's refund made pursuant to section 6402(c) or (d) shall not be subject to review by any court of the United States or by the Service in an administrative proceeding. No action brought against the United States to recover the amount of this reduction shall be considered to be a suit for refund of tax. Any legal, equitable, or administrative action by any person seeking to recover the amount of the reduction of the overpayment must be taken against the Federal agency to which the amount of the reduction was paid. Any action which is otherwise available with respect to recoveries of overpayments of benefits under section 204 of the Social Security Act must be taken against the Secretary of Health and Human Services.

(m) *Access to and use of confidential tax information.*—Access to and use of confidential tax information in connection with the tax refund offset program are restricted by section 6103 of the Code. However, section 6103(l)(10) permits Federal officers and employees of agencies participating in the tax refund offset program to have access to and use of confidential tax information. Agencies receiving such information are subject to the safeguard, recordkeeping, and reporting requirements of section 6103(p)(4) and the regulations thereunder. The agency shall inform its officers and employees who access or use confidential tax information of the restrictions and penalties under the Internal Revenue Code for misuse of confidential tax information.

(n) *Effective dates.*—This section applies to refunds payable under section 6402 after April 15, 1992, and on or before January 1, 1998. For the rules applicable after January 1, 1998, see 31 CFR part 285. [Reg. § 301.6402-6.]

☐ [*T.D.* 8413, 4-14-92. *Amended by T.D.* 8837, 9-3-99.]

⟫⟫→ *Caution: AUTHORITY: The provisions of 31 CFR Part 285 are issued under the Debt Collection Improvement Act of 1996 (P.L. 104-134), 110 Stat. 1321-358 et seq., codified at 31 U.S.C. 3720A.*

[Reg. § 285.1]

§ 285.1. Collection of past-due support by administrative offset.—(a) *Definitions.*—For purposes of this section:

Administrative offset means withholding funds payable by the United States (including funds payable by the United States on behalf of a State government) to, or held by the United States for, a person to satisfy a debt.

⫸→ *Caution: AUTHORITY: The provisions of 31 CFR Part 285 are issued under the Debt Collection Improvement Act of 1996 (P.L. 104-134), 110 Stat. 1321-358 et seq., codified at 31 U.S.C. 3720A.*

Debt as used in this section is synonymous with the term past-due support.

Disbursing official includes an official who has authority to disburse public money pursuant to 31 U.S.C. 3321 or another Federal law.

FMS means the Financial Management Service, a bureau of the Department of the Treasury. FMS is the designee of the Secretary of the Treasury for all matters concerning this section, unless otherwise specified.

HHS means the Department of Health and Human Services, Office of Child Support Enforcement.

Past-due support means the amount of support determined under a court order, or an order of an administrative procedure established under State law, for support and maintenance of a child, or of a child and the parent with whom the child is living, which has not been paid. The term child as used in this definition is not limited to minor children.

Past-due support being enforced by the State there has been an assignment of the support rights to the State, or the State making the request for offset is providing services to individuals pursuant to 42 U.S.C. 654(5) (section 454(5) of the Social Security Act), or the State is enforcing support pursuant to a cooperative agreement with or by an Indian tribal government.

State means the several States of the United States. The term State also includes the District of Columbia, American Samoa, Guam, the United States Virgin Islands, the Commonwealth of the Northern Mariana Islands, and the Commonwealth of Puerto Rico.

Secretary means the Secretary of the Treasury.

(b) *General Rule.*—FMS may enter into a reciprocal agreement with a State for the collection of past-due support being enforced by the State by administrative offset from certain Federal payments. Upon notification of past-due support either directly from a State which has entered into such an agreement or from HHS, disbursing officials of FMS or any other disbursing official of the United States shall offset Federal payments which are subject to offset under this section, to collect past-due support. The amount offset, minus the offset fee, shall be forwarded to the State to be distributed in accordance with applicable laws and procedures.

(c) *Agreements.*—FMS may enter into reciprocal agreements with States for disbursing officials of FMS and any other Federal disbursing official to offset certain Federal payments to collect past-due support being enforced by the State. The agreement shall contain any requirements which FMS considers appropriate to facilitate the offset and prevent duplicative efforts and shall require States to prescribe procedures governing the collection of past-due support by Federal administrative offset. For purposes of this section, reciprocal means of mutual benefit. An agreement between FMS and a State to collect past-due support by offsetting Federal payments will be considered of mutual benefit and it is not required that States conduct administrative offsets to collect debts owed to the Federal Government. States which have entered into an agreement with FMS pursuant to this section may thereafter request, in the manner prescribed herein, that an offset be performed. Such requests shall be made by the appropriate State disbursing official which, for purposes of this section, means an appropriate official of the State agency which administers or supervises the administration of the State plan under Title IV-D of the Social Security Act.

(d) *Notification to FMS of past-due support.*—(1) States notifying FMS of past-due support must do so in the manner and format prescribed by FMS. States notifying HHS of past-due support must do so in the manner and format prescribed by HHS. HHS shall notify FMS of all past-due support referred to HHS by States for collection by administrative offset provided that the requirements of paragraphs (d)(3) and (h) of this section have been met.

(2) When a State has knowledge that past-due support is being enforced by more than one State, the State notifying FMS or HHS of the past-due support must inform any other State involved in enforcing the past-due support when it refers the debt for offset and when it receives the offset amount.

(3) The notification of past-due support must be accompanied by a certification that the debt is past-due, legally enforceable, and that the State has complied with all the requirements as set forth in paragraph (h) of this section and with any requirements imposed by State law or procedure. For debts so certified, the Secretary may waive sections 552a (o) and (p) of Title 5, United States Code, where applicable, in accordance with the Secretary's authority under 31 U.S.C. 3716(f).

(4) FMS may reject a notification of past-due support which does not comply with the requirements of this section. The State will be notified of the rejection along with the reason for the rejection.

(e) *Minimum amount of past-due support.*—FMS will reject a notification of past-due support where the past-due support owed is less than $25.00. This amount may be adjusted from time to time by FMS to ensure that the cost of collection does not exceed the debt.

(f) *Limitations.*—Debts properly submitted to FMS for administrative offset will remain subject to collection by administrative offset until withdrawn by the State provided the debt remains past-due and legally enforceable.

(g) *Notification of changes in status of debt.*—The State notifying FMS or HHS of past-due support shall, in the manner and in the time frames provided by FMS or HHS, notify FMS or HHS of

>>> Caution: *AUTHORITY: The provisions of 31 CFR Part 285 are issued under the Debt Collection Improvement Act of 1996 (P.L. 104-134), 110 Stat. 1321-358 et seq., codified at 31 U.S.C. 3720A.*

deletions or decreases in the amount of a debt referred for collection by administrative offset. The State may notify FMS or HHS of any increases in the amount of a debt referred for collection by administrative offset provided the State has complied with the requirements of paragraph (h) of this section with regard to those amounts.

(h) *Advance notification of intent to collect by administrative offset.*—(1) The State, or FMS or HHS on behalf of the State, if the State requests and FMS or HHS agrees, shall send a written notification, at least 30 days in advance of referral of the debt for offset, to the individual owing past-due support, informing the individual that the State intends to refer the debt for collection by administrative offset against Federal payments. The notice must also inform the individual of:

(i) The nature and amount of the debt; and

(ii) The right to an administrative review by the State referring the debt or, upon the request of the individual, by the State with the order upon which the referral was based, of the determination of the State with respect to the debt and of the procedures and time frames established by the State for such reviews.

(2) Prior to referring a debt to FMS for collection by administrative offset, States must provide individuals with a reasonable opportunity to exercise the rights enumerated in paragraph (h)(1) of this section in accordance with procedures prescribed by the State.

(i) *Payments subject to offset.*—Federal payments subject to offset under this section include all Federal payments except:

(1) Payments due to an individual under

(i) Title IV of the Higher Education Act of 1965;

(ii) The Social Security Act;

(iii) Part B of the Black Lung Benefits Act;

(iv) Any law administered by the Railroad Retirement Board;

(2) Payments which the Secretary determines are exempt from offset in accordance with paragraph (k) of this section;

(3) Payments from which collection of past-due support by administrative offset is expressly prohibited by law;

(4) Payments made under the Internal Revenue Code of 1986 (except that tax refund payments are subject to offset under separate authority); and

(5) Payments made under the tariff laws of the United States.

(j) *Special provisions applicable to Federal salary payments.*—(1) Unless a lower maximum offset limitation is provided by applicable State law, the maximum part of a Federal salary payment per pay period subject to offset to collect past-due support shall not exceed those amounts set forth at section 1673(b)(2)(A) and (B) of Title 15, United States Code, as follows:

(i) Fifty (50%) percent of the debtor's aggregate disposable earnings for any pay period, where the debtor asserts by affidavit, or by other acceptable evidence, that he/she is supporting a spouse and/or dependent child, other than the former spouse and/or child for whom support is being collected, except that an additional five (5%) percent will apply if it appears that such earnings are to enforce past-due support for a period which is twelve (12) weeks or more prior to the pay period to which the offset applies. A debtor shall be considered to be supporting a spouse and/or dependent child only if the debtor provides over half of the spouse's and/or dependent child's support.

(ii) Sixty (60%) percent of the debtor's aggregate disposable earnings for any pay period where the debtor fails to assert by affidavit or establish by other acceptable evidence that he/she is supporting a spouse and/or dependent child, other than a former spouse and/or child for whom support is being collected, except that an additional five (5%) percent will apply if it appears that such earnings are to enforce past-due support for a period which is twelve (12) weeks or more prior to the pay period to which the offset applies.

(2) The maximum allowable offset amount shall be reduced by the amount of any deductions in pay resulting from a garnishment order for support. Nothing in this rule is intended to alter rules applicable to processing garnishment orders for child support and/or alimony.

(3) Federal salary payments subject to offset for the collection of past-due support include current basic pay, special pay, incentive pay, retainer pay, overtime, or in the case of an employee not entitled to basic pay, other authorized pay. Aggregate disposable earnings for purposes of determining the maximum amounts which may be offset under paragraph (j)(1) of this section is Federal salary pay remaining after the deduction of:

(i) Any amount required by law to be withheld;

(ii) Amounts properly withheld for Federal, State or local income tax purposes;

(iii) Amounts deducted as health insurance premiums;

(iv) Amounts deducted as normal retirement contributions, not including amounts deducted for supplementary coverage; and

(v) Amounts deducted as normal life insurance premiums not including amounts deducted for supplementary coverage.

(4) At least 30 days in advance of offset, the disbursing official shall send written notice to the debtor of the maximum offset limitations described in paragraph (j)(1) of this section. The notice shall include a request that the debtor submit supporting affidavits or other documentation necessary to determine the applicable off-

⟫⟫→ *Caution: AUTHORITY: The provisions of 31 CFR Part 285 are issued under the Debt Collection Improvement Act of 1996 (P.L. 104-134), 110 Stat. 1321-358 et seq., codified at 31 U.S.C. 3720A.*

set percentage limitation. The notice shall also inform the debtor of the percentage that will be deducted if he/she fails to submit the requested documentation.

(5) At the time the past-due support debt is submitted for offset, the State shall advise FMS or HHS if the maximum amount of a Federal salary payment that may be offset is less than the amount described under this paragraph.

(k) *Payments exempt from administrative offset to collect past-due support being enforced by a State.*— The Secretary will exempt from administrative offset under this part payments made under means-tested programs when requested by the head of the Federal agency which administers the program. For purposes of this section, means-tested programs are programs for which eligibility is based on a determination that income and/or assets of the beneficiary are inadequate to provide the beneficiary with an adequate standard of living without program assistance. The Secretary may exempt from administrative offset under this section any other class or type of payment upon the written request of the head of the agency which authorizes the payments. In determining whether or not to grant such exemptions, the Secretary shall give due consideration to whether administrative offset would tend to interfere substantially with or defeat the purposes of the payment agency's program.

(l) *Fees.*—A fee which FMS has determined to be sufficient to reimburse FMS for the full cost of the offset procedure, shall be deducted from each offset amount. FMS will notify the States, annually and in advance, of the amount of the fee to be charged for each offset.

(m) *Offsetting payments.*—(1) *Conducting the offset.*—Disbursing officials of the Department of the Treasury, the Department of Defense, the United States Postal Service, or any other Government corporation, any disbursing official of the United States designated by the Secretary, or any disbursing official of an executive department or agency that disburses Federal payments shall offset payments subject to offset under this section to satisfy, in whole or part, a debt owed by the payee. Disbursing officials shall compare payment certification records with records of debts submitted to FMS for collection by administrative offset. A match will occur when the taxpayer identifying number and name control of a payment record are the same as the taxpayer identifying number and name control of a debt record. The taxpayer identifying number for an individual is the individual's social security number. When a match occurs and all other requirements for offset have been met, the disbursing official shall offset the payment to satisfy, in whole or part, the debt. Any amounts not offset shall be paid to the payee. The amount that can be offset from a single payment is the lesser of the amount of the debt (including inter-

est, penalties, and administrative costs); the amount of the payment; or the amount of the payment available for offset if a statute or regulation prohibits offset of the entire amount. Debts remain subject to collection by offset until paid in full.

(2) *Disposition of amounts collected.*—FMS will transmit amounts collected for debts, less fees charged under paragraph (l) of this section, to HHS or to the appropriate State. If FMS learns that an erroneous offset payment has been made to HHS or any State, FMS will notify HHS or the appropriate State that an erroneous offset payment has been made. FMS may deduct the amount of the erroneous offset payment from amounts payable to HHS or the State, as the case may be. Alternatively, upon FMS' request, the State shall return promptly to the affected payee or FMS an amount equal to the amount of the erroneous payment (unless the State previously has paid such amounts, or any portion of such amounts, to the affected payee). HHS and States shall notify FMS any time HHS or a State returns an erroneous offset payment to an affected payee. FMS and HHS, or the appropriate State, will adjust their debtor records accordingly.

(n) *Administrative offset priorities.*—When a payee/debtor owes more than one debt which has been referred to FMS for collection by administrative offset, any offset by a disbursing official will be applied first to past-due support assigned to a State and will be applied to any other past-due support after any other reductions allowed by law.

(o) *Notification of offset.*—(1) Disbursing officials of FMS or any other disbursing official which conducts an offset will notify the payee in writing of the occurrence of the offset to satisfy past-due support. The notice shall inform the payee of the type and amount of the payment that was offset; the identity of the State which requested the offset; and a contact point within the State that will handle concerns regarding the offset. Disbursing officials shall not be liable for failure to provide this notice.

(2) Disbursing officials of FMS or any other disbursing official which conducts an offset under this section will share with HHS, upon request by the Secretary of HHS, information contained in payment certification records of persons who are delinquent in child support obligations that would assist in the collection of such debts. When no offset is conducted, disbursing officials of FMS or any other disbursing official, will provide such information to HHS to the extent such information is available from offset activities conducted by FMS and other disbursing officials.

(p) *Liability of disbursing officials and payment agencies.*—Neither the disbursing official nor the agency authorizing the payment shall be liable for the amount of the administrative offset on

»»→ *Caution: AUTHORITY: The provisions of 31 CFR Part 285 are issued under the Debt Collection Improvement Act of 1996 (P.L. 104-134), 110 Stat. 1321-358 et seq., codified at 31 U.S.C. 3720A.*

the basis that the underlying obligation, represented by the payment before the administrative offset was taken, was not satisfied. Disbursing officials will notify the agency authorizing the payment that the offset has occurred so that the agency authorizing the payment may direct any inquiries concerning the offset to the appropriate State. [Reg. § 285.1.]

☐ [*Final Rule*, 8-27-98.]

[Reg. § 285.2]

§ 285.2. Offset of tax refund payments to collect past-due, legally enforceable nontax debt.—(a) *Definitions.*—For purposes of this section:

Creditor agency means a Federal agency owed a claim that seeks to collect that claim through tax refund offset.

Debt or *claim* refers to an amount of money, funds, or property which has been determined by an agency official to be due the United States from any person, organization, or entity, except another Federal agency. For the purposes of this section, the terms "claim" and "debt" are synonymous and interchangeable and includes debt administered by a third party acting as an agent for the Federal Government.

Debtor means a person who owes a debt or claim. The term "person" includes any individual, organization or entity, except another Federal agency.

FMS means the Financial Management Service, a bureau of the Department of the Treasury.

IRS means the Internal Revenue Service, a bureau of the Department of the Treasury.

Tax refund offset means withholding or reducing a tax refund payment by an amount necessary to satisfy a debt owed by the payee(s) of a tax refund payment.

Tax refund payment means any overpayment of Federal taxes to be refunded to the person making the overpayment after the IRS makes the appropriate credits as provided in 26 U.S.C. 6402(a) and 26 CFR 6402-3(a)(6)(i) for any liabilities for any tax on the part of the person who made the overpayment.

(b) *General rule.*—(1) A Federal agency (as defined in 26 U.S.C. 6402(g)) that is owed by a person a past-due, legally enforceable nontax debt shall notify FMS of the amount of such debt for collection by tax refund offset. However, any agency subject to section 9 of the Act of May 18, 1933 (16 U.S.C. 831h) owed such a debt may, but is not required to, notify FMS of the amount of such debt for collection by tax refund offset.

(2) FMS will compare tax refund payment records, as certified by the IRS, with records of debts submitted to FMS. A match will occur when the taxpayer identifying number (as that term is used in 26 U.S.C. 6109) and name (or derivation of the name, known as a "name control") of a payment certification record are the same as the taxpayer identifying number and name control of a debtor record. When a match occurs and all other requirements for tax refund offset have been met, FMS will reduce the amount of any tax refund payment payable to a debtor by the amount of any past-due, legally enforceable debt owed by the debtor. Any amounts not offset will be paid to the payee(s) listed in the payment certification record.

(3) This section does not apply to any debt or claim arising under the Internal Revenue Code.

(4)(i) This section applies to Federal Old Age, Survivors and Disability Insurance (OASDI) overpayments provided the requirements of 31 U.S.C. 3720A(f)(1) and (2) are met with respect to such overpayments.

(ii) For purposes of this section, "OASDI overpayment" means any overpayment of benefits made to an individual under title II of the Social Security Act (42 U.S.C. 401 et seq.).

(5) A creditor agency is not precluded from using debt collection procedures, such as wage garnishment, to collect debts that have been submitted to FMS for purposes of offset under this part. Such debt collection procedures may be used separately or in conjunction with offset collection procedures.

(c) *Regulations.*—Prior to submitting debts to FMS for collection by tax refund offset, Federal agencies shall promulgate temporary or final regulations under 31 U.S.C. 3716 and 31 U.S.C. 3720A, governing the agencies' authority to collect debts by administrative offset, in general, and offset of tax refund payments, in particular.

(d) *Agency certification and referral of debt.*—(1) *Past-due, legally enforceable debt eligible for tax refund offset.*—For purposes of this section, when a Federal agency refers a past-due, legally enforceable debt to FMS for tax refund offset, the agency will certify to FMS that:

(i) The debt is past-due and legally enforceable in the amount submitted to FMS and that the agency will ensure that collections are properly credited to the debt;

(ii) Except in the case of a judgment debt or as otherwise allowed by law, the debt is referred for offset within ten years after the agency's right of action accrues;

(iii) The creditor agency has made reasonable efforts to obtain payment of the debt in that the agency has:

(A) Submitted the debt to FMS for collection by administrative offset and complied with the provisions of 31 U.S.C. 3716(a) and related regulations, to the extent that collection of the debt by administrative offset is not prohibited by statute;

(B) Notified, or has made a reasonable attempt to notify, the debtor that the debt is past-due, and unless repaid within 60 days after the date of the notice, will be referred to FMS for tax refund offset;

>>>→ *Caution: AUTHORITY: The provisions of 31 CFR Part 285 are issued under the Debt Collection Improvement Act of 1996 (P.L. 104-134), 110 Stat. 1321-358 et seq., codified at 31 U.S.C. 3720A.*

(C) Given the debtor at least 60 days to present evidence that all or part of the debt is not past-due or legally enforceable, considered any evidence presented by the debtor, and determined that the debt is past-due and legally enforceable; and

(D) Provided the debtor with an opportunity to make a written agreement to repay the amount of the debt;

(iv) The debt is at least $25; and

(v) In the case of an OASDI overpayment—

(A) The individual is not currently entitled to monthly insurance benefits under title II of the Social Security Act (42 U.S.C. 401 et seq.);

(B) The notice describes conditions under which the Commissioner of Social Security is required to waive recovery of the overpayment, as provided under 42 U.S.C. 404(b); and

(C) If the debtor files a request for a waiver under 42 U.S.C. 404(b) within the 60-day notice period, the agency has considered the debtor's request.

(2) *Pre-offset notice and consideration of evidence for past-due, legally enforceable debt.*—(i) For purposes of paragraph (d)(1)(iii)(B) of this section, a creditor agency has made a reasonable attempt to notify the debtor if the agency uses the current address information contained in the agency's records related to the debt. Agencies may, but are not required to, obtain address information from the IRS pursuant to 26 U.S.C. 6103(m)(2), (4), or (5).

(ii) For purposes of paragraph (d)(1)(iii)(C) of this section, if the evidence presented by the debtor is considered by an agent of the creditor agency, or other entities or persons acting on the agency's behalf, the debtor must be accorded at least 30 days from the date the agent or other entity or person determines that all or part of the debt is past-due and legally enforceable to request review by an officer or employee of the agency of any unresolved dispute. The agency must then notify the debtor of its decision.

(3) *Referral of past-due, legally enforceable debt.*—A Federal agency will submit past-due, legally enforceable debt information for tax refund offset to FMS in the time and manner prescribed by FMS. For each debt, the creditor agency will include the following information:

(i) The name and taxpayer identifying number (as defined in 26 U.S.C. 6109) of the debtor who is responsible for the debt;

(ii) The amount of such past-due and legally enforceable debt;

(iii) The date on which the debt became past-due;

(iv) The designation of the Federal agency or subagency referring the debt; and

(v) In the case of an OASDI overpayment, a certification by the Commissioner of Social Security designating whether the amount payable to the agency is to be deposited in either the Federal Old-Age and Survivors Insurance Trust Fund or the Federal Disability Insurance Trust Fund, but not both.

(4) *Correcting and updating referral.*—If, after referring a past-due, legally enforceable debt to FMS as provided in paragraph (d)(3) of this section, a creditor agency determines that an error has been made with respect to the information transmitted to FMS, or if an agency receives a payment or credits a payment to the account of a debtor referred to FMS for offset, or if the debt amount is otherwise incorrect, the agency shall promptly notify FMS and make the appropriate correction of the agency's records. Creditor agencies will provide certification as required under paragraph (d)(1) of this section for any increases to amounts owed.

(5) FMS may reject a certification which does not comply with the requirements of paragraph (d)(1) of this section. upon notification of the rejection and the reason for the rejection, a creditor agency may resubmit the debt with a corrected certification.

(e) *Priorities for offset.*—(1) A tax refund payment shall be reduced first by the amount of any past-due support assigned to a State under section 402(a)(26) or section 471(a)(17) of the Social Security Act (42 U.S.C. 602(a)(26) or 42 U.S.C. 671(a)(17)) which is to be offset under 26 U.S.C. 6402(c), 42 U.S.C. 664 and the regulations thereunder; second, by the amount of any past-due, legally enforceable debt owed to a Federal agency which is to be offset under 26 U.S.C. 6402(d), 31 U.S.C. 3720A and this section; and third, by the amount of any qualifying past-due support not assigned to a State which is to be offset under 26 U.S.C. 6402(c), 42 U.S.C. 664 and the regulations thereunder.

(2) If a debtor owes more than one past-due, legally enforceable debt to a Federal agency or agencies, the tax refund payment shall be credited against the debts in the order in which the debts accrued. A debt shall be considered to have accrued at the time at which the agency determines that the debt became past due.

(3) Reduction of the tax refund payment pursuant to 26 U.S.C. 6402(a), (c), and (d) shall occur prior to crediting the overpayment to any future liability for an internal revenue tax. Any amount remaining after tax refund offset under 26 U.S.C. 6402(a), (c), and (d) shall be refunded to the taxpayer, or applied to estimated tax, if elected by the taxpayer pursuant to IRS regulations.

(f) *Post-offset notice to the debtor, the creditor agency, and the IRS.*—(1)(i) FMS will notify the payee(s) to whom the tax refund payment is due, in writing of:

(A) The amount and date of the offset to satisfy a past-due, legally enforceable nontax debt;

Reg. §285.2(f)(1)(i)(A)

⫸→ *Caution: AUTHORITY: The provisions of 31 CFR Part 285 are issued under the Debt Collection Improvement Act of 1996 (P.L. 104-134), 110 Stat. 1321-358 et seq., codified at 31 U.S.C. 3720A.*

(B) The creditor agency to which this amount has been paid or credited; and

(C) A contact point within the creditor agency that will handle concerns or questions regarding the offset.

(ii) The notice in paragraph (f)(1)(i) of this section will also advise any non-debtor spouse who may have filed a joint tax return with the debtor of the steps which a non-debtor spouse may take in order to secure his or her proper share of the tax refund. See paragraph (g) of this section.

(2) FMS will advise each creditor agency of the names, mailing addresses, and identifying numbers of the debtors from whom amounts of past-due, legally enforceable debt were collected and of the amounts collected from each debtor for that agency. FMS will not advise the creditor agency of the source of payment from which such amounts were collected. If a payment from which an amount of past-due, legally enforceable debt is to be withheld is payable to two individual payees, FMS will notify the creditor agency and furnish the name and address of each payee to whom the payment was payable.

(3) At least weekly, FMS will notify the IRS of the names and taxpayer identifying numbers of the debtors from whom amounts of past-due, legally enforceable debt were collected and the amounts collected from each debtor.

(g) *Offset made with regard to a tax refund payment based upon joint return.*—If the person filing a joint return with a debtor owing the past-due, legally enforceable debt takes appropriate action to secure his or her proper share of a tax refund from which an offset was made, the IRS will pay the person his or her share of the refund and request that FMS deduct that amount from amounts payable to the creditor agency. FMS and the creditor agency will adjust their debtor records accordingly.

(h) *Disposition of amounts collected.*—FMS will transmit amounts collected for past-due, legally enforceable debts, less fees charged under paragraph (i) of this section, to the creditor agency's account. If an erroneous payment is made to any agency, FMS will notify the creditor agency that an erroneous payment has been made. The agency shall pay promptly to FMS an amount equal to the amount of the erroneous payment (without regard to whether any other amounts payable to such agency have been paid).

(i) *Fees.*—The creditor agency will reimburse FMS and the IRS for the full cost of administering the tax refund offset program. FMS will deduct the fees from amounts collected prior to disposition and transmit a portion of the fees deducted to reimburse the IRS for its share of the cost of administering the tax refund offset program. To the extent allowed by law, creditor agencies may add the offset fees to the debt.

(j) *Review of tax refund offsets.*—Any reduction of a taxpayer's refund made pursuant to 26 U.S.C. 6402(d) shall not be subject to review by any court of the United States or by the Secretary of the Treasury, FMS or IRS in an administrative proceeding. No action brought against the United States to recover the amount of this reduction shall be considered to be a suit for refund of tax. Any legal, equitable, or administrative action by any person seeking to recover the amount of the reduction of the overpayment must be taken against the Federal creditor agency to which the amount of the reduction was paid. Any action which is otherwise available with respect to recoveries of overpayments of benefits under 42 U.S.C. 404 must be taken against the Commissioner of Social Security.

(k) *Access to and use of confidential tax information.*—Access to and use of confidential tax information in connection with the tax refund offset program are restricted by 26 U.S.C. 6103. Generally, agencies will not receive confidential tax information from FMS. To the extent such information is received, agencies are subject to the safeguard, recordkeeping, and reporting requirements of 26 U.S.C. 6103(p)(4) and the regulations thereunder. The agency shall inform its officers and employees who access or use confidential tax information of the restrictions and penalties under the Internal Revenue Code for misuse of confidential tax information.

(l) *Effective date.*—This section applies to tax refund payments payable under 26 U.S.C. 6402 after January 1, 1998. [Reg. §285.2.]

☐ [*Final Rule*, 8-27-98.]

[Reg. §285.3]

§285.3. Offset of tax refund payments to collect past-due support.—(a) *Definitions.*—For purposes of this section:

Debt as used in this section is synonymous with the term past-due support unless otherwise indicated.

Debtor as used in this section means a person who owes past-due support.

FMS means the Financial Management Service, a bureau of the Department of the Treasury.

HHS means the Department of Health and Human Services, Office of Child Support Enforcement.

IRS means the Internal Revenue Service, a bureau of the Department of the Treasury.

Past-due support means the amount of support, determined under a court order, or an order of an administrative process established under State law, for support and maintenance of a child, or of a child and the parent with whom the child is living, which has not been paid, as defined in 42 U.S.C. 664(c).

State means the several States of the United States. The term "State" also includes the District of Columbia, American Samoa, Guam, the United States Virgin Islands, the Commonwealth

≫→ *Caution: AUTHORITY: The provisions of 31 CFR Part 285 are issued under the Debt Collection Improvement Act of 1996 (P.L. 104-134), 110 Stat. 1321-358 et seq., codified at 31 U.S.C. 3720A.*

of the Northern Mariana Islands, and the Commonwealth of Puerto Rico.

Tax refund offset means withholding or reducing a tax refund payment by an amount necessary to satisfy a debt owed by the payee(s) of a tax refund payment.

Tax refund payment means any overpayment of Federal taxes to be refunded to the person making the overpayment after the IRS makes the appropriate credits as provided in 26 U.S.C. 6402(a) and 26 CFR 6402-3(a)(6)(i) for any liabilities for any Federal tax on the part of the person who made the overpayment.

(b) *General rule.*—(1) Past-due support will be collected by tax refund offset upon notification to FMS in accordance with 26 U.S.C. 6402(c), 42 U.S.C. 664 and this section. Collection by offset under 26 U.S.C. 6402(c) is a collection procedure separate from the collection procedures provided by 26 U.S.C. 6305 and 26 CFR 301.6305-1, relating to the assessment and collection of certain child and spousal support liabilities. Tax refund offset may be used separately or in conjunction with the collection procedures provided in 26 U.S.C. 6305, as well as other collection procedures.

(2) FMS will compare tax refund payment records, as certified by the IRS, with records of debts submitted to FMS. A match will occur when the taxpayer identifying number (as that term is used in 26 U.S.C. 6109) and name of a payment certification record are the same as the taxpayer identifying number and name of a delinquent debtor record. When a match occurs and all other requirements for tax refund offset have been met, FMS will reduce the amount of any tax refund payment payable to a debtor by the amount of any past-due support debt owed by the debtor. Any amounts not offset will be paid to the payee(s) listed in the payment certification record.

(c) *Notification of past-due support.*—(1) *Past-due support eligible for tax refund offset.*—Past-due support qualifies for tax refund offset if:

(i)(A) There has been an assignment of the support obligation to a State and the amount of past-due support is not less than $25.00, or such higher amount as HHS rules may allow, whichever is greater; or

(B) A State agency is providing support collection services under 42 U.S.C. 654(4) and the amount of past-due support is not less than $500.00; and

(ii) A notification of liability for past-due support has been received by FMS as prescribed by paragraphs (c)(2) or (c)(3) of this section.

(2) *Notification of liability for past-due support and transmission of information to FMS by HHS.*—States notifying HHS of past-due support shall do so in the manner and format prescribed by HHS. The notification of liability shall be accompanied by a certification that the State has complied with the requirements contained in paragraph (c)(4) of this section and with any requirements applicable to the offset of Federal tax refunds to collect past-due support imposed by State law or procedures. HHS shall consolidate and transmit to FMS the information contained in the notifications of liability for past-due support submitted by the States provided that the State has certified that the requirements of paragraph (c)(4) of this section have been met.

(3) *Notification of liability for past-due support transmitted directly to FMS by States.*—States must notify HHS of past-due support in accordance with the provisions of paragraph (c)(2) of this section unless HHS rules authorize notification to FMS directly. If authorized by HHS rules, States may notify FMS directly of past-due support. States notifying FMS directly of past-due support shall do so in the manner and format prescribed by FMS. The notification of liability shall be accompanied by a certification that the State has complied with the requirements contained in paragraph (c)(4) of this section and with any requirements applicable to the offset of Federal tax refunds to collect past-due support imposed by State law or procedures. FMS may reject a notification of past-due support which does not comply with the requirements of this section. Upon notification of the rejection and the reason for rejection, the State may resubmit a corrected notification.

(4) *Advance notification to debtor of intent to collect by tax refund offset.*—The State, or HHS if the State requests and HHS agrees, is required to provide a written notification to the debtor, pursuant to the provisions of 42 U.S.C. 664(a)(3) and 45 CFR 303.72(e), informing the debtor that the State intends to refer the debt for collection by tax refund offset. The notice also shall:

(i) Instruct the debtor of the steps which may be taken to contest the State's determination that past-due support is owed or the amount of the past-due support;

(ii) Advise any non-debtor who may file a joint tax return with the debtor of the steps which a non-debtor spouse may take in order to secure his or her proper share of the tax refund; and

(iii) In cases when a debt is being enforced by more than one State, advise the debtor of his or her opportunities to request a review with the State enforcing collection or the State issuing the support order as prescribed by the provisions of 45 CFR 303.72(g).

(5) *Correcting and updating notification.*—The State shall, in the manner and in the time frames provided by FMS or HHS, notify FMS or HHS of any deletion or net decrease in the amount of past-due support referred to FMS, or HHS as the case may be, for collection by tax refund offset. The State may notify FMS or HHS of any increases in the amount of the debt referred to FMS for collection by tax refund offset provided that the State has complied with the requirements of

»»→ *Caution: AUTHORITY: The provisions of 31 CFR Part 285 are issued under the Debt Collection Improvement Act of 1996 (P.L. 104-134), 110 Stat. 1321-358 et seq., codified at 31 U.S.C. 3720A.*

paragraph (c)(4) of this section with regard to those debts.

(6) *Collection of past-due support enforced by multiple States.*—When a State has knowledge that the debt is being enforced by more than one State, the State notifying FMS, or HHS as the case may be, of the debt shall inform any such other State involved in enforcing the debt when it receives the offset amount.

(d) *Priorities for offset.*—(1) As provided in 26 U.S.C. 6402 as amended, a tax refund payment shall be reduced in the following order of priority:

(i) First by the amount of any past-due support assigned to a State (welfare cases) which is to be offset under 26 U.S.C. 6402(c), 42 U.S.C. 664 and this section;

(ii) Second, by the amount of any past-due, legally enforceable debt owed to a Federal agency which is to be offset under 26 U.S.C. 6402(d), 31 U.S.C. 3720A and § 285.2 of this part;

(iii) Third, by the amount of any qualifying past-due support not assigned to a State (non-welfare cases) which is to be offset under 26 U.S.C. 6402(c), 42 U.S.C. 664 and this section; and

(iv) Fourth, by the amount of any past-due, legally enforceable State income tax obligation which is to be offset under 26 U.S.C. 6402(e).

(2) Reduction of the tax refund payment pursuant to 26 U.S.C. 6402(a), (c), (d), and (e) shall occur prior to crediting the overpayment to any future liability for an internal revenue tax. Any amount remaining after tax refund offset under 26 U.S.C. 6402(a), (c), (d), and (e) shall be refunded to the taxpayer, or applied to estimated tax, if elected by the taxpayer pursuant to IRS regulations.

(e) *Post-offset notice.*—(1)(i) FMS shall notify the debtor in writing of:

(A) The amount and date of the offset to satisfy past-due support;

(B) The State to which this amount has been paid or credited; and

(C) A contact point within the State that will handle concerns or questions regarding the offset.

(ii) The notice in paragraph (e)(1)(i) of this section also will advise any non-debtor who may have filed a joint tax return with the debtor of the steps which a non-debtor spouse may take in order to secure his or her proper share of the tax refund. See paragraph (f) of this section.

(2) FMS will advise HHS of the names, mailing addresses, and identifying numbers of the debtors from whom amounts of past-due support were collected, of the amounts collected from each debtor through tax refund offset, the names of any non-debtor spouses who may have filed a joint return with the debtor, and of the State on whose behalf each collection was made. Alternatively, FMS will provide such information to each State that refers debts directly to

FMS. FMS will inform HHS and each State that the payment source is a tax refund payment.

(3) At least weekly, FMS will notify the IRS of the names and taxpayer identifying numbers of the debtors from whom amounts owed for past-due support were collected from tax refund offsets and the amounts collected from each debtor.

(4) At such time and in such manner as FMS and HHS agree, but no less than annually, FMS will advise HHS of the States which have furnished notices of past-due support, the number of cases in each State with respect to which such notices have been furnished, the amount of past-due support sought to be collected by each State, and the amount of such tax refund offset collections actually made in the case of each State. As FMS and HHS may agree, FMS may provide additional offset-related information about States which have furnished notices of past-due support.

(f) *Offset made with regard to a tax refund payment based upon joint return.*—If the person filing a joint return with a debtor owing the past-due support takes appropriate action to secure his or her proper share of a tax refund from which an offset was made, the IRS will pay the person his or her share of the refund and request that FMS deduct that amount from amounts payable to HHS or the State, as the case may be. FMS and HHS, or the appropriate State, will adjust their debtor records accordingly.

(g) *Disposition of amounts collected.*—FMS will transmit amounts collected for debts, less fees charged under paragraph (h) of this section, to HHS or to the appropriate State. If FMS learns that an erroneous offset payment is made to HHS or any State, FMS will notify HHS or the appropriate State that an erroneous offset payment has been made. FMS may deduct the amount of the erroneous offset payment from amounts payable to HHS or the State, as the case may be. Alternatively, upon FMS' request, the State shall return promptly to the affected taxpayer or FMS an amount equal to the amount of the erroneous payment (unless the State previously has paid such amounts, or any portion of such amounts, to the affected taxpayer). HHS and States shall notify FMS any time HHS or a State returns an erroneous offset payment to an affected taxpayer. FMS and HHS, or the appropriate State, will adjust their debtor records accordingly.

(h) *Fees.*—The State will pay a fee to FMS for the full cost of administering the tax refund offset program. The fee (not to exceed $25 per case submitted) will be established annually in such amount as FMS and HHS agree to be sufficient to reimburse FMS for the full cost of the offset procedure. FMS will deduct the fees from amounts collected prior to disposition and transmit a portion of the fees deducted to reimburse the IRS for its share of the cost of administering

>>→ *Caution: AUTHORITY: The provisions of 31 CFR Part 285 are issued under the Debt Collection Improvement Act of 1996 (P.L. 104-134), 110 Stat. 1321-358 et seq., codified at 31 U.S.C. 3720A.*

the tax refund offset program. Fees will be charged only for actual tax refund offsets completed.

(i) *Review of tax refund offsets.*—In accordance with 26 U.S.C. 6402(f), any reduction of a taxpayer's refund made pursuant to 26 U.S.C. 6402(c), (d), or (e) shall not be subject to review by any court of the United States or by the Secretary of the Treasury, FMS or IRS in an administrative proceeding. No action brought against the United States to recover the amount of this reduction shall be considered to be a suit for refund of tax.

(j) *Access to and use of confidential tax information.*—Access to and use of confidential tax information in connection with the tax refund offset program is permitted to the extent necessary in establishing appropriate agency records, locating any person with respect to whom a reduction under 26 U.S.C. 6402(c) is sought for purposes of collecting the debt, and in the defense of any litigation or administrative procedure ensuing from a reduction made under section 6402(c).

(k) *Effective date.*—This section applies to tax refund payments payable under 26 U.S.C. 6402 after January 1, 1999. [Reg. § 285.3.]

☐ [*Final Rule*, 12-29-98. *Amended by Final Rule*, 10-19-2007.]

[Reg. § 285.8]

§ 285.8. Offset of tax refund payments to collect state income tax obligations.—
(a) *Definitions.*—For purposes of this section:

Debt as used in this section means past-due, legally enforceable State income tax obligation unless otherwise indicated.

Debtor as used in this section means a person who owes a state income tax obligation.

FMS means the Financial Management Service, a bureau of the Department of the Treasury.

IRS means the Internal Revenue Service, a bureau of the Department of the Treasury.

Past-due, legally enforceable State income tax obligation means a debt which resulted from:

(1) A judgment rendered by a court of competent jurisdiction which has determined an amount of State income tax to be due,

(2) A determination after an administrative hearing which has determined an amount of state income tax to be due and which is no longer subject to judicial review, or

(3) A State income tax assessment (including self-assessments) which has become final in accordance with State law but not collected and which has not been delinquent for more than 10 years.

State means the several States of the United States. The term "State" also includes the District of Columbia, American Samoa, Guam, the United States Virgin Islands, the Commonwealth of the Northern Mariana Islands, and the Commonwealth of Puerto Rico.

State income tax obligation means State income tax obligations as determined under State law. For purposes of this section, State income tax obligation includes any local income tax administered by the chief tax administration agency of the State.

Tax refund offset means withholding or reducing a tax refund overpayment by an amount necessary to satisfy a debt owed by the payee(s).

Tax refund payment means any overpayment of Federal taxes to be refunded to the person making the overpayment after the IRS makes the appropriate credits as provided in 26 U.S.C. 6402(a) and 26 CFR 6402-3(a)(6)(i) for any liabilities for any Federal tax on the part of the person who made the overpayment.

(b) *General rule.*—(1) FMS will collect past-due, legally enforceable State income tax obligations by tax refund offset upon notification to FMS of a past-due, legally enforceable State income tax obligation in accordance with 26 U.S.C. 6402(e) and this section.

(2) FMS will compare tax refund payment records, as certified by the IRS, with records of debts submitted to FMS. A match will occur when the taxpayer identifying number (as that term is used in 26 U.S.C. 6109) and name on a payment certification record are the same as the taxpayer identifying number and name on a delinquent debtor record. When a match occurs and all other requirements for tax refund offset have been met, FMS will reduce the amount of any tax refund payment payable to a debtor by the amount of any past-due, legally enforceable State income tax obligation owed by the debtor. Any amounts not offset will be paid to the payee(s) listed in the payment certification record.

(3) FMS only will offset a tax refund payment if the address shown on the Federal tax return for the taxable year of the overpayment is an address within the State seeking the offset.

(c) *Notification of past-due, legally enforceable State income tax obligations.*—(1) *Notification to FMS of past-due, legally enforceable State income tax obligations.*—States notifying FMS of state income tax obligations shall do so in the manner and format prescribed by FMS. The notification of liability must be accompanied by a certification that the debt is past-due and legally enforceable and that the State has complied with the requirements contained in paragraph (c)(3) of this section and with any requirements applicable to the offset of Federal tax refunds to collect past-due, legally enforceable State income tax obligations imposed by State law or procedures. The certification must specifically state that none of the debts submitted for collection by offset are debts owed by an individual who has claimed immunity from state taxation by reason of being an enrolled member of an Indian tribe who lives on a reservation and derives all of his or her income from that reservation unless such claim has been

Reg. § 285.8(c)(1)

>>>→ *Caution: AUTHORITY: The provisions of 31 CFR Part 285 are issued under the Debt Collection Improvement Act of 1996 (P.L. 104-134), 110 Stat. 1321-358 et seq., codified at 31 U.S.C. 3720A.*

adjudicated de novo on its merits in accordance with paragraph (c)(3). FMS may reject a notification of past-due, legally enforceable State income tax obligations which do not comply with the requirements of this section. Upon notification of the rejection and the reason for rejection, the State may resubmit a corrected notification.

(2) *Minimum amount of past-due, legally enforceable State income tax obligations that may be submitted.*—FMS only will accept notification of past-due, legally enforceable State income tax obligations of $25 or more or such higher amounts as determined by FMS. States will be notified annually of any changes in the minimum debt amount.

(3)(i) *Advance notification to the debtor of the State's intent to collect by Federal tax refund offset.*— The State is required to provide a written notification to the debtor by certified mail, return receipt requested, informing the debtor that the State intends to refer the debt for collection by tax refund offset. The notice must also give the debtor at least 60 days to present evidence, in accordance with procedures established by the State, that all or part of the debt is not past-due or not legally enforceable.

(ii) *Determination.*—The State must, in accordance with procedures established by the State, consider any evidence presented by a debtor in response to the notice described in paragraph (c)(3)(i) of this section and determine whether an amount of such debt is past-due and legally enforceable. In those cases where a debtor claims that he or she is immune from State taxation by reason of being an enrolled member of an Indian tribe who lives on a reservation and derives all of his or her income from that reservation, State procedures shall include consideration of such claims de novo on the merits unless such claims have been previously adjudicated by a court of competent jurisdiction. States shall, upon request from the Secretary of the Treasury, make such procedures available to the Secretary of the Treasury for review.

(iii) *Reasonable efforts.*—Prior to submitting a debt to FMS for collection by tax refund offset the State must make reasonable efforts to collect the debt. Reasonable efforts include making written demand on the debtor for payment and complying with any other prerequisites to offset established by the State.

(4) *Correcting and updating notification.*—The State shall, in the manner and in the time frames provided by FMS, notify FMS of any deletion or decrease in the amount of past-due, legally enforceable State income tax obligation referred to FMS for collection by tax refund offset. The State may notify FMS of any increases in the amount of the debt referred to FMS for collection by tax refund offset provided that the State has complied with the requirements of paragraph (c)(3) of this section with regard to those debts.

(d) *Priorities for offset.*—(1) As provided in 26 U.S.C. 6402, a tax refund payment shall be reduced first by the amount of any past-due support assigned to a State; second, by the amount of any past-due, legally enforceable debt owed to a Federal agency; third, by the amount of any qualifying past-due support not assigned to a State and fourth, by any past-due, legally enforceable State income tax obligation.

(2) Reduction of the tax refund payment pursuant to 26 U.S.C. 6402(a), (c), (d) and (e) shall occur prior to crediting the overpayment to any future liability for an internal revenue tax. Any amount remaining after tax refund offset under 26 U.S.C. 6402(a), (c), (d) and (e) shall be refunded to the taxpayer, or applied to estimated tax, if elected by the taxpayer pursuant to IRS regulations.

(3) If FMS receives notice from a State of more than one debt subject to this section that is owed by a debtor to the State, any overpayment by the debtor shall be applied against such debts in the order in which such debts accrued.

(e) *Post-offset notice.*—(1) When an offset occurs, FMS shall notify the debtor in writing of:

(i) The amount and date of the offset and that the purpose of the offset was to satisfy a past-due, legally enforceable State income tax obligation;

(ii) The State to which this amount has been paid or credited; and

(iii) A contact point within the State that will handle concerns or questions regarding the offset.

(2) The notice in paragraph (e)(1) of this section also will advise any non-debtor spouse who may have filed a joint return with the debtor of the steps which the non-debtor spouse may take in order to secure his or her proper share of the tax refund. See paragraph (f) of this section.

(3) FMS will advise States of the names, mailing addresses, and taxpayer identifying numbers of the debtors from whom amounts of state income tax obligations were collected, and of the amounts collected from each debtor through tax refund offset.

(4) At least weekly, FMS will notify the IRS of the names and taxpayer identifying numbers of the debtors from whom amounts owed for past-due, legally enforceable State income tax obligations were collected from tax refund offsets and the amounts collected from each debtor.

(f) *Offset made with regard to a tax refund payment based upon joint return.*—If the person filing a joint return with a debtor owing the past-due, legally enforceable State income tax obligation takes appropriate action to secure his or her proper share of a tax refund from which an offset was made, the IRS will pay the person his or her share of the refund and request that FMS deduct that amount from future amounts payable to the State or that FMS otherwise obtain the funds

⫸→ *Caution: AUTHORITY: The provisions of 31 CFR Part 285 are issued under the Debt Collection Improvement Act of 1996 (P.L. 104-134), 110 Stat. 1321-358 et seq., codified at 31 U.S.C. 3720A.*

back from the State. FMS, or the appropriate State, will adjust their debtor records accordingly.

(g) *Disposition of amounts collected.*—FMS will transmit amounts collected for debts, less fees charged under paragraph (h) of this section, to the appropriate State. If FMS learns that an erroneous offset payment is made to any State, FMS will notify the appropriate State that an erroneous offset payment has been made. FMS may deduct the amount of the erroneous offset payment from future amounts payable to the State. Alternatively, upon FMS' request, the State shall return promptly to the affected taxpayer or FMS an amount equal to the amount of the erroneous payment (unless the State previously has paid such amounts, or any portion of such amounts, to the affected taxpayer). States shall notify FMS any time a State returns an erroneous offset payment to an affected taxpayer. FMS, or the appropriate State, will adjust their debtor records accordingly.

(h) *Fees.*—The State will pay a fee to FMS to cover the full cost of offsets taken. The fee will be established annually in such amount as FMS determines to be sufficient to reimburse FMS for the full cost of the offset procedure. FMS will deduct the fees from amounts collected prior to disposition and transmit a portion of the fees deducted to reimburse the IRS for its share of the cost of administering the tax refund offset program for purposes of collecting past-due, legally enforceable State income tax obligations reported to FMS by the States. Fees will be charged only for actual tax refund offsets completed.

(i) *Review of tax refund offsets.*—In accordance with 26 U.S.C. 6402(f), any reduction of a taxpayer's refund made pursuant to 26 U.S.C. 6402(e) shall not be subject to review by any court of the United States or by the Secretary of the Treasury, FMS or IRS in an administrative proceeding. No action brought against the United States to recover the amount of this reduction shall be considered to be a suit for refund of tax. This subsection does not preclude any legal, equitable, or administrative action against the State to which the amount of such reduction was paid.

(j) *Access to and use of confidential tax information.*—Access to and use of confidential tax information in connection with the tax refund offset program is permitted to the extent necessary in establishing appropriate agency records, locating any person with respect to whom a reduction under 26 U.S.C. 6402(e) is sought for purposes of collecting the debt, and in the defense of any litigation or administrative procedure ensuing from a reduction made under section 6402(e).

(k) *Effective date.*—This section applies to tax refund payments payable under 26 U.S.C. 6402 beginning January 1, 2000. [Reg. § 285.8.]

☐ [*Interim Rule, 12-17-99. Final Rule, 1-25-2005.*]

[Reg. § 301.6402-7]

§ 301.6402-7. Claims for refunds and applications for tentative carryback adjustments involving consolidated groups that include insolvent financial institutions.—(a) *In general.*—(1) *Overview.*—Section 6402(i) authorizes the Secretary to issue regulations providing for the payment of a refund directly to the statutory or court-appointed fiduciary of an insolvent corporation that was a subsidiary in a consolidated group, to the extent the Secretary determines that the refund is attributable to losses or credits of the insolvent corporation. This section provides rules for the payment of refunds and tentative carryback adjustments to the fiduciary of an insolvent financial institution that was a subsidiary in a consolidated group.

(2) *Notice.*—This section provides notice to the common parent of a consolidated group of which an insolvent financial institution is or was a member that—

(i) The fiduciary for the institution may, in addition to the common parent, act as agent for the group in certain matters relating to the tax liability of the group in the year in which a loss arose and for the year to which a claim for refund or application for tentative carryback adjustment relates; and

(ii) The Internal Revenue Service may deal directly with the common parent or the fiduciary (or both) as agent for the group to the extent provided in this section.

(b) *Definitions.*—For purposes of this section, the following terms have the meanings set forth below:

(1) *Carryback year group.*—A carryback year group is a consolidated group of which a corporation that is or becomes an insolvent financial institution is a member during a consolidated carryback year.

(2) *Consolidated carryback year.*—A consolidated carryback year is a consolidated return year to which a loss arising in a loss year is carried back.

(3) *Fiduciary.*—A fiduciary is—

(i) The Federal Deposit Insurance Corporation;

(ii) The Resolution Trust Corporation; or

(iii) Any other entity established by federal law, or a federal agency, that is identified by the Commissioner in a revenue ruling or revenue procedure as a fiduciary for purposes of this section;

in its capacity as an authorized receiver or conservator of an insolvent financial institution.

(4) *Insolvent Financial Institution.*—An insolvent financial institution (an institution) is a bank or domestic building and loan association for which the fiduciary is authorized to act as a receiver or conservator—

(i) On the ground that the institution is insolvent within the meaning of 12 U.S.C. 191, 12 U.S.C. 1821(c)(5)(A), 12 U.S.C. 1464(d)(2)(A)(i), or 12 U.S.C. 1464(d)(2)(C)(i) or any applicable state law (or any successor statute which adopts a substantially similar standard); or

(ii) On grounds other than insolvency, provided that the institution is insolvent within the meaning of paragraph (b)(4)(i) of this section at any time after commencement of the conservatorship or receivership.

A reference to an institution under these regulations includes, as the context requires, a reference to predecessors and successors of the institution.

(5) *Loss year.*—A loss year is a taxable year for which any member or former member of the carryback year group claims a loss that may be carried back.

(6) *Loss year group.*—A loss year group is a consolidated group of which a corporation that is or becomes an insolvent financial institution is a member during a loss year.

(7) *Procedure effective date.*—The procedure effective date is the day on which the Internal Revenue Service has processed the notice described in paragraph (d)(1) of this section to the extent necessary for all Internal Revenue Service Centers to have access to information indicating that—

(i) Appropriate notice to the Internal Revenue Service has been filed; and

(ii) Payments with respect to losses of an institution are to be paid in accordance with the procedures set forth in this section.

(8) *Definitions in § 1.1502-1.*—Unless otherwise provided, the definitions contained in § 1.1502-1 of this chapter apply in this section.

(c) *Deemed agency status of fiduciary.*—(1) *In general.*—Notwithstanding the general treatment of a common parent as the agent of a group under §§ 1.1502-77 and 1.1502-78 of this chapter, if the fiduciary satisfies the notice requirements of paragraph (d)(1) of this section, the fiduciary may also be deemed to be an agent under §§ 1.1502-77 and 1.1502-78 of this chapter—

(i) Of the loss year group (if any) for purposes of filing a consolidated return for the loss year;

(ii) Of the carryback year group for purposes of filing a claim for refund or an application for a tentative carryback adjustment for the consolidated carryback year under paragraph (e) of this section and receiving payments of any refund or tentative carryback adjustment under paragraph (g) of this section; and

(iii) Of the carryback year group, the loss year group or any other group of which the institution is a member for any matter pertaining to the determination of the refund or tentative carryback adjustment, but only to the extent provided in paragraph (c)(2) of this section.

(2) *Limitation.*—The fiduciary may act as an agent for matters described in paragraph (c)(1)(iii) of this section only to the extent—

(i) Authorized by the district director, in his/her sole discretion, after receiving a written request from the fiduciary; or

(ii) Requested by the Internal Revenue Service under paragraph (f)(3) of this section.

(d) *Notice requirements.*—(1) *Notice to the Internal Revenue Service.*—To satisfy the notice requirement of this paragraph (d)(1), the fiduciary must file Form 56-F, Notice Concerning Fiduciary Relationship of Financial Institution, with the Internal Revenue Service Center indicated on the form. However, in its sole discretion, the Internal Revenue Service may treat notice to it in any other manner as satisfying the notice requirement under this paragraph (d)(1).

(2) *Notice to the common parent.*—(i) *Form 56-F.*—The fiduciary must send a copy of the Form 56-F filed with the Internal Revenue Service Center or any other notice provided to the Service under paragraph (d)(1) of this section to the common parent of the loss year group (if any) and the common parent of all carryback year groups (if different from the loss year group).

(ii) *Claim for refund and loss year return.*—If a claim for refund is filed by the fiduciary in accordance with paragraph (e)(1) of this section, the fiduciary must provide a copy of the claim for refund to the common parent of the carryback year group. If a loss year return is filed by the fiduciary in accordance with paragraph (e)(3) of this section, the fiduciary must provide a copy of the loss year return to the common parent of the loss year group (if any).

(iii) *Additional information.*—The fiduciary must provide to the affected common parent a copy of the request for agency status referred to in paragraphs (c)(2)(i) and (ii) of this section, and a copy of any additional information submitted to the Internal Revenue Service as agent under paragraph (c)(1)(iii) of this section.

(e) *Filing requirements of the fiduciary.*—(1) *Claim for refund by the fiduciary.*—If the fiduciary accepts a claim for refund filed by the common parent, the fiduciary may claim a refund under this section by filing a copy of the common parent's claim for refund. If no claim for refund is filed by the common parent for the consolidated carryback year or the fiduciary does not accept a claim for refund filed by the common parent, the fiduciary may claim a refund under this section by filing its own claim for refund under section 6402, based on all information pertaining to the institution and all information pertaining to other members of the carryback year group and the loss year group to which the fiduciary has reasonable access. Any claim for refund filed by the fiduciary under this paragraph (e)(1) must contain the title "Claim for refund under section 6402(i) of the Code" at the top of the first page of the claim, and the following must be attached to the claim:

(i) The name and employer identification number of the institution that was a member of the carryback year group;

(ii) The name of the fiduciary;

(iii) A schedule demonstrating that the amount of the refund claimed by the fiduciary is determined in accordance with paragraph (g) of this section;

(iv) A representation that the institution is an insolvent financial institution as defined in paragraph (b)(4) of this section;

(v) A representation that the fiduciary has satisfied the requirements set forth in paragraphs (d)(2)(i) and (ii) of this section; and

(vi) A statement executed by an authorized representative of the fiduciary and any paid preparer utilized by the fiduciary that provides "Under penalties of perjury, I declare that I have examined the items listed in section 301.6402-7T(e)(1)(i) through (v), including accompanying schedules and statements, and to the best of my knowledge and belief, they are true, correct, and complete. Declaration of preparer (other than fiduciary) is based on all information of which the preparer has any knowledge."

(2) *Application for tentative carryback adjustment pursuant to section 6411.*—Notwithstanding section 6411 and § 1.1502-78 of this chapter, an application for a tentative carryback adjustment must be signed by both the common parent of the carryback year group and the fiduciary if the payment with respect to the tentative carryback adjustment is not made before the procedure effective date (whether or not the application was filed before the procedure effective date). Any application for a tentative carryback adjustment filed under this paragraph (e)(2) must contain the title "Application for tentative carryback adjustment under section 6402(i) of the Code" at the top of the first page of the application. In addition, the following must be attached to the application:

(i) The name and employer identification number of the institution that was a member of the carryback year group;

(ii) The name of the fiduciary;

(iii) A schedule demonstrating that the amount claimed by the fiduciary is determined in accordance with paragraph (g) of this section;

(iv) A representation that the institution is an insolvent financial institution as defined in paragraph (b)(4) of this section; and

(v) A representation that the fiduciary has satisfied the requirements set forth in paragraph (d)(2)(i) of this section.

(3) *Loss year return by the fiduciary.*—If the institution is a member of a loss year group, and either the common parent does not file a loss year return or the fiduciary does not accept the loss year return filed by the common parent, the fiduciary may file a loss year return with respect to the loss year group. A loss year return can

only be filed by the fiduciary in conjunction with the filing of a claim for refund under paragraph (e)(1). The return must be based on all information pertaining to the institution and all information pertaining to other members to which the fiduciary has reasonable access. Any return filed by the fiduciary under this paragraph (e)(3) must contain the title "Loss year return under section 6402(i) of the Code" at the top of the first page of the return, and the following must be attached to the return:

(i) The name and employer identification number of the institution that is a member of the loss year group;

(ii) The name of the fiduciary;

(iii) A representation that the institution is an insolvent financial institution as defined in paragraph (b)(4) of this section; and

(iv) A representation that the fiduciary has satisfied the requirements set forth in paragraphs (d)(2)(i) and (ii) of this section.

(4) *Additional information.*—If the fiduciary files additional information under paragraph (c)(1)(iii) of this section, the fiduciary must attach a representation that it has satisfied the requirements set forth in paragraph (d)(2)(iii) of this section.

(5) *Election to waive carryback.*—Any election filed after December 30, 1991 by the common parent of a loss year group under section 172(b)(3) to relinquish the entire carryback period with respect to a consolidated net operating loss arising in a loss year is not effective with respect to the portion of the consolidated net operating loss attributable to a subsidiary that is an institution. Instead, the fiduciary may make the election under section 172(b)(3) with respect to the portion attributable to the institution after the notice described in paragraph (d)(1) of this section is filed. For purposes of this paragraph section is filed. For purposes of this paragraph (e)(5), the portion attributable to an institution is determined under the principles of paragraph (g)(2)(ii) of this section.

(f) *Processing and reconciliation of information by the Internal Revenue Service.*—(1) *Loss year return if the insolvent financial institution is a member of a loss year group.*—The Internal Revenue Service may, in its sole discretion, adjust a loss year return filed by the common parent of a loss year group to take into account information filed by the fiduciary in accordance with paragraph (e) of this section, or accept or adjust a loss year return for the loss year group filed by the fiduciary. Nothing in this section relieves the common parent of a loss year group of its duty to file a consolidated return taking into account an institution's items of income, gain, loss, deduction, and credit for any taxable year, or obligates the Internal Revenue Service to accept a return filed by the fiduciary as the return of the loss year group.

(2) *Claim for refund with respect to consolidated carryback year.*—The Internal Revenue Service

may, in its sole discretion, adjust a claim for refund filed by the common parent of a carryback year group to take into account information filed by the fiduciary in accordance with paragraph (e) of this section, or accept or adjust a claim for refund for the carryback year group filed by the fiduciary. Nothing in this section obligates the Internal Revenue Service to pay a claim for refund, or to accept a claim for refund, filed by the fiduciary as a claim for refund for the carryback year group.

(3) *Additional information.*—In determining the amount of any refund that may be paid to the fiduciary under paragraph (g) of this section, the Internal Revenue Service may, in its sole discretion, take into account any information that the Internal Revenue Service deems relevant and may require the fiduciary to file any additional information the Internal Revenue Service deems appropriate.

(g) *Payment of a refund or a tentative carryback adjustment to fiduciary.*—(1) *In general.*—If a claim for refund or an application for a tentative carryback adjustment is filed for the consolidated carryback year in accordance with paragraph (e) of this section, the Internal Revenue Service may, in its sole discretion, pay to the fiduciary all or any portion of the refund or tentative carryback adjustment that the Internal Revenue Service determines under this section to be attributable to the net operating losses of the institution. Nothing in this section obligates the Internal Revenue Service to pay to the fiduciary all or any portion of a claim for refund or application for tentative carryback adjustment.

(2) *Portion of refund or tentative carryback adjustment attributable to the net operating loss of an insolvent financial institution.*—(i) *In general.*—The portion of a refund or tentative carryback adjustment attributable to a net operating loss of an institution that is carried to a consolidated carryback year is determined based on the absorption, as described in paragraph (g)(2)(iii) of this section, of the institution's net operating loss carried to the consolidated carryback year.

(ii) *Member's net operating loss.*—If the loss year is a consolidated return year, references in this section to the net operating loss of a member of the loss year group is a reference to the portion of the loss year group's consolidated net operating loss attributable to the member. The consolidated net operating loss for a taxable year that is attributable to a member is determined by a fraction, the numerator of which is the separate net operating loss of the member for the year of the loss and the denominator of which is the sum of the separate net operating losses for that year of all members having such losses. For this purpose, the separate net operating loss of a member is determined by computing the consolidated net operating loss by taking into account only the member's items of income, gain, deduction, and loss, including the member's losses and deductions actually absorbed by the group in the

taxable year (whether or not absorbed by the member).

(iii) *Absorption of net operating losses.*—The absorption of net operating losses generally is determined under applicable principles of the Code and regulations, including the principles of section 172 and § 1.1502-21(b) or 1.1502-21A(b) (as appropriate) of this chapter. Notwithstanding any contrary rule or principle of the Code or regulations, if an institution and another member of the carryback year group have net operating losses that arise in taxable years ending on the same date and are carried to the same consolidated carryback year, the carryback year group's consolidated taxable income for that year is treated as offset first by the loss attributable to the institution to the extent thereof.

(3) *Examples.*—For purposes of the examples in this section, all groups file consolidated returns, all corporations have calendar taxable years, the facts set forth the only corporate activity, the fiduciary has met the notice and filing requirements of this section, and the common parent has filed a return for the loss year and a claim for refund. The principles of this paragraph (g) are illustrated by the following examples.

Example 1. Absorption of net operating losses.

(a) P owns all the stock of S1, an insolvent financial institution, and S2, a corporation that is not a financial institution. For Year 1, P, S1, and S2 each have $50 of income, and the P group's consolidated taxable income is $150. On May 31 of Year 2, S1 becomes insolvent and is placed in receivership under the supervision of a fiduciary. For Year 2, the P group has a consolidated net operating loss of $200, of which $100 is attributable to S1 and $100 is attributable to S2.

(b) Under paragraph (g)(2)(iii) of this section, the $150 of consolidated taxable income for Year 1 is offset first by the $100 portion of the consolidated net operating loss for Year 2 attributable to S1. The remaining $50 is treated as offset by $50 of the $100 of consolidated net operating loss attributable to S2. Thus, the refund attributable to $100 of the loss may be payable to the fiduciary and the refund attributable to $50 of the loss may be payable to P. The remaining $50 consolidated net operating loss, available to be carried forward, is entirely attributable to S2.

Example 2. Separate return net operating loss. The facts are the same as in *Example 1*, except that S1 left the P group at the end of Year 1 and its $100 of loss in Year 2 is incurred in a separate return limitation year. Under paragraph (g)(2)(iii) of this section, the generally applicable absorption principles of section 172 and § 1.1502-21 of this chapter apply. Although S1 and S2 are carrying back losses to Year 1 from taxable years ending on the same date (Year 2), S1's loss is subject to a $50 limitation under § 1.1502-21(c) of this chapter and only $50 of S1's loss is absorbed before S2's net operating loss. Therefore, the refund attributable to $50 of the net operating loss of S1 may be payable to the fiduciary, and the refund attributable to $100 of the net operating loss of S2 may be payable to P. The remaining $50 net operating loss of S1 is available to be carried forward.

(4) *Refund or tentative carryback adjustment allocation agreement.*—The determination of the portion of any refund or tentative carryback adjustment payable to the fiduciary under this paragraph (g) shall be made without regard to—

(i) Any agreement among the members of the consolidated group; or

(ii) Whether the fiduciary is otherwise entitled to any portion of the refund or tentative carryback adjustment under applicable law.

(h) *Credits, net capital losses, and subgroups.*— (1) *Credits and net capital losses.*—(i) *In general.*— The principles of this section also apply to credits and net capital losses, with appropriate adjustments to reflect differences between the rules applicable to net operating losses and those applicable to credits and net capital losses.

(ii) *Example.*—The principles of this paragraph (h)(1) are illustrated by the following example.

Example. Net capital loss. (a) P owns all the stock of S1, an insolvent financial institution, and S2, a corporation that is not a financial institution. For Year 1, P, S1, and S2 each have $50 of capital gain, and the P group's consolidated capital gain net income is $150. On May 31 of Year 2, S1 becomes insolvent and is placed in receivership under the supervision of a fiduciary. For Year 2, the P group has a consolidated net operating loss of $100 that is attributable to S1, and a consolidated net capital loss of $100 that is attributable to S2.

(b) Under paragraphs (g)(2)(iii) and (h)(1) of this section, the generally applicable absorption principles of sections 172 and 1212 and §§1.1502-21(b) and 1.1502-22(b) of this chapter apply. Consequently, S2's capital loss is absorbed before S1's net operating loss. Therefore, the $150 of consolidated capital gain net income is offset first by S2's $100 capital loss and the remaining $50 by S1's net operating loss. The refund attributable to $50 of the net operating loss may be payable to the fiduciary, and the refund attributable to the $100 of capital loss may be payable to P. The remaining $50 consolidated net operating loss available to be carried forward is entirely attributable to S1.

(2) *Insolvent financial institution subgroup.*— (i) *In general.*—The principles of this section apply to all members included in an insolvent financial institution subgroup with appropriate adjustments to reflect differences resulting from the application to more than one corporation in a group. Unless otherwise determined by the Internal Revenue Service in its sole discretion, an insolvent financial institution subgroup is composed of an insolvent financial institution and those other members of a loss year group that, at any time during the conservatorship or receiver-

ship of the institution, bear the same relationship to the institution that the members of a group bear to their common parent under section 1504(a)(1).

(ii) *Examples.*—The principles of this paragraph (h)(2) are illustrated by the following examples.

Example 1. Loss of other subgroup members. (a) S1 is a financial institution, and P, S2, and S3 are not financial institutions. P owns all the stock of S1, S1 owns all the stock of S2, and the stock of S3 is owned 20 percent by S2 and 80 percent by P. For Year 1, P, S1, and S2 each have $100 of income, S3 has no income or loss, and the P group's consolidated taxable income is $300. On May 31 of Year 2, S1 becomes insolvent and is placed in receivership under the supervision of a fiduciary. For Year 2, the P group has a consolidated net operating loss of $300, of which $200 is attributable to S1 and $100 is attributable to S2.

(b) S1 and S2 compose a subgroup because S2 bears the same relationship to S1 that the member of a group bears to its common parent under section 1504(a). S3 is not included in the subgroup because it is not connected to S1 through 80 percent stock ownership as described in section 1504(a).

(c) Because S1 and S2 are members of a subgroup, a claim for refund under paragraph (e) of this section must be based on the aggregate consolidated net operating loss of both S1 and S2. Under paragraph (e)(5) of this section, P may not elect under section 172(b)(3) to relinquish the entire carryback period with respect to the $300 of consolidated net operating loss arising in Year 2 that is attributable to S1 and S2. Any refund payable under paragraph (g)(1) of this section with respect to the $300 loss of S1 and S2 may be paid by the Internal Revenue Service directly to the fiduciary.

Example 2. Income of other subgroup members. (a) The facts are the same as in *Example 1*, except that S2 has $100 of income in Year 2 rather than $100 of loss. Any refund payable under paragraph (g) of this section with respect to the loss of S1 in Year 2 must take into account the income of S2, and therefore the refund will be based on a $100 loss of the subgroup.

(b) Although P and S3 are not members included in the subgroup, the loss year return and the claim for refund filed by the fiduciary under paragraph (e) of this section must be completed based on all information to which the fiduciary has reasonable access. Under paragraph (e)(3) of this section, if P does not file a loss year return that is accepted by S1, and S1 has reasonable access to information indicating that P and S3 have income in Year 2, S1 must take that income into account in filing the P group's return for Year 2 and reduce the amount of S1's loss that may be carried to Year 1 accordingly. However, if P or S3 has a loss in Year 2, any refund attributable to that loss will not be paid to the fiduciary.

(i) [Reserved]

(j) *Determination of ownership.*—This section determines the party to whom a refund or tentative carryback adjustment will be paid but is not determinative of ownership of any such amount among current or former members of a consolidated group (including the institution).

(k) *Liability of the Government.*—Any refund or tentative carryback adjustment paid to the fiduciary discharges any liability of the Government to the same extent as payment to the common parent under § 1.1502-77 or § 1.1502-78 of this chapter. Furthermore, any refund or tentative carryback adjustment paid to the fiduciary is considered a payment to all members of the carryback year group. Any determination made by the Internal Revenue Service under this section to pay a refund or tentative carryback adjustment to a fiduciary or the common parent may not be challenged by the common parent, any member of the group, or the fiduciary.

(l) *Effective dates.*—This section applies to refunds and tentative carryback adjustments paid after December 30, 1991. [Reg. § 301.6402-7.]

☐ [*T.D.* 8387, 12-30-91. *Redesignated and amended by T.D.* 8446, 11-5-92. *Amended by T.D.* 8677, 6-26-96 *and T.D.* 8823, 6-25-99.]

[Reg. § 31.6402(a)-1]

§ 31.6402(a)-1. Credit or refunds.—(a) *In general.*—For regulations under section 6402 of special application to credits or refunds of employment taxes, see § § 31.6402(a)-2, 31.6402(a)-3, and 31.6414-1. For regulations under section 6402 of general application to credits or refunds, see § § 301.6402-1 and 301.6402-2. For provisions relating to adjustments without interest of overpayments of taxes under the Federal Insurance Contributions Act or the Railroad Retirement Tax Act or income tax withholding, see § § 31.6413(a)-1 and 31.6413(a)-2.

(b) *Period of limitation.*—For the period of limitation upon credit or refund of taxes imposed by the Internal Revenue Code of 1954, see § 301.6511(a)-1 of this chapter (Regulations on Procedure and Administration). For the period of limitation upon credit or refund of any tax imposed by the Internal Revenue Code of 1939, see the regulations applicable with respect to such tax. [Reg. § 31.6402(a)-1.]

☐ [*T.D.* 6472, 6-22-60. *Amended by T.D.* 9405, 6-30-2008.]

[Reg. § 31.6402(a)-2]

§ 31.6402(a)-2. Credit or refund of tax under Federal Insurance Contributions Act or Railroad Retirement Tax Act.—(a) *Claim by person who paid tax to IRS.*—(1) *In general.*—(i) Except as provided in paragraph (a)(1)(iii) of this section, any person may file a claim for credit or refund for an overpayment (except to the extent that the overpayment must be credited pursuant to § 31.3503-1) if the person paid to the Internal Revenue Service (IRS) more than the correct amount of employee Federal Insurance Contributions Act (FICA) tax under section 3101 or employer FICA tax under section 3111, employee Railroad Retirement Tax Act (RRTA) tax under section 3201, employee representative RRTA tax under section 3211, or employer RRTA tax under section 3221, or interest, addition to the tax, additional amount, or penalty with respect to any such tax.

(ii) Except as provided in paragraph (a)(1)(iii) of this section, the claim for credit or refund must be made in the manner and subject to the conditions stated in this section. The claim for credit or refund must be filed on the form prescribed by the IRS and must designate the return period to which the claim relates, explain in detail the grounds and facts relied upon to support the claim, and set forth such other information as may be required by this section and by the instructions relating to the form used to make such claim. No refund or credit pursuant to this section for employer tax will be allowed unless the employer has first repaid or reimbursed its employee or has secured the employee's consent to the allowance of the claim for refund and includes a claim for the refund of such employee tax. However, this requirement does not apply to the extent that the taxes were not withheld from the employee or, after the employer makes reasonable efforts to repay or reimburse the employee or secure the employee's consent, the employer cannot locate the employee or the employee will not provide consent. No refund or credit of employee FICA or RRTA tax overcollected in an earlier year will be allowed if the employee has claimed a refund or credit of the amount of the overcollection which has not been rejected or if the employee has taken the amount of such tax into account in claiming a credit against or refund of the employee's income tax, including instances in which the employee has included an overcollection of employee FICA or RRTA tax in computing a special refund (see § 31.6413(c)-1).

(iii) *Additional Medicare Tax.*—No refund or credit to the employer will be allowed for the amount of any overpayment of Additional Medicare Tax imposed under section 3101(b)(2) or section 3201(a) (as calculated under section 3101(b)(2)), which the employer deducted or withheld from an employee.

(iv) For adjustments without interest of overpayments of FICA or RRTA taxes, including Additional Medicare Tax, see § 31.6413(a)-2.

(v) For corrections of FICA and RRTA tax paid under the wrong chapter, see § 31.6205-1(b)(2)(ii) and (b)(2)(iii) and § 31.3503-1.

(vi) For provisions related to furnishing employee statements and corrected employee statements reporting wages and withheld taxes, see sections 6041 and 6051 and § § 1.6041-2 and 31.6051-1. For provisions relating to filing information returns and corrected information returns reporting wages and withheld taxes, see sections 6041 and 6051 and § § 1.6041-2 and 31.6051-2.

(vii) For the period of limitations on credit or refund of taxes, see § 301.6511(a)-1.

(2) *Statements supporting employer's claims for employee tax.*—(i) Every employer who files a claim for refund or credit of employee FICA tax under section 3101 or employee RRTA tax under section 3201 collected from an employee must certify as part of the claim process that the employer has repaid or reimbursed the tax to its employee or has secured the employee's written consent to allowance of the filing of the claim for refund except to the extent that the taxes were not withheld from the employee. The employer must retain as part of its records the written receipt of the employee showing the date and amount of the repayment, evidence of reimbursement, or the written consent of the employee, whichever is used in support of the claim.

(ii) Every employer who files a claim for refund or credit of employee FICA tax under section 3101 or employee RRTA tax under section 3201 collected from an employee in a calendar year prior to the year in which the credit or refund is claimed, also must certify as part of the claim process that the employer has obtained the employee's written statement that the employee has not claimed refund or credit of the amount of the overcollection, or if so, such claim has been rejected, and that the employee will not claim refund or credit of the amount. The employer must retain the employee's written statement as part of the employer's records.

(b) *Claim by employee.*—(1) *In general.*—Except as provided in (b)(3) of this section, if more than the correct amount of employee tax under section 3101 or section 3201 is collected by an employer from an employee and paid to the IRS, the employee may file a claim for refund of the overpayment if—

(i) The employee does not receive repayment or reimbursement in any manner from the employer and does not authorize the employer to file a claim and receive refund or credit,

(ii) The overcollection cannot be corrected under § 31.3503-1, and

(iii) In the case of overpaid employee social security tax due to having received wages or compensation from multiple employers, the employee has not taken the overcollection into account in claiming a credit against, or refund of, his or her income tax, or if so, such claim has been rejected. See § 31.6413(c)-1.

(2) *Statements supporting employee's claim.*—(i) Except as provided in (b)(3) of this section, each employee who makes a claim under paragraph (b)(1) of this section shall submit with such claim a statement setting forth (a) the extent, if any, to which the employer has repaid or reimbursed the employee in any manner for the overcollection, and (b) the amount, if any, of credit or refund of such overpayment claimed by the employer or authorized by the employee to be claimed by the employer. The employee shall obtain such statement, if possible, from the employer, who should include in such statement the fact that it is made in support of a claim against the United States to be filed by the employee for refund of employee tax paid by such employer to the IRS. If the employer's statement is not submitted with the claim, the employee shall make the statement to the best of his or her knowledge and belief, and shall include therein an explanation of his or her inability to obtain the statement from the employer.

(ii) Except as provided in paragraph (b)(3) of this section, each individual who makes a claim under paragraph (b)(1) of this section also shall submit with such claim a statement setting forth whether the individual has taken the amount of the overcollection into account in claiming a credit against, or refund of, his or her income tax, and the amount, if any, so claimed (see § 31.6413(c)-1).

(3) *Additional Medicare Tax.*—(i) If more than the correct amount of Additional Medicare Tax under section 3101(b)(2) or section 3201(a) (as calculated under section 3101(b)(2)), is collected by an employer from an employee and paid to the IRS, the employee may file a claim for refund of the overpayment and receive a refund or credit if the overcollection cannot be corrected under § 31.3503-1 and if the employee has not received repayment or reimbursement from the employer in the context of an interest-free adjustment. The claim for refund shall be made on Form 1040, "U.S. Individual Income Tax Return," by taking the overcollection into account in claiming a credit against, or refund of, tax. The form to be used by residents of the U.S. Virgin Islands, Guam, American Samoa, or the Northern Mariana Islands is Form 1040-SS, "U.S. Self-Employment Tax Return (Including Additional Child Tax Credit for Bona Fide Residents of Puerto Rico)." The form to be used by residents of Puerto Rico is either Form 1040-SS or Form 1040-PR, "Planilla para la Declaración de la Contribución Federal sobre el Trabajo por Cuenta Propia (Incluyendo el Crédito Tributario Adicional por Hijos para Residentes Bona Fide de Puerto Rico)." The employee may not authorize the employer to claim the credit or refund for the employee. See § 31.6402(a)-2(a)(1)(iii).

(ii) In the case of an overpayment of Additional Medicare Tax under section 3101(b)(2) or section 3201(a) for a taxable year of an individual for which a Form 1040 (or other applicable return in the Form 1040 series) has been filed, a claim for refund shall be made by the individual on Form 1040X, "Amended U.S. Individual Income Tax Return."

(c) *Effective/applicability date.*—This section applies to claims for refund filed on or after November 29, 2013. [Reg. § 31.6402(a)-2.]

☐ [T.D. 6472, 6-22-60. *Amended by* T.D. 9405, 6-30-2008 *and* T.D. 9645, 11-26-2013.]

Reg. § 31.6402(a)-2(c)

[Reg. § 31.6402(a)-3]

§ 31.6402(a)-3. Refund of Federal unemployment tax.—Any person who pays to the district director more than the correct amount of—

(a) Tax under section 3301 of the Federal Unemployment Tax Act or a corresponding provision of prior law, or

(b) Interest, addition to the tax, additional amount, or penalty with respect to such tax,

may file a claim for refund of the overpayment, in the manner and subject to the conditions stated in § 301.6402-2 of this chapter (Regulations on Procedure and Administration) [¶ 11,260.85]. See § 31.6413(d) and the corresponding section of prior law for provisions which bar the allowance or payment of interest on the amount of any refund based on credit allowable for contributions paid under the unemployment compensation law of a State. [Reg. § 31.6402(a)-3.]

☐ [*T.D.* 6472, 6-22-60.]

[Reg. § 301.6403-1]

§ 301.6403-1. Overpayment of installment.— If any installment of tax is overpaid, the overpayment shall first be applied against any outstanding installments of such tax. If the overpayment exceeds the correct amount of tax due, the overpayment shall be credited or refunded as provided in section 6402 and §§ 301.6402-1 to 301.6402-4, inclusive. [Reg. § 301.6403-1.]

☐ [*T.D.* 6119, 12-31-54. *Amended by T.D.* 6498, 10-24-60.]

[Reg. § 31.6404(a)-1]

§ 31.6404(a)-1. Abatements.—For regulations under section 6404 of general application to the abatement of taxes, see § 301.6404-1 of this chapter(Regulations on Procedure and Administration). Every claim filed by an employer for abatement of employee tax under section 3101 or section 3201, or a corresponding provision of prior law, shall be made in the manner and subject to the conditions stated in paragraphs (a)(2) and (c) of § 31.6402(a)-2, as if the claim for abatement were a claim for refund. [Reg. § 31.6404(a)-1.]

☐ [*T.D.* 6472, 6-22-60.]

[Reg. § 301.6404-0]

§ 301.6404-0. Table of contents.—This section lists the paragraphs contained in §§ 301.6404-1 through 301.6404-4.

(ii) Effect of gross misstatement.

(5) Listed transactions and undisclosed reportable transactions.

(i) In general.

(ii) Special rule for certain listed or undisclosed reportable transactions.

(A) Participant in a settlement initiative.

(1) Participant in a settlement initiative who as of January 23, 2006, had not reached agreement with the IRS.

(2) Participant in a settlement initiative who, as of January 23, 2006, had reached agreement with the IRS.

(B) Taxpayer acting in good faith.

(1) In general.

(2) Presumption.

(3) Examples.

(C) Closed transactions.

(c) Special rules.

(1) Tentative carryback and refund adjustments.

(2) Election under section 183(e).

(i) In general.

(ii) Example.

(d) Effective/applicability date.

[Reg. § 301.6404-0.]

□ [*T.D. 8254, 5-12-89. Redesignated and amended by T.D. 8299, 4-16-90. Amended by T.D. 9488, 6-15-2010 and T.D. 9545, 8-19-2011.*]

[Reg. § 301.6404-1]

§ 301.6404-1. Abatements.—(a) The district director or the director of the regional service center may abate any assessment, or unpaid portion thereof, if the assessment is in excess of the correct tax liability, if the assessment is made subsequent to the expiration of the period of limitations applicable thereto, or if the assessment has been erroneously or illegally made.

(b) No claim for abatement may be filed with respect to income, estate, or gift tax.

(c) Except in case of income, estate, or gift tax, if more than the correct amount of tax, interest, additional amount, addition to the tax, or assessable penalty is assessed but not paid to the district director, the person against whom the assessment is made may file a claim for abatement of such overassessment. Each claim for abatement under this section shall be made on Form 843. In the case of a claim filed prior to April 15, 1968, the claim shall be filed in the office of the internal revenue officer by whom the tax was assessed or with the assistant regional commissioner (alcohol, tobacco, and firearms) where the regulations respecting the particular tax to which the claim relates specifically require the claim to be filed with that officer. Except as provided in paragraph (b) of § 301.6091-1 (relating to hand-carried documents), in the case of a claim filed after April 14, 1968, the claim shall be filed (1) with the Director of International Operations if the tax was assessed by him, or (2) with the assistant regional commissioner (alcohol, tobacco, and firearms) where the regulations respecting the particular tax to which the claim relates specifically require the claim to be filed with that officer; otherwise, the claim shall be filed with the service center serving the internal revenue district in which the tax was assessed. Form 843 shall be made in accordance with the instructions relating to such form.

(d) The Commissioner may issue uniform instructions to district directors authorizing them, to the extent permitted in such instructions, to abate amounts the collection of which is not warranted because of the administration and collection costs. [Reg. § 301.6404-1.]

□ [*T.D. 6119, 12-31-54. Amended by T.D. 6585, 12-27-61; T.D. 6950, 4-3-68; T.D. 7008, 2-28-69 and T.D. 7188, 6-28-72.*]

[Reg. § 301.6404-2]

§ 301.6404-2. Abatement of interest.—(a) *In general.*—(1) Section 6404(e)(1) provides that the Commissioner may (in the Commissioner's discretion) abate the assessment of all or any part of interest on any—

(i) Deficiency (as defined in section 6211(a), relating to income, estate, gift, generation-skipping, and certain excise taxes) attributable in whole or in part to any unreasonable error or delay by an officer or employee of the Internal Revenue Service (IRS) (acting in an official capacity) in performing a ministerial or managerial act; or

(ii) Payment of any tax described in section 6212(a) (relating to income, estate, gift, generation-skipping, and certain excise taxes) to the extent that any unreasonable error or delay in payment is attributable to an officer or employee of the IRS (acting in an official capacity) being erroneous or dilatory in performing a ministerial or managerial act.

(2) An error or delay in performing a ministerial or managerial act will be taken into account only if no significant aspect of the error or delay is attributable to the taxpayer involved or to a person related to the taxpayer within the meaning of section 267(b) or section 707(b)(1). Moreover, an error or delay in performing a ministerial or managerial act will be taken into account only if it occurs after the IRS has contacted the taxpayer in writing with respect to the deficiency or payment. For purposes of this paragraph (a)(2), no significant aspect of the error or delay is attributable to the taxpayer merely because the taxpayer consents to extend the period of limitations.

(b) *Definitions.*—(1) *Managerial act.*—means an administrative act that occurs during the processing of a taxpayer's case involving the temporary or permanent loss of records or the exercise of judgment or discretion relating to management of personnel. A decision concerning the proper application of federal tax law (or other federal or state law) is not a managerial act. Further, a general administrative decision, such as the IRS's decision on how to organize the processing of tax returns or its delay in implementing an improved computer system, is not a managerial act for which interest can be abated under paragraph (a) of this section.

(2) *Ministerial act*.—means a procedural or mechanical act that does not involve the exercise of judgment or discretion, and that occurs during the processing of a taxpayer's case after all prerequisites to the act, such as conferences and review by supervisors, have taken place. A decision concerning the proper application of federal tax law (or other federal or state law) is not a ministerial act.

(c) *Examples*.—The following examples illustrate the provisions of paragraphs (b)(1) and (2) of this section. Unless otherwise stated, for purposes of the examples, no significant aspect of any error or delay is attributable to the taxpayer, and the IRS has contacted the taxpayer in writing with respect to the deficiency or payment. The examples are as follows:

Example 1. A taxpayer moves from one state to another before the IRS selects the taxpayer's income tax return for examination. A letter explaining that the return has been selected for examination is sent to the taxpayer's old address and then forwarded to the new address. The taxpayer timely responds, asking that the audit be transferred to the IRS's district office that is nearest the new address. The group manager timely approves the request. After the request for transfer has been approved, the transfer of the case is a ministerial act. The Commissioner may (in the Commissioner's discretion) abate interest attributable to any unreasonable delay in transferring the case.

Example 2. An examination of a taxpayer's income tax return reveals a deficiency with respect to which a notice of deficiency will be issued. The taxpayer and the IRS identify all agreed and unagreed issues, the notice is prepared and reviewed (including review by District Counsel, if necessary), and any other relevant prerequisites are completed. The issuance of the notice of deficiency is a ministerial act. The Commissioner may (in the Commissioner's discretion) abate interest attributable to any unreasonable delay in issuing the notice.

Example 3. A revenue agent is sent to a training course for an extended period of time, and the agent's supervisor decides not to reassign the agent's cases. During the training course, no work is done on the cases assigned to the agent. The decision to send the revenue agent to the training course and the decision not to reassign the agent's cases are not ministerial acts; however, both decisions are managerial acts. The Commissioner may (in the Commissioner's discretion) abate interest attributable to any unreasonable delay resulting from these decisions.

Example 4. A taxpayer appears for an office audit and submits all necessary documentation and information. The auditor tells the taxpayer that the taxpayer will receive a copy of the audit report. However, before the report is prepared, the auditor is permanently reassigned to another group. An extended period of time passes before the auditor's cases are reassigned. The decision to reassign the auditor and the decision not to reassign the auditor's cases are not ministerial acts; however, they are managerial acts. The Commissioner may (in the Commissioner's discretion) abate interest attributable to any unreasonable delay resulting from these decisions.

Example 5. A taxpayer is notified that the IRS intends to audit the taxpayer's income tax return. The agent assigned to the case is granted sick leave for an extended period of time, and the taxpayer's case is not reassigned. The decision to grant sick leave and the decision not to reassign the taxpayer's case to another agent are not ministerial acts; however, they are managerial acts. The Commissioner may (in the Commissioner's discretion) abate interest attributable to any unreasonable delay caused by these decisions.

Example 6. A revenue agent has completed an examination of the income tax return of a taxpayer. There are issues that are not agreed upon between the taxpayer and the IRS. Before the notice of deficiency is prepared and reviewed, a clerical employee misplaces the taxpayer's case file. The act of misplacing the case file is a managerial act. The Commissioner may (in the Commissioner's discretion) abate interest attributable to any unreasonable delay resulting from the file being misplaced.

Example 7. A taxpayer invests in a tax shelter and reports a loss from the tax shelter on the taxpayer's income tax return. IRS personnel conduct an extensive examination of the tax shelter, and the processing of the taxpayer's case is delayed because of that examination. The decision to delay the processing of the taxpayer's case until the completion of the examination of the tax shelter is a decision on how to organize the processing of tax returns. This is a general administrative decision. Consequently, interest attributable to a delay caused by this decision cannot be abated under paragraph (a) of this section.

Example 8. A taxpayer claims a loss on the taxpayer's income tax return and is notified that the IRS intends to examine the return. However, a decision is made not to commence the examination of the taxpayer's return until the processing of another return, for which the statute of limitations is about to expire, is completed. The decision on how to prioritize the processing of returns based on the expiration of the statute of limitations is a general administrative decision. Consequently, interest attributable to a delay caused by this decision cannot be abated under paragraph (a) of this section.

Example 9. During the examination of an income tax return, there is disagreement between the taxpayer and the revenue agent regarding certain itemized deductions claimed by the taxpayer on the return. To resolve the issue, advice is requested in a timely manner from the Office of Chief Counsel on a substantive issue of federal tax law. The decision to request advice is a decision concerning the proper application of federal tax law; it is neither a ministerial nor a managerial act. Consequently, interest attributable to a delay resulting from the decision to request advice cannot be abated under paragraph (a) of this section.

Example 10. The facts are the same as in *Example 9* except the attorney who is assigned to respond to the request for advice is granted leave for an extended period of time. The case is not reassigned during the attorney's absence. The decision to grant leave and the decision not to reassign the taxpayer's case to another attorney are not ministerial acts; however, they are managerial acts. The Commissioner may (in the Commissioner's discretion) abate interest attributable to any unreasonable delay caused by these decisions.

Example 11. A taxpayer contacts an IRS employee and requests information with respect to the amount due to satisfy the taxpayer's income tax liability for a particular taxable year. Because the employee fails to access the most recent data, the employee gives the taxpayer an incorrect amount due. As a result, the taxpayer pays less than the amount required to satisfy the tax liability. Accessing the most recent data is a ministerial act. The Commissioner may (in the Commissioner's discretion) abate interest attributable to any unreasonable error or delay arising from giving the taxpayer an incorrect amount due to satisfy the taxpayer's income tax liability.

Example 12. A taxpayer contacts an IRS employee and requests information with respect to the amount due to satisfy the taxpayer's income tax liability for a particular taxable year. To determine the current amount due, the employee must interpret complex provisions of federal tax law involving net operating loss carrybacks and foreign tax credits. Because the employee incorrectly interprets these provisions, the employee gives the taxpayer an incorrect amount due. As a result, the taxpayer pays less than the amount required to satisfy the tax liability. Interpreting complex provisions of federal tax law is neither a ministerial nor a managerial act. Consequently, interest attributable to an error or delay arising from giving the taxpayer an incorrect amount due to satisfy the taxpayer's income tax liability in this situation cannot be abated under paragraph (a) of this section.

Example 13. A taxpayer moves from one state to another after the IRS has undertaken an examination of the taxpayer's income tax return. The taxpayer asks that the audit be transferred to the IRS's district office that is nearest the new address. The group manager approves the request, and the case is transferred. Thereafter, the taxpayer moves to yet another state, and once again asks that the audit be transferred to the IRS's district office that is nearest that new address. The group manager approves the request, and the case is again transferred. The agent then assigned to the case is granted sick leave for an extended period of time, and the taxpayer's case is not reassigned. The taxpayer's repeated moves

result in a delay in the completion of the examination. Under paragraph (a)(2) of this section, interest attributable to this delay cannot be abated because a significant aspect of this delay is attributable to the taxpayer. However, as in *Example 5*, the Commissioner may (in the Commissioner's discretion) abate interest attributable to any unreasonable delay caused by the managerial decisions to grant sick leave and not to reassign the taxpayer's case to another agent.

(d) *Effective dates.*—(1) *In general.*—Except as provided in paragraph (d)(2) of this section, the provisions of this section apply to interest accruing with respect to deficiencies or payments of any tax described in section 6212(a) for taxable years beginning after July 30, 1996.

(2) *Special rules.*—(i) *Estate tax.*—The provisions of this section apply to interest accruing with respect to deficiencies or payments of—

(A) Estate tax imposed under section 2001 on estates of decedents dying after July 30, 1996;

(B) The additional estate tax imposed under sections 2032A(c) and 2056A(b)(1)(B) in the case of taxable events occurring after July 30, 1996; and

(C) The additional estate tax imposed under section 2056A(b)(1)(A) in the case of taxable events occurring after December 31, 1996.

(ii) *Gift tax.*—The provisions of this section apply to interest accruing with respect to deficiencies or payments of gift tax imposed under chapter 12 on gifts made after December 31, 1996.

(iii) *Generation-skipping transfer tax.*—The provisions of this section apply to interest accruing with respect to deficiencies or payments of generation-skipping transfer tax imposed under chapter 13—

(A) On direct skips occurring at death, if the transferor dies after July 30, 1996; and

(B) On inter vivos direct skips, and all taxable terminations and taxable distributions occurring after December 31, 1996. [Reg. §301.6404-2.]

☐ [*T.D.* 8789; 12-17-98.]

[Reg. §301.6404-3]

§301.6404-3. Abatement of penalty or addition to tax attributable to erroneous written advice of the Internal Revenue Service.— (a) *General rule.*—Any portion of any penalty or addition to tax that is attributable to erroneous advice furnished to the taxpayer in writing by an officer or employee of the Internal Revenue Service (Service), acting in his or her official capacity, shall be abated, provided the requirements of paragraph(b) of this section are met.

(b) *Requirements.*—(1) *In general.*—Paragraph (a) of this section shall apply only if—

(i) The written advice was reasonably relied upon by the taxpayer;

(ii) The advice was issued in response to a specific written request for advice by the taxpayer; and

(iii) The taxpayer requesting advice provided adequate and accurate information.

(2) *Advice was reasonably relied upon.*—(i) *In general.*—The written advice from the Service must have been reasonably relied upon by the taxpayer in order for any penalty to be abated under paragraph (a) of this section.

(ii) *Advice relating to a tax return.*—In the case of written advice from the Service that relates to an item included on a federal tax return of a taxpayer, if such advice is received by the taxpayer subsequent to the date on which the taxpayer filed such return, the taxpayer shall not be considered to have reasonably relied upon such written advice for purposes of this section, except as provided in paragraph (b)(2)(iii) of this section.

(iii) *Amended returns.*—If a taxpayer files an amended federal tax return that conforms with written advice received by the taxpayer from the Service, the taxpayer will be considered to have reasonably relied upon the advice for purposes of the position set forth in the amended return.

(iv) *Advice not related to a tax return.*—In the case of written advice that does not relate to an item included on a federal tax return (for example, the payment of estimated taxes), if such written advice is received by the taxpayer subsequent to the act or omission of the taxpayer that is the basis for the penalty or addition of tax, then the taxpayer shall not be considered to have reasonably relied upon such written advice for purposes of this section.

(v) *Period of reliance.*—If the written advice received by the taxpayer relates to a continuing action or series of actions, the taxpayer may rely on that advice until the taxpayer is put on notice that the advice is no longer consistent with Service position and, thus, no longer valid. For purposes of this section, the taxpayer will be put on notice that written advice is no longer valid if the taxpayer receives correspondence from the Service stating that the advice no longer represents Service position. Further, any of the following events, occurring subsequent to the issuance of the advice, that set forth a position that is inconsistent with the written advice received from the Service shall be deemed to put the taxpayer on notice that the advice is no longer valid—

(A) Enactment of legislation or ratification of a tax treaty;

(B) A decision of the United States Supreme Court;

(C) The issuance of temporary or final regulations; or

(D) The issuance of a revenue ruling, a revenue procedure, or other statement published in the Internal Revenue Bulletin.

(3) *Advice was in response to written request.*—No abatement under paragraph (a) of this section shall be allowed unless the penalty or addition to tax is attributable to advice issued in response to a specific written request for advice by the taxpayer. For purposes of the preceding sentence, a written request from a representative of the taxpayer shall be considered a written request by the taxpayer only if—

(i) The taxpayer's representative is an attorney, a certified public accountant, an enrolled agent, an enrolled actuary, or any other person permitted to represent the taxpayer before the Service and who is not disbarred or suspended from practice before the Service; and

(ii) The written request for advice either is accompanied by a power of attorney that is signed by the taxpayer and that authorizes the representative to represent the taxpayer for purposes of the request, or such a power of attorney is currently on file with the Service.

(4) *Taxpayer's information must be adequate and accurate.*—No abatement under paragraph (a) of this section shall be allowed with respect to any portion of any penalty or addition to tax that resulted because the taxpayer requesting the advice did not provide the Service with adequate and accurate information. The Service has no obligation to verify or correct the taxpayer's submitted information.

(c) *Definitions.*—(1) *Advice.*—For purposes of section 6404(f) and the regulations thereunder, a written response issued to a taxpayer by an officer or employee of the Service shall constitute "advice" if, and only if, the response applies the tax laws to the specific facts submitted in writing by the taxpayer and provides a conclusion regarding the tax treatment to be accorded the taxpayer upon the application of the tax law to those facts.

(2) *Penalty and addition to tax.*—For purposes of section 6404(f) and the regulations thereunder, the terms "penalty" and "addition to tax" refer to any liability of a particular taxpayer imposed under Subtitle F, Chapter 68, Subchapter A and Subchapter B of the Internal Revenue Code, and the liabilities imposed by sections 6038(b), 6038(c), 6038A(d), 6038B(b), 6039E(c), and 6332(d)(2). In addition, the terms "penalty" and "addition to tax" shall include any liability resulting from the application of other provisions of the Code where the Commissioner of Internal Revenue has designated by regulation, revenue ruling, or other guidance published in the Internal Revenue Bulletin that such provision shall be considered a penalty or addition to tax for purposes of section 6404(f). The terms "penalty" and "addition to tax" shall also include interest imposed with respect to any penalty or addition to tax.

(d) *Procedures for abatement.*—Taxpayers entitled to an abatement of a penalty or addition to tax pursuant to section 6404(f) and this section should complete and file Form 843. If the erroneous advice received relates to an item on a federal tax return, taxpayers should submit Form 843 to the Internal Revenue Service Center where the return was filed. If the advice does not relate to an item on a federal tax return, the taxpayer should submit Form 843 to the Service Center where the taxpayer's return was filed for the taxable year in which the taxpayer relied on the erroneous advice. At the top of Form 843 taxpayers should write, "Abatement of penalty or addition to tax pursuant to section 6404(f)." Further, taxpayers must state on Form 843 whether the penalty or addition to tax has been paid. Taxpayers must submit, with Form 843, copies of the following—

(1) The taxpayer's written request for advice;

(2) The erroneous written advice furnished by the Service to the taxpayer and relied on by the taxpayer; and

(3) The report (if any) of tax adjustments that identifies the penalty or addition to tax and the item relating to the erroneous written advice.

(e) *Period for requesting abatement.*—An abatement of any penalty or addition to tax pursuant to section 6404(f) and this section shall be allowed only if the request for abatement described in paragraph (d) of this section is submitted within the period allowed for collection of such penalty or addition to tax, or, if the penalty or addition to tax has been paid, the period allowed for claiming a credit or refund of such penalty or addition to tax.

(f) *Examples.*—The following examples illustrate the application of section 6404(f) of the Code and the regulations thereunder:

Example 1. In February 1989, an individual submitted a written request for advice to an Internal Revenue Service Center and included adequate and accurate information to consider the request. The question posed by the taxpayer concerned whether a certain amount was includible in income on the taxpayer's 1989 federal income tax return. An employee of the Service Center issued the taxpayer a written response that concluded that based on the specific facts submitted by the taxpayer, the amount was not includible in income on the taxpayer's 1989 return. Since the response provided a conclusion regarding the tax treatment accorded the taxpayer on the basis of the facts submitted, the response constitutes "advice" for purposes of section 6404(f). The taxpayer filed his 1989 return and, relying on the Service's advice, did not include the item in income. Upon examination, it was determined that the item should have been included in income on the taxpayer's 1989 return. Because the taxpayer reasonably relied upon erroneous written advice from the Service, any penalty or addition to tax attributable to the erroneous advice will be abated by the Service. However, the erroneous advice will not affect the amount of any taxes and interest owed by the taxpayer (except to the extent interest relates to a penalty or addition to tax attributable to the erroneous advice) due to the fact that the item was not included in income.

Example 2. In March 1989, an individual submitted a written request to the National Office of the Internal Revenue Service regarding whether a certain activity constitutes a passive activity within the meaning of section 469 of the Code. The request did not meet the procedural requirements set forth by the National Office for consideration of the submission as a private letter ruling request and, thus, was not treated as such by the Service. The Service furnished the taxpayer with a written response that transmitted various published provisions of section 469 and the regulations thereunder relevant to the determination of whether an activity is passive within the meaning of those provisions. The Service also included a Publication regarding the tax treatment of passive activities. However, the Service's response contained no opinion or determination regarding whether the taxpayer's described activity was or was not passive under section 469. The Service's response is not advice within the meaning of section 6404(f), and cannot be relied upon for purposes of an abatement of a portion of a penalty or addition to tax under that section.

Example 3. On April 1, 1989, an individual submitted a written request for advice to an Internal Revenue Service Center. The advice related to an item included on a federal tax return. The individual filed a federal income tax return with the appropriate Service Center on April 15, 1989. Subsequently, on May 1, 1989, the individual received advice from the Service Center concerning the written request made on April 1. Because the individual filed his tax return prior to the date on which written advice from the Service was received, the individual did not rely on the Service's written advice for purposes of section 6404(f). If, however, the individual amends his tax return to conform with the written advice received from the Service, the individual will be considered to have reasonably relied upon the Service's advice.

Example 4. Individual A, on May 1, 1989, received advice from the Service that concluded that interest paid by the taxpayer with respect to a specific loan was interest paid or accrued in connection with a trade or business, within the meaning of section 163(h)(2)(A) of the Code. The advice relates to a continuing action. Therefore, provided the facts submitted by the taxpayer to obtain the advice remain adequate and accurate (that is, the circumstances relating to the indebtedness do not change), Individual A may rely on the Service's advice for subsequent taxable years until the individual is put on notice that the advice no longer represents Service position and, thus, is no longer valid.

Example 5. An individual, on June 1, 1989, received advice from the Service that concluded that no gain or loss would be recognized with respect to a transfer of property to his spouse under section 1041. The advice does not relate to a continuing action. Therefore, the taxpayer may not rely on the advice of the Service for transfers other than the transfer discussed in the taxpayer's written request for advice.

(g) *Effective date.*—Section 6404(f) shall apply with respect to advice requested on or after January 1, 1989. [Reg. § 301.6404-3.]

☐ [*T.D.* 8254, 5-12-89. *Redesignated and amended by T.D.* 8299, 4-16-90.]

[Reg. § 301.6404-4]

§ 301.6404-4. Suspension of interest and certain penalties when the Internal Revenue Service does not timely contact the taxpayer.—
(a) *Suspension.*—(1) *In general.*—Except as provided in paragraph (b) of this section, if an individual taxpayer files a return of tax imposed by subtitle A on or before the due date for the return (including extensions) and the Internal Revenue Service does not timely provide the taxpayer with a notice specifically stating the amount of any increased liability and the basis for that liability, then the IRS must suspend the imposition of any interest, penalty, addition to tax, or additional amount, with respect to any failure relating to the return that is computed by reference to the period of time the failure continues to exist and that is properly allocable to the suspension period. The notice described in this paragraph (a) is timely if provided before the close of the 18- month period (36-month period in the case of notices provided after November 25, 2007, subject to the provisions of paragraph (a)(5)) beginning on the later of the date on which the return is filed or the due date of the return without regard to extensions.

(2) *Treatment of amended returns and other documents.*—(i) *Amended returns filed on or after December 21, 2005, that show an increase in tax liability.*—If a taxpayer, on or after December 21, 2005, provides to the IRS an amended return or one or more other signed written documents showing an increase in tax liability, the date on which the return was filed will, for purposes of this paragraph (a), be the date on which the last of the documents was provided. Documents described in this paragraph (a)(2)(i) are provided on the date that they are received by the IRS.

(ii) *Amended returns that show a decrease in tax liability.*—If a taxpayer provides to the IRS an amended return or other signed written document that shows a decrease in tax liability, any interest, penalty, addition to tax, or additional amount will not be suspended if the IRS at any time proposes to adjust the changed item or items on the amended return or other signed written document.

(iii) *Amended returns and other documents as notice.*—(A) As to the items reported, an amended return or one or more other signed written documents showing that the taxpayer owes an additional amount of tax for the taxable year serves as the notice described in paragraph (a)(1) of this section with respect to the items reported on the amended return.

(B) *Example.*—An individual taxpayer timely files a Federal income tax return for taxable year 2008 on April 15, 2009. On January 19, 2010, the taxpayer mails to the IRS an amended return reporting an additional item of income and an increased tax liability for taxable year 2008. The IRS receives the amended return on January 21, 2010. The amended return will be treated for purposes of this paragraph (a) as filed on January 21, 2010, the date the IRS received it. Pursuant to paragraph (a)(2)(iii) of this section, the amended return serves as the notice described in paragraph (a)(1) of this section with respect to the item reported on the amended return. Accordingly, because the filing of the amended return and the provision of notice occur simultaneously, no suspension of any interest, penalty, addition to tax or additional amount will occur under this paragraph (a) with respect to the item reported on the amended return.

(iv) *Joint return after filing separate return.*—A joint return filed under section 6013(b) is subject to the rules for amended returns described in this paragraph (a)(2). The IRS will not suspend any interest, penalty, addition to tax, or additional amount on a joint return filed under section 6013(b) after the filing of a separate return unless each spouse's separate return, if required to be filed, was timely.

(3) *Separate application.*—This paragraph (a) shall be applied separately with respect to each item or adjustment.

(4) *Duration of suspension period.*—The suspension period described in paragraph (a)(1) of this section begins the day after the close of the 18-month period (36-month period, in the case of notices provided after November 25, 2007, subject to the provisions of paragraph (a)(5)) beginning on the later of the date on which the return is filed or the due date of the return without regard to extensions. The suspension period ends 21 days after the earlier of the date on which the IRS mails the required notice to the taxpayer's last known address, the date on which the required notice is hand-delivered to the taxpayer, or the date on which the IRS receives an amended return or other signed written document showing an increased tax liability.

(5) *Certain notices provided on or after November 26, 2007.*—If the IRS provides the notice described in paragraph (a)(1) of this section to a taxpayer on or after November 26, 2007, and the notice relates to an individual Federal income tax return that was timely filed before that date, the following rules will apply:

(i) *Eighteen-month period has closed.*—If, as of November 25, 2007, the 18-month period described in paragraph (a)(1) of this section has closed and the IRS has not provided the taxpayer with the notice described in that paragraph (a)(1), the suspension described in paragraph (a)(1) of this section will begin on the day after the close of the 18-month period. The suspension will end on the date that is 21 days after the notice is provided.

(ii) *All other cases.*—In all other cases, the suspension described in paragraph (a)(1) of this section will begin on the day after the close of the 36-month period described in that paragraph (a)(1) and end on the date that is 21 days after the notice described in paragraph (a)(1) of this section is provided.

(6) *Examples.*—The following examples, which assume that no exceptions in section 6404(g)(2) to the general rule of suspension apply, illustrate the rules of this paragraph (a).

Example 1. An individual taxpayer timely files a Federal income tax return for taxable year 2005 on April 17, 2006. On December 11, 2007, the taxpayer mails to the IRS an amended return reporting an additional item of income and an increased tax liability for taxable year 2005. The IRS receives the amended return on December 13, 2007. On January 16, 2008, the IRS provides the taxpayer with a notice stating that the taxpayer has an additional tax liability based on the disallowance of a deduction the taxpayer claimed on his original return and did not change on his amended return. The date the amended return was received substitutes for the date that the original return was filed with respect to the additional item of tax liability reported on the amended return. Thus, the IRS will not suspend any interest, penalty, addition to tax, or additional amount with respect to the additional item of income and the increased tax liability reported on the amended return. The suspension period for the additional tax liability based on the IRS's disallowance of the deduction begins on October 17, 2007, so the IRS will suspend any interest, penalty, addition to tax, and additional amount with respect to the disallowed deduction and additional tax liability from that date through February 6, 2008, which is 21 days after the IRS provided notice of the additional tax liability and the basis for that liability. The suspension period in this example begins 18 months after filing the return (not 36 months) because, as of November 25, 2007, the 18-month period beginning on the date the return was filed had closed without the IRS giving notice of the additional liability. Thus, under the rules in paragraph (a)(5) of this section, the suspension period begins 18 months from the April 17, 2006 return filing date.

Example 2. An individual taxpayer files a Federal income tax return for taxable year 2008 on April 15, 2009. The taxpayer consents to extend the time within which the IRS may assess any tax due on the return until June 30, 2013. On December 20, 2012, the IRS provides a notice to the taxpayer specifically stating the taxpayer's liability and the basis for the liability. The suspension period for the liability identified by the IRS begins on April 15, 2012, so the IRS will suspend any interest, penalty, addition to tax, and additional amount with respect to that liability from that date through January 10, 2013, which is 21 days after the IRS provided notice of

the additional tax liability and the basis for that liability.

(7) *Notice of liability and the basis for the liability.*—(i) *In general.*—Notice to the taxpayer must be in writing and specifically state the amount of the liability and the basis for the liability. The notice must provide the taxpayer with sufficient information to identify which items of income, deduction, loss, or credit the IRS has adjusted or proposes to adjust, and the reason for that adjustment. Notice of the reason for the adjustment does not require a detailed explanation or a citation to any Internal Revenue Code section or other legal authority. The IRS need not incorporate all of the information necessary to satisfy the notice requirement within a single document or provide all of the information at the same time. Documents that may contain information sufficient to constitute notice, either alone or in conjunction with other documents, include, but are not limited to, statutory notices of deficiency; examination reports (for example, Form 4549, *Income Tax Examination Changes* or Form 886-A, *Explanation of Items*); Form 870, *Waiver of Restriction on Assessments and Collection of Deficiency in Tax and Acceptance of Overassessment*; notices of proposed deficiency that allow the taxpayer an opportunity for review in the Office of Appeals (30-day letters); notices pursuant to section 6213(b) (mathematical or clerical errors); and notice and demand for payment of a jeopardy assessment under section 6861.

(ii) *Tax attributable to TEFRA partnership items.*—Notice to the partner or the tax matters partner (TMP) of a partnership subject to the unified audit and litigation procedures of subchapter C of chapter 63 of subtitle F of the Internal Revenue Code (TEFRA partnership procedures) that provides specific information about the basis for the adjustments to partnership items is sufficient notice if a partner could reasonably compute the specific tax attributable to the partnership item based on the proposed adjustments as applied to the partner's individual tax situation. Documents provided by the IRS during a TEFRA partnership proceeding that may contain information sufficient to satisfy the notice requirements include, but are not limited to, a Notice of Final Partnership Administrative Adjustment (FPAA); examination reports (for example, Form 4605-A or Form 886-A); or a letter that allows the partners an opportunity for review in the Office of Appeals (60-day letter).

(iii) *Examples.*—The following examples illustrate the rules of this paragraph (a)(7).

Example 1. During an audit of Taxpayer A's 2005 taxable year return, the IRS questions a charitable deduction claimed on the return. The IRS provides A with a 30-day letter that proposes to disallow the charitable contribution deduction resulting in a deficiency of $1,000 and informs A that A may file a written protest of the proposed disallowance with the Office of Appeals within 30 days. The letter includes as an attachment a copy of the revenue agent's report that states, "It has not been established that the amount shown on your return as a charitable contribution was paid during the tax year. Therefore, this deduction is not allowable." The information in the 30-day letter and attachment provides A with notice of the specific amount of the liability and the basis for that liability as described in this paragraph (a)(7).

Example 2. Taxpayer B is a partner in partnership P, a TEFRA partnership for taxable year 2005. B claims a distributive share of partnership income on B's Federal income tax return for 2005 timely filed on April 17, 2006. On October 1, 2007, during the course of a partnership audit of P for taxable year 2005, the IRS provides P's TMP with a 60-day letter proposing to adjust P's income by $10,000. The IRS previously had provided the TMP with a copy of the examination report explaining that the adjustment was based on $10,000 of unreported net income. On October 31, 2007, P's TMP informs B of the proposed adjustment as required by § 301.6223(g)-1(b). By accounting for B's distributive share of the $10,000 of unreported income from P with B's other income tax items, B can determine B's tax attributable to the $10,000 partnership adjustment. The information in the 60-day letter and the examination report allows B to compute the specific amount of the liability attributable to the adjustment to the partnership item and the basis for that adjustment and therefore satisfies the notice requirement of paragraph (a). Because the IRS provided that notice to the TMP, B's agent under the TEFRA partnership provisions, within 18 months of the April 17, 2006 filing date of B's return, any interest, penalty, addition to tax, or additional amount with respect to B's tax liability attributable to B's distributive share of the $10,000 of unreported partnership income will not be suspended under section 6404(g).

(8) *Providing notice.*—(i) *In general.*—The IRS may provide notice by mail or in person to the taxpayer or the taxpayer's representative. If the IRS mails the notice, it must be sent to the taxpayer's last known address under rules similar to section 6212(b), except that certified or registered mail is not required. Notice is considered provided as of the date of mailing or delivery in person.

(ii) *Providing notice in TEFRA partnership proceedings.*—In the case of TEFRA partnership proceedings, the IRS must provide notice of final partnership administrative adjustments (FPAA) by mail to those partners specified in section 6223. Within 60 days of an FPAA being mailed, the TMP is required to forward notice of the FPAA to those partners not entitled to direct notice from the IRS under section 6223. Certain partners with small interests in partnerships with more than 100 partners may form a Notice Group and designate a partner to receive the FPAA on their behalf. The IRS may provide other information after the beginning of the partnership administrative proceeding to the TMP who, in turn, must provide that information to the partners specified in § 301.6223(g)-1 within

30 days of receipt. Pass-thru partners who receive notices and other information from the IRS or the TMP must forward that notice or information within 30 days to those holding an interest through the pass-thru partner. Information provided by the IRS to the TMP is deemed to be notice for purposes of this section to those partners specified in § 301.6223(g)-1 as of the date the IRS provides that notice to the TMP. A similar rule applies to notice provided to the designated partner of a Notice Group, and to notice provided to a pass-thru partner. In the foregoing situations, the TMP, designated partner, and pass-thru partner are agents for direct and indirect partners. Consequently, notice to these agents is deemed to be notice to the partners for whom they act.

(b) *Exceptions.*—(1) *Failure to file tax return or to pay tax.*—Paragraph (a) of this section does not apply to any penalty imposed by section 6651.

(2) *Fraud.*—Paragraph (a) of this section does not apply to any interest, penalty, addition to tax, or additional amount for a year involving a false or fraudulent return. If a taxpayer files a fraudulent return for a particular year, paragraph (a) of this section may apply to any other tax year of the taxpayer that does not involve fraud. Fraud affecting a particular item on a return precludes paragraph (a) of this section from applying to any other items on that return.

(3) *Tax shown on return.*—Paragraph (a) of this section does not apply to any interest, penalty, addition to tax, or additional amount with respect to any tax liability shown on a return.

(4) *Gross misstatement.*—(i) *Description.*—Paragraph (a) of this section does not apply to any interest, penalty, addition to tax, or additional amount with respect to a gross misstatement. A *gross misstatement* for purposes of this paragraph (b) means:

(A) a substantial omission of income as described in section 6501(e)(1) or section 6229(c)(2);

(B) a gross valuation misstatement within the meaning of section 6662(h)(2)(A) and (B); or

(C) a misstatement to which the penalty under section 6702(a) applies.

(ii) *Effect of gross misstatement.*—If a gross misstatement occurs, then paragraph (a) of this section does not apply to any interest, penalty, addition to tax, or additional amount with respect to any items of income omitted from the return and with respect to overstated deductions, even though one or more of the omitted items would not constitute a substantial omission, gross valuation misstatement, or misstatement to which section 6702(a) applies.

(5) *Listed transactions and undisclosed reportable transactions.*—(i) *In general.*—The general rule of suspension under section 6404(g)(1) does not apply to any interest, penalty, addition to tax, or additional amount with respect to any listed transaction as defined in section 6707A(c) or any

undisclosed reportable transaction. For purposes of this section, an *undisclosed reportable transaction* is a reportable transaction described in the regulations under section 6011 that is not adequately disclosed under those regulations and that is not a listed transaction. The date that the IRS provides notice to the taxpayer specifically stating the taxpayer's liability regarding a listed transaction or an undisclosed reportable transaction and the basis for that liability is the controlling date for determining whether the transaction is a listed transaction or an undisclosed reportable transaction for purposes of the suspension rules under section 6404(g).

(ii) *Special rule for certain listed or undisclosed reportable transactions.*—With respect to interest relating to listed transactions and undisclosed reportable transactions accruing on or before October 3, 2004, the exception to the general rule of interest suspension will not apply to a taxpayer who is a participant in a settlement initiative with respect to that transaction, to any transaction in which the taxpayer has acted reasonably and in good faith, or to a closed transaction. For purposes of this special rule, a "participant in a settlement initiative," a "taxpayer acting in good faith," and a "closed transaction" have the following meanings:

(A) *Participant in a settlement initiative.*—(1) *Participant in a settlement initiative who, as of January 23, 2006, had not reached agreement with the IRS.*—A *participant in a settlement initiative* includes a taxpayer who, as of January 23, 2006, was participating in a settlement initiative described in Internal Revenue Service Announcement 2005-80, 2005-2 C.B. 967. See § 601.601(d)(2)(ii)(b) of this chapter. A taxpayer participates in the initiative by complying with Section 5 of the Announcement. A taxpayer is not a participant in a settlement initiative if, after January 23, 2006, the taxpayer withdraws from or terminates participation in the initiative, or the IRS determines that a settlement agreement will not be reached under the initiative within a reasonable period of time.

(2) *Participant in a settlement initiative who, as of January 23, 2006, had reached agreement with the IRS.*—A *participant in a settlement initiative* is a taxpayer who, as of January 23, 2006, had entered into a settlement agreement under Announcement 2005-80 or any other prior or contemporaneous settlement initiative either offered through published guidance or, if the initiative was not formally published, direct contact with taxpayers known to have participated in a tax shelter promotion.

(B) *Taxpayer acting in good faith .*—(1) *In general.*—The IRS may suspend interest relating to a listed transaction or an undisclosed reportable transaction accruing on or before October 3, 2004, if the taxpayer has acted reasonably and in good faith. The IRS's determination of whether a taxpayer has acted reasonably and in good faith will take into account all the facts and circumstances surrounding the transaction. The facts

and circumstances include, but are not limited to, whether the taxpayer disclosed the transaction and the taxpayer's course of conduct after being identified as participating in the transaction, including the taxpayer's response to opportunities afforded to the taxpayer to settle the transaction, and whether the taxpayer engaged in unreasonable delay at any stage of the matter.

(2) *Presumption.*—If a taxpayer and the IRS promptly enter into a settlement agreement with respect to a transaction on terms proposed by the IRS or, in the event of atypical facts and circumstances, on terms more favorable to the taxpayer, and the taxpayer has complied with the terms of that agreement without unreasonable delay, the taxpayer will be presumed to have acted reasonably and in good faith except in rare and unusual circumstances. Rare and unusual circumstances must involve specific actions involving harm to tax administration. Even if a taxpayer does not qualify for the presumption described in this paragraph (b)(5)(iii)(B)(2), the taxpayer may still be granted interest suspension under the general facts and circumstances test set forth in paragraph (b)(5)(iii)(B)(1) of this section.

(3) *Examples.*—The following examples illustrate the rules the IRS uses in determining whether a taxpayer has acted reasonably and in good faith.

Example 1. The taxpayer participated in a listed transaction. The IRS, in a letter sent directly to the taxpayer in July 2005, proposed a settlement of the transaction. The taxpayer informed the IRS of his interest in the settlement within the prescribed time period. The revenue agent assigned to the taxpayer's case was not able to calculate the taxpayer's liability under the settlement or tender a closing agreement to the taxpayer until March 2006. The taxpayer promptly executed the closing agreement and returned it to the IRS with a proposal for arrangements to pay the agreed-upon liability. The IRS agreed with the proposed arrangements for full payment. For purposes of the application of section 6404(g)(2)(E), the taxpayer has acted reasonably and in good faith. Interest accruing on or before October 3, 2004, relating to the transaction in which the taxpayer participated will be suspended.

Example 2. The facts are the same as in *Example 1*, except that the letter was sent by the IRS in February 2006, and the closing agreement was tendered to the taxpayer in April 2006. For purposes of the application of section 6404(g)(2)(E), the taxpayer has acted reasonably and in good faith. Interest accruing on or before October 3, 2004, relating to the transaction in which the taxpayer participated will be suspended.

Example 3. The taxpayer participated in a listed transaction. In response to an offer of settlement extended by the IRS in August 2005, the taxpayer informed the IRS of her interest in entering into a closing agreement on the terms proposed by the IRS. The revenue agent assigned to the transaction calculated the taxpayer's liability under the settlement and tendered a closing agreement to the taxpayer in November 2005. The taxpayer executed the closing agreement but failed to make any arrangement for payment of the agreed-upon liability stated in the closing agreement. Taking into account all the facts and circumstances surrounding the transaction, the taxpayer did not act reasonably and in good faith. Interest accruing on or before October 3, 2004, relating to the transaction in which the taxpayer participated will not be suspended.

Example 4. The taxpayer participated in a listed transaction. In a letter sent by the IRS directly to the taxpayer in July 2005, the IRS extended an offer of settlement. The July 2005 letter informed the taxpayer that, absent atypical facts and circumstances, the taxpayer should not expect resolution of the tax issues on more favorable terms than proposed in the letter. The taxpayer declined the proposed settlement terms of the letter and proceeded to Appeals to present what the taxpayer claimed were atypical facts and circumstances. The administrative file did not contain sufficient information bearing on atypical facts and circumstances, and the taxpayer failed to provide additional information when requested by Appeals to explain how the transaction originally proposed to the taxpayer differed in structure or types of tax benefits claimed, from the transaction as implemented by the taxpayer. Appeals determined that the taxpayer's facts and circumstances were not significantly different from those of other taxpayers who participated in that listed transaction and thus, were not atypical. In September 2006, the taxpayer and Appeals entered into a closing agreement on terms consistent with those originally proposed in the July 2005 letter. The taxpayer has complied with the terms of that closing agreement. For purposes of the application of section 6404(g)(2)(E), this taxpayer is not presumed to have acted reasonably and in good faith; instead, the IRS will apply the general rule to determine whether to suspend interest accruing on or before October 3, 2004, relating to the transaction in which the taxpayer participated.

Example 5. The facts are the same as in *Example 4*, except that Appeals agrees that atypical facts were present that warrant additional concessions by the government. A settlement is reached on terms more favorable to the taxpayer than those proposed in the July 2005 letter. For purposes of the application of section 6404(g)(2)(E), this taxpayer is presumed to have acted reasonably and in good faith, and absent evidence of rare or unusual circumstances harmful to tax administration, is eligible for suspension of interest accruing on or before October 3, 2004, relating to the transaction in which the taxpayer participated.

(C) *Closed transactions.*—A transaction is considered closed for purposes of this clause if, as of December 14, 2005, the assessment of all federal income taxes for the taxable year in which the tax liability to which the interest relates is prevented by the operation of any law or rule of law, or a closing agreement under section 7121 has been entered into with respect to the tax liability arising in connection with the transaction.

(c) *Special rules.*—(1) *Tentative carryback and refund adjustments.*—If an amount applied, credited or refunded under section 6411 exceeds the overassessment properly attributable to a tentative carryback or refund adjustment, any interest, penalty, addition to tax, or additional amount with respect to the excess will not be suspended.

(2) *Election under section 183(e).*—(i) *In general.*—If a taxpayer elects under section 183(e) to defer the determination of whether the presumption that an activity is engaged in for profit applies, the 18-month (or 36-month) notification period described in paragraph (a)(1) of this section will be tolled for the period to which the election applies. If the 18-month (or 36-month) notification period has passed as of the date the section 183(e) election is made, the suspension period described in paragraph (a)(4) of this section will be tolled for the period to which the election applies and will resume the day after the tolling period ends. Tolling will begin on the date the election is made and end on the later of the date the return for the last taxable year to which the election applies is filed or is due without regard to extensions.

(ii) *Example.*—In taxable year 2007, taxpayer begins training and showing horses. On January 4, 2011, the taxpayer elects under section 183(e) to defer the determination of whether the horse-related activity will be presumed (under section 183(d)) to be engaged in for profit. Accordingly, under section 183(e)(1), a determination of whether the section 183(d) presumption applies will not occur before the close of the 2013 taxable year. Assume that in 2014, the IRS is considering issuing a notice of deficiency for taxable year 2009 regarding tax deductions claimed for the horse-related activity. Pursuant to paragraph (c)(2)(i) of this section, the 36-month notification period under paragraph (a)(1) of this section will be tolled with respect to taxable year 2009 for the period to which the section 183(e) election applies. This tolling of the notification period begins on January 4, 2011 (the date the taxpayer made the section 183(e) election) and ends on the later of April 15, 2014, or the date the taxpayer's return for taxable year 2013 is filed.

(d) *Effective/Applicability date.*—Paragraph (b)(5) of these regulations applies to interest relating to listed transactions and undisclosed reportable transactions accruing before, on, or after October 3, 2004. Paragraphs (a), (b)(1) through (b)(4), and (c) are effective on August 22, 2011. [Reg. § 301.6404-4.]

☐ [*T.D.* 9488, 6-15-2010. *Amended by T.D.* 9545, 8-19-2011.]

[Reg. § 301.6405-1]

§ 301.6405-1. Reports of refunds and credits.—Section 6405 requires that a report be made to the Joint Committee on Taxation of proposed refunds or credits in excess of $100,000 of any income tax (including any qualified State individual income tax collected by the Federal Government), war profits tax, excess profits tax, estate tax, or gift tax. An exception is provided under which refunds and credits made after July 1, 1972, and attributable to an election under section 165(h) to deduct a disaster loss for the taxable year in which the disaster occurred, may be made prior to the submission of such report to the Joint Committee on Taxation. [Reg. § 301.6405-1.]

☐ [*T.D. 6119, 12-31-54. Amended by T.D. 7224, 12-5-72 and T.D. 7577, 12-19-78.*]

[Reg. § 301.6407-1]

§ 301.6407-1. Date of allowance of refund or credit.—The date on which the district director or the director of the regional service center, or an authorized certifying officer designated by either of them, first certifies the allowance of an overassessment in respect of any internal revenue tax shall be considered as the date of allowance of refund or credit in respect of such tax. [Reg. § 301.6407-1.]

☐ [*T.D. 6119, 12-31-54. Amended by T.D. 6585, 12-27-61.*]

RULES OF SPECIAL APPLICATION

[Reg. § 1.6411-1]

§ 1.6411-1. Tentative carryback adjustments.—(a) *In general.*—Any taxpayer who has a net operating loss under section 172, a net capital loss under section 1211(a) which is a carryback under section 1212, or an unused investment credit under section 46, may file an application under section 6411 for a tentative carryback adjustment of the taxes for taxable years prior to the taxable year of the net operating or capital loss or the unused credit, whichever is applicable, which are affected by the net operating loss carryback, the capital loss carryback, or the unused investment credit carryback, resulting from such loss or unused credit. The regulations under section 6411 shall apply with respect to investment credit carrybacks for taxable years ending after December 31, 1961, but only with respect to applications for tentative carryback adjustments for investment credit carrybacks filed after November 2, 1966. The right to file an application for a tentative carryback adjustment is not limited to corporations, but is available to any taxpayer otherwise entitled to carry back a loss or unused credit. A corporation may file an application for a tentative carryback adjustment even though it has not extended the time for payment of tax under section 6164. In determining any decrease in tax under §§ 1.6411-1 through 1.6411-4, the decrease in tax is determined net of any increase in the tax imposed by section 56 (relating to the minimum tax for tax preferences).

(b) *Contents of application.*—(1) The application for a tentative carryback adjustment shall be filed, in the case of a corporation, on Form 1139, and in the case of taxpayers other than corporations, on Form 1045. The application shall be filled out in accordance with the instructions accompanying the form, and all information required by the form and the instructions must be furnished by the taxpayer.

(2) An application for a tentative carryback adjustment does not constitute a claim for credit or refund. If such application is disallowed by the district director or director of a service center

in whole or in part, no suit may be maintained in any court for the recovery of any tax based on such application. The filing of an application for a tentative carryback adjustment will not constitute the filing of a claim for credit or refund within the meaning of section 6511 for purposes of determining whether a claim for credit or refund was filed prior to the expiration of the applicable period of limitation. The taxpayer, however, may file a claim for credit or refund under section 6402 at any time prior to the expiration of the applicable period of limitation, and may maintain a suit based on such claim if it is disallowed or if the district director or director of a service center does not act on the claim within six months from the date it is filed. Such claim may be filed before, simultaneously with, or after the filing of the application for a tentative carryback adjustment. A claim for credit or refund under section 6402 filed after the filing of an application for a tentative carryback adjustment is not to be considered as an amendment of such application. Such claim, however, in proper cases may constitute an amendment to a prior claim filed under section 6402.

(c) *Time and place for filing application.*—Except as otherwise provided in this paragraph the application for a tentative carryback adjustment shall be filed on or after the date of the filing of the return for the taxable year of the net operating loss, net capital loss, or unused investment credit and shall be filed within a period of twelve months from the end of such taxable year. With respect to any portion of an investment credit carryback from a taxable year attributable to a net operating loss carryback or a capital loss carryback from a subsequent taxable year, the twelve-month period shall be measured from the end of such subsequent taxable year. In the case of an application for a tentative carryback adjustment attributable to the carryback of an unused investment credit, the twelve-month period for filing shall not expire before the close of December 31, 1966. Any application filed prior to the date on which the return for the taxable year of the loss or unused credit is filed shall be considered to have been filed on the date such return is filed. In the case of an application filed before April 15, 1968, the application shall be filed with the internal revenue officer to whom the tax was paid or by whom the assessment was made. Except as provided in paragraph (b) of §301.6091-1 (relating to hand-carried documents), in the case of an application filed after April 14, 1968, if the tax was paid to the Director of International Operations, the application shall be filed with him; otherwise the application shall be filed with the internal revenue office with which the return was filed. [Reg. §1.6411-1.]

☐ [T.D. 6364, 2-13-59. *Amended by T.D. 6862*, 11-17-65, *T.D.* 6950, 4-3-68, *T.D.* 7301, 1-3-74, *T.D.* 7564, 9-11-78 *and T.D.* 8107, 12-1-86.]

[Reg. §5.6411-1]

§5.6411-1. Tentative refund under claim of right adjustment (Temporary).—(a) *Effective date.*—This section applies to applications for tentative refunds filed after November 5, 1978, under section 6411(d).

(b) *In general.*—Section 6411(d) allows taxpayers to apply for a tentative refund of amounts treated under section 1341(b)(1) as an overpayment of tax under a claim of right adjustment. This section contains rules for filing an application for this tentative refund. The computation of amounts treated as an overpayment must be made in accordance with section 1341 and the regulations under that section.

(c) *Method of applying for tentative refund.*—(1) *In general.*—For a corporation, the application is made by filing Form 1139. For taxpayers other than corporations, the application is made by filing Form 1045. The application must be made by filing those forms even if the taxpayer is not applying for a tentative carryback adjustment under section 6411(a). If the taxpayer files the form to apply for the section 6411(d) tentative refund only, it may disregard those lines on the form used to compute the section 6411(a) carryback adjustment. If the taxpayer has a carryback of a net operating loss, credit, or capital loss for the taxable year (determined without the deduction described in section 1341(a)(2)) and applies for both the section 6411(a) tentative carryback adjustment and the section 6411(d) tentative refund, an ordering rule applies. The taxpayer must take into account any adjustments made in applying for the tentative carryback adjustment under section 6411(a) before determining the amount of the overpayment for which an application under section 6411(d) is being made. The taxpayer must attach to the form a separate schedule containing the information required under paragraph (d) of this section.

(2) *Applications made before.*—February 7, 1980. Applications made before February 7, 1980 that are made under penalties of perjury will be considered meeting the requirements of this section if made by filing a separate statement whether or not it is attached to Form 1139 or 1045. This application, however, must contain the information required under paragraph (d) of this section (other than paragraph (d)(2)).

(d) *Information required.*—(1) *In general.*—The application must contain (i) the taxpayer's name, address, and identification number and (ii) the information set forth in paragraph (d)(2) and (3) of this section, determined in accordance with section 1341 and the regulations under that section. For example, the decrease in tax under paragraph (d)(3)(iii) of this section is determined under §1.1341-1(d)(4).

(2) *Computation under section 1341(a)(4).*—The application must contain the following information related to the computation under section 1341(a)(4):

(i) The amount of income restored by the taxpayer to another during the taxable year and the amount of the corresponding deduction described in section 1341(a)(2);

(ii) The tax for the taxable year computed with the deduction described in section 1341(a)(2); and

(iii) The tax for each prior taxable year (determined before adjustment under section 1341) to which any net operating loss described in section 1341(b)(4)(A) may be carried and the decrease in tax for each of those years that results from the carryback of that loss.

(3) *Computation under section 1341(a)(5).*—The application must contain the following information related to the computation under section 1341(a)(5):

(i) The tax for the taxable year without the deduction described in section 1341(a)(2);

(ii) The tax for each prior taxable year (determined before adjustment under section 1341) for which a decrease in tax is computed under section 1341(a)(5)(B);

(iii) The decrease in tax for each prior taxable year computed under section 1341(a)(5)(B), including any decrease resulting from a net operating loss or capital loss described in section 1341(b)(4)(B); and

(iv) The amount treated as an overpayment of tax under section 1341(b)(1).

(e) *Time and place for filing.*—The application must be filed no earlier than the date of filing the return for the taxable year of restoration and no later than the date 12 months from the last day of that taxable year. The application must be filed with the Internal Revenue Service Center (or other office) where the taxpayer filed its return for the taxable year of restoration.

(f) *Not a claim for credit or refund.*—An application for tentative refund under section 6411(d) is not a claim for credit or refund. The principles of paragraph (b)(2) of §1.6411-1 apply in determining the effect of an application for a tentative refund. For example, the filing of an application for tentative refund under section 6411(d) is not a claim for credit or refund in determining whether a claim for credit or refund was timely filed. [Temporary Reg. §5.6411-1.]

☐ [*T.D.* 7672, 2-6-80.]

[Reg. § 301.6411-1]

§ 301.6411-1. Tentative carryback adjustments.—For regulations under this section 6411, see §§ 1.6411-1 to 1.6411-4, inclusive, of this chapter (Income Tax Regulations). [Reg. § 301.6411-1.]

☐ [T.D. 6119, 12-31-54. Amended by T.D. 6498, 10-24-60.]

[Reg. § 1.6411-2]

§ 1.6411-2. Computation of tentative carryback adjustment.—(a) *Tax previously determined.*—The taxpayer is to determine the amount of decrease, attributable to the carryback, in tax previously determined for each taxable year before the taxable year of the net operating loss, net capital loss, or unused investment credit. The tax previously determined is to be ascertained in accordance with the method prescribed in section 1314(a). Thus, the tax previously determined will be the tax shown on the return as filed, increased by any amounts assessed (or collected without assessment) as deficiencies before the date of the filing of the application for a tentative carryback adjustment, and decreased by any amounts abated, credited, refunded, or otherwise repaid prior to that date. Any items as to which the Commissioner and the taxpayer are in disagreement at the time of the filing of the application shall, for purposes of § 1.6411-2, be taken into account in ascertaining the tax previously determined only if, and to the extent that, they were reported on the return, or were reflected in any amounts assessed (or collected without assessment) as deficiencies, or in any amounts abated, credited, refunded, or otherwise repaid, before the date of filing the application. The tax previously determined, therefore, will reflect the foreign tax credit and the credit for tax withheld at source provided in section 33.

(b) *Decrease attributable to carryback.*—After ascertaining the tax previously determined in the manner described in paragraph (a) of this section, the taxpayer shall determine the decrease in tax previously determined attributable to the carryback and any related adjustments on the basis of the items of tax taken into account in computing the tax previously determined. In determining any decrease attributable to the carryback or any related adjustment, items shall be taken into account under this subsection only to the extent that they were reported on the return, or were reflected in amounts assessed (or collected without assessment) as deficiencies, or in amounts abated, credited, refunded, or otherwise repaid, before the date of filing the application for a tentative carryback adjustment. If the Commissioner and the taxpayer are in disagreement as to the proper treatment of any item, it shall be assumed, for purposes of determining the decrease in the tax previously determined, that the item was reported correctly by the taxpayer unless, and to the extent that, the disagreement has resulted in the assessment of a deficiency (or the collection of an amount without an assessment), or the allowing or making of an abatement, credit, refund, or other repayment, before the date of filing the application. Thus, if the taxpayer claimed a deduction on its return of $50,000 for salaries paid its officers but the Commissioner proposes that the deduction should not exceed $20,000, and the Commissioner and the taxpayer have not agreed on the amount properly deductible before the date the application for a tentative carryback adjustment is filed, $50,000 shall be considered as the amount properly deductible for purposes of determining the decrease in tax previously determined in respect of the application for a tentative carryback adjustment. In determining the decrease in tax previously determined, any items that are affected by the carryback must be adjusted to reflect the carryback. Thus, unless otherwise provided, any deduction limited, for example, by adjusted gross income, such as the deduction for medical, dental, etc., expenses, is to be recomputed on the basis of the adjusted gross income as affected by the carryback. See § 1.6411-3(d) for rules on the application of the decrease in tax to any tax liability.

(c) *Effective/applicability date.*—These regulations apply with respect to applications for tentative refund filed on or after August 27, 2007. [Reg. § 1.6411-2.]

☐ [T.D. 6364, 2-13-59. Amended by T.D. 7301, 1-3-74; T.D. 9355, 8–24–2007 and T.D. 9499, 8-23-2010.]

[Reg. § 1.6411-3]

§ 1.6411-3. Allowance of adjustments.—(a) *Time prescribed.*—The Commissioner shall act upon any application for a tentative carryback adjustment filed under section 6411(a) within a period of 90 days from whichever of the following two dates is the later:

(1) The date the application is filed; or

(2) The last day of the month in which falls the last date prescribed by law (including any extension of time granted the taxpayer) for filing the return for the taxable year of the net operating loss, net capital loss, or unused investment credit from which the carryback results.

(b) *Examination.*—Within the 90-day period described in paragraph (a) of this section, the Commissioner shall make, to the extent deemed practicable within this period, an examination of the application to discover omissions and errors of computation. The Commissioner shall determine within this period the decrease in tax previously determined, affected by the carryback or any related adjustments, upon the basis of the application and examination. The decrease shall be determined in the same manner as that provided in section 1314(a) for the determination by the taxpayer of the decrease in taxes previously determined, which must be set forth in the application for a tentative carryback adjustment. The Commissioner, may correct any errors of computation or omissions discovered upon examination of the application. In determining the decrease in tax previously determined which is affected by the carryback or any related adjustment, the Commissioner may correct any mathematical error appearing on the application and may correct any modification required by the law and incorrectly made by the taxpayer in computing the net operating loss, net capital loss, or unused investment credit, the resulting carrybacks, or the net operating loss deduction, capital loss deduction, or investment credit allowable. If the required modification has not been made by the taxpayer and the Commissioner has the necessary information to make the modification within the 90-day period, the Commissioner may, in the Commissioner's discretion, make the modification. In determining the decrease, the Commissioner will not, for example, change the amount claimed on the return as a deduction for depreciation because the Commissioner believes that the taxpayer has claimed an excessive amount; and the Commissioner will not include in gross income any amount not so included by the taxpayer, even though the Commissioner believes that the amount is subject to tax and properly should be included in gross income.

(c) *Disallowance in whole or in part.*—If the Commissioner finds that an application for a tentative carryback adjustment contains material omissions or errors of computation, the Commissioner may disallow the application in whole or in part without further action. If the Commissioner deems that any error of computation can be corrected within the 90-day period, the Commissioner may do so and allow the application in whole or in part. The Commissioner's determination as to whether the Commissioner can correct any error of computation within the 90-day period shall be conclusive. The Commissioner's action in disallowing, in whole or in part, any application for a tentative carryback adjustment shall be final and may not be challenged in any proceeding. The taxpayer may, however, file a claim for credit or refund under section 6402, and may maintain a suit based on the claim if the claim is disallowed or if the Commissioner does not act upon the claim within 6 months from the date it is filed.

(d) *Application of decrease.*—(1) Each decrease determined by the Commissioner in any previously determined tax that is affected by the carryback or any related adjustments shall first be applied against any unpaid amount of the tax with respect to which such decrease was determined. The unpaid amount of tax may include one or more of the following:

(i) An amount with respect to which the taxpayer is delinquent;

(ii) An amount the time for payment of which has been extended under section 6164 and which is due and payable on or after the date of the allowance of the decrease;

(iii) An amount (not including an amount the time for payment of which has been ex-

tended under section 6164) which is due and payable on or after the date of the allowance of the decrease, including any assessed liabilities, unassessed liabilities determined in a statutory notice of deficiency, unassessed liabilities identified in a proof of claim filed in a bankruptcy proceeding, and other unassessed liabilities in rare and unusual circumstances.

(2) If the unpaid amount of tax includes more than one unpaid amount, the Commissioner may determine against which amount or amounts, and in what proportion, the decrease is to be applied. In general, however, the decrease will be applied against any amounts described in paragraphs (d)(1)(i) through (iii) of this section in the order named. If there are several amounts of the type described in paragraph (d)(1)(iii) of this section, any amount of the decrease that is to be applied against the amount will be applied by assuming that the tax previously determined minus the amount of the decrease to be so applied is "the tax" and that the taxpayer had elected to pay the tax in installments. The unpaid amount of tax against which a decrease may be applied under paragraph (d)(1) of this section may not include any amount of tax for any taxable year other than the year of the decrease. After making the application, the Commissioner will credit any remainder of the decrease against any unsatisfied amount of any tax for the taxable year immediately preceding the taxable year of the net operating loss, capital loss, or unused investment credit, the time for payment of which has been extended under section 6164.

(3) Any remainder of the decrease after the application and credits may, within the 90-day period, in the discretion of the Commissioner, be credited against any tax liability or installment thereof then due from the taxpayer (including assessed liabilities, unassessed liabilities determined in a statutory notice of deficiency, unassessed liabilities identified in a proof of claim filed in a bankruptcy proceeding, and other unassessed liabilities in rare and unusual circumstances), and, if not so credited, shall be refunded to the taxpayer within the 90-day period.

(e) *Effective/applicability date.*—These regulations apply with respect to applications for tentative refund filed on or after August 27, 2007. [Reg. § 1.6411-3.]

☐ [T.D. 6364, 2-13-59. *Amended by T.D.* 6950, 4-3-68; *T.D.* 7301, 1-3-74; *T.D.* 9355, 8-24-2007 *and T.D.* 9499, 8-23-2010.]

[Reg. § 1.6411-4]

§ 1.6411-4. Consolidated groups.—For further rules applicable to consolidated groups, see § 1.1502-78. For further rules applicable to consolidated groups that include insolvent financial institutions, see § 301.6402-7 of this chapter. [Reg. § 1.6411-4.]

☐ [T.D. 6364, 2-13-59. *Amended by T.D.* 7244, 12-29-72; *T.D.* 8387, 12-30-91 *and T.D.* 8446, 11-5-92.]

[Reg. §48.6412-1]

§48.6412-1. Floor stocks credit or refund.—
(a) *In general.*—This section sets forth the procedures to be followed in claiming the credit or refund authorized by section 6412 for manufacturers excise taxes paid in respect of certain articles held by dealers as floor stocks on October 1, 1988. See §48.6412-2 for definitions of the following terms when used in this section: "floor stocks", "inventory date", "dealer", "held by a dealer", "old rate", "new rate", "dealer request limitation date", "claim limitation date", and "tax paid". See §48.6412-3 for determining the amount of tax paid on articles that are held as floor stocks. The manufacturers excise taxes for which credit or refund may be claimed under this section are those imposed by section 4071, relating to tires of the type used on highway vehicles; and section 4081, relating to gasoline. For definition of the term "highway vehicle", see §48.4061(a)-1(d).

(b) *Computation of the amount of floor stocks credit or refund.*—The amount of floor stocks credit or refund which may be claimed by the manufacturer under section 6412(a)(1) may not exceed an amount equal to the difference between the tax paid by the manufacturer on the sale of the article and the amount of tax made applicable to the article on the inventory date. No interest is allowable with respect to any amount of tax credited or refunded under section 6412 and this section. In applying the floor stocks credit or refund provisions, the date on which the manufacturer paid the tax with respect to the article held as floor stocks is not relevant. Thus, the period of limitations provided in section 6511 with respect to claims for credit or refund does not apply; however, see paragraph (f) of this section. For definition of the term "manufacturer", see §48.0-2(a)(4).

(c) *Limitation.*—Except as provided in §48.6412-3, no credit or refund is allowable under this section for an amount paid as tax which may be credited or refunded under any provisions of law other than section 6412(a)(1), or which was allowable as a credit or refund under section 6412 with respect to an earlier inventory date.

(d) *Relationship between credits or refunds for floor stocks and credits or refunds for price readjustments.*—The amount which may be credited or refunded for floor stocks and for price readjustments on an article may not in the aggregate exceed the tax paid in respect of the article. A credit or refund computed on the basis of the old tax rate will be allowed with respect to a price readjustment of an article on which a floor stock credit or refund was allowed, but only if the amount of the floor stock credit or refund otherwise allowable was reduced by taking into account such price readjustment, as determined under §48.6412-3(e). The manufacturer must keep readily available for inspection sufficient records to enable examining officers of the Internal Revenue Service to ascertain the correctness of any claim for credit or refund for a price readjustment of an article on which a floor stock refund was claimed.

(e) *Participation of dealers.*—(1) *Request by dealer.*—On or before the dealer request limitation date, a dealer may submit to a manufacturer a request with respect to a credit or refund allowable under this section for tax paid by the manufacturer with respect to articles held by the dealer as floor stocks. This request may be submitted directly to the manufacturer, or it may be submitted to him indirectly through another dealer in the distribution chain if the request is received by the manufacturer or an authorized agent of the manufacturer on or before the dealer request limitation date.

(2) *Requirements for claim by manufacturer.*—No amount of credit or refund under this section may be claimed by a manufacturer with respect to articles held by a dealer as floor stocks unless—

(i) The claim for the amount is based upon a request submitted by the dealer to the claimant on or before the dealer request limitation date;

(ii) The amount is paid by the claimant to the dealer, or the dealer's written consent to allowance of the credit or refund has been received by the claimant, on or before the claim limitation date; and

(iii) The request by the dealer is supported by an inventory statement, made under the penalties of perjury and signed by the dealer or by the dealer's authorized representative, setting forth the following information:

(A) The name and address of the dealer and of the applicable manufacturer (if the name and address of the applicable manufacturer is unknown to the dealer, these items may be added by any person in the chain of distribution);

(B) The identification number, if any, of the article, such as a serial, stock, model, type, or class number, or some other suitable means of identification;

(C) A brief description of the article, such as its common name or designation; and

(D) The quantity of articles held by the dealer as floor stocks on the inventory date.

(3) *Actual manufacturer unknown.*—If a dealer addresses a request to the person, who from markings on the article the dealer presumes to be the manufacturer, the request may be treated as made to the actual manufacturer if the actual manufacturer accepts the dealer's request.

(4) *Payment to dealer by claimant.*—Payment may be made directly to the dealer or to the dealer's authorized agent or representative by the claimant or by the claimant's authorized agent or representative. If a claimant pays a dealer through the claimant's agent or representative, the evidence must show that the dealer actually received the payment. If a dealer authorizes the claimant to pay the dealer through the dealer's agent or representative, evidence show-

ing receipt of the payment by the agent or representative will be accepted as proof of actual payment to the dealer. Payment shall be made, at the manufacturer's option, in cash, by check, or by credit to the dealer's account as maintained by the claimant. The amount of the payment which may be made by crediting the dealer's account may not exceed the undisputed debit balance due at the time the credit is made. However, payment may be made in merchandise at the dealer's option with the concurrence of the manufacturer.

(5) *Date of performance.*—The date on which any act described in this paragraph (e) is performed by an agent or representative on behalf of a claimant or dealer is deemed to be the date on which the act is performed by the principal.

(6) *Record of inventories.*—For provisions relating to the record of a dealer's inventories to be kept by the claimant, see paragraph (g) of this section.

(7) *Sample written consent.*—No particular form is prescribed or required for the written consent of the dealer described in paragraph (e)(2)(ii) of this section. However, the following is an example of an acceptable consent statement by a dealer:

Consent Statement of Dealer

(For use by dealer in requesting manufacturer, producer, or importer to obtain credit under section 6412 of the Internal Revenue Code of 1954 with respect to floor stocks.)

I hereby consent to the allowance to the manufacturer, producer, or importer of the floor stocks credit or refund of the excise tax imposed by the Internal Revenue Code of 1954 with respect to the articles in my inventory on_____

(Name)

By_____

(Signature of Officer)

_____

(Title)

_____

(Date)

(f) *Procedure for claiming credit or refund.*—(1) *In general.*—Each claim for credit or refund under this section shall be filed on or before the applicable claim limitation date, in the manner and subject to the conditions stated in this section and in §301.6402-2 of this chapter (Regulations on Procedure and Administration). Either credit or refund, or a combination thereof, may be claimed, but the amount which may be claimed as a credit on a return shall not exceed the total tax liability shown on the return, reduced by the amount of any deposits made under §48.6302(c)-1 with respect to the return and by any amount of credit claimed on the return pursuant to any provision of law other than section 6412. If the total amount which may be claimed exceeds the amount that may be claimed as credit on a return, the excess amount may be claimed on or before the applicable claim

limitation date either as a refund or as a credit on a subsequent return. If credit is claimed the amount of the credit shall be entered as a credit on a timely filed return of tax. The statement described in paragraph (f)(2) of this section must show the amount and date of each previous and concurrent claim for credit or refund under this section and indicate whether any future claims are expected to be filed.

(2) *Supporting evidence to be submitted by the manufacturer.*—No credit or refund shall be allowed under this section unless there is submitted, in support of the claim for credit or refund, a statement signed by the person making the claim, that describes in general terms the articles covered by the claim, sets forth the method of computing the amount claimed (including a description of any procedures used pursuant to §48.6412-3), and states that—

(i) The claimant paid to the district director or the director of the internal revenue service center the tax for which credit or refund is claimed;

(ii) The total amount claimed represents payments requested by dealers before the dealer request limitation date;

(iii) The total amount claimed either was paid by the claimant to the dealers, or the claimant received the written consent of the dealers to the allowance of the amount claimed;

(iv) The claimant has in his possession, and available for inspection by internal revenue officers, the evidence with respect to inventories required by paragraph (g)(2) of this section, and any written consents referred to in paragraph (f)(2)(iii) of this section; and

(v) No other claim for credit or refund under this section has been or will be made by the claimant with respect to any amount covered by the claim.

(g) *Evidence to be retained in the manufacturer's records.*—Every person filing a claim for credit or refund pursuant to this section shall support the claim by keeping as part of the claimant's records—

(1) The dealer's inventory statements required by paragraph (e)(2)(iii) of this section, to the extent that the articles are covered by the claim;

(2) Records, in respect of the articles held by each dealer, showing—

(i) The name and address of the dealer.

(ii) The quantities of each article held by the dealer as floor stocks by taxable category, for example, by model or type number.

(iii) The amount of tax considered to be paid by the manufacturer with respect to each article held by the dealer, as determined under §48.6412-3,

(iv) The amount of tax, if any, which the claimant would pay on the sale of each article held by the dealer if the tax were computed at the new rate,

(v) The total amount of reimbursement due the dealer.

(vi) The date on which the claimant received from the dealer the request described in paragraph (e)(1) of this section, but only if payment was not made to the dealer before the dealer request limitation date, and

(vii) The date and amount of each payment to a dealer, or the date of receipt by the claimant from the dealer of a written consent, as set forth in paragraph (e)(2)(ii) of this section; and

(3) Any such written consent received from a dealer.

(h) *Special rules where the presumed manufacturer is the agent of the actual manufacturer.*—For purposes of this section, if a manufacturer sells articles tax-paid to a second manufacturer for resale by the second manufacturer under its own brand name, the second manufacturer may perform any acts and keep any records which are a prerequisite to the first manufacturer's filing a claim for floor stocks credit or refund with respect to the articles. If such a procedure is followed, the claim filed by the first manufacturer shall include a statement indicating the name and address of the second manufacturer and the amount of its claim which relates to articles sold to the second manufacturer.

(i) *Effect on other claims for credit or refund.*—If a claim for credit or refund is made pursuant to section 6416 and the regulations thereunder, relating in part to returned sales, sales for export or for exempt use, sales to States, etc., with respect to a tax imposed by section 4071 or section 4081, and if the claim is made with respect to articles sold by the claimant before the date on which the tax is reduced in rate or terminated, the claim shall be based on the new rate of tax unless the claimant can establish that the tax was imposed at the old rate and that no refund or credit under this section was allowed with respect to the articles. See, however, paragraph (d) of this section.

(j) *Other applicable provisions.*—All provisions of law, including penalties, applicable in respect of the taxes imposed by sections 4071 and 4081 shall, insofar as applicable and not inconsistent with section 6412, apply in respect to the credits and refunds provided for in section 6412 to the same extent as if the credits or refunds constituted overpayments of the taxes. For provisions under which timely mailing is treated as timely filing, and for provisions applicable to the time for performance of acts when the last day falls on Saturday, Sunday, or a legal holiday, see §§ 301.7502-1 and 301.7503-1, respectively, of this chapter (Regulations on Procedure and Administration). [Reg. § 48.6412-1.]

☐ [*T.D.* 8043, 8-8-85.]

[Reg. § 48.6412-2]

§ 48.6412-2. Definitions for purposes of floor stocks credit or refund.—For purposes of section 6412 and the regulations thereunder—

(a) *Floor stocks.*—The term "floor stocks" means any article subject to the tax imposed by section 4071 or section 4081 which—

(1) Is sold by the manufacturer (otherwise than in a tax-free sale) before October 1, 1988,

(2) Is held by a dealer at the first moment on October 1, 1988, and has not been used, and

(3) Is intended for sale.

However, the term "floor stocks" does not include gasoline in retail stocks held at the place where intended to be sold at retail, nor with respect to gasoline held for sale by a producer or importer of gasoline.

(b) *Inventory date.*—The term "inventory date" means the first moment on the date on which an article is treated as floor stocks within the meaning of paragraph (a) of this section.

(c) *Dealer.*—The term "dealer" includes a wholesaler, jobber, distributor, or retailer.

(d) *Held by a dealer.*—(1) *In general.*—(i) An article is considered as "held by a dealer" if title to the article has passed to the dealer (whether or not delivery to the dealer has been made), and if, for purposes of consumption, title to or possession of the article has not at any time been transferred to any person other than a dealer.

(ii) Floor samples, demonstrators, and articles undergoing repair (whether or not on the dealer's premises) that are carried in stock to be sold as new articles, and articles purchased tax-paid by a manufacturer or a sales subsidiary and held by the person on the inventory date for resale as such, will be considered as unused and held by a dealer, if title to or possession of the article has not at any time been transferred to any person for purposes of consumption.

(iii) Articles sold by a dealer to a consumer before the inventory date and thereafter repossessed by the dealer, and articles purchased tax-paid by a manufacturer for use in further manufacture within the meaning of section 4221(d)(6), will not be considered as held by a dealer.

(iv) The determination as to the time title or possession passes for purposes of consumption shall be made under applicable local law.

(2) *Examples.*—The application of this paragraph (d) may be illustrated by the following examples:

Example (1). If, under local law, title to an article sold by a dealer under a conditional sales contract is in the dealer on the inventory date, but the consumer has physical possession of the article on that date, the article is not considered as held by the dealer.

Example (2). If, under local law, title to an article is in the consumer on the inventory date because the article is specifically identified with a contract, but on that date the dealer still has physical possession of the article, for example, in his will-call department, the article is not considered as held by the dealer on that date because title to the article has passed to the consumer for purposes of consumption.

Example (3). If, under local law, title to an article is in the consumer on the inventory date because the dealer transferred the article to a common carrier for delivery to the consumer, the article in transit is not considered as held by the dealer on that date because title has passed to the consumer for purposes of consumption, even though neither the dealer nor the consumer has physical possession of the article.

Example (4). If, under local law, title to an article is in the dealer on the inventory date and does not pass to the consumer until delivery by a common carrier, the article in transit shall be considered as held by the dealer on that date because neither the title nor possession has passed to the consumer for purposes of consumption.

Example (5). If an article has been mortgaged or otherwise hypothecated by a dealer as security for a loan and, under local law, title to the article is in the creditor on the inventory date, and physical possession is in the dealer, the article shall be considered as held by the dealer on that date because neither title nor possession has passed to the consumer for purposes of consumption.

(e) *Old rate*.—The term "old rate" means the rate of tax in effect with respect to the sale of an article before the date designated in paragraph (a) or (b) of this section on which the tax is reduced in rate or is terminated.

(f) *New rate*.—The term "new rate" means the rate of tax, if any, in effect with respect to the sale of an article on the date designated in paragraph (a) or (b) of this section on which the tax is reduced in rate or is terminated.

(g) *Dealer request limitation date*.—The term "dealer request limitation date" is the date prescribed by section 6412(a)(1) before which the request on which the manufacturer's claim is based must be submitted to the manufacturer by the dealer who held the floor stocks on the inventory date. In the case of an article held by a dealer on October 1, 1988, the dealer request limitation date is January 1, 1989.

(h) *Claim limitation date*.—The term "claim limitation date" means the last date prescribed by section 6412(a)(1) on which refund or credit with respect to floor stocks may be claimed by a manufacturer. In the case of an article held by a dealer on October 1, 1988, the claim limitation date is March 31, 1989.

(i) *Tax paid*.—A tax is considered paid if it was paid or was offset by an allowable credit on the return on which it was reported. [Reg. § 48.6412-2.]

☐ [*T.D.* 8043, 8-8-85.]

[Reg. § 48.6412-3]

§ 48.6412-3. Amount of tax paid on each article.—(a) *General rule*.—For purposes of making the claim for credit or refund under § 48.6412-1 in respect of floor stocks held by a dealer, the tax paid on each article must be separately computed. If desired, the procedures set forth in paragraphs (b) through (g) of this section may be used in making the computation. The procedure used in determining the tax paid on an article must also be used in determining the amount of tax, if any, made applicable to the article on the effective date of reduction or repeal of the tax involved. Prior approval of the Internal Revenue Service for the method of computation need not be obtained and should not be requested.

(b) *Selling price*.—In determining the price of an article on which the tax paid is to be computed, the average of the gross selling prices of identical articles sold during a representative period may be used. For example, truck chassis of the same model that are sold by the manufacturer with the same equipment and accessories are identical articles whose selling prices may be computed on the basis of an average.

(c) *Transportation charges*.—In determining the price of an article on which the tax paid is to be computed, the average of the exclusions authorized by section 4216(a) for transportation, delivery, insurance, installation, etc., for a reasonable category of articles during a representative period may be used.

(d) *Credits for tax paid on inner tubes*.—The average of the credits authorized by section 6416(c) for tax paid on tires or inner tubes may be averaged for a reasonable category of articles during a representative period. The credits shall be subtracted from the gross excise tax to arrive at the net excise tax paid.

(e) *Price readjustments*.—(1) In determining the price on which the tax paid is to be computed, there must be taken into account any price readjustments with respect to which the manufacturer has filed a claim for credit or refund under section 6416(b). Other price readjustments which have been, or are reasonably expected to be, made with respect to the article may, at the option of the manufacturer, be taken into account in computing the price of the article.

(2) Price readjustments which cannot be attributed to specific articles as of the inventory date (as, for example, a price readjustment of a flat dollar amount which is made to dealers who meet a sales quota) may be taken into account on the basis of an average of the adjustments which is computed for a reasonable category of articles over a representative period.

(3) Price readjustments related to specific items (as, for example, an automatic rebate of a specific percentage of the price of each unit sold to a dealer) may not be averaged, and in such a case only the actual price readjustment attributable to a particular article may be taken into account in computing the tax on that article.

(4) If, because of the facts in a case, a price readjustment can be attributed to specific articles for purposes of consumer refunds but cannot be attributed to specific articles for purposes of floor stocks credits or refunds, the price adjustment may be averaged for purposes of both consumer refunds and floor stocks credits and refunds.

(f) *Representative period.*—A period will be considered a representative period if—

(1) It covers (i) at least four consecutive calendar quarters, the last of which ends with a period of six calendar months immediately preceding the effective date of the tax reduction or repeal involved or (ii) any other period of time which the taxpayer can demonstrate constitutes a representative period for the particular category, and

(2) The number of articles in the category involved sold by the manufacturer during the period either (i) equals or exceeds the number of articles in the category to which the average amount is to be applied or (ii) can be demonstrated by the taxpayer to be a representative quantity.

(g) *Reasonable category.*—Examples of a reasonable category of articles are articles that are identified by a common stock or class number or which are of the same model, class, or line. For the purpose of averaging exclusions, another example of a reasonable category of articles is a grouping of articles that are shipped in the same container. If a manufacturer sells articles bearing his own trademark and also sells articles as private brands, separate computations of the two brands must be made under this section. [Reg. § 48.6412-3.]

☐ *[T.D. 8043, 8-8-85.]*

[Reg. § 301.6413-1]

§ 301.6413-1. Special rules applicable to certain employment taxes.—For regulations under section 6413, see §§ 31.6413(a)-1 to 31.6413(c)-1, inclusive, of this chapter (Employment Tax Regulations). [Reg. § 301.6413-1.]

☐ *[T.D. 6498, 10-24-60.]*

[Reg. § 31.6413(a)-1]

§ 31.6413(a)-1. Repayment or reimbursement by employer of tax erroneously collected from employee.—(a) *Federal Insurance Contributions Act and Railroad Retirement Tax Act.*—(1) *Overcollection ascertained before return is filed.*—(i) If an employer during any return period collects from an employee more than the correct amount of employee Federal Insurance Contributions Act (FICA) tax under section 3101 or employee Railroad Retirement Tax Act (RRTA) tax under section 3201, and if the employer ascertains the error before filing the return on which the employee tax is required to be reported, repays or reimburses the amount of the overcollection to the employee before filing the return for such return period, and obtains and keeps as part of its records the written receipt of the employee showing the date and amount of the repayment or evidence of reimbursement, the employer shall not report on any return or pay to the IRS the amount of the overcollection.

(ii) Any overcollection not repaid or reimbursed to the employee as provided in paragraph (a)(1)(i) of this section shall be reported and paid to the IRS on the return for reporting such tax for the return period in which the overcollection is made. However, the reporting and payment of the overcollection may subsequently be treated as an overpayment error ascertained after the return is filed for purposes of paragraph (a)(2) of this section.

(iii) For purposes of this paragraph (a)(1), an error is ascertained when the employer has sufficient knowledge of the error to be able to correct it.

(2) *Error ascertained after return is filed.*—(i) Except as provided in paragraph (a)(2)(ii) of this section, if an employer files a return for a return period on which FICA tax or RRTA tax is reported, collects from an employee and pays to the IRS more than the correct amount of the employee FICA or RRTA tax, and if the employer ascertains the error after filing the return and within the applicable period of limitations on credit or refund, the employer shall repay or reimburse the employee in the amount of the overcollection prior to the expiration of such limitations period. However, this paragraph (a)(2) does not apply to the extent that, after reasonable efforts, the employer cannot locate the employee, or the employee does not provide the employer with the written statement required by § 31.6413(a)-1(a)(2)(iv). This paragraph (a)(2) has no application in any case in which an overcollection is made the subject of a claim by the employer for refund or credit under the procedure provided in § 31.6402(a)-2.

(ii) If an employer files a return for a return period on which Additional Medicare Tax under section 3101(b)(2) or section 3201(a) is reported, collects from an employee and pays to the IRS more than the correct amount of Additional Medicare Tax required to be withheld from wages or compensation, and if the employer ascertains the error after filing the return but before the end of the calendar year in which the wages or compensation were paid, the employer shall repay or reimburse the employee in the amount of the overcollection prior to the end of the calendar year. However, this paragraph does not apply to the extent that, after reasonable efforts, the employer cannot locate the employee.

(iii) If the employer repays the amount of the overcollection to an employee, the employer shall obtain and keep as part of its records the written receipt of the employee, showing the date and amount of the repayment.

(iv) If the employer reimburses the amount of the overcollection to an employee, the employer shall keep as part of its records evidence of reimbursement. However, for purposes of overcollected Additional Medicare Tax under section 3101(b)(2) or section 3201(a), the employer shall reimburse the employee by applying the amount of the overcollection against the employee FICA or RRTA tax which attaches to wages or compensation paid by the employer to the employee in the calendar year in which the overcollection is made. The employer shall reimburse the employee by applying the amount of the overcollection against the employee FICA or RRTA tax which attaches to wages or compensation paid by the employer to the employee prior to the expiration of the applicable period of limitations on credit or refund. If the amount of the overcollection exceeds the amount so applied against such employee tax, the excess amount shall be repaid to the employee as required by this section.

(v) If, in any calendar year, an employer repays or reimburses an employee in the amount of an overcollection of employee FICA or RRTA tax that was collected from the employee in a prior calendar year, the employer shall obtain from the employee and keep as part of its records a written statement that the employee has not claimed refund or credit of the amount of the overcollection, or if so, such claim has been rejected, and that the employee will not claim refund or credit of such amount. For this purpose, a claim for refund or credit by the employee includes instances in which the employee has included an overcollection of employee FICA or RRTA tax in computing a special refund (see § 31.6413(c)-1. This paragraph (a)(2)(v) does not apply for purposes of overcollected Additional Medicare Tax under section 3101(b)(2) or section 3201(a) which must be repaid or reimbursed to the employee in the calendar year in which the overcollection is made.

(vi) For purposes of this paragraph (a)(2), an error is ascertained when the employer has sufficient knowledge of the error to be able to correct it.

(vii) For the period of limitations on credit or refund of taxes, see § 301.6511(a)-1.

(viii) For corrections of FICA and RRTA tax paid under the wrong chapter, see § 31.6205-1(b)(2)(ii) and (iii) and § 31.3503-1.

(b) *Income tax withheld from wages.*— (1) *Overcollection ascertained before return is filed.*—(i) If an employer during any return period collects from an employee more than the correct amount of tax required to be withheld from wages under section 3402, and if the employer ascertains the error before filing the return on which such tax is required to be reported, repays or reimburses the amount of the overcollection to the employee before filing the return for such return period and before the end of the calendar year in which the overcollection was made, and obtains and keeps as part of its records the written receipt of the employee showing the date and amount of the repayment or evidence of reimbursement, the employer shall not report on any return or pay to the IRS the amount of the overcollection.

(ii) Any overcollection not repaid or reimbursed to the employee as provided in paragraph (b)(1)(i) of this section shall be reported and paid to the IRS on the return for reporting such tax for the return period in which the overcollection is made. However, the reporting and payment of the overcollection may subsequently be treated as an overpayment error ascertained after the return is filed for purposes of paragraph (b)(2) of this section.

(iii) For purposes of this paragraph (b)(1), an error is ascertained when the employer has sufficient knowledge of the error to be able to correct it.

(2) *Error ascertained after return is filed.*— (i) If an employer files a return for a return period on which tax required to be withheld from wages is reported, collects from an employee and pays to the IRS more than the correct amount of the tax required to be withheld from wages, and if the employer ascertains the error after filing the return but before the end of the calendar year in which the wages were paid, the employer shall repay or reimburse the employee in the amount of the overcollection prior to the end of the calendar year. However, this paragraph does not apply to the extent that, after reasonable efforts, the employer cannot locate the employee.

(ii) If the employer repays the amount of the overcollection to an employee, the employer shall obtain and keep as part of its records the written receipt of the employee, showing the date and amount of the repayment.

(iii) If the employer reimburses the amount of the overcollection to an employee, the employer shall keep as part of its records evidence of reimbursement. The employer shall reimburse the employee by applying the amount of the overcollection against the tax under section 3402, which otherwise would be required to be withheld from wages paid by the employer to the employee in the calendar year in which the overcollection is made. If the amount of the overcollection exceeds the amount so applied against such tax, the excess amount shall be repaid to the employee as required by this section.

(iv) For purposes of this paragraph (b)(2), an error is ascertained when the employer has sufficient knowledge of the error to be able to correct it.

(c) *Effective/applicability date.*—Paragraph (a) of this section applies to adjusted returns filed on or after November 29, 2013. [Reg. § 31.6413(a)-1.]

☐ [*T.D.* 6472, 6-22-60. *Amended by T.D.* 9405, 6-30-2008 *and T.D.* 9645, 11-26-2013.]

[Reg. § 31.6413(a)-2]

§ 31.6413(a)-2. Adjustments of overpayments.—(a) *In general.*—(1) An employer who has overcollected or overpaid employee Federal Insurance Contributions Act (FICA) tax under section 3101 or employer FICA tax under section 3111, employee Railroad Retirement Tax (RRTA) tax under section 3201 or employer RRTA tax under section 3221, or income tax required under section 3402 to be withheld, and has repaid or reimbursed the amount of the overcollection of such tax to the employee, shall correct such error as provided in this section. However, this section only applies to overcollected or overpaid Additional Medicare Tax under section 3101(b)(2) or section 3201(a) if the employer has repaid or reimbursed the amount of the overcollection of such tax to the employee in the year in which the overcollection was made. Such correction may constitute an interest-free adjustment as provided in paragraph (b) or (c) of this section.

(2) Every correction under this section of an overpayment of tax shall be made on the form prescribed by the IRS that corresponds to the return being corrected. The form, filed in accordance with this section and the instructions, will constitute an adjusted return for the return period being corrected.

(3) Every adjusted return on which an overpayment is corrected pursuant to this section shall certify that the employer has repaid or reimbursed its employee, except where taxes were not withheld from the employee or where, after reasonable efforts, the employer cannot locate the employee. Every adjusted return shall designate the return period in which the error was ascertained and the return period being corrected, explain in detail the grounds and facts relied upon to support the correction, and set forth such other information as may be required by this section and §31.6413(a)-1 and by the instructions relating to the adjusted return. Every adjusted return, filed by an employer, for overpayment of employee FICA tax under section 3101 or employee RRTA tax under section 3201 collected from an employee in a calendar year prior to the year in which the adjusted return is filed, must also certify that the employer has obtained the employee's written statement that the employee has not claimed refund or credit of the amount of the overcollection, or if so, such claim has been rejected, and that the employee will not claim refund or credit of the amount.

(4) For purposes of this section, an error is ascertained when the employer has sufficient knowledge of the error to be able to correct it.

(5) For provisions related to furnishing employee statements and corrected employee statements reporting wages and withheld taxes, see sections 6041 and 6051 and §§1.6041-2 and 31.6051-1. For provisions relating to filing information returns and corrected information returns reporting wages and withheld taxes, see sections 6041 and 6051 and §§1.6041-2 and 31.6051-2.

(b) *Federal Insurance Contributions Act and Railroad Retirement Tax Act.*—(1) *Overcollection ascertained before return is filed.*—If an employer collects more than the correct amount of employee FICA or RRTA tax from an employee, and if the employer ascertains the error before filing the return on which the employee tax with respect to such wages or compensation is required to be reported, and repays or reimburses the employee under §31.6413(a)-1(a)(1), the employer shall not report on any return or pay to the IRS the amount of the overcollection. If the employer does not repay or reimburse the amount of the overcollection under §31.6413(a)-1(a)(1) before filing the return, the employer must report the amount of the overcollection on the return. However, the payment of the overcollection may subsequently be treated as an overpayment error ascertained after the return is filed for purposes of paragraph (b)(2) of this section.

(2) *Error ascertained after return is filed.*—(i) *Employee tax.*—If an employer files a return for a return period on which FICA tax or RRTA tax is required to be reported and reports on the return more than the correct amount of employee FICA or RRTA tax, and if the employer ascertains the error after filing the return, and repays or reimburses the employee the amount of the overcollection of employee tax, as provided in §31.6413(a)-1(a)(2), the employer may correct the error through an interest-free adjustment as provided in this section. The employer shall adjust the overpayment of tax by reporting the overpayment on an adjusted return for the return period in which the wages or compensation was paid, accompanied by a detailed explanation of the amount being reported on the adjusted return as required by paragraph (a)(3) of this section. However, for purposes of Additional Medicare Tax under section 3101(b)(2) or section 3201(a), if the amount of the overcollection is not repaid or reimbursed to the employee under §31.6413(a)-1(a)(2)(ii), there is no overpayment to be adjusted under this section and the employer may only adjust an overpayment of such tax attributable to an administrative error, that is, an error involving the inaccurate reporting of the amount withheld, pursuant to this section. Except as provided in paragraph (d) of this section, the reporting of the overpayment on an adjusted return constitutes an adjustment within the meaning of this section only if the adjusted return is filed before the expiration of the period of limitations on credit or refund. The employer shall take the adjusted amount as a credit towards payment of employment tax liabilities for the return period in which the adjusted return is filed unless the IRS notifies the employer that the adjustment is not permitted under paragraph (d) of this section.

(ii) *Employer tax.*—If an employer files a return for a return period on which FICA or RRTA tax is required to be reported and reports on the return more than the correct amount of employer FICA or RRTA tax, and if the employer ascertains the error after filing the return, the employer may correct the error through an interest-free adjustment as provided in this section. The employer must first repay or reimburse the employee the amount of any overcollection of employee tax, if any, as required by §31.6413(a)-1(a)(2), before making the adjustment for the employer tax. The employer shall adjust the overpayment of tax by reporting the overpayment on an adjusted return for the return period in which the wages or compensation was paid, accompanied by a detailed explanation of the amount being reported on the adjusted return as required by paragraph (a)(3) of this section. Except as provided in paragraph (d) of this section, the reporting of the overpayment on an adjusted return constitutes an adjustment within the meaning of this section only if the adjusted return is filed before the expiration of the period of limitations on credit or refund. The employer shall take the adjusted amount as a credit towards payment of employment tax liabilities for the return period in which the adjusted return is filed unless the IRS notifies the employer that the adjustment is not permitted under paragraph (d) of this section.

(c) *Income tax withheld from wages.*— (1) *Overcollection ascertained before return is filed.*—If an employer collects more than the correct amount of income tax required to be withheld from wages, and if the employer ascertains the error before filing the return on which the tax is required to be reported, and repays or reimburses the employee under §31.6413(a)-1(b)(1), the employer shall not report on any return or pay to the IRS the amount of the overcollection. If the employer does not repay or reimburse the amount of the overcollection under §31.6413(a)-1(b)(1) before filing the return, the employer must report the amount of the overcollection on the return. However, the reporting and payment of the overcollection may subsequently be treated as an overpayment error ascertained after the return is filed for purposes of paragraph (c)(2) of this section.

(2) *Error ascertained after return is filed.*—If an employer files a return for a return period on which income tax required to be withheld from wages is required to be reported and reports on the return more than the correct amount of income tax required to be withheld, and if the employer ascertains the error after filing the return, and repays or reimburses the employee in the amount of the overcollection as provided in §31.6413(a)-1(b)(2), the employer may correct the error through an interest-free adjustment as provided in this section. The employer shall adjust the overpayment of tax by reporting the overpayment on an adjusted return for the return period in which the wages were paid, accompanied by a detailed explanation of the amount being reported on the adjusted return as required in paragraph (a)(3) of this section. Except as provided in paragraph (d) of this section, the reporting of the overpayment on an adjusted return constitutes an adjustment within the meaning of this section. If the amount of the overcollection is not repaid or reimbursed to the employee under §31.6413(a)-1(b)(2), there is no overpayment to be adjusted under this section. However, the employer may adjust an overpayment of tax attributable to an administrative error, that is, an error involving the inaccurate reporting of the amount withheld, pursuant to this section. The employer shall take the adjusted amount as a credit towards payment of employment tax liabilities for the return period in which the adjusted return is filed unless the IRS notifies the employer that the adjustment is not permitted under paragraph (d) of this section.

(d) *Adjustments not permitted.*—(1) *In general.*—If an adjustment cannot be made, a claim for refund or credit may be filed in accordance with §31.6402(a)-2 or §31.6414-1.

(2) *90-day exception.*—No adjustment in respect of an overpayment may be made if the overpayment relates to a return period for which the period of limitations on credit or refund of such overpayment will expire within 90 days of filing the adjusted return.

(3) *No adjustment after claim for refund filed.*— No adjustment in respect of an overpayment may be made after the filing of a claim for credit or refund of such overpayment under §31.6402(a)-2.

(4) *No adjustment after IRS notification.*—No adjustment may be made upon notification by the IRS that the adjustment is not permitted.

(e) *Effective/applicability date.*—Paragraphs (a) and (b) of this section apply to adjusted returns filed on or after November 29, 2013. [Reg. §31.6413(a)-2.]

☐ [T.D. 6472, 6-22-60. *Amended by* T.D. 9405, 6-30-2008 *and* T.D. 9645, 11-26-2013 (*corrected* 1-28-2014).]

[Reg. §31.6413(a)-3]

§31.6413(a)-3. Repayment by payor of tax erroneously collected from payee.—(a) *In general.*—(1) *Erroneous withholding under section 3406 of the Internal Revenue Code.*—If a payor or broker withholds under section 3406 from a payee in error or withholds more than the proper amount of the tax under section 3406, the payor or broker may refund the amount erroneously withheld as provided in section 6413 and this section. A payor or broker will be considered to have withheld erroneously under section 3406 only if the amount is withheld because of an error by the payor or broker (e.g., an error in flagging or identifying an account that is subject to withholding under section 3406). The payor or broker may, in its discretion, treat the amount withheld as an amount erroneously withheld and refund it to the payee if—

(i) The payor or broker requires a payee described in §31.3406(g)-1(a) or described in a provision of the Internal Revenue Code requiring the reporting of a payment subject to withholding under section 3406 to certify that it is an exempt recipient, the payee fails to make the required certification, and the payor or broker subsequently withholds under section 3406 from a payment to the payee;

(ii) The payor or broker does not require the payee to certify concerning its exempt status and the payor or broker withholds under section 3406;

(iii) The payor or broker withholds under section 3406 from a payee after the payee provides a taxpayer identification number or required certification (including the documentation described in §1.1441-1(e)(1)(ii), 1.6045-1(g)(3), or 1.6049-5(c) of this chapter) to the payor, but before the payor or broker treats the number or required certification as having been received under § 31.3406(e)-1(b); or

(iv) The amount is withheld because a payor imposed backup withholding on a payment made to a person because the payee failed to furnish the documentation described in § 1.1441-1(e)(1)(ii) of this chapter and the payee subsequently furnishes, completes, or corrects the documentation. The documentation must be furnished, completed, or corrected prior to the end of the calendar year in which the payment is made and prior to the time the payor furnishes a Form 1099 to the payee with respect to the payment for which the withholding erroneously occurred.

(2) For purposes of paragraph (a)(1) of this section (other than erroneous withholding occurring under the circumstances described in paragraph (a)(1)(iv) of this section), if a payor or broker withholds because the payor or broker has not received a taxpayer identifying number or required certification and the payee subsequently provides a taxpayer identifying number or a required certification to the payor, the payor or broker may not refund the amount to the payee.

(b) *Refunding amounts erroneously withheld.*—(1) *Time and manner.*—If a payor or broker withholds under section 3406 from a payee in error (including withholding more than the correct amount, as described in paragraph (a) of this section), the payor or broker may refund the amount erroneously withheld to the payee if the refund is made prior to the end of the calendar year and prior to the time the payor or broker furnishes a Form 1099 to the payee with respect to the payment for which the erroneous withholding occurred. If the amount of the erroneous withholding is refunded to the payee, the payor or broker must—

(i) Keep as part of its records a receipt showing the date and amount of refund and must provide a copy of the receipt to the payee (a canceled check or an entry in a statement is sufficient, provided that the check or statement contains a specific notation that it is a refund of tax erroneously withheld);

(ii) Not report on a Form 1099 as tax withheld any amount which the payor or broker has refunded to a payee; and

(iii) Not deposit the amount erroneously withheld if the payor or broker has not deposited the amount of the tax prior to the time that the refund is made to the payee.

(2) *Adjustment after the deposit of the tax.*—(i) *In general.*—Except as provided in paragraph (b)(2)(ii) of this section, if the amount erroneously withheld has been deposited prior to the time that the refund is made to the payee, the payor or broker may adjust any subsequent deposit of the tax collected under chapter 24 of the Internal Revenue Code that the payor or broker is required to make in the amount of the tax that has been refunded to the payee.

(ii) *Erroneous withholding from a payee that is a foreign person.*—Where a payor withholds in error from a payee that is a nonresident alien or foreign person, as described in paragraph (a)(1)(iv) of this section, the payor may refund some or all of the amount subject to backup withholding under section 3406. A refund may be paid in accordance with the requirements of this paragraph (b)(2)(ii) where the documentation is furnished, completed, or corrected prior to the end of the calendar year in which the payment is made and prior to the time the payor furnishes a Form 1099 to the payee with respect to the payment for which the withholding erroneously occurred. The amount of the refund will be the amount erroneously withheld less the amount of tax required to be withheld, if any, under chapter 3 of the Internal Revenue Code and the regulations under that chapter. With respect to the amount of the payment to the foreign person and the amount of tax required to be withheld under chapter 3 of the Internal Revenue Code (and the regulations thereunder), returns must be made in accordance with the requirements of § 1.1461-1(b) and (c) of this chapter. [Reg. § 31.6413(a)-3.]

☐ [*T.D. 8637*, 12-20-95. *Amended by T.D. 8734*, 10-6-97 (T.D. 8804 delayed the effective date of T.D. 8734 from January 1, 1999, to January 1, 2000; T.D. 8856 further delayed the effective date of T.D. 8734 until January 1, 2001).]

[Reg. § 31.6413(b)-1]

§ 31.6413(b)-1. Overpayments of certain employment taxes.—For provisions relating to the adjustment of overpayments of tax imposed by section 3101, 3111, 3201, 3221, or 3402, see § 31.6413(a)-2. For provisions relating to refunds of tax imposed by section 3101, 3111, 3201, or 3221, see §§ 31.6402(a)-1 and 31.6402(a)-2. For provisions relating to refunds of tax imposed by section 3402, see §§ 31.6402(a)-1 and 31.6414-1. [Reg. § 31.6413(b)-1.]

☐ [*T.D. 6472*, 6-22-60.]

[Reg. § 31.6413(c)-1]

§ 31.6413(c)-1. Special refunds.—(a) *Who may make claims.*—(1) *In general.*—(i) If an employee receives wages, as defined in section 3121(a), from two or more employers in any calendar year:

(a) After 1954 and before 1959 in excess of $4,200,

(b) After 1958 and before 1966 in excess of $4,800,

(c) After 1965 and before 1968 in excess of $6,600, or

(d) After 1967 in excess of $7,800,

(e) After 1971 and before 1973 in excess of $9,000,

(f) After 1972 and before 1974 in excess of $10,800,

(g) After 1973 and before 1975 in excess of $13,200, or

(h) After 1974 in excess of the contribution and benefit base (as determined under section 230 of the Social Security Act) which is effective with respect to such year,

the employee shall be entitled to a special refund of the amount, if any, by which the employee tax imposed by section 3101 with respect to such wages and deducted therefrom (whether or not paid) exceeds the employee tax with respect to the amount specified in (a) through (h) of this subdivision for the calendar year in question. Employee tax imposed by section 3101 with respect to tips reported by an employee to his employer and collected by the employer from funds turned over by the employee to the employer (see section 3102(c)) shall be treated, for purposes of this paragraph, as employee tax deducted from wages received by the employee. If the employee is required to file an income tax return for such calendar year (or for his last taxable year beginning in such calendar year) he may obtain the benefit of the special refund only by claiming credit as provided in § 1.31-2 of this chapter (Income Tax Regulations).

(ii) The application of this subparagraph may be illustrated by the following examples:

Example (1). Employee A in the calendar year 1968 receives taxable wages in the amount of $5,000 from each of his employers, B, C, and D, for services performed during such year (or at any time after 1936), or a total of $15,000. Employee tax (computed at 4.4 percent, the aggregate employee tax rate in effect in 1968) is deducted from A's wages in the amount of $220 by B and $220 by C, or a total of $440. Employer D pays employee tax in the amount of $220 without deducting such tax from A's wages. The employee tax with respect to the first $7,800 of such wages is $343.20. A is entitled to a special refund of $96.80 ($440 minus $343.20). The $5,000 of wages received from employer D and the $220 of employee tax paid with respect thereto have no bearing in computing A's special refund since such tax was not deducted from his wages.

Example (2). Employee E in the calendar year 1968 performs services for employers F and G, for which E is entitled to wages of $7,800 from each employer, or a total of $15,600. On account of such services, E in 1967 received an advance payment of $1,800 of wages from F; and in 1968, receives wages in the amount of $6,000 from F and $7,800 from G. Employee tax was deducted as follows: In 1967, $79.20 ($1,800 × 4.4%, the aggregate employee tax rate in effect in 1967) by employer F; and in 1968, $264.00 ($6,000 × 4.4%, the aggregate employee tax rate in effect in 1968) by employer F, and $343.20 ($7,800 × 4.4%) by employer G. Thus, E in the calendar year 1968 received $13,800 in wages from which $607.20 of employee tax was deducted. The amount of employee tax with respect to the first $7,800 of such wages received in 1968 is $343.20. E is entitled to a special refund of $264.00 ($607.20 minus $343.20). The $1,800 advance of wages received in 1967 from F, and the $79.20 of employee tax with respect thereto, have no bearing in computing E's special refund for 1968, because the wages were not received in 1968. Such amounts could not form the basis for a special refund

unless E during 1967 received from F and at least one more employer wages totaling more than $6,000.

(2) *Federal employees.*—For purposes of special refunds of employee tax, each head of a Federal agency or of a wholly-owned instrumentality of the United States who makes a return pursuant to section 3122 (and each agent designated by a head of a Federal agency or instrumentality who makes a return pursuant to such section) is considered a separate employer. For such purposes, the term "wages" includes the amount which each such head (or agent) determines to constitute wages paid an employee, but not in excess of the amount specified in subparagraph (1)(i)(a) through (h) of this paragraph for the calendar year in question. For example, if wages received by an employee during calendar year 1974 are reportable by two or more agents of one or more Federal agencies and the amount of such wages is in excess of $13,200 the employee shall be entitled to a special refund of the amount, if any, by which the employee tax imposed with respect to such wages and deducted therefrom exceeds the employee tax with respect to the first $13,200 of such wages. Moreover, if an employee receives wages during any calendar year from an agency or wholly-owned instrumentality of the United States and from one or more other employers, either private or governmental, the total amount of such wages shall be taken into account for purposes of the special refund provisions.

(3) *State employees.*—For purposes of special refunds of employee tax, the term "wages" includes such remuneration for services covered by an agreement made pursuant to section 218 of the Social Security Act, relating to voluntary agreements for coverage of employees of State and local governments, as would be wages if such services constituted employment (see § 31.3121(a)-1 of Subpart B of the regulations in this part, relating to wages); the term "employer" includes a State or any political subdivision thereof, or any instrumentality of any one or more of the foregoing; and the term "tax" or "tax imposed by section 3101" includes an amount equivalent to the employee tax which would be imposed by section 3101 if such services constituted employment. The provisions of subparagraph (1) of this paragraph are applicable whether or not any amount deducted from an employee's remuneration as a result of an agreement made pursuant to section 218 of the Social Security Act has been paid pursuant to such agreement. Thus, the special refund provisions are applicable to amounts equivalent to employee tax deducted from employees' remuneration by States, political subdivisions, or instrumentalities by reason of agreements made under section 218 of the Social Security Act. Moreover, if during any calendar year an employee receives remuneration for services covered by such an agreement and during the same calendar year receives wages from one or more other employers, either private or governmental,

Reg. § 31.6413(c)-1(a)(1)(ii)

the total amount of such remuneration and wages shall be taken into account for purposes of the special refund provisions.

(4) *Employees of certain foreign corporations.*— For purposes of special refunds of employee tax, the term "wages" includes such remuneration for services covered by an agreement made pursuant to section 3121(l), relating to agreements for coverage of employees of certain foreign corporations, as would be wages if such services constituted employment (see §31.3121(a)-1 of Subpart B of the regulations in this part, relating to wages); the term "employer" includes any domestic corporation which has entered into an agreement pursuant to section 3121(l); and the term "tax" or "tax imposed by section 3101" includes, in the case of services covered by an agreement entered into pursuant to section 3121(l), an amount equivalent to the employee tax which would be imposed by section 3101 if such services constituted employment. The provisions of subparagraph (1) of this paragraph are applicable whether or not any amount deducted from the employee's remuneration by reason of such agreement has been paid to the district director. Thus, the special refund provisions are applicable to amounts equivalent to employee tax deducted from employees' remuneration by reason of agreements made under section 3121(l). A domestic corporation which enters into an agreement pursuant to section 3121(l) shall, for purposes of this paragraph, be considered an employer in its capacity as a party to such agreement separate and distinct from its identity as an employer employing individuals on its own account (see section 3121(l)(9)). If during any calendar year an employee receives remuneration for services covered by such an agreement and during the same calendar year receives wages for services in employment, the total amount of such remuneration and wages shall be taken into account for purposes of the special refund provisions. For provisions relating to agreements entered into under section 3121(l), see the regulations in Part 36 of this chapter (Regulations on Contract Coverage of Employees of Foreign Subsidiaries).

(5) *Governmental employees in American Samoa.*—For purposes of special refunds of employee tax, the Governor of American Samoa and each agent designated by him who makes a return pursuant to section 3125(b) (see §31.3125) is considered a separate employer. For such purposes, the term "wages" includes the amount which the Governor (or any agent) determines to constitute wages paid an employee, but not in excess of the amount specified in subparagraph (1)(i) (*a*) through (*h*) of this paragraph for the calendar year in question. For example, if wages received by an employee during calendar year 1974 are reportable by two or more agents pursuant to section 3125(b) and the total amount of such wages is in excess of $13,200, the employee shall be entitled to a special refund of the amount, if any, by which the employee tax imposed with respect to such wages and deducted

therefrom exceeds the employee tax with respect to the first $13,200 of such wages. Moreover, if an employee receives wages during any calendar year from the Government of American Samoa, from a political subdivision thereof, or from any wholly-owned instrumentality of such government or political subdivision and from one or more other employers, either private or governmental, the total amount of such wages shall be taken into account for purposes of the special refund provisions.

(6) *Governmental employees in the District of Columbia.*—For purposes of special refunds of employee tax, the Commissioner of the District of Columbia (or, prior to the transfer of functions pursuant to Reorganization Plan No. 3 of 1967 (81 Stat. 948), the Commissioners of the District of Columbia) and each agent designated by him who makes a return pursuant to section 3125(c) (see §31.3125) is considered a separate employer. For such purposes, the term "wages" includes the amount which the Commissioner (or any agent) determines to constitute wages paid an employee, but not in excess of the amount specified in subparagraph (1)(i) (*a*) through (*h*) of this paragraph for the calendar year in question. For example, if wages received by an employee during calendar year 1974 are reportable by two or more agents pursuant to section 3125(c) and the total amount of such wages is in excess of $13,200 the employee shall be entitled to a special refund of the amount, if any, by which the employee tax imposed with respect to such wages and deducted therefrom exceeds the employee tax with respect to the first $13,200 of such wages. Moreover, if an employee receives wages during any calendar year from the Government of the District of Columbia or from a wholly-owned instrumentality thereof and from one or more other employers, either private or governmental, the total amount of such wages shall be taken into account for purposes of the special refund provisions.

(b) *Claims for special refund.*—(1) *In general.*— An employee who is entitled to a special refund under section 6413(c) may claim such refund under the provisions of this section only if the employee is not entitled to claim the amount thereof as a credit against income tax as provided in §1.31-2 of this chapter (Income Tax Regulations). Each claim under this section shall be made with respect to wages received within one calendar year (regardless of the year or years after 1936 during which the services were performed for which such wages are received), and shall be filed after the close of such year.

(2) *Form of claim.*—Each claim for special refund under this section shall be made on Form 843, in accordance with the regulations in this subpart and the instructions relating to such form. In the case of a claim filed prior to April 15, 1968, the claim shall be filed with the district director for the internal revenue district in which the employee resides or, if the employee does not reside in any internal revenue district, with

Reg. §31.6413(c)-1(b)(2)

the District Director, Baltimore, Md. 21202. Except as provided in paragraph (b) of § 301.6091-1 (relating to hand-carried documents), in the case of a claim filed after April 14, 1968, the claim shall be filed with the service center serving such internal revenue district. However, in the case of an employee who does not reside in any internal revenue district and who is outside the United States, the claim shall be filed with the Director of International Operations, U.S. Internal Revenue Service, Washington, D.C. 20225, unless the employee resides in Puerto Rico or the Virgin Islands, in which case the claim shall be filed with the Director of International Operations, U.S. Internal Revenue Service, Hato Rey, Puerto Rico 00917. The claim shall include the employee's account number and the following information with respect to each employer from whom he received wages during the calendar year: (i) The name and address of such employer, (ii) the amount of wages received during the calendar year to which the claim relates, and (iii) the amount of employee tax collected by the employer from the employee with respect to such wages. Other information may be required but should be submitted only upon request.

(3) *Period of limitation.*—For the period of limitation upon special refund of employee tax imposed by section 3101, see § 301.6511(a)-1 of this chapter (Regulations on Procedure and Administration).

(c) *Special refunds with respect to compensation as defined in the Railroad Retirement Tax Act.*—(1) *In general.*—In the case of any individual who, during any calendar year after 1967, receives wages (as defined by section 3121(a)) from one or more employers and also receives compensation (as defined by section 3231(e)) which is subject to the tax imposed on employees by section 3201 or the tax imposed on employee representatives by section 3211 such compensation shall, solely for purposes of applying section 6413(c)(1) and this section with respect to the hospital insurance tax imposed by section 3101(b), be treated as wages (as defined by section 3121(a)) received from an employer with respect to which the hospital insurance tax imposed by section 3101(b) was deducted. For purposes of this section, compensation received shall be determined under the principles provided in chapter 22 of the Code and the regulations thereunder (see section 3231(e) and § 31.3231(e)-1). Therefore, compensation paid for time lost shall be deemed earned and received for purposes of this section in the month in which such time is lost, and compensation which is earned during the period for which a return of taxes under chapter 22 is required to be made and which is payable during the calendar month following such period shall be deemed to have been received for purposes of this section during such period only. Further, compensation is deemed to have been earned and received when an employee or employee representative performs services for which he is paid, or for which there is a present or future obligation to pay, regardless of the time

at which payment is made or deemed to be made.

(2) *Example.*—The application of this paragraph may be illustrated by the following example.

Example. Employee A rendered services to X during 1973 for which he was paid compensation at the monthly rate of $650 which was taxable under the Railroad Retirement Tax Act. A was paid $550 by X in January 1973 which was earned and deemed received in December 1972 and $650 in January of 1974 which was earned and deemed received in December of 1973. A also earned and received wages in 1973 from employer Y, which were subject to the employee tax under the Federal Insurance Contributions Act, in the amount of $6,000. A paid hospital insurance tax on $13,800 ($7,800 compensation from X including $650 earned and deemed received in December 1973 but paid in January 1974 and not including $550 paid in January 1973 but earned and deemed received in December 1972, $6,000 compensation from Y) received or deemed received or earned in 1973. For purposes of the hospital insurance tax imposed by section 3101(b), these amounts are all wages received from an employer in 1973. Therefore, A is entitled to a special refund for 1973 under section 6413(c) and this section of $30 (1.0% × $13,800—1.0% × $10,800). [Reg. § 31.6413(c)-1.]

☐ [T.D. 6472, 6-22-60. *Amended by* T.D. 6950, 4-3-68; T.D. 6983, 12-3-68 *and* T.D. 7374, 7-23-75 (*corrected* 9-24-2004).]

[Reg. § 1.6414-1]

§ 1.6414-1. Credit or refund of tax withheld on nonresident aliens and foreign corporations.—(a) *In general.*—Any withholding agent who for the calendar year pays more than the correct amount of—

(1) Tax required to be withheld under chapter 3 of the Code, or

(2) Interest, addition to the tax, additional amount, or penalty with respect to such tax, may file a claim for credit or refund of the overpayment in the manner and subject to the conditions stated in the Procedure and Administration Regulations (Part 301 of this chapter) under section 6402, or may claim credit for the overpayment as provided in paragraph (b) of this section. With respect to the payment of withholding tax under section 1446, this section shall only apply to a publicly traded partnership described in § 1.1446-4. See § 1.1446-3(d)(2)(iv) for rules regarding refunds to a withholding agent under section 1446.

(b) *Claim for credit on Form 1042.*—The withholding agent may claim credit of an overpayment described in paragraph (a) of this section for any calendar year by showing the amount of overpayment on the return on Form 1042 for such calendar year, which shall constitute a claim for credit under this paragraph. The claim for credit shall be evidenced by a statement on the return setting forth the amount determined as an overpayment and showing such other information as may be required by the instructions relating to the return. The amount claimed as a credit may be applied, to the extent it has not been applied under §1.1461-2(b), by the withholding agent to reduce the amount of a payment or deposit of tax required by §1.1461-1 or §1.6302-2(a) for any payment period occurring in the calendar year following the calendar year of overwithholding. The amount so claimed as a credit shall also be entered on the annual return on Form 1042 for the calendar year following the calendar year of overwithholding and shall be applied as a payment on account of the tax shown on such form. If the withholding agent files a claim for credit or refund of the overpayment on Form 843 in accordance with §301.6402-2 of this chapter (Procedure and Administration Regulations), or a claim for refund of the overpayment on Form 1042 in accordance with §301.6402-3 of such chapter, he may not claim credit for the overpayment under this paragraph.

(c) *Overpayment of amounts actually withheld.*— No credit or refund to the withholding agent shall be allowed for the amount of any overpayment of tax which, after taking into account paragraph (b) of §1.1464-1, the withholding agent has actually withheld from an item of income under chapter 3 of the Code.

(d) *Effective/Applicability date.*—The last two sentences of paragraph (a) of this section shall apply to partnership taxable years beginning after April 29, 2008. [Reg. §1.6414-1.]

☐ [*T.D. 6922, 6-16-67. Amended by T.D. 9394, 4-28-2008.*]

[Reg. §31.6414-1]

§31.6414-1. Credit or refund of income tax withheld from wages.—

⋙→ *Caution: Reg. §31.6414-1(a), below, prior to amendment by T.D. 9405, is applicable to any error ascertained before January 1, 2008.*

(a) *In general.*—Any employer who pays to the district director more than the correct amount of—

(1) Tax under section 3402 or a corresponding provision of prior law, or

(2) Interest, addition to the tax, additional amount, or penalty with respect to such tax, may file a claim for refund of the overpayment or may claim credit for such overpayment, in the manner and subject to the conditions stated in this section and §301.6402-2 of this chapter (Regulations on Procedure and Administration). If credit is claimed pursuant to this section, the amount thereof shall be claimed by entering such amount as a deduction on a return of tax under section 3402 filed by the employer. If credit is taken pursuant to this section, a claim on Form 843 is not required, but the return on which the credit is claimed shall have attached as a part thereof a statement, which shall constitute the claim for credit, setting forth in detail the grounds and facts relied upon in support of the credit, and showing such other information

as is required by the regulations in this subpart and by the instructions relating to the return. No refund or credit to the employer shall be allowed under this section for the amount of any overpayment of tax which the employer deducted or withheld from an employee.

⋙→ *Caution: Reg. §31.6414-1(a), below, as amended by T.D. 9405, is applicable to any error ascertained on or after January 1, 2008.*

(a) *In general.*—(1) Any employer who pays to the IRS more than the correct amount of income tax required to be withheld from wages under section 3402 or interest, addition to the tax, additional amount, or penalty with respect to such tax, may file a claim for refund of the overpayment in the manner and subject to the conditions stated in this section on the form prescribed by the IRS. The claim for refund must designate the return period to which the claim relates, explain in detail the grounds and facts relied upon to support the claim, and set forth such other information as may be required by the regulations in this section and by the instructions relating to the form used to make such claim. No refund to the employer will be allowed under this section for the amount of any overpayment of tax which the employer deducted or withheld from an employee.

(2) For provisions related to furnishing employee statements and corrected employee statements reporting wages and withheld taxes, see sections 6041 and 6051 and §§1.6041-2 and 31.6051-1. For provisions relating to filing information returns and corrected information returns reporting wages and withheld taxes, see sections 6041 and 6051 and §§1.6041-2 and 31.6051-2.

(3) For interest-free adjustments of overpayments of income tax withheld from wages, see §31.6413(a)-2.

(b) *Period of limitation.*—For the period of limitation upon credit or refund of taxes imposed by the Internal Revenue Code of 1954, see §301.6511(a)-1 of this chapter (Regulations on Procedure and Administration). For the period of limitation upon credit or refund of any tax imposed by the Internal Revenue Code of 1939, see the regulations applicable with respect to such tax. [Reg. §31.6414-1.]

☐ [*T.D. 6472, 6-22-60. Amended by T.D. 9405, 6-30-2008.*]

[Reg. §301.6414-1]

§301.6414-1. Income tax withheld.—For regulations under section 6414, see §31.6414-1 of this chapter (Employment Tax Regulations). [Reg. §301.6414-1.]

☐ [*T.D. 6119, 12-31-54. Amended by T.D. 6498, 10-24-60 and T.D. 6922, 6-16-67.*]

[Reg. §48.6416(a)-1]

§48.6416(a)-1. Claims for credit or refund of overpayments of taxes on special fuels and manufacturers taxes.—Any claims for credit or refund of an overpayment of a tax imposed by chapter 31 or chapter 32 shall be made in accor-

dance with the applicable provisions of this subpart and the applicable provisions of § 301.6402-2 of this chapter (Regulations on Procedure and Administration). A claim on Form 843 is not required in the case of a claim for credit, but the amount of the credit shall be claimed by entering that amount as a credit on a return of tax under this subpart filed by the person making the claim. In this regard, see § 48.6416(f)-1. [Reg. § 48.6416(a)-1.]

□ [*T.D. 6650. Amended by T.D. 8043, 8-8-85.*]

[Reg. § 48.6416(a)-2]

§ 48.6416(a)-2. Credit or refund of tax on special fuels.—(a) *Overpayments not described in section 6416(b)(2).*—(1) *Claims included.*—This paragraph applies only to claims for credit or refund of an overpayment of tax imposed by section 4041(a)(1)(A) (relating to tax on the sale of diesel fuel), section 4041(a)(2)(A) (relating to tax on the sale of special motor fuels), section 4041(c)(1)(A) (relating to tax on the sale of fuel for use in noncommercial aviation), or section 4041(c)(2)(A) (relating to the tax on sale of gasoline for use in noncommmercial aviation). It does not apply, however, to a claim for credit or refund of any overpayment described in paragraph (b) of this section which arises by reason of the application of section 6416(b)(2).

(2) *Supporting evidence required.*—No credit or refund of any overpayment to which this paragraph (a) applies shall be allowed unless the person who paid the tax submits with the claim a written consent of the ultimate purchaser to the allowance of the credit or refund, or submits with the claim a statement, supported by sufficient available evidence, asserting that—

(i) The person has neither included the tax in the price of the fuel with respect to which it was imposed nor collected the amount of the tax from a vendee, and identifying the nature of the evidence available to establish these facts, or

(ii) The person has repaid the amount of the tax to the ultimate purchaser of the fuel.

(3) *Ultimate purchaser.*—The term "ultimate purchaser", as used in paragraph (a)(2) of this section, means the vendee to whom the fuel was sold tax-paid by the person claiming credit or refund.

(b) *Overpayments determined under section 6416(b)(2).*—(1) *Claims included.*—This paragraph applies only to claims for credit or refund of amounts paid as tax under section 4041(a)(1)(A) (relating to tax on the sale of diesel fuel) or section 4041(a)(2)(A) (relating to tax on the sale of special motor fuels) that are determined to be overpayments by reason of section 6416(b)(2) (relating to tax payments in respect of certain uses, sales, or resales of a taxable article).

(2) *Supporting evidence required.*—No credit or refund of an overpayment to which this paragraph (b) applies shall be allowed unless the

person who paid the tax submits with the claim a statement, supported by sufficient available evidence, asserting that—

(i) The person has neither included the tax in the price of the fuel with respect to which it was imposed nor collected the amount of the tax from a vendee, and identifying the nature of the evidence available to establish these facts, or

(ii) The person has repaid, or agreed to repay, the amount of the tax to the ultimate vendor of the fuel, or

(iii) The person has secured, and will submit upon request of the Service, the written consent of the ultimate vendor to the allowance of the credit or refund.

(3) *Ultimate vendor.*—The term "ultimate vendor", as used in paragraph (b)(2) of this section, means the seller making the sale which gives rise to the overpayment or which last precedes the exportation or use which gives rise to the overpayment.

(c) *Nonapplication to tax on use of special fuels.*—This section shall not have any effect on overpayments of tax under section 4041(a)(1)(B) (relating to tax on the use of diesel fuel), section 4041(a)(2)(B) (relating to tax on the use of special motor fuels), section 4041(c)(1)(B) (relating to tax on the use of fuel other than gasoline in noncommercial aviation), section 4041(c)(2)(B) (relating to tax on the use of gasoline in noncommercial aviation), or section 4042 (relating to tax on fuel used in commercial transportation on inland waterways). [Reg. § 48.6416(a)-2.]

□ [*T.D. 8043, 8-8-85.*]

[Reg. § 48.6416(a)-3]

§ 48.6416(a)-3. Credit or refund of manufacturers tax under chapter 32.—(a) *Overpayments not described in section 6416(b)(3)(C) or (4) (prior to April 1, 1983) and section 6416(b)(2).*—(1) *Claims included.*—This paragraph applies only to claims for credit or refund of an overpayment of manufacturers tax imposed by chapter 32. It does not apply, however, to a claim for credit or refund on any overpayment described in paragraph (b) of this section which arises by reason of the application of section 6416(b)(2), (3)(C), or (4).

(2) *Supporting evidence required.*—No credit or refund of any overpayment to which this paragraph (a) applies shall be allowed unless the person who paid the tax submits with the claim a written consent of the ultimate purchaser to the allowance of the credit or refund, or submits with the claim a statement, supported by sufficient available evidence, asserting that—

(i) The person has neither included the tax in the price of the article with respect to which it was imposed nor collected the amount of the tax from a vendee, and identifying the nature of the evidence available to establish these facts, or

(ii) The person has repaid the amount of the tax to the ultimate purchaser of the article.

(3) *Ultimate purchaser.*—(1) *General rule.*—The term "ultimate purchaser", as used in paragraph (a)(2) of this section, means the person who purchased the article for consumption, or for use in the manufacture of other articles and not for resale in the form in which purchased.

(ii) *Special rule under section 6416(a)(3).*—(A) *Conditions to be met.*—If tax under chapter 32 is paid in respect of an article and the Commissioner determines that the article is not subject to tax under chapter 32, the term "ultimate purchaser", as used in paragraph (a)(2) of this section, includes any wholesaler, jobber, distributor, or retailer who, on the 15th day after the date of the determination, holds for sale any such article with respect to which tax has been paid, if the claim for credit or refund of the overpayment in respect of the articles held for sale by the wholesaler, jobber, distributor, or retailer is filed on or before the date on which the person who paid the tax is required to file a return for the period ending with the first calendar quarter which begins more than 60 days after the date of the determination by the Commissioner.

(B) *Supporting statement.*—A claim for credit or refund of an overpayment of tax in respect of an article as to which a wholesaler, jobber, distributor, or retailer is the ultimate purchaser, as provided in this paragraph (a)(3)(ii), must be supported by a statement that the person filing the claim has a statement, by each wholesaler, jobber, distributor, or retailer whose articles are covered by the claim, showing total inventory, by model number and quantity, of all such articles purchased tax-paid and held for sale as of 12:01 a.m. of the 15th day after the date of the determination by the Commissioner that the article is not subject to tax under chapter 32.

(C) *Inventory requirement.*—The inventory shall not include any such article title to which, or possession of which, has previously been transferred to any person for purposes of consumption unless the entire purchase price was repaid to the person or credited to the person's account and the sale was rescinded or any such article purchased by the wholesaler, jobber, distributor, or retailer as a component part of, or on or in connection with, another article. An article in transit at the first moment of the 15th day after the date of the determination is regarded as being held by the person to whom it was shipped, except that if title to the article does not pass until delivered to the person the article is deemed to be held by the shipper.

(b) *Overpayments described in section 6416(b)(3)(C) or (4) (prior to April 1, 1983) and section 6416(b)(2).*—(1) *Claims included.*—This paragraph applies only to claims for credit or refund of amounts paid as tax under chapter 32 that are determined to be overpayments by reason of section 6416(b)(2) (relating to tax payments in respect of certain uses, sales, or resales of a taxable article), section 6416(b)(3)(C) (relating to tax-paid tires or inner tubes used for fur-

ther manufacture), or section 6416(b)(4) (relating to tires or inner tubes used by the manufacturer on another manufactured article).

(2) *Supporting evidence required.*—No credit or refund of an overpayment to which this paragraph (b) applies shall be allowed unless the person who paid the tax submits with the claim a statement, supported by sufficient available evidence, asserting that—

(i) The person neither included the tax in the price of the article with respect to which it was imposed nor collected the amount of the tax from a vendee, and identifying the nature of the evidence available to establish these facts, or

(ii) The person repaid, or agreed to repay, the amount of the tax to the ultimate vendor of the article, or

(iii) The person has secured, and will submit upon request of the Service, the written consent of the ultimate vendor to the allowance of the credit or refund.

(3) *Ultimate vendor.*—(i) *General rule.*—The term "ultimate vendor", as used in paragraph (b)(2) of this section, means the seller making the sale which gives rise to the overpayment or which last precedes the exportation or use which has given rise to the overpayment.

(ii) *Special rule under section 6416(a)(3)(B) prior to revision by the Highway Revenue Act of 1982.*—In the case of an overpayment determined under section 6416(b)(2)(F), (3)(C), or (4) in respect of tires or inner tubes, where the taxable article is used as a component part of, or sold on or in connection with or with the sale of, a second article which is exported, sold to a nonprofit educational organization for its exclusive use, sold to a State or local government for the exclusive use of a State or local government or used or sold for use as supplies for vessels or aircraft, the term "ultimate vendor", as used in paragraph (b)(2) of this section, means the ultimate vendor of the second article.

(c) *Overpayments not included.*—This section does not apply to any overpayment determined under section 6416(b)(1) (relating to price readjustments), section 6416(b)(3)(A) (relating to certain cases in which refund or credit is allowable to the manufacturer who uses, in the further manufacture of a second article, a taxable article purchased by the manufacturer tax-paid), section 6416(b)(3)(B) prior to April 1, 1983 (relating to parts or accessories taxable under section 4061(b) and used by a subsequent manufacturer or producer as material or a component part of any other article manufactured or produced by him), section 6416(b)(4) after March 31, 1983 (relating to tires), section 6416(b)(5) (relating to the return to the seller of certain installment accounts which the seller had previously sold) or section 6416(b)(6) (relating to truck chassis, bodies, and semi-trailers used for further manufacture). In this regard, see §§ 48.6416(b)(1)-1, 48.6416(b)(3)-1, and 48.6416(b)(5)-1. [Reg. § 48.6416(a)-3.]

Reg. § 48.6416(a)-3(c)

☐ [*T.D. 8043, 8-8-85. Amended by T.D. 8748,* 12-31-97 *(corrected 3-30-98).*]

[Reg. § 48.6416(b)(1)-1]

§ 48.6416(b)(1)-1. Price readjustments causing overpayments of manufacturers tax.—In the case of any payment of tax under chapter 32 that is determined to be an overpayment by reason of a price readjustment within the meaning of section 6416(b)(1) and § 48.6416(b)(1)-2 or § 48.6416(b)(1)-3, the person who paid the tax may file a claim for refund of the overpayment or may claim credit for the overpayment on any return of tax under this subpart which the person subsequently files. Price readjustments may not be anticipated. However, if the readjustment has actually been made before the return is filed for the period in which the sale was made, the tax to be reported in respect of the sale may, at the election of the taxpayer, be based either (a) on the price as so readjusted or (b) on the original sale price and a credit or refund claimed in respect of the price readjustment. A price readjustment will be deemed to have been made at the time when the amount of the readjustment has been refunded to the vendor or the vendor has been informed that the vendor's account has been credited with the amount. No interest shall be paid on any credit or refund allowed under this section. For provisions relating to the evidence required in support of a claim for credit or refund, see § 301.6402-2 of this chapter (Regulations on Procedure and Administration), § 48.6416(a)-3(a)(2), and § 48.6416(b)(1)-4. For provisions authorizing the taking of a credit in lieu of filing a claim for refund, see section 6416(d) and § 48.6416(f)-1. [Reg. § 48.6416(b)(1)-1.]

☐ [*T.D. 8043, 8-8-85.*]

[Reg. § 48.6416(b)(1)-2]

§ 48.6416(b)(1)-2. Determination of price readjustments.—(a) *In general.*—(1) *Rules of usual application.*—(i) *Amount treated as overpayment.*—If the tax imposed by chapter 32 has been paid and thereafter the price of the article on which the tax was based is readjusted, that part of the tax which is proportionate to the part of the price which is repaid or credited to the purchaser is considered to be an overpayment. A readjustment of price to the purchaser may occur by reason of—

(A) The return of the article,

(B) The repossession of the article,

(C) The return or repossession of the covering or container of the article, or

(D) A bona fide discount, rebate, or allowance against the price at which the article was sold.

(ii) *Requirements of price readjustment.*—A price readjustment will not be deemed to have been made unless the person who paid the tax either—

(A) Repays part or all of the purchase price in cash to the vendee,

(B) Credits the vendee's account for part or all of the purchase price, or

(C) Directly or indirectly reimburses a third party for part or all of the purchase price for the direct benefit of the vendee. In addition, to be deemed a price readjustment, the payment or credit must be contractually or economically related to the taxable sale that the payment or credit purports to adjust. Thus, commissions or bonuses paid to a manufacturer's own agents or salesperson for selling the manufacturer's taxable products are not price readjustments for purposes of this section, since those commissions or bonuses are not paid or credited either to the manufacturer's vendee or to a third party for the vendee's benefit. On the other hand, a bonus paid by the manufacturer to a dealer's salesperson for negotiating the sale of a taxable article previously sold to the dealer by the manufacturer is considered to be a readjustment of the price on the original sale of the taxable article, regardless of whether the payment to the salesperson is made directly by the manufacturer or to the salesperson through the dealer. In such a case, the payment is related to the sale of a taxable article and is made for the benefit of the dealer because it is made to the dealer's salesperson to encourage the sale of a product owned by the dealer. Similarly, payments or credits made by a manufacturer to a vendee as reimbursement of interest expense incurred by the vendee in connection with a so-called "free flooring" arrangement for the purchase of taxable articles is a price readjustment, regardless of whether the payment or credit is made directly to the vendee or to the vendee's creditor on behalf of the vendee.

(iii) *Limitation on credit or refund.*—The credit or refund allowable by reason of a price readjustment in respect of the sale of a taxable article may not exceed an amount which bears the same ratio to the total tax originally due and payable on the article as the amount of the tax-included readjustment bears to the original tax-included sale price of the article.

Example. A manufacturer sells a taxable article for $100 plus $10 excise tax, and reports and pays tax liability accordingly. Thereafter, the manufacturer credits the customer's account for $11 (tax included) in readjustment of the original sale price. The overpayment of tax is $1, determined as follows:

$$\frac{\text{Tax-included readjustment}}{\text{Tax-included sale price}} \times \begin{array}{c}\text{Original}\\ \text{tax due}\end{array} = \begin{array}{c}\text{Tax}\\ \text{overpayment.}\end{array}$$

$$\frac{\$11}{\$110} \times \$10 = \$1 \text{ tax overpaid.}$$

(2) *Rules of special application.*—(i) *Constructive sale price.*—If, in the case of a taxable sale, the tax imposed by chapter 32 is based on a constructive sale price determined under any paragraph of section 4216(b) and the

regulations thereunder, as determined without reference to section 4218, then any price readjustment made with respect to the sale may be taken into account under this section only to the extent that the price readjustment reduces the actual sale price of the article below the constructive sale price.

Example. (A) A manufacturer sells a taxable article at retail for $110 tax included. Under section 4216(b)(1) the constructive sale price (tax included) of the article is determined to be $93. Thereafter, the manufacturer grants an allowance of $10 to the purchaser, which reduces the actual selling price (tax included) to $100. Since the readjustment price still exceeds the amounts of the constructive sale price, this readjustment is not recognized as a price readjustment under this section.

(B) Subsequently, the manufacturer extends to the purchaser an additional price allowance of $10, thereby reducing the actual sale price to $90. Since the actual sale price is now $3 less than the constructive sale price of $93, the manufacturer has overpaid by the amount of tax attributable to the $3. Assuming the tax rate involved is 10 percent, and the prices involved are tax-included, the overpayment of tax would be $0.27, determined as follows:

$$\frac{\text{percentage tax rate}}{100 \text{ plus percentage tax rate}} \times \frac{\text{tax-included}}{\text{readjustment}} = \frac{\text{tax}}{\text{overpayment}}$$

$$\frac{10}{110} \times \$3 = \$0.27).$$

(ii) *Price determined under section 4223(b)(2).*—If a manufacturer (within the meaning of section 4223(a)) to whom an article is sold or resold free of tax in accordance with the provisions of section 4221(a)(1) for use in further manufacture diverts the article to a taxable use or sells it in a taxable sale, and pursuant to the provisions of section 4223(b)(2) computes the tax liability in respect of the use or sale on the price for which the article was sold to the manufacturer or on the price at which the article was sold by the actual manufacturer, a reduction of the price on which the tax was based does not result in an overpayment within the meaning of section 6416(b)(1) or this section. Moreover, if a manufacturer purchases an article tax free and computes the tax in respect of a subsequent sale of the article pursuant to the provisions of section 4223(b)(2), an overpayment does not arise by reason of readjustment of the price for which the article was sold by the manufacturer except where the readjustment results from the return or repossession of the article by the manufacturer, and all of the purchase price is refunded by the manufacturer. See, however, paragraph (b)(4) of this section as to repurchased articles.

(b) *Return of an article.*—(1) *Price, readjustment.*—If a taxable article is returned to the manufacturer who paid the tax imposed by chapter 32 on the sale of the article, a price readjustment giving rise to an overpayment results—

(i) If the article is returned before use, and all of the purchase price is repaid to the vendee of credited to the vendee's account, or

(ii) If the article is returned under an express or implied warranty as to quality or service, and all or a part of the purchase price is repaid to the vendee or credited to the vendee's account, or

(iii) If title is still in the seller, as, for example, in the case of certain installment sales contracts, and all or a part of the purchase price is repaid to the vendee or credited to the vendee's account.

(2) *Return of purchase price.*—For purposes of paragraph (b)(1) of this section, if all of the purchase price of an article has been returned to the vendee, except for an amount retained by the manufacturer pursuant to contract as reimbursement of expense incurred in connection with the sale (such as a handling or restocking charge), all of the purchase price is considered to have been returned to the vendee.

(3) *Taxability of subsequent sale or use.*—If, under any of the conditions described in paragraph (b)(1) of this section, an article is returned to the manufacturer who paid the tax and all of the purchase price is returned to the vendee, the sale is considered to have been rescinded. Any subsequent sale or use of the article by the manufacturer will be considered to be an original sale or use of the article by the manufacturer which is subject to tax under chapter 32 unless otherwise exempt. If under any such condition an article is returned to the manufacturer who paid the tax and only part of the purchase price is returned to the vendee, a subsequent sale of the article by the manufacturer will be subject to tax to the extent that the sale price exceeds the adjusted sale price of the first taxable sale.

(4) *Treatment of other transactions as repurchases.*—Except as provided in paragraph (b)(1) of this section, a price readjustment will not result when a taxable article is returned to the manufacturer who paid the tax on the sale of the article, even though all or a part of the purchase price is repaid to the vendee or credited to the vendee's account, since such a transaction will be considered to be a repurchase of the article by the manufacturer.

(c) *Repossession of an article.*—If a taxable article is repossessed by the manufacturer who paid the tax imposed by chapter 32 on the sale of the article, and all or a part of the purchase price is repaid to the vendee or credited to the vendee's account, a price readjustment giving rise to an overpayment will result. However, if the manufacturer later resells the repossessed article for a price in excess of the original adjusted sale price, the manufacturer will be liable for tax under chapter 32 to the extent that the resale price exceeds the original adjusted sale price.

(d) *Return or repossession of covering or container.*—If the covering or container of a taxable article is returned to, or repossessed by the manufacturer who paid the tax imposed by chapter 32 on the sale of the article, and all or a portion of the purchase price is repaid to the vendee or credited to the vendee's account by reason of the return or repossession of the covering or container, a price adjustment giving rise to an overpayment will result. If a taxable article is considered to have been repurchased, as provided in paragraph (b)(4) of this section, and the covering or container accompanies the taxable article as part of the transaction, the covering or container will also be considered to have been repurchased.

(e) *Bona fide discounts, rebates, or allowances.*—(1) *In general.*—Except as provided in § 48.6416(b)(1)-3 (relating to readjustments in respect of local advertising), the basic consideration in determining, for purposes of this section, whether a bona fide discount, rebate, or allowance has been made is whether the price actually paid by, or charged against, the purchaser has in fact been reduced by subsequent transactions between the parties. Generally, the price will be considered to have been readjusted by reason of a bona fide discount, rebate, or allowance, only if the manufacturer who made the taxable sale repays a part of the purchase price in cash to the vendee, or credits the vendee's account, or directly or indirectly reimburses a third party for part or all of the purchase price for the direct benefit of the vendee, in consideration of factors which, if taken into account at the time of the original transaction, would have resulted at that time in a lower sale price. For example, a price readjustment will be considered to have been made when a bona fide discount, rebate, or allowance is given in consideration of such factors as prompt payment, quantity buying over a specified period, the vendee's inventory of an article when new models are introduced, or a general price reduction affecting articles held in stock by the vendee as of a certain date. On the other hand, repayments made to the vendee do not effectuate price readjustments if given in consideration of circumstances under which the vendee has incurred, or is required to incur, an expense which, if treated as a separate item in the original transaction, would have been includible in the price of the article for purposes of computing the tax.

Examples. The provisions of paragraph (e)(1) of this section may be illustrated by the following examples:

Example (1). B, a manufacturer of fishing rods, bills its distributors in a specific amount per fishing rods purchased by them. Thereafter, B issues to each distributor a credit memorandum in the amount of X dollars for each demonstration by the distributor of the fishing rods at a sporting goods exhibition. The credit which B allows the distributor for demonstration of B's product does not effect a readjustment of price.

Example (2). C, a manufacturer of automobiles, bills its dealers in a specified amount per automobile purchased by them. Thereafter, C remits to the dealer X dollars of the original sale price for each automobile sold by the dealer in the last month of the model year. An additional amount of Y dollars is paid to the dealer upon a showing by the dealer that the dealer has paid Y dollars to the salesperson who made the sale. In this case, the X dollars paid to the dealer by C constitutes a bona fide discount, rebate, or allowance since payment of such amount is in the nature of a price reduction by reason of the dealer's inventory when new models are introduced. In addition, the Y dollars paid to the dealer in reimbursement for the amount paid by the dealer to the salesperson who made the sale, also constitutes a bona fide discount, rebate, or allowance.

(2) *Inability to collect price.*—A charge-off of an amount outstanding in an open account, due to inability to collect, is not a bona fide discount, rebate, or allowance and does not, in and of itself, give rise to a price readjustment within the meaning of this section.

(3) *Loss or damage in transit.*—If title to an article has passed to the vendee, the subsequent loss, damage, or destruction of the article while in the possession of a carrier for delivery to the vendee does not, in and of itself, affect the price at which the article was sold. However, if the article was sold under a contract providing that if the article was lost, damaged, or destroyed in transit, title would revert to the vendor and the vendor would reimburse the vendee in full for the sale price, then the original sale is considered to have been rescinded. The vendor is entitled to credit or refund of the tax paid upon reimbursement of the full tax-included sale price to the vendee. [Reg. § 48.6416(b)(1)-2.]

☐ [*T.D.* 8043, 8-8-85.]

[Reg. § 48.6416(b)(1)-3]

§ 48.6416(b)(1)-3. Readjustment for local advertising charges.—(a) *In general.*—If a manufacturer has paid the tax imposed by chapter 32 on the price of any article sold by the manufacturer and thereafter has repaid a portion of the price to the purchaser or any subsequent vendee in reimbursement of expenses for local advertising of the article or any other article sold by the manufacturer which is taxable at the same rate under the same section of chapter 32, the reimbursement will be considered a price readjustment constituting an overpayment which the manufacturer may claim as a credit or refund. The amount of the reimbursement may not, however, exceed the limitation provided by section 4216(e)(2) and § 48.4216(e)-2, determined as of the close of the calendar quarter in which the reimbursement is made or as of the close of any subsequent calendar quarter of the same calendar year in which it is made. The term "local advertisement", as used in this section, has the same meaning as prescribed by section 4216(e)(4) and includes generally, advertising which is broadcast over a radio station or television station, or appears in a newspaper or magazine, or is displayed by means of an outdoor advertising sign or poster.

(b) *Local advertising charges excluded from taxable price in one year but repaid in following year.*— (1) *Determination of price readjustments for year in which charge is repaid.*—If the tax imposed by chapter 32 was paid with respect to local advertising charges that were excluded in computing the taxable price of an article sold in any calendar year but are not repaid to the manufacturer's purchaser or any subsequent vendee before May 1 of the following calendar year, the subsequent repayment of those charges by the manufacturer in reimbursement of expenses for local advertising will be considered a price readjustment constituting an overpayment which the manufacturer may claim as a credit or refund. The amount of the reimbursement may not, however, exceed the limitation provided by section 4216(e)(2) and §48.4216(e)-(2), determined as of the close of the calendar quarter in which the reimbursement is made or as of the close of any subsequent calendar quarter of the same calendar year in which it is made.

(2) *Redetermination of price readjustments for year in which charge was made.*—If the tax imposed by chapter 32 was paid with respect to local advertising charges that were excluded in computing the taxable price of an article sold in any calendar year but are not repaid to the manufacturer's purchaser or any subsequent vendor before May 1 of the following calendar year, the manufacturer may make a redetermination, in respect of the calendar year in which the charge was made, of the price readjustments constituting an overpayment which the manufacturer may claim as a credit or refund. This redetermination may be made by excluding the local advertising charges made in the calendar year that became taxable as of May 1 of the following calendar year. [Reg. §48.6416(b)(1)-3.]

☐ [*T.D.* 8043, 8-8-85.]

[Reg. §48.6416(b)(1)-4]

§48.6416(b)(1)-4. Supporting evidence required in case of price readjustments.—No credit or refund of an overpayment arising by reason of a price readjustment described in §48.6416(b)(1)-2 or §48.6416(b)(1)-3 shall be allowed unless the manufacturer who paid the tax submits a statement, supported by sufficient available evidence—

(a) Describing the circumstances which gave rise to the price readjustment,

(b) Identifying the article in respect of which the price readjustment was allowed,

(c) Showing the price at which the article was sold, the amount of tax paid in respect of the article, and the date on which the tax was paid,

(d) Giving the name and address of the purchaser to whom the article was sold, and

(e) Showing the amount repaid to the purchaser or credited to the purchaser's account. [Reg. §48.6416(b)(1)-4.]

☐ [*T.D.* 8043, 8-8-85.]

[Reg. §48.6416(b)(2)-1]

§48.6416(b)(2)-1. Certain exportations, uses, sales, or resales causing overpayments of tax.— In the case of any payment of tax under section 4041(a)(1) or (a)(2) or under chapter 32 (diesel fuel and special fuels tax) (manufacturers tax) that is determined to be an overpayment by reason of certain exportations, uses, sales, or resales described in section 6416(b)(2) and §48.6416(b)(2)-2, the person who paid the tax may file a claim for refund of the overpayment or, in the case of overpayments under chapter 32, may claim credit for the overpayment on any return of tax under this subpart which the person subsequently files. However, under the circumstances described in section 6416(c) and §48.6416(e)-1, the overpayments under chapter 32 may be refunded to an exporter or shipper. No interest shall be paid on any credit or refund allowed under this section. For provisions relating to the evidence required in support of a claim for credit or refund under this section, see §301.6402-2 of this chapter (Regulations on Procedure and Administration) and §§48.6416(b)(2)-3 and 48.6416(b)(2)-4. For provisions authorizing the taking of a credit in lieu of filing a claim for refund, see section 6416(d) and §48.6416(f)-1. [Reg. §48.6416(b)(2)-1.]

☐ [*T.D.* 8043, 8-8-85. *Amended by T.D.* 8879, 3-30-2000.]

[Reg. §48.6416(b)(2)-2]

§48.6416(b)(2)-2. Exportations, uses, sales, and resales included.—(a) *In general.*—The tax paid under chapter 32 (or under section 4041(a) or (d) in respect of sales or under section 4051) with respect to any article is considered to be an overpayment in the case of any exportation, use, sale, or resale described in this section. This section applies only in those cases in which the exportation, use, sale, or resale (or any combination thereof) referred to in this section occurs before any other use. In addition, the following restrictions must be taken into account in applying the regulations under section 6416(b)(2):

(1) Sections 6416(b)(2)(C) and (D) do not apply to any tax paid under section 4064 (gas guzzler tax).

(2) Sections 6416(b)(2)(B), (C), and (D) do not apply to any tax paid under section 4131 (vaccine tax) and section 6416(b)(2)(A) applies only to the extent prescribed in paragraph (b)(2) of this section.

(3) Section 6416(b)(2) does not apply to any tax paid under section 4041(a)(1) or 4081 on diesel fuel or kerosene, section 4091 (aviation fuel tax), or section 4121 (coal tax).

(4) Beginning on January 1, 2013, sections 6416(b)(2)(B), (C), (D), and (E) do not apply to any tax paid under section 4191 (medical device tax).

(b) *Exportation of tax-paid articles.*—(1) *In general.*—Subject to the limitations of section 6416(b)(2) and paragraph (b)(2) of this section, tax paid under chapter 31 or 32 on the sale of any article will be considered to be an overpayment under section 6416(b)(2)(A) if the article is exported by any person. Except in the case of articles subject to the tax imposed by section 4061(a) prior to April 1, 1983, it is immaterial for purposes of this paragraph (b), whether the person who made the taxable sale had knowledge at the time of the sale that the article or fuel was being purchased for export to a foreign country or shipment to a possession of the United States. See § 48.6416(e)-1 for the circumstances under which a claim for refund by reason of the exportation of an article may be claimed by the exporter or shipper, rather than by the person who paid the tax. For definition of the term "possession of the United States", see § 48.0-2(a)(11).

(2) *Rule for exportation of vaccines.*—Paragraph (b)(1) of this section applies to tax paid under section 4131 on the sale of a vaccine, but only if the sale by the manufacturer occurs after August 10, 1993, and, in the case of vaccine sold to the United States or any of its agencies or instrumentalities, the condition of § 48.4221-3(e)(2) is satisfied.

(c) *Supplies for vessels or aircraft.*—A payment of tax under chapter 32 on the sale of any article, or under section 4041(a)(1) or (a)(2) on the sale of diesel fuel or special motor fuel, will be considered to be an overpayment under section 6416(b)(2)(B) if the article or fuel is used by any person, or is sold by any person for use by the purchaser, as supplies for vessels or aircraft.

The term "supplies for vessels or aircraft", as used in this paragraph, has the same meaning as when used in sections 4041(g), 4221(a)(3), 4221(d)(3), and 4221(e)(1), and the regulations thereunder.

(d) *Use by State or local government.*—A payment of tax under chapter 32 on the sale of any article, or under section 4041(a)(1) or (a)(2) on the sale of diesel fuel or special motor fuel, will be considered to be an overpayment under section 6416(b)(2)(C) if the article of fuel is sold by any person to a State, any political subdivision thereof, or the District of Columbia for the exclusive use of a State, any political subdivision thereof, or the District of Columbia. For provisions relating to tax-free sales to a State, any political subdivision thereof, or the District of Columbia, see section 4221(a)(4) and the regulations thereunder.

(e) *Use by nonprofit educational organization.*—A payment of tax under chapter 32 on the sale of any article, or under section 4041(a)(1) or (a)(2) on the sale of diesel fuel or special motor fuel, will be considered to be an overpayment under section 6416(b)(2)(D) if the article or fuel is sold by any person to a nonprofit educational organization for its exclusive use. The term "nonprofit educational organization", as used in this para-

graph (e), has the same meaning as when used in section 4221(a)(5) or (d)(5), whichever applies, and the regulations thereunder.

(f) *Tax-paid tires or inner tubes resold for use in further manufacture.*—A payment of tax under section 4071 on the sale of a tire or, prior to January 1, 1984, on the sale of an inner tube will be considered to be an overpayment under section 6416(b)(2)(E) if—

(1) The tire or inner tube is, after the original sale of the article by the manufacturer, resold by any person to another manufacturer;

(2) The other manufacturer sells the tire or inner tube on or in connection with, or with the sale of, any other article manufactured or produced by the other manufacturer, and

(3) That other article is by any person either—

(i) Exported to a foreign country or to a possession of the United States,

(ii) Sold to a State, any political subdivision thereof, or the District of Columbia for the exclusive use of a State, any political subdivision thereof, or the District of Columbia,

(iii) Sold to a nonprofit educational organization for its exclusive use, or

(iv) Used or sold for use as supplies for vessels or aircraft.

The overpayment described in this paragraph (f) is to be distinguished from the overpayment described in section 6416(b)(3)(C) prior to amendment by the Highway Revenue Act of 1982 and section 6416(b)(3) as amended by the Highway Revenue Act of 1982, and § 48.6416(b)(3)-2(d) in that the overpayment here described arises from a "resale" for the use described in this paragraph, while the section 6416(b)(3)(C) overpayment arises from the "use" of tires or inner tubes in the manufacture of other articles by a subsequent manufacturer who purchases tax-paid tires or tubes and disposes of finished articles on the basis of one of the exemptions set forth in section 6416(B)[b](3)(C). A manufacturer claiming a credit or refund under this paragraph (f) must have substantially the same information available in support of the claim as is required under § 48.4221-7(c)(2) in support of exempt sales of tires or inner tubes under the provisions of section 4221(e)(2), except that none of the parties involved need be registered under section 4222. [Reg. § 48.6416(b)(2)-2.]

☐ [*T.D.* 8043, 8-8-85. *Amended by T.D.* 8561, 8-19-94; *T.D.* 8659, 3-13-96 *T.D.* 8879, 3-30-2000 *and T.D.* 9604, 12-5-2012.]

[Reg. § 48.6416(b)(2)-3]

§ 48.6416(b)(2)-3. Supporting evidence required in case of manufacturers tax involving exportations, uses, sales, or resales.— (a) *Evidence to be submitted by claimant.*—No claim for credit or refund of an overpayment, within the meaning of section 6416(b)(2) and § 48.6416(b)(2)-2, of tax under chapter 32 shall be allowed unless the person who paid the tax submits with the claim the evidence required by paragraph (b)(2) of §48.6416(a)-3 and a statement, supported by sufficient available evidence—

(1) Showing the amount claimed in respect of each category of exportations, uses, sales, or resales on which the claim is based and which give rise to a right of credit or refund under section 6416(b)(2) and §48.6416(b)(2)-1,

(2) Identifying the article, both as to nature and quantity, in respect of which credit or refund is claimed,

(3) Showing the amount of tax paid in respect of the article or articles and the dates of payment, and

(4) In the case of an overpayment determined under section 6416(b)(2)(A) and paragraph (b) of §48.6416(b)(2)-2 in respect of an article which was taxable prior to April 1, 1983, under section 4061(a), indicating that, pursuant to section 6416(g), the person claiming a credit or refund possessed at the time that person shipped the article or at the time title to the article passed to the vendee, whichever is earlier, evidence that the article was to be exported to a foreign country or shipped to a possession of the United States, or

(5) In the case of any overpayment other than an overpayment determined under section 6416(b)(2)(E) and paragraph (f) of §48.6416(b)(2)-2, indicating that the person claiming a credit or refund possesses evidence (as set forth in paragraph (b)(1) of this section) that the article has been exported, or has been used, sold, or resold in a manner or for a purpose which gives rise to an overpayment within the meaning of section 6416(b)(2) and §48.6416(b)(2)-2, or

(6) In the case of an overpayment determined under section 6416(b)(2)(E) and paragraph (f) of §48.6416(b)(2)-2, relating to a tax-paid tire or inner tube sold on or in connection with, or with the sale of, a second article that has been manufactured, indicating that the person claiming a credit or refund possesses (i) evidence (as set forth in paragraph (b)(2) of this section) that the second article has been exported, or has been used or sold as provided in §48.6416(b)(2)-2(f), and (ii) a statement, executed and signed by the ultimate purchaser of the tire or inner tube, that the ultimate purchaser purchased the tire or inner tube from a person other than the person who paid the tax on the sale of the tire or inner tube.

(b) *Evidence required to be in possession of claimant.*—(1) *Evidence required under paragraph (a)(5).*—(i) *In general.*—The evidence required to be retained by the person who paid the tax, as provided in paragraph (a)(5) of this section must, in the case of an article exported, consist of proof of exportation in the form prescribed in the regulations under section 4221 or must, in the case of other articles sold tax-paid by that person, consist of a certificate, executed and signed by the ultimate purchaser of the article, in the form prescribed in paragraph (b)(1)(ii) of this section.

However, if the article to which the claim relates has passed through a chain of sales from the person who paid the tax to the ultimate purchaser, the evidence required to be retained by the person who paid the tax may consist of a certificate, executed and signed by the ultimate vendor of the article, in the form provided in paragraph (b)(1)(iii) of this section, rather than the proof of exportation itself or the certificate of the ultimate purchaser.

(ii) *Certificate of ultimate purchaser.*

(A) The certificate executed and signed by the ultimate purchaser of the article to which the claim relates must identify the article, both as to nature and quantity; show the address of the ultimate purchaser of the article, and the name and address of the ultimate vendor of the article; and describe the use actually made of the article in sufficient detail to establish that credit or refund is due, except that the use to be made of the article must be described in lieu of actual use if the claim is made by reason of the sale or resale of an article for a specified use which gives rise to the overpayment.

(B) If the certificate sets forth the use to be made of any article, rather than its actual use, it must show that the ultimate purchaser has agreed to notify the claimant if the article is not in fact used as specified in the certificate.

(C) The certificate must also contain a statement that the ultimate purchaser understands that the ultimate purchaser and any other party may, for fraudulent use of the certificate, be subject under section 7201 to a fine of not more than $10,000, or imprisonment for not more than 5 years, or both, together with the costs of prosecution.

(D) A purchase order will be acceptable in lieu of a separate certificate of the ultimate purchaser if it contains all the information required by this paragraph (b)(1)(ii).

(iii) *Certificate of ultimate vendor.*—Any certificate executed and signed by an ultimate vendor as evidence to be retained by the person who paid the tax, as provided in paragraph (a)(5) of this section, may be executed with respect to any one or more overpayments by the person which arose under section 6416(b)(2) and §§48.6416(b)(2)-2 by reason of exportations, uses, sales or resales, occurring within any period of not more than 12 consecutive calendar quarters, the beginning and ending dates of which are specified in the certificate.

The certificate must be in substantially the following form:

Statement of Ultimate Vendor

(For use in claiming credit or refund of overpayment determined under section 6416(b)(2) (other than section 6416(b)(2)(E) of the Internal Revenue Code.)

The undersigned or the . . . . (Name of ultimate vendor if other than undersigned) of which the undersigned is . . . . (Title), is the ultimate vendor of the article specified below or on the reverse side hereof.

The article was purchased by the ultimate vendor tax-paid and was thereafter exported, used, sold, or resold (as indicated below or on the reverse side hereof). The ultimate vendor possesses . . . . (Proof of exportation in respect of the article, or a certificate as to use executed by the ultimate purchaser of the article) The . . . . (Proof of exportation or certificate) (1) is retained by the ultimate vendor, (2) will, upon request, be forwarded to . . . . (Name or person who paid the tax) at any time within 3 years from the date of this statement for use by that person to establish that credit or refund is due in respect of the article, and (3) will otherwise be held by the ultimate vendor for the required 3-year period. According to the best knowledge and belief of the undersigned, no statement in respect of the . . . . (Proof of exportation or certificate) has previously been executed, and the undersigned understands that the fraudulent use of this statement may, under section 7201, subject the undersigned or any other party making such fraudulent use to a fine of not more than $10,000, or imprisonment for not more than 5 years, or both, together with the costs of prosecution.

. . . . (Signature)
. . . . (Address)
. . . . (Date)

Vendor's invoice	Articles	Date of resale	Quantity	Exported or use made or to be made (specify)

(2) *Evidence required under paragraph (a)(6).*— (i) *In general.*—The evidence required to be retained by the person who paid the tax, as provided in paragraph (a)(6) of this section, must, in the case of an exportation of the second article, consist of proof of exportation of the second article in the form prescribed in the regulations under section 4221 or must, in other cases, consist of a certificate, executed and signed by the ultimate purchaser of the second article, in the form prescribed in paragraph (b)(2)(ii) of this section. However, the evidence required to be retained by the person who paid the tax may consist of a certificate, executed and signed by the ultimate vendor of the second article, in the form provided in paragraph (b)(2)(iii) of this section, rather than the proof of exportation itself or the certificate of the ultimate purchaser.

(ii) *Certificate of ultimate purchaser.*—The certificate of the ultimate purchaser of the second article must contain the same information as that required in paragraph (b)(1)(ii) of this section, except that the information must be furnished in respect of the second article, rather than the article to which the claims relates.

(iii) *Certificate of ultimate vendor.*—Any certificate executed and signed by an ultimate vendor as evidence to be retained by the person who paid the tax, as provided in paragraph (a)(6) of this section, may be executed with respect to any one of more overpayments by that person which arose under section 6416(b)(2)(E) and § 48.6416(b)(2)-2(f) by reason of exportations, uses, sales, or resales of a second article

occurring within any period of not more than 12 consecutive calendar quarters, the beginning and ending dates of which are specified in the certificate. The certificate must be in substantially the following form:

STATEMENT OF ULTIMATE VENDOR

(For use in claiming credit or refund of overpayment determined under section 6416(b)(2)(E) Internal Revenue Code, involving tires or inner tubes sold on or with another article) The undersigned or the . . . . (Name of ultimate vendor of second article if other than undersigned) of which the undersigned is . . . . (Title), is the ultimate vendor of an article, specified below or on the reverse side hereof, on which or with which a tax-paid tire or inner tube was sold. The ultimate vendor possesses . . . . (Proof of exportation in respect of the article on which or with which the tire or inner tube was sold, or a certificate as to use of the article executed by the ultimate purchaser of the article) The . . . . (Proof of exportation or certificate) (1) is retained by the ultimate vendor, (2) will, upon request, be forwarded to . . . . (Name of person who paid the tax on the tire or inner tube) at any time within 3 years from the date of this statement for use in establishing that credit or refund is due in respect of the tire or inner tube, and (3) will otherwise be held by the ultimate vendor for the required 3-year period. According to the best knowledge and belief of the undersigned, no statement in respect of the . . . . (Proof of exportation or certificate) has previously been executed, and the undersigned understands that the fraudulent use of this statement may, under section 7201, subject the undersigned or any other party making such fraudulent use to a fine of not more than $10,000, or imprisonment for not more than 5 years, or both, together with the costs of prosecution.

. . . . (Signature)
. . . . (Address)
. . . . (Date)

Tires or inner tubes (specify and state quantity)	Vendor's invoice on second article	Second article (specify and state quantity)	Date of sale of second article	Exported or use made of or to be made (specify in respect of second article)

(3) *Repayment or consent of ultimate vendor.*— If the person claiming credit or refund of an overpayment to which this section applies has repaid, or agreed to repay, the amount of the overpayment to the ultimate vendor or if the ultimate vendor consents to the allowance of the credit or refund, a statement to that effect, signed by the ultimate vendor, must be shown on, or made a part of, the evidence required under this section to be retained by the person claiming the credit or refund. In this regard, see § 48.6416(a)-3(b)(2). [Reg. § 48.6416(b)(2)-3.]

☐ [*T.D.* 8043, 8-8-85.]

[Reg. § 48.6416(b)(2)-4]

§ 48.6416(b)(2)-4. Supporting evidence required in case of special fuels tax involving exportations, uses, sales, or resales of special fuels.—(a) *Evidence to be submitted by claimant.*—No claim for credit or refund of an overpayment, within the meaning of section 6416(b)(2) and § 48.6416(b)(2)-2 of tax under section 4041(a)(1) or (a)(2) shall be allowed unless the person who paid the tax submits with the claim the evidence required by paragraph (b)(2) of § 48.6416(a)-2 and a statement, supported by sufficient available evidence—

(1) Showing the amount claimed in respect of each category of exportations, uses, sales, or resales on which the claim is based and which give rise to right of credit or refund under section 6416(b)(2) and § 48.6416(b)(2)-1,

(2) Identifying the fuel, both as to nature and quantity, in respect of which credit or refund is claimed,

(3) Showing the amount of tax paid in respect of the fuel and the dates of payment, and

(4) Indicating that the fuel has been exported, or has been used, sold, or resold in a manner or for a purpose which gives rise to an overpayment within the meaning of section 6416(b)(2) and § 48.6416(b)(2)-2.

(b) *Evidence required to be in possession of claimant.*—(1) The evidence required to be retained by the person who paid the tax, as provided in paragraph (a)(4) of this section, must, in the case of fuel exported, consist of proof of exportation or must, in the case of other fuel sold tax-paid by that person, consist of a certificate, executed and signed by the person who purchased the fuel in a resale or for the use which gave rise to the overpayment.

(2) The certificate must identify the fuel, both as to nature and quantity, in respect of which credit or refund is claimed; show the address of the purchaser; show the name and address of the person from whom the fuel was purchased and the date or dates on which the fuel was purchased; and show that the fuel was resold and the date of the resale.

(3) If the claim is not based on resale of the fuel, the certificate must describe the use actually made of the fuel in sufficient detail to establish that credit or refund is due. However, the use to be made of the fuel must be described in lieu of actual use if the claim is made by reason of the sale of the fuel for a specified use which gives rise to an overpayment under § 48.6416(b)(2)-2.

(4) If the certificate sets forth the use to be made of the fuel, rather than its actual use, it must show that the purchaser has agreed to notify the claimant if the fuel is not in fact used as specified in the certificate.

(5) The certificate must also contain a statement that the purchaser has not previously executed a certificate in respect of the fuel and understands that any party may, for fraudulent use of the certificate, be subject under section 7201 to a fine of not more than $10,000, or imprisonment for not more than 5 years, or both, together with the costs of prosecution. [Reg. § 48.6416(b)(2)-4.]

☐ [*T.D.* 8043, 8-8-85.]

[Reg. § 48.6416(b)(3)-1]

§ 48.6416(b)(3)-1. Tax-paid articles used for further manufacture and causing overpayments of tax.—In the case of any payment of tax under chapter 32 that is determined to be an overpayment under section 6416(b)(3) and § 48.6416(b)(3)-2 by reason of the sale of an article(other than coal taxable under section 4121), directly or indirectly, by the manufacturer of the article to a subsequent manufacturer who uses the article in further manufacture of a second article or who sells the article with, or as a part of, the second article manufactured or produced by the subsequent manufacturer, the subsequent manufacturer may file claim for refund of the overpayment or may claim credit for the overpayment on any return of tax under this subpart subsequently filed. No interest shall be paid on any credit or refund allowed under this section. For provisions relating to the evidence required in support of a claim for credit or refund, see § 301.6402-2 of this chapter (Regulations on Procedure and Administration) and § § 48.6416(a)-3 and 48.6416(b)(3)-3. For provisions authorizing the taking of a credit in lieu of filing a claim for refund, see section 6416(d) and § 48.6416(f)-1. [Reg. § 48.6416(b)(3)-1.]

☐ [*T.D.* 8043, 8-8-85.]

[Reg. § 48.6416(b)(3)-2]

§ 48.6416(b)(3)-2. Further manufacture included.—(a) *In general.*—The payment of tax imposed by chapter 32 on the sale of any article (other than coal taxable under section 4121) by a manufacturer of the article will be considered to be an overpayment by reason of any use in further manufacture, or sale as part of a second manufactured article, described in any one of paragraphs (b) through (f) of this section. This section applies in those cases where the exportation, use, or sale (or any combination of those activities) referred to in any one or more of those paragraphs occurs before any other use. For provisions relating to overpayments arising by reason of resales of tax-paid articles for use in further manufacture as provided in this section, see section 6416(b)(2)(E) and paragraph (f) of § 48.6416(b)(2)-2.

(b) *Use of tax-paid articles in further manufacture described in section 6416(b)(3)(A).*—A payment of tax under chapter 32 on the sale of any article (other than coal taxable under section 4121), directly or indirectly, by the manufacturer of the article to a subsequent manufacturer will be considered to be an overpayment under section 6416(b)(3)(A) if the article is used by the subsequent manufacturer as material in the manufacture or production of, or as a component part of, a second article manufactured or produced by the subsequent manufacturer which is—

(1) Taxable under chapter 32, or

(2) An automobile bus chassis or an automobile bus body.

For this purpose it is immaterial whether the second article is sold or otherwise disposed of, or if sold, whether the sale is a taxable sale. Any article to which this paragraph (b) applies which would have been used in the manufacture or production of a second article, except for the fact that it was broken or rendered useless in the process of manufacturing or producing the second article, will be considered to have been used as a component part of the second article. This paragraph (b) does not apply to articles sold and used as provided in any of paragraphs (c) through (f) of this section.

(c) *Use of truck, bus, etc., parts or accessories.*—A payment of tax under section 4061(b) on the sale prior to January 7, 1983, of any truck, bus, etc., part or accessory, directly or indirectly, by the manufacturer of the article to a subsequent manufacturer will be considered to be an overpayment under section 6416(b)(3)(B) if the part or accessory is used by the subsequent manufacturer as material in the manufacture or production of or as a component part of, a second article manufactured or produced by the subsequent manufacturer. For this purpose it is immaterial whether the second article is or is not taxable under chapter 32. Any article to which this paragraph (c) applies which would have been used in the manufacture or production of a second article, except for the fact that it was broken or rendered useless in the process of manufacturing or producing the second article, will be considered to have been used as a component part of the second article.

(d) *Tax-paid tires or inner tubes used in further manufacture.*—(1) A payment of tax under section 4071 on the sale prior to January 1, 1984, of a tire or inner tube, directly or indirectly, by the manufacturer of the article to a subsequent manufacturer will be considered to be an overpayment under section 6416(b)(3)(C) if the subsequent manufacturer sells the tire or inner tube on or in connection with, or with the sale of, any other article manufactured or produced by the subsequent manufacturer and if the other article is—

(i) An automobile bus chassis or automobile bus body, or

(ii) By any person (A) exported to a foreign country or to a possession of the United States, (B) sold to a State, any political subdivision thereof, or the District of Columbia for the exclusive use of a State, any political subdivision thereof, or the District of Columbia, (C) sold to a nonprofit educational organization for its exclusive use, or (D) used or sold for use as supplies to vessels or aircraft.

For tax-paid tires used in further manufacture after December 31, 1983, see section 6416 (b)(3)(A) and the regulations thereunder.

(2) The overpayment in this paragraph (d) is to be distinguished from that overpayment described in section 6416(b)(2)(E) and

§ 48.6416(b)(2)-2(f) in that this overpayment arises from the "use" described in this paragraph, whereas the overpayment under section 6416(b)(2)(E) arises from the "resale" of tax-paid tires or inner tubes by any person to a subsequent manufacturer who disposes of the articles on or in connection with, or with the sale of, a second article manufactured or produced by the subsequent manufacturer which is disposed of on the basis of one of the exemptions set forth in section 6416(b)(3)(C).

(3) If the second article is exported or shipped as provided in this paragraph (d), it is immaterial whether the subsequent manufacturer sold the article with the knowledge that it would be exported or shipped.

(4) An overpayment arises under paragraph (d)(1) of this section only if the tire or inner tube constitutes a part of, or is associated with, the second article at the time the second article is exported, shipped, sold, used, or sold for use, as prescribed in this paragraph.

(5) For definition of certain terms used in this paragraph, see section 4221 and the regulations thereunder.

(6) For provisions relating to overpayments arising by reason of tires or inner tubes sold tax-paid by the manufacturer of the same, on or in connection with, or with the sale of, any article manufactured or produced by that manufacturer and exported, sold, or used or sold for use, as provided in this paragraph (d), see section 6416(b)(4).

(7) For provisions relating to credit allowable in respect of tires and inner tubes sold on or in connection with, or with the sale of, another article taxable under chapter 32, prior to January 1, 1984, see section 6416(c) and § 48.6416(c)-1.

(8) If a second article referred to in paragraph (d)(1) of this section is sold for a use described in that paragraph and is not so used, this paragraph (d) is in all respects inapplicable.

(e) *Use of bicycle tires or tubes in further manufacture.*—A payment of tax under section 4071 on the sale, prior to January 1, 1984, of a bicycle or tricycle tire or inner tube, directly or indirectly, by the manufacturer of the same to a subsequent manufacturer will be considered to be an overpayment under section 6416(b)(3)(E) if the tire or tube is used by the subsequent manufacturer as material in the manufacture or production of, or as a component part of, a bicycle or tricycle manufactured or produced by the subsequent manufacturer which is not a rebuilt or reconditioned bicycle or tricycle. For definition of the term "bicycle tire", see section 4221(e)(4)(B) and the regulations thereunder.

(f) *Use of gasoline in further manufacture.*—A payment of tax under section 4081 on the sale of gasoline, directly or indirectly, by the manufacturer of the same to a subsequent manufacturer will be considered an overpayment under section 6416(b)(3)(B) if the gasoline is used for nonfuel purposes by the subsequent manufacturer as a material in the manufacture or production of any other article manufactured or produced by the subsequent manufacturer. For this purpose it is immaterial whether the other article is or is not taxable under chapter 32. For provisions relating to the use of gasoline for nonfuel purposes, see section 4221 and the regulations thereunder. [Reg. § 48.6416(b)(3)-2.]

☐ [*T.D. 8043, 8-8-85. Amended by T.D. 8748, 12-31-97 (corrected 3-30-98).*]

[Reg. § 48.6416(b)(3)-3]

§ 48.6416(b)(3)-3. Supporting evidence required in case of tax-paid articles used for further manufacture.—(a) *Evidence to be submitted by claimant.*—No claim for credit or refund of an overpayment, within the meaning of section 6416(b)(3) and § 48.6416(b)(3)-2 shall be allowed unless the subsequent manufacturer submits with the claim the evidence required by § 48.6416(a)-3, *and* a statement, supported by sufficient available evidence—

(1) Showing the amount claimed in respect of each category of exportations, uses, or sales on which the claim is based and which give rise to a right of credit or refund under section 6416(b)(3) and § 48.6416(b)(3)-1,

(2) Showing the name and address of the manufacturer, producer, or importer of the article in respect of which credit or refund is claimed,

(3) Identifying the article, both as to nature and quantity, in respect of which credit or refund is claimed,

(4) Showing the amount of tax paid in respect of the article by the manufacturer or producer of the article and the date of payment,

(5) Indicating that the article was used by the claimant as material in the manufacture or production of, or as a component part of, a second article manufactured or produced by the manufacturer or was sold on or in connection with, or with the sale of, a second article manufactured or produced by the manufacturer,

(6) Identifying the second article, both as to nature and quantity, and

(7) In the case of an overpayment determined under section 6416(b)(3)(C) as it existed prior to January 1, 1984, and paragraph (d)(1) of § 48.6416(b)(3)-2 in respect of a tire or inner tube taxable under section 4071, indicating that the manufacturer has evidence available (as set forth in paragraph (b) of this section) that the second article is an automobile bus chassis or automobile bus body, or has been exported, used, or sold as provided in section 6416(b)(3)(C)(ii) and § 48.6416(b)(3)-2(d)(1)(ii).

(b) *Evidence required to be in possession of claimant.*—(1) *In general.*—The evidence required to be retained by the person claiming credit or refund, as provided in paragraph (a)(7) of this section, must, in the case of an exportation of the second article, consist of proof of exportation of the second article in the form prescribed in the regulations under section 4221, or must, in other cases (except when the second article is an auto-

mobile bus chassis or automobile bus body), consist of a certificate, executed and signed by the ultimate purchaser of the second article, in the form prescribed in paragraph (b)(2) of this section. However, if the second article has passed through a chain of sales from the manufacturer of the second article to the ultimate purchaser of the second article, the evidence may consist of a certificate, executed and signed by the ultimate vendor of the second article, in the form provided in paragraph (b)(3) of this section, rather than the proof of exportation itself of the second article or the certificate of the ultimate purchaser of the second article.

(2) *Certificate of ultimate purchaser of second article.*—The certificate executed and signed by the ultimate purchaser of the second article must contain the same information as that required in paragraph (b)(1)(ii) of § 48.6416(b)(2)-3, except that the information must be furnished in respect of the second article, rather than the article to which the claim relates.

(3) *Certificate of ultimate vendor of second article.*—Any certificate executed and signed by an ultimate vendor as evidence to be retained by the person claiming credit or refund must be executed in the same form and manner as that provided in paragraph (b)(2)(iii) and § 48.6416(b)(2)-3.

(4) *Repayment or consent of ultimate vendor.*—If the person claiming credit or refund of an overpayment to which this section applies has repaid, or agreed to repay, the amount of the overpayment to the ultimate vendor or if the ultimate vendor consents to the allowance of the credit or refund, a statement to that effect, signed by the ultimate vendor, must be shown on, or made a part of, the evidence required to be retained by the person claiming the credit or refund. In this regard, see § 48.6416(a)-3(b)(2). [Reg. § 48.6416(b)(3)-3.]

☐ [*T.D. 8043, 8-8-85.*]

[Reg. § 48.6416(b)(5)-1]

§ 48.6416(b)(5)-1. Return of installment accounts causing overpayments of tax.—(a) *In general.*—In the case of any payment of tax under section 4216(d)(1) in respect of the sale of any installment account that is determined to be an overpayment under section 6416(b)(5) and paragraph(b) of this section upon return of the installment account, the person who paid the tax may file a claim for refund of the overpayment or may claim credit for the overpayment on any return of tax under this subpart which that person subsequently files. No interest shall be paid on any credit or refund allowed under this section. For provisions relating to the evidence required in support of a claim for credit or refund under this section, see § 301.6402-2 of this chapter (Regulations on Procedure and Administration) and paragraph(c) of this section. For provisions authorizing the taking of a credit in lieu of filing a claim for refund, see section 6416(d) and § 48.6416(f)-1.

(b) *Overpayment of tax allocable to repaid consideration.*—The payment of tax imposed by section 4216(d)(1) on the sale of an installment account by the manufacturer will be considered to be an overpayment under section 6416(b)(5) to the extent of the tax allocable to any consideration repaid or credited to the purchaser of the installment account upon the return of the account to the manufacturer pursuant to the agreement under which the account originally was sold, if the readjustment of the consideration occurs pursuant to the provisions of the agreement. The tax allocable to the repaid or credited consideration is the amount which bears the same ratio to the total tax paid under section 4216(d)(1) with respect to the installment account as the amount of consideration repaid or credited to the purchaser bears to the total consideration for which the account was sold. This paragraph (b) does not apply where an installment account is originally sold pursuant to the order of, or subject to the approval of, a court of competent jurisdiction in a bankruptcy or insolvency proceeding.

(c) *Evidence to be submitted by claimant.*—No claim for credit of refund of an overpayment, within the meaning of section 6416(b)(5) and paragraph (b) of this section, of tax under section 4216(d)(1) shall be allowed unless the person who paid the tax submits with the claim a statement supported by sufficient available evidence, indicating—

(1) The name and address of the person to whom the installment account was sold,

(2) The amount of tax due under section 4216(d)(1) by reason of the sale of the installment account, the amount of the tax paid under section 4216(d)(1) with respect to the sale, and the date of payment,

(3) The amount for which the installment account was sold,

(4) The amount which was repaid or credited to the purchaser of the account by reason of the return of the account to the person claiming the credit or refund, and

(5)(i) The fact that the amount repaid or credited to the purchaser of the account was so repaid or credited pursuant to the agreement under which the account was sold, and

(ii) The fact that the account was returned to the manufacturer pursuant to that agreement. [Reg. § 48.6416(b)(5)-1.]

☐ [T.D. 8043, 8-8-85.]

[Reg. § 48.6416(c)-1]

§ 48.6416(c)-1. Credit for tax paid on tires or, prior to January 1, 1984, inner tubes.— (a) *Allowance of credit against tax on sale of taxable article.*—If tax has been paid under section 4071 on the sale, or under section 4218 on the use, of a tire or inner tube, and the manufacturer of another article taxable under chapter 32 sells the tire or inner tube on or in connection with the sale of that other article, a credit in respect of the tire or inner tube is allowable under section 6416(c) against the tax imposed on the sale of that other article. The amount of the credit is to

be determined as provided in paragraph (b) or (c) of this section.

(b) *Tires or tubes purchased by manufacturer of the other article.*—If the manufacturer of the other article purchased the tire or inner tube tax-paid, the amount of the credit shall be determined by applying to the purchase price of the tire or inner tube the percentage rate of tax applicable to the sale of the other article. For this purpose, the purchase price shall be determined by including any tax passed on to the manufacturer and, in the case of a tire, by excluding any part of the price attributable to the metal rim or rim base. For example, if the selling price of an automobile truck is $24,000, tax equivalent to 10 percent of the price (*i.e.,* $2,400) is imposed under section 4601(a) on the sale (before April 1, 1983) of the automobile truck. If the tires or inner tubes sold on or in connection with the automobile truck are purchased by the manufacturer of the automobile truck for $1,500 (computed as provided in this paragraph) a credit of $150 (10 percent of $1,500) is allowable against the tax imposed on the sale of the automobile truck.

(c) *Tires or tubes manufactured by manufacturer or other articles.*—If the manufacturer of the other article is also the manufacturer of the tire or inner tube and incurs tax liability under section 4218 on the use by that manufacturer of the tire or inner tube, the amount of the credit shall be determined by applying to the fair market price of the tire or inner tube, the percentage rate of tax applicable to the sale of the other article. For this purpose, the fair market price of the tire or inner tube shall be the price at which the same or similar tires or inner tubes are sold by manufacturers of tires or inner tubes in the ordinary course of trade, as determined by the Commissioner, and by excluding, in the case of a tire, any part of the price attributable to the metal rim or rim base. The determination of the Commissioner shall be made in the same manner as determinations made under section 4218.

(d) *Other applicable rules.*—(1) For purposes of this section, the term "manufacturer" includes the original manufacturer of the other article and any succeeding purchaser of the article who further manufactures the article so as to become liable as a manufacturer of an article taxable under chapter 32. Therefore, the credit provided by section 6416(c) and this section is available both to the original manufacturer of the other article and also to every succeeding purchaser of that article who sells that article on or in connection with, or with the sale of, another article taxable under chapter 32.

(2) No interest shall be paid on any credit allowed under this section.

(3) If credit is not claimed under this section against the tax applicable to the sale of the other article, the manufacturer of the other article may claim refund of an amount equivalent to the credit or may claim credit on any return of tax under this subpart subsequently filed. [Reg. § 48.6416(c)-1.]

☐ [T.D. 6650. *Amended by T.D. 8043, 8-8-85.*]

[Reg. §48.6416(e)-1]

§48.6416(e)-1. Refund to exporter or shipper.—(a) *In general.*—Any payment of tax imposed by section 4041, 4051 or chapter 32 that is determined to be an overpayment within the meaning of section 6416(b)(2)(A) or (E), section 6416(b)(3)(C) (prior to January 7, 1983), or section 6416(b)(4) and the regulations thereunder, by reason of the exportation of any article may be refunded to the exporter or shipper of the article pursuant to section 6416(c) of this section, if—

(1) The exporter or shipper files a claim for refund of the overpayment, and

(2) The person who paid the tax waives the right to claim credit or refund of the tax.

No interest shall be paid on any refund allowed under this section. For provisions relating to the evidence required in support of a claim under this paragraph (a), see §301.6402 of this chapter (Regulations on Procedure and Administration) and paragraph (b) of this section.

(b) *Supporting evidence required.*—No claim for refund of any overpayment of tax to which this section applies shall be allowed unless the exporter or shipper submits with that claim proof of exportation in the form prescribed by the regulations under section 4221, and a statement, signed by the person who paid the tax, showing—

(1) That the person who paid the tax waives the right to claim credit or refund of the tax,

(2) In the case of an overpayment determined under section 6416(b)(2)(A) and paragraph (b) of §48.6416(b)(2)-2 in respect of a truck, bus, tractor, etc., taxable under section 4061(a), that, pursuant to section 6416(g), the person who paid the tax possessed at the time that person shipped the article or at the time title to the article passed to that person's vendee, whichever is earlier, evidence that the article was to be exported to a foreign country or shipped to a possession of the United States,

(3) The amount of tax paid on the sale of the article and the date of payment, and

(4) The internal revenue service office to which the tax was paid. [Reg. §48.6416(e)-1.]

☐ [*T.D. 6650. Amended by T.D. 8043, 8-8-85.*]

[Reg. §48.6416(f)-1]

§48.6416(f)-1. Credit on returns.—Any person entitled to claim refund of any overpayment of tax imposed by section 4041, 4042, 4051 or chapter 32 may, in lieu of claiming refund of the overpayment, claim credit for the overpayment on any return of tax under this subpart subsequently filed. Any such credit claimed on a return must be supported by the evidence prescribed in the applicable regulations in this subpart and §301.6402 of this chapter (Regulations on Procedure and Administration). [Reg. §48.6416(f)-1.]

☐ [*T.D. 6650. Amended by T.D. 8043, 8-8-85.*]

[Reg. §48.6416(h)-1]

§48.6416(h)-1. Accounting procedures for like articles.—(a) *Identification of manufacturer.*—

In applying section 6416 and the regulations thereunder, a person who has purchased like articles from various manufacturers may determine the particular manufacturer from whom that person purchased any one of those articles by a first-in-first-out (FIFO) method, by a last-in-first-out (LIFO) method, or by any other consistent method been approved by the district director. For the first year for which a person makes a determination under this section, the person may adopt any one of the following methods without securing prior approval by the district director.

(1) FIFO method.

(2) LIFO method.

(3) Any method by which the actual manufacturer of the article is in fact identified.

Any other method of determining the manufacturer of a particular article must be approved by the district director before its adoption. After any method for identifying the manufacturer has been properly adopted, it may not be changed without first securing the consent of the district director.

(b) *Determining amount of tax paid.*—In applying section 6416 and the regulations thereunder, if the identity of the manufacturer of any article has been determined by a person pursuant to a method prescribed in paragraph (a) of this section, that manufacturer of the article must determine the tax paid under chapter 32 with respect to that article consistently with the method used in identifying the manufacturer. [Reg. §48.6416(h)-1.]

☐ [*T.D. 6650. Amended by T.D. 8043, 8-8-85.*]

[Reg. §44.6419-1]

§44.6419-1. Credit or refund generally.—(a) *Overpayment of wagering tax; in general.*—If a person overpays the tax imposed under section 4401, he may either file a claim for refund on Form 843 or take credit for such overpayment against the tax due on a subsequent monthly return. A complete statement of the facts involving the overpayment shall be attached either to the claim or to the return on which the credit is claimed. Every claim for refund shall be supported by evidence showing the name and address of the taxpayer, the date of payment of the tax, and the amount of such tax. A credit taken on a return shall be supported by evidence of the same character.

(b) *Statement supporting credit or refund.*—No credit or refund shall be allowed whether in pursuance of a court decision or otherwise unless the taxpayer files a statement explaining satisfactorily the reason for claiming the credit or refund and establishing (1) that he has not collected (whether as a separate charge or otherwise) the amount of the tax from the person who placed the wager on which the tax was imposed, or (2) that he has either repaid the amount of the tax to the person who placed the wager or has secured the written consent of such person to the allowance of the credit or refund. In the latter case, the written consent of the person who placed the wager shall accompany the statement filed with the credit or refund claim. The statement supporting the credit or refund claim shall also show whether any previous claim for credit or refund covering the amount involved, or any part thereof, has been filed. If the overpayment of tax relates to a laid-off wager accepted by the taxpayer, no credit or refund shall be allowed or made unless the taxpayer complies with the provisions of the first sentence of this paragraph, not only as to the person who placed the laid-off wager, but also with respect to the person who placed the original wager.

(c) *Limitation on credit or refund.*—No claim for credit or refund of tax shall be allowed unless presented within the period of limitations prescribed in section 6511. (For regulations under section 6511, see the Regulations on Procedure and Administration (Part 301 of this Chapter).) [Reg. § 44.6419-1.]

☐ [*T.D.* 6370.]

[Reg. § 44.6419-2]

§ 44.6419-2. Credit or refund on wagers laid off by taxpayer.—(a) *Laid-off wagers; in general.*—If a taxpayer accepts a wager and lays off all or a part thereof with another person who is liable for tax under section 4401 with respect to such laid-off wager, a credit may be allowed to such taxpayer in the amount of the tax due with respect to the amount of the wager so laid off, provided there is attached to the return for the month during which the wager was accepted

and laid off by him the certificate prescribed in paragraph (d) of this section.

(b) *Claim for refund.*—If a taxpayer has paid the tax with respect to a wager laid off by him, he may file a claim for refund of such tax on Form 843 or take a credit for the tax paid by him against the tax shown to be due on any subsequent monthly return. If a refund is claimed, Form 843 shall be completed in accordance with the instructions thereon and, in addition, there shall be attached to such form a statement setting forth the reason for claiming the refund, the month in which such tax was paid, the date of payment, and whether any previous claim for refund covering the amount involved or any part thereof has been filed. There shall also be attached to the Form 843 the certificate prescribed below. In the case of a credit, the statement and certificate shall be attached to the monthly return on which the credit is claimed.

(c) *Credit or refund not allowed.*—No credit or refund will be allowed under this section if the wager is laid off with a person or organization not liable for tax under section 4401 with respect to such laid-off wager. No interest shall be allowed on any amount of tax credited or refunded under this section.

(d) *Certificate required.*—The certificate prescribed for use in support of a credit or refund with respect to a laid-off wager shall be in the following form:

CERTIFICATE

(In support of credit or refund with respect to laid-off wagers under section 6419(b) of the Internal Revenue Code.) I hereby certify that I, or the . . . . (Corporation, partnership, or syndicate) of which I am an officer or member, doing business at . . . . (Address), registered with the District Director of Internal Revenue at . . . ., under Registration No. . . . . as a person accepting wagers within the meaning of section 4401 of the Internal Revenue Code, accepted laid-off wagers, in the amounts and on the dates indicated below, from . . . . (Name), ... (Address), during the month of . . . ., 19 . . . . .

DATE	AMOUNT OF LAID-OFF WAGER	SUBJECT OF LAID-OFF WAGER (Identify horse and track, particular contest, or contestant, etc.)
. . . .	. . . .	. . . .
. . . .	. . . .	. . . .
. . . .	. . . .	. . . .
. . . .	. . . .	. . . .

(Attach supplemental sheets for additional entries, if necessary.)

The undersigned further certifies that he, or the corporation, partnership, or syndicate of which he is a member, will make return of and account for the tax, under section 4401 of the Internal Revenue Code, with respect to the laid-off wagers so accepted.

It is understood by the undersigned that this certificate is given for the purpose of enabling the person from whom the laid-off wagers were accepted to claim credit with respect to the tax due on such laid-off wagers or to claim credit or refund of the tax, if any, paid on such laid-off wagers.

It is further understood that the fraudulent use of this certificate will subject the undersigned and all guilty parties to a fine of not more than $10,000 or to imprisonment for not more than five years, or both, together with costs of prosecution.

(Signed) . . . . (Date) . . . .

(Title) . . . .

(Owner, President, Partner, Member, etc.)

[Reg. § 44.6419-2.]

☐ [*T.D.* 6370.]

Reg. § 44.6419-1(c)

[Reg. § 48.6420-1]

§ 48.6420-1. Credits or payments to ultimate purchaser of gasoline used on a farm.—(a) *In general.*—If gasoline is used on a farm for farming purposes after June 30, 1965, a credit (under the circumstances described in paragraph (b) of this section) or a payment (under the circumstances described in paragraph (c) of this section) in respect of the gasoline shall be allowed or made to the ultimate purchaser of the gasoline in an amount determined by multiplying (1) the number of gallons of gasoline so used by (2) the rate of tax on gasoline under section 4081 that applied on the date the gasoline was purchased by the ultimate purchaser. No interest shall be paid on any payment, allowed under paragraph (c) of this section. However, interest may be paid on any overpayment (as defined by section 6401) arising from a credit allowed under paragraph (b) of this section. See section 34(a), relating to credit for certain uses of gasoline and special fuels (and lubricating oil used prior to January 7, 1983). See § 48.6420-2 for the time within which a claim for credit or payment must be made. See section 4081 and the regulations thereunder for the rates of tax on gasoline. See § 48.6420-2 for meaning of the terms "Used on a farm for farming purposes," "farm," "gasoline," "ultimate purchaser," and "taxable year."

(b) *Allowance of income tax credit in lieu of payment.*—With respect to persons subject to income tax, repayment of the tax paid under section 4081 on gasoline used on a farm for farming purposes may be obtained only by claiming a credit for the amount of this tax against the income tax imposed by subtitle A of the Code. The amount of the credit shall be an amount equal to the payment which would be made under section 6420 with respect to gasoline used during the taxable year on a farm for farming purposes if section 6420(g)(1) and paragraph (c) of this section did not apply. See section 34(a)(1).

(c) *Allowance of payment.*—Payments in respect of gasoline upon which tax was paid under section 4081 that is used on a farm for farming purposes shall be made only to—

(1) The United States or agency or instrumentality thereof, a State, a political subdivision of a State, or an agency or instrumentality of one or more States or political subdivisions of a State, or the District of Columbia, or

(2) An organization which is exempt from tax under section 501(a) and is not required to make a return of the income tax imposed under subtitle A for its taxable year.

(d) *Use of gasoline.*—(1) The credit or payment described in paragraph (a) of this section is allowable only in respect of gasoline used on a farm in the United States for farming purposes. The credit or payment is not allowable with respect to gasoline used for nonfarming purposes, or gasoline used off a farm, regardless of the nature of the use. If a vehicle or other equipment is used both on a farm and off the farm, or if it is used on a farm both for farming and nonfarming purposes, the credit or payment is allowable only with respect to that portion of the

gasoline which was "used on a farm for farming purposes" as defined in paragraph (a) of § 48.6420-4. In determining if this requirement is met, neither the type of equipment or vehicle used nor its registration for highway use is material. However, the actual use of the equipment or vehicle and the place where it is used are material. For example, if a truck used on a farm for farming purposes is also used on the highways, gasoline used in connection with operating the truck on the highways is not taken into account in computing the credit or payment.

(2) For purposes of determining the allowable credit or payment in respect of gasoline used on a farm for farming purposes, gasoline on hand shall be considered used in the order in which it was purchased. Thus, if the owner, tenant, or operator of a farm has on hand gasoline acquired in two purchases made at different times and subject to different rates of tax, in determining credit or payment for gasoline used on a farm for farming purposes, it will be assumed that the gasoline purchased first was the first gasoline used, and the rate applicable to that purchase will apply in determining the credit or payment, until all that gasoline is accounted for. [Reg. § 48.6420-1.]

☐ [*T.D.* 8043, 8-8-85.]

[Reg. § 48.6420-2]

§ 48.6420-2. Time for filing claim for credit or payment.—(a) *In general.*—A claim for credit or payment described in § 48.6420-1 with respect to gasoline used after June 30, 1965, on a farm for farming purposes, shall cover only gasoline used during the taxable year on a farm for farming purposes. Therefore, gasoline on hand at the end of a taxable year as, for example, in fuel supply tanks of farm machinery or in storage tanks or drums, must be excluded from a claim filed for that taxable year (but may be included in a claim filed for a later taxable year if used during that later year on a farm for farming purposes). Gasoline used during a taxable year may be covered by a claim filed for that taxable year although the gasoline was not paid for at the time the claim is filed. For purposes of applying this section, a governmental unit or exempt organization described in § 48.6420-1(c) is considered to have as its taxable year, the calendar year or fiscal year on the basis of which it regularly keeps its books; see paragraph (h) of this section.

(b) *Time for filing.*—(1) A claim for credit with respect to gasoline used on a farm for farming purposes shall not be allowed unless it is filed no later than the time prescribed by section 6511 and the regulations thereunder for filing a claim for credit or refund of income tax for the particular taxable year.

(2) A claim for payment of a governmental unit or exempt organization described in § 48.6420-1(c) must be filed no later than 3 years following the close of its taxable year. (See paragraph (h) of this section.)

(3) See § 301.7502-1 of this chapter (Regulations on Procedure and Administration) for provisions treating timely mailing as timely filing and § 301.7502-1 of this chapter for time for per-

formance of an act where the last day falls on Saturday, Sunday, or a legal holiday.

(c) *Limit of one claim per taxable year.*—Not more than one claim may be filed under section 6420 by any person with respect to gasoline used during the same taxable year.

(d) *Form and content of claim.*—(1) *Claim for credit.*—(i) The claim for credit with respect to gasoline used on a farm for farming purposes must be made by attaching a Form 4136 to the income tax return of an individual or a corporation. Form 4136 must be executed in accordance with the instructions prescribed for the preparation of the form. A partnership may not file Form 4136. When a partnership files Form 1065, U.S. Partnership Return of Income, it must include a statement showing how many gallons of gasoline are allocated to each partner and use made of the gasoline.

(ii) If an individual dies during the taxable year, the claim for credit may be made only for that portion of the individual's taxable year ending with the date of death. If a sole proprietorship, a partnership or corporation is terminated or liquidated during the taxable year, the claim for credit may be made only for the portion of its year ending with the date of the termination or liquidation.

(2) *Claim for payment.*—The claim for payment with respect to gasoline used on a farm for farming purposes by a governmental unit or exempt organization described in §48.6420-1(c) must be made on Form 843 in accordance with the instructions prescribed for the preparation of the form. The claim by such a unit or organization must be filed with the service center for the internal revenue region in which the principal place of business or principal office of the claimant is located. [Reg. §48.6420-2.]

☐ [*T.D.* 8043, 8-8-85.]

[Reg. §48.6420-3]

§48.6420-3. Exempt sales; other payments or refunds available.—(a) *Exempt sales.*—Credits or payments are allowable only for gasoline that was sold by the producer or importer in a transaction that was subject to tax under section 4081. No credit or payment shall be allowed or made under §48.6420-1 with respect to gasoline which was exempt from the tax imposed by section 4081. For example, a State or local government may not file a claim with respect to any gasoline which it purchased tax free from the producer, even though the State or local government used the gasoline on a farm for farming purposes. Similarly, payment may not be made with respect to gasoline purchased by a State tax free for its exclusive use, as provided in section 4221,

which is used on a State prison farm for farming purposes.

(b) *Other payments or refunds available.*—Any amount which, without regard to the second sentence of section 6420(d) and this paragraph (b), would be allowable as a credit or payable to any person under §48.6420-1 with respect to any gasoline is reduced by any other amount which is allowable as a credit or payable under section 6420, or is refundable under any other provision of the Code, to any person with respect to the same gasoline. Thus, a person who is the ultimate purchaser of gasoline may not file a claim for credit or payment with respect to that gasoline if another person is entitled to claim a payment, credit, or refund with respect to the same gasoline. For example, a State or local government may not file a claim for payment if it has executed, or intends to execute, a written consent to enable the producer to claim a credit or refund for the tax that was paid. See, for example, §§48.6416(a)-3(b)(2), 48.6416(b)(2)-2(d), and 48.6416(b)(2)-3(b)(1). [Reg. §48.6420-3.]

☐ [*T.D.* 8043, 8-8-85.]

[Reg. §48.6420-4]

§48.6420-4. Meaning of terms.—For purposes of the regulations under section 6420, unless otherwise expressly indicated—

(a) *Used on a farm for farming purposes.*—The term "used on a farm for farming purposes" applies only to gasoline which is used (1) in carrying on a trade or business of farming, (2) on a farm in the United States, and (3) for farming purposes. Gasoline used in an aircraft will qualify if its use otherwise satisfies these requirements. For the meaning of the term "trade or business of farming," see paragraph (b) of this section. For the definition of the term "farm," see paragraph (c) of this section. For the definition of the term "farming purposes," see paragraphs (d) through (g) of this section. The term "United States" has the meaning assigned to it by section 7701(a)(9).

(b) *Trade or business of farming.*—A person will be considered to be engaged in the trade or business of farming if the person cultivates, operates, or manages a farm for gain or profit, either as an owner or a tenant. A person engaged in forestry or the growing of timber is not thereby engaged in the trade or business of farming. A person who operates a garden plot, orchard, or farm for the primary purpose of growing produce for the person's own use is not considered to be engaged in the trade or business of farming. Generally, the operation of a farm does not constitute the carrying on of a trade or business if the farm is occupied by a person primarily for residential purposes or is used primarily for pleasure, such as for the entertainment of guests or as a hobby.

(c) *Farm.*—The term "farm" is used in its ordinary and accepted sense, and generally means land used for the production of crops, fruits, or other agricultural products or for the sustenance of livestock or poultry. The term "livestock" includes cattle, hogs, horses, mules, donkeys, sheep, goats, and captive fur-bearing animals. The term "poultry" includes chickens, turkeys, geese, ducks, and pigeons. Thus, a farm includes livestock, dairy, poultry, fish, fruit, fur-bearing animals, and truck farms, plantations, ranches, nurseries, ranges, orchards, feed yards for fattening cattle, and greenhouses and other similar structures used primarily for the raising of agricultural or horticultural commodities. Greenhouses and other similar structures that are used primarily for purposes other than the raising of agricultural or horticultural commodities do not constitute farms, as, for example, structures that are used primarily for the display, storage, fabrication, or sale of wreaths, corsages, and bouquets. A fish farm is an area where fish are grown or raised, as opposed to merely caught or harvested.

(d) *Gasoline used in cultivating, raising, or harvesting.*—Gasoline is used for "farming purposes" when it is used on a farm by the owner, tenant, or operator of the farm in connection with cultivating the soil, raising or harvesting any agricultural or horticultural commodity, or raising, shearing, feeding, caring for, training, or managing livestock, poultry, bees, or wildlife. Examples of operations which are considered to be operations for "farming purposes" within the meaning of this paragraph include plowing, seeding, fertilizing, weed killing, corn or cotton picking, threshing, combining, baling, silo filling, and chopping silage.

(e) *Gasoline used in handling, packing, or storing.*—(1) Gasoline is used for "farming purposes" when it is used by the owner, tenant, or operator of the farm in handling, drying, packing, grading, or storing any agricultural or horticultural commodity in its unmanufactured state, but only if the owner, tenant, or operator produced more than one-half of the commodity which was so treated during the taxable year for which claim for credit or payment is filed.

(2) Gasoline used in connection with canning, freezing, packaging, or processing operations will not be considered to be used for farming purposes, even though these operations are performed on a farm. Thus, for example, although gasoline used on a farm in connection with the production or harvesting of maple sap or oleoresin from a living tree is considered to be used for farming purposes under paragraph (d) of this section, gasoline used in the processing of maple sap into maple syrup or maple sugar or used in the processing of oleoresin into gum spirits of turpentine or gum resin is not used for

farming purposes, even though these processing operations are conducted on a farm.

(3) Gasoline used in connection with processing operations which change a commodity from its raw or natural state, or operations performed with respect to a commodity after its character has been changed from its raw or natural state by a processing operation, will not be considered to be used for farming purposes. For example, gasoline used for the extraction of juices from fruits or vegetables is used in a processing operation which changes the character of the fruits or vegetables from their raw or natural state and will not be considered to be used for "farming purposes."

(4) The term "commodity," as used in this paragraph (e), refers to a single agricultural or horticultural product. For example, all apples are treated as a single commodity while apples and peaches are treated as two separate commodities. Operations with respect to each commodity are to be considered separately in applying the "one-half" production test described in paragraph (e)(1) of this section.

(f) *Gasoline used in planting, cultivating, or caring for trees.*—Gasoline is used "for farming purposes" when it is used by the owner, tenant, or operator of the farm in connection with the planting, cultivating, caring for, or cutting of trees that is incidental to the farming operations of the farm on which it is performed or incidental to the farming operations of the owner, tenant, or operator of the farm, or in connection with the preparation (other than milling) of trees for market that is incidental to these farming operations. These operations include the felling of trees and cutting them into logs or firewood but do not include sawing logs into lumber, chipping, or other milling operations. Operations of the prescribed character will be considered incidental to farming operations only if they are of a minor nature in comparison with the total farming operations involved. Therefore, a tree farmer or timber grower may not claim credit or payment under §48.6420-1 with respect to gasoline used in connection with the trade or business of tree farming or timber growing.

(g) *Gasoline used in the maintenance of a farm or farm equipment.*—Gasoline is used "for farming purposes" when it is used by the owner, tenant, or operator of a farm in connection with the operation, management, conservation, improvement, or maintenance of the farm and its tools and equipment. The activities included are those which contribute in any way to the conduct of the farm as such, as distinguished from any other enterprise in which the owner, tenant, or operator may be engaged. Examples of included operations are clearing land, repairing fences and farm buildings, building terraces or irrigation ditches, cleaning tools or farm machinery, and painting farm buildings. Since the gasoline must be used by the owner, tenant, or operator of the farm to which the operations relate, gasoline used by an organization which contracts with a farmer to renovate his farm properties is not used for farming purposes. Gasoline used in a gasoline powered lawn mower for maintaining a lawn is not used for farming purposes.

(h) *Taxable year.*—The "taxable year" of a governmental unit or tax-exempt organization described in § 48.6420-1(c) is the calendar or fiscal year on the basis of which it regularly keeps its books. The "taxable year" of persons subject to income tax shall have the meaning as it has under section 7701 (a)(23).

(i) *Gasoline.*—The term "gasoline" has the same meaning given to this term by section 4082(b) and the regulations thereunder.

(j) *Ultimate purchaser.*—The term "ultimate purchaser" includes only a person who is an owner, tenant, or operator of a farm. A person who is an owner, tenant, or operator of a farm is an ultimate purchaser of gasoline only with respect to such gasoline as is purchased by the person and used for farming purposes on a farm of which the person is the owner, tenant, or operator. Thus the owner of a farm who purchases gasoline which is used on the farm by its owner, tenant, or operator for farming purposes is generally the ultimate purchaser of the gasoline. If, however, the cost of gasoline supplied by an owner, tenant, or operator of a farm, is by agreement or other arrangement borne by a second person who is an owner, or operator of the farm, the second person who bore the cost of the gasoline is considered to be the ultimate purchaser of the gasoline.

(k) *Certain farming use by persons other than the owner, tenant or operator.*—(1) *In general.*—Except as provided in paragraph (1) of this section, the owner, tenant, or operator of a farm on which gasoline is used by any other person for the purposes described in section 6420(c)(3)(A) and paragraph (d) of this section (relating to gasoline used in cultivating, raising, or harvesting) will be treated, for the purposes of § 48.6420-1(a), as the ultimate purchaser who used the gasoline on the farm for farming purposes.

(2) *Example.*—The rule of paragraph (k)(1) of this section may be illustrated by the following example.

Example. Farmer A hired custom operator B to cultivate the soil on A's farm. B used 200 gallons of gasoline which B had purchased in performing the work on A's farm. In addition, A hired Farmer C to do some plowing on A's farm, using C's own tractor and 50 gallons of gasoline which C had purchased. A is deemed to be the ultimate purchaser and user of the gasoline used on A's farm by B and C, and A is entitled to take a credit in respect of the gasoline. Accordingly, no credit in respect to the gasoline may be taken by either B or C.

(l) *Aerial applicators treated as ultimate purchasers.*—(1) *General rule.*—Section 6420(c)(3)(A) provides that only the owner, tenant, or operator of a farm is entitled to be treated as a user and ultimate purchaser. Section 6420(c)(4) provides that, under section 6420(c)(3)(A), an aerial appli-

cator or other applicator is entitled to be treated as the user and ultimate purchaser of gasoline used by it on a farm for the purposes described in section 6420(c)(3)(A), but only if the owner, tenant, or operator who is otherwise entitled to treatment as the user and ultimate purchaser waives the right to credit or payment. See paragraph (l)(2) of this section.

(2) *Form and manner of waiver.*—To waive the right to be treated as user and ultimate purchaser of gasoline which is used on a farm by an aerial applicator or other applicator, the owner, tenant, or operator of a farm who is otherwise entitled to treatment as user and ultimate purchaser must execute an irrevocable written agreement (as here described) no later than the date on which the aerial applicator or other applicator claiming the credit or payment files its return for the taxable year in which the gasoline is used. The agreement must identify the period for which the owner, tenant, or operator waives the right to credit or payment. The effective period of the waiver cannot extend beyond the last day of the taxable year of the owner, tenant, or operator of the farm on which the gasoline was used. If the owner, tenant, or operator's taxable year extends beyond the taxable year of the applicator, the applicator can only claim a credit or payment for periods included in the applicator's taxable year. Periods after the last day of the applicator's taxable year which are included under the agreement must be claimed on the applicator's return for the next succeeding taxable year. The waiver may be in the form shown under paragraph (l)(6) of this section or in any other form that meets the requirements of this paragraph and clearly states that the owner, tenant, or operator of the farm knowingly waives the right to receive the credit or payment.

(3) *Agreement included on aerial applicator's invoice.*—The agreement waiving a right to receive a credit or payment under section 6420 may be a separate document or may appear on the invoice for aerial application services or other unrelated document from the aerial applicator to the owner, tenant, or operator of the farm. If the waiver agreement appears on an invoice or other unrelated document, however, it must be printed in a section of the invoice or other document clearly set off from all other material contained in the invoice or other document, and it must be printed in type sufficiently large to put the owner, tenant, or operator of the farm on notice that the person has waived the right to receive a credit or payment under section 6420. Additionally, if the waiver agreement appears as part of any invoice or other unrelated document, it must be executed separately from any other item included in the invoice or other document which requires the owner, tenant, or operator's signature.

(4) *Copies of agreement waiving right to credit or payment.*—No copies of any agreement waiving a right to credits or payments under section 6420 are to be submitted to the Internal Revenue

Service unless a request is made by the Service to the taxpayer for the waivers. Aerial applicators must, however, retain copies of all waivers, and a copy of each waiver must be supplied by the aerial applicator to the owner, tenant, or operator of the farm who waives the right to receive a credit or payment. See regulations § 48.6420-6 for general requirements for records to be kept.

(5) *Waiver on behalf of owner, tenant, or operator of farm.*—An agent of the owner, tenant, or operator of a farm who is expressly authorized to act on behalf of and to bind the owner, tenant, or operator may waive that person's rights to a credit or payment under section 6420 by signing the waiver on the person's behalf.

(6) *Sample form of agreement.*—While no specific form is required for an effective waiver, an acceptable form waiving the right to receive a credit or payment under section 6420 follows:

I hereby waive my right as owner/tenant/operator of a farm located at . . . . (address) . . . . to receive credit or payment from the United States for gasoline used by . . . . (aerial applicator) . . . . on the farm in connection with cultivating the soil, or the raising or harvesting of any agricultural or horticultural commodity. This waiver applies to gasoline used during the period . . . ., both dates inclusive. I understand that by signing this waiver, I give up my right to claim any credit or payment for gasoline by the aerial applicator during the period indicated, and I acknowledge that I have not previously claimed any credit for that gasoline.

. . . .
(Signature of Owner/Tenant/Operator)
[Reg. § 48.6420-4.]

☐ [*T.D.* 8043, 8-8-85. *Amended by T.D.* 8152, 8-27-87.]

[Reg. § 48.6420-5]

§ 48.6420-5. Applicable laws.—(a) *Penalties, excessive claims, etc.*—All provisions of law, including penalties, applicable in respect of the tax imposed by section 4081 shall, to the extent applicable and consistent with section 6420, apply in respect of the payments provided for in section 6420 to the same extent as if these payments were refunds of overpayments of the tax imposed on the sale of gasoline under section 4081. For special rules applicable to the assessment and collection of amounts constituting excessive payments under section 6420, see section 6206 and the regulations thereunder. For the civil penalty assessable in the case of excessive claims under section 6420, see section 6675 and the regulations thereunder. For the treatment as an overpayment of an amount allowable as an excessive credit under section 39 with respect to amounts payable under section 6420, see section 6401(b).

(b) *Examination of books and witnesses.*—For the purpose of ascertaining (1) the correctness of any claim made under section 6420 or (2) the correctness of any credit or payment made in respect of the claim, the Commissioner shall have the same

authority granted by paragraphs (1), (2), and (3) of section 7602, relating to examination of books and witnesses, as if the person claiming credit or payment under section 6420 were the person liable for tax.

(c) *Fractional part of a dollar.*—Section 6420(e)(3) provides that section 7504, relating to fractional parts of a dollar, shall not apply with respect to the allowance of any amount as a credit or payment under section 6420. Accordingly, credits or payments authorized by section 6420 shall be made in the exact amount to which the claimant is entitled and shall not be rounded to the nearest whole dollar amount. [Reg. § 48.6420-5.]

☐ [*T.D.* 8043, 8-8-85.]

[Reg. § 48.6420-6]

§ 48.6420-6. Records to be kept in substantiation of credits or payments.—(a) *In general.*—Every person making a claim for credit or payment under section 6420 must keep records sufficient to enable the district director to determine whether the person is entitled to credit or payment under section 6420 and, if so, the amount of the credit or payment. No particular form is prescribed for keeping the records, but the records must include a copy of the income tax return or claim and a copy of any statement or document submitted with the return or claim. The records must also show with respect to the taxable year covered by the claim—

(1) The number of gallons of gasoline purchased and the dates of purchase,

(2) The name and address of each vendor from whom gasoline was purchased and the total number of gallons purchased from each,

(3) The number of gallons of gasoline purchased by the claimant and used during the taxable year for farming purposes on a farm of which the claimant is the owner, tenant, or operator,

(4) The number of gallons of gasoline used during the taxable year for the purposes described in section 6420(c)(3)(A) and § 48.6420-4(d) (relating to cultivating, raising, or harvesting) by a person other than the owner, tenant, or operator on a farm of which the claimant is the owner, tenant, or operator, and

(5) Other information as necessary to establish the correctness of the claim.

(b) *Acceptable records.*—(1) Evidence of purchases of gasoline, and the purposes for which it was used, to substantiate claims may include paid duplicate sales invoices or tickets from the gasoline dealer or other vendor, and detailed records of all fuel used which show the amount consumed on a farm for farming purposes and the amount used for other purposes.

(2) Records maintained for Federal or State income tax purposes, or to support claims for refund of a State tax on gasoline, may be used to the extent that they contain the information necessary to substantiate the accuracy of the claim for credit under section 6420. However, the

records must show separately the number of gallons of gasoline used on a farm for farming purposes.

(3) If trucks or other vehicles are used both on and off the farm, an allocation of gasoline used in the vehicle will be required to show separately the number of gallons of gasoline used on a farm for farming purposes in respect of which the claim is made.

(4) If the owner, tenant, or operator is entitled under section 6420(c)(4)(A) to claim credit or payment in respect of gasoline used on the person's farm by another person other than an owner, tenant, or operator of the farm for a purpose described in section 6420(c)(3)(A) and §48.6420-4(d), the claimant must have records showing (i) the name and address of the person who performed the farming operation, (ii) a description of the type of work (such as plowing, threshing, combining, etc.) and the type of equipment used, (iii) the date or dates on which the work was done, and (iv) the number of gallons of gasoline so used on the claimant's farm.

(c) *Place and period for keeping records.*—(1) All records required by this section must be kept by the claimant at a convenient and safe location within the United States which is accessible to internal revenue officers and shall during normal business hours be available for inspection by internal revenue officers. If the claimant has a principal place of business in the United States, the records must be kept at that place of business.

(2) Records required to substantiate a claim under section 6420 must be maintained for a period of at least 3 years from the last date prescribed for the filing of the claim for credit or payment. [Reg. §48.6420-6.]

☐ [*T.D.* 8043, 8-8-85.]

[Reg. §48.6420(a)-2]

§48.6420(a)-2. Gasoline includible in claim.—Payment may be claimed under section 6420 only in respect of gasoline used on a farm in the United States for farming purposes. No payment is allowable under section 6420 with respect to gasoline used for nonfarming purposes, or gasoline used off a farm, regardless of the nature of such use. If a vehicle or other equipment is used both on a farm and off the farm, or if it is used on a farm both for farming and nonfarming purposes, payment is allowable only with respect to that portion of the gasoline which was "used on a farm for farming purposes" as defined in paragraph (a) of §48.6420(c)-1. The type of equipment or vehicle and whether or not it is registered for highway use is immaterial. However, the actual use of the equipment or vehicle and place where it is used are material. For example, if a truck used on a farm for farming purposes is also used on the highways (even though in connection with operating the farm), the gasoline used in operating the truck on the highways is not to be taken into account in computing the payment for which a claim is filed, since such gasoline was used off the farm. [Reg. §48.6420(a)-2.]

☐ [*T.D.* 6433, 12-22-59.]

[Reg. §48.6421-0]

§48.6421-0. Off-highway business use.—For purposes of the regulations under section 6421, after March 31, 1983, the term "off-highway business use" is used in lieu of the term "qualified business use" and has the same meaning as "qualified business use" under §48.6421-4(b). [Reg. §48.6421-0.]

☐ [*T.D.* 8043, 8-8-85.]

[Reg. §48.6421-1]

§48.6421-1. Credits or payments to ultimate purchaser of gasoline used for certain nonhighway purposes.—(a) *In general.*—(1) If gasoline is used in a qualified business use or as fuel in an aircraft (other than aircraft in noncommercial aviation), a credit (under the circumstances described in paragraph (b) of this section) or a payment (under the circumstances described in paragraph (c) of this section) in respect of the gasoline shall be allowed or made to the ultimate purchaser of the gasoline. For gasoline used in a qualified business use prior to April 1, 1983, the credit or payment under this section shall be an amount equal to 1 cent for each gallon of gasoline so used on which the tax was paid at the rate of 3 cents a gallon and 2 cents for each gallon of gasoline so used on which the tax was paid at the rate of 4 cents a gallon. For gasoline used in an off-highway business use after March 31, 1983, the credit or payment under this section shall be an amount equal to the amount determined by multiplying the number of gallons so used by the rate at which tax was imposed on such gasoline under section 4081. For gasoline used as a fuel in an aircraft (other than aircraft in noncommercial aviation) the credit or payment under this section shall be an amount equal to the amount determined by multiplying the number of gallons so used by the rate at which tax was imposed on the gasoline under section 4081. No interest shall be paid on any payment allowed under paragraph (c) of this section. However, interest may be paid on any overpayment (as defined by section 6401) arising from a credit allowed under paragraph (b) of this section. See section 34(a), relating to credit for certain uses of gasoline and special fuels (and lubricating oil used prior to January 7, 1983). See §48.6421-3 for the time within which a claim for credit or payment must be made under this section. See §48.6421-4 for the meaning of the terms "gasoline," "qualified business use," "noncommercial aviation," and "taxable year."

(2) For purposes of determining the allowable credit or payment in respect of gasoline used in a qualified business use or as fuel in an aircraft (other than aircraft in noncommercial aviation), gasoline on hand shall be considered used in the order in which it was purchased. Thus, if the ultimate purchaser has on hand gasoline acquired in two purchases made at different times

and subject to different rates of tax, in determining credit or payment for the gasoline used in a qualified business use or as fuel in an aircraft (other than aircraft in noncommercial aviation), it will be assumed that the gasoline first purchased was the first gasoline used, and the rate applicable to that purchase will apply in determining the credit or payment, until all that gasoline is accounted for.

(b) *Allowance of income tax credit in lieu of payment.*—Except as provided in paragraph (c) of this section, repayment under this section of the tax paid under section 4081 on gasoline used in a qualified business use or as a fuel in an aircraft (other than aircraft in noncommercial aviation) by a person subject to income tax may be obtained only by claiming a credit for the amount of this tax against the tax imposed by subtitle A of the Code. The amount of the credit shall be an amount equal to the payment which would be made under section 6421 with respect to gasoline used during the taxable year in a qualified business use or as a fuel in an aircraft (other than aircraft in noncommercial aviation) if section 6421(i) and paragraph (c) of this section did not apply. See section 34(a)(2).

(c) *Allowance of payment.*—Payments in respect of gasoline upon which tax was paid under section 4081 that is used in a qualified business use or as a fuel in an aircraft (other than aircraft in noncommercial aviation) shall be made only to—

(1) The United States or any agency or instrumentality thereof, a State, a political subdivision of a State, or an agency or instrumentality of one or more State political subdivisions of a State, or the District of Columbia,

(2) An organization which is exempt from tax under section 501(a) and is not required to make a return of the income tax imposed under subtitle A for its taxable year, or

(3) A person described in section 6421(c)(2) to whom $1,000 or more is payable (without regard to paragraph (b) of this section) under this section with respect to gasoline used during any of the first three quarters of the person's taxable year.

(d) *Dual use of gasoline.*—(1) No credit or payment may be claimed in respect of gasoline used in a highway vehicle used in a trade or business or for the production of income solely by reason of the fact that the propulsion motor in the vehicle is also used for a purpose other than the propulsion of the vehicle. Thus, if the propulsion motor of a highway vehicle (used in a trade or business or for the production of income) also operates special equipment, such as a mixing unit on a concrete mixer truck or a pump for discharging fuel from a tank truck, by means of a power takeoff or power transfer, no credit or payment may be claimed in respect of the gasoline used to operate the special equipment, even though the special equipment is mounted on the highway vehicle.

(2) If a highway vehicle is equipped with a separate motor to operate the special equipment used in a trade or business or for the production of income, such as a refrigeration unit, pump, generator, or mixing unit, credit or payment may be claimed in respect of the gasoline used in the separate motor.

(3) If gasoline used in a separate motor is drawn from the same tank as the one which supplies gasoline for the propulsion of the highway vehicle, the determination as to the quantity of gasoline used in the separate motor operating the special equipment must be based on operating experience and supported by records.

(4) Devices to measure the number of miles the highway vehicle has traveled, such as hubometers, may be used in making a preliminary determination of the number of gallons of gasoline used to propel the vehicle. In order to make a final determination of the number of gallons of gasoline used to propel the vehicle, there must be added to this preliminary determination the number of gallons of gasoline consumed while idling or warming up the motor preparatory to propelling the vehicle.

(e) *Gasoline lost or destroyed.*—Gasoline lost or destroyed through spillage, fire, or other casualty is not considered to have been "used" in a qualified business use or as fuel in an aircraft (other than aircraft in noncommercial aviation) and, accordingly, credit or payment in respect of the gasoline may not be claimed.

(f) *Supporting evidence required.*—Each claim under this section for credit or payment must include a statement showing—

(1) The total number of gallons of gasoline purchased and used during the period covered by the claim in a qualified business use multiplied by the rate of payment allowable in respect of the gasoline. (For the rate of payment allowable, see paragraph (a)(1) of this section.)

(2) The total number of gallons of gasoline purchased and used during the period covered by the claim for use as fuel in an aircraft (other than aircraft in noncommercial aviation) multiplied by the rate of payment allowable in respect of the gasoline.

(3) The purpose or purposes for which the gasoline was used, determined by reference to general categories, and the amount used for each purpose; and

(4) If a claim on Form 843 is being filed, the internal revenue district or service center with which the claimant last filed an income tax return (if any). [Reg. § 48.6421-1.]

☐ [*T.D.* 8043, 8-8-85.]

[Reg. § 48.6421-2]

§ 48.6421-2. Credits or payments to ultimate purchasers of gasoline used in intercity, local, or school buses.—(a) *In general.*—If gasoline is used in an intercity or local bus while engaged in furnishing (for compensation) passenger land transportation available to the general public or in a school bus engaged in the transportation of students or employees of schools, a credit (under the circumstances described in paragraph (b) of this section) or a payment (under the circumstances described in paragraph (c) of this section) in respect to the gasoline shall be allowed or made to the ultimate purchaser of the gasoline. The credit or payment under this section shall be an amount equal to the product of the number of gallons of gasoline so used multiplied by the rate at which tax was imposed on the gasoline by section 4081. No interest shall be paid on any payment allowed under paragraph (c) of this section. However, interest may be paid on an overpayment(as defined by section 6401) arising from a credit allowed under paragraph (b) of this section. See section 34(a) relating to credit for certain uses of gasoline and special fuels, (and lubricating oil used prior to January 7, 1983). See § 48.6421-3 for the time within which a claim for credit or payment must be made under this section. See § 48.6421-4 for the meaning of "gasoline."

(b) *Allowance of income tax credit.*—Except as provided in paragraph (c) of this section, repayment under this section of the tax paid under section 4081 of gasoline used while engaged in furnishing (for compensation) passenger land transportation available to the general public or in school bus transportation operations by a person subject to income tax may be obtained only by claiming a credit for the amount of this tax against the tax imposed by subtitle A of the Code. The amount of the credit shall be an amount equal to the payment which would be made under section 6421 with respect to gasoline used during the taxable year for this passenger land transportation or school bus operations if section 6421(i) and paragraph (c) of this section did not apply. See section 34(a)(2).

(c) *Allowance of payment.*—Payments in respect of gasoline upon which tax was paid under section 4081 that is used while engaged in furnishing (for compensation) passenger land transportation available to the general public or in school bus transportation operations shall be made only to—

(1) The United States or any agency or instrumentality thereof, a State, or political subdivision of a State, or an agency or instrumentality of one or more States or political subdivisions of a State, or the District of Columbia,

(2) An organization which is exempt from tax under section 501(a) and is not required to make a return of the income tax imposed under subtitle A for its taxable year, or

(3) A person described in section 6421(c)(2) to whom $1,000 or more is payable (without regard to paragraph (b) of this section) under this section with respect to gasoline used during any of the first three quarters of the person's taxable year.

(d) *Supporting evidence required.*—Each claim under this section for credit or payment must include a statement showing—

(1) The total number of gallons of gasoline purchased and used during the period covered

by the claim for each intercity or local bus while engaged in furnishing (for compensation) passenger land transportation available to the general public multiplied by the rate at which tax was imposed on the gasoline by section 4081.

(2) The total number of gallons of gasoline purchased and used in each bus while engaged in school bus transportation operations multiplied by the rate at which tax was imposed on the gasoline by section 4081, and

(3) If a claim on Form 843 is being filed, the internal revenue district or service center with which the claimant last filed an income tax return (if any). [Reg. § 48.6421-2.]

☐ [*T.D.* 8043, 8-8-85. *Amended by T.D.* 8879, 3-30-2000.]

[Reg. § 48.6421-3]

§ 48.6421-3. Time for filing claim for credit or payment.—(a) *In general.*—A claim for credit or payment described in § 48.6421-1 with respect to gasoline used in a qualified business use or as a fuel in an aircraft (other than aircraft in noncommercial aviation) or in § 48.6421-2 with respect to gasoline used either in an intercity or local bus while engaged in furnishing (for compensation) passenger land transportation available to the general public or in school bus transportation operations, shall cover only gasoline used during the taxable year, or when paragraph (b)(2) of this section applies, gasoline used during the calendar quarter. Therefore, gasoline on hand at the end of a taxable year, or, if applicable, a calendar quarter, such as gasoline in fuel supply tanks of vehicles or in storage tanks or drums, must be excluded from a claim filed for the taxable year or calendar quarter, as the case may be. However, this gasoline may be included in a claim filed for a later taxable year or a later calendar quarter if it is used during that later year or quarter in a qualified business use, as fuel in an aircraft (other than aircraft in noncommercial aviation), or in intercity, local, or school buses. Gasoline used during the taxable year or calendar quarter may be covered by the claim for that period although the gasoline was not paid for at the time the claim is filed. For purposes of applying this section, a governmental unit or exempt organization described in § 48.6421-1(c) or § 48.6421-2(c) is considered to have as its taxable year, the calendar year or fiscal year on the basis of which it regularly keeps its books; see § 48.6421-4(g).

(b) *Time for filing.*—(1) *Annual claims.*—(i) A claim under this section for credit or payment with respect to gasoline shall not be allowed unless it is filed no later than the time prescribed by section 6511 and the regulations thereunder for filing a claim for credit or refund of income tax for the particular taxable year.

(ii) A claim for payment of a governmental unit or exempt organization described in § 48.6421-1(c) or § 48.6421-2(c) must be filed no later than 3 years following the close of its taxable year (see § 48.6421-4).

(2) *Quarterly claims.*—A claim for payment of $1,000 or more in respect of gasoline used during any of the first three quarters of the taxable year, filed either under § 48.6421-1(c)(3) in respect of gasoline used in a qualified business use or as a fuel in an aircraft (other than aircraft used in noncommercial aviation) or under § 48.6421-2(c)(3) in respect of gasoline used while engaged in furnishing (for compensation) passenger land transportation available to the general public or in school bus operations, shall not be allowed unless the claim is filed on or before the last day of the first calendar quarter for which the claim is filed. No quarterly claim may be filed for the last calendar quarter of the taxable year. Amounts for which payment is disallowed under this paragraph (b)(2) merely because the claim was not filed on time may be included in an annual claim filed under paragraph (b)(1) of this section, but other amounts for which a claim for payment has been filed under this paragraph (b)(2) may not be included in an annual claim filed under paragraph (b)(1) of this section.

(3) *Other applicable rules.*—See § 301.7502-1 of this chapter (Regulations on Procedure and Administration) for provisions treating timely mailing as timely filing and § 301.7503-1 of this chapter for time for performance of an act where the last day falls on Saturday, Sunday, or a legal holiday.

(c) *Limit on claims per taxable year.*—Not more than one claim may be filed under § 48.6421-1 or § 48.6421-2 by any person with respect to gasoline used during any taxable year, except to the extent that quarterly claims may be filed under paragraph (b)(2) of this section with respect to any calendar quarter (other than the last calendar quarter) of the taxable year.

(d) *Form and content of claim.*—(1) *Claim for credit.*—The claim for credit to which this section applies must be made by attaching a Form 4136 to the income tax return of an individual or a corporation. Form 4136 must be executed in accordance with the instructions prescribed for the preparation of the form. A partnership may not file Form 4136. When a partnership files Form 1065, U.S. Partnership Return of Income, it must include a statement showing how many gallons are allocated to each partner and the use made of the gasoline.

(2) *Claim for payment.*—The claim for payment to which this section applies must be made on Form 8849 (or on such other form as the Commissioner may designate) in aaccordance with the instructions prescribed for the preparation of the form. Each form must designate the taxable year, or calendar quarter, for which it is filed.

(3) *Death or termination.*—(i) If an individual dies, or if a sole proprietorship, partnership, or corporation is terminated or liquidated, during the taxable year, the claim for credit or payment may be filed in respect of gasoline used during the short taxable year in the same manner as is provided for gasoline used in a full taxable year. Those months which constitute a quarter of a full taxable year will constitute the same quarter of the short taxable year. For example, if a corporation using the calendar year is liquidated on September 30, 1982, and is entitled to $900 under § 48.6421-1 in respect of gasoline used in a qualified business use for the calendar quarters ending June 30 and September 30, it may file a claim for payment in respect of the gasoline used during the calendar quarters ending June 30, and September 30, 1981, and take a credit of $900 on its income tax return for the short taxable year in respect of the gasoline used during the calendar quarter ending March 31, 1982.

(ii) A claim for payment on behalf of a decedent may be filed by the decedent's executor, administrator, or any other person charged with responsibility for the decedent's affairs. Such a claim must be accompanied by copies of the letters testamentary, letters of administration, or, in the case of a claim filed by other than the executor or administrator, the information called for in Form 1310 (Statement of Person Claiming Refund Due a Deceased Taxpayer). The claim may cover only gasoline in respect of which the decedent would have been entitled to claim payment. For example, if an individual dies on July 15, 1982, prior to claiming payment under § 48.6421-1 or $1,000 or more applicable to gasoline purchased and used in a qualified business use during the calendar quarter ending June 30, 1982, the decedent's executor or other legal representative may file a claim for payment covering that calendar quarter, and take the credit provided by section 39(a)(2) against the decedent's income tax on the income tax return for the short taxable year in respect of gasoline purchased by the decedent and so used during the period from July 1, 1982, to July 15, 1982, the date of death.

(e) *Restrictions on claims for credit or payment.*—Credits or payments are allowable only in respect of gasoline that was sold by the producer or importer in a transaction that was subject to tax under section 4081. For example, a State or local government may not file a claim with respect to any gasoline which it purchased tax free from the producer, even though the State or local government used the gasoline as a fuel for the purposes described in paragraph (a) of this section. Similarly, a governmental unit or tax-exempt organization that is the ultimate purchaser of gasoline may not file a claim for payment if it is known that another person is entitled to claim credit, payment, or refund with respect to the same gasoline. For example, a State or local government may not file a claim for payment if it has executed, or intends to execute, a written consent, or other documentation, to enable the producer to claim credit or refund for the tax that was paid. See, for example, § § 48.6416(a)-3 and 48.6416(b)(2)-3(b)(1). [Reg. § 48.6421-3.]

☐ [*T.D. 8043, 8-8-85. Amended by T.D. 8659, 3-13-96 and T.D. 8748, 12-31-97.*]

[Reg. §48.6421-4]

§48.6421-4. Meaning of terms.—For purposes of the regulations under section 6421, unless otherwise expressly indicated—

(a) *Gasoline.*—The term "gasoline" has the same meaning given to such term by section 4082(b) and regulations thereunder.

(b) *Qualified business use.*—(1) The term "qualified business use" means any use by a person in a trade or business of the person or in an activity of the person described in section 212 (relating to production of income) otherwise than as a fuel in a highway vehicle—

　　(i) That at the time of the use is registered, or is required to be registered, for highway use under the laws of any state, the District of Columbia, or a foreign country, or

　　(ii) That, in the case of a highway vehicle owned by the United States, is used on the highway.
The term "qualified business use" does not include any use in a motorboat, other than a vessel used in the fisheries or whaling business. See paragraph (c) of this section for the definition of "highway vehicle." See paragraph (d) of this section for the definition of "highway."

(2) Any highway vehicle operated under a dealer's tag, license, or permit will be considered to be registered. A highway vehicle is not considered to be "registered" solely because there has been issued a special permit for operation of the vehicle at particular times and under specified conditions. However, a highway vehicle that is required to be registered and that is also issued a special permit for operation of the vehicle under specified conditions, such as carrying an oversize load, is still considered to be "registered."

(3) Nonbusiness, off-highway use of gasoline by such vehicles and equipment as minibikes, snowmobiles, power lawn mowers, chain saws, and other yard equipment does not qualify as gasoline used in a qualified business use.

(4) Examples of gasoline used in a qualified business use include (i) gasoline used (in a trade or business or for the production of income) in stationary engines to operate pumps, generators, compressors, and power saws; (ii) gasoline used (in a trade or business or for the production of income) for cleaning purposes; (iii) gasoline used (in a trade or business or for the production of income) in forklift trucks, bulldozers, and earthmovers; and (iv) gasoline used by a nonhighway vehicle in connection with the trade or business of construction, mining or logging.

(5) *Illustration.*—The application of this paragraph (b) may be illustrated by the following example.
Example. M Corporation, a logging company, files its income tax return on the basis of the calendar year. During 1982, the company used 20,000 gallons of gasoline in its logging business. Of this amount, 12,000 gallons were used as fuel in registered highway vehicles which were operated both on the public highways and on the company's private roads. Of the remaining 8,000 gallons, 6,000 were used in nonhighway vehicles, such as tractors and bulldozers, and 2,000 gallons were used in highway vehicles, such as heavy trucks which, at the time of use, were neither registered nor required to be registered under state law for highway use by reason of being operated entirely on the company's property. As the ultimate purchaser, M may take a credit on its income tax return for 1982 under this section in respect of the 6,000 gallons used in the nonhighway vehicles and the 2,000 gallons used in the unregistered highway vehicles. However, no credit may be allowed with respect to the 12,000 gallons used in the registered highway vehicles even though a portion of this gasoline was used in operating the vehicles on the company's own property.

(c) *Highway vehicle.*—The term "highway vehicle" has the same meaning assigned to this term under §48.4061(a)-1(d).

(d) *Highway.*—The term "highway" includes any road, whether a Federal highway, State highway, city street, or otherwise, in the United States which is not a private roadway.

(e) *Noncommercial aviation.*—The term "noncommercial aviation" has the same meaning given to such term by section 4041(c)(4).

(f) *Calendar quarter.*—The term "calendar quarter" means a period of three calendar months ending on March 31, June 30, and September 30, or December 31.

(g) *Taxable year.*—The "taxable year" of a governmental unit or tax-exempt organization described in §48.6421-1(c) or §48.6421-2(c) is the calendar or fiscal year on the basis of which it regularly keeps its books. The "taxable year" of persons subject to income tax shall have the meaning it has under section 7701(a)(23). [Reg. §48.6421-4.]

☐ [*T.D. 8043, 8-8-85.*]

[Reg. §48.6421-5]

§48.6421-5. Exempt sales; other payments or refunds available.—(a) *Exempt sales.*—No credit or payment shall be allowed or made under §48.6421-1 or §48.6421-2 with respect to gasoline which was exempt from the tax imposed by section 4081. For example, credit or payment may not be allowed or made with respect to gasoline purchased tax free for use as supplies for certain vessels and airplanes, or with respect to gasoline purchased by a State tax free for its exclusive use, as provided in section 4221.

(b) *Other payments or refunds available.*—Any amount which, without regard to the second sentence of section 6421(e)(1) and this paragraph (b), would be allowable as a credit or payable to any person under §48.6421-1 or §48.6421-2 is reduced by any other amount which is allowable as a credit or payable under section 6421, or is refundable under any other provision of the Code, to any person with respect to the same gasoline.

(c) *Gasoline used on farms.*—Payments with respect to gasoline used on a farm for farming purposes shall be claimed under section 6420 and § 48.6420-1, and no claim in respect of that gasoline may be made under section 6421 and the regulations thereunder. [Reg. § 48.6421-5.]

☐ [T.D. 8043, 8-8-85.]

[Reg. § 48.6421-6]

§ 48.6421-6. Applicable laws.—(a) *Penalties, excessive claims, etc.*—All provisions of law, including penalties, applicable in respect of the tax imposed by section 4081 shall, to the extent applicable and consistent with section 6421, apply in respect of the payments provided for in section 6421 to the same extent as if these payments were refunds of overpayments of the tax imposed on the sale of gasoline by section 4081. For special rules applicable to the assessment and collection of amounts constituting excessive payments under section 6421, see section 6206 and the regulations thereunder. For the civil penalty assessable in the case of excessive claims under section 6421, see section 6675 and the regulations thereunder. For the treatment as an overpayment of an amount allowable as an excessive credit under section 34 (section 39 of the Internal Revenue Code of 1954 prior to its revision by the Tax Reform Act of 1984) with respect to amounts payable under section 6421, see section 6401(b).

(b) *Examination of books and witnesses.*—For the purpose of ascertaining (1) the correctness of any claim made under section 6421 or (2) the correctness of any credit or payment made in respect of the claim, the Commissioner shall have the same authority granted by paragraphs (1), (2), and (3) of section 7602, relating to examination of books and witnesses, as if the person claiming credits or payment under section 6421 were the person liable for tax. [Reg. § 48.6421-6.]

☐ [T.D. 8043, 8-8-85.]

[Reg. § 48.6421-7]

§ 48.6421-7. Records to be kept in substantiation of credits or payments.—(a) *In general.*—Every person making a claim for credit or payment under section 6421 must keep records sufficient to enable the district director to determine whether the person is entitled to credit or payment under section 6421 and, if so, the amount of the credit or payment. No particular form is prescribed for keeping the records, but the records must include a copy of any statement or document submitted with the return or claim. The records must also show with respect to the period covered by the claim—

(1) The number of gallons of gasoline purchased and the dates of purchase,

(2) The name and address of each vendor from whom gasoline was purchased and the total number of gallons purchased from each,

(3) The number of gallons of gasoline purchased by the claimant and used during the period covered by the claim for nonhighway purposes or in intercity, local or school buses,

(4) Other information as necessary to establish the correctness of the claim.

(b) *Acceptable records.*—(1) Evidence of purchases of gasoline, and the purposes for which it was used, to substantiate claims may include paid duplicate sales invoices or tickets from the gasoline dealer or other vendor, and detailed records of all fuel used which show the amount used for the prescribed purpose and the amount used for other purposes.

(2) Records maintained for Federal or State income tax purposes, or to support claims for refund of a State tax on gasoline, may be used to the extent that they contain the information necessary to substantiate the accuracy of the claim for credit under section 6421. However, the records must show separately the number of gallons of gasoline used for nonhighway purposes or in intercity, local, or school buses during the period covered by the claim.

(c) *Place and period for keeping records.*—(1) All records required by this section must be kept by the claimant at a convenient and safe location within the United States which is accessible to internal revenue officers and shall during normal business hours be available for inspection by internal revenue officers. If the claimant has a principal place of business in the United States, the records must be kept at that place of business.

(2) Records required to substantiate a claim under section 6421 must be maintained for a period of at least 3 years from the last date prescribed for the filing of the claim for credit or payment. [Reg. § 48.6421-7.]

☐ [T.D. 8043, 8-8-85.]

[Reg. § 1.6425-1]

§ 1.6425-1. Adjustment of overpayment of estimated income tax by corporation.—(a) *In general.*—Any corporation which has made an overpayment of estimated income tax for a taxable year beginning after December 31, 1967, may file an application for an adjustment of such overpayment. The right to file an application for an adjustment of overpayment of estimated income tax is limited to corporations.

(b) *Contents of application.*—(1) The application for an adjustment of overpayment of estimated income tax shall be filed on Form 4466. The application shall be filled out in accordance with the instructions accompanying the form, and all information required by the form and instructions must be furnished by the corporation. The application shall be verified in the manner prescribed by section 6065 as in the case of a return of the corporation.

(2) An application for an adjustment of overpayment of estimated income tax does not constitute a claim for credit or refund. If such application is disallowed by the district director, or director of a service center, in whole or in part, no suit may be maintained in any court for the recovery of any tax based on such application. The filing of an application for an adjustment of overpayment of estimated income tax will not constitute the filing of a claim for credit or refund within the meaning of section 6511 for the purpose of determining whether a claim for refund was filed prior to the expiration of the applicable period of limitation. The corporation, however, may file a claim for credit or refund under section 6402 at any time prior to the expiration of the applicable period of limitation and may maintain a suit based on such claim if it is disallowed or if the district director, or director of a service center, does not act on the claim within six months from the date it is filed. Such claim may be filed before, simultaneously with, or after the filing of the application for the adjustment of overpayment of estimated tax. A claim for credit or refund under section 6402 filed after the filing of an application for an adjustment of overpayment of estimated income tax is not to be considered an amendment of such application. Such claim, however, in proper cases, may constitute an amendment to a prior claim filed under section 6402.

(c) *Time and place for filing application.*—(1) The application for an adjustment of overpayment of estimated income tax shall be filed after the last day of the taxable year and on or before the fifteenth day of the third month thereafter, or before the date on which the corporation first files its income tax return for such taxable year (whether or not it subsequently amends the return), whichever is earlier.

(2) Except as provided in paragraph (b)(2) of §301.6091-1 (relating to hand-carried documents), the application on Form 4466 shall be filed with the internal revenue officer designated in instructions applicable to such form. [Reg. §1.6425-1.]

☐ [*T.D.* 7059, 9-16-70.]

[Reg. §301.6425-1]

§301.6425-1. Adjustment of overpayment of estimated income tax by corporation.—For regulations under section 6425, see §§1.6425-1 to 1.6425-3, inclusive, of this chapter (Income Tax Regulations). [Reg. §301.6425-1.]

☐ [*T.D.* 7059, 9-16-70.]

[Reg. §1.6425-2]

§1.6425-2. Computation of adjustment of overpayment of estimated tax.—(a) Income tax liability defined. For purposes of §1.6425-1, this section, §§1.6425-3 and 1.6655-7, relating to excessive adjustment, the term income tax liability means the excess of—

(1) The sum of—

(i) The tax imposed by section 11 or 1201(a), or subchapter L of chapter 1 of the Internal Revenue Code, whichever is applicable; plus

(ii) The tax imposed by section 55; over

(2) The credits against tax provided by part IV of subchapter A of chapter 1 of the Internal Revenue Code.

(b) *Computation of adjustment.*—The amount of an adjustment under section 6425 is an amount equal to the excess of the estimated income tax paid by the corporation during the taxable year over the amount which, at the time of filing Form 4466, the corporation estimates as its income tax liability for the taxable year.

(c) *Effective/applicability date.*—Paragraph (a) of this section is applicable to applications for adjustments of overpayments of estimated income tax that are filed in taxable years beginning after September 6, 2007. [Reg. §1.6425-2.]

☐ [*T.D.* 7059, 9-16-70. *Amended by T.D.* 9347, 8-6-2007.]

[Reg. §1.6425-3]

§1.6425-3. Allowance of adjustments.—(a) *Limitation.*—No application under section 6425 shall be allowed unless the amount of the adjustment is (1) at least 10 percent of the amount which, at the time of filing Form 4466 the corporation estimates as its income tax liability for the taxable year, *and* (2) at least $500.

(b) *Time prescribed.*—The Internal Revenue Service shall act upon an application for an adjustment of overpayment of estimated income tax within a period of 45 days from the date on which such application is filed.

(c) *Examination.*—Within the 45-day period described in paragraph (b) of this section, the Internal Revenue Service shall make, to the extent it deems practicable in such period, a limited examination of the application to discover omissions and errors therein. The Service shall verify the calculation of the adjustment, which calculation must be set forth by the corporation in the application for such adjustment, in the manner provided in section 6425(c)(2) for the determination by the corporation of such adjustment. The Service, however, may correct any material error or omission that is discovered upon examination of the application. In determining the adjustment, the Service may correct any mathematical error appearing on the application, and it may likewise make any modification required by the law to correct the corporation's computation of the adjustment. If the required modification has not been made by the corporation and the Service has available the necessary information to make such modification within the 45-day period, it may make such modification. The examination of the application and the allowance of the adjustment shall not prejudice any right of the Service to claim later that the adjustment was improper.

(d) *Disallowance in whole or in part.*—If the Internal Revenue Service finds that an application for an adjustment of overpayment of estimated tax contains material omissions or errors, the Service may disallow such application in whole or in part without further action. If, however, the Service deems that any omission or error can be corrected by it within the 45-day period, it may do so and allow the application in whole or in part. In the case of a disallowance or modification, the Service shall notify the corporation of such action. The Service's determination as to whether it can correct any omission or error shall be conclusive. Similarly, its action in disallowing, in whole or in part, any application for an adjustment of overpayment of estimated income tax shall be final and may not be challenged in any proceeding. The corporation in such case, however, may file a claim for credit or refund under section 6402, and may maintain a suit based on such claim if it is disallowed or if the Service does not act upon the claim within six months from the date it is filed.

(e) *Application of adjustment.*—If the Internal Revenue Service allows the adjustment, it may first credit the amount of the adjustment against any liability in respect of an internal revenue tax on the part of the corporation which is due and payable on the date of the allowance of the adjustment before making payment of the balance to the corporation. In such a case, the Service shall notify the corporation of the credit, and refund the balance of the adjustment.

(f) *Effect of adjustment.*—(1) For purposes of all sections of the Internal Revenue Code except section 6655, relating to additions to tax for failure to pay estimated income tax, any adjustment under section 6425 is to be treated as a reduction of prior estimated tax payments as of the date the credit is allowed or the refund is paid. For the purpose of sections 6655(a) through (g), (i), and (j), credit or refund of an adjustment is to be treated as if not made in determining whether there has been any underpayment of estimated income tax and, if there is an underpayment, the period during which the underpayment existed. However, an excessive adjustment under section 6425 is taken into account in applying the addition to tax under section 6655(h).

(2) For the effect of an excessive adjustment under section 6425, see § 1.6655-7.

(3) Effective/applicability date: This paragraph (f) is applicable to applications for adjustments of overpayments of estimated income tax that are filed in taxable years beginning after September 6, 2007. [Reg. § 1.6425-3.]

☐ [*T.D.* 7059, 9-16-70. *Amended by T.D.* 9347, 8-6-2007.]

[Reg. § 48.6427-0]

§ 48.6427-0. **Off-highway business use.**—For purposes of the regulations under section 6427, after March 31, 1983, the term "off-highway business use" is used in lieu of the term "qualified business use" and has the same meaning as "qualified business use" under § 48.6421-1(b). [Reg. § 48.6427-0.]

☐ [*T.D.* 8043, 8-8-85.]

[Reg. § 48.6427-1]

§ 48.6427-1. **Credit or payments to purchaser of special fuels resold or used for nontaxable, farming, or other purposes.**—(a) *Amount of repayment.*—(1) *Nontaxable or other uses.*—(i) If tax has been paid under section 4041(a)(1) on the sale of diesel fuel for use as a fuel in a diesel-powered highway vehicle or under section 4041(a)(2) on the sale of special motor fuel for use as a fuel in a motor vehicle or a motorboat and the fuel is used by the purchaser for a nontaxable purpose or for a purpose taxable at a lower rate than the purposes for which sold, a credit (under the circumstances described in paragraph (b) of this section) or a payment (under the circumstances described in paragraph (c) of this section) in respect of the fuel shall be allowed or made to the purchaser of the fuel in an amount equal to—

(A) The amount of the tax imposed on the sale of the fuel to the purchaser if the purchaser resells the fuel, or

(B) If the purchaser uses the fuel, the amount of tax imposed on the sale of the fuel to the purchaser, less the amount of tax, if any, that would have been imposed on the purchaser's use of the fuel if no tax had been imposed on the sale of the fuel to the purchaser.

(ii) For purposes of paragraph (a)(1)(i) of this section, and for the regulations under section 6427 applying such paragraph, tax imposed on the sale of fuel will be treated as an overpayment by the purchaser if the person resells the fuel or uses it for a nontaxable purpose or for a purpose taxable at a lower rate than that for which sold to the purchaser. Thus, for example, special motor fuel which was sold tax paid to the purchaser for use otherwise than in a qualified business use in a motor vehicle will qualify for the payment under section 6427 if the purchaser uses it as a fuel in a qualified business use.

(2) *Used for farming purposes.*—(i) If tax has been paid under section 4041(a)(1) on the sale of diesel fuel for use as a fuel in a diesel-powered highway vehicle, or under section 4041(a)(2) on the sale of special motor fuel for use as a fuel in a motor vehicle or a motor boat and the fuel is used on a farm for farming purposes, a credit (under the circumstances described in paragraph (b) of this section) or a payment (under the circumstances described in paragraph (c)(1) or (2) of this section) in respect of the fuel shall be allowed or made to the purchaser of the fuel in an amount equal to the amount of tax that was imposed under section 4041 on the sale of the fuel. The provisions of section 6420(c)(1), (2), and (3) and § 48.6420-4 shall apply under this paragraph (a)(2) in determining whether the fuel is used on a farm for farming purposes.

(ii) The term "purchaser," as used in paragraph (a)(2)(i) of this section, includes only a person who is an owner, tenant, or operator of a farm. A person who is owner, tenant, or operator of a farm is a purchaser of fuel only with respect to such fuel as is purchased by the person and used for farming purposes on a farm of which the person is the owner, tenant, or operator. Thus, the owner of a farm who purchases fuel which is used on the farm by its owner, tenant, or operator for farming purposes is generally the purchaser of the fuel. If, however, the cost of fuel supplied by an owner, tenant, or operator of a farm, is by agreement or other arrangement borne by a second person who is an owner, tenant, or operator of the farm, the second person who bore the cost of the fuel is considered to be the purchaser of the fuel.

(iii) Except as provided in paragraph (a)(2)(iv) of this section, if fuel is used on a farm by any person other than the owner, tenant, or operator for the purposes described in section 6420(c)(3)(A) and § 48.6420-4(d) (relating to gasoline used in cultivating, raising, or harvesting), the owner, tenant, or operator (as the case may be) will be treated for the purposes of § 48.6427-1(a)(2)(i) as the purchaser who used the fuel on the farm for farming purposes.

(iv) Section 6427(c) provides that an aerial applicator or other applicator is entitled to be treated as the user and ultimate purchaser of fuel that the applicator uses on a farm for the purposes described in section 6420(c)(3)(A), but only if the owner, tenant, or operator of the farm who is otherwise entitled to be treated as the ultimate purchaser waives the right to credit or payment. The rules contained in section 6420 and the regulations under the section regarding waivers by owners, tenants, and operators of farms of their rights to payments under section 6420 for gasoline used by aerial applicators on a farm for farming purposes apply to waivers under this section.

(3) *Definitions, uses, and other rules.*—(i) No interest shall be paid on any payment allowed under paragraph (c) of this section. However, interest may be paid on any overpayment (as defined by section 6401) arising from a credit. See section 34(a), relating to credit for certain uses of gasoline and special fuels. See section 39(a) of the Internal Revenue Code of 1954 prior to its revision by the Highways Revenue Act of 1982, relating to credit for certain uses of lubricating oil. See section 6611, relating to interest on overpayments.

(ii) See § 48.6427-3 for the time within which a claim for credit or payment must be made under this section.

(iii) See § 48.6420-4 for the meaning of the terms "used on a farm for farming purposes" and "farm." The term "gasoline" has the same meaning given to this term by section 4082(b) and the regulations thereunder. For the meaning of the terms "diesel fuel," "special motor fuel," "motor vehicle," "highway vehicle," and "registered" see section 4041 and the regulations thereunder. The term "fuel" means diesel fuel, special motor fuel, or gasoline, as the context requires. Where appropriate, the term "use" includes a resale. See § 48.6421-4 for the meaning of "calendar quarter" and "taxable year".

(iv) For purposes of determining the allowable credit or payment in respect of fuel used for nontaxable purposes, on a farm for farming purposes, or for purposes taxable at a lower rate, fuel on hand shall be considered used in the order in which it was purchased. Thus, if the purchaser made purchases at different times and subject to different rates of tax, then in determining credit or payment for fuel used for a described purpose, it will be assumed that the fuel first purchased was the first fuel used, and the rate applicable to that purchase will appy in determining the credit of payment, until all of that fuel is accounted for.

(v) Fuel lost or destroyed through spillage, fire, or other casualty is not considered to have been "used" within the meaning of this section, and, accordingly, no credit or payment of the tax paid on the sale of the fuel may be made under this section.

(b) *Allowance of income tax credit in lieu of payment.*—Except as provided in paragraph (c) of this section, repayment under this section of the tax paid under section 4041 on fuel used by a person subject to income tax may be obtained only by claiming a credit for the amount of this tax against the tax imposed by subtitle A of the Code. The amount of the credit shall be an amount equal to the payment which would be made under section 6427 with respect to fuel used during the taxable year for nontaxable purposes on a farm for farming purposes, or for purposes taxable at a lower rate, if section 6427(i) and paragraph (c) of this section did not apply. See section 34(a)(3).

(c) *Allowance of payment.*—Payments in respect of fuel upon which tax was paid under section 4041 that is used for nontaxable purposes, on a farm for farming purposes, or for purposes taxable at a lower rate, shall be made only to—

(1) The United States or any agency or instrumentality thereof, a State, a political subdivision of a State, or an agency or instrumentality of one or more States or political subdivisions of a State, or the District of Columbia,

(2) An organization which is exempt from tax under section 501(a) and is not required to make a return of the income tax imposed under subtitle A for its taxable year, or

(3) In the case of fuel used for nontaxable purposes to which section 6427(a) applies, to a person described in section 6427(g)(2) to whom $1,000 or more is payable (without regard to paragraph (b) of this section) under this section with respect to fuel used during any of the first three quarters of his taxable year.

(d) *Dual use of fuel.*—The principles set forth in § 48.4041-7, relating to dual use of fuel, for determining whether liability is incurred under section 4041 at the time of sale of the fuel, are equally applicable in determining whether a credit or payment is to be allowed under this section. Thus, if diesel fuel or special motor fuel used in a separate motor is drawn from the same tank as the one which supplies fuel for the propulsion of the vehicle, a reasonable determination of the quantity of the fuel used in the separate motor will be acceptable for purposes of computing the payment or credit under this section. The determination must be based, however, on the operating experience of the person using the fuel, and a statement, signed by the person, evidencing the operating experience must be maintained as a part of the records of the person claiming the payment or credit.

(e) *Supporting evidence required.*—Each claim under this section for credit or payment must include a statement showing—

(1) The total number of gallons of fuel purchased and used for nontaxable or farming purposes during the period covered by the claim, multiplied by the rate of payment allowable under this section with respect to such fuel;

(2) The purpose or purposes for which the fuel was used, determined by reference to general categories, and the amount used for each of the purposes; and

(3) If a claim on Form 843 is being filed, the internal revenue district or service center with which the claimant last filed an income tax return, (if any).

(f) *Illustrations.*—The application of this section may be illustrated by the following example:

Example. Special motor fuel was sold for use as fuel in a highway vehicle that was registered for highway use. Tax was imposed on the sale at the rate of 9 cents a gallon under section 4041(a)(2). The special motor fuel was eventually used by the purchaser in a qualified business use. The credit or payment of tax is to be computed as follows:

	Cents per gallon
Rate at which tax was paid	9
Less: Rate at which tax would have been imposed on a qualified business use under sec. 4041(b).	0
Net credit or payment under sec. 6427(a) . .	9

[Reg. § 48.6427-1.]

☐ [*T.D.* 8043, 8-8-85.]

[Reg. § 48.6427-2]

§ 48.6427-2. Credits or payments to purchaser of diesel or special motor fuels used in intercity, local, or school buses.—(a) *In general.*—(1) If tax has been paid under section 4041(a)(1) on the sale of diesel fuel for use as a fuel in a diesel-powered highway vehicle or under section 4041(a)(2) on the sale of special motor fuel for use as a fuel in a motor vehicle or a motorboat and the fuel is used by the purchaser in an intercity or local bus while engaged in furnishing (for compensation) passenger land transportation available to the general public or in a school bus in the transportation of students and employees of schools, a credit (under the circumstances described in paragraph (b) of this section) or a payment (under the circumstances described in paragraph (c) of this section) in respect of the fuel so used shall be allowed or made to the purchaser of the fuel. The credit or payment under this section shall be an amount equal to the product of the number of gallons of fuel so used multiplied by the rate at which tax was imposed on the fuel by section 4041(a)(1) or section 4041(a)(2), reduced as limited by section 6427(b)(2). No interest shall be paid on any payment allowed under paragraph (c) of this section. However, interest may be paid on any overpayment (as defined by section 6401) arising from a credit. See section 34(a), relating to credit for certain uses of gasoline and special fuels, (and lubricating oil prior to January 7, 1983). See section 6611, relating to interest on overpayments. See § 48.6427-3 for the time within which a claim for credit or payment must be made under this section.

(2) The terms "diesel fuel" and "special motor fuel" have the same meaning as in section 4041 and the regulations thereunder. The term "fuel" means diesel fuel and special motor fuel. See § 48.6421-4 for the meaning of "calendar quarter" and "taxable year."

(b) *Allowance of income tax credit.*—Except as provided in paragraph (c) of this section, repayment under this section of the tax paid under section 4041(a)(1) or section 4041(a)(2) on diesel or special motor fuel used while engaged in furnishing (for compensation) passenger land transportation available to the general public or in school bus transportation operations by a person subject to income tax may be obtained only by claiming a credit for the amount of this tax against the tax imposed by subtitle A of the Code. The amount of the credit shall be an amount equal to the payment which would be made under section 6427 with respect to fuel used during the taxable year for passenger land transportation or school bus operations if section 6427(i) and paragraph (c) of this section did not apply. See section 34(a)(3).

(c) *Allowance of payment.*—Payments in respect of diesel or special motor fuel upon which tax was paid under section 4041(a)(1) or section 4041(a)(2) that is used while engaged in furnishing (for compensation) passenger land transportation available to the general public or in school bus transportation operations shall be made only to—

(1) The United States or any agency or instrumentality thereof, a State, a political subdivision of a State, or an agency or instrumentality of one or more States or political subdivisions of a State, or the District of Columbia.

(2) An organization which is exempt from tax under section 501(a) and is not required to make a return of the income tax imposed under subtitle A for its taxable year, or

(3) A person described in section 6427(g)(2) to whom $1,000 or more is payable (without regard to paragraph (b) of this section) under this section with respect to fuel used during any of the first three quarters of the person's taxable year.

(d) *Supporting evidence required.*—Each claim under this section for credit or payment must include a statement showing—

(1) The total number of gallons of fuel purchased and used in each intercity or local bus while engaged in furnishing (for compensation) passenger land transportation available to the general public multiplied by the rate at which tax was imposed on the fuel by section 4041(a)(1) or section 4041(a)(2). See, however, section 6427(b)(2) with respect to the limitation on the amount of credit for buses other than qualified local buses.

(2) The total number of gallons of fuel purchased and used in each bus while engaged in school bus transportation operations multiplied by the rate at which tax was imposed on the fuel by subsection (a)(1) or (a)(2) of section 4041. See, however, section 6427(b)(2) with respect to the limitation on the amount of credit for buses other than qualified local buses.

(3) If a claim on Form 843 is being filed, the internal revenue district or service center with which the purchaser last filed an income tax return (if any). [Reg. § 48.6427-2.]

☐ [*T.D.* 8043, 8-8-85.]

[Reg. § 48.6427-3]

§ 48.6427-3. Time for filing claim for credit or payment.—(a) *In general.*—A claim for credit or payment described in § 48.6427-1 with respect to fuel used for nontaxable, farming, or other purposes taxable at a lower rate or in § 48.6427-2 with respect to fuel used either in an intercity or local bus while engaged in furnishing (for compensation) passenger land transportation available to the general public or in school bus transportation operations shall cover only fuel used during the taxable year, or when paragraph (b)(2) of this section applies, used during the calendar quarter. Therefore, fuel on hand at the end of a taxable year, or, if applicable, a calendar quarter, such as fuel in supply tanks of vehicles or in storage tanks or drums, must be excluded from a claim filed for the taxable year or calendar quarter, as the case may be. However, this fuel may be included in a claim filed for a later taxable year or a later calendar quarter if it is used during that later year or quarter for nontaxable or farming purposes, or in an intercity or local bus while engaged in furnishing (for compensation) passenger land transportation available to the general public or in school bus transportation operations. Fuel used during the taxable year or calendar quarter may be covered by the claim for that period although the fuel has not been paid for at the time the claim is filed. The purposes of applying this section, a governmental unit or exempt organization described in § 48.6427-1(c) or § 48.6427-2(c) is considered to have as its taxable year the calendar year or fiscal year on the basis of which it regularly keeps its books; see § 48.6421-4.

(b) *Time for filing.*—(1) *Annual claims.*—(i) A claim under this section for credit or payment with respect to fuel used during a taxable year shall not be allowed unless it is filed no later than the time prescribed by section 6511 and the regulations thereunder for filing a claim for credit or refund of income tax for the particular taxable year.

(ii) A claim for payment of a governmental unit or exempt organization described in § 48.6427-1(c) or unit or exempt organization described in § 48.6427-2(c), must be filed no later than 3 years following the close of its taxable year. See § 48.6421-4.

(2) *Quarterly claims.*—A claim for payment of $1,000 or more in respect to fuel used during any of the first three quarters of the taxable year, filed either under § 48.6427-1(c)(3) in respect of fuel used for nontaxable purposes or for purposes taxable at a lower rate, or under § 48.6427-2(c)(3) in respect of fuel used while engaged in furnishing (for compensation) passenger land transportation available to the general public or in school bus transportation operations, shall not be allowed unless the claim is filed on or before the last day of the first calendar quarter following the calendar quarter for which the claim is filed. No quarterly claim may be filed for the last calendar quarter of the taxable year. Amount for which payment is disallowed under this paragraph (b)(2) merely because the claim was not filed on time may be included in an annual claim filed under paragraph (b)(1) of this section, but other amounts for which a claim for payment has been filed under this paragraph (b)(2) may not be included in an annual claim filed under paragraph (b)(1) of this section.

(3) *Other applicable rules.*—See § 301.7502-1 of this chapter (Regulations on Procedure and Administration) for provisions treating timely mailing as timely filing and § 301.7503-1 of this chapter for time for performance of an act where the last day falls on Saturday, Sunday, or a legal holiday.

(c) *Limit on claims per taxable year.*—Not more than one claim may be filed under § 48.6427-1 or § 48.6427-2 by any person with respect to fuel used during any taxable year, except to the extent that quarterly claims may be filed under paragraph (b)(2) of this section with respect to any calendar quarter (other than the last calendar quarter) of the taxable year.

(d) *Form and content of claim.*—(1) *Claim for credit.*—The claim for credit to which this section applies must be made by attaching a Form 4136, to the income tax return of an individual or a corporation. Form 4136 must be executed in accordance with the instructions prescribed for the preparation of the form. A partnership may not file Form 4136. When a partnership files Form 1065, U.S. Partnership Return of Income, it must include a statement showing how many gallons of fuel are allocated to each partner and the use made of the fuel.

(2) *Claim for payment.*—The claim for payment to which this section applies must be made

on Form 8849 (or on such other form as the Commissioner may designate) in accordance with the instructions prescribed for the preparation of the form. Each form must designate the taxable year, or calendar quarter, for which it is filed.

(3) *Death or termination.*—(i) If an individual dies, or if a sole proprietorship, partnership, or corporation is terminated or liquidated, during the taxable year, the claim for credit or payment may be filed in respect of fuel used during the short taxable year in the same manner as is provided for fuel used in a full taxable year. Those months which constitute a quarter of a full taxable year will constitute the same quarter of the short taxable year. For example, if a corporation using the calendar year is liquidated on September 30, 1982, and is entitled to $900 under § 48.6427-1 in respect of fuel used for nontaxable purposes for the calendar quarter ending March 31 and is also entitled to payments of $1,500 for each of the calendar quarters ending June 30 and September 30, it may file a claim for payment in respect of the fuel used for nontaxable purposes during the calendar quarters ending June 30, and September 30, 1982, and take a credit of $900 on its income tax return for the short taxable year in respect of the fuel used during the calendar quarter ending March 31, 1982.

(ii) A claim for payment on behalf of a decedent may be filed by the decedent's executor, administrator, or any other person charged with responsibility for the decedent's affairs. Such a claim must be accompanied by copies of the letters testamentary, letters of administration, or, in the case of a claim filed by other than the executor or administrator, the information called for in Form 1310 (Statement of Person Claiming Refund Due a Deceased Taxpayer). The claim may cover only fuel in respect of which the decedent would have been entitled to claim payments. For example, if an individual dies on July 15, 1982, prior to claiming payment under § 48.6427-1 of $1,000 or more applicable to fuel purchased and used for nontaxable purposes during the calendar quarter ending June 30, 1982, the decedent's executor or other legal representative may file a claim for payment covering that calendar quarter, and take the credit provided by section 39(a)(3) against the decedent's income tax on the income tax return for the short taxable year in respect of fuel purchased by the decedent and so used during the period from July 1, 1982, to July 15, 1982, the date of death.

(e) *Restrictions on claims for credit or payment.*—Credits or payments are allowable only in respect of fuel that was sold by the producer or importer in a transaction that was subject to tax under section 4041. For example, a State or local government may not file a claim with respect to any fuel which it purchased tax free from the producer, even though the State or local government used the fuel for the purposes described in paragraph (a) of this section. Similarly, a State or local government may not file a claim with respect to the use of fuel if it is known that another person is entitled to claim a payment, credit, or refund with respect to the same fuel. For example, a State or local government may not file a claim in respect of tax-paid fuel that has been resold by the purchaser to the State or local government. [Reg. § 48.6427-3.]

☐ [*T.D. 8043, 8-8-85. Amended by T.D. 8659, 3-13-96 and T.D. 8748, 12-31-97.*]

[Reg. § 48.6427-4]

§ 48.6427-4. **Applicable laws.**—(a) *Penalties, excessive claims, etc.*—All provisions of law, including penalties, applicable in respect of the tax imposed by section 4041 shall, to the extent applicable and consistent with section 6427, apply in respect of the payments provided for in section 6427 to the same extent as if these payments constituted refunds of overpayments of the tax imposed on the sale of fuels by section 4041. For special rules applicable to the assessment and collection of amounts constituting excessive payments under section 6427, see section 6206 and the regulations thereunder. For the civil penalty assessable in the case of excessive claims under section 6427, see section 6675 and the regulations thereunder. For the treatment as an overpayment of an amount allowable as an excessive credit under section 34 with respect to amounts payable under section 6427, see section 6401(b).

(b) *Examination of books and witnesses.*—For the purpose of ascertaining (1) the correctness of any claim made under section 6427 or (2) the correctness of any credit or payment made in respect of the claim, the Commissioner shall have the same authority granted by paragraphs (1), (2), and (3) of section 7602, relating to examination of books and witnesses, as if the person claiming credit or payment under section 6427 were the person liable for tax. [Reg. § 48.6427-4.]

☐ [*T.D. 8043, 8-8-85.*]

[Reg. § 48.6427-5]

§ 48.6427-5. **Records to be kept in substantiation of credits or payments.**—(a) *In general.*—Every person making a claim for credit or payment under section 6427 must keep records sufficient to enable the district director to determine whether the person is entitled to credit or payment under such section and, if so, the amount of the credit or payment. No particular form is prescribed for keeping the records, but the records must include a copy of the income tax return or claim and a copy of any statement or document submitted with the return or claim. The records must also show with respect to the period covered by the claim—

(1) The number of gallons of fuel purchased and the dates of purchase,

(2) The name and address of each vendor from whom fuel was purchased and the total number of gallons purchased from each,

(3) The number of gallons of fuel purchased by the claimant and used during the period covered by the claim for nontaxable purposes, farming purposes, for other purposes taxable at a lower rate, in local, intercity, or school buses, and

(4) Other information as necessary to establish the correctness of the claim.

(b) *Acceptable records.*—(1) Evidence of purchases of fuel, and the purposes for which it was used, to substantiate claims may include paid duplicate sales invoices or tickets from the fuel dealer or other vendor, and detailed records of all fuel used which show the amount used the prescribed purpose and the amount used for other purposes.

(2) Records maintained for Federal or State income tax purposes, or to support claims for refund of a State tax on fuel, may be used to the extent that they contain the information necessary to substantiate the accuracy of the claim for credit under section 6427. However, the records must show separately the number of gallons of fuel used for nontaxable purposes, farming purposes, other purposes, taxable at a lower rate, or in intercity, local, or school buses during the period covered by the claim.

(c) *Place and period for keeping records.*—(1) All records required by this section must be kept by the claimant at a convenient and safe location within the United States which is accessible to internal revenue officers and shall during normal business hours be available for inspection by internal revenue officers. If the claimant has a principal place of business in the United States, the records must be kept at that place of business.

(2) Records required to substantiate a claim under section 6427 must be maintained for a period of at least 3 years from the last date prescribed for the filing of the claim for credit or payment. [Reg. § 48.6427-5.]

☐ [*T.D.* 8043, 8-8-85.]

[Reg. § 48.6427-6]

§ 48.6427-6. Limitation on credit or refund of tax paid on fuel used in intercity, local or school buses after July 31, 1984.—(a) *Limitation on amount of credit or refund.*—(1) *In general.*—In the case of fuel sold or used after July 31, 1984, on which tax was imposed under section 4041(a), the amount of credit or refund under section 6427(b)(1) shall not exceed 12 cents per gallon except where fuel is used in a bus while such bus is being operated as a "qualified local bus" in which case the credit or refund shall be the full amount of tax paid under section 4041(a) on such fuel.

(2) *Qualified local bus.*—A bus is considered to be operated as a "qualified local bus" if such bus—

(i) Is engaged in furnishing (for compensation) intracity passenger land transportation that is available to the general public and is scheduled and along regular routes,

(ii) Has a seating capacity of at least 20 adults (not including the driver), and

(iii) Is under contract with (or is receiving more than a nominal subsidy from) any State or local government (as defined in section 4221(d)(4)) to furnish such transportation.

A company that operates qualified local buses is eligible for a full refund or credit only with respect to fuel used while such buses are operating as qualified local buses. For example, a company that operates its buses along subsidized intracity routes and also on intercity or unsubsidized intracity routes may obtain a full refund or credit only with respect to fuel used while operating the subsidized intracity routes.

(b) *Meaning of terms.*—(1) *Contract with a State or local government.*—A bus is under contract with a State or local government only if the contract imposes a bona fide obligation on the operator of the bus to furnish the transportation to which the contract relates.

(2) *More than a nominal subsidy.*—A subsidy is more than nominal if the subsidy is reasonably expected to exceed an amount equal to 3 cents multiplied by the number of gallons of fuel used while operating on subsidized routes.

(3) *Intracity passenger land transportation.*—The term "intracity passenger land transportation" means the land transportation of passengers to and from points located within the same metropolitan area. The term includes transportation along routes that cross State, city or county boundaries provided such routes remain within the metropolitan area. [Reg. § 48.6427-6.]

☐ [*T.D.* 8027, 5-23-85.]

[Reg. § 48.6427-8]

§ 48.6427-8. Diesel fuel and kerosene; claims by ultimate purchasers.—(a) *Overview.*—This section provides rules under which ultimate purchasers of taxed diesel fuel and kerosene may claim the income tax credits or payments allowed by section 6427(l). Generally, these claims relate to diesel fuel and kerosene used in nontaxable uses. Claims relating to diesel fuel and kerosene sold for use on a farm for farming purposes and by a State are made by registered ultimate vendors under § 48.6427-9; claims relating to kerosene sold from a blocked pump are made by registered ultimate vendors (blocked pump) under § 48.6427-10; and claims relating to kerosene sold during certain periods of extreme cold for blending with diesel fuel to be used for heating purposes are made by registered ultimate vendors (blending) under § 48.6427-11.

(b) *Conditions to allowance of credit or payment.*—(1) *In general.*—Except as provided in section 6427(l)(5), a claim for an income tax credit or payment with respect to diesel fuel or kerosene is allowed under section 6427(l) only if—

(i) Tax was imposed by section 4081 on the diesel fuel or kerosene to which the claim relates;

(ii) The claimant produced or bought the diesel fuel or kerosene and did not sell it in the United States;

(iii) The claimant has filed a timely claim for a credit or payment that contains the information required under paragraph (d) of this section;

(iv) The diesel fuel or kerosene was not bought under a certificate described in § 48.6427-9(e)(2) (relating to Certificate of Farming Use or State Use);

(v) The diesel fuel or kerosene was not used on a farm for farming purposes (as defined in § 48.6420-4) or by a State;

(vi) With respect to kerosene, the kerosene was not sold from a blocked pump or sold for blending with diesel fuel under the conditions described in § 48.6427-11; and

(vii) The diesel fuel or kerosene was either—

(A) Used in a use described in § 48.4082-4(c)(3) through (c)(8);

(B) Exported;

(C) Used other than as a fuel in a propulsion engine of a diesel-powered highway vehicle; or

(D) Used as a fuel in the propulsion engine of a diesel-powered bus if the bus was engaged in a use described in section 6427(b)(1) (after the application of section 6427(b)(3)).

(2) *Examples*.—The following examples illustrate this paragraph (b).

Example 1. (i) In September 2000, F bought 250 gallons of undyed diesel fuel. In October 2000, F used 200 gallons of the fuel in a farm tractor. This use qualifies as use on a farm for farming purposes (as defined in § 48.6420-4). The farm tractor is not a diesel-powered highway vehicle (as defined in § 48.4081-1(b)). F used the remaining 50 gallons to heat F's residence. F filed a complete and timely claim for a credit relating to the 250 gallons.

(ii) A credit or payment is not allowable to F with respect to the 200 gallons of diesel fuel used in the farm tractor. Even though this fuel was used other than as a fuel in a propulsion engine of a diesel-powered highway vehicle (thus meeting the condition in paragraph (b)(1)(vii)(C) of this section), the condition in paragraph (b)(1)(v) of this section is not satisfied because the fuel was used on a farm for farming purposes.

(iii) A credit is allowable to F with respect to the 50 gallons F used for heating purposes because the conditions in paragraph (b)(1) of this section have been met. F used this fuel other than as a fuel in a propulsion engine of a diesel-powered highway vehicle and the use of the fuel for residential heating is not use on a farm for farming purposes.

Example 2. (i) In September 2000, W, a wholesale distributor, sold 3,500 gallons of diesel fuel on which tax has been imposed to C, a construction company located in the United States. W's selling price to C did not include an amount equal to the federal excise tax on the fuel. C used the fuel other than as a fuel in a propulsion engine of a diesel-powered highway

vehicle. Both W and C file a complete and timely claim for a credit relating to the fuel.

(ii) Because W resold the fuel in the United States, the condition of paragraph (b)(1)(ii) of this section is not met. Thus, W is not allowed a credit or payment with respect to the fuel.

(iii) C is eligible for a credit or payment with respect to the fuel because the conditions to allowance in paragraph (b)(1) of this section have been met. The conditions to allowance do not include a requirement that C buy the fuel at a price that includes the amount of the tax.

(c) *Form of claim*.—Each claim for an income tax credit under this section must be made on Form 4136 (or on such other form as the Commissioner may designate) in accordance with the instructions for that form. Each claim for a payment under this section must be made on Form 8849 (or on such other form as the Commissioner may designate) in accordance with the instructions for that form.

(d) *Content of claim*.—Each claim for a credit or payment under this section must contain the following information with respect to all the diesel fuel or kerosene covered by the claim:

(1) The total number of gallons.

(2) A statement by the claimant that—

(i) The diesel fuel or kerosene did not contain visible evidence of dye; or

(ii) In the case of diesel fuel or kerosene that contains visible evidence of dye, explains the circumstances under which tax was imposed on that fuel.

(3) The use made of the diesel fuel or kerosene covered by the claim described by reference to specific categories listed in paragraph (b)(1)(vii) of this section (such as use in a qualified local bus or the exclusive use of a nonprofit educational organization).

(4) If the diesel fuel or kerosene covered by the claim was exported, a declaration that the claimant has proof of exportation (as described in § 48.4221-3(d)(1)).

(5) A declaration that the claimant has in its possession the name and address of the person(s) that sold the diesel fuel or kerosene to the claimant and the date(s) of the purchase(s).

(e) *Time and place for filing claim*.—For rules relating to the time for filing a claim under section 6427, see section 6427(i). A claim under this section is not filed unless it contains all the information required by paragraph (d) of this section and is filed at the place required by the form.

(f) *Effective date*.—This section is applicable with respect to diesel fuel after December 31, 1993, except for paragraph (b)(1)(iv) of this section, which is applicable to diesel fuel bought by ultimate purchasers after June 30, 1994. This section is applicable with respect to kerosene after June 30, 1998. [Reg. § 48.6427-8.]

☐ [*T.D.* 8659, 3-13-96. *Amended by T.D.* 8879, 3-30-2000 *and T.D.* 9051, 4-1-2003.]

Reg. § 48.6427-8(f)

[Reg. §48.6427-9]

§48.6427-9. Diesel fuel and kerosene; claims by registered ultimate vendors (farming and State use).—(a) *Overview.*—This section provides rules under which certain registered ultimate vendors of taxed diesel fuel and kerosene may claim the income tax credits or payments allowed by section 6427(l)(5)(A). These claims relate to diesel fuel and kerosene sold for use on a farm for farming purposes and by a State. Claims relating to diesel fuel and kerosene used for other nontaxable purposes are made by ultimate purchasers under §48.6427-8; claims relating to kerosene sold from a blocked pump are made by registered ultimate vendors (blocked pump) under §48.6427-10; and claims relating to kerosene sold during certain periods of extreme cold for blending with diesel fuel to be used for heating purposes are made by registered ultimate vendors (blending) under §48.6427-11.

(b) *Definitions.*—(1) An *ultimate vendor*, as used in this section, is a person that sells undyed diesel fuel or undyed kerosene to—

(i) The owner, tenant, or operator of a farm for use by such person on a farm for farming purposes (as defined in §48.6420-4);

(ii) A person other than the owner, tenant, or operator of a farm for use by such person for any of the purposes described in §48.6420-4(d) (relating to cultivating, raising, or harvesting); or

(iii) Any State for its exclusive use.

(2) A *registered ultimate vendor* is an ultimate vendor that is registered under section 4101 as an ultimate vendor.

(c) *Conditions to allowance of credit or payment.*—A claim for an income tax credit or payment with respect to diesel fuel or kerosene is allowed by section 6427(l)(5)(A) only if—

(1) Tax was imposed by section 4081 on the diesel fuel or kerosene to which the claim relates;

(2) The claimant sold the diesel fuel or kerosene to—

(i) The owner, tenant, or operator of a farm for use by such person on a farm for farming purposes (as defined in §48.6420-4);

(ii) A person other than the owner, tenant, or operator of a farm for use by such person for any of the purposes described in §48.6420-4(d) (relating to cultivating, raising, or harvesting); or

(iii) Any State for its exclusive use;

(3) The claimant is a registered ultimate vendor; and

(4) The claimant has filed a timely claim for a credit or payment that contains the information required under paragraph (e) of this section.

(d) *Form of claim.*—Each claim for an income tax credit under this section must be made on Form 4136 (or on such other form as the Commissioner may designate) in accordance with the instructions for that form. Each claim for a payment under this section must be made on Form 8849 (or on such other form as the Commissioner

may designate) in accordance with the instructions for that form.

(e) *Content of claim.*—(1) *In general.*—Each claim for credit or payment under this section must contain the following information with respect to all the diesel fuel or kerosene covered by the claim:

(i) The total number of gallons.

(ii) A statement by the claimant that—

(A) The diesel fuel or kerosene did not contain visible evidence of dye; or

(B) In the case of diesel fuel or kerosene that contains visible evidence of dye, explains the circumstances under which tax was imposed on that fuel.

(iii) The claimant's registration number.

(iv) The name and taxpayer identification number of each person that bought diesel fuel or kerosene from the claimant in a transaction described in paragraph (c)(2) of this section and the number of gallons that the claimant sold to that person.

(v) A statement that the claimant—

(A) Has not included the amount of the tax in its sales price of the diesel fuel or kerosene and has not collected the amount of tax from its buyer;

(B) Has repaid the amount of the tax to the ultimate purchaser of the fuel; or

(C) Has obtained the written consent of its buyer to the allowance of the claim.

(vi) A statement that the claimant has in its possession an unexpired certificate described in paragraph (e)(2) of this section and the claimant has no reason to believe any information in the certificate is false.

(2) *Certificate.*—(i) *In general.*—The certificate to be provided to the ultimate vendor consists of a statement that is signed under penalties of perjury by a person with authority to bind the buyer, is in substantially the same form as the model certificate provided in paragraph (e)(2)(ii) of this section, and contains all information necessary to complete such model certificate. A new certificate must be given if any information in the current certificate changes. The certificate may be included as part of any business records normally used to document a sale. The certificate expires on the earlier of the following dates:

(A) The date one year after the effective date of the certificate.

(B) The date a new certificate is provided to the seller.

(ii) *Model certificate.*

CERTIFICATE OF FARMING USE OR STATE USE

(To support vendor's claim for a credit or payment under section 6427 of the Internal Revenue Code.)

_____

Name, address, and employer identification number of vendor

The undersigned buyer ("Buyer") hereby certifies the following under penalties of perjury:

Buyer will use the diesel fuel or kerosene to which this certificate relates—(check one)

___ On a farm for farming purposes (as defined in § 48.6420-4(c) of the Manufacturers and Retailers Excise Tax Regulations) and Buyer is the owner, tenant, or operator of the farm on which the fuel will be used;

___ On a farm (as defined in § 48.6420-4(c)) for any of the purposes described in paragraph (d) of that section (relating to cultivating, raising, or harvesting) and Buyer is a person that is not the owner, tenant, or operator of the farm on which the fuel will be used; or

___ For the exclusive use of a State or local government, or the District of Columbia.

This certificate applies to the following (complete as applicable):

If this is a single purchase certificate, check here ___ and enter:

1. Invoice or delivery ticket number _____
2. ___ (number of gallons)

If this is a certificate covering all purchases under a specified account or order number, check here ___ and enter:

1. Effective date _____
2. Expiration date _____
(period not to exceed 1 year after the effective date)
3. Buyer account or order number _____

Buyer will provide a new certificate to the vendor if any information in this certificate changes.

If Buyer uses the diesel fuel or kerosene to which this certificate relates for a purpose other than stated in the certificate Buyer will be liable for tax.

Buyer understands that the fraudulent use of this certificate may subject Buyer and all parties making such fraudulent use of this certificate to a fine or imprisonment, or both, together with the costs of prosecution.

_____
Printed or typed name of person signing

_____
Title of person signing

_____
Name of Buyer

_____
Employer identification number

_____
Address of Buyer

_____
Signature and date signed

(f) *Time and place for filing claim.*—For rules relating to the time for filing a claim under section 6427, see section 6427(i). A claim under this section is not filed unless it contains all the information required by paragraph (e) of this section and is filed at the place required by the form.

(g) *Effective date.*—This section is applicable with respect to diesel fuel after December 31, 1993, and with respect to kerosene after June 30, 1998. [Reg. § 48.6427-9.]

☐ [*T.D.* 8659, 3-13-96. *Amended by T.D.* 8879, 3-30-2000.]

[Reg. § 48.6427-10]

§ 48.6427-10. Kerosene; claims by registered ultimate vendors (blocked pumps).—(a) *Overview.*—This section provides rules under which certain registered ultimate vendors of taxed kerosene may claim the income tax credits or payments allowed by section 6427(l)(5)(B)(i). These claims relate to kerosene sold from a blocked pump. Claims relating to kerosene sold for use on a farm for farming purposes and by a State are made by registered ultimate vendors under § 48.6427-9; claims relating to kerosene sold during certain periods of extreme cold for blending with diesel fuel to be used for heating purposes are made by registered ultimate vendors (blending) under § 48.6427-11; and claims relating to kerosene used for nontaxable purposes are made by ultimate purchasers under § 48.6427-8.

(b) *Definitions.*—The following definitions apply to this section:

(1) A *blocked pump* is a fuel pump that—

(i) Is used to dispense undyed kerosene that is sold at retail for use by the buyer in any nontaxable use;

(ii) Is at a fixed location;

(iii) Is identified with a legible and conspicuous notice stating *"UNDYED UNTAXED KEROSENE, NONTAXABLE USE ONLY"*; and

(iv)(A) Cannot reasonably be used to dispense fuel directly into the fuel supply tank of a diesel-powered highway vehicle or diesel-powered train (because, for example, of its distance from a road surface or train track or the length of its delivery hose); or

(B) Is locked by the vendor after each sale and unlocked by the vendor only in response to a request by a buyer for undyed kerosene for use other than as a fuel in a diesel-powered highway vehicle or diesel-powered train.

(2) A *registered ultimate vendor (blocked pump)* is a person that is registered under section 4101 as an ultimate vendor (blocked pump).

(3) An *ultimate vendor (blocked pump)* is a person that sells undyed kerosene from a blocked pump.

(c) *Conditions to allowance of credit or payment.*—A claim for an income tax credit or payment with respect to undyed kerosene is allowed by section 6427(l)(5)(B)(i) only if—

(1) Tax was imposed by section 4081 on the kerosene to which the claim relates;

(2) The claimant sold the kerosene from a blocked pump for its buyer's use other than as a fuel in a diesel-powered highway vehicle or diesel-powered train and the claimant has no reason to believe that the kerosene will not be so used;

(3) The claimant is a registered ultimate vendor (blocked pump);

(4) With respect to each sale of more than five gallons of kerosene from a blocked pump that does not meet the conditions of paragraph (b)(1)(iv)(A) of this section, the claimant has in its possession the date of the sale, name and address of the buyer, and the number of gallons sold to the buyer; and

(5) The claimant has filed a timely claim for a credit or payment that contains the information required under paragraph (e) of this section.

(d) *Form of claim.*—Each claim for an income tax credit under this section must be made on Form 4136 (or such other form as the Commissioner may designate) in accordance with the instructions for that form. Each claim for a payment under this section must be made on Form 8849 (or such other form as the Commissioner may designate) in accordance with the instructions for that form.

(e) *Content of claim.*—Each claim for a credit or payment under this section must contain the following information with respect to all of the kerosene covered by the claim:

(1) The claimant's ultimate vendor (blocked pump) registration number.

(2) The total number of gallons.

(3) A statement by the claimant that—

(i) The kerosene did not contain visible evidence of dye; or

(ii) In the case of kerosene that contains visible evidence of dye, explains the circumstances under which tax was imposed on that kerosene.

(4) With respect to each sale of more than five gallons of kerosene from a blocked pump that does not meet the conditions of paragraph (b)(1)(iv)(A) of this section, a statement by the claimant that it has in its possession the date of the sale, name and address of the buyer, and the number of gallons sold to the buyer.

(5) A statement by the claimant that it—

(i) Has not included the amount of the tax in its sales price of the kerosene and has not collected the amount of the tax from its buyer;

(ii) Has repaid the amount of the tax to its buyer; or

(iii) Has obtained the written consent of its buyer to the allowance of the claim.

(f) *Time and place for filing claim.*—For rules relating to the time for filing a claim under section 6427, see section 6427(i). A claim under this section is not filed unless it contains all the information required by paragraph (e) of this section and is filed at the place required by the form.

(g) *Cross reference.*—For a rule prohibiting a registered ultimate vendor (blocked pump) from delivering kerosene from a blocked pump into the fuel supply tank of a diesel-powered highway vehicle or diesel-powered train, see §48.4101-1(h)(2)(iv).

(h) *Effective date.*—This section is applicable after March 30, 2000. [Reg. §48.6427-10.]

☐ [T.D. 8879, 3-30-2000.]

[Reg. §48.6427-11]

§48.6427-11. Kerosene; claims by registered ultimate vendors (blending).—(a) *Overview.*—

This section provides rules under which certain registered ultimate vendors of taxed kerosene may claim the income tax credits or payments allowed by section 6427(l)(5)(B)(ii). These claims relate to kerosene sold during certain periods of extreme cold for blending with diesel fuel to be used for heating purposes. Claims relating to kerosene sold for use on a farm for farming purposes and by a State are made by registered ultimate vendors under §48.6427-9; claims relating to kerosene sold from a blocked pump for nontaxable uses are made by registered ultimate vendors (blocked pump) under §48.6427-10; and other claims relating to kerosene used for nontaxable purposes are made by ultimate purchasers under §48.6427-8.

(b) *Definitions.*—The following definitions apply to this section:

(1) A *declaration of extreme cold* is a declaration by the Commissioner that a specific geographic area (such as a state or a county within a state) is affected by extremely or unseasonably cold weather conditions. A declaration will be in effect during the period determined by the Commissioner.

(2) A *cold weather blend* is a blend of kerosene and diesel fuel that is produced in an area described in a declaration of extreme cold and that is sold for use or used for heating purposes.

(3) A *registered ultimate vendor (blending)* is a taxable fuel registrant, a registered ultimate vendor, or a registered ultimate vendor (blocked pump).

(c) *Conditions to allowance of credit or payment.*—A claim for an income tax credit or payment with respect to kerosene is allowed by section 6427(l)(5)(B)(ii) only if—

(1) Tax was imposed by section 4081 on the kerosene to which the claim relates;

(2) The claimant sold the kerosene in an area described in a declaration of extreme cold for the production of a cold weather blend;

(3) The claimant is a registered ultimate vendor (blending); and

(4) The claimant has filed a timely claim for an income tax credit or payment that contains the information required under paragraph (e) of this section.

(d) *Form of claim.*—Each claim for an income tax credit under this section must be made on Form 4136 (or such other form as the Commissioner may designate) in accordance with the instructions for that form. Each claim for a payment under this section must be made on Form 8849 (or such other form as the Commissioner may designate) in accordance with the instructions for that form.

(e) *Content of claim.*—(1) *In general.*—Each claim for credit or payment under this section must contain the following information with respect to all of the kerosene covered by the claim:

(i) The claimant's registration number.

(ii) The total number of gallons.

(iii) A statement by the claimant that—

(A) The kerosene did not contain visible evidence of dye; or

(B) In the case of kerosene that contains visible evidence of dye, explains the circumstances under which tax was imposed on that kerosene.

(iv) A statement by the claimant that it—

(A) Has not included the amount of the tax in its sales price of the kerosene and has not collected the amount of the tax from its buyer;

(B) Has repaid the amount of the tax to its buyer; or

(C) Has obtained the written consent of its buyer to the allowance of the claim.

(v) A statement that the claimant has in its possession an unexpired certificate described in paragraph (e)(2) of this section and the claimant has no reason to believe any information in the certificate is false.

(2) *Certificate.*—(i) *In general.*—The certificate described in this paragraph (e) is a statement by a buyer that is signed under penalties of perjury by a person with authority to bind the buyer, is in substantially the same form as the model certificate provided in paragraph (e)(2)(iii) of this section, and contains all information necessary to complete the model certificate. A certificate must be given for each purchase of kerosene. The certificate may be included as part of any business records normally used to document a sale.

(ii) *Withdrawal of the right to provide a certificate.*—The Internal Revenue Service may withdraw the right of a buyer of kerosene to provide a certificate under this section if the buyer uses the kerosene to which a certificate relates other than for producing a cold weather blend. The Internal Revenue Service may notify any seller to whom the buyer has provided a certificate that the buyer's right to provide a certificate has been withdrawn.

(iii) *Model certificate.*

CERTIFICATE OF BUYER FOR PRODUCTION OF A COLD WEATHER BLEND

(To support vendor's claim for a credit or payment under section 6427 of the Internal Revenue Code.)

_____ (Buyer) certifies the following under penalties of perjury:

Name of Buyer

The kerosene to which this certificate applies will be used by Buyer to produce a blend of kerosene and diesel fuel in an area described in a declaration of extreme cold and the blend will be sold for use or used for heating purposes. This certificate applies to ___ percent of Buyer's purchases from _____ (name, address, and employer identification number of seller) on invoice or delivery ticket number _____.

If Buyer violates the terms of this certificate, the Internal Revenue Service may withdraw Buyer's right to provide a certificate.

Buyer has not been notified by the Internal Revenue Service that its right to provide a certificate has been withdrawn.

Buyer understands that the fraudulent use of this certificate may subject Buyer and all parties making such fraudulent use of this certificate to a fine or imprisonment, or both, together with the costs of prosecution.

_____

Printed or typed name of person signing

_____

Title of person signing

_____

Employer identification number

_____

Address of Buyer

_____

Signature and date signed

(f) *Time and place for filing claim.*—For rules relating to the time for filing a claim under section 6427, see section 6427(i). A claim under this section is not filed unless it contains all the information required by paragraph (e) of this section and is filed at the place required by the form.

(g) *Effective date.*—This section is applicable after March 30, 2000. [Reg. § 48.6427-11.]

☐ [*T.D.* 8879, 3-30-2000 (*corrected* 5-5-2000).]

Limitations

LIMITATIONS ON ASSESSMENT AND COLLECTION

[Reg. § 301.6501(a)-1]

§ 301.6501(a)-1. Period of limitations upon assessment and collection.—(a) The amount of any tax imposed by the Internal Revenue Code (other than a tax collected by means of stamps) shall be assessed within 3 years after the return was filed. For rules applicable in cases where the return is filed prior to the due date thereof, see section 6501(b). In the case of taxes payable by stamp, assessment shall be made at any time after the tax became due and before the expiration of 3 years after the date on which any part of the tax was paid. For exceptions and additional rules, see subsections (b) to (g) of section 6501, and for cross references to other provisions relating to limitations on assessment and collection, see sections 6501(h) and 6504.

(b) No proceeding in court without assessment for the collection of any tax shall be begun after the expiration of the applicable period for the assessment of such tax. [Reg. § 301.6501(a)-1.]

☐ [*T.D. 6172, 5-2-56. Amended by T.D. 6425, 11-10-59 and T.D. 6498, 10-24-60.*]

[Reg. § 301.6501(b)-1]

§ 301.6501(b)-1. Time return deemed filed for purposes of determining limitations.—(a) *Early return.*—Any return, other than a return of tax referred to in paragraph (b) of this section, filed before the last day prescribed by law or regulations for the filing thereof (determined without regard to any extension of time for filing) shall be considered as filed on such last day.

(b) *Returns of social security tax and of income tax withholding.*—If a return on or after November 13, 1966, of tax imposed by chapter 3 of the Code (relating to withholding of tax on nonresident aliens and foreign corporations and tax-free covenant bonds), or if a return of tax imposed by chapter 21 of the Code (relating to the Federal Insurance Contributions Act) or by chapter 24 of the Code (relating to collection of income tax at source on wages), for any period ending with or within a calendar year is filed before April 15 of the succeeding calendar year, such return shall be deemed filed on April 15 of such succeeding calendar year. For example, if quarterly returns of the tax imposed by chapter 24 of the Code are filed for the four quarters of 1955 on April 30, July 31, and October 31, 1955, and on January 31, 1956, the period of limitation for assessment with respect to the tax required to be reported on such return is measured from April 15, 1956. However, if any of such returns is filed after April 15, 1956, the period of limitation for assessment of the tax required to be reported on that return is measured from the date it is in fact filed.

(c) *Returns executed by district directors or other internal revenue officers.*—The execution of a return by a district director or other authorized internal revenue officer or employee under the authority of section 6020(b) shall not start the running of the statutory period of limitations on assessment and collection. [Reg. § 301.6501(b)-1.]

☐ [*T.D. 6172, 5-2-56. Amended by T.D. 6498, 10-24-60 and T.D. 6922, 6-16-67.*]

[Reg. § 301.6501(c)-1]

§ 301.6501(c)-1. Exceptions to general period of limitations on assessment and collection.—

(a) *False return.*—In the case of a false or fraudulent return with intent to evade any tax, the tax may be assessed, or a proceeding in court for the collection of such tax may be begun without assessment, at any time after such false or fraudulent return is filed.

(b) *Willful attempt to evade tax.*—In the case of a willful attempt in any manner to defeat or evade any tax imposed by the Code (other than a tax imposed by subtitle A or B, relating to income, estate, or gift taxes), the tax may be assessed, or a proceeding in court for the collection of such tax may be begun without assessment, at any time.

(c) *No return.*—In the case of a failure to file a return, the tax may be assessed, or a proceeding in court for the collection of such tax may be begun without assesment, at any time after the date prescribed for filing the return. For special rules relating to filing a return for chapter 42 and similar taxes, see § § 301.6501(n)-1, 301.6501(n)-2, and 301.6501(n)-3.

(d) *Extension by agreement.*—The time prescribed by section 6501 for the assessment of any tax (other than the estate tax imposed by chapter 11 of the Code) may, prior to the expiration of such time, be extended for any period of time agreed upon in writing by the taxpayer and the district director or an assistant regional commissioner. The extension shall become effective when the agreement has been executed by both parties. The period agreed upon may be extended by subsequent agreements in writing made before the expiration of the period previously agreed upon.

(e) *Gifts subject to chapter 14 of the Internal Revenue Code not adequately disclosed on the return.*—(1) *In general.*—If any transfer of property subject to the special valuation rules of section 2701 or section 2702, or if the occurrence of any taxable event described in section § 25.2704-4 of this chapter, is not adequately shown on a return of tax imposed by chapter 12 of subtitle B of the Internal Revenue Code (without regard to section 2503(b)), any tax imposed by chapter 12 of subtitle B of the Code on the transfer or resulting from the taxable event may be assessed, or a proceeding in court for the collection of the appropriate tax may be begun without assessment, at any time.

(2) *Adequately shown.*—A transfer of property valued under the rules of section 2701 or section 2702 or any taxable event described in § 25.2701-4 of this chapter will be considered adequately shown on a return of tax imposed by chapter 12 of subtitle B of the Internal Revenue Code only if, with respect to the entire transaction or series of transactions (including any

transaction that affected the transferred interest) of which the transfer (or taxable event) was a part, the return provides:

(i) A description of the transactions, including a description of transferred and retained interests and the method (or methods) used to value each;

(ii) The identity of, and relationship between, the transferor, transferee, all other persons participating in the transactions, and all parties related to the transferor holding an equity interest in any entity involved in the transaction; and

(iii) A detailed description (including all actuarial factors and discount rates used) of the method used to determine the amount of the gift arising from the transfer (or taxable event), including, in the case of an equity interest that is not actively traded, the financial and other data used in determining value. Financial data should generally include balance sheets and statements of net earnings, operating results, and dividends paid for each of the 5 years immediately before the valuation date.

(3) *Effective date.*—The provisions of this paragraph (e) are effective as of January 28, 1992. In determining whether a transfer or taxable event is adequately shown on a gift tax return filed prior to that date, taxpayers may rely on any reasonable interpretation of the statutory provisions. For these purposes, the provisions of the proposed regulations and the final regulations are considered a reasonable interpretation of the statutory provisions.

(f) *Gifts made after December 31, 1996, not adequately disclosed on the return.*—(1) *In general.*—If a transfer of property, other than a transfer described in paragraph (e) of this section, is not adequately disclosed on a gift tax return (Form 709, "United States Gift (and Generation-Skipping Transfer) Tax Return"), or in a statement attached to the return, filed for the calendar period in which the transfer occurs, then any gift tax imposed by chapter 12 of subtitle B of the Internal Revenue Code on the transfer may be assessed, or a proceeding in court for the collection of the appropriate tax may be begun without assessment, at any time.

(2) *Adequate disclosure of transfers of property reported as gifts.*—A transfer will be adequately disclosed on the return only if it is reported in a manner adequate to apprise the Internal Revenue Service of the nature of the gift and the basis for the value so reported. Transfers reported on the gift tax return as transfers of property by gift will be considered adequately disclosed under this paragraph (f)(2) if the return (or a statement attached to the return) provides the following information—

(i) A description of the transferred property and any consideration received by the transferor;

(ii) The identity of, and relationship between, the transferor and each transferee;

(iii) If the property is transferred in trust, the trust's tax identification number and a brief description of the terms of the trust, or in lieu of a brief description of the trust terms, a copy of the trust instrument;

(iv) Except as provided in § 301.6501-1(f)(3), a detailed description of the method used to determine the fair market value of property transferred, including any financial data (for example, balance sheets, etc. with explanations of any adjustments) that were utilized in determining the value of the interest, any restrictions on the transferred property that were considered in determining the fair market value of the property, and a description of any discounts, such as discounts for blockage, minority or fractional interests, and lack of marketability, claimed in valuing the property. In the case of a transfer of an interest that is actively traded on an established exchange, such as the New York Stock Exchange, the American Stock Exchange, the NASDAQ National Market, or a regional exchange in which quotations are published on a daily basis, including recognized foreign exchanges, recitation of the exchange where the interest is listed, the CUSIP number of the security, and the mean between the highest and lowest quoted selling prices on the applicable valuation date will satisfy all of the requirements of this paragraph (f)(2)(iv). In the case of the transfer of an interest in an entity (for example, a corporation or partnership) that is not actively traded, a description must be provided of any discount claimed in valuing the interests in the entity or any assets owned by such entity. In addition, if the value of the entity or of the interests in the entity is properly determined based on the net value of the assets held by the entity, a statement must be provided regarding the fair market value of 100 percent of the entity (determined without regard to any discounts in valuing the entity or any assets owned by the entity), the pro rata portion of the entity subject to the transfer, and the fair market value of the transferred interest as reported on the return. If 100 percent of the value of the entity is not disclosed, the taxpayer bears the burden of demonstrating that the fair market value of the entity is properly determined by a method other than a method based on the net value of the assets held by the entity. If the entity that is the subject of the transfer owns an interest in another non-actively traded entity (either directly or through ownership of an entity), the information required in this paragraph (f)(2)(iv) must be provided for each entity if the information is relevant and material in determining the value of the interest; and

(v) A statement describing any position taken that is contrary to any proposed, temporary or final Treasury regulations or revenue rulings published at the time of the transfer (see § 601.601(d)(2) of this chapter).

(3) *Submission of appraisals in lieu of the information required under paragraph (f)(2)(iv) of this section.*—The requirements of paragraph

(f)(2)(iv) of this section will be satisfied if the donor submits an appraisal of the transferred property that meets the following requirements—

(i) The appraisal is prepared by an appraiser who satisfies all of the following requirements:

(A) The appraiser is an individual who holds himself or herself out to the public as an appraiser or performs appraisals on a regular basis.

(B) Because of the appraiser's qualifications, as described in the appraisal that details the appraiser's background, experience, education, and membership, if any, in professional appraisal associations, the appraiser is qualified to make appraisals of the type of property being valued.

(C) The appraiser is not the donor or the donee of the property or a member of the family of the donor or donee, as defined in section 2032A(e)(2), or any person employed by the donor, the donee, or a member of the family of either; and

(ii) The appraisal contains all of the following:

(A) The date of the transfer, the date on which the transferred property was appraised, and the purpose of the appraisal.

(B) A description of the property.

(C) A description of the appraisal process employed.

(D) A description of the assumptions, hypothetical conditions, and any limiting conditions and restrictions on the transferred property that affect the analyses, opinions, and conclusions.

(E) The information considered in determining the appraised value, including in the case of an ownership interest in a business, all financial data that was used in determining the value of the interest that is sufficiently detailed so that another person can replicate the process and arrive at the appraised value.

(F) The appraisal procedures followed, and the reasoning that supports the analyses, opinions, and conclusions.

(G) The valuation method utilized, the rationale for the valuation method, and the procedure used in determining the fair market value of the asset transferred.

(H) The specific basis for the valuation, such as specific comparable sales or transactions, sales of similar interests, asset-based approaches, merger-acquisition transactions, etc.

(4) *Adequate disclosure of non-gift completed transfers or transactions.*—Completed transfers to members of the transferor's family, as defined in section 2032A(e)(2), that are made in the ordinary course of operating a business are deemed to be adequately disclosed under paragraph (f)(2) of this section, even if the transfer is not reported on a gift tax return, provided the transfer is properly reported by all parties for income tax purposes. For example, in the case of salary paid to a family member employed in a family owned business, the transfer will be treated as adequately disclosed for gift tax purposes if the item is properly reported by the business and the family member on their income tax returns. For purposes of this paragraph (f)(4), any other completed transfer that is reported, in its entirety, as not constituting a transfer by gift will be considered adequately disclosed under paragraph (f)(2) of this section only if the following information is provided on, or attached to, the return—

(i) The information required for adequate disclosure under paragraphs (f)(2)(i), (ii), (iii) and (v) of this section; and

(ii) An explanation as to why the transfer is not a transfer by gift under chapter 12 of the Internal Revenue Code.

(5) *Adequate disclosure of incomplete transfers.*—Adequate disclosure of a transfer that is reported as a completed gift on the gift tax return will commence the running of the period of limitations for assessment of gift tax on the transfer, even if the transfer is ultimately determined to be an incomplete gift for purposes of § 25.2511-2 of this chapter. For example, if an incomplete gift is reported as a completed gift on the gift tax return and is adequately disclosed, the period for assessment of the gift tax will begin to run when the return is filed, as determined under section 6501(b). Further, once the period of assessment for gift tax expires, the transfer will be subject to inclusion in the donor's gross estate for estate tax purposes only to the extent that a completed gift would be so included. On the other hand, if the transfer is reported as an incomplete gift whether or not adequately disclosed, the period for assessing a gift tax with respect to the transfer will not commence to run even if the transfer is ultimately determined to be a completed gift. In that situation, the gift tax with respect to the transfer may be assessed at any time, up until three years after the donor files a return reporting the transfer as a completed gift with adequate disclosure.

(6) *Treatment of split gifts.*—If a husband and wife elect under section 2513 to treat a gift made to a third party as made one-half by each spouse, the requirements of this paragraph (f) will be satisfied with respect to the gift deemed made by the consenting spouse if the return filed by the donor spouse (the spouse that transferred the property) satisfies the requirements of this paragraph (f) with respect to that gift.

(7) *Examples.*—The following examples illustrate the rules of this paragraph (f):

Example 1. (i) *Facts.* In 2001, A transfers 100 shares of common stock of XYZ Corporation to A's child. The common stock of XYZ Corporation is actively traded on a major stock exchange. For gift tax purposes, the fair market value of one share of XYZ common stock on the date of the transfer, determined in accordance with § 25.2512-2(b) of this chapter (based on the mean between the highest and lowest quoted selling prices), is $150.00. On A's Federal gift tax return,

Reg. § 301.6501(c)-1(f)(3)(i)

Form 709, for the 2001 calendar year, A reports the gift to A's child of 100 shares of common stock of XYZ Corporation with a value for gift tax purposes of $15,000. A specifies the date of the transfer, recites that the stock is publicly traded, identifies the stock exchange on which the stock is traded, lists the stock's CUSIP number, and lists the mean between the highest and lowest quoted selling prices for the date of transfer.

(ii) *Application of the adequate disclosure standard.* A has adequately disclosed the transfer. Therefore, the period of assessment for the transfer under section 6501 will run from the time the return is filed (as determined under section 6501(b)).

Example 2. (i) *Facts.* On December 30, 2001, A transfers closely-held stock to B, A's child. A determined that the value of the transferred stock, on December 30, 2001, was $9,000. A made no other transfers to B, or any other donee, during 2001. On A's Federal gift tax return, Form 709, for the 2001 calendar year, A provides the information required under paragraph (f)(2) of this section such that the transfer is adequately disclosed. A claims an annual exclusion under section 2503(b) for the transfer.

(ii) *Application of the adequate disclosure standard.* Because the transfer is adequately disclosed under paragraph (f)(2) of this section, the period of assessment for the transfer will expire as prescribed by section 6501(b), notwithstanding that if A's valuation of the closely-held stock was correct, A was not required to file a gift tax return reporting the transfer under section 6019. After the period of assessment has expired on the transfer, the Internal Revenue Service is precluded from redetermining the amount of the gift for purposes of assessing gift tax or for purposes of determining the estate tax liability. Therefore, the amount of the gift as reported on A's 2001 Federal gift tax return may not be redetermined for purposes of determining A's prior taxable gifts (for gift tax purposes) or A's adjusted taxable gifts (for estate tax purposes).

Example 3. (i) *Facts.* A owns 100 percent of the common stock of X, a closely-held corporation. X does not hold an interest in any other entity that is not actively traded. In 2001, A transfers 20 percent of the X stock to B and C, A's children, in a transfer that is not subject to the special valuation rules of section 2701. The transfer is made outright with no restrictions on ownership rights, including voting rights and the right to transfer the stock. Based on generally applicable valuation principles, the value of X would be determined based on the net value of the assets owned by X. The reported value of the transferred stock incorporates the use of minority discounts and lack of marketability discounts. No other discounts were used in arriving at the fair market value of the transferred stock or any assets owned by X. On A's Federal gift tax return, Form 709, for the 2001 calendar year, A provides the information required under paragraph (f)(2) of this section including a statement reporting the fair market value of 100 percent of

X (before taking into account any discounts), the pro rata portion of X subject to the transfer, and the reported value of the transfer. A also attaches a statement regarding the determination of value that includes a discussion of the discounts claimed and how the discounts were determined.

(ii) *Application of the adequate disclosure standard.* A has provided sufficient information such that the transfer will be considered adequately disclosed and the period of assessment for the transfer under section 6501 will run from the time the return is filed (as determined under section 6501(b)).

Example 4. (i) *Facts.* A owns a 70 percent limited partnership interest in PS. PS owns 40 percent of the stock in X, a closely-held corporation. The assets of X include a 50 percent general partnership interest in PB. PB owns an interest in commercial real property. None of the entities (PS, X, or PB) is actively traded and, based on generally applicable valuation principles, the value of each entity would be determined based on the net value of the assets owned by each entity. In 2001, A transfers a 25 percent limited partnership interest in PS to B, A's child. On the Federal gift tax return, Form 709, for the 2001 calendar year, A reports the transfer of the 25 percent limited partnership interest in PS and that the fair market value of 100 percent of PS is $y and that the value of 25 percent of PS is $z, reflecting marketability and minority discounts with respect to the 25 percent interest. However, A does not disclose that PS owns 40 percent of X, and that X owns 50 percent of PB and that, in arriving at the $y fair market value of 100 percent of PS, discounts were claimed in valuing PS's interest in X, X's interest in PB, and PB's interest in the commercial real property.

(ii) *Application of the adequate disclosure standard.* The information on the lower tiered entities is relevant and material in determining the value of the transferred interest in PS. Accordingly, because A has failed to comply with requirements of paragraph (f)(2)(iv) of this section regarding PS's interest in X, X's interest in PB, and PB's interest in the commercial real property, the transfer will not be considered adequately disclosed and the period of assessment for the transfer under section 6501 will remain open indefinitely.

Example 5. The facts are the same as in *Example 4* except that A submits, with the Federal tax return, an appraisal of the 25 percent limited partnership interest in PS that satisfies the requirements of paragraph (f)(3) of this section in lieu of the information required in paragraph (f)(2)(iv) of this section. Assuming the other requirements of paragraph (f)(2) of this section are satisfied, the transfer is considered adequately disclosed and the period for assessment for the transfer under section 6501 will run from the time the return is filed (as determined under section 6501(b) of this chapter).

Example 6. A owns 100 percent of the stock of X Corporation, a company actively engaged in a manufacturing business. B, A's child, is an employee of X and receives an annual salary paid in the ordinary course of operating X Corporation. B reports the annual salary as income on B's income tax returns. In 2001, A transfers property to family members and files a Federal gift tax return reporting the transfers. However, A does not disclose the 2001 salary payments made to B. Because the salary payments were reported as income on B's income tax return, the salary payments are deemed to be adequately disclosed. The transfer of property to family members, other than the salary payments to B, reported on the gift tax return must satisfy the adequate disclosure requirements under paragraph (f)(2) of this section in order for the period of assessment under section 6501 to commence to run with respect to those transfers.

(8) *Effective date.*—This paragraph (f) is applicable to gifts made after December 31, 1996, for which the gift tax return for such calendar year is filed after December 3, 1999.

(g) *Listed transactions.*—(1) *In general.*—If a taxpayer is required to disclose a listed transaction under section 6011 and the regulations thereunder and does not do so in the time and manner required, then the time to assess any tax attributable to that listed transaction for the taxable year(s) to which the failure to disclose relates (as defined in paragraph (g)(3)(iii) of this section) will not expire before the earlier of one year after the date on which the taxpayer makes the disclosure described in paragraph (g)(5) of this section or one year after the date on which a material advisor makes a disclosure described in paragraph (g)(6) of this section. In no case will the operation of this paragraph (g) cause the period of limitations on assessment to expire any earlier than the period that would have otherwise applied under this section determined without regard to this paragraph (g)(1).

(2) *Limitations period if paragraph (g)(5) or (g)(6) is satisfied.*—If one of the disclosure provisions described in paragraphs (g)(5) or (6) of this section is satisfied, then the tax attributable to the listed transaction may be assessed at any time before the expiration of the limitations period that would have otherwise applied under this section (determined without regard to paragraph (g)(1) of this section) or the period ending one year after the date that one of the disclosure provisions described in paragraphs (g)(5) or (6) of this section was satisfied, whichever is later. If both disclosure provisions are satisfied, the one-year period will begin on the earlier of the dates on which the provisions were satisfied. Paragraph (g)(1) of this section does not apply to any period of limitations on assessment that expired before the date on which the failure to disclose the listed transaction under section 6011 occurred.

(3) *Definitions.*—(i) *Listed transaction.*—The term *listed transaction* means a transaction described in section 6707A(c)(2) of the Code and § 1.6011-4(b)(2) of this chapter.

(ii) *Material advisor.*—The term *material advisor* means a person described in section 6111(b)(1) of the Code and § 301.6111-3(b) of this chapter.

(iii) *Taxable year(s) to which the failure to disclose relates.*—The *taxable year(s) to which the failure to disclose relates* are each taxable year that the taxpayer participated (as defined under section 6011 and the regulations thereunder) in a transaction that was identified as a listed transaction and the taxpayer failed to disclose the listed transaction as required under section 6011. If the taxable year in which the taxpayer participated in the listed transaction is different from the taxable year in which the taxpayer is required to disclose the listed transaction under section 6011, the taxable year(s) to which the failure to disclose relates are each taxable year that the taxpayer participated in the transaction.

(4) *Application of paragraph with respect to pass-through entities.*—In the case of taxpayers who are partners in partnerships, shareholders in S corporations, or beneficiaries of trusts and are required to disclose a listed transaction under section 6011 and the regulations thereunder, paragraph (g)(1) of this section will apply to a particular partner, shareholder, or beneficiary if that particular partner, shareholder, or beneficiary does not disclose within the time and in the form and manner provided by section 6011 and § 1.6011-4(d) and (e), regardless of whether the partnership, S corporation, or trust or another partner, shareholder, or beneficiary discloses in accordance with section 6011 and the regulations thereunder. Similarly, because paragraph (g)(1) of this section applies on a taxpayer-by-taxpayer basis, the failure of a partnership, S corporation, or trust that has a disclosure obligation under section 6011 and that does not disclose within the time or in the form and manner provided by § 1.6011-4(d) and (e) will not cause paragraph (g)(1) of this section to apply to a partner, shareholder or beneficiary of the entity. Instead, the application of paragraph (g)(1) of this section to a partner, shareholder, or beneficiary will be determined based on whether the particular partner, shareholder, or beneficiary satisfied their disclosure obligation under section 6011 and the regulations thereunder.

(5) *Taxpayer's disclosure of a listed transaction that the taxpayer did not properly disclose under section 6011.*—(i) *In general.*—(A) *Method of disclosure.*—The taxpayer must complete the most current version of Form 8886, "Reportable Transaction Disclosure Statement" (or successor form), available on the date the taxpayer attempts to satisfy this paragraph (g)(5) in accordance with § 1.6011-4(d) and the instructions to the Form in effect on that date. The taxpayer must indicate on the Form 8886 that the form is being submitted for purposes of section 6501(c)(10) and the tax return(s) and taxable year(s) for which the taxpayer is making a section 6501(c)(10) disclosure. Disclosure under this paragraph (g)(5) will only be effective for the tax return(s) and taxable

year(s) that the taxpayer specifies on the Form 8886 that he or she is attempting to disclose for purposes of section 6501(c)(10). If the Form 8886 contains a line for this purpose, then the taxpayer must complete the line in accordance with the instructions to that form. Otherwise, the taxpayer must include on the top of Page 1 of the Form 8886, and each copy of the form, the following statement: "*Section 6501(c)(10) Disclosure*" followed by the tax return(s) and taxable year(s) for which the taxpayer is making a section 6501(c)(10) disclosure. For example, if the taxpayer did not properly disclose its participation in a listed transaction the tax consequences of which were reflected on the taxpayer's Form 1040 for the 2005 taxable year, the taxpayer must include the following statement: "*Section 6501(c)(10) Disclosure; 2005 Form 1040*" on the form. The taxpayer must submit the properly completed Form 8886 and a cover letter, which must be completed in accordance with the requirements set forth in paragraph (g)(5)(i)(B) of this section, to the Office of Tax Shelter Analysis (OTSA). The taxpayer is permitted, but not required, to file an amended return with the Form 8886 and cover letter. Separate Forms 8886 and separate cover letters must be submitted for each listed transaction the taxpayer did not properly disclose under section 6011. If the taxpayer participated in one listed transaction over multiple years, the taxpayer may submit one Form 8886 (or successor form) and cover letter and indicate on that form all of the tax returns and taxable years for which the taxpayer is making a section 6501(c)(10) disclosure. If a taxpayer participated in more than one listed transaction, then the taxpayer must submit separate Forms 8886 (or successor form) for each listed transaction, unless the listed transactions are the same or substantially similar, in which case all the listed transactions may be reported on one Form 8886.

(B) *Cover letter.*—*(1)* A cover letter to which a Form 8886 is to be attached must identify the tax return(s) and taxable year(s) for which the taxpayer is making a section 6501(c)(10) disclosure and include the following statement signed under penalties of perjury by the taxpayer:

> Under penalties of perjury, I declare that I have examined this reportable transaction disclosure statement and, to the best of my knowledge and belief, this reportable transaction disclosure statement is true, correct, and complete.

(2) If the Form 8886 is prepared by a paid preparer, in addition to the statement under penalties of perjury signed by the taxpayer, the Form 8886 must also include the following statement signed under penalties of perjury by the paid preparer.

> Under penalties of perjury, I declare that I have

examined this reportable transaction disclosure statement and, to the best of my knowledge and belief, this reportable transaction disclosure statement is true, correct, and complete. This declaration is based on all information of which I, as paid preparer, have any knowledge.

(C) *Taxpayer under examination or Appeals consideration.*—A taxpayer making a disclosure under paragraph (g)(5) of this section with respect to a taxable year under examination or Appeals consideration by the IRS must satisfy the requirements of paragraphs (g)(5)(i)(A) and (B) of this section and also submit a copy of the submission to the IRS examiner or Appeals officer examining or considering the taxable year(s) to which the disclosure under this paragraph (g) relates.

(D) *Date the one-year period will begin to run if paragraph (g)(5) satisfied.*—Unless an earlier expiration is provided for in paragraph (g)(6) of this section, the time to assess tax under this paragraph (g) will not expire before one year after the date on which the Secretary is furnished the information from the taxpayer that satisfies all of the requirements of paragraphs (g)(5)(i)(A) and (B) of this section and, if applicable, paragraph (g)(5)(i)(C) of this section. If the taxpayer does not satisfy all of the requirements on the same date, the one-year period will begin on the date that the IRS is furnished the information that, together with prior disclosures of information, satisfies the requirements of this paragraph (g)(5). For purposes of this paragraph (g)(5), the information is deemed furnished on the date the IRS receives the information.

(ii) *Exception for returns other than annual returns.*—The IRS may prescribe alternative procedures to satisfy the requirements of this paragraph (g)(5) in a revenue procedure, notice, or other guidance published in the Internal Revenue Bulletin for circumstances involving returns other than annual returns.

(6) *Material advisor's disclosure of a listed transaction not properly disclosed by a taxpayer under section 6011.*—(i) *In general.*—In response to a written request of the IRS under section 6112, a material advisor with respect to a listed transaction must furnish to the IRS the information described in section 6112 and § 301.6112-1(b) in the form and manner prescribed by section 6112 and § 301.6112-1(e). If the information the material advisor furnishes identifies the taxpayer as a person who entered into the listed transaction, regardless of whether the material advisor provides the information before or after the taxpayer's failure to disclose the listed transaction under section 6011, then the requirements of this paragraph (g)(6) will be satisfied for that taxpayer. The requirements of this paragraph (g)(6)

will be considered satisfied even if the material advisor furnishes the information required under section 6112 to the IRS after the date prescribed in section 6708 or published guidance relating to section 6708.

(ii) *Paragraph (g)(6) not satisfied.*— (A) *Information not furnished by a material advisor or a person permitted to act on behalf of the material advisor.*—The requirements of this paragraph (g)(6) are not satisfied for a taxpayer unless the information is furnished by—

(1) A person who is a material advisor (as defined in paragraph (g)(3)(ii) of this section) with respect to the taxpayer,

(2) A person who is providing the information pursuant to § 301.6112-1(d) on behalf of a dissolved or liquidated material advisor with respect to the taxpayer, or

(3) a person who is providing the information on behalf of a material advisor with respect to the taxpayer under a designation agreement in accordance with § 301.6112-1(f).

(B) *No written request by IRS.*—The requirements of this paragraph (g)(6) are not satisfied unless the information is furnished in response to a written request made by the IRS to the material advisor under section 6112 (except as provided in § 301.6112-1(d) with respect to a list furnished to OTSA within 60 days after dissolution or liquidation of a material advisor).

(C) *Information furnished does not identify the taxpayer.*—The requirements of this paragraph (g)(6) are not satisfied for a taxpayer unless the information furnished identifies the taxpayer as a person who entered into the listed transaction.

(iii) *Date the one-year period will begin if paragraph (g)(6) is satisfied.*—Unless an earlier expiration is provided for in paragraph (g)(5) of this section, the time to assess tax under this paragraph (g) will expire one year after the date on which the material advisor satisfies the requirements of paragraph (g)(6)(i) of this section with respect to the taxpayer. For purposes of this paragraph (g)(6), information is deemed to be furnished on the date that, in response to a request under section 6112, the IRS receives the information from a material advisor that satisfies the requirements of paragraph (g)(6)(i) of this section with respect to the taxpayer.

(7) *Tax assessable under this section.*—If the period of limitations on assessment for a taxable year remains open under this section, the Secretary has authority to assess any tax with respect to the listed transaction in that year. This includes, but is not limited to, adjustments made to the tax consequences claimed on the return plus interest, additions to tax, additional amounts, and penalties that are related to the listed transaction or adjustments made to the tax consequences. This also includes any item to the extent the item is affected by the listed transaction even if it is unrelated to the listed transaction. An example of an item affected by, but

unrelated to, a listed transaction is the threshold for the medical expense deduction under section 213 that varies if there is a change in an individual's adjusted gross income. An example of a penalty related to the listed transaction is the penalty under section 6707A for failure to file the disclosure statement reporting the taxpayer's participation in the listed transaction. Examples of penalties related to the adjustments made to the tax consequences are the accuracy-related penalties under sections 6662 and 6662A.

(8) *Examples.*—The rules of this paragraph (g) are illustrated by the following examples:

Example 1. No requirement to disclose under section 6011. P, an individual, is a partner in a partnership that entered into a transaction in 2001 that was the same as or substantially similar to the transaction identified as a listed transaction in Notice 2000-44 (2000-2 CB 255). P claimed a loss from the transaction on his Form 1040 for the tax year 2001. P filed the Form 1040 prior to June 14, 2002. P did not disclose his participation in the listed transaction because P was not required to disclose the transaction under the applicable section 6011 regulations (TD 8961), which were effective for any transaction entered into before January 1, 2001 and any transaction entered into on or after January 1, 2001 that was reported on a return of the taxpayer filed on or before June 14, 2002. Although the transaction was a listed transaction and P did not disclose the transaction, P had no obligation to include on any return or statement any information with respect to a listed transaction within the meaning of section 6501(c)(10) because TD 8961 only applied to corporations, not individuals. Accordingly, section 6501(c)(10) does not apply.

Example 2. Taxable year to which the failure to disclose relates when transaction is identified as a listed transaction after first year of participation and the transaction must be disclosed with the return next filed. (i) On December 30, 2003, Y, a corporation, enters into a transaction that at the time is not a reportable transaction. On March 15, 2004, Y timely files its 2003 Form 1120, reporting the tax consequences from the transaction. On April 1, 2004, the IRS issues Notice 2004-31 that identifies the transaction as a listed transaction. Y also reports tax consequences from the transaction on its 2004 Form 1120, which it timely filed on March 15, 2005. Y did not attach a completed Form 8886 to its 2004 Form 1120 and did not send a copy of the form to OTSA. The general three-year period of limitations on assessment for Y's 2003 and 2004 taxable years would expire on March 15, 2007, and March 17, 2008, respectively.

(ii) The period of limitations on assessment for Y's 2003 taxable year was open on the date the transaction was identified as a listed transaction. Under the applicable section 6011 regulations (TD 9108), which were effective for transactions entered into before August 3, 2007, Y should have disclosed its participation in the transaction with its next filed return, which was its 2004 Form 1120, but Y did not disclose its participation. Y's failure to disclose with the 2004 Form 1120 relates to taxable years 2003 and 2004. Section 6501(c)(10) operates to keep the period of limitations on assessment open for the 2003 and 2004 taxable years with respect to the listed transaction until at least one year after the date Y satisfies the requirements of paragraph (g)(5) of this section or a material advisor satisfies the requirements of paragraph (g)(6) of this section with respect to Y.

Example 3. Taxable year to which the failure to disclose relates when transaction is identified as a listed transaction after the first year of participation and the transaction must be disclosed 90 days after the transaction became a listed transaction. (i) In January 2015, A, a calendar year taxpayer, enters into a transaction that at the time is not a listed transaction. A reports the tax consequences from the transaction on its individual income tax return for 2015 timely filed on April 15, 2016. The time for the IRS to assess tax against A under the general three-year period of limitations for A's 2015 taxable year would expire on April 15, 2019. A only participated in the transaction in 2015. On March 7, 2017, the IRS identifies the transaction as a listed transaction. A does not file the Form 8886 with OTSA by June 5, 2017.

(ii) The period of limitations on assessment for A's 2015 taxable year was open on the date the transaction was identified as a listed transaction. Under the current section 6011 regulations (TD 9350) which are effective for transactions entered into on or after August 3, 2007, A must disclose its participation in the transaction by filing a completed Form 8886 with OTSA on or before June 5, 2017, which is 90 days after the date the transaction became a listed transaction. A did not disclose the transaction as required. A's failure to disclose relates to taxable year 2015 even though the obligation to disclose did not arise until 2017. Section 6501(c)(10) operates to keep the period of limitations on assessment open for the 2015 taxable year with respect to the listed transaction until at least one year after the date A satisfies the requirements of paragraph (g)(5) of this section or a material advisor satisfies the requirements of paragraph (g)(6) of this section with respect to A.

Example 4. Requirements of paragraph (g)(6) satisfied. Same facts as *Example 3*, except that on April 5, 2019, the IRS hand delivers to Advisor J, who is a material advisor, a section 6112 request related to the listed transaction. Advisor J furnishes the required list with all the information required by section 6112 and §301.6112-1, including all the information required with respect to A, to the IRS on May 8, 2019. The submission satisfies the requirements of paragraph (g)(6) even though Advisor J furnishes the information outside of the 20-business-day period provided in section 6708. Accordingly, under section 6501(c)(10), the period of limitations with respect to A's taxable year 2015 will end on May 8, 2020, one year after the IRS received the required information, unless the period of limitations remains open under another exception. Any tax

for the 2015 taxable year not attributable to the listed transaction must be assessed by April 15, 2019.

Example 5. Requirements of paragraph (g)(5) also satisfied. Same facts as *Examples 3 and 4*, except that on May 23, 2019, A files a properly completed Form 8886 and signed cover letter with OTSA both identifying that the section 6501(c)(10) disclosure relates to A's Form 1040 for 2015. A satisfied the requirements of paragraph (g)(5) of this section as of May 23, 2019. Because the requirements of paragraph (g)(6) were satisfied first as described in *Example 4*, under section 6501(c)(10) the period of limitations will end on May 8, 2020 (one year after the requirements of paragraph (g)(6) were satisfied) instead of May 23, 2020 (one year after the requirements of paragraph (g)(5) were satisfied). Any tax for the 2015 taxable year not attributable to the listed transaction must be assessed by April 15, 2019.

Example 6. Period to assess tax remains open under another exception. Same facts as *Examples 3, 4, and 5*, except that on April 1, 2019, A signed Form 872, consenting to extend, without restriction, its period of limitations on assessment for taxable year 2015 under section 6501(c)(4) until July 15, 2020. In that case, although under section 6501(c)(10) the period of limitations would otherwise expire on May 8, 2020, the IRS may assess tax with respect to the listed transaction (as well as any other item on the return covered by the Form 872 extension) at any time up to and including July 15, 2020, pursuant to section 6501(c)(4). Section 6501(c)(10) operates to extend the assessment period but not to shorten any other applicable assessment period.

Example 7. Requirements of (g)(5) not satisfied. In 2015, X, a corporation, enters into a listed transaction. On March 15, 2016, X timely files its 2015 Form 1120, reporting the tax consequences from the transaction. X does not disclose the transaction as required under section 6011 when it files its 2015 return. The failure to disclose relates to taxable year 2015. On February 13, 2017, X completes and files a Form 8886 with respect to the listed transaction with OTSA but does not submit a cover letter, as required. The requirements of paragraph (g)(5) of this section have not been satisfied. Therefore, the time to assess tax against X with respect to the transaction for taxable year 2015 remains open under section 6501(c)(10).

Example 8. Section 6501(c)(10) applies to keep one partner's period of limitations on assessment open. T and S are partners in a partnership, TS, that enters into a listed transaction in 2015. T and S each receive a Schedule K-1 from TS on April 11, 2016. On April 15, 2016, TS, T and S each file their 2015 returns. Under the applicable section 6011 regulations, TS, T, and S each are required to disclose the transaction. TS attaches a completed Form 8886 to its 2015 Form 1065 and sends a copy of Form 8886 to OTSA. Neither T nor S files a disclosure statement with their respective returns nor sends a copy to OTSA on April 15, 2016. On May 17, 2016, T timely files a completed Form 8886 with OTSA pursuant to § 1.6011-4(e)(1). T's disclosure is timely because T received the Schedule K-1 within 10 calendar days before the due date of the return and, thus, T had 60 calendar days to file Form 8886 with OTSA. TS and T properly disclosed the transaction in accordance with the applicable regulations under section 6011, but S did not. S's failure to disclose relates to taxable year 2015. The time to assess tax with respect to the transaction against S for 2015 remains open under section 6501(c)(10) even though TS and T disclosed the transaction.

Example 9. Section 6501(c)(10) satisfied before expiration of three-year period of limitations under section 6501(a). Same facts as *Example 8*, except that on August 26, 2016, S satisfies the requirements of paragraph (g)(5) of this section. No material advisor satisfied the requirements of paragraph (g)(6) of this section with respect to S on a date earlier than August 26, 2016. Under section 6501(c)(10), the period of time in which the IRS may assess tax against S with respect to the listed transaction would expire no earlier than August 26, 2017, one year after the date S satisfied the requirements of paragraph (g)(5). As the general three-year period of limitations on assessment under section 6501(a) does not expire until April 15, 2019, the IRS will have until that date to assess any tax with respect to the listed transaction.

Example 10. No section 6112 request. B, a calendar year taxpayer, entered into a listed transaction in 2015. B did not comply with the applicable disclosure requirements under section 6011 for taxable year 2015; therefore, section 6501(c)(10) applies to keep the period of limitations on assessment open with respect to the tax related to the transaction until at least one year after B satisfies the requirements of paragraph (g)(5) of this section or a material advisor satisfies the requirements of paragraph (g)(6) of this section with respect to B. In June 2016, the IRS conducts a section 6700 investigation of Advisor K, who is a material advisor to B with respect to the listed transaction. During the course of the investigation, the IRS obtains the name, address, and TIN of all of Advisor K's clients who engaged in the transaction, including B. The information provided does not satisfy the requirements of paragraph (g)(6) with respect to B because the information was not provided pursuant to a section 6112 request. Therefore, the time to assess tax against B with respect to the transaction for taxable year 2015 remains open under section 6501(c)(10).

Example 11. Section 6112 request but the requirements of paragraph (g)(6) are not satisfied with respect to B. Same facts as *Example 10*, except that on January 9, 2017, the IRS sends by certified mail a section 6112 request to Advisor L, who is another material advisor to B with respect to the listed transaction. Advisor L furnishes some of the information required under section 6112 and § 301.6112-1 to the IRS for inspection on January 17, 2017. The list includes information with respect to many clients of Advisor L, but it does not include any information with respect to B. The submission does not satisfy the requirements of paragraph (g)(6) of this section with respect to B. Therefore, the time to assess tax against B with respect to the transaction for taxable year 2015 remains open under section 6501(c)(10).

Example 12. Section 6112 submission made before taxpayer failed to disclose a listed transaction. Advisor M, who is a material advisor, advises C, an individual, in 2015 with respect to a transaction that is not a reportable transaction at that time. C files its return claiming the tax consequences of the transaction on April 15, 2016. The time for the IRS to assess tax against C under the general three-year period of limitations for C's 2015 taxable year would expire on April 15, 2019. The IRS identifies the transaction as a listed transaction on November 3, 2017. On December 7, 2017, the IRS hand delivers to Advisor M a section 6112 request related to the transaction. Advisor M furnishes the information to the IRS on December 29, 2017. The information contains all the required information with respect to Advisor M's clients, including C. C does not disclose the transaction on or before February 1, 2018, as required under section 6011 and the regulations under section 6011. Advisor M's submission under section 6112 satisfies the requirements of paragraph (g)(6) of this section even though it occurred prior to C's failure to disclose the listed transaction. Thus, under section 6501(c)(10), the period of limitations to assess tax against C with respect to the listed transaction will end on December 29, 2018 (one year after the requirements of paragraph (g)(6) of this section were satisfied), unless the period of limitations remains open under another exception.

Example 13. Transaction removed from the category of listed transactions after taxpayer failed to disclose. D, a calendar year taxpayer, entered into a listed transaction in 2015. D did not comply with the applicable disclosure requirements under section 6011 for taxable year 2015; therefore, section 6501(c)(10) applies to keep the period of limitations on assessment open with respect to the tax related to the transaction until at least one year after D satisfies the requirements of paragraph (g)(5) of this section or a material advisor satisfies the requirements of paragraph (g)(6) of this section with respect to D. In 2017, the IRS removes the transaction from the category of listed transactions because of a change in law. Section 6501(c)(10) continues to apply to keep the period of limitations on assessment open for D's taxable year 2015.

Example 14. Taxes assessed with respect to the listed transaction. (i) F, an individual, enters into a listed transaction in 2015. F files its 2015 Form 1040 on April 15, 2016, but does not disclose his participation in the listed transaction in accordance with section 6011 and the regulations under section 6011. F's failure to disclose relates to taxable year 2015. Thus, section 6501(c)(10) applies to keep the period of limitations on assessment open with respect to the tax related to the listed transaction for taxable year 2015 until at least one year after the date F satisfies the requirements of paragraph (g)(5) of this section or a material advisor satisfies the requirements of paragraph (g)(6) of this section with respect to F.

(ii) On July 2, 2020, the IRS completes an examination of F's 2015 taxable year and disallows the tax consequences claimed as a result of the listed transaction. The disallowance of a loss increased F's adjusted gross income. Due to the increase of F's adjusted gross income, certain credits, such as the child tax credit, and exemption deductions were disallowed or reduced because of limitations based on adjusted gross income. In addition, F now is liable for the alternative minimum tax. The examination also uncovered that F claimed two deductions on Schedule C to which F was not entitled. Under section 6501(c)(10), the IRS can timely issue a statutory notice of deficiency (and assess in due course) against F for the deficiency resulting from (1) disallowing the loss, (2) disallowing the credits and exemptions to which F was not entitled based on F's increased adjusted gross income, and (3) being liable for the alternative minimum tax. In addition, the IRS can assess any interest and applicable penalties related to those adjustments, such as the accuracy-related penalty under sections 6662 and 6662A and the penalty under section 6707A for F's failure to disclose the transaction as required under section 6011 and the regulations under section 6011. The IRS cannot, however, pursuant to section 6501(c)(10), assess the increase in tax that would result from disallowing the two deductions on F's Schedule C because those deductions are not related to, or affected by, the adjustments concerning the listed transaction.

(9) *Effective/applicability date.*—The rules of this paragraph (g) apply to taxable years with respect to which the period of limitations on assessment under section 6501 (including subsection (c)(10)) did not expire before March 31, 2015. [Reg. § 301.6501(c)-1.]

☐ *[T.D. 6172, 5-2-56. Amended by T.D. 6498, 10-24-60; T.D. 7838, 10-5-82; T.D. 8395, 1-28-92, T.D. 8845, 12-2-99 (corrected 1-6-2000) and T.D. 9718, 3-30-15 (corrected 4-27-2015).]*

[Reg. § 301.6501(d)-1]

§ 301.6501(d)-1. Request for prompt assessment.—(a) Except as otherwise provided in section 6501(c), (e), or (f), any tax for which a return is required and for which:

(1) A decedent or an estate of a decedent may be liable, other than the estate tax imposed by chapter 11 of the Code, or

(2) A corporation which is contemplating dissolution, is in the process of dissolution, or has been dissolved, may be liable,

shall be assessed, or a proceeding in court without assessment for the collection of such tax shall be begun, within 18 months after the receipt of a written request for prompt assessment thereof.

(b) The executor, administrator, or other fiduciary representing the estate of the decedent, or the corporation, or the fiduciary representing the dissolved corporation, as the case may be, shall, after the return in question has been filed, file the request for prompt assessment in writing with the district director for the internal revenue district in which such return was filed. The request, in order to be effective, must be transmitted separately from any other document, must set forth the classes of tax and the taxable periods for which the prompt assessment is requested, and must clearly indicate that it is a request for prompt assessment under the provisions of section 6501(d). The effect of such a request is to limit the time in which an assessment of tax may be made, or a proceeding in court without assessment for collection of tax may be begun, to a period of 18 months from the date the request is filed with the proper district director. The request does not extend the time within which an assessment may be made, or a proceeding in court without assessment may be begun, beyond 3 years from the date the return was filed. This special period of limitations will not apply to any return filed after a request for prompt assessment has been made unless an additional request is filed in the manner provided herein.

(c) In the case of a corporation the 18-month period shall not apply unless:

(1) The written request notifies the district director that the corporation contemplates dissolution at or before the expiration of such 18-month period; the dissolution is in good faith begun before the expiration of such 18-month period; and the dissolution so begun is completed either before or after the expiration of such 18-month period; or

(2) The written request notifies the district director that a dissolution has in good faith been begun, and the dissolution is completed either before or after the expiration of such 18-month period; or

(3) A dissolution has been completed at the time the written request is made. [Reg. § 301.6501(d)-1.]

☐ *[T.D. 6172, 5-2-56. Amended by T.D. 6425, 11-10-59 and T.D. 6498, 10-24-60.]*

[Reg. § 301.6501(e)-1]

§ 301.6501(e)-1. Omission from return.—(a) *Income taxes.*—(1) *General rule.*—(i) If a taxpayer omits from the gross income stated in the return of a tax imposed by subtitle A of the Internal Revenue Code an amount properly includible therein that is in excess of 25 percent of the gross income so stated, the tax may be assessed, or a proceeding in court for the collection of that tax may be begun without assessment, at any time within 6 years after the return was filed.

(ii) For purposes of paragraph (a)(1)(i) of this section, the term *gross income*, as it relates to a trade or business, means the total of the amounts received or accrued from the sale of goods or services, to the extent required to be shown on the return, without reduction for the cost of those goods or services.

(iii) For purposes of paragraph (a)(1)(i) of this section, the term *gross income*, as it relates to any income other than from the sale of goods or services in a trade or business, has the same meaning as provided under section 61(a), and includes the total of the amounts received or accrued, to the extent required to be shown on the return. In the case of amounts received or accrued that relate to the disposition of property, and except as provided in paragraph (a)(1)(ii) of this section, *gross income* means the excess of the amount realized from the disposition of the property over the unrecovered cost or other basis of the property. Consequently, except as provided in paragraph (a)(1)(ii) of this section, an understated amount of gross income resulting from an overstatement of unrecovered cost or other basis constitutes an omission from gross income for purposes of section 6501(e)(1)(A)(i).

(iv) An amount shall not be considered as omitted from gross income if information sufficient to apprise the Commissioner of the nature and amount of the item is disclosed in the return, including any schedule or statement attached to the return.

(2) [Reserved]

(b) *Estate and gift taxes.*—(1) If the taxpayer omits from the gross estate as stated in the estate tax return, or from the total amount of the gifts made during the period for which the gift tax return was filed (see §25.6019-1 of this chapter) as stated in the gift tax return, an item or items properly includible therein the amount of which is in excess of 25 percent of the gross estate as stated in the estate tax return, or 25 percent of the total amount of the gifts as stated in the gift tax return, the tax may be assessed, or a proceeding in court for the collection thereof may be begun without assessment, at any time within 6 years after the estate tax or gift tax return, as applicable, was filed.

(2) For purposes of this paragraph (b), an item disclosed in the return or in any schedule or statement attached to the return in a manner sufficient to apprise the Commissioner of the nature and amount thereof shall not be taken into account in determining items omitted from the gross estate or total gifts, as the case may be. Further, there shall not be taken into account in computing the 25 percent omission from the gross estate stated in the estate tax return or from the total gifts stated in the gift tax return, any increases in the valuation of assets disclosed on the return.

(c) *Excise taxes.*—(1) *In general.*—If the taxpayer omits from a return of a tax imposed under a provision of subtitle D an amount properly includible thereon, which amount is in excess of 25 percent of the amount of tax reported thereon, the tax may be assessed or a proceeding in court for the collection thereof may be begun without assessment, at any time within 6 years after the return was filed. For special rules relating to chapter 41, 42, 43 and 44 taxes, see paragraphs (c)(2), (3), (4), and (5) of this section.

(2) *Chapter 41 excise taxes.*—If an organization discloses an expenditure in its return (or in a schedule or statement attached thereto) in a manner sufficient to apprise the Commissioner of the existence and nature of the expenditure, the three-year limitation on assessment and collection described in section 6501(a) shall apply with respect to any tax under chapter 41 arising from the expenditure. If a taxpayer fails to so disclose an expenditure in its return (or in a schedule or statement attached thereto), the tax arising from the expenditure not so disclosed may be assessed, or a proceeding in court for the collection of the tax may be begun without assessment, at any time within 6 years after the return was filed.

(3) *Chapter 42 excise taxes.*—(i) If a private foundation omits from its annual return with respect to the tax imposed by section 4940 an amount of tax properly includible therein that is in excess of 25 percent of the amount of tax imposed by section 4940 that is reported on the return, the tax may be assessed, or a proceeding in court for the collection of the tax may be begun without assessment, at any time within 6 years after the return was filed. If a private foundation discloses in its return (or in a schedule or statement attached thereto) the nature, source, and amount of any income giving rise to any omitted tax, the tax arising from the income shall be counted as reported on the return in computing whether the foundation has omitted more than 25 percent of the tax reported on its return.

(ii) If a private foundation, trust, or other organization (as the case may be) discloses an item in its return (or in a schedule or statement attached thereto) in a manner sufficient to apprise the Commissioner of the existence and nature of the item, the three-year limitation on assessment and collection described in section 6501(a) shall apply with respect to any tax imposed under sections 4941(a), 4942(a), 4943(a), 4944(a), 4945(a), 4951(a), 4952(a), 4953 and 4958, arising from any transaction disclosed by the item. If a private foundation, trust, or other organization (as the case may be) fails to so disclose an item in its return (or in a schedule or statement attached thereto), the tax arising from any transaction not so disclosed may be assessed or a proceeding in court for the collection of the tax may be begun without assessment, at any time within 6 years after the return was filed.

(4) *Chapter 43 excise taxes.*—If a taxpayer discloses an item in its return (or in a schedule or statement attached thereto) in a manner sufficient to apprise the Commissioner of the existence and nature of the item, the three-year limitation on assessment and collection described in section 6501(a) shall apply with respect to any tax imposed under sections 4971(a), 4972, 4973,4974 and 4975(a), arising from any transaction disclosed by the item. If a taxpayer fails to so disclose an item in its return (or in a schedule or statement attached thereto), the tax arising from any transaction not so disclosed may be assessed, or a proceeding in court for the

collection of the tax may be begun without assessment, at any time within 6 years after the return was filed. The applicable return for the tax under sections 4971, 4972, 4973 and 4974, is the return designated by the Commissioner for reporting the respective tax. The applicable return for the tax under section 4975 is the return filed by the plan used to report the act giving rise to the tax.

(5) *Chapter 44 excise taxes.*—If a real estate investment trust omits from its annual return with respect to the tax imposed by section 4981 an amount of tax properly includible therein that is in excess of 25 percent of the amount of tax imposed by section 4981 that is reported on the return, the tax may be assessed, or a proceeding in court for the collection of the tax may be begun without assessment, at any time within 6 years after the return was filed. If a real estate investment trust discloses in its return (or in a schedule or statement attached thereto) the nature, source, and amount of any income giving rise to any omitted tax, the tax arising from the income shall be counted as reported on the return in computing whether the trust has omitted more than 25 percent of the tax reported on its return.

(d) *Exception.*—The provisions of this section do not limit the application of section 6501(c).

(e) *Effective/applicability date.*—(1) *Income taxes.*—Paragraph (a) of this section applies to taxable years with respect to which the period for assessing tax was open on or after September 24, 2009.

(2) *Estate, gift and excise taxes.*—Paragraphs (b) through (d) of this section continue to apply as they did prior to being removed inadvertently on September 28, 2009. Specifically, paragraph (b) of this section applies to returns filed on or after May 2, 1956, except for the amendment to paragraph (b)(1) of this section that applies to returns filed on or after December 29, 1972. Paragraph (c) of this section applies to returns filed on or after October 7, 1982, except for the amendment to paragraph (c)(3)(ii) of this section that applies to returns filed on or after January 10, 2001. Paragraph (d) of this section applies to returns filed on or after May 2, 1956. [Reg. § 301.6501(e)-1.]

☐ [*T.D.* 9511, 12-14-2010.]

[Reg. § 301.6501(f)-1]

§ 301.6501(f)-1. Personal holding company tax.—If a corporation which is a personal holding company for any taxable year fails to file with its income tax return for such year a schedule setting forth the items of gross income described in section 543(a) received by the corporation during such year, and the names and addresses of the individuals who owned, within the meaning of section 544, at any time during the last half of such taxable year, more than 50 percent in value of the outstanding capital stock of the corporation, the personal holding company tax for such year may be assessed, or a

proceeding in court for the collection thereof may be begun without assessment, at any time within 6 years after the return for such year was filed. [Reg. § 301.6501(f)-1.]

☐ [*T.D.* 6172, 5-2-56.]

[Reg. § 301.6501(g)-1]

§ 301.6501(g)-1. Certain income tax returns of corporations.—(a) *Trusts or partnerships.*—If a taxpayer determines in good faith that it is a trust or partnership and files a return as such under subtitle A of the Code, and if the taxpayer is later held to be a corporation for the taxable year for which the return was filed, such return shall be deemed to be the return of the corporation for the purpose of section 6501.

(b) *Exempt organizations.*—If a taxpayer determines in good faith that it is an exempt organization and files a return as such under section 6033, and if the taxpayer is later held to be a taxable organization for the taxable year for which the return was filed, such return shall be deemed to be the return of the organization for the purpose of section 6501.

(c) *DISC.*—If a corporation determines in good faith that it is a DISC (as defined in section 992(a)(1)) for a taxable year and files a return as such pursuant to section 6011(c)(2), and if the corporation is thereafter held to be a corporation which is not a DISC for the taxable year for which the return was filed, then—

(1) Such return shall be deemed to be the return of the corporation for the purpose of section 6501.

(2) Such return if filed within the time required by section 6072(b) for filing a DISC return shall be deemed to be filed within the time required by section 6072(b) for filing of a return by a corporation which is not a DISC, and

(3) Interest on underpayment and overpayments allowed by chapter 67 of the Code and additions to the tax, additional amounts and assessable penalties allowed by Chapter 68 of the Code, when determined by reference to the time for filing of a return, shall be determined by reference to the time required by section 6072(b) for filing of a return by a DISC. [Reg. § 301.6501(g)-1.]

☐ [*T.D.* 6172, 5-2-56. *Amended by T.D.* 6498, 10-24-60 *and T.D.* 7533, 2-14-78.]

[Reg. § 301.6501(h)-1]

§ 301.6501(h)-1. Net operating loss or capital loss carrybacks.—In the case of a deficiency attributable to the application to the taxpayer of a net operating loss or capital loss carryback (including deficiencies which may be assessed pursuant to the provisions of section 6213(b)(2)), such deficiency may be assessed at any time before the expiration of the period within which a deficiency for the taxable year of the net operating loss or net capital loss which results in such carryback may be assessed. In the case of a deficiency attributable to the application of a net operating loss carryback, such deficiency may be assessed within 18 months after the date on which the taxpayer files in accordance with section 172(b)(3) a copy of the certification (with respect to such taxable year) issued under section 317 of the Trade Expansion Act of 1962, if later than the date prescribed by the preceding sentence. [Reg. § 301.6501(h)-1.]

☐ [*T.D.* 6425, 11-10-59. *Amended by T.D.* 6730, 5-7-64 *and T.D.* 7301, 1-3-74.]

[Reg. § 301.6501(i)-1]

§ 301.6501(i)-1. Foreign tax carrybacks; taxable years beginning after December 31, 1957.— With respect to taxable years beginning after December 31, 1957, a deficiency attributable to the application to the taxpayer of a carryback under section 904(d) (relating to carryback and carryover of excess foreign taxes), may be assessed at any time before the expiration of one year after the expiration of the period within which a deficiency may be assessed for the taxable year of the excess taxes described in section 904(d) which result in such carryback. [Reg. § 301.6501(i)-1.]

☐ [*T.D.* 6555, 3-14-61.]

[Reg. § 301.6501(j)-1]

§ 301.6501(j)-1. Investment credit carryback; taxable years ending after December 31, 1961.— With respect to taxable years ending after December 31, 1961, a deficiency attributable to the application to the taxpayer of an investment credit carryback may be assessed at any time before the expiration of the period within which a deficiency for the taxable year of the unused investment credit which results in such carryback may be assessed, or, with respect to any portion of an investment credit carryback from a taxable year attributable to a net operating loss or capital loss carryback from a subsequent taxable year, at any time before the expiration of the period within which a deficiency for such subsequent taxable year may be assessed. For purposes of this section a deficiency shall include a deficiency which may be assessed pursuant to the provisions of section 6213(b)(2), but only those arising with respect to applications for tentative carryback adjustments filed after November 2, 1966. [Reg. § 301.6501(j)-1.]

☐ [*T.D.* 7301, 1-3-74.]

[Reg. § 301.6501(m)-1]

§ 301.6501(m)-1. Tentative carryback adjustment assessment period.—(a) *Period of limitation after tentative carryback adjustment.*—(1) Under section 6501(m), in a case where an amount has been applied, credited, or refunded under section 6411, by reason of a net operating loss carryback, a capital loss carryback, an investment credit carryback, or a work incentive program credit carryback to a prior taxable year, the period described in section 6501(a) of the Code for assessing a deficiency for such prior taxable year is extended to include the period described in section 6501(h), (j) or (o), whichever is applicable; except that the amount which may be as-

sessed solely by reason of section 6501(m) may not exceed the amount so applied, credited, or refunded under section 6411, reduced by any amount which may be assessed solely by reason of section 6501(h), (j) or (o), as the case may be.

(2) The application of this paragraph may be illustrated by the following example:

Example. Assume that M Corporation, which claims an unused investment credit of $50,000 for the calendar year 1968, files an application under section 6411 of the Code for an adjustment of its tax for 1965, and receives a refund of $50,000 in 1969. In 1971, it is determined that the amount of the unused investment credit for 1968 is $30,000 rather than $50,000. Moreover, it is determined that M Corporation would have owed $40,000 of additional tax for 1965 if it had properly reported certain income which it failed to include in its 1965 return. Assuming that M Corporation filed its 1968 return on March 15, 1969, and that the 3-year period described in section 6501(a) has not been extended, the period prescribed in section 6501(j) for assessing the excessive amount refunded, $20,000 (*i.e.*, $50,000, original amount refunded, less $30,000, correct amount of unused investment credit), does not expire until March 15, 1972, and $20,000 may be assessed on or before such date under section 6501(j). Under section 6501(m), M Corporation may be assessed on or before March 15, 1972, an amount not in excess of $30,000 ($50,000, the amount refunded under section 6411, minus $20,000, the amount which may be assessed solely by reason of section 6501(J)).

(b) *Effective date.*—The provisions of paragraph (a) of this section apply only with respect to applications under section 6411 filed after November 2, 1966. [Reg. § 301.6501(m)-1.]

☐ [*T.D.* 7301, 1-3-74.]

[Reg. § 301.6501(n)-1]

§ 301.6501(n)-1. Special rules for chapter 42 and similar taxes.—(a) *Return filed by private foundation, plan, trust, or other organization.*— (1) A return filed by a private foundation, plan, trust, or other organization (as the case may be) with respect to any act giving rise to a tax imposed by chapter 42 (other than a tax imposed by section 4940), or by section 4975 shall be considered, for purposes of section 6501, to be the return of all persons required to file a return with respect to any such tax arising from such act, notwithstanding that all such persons have not signed the return. In the case of a private foundation that files a Form 990-PF (or a Form 5227 in the case of a nonexempt foundation described in section 4947(a)(2)), which contains questions with respect to such taxes, the filing of such form by such foundation shall constitute the filing of a return with respect to any such act, even though the foundation incorrectly answered such questions.

(2) For purposes of section 4940, the return referred to in this section is the return filed by the private foundation for the taxable year for which the tax is imposed.

(b) *Failure of private foundation, plan, trust, or other organization to file.*—The period of limitations on assessment and collection described in section 6501 does not begin with respect to any person liable for tax under chapter 42 (other than section 4940) or section 4975 arising from a given act, where the private foundation, plan, trust, or other organization (as the case may be) has not filed its required return that reports such act for the year in which the act (or failure to act) giving rise to liability for such tax occurred.

(c) *Example.*—The provisions of this section may be illustrated by the following example:

Example. In 1973 D, an individual taxpayer who was a disqualified person under the provisions of section 4946(a)(1), participated in an act of self-dealing with a private foundation and incurred a tax under section 4941(a)(1). On May 15, 1974 the private foundation files a Form 990-PF and answers all the questions thereon with regard to any acts of self-dealing (as defined in section 4941(d)) in which it may have engaged in 1973. Assuming that the foundation's return was not a false or fraudulent return nor made with the willful attempt to defeat tax, the period of limitations on assessment and collection under section 6501(a) shall start with respect to any tax under section 4941(a) or section 4941(b) imposed on D arising out of that transaction with such foundation. [Reg. § 301.6501(n)-1.]

☐ [*T.D.* 7838, 10-5-82. *Amended by T.D.* 8920, 1-9-2001.]

[Reg. § 301.6501(n)-2]

§ 301.6501(n)-2. Certain contributions to section 501(c)(3) organizations.—If a private foundation makes a contribution to a section 501(c)(3) organization as provided in section 4942(g)(3), and a deficiency of tax of such foundation occurs due to the failure of the section 501(c)(3) organization to make the distribution prescribed by section 4942(g)(3), then such deficiency may be assessed within one year after the expiration of the period within which a deficiency may be assessed for the taxable year with respect to which the contribution was made. [Reg. § 301.6501(n)-2.]

☐ [*T.D.* 7838, 10-5-82.]

[Reg. § 301.6501(n)-3]

§ 301.6501(n)-3. Certain set-asides described in section 4942(g)(2).—Where a deficiency of tax of a private foundation results from the failure of an amount set aside by such foundation for a specific project to be treated as a qualifying distribution under section 4942(g)(2)(B)(ii)(II), such deficiency may be assessed within two years after the expiration of the period within which a deficiency may be assessed for the taxable year to which the amount set aside relates. [Reg. § 301.6501(n)-3.]

☐ [*T.D.* 7838, 10-5-82.]

[Reg. § 301.6501(o)-1]

§ 301.6501(o)-1. Work incentive program credit carrybacks, taxable years beginning after December 31, 1971.—With respect to taxable years beginning after December 31, 1971, a deficiency attributable to the application to the taxpayer of a work incentive program credit carryback (including deficiencies which may be assessed pursuant to the provisions of section 6213(b)(2)) may be assessed at any time before the expiration of the period within which a deficiency for the taxable year of the unused work incentive program credit which results in such carryback may be assessed, or, with respect to any portion of a work incentive program credit carryback from a taxable year attributable to a net operating loss or capital loss carryback from a subsequent taxable year, at any time before the expiration of the period within which a deficiency for such subsequent taxable year may be assessed. [Reg. § 301.6501(o)-1.]

☐ [*T.D.* 7301, 1-3-74.]

[Reg. § 301.6501(o)-2]

§ 301.6501(o)-2. Special rules for partnership items of federally registered partnerships.—(a) *In general.*—In the case of any tax imposed by subtitle A with respect to any person, the period for assessing a deficiency attributable to any partnership item of a federally registered partnership shall not expire before the later of—

(1) The date which is 4 years after the date on which the return of the federally registered partnership for the partnership taxable year in which the item arose is filed (or, if later, the date prescribed for filing the return), or

(2) If the name or address of the person against whom the assessment is sought does not appear on the return of the federally registered partnership, the date which is 1 year after the date on which a satisfactory identifying statement is furnished in writing to the director of the service center with which the partnership return is filed. A satisfactory identifying statement is a written statement providing the name, address, and taxpayer identification number of both the partner and the partnership. The statement shall note the partnership taxable year for which the statement is furnished.

(b) *"Pass through" entity as partner.*—In the case of a partnership having a "pass through" entity (*i.e.*, partnership, electing small business corporation (as defined in section 1371(b)), trust, estate, or nominee) as a partner, the 1 year period described in paragraph (a)(2) of this section shall not begin with respect to the person to be assessed until the chain of ownership linking the taxpayer with the federally registered partnership in which the item originally arose is fully disclosed.

Example. Partnership U, a federally registered partnership, has two partners, Partnerships W and X. The partners of W are A and B, who are individuals, and T, a trust whose beneficiaries are individuals C and D. The partners of X are E, an individual, and Partnership Y whose partners are individuals F, G, and H. U and X properly disclose the identity of their partners. W, however, discloses the identity of only A and B, and Y discloses the identity of only F and G. The period of limitation described in paragraph (a) of this section for items attributable to U does not expire with respect to T, C, D, and H until one year after the chain of ownership linking these taxpayers with U is fully disclosed.

(c) *Federally registered partnership.*—(1) *In general.*—With respect to any partnership taxable year, a federally registered partnership is any partnership—

(i) Interests in which have been offered for sale at any time during the taxable year or a prior taxable year in an offering required to be registered with the Securities and Exchange Commission, or

(ii) Which, at any time during the taxable year, was subject to the annual reporting requirements of the Securities and Exchange Commission which relate to the protection of investors in the partnership.

For purposes of the preceding sentence an interest is "offered for sale" when it is the subject of an "offer for sale" as that term is used in section 2 of the Securities Act of 1933 (15 U.S.C. 77b).

(2) *Certain reporting requirements not taken into account.*—A requirement to file reports with the Securities and Exchange Commission for any purpose other than to protect investors does not cause the partnership to be treated as a federally registered partnership. For example, a brokerage firm organized as a partnership is not a federally registered partnership merely because it files reports required by the Commission for regulatory purposes.

(d) *Extension by agreement.*—(1) *In general.*—Any general partner of a federally registered partnership (or any other person authorized by the partnership) may, prior to the expiration of the limitation period described in paragraph (a) of this section, extend the period for assessing a deficiency attributable to a partnership item for any period of time agreed upon in writing. The extension shall become effective when the agreement has been executed by the district director or the service center director and shall be binding on all persons whose liability for tax imposed by subtitle A is affected in whole or in part by partnership items flowing from that partnership.

(2) *Authorization of other persons.*—The partnership may authorize persons other than the general partners to extend the period of limitation for assessing a deficiency attributable to a partnership item. This authorization shall be in writing, shall clearly identify the person being authorized and the action being authorized, and shall be signed by all the general partners. The authorization shall become effective when filed with the district director and shall remain in effect until a written revocation signed as provided in the preceding sentence is filed.

(3) *Removing authority of general partners.*—A partnership wishing to deny to some or all of the general partners the authority to execute an agreement extending the period of limitation for assessment may do so by submitting a written statement to that effect. The statement shall either identify the partners exclusively authorized to execute such an agreement or declare that one or more named partners or all partners lack the authority to execute such an agreement. The statement shall be signed by all the general partners. The statement shall become effective when filed with the district director and shall remain in effect until a statement revoking or superseding it and signed as provided in the preceding sentence is filed.

(e) *Special periods of limitation with respect to carryback of net operating loss, capital loss, etc.*—The provisions of section 6501(o) must also be taken into account in applying the various special periods of limitation prescribed in section 6501(h), (i) and (j). Thus, to the extent that a carryback is attributable to a partnership item of a federally registered partnership, the period for assessing a deficiency attributable to that carryback shall not expire before the date determined under paragraph (a) of this section with respect to the partnership taxable year in which the item arose.

(f) *Otherwise applicable limitation period.*—The special provisions of section 6501(o) and this section do not terminate any otherwise applicable period for assessing a deficiency. Thus, the fact that more than 4 years have elapsed since the filing of the partnership return for the year in issue does not prevent assessment against a partner based on partnership items if an otherwise applicable period of limitation for the partner has not yet expired.

Example. Partnership V files its return for the taxable year ending December 31, 1980, on April 15, 1981. A, a partner in Partnership V, agrees to extend the assessment period for A's taxable year ending December 31, 1980, until September 30, 1985. The partnership does not agree to any extension under section 6501(o)(3) so that the period for assessing a deficiency attributable to partnership items could expire on April 15, 1985. A deficiency may be assessed against A for 1980 at any time prior to October 1, 1985, even if that deficiency is based on partnership items.

(g) *Effective date.*—This section and § 301.6501(o)-3 are effective generally for partnership items arising in partnership taxable years beginning after December 31, 1978 and before September 4, 1982. This section shall not apply, however, to any partnership taxable year with respect to which the amendments made to Code section 6501(o) by section 402 of the Tax Equity and Fiscal Responsibility Act of 1982 are effective. See section 407(a)(3) of that Act. [Reg. § 301.6501(o)-2.]

☐ [*T.D.* 7884, 4-14-83.]

[Reg. §301.6501(o)-3]

§301.6501(o)-3. Partnership items.— (a) *Partnership item defined.*—For purposes of section 6501(o) (as it read before the enactment of the Tax Equity and Fiscal Responsibility Act of 1982), §301.6501(o)-2, and §301.6511(g)-1, the term "partnership item" means—

(1) Any item required to be taken into account for the partnership taxable year under any provision of subchapter K of chapter 1 of the Code, to the extent that the item is designated in paragraph (b) of this section as more appropriately determined at the partnership level than at the partner level, and

(2) Any other item to the extent affected by an item described in paragraph (b) of this section.

The items described in paragraph (a)(2) of this section include items related to the partnership (for example, a partner's basis in the partnership interest) as well as more general items whose computation may be affected by changes to items described in paragraph (b) of this section (for example, adjusted gross income, self-employment tax, income averaging, medical deduction, and charitable contribution deduction).

(b) *Items more appropriately determined at the partnership level.*—The following items which are required to be taken into account for the taxable year of a partnership under subchapter K of chapter 1 of the Code are more appropriately determined at the partnership level than at the partner level:

(1) The partnership aggregate and each partner's share of each of the following:

(i) Items of income, gain, loss, deduction, or credit of the partnership;

(ii) Expenditures by the partnership not deductible in computing its taxable income (for example, foreign taxes and charitable contributions);

(iii) Items of the partnership which may be tax preference items under section 57(a) for any partner;

(iv) Income of the partnership exempt from tax;

(v) Partnership liabilities (including determinations with respect to the amount of the liabilities, whether the liabilities are nonrecourse, and changes from the preceding taxable year); and

(vi) Other amounts with respect to partnership investments, transactions, and operations necessary to enable partners to compute—

(A) The credit provided by section 38;

(B) Recapture under section 47 of the credit provided by section 38;

(C) Their amounts at risk in any activity to which section 465 applies, and

(D) The depletion allowance under section 613A with respect to oil and gas wells;

(2) Guaranteed payments:

(3) Optional adjustments to the basis of partnership property pursuant to an election

under section 754 (including necessary preliminary determinations, such as the determination of a transferee partner's basis in a partnership interest); and

(4) To the extent that the determination can be made from determinations that are necessary at the partnership level with respect to an amount, the character of an amount, or the percentage interest of a partner in the partnership for purposes of the partnership books and records or for purposes of furnishing information to a partner—

(i) Contributions to the partnership;

(ii) Distributions from the partnership;

(iii) Amounts to be taken into account by a partner dealing with the partnership in a transaction to which section 707(a) applies (including the application of section 707(b));

(iv) The application to the distributee partner of section 751(b); and

(v) The application to the transferor partner of section 751(a).

(c) *Illustrations.*—This paragraph (c) illustrates the provisions of paragraph (b)(4) of this section. The factors enumerated are not exhaustive; there may be additional partnership-level determinations with respect to a determination listed in paragraph (b)(4) of this section.

(1) *Contributions.*—For purposes of its books and records, or for purposes of furnishing information to a partner, the partnership needs to determine:

(i) The character of an amount received from a partner (for example, whether it is a contribution, a loan, or a repayment of a loan);

(ii) The amount of money contributed by a partner;

(iii) The applicability of the investment company rules of section 721(b) with respect to a contribution; and

(iv) The basis to the partnership of contributed property.

To the extent that a determination with respect to a contribution can be made from these and similar partnership-level determinations, therefore, the determination is more appropriately made at the partnership level. To the extent that that determination requires other information, however, that determination is more appropriately made at the partner level. For example, it may be necessary to determine whether the contribution of the property causes recapture from the contributing partner of the credit provided under section 38 in certain circumstances in which that determination is irrelevant to the partnership.

(2) *Distributions.*—For purposes of its books and records, or for purposes of furnishing information to a partner, the partnership needs to determine:

(i) The character of an amount transferred to a partner (for example, whether it is a distribution, a loan, or a repayment of a loan);

(ii) The amount of money distributed to a partner;

(iii) The adjusted basis to the partnership of distributed property; and

(iv) The character of partnership property (for example, whether an item is inventory or a capital asset).

To the extent that a determination with respect to a contribution can be made from these and similar partnership-level determinations, therefore, the determination is more appropriately made at the partnership level. To the extent that that determination requires other information, however, that determination is more appropriately made at the partner level. Such other information would include certain factors used in determining the partner's basis for the partnership interest, such as the amount that the partner paid to acquire the partnership interest from a transferor partner if that transfer was not covered by an election under section 754.

(3) *Transactions to which section 707(a) applies.*—For purposes of its books and records, the partnership needs to determine:

(i) The amount transferred from the partnership to a partner or from a partner to the partnership in any transaction to which section 707(a) applies;

(ii) The character of such an amount (for example, whether or not it is a loan; in the case of amounts paid over time for the purchase of an asset, what portion is interest); and

(iii) The percentage of the capital interests and profits interests in the partnership owned by each partner.

To the extent that a determination with respect to a transaction to which section 707(a) applies can be made from these and similar partnership-level determinations, therefore, that determination is more appropriately made at the partnership level. To the extent that that determination requires other information, however, that determination is more appropriately made at the partner level. Examples of such other information are the cost to the partner of goods sold to the partnership and the extent to which the partner may be treated under section 267(c) as the constructive owner of a capital or profits interest actually owned by another.

(4) *Application of section 751.*—For purposes of its books and records, or for purposes of furnishing information to a partner for use in applying section 751, the partnership needs to determine:

(i) The fair market value and adjusted basis of the partnership's—

(A) Unrealized receivables (within the meaning of section 751(c)),

(B) Substantially appreciated inventory (within the meaning of section 751(d)), and

(C) Other property;

(ii) A partner's share of each of the classes of assets described in paragraph (c)(3)(i) of this section; and

(iii) Whether a distribution to a partner is a disproportionate distribution subject to section 751(b).

To the extent that a determination with respect to the application of section 751 can be made from these and similar partnership-level determinations, therefore, that determination is more appropriately made at the partnership level. To the extent that that determination requires other information, however, that determination is more appropriately made at the partner level. An example of such other information is the amount realized by a partner on the sale of a partnership interest. [Reg. § 301.6501(o)-3.]

☐ [*T.D.* 7884, 4-14-83.]

[Reg. § 301.6502-1]

§ 301.6502-1. Collection after assessment.—(a) *General rule.*—In any case in which a tax has been assessed within the applicable statutory period of limitations on assessment, a proceeding in court to collect the tax may be commenced, or a levy to collect the tax may be made, within 10 years after the date of assessment.

(b) *Agreement to extend the period of limitations on collection.*—The Secretary may enter into an agreement with a taxpayer to extend the period of limitations on collection in the following circumstances:

(1) *Extension agreement entered into in connection with an installment agreement.*—If the Secretary and the taxpayer enter into an installment agreement for the tax liability prior to the expiration of the period of limitations on collection, the Secretary and the taxpayer, at the time the installment agreement is entered into, may enter into a written agreement to extend the period of limitations on collection to a date certain. A written extension agreement entered into under this paragraph shall extend the period of limitations on collection until the 89th day after the date agreed upon in the written agreement.

(2) *Extension agreement entered into in connection with the release of a levy under section 6343.*—If the Secretary has levied on any part of the taxpayer's property prior to the expiration of the period of limitations on collection and the levy is subsequently released pursuant to section 6343 after the expiration of the period of limitations on collection, the Secretary and the taxpayer, prior to the release of the levy, may enter into a written agreement to extend the period of limitations on collection to a date certain. A written extension agreement entered into under this paragraph shall extend the period of limitations on collection until the date agreed upon in the extension agreement.

(c) *Proceeding in court for the collection of the tax.*—If a proceeding in court for the collection of a tax is begun within the period provided in paragraph (a) of this section (or within any extended period as provided in paragraph (b) of this section), the period during which the tax may be collected by levy is extended until the liability for the tax or a judgment against the taxpayer arising from the liability is satisfied or becomes unenforceable.

(d) *Effect of statutory suspensions of the period of limitations on collection if executed collection extension agreement is in effect.*—(1) Any statutory suspension of the period of limitations on collection tolls the running of the period of limitations on collection, as extended pursuant to an executed extension agreement under paragraph (b) of this section, for the amount of time set forth in the relevant statute.

(2) The following example illustrates the principle set forth in this paragraph (d):

Example. In June of 2003, the Internal Revenue Service (IRS) enters into an installment agreement with the taxpayer to provide for periodic payments of the taxpayer's timely assessed tax liabilities. At the time the installment agreement is entered into, the taxpayer and the IRS execute a written agreement to extend the period of limitations on collection. The extension agreement executed in connection with the installment agreement operates to extend the period of limitations on collection to the date agreed upon in the extension agreement, plus 89 days. Subsequently, and prior to the expiration of the extended period of limitations on collection, the taxpayer files a bankruptcy petition under chapter 7 of the Bankruptcy Code and receives a discharge from bankruptcy a few months later. Assuming the tax is not discharged in the bankruptcy, section 6503(h) of the Internal Revenue Code operates to suspend the running of the previously extended period of limitations on collection for the period of time the IRS is prohibited from collecting due to the bankruptcy proceeding, and for 6 months thereafter. The new expiration date for the IRS to collect the tax is the date agreed upon in the previously executed extension agreement, plus 89 days, plus the period during which the IRS is prohibited from collecting due to the bankruptcy proceeding, plus 6 months.

(e) *Date when levy is considered made.*—The date on which a levy on property or rights to property is considered made is the date on which the notice of seizure required under section 6335(a) is given.

(f) *Effective date.*—This section is applicable on September 6, 2006. [Reg. § 301.6502-1.]

☐ [*T.D.* 6172, 5-2-56. *Amended by T.D.* 7305, 3-14-74; *T.D.* 8391, 2-10-92 *and T.D.* 9284, 9-5-2006.]

[Reg. § 301.6503(a)-1]

§ 301.6503(a)-1. Suspension of running of period of limitation; issuance of statutory notice of deficiency.—(a) *General rule.*—(1) Upon the mailing of a notice of deficiency for income, estate, gift, chapter 41, 42, 43, or 44 tax under the provisions of section 6212, the period of limitation on assessment and collection of any deficiency is suspended for 90 days after the mailing of a notice of such deficiency if the notice of deficiency is addressed to a person within the States of the Union and the District of Columbia, or 150 days if such notice of deficiency is addressed to a person outside the States of the Union and the District of Columbia (not counting Saturday, Sunday, or a legal holiday in the District of Columbia as the 90th or 150th day), plus an additional 60 days thereafter in either case. If a proceeding in respect of the deficiency is placed on the docket of the Tax Court, the period of limitation is suspended until the decision of the Tax Court becomes final, and for an additional 60 days thereafter. If a notice of deficiency is mailed to a taxpayer within the period of limitation and the taxpayer does not appeal therefrom to the Tax Court, the notice of deficiency so given does not suspend the running of the period of limitation with respect to any additional deficiency shown to be due in a subsequent deficiency notice.

(2) This paragraph may be illustrated by the following example:

Example. A taxpayer filed a return for the calendar year 1973 on April 15, 1974; the notice of deficiency was mailed to him (at an address within the United States) on April 15, 1977; and he filed a petition with the Tax Court on July 14, 1977. The decision of the Tax Court became final on November 6, 1978. The running of the period of limitation for assessment is suspended from April 15, 1977, to January 5, 1979, which date is 60 days after the date (November 6, 1978), on which the decision became final. If in this example the taxpayer had failed to file a petition with the Tax Court, the running of the period of limitation for assessment would then be suspended from April 15, 1977 (the date of notice), to September 12, 1977 (that is, for the 90-day period in which he could file a petition with the Tax Court, and for 60 days thereafter).

(3) For provisions relating to suspension of the running of the period of limitation with respect to collection of "second tier" excise taxes (as defined in section 4963) until final resolution of a refund proceeding described in sections 4961 and 7422 for the determination of the taxpayer's liability for the second tier taxes, see § 53.4961-2(e)(4).

(b) *Corporations joining in consolidated return.*— If a notice under section 6212(a) with respect to a deficiency in tax imposed by subtitle A of the Code for any taxable year is mailed to a corporation, the suspension of the running of the period of limitations provided in section 6503(a)(1) shall apply in the case of corporations with which such corporation made a consolidated income tax return for such taxable year. Under § 1.1502-77(a) of this chapter (Income Tax Regulations), relating to consolidated returns, notices of deficiency are mailed only to the common parent. [Reg. § 301.6503(a)-1.]

☐ [*T.D.* 6172, 5-2-56. *Amended by T.D.* 6498, 10-24-60; *T.D.* 7244, 12-29-72; *T.D.* 7838, 10-5-82 *and T.D.* 8084, 5-1-86.]

[Reg. § 301.6503(b)-1]

§ 301.6503(b)-1. Suspension of running of period of limitation; assets of taxpayer in control or custody of court.—Where all or substantially all of the assets of a taxpayer are in the control or custody of the court in any proceeding before any court of the United States, or of any State of the United States, or of the District of Columbia, the period of limitations on collection after assessment prescribed in section 6502 is suspended with respect to the outstanding amount due on the assessment for the period such assets are in the control or custody of the court, and for 6 months thereafter. In the case of an estate of a decedent or an incompetent, the period of limitations on collection is suspended only for periods beginning after November 2, 1966, during which assets are in the control or custody of a court, and for 6 months thereafter. [Reg. § 301.6503(b)-1.]

☐ [*T.D. 6172, 5-2-56. Amended by T.D. 7121, 6-2-71.*]

[Reg. § 301.6503(c)-1]

§ 301.6503(c)-1. Suspension of running of period of limitation; location of property outside the United States or removal of property from the United States; taxpayer outside of United States.—(a) *Property located outside, or removed from, the United States prior to November 3, 1966.*— The running of the period of limitations on collection after assessment prescribed in section 6502 is suspended for the period of time, prior to November 3, 1966, that collection is hindered or delayed because property of the taxpayer is situated or held outside the United States or is removed from the United States. The total suspension of time under this provision shall not in the aggregate exceed 6 years. In any case in which the district director determines that collection is so hindered or delayed, he shall make and retain in the files of his office a written report which shall identify the taxpayer and the tax liability, shall show what steps were taken to collect the tax liability, shall state the grounds for his determination that property of the taxpayer is situated or held outside, or is removed from, the United States, and shall show the date on which it was first determined that collection was so hindered or delayed. The term "property" includes all property or rights to property, real or personal, tangible or intangible, belonging to the taxpayer. The suspension of the running of the period of limitations on collection shall be considered to begin on the date so determined by the district director. A copy of the report shall be mailed to the taxpayer at his last known address. For further guidance regarding the definition of last known address, see § 301.6212-2.

(b) *Taxpayer outside United States after November 2, 1966.*—The running of the period of limitations on collection after assessment prescribed in section 6502 (relating to collection after assessment) is suspended for the period after November 2, 1966, during which the taxpayer is absent from the United States if such period is a continuous period of absence from the United States extending for 6 months or more. In a case where the running of the period of limitations has been suspended under the first sentence of this paragraph and at the time of the taxpayer's return to the United States the period of limitations would expire before the expiration of 6 months from the date of his return, the period of limitations shall not expire until after 6 months from the date of the taxpayer's return. The taxpayer will be deemed to be absent from the United States for purposes of this section if he is generally and substantially absent from the United States, even though he makes casual temporary visits during the period. [Reg. § 301.6503(c)-1.]

☐ [*T.D. 6172, 5-2-56. Amended by T.D. 7121, 6-1-72. Amended by T.D. 8939, 1-11-2001.*]

[Reg. § 301.6503(d)-1]

§ 301.6503(d)-1. Suspension of running of period of limitation; extension of time for payment of estate tax.—Where an estate is granted an extension of time as provided in section 6161(a)(2) or (b)(2), or under the provisions of section 6166, for payment of any estate tax, the running of the period of limitations for collection of such tax is suspended for the period of time for which the extension is granted. [Reg. § 301.6503(d)-1.]

☐ [*T.D. 6172, 5-2-56. Amended by T.D. 6425, 11-10-59 and T.D. 6498, 10-24-60.*]

[Reg. § 301.6503(f)-1]

§ 301.6503(f)-1. Suspension of running of period of limitation; wrongful seizure of property of third-party owner and discharge of lien for substitution of value.—(a) *Wrongful seizure.*— The running of the period of limitations on collection after assessment prescribed in section 6502 (relating to collection after assessment) shall be suspended for a period equal to a period beginning on the date property (including money) is wrongfully seized or received by the appropriate official and ending on the date 30 days after the date on which the appropriate official returns the property pursuant to section 6343(b) (relating to authority to return property) or the date 30 days after the date on which a judgment secured pursuant to section 7426 (relating to civil actions by persons other than taxpayers) with respect to such property becomes final. The running of the period of limitations on collection after assessment shall be suspended under this section only with respect to the amount of such assessment which is equal to the amount of money or the value of specific property returned. This section applies in the case of property wrongfully seized or received after November 2, 1966. The following example illustrates the principles of this section:

Example. On June 1, 1968 (at which time 10 months remain before the period of limitations on collection after assessment will expire), the appropriate official wrongfully seizes $1,000 in B's account in Bank X and properly seizes $500 in taxpayer A's account in Bank Y in an attempt to satisfy A's assessed tax liability of $1,500. The appropriate official determines that the $1,000 seized in Bank X was not the property of taxpayer A and, on March 1, 1969, he returns the

$1,000 to B. As a result of the wrongful seizure, the running of the period of limitations on collection after assessment of the amount owed by taxpayer A is suspended for the 9-month period (beginning June 1, 1968, when the money was wrongfully seized and ending March 1, 1969, when the money was returned to B), plus 30 days. Therefore, the period of limitations on collection after assessment prescribed in section 6502 will not expire until February 1, 1970, which is 10 months plus 30 days after the money was returned.

(b) *Discharge of wrongful lien for substitution of value.*—If a person other than the taxpayer submits a request in writing for a certificate of discharge for a filed Federal tax lien under section 6325(b)(4), the running of the period of limitations on collection after assessment under section 6502 for any liability listed in such notice of Federal tax lien shall be suspended for a period equal to the period beginning on the date the appropriate official receives a deposit or bond in the amount specified in § 301.6325-1(b)(4)(i) and ending on the date that is 30 days after the earlier of—

(1) The date the appropriate official no longer holds, or is deemed to no longer hold, within the meaning of paragraph (b)(4)(iv) of this section, any amount as a deposit or bond by reason of taking such actions as prescribed in sections 6325(b)(4)(B) and (C); or

(2) The date the judgment secured under section 7426(b)(5) becomes final.

(c) As used in this section, the term *appropriate official* means either the official or office identified in the relevant IRS Publication or, if such official or office is not so identified, the Secretary or his delegate.

(d) *Effective/applicability date.*—This section applies to any request for a certificate of discharge made after January 31, 2008. [Reg. § 301.6503(f)-1.]

☐ [*T.D.* 7121, 6-2-71. *Amended by T.D.* 7838, 10-5-82 *and T.D.* 9378, 1-30-2008.]

[Reg. § 301.6503(g)-1]

§ 301.6503(g)-1. Suspension pending correction.—The running of the periods of limitations provided in sections 6501 and 6502 on the making of assessments, the collection by levy, or a proceeding in court in respect of any tax imposed by chapter 42 or section 507, 4971, or 4975 shall be suspended for any period described in section 507(g)(2) or during which the Commissioner has extended the time for making correction under section 4963(e)(1)(B). [Reg. § 301.6503(g)-1.]

☐ [*T.D.* 7838, 10-5-82. *Amended by T.D.* 8084, 5-1-86.]

[Reg. § 301.6503(j)-1]

§ 301.6503(j)-1. Suspension of running of period of limitations; extension in case of designated and related summonses.—(a) *General rule.*—The running of the applicable period of limitations on assessment provided for in section 6501 is suspended with respect to any return of tax by a corporation that is the subject of a designated or related summons if a court proceeding is instituted with respect to that summons.

(b) *Period of suspension.*—The period of suspension is the time during which the running of the applicable period of limitations on assessment provided for in section 6501 is suspended under section 6503(j). If a court requires any compliance with a designated or related summons by ordering that any record, document, paper, object, or items be produced, or the testimony of any person be given, the period of suspension consists of the judicial enforcement period plus 120 days. If a court does not require any compliance with a designated or related summons, the period of suspension consists of the judicial enforcement period, and the period of limitations on assessment provided in section 6501 shall not expire before the 60th day after the close of the judicial enforcement period.

(c) *Definitions.*—(1) A *designated summons* is a summons issued to a corporation (or to any other person to whom the corporation has transferred records) with respect to any return of tax by such corporation for a taxable period for which such corporation is being examined under the coordinated industry case program or any other successor to the coordinated examination program if—

(i) The Division Commissioner and the Division Counsel of the Office of Chief Counsel (or their successors) for the organizations that have jurisdiction over the corporation whose tax liability is the subject of the summons have reviewed the summons before it is issued;

(ii) The Internal Revenue Service (IRS) issues the summons at least 60 days before the day the period prescribed in section 6501 for the assessment of tax expires (determined with regard to extensions); and

(iii) The summons states that it is a designated summons for purposes of section 6503(j).

(2) A *related summons* is any summons issued that—

(i) Relates to the same return of the corporation under examination as the designated summons; and

(ii) Is issued to any person, including the person to whom the designated summons was issued, during the 30-day period that begins on the day the designated summons is issued.

(3) The *judicial enforcement period* is the period that begins on the day on which a court proceeding is instituted with respect to a designated or related summons and ends on the day on which there is a final resolution as to the summoned person's response to that summons.

(4) *Court proceeding.*—(i) *In general.*—For purposes of this section, a *court proceeding* is a proceeding filed in a United States district court either to quash a designated or related summons under section 7609(b)(2) or to enforce a desig-

nated or related summons under section 7604. A court proceeding includes any collateral proceeding, such as a civil contempt proceeding.

(ii) *Date when proceeding is no longer pending.*—A proceeding to quash or to enforce a designated or related summons is no longer pending when all appeals (including review by the Supreme Court) are disposed of or after the expiration of the period in which an appeal may be taken or a request for further review (including review by the Supreme Court) may be made. If, however, following an enforcement order, a collateral proceeding is brought challenging whether the testimony given or production made by the summoned party fully satisfied the court order and whether sanctions should be imposed against the summoned party for a failure to so testify or produce, the proceeding to quash or to enforce the summons shall include the time from which the proceeding to quash or to enforce the summons was brought until the decision in the collateral proceeding becomes final. The decision becomes final on the date when all appeals (including review by the Supreme Court) are disposed of or when all appeal periods or all periods for further review (including review by the Supreme Court) expire. A decision in a collateral proceeding becomes final when all appeals (including review by the Supreme Court) are disposed of or when all appeal periods or all periods for further review (including review by the Supreme Court) expire.

(5) *Compliance.*—(i) *In general.*—Compliance is the giving of testimony or the performance of an act or acts of production, or both, in response to a court order concerning the designated or related summons and the determination that the terms of the court order have been satisfied.

(ii) *Date compliance occurs.*—Compliance with a court order that wholly denies enforcement of a designated or related summons is deemed to occur on the date when all appeals (including review by the Supreme Court) are disposed of or when the period in which an appeal may be taken or a request for further review (including review by the Supreme Court) may be made expires. Compliance with a court order that grants enforcement, in whole or in part, of a designated or related summons, occurs on the date the IRS determines that the testimony given, or the books, papers, records, or other data produced, or both, by the summoned party fully satisfy the court order concerning the summons. The IRS will determine whether there has been full compliance within a reasonable time, given the volume and complexity of the records produced, after the later of the giving of all testimony or the production of all records requested by the summons or required by any order enforcing any part of the summons. If, following an enforcement order, collateral proceedings are brought challenging whether the production made by the summoned party fully satisfied the court order and whether sanctions should be imposed against the summoned party

for a failing to do so, the suspension of the periods of limitations shall continue until the order enforcing any part of the summons is fully complied with and the decision in the collateral proceeding becomes final. A decision in a collateral proceeding becomes final when all appeals are disposed of, the period in which an appeal may be taken has expired or the period in which a request for further review may be made has expired.

(6) *Final resolution* occurs when the designated or related summons or any order enforcing any part of the designated or related summons is fully complied with and all appeals or requests for further review are disposed of, the period in which an appeal may be taken has expired or the period in which a request for further review may be made has expired.

(d) *Special rules.*—(1) *Number of summonses that may be issued.*—(i) *Designated summons.*—Only one designated summons may be issued in connection with the examination of a specific taxable year or other period of a corporation. A designated summons may cover more than one year or other period of a corporation. The designated summons may require production of information that was previously sought in a summons (other than a designated summons) issued in the course of the examination of that particular corporation if that information was not previously produced.

(ii) *Related summonses.*—There is no restriction on the number of related summonses that may be issued in connection with the examination of a corporation. As provided in paragraph (c)(2) of this section, however, a related summons must be issued within the 30-day period that begins on the date on which the designated summons to which it relates is issued and must relate to the same return as the designated summons. A related summons may request the same information as the designated summons.

(2) *Time within which court proceedings must be brought.*—In order for the period of limitations on assessment to be suspended under section 6503(j), a court proceeding to enforce or to quash a designated or related summons must be instituted within the period of limitations on assessment provided in section 6501 that is otherwise applicable to the tax return.

(3) *Computation of suspension period if multiple court proceedings are instituted.*—If multiple court proceedings are instituted to enforce or to quash a designated or one or more related summonses concerning the same tax return, the period of limitations on assessment is suspended beginning on the date the first court proceeding is brought. The suspension shall end on the date that is the latest date on which the judicial enforcement period, plus the 120 day or 60 day period (depending on whether the court requires any compliance) as provided in paragraph (b) of this section, expires with respect to each summons.

(4) *Effect on other suspension periods.*—(i) *In general.*—Suspensions of the period of limitations under section 6501 provided for under subsections 7609(e)(1) and (e)(2) do not apply to any summons that is issued pursuant to section 6503(j). The suspension under section 6503(j) of the running of the period of limitations on assessment under section 6501 is independent of, and may run concurrent with, any other suspension of the period of limitations on assessment that applies to the tax return to which the designated or related summons relates.

(ii) *Examples.*—The rules of paragraph (d)(4)(i) of this section are illustrated by the following examples:

Example 1. The period of limitations on assessment against Corporation P, a calendar year taxpayer, for its 2007 return is scheduled to end on March 17, 2011. (Ordinarily, Corporation P's returns are filed on March 15th of the following year, but March 15, 2008, was a Saturday, and Corporation P timely filed its return on the subsequent Monday, March 17, 2008, making March 17, 2011 the last day of the period of limitations on assessment for Corporation P's 2007 tax year.) On January 4, 2011, a designated summons is issued to Corporation P concerning its 2007 return. On March 3, 2011 (14 days before the period of limitations on assessment would otherwise expire with respect to Corporation P's 2007 return), a court proceeding is brought to enforce the designated summons issued to Corporation P. On June 6, 2011, the court orders Corporation P to comply with the designated summons. Corporation P does not appeal the court's order. On September 6, 2011, agents for Corporation P deliver material that they state are the records requested by the designated summons. On October 13, 2011, a final resolution to Corporation P's response to the designated summons occurs when it is determined that Corporation P has fully complied with the court's order. The suspension period applicable with respect to the designated summons issued to Corporation P consists of the judicial enforcement period (March 3, 2011, through October 13, 2011) and an additional 120-day period under section 6503(j)(1)(B), because the court required Corporation P to comply with the designated summons. Thus, the suspension period applicable with respect to the designated summons issued to Corporation P begins on March 3, 2011, and ends on February 10, 2012. Under the facts of this *Example 1*, the period of limitations on assessment against Corporation P further extends to February 24, 2012, to account for the additional 14 days that remained on the period of limitations on assessment under section 6501 when the suspension period under section 6503(j) began.

Example 2. Assume the same facts set forth in *Example 1*, except that in addition to the issuance of the designated summons and related enforcement proceedings, on April 5, 2011, a summons concerning Corporation P's 2007 return is issued and served on individual A, a third party. This summons is not a related summons because it was not issued during the 30-day period that began on the date the designated summons was issued. The third-party summons served on individual A is subject to the notice requirements of section 7609(a). Final resolution of individual A's response to this summons does not occur until February 15, 2012. Because there is no final resolution of individual A's response to this summons by October 5, 2011, which is six months from the date of service of the summons, the period of limitations on assessment against Corporation P is suspended under section 7609(e)(2) to the date on which there is a final resolution to that response for the purposes of section 7609(e)(2). Moreover, because final resolution to the summons served on individual A does not occur until after February 10, 2012, the end of the suspension period for the designated summons, the period of limitations on assessment against Corporation P expires 14 days after the date that the final resolution as provided for in section 7609(e)(2) occurs with respect to the summons served on individual A.

(5) *Computation of 60-day period when last day of assessment period falls on a weekend or holiday.*—For purposes of paragraph (c)(1)(ii) of this section, in determining whether a designated summons has been issued at least 60 days before the date on which the period of limitations on assessment prescribed in section 6501 expires, the provisions of section 7503 apply when the last day of the assessment period falls on a Saturday, Sunday, or legal holiday.

(e) *Effective/applicability date.*—This section is applicable on July 31, 2009. [Reg. § 301.6503(j)-1.]

☐ [*T.D.* 9455, 7-30-2009.]

LIMITATIONS ON CREDIT OR REFUND

[Reg. § 301.6511(a)-1]

§ 301.6511(a)-1. Period of limitation on filing claim.—(a) In the case of any tax (other than a tax payable by stamp):

(1) If a return is filed, a claim for credit or refund of an overpayment must be filed by the taxpayer within 3 years from the time the return was filed or within 2 years from the time the tax was paid, whichever of such periods expires the later.

(2) If no return is filed, the claim for credit or refund of an overpayment must be filed by the taxpayer within 2 years from the time the tax was paid.

(b) In the case of any tax payable by means of a stamp, a claim for credit or refund of an overpayment of such tax must be filed by the taxpayer within 3 years from the time the tax was paid. For provisions relating to redemption of unused stamps, see section 6805.

(c) For limitations on allowance of credit or refund, special rules, and exceptions, see subsections (b) through (e) of section 6511. For limitations in the case of a petition to the Tax Court, see section 6512. For rules as to time return is deemed filed and tax considered paid, see section 6513. [Reg. § 301.6511(a)-1.]

☐ [*T.D.* 6172, 5-2-56. *Amended by T.D.* 6425, 11-10-59.]

[Reg. § 301.6511(b)-1]

§ 301.6511(b)-1. Limitations on allowance of credits and refunds.—(a) *Effect of filing claim.*— Unless a claim for credit or refund of an overpayment is filed within the period of limitation prescribed in section 6511(a), no credit or refund shall be allowed or made after the expiration of such period.

(b) *Limit on amount to be credited or refunded.*— (1) In the case of any tax (other than a tax payable by stamp):

(i) If a return was filed, and a claim is filed within 3 years from the time the return was filed, the amount of the credit or refund shall not exceed the portion of the tax paid within the period, immediately preceding the filing of the claim, equal to 3 years plus the period of any extension of time for filing the return.

(ii) If a return was filed, and a claim is filed after the 3-year period described in subdivision (i) of this subparagraph but within 2 years from the time the tax was paid, the amount of the credit or refund shall not exceed the portion of the tax paid within the 2 years immediately preceding the filing of the claim.

(iii) If no return was filed, but a claim is filed, the amount of the credit or refund shall not exceed the portion of the tax paid within the 2 years immediately preceding the filing of the claim.

(iv) If no claim is filed, the amount of the credit or refund allowed or made by the district director or the director of the regional service center shall not exceed the amount that would have been allowable under the preceding subdivisions of this subparagraph if a claim had been filed on the date the credit or refund is allowed.

(2) In the case of a tax payable by stamp—

(i) If a claim is filed, the amount of the credit or refund shall not exceed the portion of the tax paid within the 3 years immediately preceding the filing of the claim.

(ii) If no claim is filed, the amount of the credit or refund allowed or made by the district director or the director of the regional service center shall not exceed the portion of the tax paid within the 3 years immediately preceding the allowance of the credit or refund. [Reg. § 301.6511(b)-1.]

☐ [*T.D.* 6172, 5-2-56. *Amended by T.D.* 6425, 11-10-59, *T.D.* 6498, 10-24-60 *and T.D.* 6585, 12-27-61.]

[Reg. § 301.6511(c)-1]

§ 301.6511(c)-1. Special rules applicable in case of extension of time by agreement.— (a) *Scope.*—If, within the period prescribed in section 6511(a) for the filing of a claim for credit or refund, an agreement extending the period of assessment of a tax has been made in accordance with the provisions of section 6501(c)(4), the special rules provided in this section become applicable. This section shall not apply to any claim filed, or credit or refund allowed if no claim is filed, either (1) prior to the execution of an agreement extending the period in which assessment may be made, or (2) more than 6 months after the expiration of the period within which an assessment may be made pursuant to the agreement or any extension thereof.

(b) *Period in which claim may be filed.*—Claim for credit or refund of an overpayment may be filed, or credit or refund may be allowed if no claim is filed, at any time within which an assessment may be made pursuant to an agreement, or any extension thereof, under section 6501(c)(4), and for 6 months thereafter.

(c) *Limit on amount to be credited or refunded.*— (1) If a claim is filed within the time prescribed in paragraph (b) of this section, the amount of the credit or refund allowed or made shall not exceed the portion of the tax paid after the execution of the agreement and before the filing of the claim, plus the amount that could have been properly credited or refunded under the provisions of section 6511(b)(2) if a claim had been filed on the date of the execution of the agreement.

(2) If no claim is filed, the amount of credit or refund allowed or made within the time prescribed in paragraph (b) of this section shall not exceed the portion of the tax paid after the execution of the agreement and before the making of the credit or refund, plus the amount that could have been properly credited or refunded under the provisions of section 6511(b)(2) if a claim had been filed on the date of the execution of the agreement.

(d) *Effective date of agreement.*—The agreement referred to in this section shall become effective when signed by the taxpayer and the district director or an assistant regional commissioner. [Reg. § 301.6511(c)-1.]

☐ [*T.D.* 6172, 5-2-56. *Amended by T.D.* 6498, 10-24-60.]

[Reg. § 301.6511(d)-1]

§ 301.6511(d)-1. Overpayment of income tax on account of bad debts, worthless securities, etc.—(a)(1) If the claim for credit or refund relates to an overpayment of income tax on account of—

(i) The deductibility by the taxpayer, under section 166 or section 832(c), of a debt as a debt which became worthless, or, under section 165(g), of a loss from the worthlessness of a security, or

(ii) The effect that the deductibility of a debt or loss described in subdivision (i) of this subparagraph has on the application to the taxpayer of a carryover,

then in lieu of the 3-year period from the time the return was filed in which claim may be filed or credit or refund allowed, as prescribed in section 6511(a) or (b), the period shall be 7 years from the date prescribed by law for filing the return (determined without regard to any extension of time for filing such return) for the taxable year for which the claim is made or the credit or refund allowed or made.

(2) If the claim for credit or refund relates to an overpayment on account of the effect that the deductibility of a debt or loss, described in subparagraph (1) of this paragraph, has on the application to the taxpayer of a net operating loss carryback provided in section 172(b), the period in which claim for credit or refund may be filed shall be whichever of the following two periods expires later:

(i) Seven years from the last date prescribed for filing the return (determined without regard to any extension of time for filing such return) for the taxable year of the net operating loss which results in such carryback, or

(ii) The period which ends with the expiration of the period prescribed in section 6511(c) within which a claim for credit or refund may be filed with respect to the taxable year of the net operating loss which resulted in the carryback.

(3) In the case of a claim for credit or refund involving items described in this section, the amount of the credit or refund may exceed the portion of the tax paid within the period provided in section 6511(b)(2) or (c), whichever is applicable, to the extent of the amount of the overpayment attributable to the deductibility of items described in subparagraph (1) of this paragraph. If the claim involves an overpayment based not only on the deductibility of items described in subparagraph (1) of this paragraph but based also on other items, the credit or refund cannot exceed the sum of the following:

(i) The amount of the overpayment which is attributable to the deductibility of items described in subparagraph (1) of this paragraph, and

(ii) The balance of such overpayment up to a limit of the portion, if any, of the tax paid within the period provided in section 6511(b)(2) or (c), or within the period provided in any other applicable provision of law.

(4) If the claim involves an overpayment based not only on the deductibility of items described in subparagraph (1) of this paragraph but based also on other items, and if the claim with respect to any items is barred by the expiration of any applicable period of limitation, the portion of the overpayment attributable to the items not so barred shall be determined by treating the allowance of such items as the first adjustment to be made in computing such overpayment.

(b) If a claim for credit or refund is not filed within the applicable period described in paragraph (a) of this section, then credit or refund may be allowed or made only if claim therefor is filed or if such credit or refund is allowed within any period prescribed in section 6511(a), (b), or (c), whichever is applicable, subject to the provisions thereof limiting the amount of credit or refund in the case of a claim filed, or, if no claim was filed, in the case of credit or refund allowed within such applicable period as prescribed in section 6511(b) or (c).

(c) The provisions of this section and section 6511(d)(1) do not apply to an overpayment resulting from the deductibility of a debt that became partially worthless during the taxable year, but only to an overpayment resulting from the deductibility of a debt which became entirely worthless during such year.

(d) The provisions of paragraph (a) of this section with regard to an overpayment caused by the deductibility of a bad debt under section 166 or section 832(c), or of a loss from the worthlessness of a security under section 165(g), are likewise applicable to an overpayment caused by the effect that the deductibility of such bad debt or loss has on the application to the taxpayer of a carryover or of a carryback. [Reg. § 301.6511(d)-1.]

☐ [*T.D.* 6172, 5-2-56. *Amended by T.D.* 6425, 11-10-59.]

[Reg. § 301.6511(d)-2]

§ 301.6511(d)-2. Overpayment of income tax on account of net operating loss or capital loss carrybacks.—(a) *Special period of limitation.*— (1) If the claim for credit or refund relates to an overpayment of income tax attributable to a net operating loss carryback (provided in section 172(b)), or a capital loss carryback (provided in section 1212(a)), then in lieu of the 3-year period from the time the return was filed in which the claim may be filed or credit or refund allowed, as prescribed in section 6511(a) or (b), the period shall be whichever of the following 2 periods expires later:

(i) The period which ends with the expiration of the fifteenth day of the fortieth month (or thirty-ninth month, in the case of a corporation) following the end of the taxable year of the net operating loss or net capital loss which resulted in the carryback; or

(ii) The period which ends with the expiration of the period prescribed in section 6511(c) within which a claim for credit or refund may be filed with respect to the taxable year of the net operating loss or net capital loss which resulted in the carryback except that—

(a) With respect to an overpayment attributable to a net operating loss carryback to any year on account of a certification issued to the taxpayer under section 317 of the Trade Expansion Act of 1962, the period shall not expire before the expiration of the sixth month following the month in which such certification is issued to the taxpayer, and

(b) With respect to an overpayment attributable to the creation of, or an increase in, a net operating loss as a result of the elimination of excessive profits by a renegotiation (as defined in section 1481(a)(1)(A)), the period shall not expire before September 1, 1959, or the expiration of the twelfth month following the month in which the agreement or order for the elimination of such excessive profits becomes final, whichever is the later.

(2) In the case of a claim for credit or refund involving a net operating loss or capital loss carryback described in subparagraph (1) of this paragraph, the amount of the credit or refund may exceed the portion of the tax paid within the period provided in section 6511(b)(2) or (c), whichever is applicable, to the extent of the amount of the overpayment attributable to the carryback. If the claim involves an overpayment based not only on a net operating loss or capital loss carryback described in subparagraph (1) of this paragraph but based also on other items, the credit or refund cannot exceed the sum of the following:

(i) The amount of the overpayment which is attributable to the net operating loss or capital loss carryback, and

(ii) The balance of such overpayment up to a limit of the portion, if any, of the tax paid within the period provided in section 6511(b)(2) or (c), or within the period provided in any other applicable provision of law.

(3) If the claim involves an overpayment based not only on a net operating loss or capital loss carryback described in subparagraph (1) of this paragraph but based also on other items, and if the claim with respect to any items is barred by the expiration of any applicable period of limitation, the portion of the overpayment attributable to the items not so barred shall be determined by treating the allowance of such items as the first adjustment to be made in computing such overpayment. If a claim for credit or refund is not filed, and if credit or refund is not allowed, within the period prescribed in this paragraph, then credit or refund may be allowed or made only if claim therefor is filed, or if such credit or refund is allowed, within the period prescribed in section 6511(a), (b), or (c), whichever is applicable, subject to the provisions thereof limiting the amount of credit or refund in the case of a claim filed, or if no claim was filed, in case of credit or refund allowed, within such applicable period. For the limitations on the allowance of interest for an overpayment where credit or refund is subject to the provisions of this section, see section 6611(f).

(b) *Barred overpayments.*—(1) If the allowance of a credit or refund of an overpayment of tax attributable to a net operating loss carryback or capital loss carryback is otherwise prevented by the operation of any law or rule of law (other than section 7122, relating to compromises), such credit or refund may be allowed or made under the provisions of section 6511(d)(2)(B) if a claim therefor is filed within the period provided by section 6511(d)(2)(A) and paragraph (a) of this section for filing a claim for credit or refund of an overpayment attributable to a carryback. Similarly, if the allowance of an application, credit, or refund of a decrease in the tax determined under section 6411(b) is otherwise prevented by the operation of any law or rule of law (other than section 7122), such application, credit, or refund may be allowed or made if an application for a tentative carryback adjustment is filed within the period provided in section 6411(a). Thus, for example, even though the tax liability (not including the net operating loss deduction or capital loss carryback (or the effect of such deduction or carryback)) for a given taxable year has previously been litigated before the Tax Court, credit or refund of an overpayment may be allowed or made despite the provisions of section 6512(a), if claim for such credit or refund is filed within the period provided in section 6511(d)(2)(A) and paragraph (a) of this section. In the case of a claim for credit or refund of an overpayment attributable to a carryback, or in the case of an application for a tentative carryback adjustment, the determination of any court, including the Tax Court, in any proceeding in which the decision of the court has become final, shall be conclusive except with respect to the net operating loss deduction, and the effect of such deduction, or with respect to the determination of a short-term capital loss, and the effect of such short-term capital loss, to the extent that such deduction or short-term capital loss is affected by a carryback which was not in issue in such proceeding.

(2) For purposes of the special period of limitation for filing a claim for credit or refund of an overpayment of tax with respect to a computation year (as defined in section 1302(c)(1)) by an individual who has chosen to compute his tax under sections 1301 through 1305 (relating to income averaging), such claim is determined to relate to an overpayment attributable to a net operating loss carryback when such carryback relates to any base period year (as defined in section 1302(c)(3)). Thus, if (i) an individual has a net operating loss for a taxable year subsequent to a taxable year for which he had chosen the benefits of income averaging, and (ii) such net operating loss carryback is wholly utilized in any one or more of his base period years (which would result in an increased amount of averagable income for such computation year), the special period of limitation with respect to such individual's computation year applies and a timely claim for credit or refund with respect to the computation year may be filed. [Reg. §301.6511(d)-2.]

☐ [*T.D. 6172, 5-2-56. Amended by T.D. 6425, 11-10-59, T.D. 6498, 10-24-60, T.D. 6730, 5-7-64, T.D. 7196, 7-12-72 and T.D. 7301, 1-3-74.*]

[Reg. §301.6511(d)-3]

§301.6511(d)-3. Special rules applicable to credit against income tax for foreign taxes.— (a) *Period in which claim may be filed.*—In the case of an overpayment of income tax resulting from a credit, allowed under the provisions of section 901 or under the provisions of any treaty to which the United States is a party, for taxes paid or accrued to a foreign country or possession of the United States, a claim for credit or refund must be filed by the taxpayer within 10 years from the last date prescribed for filing the return (determined without regard to any extension of time for filing such return) for the taxable year with respect to which the claim is made. Such 10-year period shall be applied in lieu of the 3-year period prescribed in section 6511(a).

(b) *Limit on amount to be credited or refunded.*— In the case of a claim described in paragraph (a) of this section, the amount of the credit or refund allowed or made may exceed the portion of the tax paid within the period prescribed in section 6511(b) or (c), whichever is applicable, to the extent of the amount of the overpayment attributable to the allowance of a credit against income tax referred to in paragraph (a) of this section [Reg. § 301.6511(d)-3.]

☐ [*T.D.* 6172, 5-2-56.]

[Reg. § 301.6511(d)-4]

§ 301.6511(d)-4. Overpayment of income tax on account of investment credit carryback.— (a) *Special period of limitation.*—(1) If the claim for credit or refund relates to an overpayment of income tax attributable to an investment credit carryback, provided in section 46(b), then in lieu of the 3-year period from the time the return was filed in which the claim may be filed or credit refund allowed, as prescribed in section 6511(a) or (b), the period shall be whichever of the following 2 periods expires later:

(i) The period which ends with the expiration of the fifteenth day of the fortieth month (or thirty-ninth month, in the case of a corporation) following the end of the taxable year of the unused investment credit which resulted in the carryback (or, with respect to any portion of an investment credit carryback from a taxable year attributable to a net operating loss carryback or a capital loss carryback from a subsequent taxable year, the period which ends with the expiration of the fifteenth day of the fortieth month (or thirty-ninth month, in the case of a corporation) following the end of such subsequent taxable year); or

(ii) The period which ends with the expiration of the period prescribed in section 6511(c) within which a claim for credit or refund may be filed with respect to the taxable year of the unused investment credit which resulted in the carryback.

(2) In the case of a claim for credit or refund involving an investment credit carryback described in subparagraph (1) of this paragraph, the amount of the credit or refund may exceed the portion of the tax paid within the period provided in section 6511(b)(2) or (c), whichever is applicable, to the extent of the amount of the overpayment attributable to the carryback. If the claim involves an overpayment based not only

on an investment credit carryback described in subparagraph (1) of this paragraph but based also on other items, the credit or refund cannot exceed the sum of the following:

(i) The amount of the overpayment which is attributable to the investment credit carryback, and

(ii) The balance of such overpayment up to a limit of the portion, if any, of the tax paid within the period provided in section 6511(b)(2) or (c), or within the period provided in any other applicable provision of law.

(3) If the claim involves an overpayment based not only on an investment credit carryback described in subparagraph (1) of this paragraph but based also on other items, and if the claim with respect to any items is barred by the expiration of any applicable period of limitation, the portion of the overpayment attributable to the items not so barred shall be determined by treating the allowance of such items as the first adjustment to be made in computing such overpayment. If a claim for credit or refund is not filed, and if credit or refund is not allowed, within the period prescribed in this paragraph, then credit or refund may be allowed or made only if claim therefor is filed, or if such credit or refund is allowed, within the period prescribed in section 6511(a), (b), or (c), whichever is applicable, subject to the provisions thereof limiting the amount of credit or refund in the case of a claim filed, or if no claim was filed, in case of credit or refund allowed, within such applicable period. For the limitations on the allowance of interest for an overpayment where credit or refund is subject to the provisions of this section, see section 6611(f).

(b) *Barred overpayments.*—If the allowance of a credit or refund of an overpayment of tax attributable to an investment credit carryback is otherwise prevented by the operation of any law or rule of law (other than section 7122, relating to compromises), such credit or refund may be allowed or made under the provisions of section 6511(d)(4)(B) if a claim therefor is filed within the period provided by section 6511(d)(4)(A) and paragraph (a) of this section for filing a claim for credit or refund of an overpayment attributable to a carryback. In the case of a claim for credit or refund of an overpayment attributable to a carryback, the determination of any court, including the Tax Court, in any proceeding in which the decision of the court has become final, shall not be conclusive with respect to the investment credit, and the effect of such credit, to the extent that such credit is affected by a carryback which was not in issue in such proceeding. [Reg. § 301.6511(d)-4.]

☐ [*T.D.* 7301, 1-3-74.]

[Reg. § 301.6511(d)-7]

§ 301.6511(d)-7. Overpayment of income tax on account of work incentive program credit carryback.—(a) *Special period of limitation.*— (1) If the claim for credit or refund related to an overpayment of income tax attributable to a

67,150
Limitations on Credit or Refund
See p. 20,601 for regulations not amended to reflect law changes

work incentive program (WIN) credit carryback, provided in section 50A, then in lieu of the 3-year period from the time the return was filed in which the claim may be filed or credit or refund allowed, as prescribed in section 6511(a) or (b), the period shall be whichever of the following 2 periods expires later:

(i) The period which ends with the expiration of the fifteenth day of the fortieth month (or thirty-ninth month, in the case of a corporation) following the end of the taxable year of the unused WIN credit which resulted in the carryback (or, with respect to any portion of a WIN credit carryback from a taxable year attributable to a net operating loss carryback or a capital loss carryback from a subsequent taxable year, the period which ends with the expiration of the fifteenth day of the fortieth month (or thirty-ninth month in the case of a corporation) following the end of such subsequent taxable year); or

(ii) The period which ends with the expiration of the period prescribed in section 6511(c) within which a claim for credit or refund may be filed with respect to the taxable year of the unused WIN credit which resulted in the carryback.

(2) In the case of a claim for credit or refund involving a WIN credit carryback described in paragraph (a)(1) of this section, the amount of the credit or refund may exceed the portion of the tax paid within the period provided in section 6511(b)(2) or (c), whichever is applicable, to the extent of the amount of the overpayment attributable to the carryback. If the claim involves an overpayment based not only on a WIN credit carryback described in paragraph (a)(1) of this section but based also on other items, the credit or refund cannot exceed the sum of the following:

(i) The amount of the overpayment which is attributable to the WIN credit carryback, and

(ii) The balance of such overpayment up to a limit of the portion, if any, of the tax paid within the period provided in section 6511(b)(2) or (c), or within the period provided in any other applicable provision of law.

(3) If the claim involves an overpayment based not only on a WIN credit carryback described in paragraph (a)(1) of this section but based also on other items, and if the claim with respect to any items is barred by the expiration of any applicable period of limitation, the portion of the overpayment attributable to the items not so barred shall be determined by treating the allowance of such items as the first adjustment to be made in computing such overpayment. If a claim for credit or refund is not filed, and if credit or refund is not allowed, within the period prescribed in this paragraph, then credit or refund may be allowed or made only if claim therefor is filed, or if such credit or refund is allowed, within the period prescribed in section 6511(a), (b), or (c), whichever is applicable, subject to the provisions thereof limiting the amount of credit or refund in the case of a claim filed, or if no claim was filed, in case of credit or refund allowed, within such applicable period. For the

limitations on the allowance of interest for an overpayment where credit or refund is subject to the provisions of this section, see section 6611(f).

(b) *Barred overpayments.*—If the allowance of a credit or refund of an overpayment of tax attributable to a WIN credit carryback is otherwise prevented by the operation of any law or rule of law (other than section 7122, relating to compromises), such credit or refund may be allowed or made under the provisions of section 6511(d)(7)(B) if a claim therefor is filed within the period provided by section 6511(d)(7)(A) and paragraph (a) of this section for filing a claim for credit or refund of an overpayment attributable to a carryback. In the case of a claim for credit or refund of an overpayment attributable to a carryback, the determination of any court, including the Tax Court, in any proceeding in which the decision of the courts has become final, shall not be conclusive with respect to the WIN credit, and the effect of such credit, to the extent that such credit is affected by a carryback which was not in issue in such proceeding. [Reg. § 301.6511(d)-7.]

☐ [*T.D.* 7301, 1-3-74.]

[Reg. § 301.6511(f)-1]

§ 301.6511(f)-1. **Special rules for chapter 42 taxes.**—(a) *In general.*—Claims for credit or refund of an overpayment of any tax imposed by chapter 42 shall be filed by the taxpayer within 3 years from the time a return was filed by the private foundation or trust (as the case may be) with respect to such tax, or within 2 years from the time the tax was paid, whichever of such periods expire the later.

(b) *Examples.*—This section may be illustrated by the following examples:

Example (1). In 1972 D, an individual taxpayer who was a disqualified person under the provisions of section 4946(a)(1), participated in an act of self-dealing with a private foundation and incurred a tax under section 4941(a)(1). The private foundation files a Form 990-PF on May 15, 1973, and discloses thereon that it has engaged in an act of self-dealing with D. D files a Form 4720 on July 2, 1973, and pays the amount of tax imposed by section 4941(a) with respect to such act of self-dealing. For purposes of this section, the return was filed on May 15, 1973, and any claim for credit or refund by D must be filed by May 17, 1976 (May 15, 1976, was a Saturday).

Example (2). Assume the same facts as in example (1) except that D filed a Form 4720 on July 1, 1974, and pays the tax on that date. D must then file any claim for credit or refund by July 1, 1976. [Reg. § 301.6511(f)-1.]

☐ [*T.D.* 7838, 10-5-82.]

[Reg. § 301.6511(g)-1]

§ 301.6511(g)-1. **Special rule for partnership items of federally registered partnerships.**—(a) *In general.*—In the case of any tax imposed by subtitle A with respect to any person, the period for filing a claim for credit or refund of any overpayment attributable to any partnership item of a federally registered partnership shall not expire before the later of—

(1) The date which is 4 years after the date prescribed by law (including extensions thereof) for filing the partnership return for the partnership taxable year in which the item arose, or

(2) If the taxpayer or a general partner or a person authorized to act on behalf of the partnership, as provided in § 301.6501(o)-2(d), consents to extend the period for assessing a deficiency attributable to the partnership item before the date specified in paragraph (a)(1) of this section, the date 6 months after the expiration of the extension.

(b) *Limits on amount of credit or refund not applicable.*—In the case of a claim for credit or refund of any income tax overpayment attributable to any partnership item of a federally registered partnership, the limitations provided in section 6511(b)(2) and (c) shall not apply if the claim is filed within the period described in paragraph (a) of this section.

(c) *Special periods of limitation with respect to carryback of net operating loss, capital loss, etc.*—The provisions of section 6511(g) must also be taken into account in applying the various special periods of limitation prescribed in section 6511(d). Thus, to the extent that a carryback is attributable to a partnership item of a federally registered partnership, the period for filing a claim for credit or refund of any overpayment attributable to that carryback shall not expire before the date determined under paragraph (a) of this section with respect to the partnership taxable year in which the item arose.

(d) *Definitions.*—For purposes of this section, the terms "partnership item" and "federally registered partnership" have the same meaning as such terms have when used in section 6501(o), § 301.6501(o)-2(c), and § 301.6501(o)-3.

(e) *Effective date.*—The provisions of this section are effective generally for partnership items arising in partnership taxable years beginning after December 31, 1978 and before September 4, 1982. This section shall not apply, however, to any partnership taxable year with respect to which the amendments made to Code section 6511(g) by section 402 of the Tax Equity and Fiscal Responsibility Act of 1982 are effective. See section 407(a)(3) of that Act. [Reg. § 301.6511(g)-1.]

☐ [*T.D.* 7884, 4-14-83.]

[Reg. § 301.6512-1]

§ 301.6512-1. Limitations in case of petition to Tax Court.—(a) *Effect of petition to Tax Court.*—(1) *General rule.*—If a person having a right to file a petition with the Tax Court with respect to a deficiency in income, estate, gift, or excise tax imposed by subtitle A or B, or chapter 41, 42, 43, or 44 of the Code has filed such petition within the time prescribed in section 6213(a), no credit or refund of income tax for the same taxable year, of gift tax for the same calendar year or

calendar quarter, of estate tax in respect of the taxable estate of the same decedent, or of tax imposed by chapter 41, 42, 43, or 44 with respect to any act (or failure to act) to which such petition relates, in respect of which a district director or director of a service center (or a regional director of appeals) has determined the deficiency, shall be allowed or made, and no suit in any court for the recovery of any part of such tax shall be instituted by the taxpayer, except as to items set forth in paragraph (a)(2) of this section.

(2) *Exceptions.*—The exceptions to the rule stated in subparagraph (1) of this paragraph are as follows:

(i) An overpayment determined by a decision of the Tax Court which has become final;

(ii) Any amount collected in excess of an amount computed in accordance with the decision of the Tax Court which has become final; and

(iii) Any amount collected after the expiration of the period of limitation upon levying or beginning a proceeding in court for collection.

(b) *Overpayment determined by Tax Court.*—If the Tax Court finds that there is no deficiency and further finds that the taxpayer has made an overpayment of income tax for the same taxable year, of gift tax for the same calendar year or calendar quarter, of estate tax in respect of the taxable estate of the same decedent, or of tax imposed by chapter 41, 42, 43, or 44 with respect to any act (or failure to act) to which such petition relates, in respect of which a district director, or director of a service center (or a regional director of appeals) has determined the deficiency, or finds that there is a deficiency but that the taxpayer had made an overpayment of such tax, the overpayment determined by the Tax Court shall be credited or refunded to the taxpayer when the decision of the Tax Court has become final. (See section 7481, relating to the date when a Tax Court decision becomes final.) No such credit or refund shall be allowed or made of any portion of the tax unless the Tax Court determines as part of its decision that such portion was paid—

(1) After the mailing of the notice of deficiency, or

(2) Within the period which would be applicable under section 6511(b)(2), (c), (d), or (g) (see § § 301.6511(b)-1, 301.6511(c)-1, 301.6511(d)-1, 301.6511(d)-2, and 301.6511(d)-3), if on the date of the mailing of the notice of deficiency a claim had been filed (whether or not filed) stating the grounds upon which the Tax Court finds that there is an overpayment.

(c) *Jeopardy assessments.*—In the case of a jeopardy assessment made under section 6861(a), if the amount which should have been assessed as determined by a decision of the Tax Court which has become final is less than the amount already collected, the excess payment shall be credited or refunded subject to a determination being made by the Tax Court with respect to the time of payment as stated in paragraph (b) of this section.

(d) *Disallowance of deficiency by reviewing court.*—If the amount of the deficiency determined by the Tax Court (in a case where collection has not been stayed by the filing of a bond) is disallowed in whole or in part by the reviewing court, then the overpayment resulting from such disallowance shall be credited or refunded without the making of claim therefor, subject to a determination being made by the Tax Court with respect to the time of payment as stated in paragraph (b) of this section. (See section 7481, relating to date Tax Court decision becomes final.)

(e) *Collection in excess of amount determined by Tax Court.*—Where the amount collected is in excess of the amount computed in accordance with the decision of the Tax Court which has become final, the excess payment shall be credited or refunded within the period of limitation provided in section 6511.

(f) *Collection after expiration of statutory period.*—Where an amount is collected after the statutory period of limitation upon the beginning of levy or a proceeding in court for collection has expired (see section 6502, relating to collection after assessment), the taxpayer may file a claim for refund of the amount so collected within the period of limitation provided in section 6511. In any such case, the decision of the Tax Court as to whether the statutory period upon collection of the tax expired before notice of the deficiency was mailed shall, when the decision becomes final, be conclusive. [Reg. § 301.6512-1.]

☐ [*T.D. 6172, 5-2-56. Amended by T.D. 7238, 12-28-72 and T.D. 7838, 10-5-82.*]

[Reg. § 301.6513-1]

§ 301.6513-1. Time return deemed filed and tax considered paid.—(a) *Early return or advance payment of tax.*—For purposes of section 6511, a return filed before the last day prescribed by law or regulations for the filing thereof shall be considered as filed on such last day. For purposes of section 6511(b)(2) and (c) and section 6512, payment of any portion of the tax made before the last day prescribed for payment shall be considered made on such last day. An extension of time for filing a return or for paying any tax, or an election to pay any tax in installments, shall not be given any effect in determining under this section the last day prescribed for filing a return or paying any tax.

(b) *Prepaid income tax.*—For purposes of section 6511 (relating to limitations on credit or refund) or section 6512 (relating to limitations in case of petition to Tax Court)—

(1) Any tax actually deducted and withheld at the source during any calendar year under chapter 24 of the Code (relating to collection of income tax at source on wages) shall, in respect of the recipient of the income, be deemed to have been paid by him on the 15th day of the fourth month following the close of his taxable year

with respect to which such tax is allowable as a credit under section 31 (relating to tax withheld on wages),

(2) Any amount paid as estimated income tax for any taxable year shall be deemed to have been paid on the last day prescribed for filing the income tax return under section 6012 for such taxable year (determined without regard to any extension of time for filing such return), and

(3) Any tax withheld at the source on or after November 13, 1966, under chapter 3 of the Code (relating to tax withheld on nonresident aliens and foreign corporations and tax-free covenant bonds) shall, in respect of the recipient of the income, be deemed to have been paid by such recipient on the last day prescribed for filing his income tax return under section 6012 for the taxable year (determined without regard to any extension of time for filing such return) with respect to which such tax is allowable as a credit under section 1462 (relating to withheld tax as credit to recipient of income).

Subparagraph (3) of this paragraph shall apply even though the recipient of the income has been granted under section 6012 and the regulations thereunder an exemption from the requirement of making an income tax return for the taxable year.

(c) *Return and payment of social security taxes and income tax withholding.*—Notwithstanding paragraph (a) of this section, if a return (or payment) on or after November 13, 1966, of tax imposed by chapter 3 of the Code (relating to withholding of tax on nonresident aliens and foreign corporations and tax-free covenant bonds), or if a return (or payment) of tax imposed by chapter 21 of the Code (relating to the Federal Insurance Contributions Act) or by chapter 24 of the Code (relating to the collection of income tax at source on wages), for any period ending with or within a calendar year is filed or paid before April 15 of the succeeding calendar year, for purposes of section 6511 (relating to limitations on credit or refund) the return shall be considered filed, or the tax considered paid, on April 15 of such succeeding calendar year.

(d) *Overpayment of income tax credited to estimated tax.*—If a taxpayer elects under the provisions of section 6402(b) to credit an overpayment of income tax for a taxable year against estimated tax for the succeeding taxable year, the amount so credited shall be considered a payment of income tax for such succeeding taxable year (whether or not claimed as a credit on the estimated tax return for such succeeding taxable year). If the treatment of such amount as a payment of income tax for the succeeding taxable year results in an overpayment for such succeeding taxable year, the period of limitations applicable to such overpayment is determined by reference to that taxable year. An election so to credit an overpayment of income tax precludes the allowance of a claim for credit or refund of such overpayment for the taxable year in which the overpayment arises. [Reg. § 301.6513-1.]

☐ [*T.D. 6172*, 5-2-56. *Amended by T.D. 6498*, 10-24-60 *and T.D. 6922*, 6-16-67.]

[Reg. § 301.6514(a)-1]

§ 301.6514(a)-1. Credits or refunds after period of limitation.—(a) A refund of any portion of any internal revenue tax (or any interest, additional amount, addition to the tax, or assessable penalty) shall be considered erroneous and a credit of any such portion shall be considered void:

(1) If made after the expiration of the period of limitation prescribed by section 6511 for filing claim therefor, unless prior to the expiration of such period claim was filed, or

(2) In the case of a timely claim, if the credit or refund was made after the expiration of the period of limitation prescribed by section 6532(a) for the filing of suit, unless prior to the expiration of such period suit was begun.

(b) For procedure by the United States to recover erroneous refunds, see sections 6532(b) and 7405. [Reg. § 301.6514(a)-1.]

☐ [*T.D.* 6172, 5-2-56. *Amended by T.D.* 6498, 10-24-60.]

[Reg. § 301.6514(b)-1]

§ 301.6514(b)-1. Credit against barred liability.—Any credit against a liability in respect of any taxable year shall be void if the collection of such liability would be barred by the applicable statute of limitations at the time such credit is made. [Reg. § 301.6514(b)-1.]

☐ [*T.D.* 6172, 5-2-56.]

MITIGATION OF EFFECT OF PERIOD OF LIMITATIONS

[Reg. § 301.6521-1]

§ 301.6521-1. Mitigation of effect of limitation in case of related employee social security tax and self-employment tax.—(a) Section 6521 may be applied in the correction of a certain type of error involving both the tax on self-employment income under section 1401 and the employee tax under section 3101 if the correction of the error as to one tax is, on the date the correction is authorized, prevented in whole or in part by the operation of any law or rule of law other than section 7122, relating to compromises. Examples of such law are sections 6212(c), 6401(a), 6501, 6511, 6512(a), 6514, 6532, 6901(c), (d) and (e), 7121, and 7459(e).

(b) If the liability for either tax with respect to which the error was made has been compromised under section 7122, the provisions of section 6521 limiting the correction with respect to the other tax do not apply.

(c) Section 6521 is not applicable if, on the date of the authorization, correction of the effect of the error is permissible as to both taxes without recourse to such section.

(d) If, because an amount of wages, as defined in section 3121(a), is erroneously treated as self-employment income, as defined in section 1402(b), or an amount of self-employment income is erroneously treated as wages, it is necessary in correcting the error to assess the correct tax and give a credit or refund for the amount of the tax erroneously paid, and if either, but not both, of such adjustments is prevented by any law or rule of law (other than section 7122), the amount of the assessment, or the amount of the credit or refund, authorized shall reflect the adjustment which would be made in respect of the other tax (either the tax on self-employment income under section 1401 or the employee tax under section 3101) but for the operation of such law or rule of law. For example, assume that during 1955 A paid $10 as tax on an amount erroneously treated as "wages", when such amount was actually self-employment income, and that credit or refund of the $10 is not barred. A should have paid a self-employment tax of $15 on the amount. If the assessment of the correct tax, that is, $15, is barred by the statute of limitations, no credit or refund of the $10 shall be made without offsetting against such $10 the $15, assessment of which is barred. Thus, no credit or refund in respect of the $10 can be made.

(e) As another example, assume that during 1955 a taxpayer reports wages of $4,200 and net earnings from self-employment of $900. By reason of the limitations of section 1402(b) he shows no self-employment income. Assume further that by reason of a final decision by the Tax Court of the United States, further adjustments to the taxpayer's income tax liability are barred. The question of the amount of his wages, as defined in section 3121, was not in issue in the Tax Court litigation, but it is subsequently determined (within the period of limitations applicable under the Federal Insurance Contributions Act) that $700 of the $4,200 reported as wages was not for employment as defined in section 3121(b). Therefore, the taxpayer is entitled to the allowance of a refund of the $14 tax paid on such remuneration under section 3101. The reduction of his wages from $4,200 to $3,500 would result in the determination of $700 self-employment income, the tax on which is $21 for the year. Under section 6521, the overpayment of $14 would be offset by the barred deficiency of $21, thus eliminating the refund otherwise allowable. If the facts were changed so that the taxpayer erroneously paid tax on self-employment income of $700, having been taxed on only $3,500 as wages, and within the period of limitations applicable under the Federal Insurance Contributions Act, it is determined that his wages were $4,200, the tax of $14 under section 3101, otherwise collectible, would be eliminated by offsetting under section 6521 the barred overpayment

Reg. § 301.6521-1(e)

of $21. The balance of the barred overpayment, $7, cannot be credited or refunded.

(f) Another illustration of the operation of section 6521 is the case of a taxpayer who, for 1955, is erroneously taxed on $2,500 as wages, the tax on which is $50, and who reports no self-employment income. After the period of limitations has run on the refund of the tax under the Federal Insurance Contributions Act, it is determined that the amount treated as wages should have been reported as net earnings from self-employment. The taxpayer's self-employment income would then be $2,500 and the tax thereon would be $75. Assume that the period of limitations applicable to subtitle A of the Code has not expired, and that a notice of deficiency may properly be issued. Under section 6521, the amount of the deficiency of $75 must be reduced by the barred overpayment of $50. [Reg. § 301.6521-1.]

☐ [T.D. 6172, 5-2-56. *Amended by T.D. 6498*, 10-24-60.]

[Reg. § 301.6521-2]

§ 301.6521-2. Law applicable in determination of error.—The question of whether there was an erroneous treatment of self-employment income or of wages is determined under the provisions of law and regulations applicable with respect to the year or other taxable period as to which the error was made. The fact that the error was in pursuance of an interpretation, either judicial or administrative, accorded such provisions of law and regulations at the time the action involved was taken is not necessarily determinative of this question. For example, if a later judicial decision authoritatively alters such interpretation so that such action is contrary to the applicable provisions of the law and regulations as later interpreted, the error comes within the scope of section 6521. [Reg. § 301.6521-2.]

☐ [T.D. 6172, 5-2-56.]

PERIODS OF LIMITATION IN JUDICIAL PROCEEDINGS

[Reg. § 301.6532-1]

§ 301.6532-1. Periods of limitation on suits by taxpayers.—(a) No suit or proceeding under section 7422(a) for the recovery of any internal revenue tax, penalty, or other sum shall be begun until whichever of the following first occurs:

(1) The expiration of 6 months from the date of the filing of the claim for credit or refund, or

(2) A decision is rendered on such claim prior to the expiration of 6 months after the filing thereof.

Except as provided in paragraph (b) of this section, no suit or proceeding for the recovery of any internal revenue tax, penalty, or other sum may be brought after the expiration of 2 years from the date of mailing by registered mail prior to September 3, 1958, or by either registered or certified mail on or after September 3, 1958, by a district director, a director of an internal revenue service center, or an assistant regional commissioner to a taxpayer of a notice of disallowance of the part of the claim to which the suit or proceeding relates.

(b) The 2-year period described in paragraph (a) of this section may be extended if an agreement to extend the running of the period of limitations is executed. The agreement must be signed by the taxpayer or by an attorney, agent, trustee, or other fiduciary on behalf of the taxpayer. If the agreement is signed by a person other than the taxpayer, it shall be accompanied by an authenticated copy of the power of attorney or other legal evidence of the authority of such person to act on behalf of the taxpayer. If the taxpayer is a corporation, the agreement should be signed with the corporate name followed by the signature of a duly authorized officer of the corporation. The agreement will not be effective until signed by a district director, a

director of an internal revenue service center, or an assistant regional commissioner.

(c) The taxpayer may sign a waiver of the requirement that he be mailed a notice of disallowance. Such waiver is irrevocable and will commence the running of the 2-year period described in paragraph (a) of this section on the date the waiver is filed. The waiver shall set forth:

(1) The type of tax and the taxable period covered by the taxpayer's claim for refund;

(2) The amount of the claim;

(3) The amount of the claim disallowed;

(4) A statement that the taxpayer agrees the filing of the waiver will commence the running of the 2-year period provided for in section 6532(a)(1) as if a notice of disallowance had been sent the taxpayer by either registered or certified mail.

The filing of such a waiver prior to the expiration of 6 months from the date the claim was filed does not permit the filing of a suit for refund prior to the time specified in section 6532(a)(1) and paragraph (a) of this section.

(d) Any consideration, reconsideration, or other action with respect to a claim after the mailing by registered mail prior to September 3, 1958, or by either registered or certified mail on or after September 3, 1958, of a notice of disallowance or after the execution of a waiver referred to in paragraph (c) of this section, shall not extend the period for bringing suit or other proceeding under section 7422(a). [Reg. § 301.6532-1.]

☐ [T.D. 6172, 5-2-56. *Amended by T.D. 6425*, 11-10-59 *and T.D. 6827, 6-16-65.*]

[Reg. § 301.6532-2]

§ 301.6532-2. Periods of limitation on suits by the United States.—The United States may not recover any erroneous refund by civil action under section 7405 unless such action is begun within 2 years after the making of such refund. However, if any part of the refund was induced by fraud or misrepresentation of a material fact, the action to recover the erroneous refund may be brought at any time within 5 years from the date the refund was made. [Reg. § 301.6532-2.]

☐ [*T.D.* 6172, 5-2-56.]

[Reg. § 301.6532-3]

§ 301.6532-3. Periods of limitation on suits by persons other than taxpayers.—(a) *General rule.*—No suit or proceeding, except as otherwise provided in section 6532(c)(2) and paragraph (b) of this section, under section 7426 and § 301.7426-1 relating to civil actions by persons other than taxpayers, shall be begun after the expiration of 9 months from the date of levy or agreement under section 6325(b)(3) giving rise to such action.

(b) *Period when claim is filed.*—The 9-month period prescribed in section 6532(c)(1) and paragraph (a) of this section shall be extended to the shorter of,

(1) 12 months from the date of filing by a third party of a written request under § 301.6343-1(b)(2) for the return of property wrongfully levied upon, or

(2) 6 months from the date of mailing by registered or certified mail by the district director to the party claimant of a notice of disallowance of the part of the request to which the action relates.

A request which, under § 301.6343-1(b)(3), is not considered adequate does not extend the 9-month period described in paragraph (a) of this section.

(c) *Examples.*—The provisions of this section may be illustrated by the following examples:

Example (1). On June 1, 1970, a tax is assessed against A with respect to his delinquent tax liability. On July 19, 1970, a levy is wrongfully made upon certain tangible personal property of B's which is in A's possession at that time. On July 20, 1970, notice of seizure is given to A. Thus, under section 6502(b), July 20, 1970, is the date on which the levy is considered to be made. Unless a request for the return of property is sooner made to extend the 9-month period, no suit or proceeding under section 7426 may be begun by B after April 20, 1971, which is 9 months from the date of levy.

Example (2). Assume the same facts as in the preceding example except that, on August 3, 1970, B properly files a request for the return of his property wrongfully levied upon. Assume further that the district director mails, on March 1, 1971, a notice of disallowance of B's request for the return of the property. No suit or proceeding under section 7426 may be begun by B after August 3, 1971, which is 12 months from the date of filing a request for the return of property wrongfully levied upon.

Example (3). Assume the same facts as in the preceding example except that the notice of disallowance of B's request for the return of property wrongfully levied upon is mailed to B on November 12, 1970. Since the 6-month period from the mailing of the notice of disallowance expires before the 12-month period from the date of filing the request for the return of property which ends on August 3, 1971, no suit or proceeding under section 7426 may be begun by B after May 12, 1971, which is 6 months from the date of mailing the notice of disallowance. [Reg. § 301.6532-3.]

☐ [*T.D.* 7305, 3-14-74.]

Interest

INTEREST ON UNDERPAYMENTS

See p. 20,601 for regulations not amended to reflect law changes

[Reg. § 20.6601-1]

§ 20.6601-1. Interest on underpayment, nonpayment, or extensions of time for payment, of tax.—For regulations concerning interest on underpayments, etc., see § 301.6601-1 of this chapter (Regulations on Procedure and Administration). [Reg. § 20.6601-1.]

☐ [*T.D.* 6296, 6-23-58.]

[Reg. § 25.6601-1]

§ 25.6601-1. Interest on underpayment, nonpayment, or extensions of time for payment, of tax.—For regulations concerning interest on underpayment, nonpayment, or extensions of time for payment of tax, see § 301.6601-1 of this chapter (Regulations on Procedure and Administration). [Reg. § 25.6601-1.]

☐ [*T.D.* 6334, 10-14-58.]

[Reg. § 53.6601-1]

§ 53.6601-1. Interest on underpayment, nonpayment, or extensions of time for payment, of

tax.—For regulations concerning interest on underpayment, nonpayment, or extensions of time for payment of tax, see § 301.6601-1 of this chapter (Regulations on Procedure and Administration). [Reg. § 53.6601-1.]

☐ [*T.D.* 7368, 7-15-75.]

[Reg. § 301.6601-1]

§ 301.6601-1. Interest on underpayments.—(a) *General rule.*—(1) Interest at the annual rate referred to in the regulations under section 6621 shall be paid on any unpaid amount of tax from the last date prescribed for payment of the tax (determined without regard to any extension of time for payment) to the date on which payment is received.

(2) For provisions requiring the payment of interest during the period occurring before July 1, 1975, see section 6601(a) prior to its amendment by section 7 of the Act of Jan. 3, 1975 (Pub. L. 93-625, 88 Stat. 2115).

(b) *Satisfaction by credits made after December 31, 1957.*—(1) *In general.*—If any portion of a tax is satisfied by the credit of an overpayment after December 31, 1957, interest shall not be imposed under section 6601 on such portion of the tax for any period during which interest on the overpayment would have been allowable if the overpayment had been refunded.

(2) *Examples.*—The provisions of this paragraph may be illustrated by the following examples:

Example (1). An examination of A's income tax returns for the calendar years 1955 and 1956 discloses an underpayment of $800 for 1955 and an overpayment of $500 for 1956. Interest under section 6601(a) ordinarily accrues on the underpayment of $800 from April 15, 1956, to the date of payment. However, the 1956 overpayment of $500 is credited after December 31, 1957, against the underpayment in accordance with the provisions of section 6402(a) and §301.6402-1. Under such circumstances interest on the $800 underpayment runs from April 15, 1956, the last date prescribed for payment of the 1955 tax, to April 15, 1957, the date the overpayment of $500 was made. Since interest would have been allowed on the overpayment, if refunded, from April 15, 1957, to a date not more than 30 days prior to the date of the refund check, no interest is imposed after April 15, 1957, on $500, the portion of the underpayment satisfied by credit. Interest continues to run, however, on $300 (the $800 underpayment for 1955 less the $500 overpayment for 1956) to the date of payment.

Example (2). An examination of A's income tax returns for the calendar years 1956 and 1957 discloses an overpayment, occurring on April 15, 1957, of $700 for 1956 and an underpayment of $400 for 1957. After April 15, 1958, the last date prescribed for payment of the 1957 tax, the district director credits $400 of the overpayment against the underpayment. In such a case, interest will accrue upon the overpayment of $700 from April 15, 1957, to April 15, 1958, the due date of the amount against which the credit is taken. Interest will also accrue under section 6611 upon $300 ($700 overpayment less $400 underpayment) from April 15, 1958, to a date not more than 30 days prior to the date of the refund check. Since a refund of the portion of the overpayment credited against the underpayment would have resulted in interest running upon such portion from April 15, 1958, to a date not more than 30 days prior to the date of the refund check, no interest is imposed upon the underpayment.

(c) *Last date prescribed for payment.*—(1) In determining the last date prescribed for payment, any extension of time granted for payment of tax (including any postponement elected under section 6163(a)) shall be disregarded. The granting of an extension of time for the payment of tax does not relieve the taxpayer from liability for the payment of interest thereon during the period of the extension. Thus, except as provided in paragraph (b) of this section, interest at the annual rate referred to in the regulations under section 6621 is payable on any unpaid portion of the tax for the period during which such portion remains unpaid by reason of an extension of time for the payment thereof.

(2)(i) If a tax or portion thereof is payable in installments in accordance with an election made under section 6152(a) or 6156(a), the last date prescribed for payment of any installment of such tax or portion thereof shall be determined under the provisions of section 6152(b) or 6156(b), as the case may be, and interest shall run on any unpaid installment from such last date to the date on which payment is received. However in the event installment privileges are terminated for failure to pay an installment when due as provided by section 6152(d) and the time for the payment of any remaining installment is accelerated by the issuance of a notice and demand therefor, interest shall run on such unpaid installment from the date of the notice and demand to the date on which payment is received. But see section 6601(e)(4).

(ii) If the tax shown on a return is payable in installments, interest will run on any tax not shown on the return from the last date prescribed for payment of the first installment. If a deficiency is prorated to any unpaid installments, in accordance with section 6152(c), interest shall run on such prorated amounts from the date prescribed for the payment of the first installment to the date on which payment is received.

(3) If, by reason of jeopardy, a notice and demand for payment of any tax is issued before the last date otherwise prescribed for payment, such last date shall nevertheless be used for the purpose of the interest computation, and no interest shall be imposed for the period commencing with the date of the issuance of the notice and demand and ending on such last date. If the tax is not paid on or before such last date, interest will automatically accrue from such last date to the date on which payment is received.

(4) In the case of taxes payable by stamp and in all other cases where the last date for payment of the tax is not otherwise prescribed, such last date for the purpose of the interest computation shall be deemed to be the date on which the liability for the tax arose. However, such last date shall in no event be later than the date of issuance of a notice and demand for the tax.

(d) *Suspension of interest; waiver of restrictions on assessment.*—In the case of a deficiency determined by a district director (or an assistant regional commissioner, appellate) with respect to any income, estate, gift, or chapter 41, 42, 43, or 44 tax, if the taxpayer files with such internal revenue officer an agreement waiving the restrictions on assessment of such deficiency, and if notice and demand for payment of such deficiency is not made within 30 days after the filing of such waiver, no interest shall be imposed on the deficiency for the period beginning immediately after such 30th day and ending on the date notice and demand is made. In the case of an agreement with respect to a portion of the deficiency, the rules as set forth in this paragraph are applicable only to that portion of the deficiency to which the agreement relates.

(e) *Income tax reduced by carryback.*—(1) The carryback of a net operating loss, net capital loss, investment credit, or a work incentive program (WIN) credit shall not affect the computation of interest on any income tax for the period commencing with the last day prescribed for the payment of such tax and ending with the last day of the taxable year in which the loss or credit arises. For example, if the carryback of a net operating loss, a net capital loss, an investment credit, or a WIN credit to a prior taxable period eliminates or reduces a deficiency in income tax for that period, the full amount of the deficiency will nevertheless bear interest at the annual rate referred to in the regulations under section 6621 from the last date prescribed for payment of such tax until the last day of the taxable year in which the loss or credit arose. Interest will continue to run beyond such last day on any portion of the deficiency which is not eliminated by the carryback. With respect to any portion of an investment credit carryback or a WIN credit carryback from a taxable year attributable to a net operating loss carryback or a capital loss carryback from a subsequent taxable year, such investment credit carryback or WIN credit carryback shall not affect the computation of interest on any income tax for the period commencing with the last day prescribed for the payment of such tax and ending with the last day of such subsequent taxable year.

(2) Where an extension of time for payment of income tax has been granted under section 6164 to a corporation expecting a net operating loss carryback or a net capital loss carryback, interest is payable at the annual rate established under section 6621 on the amount of such unpaid tax from the last date prescribed for payment thereof without regard to such extension.

(3) Where there has been an allowance of an overpayment attributable to a net operating loss carryback, a capital loss carryback, or an investment credit carryback and all or part of such allowance is later determined to be excessive, interest shall be computed on the excessive amount from the last day of the year in which the net operating loss, net capital loss, or investment credit arose until the date on which the repayment of such excessive amount is received. Where there has been an allowance of an overpayment with respect to any portion of an in-

vestment credit carryback from a taxable year attributable to a net operating loss carryback or a capital loss carryback from a subsequent taxable year and all or part of such allowance is later determined to be excessive, interest shall be computed on the excessive amount from the last day of such subsequent taxable year until the date on which the repayment of such excessive amount is received.

(f) *Applicable rules.*—(1) Any interest prescribed by section 6601 shall be assessed and collected in the same manner as tax and shall be paid upon notice and demand by the district director or the director of the regional service center. Any reference in the Code (except in subchapter B, chapter 63, relating to deficiency procedures) to any tax imposed by the Code shall be deemed also to refer to the interest imposed by section 6601 on such tax. Interest on a tax may be assessed and collected at any time within the period of limitation on collection after assessment of the tax to which it relates. For rules relating to the period of limitation on collection after assessment, see section 6502.

(2) No interest under section 6601 shall be payable on any interest provided by such section. This paragraph (f)(2) shall not apply after December 31, 1982, with respect to interest accruing after such date, or accrued but unpaid on such date. See § 301.6622-1.

(3) Interest will not be imposed on any assessable penalty, addition to the tax (other than an addition to tax described in section 6601(e)(2)(B)), or additional amount if the amount is paid within 21 calendar days (10 business days if the amount assessed and shown on the notice and demand equals or exceeds $100,000) from the date of the notice and demand. If interest is imposed, it will be imposed only for the period from the date of the notice and demand to the date on which payment is received. This paragraph (f)(3) is applicable with respect to any notice and demand made after December 31, 1996.

(4) If notice and demand is made after December 31, 1996, for any amount and the amount is paid within 21 calendar days (10 business days if the amount assessed and shown on the notice and demand equals or exceeds $100,000) from the date of the notice and demand, interest will not be imposed for the period after the date of the notice and demand.

(5) For purposes of paragraphs (f)(3) and (4) of this section—

(i) The term *business day* means any day other than a Saturday, Sunday, legal holiday in the District of Columbia, or a statewide legal holiday in the state where the taxpayer resides or where the taxpayer's principal place of business is located. With respect to the tenth business day (after taking into account the first sentence of this paragraph (f)(5)(i)), see section 7503 relating to time for performance of acts where the last day falls on a statewide legal holiday in the state where the act is required to be performed.

Reg. § 301.6601-1(f)(5)(i)

(ii) The term *calendar day* means any day. With respect to the twenty-first calendar day, see section 7503 relating to time for performance of acts where the last day falls on a Saturday, Sunday, or legal holiday.

(6) No interest shall be imposed for failure to pay estimated tax as required by section 59 of the Internal Revenue Code of 1939 or section 6153 or 6154 of the Internal Revenue Code of 1954. [Reg. §301.6601-1.]

☐ [*T.D. 6234, 5-21-57. Amended by T.D. 6425, 11-10-59, T.D. 6498, 10-24-60, T.D. 6585, 12-27-61, T.D. 6730, 5-7-64, T.D. 7238, 12-28-72, T.D. 7301, 1-3-74, T.D. 7384, 10-21-75, T.D. 7838, 10-5-82; T.D. 7907, 8-22-83 and T.D. 8725, 7-21-97.*]

[Reg. §301.6602-1]

§301.6602-1. Interest on erroneous refund recoverable by suit.—Any portion of an internal revenue tax (or any interest, assessable penalty, additional amount, or addition to tax) which has been erroneously refunded, and which is recoverable by a civil action pursuant to section 7405, shall bear interest at the annual rate referred to in the regulations under section 6621 from the date of the payment of the refund. [Reg. §301.6602-1.]

☐ [*T.D. 6234, 5-21-57. Amended by T.D. 7384, 10-21-75.*]

INTEREST ON OVERPAYMENTS

[Reg. §301.6611-1]

§301.6611-1. Interest on overpayments.— (a) *General rule.*—Except as otherwise provided, interest shall be allowed on any overpayment of any tax at the annual rate referred to in the regulations under section 6621 from the date of overpayment of the tax.

(b) *Date of overpayment.*—Except as provided in section 6401(a), relating to assessment and collection after the expiration of the applicable period of limitation, there can be no overpayment of tax until the entire tax liability has been satisfied. Therefore, the dates of overpayment of any tax are the date of payment of the first amount which (when added to previous payments) is in excess of the tax liability (including any interest, addition to the tax, or additional amount) and the dates of payment of all amounts subsequently paid with respect to such tax liability. For rules relating to the determination of the date of payment in the case of an advance payment of tax, a payment of estimated tax, and a credit for income tax withholding, see paragraph (d) of this section.

(c) *Examples.*—The application of paragraph (b) may be illustrated by the following examples:

Example (1). Corporation X files an income tax return on March 15, 1955, for the calendar year 1954 disclosing a tax liability of $1,000 and elects to pay the tax in installments. Subsequent to payment of the final installment, the correct tax liability is determined to be $900.

Tax liability

Assessed	$1,000
Correct liability	900
Overassessment	100

Record of payments

March 15, 1955	$500
June 15, 1955	500

Since the correct liability in this case is $900, the payment of $500 made on March 15, 1955, and $400 of the payment made on June 15, 1955, are applied in satisfaction of the tax liability. The balance of the payment made on June 15, 1955 ($100) constitutes the amount of the overpayment, and the date on which such payment was made would be the date of the overpayment from which interest would be computed.

Example (2). Corporation Y files an income tax return for the calendar year 1954 on March 15, 1955, disclosing a tax liability of $50,000, and elects to pay the tax in installments. On October 15, 1956, a deficiency in the amount of $10,000 is assessed and is paid in equal amounts on November 15 and November 26, 1956. On April 15, 1957, it is determined that the correct tax liability of the taxpayer for 1954 is only $35,000.

Tax liability

Original assessment	$50,000
Deficiency assessment	10,000
Total assessed	60,000
Correct liability	35,000
Overassessment	25,000

Record of payments

March 15, 1955	$25,000
June 15, 1955	25,000
November 15, 1956	5,000
November 26, 1956	5,000

Since the correct liability in this case is $35,000, the entire payment of $25,000 made on March 15, 1955, and $10,000 of the payment made on June 15, 1955, are applied in satisfaction of the tax liability. The balance of the payment made on June 15, 1955 ($15,000), plus the amounts paid on November 15 ($5,000), and November 26, 1956 ($5,000), constitute the amount of the overpayment. The dates of the overpayments from which interest would be computed are as follows:

Date	Amount of overpayment
June 15, 1955	$15,000
November 15, 1956	5,000
November 26, 1956	5,000

The amount of any interest paid with respect to the deficiency of $10,000 is also an overpayment.

(d) *Advance payment of tax, payment of estimated tax, and credit for income tax withholding.*—In the case of an advance payment of tax, a payment of estimated income tax, or a credit for income tax withholding, the provisions of section 6513 (except the provisions of subsection (c) thereof), applicable in determining the date of payment of tax for purposes of the period of limitations on credit or refund, shall apply in determining the date of overpayment for purposes of computing interest thereon.

(e) *Refund of income tax caused by carryback.*—If any overpayment of tax imposed by subtitle A of the Code results from the carryback of a net operating loss, a net capital loss, an investment credit, or a work incentive (WIN) credit, such overpayment, for purposes of this section, shall be deemed not to have been made prior to the end of the taxable year in which the loss or credit arises, or, with respect to any portion of an investment credit carryback or a WIN credit carryback from a taxable year attributable to a net operating loss carryback or a capital loss carryback from a subsequent taxable year, such overpayment shall be deemed not to have been made prior to the close of such subsequent taxable year.

(f) *Refund of income tax caused by carryback of foreign taxes.*—For purposes of paragraph (a) of this section, any overpayment of tax resulting from a carryback of tax paid or accrued to foreign countries or possessions of the United States shall be deemed not to have been paid or accrued before the close of the taxable year under subtitle F of the Code of 1954 in which such taxes were in fact paid or accrued.

(g) *Period for which interest allowable in case of refunds.*—If an overpayment of tax is refunded, interest shall be allowed from the date of the overpayment to a date determined by the district director or the director of the regional service center, which shall be not more than 30 days prior to the date of the refund check. The acceptance of a refund check shall not deprive the taxpayer of the right to make a claim for any additional overpayment and interest thereon, provided the claim is made within the applicable period of limitation. However, if a taxpayer does not accept a refund check, no additional interest on the amount of the overpayment included in such check shall be allowed.

(h) *Period for which interest allowable in case of credits.*—(1) *General rule.*—If an overpayment of tax is credited, interest shall be allowed from the date of overpayment to the due date (as determined under subparagraph (2) of this paragraph) of the amount against which such overpayment is credited.

(2) *Determination of due date.*—(i) *In general.*—The term "due date", as used in this section, means the last day fixed by law or regulations for the payment of the tax (determined without regard to any extension of time), and not the date on which the district director or the director of the regional service center makes demand for the payment of the tax. Therefore, the due date of a tax (other than an additional assessment subject to the special rule provided by subdivision (iv) of this subparagraph) is the date fixed for the payment of the tax or the several installments thereof.

(ii) *Tax payable in installments.*—(a) *In general.*—In the case of a credit against a tax, where the taxpayer had properly elected to pay the tax in installments, the due date is the date prescribed for the payment of the installment against which the credit is applied.

(b) *Delinquent installment.*—If the taxpayer is delinquent in payment of an installment of tax and the notice and demand has been issued for the payment of the delinquent installment and the remaining installments, the due date of each remaining installment shall then be the date of such notice and demand.

(iii) *Tax or installment not yet due.*—If a taxpayer agrees to the crediting of an overpayment against tax or an installment of tax and the schedule of allowance is signed prior to the date on which such tax or installment would otherwise become due, then the due date of such tax or installment shall be the date on which such schedule is signed.

(iv) *Additional assessment satisfied by credit before January 1, 1958.*—In the case of a credit made before January 1, 1958, against an additional assessment, the due date of the tax satisfied by the credit is the date the additional assessment was made. For purposes of this subdivision, the term "additional assessment" means a further assessment of a tax of the same character previously paid in part, and includes the assessment of a deficiency as defined in section 6211.

(v) *Interest.*—In the case of a credit against interest that accrues for any period ending prior to January 1, 1983, the due date is the earlier of the date of assessment of such interest or December 31, 1982. In the case of a credit against interest that accrues for any period beginning on or after December 31, 1982, such interest is due as it economically accrues on a daily basis, rather than when it is assessed.

(vi) *Additional amount, addition to the tax, or assessable penalty.*—In the case of a credit against an additional amount, addition to the tax, or assessable penalty, the due date is the earlier of the date of assessment or the date from which such amount would bear interest if not satisfied by payment or credit.

(vii) *Estimated income tax for succeeding year.*—If the taxpayer elects to have all or part of the overpayment shown by his return applied to his estimated tax for his succeeding taxable year, no interest shall be allowed on such portion of the overpayment credited and such amount shall be applied as a payment on account of the estimated tax for such year or the installments thereof.

(i) [Reserved.]

(j) *Refund of overpayment.*—No interest shall be allowed on any overpayment of tax imposed by subtitle A of the Code if such overpayment is refunded—

Reg. §301.6611-1(j)

(1) In the case of a return filed on or before the last date prescribed for filing the return of such tax (determined without regard to any extension of time for filing such return), within 45 days after such last date, or

(2) After December 17, 1966, in the case of a return filed after the last day prescribed for filing the return, within 45 days after the date on which the return is filed.

However, in the case of any overpayment of tax by an individual (other than an estate or trust and other than a nonresident alien individual) for a taxable year beginning in 1974, "60 days" shall be substituted for "45 days" each place it appears in this paragraph.

(k) *Effective date.*—Paragraphs (h)(2)(v) and (h)(2)(vi) of this section are effective for credits made on or after August 25, 1992. [Reg. §301.6611-1.]

☐ [*T.D. 6234, 5-21-57. Amended by T.D. 6425,* 11-10-59; *T.D. 6498, 10-24-60; T.D. 6585, 12-27-61; T.D. 6730, 5-7-64; T.D. 7301, 1-3-74; T.D. 7384,* 10-21-75 *and T.D. 8524, 3-2-94.*]

DETERMINATION OF INTEREST RATE; COMPOUNDING OF INTEREST

[Reg. §301.6621-1]

§301.6621-1. Interest rate.—(a) *In general.*—The interest rate established under section 6621 shall be—

(1) On amounts outstanding before July 1, 1975, 6 percent per annum (or 4 percent in the case of certain extensions of time for payment of

After	And before
June 30, 1975	February 1, 1976
January 31, 1976	February 1, 1978
January 31, 1978	February 1, 1980
January 31, 1980	February 1, 1982
January 31, 1982	January 1, 1983

(3) On amounts outstanding after December 31, 1982, the adjusted rate established by the Commissioner under section 6621(b). This adjusted rate shall be published by the Commissioner in a Revenue Ruling. See §301.6622-1 for application of daily compounding in determining interest accruing after December 31, 1982. Because interest accruing after December 31, 1982, accrues at the prescribed rate per annum compounded daily, the effective annual percentage rate of interest will exceed the prescribed rate of interest.

(b) [Reserved]

(c) *Applicability of interest rate.*—(1) *Computation.*—Interest and additions to tax on any amount outstanding on a specific day shall be computed at the annual rate applicable on such day.

(2) *Additions to tax.*—Additions to tax under any section of the Code that refers to the annual rate established under this section, including sections 644(a)(2)(B), 4497(c)(2), 6654(a), and 6655(a) and (g), shall be computed at the same rate per annum as the interest rate set forth under paragraph (a) of this section.

(3) *Interest.*—Interest provided for under any section of the Code that refers to the annual rate established under this section, including sections 47(d)(3)(G), 167(q), 6332(c)(1), 6343(c), 6601(a), 6602, 6611(a), 7426(g), and section 1961(c)(1) or 2411 of Title 28 of the United States Code, shall be computed at the rate per annum set forth under paragraph (a) of this section.

taxes as provided in sections 6601(b) and (j) prior to amendment by section 7(b) of the Act of Jan. 3, 1975 (Pub. L. 93-625, 88 Stat. 2115), and certain overpayments of the unrelated business income tax as provided in section 514(b)(3)(D), prior to its amendment by such Act).

(2) On amounts outstanding—

	Rate per annum (percent)
	9 percent
	7 percent
	6 percent
	12 percent
	20 percent

(d) *Examples.*—The provisions of this section may be illustrated by the following examples. Example (6) illustrates the computation of interest for interest accruing after December 31, 1982.

Example (1). A, an individual, files an income tax return for the calendar year 1974 on April 15, 1975, showing a tax due of $1,000. A pays the $1,000 on September 1, 1975. Pursuant to section 6601(a), interest on the underpayment of $1,000 is computed at the rate of 6 percent per annum from April 15, 1975, to June 30, 1975, a total of 76 days. Interest for 63 days, from June 30, 1975, to September 1, 1975, shall be computed at the rate of 9 percent per annum.

Example (2). An executor of an estate is granted, in accordance with section 6161(a)(2)(A), a two-year extension of time for payment of the estate tax shown on the estate tax return, which tax was otherwise due on January 15, 1974. The tax is paid on January 15, 1976. Interest on the underpayment shall be computed at the rate of 4 percent per annum from January 15, 1974, to June 30, 1975, and at the rate of 9 percent per annum from June 30, 1975, to January 15, 1976.

Example (3). X, a corporation, files its 1973 corporate income tax return on March 15, 1974, and pays the balance of tax due shown thereon. On August 1, 1975, an assessment of a deficiency is made against X with respect to such tax. The deficiency is paid on October 1, 1975. Interest at the rate of 6 percent per annum is due on the deficiency from March 15, 1974, the due date of the return, to June 30, 1975, and at the rate of 9 percent per annum from June 30, 1975, to October 1, 1975.

Example (4). Y, an individual, files an amended individual income tax return on October 1, 1975, for the refund of an overpayment of income tax Y made on April 15, 1975. Interest is allowed on the overpayment to December 1, 1975. Pursuant to section 6611(a), interest is computed at the rate of 6 percent per annum from April 15, 1975, the date of overpayment, to June 30, 1975. Interest from June 30, 1975, to December 1, 1975, shall be computed at the rate of 9 percent per annum.

Example (5). A, an individual, is liable for an addition to tax under section 6654 for the underpayment of estimated tax from April 15, 1975 until January 15, 1976. The addition to tax shall be computed at the annual rate of 6 percent per annum from April 15, 1975, to June 30, 1975, and at the annual rate of 9 percent per annum from June 30, 1975, to January 15, 1976.

Example (6). B, an individual, files an income tax return for calendar year 1980 on April 15, 1981, showing a tax due of $1,000. B pays the $1,000 on March 1, 1983. Under section 6601(a), interest on the $1,000 underpayment is due from April 15, 1981, to March 1, 1983. Such interest is computed at the rate of 12 percent per annum, simple interest, from April 15, 1981, to January 31, 1982, and at the rate of 20 percent per annum, simple interest, from January 31, 1982, to December 31, 1982, and at the rate of 16 percent per annum, compounded daily, from December 31, 1982, to March 1, 1983. The total simple interest accrued but unpaid at the end of December 31, 1982, is combined with the $1,000 underpayment for purposes of determining the amount of daily compounded interest to be charged from December 31, 1982, to March 1, 1983. [Reg. § 301.6621-1.]

☐ [*T.D. 7384, 10-21-75. Amended by T.D. 7907, 8-22-83.*]

[Reg. § 301.6621-2T]

§ 301.6621-2T. Questions and answers relating to the increased rate of interest on substantial underpayments attributable to certain tax motivated transactions (Temporary).—The following questions and answers relate to the increased rate of interest on substantial underpayments attributable to certain tax motivated transactions as provided in section 6621(d) of the Internal Revenue Code of 1954, as added by section 144 of the Tax Reform Act of 1984 (Pub. L. 98-369, 98 Stat. 682):

Q-1. What is the annual interest rate under section 6621 for purposes of computing the amount of interest that must be paid under section 6601 (relating to interest on underpayments)?

A-1. In general, the annual interest rate for purposes of section 6601 is the adjusted rate of interest established under section 6621(b) and § 301.6621-1 ("adjusted rate"). If, however, a tax motivated underpayment (as defined in A-2 of this section) for a taxable year is substantial (as defined in A-7 of this section), section 6621(d) provides that the annual rate of interest with respect to the tax motivated underpayment is

120 percent of the adjusted rate ("120 percent rate"), rounded to the nearest tenth of a percent.

Q-2. What is a tax motivated underpayment?

A-2. A tax motivated underpayment is the portion of a deficiency (as defined in section 6211) of tax imposed by subtitle A (income taxes) that is attributable to any of the following tax motivated transactions:

(1) Any instance in which the value of any property, or the adjusted basis of any property, claimed on a return is 150 percent or more of the amount determined to be the correct amount of such valuation or adjusted basis (*i.e.*, a valuation overstatement within the meaning of section 6659(c)(1));

(2) Any loss disallowed for any period by reason of section 465(a) or any amount included in gross income by reason of section 465(e);

(3) Any credit disallowed for any period by reason of section 46(c)(8) or section 48(d)(6);

(4) Any loss disallowed for any period with respect to a straddle, as defined in section 1092(c), but without regard to sections 1092(d) and (e);

(5) Any use of an accounting method that may result in a substantial distortion of income for any period (see A-3 of this section); and

(6) Any deduction disallowed with respect to any other tax motivated transaction (see A-4 of this section).

Q-3. What accounting methods may result in a substantial distortion of income for any period under A-2(5) of this section?

A-3. A deduction or credit disallowed, or income included, in any of the circumstances listed below shall be treated as attributable to the use of an accounting method that may result in a substantial distortion of income and shall thus be a tax motivated transaction that results in a tax motivated underpayment:

(1) Any deduction disallowed for any period by reason of section 464 or section 278(b), relating to certain expenses of farming syndicates;

(2) In the case of a taxpayer who computes taxable income using the cash receipts and disbursements method of accounting, any interest deduction disallowed for any period by reason of section 461(g), relating to prepaid interest, provided the interest is not paid with respect to indebtedness incurred in connection with (i) the purchase, refinancing, or improvement of the principal residence of the taxpayer, or (ii) the purchase of consumer goods by the taxpayer;

(3) Any interest deduction disallowed for any period because the amount of the claimed deduction was computed using a method resulting in an amount of interest for a period that exceeds the true cost of the indebtedness for the period computed by applying the effective rate of interest on the loan to the unpaid balance of the loan for that period (*i.e.*, the economic accrual of interest for the period), provided the interest is not accrued with respect to indebtedness incurred in connection with (i) the purchase, refinancing, or improvement of the principal residence of the taxpayer, or (ii) the purchase of consumer goods

by the taxpayer (see Rev. Rul. 83-84, 1983-1 C.B. 97, and sections 163(e), 446(b), and 483);

(4) Any deduction disallowed for any period under section 709, relating to organization or syndication expenditures of a partnership;

(5) In the case of any expenditure described in section 248(b) that was incurred by an S corporation, any deduction disallowed because it exceeds the amount allowable under section 248, relating to organizational expenditures;

(6) Any deduction disallowed for any period under section 267(a), relating to transactions between related taxpayers;

(7) Any deduction disallowed for any period, or any income required to be included for any period, under section 467, relating to certain payments for the use of property or services;

(8) Any deduction disallowed for any period under section 461(i), relating to certain deductions of tax shelters; and

(9) In the case of a taxpayer who computes taxable income using the cash receipts and disbursements method of accounting, any deduction disallowed for any period because (i) the expenditure resulting in the deduction was a deposit rather than a payment, (ii) the expenditure was prepaid for tax avoidance purposes and not for a business purpose, or (iii) the deduction resulted in a material distortion of income (see, *e.g.*, Rev. Rul. 79-229, 1979-2 C.B. 210).

Q-4. Are any transactions other than those specified in A-2 of this section and those involving the use of accounting methods under circumstances specified in A-3 of this section considered tax motivated transactions under A-2(6) of this section?

A-4. Yes. Deductions disallowed under the following provisions are considered to be attributable to tax motivated transactions:

(1) Any deduction disallowed for any period under section 183, relating to an activity engaged in by an individual or an S corporation that is not engaged in for profit, and

(2) Any deduction disallowed for any period under section 165(c)(2), relating to any transaction not entered into for profit.

Q-5. How is the amount of a tax motivated underpayment determined?

A-5. Except as provided in A-6 of this section, the amount of a tax motivated underpayment is determined in the following manner:

(1) Calculate the amount of the tax liability for the taxable year as if all items of income, gain, loss, deduction, or credit, had been reported properly on the income tax return of the taxpayer ("total tax liability"); and

(2) Without taking into account any adjustments to items of income, gain, loss, deductions, or credit that are attributable to tax motivated transactions (as defined in A-2 through A-4 of this section), calculate the amount of the tax liability for the taxable year as if all other items of income, gain, loss, deduction, or credit had been reported properly on the income tax return of the taxpayer ("tax liability without regard to tax motivated transactions").

(3) The difference between the total tax liability and the tax liability without regard to tax motivated transactions is the amount of the tax motivated underpayment.

Example. Taxpayer A, a calendar year taxpayer, files his 1984 income tax return reporting $70,000 of taxable income and $23,171 of tax liability. On January 20, 1986, A enters into a closing agreement with the Internal Revenue Service that includes the following adjustments:

Section 162 deduction disallowed (not tax motivated)	$7,500
Loss disallowed under section 465 (tax motivated—see A-2(2) of this section)	$5,000
Section 170 deduction disallowed because of a valuation overstatement (tax motivated—see A-2(1) of this section)	$10,000
Loss disallowed with respect to a straddle as defined in section 1092(c) (tax motivated—see A-2 (4) of this section)	$7,000
Other adjustments (none of which are tax motivated)	$4,000

The tax motivated underpayment is determined in the following manner:

1. $70,000 + 33,500	reported taxable income (add all adjustments to items of income, gain, loss, deduction, or credit (including tax motivated transactions subject to section 6621 (d)))
$103,500	tax = $39,685 ("total tax liability")
2. $ 70,000 + 11,500	reported taxable income (add adjustments to items of income, gain, loss, deduction, or credit other than those with respect to items that are tax motivated)
$ 81,500	tax = $28,691 ("tax liability without regard to tax motivated transactions")

The tax motivated underpayment (*i.e.*, the underpayment attributable to tax motivated transactions) is $10,994 ($39,685 – $28,691). Accordingly, the interest on $10,994 would be computed at the 120 percent rate.

The remainder of the underpayment (*i.e.*, the underpayment not attributable to tax motivated transactions) is $5,520 ($28,691 (tax liability without regard to tax motivated items) – $23,171 (tax paid with return)). The interest on $5,520 would be computed at the adjusted rate.

Q-6: How are the amounts of the tax motivated underpayment and the underpayment attributable to fraud or negligence determined if all or a portion of the taxpayer's underpayment is attributable to one or more tax motivated transactions and all or a portion is subject to the addition to tax imposed by section 6653(a)(2) (in the case of an underpayment attributable to negligence or intentional disregard) or section 6653(b)(2) (in the case of an underpayment attributable to fraud)?

A-6: If all or a portion of the taxpayer's underpayment is attributable to tax motivated transactions, and all or a portion is attributable

Reg. §301.6621-2T

to fraudulent or negligent items (*i.e.*, items that result in an underpayment subject to the addition to tax imposed by section 6653(a)(2) or (b)(2)), the amount of the tax motivated underpayment and the underpayment attributable to fraud or negligence is determined in the following manner:

(1) Determine the following amounts:

(i) The tax liability for the taxable year of the taxpayer as if all items of income, gain, loss, deduction, or credit had been reported properly on the income tax return of the taxpayer ("total tax liability");

(ii) The tax liability for the taxable year of the taxpayer as if all items of income, gain, loss, deduction, or credit without taking into account adjustments to items of income, gain, loss, deduction, or credit that are both (a) attributable to tax motivated transactions and (b) subject to section 6653(a)(2) or section 6653(b)(2), had been reported properly on the income tax return of the taxpayer ("tax liability without regard to fraudulent or negligent tax motivated items");

(iii) The tax liability for the taxable year of the taxpayer as if all items of income, gain, loss, deduction, or credit, without taking into account adjustments to items of income, gain, loss, deduction, or credit that are subject to section 6653(a)(2) or section 6653(b)(2), had been reported properly on the income tax return of the taxpayer ("tax liability without regard to fraudulent or negligent items");

(iv) The tax liability for the taxable year of the taxpayer as if all items of income, gain, loss, deduction, or credit, without taking into account adjustments to items of income, gain, loss, deduction, or credit that are either subject to section 6653(a)(2) or section 6653(b)(2) or attributable to tax motivated transactions, had been reported properly on the income tax return of the taxpayer ("tax liability without regard to tax motivated or fraudulent or negligent items").

(2) The tax motivated underpayment attributable to fraudulent or negligent items is the excess of the total tax liability over the tax liability determined without regard to fraudulent or negligent tax motivated items ((i)-(ii)).

(3) The tax motivated underpayment is the sum of (a) the tax motivated underpayment attributable to fraudulent or negligent items ((i)-(ii)) plus (b) the excess of the tax liability without regard to fraudulent or negligent items over the tax liability without regard to tax motivated or fraudulent or negligent items ((iii)-(iv)). Interest on this underpayment is computed at the 120 percent rate.

(4) The underpayment attributable to fraudulent or negligent items is the excess of the total tax liability over the tax liability without regard to fraudulent or negligent items ((i)-(iii)). The section 6653 addition to tax is 50 percent of the interest on this underpayment computed at the 120 percent rate on an amount equal to the tax motivated underpayment attributable to fraudulent or negligent items (computed in (2)) and at the adjusted rate on the remainder.

Example. Taxpayer A, a calendar year taxpayer, files his 1984 income tax return reporting $70,000 of taxable income and $23,171 of tax liability. On January 20, 1986, A enters into a closing agreement with the Internal Revenue Service that includes the following adjustments:

Section 162 deduction disallowed (not tax motivated but fraudulent or negligent)	$7,500
Loss disallowed under section 465(a) (tax motivated—see A-2(2) of this section—and fraudulent or negligent)	$5,000
Section 170 deduction disallowed because of a valuation overstatement (tax motivated—see A-2(1) of this section—but not fraudulent or negligent)	$10,000
Loss disallowed with respect to a straddle as defined in section 1092(c) (tax motivated—see A-2(4) of this section—but not fraudulent or negligent)	$7,000
Other adjustments (none of which are tax motivated or fraudulent or negligent)	$4,000

The tax motivated underpayment is determined in the following manner:

(1)(i)	$ 70,000	reported taxable income
	+ 33,500	(add all adjustments)
	$103,500	tax = $39,685 ("total tax liability")
(ii)	$ 70,000	reported taxable income
	+ 28,500	(all adjustments other than those with respect to items that are both tax motivated and fraudulent or negligent)
	$ 98,500	tax = $37,185 ("tax liability without regard to fraudulent or negligent tax motivated items")
(iii)	$ 70,000	reported taxable income
	+ 21,000	(all adjustments other than those with respect to items that are fraudulent or negligent)
	$ 91,000	tax = $33,435 ("tax liability without regard to fraudulent or negligent items")
(iv)	$ 70,000	reported taxable income
	+ 4,000	(all adjustments other than those with respect to items that are either tax motivated or fraudulent or negligent)
	$ 74,000	tax = $25,091 ("tax liability without regard to tax motivated or fraudulent or negligent items")

(2) The tax motivated underpayment attributable to fraudulent or negligent items is $2,500 ((i)-(ii) or $39,685-$37,185).

(3) The tax motivated underpayment is $10,844 ((2) + (iii) − (iv)) or $2,500 + ($33,435 − $25,091)). Interest on $10,844 is computed at the 120 percent rate.

(4) The underpayment attributable to fraudulent or negligent items is $6,250 ((i) − (iii) or $39,685 − $33,435). The section 6653 addition to tax is 50 percent of the interest on $6,250, com-

puted at the 120 percent rate on an amount equal to the tax motivated underpayment attributable to fraudulent or negligent items ($2,500) and at the adjusted rate on the remainder ($3,750).

(5) In summary, therefore, the total underpayment is $16,514 (total tax liability ($39,685) less reported tax liability ($23,171)) of which $10,844 accrues interest at the 120 percent rate and $5,670 ($16,514 − $10,844) accrues interest at the adjusted rate. In addition, $6,250 of the underpayment is subject to the section 6653(a)(2) or section 6653(b)(2) addition to tax. The underlying interest, upon which the addition to tax is based, is computed using the 120 percent rate for the portion of the underpayment subject to section 6621(d) ($2,500) and the adjusted rate for the portion that is not subject to section 6621(d) ($3,750).

Q-7. Does the 120 percent rate apply to all tax motivated underpayments?

A-7. No. The 120 percent rate applies only if the tax motivated underpayment for the taxable year is substantial. A tax motivated underpayment is substantial only if it exceeds $1,000. If, for example, a taxpayer has a $600 underpayment attributable to a valuation overstatement (within the meaning of section 6659(c)(1)) and a $500 underpayment attributable to a loss disallowed under section 465(a), the amount of the tax motivated underpayment is $1,100. Because the amount of the tax motivated underpayment is thus substantial, the 120 percent rate applies.

Q-8. How do carryovers affect the amount of the tax motivated underpayment and the amount of the underpayment attributable to fraudulent or negligent items?

A-8. For purposes of A-5 and A-6 of this section, a net operating loss carryover, capital loss carryover, or credit carryover is treated as a deduction or credit in the year in which taken into account. In any computation of tax liability required under A-5 or A-6 of this section (i.e., total tax liability, tax liability without regard to tax motivated transactions, etc.), the amount of such deduction or credit is the amount of the carryover determined as if the taxpayer had properly reported in each taxable year all items of income, gain, loss, deduction, or credit affecting the amount of the carryover other than adjustments of a type not taken into account in such computation of tax liability. A net operating loss carryback, capital loss carryback, or credit carryback is not taken into account, however, in determining the amount of the tax motivated underpayment or the amount of the underpayment attributable to fraud or negligence for periods before the last date prescribed for filing the income tax return for the taxable year in which the carryback arises (determined without regard to extensions).

Q-9. What amount is subject to the 120 percent rate if the amount of a taxpayer's unpaid tax for a year is less than the taxpayer's substantial tax motivated underpayment?

A-9. The 120 percent rate applies with respect to the lesser of—

(1) The amount of unpaid tax for the taxable year determined in accordance with § 301.6601-1; or

(2) The substantial tax motivated underpayment for the taxable year.

Q-10. What is the effective date for the 120 percent rate?

A-10. The 120 percent rate applies to interest accruing on a deficiency attributable to a substantial tax motivated underpayment after December 31, 1984, including interest accruing with respect to transactions described in A-3 and A-4 of this section, regardless of the date prescribed for payment of the tax.

Example. Taxpayer A files his income tax return on April 15, 1983 (the last date prescribed for payment of tax for taxable year 1982 under section 6601). In January 1985, Taxpayer A files a petition in the Tax Court in response to a statutory notice of deficiency for taxable year 1982, which includes a tax motivated underpayment of $10,000. In September 1986, the Tax Court enters a decision for the Internal Revenue Service. Under section 6601, interest accrues at the adjusted rate, compounded daily, on tax motivated underpayments outstanding before January 1, 1985, and at the 120 percent rate, compounded daily, on amounts outstanding after December 31, 1984. The underpayment that is subject to the 120 percent rate includes both the $10,000 tax motivated underpayment and the interest that accrued on the underpayment at the adjusted rate from April 16, 1983, through December 31, 1984.

Q-11. Can a taxpayer stop the running of interest on a tax motivated underpayment by application of a remittance?

A-11. Yes. The running of interest on a tax liability stops on the date the remittance (either a payment of tax or a deposit in the nature of a cash bond) is received by the Internal Revenue Service, regardless of when the liability is assessed or the remittance is actually applied against the taxpayer's account. A taxpayer must make a remittance for both the tax liability and the interest that has accrued as of the date of remittance to stop the running of interest on both the tax liability and the accrued interest with respect to the liability. (See Rev. Proc. 84-58.) Taxpayers cannot make partial remittances applicable only to tax motivated underpayments. Under A-9 of this section, the 120 percent rate applies to the amount of unpaid tax to the extent that amount does not exceed the tax motivated underpayment. Therefore, a partial remittance is applied first to any tax due that is not attributable to a tax motivated underpayment. The excess of the partial remittance over tax that is not attributable to a tax motivated underpayment, if any, will then be applied to tax due that is attributable to a tax motivated underpayment.

Q-12. Does the 120 percent rate apply to interest accruing on interest, penalties, additional amounts, or additions to tax as provided in section 6601(e)(2)?

A-12. The 120 percent rate applies only to taxes imposed by subtitle A (income taxes) and to interest accrued with respect to such taxes. The penalties, additional amounts, and additions to tax specified in section 6601(e)(2) are not imposed by subtitle A and are not, therefore, included in the amount of a tax motivated underpayment. They are, however, included in the amount of unpaid tax for purposes of A-9 of this section.

Example. Taxpayer A, for taxable year 1984, has a $10,000 tax motivated underpayment and a $2,000 addition to tax for a total unpaid tax of $12,000. If A makes a $5,000 payment of tax, he will still have a $10,000 tax motivated underpayment but will now have only $7,000 of unpaid tax. Pursuant to A-9 of this section, therefore, the 120 percent rate would apply to the $7,000 of unpaid tax. [Temporary Reg. § 301.6621-2T.]

☐ [*T.D.* 7998, 12-26-84.]

[Reg. § 301.6621-3]

§ 301.6621-3. Higher interest rate payable on large corporate underpayments.—(a) *In general.*—Section 6621 establishes the interest rate for purposes of computing the amount of interest that must be paid under section 6601, relating to interest on underpayments of tax. Section 6621(a)(2) provides that the underpayment rate is the sum of the Federal short-term rate (determined under section 6621(b)) plus 3 percentage points. That underpayment rate is referred to hereinafter as the "section 6621(a)(2) rate." Section 6621(c) and this section, however, provide that the underpayment rate on any large corporate underpayment is the sum of the Federal short-term rate (determined under section 6621(b)) plus 5 percentage points. This higher underpayment rate is referred to hereinafter as the "section 6621(c) rate." The section 6621(c) rate applies only for periods after the applicable date (as determined in paragraph (c) of this section).

(b) *Large corporate underpayment.*—(1) *Defined.*—For purposes of section 6621(c) and this section, "large corporate underpayment" means any underpayment of a tax by a C corporation for any taxable period if the amount of the threshold underpayment of the tax (as defined in paragraph (b)(2)(ii) of this section) for that taxable period exceeds $100,000.

(2) *Underpayment of a tax.*—(i) *In general.*—As used in section 6621(c) and this section, "underpayment of a tax" means the excess of a tax imposed by the Internal Revenue Code over the amount of such tax paid on or before the last date prescribed for payment. Except as provided in paragraph (b)(2)(ii) of this section, "tax" for such purposes includes interest, penalties, additional amounts, and additions to tax. *See* sections 6601(e)(1), 6665(a), and 6671(a). Thus, the section 6621(c) rate generally applies to any interest, penalties, additional amounts, and additions to

tax, as well as to the underlying tax with respect to which such amounts are imposed.

(ii) *Threshold underpayment of a tax.*—Solely for purposes of this section and not for any other purpose under section 6621(c) or elsewhere in the interpretation or administration of the federal tax laws, a "threshold underpayment of a tax" is the excess of a tax imposed by the Internal Revenue Code (exclusive of interest, penalties, additional amounts, and additions to tax) for the taxable period over the amount of such tax paid on or before the last date prescribed for payment. Thus, any payments made after the last date prescribed for payment (for example, by way of an amended return) will not affect the existence of a threshold underpayment. In determining whether there is a threshold underpayment, different types of taxes (such as income tax and FICA tax) and amounts that relate to different taxable periods are not added together.

(iii) *When determined.*—(A) *In general.*—The existence of a threshold underpayment of a tax and the amount of a large corporate underpayment are generally determined only when an assessment is made with respect to the taxable period. Thus, the amount of a deficiency or proposed deficiency set forth in a letter or notice pursuant to which the applicable date is determined (under paragraph (c) of this section) does not determine whether there is a large corporate underpayment.

(B) *Judicial determinations.*—Notwithstanding any prior assessment made with respect to a taxable period, the section 6621(c) rate does not apply if, after a federal court determines the taxpayer's liability for a period, the threshold underpayment for that taxable period does not exceed $100,000. See *Example 3* in paragraph (d) of this section.

(iv) *Special rule.*—The section 6621(c) rate is not used to compute the interest charges that a taxpayer timely assesses against itself in return for using a method of tax accounting or reporting that defers the payment of tax, such as the interest charges relating to passive foreign investment companies under section 1291(c) and installment obligations of nondealers under section 453A(c). However, to the extent such charges are not paid on or before the last date prescribed for payment and therefore become part of an underpayment of a tax, the section 6621(c) rate will apply to such amounts for periods after the applicable date (as determined in paragraph (c) of this section).

(3) *C corporation defined.*—For purposes of section 6621(c)(3)(A) and this section, "C corporation" means, with respect to any taxable period, a corporation that is a C corporation during any part of the taxable period. Interest on a large corporate underpayment for a taxable period continues to be imposed at the section 6621(c) rate even if during or after the taxable period—

(i) The taxpayer ceases to be a C corporation; or

(ii) The underpayment becomes the liability of a successor or transferee that is not a C corporation.

(4) *Taxable period.*—For purposes of section 6621(c) and this section, the "taxable period" is the taxable year in the case of any tax imposed by subtitle A of the Internal Revenue Code. In the case of any other tax, the "taxable period" is the period ·to which the underpayment relates. For example, the taxable period for an underpayment of FICA taxes is the calendar quarter. If the underpayment does not relate to a particular period (for example, in the case of certain transactional excise taxes), the "taxable period" is the period covered by a return on which the tax is required to be shown.

(5) *Last date prescribed for payment.*—For purposes of this section, the "last date prescribed for payment" means the last date prescribed for payment as determined, without regard to any extension of time, under section 6601(b).

(c) *Applicable date.*—(1) *In general.*—The section 6621(c) rate applies only to periods after the applicable date. Pursuant to the effective date of section 6621(c) and paragraph (e) of this section, however, the section 6621(c) rate will not apply prior to January 1, 1991, even if the applicable date is prior to December 31, 1990. A letter or notice relating to a particular type of tax creates an applicable date only for that type of tax. For example, a letter or notice with respect to FUTA tax will not create an applicable date with respect to income tax for the same taxable year.

(2) *When deficiency procedures apply.*—The applicable date, in the case of any underpayment of a tax to which the deficiency procedures of subchapter B of Chapter 63 of the Internal Revenue Code apply, is the 30th day after the earlier of—

(i) The date on which the Service sends the taxpayer the first letter of proposed deficiency that allows the taxpayer an opportunity for administrative review in the Service's Office of Appeals (commonly called a "30-day letter"); or

(ii) The date on which the Service sends a deficiency notice under section 6212 of the Internal Revenue Code (commonly called a "90-day letter").

(3) *When deficiency procedures do not apply.*—The applicable date, in the case of any underpayment of a tax to which the deficiency procedures do not apply, is the 30th day after the date on which the Service sends the first letter or notice that notifies the taxpayer of an assessment or proposed assessment of the tax. In the case of income taxes, for example, the deficiency procedures do not apply to amounts shown as due on the taxpayer's return if the taxpayer fails to remit the full amount on or before the last date prescribed for payment, and to amounts attributable to mathematical or clerical errors on a return (unless a request for abatement is filed by the taxpayer under section 6213(b)). Because no 30-day letter or 90-day letter is issued to the taxpayer in such cases, the applicable date is the 30th day after the date on which an assessment notice under section 6303 of the Internal Revenue Code is sent.

(4) *Partnership items.*—For purposes of section 6621(c) and this paragraph (c), 60-day letters and the notices described in sections 6223(a)(1) and 6223(a)(2) (relating to administrative proceedings at the partnership level) are not treated as letters of proposed deficiency that allow the taxpayer an opportunity for administrative review in the Service's Office of Appeals, deficiency notices under section 6212 of the Internal Revenue Code, or letters or notices that notify the taxpayer of an assessment or proposed assessment of the tax. Thus, in the absence of any other letter or notice described in paragraph (c)(2) or (c)(3) of this section that establishes an earlier applicable date, the applicable date in the case of any underpayment of a tax attributable, in whole or in part, to a partnership item (as defined in section 6231(a)(3)) is the 30th day after the date on which the Service sends the first letter or notice that notifies the taxpayer of an assessment of the tax.

(5) *Exception for payment of amount shown as due.*—(i) *In general.*—A letter or notice will be disregarded for purposes of determining the applicable date if the taxpayer makes a payment equal to the amount shown as due in the letter or notice within 30 days from the date that the Service sends the letter or notice.

(ii) *Special transition rule.*—A letter or notice sent by the Service prior to January 1, 1991, will be disregarded by the Service for purposes of determining the applicable date if the taxpayer makes a payment on or before January 31, 1991, equal to the amount shown as due in the letter or notice plus a reasonable estimate of the interest payable on such amount computed by applying the section 6621(a)(2) rate. If the taxpayer has received two or more letters or notices with respect to the same tax for the same taxable period and pays the amount shown as due in the last letter or notice sent prior to December 19, 1990, (plus a reasonable estimate of the interest), all of the prior letters and notices with respect to the same tax for the same taxable period will be disregarded under this paragraph (c)(5)(ii). In the case of an assessment notice, the payment of the amount of interest shown as due on the last assessment notice sent to the taxpayer prior to December 19, 1990, will be treated as a payment of a reasonable estimate of the interest payable on the amount shown in that assessment notice or in any prior assessment notice sent with respect to the same tax for the same taxable period. The special transition rule in this paragraph (c)(5)(ii) applies even if the payment is not made within 30 days of the date on which the Service sent the letter or notice.

Reg. §301.6621-3(b)(3)(i)

(iii) *Amount shown as due.*—For purposes of section 6621(c)(2)(B)(ii) and this paragraph (c)(5), the "amount shown as due" in any letter or notice means the total amount of tax, as well as any interest, penalties, additional amounts, and additions to tax that are set forth in the letter or notice. A deposit in the nature of a cash bond will not be considered a payment of the amount shown as due.

(6) *Exception for withdrawn letters and notices.*—(i) *Letters of proposed deficiency.*—A letter of proposed deficiency will be disregarded for purposes of determining the applicable date if the letter of proposed deficiency is issued as a result of an administrative error either to the wrong taxpayer or for the wrong taxable period.

(ii) *Deficiency notices.*—A deficiency notice under section 6212 of the Internal Revenue Code will be disregarded for purposes of determining the applicable date if the deficiency notice is rescinded under section 6212(d).

(iii) *Assessment letters and notices.*—A letter or notice that notifies the taxpayer of an assessment or proposed assessment of tax will be disregarded for purposes of determining the applicable date if the full amount of tax assessed is subsequently abated.

(d) *Examples.*—The application of this section may be illustrated by the following examples.

Example 1. V, a C corporation, timely files Form 941 on January 31, 1991, for the fourth quarter of 1990. On September 1, 1992, the Service sends V a section 6303 notice and demand reflecting an additional FICA tax liability for that quarter of $90,000. Interest computed at the section 6621(a)(2) rate totals $15,000 as of September 1, 1992. Accordingly, V's underpayment of FICA tax for the fourth quarter of 1990 exceeds $100,000. However, V's $90,000 threshold underpayment of FICA tax for that taxable period is less than $100,000, so that the section 6621(c) rate will not apply to the underpayment for that taxable period.

Example 2. (i) W, a C corporation, timely files its 1990 income tax return on March 15, 1991, showing a liability of $95,000, of which W pays only $35,000 with the return. On June 1, 1991, the Service sends W an assessment notice reflecting the balance due of $60,000 plus interest computed at the section 6621(a)(2) rate. W pays all amounts due on August 1, 1991. On July 1, 1993, the Service sends W a 90-day letter (without having sent a 30-day letter) reflecting an additional income tax deficiency of $85,000 for the taxable year 1990. W files a petition in the Tax Court within 90 days. In 1995, the Tax Court determines a $50,000 income tax deficiency (exclusive of interest, penalties, additional amounts, and additions to tax) for 1990, which the Service promptly assesses against W.

(ii) As a result of the combination of the failure to timely pay the $60,000 of income tax reported as due on the return and the Tax Court's determination of an additional deficiency of $50,000, W's threshold underpayment of income tax for

1990 is $110,000. Because W is a C corporation and the threshold underpayment for 1990 exceeds $100,000, the section 6621(c) rate applies to W's 1990 large corporate underpayment for periods after the applicable date.

(iii) The applicable date is July 1, 1991, the 30th day after the date on which the Service sent W the first assessment notice.

(iv) From March 16, 1991, through July 1, 1991, interest on W's 1990 underpayment of income tax (including any interest, penalties, additional amounts, and additions to tax) is computed at the section 6621(a)(2) rate. From July 2, 1991, such interest is computed at the section 6621(c) rate.

(v) If W had paid the amount shown as due on the June 1, 1991, assessment notice on or before June 30, 1991, instead of on August 1, 1991, the applicable date would have been July 31, 1993.

(vi) Assume that W had paid the amount shown as due on the June 1, 1991, assessment notice on or before June 30, 1991. If W had made a $40,000 deposit in the nature of a cash bond on July 15, 1993, the applicable date would be July 31, 1993. Moreover, the deposit would have no effect on the existence or amount of W's threshold underpayment or large corporate underpayment for 1990. In such a case, however, when the Service assesses the amount due from W in 1995, the deposit would be treated as a payment made as of July 15, 1993, for purposes of computing interest due after that date. As a result, interest would accrue after July 15, 1993, (at the section 6621(c) rate) only on the portion of W's 1990 underpayment that exceeds the $40,000 deposit amount.

Example 3. (i) X, a C corporation, filed its 1989 income tax return on September 17, 1990, pursuant to an automatic extension. X enclosed payment of the $7,500 balance reported on the return as due (plus interest). On January 1, 1992, the Service sends X a written notification that X's 1989 income tax return is being examined. This written notification also contains a request that X provide supplemental information with respect to particular deductions totalling $1.5 million. On July 1, 1993, the Service sends X a 30-day letter proposing a $450,000 deficiency (without any reference to penalties, additional amounts, additions to tax, and interest) with respect to 1989. On December 15, 1993, the Service sends X a 90-day letter asserting a deficiency of $300,000 (excluding penalties, additional amounts, additions to tax, and other interest). X does not file a Tax Court petition and the Service assesses the $300,000 (plus interest and penalties) on April 1, 1994. On April 5, 1994, X pays the full amount assessed. Thereafter, X timely files an administrative claim for refund and a refund suit in federal district court for the amounts assessed on April 1, 1994. On September 30, 1995, the federal district court determines that, exclusive of interest and penalties, X overpaid its 1989 income tax by $250,000.

(ii) The April 1, 1994, assessment establishes at that time that X's threshold underpayment of

Reg. §301.6621-3(d)

income tax for 1989 is $300,000. Because X is a C corporation and the threshold underpayment for 1989 exceeds $100,000, X's underpayment of income tax for 1989 is a large corporate underpayment to which the section 6621(c) rate applies for periods after the applicable date. X's decision to file a refund claim does not affect, in and of itself, either the existence of a threshold underpayment or the amount of X's large corporate underpayment.

(iii) For purposes of determining the amount of interest to assess on April 1, 1994, the applicable date is July 31, 1993, the 30th day after the date on which the Service sent X a 30-day letter. The January 1, 1992, notice of examination and request for additional information has no effect on the applicable date. Similarly, the September 30, 1995, federal district court decision has no effect on the applicable date.

(iv) From March 16, 1990, through July 31, 1993, interest on X's 1989 underpayment of income tax (including any interest, penalties, additional amounts, and additions to tax) is computed at the section 6621(a)(2) rate. From August 1, 1993, through April 5, 1994, such interest is computed at the section 6621(c) rate.

(v) Because of the federal district court's decision that X's underpayment, exclusive of interest and penalties, was only $50,000, X does not have a large corporate underpayment of income tax for 1989. Thus, the interest X paid with respect to the remaining $250,000 in taxes (exclusive of interest and penalties) becomes part of the overpayment and will be refunded. In addition, any interest computed at the section 6621(c) rate for the period from August 1, 1993, through April 5, 1994, should be recomputed at the section 6621(a)(2) rate and the difference refunded.

Example 4. (i) Y, a C corporation, timely filed its 1989 income tax return on March 15, 1990, and enclosed payment of the amount reported on the return as due. On May 1, 1990, the Service sent to Y an assessment notice for $1,000 resulting from a math error on Y's return. Y did not request an abatement of the assessment pursuant to section 6213(b). Instead, Y paid the $1,000, plus interest, on July 31, 1990. On March 31, 1992, the Service sends Y a 90-day letter showing an income tax deficiency for 1989 of $125,000 (exclusive of interest, penalties, additional amounts, and additions to tax). No 30-day letter had been issued previously to Y in connection with its 1989 taxable year. Y does not file a petition with the Tax Court, but files an amended return for 1989 on April 15, 1992, showing $30,000 of tax due. Y pays this amount (plus interest from March 15, 1990, computed at the section 6621(a)(2) rate) with the amended return. Shortly thereafter, the Service assesses the $125,000 deficiency (plus interest) and credits the April 15, 1992, payment against the assessment.

(ii) Y's threshold underpayment for 1989 is $125,000 notwithstanding Y's April 15, 1992, payment of $30,000. Because Y is a C corporation and the threshold underpayment for 1989 exceeds $100,000, Y has a large corporate underpayment of income tax for the taxable period 1989 to which the section 6621(c) rate applies for periods after the applicable date.

(iii) Because Y paid the $1,000 amount shown as due on the math error assessment notice (plus interest) on or before January 31, 1991, the applicable date is April 30, 1992, the 30th day after the 90-day letter is sent.

(iv) From March 16, 1990, through April 30, 1992, interest is computed on Y's underpayment of income tax (including any interest, penalties, additional amounts, and additions to tax) at the section 6621(a)(2) rate. From May 1, 1992, such interest is computed at the section 6621(c) rate.

(v) If Y had not paid the $1,000 amount shown as due on the math error assessment notice (plus interest) on or before January 31, 1991, the applicable date would have been May 31, 1990, and interest would be computed at the section 6621(c) rate beginning on January 1, 1991. If, however, Y had timely requested an abatement of the assessment under section 6213(b), the applicable date would be April 30, 1992.

Example 5. (i) Effective January 1, 1993, Y converts from a C corporation to an S corporation. On January 31, 1993, Y files its 1992 FUTA tax return and encloses a payment equal to the amount reported as due on the return. On March 15, 1993, Y files its 1992 income tax return and encloses a payment equal to the amount reported as due on the return. On August 1, 1993, the Service sends to Y an assessment notice for $150,000 of FUTA tax, plus interest, with respect to calendar year 1992. Y pays the full amount shown as due in the assessment notice on August 7, 1993. On January 1, 1995, Y files an amended income tax return for 1992 showing $15,000 of tax due. Y pays this amount with the amended return. On February 10, 1995, the Service sends Y an assessment notice for the interest payable on the $15,000. Y pays this interest on February 13, 1995.

(ii) Y's threshold underpayment of FUTA tax for 1992 is $150,000. Because Y was a C corporation in 1992 and the threshold underpayment of FUTA tax for 1992 exceeds $100,000, Y has a large corporate underpayment of FUTA tax. However, Y's threshold underpayment of income tax for the same taxable period (*i.e.*, calendar 1992) is $15,000, so that Y does not have a large corporate underpayment of income tax for that year.

(iii) Because Y pays within 30 days the amount shown as due on the August 1, 1993, assessment notice, there is no applicable date with respect to the large corporate underpayment of FUTA tax for 1992.

(iv) All of the interest payable with respect to the 1992 underpayments of FUTA and income taxes is computed at the section 6621(a)(2) rate.

(v) If Y had not paid the amount shown as due on the August 1, 1993, FUTA tax assessment notice within 30 days, the applicable date would have been August 31, 1993, (the 30th day after the assessment notice is sent). Thus, interest would have been computed at the section 6621(c) rate after that date, even though Y is not at that time a C corporation.

(vi) If the amended 1992 income tax return Y files on January 1, 1995, had shown $115,000 of tax due instead of $15,000, Y's threshold underpayment of income tax for 1992 would have been $115,000. Because Y was a C corporation in 1992 and the threshold underpayment of income tax for that year would have exceeded $100,000, Y would have a large corporate underpayment of income tax for that year. However, because Y would have paid the amount shown as due in the February 10, 1995, assessment notice within 30 days of when that assessment notice was sent, there would have been no applicable date with respect to that large corporate underpayment and the section 6621(c) rate would have not applied.

Example 6. (i) On August 1, 1990, the Service sent to Z, a C corporation, an assessment notice for $200,000 of income tax, plus $30,000 in interest and penalties, with respect to calendar year 1988. Subsequent assessment notices were sent to Z on September 12, 1990, October 10, 1990, and November 14, 1990, each including additional interest. The November 14, 1990, assessment notice provided that the total amount of tax, interest and penalties due was $242,000. On December 31, 1990, Z pays $230,000. On February 13, 1991, the Service sends Z an assessment notice for the remaining balance (plus additional interest thereon). On December 31, 1991, Z pays all amounts owed as of that date in connection with its 1988 income tax liability.

(ii) Z's threshold underpayment of income tax for 1988 is $200,000. Because Z is a C corporation and its threshold underpayment of income tax for 1988 exceeds $100,000, Z has a large corporate underpayment for 1988 to which the section 6621(c) rate applies for periods after the applicable date.

(iii) Notwithstanding Z's payment of $230,000 on December 31, 1990, the applicable date with respect to the large corporate underpayment of 1988 income tax is August 31, 1990, the 30th day after the date on which the Service sent the first assessment notice.

(iv) From March 16, 1989, to December 31, 1990, interest is computed on Z's underpayment of income tax (including any interest, penalties, additional amounts and additions to tax) at the section 6621(a)(2) rate. From January 1, 1991, through December 31, 1991, interest is computed on that underpayment at the section 6621(c) rate.

(v) If Z had paid on or before January 31, 1991, the full $242,000 shown as due on the November 14, 1990, assessment notice, the applicable date with respect to any remaining unpaid interest would have been March 15, 1991, the 30th day after the Service sent the February 13, 1991, assessments notice.

(vi) The same result as in paragraph (v) of this *Example 6* would apply if the November 14, 1990, assessment notice had provided that only $150,000 was due with respect to calendar year 1988 (as a result of a correction by the Service of an error in its original August 1, 1990, assessment, and not as a result of any payment by Z), and if Z had paid that $150,000 on or before January 31, 1991.

(e) *Effective Date.*—Section 6621(c) and this section are effective for determining interest for periods after December 31, 1990, regardless of the taxable period to which the underlying tax may relate and even if the applicable date is prior to December 31, 1990. [Reg. § 301.6621-3.]

☐ [*T.D.* 8447, 11-10-92.]

[Reg. § 301.6622-1]

§ 301.6622-1. Interest compounded daily.— (a) *General rule.*—Effective for interest accruing after December 31, 1982, in computing the amount of any interest required to be paid under the Internal Revenue Code of 1954 or sections 1961(c)(1) or 2411 of Title 28, United States Code, by the Commissioner or by the taxpayer, or in computing any other amount determined by reference to such amount of interest, or by reference to the interest rate established under section 6621, such interest or such other amount shall be compounded daily by dividing such rate of interest by 365 (366 in a leap year) and compounding such daily interest rate each day.

(b) *Exception.*—Paragraph (a) of this section shall not apply for purposes of determining the amount of any addition to tax under sections 6654 or 6655 (relating to failure to pay estimated income tax).

(c) *Applicability to unpaid amounts on December 31, 1982.*—(1) *In general.*—The unpaid interest (or other amount) that shall be compounded daily includes the interest (or other amount) accrued but unpaid on December 31, 1982.

(2) *Illustration.*—The provisions of this (c) may be illustrated by the following example.

Example. Individual A files a tax return for calendar year 1981 on April 15, 1982, showing a tax due of $10,000. A pays $10,000 on December 31, 1982, but A does not pay any interest with respect to this underpayment until March 1, 1983, on which date A paid all amounts of interest with respect to the $10,000 underpayment of tax. On December 31, 1982, A's unsatisfied interest liability was $1,424.66 ($10,000 × 20 percent × 260/365 days). Interest, compounded daily, accrues on this unsatisfied interest obligation beginning on January 1, 1983, until March 1, 1983, the date the total interest obligation is satisfied. On March 1, 1983, the total interest obligation is $1,462.62, computed as follows:

Item	Amount
Unpaid tax at December 31, 1982 . . .	—0—
Unpaid interest at December 31, 1982	$1,424.66
Total unsatisfied obligation at December 31, 1982	$1,424.66
Interest from December 31, 1982, to March 1, 1983, at 16 percent per year compounded daily	$37.96
Total due, March 1, 1983	$1,462.62

[Reg. § 301.6622-1.]

☐ [*T.D.* 7907, 8-22-83.]

Additions to the Tax, Additional Amounts, and Assessable Penalties

ADDITIONS TO TAX AND ADDITIONAL AMOUNTS

See p. 20,601 for regulations not amended to reflect law changes

[Reg. §53.6651-1]

§53.6651-1. Failure to file tax return or to pay tax.—(a) *General rules.*—For general rules relating to the failure to file tax return or to pay tax, see the regulations under section 6651 contained in Part 301 of this chapter (Regulations on Procedure and Administration).

(b) *Special rule where foundation files return.*—(1) Except as provided in paragraph (b)(2) of this section, in the case of tax imposed by section 4941(a)(1) on any disqualified person, reasonable cause shall be presumed, for purposes of section 6651(a)(1), where the private foundation or trust described in section 4947(a)(2) files a return in good faith and such return indicates no tax liability with respect to such tax on the part of such disqualified person.

(2) Paragraph (b)(1) of this section shall not apply where the disqualified person knew of facts which, if known by the foundation, would have precluded the foundation from making the return, as filed, in good faith. [Reg. §53.6651-1.]

□ [T.D. 7368, 7-15-75.]

[Reg. §301.6651-1]

§301.6651-1. Failure to file tax return or to pay tax.—(a) *Addition to the tax.*—(1) *Failure to file tax return.*—In case of failure to file a return required under authority of—

(i) Subchapter A, chapter 61 of the Code, relating to returns and records (other than sections 6015 and 6016, relating to declarations of estimated tax, and part III thereof, relating to information returns);

(ii) Subchapter A, chapter 51 of the Code, relating to distilled spirits, wines, and beer;

(iii) Subchapter A, chapter 52 of the Code, relating to cigars, cigarettes, and cigarette papers and tubes; or

(iv) Subchapter A, chapter 53 of the Code, relating to machine guns, destructive devices, and certain other firearms; and

The regulations thereunder, on or before the date prescribed for filing (determined with regard to any extension of time for such filing), there shall be added to the tax required to be shown on the return the amount specified below unless the failure to file the return within the prescribed time is shown to the satisfaction of the district director, the director of the service center, or, as provided in paragraph (c) of this section, the Assistant Regional Commissioner (Alcohol, Tobacco and Firearms), to be due to reasonable cause and not to willful neglect. The amount to be added to the tax is 5 percent thereof if the failure is for not more than 1 month, with an additional 5 percent for each additional month

or fraction thereof during which the failure continues, but not to exceed 25 percent in the aggregate. The amount of any addition under this subparagraph shall be reduced by the amount of the addition under subparagraph (2) of this paragraph for any month to which an addition to tax applies under both subparagraphs (1) and (2) of this paragraph (a).

(2) *Failure to pay tax shown on return.*—In case of failure to pay the amount shown as tax on any return (required to be filed after December 31, 1969, without regard to any extension of time for filing thereof) specified in subparagraph (1) of this paragraph on or before the date prescribed for payment of such tax (determined with regard to any extension of time for payment), there shall be added to the tax shown on the return the amount specified below unless the failure to pay the tax within the prescribed time is shown to the satisfaction of the district director or the director of the service center to be due to reasonable cause and not to willful neglect. Except as provided in paragraph (a)(4) of this section, the amount to be added to the tax is 0.5 percent of the amount of tax shown on the return if the failure is for not more than 1 month, with an additional 0.5 percent for each additional month or fraction thereof during which the failure continues, but not to exceed 25 percent in the aggregate.

(3) *Failure to pay tax not shown on return.*—In the case of failure to pay any amount of any tax required to be shown on a return specified in paragraph (a)(1) of this section that is not so shown (including an assessment made pursuant to section 6213(b)) within 21 calendar days from the date of the notice and demand (10 business days if the amount assessed and shown on the notice and demand equals or exceeds $100,000) with respect to any notice and demand made after December 31, 1996, there will be added to the amount stated in the notice and demand the amount specified below unless the failure to pay the tax within the prescribed time is shown to the satisfaction of the district director or the director of the service center to be due to reasonable cause and not to willful neglect. Except as provided in paragraph (a)(4) of this section, the amount to be added to the tax is 0.5 percent of the amount stated in the notice and demand if the failure is for not more than 1 month, with an additional 0.5 percent for each additional month or fraction thereof during which the failure continues, but not to exceed 25 percent in the aggregate. For purposes of this paragraph (a)(3), see §301.6601-1(f)(5) for the definition of *calendar day* and *business day.*

(4) *Reduction of failure to pay penalty during the period an installment agreement is in effect.*— (i) *In general.*—In the case of a return filed by an individual on or before the due date for the return (including extensions)—

(A) The amount added to tax for a month or fraction thereof is determined by using 0.25 percent instead of 0.5 percent under paragraph (a)(2) of this section if at any time during the month an installment agreement under section 6159 is in effect for the payment of such tax; and

(B) The amount added to tax for a month or fraction thereof is determined by using 0.25 percent instead of 0.5 percent under paragraph (a)(3) of this section if at any time during the month an installment agreement under section 6159 is in effect for the payment of such tax.

(ii) *Effective date.*—This paragraph (a)(4) applies for purposes of determining additions to tax for months beginning after December 31, 1999.

(b) *Month defined.*—(1) If the date prescribed for filing the return or paying tax is the last day of a calendar month, each succeeding calendar month or fraction thereof during which the failure to file or pay tax continues shall constitute a month for purposes of section 6651.

(2) If the date prescribed for filing the return or paying tax is a date other than the last day of a calendar month, the period which terminates with the date numerically corresponding thereto in the succeeding calendar month and each such successive period shall constitute a month for purposes of section 6651. If, in the month of February, there is no date corresponding to the date prescribed for filing the return or paying tax, the period from such date in January through the last day of February shall constitute a month for purposes of section 6651. Thus, if a return is due on January 30, the first month shall end on February 28 (or 29 if a leap year), and the succeeding months shall end on March 30, April 30, etc.

(3) If a return is not timely filed or tax is not timely paid, the fact that the date prescribed for filing the return or paying tax, or the corresponding date in any succeeding calendar month, falls on a Saturday, Sunday, or a legal holiday is immaterial in determining the number of months for which the addition to the tax under section 6651 applies.

(c) *Showing of reasonable cause.*—(1) Except as provided in subparagraphs (3) and (4) of this paragraph, a taxpayer who wishes to avoid the addition to the tax for failure to file a tax return or pay tax must make an affirmative showing of all facts alleged as a reasonable cause for his failure to file such return or pay such tax on time in the form of a written statement containing a declaration that it is made under penalties of perjury. Such statement should be filed with the district director or the director of the service center with whom the return is required to be filed; *Provided,* That where special tax return of liquor dealers are delivered to an alcohol, tobacco and firearms officer working under the supervision of the Regional Director, Bureau of Alcohol, Tobacco and Firearms, such statement may be delivered with the return. If the district director, the director of the service center, or, where applicable, the Regional Director, Bureau of Alcohol, Tobacco and Firearms, determines that the delinquency was due to a reasonable cause and not to willful neglect, the addition to the tax will not be assessed. If the taxpayer exercised ordinary business care and prudence and was nevertheless unable to file the return within the prescribed time, then the delay is due to a reasonable cause. A failure to pay will be considered to be due to reasonable cause to the extent that the taxpayer has made a satisfactory showing that he exercised ordinary business care and prudence in providing for payment of his tax liability and was nevertheless either unable to pay the tax or would suffer an undue hardship (as described in §1.6161-1(b) of this chapter) if he paid on the due date. In determining whether the taxpayer was unable to pay the tax in spite of the exercise of ordinary business care and prudence in providing for payment of his tax liability, consideration will be given to all the facts and circumstances of the taxpayer's financial situation, including the amount and nature of the taxpayer's expenditures in light of the income (or other amounts) he could, at the time of such expenditures, reasonably expect to receive prior to the date prescribed for the payment of the tax. Thus, for example, a taxpayer who incurs lavish or extravagant living expenses in an amount such that the remainder of his assets and anticipated income will be insufficient to pay his tax, has not exercised ordinary business care and prudence in providing for the payment of his tax liability. Further, a taxpayer who invests funds in speculative or illiquid assets has not exercised ordinary business care and prudence in providing for the payment of his tax liability unless, at the time of the investment, the remainder of the taxpayer's assets and estimated income will be sufficient to pay his tax or it can be reasonably foreseen that the speculative or illiquid investment made by the taxpayer can be utilized (by sale or as security for a loan) to realize sufficient funds to satisfy the tax liability. A taxpayer will be considered to have exercised ordinary business care and prudence if he made reasonable efforts to conserve sufficient assets in marketable form to satisfy his tax liability and nevertheless was unable to pay all or a portion of the tax when it became due.

(2) In determining if the taxpayer exercised ordinary business care and prudence in providing for the payment of his tax liability, consideration will be given to the nature of the tax which the taxpayer has failed to pay. Thus, for example, facts and circumstances which, because of the taxpayer's efforts to conserve assets in marketable form, may constitute reasonable cause for nonpayment of income taxes may not constitute reasonable cause for failure to pay over

taxes described in section 7501 that are collected or withheld from any other person.

(3) If, for a taxable year ending on or after December 31, 1995, an individual taxpayer satisfies the requirement of §1.6081-4(a) of this chapter (relating to automatic extension of time for filing an individual income tax return), reasonable cause will be presumed, for the period of the extension of time to file, with respect to any underpayment of tax if—

(i) The excess of the amount of tax shown on the individual income tax return over the amount of tax paid on or before the regular due date of the return (by virtue of tax withheld by the employer, estimated tax payments, and any payment with an application for extension of time to file pursuant to §1.6081-4 of this chapter) is no greater than 10 percent of the amount of tax shown on the individual income tax return; and

(ii) Any balance due shown on the individual income tax return is remitted with the return.

(4) If, for a taxable year ending on or after December 31, 1972, a corporate taxpayer satisfies the requirements of §1.6081-3(a) (relating to an automatic extension of time for filing a corporation income tax return), reasonable cause shall be presumed, for the period of the extension of time to file, with respect to any underpayment of tax if—

(i) The amount of tax (determined without regard to any pre-payment thereof) shown on Form 7004, or the amount of tax paid on or before the regular due date of the return, is at least 90 percent of the amount of tax shown on the taxpayer's Form 1120, and

(ii) Any balance due shown on the Form 1120 is paid on, or before the due date of the return, including any extensions of time for filing.

(d) *Penalty imposed on net amount due.*— (1) *Credits against the tax.*—The amount of tax required to be shown on the return for purposes of section 6651(a)(1) and the amount shown as tax on the return for purposes of section 6651(a)(2) shall be reduced by the amount of any part of the tax which is paid on or before the date prescribed for payment of the tax and by the amount of any credit against the tax which may be claimed on the return.

(2) *Partial payments.*—(i) The amount of tax required to be shown on the return for purposes of section 6651(a)(2) shall, for the purpose of computing the addition for any month, be reduced by the amount of any part of the tax which is paid after the date prescribed for payment and on or before the first day of such month.

(ii) The amount of tax stated in the notice and demand for purposes of section 6651(a)(3) shall, for the purpose of computing the addition for any month, be reduced by the amount of any part of the tax which is paid before the first day of such month.

(e) *No addition to tax if fraud penalty assessed.*— No addition to the tax under section 6651 shall

be assessed with respect to an underpayment of tax if a 50-percent addition to the tax for fraud is assessed with respect to the same underpayment under section 6653(b). See section 6653(d).

(f) *Examples.*—The provisions of this section may be illustrated by the following examples:

Example (1). (a) Under section 6072(a), income tax returns of individuals on a calendar year basis must be filed on or before the 15th day of April following the close of the calendar year. Assume an individual filed his income tax return for the calendar year 1969 on July 20, 1970, and the failure to file on or before the prescribed date is not due to reasonable cause. The tax shown on the return is $800 and a deficiency of $200 is subsequently assessed, making the tax required to be shown on the return, $1,000. Of this amount, $300 has been paid by withholding from wages and $400 has been paid as estimated tax. The balance due as shown on the return of $100 ($800 shown as tax on the return less $700 previously paid) is paid on August 21, 1970. The failure to pay on or before the prescribed date is not due to reasonable cause. There will be imposed, in addition to interest, an additional amount under section 6651(a)(2) of $2.50, which is 2.5 percent (2% for the 4 months from April 16 through August 15, and 0.5% for the fractional part of the month from August 16 through August 21) of the net amount due as shown on the return of $100 ($800 shown on the return less $700 paid on or before April 15). There will also be imposed an additional amount under section 6651(a)(1) of $58, determined as follows:

20 percent (5% per month for the 3 months from April 16 through July 15 and 5% for the fractional part of the month from July 16 through July 20) of the net amount due of $300 ($1,000 required to be shown on the return less $700 paid on or before April 15)	$60
Reduced by the amount of the addition imposed under section 6651(a)(2) for those months	2
Addition to tax under section 6651(a)(1) .	$58

(b) A notice and demand for the $200 deficiency is issued on January 8, 1971, but the taxpayer does not pay the deficiency until December 23, 1971. In addition to interest there will be imposed an additional amount under section 6651(a)(3) of $10, determined as follows:

Addition computed without regard to limitation:	
6 percent (5¹/₂% for the 11 months from January 19, 1971, through December 18, 1971, and 0.5% for the fractional part of the month from December 19 through December 23) of the amount stated in the notice and demand ($200)	$12
Limitation on addition:	
25 percent of the amount stated in the notice and demand ($200)	$50

Reduced by the part of the addition under section 6651(a)(1) for failure to file attributable to the $200 deficiency (20% of $200) $40

Maximum amount of the addition under section 6651(a)(3) $10

Example (2). An individual files his income tax return for the calendar year 1969 on December 2, 1970, and such delinquency is not due to reasonable cause. The balance due, as shown on the return, of $500 is paid when the return is filed on December 2, 1970. In addition to interest and the addition for failure to pay under section 6651(a)(2) of $20, (8 months at 0.5% per month, 4%) there will also be imposed an additional amount under section 6651(a)(1) of $112.50, determined as follows:

Penalty at 5% for maximum of 5 months, 25% of $500 . . . . $125.00
Less reduction for the amount of the addition under section 6651(a)(2):
Amount imposed under section 6651(a)(2) for failure to pay for the months in which there is also an addition for failure to file—$2^{1}/2$ percent for the 5 months April 16 through September 15 of the net amount due ($500) $12.50
Addition to tax under section 6651(a)(1) $112.50

(g) *Treatment of returns prepared by the Secretary.*—(1). *In general.*—A return prepared by the Secretary under section 6020(b) will be disregarded for purposes of determining the amount of the addition to tax for failure to file any return pursuant to paragraph (a)(1) of this section. However, the return prepared by the Secretary will be treated as a return filed by the taxpayer for purposes of determining the amount of the addition to tax for failure to pay the tax shown on any return and for failure to pay the tax required to be shown on a return that is not so shown pursuant to paragraphs (a)(2) and (3) of this section, respectively.

(2) *Effective date.*—This paragraph (g) applies to returns the due date for which (determined without regard to extensions) is after July 30, 1996. [Reg. § 301.6651-1.]

☐ [T.D. 6268, 11-15-75. *Amended by T.D. 6498, 10-24-60; T.D. 6585, 7-21-71; T.D. 7160, 2-1-72; T.D. 7260, 2-9-73; T.D. 8651, 1-3-96; T.D. 8703, 12-30-96; T.D. 8725, 7-21-97; T.D. 8895, 8-17-2000 and T.D. 9163, 12-6-2004.]*

[Reg. § 301.6652-1]

§ 301.6652-1. Failure to file certain information returns.—(a) *Returns with respect to payments made in calendar years after 1962.*—(1) *Payments of dividends, interest, or patronage dividends aggregating $10 or more.*—In the case of each failure to file a statement required by—

(i) Section 6042(a)(1), relating to information returns with respect to payments of dividends aggregating $10 or more in a calendar year, in effect with respect to payments made after December 31, 1962,

(ii) Section 6044(a)(1), relating to information returns with respect to certain payments by cooperatives aggregating $10 or more in a calendar year, in effect with respect to payments made on or after the first day of the first taxable year of the cooperative beginning after December 31, 1962, with respect to patronage occurring on or after such first day, or

(iii) Section 6049(a)(1), relating to information returns with respect to payments of interest aggregating $10 or more in a calendar year, in effect with respect to payments made after December 31, 1962, and the regulations under such section, within the time prescribed for filing such statement (determined with regard to any extension of time for filing), there shall be paid by the person failing to so file the statement $10 for each such statement not so filed. However, the total amount imposed on the delinquent person for all such failures under section 6652(a) and this section during any calendar year shall not exceed $25,000.

(2) *Other payments; statements with respect to tips.*—In the case of each failure—

(i) To file a statement of a payment made to another person required under authority of section 6041, relating to information returns with respect to certain information at source, or section 6051(d), relating to information returns with respect to payments of wages as defined in section 3401(a), or section 6050A(a), relating to information returns with respect to remuneration of certain crew members defined in section 3121(b)(20), or

(ii) To furnish a statement required under authority of section 6053(b), relating to statements furnished by employers with respect to tips, or section 6050A(b), relating to statements furnished by fishing boat operators with respect to remuneration of certain crew members, within the time prescribed by regulations under those sections for filing such statements (determined with regard to any extension of time for filing), there shall be paid by the person failing to so file the statement $1 for each such statement not so filed. However, the total amount imposed on the delinquent person for all such failure during any calendar year shall not exceed $1,000.

(b) *Returns with respect to payments made in calendar years before 1963 and to certain payments by cooperatives after 1962.*—In the case of each failure to file a statement, with respect to a payment to another person, required under authority of—

(1) Section 6041, relating to information returns with respect to certain information at source, in effect with respect to payments made before 1963,

(2) Section 6042(1), relating to information returns with respect to payments of corporate dividends, in effect with respect to payments made before 1963,

(3) Section 6044, relating to information returns with respect to payments of patronage dividends, in effect with respect to payments made by a cooperative with respect to patronage occurring before the first day of the first taxable year of the cooperative beginning after December 31, 1962, or

(4) Section 6051(d), relating to information returns with respect to payments of wages as defined in section 3401(a), in effect with respect to payments made before 1963, and the regulations under such section, within the time prescribed for filing such statement (determined with regard to any extension of time for filing), there shall be paid by the person failing to so file such statement $1 for each such statement not so filed. However, the total amount imposed on the delinquent person for all such failures during any calendar year shall not exceed $1,000.

(c) *Returns with respect to reporting payments of wages in the form of group-term life insurance provided in a calendar year after December 31, 1963.*—In the case of each failure to file a return required by section 6052(a), relating to reporting payment of wages in the form of group-term life insurance provided for any employee on his life in a calendar year after December 31, 1963, and the regulations under such section, within the time prescribed for filing such return (determined with regard to any extension of time for filing), there shall be paid by the person failing to so file such return $10 for each such return not so filed. However, the total amount imposed on the delinquent person for all such failures under section 6652(a) and this section during any calendar year shall not exceed $25,000.

(d) *Returns with respect to transfer of stock or record title thereto pursuant to options exercised on or after January 1, 1964.*—In the case of each failure to file a statement of the transfer of stock or of record title thereto as required by section 6039(a) and the regulations under such section within the time prescribed for filing such statement (determined with regard to any extension of time for filing), there shall be paid by the corporation failing to so file such statement, $10 for each such statement not so filed. However, the total amount imposed on the delinquent corporation for all such failures under section 6652(a) and this section during any calendar year shall not exceed $25,000.

(e) *Manner of payment.*—The amount imposed under subsection (a), (b), or (c) of section 6652 and this section on any person shall be paid in the same manner as tax upon the issuance of a notice and demand therefor.

(f) *Showing of reasonable cause.*—The amount imposed by subsection (a), (b), or (c) of section 6652 shall not apply with respect to a failure to file a statement within the time prescribed if it is established to the satisfaction of the district di-

rector or the director of the internal revenue service center that such failure was due to reasonable cause and not to willful neglect. An affirmative showing of reasonable cause must be made in the form of a written statement, containing a declaration that it is made under the penalties of perjury, setting forth all the facts alleged as a reasonable cause.

(g) *Alcohol and tobacco taxes.*—For penalties for failure to file certain information returns with respect to alcohol and tobacco taxes, see, generally, subtitle E of the Code.

(h) *Tips.*—For regulations under section 6652(c) in respect of failure to report tips, see §31.6652-1 of this chapter (Employment Tax Regulations). [Reg. §301.6652-1.]

☐ [*T.D.* 6268, 11-15-57. *Amended by T.D.* 6425, 11-10-59; *T.D.* 6585, 12-27-61; *T.D.* 6628, 12-27-62; *T.D.* 6887, 6-23-66; *T.D.* 7001, 1-17-69; *T.D.* 7127, 6-14-71 *and T.D.* 7716, 8-26-80.]

[Reg. §301.6652-2]

§301.6652-2. Failure by exempt organizations and certain nonexempt organizations to file certain returns or to comply with section 6104(d) for taxable years beginning after December 31, 1969.—(a) *Exempt organization or trust.*—In the case of a failure to file a return required by—

(1) Section 6033, relating to returns by exempt organizations, trusts described in section 4947(a)(1) and nonexempt private foundations,

(2) Section 6034, relating to returns by certain trusts, or

(3) Section 6043(b), relating to returns regarding the liquidation, dissolution, termination, or substantial contraction of an exempt organization, within the time and in the manner prescribed for filing such return (determined with regard to any extension of time for filing), unless it is shown that such failure is due to reasonable cause, there shall be paid by the exempt organization or trust failing to file such return $10 for each day during which such failure continues. However, the total amount imposed on any exempt organization or trust under this paragraph for such failure with regard to any one return shall not exceed $5,000.

(b) *Managers.*—If an exempt organization or trust fails to file under section 6652(d)(1), the Commissioner may, by written demand, request that such organization or trust file the delinquent return within 90 days after the date of mailing of such demand, or within such additional period as the Commissioner shall determine is reasonable under the circumstances. If such organization or trust does not so file on or before the date specified in such demand, there shall be paid by the person or persons responsible for such failure to file $10 for each day after such date during which such failure continues, unless it is shown that such failure is due to reasonable cause. However, the total amount imposed under this paragraph on all persons responsible for such failure with regard to any one return shall not exceed $5,000.

(c) *Public inspection of private foundations' annual returns.*—(1) *In general.*—In the case of a failure to comply with the requirements of section 6104(d), relating to public inspection of private foundations' annual returns, within the time and in the manner prescribed for complying with section 6104(d), unless it is shown that such failure is due to reasonable cause, there shall be paid by the person or persons responsible for failing to comply with section 6104(d) $10 for each day during which such failure continues. However, the total amount imposed under this subparagraph on all persons responsible for any such failure with regard to any one annual return shall not exceed $5,000.

(2) *Amount imposed.*—The amount imposed under section 6652(d)(3) is $10 per day for a failure to comply with section 6104(d). For example, assume that an annual return must be filed by private foundation X on or before May 15, 1982, for the calendar year 1981. The foundation without reasonable cause does not comply with section 6104(d) by publishing notice of the availability of the annual return until July 30, 1982. In this case, the person failing to comply with section 6104(d) within the prescribed time is required to pay $760 for complying with section 6104(d) 76 days late.

(3) *Cross reference.*—For the penalty for willful failure to comply with section 6104(d), see § 301.6685-1.

(d) *Special rules.*—For purposes of section 6652(d) and this section—

(1) *Person.*—The term "person" means any officer, director, trustee, employee, member, or other individual whose duty it is to perform the act in respect of which the violation occurs.

(2) *Liability.*—If more than one person (as defined in subparagraph (1) of this paragraph) is liable for a failure to file or to comply with section 6652(d)(2) or (3), all such persons shall be jointly and severally liable with respect to such failure.

(e) *Manner of payment.*—The amount imposed under section 6652(d) and this section on any exempt organization, trust, or person (as defined in paragraph (d)(1) of this section) shall be paid in the same manner as tax upon the issuance of a notice and demand therefor.

(f) *Showing of reasonable cause.*—No amount imposed by section 6652(d) shall apply with respect to a failure to file or comply under this section if it is established to the satisfaction of the district director or director of the internal revenue service center that such failure was due to reasonable cause. An affirmative showing of reasonable cause must be made in the form of a written statement containing a declaration by the appropriate person (as defined in paragraph (d)(1) of this section), or, in his absence, by any officer, director, or trustee of the organization, that the statement is made under the penalties of

perjury, setting forth all the facts alleged as reasonable cause.

(g) *Group returns.*—If a central organization is authorized to file a group return on behalf of two or more of its local organizations for the taxable year in accordance with paragraph (d) of § 1.6033-2 (Income Tax Regulations), the responsibility for timely filing of such a return is placed upon the central organization for purposes of this section. Consequently, the amount imposed by section 6652(d)(1) for failure to file the group return shall be paid by the central organization and the amount imposed by section 6652(d)(2) for failure to file the group return within the time prescribed by the Commissioner shall be paid by the person or persons responsible for filing the group return.

(h) *Effective date.*—This section shall apply for taxable years beginning after December 31, 1969. [Reg. § 301.6652-2.]

☐ *[T.D. 7127, 6-14-71. Amended by T.D. 8026, 5-17-85.]*

[Reg. § 301.6652-3]

§ 301.6652-3. Failure to file information with respect to employee retirement benefit plan.— (a) *Amount imposed.*—(1) *Annual registration statement.*—The plan administrator (within the meaning of section 414(g)) of an employee retirement benefit plan defined in § 301.6057-1(a)(3) is liable for the amount imposed by section 6652(e)(1) in each case in which there is a failure to file information relating to the deferred vested retirement benefit of a plan participant, as required by section 6057(a) and § 301.6057-1, at the time and place and in the manner prescribed therefor (determined without regard to any extension of time for filing). The amount imposed by section 6652(e)(1) on the plan administrator is $1 for each participant with respect to whom there is a failure to file the required information, multiplied by the number of days during which the failure continues. However, the total amount imposed by section 6652(e)(1) on the plan administrator with respect to a failure to file on behalf of a plan for a plan year shall not exceed $5,000.

(2) *Notification of change in status.*—The plan administrator (within the meaning of section 411(g)) of an employee retirement benefit plan defined in § 301.6057-1(a)(3) is liable for the amount imposed by section 6652(e)(2) in each case in which there is a failure to file a notification of a change in plan status, as described in section 6057(b) and § 301.6057-2, at the time and place and in the manner prescribed therefor (determined without regard to any extension of time for filing). The amount imposed by section 6652(e)(2) on the plan administrator is $1 for each day during which the failure to so file a notification of a change in plan status continues. However, the total amount imposed by section 6652(e)(2) on the plan administrator with respect

to a failure to file a notification of a change in plan status shall not exceed $1,000.

(3) *Annual return of funded plan of deferred compensation.*—Under section 6652(f) the amount described in this subparagraph is imposed in each case in which there is a failure to file the annual return described in section 6058(a) on behalf of a plan described in § 301.6058-1(a) at the time and in the manner prescribed therefor (determined with regard to any extension of time for filing). The employer maintaining the plan is liable for the amount imposed with respect to a failure to so file the annual return in each case in which the employer must file the return under § 301.6058-1(a). The plan administrator (within the meaning of section 414(g)) is liable for the amount imposed in each case in which the plan administrator must file the return under § 301.6058-1(a). In the case of an individual retirement account or annuity described in section 408, the individual described in § 301.6058-1(d)(2) who must file the annual return under § 301.6058-1(d) is liable for the amount imposed with respect to a failure to so file the annual return. The amount imposed is $10 for each day during which the failure to file the annual return on behalf of a plan for a year continues. However, the total amount imposed with respect to a failure to file on behalf of a plan for any year shall not exceed $5,000.

(4) *Actuarial statement in case of mergers.*— The plan administrator (within the meaning of section 414(g)) is liable for an amount imposed by section 6652(f) in each case in which there is a failure to file the actuarial statement described in section 6058(b) at the time and in the manner prescribed therefor (determined with regard to any extension of time for filing). The amount imposed by section 6652(f) on the plan administrator is $10 for each day during which the failure to file the statement with respect to a merger, consolidation or transfer of assets or liabilities continues. However, the amount imposed by section 6652(f) on the plan administrator with respect to a failure to file the statement with respect to a merger, consolidation or transfer shall not exceed $5,000.

(5) *Information relating to certain trusts and annuity and bond purchase plans.*—Under section 6652(f) the amount described in this subparagraph is imposed in each case in which there is a failure to file a return or statement required by section 6047 at the time and in the manner prescribed therefor in § 1.6047-1 (determined without regard to any extension of time for filing). The amount is imposed upon the trustee of a trust described in section 401(a), custodian of a custodial account or issuer of an annuity contract, as the case may be (see § 1.6047-1(a)(1) (i) and (ii)). The amount imposed by section 6652(f) is $10 for each day during which the failure to file with respect to a payee for a calendar year continues. However, the amount imposed with respect to a failure to file with respect to a payee for a calendar year shall not exceed $5,000.

(b) *Showing of reasonable cause.*—(1) No amount imposed by section 6652(e) shall apply with respect to a failure to file information relating to the deferred vested retirement benefit of a plan participant under section 6057(a), or a failure to give notice of a change in plan status under section 6057(b), if it is established to the satisfaction of the director of the internal revenue service center at which the information or notice is required to be filed that the failure was due to reasonable cause.

(2) No amount imposed by section 6652(f) shall apply with respect to a failure to file a return or statement required by section 6058 or 6047, or a failure to provide material items of information called for on such a return or statement, if it is established to the satisfaction of the appropriate district director or the director of the internal revenue service center at which the return or statement is required to be filed that the failure was due to reasonable cause.

(3) An affirmative showing of reasonable cause must be made in the form of a written statement setting forth all the facts alleged as reasonable cause. The statement must contain a declaration by the appropriate individual that the statement is made under the penalties of perjury.

(c) *Joint liability.*—If more than one person is responsible for a failure to comply with sections 6057(a) or (b) or section 6058(a) or (b) or section 6047, all such persons shall be jointly and severally liable with respect to the failure.

(d) *Manner of payment.*—An amount imposed under section 6652(e) or (f) and this section shall be paid in the same manner as a tax upon the issuance of notice and demand therefor.

(e) *Effective dates.*—(1) *Annual registration statement.*—With respect to the annual registration statement described in section 6057(a), this section is effective—

(i) In the case of a plan to which only one employer contributes, for plan years beginning after December 31, 1975, with respect to participants who separate from service covered by the plan in plan years beginning after that date, and

(ii) In the case of a plan to which more than one employer contributes, for plan years beginning after December 31, 1977, and with respect to participants who complete two consecutive one-year breaks in service under the plan in service computation periods beginning after December 31, 1974.

(2) *Notification of change in status.*—With respect to the notification of change in plan status required by section 6057(b), this section is effective with respect to a change in status occurring within plan years beginning after December 31, 1975.

(3) *Annual return of employee benefit plan.*— With respect to the annual return of employee benefit plan required by section 6058(a), this section is effective for plan years beginning after September 2, 1974.

Reg. § 301.6652-3(a)(3)

(4) *Actuarial statement in case of mergers.*—With respect to the actuarial statement required by section 6058(b), this section is effective with respect to mergers, consolidations or transfers of assets or liabilities occurring after September 2, 1974.

(5) *Information relating to certain trusts and annuity and bond purchase plans.*—With respect to reports or statements required to be filed by section 6047 and the regulations thereunder, this section is effective with respect to calendar years ending after September 2, 1974. [Reg. §301.6652-3.]

☐ [*T.D.* 7561, 8-24-78.]

[Reg. §6a.6652(g)-1]

§6a.6652(g)-1. Failure to make return or furnish statement required under section 6039C (Temporary).—(a) *Amount imposed.*—In the case of each failure to meet the requirements of—

(1) Section 6039C, relating to information returns with respect to United States real property interests, or

(2) Section 6039C(b)(3), relating to statements to be provided to substantial investors in United States real property interests, on or before the date prescribed therefor (determined with regard to any extension of time for filing), the person failing to meet such requirement shall pay $25 for each day during which such failure continues.

(b) *Limitation.*—(1) *Domestic Corporations and Nominees.*—The maximum penalty which may be imposed under paragraph (a) of this section on a domestic corporation or nominee for failure to meet the requirements of section 6039C(a) for any calendar year is $25,000.

(2) *Partnerships, Trusts, Estates and Foreign Corporations.*—The maximum penalty which may be imposed on a partnership, trust, estate or foreign corporation for failure to meet the requirements of section 6039C(b) for any calendar year is $25,000.

(3) *Foreign persons holding U.S. real property interests and nominees.*—The maximum penalty which may be imposed on a foreign person holding a U.S. real property interest or on a nominee holding a U.S. real property interest for a foreign person for failure to meet the requirements of section 6039C(c) for any calendar year is the lesser of $25,000 or 5 percent of the aggregate of the fair market value of the U.S. real property interests owned by such person at any time during such calendar year.

(c) *Definitions.*—(1) *Fair market value.*—The term "fair market value" as used in this section is defined in §6a.897-1 (in the *Federal Register* 47 FR 41541).

(2) *Failure.*—The term "failure to meet the requirements of section 6039C" includes the failure to file a return for any calendar year on the date prescribed therefor (determined with regard to any extension of time for such filing), or the

omission on a return of one or more items of information required by section 6039C and the regulations thereunder to be provided on the return. It also includes the failure to furnish a statement required by section 6039C(b)(3). The failure to furnish a return required under section 6039C(b)(1) and the failure to furnish a statement to a substantial investor as required by section 6039C(b)(3), are separate failures for purposes of paragraph (a) of this section. Also, each failure to provide a statement to each substantial investor is a separate failure for purposes of paragraph (a). Thus, if an entity has 100 substantial investors as defined in section 6039C and fails to furnish any of the required statements to substantial investors, there are 100 separate failures to furnish the required statement.

(3) *Aggregate of the fair market value of the United States real property interests.*—The "aggregate of the fair market value of the U.S. real property interests" is the total of the fair market values of each U.S. real property interest owned at any time during the calendar year. Fair market value is determined as of December 31 of such year for property held at the end of the year and on the date of disposition for property disposed of during the year.

(d) *Attribution of ownership.*—For purposes of calculating the penalty limitation under §6a.6652(g)-1(b)(3) with respect to failure to meet the requirements of section 6039C(c), U.S. real property interests held by a partnership, trust, or estate shall be treated as owned proportionately by its partners or beneficiaries.

(e) *Exceptions.*—(1) *Provision of security.*—If a person otherwise required by section 6039C to file a return for a calendar year or furnish a statement to a substantial investor complies with the requirements of §6a.6039C-5 relating to furnishing security in lieu of filing such return, or its exempt, by virtue of §6a.6039C-5(f), from filing a return for such year with respect to its U.S. real property interests held, no penalty will be imposed under paragraph (a) of this section for failure to file such return or furnish such statement.

(2) *Showing of reasonable cause.*—No amount shall be imposed under paragraph (a) of this section for a failure described in such paragraph if it is established to the satisfaction of the director of the Internal Revenue Service Center, 11601 Roosevelt Boulevard, Philadelphia, Pennsylvania 19155 or in the case of returns concerning the Virgin Islands, the Commissioner of the Bureau of Internal Revenue, Tax Division, Charlotte Amalie, St. Thomas, V.I. 00801, that such failure is due to reasonable cause and not to willful neglect. An affirmative showing of reasonable cause must be made in the form of a written statement, made under the penalties of perjury, containing a declaration by the person failing to make a return or furnish a statement under section 6039C setting forth all the facts alleged as reasonable cause. Whether reasonable cause is shown may depend upon the subsection of sec-

tion 6039C under which the failure occurs. However, the fact that stock of a foreign corporation, or any other interest in any entity to which this section applies, is registered in bearer form does not constitute reasonable cause under this paragraph (e)(2) for failure to comply with the requirements of section 6039C(b). Also, the fact that disclosure of ownership would contravene a secrecy law of any country does not constitute reasonable cause for failure to comply with the requirements of section 6039C(b). Where a return has been filed and there is an omission of one or more items of information required by section 6039C and the regulations thereunder, one of the facts to be considered in determining whether such failure is due to reasonable cause is the materialty of the item omitted.

(3) *Spouse or parent already filed with respect to same property.*—If an individual files a return with respect to all U.S. real property interests held by such individual in accordance with §6a.6039C-4(b), no penalty shall be imposed

under this section on such individual's spouse or minor child for failure to file a return under §6a.6039C-4 with respect to the same property.

(f) *Manner of payment.*—The amount imposed under paragraph (a) of this section on any person shall be paid in the same manner as tax upon the issuance of a notice and demand therefor.

(g) *Examples.*—The provisions of this section may be illustrated by the following examples:

Example (1). Domestic corporation X is required under section 6039C(a) to make a return for calendar year 1982. X does not file such return on or before May 15, 1983 as required under §6a.6039C-1(c). The failure to file the return for calendar year 1982 continues throughout calendar years 1983, 1984, 1985, and 1986. The failure to file is not due to reasonable cause and no security has been furnished in lieu of filing. The maximum penalty which can be imposed on X for failure to file the 1982 return is $25,000, determined as follows:

	Penalty incurred in given year	Cumulative penalty for failure to file 1982 return
Total penalty incurred in 1983: ($25 per day × 230 days)	$5,750	$5,750
Total penalty incurred in 1984 (a leap year): ($25 per day × 366 days)	$9,150	$14,900
Total penalty incurred in 1985: ($25 per day × 365 days)	$9,125	$24,025
Total penalty incurred in 1986: (lesser of $25 per day × 365 days or $975 (remaining penalty which may be imposed))	$975	$25,000

Example (2). The facts are the same as in example (1) except that X also fails to file a return under section 6039C(a) for calendar year 1983. The failure to file its return for calendar year 1983 continues throughout calendar years 1984, 1985, 1986 and 1987. The total penalty which

may be imposed on X for failure to file its return for calendar year 1983 is $25,000. The amount of penalty which can be imposed on X in calendar years 1984, 1985, 1986 and 1987 is determined as follows:

	Penalty for 1982 failure	Penalty for 1983 failure	Total Penalty for given year
Penalty incurred in 1984 (a leap year):			
for failure to file 1982 return ($25 per day × 366 days)	$9,150		
for failure to file 1983 return ($25 per day × 230 days)		$5,750	
Total			$14,900
Penalty incurred in 1985:			
for failure to file 1982 return ($25 per day × 365 days)	$9,125		
for failure to file 1983 return ($25 per day × 365 days)		$9,125	
Total			$18,250
Penalty incurred in 1986:			
for failure to file 1982 return (lesser of $25 per day × 365 days or $975 (remaining penalty which may be imposed))	$975		
for failure to file 1983 return ($25 per day × 365 days)		$9,125	
Total			$10,100
Penalty incurred in 1987:			
for failure to file 1983 return (lesser of $25 per day × 365 days or $1,000 (remaining penalty which may be imposed))		$1,000	
Total			$1,000

Example (3). Foreign corporation Y is required under section 6039C(b)(1) to make a return for calendar year 1982. In addition, Y is required under section 6039C(b)(3) to furnish statements to each substantial investor in U.S. real property interests. Y has 10 such substantial investors. Y

does not file such return on or before May 15, 1983 as required under §6a.6039C-1(c), nor does it furnish the required statements on or before January 31, 1983 as required under §6a.6039C-3(h). The failure to file the return for calendar year 1982 and to furnish the required

Reg. §6a.6652(g)-1(e)(3)

statements for 1982 continues throughout calendar years 1984 and 1985. The failure to meet the requirements of section 6039C(b) are not due to reasonable cause and no security has been furnished in lieu of filing. The total penalty which can be imposed on Y for failure to file the return

Penalty incurred in 1982:

for failure to file return ($25 per day × 230 days) $5,750

for each failure to furnish a statement required by section 6039C(b)(3) ($25 per day × 10 statements × the 334 days from February 1, 1983 to December 31, 1983 ($83,500) but not more than $19,250 (which when added to $5,750 would total $25,000)) $19,250

Total $25,000

Since Y has incurred the maximum penalty for failure to file its return and statements required for 1982 by the end of calendar year 1983, no further penalty for these failures is imposed.

Example (4). Under section 6039C(c) foreign person Y is required to make a return for calendar year 1982. Y does not file such return on May 15, 1983 and the failure is not due to reasonable cause. No security has been furnished in lieu of filing. All properties owned by Y in 1982 are U.S. real property interests. Y purchased property M in January 1982 when its fair market value was $10,000. In March, Y purchased property N when its fair market value was $15,000. In November, Y sold property M for $20,000. The fair market value of property N on December 31, 1982, was $20,000. The total of the fair market values of M and N (M as of the date of its sale and N as of December 31, 1982) is $40,000. The maximum penalty which may be imposed on Y for failure to meet the requirements of section 6039C(c) for any calendar year is the lesser of $25,000 or 5 percent of the aggregate of the fair market values of the U.S. real property interests owned by Y at any time during such calendar year. Since $2,000 (5 percent of $40,000) is less than $5,750 ($25 times 230 days, the number of days in calendar year 1983 for which the failure continues), the maximum penalty which may be imposed on Y in 1983 is $2,000. Since the maximum penalty for the failure to file the 1982 return is incurred in 1983, no amount may be imposed for Y's continuing failure to file the return for calendar year 1982 during calendar years after 1983.

(h) *Effective date.*—This section shall apply to 1980 and subsequent calendar years. The calendar year 1980 shall be treated as beginning on June 19, 1980 and ending on December 31, 1980. [Temporary Reg. § 6a.6652(g)-1.]

□ [*T.D.* 7866, 1-1-83.]

[Reg. § 301.6653-1]

§ 301.6653-1. Failure to pay tax.— (a) *Negligence or intentional disregard of rules and regulations with respect to income or gift taxes.*—If any part of any underpayment, as defined in section 6653(c)(1) and paragraph (c)(1) of this section, of any income tax imposed by subtitle A or gift tax imposed by chapter 12 of subtitle B, of the Code, is due to negligence or intentional disregard of rules and regulations, but without intent to defraud, there shall be added to the tax

and statements required under section 6039C(b) for calendar year 1982 is $25,000. The amount of penalty incurred by Y in calendar year 1983 for failure to file the return and statements for calendar year 1982 is $25,000, determined as follows:

an amount equal to 5 percent of the underpayment.

(b) *Fraud.*—(1) If any part of any underpayment of tax, as defined in section 6653(c) and paragraph (c) of this section, required to be shown on a return is due to fraud, there shall be added to the tax an amount equal to 50 percent of the underpayment.

(2) If a 50 percent addition to the tax for fraud is assessed under section 6653(b) with respect to an underpayment—

(i) The addition to the tax under section 6651, relating to failure to file a tax return, will not be assessed with respect to the same underpayment, and

(ii) In the case of the income taxes imposed by subtitle A and the gift tax imposed by chapter 12 of subtitle B, the 5 percent addition to the tax under section 6653(a), relating to negligence and intentional disregard of rules and regulations, will not be assessed with respect to the same underpayment.

(c) *Definition of underpayment.*—(1) *Income, estate, gift, and chapter 41, 42, 43, and 44 taxes.*—In the case of income, estate, gift, and chapter 41, 42, 43, and 44 taxes, an underpayment for purposes of section 6653 and this section is—

(i) The total amount of all deficiencies as defined in section 6211, if a return was filed on or before the last date (determined with regard to any extension of time) prescribed for filing such return, or

(ii) The amount of the tax imposed by subtitle A or B, or chapter 41, 42, 43, or 44, as the case may be, if a return was not filed on or before the last date (determined with regard to any extension of time) prescribed for filing such return.

However, for purposes of paragraph (c)(1)(i) of this section, any amount of additional tax shown on the amended return, so called, filed after the due date of the return is a deficiency.

(2) *Other taxes.*—In the case of any tax other than an income, estate, gift or chapter 41, 42, 43, or 44 tax, an underpayment for purposes of section 6653 and this section is the amount by which the tax imposed exceeds—

(i) In the case of any tax with respect to which the taxpayer is required to file a return, the sum of (*a*) the amount shown as tax by the taxpayer upon his return filed in respect of such tax, but only if the return is filed on or before the

67,180
Additions to Tax and Additional Amounts
See p. 20,601 for regulations not amended to reflect law changes

last date (determined with regard to any extension of time) prescribed for filing such return, plus (b) any amount not shown on a return filed by the taxpayer which is paid in respect of such tax prior to the date prescribed for filing the return. The "amount shown as tax by the taxpayer upon his return" for the purposes of this subparagraph shall be determined without regard to any credit for an overpayment for any prior tax return period, and without regard to any adjustment made under section 6205(a), or section 6413(a), relating to special rules applicable to certain employment taxes.

(ii) In the case of any tax payable by stamp, the amount paid (on or before the date prescribed for payment) in respect of such tax. The amounts specified in subdivisions (i) and (ii) of this subparagraph shall be reduced, for purposes of determining the amount of the underpayment, by the amount of any rebates made. For purposes of this subparagraph, the term "rebates" means so much of an abatement, credit, refund, or other repayment as was made on the ground that the tax imposed was less than the excess of the amount specified in subdivision (i) or (ii) of this subparagraph, whichever is applicable, over any rebates previously made.

(d) *No delinquency penalty if fraud assessed.*— See paragraph (b)(2) of this section.

(e) *Failure to pay stamp tax.*—Any person (as defined in section 6671(b)) who willfully fails to pay any tax payable by stamp, coupons, tickets, books or other devices or methods prescribed by the Code or regulations promulgated thereunder, or willfully attempts in any manner to evade or defeat any such tax or the payment thereof, shall, in addition to other penalties provided by law, be liable to a penalty of 50 percent of the total amount of the underpayment of the tax.

(f) *Joint returns.*—No person filing a joint return shall be held liable for a fraud penalty except for his own personal fraudulent conduct. Thus, for the fraud penalty to apply to a taxpayer who files a joint return some part of the underpayment in such return must be due to the fraud of such taxpayer. A taxpayer shall not be subject to the fraud penalty solely by reason of the fraud of a spouse and his filing of a joint return with such spouse. [Reg. § 301.6653-1.]

□ [*T.D. 6286, 11-15-57. Amended by T.D. 6498, 10-24-60, T.D. 7320, 8-5-74, T.D. 7498, 7-12-77 and T.D. 7838, 10-5-82.*]

[Reg. § 1.6654-1]

§ 1.6654-1. Addition to the tax in the case of an individual.—(a) *In general.*—(1) Section 6654 imposes an addition to the taxes under chapters 1 and 2 of the Code in the case of any underpayment of estimated tax by an individual (with certain exceptions described in section 6654(d)), including any underpayment of estimated qualified State individual income taxes which are treated pursuant to section 6361(a) as if they were imposed by chapter 1. This addition to the

tax is in addition to any applicable criminal penalties and is imposed whether or not there was reasonable cause for the underpayment. The amount of the underpayment for any installment date is the excess of—

(i) The following percentages of the tax shown on the return for the taxable year or, if no return was filed, of the tax for such year, divided by the number of installment dates prescribed for such taxable year:

(A) 80 percent in the case of taxable years beginning after December 31, 1966, of individuals not referred to in section 6073(b) (relating to income from farming or fishing);

(B) 70 percent in the case of taxable years beginning before January 1, 1967, of such individuals; and

(C) 66²⁄₃ percent in the case of individuals referred to in section 6073(b); over

(ii) The amount, if any, of the installment paid on or before the last day prescribed for such payment.

(2) The amount of the addition is determined at the annual rate referred to in the regulations under section 6621 upon the underpayment of any installment of estimated tax for the period from the date such installment is required to be paid until the 15th day of the fourth month following the close of the taxable year, or the date such underpayment is paid, whichever is earlier. For purposes of determining the period of the underpayment (i) the date prescribed for the payment of any installment of estimated tax shall be determined without regard to any extension of time, and (ii) a payment of estimated tax on any installment date, to the extent that it exceeds the amount of the installment determined under subparagraph (1)(i) of this paragraph for such installment date, shall be considered a payment of any previous underpayment.

(3) In determining the amount of the installment paid on or before the last day prescribed for payment thereof, the estimated tax shall be computed without any reduction for the amount which the taxpayer estimates as his credit under section 31 (relating to tax withheld at source on wages), and the amount of such credit shall be deemed a payment of estimated tax. An equal part of the amount of such credit shall be deemed paid on each installment date (determined under section 6153) for the taxable year unless the taxpayer establishes the dates on which all amounts were actually withheld. In the latter case, all amounts withheld shall be considered as payments of estimated tax on the dates such amounts were actually withheld. Under section 31 the entire amount withheld during a calendar year is allowed as a credit against the tax for the taxable year which begins in such calendar year. However, where more than one taxable year begins in any calendar year no portion of the amount withheld during the calendar year will be treated as a payment of estimated tax for any taxable year other than the last taxable year beginning in such calendar year. The

rules prescribed in this subparagraph for determining the time as of which the amount withheld shall be deemed paid are applicable even though such amount was withheld during a taxable year preceding that for which the credit is allowed.

(4) The term "tax" when used in subparagraph (1)(i) of this paragraph shall mean—

(i) The tax imposed by chapter 1 of the Code (other than by section 56 or, for taxable years ending before September 30, 1968, the tax surcharge imposed by section 51), including any qualified State individual income taxes which are treated pursuant to section 6361(a) as if they were imposed by chapter 1, plus

(ii) For taxable years beginning after December 31, 1966, the tax imposed by chapter 2 of the Code, minus

(iii) All credits allowed by part IV, subchapter A of chapter 1, except the credit provided by section 31, relating to tax withheld at source on wages, minus

(iv) In the case of an individual who is subject to one or more qualified State individual incomes taxes, the sum of the credits allowed against such taxes pursuant to section 6362(b)(2)(B) or (C) or section 6362(c)(4) and paragraph (c) of § 301.6362-4 of this chapter (Regulations on Procedure and Administration) (relating to the credit for income taxes of other States or political subdivisions thereof) and paragraph (c)(2) of § 301.6361-1 (relating to the credit for tax withheld from wages on account of qualified State individual income taxes), and minus

(v) For taxable years ending after February 29, 1980, the individual's overpayment of windfall profit tax imposed by section 4986 of the Code for the taxable year. For this purpose, the amount of such overpayment is the sum of (A) the amount by which such individual's aggregate windfall profit tax liability for the taxable year as producer of crude oil is exceeded by withholding of windfall profit tax for the taxable year, and (B) any amount treated under section 6429 or 6430 as an overpayment of windfall profit tax for crude oil removed during the taxable year. The deemed payment date in section 4995(a)(4)(B) for the amount of windfall profit tax withheld with respect to payment for crude oil shall have no effect in the determination of the overpayment of windfall profit tax.

(b) *Statement relating to underpayment.*—If there has been an underpayment of estimated tax as of any installment date prescribed for its payment and the taxpayer believes that one or more of the exceptions described in § 1.6654-2 precludes the assertion of the addition to the tax under section 6654, he should attach to his income tax return for the taxable year a Form 2210 showing the applicability of any exception upon which he relies.

(c) *Examples.*—The method prescribed in paragraph (a) of this section for computing the addition to the tax may be illustrated by the following examples:

Example (1). An individual taxpayer files his return for the calendar year 1972 on April 15, 1973 showing a tax (income and self-employment tax) of $30,000. He had paid a total of $20,000 of estimated tax in four installments of $5,000 on each of the four installment dates prescribed for such year. No other payments were made prior to the date the return was filed. Since the amount of each installment paid by the last date prescribed for payment thereof is less than one-quarter of 80 percent of the tax shown on the return, the addition to the tax is applicable in respect of the underpayment existing as of each installment date and is computed as follows:

(1) Amount of tax shown on return	$30,000
(2) 80 percent of item (1)	24,000
(3) One-fourth of item (2)	$6,000
(4) Deduct amount paid on each installment date	$5,000
(5) Amount of underpayment for each installment date (item (3) minus item (4))	$1,000
(6) Addition to the tax:	
1st installment—period 4-15-72 to 4-15-73	$60
2nd installment—period 6-15-72 to 4-15-73	50
3rd installment—period 9-15-72 to 4-15-73	35
4th installment—period 1-15-73 to 4-15-73	15
Total	$160

Example (2). An individual taxpayer files his return for the calendar year 1955 on April 15, 1956, showing a tax of $30,000. The requirements of section 6015(a) were first met after April 1 and before June 2, 1955, and a total of $18,000 of estimated tax was paid in three equal installments of $6,000 on each of the three installment dates prescribed for such year. Since the amount of each installment paid by the last date prescribed for payment thereof is less than one-third of 70 percent of the tax shown on the return, the addition to the tax is applicable in respect of the underpayment existing as of each installment date and is computed as follows:

(1) Amount of tax shown on return	$30,000
(2) 70 percent of item (1)	21,000
(3) One-third of item (2)	$7,000
(4) Deduct amount paid on each installment date	6,000
(5) Amount of underpayment for each installment date (item (3) minus item (4))	$1,000
(6) Addition to the tax:	

1st installment—period 6/15/55 to 4/15/56	$50
2nd installment—period 9/15/55 to 4/15/56	35
3rd installment—period 1/15/56 to 4/15/56	15
Total	$100

[Reg. §1.6654-1.]

☐ [T.D. 6267, 11-13-57. *Amended by T.D. 6678*, 9-30-63, *T.D. 7384*, 10-21-75, *T.D. 7427*, 8-9-76, *T.D. 7577*, 12-19-78 *and T.D. 8016*, 3-25-85.]

[Reg. §301.6654-1]

§301.6654-1. Failure by individual to pay estimated income tax.—For regulations under section 6654, see §§1.6654-1 to 1.6654-5, inclusive, of this chapter (Income Tax Regulations). [Reg. §301.6654-1.]

☐ [T.D. 6268, 11-15-57. *Republished in T.D.* 6498, 10-24-60. *Amended by T.D. 7282*, 7-16-73.]

[Reg. §1.6654-2]

§1.6654-2. Exceptions to imposition of the addition to the tax in the case of individuals.—(a) *In general.*—The addition to the tax under section 6654 will not be imposed for any underpayment of any installment of estimated tax if, on or before the date prescribed for payment of the installment, the total amount of all payments of estimated tax made equals or exceeds the lesser of the amount in §1.6654-2(a)(1) or the amount in §1.6654-2(a)(2).

(1)(i) The amount which would have been required to be paid on or before the date prescribed for payment if the estimated tax were the tax shown on the return for the preceding taxable year, provided that the preceding taxable year was a year of 12 months and a return showing a liability for tax was filed for such year. However, this subparagraph shall not apply with respect to any taxable year which ends on or after September 30, 1968, for which a tax is imposed by section 51 (relating to tax surcharge), in the case of a payment of estimated tax the time prescribed for payment of which is on or after September 15, 1968.

(ii) *Special rule for taxable years beginning in 2009.*—For any taxable year beginning in 2009, for a qualified individual, the amount described in paragraph (a)(1)(i) of this section is reduced to 90 percent of that amount.

(A) *Qualified individual* means any individual whose adjusted gross income shown on the individual's return for the preceding taxable year is less than $500,000 and who certifies, as prescribed in paragraph (a)(1)(ii)(D) of this section, that more than 50 percent of the gross income shown on the return for the preceding taxable year was income from a small business.

(B) *Income from a small business* means income from the operation of a bona fide trade or business of which the individual was an owner during calendar year 2009, and that on average had fewer than 500 employees in calendar year 2008.

(C) The trade or business may be organized as, or take the legal form of, a corporation, partnership, limited liability company, or sole proprietorship.

(D) A qualified individual shall file a certification of the individual's qualification in the manner and at the time prescribed by the Internal Revenue Service in forms, publications, or other guidance.

(2) The amount which would have been required to be paid on or before the date prescribed for payment if the estimated tax were an amount equal to a percentage of the tax computed by placing on an annual basis the taxable income for the calendar months in the taxable year ending before the month in which the installment is required to be paid. That percentage is 80 percent in the case of taxable years beginning after December 31, 1966, of individuals not referred to in section 6073(b) (relating to income from farming or fishing), 70 percent in the case of taxable years beginning before January 1, 1967, of such individuals, and 66⅔ percent in the case [of] individuals referred to in section 6073(b). With respect to taxable years beginning after December 31, 1966, the adjusted self-employment income shall be taken into account in determining the amount referred to in this subparagraph if net earnings from self-employment (as defined in section 1402(a)) for the taxable year equal or exceed $400. For purposes of this subparagraph—

(i) Taxable income shall be placed on an annualized basis—

(A) For taxable years beginning after 1976, by—

(1) Multiplying by 12 (or the number of months in the taxable year if less than 12) the adjusted gross income and the itemized deductions for the calendar months in the taxable year ending before the month in which the installment is required to be paid,

(2) Dividing the resulting amounts by the number of such calendar months,

(3) Increasing the amount of the annualized adjusted gross income by the unused zero bracket amount, if any, determined by reference to the annualized itemized deductions, or decreasing the amount of the annualized adjusted gross income by the excess itemized deductions, if any, determined by reference to the annualized itemized deductions (the amount resulting under this step is annualized tax table income), and

(4) Deducting from the annualized tax table income the deduction for personal exemptions (such personal exemptions being determined as of the date prescribed for payment of the installment).

If the taxpayer would be eligible to use the tax tables on the basis of annualized tax table income, the amount which would have been required to be paid for purposes of this subparagraph may be determined by applying the tax tables to annualized tax table income, the amount resulting under (3).

(B) For taxable years beginning before 1977, by—

(1) Multiplying by 12 (or the number of months in the taxable year if less than 12) the taxable income (computed without the standard deduction and without the deduction for personal exemptions), or the adjusted gross income if the standard deduction is to be used for the calendar months in the taxable year ending before the month in which the installment is required to be paid,

(2) Dividing the resulting amount by the number of such calendar months, and

(3) Deducting from such amount the standard deduction, if applicable, and the deduction for personal exemptions (such personal exemptions being determined as of the date prescribed for payment of the installment).

(ii) The term "adjusted self-employment income" means—

(A) The net earnings from self-employment (as defined in section 1402(a)) for the calendar months in the taxable year ending before the month in which the installment is required to be paid, computed as if such months constituted the taxable year, but not more than

(B) The excess of—

(1) For taxable years beginning after 1966, $6,600,

(2) For taxable years beginning after 1971, $9,000,

(3) For taxable years beginning after 1972, $10,800,

(4) For taxable years beginning after 1973, $13,200 and

(5) For taxable years beginning after 1974, an amount equal to the contribution and benefit base (as determined under section 230 of the Social Security Act) which is effective for the calendar year in which the taxable year begins,

over the amount of the wages (within the meaning of section 1402(b)) for such calendar months placed on an annual basis. For this purpose, wages are annualized by multiplying by 12 (or the number of months in the taxable year in the case of a taxable year of less than 12 months) the wages for such calendar months and dividing the resulting amount by the number of such months.

(3) An amount equal to 90 percent of the tax computed, at the rates applicable to the taxable year, on the basis of the actual taxable income for the calendar months in the taxable year ending before the month in which the installment is required to be paid, as if such months constituted the entire taxable year. For taxable years beginning after December 31, 1966, such computation shall include the tax imposed by chapter 2 on the actual self-employment income for such months. For purposes of the subparagraph, the term "actual self-employment income" means—

(i) The net earnings from self-employment (as defined in section 1402(a)) for such

calendar months, computed as if such months constituted the taxable year, but not more than

(ii) The excess of—

(A) For taxable years beginning after 1966, $6,600,

(B) For taxable years beginning after 1971, $9,000,

(C) For taxable years beginning after 1972, $10,800,

(D) For taxable years beginning after 1973, $13,200, and

(E) For taxable years beginning after 1974, an amount equal to the contribution and benefit base (as determined under section 230 of the Social Security Act) which is effective for the calendar year in which the taxable year begins,

over the amount of wages (within the meaning of section 1402(b)) for such months.

(4) The amount which would have been required to be paid on or before the date prescribed for payment if the estimated tax were an amount equal to a tax determined on the basis of the tax rates and the taxpayer's status with respect to personal exemptions under section 151 for the taxable year, but otherwise on the basis of the facts shown on the return for the preceding taxable year and the law applicable to such year, in the case of an individual required to file a return for such preceding taxable year.

In the case of a taxpayer whose taxable year consists of 52 or 53 weeks in accordance with section 441(f), the rules prescribed by § 1.441-2(c) shall be applicable in determining, for purposes of subparagraph (1) of this paragraph, whether a taxable year was a year of 12 months and, for purposes of subparagraphs (2) and (3) of this paragraph, the number of calendar months in a taxable year preceding the date prescribed for payment of an installment of estimated tax. For the rules to be applied in determining taxable income for any period described in subparagraphs (2) and (3) of this paragraph in the case of a taxpayer who employs accounting periods (e.g., thirteen 4-week periods or four 13-week periods) none of which terminates with the end of the applicable period described in subparagraph (2) or (3) of this paragraph, see paragraph (a)(5) of § 1.6655-2.

(b) *Meaning of terms.*—As used in this section and § 1.6654-3—

(1) The term "tax" means—

(i) The tax imposed by chapter 1 of the Code (other than by section 56), including any qualified State individual income taxes which are treated pursuant to section 6361(a) as if they were imposed by chapter 1, plus

(ii) For taxable years beginning after December 31, 1966, the tax imposed by chapter 2 of the Code, minus

(iii) The credits against tax allowed by part IV, subchapter A, chapter 1 of the Code, other than the credit against tax provided by section 31 (relating to tax withheld on wages), and without reduction for any payments of estimated tax, minus

Reg. § 1.6654-2(b)(1)(iii)

(iv) In the case of an individual who is subject to one or more qualified State individual income taxes, the sum of the credits allowed against such taxes pursuant to section 6262(b)(2)(B) or (C) or section 6262(c)(4) and paragraph (c) of §301.6362-4 of this chapter (Regulations on Procedure and Administration) (relating to the credit for income taxes of other States or political subdivisions thereof) and paragraph (c)(2) of §301.6361-1 (relating to the credit for tax withheld from wages on account of qualified State individual income taxes), and minus

(v) For taxable years ending after February 29, 1980, the individual's overpayment of windfall profit tax imposed by section 4986 of the Code for the taxable year. For this purpose, the amount of such overpayment is the sum of (A) the amount by which such individual's aggregate windfall profit tax liability for the taxable year as producer of crude oil is exceeded by withholding of windfall profit tax for the taxable year, and (B) any amount treated under section 6429 or 6430 as an overpayment of windfall profit tax for crude oil removed during the taxable year. The deemed payment date in section 4995(a)(4)(B) for the amount of windfall profit tax withheld with respect to payments for crude oil shall have no effect in the determination of the overpayment of windfall profit tax.

(2) The credits against tax allowed by part IV, subchapter A, chapter 1 of the Code, are—

(i) In the case of the exception described in paragraph (a)(1) of this section, the credits shown on the return for the preceding taxable year,

(ii) In the case of the exceptions described in paragraph (a)(2) and (3) of this section, the credits computed under the law and rates applicable to the current taxable year, and

(iii) In the case of the exception described in paragraph (a)(4) of this section, the credits shown on the return for the preceding taxable year, except that if the amount of any such credit would be affected by any change in rates or status with respect to personal exemptions, the credits shall be determined by reference to the rates and status applicable to the current taxable year.
A change in rate may be either a change in the rate of tax, such as a change in the rate of tax imposed by section 1 or section 1401, or a change in a percentage affecting the computation of a credit, such as a change in the rate of withholding under chapter 3 of the Code or a change in the percentage of a qualified investment which is specified in section 46 for use in determining the amount of the investment credit allowed by section 38.

(3) The term "return for the preceding taxable year" means the income tax return for such year which is required by section 6012(a)(1) and, in the case of taxable years beginning after December 31, 1966, the self-employment tax return for such year which is required by section 6017.

(c) *Examples.*—The following examples illustrate the application of the exceptions to the imposition of the addition to the tax for an underpayment of estimated tax, in the case of an individual whose taxable year is the calendar year:

Example (1). A, a married man with one child and a dependent parent, files a joint return with his spouse, B, for 1955 on April 15, 1956, showing taxable income of $44,000 and a tax of $16,760. A and B had filed a joint declaration of estimated tax on April 15, 1955, showing an estimated tax of $10,000 which was paid in four equal installments of $2,500 each on April 15, June 15, and September 15, 1955, and January 15, 1956. The balance of $6,760 was paid with the return. A and B have an underpayment of estimated tax of $433 ($\frac{1}{4}$ of 70 percent of $16,760, less $2,500) for each installment date. The 1954 calendar year return of A and B showed a liability of $10,000. Since the total amount of estimated tax paid by each installment date equalled the amount that would have been required to be paid on or before each of such dates if the estimated tax were the tax shown on the return for the preceding year, the exception described in paragraph (a)(1) of this section applies and no addition to the tax will be imposed.

Example (2). Assume the same facts as in example (1), except that the joint return of A and B for 1954 showed taxable income of $32,000 and a tax liability of $10,400. Assume further that only two personal exemptions under section 151 appeared on the 1954 return. The exception described in paragraph (a)(1) of this section would not apply. However, A and B are entitled to four exemptions under section 151 for 1955. Taxable income for 1954 based on four exemptions, but otherwise on the basis of the facts shown on the 1954 return, would be $30,800. The tax on such amount in the case of a joint return would be $9,836. Since the total amount of estimated tax paid by each installment date exceeds the amount which would have been required to be paid on or before each of such dates if the estimated tax were $9,836, the exception described in paragraph (a)(4) of this section applies and no addition to the tax will be imposed.

Example (3). C, who is self-employed (other than as a farmer or fisherman), has annualized taxable income of $6,900 for the period January 1, 1967, through August 31, 1967, the income tax on which is $1,171. For the same period his net earnings from self-employment are $5,000 and his wages are $2,000. The estimated tax payments made by C for 1967 on or before September 15, 1967, total $1,200. For the purposes of the exception described in paragraph (a)(2) of this section, the adjusted self-employment income is $3,600, computed as follows:

(1) Net earnings from self-employment . . .	$5,000
(2) $6,600 minus annualized wages ($6,600 – 3,000 ($2,000 × 12 ÷ 8))	3,600
(3) Lesser of (1) or (2)	3,600

The tax on C's adjusted self-employment income would be $230.40 ($3,600 × 6.4 percent). Since the total amount of estimated tax paid on or before September 15, 1967, exceeds $1,121.12, that is, 80 percent of $1,401.40 ($1,171 + 230.40), the exception described in paragraph (a)(2) of this section applies and no addition to tax will be imposed.

Example (4). D, who is self-employed (other than as a farmer or fisherman), has actual taxable income of $3,800 for the period January 1, 1967, through August 31, 1967, the income tax on which is $586. For the same period his net earnings from self-employment are $5,000 and his wages are $2,000. The estimated tax payments made by D for 1967 on or before September 15, 1967, total $840. For the purposes of the exception described in paragraph (a)(3) of this section, the actual self-employment income for this period is $4,600, computed as follows:

(1) Net earnings from self-employment	$5,000
(2) $6,600 minus wages ($6,600 − 2,000)	4,600
(3) Lesser of (1) or (2)	4,600

The tax on D's actual self-employment income would be $294.40 ($4,600 × 6.4 percent). Since the total amount of estimated tax paid by September 15, 1967, exceeds $792.36, that is, 90 percent of $880.40 ($586 + 294.40); the exception described in paragraph (a)(3) of this section applies and no addition to tax will be imposed.

Example (5). E and F, his spouse, filed a joint return for the calendar year 1967 showing a tax liability of $10,000. The liability, attributable primarily to income received during the last quarter of the year, included both income and self-employment tax. Their aggregate payments of estimated tax on or before September 15, 1967, total $1,350, representing three installments of $450 paid on each of the first three installment dates prescribed for the taxable year. Since each installment paid, $450, was less than $2,000 ($\frac{1}{4}$ of 80 percent of $10,000), there was an underpayment on each of the installment dates. Assume that the exceptions described in paragraph (a)(1) and (4) of this section do not apply. Actual taxable income for the three months ending March 31, 1967, was $2,000 and for the five months ending May 31, 1967, was $4,500. Actual self-employment income, for the same periods, was $2,000 and $4,000, respectively. Since the amounts paid by the April 15 and June 15 installment dates, $450 and $900, respectively, exceed $376.20 and $873.90, respectively (90 percent of the income tax on the actual taxable income of $2,000 and $4,500, respectively, determined on the basis of a joint return, and the self-employment tax on the actual self-employment income of $2,000 and $4,000, respectively), the exception described in paragraph (a)(3) of this section applies and no addition to the tax will be imposed for the underpayments on the April 15 and June 15 installment dates. For the eight months ending August 31, 1967, actual taxable income, assuming E and F did not elect to use the standard deduction, was $7,500; net earnings from self-employment were $6,000; and wages were $2,700. Since the total amount paid by the September 15 installment date, $1,350, was less than $1,381.14 (90 percent of the income tax on the actual taxable income of $7,500 determined on the basis of a joint return and the self-employment tax on actual self-employment income of $3,900 ($6,600 − 2,700)), the exception described

in paragraph (a)(3) of this section does not apply to the September 15 installment. Furthermore, the exception described in paragraph (a)(2) of this section does not apply, as illustrated by the following computation:

(1)	Income tax:	
	Taxable income for the period ending August 31, 1967 (without deduction for personal exemptions) on an annual basis ($8,700 × 12 ÷ 8)	$13,050.00
	Deduction for two personal exemptions	1,200.00
		11,850.00
	Tax on $11,850 (on the basis of a joint return)	2,227.00
(2)	Self-employment tax:	
	Net earnings from self-employment	6,000.00
	Adjusted self-employment income ($6,600 − 4,050 annualized wages ($2,700 × 12 ÷ 8))	2,550.00
	Tax on adjusted self-employment income ($2,550 × 6.4 percent)	163.20
(3)	Total tax ($2,227.00 + 163.20)	$2,390.20
(4)	$\frac{3}{4}$ of 80 percent of $2,390.20	1,434.12
	Amount paid by Sept. 15, 1967	1,350.00

An addition to the tax will thus be imposed for the underpayment of $1,550 ($2,000 − 450) on the September 15 installment.

Example (6). Assume the same facts as in example (5) and assume further that adjusted gross income for the eight months ending August 31, 1967, was $9,200 and the amount of deductions (other than the deduction for personal exemptions) not allowable in determining adjusted gross income aggregated only $500. If E and F elect, they may use the standard deduction in computing the tax for purposes of the exceptions described in paragraph (a)(2) and (3) of this section. Taxable income for purposes of the exception described in paragraph (a)(3) of this section would be reduced to $7,080 ($9,200 less $1,200 for two personal exemptions and $920 for the standard deduction). The income tax thereon is $1,205.20; income tax and self-employment tax total $1,454.80 ($1,205.20 + $249.60 ($3,900 × 6.4 percent)). Since the amount paid by the September 15 installment date, $1,350, exceeds $1,309.32 (90 percent of $1,454.80), the exception described in paragraph (a)(3) of this section applies. However, the exception described in paragraph (a)(2) of this section does not apply, as illustrated by the following computation:

Adjusted gross income for the period ending August 31, 1967	$9,200.00
Adjusted gross income annualized ($9,200 × 12 ÷ 8)	13,800.00
Taxable income annualized ($13,800 minus $1,200 for two personal exemptions and $1,000 for the standard deduction)	11,600.00
Income tax on $11,600 (on basis of a joint return)	2,172.00

Self-employment tax on adjusted self-employment income ($2,550 × 6.4 percent)	163.20
Total tax ($2,172.00 + 163.20)	$2,355.20
³/4 of 80 percent of $2,335.20	1,401.12
Amount paid by Sept. 15, 1967	1,350.00

Example (7). G was a married individual, 73 years of age, who filed a joint return with his wife, H, for the calendar year 1956. H, who was 70 years of age, had no income during the year. G had taxable income in the amount of $7,000 for the eight-month period ending on August 31, 1956, which included $2,000 of dividend income (after excluding $50 under section 116) and $900 of rental income. The $7,000 figure also reflected a deduction of $2,400 for personal exemptions ($600 × 4), since G and H are both over 65 years of age. The application of the exception described in paragraph (a)(2) of this section to an underpayment of estimated tax on the September 15 installment date may be illustrated by the following computation:

Taxable income for the period ending August 31, 1956 (without deduction for personal exemptions) on an annual basis ($9,400 × 12 ÷ 8) . . .	$14,100.00
Deduction for personal exemptions . .	2,400.00
Taxable income on an annual basis . . .	11,700.00
Tax (on the basis of a joint return) . .	2,642.00
Dividends received for 8-month period	2,050.00
Less: Amount excluded from gross income under section 116	50.00
Dividends included in gross income . .	2,000.00
Dividend income annualized ($2,000 × 12 ÷ 8)	3,000.00
Dividends received credit under section 34 (4 percent of $3,000)	120.00
Tax less dividends received credit . . .	2,522.00
Retirement income (as defined in section 37(c)) includes:	
Dividend income (to extent included in gross income)	2,000.00
Rental income	900.00
Total retirement income	$2,000.00
Limit on amount of retirement income under section 37(d)	1,200.00
Retirement income credit under section 37 (20 percent of $1,200)	240.00
Tax less credits under section 34 and section 37	2,282.00
Amount determined under the exception described in paragraph (a)(2) of this section (³/4 of 70 percent of $2,282)	1,198.05

Example (8). C, an unmarried individual for whom another taxpayer is entitled to a deduction under section 151(e), has adjusted gross income of $4,000 for the period January 1, 1977, through August 31, 1977. All of C's income is nonexempt interest. For the same period C, who is entitled to one personal exemption, has itemized deductions amounting to $300. C is entitled to no credits other than the general tax credit. C filed a declaration of estimated tax on April 15, 1977, and on or before September 15, 1977, makes estimated tax payments for 1977 which

total $460. For purposes of determining whether the exception described in paragraph (a)(2) of this section applies, the following computations are necessary:

Adjusted gross income for the period ending August 31, 1977, on an annual basis ($4,000 × 12 ÷ 8) .		$6,000
Itemized deductions for the period ending August 31, 1977, on an annual basis ($300 × 12 ÷ 8) . . .		450
Unused zero bracket amount computation required under section 63(e)(1)(D):		
Zero bracket amount . . .	$2,200	
Annualized itemized deductions	450	
Unused zero bracket amount	$1,750	
Annualized adjusted gross income		6,000
Plus: unused zero bracket amount		1,750
Annualized tax table income		$7,750
Tax from tables		757
Amount specified in paragraph (a)(2) of this section (³/4 × 80% × $757) .		
. . . .		454.20

The exception described in paragraph (a)(2) applies, and no addition to tax will be imposed.

Example (9). D, an unmarried taxpayer entitled to one exemption, has adjusted gross income of $16,000 and itemized deductions of $2,000 for the period January 1, 1977, through August 31, 1977. D has no net earnings from self-employment and is entitled to no credits other than the general tax credit. D files a declaration of estimated tax on April 15, 1977, and on or before September 15, 1977, makes estimated tax payments for 1977 which total $3,000. For purposes of determining whether the exception in paragraph (a)(2) of this section applies, the following computations are necessary:

Adjusted gross income for the period ending August 31, 1977, on an annual basis ($16,000 × 12 ÷ 8)		$24,000
Itemized deductions for the period ending August 31, 1977, on an annual basis ($2,000 × 12 ÷ 8)		3,000
Annualized itemized deductions	$3,000	
Minus: zero bracket amount . .	2,200	
Excess itemized deductions . .	$ 800	
Annualized adjusted gross income . . .		24,000
Minus: excess itemized deductions . . .		800
Annualized tax table income		23,200
Minus: Personal exemption		750
Annualized taxable income		$22,450
Tax under section 1(c) on annualized taxable income . . .		5,325
Minus: general tax credit		180
Total		$5,145
Amount specified in paragraph (a)(2) of this section (³/4 × 80% ×$5,145)		3,087

The exception described in paragraph (a)(2) does not apply.

(d) *Determination of taxable income for installment periods.*—(1) *In general.*—(i) In determining the applicability of the exceptions described in paragraph (a)(2) and (3) of this section, there must be an accurate determination of the amount of income and deductions for the calendar months in the taxable year preceding the installment date as of which the determination is made, that is, for the period terminating with the last day of the third, fifth, or eighth month of the taxable year. For example, a taxpayer distributes year-end bonuses to his employees but does not determine the amount of the bonuses until the last month of the taxable year. He may not deduct any portion of such year-end bonuses in determining his taxable income for any installment period other than the final installment period for the taxable year, since deductions are not allowable until paid or accrued, depending on the taxpayer's method of accounting.

(ii) If a taxpayer on an accrual method of accounting wishes to use either of the exceptions described in paragraph (a)(2) and (3) of this section, he must establish the amount of income and deductions for each applicable period. If his income is derived from a business in which the production, purchase, or sale of merchandise is an income-producing factor requiring the use of inventories, he will be unable to determine accurately the amount of his taxable income for the applicable period unless he can establish, with reasonable accuracy, his cost of goods sold for the applicable installment period. The cost of goods sold for such period shall be considered, unless a more exact determination is available, as such part of the cost of goods sold during the entire taxable year as the gross receipts from sales for such installment period is of gross receipts from sales for the entire taxable year.

(2) *Members of partnerships.*—The provisions of this subparagraph shall apply in determining the applicability of the exceptions described in paragraph (a)(2) and (3) of this section to an underpayment of estimated tax by a taxpayer who is a member of a partnership.

(i) For purposes of determining taxable income, there shall be taken into account—

(A) The partner's distributive share of partnership items set forth under section 702,

(B) The amount of any guaranteed payments under section 707(c), and

(C) Gains or losses on partnership distributions which are treated as gains or losses on sales of property.

(ii) For purposes of determining net earnings from self-employment (for taxable years beginning after December 31, 1966) there shall be taken into account—

(A) The partner's distributive share of income or loss, described in section 702(a)(9), subject to the special rules set forth in section 1402(a) and §§1.1402(a)-1 to 1.1402(a)-16, inclusive, and

(B) The amount of any guaranteed payments under section 707(c), except for payments received from a partnership not engaged in a trade or business within the meaning of section 1402(c) and §1.1402(c)-1.

In determining a partner's taxable income and, for taxable years beginning after December 31, 1966, net earnings from self-employment, for the months in his taxable year which precede the month in which the installment date falls, the partner shall take into account items set forth in sections 702 and 1402(a) for any partnership taxable year ending with or within his taxable year to the extent that such items are attributable to months in such partnership taxable year which precede the month in which the installment date falls. For special rules used in computing a partner's net earnings from self-employment in the case of the termination of his taxable year as a result of death, see section 1402(f) and §1.1402(f)-1. In addition, a partner shall include in his taxable income and, for taxable years beginning after December 31, 1966, net earnings from self-employment, for the months in his taxable year which precede the month in which the installment date falls guaranteed payments from the partnership to the extent that such guaranteed payments are includible in his taxable income for such months. See section 706(a), section 707(c), paragraph (c) of §1.707-1 and section 1402(a).

(iii) The provisions of subdivision (i)(A) and (B) and subdivision (ii) of this subparagraph may be illustrated by the following examples:

Example (1). A, whose taxable year is the calendar year, is a member of a partnership whose taxable year ends on January 31. A must take into account, in determining his taxable income for the installment due on April 15, 1973, all of his distributive share of partnership items described in section 702 and the amount of any guaranteed payments made to him which were deductible by the partnership in the partnership taxable year beginning on February 1, 1972, and ending on January 31, 1973. A must take into account, in determining his net earnings from self-employment, his distributive share of partnership income or loss described in section 702(a)(9), subject to the special rules set forth in section 1402(a) and §§1.1402(a)-1 to 1.1402(a)-16, inclusive.

Example (2). Assume that the taxable year of the partnership of which A, a calendar year taxpayer, is a member ends on June 30. A must take into account in the determination of his taxable income and net earnings from self-employment for the installment due on April 15, 1973, his distributive share of partnership items for the period July 1, 1972, through March 31, 1973; for the installment due on June 15, 1973, he must take into account such amounts for the period July 1, 1972, through May 31, 1973; and for the installment due on September 15, 1973, he must take into account such amounts for the entire partnership taxable year of July 1, 1972, through June 30, 1973 (the date on which the partnership taxable year ends).

(3) *Beneficiaries of estates and trusts.*—In determining the applicability of the exceptions described in paragraph (a)(2) and (3) of this section as of any installment date, the beneficiary of an estate or trust must take into account his distributable share of income from the estate or trust for the applicable period (whether or not actually distributed) if the trust or estate is required to distribute income to him currently. If the estate or trust is not required to distribute income currently, only the amounts actually distributed to the beneficiary during such period must be taken into account. If the taxable year of the beneficiary and the taxable year of the estate or trust are different, there shall be taken into account the beneficiary's distributable share of income, or the amount actually distributed to him as the case may be, during the months in the taxable year of the estate or trust ending within the taxable year of the beneficiary which precede the month in which the installment date falls. See subparagraph (2) of this paragraph for examples of a similar rule which is applied when a partner and the partnership of which he is a member have different taxable years.

(e) *Special rule in case of change from joint return or separate return for the preceding taxable year.*—(1) *Joint return to separate returns.*—In determining the applicability of the exceptions described in paragraph (a)(1) and (4) of this section to an underpayment of estimated tax, a taxpayer filing a separate return who filed a joint return for the preceding taxable year shall be subject to the following rule: The tax—

    (i) Shown on the return for the preceding taxable year, or

    (ii) Based on the tax rates and personal exemptions for the current taxable year but otherwise determined on the basis of the facts shown on the return for the preceding taxable year, and the law applicable to such year, shall be that portion of the tax which bears the same ratio to the whole of the tax as the amount of the tax for which the taxpayer would have been liable bears to the sum of the taxes for which the taxpayer and his spouse would have been liable had each spouse filed a separate return for the preceding taxable year. For rules with respect to the allocation of joint payments of estimated tax, see § 1.6654-2(e)(5).

(2) *Examples.*—The rule in paragraph (1) of this paragraph may be illustrated by the following examples:

Example (1). H and W filed a joint return for the calendar year 1955 showing taxable income of $20,000 and a tax of $5,280. Of the $20,000 taxable income, $18,000 was attributable to H, and $2,000 was attributable to W. H and W filed separate returns for 1956. The tax shown on the return for the preceding taxable year, for purposes of determining the applicability of the exception described in paragraph (a)(1) of this section to an underpayment of estimated tax by H for 1956, is determined as follows:

Taxable income of H for 1955	$18,000
Tax on $18,000 (on basis of separate return)	
. . . .	6,200
Taxable income of W for 1955	2,000
Tax on $2,000 (on basis of separate return)	
. . . .	400
Aggregate tax of H and W (on basis of separate returns)	6,600
Portion of 1955 tax shown on joint return attributable to H (6200/6600 × 5280)	4,960

Example (2). Assume the same facts as in example (1) and that H and W file a joint declaration of estimated tax for 1956 and pay estimated tax in amounts determined on the basis of their eligibility for three rather than two exemptions for 1956. H and W ultimately file separate income tax returns for 1956. Assume further that the exception described in paragraph (a)(1) of this section does not apply. The tax based on the tax rates and personal exemptions for 1956 but otherwise determined on the basis of the facts shown on the return for 1955 and the law applicable to 1955, for purposes of determining the applicability of the exception described in paragraph (a)(4) of this section to an underpayment of estimated tax by H for 1956, is determined as follows:

Taxable income of H and W for 1955 based on additional personal exemption for 1956	$19,400
Tax on 1955 income based on joint return rate for 1956	5,076
Portion of 1955 tax attributable to H (computed as in example (1) but allowing benefit of additional exemption to H)	5,900/6,300
Portion of tax attributable to H based on tax rates and personal exemptions for 1956 but otherwise on facts on 1955 return ($5,900/6,300 × $5,076)	
. . . .	4,754

Example (3). Assume that H and W had the same taxable income in 1972 as in 1955, and that they filed a joint return for 1972 and separate returns for 1973. Assume further that H's taxable income for 1972 included net earnings from self-employment in excess of the $9,000 maximum base for the self-employment tax for 1972, and that the joint return filed by H and W for 1972 showed tax under chapter 1 (other than section 56) and tax under chapter 2 totaling $5,055. The tax shown on the return for 1972, for purposes of determining the applicability of the exception described in paragraph (a)(1) of this section to an underpayment of estimated tax by H for 1973, is determined as follows:

Taxable income of H for 1972	$18,000
Chapter 1 tax (other than section 56 tax) on $18,000 (on basis of separate return)	5,170
Self-employment income of H for 1972	
. . . .	9,000
Chapter 2 tax on $9,000	675
Total of such taxes	$5,845
Taxable income of W for 1972	2,000

Chapter 1 tax (other than section 56 tax) on $2,000 (on basis of separate return)	310
Aggregate tax of H and W (on basis of separate returns)	6,155
Portion of 1972 tax shown on joint return attributable to H (5845/6155 × $5,055)	4,800.40

(3) *Separate return to joint return.*—In the case of a taxpayer who files a joint return for the taxable year with respect to which there is an underpayment of estimated tax and who filed a separate return for the preceding taxable year—

　　(i) The tax shown on the return for the preceding taxable year, for purposes of determining the applicability of the exception described in paragraph (a)(1) of this section, shall be the sum of both the tax shown on the return of the taxpayer and the tax shown on the return of the taxpayer's spouse for such preceding year, and

　　(ii) The facts shown on both the taxpayer's return and the return of his spouse for the preceding taxable year shall be taken into account for purposes of determining the applicability of the exception described in paragraph (a)(4) of this section.

(4) *Example.*—The rules described in subparagraph (3) of this paragraph may be illustrated by the following example:

Example. H and W filed separate income tax returns for the calendar year 1954 showing tax liabilities of $2,640 and $350, respectively. In 1955 they married and participated in the filing of a joint return for that year. Thus, for the purpose of determining the applicability of the exceptions described in paragraph (a)(1) and (4) of this section to an underpayment of estimated tax for the year 1955, the tax shown on the return for the preceding taxable year is $2,990 ($2,640 plus $350).

(5) *Joint payments of estimated tax.*—(i) *In general.*—A husband and wife may make a joint payment of estimated tax even though they are not living together. However, a joint payment of estimated tax may not be made if the husband and wife are separated under a decree of divorce or of separate maintenance. A joint payment of estimated tax may not be made if the taxpayer's spouse is a nonresident alien (including a nonresident alien who is a bona fide resident of Puerto Rico or a possession to which section 931 applies during the entire taxable year), unless an election is in effect for the taxable year under section 6013(g) or (h) and the regulations. In addition, a joint payment of estimated tax may not be made if the taxpayer's spouse has a taxable year different from that of the taxpayer. If a joint payment of estimated tax is made, the amount estimated as the income tax imposed by chapter 1 of the Internal Revenue Code must be computed on the aggregate estimated taxable income of the spouses (see section 6013(d)(3) and §1.2-1), whereas, if applicable, the amount estimated as the self-employment tax imposed by chapter 2 of the Internal Revenue Code must be computed on the separate estimated self-employment income of each spouse. See sections 1401 and 1402 and §1.6017-1(b)(1). The liability with respect to the estimated tax, in the case of a joint payment, shall be joint and several.

　　(ii) *Application to separate returns.*—(A) Although a husband and wife may make a joint payment of estimated tax, they, nevertheless, can file separate returns. If they make a joint payment of estimated tax and file separate returns for the same taxable year with respect to which the joint payment was made, the payment made on account of the estimated tax for that taxable year may be treated as a payment on account of the tax liability of either the husband or wife for the taxable year, or may be divided between them in such manner as they may agree.

　　(B) In the event the husband and wife fail to agree to a division of the estimated tax payment, such payment shall be allocated between them in accordance with the following rule. The portion of such payment to be allocated to a taxpayer shall be that portion of the aggregate of all such payments as the amount of tax imposed by chapter 1 of the Internal Revenue Code shown on the separate return of the taxpayer (plus, if applicable, the amount of tax imposed by chapter 2 of the Internal Revenue Code shown on the return of the taxpayer) bears to the sum of the taxes imposed by chapter 1 of the Internal Revenue Code shown on the separate returns of the taxpayer and the spouse (plus, if applicable, the sum of the taxes imposed by chapter 2 of the Internal Revenue Code shown on the separate returns of the taxpayer and the spouse).

(6) *Example.*—The rule described in paragraph (e)(5) of this section may be illustrated by the following example:

Example. (i) H and W make a joint payment of estimated tax of $19,500 for the taxable year. H and W subsequently file separate returns for the taxable year showing tax imposed by chapter 1 of the Internal Revenue Code in the amount of $11,500 and $8,000, respectively. In addition, H's return shows a tax imposed by chapter 2 of the Internal Revenue Code in the amount of $500. H and W fail to agree to a division of the estimated tax paid. The amount of the aggregate estimated tax payments allocated to H is determined as follows:

(A) Chapter 1 tax shown on H's return	$11,500
(B) Plus: Amount of tax imposed by chapter 2 shown on H's return	$500
(C) Total taxes imposed by chapter 1 and by chapter 2 shown on H's return	$12,000
(D) Amount of tax imposed by chapter 1 shown on W's return	$8,000

(E) Total taxes imposed by chapter 1 and by chapter 2 on both H's and W's returns	$20,000
(F) Proportion of taxes shown on H's return to total amount of taxes shown on both H's and W's returns	($12,000/$20,000) 60%
(G) Amount of estimated tax payments allocated to H (60% of $19,500)	$11,700

(ii) Accordingly, H's return would show a balance due in the amount of $300 ($12,000 taxes shown less $11,700 estimated tax allocated).

(7) *Death of spouse.*—(i) A joint payment of estimated tax may not be made after the death of either the husband or wife. However, if it is reasonable for a surviving spouse to assume that there will be filed a joint return for himself and the deceased spouse for his taxable year and the last taxable year of the deceased spouse, he may, in making a separate payment of estimated tax for his taxable year which includes the period comprising such last taxable year of his spouse, estimate the amount of the tax imposed by chapter 1 of the Internal Revenue Code on his and his spouse's taxable income on an aggregate basis and compute his estimated tax with respect to chapter 1 tax in the same manner as though a joint return had been filed.

(ii) If a husband and wife make a joint payment of estimated tax and thereafter one spouse dies, no further payments of joint estimated tax liability are required from the estate of the decedent. The surviving spouse, however, shall be liable for the payment of any subsequent installments of the joint estimated tax. For the purpose of making an amended payment of estimated tax by the surviving spouse, and the allocation of payments made pursuant to a joint payment of estimated tax between the surviving spouse and the legal representative of the decedent in the event a joint return is not filed, the payment of estimated tax may be divided between the decedent and the surviving spouse in such proportion as the surviving spouse and the legal representative of the decedent may agree.

(iii) If the surviving spouse and the legal representative of the decedent fail to agree to a division of a payment, such payment shall be allocated in accordance with the following rule. The portion of such payment to be allocated to the surviving spouse shall be that portion of the aggregate amount of such payments as the amount of tax imposed by chapter 1 of the Internal Revenue Code shown on the separate return of the surviving spouse (plus, if applicable, the amount of tax imposed by chapter 2 of the Internal Revenue Code shown on the return of the surviving spouse) bears to the sum imposed by chapter 1 of the Internal Revenue Code shown on the separate returns of the surviving spouse and of the decedent (plus, if applicable, the sum of the taxes imposed by chapter 2 of the Internal Revenue Code shown on the returns of the surviving spouse and of the decedent); and the balance of such payments shall be allocated to the decedent. This rule may be illustrated by analogizing the surviving spouse described in this rule to H in the example contained in para-

graph (e)(6) of this section and the decedent in this rule to W in that example.

(f) *Effective/applicability date.*—Paragraph (a)(1)(ii) of this section applies to any taxable year beginning in 2009 and does not apply to any taxable years beginning before or after 2009. [Reg. § 1.6654-2.]

☐ [*T.D.* 6267, 11-13-57. *Amended by T.D.* 6678, 9-30-63; *T.D.* 6777, 12-15-64; *T.D.* 7282, 7-16-73; *T.D.* 7427, 8-9-76; *T.D.* 7577, 12-19-78; *T.D.* 7585, 1-3-79; *T.D.* 8016, 3-25-85; *T.D.* 8996, 5-16-2002, *T.D.* 9224, 9-1-2005; *T.D.* 9480, 2-26-2010 *and T.D.* 9613, 2-25-2013.]

[Reg. § 1.6654-3]

§ 1.6654-3. Short taxable years of individuals.—(a) *In general.*—The provisions of section 6654, with certain modifications relating to the application of section 6654(d), which are explained in paragraph (b) of this section, are applicable in the case of a short taxable year.

(b) *Rules as to application of section 6654(d).*— (1) In any case in which the taxable year for which an underpayment of estimated tax exists is a short taxable year due to a change in annual accounting periods, in determining the tax—

(i) Shown on the return for the preceding taxable year (for purposes of section 6654(d)(1)(A)), or

(ii) Based on the personal exemptions and rates for the current taxable year but otherwise on the basis of the facts shown on the return for the preceding taxable year, and the law applicable to such year (for purposes of section 6654(d)(4)),

the tax will be reduced by multiplying it by the number of months in the short taxable year and dividing the resulting amount by 12.

(2) If the taxable year for which an underpayment of estimated tax exists is a short taxable year due to a change in annual accounting periods, in annualizing the income for the months in the taxable year preceding an installment date, for purposes of section 6654(d)(2), the personal exemptions allowed as deductions under section 151 shall be reduced to the same extent that they are reduced under section 443(c) in computing the tax for a short taxable year.

(3) If "the preceding taxable year" referred to in section 6654(d)(4) was a short taxable year, for purposes of determining the applicability of the exception described in section 6654(d)(4), the tax, computed on the basis of the facts shown on the return for the preceding year, shall be the tax computed on the annual basis in the manner described in section 443(b)(1) (prior to its reduction in the manner described in the last sentence thereof). If the tax rates or the taxpayer's status with respect to personal exemptions for the taxa-

Additions to Tax and Additional Amounts
67,191
See p. 20,601 for regulations not amended to reflect law changes

ble year with respect to which the underpayment occurs differs from such rates or status applicable to the preceding taxable year, the tax determined in accordance with this subparagraph shall be recomputed to reflect the rates and status applicable to the year with respect to which the underpayment occurs. [Reg. §1.6654-3.]

☐ [T.D. 6267, 11-13-57. Amended by T.D. 7427, 8-9-76 and T.D. 9224, 9-1-2005.]

[Reg. §1.6654-4]

§1.6654-4. **Waiver of penalty for underpayment of 1971 estimated tax by an individual.**— [This regulation is obsolete and is no longer reproduced.]

[Reg. §1.6654-5]

§1.6654-5. **Payments of estimated tax.**—(a) *In general.*—A payment of estimated tax by an individual shall be determined on Form 1040-ES. For the purpose of determining the estimated tax, the amount of gross income which the taxpayer can reasonably expect to receive or accrue, depending upon the method of accounting upon which taxable income is computed, and the amount of the estimated allowable deductions and credits to be taken into account in computing the amount of estimated tax, shall be determined upon the basis of the facts and circumstances existing at the time prescribed for determining the estimated tax, as well as those reasonably to be anticipated for the taxable year. If, therefore, the taxpayer is employed at the date prescribed for making an estimated tax payment at a given wage or salary, the taxpayer should presume, in the absence of circumstances indicating the contrary, for the purpose of the estimated tax payment that such employment will continue to the end of the taxable year at the wage or salary received by the taxpayer as of such date. In the case of income other than wages and salary, the regularity in the payment of income, such as dividends, interest, rents, royalties, and income arising from estates and trusts is a factor to be taken into consideration. Thus, if the taxpayer owns shares of stock in a corporation, and dividends have been paid regularly for several years upon the stock, the taxpayer should, in the absence of information indicating a change in the dividend policy, include the prospective dividends from the corporation for the taxable year as well as those actually received in such year prior to determining the estimated tax. In the case of a taxpayer engaged in business on his own account, there shall be made an estimate of gross income and deductions and credits in the light of the best available information affecting the trade, business, or profession.

(b) *Computation of estimated tax.*—In computing the estimated tax the taxpayer should take into account the taxes, credits, and other amounts listed in §1.6654-1(a)(4). [Reg. §1.6654-5.]

☐ [T.D. 9224, 9-1-2005.]

[Reg. §1.6654-6]

§1.6654-6. **Nonresident alien individuals.**— (a) *In general.*—A nonresident alien individual is required to make a payment of estimated tax if that individual's gross income meets the requirements of section 6654 and §1.6654-1. In making the determination under section 6654 as to whether the amount of the gross income of a nonresident alien individual is such as to require making a payment of estimated income tax, only the filing status relating to a single individual (other than a head of household) or to a married individual not entitled to file a joint return shall apply, unless an election is in effect for the taxable year under section 6013(g) or (h) and the regulations.

(b) *Determination of gross income.*—To determine the gross income of a nonresident alien individual who is not, or does not expect to be, a bona fide resident of Puerto Rico or a possession to which section 931 applies during the entire taxable year, see section 872 and §§1.872-1 and 1.872-2. To determine the gross income of a nonresident alien individual who is, or expects to be, a bona fide resident of Puerto Rico or a possession to which section 931 applies during the entire taxable year, see section 876 and the regulations. For rules for determining whether an individual is a bona fide resident of a United States possession (including Puerto Rico), see section 937 and the regulations. [Reg. §1.6654-6.]

☐ [T.D. 9224, 9-1-2005.]

[Reg. §1.6654-7]

§1.6654-7. **Applicability.**—Section 6654 is applicable only with respect to taxable years beginning after December 31, 1954. Section 294(d) of the Internal Revenue Code of 1939 shall continue in force with respect to taxable years beginning before January 1, 1955. [Reg. §1.6654-7.]

☐ [T.D. 6267, 11-13-57. Amended by T.D. 7282, 7-16-73. Redesignated by T.D. 9224, 9-1-2005.]

[Reg. §1.6655-0]

§1.6655-0. **Table of contents.**—This section lists the table of contents for §§1.6655-1 through 1.6655-7.

§1.6655-1. Addition to the tax in the case of a corporation.

(a) In general.
(b) Amount of underpayment.
(c) Period of the underpayment.
(d) Amount of required installment.
(1) In general.
(2) Exception.
(e) Large corporation required to pay 100 percent of current year tax.
(1) In general.
(2) May use last year's tax for first installment.
(f) Required installment due dates.
(1) Number of required installments.
(2) Time for payment of installments.
(i) Calendar year.

(ii) Fiscal year.

(iii) Short taxable year.

(iv) Partial month.

(g) Definitions.

(h) Special rules for consolidated returns.

(i) Overpayments applied to subsequent taxable year's estimated tax.

(1) In general.

(2) Subsequent examinations.

(j) Examples.

(k) Effective/applicability date.

§1.6655-2. *Annualized income installment method.*

(a) In general.

(b) Determination of annualized income installment—in general.

(c) Special rules.

(1) Applicable percentage.

(2) Partial month.

(3) Annualization period not a short taxable year.

(d) Election of different annualization periods.

(e) 52-53 week taxable year.

(f) Determination of taxable income for an annualization period.

(1) In general.

(i) Items of income.

(ii) Items of deduction.

(iii) Losses.

(2) Certain deductions required to be allocated in a reasonably accurate manner.

(i) In general.

(ii) Application of the reasonably accurate manner requirement to certain charitable contributions, recurring items, and 12-month rule items.

(iii) Reasonably accurate manner defined.

(iv) Special rule for certain real property tax liabilities.

(v) Examples.

(3) Special rules.

(i) Advance payments.

(A) Advance payments under §1.451-5(b)(1)(ii).

(B) Advance payments under Rev. Proc. 2004-34.

(ii) Extraordinary items.

(A) In general.

(B) De minimis extraordinary items.

(C) Special rules for net operating loss deductions and section 481(a) adjustments.

(iii) Credits.

(A) Current year credits.

(B) Credit carryovers.

(iv) Depreciation and amortization.

(A) Estimated annual depreciation and amortization.

(B) Safe harbors.

(1) Proportionate depreciation allowance.

(2) 90 percent of preceding year's depreciation.

(3) Safe harbor operational rules.

(C) Short taxable years.

(v) Distributive share of items

(A) Member of partnership.

(B) Treatment of subpart F income and income under section 936(h).

(1) General rule.

(2) Prior year safe harbor.

(i) General rule.

(ii) Special rule for noncontrolling shareholder.

(C) Dividends from closely held real estate investment trust.

(1) General rule.

(2) Closely held real estate investment trust.

(D) Other passthrough entities.

(vi) Alternative minimum taxable income exemption amount.

(vii) Examples.

(g) Items that substantially affect taxable income but cannot be determined accurately by the installment due date.

(1) In general.

(2) Example.

(h) Effective/applicability date.

§1.6655-3. *Adjusted seasonal installment method.*

(a) In general.

(b) Limitation on application of section.

(c) Determination of amount.

(d) Special rules.

(1) Base period percentage.

(2) Filing month.

(3) Application of the rules related to the annualized income installment method to the adjusted seasonal installment method.

(4) Alternative minimum tax.

(e) Example.

(f) Effective/applicability date.

§1.6655-4. *Large corporations.*

(a) Large corporation defined.

(b) Testing period.

(c) Computation of taxable income during testing period.

(1) Short taxable year.

(2) Computation of taxable income in taxable year when there occurs a transaction to which section 381 applies.

(d) Members of controlled group.

(1) In general.

(2) Aggregation.

(3) Allocation rule.

(4) Controlled group members.

(e) Effect on a corporation's taxable income of items that may be carried back or carried over from any other taxable year.

(f) Consolidated returns. [Reserved]

(g) Example.

(h) Effective/applicability date.

§ 1.6655-5. *Short taxable year.*
   (a) In general.
   (b) Exception to payment of estimated tax.
   (c) Installment due dates.
      (1) In general.
         (i) Taxable year of at least four months but less than twelve months.
         (ii) Exceptions.
      (2) Early termination of taxable year.
         (i) In general.
         (ii) Exception.
   (d) Amount due for required installment.
      (1) In general.
      (2) Tax shown on the return for the preceding taxable year.
      (3) Applicable percentage.
      (4) Applicable percentage for installment period in which taxpayer does not reasonably expect that the taxable year will be an early termination year.
   (e) Examples.
   (f) 52 or 53 week taxable year.
   (g) Use of annualized income or seasonal installment method.
      (1) In general.
      (2) Computation of annualized income installment.
      (3) Annualization period for final required installment.
      (4) Examples.
   (h) Effective/applicability date.

§ 1.6655-6. *Methods of accounting.*
   (a) In general.
   (b) Accounting method changes.
   (c) Examples.
   (d) Effective/applicability date.

§ 1.6655-7. *Addition to tax on account of excessive adjustment under section 6425.*
[Reg. § 1.6655-0.]

□ [T.D. 9347, 8-6-2007.]

[Reg. § 1.6655-1.]

§ 1.6655-1. Addition to the tax in the case of a corporation.—(a) *In general.*—Section 6655 imposes an addition to the tax under chapter 1 of the Internal Revenue Code in the case of any underpayment of estimated tax by a corporation. An addition to tax due to the underpayment of estimated taxes is determined by applying the underpayment rate established under section 6621 to the amount of the underpayment, for the period of the underpayment. This addition to the tax is in addition to any applicable criminal penalties and is imposed whether or not there was reasonable cause for the underpayment.

(b) *Amount of underpayment.*—The amount of the underpayment for any required installment is the excess of—
   (1) The required installment; over
   (2) The amount, if any, of the installment paid on or before the last date prescribed for such payment.

(c) *Period of the underpayment.*—The period of the underpayment of any required installment runs from the date the installment was required to be paid to the 15th day of the 3rd month following the close of the taxable year, or to the date such underpayment is paid, whichever is earlier. For purposes of determining the period of the underpayment a payment of estimated tax will be credited against unpaid required installments in the order in which such installments are required to be paid.

(d) *Amount of required installment.*—(1) *In general.*—Except as otherwise provided in this section and §§ 1.6655-2 through 1.6655-7, the amount of any required installment is 25 percent of the lesser of—

   (i) 100 percent of the tax shown on the return for the taxable year (or, if no return is filed, 100 percent of the tax for such year); or

   (ii) 100 percent of the tax shown on the return for the preceding taxable year.

(2) *Exception.*—This paragraph (d)(1)(ii) does not apply if the preceding taxable year was not a taxable year of 12 months or the corporation did not file a return for the preceding taxable year showing a liability for tax.

(e) *Large corporation required to pay 100 percent of current year tax.*—(1) *In general.*—Except as provided in paragraph (e)(2) of this section, paragraph (d)(1)(ii) of this section does not apply in the case of a large corporation (as defined in § 1.6655-4).

(2) *May use last year's tax for first installment.*—Paragraph (e)(1) of this section does not apply for purposes of determining the amount of the 1st required installment for any taxable year. Any reduction in such 1st installment by reason of the preceding sentence is recaptured by increasing the amount of the next required installment determined under paragraph (d)(1)(i) of this section by the amount of such reduction and, if the next required installment is reduced by use of the annualized income installment method under § 1.6655-2 or the adjusted seasonal installment method under § 1.6655-3, by increasing subsequent required installments determined under paragraph (d)(1)(i) of this section to the extent that the reduction has not previously been recaptured.

(f) *Required installment due dates.*—(1) *Number of required installments.*—Unless otherwise provided, corporations must make 4 required installments for each taxable year.

(2) *Time for payment of installments.*—(i) *Calendar year.*—Unless otherwise provided, in the case of a calendar year taxpayer, the due dates of the required installments are as follows:

1st	April 15
2nd	June 15
3rd	September 15
4th	December 15

(ii) *Fiscal year.*—In the case of a taxpayer other than a calendar year taxpayer, the due dates of the required installments are as follows:

1st . . .	15th day of 4th month of the taxable year
2nd . .	15th day of 6th month of the taxable year
3rd . . .	15th day of 9th month of the taxable year
4th . . .	15th day of 12th month of the taxable year

(iii) *Short taxable year.*—See § 1.6655-5 for rules regarding required installments for corporations with a short taxable year.

(iv) *Partial month.*—Except as otherwise provided, for purposes of determining the due date of any required installment, a partial month is treated as a full month.

(g) *Definitions.*—(1) The term tax as used in this section and § § 1.6655-2 through 1.6655-7 means the excess of—

(i) The sum of—

(A) The tax imposed by section 11, section 1201(a), or subchapter L of chapter 1 of the Internal Revenue Code, whichever is applicable;

(B) The tax imposed by section 55; plus

(C) The tax imposed by section 887; over

(ii) The credits against tax provided by part IV of subchapter A of chapter 1 of the Internal Revenue Code.

(2)(i) In the case of a foreign corporation subject to taxation under section 11, section 1201(a), or subchapter L of chapter 1 of the Internal Revenue Code, the tax imposed by section 881 is treated as a tax imposed by section 11.

(ii) In the case of a partnership that is treated, pursuant to regulations issued under section 1446(f)(2), as a corporation for purposes of this section, the tax imposed by section 1446 is treated as a tax imposed by section 11.

(iii) Unless otherwise provided in the Internal Revenue Code or Treasury regulations, for purposes of the definition of "tax" as used in this section, a recapture of tax, such as a recapture provided by section 50(a)(1)(A), and any other similar provision, is not considered to be a tax imposed by section 11.

(iv) For the purposes of paragraph (d) of this section, the return for the preceding taxable year is the Federal income tax return for such taxable year that is required by section 6012(a)(2). However, if an amended Federal income tax return has been filed before the due date of an installment, then the return for the preceding taxable year is the Federal income tax return as amended. If an amended Federal income tax return has been filed on or after the due date for an installment, then the return for the preceding taxable year does not include for such installment period the Federal income tax return as amended subsequent to the due date for such installment. Paragraph (d) of this section will apply without regard to whether the taxpayer's Federal income tax return for the preceding taxable year is filed in a timely manner.

(h) *Special rules for consolidated returns.*—For special rules relating to the determination of the amount of the underpayment in the case of a corporation whose income is included in a consolidated return, see § 1.1502-5(b).

(i) *Overpayments applied to subsequent taxable year's estimated tax.*—(1) *In general.*—If a taxpayer elects under the provisions of sections 6402(b) and 6513(d) and the regulations to apply an overpayment in year one against the estimated tax liability for year two, the overpayment will be applied to the required installment payments for year two in the order due and to the extent necessary to satisfy such installments, similar to the manner in which an actual overpayment of one installment is carried forward to the next installment. No interest is accrued or paid on an overpayment if the election to apply the overpayment against estimated tax is made.

(2) *Subsequent examinations.*—If a deficiency is determined in an examination of a return for a taxable year that originally reflected an overpayment that was applied against estimated tax for the succeeding taxable year, interest on the deficiency will not begin to accrue on an amount applied until that amount is used to satisfy a required estimated tax payment in such taxable year. Regardless of whether the taxpayer anticipated the application of such overpayment from the prior taxable year in calculating and paying its required estimated tax installment liabilities for the current taxable year, the subsequently determined underpayment and interest computation thereon will not change the taxpayer's original election to apply the overpayment against the estimated tax liability of the succeeding taxable year. Any changes to the usage of the original overpayment from the prior taxable year are hypothetical only and solely for the purpose of computing deficiency interest. Overpayment interest will not be impacted. For further guidance, see Rev. Rul. 99-40 (1999-2 CB 441), (see § 601.601(d)(2)(ii)(b) of this chapter).

(j) *Examples.*—The method prescribed in paragraphs (d) through (g) of this section is illustrated by the following examples:

Example 1. (i) X, a calendar year corporation, estimates its tax liability for its taxable year ending December 31, 2009, will be $85,000. X is not a large corporation as defined in section 6655(g)(2) and § 1.6655-4. X reported a liability of $74,900 on its return for the taxable year ended December 31, 2008, with no credits against tax. X paid four installments of estimated tax, each in the amount of $18,725 (25 percent of $74,900), on April 15, 2009, June 15, 2009, September 15, 2009, and December 15, 2009, respectively. X reported a tax liability of $88,900 on its return due March 15, 2010. X had a $5,000 credit against tax for tax year 2009 as provided by part IV of subchapter A of chapter 1 of the Internal Revenue Code. X did not underpay its estimated tax for tax year 2009 for any of the four installments, determined as follows:

(A) Tax as defined in paragraph (g) of this section for 2009 ($88,900-$5,000) = $83,900

(B) Tax as defined in paragraph (g) of this section for 2008 = $74,900

(C) 100% of the lesser of this paragraph (j), *Example 1* (i)(A) or (i)(B) = $74,900

(D) Amount of estimated tax required to be paid on or before each installment date (25% of $74,900) = $18,725

(E) Deduct amount paid on or before each installment date = $18,725

(F) Amount of underpayment for each installment date = $0

(ii) [Reserved].

Example 2. (i) *Facts.* Y, a calendar year corporation, estimates its tax liability for its taxable year ending December 31, 2009, will be $70,000. Y is not a large corporation as defined in section 6655(g)(2) and § 1.6655-4. Y reported a Federal income tax liability of $90,000 for its taxable year ending December 31, 2008. Y paid no installment of estimated tax on or before April 15, 2009, June 15, 2009, or September 15, 2009, but made a payment of $63,000 on December 15, 2009. On March 15, 2010, Y filed its income tax return showing a tax of $70,000. Y had no credits against tax for tax year 2009. Of the $63,000 paid by Y on December 15, 2009, $17,500 is applied to each of the first three installments due on April 15, June 15, and September 15, 2009, and the remaining $10,500 is applied to the fourth installment. Y has an underpayment of estimated tax for each of the first three installments of $17,500 and for the fourth installment of $7,000. The addition to tax under section 6655(a) is computed as follows:

(A) Tax as defined in paragraph (g) of this section for 2009 = $70,000

(B) Tax as defined in paragraph (g) of this section for 2008 = $90,000

(C) 100% of the lesser of this paragraph (j), *Example 2* (i)(A) or (i)(B) = $70,000

(D) Amount of estimated tax required to be paid on or before each installment date (25% of $70,000) = $17,500

(E) Amount paid on or before the first, second, and third installment dates = $0

(F) Amount paid on or before the fourth installment date = $63,000

(G) Amount of underpayment for each of the first, second, and third installment dates = $17,500

(H) Amount of underpayment for the fourth installment date = $7,000

(ii) *Addition to tax.* Assuming that neither the annualized income installment method nor the adjusted seasonal installment method described in §§ 1.6655-2 and 1.6655-3 would result in a lower payment for any installment period, and the addition to tax is computed under section 6621(a)(2) at the rate of 8 percent per annum for the applicable periods of underpayment, the addition to tax is determined as follows:

(A) First installment (underpayment period 4-16-09 through 12-15-09), computed as 244/365 × $17,500 × 8% = $936

(B) Second installment (underpayment period 6-16-09 through 12-15-09), computed as 183/365 × $17,500 × 8% = $702

(C) Third installment (underpayment period 9-16-09 through 12-15-09), computed as 91/365 × $17,500 × 8% = $349

(D) Fourth installment (underpayment period 12-16-09 through 3-15-10), computed as 90/365 × $7,000 × 8% = $138

(E) Total of this paragraph (j), *Example 2* (ii)(A) through (D) = $2,125

(k) *Effective/applicability date.*—This section applies to taxable years beginning after September 6, 2007. [Reg. § 1.6655-1.]

☐ [*T.D. 6267, 11-13-57. Amended by T.D. 6768, 11-3-64, T.D. 7244, 12-29-72; T.D. 7384, 10-21-75 and T.D. 9347, 8-6-2007.*]

[Reg. § 301.6655-1]

§ 301.6655-1. Failure by corporation to pay estimated income tax.—(a) For regulations under section 6655, see §§ 1.6655-1 through 1.6655-7 of this chapter.

(b) Effective/applicability date: This section applies to taxable years beginning after September 6, 2007. [Reg. § 301.6655-1.]

☐ [*T.D. 6268, 11-15-57. Amended by T.D. 6498, 10-24-60; T.D. 7059, 9-16-70 and T.D. 9347, 8-6-2007.*]

[Reg. § 1.6655-2]

§ 1.6655-2. Annualized income installment method.—(a) *In general.*—In the case of any required installment, if the corporation establishes that the annualized income installment determined under this section, or the adjusted seasonal installment determined under § 1.6655-3, is less than the amount determined under § 1.6655-1—

(1) The amount of such required installment is the annualized income installment (or, if less, the adjusted seasonal installment); and

(2) Any reduction in a required installment resulting from the application of this section will be recaptured by increasing the amount of the next required installment determined under § 1.6655-1 by the amount of such reduction (and, if the next required installment is similarly reduced, by increasing subsequent required installments to the extent that the reduction has not previously been recaptured).

(b) *Determination of annualized income installment—in general.*—In the case of any required installment, the annualized income installment is the excess (if any) of—

(1) The product of the applicable percentage and the tax (after reducing the annualized tax by the amount of any allowable credits) for the taxable year computed by annualizing the taxable income and alternative minimum taxable income—

(i) For the first 3 months of the taxable year, in the case of the first required installment;

(ii) For the first 3 months of the taxable year, in the case of the second required installment;

(iii) For the first 6 months of the taxable year, in the case of the third required installment; and

(iv) For the first 9 months of the taxable year, in the case of the fourth required installment; over

(2) The aggregate amount of any prior required installments for the taxable year.

(c) *Special rules.*—(1) *Applicable percentage.*—Except as otherwise provided in § 1.6655-5(d) with respect to short taxable years—

In the case of the following required installments:	The applicable percentage is:
1st	25%
2nd	50%
3rd	75%
4th	100%

(2) *Partial month.*—Except as otherwise provided, for purposes of paragraph (b) of this section a partial month is treated as a month.

(3) *Annualization period not a short taxable year.*—An annualization period is not treated as a short taxable year for purposes of determining the taxable income of an annualization period.

(d) *Election of different annualization periods.*—(1) If the taxpayer timely files Form 8842, "Election to Use Different Annualization Periods for Corporate Estimated Tax," in accordance with section 6655(e)(2)(C)(iii), and elects Option 1—

(i) Paragraph (b)(1)(i) of this section will be applied by using the language "2 months" instead of "3 months";

(ii) Paragraph (b)(1)(ii) of this section will be applied by using the language "4 months" instead of "3 months";

(iii) Paragraph (b)(1)(iii) of this section will be applied by using the language "7 months" instead of "6 months"; and

(iv) Paragraph (b)(1)(iv) of this section will be applied by using the language "10 months" instead of "9 months".

(2) If the taxpayer timely files Form 8842, in accordance with section 6655(e)(2)(C)(iii), and elects Option 2—

(i) Paragraph (b)(1)(ii) of this section will be applied by using the language "5 months" instead of "3 months";

(ii) Paragraph (b)(1)(iii) of this section will be applied by using the language "8 months" instead of "6 months"; and

(iii) Paragraph (b)(1)(iv) of this section will be applied by using the language "11 months" instead of "9 months".

(3) The application of the annualized income installment method is illustrated by the following example:

Example. (i) ABC, a calendar year corporation, had a taxable year of less than twelve months for tax year 2008 and no credits against tax for tax year 2009. ABC made an estimated tax payment of $15,000 on the installment dates of April 15, 2009, June 15, 2009, September 15, 2009, and December 15, 2009, respectively. Assume that, under paragraph (d)(1) of this section, ABC elected Option 1 by timely filing Form 8842, in accordance with section 6655(e)(2)(C)(iii), and determined that its taxable income for the first 2, 4, 7 and 10 months was $25,000, $64,000, $125,000, and $175,000 respectively. The income for each period is annualized as follows:

$25,000 × 12/2 = $150,000

$64,000 × 12/4 = $192,000

$125,000 × 12/7 = $214,286

$175,000 × 12/10 = $210,000

(ii)(A) To determine whether the installment payment made on April 15, 2009, equals or exceeds the amount that would have been required to have been paid if the estimated tax were equal to 100 percent of the tax computed on the annualized income for the 2-month period, the following computation is necessary:

(1) Annualized income for the 2 month period = $150,000

(2) Tax on this paragraph (d)(3), *Example* (ii)(A)(1) = $41,750

(3) 100% of this paragraph (d)(3), *Example* (ii)(A)(2) = $41,750

(4) 25% of this paragraph (d)(3), *Example* (ii)(A)(3) = $10,438

(B) Because the total amount of estimated tax that was timely paid on or before the first installment date ($15,000) exceeds the amount required to be paid on or before this date if the estimated tax were 100 percent of the tax determined by placing on an annualized basis the taxable income for the first 2-month period ($10,438), the exception described in paragraphs (a) and (b) of this section applies, and no addition to tax will be imposed for the installment due on April 15, 2009.

(iii)(A) To determine whether the installment payments made on or before June 15, 2009, equal or exceed the amount that would have been required to have been paid if the estimated tax were equal to 100 percent of the tax computed on the annualized income for the 4-month period, the following computation is necessary:

(1) Annualized income for the 4 month period = $192,000

(2) Tax on this paragraph (d)(3), *Example* (iii)(A)(1) = $58,130

(3) 100% of this paragraph (d)(3), *Example* (iii)(A)(2) = $58,130

(4) 50% of this paragraph (d)(3), *Example* (iii)(A)(3) less $10,438 (amount due with the first installment) = $18,627

(B) Because the total amount of estimated tax actually paid on or before the second installment date ($19,562 ($15,000 second required installment payment plus $4,562 overpayment of first required installment)) exceeds the amount required to be paid on or before this date if the estimated tax were 100 percent of the tax determined by placing on an annualized basis the taxable income for the first 4-month period ($18,627), the exception described in paragraphs (a) and (b) of this section applies, and no addition to tax will be imposed for the installment due on June 15, 2009.

(iv)(A) To determine whether the installment payments made on or before September 15, 2009, equal or exceed the amount that would have been required to have been paid if the estimated tax were equal to 100 percent of the tax computed on the annualized income for the 7-month period, the following computation is necessary:

(1) Annualized income for the 7 month period = $214,286

(2) Tax on this paragraph (d)(3), *Example* (iv)(A)(1) = $66,821

(3) 100% of this paragraph (d)(3), *Example* (iv)(A)(2) = $66,821

(4) 75% of this paragraph (d)(3), *Example* (iv)(A)(3) less $29,065 (amount due with the first and second installment) = $21,051

(B) Because the total amount of estimated tax actually paid on or before the third installment date ($15,935 ($15,000 third required installment payment plus $935 overpayment of second required installment)) does not equal or exceed the amount required to be paid on or before this date if the estimated tax were 100 percent of the tax determined by placing on an annualized basis the taxable income for the first 7-month period ($21,051), the exception described in paragraphs (a) and (b) of this section does not apply, and an addition to tax will be imposed with respect to the underpayment of the September 15, 2009, installment unless another exception applies to this installment payment.

(v)(A) To determine whether the installment payments made on or before December 15, 2009, equal or exceed the amount that would have been required to have been paid if the estimated tax were equal to 100 percent of the tax computed on the annualized income for the 10-month period, the following computation is necessary:

(1) Annualized income for the 10 month period = $210,000

(2) Tax on this paragraph (d)(3), *Example* (v)(A)(1) = $65,150

(3) 100% of this paragraph (d)(3), *Example* (v)(A)(2) = $65,150

(4) 100% of this paragraph (d)(3), *Example* (v)(A)(3) less $50,116 (amount due with the first, second and third installment) = $15,034

(B) Because the total amount of estimated tax payments made on or before the fourth installment date that is available to be applied to the estimated tax due for the fourth installment ($9,884 ($15,000 fourth required installment payment less $5,116 underpayment for the third installment of estimated tax ($21,051 third installment of estimated tax due less $15,935 payments available to be applied to the third installment of estimated tax))) does not equal or exceed the amount required to be paid on or before this date if the estimated tax were 100 percent of the tax determined by placing on an annualized basis the taxable income for the first 10-month period ($15,034), the exception described in paragraphs (a) and (b) of this section does not apply, and an addition to tax will be imposed with respect to the underpayment of the December 15, 2009, installment unless another exception applies to this installment payment.

(vi) Assuming that no other exceptions apply and the addition to tax is computed under section 6621(a)(2) at the rate of 8 percent per annum for the applicable periods of underpayment, the amount of the addition to tax is as follows:

(A) First installment (no underpayment) = $0

(B) Second installment (no underpayment) = $0

(C) Third installment (underpayment period 9-16-09 through 12-15-09), computed as $91/365 \times \$5,116 \times 8\% = \$102$

(D) Fourth installment (underpayment period 12-16-09 through 3-15-10), computed as $90/365 \times \$5,150 \times 8\% = \$102$

(E) Total of this paragraph (d)(3), *Example* (vi)(A) through (D) = $204

(e) *52-53 week taxable year.*—(1) Generally, except as provided in the alternative rule in paragraph (e)(4) of this section, in the case of a taxpayer whose taxable year constitutes 52 or 53 weeks in accordance with section 441(f), the rules prescribed by §1.441-2 are applicable in determining—

(i) Whether a taxable year is a taxable year of 12 months; and

(ii) When the 2-, 3-,4-, 5-, 6-, 7-, 8-, 9-, 10-, or 11-month period (whichever is applicable) commences and ends for purposes of paragraphs (b)(1), (d)(1) and (d)(2) of this section.

(2) If a taxpayer employs four 13-week periods or thirteen 4-week accounting periods and the end of any accounting period employed by the taxpayer does not correspond to the end of the 2-, 3-,4-, 5-, 6-, 7-, 8-, 9-, 10-, or 11-month period (whichever is applicable), then, provided the taxpayer has at least one full 4-week or 13-week accounting period, as appropriate, within the applicable period, annualized taxable income for the applicable period is—

(i) $[(x/(y*13))*z]$, in the case of a taxpayer using four 13-week periods, if—

(A) x = Taxable income for the number of full 13-week periods in the applicable period;

(B) y = The number of full 13-week periods in the applicable period; and

(C) z = The number of weeks in the taxable year; or

(ii) $[(x/(y*4))*z]$, in the case of a taxpayer using thirteen 4-week periods, if—

(A) x = Taxable income for the number of full 4-week periods in the applicable period;

(B) y = The number of full 4-week periods in the applicable period; and

(C) z = The number of weeks in the taxable year.

(3) If a taxpayer employs four 13-week periods and the taxpayer does not have at least one 13-week period within the applicable 2-, 3-, 4-, 5-, 6-, 7-, 8-, 9-, 10-, or 11-month period, the taxpayer is permitted to determine annualized taxable income for the applicable period based upon—

(i) The taxable income for the number of weeks in the applicable period; or

(ii) The taxable income for the full 13-week periods that end before the due date of the required installment.

(4) As an alternative to using the 52/53 week taxable year rules provided in paragraphs (e)(1), (e)(2), and (e)(3) of this section, a taxpayer whose taxable year constitutes 52 or 53 weeks in accordance with section 441(f) may base its annualization period on the month that ends closest to the end of its applicable 4-week period or 13-week period that ends within the applicable annualization period. This alternative may only be used if it is used for determining annualization periods for all required installments for the taxable year.

(5) The following examples illustrate the rules of this paragraph (e):

Example 1. Corporation ABC, an accrual method taxpayer, uses a 52/53 week year-end ending on the last Friday in December and uses four thirteen-week periods. For its year beginning December 28, 2007, ABC uses the annualized income installment method under section 6655(e)(2)(A)(i) to calculate all of its required installments. For purposes of computing its first and second required installments, the first 3 months of A's taxable year under paragraph (b)(1)(i) of this section will end on March 28th, the thirteenth Friday of ABC's taxable year. For purposes of its third required installment, the first 6 months of ABC's taxable year will end on June 27th, the twenty-sixth Friday of ABC's taxable year. For purposes of its fourth required installment, the first 9 months of ABC's taxable year will end on September 26th, the thirty-ninth Friday of ABC's taxable year.

Example 2. Same facts as *Example 1* except that ABC uses thirteen four-week periods and there are 52 weeks during ABC's taxable year beginning December 28, 2007, and ending December 26, 2008. For purposes of computing ABC's first and second required installments, ABC's annualized taxable income for the first three months will be the taxable income for the first three four-week periods of ABC's taxable year (December 28, 2007, through March 21, 2008) divided by 12 (number of full four-week periods in the first three months (3) multiplied by 4) and multiplied by 52 (the number of weeks in the taxable year). For purposes of computing ABC's third required installment, ABC's annualized taxable income for the first six months will be the taxable income for the first six four-week

periods of ABC's taxable year (December 28, 2007, through June 13, 2008) divided by 24 and multiplied by 52. For purposes of computing ABC's fourth required installment, ABC's annualized taxable income for the first nine months will be the taxable income for the first nine four-week periods of ABC's taxable year (December 28, 2007, through September 5, 2008) divided by 36 and multiplied by 52.

Example 3. Same facts as *Example 1* except that ABC uses the alternative method under paragraph (e)(4) of this section for computing its required installments for 2008. For purposes of computing its first and second required installments, the first three months of ABC's taxable year under paragraph (b)(1)(i) of this section will end on March 31, 2008, the month that ends closest to the end of ABC's applicable thirteen-week period for the first and second required installments. For purposes of ABC's third required installment, the first six months of ABC's taxable year will end on June 30, 2008, the month that ends closest to the end of ABC's applicable thirteen-week period for the third required installment. For purposes of ABC's fourth required installment, the first nine months of ABC's taxable year will end on September 30, 2008, the month that ends closest to the end of ABC's applicable thirteen-week period for the fourth required installment.

(f) *Determination of taxable income for an annualization period.*—(1) *In general.*—This paragraph (f) applies for purposes of determining the applicability of the exception described in paragraphs (a) and (b) of this section (relating to the annualization of income) and the exception described in § 1.6655-3 (relating to annualization of income for corporations with seasonal income). An item of income, deduction, gain or loss is to be taken into account in determining the taxable income and alternative minimum taxable income (and applicable tax and alternative minimum tax) for an annualization period in the manner provided in this paragraph (f). An item may not be taken into account in determining taxable income for any annualization period unless the item is properly taken into account by the last day of that annualization period and the item is properly taken into account in determining the taxpayer's taxable income and alternative minimum taxable income (and applicable tax and alternative minimum tax) for the taxable year that includes the annualization period.

(i) *Items of income.*—An item of income is taken into account in the annualization period in which the item is properly includible under the method of accounting employed by the taxpayer with respect to the item and in accordance with the appropriate provision of the Internal Revenue Code (for example, section 451 for accrual method taxpayers, section 453 for installment sales or section 460 for long-term contracts).

(ii) *Items of deduction.*—An item of deduction is taken into account in the annualization period in which the item is properly deductible under the method of accounting employed by the taxpayer with respect to the item and in accordance with the appropriate provision of the Internal Revenue Code (for example, under the cash receipts and disbursements method of accounting, the deduction must be paid under § 1.461-1(a)(1) and be otherwise deductible in computing taxable income; under an accrual method of accounting, the deduction must be incurred under § 1.461-1(a)(2) and be otherwise deductible in computing taxable income). Section 170(a)(2) and § 1.170A-11(b) (charitable contributions by accrual method corporations) and § 1.461-5 (recurring item exception) may not be taken into consideration by an accrual method taxpayer in any annualization period in determining whether an item of deduction has been incurred under § 1.461-1(a)(2) during that annualization period.

(iii) *Losses.*—An item of loss is to be taken into account during the annualization period in which events have occurred that permit the loss to be taken into account under the appropriate provision of the Internal Revenue Code.

(2) *Certain deductions required to be allocated in a reasonably accurate manner.*—(i) *In general.*— The following deductions allowed for a taxable year must be allocated throughout the taxable year in a reasonably accurate manner (as defined in paragraph (f)(2)(iii) of this section), regardless of the annualization period in which the item is paid or incurred:

(A) Real property tax deductions.

(B) Employee and independent contractor bonus compensation deductions (including the employer's share of employment taxes related to such compensation).

(C) Deductions under sections 404 (deferred compensation) and 419 (welfare benefit funds).

(D) Items allowed as a deduction for the taxable year by reason of section 170(a)(2) and § 1.170A-11(b) (certain charitable contributions by accrual method corporations), § 1.461-5 (recurring item exception) or § 1.263(a)-4(f) (12-month rule).

(E) Items of deduction designated by the Secretary by publication in the Internal Revenue Bulletin (see § 601.601(d)(2)(ii)(b) of this chapter).

(ii) Application of the reasonably accurate manner requirement to certain charitable contributions, recurring items, and 12-month rule items. For purposes of paragraph (f)(2)(i)(D) of this section, the total amount of the item deducted in the computation of taxable income for the taxable year must be allocated in a reasonably accurate manner, notwithstanding the fact that section 170(a)(2) and § 1.170A-11(b), § 1.461-5, or § 1.263(a)-4(f) applies to only a portion of the total amount of the item deducted for the taxable year. For example, if a portion of a taxpayer's rebate liabilities are deducted in the computation of taxable income under the recurring item exception, all rebate liabilities de-

ducted in the computation of taxable income for the taxable year must be allocated in a reasonably accurate manner.

(iii) *Reasonably accurate manner defined.*— (A) An item is allocated throughout the taxable year in a reasonably accurate manner if the item is allocated ratably throughout the taxable year or if the allocation provides a reasonably accurate estimate of taxable income for the taxable year based upon the facts known as of the end of the annualization period. In determining that an allocation of an item provides a reasonably accurate estimate of taxable income for the taxable year, relevant considerations include—

(1) The extent to which the allocation is consistent with the taxpayer's accounting for the item on its non-tax books and records;

(2) The extent to which the allocable portion of the item becomes fixed and determinable (under § 1.461-1(a)(2)) during the applicable annualization period; and

(3) The extent to which the allocation, if compared to the ratable allocation of the item, results in a better matching of the item of deduction to revenue, earnings, the use of property or the provision of services occurring during the annualization period.

(B) None of the relevant considerations above override the general requirement that the allocation must be done in a reasonably accurate manner based upon the facts known as of the end of the annualization period. For example, the fact that a liability for an annual expense becomes fixed and determinable during an annualization period will not establish that allocating all of the expense to that annualization period has been done in a reasonably accurate manner if the facts known as of the end of the annualization period indicate otherwise.

(iv) *Special rule for certain real property tax liabilities.*—Notwithstanding paragraph (f)(2)(iii) of this section, real property tax liabilities for which an election under section 461(c) is in effect must be allocated ratably throughout the taxable year for purposes of this section.

(v) *Examples.*—Unless otherwise stated, the following examples assume that the taxpayer uses the 3-3-6-9 annualization period:

Example 1. (i) Corporation ABC, a calendar year taxpayer, uses an accrual method of accounting and the annualized income installment method under section 6655(e)(2)(A)(i) to calculate all of its required installment payments for its 2008 taxable year. ABC has adopted a plan under which ABC pays an annual bonus to its employees. As of March 31, 2008, ABC estimates that it will pay a year-end bonus of $500,000 to its employees if earnings remain constant throughout the tax year. ABC does not pay any of the estimated bonus liability as of March 31, 2008. On October 31, 2008, ABC declares a $600,000 bonus to its employees which is paid out on November 15, 2008, and properly deducted in ABC's December 31, 2008, tax year. No

Reg. § 1.6655-2(f)(2)(v)

other bonus liabilities are incurred by ABC during the tax year.

(ii) Under the general rule provided in paragraph (f)(2)(i) of this section, ABC is required to allocate its employee bonus liability in a reasonably accurate manner for annualization purposes. Under paragraph (f)(2)(iii) of this section, ABC's employee bonus liability will be deemed to be allocated in a reasonably accurate manner if the item is allocated ratably throughout the taxable year. Therefore, ABC is permitted to recognize a $150,000 bonus deduction (one quarter of the $600,000 bonus liability properly recognized by ABC in the tax year ending December 31, 2008) in the first annualization period ending March 31, 2008.

Example 2. (i) Corporation ABC, a calendar year taxpayer, uses an accrual method of accounting and the annualized income installment method under section 6655(e)(2)(A)(i) to calculate all of its required installment payments for its 2008 taxable year. ABC has adopted a plan under which ABC pays an annual bonus to its employees. ABC's employee bonus plan generally calls for an annual bonus equal to 2% of earnings. A bonus reserve for this amount is reported each quarter in ABC's non-tax books and records. ABC's quarterly revenues throughout the year are $10,000,000; $6,000,000; $7,000,000; and $7,000,000 respectively. As of March 31, 2008, ABC estimates that it will pay a year-end bonus of $800,000 ($10,000,000 × 4 × 2%) to its employees if earnings remain constant throughout the year. ABC does not pay any of the estimated bonus payment as of March 31, 2008. On December 31, 2008, ABC declares a $600,000 bonus to its employees which is paid out on January 15, 2009, and properly deducted in ABC's December 31, 2008, tax year.

(ii) Under the general rule provided in paragraph (f)(2)(i) of this section, ABC must allocate its employee bonus liability in a reasonably accurate manner for annualization purposes. Under paragraph (f)(2)(iii) of this section, ABC's employee bonus liability will be deemed to be allocated in a reasonably accurate manner if the allocation provides a reasonable estimate of taxable income based upon the facts known as of the end of the annualization period. Based upon its earnings activities and other information available as of March 31, 2008, ABC estimated that its total deduction for employee bonuses for the taxable year ending December 31, 2008, would be $800,000 ($10,000,000 first quarter earnings × 4 × 2%). Allocating $200,000 ($10,000,000 × 2%) of ABC's annual bonus liability of $600,000 to ABC's first quarter based upon earnings during the quarter represents a better matching of ABC's bonus expense to earnings in the quarter as compared to allocating $150,000 to ABC's first quarter under a ratable accrual method and is consistent with the allocation provided in ABC's non-tax books and records. Accordingly, allocating ABC's employee bonus deductions based upon ABC's earnings will be considered allocated in a reasonably accurate manner.

Example 3. (i) Corporation ABC, a calendar year taxpayer, uses an accrual method of accounting and the annualized income installment method under section 6655(e)(2)(A)(i) to calculate all of its required installment payments for its 2008 taxable year. ABC has adopted a plan under which ABC pays a bonus to its employees each quarter based upon earnings for that quarter. On March 31, 2008, ABC pays out $2,000,000 to its employees as a quarterly bonus based upon the earnings of ABC for the period January 1, 2008, through March 31, 2008. The $2,000,000 bonus is recognized as an expense on ABC's audited financial statements in the quarter ending March 31, 2008. As of March 31, 2008, ABC anticipates that its earnings will continue throughout the year resulting in future quarterly bonus payments in 2008 similar to the $2,000,000 first quarter payment.

(ii) Under the general rule provided in paragraph (f)(2)(i) of this section, ABC is required to allocate its employee bonus liability in a reasonably accurate manner for annualization purposes. Under paragraph (f)(2)(iii) of this section, ABC's employee bonus liability will be deemed to be allocated in a reasonably accurate manner if the item is allocated ratably throughout the taxable year. Therefore, ABC may recognize a $500,000 bonus deduction (one quarter of the $2,000,000 bonus liability properly recognized by ABC in the tax year ending December 31, 2008) in the first annualization period ending March 31, 2008 (as well as one quarter of any additional bonus liability properly recognized by ABC in the tax year ending December 31, 2008).

(iii) In addition, paragraph (f)(2)(iii) of this section provides that an allocation will be considered reasonable if the allocation provides an accurate estimate of taxable income for the taxable year based upon the facts known as of the end of the annualization period. Based upon its earnings activities and other information available as of March 31, 2008, ABC estimates that its total deduction for employee bonuses for the taxable year ending December 31, 2008, would be $8,000,000. In addition, the $2,000,000 bonus liability became fixed and determinable during the first quarter. Allocating $2,000,000 to ABC's first quarter earnings is also consistent with ABC's non-tax books and records and represents a better matching of ABC's bonus expense to earnings in the quarter as compared to a ratable accrual. Accordingly, allocating ABC's bonus liability based upon earnings will be considered a reasonably accurate manner for estimated tax purposes.

Example 4. (i) Corporation ABC, a calendar year taxpayer, uses an accrual method of accounting with the recurring item exception and the annualized income installment method under section 6655(e)(2)(A)(i) to calculate all of its required installment payments for its 2009 taxable year. ABC regularly incurs rebate obligations related to the sale of its products. Rebate coupons that are received and validated by ABC are generally paid in the following month. During the tax year ending December 31, 2009, ABC received, validated and paid $400,000 in rebates. In addition, as of the end of December 31, 2009, ABC had received and validated $100,000 in rebate claims that were paid in January of 2010 and deducted in ABC's December 31, 2009, tax year under the recurring item exception. Therefore, ABC properly recognized a $500,000 rebate liability deduction on ABC's December 31, 2009, tax return.

(ii) Under the rule provided in paragraph (f)(2)(ii) of this section, an item must be allocated in a reasonably accurate manner if any portion of the item is deducted under the recurring item exception. Therefore, ABC will be required to allocate its entire $500,000 rebate liability deduction in a reasonably accurate manner as defined in paragraph (f)(2)(iii) of this section.

(3) *Special rules.*—(i) *Advance payments.*— (A) *Advance payments under §1.451-5(b)(1)(ii).*— An advance payment for which the taxpayer uses the method of accounting provided in §1.451-5(b)(1)(ii) is includible in computing taxable income for an annualization period in accordance with that method of accounting except that, if §1.451-5(c) applies, any amount not included in computing taxable income by the end of the second taxable year following the year in which substantial advance payments are received, and not previously included in accordance with the taxpayer's accrual method of accounting, is includible in computing taxable income on the last day of such second taxable year.

(B) *Advance payments under Rev. Proc. 2004-3.*—An advance payment for which the taxpayer uses the Deferral Method provided in section 5.02 of Rev. Proc. 2004-34 (2004-1 CB 991), (see §601.601(d)(2)(ii)(b) of this chapter) is includible in computing taxable income for an annualization period in accordance with that method of accounting, except that any amount not included in computing taxable income by the end of the taxable year succeeding the taxable year of receipt is includible in computing taxable income on the last day of such succeeding taxable year.

(ii) *Extraordinary items.*—(A) *In general.*— In general, extraordinary items must be taken into account after annualizing the taxable income for the annualization period. For purposes of the preceding sentence an extraordinary item is any item identified in §1.1502-76(b)(2)(ii)(C) (1), (2), (3), (4), (7), and (8), a net operating loss carryover, a section 481(a) adjustment, net gain or loss from the disposition of 25 percent or more of the fair market value of a taxpayer's business assets during a taxable year, and any other item designated by the Secretary by publication in the Internal Revenue Bulletin (see §601.601(d)(2)(ii)(b) of this chapter).

(B) *De minimis extraordinary items.*—A taxpayer may treat any de minimis extraordinary item, other than a net operating loss carryover or section 481(a) adjustment, as an item under the general rule of paragraph (f)(1) of this section rather than an extraordinary item as provided for in paragraph (f)(3)(ii) of this section. A de minimis extraordinary item is any item identified in paragraph (f)(3)(ii)(A) of this section resulting from a transaction in which the total extraordinary items resulting from such transaction is less than $1,000,000.

(C) *Special rule for net operating loss deductions and section 481(a) adjustments.*—For purposes of paragraph (f)(3)(ii) of this section, a taxpayer must treat a net operating loss deduction and section 481(a) adjustment as extraordinary items arising on the first day of the tax year in which the item is taken into account in determining taxable income. Notwithstanding the preceding sentence, a taxpayer may choose to treat the portion of a section 481(a) adjustment recognized during the tax year of the accounting method change as an extraordinary item arising on the date the Form 3115, "Application for Change in Accounting Method," requesting the change was filed with the national office of the Internal Revenue Service.

(iii) *Credits.*—(A) *Current year credits.*— With respect to a current year credit, the items upon which the credit is computed are annualized, the amount of the credit is computed based on the annualized items, and the amount of the credit is deducted from the annualized tax. For example, for an annualization period consisting of three months in a full 12-month taxable year, the items upon which the credit is based that are taken into account for the three month period are multiplied by four, the credit is determined based on the annualized amount of the items, and the credit reduces the annualized tax.

(B) *Credit carryovers.*—Any credit carryover to the current taxable year is taken into account in computing an annualized income installment only after annualizing the taxable income for the annualization period and computing the applicable tax, and before applying the applicable percentage.

(iv) *Depreciation and amortization.*— (A) *Estimated annual depreciation and amortization.*—In general, in determining taxable income for any annualization period, a proportionate amount of the taxpayer's estimated annual depreciation and amortization (depreciation) expense may be taken into account. For purposes of the preceding sentence, estimated annual depreciation expense is the estimated depreciation expense to be properly taken into account in determining the taxpayer's taxable income for the taxable year. In determining the estimated annual depreciation expense, a taxpayer may take into account purchases, sales or other dispositions, changes in use, additional first-year depreciation and expense deductions and section 179 or any similar provision, and other events that, based on all the relevant information available as of the last day of the annualization period (such as capital spending budgets, financial statement data and projections, or similar reports that provide evidence of the taxpayer's capital spending plans for the current taxable year), are reasonably expected to occur or apply during the taxable year.

(B) *Safe harbors.*—(1) *Proportionate depreciation allowance.*—In determining taxable income for any annualization period, in lieu of the rule provided in paragraph (f)(3)(iv)(A) of this section a taxpayer may take into account a proportionate amount of the depreciation and amortization (depreciation) expense, including special depreciation and expense deductions such as those provided for in section 168(k) and section 179 or any similar provision, allowed for the taxable year from—

(i) Assets that were in service on the last day of the prior taxable year, are in service on the first day of the current taxable year, and that have not been disposed of during the annualization period;

(ii) Assets placed in service during the annualization period and have not been disposed of during that period; and

(iii) Assets that were in service on the last day of the prior taxable year and that are disposed of during the annualization period.

(2) *90 percent of preceding year's depreciation.*—In determining taxable income for any annualization period, in lieu of the general rule provided in paragraph (f)(3)(iv)(A) of this section, a proportionate amount of 90 percent of the amount of depreciation and amortization (depreciation) expense taken on the taxpayer's Federal income tax return for the preceding taxable year may be taken into account. If the taxpayer's preceding taxable year is less than 12 months (a short taxable year), the amount of depreciation expense taken into account is annualized by multiplying the depreciation and amortization for the short taxable year by 12, and dividing the result by the number of months in the short taxable year.

(3) *Safe harbor operational rules.*—If a taxpayer selects one of the two safe harbors provided in paragraph (f)(3)(iv)(B)(1) or paragraph (f)(3)(iv)(B)(2) of this section, the taxpayer must use that safe harbor for all depreciation expenses within the annualization period for the annualized income installment. However, a taxpayer may use either the method provided for in paragraph (f)(3)(iv)(A) of this section or a method provided for in this paragraph (f)(3)(iv)(B) of this section for each annualized income installment during the taxable year. For example, a taxpayer may use the safe harbor provided in paragraph (f)(3)(iv)(B)(1) of this section for its first annualized income installment and may use the general rule provided in paragraph (f)(3)(iv)(A) of this section for its second annualized income installment.

(C) *Short taxable years.*—If the taxable year is, or will be, a short taxable year (based on all relevant information available as of the last day of the annualization period), annual depreciation expense is computed using the rules applicable for computing depreciation during a short taxable year for purposes of determining the annual depreciation expense to be allocated to an annualization period. For this purpose, the rules applicable for computing depreciation during a short taxable year are applied on the basis of the date the taxable year is expected to end based on all relevant information available as of the last day of the annualization period. See Rev. Proc. 89-15 (1989-1 CB 816) for computing depreciation expense under section 168 (see § 601.601(d)(2)(ii)(b) of this chapter). An annualization period is not treated as a short taxable year for purposes of determining the depreciation expense for an annualization period. See paragraph (c)(3) of this section.

(v) *Distributive share of items.*—(A) *Member of partnership.*—In determining a partner's distributive share of partnership items that must be taken into account during an annualization period, the rules set forth in § 1.6654-2(d)(2) are applicable.

(B) *Treatment of subpart F income and income under section 936(h).*—(1) *General rule.*—Any amounts required to be included in gross income under section 936(h) or section 951(a), and credits properly allocable thereto, are taken into account in computing any annualized income installment in a manner similar to the manner under which partnership inclusions, and credits properly allocable thereto, are taken into account in accordance with paragraph (f)(3)(v)(A) of this section.

(2) *Prior year safe harbor.*—(i) *General rule.*—If a taxpayer elects to have the safe harbor in this paragraph (f)(3)(v)(B)(2) apply for any taxable year, then paragraph (f)(3)(v)(B)(1) of this section does not apply; and, for purposes of computing any annualized income installment for the taxable year, the taxpayer is treated as having received ratably during the taxable year items of income and credit described in paragraph (f)(3)(v)(B)(1) of this section in an amount equal to 115 percent of the amount of such items shown on the return of the taxpayer for the preceding taxable year (the second preceding taxable year in the case of the first and second required installments for such taxable year).

(ii) *Special rule for noncontrolling shareholder.*—If a taxpayer making the election under paragraph (f)(3)(v)(B)(2)(i) of this section is a noncontrolling shareholder of a corporation, paragraph (f)(3)(v)(B)(2)(i) of this section is applied with respect to items of such corporation by substituting "100 percent" for "115 percent". For purposes of paragraph (f)(3)(v)(B)(2)(ii) of this section, the term noncontrolling shareholder means, with respect to any corporation, a shareholder that, as of the beginning of the taxable year for which the installment is being made, does not own within the meaning of section 958(a), and is not treated as owning within the meaning of section 958(b), more than 50 percent by vote or value of the stock in the corporation.

(C) *Dividends from closely held real estate investment trust.*—(1) *General rule.*—Any dividend received from a closely held real estate investment trust by any person that owns, after the application of section 856(d)(5), 10 percent or more by vote or value of the stock or beneficial interests in the trust is taken into account in computing annualized income installments in a manner similar to the manner under which partnership income inclusions are taken into account.

˙(2) *Closely held real estate investment trust.*—For purposes of paragraph (f)(3)(v)(C)(1) of this section, the term closely held real estate investment trust means a real estate investment trust with respect to which 5 or fewer persons own, after the application of section 856(d)(5), 50 percent or more by vote or value of the stock or beneficial interests in the trust.

(D) *Other passthrough entities.*—A taxpayer's distributive share of items from a passthrough entity, other than those described in paragraphs (f)(3)(v)(A) and (f)(3)(v)(C) of this section, is taken into account in computing any annualized income installment in a manner similar to the manner under which partnership items are taken into account under paragraph (f)(3)(v)(A) of this section.

(vi) *Alternative minimum taxable income exemption amount.*—The alternative minimum taxable income exemption amount provided by section 55(d)(2) is applied after the alternative minimum taxable income for the annualization period is annualized.

(vii) *Examples.*—The provisions of this paragraph (f) are illustrated by the following examples. Unless otherwise stated, the following examples assume that the taxpayer uses the 3-3-6-9 annualization period.

Example 1. Expense paid or incurred in the installment period. Corporation ABC, a calendar year taxpayer, uses an accrual method of accounting and the annualized income installment method under section 6655(e)(2)(A)(i) to calculate all of its required installment payments for its 2008 taxable year. ABC has licensed technology from Corporation XYZ. Pursuant to the license agreement, ABC pays a license fee to XYZ equal to $.01 for every dollar of gross receipts earned by ABC. For 2008, ABC projects gross receipts of $200,000,000, of which $100,000,000 is earned by March 31, 2008. Pursuant to paragraph (f)(1) of this section, a license fee expense of $1,000,000 ($100,000,000 × $.01) is incurred by March 31, 2008, and may be taken into account for purposes of determining the taxable income to be annualized in computing ABC's first annualized income installment.

Example 2. Expense not paid or incurred in the installment period. Same facts as *Example 1* except that ABC does not earn any gross receipts by March 31, 2008. In accordance with paragraph (f)(1) of this section, because the license fee expense was not incurred under § 1.461-1(a)(2) by the last day of the annualization period, no li-

cense fee expense is taken into account for purposes of determining the taxable income to be annualized in computing ABC's first annualized income installment, which is based on the income and deductions from the first three months of the taxable year.

Example 3. Bad debt expense. Corporation ABC, a calendar year taxpayer, uses an accrual method of accounting and the annualized income installment method under section 6655(e)(2)(A)(i) to calculate all of its required installment payments for its 2008 taxable year. As of December 31, 2007, ABC had a $100,000 account receivable due from XYZ related to the sale of goods from ABC to XYZ during 2007. On March 30, 2008, ABC determined that its receivable from XYZ was worthless under section 166 and the regulations. No other receivables were determined to be worthless between January 1, 2008, and March 31, 2008. In accordance with paragraph (f)(1) of this section, a $100,000 bad debt write-off is taken into account for purposes of determining the taxable income to be annualized in computing ABC's first annualized income installment.

Example 4. Bad debt expense. Same facts as *Example 3* except that ABC determines that the receivable from XYZ was worthless under section 166 and the regulations on April 10, 2008. As of March 31, 2008, ABC had not determined that any receivables were worthless under section 166 and the regulations. In accordance with paragraph (f)(1) of this section, the $100,000 bad debt expense attributable to the receivable from XYZ is not taken into account for purposes of determining the taxable income to be annualized in computing ABC's first annualized income installment, which is based on the income and deductions from the first three months of the taxable year, because the receivable from XYZ became worthless after the last day of the annualization period.

Example 5. Employer deductions under section 404 and 419. (i) Corporation ABC, a calendar year taxpayer, uses an accrual method of accounting and uses the annualized income installment method under section 6655(e)(2)(A)(i) to calculate all of its required installment payments for its 2008 taxable year. On March 1, 2008, the board of directors of ABC makes a binding, irrevocable commitment to fund a minimum contribution of $10,000,000 to ABC's qualified retirement plan by March 14, 2009. ABC remits a $1,000,000 payment to the retirement plan on March 1, 2008, and a $9,000,000 payment on March 3, 2009. ABC does not incur any other related retirement plan deductions during its 2008 taxable year.

(ii) Under the rule provided in paragraph (f)(2)(i) of this section, ABC's employer deduction for payment made to the qualified plan must be allocated throughout the tax year for estimated tax purposes in a reasonably accurate manner. Therefore, ABC will not be permitted to allocate the $10,000,000 deduction to its first installment period. Under paragraph (f)(2)(iii) of this section, ABC's qualified plan deduction will be deemed to be allocated in a reasonably accurate manner if the item is allocated ratably throughout the taxable year. Therefore, ABC will be permitted to allocate $2,500,000 of its qualified plan deduction in its first installment period.

Example 6. Prepaid expense. (i) Corporation ABC, a calendar year taxpayer, uses an accrual method of accounting and does not capitalize qualifying costs under the exception provided for in § 1.263(a)-4(f). ABC uses the annualized income installment method under section 6655(e)(2)(A)(i) to calculate all of its required installment payments for its 2008 taxable year. On July 1, 2008, ABC purchases an annual business license from State X which permits ABC to operate its business in State X from July 1, 2008, through June 30, 2009. An annual payment of $12,000 is due on July 1, 2008, and ABC pays the fee on this date. ABC has not elected out of the 12-month rule provided by § 1.263(a)-4(f) and therefore ABC is not required to capitalize any amount paid for the license and will recognize a $12,000 deduction for the tax year ending December 31, 2008, with respect to this license.

(ii) Under the rule provided in paragraph (f)(2)(ii) of this section, ABC's $12,000 business license expense must be allocated in a reasonably accurate manner because ABC utilizes the 12-month rule exception provided for in the § 1.263(a)-4(f). Under paragraph (f)(2)(iii) of this section, ABC's deduction will be deemed to be allocated in a reasonably accurate manner if the item is allocated ratably throughout the taxable year. Therefore, ABC will be permitted to allocate $3,000 of its business license deduction in its first installment period.

Example 7. Real property tax liability. (i) Corporation ABC, a calendar year taxpayer, uses an accrual method of accounting and the annualized income installment method under section 6655(e)(2)(A)(i) to calculate all of its required installment payments for its 2008 taxable year. ABC owns real property in State Y and uses the real property in its trade or business. ABC incurs a $400,000 deduction for State Y real estate taxes during ABC's December 31, 2008, taxable year. ABC has elected to recognize its real property taxes ratably under section 461(c).

(ii) Under the rule provided in paragraph (f)(2)(i) of this section, ABC's $400,000 real property tax liabilities must be allocated in a reasonably accurate manner. However, paragraph (f)(2)(iv) of this section provides that with respect to real property taxes for which an election has been made under section 461(c), ratable accrual is the only method which will be considered a reasonably accurate method. Therefore, ABC will be required to allocate its $400,000 real property taxes ratably for estimated tax purposes and thus $100,000 will be allocated to the ABC's first annualized income installment.

Example 8. NOL (Net Operating Loss) deduction. Corporation ABC, a calendar year taxpayer, uses an accrual method of accounting and the annualized income installment method under

section 6655(e)(2)(A)(i) to calculate all of its required installment payments for its 2008 taxable year. ABC has a net operating loss carryover to 2008 of $2,000,000. ABC's taxable income from January 1, 2008, through March 31, 2008, without regard to any net operating loss deduction, is $1,500,000 (pre-NOL taxable income). Under the special rule for net operating loss deductions provided in paragraph (f)(3)(ii) of this section, the NOL deduction is treated as an extraordinary item incurred on the first day of ABC's December 31, 2008, tax year. Therefore, the NOL deduction is taken into account after annualization for purposes of determining ABC's first annualized income installment.

Example 9. Advance payment. (i) Corporation ABC, a calendar year taxpayer, uses an accrual method of accounting and the annualized income installment method under section 6655(e)(2)(A)(i) to calculate all of its required installment payments for its 2008 and 2009 taxable years. ABC is in the business of giving dancing lessons and receives advance payments. For Federal income tax purposes, ABC uses the Deferral Method provided in section 5.02 of Rev. Proc. 2004-34 for the advance payments it receives for dance lessons. On November 1, 2008, ABC receives an advance payment of $2,400 for a 2-year contract commencing on November 1, 2008, and providing for up to 24 individual, 1-hour lessons. ABC provides 2 lessons in 2008, 12 lessons in 2009, and 10 lessons in 2010. ABC recognizes $200 in revenues in its financial statements for the last quarter of 2008. ABC recognizes $300 in revenues in its financial statements for each quarter of 2009 for a total of $1,200 in 2009. ABC recognizes the remaining $1,000 in revenues in its financial statements during 2010. For tax purposes, ABC recognizes $200 into revenue in 2008 and $2,200 into revenue in 2009 under Rev. Proc. 2004-34. See § 601.601(d)(2)(ii)(b).

(ii) Pursuant to paragraph (f)(3)(i)(B) of this section, ABC is not required to take into account any of the advance payment for purposes of computing any required installment payment for ABC's 2008 taxable year because no part of the $2,400 advance payment was recognized as income in ABC's financial statements during the first nine months of ABC's 2008 taxable year. In 2009, ABC must take into account $300 of revenue for purposes of computing its first and second required installment payments, $600 of revenue for purposes of computing its third required installment payment and $900 for purposes of computing its fourth required installment payment. Pursuant to paragraph (f)(3)(i)(B) of this section, the remaining deferred revenue is recognized on December 31, 2009, for purposes of computing ABC's annualized income installments for 2009.

Example 10. Section 481(a) adjustment. Corporation ABC, a calendar year taxpayer, uses an accrual method of accounting and the annualized income installment method under section 6655(e)(2)(A)(i) to calculate all of its required installment payments for its 2008 taxable year.

Reg. § 1.6655-2(f)(3)(vii)

On December 20, 2008, ABC files a Form 3115 requesting permission to change its method of accounting. The requested change results in a negative section 481(a) adjustment of $80,000. ABC subsequently receives the consent of the Commissioner to make the change and therefore, the negative $80,000 section 481(a) adjustment is properly recognized in ABC's tax return for the year ending December 31, 2008. Under paragraph (f)(3)(ii) of this section ABC is permitted to recognize the negative $80,000 section 481(a) adjustment as an extraordinary item occurring on January 1, 2008 (the first day of ABC's December 31, 2008, tax year), or December 20, 2008 (the date ABC filed the Form 3115). ABC chooses to recognize the negative $80,000 section 481(a) adjustment as an extraordinary item occurring in January 1, 2008. Accordingly, $80,000 of the negative section 481(a) adjustment is taken into account after annualization for purposes of determining ABC's first annualized income installment. In addition, under § 1.6655-6(b), ABC is required to use its new method of accounting as of January 1, 2008 for estimated tax purposes, consistent with the recognition of the section 481(a) adjustment for estimated tax purposes. Therefore, ABC will be required to use the new method of accounting in determining taxable income to be annualized in computing ABC's first annualized income installment.

Example 11. Section 481(a) adjustment. Corporation ABC, a calendar year taxpayer, uses an accrual method of accounting and uses the annualized income installment method under section 6655(e)(2)(A)(i) to calculate all of its required installment payments for its 2008 taxable year. On June 15, 2008, ABC files a Form 3115 requesting permission to change its method of accounting. The requested change results in a positive section 481(a) adjustment of $240,000. ABC subsequently receives the consent of the Commissioner to make the change and therefore, $60,000 of the section 481(a) adjustment (one quarter of the positive $240,000 section 481(a) adjustment) is properly recognized in ABC's tax return for the year ending December 31, 2008. Under paragraph (f)(3)(ii) of this section, ABC is permitted to recognize the positive $60,000 section 481(a) adjustment as an extraordinary item occurring on January 1, 2008 (the first day of ABC's December 31, 2008, tax year), or June 15, 2008 (the date ABC filed the Form 3115). ABC chooses to recognize the positive $60,000 section 481(a) adjustment as an extraordinary item occurring on June 15, 2008. Accordingly, the $60,000 positive section 481(a) adjustment is not taken into account for purposes of determining ABC's first annualized income installment. However, in all futures years any portion of the section 481(a) adjustment related to this change in method of accounting will be treated as an extraordinary item occurring on the first day of the tax year under paragraph (f)(3)(ii) of this section. In addition, under § 1.6655-6(b), ABC is required to use its new method of accounting as of June 15, 2008 for estimated tax purposes, consistent with the recognition of the section 481(a) adjustment for

estimated tax purposes. Therefore, ABC will be required to use the new method of accounting (as of the beginning of the tax year) for purposes of determining taxable income to be annualized in computing ABC's third and fourth annualized income installments (which are based upon annualization periods that include June 15, 2008.)

Example 12. Extraordinary item. Corporation ABC, a calendar year taxpayer, uses an accrual method of accounting and the annualized income installment method under section 6655(e)(2)(A)(i) to calculate all of its required installment payments for its 2008 taxable year. On May 10, 2008, ABC reaches a settlement agreement with XYZ over a tort action filed by ABC. As a result, ABC receives a payment of $10,000,000 on June 15, 2006, that is recognized as income by ABC. The settlement of a tort action is an extraordinary item defined in paragraph (f)(3)(ii)(A) of this section. Accordingly, the $10,000,000 of income will be taken into account by ABC on May 10, 2008, for purposes of computing ABC's annualized income installments for 2008. Therefore, the $10,000,000 settlement will only be taken into account in computing ABC's third and fourth annualized income installments (which are based upon annualization periods that include May 10, 2008.) In addition, the $10,000,000 settlement income will be taken into account as an extraordinary item of income after annualization for purposes of determining ABC's third and fourth annualized installment payments.

Example 13. Credit carryover. Corporation ABC, a calendar year taxpayer, uses an accrual method of accounting and the annualized income installment method under section 6655(e)(2)(A)(i) to calculate all of its required installment payments for its 2008 taxable year. ABC projects its annualized tax for its 2008 taxable year, based on annualizing ABC's taxable income for its first annualization period from January 1, 2008, through March 31, 2008, to be $1,500,000 before reduction for any credits. ABC has an unused section 38 credit from 2007 for increasing research activities from 2007 of $500,000 that is carried over to 2008. For purposes of determining ABC's first annualized income installment, ABC's annualized tax for 2008 is $1,000,000, determined as the tax for the taxable year computed by placing on an annualized basis ABC's taxable income from its first annualization period from January 1, 2008, through March 31, 2008 ($1,500,000) reduced by the $500,000 credit carryover from 2007. Therefore, ABC's first required installment payment for 2008 is $250,000 ($1,000,000 × 25%).

Example 14. Current year credit. Corporation ABC, a calendar year taxpayer, uses an accrual method of accounting and the annualized income installment method under section 6655(e)(2)(A)(i) to calculate all of its required installment payments for its 2008 taxable year. ABC projects its annualized tax for its 2008 taxable year, based on annualizing ABC's taxable income for its first annualization period from January 1, 2008, through March 31, 2008, to be

$2,000,000 before reduction for any credits. ABC has historically earned a section 41 credit for increasing research activities and, for 2008, ABC estimates that it will earn a credit for increasing research activities under section 41 of $1,200,000. However, pursuant to paragraph (f)(3)(iii) of this section, if ABC were to annualize all components involved in computing the current year credit based on ABC's activity from January 1, 2008, through March 31, 2008, ABC would generate a credit of $1,600,000 for 2008. For purposes of determining ABC's first annualized income installment, ABC's annualized tax for 2008 is $400,000, determined as the tax for the 2008 taxable year ($2,000,000) computed by placing on an annualized basis ABC's taxable income from its first annualization period January 1, 2008, through March 31, 2008, reduced by a $1,600,000 current year section 41 credit from increasing research activities. Therefore, ABC's first required installment payment for 2008 is $100,000 ($400,000 × 25%).

Example 15. Current year credit. Same facts as *Example 14* except that ABC does not begin any research activities until April 3, 2008, and will not incur any research expenses described in paragraph (f)(1)(ii) of this section. As a result, if ABC were to annualize all components involved in computing the current year credit based on ABC's activity from January 1, 2008, through March 31, 2008, ABC would generate no section 41 research credit for purposes of determining its first annualized income installment. Pursuant to paragraph (f)(3)(iii) of this section, ABC cannot take into account any credit for its first annualization period because ABC did not incur any qualified research expenses by the last day of the first annualization period. Accordingly, for purposes of determining ABC's first annualized income installment, ABC's annualized tax for its first annualization period January 1, 2008, through March 31, 2008, is $2,000,000. Therefore, ABC's first required installment payment for 2008 is $500,000 ($2,000,000 × 25%).

Example 16. Depreciation and amortization expense. Corporation ABC, a calendar year taxpayer that began business on January 2, 2007, adopted an accrual method of accounting and will use the annualized income installment method under section 6655(e)(2)(A)(i) to calculate all of its required installment payments for its 2008 taxable year. On January 2, 2007, ABC purchased and placed in service a tangible depreciable asset that costs $50,000 and is 5-year property under section 168(e). ABC depreciates its 5-year property placed in service in 2007 under the general depreciation system using the 200-percent declining balance method, a 5-year recovery period, and the half year convention. On January 2, 2008, ABC purchased and placed in service qualified Gulf Opportunity Zone property (GO Zone property) that costs $30,000 and is 5-year property under section 168(e). ABC will depreciate its 5-year property placed in service in 2008 under the general depreciation system using the 200-percent declining balance method, a 5-year recovery period, and the half-year con-

vention. ABC will deduct the 50% additional first year depreciation deduction under section 1400N(d) with respect to the GO Zone property. For tax year 2007, ABC takes a depreciation deduction under section 168 of $10,000 ($50,000 × 20% = $10,000). ABC does not anticipate being subject to the mid-quarter convention for the 2008 taxable year, does not anticipate making any depreciation elections for any class of property, does not anticipate making a section 179 election, does not anticipate any sales or other dispositions of depreciable property, and no events have occurred, nor does ABC know, based on all relevant information available as of the due date of ABC's first required installment for 2008, of any event that will occur to cause ABC's 2008 taxable year to be a short taxable year. The optional amounts of depreciation expense ABC may take into account for its first annualized income installment for its 2008 taxable year are determined as follows:

(i) *General rule—Estimated annual depreciation.* In accordance with the general rule provided in paragraph (f)(3)(iv)(A) of this section, ABC may take a depreciation expense of $8,500 ($34,000 × 3/12 = $8,500) into account in computing ABC's January 1, 2008, through March 31, 2008, taxable income. ABC's estimated annual depreciation expense for 2008 of $34,000 is computed as follows: $15,000 for the 50% additional first year depreciation deduction under section 1400N(d) ($30,000 × 50% = $15,000) plus annual depreciation of $16,000 ($40,000 × 40% = $16,000) and $3,000 ($15,000 × 20% = $3,000). Under paragraphs (c)(3) and (f)(3)(iv)(C) of this section, ABC may not consider its first annualization period to be a short taxable year for purposes of determining the depreciation allowance for such annualization period.

(ii) *Safe Harbor—Proportionate depreciation allowance.* In accordance with the safe harbor provided in paragraph (f)(3)(iv)(B)(1) of this section, ABC may take a depreciation expense of $8,500 ($34,000 × 3/12 = $8,500) into account in computing ABC's January 1, 2008, through March 31, 2008, taxable income based on annual depreciation expense for 2008 of $34,000, computed as follows: $15,000 for the 50% additional first year depreciation deduction under section 1400N(d) ($30,000 × 50% = $15,000) plus annual depreciation of $16,000 ($40,000 × 40% = $16,000) and $3,000 ($15,000 × 20% = $3,000). Under paragraphs (c)(3) and (f)(3)(iv)(C) of this section, ABC may not consider its first annualization period to be a short taxable year for purposes of determining the depreciation allowance for such annualization period.

(iii) *Safe Harbor—90 percent of preceding year's depreciation.* In accordance with the safe harbor in paragraph (f)(3)(iv)(B)(2) of this section, ABC may take a depreciation expense of $2,250 ($10,000 prior year's depreciation × 90% = $9,000 × 3/12 = $2,250) into account in computing ABC's January 1, 2008, through March 31, 2008, taxable income. Under paragraphs (c)(3) and (f)(3)(iv)(C) of this section, ABC may not consider its first annualization period to be a short taxable year for purposes of determining the depreciation allowance for such annualization period.

(g) *Items that substantially affect taxable income but cannot be determined accurately by the installment due date.*—(1) *In general.*—In determining the applicability of the annualization exceptions described in paragraphs (a) and (b) of this section and § 1.6655-3, reasonable estimates may be made from existing data for items that substantially affect income if the amount of such items cannot be determined accurately by the installment due date. This paragraph (g) applies only to the inflation index for taxpayers using the dollar-value LIFO (last-in, first-out) inventory method, adjustments required under section 263A, the computation of a taxpayer's section 199 deduction, intercompany adjustments for taxpayers that file consolidated returns, the liquidation of a LIFO layer at the installment date that the taxpayer reasonably believes will be replaced at the end of the year, deferred gain on a qualifying conversion or exchange of property under sections 1031 and 1033 that the taxpayer reasonably believes will be replaced with qualifying replacement property, and any other item designated by the Secretary by publication in the Internal Revenue Bulletin (see § 601.601(d)(2)(ii)(b) of this chapter).

(2) *Example.*—The following example illustrates the rules of this paragraph (g):

Example. Section 199 deduction. Corporation ABC, a calendar year taxpayer, uses an accrual method of accounting and the annualized income installment method under section 6655(e)(2)(A)(i) to calculate all of its required installment payments for its 2008 taxable year. ABC engages in production activities that generate qualified production activities income (QPAI), as defined in § 1.199-1(c), and projects taxable income of $50,000 for its first annualization period from January 1, 2008, through March 31, 2008, without taking into account the section 199 deduction. During its first annualization period from January 1, 2008, through March 31, 2008, ABC incurs W-2 wages allocable to domestic production gross receipts pursuant to section 199(b)(2) of $10,000. Pursuant to paragraph (g)(1) of this section, ABC is permitted to take into account its estimated section 199 deduction before annualizing taxable income based on the lesser of its estimated QPAI or taxable income and W-2 wages for its first installment period for 2008. For the first installment period in 2008, ABC is permitted to recognize a deduction under section 199 of $3,000 ($50,000 × .06 = $3,000) subject to the wage limitation of $5,000 (50 percent of $10,000 of W-2 wages incurred during the first installment period). Accordingly, ABC's annualized income for the first installment for 2008 is $188,000 (($50,000 - $3,000) × 12/3 = $188,000). The tax on $188,000 is $56,570 and ABC's first required installment for 2008 is $14,143 ($56,570 × .25 = $14,143).

(h) *Effective/applicability date.*—This section applies to taxable years beginning after September 6, 2007. [Reg. § 1.6655-2.]

☐ [*T.D.* 6267, 11-13-57. *Amended by T.D.* 6293, 5-20-58; *T.D.* 6768, 11-3-64; *T.D.* 8996, 5-16-2002 and *T.D.* 9347, 8-6-2007 (*corrected* 9-19-2007).]

[Reg. § 1.6655-2T]

§ 1.6655-2T. Safe harbor for certain installments of tax due before July 1, 1987 (temporary).—(a) *Applicability.*—(1) *Safe harbor.*—The safe harbor provided by paragraph (b) of this section applies only to installment payments of corporate estimated tax required to be made before July 1, 1987, for taxable years beginning in 1987.

(2) *Subsequent payment.*—The requirement that a corporation using the safe harbor provided by this section make a timely subsequent installment payment in accordance with paragraph (c) of this section applies with respect to the corporation's first installment payment ("the subsequent installment payment") of estimated tax required to be made after the last payment computed under the safe harbor rule.

(3) *Section inapplicable to new corporation.*— This section shall not apply in the case of any corporation whose first taxable year began after December 31, 1986.

(b) *Safe harbor for use of annualization exception.*—(1) *In general.*—A corporation computing an installment payment of estimated tax using the annualization exception provided in section 6655(d)(3) will not be subject to an addition to tax under section 6655 with respect to an installment payment of estimated tax that satisfies the requirements of this paragraph (b), except as provided in paragraph (c) of this section. For purposes of this paragraph (b)—

(i) A corporation shall assume that its annualized taxable income for the current year equals or exceeds 120 percent of the taxable income shown on its return for the preceding taxable year, and

(ii) The term "tax" as used in section 6655(d)(3) shall be defined by reference to section 6655(f) without regard to section 6655(f)(1)(B) and (C) (that is, without regard to the alternative minimum tax imposed by section 55 or the environmental tax imposed by section 59A).

(2) *Special rules for determining taxable income for preceding year.*—For purposes of paragraph (b)(1)(i) of this section, the taxable income shown on the return of the corporation for its preceding taxable year shall be—

(i) Adjusted to eliminate any net operating loss deduction taken into account in that preceding year, and

(ii) Annualized, if that preceding year was of less than 12 months.

(3) *Credits taken into account.*—(i) *In general.*—In computing the amount of an installment payment under paragraph (b)(1) of this

section, the corporation may take into account any credits against tax that are permitted to be taken into account under section 6655(d)(3) for the current taxable year.

(ii) *Foreign tax credit.*—For purposes of paragraph (b)(3)(i) of this section, the amount of foreign tax credit that is permitted to be taken into account for the current taxable year is equal to the foreign tax credit allowed for the preceding taxable year multiplied by the fraction specified in the following sentence. The numerator of the fraction is the highest tax rate applicable for the taxable year under section 11, as adjusted under section 15, and the denominator is 46 percent. This alternative computation of the foreign tax credit is applicable only for purposes of computing a safe harbor installment payment under paragraph (b) of this section and cannot be applied for other estimated tax purposes.

(4) *Net operating loss carryover.*—A corporation that has a net operating loss carryover as of the first day of the taxable year for which the estimated tax is being paid may use that carryover to reduce the annualized taxable income referred to in paragraph (b)(1)(i) of this section. For example, if a corporation with a net operating loss carryover of $3,000 had taxable income of $10,000 in 1986, it may use the carryover to reduce its annualized taxable income to $9,000 (($10,000 × 120%) − $3,000).

(c) *Corporation must bring aggregate payments to required level through timely subsequent installment.*—(1) *In general.*—A corporation using the safe harbor provided by paragraph (b) of this section shall make a timely subsequent installment payment of estimated tax in an amount sufficient to satisfy the requirements of either paragraph (c)(3) or paragraph (c)(4) of this section.

(2) *Applicable percentage.*—For purposes of this paragraph (c), the applicable percentage is—

(i) 45 percent (50 percent × 90 percent), if the subsequent installment payment is the second installment payment for the taxable year, or

(ii) 67.5 percent (75 percent × 90 percent), if the subsequent installment payment is the third installment payment for the taxable year.

(3) *Annualization exception.*—The subsequent installment payment of a corporation satisfies the requirements of this paragraph (c)(3) if the amount of the payment is sufficient to satisfy the requirements of section 6655(d)(3) with respect to all applicable taxes specified in section 6655(f). Thus, the corporation must determine its annualized taxable income under section 6655(d)(3)(A)(ii) or (iii), whichever is applicable, and compute the resulting tax. The resulting tax shall include the alternative minimum tax under section 55 and the environmental tax under section 59A and may take credits into account to the extent permitted under section 6655(d)(3). The sum of this subsequent installment payment and the earlier installment payment or payments of the corporation must equal or exceed the appli-

cable percentage of the tax so computed. In determining whether the corporation has satisfied the requirements of section 6655(d)(3)(A)(ii) or (iii) with respect to the subsequent installment, the safe harbor provided in paragraph (b)(1) of this section shall not apply.

(4) *Installment payments equal to applicable percentage of tax shown on return.*—The subsequent installment payment of a corporation satisfies the requirement of this paragraph (c)(4) if the sum of that payment and the earlier installment payment or payments of the corporation equals or exceeds the applicable percentage of the tax shown on the return of the corporation for the taxable year to which the installment payments relate. The tax shown on the return includes all taxes specified in section 6655(f).

(5) *Consequence of corporation's failure to satisfy requirements for subsequent installment.*—(i) *In general.*—If a corporation fails to satisfy the requirements set out in this paragraph (c), the corporation shall lose the benefit of the safe harbor provided by paragraph (b)(1) of this section.

(ii) *Limit on penalty.*—The aggregate underpayment penalty with respect to any installment payment or payments for which a corporation loses the benefit of the safe harbor under paragraph (c)(5)(i) of this section shall be limited to the "shortfall penalty amount." The shortfall penalty amount is the penalty that would be imposed under section 6655(a) if there were an underpayment of the subsequent installment payment equal to the excess of—

(A) The amount required to be paid, as determined under this paragraph (c), on or before the due date of the subsequent installment payment, over

(B) The amount actually paid on or before such date with respect to the subsequent installment payment.

For purposes of this determination, the period of the underpayment shall run from the due date of the subsequent installment payment until the earlier of the dates specified in section 6655(c)(1) or (2).

(iii) *Example.*—The provisions of this paragraph (c)(5) may be illustrated by the following example:

Example. Corporation M, which uses the calendar year as its taxable year, relies on the safe harbor provided by paragraph (b) of this section for its first two installment payments of estimated tax for 1987. M is required by this paragraph (c) to make a timely subsequent installment payment of $1,000,000 by September 15, 1987, but M's actual installment payment by that date is only $990,000. Because of this shortfall, M loses the benefit of the safe harbor and is subject to underpayment penalties with respect to the first two installments. The aggregate penalties with respect to those two installments, however, cannot exceed the amount of the underpayment penalty to which M would be subject if there were an underpayment of $10,000 with respect to the September 15, 1987, installment payment. Such penalties are independent of any penalty that may apply with respect to M's third installment payment under the normal rules of section 6655.

(d) *Example.*—The provisions of this section may be illustrated by the following example:

Example. (i) Corporation X (which is not a life insurance company) uses as its taxable year a fiscal year ending on January 31 and is required to pay an installment of estimated income tax by May 15, 1987, for its taxable year beginning on February 1, 1987. On its return for the taxable year ending January 31, 1987, which was a year of 12 months, X reported taxable income of $10,000,000 ($9,000,000 of which was ordinary income and $1,000,000 of which was net capital gain) and did not claim any net operating loss deduction. As of February 1, 1987, X has no net operating loss carryforwards and no credit carryforwards. X has no credits against tax that are permitted to be taken into account under section 6655(d)(3) for 1987. If X uses the safe harbor provided in paragraph (b)(1) of this section, X must make by May 15, 1987, an installment payment of estimated tax of at least $1,037,836, computed as follows:

(1) Taxable income shown on return for taxable year ending on January 31, 1987 . . . . $10,000,000

(2) Annualized taxable income for taxable year ending January 31, 1988, determined pursuant to paragraph (b)(1) of this section (Item (1) × 120%) $12,000,000

    (Note: 120% × ordinary income of $9,000,000 = $10,800,000; 120% × net capital gain of $1,000,000 = $1,200,000)

(3) Tax on annualized taxable income (Item 2) using rates under section 11 and 1201, taking into account section 15, applicable to the taxable year ending January 31, 1988 . . . $4,612,603

(4) Amount described in section 6655(d)(3)(A)(i) (Item (3) × 22.5%) $1,037,836

(ii) To preclude imposition of an addition to tax under section 6655 with respect to its May 15, 1987, installment payment, X must make by July 15, 1987, a second installment payment of estimated tax sufficient to bring its aggregate payments to the minimum level required under paragraph (c) of this section.

(iii) X may satisfy the requirements of paragraph (c)(3) of this section by making a second installment payment sufficient to bring X within the exception provided in section 6655(d)(3). Thus, if X determines under that section that the aggregate of X's installment payments of estimated tax by July 15, 1987, must equal at least $3,000,000, X may obtain the benefit of the safe harbor provided in paragraph (b)(1) of this section with respect to the May 15, 1987, installment

payment by making a timely second installment payment of $1,962,164 ($3,000,000 − $1,037,836).

(iv) Even if X fails to satisfy the requirements of paragraph (c)(3) of this section, X may obtain the benefit of the safe harbor for the May 15, 1987, installment payment if X's second installment payment, when aggregated with the first payment, equals at least 45 percent of the tax (including the alternative minimum tax under section 55 and the environmental tax under section 59A) shown on X's return for X's taxable year beginning on February 1, 1987. Thus, if the tax shown on that return is $6,000,000, X's second installment payment under paragraph (c)(4) of this section must be at least $1,662,164, computed as follows:

45 percent of $6,000,000	=	$2,700,000
less first payment		1,037,836
Minimum second installment		$1,662,164

[Temporary Reg. § 1.6655-2T.]

  ☐ [*T.D.* 8132, 3-24-87.]

[Reg. § 1.6655-3]

§ 1.6655-3. Adjusted seasonal installment method.—(a) *In general.*—In the case of any required installment, the amount of the adjusted seasonal installment is the excess (if any) of—

(1) 100 percent of the amount determined under paragraph (c) of this section; over

(2) The aggregate amount of all prior required installments for the taxable year.

(b) *Limitation on application of section.*—This section applies only if the base period percentage (as defined in section 6655(e)(3)(D)(i) and paragraph (d)(1) of this section) for any six consecutive months of the taxable year equals or exceeds seventy percent.

(c) *Determination of amount.*—The amount determined under this paragraph (c) for any installment will be determined in the following manner—

(1) Take the taxable income for all months during the taxable year preceding the filing month;

(2) Divide such amount by the base period percentage for all months during the taxable year preceding the filing month;

(3) Determine the tax on the amount determined under paragraph (c)(2) of this section; and

(4) Multiply the tax computed under paragraph (c)(3) of this section by the base period percentage for the filing month and all months during the taxable year preceding the filing month.

(d) *Special rules.*—(1) *Base period percentage.*—The base period percentage for any period of months is the average percent that the taxable income for the corresponding months in each of the three preceding taxable years bears to the taxable income for the three preceding taxable years. If there is no taxable income for the corresponding months, taxable income for this purpose is zero.

(2) *Filing month.*—The term filing month means the month in which the installment is required to be paid.

(3) *Application of the rules related to the annualized income installment method to the adjusted seasonal installment method.*—The rules governing the computation of taxable income (and resulting tax) for purposes of determining any required installment payment of estimated tax under the annualized income installment method under § 1.6655-2 apply to the computation of taxable income (and resulting tax) for purposes of determining any required installment payment of estimated tax under the adjusted seasonal installment method.

(4) *Alternative minimum tax.*—The amount determined under paragraph (c) of this section must properly take into account the amount of any alternative minimum tax under section 55 that would apply for the period of the computation. The amount of any alternative minimum tax that would apply is determined by applying to alternative minimum taxable income, tentative minimum tax, and alternative minimum tax, the rules described in paragraph (c) of this section for taxable income and tax.

(e) *Example.*—The provisions of this section may be illustrated by the following example:

Example. (i) X, a corporation that reports on a calendar year basis, expects to have an estimated tax liability of $1,200,000 for its taxable year ending December 31, 2009. On its 2008 tax return, X reports a tax liability of $652,800. X pays four installments of estimated tax, each in the amount of $250,000, $250,000, $250,000, and $450,000 on April 15, 2009, June 15, 2009, September 15, 2009, and December 15, 2009, respectively. X reports a tax liability of $1,152,600 on its return due March 15, 2010, with no credits against tax. Under the general provision of section 6655(b) and section 6655(d), there was an underpayment in the amount of $76,300 for the second installment through September 15, 2009, and $114,450 for the third installment through December 15, 2009, determined as follows:

(A) Tax as defined in section 6655(g) = $1,152,600

(B) 100% of this paragraph (e), *Example* (i)(A) = $1,152,600

(C) Amount of estimated tax required to be paid on or before the first installment (25% of $652,800) = $163,200

(D) Deduction of amount timely paid on or before the first installment due date under the general rule of section 6655(b) = $250,000

(E) Amount of overpaid estimated tax for the first installment date = $86,800

(F) Amount of estimated tax required to be paid on or before the second installment (25% of $1,152,600 plus the recapture amount under section 6655(d)(2)(B) of $124,950 (25% of $1,152,600 less $163,200)) = $413,100

(G) Deduction of amount paid on or before the due date of the second installment less amount applied towards the first installment under the general rule of section 6655(b) ($250,000 paid in each of the first and second installments less this paragraph (e), *Example* (i)(C)) = $336,800

(H) Amount of underpayment for the second installment date = $76,300

(I) Amount of estimated tax required to be paid on or before the third installment (25% of $1,152,600) = $288,150

(J) Deduction of amount paid on or before the due date of the third installment less amount applied towards the first and second installments under the general rule of section 6655(b) ($250,000 paid in each of the first, second, and third installments less this paragraph (e), *Example* (i)(C) less this paragraph (e), *Example* (i)(F)) = $173,700

(K) Amount of underpayment for the third installment date = $114,450

(L) Amount of estimated tax required to be paid on or before the fourth installment (25% of $1,152,600) = $288,150

(M) Deduction of amount paid on or before the due date of the fourth installment less amount applied towards the first, second, and third installments under the general rule of section 6655(b) ($250,000 paid in each of the first, second, and third installments plus $450,000 paid in the fourth installment less this paragraph (e), *Example* (i)(C) less this paragraph (e), *Example* (i)(F) less this paragraph (e), *Example* (i)(I)) = $335,550

(N) Amount of overpaid estimated tax for the fourth installment date = $47,400

(ii) X wants to determine if it qualifies for the adjusted seasonal installment method. X determines that its monthly taxable income for the preceding three taxable years and for the current taxable year 2009 is as follows:

January	February	March	April	May	June
2006					
$100,000	$90,000	$80,000	$70,000	$60,000	$20,000
2007					
200,000	170,000	170,000	130,000	125,000	45,000
2008					
410,000	350,000	330,000	270,000	240,000	80,000

Reg. §1.6655-3(d)(2)

2009					
600,000	680,000	650,000	560,000	460,000	170,000
July	August	September	October	November	December
2006					
$10,000	$10,000	$10,000	$10,000	$10,000	$10,000
2007					
21,000	19,000	20,000	20,000	20,000	20,000
2008					
40,000	40,000	40,000	40,000	40,000	40,000
2009					
70,000	60,000	50,000	40,000	30,000	20,000

(iii) X must initially determine if its base period percentage for the same 6 consecutive months of the 3 preceding taxable years equals or exceeds 70 percent (see section 6655(e)(3) and paragraphs (b) and (c) of this section). By using its taxable income for the first 6 months of 2006, 2007, and 2008, X qualifies for the adjusted seasonal installment method because its base period percentage is 87.5 percent (which exceeds 70 percent) computed as follows:

(A) Taxable income for first 6 months of 2006 = $420,000

(B) Total taxable income for 2006 = $480,000

(C) Divide this paragraph (e), *Example* (iii)(A) by this paragraph (e), *Example* (iii)(B) = .875

(D) Taxable income for first 6 months of 2007 = $840,000

(E) Total taxable income for 2007 = $960,000

(F) Divide this paragraph (e), *Example* (iii)(D) by this paragraph (e), *Example* (iii)(E) = .875

(G) Taxable income for first 6 months of 2008 = $1,680,000

(H) Total taxable income for 2008 = $1,920,000

(I) Divide this paragraph (e), *Example* (iii)(G) by this paragraph (e), *Example* (iii)(H) = .875

(J) Add this paragraph (e), *Example* (iii)(C), (F), and (I) = $2.625

(K) Divide this paragraph (e), *Example* (iii)(J) by 3 = .875

(iv) To determine the amount of the first installment under the rules of section 6655(e)(3) and paragraph (a) of this section, the following computation is necessary:

(A) Taxable income for first 3 months of 2009 = $1,930,000

(B) Taxable income for first 3 months of 2006 ($270,000) divided by total taxable income for 2006 ($480,000) = .5625

(C) Taxable income for first 3 months of 2007 ($540,000) divided by total taxable income for 2007 ($960,000) = .5625

(D) Taxable income for first 3 months of 2008 ($1,090,000) divided by total taxable income for 2008 ($1,920,000) = .5677

(E) Add this paragraph (e), *Example* (iv)(B), (C), and (D) and divide by 3 = .5642

(F) Divide this paragraph (e), *Example* (iv)(A) by this paragraph (e), *Example* (iv)(E) = $3,420,773

(G) Determine the tax on this paragraph (e), *Example* (iv)(F) = $1,163,049

(H) Taxable income for first 4 months of 2006 ($340,000) divided by total taxable income for 2006 ($480,000) = .7083

(I) Taxable income for first 4 months of 2007 ($670,000) divided by total taxable income for 2007 ($960,000) = .6979

(J) Taxable income for first 4 months of 2008 ($1,360,000) divided by total taxable income for 2008 (1,920,000) = .7083

(K) Add this paragraph (e), *Example* (iv)(H), (I), and (J) and divide by 3 = .7048

(L) Multiply this paragraph (e), *Example* (iv)(G) by this paragraph (e), *Example* (iv)(K) = $819,717

(M) 100% of this paragraph (e), *Example* (iv)(L) = $819,717

(N) Amount of all prior required installments for 2009 = $0

(O) Amount of adjusted seasonal installment for the first installment payment (this paragraph (e), *Example* (iv)(M) less this paragraph (e), *Example* (iv)(N)) = $819,717

(v) To determine the amount of the second installment under the rules of section 6655(e)(3) and paragraph (a) of this section, the following computation is necessary:

(A) Taxable income for first 5 months of 2009 = $2,950,000

(B) Taxable income for first 5 months of 2006 ($400,000) divided by total taxable income for 2006 ($480,000) = .8333

(C) Taxable income for first 5 months of 2007 ($795,000) divided by total taxable income for 2007 ($960,000) = .8281

(D) Taxable income for first 5 months of 2008 ($1,600,000) divided by total taxable income for 2008 ($1,920,000) = .8333

(E) Add this paragraph (e), *Example* (v)(B), (C), and (D) and divide by 3 = .8316

(F) Divide this paragraph (e), *Example* (v)(A) by this paragraph (e), *Example* (v)(E) = $3,547,379

(G) Determine the tax on this paragraph (e), *Example* (v)(F) = $1,206,109

(H) Taxable income for first 6 months of 2006 ($420,000) divided by total taxable income for 2006 ($480,000) = .875

(I) Taxable income for first 6 months of 2007 ($840,000) divided by total taxable income for 2007 ($960,000) = .875

(J) Taxable income for first 6 months of 2008 ($1,680,000) divided by total taxable income for 2008 ($1,920,000) = .875

(K) Add this paragraph (e), *Example* (v)(H), (I), and (J) and divide by 3 = .875

(L) Multiply this paragraph (e), *Example* (v)(G) by this paragraph (e), *Example* (v)(K) = $1,055,345

(M) 100% of this paragraph (e), *Example* (v)(L) = $1,055,345

(N) Amount of all prior required installments for 2009 = $163,200

(O) Amount of adjusted seasonal installment for the second installment payment (this paragraph (e), *Example* (v)(M) less this paragraph (e), *Example* (v)(N)) = $892,145

(vi) To determine the amount of the third installment under the rules of section 6655(e)(3) and paragraph (a) of this section, the following computation is necessary:

(A) Taxable income for first 8 months of 2009 = $3,250,000

(B) Taxable income for first 8 months of 2006 ($440,000) divided by total taxable income for 2006 ($480,000) = .9167

(C) Taxable income for first 8 months of 2007 ($880,000) divided by total taxable income for 2007 ($960,000) = .9167

(D) Taxable income for first 8 months of 2008 ($1,760,000) divided by total taxable income for 2008 ($1,920,000) = .9167

(E) Add this paragraph (e), *Example* (vi)(B), (C), and (D) and divide by 3 = .9167

(F) Divide this paragraph (e), *Example* (vi)(A) by this paragraph (e), *Example* (vi)(E) = $3,545,326

(G) Determine the tax on this paragraph (e), *Example* (vi)(F) = $1,205,411

(H) Taxable income for first 9 months of 2006 ($450,000) divided by total taxable income for 2006 ($480,000) = .9375

(I) Taxable income for first 9 months of 2007 ($900,000) divided by total taxable income for 2007 ($960,000) = .9375

(J) Taxable income for first 9 months of 2008 ($1,800,000) divided by total taxable income for 2008 ($1,920,000) = .9375

(K) Add this paragraph (e), *Example* (vi)(H), (I), and (J) and divide by 3 = .9375

(L) Multiply this paragraph (e), *Example* (vi)(G) by this paragraph (e), *Example* (vi)(K) = $1,130,073

(M) 100% of this paragraph (e), *Example* (vi)(L) = $1,130,073

(N) Amount of all prior required installments for 2009 = $576,300

(O) Amount of adjusted seasonal installment for the third installment payment (this paragraph (e), *Example* (vi)(M) less this paragraph (e), *Example* (vi)(N)) = $553,773

(vii) To determine the amount of the fourth installment under the rules of section 6655(e)(3) and paragraph (a) of this section, the following computation is necessary:

(A) Taxable income for first 11 months of 2009 = $3,370,000

(B) Taxable income for first 11 months of 2006 ($470,000) divided by total taxable income for 2006 ($480,000) = .9792

(C) Taxable income for first 11 months of 2007 ($940,000) divided by total taxable income for 2007 ($960,000) = .9792

(D) Taxable income for first 11 months of 2008 ($1,880,000) divided by total taxable income for 2008 ($1,920,000) = .9792

(E) Add this paragraph (e), *Example* (vii)(B), (C), and (D) and divide by 3 = .9792

(F) Divide this paragraph (e), *Example* (vii)(A) by this paragraph (e), *Example* (vii)(E) = $3,441,585

(G) Determine the tax on this paragraph (e), *Example* (vii)(F) = $1,170,139

(H) Taxable income for first 12 months of 2006 ($480,000) divided by total taxable income for 2006 ($480,000) = 1.0000

(I) Taxable income for first 12 months of 2007 ($960,000) divided by total taxable income for 2007 ($960,000) = 1.0000

(J) Taxable income for first 12 months of 2008 ($1,920,000) divided by total taxable income for 2008 ($1,920,000) = 1.0000

(K) Add this paragraph (e), *Example* (vii)(H), (I), and (J) and divide by 3 = 1.0000

(L) Multiply this paragraph (e), *Example* (vii)(G) by this paragraph (e), *Example* (vi)(K) = $1,170,139

(M) 100% of this paragraph (e), *Example* (vii)(L) = $1,170,139

(N) Amount of all prior required installments for 2009 = $864,450

(O) Amount of adjusted seasonal installment for the fourth installment payment (this paragraph (e), *Example* (vii)(M) less this paragraph (e), *Example* (vii)(N)) = $305,689

(viii) Because the total amount of each required estimated tax payment determined under section 6655(e)(3) and paragraph (a) of this section exceeds the amount of each required estimated tax payment determined under section 6655(d) and §1.6655-1(d) and (e), the exception described in section 6655(e) and this section does not apply and the addition to the tax with respect to the underpayment for the June 15, 2009, and September 15, 2009, installments will be imposed unless another exception (for example, see section 6655(e)(2)) applies with respect to these installments.

(f) *Effective/applicability date.*—This section applies to taxable years beginning after September 6, 2007. [Reg. §1.6655-3.]

☐ [*T.D. 6267, 11-13-57. Amended by T.D. 9347, 8-6-2007.*]

[Reg. §1.6655-4]

§1.6655-4. **Large corporations.**—(a) *Large corporation defined.*—The term large corporation means any corporation (or a predecessor corporation) that had taxable income of at least $1,000,000 for any taxable year during the testing period. For purposes of this section, a predecessor corporation is the distributor or transferor corporation in a transaction to which section 381 (relating to carryovers in certain corporate acquisitions) applies.

(b) *Testing period.*—For purposes of paragraph (a) of this section, the term testing period means the 3 taxable years immediately preceding the taxable year for which estimated tax is being determined (the current taxable year) or, if less, the number of taxable years the taxpayer has been in existence.

(c) *Computation of taxable income during testing period.*—(1) *Short taxable year.*—In the case of a corporation (or predecessor corporation) that had a short taxable year during the testing period, for purposes of determining whether the $1,000,000 amount referred to in paragraph (a) of this section is equaled or exceeded, the taxable income for the short taxable year is computed by—

(i) Multiplying the taxable income for the short taxable year by 12; and

(ii) Dividing the resulting amount by the number of months in the short taxable year.

(2) *Computation of taxable income in taxable year when there occurs a transaction to which section 381 applies.*—(i) For purposes of determining whether an acquiring corporation had taxable income of $1,000,000 or more for a taxable year in which a section 381 transaction occurs, the acquiring corporation's taxable income will be the sum of—

(A) The taxable income of the acquiring corporation for its taxable year; plus

(B) The taxable income (or loss) of the distributor or transferor corporation for that portion of its taxable year corresponding to the acquiring corporation's taxable year up to and including the date of distribution or transfer (as defined in § 1.381(b)-1(b)).

(ii) For purposes of determining whether a transferor or distributor corporation had taxable income of $1,000,000 or more for a taxable year in which a section 381 transaction occurs, the distributor or transferor corporation's taxable income (or loss) is reduced by the amount of taxable income (or loss) that is included in the acquiring corporation's taxable income for the taxable year in which the distribution or transfer (as defined in § 1.381(b)-1(b)) occurs, as described in paragraph (c)(2)(i)(B) of this section.

(d) *Members of controlled group.*—(1) *In general.*—For purposes of applying paragraph (a) of this section, the taxable income of members of a controlled group of corporations (as defined in section 1563(a)) must be aggregated for each year of the testing period. The provisions of this section do not apply to a controlled group for any taxable year in which the aggregate taxable income of the members of the controlled group is less than $1,000,000.

(2) *Aggregation.*—For purposes of paragraph (d)(1) of this section, a taxable loss of any member of the controlled group for a taxable year during the testing period is not taken into account.

(3) *Allocation rule.*—If the aggregate taxable income of members of a controlled group computed pursuant to paragraph (d)(1) of this section exceeds $1,000,000 during the testing period, the $1,000,000 amount that is relevant for purposes of determining, under paragraph (a)(1) of this section, whether a corporation is a large corporation is divided equally among the component members of such group (including component members excluded pursuant to paragraph (d)(2) of this section) unless all of such component members consent to an apportionment plan providing for an alternative allocation of such amount. The procedure for making and filing this plan will be the same as the procedure used for making and filing an apportionment plan under section 1561. See section 1561 and the regulations.

(4) *Controlled group members.*—(i) In the case of any corporation that was a member of a controlled group of corporations at any time during the testing period but is not a member of such group during the taxable year involved, the taxable income of the former member for the testing period is determined as if such corporation were not a member of a group at any time during that period. With respect to the controlled group, the taxable income of its former member will not be taken into account in determining such group's taxable income for any taxable year during the testing period for purposes of applying paragraph (a)(1) of this section.

(ii) For purposes of paragraph (d)(4)(i) of this section, the determination of whether a corporation is a member of a controlled group during the testing period is based on whether the corporation was a member of the controlled group on the last day of the month preceding the due date of the required installment.

(e) *Effect on a corporation's taxable income of items that may be carried back or carried over from any other taxable year.*—In determining whether a corporation (or predecessor corporation) is a large corporation for its current taxable year, items that could offset taxable income during a taxable year included in the testing period (for example, those described in sections 172 and 1212) are not to be taken into account and the taxable income of a corporation for any taxable year during the testing period is determined without regard to items carried back or carried over from any other taxable year.

(f) *Consolidated returns.*—[Reserved].

(g) *Example.*—The provisions of this section may be illustrated by the following example:

Example. Y Corporation and Z Corporation are calendar year taxpayers. In 2008, Z acquires all of the assets of Y in a transaction to which section 381 applies. Z's taxable income for both 2006 and

Reg. § 1.6655-4(g)

2007 was less than $1,000,000. Y's taxable income for 2008 is determined under paragraph (c)(2) of this section to be $300,000 for that portion of Y's taxable year corresponding to Z's taxable year up to and including the date of transfer. Z's taxable income for 2008 is $800,000. Under the provisions of paragraph (c)(2) of this section, Z's 2008 taxable income for purposes of determining whether it is a large corporation for taxable year 2009 is $1,100,000 ($800,000 + $300,000). Thus, Z is a large corporation for the 2009 taxable year. In addition, if Z's 2008 taxable income, as determined under paragraph (c)(2) of this section, had been less than $1,000,000 but Y's taxable income in 2006 or 2007 had been $1,000,000 or more, Z would be a large corporation for taxable year 2009 because Y is a predecessor corporation.

(h) *Effective/applicability date.*—This section applies to taxable years beginning after September 6, 2007. [Reg. § 1.6655–4.]

☐ [*T.D. 9347, 8-6-2007.*]

[Reg. § 1.6655-5]

§ 1.6655-5. Short taxable year.—(a) *In general.*—Except as otherwise provided in this section, the provisions of section 6655 and these regulations are applicable in the case of a short taxable year (including an initial taxable year) for which a payment of estimated tax is required to be made.

(b) *Exception to payment of estimated tax.*—In the case of a short taxable year, no payment of estimated tax is required if—

(1) The short taxable year is a period of less than 4 full calendar months; or

(2) The tax shown on the return for such taxable year (or, if no return is filed, the tax) is less than $500.

(c) *Installment due dates.*—(1) *In general.*—(i) *Taxable year of at least four months but less than twelve months.*—Except as otherwise provided, in the case of a short taxable year, if such year results in a taxable year of four or more full calendar months but less than twelve full calendar months, the due dates prescribed in § 1.6655-1(f)(2) apply.

(ii) *Exceptions.*—(A) If the date determined under paragraph (c)(1)(i) of this section for the first required installment due during the taxpayer's short taxable year is earlier than the 15th day of the fourth month of the taxpayer's short taxable year, the taxpayer's first required installment is due on the first due date otherwise determined under paragraph (c)(1)(i) of this section that is on or after the 15th day of the fourth month of the short taxable year.

(B) A taxpayer with an initial short taxable year may make estimated tax payments as though it were a calendar year taxpayer until it files its tax return for its initial taxable year and will not be subject to an addition to tax under section 6655 for making estimated tax payments as though it were a calendar year taxpayer for the period beginning with its initial short taxable

year to the time it files its tax return for its initial short taxable year if, when filing its tax return for its initial short taxable year, the taxpayer chooses to be a fiscal year taxpayer.

(2) *Early termination of taxable year.*—(i) *In general.*—Except as provided in paragraph (c)(2)(ii) of this section, if a taxable year ends early (for example, as a result of an acquisition or a change in taxable year), the due date for the final required installment is the date that would have been the due date of the next required installment if the event that gave rise to the short taxable year had not occurred.

(ii) *Exception.*—If the date determined under paragraph (c)(2)(i) of this section is within thirty days of the last day of the short taxable year, the due date for the final required installment is the fifteenth day of the second month following the month that includes the last day of the short taxable year.

(d) *Amount due for required installment.*—(1) *In general.*—The amount due for any required installment determined under section 6655(d)(1)(B)(i) for a short taxable year is 100% of the required annual payment for the short taxable year divided by the number of required installments due (as determined under this section) for the short taxable year.

(2) *Tax shown on the return for the preceding taxable year.*—If the current taxable year is a short taxable year, the amount due for any required installment determined under section 6655(d)(1)(B)(ii) is determined in the following manner—

(i) Take 100% of the tax shown on the return of the corporation for the preceding taxable year;

(ii) Multiply such amount by the number of full calendar months in the current short taxable year and divide by 12; and

(iii) Divide the amount determined under paragraph (d)(2)(ii) of this section by the number of required installments due (as determined under this section) for the current short taxable year.

(3) *Applicable percentage.*—In the case of any required installment determined under section 6655(e), the applicable percentage under section 6655(e)(2)(B)(ii) is—

(i) 25%, 50%, 75%, and 100% for the first, second, third, and fourth (last) required installments, respectively, if the taxpayer will have four required installments due for the short taxable year;

(ii) 33.33%, 66.67%, and 100% for the first, second, and third (last) required installments, respectively, if the taxpayer will have three required installments due for the short taxable year;

(iii) 50% and 100% for the first and second (last) required installments, respectively, if the taxpayer will have two required installments due for the short taxable year; or

(iv) 100% for the first (and last) required installment if the taxpayer will have one required installment for the short taxable year.

(4) *Applicable percentage for installment period in which taxpayer does not reasonably expect that the taxable year will be an early termination year.*—In the case of any required installment determined under section 6655(e) in which the taxpayer does not reasonably expect that the taxable year will be an early termination year, the applicable percentage under section 6655(e)(2)(B)(ii) is the applicable percentage provided by paragraph (d)(3)(i) of this section with the remaining balance of the estimated tax payment for the year due with the final installment.

(e) *Examples.*—The following examples illustrate the rules of this section:

Example 1. Short year of less than 4 months. Corporation A is a calendar year taxpayer that was acquired by corporation B, a member of a consolidated group (as defined in §1.1502-1(h)) on April 16, 2009, resulting in A having a short taxable year from January 1, 2009, through April 16, 2009. Because A has a taxable year of less than four full calendar months, no estimated tax payments are required by A for the short taxable year.

Example 2. Initial short year with four required installments. Corporation B began business on January 9, 2009, and adopted a calendar year as its taxable year. B computes its required installments based on 100 percent of the tax shown on the return for the taxable year in accordance with section 6655(d)(1)(B)(i). Pursuant to §1.6655-1(f)(2)(i), the due dates of B's required installments for B's initial taxable year from January 9, 2009, through December 31, 2009, are April 15, 2009, June 15, 2009, September 15, 2009, and December 15, 2009. Pursuant to paragraph (d)(1) of this section, the amount due with each required installment is 25% of the required annual payment for B's first required installment, 50% of the required annual payment for B's second required installment, 75% of the required annual payment for B's third required installment, and 100% of the required annual payment for B's fourth required installment.

Example 3. Initial short year with three required installments. Corporation C began business on February 12, 2009, and adopted a calendar year as its taxable year. C computes its required installments based on 100 percent of the tax shown on the return for the taxable year in accordance with section 6655(d)(1)(B)(i). Pursuant to §1.6655-1(f)(2)(i), the due dates of C's required installments for C's initial taxable year from February 12, 2009, through December 31, 2009, are April 15, 2009, June 15, 2009, September 15, 2009, and December 15, 2009. However, in accordance with paragraph (c)(1)(ii)(A) of this section, C's first required installment is due June 15, 2009, because April 15, 2009, is earlier than the fifteenth day of the fourth month of C's taxable year. As a result, C's second required installment is due September 15, 2009, and C's third (and last) installment is due December 15, 2009. Pur-

suant to paragraph (d)(1) of this section, the amount due with each required installment is 33.33% of the required annual payment for C's first required installment, 66.67% of the required annual payment for C's second required installment, and 100% of the required annual payment for C's third (and last) required installment.

Example 4. Initial short year with two required installments. Same facts as *Example 3* except C began business on April 10, 2009. In accordance with paragraph (c)(1)(ii)(A) of this section, C's first required installment is due September 15, 2009, because April 15, 2009, and June 15, 2009, are earlier than the fifteenth day of the fourth month of C's taxable year. As a result, C's second (and last) required installment is due December 15, 2009. Pursuant to paragraph (d)(1) of this section, the amount due with each required installment is 50% of the required annual payment for C's first required installment, and 100% of the required annual payment for C's second (and last) required installment.

Example 5. Initial short year for fiscal year taxpayer with two required installments. Corporation D began business on February 12, 2009, and adopted a fiscal year ending October 31 as its taxable year. D computes its required installments based on 100 percent of the tax shown on the return for the taxable year in accordance with section 6655(d)(1)(B)(i). Pursuant to §1.6655-1(f)(2)(ii), the due dates of D's required installments for D's initial taxable year from February 12, 2009, through October 31, 2009, are February 15, 2009, April 15, 2009, July 15, 2009, and October 15, 2009. However, in accordance with paragraph (c)(1)(ii)(A) of this section, D's first required installment is due July 15, 2009, because February 15, 2009, and April 15, 2009, are earlier than the fifteenth day of the fourth month of D's taxable year. As a result, D's second (and last) installment is due October 15, 2009. Pursuant to paragraph (d)(1) of this section, the amount due with each required installment is 50% of the required annual payment for D's first required installment, and 100% of the required annual payment for D's second (and last) required installment.

Example 6. Initial short year for fiscal year taxpayer with one required installment. Same facts as *Example 5* except D corporation began business on May 11, 2009. In accordance with paragraph (c)(1)(ii)(A) of this section, D's first (and last) installment is due October 15, 2009, because July 15, 2009, is earlier than the fifteenth day of the fourth month of D's taxable year. Pursuant to paragraph (d)(1) of this section, the amount due with D's required installment is 100% of the required annual payment, computed as 100% divided by the number of required installments due for the short taxable year.

Example 7. Short termination year with three required installments. Corporation E is a calendar year taxpayer that computes its required installments based on 100 percent of the tax shown on the return for the taxable year in accordance with section 6655(d)(1)(B)(i). E computes its 2009 required installments based on a projected 2009 total tax liability of $600,000. On July 31, 2009, E is acquired by corporation F, a member of a consolidated group (as defined in § 1.1502-1(h)), resulting in E having a short taxable year from January 1, 2009, through July 31, 2009. E determines that its total tax liability for the short period is $350,000. The due dates for E's first and second required installments are April 15, 2009, and June 15, 2009, respectively. Pursuant to section 6655(d)(1)(A), E paid $150,000 with each required installment. Pursuant to paragraph (c)(2) of this section, E's third (and last) required installment of estimated tax is due on September 15, 2009, and the percentage of the required annual payment due with such installment is 100% pursuant to paragraph (d)(1) of this section. Accordingly, E is required to pay $50,000 with its final required installment on September 15, 2009 ($350,000 total tax liability for the short taxable year less prior installment payments of $300,000).

Example 8. Unexpected short termination year with three required installments using the annualization method. Same facts as *Example 7* except that E uses the annualized income installment method under section 6655(e)(2)(A)(i) to calculate all of its required installment payments for its 2009 taxable year. In addition, E does not reasonably expect until July 28, 2009, that it will have a short termination year caused by E being acquired by F on July 31, 2009. Had E known about its acquisition by F in the first quarter of 2009, E's applicable percentages for computing the amount of its three required installments would be 33.33%, 66.67%, and 100% for the first, second, and third (last) required installments, respectively, pursuant to paragraph (d)(3)(ii) of this section. However, because E had an unexpected short termination year that E was not aware of until after its second required installment payment, E's applicable percentages for computing the amount of its three required installment are 25%, 50%, and 100% for the first, second, and third (last) required installments, respectively, pursuant to paragraph (d)(4) of this section.

Example 9. Short termination year ending within 30 days of the regular final installment due date. Same facts as *Example 7* except that E is acquired by F on August 31, 2009. Pursuant to paragraph (c)(2)(ii) of this section, E's third (and last) required installment of estimated tax is due on October 15, 2009, because September 15, 2009, the date that would have been the due date of E's next required installment if F's acquisition of E had not occurred, is within thirty days of the last day of E's short taxable year, and 100% of the required annual payment is due with such installment.

Example 10. Short termination year ending within 30 days of the regular final installment due date. Corporation F is a calendar year taxpayer that computes its required installments based on 100 percent of the tax shown on the return for the taxable year in accordance with section 6655(d)(1)(B)(i). F computes its 2009 estimated tax payments based on a projected 2009 total tax liability of $900,000. On December 3, 2009, F is acquired by corporation G, a member of a consolidated group (as defined in § 1.1502-2(h)), resulting in F having a short taxable year from January 1, 2009, through December 3, 2009. F determined its total tax liability for the short period to be $800,000. The due dates for F's first, second, and third required installments are April 15, 2009, June 15, 2009, and September 15, 2009, respectively. Pursuant to section 6655(d)(1)(A), F paid $225,000 with each required installment. Pursuant to paragraph (c)(2)(ii) of this section, F's fourth (and last) required installment of estimated tax is due on February 15, 2010, and the percentage of the required annual payment due with such installment is 100% pursuant to paragraph (d)(1) of this section. However, because the due date for the fourth required installment falls on a legal holiday, F's required installment payment will be timely if paid on or before the first business day following the actual due date of the fourth required installment, that is, February 16, 2010. Accordingly, F is required to pay $125,000 with its final required installment on February 16, 2010 ($800,000 total tax liability for the short taxable year less prior installment payments of $675,000).

Example 11. Short termination year using the tax shown on the return for the preceding taxable year. Corporation G, a calendar year taxpayer, reported a tax liability of $75,000 on its return for the taxable year ending December 31, 2008, and is not a large corporation as defined in section 6655(g). On July 31, 2009, G makes a final distribution of its assets, in connection with a plan of complete liquidation, resulting in a short taxable year from January 1, 2009, through July 31, 2009. To satisfy the requirements of the exception described in section 6655(d)(1)(B)(ii) for payments determined by reference to the tax shown on the return of the corporation for the preceding taxable year, pursuant to paragraph (d)(2) of this section, G must pay in a proportionate amount of its 2008 tax liability based on the number of months in the current taxable year. Accordingly, G must pay $43,750 ($75,000 X 7/12) through payments of estimated tax payments in 2009, with $14,583 due on April 15, 2009, June 15, 2009, and September 15, 2009.

Example 12. Short termination year using the tax shown on the return for the preceding taxable year. Same facts as *Example 11* except that G makes a final distribution of its assets, in connection with a plan of complete liquidation, on October 1, 2009, resulting in a short taxable year from January 1, 2009, through October 1, 2009. To satisfy the requirements of the exception described in section 6655(d)(1)(B)(ii), G must pay $56,250 ($75,000 x 9/12) through payments of estimated tax in 2009, with $14,063 due on April 15, 2009, June 15, 2009, September 15, 2009, and December 15, 2009, respectively.

Example 13. Short initial year with three required installments resulting in an underpayment. (i) Corporation H began business on February 17, 2009, and adopted a calendar year. H computes its required installments based on 100 percent of the tax shown on the return for the taxable year in accordance with section 6655(d)(1)(B)(i). H estimated at the beginning of its short taxable year that its estimated tax liability for short taxable year February 17, 2009, through December 31, 2009, would be $180,000. H paid its first required installment of estimated tax of $60,000 on June 15, 2009, its second required installment of estimated tax of $60,000 on September 15, 2009, and its third (and last) required installment of estimated tax of $60,000 on December 15, 2009 ($180,000 total estimated tax liability for the short taxable year less prior installment payments of $120,000). H reported a tax liability of $240,000 on its return for the short period February 17, 2009, through December 31, 2009, with no credits against tax. There was an underpayment in the amount of $20,000 on the first installment date through September 15, 2009, $40,000 on the second installment date through December 15, 2009, and $60,000 on the third (and last) installment date through March 15, 2010, determined as follows:

(A) Tax as defined in section 6655(d)(1)(B)(i) = $240,000

(B) 100% of this paragraph (e), *Example 13* (A) = $240,000

(C) Amount of estimated tax required to be paid by the first installment date (33.33% of $240,000) = $80,000

(D) Amount of estimated tax required to be paid by the second installment date (66.67% of $240,000 less $80,000 (amount due with first installment)) = $80,000

(E) Amount of estimated tax required to be paid by the third installment date (100% of $240,000 less $160,000 (amount due with first and second installment)) = $80,000

(F) Deduction of amount paid on or before the first installment date = $60,000

(G) Amount of underpayment for the first installment date (this paragraph (e), *Example 13* (i)(C) minus this paragraph (e), *Example 13* (i)(F)) = $20,000

(H) Deduction of amount available for the second installment date ($60,000 second installment payment less this paragraph (e), *Example 13* (i)(G) applied towards the first installment underpayment) = $40,000

(I) Amount of underpayment for the second installment date (this paragraph (e), *Example 13* (i)(D) minus this paragraph (e), *Example 13* (i)(H)) = $40,000

(J) Deduction of amount available for the third installment date ($60,000 third installment payment less this paragraph (e), *Example 13* (i)(I) applied towards the second installment underpayment) = $20,000

(K) Amount of underpayment for the third installment date (this paragraph (e), *Example 1* (i)(E) minus this paragraph (e), *Example 13* (i)(J)) = $60,000

(ii) [Reserved].

(f) *52 or 53 week taxable year.*—For purposes of this section a taxable year of 52 or 53 weeks is deemed a period of 12 months in the case of a corporation that computes its taxable income in accordance with the election permitted by section 441(f).

(g) *Use of annualized income or seasonal installment method.*—(1) *In general.*—Regardless of the annual accounting period used by a corporation (for example, calendar year, fiscal year) the taxpayer may use the method described in § 1.6655-2 (annualized income installment method) or § 1.6655-3 (adjusted seasonal installment method) to compute its required installments of estimated tax when the current taxable year is a short taxable year.

(2) *Computation of annualized income installment.*—To the extent a short taxable year includes an annualization period elected by the taxpayer, the taxpayer computes its annualized income installment by determining the tax on the basis of such annualized income for the annualization period, divided by 12, multiplied by the number of months in the short taxable year, and multiplied by the applicable percentage for the required installment.

(3) *Annualization period for final required installment.*—For purposes of determining the final required installment (as described in paragraph (c)(2) of this section) for a short taxable year, annualized taxable income is determined by placing on an annualized basis the taxable income for the last complete annualization period that occurs within the short taxable year.

(4) *Examples.*—The provisions of paragraph (g) of this section may be illustrated by the following examples:

Example 1. Corporation X began business on February 12, 2009, and adopted a calendar year as its taxable year. X adopts an accrual method of accounting and uses the annualized income installment method under section 6655(e)(2)(A)(i) to calculate all of its required installment payments for its 2009 taxable year. Pursuant to § 1.6655-1(f)(2)(i), the due dates of X's required installments for X's initial taxable year from February 12, 2009, through December 31, 2009, are April 15, 2009, June 15, 2009, September 15, 2009, and December 15, 2009. However, in accordance with paragraph (c)(1)(ii)(A) of this section, X's first required installment is due June 15, 2009. As a result, X's second required installment is due September 15, 2009, and X's third (and last) required installment is due December 15, 2009. The amount of X's first and second required installments are each based on annualizing X's taxable income from February 12, 2009, through April 30, 2009, (the first three months of X's taxable year) and X's third (and last) required installment is based on annualizing X's taxable income from February 12, 2009, through July 31, 2009 (the first six months of X's taxable year). Because X will have three required installments due for its short taxable year, pursuant to paragraph (d)(3)(ii) of this section, the applicable percentage is 33.33% for X's first required installment, 66.67% for X's second required installment, and 100% for X's third (and last) required installment.

Example 2. (i) Y, a calendar year corporation, made a final distribution of its assets, in connection with a plan of complete liquidation, on August 3, 2009. Y filed a timely election to use the alternative annualization periods described under section 6655(e)(2)(C)(i) and determined that its taxable income for the first 2, 4 and 7 months of the taxable year was $25,000, $50,000 and $140,000. The due dates for Y's required installments for its short taxable year January 1, 2009, through August 3, 2009, are April 15, 2009, June 15, 2009, and September 15, 2009. Y made installment payments of $10,000, $10,000, and $20,000, respectively, on April 15, 2009, June 15, 2009, and September 15, 2009. The taxable income for each period is annualized as follows:

$25,000 X 12/2 = $150,000

$50,000 X 12/4 = $150,000

$140,000 x 12/7 = $240,000

(ii)(A) To determine whether the first required installment equals or exceeds the amount that would have been required to have been paid if the estimated tax were equal to one hundred percent of the tax computed on the annualized income for the 2-month period taking into account the number of months in the short taxable year, the following computation is necessary:

(1) Annualized income for the 2 month period = $150,000

(2) Tax on this paragraph (g)(4), Example 2 (ii)(A)(1) = $41,750

(3) Tax determined under this paragraph (g)(4), Example 2 (ii)(A)(2) divided by 12 multiplied by 7 (the number of months in the short taxable year) = $24,354

(4) 100% of this paragraph (g)(4), Example 2 (ii)(A)(3) = $24,354

(5) 33.33% of this paragraph (g)(4), Example 2 (ii)(A)(4) = $ 8,117

(B) Because the total amount of estimated tax that is timely paid on or before the first installment date ($10,000) exceeds the amount required to be paid on or before this date if the estimated tax were one hundred percent of the tax determined by placing on an annualized basis the taxable income for the first 2-month period taking into account the number of months in the short taxable year, the exception described in § 1.6655-2(a) applies and no addition to tax will be imposed for the installment due on April 15, 2009.

(iii)(A) To determine whether the required installments made on or before June 15, 2009, equal or exceed the amount that would have been required to have been paid if the estimated tax were equal to one hundred percent of the tax computed on the annualized income for the 4-month period taking into account the number of months in the short taxable year, the following computation is necessary:

(1) Annualized income for the 4 month period = $150,000

(2) Tax on this paragraph (g)(4), Example 2 (iii)(A)(1) = $41,750

(3) Tax determined under this paragraph (g)(4), Example 2 (iii)(A)(2) divided by 12 multiplied by 7 (the number of months in the short taxable year) = $24,354

(4) 100% of this paragraph (g)(4), Example 2 (iii)(A)(3) = $24,354

(5) 66.67% of this paragraph (g)(4), Example 2 (iii)(A)(4) less $8,117 (amount due with first installment) = $8,120

(B) Because the total amount of estimated tax available to apply towards the amount due for the second installment ($11,883 ($10,000 paid on the second installment date plus $1,883 overpayment of the first installment)) exceeds the amount required to be paid on or before this date if the estimated tax were one hundred percent of the tax determined by placing on an annualized basis the taxable income for the first 4-month period for the taxable year taking into account the number of months in the short taxable year, the exception described in § 1.6655-2(a) applies and no addition to tax will be imposed for the installment due on June 15, 2009.

(iv)(A) Pursuant to paragraph (c) and (d) of this section, the final required installment is due by September 15, 2009, and the applicable percentage due for the final required installment is 100%. To determine whether the installment payments made on or before September 15, 2009, equal or exceed the amount that would have been required to have been paid if the estimated tax were equal to one hundred percent of the tax computed on the annualized income for the 7-month period taking into account the number of months in the short taxable year, the following computation is necessary:

(1) Annualized income for the 7 month period = $240,000

(2) Tax on this paragraph (g)(4), Example 2 (iv)(A)(1) = $76,850

(3) Tax determined under this paragraph (g)(4), Example 2 (iv)(A)(2) divided by 12 multiplied by 7 (the number of months in the short taxable year) = $44,829

(4) 100% of this paragraph (g)(4), Example 2 (iv)(A)(3) = $44,829

(5) 100% of this paragraph (g)(4), Example 2 (iv)(A)(4) less $16,237 (amount due with first and second installment) = $28,592

(B) Because the total amount of estimated tax available to apply towards the amount due for the final installment ($23,763 ($20,000 that is timely paid on the third installment date plus $3,763 overpayment of the second installment)) does not exceed the amount required to be paid on or before this date if the estimated tax were one hundred percent of the tax determined by placing on an annualized basis the taxable income for the first 7-month period for the taxable year taking into account the number of months in the short taxable year, the exception described in § 1.6655-2(a) does not apply and an addition to tax will be imposed for the final installment due on September 15, 2009, unless another exception (for example, see section 6655(e)(3)) applies with respect to these installments.

(h) *Effective/applicability date.*—This section applies to taxable years beginning after September 6, 2007. [Reg. § 1.6655-5.]

☐ [*T.D.* 9347, 8-6-2007.]

[Reg. § 1.6655-6]

§ 1.6655-6. Methods of accounting.—(a) *In general.*—In computing any required installment, a corporation must use the methods of accounting used in computing taxable income for the taxable year for which estimated tax is being determined (the current taxable year).

(b) *Accounting method changes.*—A taxpayer that changes its method of accounting with the consent of the Commissioner for the current taxable year must use the new method of accounting (as of the beginning of the taxable year) in the determination of taxable income for annualization periods ending on or after the date the related section 481(a) adjustment is treated as arising. See § 1.6655-2(f)(3)(ii)(C) for the date a section 481(a) adjustment is treated as arising. If the change in method of accounting does not result in a section 481(a) adjustment, the taxpayer may choose to use the new method of accounting (as of the beginning of the taxable year) in the determination of taxable income for all annualization periods during the year of change or only those annualization periods ending on or after the date the Form 3115 "Application for Change in Accounting Method" was filed with the national office of the Internal Revenue Service. This paragraph (b) only applies to the extent a taxpayer changes a method of accounting for the taxable year with the consent of the Commissioner. Therefore, a taxpayer may be subject to a section 6655 addition to tax for an underpayment of estimated tax if an underpayment results from a change in a method of accounting the taxpayer anticipates making for the taxable year but for which the consent of the Commissioner is not subsequently received.

(c) *Examples.*—The following examples illustrate the rules of this section:

Example 1. Accounting method used in computing taxable income for the taxable year. Corporation ABC, a calendar year taxpayer, uses an accrual method of accounting and the annualization method under section 6655(e)(2)(A)(i) to calculate all of its 2008 required installments. ABC receives advance payments each taxable year with respect to agreements for the sale of goods properly includible in ABC's inventory. The advance payments received by ABC qualify for deferral under § 1.451-5(c). Although ABC is eligible to defer the advance payments in accordance with § 1.451-5(c), ABC's method of accounting with respect to the advance payments is to include the advance payments in income when received and ABC does not change its accounting method for advance payments for the 2008 taxable year. ABC must use its current method of recognizing advance payments as income in the year received for purposes of computing its 2008 required installments.

Example 2. Change of accounting method. Corporation ABC, a calendar year taxpayer, uses an accrual method of accounting and the annualization method under section 6655(e)(2)(A)(i) to calculate all of its 2008 required installments. On June 15, 2008, ABC files a Form 3115 requesting permission to change its method of accounting for future litigation reserves for the tax year ending December 31, 2008. On February 15, 2009, ABC receives consent from the Commissioner to make the change for the tax year ending December 31, 2008. The change results in a positive section 481(a) adjustment of $100,000. Under the provisions of § 1.6655-2(f)(3)(ii) ABC chooses to treat the section 481(a) adjustment as arising on the date the Form 3115 is filed with the national office of the Internal Revenue Service. Therefore, ABC is required to use the new method of accounting (as of the beginning of the year) in the determination of taxable income for annualization periods ending on or after June 15, 2008.

(d) *Effective/applicability date.*—This section applies to taxable years beginning after September 6, 2007. [Reg. § 1.6655-6.]

☐ [*T.D.* 9347, 8-6-2007.]

[Reg. § 1.6655-7]

§ 1.6655-7. Addition to tax on account of excessive adjustment under section 6425.—(a) Section 6655(h) imposes an addition to the tax under chapter 1 of the Internal Revenue Code in the case of any excessive amount (as defined in paragraph (c) of this section) of an adjustment under section 6425 that is made before the 15th day of the third month following the close of a taxable year beginning after December 31, 1967. This addition to tax is imposed whether or not there was reasonable cause for an excessive adjustment.

(b) If the amount of an adjustment under section 6425 is excessive, there shall be added to the tax under chapter 1 of the Internal Revenue Code for the taxable year an amount determined at the annual rate referred to in the regulations under section 6621 upon the excessive amount from the date on which the credit is allowed or refund paid to the 15th day of the third month following the close of the taxable year. A refund is paid on the date it is allowed under section 6407.

(c) The excessive amount is equal to the lesser of the amount of the adjustment or the amount by which—

(1) The income tax liability (as defined in section 6425(c)) for the taxable year, as shown on the return for the taxable year; exceeds

(2) The estimated income tax paid during the taxable year, reduced by the amount of the adjustment.

(d) The computation of the addition to the tax imposed by section 6425 is made independent of, and does not affect the computation of, any addition to the tax that a corporation may otherwise owe for an underpayment of an installment of estimated tax.

(e) The following example illustrates the rules of this section:

Example. (i) Corporation X, a calendar year taxpayer, had an underpayment as defined in section 6655(b), for its fourth installment of estimated tax that was due on December 15, 2009, in the amount of $10,000. On January 4, 2010, X filed an application for adjustment of overpayment of estimated income tax for 2009 in the amount of $20,000.

(ii) On February 16, 2010, the Internal Revenue Service, in response to the application, refunded $20,000 to X. On March 15, 2010, X filed its 2009 tax return and made a payment in settlement of its total tax liability. Assuming that the addition to tax is computed under section 6621(a)(2) at a rate of 8% per annum for the applicable periods of underpayment, under section 6655(a), X is subject to an addition to tax in the amount of $197 (90/365 X $10,000 X 8%) on account of X's December 15, 2009, underpayment. Under section 6655(h), X is subject to an addition to tax in the amount of $118 (27/365 X $20,000 X 8%) on account of X's excessive adjustment under section 6425. In determining the amount of the addition to tax under section 6655(a) for failure to pay estimated income tax, the excessive adjustment under section 6425 is not taken into account.

(f) An adjustment is generally to be treated as a reduction of estimated income tax paid as of the date of the adjustment. However, for purposes of §§ 1.6655-1 through 1.6655-6, the adjustment is to be treated as if not made in determining whether there has been any underpayment of estimated income tax and, if there is an underpayment, the period during which the underpayment existed.

(g) Effective/applicability date: This section applies to taxable years beginning after September 6, 2007. [Reg. § 1.6655-7.]

☐ [*T.D. 7059, 9-16-70. Amended by T.D. 7384, 10-21-75. Redesignated and amended by T.D. 9347, 8-6-2007.*]

[Reg. § 1.6655(e)-1]

§1.6655(e)-1. Time and manner for making election under the Omnibus Budget Reconciliation Act of 1993.—(a) *Description.*—Section 6655(e)(2)(C), as added by section 13225 of the Omnibus Budget Reconciliation Act of 1993 (Public Law 103-66, 107 Stat. 486), allows a corporate taxpayer to make an annual election to use a different annualization period to determine annualized income for purposes of paying any required installment of estimated income tax for a taxable year beginning after December 31, 1993.

(b) *Time and manner for making the election.*— An election under section 6655(e)(2)(C) must be made on or before the date required for the payment of the first required installment for the taxable year. For a calendar or fiscal year corporation, Form 8842, Election to Use Different Annualization Periods for Corporate Estimated Tax,

must be filed by the 15th day of the 4th month of the taxable year for which the election is to apply. Form 8842 must be filed with the Internal Revenue Service Center where the corporation files its income tax return.

(c) *Revocability of election.*—The election described in this section is irrevocable.

(d) *Effective date.*—The rules set forth in this section are effective December 12, 1996. [Reg. § 1.6655(e)-1.]

☐ [*T.D. 8688, 12-11-96.*]

[Reg. § 301.6656-1]

§301.6656-1. Abatement of penalty.— (a) *Exception for first time depositors of employment taxes.*—(1) *Waiver.*—The Secretary will generally waive the penalty imposed by section 6656(a) on a person's failure to deposit any employment tax under subtitle C of the Internal Revenue Code if—

(i) The failure is inadvertent;

(ii) The person meets the requirements referred to in section 7430(c)(4)(A)(ii) (relating to the net worth requirements applicable for awards of attorney's fees);

(iii) The failure occurs during the first quarter that the person is required to deposit any employment tax; and

(iv) The return of the tax is filed on or before the due date.

(2) *Inadvertent failure.*—For purposes of paragraph (a)(1)(i) of this section, the Secretary will determine if a failure to deposit is inadvertent based on all the facts and circumstances.

(b) *Deposit sent to Secretary.*—The Secretary may abate the penalty imposed by section 6656(a) if the first time a taxpayer is required to make a deposit, the amount required to be deposited is inadvertently sent to the Secretary rather than deposited by electronic funds transfer.

(c) *Effective/applicability date.*—This section applies to deposits and payments made after December 31, 2010. [Reg. § 301.6656-1.]

☐ [*T.D. 8725, 7-21-97. Redesignated by T.D. 8947, 6-14-2001. Amended by T.D. 9507, 12-2-2010.*]

[Reg. § 301.6657-1]

§301.6657-1. Bad checks.—(a) *In general.*— Except as provided in paragraph (b) of this section, if a check or money order is tendered in the payment of any amount receivable under the Code, and such check or money order is not paid upon presentment, a penalty of one percent of the amount of the check or money order, in addition to any other penalties provided by law, shall be paid by the person who tendered such check or money order. If, however, the amount of the check or money order is less than $500, the penalty shall be $5 or the amount of the check or money order, whichever amount is the lesser.

Such penalty shall be paid in the same manner as tax upon the issuance of a notice and demand therefor.

(b) *Reasonable cause.*—If payment is refused upon presentment of any check or money order and the person who tendered such check or money order establishes to the satisfaction of the district director that it was tendered in good faith with reasonable cause to believe that it would be duly paid, the penalty set forth in paragraph (a) of this section shall not apply. [Reg. § 301.6657-1.]

☐ [*T.D.* 6268, 11-15-57. *Amended by T.D.* 6586, 12-27-61.]

[Reg. § 301.6659-1]

§ 301.6659-1. Applicable rules.—(a) *Additions treated as tax.*—Except as otherwise provided in the Code, any reference in the Code to "tax" shall be deemed also to be a reference to any addition to the tax, additional amount, or penalty imposed by chapter 68 of the Code with respect to such tax. Such additions to the tax, additional amounts, and penalties shall become payable upon notice and demand therefor and shall be assessed, collected, and paid in the same manner as taxes.

(b) *Additions to tax for failure to file return or pay tax.*—Any addition under section 6651 or section 6653 to a tax shall be considered a part of such tax for the purpose of the assessment and collection of such tax. For applicability of deficiency procedures to additions to the tax, see paragraph (c) of this section.

(c) *Deficiency procedures.*—(1) *Addition to the tax for failure to file tax return.*—Subchapter B, chapter 63, of the Code (deficiency procedures) applies to the additions to the income, estate, and gift taxes imposed by section 6651 for failure to file a tax return to the same extent that it applies to such taxes. Accordingly, if there is a deficiency (as defined in section 6211) in the tax (apart from the addition to the tax) where a return has not been timely filed, deficiency procedures apply to the addition to the tax under section 6651. If there is no deficiency in the tax where a return has not been timely filed, the addition to the tax under section 6651 may be assessed and collected without deficiency procedures. The provisions of this subparagraph may be illustrated by the following examples:

Example (1). A filed his income tax return for the calendar year 1955 on May 15, 1956, not having been granted an extension of time for such filing. His failure to file on time was not due to reasonable cause. The return showed a liability of $1,000 and it was determined that A is liable under section 6651 for an addition to such tax of $50 (5 percent a month for 1 month). The provisions of subchapter B of chapter 63 (deficiency procedures) do not apply to the assessment and collection of the addition to the tax since such provisions are not applicable to the tax with respect to which such addition was asserted, there being no statutory deficiency for purposes of section 6211.

Example (2). Assume the same facts as in Example (1) and assume further that a deficiency of $500 in tax and a further $25 addition to the tax under section 6651 is asserted against A for the calendar year 1955. Thus, the total addition to the tax under section 6651 is $75. Since the provisions of subchapter B of chapter 63 are applicable to the $500 deficiency, they likewise apply to the $25 addition to the tax asserted with respect to such deficiency (but not to the $50 addition to the tax under example (1)).

(2) *Additions to the tax for negligence or fraud.*—Subchapter B of chapter 63 (deficiency procedures) applies to all additions to the income, estate, and gift taxes imposed by section 6653(a) and (b) for negligence and fraud.

(3) *Additions to tax for failure to pay estimated income taxes.*—(i) *Return filed by taxpayer.*—The addition to the tax for underpayment of estimated income tax imposed by section 6654 (relating to failure by individuals to pay estimated income tax) or section 6655 (relating to failure by corporations to pay estimated income tax) is determined by reference to the tax shown on the return if a return is filed. Therefore, such addition may be assessed and collected without regard to the provisions of subchapter B of chapter 63 (deficiency procedures) if a return is filed since such provisions are not applicable to the assessment of the tax shown on the return. Further, since the additions to the tax imposed by section 6654 or 6655 are determined solely by reference to the amount of tax shown on the return if a return is filed, the assertion of a deficiency with respect to any tax not shown on such return will not make the provisions of subchapter B of chapter 63 (deficiency procedures) apply to the assessment and collection of any additions to the tax under section 6654 or 6655.

(ii) *No return filed by taxpayer.*—If the taxpayer has not filed a return and his entire income tax liability is asserted as a deficiency to which the provisions of subchapter B of chapter 63 apply, such provisions likewise will apply to any addition to such tax imposed by section 6654 or 6655. [Reg. § 301.6659-1.]

☐ [*T.D.* 6268, 11-16-57. *Amended by T.D.* 6498, 10-24-60 *and T.D.* 7838, 10-5-82.]

[Reg. § 1.6662-0]

§ 1.6662-0. Table of contents.—This section lists the captions that appear in §§ 1.6662-1 through 1.6662-7.

(d) Effective dates.

  (1) Returns due before January 1, 1994.

  (2) Returns due after December 31, 1993.

  (3) Special rules for tax shelter items.

  (4) Special rule for reasonable basis.

  (5) Returns filed after December 31, 2002.

§1.6662-3. Negligence or disregard of rules or regulations.

(a) In general.

(b) Definitions and rules.

  (1) Negligence.

  (2) Disregard of rules or regulations.

  (3) Reasonable basis.

(c) Exception for adequate disclosure.

  (1) In general.

  (2) Method of disclosure.

(d) Special rules in the case of carrybacks and carryovers.

  (1) In general.

  (2) Transition rule for carrybacks to pre-1990 years.

  (3) Example.

§1.6662-4. Substantial understatement of income tax.

(a) In general.

(b) Definitions and computational rules.

  (1) Substantial.

  (2) Understatement.

  (3) Amount of the tax required to be shown on the return.

  (4) Amount of the tax imposed which is shown on the return.

  (5) Rebate.

  (6) Examples.

(c) Special rules in the case of carrybacks and carryovers.

  (1) In general.

  (2) Understatements for carryback years not reduced by amount of carrybacks.

  (3) Tainted items defined.

    (i) In general.

    (ii) Tax shelter items.

  (4) Transition rule for carrybacks to pre-1990 years.

  (5) Examples.

(d) Substantial authority.

  (1) Effect of having substantial authority.

  (2) Substantial authority standard.

  (3) Determination of whether substantial authority is present.

    (i) Evaluation of authorities.

    (ii) Nature of analysis.

    (iii) Types of authority.

    (iv) Special rules.

      (A) Written determinations.

      (B) Taxpayer's jurisdiction.

      (C) When substantial authority determined.

    (v) Substantial authority for tax returns due before January 1, 1990.

(e) Disclosure of certain information.

  (1) Effect of adequate disclosure.

  (2) Circumstances where disclosure will not have an effect.

  (3) Restriction for corporations.

(f) Method of making adequate disclosure.

  (1) Disclosure statement.

  (2) Disclosure on return.

  (3) Recurring item.

  (4) Carrybacks and carryovers.

  (5) Pass-through entities.

(g) Items relating to tax shelters.

  (1) In general.

    (i) Noncorporate taxpayers.

    (ii) Corporate taxpayers.

      (A) In general.

      (B) Special rule for transactions occurring prior to December 9, 1994.

    (iii) Disclosure irrelevant.

    (iv) Cross-reference.

  (2) Tax shelter.

    (i) In general.

    (ii) Principal purpose.

  (3) Tax shelter item.

  (4) Reasonable belief.

    (i) In general.

    (ii) Facts and circumstances; reliance on professional tax advisor.

  (5) Pass-through entities.

§1.6662-5. Substantial and gross valuation misstatements under chapter 1.

(a) In general.

(b) Dollar limitation.

(c) Special rules in the case of carrybacks and carryovers.

  (1) In general.

  (2) Transition rule for carrybacks to pre-1990 years.

(d) Examples.

(e) Definitions.

  (1) Substantial valuation misstatement.

  (2) Gross valuation misstatement.

  (3) Property.

(f) Multiple valuation misstatements on a return.

  (1) Determination of whether valuation misstatements are substantial or gross.

  (2) Application of dollar limitation.

(g) Property with a value or adjusted basis of zero.

(h) Pass-through entities.

  (1) In general.

  (2) Example.

(i) [Reserved]

(j) Transactions between persons described in section 482 and net section 482 transfer price adjustments. [Reserved]

(k) Returns affected.

§1.6662-5T. Substantial and gross valuation misstatements under chapter 1 (Temporary).

(a) through (e)(3) [Reserved].

  (e)(4) Tests related to section 482.

    (i) Substantial valuation misstatement.

    (ii) Gross valuation misstatement.

(iii) Property.

(f) through (i) [Reserved].

(j) Transactions between persons described in section 482 and net section 482 transfer price adjustments.

§ 1.6662-6. *Transactions between persons described in section 482 and net section 482 transfer price adjustments.*

(a) In general.

(1) Purpose and scope.

(2) Reported results.

(3) Identical terms used in the section 482 regulations.

(b) The transactional penalty.

(1) Substantial valuation misstatement.

(2) Gross valuation misstatement.

(3) Reasonable cause and good faith.

(c) Net adjustment penalty.

(1) Net section 482 adjustment.

(2) Substantial valuation misstatement.

(3) Gross valuation misstatement.

(4) Setoff allocation rule.

(5) Gross receipts.

(6) Coordination with reasonable cause exception under section 6664(c).

(7) Examples.

(d) Amounts excluded from net section 482 adjustments.

(1) In general.

(2) Application of a specified section 482 method.

(i) In general.

(ii) Specified method requirement.

(iii) Documentation requirement.

(A) In general.

(B) Principal documents.

(C) Background documents.

(3) Application of an unspecified method.

(i) In general.

(ii) Unspecified method requirement.

(A) In general.

(B) Specified method potentially applicable.

(C) No specified method applicable.

(iii) Documentation requirement.

(A) In general.

(B) Principal and background documents.

(4) Certain foreign to foreign transactions.

(5) Special rule.

(6) Examples.

(e) Special rules in the case of carrybacks and carryovers.

(f) Rules for coordinating between the transactional penalty and the net adjustment penalty.

(1) Coordination of a net section 482 adjustment subject to the net adjustment penalty and a gross valuation misstatement subject to the transactional penalty.

(2) Coordination of net section 482 adjustment subject to the net adjustment penalty and substantial valuation misstatements subject to the transactional penalty.

(3) Examples.

(g) Effective date.

§ 1.6662-7. *Omnibus Budget Reconciliation Act of 1993 changes to the accuracy-related penalty.*

(a) Scope.

(b) No disclosure exception for negligence penalty.

(c) Disclosure standard for other penalties is reasonable basis.

(d) Reasonable basis.

[Reg. § 1.6662-0.]

☐ *[T.D. 8381, 12-30-91. Amended by T.D. 8519, 1-27-94; T.D. 8533, 3-14-94; T.D. 8551, 7-5-94; T.D. 8617, 8-31-95; T.D. 8656, 2-8-96; T.D. 8790, 12-1-98 and T.D. 9109, 12-29-2003.]*

[Reg. § 1.6662-1]

§ 1.6662-1. Overview of the accuracy-related penalty.—Section 6662 imposes an accuracy-related penalty on any portion of an underpayment of tax required to be shown on a return that is attributable to one or more of the following:

(a) Negligence or disregard of rules or regulations;

(b) Any substantial understatement of income tax;

(c) Any substantial valuation misstatement under chapter 1;

(d) Any substantial overstatement of pension liabilities; or

(e) Any substantial estate or gift tax valuation understatement.

Sections 1.6662-1 through 1.6662-5 address only the first three components of the accuracy-related penalty, *i.e.*, the penalties for negligence or disregard of rules or regulations, substantial understatements of income tax, and substantial (or gross) valuation misstatements under chapter 1. The penalties for disregard of rules or regulations and for a substantial understatement of income tax may be avoided by adequately disclosing certain information as provided in § 1.6662-3(c) and § § 1.6662-4(e) and (f), respectively. The penalties for negligence and for a substantial (or gross) valuation misstatement under chapter 1 may not be avoided by disclosure. No accuracy-related penalty may be imposed on any portion of an underpayment if there was reasonable cause for, and the taxpayer acted in good faith with respect to, such portion. The reasonable cause and good faith exception to the accuracy-related penalty is set forth in § 1.6664-4. [Reg. § 1.6662-1.]

☐ *[T.D. 8381, 12-30-91. Amended by T.D. 8617, 8-31-95.]*

[Reg. § 1.6662-2]

§ 1.6662-2. Accuracy-related penalty.—(a) *In general.*—Section 6662(a) imposes an accuracy-related penalty on any portion of an underpayment of tax (as defined in section 6664(a) and § 1.6664-2) required to be shown on a return if such portion is attributable to one or more of the following types of misconduct:

(1) Negligence or disregard of rules or regulations (see § 1.6662-3);

(2) Any substantial understatement of income tax (see § 1.6662-4); or

(3) Any substantial (or gross) valuation misstatement under chapter 1 ("substantial valuation misstatement" or "gross valuation misstatement"), provided the applicable dollar limitation set forth in section 6662(e)(2) is satisfied (see § 1.6662-5).

The accuracy-related penalty applies only in cases in which a return of tax is filed, except that the penalty does not apply in the case of a return prepared by the Secretary under the authority of section 6020(b). The accuracy-related penalty under section 6662 and the penalty under section 6651 for failure to timely file a return of tax may both be imposed on the same portion of an underpayment if a return is filed, but is filed late. The fact that a return is filed late, however, is not taken into account in determining whether an accuracy-related penalty should be imposed. No accuracy-related penalty may be imposed on any portion of an underpayment of tax on which the fraud penalty set forth in section 6663 is imposed.

(b) *Amount of penalty.*—(1) *In general.*—The amount of the accuracy-related penalty is 20 percent of the portion of an underpayment of tax required to be shown on a return that is attributable to any of the types of misconduct listed in paragraphs (a)(1) through (a)(3) of this section, except as provided in paragraph (b)(2) of this section.

(2) *Increase in penalty for gross valuation misstatement.*—In the case of a gross valuation misstatement, as defined in section 6662(h)(2) and § 1.6662-5(e)(2), the amount of the accuracy-related penalty is 40 percent of the portion of an underpayment of tax required to be shown on a return that is attributable to the gross valuation misstatement, provided the applicable dollar limitation set forth in section 6662(e)(2) is satisfied.

(c) *No stacking of accuracy-related penalty components.*—The maximum accuracy-related penalty imposed on a portion of an underpayment may not exceed 20 percent of such portion (40 percent of the portion attributable to a gross valuation misstatement), notwithstanding that such portion is attributable to more than one of the types of misconduct described in paragraph (a) of this section. For example, if a portion of an underpayment of tax required to be shown on a return is attributable both to negligence and a substantial understatement of income tax, the maximum accuracy-related penalty is 20 percent of such portion. Similarly, the maximum accuracy-related penalty imposed on any portion of an underpayment that is attributable both to negligence and a gross valuation misstatement is 40 percent of such portion.

(d) *Effective dates.*—(1) *Returns due before January 1, 1994.*—Section 1.6662-3(c) and §§ 1.6662-4(e) and (f) (relating to methods of making adequate disclosure) (as contained in 26 CFR part 1 revised April 1, 1995) apply to returns the due date of which (determined without regard to extensions of time for filing) is after December 31, 1991, but before January 1, 1994. Except as provided in the preceding sentence and in paragraphs (d)(2), (3), and (4) of this section, §§ 1.6662-1 through 1.6662-5 apply to returns the due date of which (determined without regard to extensions of time for filing) is after December 31, 1989, but before January 1, 1994. To the extent the provisions of these regulations were not reflected in the statute as amended by the Omnibus Budget Reconciliation Act of 1989 (OBRA 1989), in Notice 90-20, 1990-1 C.B. 328, or in rules and regulations in effect prior to March 4, 1991 (to the extent not inconsistent with the statute as amended by OBRA 1989), these regulations will not be adversely applied to a taxpayer who took a position based upon such prior rules on a return filed before January 1, 1992.

(2) *Returns due after December 31, 1993.*—Except as provided in paragraphs (d)(3), (4) and (5) of this section and the last sentence of this paragraph (d)(2), the provisions of §§ 1.6662-1 through 1.6662-4 and § 1.6662-7 (as revised to reflect the changes made to the accuracy-related penalty by the Omnibus Budget Reconciliation Act of 1993) and of § 1.6662-5 apply to returns the due date of which (determined without regard to extensions of time for filing) is after December 31, 1993. These changes include raising the disclosure standard for the penalties for disregarding rules or regulations and for a substantial understatement of income tax from not frivolous to reasonable basis, eliminating the disclosure exception for the negligence penalty, and providing guidance on the meaning of reasonable basis. The Omnibus Budget Reconciliation Act of 1993 changes relating to the penalties for negligence or disregard of rules or regulations will not apply to returns (including qualified amended returns) that are filed on or before March 14, 1994, but the provisions of §§ 1.6662-1 through 1.6662-3 (as contained in 26 CFR part 1 revised April 1, 1995) relating to those penalties will apply to such returns.

(3) *Special rules for tax shelter items.*—Sections 1.6662-4(g)(1) and 1.6662-4(g)(4) apply to returns the due date of which (determined without regard to extensions of time for filing) is after September 1, 1995. Except as provided in the last sentence of this paragraph (d)(3), §§ 1.6662-4(g)(1) and 1.6662-4(g)(4) (as contained in 26 CFR part 1 revised April 1, 1995) apply to returns the due date of which (determined without regard to extensions of time for filing) is on or before September 1, 1995, and after December 31, 1989. For transactions occurring after December 8, 1994, §§ 1.6662-4(g)(1) and 1.6662-4(g)(2) (as contained in 26 CFR part 1 revised April 1, 1995) are applied taking into account the

changes made to section 6662(d)(2)(C) (relating to the substantial understatement penalty for tax shelter items of corporations) by section 744 of Title VII of the Uruguay Round Agreements Act, Pub. L. 103-465 (108 Stat. 4809).

(4) *Special rules for reasonable basis.*—Section 1.6662-3(b)(3) applies to returns filed on or after December 2, 1998.

(5) *For returns filed after December 31, 2002.*—Sections 1.6662-3(a), 1.6662-3(b)(2) and 1.6662-3(c)(1) (relating to adequate disclosure) apply to returns filed after December 31, 2002, with respect to transactions entered into on or after January 1, 2003. Except as provided in paragraph (d)(1) of this section, §§1.6662-3(a), 1.6662-3(b)(2) and 1.6662-3(c)(1) (as contained in 26 CFR part 1 revised April 1, 2003) apply to returns filed with respect to transactions entered into prior to January 1, 2003. [Reg. §1.6662-2.]

[*T.D. 8381, 12-30-91. Amended by T.D. 8617, 8-31-95; T.D. 8790, 12-1-98 and T.D. 9109, 12-29-2003.*]

[Reg. §1.6662-3]

§1.6662-3. Negligence or disregard of rules or regulations.—(a) *In general.*—If any portion of an underpayment, as defined in section 6664(a) and §1.6664-2, of any income tax imposed under subtitle A of the Internal Revenue Code that is required to be shown on a return is attributable to negligence or disregard of rules or regulations, there is added to the tax an amount equal to 20 percent of such portion. The penalty for disregarding rules or regulations does not apply, however, if the requirements of paragraph (c)(1) of this section are satisfied and the position in question is adequately disclosed as provided in paragraph (c)(2) of this section (and, if the position relates to a reportable transaction as defined in §1.6011-4(b) (or §1.6011-4T(b), as applicable), the transaction is disclosed in accordance with §1.6011-4 (or §1.6011-4T, as applicable)), or to the extent that the reasonable cause and good faith exception to this penalty set forth in §1.6664-4 applies. In addition, if a position with respect to an item (other than with respect to a reportable transaction, as defined in §1.6011-4(b) or §1.6011-4T(b), as applicable) is contrary to a revenue ruling or notice (other than a notice of proposed rulemaking) issued by the Internal Revenue Service and published in the Internal Revenue Bulletin (see §601.601(d)(2) of this chapter), this penalty does not apply if the position has a realistic possibility of being sustained on its merits. See §1.6694-2(b) of the income tax return preparer penalty regulations for a description of the realistic possibility standard.

(b) *Definitions and rules.*—(1) *Negligence.*—The term "negligence" includes any failure to make a reasonable attempt to comply with the provisions of the internal revenue laws or to exercise ordinary and reasonable care in the preparation of a tax return. "Negligence" also includes any failure by the taxpayer to keep adequate books and records or to substantiate items properly. A return position that has a reasonable basis as defined in paragraph (b)(3) of this section is not attributable to negligence. Negligence is strongly indicated where—

(i) A taxpayer fails to include on an income tax return an amount of income shown on an information return, as defined in section 6724(d)(1);

(ii) A taxpayer fails to make a reasonable attempt to ascertain the correctness of a deduction, credit or exclusion on a return which would seem to a reasonable and prudent person to be "too good to be true" under the circumstances;

(iii) A partner fails to comply with the requirements of section 6222, which requires that a partner treat partnership items on its return in a manner that is consistent with the treatment of such items on the partnership return (or notify the Secretary of the inconsistency); or

(iv) A shareholder fails to comply with the requirements of section 6242, which requires that an S corporation shareholder treat subchapter S items on its return in a manner that is consistent with the treatment of such items on the corporation's return (or notify the Secretary of the inconsistency).

(2) *Disregard of rules or regulations.*—The term "disregard" includes any careless, reckless or intentional disregard of rules or regulations. The term "rules or regulations" includes the provisions of the Internal Revenue Code, temporary or final Treasury regulations issued under the Code, and revenue rulings or notices (other than notices of proposed rulemaking) issued by the Internal Revenue Service and published in the Internal Revenue Bulletin. A disregard of rules or regulations is "careless" if the taxpayer does not exercise reasonable diligence to determine the correctness of a return position that is contrary to the rule or regulation. A disregard is "reckless" if the taxpayer makes little or no effort to determine whether a rule or regulation exists, under circumstances which demonstrate a substantial deviation from the standard of conduct that a reasonable person would observe. A disregard is "intentional" if the taxpayer knows of the rule or regulation that is disregarded. Nevertheless, a taxpayer who takes a position (other than with respect to a reportable transaction, as defined in §1.6011-4(b) or §1.6011-4T(b), as applicable) contrary to a revenue ruling or notice has not disregarded the ruling or notice if the contrary position has a realistic possibility of being sustained on its merits.

(3) *Reasonable basis.*—Reasonable basis is a relatively high standard of tax reporting, that is, significantly higher than not frivolous or not patently improper. The reasonable basis standard is not satisfied by a return position that is merely arguable or that is merely a colorable claim. If a return position is reasonably based on one or more of the authorities set forth in §1.6662-4(d)(3)(iii) (taking into account the relevance and persuasiveness of the authorities, and subsequent developments), the return position

will generally satisfy the reasonable basis standard even though it may not satisfy the substantial authority standard as defined in § 1.6662-4(d)(2). (See § 1.6662-4(d)(3)(ii) for rules with respect to relevance, persuasiveness, subsequent developments, and use of a well-reasoned construction of an applicable statutory provision for purposes of the substantial understatement penalty.) In addition, the reasonable cause and good faith exception in § 1.6664-4 may provide relief from the penalty for negligence or disregard of rules or regulations, even if a return position does not satisfy the reasonable basis standard.

(c) *Exception for adequate disclosure.*—(1) *In general.*—No penalty under section 6662(b)(1) may be imposed on any portion of an underpayment that is attributable to a position contrary to a rule or regulation if the position is disclosed in accordance with the rules of paragraph (c)(2) of this section (and, if the position relates to a reportable transaction as defined in § 1.6011-4(b) (or § 1.6011-4T(b), as applicable), the transaction is disclosed in accordance with § 1.6011-4 (or § 1.6011-4T, as applicable)) and, in case of a position contrary to a regulation, the position represents a good faith challenge to the validity of the regulation. This disclosure exception does not apply, however, in the case of a position that does not have a reasonable basis or where the taxpayer fails to keep adequate books and records or to substantiate items properly.

(2) *Method of disclosure.*—Disclosure is adequate for purposes of the penalty for disregarding rules or regulations if made in accordance with the provisions of § § 1.6662-4(f)(1), (3), (4) and (5), which permit disclosure on a properly completed and filed Form 8275 or 8275-R, as appropriate. In addition, the statutory or regulatory provision or ruling in question must be adequately identified on the Form 8275 or 8275-R, as appropriate. The provisions of § 1.6662-4(f)(2), which permit disclosure in accordance with an annual revenue procedure for purposes of the substantial understatement penalty, do not apply for purposes of this section.

(d) *Special rules in the case of carrybacks and carryovers*—.—(1) *In general.*—The penalty for negligence or disregard of rules or regulations applies to any portion of an underpayment for a year to which a loss, deduction or credit is carried, which portion is attributable to negligence or disregard of rules or regulations in the year in which the carryback or carryover of the loss, deduction or credit arises (the "loss or credit year").

(2) *Transition rule for carrybacks to pre-1990 years.*—A 20 percent penalty under section 6662(b)(1) is imposed on any portion of an underpayment for a carryback year, the return for which is due (without regard to extensions) before January 1, 1990, if—

(i) That portion is attributable to negligence or disregard of rules or regulations in a loss or credit year; and

(ii) The return for the loss or credit year is due (without regard to extensions) after December 31, 1989.

(3) *Example.*—The following example illustrates the provisions of paragraph (d) of this section. This example does not take into account the reasonable cause exception under § 1.6664-4.

Example. Corporation M is a C corporation. In 1990, M had a loss of $200,000 before taking into account a deduction of $350,000 that M claimed as an expense in careless disregard of the capitalization requirements of section 263 of the Code. M failed to make adequate disclosure of the item for 1990. M reported a $550,000 loss for 1990 and carried back the loss to 1987 and 1988. M had reported taxable income of $400,000 for 1987 and $200,000 for 1988, before application of the carryback. The carryback eliminated all of M's taxable income for 1987 and $150,000 of taxable income for 1988. After disallowance of the $350,000 expense deduction and allowance of a $35,000 depreciation deduction with respect to the capitalized amount, the correct loss for 1990 was determined to be $235,000. Because there is no underpayment for 1990, the penalty for negligence or disregard of rules or regulations does not apply for 1990. However, as a result of the 1990 adjustments, the loss carried back to 1987 is reduced from $550,000 to $235,000. After application of the $235,000 carryback, M has taxable income of $165,000 for 1987 and $200,000 for 1988. This adjustment results in underpayments for 1987 and 1988 that are attributable to the disregard of rules or regulations on the 1990 return. Therefore, the 20 percent penalty rate applies to the 1987 and 1988 underpayments attributable to the disallowed carryback. [Reg. § 1.6662-3.]

□ [*T.D.* 8381, 12-30-91. *Amended by T.D.* 8617, 8-31-95; *T.D.* 8790, 12-1-98 *and `T.D.* 9109, 12-29-2003.]

[Reg. § 1.6662-4]

§ 1.6662-4. Substantial understatement of income tax.—(a) *In general.*—If any portion of an underpayment, as defined in section 6664(a) and § 1.6664-2, of any income tax imposed under subtitle A of the Code that is required to be shown on a return is attributable to a substantial understatement of such income tax, there is added to the tax an amount equal to 20 percent of such portion. Except in the case of any item attributable to a tax shelter (as defined in paragraph (g)(2) of this section), an understatement is reduced by the portion of the understatement that is attributable to the tax treatment of an item for which there is substantial authority, or with respect to which there is adequate disclosure. General rules for determining the amount of an understatement are set forth in paragraph (b) of this section and more specific rules in the case of carrybacks and carryovers are set forth in paragraph (c) of this section. The rules for determining when substantial authority exists are set forth in § 1.6662-4(d). The rules for determining when there is adequate disclosure are set forth in

§ 1.6662-4(e) and (f). This penalty does not apply to the extent that the reasonable cause and good faith exception to this penalty set forth in § 1.6664-4 applies.

(b) *Definitions and computational rules.*—(1) *Substantial.*—An understatement (as defined in paragraph (b)(2) of this section) is "substantial" if it exceeds the greater of—

(i) 10 percent of the tax required to be shown on the return for the taxable year (as defined in paragraph (b)(3) of this section); or

(ii) $5,000 ($10,000 in the case of a corporation other than an S corporation (as defined in section 1361(a)(1)) or a personal holding company (as defined in section 542)).

(2) *Understatement.*—Except as provided in paragraph (c)(2) of this section (relating to special rules for carrybacks), the term "understatement" means the excess of—

(i) The amount of the tax required to be shown on the return for the taxable year (as defined in paragraph (b)(3) of this section), over

(ii) The amount of the tax imposed which is shown on the return for the taxable year (as defined in paragraph (b)(4) of this section), reduced by any rebate (as defined in paragraph (b)(5) of this section).

The definition of understatement also may be expressed as—

$$\text{Understatement} = X - (Y - Z)$$

where X = the amount of the tax required to be shown on the return; Y = the amount of the tax imposed which is shown on the return; and Z = any rebate.

(3) *Amount of the tax required to be shown on the return.*—The "amount of the tax required to be shown on the return" for the taxable year has the same meaning as the "amount of income tax imposed" as defined in § 1.6664-2(b).

(4) *Amount of the tax imposed which is shown on the return.*—The "amount of the tax imposed which is shown on the return" for the taxable year has the same meaning as the "amount shown as the tax by the taxpayer on his return," as defined in § 1.6664-2(c), except that—

(i) There is no reduction for the excess of the amount described in § 1.6664-2(c)(1)(i) over the amount described in § 1.6664-2(c)(1)(ii), and

(ii) The tax liability shown by the taxpayer on his return is recomputed as if the following items had been reported properly:

(A) Items (other than tax shelter items as defined in § 1.6662-4(g)(3)) for which there is substantial authority for the treatment claimed (as provided in § 1.6662-4(d)).

(B) Items (other than tax shelter items as defined in § 1.6662-4(g)(3)) with respect to which there is adequate disclosure (as provided in § 1.6662-4(e) and (f)).

(C) Tax shelter items (as defined in § 1.6662-4(g)(3)) for which there is substantial authority for the treatment claimed (as provided in § 1.6662-4(d)), and with respect to which the taxpayer reasonably believed that the tax treat-

ment of the items was more likely than not the proper tax treatment (as provided in § 1.6662-4(g)(4)).

(5) *Rebate.*—The term "rebate" has the meaning set forth in § 1.6664-2(e), except that—

(i) "Amounts not so shown previously assessed (or collected without assessment)" includes only amounts not so shown previously assessed (or collected without assessment) as a deficiency, and

(ii) The amount of the rebate is determined as if any items to which the rebate is attributable that are described in paragraph (b)(4) of this section had received the proper tax treatment.

(6) *Examples.*—The following examples illustrate the provisions of paragraph (b) of this section. These examples do not take into account the reasonable cause exception under § 1.6664-4:

Example 1. In 1990, Individual A, a calendar year taxpayer, files a return for 1989, which shows taxable income of $18,200 and tax liability of $2,734. Subsequent adjustments on audit for 1989 increase taxable income to $51,500 and tax liability to $12,339. There was substantial authority for an item resulting in an adjustment that increases taxable income by $5,300. The item is not a tax shelter item. In computing the amount of the understatement, the amount of tax shown on A's return is determined as if the item for which there was substantial authority had been given the proper tax treatment. Thus, the amount of tax that is treated as shown on A's return is $4,176, i.e., the tax on $23,500 ($18,200 taxable income actually shown on A's return plus $5,300, the amount of the adjustment for which there was substantial authority). The amount of the understatement is $8,163, i.e., $12,339 (the amount of tax required to be shown) less $4,176 (the amount of tax treated as shown on A's return after adjustment for the item for which there was substantial authority). Because the $8,163 understatement exceeds the greater of 10 percent of the tax required to be shown on the return for the year, i.e., $1,234 ($12,339 × .10) or $5,000, A has a substantial understatement of income tax for the year.

Example 2. Individual B, a calendar year taxpayer, files a return for 1990 that fails to include income reported on an information return, Form 1099, that was furnished to B. The Service detects this omission through its document matching program and assesses $3,000 in unreported tax liability. B's return is later examined and as a result of the examination the Service makes an adjustment to B's return of $4,000 in additional tax liability. Assuming there was neither substantial authority nor adequate disclosure with respect to the items adjusted, there is an understatement of $7,000 with respect to B's return. There is also an underpayment of $7,000. (See § 1.6664-2.) The amount of the understatement is not reduced by imposition of a negligence penalty on the $3,000 portion of the underpayment that is attributable to the unreported income.

Reg. § 1.6662-4(b)(6)

However, if the Service does impose the negligence penalty on this $3,000 portion, the Service may only impose the substantial understatement penalty on the remaining $4,000 portion of the underpayment. (See § 1.6662-2(c), which prohibits stacking of accuracy-related penalty components.)

(c) *Special rules in the case of carrybacks and carryovers.*—(1) *In general.*—The penalty for a substantial understatement of income tax applies to any portion of an underpayment for a year to which a loss, deduction or credit is carried that is attributable to a "tainted item" for the year in which the carryback or carryover of the loss, deduction or credit arises (the "loss or credit year"). The determination of whether an understatement is substantial for a carryback or carryover year is made with respect to the return of the carryback or carryover year. "Tainted items" are taken into account with items arising in a carryback or carryover year to determine whether the understatement is substantial for that year.

(2) *Understatements for carryback years not reduced by amount of carrybacks.*—The amount of an understatement for a carryback year is not reduced on account of a carryback of a loss, deduction or credit to that year.

(3) *Tainted items defined.*—(i) *In general.*—Except in the case of a tax shelter item (as defined in paragraph (g)(3) of this section), a "tainted item" is any item for which there is neither substantial authority nor adequate disclosure with respect to the loss or credit year.

(ii) *Tax shelter items.*—In the case of a tax shelter item (as defined in paragraph (g)(3) of this section), a "tainted item" is any item for which there is not, with respect to the loss or credit year, both substantial authority and a reasonable belief that the tax treatment is more likely than not the proper treatment.

(4) *Transition rule for carrybacks to pre-1990 years.*—A 20 percent penalty under section 6662(b)(2) is imposed on any portion of an underpayment for a carryback year, the return for which is due (without regard to extensions) before January 1, 1990, if—

(i) That portion is attributable to one or more "tainted items" (as defined in paragraph (c)(3) of this section) arising in a loss or credit year; and

(ii) The return for the loss or credit year is due (without regard to extensions) after December 31, 1989.

The preceding sentence applies only if the understatement in the carryback year is substantial. See *Example 2* in paragraph (c)(5) of this section.

(5) *Examples.*—The following examples illustrate the rules of paragraph (c) of this section regarding carrybacks and carryovers. These examples do not take into account the reasonable cause exception under § 1.6664-4.

Example 1. (i) Corporation N, a calendar year taxpayer, is a C corporation. N was formed on January 1, 1987, and timely filed the following income tax returns:

Tax Year	1987	1988	1989	1990
Taxable Income	$30,000	$100,000	($300,000)	$50,000 (Before NOLCO)
Tax Liability	$4,575	$22,250	–0–	$ 7,500 (Before NOLCO)

(ii) During 1990, N files Form 1139, Corporation Application for Tentative Refund, to carry back the NOL generated in 1989 (NOLCB). N received refunds of $4,575 for 1987 and $22,250 for 1988.

(iii) For tax year 1990, N carries over $50,000 of the 1989 loss to offset $50,000 of income earned in 1990 and reduce taxable income to zero. N would have reported $7,500 of tax liability for 1990 if it were not for use of the net operating loss carryover (NOLCO). N assumes there is a remaining NOLCO of $120,000 to be applied for tax year 1991.

(iv) In June 1991, the Service completes its examination of the 1989 loss year return and makes the following adjustment:

Taxable income per 1989 return	($300,000)
Adjustment: Unreported income	310,000
Corrected taxable income	$ 10,000
Corrected tax liability	$1,500

(v) There was not substantial authority for N's treatment of the items comprising the 1989 adjustment and N did not make adequate disclosure.

(vi) As a result of the adjustment to the 1989 return, N had an understatement of $4,575 for tax year 1987; an understatement of $22,250 for tax year 1988; an understatement of $1,500 for tax year 1989; and an understatement of $7,500 for tax year 1990. Only the $22,250 understatement for 1988 is a substantial understatement, i.e., it exceeds the greater of (a) $2,225 (10 percent of the tax required to be shown on the return for the taxable year (.10 × $22,250)) or (b) $10,000. The underpayment for 1988 is subject to a penalty rate of 20 percent.

Example 2. The facts are the same as in *Example 1*, except that in addition to examining the 1989 return, the Service also examines the 1987 return and makes an adjustment that results in an understatement. (This adjustment is unrelated to the adjustment on the 1987 return for the disallowance of the NOLCB from 1989.) If the understatement resulting from the adjustment to the 1987 return, when combined with the understatement resulting from the disallowance of the NOLCB from 1989, exceeds the greater of (a) 10 percent of the tax required to be shown on the return for 1987 or (b) $10,000, the underpayment for 1987 will also be subject to a substantial understatement penalty. The portion of the underpayment attributable to the adjustment unrelated to the disallowance of the NOLCB will be subject to a penalty rate of 25 percent under former section 6661. The portion of the underpayment attributable to the disallowance of the NOLCB will be subject to a penalty rate of 20 percent under section 6662.

Example 3. Individual P, a calendar year single taxpayer, files his 1990 return reporting taxable income of $10,000 and a tax liability of $1,504. An examination of the 1990 return results in an adjustment for unreported income of $25,000. There was not substantial authority for P's failure to report the income, and P did not make adequate disclosure with respect to the unreported income. P's correct tax liability for 1990 is determined to be $7,279, resulting in an understatement of $5,775 (the difference between the amount of tax required to be shown on the return ($7,279) and the tax shown on the return ($1,504)). Because the understatement exceeds the greater of (a) $728 (10 percent of the tax required to be shown on the return (.10 × $7,279)) or (b) $5,000, the understatement is substantial. Subsequently, P files his 1993 return showing a net operating loss. The loss is carried back to his 1990 return, reducing his taxable income for 1990 to zero. However, the amount of the understatement for 1990 is not reduced on account of the NOLCB to that year. P is subject to the 20 percent penalty rate under section 6662 on the underpayment attributable to the substantial understatement for 1990, notwithstanding that the tax required to be shown on the return for that year, after application of the NOLCB, is zero.

(d) *Substantial authority.*—(1) *Effect of having substantial authority.*—If there is substantial authority for the tax treatment of an item, the item is treated as if it were shown properly on the return for the taxable year in computing the amount of the tax shown on the return. Thus, for purposes of section 6662(d), the tax attributable to the item is not included in the understatement for that year. (For special rules relating to tax shelter items see § 1.6662-4(g).)

(2) *Substantial authority standard.*—The substantial authority standard is an objective standard involving an analysis of the law and application of the law to relevant facts. The substantial authority standard is less stringent than the more likely than not standard (the standard that is met when there is a greater than 50-percent likelihood of the position being upheld), but more stringent than the reasonable basis standard as defined in § 1.6662-3(b)(3). The possibility that a return will not be audited or, if audited, that an item will not be raised on audit, is not relevant in determining whether the substantial authority standard (or the reasonable basis standard) is satisfied.

(3) *Determination of whether substantial authority is present.*—(i) *Evaluation of authorities.*—There is substantial authority for the tax treatment of an item only if the weight of the authorities supporting the treatment is substantial in relation to the weight of authorities supporting contrary treatment. All authorities relevant to the tax treatment of an item, including the authorities contrary to the treatment, are taken into account in determining whether substantial authority exists. The weight of authorities is determined in light of the pertinent facts and circumstances in the manner prescribed by paragraph (d)(3)(ii) of this section. There may be substantial authority for more than one position with respect to the same item. Because the substantial authority standard is an objective standard, the taxpayer's belief that there is substantial authority for the tax treatment of an item is not relevant in determining whether there is substantial authority for that treatment.

(ii) *Nature of analysis.*—The weight accorded an authority depends on its relevance and persuasiveness, and the type of document providing the authority. For example, a case or revenue ruling having some facts in common with the tax treatment at issue is not particularly relevant if the authority is materially distinguishable on its facts, or is otherwise inapplicable to the tax treatment at issue. An authority that merely states a conclusion ordinarily is less persuasive than one that reaches its conclusion by cogently relating the applicable law to pertinent facts. The weight of an authority from which information has been deleted, such as a private letter ruling, is diminished to the extent that the deleted information may have affected the authority's conclusions. The type of document also must be considered. For example, a revenue ruling is accorded greater weight than a private letter ruling addressing the same issue. An older private letter ruling, technical advice memorandum, general counsel memorandum or action on decision generally must be accorded less weight than a more recent one. Any document described in the preceding sentence that is more than 10 years old generally is accorded very little weight. However, the persuasiveness and relevance of a document, viewed in light of subsequent developments, should be taken into account along with the age of the document. There may be substantial authority for the tax treatment of an item despite the absence of certain types of authority. Thus, a taxpayer may have substantial authority for a position that is supported only by a well-reasoned construction of the applicable statutory provision.

(iii) *Types of authority.*—Except in cases described in paragraph (d)(3)(iv) of this section concerning written determinations, only the following are authority for purposes of determining whether there is substantial authority for the tax treatment of an item: applicable provisions of the Internal Revenue Code and other statutory provisions; proposed, temporary and final regulations construing such statutes; revenue rulings and revenue procedures; tax treaties and regulations thereunder, and Treasury Department and other official explanations of such treaties; court cases; congressional intent as reflected in committee reports, joint explanatory statements of managers included in conference committee reports, and floor statements made prior to enactment by one of a bill's managers; General Explanations of tax legislation prepared by the Joint Committee on Taxation (the Blue Book); private letter rulings and technical advice memoranda issued after October 31, 1976; actions on decisions and general counsel memoranda issued after March 12, 1981 (as well as general counsel memoranda published in pre-1955 volumes of the Cumulative Bulletin); Internal Revenue Service information or press releases; and notices, announcements and other administrative pronouncements published by the Service in the Internal Revenue Bulletin. Conclusions reached in treatises, legal periodicals, legal opinions or opinions rendered by tax professionals are not authority. The authorities underlying such expressions of opinion where applicable to the facts of a particular case, however, may give rise to substantial authority for the tax treatment of an item. Notwithstanding the preceding list of authorities, an authority does not continue to be an authority to the extent it is overruled or modified, implicitly or explicitly, by a body with the power to overrule or modify the earlier authority. In the case of court decisions, for example, a district court opinion on an issue is not an authority if overruled or reversed by the United States Court of Appeals for such district. However, a Tax Court opinion is not considered to be overruled or modified by a court of appeals to which a taxpayer does not have a right of appeal, unless the Tax Court adopts the holding of the court of appeals. Similarly, a private letter ruling is not authority if revoked or if inconsistent with a subsequent proposed regulation, revenue ruling or other administrative pronouncement published in the Internal Revenue Bulletin.

(iv) *Special rules.*—(A) *Written determinations.*—There is substantial authority for the tax treatment of an item by a taxpayer if the treatment is supported by the conclusion of a ruling or a determination letter (as defined in §301.6110-2(d) and (e)) issued to the taxpayer, by the conclusion of a technical advice memorandum in which the taxpayer is named, or by an affirmative statement in a revenue agent's report with respect to a prior taxable year of the taxpayer ("written determinations"). The preceding sentence does not apply, however, if—

(1) There was a misstatement or omission of a material fact or the facts that subsequently develop are materially different from the facts on which the written determination was based, or

(2) The written determination was modified or revoked after the date of issuance by—

(i) A notice to the taxpayer to whom the written determination was issued,

(ii) The enactment of legislation or ratification of a tax treaty,

(iii) A decision of the United States Supreme Court,

(iv) The issuance of temporary or final regulations, or

(v) The issuance of a revenue ruling, revenue procedure, or other statement published in the Internal Revenue Bulletin.

Except in the case of a written determination that is modified or revoked on account of §1.6662-4(d)(3)(iv)(A)(1), a written determination that is modified or revoked as described in §1.6662-4(d)(3)(iv)(A)(2) ceases to be authority on the date, and to the extent, it is so modified or revoked. See section 6404(f) for rules which require the Secretary to abate a penalty that is attributable to erroneous written advice furnished to a taxpayer by an officer or employee of the Internal Revenue Service.

(B) *Taxpayer's jurisdiction.*—The applicability of court cases to the taxpayer by reason of the taxpayer's residence in a particular jurisdiction is not taken into account in determining whether there is substantial authority for the tax treatment of an item. Notwithstanding the preceding sentence, there is substantial authority for the tax treatment of an item if the treatment is supported by controlling precedent of a United States Court of Appeals to which the taxpayer has a right of appeal with respect to the item.

(C) *When substantial authority determined.*—There is substantial authority for the tax treatment of an item if there is substantial authority at the time the return containing the item is filed or there was substantial authority on the last day of the taxable year to which the return relates.

(v) *Substantial authority for tax returns due before January 1, 1990.*—There is substantial authority for the tax treatment of an item on a return that is due (without regard to extensions) after December 31, 1982 and before January 1, 1990, if there is substantial authority for such treatment under either the provisions of paragraph (d)(3)(iii) of this section (which set forth an expanded list of authorities) or of §1.6661-3(b)(2) (which set forth a narrower list of authorities). Under either list of authorities, authorities both for and against the position must be taken into account.

(e) *Disclosure of certain information.*—(1) *Effect of adequate disclosure.*—Items for which there is adequate disclosure as provided in this paragraph (e) and in paragraph (f) of this section are treated as if such items were shown properly on the return for the taxable year in computing the amount of the tax shown on the return. Thus, for purposes of section 6662(d), the tax attributable to such items is not included in the understatement for that year.

(2) *Circumstances where disclosure will not have an effect.*—The rules of paragraph (e)(1) of this section do not apply where the item or position on the return —

(i) Does not have a reasonable basis (as defined in § 1.6662-3(b)(3));

(ii) Is attributable to a tax shelter (as defined in section 6662(d)(2)(C)(iii) and paragraph (g)(2) of this section); or

(iii) Is not properly substantiated, or the taxpayer failed to keep adequate books and records with respect to the item or position.

(3) *Restriction for corporations.*—For purposes of paragraph (e)(2)(i) of this section, a corporation will not be treated as having a reasonable basis for its tax treatment of an item attributable to a multi-party financing transaction entered into after August 5, 1997, if the treatment does not clearly reflect the income of the corporation.

(f) *Method of making adequate disclosure.*— (1) *Disclosure statement.*—Disclosure is adequate with respect to an item (or group of similar items, such as amounts paid or incurred for supplies by a taxpayer engaged in business) or a position on a return if the disclosure is made on a properly completed form attached to the return or to a qualified amended return (as defined in § 1.6664-2(c)(3)) for the taxable year. In the case of an item or position other than one that is contrary to a regulation, disclosure must be made on Form 8275 (Disclosure Statement); in the case of a position contrary to a regulation, disclosure must be made on Form 8275-R (Regulation Disclosure Statement).

(2) *Disclosure on return.*—The Commissioner may by annual revenue procedure (or otherwise) prescribe the circumstances under which disclosure of information on a return (or qualified amended return) in accordance with applicable forms and instructions is adequate. If the revenue procedure does not include an item, disclosure is adequate with respect to that item only if made on a properly completed Form 8275 or 8275-R, as appropriate, attached to the return for the year or to a qualified amended return.

(3) *Recurring item.*—Disclosure with respect to a recurring item, such as the basis of recovery property, must be made for each taxable year in which the item is taken into account.

(4) *Carrybacks and carryovers.*—Disclosure is adequate with respect to an item which is included in any loss, deduction or credit that is carried to another year only if made in connection with the return (or qualified amended return) for the taxable year in which the carryback or carryover arises (the "loss or credit year"). Disclosure is not also required in connection with the return for the taxable year in which the carryback or carryover is taken into account.

(5) *Pass-through entities.*—Disclosure in the case of items attributable to a pass-through entity (pass-through items) is made with respect to the return of the entity, except as provided in this paragraph (f)(5). Thus, disclosure in the case of pass-through items must be made on a Form 8275 or 8275-R, as appropriate, attached to the return (or qualified amended return) of the entity, or on the entity's return in accordance with the revenue procedure described in paragraph (f)(2) of this section, if applicable. A taxpayer (i.e., partner, shareholder, beneficiary, or holder of a residual interest in a REMIC) also may make adequate disclosure with respect to a pass-through item, however, if the taxpayer files a properly completed Form 8275 or 8275-R, as appropriate, in duplicate, one copy attached to the taxpayer's return (or qualified amended return) and the other copy filed with the Internal Revenue Service Center with which the return of the entity is required to be filed. Each Form 8275 or 8275-R, as appropriate, filed by the taxpayer should relate to the pass-through items of only one entity. For purposes of this paragraph (f)(5), a pass-through entity is a partnership, S corporation (as defined in section 1361(a)(1)), estate, trust, regulated investment company (as defined in section 851(a)), real estate investment trust (as defined in section 856(a)), or real estate mortgage investment conduit ("REMIC") (as defined in section 860D(a)).

(g) *Items relating to tax shelters.*—(1) *In general.*—(i) *Noncorporate taxpayers.*—Tax shelter items (as defined in paragraph (g)(3) of this section) of a taxpayer other than a corporation are treated for purposes of this section as if such items were shown properly on the return for a taxable year in computing the amount of the tax shown on the return, and thus the tax attributable to such items is not included in the understatement for the year, if—

(A) There is substantial authority (as provided in paragraph (d) of this section) for the tax treatment of that item; and

(B) The taxpayer reasonably believed at the time the return was filed that the tax treatment of that item was more likely than not the proper treatment.

(ii) *Corporate taxpayers.*—(A) *In general.*— Except as provided in paragraph (g)(1)(ii)(B) of this section, all tax shelter items (as defined in paragraph (g)(3) of this section) of a corporation are taken into account in computing the amount of any understatement.

(B) *Special rule for transactions occurring prior to December 9, 1994.*—The tax shelter items of a corporation arising in connection with transactions occurring prior to December 9, 1994 are treated for purposes of this section as if such items were shown properly on the return if the requirements of paragraph (g)(1)(i) are satisfied with respect to such items.

(iii) *Disclosure irrelevant.*—Disclosure made with respect to a tax shelter item of either a corporate or noncorporate taxpayer does not affect the amount of an understatement.

(iv) *Cross-reference.*—See §1.6664-4(f) for certain rules regarding the availability of the reasonable cause and good faith exception to the substantial understatement penalty with respect to tax shelter items of corporations.

(2) *Tax shelter.*—(i) *In general.*—For purposes of section 6662(d), the term "tax shelter" means—

    (A) A partnership or other entity (such as a corporation or trust),

    (B) An investment plan or arrangement, or

    (C) Any other plan or arrangement,

if the principal purpose of the entity, plan or arrangement, based on objective evidence, is to avoid or evade Federal income tax. The principal purpose of an entity, plan or arrangement is to avoid or evade Federal income tax if that purpose exceeds any other purpose. Typical of tax shelters are transactions structured with little or no motive for the realization of economic gain, and transactions that utilize the mismatching of income and deductions, overvalued assets or assets with values subject to substantial uncertainty, certain nonrecourse financing, financing techniques that do not conform to standard commercial business practices, or the mischaracterization of the substance of the transaction. The existence of economic substance does not of itself establish that a transaction is not a tax shelter if the transaction includes other characteristics that indicate it is a tax shelter.

(ii) *Principal purpose.*—The principal purpose of an entity, plan or arrangement is not to avoid or evade Federal income tax if the entity, plan or arrangement has as its purpose the claiming of exclusions from income, accelerated deductions or other tax benefits in a manner consistent with the statute and Congressional purpose. For example, an entity, plan or arrangement does not have as its principal purpose the avoidance or evasion of Federal income tax solely as a result of the following uses of tax benefits provided by the Internal Revenue Code: the purchasing or holding of an obligation bearing interest that is excluded from gross income under section 103; taking an accelerated depreciation allowance under section 168; taking the percentage depletion allowance under section 613 or section 613A; deducting intangible drilling and development costs as expenses under section 263(c); establishing a qualified retirement plan under sections 401-409; claiming the possession tax credit under section 936; or claiming tax benefits available by reason of an election under section 992 to be taxed as a domestic international sales corporation ("DISC"), under section 927(f)(1) to be taxed as a foreign sales corporation ("FSC"), or under section 1362 to be taxed as an S corporation.

(3) *Tax shelter item.*—An item of income, gain, loss, deduction or credit is a "tax shelter item" if the item is directly or indirectly attributable to the principal purpose of a tax shelter to avoid or evade Federal income tax. Thus, if a partnership is established for the principal purpose of avoiding or evading Federal income tax by acquiring and overstating the basis of property for purposes of claiming accelerated depreciation, the depreciation with respect to the property is a tax shelter item. However, a deduction claimed in connection with a separate transaction carried on by the same partnership is not a tax shelter item if the transaction does not constitute a plan or arrangement the principal purpose of which is to avoid or evade tax.

(4) *Reasonable belief.*—(i) *In general.*—For purposes of section 6662(d) and paragraph (g)(1)(i)(B) of this section (pertaining to tax shelter items of noncorporate taxpayers), a taxpayer is considered reasonably to believe that the tax treatment of an item is more likely than not the proper tax treatment if (without taking into account the possibility that a return will not be audited, that an issue will not be raised on audit, or that an issue will be settled)—

    (A) The taxpayer analyzes the pertinent facts and authorities in the manner described in paragraph (d)(3)(ii) of this section, and in reliance upon that analysis, reasonably concludes in good faith that there is a greater than 50-percent likelihood that the tax treatment of the item will be upheld if challenged by the Internal Revenue Service; or

    (B) The taxpayer reasonably relies in good faith on the opinion of a professional tax advisor, if the opinion is based on the tax advisor's analysis of the pertinent facts and authorities in the manner described in paragraph (d)(3)(ii) of this section and unambiguously states that the tax advisor concludes that there is a greater than 50-percent likelihood that the tax treatment of the item will be upheld if challenged by the Internal Revenue Service.

(ii) *Facts and circumstances; reliance on professional tax advisor.*—All facts and circumstances must be taken into account in determining whether a taxpayer satisfies the requirements of paragraph (g)(4)(i) of this section. However, in no event will a taxpayer be considered to have reasonably relied in good faith on the opinion of a professional tax advisor for purposes of paragraph (g)(4)(i)(B) of this section unless the requirements of §1.6664-4(c)(1) are met. The fact that the requirements of §1.6664-4(c)(1) are satisfied will not necessarily establish that the taxpayer reasonably relied on the opinion in good faith. For example, reliance may not be reasonable or in good faith if the taxpayer knew, or should have known, that the advisor lacked knowledge in the relevant aspects of Federal tax law.

(5) *Pass-through entities.*—In the case of tax shelter items attributable to a pass-through entity, the actions described in paragraphs (g)(4)(i)(A) and (B) of this section, if taken by the entity, are deemed to have been taken by the

taxpayer and are considered in determining whether the taxpayer reasonably believed that the tax treatment of an item was more likely than not the proper tax treatment. [Reg. §1.6662-4.]

☐ [*T.D. 8381, 12-30-91. Amended by T.D. 8617, 8-31-95; T.D. 8790, 12-1-98 and T.D. 9109, 12-29-2003.*]

[Reg. §1.6662-5]

§1.6662-5. Substantial and gross valuation misstatements under chapter 1.—(a) *In general.*—If any portion of an underpayment, as defined in section 6664(a) and §1.6664-2, of any income tax imposed under chapter 1 of subtitle A of the Code that is required to be shown on a return is attributable to a substantial valuation misstatement under chapter 1 ("substantial valuation misstatement"), there is added to the tax an amount equal to 20 percent of such portion. Section 6662(h) increases the penalty to 40 percent in the case of a gross valuation misstatement under chapter 1 ("gross valuation misstatement"). No penalty under section 6662(b)(3) is imposed, however, on a portion of an underpayment that is attributable to a substantial or gross valuation misstatement unless the aggregate of all portions of the underpayment attributable to substantial or gross valuation misstatements exceeds the applicable dollar limitation ($5,000 or $10,000), as provided in section 6662(e)(2) and paragraphs (b) and (f)(2) of this section. This penalty also does not apply to the extent that the reasonable cause and good faith exception to this penalty set forth in §1.6664-4 applies. There is no disclosure exception to this penalty.

(b) *Dollar limitation.*—No penalty may be imposed under section 6662(b)(3) for a taxable year unless the portion of the underpayment for that year that is attributable to substantial or gross valuation misstatements exceeds $5,000 ($10,000 in the case of a corporation other than an S corporation (as defined in section 1361(a)(1)) or a personal holding company (as defined in section 542)). This limitation is applied separately to each taxable year for which there is a substantial or gross valuation misstatement.

(c) *Special rules in the case of carrybacks and carryovers.*—(1) *In general.*—The penalty for a substantial or gross valuation misstatement applies to any portion of an underpayment for a year to which a loss, deduction or credit is carried that is attributable to a substantial or gross valuation misstatement for the year in which the carryback or carryover of the loss, deduction or credit arises (the "loss or credit year"), provided that the applicable dollar limitation set forth in section 6662(e)(2) is satisfied in the carryback or carryover year.

(2) *Transition rule for carrybacks to pre-1990 years.*—The penalty under section 6662(b)(3) is imposed on any portion of an underpayment for a carryback year, the return for which is due (without regard to extensions) before January 1, 1990, if—

(i) That portion is attributable to a substantial or gross valuation misstatement for a loss or credit year; and

(ii) The return for the loss or credit year is due (without regard to extensions) after December 31, 1989.

The preceding sentence applies only if the underpayment for the carryback year exceeds the applicable dollar limitation ($5,000, or $10,000 for most corporations). See *Example 3* in paragraph (d) of this section.

(d) *Examples.*—The following examples illustrate the provisions of paragraphs (b) and (c) of this section. These examples do not take into account the reasonable cause exception under §1.6664-4.

Example 1. Corporation Q is a C corporation. In 1990, the first year of its existence, Q had taxable income of $200,000 without considering depreciation of a particular asset. On its calendar year 1990 return, Q overstated its basis in this asset by an amount that caused a substantial valuation misstatement. The overstated basis resulted in depreciation claimed of $350,000, which was $250,000 more than the $100,000 allowable. Thus, on its 1990 return, Q showed a loss of $150,000. In 1991, Q had taxable income of $450,000 before application of the loss carryover, and Q claimed a carryover loss deduction under section 172 of $150,000, resulting in taxable income of $300,000 for 1991. Upon audit of the 1990 return, the basis of the asset was corrected, resulting in an adjustment of $250,000. For 1990, the underpayment resulting from the $100,000 taxable income (−$150,000 + $250,000) is attributable to the valuation misstatement. Assuming the underpayment resulting from the $100,000 taxable income exceeds the $10,000 limitation, the penalty will be imposed in 1990. For 1991, the elimination of the loss carryover results in additional taxable income of $150,000. The underpayment for 1991 resulting from that adjustment is also attributable to the substantial valuation misstatement on the 1990 return. Assuming the underpayment resulting from the $150,000 additional taxable income for 1991 exceeds the $10,000 limitation, the substantial valuation misstatement penalty also will be imposed for that year.

Example 2. (i) Corporation T is a C corporation. In 1990, the first year of its existence, T had a loss of $3,000,000 without considering depreciation of its major asset. On its calendar year 1990 return, T overstated its basis in this asset in an amount that caused a substantial valuation misstatement. This overstatement resulted in depreciation claimed of $3,500,000, which was $2,500,000 more than the $1,000,000 allowable. Thus, on its 1990 return, T showed a loss of $6,500,000. In 1991, T had taxable income of $4,500,000 before application of the carryover loss, but claimed a carryover loss deduction under section 172 in the amount of $4,500,000, resulting in taxable income of zero for that year and leaving a $2,000,000 carryover available. Upon audit of the 1990 return, the basis of the asset was corrected, resulting in an adjustment of $2,500,000.

(ii) For 1990, the underpayment is still zero (−$6,500,000 + $2,500,000 = − $4,000,000). Thus, the penalty does not apply in 1990. The loss for 1990 is reduced to $4,000,000.

(iii) For 1991, there is additional taxable income of $500,000 as a result of the reduction of the carryover loss ($4,500,000 reported income before carryover loss minus corrected carryover loss of $4,000,000 = $500,000). The underpayment for 1991 resulting from reduction of the carryover loss is attributable to the valuation misstatement on the 1990 return. Assuming the underpayment resulting from the $500,000 additional taxable income exceeds the $10,000 limitation, the substantial valuation misstatement penalty will be imposed in 1991.

Example 3. Corporation V is a C corporation. In 1990, V had a loss of $100,000 without considering depreciation of a particular asset which it had fully depreciated in earlier years. V had a depreciable basis in the asset of zero, but on its 1990 calendar year return erroneously claimed a basis in the asset of $1,250,000 and depreciation of $250,000. V reported a $350,000 loss for the year 1990, and carried back the loss to the 1987 and 1988 tax years. V had reported taxable income of $300,000 in 1987 and $200,000 in 1988, before application of the carryback. The $350,000 carryback eliminated all taxable income for 1987, and $50,000 of the taxable income for 1988. After disallowance of the $250,000 depreciation deduction for 1990, V still had a loss of $100,000. Because there is no underpayment for 1990, no valuation misstatement penalty is imposed for 1990. However, as a result of the 1990 depreciation adjustment, the carryback to 1987 is reduced from $350,000 to $100,000. After absorption of the $100,000 carryback, V has taxable income of $200,000 for 1987. This adjustment results in an underpayment for 1987 that is attributable to the valuation misstatement on the 1990 return. The valuation misstatement for 1990 is a gross valuation misstatement because the correct adjusted basis of the depreciated asset was zero. (See paragraph (e)(2) of this section.) Therefore, the 40 percent penalty rate applies to the 1987 underpayment attributable to the 1990 misstatement, provided that this underpayment exceeds $10,000. The adjustment also results in the elimination of any loss carryback to 1988 resulting in an increase in taxable income for 1988 of $50,000. Assuming the underpayment resulting from this additional $50,000 of income exceeds $10,000, the gross valuation misstatement penalty is imposed on the underpayment for 1988.

(e) *Definitions.*—(1) *Substantial valuation misstatement.*—There is a substantial valuation misstatement if the value or adjusted basis of any property claimed on a return of tax imposed under chapter 1 is 200 percent or more of the correct amount.

(2) *Gross valuation misstatement.*—There is a gross valuation misstatement if the value or adjusted basis of any property claimed on a return of tax imposed under chapter 1 is 400 percent or more of the correct amount.

(3) *Property.*—For purposes of this section, the term "property" refers to both tangible and intangible property. Tangible property includes property such as land, buildings, fixtures and inventory. Intangible property includes property such as goodwill, covenants not to compete, leaseholds, patents, contract rights, debts and choses in action.

(f) *Multiple valuation misstatements on a return.*—(1) *Determination of whether valuation misstatements are substantial or gross.*—The determination of whether there is a substantial or gross valuation misstatement on a return is made on a property-by-property basis. Assume, for example, that property A has a value of 60 but a taxpayer claims a value of 110, and that property B has a value of 40 but the taxpayer claims a value of 100. Because the claimed and correct values are compared on a property-by-property basis, there is a substantial valuation misstatement with respect to property B, but not with respect to property A, even though the claimed values (210) are 200 percent or more of the correct values (100) when compared on an aggregate basis.

(2) *Application of dollar limitation.*—For purposes of applying the dollar limitation set forth in section 6662(e)(2), the determination of the portion of an underpayment that is attributable to a substantial or gross valuation misstatement is made by aggregating all portions of the underpayment attributable to substantial or gross valuation misstatements. Assume, for example, that the value claimed for property C on a return is 250 percent of the correct value, and that the value claimed for property D on the return is 400 percent of the correct value. Because the portions of an underpayment that are attributable to a substantial or gross valuation misstatement on a return are aggregated in applying the dollar limitation, the dollar limitation is satisfied if the portion of the underpayment that is attributable to the misstatement of the value of property C, when aggregated with the portion of the underpayment that is attributable to the misstatement of the value of property D, exceeds $5,000 ($10,000 in the case of most corporations).

(g) *Property with a value or adjusted basis of zero.*—The value or adjusted basis claimed on a return of any property with a correct value or adjusted basis of zero is considered to be 400 percent or more of the correct amount. There is a gross valuation misstatement with respect to such property, therefore, and the applicable penalty rate is 40 percent.

(h) *Pass-through entities.*—(1) *In general.*—The determination of whether there is a substantial or gross valuation misstatement in the case of a return of a pass-through entity (as defined in § 1.6662-4(f)(5)) is made at the entity level. However, the dollar limitation ($5,000 or $10,000, as the case may be) is applied at the taxpayer level (*i.e.*, with respect to the return of the shareholder, partner, beneficiary, or holder of a residual interest in a REMIC).

(2) *Example.*—The rules of paragraph (h)(1) of this section may be illustrated by the following example.

Example. Partnership P has two partners, individuals A and B. P claims a $40,000 basis in a depreciable asset which, in fact, has a basis of $15,000. The determination that there is a substantial valuation misstatement is made solely with reference to P by comparing the $40,000 basis claimed by P with P's correct basis of $15,000. However, the determination of whether the $5,000 threshold for application of the penalty has been reached is made separately for each partner. With respect to partner A, the penalty will apply if the portion of A's underpayment attributable to the passthrough of the depreciation deduction, when aggregated with any other portions of A's underpayment also attributable to substantial or gross valuation misstatements, exceeds $5,000 (assuming there is not reasonable cause for the misstatements (*see* § 1.6664-4(c)).

(i) [Reserved]

(j) *Transactions between persons described in section 482 and net section 482 transfer price adjustments.*—[Reserved]

(k) *Returns affected.*—Except in the case of rules relating to transactions between persons described in section 482 and net section 482 transfer price adjustments, the provisions of section 6662(b)(3) apply to returns due (without regard to extensions of time to file) after December 31, 1989, notwithstanding that the original substantial or gross valuation misstatement occurred on a return that was due (without regard to extensions) before January 1, 1990. Assume, for example, that a calendar year corporation claimed a deduction on its 1990 return for depreciation of an asset with a basis of X. Also assume that it had reported the same basis for computing depreciation on its returns for the preceding 5 years and that the basis shown on the return each year was 200 percent or more of the correct basis. The corporation may be subject to a penalty for substantial valuation misstatements on its 1989 and 1990 returns, even though the original misstatement occurred prior to the effective date of sections 6662(b)(3) and (e). [Reg. § 1.6662-5.]

☐ [*T.D.* 8381, 12-30-91.]

[Reg. § 1.6662-5T]

§ 1.6662-5T. Substantial and gross valuation misstatements under chapter 1 (Temporary).—(a) through (e)(3) [Reserved]. For further information, see § 1.6662-5(a) through (e)(3).

(e)(4) *Tests related to section 482.*—(i) *Substantial valuation misstatement.*—There is a substantial valuation misstatement if there is a misstatement described in § 1.6662-6(b)(1) or (c)(1) (concerning substantial valuation misstatements pertaining to transactions between related persons).

(ii) *Gross valuation misstatement.*—There is a gross valuation misstatement if there is a misstatement described in § 1.6662-6(b)(2) or (c)(2) (concerning gross valuation misstatements pertaining to transactions between related persons).

(iii) *Property.*—For purposes of this section, the term *property* refers to both tangible and intangible property. Tangible property includes property such as money, land, buildings, fixtures and inventory. Intangible property includes property such as goodwill, covenants not to compete, leaseholds, patents, contract rights, debts, choses in action, and any other item of intangible property described in § 1.482-4(b).

(f) through (h) [Reserved] For further information, see § 1.6662-5(f) through (h).

(i) [Reserved].

(j) *Transactions between persons described in section 482 and net section 482 transfer price adjustments.*—For rules relating to the penalty imposed with respect to a substantial or gross valuation misstatement arising from a section 482 allocation, see § 1.6662-6. [Temporary Reg. § 1.6662-5T.]

☐ [*T.D.* 8519, 1-27-94. *Amended by T.D.* 8656, 2-8-96.]

[Reg. § 1.6662-6]

§ 1.6662-6. Transactions between persons described in section 482 and net section 482 transfer price adjustments.—(a) *In general.*—(1) *Purpose and scope.*—Pursuant to section 6662(e) a penalty is imposed on any underpayment attributable to a substantial valuation misstatement pertaining to either a transaction between persons described in section 482 (the transactional penalty) or a net section 482 transfer price adjustment (the net adjustment penalty). The penalty is equal to 20 percent of the underpayment of tax attributable to that substantial valuation misstatement. Pursuant to section 6662(h) the penalty is increased to 40 percent of the underpayment in the case of a gross valuation misstatement with respect to either penalty. Paragraph(b) of this section provides specific rules related to the transactional penalty. Paragraph (c) of this section provides specific rules related to the net adjustment penalty, and paragraph (d) of this section describes amounts that will be excluded for purposes of calculating the net adjustment penalty. Paragraph (e) of this section sets forth special rules in the case of carrybacks and carryovers. Paragraph (f) of this section provides coordination rules between penalties. Paragraph (g) of this section provides the effective date of this section.

(2) *Reported results.*—Whether an underpayment is attributable to a substantial or gross valuation misstatement must be determined from the results of controlled transactions that are reported on an income tax return, regardless of whether the amount reported differs from the transaction price initially reflected in the taxpayer's books and records. The results of controlled transactions that are reported on an

amended return will be used only if the amended return is filed before the Internal Revenue Service has contacted the taxpayer regarding the corresponding original return. A written statement furnished by a taxpayer subject to the Coordinated Examination Program or a written statement furnished by the taxpayer when electing Accelerated Issue Resolution or similar procedures will be considered an amended return for purposes of this section if it satisfies either the requirements of a qualified amended return for purposes of § 1.6664-2(c)(3) or such requirements as the Commissioner may prescribe by revenue procedure. In the case of a taxpayer that is a member of a consolidated group, the rules of this paragraph (a)(2) apply to the consolidated income tax return of the group.

(3) *Identical terms used in the section 482 regulations.*—For purposes of this section, the terms used in this section shall have the same meaning as identical terms used in regulations under section 482.

(b) *The transactional penalty.*—(1) *Substantial valuation misstatement.*—In the case of any transaction between related persons, there is a substantial valuation misstatement if the price for any property or services (or for the use of property) claimed on any return is 200 percent or more (or 50 percent or less) of the amount determined under section 482 to be the correct price.

(2) *Gross valuation misstatement.*—In the case of any transaction between related persons, there is a gross valuation misstatement if the price for any property or services (or for the use of property) claimed on any return is 400 percent or more (or 25 percent or less) of the amount determined under section 482 to be the correct price.

(3) *Reasonable cause and good faith.*—Pursuant to section 6664(c), the transactional penalty will not be imposed on any portion of an underpayment with respect to which the requirements of § 1.6664-4 are met. In applying the provisions of § 1.6664-4 in a case in which the taxpayer has relied on professional analysis in determining its transfer pricing, whether the professional is an employee of, or related to, the taxpayer is not determinative in evaluating whether the taxpayer reasonably relied in good faith on advice. A taxpayer that meets the requirements of paragraph (d) of this section with respect to an allocation under section 482 will be treated as having established that there was reasonable cause and good faith with respect to that item for purposes of § 1.6664-4. If a substantial or gross valuation misstatement under the transactional penalty also constitutes (or is part of) a substantial or gross valuation misstatement under the net adjustment penalty, then the rules of paragraph (d) of this section (and not the rules of § 1.6664-4) will be applied to determine whether the adjustment is excluded from calculation of the net section 482 adjustment.

(c) *Net adjustment penalty.*—(1) *Net section 482 adjustment.*—For purposes of this section, the term *net section 482 adjustment* means the sum of all increases in the taxable income of a taxpayer for a taxable year resulting from allocations under section 482 (determined without regard to any amount carried to such taxable year from another taxable year) less any decreases in taxable income attributable to collateral adjustments as described in § 1.482-1(g). For purposes of this section, amounts that meet the requirements of paragraph (d) of this section will be excluded from the calculation of the net section 482 adjustment. Substantial and gross valuation misstatements that are subject to the transactional penalty under paragraph (b)(1) or (2) of this section are included in determining the amount of the net section 482 adjustment. See paragraph (f) of this section for coordination rules between penalties.

(2) *Substantial valuation misstatement.*—There is a substantial valuation misstatement if a net section 482 adjustment is greater than the lesser of 5 million dollars or ten percent of gross receipts.

(3) *Gross valuation misstatement.*—There is a gross valuation misstatement if a net section 482 adjustment is greater than the lesser of 20 million dollars or twenty percent of gross receipts.

(4) *Setoff allocation rule.*—If a taxpayer meets the requirements of paragraph (d) of this section with respect to some, but not all of the allocations made under section 482, then for purposes of determining the net section 482 adjustment, setoffs, as taken into account under § 1.482-1(g)(4), must be applied ratably against all such allocations. The following example illustrates the principle of this paragraph (c)(4):

Example. (i) The Internal Revenue Service makes the following section 482 adjustments for the taxable year:

(1)	Attributable to an increase in gross income because of an increase in royalty payments	$9,000,000
(2)	Attributable to an increase in sales proceeds due to a decrease in the profit margin of a related buyer . . .	6,000,000
(3)	Because of a setoff under § 1.482-1(g)(4)	(5,000,000)
	Total section 482 adjustments	10,000,000

(ii) The taxpayer meets the requirements of paragraph (d) with respect to adjustment number one, but not with respect to adjustment number two. The five million dollar setoff will be allocated ratably against the nine million dollar adjustment ($9,000,000/$15,000,000 x $5,000,000 = $3,000,000) and the six million dollar adjustment ($6,000,000/$15,000,000 x $5,000,000 = $2,000,000). Accordingly, in determining the net section 482 adjustment, the nine million dollar adjustment is reduced to six million dollars ($9,000,000 - $3,000,000) and the six million dollar adjustment is reduced to four million dollars ($6,000,000 - $2,000,000). Therefore, the net section 482 adjustment equals four million dollars.

(5) *Gross receipts.*—For purposes of this section, gross receipts must be computed pursuant to the rules contained in §1.448-1T(f)(2)(iv), as adjusted to reflect allocations under section 482.

(6) *Coordination with reasonable cause exception under section 6664(c).*—Pursuant to section 6662(e)(3)(D), a taxpayer will be treated as having reasonable cause under section 6664(c) for any portion of an underpayment attributable to a net section 482 adjustment only if the taxpayer meets the requirements of paragraph (d) of this section with respect to that portion.

(7) *Examples.*—The principles of this paragraph (c) are illustrated by the following examples:

Example 1. (i) The Internal Revenue Service makes the following section 482 adjustments for the taxable year:

(1) Attributable to an increase in gross income because of an increase in royalty payments .	$2,000,000
(2) Attributable to an increase in sales proceeds due to a decrease in the profit margin of a related buyer	2,500,000
(3) Attributable to a decrease in the cost of goods sold because of a decrease in the cost plus mark-up of a related seller	2,000,000
Total section 482 adjustments .	6,500,000

(ii) None of the adjustments are excluded under paragraph (d) of this section. The net section 482 adjustment ($6.5 million) is greater than five million dollars. Therefore, there is a substantial valuation misstatement.

Example 2. (i) The Internal Revenue Service makes the following section 482 adjustments for the taxable year:

(1) Attributable to an increase in gross income because of an increase in royalty payments .	$11,000,000
(2) Attributable to an increase in sales proceeds due to a decrease in the profit margin of a related buyer	2,000,000
(3) Because of a setoff under §1.482-1(g)(4)	(9,000,000)
Total section 482 adjustments .	4,000,000

(ii) The taxpayer has gross receipts of sixty million dollars after taking into account all section 482 adjustments. None of the adjustments are excluded under paragraph (d) of this section. The net section 482 adjustment ($4 million) is less than the lesser of five million dollars or ten percent of gross receipts ($60 million × 10% = $6 million). Therefore, there is no substantial valuation misstatement.

Example 3. (i) The Internal Revenue Service makes the following section 482 adjustments to the income of an affiliated group that files a consolidated return for the taxable year:

(1) Attributable to Member A . . .	$1,500,000
(2) Attributable to Member B . . .	1,000,000
(3) Attributable to Member C . . .	2,000,000
Total section 482 adjustments .	4,500,000

(ii) Members A, B, and C have gross receipts of 20 million dollars, 12 million dollars, and 11 million dollars, respectively. Thus, the total gross receipts are 43 million dollars. None of the adjustments are excluded under paragraph (d) of this section. The net section 482 adjustment ($4.5 million) is greater than the lesser of five million dollars or ten percent of gross receipts ($43 million x 10% = $4.3 million). Therefore, there is a substantial valuation misstatement.

Example 4. (i) The Internal Revenue Service makes the following section 482 adjustments to the income of an affiliated group that files a consolidated return for the taxable year:

(1)	Attributable to Member A	$1,500,000
(2)	Attributable to Member B	3,000,000
(3)	Attributable to Member C	2,500,000
	Total section 482 adjustments	7,000,000

(ii) Members A, B, and C have gross receipts of 20 million dollars, 35 million dollars, and 40 million dollars, respectively. Thus, the total gross receipts are 95 million dollars. None of the adjustments are excluded under paragraph (d) of this section. The net section 482 adjustment (7 million dollars) is greater than the lesser of five million dollars or ten percent of gross receipts ($95 million × 10% = $9.5 million). Therefore, there is a substantial valuation misstatement.

Example 5. (i) The Internal Revenue Service makes the following section 482 adjustments to the income of an affiliated group that files a consolidated return for the taxable year:

(1) Attributable to Member A . . .	$2,000,000
(2) Attributable to Member B . . .	1,000,000
(3) Attributable to Member C . . .	1,500,000
Total section 482 adjustments .	4,500,000

(ii) Members A, B, and C have gross receipts of 10 million dollars, 35 million dollars, and 40 million dollars, respectively. Thus, the total gross receipts are 85 million dollars. None of the adjustments are excluded under paragraph (d) of this section. The net section 482 adjustment ($4.5 million) is less than the lesser of five million dollars or ten percent of gross receipts ($85 million x 10% = $8.5 million). Therefore, there is no substantial valuation misstatement even though individual member A's adjustment ($2 million) is greater than ten percent of its individual gross receipts ($10 million x 10% = $1 million).

(d) *Amounts excluded from net section 482 adjustments.*—(1) *In general.*—An amount is excluded from the calculation of a net section 482 adjustment if the requirements of paragraph (d)(2), (3), or (4) of this section are met with respect to that amount.

(2) *Application of a specified section 482 method.*—(i) *In general.*—An amount is excluded from the calculation of a net section 482 adjustment if the taxpayer establishes that both the specified method and documentation requirements of this paragraph (d)(2) are met with respect to that amount. For purposes of this paragraph (d), a method will be considered a specified method if it is described in the regulations under section 482 and the method applies

Reg. §1.6662-6(d)(2)(i)

to transactions of the type under review. An unspecified method is not considered a specified method. See § § 1.482–3(e) and 1.482–4(d).

(ii) *Specified method requirement.*—(A) The specified method requirement is met if the taxpayer selects and applies a specified method in a reasonable manner. The taxpayer's selection and application of a specified method is reasonable only if, given the available data and the applicable pricing methods, the taxpayer reasonably concluded that the method (and its application of that method) provided the most reliable measure of an arm's length result under the principles of the best method rule of § 1.482–1(c). A taxpayer can reasonably conclude that a specified method provided the most reliable measure of an arm's length result only if it has made a reasonable effort to evaluate the potential applicability of the other specified methods in a manner consistent with the principles of the best method rule. The extent of this evaluation generally will depend on the nature of the available data, and it may vary from case to case and from method to method. This evaluation may not entail an exhaustive analysis or detailed application of each method. Rather, after a reasonably thorough search for relevant data, the taxpayer should consider which method would provide the most reliable measure of an arm's length result given that data. The nature of the available data may enable the taxpayer to conclude reasonably that a particular specified method provides a more reliable measure of an arm's length result than one or more of the other specified methods, and accordingly no further consideration of such other specified methods is needed. Further, it is not necessary for a taxpayer to conclude that the selected specified method provides a more reliable measure of an arm's length result than any unspecified method. For examples illustrating the selection of a specified method consistent with this paragraph (d)(2)(ii), see § 1.482–8. Whether the taxpayer's conclusion was reasonable must be determined from all the facts and circumstances. The factors relevant to this determination include the following:

(1) The experience and knowledge of the taxpayer, including all members of the taxpayer's controlled group.

(2) The extent to which reliable data was available and the data was analyzed in a reasonable manner. A taxpayer must engage in a reasonably thorough search for the data necessary to determine which method should be selected and how it should be applied. In determining the scope of a reasonably thorough search for data, the expense of additional efforts to locate new data may be weighed against the likelihood of finding additional data that would improve the reliability of the results and the amount by which any new data would change the taxpayer's taxable income. Furthermore, a taxpayer must use the most current reliable data that is available before the end of the taxable year in question. Although the taxpayer is not required to search for relevant data after the end

of the taxable year, the taxpayer must maintain as a principal document described in paragraph (d)(2)(iii)(B)(9) of this section any relevant data it obtains after the end of the taxable year but before the return is filed, if that data would help determine whether the taxpayer has reported its true taxable income.

(3) The extent to which the taxpayer followed the relevant requirements set forth in regulations under section 482 with respect to the application of the method.

(4) The extent to which the taxpayer reasonably relied on a study or other analysis performed by a professional qualified to conduct such a study or analysis, including an attorney, accountant, or economist. Whether the professional is an employee of, or related to, the taxpayer is not determinative in evaluating the reliability of that study or analysis, as long as the study or analysis is objective, thorough, and well reasoned. Such reliance is reasonable only if the taxpayer disclosed to the professional all relevant information regarding the controlled transactions at issue. A study or analysis that was reasonably relied upon in a prior year may reasonably be relied upon in the current year if the relevant facts and circumstances have not changed or if the study or analysis has been appropriately modified to reflect any change in facts and circumstances.

(5) If the taxpayer attempted to determine an arm's length result by using more than one uncontrolled comparable, whether the taxpayer arbitrarily selected a result that corresponds to an extreme point in the range of results derived from the uncontrolled comparables. Such a result generally would not likely be closest to an arm's length result. If the uncontrolled comparables that the taxpayer uses to determine an arm's length result are described in § 1.482–1(e)(2)(iii)(B), one reasonable method of selecting a point in the range would be that provided in § 1.482–1(e)(3).

(6) The extent to which the taxpayer relied on a transfer pricing methodology developed and applied pursuant to an Advance Pricing Agreement for a prior taxable year, or specifically approved by the Internal Revenue Service pursuant to a transfer pricing audit of the transactions at issue for a prior taxable year, provided that the taxpayer applied the approved method reasonably and consistently with its prior application, and the facts and circumstances surrounding the use of the method have not materially changed since the time of the IRS's action, or if the facts and circumstances have changed in a way that materially affects the reliability of the results, the taxpayer makes appropriate adjustments to reflect such changes.

(7) The size of a net transfer pricing adjustment in relation to the size of the controlled transaction out of which the adjustment arose.

(B) *Services cost method.*—A taxpayer's selection of the services cost method for certain services, described in § 1.482–9(b), and its application of that method to a controlled services transaction will be considered reasonable for purposes of the specified method requirement only if the taxpayer reasonably allocated and apportioned costs in accordance with § 1.482-9(k), and reasonably concluded that the controlled services transaction satisfies the requirements described in § 1.482-9(b)(2). Whether the taxpayer's conclusion was reasonable must be determined from all the facts and circumstances. The factors relevant to this determination include those described in paragraph (d)(2)(ii)(A) of this section, to the extent applicable.

(iii) *Documentation requirement.*—(A) *In general.*—The documentation requirement of this paragraph (d)(2)(iii) is met if the taxpayer maintains sufficient documentation to establish that the taxpayer reasonably concluded that, given the available data and the applicable pricing methods, the method (and its application of that method) provided the most reliable measure of an arm's length result under the principles of the best method rule in § 1.482-1(c), and provides that documentation to the Internal Revenue Service within 30 days of a request for it in connection with an examination of the taxable year to which the documentation relates. With the exception of the documentation described in paragraphs (d)(2)(iii)(B)(9) and (10) of this section, that documentation must be in existence when the return is filed. The district director may, in his discretion, excuse a minor or inadvertent failure to provide required documents, but only if the taxpayer has made a good faith effort to comply, and the taxpayer promptly remedies the failure when it becomes known. The required documentation is divided into two categories, principal documents and background documents as described in paragraphs (d)(2)(iii)(B) and (C) of this section.

(B) *Principal documents.*—The principal documents should accurately and completely describe the basic transfer pricing analysis conducted by the taxpayer. The documentation must include the following—

(1) An overview of the taxpayer's business, including an analysis of the economic and legal factors that affect the pricing of its property or services;

(2) A description of the taxpayer's organizational structure (including an organization chart) covering all related parties engaged in transactions potentially relevant under section 482, including foreign affiliates whose transactions directly or indirectly affect the pricing of property or services in the United States;

(3) Any documentation explicitly required by the regulations under section 482;

(4) A description of the method selected and an explanation of why that method was selected, including an evaluation of whether the regulatory conditions and requirements for application of that method, if any, were met;

(5) A description of the alternative methods that were considered and an explanation of why they were not selected;

(6) A description of the controlled transactions (including the terms of sale) and any internal data used to analyze those transactions. For example, if a profit split method is applied, the documentation must include a schedule providing the total income, costs, and assets (with adjustments for different accounting practices and currencies) for each controlled taxpayer participating in the relevant business activity and detailing the allocations of such items to that activity. Similarly, if a cost-based method (such as the cost plus method, the services cost method for certain services, or a comparable profits method with a cost-based profit level indicator) is applied, the documentation must include a description of the manner in which relevant costs are determined and are allocated and apportioned to the relevant controlled transaction.

(7) A description of the comparables that were used, how comparability was evaluated, and what (if any) adjustments were made;

(8) An explanation of the economic analysis and projections relied upon in developing the method. For example, if a profit split method is applied, the taxpayer must provide an explanation of the analysis undertaken to determine how the profits would be split;

(9) A description or summary of any relevant data that the taxpayer obtains after the end of the tax year and before filing a tax return, which would help determine if a taxpayer selected and applied a specified method in a reasonable manner; and

(10) A general index of the principal and background documents and a description of the recordkeeping system used for cataloging and accessing those documents.

(C) *Background documents.*—The assumptions, conclusions, and positions contained in principal documents ordinarily will be based on, and supported by, additional background documents. Documents that support the principal documentation may include the documents listed in § 1.6038A-3(c) that are not otherwise described in paragraph (d)(2)(iii)(B) of this section. Every document listed in those regulations may not be relevant to pricing determinations under the taxpayer's specific facts and circumstances and, therefore, each of those documents need not be maintained in all circumstances. Moreover, other documents not listed in those regulations may be necessary to establish that the taxpayer's method was selected and applied in the way that provided the most reliable measure of an arm's length result under the principles of the best method rule in § 1.482-1(c). Background documents need not be provided to the Internal Revenue Service in response to a request for principal documents. If the Internal Revenue Service subsequently requests background documents, a taxpayer must provide that documentation to the Internal Revenue Service within 30 days of the request. However, the district director may, in his discretion, extend the period for producing the background documentation.

(D) Satisfaction of the documentation requirements described in §1.482-7(k)(2) for the purpose of complying with the rules for CSAs under §1.482-7 also satisfies all of the documentation requirements listed in paragraph (d)(2)(iii)(B) of this section, except the requirements listed in paragraphs (d)(2)(iii)(B)(2) and (10) of this section, with respect to CSTs and PCTs described in §1.482-7(b)(1)(i) and (ii), provided that the documentation also satisfies the requirements of paragraph (d)(2)(iii)(A) of this section.

(3) *Application of an unspecified method.*— (i) *In general.*—An adjustment is excluded from the calculation of a net section 482 adjustment if the taxpayer establishes that both the unspecified method and documentation requirements of this paragraph (d)(3) are met with respect to that amount.

(ii) *Unspecified method requirement.*— (A) *In general.*—If a method other than a specified method was applied, the unspecified method requirement is met if the requirements of paragraph (d)(3)(ii)(B) or (C) of this section, as appropriate, are met.

(B) *Specified method potentially applicable.*—If the transaction is of a type for which methods are specified in the regulations under section 482, then a taxpayer will be considered to have met the unspecified method requirement if the taxpayer reasonably concludes, given the available data, that none of the specified methods was likely to provide a reliable measure of an arm's length result, and that it selected and applied an unspecified method in a way that would likely provide a reliable measure of an arm's length result. A taxpayer can reasonably conclude that no specified method was likely to provide a reliable measure of an arm's length result only if it has made a reasonable effort to evaluate the potential applicability of the specified methods in a manner consistent with the principles of the best method rule. However, it is not necessary for a taxpayer to conclude that the selected method provides a more reliable measure of an arm's length result than any other unspecified method. Whether the taxpayer's conclusion was reasonable must be determined from all the facts and circumstances. The factors relevant to this conclusion include those set forth in paragraph (d)(2)(ii) of this section.

(C) *No specified method applicable.*—If the transaction is of a type for which no methods are specified in the regulations under section 482, then a taxpayer will be considered to have met the unspecified method requirement if it selected and applied an unspecified method in a reasonable manner. For purposes of this paragraph (d)(3)(ii)(C), a taxpayer's selection and application is reasonable if the taxpayer reasonably concludes that the method (and its application of

that method) provided the most reliable measure of an arm's length result under the principles of the best method rule in §1.482-1(c). However, it is not necessary for a taxpayer to conclude that the selected method provides a more reliable measure of an arm's length result than any other unspecified method. Whether the taxpayer's conclusion was reasonable must be determined from all the facts and circumstances. The factors relevant to this conclusion include those set forth in paragraph (d)(2)(ii) of this section.

(iii) *Documentation requirement.*—(A) *In general.*—The documentation requirement of this paragraph (d)(3) is met if the taxpayer maintains sufficient documentation to establish that the unspecified method requirement of paragraph (d)(3)(ii) of this section is met and provides that documentation to the Internal Revenue Service within 30 days of a request for it. That documentation must be in existence when the return is filed. The district director may, in his discretion, excuse a minor or inadvertent failure to provide required documents, but only if the taxpayer has made a good faith effort to comply, and the taxpayer promptly remedies the failure when it becomes known.

(B) *Principal and background documents.*—See paragraphs (d)(2)(iii)(B) and (C) of this section for rules regarding these two categories of required documentation.

(4) *Certain foreign to foreign transactions.*— For purposes of calculating a net section 482 adjustment, any increase in taxable income resulting from an allocation under section 482 that is attributable to any controlled transaction solely between foreign corporations will be excluded unless the treatment of that transaction affects the determination of either corporation's income from sources within the United States or taxable income effectively connected with the conduct of a trade or business within the United States.

(5) *Special rule.*—If the regular tax (as defined in section 55(c)) imposed on the taxpayer is determined by reference to an amount other than taxable income, that amount shall be treated as the taxable income of the taxpayer for purposes of section 6662(e)(3). Accordingly, for taxpayers whose regular tax is determined by reference to an amount other than taxable income, the increase in that amount resulting from section 482 allocations is the taxpayer's net section 482 adjustment.

(6) *Examples.*—The principles of this paragraph (d) are illustrated by the following examples:

Example 1. (i) The Internal Revenue Service makes the following section 482 adjustments for the taxable year:

(1) Attributable to an increase in gross income because of an increase in royalty payments $9,000,000

(2) Not a 200 percent or 400 percent adjustment 2,000,000

(3) Attributable to a decrease in the cost of goods sold because of a decrease in the cost plus mark-up of a realted seller   9,000,000

Total section 482 adjustments .   20,000,000

(ii) The taxpayer has gross receipts of 75 million dollars after all section 482 adjustments. The taxpayer establishes that for adjustments number one and three, it applied a transfer pricing method specified in section 482, the selection and application of the method was reasonable, it documented the pricing analysis, and turned that documentation over to the IRS within 30 days of a request. Accordingly, eighteen million dollars is excluded from the calculation of the net section 482 adjustment. Because the net section 482 adjustment is two million dollars, there is no substantial valuation misstatement.

Example 2. (i) The Internal Revenue Service makes the following section 482 adjustments for the taxable year:

(1) Attributable to an increase in gross income because of an increase in royalty payments . $9,000,000

(2) Attributable to an adjustment that is 200 percent or more of the correct section 482 price . .   2,000,000

(3) Attributable to a decrease in the cost of goods sold because of a decrease in the cost plus mark-up of a related seller   9,000,000

Total section 482 adjustments .   20,000,000

(ii) The taxpayer has gross receipts of 75 million dollars after all section 482 adjustments. The taxpayer establishes that for adjustments number one and three it applied a transfer pricing method specified in section 482, the selection and application of the method was reasonable, it documented that analysis, and turned the documentation over to the IRS within 30 days. Accordingly, eighteen million dollars is excluded from the calculation of the section 482 transfer pricing adjustments for purposes of applying the five million dollar or 10% of gross receipts test. Because the net section 482 adjustment is only two million dollars, the taxpayer is not subject to the net adjustment penalty. However, the taxpayer may be subject to the transactional penalty on the underpayment of tax attributable to the two million dollar adjustment.

Example 3. CFC1 and CFC2 are controlled foreign corporations within the meaning of section 957. Applying section 482, the IRS disallows a deduction for 25 million dollars of the interest that CFC1 paid to CFC2, which results in CFC1's U.S. shareholder having a subpart F inclusion in excess of five million dollars. No other adjustments under section 482 are made with respect to the controlled taxpayers. However, the increase has no effect upon the determination of CFC1's or CFC2's income from sources within the United States or taxable income effectively connected with the conduct of a trade or business within the United States. Accordingly, there is no substantial valuation misstatement.

(e) *Special rules in the case of carrybacks and carryovers.*—If there is a substantial or gross valuation misstatement for a taxable year that gives rise to a loss, deduction or credit that is carried to another taxable year, the transactional penalty and the net adjustment penalty will be imposed on any resulting underpayment of tax in that other taxable year. In determining whether there is a substantial or gross valuation misstatement for a taxable year, no amount carried from another taxable year shall be included. The following example illustrates the principle of this paragraph (e):

Example. The Internal Revenue Service makes a section 482 adjustment of six million dollars in taxable year 1, no portion of which is excluded under paragraph (d) of this section. The taxpayer's income tax return for year 1 reported a loss of three million dollars, which was carried to taxpayer's year 2 income tax return and used to reduce income taxes otherwise due with respect to year 2. A determination is made that the six million dollar allocation constitutes a substantial valuation misstatement, and a penalty is imposed on the underpayment of tax in year 1 attributable to the substantial valuation misstatement and on the underpayment of tax in year 2 attributable to the disallowance of the net operating loss in year 2. For purposes of determining whether there is a substantial or gross valuation misstatement for year 2, the three million dollar reduction of the net operating loss will not be added to any section 482 adjustments made with respect to year 2.

(f) *Rules for coordinating between the transactional penalty and the net adjustment penalty.*— (1) *Coordination of a net section 482 adjustment subject to the net adjustment penalty and a gross valuation misstatement subject to the transactional penalty.*—In determining whether a net section 482 adjustment exceeds five million dollars or 10 percent of gross receipts, an adjustment attributable to a substantial or gross valuation misstatement that is subject to the transactional penalty will be taken into account. If the net section 482 adjustment exceeds five million dollars or ten percent of gross receipts, any portion of such amount that is attributable to a gross valuation misstatement will be subject to the transactional penalty at the forty percent rate, but will not also be subject to net adjustment penalty at a twenty percent rate. The remaining amount is subject to the net adjustment penalty at the twenty percent rate, even if such amount is less than the lesser of five million dollars or ten percent of gross receipts.

(2) *Coordination of net section 482 adjustment subject to the net adjustment penalty and substantial valuation misstatements subject to the transactional penalty.*—If the net section 482 adjustment exceeds twenty million dollars or 20 percent of gross receipts, the entire amount of the adjustment is subject to the net adjustment penalty at a forty percent rate. No portion of the adjustment is subject to the transactional penalty at a twenty percent rate.

Reg. § 1.6662-6(f)(2)

(3) *Examples.*—The following examples illustrate the principles of this paragraph (f):

Example 1. (i) Applying section 482, the Internal Revenue Service makes the following adjustments for the taxable year:

(1) Attributable to an adjustment that is 400 percent or more of the correct section 482 arm's length result	$2,000,000
(2) Not a 200 or 400 percent adjustment	2,500,000
Total	4,500,000

(ii) The taxpayer has gross receipts of 75 million dollars after all section 482 adjustments. None of the adjustments is excluded under paragraph (d) (Amounts excluded from net section 482 adjustments) of this section, in determining the five million dollar or 10% of gross receipts test under section 6662(e)(1)(B)(ii). The net section 482 adjustment (4.5 million dollars) is less than the lesser of five million dollars or ten percent of gross receipts ($75 million × 10% = $7.5 million). Thus, there is no substantial valuation misstatement. However, the two million dollar adjustment is attributable to a gross valuation misstatement. Accordingly, the taxpayer may be subject to a penalty, under section 6662(h), equal to 40 percent of the underpayment of tax attributable to the gross valuation misstatement of two million dollars. The 2.5 million dollar adjustment is not subject to a penalty under section 6662(b)(3).

Example 2. The facts are the same as in *Example 1*, except the taxpayer has gross receipts of 40 million dollars. The net section 482 adjustment ($4.5 million) is greater than the lesser of five million dollars or ten percent of gross receipts ($40 million × 10% = $4 million). Thus, the five million dollar or 10% of gross receipts test has been met. The two million dollar adjustment is attributable to a gross valuation misstatement. Accordingly, the taxpayer is subject to a penalty, under section 6662(h), equal to 40 percent of the underpayment of tax attributable to the gross valuation misstatement of two million dollars. The 2.5 million dollar adjustment is subject to a penalty under sections 6662(a) and 6662(b)(3), equal to 20 percent of the underpayment of tax attributable to the substantial valuation misstatement.

Example 3. (i) Applying section 482, the Internal Revenue Service makes the following transfer pricing adjustments for the taxable year:

(1) Attributable to an adjustment that is 400 percent or more of the correct section 482 arm's length result	$6,000,000
(2) Not a 200 or 400 percent adjustment	15,000,000
Total	21,000,000

(ii) None of the adjustments are excluded under paragraph (d) (Amounts excluded from net section 482 adjustments) in determining the twenty million dollar or 20% of gross receipts test under section 6662(h). The net section 482 adjustment (21 million dollars) is greater than twenty million dollars and thus constitutes a gross valuation misstatement. Accordingly, the total adjustment is subject to the net adjustment penalty equal to 40 percent of the underpayment of tax attributable to the 21 million dollar gross valuation misstatement. The six million dollar adjustment will not be separately included for purposes of any additional penalty under section 6662.

(g) *Effective/applicability date.*—(1) *In general.*—This section is generally applicable on February 9, 1996. However, taxpayers may elect to apply this section to all open taxable years beginning after December 31, 1993.

(2) *Special rules.*—The provisions of paragraphs (d)(2)(ii)(B), (d)(2)(iii)(B)(4) and (d)(2)(iii)(B)(6) of this section are applicable for taxable years beginning after July 31, 2009. However, taxpayers may elect to apply the provisions of paragraphs (d)(2)(ii)(B), (d)(2)(iii)(B)(4) and (d)(2)(iii)(B)(6) of this section to earlier taxable years in accordance with the rules set forth in § 1.482-9(n)(2). [Reg. § 1.6662-6.]

☐ [*T.D.* 8656, 2-8-96. *Amended by T.D.* 9278, 7-31-2006; *T.D.* 9441, 12-31-2008; *T.D.* 9456, 7-31-2009 *and T.D.* 9568, 12-16-2011.]

[Reg. § 1.6662-7]

§ 1.6662-7. Omnibus Budget Reconciliation Act of 1993 changes to the accuracy-related penalty.—(a) *Scope.*—The Omnibus Budget Reconciliation Act of 1993 made certain changes to the accuracy-related penalty in section 6662. This section provides rules reflecting those changes.

(b) *No disclosure exception for negligence penalty.*—The penalty for negligence in section 6662(b)(1) may not be avoided by disclosure of a return position.

(c) *Disclosure standard for other penalties is reasonable basis.*—The penalties for disregarding rules or regulations in section 6662(b)(1) and for a substantial understatement of income tax in section 6662(b)(2) may be avoided by adequate disclosure of a return position only if the position has at least a reasonable basis. See § 1.6662-3(c) and § § 1.6662-4(e) and (f) for other applicable disclosure rules.

(d) *Reasonable basis.*—For purposes of § § 1.6662-3(c) and 1.6662-4(e) and (f) (relating to methods of making adequate disclosure), the provisions of § 1.6662-3(b)(3) apply in determining whether a return position has a reasonable basis. [Reg. § 1.6662-7.]

☐ [*T.D.* 8617, 8-31-95. *Amended by T.D.* 8790, 12-1-98.]

[Reg. § 1.6664-0]

§ 1.6664-0. Table of contents.—This section lists the captions in § § 1.6664-1 through 1.6664-4T.

§ 1.6664-1. Accuracy-related and fraud penalties; definitions, effective date and special rules.

(a) In general.

(b) Effective date.

(1) In general.

(2) Reasonable cause and good faith exception to section 6662 penalties.

(i) For returns due after September 1, 1995.

(ii) For returns filed after December 31, 2002.

(3) Qualified amended returns.

§1.6664-2. Underpayment.

(a) Underpayment defined.

(b) Amount of income tax imposed.

(c) Amount shown as the tax by the taxpayer on his return.

(1) Defined.

(2) Effect of qualified amended return.

(3) Qualified amended return defined.

(i) General rule.

(ii) Undisclosed listed transactions.

(4) Special rules.

(5) Examples.

(d) Amounts not so shown previously assessed (or collected without assessment).

(e) Rebates.

(f) Underpayments for certain carryback years not reduced by amount of carrybacks.

(g) Examples.

§1.6664-3. Ordering rules for determining the total amount of penalties imposed.

(a) In general.

(b) Order in which adjustments are taken into account.

(c) Manner in which unclaimed prepayment credits are allocated.

(d) Examples.

§1.6664-4. Reasonable cause and good faith exception to section 6662 penalties.

(a) In general.

(b) Facts and circumstances taken into account.

(1) In general.

(2) Examples.

(c) Reliance on opinion or advice.

(1) Fact and circumstances; minimum requirements.

(i) All facts and circumstances considered.

(ii) No unreasonable assumptions.

(iii) Reliance on the invalidity of a regulation.

(2) Advice defined.

(3) Cross-reference.

(d) Underpayments attributable to reportable transactions.

(e) Pass-through items.

(f) Special rules for substantial understatement penalty attributable to the tax shelter items of corporations.

(1) In general; facts and circumstances.

(2) Reasonable cause based on legal justification.

(i) Minimum requirements.

(A) Authority requirement.

(B) Belief requirement.

(ii) Legal justification defined.

(3) Minimum requirements not dispositive.

(4) Other factors.

(g) Transactions between persons described in section 482 and net section 482 transfer price adjustments. [Reserved]

(h) Valuation misstatements of charitable deduction property.

(1) In general.

(2) Definitions.

(3) Special rules.

(i) Charitable deduction property.

(ii) Qualified appraisal.

(iii) Qualified appraiser.

§1.6664-4T. Reasonable cause and good faith exception to section 6662 penalties.

(a) through (c) [Reserved]

(d) Transactions between persons described in section 482 and net section 482 transfer price adjustments.

[Reg. §1.6664-0.]

☐ [T.D. 8381, 12-30-91. Amended by T.D. 8519, 1-27-94; T.D. 8617, 8-31-95; T.D. 8656, 2-8-96; T.D. 8790, 12-1-98; T.D. 9109, 12-29-2003 and T.D. 9309, 1-8-2007.]

[Reg. §1.6664-1]

§1.6664-1. Accuracy-related and fraud penalties; definitions, effective date and special rules.—(a) In general.—Section 6664(a) defines the term "underpayment" for purposes of the accuracy-related penalty under section 6662 and the fraud penalty under section 6663. The definition of "underpayment" of income taxes imposed under subtitle A is set forth in §1.6664-2. Ordering rules for computing the total amount of accuracy-related and fraud penalties imposed with respect to a return are set forth in §1.6664-3. Section 6664(c) provides a reasonable cause and good faith exception to the accuracy-related penalty. Rules relating to the reasonable cause and good faith exception are set forth in §1.6664-4.

(b) Effective date.—(1) In general.—Sections 1.6664-1 through 1.6664-3 apply to returns the due date of which (determined without regard to extensions of time for filing) is after December 31, 1989.

(2) Reasonable cause and good faith exception to section 6662 penalties.—(i) For returns due after September 1, 1995.—Section 1.6664-4 applies to returns the due date of which (determined without regard to extensions of time for filing) is after September 1, 1995. Except as provided in the last sentence of this paragraph (b)(2), §1.6664-4 (as contained in 26 CFR part 1 revised April 1, 1995) applies to returns the due date of which (determined without regard to extensions of time for filing) is on or before September 1, 1995, and after December 31, 1989. For transactions occurring after December 8, 1994, §1.6664-4 (as contained in 26 CFR part 1 revised April 1, 1995) is

applied taking into account the changes made to section 6662(d)(2)(C) (relating to the substantial understatement penalty for tax shelter items of corporations) by section 744 of Title VII of the Uruguay Round Agreements Act, Pub. L. 103-465 (108 Stat. 4809).

(ii) *For returns filed after December 31, 2002.*—Sections 1.6664-4(c) (relating to relying on opinion or advice) and (d) (relating to underpayments attributable to reportable transactions) apply to returns filed after December 31, 2002, with respect to transactions entered into on or after January 1, 2003. Except as provided in paragraph (b)(2)(i) of this section, § 1.6664-4 (as contained in 26 CFR part 1 revised April 1, 2003) applies to returns filed with respect to transactions entered into before January 1, 2003.

(3) *Qualified amended returns.*—Sections 1.6664-2(c)(1), (c) (2), (c) (3) (i) (A), (c) (3) (i) (B), (c) (3) (i) (C), (c) (3) (i) (D) (2), (c)(3)(i)(E), and (c)(4) are applicable for amended returns and requests for administrative adjustment filed on or after March 2, 2005. Sections 1.6664-2(c)(3)(i)(D)(1) and (c)(3)(ii)(B) and (C) are applicable for amended returns and requests for administrative adjustment filed on or after April 30, 2004. The applicability date for § 1.6664-2(c)(3)(ii)(A) varies depending upon which event occurs under § 1.6664-2(c)(3)(i). For purposes of § 1.6664-2(c)(3)(ii)(A), the date described in § 1.6664-2(c)(3)(i)(D)(1) is applicable for amended returns and requests for administrative adjustment filed on or after April 30, 2004. For purposes of § 1.6664-2(c)(3)(ii)(A), the dates described in § 1.6664-2(c)(3)(i)(A), (B), (C), (D)(2), and (E) are applicable for amended returns and requests for administrative adjustment filed on or after March 2, 2005. Section 1.6664-2(c)(1) through (c)(3), as contained in 26 CFR part 1 revised as of April 1, 2004 and as modified by Notice 2004-38, 2004-1 C.B. 949, applies with respect to returns and requests for administrative adjustment filed on or after April 30, 2004 and before March 2, 2005. Section 1.6664-2(c)(1) through (3), as contained in 26 CFR part 1 revised as of April 30, 2004, applies with respect to returns and requests for administrative adjustment filed before April 30, 2004. [Reg. § 1.6664-1.]

☐ [*T.D. 8381, 12-30-91. Amended by T.D. 8617, 8-31-95; T.D. 9109, 12-29-2003 and T.D. 9309, 1-8-2007.*]

[Reg. § 1.6664-2]

§ 1.6664-2, Underpayment.—
(a) *Underpayment defined.*—In the case of income taxes imposed under subtitle A, an underpayment for purposes of section 6662, relating to the accuracy-related penalty, and section 6663, relating to the fraud penalty, means the amount by which any income tax imposed under this subtitle (as defined in paragraph (b) of the section) exceeds the excess of—

(1) The sum of—

(i) The amount shown as the tax by the taxpayer on his return (as defined in paragraph (c) of this section), plus

(ii) Amounts not so shown previously assessed (or collected without assessment) (as defined in paragraph (d) of this section), over

(2) The amount of rebates made (as defined in paragraph (e) of this section).
The definition of underpayment also may be expressed as—

$$Underpayment = W - (X + Y - Z),$$

where W = the amount of income tax imposed; X = the amount shown as the tax by the taxpayer on his return; Y = amounts not so shown previously assessed (or collected without assessment); and Z = the amount of rebates made.

(b) *Amount of income tax imposed.*—For purposes of paragraph (a) of this section, the "amount of income tax imposed" is the amount of tax imposed on the taxpayer under subtitle A for the taxable year, determined without regard to—

(1) The credits for tax withheld under sections 31 (relating to tax withheld on wages) and 33 (relating to tax withheld at source on nonresident aliens and foreign corporations);

(2) Payments of tax or estimated tax by the taxpayer;

(3) Any credit resulting from the collection of amounts assessed under section 6851 as the result of a termination assessment, or section 6861 as the result of a jeopardy assessment; and

(4) Any tax that the taxpayer is not required to assess on the return (such as the tax imposed by section 531 on the accumulated taxable income of a corporation).

(c) *Amount shown as the tax by the taxpayer on his return.*—(1) *Defined.*—For purposes of paragraph (a) of this section, the amount shown as the tax by the taxpayer on his return is the tax liability shown by the taxpayer on his return, determined without regard to the items listed in paragraphs (b)(1), (2), and (3) of this section, except that it is reduced by the excess of—

(i) The amounts shown by the taxpayer on his return as credits for tax withheld under section 31 (relating to tax withheld on wages) and section 33 (relating to tax withheld at source on nonresident aliens and foreign corporations), as payments of estimated tax, or as any other payments made by the taxpayer with respect to a taxable year before filing the return for such taxable year, over

(ii) The amounts actually withheld, actually paid as estimated tax, or actually paid with respect to a taxable year before the return is filed for such taxable year.

(2) *Effect of qualified amended return.*—The amount shown as the tax by the taxpayer on his return includes an amount shown as additional tax on a qualified amended return (as defined in paragraph (c)(3) of this section), except that such amount is not included if it relates to a fraudulent position on the original return.

(3) *Qualified amended return defined.*— (i) *General rule.*—A qualified amended return is an amended return, or a timely request for an administrative adjustment under section 6227, filed after the due date of the return for the taxable year (determined with regard to extensions of time to file) and before the earliest of—

(A) The date the taxpayer is first contacted by the Internal Revenue Service (IRS) concerning any examination (including a criminal investigation) with respect to the return;

(B) The date any person is first contacted by the IRS concerning an examination of that person under section 6700 (relating to the penalty for promoting abusive tax shelters) for an activity with respect to which the taxpayer claimed any tax benefit on the return directly or indirectly through the entity, plan or arrangement described in section 6700(a)(1)(A);

(C) In the case of a pass-through item (as defined in § 1.6662-4(f)(5)), the date the pass-through entity (as defined in § 1.6662-4(f)(5)) is first contacted by the IRS in connection with an examination of the return to which the pass-through item relates;

(D)*(1)* The date on which the IRS serves a summons described in section 7609(f) relating to the tax liability of a person, group, or class that includes the taxpayer (or pass-through entity of which the taxpayer is a partner, shareholder, beneficiary, or holder of a residual interest in a REMIC) with respect to an activity for which the taxpayer claimed any tax benefit on the return directly or indirectly.

(2) The rule in paragraph (c)(3)(i)(D)(1) of this section applies to any return on which the taxpayer claimed a direct or indirect tax benefit from the type of activity that is the subject of the summons, regardless of whether the summons seeks the production of information for the taxable period covered by such return; and

(E) The date on which the Commissioner announces by revenue ruling, revenue procedure, notice, or announcement, to be published in the Internal Revenue Bulletin (see § 601.601(d)(2) of this chapter), a settlement initiative to compromise or waive penalties, in whole or in part, with respect to a listed transaction. This rule applies only to a taxpayer who participated in the listed transaction and for the taxable year(s) in which the taxpayer claimed any direct or indirect tax benefits from the listed transaction. The Commissioner may waive the requirements of this paragraph or identify a later date by which a taxpayer who participated in the listed transaction must file a qualified amended return in the published guidance announcing the listed transaction settlement initiative.

(ii) *Undisclosed listed transactions.*—An undisclosed listed transaction is a transaction that is the same as, or substantially similar to, a listed transaction within the meaning of § 1.6011-4(b)(2) (regardless of whether § 1.6011-4 requires the taxpayer to disclose the transaction) and was neither previously disclosed by the taxpayer within the meaning of § 1.6011-4 or § 1.6011-4T, nor disclosed under Announcement 2002-2 (2002-1 C.B. 304), (see § 601.601(d)(2)(ii) of this chapter) by the deadline therein. In the case of an undisclosed listed transaction for which a taxpayer claims any direct or indirect tax benefits on its return (regardless of whether the transaction was a listed transaction at the time the return was filed), an amended return or request for administrative adjustment under section 6227 will not be a qualified amended return if filed on or after the earliest of—

(A) The dates described in paragraph (c)(3)(i) of this section;

(B) The date on which the IRS first contacts any person regarding an examination of that person's liability under section 6707(a) with respect to the undisclosed listed transaction of the taxpayer; or

(C) The date on which the IRS requests, from any person who made a tax statement to or for the benefit of the taxpayer or from any person who gave the taxpayer material aid, assistance, or advice as described in section 6111(b)(1)(A)(i) with respect to the taxpayer, the information required to be included on a list under section 6112 relating to a transaction that was the same as, or substantially similar to, the undisclosed listed transaction, regardless of whether the taxpayer's information is required to be included on that list.

(4) *Special rules.*—(i) A qualified amended return includes an amended return that is filed to disclose information pursuant to § 1.6662-3(c) or § 1.6662-4(e) and (f) even though it does not report any additional tax liability. See § 1.6662-3(c), § 1.6662-4(f), and § 1.6664-4(c) for rules relating to adequate disclosure.

(ii) The Commissioner may by revenue procedure prescribe the manner in which the rules of paragraph (c) of this section regarding qualified amended returns apply to particular classes of taxpayers.

(5) *Examples.* The following examples illustrate the provisions of paragraphs (c)(3) and (c)(4) of this section:

Example 1. T, an individual taxpayer, claimed tax benefits on its 2002 Federal income tax return from a transaction that is substantially similar to the transaction identified as a listed transaction in Notice 2002-65, 2002-2 C.B. 690 (Partnership Entity Straddle Tax Shelter). T did not disclose his participation in this transaction on a Form 8886, "Reportable Transaction Disclosure Statement," as required by § 1.6011-4. On June 30, 2004, the IRS requested from P, T's material advisor, an investor list required to be maintained under section 6112. The section 6112 request, however, related to the type of transaction described in Notice 2003-81, 2003-2 C.B. 1223 (Tax Avoidance Using Offsetting Foreign Currency Option Contracts). T did not participate in (within the meaning of § 1.6011-4(c)) a transaction described in Notice 2003-81. T may file a qualified amended return relating to the transaction described in Notice 2002-65 because

T did not claim a tax benefit with respect to the listed transaction described in Notice 2003-81, which is the subject of the section 6112 request.

Example 2. The facts are the same as in *Example 1*, except that T's 2002 Federal income tax return reflected T's participation in the transaction described in Notice 2003-81. As of June 30, 2004, T may not file a qualified amended return for the 2002 tax year.

Example 3. (i) Corporation X claimed tax benefits from a transaction on its 2002 Federal income tax return. In October 2004, the IRS and Treasury Department identified the transaction as a listed transaction. In December 2004, the IRS contacted P concerning an examination of P's liability under section 6707(a) (as in effect prior to the amendment to section 6707 by section 816 of the American Jobs Creation Act of 2004 (the Jobs Act), Public Law 108-357 (118 Stat. 1418)). P is the organizer of a section 6111 tax shelter (as in effect prior to the amendment to section 6111 by section 815 of the Jobs Act) who provided representations to X regarding tax benefits from the transaction, and the IRS has contacted P about the failure to register that transaction. Three days later, X filed an amended return.

(ii) X's amended return is not a qualified amended return, because X did not disclose the transaction before the IRS contacted P. X's amended return would have been a qualified amended return if it was submitted prior to the date on which the IRS contacted P.

Example 4. The facts are the same as in *Example 3* except that, instead of contacting P concerning an examination under section 6707(a), in December 2004, the IRS served P with a John Doe summons described in section 7609(f) relating to the tax liability of participants in the type of transaction for which X claimed tax benefits on its return. X cannot file a qualified amended return after the John Doe summons has been served regardless of when, or whether, the transaction becomes a listed transaction.

Example 5. On November 30, 2003, the IRS served a John Doe summons described in section 7609(f) on Corporation Y, a credit card company. The summons requested the identity of, and information concerning, United States taxpayers who, during the taxable years 2001 and 2002, had signature authority over Corporation Y's credit cards issued by, through, or on behalf of certain offshore financial institutions. Corporation Y complied with the summons, and identified, among others, Taxpayer B. On May 31, 2004, before the IRS first contacted Taxpayer B concerning an examination of Taxpayer B's Federal income tax return for the taxable year 2002, Taxpayer B filed an amended return for that taxable year, that showed an increase in Taxpayer B's Federal income tax liability. Under paragraph (c)(3)(i)(D) of this section, the amended return is not a qualified amended return because it was not filed before the John Doe summons was served on Corporation Y.

Example 6. The facts are the same as in *Example 5*. Taxpayer B continued to maintain the offshore credit card account through 2003 and filed an original tax return for the 2003 taxable year claiming tax benefits attributable to the existence of the account. On March 21, 2005, Taxpayer B

filed an amended return for the taxable year 2003, that showed an increase in Taxpayer B's Federal income tax liability. Under paragraph (c)(3)(i)(D) of this section, the amended return is not a qualified amended return because it was not filed before the John Doe summons for 2001 and 2002 was served on Corporation Y, and the return reflects benefits from the type of activity that is the subject of the John Doe summons.

Example 7. (i) On November 30, 2003, the IRS served a John Doe summons described in section 7609(f) on Corporation Y, a credit card company. The summons requested the identity of, and information concerning, United States taxpayers who, during the taxable years 2001 and 2002, had signature authority over Corporation Y's credit cards issued by, through, or on behalf of certain offshore financial institutions. Taxpayer C did not have signature authority over any of Corporation Y's credit cards during either 2001 or 2002 and, therefore, was not a person described in the John Doe summons.

(ii) In 2003, Taxpayer C first acquired signature authority over a Corporation Y credit card issued by an offshore financial institution. Because Taxpayer C did not have signature authority during 2001 or 2002 over a Corporation Y credit card issued by an offshore financial institution, and was therefore not covered by the John Doe summons served on November 30, 2003, Taxpayer C's ability to file a qualified amended return for the 2003 taxable year is not limited by paragraph (c)(3)(i)(D) of this section.

(d) *Amounts not so shown previously assessed (or collected without assessment).*—For purposes of paragraph (a) of this section, "amounts not so shown previously assessed" means only amounts assessed before the return is filed that were not shown on the return, such as termination assessments under section 6851 and jeopardy assessments under section 6861 made prior to the filing of the return for the taxable year. For purposes of paragraph (a) of this section, the amount "collected without assessment" is the amount by which the total of the credits allowable under section 31 (relating to tax withheld on wages) and section 33 (relating to tax withheld at source on nonresident aliens and foreign corporations), estimated tax payments, and other payments in satisfaction of tax liability made before the return is filed, exceed the tax shown on the return (provided such excess has not been refunded or allowed as a credit to the taxpayer).

(e) *Rebates.*—The term "rebate" means so much of an abatement credit, refund or other repayment, as was made on the ground that the tax imposed was less than the excess of—

(1) The sum of—

(i) The amount shown as the tax by the taxpayer on his return, plus

(ii) Amounts not so shown previously assessed (or collected without assessment), over

(2) Rebates previously made.

(f) *Underpayments for certain carryback years not reduced by amount of carrybacks.*—The amount of an underpayment for a taxable year that is attributable to conduct proscribed by sections 6662 or 6663 is not reduced on account of a carryback of a loss, deduction or credit to that year. Such

Additions to Tax and Additional Amounts
67,247
See p. 20,601 for regulations not amended to reflect law changes

conduct includes negligence or disregard of rules or regulations; a substantial understatement of income tax; and a substantial (or gross) valuation misstatement under chapter 1, provided that the applicable dollar limitation is satisfied for the carryback year.

(g) *Examples.*—The following examples illustrate this section:

Example 1. Taxpayer's 1990 return showed a tax liability of $18,000. Taxpayer had no amounts previously assessed (or collected without assessment) and received no rebates of tax. Taxpayer claimed a credit in the amount of $23,000 for income tax withheld under section 3402, which resulted in a refund received of $5,000. It is later determined that the taxpayer should have reported additional income and that the correct tax for the taxable year is $25,500. There is an underpayment of $7,500, determined as follows:

Tax imposed under subtitle A		$25,500
Tax shown on return	$18,000	
Tax previously assessed (or collected without assessment)	None	
Amount of rebates made . . .	None	
Balance		$18,000
Underpayment		$7,500

Example 2. The facts are the same as in *Example 1* except that the taxpayer failed to claim on the return a credit of $1,500 for income tax withheld. This $1,500 constitutes an amount collected without assessment as defined in paragraph (d) of this section. The underpayment is $6,000, determined as follows:

Tax imposed under subtitle A		$25,500
Tax shown on return	$18,000	
Tax previously assessed (or collected without assessment)	1,500	
Amount of rebates made . . .	None	
Balance		$19,500
Underpayment		$6,000

Example 3. On Form 1040 filed for tax year 1990, taxpayer reported a tax liability of $10,000, estimated tax payments of $15,000, and received a refund of $5,000. Estimated tax payments actually made with respect to tax year 1990 were only $7,000. For purposes of determining the amount of underpayment subject to a penalty under section 6662 or section 6663, the tax shown on the return is $2,000 (reported tax liability of $10,000 reduced by the overstated estimated tax of $8,000 ($15,000 − $7,000)). The underpayment is $8,000, determined as follows:

Tax imposed under subtitle A		$10,000
Tax shown on return	$2,000	
Tax previously assessed (or collected without assessment)	None	
Amount of rebates made	None	
Balance		$2,000
Underpayment		$8,000

[Reg. § 1.6664-2.]

☐ [*T.D.* 8381, 12-30-91. *Amended by T.D.* 9186, 3-1-2005 *and T.D.* 9309, 1-8-2007.]

[Reg. § 1.6664-3]

§ 1.6664-3. Ordering rules for determining the total amount of penalties imposed.—(a) *In general.*—This section provides rules for determining the order in which adjustments to a return are taken into account for the purpose of computing the total amount of penalties imposed under sections 6662 and 6663, where—

(1) There is at least one adjustment with respect to which no penalty has been imposed and at least one with respect to which a penalty has been imposed, or

(2) There are at least two adjustments with respect to which penalties have been imposed and they have been imposed at different rates.

This section also provides rules for allocating unclaimed prepayment credits to adjustments to a return.

(b) *Order in which adjustments are taken into account.*—In computing the portions of an underpayment subject to penalties imposed under sections 6662 and 6663, adjustments to a return are considered made in the following order:

(1) Those with respect to which no penalties have been imposed.

(2) Those with respect to which a penalty has been imposed at a 20 percent rate (*i.e.*, a penalty for negligence or disregard of rules or regulations, substantial understatement of income tax, or substantial valuation misstatement, under sections 6662(b)(1) through 6662(b)(3), respectively).

(3) Those with respect to which a penalty has been imposed at a 40 percent rate (*i.e.*, a penalty for a gross valuation misstatement under sections 6662(b)(3) and (h)).

(4) Those with respect to which a penalty has been imposed at a 75 percent rate (*i.e.*, a penalty for fraud under section 6663).

(c) *Manner in which unclaimed prepayment credits are allocated.*—Any income tax withholding or other payment made before a return was filed, that was neither claimed on the return nor previously allowed as a credit against the tax liability for the taxable year (an "unclaimed prepayment credit"), is allocated as follows—

(1) If an unclaimed prepayment credit is allocable to a particular adjustment, such credit is applied in full in determining the amount of the underpayment resulting from such adjustment.

(2) If an unclaimed prepayment credit is not allocable to a particular adjustment, such credit is applied in accordance with the ordering rules set forth in paragraph (b) of this section.

(d) *Examples.*—The following examples illustrate the rules of this § 1.6664-3. These examples do not take into account the reasonable cause exception to the accuracy-related penalty under §1.6664-4.

Example 1. A and B, husband and wife, filed a joint federal income tax return for calendar year 1989, reporting taxable income of $15,800 and a tax liability of $2,374. A and B had no amounts previously assessed (or collected without assessment) and no rebates had been made. Subsequently, the return was examined and the following adjustments and penalties were agreed to:

Adjustment #1 (No penalty imposed)	$1,000
Adjustment #2 (Substantial understatement penalty imposed) ..	40,000
Adjustment # 3 (Civil fraud penalty imposed)	45,000
Total adjustments	$86,000
Taxable income shown on return . . .	15,800
Taxable income as corrected	$101,800

Computation of underpayment:

Tax imposed by subtitle A		$25,828
Tax shown on return	$2,374	
Previous assessments	None	
Rebates	None	
Balance		$2,374
Underpayment		$23,454

Computation of the portions of the underpayment on which penalties under section 6662(b)(2) and section 6663 are imposed:

Step 1 Determine the portion, if any, of the underpayment on which no accuracy-related or fraud penalty is imposed:

Taxable income shown on return	$15,800
Adjustment #1	1,000
"Adjusted" taxable income	$16,800
Tax on "adjusted" taxable income	$2,524
Tax shown on return	2,374
Portion of underpayment on which no penalty is imposed	$150

Step 2 Determine the portion, if any, of the underpayment on which a penalty of 20 percent is imposed:

"Adjusted" taxable income from step 1 . .	$16,800
Adjustment #2	40,000
"Adjusted" taxable income	$56,800
Tax on "adjusted" taxable income	$11,880
Tax on "adjusted" taxable income from step 1	2,524
Portion of underpayment on which 20 percent penalty is imposed	$9,356

Step 3 Determine the portion, if any, of the underpayment on which a penalty of 75 percent is imposed:

Total underpayment		$23,454
Less the sum of the portions of such underpayment determined in:		
Step 1	$150	
Step 2	$9,356	
Total		$9,506

Portion of underpayment on which 75 percent penalty is imposed $13,948

Example 2. The facts are the same as in *Example 1* except that the taxpayers failed to claim on their return a credit of $1,500 for income tax withheld on unreported additional income that resulted in Adjustment #2. Because the unclaimed prepayment credit is allocable to Adjustment #2, the portion of the underpayment attributable to that adjustment is $7,856 ($9,356 – $1,500). The portions of the underpayment attributable to Adjustments #1 and #3 remain the same.

Example 3. The facts are the same as in *Example 1* except that the taxpayers made a timely estimated tax payment of $1,500 for 1989 which they failed to claim (and which the Service had not previously allowed). This unclaimed prepayment credit is not allocable to any particular adjustment. Therefore, the credit is allocated first to the portion of the underpayment on which no penalty is imposed ($150). The remaining amount ($1,350) is allocated next to the 20 percent penalty portion of the underpayment ($9,356). Thus, the portion of the underpayment that is not penalized is zero ($150 – $150), the portion subject to a 20 percent penalty is $8,006 ($9,356 – $1,350) and the portion subject to a 75 percent penalty is unchanged at $13,948. [Reg. § 1.6664-3.]

☐ [*T.D.* 8381, 12-30-91.]

[Reg. § 1.6664-4]

§ 1.6664-4. Reasonable cause and good faith exception to section 6662 penalties.—(a) *In general.*—No penalty may be imposed under section 6662 with respect to any portion of an underpayment upon a showing by the taxpayer that there was reasonable cause for, and the taxpayer acted in good faith with respect to, such portion. Rules for determining whether the reasonable cause and good faith exception applies are set forth in paragraphs (b) through (h) of this section.

(b) *Facts and circumstances taken into account.*—(1) *In general.*—The determination of whether a taxpayer acted with reasonable cause and in good faith is made on a case-by-case basis, taking into account all pertinent facts and circumstances. (See paragraph (e) of this section for certain rules relating to a substantial understatement penalty attributable to tax shelter items of corporations.) Generally, the most important factor is the extent of the taxpayer's effort to assess the taxpayer's proper tax liability. Circumstances that may indicate reasonable cause and good faith include an honest misunderstanding of fact or law that is reasonable in light of all of the facts and circumstances, including the experience, knowledge, and education of the taxpayer. An isolated computational or transcriptional error generally is not inconsistent with reasonable cause and good faith. Reliance on an information return or on the advice of a professional tax advisor or an appraiser does not necessarily demonstrate reasonable cause and good faith. Similarly, reasonable cause and good faith is not necessarily indicated by reliance on facts that, unknown to the taxpayer, are incorrect. Reliance on an information return, professional advice, or other facts, however, constitutes reasonable cause and good faith if, under all the circumstances, such reliance was reasonable and the taxpayer acted in good faith. (See paragraph (c) of this section for certain rules relating to reliance on the advice of others.) For example, reliance on erroneous information (such as an error relating to the cost or adjusted basis of property, the date property was placed in service, or the amount of opening or closing inventory) inadvertently included in data compiled by the various divisions of a multidivisional corporation or in financial books and records prepared by those divisions generally indicates reasonable cause and good faith, provided the corporation employed internal controls and procedures, reasonable under the circumstances, that were designed to identify such factual errors. Reasonable cause and good faith ordinarily is not indicated by the mere fact that there is an appraisal of the value of property. Other factors to consider include the methodology and assumptions underlying the appraisal, the appraised value, the relationship between appraised value and purchase price, the circumstances under which the appraisal was obtained, and the appraiser's relationship to the taxpayer or to the activity in which the property is used. (See paragraph (g) of this section for certain rules relating to appraisals for charitable deduction property.) A taxpayer's reliance on erroneous information reported on a Form W-2, Form 1099, or other information return indicates reasonable cause and good faith, provided the taxpayer did not know or have reason to know that the information was incorrect. Generally, a taxpayer knows, or has reason to know, that the information on an information return is incorrect if such information is inconsistent with other information reported or otherwise furnished to the taxpayer, or with the taxpayer's knowledge of the transaction. This knowledge includes, for example, the taxpayer's knowledge of the terms of his employment relationship or of the rate of return on a payor's obligation.

(2) *Examples.*—The following examples illustrate this paragraph (b). They do not involve tax shelter items. (See paragraph (e) of this section for certain rules relating to the substantial understatement penalty attributable to the tax shelter items of corporations.)

Example 1. A, an individual calendar year taxpayer, engages B, a professional tax advisor, to give A advice concerning the deductibility of certain state and local taxes. A provides B with full details concerning the taxes at issue. B advises A that the taxes are fully deductible. A, in preparing his own tax return, claims a deduction for the taxes. Absent other facts, and assuming the facts and circumstances surrounding B's advice and A's reliance on such advice satisfy the requirements of paragraph (c) of this section, A is considered to have demonstrated good faith by seeking the advice of a professional tax advisor, and to have shown reasonable cause for any underpayment attributable to the deduction claimed for the taxes. However, if A had sought advice from someone that A knew, or should have known, lacked knowledge in the relevant aspects of Federal tax law, or if other facts demonstrate that A failed to act reasonably or in good faith, A would not be considered to have shown reasonable cause or to have acted in good faith.

Example 2. C, an individual, sought advice from D, a friend who was not a tax professional, as to how C might reduce his Federal tax obligations. D advised C that, for a nominal investment in Corporation X, D had received certain tax benefits which virtually eliminated D's Federal tax liability. D also named other investors who had received similar benefits. Without further inquiry, C invested in X and claimed the benefits that he had been assured by D were due him. In this case, C did not make any good faith attempt to ascertain the correctness of what D had advised him concerning his tax matters, and is not considered to have reasonable cause for the underpayment attributable to the benefits claimed.

Example 3. E, an individual, worked for Company X doing odd jobs and filling in for other employees when necessary. E worked irregular hours and was paid by the hour. The amount of E's pay check differed from week to week. The Form W-2 furnished to E reflected wages for 1990 in the amount of $29,729. It did not, however, include compensation of $1,467 paid for some hours E worked. Relying on the Form W-2, E filed a return reporting wages of $29,729. E had no reason to know that the amount reported on the Form W-2 was incorrect. Under the circumstances, E is considered to have acted in good faith in relying on the Form W-2 and to have reasonable cause for the underpayment attributable to the unreported wages.

Example 4. H, an individual, did not enjoy preparing his tax returns and procrastinated in doing so until April 15th. On April 15th, H hurriedly gathered together his tax records and materials, prepared a return, and mailed it before midnight. The return contained numerous errors, some of which were in H's favor and some of which were not. The net result of all the adjustments, however, was an underpayment of tax by H. Under these circumstances, H is not considered to have reasonable cause for the underpayment or to have acted in good faith in attempting to file an accurate return.

(c) *Reliance on opinion or advice.*—(1) *Facts and circumstances; minimum requirements.*—All facts and circumstances must be taken into account in determining whether a taxpayer has reasonably relied in good faith on advice (including the opinion of a professional tax advisor) as to the treatment of the taxpayer (or any entity, plan, or arrangement) under Federal tax law. For example, the taxpayer's education, sophistication and business experience will be relevant in determining whether the taxpayer's reliance on tax advice was reasonable and made in good faith. In no event will a taxpayer be considered to have reasonably relied in good faith on advice (including an opinion) unless the requirements of this paragraph (c)(1) are satisfied. The fact that these requirements are satisfied, however, will not necessarily establish that the taxpayer reasonably relied on the advice (including the opinion of a tax advisor) in good faith. For example, reliance may not be reasonable or in good faith if the taxpayer knew, or reasonably should have known, that the advisor lacked knowledge in the relevant aspects of Federal tax law.

(i) *All facts and circumstances considered.*— The advice must be based upon all pertinent facts and circumstances and the law as it relates to those facts and circumstances. For example, the advice must take into account the taxpayer's purposes (and the relative weight of such purposes) for entering into a transaction and for structuring a transaction in a particular manner. In addition, the requirements of this paragraph (c)(1) are not satisfied if the taxpayer fails to disclose a fact that it knows, or reasonably should know, to be relevant to the proper tax treatment of an item.

(ii) *No unreasonable assumptions.*—The advice must not be based on unreasonable factual or legal assumptions (including assumptions as to future events) and must not unreasonably rely on the representations, statements, findings, or agreements of the taxpayer or any other person. For example, the advice must not be based upon a representation or assumption which the taxpayer knows, or has reason to know, is unlikely to be true, such as an inaccurate representation or assumption as to the taxpayer's purposes for entering into a transaction or for structuring a transaction in a particular manner.

(iii) *Reliance on the invalidity of a regulation.*—A taxpayer may not rely on an opinion or advice that a regulation is invalid to establish that the taxpayer acted with reasonable cause and good faith unless the taxpayer adequately disclosed, in accordance with § 1.6662-3(c)(2), the position that the regulation in question is invalid.

(2) *Advice defined.*—Advice is any communication, including the opinion of a professional tax advisor, setting forth the analysis or conclusion of a person, other than the taxpayer, provided to (or for the benefit of) the taxpayer and on which the taxpayer relies, directly or indirectly, with respect to the imposition of the section 6662 accuracy-related penalty. Advice does not have to be in any particular form.

(3) *Cross-reference.*—For rules applicable to advisors, see e.g., § § 1.6694-1 through 1.6694-3 (regarding preparer penalties), 31 CFR 10.22 (regarding diligence as to accuracy), 31 CFR 10.33 (regarding tax shelter opinions), and 31 CFR 10.34 (regarding standards for advising with respect to tax return positions and for preparing or signing returns).

(d) *Underpayments attributable to reportable transactions.*—If any portion of an underpayment is attributable to a reportable transaction, as defined in § 1.6011-4(b) (or § 1.6011-4T(b), as applicable), then failure by the taxpayer to disclose

the transaction in accordance with § 1.6011-4 (or § 1.6011-4T, as applicable) is a strong indication that the taxpayer did not act in good faith with respect to the portion of the underpayment attributable to the reportable transaction.

(e) *Pass-through items.*—The determination of whether a taxpayer acted with reasonable cause and in good faith with respect to an underpayment that is related to an item reflected on the return of a pass-through entity is made on the basis of all pertinent facts and circumstances, including the taxpayer's own actions, as well as the actions of the pass-through entity.

(f) *Special rules for substantial understatement penalty attributable to tax shelter items of corporations.*—(1) *In general; facts and circumstances.*— The determination of whether a corporation acted with reasonable cause and in good faith in its treatment of a tax shelter item (as defined in § 1.6662-4(g)(3)) is based on all pertinent facts and circumstances. Paragraphs (f)(2), (3), and (4) of this section set forth rules that apply, in the case of a penalty attributable to a substantial understatement of income tax (within the meaning of section 6662(d)), in determining whether a corporation acted with reasonable cause and in good faith with respect to a tax shelter item.

(2) *Reasonable cause based on legal justification.*—(i) *Minimum requirements.*—A corporation's legal justification (as defined in paragraph (f)(2)(ii) of this section) may be taken into account, as appropriate, in establishing that the corporation acted with reasonable cause and in good faith in its treatment of a tax shelter item only if the authority requirement of paragraph (f)(2)(i)(A) of this section and the belief requirement of paragraph (f)(2)(i)(B) of this section are satisfied (the minimum requirements). Thus, a failure to satisfy the minimum requirements will preclude a finding of reasonable cause and good faith based (in whole or in part) on the corporation's legal justification.

(A) *Authority requirement.*—The authority requirement is satisfied only if there is substantial authority (within the meaning of § 1.6662-4(d)) for the tax treatment of the item.

(B) *Belief requirement.*—The belief requirement is satisfied only if, based on all facts and circumstances, the corporation reasonably believed, at the time the return was filed, that the tax treatment of the item was more likely than not the proper treatment. For purposes of the preceding sentence, a corporation is considered reasonably to believe that the tax treatment of an item is more likely than not the proper-tax treatment if (without taking into account the possibility that a return will not be audited, that an issue will not be raised on audit, or that an issue will be settled)—

(1) The corporation analyzes the pertinent facts and authorities in the manner described in § 1.6662-4(d)(3)(ii), and in reliance upon that analysis, reasonably concludes in good

faith that there is a greater than 50-percent likelihood that the tax treatment of the item will be upheld if challenged by the Internal Revenue Service; or

(2) The corporation reasonably relies in good faith on the opinion of a professional tax advisor, if the opinion is based on the tax advisor's analysis of the pertinent facts and authorities in the manner described in § 1.6662-4(d)(3)(ii) and unambiguously states that the tax advisor concludes that there is a greater than 50-percent likelihood that the tax treatment of the item will be upheld if challenged by the Internal Revenue Service. (For this purpose, the requirements of paragraph (c) of this section must be met with respect to the opinion of a professional tax advisor.)

(ii) *Legal justification defined.*—For purposes of this paragraph (f), *legal justification* includes any justification relating to the treatment or characterization under the Federal tax law of the tax shelter item or of the entity, plan, or arrangement that gave rise to the item. Thus, a taxpayer's belief (whether independently formed or based on the advice of others) as to the merits of the taxpayer's underlying position is a legal justification.

(3) *Minimum requirements not dispositive.*—Satisfaction of the minimum requirements of paragraph (f)(2) of this section is an important factor to be considered in determining whether a corporate taxpayer acted with reasonable cause and in good faith, but is not necessarily dispositive. For example, depending on the circumstances, satisfaction of the minimum requirements may not be dispositive if the taxpayer's participation in the tax shelter lacked significant business purpose, if the taxpayer claimed tax benefits that are unreasonable in comparison to the taxpayer's investment in the tax shelter, or if the taxpayer agreed with the organizer or promoter of the tax shelter that the taxpayer would protect the confidentiality of the tax aspects of the structure of the tax shelter.

(4) *Other factors.*—Facts and circumstances other than a corporation's legal justification may be taken into account, as appropriate, in determining whether the corporation acted with reasonable cause and in good faith with respect to a tax shelter item regardless of whether the minimum requirements of paragraph (f)(2) of this section are satisfied.

(g) *Transactions between persons described in section 482 and net section 482 transfer price adjustments.*—[Reserved]

(h) *Valuation misstatements of charitable deduction property.*—(1) *In general.*—There may be reasonable cause and good faith with respect to a portion of an underpayment that is attributable to a substantial (or gross) valuation misstatement of charitable deduction property (as defined in paragraph (h)(2) of this section) only if—

(i) The claimed value of the property was based on a qualified appraisal (as defined in paragraph (h)(2) of this section) by a qualified appraiser (as defined in paragraph (h)(2) of this section); and

(ii) In addition to obtaining a qualified appraisal, the taxpayer made a good faith investigation of the value of the contributed property.

(2) *Definitions.*—For purposes of this paragraph (h):

Charitable deduction property means any property (other than money or publicly traded securities, as defined in § 1.170A-13(c)(7)(xi)) contributed by the taxpayer in a contribution for which a deduction was claimed under section 170.

Qualified appraisal means a qualified appraisal as defined in § 1.170A-13(c)(3).

Qualified appraiser means a qualified appraiser as defined in § 1.170A-13(c)(5).

(3) *Special rules.*—The rules of this paragraph (h) apply regardless of whether § 1.170A-13 permits a taxpayer to claim a charitable contribution deduction for the property without obtaining a qualified appraisal. The rules of this paragraph (h) apply in addition to the generally applicable rules concerning reasonable cause and good faith. [Reg. § 1.6664-4.]

☐ [*T.D.* 8381, 12-30-91. *Amended by T.D.* 8617, 8-31-95; *T.D.* 8790, 12-1-98 *and T.D.* 9109, 12-29-2003.]

[Reg. § 1.6664-4T]

§ 1.6664-4T. Reasonable cause and good faith exception to section 6662 penalties.—(a) through (e) [Reserved].

(f) *Transactions between persons described in section 482 and net section 482 transfer price adjustments.*—For purposes of applying the reasonable cause and good faith exception of section 6664(c) to net section 482 adjustments, the rules of § 1.6662-6(d) apply. A taxpayer that does not satisfy the rules of § 1.6662-6(d) for a net section 482 adjustment cannot satisfy the reasonable cause and good faith exception under section 6664(c). The rules of this section apply to underpayments subject to the transactional penalty in § 1.6662-6(b). If the standards of the net section 482 penalty exclusion provisions under § 1.6662-6(d) are met with respect to such underpayments, then the taxpayer will be considered to have acted with reasonable cause and good faith for purposes of this section. [Temporary Reg. § 1.6664-4T.]

☐ [*T.D.* 8519, 1-27-94. *Amended by T.D.* 8656, 2-8-96.]

ASSESSABLE PENALTIES

General Provisions

[Reg. § 301.6671-1]

§ 301.6671-1. Rules for application of assessable penalties.—(a) *Penalty assessed as tax.*—The penalties and liabilities provided by subchapter B, chapter 68, of the Code (sections 6671 to 6675, inclusive) shall be paid upon notice and demand by the district director or the director of the regional service center and shall be assessed and collected in the same manner as taxes. Except as otherwise provided, any reference in the Code to "tax" imposed thereunder shall also be deemed to refer to the penalties and liabilities provided by subchapter B of chapter 68.

(b) *Person defined.*—For purposes of subchapter B of chapter 68, the term "person" includes an officer or employee of a corporation, or a member or employee of a partnership, who as such officer, employee, or member is under a duty to perform the act in respect of which the violation occurs. [Reg. § 301.6671-1.]

☐ [T.D. 6268, 11-15-57. *Amended by T.D.* 6498, 10-24-60 *and T.D.* 6585, 12-27-61.]

[Reg. § 301.6672-1]

§ 301.6672-1. Failure to collect and pay over tax, or attempt to evade or defeat tax.—Any person required to collect, truthfully account for, and pay over any tax imposed by the Code who willfully fails to collect such tax, or truthfully account for and pay over such tax, or willfully attempts in any manner to evade or defeat any such tax or the payment thereof, shall, in addition to other penalties, be liable to a penalty equal to the total amount of the tax evaded, or not collected, or not accounted for and paid over. The penalty imposed by section 6672 applies only to the collection, accounting for, or payment over of taxes imposed on a person other than the person who is required to collect, account for, and pay over such taxes. No penalty under section 6653, relating to failure to pay tax, shall be imposed for any offense to which this section is applicable. For further guidance regarding the determination of the proper address for mailing the notice required under section 6672(b)(1), see § 301.6212-2. [Reg. § 301.6672-1.]

☐ [T.D. 6268, 11-15-57. *Amended by T.D.* 8939, 1-11-2001.]

[Reg. § 301.6673-1]

§ 301.6673-1. Damages assessable for instituting proceedings before the Tax Court merely for delay.—Any damages awarded to the United States by the Tax Court under section 6673 against a taxpayer for instituting proceedings before the Tax Court merely for delay shall be assessed at the same time as the deficiency and shall be paid upon notice and demand from the district director or the director of the regional service center and shall be collected as a part of the tax. [Reg. § 301.6673-1.]

☐ [T.D. 6268, 11-15-57. *Amended by T.D.* 6585, 12-27-61.]

[Reg. § 31.6674-1]

§ 31.6674-1. Penalties for fraudulent statement or failure to furnish statement.—Any person required to furnish a statement to an employee under the provisions of section 6051 or 6053(b) is subject to a civil penalty for willful failure to furnish such statement in the manner, at the time, and showing the information required under such section (or § 31.6051-1 or § 31.6053-2), or for willfully furnishing a false or fraudulent statement to an employee. The penalty for each such violation is $50, which shall be assessed and collected in the same manner as the tax imposed on employers under the Federal Insurance Contributions Act. See section 7204 for criminal penalty. [Reg. § 31.6674-1.]

☐ [T.D. 6472, 6-22-60. *Amended by T.D.* 7001, 1-17-69.]

[Reg. § 301.6674-1]

§ 301.6674-1. Fraudulent statement or failure to furnish statement to employee.—For regulations under section 6674, see § 31.6674-1 of this chapter (Employment Tax Regulations). [Reg. § 301.6674-1.]

☐ [T.D. 6268, 11-15-57. *Amended by T.D.* 6498, 10-24-60.]

[Reg. § 301.6678-1]

§ 301.6678-1. Failure to furnish statements.—(a) *In general.*—In the case of each failure to furnish a statement required—

(1) Under section 6042(c) and § 1.6042-4 to a person with respect to whom a return has been made under section 6042(a)(1), relating to information returns with respect to payments of dividends aggregating $10 or more in a calendar year,

(2) Under section 6044(e) and § 1.6044-5 to a person with respect to whom a return has been made under section 6044(a)(1), relating to information returns with respect to certain payments by cooperatives aggregating $10 or more in a calendar year,

(3) Under section 6049(c) and § 1.6049-3 to a person with respect to whom a return has been made under section 6049(a)(1), relating to information returns with respect to payments of interest aggregating $10 or more in a calendar year,

(4) Under section 6039(b) and § 1.6039-2 to a person with respect to whom a return has been made under section 6039(a), relating to information returns with respect to certain stock option transactions occurring in a calendar year, or

(5) Under section 6052(b) and § 1.6052-2 to a person with respect to whom a return has been made under section 6052(a), relating to information returns with respect to payment of wages in

the form of group-term life insurance provided for an employee on his life,

within the time prescribed for furnishing such statement (determined with regard to any extension of time for furnishing), there shall be paid by the person failing to so furnish the statement $10 for each such statement not so furnished. However, the total amount imposed on the delinquent person for all such failures during a calendar year shall not exceed $25,000.

(b) *Manner of payment.*—The penalty imposed under section 6678 and this section on any person shall be paid in the same manner as tax upon the issuance of a notice and demand therefor.

(c) *Showing of reasonable cause.*—The penalty imposed by section 6678 shall not apply with respect to a failure to furnish a statement within the time prescribed if it is established to the satisfaction of the district director or the director of the regional service center that such failure was due to reasonable cause and not to willful neglect. An affirmative showing of reasonable cause must be made in the form of a written statement, containing a declaration that it is made under the penalties of perjury, setting forth all the facts alleged as a reasonable cause. [Reg. § 301.6678-1.]

☐ [*T.D.* 6628, 12-27-62. *Amended by T.D.* 6887, 6-23-66.]

[Reg. § 301.6679-1]

§ 301.6679-1. Failure to file returns, etc. with respect to foreign corporations or foreign partnerships for taxable years beginning after September 3, 1982.—(a) *Civil penalty.*—(1) *In general.*—In addition to any criminal penalty provided by law, each United States citizen, resident or person filing a separate or joint information return, or on whose behalf a return is filed, pursuant to sections 6035, 6046, or 6046A, and the regulations thereunder, who fails to file such a return within the time provided, or who files a return which does not show the required information, shall pay a penalty of $1,000, unless such failure is shown to be due to reasonable cause.

(2) *Joint return.*—The penalty imposed by section 6679 and this section shall apply to each United States citizen, resident, or person filing a joint return pursuant to the provisions of section 6035, 6046, or 6046A, which does not show the required information.

(3) *Showing of reasonable cause.*—The district director, the director of the Internal Revenue service center, and the Director of International Operations are authorized to make the determination that such failure was due to a reasonable cause and that, accordingly, the penalty imposed by section 6679 shall not apply. An affirmative showing of reasonable cause must be made in the form of a written statement, containing a declaration that it is made under the penalties of perjury, setting forth all the facts alleged as a reasonable cause. If the taxpayer exercises ordinary business care and prudence and is never-

theless unable to furnish any item of information required under section 6035, 6046, or 6046A and the regulations thereunder, such failure shall be considered due to a reasonable cause. In determining the extent of a taxpayer's ability to obtain information, the percentage of stock owned by such taxpayer and the nature of the other interests in the foreign corporation will be considered.

(b) *Deficiency procedures not to apply.*—The penalty imposed by section 6679 may be assessed and collected without regard to the deficiency procedures provided by subchapter B of chapter 63 of the Code. [Reg. § 301.6679-1.]

☐ [*T.D.* 6623, 11-30-62. *Amended by T.D.* 7288, 9-28-73; *T.D.* 7542, 4-28-78 *and T.D.* 8028, 6-3-85.]

[Reg. § 31.6682-1]

§ 31.6682-1. False information with respect to withholding.—(a) *Civil penalty.*—If any individual makes a statement under section 3402 (relating to income tax collected at source) which results in a lesser amount of income tax actually deducted and withheld than is properly allowable under section 3402 and, at the time the statement was made, there was no reasonable basis for the statement, the individual shall pay a penalty of $500 for the statement. There was a reasonable basis for a statement of the number of exemptions an individual claimed on a Form W-4, if the individual properly completed the Form W-4 by taking into account only allowable amounts for items which are allowable and by computing the number of exemptions in accordance with the instructions on the Form W-4. This penalty is in addition to any criminal penalty provided by law. This penalty may be assessed at any time after the statement is made, until the expiration of the applicable statute of limitations.

(b) *Deficiency procedures not to apply.*—The civil penalty imposed by section 6682 may be assessed and collected without regard to the deficiency procedures provided by subchapter B of chapter 63 of the Code. [Reg. § 31.6682-1.]

☐ [*T.D.* 7963, 7-13-84.]

[Reg. § 301.6682-1]

§ 301.6682-1. False information with respect to withholding allowances based on itemized deductions.—For regulations under section 6682, see § 31.6682-1 of this chapter (Employment Tax Regulations). [Reg. § 301.6682-1.]

☐ [*T.D.* 7065, 10-22-70.]

[Reg. § 301.6684-1]

§ 301.6684-1. Assessable penalties with respect to liability for tax under chapter 42.—(a) *In general.*—If any person (as defined in section 7701(a)(1)) becomes liable for tax under any section of chapter 42 (other than section 4940 or 4948(a)), relating to private foundations, by reason of any act or failure to act which is not due to reasonable cause and either—

(1) Such person has theretofore (at any time) been liable for tax under any section of such chapter (other than section 4940 or 4948(a)), or

(2) Such act or failure to act is both willful and flagrant,

then such person shall be liable for a penalty equal to the amount of such tax.

(b) *Showing of reasonable cause.*—The penalty imposed by section 6684 shall not apply to any person with respect to a violation of any section of chapter 42 if it is established to the satisfaction of the district director or director of the internal revenue service center that such violation was due to reasonable cause. An affirmative showing of reasonable cause must be made in the form of a written statement, containing a declaration by such person that it is made under the penalties of perjury, setting forth all the facts alleged as reasonable cause.

(c) *Willful and flagrant.*—For purposes of this section, the term "willful and flagrant" has the same meaning as such term possesses in section 507(a)(2)(A) and the regulations thereunder.

(d) *Effective date.*—This section shall take effect on January 1, 1970. [Reg. § 301.6684-1.]

☐ [*T.D. 7127, 6-14-71.*]

[Reg. § 301.6685-1]

§ 301.6685-1. Assessable penalties with respect to private foundations' failure to comply with section 6104(d).—(a) *In general.*—In addition to the penalty imposed by section 7207, relating to fraudulent returns, statements, or other documents, any person (as defined in paragraph (b) of this section) who is required to comply with the requirements of section 6104(d), relating to public inspection of private foundations' annual returns, and who fails so to comply, if such failure is willful, shall pay a penalty of $1,000 with respect to each such return with respect to which there is a failure so to comply.

(b) *Person.*—For purposes of this section, the term "person" means any officer, director, trustee, employee, member, or other individual whose duty it is to perform the act in respect of which the failure occurs.

(c) *Effective date.*—This section shall take effect on January 1, 1970.

(d) *Cross reference.*—For the amount imposed for failure to comply with section 6104(d), see paragraph (c) of § 301.6652-2. [Reg. § 301.6685-1.]

☐ [*T.D. 7127, 6-14-71. Amended by T.D. 8026, 5-17-85.*]

[Reg. § 301.6686-1]

§ 301.6686-1. Failure of DISC to file returns.—(a) *In general.*—In addition to the penalty imposed by section 7203 (relating to willful failure to file a return, supply information, or pay tax) any person who is required to supply information or to file a return under section 6011(c) (relating to records and returns of DISC's) and who fails to supply such information or file such return at the time prescribed in sections 6072(b) and 1.6072-2(e) shall pay a penalty of $100 for each failure to supply information (provided that the total amount imposed on the delinquent person for all such failures during a calendar year shall not exceed $25,000) and a penalty of $1,000 with respect to each failure to file a return, unless it is shown that such failure is due to a reasonable cause.

(b) *Showing of reasonable cause.*—The penalty imposed by section 6686 shall not apply to any person with respect to a failure to supply information, or to file a return, under section 6011(c) if it is established to the satisfaction of the district director or director of the Internal Revenue Service Center that such failure was due to reasonable cause. An affirmative showing of reasonable cause must be made in the form of a written statement, which contains a declaration by such person that the statement is made under the penalties of perjury, and sets forth all the facts alleged as reasonable cause. [Reg. § 301.6686-1.]

☐ [*T.D. 7533, 2-14-78.*]

[Reg. § 301.6688-1]

§ 301.6688-1. Assessable penalties with respect to information required to be furnished with respect to possessions.—(a) *In general.*—Each individual described in section 7654(a) who is subject to an information reporting requirement promulgated under the authority of section 937(c) or 7654 and who fails to fully satisfy such requirement within the time prescribed for reporting such information must, in addition to any criminal penalty provided by law, pay a penalty of $1000 for each such failure. Information reporting requirements promulgated under the authority of sections 937(c) and 7654(e) include the requirement for an individual to file Form 8898, "Statement for Individuals who Begin or End Bona Fide Residence in a U.S. Possession," under § 1.937-1(h) of this chapter, to report that he or she became or ceased to be a bona fide resident of a possession.

(b) *Manner of payment.*—The penalty set forth in paragraph (a) of this section must be paid in the same manner as tax upon the issuance of a notice and demand for the penalty.

(c) *Reasonable cause.*—(1) *In general.*—The penalty set forth in paragraph (a) of this section will not apply if it is established to the satisfaction of the *Commissioner* that the failure to file the information return or furnish the information within the prescribed time was due to reasonable cause and not to willful neglect. An individual who wishes to avoid the penalty must make an affirmative showing of all facts alleged as a reasonable cause for failure to file the information return on time, or furnish the information on time, in the form of a written statement containing a declaration that it is made under penalties of perjury. This statement must be filed with Internal Revenue Service Center where Form 8898 must be filed. In determining whether there was reasonable cause for failure to furnish the required information, account will be taken of the fact that the individual was unable to furnish the required information in spite of the exercise of ordinary business care and prudence in his effort to furnish the information. An individual will be considered to have exercised ordinary business care and prudence in his effort to furnish the required information if he made reasonable efforts to furnish the information but was unable to do so because of a lack of sufficient facts on which to make a proper determination.

(d) *Effective/applicability date.*—This section applies to taxable years ending after April 9, 2008. [Reg. § 301.6688-1.]

☐ [*T.D.* 7385, 10-18-75. *Amended by T.D.* 9194, 4-6-2005 *and T.D.* 9391, 4-4-2008 (*corrected* 5-13-2008).]

[Reg. § 301.6689-1T]

§ 301.6689-1T. Failure to file notice of redetermination of foreign tax (Temporary).— (a) *Application of civil penalty.*—If a foreign tax redetermination was made with respect to taxes for which the taxpayer previously claimed the foreign tax credit, and the taxpayer failed to notify the Service on or before the date prescribed in regulations under section 905(c) or in regulations under section 404A(g)(2) for giving notice of a foreign tax redetermination, then, unless paragraph (d) of this section applies, there shall be added to the deficiency attributable to such redetermination an amount determined under paragraph (b) of this section. Subchapter B of chapter 63 of the Internal Revenue Code (relating to deficiency proceedings) shall not apply with respect to the assessment of the amount of the penalty.

(b) *Amount of penalty.*—The amount of the penalty shall be equal to—

(1) Five percent of the deficiency if the failure is for not more than one month, plus

(2) An additional five percent of the deficiency for each month (or fraction thereof) during which the failure continues, but not to exceed in the aggregate twenty-five percent of the deficiency. If the penalty imposed under paragraph (a) of this section applies, then the penalty imposed under section 6653(a), relating to failure to pay by reason of negligent or intentional disregard of rules and regulations, shall not apply.

(c) *Foreign tax redetermination defined.*—For purposes of this section, a foreign tax redetermination is any redetermination for which a notice is required under section 905(c) and the regulations thereunder, or section 404A(g)(2) and the regulations thereunder.

(d) *Reasonable cause.*—The penalty set forth in this section shall not apply if it is established to the satisfaction of the Service that the failure to file the notification within the prescribed time was due to reasonable cause and not due to willful neglect. An affirmative showing of reasonable cause must be made in the form of a written statement that sets forth all the facts alleged as reasonable cause for the failure to file the notification on time and that contains a declaration by the taxpayer that the statement is made under the penalties of perjury. This statement must be filed with the service center in which the notification was required to be filed. The taxpayer must file this statement with the notice required under section 905(c) and the regulations thereunder or section 404A(g)(2) and the regulations thereunder. If the taxpayer exercised ordinary business care and prudence and was nevertheless unable to file the notification within the prescribed time, then the delay will be considered to be due to reasonable cause and not willful neglect.

(e) *Effective/applicability date.*—(1) *In general.*—This section applies to foreign tax redeterminations (as defined in § 1.905-3T(c) of this chapter) occurring in taxable years of United States taxpayers beginning on or after November 7, 2007, and in the three immediately preceding taxable years. For corresponding rules applicable to foreign tax redeterminations occurring in earlier taxable years of United States taxpayers, see 26 CFR 301.6689-1T (as contained in 26 CFR part 301, revised as of April 1, 2007).

(2) *Expiration date.*—The applicability of this section expires on or before November 5, 2010. [Temporary Reg. § 301.6689-1T.]

☐ [*T.D.* 8210, 6-22-88. *Amended by T.D.* 9362, 11-6-2007.]

[Reg. § 301.6690-1]

§ 301.6690-1. Penalty for fraudulent statement or failure to furnish statement to plan participant.—(a) *Penalty.*—Any plan administrator required by section 6057(e) and § 301.6058-1(d) to furnish a statement of deferred vested retirement benefit to a plan participant is subject to a penalty of $50 in each case in which the administrator (1) willfully fails to furnish the statement to the participant in the manner, at the time, and showing the information required by section 6057(e) and § 301.6057-1(e) or (2) willfully furnishes a false or fraudulent statement to the participant. The penalty shall be assessed and collected in the same manner as the tax imposed on employers under the Federal Insurance Contributions Act.

(b) *Effective date.*—This section shall take effect on September 2, 1974. [Reg. § 301.6690-1.]

☐ [*T.D.* 7561, 8-24-78.]

[Reg. § 301.6692-1]

§ 301.6692-1. Failure to file actuarial report.— (a) *Penalty.*—In each case in which the plan administrator (within the meaning of section 414(g)) of a defined benefit plan to which the minimum funding standards of section 412 apply fails to file the actuarial report described in section 6059 and § 301.6059-1 within the time prescribed, the plan administrator shall pay a penalty of $1,000. A failure to provide a material item of information called for in the actuarial report is considered a failure to file the report. For this purpose, the signature of an enrolled actuary (see §301.6059-1(d)) is considered a material item of information. Further, for any report filed for a plan year ending after January 25, 1982, if the actuary seeks to materially qualify a statement required by §301.6059-1(c)(4) or (5) there is a failure to provide a material item of information called for in the report. For rules relating to statements not considered as materially qualifying the required statements, see §301.6059-1(d).

(b) *Failure to make actuarial valuation.*—Section 412(c)(9) and the regulations thereunder prescribe the time for making an actuarial valuation of a defined benefit plan. For purposes of this section, the failure to base information called for in the actuarial report upon an actuarial valuation of the plan which is made within the time prescribed by section 412(c)(9) and the regulations thereunder is considered a failure to file the actuarial report.

(c) *Showing of reasonable cause.*—The penalty imposed by this section does not apply if it is established to the satisfaction of the appropriate district director or the director of the Internal Revenue Service Center at which the actuarial report is required to be filed that the failure to file the report was due to reasonable cause. An affirmative showing of reasonable cause must be made in the form of a written statement setting forth all the facts alleged as reasonable cause. The statement must contain a declaration by the appropriate individual that the statement is made under the penalties of perjury.

(d) *Joint liability.*—If more than one person is responsible as a plan administrator for a failure to file the actuarial report, all such persons are jointly and severally liable with respect to the failure.

(e) *Manner of payment.*—The penalty imposed for the failure to file an actuarial report shall be paid in the same manner as a tax upon the issuance of notice and demand therefor.

(f) *Effective dates.*—In the case of a plan in existence on January 1, 1974, this section is effective beginning with the first plan year beginning after December 31, 1975, for which the minimum funding standards of section 412 apply to the plan. In the case of a plan not in existence on January 1, 1974, this section is effective beginning with the first plan year beginning after September 2, 1974, for which the minimum funding standards apply to the plan. [Reg. §301.6692-1.]

    ☐ [*T.D. 7798,* 11-23-81.]

[Reg. §301.6693-1]

§301.6693-1. Penalty for failure to provide reports and documents concerning individual retirement accounts or annuities.—(a) *In general.*—(1) *Annual reports, etc.*—The trustee of an individual retirement account described in sec-

tion 408(a), or the issuer of an individual retirement annuity described in section 408(b), who fails to furnish or file a report or any other document required under section 408(i) and §1.408-5 within the time and in the manner prescribed for furnishing or filing such item shall pay a penalty of $10 for each failure unless it is shown that such failure is due to reasonable cause.

(2) *Disclosure statements.*—The trustee of an individual retirement account described in section 408(a), or the issuer of an individual retirement annuity described in section 408(b), who fails to furnish or file a disclosure statement, a governing instrument, an amendment to either, or any other document required under section 408(i) and §1.408-6, within the time and in the manner prescribed for furnishing or filing such item, shall pay a penalty of $10 for each failure unless it is shown that such failure is due to reasonable cause.

(b) *Showing of reasonable cause.*—The penalty imposed by section 6693 shall not apply to any person with respect to a failure to furnish or file a report, statement, or other document within the time and in the manner prescribed if it is established to the satisfaction of the district director that such failure was due to reasonable cause. An affirmative showing of reasonable cause must be made in the form of a written statement, containing a declaration by such person that it is made under the penalties of perjury and setting forth all the facts alleged to constitute reasonable cause.

(c) *Deficiency procedures not to apply.*—The penalty imposed by section 6693 may be assessed and collected without regard to the deficiency procedures provided by subchapter B of chapter 63 of the Code.

(d) *Other penalties.*—The penalties of section 6693 and this section are in lieu of any penalty imposed by section 6652(f) for violation of section 6047(d), with respect to any failure to furnish or file described in this section.

(e) *Effective date.*—This section shall take effect on January 1, 1975. [Reg. §301.6693-1.]

    ☐ [*T.D. 7730,* 10-31-80.]

[Reg. §1.6694-0]

§1.6694-0. Table of contents.—This section lists the captions that appear in §§1.6694-1 through 1.6694-4.

(4) Responsibility of signing and nonsigning tax return preparer.

(5) Tax return preparer and firm responsibility.

(6) Examples.

(c) Understatement of liability.

(d) Abatement of penalty where taxpayer's liability not understated.

(e) Verification of information furnished by taxpayer or other third party.

(1) In general.

(2) Verification of information on previously filed returns.

(3) Examples.

(f) Income derived (or to be derived) with respect to the return or claim for refund.

(1) In general.

(2) Compensation.

(i) Multiple engagements.

(ii) Reasonable allocation.

(iii) Fee refunds.

(iv) Reduction of compensation.

(3) Individual and firm allocation.

(4) Examples.

(g) Effective/applicability date.

§1.6694-2 Penalty for understatement due to an unreasonable position.

(a) In general.

(1) Proscribed conduct.

(2) Special rule for corporations, partnerships, and other firms.

(b) Reasonable to believe that the position would more likely than not be sustained on its merits.

(1) In general.

(2) Authorities.

(3) Written determinations.

(4) Taxpayer's jurisdiction.

(5) When "more likely than not" standard must be satisfied.

(c) Substantial authority.

(d) Exception for adequate disclosure of positions with a reasonable basis.

(1) In general.

(2) Reasonable basis.

(3) Adequate disclosure.

(i) Signing tax return preparers.

(ii) Nonsigning tax return preparers.

(A) Advice to taxpayers.

(B) Advice to another tax return preparer.

(iii) Requirements for advice.

(iv) Pass-through entities.

(v) Examples.

(e) Exception for reasonable cause and good faith.

(1) Nature of the error causing the understatement.

(2) Frequency of errors.

(3) Materiality of errors.

(4) Tax return preparer's normal office practice.

(5) Reliance on advice of others.

(6) Reliance on generally accepted administrative or industry practice.

(f) Effective/applicability date.

§1.6694-3 Penalty for understatement due to willful, reckless, or intentional conduct.

(a) In general.

(1) Proscribed conduct.

(2) Special rule for corporations, partnerships, and other firms.

(b) Willful attempt to understate liability.

(c) Reckless or intentional disregard.

(d) Examples.

(e) Rules or regulations.

(f) Section 6694(b) penalty reduced by section 6694(a) penalty.

(g) Effective/applicability date.

§1.6694-4 Extension of period of collection when tax return preparer pays 15 percent of a penalty for understatement of taxpayer's liability and certain other procedural matters.

(a) In general.

(b) Tax return preparer must bring suit in district court to determine liability for penalty.

(c) Suspension of running of period of limitations on collection.

(d) Effective/applicability date.

[Reg. §1.6694-0.]

☐ *T.D. 8382, 12-30-91. Amended by T.D. 9436, 12-15-2008.*]

[Reg. §1.6694-1]

§1.6694-1. Section 6694 penalties applicable to tax return preparers.—(a) *Overview.*—(1) *In general.*—Sections 6694(a) and (b) impose penalties on tax return preparers for conduct giving rise to certain understatements of liability on a return (including an amended or adjusted return) or claim for refund. For positions other than those with respect to tax shelters (as defined in section 6662(d)(2)(C)(ii)) and reportable transactions to which section 6662A applies, the section 6694(a) penalty is imposed in an amount equal to the greater of $1,000 or 50 percent of the income derived (or to be derived) by the tax return preparer for an understatement of tax liability that is due to an undisclosed position for which the tax return preparer did not have substantial authority or due to a disclosed position for which there is no reasonable basis. For positions with respect to tax shelters (as defined in section 6662(d)(2)(C)(ii)) or reportable transactions to which section 6662A applies, the section 6694(a) penalty is imposed in an amount equal to the greater of $1,000 or 50 percent of the income derived (or to be derived) by the tax return preparer for an understatement of tax liability for which it is not reasonable to believe that the position would more likely than not be sustained on its merits. The section 6694(b) penalty is imposed in an amount equal to the greater of $5,000 or 50 percent of the income derived (or to be derived) by the tax return preparer for an understatement of liability with respect to tax that is due to a willful attempt to understate tax liability or that is due to reckless or intentional disregard of rules or regulations. Refer to §1.6694-2 for rules relating to the penalty under section 6694(a). Refer to §1.6694-3 for rules relating to the penalty under section 6694(b).

(2) *Date return is deemed prepared.*—For purposes of the penalties under section 6694, a return or claim for refund is deemed prepared on the date it is signed by the tax return preparer. If a signing tax return preparer within the meaning of §301.7701-15(b)(1) of this chapter fails to sign the return, the return or claim for refund is deemed prepared on the date the return or claim is filed. See §1.6695-1 of this section. In the case of a nonsigning tax return preparer within the meaning of §301.7701-15(b)(2) of this chapter, the relevant date is the date the nonsigning tax return preparer provides the tax advice with respect to the position giving rise to the understatement. This date will be determined based on all the facts and circumstances.

(b) *Tax return preparer.*—(1) *In general.*—For purposes of this section, "tax return preparer" means any person who is a tax return preparer within the meaning of section 7701(a)(36) and §301.7701-15 of this chapter. An individual is a tax return preparer subject to section 6694 if the individual is primarily responsible for the position(s) on the return or claim for refund giving rise to an understatement. See §301.7701-15(b)(3). There is only one individual within a firm who is primarily responsible for each position on the return or claim for refund giving rise to an understatement. In the course of identifying the individual who is primarily responsible for the position, the Internal Revenue Service (IRS) may advise multiple individuals within the firm that it may be concluded that they are the individual within the firm who is primarily responsible. In some circumstances, there may be more than one tax return preparer who is primarily responsible for the position(s) giving rise to an understatement if multiple tax return preparers are employed by, or associated with, different firms.

(2) *Responsibility of signing tax return preparer.*—If there is a signing tax return preparer within the meaning of §301.7701-15(b)(1) of this chapter within a firm, the signing tax return preparer generally will be considered the person who is primarily responsible for all of the positions on the return or claim for refund giving rise to an understatement unless, based upon credible information from any source, it is concluded that the signing tax return preparer is not primarily responsible for the position(s) on the return or claim for refund giving rise to an understatement. In that case, a nonsigning tax return preparer within the signing tax return preparer's firm (as determined in paragraph (b)(3) of this section) will be considered the tax return preparer who is primarily responsible for the position(s) on the return or claim for refund giving rise to an understatement.

(3) *Responsibility of nonsigning tax return preparer.*—If there is no signing tax return

preparer within the meaning of §301.7701-15(b)(1) of this chapter for the return or claim for refund within the firm or if, after the application of paragraph (b)(2) of this section, it is concluded that the signing tax return preparer is not primarily responsible for the position, the nonsigning tax return preparer within the meaning of §301.7701-15(b)(2) of this chapter within the firm with overall supervisory responsibility for the position(s) giving rise to the understatement generally will be considered the tax return preparer who is primarily responsible for the position for purposes of section 6694 unless, based upon credible information from any source, it is concluded that another nonsigning tax return preparer within that firm is primarily responsible for the position(s) on the return or claim for refund giving rise to the understatement.

(4) *Responsibility of signing and nonsigning tax return preparer.*—If the information presented would support a finding that, within a firm, either the signing tax return preparer or a nonsigning tax return preparer is primarily responsible for the position(s) giving rise to the understatement, the penalty may be assessed against either one of the individuals, but not both, as the primarily responsible tax return preparer.

(5) *Tax return preparer and firm responsibility.*—To the extent provided in §§1.6694-2(a)(2) and 1.6694-3(a)(2), an individual and the firm that employs the individual, or the firm of which the individual is a partner, member, shareholder, or other equity holder, both may be subject to penalty under section 6694 with respect to the position(s) on the return or claim for refund giving rise to an understatement. If an individual (other than the sole proprietor) who is employed by a sole proprietorship is subject to penalty under section 6694, the sole proprietorship is considered a "firm" for purposes of this paragraph (b).

(6) *Examples.*—The provisions of paragraph (b) of this section are illustrated by the following examples:

Example 1. Attorney A provides advice to Client C concerning the proper treatment of an item with respect to which all events have occurred on C's tax return. In preparation for providing that advice, A seeks advice regarding the proper treatment of the item from Attorney B, who is within the same firm as A, but A is the attorney who signs C's return as a tax return preparer. B provides advice on the treatment of the item upon which A relies. B's advice is reflected on C's tax return but no disclosure was made in accordance with §1.6694-2(d)(3). The advice constitutes preparation of a substantial portion of the return within the meaning of §301.7701-15(b)(3). The IRS later challenges the position taken on the tax return, giving rise to an understatement of liability. For purposes of the regulations under section 6694, A is initially considered the tax return preparer with respect to

Reg. §1.6694-1(a)(2)

C's return, and the IRS advises A that A may be subject to the penalty under section 6694 with respect to C's return. Based upon information received from A or another source, it may be concluded that B, rather than A, had primary responsibility for the position taken on the return that gave rise to the understatement and may be subject to penalty under section 6694 instead of A.

Example 2. Same as *Example 1*, except that neither Attorney A nor any other source produce credible information that Attorney B had primary responsibility for the position on the return giving rise to an understatement. Attorney A is the tax return preparer who may be subject to penalty under section 6694 with respect to C's return.

Example 3. Same as *Example 1*, except that neither Attorney A nor any other attorney within A's firm signs Client C's return as a tax return preparer. Attorney B is the nonsigning tax return preparer within the firm with overall supervisory responsibility for the position giving rise to an understatement. Accordingly, B is the tax return preparer who is primarily responsible for the position on C's return giving rise to an understatement and may be subject to penalty under section 6694.

Example 4. Same as *Example 1*, except Attorney D, who works for a different firm than A, also provides advice on the same position upon which A relies. It may be concluded that D is also primarily responsible for the position on the return and may be subject to penalty under section 6694.

Example 5. Same as *Example 1*, except Attorney B is able to present credible information that A is also responsible for the position on C's return giving rise to an understatement. The IRS may conclude between A and B, the two responsible persons for the position, who is primarily responsible and may assess a section 6694 penalty against A or B, but not both, as the primarily responsible tax return preparer.

(c) *Understatement of liability.*—For purposes of this section, an "understatement of liability" exists if, viewing the return or claim for refund as a whole, there is an understatement of the net amount payable with respect to any tax imposed by the Internal Revenue Code (Code), or an overstatement of the net amount creditable or refundable with respect to any tax imposed by the Code. The net amount payable in a taxable year with respect to the return for which the tax return preparer engaged in conduct proscribed by section 6694 is not reduced by any carryback. Tax imposed by the Code does not include additions to the tax, additional amounts, and assessable penalties imposed by subchapter 68 of the Code. Except as provided in paragraph (d) of this section, the determination of whether an understatement of liability exists may be made in a proceeding involving the tax return preparer that is separate and apart from any proceeding involving the taxpayer.

(d) *Abatement of penalty where taxpayer's liability not understated.*—If a penalty under section 6694(a) or (b) concerning a return or claim for refund has been assessed against one or more tax return preparers, and if it is established at any time in a final administrative determination or a final judicial decision that there was no understatement of liability relating to the position(s) on the return or claim for refund, then—

(1) The assessment shall be abated; and

(2) If any amount of the penalty was paid, that amount shall be refunded to the person or persons who so paid, as if the payment were an overpayment of tax, without consideration of any period of limitations.

(e) *Verification of information furnished by taxpayer or other party.*—(1) *In general.*—For purposes of sections 6694(a) and (b) (including demonstrating that a position complied with relevant standards under section 6694(a) and demonstrating reasonable cause and good faith under §1.6694-2(e)), the tax return preparer generally may rely in good faith without verification upon information furnished by the taxpayer. A tax return preparer also may rely in good faith and without verification upon information and advice furnished by another advisor, another tax return preparer or other party (including another advisor or tax return preparer at the tax return preparer's firm). The tax return preparer is not required to audit, examine or review books and records, business operations, documents, or other evidence to verify independently information provided by the taxpayer, advisor, other tax return preparer, or other party. The tax return preparer, however, may not ignore the implications of information furnished to the tax return preparer or actually known by the tax return preparer. The tax return preparer must make reasonable inquiries if the information as furnished appears to be incorrect or incomplete. Additionally, some provisions of the Code or regulations require that specific facts and circumstances exist (for example, that the taxpayer maintain specific documents) before a deduction or credit may be claimed. The tax return preparer must make appropriate inquiries to determine the existence of facts and circumstances required by a Code section or regulation as a condition of the claiming of a deduction or credit.

(2) *Verification of information on previously filed returns.*—For purposes of section 6694(a) and (b) (including meeting the reasonable to believe that the position would more likely than not be sustained on its merits and reasonable basis standards in §§1.6694-2(b) and (d)(2), and demonstrating reasonable cause and good faith under §1.6694-2(e)), a tax return preparer may rely in good faith without verification upon a tax return that has been previously prepared by a taxpayer or another tax return preparer and filed with the IRS. For example, a tax return preparer who prepares an amended return (including a claim for refund) need not verify the positions on the original return. The tax return preparer,

however, may not ignore the implications of information furnished to the tax return preparer or actually known by the tax return preparer. The tax return preparer must make reasonable inquiries if the information as furnished appears to be incorrect or incomplete. The tax return preparer must confirm that the position being relied upon has not been adjusted by examination or otherwise.

(3) *Examples.*—The provisions of this paragraph (e) are illustrated by the following examples:

Example 1. During an interview conducted by Preparer E, a taxpayer stated that he had made a charitable contribution of real estate in the amount of $50,000 during the tax year, when in fact he had not made this charitable contribution. E did not inquire about the existence of a qualified appraisal or complete a Form 8283, Noncash Charitable Contributions, in accordance with the reporting and substantiation requirements under section 170(f)(11). E reported a deduction on the tax return for the charitable contribution, which resulted in an understatement of liability for tax, and signed the tax return as the tax return preparer. E is subject to a penalty under section 6694.

Example 2. While preparing the 2008 tax return for an individual taxpayer, Preparer F realizes that the taxpayer did not provide a Form 1099-INT, "Interest Income", for a bank account that produced significant taxable income in 2007. When F inquired about any other income, the taxpayer furnished the Form 1099-INT to F for use in preparation of the 2008 tax return. F did not know that the taxpayer owned an additional bank account that generated taxable income for 2008, and the taxpayer did not reveal this information to the tax return preparer notwithstanding F's general inquiry about any other income. F signed the taxpayer's return as the tax return preparer. F is not subject to a penalty under section 6694.

Example 3. In preparing a tax return, for purposes of determining the deductibility of a contribution by an employer for a qualified pension plan, Accountant G relies on a computation of the section 404 limit on deductible amounts made by the enrolled actuary for the plan. On the basis of this calculation, G completed and signed the tax return. It is later determined that there is an understatement of liability for tax that resulted from the overstatement of the section 404 limit on deductible amounts made by the actuary. G had no reason to believe that the actuary's calculation of the limit on deductible contributions was incorrect or incomplete, and the calculation appeared reasonable on its face. G was also not aware at the time the return was prepared of any reason why the actuary did not know all of the relevant facts or that the calculation of the limit on deductible contributions was no longer reliable due to developments in the law since the time the calculation was given. G is not subject to a penalty under section 6694. The actuary, however, may be subject to penalty under section 6694 if the calculation provided by the actuary constitutes a substantial portion of

the tax return within the meaning of §301.7701-15(b)(3) of this chapter.

(f) *Income derived (or to be derived) with respect to the return or claim for refund.*—(1) *In general.*— For purposes of sections 6694(a) and (b), *income derived (or to be derived)* means all compensation the tax return preparer receives or expects to receive with respect to the engagement of preparing the return or claim for refund or providing tax advice (including research and consultation) with respect to the position(s) taken on the return or claim for refund that gave rise to the understatement. In the situation of a tax return preparer who is not compensated directly by the taxpayer, but rather by a firm that employs the tax return preparer or with which the tax return preparer is associated, *income derived (or to be derived)* means all compensation the tax return preparer receives from the firm that can be reasonably allocated to the engagement of preparing the return or claim for refund or providing tax advice (including research and consultation) with respect to the position(s) taken on the return or claim for refund that gave rise to the understatement. In the situation where a firm that employs the individual tax return preparer (or the firm of which the individual tax return preparer is a partner, member, shareholder, or other equity holder) is subject to a penalty under section 6694(a) or (b) pursuant to the provisions in §§1.6694-2(a)(2) or 1.6694-3(a)(2), *income derived (or to be derived)* means all compensation the firm receives or expects to receive with respect to the engagement of preparing the return or claim for refund or providing tax advice (including research and consultation) with respect to the position(s) taken on the return or claim for refund that gave rise to the understatement.

(2) *Compensation.*—(i) *Multiple engagements.*—For purposes of applying paragraph (f)(1) of this section, if the tax return preparer or the tax return preparer's firm has multiple engagements related to the same return or claim for refund, only those engagements relating to the position(s) taken on the return or claim for refund that gave rise to the understatement are considered for purposes of calculating the income derived (or to be derived) with respect to the return or claim for refund.

(ii) *Reasonable allocation.*—For purposes of applying paragraph (f)(1) of this section, only compensation for tax advice that is given with respect to events that have occurred at the time the advice is rendered and that relates to the position(s) giving rise to the understatement will be taken into account for purposes of calculating the section 6694(a) and (b) penalties. If a lump sum fee is received that includes amounts not taken into account under the preceding sentence, the amount of income derived will be based on a reasonable allocation of the lump sum fee between the tax advice giving rise to the penalty and the advice that does not give rise to the penalty.

(iii) *Fee refunds.*—For purposes of applying paragraph (f)(1) of this section, a refund to the taxpayer of all or part of the amount paid to the tax return preparer or the tax return preparer's firm will not reduce the amount of the section 6694 penalty assessed. A refund in this context does not include a discounted fee or alternative billing arrangement for the services provided.

(iv) *Reduction of compensation.*—For purposes of applying paragraph (f)(1) of this section, it may be concluded based upon information provided by the tax return preparer or the tax return preparer's firm that an appropriate allocation of compensation attributable to the position(s) giving rise to the understatement on the return or claim for refund is less than the total amount of compensation associated with the engagement. For example, the number of hours of the engagement spent on the position(s) giving rise to the understatement may be less than the total hours associated with the engagement. If this is concluded, the amount of the penalty will be calculated based upon the compensation attributable to the position(s) giving rise to the understatement. Otherwise, the total amount of compensation from the engagement will be the amount of income derived for purposes of calculating the penalty under section 6694.

(3) *Individual and firm allocation.*—If both an individual within a firm and a firm that employs the individual (or the firm of which the individual is a partner, member, shareholder, or other equity holder) are subject to a penalty under section 6694(a) or (b) pursuant to the provisions in §§ 1.6694-2(a)(2) or 1.6694-3(a)(2), the amount of penalties assessed against the individual and the firm shall not exceed 50 percent of the income derived (or to be derived) by the firm from the engagement of preparing the return or claim for refund or providing tax advice (including research and consultation) with respect to the position(s) taken on the return or claim for refund that gave rise to the understatement. The portion of the total amount of the penalty assessed against the individual tax return preparer shall not exceed 50 percent of the individual's compensation as determined under paragraphs (f)(1) and (2) of this section.

(4) *Examples.*—The provisions of this paragraph (f) are illustrated by the following examples:

Example 1. Signing Tax Return Preparer H is engaged by a taxpayer and paid a total of $21,000. Of this amount, $20,000 relates to research and consultation regarding a transaction that is later reported on a return, and $1,000 is for the activities relating to the preparation of the return. Based on H's hourly rates, a reasonable allocation of the amount of compensation related to the advice rendered prior to the occurrence of events that are the subject of the advice is $5,000. The remaining compensation of $16,000 is considered to be compensation related to the advice rendered after the occurrence of events that are the subject of the advice and return preparation. The income derived by H with respect to the

return for purposes of computing the penalty under section 6694(a) is $16,000, and the amount of the penalty imposed under section 6694(a) is $8,000.

Example 2. Accountants I, J, and K are employed by Firm L. I is a principal manager of Firm L and provides corporate tax advice for the taxpayer after all events have occurred subject to an engagement for corporate tax advice. J provides international tax advice for the taxpayer after all events have occurred subject to a different engagement for international tax advice. K prepares and signs the taxpayer's return under a general tax services engagement. I's advice is the source of an understatement on the return and the advice constitutes preparation of a substantial portion of the return within the meaning of § 301.7701-15(b) of this chapter. I is the nonsigning tax return preparer within the firm with overall supervisory responsibility for the position on the taxpayer's return giving rise to an understatement. Thus, I is the tax return preparer who is primarily responsible for the position on the taxpayer's return giving rise to the understatement. Because K's signature as the signing tax return preparer is on the return, the IRS advises K that K may be subject to the section 6694(a) penalty. K provides credible information that I is the tax return preparer with primary responsibility for the position that gave rise to the understatement. The IRS, therefore, assesses the section 6694 penalty against I. The portion of the total amount of the penalty allocable to I does not exceed 50 percent of that part of I's compensation that is attributable to the corporate tax advice engagement. In the event that Firm L is also liable under the provisions in § 1.6694-2(a)(2), the IRS assesses the section 6694 penalty in an amount not exceeding 50 percent of Firm L's firm compensation based on the engagement relating to the corporate tax advice services provided by I where there is no applicable reduction in compensation pursuant to § 1.6694-1(f)(2)(iii).

Example 3. Same facts as *Example 2*, except that I provides the advice on the corporate matter when the events have not yet occurred. I's advice is the cause of an understatement position on the return, but I is not a tax return preparer pursuant to § 301.7701-15(b)(2) or (3) of this chapter. K is not limited to reliance on persons who provide post-transactional advice if such reliance is reasonable and in good faith. Further, K has reasonable cause because K relied on I for the advice on the corporate tax matter. I, K and Firm L are not liable for the section 6694 penalty.

Example 4. Attorney M is an employee of Firm N with a salary of $75,000 per year. M performs tax preparation work for Client O. Client O's return contains a position that results in an understatement subject to the section 6694 penalty. M spent 100 hours on the position (out of a total 2,000 billed during the year). The total fees earned by Firm N with respect to the position reflected on Client O's return are $50,000. If M is subject to the penalty, the penalty amount computed under the 50 percent of income standard is .5 × (100/2000) × $75,000 = $1,875. If Firm N is subject to the penalty, the penalty amount computed under the 50% of income standard is .5 × $50,000 = $25,000, less any penalty amount imposed against M. If a penalty of $1,875 was assessed against M and Firm N was subject to the penalty, a penalty of $23,125 would be the amount of penalty assessed against Firm N.

(g) *Effective/applicability date.*—This section is applicable to returns and claims for refund filed, and advice provided, after December 31, 2008. [Reg. § 1.6694-1.]

☐ [*T.D.* 7519. *Amended by T.D.* 7572, 11-15-78; *T.D.* 8382, 12-30-91 *and T.D.* 9436, 12-15-2008 (*corrected* 1-28-2009).]

[Reg. § 20.6694-1]

§ 20.6694-1. Section 6694 penalties applicable to tax return preparer.—(a) *In general.*—For general definitions regarding section 6694 penalties applicable to preparers of estate tax returns or claims for refund, see § 1.6694-1 of this chapter.

(b) *Effective/applicability date.*—Paragraph (a) of this section is applicable to returns and claims for refund filed, and advice provided, after December 31, 2008. [Reg. § 20.6694-1.]

☐ [*T.D.* 9436, 12-15-2008 (*corrected* 1-28-2009).]

[Reg. § 25.6694-1]

§ 25.6694-1. Section 6694 penalties applicable to tax return preparer.—(a) *In general.*—For general definitions regarding section 6694 penalties applicable to preparers of gift tax returns or claims for refund, see § 1.6694-1 of this chapter.

(b) *Effective/applicability date.*—Paragraph (a) of this section is applicable to returns and claims for refund filed, and advice provided, after December 31, 2008. [Reg. § 25.6694-1.]

☐ [*T.D.* 9436, 12-15-2008 (*corrected* 1-28-2009).]

[Reg. § 26.6694-1]

§ 26.6694-1. Section 6694 penalties applicable to tax return preparer.—(a) *In general.*—For general definitions regarding section 6694 penalties applicable to preparers of generation-skipping transfer tax returns or claims for refund, see § 1.6694-1 of this chapter.

(b) *Effective/applicability date.*—Paragraph (a) of this section is applicable to returns and claims for refund filed, and advice provided, after December 31, 2008. [Reg. § 26.6694-1.]

☐ [*T.D.* 9436, 12-15-2008 (*corrected* 1-28-2009).]

[Reg. § 31.6694-1]

§ 31.6694-1. Section 6694 penalties applicable to tax return preparer.—(a) *In general.*—For general definitions regarding section 6694 penalties applicable to preparers of employment tax returns or claims for refund of employment tax under chapters 21 through 25 of subtitle C of the Internal Revenue Code, see § 1.6694-1 of this chapter.

(b) *Effective/applicability date.*—Paragraph (a) of this section is applicable to returns and claims for refund filed, and advice provided, after December 31, 2008. [Reg. § 31.6694-1.]

☐ [*T.D.* 9436, 12-15-2008 (*corrected* 1-28-2009).]

[Reg. § 40.6694-1]

§ 40.6694-1. Section 6694 penalties applicable to tax return preparer.—(a) *In general.*—For general definitions regarding section 6694 penalties applicable to preparers of returns or claims for refund of any tax to which this part 40 applies, see § 1.6694-1 of this chapter.

(b) *Effective/applicability date.*—This section is applicable to returns and claims for refund filed, and advice provided, after December 31, 2008. [Reg. § 40.6694-1.]

☐ [*T.D.* 9436, 12-15-2008 (*corrected* 1-28-2009).]

[Reg. § 41.6694-1]

§ 41.6694-1. Section 6694 penalties applicable to tax return preparer.—(a) *In general.*—For general definitions regarding section 6694 penalties applicable to preparers of tax returns or claims for refund, see § 1.6694-1 of this chapter.

(b) *Effective/applicability date.*—This section is applicable to returns and claims for refund filed, and advice provided, after December 31, 2008. [Reg. § 41.6694-1.]

☐ [*T.D.* 9436, 12-15-2008.]

[Reg. § 44.6694-1]

§ 44.6694-1. Section 6694 penalties applicable to tax return preparer.—(a) *In general.*—For general definitions regarding section 6694 penalties applicable to preparers of wagering tax returns or claims for refund under sections 4401 or 4411, see § 1.6694-1 of this chapter.

(b) *Effective/applicability date.*—This section is applicable to returns and claims for refund filed, and advice provided, after December 31, 2008. [Reg. § 44.6694-1.]

☐ [*T.D.* 9436, 12-15-2008.]

[Reg. § 53.6694-1]

§ 53.6694-1. Section 6694 penalties applicable to tax return preparer.—(a) *In general.*—For general definitions regarding section 6694 penalties applicable to preparers of tax returns or claims for refund under Chapter 42 of the Internal Revenue Code, see § 1.6694-1 of this chapter.

(b) *Effective/applicability date.*—Paragraph (a) of this section is applicable to returns and claims for refund filed, and advice provided, after December 31, 2008. [Reg. § 53.6694-1.]

☐ [*T.D.* 9436, 12-15-2008.]

[Reg. § 54.6694-1]

§ 54.6694-1. Section 6694 penalties applicable to tax return preparer.—(a) *In general.*—For general definitions regarding section 6694 penalties applicable to preparers of tax returns or claims for refund of tax under Chapter 43 of subtitle D, see § 1.6694-1 of this chapter.

(b) *Effective/applicability date.*—Paragraph (a) of this section is applicable to returns and claims for refund filed, and advice provided, after December 31, 2008. [Reg. § 54.6694-1.]

☐ [*T.D.* 9436, 12-15-2008.]

[Reg. § 55.6694-1]

§ 55.6694-1. Section 6694 penalties applicable to tax return preparer.—(a) *In general.*—For general definitions regarding section 6694 penalties applicable to preparers of tax returns or claims for refund of tax under chapter 44 of Subtitle D see § 1.6694-1 of this chapter.

(b) *Effective/applicability date.*—Paragraph (a) of this section is applicable to returns and claims for refund filed, and advice provided, after December 31, 2008. [Reg. § 55.6694-1.]

☐ [*T.D.* 9436, 12-15-2008.]

[Reg. § 56.6694-1]

§ 56.6694-1. Section 6694 penalties applicable to tax return preparer.—(a) *In general.*—For general definitions regarding section 6694 penalties applicable to preparers of tax returns or claims for refund of tax under chapter 41 of subtitle D see § 1.6694-1 of this chapter.

(b) *Effective/applicability date.*—Paragraph (a) of this section is applicable to returns and claims for refund filed, and advice provided, after December 31, 2008. [Reg. § 56.6694-1.]

☐ [*T.D.* 9436, 12-15-2008.]

[Reg. § 156.6694-1]

§ 156.6694-1. Section 6694 penalties applicable to tax return preparer.—(a) *In general.*—For general definitions regarding section 6694 penalties applicable to preparers of tax returns or claims for refund for tax under section 5881 of the Internal Revenue Code, see § 1.6694-1 of this chapter.

(b) *Effective/applicability date.*—Paragraph (a) of this section is applicable to returns and claims for refund filed, and advice provided, after December 31, 2008. [Reg. § 156.6694-1.]

☐ [*T.D.* 9436, 12-15-2008.]

[Reg. § 157.6694-1]

§ 157.6694-1. Section 6694 penalties applicable to tax return preparer.—(a) *In general.*—For general definitions regarding section 6694 penalties applicable to preparers of tax returns or claims for refund for tax under section 5891 of the Internal Revenue Code see § 1.6694-1 of this chapter.

(b) *Effective/applicability date.*—Paragraph (a) of this section is applicable to returns and claims

for refund filed, and advice provided, after December 31, 2008. [Reg. § 157.6694-1.]

☐ [*T.D.* 9436, 12-15-2008.]

[Reg. § 1.6694-2]

§ 1.6694-2. Penalty for understatement due to an unreasonable position.—(a) *In general.*—(1) *Proscribed conduct.*—Except as otherwise provided in this section, a tax return preparer is liable for a penalty under section 6694(a) equal to the greater of $1,000 or 50 percent of the income derived (or to be derived) by the tax return preparer for any return or claim for refund that it prepares that results in an understatement of liability due to a position if the tax return preparer knew (or reasonably should have known) of the position and either—

(i) The position is with respect to a tax shelter (as defined in section 6662(d)(2)(C)(ii)) or a reportable transaction to which section 6662A applies, and it was not reasonable to believe that the position would more likely than not be sustained on its merits;

(ii) The position was not disclosed as provided in this section, the position is not with respect to a tax shelter (as defined in section 6662(d)(2)(C)(ii)) or a reportable transaction to which section 6662A applies, and there was not substantial authority for the position; or

(iii) The position (other than a position with respect to a tax shelter or a reportable transaction to which section 6662A applies) was disclosed as provided in this section but there was no reasonable basis for the position.

(2) *Special rule for corporations, partnerships, and other firms.*—A firm that employs a tax return preparer subject to a penalty under section 6694(a) (or a firm of which the individual tax return preparer is a partner, member, shareholder or other equity holder) is also subject to penalty if, and only if—

(i) One or more members of the principal management (or principal officers) of the firm or a branch office participated in or knew of the conduct proscribed by section 6694(a);

(ii) The corporation, partnership, or other firm entity failed to provide reasonable and appropriate procedures for review of the position for which the penalty is imposed; or

(iii) The corporation, partnership, or other firm entity disregarded its reasonable and appropriate review procedures through willfulness, recklessness, or gross indifference (including ignoring facts that would lead a person of reasonable prudence and competence to investigate or ascertain) in the formulation of the advice, or the preparation of the return or claim for refund, that included the position for which the penalty is imposed.

(b) *Reasonable to believe that the position would more likely than not be sustained on its merits.*—(1) *In general.*—If a position is with respect to a tax shelter (as defined in section 6662(d)(2)(C)(ii)) or a reportable transaction to which section 6662A applies, it is "reasonable to believe that a position would more likely than not be sustained on its merits" if the tax return preparer analyzes the pertinent facts and authorities and, in reliance upon that analysis, reasonably concludes in good faith that the position has a greater than 50 percent likelihood of being sustained on its merits. In reaching this conclusion, the possibility that the position will not be challenged by the Internal Revenue Service (IRS) (for example, because the taxpayer's return may not be audited or because the issue may not be raised on audit) is not to be taken into account. The analysis prescribed by §1.6662-4(d)(3)(ii) (or any successor provision) for purposes of determining whether substantial authority is present applies for purposes of determining whether the more likely than not standard is satisfied. Whether a tax return preparer meets this standard will be determined based upon all facts and circumstances, including the tax return preparer's diligence. In determining the level of diligence in a particular situation, the tax return preparer's experience with the area of Federal tax law and familiarity with the taxpayer's affairs, as well as the complexity of the issues and facts, will be taken into account. A tax return preparer may reasonably believe that a position more likely than not would be sustained on its merits despite the absence of other types of authority if the position is supported by a well-reasoned construction of the applicable statutory provision. For purposes of determining whether it is reasonable to believe that the position would more likely than not be sustained on the merits, a tax return preparer may rely in good faith without verification upon information furnished by the taxpayer and information and advice furnished by another advisor, another tax return preparer, or other party (including another advisor or tax return preparer at the tax return preparer's firm), as provided in §§1.6694-1(e) and 1.6694-2(e)(5).

(2) *Authorities.*—The authorities considered in determining whether a position satisfies the more likely than not standard are those authorities provided in §1.6662-4(d)(3)(iii) (or any successor provision).

(3) *Written determinations.*—The tax return preparer may avoid the section 6694(a) penalty by taking the position that the tax return preparer reasonably believed that the taxpayer's position satisfies the "more likely than not" standard if the taxpayer is the subject of a "written determination" as provided in §1.6662-4(d)(3)(iv)(A).

(4) *Taxpayer's jurisdiction.*—The applicability of court cases to the taxpayer by reason of the taxpayer's residence in a particular jurisdiction is not taken into account in determining whether it is reasonable to believe that the position would more likely than not be sustained on the merits. Notwithstanding the preceding sentence, the tax return preparer may reasonably believe that the position would more likely than not be sustained on the merits if the position is supported by

controlling precedent of a United States Court of Appeals to which the taxpayer has a right of appeal with respect to the item.

(5) *When "more likely than not" standard must be satisfied.*—For purposes of this section, the requirement that a position satisfies the "more likely than not" standard must be satisfied on the date the return is deemed prepared, as prescribed by §1.6694-1(a)(2).

(c) [Reserved].

(d) *Exception for adequate disclosure of positions with a reasonable basis.*—(1) *In general.*—The section 6694(a) penalty will not be imposed on a tax return preparer if the position taken (other than a position with respect to a tax shelter or a reportable transaction to which section 6662A applies) has a reasonable basis and is adequately disclosed within the meaning of paragraph (c)(3) of this section. For an exception to the section 6694(a) penalty for reasonable cause and good faith, see paragraph (e) of this section.

(2) *Reasonable basis.*—For purposes of this section, "reasonable basis" has the same meaning as in §1.6662-3(b)(3) or any successor provision of the accuracy-related penalty regulations. For purposes of determining whether the tax return preparer has a reasonable basis for a position, a tax return preparer may rely in good faith without verification upon information furnished by the taxpayer and information and advice furnished by another advisor, another tax return preparer, or other party (including another advisor or tax return preparer at the tax return preparer's firm), as provided in §§1.6694-1(e) and 1.6694-2(e)(5).

(3) *Adequate disclosure.*—(i) *Signing tax return preparers.*—In the case of a signing tax return preparer within the meaning of §301.7701-15(b)(1) of this chapter, disclosure of a position (other than a position with respect to a tax shelter or a reportable transaction to which section 6662A applies) for which there is a reasonable basis but for which there is not substantial authority is adequate if the tax return preparer meets any of the following standards:

(A) The position is disclosed in accordance with §1.6662-4(f) (which permits disclosure on a properly completed and filed Form 8275, "Disclosure Statement," or Form 8275-R, "Regulation Disclosure Statement," as appropriate, or on the tax return in accordance with the annual revenue procedure described in §1.6662-4(f)(2));

(B) The tax return preparer provides the taxpayer with the prepared tax return that includes the disclosure in accordance with §1.6662-4(f); or

(C) For returns or claims for refund that are subject to penalties pursuant to section 6662 other than the accuracy-related penalty attributable to a substantial understatement of income tax under section 6662(b)(2) and (d), the tax return preparer advises the taxpayer of the penalty standards applicable to the taxpayer under section 6662. The tax return preparer must also contemporaneously document the advice in the tax return preparer's files.

(ii) *Nonsigning tax return preparers.*—In the case of a nonsigning tax return preparer within the meaning of § 301.7701-15(b)(2) of this chapter, disclosure of a position (other than a position with respect to a tax shelter or a reportable transaction to which section 6662A applies) that satisfies the reasonable basis standard but does not satisfy the substantial authority standard is adequate if the position is disclosed in accordance with § 1.6662-4(f) (which permits disclosure on a properly completed and filed Form 8275 or Form 8275-R, as applicable, or on the return in accordance with an annual revenue procedure described in § 1.6662-4(f)(2)). In addition, disclosure of a position is adequate in the case of a nonsigning tax return preparer if, with respect to that position, the tax return preparer complies with the provisions of paragraph (d)(3)(ii)(A) or (B) of this section, whichever is applicable.

(A) *Advice to taxpayers.*—If a nonsigning tax return preparer provides advice to the taxpayer with respect to a position (other than a position with respect to a tax shelter or a reportable transaction to which section 6662A applies) for which there is a reasonable basis but for which there is not substantial authority, disclosure of that position is adequate if the tax return preparer advises the taxpayer of any opportunity to avoid penalties under section 6662 that could apply to the position, if relevant, and of the standards for disclosure to the extent applicable. The tax return preparer must also contemporaneously document the advice in the tax return preparer's files. The contemporaneous documentation should reflect that the affected taxpayer has been advised by a tax return preparer in the firm of the potential penalties and the opportunity to avoid penalty through disclosure.

(B) *Advice to another tax return preparer.*—If a nonsigning tax return preparer provides advice to another tax return preparer with respect to a position (other than a position with respect to a tax shelter or a reportable transaction to which section 6662A applies) for which there is a reasonable basis but for which there is not substantial authority, disclosure of that position is adequate if the tax return preparer advises the other tax return preparer that disclosure under section 6694(a) may be required. The tax return preparer must also contemporaneously document the advice in the tax return preparer's files. The contemporaneous documentation should reflect that the tax return preparer outside the firm has been advised that disclosure under section 6694(a) may be required. If the advice is to another nonsigning tax return preparer within the same firm, contemporaneous documentation is satisfied if there is a single instance of contemporaneous documentation within the firm.

(iii) *Requirements for advice.*—For purposes of satisfying the disclosure standards of paragraphs (d)(3)(i)(C) and (ii) of this section, each return position for which there is a reasonable basis but for which there is not substantial authority must be addressed by the tax return preparer. The advice to the taxpayer with respect to each position, therefore, must be particular to the taxpayer and tailored to the taxpayer's facts and circumstances. The tax return preparer is required to contemporaneously document the fact that the advice was provided. There is no general pro forma language or special format required for a tax return preparer to comply with these rules. A general disclaimer will not satisfy the requirement that the tax return preparer provide and contemporaneously document advice regarding the likelihood that a position will be sustained on the merits and the potential application of penalties as a result of that position. Tax return preparers, however, may rely on established forms or templates in advising clients regarding the operation of the penalty provisions of the Internal Revenue Code. A tax return preparer may choose to comply with the documentation standard in one document addressing each position or in multiple documents addressing all of the positions.

(iv) *Pass-through entities.*—Disclosure in the case of items attributable to a pass-through entity is adequate if made at the entity level in accordance with the rules in § 1.6662-4(f)(5) or at the entity level in accordance with the rules in paragraphs (d)(3)(i) or (ii) of this section.

(v) *Examples.*—The provisions of paragraph (d)(3) of this section are illustrated by the following examples:

Example 1. An individual taxpayer hires Accountant R to prepare its income tax return. A particular position taken on the tax return does not have substantial authority although there is a reasonable basis for the position. The position is not with respect to a tax shelter or a reportable transaction to which section 6662A applies. R prepares and signs the tax return and provides the taxpayer with the prepared tax return that includes the Form 8275, "Disclosure Statement," disclosing the position taken on the tax return. The individual taxpayer signs and files the tax return without disclosing the position. The IRS later challenges the position taken on the tax return, resulting in an understatement of liability. R is not subject to a penalty under section 6694.

Example 2. Attorney S advises a large corporate taxpayer concerning the proper treatment of complex entries on the corporate taxpayer's tax return. S has reason to know that the tax attributable to the entries is a substantial portion of the tax required to be shown on the tax return within the meaning of § 301.7701-15(b)(3). When providing the advice, S concludes that one position does not have substantial authority, although the position meets the reasonable basis standard. The position is not with respect to a tax shelter or a reportable transaction to which section 6662A applies. S advises the corporate taxpayer that the position lacks substantial authority and the taxpayer may be subject to an accuracy-related penalty under section 6662 unless the position is disclosed in a disclosure statement included in the return. S also documents the fact that this advice was contemporaneously provided to the corporate taxpayer at the time the advice was provided. Neither S nor any other attorney within S's firm signs the corporate taxpayer's return as a tax return preparer, but the advice by S constitutes preparation of a substantial portion of the tax return, and S is the individual with overall supervisory responsibility for the position giving rise to the understatement. Thus, S is a tax return preparer for purposes of section 6694. S, however, will not be subject to a penalty under section 6694.

(e) *Exception for reasonable cause and good faith.*—The penalty under section 6694(a) will not be imposed if, considering all the facts and circumstances, it is determined that the understatement was due to reasonable cause and that the tax return preparer acted in good faith. Factors to consider include:

(1) *Nature of the error causing the understatement.*—The error resulted from a provision that was complex, uncommon, or highly technical, and a competent tax return preparer of tax returns or claims for refund of the type at issue reasonably could have made the error. The reasonable cause and good faith exception, however, does not apply to an error that would have been apparent from a general review of the return or claim for refund by the tax return preparer.

(2) *Frequency of errors.*—The understatement was the result of an isolated error (such as an inadvertent mathematical or clerical error) rather than a number of errors. Although the reasonable cause and good faith exception generally applies to an isolated error, it does not apply if the isolated error is so obvious, flagrant, or material that it should have been discovered during a review of the return or claim for refund. Furthermore, the reasonable cause and good faith exception does not apply if there is a pattern of errors on a return or claim for refund even though any one error, in isolation, would have qualified for the reasonable cause and good faith exception.

(3) *Materiality of errors.*—The understatement was not material in relation to the correct tax liability. The reasonable cause and good faith exception generally applies if the understatement is of a relatively immaterial amount. Nevertheless, even an immaterial understatement may not qualify for the reasonable cause and good faith exception if the error or errors creating the understatement are sufficiently obvious or numerous.

(4) *Tax return preparer's normal office practice.*—The tax return preparer's normal office practice, when considered together with other facts and circumstances, such as the knowledge of the tax return preparer, indicates that the error in question would occur rarely and the normal office practice was followed in preparing the return or claim for refund in question. Such a normal office practice must be a system for promoting accuracy and consistency in the preparation of returns or claims for refund and generally would include, in the case of a signing tax return preparer, checklists, methods for obtaining necessary information from the taxpayer, a review of the prior year's return, and review procedures. Notwithstanding these rules, the reasonable cause and good faith exception does not apply if there is a flagrant error on a return or claim for refund, a pattern of errors on a return or claim for refund, or a repetition of the same or similar errors on numerous returns or claims for refund.

(5) *Reliance on advice of others.*—For purposes of demonstrating reasonable cause and good faith, a tax return preparer may rely without verification upon advice and information furnished by the taxpayer and information and advice furnished by another advisor, another tax return preparer or other party, as provided in § 1.6694-1(e). The tax return preparer may rely in good faith on the advice of, or schedules or other documents prepared by, the taxpayer, another advisor, another tax return preparer, or other party (including another advisor or tax return preparer at the tax return preparer's firm), who the tax return preparer had reason to believe was competent to render the advice or other information. The advice or information may be written or oral, but in either case the burden of establishing that the advice or information was received is on the tax return preparer. A tax return preparer is not considered to have relied in good faith if—

(i) The advice or information is unreasonable on its face;

(ii) The tax return preparer knew or should have known that the other party providing the advice or information was not aware of all relevant facts; or

(iii) The tax return preparer knew or should have known (given the nature of the tax return preparer's practice), at the time the return or claim for refund was prepared, that the advice or information was no longer reliable due to developments in the law since the time the advice was given.

(6) *Reliance on generally accepted administrative or industry practice.*—The tax return preparer reasonably relied in good faith on generally accepted administrative or industry practice in taking the position that resulted in the understatement. A tax return preparer is not considered to have relied in good faith if the tax return preparer knew or should have known (given the nature of the tax return preparer's practice), at the time the return or claim for refund was prepared, that the administrative or industry practice was no longer reliable due to developments in the law or IRS administrative practice since the time the practice was developed.

Reg. § 1.6694-2(e)

(f) *Effective/applicability date.*—This section is applicable to returns and claims for refund filed, and advice provided, after December 31, 2008. [Reg. § 1.6694-2.]

☐ [*T.D.* 7519, 11-17-77. *Amended by T.D.* 8382, 12-30-91 *and T.D.* 9436, 12-15-2008 (*corrected* 1-28-2009).]

[Reg. § 20.6694-2]

§ 20.6694-2. Penalties for understatement due to an unreasonable position.—(a) *In general.*—A person who is a tax return preparer of any return or claim for refund of estate tax under chapter 11 of subtitle B of the Internal Revenue Code (Code) shall be subject to penalties under section 6694(a) of the Code in the manner stated in § 1.6694-2 of this chapter.

(b) *Effective/applicability date.*—This section is applicable to returns and claims for refund filed, and advice provided, after December 31, 2008. [Reg. § 20.6694-2.]

☐ [*T.D.* 9436, 12-15-2008.]

[Reg. § 25.6694-2]

§ 25.6694-2. Penalties for understatement due to an unreasonable position.—(a) *In general.*—A person who is a tax return preparer of any return or claim for refund of gift tax under chapter 12 of subtitle B of the Internal Revenue Code (Code) shall be subject to penalties under section 6694(a) of the Code in the manner stated in § 1.6694-2 of this chapter.

(b) *Effective/applicability date.*—This section is applicable to returns and claims for refund filed, and advice provided, after December 31, 2008. [Reg. § 25.6694-2.]

☐ [*T.D.* 9436, 12-15-2008.]

[Reg. § 26.6694-2]

§ 26.6694-2. Penalties for understatement due to an unreasonable position.—(a) *In general.*—A person who is a tax return preparer of any return or claim for refund of generationskipping transfer tax under chapter 13 of subtitle B of the Internal Revenue Code (Code) shall be subject to penalties under section 6694(a) of the Code in the manner stated in § 1.6694-2 of this chapter.

(b) *Effective/applicability date.*—This section is applicable to returns and claims for refund filed, and advice provided, after December 31, 2008. [Reg. § 26.6694-2.]

☐ [*T.D.* 9436, 12-15-2008.]

[Reg. § 31.6694-2]

§ 31.6694-2. Penalties for understatement due to an unreasonable position.—(a) *In general.*—A person who is a tax return preparer of any return or claim for refund of employment tax under chapters 21 through 25 of subtitle C of the Internal Revenue Code (Code) shall be subject to penalties under section 6694(a) of the Code in the manner stated in § 1.6694-2 of this chapter.

(b) *Effective/applicability date.*—This section is applicable to returns and claims for refund filed, and advice provided, after December 31, 2008. [Reg. § 31.6694-2.]

☐ [*T.D.* 9436, 12-15-2008.]

[Reg. § 40.6694-2]

§ 40.6694-2. Penalties for understatement due to an unreasonable position.—(a) *In general.*—A person who is a tax return preparer of any return or claim for refund of any tax to which this part 40 applies shall be subject to penalties under section 6694(a) in the manner stated in § 1.6694-2 of this chapter.

(b) *Effective/applicability date.*—This section is applicable to returns and claims for refund filed, and advice provided, after December 31, 2008. [Reg. § 40.6694-2.]

☐ [*T.D.* 9436, 12-15-2008 (*corrected* 1-28-2009).]

[Reg. § 41.6694-2]

§ 41.6694-2. Penalties for understatement due to an unreasonable position.—(a) *In general.*—A person who is a tax return preparer of any return or claim for refund of excise tax under section 4481 shall be subject to penalties under section 6694(a) in the manner stated in § 1.6694-2 of this chapter.

(b) *Effective/applicability date.*—This section is applicable to returns and claims for refund filed, and advice provided, after December 31, 2008. [Reg. § 41.6694-2.]

☐ [*T.D.* 9436, 12-15-2008.]

[Reg. § 44.6694-2]

§ 44.6694-2. Penalties for understatement due to an unreasonable position.—(a) *In general.*—A person who is a tax return preparer of any return or claim for refund of tax on wagers under sections 4401 or 4411 shall be subject to penalties under section 6694(a) in the manner stated in § 1.6694-2 of this chapter.

(b) *Effective/applicability date.*—This section is applicable to returns and claims for refund filed, and advice provided, after December 31, 2008. [Reg. § 44.6694-2.]

☐ [*T.D.* 9436, 12-15-2008.]

[Reg. § 53.6694-2]

§ 53.6694-2. Penalties for understatement due to an unreasonable position.—(a) *In general.*—A person who is a tax return preparer of any return or claim for refund of tax under Chapter 42 of the Internal Revenue Code (Code) shall be subject to penalties under section 6694(a) of the Code in the manner stated in § 1.6694-2 of this chapter.

(b) *Effective/applicability date.*—This section is applicable to returns and claims for refund filed, and advice provided, after December 31, 2008. [Reg. § 53.6694-2.]

☐ [*T.D.* 9436, 12-15-2008.]

[Reg. § 54.6694-2]

§ 54.6694-2. Penalties for understatement due to an unreasonable position.—(a) *In general.*—A person who is a tax return preparer of any return or claim for refund of tax under chapter 43 of subtitle D of the Internal Revenue Code (Code) shall be subject to penalties under section 6694(a) of the Code in the manner stated in § 1.6694-2 of this chapter.

(b) *Effective/applicability date.*—This section is applicable to returns and claims for refund filed, and advice provided, after December 31, 2008. [Reg. § 54.6694-2.]

☐ [*T.D.* 9436, 12-15-2008.]

[Reg. § 55.6694-2]

§ 55.6694-2. Penalties for understatement due to an unreasonable position.—(a) *In general.*—A person who is a tax return preparer of any return or claim for refund of excise tax under chapter 44 of subtitle D of the Internal Revenue Code (Code) shall be subject to penalties under section 6694(a) of the Code in the manner stated in § 1.6694-2 of this chapter.

(b) *Effective/applicability date.*—This section is applicable to returns and claims for refund filed, and advice provided, after December 31, 2008. [Reg. § 55.6694-2.]

☐ [*T.D.* 9436, 12-15-2008.]

[Reg. § 56.6694-2]

§ 56.6694-2. Penalties for understatement due to an unreasonable position.—(a) *In general.*—A person who is a tax return preparer of any return or claim for refund of excise tax under chapter 41 of subtitle D of the Internal Revenue Code (Code) shall be subject to penalties under section 6694(a) of the Code in the manner stated in § 1.6694-2 of this chapter.

(b) *Effective/applicability date.*—This section is applicable to returns and claims for refund filed, and advice provided, after December 31, 2008. [Reg. § 56.6694-2.]

☐ [*T.D.* 9436, 12-15-2008.]

[Reg. § 156.6694-2]

§ 156.6694-2. Penalties for understatement due to an unreasonable position.—(a) *In general.*—A person who is a tax return preparer of any return or claim for refund of tax under section 5881 of the Internal Revenue Code (Code) shall be subject to penalties under section 6694(a) of the Code in the manner stated in § 1.6694-2 of this chapter.

(b) *Effective/applicability date.*—This section is applicable to returns and claims for refund filed, and advice provided, after December 31, 2008. [Reg. § 156.6694-2.]

☐ [*T.D.* 9436, 12-15-2008.]

[Reg. § 157.6694-2]

§ 157.6694-2. Penalties for understatement due to an unreasonable position.—(a) *In general.*—A person who is a tax return preparer of any return or claim for refund of tax under section 5891 of the Internal Revenue Code (Code) shall be subject to penalties under section 6694(a) of the Code in the manner stated in § 1.6694-2 of this chapter.

(b) *Effective/applicability date.*—This section is applicable to returns and claims for refund filed, and advice provided, after December 31, 2008. [Reg. § 157.6694-2.]

☐ [*T.D.* 9436, 12-15-2008.]

[Reg. § 1.6694-3]

§ 1.6694-3. Penalty for understatement due to willful, reckless, or intentional conduct.—(a) *In general.*—(1) *Proscribed conduct.*—A tax return preparer is liable for a penalty under section 6694(b) equal to the greater of $5,000 or 50 percent of the income derived (or to be derived) by the tax return preparer if any part of an understatement of liability for a return or claim for refund that is prepared is due to—

(i) A willful attempt by a tax return preparer to understate in any manner the liability for tax on the return or claim for refund; or

(ii) Any reckless or intentional disregard of rules or regulations by a tax return preparer.

(2) *Special rule for corporations, partnerships, and other firms.*—A firm that employs a tax return preparer subject to a penalty under section 6694(b) (or a firm of which the individual tax return preparer is a partner, member, shareholder or other equity holder) is also subject to penalty if, and only if—

(i) One or more members of the principal management (or principal officers) of the firm or a branch office participated in or knew of the conduct proscribed by section 6694(b);

(ii) The corporation, partnership, or other firm entity failed to provide reasonable and appropriate procedures for review of the position for which the penalty is imposed; or

(iii) The corporation, partnership, or other firm entity disregarded its reasonable and appropriate review procedures through willfulness, recklessness, or gross indifference (including ignoring facts that would lead a person of reasonable prudence and competence to investigate or ascertain) in the formulation of the advice, or the preparation of the return or claim for refund, that included the position for which the penalty is imposed.

(b) *Willful attempt to understate liability.*—A preparer is considered to have willfully attempted to understate liability if the preparer disregards, in an attempt wrongfully to reduce the tax liability of the taxpayer, information furnished by the taxpayer or other persons. For example, if a preparer disregards information concerning certain items of taxable income furnished by the taxpayer or other persons, the preparer is subject to the penalty. Similarly, if a taxpayer states to a preparer that the taxpayer has only two dependents, and the preparer reports six dependents on the return, the preparer is subject to the penalty.

(c) *Reckless or intentional disregard.*—(1) Except as provided in paragraphs (c)(2) and (c)(3) of this section, a preparer is considered to have recklessly or intentionally disregarded a rule or regulation if the preparer takes a position on the return or claim for refund that is contrary to a rule or regulation (as defined in paragraph (f)[(e)] of this section) and the preparer knows of, or is reckless in not knowing of, the rule or regulation in question. A preparer is reckless in not knowing of a rule or regulation if the preparer makes little or no effort to determine whether a rule or regulation exists, under circumstances which demonstrate a substantial deviation from the standard of conduct that a reasonable preparer would observe in the situation.

(2) A tax return preparer is not considered to have recklessly or intentionally disregarded a rule or regulation if the position contrary to the rule or regulation has a reasonable basis as defined in § 1.6694-2(d)(2) and is adequately disclosed in accordance with § § 1.6694-2(d)(3)(i)(A) or (C) or 1.6694-2(d)(3)(ii). In the case of a position contrary to a regulation, the position must represent a good faith challenge to the validity of the regulation and, when disclosed in accordance with § § 1.6694-2(d)(3)(i)(A) or (C) or 1.6694-2(d)(3)(ii), the tax return preparer must identify the regulation being challenged. For purposes of this section, disclosure on the return in accordance with an annual revenue procedure under § 1.6662-4(f)(2) is not applicable.

(3) In the case of a position contrary to a revenue ruling or notice (other than a notice of proposed rulemaking) published by the Internal Revenue Service in the Internal Revenue Bulletin, a tax return preparer also is not considered to have recklessly or intentionally disregarded the ruling or notice if the position meets the substantial authority standard described in § 1.6662-4(d) and is not with respect to a reportable transaction to which section 6662A applies.

(d) *Examples.*—The provisions of paragraphs (b) and (c) of this section are illustrated by the following examples:

Example 1. A taxpayer provided Preparer T with detailed check registers reflecting personal and business expenses. One of the expenses was for domestic help, and this expense was identified as personal on the check register. T knowingly deducted the expenses of the taxpayer's domestic help as wages paid in the taxpayer's business. T is subject to the penalty under section 6694(b).

Example 2. A taxpayer provided Preparer U with detailed check registers to compute the taxpayer's expenses. U, however, knowingly overstated the expenses on the return. After adjustments by the examiner, the tax liability increased significantly. Because U disregarded information provided in the check registers, U is subject to the penalty under section 6694(b).

Example 3. Preparer V prepares a taxpayer's return in 2009 and encounters certain expenses incurred in the purchase of a business. Final regulations provide that such expenses incurred in the purchase of a business must be capitalized. One U.S. Tax Court case decided in 2006 has expressly invalidated that portion of the regulations. There are no courts that ruled favorably with respect to the validity of that portion of the regulations and there are no other authorities existing on the issue. Under these facts, V will have a reasonable basis for the position as defined in § 1.6694-2(d)(2) and will not be subject to the section 6694(b) penalty if the position is adequately disclosed in accordance with paragraph (c)(2) of this section because the position represents a good faith challenge to the validity of the regulations.

(e) *Rules or regulations.*—The term *rules or regulations* includes the provisions of the Internal Revenue Code (Code), temporary or final Treasury regulations issued under the Code, and revenue rulings or notices (other than notices of proposed rulemaking) issued by the Internal Revenue Service and published in the Internal Revenue Bulletin.

(f) *Section 6694(b) penalty reduced by section 6694(a) penalty.*—The amount of any penalty to which a tax return preparer may be subject under section 6694(b) for a return or claim for refund is reduced by any amount assessed and collected against the tax return preparer under section 6694(a) for the same position on a return or claim for refund.

(g) *Effective/applicability date.*—This section is applicable to returns and claims for refund filed, and advice provided, after December 31, 2008.

(h) *Burden of proof.*—In any proceeding with respect to the penalty imposed by section 6694(b), the Government bears the burden of proof on the issue of whether the preparer willfully attempted to understate the liability for tax. See section 7427. The preparer bears the burden of proof on such other issues as whether—

(1) The preparer recklessly or intentionally disregarded a rule or regulation;

(2) A position contrary to a regulation represents a good faith challenge to the validity of the regulation; and

(3) Disclosure was adequately made in accordance with paragraph (e) of this section. [Reg. § 1.6694-3.]

☐ [*T.D.* 8382, 12-30-91. *Amended by T.D.* 9436, 12-15-2008 (*corrected* 1-28-2009).]

[Reg. § 20.6694-3]

§ 20.6694-3. Penalty for understatement due to willful, reckless, or intentional conduct.— (a) *In general.*—A person who is a tax return preparer of any return or claim for refund of estate tax under chapter 11 of subtitle B of the Internal Revenue Code (Code) shall be subject to penalties under section 6694(b) of the Code in the manner stated in § 1.6694-3 of this chapter.

(b) *Effective/applicability date.*—This section is applicable to returns and claims for refund filed, and advice provided, after December 31, 2008. [Reg. § 20.6694-3.]

☐ [*T.D.* 9436, 12-15-2008.]

[Reg. § 25.6694-3]

§ 25.6694-3. Penalty for understatement due to willful, reckless, or intentional conduct.— (a) *In general.*—A person who is a tax return preparer of any return or claim for refund of gift tax under chapter 12 of subtitle B of the Internal Revenue Code (Code) shall be subject to penalties under section 6694(b) of the Code in the manner stated in § 1.6694-3 of this chapter.

(b) *Effective/applicability date.*—This section is applicable to returns and claims for refund filed, and advice provided, after December 31, 2008. [Reg. § 25.6694-3.]

☐ [*T.D.* 9436, 12-15-2008.]

[Reg. § 26.6694-3]

§ 26.6694-3. Penalty for understatement due to willful, reckless, or intentional conduct.— (a) *In general.*—A person who is a tax return preparer of any return or claim for refund of generation-skipping transfer tax under chapter 13 of subtitle B of the Internal Revenue Code (Code) shall be subject to penalties under section 6694(b) of the Code in the manner stated in § 1.6694-3 of this chapter.

(b) *Effective/applicability date.*—This section is applicable to returns and claims for refund filed, and advice provided, after December 31, 2008. [Reg. § 26.6694-3.]

☐ [*T.D.* 9436, 12-15-2008.]

[Reg. § 31.6694-3]

§ 31.6694-3. Penalty for understatement due to willful, reckless, or intentional conduct.— (a) *In general.*—A person who is a tax return preparer of any return or claim for refund of employment tax under chapters 21 through 25 of subtitle C of the Internal Revenue Code (Code) shall be subject to penalties under section 6694(b) of the Code in the manner stated in § 1.6694-3 of this chapter.

(b) *Effective/applicability date.*—This section is applicable to returns and claims for refund filed, and advice provided, after December 31, 2008. [Reg. § 31.6694-3.]

☐ [*T.D.* 9436, 12-15-2008 (*corrected* 1-28-2009).]

[Reg. § 40.6694-3]

§ 40.6694-3. Penalty for understatement due to willful, reckless, or intentional conduct.— (a) *In general.*—A person who is a tax return preparer of any return or claim for refund of any tax to which this part 40 applies shall be subject to penalties under section 6694(b) in the manner stated in § 1.6694-3 of this chapter.

(b) *Effective/applicability date.*—This section is applicable to returns and claims for refund filed,

and advice provided, after December 31, 2008. [Reg. § 40.6694-3.]

☐ [*T.D.* 9436, 12-15-2008 (*corrected* 1-28-2009).]

[Reg. § 41.6694-3]

§ 41.6694-3. Penalty for understatement due to willful, reckless, or intentional conduct.— (a) *In general.*—A person who is a tax return preparer of any return or claim for refund of excise tax under section 4481 shall be subject to penalties under section 6694(b) in the manner stated in § 1.6694-3 of this chapter.

(b) *Effective/applicability date.*—This section is applicable to returns and claims for refund filed, and advice provided, after December 31, 2008. [Reg. § 41.6694-3.]

☐ [*T.D.* 9436, 12-15-2008.]

[Reg. § 44.6694-3]

§ 44.6694-3. Penalty for understatement due to willful, reckless, or intentional conduct.— (a) *In general.*—A person who is a tax return preparer of any return or claim for refund of tax on wagers under sections 4401 or 4411 shall be subject to penalties under section 6694(b) in the manner stated in § 1.6694-3 of this chapter.

(b) *Effective/applicability date.*—This section is applicable to returns and claims for refund filed, and advice provided, after December 31, 2008. [Reg. § 44.6694-3.]

☐ [*T.D.* 9436, 12-15-2008.]

[Reg. § 53.6694-3]

§ 53.6694-3. Penalty for understatement due to willful, reckless, or intentional conduct.— (a) *In general.*—A person who is a tax return preparer of any return or claim for refund of tax under Chapter 42 of the Internal Revenue Code (Code) shall be subject to penalties under section 6694(b) of the Code in the manner stated in § 1.6694-3 of this chapter.

(b) *Effective/applicability date.*—This section is applicable to returns and claims for refund filed, and advice provided, after December 31, 2008. [Reg. § 53.6694-3.]

☐ [*T.D.* 9436, 12-15-2008.]

[Reg. § 54.6694-3]

§ 54.6694-3. Penalty for understatement due to willful, reckless, or intentional conduct.— (a) *In general.*—A person who is a tax return preparer of any return or claim for refund of excise tax under chapter 43 of subtitle D of the Internal Revenue Code (Code) shall be subject to penalties under section 6694(b) of the Code in the manner stated in § 1.6694-3 of this chapter.

(b) *Effective/applicability date.*—This section is applicable to returns and claims for refund filed, and advice provided, after December 31, 2008. [Reg. § 54.6694-3.]

☐ [*T.D.* 9436, 12-15-2008.]

[Reg. §55.6694-3]

§55.6694-3. Penalty for understatement due to willful, reckless, or intentional conduct.— (a) *In general.*—A person who is a tax return preparer of any return or claim for refund of tax under chapter 44 of subtitle D of the Internal Revenue Code (Code) shall be subject to penalties under section 6694(b) of the Code in the manner stated in §1.6694-3 of this chapter.

(b) *Effective/applicability date.*—This section is applicable to returns and claims for refund filed, and advice provided, after December 31, 2008. [Reg. §55.6694-3.]

☐ [*T.D.* 9436, 12-15-2008.]

[Reg. §56.6694-3]

§56.6694-3. Penalty for understatement due to willful, reckless, or intentional conduct.— (a) *In general.*—A person who is a tax return preparer of any return or claim for refund of tax under chapter 41 of subtitle D of the Internal Revenue Code (Code) shall be subject to penalties under section 6694(b) of the Code in the manner stated in §1.6694-3 of this chapter.

(b) *Effective/applicability date.*—This section is applicable to returns and claims for refund filed, and advice provided, after December 31, 2008. [Reg. §56.6694-3.]

☐ [*T.D.* 9436, 12-15-2008.]

[Reg. §156.6694-3]

§156.6694-3. Penalty for understatement due to willful, reckless, or intentional conduct.— (a) *In general.*—A person who is a tax return preparer of any return or claim for refund of tax under section 5881 of the Internal Revenue Code (Code) shall be subject to penalties under section 6694(b) of the Code in the manner stated in §1.6694-3 of this chapter.

(b) *Effective/applicability date.*—This section is applicable to returns and claims for refund filed, and advice provided, after December 31, 2008. [Reg. §156.6694-3.]

☐ [*T.D.* 9436, 12-15-2008.]

[Reg. §157.6694-3]

§157.6694-3. Penalty for understatement due to willful, reckless, or intentional conduct.— (a) *In general.*—A person who is a tax return preparer of any return or claim for refund of tax under section 5891 of the Internal Revenue Code (Code) shall be subject to penalties under section 6694(b) of the Code in the manner stated in §1.6694-3 of this chapter.

(b) *Effective/applicability date.*—This section is applicable to returns and claims for refund filed, and advice provided, after December 31, 2008. [Reg. §157.6694-3.]

☐ [*T.D.* 9436, 12-15-2008.]

[Reg. §1.6694-4]

§1.6694-4. Extension of period of collection when tax return preparer pays 15 percent of a penalty for understatement of taxpayer's liability and certain other procedural matters.— (a) *In general.*—(1) The Internal Revenue Service (IRS) will investigate the preparation by a tax return preparer of a return of tax under the Internal Revenue Code (Code) or claim for refund of tax under the Code as described in §301.7701-15(b)(4) of this chapter, and will send a report of the examination to the tax return preparer before the assessment of either—

(i) A penalty for understating tax liability due to a position for which either it was not reasonable to believe that the position would more likely than not be sustained on its merits under section 6694(a) or no substantial authority, as applicable (or not a reasonable basis for disclosed positions); or

(ii) A penalty for willful understatement of liability or reckless or intentional disregard of rules or regulations under section 6694(b).

(2) Unless the period of limitations (if any) under section 6696(d) may expire without adequate opportunity for assessment, the IRS will also send, before assessment of either penalty, a 30-day letter to the tax return preparer notifying him of the proposed penalty or penalties and offering an opportunity to the tax return preparer to request further administrative consideration and a final administrative determination by the IRS concerning the assessment. If the tax return preparer then makes a timely request, assessment may not be made until the IRS makes a final administrative determination adverse to the tax return preparer.

(3) If the IRS assesses either of the two penalties described in section 6694(a) and section 6694(b), it will send to the tax return preparer a statement of notice and demand, separate from any notice of a tax deficiency, for payment of the amount assessed.

(4) Within 30 days after the day on which notice and demand of either of the two penalties described in section 6694(a) and section 6694(b) is made against the tax return preparer, the tax return preparer must either—

(i) Pay the entire amount assessed (and may file a claim for refund of the amount paid at any time not later than 3 years after the date of payment); or

(ii) Pay an amount which is not less than 15 percent of the entire amount assessed with respect to each return or claim for refund and file a claim for refund of the amount paid.

(5) If the tax return preparer pays an amount and files a claim for refund under paragraph (a)(4)(ii) of this section, the IRS may not make, begin, or prosecute a levy or proceeding in court for collection of the unpaid remainder of the amount assessed until the later of—

(i) A date which is more than 30 days after the earlier of—

(A) The day on which the tax return preparer's claim for refund is denied; or

(B) The expiration of 6 months after the day on which the tax return preparer filed the claim for refund; and

Reg. §1.6694-4(a)(5)(i)(B)

(ii) Final resolution of any proceeding begun as provided in paragraph (b) of this section.

(6) The IRS may counterclaim in any proceeding begun as provided in paragraph (b) of this section for the unpaid remainder of the amount assessed. Final resolution of a proceeding includes any settlement between the IRS and the tax return preparer, any final determination by a court (for which the period for appeal, if any, has expired) and, generally, the types of determinations provided under section 1313(a) (relating to taxpayer deficiencies). Notwithstanding section 7421(a) (relating to suits to restrain assessment or collection), the beginning of a levy or proceeding in court by the IRS in contravention of paragraph (a)(5) of this section may be enjoined by a proceeding in the proper court.

(b) *Preparer must bring suit in district court to determine liability for penalty.*—The IRS may proceed with collection of the amount of the penalty not paid under paragraph (a)(4)(ii) of this section if the preparer fails to begin a proceeding for refund in the appropriate United States district court within 30 days after the earlier of—

(1) The day on which the preparer's claim for refund filed under paragraph (a)(4)(ii) of this section is denied; or

(2) The expiration of 6 months after the day on which the preparer filed the claim for refund.

(c) *Suspension of running of period of limitations on collection.*—The running of the period of limitations provided in section 6502 on the collection by levy or by a proceeding in court of the unpaid amount of a penalty or penalties described in section 6694(a) or section 6694(b) is suspended for the period during which the IRS, under paragraph (a)(5) of this section, may not collect the unpaid amount of the penalty or penalties by levy or a proceeding in court.

(d) *Effective/applicability date.*—This section is applicable to returns and claims for refund filed, and advice provided, after December 31, 2008. [Reg. § 1.6694-4.]

□ [*T.D.* 8382, 12-30-91. *Amended by T.D.* 9436, 12-15-2008.]

[Reg. § 20.6694-4]

§ 20.6694-4. Extension of period of collection when preparer pays 15 percent of a penalty for understatement of taxpayer's liability and certain other procedural matters.—(a) *In general.*— For rules relating to the extension of the period of collection when a tax return preparer who prepared a return or claim for refund for estate tax under chapter 11 of subtitle B of the Internal Revenue Code pays 15 percent of a penalty for understatement of the taxpayer's liability, and procedural matters relating to the investigation, assessment and collection of the penalties under sections 6694(a) and (b), the rules under § 1.6694-4 of this chapter will apply.

(b) *Effective/applicability date.*—This section is applicable to returns and claims for refund filed, and advice provided, after December 31, 2008. [Reg. § 20.6694-4.]

□ [*T.D.* 9436, 12-15-2008.]

[Reg. § 25.6694-4]

§ 25.6694-4. Extension of period of collection when tax return preparer pays 15 percent of a penalty for understatement of taxpayer's liability and certain other procedural matters.— (a) *In general.*—For rules for the extension of period of collection when a tax return preparer who prepared a return or claim for refund for gift tax under chapter 12 of subtitle B of the Internal Revenue Code pays 15 percent of a penalty for understatement of taxpayer's liability, and procedural matters relating to the investigation, assessment and collection of the penalties under section 6694(a) and (b), the rules under § 1.6694-4 of this chapter will apply.

(b) *Effective/applicability date.*—This section is applicable to returns and claims for refund filed, and advice provided, after December 31, 2008. [Reg. § 25.6694-4.]

□ [*T.D.* 9436, 12-15-2008.]

[Reg. § 26.6694-4]

§ 26.6694-4. Extension of period of collection when preparer pays 15 percent of a penalty for understatement of taxpayer's liability and certain other procedural matters.—(a) *In general.*— For rules relating to the extension of period of collection when a tax return preparer who prepared a return or claim for refund for generation-skipping transfer tax under chapter 13 of subtitle B of the Internal Revenue Code pays 15 percent of a penalty for understatement of taxpayer's liability, and procedural matters relating to the investigation, assessment and collection of the penalties under section 6694(a) and (b), the rules under § 1.6694-4 of this chapter will apply.

(b) *Effective/applicability date.*—This section is applicable to returns and claims for refund filed, and advice provided, after December 31, 2008. [Reg. § 26.6694-4.]

□ [*T.D.* 9436, 12-15-2008.]

[Reg. § 31.6694-4]

§ 31.6694-4. Extension of period of collection when tax return preparer pays 15 percent of a penalty for understatement of taxpayer's liability and certain other procedural matters.— (a) *In general.*—For rules relating to the extension of period of collection when a tax return preparer who prepared a return or claim for refund for employment tax under chapters 21 through 25 of subtitle C of the Internal Revenue Code pays 15 percent of a penalty for understatement of taxpayer's liability and procedural matters relating to the investigation, assessment and collection of the penalties under section 6694(a) and (b), the rules under § 1.6694-4 of this chapter will apply.

(b) *Effective/applicability date.*—This section is applicable to returns and claims for refund filed, and advice provided, after December 31, 2008. [Reg. § 31.6694-4.]

□ [*T.D.* 9436, 12-15-2008.]

[Reg. § 40.6694-4]

§ 40.6694-4. Extension of period of collection when tax return preparer pays 15 percent of a penalty for understatement of taxpayer's liabil-

ity and certain other procedural matters.—(a) *In general.*—For rules relating to the extension of period of collection when a tax return preparer who prepared a return or claim for refund of any tax to which this part 40 applies pays 15 percent of a penalty for understatement of taxpayer's liability and procedural matters relating to the investigation, assessment and collection of the penalties under section 6694(a) and (b), the rules under § 1.6694-4 of this chapter will apply.

(b) *Effective/applicability date.*—This section is applicable to returns and claims for refund filed, and advice provided, after December 31, 2008. [Reg. § 40.6694-4.]

☐ [*T.D.* 9436, 12-15-2008 (*corrected* 1-28-2009).]

[Reg. § 41.6694-4]

§ 41.6694-4. Extension of period of collection when preparer pays 15 percent of a penalty for understatement of taxpayer's liability and certain other procedural matters.—(a) *In general.*—For rules relating to the extension of period of collection when a tax return preparer who prepared a return or claim for refund for excise tax under section 4481 pays 15 percent of a penalty for understatement of taxpayer's liability, and procedural matters relating to the investigation, assessment and collection of the penalties under section 6694(a) and (b), the rules under § 1.6694-4 of this chapter will apply.

(b) *Effective/applicability date.*—This section is applicable to returns and claims for refund filed, and advice provided, after December 31, 2008. [Reg. § 41.6694-4.]

☐ [*T.D.* 9436, 12-15-2008.]

[Reg. § 44.6694-4]

§ 44.6694-4. Extension of period of collection when preparer pays 15 percent of a penalty for understatement of taxpayer's liability and certain other procedural matters.—(a) *In general.*—For rules relating to the extension of period of collection when a tax return preparer who prepared a return or claim for refund for tax on wagers under sections 4401 or 4411 pays 15 percent of a penalty for understatement of taxpayer's liability and procedural matters relating to the investigation, assessment and collection of the penalties under section 6694(a) and (b), the rules under § 1.6694-4 of this chapter will apply.

(b) *Effective/applicability date.*—This section is applicable to returns and claims for refund filed, and advice provided, after December 31, 2008. [Reg. § 44.6694-4.]

☐ [*T.D.* 9436, 12-15-2008.]

[Reg. § 53.6694-4]

§ 53.6694-4. Extension of period of collection when tax return preparer pays 15 percent of a penalty for understatement of taxpayer's liability and certain other procedural matters.—(a) *In general.*—For rules relating to the extension of period of collection when a tax return preparer who prepared a return or claim for refund of tax under Chapter 42 of the Internal Revenue Code pays 15 percent of a penalty for understatement of taxpayer's liability and procedural matters relating to the investigation, assessment and collection of the penalties under section 6694(a) and (b), the rules under § 1.6694-4 of this chapter will apply.

(b) *Effective/applicability date.*—This section is applicable to returns and claims for refund filed, and advice provided, after December 31, 2008. [Reg. § 53.6694-4.]

☐ [*T.D.* 9436, 12-15-2008.]

[Reg. § 54.6694-4]

§ 54.6694-4. Extension of period of collection when tax return preparer pays 15 percent of a penalty for understatement of taxpayer's liability and certain other procedural matters.—(a) *In general.*—For rules relating to the extension of period of collection when a tax return preparer who prepared a return or claim for refund for tax under chapter 43 of subtitle D of the Internal Revenue Code pays 15 percent of a penalty for understatement of taxpayer's liability, and procedural matters relating to the investigation, assessment and collection of the penalties under section 6694(a) and (b), the rules under § 1.6694-4 of this chapter will apply.

(b) *Effective/applicability date.*—This section is applicable to returns and claims for refund filed, and advice provided, after December 31, 2008. [Reg. § 54.6694-4.]

☐ [*T.D.* 9436, 12-15-2008.]

[Reg. § 55.6694-4]

§ 55.6694-4. Extension of period of collection when tax return preparer pays 15 percent of a penalty for understatement of taxpayer's liability and certain other procedural matters.—(a) *In general.*—For rules relating to the extension of period of collection when a tax return preparer who prepared a return or claim for refund for excise tax under chapter 44 of subtitle D of the Internal Revenue Code pays 15 percent of a penalty for understatement of taxpayer's liability and procedural matters relating to the investigation, assessment and collection of the penalties under section 6694(a) and (b), the rules under § 1.6694-4 of this chapter will apply.

(b) *Effective/applicability date.*—This section is applicable to returns and claims for refund filed, and advice provided, after December 31, 2008. [Reg. § 55.6694-4.]

☐ [*T.D.* 9436, 12-15-2008.]

[Reg. §56.6694-4]

§56.6694-4. Extension of period of collection when tax return preparer pays 15 percent of a penalty for understatement of taxpayer's liability and certain other procedural matters.— (a) *In general.*—For rules relating to the extension of period of collection when a tax return preparer who prepared a return or claim for refund for tax under chapter 41 of subtitle D of the Internal Revenue Code pays 15 percent of a penalty for understatement of taxpayer's liability and procedural matters relating to the investigation, assessment and collection of the penalties under section 6694(a) and (b), the rules under §1.6694-4 of this chapter will apply.

(b) *Effective/applicability date.*—This section is applicable to returns and claims for refund filed, and advice provided, after December 31, 2008. [Reg. §56.6694-4.]

☐ [*T.D.* 9436, 12-15-2008.]

[Reg. §156.6694-4]

§156.6694-4. Extension of period of collection when tax return preparer pays 15 percent of a penalty for understatement of taxpayer's liability and certain other procedural matters.— (a) *In general.*—For rules relating to the extension of period of collection when a tax return preparer who prepared a return or claim for refund for tax under section 5881 of the Internal Revenue Code pays 15 percent of a penalty for understatement of taxpayer's liability and procedural matters relating to the investigation, assessment and collection of the penalties under section 6694(a) and (b), the rules under §1.6694-4 of this chapter will apply.

(b) *Effective/applicability date.*—This section is applicable to returns and claims for refund filed, and advice provided, after December 31, 2008. [Reg. §156.6694-4.]

☐ [*T.D.* 9436, 12-15-2008.]

[Reg. §157.6694-4]

§157.6694-4. Extension of period of collection when preparer pays 15 percent of a penalty for understatement of taxpayer's liability and certain other procedural matters.—(a) *In general.*—For rules relating to the extension of period of collection when a tax return preparer who prepared a return or claim for refund for tax under section 5891 of the Internal Revenue Code pays 15 percent of a penalty for understatement of taxpayer's liability and procedural matters relating to the investigation, assessment and collection of the penalties under section 6694(a) and (b), the rules under §1.6694-4 of this chapter will apply.

(b) *Effective/applicability date.*—This section is applicable to returns and claims for refund filed, and advice provided, after December 31, 2008. [Reg. §157.6694-4.]

☐ [*T.D.* 9436, 12-15-2008.]

[Reg. §1.6695-1]

§1.6695-1. Other assessable penalties with respect to the preparation of tax returns for other persons.—(a) *Failure to furnish copy to taxpayer.*—(1) A person who is a signing tax return preparer as described in §301.7701-15(b)(1) of this chapter of any return of tax or claim for refund of tax under the Internal Revenue Code (Code), and who fails to satisfy the requirements imposed by section 6107(a) and §1.6107-1(a) to furnish a copy of the return or claim for refund to the taxpayer (or nontaxable entity), shall be subject to a penalty of $50 for such failure, with a maximum penalty of $25,000 per person imposed with respect to each calendar year, unless it is shown that the failure is due to reasonable cause and not due to willful neglect.

(2) No penalty may be imposed under section 6695(a) and paragraph (a)(1) of this section upon a tax return preparer who furnishes a copy of the return or claim for refund to taxpayers who—

(i) Hold an elected or politically appointed position with the government of the United States or a state or political subdivision thereof; and

(ii) In order faithfully to carry out their official duties, have so arranged their affairs that they have less than full knowledge of the property that they hold or of the debts for which they are responsible, if information is deleted from the copy in order to preserve or maintain this arrangement.

(b) *Failure to sign return.*—(1) An individual who is a signing tax return preparer as described in §301.7701-15(b)(1) of this chapter with respect to a return of tax or claim for refund of tax under the Code as described in §301.7701-15(b)(4) that is not signed electronically shall sign the return or claim for refund after it is completed and before it is presented to the taxpayer (or nontaxable entity) for signature. For rules covering electronically signed returns, see paragraph (b)(2) of this section. If the signing tax return preparer is unavailable for signature, another tax return preparer shall review the entire preparation of the return or claim for refund, and then shall sign the return or claim for refund. The tax return preparer shall sign the return in the manner prescribed by the Commissioner in forms, instructions, or other appropriate guidance.

(2) In the case of electronically signed tax returns, the signing tax return preparer need not sign the return prior to presenting a completed copy of the return to the taxpayer. The signing tax return preparer, however, must furnish all of the information that will be transmitted as the electronically signed tax return to the taxpayer contemporaneously with furnishing the Form 8879, "IRS e-file Signature Authorization," or other similar Internal Revenue Service (IRS) e-file signature form. The information may be furnished on a replica of an official form. The signing tax return preparer shall electronically sign the return in the manner prescribed by the Commissioner in forms, instructions, or other appropriate guidance.

(3) An individual required by this paragraph (b) to sign a return or claim for refund shall be subject to a penalty of $50 for each failure to sign, with a maximum of $25,000 per person imposed with respect to each calendar year, unless it is shown that the failure is due to reasonable cause and not due to willful neglect.

If the tax return preparer asserts reasonable cause for failure to sign, the IRS will require a written statement to substantiate the tax return preparer's claim of reasonable cause. For purposes of this paragraph (b), reasonable cause is a cause that arises despite ordinary care and prudence exercised by the individual tax return preparer.

(4) *Examples.*—The application of this paragraph (b) is illustrated by the following examples:

Example 1. Law Firm A employs B, a lawyer, to prepare for compensation estate tax returns and claims for refund of taxes. Firm A is engaged by C to prepare a Federal estate tax return. Firm A assigns B to prepare the return. B obtains the information necessary for completing the return from C and makes determinations with respect to the proper application of the tax laws to such information in order to determine the estate's tax liability. B then forwards such information to D, a computer tax service that performs the mathematical computations and prints the return by means of computer processing. D then sends the completed estate tax return to B who reviews the accuracy of the return. B is the individual tax return preparer who is primarily responsible for the overall accuracy of the estate tax return. B must sign the return as tax return preparer in order to not be subject to the section 6695(b) penalty.

Example 2. Partnership E is a national accounting firm that prepares returns and claims for refund of taxes for compensation. F and G, employees of Partnership E, are involved in preparing the Form 990-T, Exempt Organization Business Income Tax Return, for H, a tax exempt organization. After they complete the return, including the gathering of the necessary information, analyzing the proper application of the tax laws to such information, and the performance of the necessary mathematical computations, I, a supervisory employee of Partnership E, reviews the return. As part of this review, I reviews the information provided and the application of the tax laws to this information. The mathematical computations and carriedforward amounts are reviewed by J, an employee of Partnership E. The policies and practices of Partnership E require that K, a partner, finally review the return. The scope of K's review includes reviewing the information provided and applying to this information his knowledge of H's affairs, observing that Partnership E's policies and practices have been followed, and making the final determination with respect to the proper application of the tax laws to determine H's tax liability. K may or may not exercise these responsibilities, or may exercise them to a greater or lesser extent, depending on the degree of complexity of the return, his confidence in I (or F and G), and other factors. K is the individual tax return preparer who is primarily responsible for the overall accuracy of H's return. K must sign the return as tax return preparer in order to not be subject to the section 6695(b) penalty.

Example 3. L corporation maintains an office in Seattle, Washington, for the purpose of preparing partnership returns for compensation. L makes compensatory arrangements with individuals (but provides no working facilities) in several states to collect information from partners of a partnership and to make decisions with respect to the proper application of the tax laws to the information in order to prepare the partnership return and calculate the partnership's distributive items. M, an individual, who has such an arrangement in Los Angeles with L, collects information from N, the general partner of a partnership, and completes a worksheet kit supplied by L that is stamped with M's name and an identification number assigned to M by L. In this process, M classifies this information in appropriate categories for the preparation of the partnership return. The completed worksheet kit signed by M is then mailed to L. O, an employee in L's office, reviews the worksheet kit to make sure it was properly completed. O does not review the information obtained from N for its validity or accuracy. O may, but did not, make the final decision with respect to the proper application of tax laws to the information provided. The data from the worksheet is entered into a computer and the return form is completed. The return is prepared for submission to N with filing instructions. M is the individual tax return preparer primarily responsible for the overall accuracy of the partnership return. M must sign the return as tax return preparer in order to not be subject to the section 6695(b) penalty.

Example 4. P employs R, S, and T to prepare gift tax returns for taxpayers. After R and S have collected the information from a taxpayer and applied the tax laws to the information, the return form is completed by a computer service. On the day the returns prepared by R and S are ready for their signatures, R is away from the city for 1 week on another assignment and S is on detail to another office in the same city for the day. T may sign the gift tax returns prepared by R, provided that T reviews the information obtained by R relative to the taxpayer, and T reviews the preparation of each return prepared by R. T may not sign the returns prepared by S because S is available.

(5) *Effective/applicability date.*—This paragraph (b) is applicable to returns and claims for refund filed after December 31, 2008.

(c) *Failure to furnish identifying number.*—(1) A person who is a signing tax return preparer as described in §301.7701-15(b)(1) of this chapter of any return of tax under the Code or claim for refund of tax under the Code, and who fails to satisfy the requirement of section 6109(a)(4) and § 1.6109-2(a) to furnish one or more identifying numbers of signing tax return preparers or persons employing the signing tax return preparer (or with which the signing tax return preparer is associated) on a return or claim for refund after it is completed and before it is presented to the taxpayer (or nontaxable entity) for signature shall be subject to a penalty of $50 for each failure, with a maximum of $25,000 per person imposed with respect to each calendar year, unless it is shown that the failure is due to reasonable cause and not due to willful neglect.

(2) No more than one penalty of $50 may be imposed under section 6695(c) and paragraph (c)(1) of this section with respect to a single return or claim for refund.

(d) *Failure to retain copy or record.*—(1) A person who is a signing tax return preparer as described in § 301.7701-15(b)(1) of this chapter of any return of tax under the Code or claim for refund of tax under the Code, and who fails to satisfy the requirements imposed upon him or her by section 6107(b) and § 1.6107-1(b) and (c) (other than the record requirement described in both § 1.6107-1(b)(2) and (3)) to retain and make available for inspection a copy of the return or claim for refund, or to include the return or claim for refund in a record of returns and claims for refund and make the record available for inspection, shall be subject to a penalty of $50 for the failure, unless it is shown that the failure is due to reasonable cause and not due to willful neglect.

(2) A person may not, for returns or claims for refund presented to the taxpayers (or nontaxable entities) during each calendar year, be subject to more than $25,000 in penalties under section 6695(d) and paragraph (d)(1) of this section.

(e) *Failure to file correct information returns.*—A person who is subject to the reporting requirements of section 6060 and § 1.6060-1 and who fails to satisfy these requirements shall pay a penalty of $50 for each such failure, with a maximum of $25,000 per person imposed for each calendar year, unless such failure was due to reasonable cause and not due to willful neglect.

(f) *Negotiation of check.*—(1) No person who is a tax return preparer as described in § 301.7701-15 of this chapter may endorse or otherwise negotiate, directly or through an agent, a check (including an electronic version of a check) for the refund of tax under the Code that is issued to a taxpayer other than the tax return preparer if the person was a tax return preparer of the return or claim for refund which gave rise to the refund check. A tax return preparer will not be considered to have endorsed or otherwise negotiated a check for purposes of this paragraph (f)(1) solely as a result of having affixed the taxpayer's name to a refund check for the purpose of depositing the check into an account in the name of the taxpayer or in the joint names

of the taxpayer and one or more other persons (excluding the tax return preparer) if authorized by the taxpayer or the taxpayer's recognized representative.

(2) Section 6695(f) and paragraphs (f)(1) and (3) of this section do not apply to a tax return preparer-bank that—

(i) Cashes a refund check and remits all of the cash to the taxpayer or accepts a refund check for deposit in full to a taxpayer's account, so long as the bank does not initially endorse or negotiate the check (unless the bank has made a loan to the taxpayer on the basis of the anticipated refund); or

(ii) Endorses a refund check for deposit in full to a taxpayer's account pursuant to a written authorization of the taxpayer (unless the bank has made a loan to the taxpayer on the basis of the anticipated refund).

(3) A tax return preparer-bank may also subsequently endorse or negotiate a refund check as a part of the checkclearing process through the financial system after initial endorsement or negotiation.

(4) The tax return preparer shall be subject to a penalty of $500 for each endorsement or negotiation of a check prohibited under section 6695(f) and paragraph (f)(1) of this section.

(g) *Effective/applicability date.*—This section is applicable to returns and claims for refund filed after December 31, 2008. [Reg. § 1.6695-1.]

☐ [T.D. 7519, 11-17-77. *Amended by T.D. 7640,* 8-21-79; *T.D. 8549, 6-28-94; T.D. 8689, 12-11-96; T.D. 8803, 12-30-98; T.D. 8893, 7-17-2000; T.D. 9053, 4-23-2003; T.D. 9119, 3-24-2004 and T.D. 9436, 12-15-2008 (corrected 1-28-2009).*]

[Reg. § 20.6695-1]

§ 20.6695-1. Other assessable penalties with respect to the preparation of tax returns for other persons.—(a) *In general.*—A person who is a tax return preparer of any return or claim for refund of estate tax under chapter 11 of subtitle B of the Internal Revenue Code (Code) shall be subject to penalties for failure to furnish a copy to the taxpayer under section 6695(a) of the Code, failure to sign the return under section 6695(b) of the Code, failure to furnish an identification number under section 6695(c) of the Code, failure to retain a copy or list under section 6695(d) of the Code, failure to file a correct information return under section 6695(e) of the Code, and negotiation of a check under section 6695(f) of the Code, in the manner stated in § 1.6695-1 of this chapter.

(b) *Effective/applicability date.*—This section is applicable to returns and claims for refund filed after December 31, 2008. [Reg. § 20.6695-1.]

☐ [T.D. 9436, 12-15-2008.]

[Reg. § 25.6695-1]

§ 25.6695-1. Other assessable penalties with respect to the preparation of tax returns for other persons.—(a) *In general.*—A person who is a tax return preparer of any return or claim for refund of gift tax under chapter 12 of subtitle B of the Internal Revenue Code (Code) shall be subject to penalties for failure to furnish a copy to the taxpayer under section 6695(a) of the Code, failure to sign the return under section 6695(b) of the Code, failure to furnish an identification number under section 6695(c) of the Code, failure to retain a copy or list under section 6695(d) of the Code, failure to file a correct information return under section 6695(e) of the Code, and negotiation of a check under section 6695(f) of the Code, in the manner stated in § 1.6695-1 of this chapter.

(b) *Effective/applicability date.*—This section is applicable to returns and claims for refund filed after December 31, 2008. [Reg. § 25.6695-1.]

☐ [*T.D.* 9436, 12-15-2008.]

[Reg. § 26.6695-1]

§ 26.6695-1. Other assessable penalties with respect to the preparation of tax returns for other persons.—(a) *In general.*—A person who is a tax return preparer of any return or claim for refund of generation-skipping transfer tax under chapter 13 of subtitle B of the Internal Revenue Code (Code) shall be subject to penalties for failure to furnish a copy to the taxpayer under section 6695(a) of the Code, failure to sign the return under section 6695(b) of the Code, failure to furnish an identification number under section 6695(c) of the Code, failure to retain a copy or list under section 6695(d) of the Code, failure to file a correct information return under section 6695(e) of the Code, and negotiation of a check under section 6695(f) of the Code, in the manner stated in § 1.6695-1 of this chapter.

(b) *Effective/applicability date.*—This section is applicable to returns and claims for refund filed after December 31, 2008. [Reg. § 26.6695-1.]

☐ [*T.D.* 9436, 12-15-2008.]

[Reg. § 31.6695-1]

§ 31.6695-1. Other assessable penalties with respect to the preparation of tax returns for other persons.—(a) *In general.*—A person who is a tax return preparer of any return or claim for refund of employment tax under chapters 21 through 25 of subtitle C of the Internal Revenue Code (Code) shall be subject to penalties for failure to furnish a copy to the taxpayer under section 6695(a) of the Code, failure to sign the return under section 6695(b) of the Code, failure to furnish an identification number under section 6695(c) of the Code, failure to retain a copy or list under section 6695(d) of the Code, failure to file a correct information return under section 6695(e) of the Code, and negotiation of a check under section 6695(f) of the Code, in the manner stated in § 1.6695-1 of this chapter.

(b) *Effective/applicability date.*—This section is applicable to returns and claims for refund filed after December 31, 2008. [Reg. § 31.6695-1.]

☐ [*T.D.* 9436, 12-15-2008.]

[Reg. § 40.6695-1]

§ 40.6695-1. Other assessable penalties with respect to the preparation of tax returns for other persons.—(a) *In general.*—A person who is a tax return preparer of any return or claim for refund of any tax to which this part 40 applies shall be subject to penalties for failure to furnish a copy to the taxpayer under section 6695(a) of the Internal Revenue Code (Code), failure to sign the return under section 6695(b) of the Code, failure to furnish an identification number under section 6695(c) of the Code, failure to retain a copy or list under section 6695(d) of the Code, failure to file a correct information return under section 6695(e) of the Code, and negotiation of a check under section 6695(f) of the Code, in the manner stated in § 6695-1 of this chapter.

(b) *Effective/applicability date.*—This section is applicable for returns and claims for refund filed after December 31, 2008. [Reg. § 40.6695-1.]

☐ [*T.D.* 9436, 12-15-2008 (*corrected* 1-28-2009).]

[Reg. § 41.6695-1]

§ 41.6695-1. Other assessable penalties with respect to the preparation of tax returns for other persons.—(a) *In general.*—A person who is a tax return preparer of any return or claim for refund of excise tax under section 4481 of the Internal Revenue Code (Code) shall be subject to penalties for failure to furnish a copy to the taxpayer under section 6695(a) of the Code, failure to sign a return under section 6695(b) of the Code, failure to furnish an identification number under section 6695(c) of the Code, failure to retain a copy or list under section 6695(d) of the Code, failure to file a correct information return under section 6695(e) of the Code, and negotiation of a check under section 6695(f) of the Code, in the manner stated in § 6695-1 of this chapter.

(b) *Effective/applicability date.*—This section is applicable to returns and claims for refund filed after December 31, 2008. [Reg. § 41.6695-1.]

☐ [*T.D.* 9436, 12-15-2008 (*corrected* 1-28-2009).]

[Reg. § 44.6695-1]

§ 44.6695-1. Other assessable penalties with respect to the preparation of tax returns for other persons.—(a) *In general.*—A person who is a tax return preparer of any return or claim for refund of tax on wagers under sections 4401 or 4411 of the Internal Revenue Code (Code) shall be subject to penalties for failure to furnish a copy to the taxpayer under section 6695(a) of the Code, failure to sign the return under section 6695(b) of the Code, failure to furnish an identification number under section 6695(c) of the Code, failure to retain a copy or list under section 6695(d) of the Code, failure to file a correct information return under section 6695(e) of the Code, and negotiation of a check under section 6695(f) of the Code, in the manner stated in § 6695-1 of this chapter.

(b) *Effective/applicability date.*—This section is applicable to returns and claims for refund filed after December 31, 2008. [Reg. § 44.6695-1.]

☐ [*T.D.* 9436, 12-15-2008 (*corrected* 1-28-2009).]

[Reg. § 53.6695-1]

§ 53.6695-1. Other assessable penalties with respect to the preparation of tax returns or claims for refund for other persons..—(a) *In general.*—A person who is a tax return preparer of any return or claim for refund of tax under Chapter 42 of the Internal Revenue Code (Code) shall be subject to penalties for failure to furnish a copy to the taxpayer under section 6695(a) of the Code, failure to sign the return under section 6695(b) of the Code, failure to furnish an identification number under section 6695(c) of the Code, failure to retain a copy or list under section 6695(d) of the Code, failure to file a correct information return under section 6695(e) of the Code, and negotiation of a check under section 6695(f) of the Code, in the manner stated in § 1.6695-1 of this chapter.

(b) *Effective/applicability date.*—This section is applicable to returns and claims for refund filed after December 31, 2008. [Reg. § 53.6695-1.]

☐ [*T.D.* 9436, 12-15-2008.]

[Reg. § 54.6695-1]

§ 54.6695-1. Other assessable penalties with respect to the preparation of tax returns for other persons.—(a) *In general.*—A person who is a tax return preparer of any return or claim for refund of tax under chapter 43 of subtitle D of the Internal Revenue Code (Code) shall be subject to penalties for failure to furnish a copy to the taxpayer under section 6695(a) of the Code, failure to sign the return under section 6695(b) of the Code, failure to furnish an identification number under section 6695(c) of the Code, failure to retain a copy or list under section 6695(d) of the Code, failure to file a correct information return under section 6695(e) of the Code, and negotiation of a check under section 6695(f) of the Code, in the manner stated in § 1.6695-1 of this chapter.

(b) *Effective/applicability date.*—This section is applicable to returns and claims for refund filed after December 31, 2008. [Reg. § 54.6695-1.]

☐ [*T.D.* 9436, 12-15-2008.]

[Reg. § 55.6695-1]

§ 55.6695-1. Other assessable penalties with respect to the preparation of tax returns or claims for refund for other persons.—(a) *In general.*—A person who is a tax return preparer of any return or claim for refund of tax under chapter 44 of subtitle D of the Internal Revenue Code (Code) shall be subject to penalties for failure to furnish a copy to the taxpayer under section 6695(a) of the Code, failure to sign the return under section 6695(b) of the Code, failure to furnish an identification number under section 6695(c) of the Code, failure to retain a copy or list under section 6695(d) of the Code, failure to file

a correct information return under section 6695(e) of the Code, and negotiation of a check under section 6695(f) of the Code, in the manner stated in § 1.6695-1 of this chapter.

(b) *Effective/applicability date.*—This section is applicable to returns and claims for refund filed after December 31, 2008. [Reg. § 55.6695-1.]

☐ [*T.D.* 9436, 12-15-2008.]

[Reg. § 56.6695-1]

§ 56.6695-1. Other assessable penalties with respect to the preparation of tax returns or claims for refund for other persons.—(a) *In general.*—A person who is a tax return preparer of any return or claim for refund of tax under chapter 41 of subtitle D of the Internal Revenue Code (Code) shall be subject to penalties for failure to furnish a copy to the taxpayer under section 6695(a) of the Code, failure to sign the return under section 6695(b) of the Code, failure to furnish an identification number under section 6695(c) of the Code, failure to retain a copy or list under section 6695(d) of the Code, failure to file a correct information return under section 6695(e) of the Code, and negotiation of a check under section 6695(f) of the Code, in the manner stated in § 1.6695-1 of this chapter.

(b) *Effective/applicability date.*—This section is applicable to returns and claims for refund filed after December 31, 2008. [Reg. § 56.6695-1.]

☐ [*T.D.* 9436, 12-15-2008.]

[Reg. § 156.6695-1]

§ 156.6695-1. Other assessable penalties with respect to the preparation of tax returns or claims for refund for other persons.—(a) *In general.*—A person who is a tax return preparer of any return or claim for refund of tax under section 5881 of the Internal Revenue Code (Code) shall be subject to penalties for failure to furnish a copy to the taxpayer under section 6695(a) of the Code, failure to sign the return under section 6695(b) of the Code, failure to furnish an identification number under section 6695(c) of the Code, failure to retain a copy or list under section 6695(d) of the Code, failure to file a correct information return under section 6695(e) of the Code, and negotiation of a check under section 6695(f) of the Code, in the manner stated in § 1.6695-1 of this chapter.

(b) *Effective/applicability date.*—This section is applicable to returns and claims for refund filed after December 31, 2008. [Reg. § 156.6695-1.]

☐ [*T.D.* 9436, 12-15-2008.]

[Reg. § 157.6695-1]

§ 157.6695-1. Other assessable penalties with respect to the preparation of tax returns or claims for refund for other persons.—(a) *In general.*—A person who is a tax return preparer of any return or claim for refund of tax under section 5891 of the Internal Revenue Code (Code) shall be subject to penalties for failure to furnish a copy to the taxpayer under section 6695(a) of the Code, failure to sign the return under section 6695(b) of the Code, failure to furnish an identification number under section 6695(c) of the Code, failure to retain a copy or list under section 6695(d) of the Code, failure to file a correct information return under section 6695(e) of the Code, and negotiation of a check under section 6695(f) of the Code, in the manner stated in § 1.6695-1 of this chapter.

(b) *Effective/applicability date.*—This section is applicable to returns and claims for refund filed after December 31, 2008. [Reg. § 157.6695-1.]

☐ *[T.D. 9436, 12-15-2008.]*

[Reg. § 1.6695-2]

§ 1.6695-2. Tax return preparer due diligence requirements for certain credits.— (a) [Reserved]. For further guidance regarding the penalty for failure to meet due diligence requirements with respect to certain credits, see § 1.6695-2T(a).

(b) *Due diligence requirements.*—A preparer must satisfy the following due diligence requirements:

(1) *Completion and submission of Form 8867.*— (i) [Reserved]. For further guidance regarding the completion of Form 8867, see § 1.6695-2T(b)(1)(i).

(A) In the case of a signing tax return preparer electronically filing the tax return or claim for refund, must electronically file the completed Form 8867 (or successor form) with the tax return or claim for refund;

(B) In the case of a signing tax return preparer not electronically filing the tax return or claim for refund, must provide the taxpayer with the completed Form 8867 (or successor form) for inclusion with the filed tax return or claim for refund; or

(C) In the case of a nonsigning tax return preparer, must provide the signing tax return preparer with the completed Form 8867 (or successor form), in either electronic or non-electronic format, for inclusion with the filed tax return or claim for refund.

(ii) [Reserved]. For further guidance regarding the information used to complete the Form 8867, see 1.6695-2T(b)(1)(ii).

(2) [Reserved]. For further guidance regarding computation, see § 1.6695-2T(b)(2).

(3) *Knowledge.*—(i) [Reserved]. For further guidance regarding the knowledge requirement, see § 1.6695-2T(b)(3)(i).

(ii) [Reserved]. For current examples, see § 1.6695-2T(b)(3)(ii).

(4) *Retention of records.*—(i) The tax return preparer must retain—

(A) A copy of the completed Form 8867 (or successor form);

(B) [Reserved]. For further guidance on the retention of records, see § 1.6695-2T(b)(4)(i)(B).

(C) [Reserved]. For further guidance on the retention of records, see § 1.6695-2T(b)(4)(i)(C).

(ii) The items in paragraph (b)(4)(i) of this section must be retained for three years from the latest of the following dates, as applicable:

(A) The due date of the tax return (determined without regard to any extension of time for filing);

(B) In the case of a signing tax return preparer electronically filing the tax return or claim for refund, the date the tax return or claim for refund was filed;

(C) In the case of a signing tax return preparer not electronically filing the tax return or claim for refund, the date the tax return or claim for refund was presented to the taxpayer for signature; or

(D) In the case of a nonsigning tax return preparer, the date the nonsigning tax return preparer submitted to the signing tax return preparer that portion of the tax return or claim for refund for which the nonsigning tax return preparer was responsible.

(iii) The items in paragraph (b)(4)(i) of this section may be retained on paper or electronically in the manner prescribed in applicable regulations, revenue rulings, revenue procedures, or other appropriate guidance (see § 601.601(d)(2) of this chapter).

(c) *Special rule for firms.*—A firm that employs a tax return preparer subject to a penalty under section 6695(g) is also subject to penalty if, and only if—

(1) One or more members of the principal management (or principal officers) of the firm or a branch office participated in or, prior to the time the return was filed, knew of the failure to comply with the due diligence requirements of this section;

(2) The firm failed to establish reasonable and appropriate procedures to ensure compliance with the due diligence requirements of this section; or

(3) [Reserved]. For further guidance on the special rule for firms, see § 1.6695-2T(c)(3).

(d) *Exception to penalty.*—The section 6695(g) penalty will not be applied with respect to a particular tax return or claim for refund if the tax return preparer can demonstrate to the satisfaction of the IRS that, considering all the facts and circumstances, the tax return preparer's normal office procedures are reasonably designed and routinely followed to ensure compliance with the due diligence requirements of paragraph (b) of this section, and the failure to meet the due diligence requirements of paragraph (b) of this section with respect to the particular tax return or claim for refund was isolated and inadvertent. The preceding sentence does not apply to a firm that is subject to the penalty as a result of paragraph (c) of this section.

(e) *Effective/applicability date.*—This section applies to tax returns and claims for refund for tax years ending on or after December 31, 2011. [Reg. § 1.6695-2.]

☐ *[T.D. 8905, 10-16-2000. Amended by T.D. 9436, 12-15-2008, T.D. 9570, 12-19-2011 and T.D. 9799, 12-2-2016.]*

[Reg. § 1.6695-2T]

§ 1.6695-2T. Tax return preparer due diligence requirements for certain credits (Temporary).—(a) *Penalty for failure to meet due diligence* *requirements.*—(1) *In general.*—A person who is a tax return preparer (as defined in section 7701(a)(36)) of a tax return or claim for refund under the Internal Revenue Code with respect to determining the eligibility for, or the amount of, the child tax credit (CTC) and additional child tax credit (ACTC) under section 24, the American opportunity tax credit (AOTC) under section 25A(i), or the earned income credit (EIC) under section 32 and who fails to satisfy the due diligence requirements of paragraph (b) of this section will be subject to a penalty as prescribed in section 6695(g) (indexed for inflation under section 6695(h)) for each failure. A separate penalty applies with respect to each credit claimed on a return or claim for refund for which the due diligence requirements of this section are not satisfied and for which the exception to penalty provided by paragraph (d) of this section does not apply.

(2) *Examples.*—The provisions of paragraph (a)(1) of this section are illustrated by the following examples:

Example 1. Preparer A prepares a federal income tax return for a taxpayer claiming the CTC and the AOTC. Preparer A did not meet the due diligence requirements under this section with respect to the CTC or the AOTC claimed on the taxpayer's return. Unless the exception to penalty provided by paragraph (d) of this section applies, Preparer A is subject to two penalties under section 6695(g): one for failure to meet the due diligence requirements for the CTC and a second penalty for failure to meet the due diligence requirements for the AOTC.

Example 2. Preparer B prepares a federal income tax return for a taxpayer claiming the CTC and the AOTC. Preparer B did not meet the due diligence requirements under this section with respect to the CTC claimed on the taxpayer's return, but Preparer B did meet the due diligence requirements under this section with respect to the AOTC claimed on the taxpayer's return. Unless the exception to penalty provided by paragraph (d) of this section applies, Preparer B is subject to one penalty under section 6695(g) for the failure to meet the due diligence requirements for the CTC. Preparer B is not subject to a penalty under section 6695(g) for failure to meet the due diligence requirements for the AOTC.

(b) [Reserved]. For further guidance, see § 1.6695-2(b).

(1) *Completion and submission of Form 8867.*—(i) The tax return preparer must complete Form 8867, "Paid Preparer's Due Diligence Checklist," or such other form and such other information as may be prescribed by the Internal Revenue Service (IRS), and—

(A) through (C) [Reserved]. For further guidance, see § 1.6695-2(b)(1)(i)(A) through (C).

(ii) The tax return preparer's completion of Form 8867 must be based on information provided by the taxpayer to the tax return preparer or otherwise reasonably obtained or known by the tax return preparer.

(2) *Computation of credit or credits.*—(i) When computing the amount of a credit described in paragraph (a) of this section to be claimed on a return or claim for refund, the tax return preparer must either—

(A) Complete the worksheet in the Form 1040, 1040A, 1040EZ, and/or Form 8863 instructions or such other form including such other information as may be prescribed by the IRS applicable to each credit described in paragraph (a) of this section claimed on the return or claim for refund; or

(B) Otherwise record in one or more documents in the tax return preparer's paper or electronic files the tax return preparer's computation of the credit or credits claimed on the return or claim for refund, including the method and information used to make the computations.

(ii) The tax return preparer's completion of an applicable worksheet described in paragraph (b)(2)(i)(A) of this section (or other record of the tax return preparer's computation of the credit or credits permitted under paragraph (b)(2)(i)(B) of this section) must be based on information provided by the taxpayer to the tax return preparer or otherwise reasonably obtained or known by the tax return preparer.

(3) *Knowledge.*—(i) *In general.*—The tax return preparer must not know, or have reason to know, that any information used by the tax return preparer in determining the taxpayer's eligibility for, or the amount of, any credit described in paragraph (a) of this section and claimed on the return or claim for refund is incorrect. The tax return preparer may not ignore the implications of information furnished to, or known by, the tax return preparer, and must make reasonable inquiries if a reasonable and well-informed tax return preparer knowledgeable in the law would conclude that the information furnished to the tax return preparer appears to be incorrect, inconsistent, or incomplete. The tax return preparer must also contemporaneously document in the files any inquiries made and the responses to those inquiries.

(ii) *Examples.*—The provisions of paragraph (b)(3)(i) of this section are illustrated by the following examples:

Example 1. In 2018, Q, a 22 year-old taxpayer, engages Preparer C to prepare Q's 2017 federal income tax return. Q completes Preparer C's standard intake questionnaire and states that she has never been married and has two sons, ages 10 and 11. Based on the intake sheet and other information that Q provides, including in-

Reg. § 1.6695-2T(a)(1)

formation that shows that the boys lived with Q throughout 2017, Preparer C believes that Q may be eligible to claim each boy as a qualifying child for purposes of the EIC and the CTC. However, Q provides no information to Preparer C, and Preparer C does not have any information from other sources, to verify the relationship between Q and the boys. To meet the knowledge requirement in paragraph (b)(3) of this section, Preparer C must make reasonable inquiries to determine whether each boy is a qualifying child of Q for purposes of the EIC and the CTC, including reasonable inquiries to verify Q's relationship to the boys, and Preparer C must contemporaneously document these inquiries and the responses.

Example 2. Assume the same facts as in *Example 1* of this paragraph (b)(3)(ii). In addition, as part of preparing Q's 2017 federal income tax return, Preparer C made sufficient reasonable inquiries to verify that the boys were Q's legally adopted children. In 2019, Q engages Preparer C to prepare her 2018 federal income tax return. When preparing Q's 2018 federal income tax return, Preparer C is not required to make additional inquiries to determine the boys relationship to Q for purposes of the knowledge requirement in paragraph (b)(3) of this section.

Example 3. In 2018, R, an 18 year-old taxpayer, engages Preparer D to prepare R's 2017 federal income tax return. R completes Preparer D's standard intake questionnaire and states that she has never been married, has one child, an infant, and that she and her infant lived with R's parents during part of the 2017 tax year. R also provides Preparer D with a Form W-2 showing that she earned $10,000 during 2017. R provides no other documents or information showing that R earned any other income during the tax year. Based on the intake sheet and other information that R provides, Preparer D believes that R may be eligible to claim the infant as a qualifying child for the EIC and the CTC. To meet the knowledge requirement in paragraph (b)(3) of this section, Preparer D must make reasonable inquiries to determine whether R is eligible to claim these credits, including reasonable inquiries to verify that R is not a qualifying child of her parents (which would make R ineligible to claim the EIC) or a dependent of her parents (which would make R ineligible to claim the CTC), and Preparer D must contemporaneously document these inquiries and the responses.

Example 4. The facts are the same as the facts in *Example 3* of this paragraph (b)(3)(ii). In addition, Preparer D previously prepared the 2017 joint federal income tax return for R's parents. Based on information provided by R's parents, Preparer D has determined that R is not eligible to be claimed as a dependent or as a qualifying child for purposes of the EIC or CTC on R's parents' return. Therefore, for purposes of the knowledge requirement in paragraph (b)(3) of this section, Preparer D is not required to make additional inquiries to determine that R is not her parents' qualifying child or dependent.

Example 5. In 2018, S engages Preparer E to prepare his 2017 federal income tax return. During Preparer E's standard intake interview, S states that he has never been married and his niece and nephew lived with him for part of the 2017 tax year. Preparer E believes S may be eligible to claim each of these children as a qualifying child for purposes of the EIC and the CTC. To meet the knowledge requirement in paragraph (b)(3) of this section, Preparer E must make reasonable inquiries to determine whether each child is a qualifying child for purposes of the EIC and the CTC, including reasonable inquiries about the children's parents and the children's residency, and Preparer E must contemporaneously document these inquiries and the responses.

Example 6. W engages Preparer F to prepare her federal income tax return. During Preparer F's standard intake interview, W states that she is 50 years old, has never been married, and has no children. W further states to Preparer F that during the tax year she was self-employed, earned $10,000 from her business, and had no business expenses or other income. Preparer F believes W may be eligible for the EIC. To meet the knowledge requirement in paragraph (b)(3) of this section, Preparer F must make reasonable inquiries to determine whether W is eligible for the EIC, including reasonable inquiries to determine whether W's business income and expenses are correct, and Preparer F must contemporaneously document these inquiries and the responses.

Example 7. Y, who is 32 years old, engages Preparer G to prepare his federal income tax return. Y completes Preparer G's standard intake questionnaire and states that he has never been married. As part of Preparer G's client intake process, Y provides Preparer G with a copy of the Form 1098-T Y received showing that University M billed $4,000 of qualified tuition and related expenses for Y's enrollment or attendance at the university and that Y was at least a half-time undergraduate student. Preparer G believes that Y may be eligible for the AOTC. To meet the knowledge requirements in paragraph (b)(3) of this section, Preparer G must make reasonable inquiries to determine whether Y is eligible for the AOTC, as Form 1098-T does not contain all the information needed to determine eligibility for the AOTC or to calculate the amount of the credit if Y is eligible, and contemporaneously document these inquiries and the responses.

(4) *Retention of records.*—(i) [Reserved]. For further guidance, see § 1.6695-2(b)(4)(i).

(A) [Reserved]. For further guidance, see § 1.6695-2(b)(4)(i)(A).

(B) A copy of each completed worksheet required under paragraph (b)(2)(i)(A) of this section (or other record of the tax return preparer's computation permitted under paragraph (b)(2)(i)(B) of this section); and

(C) A record of how and when the information used to complete Form 8867 and the

Reg. § 1.6695-2T(b)(4)(i)(C)

applicable worksheets required under paragraph (b)(2)(i)(A) of this section (or other record of the tax return preparer's computation permitted under paragraph (b)(2)(i)(B) of this section) was obtained by the tax return preparer, including the identity of any person furnishing the information, as well as a copy of any document that was provided by the taxpayer and on which the tax return preparer relied to complete Form 8867 and/or an applicable worksheet required under paragraph (b)(2)(i)(A) of this section (or other record of the tax return preparer's computation permitted under paragraph (b)(2)(i)(B) of this section).

(ii) through (iii) [Reserved]. For further guidance, see § 1.6695-2(b)(4)(ii) through (iii).

(c) [Reserved]. For further guidance, see § 1.6695-2(c).

(1) through (2) [Reserved]. For further guidance, see § 1.6695-2(c)(1) through (2).

(3) The firm disregarded its reasonable and appropriate compliance procedures through willfulness, recklessness, or gross indifference (including ignoring facts that would lead a person of reasonable prudence and competence to investigate) in the preparation of the tax return or claim for refund with respect to which the penalty is imposed.

(d) [Reserved]. For further guidance, see § 1.6695-2(d).

(e) *Applicability date.*—This section applies to tax returns and claims for refund prepared on or after December 5, 2016 with respect to tax years beginning after December 31, 2015. For returns and claims for refund prepared before December 5, 2016 with respect to tax years beginning before January 1, 2016, the rules that apply are contained in § 1.6695-2 in effect prior to December 5, 2016. (See 26 CFR part 1 revised as of April 2016).

(f) *Expiration date.*—This section will expire on December 5, 2019. [Temporary Reg. § 1.6695-2T.]

☐ *T.D. 9799, 12-2-2016.*]

[Reg. § 1.6696-1]

§ 1.6696-1. Claims for credit or refund by tax return preparers or appraisers.—(a) *Notice and demand.*—(1) The Internal Revenue Service (IRS) shall issue to each tax return preparer or appraiser one or more statements of notice and demand for payment for all penalties assessed against the tax return preparer or appraiser under section 6694 and § 1.6694-1, under section 6695 and § 1.6695-1, or under section 6695A (and any subsequently issued regulations).

(2) For the definition of the term "tax return preparer", see section 7701(a)(36) and § 301.7701-15 of this chapter. A person who prepares a claim for credit or refund under this section for another person, however, is not, with respect to that preparation, a tax return preparer as defined in section 7701(a)(36) and § 301.7701-15 of this chapter.

(b) *Claim filed by tax return preparer or appraiser.*—A claim for credit or refund of a penalty (or penalties) assessed against a tax return preparer or appraiser under section 6694 and § 1.6694-1, under section 6695 and § 1.6695-1, or under section 6695A (and any subsequently issued regulations) may be filed under this section only by the tax return preparer or the appraiser (or the tax return preparer's or appraiser's estate) against whom the penalty (or penalties) is assessed and not by, for example, the tax return preparer's or appraiser's employer. This paragraph (b) is not intended, however, to impose any restrictions on the preparation of this claim for credit or refund. The claim may be prepared by the tax return preparer's or appraiser's employer or by other persons. In all cases, however, the claim for credit or refund shall contain the information specified in paragraph (d) of this section and, as required by paragraph (d) of this section, shall be verified by a written declaration by the tax return preparer or appraiser that the information is provided under penalty of perjury.

(c) *Separation and consolidation of claims.*—(1) Unless paragraph (c)(2) of this section applies, a tax return preparer shall file a separate claim for each penalty assessed in each statement of notice and demand issued to the tax return preparer.

(2) A tax return preparer may file one or more consolidated claims for any or all penalties imposed on the tax return preparer by a single IRS campus or office under section 6695(a) and § 1.6695-1(a) (relating to failure to furnish copy of return to taxpayer), section 6695(b) and § 1.6695-1(b) (relating to failure to sign), section 6695(c) and § 1.6695-1(c) (relating to failure to furnish identifying number), or under section 6695(d) and § 1.6695-1(d) (relating to failure to retain copy of return or record), whether the penalties are asserted on a single or on separate statements of notice and demand. In addition, a tax return preparer may file one consolidated claim for any or all penalties imposed on the tax return preparer by a single IRS campus or office under section 6695(e) and § 1.6695-1(e) (relating to failure to file correct information return), which are asserted on a single statement of notice and demand.

(d) *Content of claim.*—Each claim for credit or refund for any penalty (or penalties) paid by a tax return preparer under section 6694 and § 1.6694-1, or under section 6695 and § 1.6695-1, or paid by an appraiser under section 6695A (and any subsequently issued regulations) shall include the following information, verified by a written declaration by the tax return preparer or appraiser that the information is provided under penalty of perjury:

(1) The tax return preparer's or appraiser's name.

(2) The tax return preparer's or appraiser's identification number. If the tax return preparer or appraiser is—

(i) An individual (not described in paragraph (d)(2)(iii) of this section) who is a citizen or resident of the United States, the tax return preparer's or appraiser's social security account number (or such alternative number as may be prescribed by the IRS in forms, instructions, or other appropriate guidance) shall be provided;

(ii) An individual who is not a citizen or resident of the United States and also was not employed by another tax return preparer or appraiser to prepare the document (or documents) with respect to which the penalty (or penalties) was assessed, the tax return preparer's or appraiser's employer identification number shall be provided; or

(iii) A person (whether an individual, corporation, or partnership) that employed one or more persons to prepare the document (or documents) with respect to which the penalty (or penalties) was assessed, the tax return preparer's or appraiser's employer identification number shall be provided.

(3) The tax return preparer's or appraiser's address where the IRS mailed the statement (or statements) of notice and demand and, if different, the tax return preparer's or appraiser's address shown on the document (or documents) with respect to which the penalty (or penalties) was assessed.

(4)(i) The address of the IRS campus or office that issued the statement (or statements) of notice and demand for payment of the penalty (or penalties).

(ii) The date (or dates) and identifying number (or numbers) of the statement (or statements) of notice and demand.

(5)(i) The identification, by amount, type, and document to which related, of each penalty included in the claim. Each document referred to in the preceding sentence shall be identified by the form title or number, by the taxpayer's (or nontaxable entity's) name and taxpayer identification number, and by the taxable year to which the document relates.

(ii) The date (or dates) of payment of the amount (or amounts) of the penalty (or penalties) included in the claim.

(iii) The total amount claimed.

(6) A statement setting forth in detail—

(i) Each ground upon which each penalty overpayment claim is based; and

(ii) Facts sufficient to apprise the IRS of the exact basis of each such claim.

(e) *Form for filing claim.*—Notwithstanding § 301.6402-2(c) of this chapter, Form 6118, "Claim for Refund of Tax Return Preparer and Promoter Penalties," is the form prescribed for making a claim as provided in this section with respect to penalties under sections 6694 and 6695. Form 843, Claim for Refund and Request for Abatement, is the form prescribed for making a claim as provided in this section with respect to a penalty under section 6695A.

(f) *Place for filing claim.*—A claim filed under this section shall be filed with the IRS campus or office that issued to the tax return preparer or appraiser the statement (or statements) of notice

and demand for payment of the penalty (or penalties) included in the claim.

(g) *Time for filing claim.*—(1)(i) Except as provided in section 6694(c)(1) and § 1.6694-4(a)(4)(ii) and (5), and in section 6694(d) and § 1.6694-1(d):

(A) A claim for a penalty paid by a tax return preparer under section 6694 and § 1.6694-1, or under section 6695 and § 1.6695-1, or by an appraiser under section 6695A (and any subsequently issued regulations) shall be filed within three years from the date the payment was made.

(B) A consolidated claim, permitted under paragraph (c)(2) of this section, shall be filed within three years from the first date of payment of any penalty included in the claim.

(ii) For purposes of this paragraph (g)(1), payment is considered made on the date payment is received by the IRS or, if applicable, on the date an amount is credited in satisfaction of the penalty.

(2) For purposes of determining whether a claim is timely filed, the rules under sections 7502 and 7503 and the provisions of §§ 1.7502-1, 1.7502-2, and 1.7503-1 apply.

(h) *Application of refund to outstanding liability of tax return preparer or appraiser.*—The IRS may, within the applicable period of limitations, credit any amount of an overpayment by a tax return preparer or appraiser of a penalty (or penalties) paid under section 6694 and § 1.6694-1, under section 6695 and § 1.6695-1, or under section 6695A (and any subsequently issued regulations) against any outstanding liability for any tax (or for any interest, additional amount, addition to the tax, or assessable penalty) owed by the tax return preparer or appraiser making the overpayment. If a portion of an overpayment is so credited, only the balance will be refunded to the tax return preparer or appraiser.

(i) *Interest.*—(1) Section 6611 and § 301.6611-1 of this chapter apply to the payment by the IRS of interest on an overpayment by a tax return preparer or appraiser of a penalty (or penalties) paid under section 6694 and § 1.6694-1, under section 6695 and § 1.6695-1, or under section 6695A (and any subsequently issued regulations).

(2) Section 6601 and § 301.6601-1 of this chapter apply to the payment of interest by a tax return preparer or appraiser to the IRS on any penalty (or penalties) assessed against the tax return preparer under section 6694 and § 1.6694-1, under section 6695 and § 1.6695-1, or under section 6695A (and any subsequently issued regulations).

(j) *Suits for refund of penalty.*—(1) A tax return preparer or appraiser may not maintain a civil action for the recovery of any penalty paid under section 6694 and § 1.6694-1, under section 6695 and § 1.6695-1, or under section 6695A(and any subsequently issued regulations), unless the tax return preparer or appraiser has previously filed a claim for credit or refund of the penalty as provided in this section (and the court has jurisdiction of the proceeding). See sections 6694(c) and 7422.

(2)(i) Except as provided in section 6694(c)(2) and § 1.6694-4(b), the periods of limitation contained in section 6532 and § 301.6532-1 of this chapter apply to a tax return preparer's or appraiser's suit for the recovery of any penalty paid under section 6694 and § 1.6694-1, under section 6695 and § 1.6695-1, or under section 6695A (and any subsequently issued regulations).

(ii) The rules under section 7503 and § 301.7503-1 of this chapter apply to the timely commencement by a tax return preparer or appraiser of a suit for the recovery of any penalty paid under section 6694 and § 1.6694-1, under section 6695 and § 1.6695-1, or under section 6695A (and any subsequently issued regulations).

(k) *Effective/applicability date.*—This section is applicable to returns and claims for refund filed, and advice provided, after December 31, 2008. [Reg. § 1.6696-1.]

☐ [*T.D.* 7621, 5-11-79. *Amended by T.D.* 9436, 12-15-2008 (*corrected* 1-28-2009).]

[Reg. § 20.6696-1]

§ 20.6696-1. Claims for credit or refund by tax return preparers or appraisers.—(a) *In general.*—For rules for claims for credit or refund by a tax return preparer who prepared a return or claim for refund for estate tax under chapter 11 of subtitle B of the Internal Revenue Code, or by an appraiser that prepared an appraisal in connection with such a return or claim for refund under section 6695A, the rules under § 1.6696-1 of this chapter will apply.

(b) *Effective/applicability date.*—This section is applicable to returns and claims for refund filed, and advice provided, after December 31, 2008. [Reg. § 20.6696-1.]

☐ [*T.D.* 9436, 12-15-2008.]

[Reg. § 25.6696-1]

§ 25.6696-1. Claims for credit or refund by tax return preparers.—(a) *In general.*—For rules for claims for credit or refund by a tax return preparer who prepared a return or claim for refund for gift tax under chapter 12 of subtitle B of the Internal Revenue Code, or by an appraiser that prepared an appraisal in connection with such a return or claim for refund under section 6695A, the rules under § 1.6696-1 of this chapter will apply.

(b) *Effective/applicability date.*—This section is applicable to returns and claims for refund filed, and advice provided, after December 31, 2008. [Reg. § 25.6696-1.]

☐ [*T.D.* 9436, 12-15-2008.]

[Reg. § 26.6696-1]

§ 26.6696-1. Claims for credit or refund by tax return preparers.—(a) *In general.*—For rules for

claims for credit or refund by a tax return preparer who prepared a return or claim for refund for generation-skipping transfer tax under chapter 13 of subtitle B of the Internal Revenue Code, or by an appraiser that prepared an appraisal in connection with such a return or claim for refund under section 6695A, the rules under § 1.6696-1 of this chapter will apply.

(b) *Effective/applicability date.*—This section is applicable to returns and claims for refund filed, and advice provided, after December 31, 2008. [Reg. § 26.6696-1.]

☐ [*T.D.* 9436, 12-15-2008.]

[Reg. § 31.6696-1]

§ 31.6696-1. Claims for credit or refund by tax return preparers.—(a) *In general.*—For rules for claims for credit or refund by a tax return preparer who prepared a return or claim for refund for employment tax under chapters 21 through 25 of subtitle C of the Internal Revenue Code, the rules under § 1.6696-1 of this chapter will apply.

(b) *Effective/applicability date.*—This section is applicable to returns and claims for refund filed, and advice provided, after December 31, 2008. [Reg. § 31.6696-1.]

☐ [*T.D.* 9436, 12-15-2008.]

[Reg. § 40.6696-1]

§ 40.6696-1. Claims for credit or refund by tax return preparers.—(a) *In general.*—The rules under § 1.6696-1 of this chapter will apply for claims for credit or refund by a tax return preparer who prepared a return or claim for refund of any tax to which this part 40 applies.

(b) *Effective/applicability date.*—This section is applicable to returns and claims for refund filed, and advice provided, after December 31, 2008. [Reg. § 40.6696-1.]

☐ [*T.D.* 9436, 12-15-2008 (*corrected* 1-28-2009).]

[Reg. § 41.6696-1]

§ 41.6696-1. Claims for credit or refund by tax return preparers.—(a) *In general.*—For rules for claims for credit or refund by a tax return preparer who prepared a return or claim for refund for excise tax under section 4481, the rules under § 1.6696-1 of this chapter will apply.

(b) *Effective/applicability date.*—This section is applicable to returns and claims for refund filed, and advice provided, after December 31, 2008. [Reg. § 41.6696-1.]

☐ [*T.D.* 9436, 12-15-2008.]

[Reg. § 44.6696-1]

§ 44.6696-1. Claims for credit or refund by tax return preparers.—(a) *In general.*—For rules for claims for credit or refund by a tax return preparer who prepared a return or claim for refund for tax on wagers under sections 4401 or 4411, the rules under § 1.6696-1 of this chapter will apply.

(b) *Effective/applicability date.*—This section is applicable to returns and claims for refund filed, and advice provided, after December 31, 2008. [Reg. § 44.6696-1.]

☐ [*T.D.* 9436, 12-15-2008.]

[Reg. § 53.6696-1]

§ 53.6696-1. Claims for credit or refund by tax return preparers.—(a) *In general.*—For rules for claims for credit or refund by a tax return preparer who prepared a return or claim for refund for tax under Chapter 42 of the Internal Revenue Code, the rules under § 1.6696-1 of this chapter will apply.

(b) *Effective/applicability date.*—This section is applicable to returns and claims for refund filed, and advice provided, after December 31, 2008. [Reg. § 53.6696-1.]

☐ [*T.D.* 9436, 12-15-2008.]

[Reg. § 54.6696-1]

§ 54.6696-1. Claims for credit or refund by tax return preparers.—(a) *In general.*—For rules for claims for credit or refund by a tax return preparer who prepared a return or claim for refund for excise tax under chapter 43 of subtitle D of the Internal Revenue Code, the rules under § 1.6696-1 of this chapter will apply.

(b) *Effective/applicability date.*—This section is applicable to returns and claims for refund filed, and advice provided, after December 31, 2008. [Reg. § 54.6696-1.]

☐ [*T.D.* 9436, 12-15-2008.]

[Reg. § 55.6696-1]

§ 55.6696-1. Claims for credit or refund by tax return preparers.—(a) *In general.*—For rules for claims for credit or refund by a tax return preparer who prepared a return or claim for refund for tax under chapter 44 of subtitle D of the Internal Revenue Code, the rules under § 1.6696-1 of this chapter will apply.

(b) *Effective/applicability date.*—This section is applicable to returns and claims for refund filed, and advice provided, after December 31, 2008. [Reg. § 55.6696-1.]

☐ [*T.D.* 9436, 12-15-2008.]

[Reg. § 56.6696-1]

§ 56.6696-1. Claims for credit or refund by tax return preparers.—(a) *In general.*—For rules relating to claims for credit or refund by a tax return preparer who prepared a return or claim for refund for tax under chapter 41 of subtitle D of the Internal Revenue Code, the rules under § 1.6696-1 of this chapter will apply.

(b) *Effective/applicability date.*—This section is applicable to returns and claims for refund filed, and advice provided, after December 31, 2008. [Reg. § 56.6696-1.]

☐ [*T.D.* 9436, 12-15-2008.]

[Reg. § 156.6696-1]

§ 156.6696-1. Claims for credit or refund by tax return preparers.—(a) *In general.*—For rules for claims for credit or refund by a tax return preparer who prepared a return or claim for refund for tax under section 5881 of the Internal Revenue Code, the rules under § 1.6696-1 of this chapter will apply.

(b) *Effective/applicability date.*—This section is applicable to returns and claims for refund filed, and advice provided, after December 31, 2008. [Reg. § 156.6696-1.]

☐ [*T.D.* 9436, 12-15-2008.]

[Reg. § 157.6696-1]

§ 157.6696-1. Claims for credit or refund by tax return preparers.—(a) *In general.*—For rules for claims for credit or refund by a tax return preparer who prepared a return or claim for refund for tax under section 5891 of the Internal Revenue Code, the rules under § 1.6696-1 of this chapter will apply.

(b) *Effective/applicability date.*—This section is applicable to returns and claims for refund filed, and advice provided, after December 31, 2008. [Reg. § 157.6696-1.]

☐ [*T.D.* 9436, 12-15-2008.]

[Reg. § 301.6707-1]

§ 301.6707-1. Failure to furnish information regarding reportable transactions.—(a)(1) *In general.*—A material advisor who is required to file a return under section 6111(a) of the Internal Revenue Code (Code) with respect to any reportable transaction who fails to file a timely return in accordance with § 301.6111-3(e) or who files a return with false or incomplete information with respect to the reportable transaction will be subject to a penalty. A material advisor who fails to file a timely return or who files a false or incomplete return with respect to more than one reportable transaction will be subject to a separate section 6707 penalty for each transaction.

(i) *Reportable transactions.*—The amount of the penalty for failing to timely file a return under section 6111(a), or filing the return with false or incomplete information with respect to any reportable transaction other than a listed transaction is $50,000.

(ii) *Listed transactions.*—(A) *In general.*—The amount of the penalty for failing to timely file a return under section 6111(a), or filing the return with false or incomplete information with respect to a listed transaction is the greater of $200,000 or 50 percent of the gross income derived by the material advisor with respect to aid, assistance, or advice that is provided with respect to the listed transaction before the date the return is filed under section 6111.

(B) *Intentional action or failure.*—If the failure or action subject to the penalty is with respect to a listed transaction and is intentional, the penalty is the greater of $200,000 or 75 percent of the gross income derived by the material advisor with respect to aid, assistance, or advice that is provided with respect to the listed transaction before the date the return is filed under section 6111.

(C) *Transaction that is both a listed transaction and reportable transaction other than a listed transaction.*—In the case of a penalty imposed under section 6707 with respect to a transaction that is both a listed transaction and a reportable transaction other than a listed transaction, the penalty under this paragraph (a)(1)(ii), and not the penalty under paragraph (a)(1)(i) of this section, will apply.

(2) *Gross income derived by the material advisor.*—For purposes of calculating the amount of the penalty with respect to a listed transaction, the gross income derived by the material advisor will be determined in accordance with § 301.6111-3(b)(3)(ii) of this chapter. If a person is a material advisor with regard to more than one type of listed transaction, the gross income derived from each type of listed transaction will be considered separately and will not be aggregated to determine the amount of any section 6707 penalty for failing to make a proper return under section 6111(a). Further, only gross income derived from listed transactions for which the advisor is a material advisor under section 6111 is taken into account for purposes of computing the penalty.

(b) *Definitions.*—(1) *Derive.*—The term "derive" is defined in § 301.6111-3(c)(3).

(2) *False information.*—For purposes of this section, the term "false information: means information provided on a Form 8918, "Material Advisor Disclosure Statement" (or successor form), filed with the Internal Revenue Service (IRS) that is untrue or incorrect when the Form 8918 (or successor form) was filed. False information does not include information provided on a Form 8918 (or successor form) filed with the IRS that is immaterial or that is untrue or incorrect due to a mistake or accident after the exercise of reasonable care.

(3) *Incomplete information.*—For purposes of this section, the term "incomplete information" means a Form 8918 (or successor form) filed with the IRS that does not provide the information required under § 301.6111-3(d). A Form 8918 (or successor form) filed with the IRS will not be considered incomplete when the information not provided on the form is immaterial or was not provided due to mistake or accident after the exercise of reasonable care. Whether information is immaterial will be determined based upon the facts and circumstances surrounding each failure to file or filing of an incomplete return. A material advisor who completes the form to the best of the material advisor's ability and knowledge after the exercise of reasonable effort to obtain the information will not be considered to have filed incomplete information within the meaning of this section. A Form 8918 (or successor form)

will be considered to provide incomplete information when it omits information required to be provided under § 301.6111-3(d) or contains a statement that the omitted information will be provided upon request.

(4) *Intentional.*—For purposes of this section, the failure to timely file a return or the submission of a return with false or incomplete information is intentional if—

(i) The material advisor knew of the obligation to file a return and knowingly did not timely file a return with the IRS; or

(ii) The material advisor filed a return knowing that it was false or incomplete.

(5) *Listed transaction.*—The term "listed transaction" is defined in section 6707A(c)(2) of the Code and § 1.6011-4(b)(2) of this chapter.

(6) *Material Advisor.*—The term "material advisor" is defined in section 6111(b)(1) of the Code and § 301.6111-3(b).

(7) *Reportable transaction.*—The term "reportable transaction" is defined in section 6707A(c)(1) of the Code and § 1.6011-4(b)(1) of this chapter.

(c) *Assessment of penalty.*—(1) *Intentional failure determined based on all the facts and circumstances.*—Whether a material advisor intentionally failed to timely file a return or intentionally filed a false or incomplete return will be determined based upon all the facts and circumstances surrounding the non-filing or filing of a false and/or incomplete return. The higher penalty under the flush language of section 6707(b)(2) will not apply to any material advisor whose failure to timely file or whose furnishing of false or incomplete information was unintentional. The failure to timely file a return, or filing a return with false or incomplete information, will be considered unintentional if the material advisor subsequently files a true and complete return prior to the earlier of the date that any taxpayer files a Form 8886, "Reportable Transaction Disclosure Statement" (or successor form) identifying the material advisor with respect to the reportable transaction in question, or the date the IRS contacts the material advisor concerning the reportable transaction.

(2) *Individual liability in the case of more than one material advisor.*—If there is more than one material advisor who is responsible for filing a return under section 6111 with respect to the same reportable transaction, a separate penalty under section 6707 may be assessed against each material advisor who fails to timely file or files a return with false or incomplete information. The determination of whether the failure or action subject to the penalty is intentional will be made individually for each material advisor.

(3) *Designation agreements.*—A material advisor who is required to file a return under section 6111 and who is a party to a designation agreement within the meaning of § 301.6111-3(f) is subject to a penalty under section 6707 if the

designated material advisor fails to file a return timely or files a return with false or incomplete information. In the case of a listed transaction, if the designated material advisor fails to file a return timely, or files a return with false or incomplete information, the nondesignated material advisor who is a party to the designation agreement will not be treated as intentionally failing to file the return, or intentionally filing a return with false or incomplete information, unless the nondesignated material advisor knew or should have known that the designated material advisor would fail to file a true and complete return timely.

(d) *Examples.*—The rules of paragraphs (a) through (c) of this section are illustrated by the following examples:

Example 1. Advisor A becomes a material advisor as defined under section 6111(b)(1) and § 301.6111-3(b) in the fourth quarter of 2014 with respect to a reportable transaction other than a listed transaction, and Advisor B also becomes a material advisor in the same quarter with respect to the same reportable transaction. Advisors A and B fail to timely file the Form 8918 with respect to the reportable transaction. Under paragraph (a)(1)(ii) of this section, the penalty for failure by a material advisor to timely disclose a reportable transaction other than a listed transaction is $50,000. Because the section 6707 penalty applies to each material advisor independently under paragraph (c)(2) of this section, Advisors A and B each are subject to a section 6707 penalty of $50,000.

Example 2. Same as *Example 1*, except that Advisor B timely files the Form 8918. Advisors A and B did not enter into a designation agreement. Accordingly, paragraph (c)(3) of this section does not apply and only Advisor A is subject to a $50,000 section 6707 penalty.

Example 3. Advisor C becomes a material advisor to Client X on January 5, 2015, with respect to a listed transaction. Advisor C derives $400,000 in gross income from his advice to Client X because he expects to receive that amount from Client X, even though he has not yet received that amount. On January 5, 2016, Advisor C becomes a material advisor to Client Y with respect to the same type of listed transaction. Advisor C derives $100,000 in gross income from his advice to Client Y because he expects to receive that amount from Client Y, even though he has not yet received that amount. At no time did Advisor C file a Form 8918 to disclose the listed transaction. For purposes of this example, assume that Advisor C's failure to file a Form 8918 was unintentional. Therefore, under paragraph (c)(2) of this section, Advisor C is subject to a section 6707 penalty based on the gross income derived from Client X and Client Y. Accordingly, Advisor C is subject to a penalty of $250,000 (50 percent of $500,000, the gross income derived from Clients X and Y).

Example 4. Same as *Example 3*, except that the gross income Advisor C expects to receive from his advice to Client Y (a C corporation) is $20,000. Because the material advisor fee threshold is not satisfied with respect to Client Y, Advisor C is not a material advisor to Client Y with respect to the listed transaction. Advisor C is, however, a material advisor with respect to Client X with respect to the same listed transaction. Therefore, Advisor C is subject to a section 6707 penalty with respect to the failure to timely file a Form 8918 disclosing the listed transaction. Although Advisor C provided advice with respect to two transactions that are the same type of listed transaction, Advisor C was only a material advisor with respect to advice provided to Client X. Therefore, under paragraph (c)(2) of this section Advisor C is subject to a section 6707 penalty based only on the gross income derived from Client X. Accordingly, Advisor C is subject to a penalty of $200,000 (50 percent of $400,000, the gross income derived from Client X).

Example 5. Same as *Example 3*, except that Advisor C files a Form 8918 disclosing the listed transaction on November 16, 2015. Because Advisor C becomes a material advisor to Client X on January 5, 2015, the Form 8918 is required to be filed on or before April 30, 2015 (the last day of the month that follows the end of the calendar quarter in which the advisor became a material advisor with regard to the reportable transaction). See § 301.6111-3(e). Therefore, Advisor C did not timely file the Form 8918. Advisor C is subject to a $200,000 penalty under section 6707 for his unintentional failure because, as of the date he filed the Form 8918, the gross income Advisor C had received or expected to receive with respect to advice relating to a listed transaction that was not disclosed only included $400,000 of gross income for advice to Client X. By the time that Advisor C provides advice to Client Y on January 5, 2016, Advisor C has disclosed the listed transaction.

Example 6. Same as *Example 3*, except that Advisor C files the Form 8918 on February 16, 2016, disclosing the listed transaction. Because Advisor C first becomes a material advisor with respect to the listed transaction on January 5, 2015, the Form 8918 is required to be filed on or before April 30, 2015 regardless of the fact that Advisor C is also a material advisor to a second client, Client Y, with respect to the same listed transaction. This is because under the facts of *Example 3*, Advisor C "becomes" a material advisor on January 5, 2015. The date on which a material advisor "becomes" a material advisor is determinative of the due date for the Form 8918 under § 301.6111-3(e). Therefore, when Advisor C files the Form 8918 on February 16, 2016, the form is not timely filed under section 6111. Under paragraph (c)(2) of this section, Advisor C is subject to a penalty under section 6707 of $250,000 (50 percent of $500,000) because, as of the date that the Form 8918 was filed, the gross income that Advisor C received or expected to receive as a material advisor with respect to a listed transaction that was not disclosed included gross income for advice to both Client X ($400,000) and Client Y ($100,000).

Reg. § 301.6707-1(d)

Example 7. Advisor D becomes a material advisor as defined under section 6111(b)(1) and §301.6111-3(b) in the first quarter of 2016 with respect to a reportable transaction other than a listed transaction. Advisor D does not file a Form 8918 by April 30, 2016. The transaction is then identified as a listed transaction in published guidance on July 7, 2016. Advisor D knew that he had a new obligation to file a Form 8918 by October 31, 2016, and intentionally fails to file the Form 8918. Advisor D is subject to only one penalty, in the amount of the greater of $200,000, or 75 percent of the gross income he derived from the transaction, for intentionally failing to disclose the listed transaction in accordance with §301.6111-3(d)(1) and (e).

Example 8. Same as *Example 7*, except that Advisor D filed a Form 8918 disclosing the listed transaction on October 15, 2016. As a result of that disclosure, Advisor D is not subject to the section 6707 penalty amount described in §301.6707-1(a)(1)(ii). However, because Advisor D did not timely file a Form 8918 by April 30, 2016, the due date for the Form 8918 with respect to the reportable transaction for which Advisor D became a material advisor in the first quarter of 2016, Advisor D is subject to a section 6707 penalty of $50,000 as described in §301.6707-1(a)(1)(i). The disclosure of the listed transaction does not correct Advisor D's initial failure to disclose the reportable transaction by April 30, 2016.

(e) *Rescission authority.*—(1) *In general.*—The Commissioner (or the Commissioner's delegate) may rescind the section 6707 penalty if—

(i) The violation relates to a reportable transaction that is not a listed transaction; and

(ii) Rescinding the penalty would promote compliance with the requirements of the Code and effective tax administration.

(2) *Requesting rescission.*—The Secretary may prescribe the procedures for a material advisor to request rescission of a section 6707 penalty by guidance published in the Internal Revenue Bulletin.

(3) *Factors that weigh in favor of granting rescission.*—In determining whether rescission would promote compliance with the requirements of the Code and effective tax administration, the Commissioner (or the Commissioner's delegate) will take into account the following list of factors that weigh in favor of granting rescission. This is not an exclusive list, and no single factor will be determinative of whether to grant rescission in any particular case. Rather, the Commissioner (or the Commissioner's delegate) will consider and weigh all relevant factors, regardless of whether the factor is included in this list.

(i) The material advisor, upon becoming aware of the failure to disclose a reportable transaction in accordance with section 6111 and the regulations thereunder, filed a complete and proper, albeit untimely, Form 8918 (or successor form). This factor weighs in favor of rescission if

circumstances suggest that the material advisor did not delay in filing an untimely but properly completed Form 8918 (or successor form) until after the IRS had taken steps to identify the person as a material advisor with respect to the reportable transaction. For instance, this factor will weigh strongly in favor of rescission if the material advisor files the Form 8918 (or successor form) prior to the date the IRS contacts the material advisor concerning the reportable transaction. However, this factor will not weigh in favor of rescission if the facts and circumstances indicate that the material advisor delayed filing the Form 8918 (or successor form) until after a taxpayer files a Form 8886 (or successor form) identifying the material advisor with respect to the reportable transaction in question.

(ii) The material advisor's failure to disclose the reportable transaction properly was due to an unintentional mistake of fact that existed despite the material advisor's reasonable attempts to ascertain the correct facts with respect to the transaction.

(iii) The material advisor has an established history of properly disclosing other reportable transactions and complying with other tax laws, including compliance with any requests made by the IRS under section 6112, if applicable.

(iv) The material advisor demonstrates that the failure to include on any return or statement any information required to be disclosed under section 6111 arose from events beyond the material advisor's control.

(v) The material advisor cooperates with the IRS by providing timely information with respect to the transaction at issue that the Commissioner (or the Commissioner's delegate) may request in consideration of the rescission request. In considering whether a material advisor cooperates with the IRS, the Commissioner (or the Commissioner's delegate) will take into account whether the material advisor meets the deadlines described in guidance published in the Internal Revenue Bulletin for complying with requests for additional information.

(vi) Assessment of the penalty weighs against equity and good conscience, including whether the material advisor demonstrates that there was reasonable cause for, and the material advisor acted in good faith with respect to, the failure to timely file or to include on any return any information required to be disclosed under section 6111. An important factor in determining reasonable cause and good faith is the extent of the material advisor's efforts to determine whether there was a requirement to file the return required under section 6111. The presence of reasonable cause, however, will not necessarily be determinative of whether to grant rescission.

(4) *Absence of favorable factors weighs against rescission.*—The absence of facts establishing the factors described in paragraph (e)(3) of this section weighs against granting rescission. The presence or absence of any one of these factors,

however, will not necessarily be determinative of whether to grant rescission; rather the determination will be made in consideration of all of the factors and any other facts and circumstances.

(5) *Factors not considered.*—In determining whether to grant rescission, the Commissioner (or the Commissioner's delegate) will not consider doubt as to collectability of, or liability for, the penalties (except that the Commissioner (or the Commissioner's delegate) may consider doubt as to liability to the extent it is a factor in the determination of reasonable cause and good faith).

(f) *Effective/applicability date.*—The rules of this section apply to returns the due date for which is after July 31, 2014. [Reg. § 301.6707-1.]

☐ [*T.D. 9686, 7-30-2014.*]

[Reg. § 301.6707A-1]

§ 301.6707A-1. Failure to include on any return or statement any information required to be disclosed under section 6011 with respect to a reportable transaction.—(a) *In general.*—Any person who fails to include on any return or statement any information required to be disclosed under section 6011 with respect to a reportable transaction may be subject to a monetary penalty. Subject to maximum and minimum limits, the penalty for failure to include information with respect to any reportable transaction is 75 percent of the decrease in tax shown on the return as a result of the transaction or the decrease that would have resulted from the transaction if it were respected for Federal tax purposes. The penalty for failure to include information with respect to a listed transaction shall not exceed $100,000 for a natural person and $200,000 for all other persons. The penalty for failure to include information with respect to any other reportable transaction shall not exceed $10,000 for a natural person and $50,000 for all other persons. The penalty with respect to any reportable transaction shall not be less than $5,000 for a natural person and $10,000 for all other persons. The section 6707A penalty is in addition to any other penalty that may be imposed.

(b) *Definitions.*—(1) *Reportable transaction.*—The term "reportable transaction" is defined in section 6707A(c)(1) of the Code and § 1.6011-4(b)(1) of this chapter.

(2) *Listed transaction.*—The term "listed transaction" is defined in section 6707A(c)(2) of the Code and § 1.6011-4(b)(2) of this chapter.

(c) *Assessment of the penalty.*—(1) *In general.*—The Internal Revenue Service may assess a penalty under section 6707A with respect to each failure to disclose a reportable transaction within the time and in the form and manner provided by § § 1.6011-4(d) and 1.6011-4(e) of this chapter or pursuant to the time, form, and manner stated in other published guidance. Section 1.6011-4(e) provides, in part, that a taxpayer must attach a

disclosure statement to the taxpayer's return for each taxable year for which the taxpayer participates in a reportable transaction. A taxpayer also must attach a disclosure statement to each amended return that reflects the taxpayer's participation in a reportable transaction and, if a reportable transaction results in a loss that is carried back to a prior year, a taxpayer must attach a disclosure statement to the taxpayer's application for tentative refund or amended return for that prior year. In addition, a copy of the disclosure statement must be sent to the IRS Office of Tax Shelter Analysis (OTSA) at the same time that any disclosure statement is first filed by the taxpayer pertaining to a particular reportable transaction. Nonetheless, a taxpayer who is required to disclose a transaction by filing Form 8886, "Reportable Transaction Disclosure Statement," (or successor form) with a return (including an amended return or application for tentative refund) and who is also required to disclose the transaction by filing that form with OTSA, is subject to only a single section 6707A penalty for failure to make either one or both of those disclosures. If section 6011 and the regulations thereunder require a disclosure statement to be filed at the time that a return is filed, the disclosure statement is considered to be timely filed if it is filed at the same time as the return, even if the return is filed untimely after its due date (including extensions).

(2) *Examples.*—The rules of paragraph (c)(1) of this section are illustrated by the following examples:

Example 1. Taxpayer T is required to attach a Form 8886 to its return for the 2008 taxable year and to send a copy of the Form 8886 to OTSA at the time it files its return. Taxpayer T fails to attach the Form 8886 to its return and fails to send a copy of the Form 8886 to OTSA. Taxpayer T is subject to a single penalty under section 6707A for failure to disclose because Taxpayer T failed to comply with the disclosure requirements of section 6011 as described in § § 1.6011-4(d) and 1.6011-4(e) of this chapter. A penalty under section 6707A also would apply if Taxpayer T had failed to comply with only one of the two requirements.

Example 2. Same as *Example 1*, except that Taxpayer T also subsequently files an amended return for 2008 that reflects Taxpayer T's participation in the reportable transaction described in *Example 1*. Taxpayer T fails to attach a Form 8886 to the amended return as required by § 1.6011-4(e)(1) of this chapter. Taxpayer T is subject to an additional penalty under section 6707A for failing to disclose a reportable transaction on the amended return for 2008.

Example 3. In November 2009, Taxpayer U participates in a reportable transaction resulting in a loss. On March 15, 2010, Taxpayer U files its 2009 return, on which it reports the loss and to which it fails to attach a Form 8886. One month later, Taxpayer U files an amended return for 2008, on which it carries back the loss and to which it fails to attach a Form 8886. Section

1.6011-4(e)(1) of this chapter requires Taxpayer U to attach a Form 8886 to its amended return for the 2008 taxable year. Taxpayer U is subject to two penalties under section 6707A: one for the failure to attach Form 8886 to its amended return for 2008 and another for the failure to attach Form 8886 to its 2009 return.

Example 4. Taxpayer V participates in a non-listed reportable transaction and is required to attach a Form 8886 to its return for the 2009 taxable year that is due on March 15, 2010. Taxpayer V timely files its return but fails to attach the Form 8886 to its return. After the due date of Taxpayer V's return and without an extension of time to file, Taxpayer V files an amended return relating to the 2009 taxable year to which Taxpayer V attaches the Form 8886. Taxpayer V is subject to a penalty under section 6707A for failure to disclose because Taxpayer V failed to comply with the disclosure requirements of section 6011 (described in § 1.6011-4(e)(1) of this chapter) by not attaching a Form 8886 to its original return for the 2009 taxable year that was timely filed on or before the due date of March 15, 2010. An additional penalty under section 6707A would apply if Taxpayer V had failed to attach a Form 8886 to its amended return.

Example 5. Shareholder W, a shareholder in an S Corporation, receives a timely Schedule K-1, "Shareholder's Share of Income, Deductions, Credits, etc.," on April 10, 2009, and determines that she is required to attach a Form 8886 to her individual income tax return for the 2008 taxable year. Shareholder W fails to attach the Form 8886 to her 2008 individual income tax return but files a proper and complete Form 8886 with OTSA on June 12, 2009. Section 1.6011-4(e)(1) of this chapter provides that if a taxpayer who is a partner in a partnership, a shareholder in an S corporation, or a beneficiary of a trust receives a timely Schedule K-1 less than 10 calendar days before the due date of the taxpayer's return (including extensions) and, based on receipt of the timely Schedule K-1, the taxpayer determines that the taxpayer participated in a reportable transaction, the disclosure statement will not be considered late if the taxpayer discloses the reportable transaction by filing a disclosure statement with OTSA within 60 calendar days after the due date of the taxpayer's return (including extensions). Accordingly, Shareholder W is not subject to a penalty under section 6707A for failure to disclose.

Example 6. In July 2008, Taxpayer X participates in Transaction Z, a transaction that is not reportable as of April 15, 2009, the date Taxpayer X files his individual income tax return for 2008. On July 15, 2009, Transaction Z is identified as a transaction of interest. Section 1.6011-4(e)(2)(i) of this chapter provides that if a transaction that is not otherwise a reportable transaction becomes a listed transaction or a transaction of interest after the taxpayer has filed a tax return (including an amended return) reflecting the taxpayer's participation in the listed transaction or transaction of interest and before the end of the period of limitations for assessment of tax for any taxable year

in which the taxpayer participated in the listed transaction or transaction of interest, then a disclosure statement must be filed with OTSA within 90 calendar days after the date on which the transaction became a listed transaction or transaction of interest, regardless of whether the taxpayer participated in the transaction in the year the transaction became a listed transaction or a transaction of interest. Taxpayer X fails to file a Form 8886 with OTSA by October 13, 2009, 90 calendar days after the date that the transaction was identified as a transaction of interest. Accordingly, Taxpayer X is subject to a penalty under section 6707A.

Example 7. Taxpayer Y is required to attach a Form 8886 to its return for the 2008 taxable year with respect to participation in a listed transaction. Taxpayer Y attaches the Form 8886 to its timely filed return. The Form 8886, however, does not describe all of the potential tax benefits expected to result from this transaction and states that information will be provided upon request. Because the Form 8886 does not describe all of the potential tax benefits expected to result from the transaction and merely provides that the information will be provided upon request, the Form 8886 filed by Taxpayer Y is incomplete and does not satisfy the requirements set forth in § 1.6011-4(d) of this chapter. Taxpayer Y is subject to a penalty under section 6707A for failure to disclose in the appropriate manner.

(d) *Rescission authority.*—(1) *In general.*—The Commissioner (or the Commissioner's delegate) may rescind the section 6707A penalty if—

　　(i) The violation relates to a reportable transaction that is not a listed transaction; and

　　(ii) Rescinding the penalty would promote compliance with the requirements of the Code and effective tax administration.

(2) *Requesting rescission.*—The Secretary may prescribe the procedures for a taxpayer to request rescission of a section 6707A penalty with respect to a reportable transaction other than a listed transaction by publishing a revenue procedure or other guidance in the Internal Revenue Bulletin.

(3) *Factors that weigh in favor of granting rescission.*—In determining whether rescission would promote compliance with the requirements of the Internal Revenue Code and effective tax administration, the Commissioner (or the Commissioner's delegate) will take into account the following list of factors that weigh in favor of granting rescission. This is not an exclusive list and no single factor will be determinative of whether to grant rescission in any particular case. Rather, the Commissioner (or the Commissioner's delegate) will consider and weigh all relevant factors, regardless of whether the factor is included in this list.

　　(i) The taxpayer, upon becoming aware that it failed, in whole or in part, to disclose a reportable transaction in accordance with the requirements of § 1.6011-4 of this chapter, filed a complete and proper, albeit untimely, Form 8886 (or successor form), as required by § 1.6011-4. If the penalty is due to the taxpayer's failure to file Form 8886 (or successor form) with a return (including an amended return or application for tentative refund), in order for an untimely disclosure to weigh in favor of rescission, the taxpayer must file an amended return with the appropriate Service Center and attach a complete and proper Form 8886 (or successor form) to that amended return. The amended return filed with the untimely Form 8886 (or successor form) must not reflect any other changes to the return (including an amended return or application for tentative refund) that it amends, and the taxpayer must, in the space provided for an explanation of changes on the amended return, state the reason for filing the amended return. If the penalty is due to the taxpayer's failure to file Form 8886 (or successor form) with OTSA, in order for an untimely disclosure to weigh in favor of rescission, the taxpayer must file a complete and proper Form 8886 (or successor form) with OTSA. If the taxpayer fails to file a complete and proper Form 8886 (or successor form) with the return (including an amended return or application for tentative refund) and also fails to file a copy of the complete and proper Form 8886 (or successor form) with OTSA, incurring one penalty for both failures, then the taxpayer must, in the manner prescribed in this paragraph (d)(3)(i), file complete and proper Forms 8886 with both the Service Center and OTSA in order for the untimely disclosures to weigh in favor of rescission. This factor will weigh heavily in favor of rescission provided that—

(A) The taxpayer files the Form 8886 prior to the date the IRS first contacts the taxpayer (including contacts by the IRS with any partnership in which the taxpayer is a partner, any S corporation in which the taxpayer is a shareholder, or any trust in which the taxpayer is a beneficiary) concerning a tax examination for the tax period in which the taxpayer participated in the reportable transaction; and

(B) Other circumstances suggest that the taxpayer did not delay filing an untimely but properly completed Form 8886 until after the IRS had taken steps to identify the taxpayer's participation in the reportable transaction in question.

(ii) The failure, in whole or in part, to disclose in accordance with the requirements of § 1.6011-4 of this chapter was due to an unintentional mistake of fact that existed despite the taxpayer's reasonable attempts to ascertain the correct facts with respect to the transaction.

(iii) The taxpayer has an established history of properly disclosing other reportable transactions and complying with other tax laws.

(iv) The taxpayer demonstrates that the failure to include on any return or statement any information required to be disclosed under section 6011 arose from events beyond the taxpayer's control.

(v) The taxpayer cooperates with the IRS by providing timely information with respect to the transaction at issue that the Commissioner

(or the Commissioner's delegate) may request in consideration of the rescission request. In considering whether a taxpayer cooperates with the IRS, the Commissioner (or the Commissioner's delegate) will take into account whether the taxpayer meets the deadlines described in Rev. Proc. 2007-21 (2007-1 CB 613) (or successor document) (see § 601.601(d)(2)(ii)(b) of this chapter) for complying with requests for additional information.

(vi) Assessment of the penalty weighs against equity and good conscience, including whether the taxpayer demonstrates that there was reasonable cause for, and the taxpayer acted in good faith with respect to, the failure to timely file or to include on any return any information required to be disclosed under section 6011. An important factor in determining reasonable cause and good faith is the extent of the taxpayer's efforts to ensure that persons who prepared the taxpayer's return were informed of the taxpayer's participation in the reportable transactions; this factor will be disregarded, however, if the persons who prepared the taxpayer's return were material advisors with respect to the reportable transaction. The presence of reasonable cause, however, will not necessarily be determinative of whether to grant rescission.

(4) *Absence of favorable factors weighs against rescission.*—The absence of facts establishing the factors described in paragraph (d)(3) of this section weighs against granting rescission. The absence of any one of these factors, however, will not necessarily be determinative of whether to grant rescission.

(5) *Factors not considered.*—In determining whether to grant rescission, the Commissioner (or the Commissioner's delegate) will not consider collectability of, or doubt as to liability for, the penalties (except that the Commissioner may consider doubt as to liability to the extent it is a factor in the determination of reasonable cause and good faith).

(6) *Example.*—The following example illustrates the rules of paragraph (d)(3) of this section:

Example. In 2008, Taxpayer Z participated in a nonlisted reportable transaction for the first time. Under § 1.6011-4(e)(1) of this chapter, he was required to attach a complete and proper Form 8886 to his 2008 return, due on April 15, 2009, and to file a copy of the Form 8886 with OTSA. Taxpayer Z timely filed his 2008 return but failed to attach a Form 8886 to his return or file a Form 8886 with OTSA. On June 1, 2009, Taxpayer Z discovered his error. On June 8, 2009, Taxpayer Z filed an amended return for tax year 2008 and attached a complete and proper Form 8886 that disclosed his participation in the reportable transaction. The amended return reflected no changes from the original return and explained that the sole purpose of the amended return was to correct Taxpayer Z's failure to file a Form 8886 with his original return. On June 8, 2009, Taxpayer Z also filed a copy of the complete and proper Form 8886 with OTSA. The IRS later notified Taxpayer Z that he was subject to a penalty under section 6707A because he failed to comply with the disclosure requirements of section 6011 by not attaching Form 8886 to his return for the 2008 taxable year. The IRS properly assessed the penalty under section 6707A and, on October 15, 2010, issued notice and demand. On November 1, 2010, in accordance with Rev. Proc. 2007-21, Taxpayer Z submitted a written request for rescission of the assessed penalty. The fact that Taxpayer Z filed an untimely Form 8886 shortly after discovery of his error but before the IRS first contacted him concerning his return for the 2008 taxable year will weigh heavily in favor of rescission.

(e) *Reports to the Securities and Exchange Commission (SEC).*—(1) *In general.*—Under section 6707A(e), a taxpayer who is required to file periodic reports under section 13 or section 15(d) of the Securities Exchange Act of 1934 (or is required to be consolidated with another person for purposes of these reports) must disclose in certain reports, as provided in revenue procedures or other guidance published pursuant to paragraph (e)(2) of this section, the requirement to pay each of the following penalties:

(i) The penalty imposed by section 6707A(a) for failure to disclose a listed transaction.

(ii) The accuracy-related penalty imposed by section 6662A(a) at the 30-percent rate determined under section 6662A(c) for a reportable transaction understatement with respect to which the relevant facts affecting the tax treatment of the reportable transaction were not adequately disclosed in accordance with regulations prescribed under section 6011.

(iii) The accuracy-related penalty imposed by section 6662(a) at the 40-percent rate determined under section 6662(h) for a gross valuation misstatement, if the taxpayer (but for the exclusionary rule of section 6662A(e)(2)(C)(ii)) would have been subject to the accuracy-related penalty under section 6662A(a) at the 30-percent rate determined under section 6662A(c).

(iv) The penalty described in paragraph (e)(3) of this section for failure to disclose in periodic reports filed with the SEC the requirement to pay any of the penalties described in paragraphs (e)(1)(i) through (e)(1)(iii) or paragraph (e)(3) of this section.

(2) *Manner and content of disclosure.*—The Secretary may, by publishing a revenue procedure or other guidance in the Internal Revenue Bulletin, prescribe the manner in which the disclosure under paragraph (e)(1) of this section must be made, including identification of the specific SEC form and section thereof in which the taxpayer must make the disclosure as well as specification of the timing and contents of the disclosure.

(3) *Penalty for failure to disclose in SEC filings.*—Any taxpayer who is required to file periodic reports under section 13 or section 15(d) of the Securities Exchange Act of 1934 (or is required to file consolidated reports with another person) may be subject to a penalty under section 6707A(b) for each failure to disclose the requirement to pay a penalty identified in paragraphs (e)(1)(i) through (e)(1)(iii) of this section in the manner specified by revenue procedure or other guidance published in the Internal Revenue Bulletin. The taxpayer also may be subject to an additional penalty under section 6707A(b) for each failure to disclose a penalty arising under this section in the manner specified by revenue procedure or other guidance published in the Internal Revenue Bulletin. The penalty provided by this paragraph (e)(3) will be rescinded if the IRS rescinds in full the penalty for failing to disclose under section 6011 the reportable transaction underlying the penalty provided by this section. Otherwise, the penalty provided by this paragraph (e)(3) is not subject to rescission.

(f) *Effective/applicability date.*—(1) The rules of this section apply to disclosure statements that are due after September 11, 2008.

(2) The penalty calculations set forth in paragraph (a) of this section apply to penalties assessed after December 31, 2006. [Reg. §301.6707A-1].

☐ [*T.D.* 9550, 9-1-2011.]

[Reg. §301.6708-1]

§301.6708-1. Failure to maintain lists of advisees with respect to reportable transactions.— (a) *In general.*—Any person who is required to maintain a list under section 6112 who, upon written request for the list, fails to make the list available to the Secretary within 20 business days after the date of the request shall be subject to a penalty in the amount of $10,000 for each subsequent calendar day on which the person fails to furnish a list containing the information and in the form required by section 6112 and its corresponding regulations. The penalty will not be imposed on any particular day or days for which the person establishes that the failure to comply on that day is due to reasonable cause.

(b) *Calculation of the 20-business-day period.*— The 20-business-day period shall begin on the first business day after the earliest of the date that the IRS—

(1) Mails a request for the list required to be maintained under section 6112(a) by certified or registered mail to the person required to maintain the list;

(2) Hand delivers the written request to the person required to maintain the list; or

(3) Leaves the written request with an individual 18 years old or older at the usual place of business of the person required to maintain the list.

(c) *Making a list available.*—(1) A person who is required to maintain a list required by section 6112 may make the list available by mailing or delivering it to the IRS within 20 business days after the date of the list request. Section 7502 and the regulations thereunder shall apply to this section.

(2) A person who is required to maintain a list required by section 6112 may also make the list available to the IRS by making it available for inspection and copying during normal business hours, as provided by section 6112, or by another agreed-upon method, on an agreed-upon date that falls within the 20-business-day period following the list request.

(3) *Extension.*—(i) *In general.*—Upon a showing of good cause by the person prior to the expiration of the 20-business-day period following a list request, the IRS may, in its discretion, agree to extend the period within which to make all or part of the list available. For purposes of this paragraph, "good cause" is shown if the person establishes that the 20-business-day deadline cannot reasonably be met despite diligent efforts by the person to maintain the materials constituting a list and to make that list available to the IRS in the time and manner required by the Secretary under section 6112.

(ii) *Requesting an extension.*—Any request for an extension of the 20-business-day period must be made in writing to the person at the IRS who requested the list. The person requesting an extension must briefly describe the information and documents that comprise the list as required by section 6112; explain the circumstances that would warrant additional time; propose a schedule to complete the production of the list; state that to the best of the person's knowledge, as of the date of the list request, all information and records relating to the list under the person's possession, custody, or control had been maintained in accordance with procedures and policies that are consistent with sections 6001 and 6112 of the Internal Revenue Code; and state that the extension request is not being made to avoid the person's list maintenance obligations imposed by section 6112 and its corresponding regulations. The IRS may, in its discretion, grant the person's extension request in full or in part. The IRS will consider whether granting an extension may impair its ability to make a timely assessment against any of the participants in the transaction associated with the requested list. The IRS will not grant an extension if it determines that a significant reason for the extension request is to delay producing the list. A pending extension request by itself does not constitute reasonable cause for purposes of section 6708.

(4) *Examples.*—The following examples illustrate paragraph (c)(3)(i) and (ii) of this section. These examples are intended to illustrate how the facts and circumstances in paragraph (c)(3)(i) and (ii) of this section may apply; in any given case, however, all of the facts and circumstances must be analyzed.

Example 1. (i) Firm A is a large law firm that is a material advisor. Firm A conducts annual sessions to educate its professionals about reportable transactions and the firm's obligations related to those reportable transactions. Firm A instructs its professionals to provide information on tax engagements that involve reportable transactions and to provide the documents required to be maintained under sections 6001 and 6112 to Firm A's compliance officer for list maintenance purposes. Firm A's policy provides that, for each engagement involving a reportable transaction, one firm professional will send an email to the firm's compliance officer about the engagement and then direct a subordinate to send the documents required to be maintained to the firm's compliance officer. Firm A has policies and procedures in place to monitor compliance with these rules and to address non-compliance.

(ii) Firm A receives a request from the IRS for a section 6112 list. In compiling its list to turn over to the IRS during the 20-business-day period following the list request, Firm A discovers that, with respect to one reportable transaction, a subordinate did not provide the documentation required by Firm A's policy. In addition, Firm A experiences difficulty locating the required documents as both the professional and the subordinate who worked on the matter are no longer employed by Firm A, requiring the firm to undertake an extensive search for the information responsive to the list request. Firm A also seeks the information from the firm's clients. Despite these efforts, Firm A reasonably determined that it will not be able to respond timely to the request. Within the 20-business-day period, Firm A notifies the IRS, in writing, of the difficulties it is experiencing and requests an additional 10 business days to locate and produce the information for this one transaction. Within the 20-business-day period, Firm A makes all other required list information available to the IRS, together with a description of the information that is being searched for, all statements required by these regulations, and a proposed schedule to produce the missing information.

(iii) Under these circumstances, Firm A demonstrated that it could not reasonably make the portion of the list relating to the one transaction available within the 20-business-day period and thus qualified for an extension. Firm A had established policies and procedures reasonably designed and implemented to ensure and monitor compliance with the requirements of section 6112 and address non-compliance. Because the facts and circumstances indicate that Firm A made diligent efforts to maintain the materials constituting the list in a readily accessible form and as otherwise required under section 6112, the requested 10-business-day extension with respect to the portion of the list relating to the one transaction where records were not maintained in accordance with the firm's policies and procedures should be granted.

Example 2. (i) Assume the same facts set forth in example one, except that, in the process of compiling the list to comply with the list maintenance request, Firm A first becomes aware that a firm professional did not send an email to the firm's compliance officer about a

Reg. § 301.6708-1(c)(4)

transaction subject to the list maintenance request and did not direct a subordinate to send to the firm's compliance officer the information required to be maintained with respect to the transaction. Assume further that Firm A had a robust section 6112 compliance monitoring program in place and despite this, the firm did not know that the professional did not follow firm policies and procedures with respect to this transaction. The professional who worked on the matter is no longer employed by Firm A, causing Firm A difficulty in locating the required information and in ascertaining whether the professional in question failed to comply with Firm A's list maintenance policies with respect to any other reportable transactions. Firm A is searching its records to locate information responsive to the list request and to ensure that no other reportable transactions were omitted from the list. Firm A estimates that it will take an additional 20 business days after the 20th business day to retrieve the missing information and provide IRS with the additional information responsive to the list request. Within the 20-business-day period, Firm A notifies the IRS, in writing, of the difficulties it is experiencing and requests an additional 20 business days to locate and produce the information for this one transaction and for any other reportable transactions omitted from the list as a result of the inaction by the professional in question. Within the 20-business-day period, Firm A makes all other required list information available to the IRS, together with a description of the information that is being searched for, all statements required by these regulations, and a proposed schedule to produce the missing documents.

(ii) Under these facts and circumstances, Firm A demonstrated that it could not reasonably, within the 20-business-day period, make available the portion of the list relating to one or possibly more transactions omitted from the list because of the inaction of the professional in question. Firm A therefore qualifies for an extension. Firm A had established policies and procedures reasonably designed and implemented to ensure and monitor compliance with the requirements of section 6112 and address non-compliance. Because the facts and circumstances indicate that Firm A made diligent efforts to maintain the materials constituting the list in a readily accessible form and as otherwise required under section 6112, the requested 20-business-day extension with respect to the portion of the list relating to the one known omitted transaction and to any other omitted reportable transactions resulting from the inaction of the professional in question should be granted.

(d) *Failure to make list available.*—A failure to make the list available includes any failure to furnish the requested list to the IRS in a timely manner and in the form required under section 6112 and its corresponding regulations. Examples of failures to make a list available include instances in which a person fails to furnish any list; furnishes an incomplete list; or furnishes a list, whether or not complete, after the time required by this section.

(e) *Computation of penalty.*—(1) *In general.*—The penalty imposed by section 6708 accrues daily, beginning on the first calendar day after the expiration of the 20-business-day period following a written list request, and continues for each calendar day thereafter until the person's failure to furnish a list in the form required by section 6112 and its corresponding regulations ends. If the list is delivered or mailed to the IRS outside of the 20-business-day period, the penalty shall not apply on the day the list is delivered to the IRS or, if the list is mailed, the day the list is received by the IRS.

(2) *Computation of penalty after grant of extension.*—If the IRS grants an extension of the 20-business-day period pursuant to paragraph (c)(3) of this section, the penalty imposed by section 6708 accrues daily, beginning on the first calendar day after the extension period expires, and continues for each calendar day thereafter until the person's failure to furnish a list in the form required by section 6112 and its corresponding regulations ends. If the list is delivered or mailed to the IRS outside of the period of extension, the penalty shall not apply on the day the list is delivered to the IRS or, if the list is mailed, the day the list is received by the IRS.

(3) *Designation agreements and concurrent application of penalty.*—If material advisors with respect to the same reportable transaction enter into a designation agreement pursuant to section 6112(b)(2) and §301.6112-1(f), separate penalties will be imposed on designated material advisors and nondesignated material advisors who are parties to the designation agreement for their respective periods of failure or noncompliance with a list request. A penalty will continue to accrue against a material advisor who is a party to a designation agreement until such time when a list complying with the requirements of section 6112 and its corresponding regulations is furnished by that material advisor or any other material advisor who is a party to the designation agreement.

(4) *Example.*—The following example illustrates paragraph (e) of this section.

Example. The IRS hand delivers a written request for the list required to be maintained under section 6112 to Firm B, a material advisor, on Friday, March 10, 2017. Firm B must make the list available to the IRS on or before Friday, April 7, 2017, the 20th business day after the request was hand delivered. If Firm B fails to make the list available to the IRS by that day, absent reasonable cause or the IRS's grant of an extension of the response time, the $10,000-per-day penalty begins on Saturday, April 8, 2017. The $10,000 per day penalty will continue for each subsequent calendar day until Firm B makes the complete list available, except for those days for which Firm B demonstrates reasonable cause. If Firm B hand delivers a complete copy of the requested list to the IRS on the morning of Tuesday, April 11, 2017, absent reasonable cause or the IRS's prior grant of an extension for the response time, a penalty of $30,000 will be imposed upon Firm B (for April 8, 9, and 10). See paragraphs (g) and (h) of this section for an explanation of reasonable cause.

(f) *Definitions.*—For purposes of this section, the following definitions apply:

(1) *Material advisor* means a person described in section 6111 and §301.6111-3(b).

(2) *Business day* means every calendar day other than a Saturday, Sunday, or legal holiday within the meaning of section 7503.

(3) *Reportable transaction* means a transaction described in section 6707A(c)(1) and section 1.6011-4(b)(1).

(4) *Listed transaction* means a transaction described in section 6707A(c)(2) and §1.6011-4(b)(2) of this chapter.

(g) *Reasonable cause – general applicability.*—(1) *Overview.*—The section 6708 penalty will not be imposed for any day or days for which the person shows that the failure to make a complete list available to the IRS was due to reasonable cause. The determination of whether a person had reasonable cause is made on a case-by-case and day-by-day basis, taking into account all the relevant facts and circumstances. Facts and circumstances relevant to a material advisor's reasonable cause for failing to make available the list on a specific day include facts and circumstances arising after the request for the list. The person's showing of reasonable cause should relate to each specific day or days for which the person failed to make available the requested list. Factors establishing reasonable cause include, but are not limited to, factors identified in paragraphs (g) and (h) of this section.

(2) *Good-faith factors.*—The most important factors to establish reasonable cause are those that reflect the extent of the person's good-faith efforts to comply with section 6112. The following factors, which are not exclusive, will be considered in determining whether a person has made a good-faith effort to comply with the section 6112 requirements:

(i) The person's efforts to determine or assess its status as a material advisor as defined by section 6111;

(ii) The person's efforts to determine the information and documentation required to be maintained under section 6112;

(iii) The person's efforts to meet its obligations to maintain a readily producible list as required by section 6112;

(iv) The person's efforts, upon receiving the list request, to make the list available to the IRS within the 20-business-day period (or extended period) under paragraphs (a), (b), and (c)(3) of this section; and

(v) The person's efforts to ensure that the list furnished to the IRS is accurate and complete.

(3) *Ordinary business care.*—The exercise of ordinary business care may constitute reasonable cause. To show ordinary business care, the person may, for example, show that the person established, and adhered to, procedures reasonably designed and implemented to ensure compliance with the section 6112 requirements. In all instances when ordinary business care is claimed as constituting reasonable cause, a person must show that the person took immediate steps, upon discovering any failure relating to the list, to correct the failure. A person's failure to take immediate steps to correct a failure related to the list upon discovering the failure is a factor weighing against a conclusion that the person exercised ordinary business care. Notwithstanding the occurrence of an isolated and inadvertent failure, a person still may be able to demonstrate that the person exercised ordinary business care, considering all the relevant facts and circumstances, but only if the person had established and adhered to procedures reasonably designed and implemented to ensure compliance with the section 6112 requirements.

(4) *Supervening events.*—A person may establish reasonable cause for one or more days for which, considering all the relevant facts and circumstances, the failure to timely furnish the list required by section 6112 was due solely to a supervening event beyond the person's control. Events beyond a person's control may include fire, flood, storm, or other casualty; illness; theft; or other similarly unexpected event that damages or impairs the person's relevant business records or system for processing and providing these records, or that affects the person's ability to maintain the section 6112 list or make it available to the IRS. Reasonable cause may be established only for the period that a person who exercised ordinary business care would need to provide the list from alternative records in existence, or make the list available, under the specific facts and circumstances.

(5) *Reliance on opinion or advice.*—(i) *In general.*—A person may rely on an independent tax professional's advice to establish reasonable cause. The reliance, however, must be reasonable and in good faith, in light of all the other facts and circumstances. For a person to be considered to have relied on the advice, the advice must have been received by the person before the date the list is required to be made available to the IRS. If the person received advice from an independent tax professional, the person's reliance on that advice will be considered reasonable only if the independent tax professional reasonably believed that it is more likely than not that the person does not have an obligation imposed by section 6112. For example, this advice may conclude that the person is not a material advisor; that the transaction upon which the person provided material aid, assistance, or advice is not a reportable transaction for which a list was required to be maintained as of the date of the advice; that the information and documents to be produced constitute the required list; or that

the information or documents withheld by the person are not required to be produced. The advice must also take into account and consider all relevant facts and circumstances, not rely on unreasonable legal or factual assumptions, not rely on or take into account the possibility that a list request may not be made, and not rely on unreasonable representations or statements of the person seeking the advice. Advice from a tax professional who is not independent may be considered in determining reasonable cause if, in light of and in relation to all the other facts and circumstances, taking into account such advice is reasonable. However, by itself, advice from a tax professional who is not independent is not sufficient to establish reasonable cause. Independent tax professional advice is not required to establish reasonable cause and the failure to obtain advice from an independent tax professional does not preclude a finding of reasonable cause if, based on the totality of all of the relevant facts and circumstances, reasonable cause has been established.

(ii) *Independent tax professional.*—For purposes of this section, an independent tax professional is a person who is knowledgeable in the relevant aspects of Federal tax law and who is not a material advisor with respect to the specific transaction that is the subject of the list request. For advice related to a listed transaction, a person who is a material advisor with respect to any transaction that is the same as or substantially similar to the type of transaction that is the subject of the list request will not be considered an independent tax professional.

(6) *Examples.*—The following examples illustrate this paragraph (g). These examples are intended to illustrate how the facts and circumstances in paragraphs (g)(2) through (g)(5) of this section may apply; in any given case, however, all of the facts and circumstances must be analyzed.

Example 1. On August 11, 2017, the IRS sends a list request via certified mail to Firm C, a material advisor. Firm C consists of a sole practitioner, X, who is away from the office on vacation on this date. X has arranged for a colleague, Y, to review Firm C's mail, email, and telephone messages daily during his absence. X returns to the office the day after his vacation ends, on September 5, 2017, and immediately contacts the IRS to notify it of his absence. Firm C makes a complete list available to the IRS on September 19, 2017, 10 business days after he has returned from vacation. Firm C establishes that X was on vacation at the time the list request was sent to Firm C, and Firm C promptly furnished the requested list in a manner and time period reflecting ordinary business care and prudence upon X's return to the office. Under these circumstances, Firm C is considered to have made a good-faith effort to comply with the section 6112 requirements. Firm C has established reasonable cause for the entire period between the expiration of the 20-business-day period following the list request and the date the list was made available to the IRS. See paragraphs (g)(2) and (3) of this section.

Example 2. On March 3, 2017, the IRS hand delivers to Firm D, a material advisor, a list request related to a transaction believed by the IRS to have been implemented in November 2008 by a group of Firm D's clients (the advisees). Firm D's involvement in the transaction included implementing the transaction on behalf of some but not all of the advisees. Firm D timely makes the requested list available to the IRS. Upon review, the IRS determines that the information furnished by Firm D appears to be accurate, but the IRS believes that some of the information is incomplete because it does not contain information about certain individuals who were identified through other investigative means as Firm D's clients who may have engaged in the transaction. In response to a follow-up inquiry by the IRS, Firm D establishes, however, that it is not a material advisor with respect to these taxpayers. Under these circumstances, Firm D has furnished the list as required by section 6112. Because the list was complete when furnished, Firm D need not make a showing of reasonable cause. See paragraph (g)(1) of this section.

Example 3. The IRS sends a list request by certified mail to Firm E, a material advisor. Firm E maintains the materials responsive to the list request on a portable data storage device. Under Firm E's established procedures for maintaining section 6112 lists, once the transaction is completed, paper documents are scanned and saved electronically according to Firm E's records management procedures. Under Firm E's records management procedures, after the scanning process is completed, Firm E sends the paper documents to an off-site storage facility. Three days before the 20th business day following the date of the written request, the electronic data is permanently destroyed. Firm E contacts the IRS representative listed as a contact person on the section 6112 list request to advise him that the relevant data was permanently destroyed. Firm E establishes that it exercised ordinary business care but that the data was nevertheless destroyed due to circumstances outside of its control. Under these circumstances, Firm E has reasonable cause for the period of time that Firm E cannot respond to the list request due to circumstances out of Firm E's control. The reasonable cause exception, however, will only be available to Firm E for the period of time that a person who exercises ordinary business care would need to obtain the materials that are part of the list, including in this case paper documents from the off-site storage facility, and furnish the list to the IRS. See paragraphs (g)(3) and (4) of section.

Example 4. On February 2, 2017, the IRS hand delivers a list request to Firm F, a material advisor. Firm F filed with the IRS the disclosure statement required by section 6111 for the reportable transaction that is the subject of the list request but did not maintain the section 6112 list documentation in a readily accessible format after filing the section 6111 statement. On March 3, 2017, the 20th business day (due to the Presidents' Day holiday) after the list request is delivered to Firm F, Firm F contacts the IRS to ask for additional time to comply with the list request, stating that it could not gather the list information together in 20 business days. Because Firm F is not able to show that it made diligent efforts to maintain the materials constituting the list in a readily accessible form, the IRS should not grant Firm F an extension of time. See paragraph (c)(3) of this section. Further, Firm F does not have reasonable cause because it has failed to demonstrate a good-faith effort to comply with the section 6112 requirements and ordinary business care. See paragraphs (g)(2) and (3) of this section.

Example 5. On August 11, 2017, the IRS sends a list request, via certified mail, to Firm G, a material advisor. Firm G consists of a sole practitioner, P. Firm G maintains the materials responsive to the list request electronically. Generally, under Firm G's records management procedures, once a transaction is completed, the documents related to that transaction are scanned and then saved electronically consistent with IRS guidance on maintaining books and records in electronic form. P is aware of the list request but ignores it. On September 24, 2017, the 13th calendar day after the 20-business-day period following the list request (due to the Labor Day holiday), P suffers a temporary but debilitating illness that lasts 22 days. Following the illness, P immediately returns to work. After returning to work, P continues to ignore the list request. In this situation, the facts and circumstances indicate that Firm G does not have reasonable cause for any day in which there was a failure to make the list available to the IRS, including the 22 days due to the intervening event, because the failure was not due solely to the supervening event occurring on September 24, 2017. Firm G did not make a good-faith effort to make the list available to the IRS before or after the supervening event occurred. Firm G is liable for the $10,000 per day penalty from the first day following the expiration of the 20-business-day period until but not including the day that Firm G furnishes the list to the IRS. See paragraphs (g)(2) and (4) of this section.

Example 6. On August 11, 2017, the IRS sends a list request, via certified mail, to Firm H, a material advisor. Firm H, consists of a sole practitioner, P. Firm H maintains the materials responsive to the list request electronically. Generally, under Firm H's records management procedures, once the transaction is completed, the documents are scanned and then saved electronically consistent with IRS guidance on maintaining books and records in electronic form. P is aware of the list request and begins compiling the documents to respond to the IRS within the 20–business-day period ending on September 11, 2017 (due to the Labor Day holiday). Before responding to the list request, P suffers a temporary but debilitating illness on September 3, 2017, that lasts through September 19, 2017. Upon returning to work on September 20, 2017,

P contacts the IRS to explain that P experienced a temporary but debilitating illness from September 3, 2017, through September 19, 2017, and that P has returned to the office and intends to furnish the list to the IRS within a short period of time. Firm H furnishes the list to the IRS on September 22, 2017. In this situation, the facts and circumstances indicate that Firm H has reasonable cause for the period from September 12, 2017 until September 21, 2017, attributable to P's illness. The failure to furnish the list in a timely fashion was solely attributable to the supervening event occurring on September 3, 2017, and Firm H promptly furnished the requested list in a manner and time period reflecting ordinary business care upon P's return to the office. Firm H is considered to have made a good-faith effort to comply with the section 6112 requirements. Firm H has established reasonable cause for the entire period between the expiration of the 20-business-day period following the list request and the date Firm H furnished the list to the IRS. See paragraphs (g)(2) and (4) of this section.

Example 7. Firm I receives a list request for transactions that are the same or substantially similar to the listed transaction described in Notice 2002-21, 2002-1 CB 730. Firm I will be considered a material advisor with respect to a particular transaction for which it provided advice if the transaction is the same as or substantially similar to the transaction described in Notice 2002-21. Firm I, however, is unsure whether the transaction is the same as or substantially similar to the transaction described in this Notice. Firm I obtains an opinion from Firm L, a law firm, on this issue. P, a partner in Firm L, provided tax advice to clients who invested in other Notice 2002-21 transactions, including how to report the purported tax benefits from the transaction on their income tax returns, and Firm L is a material advisor with respect to those transactions. Because Firm L is a material advisor with respect to the type of transaction that is the same as or substantially similar to the transaction described in Notice 2002-21, Firm L is not considered an independent tax professional under paragraph (g)(5)(ii) of this section. Therefore, Firm I cannot rely on advice provided by Firm L to establish reasonable cause under this paragraph (g). The IRS may consider Firm L's advice in determining reasonable cause in light of other facts and circumstances, but Firm L's advice, without more, is not sufficient to establish reasonable cause because P is not an independent tax professional under paragraph (g)(5)(ii) of this section.

Example 8. Firm J, a law firm, provides advice to various clients of the firm regarding the potential tax benefits of a reportable transaction under § 1.6011-4(b)(5) of this chapter (involving a section 165 loss) and is a material advisor with respect to that transaction. Firm J also provides advice to Firm M, an accounting firm, regarding the same transaction. Firm M then advises various Firm M clients regarding this same transaction, and is a material advisor. The transaction is not a listed transaction. Firm N, a law firm that is not associated with Firm J and has not provided advice with respect to the same transaction to Firm M, has provided advice to its own clients regarding other transactions subject to § 1.6011-4(b)(5) of this chapter, but not the particular transaction that was the subject of Firm J's advice to Firm M. The IRS hand delivers a list request to Firm M, the subject of which is the transaction regarding which Firm J provided advice to Firm M. Before the expiration of the 20-business-day period, Firm M seeks advice from Firm J and Firm N about the propriety of withholding certain documents related to the transaction. Because Firm J provided advice with respect to the particular transaction that is the subject of the list request, Firm J is not an independent tax professional under paragraph (g)(5)(ii) of this section. Although Firm N has provided advice on a transaction that is considered a reportable transaction under § 1.6011-4(b)(5) of this chapter, Firm N is considered to be an independent tax professional under paragraph (g)(5)(ii) of this section because Firm N did not provide material assistance with respect to the particular transaction that is the subject of the list request.

(h) *Reasonable cause – special considerations.—* (1) *Material advisor no longer in existence.*—If a material advisor has dissolved, been liquidated, or otherwise is no longer in existence, the person required by section 6112 to maintain the list (the "responsible person") is subject to the penalty for failing to make the list available. In considering whether a responsible person or successor in interest has reasonable cause for any failure to timely make the list available to the IRS, the IRS will consider all of the facts and circumstances, including those facts and circumstances relating to the dissolution, liquidation, and winding up of the original material advisor's business and any efforts the original material advisor made to comply with the section 6112 requirements before the dissolution or liquidation. When appropriate or applicable, due diligence, if any, performed by a responsible person or successor in interest will be considered, and due consideration will be given for acts taken by that person to minimize the potential for violating the section 6112 requirements.

(2) *Review by IRS.*—Whether reasonable cause exists for a period of time will be determined based on all the relevant facts and circumstances, including facts and circumstances arising after the request for the list. If a material advisor establishes that, in its efforts to comply with the provisions of section 6112 and its corresponding regulations, it acted in good faith, as defined in paragraph (g)(2) of this section, the material advisor will be deemed to have reasonable cause for the periods of time the IRS takes to review a furnished list for compliance with the section 6112 requirements and to inform the material advisor of any identified failures in the list. If the material advisor does not establish that it acted in good faith the IRS will not consider the

time it takes to review the list or inform the material advisor of identified failures as a factor in determining whether the material advisor has reasonable cause for that period.

(3) *Examples.*—The following examples illustrate paragraph (h)(2) of this section.

Example 1. On February 2, 2017, the IRS hand delivers a list request to Firm O, a material advisor. On March 3, 2017, the 20th business day (due to the Presidents' Day holiday) after the list request is delivered to Firm O, Firm O sends a list to the IRS that was contemporaneously prepared after Firm O issued advice with respect to the reportable transaction and continuously maintained in accordance with the requirements of section 6112 and the related regulations. Before sending the list, a supervisor at Firm O carefully reviewed the list to verify that it was comprehensive and accurate. The IRS completes its review on March 23, 2017, and determines that the list is not complete because Firm O furnished a draft copy of the tax opinion, rather than the final document, which Firm O had mistakenly misfiled. After Firm O is notified of the missing information, Firm O immediately furnishes a complete copy of the final version of the tax opinion. Firm O made a good-faith effort to comply with the section 6112 requirements, including its efforts to ensure that the list that was furnished to the IRS was accurate and complete. Firm O has reasonable cause for the entire period between the expiration of the 20-business-day period following the list request and the date it furnished the complete list to the IRS.

Example 2. On February 2, 2017, the IRS hand delivers a list request to Firm P, a material advisor. Firm P's involvement in the reportable transaction included implementing the transaction on behalf of some but not all of Firm P's clients. On March 3, 2017, the 20th business day (due to the Presidents' Day holiday) after the list request is delivered to Firm P, Firm P sends the list to the IRS. The IRS completes its review on March 23, 2017. The IRS believes the client list is incomplete because it does not contain information about certain individuals who were identified through other investigative means as clients of Firm P who may have engaged in the transaction. On March 27, 2017, in response to a follow-up inquiry by the IRS, Firm P establishes that it is not a material advisor with respect to these taxpayers. Therefore, the March 3, 2017 list was complete and accurate when first furnished. Under these circumstances, Firm P has timely furnished the list as required by section 6112. Because Firm P complied with the requirements of section 6112 no penalty applies, and Firm P does not need to establish reasonable cause for the period from March 4, 2017, through March 27, 2017, when the IRS was reviewing the list.

Example 3. On February 2, 2017, the IRS hand delivers a list request to Firm Q, a material advisor. On March 3, 2017, the 20th business day (due to the Presidents' Day holiday) after the list request is delivered to Firm Q, Firm Q sends the list to the IRS. Firm Q had not maintained a list contemporaneously after issuing the advice with respect to the reportable transaction, and created the list during the 20 business days before providing the list to the IRS. To meet the 20-business-day deadline, a supervisor did not review the final list before sending it to the IRS. The IRS completes its review on March 23, 2017, and determines that the list is not complete because it does not include 15 persons for whom Firm Q acted as a material advisor with respect to the reportable transaction. Firm Q furnishes the additional information on March 27, 2017. Because Firm Q is not able to show that it made diligent efforts to maintain the materials constituting the list in a readily accessible form and that it made a reasonable effort to ensure that the list that was furnished to the IRS was accurate and complete, Firm Q cannot establish that it exhibited a good-faith effort to comply with the section 6112 requirements. Firm Q does not have reasonable cause for its failure to furnish the complete list from March 4, 2017, through March 26, 2017.

Example 4. Within the 20-business-day period following a list request, Firm R sends four boxes of documents comprising the required list to the IRS using a commercial delivery service. The IRS receives only three of the boxes because box 4 was erroneously self-addressed using Firm R's office address. Box 4 arrives at Firm R's office on January 6, 2017, the 2nd calendar day after the 20th business day after the list request was made. Firm R immediately recognizes its clerical error, promptly contacts the IRS, and resends the original and unopened box 4, properly addressed, to the IRS together with documentation supporting the error. The IRS receives box 4 on January 9, 2017. Under these circumstances, Firm R has reasonable cause for the late delivery of box 4 because it made a good-faith attempt to timely comply with the list request and immediately corrected an inadvertent error upon its discovery. As a result, no penalty will be imposed based on the delay in providing box 4. If, after inspection, the IRS determines that, even with the contents of box 4, the list is incomplete or defective, Firm R must establish reasonable cause for the incomplete nature of the list or the defect to avoid imposition of a penalty for the period beginning January 5, 2017, until but not including the day that Firm R furnishes the list to the IRS.

Example 5. (i) Firm S is a large law firm that is a material advisor. Firm S conducts annual sessions to educate its professionals about reportable transactions and the firm's obligations related to those reportable transactions. Firm S instructs its professionals to provide information on tax engagements that involve reportable transactions and to provide the documents required to be maintained under section 6112 to Firm S's compliance officer for list maintenance purposes. Firm S's policy provides that, for each engagement involving a reportable transaction, one firm professional will send an email to the firm's compliance officer about the engagement and then direct a subordinate to send to the firm's compliance officer the documents required to be maintained.

(ii) Firm S receives a request from the IRS for a section 6112 list. In compiling its list to turn over to the IRS during the 20-business-day period, Firm S asks all professionals to ensure that they have reported all engagements involving a reportable transaction to the firm's compliance officer. Before submission to the IRS, a Firm S supervisor reviews the list to ensure completeness. Firm S has no reason to know of any deficiencies, and in compiling its list, Firm S discovers no deficiencies.

(iii) Upon review of the list, the IRS determines that the information furnished by Firm S appears to be accurate, but the IRS believes that some of the information is incomplete because it does not contain information about an individual who may have engaged in the transaction and who was identified through other investigative means as Firm S's client. In response to a follow-up inquiry by the IRS, Firm S immediately reviews its files and discovers that a former Firm S professional, who is no longer employed by Firm S, provided material advice to the individual with respect to carrying out a reportable transaction, but did not send an email to the firm's compliance officer about the transaction or direct a subordinate to send the documents required to be maintained to the firm's compliance officer. Firm S immediately furnishes the missing information and documents related to the identified omission to the IRS.

(iv) Firm S establishes that the professional in question ordinarily complied with Firm S's list maintenance procedures and that Firm S had no reason to know of this one omission or to suspect that the professional had failed to report any reportable transactions to the firm's compliance officer in accordance with the firm's policies. Firm S also immediately undertakes a thorough search of its electronic and paper files to locate any additional reportable transactions relating to the professional in question that may have been omitted from the list. Under these circumstances, Firm S has demonstrated that it has acted in good faith in its efforts to comply with section 6112 and is deemed to have reasonable cause for the period of time the IRS took to review the furnished list and to inform the material advisor of the identified failure in the list. See paragraph (h)(2) of this section. The reasonable cause exception, however, will only be available to Firm S with respect to the omission identified by the IRS for the period of time that a person who exercises ordinary business care would need to obtain the information and documents related to the identified omission. See paragraph (g)(3) of this section. With respect to any other omissions related to the same professional and not identified by the IRS, the reasonable cause exception will only be available to Firm S for the period of time that a person who exercises ordinary business care would need to ascertain whether any other reportable transactions were omitted from the list and to obtain the

Reg. § 301.6708-1(h)(3)

information and documents related to any such omissions. See paragraph (g)(3) of this section.

(i) *Effective/applicability date.*—This section applies to all requests for lists required to be maintained under section 6112, including lists that persons were required to maintain under section 6112(a) as in effect before October 22, 2004, made on or after April 28, 2016. [Reg. § 301.6708-1.]

☐ [T.D. 9764, 4-27-2016.]

[Reg. § 301.6708-1T]

§ 301.6708-1T. Failure to maintain list of investors in potentially abusive tax shelters (Temporary).—The following questions and answers issued under section 6708 of the Internal Revenue Code of 1954, as added by section 142 of the Tax Reform Act of 1984 (Pub. L. No. 98-369; 98 Stat. 683), relate to the penalty for failure to maintain a list of investors in potentially abusive tax shelters.

Q-1. What penalties are provided with respect to the failure properly to maintain a list of persons who acquire interests in potentially abusive tax shelters?

A-1. Any organizer (as defined in A-5 of § 301.6112-1T) of a tax shelter (as defined in A-3 of § 301.6112-1T) or seller (as defined in A-6 of § 301.6112-1T) of interests in a tax shelter who fails to meet any requirement imposed by section 6112 regarding the requirement to maintain a list of persons who have acquired interests in a tax shelter shall pay a penalty of $50 for each investor with respect to whom there is such a failure, unless it is shown that the failure is due to reasonable cause and not due to willful neglect. For example, if an organizer who is required to maintain a list identifying each of 100 persons who acquired interests in a tax shelter fails to maintain the list, the organizer will be liable for a penalty of $5,000 ($50 × 100 persons), unless the organizer can show the failure was due to reasonable cause and not due to willful neglect. As another example, if a seller is required to maintain a list identifying each of 100 persons who acquired interests in a tax shelter from the seller and fails properly to maintain such list by omitting the TIN of each person, the seller will be liable for a penalty of $5,000 ($50 × 100 persons), unless the seller can show the failure was due to reasonable cause and not due to willful neglect.

Q-2. If an organizer or seller properly maintains a list, but fails to make the list available to the Internal Revenue Service upon request, will the organizer or seller be subject to a penalty?

A-2. Yes. A penalty applies if an organizer or seller fails to meet any requirement imposed by section 6112, including the requirement, upon request, to make the list available to the Internal Revenue Service as soon as practicable, but in any event within 10 calendar days. (See A-21 of § 301.6112-1T). The amount of the penalty is $50 for each person required to be on the list at the time of the request by the Internal Revenue Service. Assume, for example, that an organizer of a tax shelter properly maintains a list of 200 persons who have acquired interests in a tax shelter and that the Internal Revenue Service requests the organizer to provide the list. If the organizer fails to provide the list to the Internal Revenue

Service as soon as practicable (as required by A-21 of § 301.6112-1T), or in a form that enables the Internal Revenue Service to obtain the required information without undue delay or difficulty (as required by A-16 of § 301.6112-1T), the organizer will be liable for a penalty of $10,000 ($50 × 200 persons), unless the organizer can show that the failure to provide the list was due to reasonable cause and not to willful neglect.

Q-3. If an organizer or seller is required to maintain lists for more than one tax shelter in which the same person has acquired interests, how does the penalty apply if the organizer or seller fails to identify the person on each of the lists?

A-3. A separate $50 penalty applies with respect to the list for each tax shelter on which the person who acquired interests is not identified.

Q-4. Is there a limitation on the amount of the penalty imposed on a seller or organizer required to maintain a list of persons who have acquired interests in a tax shelter?

A-4. Yes. The maximum penalty that may be imposed on a person for any calendar year may not exceed $50,000.

Q-5. How does the calendar year limitation apply?

A-5. A separate $50,000 limitation applies to each calendar year in which a failure occurs, and to each tax shelter for which a list is required to be maintained. See A-6 of this section for special rules for determining how the $50,000 limitation applies to a designated person who fails properly to maintain a list of investors.

Example (1). Assume that A, an organizer of a tax shelter, fails to maintain and to provide to the Internal Revenue Service a list of 900 persons who acquired interests in the tax shelter in 1986. In addition, assume that A again fails to maintain and to provide the list of 900 investors upon request in 1987. A is subject to a penalty of $45,000 (900 persons × $50) for each calendar year in which there is a failure to comply with the requirements of section 6112. Thus, A is subject to $45,000 in penalties for the failures to maintain and to provide the list in 1986, and $45,000 in penalties for the failures to maintain and to provide the list in 1987, unless A can show reasonable cause for the failures.

Example (2). Assume that B, an organizer of Tax Shelter I, fails to provide a list of 1,500 persons who acquired interests in the tax shelter to the Internal Revenue Service upon request in 1987. Assume also that B, an organizer of Tax Shelter II, fails to provide a list of 2,000 persons who acquired interests in Tax Shelter II to the Internal Revenue Service upon request in 1987. Because the $50,000 calendar year limitation applies separately with respect to each tax shelter for which a list must be maintained, B is subject to a penalty of $50,000 for failing to provide the list for Tax Shelter I in 1987 and a $50,000 penalty for failing to provide the list for Tax Shelter II in 1987.

Q-6. How does the penalty apply to a designated person?

A-6. Separate penalties, each with its own $50,000 calendar year limitation, apply with respect to the portion of the list kept by the designated person in that person's capacity as organizer and to each portion of the list kept by the designated person in that person's capacity as the designated person with respect to each organizer and seller who signed the agreement under A-12 of § 301.6112-1T and for whom the designated person is responsible for complying with the requirements of section 6112.

Example. Assume that X, an organizer and seller, sells interests in a tax shelter directly to 750 investors in 1985. In addition, assume that A, an agent of X, negotiates for X sales of interests in the tax shelter to an additional 500 persons in 1985. If no agreement to designate X is made pursuant to A-11 of § 301.6112-1T, X would be required to maintain a list of the 1,250 investors who acquired interests in the tax shelter (see paragraph (a) of A-8 of § 301.6112-1T) and A would be required to maintain a list of the 500 persons who acquired interests through A (see A-10 of § 301.6112-1T). If, therefore, neither X nor A complied with the requirements of section 6112 in 1985, X would be liable for $50,000 in penalties ($50 × 1,250 investors, subject to the $50,000 maximum) and A would be liable for $25,000 in penalties ($50 × 500 investors). Assume, however, that X and A enter into a written agreement to designate X to maintain the list for the tax shelter. Pursuant to that agreement, A submits to X all of the required information regarding the sales to the 500 persons otherwise required to be maintained on A's list and provides the notice required by A-13 of § 301.6112-1T to each person. In 1986, X fails to provide any list of investors to the Internal Revenue Service upon request. For calendar year 1986, X is liable for penalties of $50,000 in in X's capacity as an organizer ($50 × 1,250 persons, subject to the $50,000 maximum). In addition, X, as the person designated to maintain the list for A, is liable for penalties of $25,000 for failing properly to maintain A's list of investors ($50 × 500 persons). A would not be liable for any penalties.

Q-7. If an organizer or seller is subject to a penalty with respect to a tax shelter under section 6708, may the organizer or seller also be liable for other fines or penalties with respect to the tax shelter?

A-7. Yes. The penalty imposed by section 6708 is in addition to any other penalty provided by law. If, for example, an organizer of a tax shelter is subject to a penalty under section 6700 for promoting an abusive tax shelter, the organizer also would be liable for any applicable penalties for failing properly to maintain a list for the tax shelter. Similarly, if an organizer or seller fails to furnish a list upon request by the Internal Revenue Service, the organizer or seller may be subject both to the fine under section 7203 for the willful failure to supply information, and to the penalty for failing properly to maintain a list for the tax shelter.

Q-8. When is the penalty under section 6708 effective?

A-8. The penalty under section 6708 applies with respect to any interest in a tax shelter which is required to be included on a list under section 6112. See A-22 of § 301.6112-1T.

[Temporary Reg. § 301.6708-1T.]

☐ [*T.D.* 7969, 8-24-84.]

[Reg. § 1.6709-1T]

§ 1.6709-1T. Penalties with respect to mortgage credit certificates.—(a) *Material misstatement.*—(1) *Negligence.*—If any person makes a material misstatement in any affidavit or other statement under penalty of perjury made with respect to the issuance of a mortgage credit certificate and such misstatement is due to the negligence of that person, that person shall pay a penalty of $1,000 for each mortgage credit certificate with respect to which that misstatement was made.

(2) *Fraud.*—If a misstatement described in subparagraph (1) is due to fraud on the part of the person making the misstatement, that person shall pay a penalty of $10,000 for each mortgage credit certificate with respect to which the fraudulent misstatement was made. The penalty imposed by this paragraph (a)(2) is in addition to any criminal penalty.

(b) *Reports.*—(1) Any person required by § 1.25-8T to file a report with respect to any mortgage credit certificate who fails to file the report at the time and in the manner required by § 1.25-8T shall pay a penalty of $200 for each mortgage credit certificate with respect to which that failure occurred. The preceding sentence shall not apply if it is shown that such failure is due to reasonable cause and not to willful neglect.

(2) In the case of any report required under § 1.25-8T(b), the aggregate amount of the penalty imposed by this paragraph shall not exceed $2,000. [Temporary Reg. § 1.6709-1T.]

☐ [*T.D.* 8023, 5-3-85.]

[Reg. § 301.6712-1]

§ 301.6712-1. Failure to disclose treaty-based return positions.—(a) *Penalty imposed.*—A taxpayer who fails in a material way to disclose one or more positions taken for a taxable year, as required by section 6114 and the regulations thereunder, is subject to a separate penalty for each failure to disclose a position taken with respect to each separate payment or separate income item in the amount of—

(1) For a corporation taxable as such under the Code, $10,000; or

(2) For all other taxpayers, $1,000.

The penalty imposed by this section may be imposed more than once for a single taxable year if a taxpayer has failed to disclose one or more positions taken with respect to more than one separate payment or separate income item and may be imposed in addition to any other penalty imposed by law. For this purpose, separate payments or income items of the same type (*e.g.*, interest payments) received from the same ultimate payor (*e.g.*, the obligor on the note) will be treated as separate payments or income items (and not aggregated). However, for purposes of determining the number of separate penalties to be imposed under this section, the District Director shall have the discretion to aggregate separate payments or income items, in whole or in part, in accordance with the rules for aggregation of such items for purposes of reporting, as described in § 301.6114-1(d).

(b) *Penalty waived.*—Pursuant to the authority contained in section 6712 (b) of the Code, the penalty imposed by paragraph (a) of this section may be waived, in whole or in part, if it is established to the satisfaction of the Assistant Commissioner (International), the district director or the director of the Internal Revenue Service Center that the taxpayer's failure to disclose the required information was not due to willful neglect. An affirmative showing of lack of willful neglect must be made in the form of a written statement that sets forth all the facts alleged to show lack of willful neglect and contains a declaration by such person that the statement is made under the penalties of perjury.

(c) *Manner of payment.*—The penalty set forth in paragraph (a) of this section shall be paid in the same manner as tax upon the issuance of a notice and demand thereof.

(d) *Effective date.*—This section is effective for taxable years of the taxpayer for which the due date for filing returns (without extension) occurs after December 31, 1988. [Reg. § 301.6712-1.]

☐ [*T.D. 8292, 3-13-90.*]

§ 48.6715-1. Penalty for misuse of dyed fuel.—(a) *In general.*—If any person willfully alters, or attempts to alter, the strength or composition of any dye or marking done pursuant to § 48.4082-1 in any dyed fuel, then section 6715(a)(3) provides that such person shall pay a penalty in addition to any tax. The penalty imposed by section 6715(a)(3) will not apply in the following cases:

(1) Diesel fuel or kerosene that satisfies the dyeing and marking requirements of § 48.4082-1(b) and (c) is blended with any undyed liquid and the resulting product satisfies the dyeing and marking requirements of § 48.4082-1(b) and (c).

(2) Diesel fuel or kerosene that satisfies the dyeing and marking requirements of § 48.4082-1(b) and (c) is blended with any other liquid (other than diesel fuel or kerosene) that contains the type and amount of dye and marker required for diesel fuel or kerosene dyed and marked in accordance with § 48.4082-1(b) and (c).

(3) The alteration or attempted alteration occurs in an exempt area of Alaska after September 30, 1996.

(4) Diesel fuel or kerosene that does not satisfy the dyeing and marking requirements of § 48.4082-1(b) and (c) is blended with diesel fuel or kerosene that satisfies the dyeing and marking requirements of § 48.4082-1(b) and (c) and the blending occurs as part of a use described in § 48.4082-4(c) or § 48.6427-8(b)(1)(vii)(C) or (D).

(b) *Effective date.*—This section is effective January 1, 1994. [Reg. § 48.6715-1.]

☐ [*T.D. 8659, 3-13-96. Amended by T.D. 8685, 11-8-96; T.D. 8748, 12-31-97 and T.D. 8879, 3-30-2000.*]

Failure to File Certain Information Returns or Statements

§ 301.6721-0. Table of contents.—

In order to facilitate the use of §§ 301.6721-1 through 6724-1, this § 301.6721-0 lists the paragraph headings contained in these sections.

(f) Higher penalty for intentional disregard of requirement to file timely correct information returns.

(1) Application of section 6721(e).

(2) Meaning of "intentional disregard."

(3) Facts and circumstances considered.

(4) Amount of the penalty.

(5) Computation of the penalty; aggregate dollar amount of the items required to be reported correctly.

(6) Examples.

(g) Definitions.

(1) Information return.

(2) Statements.

(3) Returns.

(4) Other items.

(5) Payee.

(6) Filer.

§ 301.6722-1. *Failure to furnish correct payee statements.*

(a) Imposition of penalty.

(1) General rule.

(2) Failures subject to the penalty.

(b) Exception for inconsequential errors or omissions.

(1) In general.

(2) Errors or omissions that are never inconsequential.

(3) Examples.

(c) Higher penalty for intentional disregard of requirement to furnish timely correct payee statements.

(1) Application of section 6722(c).

(2) Amount of the penalty.

(3) Computation of the penalty; aggregate dollar amount of items required to be shown correctly.

(d) Definitions.

(1) Payee.

(2) Payee statement.

(3) Other items.

§ 301.6723-1. *Failure to comply with other information reporting requirements.*

(a) Imposition of penalty.

(1) General rule.

(2) Failures subject to the penalty.

(3) Exception for inconsequential errors or omissions.

(4) Specified information reporting requirement defined.

(b) Examples.

§ 301.6724-1. *Reasonable cause.*

(a) Waiver of the penalty.

(1) General rule.

(2) Reasonable cause defined.

(b) Significant mitigating factors.

(c) Events beyond the filer's control.

(1) In general.

(2) Unavailability of the relevant business records.

(3) Undue economic hardship relating to filing on magnetic media.

(4) Actions of the Internal Revenue Service.

(5) Actions of agent—imputed reasonable cause.

(6) Actions of the payee or any other person.

(d) Responsible manner.

(1) In general.

(2) Special rule for filers seeking a waiver pursuant to paragraph (c)(6) of this section.

(e) Acting in a responsible manner—special rules for missing TINs.

(1) In general.

(i) Initial solicitation.

(ii) First annual solicitation.

(iii) Second annual solicitation.

(iv) Additional requirements.

(v) Failures to which a solicitation relates.

(vi) Exceptions and limitations.

(2) Manner of making annual solicitations—by mail or telephone.

(i) By mail.

(ii) By telephone.

(f) Acting in a responsible manner—special rules for incorrect TINs.

(1) In general.

(i) Initial solicitation.

(ii) First annual solicitation.

(iii) Second annual solicitation.

(iv) Additional requirements.

(2) Manner of making annual solicitation if notified pursuant to section 3406(a)(1)(B) and the regulations thereunder.

(3) Manner of making annual solicitation if notified pursuant to section 6721.

(4) Failures to which a solicitation relates.

(5) Exceptions and limitations.

(g) Due diligence safe harbor.

(1) In general.

(2) Special rules relating to TINs.

(3) Effective dates.

(h) Transitional rules for information returns required to be filed (or payee statements required to be furnished) after December 31, 1989 (without regard to extensions), and on or before April 22, 1991.

(1) In general.

(2) Special rule on TINs.

(i) [Reserved].

(j) Failures to which this section relates.

(k) Examples.

(l) [Reserved].

(m) Procedure for seeking a waiver.

(n) Manner of payment.

[Reg. § 301.6721-0.]

☐ [*T.D. 8386, 12-27-91. Amended by T.D. 8734,* 10-6-97 (T.D. 8804 delayed the effective date of T.D. 8734 from January 1, 1999, to January 1, 2000; T.D. 8856 further delayed the effective date of T.D. 8734 until January 1, 2001).]

Reg. § 301.6721-0

[Reg. § 301.6721-1]

§ 301.6721-1. Failure to file correct information returns.—(a) *Imposition of penalty.*—(1) *General rule.*—A penalty of $50 is imposed for each information return (as defined in section 6724(d)(1) and paragraph (g) of this section) with respect to which a failure (as defined in section 6721(a)(2) and paragraph (a)(2) of this section) occurs. No more than one penalty will be imposed under this paragraph (a)(1) with respect to a single information return even though there may be more than one failure with respect to such return. The total amount imposed on any person for all failures during any calendar year with respect to all information returns shall not exceed $250,000. See paragraph (b) of this section for a reduction in the penalty when the failures are corrected within specified periods. See paragraph (c) of this section for an exception to the penalty for inconsequential errors or omissions. See paragraph (d) of this section for an exception to the penalty for a *de minimis* number of failures. See paragraph (e) of this section for lower limitations to the $250,000 maximum penalty. See paragraph (f) of this section for higher penalties when a failure is due to intentional disregard of the requirement to file timely correct information returns. See paragraph (a)(1) of § 301.6724-1 for waiver of the penalty for a failure that is due to reasonable cause.

(2) *Failures subject to the penalty.*—The failures to which section 6721(a) and paragraph (a)(1) of this section apply are—

(i) A failure to file an information return on or before the required filing date ("failure to file timely"), and

(ii) A failure to include all of the information required to be shown on the return or the inclusion of incorrect information ("failure to include correct information"). A failure to file timely includes a failure to file in the required manner, for example, on magnetic media or in other machine-readable form as provided under section 6011(e). However, no penalty is imposed under paragraph (a)(1) of this section solely by reason of any failure to comply with the requirements of section 6011(e)(2), except to the extent that such a failure occurs with respect to more than 250 information returns (the 250-threshold requirement) or in the case of a partnership with more than 100 partners, more than 100 information returns (the 100-threshold requirement) (collectively, the threshold requirements). Each Schedule K-1 considered in applying the 100-threshold requirement will be treated as a separate information return. These threshold requirements apply separately to each type of information return required to be filed. Further, these threshold requirements apply separately to original and corrected returns. Thus, for example, if a filer files 300 returns on Form 1099-DIV and later files 70 corrected returns on Form 1099-DIV, the corrected returns may be filed either on the prescribed paper form (because they fall below the 250-threshold requirement) or on

magnetic media or other machine-readable form. Filers who are required to file information returns on magnetic media and who file such information returns electronically are considered to have satisfied the magnetic media filing requirement. Except as provided in paragraph (c)(1) of this section, a failure to include correct information encompasses a failure to include the information required by applicable information reporting statutes or by any administrative pronouncements issued thereunder (such as regulations, revenue rulings, revenue procedures, or information reporting forms and form instructions). A failure to include information in the correct format may be either a failure to file timely an information return or a failure to include correct information on an information return. For example, an error on a magnetic media submission to the Internal Revenue Service that prevents processing by the Internal Revenue Service may constitute a failure to file timely. However, if information is set forth on the wrong field of the magnetic media submission, such an error may constitute a failure to file timely or a failure to include correct information, depending upon the extent of the failure.

(b) *Reduction in the penalty when a correction is made within specified periods.*—(1) *Correction within 30 days.*—The penalty imposed under section 6721(a) for a failure to file timely or for a failure to include correct information shall be $15 in lieu of $50 if the failure is corrected on or before the 30th day after the required filing date ("within 30 days"). The total amount imposed on a person for all failures during any calendar year that are corrected within 30 days shall not exceed $75,000.

(2) *Correction after 30 days but on or before August 1.*—The penalty imposed under section 6721(a) for a failure to file timely or for a failure to include correct information shall be $30 in lieu of $50 if the failure is corrected after the 30-day period described in paragraph (b)(1) of this section but on or before August 1 of the year in which the required filing date occurs ("after 30 days but on or before August 1"). (See paragraph (b)(6) of this section for an exception to the provisions of this paragraph (b)(2) for returns that are not due on February 28 or March 15.) The total amount imposed on a person for all failures during any calendar year corrected after 30 days but on or before August 1 shall not exceed $150,000.

(3) *Required filing date defined.*—The term "required filing date" means the date prescribed for filing an information return with the Internal Revenue Service (or the Social Security Administration in the case of Forms W-2) determined with regard to any extension of time for filing.

(4) *Penalty amount for return with multiple failures.*—If a return is subject to a penalty for more than one failure, and the penalty amounts for the failures differ, the higher penalty amount will be imposed.

(5) *Examples.*—The provisions of paragraphs (a) and (b)(1) through (4) of this section may be illustrated by the following examples. These examples do not take into account any possible application of the *de minimis* exception under paragraph (d) of this section, the lower small business limitations under paragraph (e) of this section, the penalty for intentional disregard under paragraph (f) of this section, or the reasonable cause waiver under paragraph (a) of § 301.6724-1:

Example 1. Corporation R fails to file timely 11,000 Forms 1099-MISC (relating to miscellaneous income) for the 1990 calendar year. Five thousand of these returns are filed with correct information within 30 days, and 6,000 after 30 days but on or before August 1, 1991. For the same year R fails to file timely 400 Forms 1099-INT (relating to payments of interest) which R eventually files on September 28, 1991, after the period for reduction of the penalty has elapsed. R is subject to a penalty of $20,000 for the 400 forms which were not filed by August 1 ($50 × 400 = $20,000), $150,000 for the 6,000 forms filed after 30 days ($30 × 6,000 = $180,000, limited to $150,000 under paragraph (b)(2) of this section), and $75,000 for the 5,000 forms filed within 30 days ($15 × 5,000 = $75,000), for a total penalty of $245,000.

Example 2. Corporation T fails to file timely 6,000 Forms 1099-MISC for the 1990 calendar year. T files the 6000 Forms 1099-MISC on September 1, 1991. Because T does not correct the failure by August 1, 1991, T is subject to a penalty of $250,000, the maximum penalty under paragraph (a) of this section. Without the limitation of paragraph (a), T would be subject to a $300,000 penalty ($50 × 6,000 = $300,000).

Example 3. Corporation U files timely 300 Forms 1099-MISC on paper for the 1990 calendar year with correct information. Under section 6011(e)(2) a person required to file at least 250 returns during a calendar year must file those returns on magnetic media. U does not correct its failures to file these returns on magnetic media by August 1, 1991. It is therefore subject to a penalty for a failure to file timely under paragraph (a)(2) of this section. However, pursuant to section 6724(c) and paragraph (a)(2) of this section, the penalty for a failure to file timely on magnetic media applies only to the extent the number of returns exceeds 250. As U was required to file 300 returns on magnetic media, U is subject to a penalty of $2,500 for 50 returns ($50 × 50 = $2,500).

Example 4. Corporation V files 300 Forms 1099-MISC on paper for the 1990 calendar year. The forms were filed on March 15, 1991, rather than on the required filing date of February 28, 1991. Under section 6011(e)(2), a person required to file at least 250 returns during a calendar year must file those returns on magnetic media. V does not correctly file these returns on magnetic media by August 1, 1991. V is subject to a penalty of $3,750 for filing 250 of the returns late ($15 × 250) and $2,500 for failing to file 50 re-

turns on magnetic media ($50 × 50) for a total penalty of $6,250.

(6) *Application to returns not due on February 28 or March 15.*—For returns that are not due on February 28 or March 15 (for example, Forms 8300 reporting certain cash payments of $10,000 or more), the penalty is $15 if the failure is corrected within 30 days. If the failure is corrected after 30 days, the penalty is $50 rather than $30. There is no period during which the penalty is reduced to $30 under paragraph (b)(2) of this section.

(c) *Exception for inconsequential errors or omissions.*—(1) *In general.*—An inconsequential error or omission is not considered a failure to include correct information. For purposes of this paragraph (c)(1), the term "inconsequential error or omission" means any failure that does not prevent or hinder the Internal Revenue Service from processing the return, from correlating the information required to be shown on the return with the information shown on the payee's tax return, or from otherwise putting the return to its intended use. See paragraph (g)(5) of this section for the definition of "payee."

(2) *Errors or omissions that are never inconsequential.*—Errors or omissions relating to the following are never inconsequential—

(i) A taxpayer identification number;

(ii) A surname of a payee (*i.e.*, the person required to be furnished a copy of the information set forth on an information return); and

(iii) Any monetary amounts.

The Internal Revenue Service may, by administrative pronouncement, specify other types of errors or omissions that are never inconsequential.

(3) *Examples.*—The provisions of this paragraph (c) may be illustrated by the following examples, which do not take into account any possible application of the penalty for intentional disregard under paragraph (f) of this section or the reasonable cause waiver under paragraph (a) of § 301.6724-1:

Example 1. A filer files a Form 1099-MISC (relating to miscellaneous income) with the Internal Revenue Service. The Form 1099-MISC is complete and correct except that the word "street" is misspelled in the payee's address. The error does not prevent or hinder the Internal Revenue Service from processing the return, from correlating the information required to be shown on the return with the information shown on the payee's tax return, or from otherwise putting the return to its intended use. Therefore, no penalty is imposed under paragraph (a) of this section.

Example 2. A filer files a Form 1099-MISC with the Internal Revenue Service. The Form 1099-MISC is complete and correct except that the payee's first name, William, is misspelled as "Willaim." The error does not prevent or hinder the Internal Revenue Service from processing the return, from correlating the information required

Reg. § 301.6721-1(c)(3)

to be shown on the return with the information shown on the payee's tax return, or from otherwise putting the return to its intended use. See paragraph (c)(2) of this section. Therefore, no penalty is imposed under paragraph (a) of this section.

Example 3. A filer files a Form 1099-MISC with the Internal Revenue Service. The Form 1099-MISC is complete and correct except that the payee's name, "John Doe," is misspelled as "John Ode." Under paragraph (c)(2) of this section, supplying an incorrect surname for a payee is never considered an inconsequential error. Therefore, a penalty is imposed under paragraph (a) of this section.

(d) *Exception for a de minimis number of failures.*—(1) *Requirements.*—The penalty under paragraph (a) of this section is not imposed for a *de minimis* number of failures to include correct information if the filer corrects such failures on or before August 1 of the year in which the required filing date occurs. (See paragraph (d)(4) of this section for special rules relating to returns that are not due on February 28 or March 15.)

(2) *Calculation of the de minimis exception.*—The number of returns to which the *de minimis* exception applies for any calendar year shall not exceed the greater of 10 or one-half of one percent of the total number of all information returns the filer is required to file during the year. If the number of returns on which the filer fails to include correct information exceeds the number of returns to which the *de minimis* exception applies, the *de minimis* exception applies to those returns that will afford the filer the greatest reduction in penalty. The *de minimis* exception applies to failures to include correct information that exist after the application (if any) of the waiver for reasonable cause under section 6724(a) and § 301.6724-1. Returns to which the *de minimis* exception applies are treated as having been originally filed with correct information.

(3) *Examples.*—The provisions of this paragraph (d) may be illustrated by the following examples. In each of the examples, the failures to file and to include correct information are subject to penalty under paragraph (a) of this section. The examples do not take into account any possible application of paragraph (f) of this section or the reasonable cause waiver under paragraph (a) of § 301.6724-1 of this section.

Example 1. Corporation T files timely 10,000 Forms 1099-INT (relating to payments of interest) for 1990 by February 28, 1991. The 10,000 returns are all the information returns that T is required to file during the 1991 calendar year. Of the returns filed, 70 contained incorrect information. T corrects the failures on July 12, 1991. No penalty is imposed for 50 of the failures (i.e., the greater of 10 or .005 × 10,000 = 50) even though the total failures, 70, exceed the number to which the *de minimis* exception may apply. The $30 penalty under paragraph (b)(2) of this section is imposed, in lieu of $50, for the remaining 20 failures, which were corrected after 30 days but on or before August 1, resulting in a total penalty of $600 ($30 × 20 = $600).

Example 2. Corporation U files timely 9,500 Forms 1099-INT for 1990 by February 28, 1991, the required filing date. Fifty of these returns contain incorrect information with respect to which U files correct information on August 1, 1991. U also files 500 Forms 1099-INT for 1990 on August 30, 1991, after the required filing date. The 10,000 returns are all the information returns that U is required to file during the 1991 calendar year. The calculation of the *de minimis* exception is based on the 10,000 returns required to be filed during the 1991 calendar year even though 500 of the returns filed during the year were not filed timely. Therefore, the number of failures for which the *de minimis* exception applies is 50, and accordingly no penalty is imposed for the 50 Forms 1099-INT that were corrected on August 1, 1991. However, the $50 penalty under paragraph (a)(1) of this section is imposed for each failure to file timely, resulting in a total penalty of $25,000 ($50 × 500 = $25,000).

Example 3. Corporation V files timely 9,950 Forms 1099-INT for 1990 by February 28, 1991. However, V fails to file timely 50 of its Forms 1099-INT. The 10,000 returns are all the information returns that V is required to file during the 1991 calendar year. Upon discovering the error, V files the 50 returns within 30 days of February 28, 1991. The 50 returns are complete and correct except that V fails to include the taxpayer identification numbers of the payees on the returns. V files corrected returns on August 1, 1991. Absent application of the *de minimis* exception, the penalty imposed for the failure to include correct information would be $1,500 ($30 × 50 = $1,500). Because the incorrect returns are corrected on August 1, the 50 forms are treated under the *de minimis* exception as originally filed with correct information, and therefore no penalty is imposed under paragraph (a) of this section for the failure to include correct information. Nevertheless, the penalty under paragraph (a) of this section is imposed for the failure to file timely the 50 returns because the *de minimis* exception does not apply to the penalty for the failure to file timely. Hence, a penalty of $750 ($15 × 50 = $750) is imposed.

Example 4. Corporation W files timely 100 Forms 1099-DIV and files an additional 50 Forms 1099-DIV late, but within 30 days of February 28, 1991. These are all the information returns that W was required to file during the 1991 calendar year. W discovers errors on 10 of the returns that were filed timely, and on 5 of the returns that were filed late. W corrects all the errors on August 1. The *de minimis* exception applies to 10 of the corrected returns. The exception will be allocated to the 10 returns that were filed timely with incorrect information because that allocation is most favorable to W (i.e., applying the exception to a return filed late with incorrect information would save W $15, by reducing the penalty on that return from $30 to $15, but applying the exception to a return filed timely would save W $30, by reducing the penalty on that return from $30 to $0). (See paragraph (b)(4) of this section.)

(4) *Nonapplication to returns not due on February 28 or March 15.*—The exception for a *de*

minimis number of failures provided in paragraph (d)(1) of this section does not apply to failures with respect to returns that are not due on February 28 or March 15 (for example, Forms 8300 reporting certain cash payments of $10,000 or more). Nevertheless, the returns that are not due on February 28 or March 15 are included in the total number of all information returns that the filer is required to file during a year for purposes of calculating the number of the returns subject to the de minimis exception under paragraph (d)(2) of this section.

(e) *Lower limitations on the $250,000 maximum penalty amount with respect to persons with gross receipts of not more than $5,000,000.*—(1) *In general.*—If a person meets the gross receipts test (as defined in paragraph (e)(2) of this section) for any calendar year, the total amount of the penalty imposed on such person for all failures described in section 6721(a)(2) and paragraph (a)(2) of this section during such calendar year shall not exceed $100,000. The total amount of the penalty imposed under paragraph (b)(1) of this section for failures corrected within 30 days shall not exceed $25,000 for such calendar year. The total amount of the penalty imposed under paragraph (b)(2) of this section for failures corrected after 30 days but on or before August 1 shall not exceed $50,000 for such calendar year.

(2) *Gross receipts test.*—A person meets the gross receipts test for any calendar year if the average annual gross receipts for such person for the three most recent taxable years ending before such calendar year do not exceed $5,000,000. For purposes of determining the amount of gross receipts during the three most recent taxable years, the rules of section 448(c)(2) and (3) shall apply.

(f) *Higher penalty for intentional disregard of requirement to file timely correct information returns.*—(1) *Application of section 6721(e).*—If a failure is due to intentional disregard of the requirement to file timely or to include correct information on a return as described in paragraph (g) of this section, the amount of the penalty imposed under paragraph (a) of this section shall be determined under paragraph (f)(4) of this section.

(2) *Meaning of "intentional disregard."*—A failure is due to intentional disregard if it is a knowing or willful—

(i) Failure to file timely, or

(ii) Failure to include correct information.

Whether a person knowingly or willfully fails to file timely or fails to include correct information is determined on the basis of all the facts and circumstances in the particular case.

(3) *Facts and circumstances considered.*—The facts and circumstances that are considered in determining whether a failure is due to intentional disregard include, but are not limited to—

(i) Whether the failure to file timely or the failure to include correct information is part of a pattern of conduct by the person who filed the return of repeatedly failing to file timely or repeatedly failing to include correct information;

(ii) Whether correction was promptly made upon discovery of the failure;

(iii) Whether the filer corrects a failure to file or a failure to include correct information within 30 days after the date of any written request from the Internal Revenue Service to file or to correct; and

(iv) Whether the amount of the information reporting penalties is less than the cost of complying with the requirement to file timely or to include correct information on an information return.

(4) *Amount of the penalty.*—If one or more failures to file timely or to include correct information are due to intentional disregard of the requirement to file timely or to include correct information, then, with respect to each such failure determined under this paragraph (f)—

(i) Paragraphs (b), (d), and (e) of this section shall not apply;

(ii) The $250,000 limitation under paragraph (a) of this section shall not apply, and the penalty under this paragraph (f) shall not be taken into account in applying the $250,000 limitation (or any similar limitation under paragraph (b) or (e) of this section) to penalties not determined under this paragraph (f);

(iii) The penalty imposed under paragraph (a) of this section shall be $100 or, if greater, the statutory percentage; and

(iv) The term "statutory percentage" means—

(A) In the case of a return other than a return required under section 6045(a), 6041A(b), 6050H, 6050I (for amounts received after November 5, 1990), 6050J, 6050K, or 6050L, 10 percent of the aggregate dollar amount of the items required to be reported correctly,

(B) In the case of a return required to be filed by section 6045(a), 6050K, or 6050L, 5 percent of the aggregate dollar amount of the items required to be reported correctly, or

(C) In the case of a return required to be filed under section 6050I(a) with respect to amounts received after November 5, 1990, for any transaction (or related transactions), the greater of $25,000 or the amount of cash (within the meaning of section 6050I(d)) received in such transaction to the extent the amount of such cash does not exceed $100,000.

(5) *Computation of the penalty; aggregate dollar amount of the items required to be reported correctly.*—The aggregate dollar amount used in computing the penalty under this paragraph (f) is the amount that is not reported or is reported incorrectly. If the intentional disregard relates to a dollar amount, the statutory percentage is applied to the difference between the dollar

amount reported and the amount required to be reported correctly. If the intentional disregard relates to any other item on the return, the statutory percentage is applied to the aggregate amount of items required to be reported correctly. In determining the aggregate amount of items required to be reported correctly, no item shall be taken into account more than once. For example, if a filer willfully fails to file a Form 1099-INT on which $800 of interest and $160 of Federal income tax withheld (*i.e.,* backup withholding) is required to be reported, only the $800 amount is taken into account in computing the penalty.

(6) *Examples.*—The provisions of this paragraph (f) may be illustrated by the following examples:

Example 1. On December 1, 1990, Automobile dealer P receives $55,000 from an individual for the purchase of an automobile in a transaction subject to reporting under section 6050I. The individual presents documents to P that identify him as "John Doe." However, P completes the Form 8300 (relating to cash received in a trade or business) and reflects the name of a cartoon character as the payor. Because P knew at the time of filing the Form 8300 that the payor's name was not the name of the cartoon character, he willfully failed to include correct information as described under paragraph (f)(2) of this section. Therefore, the penalty under paragraph (f)(4) of this section is imposed for the intentional disregard of the requirement to include correct information. The amount used in computing the penalty under paragraph (f)(5) of this section is $55,000 (*i.e.,* the amount required to be reported on the return with respect to which the payee is not correctly identified). The amount of the penalty determined under paragraph (f)(4)(ii)(C) of this section is $55,000 (*i.e.,* the greater of $25,000 or the amount of cash received in the transaction up to $100,000).

Example 2. On December 1, 1990, Individual B contacts his agent, F, to act as his intermediary in the purchase of an automobile. B gives F $20,000 and requests F to purchase the automobile in F's name, which F does. F prepares the Form 8300 as required under section 6050I, but in the area designated for the name of the payor, F writes "confidential." Because F knew at the time the return was filed that it contained incomplete information, the penalty under paragraph (f)(4) of this section is imposed for the intentional disregard of the requirement to include correct information. The amount used in computing the penalty under paragraph (f)(5) of this section is $20,000 (*i.e.,* the amount required to be reported on the return with respect to which the payee is not correctly identified). The amount of the penalty determined under paragraph (f)(4)(ii)(C) of this section is $25,000 (*i.e.,* the greater of $25,000 or the amount of cash received in the transaction up to $100,000).

Example 3. Corporation M deliberately does not include $5,000 of dividends on a Form 1099-DIV (relating to payments of dividends) on which a total of $200,000 (including the $5,000 dividends) is required to be reported under section 6042(a). Because the failure was deliberate, Corporation M's failure is due to intentional disregard of the requirement to include correct information. Accordingly, the amount of the penalty imposed under paragraph (a) is determined under paragraph (f)(4) of this section. Because the Form 1099-DIV is required to be filed under section 6042(a), under paragraph (f)(4)(ii)(A) the amount of the penalty with respect to such failure is 10 percent of the aggregate dollar amount of the items that were required to be but that were not reported correctly. Under paragraph (f)(5) of this section, $5,000 is the difference between the dollar amount reported and the amount required to be reported correctly. Therefore, the amount of the penalty is $500 ($5,000 × .10 = $500).

Example 4. Form 8027 requires certain large food and beverage establishments to report certain information with respect to tips. The form requires (among other things) that the establishment report its gross receipts from food and beverage operations. Establishment A, in intentional disregard of the information reporting requirement, reported gross receipts of $1,000,000, when the correct amount was $1,500,000. The significance of the gross receipts reporting requirement is that section 6053(c)(3)(A) requires an establishment to allocate as tips among its employees the excess of 8 percent of its gross receipts over the aggregate amount reported by employees to the establishment as tips under section 6053(a). A's misstatement of its gross receipts caused A to show $80,000 on the Form 8027 as 8 percent of its gross receipts, rather than the correct amount of $120,000. A correctly reported the amount of tips reported to it by employees under section 6053(a) as $80,000. Thus A reported the excess of 8 percent of its gross receipts over tips reported to it as zero, rather than as the correct amount of $40,000. The requirement of reporting gross receipts is considered merely a step in the computation of the excess of 8 percent of gross receipts over tips reported to A under section 6053(a), so that the penalty for intentional disregard will be $4,000 (*i.e.,* 10 percent of the difference between the $40,000 required to be reported as the excess of 8 percent of gross receipts over tips reported under section 6053(a), and the zero amount actually reported).

(g) *Definitions.*—(1) *Information return.*—For purposes of this section the term "information return" means any statement described in paragraph (g)(2) of this section, any return described in paragraph (g)(3) of this section, and any other items described in paragraph (g)(4) of this section.

(2) *Statements.*—The statements subject to this section are the statements required by—

(i) Section 6041(a) or (b) (relating to certain information at source, generally reported on Form 1099-MISC, "Miscellaneous Income"; Form W-2, "Wage and Tax Statement"; Form W-2G,

"Certain Gambling Winnings"; and Form 1099-INT, "Interest Income");

(ii) Section 6042(a)(1) (relating to payments of dividends, generally reported on Form 1099-DIV, "Dividends and Distributions");

(iii) Section 6044(a)(1) (relating to payments of patronage dividends, generally reported on Form 1099-PATR, "Taxable Distributions Received From Cooperatives");

(iv) Section 6049(a) (relating to payments of interest, generally reported on Form 1099-INT or Form 1099-OID, "Original Issue Discount");

(v) Section 6050A(a) (relating to reporting requirements of certain fishing boat operators, generally reported on Form 1099-MISC);

(vi) Section 6050N(a) (relating to payments of royalties, generally reported on Form 1099-MISC);

(vii) Section 6051(d) (relating to information returns with respect to income tax withheld, generally reported on Form W-2);

(viii) Section 6050R (relating to returns relating to certain purchases of fish, generally reported on Form 1099-MISC);

(ix) Section 110(d) (relating to qualified lessee construction allowances for shortterm leases, generally reported by attaching a statement to an income tax return);

(x) Section 408(i) (relating to reports with respect to individual retirement accounts or annuities on Form 1099-R, "Distributions From Pensions, Annuities, Retirement or Profit-Sharing Plans, IRAs, Insurance Contracts, etc."); or

(xi) Section 6047(d) (relating to reports by employers, plan administrators, etc., on Form 1099-R).

(3) *Returns.*—The returns subject to this section are the returns required by—

(i) Section 6041A(a) or (b) (relating to returns of direct sellers, generally reported on Form 1099-MISC);

(ii) Section 6043A(a) (relating to returns relating to taxable mergers and acquisitions);

(iii) Section 6045(a) or (d) (relating to returns of brokers, generally reported on Form 1099-B, "Proceeds From Broker and Barter Exchange Transactions," for broker transactions; Form 1099-S, "Proceeds From Real Estate Transactions," for gross proceeds from the sale or exchange of real estate; and Form 1099-MISC for certain substitute payments and payments to attorneys);

(iv) Section 6045B(a) (relating to returns relating to actions affecting basis of specified securities);

(v) Section 6050H(a) or (h)(1) (relating to mortgage interest received in trade or business from individuals, generally reported on Form 1098, "Mortgage Interest Statement");

(vi) Section 6050I(a) or (g)(1) (relating to cash received in trade or business, etc., generally reported on Form 8300, "Report of Cash Payments Over $10,000 Received In a Trade or Business");

(vii) Section 6050J(a) (relating to foreclosures and abandonments of security, generally reported on Form 1099-A, "Acquisition or Abandonment of Secured Property");

(viii) Section 6050K(a) (relating to exchanges of certain partnership interests, generally reported on Form 8308, "Report of a Sale or Exchange of Certain Partnership Interests");

(ix) Section 6050L(a) (relating to returns relating to certain dispositions of donated property, generally reported on Form 8282, "Donee Information Return");

(x) Section 6050P (relating to returns relating to the cancellation of indebtedness by certain financial entities, generally reported on Form 1099-C, "Cancellation of Debt");

(xi) Section 6050Q (relating to certain long-term care benefits, generally reported on Form 1099-LTC, "Long-Term Care and Accelerated Death Benefits");

(xii) Section 6050S (relating to returns relating to payments for qualified tuition and related expenses, generally reported on Form 1098-E, "Student Loan Interest Statement," or Form 1098-T, "Tuition Statement");

(xiii) Section 6050T (relating to returns relating to credit for health insurance costs of eligible individuals, generally reported on Form 1099-H, "Health Coverage Tax Credit (HCTC) Advance Payments");

(xiv) Section 6052(a) (relating to reporting payment of wages in the form of group-life insurance, generally reported on Form W-2);

(xv) Section 6050V (relating to returns relating to applicable insurance contracts in which certain exempt organizations hold interests, generally reported on Form 8921, "Applicable Insurance Contract Information Return");

(xvi) Section 6053(c)(1) (relating to reporting with respect to certain tips, generally reported on Form 8027, "Employer's Annual Information Return of Tip Income and Allocated Tips");

(xvii) Section 1060(b) (relating to reporting requirements of transferors and transferees in certain asset acquisitions, generally reported on Form 8594, "Asset Acquisition Statement"), or section 1060(e) (relating to information required in the case of certain transfers of interests in entities (effective for acquisitions after October 9, 1990, except any acquisition pursuant to a written binding contract in effect on October 9, 1990, and at all times thereafter before such acquisition));

(xviii) Section 4101(d) (relating to information reporting with respect to fuel oils (effective for information returns required to be filed after November 30, 1990));

(xix) Section 338(h)(10)(C) (relating to information required to be furnished to the Secretary in case of elective recognition of gain or loss (effective for acquisitions after October 9, 1990, except any acquisition pursuant to a written binding contract in effect on October 9, 1990, and at all times thereafter before such acquisition));

Reg. §301.6721-1(g)(3)(xix)

(xx) Section 264(f)(5)(A)(iv) (relating to reporting with respect to certain life insurance and annuity contracts);

(xxi) Section 6050U (relating to charges or payments for qualified long-term care insurance contracts under combined arrangements, generally reported on Form 1099-R);

(xxii) Section 6039(a) (relating to returns required with respect to certain options);

(xxiii) Section 6050W (relating to information returns with respect to payments made in settlement of payment card and third party network transactions);

(xxiv) Section 6055 (relating to information returns reporting minimum essential coverage); or

(xxv) Section 6056 (relating to information returns reporting on offers of health insurance coverage by applicable large employer members).

(4) *Other items.*—The term *information return* also includes any form, statement, or schedule required to be filed with the Internal Revenue Service with respect to any amount from which tax is required to be deducted and withheld under chapter 3 of the Internal Revenue Code (or from which tax would be required to be so deducted and withheld but for an exemption under the Internal Revenue Code or any treaty obligation of the United States), generally Forms 1042-S, "Foreign Person's U.S. Source Income Subject to Withholding," and 8805, "Foreign Partner's Information Statement of Section 1446 Withholding Tax." The provisions of this paragraph (g)(4) referring to Form 8805, shall apply to partnership taxable years beginning after May 18, 2005, or such earlier time as the regulations under §§1.1446-1 through 1.1446-5 of this chapter apply by reason of an election under §1.1446-7 of this chapter.

(5) *Payee.*—For purposes of section 6721 the term "payee" means any person who is required to receive a copy of the information set forth on an information return by the filer of the return as defined in section 6724(d)(1).

(6) *Filer.*—For purposes of this section the term "filer" means a person that is required to file an information return as defined in paragraph (g)(1) of this section under the applicable information reporting section described in paragraph (g)(2) through (4) of this section. [Reg. §301.6721-1.]

☐ [T.D. 8386, 12-27-91. *Amended by* T.D. 8843, 11-10-99; T.D. 9200, 5-13-2005; T.D. 9496, 8-13-2010; T.D. 9504, 10-12-2010 *and* T.D. 9660, 3-5-2014.]

[Reg. §301.6722-1]

§301.6722-1. Failure to furnish correct payee statements.—(a) *Imposition of penalty.*—(1) *General rule.*—A penalty of $50 is imposed for each payee statement (as defined in section 6724(d)(2)) with respect to which a failure (as defined in section 6722(a) and paragraph (a)(2)

of this section) occurs. No more than one penalty will be imposed under this paragraph (a) with respect to a single payee statement even though there may be more than one failure with respect to such statement. However, the penalty shall apply to failures on composite substitute payee statements as though each type of payment and other required information were furnished on separate statements. A "composite substitute payee statement" is a single document created by a filer to reflect several types of payments made to the same payee. The total amount imposed on any person for all failures during any calendar year with respect to all payee statements shall not exceed $100,000. See section 6722(c) and paragraph(c) of this section for higher penalties when a failure is due to intentional disregard of the requirement to furnish timely correct payee statements. See paragraph (a)(1) of §301.6724-1 for a waiver of the penalty for a failure that is due to reasonable cause.

(2) *Failures subject to the penalty.*—The failures to which section 6722(a) and paragraph (a)(1) of this section apply are—

(i) A failure to furnish a payee statement on or before the prescribed date therefor to the person to whom such statement is required to be furnished ("failure to furnish timely"), and

(ii) A failure to include all of the information required to be shown on a payee statement or the inclusion of incorrect information ("failure to include correct information").

A failure to furnish timely includes a failure to furnish a written statement to the payee in a statement mailing as required under sections 6042(c), 6044(e), 6049(c), and 6050N(b), as well as a failure to furnish the statement on a form acceptable to the Internal Revenue Service. Except as provided in paragraph (b) of this section, a failure to include correct information encompasses a failure to include the information required by applicable information reporting statutes or by any administrative pronouncements issued thereunder (such as regulations, revenue rulings, revenue procedures, or information reporting forms).

(b) *Exception for inconsequential errors or omissions.*—(1) *In general.*—An inconsequential error or omission is not considered a failure to include correct information. For purposes of this paragraph (b), the term "inconsequential error or omission" means any failure that cannot reasonably be expected to prevent or hinder the payee from timely receiving correct information and reporting it on his or her return or from otherwise putting the statement to its intended use.

(2) *Errors or omissions that are never inconsequential.*—Errors or omissions relating to the following are never inconsequential:

(i) A dollar amount,

(ii) The significant items in the address of a payee, which is the address provided by the payee to the filer,

(iii) The appropriate form for the information provided (*i.e.*, whether or not the form is an acceptable substitute for an official form of the Internal Revenue Service), and

    (iv) The manner of furnishing a statement required under sections 6042(c), 6044(e), 6049(e), and 6050N(b).

    The Internal Revenue Service may, by administrative pronouncement, specify other types of errors or omissions that are never inconsequential.

    (3) *Examples.*—The provisions of this paragraph (b) may be illustrated by the following examples which do not take into account any possible application of the penalty for intentional disregard under paragraph (c) of this section or the reasonable cause waiver under paragraph (a) of § 301.6724-1:

    Example 1. A payor furnishes a statement with respect to a Form 1099-MISC (relating to miscellaneous income). The payee statement is complete and correct, except the word "boulevard" is misspelled in the payee's address. The error cannot reasonably be expected to prevent or hinder the payee from timely receiving correct information and reporting it on his or her tax return or from otherwise putting the statement to its intended use. Therefore, no penalty is imposed under paragraph (a) of this section.

    Example 2. Assume the same facts as in *Example 1*, except that the only error on the payee statement is that the payee's street address, 4821 Grant Boulevard, is reported incorrectly as 8421 Grant Boulevard. A penalty is imposed under paragraph (a) of this section with respect to the payee statement because the error can reasonably be expected to prevent or hinder the payee from timely receiving correct information and reporting it on his or her tax return or from otherwise putting the statement to its intended use.

    (c) *Higher penalty for intentional disregard of requirement to furnish timely correct payee statements.*—(1) *Application of section 6722(c).*—If a failure is due to intentional disregard of the requirement to furnish timely correct payee statements, the amount of the penalty shall be determined under paragraph (c)(2) of this section. Whether a failure is due to intentional disregard of the requirement to furnish timely correct payee statements is based upon the facts and circumstances surrounding the failure. The facts and circumstances considered include those under § 301.6721-1(f)(3), which shall apply in determining whether a failure under this section is due to intentional disregard.

    (2) *Amount of the penalty.*—If one or more failures under paragraph (a) of this section are due to intentional disregard of the requirement to furnish timely payee statements or of the requirement to include correct information, then, with respect to each such failure determined under this paragraph (c)(2)—

    (i) The $100,000 limitation under paragraph (a) of this section shall not apply and the penalty under this paragraph (c)(2) shall not be taken into account in applying the $100,000 limi-

tation to penalties not determined under this paragraph (c)(2);

    (ii) The penalty imposed under paragraph (a) of this section shall be $100 or, if greater, the statutory percentage; and

    (iii) The term "statutory percentage" means—

    (A) In the case of a payee statement other than a statement required under section 6045(b), 6041A(e) (in respect of a return required under section 6041A(b)), 6050H(d), 6050J(e), 6050K(b), or 6050L(c), 10 percent of the aggregate dollar amount of the items required to be reported correctly, or

    (B) In the case of a payee statement required under section 6045(b), 6050K(b), or 6050L(c), 5 percent of the aggregate dollar amount of the items required to be reported correctly.

    (3) *Computation of the penalty; aggregate dollar amount of items required to be shown correctly.*—The aggregate dollar amount used in computing the penalty under this paragraph (c) is the amount that is not reported or is reported incorrectly. If the intentional disregard relates to a dollar amount, the statutory percentage is applied to the difference between the dollar amount reported and the amount required to be reported correctly. If the intentional disregard relates to any other item on the return, the statutory percentage is applied to the aggregate amount of items required to be reported correctly. In determining such amount the same item shall be counted only once. For example, if a filer willfully fails to furnish a Form 1099-INT on which $800 of interest and $160 of Federal income tax withheld (*i.e.*, backup withholding) is required to be shown, only the $800 amount is taken into account in computing the penalty.

    (d) *Definitions.*—(1) *Payee.*—See § 301.6721-1(g)(5) for the definition of "payee."

    (2) *Payee statement.*—The term *payee statement* means any statement required to be furnished under—

    (i) Section 6031(b) or (c), 6034A, or 6037(b) (relating to statements furnished by certain pass-thru entities, generally a Schedule K-1 (Form 1065), "Partner's Share of Income, Deductions, Credits, etc.," for section 6031(b) or (c), a copy of the Schedule K-1 (Form 1041), "Beneficiary's Share of Income, Deductions, Credits, etc.," for section 6034A, and a copy of Schedule K-1 (Form 1120S), "Shareholder's Share of Income, Deductions, Credits, etc.," for section 6037(b));

    (ii) Section 6039(b) (relating to information required in connection with certain options);

    (iii) Section 6041(d) (relating to information at source, generally the recipient copy of Form 1099-MISC, "Miscellaneous Income"; Form W-2, "Wage and Tax Statement"; Form 1099-INT, "Interest Income"; and the winner's copies of Form W-2G, "Certain Gambling Winnings");

    (iv) Section 6041A(e) (relating to returns regarding payments of remuneration for services and direct sales, generally the recipient copy of Form 1099-MISC);

Reg. § 301.6722-1(d)(2)(iv)

(v) Section 6042(c) (relating to returns regarding payments of dividends and corporate earnings and profits, generally the recipient copy of Form 1099-DIV, "Dividends and Distributions");

(vi) Section 6043A(b) or (d) (relating to returns relating to taxable mergers and acquisitions);

(vii) Section 6044(e) (relating to returns regarding payments of patronage dividends, generally the recipient copy of Form 1099-PATR, "Taxable Distributions Received From Cooperatives");

(viii) Section 6045(b) or (d) (relating to returns of brokers, generally the recipient copy of Form 1099-B, "Proceeds From Broker and Barter Exchange Transactions," for broker transactions; the transferor copy of Form 1099-S, "Proceeds From Real Estate Transactions," for reporting proceeds from real estate transactions; and the recipient copy of Form 1099-MISC for certain substitute payments and payments to attorneys);

(ix) Section 6045A (relating to information required in connection with transfers of covered securities to brokers);

(x) Section 6045B(c) or (e) (relating to returns relating to actions affecting basis of specified securities);

(xi) Section 6049(c) (relating to returns regarding payments of interest, generally the recipient copy of Form 1099-INT or Form 1099-OID, "Original Issue Discount");

(xii) Section 6050A(b) (relating to reporting requirements of certain fishing boat operators, generally the recipient copy of Form 1099-MISC);

(xiii) Section 6050H(d) or (h)(2) (relating to returns relating to mortgage interest received in trade or business from individuals, generally the payor copy of Form 1098, "Mortgage Interest Statement");

(xiv) Section 6050I(e), (g)(4), or (g)(5) (relating to returns relating to cash received in trade or business, etc., generally a copy of Form 8300, "Report of Cash Payments Over $10,000 Received In a Trade or Business");

(xv) Section 6050J(e) (relating to returns relating to foreclosures and abandonments of security, generally the borrower copy of Form 1099-A, "Acquisition or Abandonment of Secured Property");

(xvi) Section 6050K(b) (relating to returns relating to exchanges of certain partnership interests, generally a copy of Form 8308, "Report of a Sale or Exchange of Certain Partnership Interests");

(xvii) Section 6050L(c) (relating to returns relating to certain dispositions of donated property, generally a copy of Form 8282, "Donee Information Return");

(xviii) Section 6050N(b) (relating to returns regarding payments of royalties, generally the recipient copy of Form 1099-MISC);

(xix) Section 6050P(d) (relating to returns relating to the cancellation of indebtedness by certain financial entities, generally the recipient copy of Form 1099-C, "Cancellation of Debt");

(xx) Section 6050Q(b) (relating to certain long-term care benefits, generally the policyholder and insured copies of Form 1099-LTC, "Long-Term Care and Accelerated Death Benefits");

(xxi) Section 6050R(c) (relating to returns relating to certain purchases of fish, generally the recipient copy of Form 1099-MISC);

(xxii) Section 6051 (relating to receipts for employees, generally the employee copy of Form W-2);

(xxiii) Section 6052(b) (relating to returns regarding payment of wages in the form of group-term life insurance, generally the employee copy of Form W-2);

(xxiv) Section 6053(b) or (c) (relating to reports of tips, generally the employee copy of Form W-2);

(xxv) Section 6048(b)(1)(B) (relating to foreign trust reporting requirements, generally copies of the owner and beneficiary statements of Form 3520-A, "Annual Information Return of Foreign Trust With a U.S. Owner");

(xxvi) Section 408(i) (relating to reports with respect to individual retirement plans on the recipient copies of Form 1099-R, "Distributions From Pensions, Annuities, Retirement or Profit-Sharing Plans, IRAs, Insurance Contracts, etc.");

(xxvii) Section 6047(d) (relating to reports by plan administrators on the recipient copies of Form 1099-R);

(xxviii) Section 6050S(d) (relating to returns relating to qualified tuition and related expenses, generally the borrower copy of Form 1098-E, "Student Loan Interest Statement," or the student copy of Form 1098-T, "Tuition Statement");

(xxix) Section 264(f)(5)(A)(iv) (relating to reporting with respect to certain life insurance and annuity contracts);

(xxx) Section 6050T (relating to returns relating to credit for health insurance costs of eligible individuals, generally the recipient copy of Form 1099-H, "Health Coverage Tax Credit (HCTC) Advance Payments");

(xxxi) Section 6050U (relating to charges or payments for qualified long-term care insurance contracts under combined arrangements, generally the recipient copy of Form 1099-R);

(xxxii) Section 6050W (relating to information returns with respect to payments made in settlement of payment card and third party network transactions);

(xxxiii) Section 6055 (relating to information returns reporting minimum essential coverage); or

(xxxiv) Section 6056 (relating to information returns reporting on offers of health insurance coverage by applicable large employer members).

(3) *Other items.*—The term *payee statement* also includes any form, statement, or schedule required to be furnished to the recipient of any amount from which tax is required to be deducted and withheld under chapter 3 of the Internal Revenue Code (or from which tax would be required to be so deducted and withheld but for an exemption under the Internal Revenue Code or any treaty obligation of the United States) (generally the recipient copy of Form 1042-S, "Foreign Person's U.S. Source Income subject to Withholding," or Form 8805, "Foreign Partner's Information Statement of Section 1446 Withholding Tax.")

(e) *Effective/Applicability date.*—The reference in paragraph (d)(3) of this section to Form 8805 shall apply to partnership taxable years beginning after April 29, 2008. [Reg. § 301.6722-1.]

☐ [*T.D.* 8386, 12-27-91. *Amended by T.D.* 9394, 4-28-2008; *T.D.* 9496, 8-13-2010; *T.D.* 9504, 10-12-2010 *and T.D.* 9660, 3-5-2014.]

⇛→ *Caution: Reg. § 301.6723-1A, below, is applicable to information returns and payee statements the due date for which (without regard to extensions) is after December 31, 1986, and before January 1, 1990.*

[Reg. § 301.6723-1A]

§ 301.6723-1A. Failure to include correct information.—(a) *General rule.*—If any person files an information return (as defined in section 6724(d)(1)) or furnishes a payee statement (as defined in section 6724(d)(2)) the due date for which, determined without regard to extensions, is after December 31, 1986, and before January 1, 1990, and such person fails to include all of the information required to be shown on such return or statement or includes incorrect information, such person will be considered to have failed to include correct information. For this purpose, information required to be shown on a return or statement is the information required by the applicable information reporting statute or by any administrative pronouncement issued thereunder (such as a regulation, revenue ruling, revenue procedure, or information reporting form). Except as otherwise provided in this section, any person who fails to include correct information shall pay $5 for each return or statement with respect to which such failure occurs; however, the total amount imposed on any person for all such failures during any calendar year shall not exceed $20,000. See paragraph (e) of this section regarding the higher penalties for intentional disregard of the correct information reporting requirement and for interest and dividend returns and statements.

(b) *Exception for inconsequential omissions and inaccuracies.*—(1) *Exception.*—The penalty imposed by paragraph (a) of this section will not be assessed for any failure to include correct information on an information return if the failure does not prevent or hinder the Internal Revenue Service from processing the return or from corre-

lating the information required to be shown on the return with the information shown on the payee's tax return. Similarly, the penalty imposed by paragraph (a) of this section will not be assessed for any failure to include correct information on a payee statement if the failure cannot reasonably be expected to prevent or hinder the payee from timely receiving correct information and reporting it on his or her tax return.

(2) *Examples.*—The provisions of this paragraph (b) may be illustrated by the following examples:

Example 1. A payor files a Form 1099-MISC (relating to miscellaneous income) with the Internal Revenue Service and furnishes a corresponding statement to the payee. Both the Form 1099-MISC and the payee statement are complete and correct except that the word "Street" is misspelled in the payee's address. The error does not prevent or hinder the Internal Revenue Service from processing the return or from correlating the information required to be shown on the return with the information shown on the payee's tax return. In addition, the error cannot reasonably be expected to prevent or hinder the payee from timely receiving correct information and reporting it on his or her tax return. Therefore, the penalty imposed by paragraph (a) of this section will not be assessed.

Example 2. Assume the same facts as in *Example 1*, except that the only error on the Form 1099-MISC and the payee statement is that the payee's first name, "William," is misspelled as "Willaim." The penalty imposed by paragraph (a) of this section will not be assessed, for the reasons set forth in *Example 1*.

Example 3. Assume the same facts as in *Example 1*, except that the only error on the Form 1099-MISC and the payee statement is that the payee's street address, 4821 Main Street, is incorrectly reported as 8421 Main Street. The penalty imposed by paragraph (a) of this section will not be assessed with respect to the Form 1099-MISC if the error does not prevent or hinder the Internal Revenue Service from processing the return or from correlating the information required to be shown on the return with the information shown on the payee's tax return. However, the penalty will be assessed with respect to the payee statement because the error can reasonably be expected to prevent or hinder the payee from timely receiving correct information and reporting it on his or her tax return. See paragraph (d) of this section regarding waiver of the penalty for reasonable cause or due diligence.

(c) *Exception for corrected omissions and inaccuracies.*—(1) *Exception.*—The penalty imposed by paragraph (a) of this section generally will not be assessed for a failure to include correct information on an information return or payee statement if the person who filed the return or furnished the statement corrects the failure by the earliest of—

(i) The date that is 30 days after the date that the person discovers the failure; or

(ii) The date that is 30 days after the date of a written request, from the Internal Revenue Service to the person, for corrected information; or

(iii) October 1 (March 1 for payee statements) of the calendar year in which the return or statement is due.

(2) *Limitations on exception.*—Notwithstanding paragraph (c)(1) of this section, timely correction of a failure to include correct information on a return or statement will not prevent assessment of the penalty for any failure that is part of a pattern of conduct, by the person who filed the return or furnished the statement, of repeatedly failing to include correct information. Further, correction of a failure to include correct information will not prevent assessment of the penalty for intentional disregard of the correct information reporting requirement. See paragraph (e)(1) of this section with respect to intentional disregard.

(3) *Examples.*—The provisions of this paragraph (c) may be illustrated by the following examples:

Example 1. In January 1987, Bank M prepares Forms 1099-INT (relating to interest income) with respect to interest income earned by its depositors in calendar year 1986. M timely files the forms with the Internal Revenue Service and timely furnishes copies to its depositors. On March 16, 1987, M discovers that the amount of backup withholding tax (Federal income tax withheld) was inadvertently omitted from several of the forms and payee copies. Several days later M files corrected forms with the Service and furnishes corrected copies to the affected payees. The penalty for failure to include correct information will not be due with respect to the incomplete Forms 1099-INT filed with the Internal Revenue Service, since they were corrected within 30 days after M discovered the omission and before October 1, 1987. However, the penalty will be due with respect to the incomplete copies furnished to the payees, since they were not corrected by March 1, 1987.

Example 2. In January 1987, Corporation N files Forms 1099-DIV (relating to dividends and distributions) for calendar year 1986 and furnishes copies to its shareholders. A significant number of the forms and payee copies do not include the amount of backup withholding tax. On December 1, 1987, the Internal Revenue Service provides N with a written request for corrected information. On December 15, 1987, N files corrected forms with the Service and furnishes corrected copies to the payees. The penalty for failure to include correct information will be due with respect to the incomplete forms, since they were not corrected by October 1, 1987. In addition, the penalty will be due with respect to the incomplete copies furnished to the payees, since they were not corrected by March 1, 1987. However, N's correction of the forms is a fact to be considered, along with other facts, in determining whether the higher penalty for inten-

tional failures will imposed; see paragraph (e)(1)(ii)(B) of this section.

Example 3. In January 1987, Corporation O files Forms 1099-DIV for calendar year 1986 and furnishes copies to its shareholders. O intentionally does not include the amount of backup withholding tax for any shareholder. Since the omissions represent an intentional disregard of the correct information reporting requirement, correction of the omissions will not prevent assessment of the penalty for intentional failure to include correct information.

(d) *Waiver for reasonable cause or due diligence.*—(1) *Reasonable cause.*—Except as provided in paragraph (d)(2) of this section (relating to interest or dividend returns or statements), the penalty imposed by paragraph (a) of this section will be waived for any failure to include correct information if it is established to the satisfaction of the district director or the director of the internal revenue service center that such failure was due to reasonable cause and not to willful neglect.

(2) *Due diligence.*—Paragraph (d)(1) of this section will not apply in the case of any interest or dividend return or statement (as defined in section 6724(c)(5)). However, in such a case, the penalty imposed by paragraph (a) of this section will be waived for any failure to include correct information if it is established to the satisfaction of the district director or the director of the internal revenue service center that the person otherwise liable for such penalty exercised due diligence in attempting to include such information. The requirement to exercise due diligence imposes a higher standard of conduct than required under the reasonable cause defense.

(3) *Procedure for seeking waiver.*—Reasonable cause (or due diligence) may be established only by submitting a written statement that sets forth all the facts alleged as reasonable cause (or due diligence) and makes an affirmative showing of reasonable cause (or due diligence). The statement must be signed by the person required to file the information return or furnish the payee statement to which the penalty imposed by paragraph (a) of this section relates, and must contain a declaration that it is made under the penalties of perjury. See § 301.6061-1 for rules on the signing of returns.

(e) *Higher penalties in certain cases.*—(1) *Intentional disregard of the correct information reporting requirement.*—(i) *Application of section 6723(b).*—If a person fails to include correct information on an information return and such failure is due to intentional disregard of the correct information reporting requirement, the penalty imposed by paragraph (a) of this section with respect to such return will be determined under section 6723(b). The penalty prescribed by section 6723(b) for such a return is $100 or, if greater, the amount equal to 10 percent (or, in some cases, 5 percent) of the aggregate amount of the items required to be reported correctly on the return. In the case of any penalty determined under section 6723(b),

Reg. § 301.6723-1A(c)(1)(ii)

the $20,000 limitation of paragraph (a) of this section will not apply. In addition, such penalty will not be taken into account in applying the $20,000 limitation to penalties not determined under section 6723(b).

(ii) *Meaning of intentional disregard.*—A failure to include correct information on an information return will be treated as due to intentional disregard of the correct information reporting requirement if the person who filed the return knowingly or willfully failed to include correct information at the time the return was filed. Whether a person knowingly or willfully failed to include correct information will be determined on the basis of all of the facts and circumstances in the particular case. Facts and circumstances to be considered for this purpose include, but are not limited to, the following—

(A) Whether the failure to include correct information is part of a pattern of conduct, by the person who filed the return, of repeatedly failing to include correct information on information returns;

(B) Whether the person who filed the return corrects the failure within 30 days after the date of any written request from the Internal Revenue Service for corrected information; and

(C) Whether the person who filed the return can reasonably be expected to have discovered the failure during the calendar year the return was due and, if so, whether timely correction was made.

(2) *Interest and dividend returns and statements.*—In the case of any interest or dividend return or statement (as defined in section 6724(c)(5)), the $20,000 limitation of paragraph (a) of this section will not apply. In addition, any penalty imposed by paragraph (a) of this section with respect to such a return or statement—

(i) Will not be taken into account in applying the $20,000 limitation of paragraph (a) of this section with respect to other returns or statements, and

(ii) Will not be taken into account in applying the $100,000 limitations of sections 6721(a) and 6722(a) with respect to any return or statement.

(f) *Manner of payment.*—(1) *In general.*—Except as provided in paragraph (f)(2) of this section (relating to interest and dividend returns and statements), any penalty imposed by paragraph (a) of this section shall be paid on notice and demand by the Internal Revenue Service and in the same manner as a tax liability is paid.

(2) *Self-assessment for interest and dividend returns and statements.*—Any penalty imposed by paragraph (a) of this section with respect to an interest or dividend return or statement will be assessed and collected in the same manner as an excise tax imposed by subtitle D of the Internal Revenue Code, and the deficiency procedures of subchapter B of chapter 63 of the Code will not apply. In such a case, the penalty must be self-assessed and will be due and payable on April 1

of the calendar year following the calendar year for which the return or statement is required. The penalty should be remitted with a properly executed Form 8210 (Self-Assessed Penalties Return).

(g) *Coordination with other penalties.*—(1) *Penalty for failure to supply identifying numbers.*—Pursuant to section 6723(c), no penalty shall be imposed under paragraph (a) of this section with respect to any return or statement if a penalty is imposed under section 6676 (relating to the failure to supply identifying numbers) with respect to such return or statement.

(2) *Penalty for failure to file information returns or furnish payee statements.*—No penalty shall be imposed under paragraph (a) of this section with respect to any return or statement if a penalty is imposed under section 6721 (relating to the failure to file certain information returns) or section 6722 (relating to the failure to furnish certain payee statements) with respect to such return or statement.

(3) *Examples.*—The provisions of this paragraph (g) may be illustrated by the following examples:

Example 1. Corporation P timely files Forms 1099-DIV (relating to dividends and distributions) for a calendar year and furnishes copies to its shareholders. Several of these forms and shareholder copies do not include correct taxpayer identification numbers (TINs), and Corporation P does not show that it exercised due diligence in attempting to include correct TINs; therefore, a penalty is imposed under section 6676(b) with respect to these several forms and shareholder copies. Since a penalty is imposed under section 6676, no penalty is imposed under paragraph (a) of this section with respect to the same several forms and shareholder copies.

Example 2. Corporation Q, a bank, fails to file certain required Forms 1099-INT (relating to interest income of its depositors) in a timely fashion. Corporation Q claims that it exercised due diligence in attempting to file the forms on time and that therefore no penalty under section 6721 or 6723 should apply. If the Internal Revenue Service finds that Corporation Q did not exercise due diligence and imposes the failure-to-file penalty under section 6721 with respect to the forms, no penalty will be imposed under paragraph (a) of this section.

Example 3. Corporation R files with the Internal Revenue Service a document purporting to be an information return. The document contains so many omissions and inaccuracies that its utility as an information return is minimized or eliminated. The Service imposes the failure-to-file penalty under section 6721 with respect to the document. Since the failure-to-file penalty is imposed, no penalty will be imposed under paragraph (a) of this section.

(h) *Effective date.*—The rules contained in this section are effective January 1, 1987, as applicable to information returns and payee statements the due date for which, determined without re-

Reg. §301.6723-1A(h)

gard to extensions, is after December 31, 1986, and before January 1, 1990. See section 7711 of the Omnibus Budget Reconciliation Act of 1989 (Pub. L. 101-239, 103 Stat. 2106 (1989)) for the applicable penalty for certain failures related to information returns and payee statements the due date for which, without regard to extensions, is after December 31, 1989. [Reg. § 301.6723-1A.]

☐ [*T.D.* 8344, 4-12-91.]

[Reg. § 301.6723-1]

§ 301.6723-1. Failure to comply with other information reporting requirements.— (a) *Imposition of penalty.—*(1) *General rule.—*A penalty of $50 is imposed for each failure to comply timely with a specified information reporting requirement(as defined in paragraph (a)(4) of this section) or for each failure to include correct specified information. Multiple penalties are imposed with respect to a document with failures to comply with more than one of the requirements set forth in paragraph (a)(4) of this section or multiple instances of failures to comply with any one of these requirements. Nonetheless, if a failure that occurs with respect to any requirement defined in paragraph (a)(4) of this section would be subject to a penalty under both paragraph (a)(2)(i) and paragraph (a)(2)(ii) of this section, no more than one penalty is imposed for such failure. The total amount imposed on any person for all failures during any calendar year with respect to all specified information reporting requirements shall not exceed $100,000. See paragraph (a) of § 301.6724-1 for the waiver of the penalty for a failure that is due to reasonable cause.

(2) *Failures subject to the penalty.—*The failures to which paragraph (a)(1) of this section apply are—

(i) A failure to comply timely with a specified information reporting requirement on or before the date prescribed therefor ("failure to comply timely"), and

(ii) A failure to include all the information required by a specified information reporting requirement or the inclusion of incorrect information ("failure to include correct information").

(3) *Exception for inconsequential errors or omissions.—*An inconsequential error or omission is not considered a failure to comply with a specified information reporting requirement. For purposes of paragraph (a)(3) of this section, an error or omission is considered inconsequential if it does not frustrate the purpose or use for which the information is intended.

(4) *Specified information reporting requirement defined.—*For purposes of section 6723 and this section, a "specified information reporting requirement" means—

(i) The requirement to provide the notice under section 6050X(c)(1) (relating to the requirement that a transferor notify the partnership of an exchange of a partnership interest);

(ii) Any requirement contained in the regulations under section 6109 that a person—

(A) Include his or her taxpayer identification number ("TIN") on any return, statement, or other document (other than an information return or payee statement),

(B) Include on any return, statement, or other document (other than an information return or payee statement) made with respect to another person the TIN of such person, or

(C) Furnish his or her TIN to another person;

(iii) Any requirement contained in the regulations under section 215 that a person—

(A) Furnish his or her TIN to another person, or

(B) Include on his or her return the TIN of another person; and

(iv) The requirement under section 6109(e) that a person include the TIN of any dependent on his or her return.

(b) *Examples.—*The provisions of paragraph (a) of this section may be illustrated by the following examples which do not take into account the reasonable cause waiver under section 6724(a) and paragraph (a)(1) of § 301.6724-1.

Example 1. Individual A, who has two dependents ages 7 and 9, files his 1990 Form 1040 in 1991. The Form 1040 requires him to provide the TINs of his two dependents, which A fails to do. Because A fails to comply timely with two requirements to include on his return the TIN of another person, a $50 penalty under paragraph (a) of this section is imposed on A for each of the two failures, for a total penalty of $100.

Example 2. In 1991 Individual B opens with Bank X an account which pays reportable interest under section 6049. When B opens the account, Bank X requests that B provide his TIN on a Form W-9. B does not provide his TIN as required by § 301.6109-1(b). As a result B fails to comply timely with a specified information reporting requirement under paragraph (a) of this section for furnishing his TIN to another person. Therefore, a $50 penalty is imposed on B under paragraph (a) of this section for the failure. See section 6721(a) for the penalty to which X may be subject if X files a Form 1099-INT (relating to payments of interest) for calendar year 1991 without B's TIN. See section 3406(a)(1)(A) which requires X to impose backup withholding on reportable payments of interest to B's account.

Example 3. In 1991 Individual C is a nonresident alien with an account inside the U.S. with Bank Z. The account pays interest that would be reportable under section 6049 but for the fact that it is paid to a nonresident alien. Under section 6109 and § 301.6109-1(b), Bank Z is required to request the TIN from C. C claims that he is a nonresident alien and that his account is not subject to information reporting under section 6049. Because of this, C contends he is not required to provide any TIN information. As a result of this discussion, Bank Z then requests C to provide it with a Form W-8 in order for C to certify that he is a nonresident alien which C fails to do. C fails to comply timely with a specified information reporting requirement under paragraph (a) of this section to furnish his TIN to another person. Therefore, a penalty is imposed on C under paragraph (a) of this section for the failure. See section 6721(a) for the penalty that may be imposed on Z if Z files a Form 1099-INT for calendar year 1991 without C's TIN. See section 3406(a)(1)(A) under which Z is required to impose backup withholding on reportable payment of interest to C's account.

Example 4. In 1991 Partnership D opens with Bank Y an account that pays reportable interest under section 6049. When D opens the account, Y requests the partnership's employer identification number (EIN) on a Form W-9 as required under §301.6109-1(b). The partnership provides its EIN on the Form W-9. Y files an information return with respect to D for the 1991 calendar year. Subsequently, the Internal Revenue Service later notifies Y that D's EIN is incorrect as defined under section 3406 and §35a.3406-1(a)(6). D fails to comply timely with a specified reporting requirement under paragraph (a) of this section of furnishing its correct EIN to another person. Therefore, a penalty is imposed on D under paragraph (a) of this section for the failure. See section 6721(a) for the penalty to which Y may be subject if Y files a Form 1099-INT for calendar year 1991 without D's correct EIN. See section 3406(a)(1)(B), which requires Y to impose backup withholding on reportable payments of interest to B's account when the Internal Revenue Service or a broker has notified Y that the EIN is incorrect. [Reg. §301.6723-1.]

☐ [*T.D. 8386*, 12-27-91.]

[Reg. §301.6724-1]

§301.6724-1. Reasonable cause.—(a) *Waiver of the penalty.*—(1) *General rule.*—The penalty for a failure relating to an information reporting requirement(as defined in paragraph (j) of this section) is waived if the failure is due to reasonable cause and is not due to willful neglect.

(2) *Reasonable cause defined.*—The penalty is waived for reasonable cause only if the filer establishes that either—

(i) There are significant mitigating factors with respect to the failure, as described in paragraph (b) of this section; or

(ii) The failure arose from events beyond the filer's control ("impediment"), as described in paragraph (c) of this section.

Moreover, the filer must establish that the filer acted in a responsible manner, as described in paragraph (d) of this section, both before and after the failure occurred. Thus, if the filer establishes that there are significant mitigating factors for a failure but is unable to establish that the filer acted in a responsible manner, the mitigating factors will not be sufficient to obtain a waiver of the penalty. Similarly, if the filer establishes that a failure arose from an impediment but is unable to establish that the filer acted in a responsible manner, the impediment will not be sufficient to obtain a waiver of the penalty. See paragraph (g) of this section for the reasonable cause safe harbor for persons who exercise due diligence.

(b) *Significant mitigating factors.*—In order to establish reasonable cause under this paragraph (b), the filer must satisfy paragraph (d) of this section and must show that there are significant mitigating factors for the failure. The mitigating factors include, but are not limited to—

(1) The fact that prior to the failure the filer was never required to file the particular type of return or furnish the particular type of statement with respect to which the failure occurred, or

(2) The fact that the filer has an established history of complying with the information reporting requirement with respect to which the failure occurred. In determining whether the filer has such an established history, significant consideration is given to—

(i) Whether the filer has incurred any penalty under §§301.6721-1, 301.6722-1, or 301.6723-1 in prior years for the failure (or under parallel provisions of prior law), and

(ii) If the filer has incurred any such penalty in prior years, the extent of the filer's success in lessening its error rate from year to year.

A filer may treat as a penalty not incurred any penalty under sections 6721 through 6723 that was self-assessed under section 6724(c)(3) and any penalty under section 6676(b) that was self-assessed under section 6676(d), prior to amendment or repeal by the Omnibus Budget Reconciliation Act of 1989. See paragraph (c)(5) of this section for the application of this paragraph (b) to failures attributable to the actions of a filer's agent.

(c) *Events beyond the filer's control.*—(1) *In general.*—In order to establish reasonable cause under this paragraph (c)(1), the filer must satisfy paragraph (d) of this section and must show that the failure was due to events beyond the filer's control. Events which are generally considered beyond the filer's control include but are not limited to—

(i) The unavailability of the relevant business records (as described in paragraph (c)(2) of this section),

(ii) An undue economic hardship relating to filing on magnetic media (as described in paragraph (c)(3) of this section),

(iii) Certain actions of the Internal Revenue Service (as described in paragraph (c)(4) of this section),

(iv) Certain actions of an agent (as described in paragraph (c)(5) of this section), and

(v) Certain actions of the payee or any other person providing necessary information with respect to the return or payee statement (as described in paragraph (c)(6) of this section).

(2) *Unavailability of the relevant business records.*—In order to establish reasonable cause under paragraph (c)(1) of this section due to the unavailability of the relevant business records,

the filer's business records must have been unavailable under such conditions, in such manner, and for such period as to prevent timely compliance (ordinarily at least a 2-week period prior to the due date (with regard to extensions) of the required return or the required date (with regard to extensions) for furnishing the payee statement), and the unavailability must have been caused by a supervening event. A "supervening event" includes, but is not limited to—

(i) A fire or other casualty that damages or impairs the filer's relevant business records or the filer's system for processing and filing such records;

(ii) A statutory or regulatory change that has a direct impact upon data processing and that is made so close to the time that the return or payee statement is required that, for all practical purposes, the change cannot be complied with; or

(iii) The unavoidable absence (*e.g.*, due to death or serious illness) of the person with the sole responsibility for filing a return or furnishing a payee statement.

(3) *Undue economic hardship relating to filing on magnetic media.*—In order to establish reasonable cause under paragraph (c)(1) of this section due to an undue economic hardship for filing on magnetic media, the filer must show that it failed to file on magnetic media because the filer lacked the necessary hardware. For purposes of this paragraph (c)(3), the filer will not be considered to have acted in a responsible manner under paragraph (d) of this section unless—

(i) The filer attempted on a timely basis to contract out the magnetic media filing;

(ii) The cost of filing on magnetic media was prohibitive as determined at least 45 days before the due date of the returns (without regard to extensions) (90 days for information returns the due date for which (without regard to extensions) is after December 31, 1989, and by or before February 28, 1991 (March 15, 1991, for Forms 1042S));

(iii) The cost was supported by a minimum of two cost estimates from unrelated parties; and

(iv) The filer filed the returns on paper. Reasonable cause will not ordinarily be established under this paragraph (c)(3) if a filer received a reasonable cause waiver in any prior year under paragraph (c)(1) of this section due to an undue economic hardship relating to filing on magnetic media.

(4) *Actions of the Internal Revenue Service.*—In order to establish reasonable cause under paragraph (c)(1) of this section due to certain actions of the Internal Revenue Service, a filer must show that the failure was due to the filer's reasonable reliance on erroneous written information from the Internal Revenue Service. Reasonable reliance means that the filer relied in good faith on the information. The filer shall not be considered to have relied in good faith if the

Internal Revenue Service was not aware of all the facts when it provided the information to the filer. In order to substantiate reasonable cause under this paragraph (c)(4), the filer must provide a copy of the written information provided by the Internal Revenue Service and, if applicable, the filer's written request for the information.

(5) *Actions of agent—imputed reasonable cause.*—In order to establish reasonable cause under paragraph (c)(1) of this section due to actions of an agent, the filer must show the following:

(i) The filer exercised reasonable business judgment in contracting with the agent to file timely correct returns or furnish timely correct payee statements with respect to which the failure occurred. This includes contracting with the agent and providing the proper information sufficiently in advance of the due date of the return or statement to permit timely filing of correct returns or timely furnishing of correct payee statements; and

(ii) The agent satisfied the reasonable cause criteria set forth in paragraph (b) or one of the reasonable cause criteria set forth in paragraph (c)(2) through (6) of this section.

(6) *Actions of the payee or any other person.*—In order to establish reasonable cause under paragraph (c)(1) of this section due to the actions of the payee or any other person, such as a broker as defined in section 6045(c) providing information with respect to the return or payee statement, the filer must show either—

(i) That the failure resulted from the failure of the payee, or any other person required to provide information necessary for the filer to comply with the information reporting requirements ("any other person"), to provide information to the filer, or

(ii) That the failure resulted from incorrect information provided by the payee (or any other person) upon which information the filer relied in good faith.

To substantiate reasonable cause under this paragraph (c)(6), the filer must provide documentary evidence upon request of the Internal Revenue Service showing that the failure was attributable to the payee (or any other person). See paragraph (d)(2) of this section for special rules relating to the availability of a waiver where the filer's failure relates to a taxpayer identification number (TIN), and the failure is attributable to actions of the payee described in paragraph (c)(6)(i) or (ii) of this section.

(d) *Responsible manner.*—(1) *In general.*—Acting in a responsible manner means—

(i) That the filer exercised reasonable care, which is that standard of care that a reasonably prudent person would use under the circumstances in the course of its business in determining its filing obligations and in handling account information such as account numbers and balances, and

(ii) That the filer undertook significant steps to avoid or mitigate the failure, including, where applicable—

(A) Requesting appropriate extensions of time to file, when practicable, in order to avoid the failure,

(B) Attempting to prevent an impediment or a failure, if it was foreseeable,

(C) Acting to remove an impediment or the cause of a failure, once it occurred, and

(D) Rectifying the failure as promptly as possible once the impediment was removed or the failure was discovered.

Ordinarily, a rectification is considered prompt if it is made within 30 days after the date the impediment is removed or the failure is discovered or on the earliest date thereafter on which a regular submission of corrections is made. Submissions will be considered regular only if made at intervals of 30 days or less. A failure may be rectified by filing or correcting the information return, furnishing or correcting the payee statement, or by providing or correcting the information to satisfy the specified information reporting requirement with respect to which the failure occurs. Paragraph (d)(ii)(D) of this section does not apply with respect to information the filer is prohibited from altering under specific information reporting rules. See § 1.6045-4(i)(5) of this chapter.

(2) *Special rule for filers seeking a waiver pursuant to paragraph (c)(6) of this section.*—A filer seeking a waiver for reasonable cause pursuant to paragraph (c)(6) of this section with respect to a failure resulting from a missing or an incorrect TIN will be deemed to have acted in a responsible manner in compliance with this paragraph (d) only if the filer satisfies the requirements of paragraph (e) of this section (relating to missing TINs) or paragraph (f) of this section (relating to incorrect TINs), whichever is applicable.

(e) *Acting in a responsible manner—special rules for missing TINs.*—(1) *In general.*—A filer that is seeking a waiver for reasonable cause under paragraph (c)(6) of this section will satisfy paragraph (d)(2) of this section with respect to establishing that a failure to include a TIN on an information return resulted from the failure of the payee to provide information to the filer (*i.e.*, a missing TIN) only if the filer makes the initial and, if required, the annual solicitations described in this paragraph (e) (required solicitations). For purposes of this section, a number is treated as a "missing TIN" if the number does not contain nine digits or includes one or more alpha characters (a character or symbol other than an Arabic numeral) as one of the nine digits. A solicitation means a request by the filer for the payee to furnish a correct TIN. See paragraph (f) of this section for the rules that a filer must follow to establish that the filer acted in a responsible manner with respect to providing incorrect TINs on information returns. See paragraph (e)(1)(vi)(A) of this section for alternative solicitation requirements. See paragraph (g)

of this section for the safe harbor due diligence rules. See paragraph (h) of this section for the rule applicable to failures with respect to information returns the due date for which (without regard to extensions) is after December 31, 1989, and on or before April 22, 1991.

(i) *Initial solicitation.*—An initial solicitation for a payee's correct TIN must be made at the time an account is opened. The term "account" includes accounts, relationships, and other transactions. However, a filer is not required to make an initial solicitation under this paragraph (e)(1)(i) with respect to a new account if the filer has the payee's TIN and uses that TIN for all accounts of the payee. For example, see § 31.3406(h)-3(a) of this chapter. Further, a filer is not required to make an initial solicitation under this paragraph (e)(1)(i) with respect to accounts for which the filer filed an information return subject to paragraph (h) of this section. For purposes of this section, the initial solicitation requirement is deemed to have been met with respect to accounts opened after December 31, 1989, and on or before April 22, 1991. If the account is opened in person, the initial solicitation may be made by oral or written request, such as on an account creation document. If the account is opened by mail, telephone, or other electronic means, the TIN may be requested through such communications. If the account is opened by the payee's completing and mailing an application furnished by the filer that requests the payee's TIN, the initial solicitation requirement is considered met. If a TIN is not received as a result of an initial solicitation, the filer may be required to make additional solicitations ("annual solicitations").

(ii) *First annual solicitation.*—Except as provided in paragraph (e)(1)(vi) of this section, a filer must undertake an annual solicitation if a TIN is not received as a result of an initial solicitation (or if the filer was not required to make an initial solicitation under paragraph (e)(1)(i) of this section and the filer has not received a payee's TIN). The first annual solicitation must be made on or before December 31 of the year in which the account is opened (for accounts opened before December) or January 31 of the following year (for accounts opened in the preceding December) ("annual solicitation period").

(iii) *Second annual solicitation.*—If the TIN is not received as a result of the first annual solicitation, the filer must undertake a second annual solicitation. The second annual solicitation must be made after the expiration of the annual solicitation period and on or before December 31 of the year immediately succeeding the calendar year in which the account is opened.

(iv) *Additional requirements.*—After receiving a TIN, a filer must include that TIN on any information returns the original due date of which (with regard to extensions) is after the date that the filer receives the TIN.

Reg. §301.6724-1(e)(1)(iv)

(v) *Failures to which a solicitation relates.*—The initial and first annual solicitations relate to failures on returns filed for the year in which an account is opened. The second annual solicitation relates to failures on returns filed for the year immediately following the year in which an account is opened and for succeeding calendar years.

(vi) *Exceptions and limitations.*—(A) The solicitation requirements under this paragraph (e) do not apply to the extent an information reporting provision under which a return, as defined in paragraph (g) of § 301.6721-1, is filed provides specific requirements relating to the manner or the time period in which a TIN must be solicited. In that event, the requirements of this paragraph (e) will be satisfied only if the filer complies with the manner and time period requirements of the specific information reporting provision and the provisions of this paragraph (e) to the extent applicable. Also, see section 3406(e) which provides rules on the manner and time period in which a TIN must be provided for certain accounts with respect to interest, dividends, patronage dividends, and amounts subject to broker reporting.

(B) An annual solicitation is not required to be made for a year under this paragraph (e) with respect to an account if no payments are made to the account for such year or if no return as defined in paragraph (g) of § 301.6721-1 is required to be filed for the account for the year.

(C) If a filer fails to make one (or more) of the required solicitations under paragraphs (e)(1)(i), (ii), and (iii) of this section, the filer may satisfy the requirements of this section by—

(1) Making two consecutive annual solicitations in subsequent years ("make-up solicitations"), and

(2) Satisfying paragraph (e)(1)(iv) of this section.

For example, a filer who has made none of the required solicitations may satisfy the requirements of this section by making two consecutive solicitations. In determining whether a filer has made two consecutive solicitations, years to which paragraph (e)(1)(vi)(B) of this section applies shall be disregarded. If a filer fails to make the initial solicitation under paragraph (e)(1)(i) of this section, the make-up solicitations described in this paragraph (e)(1)(vi)(C) may be made in the years in which the first and second annual solicitations are required to be made; however, the penalty will apply with respect to the year in which the filer failed to make the initial solicitation. The penalty will apply to failures with respect to years for which a required solicitation is not made and to failures with respect to all subsequent years until the filer conducts its make-up solicitations. The penalty will not apply with respect to the year in which the first make-up solicitation is made (unless it is also the year in which the filer fails to make its initial solicitation) if the second make-up solicitation is made in the following year.

(D) A financial institution is not required to make an annual solicitation by mail on accounts with "stop-mail" or "hold-mail" instructions, provided the filer furnishes the solicitation material to the payee in the same manner as it furnishes other mail.

(E) A filer is not required to make annual solicitations on accounts with respect to which the filer undertook two consecutive annual mailings by December 31, 1989, under Q/A-5 through Q/A-7B or under Q/A-56 of § 35a.9999-1 of the Temporary Employment Tax Regulations under the Interest and Dividend Tax Compliance Act of 1983, as provided under section 6676(b) (prior to its amendment by the Omnibus Budget Reconciliation Act of 1989).

(F) A filer is not required to make annual solicitations by mail on accounts with respect to which the filer has an undeliverable address, *i.e.*, where other mailings to that address have been returned to the filer because the address was incorrect and no new address has been provided to the filer.

(G) Except as provided in paragraph (e)(1)(vi)(A) and (C) of this section, no more than two annual solicitations are required under this paragraph (e) in order for a filer to establish reasonable cause.

(2) *Manner of making annual solicitations—by mail or telephone.*—(i) *By mail.*—A mail solicitation must include—

(A) A letter informing the payee that he or she must provide his or her TIN and that he or she is subject to a $50 penalty imposed by the Internal Revenue Service under section 6723 if he or she fails to furnish his or her TIN,

(B) A Form W-9 or an acceptable substitute form, as defined in § 31.3406(h)-3(a), (b), or (c) of this chapter, on which the payee may provide the TIN, and

(C) A return envelope for the payee to provide the TIN which may be, but is not required to be, postage prepaid.

(ii) *By telephone.*—An annual solicitation may be made by telephone if the solicitation procedure is reasonably designed and carried out in a manner that is conducive to obtaining the TIN. An annual solicitation is made pursuant to this paragraph (e)(2)(ii) for a failure if the filer—

(A) Completes a call to each person with a missing TIN and speaks to an adult member of the household, or to an officer of the business or the organization,

(B) Requests the TIN of the payee,

(C) Informs the payee that he or she is subject to a $50 penalty imposed by the Internal Revenue Service under section 6723 if he or she fails to furnish his or her TIN,

(D) Maintains contemporaneous records showing that the solicitation was properly made, and

(E) Provides such contemporaneous records to the Internal Revenue Service upon request.

(f) *Acting in a responsible manner—special rules for incorrect TINS.*—(1) *In general.*—A filer that is seeking a waiver for reasonable cause under paragraph (c)(6) of this section will satisfy paragraph (d)(2) of this section with respect to establishing that a failure resulted from incorrect information provided by the payee or any other person (*i.e.,* inclusion of an incorrect TIN) on an information return only if the filer makes the initial and annual solicitations described in this paragraph (f). See paragraph (e)(1) of this section for the definition of the term "solicitation." See paragraph (f)(5)(i) of this section for alternative solicitation requirements. See paragraph (g) of this section for the safe harbor due diligence rules. See paragraph (h) of this section for the rule applicable to failures with respect to information returns the due date for which (without regard to extensions) is after December 31, 1989, and on or before April 22, 1991.

(i) *Initial solicitation.*—An initial solicitation for a payee's correct TIN must be made at the time the account is opened. The term "account" includes accounts, relationships, and other transactions. However, a filer is not required to make an initial solicitation under this paragraph (f)(1)(i) with respect to a new account if the filer has the payee's TIN and uses that TIN for all accounts of the payee. For example, see § 31.3406(h)-3(a) of this chapter. Further, a filer is not required to make an initial solicitation under this paragraph (f)(1)(i) with respect to accounts for which the filer filed an information return subject to paragraph (h) of this section. For purposes of this section, the initial solicitation requirement is deemed to have been met with respect to accounts opened after December 31, 1989, and on or before April 22, 1991. No additional solicitation is required after the filer receives the TIN unless the Internal Revenue Service or, in some cases, a broker notifies the filer that the TIN is incorrect. Following such notification the filer may be required to make an annual solicitation to obtain the correct TIN as provided in paragraph (f)(1)(ii) and (iii) of this section.

(ii) *First annual solicitation.*—Except as provided in paragraph (f)(5) of this section, a filer must undertake an annual solicitation only if the payor has been notified of an incorrect TIN and such account contains the incorrect TIN at the time of the notification. The first annual solicitation must be made as required by paragraph (f)(2) or (3) of this section, whichever applies. An account contains an incorrect TIN at the time of notification if the name and number combination on the account matches the name and number combination set forth on the notice from the Internal Revenue Service or a broker. A filer may be notified of an incorrect TIN by the Internal Revenue Service or by a broker pursuant to section 3406(a)(1)(B), or by a penalty notice issued by the Internal Revenue Service pursuant to section 6721. Except as otherwise provided in this section, the annual solicitation required by this paragraph (f) must be made on or before December 31 of the year in which the filer is notified of the incorrect TIN or by January 31 of the following year if the filer is notified of an incorrect TIN in the preceding December.

(iii) *Second annual solicitation.*—A filer must undertake a second annual solicitation as required by paragraph (f)(2) or (3) of this section, whichever applies, if the filer is notified in any year following the year of the notification described in paragraph (f)(1)(ii) of this section that the account of a payee contains an incorrect TIN, as described in paragraph (f) (1)(ii) of this section.

(iv) *Additional requirements.*—Upon receipt of a TIN, a filer must include that TIN on any information returns the original due date of which (with regard to extensions) is after the date that the filer receives the TIN.

(2) *Manner of making annual solicitation if notified pursuant to section 6721.*—A filer that has been notified of an incorrect TIN by a penalty notice or other notification pursuant to section 6721 may satisfy the solicitation requirement of this paragraph (f) either by mail, in the manner set forth in paragraph (e)(2)(i) of this section; by telephone, in the manner set forth in paragraph (e)(2)(ii) of this section; or by requesting the TIN in person.

(3) *Coordination with solicitations under section 3406(a)(1)(b).*—(i) A filer that has been notified of an incorrect TIN pursuant to section 3406(a)(1)(B) (except filers to which § 31.3406(d)-5(b)(4)(i)(A) of this chapter applies) will satisfy the solicitation requirement of this paragraph (f) only if it makes a solicitation in the manner and within the time period required under § 31.3406(d)-5(d)(2)(i) or (g)(1)(ii) of this chapter, whichever applies.

(ii) A filer that has been notified of an incorrect TIN by a notice pursuant to section 6721 (except filers to which § 31.3406(d)-5(b)(4)(i)(A) of this chapter applies) is not required to make the annual solicitation of this paragraph (f) if—

(A) The filer has received an effective notice pursuant to section 3406(a)(1)(B) with respect to the same payee, either during the same calendar year or for information returns filed for the same year; and

(B) The filer makes a solicitation in the manner and within the time period required under § 31.3406(d)-5(d)(2)(i) or (g)(1)(ii) of this chapter, whichever applies, before the filer is required to make the annual solicitation of this paragraph (f).

(iii) A filer that has been notified of an incorrect TIN by a notice pursuant to section 6721 with respect to a fiduciary or nominee account to which § 31.3406(d)-5(b)(4)(i)(A) of this chapter applies is required to make the annual solicitation of this paragraph (f).

(4) *Failures to which a solicitation relates.*—The initial solicitation relates to failures on returns filed for the year an account is opened and

Reg. § 301.6724-1(f)(4)

for any succeeding year that precedes the year in which the filer receives a notification of an incorrect TIN. The first and second annual solicitations relate to failures on returns filed for the year in which a notification of an incorrect TIN is received. The second solicitation also relates to failures on returns filed for succeeding calendar years.

(5) *Exceptions and limitations.*—(i) The solicitation requirements under this paragraph (f) do not apply to the extent that an information reporting provision under which a return, as defined in paragraph (g) of § 301.6721-1, is filed provides specific requirements relating to the manner or the time period in which a TIN must be solicited. In that event, the requirements of this paragraph (f) will be satisfied only if the filer complies with the manner and time period requirement under the specific information reporting provisions and this paragraph (f), to the extent applicable.

(ii) An annual solicitation is not required to be made for a year under this paragraph (f) with respect to an account if no payments are made to the account for such year or if no return as defined in paragraph (g) of § 301.6721-1 is required to be filed for the account for such year.

(iii) If a filer fails to make one (or more) of the required solicitations under paragraph (f)(1)(i), (ii), and (iii) of this section, the filer may satisfy the requirements of this section by:

(A) Making two consecutive annual solicitations in subsequent years ("make-up solicitations"), and

(B) Satisfying paragraph (f)(1)(iv) of this section.

For example, a filer who has made none of the required solicitations may satisfy the requirements of this section by making two consecutive solicitations. In determining whether a filer has made two consecutive solicitations, years to which paragraph (f)(5)(ii) of this section applies are disregarded. If a filer fails to make the initial solicitation under paragraph (f)(1)(i) of this section, the make-up solicitations described in this paragraph (f)(5)(iii) may be made in the years in which the first and second annual solicitations are required to be made; however, the penalty will apply with respect to the year in which the filer failed to make the initial solicitation. The penalty will apply to failures in years in which a required solicitation is not made and to failures with respect to all subsequent years until the filer conducts its make-up solicitations. The penalty will not apply with respect to the year in which the first make-up solicitation is made (unless it is also the year in which the filer fails to make the initial solicitation) if the second make-up solicitation is made in the following year.

(iv) A financial institution is not required to make an annual solicitation by mail on accounts with "stop-mail" or "hold-mail" instructions, provided the filer furnishes the solicitation material to the payee in the same manner as it furnishes other mail.

(v) A filer is not required to make annual solicitations by mail on accounts with respect to which the filer has an undeliverable address, *i.e.,* where other mailings to that address have been returned to the filer because the address was incorrect and no new address has been provided to the filer.

(vi) In general, except as provided in paragraph (f)(5)(i) and (iii) of this section, no more than two annual solicitations are required under this paragraph (f) in order for a filer to establish reasonable cause. However, a filer who complies with this paragraph (f) during a calendar year after receiving a notice under section 6721 and who later during the same calendar year receives a notice pursuant to section 3406 may be required to undertake additional annual mailings in such calendar year pursuant to section 3406(a)(1)(B) in order to satisfy the annual solicitation requirement in paragraph (f)(3) of this section.

(g) *Due diligence safe harbor.*—(1) *In general.*— A filer may establish reasonable cause with respect to a failure relating to an information reporting requirement as described in paragraph (j) of this section if the filer exercises due diligence with respect to failures described in sections 6721 through 6723.

(2) *Special rules relating to TINs.*—The following questions and answers provide guidance on the exercise of due diligence for an exception to a penalty under sections 6721 through 6723 for a failure to provide a correct TIN on any information return (as defined in § 301.6721-1(g)), payee statement (as defined in § 301.6722-1(d)), document (as described in § 301.6723-1(a)(4)), or the failure merely to provide a TIN as described in § 301.6723-1(a)(4)(ii).

GENERAL RULE

Q-1. Is a payor subject to a penalty for a failure to provide a correct TIN on an information return with respect to a reportable interest or dividend payment if the payee has certified, under penalties of perjury, that the TIN furnished to the payor is the payee's correct number, the payor provided that number on an information return, and the number is later determined not to be the payee's correct number?

A-1. A payor is not subject to a penalty for failure to provide the payee's correct TIN on an information return, if the payee has certified, under penalties of perjury, that the TIN provided to the payor was his correct number, and the payor included such number on the information return before being notified by the Internal Revenue Service (IRS) (or a broker) that the number is incorrect.

DUE DILIGENCE DEFINED FOR ACCOUNTS OPENED AND INSTRUMENTS ACQUIRED AFTER DECEMBER 31, 1983

Q-2. In order for a payor of a reportable interest or dividend payment (other than in a window transaction) to be considered to have exercised due diligence in furnishing the correct TIN of a payee with respect to an account opened or an instrument acquired after December 31, 1983, what actions must the payor take?

A-2. (1) In general, the payor of an account or instrument that is not a pre-1984 account nor a window transaction must use a TIN provided by the payee under penalties of perjury on information returns filed with the IRS to satisfy the due diligence requirement. Therefore, if a payor permits a payee to open an account without obtaining the payee's TIN under penalties of perjury and files an information return with the IRS with a missing or an incorrect TIN, the payor will be liable for the $50 penalty for the year with respect to which such information return is filed. However, in its administrative discretion, the IRS will not enforce the penalty with respect to a calendar year if the certified TIN is obtained after the account is opened and before December 31 of such year, provided that the payor exercises due diligence in processing such number, i.e., the payor uses the same care in processing the TIN provided by the payee that a reasonably prudent payor would use in the course of the payor's business in handling account information such as account numbers and balances.

(2) Once notified by the IRS (or a broker) that a number is incorrect, a payor is liable for the penalty for all prior years in which an information return was filed with that particular incorrect number if the payor has not exercised due diligence with respect to such years. A pre-existing certified TIN does not constitute an exercise of due diligence after the IRS or a broker notifies the payor that the number is incorrect unless the payor undertakes the actions described in §31.3406(d)-5(d)(2)(i) of this chapter with respect to accounts receiving reportable payments described in section 3406(b)(1) and reported on information returns described in sections 6724(d)(1)(A)(i) through (iv).

Q-3. Is a payor as described in A-2 liable for the penalty if the payor obtained a certified TIN from a payee but inadvertently processed the name or number incorrectly on the information return?

A-3. Yes. The payor is liable for the penalty unless the payor exercised that degree of care in processing the TIN and name and in furnishing it on the information return that a reasonably prudent payor would use in the course of the payor's business in handling account information, such as account numbers and account balances.

SPECIAL RULES

Q-4. With respect to an instrument transferred without the assistance of a broker, is a payor liable for the penalty for filing an information return with a missing or an incorrect TIN if the payor records on its books a transfer of a readily tradable instrument in a transaction in which the payor was not a party?

A-4. Generally, a payor as described in Q-4 will be considered to have exercised due diligence with respect to a readily tradable instrument that is not part of a pre-1984 account with the payor if the payor records on its books a

transfer in which the payor was not a party. This exception applies until the calendar year in which the payor receives a certified TIN from the payee.

Q-5. Is the payor described in A-4 required to solicit the TIN of a payee of an account with a missing TIN in order to be considered as having exercised due diligence in a subsequent calendar year?

A-5. There is no requirement on the payor to solicit the TIN in order to be considered to have exercised due diligence in a subsequent calendar year under the rule set forth in A-4.

Q-6. Is a payor as described in Q-4 considered to have exercised due diligence if the payee provides a TIN to the payor (whether or not certified), the payor uses that number on the information return filed for the payee, and the number is later determined to be incorrect?

A-6. A payor as described in Q-4 who records on its books a transfer in which it was not a party is considered to have exercised due diligence under the rule set forth in A-4 where the transfer is accompanied with a TIN provided that the payor uses the same care in processing the TIN provided by a payee that a reasonably prudent payor would use in the course of the payor's business in handling account information, such as account numbers and account balances. Thus, a payor will not be liable for the penalty if the payor uses the TIN provided by the payee on information returns that it files, even if the TIN provided by the payee is later determined to be incorrect. However, a payor will not be considered as having exercised due diligence under A-4 after the IRS or a broker notifies the payor that the number is incorrect unless the payor undertakes the required additional actions described in the second paragraph of A-2.

Q-7. Is a payor liable for a penalty for filing an information return with a missing or an incorrect TIN with respect to a post-1983 account or instrument if the payor could have met the due diligence requirements but for the fact that the payor incurred an undue hardship?

A-7. A payor of a post-1983 account or instrument is not liable for a penalty under section 6721(a) for filing an information return with a missing or an incorrect TIN if the IRS determines that the payor could have satisfied the due diligence requirements but for the fact that the payor incurred an undue hardship. An undue hardship is an extraordinary or unexpected event such as the destruction of records or place of business of the payor by fire or other casualty (or the place of business of the payor's agent who under a pre-existing written contract had agreed to fulfill the payor's due diligence obligations with respect to the account subject to the penalty and there was no means for the obligations to be performed by another agent or the payor). Undue hardship will also be found to exist if the payor could have met the due diligence requirements only by incurring an extraordinary cost.

Reg. §301.6724-1(g)(2)

Q-8. How does a payor obtain a determination from the IRS that the payor has met the undue hardship exception to the penalty under section 6721(a) for the failure to include the correct TIN on an information return for the year with respect to which the payor is subject to the penalty?

A-8. A determination of undue hardship may be established only by submitting a written statement to the IRS signed under penalties of perjury that sets forth all the facts and circumstances that make an affirmative showing that the payor could have satisfied the due diligence requirements but for the occurrence of an undue hardship. Thus, the statement must describe the undue hardship and make an affirmative showing that the payor either was in the process of exercising or stood ready to exercise due diligence when the undue hardship occurred. A payor may request an undue hardship determination from the district director or the director of the Internal Revenue Service Center where the payor is required to remit the penalty under section 6721(a).

Q-9. Is a pre-1984 account or instrument of a payor that is exchanged for an account or instrument of another payor as a result of a merger of the other payor or acquisition of the accounts or instruments of such payor transformed into a post-1983 account or instrument if the merger or acquisition occurs after December 31, 1983?

A-9. No. A pre-1984 account or instrument that is exchanged for another account or instrument pursuant to a statutory merger or the acquisition of accounts or instruments is not transformed into a post-1983 account or instrument because the exchange occurs without the participation of the payee.

Q-10. May the acquiring taxpayer described in A-9 rely upon the business records and past procedures of the merged payor or the payor whose accounts or instruments were acquired in order to establish that due diligence has been exercised on the acquired pre-1984 and post-1983 accounts or instruments?

A-10. Yes. The acquiring payor may rely upon the business records and past procedures of the merged payor or of the payor whose accounts or instruments were acquired in order to establish due diligence to avoid the penalty under section 6721(a) with respect to information returns that have been or will be filed.

Q-11. To what extent may a payor rely on the due diligence rules set forth in §§ 35a.9999-1, 35a.9999-2, and 35a.9999-3 of this chapter in effect prior to January 1, 2001 (see §§ 35a.9999-1, 35a.9999-2, and 35a.9999-3 as contained in 26 CFR part 35a, revised April 1, 1999).

A-11. A payor may rely on the due diligence rules set forth in §§ 35a.9999-1, 35a.9999-2, and 35a.9999-3 of this chapter in effect prior to January 1, 2001 (see §§ 35a.9999-1, 35a.9999-2, and 35a.9999-3 as contained in 26 CFR part 35a, revised April 1, 1999) solely for the definitions of terms or phrases used in this paragraph (g)(2).

(3) *Effective dates.*—This paragraph (g) is effective for information returns (as defined in section 6724(d)(1)) required to be filed, payee statements (as defined in section 6724(d)(2)) required to be furnished, and specified information (as described in section 6724(d)(3)) required to be reported after December 31, 2000. See § 301.6724-1(g) in effect prior to January 1, 2001 (see § 301.6724-1(g) as contained in 26 CFR part 301, revised April 1, 1999) for substantially similar rules applicable prior to January 1, 2001.

(h) *Transitional rules for information returns required to be filed (or payee statements required to be furnished) after December 31, 1989 (without regard to extensions), and on or before April 22, 1991.*—(1) *In general.*—With respect to information returns required to be filed (or payee statements required to be furnished) after December 31, 1989 (without regard to extensions), and on or before April 22, 1991, a filer will be deemed to have satisfied reasonable cause if, with respect to the failure, the filer would have satisfied reasonable cause under sections 6721, 6722, or 6723 (prior to their amendment by the Omnibus Budget Reconciliation Act of 1989) and the regulations thereunder.

(2) *Special rule on TINs.*—With respect to information returns required to be filed after December 31, 1989 (without regard to extensions), and on or before April 22, 1991, which contain a missing or an incorrect TIN, a filer will be deemed to have satisfied reasonable cause if, at the time the account was opened, the filer—

(i) Exercised due diligence or fulfilled the requirements of Q/A-56 of § 35a.9999-1 of this chapter as in effect on December 31, 1989, as provided under section 6676(b) (prior to its repeal by the Omnibus Budget Reconciliation Act of 1989),

(ii) Requested the TIN according to the regulations under the section requiring the filing of the information return, but if none, under section 6109, or

(iii) Would have satisfied reasonable cause under section 6676(a) (prior to its repeal by the Omnibus Budget Reconciliation Act of 1989).

(i) [*Reserved.*]

(j) *Failures to which this section relates.*—For purposes of this section, a failure relating to an information reporting requirement means—

(1) A failure described under § 301.6721-1(a)(2) relating to the failure to file timely correct information returns as defined in section 6724(d)(1),

(2) A failure described under § 301.6722-1(a)(2) relating to the failure to furnish timely a correct payee statement as defined in section 6724(d)(2), and

(3) A failure described under § 301.6723-1(a)(2) relating to the failure to timely comply with and to include correct specified information as defined in section 6724(d)(3).

(k) *Examples.*—The provisions of this section may be illustrated by the following examples:

Example (1). (i) On August 1, 1991, Individual A, an independent contractor, establishes a relationship ("an account") with Institution L, which pays A amounts reportable under section 6041. When A opens the account L requests that A supply his TIN on the account creation document. A fails to provide his TIN. On October 1, 1991, L mails a solicitation for A's TIN that satisfies the requirement of paragraph (e)(1)(ii) of this section. A does not provide a TIN to L during 1991. L timely files an information return subject to section 6721, that does not contain A's TIN, for payments made during the 1991 calendar year with respect to A's account. A penalty is imposed on L pursuant to paragraph (a)(2) of §301.6721-1 for L's failure to file a correct information return because A's TIN was not shown on the return. The penalty will be waived, however, if L establishes that the failure was due to reasonable cause as defined in this section.

(ii) To establish reasonable cause under this section, L must satisfy both paragraphs (c)(6) and (d) of this section. The criteria for obtaining a waiver under these paragraphs are as follows:

(A) L acted in a responsible manner in attempting to satisfy the information reporting requirement as described in paragraph (d) of this section, and

(B) L demonstrates that the failure arose from events beyond L's control, as described in paragraph (c)(6) of this section.

(iii) Pursuant to paragraph (d)(2) of this section, L may demonstrate that it acted in a responsible manner only by complying with paragraph (e) of this section. Paragraph (e) of this section requires a filer to request a TIN at the time the account is opened (the initial solicitation) and, if the filer does not receive the TIN at that time, to solicit the TIN on or before December 31 of the year the account is opened (for accounts opened before December) or January 31 of the following year (for accounts in the preceding December) (the annual solicitation). Because L has performed these solicitations within the time and in the manner prescribed by paragraph (e) of this section, L has acted in a responsible manner as described in paragraph (d) of this section. L satisfies paragraph (c)(6) of this section because, under the facts, L can show that the failure was caused by A's failure to provide a TIN, an event beyond L's control. As a result, L has established reasonable cause under paragraph (a)(2) of this section. Therefore, the penalty imposed under paragraph (a)(2) of

| 1991 | 2/92 |
| account opened (solicits TIN) | 1991 return |

| 4/93 | 10/93 |
| 6721 penalty notice for 1991 return | B-notice w/respect to 1992 return |

(ii) The facts are the same as in *Example 2.* Under §31.3406(d)-5(d)(2)(i) of this chapter and paragraph (f)(3) of this section, within 15 days of the October 1992 notification of the incorrect TIN from the Internal Revenue Service, M solicits the

§301.6721-1 for the failure on the 1991 information return is waived. See section 3406(a)(1)(A) which requires L to impose backup withholding on reportable payments to A if L has not received A's TIN.

Example (2). (i) On August 1, 1991, Individual B opens an account with Bank M, which pays B interest reportable under section 6049. When B opens the account, M requests that B supply his TIN on the account creation document. B provides his TIN to M. On February 28, 1992, M includes the TIN that B provided on the Form 1099-INT for the 1991 calendar year. In October 1992 the Internal Revenue Service, pursuant to section 3406(a)(1)(B), notifies M that the 1991 return filed for B contains an incorrect TIN. In April 1993 a penalty is imposed on M pursuant to paragraph (a)(2) of §301.6721-1 for M's failure to file a correct information return for the 1991 calendar year, *i.e.,* the return did not contain B's correct TIN. The penalty will be waived, however, if M establishes that the failure was due to reasonable cause as defined in this section.

(ii) To establish reasonable cause under this section, M must satisfy the criteria in both paragraphs (c)(6) and (d) of this section. Pursuant to paragraph (d)(2) of this section, M can demonstrate that it acted in a responsible manner only if M complies with paragraph (f) of this section. Paragraph (f) of this section requires a filer to request a TIN at the time the account is opened, an initial solicitation. Under paragraph (f)(4) of this section the initial solicitation relates to failures on returns filed for the year an account is opened. Because M performed the initial solicitation in 1991 in the time and manner prescribed in paragraph (f)(1)(i) of this section and reflected the TIN received from B on the 1991 return as required by paragraph (f)(1)(iv) of this section, M has acted in a responsible manner as described in paragraph (d) of this section. M satisfies paragraph (c)(6) of this section because, under the facts, M can show that the failure was caused by B's failure to provide a correct TIN, an event beyond M's control. As a result, M has established reasonable cause under paragraph (a)(2) of this section. Therefore, the penalty imposed under paragraph (a)(2) of §301.6721-1 for the failure on the 1991 information return is waived. See section 3406(a)(1)(B) which requires M to impose backup withholding on reportable payments to B if M has not received B's correct TIN.

Example (3). (i) *Table.*

| 10/92 | 2/93 |
| B-notice w/respect to 1991 return | 1992 return filed |

| 2/93 | 4/94 |
| 1993 return filed | 6721 penalty notice for 1992 return |

correct TIN from B. B fails to respond. M timely files the return for 1992 with respect to the account setting forth B's incorrect TIN. In October 1993 the Internal Revenue Service notifies M pursuant to section 3406(a)(1)(B) that the 1992

Reg. §301.6724-1(k)

return contains an incorrect TIN. In April 1994, a penalty is imposed on M pursuant to paragraph (a)(2) of § 301.6721-1 for M's failure to include B's correct TIN on the return for 1992. The penalty will be waived, however, if M establishes that the failure was due to reasonable cause as defined in this section.

(iii) M must satisfy the reasonable cause criteria in paragraphs (c)(6) and (d) of this section. M may demonstrate that it acted in a responsible manner as required under paragraph (d) of this section only by complying with paragraph (f) of this section. Paragraph (f) of this section requires a filer to make an initial solicitation for a TIN when an account is opened. Further, a filer must make an annual solicitation for a TIN by mail within 15 business days after the date that the Internal Revenue Service notifies the filer of an

1991	2/92
account opened (solicits TIN)	1991 return filed

4/93	10/93
6721 penalty notice for 1991 return	B-notice w/respect to 1992 return

(ii) The facts are the same as in *Example 3*. M timely solicits B's TIN in October 1993, which B fails to provide. M files the return for 1993 with the incorrect TIN. In April 1995 the Internal Revenue Service informs M that the 1993 return contains an incorrect TIN. M does not solicit a TIN from B in 1994 and files a return for 1994 with B's incorrect TIN. M seeks a waiver of the penalty under paragraph (a)(2) of § 301.6721-1 for reasonable cause. M must satisfy the reasonable cause criteria in paragraphs (c)(6) and (d) of this section. Because M made the initial and two annual solicitations as required by paragraph (f) of this section, M has demonstrated that it acted in a responsible manner and is not required to solicit B's TIN in 1994. See paragraph (f)(5)(iv) of this section. M satisfies paragraph (c)(6) of this section because, under the facts, M can show that the failure was caused by B's failure to provide his correct TIN, an event beyond M's control. Therefore, M has established reasonable cause under paragraph (a)(2) of this section.

Example 5. In 1992, Mortgage Finance Company N lends money to C to purchase property

10/91	2/92
account opened (solicits TIN)	1991 return filed

4/93	10/93
6721 penalty notice	B-notice w/respect to 1992 return

(ii) On October 1, 1991, Individual E opens an account with Institution R, which pays E amounts reportable under section 6049. When E opens the account, R requests that E supply his TIN on an account creation document, which E does. Pursuant to paragraph (f)(1)(iv) of this section, R uses the TIN furnished by E on the information return filed for the 1991 calendar year. In October 1992 the Internal Revenue Service noti-

incorrect TIN pursuant to section 3406(a)(1)(B). M made the initial solicitation for the TIN in 1991 and, after being notified of the incorrect TIN in October 1992, the first annual solicitation within the time and manner prescribed by § 31.3406(d)-5(d)(2)(i) of this chapter and paragraph (f)(1)(ii) and (2) of this section. M acted in a responsible manner. M satisfies paragraph (c)(6) of this section because, under the facts, M can show that the failure was caused by B's failure to provide his correct TIN, an event beyond M's control. As a result M has established reasonable cause under paragraph (a)(2) of this section. Therefore, the penalty imposed under paragraph (a)(2) of § 301.6721-1 for the failure on the 1992 return is waived due to reasonable cause.

Example (4). (i) *Table.*

10/92	2/93
B-notice w/respect to 1991 return	1992 return filed

2/94	4/94
1993 return filed	6721 penalty notice for 1992 return

in a transaction subject to reporting under section 6050H and to section 6721. As part of the transaction, C gives N a promissory note providing for repayment of principal and the payment of interest. At the time C incurs the obligation N requests C's TIN, as required under § 1.6050H-2(f) of this chapter. C fails to provide the TIN as required by § 1.6050H-2(f) of this chapter. N sends solicitations by mail in 1992 and 1993 for the missing TIN, which C fails to provide. However, for 1994 M fails to send the solicitation required by § 1.6050H-2(f) of this chapter. N files returns for the 1992, 1993, and 1994 calendar years pursuant to section 6050H without C's TIN. Although N made the initial and the first annual solicitations in 1992 and the second annual solicitation in 1993, N did not solicit the TIN in 1994 as required under section 6050H, which requires continued annual solicitations until the TIN is obtained. Therefore, under paragraph (e)(1)(vi)(A) of this section the penalty imposed under paragraph (a) of § 301.6721-1 for the 1994 information return is not waived.

Example (6). (i) *Table.*

10/92	2/93
B-notice w/respect to 1991 return	1992 return filed

2/94	4/94
1993 return filed	6721 penalty notice for 1992 return

fies R pursuant to section 3406(a)(1)(B) that the information return filed for E for the 1991 calendar year contained an incorrect TIN. At the time R receives this notification, E's account contains the incorrect TIN. On December 31, 1992, R telephones E pursuant to paragraphs (f)(2) and (e)(2)(ii) of this section and receives different TIN information from E. R uses this information on

Reg. § 301.6724-1(k)

the return that it files timely for E for the 1992 calendar year, *i.e.*, in February 1993.

(iii) In April 1993, the Internal Revenue Service notifies R pursuant to paragraph (a)(2) of § 301.6721-1 that the information return filed for the 1991 calendar year contains an incorrect TIN. The penalty will be waived, however, if R establishes the failure was due to reasonable cause as defined in this section.

(iv) To establish reasonable cause under this section, R must satisfy the criteria in both paragraphs (c)(6) and (d)(2) of this section. Pursuant to paragraph (d)(2) of this section, R can demonstrate that it acted in a responsible manner only if it complies with paragraph (f) of this section. R solicited E's TIN at the time the account was opened (initial solicitation). Under paragraphs (d)(2) and (f)(4) of this section, the initial solicitation relates to failures on returns filed for the year in which an account is opened (*i.e.*, 1991) and for subsequent years until the calendar year in which the filer receives a notification of an incorrect TIN pursuant to section 3406. Because E failed to provide the correct TIN upon request, the failure arose from events beyond R's control as described in paragraph (c)(6) of this section. Therefore, the penalty with respect to the failure on the 1991 calendar year information return is waived due to reasonable cause.

Example (7). (i) The facts are the same as in *Example 6.* In April 1994 the Internal Revenue Service notifies R pursuant to paragraph (a)(2) of § 301.6721-1 that the information return filed for the 1992 calendar year for E contained an incorrect TIN.

(ii) To establish reasonable cause for the failure under this section, R must satisfy the criteria in both paragraphs (c)(6) and (d)(2) of this section. Pursuant to paragraph (d)(2) of this section R may establish that it acted in a responsible manner only by complying with paragraph (f) of this section. Pursuant to paragraph (f)(1)(ii) of this section, R must make an annual solicitation after being notified of an incorrect TIN if the payee's

account contains the incorrect TIN at the time of the notification. Paragraph (f)(3) of this section provides that if the filer is notified pursuant to section 3406(a)(1)(B) the time and manner of making an annual solicitation is that required under § 31.3406(d)-5(g)(1)(ii) of this chapter. Section 31.3406(d)-5(g)(1)(ii) of this chapter requires R to notify E by mail within 15 business days after the date of the notice from the Internal Revenue Service, which R failed to do. As a result, R has failed to act in a responsible manner with respect to the failure on the 1992 information return, and the penalty will not be waived due to reasonable cause.

(l) [*Reserved.*]

(m) *Procedure for seeking a waiver.*—In seeking an administrative determination that the failure was due to reasonable cause and not willful neglect, the filer must submit a written statement to the district director or the director of the Internal Revenue Service Center where the returns, as defined in section 6724(d), are required to be filed. The statement must—

(1) State the specific provision under which the waiver is being requested, *i.e.*, paragraph (b) or under paragraph (c)(2) through (6),

(2) Set forth all the facts alleged as the basis for reasonable cause,

(3) Contain the signature of the person required to file the return, and

(4) Contain a declaration that it is made under penalties of perjury.

See § 1.6061-1 of the Income Tax Regulations for the rules on the signing of returns.

(n) *Manner of payment.*—The penalty due under sections 6721 through 6723 shall be paid upon notice and demand by Internal Revenue Service, and in the same manner as a tax liability is paid. [Reg. § 301.6724-1.]

☐ [*T.D.* 8386, 12-27-91. *Amended by T.D.* 8409, 4-10-92; *T.D.* 8734, 10-6-97; *T.D.* 8804, 12-30-98; *T.D.* 8856, 12-29-99; *T.D.* 9055, 4-28-2003; *T.D.* 9136, 7-12-2004 *and T.D.* 9699, 10-24-2014.]

General Provisions Relating to Stamps

See p. 20,601 for regulations not amended to reflect law changes

[Reg. § 301.6801-1]

§ 301.6801-1. Authority for establishment, alteration, and distribution.—(a) *Establishment and alteration.*—The Commissioner may establish, and from time to time alter, renew, replace, or change the form, style, character, material, and device of any stamp, mark, or label under any provision of the law relating to internal revenue.

(b) *Preparation and distribution of forms, stamps and dies.*—The Commissioner shall prepare and distribute all the instructions, directions, forms, blanks, and stamps; and shall provide proper and sufficient adhesive stamps and other stamps

or dies for expressing and denoting the several stamp taxes. [Reg. § 301.6801-1.]

[Reg. § 301.6802-1]

§ 301.6802-1. Supply and distribution.—(a) *Postmaster General.*—The Commissioner shall furnish to the Postmaster General, without prepayment, a suitable quantity of adhesive stamps (other than the stamps on playing cards), coupons, tickets, or such other devices as may be prescribed pursuant to section 6302(b) (authorizing a discretionary method for collecting certain specified taxes) or chapter 69 of the Code, to be distributed to, and kept on sale by, the various postmasters in the United States in all post offices of the first and second classes, and such post offices of the third and fourth classes as are located in county seats or Postmaster General as necessary.

(b) *Designated depositary of the United States.*— The district director for the district in which any designated depositary of the United States is located shall furnish to such designated depositary, without prepayment, a suitable quantity of adhesive stamps to be kept on sale by the designated depositary.

(c) *State agents.*—Any person who is duly appointed and acting as agent of any State for the sale of stock transfer stamps of such State may make application to the district director for the district in which the State agent is located, to be designated for the purpose of being furnished without prepayment, for sale, stamps to be used in payment of the tax imposed by section 4301. The application shall contain the location and post office address of the State agent, and the maximum amount of stamps he desires to maintain on hand. A copy of the agent's appointment as State agent should be attached to the application. [Reg. § 301.6802-1.]

[Reg. § 301.6803-1]

§ 301.6803-1. Accounting and safeguarding.—In cases coming within the provisions of section 6802(2) and (3) and paragraphs (b) and (c) of § 301.6802-1, the district director may require a bond in such amount as he deems advisable, conditioned for the faithful return, whenever so required, of all quantities or amounts of adhesive stamps undisposed of and for the payment monthly for all quantities or amounts of adhesive stamps sold or not remaining on hand. Such bond shall be furnished in accordance with the provisions contained in section 7101 and § 301.7101-1. [Reg. § 301.6803-1.]

[Reg. § 301.6804-1]

§ 301.6804-1. Attachment and cancellation.— For provisions relating to the attachment and cancellation of specific stamps used with respect to a particular tax, see the regulations relating to such tax. [Reg. § 301.6804-1.]

[Reg. § 301.6805-1]

§ 301.6805-1. Redemption of stamps.—(a) *Authorization.*—(1) Upon receipt of satisfactory evidence of the facts by the district director or director of the service center, he may make allowance for or redeem stamps issued under the authority of any internal revenue law if—

(i) The stamps have been spoiled, destroyed, or rendered useless or unfit for the purpose intended, or

(ii) The owner of the stamps has no use therefor.

(2) If a stamp has been in use for any period of time, it may not be redeemed under section 6805. Similarly, no allowance shall be made for stamps which have been lost or stolen.

(b) *Method and conditions of allowance.*—Such allowance or redemption may be made, either by giving other stamps in lieu of the stamps so allowed for or redeemed, or by refunding the amount or value to the owner thereof, deducting therefrom, in case of repayment, the percentage, if any, allowed to the purchaser thereof. Claims for the redemption of or allowance for stamps shall be made on Form 843 and filed with the district director or director of the service center within three years from the date of the purchase of the stamps from the Government. The stamps for which redemption or allowance is claimed shall be submitted with the claim. If the stamps are destroyed or damaged to the extent that they cannot be presented for redemption or allowance, proof satisfactory to the district director or director of the service center that they have been destroyed or so damaged must accompany the claim before allowance or redemption shall be made. In any case where the actual date of purchase of the stamps from the Government cannot be established, it must be definitely shown in the claim whether they were so purchased within three years prior to the date of filing of the claim.

(c) *Time for filing claims.*—No claim for the redemption of, or allowance for, stamps shall be allowed under this section unless presented within 3 years after the purchase of such stamps from the Government.

(d) *Finality of decisions.*—The findings of fact in and the decision of the district director or director of the service center upon the merits of any claim presented under or authorized by this section, shall, in the absence of fraud or mistake in mathematical calculation, be final and not subject to revision by any accounting officer. [Reg. § 301.6805-1.]

☐ [*T.D.* 7188, 6-29-72.]

[Reg. § 301.6806-1]

§ 301.6806-1. Posting occupational tax stamps.—For provisions relating to the posting of specific stamps used with respect to a particular tax, other than a special tax under subchapter B of chapter 35, subchapter B of chapter 36, or subtitle E, see the regulations relating to such tax. For penalties for failure to post occupational tax stamps, see section 7273. [Reg. § 301.6806-1.]

☐ [*T.D.* 7188, 6-29-72.]

Jeopardy, Receiverships, Etc.

JEOPARDY

Termination of Taxable Year

See p. 20,601 for regulations not amended to reflect law changes

[Reg. § 1.6851-1]

§ 1.6851-1. Termination assessments of income tax.—(a) *Authority for making.*—(1) *In general.*—This section applies to assessments authorized by a district director under section 6851(a) (hereinafter referred to as termination assessments). The district director shall immediately authorize a termination assessment of the income tax for the current or preceding taxable year if the district director finds that a taxpayer designs to do an act which would tend to prejudice proceedings to collect the income tax for such year or years unless such proceedings are brought without delay. In addition, the district director shall immediately authorize such a termination assessment if the district director determines that the taxpayer designs to do any act which would tend to render such proceedings wholly or partially ineffective unless brought without delay. A termination assessment will be made if collection is determined to be in jeopardy because at least one of the following conditions exists:

(i) The taxpayer is or appears to be designing quickly to depart from the United States or to conceal himself or herself.

(ii) The taxpayer is or appears to be designing quickly to place his, her, or its property beyond the reach of the Government either by removing it from the United States, by concealing it, by dissipating it, or by transferring it to other persons.

(iii) The taxpayer's financial solvency is or appears to be imperiled.
Paragraph (a)(1)(iii) of this section does not include cases where the taxpayer becomes insolvent by virtue of the accrual of the proposed assessment of tax, and penalty, if any. A tax assessed under this section shall become immediately due and payable and the district director shall serve upon such taxpayer notice and demand for immediate payment of such tax.

(2) *Computation of tax.*—If a termination assessment of the income tax for the current year is made, the income tax for such year shall be computed for the period beginning on the first day of such year and ending on the day of the assessment. A credit shall be allowed for any tax for the taxable year previously assessed under section 6851. The taxpayer is entitled to a deduction for the personal exemptions (as limited in the case of certain nonresident aliens) without any proration for or because of the short taxable period.

(3) *Taxable year not affected by termination.*—Notwithstanding any termination assessment a taxpayer shall file a return in accordance with section 6012 and the regulations thereunder for the taxpayer's full taxable year. The term "full taxable year" means the taxpayer's usual annual accounting period determined without regard to any action under section 6851 and this section. The return shall show all items of gross income, deductions, and credits for such taxable year. Any tax collected as a result of a termination assessment will be applied against the tax due for the taxpayer's full taxable year. Except as provided in § 1.6851-2 (relating to departing aliens), no return is required to be filed for a terminated period other than a full taxable year.

(4) *Evidence of compliance with income tax obligations.*—Citizens of the United States or of possessions of the United States departing from the United States or its possessions will not be required to procure certificates of compliance or to present any other evidence of compliance with income tax obligations. However, for the rules relating to the furnishing of evidence of compliance with the income tax obligations by certain departing aliens, see § 1.6851-2.

(5) *Section 6851 inapplicable where section 6861 applies.*—No termination assessment for the preceding taxable year shall be made after the due date of the taxpayer's return for such year (determined with regard to extensions of time to file such return).

(b) *Notice of deficiency.*—Where notice and demand for payment (following a termination assessment) takes place after February 28, 1977, the district director shall, within 60 days after the later of—

(1) The date the taxpayer files a return for the full taxable year; or

(2) The due date of such return (determined with regard to extensions).
send the taxpayer a notice of deficiency under section 6212(a). The amount of the deficiency shall be computed in accordance with section 6211 and the regulations thereunder. In applying section 6211, the tax imposed and the amount shown upon the return shall be determined on the basis of the taxpayer's full taxable year. Thus, for example assume that on November 1, 1979, a termination assessment against A, a calendar year taxpayer, is made in the amount of $18,000. The termination assessment is for the period from January 1, 1979 through November 1, 1979. Further assume that on or before April 15, 1980, A files a form 1040 showing an income tax liability for the full year 1979 of $10,000. If the district director determines A's liability for tax for 1979 is $16,000, a notice of deficiency for

67,330
    Termination of Taxable Year
See p. 20,601 for regulations not amended to reflect law changes

$6,000 shall be sent to A on or before June 14, 1980. Assuming that the district director had collected the $18,000 assessed, $2,000 shall be refunded.

(c) *Immediate payment.*—The district director shall make demand for immediate payment of the amount of the termination assessment, and the taxpayer shall immediately pay such amount or shall immediately file the bond provided in section 6863.

(d) *Abatement.*—The provisions of §§301.6861-1(e) and 301.6861-1(f) relating to the abatement of jeopardy assessments, shall apply to assessments made under section 6851. [Reg. §1.6851-1.]

☐ [T.D. 6426, 11-30-59. *Amended by* T.D. 7575, 12-15-78.]

[Reg. §301.6851-1]

§301.6851-1. Termination of taxable year.— For regulations under section 6851, see §§1.6851-1 to 1.6851-3, inclusive, of this chapter (Income Tax Regulations). [Reg. §301.6851-1.]

☐ [T.D. 6227, 3-29-57. *Amended by* T.D. 6498, 10-24-60.]

[Reg. §1.6851-2]

§1.6851-2. Certificates of compliance with income tax laws by departing aliens.—(a) *In general.*—(1) *Requirement.*—The rules of this section are applicable, except as otherwise expressly provided, to any alien who departs from the United States or any of its possessions after January 20, 1961. Except as provided in subparagraph (2) of this paragraph, no such alien, whether resident or nonresident, may depart from the United States unless he first procures a certificate that he has complied with all of the obligations imposed upon him by the income tax laws. In order to procure such a certificate, an alien who intends to depart from the United States (i) must file with the district director for the internal revenue district in which he is located the statements or returns required by paragraph (b) of this section to be filed before obtaining such certificate, (ii) must appear before such district director if the district director deems it necessary, and (iii) must pay any taxes required under paragraph (b) of this section to be paid before obtaining the certificate. Either such certificate of compliance, properly executed, or evidence that the alien is excepted under subparagraph (2) of this paragraph from obtaining the certificate must be presented at the point of departure. An alien who presents himself at the point of departure without a certificate of compliance, or evidence establishing that such a certificate is not required, will be subject at such departure point to examination by an internal revenue officer or employee and to the completion of returns and statements and payment of taxes as required by paragraph (b) of this section.

(2) *Exceptions.*—(i) *Employees of foreign governments or international organizations.*—

(a) *Diplomatic representatives, their families and servants.*—(1) Representatives of foreign governments bearing diplomatic passports, whether accredited to the United States or other countries, and members of their households shall not, upon departure from the United States or any of its possessions, be examined as to their liability for United States income tax or be required to obtain a certificate of compliance. If a foreign government does not issue diplomatic passports but merely indicates on passports issued to members of its diplomatic service the status of the bearer as a member of such service, such passports are considered as diplomatic passports for income tax purposes.

(2) Likewise, the servant of a diplomatic representative who accompanies any individual bearing a diplomatic passport upon departure from the United States or any of its possessions shall not be required, upon such departure, to obtain a certificate of compliance or to submit to examination as to his liability for United States income tax. If the departure of such a servant from the United States or any of its possessions is not made in the company of an individual bearing a diplomatic passport, the servant is required to obtain a certificate of compliance. However, such certificate will be issued to him on Form 2063 without examination as to his income tax liability upon presentation to the district director for the internal revenue district in which the servant is located of a letter from the chief of the diplomatic mission to which the servant is attached certifying (i) that the name of the servant appears on the "White List," a list of employees of diplomatic missions, and (ii) that the servant is not obligated to the United States for any income tax, and will not be so obligated up to and including the intended date of departure.

(b) *Other employees.*—Any employee of an international organization or of a foreign government (other than a diplomatic representative to whom (a) of this subdivision applies) whose compensation for official services rendered to such organization or government is excluded from gross income under section 893 and who has received no gross income from sources within the United States, and any member of his household who has received no gross income from sources within the United States, shall not, upon departure from the United States or any of its possessions after November 30, 1962 be examined as to his liability for United States income tax or be required to obtain a certificate of compliance.

(c) *Effect of waiver.*—An alien who has filed with the Attorney General the waiver provided for under section 247(b) of the Immigration and Nationality Act (8 U.S.C. 1257(b)) is not entitled to the exception provided by this subdivision.

(ii) *Alien students, industrial trainees, and exchange visitors.*—A certificate of compliance shall not be required, and examination as to

United States income tax liability shall not be made, upon the departure from the United States or any of its possessions of—

(A) An alien student, industrial trainee, or exchange visitor, and any spouse and children of that alien, admitted solely on an F-1, F-2, H-3, H-4, J-1 or J-2 visa, who has received no gross income from sources inside the United States other than—

(1) Allowances to cover expenses incident to study or training in the United States (including expenses for travel, maintenance, and tuition);

(2) The value of any services or accommodations furnished incident to such study or training;

(3) Income derived in accordance with the employment authorizations in 8 CFR 274a.12(b) and (c) that apply to the alien's visa; or

(4) Interest on deposits described in section 871(i)(2)(A); or

(B) An alien student, and any spouse or children of that alien admitted solely on an M-1 or M-2 visa, who has received no gross income from sources inside the United States other than income derived in accordance with the employment authorization in 8 CFR 274a.12(c)(6) or interest on deposits described in section 871(i)(2)(A).

(b) *Issuance of certificate of compliance.*—(1) *In general.*—(i) Upon the departure of an alien required to secure a certificate of compliance under paragraph (a) of this section, the district director shall determine whether the departure of such alien jeopardizes the collection of any income tax for the current or the preceding taxable year, but the district director may determine that jeopardy does not exist in some cases. If the district director finds that the departure of such an alien results in jeopardy, the taxable period of the alien will be terminated, and the alien will be required to file returns and make payment of tax in accordance with subparagraph (3)(iii) of this paragraph. On the other hand, if the district director finds that the departure of the alien does not result in jeopardy, the alien will be required to file the statement on returns required by subparagraph (2) or (3)(ii) of this paragraph, but will not be required to pay income tax before the usual time for payment.

(ii) The departure of an alien who is a resident of the United States or a possession thereof (or treated as a resident under section 6013(g) or (h)) and who intends to continue such residence (or treatment as a resident) shall be treated as not resulting in jeopardy, and thus not requiring termination of his taxable period, except when the district director has information indicating that the alien intends by such departure to avoid the payment of his income tax. In the case of a nonresident alien (including a resident alien discontinuing residence), the fact that the alien intends to depart from the United States will justify termination of his taxable period unless the alien establishes to the satisfaction of the district director that he intends to return to the United States and that his departure will not jeopardize collection of the tax. The determination of whether the departure of the alien results in jeopardy will be made on examination of all the facts in the case. Evidence tending to establish that jeopardy does not result from the departure of the alien may be provided, for example, by information showing that the alien is engaged in trade or business in the United States or that he leaves sufficient property in the United States to secure payment of his income tax for the taxable year and of any income tax for the preceding year which remains unpaid.

(2) *Alien having no taxable income and resident alien whose taxable period is not terminated.*—A statement on Form 2063 shall be filed with the district director by every alien required to obtain a certificate of compliance—

(i) Who is a resident of the United States and whose taxable period is not terminated either because he has had no taxable income for the taxable year up to and including the date of his departure (and for the preceding taxable year where the period for making the income tax return for such year has not expired) or because, although he has had taxable income for such period or periods, the district director has not found that his departure jeopardizes collection of the tax on such income; or

(ii) Who is not a resident of the United States and who has had no taxable income for the taxable year up to and including the date of his departure (and for the preceding taxable year where the period for making the income tax return for such year has not expired).

Any alien described in subdivision (i) or (ii) of this subparagraph who is in default in making return of, or paying, income tax for any taxable year shall, in addition, file with the district director any returns which have not been made as required and pay to the district director the amount of any tax for which he is in default. Upon compliance by an alien with the foregoing requirements of this subparagraph, the district director shall execute and issue to the alien the certificate of compliance attached to Form 2063. The certificate of compliance so issued shall be effective for all departures of the alien during his current taxable year, subject to revocation upon any subsequent departure should the district director have reason to believe that such subsequent departure would result in jeopardy. The statement required of a resident alien under this subparagraph, if made before January 21, 1961, with respect to a departure after January 20, 1961, may be made on a Form 1040C in lieu of a Form 2063.

(3) *Nonresident alien having taxable income and resident alien whose taxable period is terminated.*—(i) *Nonresident alien having taxable income.*—Every nonresident alien required to obtain a certificate of compliance (but not described in subparagraph (2) of this paragraph) who wishes to establish that his departure does

not result in jeopardy shall furnish to the district director such information as may be required for the purpose of determining whether the departure of the alien jeopardizes collection of the income tax and thus requires termination of his taxable period.

(ii) *Nonresident alien whose taxable period is not terminated.*—Every nonresident alien described in subdivision (i) of this subparagraph whose taxable period is not terminated upon departure shall file with the district director—

(a) A return in duplicate on Form 1040C for the taxable year of his intended departure, showing income received, and reasonably expected to be received, during the entire taxable year within which the departure occurs; and

(b) Any income tax returns which have not been filed as required.

Upon compliance by the alien with the foregoing requirements of this subdivision, and the payment of any income tax for which he is in default, the district director shall execute and issue to the alien the certificate of compliance on the duplicate copy of Form 1040C. The certificate of compliance so issued shall be effective for all departures of the alien during his current taxable year, subject to revocation by the district director upon any subsequent departure if the taxable period of the alien is terminated on such subsequent departure.

(iii) *Alien (whether resident or nonresident) whose taxable period is terminated.*—Every alien required to obtain a certificate of compliance, whether resident or nonresident, whose taxable period is terminated upon departure shall file with the district director—

(a) A return in duplicate on Form 1040C for the short taxable period resulting from such termination, showing income received, and reasonably expected to be received, during the taxable year up to and including the date of departure;

(b) Where the period for filing has not expired, the return required under section 6012 and § 1.6012-1 for the preceding taxable years; and

(c) Any other income tax returns which have not been filed as required.

Upon compliance with the foregoing requirements of this subdivision, and payment of the income tax required to be shown on the returns filed pursuant to (a) and (b) of this subdivision and of any income tax due and owing for prior years, the departing alien will be issued the certificate of compliance on the duplicate copy of Form 1040C. The certificate of compliance so issued shall be effective only for the specific departure with respect to which it is issued. A departing alien may postpone payment of the tax required to be shown on the returns filed in accordance with (a) and (b) of this subdivision until the usual time of payment by furnishing a bond as provided in § 301.6863-1 of this chapter (regulations on procedure and administration).

(4) *Joint return on Form 1040C.*—A departing alien may not file a joint return on Form 1040C unless—

(i) Such alien and his spouse may reasonably be expected to be eligible to file a joint return at the normal close of their taxable periods for which the return is made; and

(ii) If the taxable period of such alien is terminated, the taxable periods of both spouses are so terminated as to end at the same time.

(5) *Annual return.*—Notwithstanding that Form 1040C has been filed for either the entire taxable year of departure or for a terminated period, the return required under section 6012 and § 1.6012-1 for such taxable year shall be filed. Any income tax paid on income shown on the return on Form 1040C shall be applied against the tax determined to be due on the income required to be shown on the subsequent return under section 6012 and § 1.6012-1. [Reg. § 1.6851-2.]

☐ [*T.D.* 6426, 11-30-59. *Amended by T.D.* 6537, 1-19-61; *T.D.* 6620, 11-29-62; *T.D.* 7575, 12-15-78; *T.D.* 7670, 1-30-80; *T.D.* 8332, 1-25-91 *and T.D.* 8526, 3-2-94.]

[Reg. § 1.6851-3]

§ 1.6851-3. Furnishing of bond to insure payment; cross reference.—See section 6863 and § 301.6863-1 of this chapter (regulations on procedure and administration) for rules relating to the furnishing of bond to stay collection. [Reg. § 1.6851-3.]

☐ [*T.D.* 6426, 11-30-59. *Amended by T.D.* 7575, 12-15-78.]

[Reg. § 301.6852-1]

§ 301.6852-1. Termination assessments of tax in the case of flagrant political expenditures of section 501(c)(3) organizations.—(a) *Authority for making.*—Any assessment under section 6852 as a result of a flagrant violation by a section 501(c)(3) organization of the prohibition against making political expenditures must be authorized by the District Director.

(b) *Determination of income tax.*—An organization shall be subject to an assessment of income tax under section 6852 only if the flagrant violation of the prohibition against making political expenditures results in revocation of the organization's tax exemption under section 501(a) because it is not described in section 501(c)(3). An organization subject to such an assessment is not liable for income taxes for any period prior to the effective date of the revocation of the organization's tax exemption.

(c) *Payment.*—Where a District Director has made a determination of income tax under paragraph (b) of this section or of section 4955 excise tax, notwithstanding any other provision of law, any tax will become immediately due and payable. The taxpayer is required to pay the amount of the assessment within 10 days after the District Director sends the notice and demand for immediate payment regardless of the filing of an administrative appeal or of a court petition. Regardless of filing an administrative appeal or of petitioning a court, enforced collection action may proceed after the 10-day payment period unless the taxpayer posts the bond described in section 6863. For purposes of collection procedures such as section 6331 (regarding levy), assessments under the authority of paragraph (a) of this section do not constitute situations in which the collection of such tax is in jeopardy and, therefore, do not suspend normal collection procedures.

(d) *Effective date.*—This section is effective December 5, 1995. [Reg. § 301.6852-1.]

☐ [*T.D.* 8628, 12-4-95.]

Jeopardy Assessments

[Reg. § 301.6861-1]

§ 301.6861-1. Jeopardy assessments of income, estate, gift, and certain excise taxes.— (a) *Authority for making.*—If a district director or director of a service center believes that the assessment or collection of a deficiency in income, estate, gift, or chapter 41, 42, 43, or 44 tax will be jeopardized by delay, then the director is required to assess such deficiency immediately, together with the interest, additional amounts, and additions to the tax provided by law. A district director will make an assessment under this section if collection is determined to be in jeopardy because at least one of the conditions described in § 1.6851-1(a)(1)(i), (ii), or (iii) (relating to termination assessments) exists. A jeopardy assessment may be made before or after the mailing of the notice of deficiency provided by section 6212. However, a jeopardy assessment for a taxable year under section 6861 cannot be made after a decision of the Tax Court with respect to such taxable year has become final (see section 7481) or after the taxpayer has filed a petition for review of the decision of the Tax Court with respect to such taxable year. In the case of a deficiency determined by a decision of the Tax Court which has become final or with respect to which the taxpayer has filed a petition for review and has not filed a bond as provided in section 7485, assessment may be made in accordance with the provisions of section 6215, without regard to section 6861.

(b) *Amount of jeopardy assessment.*—If a notice of a deficiency is mailed to the taxpayer before it is discovered that delay would jeopardize the assessment or collection of the tax, a jeopardy assessment may be made in an amount greater or less than that included in the deficiency notice. If a deficiency is assessed on account of jeopardy after the decision of the Tax Court is rendered, the jeopardy assessment may be made only with respect to the deficiency determined by the Tax Court.

(c) *Jurisdiction of Tax Court.*—If the jeopardy assessment is made before the notice in respect of the tax to which the jeopardy assessment relates has been mailed pursuant to section 6212(a), the district director shall, within 60 days after the making of the assessment, send the taxpayer a notice of deficiency pursuant to such subsection. The taxpayer may file a petition with the Tax Court for a redetermination of the amount of the deficiency within the time prescribed in section 6213(a). If the petition of the taxpayer is filed with the Tax Court, either before or after the making of the jeopardy assessment, the Commissioner, through his counsel, is required to notify the Tax Court of such assessment or of any abatement thereof, and the Tax Court has jurisdiction to redetermine the amount of the deficiency, together with all other amounts assessed at the same time in connection therewith.

(d) *Payment and collection of jeopardy assessment.*—After a jeopardy assessment has been made, the district director is required to send notice and demand to the taxpayer for the amount of the jeopardy assessment. Regardless of whether the taxpayer has filed a petition with the Tax Court, he is required to make payment of the amount of such assessment (to the extent that it has not been abated) within 10 days after the sending of notice and demand by the district director, unless before the expiration of such 10-day period he files with the district director a bond as provided in section 6863. Section 6331 provides that, if the district director makes a finding that the collection of the tax is in jeopardy, he may make demand for immediate payment of the amount of the jeopardy assessment and, in such case, the taxpayer shall immediately pay such amount or shall immediately file the bond provided in section 6863. If a petition is not filed with the Tax Court within the period prescribed in section 6213(a), the district director will be so advised, and, if collection of the deficiency has been stayed by the timely filing of a bond as provided in section 6863, he should then give notice and make demand for payment of the amount assessed plus interest. After the Tax Court has rendered its decision and such decision has become final, the district director will be notified of the action taken. He will then send notice and demand for payment of the unpaid portion of the amount determined by the Tax Court, the collection of which has been stayed by the bond. If the amount of the jeopardy assessment is less than the amount determined by the Tax Court, the difference will be assessed and collected as part of the tax upon the issuance of a notice and demand therefor. If the amount of the jeopardy assessment is in excess of the amount determined by the Tax Court, the unpaid portion of such excess will be abated. If any part of the excess amount has been paid, it will be credited or refunded to the taxpayer as provided in section 6402, without the filing of claim therefor.

Reg. § 301.6861-1(d)

(e) *Abatement of excessive assessment.*—The district director or the director of the regional service center may, at any time before the decision of the Tax Court is rendered, abate a jeopardy assessment in whole or in part if the district director believes that such assessment is excessive in amount.

(f) *Abatement if jeopardy does not exist.*—(1) The district director or the director of the regional service center may abate a jeopardy assessment in whole or in part, if it is shown to his satisfaction that jeopardy does not exist. An abatement may not be made under this paragraph after a decision of the Tax Court in respect of the deficiency has been rendered or, if no petition is filed with such court, after the expiration of the period for filing such petition.

(2) After abatement of a jeopardy assessment in whole or in part, a deficiency may be assessed and collected in the manner authorized by law as if the jeopardy assessment or part thereof so abated had not existed. If a notice of deficiency has been sent to the taxpayer before the abatement of the jeopardy assessment in whole or in part, whether such notice was sent before or after the making of the assessment, such abatement will not affect the validity of the notice or of any proceedings for redetermination based thereon. The period of limitation on the making of assessments and the beginning of levy or a proceeding in court for collection in respect of any deficiency shall be determined as if the jeopardy assessment so abated had not been made, except that the running of such period shall in any event be suspended for the period from the date of such jeopardy assessment until the expiration of the tenth day after the date on which such jeopardy assessment is abated in whole or in part. The provisions of this subparagraph may be illustrated by the following example:

Example. On March 18, 1958, 28 days before the last day of the 3-year period of limitations on assessment, a jeopardy assessment is made in respect of a proposed deficiency. On May 2, 1958, before the mailing of the notice of deficiency provided by section 6861(b), this assessment is abated. By virtue of this subparagraph, the last day of the period of limitations for the making of an assessment is June 9, 1958, that is, the thirty-eighth day after the date of the abatement. If the notice of deficiency provided for in section 6861(b) had been sent before the abatement, the running of the period of limitations on assessment would have been suspended pursuant to the provisions of section 6503(a).

(3) See section 7429 with respect to requesting the district director to review the making of the jeopardy assessment.

(g) *Special rules for chapters 42 and 43 taxes.*—For purposes of paragraph (a) of this section, the amount of a deficiency with respect to any tax imposed by section 4941(a), 4942(a), 4943(a), 4944(a), 4945(a), 4951(a), 4952(a), 4955(a), 4971(a) or 4975(a) shall include the amount of additional tax imposed by section 4941(b), 4942(b), 4943(b),

4944(b), 4945(b), 4951(b), 4952(b), 4955(b), 4971(b), or 4975(b) for failure to correct the act (or failure to act) which gave rise to liability for the initial tax. [Reg. § 301.6861-1.]

☐ [*T.D. 6227, 3-29-57. Amended by T.D. 6585, 12-27-61; T.D. 7575, 12-15-78; T.D. 7838, 10-5-82; T.D. 8084, 5-1-86 and T.D. 8628, 12-4-95.*]

[Reg. § 301.6862-1]

§ 301.6862-1. Jeopardy assessment of taxes other than income, estate, gift, and certain excise taxes.—(a) If the district director believes that the collection of any tax (other than income, estate, gift, chapter 41, 42, 43, or 44 tax) will be jeopardized by delay, the director shall, whether or not the time otherwise prescribed by law for filing the return or paying such tax has expired, immediately assess such tax, together with all interest, additional amounts and additions to the tax provided by law. A district director will make an assessment under this section if collection is determined to be in jeopardy because at least one of the conditions described in § 1.6851-1(a)(1)(i), (ii), or (iii) (relating to termination assessments) exists. For example, assume that a taxpayer incurs on January 18, 1977, liability for tax imposed by section 4061, that the last day on which return and payment of such tax is required to be made is May 2, 1977, and that on January 18, 1977 the district director determines that collection of such tax would be jeopardized by delay. In such case, the district director shall immediately assess the tax.

(b) The tax, interest, additional amounts, and additions to the tax will, upon assessment, become immediately due and payable, and the district director shall, without delay, issue a notice and demand for payment thereof in full. Upon failure or refusal to pay the amount demanded, collection thereof by levy shall be lawful without regard to the 10-day period provided in section 6331(a). However, the collection of the whole or any part of the amount of the jeopardy assessment may be stayed by timely filing with the district director a bond as provided in section 6863.

(c) See section 7429 with respect to requesting the district director to review the making of the jeopardy assessment. [Reg. § 301.6862-1.]

☐ [*T.D. 6227, 3-29-57. Amended by T.D. 7575, 12-15-78 and T.D. 7838, 10-5-82.*]

[Reg. § 301.6863-1]

§ 301.6863-1. Stay of collection of jeopardy assessments; bond to stay collection.—(a) *General rule.*—(1) The collection of an assessment under section 6851, 6861, or 6862 (referred to as a "jeopardy assessment" for purposes of this section), or under section 6852 (referred to as a political assessment for purposes of this section) of any tax may be stayed by filing with the district director a bond on the form to be furnished by the district director upon request.

(2) The bond may be filed—

(i) At any time before the time collection by levy is authorized under section 6331(a), or

(ii) After collection by levy is authorized and before levy is made on any property or rights to property, or

(iii) In the discretion of the district director, after any such levy has been made and before the expiration of the period of limitations on collection.

(3) The bond made must be in an amount equal to the portion (including interest thereon to the date of payment as calculated by the district director) of the jeopardy assessment or political assessment collection of which is sought to be stayed. See section 7101 and § 301.7101-1, relating to the form of bond and the sureties thereon. The bond shall be conditioned upon the payment of the amount (together with interest thereon), the collection of which is stayed, at the time at which, but for the making of the jeopardy assessment, such amount would be due.

(4) Upon the filing of a bond in accordance with this section, the collection of so much of the assessment as is covered by the bond will be stayed. The taxpayer may at any time waive the stay of collection of the whole or any part of the amount covered by the bond. If as a result of such waiver any part of the amount covered by the bond is paid, or if any portion of the jeopardy assessment or political assessment is abated by the district director, then the bond shall at the request of the taxpayer be proportionately reduced.

(b) *Additional conditions applicable to income, estate, gift, and chapter 41, 42, 43 and 44 tax assessments.*—In the case of a jeopardy assessment or political assessment of income, estate, gift, chapter 41, 42, 43, or 44 tax, the bond must be conditioned upon the payment of so much of the amount included therein as is not abated by a decision of the Tax Court which has become final, together with the interest on such amount. If the Tax Court determines that the amount assessed is greater than the correct amount of the tax, the bond will be proportionately reduced at the request of the taxpayer after the Tax Court renders its decision. If the bond is given before the taxpayer has filed his petition with the Tax Court, it must contain a further condition that if a petition is not filed before the expiration of the period provided in section 6213(a) for the filing of such petition the amount stayed by the bond will be paid upon notice and demand at any time after the expiration of such period, together with interest thereon at the annual rate referred to in the regulations under section 6621 from the date of the jeopardy (or political assessment) notice and demand to the date of the notice and demand made after the expiration of the period for filing petition with the Tax Court. [Reg. § 301.6863-1.]

☐ [*T.D.* 6227, 3-29-57. *Amended by T.D.* 6498, 10-24-60; *T.D.* 7384, 10-21-75; *T.D.* 7575, 12-15-78; *T.D.* 7838, 10-5-82 *and T.D.* 8628, 12-4-95.]

[Reg. § 301.6863-2]

§ 301.6863-2. Collection of jeopardy assessment; stay of sale of seized property pending Tax Court decision.—(a) *General rule.*—In the case of an assessment under section 6851, 6852, 6861, or 6862, any property seized for the collection of such assessment shall not (except as provided in paragraph (b) of this section) be sold until the latest of the following occurs:

(1) The period provided in section 7429(a)(2) to request the district director to review the action taken expires.

(2) The period provided in section 7429(b)(1) to file an action in U.S. District Court expires if a request for a redetermination is made to the district director.

(3) The U.S. District Court judgment in such action becomes final, if a civil action is begun in accordance with section 7429(b).

(4) In addition to the occurrences described in paragraphs (a)(1), (2), and (3) of this section in the case of an assessment of income, estate, gift, chapter 41, 42, 43, or 44 excise taxes, until the latest of the following occurs:

(i) The expiration of the period provided in section 6213(a) within which the taxpayer may file a petition with the Tax Court; or

(ii) The decision of the Tax Court becomes final, if a petition for redetermination is filed with the Tax Court (whether before or after the making of the assessment).

However, notwithstanding paragraph (a)(4)(i) of this section, in the case of a termination assessment under section 6851, property seized may be sold after the due date (determined with extensions) of the taxpayer's return if the taxpayer does not file a return by such date. Furthermore, for the purposes of paragraph (a)(4)(ii) of this section, a petition will not operate as a further stay of the sale of the seized property unless the taxpayer files a bond as provided in section 7485.

(b) *Exceptions.*—Notwithstanding the provisions of paragraph (a) of this section, any property seized may be sold—

(1) If the taxpayer files with the district director a written consent to the sale, or

(2) If the district director determines that the expenses of conservation and maintenance of the property will greatly reduce the net proceeds from the sale of such property, or

(3) If the property is of a type to which section 6336 (relating to sale of perishable goods) is applicable. [Reg. § 301.6863-2.]

☐ [*T.D.* 6227, 3-29-57. *Amended by T.D.* 7575, 12-15-78 *and T.D.* 8628, 12-4-95.]

Special Rules with Respect to Certain Cash

[Reg. § 301.6867-1]

§ 301.6867-1. Presumptions where owner of large amount of cash is not identified.—(a) *General rule.*—For purposes of section 6851 (relating to termination assessments) and section

6861 (relating to jeopardy assessments), if cash in excess of $10,000 is found in the physical possession of an individual who does not claim either ownership of that cash or ownership by some other person whose identity the Commissioner can readily ascertain and who acknowledges ownership of that cash as of the date the cash was found, then, it shall be presumed that—

(1) The cash represents gross income of an unknown single individual; and

(2) That the collection of tax on that income will be jeopardized by delay.

(b) *Rules for assessment.*—The Commissioner may make an assessment pursuant to section 6851 or section 6861, as appropriate, using the rules for assessment specified in this paragraph. In the case of any assessment resulting from the application of paragraph (a) of this section—

(1) The entire amount of cash is treated as taxable income for the taxable year in which the cash is found;

(2) The income is treated as taxable at the highest rate of tax specified in section 1 of the Internal Revenue Code; and

(3) Except as provided in paragraph (c), the possessor of the cash is treated (solely with respect to that cash) as the taxpayer for purposes of chapters 63 and 64 and section 7429(a)(1) of the Internal Revenue Code.

(c) *Effect of later substitution of true owner.*—(1) *In general.*—If an assessment resulting from the application of paragraph (a) of this section is later abated and replaced by an assessment against the true owner of the cash, the later assessment is treated for purposes of all laws relating to lien, levy, and collection as relating back to the date of the original assessment. Notwithstanding the preceding sentence, any notice and review provided for by section 7429 and the notice of deficiency issued to the true owner relative to the later assessment are to be made within the prescribed time limits, using the actual date of the later assessment against the true owner.

(2) *Example.*—The provisions of paragraph (c)(1) of this section may be illustrated by the following example:

Example. On June 5, 1994, A is found in possession of a bag, containing $200,000, which A claims he was holding for a friend whose name A cannot remember. Because A does not claim ownership of the cash and does not provide the name of the true owner so that the Commissioner can identify the true owner and have that person acknowledge ownership of the cash, it is presumed that the cash represents gross income of an individual for calendar year 1994, and that the collection of tax on that gross income will be jeopardized by delay. Accordingly, on June 17, 1994, a termination assessment under section 6851 is made against A, in his capacity as possessor of the cash. On June 21, 1994, the written statement of information provided for by section 7429(a)(1) is given to A. No request for review under section 7429(a)(2) is

made by the true owner within 30 days after the day on which A was furnished the written statement provided for in section 7429(a)(1). Subsequently, individual B comes to the Service and states that he is the owner of the cash. On September 2, 1994, the Service determines that B was the true owner of the cash on June 5, 1994. On September 9, 1994, the Service abates the termination assessment made against A solely as possessor of cash and, after determining that jeopardy exists, replaces it with a termination assessment under section 6851 against B. The lien against B that arises under section 6321 is treated as arising on June 17, 1994. However, within 5 days after September 9, 1994, the Service must give B the written statement of information required by section 7429(a)(1) so that B can make a request for review under section 7429(a)(2). In addition, a notice of deficiency must be sent to B within 60 days after the later of the due date or the actual filing of B's tax return for 1994, as required by section 6851(b).

(d) *Rights of possessor of cash.*—(1) *Action permitted.*—Section 6867 provides that the possessor of cash is treated as the taxpayer for purposes of chapter 63 (relating to assessment) and chapter 64 (relating to collection) of the Internal Revenue Code. Accordingly, the possessor of cash may file a petition with the United States Tax Court, within the applicable time limits, challenging the notice of deficiency issued to the possessor solely in that person's capacity as possessor of cash.

(2) *Actions not permitted.*—Section 6867 provides that the possessor of cash is treated as the taxpayer solely for purposes of section 7429(a)(1), and is entitled to the written statement of information provided for by that section. The possessor of cash is not treated as the taxpayer for purposes of sections 7429(a)(2) and 7429(b), relating to administrative and judicial review of termination and jeopardy assessments, and may not maintain an action under section 7429 for such review. The possessor of cash is not treated as the taxpayer for purposes of section 7422, relating to civil actions for refund, or chapter 65 of the Internal Revenue Code, relating to abatements, credits, and refunds, and may not institute a suit for refund in district court after the deficiency has been collected.

(e) *Rights of true owner of cash.*—(1) *Actions permitted.*—The true owner of cash may request administrative review under section 7429(a)(2) and may maintain a civil action under section 7429(b) for judicial review of an assessment under section 6851 or section 6861 made against the possessor solely in that person's capacity as possessor of cash. Such an action, however, must be preceded by a request for review under section 7429(a)(2) made by the true owner within 30 days after the day on which the possessor is furnished the written statement provided for in section 7429(a)(1). In addition, after the deficiency asserted against the possessor of cash has been levied upon, the true owner of cash may bring an action in federal district court to recover the cash, as provided in section 7426, relating to civil actions by persons other than taxpayers. See, however, section 6532(c), relating to the 9-month statute of limitations for suits under section 7426. In addition, the true owner of cash, with the permission of the court, may appear before the United States Tax Court in any proceeding that may be filed by the possessor of the cash challenging the notice of deficiency issued to the possessor solely in that person's capacity as possessor of the cash.

(2) *Actions not permitted.*—The true owner of cash may not file a petition with the United States Tax Court challenging the notice of deficiency issued to the possessor solely in that person's capacity as possessor of cash. Notwithstanding the preceding sentence, the true owner of cash may file a petition with the United States Tax Court challenging any notice of deficiency issued to the true owner following the abatement of the assessment made against the possessor of cash.

(f) *Definitions.*—For the purposes of this section and section 6867—

(1) *Cash.*—The term *cash* includes any cash equivalents.

(2) *Cash equivalent.*—(i) *In general.*—The term *cash equivalent* includes foreign currency, any bearer obligation, and any medium of exchange that is of a type that has been frequently used in illegal activities, as listed in paragraph (f)(2)(ii) of this section.

(ii) *Specific cash equivalents.*—For purposes of paragraph (f)(2)(i), the following are also cash equivalents—

(A) Coins;

(B) Precious metals;

(C) Jewelry;

(D) Precious stones;

(E) Postage stamps;

(F) Traveler's checks in any form;

(G) Negotiable instruments (including personal checks, business checks, official bank checks, cashier's checks, notes, and money orders) that are either in bearer form, endorsed without restriction, made out to a fictitious payee, or otherwise in such form that title thereto passes upon delivery;

(H) Incomplete instruments (including personal checks, business checks, official bank checks, cashier's checks, notes, and money orders) signed but with the payee's name omitted; and

(I) Securities or stock in bearer form or otherwise in such form that title thereto passes upon delivery.

(iii) *Value of cash equivalents.*—A cash equivalent is taken into account at its fair market value except in the case of a bearer obligation, in which case it is taken into account at its face value.

(3) *Possessor of cash.*—An individual is considered to be the possessor of cash if the cash is found on that individual's person or in that individual's possession or is found in any object, container, vehicle, or area under that individual's custody or control.

(4) *True owner of the cash.*—The true owner of cash is the individual who beneficially owns the cash on the date such cash is found in the physical possession of the individual described in paragraph (f)(3) of this section. An agent, bailee, or other custodian of the cash is not the true owner of cash. A true owner of cash does not include an individual who, subsequent to the date on which the cash is found in the physical possession of the individual described in paragraph (f)(3) of this section, obtains ownership of the cash by purchase, subrogation, descent, or other means.

(g) *Effective date.*—This section is effective with respect to cash found in the physical possession of an individual on or after August 3, 1995. [Reg. §301.6867-1.]

☐ [*T.D.* 8605, 8-2-95.]

RECEIVERSHIPS, ETC.

[Reg. §301.6871(a)-1]

§301.6871(a)-1. **Immediate assessment of claims for income, estate, and gift taxes in bankruptcy and receivership proceedings.**— (a) Upon (1) the adjudication of bankruptcy of any taxpayer in any liquidating proceeding, (2) the filing with a court of competent jurisdiction or (where approval is required by the Bankruptcy Act, 11 U.S.C. chs. 1-14) the approval of a petition of, or the approval of a petition against, any taxpayer in any other proceeding under the Bankruptcy Act, or (3) the appointment of any receiver for any taxpayer in a receivership proceeding before any court of the United States or of any State or Territory or of the District of Columbia, the district director shall immediately assess any deficiency of income, estate, or gift tax (together with all interest, additional amounts, or additions to the tax provided by law), determined by him, if such deficiency has not heretofore been assessed in accordance with law. Such assessment shall be made immediately, whether or not a notice of deficiency has been issued, and without regard to the restrictions upon assessments under section 6213.

(b) As used in this section and §§301.6871(a)-2 to 301.6873-1, inclusive, the term "proceeding under the Bankruptcy Act" includes a proceeding under chapters I to VII, inclusive, of the Bankruptcy Act, or under section 75 or 77 (11 U.S.C. 203, 205), or chapters X to XIII, inclusive, of such Act, or any other proceeding under the Act. [Reg. § 301.6871(a)-1.]

☐ [*T.D.* 6227, 3-29-57. *Amended by T.D.* 6425, 11-10-59 *and T.D.* 6498, 10-24-60.]

[Reg. § 301.6871(a)-2]

§ 301.6871(a)-2. Collection of assessed taxes in bankruptcy and receivership proceedings.— (a) During a proceeding under the Bankruptcy Act (11 U.S.C. chs. 1-14) or a receivership proceeding in either a Federal or State court, generally the assets of the taxpayer are under the control of the court in which such proceeding is pending, and the collection of taxes cannot be made by levying upon such assets. However, any assets which under applicable provisions of law are not under the control of the court may be subject to levy. See paragraph (b) of this section and § 301.6871(b)-1 with respect to claims for such taxes. See section 6873 with respect to collection of unpaid claims.

(b) District directors should, promptly after ascertaining the existence of any outstanding liability against a taxpayer in any proceeding under the Bankruptcy Act or in any receivership proceeding, and in any event within the time limited by the appropriate provisions of the Bankruptcy Act, or by the appropriate orders of the court in which such proceeding is pending, file proof of claim covering such liability in the court in which such proceeding is pending. Such proof of claim should be filed whether the unpaid taxes involved have been assessed or not, except in cases where the instructions of the Commissioner direct otherwise; for example, where the payment of the taxes is secured by a sufficient bond. At the same time proof of claim is filed with the bankruptcy or receivership court, the district director will send notice and demand for payment to the taxpayer, together with a copy of such proof of claim.

(c) Under sections 3466 and 3467 of the Revised Statutes (31 U.S.C. 191, 192) and section 64 of the Bankruptcy Act, 11 U.S.C. 104, taxes are entitled to the priority over other claims therein specified, and the trustee, receiver, debtor in possession, or other person designated as in control of the assets of the debtor by the court in which the proceeding under the Bankruptcy Act or receivership proceeding is pending, may be held personally liable for failure on his part to protect the priority of the Government respecting taxes of which he has notice. Sections 75(l), 77(e), 199, 337(2), 455, and 659(6) of the Bankruptcy Act (11 U.S.C. 203(l), 205(e), 599, 737(2), 855, and 1059(6)) also contain provisions with respect to the rights of the United States relative to priority of payment. For the filing of returns by a trustee in bankruptcy or by a receiver, see section 6012(b)(3) and 28 U.S.C. 960. Bankruptcy courts have jurisdiction under the Bankruptcy Act to determine all disputes regarding the amount and validity of taxes claimed in a proceeding under the Bankruptcy Act. A proceeding under the Bankruptcy Act or receivership proceeding does not discharge any portion of a claim of the United States for taxes except in the case of a proceeding under section 77 or chapter X of the Bankruptcy Act. However, the claim may be settled or compromised as in other cases in court.

(d) For the requirement that a receiver, trustee in bankruptcy, or other like fiduciary give notice as to his qualification as such, see section 6036 and the regulations thereunder. [Reg. § 301.6871(a)-2.]

☐ [*T.D.* 6227, 3-29-57. *Amended by T.D.* 6498, 10-24-60.]

[Reg. § 301.6871(b)-1]

§ 301.6871(b)-1. Claims for income, estate, and gift taxes in proceedings under the Bankruptcy Act and receivership proceedings; claim filed despite pendency of Tax Court proceedings.—(a) If it is determined that a deficiency is due in respect of income, estate, or gift tax and the taxpayer has filed a petition with the Tax Court before (1) the adjudication of bankruptcy in any liquidating proceeding, (2) the filing with a court of competent jurisdiction or (where approval is required by the Bankruptcy Act (11 U.S.C. chs. 1-14)) the approval of a petition of, or the approval of a petition against, any taxpayer in any other proceeding under the Bankruptcy Act, or (3) the appointment of a receiver, trustee, receiver, debtor in possession, or other like fiduciary, may, upon his own motion, be made a party to the Tax Court proceeding and thereafter may prosecute the appeal before the Tax Court as to that particular determination. No petition shall be filed with the Tax Court for a redetermination of the deficiency after the adjudication of bankruptcy, the filing or (where approval is required by the Bankruptcy Act) the approval of a petition of, or the approval of a petition against, any taxpayer in any other bankruptcy proceeding, or the appointment of the receiver.

(b) Even though the determination of a deficiency is pending before the Tax Court for redetermination, proof of claim for the amount of such deficiency may be filed with the court in which the proceeding under the Bankruptcy Act or receivership proceeding is pending without awaiting final decision of the Tax Court. In case of a final decision of the Tax Court before the payment or the disallowance of the claim in the proceeding under the Bankruptcy Act or receivership proceeding, a copy of the Tax Court's decision may be filed by the district director with the court in which such proceeding is pending.

(c) While a district director is required by section 6871(a) and paragraph (a) of § 301.6871(a)-1 to make immediate assessment of any deficiency, such assessment is not made as a jeopardy assessment within the meaning of section 6861, and consequently the provisions of that section do not apply to any assessment made under section 6871. Therefore, the notice of deficiency provided in section 6861(b) will not be mailed. Although such notice will not be issued, a letter will be sent to the taxpayer or to the trustee, receiver, debtor in possession, or other like fiduciary, notifying him in detail how the deficiency was computed, that he may furnish evidence showing wherein the deficiency is incorrect, and that upon request he will be granted a conference by the district director with respect to such deficiency. However, such letter will not provide for such a conference where a petition was filed with the Tax Court before (1) the adjudication of bankruptcy in a liquidating proceeding, (2) the filing with a court of competent jurisdiction or (where approval is required by the Bankruptcy Act), the approval of a petition of, or the approval of a petition against, any taxpayer in any other proceeding under the Bankruptcy Act, or (3) the appointment of a receiver. [Reg. § 301.6871(b)-1.]

☐ [*T.D.* 6227, 3-29-57. *Amended by T.D.* 6425, 11-10-59 *and T.D.* 6498, 10-24-60.]

[Reg. § 301.6872-1]

§ 301.6872-1. Suspension of running of period of limitations on assessment.—If any fiduciary in any proceeding under the Bankruptcy Act (11 U.S.C. chs. 1-14), including a trustee, receiver, or debtor in possession or a receiver in any other court proceeding is required, pursuant to section 6036, to give notice in writing to the district director of his qualification as such, then the running of the period of limitations on assessment shall be suspended from the date the proceeding is instituted to the date such notice is received by the district director, and for an additional 30 days thereafter. However, the suspension under this section of the running of the period of limitation on assessment shall in no case exceed 2 years. [Reg. § 301.6872-1.]

☐ [*T.D.* 6227, 3-29-57. *Amended by T.D.* 6948, 10-24-60.]

[Reg. § 301.6873-1]

§ 301.6873-1. Unpaid claims in bankruptcy or receivership proceedings.—(a) If any portion of the claim allowed by the court in a receivership proceeding, or in any proceeding under the Bankruptcy Act (11 U.S.C. chs. 1-14), remains unpaid after the termination of such proceeding, the district director will send notice and demand for payment thereof to the taxpayer. Such unpaid portion with interest as provided in section 6601 may be collected from the taxpayer by levy or proceeding in court within the period of limitation for collection after assessment. For the general rule as to such period of limitation, see section 6502, and for suspensions of the running of the period provided in section 6502, see, for example, section 6503. For suspensions under other provisions of law, see, for example, section 11f of the Bankruptcy Act (11 U.S.C. 29(f)). Extension of time for the payment of such unpaid amount may be granted in the same manner and subject to the same provisions and limitations as provided in section 6161(c).

(b) Section 6873 is applicable only where a claim for taxes is allowed in a receivership proceeding or in a proceeding under the Bankruptcy Act. Claims for taxes, interest, additional amounts, or additions to the tax may be collectible in equity or under other provisions of law although no claim was allowed in the proceeding because, for example, such items were not included in a proof of claim filed in the proceeding or no proof of claim was filed. Except in the case of a proceeding under section 77 or chapter X of the Bankruptcy Act, a tax or a liability in respect thereof is not discharged by a proceeding under such Act, whether or not a claim is filed in such proceeding, and provisions suspending the running of the period of limitation on the collection of taxes are applicable, whether or not a claim is filed in such proceeding. [Reg. § 301.6873-1.]

☐ [*T.D.* 6227, 3-29-57.]

Transferees and Fiduciaries

See p. 20,601 for regulations not amended to reflect law changes

[Reg. § 301.6901-1]

§ 301.6901-1. Procedure in the case of transferred assets.—(a) *Method of collection.*—(1) *Income, estate, and gift taxes.*—The amount for which a transferee of property of—

(i) A taxpayer, in the case of a tax imposed by subtitle A (relating to income taxes),

(ii) A decedent, in the case of the estate tax imposed by chapter 11 of the Code, or

(iii) A donor, in the case of the gift tax imposed by chapter 12 of the Code, is liable, at law or in equity, and the amount of the personal liability of a fiduciary under section 3467 of the Revised Statutes, as amended (31 U.S.C. 192), in respect of the payment of such taxes, whether shown on the return of the taxpayer or determined as a deficiency in the tax, shall be assessed against such transferee or fiduciary and paid and collected in the same manner and subject to the same provisions and limitations as in the case of a deficiency in the tax with respect to which such liability is incurred, except as hereinafter provided.

(2) *Other taxes.*—The liability, at law or in equity, of a transferee of property of any person liable in respect of any other tax, in any case where the liability of the transferee arises on the liquidation of a corporation or partnership, or a corporate reorganization within the meaning of section 368(a), shall be assessed against such transferee and paid and collected in the same manner and subject to the same provisions and limitations as in the case of the tax with respect

Reg. § 301.6901-1(a)(2)

to which such liability is incurred, except as hereinafter provided.

(3) *Applicable provisions.*—The provisions of the Code made applicable by section 6901(a) to the liability of a transferee or fiduciary referred to in subparagraphs (1) and (2) of this paragraph include the provisions relating to:

(i) Delinquency in payment after notice and demand and the amount of interest attaching because of such delinquency;

(ii) The authorization of distraint and proceedings in court for collection;

(iii) The prohibition of claims and suits for refund; and

(iv) In any instance in which the liability of a transferee or fiduciary is one referred to in subparagraph (1) of this paragraph, the filing of a petition with the Tax Court of the United States and the filing of a petition for review of the Tax Court's decision.

For detailed provisions relating to assessments, collections, and refunds, see chapters 63, 64, and 65 of the Code, respectively.

(b) *Definition of transferee.*—As used in this section, the term "transferee" includes an heir, legatee, devisee, distributee of an estate of a deceased person, the shareholder of a dissolved corporation, the assignee or donee of an insolvent person, the successor of a corporation, a party to a reorganization as defined in section 368, and all other classes of distributees. Such term also includes, with respect to the gift tax, a donee (without regard to the solvency of the donor) and, with respect to the estate tax, any person who, under section 6324(a)(2), is personally liable for any part of such tax.

(c) *Period of limitation on assessment.*—The period of limitation for assessment of the liability of a transferee or of a fiduciary is as follows:

(1) *Initial transferee.*—In the case of the liability of an initial transferee, one year after the expiration of the period of limitation for assessment against the taxpayer in the case of a tax imposed by subtitle A (relating to income taxes), the executor in the case of the estate tax imposed by Chapter 11, or the donor in the case of the gift tax imposed by Chapter 12, each of which for purposes of this section is referred to as the "taxpayer" (see subchapter A of Chapter 66 of the Code).

(2) *Transferee of transferee.*—In the case of the liability of a transferee of a transferee, one year after the expiration of the period of limitation for assessment against the preceding transferee, or three years after the expiration of the period of limitation for assessment against the taxpayer, whichever of such periods first expires.

(3) *Court proceeding against taxpayer or last preceding transferee.*—If, before the expiration of the period specified in subparagraph (1) or subparagraph (2) of this paragraph (whichever is applicable), a court proceeding against the taxpayer or last preceding transferee for the collec-

tion of the tax or liability in respect thereof, respectively, has been begun within the period of limitation for the commencement of such proceeding, then within one year after the return of execution in such proceeding.

(4) *Fiduciary.*—In the case of the liability of a fiduciary, not later than one year after the liability arises or not later than the expiration of the period for collection of the tax in respect of which such liability arises, whichever is the later.

(d) *Extension by agreement.*—(1) *Extension of time for assessment.*—The time prescribed by section 6901 for the assessment of the liability of a transferee or fiduciary may, prior to the expiration of such time, be extended for any period of time agreed upon in writing by the transferee or fiduciary and the district director or an assistant regional commissioner. The extension shall become effective when the agreement has been executed by both parties. The period agreed upon may be extended by subsequent agreements in writing made before the expiration of the period previously agreed upon.

(2) *Extension of time for credit or refund.*—(i) For the purpose of determining the period of limitation on credit or refund to the transferee or fiduciary of overpayments made by such transferee or fiduciary or of overpayments made by the taxpayer to which such transferee or fiduciary may be legally entitled to credit or refund, an agreement and any extension thereof referred to in subparagraph (1) of this paragraph shall be deemed an agreement and extension thereof for purposes of section 6511(c) (relating to limitations on credit or refund in case of extension of time by agreement).

(ii) For the purpose of determining the limit specified in section 6511(c)(2) on the amount of the credit or refund, if the agreement is executed after the expiration of the period of limitation for assessment against the taxpayer with reference to whom the liability of such transferee or fiduciary arises, the periods specified in section 6511(b)(2) shall be increased by the period from the date of such expiration to the date the agreement is executed. The application of this subdivision may be illustrated by the following example:

Example. Assume that Corporation A files its income tax return on March 15, 1955, for the calendar year 1954, showing a liability of $100,000 which is paid with the return. The period within which an assessment may be made against Corporation A expires on March 15, 1958. Corporation B is a transferee of Corporation A. An agreement is executed on October 9, 1958, extending beyond its normal expiration date of March 15, 1959, the period within which an assessment may be made against Corporation B. Under section 6511(c)(2) and section 6511(b)(2)(A) the portion of an overpayment, paid before the execution of an agreement extending the period for assessment, may not be credited or refunded unless paid within three years prior to the date on which the agreement is executed. However, as applied to Corporation B such 3-year period is increased under section 6901(d)(2) to include the period from March 15, 1958, to October 9, 1958, the date on which the agreement was executed.

(e) *Period of assessment against taxpayer.*—For the purpose of determining the period of limitation for assessment against a transferee or a fiduciary, if the taxpayer is deceased, or, in the case of a corporation, has terminated its existence, the period of limitation for assessment against the taxpayer shall be the period that would be in effect had the death or termination of existence not occurred.

(f) *Suspension of running of period of limitations.*—In the cases of the income, estate, and gift taxes, if a notice of the liability of a transferee or the liability of a fiduciary has been mailed to such transferee or to such fiduciary under the provisions of section 6212, then the running of the statute of limitations shall be suspended for the period during which assessment is prohibited in respect of the liability of the transferee or fiduciary (and in any event, if a proceeding in respect of the liability is placed on the docket of the Tax Court, until the decision of the Tax Court becomes final), and for 60 days thereafter. [Reg. § 301.6901-1.]

☐ *[T.D. 6246, 8-2-57. Amended by T.D. 6498, 10-24-60 and T.D. 6585, 12-27-61.]*

[Reg. § 301.6902-1]

§ 301.6902-1. Burden of proof.—In proceedings before the Tax Court the burden of proof shall be upon the Commissioner to show that a petitioner is liable as a transferee of property of a taxpayer, but not to show that the taxpayer was liable for the tax. [Reg. § 301.6902-1.]

☐ *[T.D. 6246, 8-2-57.]*

[Reg. § 301.6903-1]

§ 301.6903-1. Notice of fiduciary relationship.—(a) *Rights and obligations of fiduciary.*— Every person acting for another person in a fiduciary capacity shall give notice thereof to the district director in writing. As soon as such notice is filed with the district director such fiduciary must, except as otherwise specifically provided, assume the powers, rights, duties, and privileges of the taxpayer with respect to the taxes imposed by the Code. If the person is acting as a fiduciary for a transferee or other person subject to the liability specified in section 6901, such fiduciary is required to assume the powers, rights, duties, and privileges of the transferee or other person under that section. The amount of the tax or liability is ordinarily not collectible from the personal estate of the fiduciary but is collectible from the estate of the taxpayer or from the estate of the transferee or other person subject to the liability specified in section 6901.

(b) *Manner of notice.*—(1) *Notices filed before April 24, 2002.*—This paragraph (b)(1) applies to notices filed before April 24, 2002. The notice shall be signed by the fiduciary, and shall be filed with the Internal Revenue Service office where the return of the person for whom the fiduciary is acting is required to be filed. The notice must state the name and address of the person for whom the fiduciary is acting, and the nature of the liability of such person; that is, whether it is a liability for tax, and, if so, the type of tax, the year or years involved, or a liability at law or in equity of a transferee of property of a taxpayer, or a liability of a fiduciary under section 3467 of the Revised Statutes, as amended (31 U.S.C. 192) in respect of the payment of any tax from the estate of the taxpayer. Satisfactory evidence of the authority of the fiduciary to act for any other person in a fiduciary capacity must be filed with and made a part of the notice. If the fiduciary capacity exists by order of court, a certified copy of the order may be regarded as satisfactory evidence. When the fiduciary capacity has terminated, the fiduciary, in order to be relieved of any further duty or liability as such, must file with the Internal Revenue Service office with whom the notice of fiduciary relationship was filed written notice that the fiduciary capacity has terminated as to him, accompanied by satisfactory evidence of the termination of the fiduciary capacity. The notice of termination should state the name and address of the person, if any, who has been substituted as fiduciary. Any written notice disclosing a fiduciary relationship which has been filed with the Commissioner under the Internal Revenue Code of 1939 or any prior revenue law shall be considered as sufficient notice within the meaning of section 6903. Any satisfactory evidence of the authority of the fiduciary to act for another person already filed with the Commissioner or district director need not be resubmitted.

(2) *Notices filed on or after April 24, 2002.*— This paragraph (b)(2) applies to notices filed on or after April 24, 2002. The notice shall be signed by the fiduciary, and shall be filed with the Internal Revenue Service Center where the return of the person for whom the fiduciary is acting is required to be filed. The notice must state the name and address of the person for whom the fiduciary is acting, and the nature of the liability of such person; that is, whether it is a liability for tax, and if so, the type of tax, the year or years involved, or a liability at law or in equity of a transferee of property of a taxpayer, or a liability of a fiduciary under 31 U.S.C. 3713(b), in respect of the payment of any tax from the estate of the taxpayer. The fiduciary must retain satisfactory evidence of his or her authority to act for any other person in a fiduciary capacity as long as the evidence may become material in the administration of any internal revenue law.

(c) *Where notice is not filed.*—If the notice of the fiduciary capacity described in paragraph (b) of this section is not filed with the district director before the sending of notice of a deficiency by registered mail or certified mail to the last known address of the taxpayer (see section

6212), or the last known address of the transferee or other person subject to liability (see section 6901(g)), no notice of the deficiency will be sent to the fiduciary. For further guidance regarding the definition of last known address, see §301.6212-2. In such a case the sending of the notice to the last known address of the taxpayer, transferee, or other person, as the case may be, will be a sufficient compliance with the requirements of the Code, even though such taxpayer, transferee, or other person is deceased, or is under a legal disability, or, in the case of a corporation, has terminated its existence. Under such circumstances, if no petition is filed with the Tax Court of the United States within 90 days after the mailing of the notice (or within 150 days after mailing in the case of such a notice addressed to a person outside the States of the Union and the District of Columbia) to the taxpayer, transferee, or other person, the tax, or liability under section 6901, will be assessed immediately upon the expiration of such 90-day or 150-day period, and demand for payment will be made. See paragraph (a) of §301.6213-1 with respect to the expiration of such 90-day or 150-day period.

(d) *Definition of fiduciary.*—The term "fiduciary" is defined in section 7701(a)(6) to mean a guardian, trustee, executor, administrator, receiver, conservator, or any person acting in any fiduciary capacity for any person.

(e) *Applicability of other provisions.*—This section, relating to the provisions of section 6903, shall not be taken to abridge in any way the powers and duties of fiduciaries provided for in other sections of the Code. [Reg. §301.6903-1.]

☐ [T.D. 6246, 8-2-57. *Amended by T.D. 6498, 10-24-60; T.D. 6585, 12-27-61; T.D. 8939, 1-11-2001; T.D. 8989, 4-23-2002 and T.D. 9040, 1-30-2003.*]

[Reg. §20.6905-1]

§20.6905-1. **Discharge of executor from personal liability for decedent's income and gift taxes.**—For regulations concerning the discharge of an executor from personal liability for a decedent's income and gift taxes, see §301.6905-1 of this chapter (Regulations on Procedure and Administration). [Reg. §20.6905-1.]

☐ [T.D. 7238, 12-28-72.]

[Reg. §25.6905-1]

§25.6905-1. **Discharge of executor from personal liability for decedent's income and gift taxes.**—For regulations concerning the discharge of an executor from personal liability for a dece-dent's income and gift taxes, see §301.6905-1 of this chapter (Regulations on Procedure and Administration). [Reg. §25.6905-1.]

☐ [T.D. 7238, 12-28-72.]

[Reg. §301.6905-1]

§301.6905-1. **Discharge of executor from personal liability for decedent's income and gift taxes.**—(a) *Discharge of liability.*—With respect to decedents dying after December 31, 1970, the executor of a decedent's estate may make written application to the applicable internal revenue officer with whom the estate tax return is required to be filed, as provided in §20.6091-1 of this chapter, for a determination of the income or gift taxes imposed upon the decedent by subtitle A or by chapter 12 of the Code, and for a discharge of personal liability therefrom. If no estate tax return is required to be filed, then such application should be filed where the decedent's final income tax return is required to be filed. The application must be filed after the return with respect to such income or gift taxes is filed. Within 9 months (1 year with respect to the estate of a decedent dying before January 1, 1974) after receipt of the application, the executor shall be notified of the amount of the income or gift tax and, upon payment thereof, he will be discharged from personal liability for any deficiency in income or gift tax thereafter found to be due. If no such notification is received, the executor is discharged at the end of such 9-month (1 year with respect to the estate of a decedent dying before January 1, 1974) period from personal liability for any deficiency thereafter found to be due. The discharge of the executor under this section from personal liability applies only to him in his personal capacity and to his personal assets. The discharge is not applicable to his liability as executor to the extent of the assets of the estate in his possession or control. Further, the discharge does not operate as a release of any part of the property from the lien provided under section 6321 or the special lien provided under subsection (a) or (b) of section 6324.

(b) *Definition of "executor".*—For purposes of this section, the term "executor" means the executor or administrator of the decedent appointed, qualified, and acting within the United States.

(c) *Cross reference.*—For provisions concerning the discharge of the executor from personal liability for estate taxes imposed by chapter 11 of the Code, see section 2204 and the regulations thereunder. [Reg. §301.6905-1.]

☐ [T.D. 7238, 12-28-72.]

Licensing and Registration

See p. 20,601 for regulations not amended to reflect law changes

[Reg. §301.7001-1]

§301.7001-1. **License to collect foreign items.**—(a) *In general.*—Any bank or agent undertaking as a matter of business or for profit the collection of foreign items must obtain a license from the district director for the district in which is located its principal place of business within the United States. For definitions of the terms "foreign item" and "collection", see paragraph (b) of this section.

(b) *Definitions.*—(1) *Foreign item.*—The term "foreign item", as used in this section, means any item of interest upon the bonds of a foreign country or of a nonresident foreign corporation not having a fiscal or paying agent in the United States (including Puerto Rico as if a part of the United States), or any item of dividends upon the stock of such corporation.

(2) *Collection.*—The term "collection", as used in this section, includes the following:

(i) The payment by the licensee of the foreign item in cash;

(ii) The crediting by the licensee of the account of the person presenting the foreign item;

(iii) The tentative crediting by the licensee of the account of the person presenting the foreign item until the amount of the foreign item is received by the licensee from abroad; and

(iv) The receipt of foreign items by the licensee for the purpose of transmitting them abroad for deposits.

(c) *Application for license.*—Application for the license required by paragraph (a) of this section shall be made in writing and shall contain the following information:

(1) The name and present business of the person, partnership (including names of all partners), or corporation applying for the license;

(2) The address of the applicant's principal place of business in the United States and of any branch offices in the United States;

(3) The date on which the applicant intends to commence the collection of foreign items; and

(4) An estimate of the aggregate amount of annual collections of foreign items (in dollars).
The application shall be signed by the applicant (a partner, in the case of a partnership, or an officer, in the case of a corporation).

(d) *Issuance of license.*—The license will be issued by the district director in letter form without cost to the licensee.

(e) *Previous license holders.*—Any person who has been issued a license under the corresponding provision of the Internal Revenue Code of 1939, or any prior revenue law, is not required to renew such license under this section.

(f) *Returns of information as to foreign items.*—For provisions relating to the filing of returns as to foreign items, see section 6041(b) and § 1.6041-4 of this chapter (Income Tax Regulations). [Reg. § 301.7001-1.]

☐ [*T.D.* 6450, 2-3-60. *Amended by T.D.* 6498, 10-24-60.]

Bonds

[Reg. § 20.7101-1]

§ 20.7101-1. Form of bonds.—See paragraph (b) of § 20.6165-1 for provisions relating to the bond required in any case in which the payment of the tax attributable to a reversionary or remainder interest has been postponed under the provisions of § 20.6163-1. For further provisions relating to bonds, see § 20.6165-1 of these regulations and the regulations under section 7101 contained in Part 301 of this chapter (Regulations on Procedure and Administration). **[Reg. § 20.7101-1.]**

☐ [*T.D.* 6296, 6-23-58. *Amended by T.D.* 6600, 5-28-62.]

[Reg. § 25.7101-1]

§ 25.7101-1. Form of bonds.—For provisions relating to form of bonds, see the regulations under section 7101 contained in Part 301 of this chapter (Regulations on Procedure and Administration). **[Reg. § 25.7101-1.]**

☐ [*T.D.* 6334, 10-14-58. *Amended by T.D.* 6600, 5-28-62.]

[Reg. § 53.7101-1]

§ 53.7101-1. Form of bonds.—For provisions relating to form of bonds, see the regulations under section 7101 contained in Part 301 of this chapter (Regulations on Procedure and Administration). [Reg. § 53.7101-1.]

☐ [*T.D.* 7368, 7-15-75.]

[Reg. § 301.7101-1]

§ 301.7101-1. Form of bond and surety required.—(a) *In general.*—Any person required to furnish a bond under the provisions of the Code (other than section 6803(a)(1), relating to bonds required of certain postmasters before June 6, 1972, and section 7485, relating to bonds to stay assessment and collection of a deficiency pending review of a Tax Court decision), or under any rules or regulations prescribed under the Code, shall (except as provided in paragraph (d) of this section) execute such bond;

(1) On the appropriate form prescribed by the Internal Revenue Service (which may be obtained from the district director), and

(2) With satisfactory surety.

For provisions as to what will be considered "satisfactory surety", see paragraph (b) of this section. The bonds referred to in this paragraph shall be drawn in favor of the United States.

(b) *Satisfactory surety.*—(1) *Approved surety company or bonds or notes of the United States.*—For purposes of paragraph (a) of this section, a bond shall be considered executed with satisfactory surety if:

(i) It is executed by a surety company holding a certificate of authority from the Secretary as an acceptable surety on Federal bonds; or

(ii) It is secured by bonds or notes of the United States as provided in 6 U.S.C. 15 (see 31 CFR Part 225).

(2) *Other surety acceptable in discretion of district director.*—Unless otherwise expressly provided in the Code, or the regulations thereunder, a bond may, in the discretion of the district director, be considered executed with satisfactory surety if, in lieu of being executed or secured as provided in subparagraph (1) of this paragraph, it is—

(i) Executed by a corporate surety (other than a surety company), provided such corporate surety establishes that it is within its corporate powers to act as surety for another corporation or an individual;

(ii) Executed by two or more individual sureties, provided such individual sureties meet the conditions contained in subparagraph (3) of this paragraph;

(iii) Secured by a mortgage on real or personal property;

(iv) Secured by a certified, cashier's, or treasurer's check drawn on any bank or trust company incorporated under the laws of the United States or any State, Territory, or possession of the United States, or by a United States postal, bank, express, or telegraph money order;

(v) Secured by corporate bonds or stocks, or by bonds issued by a State or political subdivision thereof, of recognized stability; or

(vi) Secured by any other acceptable collateral.
Collateral shall be deposited with the district director or, in his discretion, with a responsible financial institution acting as escrow agent.

(3) *Conditions to be met by individual sureties.*—If a bond is executed by two or more individual sureties, the following conditions must be met by each such individual surety:

(i) He must reside within the State in which the principal place of business or legal residence of the primary obligor is located;

(ii) He must have property subject to execution of a current market value, above all encumbrances, equal to at least the penalty of the bond;

(iii) All real property which he offers as security must be located in the State in which the principal place of business or legal residence of the primary obligor is located;

(iv) He must agree not to mortgage, or otherwise encumber, any property offered as security while the bond continues in effect without first securing the permission of the district director; and

(v) He must file with the bond, and annually thereafter so long as the bond continues in effect, an affidavit as to the adequacy of his security, executed on the appropriate form furnished by the district director.
Partners may not act as sureties upon bonds of their partnership. Stockholders of a corporate principal may be accepted as sureties provided their qualifications as such are independent of their holding of the stock of the corporation.

(4) *Adequacy of surety.*—No surety or security shall be accepted if it does not adequately protect the interest of the United States.

(c) *Bonds required by Internal Revenue Code of 1939.*—This section shall also apply in the case of bonds required under the Internal Revenue Code of 1939 (other than sections 1423(b) and 1145) or under the regulations under such Code.

(d) *Bonds required under subtitle E and chapter 75 of the Internal Revenue Code of 1954.*—Bonds required under subtitle E and chapter 75, subtitle F, of the Internal Revenue Code of 1954 (or under the corresponding provisions of the Internal Revenue Code of 1939) shall be in such form and with such surety or sureties as are prescribed in the regulations in Subchapter E of this Chapter (Alcohol, Tobacco, and other Excise Taxes). [Reg. §301.7101-1.]

☐ [*T.D. 6443, 1-7-60. Amended by T.D. 6498, 10-24-60 and T.D. 7239, 12-27-72.*]

[Reg. §301.7102-1]

§301.7102-1. Single bond in lieu of multiple bonds.—(a) *In general.*—Except as provided in paragraph (b) of this section, a person who is required, or authorized, under the Internal Revenue Code of 1954 (other than sections 6803(a)(1) and 7485), or under any rules or regulations under the Code, to execute two or more bonds may, in the discretion of the district director, furnish a single bond in lieu of such two or more bonds but only if such single bond meets all the conditions and requirements prescribed for each of the separate bonds which it replaces. This section shall also apply in the case of bonds required or authorized under the Internal Revenue Code of 1939 (other than sections 1423(b) and 1145) or under the regulations under such Code.

(b) *Bonds required under subtitle E and chapter 75 of the Internal Revenue Code of 1954.*—In the case of bonds required under subtitle E and chapter 75, subtitle F, of the Internal Revenue Code of 1954 (or under the corresponding provisions of the Internal Revenue Code of 1939), a single bond will not be accepted in lieu of two or more bonds except as provided in the regulations in Subchapter E of this Chapter (Alcohol, Tobacco, and other Excise Taxes). [Reg. §301.7102-1.]

☐ [*T.D. 6443, 1-7-60. Amended by T.D. 6498, 10-24-60.*]

Closing Agreements and Compromises

See p. 20,601 for regulations not amended to reflect law changes

[Reg. §301.7121-1]

§301.7121-1. Closing agreements.—(a) *In general.*—The Commissioner may enter into a written agreement with any person relating to the liability of such person (or of the person or estate for whom he acts) in respect of any internal revenue tax for any taxable period ending prior or subsequent to the date of such agreement. A closing agreement may be entered into in any case in which there appears to be an advantage in having the case permanently and conclusively closed, or if good and sufficient reasons are shown by the taxpayer for desiring a closing agreement and it is determined by the Commissioner that the United States will sustain no disadvantage through consummation of such an agreement.

(b) *Scope of closing agreement.*—(1) *In general.*— A closing agreement may be executed even though under the agreement the taxpayer is not liable for any tax for the period to which the agreement relates. There may be a series of closing agreements relating to the tax liability for a single period.

(2) *Taxable periods ended prior to due date of closing agreement.*—Closing agreements with respect to taxable periods ended prior to the date of the agreement may relate to the total tax liability of the taxpayer or to one or more separate items affecting the tax liability of the taxpayer, as, for example, the amount of gross income, deduction for losses, depreciation, depletion, the year in which an item of income is to be included in gross income, the year in which an item of loss is to be deducted, or the value of property on a specific date. A closing agreement may also be entered into for the purpose of allowing a deficiency dividend deduction under section 547. In addition, a closing agreement constitutes a determination as defined by section 1313.

(3) *Taxable periods ending subsequent to date of closing agreement.*—Closing agreements with respect to taxable periods ending subsequent to the date of the agreement may relate to one or more separate items affecting the tax liability of the taxpayer.

(4) *Illustration.*—The provisions of this paragraph may be illustrated by the following example:

Example. A owns 500 shares of stock in the XYZ Corporation which he purchased prior to March 1, 1913. A is considering selling 200 shares of such stock but is uncertain as to the basis of the stock for the purpose of computing gain. Either prior or subsequent to the sale, a closing agreement may be entered into determining the market value of such stock as of March 1, 1913, which represents the basis for determining gain if it exceeds the adjusted basis otherwise determined as of such date. Not only may the closing agreement determine the basis for computing gain on the sale of the 200 shares of stock, but such an agreement may also determine the basis (unless or until the law is changed to require the use of some other factor to determine basis) of the remaining 300 shares of stock upon which gain will be computed in a subsequent sale.

(c) *Finality.*—A closing agreement which is approved within such time as may be stated in such agreement, or later agreed to, shall be final and conclusive, and, except upon a showing of fraud or malfeasance, or misrepresentation of a material fact—

(1) The case shall not be reopened as to the matters agreed upon or the agreement modified by any officer, employee, or agent of the United States, and

(2) In any suit, action, or proceeding, such agreement, or any determination, assessment, collection, payment, abatement, refund, or credit made in accordance therewith, shall not be annulled, modified, set aside, or disregarded.

However, a closing agreement with respect to a taxable period ending subsequent to the date of the agreement is subject to any change in, or modification of, the law enacted subsequent to the date of the agreement and made applicable to such taxable period, and each closing agreement shall so recite.

(d) *Procedure with respect to closing agreements.*—(1) *Submission of request.*—A request for a closing agreement which relates to a prior taxable period may be submitted at any time before a case with respect to the tax liability involved is docketed in the Tax Court of the United States. All closing agreements shall be executed on forms prescribed by the Internal Revenue Service. The procedure with respect to request for closing agreements shall be under such rules as may be prescribed from time to time by the Commissioner in accordance with the regulations under this section.

(2) *Collection, credit, or refund.*—Any tax or deficiency in tax determined pursuant to a closing agreement shall be assessed and collected, and any overpayment determined pursuant thereto shall be credited or refunded, in accordance with the applicable provisions of law. [Reg. § 301.7121-1.]

☐ [*T.D. 6450, 2-3-60. Amended by T.D. 6498, 10-24-60.*]

[Reg. § 301.7122-0]

§ 301.7122-0. Table of contents.—This section lists the major captions that appear in the regulations under § 301.7122-1.

§ 301.7122-1 Compromises.

(a) In general.

(b) Grounds for compromise.

(c) Special rules for the evaluation of offers to compromise.

(d) Procedures for submission and consideration of offers.

(e) Acceptance of an offer to compromise a tax liability.

(f) Rejection of an offer to compromise.

(g) Effect of offer to compromise on collection activity

(h) Deposits.

(i) Statute of limitations.

(j) Inspection with respect to accepted offers to compromise.

(k) Effective date.

[Reg. § 301.7122-0.]

☐ [*T.D.* 9007, 7-18-2002.]

[Reg. § 301.7122-1]

§ 301.7122-1. Compromises.—(a) *In general.*—(1) If the Secretary determines that there are grounds for compromise under this section, the Secretary may, at the Secretary's discretion, compromise any civil or criminal liability arising under the internal revenue laws prior to reference of a case involving such a liability to the Department of Justice for prosecution or defense.

(2) An agreement to compromise may relate to a civil or criminal liability for taxes, interest, or penalties. Unless the terms of the offer and acceptance expressly provide otherwise, acceptance of an offer to compromise a civil liability does not remit a criminal liability, nor does acceptance of an offer to compromise a criminal liability remit a civil liability.

(b) *Grounds for compromise.*—(1) *Doubt as to liability.*—Doubt as to liability exists where there is a genuine dispute as to the existence or amount of the correct tax liability under the law. Doubt as to liability does not exist where the liability has been established by a final court decision or judgment concerning the existence or amount of the liability. See paragraph (f)(4) of this section for special rules applicable to rejection of offers in cases where the Internal Revenue Service (IRS) is unable to locate the taxpayer's return or return information to verify the liability.

(2) *Doubt as to collectibility.*—Doubt as to collectibility exists in any case where the taxpayer's assets and income are less than the full amount of the liability.

(3) *Promote effective tax administration.*—(i) A compromise may be entered into to promote effective tax administration when the Secretary determines that, although collection in full could be achieved, collection of the full liability would cause the taxpayer economic hardship within the meaning of § 301.6343-1.

(ii) If there are no grounds for compromise under paragraphs (b)(1), (2), or (3)(i) of this section, the IRS may compromise to promote effective tax administration where compelling public policy or equity considerations identified by the taxpayer provide a sufficient basis for compromising the liability. Compromise will be justified only where, due to exceptional circumstances, collection of the full liability would undermine public confidence that the tax laws are being administered in a fair and equitable manner. A taxpayer proposing compromise under this paragraph (b)(3)(ii) will be expected to demonstrate circumstances that justify compromise even though a similarly situated taxpayer may have paid his liability in full.

(iii) No compromise to promote effective tax administration may be entered into if compromise of the liability would undermine compliance by taxpayers with the tax laws.

(c) *Special rules for evaluating offers to compromise.*—(1) *In general.*—Once a basis for compromise under paragraph (b) of this section has been identified, the decision to accept or reject an offer to compromise, as well as the terms and conditions agreed to, is left to the discretion of the Secretary. The determination whether to accept or reject an offer to compromise will be based upon consideration of all the facts and circumstances, including whether the circumstances of a particular case warrant acceptance of an amount that might not otherwise be acceptable under the Secretary's policies and procedures.

(2) *Doubt as to collectibility.*—(i) *Allowable Expenses.*—A determination of doubt as to collectibility will include a determination of ability to pay. In determining ability to pay, the Secretary will permit taxpayers to retain sufficient funds to pay basic living expenses. The determination of the amount of such basic living expenses will be founded upon an evaluation of the individual facts and circumstances presented by the taxpayer's case. To guide this determination, guidelines published by the Secretary on national and local living expense standards will be taken into account.

(ii) *Nonliable spouses.*—(A) *In general.*—Where a taxpayer is offering to compromise a liability for which the taxpayer's spouse has no liability, the assets and income of the nonliable spouse will not be considered in determining the amount of an adequate offer. The assets and income of a nonliable spouse may be considered, however, to the extent property has been transferred by the taxpayer to the nonliable spouse under circumstances that would permit the IRS to effect collection of the taxpayer's liability from such property (e.g., property that was conveyed in fraud of creditors), property has been transferred by the taxpayer to the nonliable spouse for the purpose of removing the property from consideration by the IRS in evaluating the compromise, or as provided in paragraph (c)(2)(ii)(B) of this section. The IRS also may request information regarding the assets and income of the nonliable spouse for the purpose of verifying the amount of and responsibility for expenses claimed by the taxpayer.

(B) *Exception.*—Where collection of the taxpayer's liability from the assets and income of the nonliable spouse is permitted by applicable state law (e.g., under state community property laws), the assets and income of the nonliable spouse will be considered in determining the amount of an adequate offer except to the extent that the taxpayer and the nonliable spouse demonstrate that collection of such assets and income would have a material and adverse impact on the standard of living of the taxpayer, the nonliable spouse, and their dependents.

(3) *Compromises to promote effective tax administration.*—(i) Factors supporting (but not conclusive of) a determination that collection would cause economic hardship within the meaning of paragraph (b)(3)(i) of this section include, but are not limited to—

(A) Taxpayer is incapable of earning a living because of a long term illness, medical condition, or disability, and it is reasonably foreseeable that taxpayer's financial resources will be exhausted providing for care and support during the course of the condition;

(B) Although taxpayer has certain monthly income, that income is exhausted each month in providing for the care of dependents with no other means of support; and

(C) Although taxpayer has certain assets, the taxpayer is unable to borrow against the equity in those assets and liquidation of those assets to pay outstanding tax liabilities would render the taxpayer unable to meet basic living expenses.

(ii) Factors supporting (but not conclusive of) a determination that compromise would undermine compliance within the meaning of paragraph (b)(3)(iii) of this section include, but are not limited to—

(A) Taxpayer has a history of noncompliance with the filing and payment requirements of the Internal Revenue Code;

(B) Taxpayer has taken deliberate actions to avoid the payment of taxes; and

(C) Taxpayer has encouraged others to refuse to comply with the tax laws.

(iii) The following examples illustrate the types of cases that may be compromised by the Secretary, at the Secretary's discretion, under the economic hardship provisions of paragraph (b)(3)(i) of this section:

Example 1. The taxpayer has assets sufficient to satisfy the tax liability. The taxpayer provides full time care and assistance to her dependent child, who has a serious long-term illness. It is expected that the taxpayer will need to use the equity in his assets to provide for adequate basic living expenses and medical care for his child. The taxpayer's overall compliance history does not weigh against compromise.

Example 2. The taxpayer is retired and his only income is from a pension. The taxpayer's only asset is a retirement account, and the funds in the account are sufficient to satisfy the liability. Liquidation of the retirement account would leave the taxpayer without an adequate means to provide for basic living expenses. The taxpayer's overall compliance history does not weigh against compromise.

Example 3. The taxpayer is disabled and lives on a fixed income that will not, after allowance of basic living expenses, permit full payment of his liability under an installment agreement. The taxpayer also owns a modest house that has been specially equipped to accommodate his disability. The taxpayer's equity in the house is sufficient to permit payment of the liability he owes. However, because of his disability and limited earning potential, the taxpayer is unable to obtain a mortgage or otherwise borrow against this equity. In addition, because the taxpayer's home has been specially equipped to accommodate his disability, forced sale of the taxpayer's residence would create severe adverse consequences for the taxpayer. The taxpayer's overall compliance history does not weigh against compromise.

(iv) The following examples illustrate the types of cases that may be compromised by the Secretary, at the Secretary's discretion, under the public policy and equity provisions of paragraph (b)(3)(ii) of this section:

Example 1. In October of 1986, the taxpayer developed a serious illness that resulted in almost continuous hospitalizations for a number of years. The taxpayer's medical condition was such that during this period the taxpayer was unable to manage any of his financial affairs. The taxpayer has not filed tax returns since that time. The taxpayer's health has now improved and he has promptly begun to attend to his tax affairs. He discovers that the IRS prepared a substitute for return for the 1986 tax year on the basis of information returns it had received and had assessed a tax deficiency. When the taxpayer discovered the liability, with penalties and interest, the tax bill is more than three times the original tax liability. The taxpayer's overall compliance history does not weigh against compromise.

Example 2. The taxpayer is a salaried sales manager at a department store who has been able to place $2,000 in a tax-deductible IRA account for each of the last two years. The taxpayer learns that he can earn a higher rate of interest on his IRA savings by moving those savings from a money management account to a certificate of deposit at a different financial institution. Prior to transferring his savings, the taxpayer submits an e-mail inquiry to the IRS at its Web Page, requesting information about the steps he must take to preserve the tax benefits he has enjoyed and to avoid penalties. The IRS responds in an answering e-mail that the taxpayer may withdraw his IRA savings from his neighborhood bank, but he must redeposit those savings in a new IRA account within 90 days. The taxpayer withdraws the funds and redeposits them in a new IRA account 63 days later. Upon audit, the taxpayer learns that he has been misinformed about the required rollover period and that he is liable for additional taxes, penalties and additions to tax for not having redeposited the amount within 60 days. Had it not been for the erroneous advice that is reflected in the taxpayer's retained copy of the IRS e-mail response to his inquiry, the taxpayer would have redeposited the amount within the required 60-day period. The taxpayer's overall compliance history does not weigh against compromise.

(d) *Procedures for submission and consideration of offers.*—(1) *In general.*—An offer to compromise a tax liability pursuant to section 7122 must be submitted according to the procedures, and in the form and manner, prescribed by the Secretary. An offer to compromise a tax liability must be made in writing, must be signed by the taxpayer under penalty of perjury, and must contain all of the information prescribed or requested by the Secretary. However, taxpayers submitting offers to compromise liabilities solely on the basis of doubt as to liability will not be required to provide financial statements.

(2) *When offers become pending and return of offers.*—An offer to compromise becomes pending when it is accepted for processing. The IRS may not accept for processing any offer to compromise a liability following reference of a case involving such liability to the Department of Justice for prosecution or defense. If an offer accepted for processing does not contain sufficient information to permit the IRS to evaluate whether the offer should be accepted, the IRS will request that the taxpayer provide the needed additional information. If the taxpayer does not submit the additional information that the IRS has requested within a reasonable time period after such a request, the IRS may return the offer to the taxpayer. The IRS may also return an offer to compromise a tax liability if it determines that the offer was submitted solely to delay collection or was otherwise non-processable. An offer returned following acceptance for processing is deemed pending only for the period between the date the offer is accepted for processing and the date the IRS returns the offer to the taxpayer. See paragraphs (f)(5)(ii) and (g)(4) of this section for rules regarding the effect of such returns of offers.

(3) *Withdrawal.*—An offer to compromise a tax liability may be withdrawn by the taxpayer or the taxpayer's representative at any time prior to the IRS' acceptance of the offer to compromise. An offer will be considered withdrawn upon the IRS' receipt of written notification of the withdrawal of the offer either by personal delivery or certified mail, or upon issuance of a letter by the IRS confirming the taxpayer's intent to withdraw the offer.

(e) *Acceptance of an offer to compromise a tax liability.*—(1) An offer to compromise has not been accepted until the IRS issues a written notification of acceptance to the taxpayer or the taxpayer's representative.

(2) As additional consideration for the acceptance of an offer to compromise, the IRS may request that taxpayer enter into any collateral agreement or post any security which is deemed necessary for the protection of the interests of the United States.

(3) Offers may be accepted when they provide for payment of compromised amounts in one or more equal or unequal installments.

(4) If the final payment on an accepted offer to compromise is contingent upon the immediate and simultaneous release of a tax lien in whole or in part, such payment must be made in accordance with the forms, instructions, or procedures prescribed by the Secretary.

(5) Acceptance of an offer to compromise will conclusively settle the liability of the taxpayer specified in the offer. Compromise with one taxpayer does not extinguish the liability of, nor prevent the IRS from taking action to collect from, any person not named in the offer who is also liable for the tax to which the compromise relates. Neither the taxpayer nor the Government will, following acceptance of an offer to compromise, be permitted to reopen the case except in instances where—

(i) False information or documents are supplied in conjunction with the offer;

(ii) The ability to pay or the assets of the taxpayer are concealed; or

(iii) A mutual mistake of material fact sufficient to cause the offer agreement to be reformed or set aside is discovered.

(6) *Opinion of Chief Counsel.*—Except as otherwise provided in this paragraph (e)(6), if an offer to compromise is accepted, there will be placed on file the opinion of the Chief Counsel for the IRS with respect to such compromise, along with the reasons therefor. However, no such opinion will be required with respect to the compromise of any civil case in which the unpaid amount of tax assessed (including any interest, additional amount, addition to the tax, or assessable penalty) is less than $50,000. Also placed on file will be a statement of—

(i) The amount of tax assessed;

(ii) The amount of interest, additional amount, addition to the tax, or assessable penalty, imposed by law on the person against whom the tax is assessed; and

(iii) The amount actually paid in accordance with the terms of the compromise.

(f) *Rejection of an offer to compromise.*—(1) An offer to compromise has not been rejected until the IRS issues a written notice to the taxpayer or his representative, advising of the rejection, the reason(s) for rejection, and the right to an appeal.

(2) The IRS may not notify a taxpayer or taxpayer's representative of the rejection of an offer to compromise until an independent administrative review of the proposed rejection is completed.

(3) No offer to compromise may be rejected solely on the basis of the amount of the offer without evaluating that offer under the provisions of this section and the Secretary's policies and procedures regarding the compromise of cases.

(4) *Offers based upon doubt as to liability.*—Offers submitted on the basis of doubt as to liability cannot be rejected solely because the IRS is unable to locate the taxpayer's return or return information for verification of the liability.

(5) *Appeal of rejection of an offer to compromise.*—(i) *In general.*—The taxpayer may administratively appeal a rejection of an offer to compromise to the IRS Office of Appeals (Appeals) if, within the 30-day period commencing the day after the date on the letter of rejection,

the taxpayer requests such an administrative review in the manner provided by the Secretary.

(ii) *Offer to compromise returned following a determination that the offer was nonprocessable, a failure by the taxpayer to provide requested information, or a determination that the offer was submitted for purposes of delay.*—Where a determination is made to return offer documents because the offer to compromise was nonprocessable, because the taxpayer failed to provide requested information, or because the IRS determined that the offer to compromise was submitted solely for purposes of delay under paragraph (d)(2) of this section, the return of the offer does not constitute a rejection of the offer for purposes of this provision and does not entitle the taxpayer to appeal the matter to Appeals under the provisions of this paragraph (f)(5). However, if the offer is returned because the taxpayer failed to provide requested financial information, the offer will not be returned until a managerial review of the proposed return is completed.

(g) *Effect of offer to compromise on collection activity.*—(1) *In general.*—The IRS will not levy against the property or rights to property of a taxpayer who submits an offer to compromise, to collect the liability that is the subject of the offer, during the period the offer is pending, for 30 days immediately following the rejection of the offer, and for any period when a timely filed appeal from the rejection is being considered by Appeals.

(2) *Revised offers submitted following rejection.*—If, following the rejection of an offer to compromise, the taxpayer makes a good faith revision of that offer and submits the revised offer within 30 days after the date of rejection, the IRS will not levy to collect from the taxpayer the liability that is the subject of the revised offer to compromise while that revised offer is pending.

(3) *Jeopardy.*—The IRS may levy to collect the liability that is the subject of an offer to compromise during the period the IRS is evaluating whether that offer will be accepted if it determines that collection of the liability is in jeopardy.

(4) *Offers to compromise determined by IRS to be nonprocessable or submitted solely for purposes of delay.*—If the IRS determines, under paragraph (d)(2) of this section, that a pending offer did not contain sufficient information to permit evaluation of whether the offer should be accepted, that the offer was submitted solely to delay collection, or that the offer was otherwise nonprocessable, then the IRS may levy to collect the liability that is the subject of that offer at any time after it returns the offer to the taxpayer.

(5) *Offsets under section 6402.*—Notwithstanding the evaluation and processing of an offer to compromise, the IRS may, in accordance with section 6402, credit any overpayments made by the taxpayer against a liability that is the subject of an offer to compromise and may offset such overpayments against other liabilities owed by the taxpayer to the extent authorized by section 6402.

(6) *Proceedings in court.*—Except as otherwise provided in this paragraph (g)(6), the IRS will not refer a case to the Department of Justice for the commencement of a proceeding in court, against a person named in a pending offer to compromise, if levy to collect the liability is prohibited by paragraph (g)(1) of this section. Without regard to whether a person is named in a pending offer to compromise, however, the IRS may authorize the Department of Justice to file a counterclaim or third-party complaint in a refund action or to join that person in any other proceeding in which liability for the tax that is the subject of the pending offer to compromise may be established or disputed, including a suit against the United States under 28 U.S.C. 2410. In addition, the United States may file a claim in any bankruptcy proceeding or insolvency action brought by or against such person.

(h) *Deposits.*—Sums submitted with an offer to compromise a liability or during the pendency of an offer to compromise are considered deposits and will not be applied to the liability until the offer is accepted unless the taxpayer provides written authorization for application of the payments. If an offer to compromise is withdrawn, is determined to be nonprocessable, or is submitted solely for purposes of delay and returned to the taxpayer, any amount tendered with the offer, including all installments paid on the offer, will be refunded without interest. If an offer is rejected, any amount tendered with the offer, including all installments paid on the offer, will be refunded, without interest, after the conclusion of any review sought by the taxpayer with Appeals. Refund will not be required if the taxpayer has agreed in writing that amounts tendered pursuant to the offer may be applied to the liability for which the offer was submitted.

(i) *Statute of limitations.*—(1) *Suspension of the statute of limitations on collection.*—The statute of limitations on collection will be suspended while levy is prohibited under paragraph (g)(1) of this section.

(2) *Extension of the statute of limitations on assessment.*—For any offer to compromise, the IRS may require, where appropriate, the extension of the statute of limitations on assessment. However, in any case where waiver of the running of the statutory period of limitations on assessment is sought, the taxpayer must be notified of the right to refuse to extend the period of limitations or to limit the extension to particular issues or particular periods of time.

(j) *Inspection with respect to accepted offers to compromise.*—For provisions relating to the inspection of returns and accepted offers to compromise, see section 6103(k)(1).

(k) *Effective date.*—This section applies to offers to compromise pending on or submitted on or after July 18, 2002. [Reg. § 301.7122-1.]

☐ [*T.D.* 9007, 7-18-2002 (*corrected* 8-19-2002).]

Reg. § 301.7122-1(k)

Crimes, Other Offenses, and Forfeitures

CRIMES

General Provisions

See p. 20,601 for regulations not amended to reflect law changes

[Reg. § 301.7207-1]

§ 301.7207-1. Fraudulent returns, statements, or other documents.—Any person who willfully delivers or discloses to any officer or employee of the Internal Revenue Service any list, return, account, statement, or other document known by him to be fraudulent or to be false as to any material matter, shall be fined not more than $1,000, or imprisoned not more than 1 year, or both. Any person required pursuant to section 6047(b) or (c) or section 6104(d), to furnish information to any officer or employee of the Internal Revenue Service or any other person who willfully furnishes to such officer or employee of the Internal Revenue Service or such other person any information known by him to be fraudulent or to be false as to any material matter shall be fined not more than $1,000, or imprisoned not more than 1 year, or both. [Reg. § 301.7207-1.]

☐ [*T.D. 6498, 10-24-60. Amended by T.D. 6677, 9-16-63, T.D. 7127, 6-14-71, and T.D. 8026, 5-17-85.*]

[Reg. § 301.7214-1]

§ 301.7214-1. Offenses by officers and employees of the United States.—Any officer or employee of the United States acting in connection with any revenue law of the United States required to make a written report under the provisions of section 7214(a)(8) shall submit such report to the Commissioner, or to a regional commissioner or district director. [Reg. § 301.7214-1.]

☐ [*T.D. 6498, 10-24-60.*]

[Reg. § 301.7216-0]

§ 301.7216-0. Table of contents.—This section lists captions contained in §§ 301.7216-1 through 301.7216-3.

§ 301.7216-1 Penalty for disclosure or use of tax return information.

(a) In general.

(b) Definitions.

(c) Gramm-Leach-Bliley Act.

(d) Effective date.

§ 301.7216-2 Permissible disclosures or uses without consent of the taxpayer.

(a) Disclosure pursuant to other provisions of the Internal Revenue Code.

(b) Disclosures to the IRS.

(c) Disclosures or uses for preparation of a taxpayer's return.

(d) Disclosures to other tax return preparers.

(e) Disclosure or use of information in the case of related taxpayers.

(f) Disclosure pursuant to an order of a court, or an administrative order, demand, request, summons or subpoena which is issued in the performance of its duties by a Federal or State agency, the United States Congress, a professional association ethics committee or board, or the Public Company Accounting Oversight Board.

(g) Disclosure for use in securing legal advice, Treasury investigations or court proceedings.

(h) Certain disclosures by attorneys and accountants.

(i) Corporate fiduciaries.

(j) Disclosure to taxpayer's fiduciary.

(k) Disclosure or use of information in preparation or audit of State or local tax returns or assisting a taxpayer with foreign country tax obligations.

(l) Payment for tax preparation services.

(m) Retention of records.

(n) Lists for solicitation of tax return preparation business.

(o) Producing statistical information in connection with tax return preparation business.

(p) Disclosure or use of information for quality, peer, or conflict reviews.

(q) Disclosure to report the commission of a crime.

(r) Disclosure of tax return information due to a tax return preparer's incapacity or death.

(s) Effective date.

§ 301.7216-3 Disclosure or use permitted only with the taxpayer's consent.

(a) In general.

(b) Timing requirements and limitations.

(c) Special rules.

(d) Effective date.

[Reg. § 301.7216-0.]

☐ [*T.D. 9375, 1-3-2008. Amended by T.D. 9478, 12-29-2009 and T.D. 9608, 12-26-2012.*]

[Reg. § 301.7216-1]

§ 301.7216-1. Penalty for disclosure or use of tax return information.—(a) *In general.*—Section 7216(a) prescribes a criminal penalty for tax return preparers who knowingly or recklessly disclose or use tax return information for a purpose other than preparing a tax return. A violation of section 7216 is a misdemeanor, with a maximum penalty of up to one year imprisonment or a fine of not more than $1,000, or both, together with the costs of prosecution. Section 7216(b) establishes exceptions to the general rule in section 7216(a) prohibiting disclosure and use. Section 7216(b) also authorizes the Secretary to promulgate regulations prescribing additional permitted disclosures and uses. Section 6713(a) prescribes a related civil penalty for disclosures and uses that constitute a violation of section 7216. The penalty for violating section 6713 is $250 for each prohibited disclosure or use, not to exceed a total of $10,000 for a calendar year. Section 6713(b) provides that the exceptions in section 7216(b) also apply to section 6713. Under section 7216(b), the provisions of section 7216(a) will not apply to any disclosure or use permitted under regulations prescribed by the Secretary.

(b) *Definitions.*—For purposes of section 7216 and §§ 301.7216-1 through 301.7216-3:

(1) *Tax return.*—The term *tax return* means any return (or amended return) of income tax imposed by chapter 1 of the Internal Revenue Code.

(2) *Tax return preparer.*—(i) *In general.*—The term *tax return preparer* means:

(A) Any person who is engaged in the business of preparing or assisting in preparing tax returns;

(B) Any person who is engaged in the business of providing auxiliary services in connection with the preparation of tax returns, including a person who develops software that is used to prepare or file a tax return and any Authorized IRS *e-file* Provider;

(C) Any person who is otherwise compensated for preparing, or assisting in preparing, a tax return for any other person; or

(D) Any individual who, as part of their duties of employment with any person described in paragraph (b)(2)(i)(A), (B), or (C) of this section performs services that assist in the preparation of, or assist in providing auxiliary services in connection with the preparation of, a tax return.

(ii) *Business of preparing returns.*—A person is engaged in the business of preparing tax returns as described in paragraph (b)(2)(i)(A) of this section if, in the course of the person's business, the person holds himself out to tax return preparers or taxpayers as a person who prepares tax returns or assists in preparing tax returns, whether or not tax return preparation is the person's sole business activity and whether or not the person charges a fee for tax return preparation services.

(iii) *Providing auxiliary services.*—A person is engaged in the business of providing auxiliary services in connection with the preparation of tax returns as described in paragraph (b)(2)(i)(B) of this section if, in the course of the person's business, the person holds himself out to tax return preparers or to taxpayers as a person who performs auxiliary services, whether or not providing the auxiliary services is the person's sole business activity and whether or not the person charges a fee for the auxiliary services. Likewise,

a person is engaged in the business of providing auxiliary services if, in the course of the person's business, the person receives a taxpayer's tax return information from another tax return preparer pursuant to the provisions of § 301.7216-2(d)(2).

(iv) *Otherwise compensated.*—A tax return preparer described in paragraph (b)(2)(i)(C) of this section includes any person who—

(A) Is compensated for preparing a tax return for another person, but not in the course of a business; or

(B) Is compensated for helping, on a casual basis, a relative, friend, or other acquaintance to prepare their tax return.

(v) *Exclusions.*—A person is not a tax return preparer merely because he leases office space to a tax return preparer, furnishes credit to a taxpayer whose tax return is prepared by a tax return preparer, furnishes information to a tax return preparer at the taxpayer's request, furnishes access (free or otherwise) to a separate person's tax return preparation website through a hyperlink on his own website, or otherwise performs some service that only incidentally relates to the preparation of tax returns.

(vi) *Examples.*—The application of § 301.7216-1(b)(2) may be illustrated by the following examples:

Example 1. Bank B is a tax return preparer within the meaning of paragraph (b)(2)(i)(A) of this section, and an Authorized IRS *e-file* Provider. B employs one individual, Q, to solicit the necessary tax return information for the preparation of a tax return; another individual, R, to prepare the return on the basis of the information that is furnished; a secretary, S, who types the information on the returns into a computer; and an administrative assistant, T, who uses a computer to file electronic versions of the tax returns. Under these circumstances, only R is a tax return preparer for purposes of section 7701(a)(36), but all four employees are tax return preparers for purposes of section 7216, as provided in paragraph (b) of this section.

Example 2. Tax return preparer P contracts with department store D to rent space in D's store. D advertises that taxpayers who use P's services may charge the cost of having their tax return prepared to their charge account with D. Under these circumstances, D is not a tax return preparer because it provides space, credit, and services only incidentally related to the preparation of tax returns.

(3) *Tax return information.*—(i) *In general.*—The term *tax return information* means any information, including, but not limited to, a taxpayer's name, address, or identifying number, which is furnished in any form or manner for, or in connection with, the preparation of a tax return of the taxpayer. This information includes information that the taxpayer furnishes to a tax return preparer and information furnished to the tax return preparer by a third party. Tax return

Reg. § 301.7216-1(b)(3)(i)

information also includes information the tax return preparer derives or generates from tax return information in connection with the preparation of a taxpayer's return.

(A) Tax return information can be provided directly by the taxpayer or by another person. Likewise, tax return information includes information received by the tax return preparer from the IRS in connection with the processing of such return, including an acknowledgment of acceptance or notice of rejection of an electronically filed return.

(B) Tax return information includes statistical compilations of tax return information, even in a form that cannot be associated with, or otherwise identify, directly or indirectly, a particular taxpayer. See §301.7216-2(o) for limited use of tax return information to make statistical compilations without taxpayer consent and to use the statistical compilations for limited purposes.

(C) Tax return information does not include information identical to any tax return information that has been furnished to a tax return preparer if the identical information was obtained otherwise than in connection with the preparation of a tax return.

(D) Information is considered "in connection with tax return preparation," and therefore tax return information, if the taxpayer would not have furnished the information to the tax return preparer but for the intention to engage, or the engagement of, the tax return preparer to prepare the tax return.

(ii) *Examples.*—The application of this paragraph (b)(3) may be illustrated by the following examples:

Example 1. Taxpayer A purchases computer software designed to assist with the preparation and filing of her income tax return. When A loads the software onto her computer, it prompts her to register her purchase of the software. In this situation, the software provider is a tax return preparer under paragraph (b)(2)(i)(B) of this section and the information that A provides to register her purchase is tax return information because she is providing it in connection with the preparation of a tax return.

Example 2. Corporation A is a brokerage firm that maintains a website through which its clients may access their accounts, trade stocks, and generally conduct a variety of financial activities. Through its website, A offers its clients free access to its own tax preparation software. Taxpayer B is a client of A and has furnished A his name, address, and other information when registering for use of A's website to use A's brokerage services. In addition, A has a record of B's brokerage account activity, including sales of stock, dividends paid, and IRA contributions made. B uses A's tax preparation software to prepare his tax return. The software populates some fields on B's return on the basis of information A already maintains in its databases. A is a tax return preparer within the meaning of paragraph (b)(2)(i)(B) of this section because it has

prepared and provided software for use in preparing tax returns. The information in A's databases that the software accesses to populate B's return, *i.e.*, the registration information and brokerage account activity, is not tax return information because A did not receive that information in connection with the preparation of a tax return. Once A uses the information to populate the return, however, the information associated with the return becomes tax return information. If A retains the information in a form in which A can identify that the information was used in connection with the preparation of a return, the information in that form is tax return information. If, however, A retains the information in a database in which A cannot identify whether the information was used in connection with the preparation of a return, then that information is not tax return information.

(4) *Use.*—(i) *In general.*—Use of tax return information includes any circumstance in which a tax return preparer refers to, or relies upon, tax return information as the basis to take or permit an action.

(ii) *Example.*—The application of this paragraph (b)(4) may be illustrated by the following example:

Example. Preparer G is a tax return preparer as defined by paragraph (b)(2)(i)(A) of this section. If G determines, upon preparing a return, that the taxpayer is eligible to make a contribution to an individual retirement account (IRA), G will ask whether the taxpayer desires to make a contribution to an IRA. G does not ask about IRAs in cases in which the taxpayer is not eligible to make a contribution. G is using tax return information when it asks whether a taxpayer is interested in making a contribution to an IRA because G is basing the inquiry upon knowledge gained from information that the taxpayer furnished in connection with the preparation of the taxpayer's return.

(5) *Disclosure.*—The term *disclosure* means the act of making tax return information known to any person in any manner whatever. To the extent that a taxpayer's use of a hyperlink results in the transmission of tax return information, this transmission of tax return information is a disclosure by the tax return preparer subject to penalty under section 7216 if not authorized by regulation.

(6) *Hyperlink.*—For purposes of section 7216, a hyperlink is a device used to transfer an individual using tax preparation software from a tax return preparer's webpage to a webpage operated by another person without the individual having to separately enter the web address of the destination page.

(7) *Request for consent.*—A request for consent includes any effort by a tax return preparer to obtain the taxpayer's consent to use or disclose the taxpayer's tax return information. The act of supplying a taxpayer with a paper or electronic form that meets the requirements of a

Reg. §301.7216-1(b)(3)(i)(A)

revenue procedure published pursuant to § 301.7216-3(a) is a request for a consent. When a tax return preparer requests a taxpayer's consent, any associated efforts of the tax return preparer, including, but not limited to, verbal or written explanations of the form, are part of the request for consent.

(c) *Gramm-Leach-Bliley Act.*—Any applicable requirements of the Gramm-Leach-Bliley Act, Public Law 106-102 (113 Stat. 1338), do not supersede, alter, or affect the requirements of section 7216 and § § 301.7216-1 through 301.7216-3. Similarly, the requirements of section 7216 and § § 301.7216-1 through 301.7216-3 do not override any requirements or restrictions of the Gramm-Leach-Bliley Act, which are in addition to the requirements or restrictions of section 7216 and § § 301.7216-1 through 301.7216-3.

(d) *Effective/applicability date.*—This section applies to disclosures or uses of tax return information occurring on or after January 1, 2009. [Reg. § 301.7216-1.]

☐ [*T.D. 7310, 3-27-74. Amended by T.D. 9375,* 1-3-2008.]

[Reg. § 301.7216-2]

§ 301.7216-2. Permissible disclosures or uses without consent of the taxpayer.—(a) *Disclosure pursuant to other provisions of the Internal Revenue Code.*—The provisions of section 7216(a) and § 301.7216-1 shall not apply to any disclosure of tax return information if the disclosure is made pursuant to any other provision of the Internal Revenue Code or the regulations thereunder.

(b) *Disclosures to the IRS.*—The provisions of section 7216(a) and § 301.7216-1 shall not apply to any disclosure of tax return information to an officer or employee of the IRS.

(c) *Disclosures or uses for preparation of a taxpayer's return.*—(1) *Updating Taxpayers' Tax Return Preparation Software.*—If a tax return preparer provides software to a taxpayer that is used in connection with the preparation or filing of a tax return, the tax return preparer may use the taxpayer's tax return information to update the taxpayer's software for the purpose of addressing changes in IRS forms, e-file specifications and administrative, regulatory and legislative guidance or to test and ensure the software's technical capabilities without the taxpayer's consent under § 301.7216-3.

(2) *Tax return preparers located within the same firm in the United States.*—If a taxpayer furnishes tax return information to a tax return preparer located within the United States, including any territory or possession of the United States, an officer, employee, or member of a tax return preparer may use the tax return information, or disclose the tax return information to another officer, employee, or member of the same tax return preparer, for the purpose of performing services that assist in the preparation of, or assist in providing auxiliary services in connection with the preparation of, the taxpayer's tax re-

turn. If an officer, employee, or member to whom the tax return information is to be disclosed is located outside of the United States or any territory or possession of the United States, the taxpayer's consent under § 301.7216-3 prior to any disclosure is required.

(3) *Furnishing tax return information to tax return preparers located outside the United States.*— If a taxpayer initially furnishes tax return information to a tax return preparer located outside of the United States or any territory or possession of the United States, an officer, employee, or member of a tax return preparer may use tax return information, or disclose any tax return information to another officer, employee, or member of the same tax return preparer, for the purpose of performing services that assist in the preparation of, or assist in providing auxiliary services in connection with the preparation of, the tax return of a taxpayer by or for whom the information was furnished without the taxpayer's consent under § 301.7216-3.

(4) *Examples.*—The following examples illustrate this paragraph (c):

Example 1. Preparer P provides tax return preparation software to Taxpayer T for T to use in the preparation of its 2009 income tax return. For the 2009 tax year, and using T's tax return information furnished while registering for the software, P would like to update the tax return preparation software that T is using to account for last minute changes made to the tax laws for the 2009 tax year. P is not required to obtain T's consent to update the tax return preparation software. P may perform a software update regardless of whether the software update will affect T's particular return preparation activities.

Example 2. T is a client of Firm, which is a tax return preparer. E, an employee at Firm's State A office, receives tax return information from T for use in preparing T's income tax return. E discloses the tax return information to P, an employee in Firm's State B office; P uses the tax return information to process T's income tax return. Firm is not required to receive T's consent under § 301.7216-3 prior to E's disclosure of T's tax return information to P because the tax return information is disclosed to an employee employed by the same tax return preparer located within the United States.

Example 3. Same facts as *Example 2* except T's tax return information is disclosed to FE who is located in Firm's Country F office. FE uses the tax return information to process T's income tax return. After processing, FE returns the processed tax return information to E in Firm's State A office. Because FE is outside of the United States, Firm is required to obtain T's consent under § 301.7216-3 prior to E's disclosure of T's tax return information to FE.

Example 4. T, Firm's client, is temporarily located in Country F. She initially furnishes her tax return information to employee FE in Firm's Country F office for the purpose of having Firm prepare her U.S. income tax return. FE makes the substantive determinations concerning T's tax liability and forwards T's tax return information to FP, an employee in Firm's Country P office, for the purpose of processing T's tax return information. FP processes the return information and forwards it to Partner at Firm's State A office in the United States for review and delivery to T. Because T initially furnished the tax return information to a tax return preparer outside of the United States, T's prior consent for disclosure or use under § 301.7216-3 was not required. An officer, employee, or member of Firm in the United States may use T's tax return information or disclose the tax return information to another officer, employee, or member of Firm without T's prior consent under § 301.7216-3 as long as any disclosure or use of T's tax return information is within the United States. Firm is required to receive T's consent under § 301.7216-3 prior to any subsequent disclosure of T's tax return information to a tax return preparer located outside of the United States.

(d) *Disclosures to other tax return preparers.*— (1) *Preparer-to-preparer disclosures.*—Except as limited in paragraph (d)(2) of this section, an officer, employee, or member of a tax return preparer may disclose tax return information of a taxpayer to another tax return preparer (other than an officer, employee, or member of the same tax return preparer) located in the United States (including any territory or possession of the United States) for the purpose of preparing or assisting in preparing a tax return, or obtaining or providing auxiliary services in connection with the preparation of any tax return, so long as the services provided are not substantive determinations or advice affecting the tax liability reported by taxpayers. A substantive determination involves an analysis, interpretation, or application of the law. The authorized disclosures permitted under this paragraph (d)(1) include one tax return preparer disclosing tax return information to another tax return preparer for the purpose of having the second tax return preparer transfer that information to, and compute the tax liability on, a tax return of the taxpayer by means of electronic, mechanical, or other form of tax return processing service. The authorized disclosures permitted under this paragraph (d)(1) also include disclosures by a tax return preparer to an Authorized IRS *e-file* Provider for the purpose of electronically filing the return with the IRS. Authorized disclosures also include disclosures by a tax return preparer to a second tax return preparer for the purpose of making information concerning the return available to the taxpayer. This would include, for example, whether the return has been accepted or rejected by the IRS, or the status of the taxpayer's refund. Except as provided in paragraph (c) of this section, a tax return preparer may not disclose tax return information to another tax return preparer for the purpose of the second tax return preparer providing substantive determinations without first receiving the taxpayer's

consent in accordance with the rules under § 301.7216-3.

(2) *Disclosures to contractors.*—A tax return preparer may disclose tax return information to a person under contract with the tax return preparer in connection with the programming, maintenance, repair, testing, or procurement of equipment or software used for purposes of tax return preparation only to the extent necessary for the person to provide the contracted services, and only if the tax return preparer ensures that all individuals who are to receive disclosures of tax return information receive a written notice that informs them of the applicability of sections 6713 and 7216 to them and describes the requirements and penalties of sections 6713 and 7216. Contractors receiving tax return information pursuant to this section are tax return preparers under section 7216 because they are performing auxiliary services in connection with tax return preparation. See § 301.7216-1(b)(2)(i)(B) and (D).

(3) *Examples.*—The following examples illustrate this paragraph (d):

Example 1. E, an employee at Firm's State A office, receives tax return information from T for Firm's use in preparing T's income tax return. E makes substantive determinations and forwards the tax return information to P, an employee at Processor; Processor is located in State B. P places the tax return information on the income tax return and furnishes the finished product to E. E is not required to receive T's prior consent under § 301.7216-3 before disclosing T's tax return information to P because Processor's services are not substantive determinations and the tax return information remained in the United States at Processor's State B office during the entire course of the tax return preparation process.

Example 2. Firm, a tax return preparer, offers income tax return preparation services. Firm's contract with its software provider, Contractor, requires Firm to periodically randomly select certain taxpayers' tax return information solely for the purpose of testing the reliability of the software sold to Firm. Under its agreement with Contractor, Firm discloses tax return information to Contractor's employee, C, who services Firm's contract without providing Contractor or C with a written notice that describes the requirements of and penalties under sections 7216 and 6713. C uses the tax return information solely for quality assurance purposes. Firm's disclosure of tax return information to C was an impermissible disclosure because Firm failed to ensure that C received a written notice that describes the requirements and penalties of sections 7216 and 6713.

Example 3. E, an employee of Firm in State A in the United States, receives tax return information from T for use in preparing T's income tax return. After E enters T's tax return information into Firm's computer, that information is stored on a computer server that is physically located in State A. Firm contracts with Contractor, located in Country F, to prepare its clients' tax returns.

FE, an employee of Contractor, uses a computer in Country F and inputs a password to view T's income tax information stored on the computer server in State A to prepare T's tax return. A computer program permits FE to view T's tax return information, but prohibits FE from downloading or printing out T's tax return information from the computer server. Because Firm is disclosing T's tax return information outside of the United States, Firm is required to obtain T's consent under §301.7216-3 prior to the disclosure to FE. As provided in §301.7216-3(b)(5), however, Firm may not obtain consent to disclose T's social security number (SSN) to a tax return preparer located outside of the United States or any territory or possession of the United States.

Example 4. A, an employee at Firm A, receives tax return information from T for Firm's use in preparing T's income tax return. A forwards the tax return information to B, an employee at another firm, Firm B, to obtain advice on the issue of whether T may claim a deduction for a certain business expense. A is required to receive T's prior consent under §301.7216-3 before disclosing T's tax return information to B because B's services involve a substantive determination affecting the tax liability that T will report.

(e) *Disclosure or use of information in the case of related taxpayers.*—(1) In preparing a tax return of a second taxpayer, a tax return preparer may use, and may disclose to the second taxpayer in the form in which it appears on the return, any tax return information that the tax return preparer obtained from a first taxpayer if—

(i) The second taxpayer is related to the first taxpayer within the meaning of paragraph (e)(2) of this section;

(ii) The first taxpayer's tax interest in the information is not adverse to the second taxpayer's tax interest in the information; and

(iii) The first taxpayer has not expressly prohibited the disclosure or use.

(2) For purposes of paragraph (e)(1)(i) of this section, a taxpayer is related to another taxpayer if they have any one of the following relationships: husband and wife, child and parent, grandchild and grandparent, partner and partnership, trust or estate and beneficiary, trust or estate and fiduciary, corporation and shareholder, or members of a controlled group of corporations as defined in section 1563.

(3) See §301.7216-3 for disclosure or use of tax return information of the taxpayer in preparing the tax return of a second taxpayer when the requirements of this paragraph are not satisfied.

(f) *Disclosure pursuant to an order of a court, or an administrative order, demand, request, summons or subpoena which is issued in the performance of its duties by a Federal or State agency, the United States Congress, a professional association ethics committee or board, or the Public Company Accounting Oversight Board.*—The provisions of section 7216(a) and §301.7216-1 will not apply to any disclosure

of tax return information if the disclosure is made pursuant to any one of the following documents:

(1) The order of any court of record, Federal, State, or local.

(2) A subpoena issued by a grand jury, Federal or State.

(3) A subpoena issued by the United States Congress.

(4) An administrative order, demand, summons or subpoena that is issued in the performance of its duties by—

(i) Any Federal agency as defined in 5 U.S.C. 551(1) and 5 U.S.C. 552(f), or

(ii) A State agency, body, or commission charged under the laws of the State or a political subdivision of the State with the licensing, registration, or regulation of tax return preparers.

(5) A written request from a professional association ethics committee or board investigating the ethical conduct of the tax return preparer.

(6) A written request from the Public Company Accounting Oversight Board in connection with an inspection under section 104 of the Sarbanes-Oxley Act of 2002, 15 U.S.C. 7214, or an investigation under section 105 of such Act, 15 U.S.C. 7215, for use in accordance with such Act.

(g) *Disclosure for use in securing legal advice, Treasury investigations or court proceedings.*—A tax return preparer may disclose tax return information—

(1) To an attorney for purposes of securing legal advice;

(2) To an employee of the Treasury Department for use in connection with any investigation of the tax return preparer (including investigations relating to the tax return preparer in its capacity as a practitioner) conducted by the IRS or the Treasury Department; or

(3) To any officer of a court for use in connection with proceedings involving the tax return preparer (including proceedings involving the tax return preparer in its capacity as a practitioner), or the return preparer's client, before the court or before any grand jury that may be convened by the court.

(h) *Certain disclosures by attorneys and accountants.*—The provisions of section 7216(a) and §301.7216-1 shall not apply to any disclosure of tax return information permitted by this paragraph (h).

(1)(i) A tax return preparer who is lawfully engaged in the practice of law or accountancy and prepares a tax return for a taxpayer may use the taxpayer's tax return information, or disclose the information to another officer, employee or member of the tax return preparer's law or accounting firm, consistent with applicable legal and ethical responsibilities, who may use the tax return information for the purpose of providing other legal or accounting services to the taxpayer. As an example, a lawyer who prepares a tax return for a taxpayer may use the tax return information of the taxpayer for, or in connection with, rendering legal services, including estate planning or administration, or preparation of trial briefs or trust instruments, for the taxpayer or the estate of the taxpayer. In addition, the lawyer who prepared the tax return may disclose the tax return information to another officer, employee or member of the same firm for the purpose of providing other legal services to the taxpayer. As another example, an accountant who prepares a tax return for a taxpayer may use the tax return information, or disclose it to another officer, employee or member of the firm, for use in connection with the preparation of books and records, working papers, or accounting statements or reports for the taxpayer. In the normal course of rendering the legal or accounting services to the taxpayer, the attorney or accountant may make the tax return information available to third parties, including stockholders, management, suppliers, or lenders, consistent with the applicable legal and ethical responsibilities, unless the taxpayer directs otherwise. For rules regarding disclosures outside of the United States, see § 301.7216-2(c) and (d).

(ii) A tax return preparer's law or accounting firm does not include any related or affiliated firms. For example, if law firm A is affiliated with law firm B, officers, employees and members of law firm A must receive a taxpayer's consent under § 301.7216-3 before disclosing the taxpayer's tax return information to an officer, employee or member of law firm B.

(2) A tax return preparer who is lawfully engaged in the practice of law or accountancy and prepares a tax return for a taxpayer may, consistent with the applicable legal and ethical responsibilities, take the tax return information into account, and may act upon it, in the course of performing legal or accounting services for a client other than the taxpayer, or disclose the information to another officer, employee or member of the tax return preparer's law or accounting firm to enable that other officer, employee or member to take the information into account, and act upon it, in the course of performing legal or accounting services for a client other than the taxpayer. This is permissible when the information is, or may be, relevant to the subject matter of the legal or accounting services for the other client, and consideration of the information by those performing the services is necessary for the proper performance of the services. In no event, however, may the tax return information be disclosed to a person who is not an officer, employee or member of the law or accounting firm, unless the disclosure is exempt from the application of section 7216(a) and § 301.7216-1 by reason of another provision of §§ 301.7216-2 or 301.7216-3.

(3) *Examples.*—The application of this paragraph may be illustrated by the following examples:

Example 1. A, a member of an accounting firm, renders an opinion on a financial statement of M Corporation that is part of a registration statement filed with the Securities and Exchange

Commission. After the registration statement is filed, but before its effective date, B, a member of the same accounting firm, prepares an income tax return for N Corporation. In the course of preparing N's income tax return, B discovers that N does business with M and concludes that the information given by N should be considered by A to determine whether the financial statement opined on by A contains an untrue statement of material fact or omits a material fact required to keep the statement from being misleading. B discloses to A the tax return information of N for this purpose. A determines that there is an omission of material fact and that an amended statement should be filed. A so advises M and the Securities and Exchange Commission. A explains that the omission was revealed as a result of confidential information that came to A's attention after the statement was filed, but A does not disclose the identity of the taxpayer or the tax return information itself. Section 7216(a) and § 301.7216-1 do not apply to B's disclosure of N's tax return information to A and A's use of the information in advising M and the Securities and Exchange Commission of the necessity for filing an amended statement. Section 7216(a) and § 301.7216-1 would apply to a disclosure of N's tax return information to M or to the Securities and Exchange Commission unless the disclosure is exempt from the application of section 7216(a) and § 301.7216-1 by reason of another provision of either this section or § 301.7216-3.

Example 2. A, a member of an accounting firm, is conducting an audit of M Corporation, and B, a member of the same accounting firm, prepares an income tax return for D, an officer of M. In the course of preparing the return, B obtains information from D indicating that D, pursuant to an arrangement with a supplier doing business with M, has been receiving from the supplier a percentage of the amounts that the supplier invoices to M. B discloses this information to A who, acting upon it, searches in the course of the audit for indications of a kickback scheme. As a result, A discovers information from audit sources that independently indicate the existence of a kickback scheme. Without revealing the tax return information A has received from B, A brings to the attention of officers of M the audit information indicating the existence of the kickback scheme. Section 7216(a) and § 301.7216-1 do not apply to B's disclosure of D's tax return information to A, A's use of D's information in the course of the audit, and A's disclosure to M of the audit information indicating the existence of the kickback scheme. Section 7216(a) and § 301.7216-1 would apply to a disclosure to M, or to any other person not an employee or member of the accounting firm, of D's tax return information furnished to B.

(i) *Corporate fiduciaries.*—A trust company, trust department of a bank, or other corporate fiduciary that prepares a tax return for a taxpayer for whom it renders fiduciary, investment, or other custodial or management services may, unless the taxpayer directs otherwise—

(1) Disclose or use the taxpayer's tax return information in the ordinary course of rendering such services to or for the taxpayer; or

(2) Make the information available to the taxpayer's attorney, accountant, or investment advisor.

(j) *Disclosure to taxpayer's fiduciary.*—If, after furnishing tax return information to a tax return preparer, the taxpayer dies or becomes incompetent, insolvent, or bankrupt, or the taxpayer's assets are placed in conservatorship or receivership, the tax return preparer may disclose the information to the duly appointed fiduciary of the taxpayer or his estate, or to the duly authorized agent of the fiduciary.

(k) *Disclosure or use of information in preparation or audit of State or local tax returns or assisting a taxpayer with foreign country tax obligations.*—The provisions of paragraphs (c) and (d) of this section shall apply to the disclosure by any tax return preparer of any tax return information in the preparation of, or in connection with the preparation of, any tax return of the taxpayer under the law of any State or political subdivision thereof, of the District of Columbia, of any territory or possession of the United States, or of a country other than the United States. The provisions of section 7216(a) and §301.7216-1 shall not apply to the use by any tax return preparer of any tax return information in the preparation of, or in connection with the preparation of, any tax return of the taxpayer under the law of any State or political subdivision thereof, of the District of Columbia, of any territory or possession of the United States, or of a country other than the United States. The provisions of section 7216(a) and §301.7216-1 shall not apply to the disclosure or use by any tax return preparer of any tax return information in the audit of, or in connection with the audit of, any tax return of the taxpayer under the law of any State or political subdivision thereof, the District of Columbia, or any territory or possession of the United States.

(l) *Payment for tax preparation services.*—A tax return preparer may use and disclose, without the taxpayer's written consent, tax return information that the taxpayer provides to the tax return preparer to pay for tax preparation services to the extent necessary to process or collect the payment. For example, if the taxpayer gives the tax return preparer a credit card to pay for tax preparation services, the tax return preparer may disclose the taxpayer's name, credit card number, credit card expiration date, and amount due for tax preparation services to the credit card company, as necessary, to process the payment. Any tax return information that the taxpayer did not give the tax return preparer for the purpose of making payment for tax preparation services may not be used or disclosed by the tax return preparer without the taxpayer's prior written consent, unless otherwise permitted under another provision of this section.

(m) *Retention of records.*—A tax return preparer may retain tax return information of a taxpayer, including copies of tax returns, in paper or electronic format, prepared on the basis of the tax return information, and may use the information in connection with the preparation of other tax returns of the taxpayer or in connection with an examination by the Internal Revenue Service of any tax return or subsequent tax litigation relating to the tax return. The provisions of paragraph (n) of this section regarding the transfer of a taxpayer list also apply to the transfer of any records and related papers to which this paragraph applies.

(n) *Lists for solicitation of tax return preparation business.*—(1) A tax return preparer, other than a person who is a tax return preparer solely because the person provides auxiliary services as defined in §301.7216-1(b)(2)(iii), may compile and maintain a separate list containing solely items of tax return information. The following items of tax return information are permissible: the names, mailing addresses, e-mail addresses, phone numbers, taxpayer entity classification (including "individual" or the specific type of business entity), and income tax return form number (for example, Form 1040-EZ) of taxpayers whose tax returns the tax return preparer has prepared or processed. The Internal Revenue Service may issue guidance, by publication in the Internal Revenue Bulletin (see §601.601(d)(2)(ii)(b) of this chapter), describing other types of information that may be included in a list compiled and maintained pursuant to this paragraph. This list may be used by the compiler solely to contact the taxpayers on the list for the purpose of providing tax information and general business or economic information or analysis for educational purposes, or soliciting additional tax return preparation services. The list may not be used to solicit any service or product other than tax return preparation services. The compiler of the list may not transfer the taxpayer list, or any part thereof, to any other person unless the transfer takes place in conjunction with the sale or other disposition of the compiler's tax return preparation business. Due diligence conducted prior to a proposed sale of a compiler's tax return preparation business is in conjunction with the sale or other disposition of a compiler's tax return preparation business and will not constitute a transfer of the list if conducted pursuant to a written agreement that requires confidentiality of the tax return information disclosed and expressly prohibits the further disclosure or use of the tax return information for any purpose other than that related to the purchase of the tax return preparation business. A person who acquires a taxpayer list, or a part thereof, in conjunction with a sale or other disposition of a tax return preparation business falls under the provisions of this paragraph with respect to the list. The term *list*, as used in this paragraph (n), includes any record or system whereby the types of information expressly authorized for inclusion in a taxpayer list pursuant to the terms of this paragraph (n) are retained. The provisions of this paragraph (n) also apply to the transfer of any records and related papers to which this paragraph (n) applies.

(2) *Examples.*—The following examples illustrate this paragraph (n):

Example 1. Preparer A is a tax return preparer as defined by §301.7216-1(b)(2)(i)(A). Preparer A's office is located in southeast Pennsylvania, and Preparer A prepares federal and state income tax returns for taxpayers who live in Pennsylvania, New Jersey, Maryland, and Delaware. Preparer A maintains a list of taxpayer clients containing the information allowed by this paragraph (n). Preparer A provides quarterly state income tax information updates to his individual taxpayer clients by e-mail or U.S. mail. To ensure that his clients only receive the information updates that are relevant to them, Preparer A uses his list to direct his outreach efforts towards the relevant clients by searching his list to filter it by zip code and income tax return form number (Form 1040 and corresponding state income tax return form number). Preparer A may use the list information in this manner without taxpayer consent because he is providing tax information for educational or informational purposes and is targeting clients based solely upon tax return information that is authorized by this paragraph (n) (by zip code, which is part of a taxpayer's address, and by income tax return form number). Without taxpayer consent, Preparer A also may deliver this information to his clients by e-mail, U.S. mail, or other method of delivery that uses only information authorized by this paragraph (n).

Example 2. Preparer B is a tax return preparer as defined by §301.7216-1(b)(2)(i)(A). Preparer B maintains a list of taxpayer clients containing the information allowed by this paragraph (n). Preparer B provides monthly federal income tax information updates in the form of a newsletter to all of her taxpayer clients by e-mail or U.S. mail. When Preparer B hires a new employee who participates or assists in tax return preparation, she announces that hire in the newsletter for the month that follows the hiring. Each announcement includes a photograph of the new employee, the employee's name, the employee's telephone number, a brief listing of the employee's qualifications, and a brief listing of the employee's employment responsibilities. Preparer B may use the tax return information described in this paragraph (n) in this manner without taxpayer consent because she is providing tax information for educational or informational purposes to provide general federal income tax information updates. Preparer B may include the new employee announcements in the form described because this is considered tax information for informational purposes, provided the announcements do not contain solicitations for non-tax return preparation services. Without taxpayer consent, Preparer B also may deliver this information to her clients by e-mail,

U.S. mail, or other method of delivery that uses only information authorized by this paragraph (n).

(o) *Producing statistical information in connection with tax return preparation business.*—(1) A tax return preparer may use tax return information, subject to the limitations specified in this paragraph (o), to produce a statistical compilation of data described in §301.7216-1(b)(3)(i)(B). The purpose for and disclosure or use of the statistical compilation requiring data acquired during the tax return preparation process must relate directly to the internal management or support of the tax return preparer's tax return preparation business, or to bona fide research or public policy discussions concerning state or federal taxation. A tax return preparer may not disclose the statistical compilation, or any part thereof, to any other person unless disclosure of the statistical compilation is anonymous as to taxpayer identity, does not disclose an aggregate figure containing data from fewer than ten tax returns, and is in direct support of the tax return preparer's tax return preparation business or of bona fide research or public policy discussions concerning state or federal taxation. A statistical compilation is anonymous as to taxpayer identity if it is in a form which cannot be associated with, or otherwise identify, directly or indirectly, a particular taxpayer. For purposes of this paragraph, marketing and advertising is in direct support of the tax return preparer's tax return preparation business provided the marketing and advertising is not false, misleading, or unduly influential. This paragraph, however, does not authorize the disclosure or use in marketing or advertising of any statistical compilations, or part thereof, that identify dollar amounts of refunds, credits, or deductions associated with tax returns, or percentages relating thereto, whether or not the data are statistical, averaged, aggregated, or anonymous. Disclosures made in support of fundraising activities conducted by volunteer return preparation programs and other organizations described in section 501(c) of the Internal Revenue Code (Code) in direct support of their tax return preparation businesses are not marketing and advertising under this paragraph. A tax return preparer who produces a statistical compilation of data described in §301.7216-1(b)(3)(i)(B) may disclose the compilation to comply with financial accounting or regulatory reporting requirements whether or not the statistical compilation is anonymous as to taxpayer identity or discloses an aggregate figure containing data from fewer than ten tax returns.

(2) A tax return preparer may not sell or exchange for value a statistical compilation of data described in §301.7216-1(b)(3)(i)(B), in whole or in part, except in conjunction with the transfer of assets made pursuant to the sale or other disposition of the tax return preparer's tax return preparation business. The provisions of paragraph (n) of this section regarding the transfer of a taxpayer list also apply to the transfer of any statistical compilations of data to which this

paragraph applies. A person who acquires a statistical compilation, or a part thereof, pursuant to the operation of this paragraph (o) or in conjunction with a sale or other disposition of a tax return preparation business is subject to the provisions of this paragraph with respect to the compilation.

(3) *Examples.*—The following examples illustrate this paragraph (o):

Example 1. Preparer A is a tax return preparer as defined by § 301.7216-1(b)(2)(i)(A). In 2009, A used tax return information to produce a statistical compilation of data for both internal management purposes and to support A's tax return preparation business. The statistical compilation included an aggregate figure containing the information that A prepared 32 S corporation tax returns in 2009. In 2010, A decided to embark upon a new marketing campaign emphasizing its experience preparing small business tax returns. In the campaign, A discloses the aggregate figure containing the number of S corporation tax returns prepared in 2009. A's disclosure does not include any information that can be associated with or identify any specific taxpayers. A may disclose the anonymous statistical compilation without taxpayer consent.

Example 2. Preparer B is a tax return preparer as defined by § 301.7216-1(b)(2)(i)(A). In 2010, in support of B's tax return preparation business, B wants to advertise that the average tax refund obtained for its clients in 2009 was $2,800. B may not disclose this information because it contains a statistical compilation reflecting average refund amounts.

Example 3. Preparer C is a tax return preparer as defined by § 301.7216-1(b)(2)(i)(A) and is a volunteer income tax assistance program. In 2010, in support of C's tax return preparation business, C submits a grant application to a charitable foundation to fund C's operations providing free tax return preparation services to low- and moderate-income families. In support of C's request, C includes anonymous statistical data consisting of aggregated figures containing data from ten or more tax returns showing that, in 2009, C provided services to 500 taxpayers, that 95 percent of the taxpayer population served by C received the Earned Income Tax Credit (EITC), and that the average amount of the EITC received was $3,300. Despite the fact that this information constitutes an average credit amount, C may disclose the information to the charitable foundation because disclosures made in support of fundraising activities conducted by volunteer income tax assistance programs and other organizations described in section 501(c) of the Code in direct support of their tax return preparation business are not considered marketing and advertising for purposes of § 301.7216-2(o)(1).

Example 4. Preparer D is a tax return preparer as defined by § 301.7216-1(b)(2)(i)(A). In December 2009, D produced an anonymous statistical compilation of tax return information obtained during the 2009 filing season. In 2010, D wants to disclose portions of the anonymous statistical compilation from aggregated figures containing data from ten or more tax returns in connection with the marketing of its financial advisory and asset planning services. D is required to receive taxpayer consent under § 301.7216-3 before disclosing the tax return information contained in the anonymous statistical compilation because the disclosure is not being made in support of D's tax return preparation business.

(p) *Disclosure or use of information for quality, peer, or conflict reviews.*—(1) The provisions of section 7216(a) and § 301.7216-1 shall not apply to any disclosure for the purpose of a quality or peer review to the extent necessary to accomplish the review. A quality or peer review is a review that is undertaken to evaluate, monitor, and improve the quality and accuracy of a tax return preparer's tax preparation, accounting, or auditing services. A quality or peer review may be conducted only by attorneys, certified public accountants, enrolled agents, and enrolled actuaries who are eligible to practice before the Internal Revenue Service. See Department of the Treasury Circular 230, 31 CFR part 10. Tax return information may also be disclosed to persons who provide administrative or support services to an individual who is conducting a quality or peer review under this paragraph (p), but only to the extent necessary for the reviewer to conduct the review. Tax return information gathered in conducting a review may be used only for purposes of a review. No tax return information identifying a taxpayer may be disclosed in any evaluative reports or recommendations that may be accessible to any person other than the reviewer or the tax return preparer being reviewed. The tax return preparer being reviewed will maintain a record of the review, including the information reviewed and the identity of the persons conducting the review. After completion of the review, no documents containing information that may identify any taxpayer by name or identification number may be retained by a reviewer or by the reviewer's administrative or support personnel.

(2) The provisions of section 7216(a) and § 301.7216-1 shall not apply to any disclosure necessary to accomplish a conflict review. A conflict review is a review undertaken to comply with requirements established by any federal, state, or local law, agency, board or commission, or by a professional association ethics committee or board, to either identify, evaluate, or monitor actual or potential legal and ethical conflicts of interest that may arise when a tax return preparer is employed or acquired by another tax return preparer, or to identify, evaluate, or monitor actual or potential legal and ethical conflicts of interest that may arise when a tax return preparer is considering engaging a new client. Tax return information gathered in conducting a conflict review may be used only for purposes of a conflict review. No tax return information identifying a taxpayer may be disclosed in any

evaluative reports or recommendations that may be accessible to any person other than those responsible for identifying, evaluating, or monitoring legal and ethical conflicts of interest. No tax return information identifying a taxpayer may be disclosed outside of the United States or a territory or possession of the United States unless the disclosing and receiving tax return preparers have procedures in place that are consistent with good business practices and designed to maintain the confidentiality of the disclosed tax return information.

(3) Any person (including administrative and support personnel) receiving tax return information in connection with a quality, peer, or conflict review is a tax return preparer for purposes of sections 7216(a) and 6713(a). Tax return information disclosed and used for purposes of a quality, peer, or conflict review shall not be disclosed or used for any other purpose.

(q) *Disclosure to report the commission of a crime.*—The provisions of section 7216(a) and § 301.7216-1 shall not apply to the disclosure of any tax return information to the proper Federal, State, or local official in order, and to the extent necessary, to inform the official of activities that may constitute, or may have constituted, a violation of any criminal law or to assist the official in investigating or prosecuting a violation of criminal law. A disclosure made in the bona fide but mistaken belief that the activities constituted a violation of criminal law is not subject to section 7216(a) and § 301.7216-1.

(r) *Disclosure of tax return information due to a tax return preparer's incapacity or death.*—In the event of incapacity or death of a tax return preparer, disclosure of tax return information may be made for the purpose of assisting the tax return preparer or his legal representative (or the representative of a deceased tax return preparer's estate) in operating the business. Any person receiving tax return information under the provisions of this paragraph (r) is a tax return preparer for purposes of sections 7216(a) and 6713(a).

(s) *Effective/applicability date.*—Paragraphs (n), (o), and (p) of this section apply to disclosures or uses of tax return information occurring on or after December 28, 2012. All other paragraphs of this section apply to disclosures or uses of tax return information occurring on or after January 1, 2009. [Reg. § 301.7216-2.]

☐ [*T.D.* 7310, 3-27-74. *Amended by T.D.* 7676, 2-20-80; *T.D.* 7708, 7-24-80; *T.D.* 7498, 3-7-84; *T.D.* 8383, 12-26-91; *T.D.* 8427, 8-17-92; *T.D.* 9375, 1-3-2008; *T.D.* 9478, 12-29-2009 *and T.D.* 9608, 12-26-2012.]

[Reg. § 301.7216-3]

§ 301.7216-3. Disclosure or use permitted only with the taxpayer's consent..—(a) *In general.*—(1) *Taxpayer consent.*—Unless section 7216 or § 301.7216-2 specifically authorizes the disclosure or use of tax return information, a tax return preparer may not disclose or use a taxpayer's tax

return information prior to obtaining a written consent from the taxpayer, as described in this section. A tax return preparer may disclose or use tax return information as the taxpayer directs as long as the preparer obtains a written consent from the taxpayer as provided in this section. The consent must be knowing and voluntary. Except as provided in paragraph (a)(2) of this section, conditioning the provision of any services on the taxpayer's furnishing consent will make the consent involuntary, and the consent will not satisfy the requirements of this section.

(2) *Taxpayer consent to a tax return preparer furnishing tax return information to another tax return preparer.*—(i) A tax return preparer may condition its provision of preparation services upon a taxpayer's consenting to disclosure of the taxpayer's tax return information to another tax return preparer for the purpose of performing services that assist in the preparation of, or provide auxiliary services in connection with the preparation of, the tax return of the taxpayer.

(ii) *Example.*—The application of this paragraph (a)(2) may be illustrated by the following example:

Example. Preparer P, who is located within the United States, is retained by Company C to provide tax return preparation services for employees of Company C. An employee of Company C, Employee E, works for C outside of the United States. To provide tax return preparation services for E, P requires the assistance of and needs to disclose E's tax return information to a tax return preparer who works for P's affiliate located in the country where E works. P may condition its provision of tax return preparation services upon E consenting to the disclosure of E's tax return information to the tax return preparer in the country where E works.

(3) *The form and contents of taxpayer consents.*—(i) *In general.*—All consents to disclose or use tax return information must satisfy the following requirements—

(A) A taxpayer's consent to a tax return preparer's disclosure or use of tax return information must include the name of the tax return preparer and the name of the taxpayer.

(B) If a taxpayer consents to a disclosure of tax return information, the consent must identify the intended purpose of the disclosure. Except as provided in § 301.7216-3(a)(3)(iii), if a taxpayer consents to a disclosure of tax return information, the consent must also identify the specific recipient (or recipients) of the tax return information. If the taxpayer consents to use of tax return information, the consent must describe the particular use authorized. For example, if the tax return preparer intends to use tax return information to generate solicitations for products or services other than tax return preparation, the consent must identify each specific type of product or service for which the tax return preparer may solicit use of the tax return information. Examples of products or services that must be identified include, but are not limited to, balance due loans, mortgage loans, mutual funds, individual retirement accounts, and life insurance.

(C) The consent must specify the tax return information to be disclosed or used by the return preparer.

(D) If a tax return preparer to whom the tax return information is to be disclosed is located outside of the United States, the taxpayer's consent under § 301.7216-3 prior to any disclosure is required. See § 301.7216-2(c) and (d).

(E) A consent to disclose or use tax return information must be signed and dated by the taxpayer.

(ii) *The form and contents of taxpayer consents with respect to taxpayers filing a return in the Form 1040 series - guidance describing additional requirements for taxpayer consents with respect to Form 1040 series filers.*—The Secretary may issue guidance, by publication in the Internal Revenue Bulletin (see § 601.601(d)(2)(ii)(b) of this chapter), describing additional requirements for tax return preparers regarding the format and content of consents to disclose and use tax return information with respect to taxpayers filing a return in the Form 1040 series, *e.g.*, Form 1040, Form 1040NR, Form 1040A, or Form 1040EZ.

(iii) *The form and contents of taxpayer consents with respect to all other taxpayers.*—A consent to disclose or use tax return information with respect to a taxpayer not filing a return in the Form 1040 series may be in any format, including an engagement letter to a client, as long as the consent complies with the requirements of § 301.7216-3(a)(3)(i). Additionally, the requirements of § 301.7216-3(c)(1) are inapplicable to consents to disclose or use tax return information with respect to taxpayers not filing a return in the Form 1040 series. Solely for purposes of a consent issued under § 301.7216-3(a)(3)(iii), in lieu of identifying specific recipients of an intended disclosure under § 301.7216-3(a)(3)(i)(B), a consent may allow disclosure to a descriptive class of entities engaged by a taxpayer or the taxpayer's affiliate for purposes of services in connection with the preparation of tax returns, audited financial statements, or other financial statements or financial information as required by a government authority, municipality or regulatory body.

(iv) *Examples.*—The application of § 301.7216-3(a)(3)(iii) may be illustrated by the following examples:

Example 1. Consistent with applicable legal and ethical responsibilities, Preparer Z sends its client, a corporation, Taxpayer C, an engagement letter. Part of the engagement letter requests the consent of Taxpayer C for the purpose of disclosing tax return information to an investment banking firm in securing long term financing for Taxpayer C. The engagement letter includes language and information that meets the requirements of § 301.7216-3(a)(3)(i), including: (I) Preparer Z's name, Taxpayer C's name, and a signature and date line for Taxpayer C; and (II) a statement that "Taxpayer C authorizes Preparer Z to disclose the portions of Taxpayer C's 2009 tax return information to the firm retained by Taxpayer C necessary for the purposes of assisting Taxpayer C secure long term financing." The engagement letter satisfies the requirements of § 301.7216-3(a)(3) for the disclosure of the information provided therein for the specific purpose stated.

Example 2. Consistent with applicable legal and ethical responsibilities, Preparer N sends its client, a corporation, Taxpayer D, an engagement letter. Part of the engagement letter requests the consent of Taxpayer D for the purpose of disclosing tax return information to Preparer N's affiliated firms located outside of the United States for the purposes of preparation of Taxpayer D's 2009 tax return. The engagement letter includes language and information that meets the requirements of § 301.7216-3(a)(3)(i), including: (I) Preparer N's name, Taxpayer D's name, and a signature and date line for Taxpayer D; (II) a statement that "Taxpayer D authorizes Preparer N to disclose Taxpayer D's 2009 tax return information to Preparer N's affiliates located outside of the United States for the purposes of assisting Preparer N prepare Taxpayer D's 2009 tax return"; and (III) a statement that, in providing consent, Taxpayer D acknowledges that its tax return information for 2009 will be disclosed to tax return preparers located abroad. The engagement letter satisfies the requirements of § 301.7216-3(a)(3) for the disclosure of the information provided therein for the specific purpose stated.

(b) *Timing requirements and limitations.*—(1) *No retroactive consent.*—A taxpayer must provide written consent before a tax return preparer discloses or uses the taxpayer's tax return information.

(2) *Time limitations on requesting consent in solicitation context.*—A tax return preparer may not request a taxpayer's consent to disclose or use tax return information for purposes of solicitation of business unrelated to tax return preparation after the tax return preparer provides a completed tax return to the taxpayer for signature.

(3) *No requests for consent after an unsuccessful request.*—With regard to tax return information for each income tax return that a tax return preparer prepares, if a taxpayer declines a request for consent to the disclosure or use of tax return information for purposes of solicitation of business unrelated to tax return preparation, the tax return preparer may not solicit from the taxpayer another consent for a purpose substantially similar to that of the rejected request.

(4) *No consent to the disclosure of a taxpayer's social security number to a return preparer outside of the United States with respect to a taxpayer filing a return in the Form 1040 Series.*—(i) *In general.*—

Except as provided in paragraph (b)(4)(ii) of this section, a tax return preparer located within the United States, including any territory or possession of the United States, may not obtain consent to disclose the taxpayer's social security number (SSN) with respect to a taxpayer filing a return in the Form 1040 Series, for example, Form 1040, Form 1040NR, Form 1040A, or Form 1040EZ, to a tax return preparer located outside of the United States or any territory or possession of the United States. Thus, if a tax return preparer located within the United States (including any territory or possession of the United States) obtains consent from an individual taxpayer to disclose tax return information to another tax return preparer located outside of the United States, as provided under §§ 301.7216-2(c) and 301.7216-2(d), the tax return preparer located in the United States may not disclose the taxpayer's SSN, and the tax return preparer must redact or otherwise mask the taxpayer's SSN before the tax return information is disclosed outside of the United States. If a tax return preparer located within the United States initially receives or obtains a taxpayer's SSN from another tax return preparer located outside of the United States, however, the tax return preparer within the United States may, without consent, retransmit the taxpayer's SSN to the tax return preparer located outside the United States that initially provided the SSN to the tax return preparer located within the United States. For purposes of this section, a tax return preparer located outside of the United States does not include a tax return preparer who is continuously and regularly employed in the United States or any territory or possession of the United States and who is in a temporary travel status outside of the United States.

(ii) *Exception.*—A tax return preparer located within the United States, including any territory or possession of the United States, may obtain consent to disclose the taxpayer's SSN to a tax return preparer located outside of the United States or any territory or possession of the United States only if the tax return preparer within the United States discloses the SSN to a tax return preparer outside of the United States through the use of an adequate data protection safeguard as defined by the Secretary in guidance published in the Internal Revenue Bulletin (see § 601.601(d)(2)(ii)(b) of this chapter) and verifies the maintenance of the adequate data pro-

tection safeguards in the request for the taxpayer's consent pursuant to the specifications described by the Secretary in guidance published in the Internal Revenue Bulletin.

(5) *Duration of consent.*—A consent document may specify the duration of the taxpayer's consent to the disclosure or use of tax return information. If a consent agreed to by the taxpayer does not specify the duration of the consent, the consent to the disclosure or use of tax return information will be effective for a period of one year from the date the taxpayer signed the consent.

(c) *Special rules.*—(1) *Multiple disclosures within a single consent form or multiple uses within a single consent form.*—A taxpayer may consent to multiple uses within the same written document, or multiple disclosures within the same written document. A single written document, however, cannot authorize both uses and disclosures; rather one written document must authorize the uses and another separate written document must authorize the disclosures. Furthermore, a consent that authorizes multiple disclosures or multiple uses must specifically and separately identify each disclosure or use. See § 301.7216-3(a)(3)(iii) for an exception to this rule for certain taxpayers.

(2) *Disclosure of entire return.*—A consent may authorize the disclosure of all information contained within a return. A consent authorizing the disclosure of an entire return must provide that the taxpayer has the ability to request a more limited disclosure of tax return information as the taxpayer may direct.

(3) *Copy of consent must be provided to taxpayer.*—The tax return preparer must provide a copy of the executed consent to the taxpayer at the time of execution. The requirements of this paragraph (c)(3) may also be satisfied by giving the taxpayer the opportunity, at the time of executing the consent, to print the completed consent or save it in electronic form.

(d) *Effective/applicability date.*—This section applies to disclosures or uses of tax return information occurring on or after January 1, 2009. [Reg. § 301.7216-3.]

☐ [*T.D. 7310, 3-27-74. Amended by T.D. 9375, 1-3-2008; T.D. 9409, 7-1-2008 and T.D. 9437, 12-15-2008.*]

Penalties Applicable to Certain Taxes

[Reg. § 301.7231-1]

§ 301.7231-1. Failure to obtain license for collection of foreign items.—For provisions relating to the obtaining of a license for the collection of foreign items, see section 7001 and § 301.7001-1. [Reg. § 301.7231-1.]

☐ [*T.D. 6498, 10-24-60.*]

[Reg. § 44.7262-1]

§ 44.7262-1. Failure to pay special tax.—Any person liable for the special tax who does any act which makes him liable for such tax, without having paid the tax, is, besides being liable for the tax, subject to a fine of not less than $1,000 and not more than $5,000. [Reg. § 44.7262-1.]

☐ [*T.D. 6370.*]

OTHER OFFENSES

[Reg. § 301.7269-1]

§ 301.7269-1. Failure to produce records.— Whoever fails to comply with any duty imposed upon him by section 6018, 6036 (in the case of an executor), or 6075(a), or, having in his possession or control any record, file, or paper, containing or supposed to contain any information concerning the estate or the decedent, or, having in his possession or control any property comprised in the gross estate of the decedent, fails to exhibit the same upon request of any officer or employee of the Internal Revenue Service who desires to examine the same in the performance of his duties under chapter 11 of the Code (relating to estate taxes) shall be liable to a penalty of not exceeding $500, to be recovered with costs of suit, in a civil action in the name of the United States. [Reg. § 301.7269-1.]

☐ [*T.D.* 6498, 10-24-60.]

[Reg. § 301.7272-1]

§ 301.7272-1. Penalty for failure to register.— (a) Any person who fails to register with the district director as required by the Code or by regulations issued thereunder shall be liable to a penalty of $50 except that on and after September 3, 1958, this section shall not apply to persons required to register under subtitle E of the Code, or persons engaging in a trade or business on which a special tax is imposed by such subtitle.

(b) For provisions relating to registration under sections 4101, 4412, 4455, 4722, 4753, and 4804(d), see the regulations relating to the particular tax. For regulations under section 7011, see § 301.7011-1. [Reg. § 301.7272-1.]

☐ [*T.D.* 6498, 10-24-60.]

FORFEITURES
Provisions Common to Forfeitures

[Reg. § 301.7304-1]

§ 301.7304-1. Penalty for fraudulently claiming drawback.—Whenever any person fraudulently claims or seeks to obtain an allowance of drawback on goods, wares, or merchandise on which no internal tax shall have been paid, or fraudulently claims any greater allowance of drawback than the tax actually paid, he shall forfeit triple the amount wrongfully or fraudulently claimed or sought to be obtained, or the sum of $500, at the election of the district director. [Reg. § 301.7304-1.]

[Reg. § 301.7321-1]

§ 301.7321-1. Seizure of property.—Any property subject to forfeiture to the United States under any provision of the Code may be seized by the district director or assistant regional commissioner(alcohol, tobacco, and firearms). Upon seizure of property by the district director he shall notify the assistant regional commissioner (alcohol, tobacco, and firearms) for the region wherein the district is located who will take charge of the property and arrange for its disposal or retention under the provisions of law and regulations applicable thereto. [Reg. § 301.7321-1.]

☐ [*T.D.* 6498, 10-24-60. *Amended by T.D.* 7188, 6-28-72.]

[Reg. § 301.7322-1]

§ 301.7322-1. Delivery of seized property to United States marshal.—Any forfeitable property which may be seized under the provisions of the Code may, at the option of the assistant regional commissioner (alcohol, tobacco, and firearms), be delivered to the United States marshal of the judicial district wherein the property was seized, and remain in the care and custody and under the control of such marshal, pending the disposal thereof as provided by law. [Reg. § 301.7322-1.]

☐ [*T.D.* 7188, 6-28-72.]

[Reg. § 301.7324-1]

§ 301.7324-1. Special disposition of perishable goods.—For regulations relating to the disposal of perishable goods, see § 172.30 of this chapter (Disposition of Seized Personal Property). [Reg. § 301.7324-1.]

☐ [*T.D.* 6498, 10-24-60.]

[Reg. § 301.7325-1]

§ 301.7325-1. Personal property valued at $2,500 or less.—For regulations relating to the forfeiture of personal property valued at $2,500 or less, see Part 172 of this chapter (Disposition of Seized Personal Property). [Reg. § 301.7325-1.]

☐ [*T.D.* 6498, 10-24-60.]

Judiciary Proceedings
CIVIL ACTIONS BY THE UNITED STATES

See p. 20,601 for regulations not amended to reflect law changes

[Reg. § 301.7401-1]

§ 301.7401-1. Authorization.—(a) *In general.*— No civil action for the collection or recovery of taxes, or of any fine, penalty, or forfeiture, shall be commenced unless the Commissioner (or the Director, Alcohol, Tobacco and Firearms Division, with respect to the provisions of subtitle E of the Code), or the Chief Counsel for the Internal Revenue Service or his delegate authorizes or sanctions the proceedings and the Attorney General or his delegate directs that the action be commenced.

Reg. § 301.7401-1(a)

(b) *Property held by banks.*—The Commissioner shall not authorize or sanction any civil action for the collection or recovery of taxes, or of any fine, penalty, or forfeiture, from any deposits held in a foreign office of a bank engaged in the banking business in the United States or a possession of the United States unless the Commissioner believes—

(1) That the taxpayer is within the jurisdiction of a United States court at the time the civil action is authorized or sanctioned and that the bank is in possession of (or obligated with respect to) deposits of the taxpayer in an office of the bank outside the United States or a possession of the United States; or

(2) That the taxpayer is not within the jurisdiction of a United States court at the time the civil action is authorized or sanctioned, that the bank is in possession of (or obligated with respect to) deposits of the taxpayer in an office outside the United States or a possession of the United States, and that such deposits consist, in whole or in part, of funds transferred from the United States or a possession of the United States in order to hinder or delay the collection of a tax imposed by the Code.

For purposes of this paragraph, the term "possession of the United States" includes Guam, the Midway Islands, the Panama Canal Zone, the Commonwealth of Puerto Rico, American Samoa, the Virgin Islands, and Wake Island. [Reg. § 301.7401-1.]

☐ [*T.D.* 6498, 10-24-60. *Amended by T.D.* 6746, 7-20-64; *T.D.* 6902, 12-13-66 *and T.D.* 7188, 6-28-72.]

[Reg. § 301.7403-1]

§ 301.7403-1. Action to enforce lien or to subject property to payment of tax.—(a) *Civil actions.*—In any case where there has been a refusal or neglect to pay any tax, or to discharge any liability in respect thereof, whether or not levy has been made, the Attorney General or his delegate, at the request of the Commissioner (or the Director, Bureau of Alcohol, Tobacco, and Firearms, or the Chief Counsel for the Bureau, with respect to the provisions of subtitle E of the Code), or the Chief Counsel for the Internal Revenue Service or his delegate, may direct a civil action to be filed in a district court of the United States to enforce the lien of the United States under the Code with respect to such tax or liability or to subject any property, of whatever nature, of the delinquent, or in which he has any right, title or interest, to the payment of such tax or liability. In any such proceeding, at the instance of the United States, the court may appoint a receiver to enforce the lien, or, upon certification by the Commissioner or the Chief Counsel for the Internal Revenue Service during the pendency of such proceedings that it is in the public interest, may appoint a receiver with all the powers of a receiver in equity.

(b) *Bid by the United States.*—If property is sold to satisfy a first lien held by the United States, the United States may bid at the sale a sum which does not exceed the amount of its lien and the expenses of the sale. See also 31 U.S.C. 195. [Reg. § 301.7403-1.]

☐ [*T.D.* 6498, 10-24-60. *Amended by T.D.* 6902, 12-13-66 *and T.D.* 7305, 3-14-74.]

[Reg. § 301.7404-1]

§ 301.7404-1. Authority to bring civil action for estate taxes.—(a) If the estate tax imposed by chapter 11 of the Code is not paid on or before the last date prescribed for payment, the district director shall proceed to collect the tax under the provisions of general law; or appropriate proceedings in the name of the United States may be commenced in any court having jurisdiction to subject the property of the decedent to be sold under the judgment or decree of the court.

(b) The remedy by action provided in section 7404 is not exclusive. The district director may proceed to collect the tax by levy, as provided in section 6331, on any or all property or rights to property of the estate, or collection may be enforced by an appropriate action against the executor, certain transferees, trustees, and beneficiaries for their personal liability. See § 20.2002-1 of this chapter (Estate Tax Regulations). [Reg. § 301.7404-1.]

☐ [*T.D.* 6498, 10-24-60.]

[Reg. § 301.7406-1]

§ 301.7406-1. Disposition of judgments and moneys received.—All judgments and moneys recovered or received for taxes, costs, forfeitures, and penalties shall be paid to the district director as collections of internal revenue taxes. [Reg. § 301.7406-1.]

☐ [*T.D.* 6498, 10-24-60.]

[Reg. § 301.7409-1]

§ 301.7409-1. Action to enjoin flagrant political expenditures of section 501(c)(3) organizations.—(a) *Letter to organization.*—When the Assistant Commissioner (Employee Plans and Exempt Organizations) concludes that a section 501(c)(3) organization has engaged in flagrant political intervention and is likely to continue to engage in political intervention that involves political expenditures, the Assistant Commissioner (Employee Plans and Exempt Organizations) shall send a letter to the organization providing it with the facts based on which the Service believes that the organization has been engaging in flagrant political intervention and is likely to continue to engage in political intervention that involves political expenditures. The organization will have 10 calendar days after the letter is sent to respond by establishing that it will immediately cease engaging in political intervention, or by providing the Service with sufficient information to refute the Service's evidence that it has been engaged in flagrant political intervention. The Internal Revenue Service will not proceed to seek an injunction under section 7409 until after the close of this 10-day response period.

(b) *Determination by Commissioner.*—If the organization does not respond within 10 calendar days to the letter under paragraph (a) of this section in a manner sufficient to dissuade the Assistant Commissioner (Employee Plans and Exempt Organizations) of the need for an injunction, the file will be forwarded to the Commissioner of Internal Revenue. The Commissioner of Internal Revenue will personally determine whether to forward to the Department of Justice a recommendation that it immediately bring an action to enjoin the organization from making further political expenditures. The Commissioner may also recommend that the court action include any other action that is appropriate in ensuring that the assets of the section 501(c)(3) organization are preserved for section 501(c)(3) purposes. The authority of the Commissioner to make the determinations described in this paragraph may not be delegated to any other persons.

(c) *Flagrant political intervention.*—For purposes of this section, *flagrant political intervention* is defined as participation in, or intervention in (including the publication and distribution of statements), any political campaign by a section 501(c)(3) organization on behalf of (or in opposition to) any candidate for public office in violation of the prohibition on such participation or intervention in section 501(c)(3) and the regulations thereunder if the participation or intervention is flagrant.

(d) *Effective date.*—This section is effective December 5, 1995. [Reg. § 301.7409-1.]

☐ [T.D. 8628, 12-4-95.]

PROCEEDINGS BY TAXPAYERS AND THIRD PARTIES

[Reg. § 301.7422-1]

§ 301.7422-1. Special rules for certain excise taxes imposed by chapter 42 or 43.—(a) *Finality of refund proceeding.*—For purposes of sections 4941, 4942, 4943, 4944, 4945, 4951, 4952, 4955, 4958, 4961, 4963, 4971, and 4975, and the regulations thereunder, a decision in a suit for refund instituted under the provisions of this section shall be final—

(1) Upon the expiration of the time allowed for filing a notice of appeal from a decision of the United States Claims Court or of the United States District Court, if no timely notice of appeal is filed; or

(2) Upon the expiration of the time allowed for filing a petition for certiorari from a decision of the United States Claims Court, or from a decision of the United States District Court, which has been affirmed or the appeal dismissed by the United States Court of Appeals, if no timely petition for certiorari is filed; or

(3) If a petition for certiorari has been filed, thirty days from the denial of such petition; or

(4) Thirty days from the date of a decision of the United States Supreme Court if no timely petition for rehearing is filed; however, if a timely petition for rehearing from such a decision is filed, and is denied, thirty days from the denial thereof; or

(5) If a decision is entered upon a rehearing or if a decision is modified or reversed as the result of a decision of a higher court, upon the expiration, with respect to the decision on rehearing or the modified or reversed decision, of periods similar to those provided in subparagraphs (1) through (4).

(b) *Right to bring action.*—With respect to any taxable event, payment of the full amount of first tier tax for the taxable period shall constitute sufficient payment in order to maintain an action under this section with respect to the second tier tax.

(c) *Limitation on suit for refund.*—No suit may be maintained under this section for the credit or refund of any tax imposed under section 4941, 4942, 4943, 4944, 4945, 4951, 4952, 4955, 4958, 4971, or 4975 with respect to any taxable event unless—

(1) No other suit has been maintained for credit or refund of any tax imposed by such sections with respect to such taxable event; and

(2) No petition has been filed in the Tax Court with respect to a deficiency in any tax imposed by such sections with respect to such taxable event.

(d) *Final determination of issues.*—For purposes of this section, any suit for the credit or refund of any tax imposed under section 4941, 4942, 4943, 4944, 4945, 4951, 4952, 4955, 4958, 4971, or 4975, together with a supplemental proceeding (if any) under section 4961(b), with respect to any taxable event, shall constitute a suit to determine all questions with respect to any other tax imposed with respect to such taxable event under such sections. Consequently, failure by the parties to the suit to bring before the Court any question described in the preceding sentence shall constitute a bar to the question.

(e) *Definitions.*—For definitions of the terms "taxable event," "first tier tax," and "second tier tax," see § 53.4963-1. [Reg. § 301.7422-1.]

☐ [T.D. 7838, 10-5-82. Amended by T.D. 8084, 5-1-86; T.D. 8628, 12-4-95 and T.D. 8920, 1-9-2001.]

[Reg. §301.7423-1]

§301.7423-1. Repayments to officers or employees.—The Commissioner is authorized to repay to any officer or employee of the United States the full amount of such sums of money as may be recovered against him in any court, for any internal revenue taxes collected by him, with the cost and expense of suit, and all damages and costs recovered against any officer or employee of the United States in any suit brought against him by reason of anything done in the official performance of his duties under the Code. [Reg. §301.7423-1.]

☐ [*T.D.* 6498, 10-24-60.]

[Reg. §301.7424-2]

§301.7424-2. Intervention.—If the United States is not a party to a civil action or suit, the United States may intervene in such action or suit to assert any lien arising under title 26 of the United States Code on the property which is the subject of such action or suit. The provisions of section 2410 of title 28 of the United States Code (except subsection (b)) and of section 1444 of title 28 of the United States Code shall apply in any case in which the United States intervenes as if the United States had originally been named a defendant in such action or suit. If the application of the United States to intervene is denied, the adjudication in such civil action or suit shall have no effect upon such lien. [Reg. §301.7424-2.]

☐ [*T.D.* 7305, 3-14-74.]

[Reg. §301.7425-1]

§301.7425-1. Discharge of liens; scope and application; judicial proceedings.—(a) *In general.*—A tax lien of the United States, or a title derived from the enforcement of a tax lien of the United States, may be discharged or divested under local law only in the manner prescribed in section 2410 of Title 28 of the United States Code or in the manner prescribed in section 7425 of the Internal Revenue Code. Section 7425(a) contains provisions relating to the discharge of a lien when the United States is not joined as a party in the judicial proceedings described in subsection (a) of section 2410 of Title 28 of the United States Code. These judicial proceedings are plenary in nature and proceed on formal pleadings. Section 7425(b) contains provisions relating to the discharge of a lien or a title derived from the enforcement of a lien in the event of a nonjudicial sale with respect to the property involved. Section 7425(c) contains special rules relating to the notice of sale requirements contained in section 7425(b). Section 301.7425-2 contains rules with respect to the nonjudicial sales described in section 7425(b). Paragraph(a) of §301.7425-3 contains rules with respect to the notice of sale provisions of section 7425(c)(1). Paragraph (b) of §301.7425-3 contains rules relating to the consent to sale provisions of section 7425(c)(2). Paragraph (c) of §301.7425-3 contains rules relating to the sale of perishable goods provisions of

section 7425(c)(3). Paragraph (d) of §301.7425-3 contains the requirements with respect to the contents of a notice of sale. Section 301.7425-4 prescribes rules with respect to the redemption of real property by the United States.

(b) *Effective date.*—The provisions of section 7425, as added by the Federal Tax Lien Act of 1966, are effective with respect to sales described in section 7425 occurring after November 2, 1966. The notice of sale provisions of section 7425(c)(1) or (3) do not apply to sales occurring after November 2, 1966, if the seller of the property performed an act before November 3, 1966, which act at the time of performance was required and effective under local law with respect to the sale. An example of such an act is publication of a notice of the sale in a local newspaper before November 3, 1966, if local law requires such publication before a sale and the publication is effective under local law. Accordingly, in such a case, it is not necessary to notify the Internal Revenue Service pursuant to the provisions of section 7425(c)(1) or (3). With respect to a notice of sale required under section 7425(c)(1) or (3)—

(1) Any notice of sale given to an office of the Internal Revenue Service or the Treasury Department during the period November 3, 1966, through December 21, 1966, shall be considered as adequate;

(2) Any notice of sale given during the period December 22, 1966, through January 31, 1968, which complies with the provisions of either—

(i) Revenue Procedure 67-25, 1967-1 C.B. 626 (based on Technical Information Release 873, dated December 22, 1966), or

(ii) Section 301.7425-3,

shall be considered as adequate; and

(3) Any notice of sale given after January 31, 1968, which complies with the provisions of §301.7425-3 shall be considered as adequate.

(c) *Judicial proceedings.*—(1) *In general.*—Section 7425(a) provides rules, where the United States is not joined as a party, to determine the effect of a judgment in any civil action or suit described in subsection (a) of section 2410 of title 28 of the United States Code (relating to joinder of the United States in certain proceedings), or a judicial sale pursuant to such a judgment, with respect to property on which the United States has or claims a lien under the provisions of this title. If the United States is improperly named as a party to a judicial proceeding, the effect is the same as if the United States were not joined.

(2) *Notice of lien filed when the proceeding is commenced.*—Where the United States is not properly joined as a party in the court proceeding and a notice of lien has been filed in accordance with section 6323(f) or (g) in the place provided by law for such filing at the time the action or suit is commenced, a judgment or judicial sale pursuant to such a judgment shall be made subject to and without disturbing the lien of the United States.

(3) *Notice of lien not filed when the proceeding is commenced.*—(i) *General rule.*—Where the United States is not joined as a party in the court proceeding and either a notice of lien has not been filed in accordance with section 6323(f) or (g) in the place provided by law for such filing at the time the action or suit is commenced, or the law makes no provision for that filing, a judgment or judicial sale pursuant to such a judgment shall have the same effect with respect to the discharge or divestment of the lien of the United States as may be provided with respect to these matters by the local law of the place where the property is situated.

(ii) *Examples.*—The provisions of subparagraph (3) may be illustrated by the following examples:

Example (1). A, the first mortgagee of an apartment building located in State Y, commenced a foreclosure action on the mortgage prior to the time that a notice of a Federal tax lien, on that building, had been filed. Under the law of Y, junior liens on real property are discharged by a judicial sale pursuant to a judgment in a foreclosure action. Therefore, the Federal tax lien on the building will be discharged by the judicial sale. This result is the same whether the tax lien arose before or after the date of commencement of the foreclosure action and whether notice of the tax lien was filed at any time after commencement of the foreclosure action.

Example (2). On January 10, 1969, B dies testate and devises Blackacre to C. At B's death, Blackacre is subject to a first mortgage held by D. Realty is subject to administration as part of a decedent's estate under the laws of State X. However, C takes possession of Blackacre with the assent of E, the executor of B's estate. On January 5, 1970, D commences a foreclosure action on the mortgage. Under the law of X, junior liens on real property are discharged by a judicial sale pursuant to a judgment in a foreclosure action. After commencement of the proceedings, an assessment for estate taxes is made and, thereafter, a notice of lien is filed in accordance with section 6323. The special lien on Blackacre, arising at the date of B's death, for estate taxes under section 6324(a) will be discharged by the judicial sale because there are no provisions for filing a notice thereof under law and junior liens are discharged by the sale under local law. The lien is discharged even though the executor failed to obtain a discharge of his personal liability under section 2204. Furthermore, the general lien on Blackacre under section 6321 will be discharged by the judicial sale because the foreclosure action was commenced prior to the time that a notice of lien was filed.

(4) *Proceeds of a judicial sale.*—If a judicial sale of property pursuant to a judgment in any civil action or suit to which the United States is not a party discharges a lien of the United States arising under the provisions of the Internal Revenue Code of 1954, the United States may claim the proceeds of the sale (exclusive of costs) prior to the time that distribution of the proceeds is ordered. The claim of the United States in such a case is treated as having the same priority with respect to the proceeds as the lien had with respect to the property which was discharged from the lien by the judicial sale. [Reg. § 301.7425-1.]

☐ [*T.D.* 7430, 5-20-75.]

[Reg. § 301.7425-2]

§ 301.7425-2. **Discharge of liens; nonjudicial sales.**—(a) *In general.*—Section 7425(b) contains provisions with respect to the effect on the interest of the United States in property in which the United States has or claims a lien, or a title derived from the enforcement of a lien, of a sale made pursuant to—

(1) An instrument creating a lien on the property sold,

(2) A confession of judgment on the obligation secured by an instrument creating a lien on the property sold, or

(3) A statutory lien on the property sold.

For purposes of this section, such a sale is referred to as a "nonjudicial sale." The term "nonjudicial sale" includes, but is not limited to, the divestment of the taxpayer's interest in property which occurs by operation of law, by public or private sale, by forfeiture, or by termination under provisions contained in a contract for a deed or a conditional sales contract. Under section 7425(b)(1), if a notice of lien is filed in accordance with section 6323(f) or (g), or the title derived from the enforcement of a lien is recorded as provided by local law, more than 30 days before the date of sale, and the appropriate district director is not given notice of the sale (in the manner prescribed in § 301.7425-3), the sale shall be made subject to and without disturbing the lien or title of the United States. Under section 7425(b)(2)(C), in any case in which notice of the sale is given to the district director not less than 25 days prior to the date of sale (in the manner prescribed in section 7425(c)(1)), the sale shall have the same effect with respect to the discharge or divestment of the lien or title as may be provided by local law with respect to other junior liens or other titles derived from the enforcement of junior liens. A nonjudicial sale pursuant to a lien which is junior to a tax lien does not divest the tax lien, even though notice of the nonjudicial sale is given to the appropriate district director. However, under the provisions of section 6325(b) and § 301.6325-1, a district director may discharge the property from a tax lien, including a tax lien which is senior to another lien upon the property.

(b) *Date of sale.*—In the case of a nonjudicial sale subject to the provisions of section 7425(b), in order to compute any period of time determined with reference to the date of sale, the date of sale shall be determined in accordance with the following rules:

(1) In the case of divestment of junior liens on property resulting directly from a public sale, the date of sale is deemed to be the date the

public sale is held, regardless of the date under local law on which junior liens on the property are divested or the title to the property is transferred,

(2) In the case of divestment of junior liens on property resulting directly from a private sale, the date of sale is deemed to be the date title to the property is transferred, regardless of the date junior liens on the property are divested under local law, and

(3) In the case of divestment of junior liens on property not resulting directly from a public or private sale, the date of sale is deemed to be the date on which junior liens on the property are divested under local law.

For provisions relating to the right of redemption of the United States, see section 7425(d) and §301.7425-4.

(c) *Examples.*—The provisions of this section may be illustrated by the following examples:

Example (1). (i) Under the law of State M, upon entry of judgment, the judgment creditor obtains a statutory lien upon the real property of the judgment debtor, and certain procedures are provided by which the judgment creditor may execute by public sale upon such real property. These procedures provide, among other things, for notification by personal service or registered or certified mail to other lien creditors, if any, and publication of a notice of the sale in a local newspaper. After the expiration of a prescribed period of time after such notification and publication, the sheriff of the county where the real property is located may sell the property at public sale. After payment of the amount bid at the public sale, the sheriff issues to the purchaser a deed to the real property, and the interests of junior lienors in the property are divested.

(ii) For purposes of this section, such an execution sale is a nonjudicial sale described in section 7425(b) because the sale is made pursuant to a statutory lien on the property sold. The date of sale, for purposes of computing a period of time determined with reference to the date of sale, is the date on which the public sale is held because junior liens on the real property are divested directly as a result of the public sale. This result obtains even though the junior liens are legally divested on a later date when the sheriff issues the deed.

Example (2). (i) Under the law of State N, mortgages on real property may contain a power of sale which authorizes the mortgagee, upon breach by the mortgagor of one of the conditions of the mortgage, to have the mortgaged property sold at public sale. This public sale must be preceded by notice by advertisement in a local newspaper, and the time, place, description of the property, and other terms of the sale must be specified. The purchaser at such a public sale obtains a title to the real property which is not subject to a right of redemption by the mortgagor and which divests the interests of the junior lienors in the property.

(ii) For purposes of this section, a sale pursuant to such a power of sale is a nonjudicial sale described in section 7425(b) because the sale is made pursuant to the mortgage instrument which created a lien on the property sold. The date of the sale, for purposes of computing a period of time determined with reference to the date of sale, is the date of the public sale because junior liens on the property are divested directly as a result of the public sale.

Example (3). Assume the same facts as in example (2) except that the purchaser at the public sale obtains a title which is defeasible by the exercise of a right of redemption in the mortgagor. The purchaser's title divests the interests of junior lienors in the property as of the time of public sale. The interests of junior lienors in the property revive if the mortgagor exercises his right of redemption. The date of the sale, for purposes of computing a period of time determined with reference to the date of sale, is the date of the public sale because junior liens on the property are divested directly as a result of the public sale although such junior liens may be revived by a subsequent redemption by the mortgagor.

Example (4). (i) Under the law of State O, upon breach by a mortgagor of real property of one of the conditions of the mortgage, the mortgagee may foreclose the mortgage by securing possession of the property by one of several procedures provided by statute. These procedures are generally referred to as "strict foreclosure." In order for a foreclosure to be effective under these procedures, a certificate attesting the fact of entry must be recorded with the proper registrar of deeds within 30 days after the mortgagee enters the property. During the one-year period following the date on which the certificate of entry is recorded, the mortgagor or a junior lienor may redeem the property by paying the mortgagee the amount of the mortgage obligation. If, during such one-year period the property is not redeemed and the mortgagee's possession is continued, the interests of the mortgagor and the junior lienors in the property are divested as of the date such one-year period expires.

(ii) For purposes of this section, such a foreclosure procedure is a nonjudicial sale described in section 7425(b) because it results in the divestment of the mortgagor's interest in the property by operation of law pursuant to the mortgage which created a lien on the property. In addition, because there is no public or private sale which directly results in the divestment of junior liens on the property, the date of sale, for purposes of computing a period of time determined with reference to the date of sale, is the date on which the one-year period following the recording of the certificate of entry expires.

Example (5). The law of State P contains a procedure which permits a county to collect a delinquent tax assessment with respect to real property by the means of a tax sale of the property. First, a notice of a public auction with respect to the tax assessment on the real property is published in a local newspaper. At the public auction, the purchaser, upon payment of the delinquent taxes and interest, obtains from the county tax collector a tax certificate with respect to the real property. Because the obtaining of this tax certificate does not directly result in the divestment of either the owner's title or junior liens with respect to the property, the public auction is not a nonjudicial sale described in section 7425(b). At any time before a tax deed with respect to the property is issued by the clerk of the county court, the owner or any holder of a lien or other interest with respect to the property may obtain the tax certificate by paying the holder of the tax certificate the amount of the taxes, interest, and costs. After a date which is two years after the date on which the tax assessment became delinquent, the holder of the tax certificate may request the clerk of the county court to have the property advertised for sale. After advertisement of the sale, the clerk of the county court conducts a public sale of the real property and the purchaser obtains a tax deed. The interests of all junior lienors in the property are divested and the property is not subject to a right of redemption under the law of State P. For purposes of this section, this public sale is considered to be a nonjudicial sale described in section 7425(b) because the sale is made pursuant to a statutory lien on the property sold. The date of the sale, for purposes of computing a period of time determined with reference to the date of sale, is the date on which the public sale is held at which the purchaser obtains a tax deed as this sale directly results in the divestment of junior liens on the property.

Example (6). The law of State Q contains a provision which permits a county to collect a delinquent tax assessment with respect to real property by the means of a tax sale of the property. After public notice is given, a "tax sale" of the real property is conducted. Upon payment of the delinquent taxes and interest, a purchaser obtains a tax certificate with respect to the real property. If there is no purchaser at the tax sale, the property is deemed to be bid in by the State. Because the obtaining of this tax certificate by a purchaser or State Q does not directly result in the divestment of either the owner's title or junior liens with respect to the property, the tax sale is not a nonjudicial sale described in section 7425(b). Following the tax sale, there is a three year period during which any person having an interest in the property may redeem the property by paying the holder of the tax certificate the amount of taxes, interest, and costs. Unless redeemed, the holder of the tax certificate may obtain an absolute title at the expiration of the period of redemption provided he serves a notice of the expiration of the redemption period upon the owner at least 60 days prior to the date of expiration. Because there is no public or private sale which directly results in the divestment of junior liens on the property, the date of sale, for purposes of computing a period of time determined with reference to the date of sale, is the date on which the holder of the tax certificate obtains absolute title. [Reg. § 301.7425-2.]

☐ [*T.D.* 7430, 8-19-76.]

[Reg. § 301.7425-3]

§ 301.7425-3. Discharge of liens; special rules.—(a) *Notice of sale requirements.*—(1) *In general.*—Except in the case of the sale of perishable goods described in paragraph (c) of this section, a notice (as described in paragraph (d) of this section) of a nonjudicial sale shall be given, in writing by registered or certified mail or by personal service, not less than 25 days prior to the date of sale (determined under the provisions of § 301.7425-2(b)), to the Internal Revenue Service (IRS) official, office and address specified in IRS Publication 786, "Instructions for Preparing a Notice of Nonjudicial Sale of Property and Application for Consent to Sale," or any successor publication. The relevant IRS publications may be downloaded from the IRS internet site at *www.irs.gov*. Under this section, a notice of sale is not effective if it is given to an office other than the office listed in the relevant publication. The provisions of sections 7502 (relating to timely mailing treated as timely filing) and 7503 (relating to time for performance of acts where the last day falls on Saturday, Sunday, or a legal holiday) apply in the case of notices required to be made under this paragraph.

(2) *Postponement of scheduled sale.*—(i) *Where notice of sale is given.*—In the event that notice of a sale is given in accordance with subparagraph (1) of this paragraph with respect to a scheduled sale which is postponed to a later time or date, the seller of the property is required to give notice of the postponement to the IRS in the same manner as is required under local law with respect to other secured creditors. For example, assume that in State M local law requires that in the event of a postponement of a scheduled foreclosure sale of real property, an oral announcement of the postponement at the place and time of the scheduled sale constitutes sufficient notice to secured creditors of the postponement. Accordingly, if at the place and time of a scheduled sale in State M an oral announcement of the postponement is made, the Internal Revenue Service is considered to have notice of the postponement for the purpose of this subparagraph.

(ii) *Where notice of sale is not given.*—In the event that—

(A) Notice of a nonjudicial sale would not be required under subparagraph (1) of this paragraph if the sale were held on the originally scheduled date,

(B) Because of a postponement of the scheduled sale, more than 30 days elapse between the originally scheduled date of the sale and the date of the sale, and

(C) A notice of lien with respect to the property to be sold is filed more than 30 days before the date of the sale,

notice of the sale is required to be given to the IRS in accordance with the provisions of subparagraph (1) of this paragraph. In any case in which notice of sale is required to be given with respect to a scheduled sale, and notice of the sale is not given, any postponement of the scheduled

Reg. § 301.7425-3(a)(2)(ii)(C)

sale does not affect the rights of the United States under section 7425(b).

(iii) *Examples.*—The provisions of subdivision (ii) of this subparagraph may be illustrated by the following examples:

Example (1). A nonjudicial sale of Blackacre, belonging to A, a delinquent taxpayer, is scheduled for December 2, 1968. As no notice of lien is filed applicable to Blackacre more than 30 days before December 2, 1968, no notice of sale is given to the IRS. On December 2, 1968, the sale of Blackacre is postponed until January 15, 1969. A notice of lien with respect to Blackacre is properly filed on January 2, 1969. The sale of Blackacre is held on Jannuary 15, 1969. Even though more than 30 days elapsed between the originally scheduled date of the sale (December 2, 1968) and the date of the sale (January 15, 1969), no notice of sale is required to be given to the IRS because the notice of lien was not filed more than 30 days before the date of the sale.

Example (2). Assume the same facts as in example (1) except that a notice of lien is filed on November 29, 1968 in accordance with section 6323. Because more than 30 days elapsed between the originally scheduled date of the sale and the date of the sale, and the notice of lien is filed (on November 29, 1968) more than 30 days before the date of the sale (January 15, 1969), notice of the sale, in accordance with the provisions of subparagraph (1) of this paragraph, is required to be given to the IRS.

Example (3). A nonjudicial sale of Whiteacre, belonging to B, a delinquent taxpayer, is scheduled for December 2, 1968. A notice of lien applicable to Whiteacre is filed on November 12, 1968 in accordance with section 6323. As the notice of lien was not filed more than 30 days before December 2, 1968, no notice of sale is given to the IRS. On December 2, 1968, the sale of Whiteacre is postponed until December 20, 1968. The sale of Whiteacre is held on December 20, 1968. Even though more than 30 days elapsed between the date notice of lien was filed (November 12, 1968) and the date of the sale (December 20, 1968), no notice of sale is required to be given to the IRS because not more than 30 days elapsed between the date of the originally scheduled sale (December 2, 1968) and the date the sale was actually held (December 20, 1968).

(b) *Consent to sale.*—(1) *In general.*—Notwithstanding the notice of sale provisions of paragraph (a) of this section, a nonjudicial sale of property shall discharge or divest the property of the lien and title of the United States if the IRS consents to the sale of the property free of the lien or title. Pursuant to section 7425(c)(2), where adequate protection is afforded the lien or title of the United States, the IRS may, in its discretion, consent with respect to the sale of property in appropriate cases. Such consent shall be effective only if given in writing and shall be subject to such limitations and conditions as the IRS may require. However, the IRS may not consent to a sale of property under this section after the date

of sale, as determined under § 301.7425-2(b). For provisions relating to the authority of the IRS to release a lien or discharge property subject to a tax lien, see section 6325 and the section 6325 regulations.

(2) *Application for consent.*—Any person desiring the IRS's consent to sell property free of a tax lien or a title derived from the enforcement of a tax lien of the United States in the property shall submit to the IRS, at the office and address specified in the relevant IRS publications, a written application, in triplicate, declaring that it is made under penalties of perjury, and requesting that such consent be given. The application shall contain the information required in the case of a notice of sale, as set forth in paragraph (d)(1) of this section, and, in addition, shall contain a statement of the reasons why the consent is desired.

(c) *Sale of perishable goods.*—(1) *In general.*—A notice (as described in paragraph (d) of this section) of a nonjudicial sale of perishable goods (as defined in paragraph (c)(2) of this section) shall be given in writing, by registered or certified mail or delivered by personal service, at any time before the sale, to the IRS official and office specified in the relevant IRS publications, at the address specified in such publications. Under this section, a notice of sale is not effective if it is given to an office other than the office listed in the relevant publication. If a notice of a nonjudicial sale is timely given in the manner described in this paragraph, the nonjudicial sale shall discharge or divest the tax lien, or a title derived from the enforcement of a tax lien, of the United States in the property. The provisions of sections 7502 (relating to timely mailing treated as timely filing) and 7503 (relating to time for performance of acts where the last day falls on Saturday, Sunday, or a legal holiday) apply in the case of notices required to be made under this paragraph. The seller of the perishable goods shall hold the proceeds (exclusive of costs) of the sale as a fund, for not less than 30 days after the date of the sale, subject to the liens and claims of the United States, in the same manner and with the same priority as the liens and claims of the United States had with respect to the property sold. If the seller fails to hold the proceeds of the sale in accordance with the provisions of this paragraph and if the IRS asserts a claim to the proceeds within 30 days after the date of sale, the seller shall be personally liable to the United States for an amount equal to the value of the interest of the United States in the fund. However, even if the proceeds of the sale are not so held by the seller, but all the other provisions of this paragraph are satisfied, the buyer of the property at the sale takes the property free of the liens and claims of the United States. In the event of a postponement of the scheduled sale of perishable goods, the seller is not required to notify the IRS of the postponement. For provisions relating to the authority of the IRS to release a lien or discharge property subject to a tax lien, see section 6325 and the regulations.

Reg. §301.7425-3(a)(2)(iii)

(2) *Definition of perishable goods.*—For the purpose of this paragraph, the term "perishable goods" means any tangible personal property which, in the reasonable view of the person selling the property, is liable to perish or become greatly reduced in price or value by keeping, or cannot be kept without great expense.

(d) *Content of notice of sale.*—(1) *In general.*— With respect to a notice of sale described in paragraph (a) or (c) of this section, the notice will be considered adequate if it contains the information described in subdivision (i), (ii), (iii), and (iv) of this subparagraph.

(i) The name and address of the person submitting the notice of sale;

(ii) A copy of each Notice of Federal Tax Lien (Form 668) affecting the property to be sold, or the following information as shown on each such Notice of Federal Tax Lien—

(A) The IRS office named thereon,

(B) The name and address of the taxpayer, and

(C) The date and place of filing of the notice;

(iii) With respect to the property to be sold, the following information—

(A) A detailed description, including location, of the property affected by the notice (in the case of real property, the street address, city, and State and the legal description contained in the title or deed to the property and, if available, a copy of the abstract of title),

(B) The date, time, place, and terms of the proposed sale of the property, and

(C) In the case of a sale of perishable property described in paragraph (c) of this section, a statement of the reasons why the property is believed to be perishable; and

(iv) The approximate amount of the principal obligation, including interest, secured by the lien sought to be enforced and a description of the other expenses (such as legal expenses, selling costs, etc.) which may be charged against the sale proceeds.

(2) *Inadequate notice.*—Except as otherwise provided in this paragraph, a notice of sale described in paragraph (a) of this section that does not contain the information described in paragraph (d)(1) of this section shall be considered inadequate by the IRS. If the IRS determines that the notice is inadequate, the IRS will give written notification of the items of information which are inadequate to the person who submitted the notice. A notice of sale that does not contain the name and address of the person submitting such notice shall be considered to be inadequate for all purposes without notification of any specific inadequacy. In any case where a notice of sale does not contain the information required under paragraph (d)(1)(ii) of this section with respect to a Notice of Federal Tax Lien, the IRS may give written notification of such omission without specification of any other inadequacy and such notice of sale shall be considered inadequate for

all purposes. In the event the IRS gives notification that the notice of sale is inadequate, a notice complying with the provisions of this section (including the requirement that the notice be given not less than 25 days prior to the sale in the case of a notice described in paragraph (a) of this section) must be given. However, in accordance with the provisions of paragraph (b)(1) of this section, in such a case the IRS may, in its discretion, consent to the sale of the property free of the lien or title of the United States even though notice of the sale is given less than 25 days prior to the sale. In any case where the person who submitted a timely notice, which indicates his name and address, does not receive more than 5 days prior to the date of sale written notification from the IRS that the notice is inadequate, the notice shall be considered adequate for purposes of this section.

(3) *Acknowledgment of notice.*—If a notice of sale described in paragraph (a) or (c) of this section is submitted in duplicate to the IRS with a written request that receipt of the notice be acknowledged and returned to the person giving the notice, this request will be honored by the IRS. The acknowledgment by the IRS will indicate the date and time of the receipt of the notice.

(4) *Disclosure of adequacy of notice.*—The IRS is authorized to disclose, to any person who has a proper interest, whether an adequate notice of sale was given under paragraph (d)(1) of this section. Any person desiring this information should submit to the IRS a written request that clearly describes the property sold or to be sold, identifies the applicable notice of lien, gives the reasons for requesting the information, and states the name and address of the person making the request. The request should be submitted to the IRS official, office and address specified in IRS Publication 4235, "Technical Services (Advisory) Group Addresses," or any successor publication. The relevant IRS publications may be downloaded from the IRS internet site at *www.irs.gov.*

(e) *Effective/applicability date.*—These regulations are effective on July 8, 2008. [Reg. § 301.7425-3.]

☐ [*T.D.* 7430, 8-19-76. *Amended by T.D.* 9344, 7-19-2007 *and T.D.* 9410, 7-7-2008.]

[Reg. § 301.7425-4]

§ 301.7425-4. Discharge of liens; redemption by United States.—(a) *Right to redeem.*—(1) *In general.*—In the case of a nonjudicial sale of real property to satisfy a lien prior to the tax lien or a title derived from the enforcement of a tax lien, the district director may redeem the property within the redemption period (as described in subparagraph (2) of this paragraph). The right of redemption of the United States exists under section 7425(d) even though the district director has consented to the sale under section 7425(c)(2) and § 301.7425-3(b). For purposes of this section, the term "nonjudicial sale" shall have the same meaning as used in paragraph (a) of § 301.7425-2.

(2) *Redemption period.*—For purposes of this section, the redemption period shall be—

(i) The period beginning with the date of the sale (as determined under paragraph (b) of § 301.7425-2) and ending with the 120th day after such date, or

(ii) The period for redemption of real property allowable, with respect to other secured creditors, under the local law of the place where the real property is located, whichever expires later. Whichever period is applicable, section 7425 and this section shall govern the amount to be paid and the procedure to be followed.

(3) *Limitations.*—In the event a sale does not ultimately discharge the property from the tax lien (whether by reason of local law or the provisions of section 7425(b)), the provisions of this section do not apply because the tax lien will continue to attach to the property after the sale. In a case in which the Internal Revenue Service is not entitled to a notice of sale under section 7425(b) and § 301.7425-3, the United States does not have a right of redemption under section 7425(d). However, in such a case, if a tax lien has attached to the property at the time of sale, the United States has the same right of redemption, if any, which is afforded to any similar creditors under the local law of the place in which the property is situated.

(b) *Amount to be paid.*—(1) *In general.*—In any case in which a district director exercises the right to redeem real property under section 7425(d), the amount to be paid is the sum of the following amounts—

(i) The actual amount paid for the property (as determined under subparagraph (2) of this paragraph) being redeemed (which, in the case of a purchaser who is the holder of the lien being foreclosed, shall include the amount of the obligation secured by such lien to the extent legally satisfied by reason of the sale);

(ii) Interest on the amount paid (described in subdivision (i) of this subparagraph) at the sale by the purchaser of the real property computed at the rate of 6 percent per annum for the period from the date of the sale (as determined under paragraph (b) of § 301.7425-2) to the date of redemption;

(iii) The amount, if any, equal to the excess of (A) the expenses necessarily incurred to maintain such property (as determined under subparagraph (3) of this paragraph) by the purchaser (and his successor in interest, if any) over (B) the income from such property realized by the purchaser (and his successor in interest, if any) plus a reasonable rental value of such property (to the extent the property is used by or with the consent of the purchaser or his successor in interest or is rented at less than its reasonable rental value); and

(iv) With respect to a redemption made after December 31, 1976, the amount, if any, of a payment made by the purchaser or his successor in interest after the foreclosure sale to a holder of a senior lien (to the extent provided under subparagraph (4) of this paragraph).

(2) *Actual amount paid.*—(i) The actual amount paid for property by a purchaser, other than the holder of the lien being foreclosed, is the amount paid by him at the sale. For purposes of this subdivision, the amount paid by the purchaser at the sale includes deferred payments upon the bid price. The actual amount paid does not include costs and expenses incurred prior to the foreclosure sale by the purchaser except to the extent such expenses are included in the amount bid and paid for the property. For example, the actual amount paid does not normally include the expenses of the purchaser such as title searches, professional fees, or interest on debt incurred to obtain funds to purchase the property.

(ii) In the case of a purchaser who is the holder of the lien being foreclosed, the actual amount paid is the sum of (A) the amount of the obligation secured by such lien to the extent legally satisfied by reason of the sale and (B) any additional amount bid and paid at the sale. For purposes of this section, a purchaser who acquires title as a result of a nonjudicial foreclosure sale is treated as the holder of the lien being foreclosed if a lien (or any interest reserved, created, or conveyed as security for the payment of a debt or fulfillment of other obligation) held by him is partially or fully satisfied by reason of the foreclosure sale. For example, a person whose title is derived from a tax deed issued under local law shall be treated as a purchaser who is the holder of the lien foreclosed in a case where a tax certificate, evidencing a lien on the property arising from the payment of property taxes, ripens into title. The amount paid by a purchaser at the sale includes deferred payments upon any portion of the bid price which is in excess of the amount of the lien being foreclosed. The actual amount paid does not include costs and expenses incurred prior to the foreclosure sale by the purchaser except to the extent such expenses are included in the amount of the lien being foreclosed which is legally satisfied by reason of the sale or in the amount bid and paid at the sale. Where the lien being foreclosed attaches to other property not subject to the foreclosure sale, the amount legally satisfied by reason of the sale does not include the amount of such lien that attaches to the other property. However, for purposes of the preceding sentence, the amount of the lien that attaches to the other property shall be considered to be equal to the amount by which the value of the other property exceeds the amount of any other senior lien on that property. Where, after the sale, the holder of the lien being foreclosed has the right to the unpaid balance of the amount due him, the amount legally satisfied by reason of the sale does not include the amount of such lien to the extent a deficiency judgment may be obtained therefor. However, for purposes of the preceding sentence, an amount, with respect to which the holder of the lien being foreclosed would otherwise have a right to a deficiency judgment, shall be considered to be legally satisfied by reason of the foreclosure sale to the extent that the holder has waived his right to a deficiency judgment prior to the foreclosure sale. For this purpose, the waiver must be in writing and legally binding upon the foreclosing lienholder as of the time the sale is concluded. If, prior to the foreclosure, payments have been made by the foreclosing lienhold to a holder of a superior lien, the payments are included in the actual amount paid to the extent they give rise to an interest which is legally satisfied by reason of the foreclosure sale.

(3) *Excess expenses incurred by purchaser.*— (i) Expenses necessarily incurred in connection with the property after the foreclosure sale and before redemption by the United States are taken into account in determining if there are excess expenses payable under subparagraph (1)(iii) of this paragraph. Expenses incurred by the purchaser prior to the foreclosure sale are not considered under this subparagraph. (See subparagraph (2)(ii) of this paragraph for circumstances under which such expenses may be included in the amount to be paid.) Expenses necessarily incurred in connection with the property include, for example, rental agent commissions, repair and maintenance expenses, utilities expenses, legal fees incurred after the foreclosure sale and prior to redemption in defending the title acquired through the foreclosure sale, and a proportionate amount of casualty insurance premiums and ad valorem taxes. Improvements made to the property are not considered as an expense unless the amounts incurred for such improvements are necessarily incurred to maintain the property.

(ii) At any time prior to the expiration of the redemption period applicable under paragraph (a)(2) of this section, the district director may, by certified or registered mail or hand delivery, request a written itemized statement of the amount claimed by the purchaser or his successor in interest to be payable under subparagraph (1)(iii) of this paragraph. Unless the purchaser or his successor in interest furnishes the written itemized statement within 15 days after the request is made by the district director, it shall be presumed that no amount is payable for expenses in excess of income and the Internal Revenue Service shall tender only the amount otherwise payable under subparagraph (1) of this paragraph. If a purchaser or his or her successor in interest has failed to furnish the written itemized statement within 15 days after the request therefor is made by the district director, or there is a disagreement as to the amount properly payable under paragraph (b)(1)(iii) of this section, or if there were additional excess expenses that were not claimed in the original itemized statement, the purchaser or his or her successor in interest may submit a written itemized statement to the district director within 30 days after the date of redemption. If the purchaser or his or her successor in interest fails to timely submit such a written itemized statement,

no amount shall be payable for expenses in excess of income.

(4) *Payments made by purchaser or his successor in interest to a senior lienor.*—(i) The amount to be paid upon a redemption by the United States made after December 31, 1976, shall include the amount of a payment made by the purchaser or his successor in interest to a holder of a senior lien to the extent a request for the reimbursement thereof (made in accordance with subdivision (ii) of this subparagraph) is approved as provided under subdivision (iii) of this subparagraph. This subparagraph applies only to a payment made after the foreclosure sale and before the redemption to a holder of a lien that was, immediately prior to the foreclosure sale, superior to the lien foreclosed. A payment of principal or interest to a senior lienor shall be taken into account. Generally, the portion, if any, of a payment which is to be held in escrow for the payment of an expense, such as hazard insurance or real property taxes, is not considered under this subparagraph. However, a payment by the escrow agent of a real property tax or special assessment lien, which was senior to the lien foreclosed, shall be considered to be a payment made by the purchaser or his successor in interest for purposes of this subparagraph. With respect to real property taxes assessed after the foreclosure sale, see subparagraph (3)(i) of this paragraph, relating to excess expenses incurred by the purchaser.

(ii) Before the expiration of the redemption period applicable under paragraph (a)(2) of this section, the district director shall, in any case where a redemption is contemplated, send notice to the purchaser (or his successor in interest of record) by certified or registered mail or hand delivery of his right under this subparagraph to request reimbursement (payable in the event the right to redeem under section 7425(d) is exercised) for a payment made to a senior lienor. No later than 15 days after the notice from the district director is sent, the request for reimbursement shall be mailed or delivered to the office specified in such notice and shall consist of—

(A) A written itemized statement, signed by the claimant, of the amount claimed with respect to a payment made to a senior lienor, together with the supporting evidence requested in the notice from the district director, and

(B) A waiver or other document that will be effective upon redemption by the United States to discharge the property from, or transfer to the United States, any interest in or lien on the property that may arise under local law with respect to the payment made to a senior lienor.

Upon a showing of reasonable cause, a district director may, in his discretion, and at any time before the expiration of the applicable period for redemption, grant an extension for a reasonable period of time to submit, amend, or supplement a request for reimbursement. Unless a request for reimbursement is timely submitted (determined with regard to any extension of time

Reg. §301.7425-4(b)(4)(ii)(B)

granted), no amount shall be payable to the purchaser or his successor in interest on account of a payment made to a senior lienor if the right to redeem under section 7425(d) is exercised. A waiver or other document submitted pursuant to this subdivision shall be treated as effective only to the extent of the amount included in the redemption price under this subparagraph. If the right to redeem is not exercised or a request for reimbursement is withdrawn, the district director shall, by certified or registered mail or hand delivery, return to the purchaser or his successor any waiver or other document submitted pursuant to this subdivision as soon as is practicable.

(iii) A request for reimbursement submitted in accordance with subdivision (ii) of this subparagraph shall be considered to be approved for the total amount claimed by the purchaser, and payable in the event the right to redeem is exercised, unless the district director sends notice to the claimant, by certified or registered mail or hand delivery, of the denial of the amount claimed within 30 days after receipt of the request or 15 days before expiration of the applicable period for redemption, whichever is later. The notification of denial shall state the grounds for denial. If such notice of denial is given, the request for reimbursement for a payment made to a senior lienor shall be treated as having been withdrawn by the purchaser or his successor and the Internal Revenue Service shall tender only the amount otherwise payable under subparagraph (1) of this paragraph. If a request for reimbursement is treated as having been withdrawn under the preceding sentence, payment for amounts described in this subparagraph may, in the discretion of the district director, be made after the redemption upon the resolution of the disagreement as to the amount properly payable under paragraph (1)(iv) of this paragraph.

(5) *Examples.*—The provisions of subparagraph (1)(i) of this paragraph may be illustrated by the following examples:

Example (1). A, a delinquent taxpayer, owns Blackacre located in State X upon which B holds a mortgage. After the mortgage is properly recorded, a notice of tax lien is filed under section 6323(f) which is applicable to Blackacre. Subsequently, A defaults on the mortgage and B forecloses on the mortgage which has an outstanding obligation in the amount of $100,000. At the foreclosure sale, B bids $50,000 and obtains title to Blackacre as a result of the sale. At the time of the foreclosure sale, Blackacre has a fair market value of $75,000. Under the laws of State X, the mortgage obligation is fully satisfied by operation of the foreclosure sale per se and the mortgagee cannot obtain a deficiency judgment. Under paragraph (b)(1)(i) of this section, the district director must pay $100,000 in order to redeem Blackacre.

Example (2). Assume the same facts as in example (1) except that under the laws of State X, the amount bid is the amount of the obligation legally satisfied as a result of the foreclosure sale, and in the case in which the amount of the obligation exceeds the amount bid, the mortgagee has the right to a judgment for the deficiency computed as the difference between the amount of the obligation and the amount bid. B does not waive, prior to the foreclosure sale, his right to a deficiency judgment. In such a case, the district director must, under paragraph (b)(1)(i) of this section, pay $50,000 in order to redeem Blackacre, whether or not B seeks a judgment for the deficiency.

Example (3). C, a delinquent taxpayer, owns Greenacre located in State Y upon which D holds a first mortgage and E holds a second mortgage. After the mortgages are properly recorded, a notice of tax lien is filed under section 6323(f) which is applicable to Greenacre. Subsequently, C defaults on both mortgages and E pays $5,000 to D, which is the portion of D's obligation which is in default. The second mortgage held by E is an outstanding obligation in the amount of $100,000. Under the laws of State Y, E may treat the amount paid to D as an addition to his second mortgage upon foreclosure by him. E forecloses upon the security interest held by him. At the foreclosure sale, E bids $50,000 and obtains title to Greenacre subject to D's mortgage as a result of the foreclosure sale. Under the laws of State Y, the mortgage obligation legally satisfied is the amount bid and E has the right to a judgment for a deficiency in the amount of $55,000 ($100,000 plus $5,000 less $50,000). In such a case, the district director must, under paragraph (b)(1)(i) of this section, pay $50,000 in order to redeem Greenacre, whether or not E seeks a judgment for the deficiency.

Example (4). The law of State Z contains a procedure which permits a county to collect a delinquent tax assessment with respect to real property by the means of a "tax sale" of the property. Pursuant to this procedure, a public auction is conducted on January 15, 1970, to collect the delinquent property taxes assessed against Whiteacre, which is owned by F. At the auction, a bid of $1,000 (representing the tax, costs, and interest due at the time of the auction) is made by G. Subsequently, G pays the amount bid to the county and obtains a tax certificate with respect to Whiteacre. Under this tax sale procedure, the obtaining of the tax certificate does not directly result in the divestment of either F's title or any junior liens on Whiteacre. On January 15, 1973, the period under this tax sale procedure during which F could have redeemed Whiteacre expires. Further, more than 30 days before January 15, 1973, a notice of tax lien affecting Whiteacre is filed under section 6323(f) with respect to F's delinquent Federal income taxes. Under the state tax sale procedure, the amount which would be required to be paid by F to G on January 15, 1973, to redeem Whiteacre is $1,350 (the $1,000 amount bid, interest of $300, and costs of $50). However, Whiteacre is not redeemed by F under the state procedure and, on January 16, 1973, G obtains a tax deed to Whiteacre. Under the law of State Z, the issuance of the tax deed results in the divestment of F's title and junior liens on Whiteacre. Thus, under §301.7425-2(b), the date of sale is January 16, 1973, for purposes of section 7425(b). The amount legally satisfied by reason of the sale is the amount G is entitled to receive, immediately prior to the expiration of the period for redemption under the law of State Z, if Whiteacre were redeemed at such time. Thus, the district director must, under paragraph (b)(1)(i) of this section pay $1,350 in order to redeem Whiteacre.

(c) *Certificate of redemption.*—(1) *In general.*—If a district director exercises the right of redemption of the United States described in paragraph (a) of this section, he shall apply to the officer designated by local law, if any, for the documents necessary to evidence the fact of redemption and to record title to the redeemed property in the name of the United States. If no such officer has been designated by local law or if the officer designated by local law fails to issue the necessary documents, the district director is authorized to issue a certificate of redemption for the property redeemed by the United States.

(2) *Filing.*—The district director shall, without delay, cause either the documents issued by the local officer or the certificate of redemption executed by the district director to be filed with the local office where certificates of redemption are generally filed. If a certificate of redemption is issued by the district director and if the State in which the real property redeemed by the United States is situated has no office with which certificates of redemption may be filed, the district director shall file the certificate of redemption in the office of the clerk of the United States district court for the judicial district in which the redeemed property is situated.

(3) *Effect of certificate of redemption.*—A certificate of redemption executed pursuant to paragraph (c)(1) of this section shall constitute *prima facie* evidence of the regularity of the redemption. When a certificate of redemption is recorded, it shall transfer to the United States all the rights, title, and interest in and to the redeemed property acquired by the person, from whom the district director redeemed the property, by virtue of the sale of the property. Therefore, if under local law the purchaser takes title free of liens junior to the lien of the foreclosing lienholder, the United States takes title free of such junior liens upon redemption of the property. If a certificate of redemption has been erroneously prepared and filed because the redemption was not effective, the district director shall issue a document revoking such certificate of redemption and such document shall be conclusively binding upon the United States against a purchaser of the property or a holder of a lien upon the property.

(4) *Application for release of right of redemption.*—Upon application of a party with a proper interest in the real property sold in a nonjudicial sale described in section 7425(b) and §301.7425-2 which real property is subject to the right of redemption of the United States described in this section, the district director may, in his discretion, release the right of redemption with respect to the property. The application for the release shall be submitted in writing to a district director and shall contain such information as the district director may require. If the district director determines that the right of redemption of the United States is without value, no amount shall be required to be paid with respect to the release of the right of redemption. [Reg. §301.7425-4.]

☐ [*T.D. 7430, 8-19-76. Amended by T.D. 8596, 6-1-95.*]

[Reg. §301.7426-1]

§301.7426-1. Civil actions by persons other than taxpayers.—(a) *Actions permitted.*— (1) *Wrongful levy.*—(i) *In general.*—If a levy has been made on property or property has been sold pursuant to a levy, any person (other than the person against whom is assessed the tax out of which such levy arose) may bring a civil action against the United States in a district court of the United States based upon such person's claim—

(A) That such person has an interest in, or lien on, such property which is senior to the interest of the United States; and

(B) That such property was wrongfully levied upon.

(ii) *Debt owed by another Federal agency.*— Section 7426 and this paragraph (a) apply when a levy is made by the Internal Revenue Service on a debt owed to a taxpayer by another Federal agency. By contrast, section 7426 and this paragraph (a) do not apply if the Internal Revenue Service requests payment from another Federal agency pursuant to a request for setoff.

(2) *Surplus proceeds.*—If property has been sold pursuant to levy, any person (other than the person against whom is assessed the tax out of which such levy arose) may bring a civil action against the United States in a district court of the United States based upon such person's claim that he—

(i) Has an interest in or lien on such property junior to that of the United States; and

(ii) Is entitled to the surplus proceeds of such sale.

(3) *Substituted sale proceeds.*—Any person who claims to be legally entitled to all or any part of the amount which is held as a fund from the sale of property pursuant to an agreement described in section 6325(b)(3) may bring a civil action against the United States in a district court of the United States to obtain the relief provided by section 7426(b)(4). It is not necessary that the claimant be a party to the agreement which provides for the substitution of the sale proceeds for the property subject to the lien.

(4) *Substitution of value.*—A person who obtains a certificate of discharge under section 6325(b)(4) with respect to any property may, within 120 days after the day on which the certificate is issued, bring a civil action against the

United States in a district court of the United States for a determination of whether the value of the interest of the United States (if any) in such property is less than the value determined by the appropriate official. A civil action under this provision shall be the exclusive judicial remedy for a person other than the taxpayer who obtains a certificate of discharge for a filed notice of Federal tax lien.

(b) *Adjudication.*—(1) *Wrongful levy.*—If the court determines that property has been wrongfully levied upon, the court may—

(i) Grant an injunction to prohibit the enforcement of such levy or to prohibit a sale of such property if such sale would irreparably injure rights in the property which are superior to the rights of the United States in such property; or

(ii) Order the return of specific property if the United States is in possession of such property; or

(iii) Grant a judgment for the amount of money levied upon; or

(iv) Grant a judgment for an amount not exceeding the amount received by the United States from the sale of such property (which, in the case of property declared purchased by the United States at a sale, shall be the greater of the minimum amount determined pursuant to section 6335(e) or the amount received by the United States from the resale of such property). For purposes of this paragraph, a levy is wrongful against a person (other than the taxpayer against whom the assessment giving rise to the levy is made) if (*a*) the levy is upon property exempt from levy under section 6334, or (*b*) the levy is upon property in which the taxpayer had no interest at the time the lien arose or thereafter, or (*c*) the levy is upon property with respect to which such person is a purchaser against whom the lien is invalid under section 6323 or 6324(a)(2) or (b), or (*d*) the levy or sale pursuant to levy will or does effectively destroy or otherwise irreparably injure such person's interest in the property which is senior to the Federal tax lien. A levy may be wrongful against a holder of a senior lien upon the taxpayer's property under certain circumstances although legal rights to enforce his interest survive the levy procedure. For example, the levy may be wrongful against such a person if the property is an obligation which is collected pursuant to the levy rather than sold and nothing thereafter remains for the senior lienholder, or the property levied upon is of such a nature that when it is sold at a public sale the property subject to the senior lien is not available for the senior lienholder as a realistic source for the enforcement of his interest. Some of the factors which should be taken into account in determining whether property remains or will remain a realistic source from which the senior lienholder may realize collection are: (*1*) the nature of the property, (*2*) the number of purchasers, (*3*) the value of each unit sold or to be sold, (*4*) whether, as a direct result of the distraint sale, the costs of realizing collection from the security

have been or will be so substantially increased as to render the security substantially valueless as a source of collection, and (5) whether the property subject to the distraint sale constitutes substantially all of the property available as security for the payment of the indebtedness to the senior lienholder.

(2) *Example.*—The provisions of subparagraph (1) of this paragraph may be illustrated by the following example:

Example. On April 10, 1972, A makes a $10,000 loan to B which is partially secured by a $5,000 obligation owed to B by C. Under local law, A's security interest in the obligation owed to B by C is protected against a subsequent judgment lien arising out of an unsecured obligation. Thus, under section 6323(h)(1), A's security interest exists as of April 10, 1972, for purposes of determining priorities against a tax lien under section 6323. On April 17, 1972, an assessment of $6,000 is made against B with respect to his delinquent Federal tax liability. Thereafter, notice of lien is filed pursuant to section 6323(f) with respect to B's delinquent tax liability. On July 10, 1972, a notice of levy is served upon C to reach the amount owed by him to B. C pays over the $5,000 obligation in satisfaction of the levy and, under local law, the obligation is discharged as to A. Because the levy effectively destroyed A's senior security interest in the obligation owed to B by C, the levy is wrongful as to A for purposes of section 7426. Under these circumstances, the levy is wrongful with respect to A even if, under local law, A may have a cause of action in contract against B for the $10,000 loan or may have a cause of action in tort against C for the amount of the $5,000 payment which defeated A's security interest in the obligation owed by C to B.

(3) *Surplus proceeds.*—If the court determines that the interest or lien of any party to an action under section 7426 was transferred to the proceeds of a sale of the property, the court may grant a judgment in an amount equal to all or any part of the amount of the surplus proceeds of such sale. The term "surplus proceeds" means those proceeds realized on a sale of property remaining after application of the provisions of section 6342(a).

(4) *Substituted sale proceeds.*—If the court determines that a party has an interest in or lien on the amount held as a fund pursuant to an agreement described in section 6325(b)(3), the court may grant a judgment in an amount equal to all or any part of the amount of such fund.

(5) *Substitution of value.*—If the court determines that the determination by the appropriate official of the value of the interest of the United States in the property exceeds the actual value of such interest, the court may grant a judgment ordering a refund of the amount deposited, or a release of the bond, to the extent that the aggregate of those amounts exceeds the value as determined by the court.

(c) *Effective date.*—Paragraph (a)(1) of this section is effective as of December 23, 1993.

(d) Paragraphs (a)(4) and (b)(5) of this section apply to any request for a certificate of discharge made after January 31, 2008. [Reg. § 301.7426-1.]

☐ [*T.D.* 7305, 3-14-74. *Amended by T.D.* 8541, 5-20-94 *and T.D.* 9378, 1-30-2008.]

[Reg. § 301.7426-2]

§ 301.7426-2. Recovery of damages in certain cases.—(a) *In general.*—In addition to remedies related to wrongful levy set forth in § 301.7426-1(b), if a district court of the United States finds in any action brought under section 7426 that any officer or employee of the Internal Revenue Service recklessly or intentionally, or by reason of negligence, disregarded any provision of this title, the United States shall be liable to the plaintiff for damages. The plaintiff has a duty to mitigate damages. The total amount of damages recoverable under this section is the lesser of $1,000,000 ($100,000 in the case of negligence), or the sum of—

(1) Actual, direct economic damages as defined in § 301.7433-1(b) sustained as a proximate result of the reckless, intentional, or negligent actions of the officer or employee, reduced by the amount of any damages awarded under § 301.7426-1(b); and

(2) Costs of the action as defined in § 301.7433-1(c).

(b) *Administrative remedies must be exhausted.*—The court may not award a judgment for damages under paragraph (a) of this section unless the court determines that the plaintiff has filed an administrative claim pursuant to paragraph (d) of this section, and has satisfied the requirements of paragraph (c) of this section.

(c) *No request for damages in a district court of the United States prior to filing an administrative claim.*—(1) Except as provided in paragraph (c)(2) of this section, no request for damages under paragraph (a) of this section shall be maintained in any district court of the United States before the earlier of the following dates—

(i) The date the decision is rendered on a claim filed in accordance with paragraph (d) of this section; or

(ii) The date that is six months after the date an administrative claim is filed in accordance with paragraph (d) of this section.

(2) If an administrative claim is filed in accordance with paragraph (d) of this section during the last six months of the period of limitations described in paragraph (f) of this section, the claimant may file an action in a district court of the United States any time after the administrative claim is filed and before the expiration of the period of limitations.

(d) *Procedures for an administrative claim.*—(1) *Manner.*—An administrative claim for the lesser of $1,000,000 ($100,000 in the case of negligence) or actual, direct economic damages as defined in § 301.7433-1(b) shall be in writing to the Area Director, Attn: Compliance Technical Support Manager of the area in which the taxpayer currently resides.

(2) *Form.*—The administrative claim shall include—

(i) The name, taxpayer identification number, current address and current home and work telephone numbers (indicating any convenient times to be contacted) of the person making the claim;

(ii) The grounds, in reasonable detail, for the claim (include copies of any available substantiating documentation or correspondence with the Internal Revenue Service);

(iii) A description of the damages incurred by the claimant filing the claim (include copies of any available substantiating documentation or evidence);

(iv) The dollar amount of the claim, including any damages that have not yet been incurred but which are reasonably foreseeable (include copies of any available substantiating documentation or evidence); and

(v) The signature of the claimant or duly authorized representative.

(3) *Duly authorized representative.*—For purposes of this paragraph (d), a duly authorized representative is any attorney, certified public accountant, enrolled actuary, or any other person permitted to represent the claimant before the Internal Revenue Service who is not disbarred or suspended from practice before the Internal Revenue Service and who has a written power of attorney executed to the claimant.

(e) *No liability for damages for any sum in excess of the dollar amount sought in the administrative claim.*—See § 301.7433-1(f).

(f) *Period of limitations.*—(1) *Time for filing.*—A civil action under paragraph (a) of this section must be brought in a district court of the United States within two years after the date the cause of action accrues.

(2) *Right of action accrues.*—A cause of action under paragraph (a) of this section accrues when the plaintiff has had a reasonable opportunity to discover all essential elements of a possible cause of action.

(g) *Recovery of costs under section 7430.*—See § 301.7433-1(h).

(h) *Effective date.*—This section is applicable March 25, 2003. [Reg. § 301.7426-2.]

☐ [*T.D.* 9050, 3-24-2003.]

[Reg. § 301.7429-1]

§ 301.7429-1. Review of jeopardy and termination assessment and jeopardy levy procedures; information to taxpayer.—Not later than 5 days after the day on which an assessment is made under section 6851(a), 6852(a), 6861(a), or 6862, or a levy is made under section 6331(a) without complying with the notice before levy provisions of section 6331(d), the district director shall provide the taxpayer a written statement setting forth the information upon which the district director relies in authorizing such assessment or levy. [Reg. § 301.7429-1.]

☐ [*T.D.* 7575, 12-15-78. *Amended by T.D.* 8453, 12-11-92.]

[Reg. §301.7429-2]

§301.7429-2. Review of jeopardy and termination assessment and jeopardy levy procedures.—(a) *Request for administrative review.*— Any request for the review of a jeopardy or termination assessment or jeopardy levy provided for by section 7429(a)(2) shall be filed with the district director within 30 days after the statement described in §301.7429-1 is given to the taxpayer. However, if no statement is given within the 5 day period described in §301.7429-1, any request for review of the jeopardy or termination assessment or jeopardy levy shall be filed within 35 days after the date such assessment or levy is made. Such request shall be in writing, shall state fully the reasons for the request, and shall be supported by such evidence as will enable the district director to make the redetermination described in section 7429(a)(3).

(b) *Administrative review.*—In determining whether the assessment is reasonable and the amount assessed is appropriate, or whether the jeopardy levy is reasonable, the district director shall take into account not only information available at the time the assessment or jeopardy levy is made but also information which subsequently becomes available.

(c) *Abatement of assessment.*—For rules relating to the abatement of assessments made under sections 6851 and 6861 see §§301.6861-1(e), 301.6861-1(f) and 1.6851-1(d) of this chapter. [Reg. §301.7429-2.]

☐ [*T.D.* 7575, 12-15-78. *Amended by T.D.* 8453, 12-11-92.]

[Reg. §301.7429-3]

§301.7429-3. Review of jeopardy and termination assessment and jeopardy levy procedures; judicial action.—(a) *Time for bringing judicial action.*—An action for judicial review described in section 7429(b) may be instituted by the taxpayer during the period beginning on the earlier of—

(1) The date the district director notifies the taxpayer of the determination described in section 7429(a)(3) and ending on the 90th day thereafter; or

(2) The 16th day after the request described in section 7429(a)(2) was made by the taxpayer and ending on the 90th day thereafter.

(b) *Extension of period for judicial review.*—The United States Government may not by itself seek an extension of the 20 day period described in section 7429(b)(3), but it may join with the taxpayer in seeking such an extension.

(c) *Jurisdiction for determination.*—In general, the United States district courts will have exclusive jurisdiction over any civil action for a determination described in section 7429(b). However, if a petition for a redetermination of a deficiency has been timely filed with the Tax Court prior to

the making of an assessment or levy that is subject to the section 7429 review procedures, and one or more of the taxes and tax periods before the Tax Court as a result of the petition is also included in the written statement that was provided to the taxpayer, then the Tax Court will have jurisdiction concurrent with the district courts over any civil action for a judicial determination with respect to all the taxes and tax periods included in the written statement. In all other cases, the appropriate United States district court continues to have exclusive jurisdiction over such an action. [Reg. §301.7429-3.]

☐ [*T.D.* 7575, 12-15-78. *Amended by T.D.* 8453, 12-11-92.]

[Reg. §301.7430-0]

§301.7430-0. Table of contents.—This section lists the captions that appear in §§301.7430-1 through 301.7430-6.

§301.7430-1 Exhaustion of administrative remedies.

(a) In general.

(b) Requirements.

(1) In general.

(2) Participates.

(3) Tax matter.

(4) Failure to agree to extension of time for assessments.

(c) Revocation of a determination that an organization is described in section 501(c)(3).

(d) Actions involving summonses, levies, liens, jeopardy and termination assessments, etc.

(e) Exception to requirement that party pursue administrative remedies.

(f) Examples.

(g) Effective date.

§301.7430-2 Requirements and procedures for recovery of reasonable administrative costs.

(a) Introduction.

(b) Requirements for recovery.

(1) Determination by the Internal Revenue Service.

(i) Jurisdiction.

(ii) Administrative proceeding.

(iii) Administrative proceeding date.

(iv) Reasonable administrative costs.

(v) Prevailing party.

(vi) Not unreasonably protracted.

(vii) Procedural requirements.

(2) Determination by court.

(c) Procedure for recovering reasonable administrative costs.

(1) In general.

(2) Where request must be filed.

(3) Contents of request.

(i) Statements.

(ii) Affidavit or affidavits.

(iii) Documentation and information.

(4) Form of request.

(5) Period for requesting costs from the Internal Revenue Service.

(6) Notice.

(7) Appeal to Tax Court.

(d) Unreasonable protraction of administrative proceeding.

(e) Examples.

§ 301.7430-3 *Administrative proceeding and administrative proceeding date.*

(a) Administrative proceeding.

(b) Collection action.

(c) Administrative proceeding date.

(1) General rule.

(2) Notice of the decision of the Internal Revenue Service Office of Appeals.

(3) Notice of deficiency.

(4) First letter of proposed deficiency that allows the taxpayer an opportunity for administrative review in the Office of Appeals.

(d) Examples.

§ 301.7430-4 *Reasonable administrative costs.*

(a) In general.

(b) Costs described.

(1) In general.

(2) Representative and specially qualified representative.

(i) Representative.

(ii) Specially qualified representative.

(3) Limitation on fees for a representative.

(i) In general.

(ii) Cost of living adjustment.

(iii) Special factor adjustment.

(A) In general.

(B) Special factor.

(C) Limited availability.

(D) Local availability of tax expertise.

(E) Difficulty of the issues.

(F) Example.

(c) Certain costs excluded.

(1) Costs not incurred in an administrative proceeding.

(2) Costs incurred in an administrative proceeding but not reasonable.

(i) In general.

(ii) Special rule for expert witness' fees on issue of prevailing market rates.

(3) Litigation costs.

(4) Examples.

(d) Pro bono representation.

(1) In general.

(2) Requirements.

(3) Nominal fee.

(4) Payment when representation provided for a nominal fee.

(5) Requirements.

(6) Hourly rate.

(7) Examples.

§ 301.7430-5 *Prevailing party.*

(a) In general.

(b) Position of the Internal Revenue Service.

(c) Examples.

(d) Substantially justified.

(1) In general.

(2) Position in courts of appeal.

(3) Examples.

(4) Included costs.

(5) Examples.

(6) Exception.

(7) Presumption.

(e) Amount in controversy.

(f) Most significant issue or set of issues presented.

(1) In general.

(2) Example.

(g) Net worth and size limitations.

(1) Individuals.

(2) Estates and trusts.

(3) Others.

(4) Special rule for charitable organizations and certain cooperatives.

(5) Special rule for TEFRA partnerships.

(6) Determining net worth.

(h) Determination of prevailing party.

(i) Examples.

§ 301.7430-6 *Effective/applicability dates.*

§ 301.7430-7 *Qualified offers.*

(a) In general.

(b) Requirements for treatment as a prevailing party based upon having made a qualified offer.

(1) In general.

(2) Liability under the last qualified offer.

(3) Liability pursuant to the judgment.

(c) Qualified offer.

(1) In general.

(2) To the United States.

(3) Specifies the offered amount.

(4) Designated at the time it is made as a qualified offer.

(5) Remains open.

(6) Last qualified offer.

(7) Qualified offer period.

(8) Interest as a contested issue.

(d) [Reserved].

(e) Examples.

(f) Effective date.

§ 301.7430-8 *Administrative costs incurred in damage actions for violations of section 362 or 524 of the Bankruptcy Code.*

(a) In general.

(b) Prevailing party.

(c) Administrative proceeding.

(d) Costs incurred after filing of bankruptcy petition.

(e) Time for filing claim for administrative costs.

(f) Effective date.

[Reg. § 301.7430-0.]

☐ [*T.D.* 8542, 6-6-94. *Amended by T.D.* 8725, 7-21-97 *and T.D.* 9756, 2-29-2016.]

Reg. § 301.7430-0

[Reg. §301.7430-1]

§301.7430-1. Exhaustion of administrative remedies.—(a) *In general.*—Section 7430(b)(1) provides that a court shall not award reasonable litigation costs in any civil tax proceeding under section 7430(a) unless the court determines that the prevailing party has exhausted the administrative remedies available to the party within the Internal Revenue Service. This section sets forth the circumstances in which such administrative remedies shall be deemed to have been exhausted.

(b) *Requirements.*—(1) *In general.*—A party has not exhausted the administrative remedies available within the Internal Revenue Service with respect to any tax matter for which an Appeals office conference is available under §§601.105 and 601.106 of this chapter (other than a tax matter described in paragraph (c) of this section) unless—

(i) The party, prior to filing a petition in the Tax Court or a civil action for refund in a court of the United States (including the Court of Federal Claims), participates, either in person or through a qualified representative described in §601.502 of this chapter, in an Appeals office conference; or

(ii) If no Appeals office conference is granted, the party, prior to the issuance of a statutory notice in the case of a petition in the Tax Court or the issuance of a notice of disallowance in the case of a civil action for refund in a court of the United States (including the Court of Federal Claims)—

(A) Requests an Appeals office conference in accordance with §§601.105 and 601.106 of this chapter or any successor published guidance; and

(B) Files a written protest if a written protest is required to obtain an Appeals office conference.

(2) *Participates.*—For purposes of this section, a party or qualified representative of the party described in §601.502 of this chapter participates in an Appeals office conference if the party or qualified representative discloses to the Appeals office all relevant information regarding the party's tax matter to the extent such information and its relevance were known or should have been known to the party or qualified representative at the time of such conference.

(3) *Tax matter.*—For purposes of this section, "tax matter" means a matter in connection with the determination, collection or refund of any tax, interest, penalty, addition to tax or additional amount under the Internal Revenue Code.

(4) *Failure to agree to extension of time for assessments.*—Any failure by the prevailing party to agree to an extension of the time for the assessment of any tax will not be taken into account for purposes of determining whether the prevailing party has exhausted the administrative remedies available to the party within the Internal Rrevenue Service.

(c) *Revocation of a determination that an organization is described in section 501(c)(3).*—A party has not exhausted the administrative remedies available within the Internal Revenue Service with respect to a revocation of a determination that it is an organization described in section 501(c)(3) unless, prior to filing a declaratory judgment action under section 7428, the party has exhausted its administrative remedies in accordance with section 7428, and any regulations, rules, and revenue procedures thereunder.

(d) *Actions involving summonses, levies, liens, jeopardy and termination assessments, etc.*—(1) A party has not exhausted the administrative remedies available within the Internal Revenue Service with respect to a matter other than one to which paragraph (b) or (c) of this section applies (including summonses, levies, liens, and jeopardy and termination assessments) unless, prior to filing an action in a court of the United States (including the Tax Court and the Court of Federal Claims)—

(i) The party follows all applicable Internal Revenue Service procedures for contesting the matter (including filing a written protest or claim, requesting an administrative appeal, and participating in an administrative hearing or conference); or

(ii) If there are no applicable Internal Revenue Service procedures, the party submits to the Area Director of the area having jurisdiction over the dispute a written claim for relief reciting facts and circumstances sufficient to show the nature of the relief requested and that the party is entitled to the requested relief, and the Area Director denies the claim for relief in writing or fails to act on the claim within a reasonable period after the claim is received by the Area Director.

(2) For purposes of paragraph (d)(1)(ii) of this section, a *reasonable period* is—

(i) The 5-day period preceding the filing of a petition to quash an administrative summons issued under section 7609;

(ii) The 5-day period preceding the filing of a wrongful levy action in which a demand for the return of property is made;

(iii) The period expressly provided for administrative review of the party's claim by an applicable provision of the Internal Revenue Code that expressly provides for the pursuit of administrative remedies (such as the 16-day period provided under section 7429(b)(1)(B) relating to review of jeopardy assessment procedures); or

(iv) The 60-day period following receipt of the claim for relief in all other cases.

(e) *Actions involving willful violations of the automatic stay under section 362 or the discharge provisions under section 524 of the Bankruptcy Code.*—(1) *Section 7433 claims.*—A party has not exhausted administrative remedies within the Internal Revenue Service with respect to asserted violations of the automatic stay under section 362 of the Bankruptcy Code or the discharge provisions under section 524 of the Bankruptcy Code unless it files an administrative claim for damages or for relief from a violation of section 362 or 524 of the Bankruptcy Code with the Chief, Local Insolvency Unit, for the judicial district in which the bankruptcy petition that is the basis for the asserted automatic stay or discharge violation was filed pursuant to § 301.7433-2(e) and satisfies the other conditions set forth in § 301.7433-2(d) prior to filing a petition under section 7433.

(2) *Section 362(h) claims.*—A party has not exhausted administrative remedies within the Internal Revenue Service with respect to asserted violations of the automatic stay under section 362 of the Bankruptcy Code unless it files an administrative claim for relief from a violation of section 362 of the Bankruptcy Code with the Chief, Local Insolvency Unit, for the judicial district in which the bankruptcy petition that is the basis for the asserted automatic stay violation was filed pursuant to § 301.7433-2(e) and satisfies the other conditions set forth in § 301.7433-2(d) prior to filing a petition under section 362(h) of the Bankruptcy Code.

(f) *Exception to requirement that party pursue administrative remedies.*—If the conditions set forth in paragraph (f)(1), (f)(2), (f)(3), or (f)(4) of this section are satisfied, a party's administrative remedies within the Internal Revenue Service shall be deemed to have been exhausted for purposes of section 7430.

(1) The Internal Revenue Service notifies the party in writing that the pursuit of administrative remedies in accordance with paragraphs (b), (c), and (d) of this section is unnecessary.

(2) In the case of a petition in the Tax Court—

(i) The party did not receive a notice of proposed deficiency (30-day letter) prior to the issuance of the statutory notice and the failure to receive such notice was not due to actions of the party (such as a failure to supply requested information or a current mailing address to the Internal Revenue Service office or service center having jurisdiction over the tax matter); and

(ii) The party does not refuse to participate in an Appeals office conference while the case is in docketed status.

(3) In the case of a civil action for refund involving a tax matter other than a tax matter described in paragraph (e)[(f)](4) of this section, the party—

(i) Participates in an Appeals office conference with respect to the tax matter prior to issuance of a statutory notice of deficiency with respect to such tax matter; or

(ii) Did not receive written notification that an Appeals office conference was available prior to issuance of a notice of disallowance and the failure to receive such a notification was not due to the actions of the party (such as the failure to supply requested information or a current mailing address to the Internal Revenue

Service office or service center having jurisdiction over the tax matter); or

(iii) Did not receive either written or oral notification that an Appeals office conference had been granted within six months from the date of the filing of the claim for refund and the failure to receive such notice was not due to actions of the party (such as the failure to supply requested information or a current mailing address to the Internal Revenue Service office or service center having jurisdiction over the tax matter).

(4) In the case of a civil action for refund involving a tax matter under sections 6703 or 6694—

(i) The party did not receive a notice of proposed disallowance prior to issuance of a notice of disallowance and the failure to receive such notice was not due to actions of the party (such as the failure to supply requested information or a current mailing address to the Internal Revenue Service office or service center having jurisdiction over the tax matter); or

(ii) During the six-month period following the day on which the party's claim for refund is filed, the party's claim for refund is not denied, and the Internal Revenue Service has failed to process the claim with due diligence.

(g) *Examples.*—The provisions of this section may be illustrated by the following examples:

Example 1. Taxpayer A exchanges property held for investment for similar property and claims that the gain on the exchange is not recognized under section 1031. The Internal Revenue Service conducts a field examination and determines that there has not been a like-kind exchange. No agreement is reached on the matter and a notice of proposed deficiency (30-day letter) is sent to A. A does not file a request for an Appeals office conference. A pays the amount of the proposed deficiency and files a claim for refund. A notice of proposed disallowance is issued by the Internal Revenue Service. A does not request an Appeals office conference and, instead, files a civil action for refund in a United States District Court. A has not exhausted the administrative remedies available within the Internal Revenue Service.

Example 2. Assume the same facts as in *Example 1* except that, after receiving the notice of proposed deficiency (30-day letter), A files a request for an Appeals office conference. No agreement is reached at the conference. A pays the amount of the proposed deficiency and files a claim for refund. A notice of proposed disallowance is issued by the Internal Revenue Service. A does not request an Appeals office conference and files a civil action for refund in a United States District Court. A has exhausted the administrative remedies available within the Internal Revenue Service.

Example 3. Assume the same facts as in *Example 1* except A first requests an Appeals office conference after A's receipt of the notice of proposed disallowance. A is granted an Appeals office conference and A participates in such conference. A has exhausted the administrative remedies available within the Internal Revenue Service.

Example 4. Taxpayer B receives a notice of proposed deficiency (30-day letter) after completion of a field examination. B provided to the Internal Revenue Service during the examination all relevant information under the taxpayer's control and all relevant legal arguments supporting the taxpayer's position. B properly requests an Appeals office conference. The Appeals office, to obtain an additional period of time to consider the tax matter, requests that B sign Form 872 to extend the time for an assessment of tax, but B declines. Appeals then denies the request for a conference and issues a notice of deficiency. B has exhausted the administrative remedies available within the Internal Revenue Service.

Example 5. Taxpayer C receives a notice of proposed deficiency (30-day letter) and a written statement that C need not file a written protest or request an Appeals office conference since a conference will not be granted. C files a petition in the Tax Court after receiving the statutory notice of deficiency. C's administrative remedies within the Internal Revenue Service are deemed to have been exhausted.

Example 6. On January 2, the Internal Revenue Service serves a summons issued under section 7609 on third-party recordkeeper D to produce records of taxpayer E. On January 5, notice of the summons is given to E. The last day on which E may file a petition in a court of the United States to quash the summons is January 25. Thereafter, E files a written claim for relief with the Internal Revenue Service office having jurisdiction over the matter together with a copy of the summons. The claim and copy are received by the Internal Revenue Service office on January 20. On January 25, E files a petition to quash the summons. E has exhausted the administrative remedies available within the Internal Revenue Service.

Example 7. A notice of Federal tax lien is filed in County M on March 3, in the name of F. On April 2, F pays the entire liability thereby satisfying the lien. On May 2, F files a written claim with the Internal Revenue Service office having jurisdiction over the tax matter demanding a certificate of release of lien. Thereafter, F provides the Internal Revenue Service office with a copy of the notice of Federal tax lien and a copy of the cancelled check in satisfaction of the lien, which are received by the district director on May 15. F's claim is deemed to have been filed on May 15. Accordingly, F must wait until after July 14 (60 days following the filing of the claim for relief on May 15) to commence an action, in order to have exhausted the administrative remedies available within the Internal Revenue Service.

Example 8. A revenue officer seizes an automobile to effect collection of G's liability on January 10. On January 22, H submits a written claim to the Internal Revenue Service office having jurisdiction over the tax matter claiming that H purchased the automobile from G for an adequate

consideration before the tax lien against G arose, and demands immediate return of the automobile. A copy of the title certificate and H's cancelled check are submitted with the claim. The claim is received by the Internal Revenue Service office on January 25. On January 30, H brings a wrongful levy action. H has exhausted the administrative remedies available within the Internal Revenue Service.

Example 9. The Internal Revenue Service issues a revenue ruling which holds that ear piercing does not affect a function or structure of the body within the meaning of section 213 and therefore is not deductible. Taxpayer I deducts the costs of ear piercing and, following an examination, receives a notice of proposed deficiency (30-day letter) disallowing the treatment of these costs. Because of the revenue ruling, I believes a conference would not aid in the resolution of the tax dispute. Accordingly, I does not request an Appeals office conference. After receiving a statutory notice of deficiency, I files a petition in the Tax Court. I has not exhausted the administrative remedies available within the Internal Revenue Service. The issuance of a revenue ruling covering the same fact situation but taking a contrary position does not constitute notification by the Internal Revenue Service to I that the pursuit of administrative remedies is unnecessary. Similarly, the issuance to I of a private letter ruling or technical advice does not constitute notification by the Internal Revenue Service that the pursuit of administrative remedies is unnecessary.

Example 10. Taxpayer J is assessed a penalty under section 6701 for aiding in the understatement of the tax liability of another person. J pays 15% of the penalty in accordance with section 6703 and files a claim for refund on June 15. J is not issued a notice of proposed disallowance and thus cannot participate in an Appeals office conference within six months of the filing of the claim for refund. J brings an action on December 23. J has exhausted the administrative remedies available within the Internal Revenue Service.

Example 11. Taxpayer K receives a notice of proposed deficiency (30-day letter) and neither requests nor participates in an Appeals office conference. The Service then issues a statutory notice of deficiency (90-day letter). Upon receiving the statutory notice, and after filing a petition with the Tax Court, K requests an Appeals office conference. K has not exhausted the administrative remedies available within the Internal Revenue Service because the request for an Appeals office conference was made after the issuance of the statutory notice.

(h) *Effective date.*—This section applies to court proceedings described in section 7430 filed in a court of the United States (including the Tax Court and the Court of Federal Claims) after May 7, 1992. [Reg. § 301.7430-1.]

☐ [*T.D. 7950, 4-16-83. Amended by T.D. 8543, 6-6-94; T.D. 8725, 7-21-97 T.D. 9050, 3-24-2003 and T.D. 9756, 2-29-2016.*]

[Reg. § 301.7430-2]

§ 301.7430-2. Requirements and procedures for recovery of reasonable administrative costs.—(a) *Introduction.*—Section 7430(a)(1) provides for the recovery, under certain circumstances, of reasonable administrative costs incurred in connection with an administrative proceeding before the Internal Revenue Service. Paragraph (b) of this section lists the requirements that a taxpayer must meet to be entitled to an award of reasonable administrative costs from the Internal Revenue Service. Paragraph (c) of this section describes the procedures that a taxpayer must follow to recover reasonable administrative costs. Paragraphs (b) and (c) apply to requests for administrative costs regarding all administrative proceedings within the Internal Revenue Service.

(b) *Requirements for recovery.*—(1) *Determination by the Internal Revenue Service.*—The Internal Revenue Service will grant a taxpayer's request for recovery of reasonable administrative costs incurred in connection with an administrative proceeding under section 7430 and this section only if—

(i) *Jurisdiction.*—The underlying substantive issues or the issue of reasonable administrative costs are not, and have never been, before any court of the United States (including the Tax Court or United States Court of Federal Claims) with jurisdiction over those issues;

(ii) *Administrative proceeding.*—The costs were incurred in connection with an administrative proceeding as defined in § 301.7430-3(a);

(iii) *Administrative proceeding date.*—The costs were incurred on or after the administrative proceeding date as defined in § 301.7430-3(c);

(iv) *Reasonable administrative costs.*—The costs were reasonable administrative costs as defined in § 301.7430-4;

(v) *Prevailing party.*—The taxpayer is a prevailing party as defined in § 301.7430-5;

(vi) *Not unreasonably protracted.*—The administrative proceeding was not unreasonably protracted by the taxpayer as discussed in paragraph (d) of this section; and

(vii) *Procedural requirements.*—The taxpayer follows the procedures set forth in paragraph (c) of this section.

(2) *Determination by court.*—Although the Internal Revenue Service will not grant a request for reasonable administrative costs where the requirements of paragraph (b)(1)(i) of this section are not met, a taxpayer may file a claim for reasonable administrative costs with the court with jurisdiction over the judicial proceeding. The court may award the taxpayer reasonable administrative costs under section 7430(a). Under section 7430(c)(4)(C)(ii), where the final determination with respect to the tax, interest, or penalty at issue is made by a court, the court

determines whether the taxpayer qualifies as a prevailing party. Thus, where the requirements of paragraph (b)(1)(i) of this section are not met, the taxpayer's only possibility of obtaining an award of reasonable administrative costs is to obtain an award of these costs from the court. In the event the court awards reasonable administrative costs, it may also award litigation costs for the reasonable costs of pursuing the claim for reasonable administrative costs, provided the requirements under section 7430 regarding an award of reasonable administrative costs are satisfied with respect to these costs. A claim filed with the court should be made in accordance with the rules of the court.

(c) *Procedure for recovering reasonable administrative costs.*—(1) *In general.*—The Internal Revenue Service will not award administrative costs under section 7430 unless the taxpayer files a written request to recover reasonable administrative costs in accordance with the provisions of this section.

(2) *Where request must be filed.*—A request required by paragraph (c)(1) of this section must be filed with the Internal Revenue Service personnel who have jurisdiction over the tax matter underlying the claim for the costs, except that requests with respect to administrative proceedings defined by § 301.7430-8(c) should be made to the Chief, Local Insolvency Unit. However, if those persons are unknown to the taxpayer making the request, the taxpayer may send the request to the Internal Revenue Service office that considered the underlying matter.

(3) *Contents of request.*—The request must be in writing and must contain the following statements, affidavits, documentation, and information with regard to the taxpayer's administrative proceeding—

(i) *Statements*—

(A) A statement that the underlying substantive issues or the issue of reasonable administrative costs are not, and have never been, before any court of the United States (including the Tax Court or United States Court of Federal Claims) with jurisdiction over those issues;

(B) A clear and concise statement of the reasons why the taxpayer alleges that the position of the Internal Revenue Service in the administrative proceeding was not substantially justified. For administrative proceedings commenced after July 30, 1996, if the taxpayer alleges that the Internal Revenue Service did not follow any applicable published guidance, the statement must identify all applicable published guidance that the taxpayer alleges that the Internal Revenue Service did not follow. For purposes of this paragraph (c)(3)(i)(B), the term applicable published guidance means final or temporary regulations, revenue rulings, revenue procedures, information releases, notices, announcements, and, if issued to the taxpayer, private letter rulings, technical advice memoranda, and determination letters. Also, for purposes of this paragraph (c)(3)(i)(B), the term administrative proceeding includes only those administrative proceedings or portions of administrative proceedings occurring on or after the administrative proceeding date as defined in §301.7430-3(c). For costs incurred after January 18, 1999, if the taxpayer alleges that the United States has lost in courts of appeal for other circuits on substantially similar issues, the taxpayer must provide, for each such case, the full name of the case, volume and pages of the reporter in which the opinion appears, the circuit in which the case was decided, and the year of the opinion;

(C) A statement sufficient to demonstrate that the taxpayer has substantially prevailed as to the amount in controversy or with respect to the most significant issue or set of issues presented in the proceeding;

(D) A statement that the taxpayer has not unreasonably protracted the portion of the administrative proceeding for which the taxpayer is requesting costs; and

(E) A statement supported by a detailed affidavit executed by the taxpayer or the taxpayer's representative that sets forth the nature and amount of each specific item of reasonable administrative costs for which the taxpayer is seeking recovery. This statement must identify whether the representation is on a pro bono basis as defined in §301.7430-4(d) and, if so, to whom payment should be made. Specifically, the statement must direct whether payment should be made to the taxpayer's representative or to the representative's employer.

(ii) *Affidavit or affidavits—*

(A) An affidavit executed by the taxpayer stating that the taxpayer meets the net worth and size limitations of §301.7430-5(f);

(B) An affidavit supporting the statement described in paragraph (c)(3)(i)(E) of this section; and

(C) For costs incurred after January 18, 1999, if more than $125 per hour (as adjusted for an increase in the cost of living pursuant to §301.7430-4(b)(3)) is claimed for the fees of a representative in connection with the administrative proceeding, an affidavit is necessary stating that a special factor described in §301.7430-4(b)(3) is applicable, such as the difficulty of the issues presented in the case or the lack of local availability of tax expertise. If a special factor is claimed based on specialized skills and distinctive knowledge as described in §301.7430-4(b)(2)(ii), the affidavit should state—

(1) Why the specialized skills and distinctive knowledge were necessary in the representation;

(2) That there is a limited availability of representatives possessing these specialized skills and distinctive knowledge; and

(3) How the representative's education and experience qualifies the representative as someone with the necessary specialized skills and distinctive knowledge.

(iii) *Documentation and information—*

(A) A copy of the billing records of the representative for the requested fees; and

(B) An address at which the taxpayer wishes to receive notice of the determination of the Internal Revenue Service with regard to the request for reasonable administrative costs.

(C) In cases of pro bono representation, time records similar to billing records, detailing the time spent and work completed, must be submitted for the requested fees.

(4) *Form of Request.*—No specific form is required for the request other than one that satisfies the requirements of paragraph (c)(3) of this section. Where practicable the required statements may be included in a single document. Similarly, where practicable, the required affidavits may be combined in a single affidavit to the extent they are to be executed by the same person.

(5) *Period for requesting costs from the Internal Revenue Service.*—To recover reasonable administrative costs pursuant to section 7430 and this section, the taxpayer must file a written request for costs within 90 days after the date the final adverse decision of the Internal Revenue Service with respect to all tax, additions to tax, interest, and penalties at issue in the administrative proceeding is mailed or otherwise furnished to the taxpayer. For purposes of this section, *interest* means the interest that is specifically at issue in the administrative proceeding independent of the taxpayer's objections to the underlying tax, additions to tax, and penalties imposed. The final decision of the Internal Revenue Service for purposes of this section is the document that resolves the taxpayer's liability with regard to all tax, additions to tax, interest, and penalties at issue in the administrative proceeding (such as a Form 870 or closing agreement), or a notice of assessment for that liability (such as the notice and demand under section 6303), whichever is earlier mailed or otherwise furnished to the taxpayer. For purposes of this section, if the 90th day falls on a Saturday, Sunday, or a legal holiday, the 90-day period shall end on the next succeeding day that is not a Saturday, Sunday, or a legal holiday as defined by section 7503.

(6) *Notice.*—The Internal Revenue Service is authorized, but not required, to notify the taxpayer of its decision to grant or deny (in whole or in part) an award for reasonable administrative costs under section 7430 and this section by certified mail or registered mail. If the Internal Revenue Service does not respond on the merits to a request by the taxpayer for an award of reasonable administrative costs filed under paragraph (c)(1) of this section within 6 months after the request is filed, the Internal Revenue Service's failure to respond may be considered by the taxpayer as a decision of the Internal Revenue Service denying an award for reasonable administrative costs.

(7) *Appeal to Tax Court.*—A taxpayer may appeal a decision by the Internal Revenue Ser-

vice denying (in whole or in part) a request for reasonable administrative costs under section 7430 and this section by filing a petition for reasonable administrative costs with the Tax Court. The petition must be in accordance with the Tax Court's Rules of Practice and Procedure and must be filed with the Tax Court after the Internal Revenue Service denies (in whole or in part) the taxpayer's request for reasonable administrative costs. Once a notice of decision denying (in whole or in part) an award for reasonable administrative costs is mailed by the Internal Revenue Service via certified mail or registered mail as required by paragraph (c)(6) of this section, a taxpayer may obtain judicial review of that decision by filing a petition for review with the Tax Court prior to the 91st day after the mailing of the notice of decision.

(d) *Unreasonable protraction of administrative proceeding.*—An award of reasonable administrative costs will not be made where the taxpayer unreasonably protracted the administrative proceeding. However, a taxpayer that unreasonably protracted only a portion of the administrative proceeding, but not other portions of the administrative proceeding, may recover reasonable administrative costs for the portion(s) of the administrative proceeding that the taxpayer did not unreasonably protract, if the requirements of paragraph (b)(1) of this section are otherwise satisfied.

(e) The following examples primarily illustrate paragraph (a) of this section:

Example 1. Taxpayer A receives a notice of proposed deficiency (30-day letter). A requests and is granted Appeals office consideration. The administrative file contains certain documents provided by A as substantiation for the tax matters at issue. Appeals determines that the information submitted is insufficient. Appeals then issues a notice of deficiency. After receiving the notice of deficiency but before the 90-day period for filing a petition with the Tax Court has expired, and before filing a petition with the Tax Court, A convinces Appeals that the information previously submitted and reviewed by Appeals is sufficient and, therefore, the notice of deficiency is incorrect and A owes no additional tax. Pursuant to section 6212(d), the notice of deficiency is rescinded. Appeals then closes the case showing a zero deficiency and mails A a notice to this effect. Assuming that Appeals did not rely on any new information provided by A in rescinding the notice of deficiency and that all of the other requirements of section 7430 are satisfied, A may recover reasonable administrative costs incurred after the date of the 30-day letter (the administrative proceeding date as defined in Treas. Reg. § 301.7430-3(c)). To recover these costs, A must file a request for administrative costs with the Appeals office personnel who settled A's tax matter, or if that person is unknown to A, with the Area Director of the area that considered the underlying matter, within 90 days after the date of mailing of the Office of

Appeals' final decision that A owes no additional tax.

Example 2. Taxpayer B files a request for an abatement of interest pursuant to section 6404 and the regulations thereunder. The Area Director issues a notice of proposed disallowance of the abatement request (akin to a 30-day letter). B requests and is granted Appeals office consideration. No agreement is reached with Appeals and the Office of Appeals issues a notice of disallowance of the abatement request. B does not file suit in the Tax Court, but instead contacts the Appeals office within 180 days after the mailing date of the notice of disallowance of the abatement request to attempt to reverse the decision. B convinces the Appeals office that the notice of disallowance is in error. The Appeals office agrees to abate the interest and mails the taxpayer a notification of this decision. The mailing date of the notification from Appeals of the decision to abate interest commences the 90-day period from which the taxpayer may request administrative costs. Assuming that Appeals did not rely on any new information provided by B in reversing its notice of disallowance, and that all of the other requirements of section 7430 are satisfied, B may recover reasonable administrative costs incurred after the date the Area Director issued the notice of proposed disallowance of the abatement request (the administrative proceeding date as defined in Treas. Reg. § 301.7430-3(c)). To recover these costs, B must file a request for costs with the Appeals office personnel who settled B's tax matter, or if that person is unknown to B, with the Area Director of the area that considered the underlying matter within 90 days after the date of mailing of the Office of Appeals' final decision that B is entitled to abatement of interest.

Example 3. Taxpayer C receives a notice of proposed adjustment and employment tax 30-day letter. C requests and is granted Appeals office consideration. The administrative file contains certain documents provided by C to support C's position in the tax matters at issue. Appeals determines that the documents submitted are insufficient. Appeals then issues a notice of determination of worker classification. After receiving the notice of determination of worker classification but before the 90-day period for filing a petition with the Tax Court has expired, C convinces Appeals that the documents previously submitted and reviewed by Appeals adequately support its position and, therefore, C owes no additional employment tax. Appeals then closes the case showing a zero tax adjustment and mails C a no-change letter. Assuming that Appeals did not rely on any new information provided by C in reversing its notice of determination of worker classification, and that all of the other requirements of section 7430 are satisfied, C may recover reasonable administrative costs incurred after the date of the notice of proposed adjustment and 30-day letter (the administrative proceeding date as defined in Treas. Reg. § 301.7430-3(c)). To recover these costs, C must file a request for administrative costs with the Appeals office personnel who settled C's tax matter, or if that person is unknown to C, with the Area Director of the area that considered the underlying matter, within 90 days after the date of mailing of the Office of Appeals' final decision that C owes no additional tax. [Reg. § 301.7430-2.]

☐ [*T.D. 8542, 6-6-94. Amended by T.D. 8725, 7-21-97 T.D. 9050, 3-24-2003 and T.D. 9756, 2-29-2016.*]

[Reg. § 301.7430-3]

§ 301.7430-3. Administrative proceeding and administrative proceeding date.— (a) *Administrative proceeding.*—For purposes of section 7430, an administrative proceeding generally means any procedure or other action before the Internal Revenue Service that is commenced after November 10, 1988. However, an administrative proceeding does not include—

(1) Proceedings involving matters of general application, including hearings on regulations, comments on forms, or proceedings involving revenue rulings or revenue procedures;

(2) Proceedings involving requests for private letter rulings or similar determinations;

(3) Proceedings involving technical advice memoranda, except those submitted after the administrative proceeding date (as defined in paragraph (c) of this section); and

(4) Proceedings in connection with collection actions (as defined in paragraph (b) of this section), including proceedings under section 7432 or 7433, except proceedings brought under section 7433(e) and § 301.7433-2 or proceedings otherwise described in § 301.7430-8(c). See § 301.7430-8.

(b) *Collection action.*—A collection action generally includes any action taken by the Internal Revenue Service to collect a tax (or any interest, additional amount, addition to tax, or penalty, together with any costs in addition to the tax) or any action taken by a taxpayer in response to the Internal Revenue Service's act or failure to act in connection with the collection of a tax (including any interest, additional amount, addition to tax, or penalty, together with any costs in addition to the tax). A collection action for purposes of section 7430 and this section includes any action taken by the Internal Revenue Service under Chapter 64 of Subtitle F to collect a tax. Collection actions also include collection due process hearings under sections 6320 and 6330 (unless the underlying tax liability is properly at issue), and those actions taken by a taxpayer to remedy the Internal Revenue Service's failure to release a lien under section 6325 or to remedy any unauthorized collection action as described by section 7433, except those collection actions described by section 7433(e). An action or procedure directly relating to a claim for refund after payment of an assessed tax is not a collection action.

(c) *Administrative proceeding date.*—(1) *General rule.*—For purposes of section 7430 and the regulations thereunder, the term *administrative proceeding date* means the earlier of—

(i) The date of the receipt by the taxpayer of the notice of the decision of the Internal Revenue Service Office of Appeals;

(ii) The date of the notice of deficiency; or

(iii) The date on which the first letter of proposed deficiency that allows the taxpayer an opportunity for administrative review in the Internal Revenue Service Office of Appeals is sent.

(2) *Notice of the decision of the Internal Revenue Service Office of Appeals.*—For purposes of section 7430 and the regulations thereunder, a notice of the decision of the Internal Revenue Service Office of Appeals is the final written document, mailed or delivered to the taxpayer, that is signed by an individual in the Office of Appeals who has been delegated the authority to settle the dispute on behalf of the Commissioner, and states or indicates that the notice is the final determination of the entire case. A notice of claim disallowance issued by the Office of Appeals is a notice of the decision of the Internal Revenue Service Office of Appeals. Solely for purposes of determining the administrative proceeding date, a notice of deficiency issued by the Office of Appeals is not a notice of the decision of the Internal Revenue Service Office of Appeals.

(3) *Notice of deficiency.*—A notice of deficiency is a notice described in section 6212(a), including a notice rescinded pursuant to section 6212(d). For purposes of determining reasonable administrative costs under section 7430 and the regulations thereunder, the following will be treated as a notice of deficiency:

(i) A notice of final partnership administrative adjustment described in section 6223(a)(2).

(ii) A notice of determination of worker classification issued pursuant to section 7436.

(iii) A final notice of determination denying innocent spouse relief issued pursuant to section 6015.

(4) *First letter of proposed deficiency that allows the taxpayer an opportunity for administrative review in the Office of Appeals.*—Generally, the first letter of proposed deficiency that allows the taxpayer an opportunity for administrative review in the Office of Appeals is the first letter issued to the taxpayer that describes the proposed adjustments and advises the taxpayer of the opportunity to contact the Office of Appeals. It also may be a claim disallowance or the first letter of determination that allows the taxpayer an opportunity for administrative review in the Office of Appeals.

(d) *Examples.*—The provisions of this section are illustrated by the following examples:

Example 1. Taxpayer A receives a notice of proposed deficiency (30-day letter). A files a request for and is granted an Appeals office conference. At the Appeals conference no agreement is reached on the tax matters at issue. The Office of Appeals then issues a notice of deficiency. Upon receiving the notice of deficiency, A does not file a petition with the Tax Court. Instead, A pays the deficiency and files a claim for refund. The claim for refund is considered by the Internal Revenue Service and the Area Director issues a notice of proposed claim disallowance. A requests and is granted Appeals office consideration. A convinces Appeals that A's claim is correct and Appeals allows A's claim. A may recover reasonable administrative costs incurred on or after the date of the notice of proposed deficiency (30-day letter), but only if the other requirements of section 7430 and the regulations thereunder are satisfied. A cannot recover costs incurred prior to the date of the 30-day letter because these costs were incurred before the administrative proceeding date.

Example 2. Taxpayer B files an individual income tax return showing a balance due. No payment is made with the return and the Internal Revenue Service assesses the amount shown on the return. The Internal Revenue Service issues a Notice Of Intent to Levy And Notice Of Your Right To A Hearing pursuant to sections 6330(a) and 6331(d). B timely requests and is granted a Collection Due Process (CDP) hearing. In connection with the CDP hearing, B enters into an installment agreement as a collection alternative. The costs that B incurred in connection with the CDP hearing were not incurred in an administrative proceeding, but rather in a collection action. Accordingly, B may not recover those costs as reasonable administrative costs under section 7430 and the regulations thereunder. [Reg. § 301.7430-3.]

☐ [*T.D. 8542,* 6-6-94. *Amended by T.D. 9050,* 3-24-2003 *and T.D. 9756,* 2-29-2016.]

[Reg. § 301.7430-4]

§ 301.7430-4. Reasonable administrative costs.—(a) *In general.*—For purposes of section 7430 and the regulations thereunder, reasonable administrative costs are any costs described in paragraph (b) of this section that are incurred in connection with an administrative proceeding (as defined in § 301.7430-3(a)) and incurred on or after the administrative proceeding date (as defined in § 301.7430-3(c)).

(b) *Costs described.*—(1) *In general.*—The costs described in this paragraph are the reasonable and necessary amount of costs incurred by the taxpayer to present the taxpayer's position with respect to the merits of the tax controversy or the recovery of reasonable administrative costs. These costs include—

(i) Any administrative fees or similar charges imposed by the Internal Revenue Service;

(ii) Reasonable expenses of expert witnesses;

(iii) Reasonable costs of any study, analysis, engineering report, test or project that is necessary for, and incurred in preparation of, the taxpayer's case; and

(iv) Reasonable fees paid or incurred for the services of a representative (as defined in paragraph (b)(2) of this section) in connection with the administrative proceeding.

(2) *Representative and specially qualified representative.*—(i) *Representative.*—A representative is a person compensated for services rendered in connection with the administrative proceeding, who is authorized to practice before the Internal Revenue Service or the Tax Court.

(ii) *Specially qualified representative.*—For purposes of paragraphs (b)(3)(iii) and (c)(2)(ii) of this section, a specially qualified representative is a representative (as defined in paragraph (b)(2)(i) of this section) possessing a distinctive knowledge or a unique and specialized skill that is necessary to adequately represent the taxpayer in the proceeding. Examples of a unique and specialized skill or distinctive knowledge would be an identifiable practice specialty such as patent law or knowledge of a foreign law or language where that specialty or knowledge is necessary to adequately represent the taxpayer in the proceeding. For purposes of this paragraph, neither knowledge of tax law nor experience in representing taxpayers before the Internal Revenue Service is considered distinctive knowledge or a unique and specialized skill. An extraordinary level of general representational knowledge and ability that is useful in all proceedings is not considered, in and of itself, distinctive knowledge or a unique and specialized skill. Specially qualified representatives also do not include those who have a distinctive knowledge of the underlying subject matter of the controversy in circumstances where that distinctive knowledge could reasonably be supplied through the use of an expert, or could readily be obtained through literature pertaining to the subject.

(3) *Limitation on fees for a representative.*—(i) *In general.*—Except as otherwise provided in this section, fees incurred after January 18, 1999, and described in paragraph (b)(1)(iv) of this section that are recoverable under section 7430 and the regulations thereunder as reasonable administrative costs may not exceed $125 per hour (as adjusted for an increase in the cost of living and, if appropriate, a special factor adjustment).

(ii) *Cost of living adjustment.*—The Internal Revenue Service will make a cost of living adjustment to the $125 per hour limitation for fees incurred in any calendar year beginning after December 31, 1996. The cost of living adjustment will be an amount equal to $125 multiplied by the cost of living adjustment determined under section 1(f)(3) for the calendar year (substituting "calendar year 1995" for "calendar year 1992" in section 1(f)(3)(B)). If the dollar limitation as adjusted by this cost of living increase is not a multiple of $10, the dollar amount will be rounded to the nearest multiple of $10 (rounding up if the amount is a multiple of $5).

(iii) *Special factor adjustment.*—(A) *In general.*—If the presence of a special factor is demonstrated by the taxpayer, the amount reimbursable is the amount of reasonable fees paid or incurred by the taxpayer in connection with the proceeding for the services of a representative as defined in paragraph (b)(2)(i) of this section.

(B) *Special factor.*—A *special factor* is a factor, other than an increase in the cost of living, that justifies an increase in the $125 per hour limitation of section 7430(c)(1)(B)(iii). The undesirability of the case, the work and the ability of counsel, the results obtained, and customary fees and awards in other cases, are factors applicable to a broad spectrum of litigation and do not constitute special factors for the purpose of increasing the $125 per hour limitation. By contrast, the limited availability of a specially qualified representative for the proceeding, the limited local availability of tax expertise, and the difficulty of the issues are special factors justifying an increase in the $125 per hour limitation.

(C) *Limited availability.*—Limited availability of a specially qualified representative is established by demonstrating that a specially qualified representative for the proceeding is not available at the $125 per hour rate (as adjusted for an increase in the cost of living). The representative's special qualification must be based on nontax expertise. Initially, this showing may be made by submission of an affidavit signed by the taxpayer or by the taxpayer's counsel, that in a case similar to the taxpayer's, a specially qualified representative that practices within a reasonable distance from the taxpayer's principal residence or principal office would normally charge a client similar to the taxpayer at a rate in excess of this amount. If the Internal Revenue Service challenges this initial showing, the taxpayer may submit additional evidence to establish the limited availability of a specially qualified representative at the rate specified above.

(D) *Limited local availability of tax expertise.*—Limited local availability of tax expertise is established by demonstrating that a representative possessing tax expertise is not available in the taxpayer's geographical area. Initially, this showing may be made by submission of an affidavit signed by the taxpayer, or by the taxpayer's counsel, that no representative possessing tax expertise practices within a reasonable distance from the taxpayer's principal residence or principal office. The higher rate charged by representatives in the geographical area is not relevant in determining whether tax expertise is locally available. If the Internal Revenue Service challenges this initial showing, the taxpayer may submit additional evidence to establish the limited local availability of a representative possessing tax expertise.

(E) *Difficulty of the issues.*—In determining whether the difficulty of the issues justifies an increase in the $125 per hour limitation on the applicable hourly rate, the Internal Revenue Service will consider the following factors:

(1) The number of different provisions of law involved in each issue.

(2) The complexity of the particular provision or provisions of law involved in each issue.

(3) The number of factual issues present in the proceeding.

(4) The complexity of the factual issues present in the proceeding.

(F) *Example.*—The provisions of this section are illustrated by the following example:

Example. Taxpayer A is represented by B, a CPA and attorney with a LL.M. Degree in Taxation with Highest Honors who regularly handles cases dealing with TEFRA partnership issues. B represents A in an administrative proceeding involving TEFRA partnership issues that is subject to the provisions of this section. Assuming A qualifies for an award of reasonable administrative costs by meeting the requirements of section 7430, the amount of the award attributable to the fees of B may not exceed the $125 per hour limitation (as adjusted for an increase in the cost of living), absent a special factor. B is not a specially qualified representative because extraordinary knowledge of the tax laws does not constitute distinctive knowledge or a unique and specialized skill constituting a special factor. A higher rate may be justified by another special factor, that is, the limited local availability of tax expertise or the difficulty of the issues.

(c) *Certain costs excluded.*—(1) *Costs not incurred in an administrative proceeding.*—Costs that are not reasonable administrative costs for purposes of section 7430 include any costs incurred in connection with a proceeding that is not an administrative proceeding within the meaning of § 301.7430-3.

(2) *Costs incurred in an administrative proceeding but not reasonable.*—(i) *In general.*—Costs incurred in an administrative proceeding that are incurred on or after the administrative proceeding date, and that are otherwise described in paragraph (b) of this section, are not recoverable unless they are reasonable in both nature and amount. For example, costs normally included in the hourly rate of the representative by the custom and usage of the representative's profession, when billed separately, are not recoverable separate and apart from the representative's hourly rate. These costs typically include costs such as secretarial and overhead expenses. In contrast, costs that are normally billed separately may be reasonable administrative costs that may be recoverable in addition to the representative's hourly rate. Therefore, necessary costs incurred for travel; expedited mail delivery; messenger service; expenses while on travel; long distance telephone calls; and necessary copying fees imposed by the Internal Revenue Service, any court, bank or other third party, when normally billed separately from the representative's hourly rate, may be reasonable administrative costs.

Reg. § 301.7430-4(b)(3)(iii)(A)

(ii) *Special Rule for Expert Witness' Fees on Issue of Prevailing Market Rates.*—Under paragraph (b)(3)(iii)(C) of this section, the taxpayer may initially establish a limited availability of specially qualified representatives for the proceeding by submission of an affidavit signed by the taxpayer or by the taxpayer's representative. The Internal Revenue Service may endeavor to rebut the affidavit submitted on this issue by demonstrating either that a specially qualified representative was not necessary to represent the taxpayer in the proceeding, that the taxpayer's representative is not a specially qualified representative or that the prevailing rate for specially qualified representatives does not exceed $125 per hour (as adjusted for an increase in the cost of living). Unless the Internal Revenue Service endeavors to demonstrate that the prevailing rate for specially qualified representatives does not exceed $125 per hour (as adjusted for an increase in the cost of living), fees for expert witnesses used to establish prevailing market rates are not included in the term reasonable administrative costs.

(3) *Litigation costs.*—Litigation costs are not reasonable administrative costs because they are not incurred in connection with an administrative proceeding. Litigation costs include—

(i) Costs incurred in connection with the preparation and filing of a petition with the United States Tax Court or in connection with the commencement of any other court proceeding; and

(ii) Costs incurred after the filing of a petition with the United States Tax Court or after the commencement of any other court proceeding.

(4) *Examples.*—The provisions of this section are illustrated by the following examples:

Example 1. After incurring fees for representation during the Internal Revenue Service's examination of A's income tax return, A receives a notice of proposed deficiency (30-day letter). A files a request for and is granted an Appeals office conference. At the conference no agreement is reached on the tax matters at issue. The Internal Revenue Service then issues a notice of deficiency. Upon receiving the notice of deficiency, A discontinues A's administrative efforts and files a petition with the Tax Court. A's costs incurred before the date of the mailing of the 30-day letter are not reasonable administrative costs because they were incurred before the administrative proceeding date. Similarly, A's costs incurred in connection with the preparation and filing of a petition with the Tax Court are litigation costs and not reasonable administrative costs.

Example 2. Assume the same facts as in *Example 1* except that after A receives the notice of deficiency, in addition to petitioning the Tax Court, A recontacts Appeals and A convinces Appeals that the information previously submitted during the review by Appeals is sufficient and, therefore, the notice of deficiency is incorrect and A owes no additional tax. The Internal Revenue Service and A agree to a stipulated decision in the Tax Court case to reflect Appeals' decision. The Tax Court enters the decision. If A seeks administrative costs, A may recover costs incurred after the date of the mailing of the 30-day letter, costs incurred in recontacting Appeals after the issuance of the notice of deficiency, and costs incurred up to the time the Tax Court petition was filed, as reasonable administrative costs, but only if the other requirements of section 7430 and the regulations thereunder are satisfied. The costs incurred before the date of the mailing of the 30-day letter are not reasonable administrative costs because they were incurred before the administrative proceeding date, as set forth in § 301.7430-3(c)(1)(iii). A's costs incurred in connection with the filing of a petition with the Tax Court are not reasonable administrative costs because those costs are litigation costs. Similarly, A's costs incurred after the filing of the petition are not reasonable administrative costs, as they are litigation costs.

(d) *Pro bono representation.*—(1) *In general.*—Fees recoverable under section 7430 and the regulations thereunder as reasonable administrative costs may exceed the attorneys' fees paid or incurred by the prevailing party if such fees are less than the reasonable attorneys' fees because an individual is representing the prevailing party on a pro bono basis. In addition to attorneys' fees, reasonable costs incurred or paid by the individual providing the pro bono representation that are normally billed separately also may be recovered under this section. The Treasury Department and the Internal Revenue Service may, in revenue rulings, notices, or other guidance published in the Internal Revenue Bulletin, provide for additional rules that apply for awards of costs for pro bono representation for purposes of this paragraph (d).

(2) *Requirements.*—Pro bono representation is established by demonstrating—

(i) Representation was provided for no fee or for a fee that (taking into account all the facts and circumstances) constitutes a nominal fee;

(ii) The representative intended to provide representation for no fee or for a nominal fee from the commencement of the representation. Intent to provide representation for no fee or for a nominal fee may be demonstrated through documentation such as a retainer agreement. An individual will not be considered to have represented a client on a pro bono basis if the facts demonstrate that the individual anticipated a fee greater than a nominal fee or provided representation on a contingency fee basis. The fact that the representative intended to seek recovery of fees under section 7430 will not prevent the representative from satisfying this requirement.

Reg. § 301.7430-4(d)(2)(ii)

(3) *Nominal fee.*—A *nominal fee* is defined as a fee that is insignificantly small or minimal. A nominal fee is a trivial payment, bearing no relation to the value of the representation provided, taking into account all the facts and circumstances.

(4) *Payment when representation provided at no charge or for a nominal fee.*—A prevailing party who receives representation at no charge or for a nominal fee and who satisfies the requirements under this section is eligible to receive reasonable fees in excess of the fees actually paid or incurred. Payment will be made to the representative or the representative's employer.

(5) *Recordkeeping.*—Contemporaneous records must be maintained, demonstrating the work performed and the time allocated to each task. These records should contain similar information to billing records.

(6) *Examples.*—The provisions of this section are illustrated by the following example:

Example 1. Taxpayer A, an attorney, files a petition with the Tax Court and pays a $60 filing fee. A appears pro se in the court proceeding. If A prevails, he will not be entitled to an award of reasonable litigation costs for his services. A is rendering services on his own behalf, not providing pro bono representation. His lost opportunity costs are not compensable under section 7430. A may recover the filing fee as a litigation cost, but only if the other requirements of section 7430 and the regulations thereunder are satisfied. [Reg. § 301.7430-4.]

☐ [*T.D.* 8542, 6-6-94. *Amended by T.D.* 8725, 7-21-97 *and T.D.* 9756, 2-29-2016.]

[Reg. § 301.7430-5]

§ 301.7430-5. Prevailing party.—(a) *In general.*—For purposes of an award of reasonable administrative costs under section 7430 in the case of administrative proceedings commenced after July 30, 1996, a taxpayer is a prevailing party (other than by reason of section 7430(c)(4)(E)) only if—

(1) At least one issue (other than recovery of administrative costs) remains in dispute as of the date that the Internal Revenue Service takes a position in the administrative proceeding, as described in paragraph (b) of this section;

(2) The position of the Internal Revenue Service was not substantially justified;

(3) The taxpayer substantially prevails as to the amount in controversy or with respect to the most significant issue or set of issues presented; and

(4) The taxpayer satisfies the net worth and size limitations referenced in paragraph (f) of this section.

(b) *Position of the Internal Revenue Service.*—The position of the Internal Revenue Service in an administrative proceeding is the position taken by the Internal Revenue Service as of the earlier of—

(1) The date of the receipt by the taxpayer of the notice of the decision of the Internal Revenue Service Office of Appeals; or

(2) The date of the notice of deficiency or any date thereafter.

(c) *Examples.*—The provisions of this section may be illustrated by the following examples:

Example 1. Taxpayer A receives a notice of proposed deficiency (30-day letter). A pays the amount of the proposed deficiency and files a claim for refund. A's claim is considered and a notice of proposed claim disallowance is issued by the Area Director. A does not request an Appeals office conference and the Area Director issues a notice of claim disallowance. A then files suit in a United States District Court. A cannot recover reasonable administrative costs because the notice of claim disallowance is not a notice of the decision of the Internal Revenue Service Office of Appeals or a notice of deficiency. Accordingly, the Internal Revenue Service has not taken a position in the administrative proceeding pursuant to section 7430(c)(7)(B).

Example 2. Taxpayer B receives a notice of proposed deficiency (30-day letter). B disputes the proposed adjustments and requests an Appeals office conference. The Appeals office determines that B has no additional tax liability. B requests administrative costs from the date of the 30-day letter. B is not the prevailing party and may not recover administrative costs because all of the proposed adjustments in the case were resolved as of the date that the Internal Revenue Service took a position in the administrative proceeding.

(d) *Substantially justified.*—(1) *In general.*—The position of the Internal Revenue Service is substantially justified if it has a reasonable basis in both fact and law. A significant factor in determining whether the position of the Internal Revenue Service is substantially justified as of a given date is whether, on or before that date, the taxpayer has presented all relevant information under the taxpayer's control and relevant legal arguments supporting the taxpayer's position to the appropriate Internal Revenue Service personnel. The appropriate Internal Revenue Service personnel are personnel responsible for reviewing the information or arguments, or personnel who would transfer the information or arguments in the normal course of procedure and administration to the personnel who are responsible.

(2) *Position in courts of appeal.*—Whether the United States has won or lost an issue substantially similar to the one in the taxpayer's case in courts of appeal for circuits other than the one to which the taxpayer's case would be appealable should be taken into consideration in determining whether the Internal Revenue Service's position was substantially justified.

(3) *Example.*—The provisions of this section (d) are illustrated by the following example:

Example. The Internal Revenue Service, in the conduct of a correspondence examination of taxpayer A's individual income tax return, requests substantiation from A of claimed medical expenses. A does not respond to the request and the Internal Revenue Service issues a notice of deficiency. After receiving the notice of deficiency, A presents sufficient information and arguments to convince a tax compliance officer that the notice of deficiency is incorrect and that A owes no tax. The revenue agent then closes the case showing no deficiency. Although A incurred costs after the issuance of the notice of deficiency, A is unable to recover these costs because, as of the date these costs were incurred, A had not presented relevant information under A's control and relevant legal arguments supporting A's position to the appropriate Internal Revenue Service personnel. Accordingly, the position of the Internal Revenue Service was substantially justified at the time the costs were incurred.

(4) *Included costs.*—(i) An award of reasonable administrative costs shall only include costs incurred on or after the administrative proceeding date as defined in section 301.7430-3(c) of this chapter.

(ii) If the Internal Revenue Service takes a position in an administrative proceeding, as defined in paragraph (b) of this section, and the position is not substantially justified, the taxpayer may be permitted to recover costs incurred before the position was taken, but not before the dates set forth in this paragraph (d)(4).

(5) *Examples.*—The provisions of this section may be illustrated by the following examples:

Example 1. Pursuant to section 6672, taxpayer D receives from the Area Director Collection Operations (Collection) a proposed assessment of trust fund taxes (Trust Fund Recovery Penalty). D requests and is granted Appeals office consideration. Appeals considers the issues and decides to uphold Collection's recommended assessment. Appeals notifies D of this decision in writing. Collection then assesses the tax and notice and demand is made. D timely pays the minimum amount required to commence a court proceeding, files a claim for refund, and furnishes the required bond. Collection disallows the claim, but Appeals, on reconsideration, reverses its original position, thus upholding D's position. If Appeals' initial determination was not substantially justified, D may recover administrative costs incurred on or after the mailing of the proposed assessment of trust fund taxes, because the proposed assessment is the first determination letter that allows the taxpayer an opportunity for administrative review in the Internal Revenue Service Office of Appeals.

Example 2. Taxpayer E receives a notice of proposed deficiency (30-day letter). E pays the amount of the proposed deficiency and files a claim for refund. E's claim is considered and a notice of proposed disallowance is issued by the Area Director. E requests and is granted Appeals office consideration. No agreement is reached with Appeals and the Office of Appeals issues a notice of claim disallowance. E does not file suit in a United States District Court but instead contacts the Appeals office to attempt to reverse the decision. E convinces the Appeals officer that the notice of claim disallowance is in error. The Appeals officer then abates the assessment. E may recover reasonable administrative costs if the position taken in the notice of claim disallowance issued by the Office of Appeals was not substantially justified and the other requirements of section 7430 and the regulations thereunder are satisfied. If so, E may recover administrative costs incurred from the mailing date of the 30-day letter because the requirements of paragraph (c)(2) of this section are met. E cannot recover the costs incurred prior to the mailing of the 30-day letter because they were incurred before the administrative proceeding date.

(6) *Exception.*—If the position of the Internal Revenue Service was substantially justified with respect to some issues in the proceeding and not substantially justified with respect to the remaining issues, any award of reasonable administrative costs to the taxpayer may be limited to only reasonable administrative costs attributable to those issues with respect to which the position of the Internal Revenue Service was not substantially justified. If the position of the Internal Revenue Service was substantially justified for only a portion of the period of the proceeding and not substantially justified for the remaining portion of the proceeding, any award of reasonable administrative costs to the taxpayer may be limited to only reasonable administrative costs attributable to that portion during which the position of the Internal Revenue Service was not substantially justified. Where an award of reasonable administrative costs is limited to that portion of the administrative proceeding during which the position of the Internal Revenue Service was not substantially justified, whether the position of the Internal Revenue Service was substantially justified is determined as of the date any cost is incurred.

(7) *Presumption.*—If the Internal Revenue Service did not follow any applicable published guidance in an administrative proceeding commenced after July 30, 1996, the position of the Internal Revenue Service, on those issues to which the guidance applies and for all periods during which the guidance was not followed, will be presumed not to be substantially justified. This presumption may be rebutted. For purposes of this paragraph (d)(7), the term *applicable published guidance* means final or temporary regulations, revenue rulings, revenue procedures, information releases, notices, and announcements published in the Internal Revenue Bulletin and, if issued to or with respect to the taxpayer, private letter rulings, technical advice memoranda, and determination letters (§ 601.601(d)(2) of this chapter). Also, for purposes of this paragraph (d)(7), the term administrative proceeding includes only those administrative proceedings or portions of administrative proceedings occur-

ring on or after the administrative proceeding date as defined in § 301.7430-3(c).

(e) *Amount in controversy.*—The amount in controversy shall include the amount in issue as of the administrative proceeding date as increased by any amounts subsequently placed in issue by any party. The amount in controversy is determined without increasing or reducing the amount in controversy for amounts of loss, deduction, or credit carried over from years not in issue.

(f) *Most significant issue or set of issues presented.*—(1) *In general.*—Where the taxpayer has not substantially prevailed with respect to the amount in controversy the taxpayer may nonetheless be a prevailing party if the taxpayer substantially prevails with respect to the most significant issue or set of issues presented. The issues presented include those raised as of the administrative proceeding date and those raised subsequently. Only in a multiple issue proceeding can a most significant issue or set of issues presented exist. However, not all multiple issue proceedings contain a most significant issue or set of issues presented. An issue or set of issues constitutes the most significant issue or set of issues presented if, despite involving a lesser dollar amount in the proceeding than the other issue or issues, it objectively represents the most significant issue or set of issues for the taxpayer or the Internal Revenue Service. This may occur because of the effect of the issue or set of issues on other transactions or other taxable years of the taxpayer or related parties.

(2) *Example.*—The provisions of this section may be illustrated by the following example:

Example. In the purchase of an ongoing business, Taxpayer F obtains from the previous owner of the business a covenant not to compete for a period of five years. On audit of F's individual income tax return for the year in which the business was acquired, the Internal Revenue Service challenges the basis assigned to the covenant not to compete and a deduction taken as a business expense for a seminar attended by F. Both parties agree that the covenant not to compete is amortizable over a period of five years; however, the Internal Revenue Service asserts that the proper basis of the covenant is $25,000, while F asserts the basis is $50,000 and claims a deduction of $10,000 in the year in which the business was acquired. F deducted $12,000 for the seminar. The Internal Revenue Service determines that the deduction for the seminar should be disallowed entirely. In the notice of deficiency, the Internal Revenue Service adjusts the amortization deduction to reflect the change to the basis of the covenant not to compete, and disallows the seminar expense. Thus, of the two adjustments determined for the year under audit, the adjustment attributable to the disallowance of the seminar is larger than that attributable to the covenant not to compete. Due to the impact on the next succeeding four years,

however, the covenant not to compete adjustment is the most significant issue to both F and the Internal Revenue Service.

(g) *Net worth and size limitations.*—(1) *Individuals.*—A taxpayer who is a natural person meets the net worth and size limitations of this paragraph if the taxpayer's net worth does not exceed two million dollars. For purposes of determining net worth, individuals filing a joint return, and jointly incurring administrative or litigation costs shall have their net worth determined jointly, with all assets and liabilities treated as joint for purposes of the net worth evaluation, and applying a joint cap of four million dollars. Individuals who file a joint return, but incur separate administrative or litigation costs, by retaining separate representation, and/ or seeking individual administrative review or petitioning the court individually, such as under section 6015, shall have their net worth determined separately, with only those assets and liabilities reasonably attributable to each spouse considered against separate caps of two million dollars per spouse.

(2) *Estates and trusts.*—An estate or a trust meets the net worth and size limitations of this paragraph if the estate or trust's net worth does not exceed two million dollars. The net worth of an estate shall be determined as of the date of the decedent's death provided the date of death is prior to the date the court proceeding is commenced. The net worth of a trust shall be determined as of the last day of the last taxable year involved in the proceeding.

(3) *Others.*—(i) A taxpayer that is a partnership, corporation, association, unit of local government, or organization (other than an organization described in paragraph (g)(4) of this section) meets the net worth and size limitations of this paragraph if, as of the administrative proceeding date:

(A) The taxpayer's net worth does not exceed seven million dollars; and

(B) The taxpayer does not have more than 500 employees.

(ii) A taxpayer who is a natural person and owns an unincorporated business is subject to the net worth and size limitations contained in paragraph (g)(3)(i) of this section if the tax at issue (or any interest, additional amount, addition to tax, or penalty, together with any costs in addition to the tax) relates directly to the business activities of the unincorporated business.

(4) *Special rule for charitable organizations and certain cooperatives.*—An organization described in section 501(c)(3) exempt from taxation under section 501(a), or a cooperative association as defined in section 15(a) of the Agricultural Marketing Act, 12 U.S.C. 1141j(a) (as in effect on October 22, 1986), meets the net worth and size limitations of this paragraph if, as of the administrative proceeding date, the organization or cooperative association does not have more than 500 employees.

Reg. § 301.7430-5(e)

(5) *Special rule for TEFRA partnership proceedings.*—(i) In cases involving partnerships subject to the unified audit and litigation procedures of subchapter C of chapter 63 of the Internal Revenue Code (TEFRA partnership cases), the TEFRA partnership meets the net worth and size limitations requirements of this paragraph (g) if, on the administrative proceeding date—

(A) The partnership's net worth does not exceed seven million dollars; and

(B) The partnership does not have more than 500 employees.

(ii) In addition, each partner requesting fees pursuant to section 7430 must meet the appropriate net worth and size limitations set forth in paragraph (g)(1), (g)(2), or (g)(3) of this section. For example, if a partner is an individual, his or her net worth must not exceed two million dollars as of the administrative proceeding date. If the partner is a corporation, its net worth must not exceed seven million dollars and it must not have more than 500 employees.

(6) *Determining net worth.*—For purposes of determining net worth under this paragraph (g), assets are valued based on the cost of their acquisition.

(h) *Determination of prevailing party.*—If the final decision with respect to the tax, interest, or penalty is made at the administrative level, the determination of whether a taxpayer is a prevailing party shall be made by agreement of the parties, or absent an agreement, by the Internal Revenue Service. See § 301.7430-2(c)(7) regarding the right to appeal the decision of the Internal Revenue Service denying (in whole or in part) a request for reasonable administrative costs to the Tax Court. [Reg. § 301.7430-5.]

☐ [*T.D.* 8542, 6-6-94. *Amended by T.D.* 8725, 7-21-97 *and T.D.* 9756, 2-29-2016.]

[Reg. § 301.7430-6]

§ 301.7430-6. Effective/applicability dates.—Sections 301.7430-2 through 301.7430-6, other than § § 301.7430-2(b)(2), (c)(3)(i)(B), (c)(3)(i)(E), (c)(3)(ii)(C), (c)(3)(iii)(C), (c)(5), (c)(7), and (e); § § 301.7430-3(c)(1), (c)(3), (c)(4), and (d); § § 301.7430-4(b)(3)(i), (b)(3)(ii), (b)(3)(iii)(B), (b)(3)(iii)(C), (b)(3)(iii)(D), (b)(3)(iii)(E), (b)(3)(iii)(F), (c)(2)(ii), (c)(4), and (d); and § § 301.7430-5(a), (b), (c)(3), (d)(2), (d)(3), (d)(4), (d)(5), (d)(7), (f)(2), (g)(1), (g)(2), (g)(3), (g)(5), and (g)(6) apply to claims for reasonable administrative costs filed with the Internal Revenue Service after December 23, 1992, with respect to costs incurred in administrative proceedings commenced after November 10, 1988. Section 301.7430-2(c)(5) is applicable to costs incurred and services performed in cases in which the petition was filed on or after March 1, 2016, except for the last two sentences, which are applicable March 23, 1993. Sections 301.7430-2(b)(2), and (c)(3)(i)(B) (except the last sentence); 301.7430-4(b)(3)(ii), (b)(3)(iii)(C) (except the first two sentences), and (c)(2)(ii) (except for references to the statutory cap as $125); and

301.7430-5(a) (except the parenthetical of 5(a) and all of 5(a)(1)), and the first and last sentence of (d)(7) are applicable for administrative proceedings commenced after July 30, 1996. Sections 301.7430-1(e), 301.7430-2(c)(2), 7430-3(a)(4) and (b) are applicable with respect to actions taken by the Internal Revenue Service after July 22, 1998. The last sentence of § 301.7430-2(c)(3)(i)(B), the first two sentences of § § 301.7430-2(b)(3)(iii)(C), § § 301.7430-2(c)(3)(i)(E), (c)(3)(ii)(C), (c)(3)(iii)(C), (c)(7), (e); 301.7430-3(c)(1), (c)(3), (c)(4), (d); Reg. § 301.7430-4(b)(3)(i),(b)(3)(iii)(B), (b)(3)(iii)(E), (b)(3)(iii)(F), (c)(2)(ii)(to the extent it references the statutory cap as $125), (c)(4), (d); the parenthetical of § 301.7430-5(a) and § § 301.7430-5(a)(1), (b), (d)(2), (d)(3), (d)(4), (d)(5), (d)(7), except the first and last sentences, (f)(2), (g)(1), (g)(2), (g)(3), (g)(5), and (g)(6)apply to costs incurred and services performed in cases in which the petition was filed on or after March 1, 2016. [Reg. § 301.7430-6.]

☐ [*T.D.* 8542, 6-6-94. *Amended by T.D.* 8725, 7-21-97, *T.D.* 9050, 3-24-2003 *and T.D.* 9756, 2-29-2016.]

[Reg. § 301.7430-7]

§ 301.7430-7. Qualified offers.—(a) *In general.*—Section 7430(c)(4)(E) (the qualified offer rule) provides that a party to a court proceeding satisfying the timely filing and net worth requirements of section 7430(c)(4)(A)(ii) shall be treated as the prevailing party if the liability of the taxpayer pursuant to the judgment in the proceeding (determined without regard to interest) is equal to or less than the liability of the taxpayer which would have been so determined if the United States had accepted the last qualified offer of the party as defined in section 7430(g). For purposes of this section, the term *judgment* means the cumulative determinations of the court concerning the adjustments at issue and litigated to a determination in the court proceeding. In making the comparison between the liability under the qualified offer and the liability under the judgment, the taxpayer's liability under the judgment is further modified by the provisions of paragraph (b)(3) of this section. The provisions of the qualified offer rule do not apply if the taxpayer's liability under the judgment, as modified by the provisions of paragraph (b)(3) of this section, is determined exclusively pursuant to a settlement, or to any proceeding in which the amount of tax liability is not in issue, including any declaratory judgment proceeding, any proceeding to enforce or quash any summons issued pursuant to the Internal Revenue Code (Code), and any action to restrain disclosure under section 6110(f). If the qualified offer rule applies to the court proceeding, the determination of whether the liability under the qualified offer would have equaled or exceeded the liability pursuant to the judgment is made by reference to the last qualified offer made with respect to the tax liability at issue in the administrative or court proceeding. An award of reasonable administrative and litigation costs under the qualified offer rule only includes those costs incurred on or after the date of the last qualified offer and is limited to those costs attributable to the adjustments at issue at the time the last qualified offer was made that were included in the court's judgment other than by reason of settlement. The qualified offer rule is inapplicable to reasonable administrative or litigation costs otherwise awarded to a taxpayer who is a prevailing party under any other provision of section 7430(c)(4). This section sets forth the requirements to be satisfied for a taxpayer to be treated as a prevailing party by reason of the taxpayer making a qualified offer, as well as the circumstances leading to the application of the exceptions, special rules, and coordination provisions of the qualified offer rule. Furthermore, this section sets forth the elements necessary for an offer to be treated as a qualified offer under section 7430(g).

(b) *Requirements for treatment as a prevailing party based upon having made a qualified offer.*— (1) *In general.*—In order to be treated as a prevailing party by reason of having made a qualified offer, the liability of the taxpayer for the type or types of tax and the taxable year or years at issue in the proceeding (as calculated pursuant to paragraph (b)(2) of this section), based on the last qualified offer (as defined in paragraph (c) of this section) made by the taxpayer in the court or administrative proceeding, must equal or exceed the liability of the taxpayer pursuant to the judgment by the court for the same type or types of tax and the same taxable year or years (as calculated pursuant to paragraph (b)(3) of this section). Furthermore, the taxpayer must meet the timely filing and net worth requirements of section 7430(c)(4)(A)(ii). If all of the adjustments subject to the last qualified offer are settled prior to the entry of the judgment by the court, the taxpayer is not a prevailing party by reason of having made a qualified offer. The taxpayer may, however, still qualify as a prevailing party if the requirements of section 7430(c)(4)(A) are met. If one or more adjustments covered by a qualified offer (see paragraph (c)(3)) are settled following a ruling by the court that substantially resolves those adjustments, then those adjustments will not be treated as having been settled prior to the entry of the judgment by the court and instead will be treated as amounts included in the judgment as a result of the court's determinations. For purposes of the preceding sentence, rulings relating to discovery, admissibility of evidence, and burden of proof are not rulings that substantially resolve adjustments covered by a qualified offer.

(2) *Liability under the last qualified offer.*—For purposes of paragraph (b)(1) of this section, the taxpayer's liability under the last qualified offer is the change in the taxpayer's liability that would have resulted if the United States had accepted the taxpayer's last qualified offer on all of the adjustments that were at issue in the administrative or court proceeding at the time that the offer was made compared to the amount shown on the return or returns (or as previously adjusted). The portion of a taxpayer's liability that is attributable to adjustments raised by either party after the making of the last qualified offer is not included in the calculation of the liability under that offer. The taxpayer's liability under the last qualified offer is calculated without regard to adjustments that the parties have stipulated will be resolved in accordance with the outcome of a separate pending Federal, state, or other judicial or administrative proceeding. For example, the parties may stipulate that the taxpayer's liability will be resolved in accordance with the outcome of an alternative dispute resolution proceeding or a separate court proceeding, such as a probate, tort liability, or trademark action. Furthermore, the taxpayer's liability under the last qualified offer is calculated without regard to interest, unless the taxpayer's liability for, or entitlement to, interest is a contested issue in the administrative or court proceeding and is one of the adjustments included in the last qualified offer.

(3) *Liability pursuant to the judgment.*—For purposes of paragraph (b)(1) of this section, the taxpayer's liability pursuant to the judgment is the change in the taxpayer's liability resulting from amounts contained in the judgment as a result of the court's determinations, and amounts contained in settlements not included in the judgment, that are attributable to all adjustments that were included in the last qualified offer compared to the amount shown on the return or returns (or as previously adjusted). This liability includes amounts attributable to adjustments included in the last qualified offer and settled by the parties prior to the entry of judgment regardless of whether those amounts are actually included in the judgment entered by the court. The taxpayer's liability pursuant to the judgment does not include amounts attributable to adjustments that are not included in the last qualified offer, even if those amounts are actually included in the judgment entered by the court. The taxpayer's liability under the judgment is calculated without regard to adjustments that the parties have stipulated will be resolved in accordance with the outcome of a separate pending Federal, state, or other judicial or administrative proceeding. Furthermore, the taxpayer's liability pursuant to the judgment is calculated without regard to interest, unless the taxpayer's liability for, or entitlement to, interest is a contested issue in the administrative or court proceeding and is one of the adjustments included in the last qualified offer. Where adjustments raised by either party subsequent to the making of the last qualified offer are included in the judgment entered by the court, or are settled prior to the court proceeding, the taxpayer's liability pursuant to the judgment is calculated by treating the subsequently raised adjustments as if they had never been raised.

(c) *Qualified offer.*—(1) *In general.*—A qualified offer is defined in section 7430(g) to mean a written offer which—

(i) Is made by the taxpayer to the United States during the qualified offer period;

(ii) Specifies the offered amount of the taxpayer's liability (determined without regard to interest, unless interest is a contested issue in the proceeding);

(iii) Is designated at the time it is made as a qualified offer for purposes of section 7430(g); and

(iv) By its terms, remains open during the period beginning on the date it is made and ending on the earliest of the date the offer is rejected, the date the trial begins, or the 90th day after the date the offer is made.

(2) *To the United States.*—(i) A qualified offer is made to the United States when it is delivered to the office or personnel within the Internal Revenue Service, Office of Appeals, Office of Chief Counsel (including field personnel) or Department of Justice that has jurisdiction over the tax matter at issue in the administrative or court proceeding. If those offices or persons are unknown to the taxpayer making the qualified offer, the taxpayer may deliver the offer to the appropriate office, as follows:

(A) If the taxpayer's initial pleading in a court proceeding has been answered, the taxpayer may deliver the offer to the office that filed the answer.

(B) If the taxpayer's petition in the Tax Court has not yet been answered, the taxpayer may deliver the offer to the Office of Chief Counsel, 1111 Constitution Avenue, NW., Washington, DC 20224.

(C) If the taxpayer's initial pleading in any Federal court, other than the Tax Court, has not yet been answered, the taxpayer may deliver the offer to the Attorney General of the United States, 950 Pennsylvania Ave., NW., Washington, DC 20530-0001. For a suit brought in a United States district court, a copy of the offer should also be delivered to the United States Attorney for the district in which the suit was brought.

(D) In any other situation, the taxpayer may deliver the offer to the office that sent the taxpayer the first letter of proposed deficiency which allows the taxpayer an opportunity for administrative review in the Internal Revenue Service Office of Appeals.

(ii) Until an offer is received by the appropriate personnel or office under this paragraph (c)(2), it is not considered to have been made, with the following exception. If the offer is deposited in the United States mail, in an envelope or other appropriate wrapper, postage prepaid, properly addressed to the appropriate personnel or office under this paragraph (c)(2), the date of the United States postmark stamped on the cover in which the offer is mailed shall be deemed to be the date of receipt of that offer by the addressee. If any offer is deposited with a designated delivery service, as defined in section 7502(f)(2), in lieu of the United States mail, the provisions of section 7502(f)(1) shall apply in determining whether that offer qualifies for this exception.

(3) *Specifies the offered amount.*—A qualified offer specifies the offered amount if it clearly specifies the amount for the liability of the taxpayer, calculated as set forth in paragraph (b)(2) of this section. The offer may be a specific dollar amount of the total liability or a percentage of the adjustments at issue in the proceeding at the time the offer is made. This amount must be with respect to all of the adjustments at issue in the administrative or court proceeding at the time the offer is made and only those adjustments. The specified amount must be an amount, the acceptance of which by the United States will fully resolve the taxpayer's liability, and only that liability (determined without regard to adjustments that the parties have stipulated will be resolved in accordance with the outcome of a separate pending Federal, state, or other judicial or administrative proceeding, or interest, unless interest is a contested issue in the proceeding) for the type or types of tax and the taxable year or years at issue in the proceeding. In cases involving multiple tax years, if adjustments in different tax years arise from separate and distinct issues such that the resolution of issues in one or more tax years will not affect the taxpayer's liability in one or more of the other tax years in the proceeding, then a qualified offer may be made for less than all of the tax years involved. A qualified offer, however, must resolve all of the issues for the tax years covered by the offer and also must cover all tax years in the proceeding affected by those issues. A tax year (affected year) is affected by an issue if the treatment of the issue in another tax year involved in the proceeding necessarily affects the treatment of the issue in the affected year.

(4) *Designated at the time it is made as a qualified offer.*—An offer is not a qualified offer unless it designates in writing at the time it is made that it is a qualified offer for purposes of section 7430(g). An offer made at a time when one or more adjustments not included in the first letter of proposed deficiency which allows the taxpayer an opportunity for administrative review in the Internal Revenue Service Office of Appeals have been raised by the taxpayer and remain unresolved, is not considered to be a qualified offer unless contemporaneously or prior to the making of the offer, the taxpayer has provided the United States with the substantiation and legal and factual arguments necessary to allow for informed consideration of the merits of those adjustments. For example, a taxpayer will be considered to have provided the United States with the necessary substantiation and legal and factual arguments if the taxpayer (or a recognized representative of the taxpayer described in §601.502 of this chapter) participates in an Appeals office conference, participates in an Area Counsel conference, or confers with the Department of Justice, and at that time, discloses all relevant information. All relevant information includes, but is not limited to, the legal and factual arguments supporting the taxpayer's position on any adjustments raised by the taxpayer

after the issuance of the first letter of proposed deficiency which allows the taxpayer an opportunity for administrative review in the Internal Revenue Service Office of Appeals. A taxpayer has disclosed all relevant information if the taxpayer has supplied sufficient information to allow informed consideration of the taxpayer's tax matter to the extent the information and its relevance were known or should have been known to the taxpayer at the time of the conference.

(5) *Remains open.*—A qualified offer must, by its terms, remain open for acceptance by the United States from the date it is made, as defined in paragraph (c)(2)(ii) of this section, until the earliest of the date it is rejected in writing by a person with authority to reject the offer, the date the trial begins, or the 90th day after being received by the United States. The offer, by its written terms, may remain open after the occurrence of one or more of the above-referenced events. Once made, the period during which a qualified offer remains open may be extended by the taxpayer prior to its expiration, but an extension cannot be used to make an offer meet the minimum period for remaining open required by this paragraph (c)(5).

(6) *Last qualified offer.*—A taxpayer may make multiple qualified offers during the qualified offer period. For purposes of the comparison under paragraph (b) of this section, the making of a qualified offer supersedes any previously made qualified offers. In making the comparison described in paragraph (b) of this section, only the qualified offer made most closely in time to the end of the qualified offer period is compared to the taxpayer's liability under the judgment.

(7) *Qualified offer period.*—To constitute a qualified offer, an offer must be made during the qualified offer period. The qualified offer period begins on the date on which the first letter of proposed deficiency which allows the taxpayer an opportunity for administrative review in the Internal Revenue Service Office of Appeals is sent to the taxpayer. For this purpose, the date of the notice of claim disallowance will begin the qualified offer period in a refund case. If there has been no notice of claim disallowance in a refund case, the qualified offer period begins on the date on which the answer or other responsive pleading is filed with the court. The qualified offer period ends on the date which is thirty days before the date the case is first set for trial. In determining when the qualified offer period ends for cases in the Tax Court and other Federal courts using calendars for trial, a case will be considered set for trial on the date scheduled for the calendar call. A case may be removed from a trial calendar at any time. Thus, a case may be removed from a trial calendar before the date that precedes by thirty days the date scheduled for that trial calendar. The qualified offer period does not end until the case remains on a trial calendar on the date that precedes by 30 days the scheduled date of the calendar call for that trial session. The qualified offer period may not be extended beyond the periods set forth in this paragraph (c)(7), although the period during which a qualified offer remains open may extend beyond the end of the qualified offer period.

(8) *Interest as a contested issue.*—To constitute a qualified offer, an offer must specify the offered amount of the taxpayer's liability (determined without regard to interest, unless interest is a contested issue in the proceeding), as provided in paragraphs (c)(1)(ii) and (c)(3) of this section. Therefore, a qualified offer generally may only include an offer to compromise tax, penalties, additions to the tax, and additional amounts. Interest may only be included in a qualified offer if interest is a contested issue in the proceeding. For purposes of this section, interest is a contested issue in the proceeding only if the court in which the proceeding could be brought would have jurisdiction to determine the amount of interest due on the underlying tax, penalties, additions to the tax, and additional amounts. Examples of proceedings in which interest might be a contested issue include proceedings in which the increased interest rate for large corporate underpayments under section 6621(c) is imposed by the Internal Revenue Service and interest abatement proceedings brought under section 6404. Interest is not a contested issue in the proceeding if the court that would have jurisdiction over the proceeding would not have jurisdiction to determine the amount or rate of interest, regardless of whether the taxpayer attempts to raise interest as an issue in the proceeding. Consequently, interest will not be a contested issue in the vast majority of tax cases because they merely involve the straightforward application of statutory interest under section 6601. Accordingly, in those cases, interest may not be included in the offer.

(d) [Reserved].

(e) *Examples.*—The following examples illustrate the provisions of this section:

Example 1. Definition of a judgment. The Internal Revenue Service (IRS) audits Taxpayer A for year X and issues a notice of proposed deficiency (30-day letter) proposing to disallow deductions 1, 2, 3, and 4. A files a protest and participates in a conference with the Internal Revenue Service Office of Appeals (Appeals). Appeals allows deduction 1, and issues a statutory notice of deficiency for deductions 2, 3, and 4. A's petition to the United States Tax Court for year X never mentions deduction 2. Prior to trial, A concedes deduction 3. After the trial, the Tax Court issues an opinion allowing A to deduct a portion of deduction 4. As used in paragraph (a) of this section, the term judgment means the cumulative determinations of the court concerning the adjustments at issue in the court proceeding. Thus, the term judgment does not include deduction 1 because it was never at issue in the court proceeding. Similarly, the term judgment does not include deduction 2 because it was not placed at issue by A in the court proceeding. Although deduction 3 was at issue in the court proceeding, it is not included in the term judgment because it was not determined by the court, but rather by concession or settlement. For purposes of section 7430(c)(4)(E), the term judgment only includes the portion of deduction 4 disallowed by the Tax Court.

Example 2. Liability under the offer and liability under the judgment. Assume the same facts as in *Example 1* except that A makes a qualified offer after the Appeals conference, which is not accepted by the IRS. A's offer is with respect to all adjustments at issue at that time. Those adjustments are deductions 2, 3, and 4. At the conclusion of the litigation, A's entitlement to an award based upon the qualified offer will depend, among other things, on a comparison of the change in A's liability for income tax for year X resulting from the judgment of the Tax Court with the change that would have resulted had the IRS accepted A's qualified offer. In making this comparison, the term judgment (as discussed in *Example 1*) is modified by including the amounts of settled or conceded adjustments that were at issue at the time the qualified offer was made. Any settled or conceded adjustments that were not at issue at the time the qualified offer was made, either because the settlement or concession occurred before the offer or because the adjustment was not raised until after the offer, are not included in the comparison. Thus, A's offer on deductions 2, 3, and 4 is compared with the change in A's liability resulting from the Tax Court's determination of deduction 4, and the concessions of issues 2 and 3 by A.

Example 3. Offer must resolve full liability. Assume the same facts as in *Example 2* except that A's offer after the Appeals conference explicitly states that it is only with respect to adjustments 2 and 3 and not with respect to adjustment 4. Even if A's liability pursuant to the judgment, calculated under paragraph (b)(3) of this section as illustrated in *Example 2*, is equal to or less than it would have been had the IRS accepted A's offer after the Appeals conference, A is not a prevailing party under section 7430(c)(4)(E). A qualified offer must include all adjustments at issue at the time the offer is made. Since A's offer excluded adjustment 4, which was an adjustment at issue at the time the offer was made, it does not constitute a qualified offer pursuant to paragraph (b)(2) of this section.

Example 4. Offer must resolve full liability. Assume the same facts as in *Example 1*, except that A makes a qualified offer that is accepted by the IRS. After the offer is accepted, A attempts to reduce the amount A will pay pursuant to the offer by applying net operating loss carryovers to the years in issue. Because the net operating losses were not at issue when the offer was made, A's offer was a qualified offer. Whether A is entitled to apply net operating losses to reduce the amount stated in the offer will depend upon the application of contract principles, local court rules, and, because net operating losses are at issue, section 6511(d) and related provisions.

Example 5. Qualified offer rule for multiple tax years, partial resolution offer is a qualified offer. Taxpayer B receives a notice of deficiency for taxable

years 2001, 2002, and 2003. For 2001, the statutory notice disallows business deductions. For 2002, the statutory notice increases income for unreported lottery winnings. For 2003, the statutory notice disallows a child care credit. B submits a qualified offer only with respect to 2002. Since the adjustments for the three tax years are separate and distinct, B may submit a qualified offer for a single year. If B's liability under the judgment is equal to or less than the qualified offer with respect to 2002, irrespective of 2001 and 2003, B is a prevailing party for 2002 for purposes of section 7430(g). Assuming B satisfies the remaining requirements of section 7430, B may recover reasonable administrative and litigation costs that are attributable to 2002 from the date of the qualified offer. To qualify for any costs with respect to 2001 or 2003, B must satisfy the requirements of section 7430(c)(4).

Example 6. Qualified offer rule for multiple tax years, partial resolution offer is not a qualified offer. Assume the same facts as in *Example 5* except that with respect to 2002, in addition to increasing B's income for the unreported lottery winnings, the statutory notice also disallows a charitable contribution deduction. B submits a settlement offer that purports to be a qualified offer, but only covers the unreported lottery winnings. B's offer is not a qualified offer because it does not address the charitable contribution issue, and thus, does not fully resolve B's liability for 2002.

Example 7. Qualified offer rule for multiple tax years, partial resolution offer is not a qualified offer. Taxpayer C receives a notice of deficiency for taxable years 2001, 2002, and 2003 adjusting the amount of a depreciation deduction due to the Internal Revenue Service's increase to the recovery period. C submits a settlement offer relating only to 2003 that purports to be a qualified offer. C's offer is not a qualified offer because the issue in the three tax years is not separable given that the treatment of the issue in one of the years necessarily affects the treatment of the issue in the other years, and C's offer only applies to one of the years in the proceeding. In cases involving multiple tax years with nonseparable tax issues affecting all tax years, an offer is not a qualified offer unless it resolves the liability for all tax years at issue in the administrative or judicial proceeding.

Example 8. Qualified offer rule inapplicable when all issues settled. Taxpayer D receives a notice of proposed deficiency (30-day letter) proposing to disallow both a personal interest deduction in the amount of $10,000 (Adjustment 1), and a charitable contribution deduction in the amount of $2,000 (Adjustment 2), and to include in income $4,000 of unreported interest income (Adjustment 3). D timely files a protest with Appeals. At the Appeals conference, D presents substantiation for the charitable contribution and presents arguments that the interest paid was deductible mortgage interest and that the interest received was held in trust for Taxpayer E. At the conference, D also provides the Appeals officer assigned to D's case a written offer to settle the case for a deficiency of $2,000, exclusive of interest. The offer states that it is a qualified offer for purposes of section 7430(g) and that it will remain open for acceptance by the IRS for a period in excess of 90 days. After considering D's substantiation and arguments, the Appeals Officer accepts the $2,000 offer to settle the case in full. Although D's offer is a qualified offer, because all three adjustments contained in the qualified offer were settled, the qualified offer rule is inapplicable.

Example 9. Qualified offer rule inapplicable when all issues contained in the qualified offer are settled; subsequently raised adjustments ignored. Assume the same facts as in *Example 8* except that D's qualified offer was for a deficiency of $1,800 and the IRS rejected that offer. Subsequently, the IRS issued a statutory notice of deficiency disallowing the three adjustments contained in *Example 8*, and, in addition, disallowing a home office expense in the amount of $5,000 (Adjustment 4). After petitioning the Tax Court, D presents the field attorney assigned to the case with a written offer, which is not designated as a qualified offer for purposes of section 7430(g), to settle the three adjustments that had been the subject of the qualified offer, plus adjustment 4, for a total deficiency of $2,500. After negotiating with D, a settlement is reached on the three adjustments that were the subject of the rejected qualified offer, for a deficiency of $1,800. Adjustment 4 is litigated in the Tax Court and the court determines that D is entitled to the full $5,000 deduction for that adjustment. Consequently, a decision is entered by the Tax Court reflecting the $1,800 settlement amount, which matches exactly the amount of D's only qualified offer in the case. Although the determined liability for adjustments 1, 2, and 3, equals that of the rejected qualified offer, because all three adjustments contained in the qualified offer were settled, the qualified offer rule is inapplicable.

Example 10. Exclusion of adjustments made after the qualified offer is made. Assume the same facts as in *Example 9* except the settlement is reached only on adjustments 1 and 2, for a liability of $1,500. Adjustments 3 and 4 are tried in the Tax Court and in accordance with the court's opinion, the taxpayer has a $300 deficiency attributable to Adjustment 3, and a $1,550 deficiency attributable to adjustment 4. Consequently, a decision is entered reflecting the $1,500 settled amount, the $300 liability on adjustment 3, and the $1,550 liability on adjustment 4. The $3,350 deficiency reflected in the Tax Court's decision exceeds the last (and only) qualified offer made by D. For purposes of determining whether D is a prevailing party as a result of having made a qualified offer in the proceeding, the liability attributable to adjustment 4, which was raised after the last qualified offer was made, is not included in the comparison of D's liability under the judgment with D's offered liability under the last qualified offer. Thus, D's $1,800 liability under the judgment, as modified for purposes of the qualified offer rule comparison, is equal to D's offered liability under the last qualified offer.

Because D's liability under the last qualified offer equals or exceeds D's liability under the judgment, as calculated under paragraph (b)(3) of this section, D is a prevailing party for purposes of section 7430. Assuming D satisfies the remaining requirements of section 7430, D may recover those reasonable administrative and litigation costs attributable to adjustment 3. To qualify for any further award of reasonable administrative and litigation costs, D must satisfy the requirements of section 7430(c)(4)(A).

Example 11. Qualified offer in a refund case. Taxpayer E timely files an amended return claiming a refund of $1,000. This refund claim results from several omitted deductions which, if allowed, would reduce E's tax liability from $10,000 to $9,000. E receives a notice of claim disallowance and files a complaint with the appropriate United States District Court. Subsequently, E makes a qualified offer for a refund of $500. The offer is rejected and after trial the court finds E is entitled to a refund of $700. The change in E's liability from the tax shown on the return that would have resulted from the acceptance of E's qualified offer is a reduction in that liability of $500. The change in E's liability from the tax shown on the return resulting from the judgment of the court is a reduction in that liability of $700. Because E's liability under the qualified offer exceeds E's liability under the judgment, E is a prevailing party for purposes of section 7430. Assuming E satisfies the remaining requirements of section 7430, E may recover those reasonable litigation costs incurred on or after the date of the qualified offer. To qualify for any further award of reasonable administrative and litigation costs E must satisfy the requirements of section 7430(c)(4)(A).

Example 12. End of qualified offer period when case is removed from Tax Court trial calendar more than 30 days before scheduled trial calendar. Taxpayer F has petitioned the Tax Court in response to the issuance of a notice of deficiency. F receives notice that the case will be heard on the July trial session in F's city of residence. The scheduled date for the calendar call for that trial session is July 1st. On May 15th, F's motion to remove the case from the July trial session and place it on the October trial session for that city is granted. The scheduled date for the calendar call for the October trial session is October 1st. On May 31st, F delivers a qualified offer to the field attorney assigned to the case. On August 31st, F delivers a revised qualified offer to the field attorney assigned to the case. Neither offer is accepted. The case is tried during the October trial session, and at some time thereafter, a decision is entered by the court. Assume the judgment in the case, as calculated under paragraph (b)(3) of this section, is greater than the amount offered, as calculated under paragraph (b)(2) of this section, in the qualified offer delivered on May 31st, but less than the amount offered, as similarly calculated, in the qualified offer delivered on August 31st. Because the qualified offer period did not end until September 1st, and the offer of August 31st otherwise satisfied the requirements of para-

Reg. § 301.7430-7(e)

graph (c) of this section, the offer delivered on August 31st is a qualified offer. Furthermore, because the August 31st qualified offer is closer in time to the end of the qualified offer period than the May 31st qualified offer, the August 31st qualified offer is the last qualified offer made by F. Consequently, the August 31st offer is the qualified offer that is compared to the judgment for purposes of determining whether F is a prevailing party under section 7430(c)(4)(E). Because F's liability under the August 31st qualified offer equals or exceeds F's liability under the judgment as calculated under paragraph (b)(3) of this section, F is a prevailing party for purposes of section 7430.

Example 13. End of qualified offer period when case is removed from Tax Court trial calendar less than 30 days before scheduled trial calendar. Assume the same facts as in *Example 12* except that F's motion was granted on June 15th. Because the qualified offer period ended on June 1st when the case remained on the July trial session on the date that preceded by 30 days the scheduled date of the calendar call for that trial session, the offer delivered on May 31st was F's last qualified offer. The August 31st offer is not a qualified offer for purposes of this rule. Consequently, F is not a prevailing party under the qualified offer rule. Therefore, F must satisfy the requirements of section 7430(c)(4)(A) to qualify for any award of reasonable administrative and litigation costs.

Example 14. When a qualified offer can be made and to whom it must be made. During the examination of Taxpayer G's return, the IRS issues a notice of deficiency without having first issued a 30-day letter. After receiving the notice of deficiency G timely petitions the Tax Court. The next day G mails an offer to the office that issued the notice of deficiency, which offer satisfies the requirements of paragraphs (c)(3) through (6) of this section. This is the only written offer made by G during the administrative or court proceeding, and by its terms it is to remain open for a period in excess of 90 days after the date of mailing to the office issuing the notice of deficiency. The office that issued the notice of deficiency transmitted the offer to the field attorney with jurisdiction over the Tax Court case. After answering the case, the field attorney refers the case to Appeals pursuant to Rev. Proc. 87-24 (1987-1 C.B. 720). See § 601.601(d)(2)(ii)(*b*) of this chapter. After careful consideration, Appeals rejects the offer and holds a conference with G during which some adjustments are settled. The remainder of the adjustments are tried in the Tax Court and G's liability resulting from the Tax Court's determinations, when added to G's liability resulting from the settled adjustments, is less than G's liability would have been under the offer rejected by Appeals. Because the Tax Court case had not yet been answered when the offer was sent, G properly mailed the offer to the office that issued the notice of deficiency. Thus, G's offer satisfied the requirements of paragraph (c)(2) of this section. Furthermore, even though G did not receive a 30-day letter, G's offer was made after the beginning of the qualified offer period, satisfying the requirements of paragraph (c)(7) of this section, because the issuance of the statutory notice provided G with notice of the IRS's determination of a deficiency, and the docketing of the case provided G with an opportunity for administrative review in the Internal Revenue Service Office of Appeals under Rev. Proc. 87-24. See § 601.601(d)(2)(ii)(*b*) of this chapter. Because G's offer satisfied all of the requirements of paragraph (c) of this section, the offer was a qualified offer and G is a prevailing party.

Example 15. Substitution of parties permitted under last qualified offer. Taxpayer H receives a 30-day letter and participates in a conference with the Office of Appeals but no agreement is reached. Subsequently, H receives a notice of deficiency and petitions the Tax Court. Upon receiving the Internal Revenue Service's answer to the petition, H sends a qualified offer to the field attorney who signed the answer, by United States mail. The qualified offer stated that it would remain open for more than 90 days. Thirty days after making the offer, H dies and, on motion under Rule 63(a) of the Tax Court's Rules of Practice and Procedure by H's personal representative, I is substituted for H as a party in the Tax Court proceeding. I makes no qualified offers to settle the case and the case proceeds to trial, with the Tax Court issuing an opinion partially in favor of I. Even though I was not a party when the qualified offer was made by H, that offer constitutes a qualified offer because by its terms, when made, it was to remain open until at least the earlier of the date it is rejected, the date of trial, or 90 days. If the liability of I under the qualified offer, as determined under paragraph (b)(2) of this section, equals or exceeds the liability under the judgment of the Tax Court, as determined under paragraph (b)(3) of this section, I will be a prevailing party for purposes of an award of reasonable litigation costs under section 7430.

Example 16. Qualified offer may not compromise interest unless it is a contested issue. Taxpayer J receives a notice of deficiency making an adjustment resulting in a deficiency in tax of $6,500 plus a penalty of $500. Interest is not a contested issue in the proceeding. Within the qualified offer period, J submits a written offer to settle the case for a deficiency of $1,000, including all taxes, penalties, and interest. The offer states that it is a qualified offer for purposes of section 7430(g) and that it will remain open for acceptance by the Internal Revenue Service for a period of 90 days. Section 7430(g)(2)(B) and paragraph (c)(3) of this section state that the amount of a qualified offer must be without regard to interest unless interest is at issue in the proceeding. Since J's offer attempts to compromise interest, which is not a contested issue in the proceeding, it is not a qualified offer.

Example 17. Qualified offer based on new defense or legal theory. Taxpayers K and L received a statutory notice of deficiency for tax year 2005, a tax year when they were married and filed a joint income tax return. Taxpayer K files a separate petition claiming innocent spouse relief and simultaneously submits an offer purporting to be a qualified offer. The offer states that K is entitled to innocent spouse relief and offers to settle the 2005 deficiency as to K. K's innocent spouse claim was not raised during K and L's audit, nor was it raised during their appeals conference. Additionally, at no time prior to or contemporaneously with submitting the offer did K file with the Internal Revenue Service a Form 8857, Request for Innocent Spouse Relief, or otherwise provide the information specified in § 1.6015-5(a) of this chapter. K's offer is not a qualified offer because K did not file a Form 8857 or otherwise provide substantiation or legal and factual arguments necessary to allow for informed consideration of the merits of the innocent spouse claim as required by paragraph (c)(4) of this section, contemporaneously with the offer or prior to making the offer.

(f) *Effective/applicability date.*—This section is applicable with respect to qualified offers made in administrative or court proceedings described in section 7430 after December 24, 2003, except that paragraph (c)(8) is effective as of March 1, 2016. [Reg. § 301.7430-7.]

☐ [T.D. 9106, 12-24-2003 (*corrected* 1-27-2004). *Amended by T.D.* 9756, 2-29-2016]

[Reg. § 301.7430-8]

§ 301.7430-8. Administrative costs incurred in damage actions for violations of section 362 or 524 of the Bankruptcy Code.—(a) *In general.*—The Internal Revenue Service may grant a taxpayer's request for recovery of reasonable administrative costs incurred in connection with the administrative proceeding before the Internal Revenue Service relating to the willful violation of section 362 or 524 of the Bankruptcy Code only if the taxpayer is a prevailing party.

(b) *Prevailing party.*—A taxpayer is a prevailing party for purposes of this section only if—

(1) The taxpayer satisfies the net worth and size limitations in paragraph (f) of § 301.7430-5;

(2) The taxpayer establishes that in connection with the collection of his or her federal tax an officer or employee of the Internal Revenue Service has willfully violated a provision of section 362 or 524 of the Bankruptcy Code; and

(3) The position of the Internal Revenue Service in the proceeding was not substantially justified.

(c) *Administrative proceeding.*—For purposes of this section, an administrative proceeding is a proceeding related to an administrative claim presented to the Internal Revenue Service seeking relief from a violation of section 362 or 524 of the Bankruptcy Code by the Internal Revenue Service or recovery of damages from the Internal Revenue Service under § 301.7433-2(e).

(d) *Costs incurred after filing of bankruptcy petition.*—Administrative costs may be recovered only if incurred on or after the date of filing of the bankruptcy petition that formed the basis for the stay on collection under Bankruptcy Code section 362 or the discharge injunction under Bankruptcy Code section 524, as the case might be.

(e) *Time for filing claim for administrative costs.*—(1) For purposes of this section, the taxpayer must file a claim for administrative costs before the Internal Revenue Service not later than 90 days after the date the Internal Revenue Service mails to the taxpayer, or otherwise notifies the taxpayer of, the decision regarding the claim for relief from or damages relating to a violation of the collection stay or the discharge injunction.

(2) If the Internal Revenue Service denies the claim for administrative costs in whole or in part, the taxpayer must file a petition with the Bankruptcy Court for administrative costs no later than 90 days after the date on which the denial of the claim for administrative costs is mailed, or otherwise furnished, to the taxpayer. If the Internal Revenue Service does not respond on the merits to a request by the taxpayer for an award of reasonable administrative costs within six months after such request is filed, the Internal Revenue Service's failure to respond may be considered by the taxpayer as a denial of an award of reasonable administrative costs.

(3) For purposes of paragraphs (e)(1) and (2) of this section, if the 90th day falls on a Saturday, Sunday, or a legal holiday, the 90-day period shall end on the next succeeding day which is not a Saturday, Sunday, or a legal holiday. The term legal holiday means a legal holiday in the District of Columbia. If the request for costs is to be filed with the Internal Revenue Service at an office of the Internal Revenue Service located outside the District of Columbia, the term legal holiday also means a statewide legal holiday in the state where such office is located.

(f) *Effective date.*—This section is applicable with respect to actions taken by the Internal Revenue Service after July 22, 1998. [Reg. § 301.7430-8.]

☐ [T.D. 9050, 3-24-2003.]

[Reg. § 301.7432-1]

§ 301.7432-1. Civil cause of action for failure to release a lien.—(a) *In general.*—If any officer or employee of the Internal Revenue Service knowingly, or by reason of negligence, fails to release a lien on property of the taxpayer in accordance with section 6325 of the Internal Revenue Code, such taxpayer may bring a civil action for damages against the United States in federal district court. The total amount of damages recoverable is the sum of:

(1) the actual, direct economic damages sustained by the taxpayer which, but for the officer's or the employee's knowing or negligent failure to release the lien under section 6325, would not have been sustained; and

(2) costs of the action.

The amount of actual, direct economic damages that are recoverable is reduced to the extent such damages reasonably could have been mitigated by the plaintiff. An action for damages filed in federal district court may not be maintained unless the taxpayer has filed an administrative claim pursuant to paragraph (f) of this section and has waited the period required under paragraph (e) of this section.

(b) *Finding of satisfaction or unenforceability.*— For purposes of this section, a finding under section 6325(a)(1) that the liability for the amount assessed, together with all interest in respect thereof, has been fully satisfied or has become legally unenforceable is treated as made on the earlier of:

(1) the date on which the district director of the district in which the taxpayer currently resides or the district in which the lien was filed finds full satisfaction or legal unenforceability; or

(2) the date on which such district director receives a request for a certificate of release of lien in accordance with § 401.6325-1(f), together with any information which is reasonably necessary for the district director to conclude that the lien has been fully satisfied or is legally unenforceable.

(c) *Actual, direct economic damages.*—(1) *Definition.*—Actual, direct economic damages are actual pecuniary damages sustained by the taxpayer that would not have been sustained but for an officer's or an employee's failure to release a lien in accordance with section 6325 of the Internal Revenue Code. Injuries such as inconvenience, emotional distress and loss of reputation are compensable only to the extent that they result in actual pecuniary damages.

(2) *Litigation costs and administrative costs not recoverable.*—Litigation costs and administrative costs described in this paragraph are not recoverable as actual, direct economic damages. Litigation costs may be recoverable under section 7430 (*see* paragraph (j) of this section) or, solely to the extent described in paragraph (d) of this section, as costs of the action.

(i) *Litigation costs.*—For purposes of this paragraph, litigation costs are any costs incurred pursuing litigation for relief from the failure to release a lien, including costs incurred pursuing a civil action in federal district court under paragraph (a) of this section. Litigation costs include the following:

(A) Court costs;

(B) Expenses of expert witnesses in connection with a court proceeding;

(C) Cost of any study, analysis, engineering report, test, or project prepared for a court proceeding; and

(D) Fees paid or incurred for the services of attorneys, or other individuals authorized to practice before the court, in connection with a court proceeding.

(ii) *Administrative costs.*—For purposes of this section, administrative costs are any costs incurred pursuing administrative relief from the failure to release a lien, including costs incurred pursuing an administrative claim for damages

under paragraph (f) of this section. The term administrative costs includes:

(A) Any administrative fees or similar charges imposed by the Internal Revenue Service; and

(B) Expenses, costs, and fees described in paragraph (c)(2)(i) of this section incurred in pursuing administrative relief.

(d) *Costs of the action.*—Costs of the action recoverable as damages under this section are limited to the following costs:

(1) Fees of the clerk and marshall;

(2) Fees of the court reporter for all or any part of the stenographic transcript necessarily obtained for use in the case;

(3) Fees and disbursements for printing and witnesses;

(4) Fees for exemplification and copies of paper necessarily obtained for use in the case;

(5) Docket fees; and

(6) Compensation of court appointed experts and interpreters.

(e) *No civil action in federal district court prior to filing an administrative claim.*—(1) Except as provided in paragraph (e)(2) of this section, no action under paragraph (a) of this section shall be maintained in any federal district court before the earlier of the following dates:

(i) The date a decision is rendered on a claim filed in accordance with paragraph (f) of this section; or

(ii) The date 30 days after the date an administrative claim is filed in accordance with paragraph (f) of this section.

(2) If an administrative claim is filed in accordance with paragraph (f) of this section during the last 30 days of the period of limitations described in paragraph (i) of this section, the taxpayer may file an action in federal district court any time after the administrative claim is filed and before the expiration of the period of limitations, without waiting for 30 days to expire or for a decision to be rendered on the claim.

(f) *Procedures for an administrative claim.*— (1) *Manner.*—An administrative claim for actual, direct economic damages as defined in paragraph (c) of this section shall be sent in writing to the district director (marked for the attention of the Chief, Special Procedures Function) in the district in which the taxpayer currently resides or the district in which the notice of federal tax lien was filed.

(2) *Form.*—The administrative claim shall include:

(i) The name, current address, current home and work telephone numbers and any convenient times to be contacted, and taxpayer identification number of the taxpayer making the claim;

(ii) A copy of the notice of federal tax lien affecting the taxpayer's property, if available;

(iii) A copy of the request for release of lien made in accordance with section 401.6325-1(f) of the Code of Federal Regulations, if applicable;

(iv) The grounds, in reasonable detail, for the claim (include copies of any available substantiating documentation or correspondence with the Internal Revenue Service);

(v) A description of the injuries incurred by the taxpayer filing the claim (include copies of any available substantiating documentation or evidence);

(vi) The dollar amount of the claim, including any damages that have not yet been incurred but that are reasonably foreseeable (include copies of any available substantiating documentation or evidence); and

(vii) The signature of the taxpayer or duly authorized representative.

For purposes of this paragraph, a duly authorized representative is any attorney, certified public accountant, enrolled actuary, or any other person permitted to represent the taxpayer before the Internal Revenue Service who is not disbarred or suspended from practice before the Internal Revenue Service and who has a written power of attorney executed by the taxpayer.

(g) *Notice of failure to release lien.*—An administrative claim under paragraph (f) of this section shall be considered a notice of failure to release a lien.

(h) *No action in federal district court for any sum in excess of the dollar amount sought in the administrative claim.*—No action for actual, direct economic damages under paragraph (a) of this section shall be instituted in federal district court for any sum in excess of the amount (already incurred and estimated) of the administrative claim filed under paragraph (f) of this section, except where the increased amount is based upon newly discovered evidence not reasonably discoverable at the time the administrative claim was filed, or upon allegation and proof of intervening facts relating to the amount of the claim.

(i) *Period of limitations.*—(1) *Time of filing.*—A civil action under paragraph (a) of this section must be brought in federal district court within 2 years after the date the cause of action accrues.

(2) *Cause of action accrues.*—A cause of action accrues when the taxpayer has had a reasonable opportunity to discover all essential elements of a possible cause of action.

(j) *Recovery of costs under section 7430.*—Reasonable litigation costs, including attorney's fees, not recoverable under this section may be recoverable under section 7430. If following the Internal Revenue Service's denial of an administrative claim on the grounds that the Internal Revenue Service did not violate section 7432(a), a taxpayer brings a civil action for damages in a district court of the United States, and establishes entitlement to damages under this section, substantially prevails with respect to the amount of damages in controversy, and meets the requirements of section 7430(c)(4)(A)(iii) (relating to notice and net worth requirements), the taxpayer will be considered a "prevailing party"

for purposes of section 7430. Such taxpayer, therefore, will generally be entitled to attorney's fees and other reasonable litigation costs not recoverable under this section. For purposes of this paragraph, if the Internal Revenue Service does not respond on the merits to an administrative claim for damages within 30 days after the claim is filed, the Internal Revenue Service's failure to respond shall be considered a denial of the administrative claim on the grounds that the Internal Revenue Service did not violate section 7432(a). Administrative costs, including attorney's fees incurred pursuing an administrative claim under paragraph (f) of this section, are not recoverable under section 7430.

(k) *Effective date.*—This section applies with respect to civil actions under section 7432 filed in federal district court after January 30, 1992. [Reg. § 301.7432-1.]

☐ [*T.D.* 8393, 1-29-92.]

[Reg. § 301.7433-1]

§ 301.7433-1. Civil cause of action for certain unauthorized collection actions.—(a) *In general.*—If, in connection with the collection of a federal tax with respect to a taxpayer, an officer or an employee of the Internal Revenue Service recklessly or intentionally, or by reason of negligence, disregards any provision of the Internal Revenue Code or any regulation promulgated under the Internal Revenue Code, such taxpayer may bring a civil action for damages against the United States in federal district court. The taxpayer has a duty to mitigate damages. The total amount of damages recoverable is the lesser of $1,000,000 ($100,000 in the case of negligence), or the sum of:

(1) the actual, direct economic damages sustained as a proximate result of the reckless or intentional actions of the officer or employee; and

(2) costs of the action.

An action for damages filed in federal district court may not be maintained unless the taxpayer has filed an administrative claim pursuant to paragraph (e) of this section, and has waited for the period required under paragraph (d) of this section.

(b) *Actual, direct economic damages.*—(1) *Definition.*—Actual, direct economic damages are actual pecuniary damages sustained by the taxpayer as the proximate result of the reckless or intentional, or negligent, actions of an officer or an employee of the Internal Revenue Service. Injuries such as inconvenience, emotional distress and loss of reputation are compensable only to the extent that they result in actual pecuniary damages.

(2) *Litigation costs and administrative costs not recoverable.*—Litigation costs and administrative costs are not recoverable as actual, direct economic damages. Litigation costs may be recoverable under section 7430 (*see* paragraph (h) of this

section) or, solely to the extent described in paragraph (c) of this section, as costs of the action.

(i) *Litigation costs.*—For purposes of this paragraph, litigation costs are any costs incurred pursuing litigation for relief from the action taken by the officer or employee of the Internal Revenue Service, including costs incurred pursuing a civil action in federal district court under paragraph (a) of this section. The term litigation costs includes the following:

(A) Court costs;

(B) Expenses of expert witnesses in connection with a court proceeding;

(C) Cost of any study, analysis, engineering report, test, or project prepared for a court proceeding; and

(D) Fees paid or incurred for the services of attorneys, or other individuals authorized to practice before the court, in connection with a court proceeding.

(ii) *Administrative costs.*—For purposes of this section, administrative costs are any costs incurred pursuing administrative relief from the action taken by an officer or employee of the Internal Revenue Service, including costs incurred pursuing an administrative claim for damages under paragraph (e) of this section. The term administrative costs includes:

(A) Any administrative fees or similar charges imposed by the Internal Revenue Service; and

(B) Expenses, costs, and fees described in paragraph (b)(2)(i) of this section incurred pursuing administrative relief.

(c) *Costs of the action.*—Costs of the action recoverable as damages under this section are limited to the following costs:

(1) Fees of the clerk and marshall;

(2) Fees of the court reporter for all or any part of the stenographic transcript necessarily obtained for use in the case;

(3) Fees and disbursements for printing and witnesses;

(4) Fees for exemplification and copies of paper necessarily obtained for use in the case;

(5) Docket fees; and

(6) Compensation of court appointed experts and interpreters.

(d) *No civil action in federal district court prior to filing an administrative claim.*—(1) Except as provided in paragraph (d)(2) of this section, no action under paragraph (a) of this section shall be maintained in any federal district court before the earlier of the following dates:

(i) The date the decision is rendered on a claim filed in accordance with paragraph (e) of this section; or

(ii) The date six months after the date an administrative claim is filed in accordance with paragraph (e) of this section.

(2) If an administrative claim is filed in accordance with paragraph (e) of this section during the last six months of the period of limitations described in paragraph (g) of this section, the taxpayer may file an action in federal district court any time after the administrative claim is filed and before the expiration of the period of limitations.

(e) *Procedures for an administrative claim.*—(1) *Manner.*—An administrative claim for the lesser of $1,000,000 ($100,000 in the case of negligence) or actual, direct economic damages as defined in paragraph (b) of this section shall be sent in writing to the Area Director, Attn: Compliance Technical Support Manager of the area in which the taxpayer currently resides.

(2) *Form.*—The administrative claim shall include:

(i) The name, current address, current home and work telephone numbers and any convenient times to be contacted, and taxpayer identification number of the taxpayer making the claim;

(ii) The grounds, in reasonable detail, for the claim (include copies of any available substantiating documentation or correspondence with the Internal Revenue Service);

(iii) A description of the injuries incurred by the taxpayer filing the claim (include copies of any available substantiating documentation or evidence);

(iv) The dollar amount of the claim, including any damages that have not yet been incurred but which are reasonably foreseeable (include copies of any available substantiating documentation or evidence); and

(v) The signature of the taxpayer or duly authorized representative.

For purposes of this paragraph, a duly authorized representative is any attorney, certified public accountant, enrolled actuary, or any other person permitted to represent the taxpayer before the Internal Revenue Service who is not disbarred or suspended from practice before the Internal Revenue Service and who has a written power of attorney executed by the taxpayer.

(f) *No action in federal district court for any sum in excess of the dollar amount sought in the administrative claim.*—No action for actual, direct economic damages under paragraph (a) of this section shall be instituted in federal district court for any sum in excess of the amount (already incurred and estimated) of the administrative claim filed under paragraph (e) of this section, except where the increased amount is based upon newly discovered evidence not reasonably discoverable at the time the administrative claim was filed, or upon allegation and proof of intervening facts relating to the amount of the claim.

(g) *Period of limitations.*—(1) *Time for filing.*—A civil action under paragraph (a) of this section must be brought in federal district court within 2 years after the date the cause of action accrues.

(2) *Right of action accrues.*—A cause of action under paragraph (a) of this section accrues when the taxpayer has had a reasonable opportunity to discover all essential elements of a possible cause of action.

Reg. § 301.7433-1(g)(2)

(h) *Recovery of costs under section 7430.*—Reasonable litigation costs, including attorney's fees, not recoverable under this section may be recoverable under section 7430. If following the Internal Revenue Service's denial of an administrative claim on the grounds that the Internal Revenue Service did not violate section 7433(a), a taxpayer brings a civil action for damages in a district court of the United States, and establishes entitlement to damages under this section, substantially prevails with respect to the amount of damages in controversy and meets the requirements of section 7430(c)(4)(A)(iii) (relating to notice and net worth requirements), the taxpayer will be considered a "prevailing party" for purposes of section 7430. Such taxpayer, therefore, will generally be entitled to attorney's fees and other reasonable litigation costs not recoverable under this section. For purposes of this paragraph, if the Internal Revenue Service does not respond on the merits to an administrative claim for damages within six months after the claim is filed, the Internal Revenue Service's failure to respond shall be considered a denial of the claim on the grounds that the Internal Revenue Service did not violate section 7433(a). Administrative costs, including attorney's fees incurred pursuing an administrative claim under paragraph (e) of this section, are not recoverable under section 7430.

(i) *Effective dates.*—The portions of this section relating to reckless or intentional acts are applicable to actions taken by Internal Revenue Service officials after July 30, 1996. The portions of this section relating to negligent acts are applicable to actions taken by the Internal Revenue Service officials after July 22, 1998. [Reg. § 301.7433-1.]

☐ [*T.D. 8392, 1-29-92. Amended by T.D. 9050,* 3-24-2003.]

[Reg. § 301.7433-2]

§ 301.7433-2. Civil cause of action for violation of section 362 or 524 of the Bankruptcy Code.—(a) *In general.*—(1) If, in connection with the collection of a federal tax with respect to a taxpayer, an officer or employee of the Internal Revenue Service willfully violates any provision of section 362 (relating to the automatic stay) or section 524 (relating to discharge) of title 11, United States Code, or any regulation promulgated under such provision, the taxpayer may file a petition for damages against the United States in Federal bankruptcy court. The taxpayer has a duty to mitigate damages. The total amount of damages recoverable under this section is the lesser of $1,000,000, or the sum of—

(i) Actual, direct economic damages sustained as a proximate result of the willful actions of the officer or employee; and

(ii) Costs of the action.

(2) An action under this section constitutes the exclusive remedy under the Internal Revenue Code for violations of sections 362 and 524 of the Bankruptcy Code. In addition, taxpayers injured by violations of section 362 of the Bankruptcy Code may maintain actions under section 362(h) of the Bankruptcy Code (relating to an individual injured by a willful violation of the stay). However, any administrative or litigation costs in connection with an action under section 362(h) may be awarded, if at all, only under section 7430 of the Internal Revenue Code.

(b) *Actual, direct economic damages.*—(1) *Definition.*—See § 301.7433-1(b)(1).

(2) *Litigation costs and administrative costs not recoverable as actual, direct economic damages.*—Litigation costs and administrative costs are not recoverable as actual, direct economic damages. These costs may be recoverable under section 7430 (see paragraph (h) of this section), or, solely to the extent described in paragraph (c) of this section, as costs of the action.

(c) *Costs of the action.*—Costs of the action recoverable as damages under this section are limited to the costs set forth in § 301.7433-1(c).

(d) *No civil action in federal bankruptcy court prior to filing an administrative claim.*—(1) *In general.*—Except as provided in paragraph (d)(2) of this section, no action under paragraph (a)(1) of this section shall be maintained in any bankruptcy court before the earlier of the following dates—

(i) The date the decision is rendered on a claim filed in accordance with paragraph (e) of this section; or

(ii) The date that is six months after the date an administrative claim is filed in accordance with paragraph (e) of this section.

(2) *When administrative claim filed in last six months of period of limitations.*—If an administrative claim is filed in accordance with paragraph (e) of this section during the last six months of the period of limitations described in paragraph (g) of this section, the taxpayer may petition the bankruptcy court any time after the administrative claim is filed and before the expiration of period of limitations.

(e) *Procedures for an administrative claim.*—(1) *Manner.*—An administrative claim for the lesser of $1,000,000 or actual, direct economic damages as defined in paragraph (b) of this section shall be sent in writing to the Chief, Local Insolvency Unit, for the judicial district in which the taxpayer filed the underlying bankruptcy case giving rise to the alleged violation.

(2) *Form.*—The administrative claim shall include—

(i) The name, taxpayer identification number, current address, and current home and work telephone numbers (with an identification of any convenient times to be contacted) of the taxpayer making the claim;

(ii) The location of the bankruptcy court in which the underlying bankruptcy case was filed and the case number of the case in which the violation occurred;

(iii) A description, in reasonable detail, of the violation (include copies of any available substantiating documentation or correspondence with the Internal Revenue Service);

(iv) A description of the injuries incurred by the taxpayer filing the claim (include copies of any available substantiating documentation or evidence);

(v) The dollar amount of the claim, including any damages that have not yet been incurred but which are reasonably foreseeable (include copies of any available documentation or evidence); and

(vi) The signature of the taxpayer or duly authorized representative.

(3) *Duly authorized representative defined.*— For purposes of this paragraph (e), a duly authorized representative is any attorney, certified public accountant, enrolled actuary, or any other person permitted to represent the taxpayer before the Internal Revenue Service who is not disbarred or suspended from practice before the Internal Revenue Service and who has a written power of attorney executed by the taxpayer.

(f) *No action in bankruptcy court for any sum in excess of the dollar amount sought in the administrative claim.*—No action for actual, direct economic damages under paragraph (a) of this section may be instituted in federal bankruptcy court for any sum in excess of the amount (already incurred and estimated) of the administrative claim filed under paragraph (e) of this section, except where the increased amount is based upon newly discovered evidence not reasonably discoverable at the time the administrative claim was filed, or upon allegation and proof of intervening facts relating to the amount of the claim.

(g) *Period of limitations.*—(1) *Time for filing.*—A petition for damages under paragraph (a) of this section must be filed in bankruptcy court within two years after the date the cause of action accrues.

(2) *Right of action accrues.*—A cause of action under paragraph (a) of this section accrues when the taxpayer has had a reasonable opportunity to discover all essential elements of a possible cause of action.

(h) *Recovery of litigation costs and administrative costs under section 7430.*—(1) *In general.*—Litiga-tion costs, as defined in § 301.7433-1(b)(2)(i), including attorneys fees, not recoverable under this section may be recoverable under section 7430 if a taxpayer challenges in whole or in part an Internal Revenue Service denial of an administrative claim for damages by filing a petition in the bankruptcy court. If, following the Internal Revenue Service's denial of an administrative claim for damages, a taxpayer files a petition in the bankruptcy court challenging that denial in whole or in part, substantially prevails with respect to the amount of damages in controversy, and meets the requirements of section 7430(c)(4)(A)(ii) (relating to net worth and size requirements), the taxpayer will be considered a prevailing party for purposes of section 7430, unless the Internal Revenue Service establishes that the position of the Internal Revenue Service in the proceeding was substantially justified. Such taxpayer will generally be entitled to attorneys' fees and other reasonable litigation costs not recoverable under this section. For purposes of this paragraph (h), if the Internal Revenue Service does not respond on the merits to an administrative claim for damages within six months after the claim is filed, the Internal Revenue Service's failure to respond will be considered a denial of the claim on the grounds that the Internal Revenue Service did not willfully violate Bankruptcy Code section 362 or 524.

(2) *Administrative costs.*—(i) *In general.*— Administrative costs, as defined in § 301.7433-1(b)(2)(ii), including attorneys' fees, not recoverable under this section may be recoverable under section 7430. See § 301.7430-8.

(ii) *Limitation regarding recoverable administrative costs.*—Administrative costs may be awarded only if incurred on or after the date of filing of the bankruptcy petition that formed the basis for the stay on collection under Bankruptcy Code section 362 or the discharge injunction under Bankruptcy Code section 524, as the case might be.

(i) *Effective date.*—This section is applicable to actions taken by the Internal Revenue Service officials after July 22, 1998. [Reg. § 301.7433-2.]

☐ [T.D. 9050, 3-24-2003.]

THE TAX COURT

Procedure

[Reg. § 301.7452-1]

§ 301.7452-1. Representation of parties.—The Commissioner shall be represented by the Chief Counsel for the Internal Revenue Service in the same manner before the Tax Court as he has heretofore been represented in proceedings before such Court. The taxpayer shall continue to be represented in accordance with the rules of practice prescribed by the Court. [Reg. § 301.7452-1.]

☐ [T.D. 6498, 10-24-60.]

[Reg. § 301.7454-1]

§ 301.7454-1. Burden of proof in fraud and transferee cases.—In any proceeding involving the issue whether the petitioner has been guilty of fraud with intent to evade tax, the burden of proof in respect of such issue shall be upon the Commissioner. [Reg. § 301.7454-1.]

☐ [T.D. 6498, 10-24-60.]

[Reg. § 301.7454-2]

§ 301.7454-2. Burden of proof in foundation manager, etc. cases.—(a) *Foundation manager.*—In any proceeding involving the issue whether a foundation manager as defined in section 4946(b) has "knowingly" participated in an act of self-dealing within the meaning of section 4941, participated in an investment which jeopardizes the carrying out of exempt purposes within the meaning of section 4944, or agreed to the making of a taxable expenditure within the meaning of section 4945 or whether an organization manager (as defined in section 4958(f)(2) has "knowingly" participated in an excess benefit transaction (as defined in section 4958(c), the burden of proof in respect of such issue shall be upon the Commissioner.

(b) *Trustee of a black lung benefit trust.*—In any proceeding involving the issue whether a trustee of a trust described in section 501(c)(21) has "knowingly" participated in an act of self-dealing within the meaning of section 4951 or agreed to the making of a taxable expenditure within the meaning of section 4952, the burden of proof in respect of such issue shall be upon the Commissioner. [Reg. § 301.7454-2.]

☐ [*T.D. 7838, 10-5-82. Amended by T.D. 8920, 1-9-2001.*]

[Reg. § 301.7456-1]

§ 301.7456-1. Administration of oaths and procurement of testimony; production of records of foreign corporations, foreign trusts or estates and nonresident alien individuals.—Upon motion and notice by the Commissioner and upon good cause shown therefor, the Tax Court or any division thereof shall order any foreign corporation, foreign trust or estate, or nonresident alien individual, who has filed a petition with the Tax Court, to produce, or, upon satisfactory proof to the Tax Court or any of its divisions that the petitioner is unable to produce, to make available to the Commissioner, and, in either case, to permit the inspection, copying, or photographing of, such books, records, documents, memoranda, correspondence and other papers, wherever situated, as the Tax Court or any of its divisions may deem relevant to the proceedings and which are in the possession, custody or control of the petitioner, or of any person directly or indirectly under his control or having control over him or subject to the same common control. [Reg. § 301.7456-1.]

☐ [*T.D. 6498, 10-24-60.*]

[Reg. § 301.7457-1]

§ 301.7457-1. Witness fees.—Any witness summoned for the Commissioner or whose deposition is taken under section 7456 shall receive the same fees and mileage as witnesses in courts of the United States. Such fees and mileage and the expense of taking any such deposition shall be paid by the Commissioner out of any moneys appropriated for the collection of internal revenue taxes, and may be paid in advance. [Reg. § 301.7457-1.]

☐ [*T.D. 6498, 10-24-60.*]

[Reg. § 301.7458-1]

§ 301.7458-1. Hearings.—Notice and opportunity to be heard upon any proceeding instituted before the Tax Court shall be given to the taxpayer and the Commissioner. If an opportunity to be heard upon the proceeding is given before a division of the Tax Court, neither the taxpayer nor the Commissioner shall be entitled to notice and opportunity to be heard before the Tax Court upon review, except upon a specific order to the chief judge. [Reg. § 301.7458-1.]

☐ [*T.D. 6498, 10-24-60.*]

[Reg. § 301.7461-1]

§ 301.7461-1. Publicity of proceedings.—All reports of the Tax Court and all evidence received by the Tax Court and its divisions, including a transcript of the stenographic report of the hearings, shall be public records open to the inspection of the public; except that after the decision of the Tax Court in any proceeding has become final the Tax Court may, upon motion of the taxpayer or the Commissioner, permit the withdrawal by the party entitled thereto of the originals of books, documents, and records, and of models, diagrams, and other exhibits, introduced in evidence before the Tax Court or any of its divisions; or the Tax Court may, on its own action, make such other disposition thereof as it deems advisable. [Reg. § 301.7461-1.]

☐ [*T.D. 6498, 10-24-60.*]

Declaratory Judgments

[Reg. § 1.7476-1]

§ 1.7476-1. Interested parties.—(a) *In general.*—(1) *Notice requirement.*—Before the Internal Revenue Service can issue an advance determination as to the qualified status of certain retirement plans, the applicant must provide the Internal Revenue Service with satisfactory evidence that such applicant has notified the persons who qualify as interested parties, under regulations prescribed under section 7476(b)(1) of the Code, of the application for such determination. See section 3001(a) of the Employee Retirement Income Security Act of 1974 (88 Stat. 995). For the rules for giving notice to interested parties, see § 1.7476-2 and paragraph (o) of § 601.201 of this chapter (Statement of Procedural Rules).

(2) *Declaratory judgments.*—Section 7476 provides a procedure for obtaining a declaratory judgment by the Tax Court with respect to the initial or continuing qualification under subchapter D of chapter 1 of the Code of a retirement plan defined in section 7476(d), in the case of an actual controversy involving:

(i) A determination by the Internal Revenue Service with respect to the initial qualification or continuing qualification under such subchapter of such a plan, or

(ii) A failure by the Internal Revenue Service to make a determination with respect to—

(A) Such initial qualification of such a plan, or

(B) Such continuing qualification of such a plan, if the controversy arises from a plan amendment or plan termination.

Under section 7476(d) the term "retirement plan" means a pension, profit-sharing, or stock bonus plan described in section 401(a), or a trust which is part of such a plan, an annuity plan described in section 403(a), or a bond purchase plan described in section 405(a). This procedure is available only to the employer, the plan administrator as defined in section 414(g), an employee who qualifies as an interested party as defined in this section, or the Pension Benefit Guaranty Corporation, where such person has an actual controversy involving a determination described in paragraph (a)(2)(i) of this section, or failure to make a determination described in paragraph (a)(2)(ii) of this section. In the case of an application for such a determination, this procedure is available only if such determination or failure to make such determination is with respect to an application described in paragraph (b)(7) of this section. In addition, in the case of such an application, if a petitioner was the applicant for the determination, the Tax Court may hold, under section 7476(b)(2), the filing of a pleading for a declaratory judgment to be premature unless the petitioner establishes to the satisfaction of the Tax Court that such petitioner has caused the interested parties to be notified in accordance with this section and § 1.7476-2.

(b) *Interested parties.*—(1) *In general.*—If paragraphs (b)(2), (3), (4), and (5) of this section do not apply, then, except as otherwise provided in paragraphs (b)(6)(i), (ii), and (iii) of this section, the following persons shall be interested parties with respect to an application for an advance determination as to the qualified status of a retirement plan:

(i) All present employees of the employer who are eligible to participate in the plan (as defined in paragraph (d)(2) of this section), and

(ii) All other present employees of the employer whose principal place of employment (as defined in paragraph (d)(3) of this section) is the same as the principal place of employment of any employee described in paragraph (b)(1)(i) of this section.

(2) *Certain plans covering a principal owner.*—Notwithstanding paragraph (b)(1) of this section, where—

(i) A principal owner (within the meaning of paragraph (d)(2) of § 1.414(c)-3) of the employer or of a common parent of the employer (where the employer is a member of a parent-subsidiary group of trades or businesses under common control under section 414(b) or (c)) is eligible to participate in the plan, and

(ii) the number of employees employed by such employer (including all employees who by reason of section 414(b) or (c) are treated as employees of such employer) is 100 or less,

then except as otherwise provided in paragraphs (b)(6)(i), (ii), and (iv) of this section, all present employees of the employer shall be interested parties with respect to an application for an advance determination as to the qualified status of the retirement plan.

(3) *Certain plan amendments.*—In the case of an application for an advance determination as to whether a plan amendment affects the continuing qualification of a plan, if—

(i) there is outstanding a favorable determination letter for a plan year to which section 410 applies, and

(ii) the amendment does not alter the participation provisions of the plan,

then paragraphs (b)(1) and (2) of this section shall not apply, and all present employees of the employer who are eligible to participate in the plan (as defined in paragraph (d)(2) of this section), shall be interested parties. For the purpose of this paragraph (b)(3), if qualification of the plan is dependent upon benefits under the plan integrating with those benefits provided under the Social Security Act or a similar program, and if such integration results in excluding any employee or could possibly result in any participant's benefit being reduced to zero or the amendment alters contributions to or the amount of benefits payable under the plan, then the amendment shall be considered to alter the participation provisions of the plan.

(4) *Collectively bargained plans.*—In the case of an application with respect to a plan described in section 413(a) (relating to collectively bargained plans), paragraphs (b)(1), (2) and (3) of this section shall not apply and all present employees covered by a collective-bargaining agreement pursuant to which the plan is maintained shall be interested parties.

(5) *Plan terminations.*—In the case of an application for an advance determination with respect to whether a plan termination affects the continuing qualification of a retirement plan, paragraphs (b)(1), (2), (3) and (4) of this section shall not apply, and all present employees with accrued benefits under the plan, all former employees with vested benefits under the plan, and all beneficiaries of deceased former employees currently receiving benefits under the plan, shall be interested parties.

(6) *Exceptions.*—(i) In the case of an application to which paragraph (b)(1) or (2) of this section applies, an employee who is not eligible to participate in the plan shall not be an interested party if such employee is excluded from consideration for purposes of section 410(b)(1) by reason of section 410(b)(2)(B) or (C).

(ii) In the case of an application to which paragraph (b)(1) or (2) of this section applies, an employee who is not eligible to participate in the plan shall not be an interested party if such plan meets the eligibility standards of section 410(b)(1)(A).

(iii) In the case of an application to which paragraph (b)(1) of this section applies, an employee who is not eligible to participate in the plan shall not be an interested party with respect to such plan if such employee is eligible to participate in any other plan of the employer with respect to which a favorable determination letter is outstanding (whether or not issued pursuant to an application to which this section applies), or in such a plan of another employer whose employees, by reason of section 414(b) or (c), are treated as employees of the employer making the application.

(iv) In the case of an application to which paragraph (b)(2) of this section applies, an employee who is not eligible to participate in the plan shall not be an interested party with respect to such plan if such employee is eligible to participate in a plan described in section 413(a) (relating to collectively bargained plans) maintained by the employer with respect to which a favorable determination letter is outstanding (whether or not issued pursuant to an application to which this section applies), or in such a plan of another employer whose employees, by reason of section 414(b) or (c), are treated as employees of the employer making the application.

(7) *Applicability.*—Paragraph (b) of this section shall only apply in the case of an application made to the Internal Revenue Service requesting an advance determination that a retirement plan as defined in section 7476(d) and paragraph (a) of this section meets the requirements for qualification for a plan year or years to which section 410 applies to such plan. See paragraph (c)(4) and (5) of this section for special rules in respect of years to which section 410 applies.

(c) *Special rules.*—For purposes of paragraph (b) of this section and §1.7476-2—

(1) *Time of determination.*—The status of an individual as an interested party and as a present employee or former employee shall be determined as of a date determined by the applicant, which date shall not be earlier than five business days before the first date on which the notice of the application is given to interested parties pursuant to §1.7476-2 nor later than the date on which such notice is given.

(2) *Controlled groups, etc.*—An individual shall be considered to be an employee of an employer if such employee is treated as that employer's employee under section 414(b) or (c).

(3) *Self-employed individuals.*—A self-employed individual shall be considered an employee.

(4) *Years to which section 410 relates.*—For purposes of paragraph (b)(7) of this section, section 410 shall be considered to apply to a plan year if an election has been made under section 1017(d) of the Employee Retirement Income Se-

curity Act of 1974 to have section 410 apply to such plan year, whether or not the election is conditioned upon the issuance by the Commissioner of a favorable determination letter.

(5) *Government, church plans, etc.*—In the case of an organization described in section 410(c)(1), section 410 will be considered to apply to a plan year of such organization for any plan year to which section 410(c)(2) applies to such plan.

(d) *Definitions.*—For the purposes of paragraph (b) of this section and §1.7476-2—

(1) *Employer.*—The term "employer" includes all employers who maintain the plan with respect to which an advance determination applies. A sole proprietor shall be considered such person's own employer and a partnership is considered to be the employer of each of the partners.

(2) *Eligible to participate.*—For purposes of this section, an employee is eligible to participate in a plan if such employee—

(i) is a participant in the plan,

(ii) would be a participant in the plan if such employee met the minimum age and service requirements of the plan or

(iii) would be a participant in the plan upon making mandatory employee contributions.
In applying this paragraph (d)(2), plan provisions (with respect to which the determination regarding qualification is to be based) not in effect on the first date on which notice is given to interested parties shall be treated as though they were in effect on such date.

(3) *Place of employment.*—A place of employment includes all worksites within a plant, installation, store, office, or similar facility. Any employee who has no principal place of employment shall be treated as though such employee's principal place of employment is that place to which such employee regularly reports to the employer.

(e) *Effective date.*—The provisions of this section apply to applications referred to in paragraph (a) of this section made on or after June 21, 1976. [Reg. §1.7476-1.]

□ [*T.D. 7421, 5-20-76. Amended by T.D. 8179, 3-1-88 and T.D. 9006, 7-18-2002.*]

[Reg. §301.7476-1]

§301.7476-1. Declaratory judgments.—See the regulations under section 7476 contained in Part 1 of this chapter (Income Tax Regulations) for provisions relating to declaratory judgments, for provisions relating to the qualification of an employee as an "interested party", and for a requirement that the applicant for an advance determination by the Internal Revenue Service of the qualification of certain retirement plans give notice of such application to interested parties. [Reg. §301.7476-1.]

□ [*T.D. 7421, 5-20-76.*]

[Reg. §1.7476-2]

§1.7476-2. Notice to interested parties.—(a) *In general.*—Any person applying to a district director for a determination described in paragraph (b)(7) of §1.7476-1 shall cause notice of the application to be given to persons who qualify as interested parties under §1.7476-1 with respect to the application, whether or not such application is received by the Internal Revenue Service before the date on which section 410 applies to the plan.

(b) *Nature of notice.*—The notice required by this section shall—

(1) Contain the information and be given within the time period prescribed in §601.201(o)(3) of this chapter; and

(2) Be given in a manner prescribed in paragraph (c) of this section.

(c) *Method of giving notice.*—(1) In the case of a present employee, former employee, or beneficiary who is an interested party, the notice may be provided by any method reasonably calculated to ensure that each interested party is notified of the application for a determination. If an interested party who is a present employee is in a unit of employees covered by a collective-bargaining agreement between employee representatives and one or more employers, notice shall also be given to the collective-bargaining representative of such interested party by any method that satisfies this paragraph. Whether the notice is provided in a manner that satisfies the requirements of this paragraph is determined on the basis of all the relevant facts and circumstances. Because the facts and circumstances differ depending on the interested party, it may be necessary to use more than one method of delivery in order to ensure timely and adequate notice to all interested parties.

(2) If the notice to interested parties is delivered using an electronic medium under an electronic system that satisfies the applicable notice requirements of §1.401(a)-21 of this chapter, the notice is deemed to be provided in a manner that satisfies the requirements of paragraph (c)(1) of this section.

(d) *Examples.*—The principles of this section are illustrated by the following examples:

Example 1. (i) Employer A is amending Plan C and applying for a determination letter. Plan C is not maintained pursuant to one or more collective bargaining agreements and is not being terminated. As part of the determination letter application process, Employer A provides the notice required under this section to interested parties. For present employees, Employer A provides the notice by posting the notice at those locations within the principal places of employment of the interested parties which are customarily used for employer notices to employees with regard to employment and employee benefit matters.

(ii) In this *Example 1,* Employer A satisfies the notice to interested parties requirement described in this section.

Example 2. (i) Employer B is amending Plan D and applying for a determination letter. As part of the determination letter application process, Employer B provides the notice required under this section to interested parties.

(ii) Employer B has multiple worksites. Employer B's employees located at worksites 1 through 4 have reasonable access to computers at their workplace. However, Employer B's employees located at worksite 5 do not have access to computers.

(iii) For present employees with reasonable access to computers (worksites 1 through 4), Employer B provides the notice by posting the notice on Employer B's web site (Internet or intranet). Employees at worksites 1 through 4 customarily receive employer notification with regard to employment and employee benefit matters from the Employer B's web site. For present employees without access to computers (worksite 5), Employer B provides the notice by posting the notice at worksite 5 in a location that is customarily used for employer notices to employees with regard to employment and employee benefit matters.

(iv) Employer B also sends the notice by e-mail to each collective-bargaining representative of interested parties who are present employees of Employer B covered by a collective-bargaining agreement between employee representatives and Employer B, using the e-mail address previously provided to Employer B by such collective-bargaining representative.

(v) In this *Example 2,* Employer B satisfies the notice to interested parties requirement described in this section.

Example 3. (i) Employer C is terminating Plan E and applying for a determination letter as to whether the plan termination affects the continuing qualification of Plan E. As part of the determination letter application process, Employer C provides the notice required under this section to interested parties.

(ii) All of Employer C's employees have reasonable access to computers. Each employee has an e-mail address where he or she can receive messages from Employer C. Employees of Employer C customarily receive employer notices regarding employment and employee benefit matters by e-mail.

(iii) For present employees, Employer C provides the notice by sending the notice by e-mail.

(iv) Employer C also sends the notice by e-mail to each collective-bargaining representative of interested parties who are present employees of Employer C covered by a collective-bargaining agreement between employee representatives and Employer C, using the e-mail address previously provided to Employer C by such collective-bargaining representative.

Reg. §1.7476-2(d)

(v) In addition, Employer C sends the notice by e-mail to each interested party who is a former employee or beneficiary, using the e-mail address previously provided to Employer C by such interested party. For any former employee or beneficiary who did not provide an e-mail address, Employer C sends the notice by regular mail to the last known address of such former employee or beneficiary.

(vi) In this *Example 3*, Employer C satisfies the notice to interested parties requirement described in this section.

(e) *Effective date.*—(1) The provisions of this section shall apply to applications referred to in § 1.7476-1 (a) made on or after January 1, 2003.

(2) For applications made on or after June 21, 1976 and before January 1, 2003, § 1.7476-2 (as it appeared in the April 1, 2002 edition of 26 CFR part 1) applies. [Reg. § 1.7476-2.]

☐ [T.D. 7421, 5-20-76. *Amended by T.D.* 9006, 7-18-2002 *and T.D.* 9294, 10-19-2006.]

[Reg. § 1.7476-3]

§ 1.7476-3. Notice of determination.—(a) *In general.*—Under section 7476(b)(5), if a district director sends to the employer, the plan administrator, an interested party with respect to the plan, or the Pension Benefit Guaranty Corporation (or in the case of certain individuals who qualify as interested parties under paragraph (b) of § 1.7476-1, to the person described under paragraph (c) of this section as the representative of such individuals) by certified or registered mail a notice of determination with respect to the qualification of a retirement plan described in section 7476(d), no proceeding for a declaratory judgment by the United States Tax Court with respect to the qualification of such plan may be initiated by such person unless the pleading initiating such proceeding is filed by such person with such Court before the ninety-first day after the day after such notice is mailed.

(b) *Address for notice of determination.*—(1) *Applicant.*—In the case of the applicant for a determination, a notice of determination referred to in section 7476(b)(5) shall be sufficient if mailed to such person at the address set forth on the application for the determination.

(2) *Interested party.*—In the case of an interested party or parties who, pursuant to section 3001(b) of the Employee Retirement Income Security Act of 1974 (88 Stat. 995), submitted a comment to a district director with respect to the qualification of the plan, a notice of determination referred to in section 7476(b)(5) shall be sufficient if mailed to the address designated in the comment as the address to which correspondence should be sent.

(c) *Representative of interested parties.*—(1) In the case of an interested party who, in accordance with section 3001(b) of the Employee Retirement Income Security Act of 1974 (88 Stat. 995), requests the Secretary of Labor to submit a comment to a district director on matters re-

specting the qualification of the plan, where pursuant to such request such Secretary does in fact submit such a comment, the Administrator of Pension and Welfare Benefit Programs, Department of Labor, shall be the representative of such interested party for purposes of receiving the notice referred to in section 7476(b)(5) with respect to those matters on which the Secretary of Labor commented.

(2) In the event a single comment with respect to the qualification of the plan is submitted to a district director by two or more interested parties, the representative designated in the comment for receipt of correspondence shall be the representative of all the interested parties submitting the comment for purposes of receiving the notice referred to in section 7476(b)(5) on behalf of all of them. Such designated representative must be either one of the interested parties who submitted the comment or a person described in paragraph (e)(6)(i), (ii) or (iii) of § 601.201 of this chapter (Statement of Procedural Rules). If one person is not designated in the comment as the representative for receipt of correspondence, a notice of determination mailed to any interested party who submitted the comment shall be notice to all the interested parties who submitted the comment for purposes of section 7476(b)(5). [Reg. § 1.7476-3.]

☐ [T.D. 7421, 5-20-76.]

[Reg. § 301.7477-1]

§ 301.7477-1. Declaratory judgments relating to the value of certain gifts for gift tax purposes.—(a) *In general.*—If the adjustment(s) proposed by the Internal Revenue Service (IRS) will not result in any deficiency in or refund of the donor's gift tax liability for the calendar year, and if the requirements contained in paragraph (d) of this section are satisfied, then the declaratory judgment procedure under section 7477 is available to the donor for determining the amount of one or more of the donor's gifts during that calendar year for Federal gift tax purposes.

(b) *Declaratory judgment procedure.*—(1) *In general.*—If a donor does not resolve a dispute with the IRS concerning the value of a transfer for gift tax purposes at the Examination level, the donor will be sent a notice of preliminary determination of value (Letter 950-G or such other document as may be utilized by the IRS for this purpose from time to time, but referred to in this section as Letter 950-G), inviting the donor to file a formal protest and to request consideration by the appropriate IRS Appeals office. See §§ 601.105 and 601.106 of this chapter. Subsequently, the donor will be sent a notice of determination of value (Letter 3569, or such other document as may be utilized from time to time by the IRS for this purpose in cases where no deficiency or refund would result, but referred to in this section as Letter 3569) if—

(i) The donor requests Appeals consideration in writing within 30 calendar days after the mailing date of the Letter 950-G, or by such later date as determined pursuant to IRS procedures, and the matter is not resolved by Appeals;

(ii) The donor does not request Appeals consideration within the time provided in paragraph (b)(1)(i) of this section; or

(iii) The IRS does not issue a Letter 950-G in circumstances described in paragraph (d)(4)(iv) of this section.

(2) *Notice of determination of value.*—The Letter 3569 will notify the donor of the adjustment(s) proposed by the IRS, and will advise the donor that the donor may contest the determination made by the IRS by filing a petition with the Tax Court before the 91st day after the date on which the Letter 3569 was mailed to the donor by the IRS.

(3) *Tax Court petition.*—If the donor does not file a timely petition with the Tax Court, the IRS determination as set forth in the Letter 3569 will be considered the final determination of value, as defined in sections 2504(c) and 2001(f). If the donor files a timely petition with the Tax Court, the Tax Court will determine whether the donor has exhausted available administrative remedies. Under section 7477, the Tax Court is not authorized to issue a declaratory judgment unless the Tax Court finds that the donor has exhausted all administrative remedies within the IRS. See paragraph (d)(4) of this section regarding the exhaustion of administrative remedies.

(c) *Adjustments subject to declaratory judgment procedure.*—The declaratory judgment procedures set forth in this section apply to adjustments involving all issues relating to the transfer, including without limitation valuation issues and legal issues involving the interpretation and application of the gift tax law.

(d) *Requirements for declaratory judgment procedure.*—(1) *In general.*—The declaratory judgment procedure provided in this section is available to a donor with respect to a transfer only if all the requirements of paragraphs (d)(2) through (5) of this section with regard to that transfer are satisfied.

(2) *Reporting.*—The transfer is shown or disclosed on the return of tax imposed by chapter 12 for the calendar year during which the transfer was made or on a statement attached to such return. For purposes of this paragraph (d)(2), the term *return of tax imposed by chapter 12* means the last gift tax return (Form 709, "United States Gift (and Generation-Skipping Transfer) Tax Return" or such other form as may be utilized for this purpose from time to time by the IRS) for the calendar year filed on or before the due date of the return, including extensions granted if any, or, if a timely return is not filed, the first gift tax return for that calendar year filed after the due date. For purposes of satisfying this requirement, the transfer need not be reported in a manner that constitutes adequate disclosure within the meaning of §301.6501(c)-1(e) or (f) (and thus for which, under §§20.2001-1(b) and 25.2504-2(b) of this chapter, the period during which the IRS

may adjust the value of the gift will not expire). The issuance of a Letter 3569 with regard to a transfer disclosed on a return does not constitute a determination by the IRS that the transfer was adequately disclosed, or otherwise cause the period of limitations on assessment to commence to run with respect to that transfer. In addition, in the case of a transfer that is shown on the return, the IRS may in its discretion defer until a later time making a determination with regard to such transfer. If the IRS exercises its discretion to defer such determination in that case, the transfer will not be addressed in the Letter 3569 (if any) sent to the donor currently, and the donor is not yet eligible for a declaratory judgment with regard to that transfer under section 7477.

(3) *IRS determination and actual controversy.*—The IRS makes a determination regarding the gift tax treatment of the transfer that results in an actual controversy. The IRS makes a determination that results in an actual controversy with respect to a transfer by mailing a Letter 3569 to the donor, thereby notifying the donor of the adjustment(s) proposed by the IRS with regard to that transfer and of the donor's rights under section 7477.

(4) *Exhaustion of administrative remedies.*—(i) *In general.*—The Tax Court determines whether the donor has exhausted all administrative remedies available within the IRS for resolving the controversy.

(ii) *Appeals office consideration.*—For purposes of this section, the IRS will consider a donor to have exhausted all administrative remedies if, prior to filing a petition in Tax Court (except as provided in paragraphs (d)(4)(iii) and (iv) of this section), the donor, or a qualified representative of the donor described in §601.502 of this chapter, timely requests consideration by Appeals and participates fully (within the meaning of paragraph (d)(4)(vi) of this section) in the Appeals consideration process. A timely request for consideration by Appeals is a written request from the donor for Appeals consideration made within 30 days after the mailing date of the Letter 950-G, or by such later date for responding to the Letter 950-G as is agreed to between the donor and the IRS.

(iii) *Request for Appeals office consideration not granted.*—If the donor, or a qualified representative of the donor described in §601.502 of this chapter, timely requests consideration by Appeals and Appeals does not grant that request, the IRS nevertheless will consider the donor to have exhausted all administrative remedies within the IRS for purposes of section 7477 upon the issuance of the Letter 3569, provided that the donor, or a qualified representative of the donor described in §601.502 of this chapter, after the filing of a petition in Tax Court for a declaratory judgment pursuant to section 7477, participates fully (within the meaning of paragraph (d)(4)(vi) of this section) in the Appeals office consideration if offered by the IRS while the case is in docketed status.

Reg. §301.7477-1(d)(4)(iii)

(iv) *No Letter 950-G issued.*—If the IRS does not issue a Letter 950-G to the donor prior to the issuance of Letter 3569, the IRS nevertheless will consider the donor to have exhausted all administrative remedies within the IRS for purposes of section 7477 upon the issuance of the Letter 3569, provided that—

(A) The IRS decision not to issue the Letter 950-G was not due to actions or inactions of the donor (such as a failure to supply requested information or a current mailing address to the Area Director having jurisdiction over the tax matter); and

(B) The donor, or a qualified representative of the donor described in § 601.502 of this chapter, after the filing of a petition in Tax Court for a declaratory judgment pursuant to section 7477, participates fully (within the meaning of paragraph (d)(4)(vi) of this section) in the Appeals office consideration if offered by the IRS while the case is in docketed status.

(v) *Failure to agree to extension of time for assessment.*—For purposes of section 7477, the donor's refusal to agree to an extension of the time under section 6501 within which gift tax with respect to the transfer at issue (if any) may be assessed will not be considered by the IRS to constitute a failure by the donor to exhaust all administrative remedies available to the donor within the IRS.

(vi) *Participation in Appeals consideration process.*—For purposes of this section, the donor or a qualified representative of the donor described in § 601.502 of this chapter participates fully in the Appeals consideration process if the donor or the qualified representative timely submits all information related to the transfer that is requested by the IRS in connection with the Appeals consideration and discloses to the Appeals office all relevant information regarding the controversy to the extent such information and its relevance is known or should be known by the donor or the qualified representative during the time the issue is under consideration by Appeals.

(5) *Timely petition in Tax Court.*—The donor files a pleading with the Tax Court requesting a declaratory judgment under section 7477. This pleading must be filed with the Tax Court before the 91st day after the date of mailing of the Letter 3569 by the IRS to the donor. The pleading must be in the form of a petition subject to Tax Court Rule 211(d).

(e) *Examples.*—The following examples illustrate the provisions of this section, and assume that in each case the Tax Court petition is filed on or after September 9, 2009. These examples, however, do not address any other situations that might affect the Tax Court's jurisdiction over the proceeding:

Example 1. Exhaustion of administrative remedies. The donor (D) timely files a Form 709, "United States Gift (and Generation-Skipping Transfer) Tax Return," on which D reports D's completed gift of closely held stock. After conducting an examination, the IRS concludes that the value of the stock on the date of the gift is greater than the value reported on the return. Because the amount of D's available applicable credit amount under section 2505 is sufficient to cover any resulting tax liability, no gift tax deficiency will result from the adjustment. D is unable to resolve the matter with the IRS examiner. The IRS sends a Letter 950-G to D informing D of the proposed adjustment. D, within 30 calendar days after the mailing date of the letter, submits a written request for Appeals consideration. During the Appeals process, D provides to the Appeals office all additional information (if any) requested by Appeals relevant to the determination of the value of the stock in a timely fashion. The Appeals office and D are unable to reach an agreement regarding the value of the stock as of the date of the gift. The Appeals office sends D a notice of determination of value (Letter 3569). For purposes of section 7477, the IRS will consider D to have exhausted all available administrative remedies within the IRS, and thus will not contest the allegation in D's petition that D has exhausted all such administrative remedies.

Example 2. Exhaustion of administrative remedies. Assume the same facts as in *Example 1*, except that D does not timely request consideration by Appeals after receiving the Letter 950-G. A Letter 3569 is mailed to D more than 30 days after the mailing of the Letter 950-G and prior to the expiration of the period of limitations for assessment of gift tax. D timely files a petition in Tax Court pursuant to section 7477. After the case is docketed, D requests Appeals consideration. In this situation, because D did not respond timely to the Letter 950-G with a written request for Appeals consideration, the IRS will not consider D to have exhausted all administrative remedies available within the IRS for purposes of section 7477 prior to filing the petition in Tax Court, and thus may contest any allegation in D's petition that D has exhausted all such administrative remedies.

Example 3. Exhaustion of administrative remedies. D timely files a Form 709 on which D reports D's completed gifts of interests in a family limited partnership. After conducting an examination, the IRS proposes to adjust the value of the gifts as reported on the return. No gift tax deficiency will result from the adjustments, however, because D has a sufficient amount of available applicable credit amount under section 2505. D declines to consent to extend the time for the assessment of gift tax with respect to the gifts at issue. Because of the pending expiration of the period of limitation on assessment within which a gift tax, if any, could be assessed, the IRS determines that there is not adequate time for Appeals consideration. Accordingly, the IRS mails to D a Letter 3569, even though a Letter 950-G had not first been issued to D. D timely files a petition in Tax Court pursuant to section 7477. After the case is docketed in Tax Court, D is offered the opportunity for Appeals to consider any dispute regarding the determination and participates fully in the Appeals consideration process. However, the Appeals office and D are unable to resolve the issue. The IRS will consider D to have exhausted all administrative remedies available within the IRS, and thus will not assert that D has not exhausted all such administrative remedies.

Example 4. Legal issue. D transfers nonvested stock options to a trust for the benefit of D's child. D timely files a Form 709 reporting the transfer as a completed gift for Federal gift tax purposes and complies with the adequate disclosure requirements for purposes of triggering the commencement of the applicable statute of limitations. Pursuant to §301.6501(c)-1(f)(5), adequate disclosure of a transfer that is reported as a completed gift on the Form 709 will commence the running of the period of limitations for assessment of gift tax on D, even if the transfer is ultimately determined to be an incomplete gift for purposes of §25.2511-2 of this chapter. After conducting an examination, the IRS concurs with the reported valuation of the stock options, but concludes that the reported transfer is not a completed gift for Federal gift tax purposes. D is unable to resolve the matter with the IRS examiner. The IRS sends a Letter 950-G to D, who timely mails a written request for Appeals consideration. Assuming that the IRS mails to D a Letter 3569 with regard to this transfer, and that D complies with the administrative procedures set forth in this section, including the exhaustion of all administrative remedies available within the IRS, then D may file a petition for declaratory judgment with the Tax Court pursuant to section 7477.

Example 5. Transfers in controversy. On April 16, 2007, D timely files a Form 709 on which D reports gifts made in 2006 of fractional interests in certain real property and of interests in a family limited partnership (FLP). However, although the gifts are disclosed on the return, the return does not contain information sufficient to constitute adequate disclosure under §301.6501(c)-1(e) or (f) for purposes of the application of the statute of limitations on assessment of gift tax with respect to the reported gifts. The IRS conducts an examination and concludes that the value of both the interests in the real property and the FLP interests on the date(s) of the transfers are greater than the values reported on the return. No gift tax deficiency will result from the adjustments because D has a sufficient amount of remaining applicable credit amount under section 2505. However, D does not agree with the adjustments. The IRS sends a Letter 950-G to D informing D of the proposed adjustments in the value of the reported gifts. D, within 30 calendar days after the mailing date of the letter, submits a written request for Appeals consideration. The Appeals office and D are unable to reach an agreement regarding the value of any of the gifts. In the exercise of its discretion, the IRS decides to resolve currently only the value of the real property interests, and to defer the resolution of the value of the FLP interests. On May 28, 2009, the Appeals office sends D a Letter 3569 addressing only the value of the gifts of interests in the real property. Because none of the gifts reported on the return filed on April 16, 2007, were adequately disclosed for purposes of §301.6501(c)-1(e) or (f), the period of limitations during which the IRS may adjust the value of those gifts has not begun to run. Accordingly, the Letter 3569 is timely mailed. If D timely files a petition in Tax Court pursuant to section 7477 with regard to the value of the interests in the real property, then, assuming the other requirements of section 7477 are satisfied with regard to those interests, the Tax Court's declaratory judgment, once it becomes final, will determine the value of the gifts of the interests in the real property. Because the IRS has not yet put the gift tax value of the interests in the FLP into controversy, the procedure under section 7477 is not yet available with regard to those gifts.

(f) *Effective/applicability date.*—This section applies to civil proceedings described in section 7477 filed in the United States Tax Court on or after September 9, 2009. [Reg. §301.7477-1.]

☐ [*T.D. 7596, 2-22-79. Amended by T.D. 7954, 5-7-84 and T.D. 9460, 9-8-2009 (corrected 10-26-2009).]*

COURT REVIEW OF TAX COURT PROCEEDINGS

[Reg. §301.7481-1]

§301.7481-1. Date when Tax Court decision becomes final; decision modified or reversed.—
(a) *Upon mandate of Supreme Court.*—Under section 7481(3)(A) of the Code, if the Supreme Court directs that the decision of the Tax Court be modified or reversed, the decision of the Tax Court rendered in accordance with the mandate of the Supreme Court shall become final upon the expiration of 30 days from the time it was rendered, unless within 30 days either the Commissioner or the taxpayer has instituted proceedings to have such decision corrected to accord with the mandate, in which event the decision of the Tax Court shall become final when so corrected.

(b) *Upon mandate of the Court of Appeals.*—Under section 7481(3)(B) of the Code, if the decision of the Tax Court is modified or reversed by the United States Court of Appeals, and if—

(i) The time allowed for filing a petition for certiorari has expired and no such petition has been duly filed, or

(ii) The petition for certiorari has been denied, or

(iii) The decision of the United States Court of Appeals has been affirmed by the Supreme Court, then the decision of the Tax Court rendered in accordance with the mandate of the United States Court of Appeals shall become final on the expiration of 30 days from the time such decision of the Tax Court was rendered, unless within such 30 days either the Commissioner or the taxpayer has instituted proceedings to have such decision corrected so that it will accord with the mandate, in which event the decision of the Tax Court shall become final when so corrected. [Reg. § 301.7481-1.]

☐ [*T.D.* 6498, 10-24-60.]

[Reg. § 301.7482-1]

§ 301.7482-1. Courts of review; venue.—Under section 7482(b)(2) of the Code, decisions of the Tax Court may be reviewed by any United States Court of Appeals which may be designated by the Commissioner and the taxpayer by stipulation in writing. [Reg. § 301.7482-1.]

☐ [*T.D.* 6498, 10-24-60.]

[Reg. § 301.7483-1]

§ 301.7483-1. Petition for review.—The decision of the Tax Court may be reviewed by a United States Court of Appeals as provided in section 7482 of the Code if a petition for such review is filed by either the Commissioner or the taxpayer within 3 months after the decision is rendered. If, however, a petition for such review is so filed by one party to the proceeding, a petition for review of the decision of the Tax Court may be filed by any other party to the proceeding within 4 months after such decision is rendered. [Reg. § 301.7483-1.]

☐ [*T.D.* 6498, 10-24-60.]

[Reg. § 301.7484-1]

§ 301.7484-1. Change of incumbent in office.—When the incumbent of the office of Commissioner changes, no substitution of the name of his successor shall be required in proceedings pending before any appellate court reviewing the action of the Tax Court. [Reg. § 301.7484-1.]

☐ [*T.D.* 6498, 10-24-60.]

Miscellaneous Provisions

See p. 20,601 for regulations not amended to reflect law changes

[Reg. § 301.7502-1]

§ 301.7502-1. Timely mailing of documents and payments treated as timely filing and paying.—(a) *General rule.*—Section 7502 provides that, if the requirements of that section are met, a document or payment is deemed to be filed or paid on the date of the postmark stamped on the envelope or other appropriate wrapper (envelope) in which the document or payment was mailed. Thus, if the envelope that contains the document or payment has a timely postmark, the document or payment is considered timely filed or paid even if it is received after the last date, or the last day of the period, prescribed for filing the document or making the payment. Section 7502 does not apply in determining whether a failure to file a return or pay a tax has continued for an additional month or fraction thereof for purposes of computing the penalties and additions to tax imposed by section 6651. Except as provided in section 7502(e) and § 301.7502-2, relating to the timely mailing of deposits, and paragraph (d) of this section, relating to electronically filed documents, section 7502 is applicable only to those documents or payments as defined in paragraph (b) of this section and only if the document or payment is mailed in accordance with paragraph (c) of this section and is delivered in accordance with paragraph (e) of this section.

(b) *Definitions.*—(1) *Document defined.*—(i) The term *document,* as used in this section, means any return, claim, statement, or other document required to be filed within a prescribed period or on or before a prescribed date under authority of any provision of the internal revenue laws, except as provided in paragraph (b) (1) (ii), (iii), or (iv) of this section.

(ii) The term does not include returns, claims, statements, or other documents that are required under any provision of the internal revenue laws or the regulations thereunder to be delivered by any method other than mailing.

(iii) The term does not include any document filed in any court other than the Tax Court, but the term does include any document filed with the Tax Court, including a petition and a notice of appeal of a decision of the Tax Court.

(iv) The term does not include any document that is mailed to an authorized financial institution under section 6302. However, see § 301.7502-2 for special rules relating to the timeliness of deposits and documents required to be filed with deposits.

(2) *Claims for refund.*—(i) *In general.*—In the case of certain taxes, a return may constitute a claim for credit or refund. Section 7502 is applicable to the determination of whether a claim for credit or refund is timely filed for purposes of section 6511(a) if the conditions of section 7502 are met, irrespective of whether the claim is also a return. For rules regarding claims for refund on late filed tax returns, see paragraph (f) of this section. Section 7502 is also applicable when a claim for credit or refund is delivered after the last day of the period specified in section 6511(b)(2)(A) or in any other corresponding provision of law relating to the limit on the amount of credit or refund that is allowable.

(ii) *Example.*—The rules of paragraph (b)(2)(i) of this section are illustrated by the following example:

Example. (A) Taxpayer A, an individual, mailed his 2004 Form 1040, "U.S. Individual Income Tax Return," on May 10, 2005, but no tax was paid at that time because the tax liability disclosed by the return had been completely satisfied by the income tax that had been withheld on A's wages. On April 15, 2008, A mails, in accordance with the requirements of this section, a Form 1040X, "Amended U.S. Individual Income Tax Return," claiming a refund of a portion of the tax that had been paid through withholding during 2004. The date of the postmark on the envelope containing the claim for refund is April 15, 2008. The claim is received by the IRS on April 18, 2008.

(B) Under section 6511(a), A's claim for refund is timely if filed within three years from May 10, 2005, the date on which A's 2004 return was filed. As a result of the limitations of section 6511(b)(2)(A), if A's claim is not filed within three years after April 15, 2005, the date on which A is deemed under section 6513 to have paid his 2004 tax, A is not entitled to any refund. Because A's claim for refund is postmarked and mailed in accordance with the requirements of this section and is delivered after the last day of the period specified in section 6511(b)(2)(A), section 7502 is applicable and the claim is deemed to have been filed on April 15, 2008.

(3) *Payment defined.*—(i) The term *payment,* as used in this section, means any payment required to be made within a prescribed period or on or before a prescribed date under the authority of any provision of the internal revenue laws, except as provided in paragraph(b)(3)(ii), (iii), (iv), or (v) of this section.

(ii) The term does not include any payment that is required under any provision of the internal revenue laws or the regulations thereunder to be delivered by any method other than mailing. See, for example, section 6302(h) and the regulations thereunder regarding electronic funds transfer.

(iii) The term does not include any payment, whether it is made in the form of currency or other medium of payment, unless it is actually received and accounted for. For example, if a check is used as the form of payment, this section does not apply unless the check is honored upon presentation.

(iv) The term does not include any payment to any court other than the Tax Court.

(v) The term does not include any deposit that is required to be made with an authorized financial institution under section 6302. However, see § 301.7502-2 for rules relating to the timeliness of deposits.

(4) *Last date or last day prescribed.*—As used in this section, the term *the last date, or the last day of the period, prescribed for filing the document or making the payment* includes any extension of time granted for that action. When the last date, or the last day of the period, prescribed for filing the document or making the payment falls on a Saturday, Sunday or legal holiday, section 7503 applies. Therefore, in applying the rules of this paragraph (b)(4), the next succeeding day that is not a Saturday, Sunday, or legal holiday is treated as the last date, or the last day of the period, prescribed for filing the document or making the payment. Also, when the last date, or the last day of the period, prescribed for filing the document or making the payment falls

within a period disregarded under section 7508 or section 7508A, the next succeeding day after the expiration of the section 7508 period or section 7508A period that is not a Saturday, Sunday, or legal holiday is treated as the last date, or the last day of the period, prescribed for filing the document or making the payment.

(c) *Mailing requirements.*—(1) *In general.*—Section 7502 does not apply unless the document or payment is mailed in accordance with the following requirements:

(i) *Envelope and address.*—The document or payment must be contained in an envelope, properly addressed to the agency, officer, or office with which the document is required to be filed or to which the payment is required to be made.

(ii) *Timely deposited in U.S. mail.*—The document or payment must be deposited within the prescribed time in the mail in the United States with sufficient postage prepaid. For this purpose, a document or payment is deposited in the mail in the United States when it is deposited with the domestic mail service of the U.S. Postal Service. The domestic mail service of the U.S. Postal Service, as defined by the Domestic Mail Manual as incorporated by reference in the postal regulations, includes mail transmitted within, among, and between the United States of America, its territories and possessions, and Army post offices (APO), fleet post offices (FPO), and the United Nations, NY. (See Domestic Mail Manual, section G011.2.1, as incorporated by reference in 39 CFR 111.1.) Section 7502 does not apply to any document or payment that is deposited with the mail service of any other country.

(iii) *Postmark.*—(A) *U.S. Postal Service postmark.*—If the postmark on the envelope is made by the U.S. Postal Service, the postmark must bear a date on or before the last date, or the last day of the period, prescribed for filing the document or making the payment. If the postmark does not bear a date on or before the last date, or the last day of the period, prescribed for filing the document or making the payment, the document or payment is considered not to be timely filed or paid, regardless of when the document or payment is deposited in the mail. Accordingly, the sender who relies upon the applicability of section 7502 assumes the risk that the postmark will bear a date on or before the last date, or the last day of the period, prescribed for filing the document or making the payment. See, however, paragraph (c)(2) of this section with respect to the use of registered mail or certified mail to avoid this risk. If the postmark on the envelope is made by the U.S. Postal Service but is not legible, the person who is required to file the document or make the payment has the burden of proving the date that the postmark was made. Furthermore, if the envelope that contains a document or payment has a timely postmark made by the U.S. Postal Service, but it is received after the time when a document

Reg. § 301.7502-1(c)(1)(iii)(A)

or payment postmarked and mailed at that time would ordinarily be received, the sender may be required to prove that it was timely mailed.

(B) *Postmark made by other than U.S. Postal Service.*—(1) *In general.*—If the postmark on the envelope is made other than by the U.S. Postal Service—

(i) The postmark so made must bear a legible date on or before the last date, or the last day of the period, prescribed for filing the document or making the payment; and

(ii) The document or payment must be received by the agency, officer, or office with which it is required to be filed not later than the time when a document or payment contained in an envelope that is properly addressed, mailed, and sent by the same class of mail would ordinarily be received if it were postmarked at the same point of origin by the U.S. Postal Service on the last date, or the last day of the period, prescribed for filing the document or making the payment.

(2) *Document or payment received late.*—If a document or payment described in paragraph (c)(1)(iii)(B)(1) is received after the time when a document or payment so mailed and so postmarked by the U.S. Postal Service would ordinarily be received, the document or payment is treated as having been received at the time when a document or payment so mailed and so postmarked would ordinarily be received if the person who is required to file the document or make the payment establishes—

(i) That it was actually deposited in the U.S. mail before the last collection of mail from the place of deposit that was postmarked (except for the metered mail) by the U.S. Postal Service on or before the last date, or the last day of the period, prescribed for filing the document or making the payment;

(ii) That the delay in receiving the document or payment was due to a delay in the transmission of the U.S. mail; and

(iii) The cause of the delay.

(3) *U.S. and non-U.S. postmarks.*—If the envelope has a postmark made by the U.S. Postal Service in addition to a postmark not so made, the postmark that was not made by the U.S. Postal Service is disregarded, and whether the envelope was mailed in accordance with this paragraph (c)(1)(iii)(B) will be determined solely by applying the rule of paragraph (c)(1)(iii)(A) of this section.

(2) *Registered or certified mail.*—If the document or payment is sent by U.S. registered mail, the date of registration of the document or payment is treated as the postmark date. If the document or payment is sent by U.S. certified mail and the sender's receipt is postmarked by the postal employee to whom the document or payment is presented, the date of the U.S. postmark on the receipt is treated as the postmark date of the document or payment. Accordingly, the risk that the document or payment will not be post-

marked on the day that it is deposited in the mail may be eliminated by the use of registered or certified mail.

(3) *Private delivery services.*—Under section 7502(f)(1), a service of a private delivery service (PDS) may be treated as an equivalent to United States mail for purposes of the postmark rule if the Commissioner determines that the service satisfies the conditions of section 7502(f)(2). Thus, the Commissioner may, in guidance published in the Internal Revenue Bulletin (see § 601.601(d)(2)(ii)(b) of this chapter), prescribe procedures and additional rules to designate a service of a PDS for purposes of the postmark rule of section 7502(a).

(d) *Electronically filed documents.*—(1) *In general.*—A document filed electronically with an electronic return transmitter (as defined in paragraph (d)(3)(i) of this section and authorized pursuant to paragraph (d)(2) of this section) in the manner and time prescribed by the Commissioner is deemed to be filed on the date of the electronic postmark (as defined in paragraph (d)(3)(ii) of this section) given by the authorized electronic return transmitter. Thus, if the electronic postmark is timely, the document is considered filed timely although it is received by the agency, officer, or office after the last date, or the last day of the period, prescribed for filing such document.

(2) *Authorized electronic return transmitters.*—The Commissioner may enter into an agreement with an electronic return transmitter or prescribe in forms, instructions, or other appropriate guidance the procedures under which the electronic return transmitter is authorized to provide taxpayers with an electronic postmark to acknowledge the date and time that the electronic return transmitter received the electronically filed document.

(3) *Definitions.*—(i) *Electronic return transmitter.*—For purposes of this paragraph (d), the term *electronic return transmitter* has the same meaning as contained in section 3.01(4) of Rev. Proc. 2000-31 (2000-31 I.R.B. 146 (July 31, 2000)) (see § 601.601(d)(2) of this chapter) or in procedures prescribed by the Commissioner.

(ii) *Electronic postmark.*—For purposes of this paragraph (d), the term *electronic postmark* means a record of the date and time (in a particular time zone) that an authorized electronic return transmitter receives the transmission of a taxpayer's electronically filed document on its host system. However, if the taxpayer and the electronic return transmitter are located in different time zones, it is the taxpayer's time zone that controls the timeliness of the electronically filed document.

(e) *Delivery.*—(1) *General rule.*—Except as provided in section 7502(f) and paragraphs (c)(3) and (d) of this section, section 7502 is not applicable unless the document or payment is delivered by U.S. mail to the agency, officer, or office with which the document is required to be filed or to which payment is required to be made.

(2) *Exceptions to actual delivery.*— (i) *Registered and certified mail.*—In the case of a document (but not a payment) sent by registered or certified mail, proof that the document was properly registered or that a postmarked certified mail sender's receipt was properly issued and that the envelope was properly addressed to the agency, officer, or office constitutes prima facie evidence that the document was delivered to the agency, officer, or office. Other than direct proof of actual delivery, proof of proper use of registered or certified mail, and proof of proper use of a duly designated PDS as provided for by paragraph (e)(2)(ii) of this section, are the exclusive means to establish prima facie evidence of delivery of a document to the agency, officer, or office with which the document is required to be filed. No other evidence of a postmark or of mailing will be prima facie evidence of delivery or raise a presumption that the document was delivered.

(ii) *Equivalents of registered and certified mail.*—Under section 7502(f)(3), the Secretary may extend the prima facie evidence of delivery rule of section 7502(c)(1)(A) to a service of a designated PDS, which is substantially equivalent to United States registered or certified mail. Thus, the Commissioner may, in guidance published in the Internal Revenue Bulletin (see § 601.601(d)(2)(ii)(b) of this chapter), prescribe procedures and additional rules to designate a service of a PDS for purposes of demonstrating prima facie evidence of delivery of a document pursuant to section 7502(c).

(f) *Claim for credit or refund on late filed tax return.*—(1) *In general.*—Generally, an original income tax return may constitute a claim for credit or refund of income tax. See § 301.6402-3(a)(5). Other original tax returns can also be considered claims for credit or refund if the liability disclosed on the return is less than the amount of tax that has been paid. If section 7502 would not apply to a return (but for the operation of paragraph (f)(2) of this section) that is also considered a claim for credit or refund because the envelope that contains the return does not have a postmark dated on or before the due date of the return, section 7502 will apply separately to the claim for credit or refund if—

(i) The date of the postmark on the envelope is within the period that is three years (plus the period of any extension of time to file) from the day the tax is paid or considered paid (see section 6513), and the claim for credit or refund is delivered after this three-year period; and

(ii) The conditions of section 7502 are otherwise met.

(2) *Filing date of late filed return.*—If the conditions of paragraph (f)(1) of this section are met, the late filed return will be deemed filed on the postmark date.

(3) *Example.*—The rules of this paragraph (f) are illustrated by the following example:

Example. (i) Taxpayer A, an individual, mailed his 2001 Form 1040, "U.S. Individual Income Tax Return," on April 15, 2005, claiming a refund of amounts paid through withholding during 2001. The date of the postmark on the envelope containing the return and claim for refund is April 15, 2005. The return and claim for refund are received by the Internal Revenue Service (IRS) on April 18, 2005. Amounts withheld in 2001 exceeded A's tax liability for 2001 and are treated as paid on April 15, 2002, pursuant to section 6513.

(ii) Even though the date of the postmark on the envelope is after the due date of the return, the claim for refund and the late filed return are treated as filed on the postmark date for purposes of this paragraph (f). Accordingly, the return will be treated as filed on April 15, 2005. In addition, the claim for refund will be treated as timely filed on April 15, 2005. Further, the entire amount of the refund attributable to withholding is allowable as a refund under section 6511(b)(2)(A).

(g) *Effective date.*—(1) *In general.*—Except as provided in paragraphs (g) (2) and (3) of this section, the rules of this section apply to any payment or document mailed and delivered in accordance with the requirements of this section in an envelope bearing a postmark dated after January 11, 2001.

(2) *Claim for credit or refund on late filed tax return.*—Paragraph (f) of this section applies to any claim for credit or refund on a late filed tax return described in paragraph (f) (1) of this section except for those claims for credit or refund which (without regard to paragraph (f) of this section) were barred by the operation of section 6532(a) or any other law or rule of law (including res judicata) as of January 11, 2001.

(3) *Electronically filed documents.*—This section applies to any electronically filed return, claim, statement, or other document transmitted to an electronic return transmitter that is authorized to provide an electronic postmark pursuant to paragraph (d) (2) of this section after January 11, 2001.

(4) *Registered or certified mail as the means to prove delivery of a document.*—Section 301.7502-1(e)(2) will apply to all documents mailed after September 21, 2004. [Reg. § 301.7502-1.]

☐ [*T.D. 6232, 5-2-57. Amended by T.D. 6292, 4-18-58; T.D. 6444, 1-14-60; T.D. 6498, 10-24-60; T.D. 8807, 1-14-99; T.D. 8932, 1-10-2001 and T.D. 9543, 8-22-2011.*]

[Reg. § 301.7503-1]

§ 301.7503-1. Time for performance of acts where last day falls on Saturday, Sunday, or legal holiday.—(a) *In general.*—Section 7503 provides that when the last day prescribed under authority of any internal revenue law for the performance of any act falls on a Saturday, Sunday, or legal holiday, such act shall be considered performed timely if performed on the next succeeding day which is not a Saturday, Sunday, or legal holiday. For this purpose, any authorized extension of time shall be included in determining the last day for performance of any act. Section 7503 is applicable only in case an act is required under authority of any internal revenue law to be performed on or before a prescribed date or within a prescribed period. For example, if the 2-year period allowed by section 6532(a)(1) to bring a suit for refund of any internal revenue tax expires on Thursday, November 23, 1995 (Thanksgiving Day), the suit will be timely if filed on Friday, November 24, 1995, in the Court of Federal Claims, or in a district court. Section 7503 applies to acts to be performed by the taxpayer (such as, the filing of any return of, and the payment of, any income, estate, or gift tax; the filing of a petition with the Tax Court for redetermination of a deficiency, or for review of a decision rendered by such Court; the filing of a claim for credit or refund of any tax) and acts to be performed by the Commissioner, a district director, or the director of a regional service center (such as, the giving of any notice with respect to, or making any demand for the payment of, any tax; the assessment or collection of any tax).

(b) *Legal holidays.*—For the purpose of section 7503, the term *legal holiday* includes the legal holidays in the District of Columbia as found in D.C. Code Ann. 28-2701. In the case of any return, statement, or other document required to be filed, or any other act required under the authority of the internal revenue laws to be performed, at an office of the Internal Revenue Service, or any other office or agency of the United States, located outside the District of Columbia but within an internal revenue district, the term *legal holiday* includes, in addition to the legal holidays in the District of Columbia, any statewide legal holiday of the state where the act is required to be performed. If the act is performed in accordance with law at an office of the Internal Revenue Service or any other office or agency of the United States located in a territory or possession of the United States, the term *legal holiday* includes, in addition to the legal holidays in the District of Columbia, any legal holiday that is recognized throughout the territory or possession in which the office is located. [Reg. § 301.7503-1.]

☐ [*T.D. 6232, 5-2-57. Amended by T.D. 6498, 10-24-60; T.D. 6585, 12-27-61; T.D. 7309, 3-27-74 and T.D. 8681, 8-13-96.*]

[Reg. § 301.7505-1]

§ 301.7505-1. **Sale of personal property acquired by the United States.**—(a) *Sale.*—(1) *In general.*—Any personal property (except bonds, notes, checks, and other securities) acquired by the United States in payment of or as security for debts arising under the internal revenue laws may be sold by the district director who acquired

such property for the United States. United States Savings Bonds shall not be sold by the district director but shall be transferred to the appropriate office of the Treasury Department for redemption. Other bonds, notes, checks, and other securities shall be disposed of in accordance with instructions issued by the Commissioner.

(2) *Time, place, manner, and terms of sale.*—The time, place, manner, and terms of sale of personal property acquired for the United States shall be as follows:

(i) *Time, notice, and place of sale.*—The property may be sold at any time after it has been acquired by the United States. A public notice of sale shall be posted at the post office nearest the place of sale and in at least two other public places. The notice shall specify the property to be sold and the time, place, manner, and conditions of sale. In addition, the district director may use such other methods of advertising as he believes will result in obtaining the highest price for the property. The place of sale shall be within the internal revenue district where the property was originally acquired by the United States. However, if the district director believes that a substantially higher price may be obtained, the sale may be held outside his district.

(ii) *Rejection of bids and adjournment of sale.*—The internal revenue officer conducting the sale reserves the right to reject any and all bids and withdraw the property from the sale. When it appears to the internal revenue officer conducting the sale that an adjournment of the sale will best serve the interest of the United States, he may order the sale adjourned from time to time. If the sale is adjourned for more than 30 days in the aggregate, public notice of the sale must again be given in accordance with subdivision (i) of this subparagraph.

(iii) *Liquidated damages.*—The notice shall state whether, in the case of default in payment of the bid price, any amount deposited with the United States will be retained as liquidated damages. In case liquidated damages are provided, the amount thereof shall not exceed $200.

(3) *Agreement to bid.*—The district director may, before giving notice of sale, solicit offers from prospective bidders and enter into agreements with such persons that they will bid at least a specified amount in case the property is offered for sale. In such cases, the district director may also require such persons to make deposits to secure the performance of their agreements. Any such deposit, but not more than $200, shall be retained as liquidated damages in case such person fails to bid the specified amount and the property is not sold for as much as the amount specified in such agreement.

(4) *Terms of payment.*—The property shall be offered for sale upon whichever of the following terms is fixed by the district director in the public notice of sale—

(i) Payment in full upon acceptance of the highest bid, without regard to the amount of such bid, or

(ii) If the aggregate price of all property purchased by a successful bidder at the sale is more than $200, an initial payment of $200 or 20 percent of the purchase price, whichever is the greater, and payment of the balance (including all costs incurred for the protection or preservation of the property subsequent to the sale and prior to final payment) within a specified period, not to exceed one month from the date of the sale.

(5) *Method of sale.*—The property may be sold either—

(i) At public auction, at which open competitive bids shall be received, or

(ii) At public sale under sealed bids.

(6) *Sales under sealed bids.*—The following rules, in addition to the other rules provided in this paragraph, shall be applicable to public sales under sealed bids:

(i) *Invitation to bidders.*—Bids shall be solicited through a public notice of sale.

(ii) *Form for use by bidders.*—A bid shall be submitted on a form which will be furnished by the district director upon request. The form shall be completed in accordance with the instructions thereon.

(iii) *Remittance with bid.*—If the total bid is $200 or less, the full amount of the bid shall be submitted therewith. If the total bid is more than $200, 20 percent of such bid or $200, whichever is greater, shall be submitted therewith. Such remittance shall be by a certified, cashier's, or treasurer's check drawn on any bank or trust company incorporated under the laws of the United States or under the laws of any State, Territory, or possession of the United States, or by a United States postal, bank, express, or telegraph money order.

(iv) *Time for receiving and opening bids.*—Each bid shall be submitted in a securely sealed envelope. The bidder shall indicate in the upper left hand corner of the envelope his name and address and the time and place of sale as announced in the public notice of sale. A bid will not be considered unless it is received by the internal revenue officer conducting the sale prior to the opening of the bids. The bids will be opened at the time and place stated in the notice of sale, or at the time fixed in the announcement of the adjournment of the sale.

(v) *Consideration of bids.*—The internal revenue officer conducting the sale shall have the right to waive any technical defects in a bid. After the opening, examination, and consideration of all bids, the internal revenue officer conducting the sale shall announce the amount of the highest bid or bids and the name of the successful bidder or bidders, unless in the opinion of the officer a higher price can be obtained for the property than has been bid. In the event the highest bids are equal in amount (and unless in the opinion of the internal revenue officer conducting the sale a higher price can be obtained for the property than has been bid), the

officer shall determine the successful bidder by drawing lots. Any remittance submitted in connection with an unsuccessful bid shall be returned to the bidder at the conclusion of the sale.

(vi) *Withdrawal of bids.*—A bid may be withdrawn on written or telegraphic request received from the bidder prior to the time fixed for opening the bids. A technical defect in a bid confers no right on the bidder for the withdrawal of his bid after it has been opened.

(7) *Payment of bid price.*—All payments for property sold pursuant to this section shall be made by cash or by a certified, cashier's, or treasurer's check drawn on any bank or trust company incorporated under the laws of the United States or under the laws of any State, Territory, or possession of the United States, or by a United States postal, bank, express, or telegraph money order. If payment in full is required upon acceptance of the highest bid, the payment shall be made at such time. If payment in full is not made at such time, the internal revenue officer conducting the sale may forthwith proceed again to sell the property in the manner provided in subparagraph (5) of this paragraph. If deferred payment is permitted, the initial payment shall be made upon acceptance of the bid, and the balance shall be paid on or before the date fixed for payment thereof. Any remittance submitted with a successful sealed bid shall be applied toward the purchase price.

(8) *Delivery and removal of personal property.*—The risk of loss is on the purchaser of the property upon acceptance of his bid. Possession of any property shall not be delivered to the purchaser until the purchase price has been paid in full. If payment of part of the purchase price for the property is deferred, the United States will retain possession of such property as security for the payment of the balance of the purchase price and, as agent for the purchaser, will cause the property to be cared for until the purchase price has been paid in full or the sale is declared null and void for failure to make full payment of the purchase price. In such case, all charges and expenses incurred in caring for the property after acceptance of the bid shall be borne by the purchaser.

(9) *Certificate of sale.*—The internal revenue officer conducting the sale shall issue a certificate of sale to the purchaser upon payment in full of the purchase price.

(b) *Accounting.*—In case of the resale of such property, the proceeds of the sale shall be paid into the Treasury as internal revenue collections, and there shall be rendered by the district director a distinct account of all charges incurred in such sale. For additional accounting rules, see section 7809 and the instructions thereunder. [Reg. § 301.7505-1.]

☐ [*T.D. 6232, 5-2-57. Amended by T.D. 7305, 3-14-75.*]

[Reg. § 301.7506-1]

§ 301.7506-1. Administration of real estate acquired by the United States.—(a) *Persons charged with.*—The district director for the internal revenue district in which the property is situated shall have charge of all real estate which is or shall become the property of the United States by judgment of forfeiture under the internal revenue laws, or which has been or shall be assigned, set off, or conveyed by purchase or otherwise to the United States in payment of debts or penalties arising under the laws relating to internal revenue, or which has been or shall be vested in the United States by mortgage, or other security for payment of such debts, or which has been redeemed by the United States, or which has been or shall be acquired by the United States in payment of or as security for debts arising under the internal revenue laws, and of all trusts created for the use of the United States in payment of such debts due the United States.

(b) *Sale.*—The district director for the internal revenue district in which the property is situated may sell any real estate owned or held by the United States as aforesaid, subject to the following rules—

(1) *Property purchases at sale under levy.*—If the property was acquired as a result of being declared purchased for the United States at a sale under section 6335, relating to sale of seized property, the property shall not be sold until after the expiration of 120 days (or 1 year in the case of such sale under levy before November 3, 1966) after such sale under levy.

(2) *Notice of sale.*—A notice of sale shall be published in some newspaper published or generally circulated within the county where the property is situated, or a notice shall be posted at the post office nearest the place where the property is situated and in at least two other public places. The notice shall specify the property to be sold and the time, place, manner and conditions of sale. In addition, the district director may use other methods of advertising and of giving notice of sale if he believes such method will enhance the possibility of obtaining a higher price for the property.

(3) *Time and place of sale.*—The time of the sale shall be not less than 20 days from the date of giving public notice of sale under subparagraph (2) of this paragraph. The place of sale shall be within the county where the property is situated. However, if the district director believes a substantially better price may be obtained, he may hold the sale outside such county.

(4) *Rejection of bids and adjournment of sale.*—The internal revenue officer conducting the sale reserves the right to reject any and all bids and withdraw the property from the sale. When it appears to the internal revenue officer conducting the sale that an adjournment of the sale will best serve the interests of the United States, he may order the sale adjourned from time to time. If the sale is adjourned for more than 30 days in the aggregate, public notice of the sale must be given again in accordance with subparagraph (2) of this paragraph.

(5) *Liquidated damages.*—The notice shall state whether, in the case of default in payment of the bid price, any amount deposited with the United States will be retained as liquidated damages. In case liquidated damages are provided, the amount thereof shall not exceed $200.

(6) *Agreement to bid.*—The district director may, before giving notice of sale, solicit offers from prospective bidders and enter into agreements with such persons that they will bid at least a specified amount in case the property is offered for sale. In such cases, the district director may also require such persons to make deposits to secure the performance of their agreements. Any such deposit, but not more than $200, shall be retained as liquidated damages in case such person fails to bid the specified amount and the property is not sold for as much as the amount specified in such agreement.

(7) *Terms.*—The property shall be offered for sale upon whichever of the following terms is fixed by the district director in the public notice of sale:

(i) Payment in full upon acceptance of the highest bid, or

(ii) If the price of the property purchased by a successful bidder at the sale is more than $200, an initial payment of $200 or 20 percent of the purchase price, whichever is the greater, and payment of the balance within a specified period, not to exceed one month from the date of the sale.

(8) *Method of sale.*—The property may be sold either—

(i) At public auction, at which open competitive bids shall be received, or

(ii) At public sale under sealed bids.

(9) *Sales under sealed bids.*—The following rules, in addition to the other rules provided in this paragraph, shall be applicable at public sales under sealed bids:

(i) *Invitation to bidders.*—Bids shall be solicited through a public notice of sale.

(ii) *Form for use by bidders.*—A bid shall be submitted on a form which will be furnished by the district director upon request. The form shall be completed in accordance with the instructions thereon.

(iii) *Remittance with bid.*—If the total bid is $200 or less, the full amount of the bid shall be submitted therewith. If the total bid is more than $200, 20 percent of such bid or $200, whichever is greater, shall be submitted therewith. Such remittance shall be by a certified, cashier's, or treasurer's check drawn on any bank or trust company incorporated under the laws of the United States or under the laws of any State, Territory, or possession of the United States, or by a United States postal, bank, express, or telegraph money order.

(iv) *Time for receiving and opening bids.*— Each bid shall be submitted in a securely sealed envelope. The bidder shall indicate in the upper left hand corner of the envelope his name and address and the time and place of sale as announced in the public notice of sale. A bid shall not be considered unless it is received by the internal revenue officer conducting the sale prior to the opening of the bids. The bids will be opened at the time and place stated in the notice of sale, or at the time fixed in the announcement of the adjournment of the sale.

(v) *Consideration of bids.*—The internal revenue officer conducting the sale shall have the right to waive any technical defects in a bid. After the opening, examination, and consideration of all bids, the internal revenue officer conducting the sale shall announce the amount of the highest bid or bids and the name of the successful bidder or bidders, unless in the opinion of the officer a higher price can be obtained for the property than has been bid. In the event the highest bids are equal in amount (and unless in the opinion of the internal revenue officer conducting the sale a higher price can be obtained for the property than has been bid), the officer shall determine the successful bidder by drawing lots. Any remittance submitted in connection with an unsuccessful bid shall be returned to the bidder at the conclusion of the sale.

(vi) *Withdrawal of bids.*—A bid may be withdrawn on written or telegraphic request received from the bidder prior to the time fixed for opening the bids. A technical defect in a bid confers no right on the bidder for the withdrawal of his bid after it has been opened.

(10) *Payment of bid price.*—All payments for property sold pursuant to this section shall be made by cash or by a certified, cashier's or treasurer's check drawn on any bank or trust company incorporated under the laws of the United States or under the laws of any State, Territory, or possession of the United States, or by a United States postal, bank, express, or telegraph money order. If payment in full is required upon acceptance of the highest bid, the payment shall be made at such time. If payment in full is not made at such time, the internal revenue officer conducting the sale may forthwith proceed again to sell the property in the manner provided in subparagraph (8) of this paragraph. If deferred payment is permitted, the initial payment shall be made upon acceptance of the bid, and the balance shall be paid on or before the date fixed for payment thereof. Any remittance submitted with a successful sealed bid shall be applied toward the purchase price.

(11) *Deed.*—Upon payment in full of the purchase price, the district director shall execute a quitclaim deed to the purchaser.

(c) *Lease.*—Until real estate is sold, the district director for the internal revenue district in which the property is situated may, in accordance with instructions issued by the Commissioner, lease such property.

(d) *Release to debtor.*—In cases where real estate has or may become the property of the United States by conveyance or otherwise, in payment of or as security for a debt arising under the laws relating to internal revenue, and such debt shall have been paid, together with the interest thereon (at the rate of one percent per month), to the United States within two years from the date of the acquisition of such real estate, the district director for the internal revenue district in which the property is located may release by deed or otherwise convey such real estate to the debtor from whom it was taken, or to his heirs or other legal representatives. If property is declared purchased by the United States under section 6335, then, for the purpose of this paragraph, the date of such declaration shall be deemed to be the date of acquisition of such real estate.

(e) *Accounting.*—The district director for the internal revenue district in which the property is situated shall, in accordance with section 7809 and the instructions thereunder, account for the proceeds of all sales or leases of the property and all expenses connected with the maintenance, sale, or lease of the property.

(f) *Authority of Commissioner.*—Notwithstanding the other paragraphs of this section, the Commissioner may, when he deems it advisable, take charge of and assume responsibility for any real estate to which this section is applicable. In such case, the Commissioner will notify in writing the district director for the internal revenue district in which the property is situated. In any case where a single parcel of real estate is situated in more than one internal revenue district, the Commissioner may designate in writing a district director who shall have charge of and be responsible for the entire property. [Reg. § 301.7506-1.]

☐ [T.D. 6232, 5-2-57. *Amended by T.D. 7027, 2-26-70 and T.D. 7305, 3-14-74.*]

[Reg. § 301.7507-1]

§ 301.7507-1. Banks and trust companies covered.—(a) Section 7507 applies to any national bank, or bank or trust company organized under State law, a substantial portion of the business of which consists of receiving deposits and making loans and discounts, and which has—

(1) Ceased to do business by reason of insolvency or bankruptcy, or

(2) Been released or discharged from its liability to its depositors for any part of their deposit claims, and the depositors have accepted in lieu thereof a lien upon its subsequent earnings

or claims against its assets either (i) segregated and held by it for benefit of the depositors or (ii) transferred to an individual or corporate trustee or agent who liquidates, holds or operates the assets for the benefit of the depositors.

(b) As used in this section and §§ 301.7507-2 to 301.7507-11, inclusive:

(1) The term "bank", unless otherwise indicated by the context, means any national bank, or bank or trust company organized under State law, within the scope of section 7507.

(2) The terms "statute of limitations" and "limitations" mean all applicable provisions of law (including section 7507) which impose, change, or affect the limitations, conditions, or requirements relative to the allowance of refunds and abatements or the assessment or collection of tax, as the case may be.

(3) The term "segregated assets" includes transferred or trusteed assets, or assets set aside or earmarked, to all or a portion of which, or the proceeds of which, the depositors are absolutely or conditionally entitled.

(4) The term *ceased to do business* means the bank no longer accepts deposits or makes loans and discounts, and is winding up its affairs and is in the process of liquidating its assets to pay depositors. A bank will not be considered to have ceased to do business on account of a transaction in which the bank—

(i) Transfers assets and liabilities to a Bridge Bank in a transfer described in § 1.597-4 of this chapter;

(ii) Transfers assets and liabilities to any person in a transaction to which section 381(a) applies or in which the transferee receives property with a transferred basis;

(iii) Transfers assets or liabilities to any person in a transaction in which Federal Financial Assistance (as defined in section 597) is provided to any party to the transaction, unless all the Federal Financial Assistance is deposit insurance under § 301.7507-9(d); or

(iv) Transfers assets or liabilities to any person in a transaction similar to any transaction described in paragraphs (b)(4)(i) through (iii) of this section. This paragraph (b)(4) applies to taxable years ending on or after April 22, 1992. [Reg. § 301.7507-1.]

☐ [*T.D.* 6232, 5-2-57. *Amended by T.D.* 6498, 10-24-60 *and T.D.* 8641, 12-20-95.]

[Reg. § 301.7507-2]

§ 301.7507-2. Scope of section generally.— (a) *Purpose.*—Section 7507 is intended to assist depositors of a bank which had ceased to do business by reason of insolvency to recover their deposits, by prohibiting collection of taxes of the bank which would diminish the assets necessary for payment of its depositors and also assist depositors of banks which are in financial difficulties but which, in certain conditions, continue in business.

(b) *Requisites of application.*—In order that section 7507 shall operate in a case where the bank

continues business it is necessary that the depositors shall agree to accept, in lieu of all or a part of their deposit claims as such, claims against segregated assets, or a lien upon subsequent earnings of the bank, or both. When such an agreement exists, no tax diminishing such assets or earnings, or both, otherwise available and necessary for payment of depositors, may be collected therefrom. If, under such an agreement, the depositors have the right also to look to the unsegregated assets of the bank for recovery, in whole or in part, the unsegregated assets are likewise, until they exceed the amount of the depositors' claims chargeable thereto, unavailable for tax collection. Any tax of such a bank, or part of any tax, which is once uncollectible under section 7507, cannot thereafter be collected except from any residue of segregated assets remaining after claims of depositors against such assets have been paid.

(c) *Interest.*—For the purposes of section 7507, depositors' claims include bona fide interest, either on the deposits as such, or on the claims accepted in lieu of deposits as such.

(d) *Limitations on immunity.*—Section 7507 is not primarily intended for the relief of banks as such. It does not prevent tax collection, from assets not necessary, or not available, for payment of depositors, from a bank within section 7507(a), at any time within the statute of limitations. In other words, the immunity of such a bank is not complete, but ceases whenever, within the statutory period for collection, it becomes possible to make collection without diminishing assets necessary for payment of depositors. In the case of a bank within section 7507(b), any immunity to which the bank is entitled is absolute except as to segregated assets. Any tax coming within such immunity may never be collected. With respect to segregated assets, such a bank is subject to the same rule as a bank within section 7507(a), that is to say, after claims of depositors against segregated assets have been paid, any surplus is subject, within the statute of limitations, to collection of any tax, due at any time, the collection of which was suspended by the section. The section is not for the relief of creditors other than depositors, although it may incidentally operate for their benefit. See § 301.7507-4 and paragraph (b) of § 301.7507-9. [Reg. § 301.7507-2.]

* ☐ [*T.D.* 6232, 5-2-57. *Amended by T.D.* 6498, 10-24-60.]

[Reg. § 301.7507-3]

§ 301.7507-3. Segregated or transferred assets.—(a) *In general.*—In a case involving segregated or transferred assets, it is not necessary, for application of section 7507, that the assets shall technically constitute a trust fund. It is sufficient that segregated assets be definitely separated from other assets of the bank and that transferred assets be definitely separated both from other assets of the bank and from other assets held or owned by the trustee or agent to whom assets of the bank have been transferred; that the bank be wholly or partially released from liability for repayment of deposits as such; and that the depositors have claims against the separated assets. Any excess of separated assets, over the amount necessary for payment of such depositors will be available for tax collection after full payment of depositors' claims under the agreement against such assets. But see § 301.7507-9.

(b) *Corporate transferees.*—Where the segregated assets are transferred to a separate corporate trustee or corporate agent, the assets and earnings therefrom are within the protection of the section, until full payment of depositors' claims against such assets and earnings, no matter by whom the stock of such corporation is held, and no matter whether the assets be liquidated or operated or held for benefit of the depositors. [Reg. § 301.7507-3.]

☐ [*T.D. 6232, 5-2-57. Amended by T.D. 6498, 10-24-60.*]

[Reg. § 301.7507-4]

§ 301.7507-4. Unsegregated assets.—(a) *Depositors' claims against assets.*—(1) Claims of depositors, to the extent that they are to be satisfied out of segregated assets, will not be considered in determining the availability of unsegregated assets for tax collection. If depositors have agreed to accept payment out of segregated assets only, collection of tax from unsegregated assets will not diminish the assets available and necessary for payment of the depositors' claims. Thus, it may be possible to collect taxes from the unsegregated assets of the bank although the segregated assets are immune under the section.

(2) If the unsegregated assets of the bank are subject to any portion of the depositors' claims, such unsegregated assets will be within the immunity of the section only to the extent necessary to satisfy the claims to which such assets are subject. Taxes will still be collectible from the unsegregated assets to the extent of the amount by which the total value of such assets exceeds the liability to depositors to be satisfied therefrom. Therefore, if, for example, in the case of a bank having a tax liability, not previously immune under the section, of $50,000, the deposit claims against the bank are in the amount of $75,000, and the assets available for satisfaction of deposit claims amount to $100,000, the $50,000 tax is collectible to the extent of the $25,000 excess of assets over deposit claims. Collection is not to be postponed until the full amount of the tax is collectible.

(b) *Depositors' claims against earnings.*—Even though under a bona fide agreement a bank has been released from depositors' claims as to unsegregated assets, if all or a portion of its earnings are subject to depositors' claims, all assets the earnings from which, in whole or part, are charged with the payment of depositors' claims, will be immune from tax collection. But see paragraph (a) of § 301.7507-5. [Reg. § 301.7507-4.]

☐ [*T.D. 6232, 5-2-57.*]

[Reg. § 301.7507-5]

§ 301.7507-5. Earnings.—(a) *Availability for tax collection.*—Earnings of a bank within section 7507(b), whether from segregated or unsegregated assets, which are necessary for, applicable to, and actually used for, payment of depositors' claims under an agreement, are within the immunity of the section. If only a portion or percentage of income from segregated or unsegregated assets is available and necessary for payment of depositors' claims, the remaining income is available for tax collection. Earnings of the bank's first fiscal year ending after the making of the agreement not applicable to payment of depositors will be assumed to be applicable for collection of any tax due prior to subsequent to execution of the agreement. Earnings of subsequent fiscal periods from unsegregated assets not applicable to depositors' claims will be assumed to be applicable to payment of taxes as to which immunity under the section has not previously attached. Earnings from segregated assets are available for collection of tax, whether previously uncollectible under the section or not, after depositors' claims against such assets have been paid in full. See paragraph (a) of § 301.7507-3 and paragraph (a) of § 301.7507-9.

(b) *Tax computation.*—The fact that earnings of a given year may be wholly or partly unavailable under section 7507 for collection of taxes does not exempt the income for that year, or any part thereof, from tax liability. The section affects collectibility only, and is not concerned with taxability. Accordingly, the taxpayer's income tax return shall correctly compute the tax liability, even though in the opinion of the taxpayer it is immune from tax collection under the section. The tax shall be determined with respect to the entire gross income and not merely with respect to the portion of the earnings out of which tax may be collected. As to establishment of immunity from tax collection see § 301.7507-7.

Example. (1) An agreement, executed in the year 1954 between a bank and its depositors, provides (i) that certain assets are to be segregated for the benefit of the depositors who have waived (as claims against unsegregated assets of the bank) a percentage of the deposits; (ii) that 40 percent of the bank's net earnings, for years beginning with 1954, from unsegregated assets, shall be paid to the depositors until the portion of their claims waived with respect to unsegregated assets of the bank has been paid; and (iii) that the unsegregated assets shall not be subject to depositors' claims. The net income of the bank for the calendar year 1954 is $10,000, $4,000 produced by the segregated, and $6,000 produced by the unsegregated assets. Such amount shall be considered the net earnings for the purpose of section 7507 in computing the portion of the earnings to be paid to depositors. The bank has an outstanding tax liability for prior years of $7,000. The income tax liability of the bank for 1954 is 30 percent of $10,000, or $3,000, making a total outstanding tax liability of $10,000. The portion of the earnings of the bank for 1954 remaining after provision for depositors is $3,600 ($6,000 less 40 percent thereof, or $2,400). It will be assumed that of the total outstanding tax liability of $10,000, $3,600 may be assessed and collected, leaving $6,400 to be collected from any excess of the segregated assets after claims of depositors against such segregated assets have been paid in full. No part of the $6,400 immune from collection from 1954 earnings may be collected thereafter from unsegregated assets of the bank or earnings therefrom, so that except for any possible surplus of the segregated assets the $6,400 is uncollectible.

(2) In the year 1955, the earnings are again $10,000, $4,000 from segregated and $6,000 from unsegregated assets, as in 1954. However, the return filed shows income of $5,000 and a tax liability of $1,500. An investigation shows the true income to be $10,000, on which the tax is $3,000. The full $3,000 will be assumed to be collectible. The $600 difference between $3,600 (the excess of earnings from unsegregated assets over the amount going to the depositors), and the $3,000 tax for 1955, is not available for collection of the tax for prior years, which became immune as described above, but may be available for collection of tax for subsequent years.

(c) No significance attaches to the selection of the years 1954 and 1955 in the example set forth in paragraph (b) of this section. The rules indicated by the example are equally applicable to subsequent or prior years not excluded by limitations. [Reg. § 301.7507-5.]

☐ [*T.D.* 6232, 5-2-57. *Amended by T.D.* 6498, 10-24-60.]

[Reg. § 301.7507-6]

§ 301.7507-6. Abatement and refund.—(a) An assessment or collection, no matter when made, if contrary to section 7507, is subject to abatement or refund within the applicable statutory period of limitations.

(b) Collection from a bank within section 7507(b) which diminishes assets necessary for payment of depositors, if made prior to agreement with depositors, is not contrary to the section, and affords no ground for refund.

(c) Any abatement or refund is subject to existing statutory periods of limitation, which periods are not suspended or extended by section 7507. In order to secure a refund of any taxes paid for any taxable year during the period of immunity the bank must file claim therefor. [Reg. § 301.7507-6.]

☐ [*T.D.* 6232, 5-2-57.]

[Reg. § 301.7507-7]

§ 301.7507-7. Establishment of immunity.—(a) The mere allegation of insolvency, or that depositors have claims against segregated or other assets or earnings, will not of itself secure immunity from tax collection. It must be affirmatively established to the satisfaction of the district director that collection of tax will be contrary to section 7507. See also § 301.7507-8.

(b) Any claim, by a bank, of immunity under section 7507(b), shall be supported by a statement, under oath or affirmation, which shall show: (1) The total of depositors' claims outstanding, and (2) separately and in detail, the amount of each of the following, and the amount of depositors' claims properly chargeable against each: (i) Segregated or transferred assets; (ii) unsegregated assets; (iii) estimated future average annual earnings and profits; (iv) amount collectible from shareholders; and (v) any other resources available for payment of depositors' claims. The detail shall show the full amount of depositors' claims chargeable against each of the items in subdivisions (i) to (v), inclusive, of this paragraph even though part or all of the amount chargeable against a particular item is also chargeable against some other item or items. There shall also be filed a copy of any agreement between the bank and its depositors, and any other agreement or document bearing on the claim of immunity. The statement shall show the basis, as "book", "market", etc., of valuation of the assets. [Reg. § 301.7507-7.]

☐ [*T.D.* 6232, 5-2-57. *Amended by T.D.* 6498, 10-24-60.]

[Reg. § 301.7507-8]

§ 301.7507-8. Procedure during immunity.—(a) *Statements to be filed.*—As long as complete or partial immunity is claimed, a bank within section 7507(b) shall file with each income tax return a statement as required by § 301.7507-7, in duplicate, and shall also file such additional statements as the district director may require. Whether or not additional statements shall be required, and the frequency thereof, will depend on the circumstances, including the financial status and apparent prospects of the bank, and the time which is available for assessment and collection. If a copy of an agreement or document has once been filed, a copy of the same agreement or document need not again be filed with a subsequent statement, if it is shown by the subsequent statement, when and where and with what return the copy was filed. In case of amendment a copy of the amendment must be filed with the return for the taxable year in which the amendment is made.

(b) *Failure to file.*—Failure of a bank to file any required statement will be treated as indicating that the bank is not entitled to immunity. [Reg. § 301.7507-8.]

☐ [*T.D.* 6232, 5-2-57.]

[Reg. § 301.7507-9]

§ 301.7507-9. Termination of immunity.—(a) *In general.*—(1) In the case of a bank within section 7507(a), immunity will end whenever, and to the extent that, taxes may be assessed and collected, within the applicable limitation periods as extended by section 7507, without diminishing the assets available and necessary for payment of depositors. Immunity of a bank within section 7507(b) is terminated, as to segregated assets, whenever claims of depositors against such assets have been paid in full. See § 301.7507-3. As to segregated assets, the termination of immunity is complete, and any balance remaining after payment of depositors is available, within statutory limitations, for collection of tax due at any time. However, taxes of the bank will be collectible from segregated assets only to the extent that the bank has a legal or equitable interest therein. Assets as to which there has been a complete conveyance for benefit of depositors, and the bank has bona fide been divested of all legal and equitable interest, are not available for collection of the bank's tax liability.

(2) As to unsegregated assets of a bank within section 7507(b), immunity terminates only as to taxes thereafter becoming due. When taxes are once immune from collection, the immunity as to unsegregated assets is absolute. But see paragraph (a) of § 301.7507-4.

(b) *General creditors.*—While the immunity from tax collection is for protection of depositors, and not for benefit of general creditors, in some cases the immunity will not end until the assets are sufficient to cover indebtedness of creditors generally. This situation will exist where under applicable law the claims of general creditors are on a parity with those of depositors, so that to pay depositors in full it is necessary to pay all creditors in full.

(c) *Shareholder liability.*—In determining the sufficiency of the assets to satisfy the depositors' claims, shareholders' liability to the extent collectible shall be treated as available assets. See § 301.7507-7.

(d) *Deposit insurance.*—Deposit insurance payable to depositors shall not be treated as an asset of the bank and shall be disregarded in determining the sufficiency of the assets to meet the claims of depositors. For taxable years ending on or after April 22, 1992, deposit insurance does not include Federal Financial Assistance (as defined in section 597) and other payments described in section 597(a) prior to its amendment by the Financial Institutions Reform, Recovery, and Enforcement Act of 1989 and, therefore, such payments must be taken into account to determine whether a bank's assets are sufficient to meet claims of depositors.

(e) *Notice by bank.*—A bank within section 7507(b), upon termination of immunity with respect to (1) earnings, (2) segregated or transferred assets, or (3) unsegregated assets, shall immediately notify the district director of internal revenue for the internal revenue district in which the taxpayer's returns were filed of such termination of immunity. See paragraph (b) of § 301.7507-8.

(f) *Payment by bank.*—As immunity terminates with respect to any assets, it will be the duty of the bank, without notice from the district director, to make payment of taxes collectible from such assets. [Reg. § 301.7507-9.]

☐ [*T.D.* 6232, 5-2-57. *Amended by T.D.* 6498, 10-24-60 *and T.D.* 8641, 12-20-95.]

[Reg. § 301.7507-10]

§ 301.7507-10. Collection of tax after termination of immunity.—If, in the case of a bank within section 7507(b), segregated assets (including earnings therefrom), in excess of those necessary for payment of outstanding deposits become available, such excess of segregated assets shall be applied toward satisfaction of accumulated outstanding taxes previously immune under the section, and not barred by the statute of limitations. But see § 301.7507-3. Where sufficient segregated or unsegregated assets are available, statutory interest shall be collected with the tax. When unsegregated assets or earnings therefrom previously immune become available for tax collection, they will be available only for collection of taxes (including interest and other additions) becoming due after immunity ceases. See the example in paragraph (b) of § 301.7507-5. [Reg. § 301.7507-10.]

☐ [*T.D.* 6232, 5-2-57. *Amended by T.D.* 6498, 10-24-60.]

[Reg. § 301.7507-11]

§ 301.7507-11. Exception of employment taxes.—The immunity granted by section 7507 does not apply to taxes imposed by chapter 21 or chapter 23 of the Code. [Reg. § 301.7507-11.]

☐ [*T.D.* 6232, 5-2-57. *Amended by T.D.* 6498, 10-24-60.]

[Reg. § 301.7508-1]

§ 301.7508-1. Time for performing certain acts postponed by reason of service in a combat zone.—(a) *General rule.*—The period of time that may be disregarded for performing certain acts under section 7508 applies to acts described in section 7508(a)(1) and to other acts specified in a revenue ruling, revenue procedure, notice, or other guidance published in the Internal Revenue Bulletin (see § 601.601(d)(2) of this chapter).

(b) *Effective date.*—This section applies to any period for performing an act that has not expired before December 30, 1999. [Reg. § 301.7508-1.]

☐ [*T.D.* 8911, 12-14-2000.]

[Reg. § 301.7508A-1]

§ 301.7508A-1. Postponement of certain tax-related deadlines by reasons of a federally declared disaster or terroristic or military action.—(a) *Scope.*—This section provides rules by which the Internal Revenue Service (IRS) may postpone deadlines for performing certain acts with respect to taxes other than taxes not administered by the IRS such as firearms tax (chapter 32, section 4181); harbor maintenance tax (chapter 36, section 4461); and alcohol and tobacco taxes (subtitle E).

(b) *Postponed deadlines.*—(1) *In general.*—In the case of a taxpayer determined by the Secretary to be affected by a federally declared disaster (as defined in section 1033(h)(3)) or a terroristic or

Reg. § 301.7508A-1(b)(1)

military action (as defined in section 692(c)(2)), the Secretary may specify a postponement period (as defined in paragraph (d)(1) of this section) of up to one year that may be disregarded in determining under the internal revenue laws, in respect of any tax liability of the affected taxpayer (as defined in paragraph (d)(1) of this section)—

    (i) Whether any or all of the acts described in paragraph (c) of this section were performed within the time prescribed;

    (ii) The amount of interest, penalty, additional amount, or addition to the tax; and

    (iii) The amount of credit or refund.

    (2) *Effect of postponement period.*—When an affected taxpayer is required to perform a tax-related act by a due date that falls within the postponement period, the affected taxpayer is eligible for postponement of time to perform the act until the last day of the period. The affected taxpayer is eligible for relief from interest, penalties, additional amounts, or additions to tax during the postponement period.

    (3) *Interaction between postponement period and extensions of time to file or pay.*—(i) *In general.*—The postponement period under section 7508A runs concurrently with extensions of time to file and pay, if any, under other sections of the Internal Revenue Code.

    (ii) *Original due date prior to, but extended due date within, the postponement period.*—When the original due date precedes the first day of the postponement period and the extended due date falls within the postponement period, the following rules apply. If an affected taxpayer received an extension of time to file, filing will be timely on or before the last day of the postponement period, and the taxpayer is eligible for relief from penalties or additions to tax related to the failure to file during the postponement period. Similarly, if an affected taxpayer received an extension of time to pay, payment will be timely on or before the last day of the postponement period, and the taxpayer is eligible for relief from interest, penalties, additions to tax, or additional amounts related to the failure to pay during the postponement period.

    (4) *Due date not extended.*—The postponement of the deadline of a tax-related act does not extend the due date for the act, but merely allows the IRS to disregard a time period of up to one year for performance of the act. To the extent that other statutes may rely on the date a return is due to be filed, the postponement period will not change the due date of the return.

    (5) *Additional relief.*—The rules of this paragraph (b) demonstrate how the IRS generally implements section 7508A. The IRS may determine, however, that additional relief to taxpayers is appropriate and may provide additional relief to the extent allowed under section 7508A. To the extent that the IRS grants additional relief, the IRS will provide specific guidance on the scope of relief in the manner provided in paragraph (e) of this section.

    (c) *Acts for which a period may be disregarded.*—(1) *Acts performed by taxpayers.*—Paragraph (b) of this section applies to the following acts performed by affected taxpayers (as defined in paragraph (d)(1) of this section)—

    (i) Filing any return of income tax, estate tax, gift tax, generation-skipping transfer tax, excise tax (other than firearms tax (chapter 32, section 4181); harbor maintenance tax (chapter 36, section 4461); and alcohol and tobacco taxes (subtitle E)), or employment tax (including income tax withheld at source and income tax imposed by subtitle C or any law superseded thereby);

    (ii) Paying any income tax, estate tax, gift tax, generation-skipping transfer tax, excise tax (other than firearms tax (chapter 32, section 4181); harbor maintenance tax (chapter 36, section 4461); and alcohol and tobacco taxes (subtitle E)), employment tax (including income tax withheld at source and income tax imposed by subtitle C or any law superseded thereby), any installment of those taxes (including payment under section 6159 relating to installment agreements), or of any other liability to the United States in respect thereof, but not including deposits of taxes pursuant to section 6302 and the regulations under section 6302;

    (iii) Making contributions to a qualified retirement plan (within the meaning of section 4974(c)) under section 219(f)(3), 404(a)(6), 404(h)(1)(B), or 404(m)(2); making distributions under section 408(d)(4); recharacterizing contributions under section 408A(d)(6); or making a rollover under section 402(c), 403(a)(4), 403(b)(8), or 408(d)(3);

    (iv) Filing a petition with the Tax Court, or for review of a decision rendered by the Tax Court;

    (v) Filing a claim for credit or refund of any tax;

    (vi) Bringing suit upon a claim for credit or refund of any tax; and

    (vii) Any other act specified in a revenue ruling, revenue procedure, notice, announcement, news release, or other guidance published in the Internal Revenue Bulletin (see § 601.601(d)(2) of this chapter).

    (2) *Acts performed by the government.*—Paragraph (b) of this section applies to the following acts performed by the government—

    (i) Assessing any tax;

    (ii) Giving or making any notice or demand for the payment of any tax, or with respect to any liability to the United States in respect of any tax;

    (iii) Collecting by the Secretary, by levy or otherwise, of the amount of any liability in respect of any tax;

    (iv) Bringing suit by the United States, or any officer on its behalf, in respect of any liability in respect of any tax;

(v) Allowing a credit or refund of any tax; and

(vi) Any other act specified in a revenue ruling, revenue procedure, notice, or other guidance published in the Internal Revenue Bulletin (see §601.601(d)(2) of this chapter).

(d) *Definitions.*—(1) *Affected taxpayer* means—

(i) Any individual whose principal residence (for purposes of section 1033(h)(4)) is located in a covered disaster area;

(ii) Any business entity or sole proprietor whose principal place of business is located in a covered disaster area;

(iii) Any individual who is a relief worker affiliated with a recognized government or philanthropic organization and who is assisting in a covered disaster area;

(iv) Any individual whose principal residence (for purposes of section 1033(h)(4)), or any business entity or sole proprietor whose principal place of business is not located in a covered disaster area, but whose records necessary to meet a deadline for an act specified in paragraph (c) of this section are maintained in a covered disaster area;

(v) Any estate or trust that has tax records necessary to meet a deadline for an act specified in paragraph (c) of this section and that are maintained in a covered disaster area;

(vi) The spouse of an affected taxpayer, solely with regard to a joint return of the husband and wife; or

(vii) Any individual, business entity, or sole proprietorship not located in a covered disaster area, but whose records necessary to meet a deadline for an act specified in paragraph (c) of this section are located in the covered disaster area;

(viii) Any individual visiting the covered disaster area who was killed or injured as a result of the disaster; or

(ix) Any other person determined by the IRS to be affected by a federally declared disaster (within the meaning of section 1033(h)(3)).

(2) *Covered disaster area* means an area of a federally declared disaster (within the meaning of section 1033(h)(3)) to which the IRS has determined paragraph (b) of this section applies.

(3) *Postponement period* means the period of time (up to one year) that the IRS postpones deadlines for performing tax-related acts under section 7508A.

(e) *Notice of postponement of certain acts.*—If a tax-related deadline is postponed under section 7508A and this section, the IRS will publish a revenue ruling, revenue procedure, notice, announcement, news release, or other guidance (see §601.601(d)(2) of this chapter) describing the acts postponed, the postponement period, and the location of the covered disaster area. Guidance under this paragraph (e) will be published as soon as practicable after the occurrence of a terrorist or military action or declaration of a federally declared disaster.

(f) *Examples.*—The rules of this section are illustrated by the following examples:

Example 1. (i) Corporation X, a calendar year taxpayer, has its principal place of business in County M in State W. Pursuant to a timely filed request for extension of time to file, Corporation X's 2008 Form 1120, "U.S. Corporation Income Tax Return," is due on September 15, 2009. Also due on September 15, 2009, is Corporation X's third quarter estimated tax payment for 2009. Corporation X's 2009 third quarter Form 720, "Quarterly Federal Excise Tax Return," and third quarter Form 941, "Employer's Quarterly Federal Tax Return," are due on October 31, 2009. In addition, Corporation X has an employment tax deposit due on September 15, 2009.

(ii) On September 1, 2009, a hurricane strikes County M in State W. On September 7, 2009, certain counties in State W (including County M) are determined to be disaster areas within the meaning of section 1033(h)(3) that are eligible for assistance by the Federal government under the Stafford Act. Also on September 7, 2009, the IRS determines that County M in State W is a covered disaster area and publishes guidance announcing that the time period for affected taxpayers to file returns, pay taxes, and perform other time-sensitive acts falling on or after September 1, 2009, and on or before November 30, 2009, has been postponed to November 30, 2009, pursuant to section 7508A.

(iii) Because Corporation X's principal place of business is in County M, Corporation X is an affected taxpayer. Accordingly, Corporation X's 2008 Form 1120 will be timely if filed on or before November 30, 2009. Corporation X's 2009 third quarter estimated tax payment will be timely if made on or before November 30, 2009. In addition, pursuant to paragraph (c) of this section, Corporation X's 2009 third quarter Form 720 and third quarter Form 941 will be timely if filed on or before November 30, 2009. However, because deposits of taxes are excluded from the scope of paragraph (c) of this section, Corporation X's employment tax deposit is due on September 15, 2009. In addition, Corporation X's deposits relating to the third quarter Form 720 are not postponed. Absent reasonable cause, Corporation X is subject to the failure to deposit penalty under section 6656 and accrual of interest.

Example 2. The facts are the same as in *Example 1*, except that because of the severity of the hurricane, the IRS determines that postponement of government acts is necessary. During 2009, Corporation X's 2005 Form 1120 is being examined by the IRS. Pursuant to a timely filed request for extension of time to file, Corporation X timely filed its 2005 Form 1120 on September 15, 2006. Without application of this section, the statute of limitation on assessment for the 2005 income tax year will expire on September 15, 2009. However, pursuant to paragraph (c) of this section, assessment of tax is one of the government acts for which up to one year may be disregarded. Because September 15, 2009, falls within the period in which government acts are postponed, the statute of limitation on assessment for Corporation X's 2005 income tax will expire on November 30, 2009. Because Corporation X did not timely file an extension of time to pay, payment of its 2005 income tax was due on March 15, 2006. As such, Corporation X will be subject to the failure to pay penalty and related interest beginning on March 15, 2006. The due date for payment of Corporation X's 2005 income tax preceded the postponement period. Therefore, Corporation X is not entitled to the suspension of interest or penalties during the disaster period with respect to its 2005 income tax liability.

Example 3. The facts are the same as in *Example 2,* except that the examination of the 2005 taxable year was completed earlier in 2009, and on July 28, 2009, the IRS mailed a statutory notice of deficiency to Corporation X. Without application of this section, Corporation X has 90 days (or until October 26, 2009) to file a petition with the Tax Court. However, pursuant to paragraph (c) of this section, filing a petition with the Tax Court is one of the taxpayer acts for which a period of up to one year may be disregarded. Because Corporation X is an affected taxpayer, Corporation X's petition to the Tax Court will be timely if filed on or before November 30, 2009, the last day of the postponement period.

Example 4. (i) H and W, individual calendar year taxpayers, intend to file a joint Form 1040, "U.S. Individual Income Tax Return," for the 2008 taxable year and are required to file a Schedule H, "Household Employment Taxes." The joint return is due on April 15, 2009. H and W's principal residence is in County M in State Q.

(ii) On April 2, 2009, a severe ice storm strikes County M. On April 5, 2009, certain counties in State Q (including County M) are determined to be disaster areas within the meaning of section 1033(h)(3) that are eligible for assistance by the Federal government under the Stafford Act. Also on April 5, 2009, the IRS determines that County M in State Q is a covered disaster area and publishes guidance announcing that the time period for affected taxpayers to file returns, pay taxes, and perform other time-sensitive acts falling on or after April 2, 2009, and on or before June 2, 2009, has been postponed to June 2, 2009.

(iii) Because H and W's principal residence is in County M, H and W are affected taxpayers. April 15, 2009, the due date for the filing of H and W's 2008 Form 1040 and Schedule H, falls within the postponement period described in the IRS published guidance. Thus, H and W's return will be timely if filed on or before June 2, 2009. If H and W request an extension of time to file under section 6081 on or before June 2, 2009, the extension is deemed to have been filed by April 15, 2009. Thus, H and W's return will be timely if filed on or before October 15, 2009.

(iv) April 15, 2009, is also the due date for the payment due on the return. This date falls within the postponement period described in the IRS published guidance. Thus, the payment of tax due with the return will be timely if paid on or before June 2, 2009, the last day of the postponement period. If H and W fail to pay the tax due on the 2008 Form 1040 by June 2, 2009, and do not receive an extension of time to pay under section 6161, H and W will be subject to failure to pay penalties and accrual of interest beginning on June 3, 2009.

Example 5. (i) H and W, residents of County D in State G, intend to file an amended return to request a refund of 2008 taxes. H and W timely filed their 2008 income tax return on April 15, 2009. Under section 6511(a), H and W's amended 2008 tax return must be filed on or before April 16, 2012 (because April 15, 2012, falls on a Sunday, H and W's amended return was due to be filed on April 16, 2012).

(ii) On April 2, 2012, an earthquake strikes County D. On April 6, 2012, certain counties in State G (including County D) are determined to be disaster areas within the meaning of section 1033(h)(3) that are eligible for assistance by the Federal government under the Stafford Act. Also on April 6, 2012, the IRS determines that County D in State G is a covered disaster area and publishes guidance announcing that the time period for affected taxpayers to file returns, pay taxes, and perform other time-sensitive acts falling on or after April 2, 2012, and on or before October 2, 2012, has been postponed to October 2, 2012.

(iii) Under paragraph (c) of this section, filing a claim for refund of tax is one of the taxpayer acts for which the IRS may disregard a period of up to one year. The postponement period for this disaster begins on April 2, 2012, and ends on October 2, 2012. Accordingly, H and W's claim for refund for 2008 taxes will be timely if filed on or before October 2, 2012. Moreover, in applying the lookback period in section 6511(b)(2)(A), which limits the amount of the allowable refund, the period from October 2, 2012, back to April 2, 2012, is disregarded under paragraph (b)(1)(iii) of this section. Thus, if the claim is filed on or before October 2, 2012, amounts deemed paid on April 15, 2009, under section 6513(b), such as estimated tax and tax withheld from wages, will have been paid within the lookback period of section 6511(b)(2)(A).

Example 6. (i) A is an unmarried, calendar year taxpayer whose principal residence is located in County W in State Q. A intends to file a Form 1040 for the 2008 taxable year. The return is due on April 15, 2009. A timely files Form 4868, "Application for Automatic Extension of Time to File U.S. Individual Income Tax Return." Due to A's timely filing of Form 4868, the extended filing deadline for A's 2008 tax return is October 15, 2009. Because A timely requested an extension of time to file, A will not be subject to the failure to file penalty under section 6651(a)(1), if A files the 2008 Form 1040 on or before October 15, 2009. However, A failed to pay the tax due on the return by April 15, 2009, and did not receive an extension of time to pay under section 6161. Absent reasonable cause, A is subject to the failure to pay penalty under section 6651(a)(2) and accrual of interest.

Reg. §301.7508A-1(f)

(ii) On September 30, 2009, a blizzard strikes County W. On October 5, 2009, certain counties in State Q (including County W) are determined to be disaster areas within the meaning of section 1033(h)(3) that are eligible for assistance by the Federal government under the Stafford Act. Also on October 5, 2009, the IRS determines that County W in State Q is a covered disaster area and announces that the time period for affected taxpayers to file returns, pay taxes, and perform other time-sensitive acts falling on or after September 30, 2009, and on or before December 2, 2009, has been postponed to December 2, 2009.

(iii) Because A's principal residence is in County W, A is an affected taxpayer. Because October 15, 2009, the extended due date to file A's 2008 Form 1040, falls within the postponement period described in the IRS's published guidance, A's return is timely if filed on or before December 2, 2009. However, the payment due date, April 15, 2009, preceded the postponement period. Thus, A will continue to be subject to failure to pay penalties and accrual of interest during the postponement period.

Example 7. (i) H and W, individual calendar year taxpayers, intend to file a joint Form 1040 for the 2008 taxable year. The joint return is due on April 15, 2009. After credits for taxes withheld on wages and estimated tax payments, H and W owe tax for the 2008 taxable year. H and W's principal residence is in County J in State W.

(ii) On March 3, 2009, severe flooding strikes County J. On March 6, 2009, certain counties in State W (including County J) are determined to be disaster areas within the meaning of section 1033(h)(3) that are eligible for assistance by the Federal government under the Stafford Act. Also on March 6, 2009, the IRS determines that County J in State W is a covered disaster area and publishes guidance announcing that the time period for affected taxpayers to file returns, pay taxes, and perform other time-sensitive acts falling on or after March 3, 2009, and on or before June 1, 2009, has been postponed to June 1, 2009.

(iii) Because H and W's principal residence is in County J, H and W are affected taxpayers. April 15, 2009, the due date for filing the 2008 joint return, falls within the postponement period described in the IRS published guidance. Therefore, H and W's joint return without extension will be timely if filed on or before June 1, 2009. Similarly, H and W's 2008 income taxes will be timely paid if paid on or before June 1, 2009.

(iv) On April 30, 2009, H and W timely file Form 4868, "Application for Automatic Extension of Time to File U.S. Individual Income Tax Return." H and W's extension will be deemed to have been filed on April 15, 2009. Thus, H and W's 2008 income tax return will be timely if filed on or before October 15, 2009.

(v) H and W did not request or receive an extension of time to pay. Therefore, the payment of tax due with the 2008 joint return will be timely if paid on or before June 1, 2009. If H and W fail to pay the tax due on the 2008 joint return by June 1, 2009, H and W will be subject to failure to pay penalties and accrual of interest beginning on June 2, 2009.

Example 8. (i) H and W, individual calendar year taxpayers, entered into an installment agreement with respect to their 2006 tax liabilities. H and W's installment agreement required H and W to make regularly scheduled installment payments on the 15th day of the month for the next 60 months. H and W's principal residence is in County K in State X.

(ii) On May 1, 2009, severe flooding strikes County K. On May 5, 2009, certain counties in State X including County K) are determined by the Federal government to be disaster areas within the meaning of section 1033(h)(3), and are eligible for assistance under the Stafford Act. Also on May 5, 2009, the IRS determines that County K in State X is a covered disaster area and publishes guidance announcing that the time period for affected taxpayers to file returns, pay taxes, and perform other time-sensitive acts falling on or after May 1, 2009, and on or before July 1, 2009, has been postponed to July 1, 2009.

(iii) Because H and W's principal residence is in County K, H and W are affected taxpayers. Pursuant to the IRS's grant of relief under section 7508A, H and W's installment agreement payments that become due during the postponement period are suspended until after the postponement period has ended. H and W will be required to resume payments no later than August 15, 2009. Skipped payments will be tacked on at the end of the installment payment period. Because the installment agreement pertains to prior year tax liabilities, interest and penalties will continue to accrue. H and W may, however, be entitled to abatement of the failure to pay penalties incurred during the postponement period upon establishing reasonable cause.

(g) *Effective/applicability date.*—This section applies to disasters declared after January 15, 2009. [Reg. § 301.7508A-1.]

☐ [*T.D.* 8911, 12-14-2000 (*corrected* 2-14-2001). *Amended by T.D.* 9443, 1-14-2009 (*corrected* 12-16-2009).]

[Reg. § 301.7510-1]

§ 301.7510-1. Exemption from tax of domestic goods purchased for the United States.—For any regulations under section 7510, see the applicable regulations with respect to the various taxes. [Reg. § 301.7510-1.]

☐ [*T.D.* 6232, 5-2-57.]

[Reg. § 301.7512-1]

§ 301.7512-1. Separate accounting for certain collected taxes.—(a) *Scope.*—The provisions of section 7512 and this section apply to—

(1) The following taxes imposed by subtitle C of the Code in respect of wages or compensation paid after February 11, 1958, for pay periods beginning after such date:

(i) The employee tax imposed by section 3101 of chapter 21 (Federal Insurance Contributions Act),

(ii) The employee tax imposed by section 3201 of chapter 22 (Railroad Retirement Tax Act), and

(iii) The income tax required to be withheld on wages by section 3402 of chapter 24 (Collection of Income Tax at Source on Wages); and

(2) The following taxes imposed by chapter 33 of the Code in respect of taxable payments made, except as otherwise specifically provided in this subparagraph, after February 11, 1958:

(i) The taxes imposed by section 4231(1), (2), and (3) on amounts paid for admissions, and the tax imposed by section 4231(6) on amounts paid for admission, refreshment, service, or merchandise, at any roof garden, cabaret, or other similar place, to the extent that such tax on amounts paid on or after January 1, 1959, is required to be collected by the proprietor of the roof garden, cabaret, or similar place from a concessionaire in such establishment,

(ii) The taxes imposed by section 4241 on amounts paid as club dues,

(iii) The taxes imposed by section 4251 on amounts paid for communications services or facilities,

(iv) The tax imposed by section 4261 on amounts paid for transportation of persons and the tax imposed by section 4271 on amounts paid before August 1, 1958, for the transportation of property, and

(v) The tax imposed by section 4286 on amounts collected for the use of safe deposit boxes.

(b) *Requirement.*—If the district director determines that any person required to collect, account for, and pay over any tax described in paragraph (a) of this section has, at the time and in the manner prescribed by law or regulations, failed to collect, truthfully account for, or pay over any such tax, or make deposits, payments, or returns of any such tax, such person, if notified to do so by the district director in accordance with section 7512 and paragraph (d) of this section, shall—

(1) Collect, at the times and in the manner provided by the law and the regulations in respect of the various taxes described in paragraph (a) of this section, all of the taxes described in such paragraph which become collectible by him after receipt of such notice;

(2) Deposit the taxes so collected, not later than the end of the second banking day after collection, with a bank, as defined in section 581, in a separate account established in accordance with paragraph (c) of this section; and

(3) Keep in such account the taxes so deposited until payment thereof is made to the United States as required by the law and the regulations in respect of such taxes.

The separate accounting requirements contained in subparagraphs (1), (2), and (3) of this paragraph are applicable, in the case of the taxes described in paragraph (a)(1) of this section, to taxes with respect to wages or compensation paid after receipt of the notice from the district director, irrespective of whether such wages or compensation was earned prior to or after receipt of the notice; and, in the case of the taxes described in paragraph (a)(2) of this section, to taxes with respect to taxable payments made after receipt of the notice from the district director, irrespective of whether the transactions with respect to which such payments were made occurred prior to or after receipt of the notice.

(c) *Trust fund account.*—The separate bank account referred to in paragraph (b) of this section shall be established under the designation, "(Name of person required to establish account), Trustee, Special Fund in Trust for U.S. under sec. 7512, I.R.C.". The taxes deposited in such account shall constitute a fund in trust for the United States payable only to the Internal Revenue Service on demand by the trustee.

(d) *Notice.*—Notice to any person requiring his compliance with the provisions of section 7512(b) and this section shall be in writing and shall be delivered in hand to such person by an internal revenue officer or employee. In the case of a trade or business carried on other than as a sole proprietorship, such as a corporation, partnership, or trust, notice delivered in hand to an officer, partner, or trustee shall be deemed to be notice delivered in hand to such corporation, partnership, or trust and to all officers, partners, trustees, and employees thereof.

(e) *Cancellation of notice.*—The district director may relieve a person to whom notice requiring separate accounting has been given pursuant to section 7512 and this section from further compliance with such separate accounting requirements whenever he is satisfied that such person will comply with all requirements of the Code and the regulations applicable, in respect of the taxes to which the notice relates, in the case of persons not required to comply with the provisions of section 7512(b). Notice of cancellation of the requirement for separate accounting shall be made in writing and shall take effect at such time as is specified in the notice of cancellation.

(f) *Penalties.*—For criminal penalty for failure to comply with any provision of section 7512, see section 7215. For criminal penalties for failure to file return, supply information, or pay tax, for failure to collect or pay over tax, and for attempt to evade or defeat tax, see sections 7203, 7202, and 7201, respectively. [Reg. § 301.7512-1.]

☐ [*T.D.* 6299, 6-30-58. *Amended by T.D.* 6444, 1-14-60.]

[Reg. § 301.7513-1]

§ 301.7513-1. Reproduction of returns and other documents.—(a) *In general.*—The Commissioner, district directors, and other authorized officers and employees of the Internal Revenue Service may contract with any Federal agency or any person to have such agency or person process films and other photoimpressions of any return, statement, document, or of any card, record, or other matter, and make reproductions from such films and photoimpressions.

(b) *Safeguards.*—(1) *By private contractor.*— Any person entering into a contract with the Internal Revenue Service for the performance of any of the services described in paragraph (a) of this section shall agree to comply, and to assume responsibility for compliance by his employees, with the following requirements:

(i) The films or photoimpressions, and reproductions made therefrom, shall be used only for the purpose of carrying out the provisions of the contract, and information contained in such material shall be treated as confidential and shall not be divulged or made known in any manner to any person except as may be necessary in the performance of the contract;

(ii) All the services shall be performed under the supervision of the person with whom the contract is made or his responsible employees;

(iii) All material received for processing and all processed and reproduced material shall be kept in a locked and fireproof compartment in a secure place when not being worked upon;

(iv) All spoilage of reproductions made from the film or photoimpressions supplied to the contractor shall be destroyed, and a statement under the penalties of perjury shall be submitted to the Internal Revenue Service that such destruction has been accomplished; and

(v) All film, photoimpressions, and reproductions made therefrom, shall be transmitted to the Internal Revenue Service by personal delivery, first-class mail, parcel post, or express.

(2) *By Federal agency.*—Any Federal agency entering into a contract with the Internal Revenue Service for the performance of any services described in paragraph (a) of this section, shall treat as confidential all material processed or reproduced pursuant to such contract.

(3) *Inspection.*—The Internal Revenue Service shall have the right to send its officers and employees into the offices and plants of Federal agencies and other contractors for inspection of the facilities and operations provided for the performance of any work contracted or to be contracted for under this section.

(4) *Criminal sanctions.*—For penalty provisions relating to the unauthorized use and disclosure of information in violation of the provisions of this section, see section 7213(c).

(c) *Legal status of reproductions.*—Section 7513 provides that any reproduction made in accordance with such section of any return, docu-

ment, or other matter shall have the same legal status as the original and requires that any such reproduction shall, if properly authenticated, be admissible in evidence in any judicial or administrative proceeding, as if it were the original, whether or not the original is in existence. [Reg. §301.7513-1.]

☐ [*T.D.* 6444, 1-14-60. *Amended by T.D.* 6498, 10-24-60.]

[Reg. §301.7514-1]

§301.7514-1. Seals of office.— (a) *Establishment of seals.*—(1) *Commissioner of Internal Revenue.*—There is hereby established in and for the office of the Commissioner of Internal Revenue an official seal. The seal is described as follows, and illustrated below: A circle within which shall appear that part of the seal of the Treasury Department represented by the shield and side wreaths. Exterior to this circle and within a circumscribed circle in the form of a rope shall appear in the upper part the words "OFFICE OF" and in the lower part the words "COMMISSIONER OF INTERNAL REVENUE."

(2) *Establishment of uniform seal.*—(i) In addition to the seals of office prescribed for those offices set forth in paragraphs (a)(3) through (8) of this section, a uniform seal for use by any office of internal revenue is established. The uniform seal is described as follows, and is illustrated in this paragraph (a)(2)(i). A circle within which shall appear that part of the seal of the Treasury Department represented by the shield with a dark background. Exterior to this circle and within a circumscribed circle forming the exterior of the seal shall appear words describing the specific office of internal revenue authorized to use the seal under this section. This paragraph (a)(2) is effective on October 27, 1995. The uniform seal is as follows:

Reg. §301.7514-1(a)(2)(i)

(ii) The uniform seal may be used by any office of internal revenue set forth in paragraphs (a)(3) through (8) of this section, and any other office designated by the Commissioner to use a seal, including the following internal revenue offices resulting from a reorganization of the IRS that will be implemented beginning October 1, 1995:

Office of Regional Commissioner for:
  Midstates Region (Dallas)
  Northeast Region (Manhattan)
  Southeast Region (Atlanta)
  Western Region (San Francisco)

Office of District Director for:
  Arkansas-Oklahoma District (Oklahoma City)
  Brooklyn District
  Central California District (San Jose)
  Connecticut-Rhode Island District (Hartford)
  Delaware-Maryland District (Baltimore)
  Georgia District (Atlanta)
  Gulf Coast District (New Orleans)
  Houston District
  Illinois District (Chicago)
  Indiana District (Indianapolis)
  Kansas-Missouri District (St. Louis)
  Kentucky-Tennessee District (Nashville)
  Los Angeles District
  Manhattan District
  Michigan District (Detroit)
  Midwest District (Milwaukee)
  New Jersey District (Newark)
  New England District (Boston)
  North Central District (St. Paul)
  North Florida District (Jacksonville)
  North-South Carolina District (Greensboro)
  North Texas District (Dallas)
  Northern California District (Oakland)
  Ohio District (Cincinnati)
  Pacific-Northwest District (Seattle)
  Pennsylvania District (Philadelphia)
  Rocky Mountain District (Denver)
  South Florida District (Fort Lauderdale)
  South Texas District (Austin)
  Southern California District (Laguna Niguel)
  Southwest District (Phoenix)
  Upstate New York District (Buffalo)
  Virginia-West Virginia District (Richmond)

Office of Director of Computing Centers in:
  Detroit   Martinsburg
  Memphis

Office of Director of Submission Processing Centers in:
  Austin   Kansas City
  Cincinnati   Ogden
  Memphis

Office of Director of Customer Service Centers in:
  Andover   Jacksonville
  Atlanta   Kansas City
  Austin   Memphis
  Baltimore   Nashville
  Brookhaven   Ogden
  Buffalo   Philadelphia
  Cincinnati   Pittsburgh
  Cleveland   Portland, OR
  Dallas   Richmond
  Denver   St. Louis
  Fresno   Seattle.
  Indianapolis

(3) *District directors of internal revenue.—* (i) There is hereby established an official seal in and for each of the offices of district director of internal revenue listed in subdivision (ii) of this subparagraph. The seal is described as follows, and one such seal is illustrated below: A circle within which shall appear that part of the seal of the Treasury Department represented by the shield and side wreaths. Exterior to this circle and within a circumscribed circle in the form of a rope shall appear in the upper part the words "DISTRICT DIRECTOR OF INTERNAL REVENUE" and in the lower part the location of the office for which the seal is established.

(ii) The offices of district director of internal revenue for which seals are established in subdivision (i) of this subparagraph are as follows:

* * *

[Asterisks represent list of District Directors' offices.]

(iii) There is hereby established an official seal in and for each of the offices of district director of internal revenue listed in paragraph (a)(2)(iv) of this section. The seal is described as follows, and one such seal is illustrated below: A circle within which shall appear that part of the seal of the Treasury Department represented by the shield. Exterior to this circle and within a circumscribed circle in the form of a rope shall appear in the upper part the words "DISTRICT DIRECTOR OF INTERNAL REVENUE" and in the lower part the location of the office for which the seal is established.

(iv) The offices of district director of internal revenue for which seals are established in paragraph (a)(2)(iii) of this section are as follows: District Director of Internal Revenue, Laguna Niguel, CA., District Director of Internal Revenue, Sacramento, CA., District Director of Internal Revenue, San Jose Dist.

(v) There is hereby established an official seal in and for the office of district director of internal revenue listed in paragraph (a)(2)(vi) of this section. The seal is described as follows, and illustrated below: A circle within which shall appear the Internal Revenue emblem. Exterior to this circle and within a circumscribed circle in the form of a rope shall appear in the upper part the words "DISTRICT DIRECTOR OF INTERNAL REVENUE" and in the lower part the location of the office for which the seal is established.

(vi) The office of district director of internal revenue for which the seal is established in paragraph (a)(2)(v) of this section is as follows:

District Director of Internal Revenue, Las Vegas, Nevada.

(4) *Assistant Commissioner (International).*— There is hereby established in and for the office of the Assistant Commissioner (International) an official seal. The seal is described as follows, and illustrated below: A circle within which shall appear that part of the seal of the Treasury Department represented by the shield and side wreaths. Exterior to this circle and within a circumscribed circle in the form of a rope shall appear in the upper part the words "ASSISTANT COMMISSIONER (INTERNATIONAL)" and in the lower part "Washington, D.C. Internal Revenue Service".

(5) *Regional commissioners of internal revenue.*—(i) There is hereby established an official seal in and for each of the offices of regional commissioner of internal revenue listed in subdivision (ii) of this subparagraph. The seal is described as follows, and one such seal is illustrated below: A circle within which shall appear that part of the seal of the Treasury Department represented by the shield and side wreaths. Exterior to this circle and within a circumscribed circle in the form of a rope shall appear in the upper part the words "REGIONAL COMMISSIONER OF INTERNAL REVENUE" and in the lower part the title of the region for which the seal is established.

Reg. §301.7514-1(a)(5)(i)

(ii) The offices of the regional commissioner of internal revenue for which seals are established in subdivision (i) of this subparagraph are as follows:

Regional Commissioner of Internal Revenue, Central Region.

Regional Commissioner of Internal Revenue, Mid-Atlantic Region.

Regional Commissioner of Internal Revenue, Midwest Region.

Regional Commissioner of Internal Revenue, North-Atlantic Region.

Regional Commissioner of Internal Revenue, Southeast Region.

Regional Commissioner of Internal Revenue, Southwest Region.

Regional Commissioner of Internal Revenue, Western Region.

(6) *Directors of internal revenue service centers.*—(i) There is hereby established an official seal in and for each of the offices of director of internal revenue service center listed in subdivision (ii) of this subparagraph. The seal is described as follows, and one such seal is illustrated below: A circle within which shall appear that part of the seal of the Treasury Department represented by the shield and side wreaths. Exterior to this circle and within a circumscribed circle in the form of a rope shall appear in the upper part the words "DIRECTOR, INTERNAL REVENUE SERVICE CENTER" and in the lower part the name of the region and the name of the principal city in or near which the service center is located.

(ii) The offices of director of internal revenue service center for which seals are established in subdivision (i) of this subparagraph are as follows:

Director, Internal Revenue Service Center, Central Region, Covington, Ky.

Director, Internal Revenue Service Center, Mid-Atlantic Region, Philadelphia, Pa.

Director, Internal Revenue Service Center, Midwest Region, Kansas City, Mo.

Director, Internal Revenue Service Center, North-Atlantic Region, Andover, Mass.

Director, Internal Revenue Service Center, North-Atlantic Region, Brookhaven, N.Y.

Director, Internal Revenue Service Center, Southeast Region, Chamblee, Ga.

Director, Internal Revenue Service Center, Southeast Region, Memphis, Tenn.

Director, Internal Revenue Service Center, Southwest Region, Austin, Tex.

Director, Internal Revenue Service Center, Western Region, Fresno, Calif.

Director, Internal Revenue Service Center, Southwest Region, Ogden, Utah.

(7) *Director of Internal Revenue Computing Center.*—There is hereby established in and for the office of the Director of the Internal Revenue Computing Center an official seal. The seal is described as follows, and illustrated below: A circle within which shall appear that part of the seal of the Treasury Department represented by the shield. Exterior to this circle and within a circumscribed circle in the form of a rope shall appear in the upper part the words "DIRECTOR, INTERNAL REVENUE SERVICE" and in the lower part "Detroit Computing Center Detroit, Michigan".

Reg. §301.7514-1(a)(5)(ii)

(8) *Director of Internal Revenue Compliance Center.*—There is hereby established in and for the office of the Director of the Internal Revenue Compliance Center an official seal. The seal is described as follows, and illustrated below: A circle within which shall appear that part of the seal of the Treasury Department represented by the shield and side wreaths. Exterior to this circle and within a circumscribed circle in the form of a rope shall appear in the upper part the words "DIRECTOR, INTERNAL REVENUE COMPLIANCE CENTER" and in the lower part "Southwest Region Austin, Tex".

(b) *Custody of seal.*—Each seal established by this section shall be in the custody of the officer for whose office such seal is established.

(c) *Use of official seal.*—Each seal of office established by this section may be affixed in lieu of the seal of the Treasury Department to any certificate or attestation required to be made by the officer for whose office such seal is established in authentication of originals and copies of books, records, papers, writings, and documents of the Internal Revenue Service in the custody of such officer, for all purposes, including the purposes of 28 U.S.C. 1733(b), Rule 44 of the Federal Rules of Civil Procedure, and Rule 27 of the Federal Rules of Criminal Procedure, except that—

(1) No such seal shall be affixed to material to be published in the Federal Register, and

(2) The seal of the office of a district director of internal revenue or the Director of International Operations shall not be affixed to the certification of copies of books, records, papers, writings, or documents in his custody in any case in which, pursuant to Executive order, Treasury decision, or Part 601 of this chapter (Statement of Procedural Rules), such copies may be furnished to applicants only by the Commissioner.

(d) *Judicial notice.*—In accordance with the provisions of section 7514, judicial notice shall be taken of the seals established under this section. [Reg. § 301.7514-1.]

☐ [*T.D.* 6422, 10-28-59. *Amended by T.D.* 6442, 1-5-60; *T.D.* 6498, 10-24-60; *T.D.* 6585, 12-27-61; *T.D.* 6626, 12-26-62; *T.D.* 6698, 12-27-63; *T.D.* 6833, 7-6-65; *T.D.* 6974, 10-2-68; *T.D.* 7147, 10-22-71, *T.D.* 8414, 4-23-92; *and T.D.* 8625, 10-26-95.]

[Reg. § 301.7516-1]

§ 301.7516-1. Training and training aids on request.—The Commissioner is authorized, within his discretion, upon written request, to admit employees and officials of any State, the Commonwealth of Puerto Rico, any possession of the United States, any political subdivision or instrumentality of any of the foregoing, the District of Columbia, or any foreign government to training courses conducted by the Internal Revenue Service, and to supply them with texts and other training aids. Requests for such training or training aids should be addressed to the Commissioner of Internal Revenue, Washington, D.C. 20224, Attention: A: T, except that requests involving officials or visitors of foreign governments should be addressed to the Commissioner of Internal Revenue, Washington, D.C. 20224, Attention: C: FA. The Commissioner may require payment from the party or parties making the request of a reasonable fee not to exceed the cost of the training and training aids supplied pursuant to such request. [Reg. § 301.7516-1.]

☐ [*T.D.* 6713, 3-23-64. *Amended by T.D.* 6790, 1-4-65.]

[Reg. § 301.7517-1]

§ 301.7517-1. Furnishing on request of statement explaining estate or gift valuation.—(a) *In general.*—Section 7517 requires the Service to furnish to a taxpayer, at the request of that taxpayer, a statement explaining the estate, gift or generation-skipping transfer valuation of any item contained on a return filed by the taxpayer as to which a determination or proposed determination of value has been made. The request must be filed no later than the latest time to file a claim for refund of the tax which is dependent on the value with respect to which the determination has been made. The request should be filed with the district director's office that has jurisdiction over the return of the taxpayer.

(b) *Effective date.*—(1) *Estates of decedents.*—Section 7517 applies to estates of decedents dying after December 31, 1976.

(2) *Gifts.*—Section 7517 applies to gifts made after December 31, 1976.

(3) *Generation-skipping transfer.*—Section 7517 applies to any generation-skipping transfer subject to chapter 13 [Reg. § 301.7517-1.]

☐ [*T.D. 7757,* 1-16-81.]

[Reg. §1.7519-0T]

§1.7519-0T. Table of contents (temporary).—This section lists the captions that appear in the temporary regulations under section 7519.

§1.7519-1T. Required payments for entities electing not to have required year (temporary).
  (a) In general.
    (1) Applicability.
    (2) Returns and required payments.
    (3) Required payment.
    (4) Examples.
  (b) Definitions and special rules.
    (1) Applicable percentage.
      (i) In general.
      (ii) Exception for certain applicable election years beginning after 1987.
      (iii) Example.
    (2) Adjusted highest section 1 rate.
      (i) General rule.
      (ii) Period for determining highest section 1 rate.
    (3) Base year.
    (4) Special rules for certain applicable election years.
      (i) First applicable election year of new entities.
      (ii) Applicable election years ending prior to the required taxable year.
    (5) Net base year income.
      (i) In general.
      (ii) Partnership net income.
        (A) In general.
        (B) Treatment of deductions and losses.
        (C) Partner limitations disregarded.
      (iii) S corporation net income.
        (A) In general.
        (B) Treatment of deductions and losses.
        (C) Shareholder limitations disregarded.
      (iv) Applicable payments.
        (A) In general.
        (B) Exceptions.
        (C) Special rule for corporation electing S status.
        (D) Special rules for certain payments.
          (1) Certain indirect payments.

          (2) Payments by a downstream controlled partnership.
            (i) In general.
            (ii) Definition of a downstream controlled partnership.
          (3) Examples.
      (v) Special rule for base year of less than twelve months.
        (A) In general.
        (B) Annualized short base year income.
      (vi) Examples.
    (c) Refunds of required payments.
    (d) Examples.

§1.7519-2T. Required payments—procedures and administration (temporary).
  (a) Payment and return required.
    (1) In general.
    (2) Return required.
      (i) In general.
      (ii) Procedure if amount for applicable election year (and all preceding years) is not greater than $500.
    (3) Time and place for filing return.
      (i) Applicable election years beginning in 1987.
        (A) Taxpayers that would otherwise file Form 720 for the second quarter of 1988.
        (B) Other taxpayers.
      (ii) Applicable election years beginning after 1987.
        (A) Return made on Form 720.
        (B) Return made on form other than Form 720.
      (iii) Special rule for back-up section 444 election.
    (4) Time and place for making required payment.
      (i) Applicable election years beginning in 1987.
      (ii) Applicable election years beginning after 1987.
      (iii) Special rule for back-up section 444 election.
    (5) Penalties for failure to pay.
    (6) Refund of required payment.
      (i) In general.
      (ii) Procedures for claiming refund.
      (iii) Interest on refund.
  (b) Assessment and collection of payment.
  (c) Termination due to willful failure.
  (d) Negligence and fraud penalties made applicable.

§1.7519-3T. Effective date (temporary).
[Temporary Reg. §1.7519-0T.]

☐ [*T.D. 8205,* 5-24-88.]

[Reg. §1.7519-1T]

§1.7519-1T. Required payments for entities electing not to have required year (temporary).—(a) *In general.*—(1) *Applicability.*—This section applies to any taxable year that a partnership or S corporation has an election under section 444 in effect (an "applicable election year").

(2) *Returns and required payments.*—For each applicable election year, a partnership or S corporation must—

(i) File a return as provided in §1.7519-2T (a)(2), and

(ii) Make a required payment (as defined in paragraph (a)(3) of this section) as provided in §1.7519-2T.

However, if the required payment for an applicable election year is not more than $500 and the partnership or S corporation has not been required to make a required payment for a prior year, the partnership or S corporation should not make a required payment for such applicable election year.

(3) *Required payment.*—The term "required payment" means, with respect to any applicable election year, an amount equal to the excess of—

(i) The product of the applicable percentage of the adjusted highest section 1 rate, multiplied by the net base year income (as defined in paragraph (b)(5) of this section) of the entity, over

(ii) The cumulative amount of required payments actually made for all preceding applicable election years (reduced by the cumulative amount of such payments refundable under section 7519(c) for all such preceding years).

Furthermore, the amount of the required payment is determined without regard to the required payment of any other partnership or S corporation. See example (3) in paragraph (d) of this section.

(4) *Examples.*—The provisions of paragraph (a) of this section may be illustrated by the following examples.

Example (1). A, a partnership, makes a section 444 election to retain its taxable year ending September 30. For A's first applicable election year, A's required payment, as defined in paragraph (a)(3) of this section, is $400. Thus, A does not have to make a required payment for that year. However, A is required to file the return prescribed by §1.7519-2T (a)(2).

Example (2). The facts are the same as in example (1), and, in addition to those facts, for A's second applicable election year, the amount determined under paragraph (a)(3)(i) of this section is $800. Because A did not actually make a required payment for A's first applicable election year, A's required payment is $800 for its second applicable election year. Since the required payment is greater than $500, A must make a required payment for its second applicable election year. Furthermore, A must file the return prescribed by §1.7519-2T (a)(2).

Example (3). The facts are the same as in example (2), and, in addition to those facts, for A's third applicable election year, the amount determined under paragraph (a)(3)(i) is $1,200. Thus, A's required payment is $400 ($1,200 determined under paragraph (a)(3)(i) of this section less $800 determined under paragraph (a)(3)(ii)

of this section). Although A's required payment for its third applicable election year is not more than $500, A must make its required payment for such year because the required payment for a preceding applicable election year exceeded $500. A must also file the return prescribed by §1.7519-2T (a)(2) for its third applicable election year.

(b) *Definitions and special rules.*—(1) *Applicable percentage.*—(i) *In general.*—Except as provided in paragraph (b)(1)(ii) of this section, the term "applicable percentage" means the percentage determined in accordance with the following table:

If the applicable election year of the partnership or S corporation begins during:	The applicable percentage is:
1987	25
1988	50
1989	75
1990 or thereafter	100

(ii) *Exception for certain applicable election years beginning after 1987.*—[Reserved.]

(iii) *Example.*—The provisions of paragraph (b) (1) of this section may be illustrated by the following example.

Example. B is a corporation that has historically used a June 30 taxable year. For its taxable year beginning July 1, 1987, B elects to be an S corporation and elects under section 1.444-1T (b)(3) to retain its June 30 taxable year. Had B changed to a calendar year, its required year under section 1378, B's shareholders would not have been entitled to the 4-year spread under section 806(e)(2)(C) of the Tax Reform Act of 1986 because B was not an S corporation for its taxable year beginning in 1986. Nevertheless, for purposes of determining the required payment for B's applicable election year beginning July 1, 1987, the applicable percentage is 25 percent.

(2) *Adjusted highest section 1 rate.*—(i) *General rule.*—For any applicable election year, the term "adjusted highest section 1 rate" means the highest rate of tax under section 1 applicable to the period defined in paragraph (b)(2)(ii) of this section, plus 1 percentage point. Notwithstanding the preceding sentence, the adjusted highest section 1 rate is 36 percent for applicable election years beginning in 1987. For purposes of this section, the highest rate of tax is determined without regard to the effect of section 1(g), relating to the phaseout of the 15-percent rate and personal exemptions.

(ii) *Period for determining highest section 1 rate.*—For purposes of paragraph (b)(2)(i) of this section, the period for determining the highest rate of tax under section 1 is the 12 month period that—

(A) Ends with the required taxable year for the applicable election year, and

(B) Includes the end of the base year.

For example, assume that a partnership's applicable election year begins on October 1, 1988 and that the required taxable year for

Reg. §1.7519-1T(b)(2)(ii)(B)

such applicable election year is December 31. Based upon these facts, the period for determining the highest section 1 rate is the 12-month period ending December 31, 1988.

(3) *Base year.*—The term "base year" means, with respect to any applicable election year, the taxable year of the partnership or S corporation preceding such applicable election year.

(4) *Special rules for certain applicable election years.*—(i) *First applicable election year of new entities.*—If an applicable election year is a partnership's or S corporation's first year in existence (*i.e.,* the partnership or S corporation is newly formed and therefore does not have a base year), the required payment for such applicable election year is zero.

(ii) *Applicable election years ending prior to the required taxable year.*—If a partnership or S corporation makes a section 444 election and the resulting applicable election year (the "first applicable election year") of the partnership or S corporation ends prior to the last day of the required year, the required payment for the first applicable election year is zero. See example (5) in paragraph (b)(5)(vi) of this section.

(5) *Net base year income.*—(i) *In general.*—Except as provided in paragraph (b)(5)(v) of this section (relating to short base years), the net base year income of a partnership or S corporation is the sum of—

(A) The deferral ratio multiplied by the partnership's or S corporation's net income for the base year, plus

(B) The excess (if any) of—

(1) The deferral ratio multiplied by the aggregate amount of applicable payments made by the partnership or S corporation during the base year, over

(2) The aggregate amount of such applicable payments made during the deferral period of the base year.

The term "deferral ratio" means the ratio which the number of months in the deferral period (as defined in §1.444-1T (b)(4)) of the applicable election year bears to 12 months.

(ii) *Partnership net income.*—For purposes of paragraph (b)(5)(i) of this section—

(A) *In general.*—The net income of the partnership is the amount (not below zero) determined by taking into account the aggregate amount of the partnership's items described in section 702(a), except for—

(1) Credits,

(2) Tax-exempt income, and

(3) Guaranteed payments under section 707(c).

(B) *Treatment of deductions and losses.*—For purposes of determining the aggregate amount of partnership items, deductions and losses are treated as negative income. Thus, for example, if under section 702(a) a partnership has $1,000 of ordinary taxable income, $500 of specially allocated deductions, and $300 of capital loss, the net income of the partnership is $200 ($1,000 – $500 – $300).

(C) *Partner limitations disregarded.*—Any limitation on the amount of a partnership item described in section 702(a) which may be taken into account for purposes of computing the taxable income of a partner shall be disregarded in computing the net income of the partnership.

(iii) *S corporation net income.*—For purposes of paragraph (b)(5)(i) of this section—

(A) *In general.*—The net income of an S corporation is the amount (not below zero) determined by taking into account the aggregate amount of the S corporation's items described in section 1366(a)(other than credits and tax-exempt income). If the S corporation was a C corporation for the base year, the taxable income of the C corporation shall be treated as the net income of the S corporation for such year.

(B) *Treatment of deductions and losses.*—For purposes of determining the aggregate amount of S corporation items, deductions and losses are treated as negative income. Thus, for example, if under section 1366(a) an S corporation has $2,000 of ordinary taxable income, $1,000 of deductions described in section 1366 (a)(1)(A) of the Code, and $500 of capital loss, the net income of the S corporation is $500 ($2,000 – $1,000 – $500).

(C) *Shareholder limitations disregarded.*—Any limitation on any amount described in section 1366(a) which may be taken into account for purposes of computing the taxable income of a shareholder shall be disregarded in computing the net income of the S corporation.

(iv) *Applicable payments.*—(A) *In general.*—The term "applicable payment" means any amount deductible in the base year that is includible at any time, directly or indirectly, in the gross income of a taxpayer that during the base year is a partner or shareholder.

(B) *Exceptions.*—The term "applicable payment" does not include any guaranteed payments under section 707(c).

(C) *Special rule for corporation electing S status.*—If an S corporation was a C corporation for the base year, the corporation shall be treated as if it were an S corporation for the base year for purposes of determining the amount of applicable payments under this section. Thus, amounts deductible by the C corporation in the base year that are includible at any time in the gross income of a taxpayer that is a shareholder during the base year are treated as if from an S corporation, and therefore within the meaning of the term "applicable payments."

(D) *Special rules for certain payments.*—(1) *Certain indirect payments.*—For purposes of paragraph (b)(5)(iv)(A) of this section, an amount is indirectly includible in the gross income of a partner or shareholder of a partnership or S corporation that has a section 444 election in effect (an electing partnership or S corporation) if the amount is includible in the gross income of—

    (i) The spouse (other than a spouse who is legally separated from the partner or shareholder under a decree of divorce or separate maintenance) or child (under age 14) of such partner or shareholder, or

    (ii) A corporation more than 50 percent (measured by fair market value) of which is owned in the aggregate by partners or shareholders (and individuals related under paragraph (b)(5)(iv)(D)(1)(i) of this section to any such partners or shareholders), of the electing partnership or S corporation, or

    (iii) A partnership more than 50 percent of the profits and capital of which is owned in the aggregate by partners or shareholders (and individuals related under paragraph (b)(5)(iv)(D)(1)(i) of this section to any such partners or shareholders), of the electing partnership or S corporation, or

    (iv) A trust more than 50 percent of the beneficial ownership of which is owned in the aggregate by partners or shareholders (and individuals related under paragraph (b)(5)(iv)(D)(1)(i) of this section to any such partners or shareholders), of the electing partnership or S corporation.

For purposes of this paragraph (b)(5)(iv)(D)(1), ownership by any person described in this paragraph (b)(5)(iv)(D)(1) shall be treated as ownership by the partners or shareholders of the electing partnership or S corporation. This paragraph (b)(5)(iv)(D)(1) does not apply to amounts deductible by a partnership or S corporation that has made a section 444 election (the "deducting partnership") and included in the gross income of a partnership or S corporation defined in paragraphs (b)(5)(iv)(D)(1)(ii) or (iii) of this section (the "including partnership"), if the including partnership has the same taxable year as the deducting partnership and the including partnership has a section 444 election in effect. Furthermore, notwithstanding the general effective date provided in §1.7519-3T, this paragraph (b)(5)(iv)(D)(1) is effective for amounts deductible on or after June 1, 1988.

    (2) *Payments by a downstream controlled partnership.—(i) In general.*—If a partnership or S corporation has made a section 444 election, any amounts deducted by a downstream controlled partnership will be considered deducted by the partnership or S corporation that has made the section 444 election for purposes of determining the applicable payments of the partnership or S corporation that has made the section 444 election.

    (ii) Definition of a downstream controlled partnership.—If a partnership or S corporation that has made a section 444 election owns more than 50 percent of a partnership's profits and capital, such owned partnership is considered a downstream controlled partnership for purposes of paragraph (b)(5)(iv)(D)(2)(i) of this section. Furthermore, if more than 50 percent of a partnership's profits and capital are owned by a downstream controlled partnership, such owned partnership is considered a downstream controlled partnership for purposes of paragraph (b)(5)(iv)(D)(2)(i) of this section.

    (3) *Examples.*—The provisions of this paragraph (b)(5)(iv)(D) may be illustrated by the following examples.

    Example (1). I1 and I2, calendar year individuals, own 100 percent of the profits and capital of C1, a partnership. In addition to owning C1, I1 and I2 also own 100 percent of the profits and capital of C2, a calendar year partnership. For its taxable years beginning February 1, 1987, 1988, and 1989, C1 has a section 444 election in effect to use a January 31 taxable year. During its base years beginning February 1, 1986, 1987, and 1988, C1 deducted $10,000, $11,000, and $12,000, respectively that was included in C2's gross income. Furthermore, of the $12,000 deducted by C1 for its taxable year beginning February 1, 1988, $7,000 was deducted during the period June 1, 1988 to January 31, 1989. Pursuant to paragraph (b)(5)(iv)(D)(1) of this section, the $7,000 deducted by C1 on or after June 1, 1988, and included in C2's gross income is considered an applicable payment for C1's base year beginning February 1, 1988. Amounts deducted by C1 prior to June 1, 1988, are not subject to paragraph (b)(5)(iv)(D)(1) of this section.

    Example (2). The facts are the same as in example (1), except that I1 and I2 own only 51 percent of C2's profits and capital. Since the two partners in C1 (*i.e.*, I1 and I2) own more than 50 percent of C2's profits and capital, C2 is considered controlled by the partners of C1 pursuant to paragraph (b)(5)(iv)(D)(1)(iii) of this section. Thus, the conclusions in example (1) are unchanged. Furthermore, if the $7,000 deducted by C1 was included in the income of a partnership more than 50 percent of the profits and capital of which is owned by C2, such $7,000 would be considered an applicable payment for its base year beginning February 1, 1988.

    Example (3). The facts are the same as in example (1), except that for its taxable years beginning February 1, 1987, 1988, and 1989, C2 has a section 444 election in effect to use a January 31 taxable year. Since both C1 and C2 have the same taxable year and both have section 444 elections in effect, paragraph (b)(5)(iv)(D)(1) of this section does not apply to the $7,000 deducted by C1 for its base year beginning February 1, 1988.

    Example (4). I3 and I4, calendar year individuals, own 100 percent of the profits and capital of C3, a partnership. C3 has made a section 444 election to retain a year ending June 30 for its taxable year beginning July 1, 1987. Furthermore, C3 owns more than 50 percent of the profits and capital of C4, a partnership that historically used a June 30 taxable year. Pursuant to §1.706-3T(b), C4 retains its year ending June 30 for its taxable year beginning July 1, 1987. For its taxable year beginning July 1, 1986, C4 deducted $20,000 that was included in I3's gross income. Pursuant to paragraph (b)(5)(iv)(D)(2) of this section, the $20,000 deducted by C4 is considered an applicable payment by C3 for its base year beginning July 1, 1986.

Example (5). The facts are the same as in example (4), except that the $20,000 deducted by C4 is included in the gross income of a calendar year partnership 100 percent owned by I3 and I4. Pursuant to paragraphs (b)(5)(iv)(D)(1) and (2) of this section, the $20,000 deducted by C4 is considered an applicable payment by C3 for its base year beginning July 1, 1986.

Example (6). The facts are the same as in example (4), except that instead of directly owning a portion of C4, C3 owns more than 50 percent of the profits and capital of C5. Furthermore, C5 owns more than 50 percent of the profits and capital of C4. Pursuant to paragraph (b)(5)(iv)(D)(2)(ii) of this section, both C5 and C4 are considered downstream controlled partnerships of C3. Thus, pursuant to paragraph (b)(5)(iv)(D)(2)(i) of this section, the $20,000 deducted by C4 is considered an applicable payment by C3 for its base year beginning July 1, 1986.

(v) *Special rule for base year of less than twelve months.*—(A) *In general.*—If a base year is a taxable year of less than twelve months (a "short base year"), net base year income for such year is an amount equal to the excess, if any, of—

(1) The deferral ratio multiplied by the annualized short base year income, over

(2) Applicable payments made during the deferral period of the applicable election year following the base year.

(B) *Annualized short base year income.*—The annualized short base year income is determined by—

(1) Increasing the net income for the short base year by applicable payments deductible in the short base year, and

(2) Multiplying the short base year income as increased in paragraph (b)(5)(v)(B)(1) of this section by twelve, and dividing the result by the number of months in the short base year.

(vi) *Examples.*—The provisions of paragraph (b)(5) of this section may be illustrated by the following examples.

Example (1). D, a partnership, is owned 10 percent by a C corporation with a September 30 taxable year and 90 percent by calendar year individuals. D has historically used a September 30 taxable year. For its taxable year beginning October 1, 1987, D makes a section 444 election to retain its September 30 taxable year. For the base year from October 1, 1986 to September 30, 1987, D has net income of $200,000 and no applicable payments. D's deferral ratio is 3/12 (the ratio of the number of months in the deferral period to 12 months). Based upon these facts, D has net base year income of $50,000 ($200,000 × 3/12).

Example (2). The facts are the same as in example (1) except that D's net income for the base year is $140,000, after applicable payments of $60,000. Of the applicable payments $15,000 were deductible during the deferral period of the base year. Based upon these facts, D has net base year income of $35,000, determined as follows:

Net income	$140,000	
multiplied by deferral ratio	× 3/12	
		$35,000
Plus the excess, if any, of applicable payments	$60,000	
multiplied by deferral ratio	× 3/12	
	$15,000	
over aggregate amount of applicable payments deductible during deferral period of base year	$15,000	—0—
Net base year income		$35,000

Example (3). The facts are the same as in example (2) except that of the $60,000 applicable payments only $10,000 are deductible during the deferral period of the base year. Based on these facts, D has net base year income of $40,000, determined as follows:

Net income	$140,000	
multiplied by deferral ratio	× 3/12	
		$35,000
plus the excess, if any, of applicable payments . .	$60,000	
multiplied by deferral ratio	× 3/12	
	$15,000	
over aggregate amount of applicable payments deductible during deferral period of base year	$10,000	
		$5,000
Net base year income		$40,000

Example (4). E is a C corporation that has historically used a January 31 taxable year. For its taxable year beginning February 1, 1987, E makes an election to be an S corporation and also makes a section 444 election to retain its January 31 taxable year. E's taxable income for the taxable year beginning February 1, 1986 to January 31, 1987 is $120,000. Pursuant to paragraph (b)(5)(iii)(A) of this section, the base year for X's first applicable election year is the taxable year beginning February 1, 1986 and ending January 31, 1987. Thus, E's net income for the base year is $120,000. During the base year, E pays its sole shareholder, A, a salary of $5,000 a month plus a $30,000 bonus on January 15, 1987. Thus, under paragraph (b)(5)(iv)(C) of this section, E's applicable payments for the base year are $90,000, of which $55,000 are applicable payments deductible during the deferral period of the base year (February 1 to December 31, 1986). Based upon these facts, E's net base year income is $137,500, determined as follows:

Net income	$120,000	
multiplied by		
deferral ratio	× 11/12	
		$110,000
plus the excess, if any, of applicable payments	$90,000	
multiplied by the deferral ratio	× 11/12	
	$82,500	
over aggregate amount of applicable payments deductible during deferral period of base year	$55,000	$27,500
Net base year income		$137,500

Example (5). E, a corporation that has historically used a taxable year ending July 31, makes an election to be an S corporation for its taxable year beginning August 1, 1987. For that year, E also makes a section 444 election to use a taxable year ending September 30. Thus, E has two applicable election years beginning in 1987, the first beginning August 1, 1987 and ending September 30, 1987, and the second beginning October 1, 1987 and ending September 30, 1988. E's required year under section 1378 is the calendar year. Because E's first applicable election year ends prior to the last day of E's required year (*i.e.*, December 31, 1987), the required payment for E's first applicable election year is zero. However, E is required to file a return for such year as provided in § 1.7519-2T.

Example (6). The facts are the same as in example (5). E's second applicable election year is the year from October 1, 1987 to September 30, 1988, and the base year for the second applicable election year is a period of less than 12 months (*i.e.*, August 1, 1987 to September 30, 1987). Thus, E must compute its net base year income using the special rule for short base years provided in paragraph (b)(5)(v) of this section. Assume E's net income for the short base year is $50,000, and E's applicable payments for the short base year are $15,000. Pursuant to paragraph (b)(5)(v)(B) of this section, E's annualized short base year net income is $390,000 ($65,000 × 12/2). Furthermore, assume E's applicable payments for the deferral period of its second applicable election year are $20,000. Based on these facts, the net base year income for the applicable election year beginning October 1, 1987 is $77,500, computed as follows:

Annualized short base year income	$390,000	
multiplied by deferral ratio	× 3/12	
		$97,500
less: applicable payments for deferral period		$20,000
Net base year income		$77,500

(c) *Refunds of required payments.*—A partnership or S corporation is entitled to make a claim for refund, in accordance with the procedures provided in § 1.7519-2T(a)(6), if—

(1) The amount specified in paragraph (a)(3)(i) of this section is less than the amount specified in paragraph (a)(3)(ii) of this section; or

(2) The partnership or S corporation terminates its section 444 election, within the meaning of § 1.444-1T(a)(5).

(d) *Examples.*—The provisions of this section may be illustrated by the following examples.

Example (1). G, a partnership, is owned 10 percent by a C corporation with a June 30 taxable year, and 90 percent by calendar year individuals. G has historically used a June 30 taxable year. For its taxable year beginning July 1, 1987, G makes a section 444 election to retain its June 30 taxable year. For the base year from July 1, 1986 to June 30, 1987, G has net income of $300,000 and no applicable payments. G's deferral ratio is 6/12 (the ratio of the number of months in the deferral period to 12 months). Based on these facts, G's net base year income is $150,000 ($300,000 × 6/12). Thus, G's required payment for its first applicable election year is $13,500 ($150,000 of net base year income multiplied by 9 percent (the product of the applicable percentage for 1987, 25 percent, and the highest section 1 rate for 1987, 36 percent)).

Example (2). The facts are the same as in example (1). In addition, G continues its section 444 election for the taxable year beginning July 1, 1988, and G's net base year income for the year beginning July 1, 1987 is $150,000. The required payment for G's second applicable election year is $8,250 ($150,000 of net base year income multiplied by 14.5 percent (the product of the applicable percentage for 1988 applicable election years, 50 percent, and the adjusted highest section 1 rate for 1988, 29 percent) less G's $13,500 required payment for the first applicable election year).

Example (3). H, a partnership with a taxable year ending September 30, desires to make a section 444 election for its taxable year beginning October 1, 1987. H is 15 percent owned by I, a partnership with a taxable year ending September 30, and 85 percent owned by calendar year individuals. Assume H and I are qualified to make section 444 elections as a result of the "same taxable year exception" provided in § 1.444-2T(e). If H and I make section 444 elections, they must each make a required payment (assuming the amount computed under paragraph (a)(3) of this section is greater than $500). Pursuant to paragraph (a)(3) of this section, the required payments of H and I are calculated independent of each other. Thus, in determining the amount of its required payment, I may not exclude its income attributable to H, even though H must also make a required payment on the same income.

Example (4). The facts are the same as in example (1) except that H is 90 percent owned by I and 10 percent owned by calendar year individuals. Pursuant to § 1.706-3T, if I makes a section 444 election to retain its taxable year ending September 30, H's required year will be September 30, because H's majority interest partner will have a September 30 taxable year. Thus, H is not required to make a section 444 election and a required payment in order to use a September 30 taxable year. I, however, must make a required payment. [Temporary Reg. § 1.7519-1T.]

☐ [T.D. 8205, 5-24-88.]

[Reg. § 1.7519-2T]

§ 1.7519-2T. Required payments—procedures and administration (temporary).—(a) *Payment and return required.*—(1) *In general.*—With respect to any taxable year for which a partnership or S corporation has a section 444 election in effect (an "applicable election year"), the partnership or S corporation shall file a return as provided in paragraphs (a)(2) and (3) of this section and make a payment, if required, as provided in paragraph (a)(4) of this section.

(2) *Return required.*—(i) *In general.*—A return showing the required payment shall be made, even if the required payment for the applicable election year is zero. For an applicable election year beginning in 1987, the return shall be made on Form 720, "Quarterly Federal Excise Tax Return." For an applicable election year beginning after 1987, the return shall also be made on Form 720 unless another form is prescribed by the Commissioner.

(ii) *Procedure if amount for applicable election year (and all preceding years) is not greater than $500.*—If a partnership or S corporation is not required to make a payment under section 7519 for an applicable election year, the partnership or S corporation should type or legibly print "zero" on the appropriate line of the prescribed form.

(3) *Time and place for filing return.*—(i) *Applicable election years beginning in 1987.*—For an applicable election year beginning in 1987, the Form 720 must be filed with the Service Center indicated by the instructions for the Form 720. The date for filing such form is as follows—

(A) *Taxpayers that would otherwise file Form 720 for the second quarter of 1988.*—Taxpayers that are required, without regard to this section, to file Form 720 for the second quarter of 1988 (*e.g.*, taxpayers reporting liability for manufacturers excise tax) must file Form 720 by the normal due date of such form for the second quarter of 1988. Thus, such taxpayers must generally file Form 720 on or before July 31, 1988. However, if such taxpayers must also report tax imposed by section 4251 (relating to communications services tax), sections 4261 and 4271 (relating to air transportation tax), or section 4986 (relating to windfall profits tax) for the second quarter of 1988, they must file Form 720 on or before August 31, 1988.

(B) *Other taxpayers.*—Taxpayers that are not described in paragraph (a)(3)(i)(A) of this section (*i.e.*, taxpayers that but for this section would not be required to file Form 720 for the second quarter of 1988) must file Form 720 on or before July 31, 1988.

(ii) *Applicable election years beginning after 1987.*—(A) *Return made on Form 720.*—[Reserved].

(B) *Return made on form other than Form 720.*—For an applicable election year beginning after 1987, the return showing the required payment is to be filed with the Service Center indicated by the instructions for the form prescribed for payment. The return must be filed on or before the date prescribed by the instructions to the form.

(iii) *Special rule for back-up section 444 election.*—See § 1.444-3T(b)(4)(iii) for a special rule that may extend the due date for filing a return required by paragraph (a)(2) of this section.

(4) *Time and place for making required payment.*—(i) *Applicable election years beginning in 1987.*—For an applicable election year beginning in 1987, the required payment is due and payable without assessment and notice on or before the date the taxpayer's Form 720 for the second quarter is due (as specified in paragraph (a)(3) of this section). The required payment must be paid by check or money order, and such check or money order must indicate the partnership's or S corporation's taxpayer identification number and must include the statement: "IRS NO. 11 PAYMENT." The check or money order must be sent, together with Form 720, to the Service Center indicated by the instructions for the Form 720.

(ii) *Applicable election years beginning after 1987.*—For an applicable election year beginning after 1987, the required payment is due and payable without assessment or notice, on or before May 15 of the calendar year following the calendar year in which the applicable election year begins.

(iii) *Special rule for back-up section 444 election.*—See § 1.444-3T(b)(4)(iii) for a special rule that may extend the due date for making a required payment.

(5) *Penalties for failure to pay.*—In the case of any failure by a partnership or S corporation to pay the required payment on or before the date prescribed in paragraph (a)(4) of this section, there shall be assessed on such partnership or S corporation a penalty of 10 percent of the underpayment. For purposes of this section, the term "underpayment" means the excess of the amount of the payment required under this section over the amount (if any) of such payment paid on or before the date prescribed in paragraph (a)(4) of this section.

(6) *Refund of required payment.*—(i) *In general.*—If a partnership or S corporation is entitled to make a claim for refund pursuant to § 1.7519-1T(c), such partnership or S corporation should file a claim for refund, as provided in

paragraph (a)(6)(ii) of this section. However, in no event shall a refund be made prior to April 15 of the second calendar year that follows the calendar year in which an applicable election year begins. For example, assume a partnership made a section 444 election to retain its taxable year for its taxable year beginning October 1, 1987, and as a result made a required payment for such year. Further assume that the partnership terminates its election for its taxable year beginning October 1, 1988. Based on these facts, the partnership will be entitled to a refund, but no earlier than April 15, 1989.

(ii) *Procedures for claiming refund.*—[Reserved].

(iii) *Interest on refund.*—No interest shall be allowed with respect to any refund of a required payment under § 1.7519-1T(c).

(b) *Assessment and collection of payment.*—A required payment shall be assessed and collected in the same manner as if it were a tax imposed by subtitle C. Furthermore, no deduction shall be allowable to a partnership or S corporation (or their owners) with respect to the required payment.

(c) *Termination due to willful failure.*—See § 1.444-1T(a)(5)(i)(C), which provides that willful failure to comply with the requirements of this section will result in the termination of the section 444 election.

(d) *Negligence and fraud penalties made applicable.*—For purposes of section 6653, relating to additions to tax for negligence and fraud, any payment required by this section shall be treated as a tax. [Temporary Reg. § 1.7519-2T.]

☐ [*T.D. 8205, 5-24-88.*]

[Reg. § 1.7519-3T]

§ 1.7519-3T. Effective date (temporary).—The provisions of §§ 1.7519-1T through 1.7519-3T are effective for taxable years beginning after December 31, 1986. [Temporary Reg. § 1.7519-3T.]

☐ [*T.D. 8205, 5-24-88.*]

[Reg. § 1.7520-1]

§ 1.7520-1. Valuation of annuities, unitrust interests, interests for life or terms of years, and remainder or reversionary interests.— (a) *General actuarial valuations.*—(1) Except as otherwise provided in this section and in § 1.7520-3 (relating to exceptions to the use of prescribed tables under certain circumstances), in the case of certain transactions after April 30, 1989, subject to income tax, the fair market value of annuities, interests for life or for a term of years (including unitrust interests), remainders, and reversions is their present value determined under this section. See § 20.2031-7(d) of this chapter (and, for periods prior to May 1, 2009, § 20.2031-7A) for the computation of the value of annuities, unitrust interests, life estates, terms for years, remainders, and reversions, other than interests described in paragraphs (a)(2) and (a)(3) of this section.

(2) For a transfer to a pooled income fund, see § 1.642(c)-6(e) (or, for periods prior to May 1, 2009, § 1.642(c)-6A) with respect to the valuation of the remainder interest.

(3) For a transfer to a charitable remainder annuity trust after April 30, 1989, see § 1.664-2 with respect to the valuation of the remainder interest. See § 1.664-4 with respect to the valuation of the remainder interest in property transferred to a charitable remainder unitrust.

(b) *Components of valuation.*—(1) *Interest rate component.*—(i) *Section 7520 interest rate.*—The section 7520 interest rate is the rate of return, rounded to the nearest two-tenths of one percent, that is equal to 120 percent of the applicable Federal mid-term rate, compounded annually, for purposes of section 1274(d)(1), for the month in which the valuation date falls. In rounding the rate to the nearest two-tenths of a percent, any rate that is midway between one two-tenths of a percent and another is rounded up to the higher of those two rates. For example, if 120 percent of the applicable Federal mid-term rate is 10.30, the section 7520 interest rate component is 10.4. The section 7520 interest rate is published monthly by the Internal Revenue Service in the Internal Revenue Bulletin (see § 601.601(d)(2)(ii)(*b*) of this chapter).

(ii) *Valuation date.*—Except as provided in § 1.7520-2, the valuation date is the date on which the transaction takes place.

(2) *Mortality component.*—The mortality component reflects the mortality data most recently available from the United States census. As new mortality data becomes available after each decennial census, the mortality component described in this section will be revised and the revised mortality component tables will be published in the regulations at that time. For transactions with valuation dates on or after May 1, 2009, the mortality component table (Table 2000CM) is contained in § 20.2031-7(d)(7) of this chapter. See § 20.2031-7A for mortality component tables applicable to transactions for which the valuation date falls before May 1, 2009.

(c) *Tables.*—The present value on the valuation date of an annuity, life estate, term of years, remainder, or reversion is computed by using the section 7520 interest rate component that is described in paragraph (b)(1) of this section and the mortality component that is described in paragraph (b)(2) of this section. Actuarial factors for determining these present values are included in tables in these regulations and in publications by the Internal Revenue Service. If a special factor is required in order to value an interest, the Internal Revenue Service will furnish the factor upon a request for a ruling. The request for a ruling must be accompanied by a recitation of the facts, including the date of birth for each measuring life and copies of relevant instruments. A request for a ruling must comply with the instructions for requesting a ruling published periodically in the Internal Revenue Bulletin (see Rev. Proc. 94-1, 1994-1 I.R.B. 10, and subsequent updates, and §§ 601.201 and 601.601(d)(2)(ii)(*b*) of this chapter) and include payment of the required user fee.

(1) *Regulation sections containing tables with interest rates between 0.2 and 14 percent for valuation dates on or after May 1, 2009.*—Section 1.642(c)-6(e)(6) contains Table S used for determining the present value of a single life remainder interest in a pooled income fund as defined in § 1.642(c)-5. See § 1.642(c)-6A for actuarial factors for one life applicable to valuation dates before May 1, 2009. Section 1.664-4(e)(6) contains Table F (payout factors) and Table D (actuarial factors used in determining the present value of a remainder interest postponed for a term of years). Section 1.664-4(e)(7) contains Table U(1) (unitrust single life remainder factors). These tables are used in determining the present value of a remainder interest in a charitable remainder unitrust as defined in § 1.664-3. See § 1.664-4A for unitrust single life remainder factors applicable to valuation dates before May 1, 2009. Section 20.2031-7(d)(6) of this chapter contains Table B (actuarial factors used in determining the present value of an interest for a term of years), Table J (term certain annuity beginning-of-interval adjustment factors), and Table K (annuity end-of-interval adjustment factors). Section 20.2031-7(d)(7) contains Table S (single life remainder factors), and Table 2000CM (mortality components). These tables are used in determining the present value of annuities, life estates, remainders, and reversions. See § 20.2031-7A for single life remainder factors for one life and mortality components applicable to valuation dates before May 1, 2009.

(2) *Internal Revenue Service publications containing tables with interest rates between 0.2 and 22 percent for valuation dates on or after May 1, 2009.*—The following documents are available, at no charge, electronically via the IRS Internet site at *www.irs.gov*:

(i) Internal Revenue Service Publication 1457, "Actuarial Valuations Version 3A" (2009). This publication includes tables of valuation factors, as well as examples that show how to compute other valuation factors, for determining the present value of annuities, life estates, terms of years, remainders, and reversions, measured by one or two lives. These factors must also be used in the valuation of interests in a charitable remainder annuity trust as defined in § 1.664-2 and a pooled income fund as defined in § 1.642(c)-5.

(ii) Internal Revenue Service Publication 1458, "Actuarial Valuations Version 3B" (2009). This publication includes term certain tables and tables of one and two life valuation factors for determining the present value of remainder interests in a charitable remainder unitrust as defined in § 1.664-3.

(iii) Internal Revenue Service Publication 1459, "Actuarial Valuations Version 3C" (2009). This publication includes tables for computing depreciation adjustment factors. See § 1.170A-12.

(d) *Effective/applicability dates.*—This section applies on and after May 1, 2009. [Reg. § 1.7520-1.]

☐ [*T.D.* 8540, 6-9-94. *Amended by T.D.* 8819, 4-29-99; *T.D.* 8886, 6-9-2000; *T.D.* 9448, 5-1-2009; *and T.D.* 9540, 8-9-2011.]

[Reg. § 20.7520-1]

§ 20.7520-1. Valuation of annuities, unitrust interests, interests for life or terms of years, and remainder or reversionary interests.— (a) *General actuarial valuations.*—(1) Except as otherwise provided in this section and in § 20.7520-3 (relating to exceptions to the use of prescribed tables under certain circumstances), in the case of estates of decedents with valuation dates after April 30, 1989, the fair market value of annuities, interests for life or for a term of years (including unitrust interests), remainders, and reversions is their present value determined under this section. See § 20.2031-7(d) (and, for periods prior to May 1, 2009, § 20.2031-7A) for the computation of the value of annuities, unitrust interests, life estates, terms for years, remainders, and reversions, other than interests described in paragraphs (a)(2) and (a)(3) of this section.

(2) In the case of a transfer to a pooled income fund, see § 1.642(c)-6(e) of this chapter (or, for periods prior to May 1, 2009, § 1.642(c)-6A) with respect to the valuation of the remainder interest.

(3) In the case of a transfer to a charitable remainder annuity trust with a valuation date after April 30, 1989, see § 1.664-2 of this chapter with respect to the valuation of the remainder interest. See § 1.664-4 of this chapter with respect to the valuation of the remainder interest in property transferred to a charitable remainder unitrust.

(b) *Components of valuation.*—(1) *Interest rate component.*—(i) *Section 7520 Interest rate.*—The section 7520 interest rate is the rate of return, rounded to the nearest two-tenths of one percent, that is equal to 120 percent of the applicable Federal mid-term rate, compounded annually, for purposes of section 1274(d)(1), for the month in which the valuation date falls. In rounding the rate to the nearest two-tenths of a percent, any rate that is midway between one two-tenths of a percent and another is rounded up to the higher of those two rates. For example, if 120 percent of the applicable Federal mid-term rate is 10.30, the section 7520 interest rate component is 10.4. The section 7520 interest rate is published monthly by the Internal Revenue Service in the Internal Revenue Bulletin (See § 601.601(d)(2)(ii)(*b*) of this chapter).

(ii) *Valuation date.*—Generally, the valuation date is the date on which the transfer takes place. For estate tax purposes, the valuation date is the date of the decedent's death, unless the executor elects the alternate valuation date in accordance with section 2032, in which event, and under the limitations prescribed in section

2032 and the regulations thereunder, the valuation date is the alternate valuation date. For special rules in the case of charitable transfers, see § 20.7520-2.

(2) *Mortality component.*—The mortality component reflects the mortality data most recently available from the United States census. As new mortality data becomes available after each decennial census, the mortality component described in this section will be revised and the revised mortality component tables will be published in the regulations at that time. For decedent's estates with valuation dates on or after May 1, 2009, the mortality component table (Table 2000CM) is contained in § 20.2031-7(d)(7). See § 20.2031-7A for mortality component tables applicable to decedent's estates with valuation dates before May 1, 2009.

(c) *Tables.*—The present value on the valuation date of an annuity, life estate, term of years, remainder, or reversion is computed by using the section 7520 interest rate component that is described in paragraph (b)(1) of this section and the mortality component that is described in paragraph (b)(2) of this section. Actuarial factors for determining these present values are included in tables in these regulations and in publications by the Internal Revenue Service. If a special factor is required in order to value an interest, the Internal Revenue Service will furnish the factor upon a request for a ruling. The request for a ruling must be accompanied by a recitation of the facts, including the date of birth for each measuring life and copies of relevant instruments. A request for a ruling must comply with the instructions for requesting a ruling published periodically in the Internal Revenue Bulletin (see Rev. Proc. 94-1, 1994-1 I.R.B. 10, and the first Rev. Proc. published each year, and § § 601.201 and 601.601(d)(2)(ii)(*b*) of this chapter) and include payment of the required user fee.

(1) *Regulation sections containing tables with interest rates between 0.2 and 14 percent for valuation dates on or after May 1, 2009.*—Section 1.642(c)-6(e)(6) of this chapter contains Table S used for determining the present value of a single life remainder interest in a pooled income fund as defined in § 1.642(c)-5. See § 1.642(c)-6A for single life remainder factors applicable to valuation dates before May 1, 2009. Section 1.664-4(e)(6) contains Table F (payout factors) and Table D (actuarial factors used in determining the present value of a remainder interest postponed for a term of years). Section 1.664-4(e)(7) contains Table U(1) (unitrust single life remainder factors). These tables are used in determining the present value of a remainder interest in a charitable remainder unitrust as defined in § 1.664-3. See § 1.664-4A for unitrust single life remainder factors applicable to valuation dates before May 1, 2009. Section 20.2031-7(d)(6) contains Table B (actuarial factors used in determining the present value of an interest for a term of years), Table K (annuity end-of-interval adjustment factors), and Table J (term certain annu-

ity beginning-of-interval adjustment factors). Section 20.2031-7(d)(7) contains Table S (single life remainder factors), and Table 2000CM (mortality components). These tables are used in determining the present value of annuities, life estates, remainders, and reversions. See § 20.2031-7A for single life remainder factors applicable to valuation dates before May 1, 2009.

(2) *Internal Revenue Service publications containing tables with interest rates between 0.2 and 22 percent for valuation dates on or after May 1, 2009.*— The following documents are available, at no charge, electronically via the IRS Internet site at *www.irs.gov*:

(i) Internal Revenue Service Publication 1457, "Actuarial Valuations Version 3A" (2009). This publication includes tables of valuation factors, as well as examples that show how to compute other valuation factors, for determining the present value of annuities, life estates, terms of years, remainders, and reversions, measured by one or two lives. These factors may also be used in the valuation of interests in a charitable remainder annuity trust as defined in § 1.664-2 of this chapter and a pooled income fund as defined in § 1.642(c)-5.

(ii) Internal Revenue Service Publication 1458, "Actuarial Valuations Version 3B" (2009). This publication includes term certain tables and tables of one and two life valuation factors for determining the present value of remainder interests in a charitable remainder unitrust as defined in § 1.664-3 of this chapter.

(iii) Internal Revenue Service Publication 1459, "Actuarial Valuations Version 3C" (2009). This publication includes tables for computing depreciation adjustment factors. See § 1.170A-12 of this chapter.

(d) *Effective/applicability dates.*—This section applies on and after May 1, 2009. [Reg. § 20.7520-1.]

☐ [*T.D. 8540, 6-9-94. Amended by T.D. 8819, 4-29-99; T.D. 8886, 6-9-2000; T.D. 9448, 5-1-2009; and T.D. 9540, 8-9-2011.*]

[Reg. § 25.7520-1]

§ 25.7520-1. Valuation of annuities, unitrust interests, interests for life or terms of years, and remainder or reversionary interests.— (a) *General actuarial valuations.*—(1) Except as otherwise provided in this section and in § 25.7520-3(b) (relating to exceptions to the use of prescribed tables under certain circumstances), in the case of certain gifts after April 30, 1989, the fair market value of annuities, interests for life or for a term of years (including unitrust interests), remainders, and reversions is their present value determined under this section. See § 20.2031-7(d) of this chapter (and, for periods prior to May 1, 2009, § 20.2031-7A) for the computation of the value of annuities, unitrust interests, life estates, terms for years, remainders, and reversions, other than interests described in paragraphs (a)(2) and (a)(3) of this section.

(2) In the case of a gift to a beneficiary of a pooled income fund, see § 1.642(c)-6(e) of this chapter (or, for periods prior to May 1, 2009, § 1.642(c)-6A) with respect to the valuation of the remainder interest.

(3) In the case of a gift to a beneficiary of a charitable remainder annuity trust after April 30, 1989, see § 1.664-2 of this chapter with respect to the valuation of the remainder interest. See § 1.664-4 of this chapter (Income Tax Regulations) with respect to the valuation of the remainder interest in property transferred to a charitable remainder unitrust.

(b) *Components of valuation.*—(1) *Interest rate component.*—(i) *Section 7520 interest rate.*—The section 7520 interest rate is the rate of return, rounded to the nearest two-tenths of one percent, that is equal to 120 percent of the applicable Federal mid-term rate, compounded annually, for purposes of section 1274(d)(1), for the month in which the valuation date falls. In rounding the rate to the nearest two-tenths of a percent, any rate that is midway between one two-tenths of a percent and another is rounded up to the higher of those two rates. For example, if 120 percent of the applicable Federal mid-term rate is 10.30, the section 7520 interest rate component is 10.4. The section 7520 interest rate is published monthly by the Internal Revenue Service in the Internal Revenue Bulletin (See § 601.601(d)(2)(ii)(*b*) of this chapter).

(ii) *Valuation date.*—Generally, the valuation date is the date on which the gift is made. For gift tax purposes, the valuation date is the date on which the gift is complete under § 25.2511-2. For special rules in the case of charitable transfers, see § 25.7520-2.

(2) *Mortality component.*—The mortality component reflects the mortality data most recently available from the United States census. As new mortality data becomes available after each decennial census, the mortality component described in this section will be revised and the revised mortality component tables will be published in the regulations at that time. For gifts with valuation dates on or after May 1, 2009, the mortality component table (Table 2000CM) is contained in § 20.2031-7(d)(7). See § 20.2031-7A of this chapter for mortality component tables applicable to gifts for which the valuation date falls before May 1, 2009.

(c) *Tables.*—The present value on the valuation date of an annuity, life estate, term of years, remainder, or reversion is computed by using the section 7520 interest rate component that is described in paragraph (b)(1) of this section and the mortality component that is described in paragraph (b)(2) of this section. Actuarial factors for determining these present values are included in tables in these regulations and in publications by the Internal Revenue Service. If a special factor is required in order to value an interest, the Internal Revenue Service will furnish the factor upon a request for a ruling. The request for a ruling must be accompanied by a recitation of the facts, including the date of birth for each measuring life and copies of relevant instruments. A request for a ruling must comply with the instructions for requesting a ruling published periodically in the Internal Revenue Bulletin (see Rev. Proc. 94-1, 1994-1 I.R.B. 10, and subsequent updates, and § § 601.201 and 601.601(d)(2)(ii)(*b*) of this chapter) and include payment of the required user fee.

(1) *Regulation sections containing tables with interest rates between 0.2 and 14 percent for valuation dates on or after May 1, 2009.*—Section 1.642(c)-6(e)(6) of this chapter contains Table S used for determining the present value of a single life remainder interest in a pooled income fund as defined in § 1.642(c)-5. See § 1.642(c)-6A for single life remainder factors applicable to valuation dates before May 1, 2009. Section 1.664-4(e)(6) contains Table F (payout factors) and Table D (actuarial factors used in determining the present value of a remainder interest postponed for a term of years). Section 1.664-4(e)(7) contains Table U(1) (unitrust single life remainder factors). These tables are used in determining the present value of a remainder interest in a charitable remainder unitrust as defined in § 1.664-3. See § 1.664-4A for unitrust single life remainder factors applicable to valuation dates before May 1, 2009. Section 20.2031-7(d)(6) of this chapter contains Table B (actuarial factors used in determining the present value of an interest for a term of years), Table K (annuity end-of-interval adjustment factors), and Table J (term certain annuity beginning-of-interval adjustment factors). Section 20.2031-7(d)(7) contains Table S (single life remainder factors), and Table 2000CM (mortality components). These tables are used in determining the present value of annuities, life estates, remainders, and reversions. See § 20.2031-7A for single life remainder factors and mortality components applicable to valuation dates before May 1, 2009.

(2) *Internal Revenue Service publications containing tables with interest rates between 0.2 and 22 percent for valuation dates on or after May 1, 2009.*—The following documents are available, at no charge, electronically via the IRS Internet site at *www.irs.gov*:

(i) Internal Revenue Service Publication 1457, "Actuarial Valuations Version 3A" (2009). This publication includes tables of valuation factors, as well as examples that show how to compute other valuation factors, for determining the present value of annuities, life estates, terms of years, remainders, and reversions, measured by one or two lives. These factors may also be used in the valuation of interests in a charitable remainder annuity trust as defined in § 1.664-2 and a pooled income fund as defined in § 1.642(c)-5 of this chapter.

(ii) Internal Revenue Service Publication 1458, "Actuarial Valuations Version 3B" (2009). This publication includes term certain tables and tables of one and two life valuation factors for determining the present value of remainder interests in a charitable remainder unitrust as defined in § 1.664-3 of this chapter.

(iii) Internal Revenue Service Publication 1459, "Actuarial Valuations Version 3C" (2009). This publication includes tables for computing depreciation adjustment factors. See § 1.170A-12 of this chapter.

(d) *Effective/applicability dates.*—This section applies on and after May 1, 2009. [Reg. § 25.7520-1.]

☐ [*T.D.* 8540, 6-9-94. *Amended by T.D.* 8819, 4-29-99 (corrected 6-21-99); *T.D.* 8886, 6-9-2000; *T.D.* 9448, 5-1-2009 *and T.D.* 9540, 8-9-2011.]

[Reg. § 1.7520-2]

§ 1.7520-2. Valuation of charitable interests.—(a) *In general.*—(1) *Valuation.*—Except as otherwise provided in this section and in § 1.7520-3 (relating to exceptions to the use of prescribed tables under certain circumstances), the fair market value of annuities, interests for life or for a term of years, remainders, and reversions for which an income tax charitable deduction is allowable is the present value of such interests determined under § 1.7520-1.

(2) *Prior-month election rule.*—If any part of the property interest transferred qualifies for an income tax charitable deduction under section 170(c), the taxpayer may elect (under paragraph (b) of this section) to compute the present value of the interest transferred by use of the section 7520 interest rate for the month during which the interest is transferred or the section 7520 interest rate component for either of the 2 months preceding the month during which the interest is transferred. Paragraph (b) of this section explains how a prior-month election is made. The interest rate for the month so elected is the applicable section 7520 interest rate. If the actuarial factor for either or both of the 2 months preceding the month during which the interst is transferred is based on a mortality experience that is different from the mortality experience at the date of the transfer and if the taxpayer elects to use the section 7520 rate for a prior month with the different mortality experience, the taxpayer must use the actuarial factor derived from the mortality experience in effect during the month of the section 7520 rate elected. All actuarial computations relating to the transfer must be made by applying the interest rate component and the mortality component of the month elected by the taxpayer.

(3) *Transfers of more than one interest in the same property.*—If a taxpayer transfers more than one interest in the same property at the same time, for purposes of valuing the transferred interests, the taxpayer must use the same interest rate and mortality component for each interest in the property transferred. If more than one interest in the same property is transferred in two or more separate transfers at different times, the value of each interest is determined by the use of the interest rate component and mortality component in effect during the month of the transfer

of that interest or, if applicable under paragraph (a)(2) of this section, either of the two months preceding the month of the transfer.

(4) *Information required with tax return.*—The following information must be attached to the income tax return (or to the amended return) if the taxpayer claims a charitable deduction for the present value of a temporary or remainder interest in property—

(i) A complete description of the interest that is transferred, including a copy of the instrument of transfer;

(ii) The valuation date of the transfer;

(iii) The names and identification numbers of the beneficiaries of the transferred interest;

(iv) The names and birthdates of any measuring lives, a description of any relevant terminal illness condition of any measuring life, and (if applicable) an explanation of how any terminal illness condition was taken into account in valuing the interest; and

(v) A computation of the deduction showing the applicable section 7520 interest rate that is used to value the transferred interest.

(5) *Place for filing returns.*—See section 6091 of the Internal Revenue Code and the regulations thereunder for the place for filing the return or other document required by this section.

(b) *Election of interest rate component.*—(1) *Time for making election.*—A taxpayer makes a prior-month election under paragraph (a)(2) of this section by attaching the information described in paragraph (b)(2) of this section to the taxpayer's income tax return or to an amended return for that year that is filed within 24 months after the later of the date the original return for the year was filed or the due date for filing the return.

(2) *Manner of making election.*—A statement that the prior-month election under section 7520(a) of the Internal Revenue Code is being made and that identifies the elected month must be attached to the income tax return (or to the amended return).

(3) *Revocability.*—The prior-month election may be revoked by filing an amended return within 24 months after the later of the date the original return of tax for the year was filed or the due date for filing the return. The revocation must be filed in the place referred to in paragraph (a)(5) of this section.

(c) *Effective dates.*—Paragraph (a) of this section is effective as of May 1, 1989. Paragraph (b) of this section is effective for elections made after June 10, 1994. [Reg. § 1.7520-2.]

☐ [*T.D.* 8540, 6-9-94.]

[Reg. § 20.7520-2]

§ 20.7520-2. Valuation of charitable interests.—(a) *In general.*—(1) *Valuation.*—Except as otherwise provided in this section and in § 20.7520-3 (relating to exceptions to the use of prescribed tables under certain circumstances), the fair market value of annuities, interests for life or for a term of years, remainders, and reversions for which an estate tax charitable deduction is allowable is the present value of such interests determined under § 20.7520-1.

(2) *Prior-month election rule.*—If any part of the property interest transferred qualifies for an estate tax charitable deduction under section 2055 or 2106, the executor may compute the present value of the transferred interest by use of the section 7520 interest rate for the month during which the interest is transferred or the section 7520 interest rate for either of the 2 months preceding the month during which the interest is transferred. Paragraph (b) of this section explains how a prior-month election is made. The interest rate for the month so elected is the applicable section 7520 interest rate. If the executor elects the alternate valuation date under section 2032 and also elects to use the section 7520 interest rate for either of the 2 months preceding the month in which the interest is transferred, the month so elected (either of the 2 months preceding the month in which the alternate valuation date falls) is the valuation date. If the actuarial factor for either or both of the 2 months preceding the month during which the interest is transferred is based on a mortality experience that is different from the mortality experience at the date of the transfer and if the executor elects to use the section 7520 rate for a prior month with the different mortality experience, the executor must use the actuarial factor derived from the mortality experience in effect during the month of the section 7520 rate elected. All actuarial computations relating to the transfer must be made by applying the interest rate component and the mortality component of the month elected by the executor.

(3) *Transfers of more than one interest in the same property.*—If a decedent's estate includes the transfer of more than one interest in the same property, the executor must, for purposes of valuing the transferred interests, use the same interest rate and mortality components for each interest in the property transferred.

(4) *Information required with tax return.*—The following information must be attached to the estate tax return (or be filed subsequently as supplemental information to the return) if the estate claims a charitable deduction for the present value of a temporary or remainder interest in property—

(i) A complete description of the interest that is transferred, including a copy of the instrument of transfer;

(ii) The valuation date of the transfer;

(iii) The names and identification numbers of the beneficiaries of the transferred interest;

(iv) The names and birthdates of any measuring lives, a description of any relevant terminal illness condition of any measuring life, and (if applicable) an explanation of how any terminal illness condition was taken into account in valuing the interest; and

(v) A computation of the deduction showing the applicable section 7520 interest rate that is used to value the transferred interest.

(5) *Place for filing returns.*—See section 6091 of the Internal Revenue Code and the regulations thereunder for the place for filing the return or other document required by this section.

(b) *Election of interest rate component.*—(1) *Time for making election.*—An executor makes a prior-month election under paragraph (a)(2) of this section by attaching the information described in paragraph (b)(2) of this section to the decedent's estate tax return or by filing a supplemental statement of the election information within 24 months after the later of the date the original estate tax return was filed or the due date for filing the return.

(2) *Manner of making election.*—A statement that the prior-month election under section 7520(a) of the Internal Revenue Code is being made and that identifies the elected month must be attached to the estate tax return (or by subsequently filing the statement as supplemental information to the return).

(3) *Revocability.*—The prior-month election may be revoked by filing a statement of supplemental information within 24 months after the later of the date the original return of tax for the decedent's estate was filed or the due date for filing the return. The revocation must be filed in the place referred to in paragraph (a)(5) of this section.

(c) *Effective dates.*—Paragraph (a) of this section is effective as of May 1, 1989. Paragraph (b) of this section is effective for elections made after June 10, 1994. [Reg. § 20.7520-2.]

☐ [*T.D.* 8540, 6-9-94.]

[Reg. § 25.7520-2]

§ 25.7520-2. Valuation of charitable interests.—(a) *In general.*—(1) *Valuation.*—Except as otherwise provided in this section and in § 25.7520-3 (relating to exceptions to the use of prescribed tables under certain circumstances), the fair market value of annuities, interests for life or for a term for years, remainders, and reversions for which a gift tax charitable deduction is allowable is the present value of such interests determined under § 25.7520-1.

(2) *Prior-month election rule.*—If any part of the property interest transferred qualifies for a gift tax charitable deduction under section 2522, the donor may elect to compute the present value of the interest transferred by use of the section 7520 interest rate for the month during which the gift is made or the section 7520 interest rate for either of the 2 months preceding the month during which the gift is made. Paragraph (b) of this section explains how a prior-month election is made. The interest rate for the month so elected is the applicable section 7520 interest

rate. If the actuarial factor for either or both of the 2 months preceding the month during which the gift is made is based on a mortality experience that is different from the mortality experience at the date of the gift and if the donor elects to use the section 7520 rate for a prior month with the different mortality experience, the donor must use the actuarial factor derived from the mortality experience in effect during the month of the section 7520 rate elected. All actuarial computations relating to the gift must be made by applying the interest rate component and the mortality component of the month elected by the donor.

(3) *Gifts of more than one interest in the same property.*—If a donor makes a gift of more than one interest in the same property at the same time, the donor must, for purposes of valuing the gifts, use the same interest rate and mortality components for the gift of each interest in the property. If the donor has made gifts of more than one interest in the same property at different times, the donor must determine the value of the gift by the use of the interest rate component and mortality component in effect during the month of that gift or, if applicable under paragraph (a)(2) of this section, either of the two months preceding the month of the gift.

(4) *Information required with tax return.*—The following information must be attached to the gift tax return (or to the amended return) if the donor claims a charitable deduction for the present value of a temporary or remainder interest in property—

(i) A complete description of the interest that is transferred, including a copy of the instrument of transfer;

(ii) The valuation date of the transfer;

(iii) The names and identification numbers of the beneficiaries of the transferred interest;

(iv) The names and birthdates of any measuring lives, a description of any relevant terminal illness condition of any measuring life, and (if applicable) an explanation of how any terminal illness condition was taken into account in valuing the interest; and

(v) A computation of the deduction showing the applicable section 7520 interest rate that is used to value the transferred interest.

(5) *Place for filing returns.*—See section 6091 of the Internal Revenue Code and the regulations thereunder for the place for filing the return or other document required by this section.

(b) *Election of interest rate component.*—(1) *Time for making election.*—A taxpayer makes a prior-month election under paragraph (a)(2) of this section by attaching the information described in paragraph (b)(2) of this section to the donor's gift tax return or to an amended return for that year that is filed within 24 months after the later of the date the original return for the year was filed or the due date for filing the return.

(2) *Manner of making election.*—A statement that the prior-month election under section

7520(a) of the Internal Revenue Code is being made and that identifies the elected month must be attached to the gift tax return (or to the amended return).

(3) *Revocability.*—The prior-month election may be revoked by filing an amended return within 24 months after the later of the date the original return of tax for that year was filed or the due date for filing the return. The revocation must be filed in the place referred to in paragraph (a)(5) of this section.

(c) *Effective dates.*—Paragraph (a) of this section is effective as of May 1, 1989. Paragraph (b) of this section is effective for elections made after June 10, 1994. [Reg. § 25.7520-2.]

☐ [*T.D.* 8540, 6-9-94.]

[Reg. § 1.7520-3]

§ 1.7520-3. Limitation on the application of section 7520.—(a) *Internal Revenue Code sections to which section 7520 does not apply.*—Section 7520 of the Internal Revenue Code does not apply for purposes of—

(1) Part I, subchapter D of subtitle A (section 401 et. seq.), relating to the income tax treatment of certain qualified plans. (However, section 7520 does apply to the estate and gift tax treatment of certain qualified plans and for purposes of determining excess accumulations under section 4980A);

(2) Sections 72 and 101(b), relating to the income taxation of life insurance, endowment, and annuity contracts, unless otherwise provided for in the regulations under sections 72, 101, and 1011 (see, particularly, § § 1.101-2(e)(1)(iii)(b)(2), and 1.1011-2(c), *Example 8*);

(3) Sections 83 and 451, unless otherwise provided for in the regulations under those sections;

(4) Section 457, relating to the valuation of deferred compensation, unless otherwise provided for in the regulations under section 457;

(5) Sections 3121(v) and 3306(r), relating to the valuation of deferred amounts, unless otherwise provided for in the regulations under those sections;

(6) Section 6058, relating to valuation statements evidencing compliance with qualified plan requirements, unless otherwise provided for in the regulations under section 6058;

(7) Section 7872, relating to income and gift taxation of interest-free loans and loans with below-market interest rates, unless otherwise provided for in the regulations under section 7872; or

(8) Section 2702(a)(2)(A), relating to the value of a nonqualified retained interest upon a transfer of an interest in trust to or for the benefit of a member of the transferor's family; and

(9) Any other sections of the Internal Revenue Code to the extent provided by the Internal Revenue Service in revenue rulings or revenue procedures. (See § § 601.201 and 601.601 of this chapter).

(b) *Other limitations on the application of section 7520.*—(1) *In general.*—(i) *Ordinary beneficial interests.*—For purposes of this section:

(A) An *ordinary annuity interest* is the right to receive a fixed dollar amount at the end of each year during one or more measuring lives or for some other defined period. A standard section 7520 annuity factor for an ordinary annuity interest represents the present worth of the right to receive $1.00 per year for a defined period, using the interest rate prescribed under section 7520 for the appropriate month. If an annuity interest is payable more often than annually or is payable at the beginning of each period, a special adjustment must be made in any computation with a standard section 7520 annuity factor.

(B) An *ordinary income interest* is the right to receive the income from, or the use of, property during one or more measuring lives or for some other defined period. A standard section 7520 income factor for an ordinary income interest represents the present worth of the right to receive the use of $1.00 for a defined period, using the interest rate prescribed under section 7520 for the appropriate month.

(C) An *ordinary remainder or reversionary interest* is the right to receive an interest in property at the end of one or more measuring lives or some other defined period. A standard section 7520 remainder factor for an ordinary remainder or reversionary interest represents the present worth of the right to receive $1.00 at the end of a defined period, using the interest rate prescribed under section 7520 for the appropriate month.

(ii) *Certain restricted beneficial interests.*—A *restricted beneficial interest* is an annuity, income, remainder, or reversionary interest that is subject to a contingency, power, or other restriction, whether the restriction is provided for by the terms of the trust, will, or other governing instrument or is caused by other circumstances. In general, a standard section 7520 annuity, income, or remainder factor may not be used to value a restricted beneficial interest. However, a special section 7520 annuity, income, or remainder factor may be used to value a restricted beneficial interest under some circumstances. See paragraph (b)(4) *Example 2* of this section, which illustrates a situation where a special section 7520 actuarial factor is needed to take into account the shorter life expectancy of the terminally ill measuring life. See §1.7520-1(c) for requesting a special factor from the Internal Revenue Service.

(iii) *Other beneficial interests.*—If, under the provisions of this paragraph (b), the interest rate and mortality components prescribed under section 7520 are not applicable in determining the value of any annuity, income, remainder, or reversionary interest, the actual fair market value of the interest (determined without regard to section 7520) is based on all of the facts and circumstances if and to the extent permitted by the Internal Revenue Code provision applicable to the property interest.

(2) *Provisions of governing instrument and other limitations on source of payment.*—(i) *Annuities.*—A standard section 7520 annuity factor may not be used to determine the present value of an annuity for a specified term of years or the life of one or more individuals unless the effect of the trust, will, or other governing instrument is to ensure that the annuity will be paid for the entire defined period. In the case of an annuity payable from a trust or other limited fund, the annuity is not considered payable for the entire defined period if, considering the applicable section 7520 interest rate at the valuation date of the transfer, the annuity is expected to exhaust the fund before the last possible annuity payment is made in full. For this purpose, it must be assumed that it is possible for each measuring life to survive until age 110. For example, for a fixed annuity payable annually at the end of each year, if the amount of the annuity payment (expressed as a percentage of the initial corpus) is less than or equal to the applicable section 7520 interest rate at the date of the transfer, the corpus is assumed to be sufficient to make all payments. If the percentage exceeds the applicable section 7520 interest rate and the annuity is for a definite term of years, multiply the annual annuity amount by the Table B term certain annuity factor, as described in §1.7520-1(c)(1), for the number of years of the defined period. If the percentage exceeds the applicable section 7520 interest rate and the annuity is payable for the life of one or more individuals, multiply the annual annuity amount by the Table B annuity factor for 110 years minus the age of the youngest individual. If the result exceeds the limited fund, the annuity may exhaust the fund, and it will be necessary to calculate a special section 7520 annuity factor that takes into account the exhaustion of the trust or fund. This computation would be modified, if appropriate, to take into account annuities with different payment terms. See §25.7520-3(b)(2)(v) *Example 5* of this chapter, which provides an illustration involving an annuity trust that is subject to exhaustion.

(ii) *Income and similar interests.*—(A) *Beneficial enjoyment.*—A standard section 7520 income factor for an ordinary income interest may not be used to determine the present value of an income or similar interest in trust for a term of years or for the life of one or more individuals unless the effect of the trust, will, or other governing instrument is to provide the income beneficiary with that degree of beneficial enjoyment of the property during the term of the income interest that the principles of the law of trusts accord to a person who is unqualifiedly designated as the income beneficiary of a trust for a similar period of time. This degree of beneficial enjoyment is provided only if it was the transferor's intent, as manifested by the provisions of the governing instrument and the surrounding circumstances, that the trust provide an income interest for the income beneficiary during the specified period of time that is consistent with the value of the trust corpus and with its preservation. In determining whether a trust arrangement evidences that intention, the treatment required or permitted with respect to individual items must be considered in relation to the entire system provided for in the administration of the subject trust. Similarly, in determining the present value of the right to use tangible property (whether or not in trust) for one or more measuring lives or for some other specified period of time, the interest rate component prescribed under section 7520 and § 1.7520-1 may not be used unless, during the specified period, the effect of the trust, will or other governing instrument is to provide the beneficiary with that degree of use, possession, and enjoyment of the property during the term of interest that applicable state law accords to a person who is unqualifiedly designated as a life tenant or term holder for a similar period of time.

(B) *Diversions of income and corpus.*—A standard section 7520 income factor for an ordinary income interest may not be used to value an income interest or similar interest in property for a term of years or for one or more measuring lives if—

(1) The trust, will, or other governing instrument requires or permits the beneficiary's income or other enjoyment to be withheld, diverted, or accumulated for another person's benefit without the consent of the income beneficiary; or

(2) The governing instrument requires or permits trust corpus to be withdrawn from the trust for another person's benefit during the income beneficiary's term of enjoyment without the consent of and accountability to the income beneficiary for such diversion.

(iii) *Remainder and reversionary interests.*—A standard section 7520 remainder interest factor for an ordinary remainder or reversionary interest may not be used to determine the present value of a remainder or reversionary interest (whether in trust or otherwise) unless, consistent with the preservation and protection that the law of trusts would provide for a person who is unqualifiedly designated as the remainder beneficiary of a trust for a similar duration, the effect of the administrative and dispositive provisions for the interest or interests that precede the remainder or reversionary interest is to assure that the property will be adequately preserved and protected (e.g., from erosion, invasion, depletion, or damage) until the remainder or reversionary interest takes effect in possession and enjoyment. This degree of preservation and protection is provided only if it was the transferor's intent, as manifested by the provisions of the arrangement and the surrounding circumstances, that the entire disposition provide the remainder or reversionary beneficiary with an undiminished interest in the property transferred at the time of the termination of the prior interest.

(iv) *Pooled income fund interests.*—In general, pooled income funds are created and administered to achieve a special rate of return. A beneficial interest in a pooled income fund is not ordinarily valued using a standard section 7520 income or remainder interest factor. The present value of a beneficial interest in a pooled income fund is determined according to rules and special remainder factors prescribed in § 1.642(c)-6 and, when applicable, the rules set forth in paragraph (b)(3) of this section, if the individual who is the measuring life is terminally ill at the time of the transfer.

(3) *Mortality component.*—The mortality component prescribed under section 7520 may not be used to determine the present value of an annuity, income interest, remainder interest, or reversionary interest if an individual who is a measuring life is terminally ill at the time of the transaction. For purposes of this paragraph (b)(3), an individual who is known to have an incurable illness or other deteriorating physical condition is considered terminally ill if there is at least a 50 percent probability that the individual will die within 1 year. However, if the individual survives for eighteen months or longer after the date of the transaction, that individual shall be presumed to have not been terminally ill at the time of the transaction unless the contrary is established by clear and convincing evidence.

(4) *Examples.*—The provisions of this paragraph (b) are illustrated by the following examples:

Example 1. Annuity funded with unproductive property. The taxpayer transfers corporation stock worth $1,000,000 to a trust. The trust provides for a 6 percent ($60,000 per year) annuity in cash or other property to be paid to a charitable organization for 25 years and for the remainder to be distributed to the donor's child. The trust specifically authorizes, but does not require, the trustee to retain the shares of stock. The section 7520 interest rate for the month of the transfer is 8.2 percent. The corporation has paid no dividends on this stock during the past 5 years, and there is no indication that this policy will change in the near future. Under applicable state law, the corporation is considered to be a sound investment that satisfies fiduciary standards. Therefore, the trust's sole investment in this corporation is not expected to adversely affect the interest of either the annuitant or the remainder beneficiary. Considering the 6 percent annuity payout rate and the 8.2 percent section 7520 interest rate, the trust corpus is considered sufficient to pay this annuity for the entire 25-year term of the trust, or even indefinitely. Although it appears that neither beneficiary would be able to compel the trustee to make the trust corpus produce investment income, the annuity interest in this case is considered to be an ordinary annuity interest, and the standard section 7520 annuity factor may be used to determine the present value of the annuity. In this case, the section 7520 annuity factor would represent the right to receive $1.00 per year for a term of 25 years.

Example 2. Terminal illness. The taxpayer transfers property worth $1,000,000 to a charitable remainder unitrust described in section 664(d)(2) and § 1.664-3. The trust provides for a fixed-percentage 7 percent unitrust benefit (each annual payment is equal to 7 percent of the trust assets as valued at the beginning of each year) to be paid quarterly to an individual beneficiary for life and for the remainder to be distributed to a charitable organization. At the time the trust is created, the individual beneficiary is age 60 and has been diagnosed with an incurable illness and there is at least a 50 percent probability of the individual dying within 1 year. Assuming the presumption in paragraph (b)(3) of this section does not apply, because there is at least a 50 percent probability that this beneficiary will die within 1 year, the standard section 7520 unitrust remainder factor for a person age 60 from the valuation tables may not be used to determine the present value of the charitable remainder interest. Instead, a special unitrust remainder factor must be computed that is based on the section 7520 interest rate and that takes into account the projection of the individual beneficiary's actual life expectancy.

(5) *Additional limitations.*—Section 7520 does not apply to the extent as may otherwise be provided by the Commissioner.

(c) *Effective date.*—Section 1.7520-3(a) is effective as of May 1, 1989. The provisions of paragraph (b) of this section are effective with respect to transactions after December 13, 1995. [Reg. § 1.7520-3.]

☐ [*T.D.* 8540, 6-9-94. *Amended by T.D.* 8630, 12-12-95.]

[Reg. § 20.7520-3]

§ 20.7520-3. Limitation on the application of section 7520.—(a) *Internal Revenue Code sections to which section 7520 does not apply.*—Section 7520 of the Internal Revenue Code does not apply for purposes of—

(1) Part I, subchapter D of subtitle A (section 401 et. seq.), relating to the income tax treatment of certain qualified plans. (However, section 7520 does apply to the estate and gift tax treatment of certain qualified plans and for purposes of determining excess accumulations under section 4980A);

(2) Sections 72 and 101(b), relating to the income taxation of life insurance, endowment, and annuity contracts, unless otherwise provided for in the regulations under sections 72, 101, and 1011 (see, particularly, §§ 1.101-2(e)(1)(iii)(b)(2), and 1.1011-2(c), *Example 8*);

(3) Sections 83 and 451, unless otherwise provided for in the regulations under those sections;

(4) Section 457, relating to the valuation of deferred compensation, unless otherwise provided for in the regulations under section 457;

(5) Sections 3121(v) and 3306(r), relating to the valuation of deferred amounts, unless otherwise provided for in the regulations under those sections;

(6) Section 6058, relating to valuation statements evidencing compliance with qualified plan requirements, unless otherwise provided for in the regulations under section 6058;

(7) Section 7872, relating to income and gift taxation of interest-free loans and loans with below-market interest rates, unless otherwise provided for in the regulations under section 7872; or

(8) Section 2702(a)(2)(A), relating to the value of a nonqualified retained interest upon a transfer of an interest in trust to or for the benefit of a member of the transferor's family; and

(9) Any other sections of the Internal Revenue Code to the extent provided by the Internal Revenue Service in revenue rulings or revenue procedures. (See §§ 601.201 and 601.601 of this chapter).

(b) *Other limitations on the application of section 7520.*—(1) *In general.*—(i) *Ordinary beneficial interests.*—For purposes of this section:

(A) An *ordinary annuity interest* is the right to receive a fixed dollar amount at the end of each year during one or more measuring lives or for some other defined period. A standard section 7520 annuity factor for an ordinary annuity interest represents the present worth of the right to receive $1.00 per year for a defined period, using the interest rate prescribed under section 7520 for the appropriate month. If an annuity interest is payable more often than annually or is payable at the beginning of each period, a special adjustment must be made in any computation with a standard section 7520 annuity factor.

(B) An *ordinary income interest* is the right to receive the income from or the use of property during one or more measuring lives or for some other defined period. A standard section 7520 income factor for an ordinary income interest represents the present worth of the right to receive the use of $1.00 for a defined period, using the interest rate prescribed under section 7520 for the appropriate month.

(C) An *ordinary remainder or reversionary interest* is the right to receive an interest in property at the end of one or more measuring lives or some other defined period. A standard section 7520 remainder factor for an ordinary remainder or reversionary interest represents the present worth of the right to receive $1.00 at the end of a defined period, using the interest rate prescribed under section 7520 for the appropriate month.

(ii) *Certain restricted beneficial interests.*—A *restricted beneficial interest* is an annuity, income, remainder, or reversionary interest that is subject to any contingency, power, or other restriction, whether the restriction is provided for by the terms of the trust, will, or other governing instrument or is caused by other circumstances. In general, a standard section 7520 annuity, income, or remainder factor may not be used to value a restricted beneficial interest. However, a special section 7520 annuity, income, or remainder factor may be used to value a restricted beneficial interest under some circumstances. See paragraphs (b)(2)(v) *Example 4* and (b)(4) *Example 1* of this section, which illustrate situations where special section 7520 actuarial factors are needed to take into account limitations on beneficial interests. See § 20.7520-1(c) for requesting a special factor from the Internal Revenue Service.

(iii) *Other beneficial interests.*—If, under the provisions of this paragraph (b), the interest rate and mortality components prescribed under section 7520 are not applicable in determining the value of any annuity, income, remainder, or reversionary interest, the actual fair market value of the interest (determined without regard to section 7520) is based on all of the facts and circumstances if and to the extent permitted by the Internal Revenue Code provision applicable to the property interest.

(2) *Provisions of governing instrument and other limitations on source of payment.*— (i) *Annuities.*—A standard section 7520 annuity factor may not be used to determine the present value of an annuity for a specified term of years or the life of one or more individuals unless the effect of the trust, will, or other governing instrument is to ensure that the annuity will be paid for the entire defined period. In the case of an annuity payable from a trust or other limited fund, the annuity is not considered payable for the entire defined period if, considering the applicable section 7520 interest rate at the valuation date of the transfer, the annuity is expected to exhaust the fund before the last possible annuity payment is made in full. For this purpose, it must be assumed that it is possible for each measuring life to survive until age 110. For example, for a fixed annuity payable annually at the end of each year, if the amount of the annuity payment (expressed as a percentage of the initial corpus) is less than or equal to the applicable section 7520 interest rate at the date of the transfer, the corpus is assumed to be sufficient to make all payments. If the percentage exceeds the applicable section 7520 interest rate and the annuity is for a definite term of years, multiply the annual annuity amount by the Table B term certain annuity factor, as described in § 20.7520-1(c)(1), for the number of years of the defined period. If the percentage exceeds the applicable section 7520 interest rate and the annuity is payable for the life of one or more individuals, multiply the annual annuity amount by the Table B annuity factor for 110 years minus the age of the youngest individual. If the result exceeds the limited fund, the annuity may exhaust the fund, and it will be necessary to calculate a special section 7520 annuity factor that takes into account the exhaustion of the trust or fund. This computation would be modified, if appropriate, to take into account annuities with different payment terms. See § 25.7520-3(b)(2)(v) *Example 5* of this chapter, which provides an

illustration involving an annuity trust that is subject to exhaustion.

(ii) *Income and similar interests.*— (A) *Beneficial enjoyment.*—A standard section 7520 income factor for an ordinary income interest may not be used to determine the present value of an income or similar interest in trust for a term of years, or for the life of one or more individuals, unless the effect of the trust, will, or other governing instrument is to provide the income beneficiary with that degree of beneficial enjoyment of the property during the term of the income interest that the principles of the law of trusts accord to a person who is unqualifiedly designated as the income beneficiary of a trust for a similar period of time. This degree of beneficial enjoyment is provided only if it was the transferor's intent, as manifested by the provisions of the governing instrument and the surrounding circumstances, that the trust provide an income interest for the income beneficiary during the specified period of time that is consistent with the value of the trust corpus and with its preservation. In determining whether a trust arrangement evidences that intention, the treatment required or permitted with respect to individual items must be considered in relation to the entire system provided for in the administration of the subject trust. Similarly, in determining the present value of the right to use tangible property (whether or not in trust) for one or more measuring lives or for some other specified period of time, the interest rate component prescribed under section 7520 and § 1.7520-1 of this chapter may not be used unless, during the specified period, the effect of the trust, will or other governing instrument is to provide the beneficiary with that degree of use, possession, and enjoyment of the property during the term of interest that applicable state law accords to a person who is unqualifiedly designated as a life tenant or term holder for a similar period of time.

(B) *Diversions of income and corpus.*—A standard section 7520 income factor for an ordinary income interest may not be used to value an income interest or similar interest in property for a term of years, or for one or more measuring lives, if—

(1) The trust, will, or other governing instrument requires or permits the beneficiary's income or other enjoyment to be withheld, diverted, or accumulated for another person's benefit without the consent of the income beneficiary; or

(2) The governing instrument requires or permits trust corpus to be withdrawn from the trust for another person's benefit without the consent of the income beneficiary during the income beneficiary's term of enjoyment and without accountability to the income beneficiary for such diversion.

(iii) *Remainder and reversionary interests.*— A standard section 7520 remainder interest factor for an ordinary remainder or reversionary interest may not be used to determine the present value of a remainder or reversionary interest (whether in trust or otherwise) unless, consistent with the preservation and protection that the law of trusts would provide for a person who is unqualifiedly designated as the remainder beneficiary of a trust for a similar duration, the effect of the administrative and dispositive provisions for the interest or interests that precede the remainder or reversionary interest is to assure that the property will be adequately preserved and protected (e.g., from erosion, invasion, depletion, or damage) until the remainder or reversionary interest takes effect in possession and enjoyment. This degree of preservation and protection is provided only if it was the transferor's intent, as manifested by the provisions of the arrangement and the surrounding circumstances, that the entire disposition provide the remainder or reversionary beneficiary with an undiminished interest in the property transferred at the time of the termination of the prior interest.

(iv) *Pooled income fund interests.*—In general, pooled income funds are created and administered to achieve a special rate of return. A beneficial interest in a pooled income fund is not ordinarily valued using a standard section 7520 income or remainder interest factor. The present value of a beneficial interest in a pooled income fund is determined according to rules and special remainder factors prescribed in § 1.642(c)-6 of this chapter and, when applicable, the rules set forth under paragraph (b)(3) of this section if the individual who is the measuring life is terminally ill at the time of the transfer.

(v) *Examples.*—The provisions of this paragraph (b)(2) are illustrated by the following examples:

Example 1. Unproductive property. A died, survived by B and C. B died two years after A. A's will provided for a bequest of corporation stock in trust under the terms of which all of the trust income was paid to B for life. After the death of B, the trust terminated and the trust property was distributed to C. The trust specifically authorized, but did not require, the trustee to retain the shares of stock. The corporation paid no dividends on this stock during the 5 years before A's death and the 2 years before B's death. There was no indication that this policy would change after A's death. Under applicable state law, the corporation is considered to be a sound investment that satisfies fiduciary standards. The facts and circumstances, including applicable state law, indicate that B did not have the legal right to compel the trustee to make the trust corpus productive in conformity with the requirements for a lifetime trust income interest under applicable local law. Therefore, B's life income interest in this case is considered nonproductive. Consequently, B's income interest may not be valued actuarially under this section.

Example 2. Beneficiary's right to make trust productive. The facts are the same as in *Example 1,* except that the trustee is not specifically authorized to retain the shares of stock. Further, the terms of the trust specifically provide that B, the life income beneficiary, may require the trustee to make the trust corpus productive consistent with income yield standards for trusts under applicable state law. Under that law, the minimum rate of income that a productive trust may produce is substantially below the section 7520 interest rate for the month of A's death. In this case, because B has the right to compel the trustee to make the trust productive for purposes of applicable local law during the beneficiary's lifetime, the income interest is considered an ordinary income interest for purposes of this paragraph, and the standard section 7520 life income interest factor may be used to determine the present value of B's income interest.

Example 3. Discretionary invasion of corpus. The decedent, A, transferred property to a trust under the terms of which all of the trust income is to be paid to A's child for life and the remainder of the trust is to be distributed to a grandchild. The trust authorizes the trustee without restriction to distribute corpus to A's surviving spouse for the spouse's comfort and happiness. In this case, because the trustee's power to invade trust corpus is unrestricted, the exercise of the power could result in the termination of the income interest at any time. Consequently, the income interest is not considered an ordinary income interest for purposes of this paragraph, and may not be valued actuarially under this section.

Example 4. Limited invasion of corpus. The decedent, A, bequeathed property to a trust under the terms of which all of the trust income is to be paid to A's child for life and the remainder is to be distributed to A's grandchild. The trust authorizes the child to withdraw up to $5,000 per year from the trust corpus. In this case, the child's power to invade trust corpus is limited to an ascertainable amount each year. Annual invasions of any amount would be expected to progressively diminish the property from which the child's income is paid. Consequently, the income interest is not considered an ordinary income interest for purposes of this paragraph, and the standard section 7520 income interest factor may not be used to determine the present value of the income interest. Nevertheless, the present value of the child's income interest is ascertainable by making a special actuarial calculation that would take into account not only the initial value of the trust corpus, the section 7520 interest rate for the month of the transfer, and the mortality component for the child's age, but also the assumption that the trust corpus will decline at the rate of $5,000 each year during the child's lifetime. The child's right to receive an amount not in excess of $5,000 per year may be separately valued in this instance and, assuming the trust corpus would not exhaust before the child would attain age 110, would be considered an ordinary annuity interest.

Example 5. Power to consume. The decedent, A, devised a life estate in 3 parcels of real estate to A's surviving spouse with the remainder to a child, or, if the child doesn't survive, to the child's estate. A also conferred upon the spouse an unrestricted power to consume the property, which includes the right to sell part or all of the property and to use the proceeds for the spouse's support, comfort, happiness, and other purposes. Any portion of the property or its sale proceeds remaining at the death of the surviving spouse is to vest by operation of law in the child at that time. The child predeceased the surviving spouse. In this case, the surviving spouse's power to consume the corpus is unrestricted, and the exercise of the power could entirely exhaust the remainder interest during the life of the spouse. Consequently, the remainder interest that is includible in the child's estate is not considered an ordinary remainder interest for purposes of this paragraph and may not be valued actuarially under this section.

(3) *Mortality component.*—(i) *Terminal illness.*—Except as provided in paragraph (b)(3)(ii) of this section, the mortality component prescribed under section 7520 may not be used to determine the present value of an annuity, income interest, remainder interest, or reversionary interest if an individual who is a measuring life is terminally ill at the time of the decedent's death. For purposes of this paragraph (b)(3), an individual who is known to have an incurable illness or other deteriorating physical condition is considered terminally ill if there is at least a 50 percent probability that the individual will die within 1 year. However, if the individual survives for eighteen months or longer after the date of the decedent's death, that individual shall be presumed to have not been terminally ill at the date of death unless the contrary is established by clear and convincing evidence.

(ii) *Terminal illness exceptions.*—In the case of the allowance of the credit for tax on a prior transfer under section 2013, if a final determination of the federal estate tax liability of the transferor's estate has been made under circumstances that required valuation of the life interest received by the transferee, the value of the property transferred, for purposes of the credit allowable to the transferee's estate, shall be the value determined previously in the transferor's estate. Otherwise, for purposes of section 2013, the provisions of paragraph (b)(3)(i) of this section shall govern in valuing the property transferred. The value of a decedent's reversionary interest under sections 2037(b) and 2042(2) shall be determined without regard to the physical condition, immediately before the decedent's death, of the individual who is the measuring life.

(iii) *Death resulting from common accidents.*—The mortality component prescribed under section 7520 may not be used to determine the present value of an annuity, income interest, remainder interest, or reversionary interest if the decedent, and the individual who is the measuring life, die as a result of a common accident or other occurrence.

(4) *Examples.*—The provisions of paragraph (b)(3) of this section are illustrated by the following examples:

Example 1. Terminal illness. The decedent bequeaths $1,000,000 to a trust under the terms of which the trustee is to pay $103,000 per year to a charitable organization during the life of the decedent's child. Upon the death of the child, the remainder in the trust is to be distributed to the decedent's grandchild. The child, who is age 60, has been diagnosed with an incurable illness, and there is at least a 50 percent probability of the child dying within 1 year. Assuming the presumption provided for in paragraph (b)(3)(i) of this section does not apply, the standard life annuity factor for a person age 60 may not be used to determine the present value of the charitable organization's annuity interest because there is at least a 50 percent probability that the child, who is the measuring life, will die within 1 year. Instead, a special section 7520 annuity factor must be computed that takes into account the projection of the child's actual life expectancy.

Example 2. Deaths resulting from common accidents, etc. The decedent's will establishes a trust to pay income to the decedent's surviving spouse for life. The will provides that, upon the spouse's death or, if the spouse fails to survive the decedent, upon the decedent's death the trust property is to pass to the decedent's children. The decedent and the decedent's spouse die simultaneously in an accident under circumstances in which it was impossible to determine who survived the other. Even if the terms of the will and applicable state law presume that the decedent died first with the result that the property interest is considered to have passed in trust for the benefit of the spouse for life, after which the remainder is to be distributed to the decedent's children, the spouse's life income interest may not be valued by use of the mortality component described under section 7520. The result would be the same even if it was established that the spouse survived the decedent.

(5) *Additional limitations.*—Section 7520 does not apply to the extent as may otherwise be provided by the Commissioner.

(c) *Effective date.*—Section § 20.7520-3(a) is effective as of May 1, 1989. The provisions of paragraph (b) of this section are effective with respect to estates of decedents dying after December 13, 1995. [Reg. § 20.7520-3.]

☐ [*T.D.* 8540, 6-9-94. *Amended by T.D.* 8630, 12-12-95.]

[Reg. § 25.7520-3]

§ 25.7520-3. Limitation on the application of section 7520.—(a) *Internal Revenue Code sections to which section 7520 does not apply.*—Section 7520 of the Internal Revenue Code does not apply for purposes of—

(1) Part I, subchapter D of subtitle A (section 401 et. seq.), relating to the income tax treatment of certain qualified plans. (However, section 7520 does apply to the estate and gift tax

treatment of certain qualified plans and for purposes of determining excess accumulations under section 4980A);

(2) Sections 72 and 101(b), relating to the income taxation of life insurance, endowment, and annuity contracts, unless otherwise provided for in the regulations under sections 72, 101, and 1011 (see, particularly, §§ 1.101-2(e)(1)(iii)(b)(2), and 1.1011-2(c), *Example* 8);

(3) Sections 83 and 451, unless otherwise provided for in the regulations under those sections;

(4) Section 457, relating to the valuation of deferred compensation, unless otherwise provided for in the regulations under section 457;

(5) Sections 3121(v) and 3306(r), relating to the valuation of deferred amounts, unless otherwise provided for in the regulations under those sections;

(6) Section 6058, relating to valuation statements evidencing compliance with qualified plan requirements, unless otherwise provided for in the regulations under section 6058;

(7) Section 7872, relating to income and gift taxation of interest-free loans and loans with below-market interest rates, unless otherwise provided for in the regulations under section 7872; or

(8) Section 2702(a)(2)(A), relating to the value of a nonqualified retained interest upon a transfer of an interest in trust to or for the benefit of a member of the transferor's family; and

(9) Any other section of the Internal Revenue Code to the extent provided by the Internal Revenue Service in revenue rulings or revenue procedures. (See §§ 601.201 and 601.601 of this chapter).

(b) *Other limitations on the application of section 7520.*—(1) *In general.*—(i) *Ordinary beneficial interests.*—For purposes of this section:

(A) An *ordinary annuity interest* is the right to receive a fixed dollar amount at the end of each year during one or more measuring lives or for some other defined period. A standard section 7520 annuity factor for an ordinary annuity interest represents the present worth of the right to receive $1.00 per year for a defined period, using the interest rate prescribed under section 7520 for the appropriate month. If an annuity interest is payable more often than annually or is payable at the beginning of each period, a special adjustment must be made in any computation with a standard section 7520 annuity factor.

(B) An *ordinary income interest* is the right to receive the income from or the use of property during one or more measuring lives or for some other defined period. A standard section 7520 income factor for an ordinary income interest represents the present worth of the right to receive the use of $1.00 for a defined period, using the interest rate prescribed under section 7520 for the appropriate month. However, in the case of certain gifts made after October 8, 1990, if

the donor does not retain a qualified annuity, unitrust, or reversionary interest, the value of any interest retained by the donor is considered to be zero if the remainder beneficiary is a member of the donor's family. See § 25.2702-2.

(C) An *ordinary remainder or reversionary interest* is the right to receive an interest in property at the end of one or more measuring lives or some other defined period. A standard section 7520 remainder factor for an ordinary remainder or reversionary interest represents the present worth of the right to receive $1.00 at the end of a defined period, using the interest rate prescribed under section 7520 for the appropriate month.

(ii) *Certain restricted beneficial interests.*—A *restricted beneficial interest* is an annuity, income, remainder, or reversionary interest that is subject to any contingency, power, or other restriction, whether the restriction is provided for by the terms of the trust, will, or other governing instrument or is caused by other circumstances. In general, a standard section 7520 annuity, income, or remainder factor may not be used to value a restricted beneficial interest. However, a special section 7520 annuity, income, or remainder factor may be used to value a restricted beneficial interest under some circumstances. See paragraphs (b)(2)(v) *Example 5* and (b)(4) of this section, which illustrate situations in which special section 7520 actuarial factors are needed to take into account limitations on beneficial interests. See § 25.7520-1(c) for requesting a special factor from the Internal Revenue Service.

(iii) *Other beneficial interests.*—If, under the provisions of this paragraph (b), the interest rate and mortality components prescribed under section 7520 are not applicable in determining the value of any annuity, income, remainder, or reversionary interest, the actual fair market value of the interest (determined without regard to section 7520) is based on all of the facts and circumstances if and to the extent permitted by the Internal Revenue Code provision applicable to the property interest.

(2) *Provisions of governing instrument and other limitations on source of payment.*—(i) *Annuities.*—A standard section 7520 annuity factor may not be used to determine the present value of an annuity for a specified term of years or the life of one or more individuals unless the effect of the trust, will, or other governing instrument is to ensure that the annuity will be paid for the entire defined period. In the case of an annuity payable from a trust or other limited fund, the annuity is not considered payable for the entire defined period if, considering the applicable section 7520 interest rate on the valuation date of the transfer, the annuity is expected to exhaust the fund before the last possible annuity payment is made in full. For this purpose, it must be assumed that it is possible for each measuring life to survive until age 110. For example, for a fixed annuity payable annually at the end of each year, if the amount of the annuity payment (expressed as a percentage of the

initial corpus) is less than or equal to the applicable section 7520 interest rate at the date of the transfer, the corpus is assumed to be sufficient to make all payments. If the percentage exceeds the applicable section 7520 interest rate and the annuity is for a definite term of years, multiply the annual annuity amount by the Table B term certain annuity factor, as described in § 25.7520-1(c)(1), for the number of years of the defined period. If the percentage exceeds the applicable section 7520 interest rate and the annuity is payable for the life of one or more individuals, multiply the annual annuity amount by the Table B annuity factor for 110 years minus the age of the youngest individual. If the result exceeds the limited fund, the annuity may exhaust the fund, and it will be necessary to calculate a special section 7520 annuity factor that takes into account the exhaustion of the trust or fund. This computation would be modified, if appropriate, to take into account annuities with different payment terms.

(ii) *Income and similar interests.*— (A) *Beneficial enjoyment.*—A standard section 7520 income factor for an ordinary income interest is not to be used to determine the present value of an income or similar interest in trust for a term of years or for the life of one or more individuals unless the effect of the trust, will, or other governing instrument is to provide the income beneficiary with that degree of beneficial enjoyment of the property during the term of the income interest that the principles of the law of trusts accord to a person who is unqualifiedly designated as the income beneficiary of a trust for a similar period of time. This degree of beneficial enjoyment is provided only if it was the transferor's intent, as manifested by the provisions of the governing instrument and the surrounding circumstances, that the trust provide an income interest for the income beneficiary during the specified period of time that is consistent with the value of the trust corpus and with its preservation. In determining whether a trust arrangement evidences that intention, the treatment required or permitted with respect to individual items must be considered in relation to the entire system provided for in the administration of the subject trust. Similarly, in determining the present value of the right to use tangible property (whether or not in trust) for one or more measuring lives or for some other specified period of time, the interest rate component prescribed under section 7520 and § 1.7520-1 of this chapter may not be used unless, during the specified period, the effect of the trust, will or other governing instrument is to provide the beneficiary with that degree of use, possession, and enjoyment of the property during the term of interest that applicable state law accords to a person who is unqualifiedly designated as a life tenant or term holder for a similar period of time.

(B) *Diversions of income and corpus.*—A standard section 7520 income factor for an ordinary income interest may not be used to value an income interest or similar interest in property for a term of years, or for one or more measuring lives, if—

(1) The trust, will, or other governing instrument requires or permits the beneficiary's income or other enjoyment to be withheld, diverted, or accumulated for another person's benefit without the consent of the income beneficiary; or

(2) The governing instrument requires or permits trust corpus to be withdrawn from the trust for another person's benefit without the consent of the income beneficiary during the income beneficiary's term of enjoyment and without accountability to the income beneficiary for such diversion.

(iii) *Remainder and reversionary interests.*— A standard section 7520 remainder interest factor for an ordinary remainder or reversionary interest may not be used to determine the present value of a remainder or reversionary interest (whether in trust or otherwise) unless, consistent with the preservation and protection that the law of trusts would provide for a person who is unqualifiedly designated as the remainder beneficiary of a trust for a similar duration, the effect of the administrative and dispositive provisions for the interest or interests that precede the remainder or reversionary interest is to assure that the property will be adequately preserved and protected (e.g., from erosion, invasion, depletion, or damage) until the remainder or reversionary interest takes effect in possession and enjoyment. This degree of preservation and protection is provided only if it was the transferor's intent, as manifested by the provisions of the arrangement and the surrounding circumstances, that the entire disposition provide the remainder or reversionary beneficiary with an undiminished interest in the property transferred at the time of the termination of the prior interest.

(iv) *Pooled income fund interests.*—In general, pooled income funds are created and administered to achieve a special rate of return. A beneficial interest in a pooled income fund is not ordinarily valued using a standard section 7520 income or remainder interest factor. The present value of a beneficial interest in a pooled income fund is determined according to rules and special remainder factors prescribed in § 1.642(c)-6 of this chapter and, when applicable, the rules set forth under paragraph (b)(3) of this section if the individual who is the measuring life is terminally ill at the time of the transfer.

(v) *Examples.*—The provisions of this paragraph (b)(2) are illustrated by the following examples:

Example 1. Unproductive property. The donor transfers corporation stock to a trust under the terms of which all of the trust income is payable to A for life. Considering the applicable federal rate under section 7520 and the appropriate life estate factor for a person A's age, the value of A's income interest, if valued under this section, would be $10,000. After A's death, the trust is to terminate and the trust property is to be distributed to B. The trust specifically authorizes, but does not require, the trustee to retain the shares of stock. The corporation has paid no dividends on this stock during the past 5 years, and there is no indication that this policy will change in the near future. Under applicable state law, the corporation is considered to be a sound investment that satisfies fiduciary standards. The facts and circumstances, including applicable state law, indicate that the income beneficiary would not have the legal right to compel the trustee to make the trust corpus productive in conformity with the requirements for a lifetime trust income interest under applicable local law. Therefore, the life income interest in this case is considered nonproductive. Consequently, A's income interest may not be valued actuarially under this section.

Example 2. Beneficiary's right to make trust productive. The facts are the same as in *Example 1*, except that the trustee is not specifically authorized to retain the shares of corporation stock. Further, the terms of the trust specifically provide that the life income beneficiary may require the trustee to make the trust corpus productive consistent with income yield standards for trusts under applicable state law. Under that law, the minimum rate of income that a productive trust may produce is substantially below the section 7520 interest rate on the valuation date. In this case, because A, the income beneficiary, has the right to compel the trustee to make the trust productive for purposes of applicable local law during A's lifetime, the income interest is considered an ordinary income interest for purposes of this paragraph, and the standard section 7520 life income factor may be used to determine the value of A's income interest. However, in the case of gifts made after October 8, 1990, if the donor was the life income beneficiary, the value of the income interest would be considered to be zero in this situation. See § 25.2702-2.

Example 3. Annuity trust funded with unproductive property. The donor, who is age 60, transfers corporation stock worth $1,000,000 to a trust. The trust will pay a 6 percent ($60,000 per year) annuity in cash or other property to the donor for 10 years or until the donor's prior death. Upon the termination of the trust, the trust property is to be distributed to the donor's child. The section 7520 rate for the month of the transfer is 8.2 percent. The corporation has paid no dividends on the stock during the past 5 years, and

there is no indication that this policy will change in the near future. Under applicable state law, the corporation is considered to be a sound investment that satisfies fiduciary standards. Therefore, the trust's sole investment in this corporation is not expected to adversely affect the interest of either the annuity beneficiary or the remainder beneficiary. Considering the 6 percent annuity payout rate and the 8.2 percent section 7520 interest rate, the trust corpus is considered sufficient to pay this annuity for the entire 10-year term of the trust, or even indefinitely. The trust specifically authorizes, but does not require, the trustee to retain the shares of stock. Although it appears that neither beneficiary would be able to compel the trustee to make the trust corpus produce investment income, the annuity interest in this case is considered to be an ordinary annuity interest, and a section 7520 annuity factor may be used to determine the present value of the annuity. In this case, the section 7520 annuity factor would represent the right to receive $1.00 per year for a term of 10 years or the prior death of a person age 60.

Example 4. Unitrust funded with unproductive property. The facts are the same as in *Example 3*, except that the donor has retained a unitrust interest equal to 7 percent of the value of the trust property, valued as of the beginning of each year. Although the trust corpus is nonincome-producing, the present value of the donor's retained unitrust interest may be determined by using the section 7520 unitrust factor for a term of years or a prior death.

Example 5. Eroding corpus in an annuity trust. (i) The donor, who is age 60 and in normal health, transfers property worth $1,000,000 to a trust on or after May 1, 2009, but before 2019. The trust will pay a 10 percent ($100,000 per year) annuity to a charitable organization for the life of the donor, payable annually at the end of each period, and the remainder then will be distributed to the donor's child. The section 7520 rate for the month of the transfer is 6.8 percent. First, it is necessary to determine whether the annuity may exhaust the corpus before all annuity payments are made. Because it is assumed that any measuring life may survive until age 110, any life annuity could require payments until the measuring life reaches age 110. Based on a section 7520 interest rate of 6.8 percent, the determination of whether the annuity may exhaust the corpus before the termination of the annuity interest is made as follows:

Age to which life annuity may continue	110
less: Age of measuring life at date of transfer	60
Number of years annuity may continue	50
Annual annuity payment	$100,000.00
times: Annuity factor for 50 years derived from Table B (1 - .037277 / .068) . . .	14.1577
Present value of term certain annuity	$1,415,770.00

(ii) Because the present value of an annuity for a term of 50 years exceeds the corpus, the annuity may exhaust the trust before all payments are made. Consequently, the annuity must

be valued as an annuity payable for a term of years or until the prior death of the annuitant, with the term of years determined by when the fund will be exhausted by the annuity payments.

(iii) The annuity factor for a term of years at 6.8 percent is derived by subtracting the applicable remainder factor in Table B (see § 20.2031-7(d)(6)) from 1.000000 and then dividing the result by .068. An annuity of $100,000 payable at the end of each year for a period that has an annuity factor of 10.0 would have a present value exactly equal to the principal available to pay the annuity over the term. The annuity factor for 17 years is 9.8999 and the annuity factor for 18 years is 10.2059. Thus, it is determined that the $1,000,000 initial transfer will be sufficient to make 17 annual payments of $100,000, but not to make the entire 18th payment. The present value of an annuity of $100,000 payable at the end of each year for 17 years is $100,000 times 9.8999 or $989,990. The remaining amount is $10,010.00. Of the initial corpus amount, $10,010.00 is not needed to make payments for 17 years, so this amount, as accumulated for 18 years, will be available for the final payment. The 18-year accumulation factor is $(1 + 0.068)^{18}$ or 3.268004, so the amount available in 18 years is $10,010.00 times 3.268004 or $32,712.72. Therefore, for purposes of analysis, the annuity payments are considered to be composed of two distinct annuity components. The two annuity components taken together must equal the total annual amount of $100,000. The first annuity component is the exact amount that the trust will have available for the final payment, $32,712.72. The second annuity component then must be $100,000 minus $32,712.72, or $67,287.28. Specifically, the initial corpus will be able to make payments of $67,287.28 per year for 17 years plus payments of $32,712.72 per year for 18 years. The total annuity is valued by adding the value of the two separate annuity components.

(iv) Based on Table H of Publication 1457, Actuarial Valuations Version 3A, which may be obtained from the IRS Internet site, the present value of an annuity of $67,287.28 per year payable for 17 years or until the prior death of a person aged 60 is $597,013.12 ($67,287.28 X 8.8726). The present value of an annuity of $32,712.72 per year payable for 18 years or until the prior death of a person aged 60 is $296,887.56 ($32,712.72 X 9.0756). Thus, the present value of the charitable annuity interest is $893,900.68 ($597,013.12 + $296,887.56).

(3) *Mortality component.*—The mortality component prescribed under section 7520 may not be used to determine the present value of an annuity, income interest, remainder interest, or reversionary interest if an individual who is a measuring life dies or is terminally ill at the time the gift is completed. For purposes of this paragraph (b)(3), an individual who is known to have an incurable illness or other deteriorating physical condition is considered terminally ill if there is at least a 50 percent probability that the individual will die within 1 year. However, if the individual survives for eighteen months or longer after the date the gift is completed, that individual shall be presumed to have not been terminally ill at the date the gift was completed unless the contrary is established by clear and convincing evidence.

(4) *Example.*—The provisions of paragraph (b)(3) of this section are illustrated by the following example:

Example. Terminal illness. The donor transfers property worth $1,000,000 to a child on or after May 1, 2009 but before 2019, in exchange for the child's promise to pay the donor $80,000 per year for the donor's life, payable annually at the end of each period. The donor is age 75 but has been diagnosed with an incurable illness and has at least a 50 percent probability of dying within 1 year. The section 7520 interest rate for the month of the transfer is 7.6 percent, and the standard annuity factor at that interest rate for a person age 75 in normal health is 6.6493 (1 - .49465 / .076). Thus, if the donor were not terminally ill, the present value of the annuity would be $531,944.00 ($80,000 X 6.6493). Assuming the presumption provided in paragraph (b)(3) of this section does not apply, because there is at least a 50 percent probability that the donor will die within 1 year, the standard section 7520 annuity factor may not be used to determine the present value of the donor's annuity interest. Instead, a special section 7520 annuity factor must be computed that takes into account the projection of the donor's actual life expectancy.

(5) *Additional limitations.*—Section 7520 does not apply to the extent as may otherwise be provided by the Commissioner.

(c) *Effective/applicability dates.*—Section 25.7520-3(a) is effective as of May 1, 1989. The provisions of paragraph (b) of this section, except *Example 5* in paragraph (b)(2)(v) and paragraph (b)(4), are effective with respect to gifts made after December 13, 1995. *Example 5* in paragraph (b)(2)(v) and paragraph (b)(4) are effective with respect to gifts made on or after May 1, 2009. [Reg. § 25.7520-3.]

☐ [*T.D.* 8540, 6-9-94. *Amended by T.D.* 8630, 12-12-95; *T.D.* 8819, 4-29-99; *T.D.* 8886, 6-9-2000; *T.D.* 9448, 5-1-2009 *and T.D.* 9540, 8-9-2011.]

[Reg. § 1.7520-4]

§ 1.7520-4. Transitional rules.—(a) *Reliance.*— If the valuation date is after April 30, 1989, and before June 10, 1994, a taxpayer can rely on Notice 89-24, 1989-1 C.B. 660, or Notice 89-60, 1989-1 C.B. 700 (See § 601.601(d)(2)(ii)(b) of this chapter), in valuing the transferred interest.

(b) *Effective date.*—This section is effective as of May 1, 1989. [Reg. § 1.7520-4.]

☐ [*T.D.* 8540, 6-9-94.]

[Reg. § 20.7520-4]

§ 20.7520-4. Transitional rules.— (a) *Reliance.*—If the valuation date is after April 30, 1989, and before June 10, 1994, an executor can rely on Notice 89-24, 1989-1 C.B. 660, or Notice 89-60, 1989-1 C.B. 700 (See

§ 601.601(d)(2)(ii)(b) of this chapter), in valuing the transferred interest.

(b) *Effective date.*—This section is effective as of May 1, 1989. [Reg. § 20.7520-4.]

☐ [*T.D.* 8540, 6-9-94.]

[Reg. § 25.7520-4]

§ **25.7520-4. Transitional rules.**—(a) *Reliance.*—If the valuation date is after April 30, 1989, and before June 10, 1994, a donor can rely on Notice 89-24, 1989-1 C.B. 660, or Notice 89-60, 1989-1 C.B. 700 (See § 601.601(d)(2)(ii)(b) of this chapter), in valuing the transferred interest.

(b) *Transfers in 1989.*—If a donor transferred an interest in property by gift after December 31, 1988, and before May 1, 1989, retaining an interest in the same property and, after April 30, 1989, and before January 1, 1990, transferred the retained interest in the property, the donor may, at the donor's option, value the transfer of the retained interest under either § 25.2512-5(d) or § 25.2512-5A(d).

(c) *Effective date.*—This section is effective as of May 1, 1989. [Reg. § 25.7520-4.]

☐ [*T.D.* 8540, 6-9-94.]

Discovery of Liability and Enforcement of Title

EXAMINATION AND INSPECTION

See p. 20,601 for regulations not amended to reflect law changes

[Reg. § 301.7601-1]

§ **301.7601-1. Canvass of districts for taxable persons and objects.**—Each district director shall, to the extent he deems it practicable, cause officers or employees under his supervision and control to proceed, from time to time, through his district and inquire after and concerning all persons therein who may be liable to pay any internal revenue tax, and all persons owning or having the care and management of any objects with respect to which any tax is imposed. [Reg. § 301.7601-1.]

☐ [*T.D.* 6421, 10-23-59. *Amended by T.D.* 7188, 6-28-72 *and T.D.* 7297, 12-18-73.]

⋙→ *Caution: The Treasury Department has identified Reg. § 301.7602-1, as amended by T.D. 9778, as a significant tax regulation that imposes an undue financial burden on U.S. taxpayers and/or adds undue complexity to the federal tax laws, pursuant to Executive Order 13789 (issued April 21, 2017) (Notice 2017-38, I.R.B. 2017-30). In a subsequent report, issued October 4, 2017, Treasury recommended planned actions that would reduce the burden of these regulations.*

[Reg. § 301.7602-1]

§ **301.7602-1. Examination of books and witnesses.**—(a) *In general.*—For the purpose of ascertaining the correctness of any return, making a return where none has been made, determining the liability of any person for any internal revenue tax (including any interest, additional amount, addition to the tax, or civil penalty) or the liability at law or in equity of any transferee or fiduciary of any person in respect of any internal revenue tax, collecting any such liability or inquiring into any offense connected with the administration or enforcement of the internal revenue laws, any authorized officer or employee of the Internal Revenue Service may examine any books, papers, records or other data which may be relevant or material to such inquiry; and take such testimony of the person concerned, under oath, as may be relevant to such inquiry.

(b) *Summons.*—(1) *In general.*—For the purposes described in § 301.7602-1(a), the Commissioner is authorized to summon the person liable for tax or required to perform the act, or any officer or employee of such person or any person having possession, custody, or care of books of accounts containing entries relating to the business of the person liable for tax or required to perform the act, or any other person deemed proper, to appear before one or more officers or employees of the Internal Revenue Service at a time and place named in the summons and to produce such books, papers, records, or other data, and to give such testimony, under oath, as may be relevant or material to such inquiry; and take such testimony of the person concerned, under oath, as may be relevant or material to such inquiry. This summons power may be used in an investigation of either civil or criminal tax-related liability. The Commissioner may designate one or more officers or employees of the IRS as the individuals before whom a person summoned pursuant to section 6420(e)(2), 6421(g)(2), 6427(j)(2), or 7602 shall appear. Any such officer or employee is authorized to take testimony under oath of the person summoned and to receive and examine books, papers, records, or other data produced in compliance with the summons.

(2) *Officer or employee of the IRS.*—For purposes of this paragraph (b), officer or employee of the IRS means all officers and employees of the United States, who are engaged in the administration and enforcement of the internal revenue laws or any other laws administered by the IRS, and who are appointed or employed by, or subject to the directions, instructions, or orders of the Secretary of the Treasury or the Secretary's delegate. An officer or employee of the IRS, for purposes of this paragraph (b), shall include an officer or employee of the Office of Chief Counsel.

(3) *Participation of a person described in section 6103(n).*—For purposes of this paragraph (b), a person authorized to receive returns or return information under section 6103(n) and §301.6103(n)-1(a) of the regulations may receive and review books, papers, records, or other data produced in compliance with a summons and, in the presence and under the guidance of an IRS officer or employee, participate fully in the interview of a witness summoned by the IRS to provide testimony under oath. Fully participating in an interview includes, but is not limited to, receipt, review, and use of summoned books, papers, records, or other data; being present during summons interviews; questioning the person providing testimony under oath; and asking a summoned person's representative to clarify an objection or assertion of privilege.

(c) *Proscription on issuing of administrative summons when a Justice Department referral is in effect.*—(1) *In general.*—The Commissioner may neither issue a summons under this title nor initiate a proceeding to enforce a previously issued summons by way of section 7604 with respect to any person whose tax liability is in issue, if a Justice Department referral is in effect with respect to that person for that liability.

(2) *Justice Department referral in effect.*—A Justice Department referral is in effect with respect to any person when:

(i) The Secretary recommends, within the meaning of this paragraph, that the Attorney General either commence a grand jury investigation of or criminal prosecution of such person for any alleged offense connected with the administration or enforcement of the internal revenue laws, or

(ii) The Attorney General (or Deputy Attorney General or Assistant Attorney General) under section 6103(h)(3)(B) requests in writing that the Secretary disclose a return of, or return information relating to, such person. The request must set forth that the need for disclosure is for the purpose of a grand jury investigation of or potential or pending criminal prosecution of such person for any alleged offense connected with the administration or enforcement of the internal revenue laws.

The referral is effective at the time the document recommending criminal prosecution or grand jury investigation is signed by the Secretary or upon the Secretary's receipt of the section 6103(h)(3)(B) request.

(3) *Cessation of Justice Department referral.*—A Justice Department referral ceases to be in effect with respect to a person:

(i) When the Secretary receives written notification from the Attorney General that the Justice Department:

(A) Will not prosecute that person for any offense connected with the administration or enforcement of the internal revenue laws that gave rise to the referral under paragraph (2)(i) of this section, or

(B) Will not authorize a grand jury investigation of that person with respect to such offense, or

(C) Will discontinue any grand jury investigation of that person with respect to such offense;

(ii) When a final disposition with respect to a criminal proceeding brought against that person has been made; or

(iii) When the Secretary receives written notification from the Attorney General, Deputy Attorney General, or an Assistant Attorney General, that the Justice Department will not prosecute such person for any offense connected with the administration or enforcement of the internal revenue laws, based upon a previous request for disclosure under section 6103(h)(3)(B).

(4) *Taxable years and taxes imposed by separate chapters of the Code treated separately.*—(i) *In general.*—For purposes of this section, each taxable period (or, if there is no taxable period, each taxable event) and each tax imposed by a separate chapter of the Code is treated separately.

(ii) *Examples.*—The following examples illustrate the application of this paragraph (c)(4):

Example (1). A Justice Department referral is in effect for D's criminal evasion of income tax for the taxable year 1979. The Commissioner may issue a summons respecting D's 1980 criminal and/or civil tax liability. The Commissioner may not issue a summons respecting D's 1979 income tax liability.

Example (2). A referral has been made to the Department of Justice for the criminal prosecution of F with regard to F's income tax liability for the taxable year 1978. The Commissioner may issue a summons respecting F's gift tax liability for the taxable year 1978.

Example (3). A referral has been made to the Department of Justice for a grand jury investigation respecting G's 1980 income tax liability. The Commissioner may issue a summons related to an investigation of G's liability for Federal Insurance Contribution Act (FICA) taxes for the taxable year 1980.

Example (4). A referral has been made to the Department of Justice respecting J's criminal evasion of windfall profit tax for all quarters of the calendar year 1982. The Commissioner may issue a summons respecting J's liability for highway motor vehicle use tax covering the same periods.

Example (5). A referral has been made to the Department of Justice for a grand jury investigation respecting L's 1983 income tax liability. The Commissioner may issue a summons related to the investigation of L's liability under sections 6700 (abusive tax shelter promoter penalty) and 7408 of the Code for his conduct during 1983.

(d) *Applicability date.*—This section is applicable after September 3, 1982, except for paragraphs (b)(1) and (2) of this section which are applicable on and after April 1, 2005 and paragraph (b)(3) of this section which applies to summons interviews conducted on or after July

14, 2016. For rules under paragraphs (b)(1) and (2) that are applicable to summonses issued on or after September 10, 2002 or under paragraph (b)(3) that are applicable to summons interviews conducted on or after June 18, 2014, see 26 CFR 301.7602-1T (revised as of April 1, 2016). [Reg. § 301.7602-1.]

☐ [*T.D. 6421*, 10-23-59. *Amended by T.D. 6498*, 10-24-60, *T.D. 7188*, 6-28-72, *T.D. 7297*, 12-18-73; *T.D. 8091*, 6-24-86; *T.D. 9015*, 9-9-2002, *T.D. 9195*, 3-31-2005 *and T.D. 9778*, 7-12-2016.]

[Reg. § 301.7602-2]

§ 301.7602-2. Third party contacts.—(a) *In general.*—Subject to the exceptions in paragraph (f) of this section, no officer or employee of the Internal Revenue Service (IRS) may contact any person other than the taxpayer with respect to the determination or collection of such taxpayer's tax liability without giving the taxpayer reasonable notice in advance that such contacts may be made. A record of persons so contacted must be made and given to the taxpayer upon the taxpayer's request.

(b) *Third-party contact defined.*—Contacts subject to section 7602(c) and this regulation shall be called "third-party contacts." A third-party contact is a communication which—

(1) Is initiated by an IRS employee;

(2) Is made to a person other than the taxpayer;

(3) Is made with respect to the determination or collection of the tax liability of such taxpayer;

(4) Discloses the identity of the taxpayer being investigated; and

(5) Discloses the association of the IRS employee with the IRS.

(c) *Elements of third-party contact explained.*— (1) *Initiation by an IRS employee.*— (i) *Explanation.*—(A) *Initiation.*—An IRS employee initiates a communication whenever it is the employee who first tries to communicate with a person other than the taxpayer. Returning unsolicited telephone calls or speaking with persons other than the taxpayer as part of an attempt to speak to the taxpayer are not initiations of third-party contacts.

(B) *IRS employee.*—For purposes of this section, an IRS employee includes all officers and employees of the IRS, the Chief Counsel of the IRS and the National Taxpayer Advocate, as well as a person described in section 6103(n), an officer or employee of such person, or a person who is subject to disclosure restrictions pursuant to a written agreement in connection with the solicitation of an agreement described in section 6103(n) and its implementing regulations. No inference about the employment or contractual relationship of such other persons with the IRS may be drawn from this regulation for any purpose other than the requirements of section 7602(c).

(ii) *Examples.*—The following examples illustrate this paragraph (c)(1):

Example 1. An IRS employee receives a message to return an unsolicited call. The employee returns the call and speaks with a person who reports information about a taxpayer who is not meeting his tax responsibilities. Later, the employee makes a second call to the person and asks for more information. The first call is not a contact initiated by an IRS employee. Just because the employee must return the call does not change the fact that it is the other person, and not the employee, who initiated the contact. The second call, however, is initiated by the employee and so meets the first element.

Example 2. An IRS employee wants to hire an appraiser to help determine the value of a taxpayer's oil and gas business. At the initial interview, the appraiser signs an agreement that prohibits him from disclosing return information of the taxpayer except as allowed by the agreement. Once hired, the appraiser initiates a contact by calling an industry expert in Houston and discusses the taxpayer's business. The IRS employee's contact with the appraiser does not meet the first element of a third-party contact because the appraiser is treated, for section 7602(c) purposes only, as an employee of the IRS. For the same reason, however, the appraiser's call to the industry expert does meet the first element of a third-party contact.

Example 3. A revenue agent trying to contact the taxpayer to discuss the taxpayer's pending examination twice calls the taxpayer's place of business. The first call is answered by a receptionist who states that the taxpayer is not available. The IRS employee leaves a message with the receptionist stating only his name and telephone number, and asks that the taxpayer call him. The second call is answered by the office answering machine, on which the IRS employee leaves the same message. Neither of these phone calls meets the first element of a third-party contact because the IRS employee is trying to initiate a communication with the taxpayer and not a person other than the taxpayer. The fact that the IRS employee must either speak with a third party (the receptionist) or leave a message on the answering machine, which may be heard by a third party, does not mean that the employee is initiating a communication with a person other than the taxpayer. Both the receptionist and the answering machine are only intermediaries in the process of reaching the taxpayer.

(2) *Person other than the taxpayer.*— (i) *Explanation.*—The phrases "person other than the taxpayer" and "third party" are used interchangeably in this section, and do not include—

(A) An officer or employee of the IRS, as defined in paragraph (c)(1)(i)(B) of this section, acting within the scope of his or her employment;

(B) Any computer database or web site regardless of where located and by whom maintained, including databases or web sites maintained on the Internet or in county courthouses, libraries, or any other real or virtual site; or

(C) A current employee, officer, or fiduciary of a taxpayer when acting within the scope of his or her employment or relationship with the taxpayer. Such employee, officer, or fiduciary shall be conclusively presumed to be acting within the scope of his or her employment or relationship during business hours on business premises.

(ii) *Examples.*—: The following examples illustrate this paragraph (c)(2):

Example 1. A revenue agent examining a taxpayer's return speaks with another revenue agent who has previously examined the same taxpayer about a recurring issue. The revenue agent has not contacted a "person other than the taxpayer" within the meaning of section 7602(c).

Example 2. A revenue agent examining a taxpayer's return speaks with one of the taxpayer's employees on business premises during business hours. The employee is conclusively presumed to be acting within the scope of his employment and is therefore not a "person other than the taxpayer" for section 7602(c) purposes.

Example 3. A revenue agent examining a corporate taxpayer's return uses a commercial online research service to research the corporate structure of the taxpayer. The revenue agent uses an IRS account, logs on with her IRS user name and password, and uses the name of the corporate taxpayer in her search terms. The revenue agent later explores several Internet web sites that may have information relevant to the examination. The searches on the commercial online research service and Internet web sites are not contacts with "persons other than the taxpayer."

(3) *With respect to the determination or collection of the tax liability of such taxpayer.*—(i) *Explanation.*—(A) *With respect to.*—A contact is "with respect to" the determination or collection of the tax liability of such taxpayer when made for the purpose of either determining or collecting a particular tax liability and when directly connected to that purpose. While a contact made for the purpose of determining a particular taxpayer's tax liability may also affect the tax liability of one or more other taxpayers, such contact is not for that reason alone a contact "with respect to" the determination or collection of those other taxpayers' tax liabilities. Contacts to determine the tax status of a pension plan under chapter 1, subchapter D (Deferred Compensation) of the Internal Revenue Code, are not "with respect to" the determination of plan participants' tax liabilities. Contacts to determine the tax status of a bond issue under chapter 1, subchapter B, Part IV (Tax Exemption Requirements for State and Local Bonds) of the Internal Revenue Code, are not "with respect to" the determination of the bondholders' tax liabilities. Contacts to determine the tax status of an organization under chapter 1, subchapter F (Exempt Organizations) of the Internal Revenue Code, are not "with respect to" the determination of the

contributors' liabilities, nor are any similar determinations "with respect to" any persons with similar relationships to the taxpayer whose tax liability is being determined or collected.

(B) *Determination or collection.*—A contact is with respect to the "determination or collection" of the tax liability of such taxpayer when made during the administrative determination or collection process. For purposes of this paragraph (c) only, the administrative determination or collection process may include any administrative action to ascertain the correctness of a return, make a return when none has been filed, or determine or collect the tax liability of any person as a transferee or fiduciary under chapter 71 of Title 26.

(C) *Tax liability.*—A *tax liability* means the liability for any tax imposed by Title 26 of the United States Code (including any interest, additional amount, addition to the tax, or penalty) and does not include the liability for any tax imposed by any other jurisdiction nor any liability imposed by other Federal statutes.

(D) *Such taxpayer.*—A contact is with respect to the determination or collection of the tax liability of "such taxpayer" when made while determining or collecting the tax liability of a particular, identified taxpayer. Contacts made during an investigation of a particular, identified taxpayer are third-party contacts only as to the particular, identified taxpayer under investigation and not as to any other taxpayer whose tax liabilities might be affected by such contacts.

(ii) *Examples.*—The following examples illustrate the operation of this paragraph (c)(3):

Example 1. As part of a compliance check on a return preparer, an IRS employee visits the preparer's office and reviews the preparer's client files to ensure that the proper forms and records have been created and maintained. This contact is not a third-party contact "with respect to" the preparer's clients because it is not for the purpose of determining the tax liability of the preparer's clients, even though the agent might discover information that would lead the agent to recommend an examination of one or more of the preparer's clients.

Example 2. A revenue agent is assigned to examine a taxpayer's return, which was prepared by a return preparer. As in all such examinations, the revenue agent asks the taxpayer routine questions about what information the taxpayer gave the preparer and what advice the preparer gave the taxpayer. As a result of the examination, the revenue agent recommends that the preparer be investigated for penalties under section 6694 or 6695. Neither the examination of the taxpayer's return nor the questions asked of the taxpayer are "with respect to" the determination of the preparer's tax liabilities within the meaning of section 7602(c) because the purpose of the contacts was to determine the taxpayer's tax liability, even though the agent discovered information that may result in a later investigation of the preparer.

Example 3. To help identify taxpayers in the florist industry who may not have filed proper returns, an IRS employee contacts a company that supplies equipment to florists and asks for a list of its customers in the past year in order to cross-check the list against filed returns. The employee later contacts the supplier for more information about one particular florist who the employee believes did not file a proper return. The first contact is not a contact with respect to the determination of the tax liability of "such taxpayer" because no particular taxpayer has been identified for investigation at the time the contact is made. The later contact, however, is with respect to the determination of the tax liability of "such taxpayer" because a particular taxpayer has been identified. The later contact is also "with respect to" the determination of that taxpayer's liability because, even though no examination has been opened on the taxpayer, the information sought could lead to an examination.

Example 4. A revenue officer, trying to collect the trust fund portion of unpaid employment taxes of a corporation, begins to investigate the liability of two corporate officers for the section 6672 Trust Fund Recovery Penalty (TFRP). The revenue officer obtains the signature cards for the corporation's bank accounts from the corporation's bank. The contact with the bank to obtain the signature cards is a contact with respect to the determination of the two identified corporate officers' tax liabilities because it is directly connected to the purpose of determining a tax liability of two identified taxpayers. It is not, however, a contact with respect to any other person not already under investigation for TFRP liability, even though the signature cards might identify other potentially liable persons.

Example 5. The IRS is asked to rule on whether a certain pension plan qualifies under section 401 so that contributions to the pension plan are excludable from the employees' incomes under section 402 and are also deductible from the employer's income under section 404. Contacts made with the plan sponsor (and with persons other than the plan sponsor) are not contacts "with respect to" the determination of the tax liabilities of the pension plan participants because the purpose of the contacts is to determine the status of the plan, even though that determination may affect the participants' tax liabilities.

Example 6(a). The IRS audits a TEFRA partnership at the partnership (entity) level pursuant to sections 6221 through 6233. The tax treatment of partnership items is at issue, but the respective tax liabilities of the partners may be affected by the results of the TEFRA partnership audit. With respect to the TEFRA partnership, contacts made with employees of the partnership acting within the scope of their duties or any partner are not section 7602(c) contacts because they are considered the equivalent of contacting the partnership. Contacts relating to the tax treatment of partnership items made with persons other than the employees of the partnership who are acting within the scope of their duties or the partners are section 7602(c) contacts with respect to the TEFRA partnership, and reasonable advance notice should be provided by sending the appropriate Letter 3164 to the partnership's tax matters partner (TMP). Individual partners who are merely affected by the partnership audit but who are not identified as subject to examination with respect to their individual tax liabilities need not be sent Letters 3164.

Example 6(b). In the course of an audit of a TEFRA partnership at the partnership (entity) level, the IRS intends to contact third parties regarding transactions between the TEFRA partnership and specific, identified partners. In addition to the partnership's TMP, the specific, identified partners should also be provided advance notice of any third-party contacts relating to such transactions.

(4) *Discloses the identity of the taxpayer being investigated.*—(i) *Explanation.*—An IRS employee discloses the taxpayer's identity whenever the employee knows or should know that the person being contacted can readily ascertain the taxpayer's identity from the information given by the employee.

(ii) *Examples.*—The following examples illustrate this paragraph (c)(4):

Example 1. A revenue agent seeking to value the taxpayer's condominium calls a real estate agent and asks for a market analysis of the taxpayer's condominium, giving the unit number of the taxpayer's condominium. The revenue agent has revealed the identity of the taxpayer, regardless of whether the revenue agent discloses the name of the taxpayer, because the real estate agent can readily ascertain the taxpayer's identity from the address given.

Example 2. A revenue officer seeking to value the taxpayer's condominium calls a real estate agent and, without identifying the taxpayer's unit, asks for the sales prices of similar units recently sold and listing prices of similar units currently on the market. The revenue officer has not revealed the identity of the taxpayer because the revenue officer has not given any information from which the real estate agent can readily ascertain the taxpayer's identity.

(5) *Discloses the association of the IRS employee with the IRS.*—An IRS employee discloses his association with the IRS whenever the employee knows or should know that the person being contacted can readily ascertain the association from the information given by the employee.

(d) *Pre-contact notice.*—(1) *In general.*—An officer or employee of the IRS may not make third-party contacts without providing reasonable notice in advance to the taxpayer that contacts may be made. The pre-contact notice may be given either orally or in writing. If written notice is given, it may be given in any manner that the IRS employee responsible for giving the notice reasonably believes will be received by the taxpayer in advance of the third-party contact. Written notice is deemed reasonable if it is—

(i) Mailed to the taxpayer's last known address;

(ii) Given in person;

(iii) Left at the taxpayer's dwelling or usual place of business; or

(iv) Actually received by the taxpayer.

(2) *Pre-contact notice not required.*—Pre-contact notice under this section need not be provided to a taxpayer for third-party contacts of which advance notice has otherwise been provided to the taxpayer pursuant to another statute, regulation or administrative procedure. For example, Collection Due Process notices sent to taxpayers pursuant to section 6330 and its regulations constitute reasonable advance notice that contacts with third parties may be made in order to effectuate a levy.

(e) *Post-contact reports.*—(1) *Requested reports.*—A taxpayer may request a record of persons contacted in any manner that the Commissioner reasonably permits. The Commissioner may set reasonable limits on how frequently taxpayer requests need be honored. The requested report may be mailed either to the taxpayer's last known address or such other address as the taxpayer specifies in the request.

(2) *Contents of record.*—(i) *In general.*—The record of persons contacted should contain information, if known to the IRS employee making the contact, which reasonably identifies the person contacted. Providing the name of the person contacted fully satisfies the requirements of this section, but this section does not require IRS employees to solicit identifying information from a person solely for the purpose of the post-contact report. The record need not contain any other information, such as the nature of the inquiry or the content of the third party's response. The record need not report multiple contacts made with the same person during a reporting period.

(ii) *Special rule for employees.*—For contacts with the employees, officers; or fiduciaries of any entity who are acting within the scope of their employment or relationship, it is sufficient to record the entity as the person contacted. A fiduciary, officer or employee shall be conclusively presumed to be acting within the scope of his employment or relationship during business hours on business premises. For purposes of this paragraph (e)(2)(ii), the term *entity* means any business (whether operated as a sole proprietorship, disregarded entity under §301.7701-2 of the regulations, or otherwise), trust, estate, partnership, association, company, corporation, or similar organization.

(3) *Post-contact record not required.*—A post-contact record under this section need not be made, or provided to a taxpayer, for third-party contacts of which the taxpayer has already been given a similar record pursuant to another statute, regulation, or administrative procedure.

(4) *Examples.*—The following examples illustrate this paragraph (e):

Example 1. An IRS employee trying to find a specific taxpayer's assets in order to collect unpaid taxes talks to the owner of a marina. The employee asks whether the taxpayer has a boat at the marina. The owner gives his name as John Doe. The employee may record the contact as being with John Doe and is not required by this regulation to collect or record any other identifying information.

Example 2. An IRS employee trying to find a specific taxpayer and his assets in order to collect unpaid taxes talks to a person at 502 Fernwood. The employee asks whether the taxpayer lives next door at 500 Fernwood, as well as where the taxpayer works, what kind of car the taxpayer drives and whether the camper parked in front of 500 Fernwood belongs to the taxpayer. The person does not disclose his name. The employee may record the contact as being with a person at 502 Fernwood. If the employee then makes the same inquiries of another person on the street in front of 500 Fernwood, and does not learn that person's name, the latter contact may be reported as being with a person on the street in front of 500 Fernwood.

Example 3. An IRS employee examining a return obtains loan documents from a bank where the taxpayer applied for a loan. After reviewing the documents, the employee talks with the loan officer at the bank who handled the application. The employee has contacted only one "person other than the taxpayer." The bank and not the loan officer is the "person other than the taxpayer" for section 7602(c) purposes. The contact with the loan officer is treated as a contact with the bank because the loan officer was an employee of the bank and was acting within the scope of her employment with the bank.

Example 4. An IRS employee issues a summons to a third party with respect to the determination of a taxpayer's liability and properly follows the procedures for such summonses under section 7609, which requires that a copy of the summons be given to the taxpayer. This third-party contact need not be maintained in a record of contacts available to the taxpayer because providing a copy of the third-party summons to the taxpayer pursuant to section 7609 satisfies the post-contact recording and reporting requirement of this section.

Example 5. An IRS employee serves a levy on a third party with respect to the collection of a taxpayer's liability. The employee provides the taxpayer with a copy of the notice of levy form that shows the identity of the third party. This third-party contact need not be maintained in a record of contacts available to the taxpayer because providing a copy of the notice of levy to the taxpayer satisfies the post-contact recording and reporting requirement of this section.

(f) *Exceptions.*—(1) *Authorized by taxpayer.*—(i) *Explanation.*—Section 7602(c) does not apply to contacts authorized by the taxpayer. A contact is "authorized" within the meaning of this section if—

Reg. §301.7602-2(f)(1)(i)

(A) The contact is with the taxpayer's authorized representative, that is, a person who is authorized to speak or act on behalf of the taxpayer, such as a person holding a power of attorney, a corporate officer, a personal representative, an executor or executrix, or an attorney representing the taxpayer; or

(B) The taxpayer or the taxpayer's authorized representative requests or approves the contact.

(ii) *No prevention or delay of contact.*—This section does not entitle any person to prevent or delay an IRS employee from contacting any individual or entity.

(2) *Jeopardy.*—(i) *Explanation.*—Section 7602(c) does not apply when the IRS employee making a contact has good cause to believe that providing the taxpayer with either a general pre-contact notice or a record of the specific person contacted may jeopardize the collection of any tax. For purposes of this section only, good cause includes a reasonable belief that providing the notice or record will lead to—

(A) Attempts by any person to conceal, remove, destroy, or alter records or assets that may be relevant to any tax examination or collection activity;

(B) Attempts by any person to prevent other persons, through intimidation, bribery, or collusion, from communicating any information that may be relevant to any tax examination or collection activity; or

(C) Attempts by any person to flee, or otherwise avoid testifying or producing records that may be relevant to any tax examination or collection activity.

(ii) *Record of contact.*—If the circumstances described in this paragraph (f)(2) exist, the IRS employee must still make a record of the person contacted, but the taxpayer need not be provided the record until it is no longer reasonable to believe that providing the record would cause the jeopardy described.

(3) *Reprisal.*—(i) *In general.*—Section 7602(c) does not apply when the IRS employee making a contact has good cause to believe that providing the taxpayer with either a general pre-contact notice or a specific record of the person being contacted may cause any person to harm any other person in any way, whether the harm is physical, economic, emotional or otherwise. A statement by the person contacted that harm may occur against any person is sufficient to constitute good cause for the IRS employee to believe that reprisal may occur. The IRS employee is not required to further question the contacted person about reprisal or otherwise make further inquiries regarding the statement.

(ii) *Examples.*—The following examples illustrate this paragraph (f)(3):

Example 1. An IRS employee seeking to collect unpaid taxes is told by the taxpayer that all the money in his and his brother's joint bank account belongs to the brother. The IRS employee contacts the brother to verify this information. The brother refuses to confirm or deny the taxpayer's statement. He states that he does not believe that reporting the contact to the taxpayer would result in harm to anyone but further states that he does not want his name reported to the taxpayer because it would appear that he gave information. This contact is not excepted from the statute merely because the brother asks that his name be left off the list of contacts.

Example 2. Assume the same facts as in *Example 1,* except that the brother states that he fears harm from the taxpayer should the taxpayer learn of the contact, even though the brother gave no information. This contact is excepted from the statute because the third party has expressed a fear of reprisal. The IRS employee is not required to make further inquiry into the nature of the brothers' relationship or otherwise question the brother's fear of reprisal.

Example 3. An IRS employee is examining a joint return of a husband and wife, who recently divorced. From reading the court divorce file, the IRS employee learns that the divorce was acrimonious and that the ex-husband once violated a restraining order issued to protect the ex-wife. This information provides good cause for the IRS employee to believe that reporting contacts which might disclose the ex-wife's location may cause reprisal against any person. Therefore, when the IRS employee contacts the ex-wife's new employer to verify salary information provided by the ex-wife, the IRS employee has good cause not to report that contact to the ex-husband, regardless of whether the new employer expresses concern about reprisal against it or its employees.

(4) *Pending criminal investigations.*—(i) *IRS criminal investigations.*—Section 7602(c) does not apply to contacts made during an investigation, or inquiry to determine whether to open an investigation, when the investigation or inquiry is—

(A) Made against a particular, identified taxpayer for the primary purpose of evaluating the potential for criminal prosecution of that taxpayer; and

(B) Made by an IRS employee whose primary duties include either identifying or investigating criminal violations of the law.

(ii) *Other criminal investigations.*—Section 7602(c) does not apply to contacts which, if reported to the taxpayer, could interfere with a known pending criminal investigation being conducted by law enforcement personnel of any local, state, Federal, foreign or other governmental entity.

(5) *Governmental entities.*—Section 7602(c) does not apply to any contact with any office of any local, state, Federal or foreign governmental entity except for contacts concerning the taxpayer's business with the government office contacted, such as the taxpayer's contracts with or employment by the office. The term *office* in-

cludes any agent or contractor of the office acting in such capacity.

(6) *Confidential informants.*—Section 7602(c) does not apply when the employee making the contact has good cause to believe that providing either the pre-contact notice or the record of the person contacted would identify a confidential informant whose identity would be protected under section 6103(h)(4).

(7) *Nonadministrative contacts.*—(i) *Explanation.*—Section 7602(c) does not apply to contacts made in the course of a pending court proceeding.

(ii) *Examples.*—The following examples illustrate this paragraph (f)(7):

Example 1. An attorney for the Office of Chief Counsel needs to contact a potential witness for an upcoming Tax Court proceeding involving the 1997 and 1998 taxable years of the taxpayer. Section 7602(c) does not apply because the contact is being made in the course of a pending court proceeding.

Example 2. While a Tax Court case is pending with respect to a taxpayer's 1997 and 1998 income tax liabilities, a revenue agent is conducting an examination of the taxpayer's excise tax liabilities for the fiscal year ending 1999. Any third-party contacts made by the revenue agent with respect to the excise tax liabilities would be subject to the requirements of section 7602(c) because the Tax Court proceeding does not involve the excise tax liabilities.

Example 3. A taxpayer files a Chapter 7 bankruptcy petition and receives a discharge. A revenue officer contacts a third party in order to determine whether the taxpayer has any exempt assets against which the IRS may take collection action to enforce its federal tax lien. At the time of the contact, the bankruptcy case has not been closed. Although the bankruptcy proceeding remains pending, the purpose of this contact relates to potential collection action by the IRS, a matter not before or related to the bankruptcy court proceeding.

(g) *Effective date.*—This section is applicable on December 18, 2002. [Reg. § 301.7602-2.]

☐ [*T.D. 9028*, 12-17-2002.]

[Reg. § 301.7603-1]

§ 301.7603-1. Service of summons.—(a) *In general.*—(1) *Hand delivery or delivery to place of abode.*—Except as otherwise provided in paragraph (a)(2) of this section, a summons issued under section 6420(e)(2), 6421(g)(2), 6427(j)(2), or 7602 shall be served by an attested copy delivered in hand to the person to whom it is directed, or left at such person's last and usual place of abode.

(2) *Summonses issued to third-party recordkeepers.*—A summons issued under section 6420(e)(2), 6421(g)(2), 6427(j)(2), or 7602 for the production of records (or testimony about such records) by a third-party recordkeeper, as described in section 7603(b)(2) and § 301.7603-2,

may also be served by certified or registered mail to the third-party recordkeeper's last known address, as defined in § 301.6212-2. If service to a third-party recordkeeper is made by certified or registered mail, the date of service is the date on which the summons is mailed.

(b) *Persons who may serve a summons.*—The officers and employees of the Internal Revenue Service whom the Commissioner has designated to carry out the authority described in § 301.7602-1(b) to issue a summons are authorized to serve a summons issued under section 6420(e)(2), 6421(g)(2), 6427(j)(2), or 7602.

(c) *Effect of certificate of service.*—The certificate of service signed by the person serving the summons shall be evidence of the facts it states on the hearing of an application for the enforcement of the summons.

(d) *Sufficiency of description of summoned records.*—When a summons requires the production of records, it shall be sufficient if such records are described with reasonable certainty.

(e) *Records.*—For purposes of this section and § 301.7603-2, the term records includes books, papers, or other data.

(f) *Effective/applicability date.*—This section is applicable on April 30, 2008. [Reg. § 301.7603-1.]

☐ [*T.D. 6421*, 10-23-59. Amended by *T.D. 7188*, 6-28-72; *T.D. 7297*, 12-18-73 and *T.D. 9395*, 4-29-2008.]

[Reg. § 301.7603-2]

§ 301.7603-2. Third-party recordkeepers.—(a) *Definitions.*—(1) *Accountant.*—A person is an accountant under section 7603(b)(2)(F) for purposes of determining whether that person is a third-party recordkeeper if, on the date the records described in the summons were created, the person was registered, licensed, or certified as an accountant under the authority of any state, commonwealth, territory, or possession of the United States, or of the District of Columbia.

(2) *Attorney.*—A person is an attorney under section 7603(b)(2)(E) for purposes of determining whether that person is a third-party recordkeeper if, on the date the records described in the summons were created, the person was registered, licensed, or certified as an attorney under the authority of any state, commonwealth, territory, or possession of the United States, or of the District of Columbia.

(3) *Credit cards.*—(i) *Person extending credit through credit cards.*—The term *person extending credit through the use of credit cards or similar devices* under section 7603(b)(2)(C) generally includes any person who issues a credit card. The term does not include a seller of goods or services who honors credit cards issued by other parties but who does not extend credit through the use of credit cards or similar devices.

(ii) *Devices similar to credit cards.*—An object is a device similar to a credit card under section 7603(b)(2)(C) only if it is physical in nature, such as a charge plate or similar device that may be tendered to obtain an extension of credit. Thus, a person who extends credit by requiring customers to sign sales slips without requiring the use of, or reference to, a physical object issued by that person is not a third-party recordkeeper under section 7603(b)(2)(C).

(iii) *Debit cards.*—A debit card is not a credit card or similar device because a debit card is not tendered to obtain an extension of credit.

(4) *Enrolled agent.*—A person is an enrolled agent under section 7603(b)(2)(I) for purposes of determining whether that person is a third-party recordkeeper if the person is enrolled as an agent authorized to practice before the Internal Revenue Service pursuant to Circular 230, 31 CFR Part 10.

(5) *Owner or developer of certain computer code and data.*—An owner or developer of computer software source code under section 7603(b)(2)(J) is a third-party recordkeeper when summoned to produce a computer software source code (as defined in section 7612(d)(2)), or an executable code and associated data described in section 7612(b)(1)(A)(ii), even if that person did not make or keep records of another person's business transactions or affairs.

(b) *When third-party recordkeeper status arises.*—(1) *In general.*—Except as provided in paragraph (a)(5) of this section, a person listed in section 7603(b)(2) is a third-party recordkeeper for purposes of section 7609(c)(2)(E) and §301.7603-1 only if the summons served on that person seeks records (or testimony regarding such records) of a third party's business transactions or affairs and such recordkeeper made or kept the records in the capacity of a third-party recordkeeper. For instance, an accountant is not a third-party recordkeeper (by reason of being an accountant) with respect to the accountant's records of a sale of property by the accountant to another person. Similarly, a credit card issuer is not a third-party recordkeeper (by reason of being a person extending credit through the use of credit cards or similar devices) with respect to—

(i) Records relating to non-credit card transactions, such as a cash sale by the issuer to a holder of the issuer's credit card; or

(ii) Records relating to transactions involving the use of another issuer's credit card.

(2) *Examples.*—The rules of paragraph (b)(1) of this section are illustrated by the following examples:

Example 1. V issues a credit card (the V card) that is honored by R, a retailer. When using the V card, C, a customer, signs a sales slip in triplicate. C, R, and V each retain one copy. Only the copy held by V is held by a third-party recordkeeper under section 7603(b)(2), even though R may issue its own credit card.

Example 2. R, a retailer, issues its own credit card (the R card) to C, a customer. When C makes a credit purchase from R using the R card,

C signs a sales slip in duplicate. C and R each retain one copy. Because R keeps the copy in its capacity as credit card issuer, as well as in its capacity as a retailer, it is a third-party recordkeeper under section 7603(b)(2) with respect to its copy of the sales slip.

(c) *Effective/applicability date.*—This section is applicable on April 30, 2008. [Reg. §301.7603-2.]

☐ [*T.D.* 9395, 4-29-2008.]

[Reg. §301.7604-1]

§301.7604-1. Enforcement of summons.—(a) *In general.*—Whenever any person summoned under section 6420(e)(2), 6421(f)(2), or 7602 neglects or refuses to obey such summons, or to produce books, papers, records, or other data, or to give testimony, as required, application may be made to the judge of the district court or to a United States commissioner for the district within which the person so summoned resides or is found for an attachment against him as for a contempt.

(b) *Persons who may apply for an attachment.*—The officers and employees of the Internal Revenue Service whom the Commissioner has designated to carry out the authority given him by §301.7602-1(b) to issue a summons are authorized to apply for an attachment as provided in paragraph (a) of this section. [Reg. §301.7604-1.]

☐ [*T.D.* 6421, 10-23-59. *Amended by T.D.* 7297, 12-18-73.]

[Reg. §301.7605-1]

§301.7605-1. Time and place of examination.—(a) *Time and place of examination to be reasonable.*—(1) *In general.*—The time and place of examination pursuant to the provisions of sections 6420(e)(2), 6421(g)(2), 6427(j)(2), or 7602 of the Internal Revenue Code are to be fixed by an officer or employee of the Internal Revenue Service, and officers and employees are to endeavor to schedule a time and place that are reasonable under the circumstances. This section sets forth general criteria for the Service to apply in determining whether a particular time and place for an examination are reasonable under the circumstances. Officers and employees should exercise sound judgment in applying these criteria to the circumstances at hand and should balance convenience of the taxpayer with the requirements of sound and efficient tax administration.

(2) *International examinations.*—Except for the provisions of paragraph (b)(2) of this section, this section does not apply to examinations that fall under the jurisdiction of the Office of the Assistant Commissioner (International).

(3) *Criminal investigations.*—Except for the provisions of paragraph (b)(2) of this section, this section does not apply to criminal investigations.

(b) *Time of examination.*—(1) *Date and time of examination.*—It is reasonable for the Service to schedule the day (or days) for an examination during a normally scheduled workday (or workdays) of the Service, during the Service's normal business hours. It is reasonable for the Service to schedule examinations throughout the year, without regard to seasonal fluctuations in the businesses of particular taxpayers or their representatives. However, the Service will work with taxpayers or their representatives to try to minimize any adverse effects in scheduling the date and time of an examination.

(2) *Date of appearance when summons is used.*—If a summons is issued under authority of section 7602(a)(2) of the Internal Revenue Code, or under the corresponding authority of sections 6420(e)(2), 6421(g)(2), or 6427(j)(2), the date fixed for appearance before an officer or employee of the Service must be no less than 10 days from the date of the summons.

(c) *Type of examination.*—(1) *In general.*—The Service will determine whether an examination will be an office examination (*i.e.*, an examination conducted at a Service office) or a field examination (*i.e.*, an examination conducted at the taxpayer's residence or place of business, or some other location that is not a Service office), based upon the complexity of the return and which form of examination will be more conducive to effective and efficient tax administration.

(2) *Office examination held in location other than Service office in case of clear need.*—The Service will grant a request to hold an office examination at a location other than a Service office in a case of clear need, such as when it would be unreasonably difficult for the taxpayer to travel to a Service office because of the taxpayer's advanced age or infirm physical condition, or when the taxpayer's books, records, and source documents are too cumbersome for the taxpayer to bring to a Service office.

(d) *Place of examination.*—(1) *In general.*—The Service generally will make an initial determination of the place for an examination, including the Internal Revenue Service district to which an examination will be assigned, based upon the address shown on the return for the period selected for examination. Requests by taxpayers to transfer the place of examination will be resolved on a case-by-case basis, using the criteria set forth in paragraph (e) of this section.

(2) *Office examinations.*—(i) *In general.*—An office examination of an individual or sole proprietorship generally is based on the residence of the individual taxpayer. An office examination of a taxpayer that is an entity generally is based on the location where the taxpayer entity's original books, records, and source documents are maintained. An office examination generally will take place at the closest Service office within the district encompassing the taxpayer's residence or at the closest Service office within the district where the taxpayer entity's books, records, and source documents are maintained. It generally is not reasonable for the Service to require a taxpayer to attend an examination at an office

within an assigned district other than the closest Service office.

(ii) *Exception.*—If the office within the assigned district closest to an individual taxpayer's residence or the location where a taxpayer entity's books, records and source documents are maintained does not have an examination group or the appropriate personnel to conduct the examination, it generally is reasonable for the Service to require the taxpayer to attend an examination at the closest Service office within the assigned district that has an examination group or the appropriate personnel.

(iii) *Travel considerations.*—In scheduling office examinations, the Service in appropriate circumstances will take into account the distance a taxpayer would have to travel.

(3) *Field examinations.*—(i) *In general.*—A field examination will generally take place at the location where the taxpayer's original books, records, and source documents pertinent to the examination are maintained. In the case of a sole proprietorship or taxpayer entity, this will usually be the taxpayer's principal place of business.

(ii) *Exception for certain small businesses.*—If an examination is scheduled by the Service at the taxpayer's place of business and the taxpayer represents to the Service in writing that conducting the examination at the place of business would essentially require the business to close or would unduly disrupt business operations, the Service, upon verification, will change the place of examination to a Service office within the district where the taxpayer's books, records, and source documents are maintained.

(iii) *Site visitations.*—Regardless of where an examination takes place, the Service may visit the taxpayer's place of business or residence to establish facts that can only be established by direct visit, such as inventory or asset verification. The Service generally will visit for these purposes on a normal workday of the Service during the Service's normal duty hours.

(e) *Requests by taxpayers to change place of examination.*—(1) *In general.*—The Service will consider, on a case-by-case basis, written requests by taxpayers or their representatives to change the place that the Service has set for an examination. In considering these requests, the Service will take into account the following factors—

(i) The location of the taxpayer's current residence;

(ii) The location of the taxpayer's current principal place of business;

(iii) The location at which the taxpayer's books, records, and source documents are maintained;

(iv) The location at which the Service can perform the examination most efficiently;

(v) The Service resources available at the location to which the taxpayer has requested a transfer; and

Reg. §301.7605-1(e)(1)(v)

(vi) Other factors that indicate that conducting the examination at a particular location could pose undue inconvenience to the taxpayer.

(2) *Circumstances in which the Service normally will permit transfers.*—A request by a taxpayer to transfer the place of examination will generally be granted under the following circumstances:

(i) *Office examination.*—(A) If the current residence of the taxpayer, in the case of an individual or sole proprietorship, or the location where the taxpayer's books, records, and source documents are maintained, in the case of a taxpayer entity, is closer to a different Service office in the same district as the office where the examination has been scheduled, the Service normally will agree to transfer the examination to the closer Service office.

(B) If the current residence of a taxpayer, in the case of an individual or sole proprietorship, or the location where a taxpayer entity's books, records, and source documents are maintained, is in a district other than the district where the examination has been scheduled, the Service normally will agree to transfer the examination to the closest Service office in the other district.

(ii) *Field examinations.*—(A) If a taxpayer does not reside at the residence where an examination has been scheduled, the Service will agree to transfer the examination to the taxpayer's current residence.

(B) If, in the case of an individual, a sole proprietorship, or a taxpayer entity, the taxpayer's books, records, and source documents are maintained at a location other than the location where the examination has been scheduled, the Service will agree to transfer the examination to the location where the taxpayer's books, records, and source documents are maintained.

(3) *Transfer for convenience of taxpayer's representative.*—The location of the place of business of a taxpayer's representative will generally not be considered in determining the place for an examination. However, the Service in its sole discretion may determine, based on the factors described in paragraph (e)(1) of this section, to transfer the place of examination to the representative's office.

(4) *Transfer within thirteen months of expiration of limitations period.*—If any applicable period of limitations on assessment or collection provided in the Internal Revenue Code will expire within thirteen months from the date of a taxpayer's request to transfer the place of an examination, the Service may require, as a condition for an otherwise permissible transfer, that the taxpayer first agree in writing to extend the limitations period for up to one year.

(5) *Transfer to office with insufficient resources.*—The Service is not required to transfer an examination to an office or district that does not have adequate resources to conduct the examination.

(f) *Safety of Service officers and employees.*—Notwithstanding any other provision of this regulation, officers and employees of the Service may decline to conduct an examination at a particular location if it appears that the possibility of physical danger may exist at that location. In these circumstances, the Service may transfer an examination to a Service office and take any other steps reasonably necessary to protect its officers and employees.

(g) *Transfers initiated by Service.*—Nothing in this section shall be interpreted as precluding the Service from initiating the transfer of an examination if the transfer would promote the effective and efficient conduct of the examination. Should a taxpayer request that such a transfer not be made, the Service will consider the request according to the principles and criteria set forth in paragraph (e) of this section.

(h) *Restrictions on examination of taxpayer.*—No taxpayer shall be subjected to unnecessary examination or investigations, and only one inspection of a taxpayer's books of account shall be made for each taxable year unless the taxpayer requests otherwise or unless an authorized internal revenue officer, after investigation, notifies the taxpayer in writing that an additional inspection is necessary. The inspection of a taxpayer's books of account pursuant to the procedures of §1.1441-4(b)(3) and (4) is not an inspection of a taxpayer's books of account for purposes of section 7605(b) and this section.

(i) *Restriction on examination of churches.*—(1) *In general.*—This section imposes certain restrictions upon the examination of the books of account and religious activities of a church or convention or association of churches for the purpose of determining whether such organization may be engaged in activities the income from which is subject to tax under section 511 as unrelated business taxable income. The purposes of these restrictions are to protect such organizations from undue interference in their internal financial affairs through unnecessary examinations to determine the existence of unrelated business taxable income, and to limit the scope of examination for this purpose to matters directly relevant to a determination of the existence or amount of such income. This section also imposes additional restrictions upon other examinations of such organizations.

(2) *Books of account.*—No examination of the books of account of an organization which claims to be a church or a convention or association of churches shall be made except after the giving of notice as provided in this subparagraph and except to the extent necessary (i) to determine the initial or continuing qualification of the organization under section 501(c)(3); (ii) to determine whether the organization qualifies as one, contributions to which are deductible under section 170, 545, 556, 642, 2055, 2106, or 2522; (iii) to obtain information for the purpose of ascertaining or verifying payments made by the organization to another person in determining the

tax liability of the recipient, such as payments of salaries, wages, or other forms of compensation; or (iv) to determine the amount of tax, if any, imposed by the Code upon such organization. No examination of the books of account of a church or convention or association of churches shall be made unless the Regional Commissioner believes that such examination is necessary and so notifies the organization in writing at least 30 days in advance of examination. The Regional Commissioner will conclude that such examination is necessary only after reasonable attempts have been made to obtain information from the books of account by written request and the Regional Commissioner has determined that the information cannot be fully or satisfactorily obtained in that manner. In any examination of a church or convention or association of churches for the purpose of determining unrelated business income tax liability pursuant to such notice, no examination of the books of account of the organization shall be made except to the extent necessary to determine such liability.

(3) *Religious activities.*—No examination of the religious activities of an organization which claims to be a church or convention or association of churches shall be made except (i) to the extent necessary to determine the initial or continuing qualification of the organization under section 501(c)(3); (ii) to determine whether the organization qualifies as one, contributions to which are deductible under section 170, 545, 556, 642, 2055, 2106, or 2522; or (iii) to determine whether the organization is a church or convention or association of churches subject to the provisions of part III of subchapter F of chapter 1. The requirements of subparagraph (2) of this paragraph that the Regional Commissioner give notice prior to examination of the books of account of an organization do not apply to an examination of the religious activities of the organization for any purpose described in this subparagraph. Once it has been determined that the organization is a church or convention or association of churches, no further examination of its religious activities may be made in connection with determining its liability, if any, for unrelated business income tax.

(4) *Effective date.*—The provisions of this paragraph shall apply to audits and examinations of taxable years beginning after December 31, 1969.

(j) *Effective date.*—Paragraphs (a) through (g) of this section, inclusive, are effective for examinations scheduled after April 2, 1993. [Reg. § 301.7605-1.]

☐ [*T.D.* 6421, 10-23-59. *Amended by T.D.* 6498, 10-24-60; *T.D.* 7146, 10-26-71; *T.D.* 7977, 9-19-84; *T.D.* 8297, 4-2-90 *and T.D.* 8469, 4-2-93.]

[Reg. § 301.7606-1]

§ 301.7606-1. Entry of premises for examination of taxable objects.—Any officer or employee of the Internal Revenue Service may, in the performance of his duty, enter in the daytime any building or place where any articles or objects subject to tax are made, produced, or kept, so far as it may be necessary for the purpose of examining said articles or objects and also enter at night any such building or place, while open, for a similar purpose. [Reg. § 301.7606-1.]

☐ [*T.D.* 6421, 10-23-59. *Amended by T.D.* 7297, 12-18-73.]

[Reg. § 301.7609-1]

§ 301.7609-1. Special procedures for third-party summonses.—(a) *In general.*—(1) Section 7609 requires the Internal Revenue Service (IRS) to follow special procedures when summoning a third party's testimony, records, or computer software source code. Except as provided in § 301.7609-2(b), the IRS must provide notice of a third-party summons to any person identified in the summons, other than the person summoned. A person entitled to notice of a third-party summons may intervene in any proceeding brought to enforce the summons or may bring a proceeding to quash the summons, regardless of whether they receive notice of the summons from the IRS pursuant to section 7609(a) and § 301.7609-2.

(2) Neither section 7609 nor the regulations hereunder limit the IRS's ability to obtain information, other than by summons, through formal or informal procedures authorized by sections 7601 and 7602.

(b) *Cross references.*—See § 301.7609-2 for rules relating to persons who must be notified of a third-party summons and exceptions to the notification requirements. See § 301.7609-3 for rules relating to the rights and duties of summoned parties. See § 301.7609-4 for rules relating to actions to quash a summons or to intervene in a summons enforcement proceeding. See § 301.7609-5 for rules relating to the suspension of periods of limitations.

(c) *Records.*—For purposes of §§ 301.7609-1 through 301.7609-5, the term *records* includes books, papers, or other data.

(d) *Effective/applicability date.*—This section is applicable on April 30, 2008. [Reg. § 301.7609-1.]

☐ [*T.D.* 7899, 7-18-83. *Amended by T.D.* 8091, 6-24-86 *and T.D.* 9395, 4-29-2008.]

[Reg. § 301.7609-2]

§ 301.7609-2. Notification of persons identified in third-party summonses.—(a) *In general.*—(1) *Persons entitled to notice.*—Except as provided in § 301.7609-2(b), the Internal Revenue Service (IRS) shall give notice of a third-party summons to any person, other than the person summoned, who is identified in the summons. The only persons so identified are the person with respect to whose liability the summons is issued and any other person identified in the description of summoned records or testimony. For example, if the IRS issues a summons to a bank with respect to the liability of C that requires the production of account records of A and B, both of whom are named in the summons, the IRS must notify A, B and C of the summons.

(2) *Time for providing notice.*—If notice is required by this paragraph, such notice must be given within three days of the date on which the summons is served on the third party, but no

later than 23 days prior to the date fixed in the summons as the date on which the examination of the summoned person or records is scheduled.

(3) *Methods for serving notice.*—Notice may be served by hand delivery to any person entitled to notice or by leaving notice at such person's last and usual place of abode. Notice also may be served by certified or registered mail to the person's last known address, as defined in §301.6212-2. If service to a person entitled to notice is made by certified or registered mail, the date of service is the date on which the notice is mailed.

(4) *Content of the notice.*—Notice required to be given to any person entitled to notice must be accompanied by a copy of the summons that has been served and must include an explanation of the right to bring a proceeding to quash the summons. The copy of the summons accompanying the notice is not required to contain the attestation that appears pursuant to section 7603 on the copy of the summons served on the summoned person.

(b) *Exceptions.*—The IRS is not required to provide notice to persons identified in the following third-party summonses:

(1) *Summons served on the taxpayer.*—The IRS is not required to provide notice of a summons served on the person with respect to whose liability the summons was issued, or any officer or employee of such person.

(2) *Existence of records.*—The IRS is not required to provide notice in the case of a summons issued to determine whether or not records of the business transactions or affairs of a person identified in the summons have been made or kept.

(3) *Numbered account or similar arrangement.*—The IRS is not required to provide notice in the case of a summons issued solely to determine the identity of a person having a numbered account or similar arrangement with a bank or other institution. An account is a numbered account or similar arrangement within the meaning of this paragraph if it is an account through which a person may authorize transactions solely through the use of a number, symbol, code name, or other device not involving the disclosure of the person's identity. The term *person having a numbered account or similar arrangement* includes the person who opened the account and any person authorized to access the account or to receive records or statements concerning it.

(4) *Summonses in aid of the collection of liabilities.*—(i) *In general.*—The IRS is not required to provide notice in the case of a summons issued in aid of the collection of liabilities. A summons is in aid of the collection of liabilities within the meaning of this paragraph if it is issued in connection with the collection of—

(A) An assessment or judgment against the person with respect to whose liability the summons is issued; or

(B) The liability determined at law or in equity of any transferee or fiduciary of a person described in paragraph (b)(4)(i)(A) of this section.

(ii) *Examples.*—The rules of paragraph (b)(4) of this section are illustrated by the following examples:

Example 1. A third-party summons is issued to a bank to determine the amount held in an account in the name of A, against whom unpaid income taxes have been assessed. Notice of the summons is not required to be given to A or any other persons identified in the summons because the summons is issued in connection with the collection of taxes that have been assessed.

Example 2. A third-party summons is issued to determine whether assessments should be made against A, who is potentially liable for a trust fund recovery penalty under section 6672 with respect to the assessed but unpaid withholding tax liability of employer E. The summons is captioned: In the matter of A. Notice of the summons must be provided to A and to any other persons identified in the summons because the summons was issued with respect to A's potential, unassessed liability under section 6672.

(5) *Summonses issued by a criminal investigator.*—The IRS is not required to provide notice in the case of a summons issued by a criminal investigator to a person other than a third-party recordkeeper, as defined in section 7603(b). For purposes of section 7609(c)(2)(E), a summons issued by a criminal investigator is any summons issued as part of a criminal investigation by an IRS officer or employee having authority to conduct a criminal investigation and to issue a summons.

(6) *John Doe summons.*—The IRS is not required to provide notice in the case of a John Doe summons issued under section 7609(f).

(7) *Summons issued pursuant to a court order to prevent spoliation of evidence.*—The IRS is not required to provide notice in the case of a summons for which a court determines there is reasonable cause to believe the giving of notice may lead to attempts to conceal, destroy, or alter records relevant to the examination, to prevent communication of information from other persons through intimidation, bribery, or collusion, or to flee to avoid prosecution, testifying, or production of records.

(c) *Effective/applicability date.*—This section is applicable on April 30, 2008. [Reg. §301.7609-2.]

☐ [T.D. 7899, 7-18-83. *Amended by* T.D. 8091, 6-24-86 *and* T.D. 9395, 4-29-2008.]

[Reg. § 301.7609-3]

§ 301.7609-3. Duty of and protection for the summoned party.—(a) *Duty of the summoned party.*—Upon receipt of a summons, the summoned party must begin to assemble the summoned records. The summoned party must be prepared to produce the summoned records on the date on which the summons states that they are to be examined, regardless of the institution or anticipated institution of a proceeding to quash or the summoned party's intervention in a proceeding to quash, as allowed under section 7609(b)(2)(C).

(b) *Disclosing summoned party not liable.*—(1) *In general.*—A summoned party, or an agent or employee thereof, who makes a disclosure of records or gives testimony as required by a summons in good faith reliance on the certificate of the Secretary (as defined in paragraph (b)(2) of this section) or an order of a court requiring production of records or giving of testimony, will not be liable for any claim arising from such disclosure brought by any customer, any party with respect to whose tax liability the summons was issued, or any other person.

(2) *Certificate of the Secretary.*—The Secretary may issue to the summoned party a certificate if the person with respect to whose liability the summons was issued expressly consents to the examination of the records summoned and the taking of testimony. The Secretary also may issue to the summoned party a certificate stating that—

(i) The 20-day period within which a person entitled to notice of the summons may institute a proceeding to quash the summons has expired; and

(ii) No proceeding has been instituted within that period.

(c) *Reimbursement of costs.*—Summoned third parties may be entitled to reimbursement of their costs of assembling and preparing to produce summoned records, to the extent allowed by section 7610 and § 301.7610-1.

(d) *Notification of suspension of periods of limitations in connection with a John Doe summons.*—(1) *Requirement of notification.*—If any periods of limitations are suspended under section 7609(e)(2) and § 301.7609-5(d) with respect to a John Doe summons described in section 7609(f), the summoned party is required under section 7609(i)(4) to provide notice of such suspension to all persons with respect to whose liability the summons was issued.

(2) *Content of notification.*—A summoned party required to notify a person of the suspension of the periods of limitations shall provide the following information to such person—

(i) A John Doe summons was served on the summoned party seeking records that may be relevant to the person's tax liability;

(ii) The date on which the summons was served;

(iii) The tax period(s) to which the summons relates;

(iv) Six months has passed since service of the summons and the summoned party's response to the summons has not been finally resolved;

(v) The periods of limitations under section 6501 (relating to assessment and collection) and section 6531 (relating to criminal prosecution), have been suspended; and

(vi) The date on which suspension of the periods of limitations under sections 6501 and 6531 began.

(3) *Time and manner of notification.*—The notification must be made in writing and may be delivered in person, by mail sent to the address last known by the summoned party, or by use of any electronic means of transmission. Notification should be made as soon as possible after the suspension of the periods of limitations begins. Failure by a summoned party to give notice of the suspension of periods of limitations as required by section 7609(i)(4) does not prevent the suspension of the periods of limitations under section 7609(e)(2).

(e) *Effective/applicability date.*—This section is applicable on April 30, 2008. [Reg. § 301.7609-3.]

☐ [*T.D. 7899, 7-18-83. Amended by T.D. 8091, 6-24-86 and T.D. 9395, 4-29-2008.*]

[Reg. § 301.7609-4]

§ 301.7609-4. Right to intervene; right to institute a proceeding to quash.—(a) *Intervention in proceeding with respect to enforcement of a summons.*—Under section 7609(b)(1), a person entitled to notice of a summons under section 7609(a) and § 301.7609-2 is entitled to intervene in any proceeding brought under section 7604 with respect to the enforcement of that summons.

(b) *Right to institute a proceeding to quash.*—(1) *In general.*—Under section 7609(b), a person entitled to notice of a summons under section 7609(a) and § 301.7609-2 may institute a proceeding to quash the summons in the United States district court for the district in which the summoned person resides or is found.

(2) *Requirements for a proceeding to quash.*—To institute a proceeding to quash a summons, a person entitled to notice of the summons must, not later than the 20th day following the day the notice of the summons was served on or mailed to such person—

(i) File a petition to quash a summons in the name of the person entitled to notice of the summons in the proper district court;

(ii) Notify the Internal Revenue Service (IRS) by sending a copy of that petition to quash by registered or certified mail to the IRS employee and office designated in the notice of summons to receive the copy; and

(iii) Notify the summoned person by sending by registered or certified mail a copy of the petition to quash to the summoned person.

(3) *Failure to give timely notice.*—If a person entitled to notice of the summons fails to give proper and timely notice to either the summoned person or the IRS in the manner described in this paragraph, that person has failed to institute a proceeding to quash and the district court lacks jurisdiction to hear the proceeding. For example, if the person entitled to notice mails a copy of the petition to the summoned person, but fails to mail a copy of the petition to the designated IRS employee and office, the person entitled to notice has failed to institute a proceeding to quash. Similarly, if the person entitled to notice mails a copy of such petition to the summoned person but, instead of sending a copy of the petition by registered or certified mail to the designated IRS employee and office, the person entitled to notice provides the designated IRS employee and office the petition by some other means, the person entitled to notice has failed to institute a proceeding to quash.

(4) *Failure to institute a proceeding to quash.*— If a person entitled to notice fails to institute a proceeding to quash within 20 days following the day the notice of the summons was served on or mailed to such person, the IRS may examine the summoned records and take summoned testimony following the 23rd day after notice of the summons was served on or mailed to the person entitled to notice.

(c) *Presumption no notice has been mailed.*—Section 7609(b)(2)(B) permits a person entitled to notice to institute a proceeding to quash by filing a petition in district court and notifying both the IRS and the summoned person. Unless the person entitled to notice has notified both the IRS and the summoned person in the appropriate manner, the person entitled to notice has failed to institute a proceeding to quash. For the purpose of permitting the IRS to examine the summoned witnesses and records, it is presumed that the notification was not timely mailed if the copy of the petition was not delivered to the summoned person or to the person and office designated to receive the notice on behalf of the IRS within three days after the close of the 20-day period allowed for instituting a proceeding to quash.

(d) *Effective/applicability date.*—This section is applicable on April 30, 2008. [Reg. § 301.7609-4.]

☐ [*T.D.* 7899, 7-18-83. *Amended by T.D.* 8091, 6-24-86 *and T.D.* 9395, 4-29-2008.]

[Reg. § 301.7609-5]

§ 301.7609-5. Suspension of periods of limitations.—(a) *In general.*—Except in the case of a summons that is a designated or related summons described in section 6503(j), the following rules relating to the suspension of certain periods of limitations apply to all third-party summonses subject to the notice requirements of section 7609(a) and to all John Doe summonses subject to the requirements of section 7609(f).

(b) *Intervention in an action to enforce the summons.*—(1) *In general.*—If a person entitled to notice of a summons under section 7609(a) and § 301.7609-2 with respect to whose liability the summons was issued, or such person's agent, nominee, or other person acting under the direction or control of the person entitled to notice, takes any action to intervene in a proceeding with respect to enforcement of such summons brought pursuant to section 7604, that person's periods of limitations under sections 6501 (relating to assessment and collection) and 6531 (relating to criminal prosecutions) for the tax period or periods that are the subject of the summons are suspended for the period during which such proceeding is pending.

(2) *Action to intervene.*—A person entitled to notice takes any action to intervene in a proceeding to enforce a summons within the meaning of § 301.7609-4(a) on the date when a motion to intervene is filed with the court.

(c) *Institution of a proceeding to quash a summons.*—(1) *In general.*—If a person entitled to notice of a summons under section 7609(a) and § 301.7609-2 with respect to whose liability the summons was issued, or such person's agent, nominee, or other person acting under the direction or control of the such person, takes any action described in § 301.7609-4(b) to institute a proceeding to quash such summons, that person's periods of limitations under sections 6501 and 6531 for the tax period or periods that are the subject of the summons are suspended for the period during which such proceeding is pending.

(2) *Action to institute a proceeding to quash a summons.*—A person entitled to notice takes any action to institute a proceeding to quash if he or she files a petition to quash the summons in any district court, regardless of whether the timely filing requirements of section 7609(b)(2)(A) or the notice requirements of section 7609(b)(2)(B) are satisfied. For example, a person entitled to notice takes an action to institute a proceeding to quash a summons for purposes of this section if that person files a petition to quash the summons in district court and notifies the summoned person by sending a copy of the petition by registered or certified mail, but fails to mail a copy of that notice to the appropriate Internal Revenue Service (IRS) person and office.

(d) *Summoned party's failure to finally resolve the response to a summons after six months from service.*—(1) *In general.*—If a third party's response to a summons for which the IRS was required to provide notice to persons identified in the summons, or to a John Doe summons described in section 7609(f), is not finally resolved within six months after the date of service of the summons, the periods of limitations are suspended under sections 6501 and 6531, for the person with respect to whose liability the summons was issued and for any person whose identity is sought to be obtained by a John Doe summons, for the tax period or periods that are the subject of the summons. The suspension shall begin on the date which is six months after the service of the summons and shall end on the date on which there is a final resolution of the summoned party's response to the summons.

(2) *Example.*—The rules of paragraph (d)(1) of this section are illustrated by the following example:

A John Doe summons is issued on April 1, 2004, to the promoter of a tax shelter and seeks the names of all participants in the shelter in order to investigate the participants' income tax liabilities for 2001 and 2002. The district court approves service of the summons on April 30, 2004, and the summons is served on the promoter on May 3, 2004. The promoter does not provide the names of the participants. The periods of limitations for the participants' income tax liabilities and criminal prosecution for 2001 and 2002 are suspended under section 7609(e)(2) beginning on November 3, 2004, the date which is six months after the date the John Doe summons was served until the date on which the promoter's response to the summons is finally resolved.

(e) *Definitions.*—(1) *Agent, nominee, etc.*—A person is the agent, nominee, or other person of a person entitled to notice under section 7609(a) and § 301.7609-2, and is acting under the direction or control of the person entitled to notice for purposes of section 7609(e)(1), if the person entitled to notice has the ability in fact or at law to cause the agent, nominee or other person, to take the actions permitted under section 7609(b).

(2) *Period during which a proceeding is pending.*—(i) *Intervention in an enforcement proceeding.*—The period during which the periods of limitations under sections 6501 and 6531 are suspended under section 7609(e)(1) begins on the date any person described in paragraph (b) of this section intervenes in an action to enforce the summons. The periods of limitations remain suspended until all appeals are disposed of, or until the expiration of the period during which an appeal may be taken or a request for further review may be made. The periods of limitations remain suspended for the period during which a proceeding is pending, regardless of compliance (or partial compliance) with the summons during that period. If, following issuance of an order to enforce a third-party summons, a collateral proceeding is brought challenging whether production made by the summoned party fully satisfied the court order and whether sanctions should be imposed against the summoned party for a failure to satisfy that order, the periods of limitations remain suspended until all appeals of the collateral proceeding are disposed of, or until the expiration of the period during which an appeal may be taken or a request for further review of the collateral proceeding may be made. Any collateral proceeding to the original proceeding shall be considered to be a continuation of the original proceeding.

(ii) *Proceeding to quash a summons.*—The period during which the periods of limitations under sections 6501 and 6531 are suspended

under section 7609(e)(1) begins on the date any person described in paragraph (c) of this section files a petition to quash the summons in district court. The periods of limitations remain suspended until all appeals are disposed of, or until expiration of the period in which an appeal may be taken or a request for further review may be made. The periods of limitations remain suspended for the period during which a proceeding is pending, regardless of compliance (or partial compliance) with the summons during that period.

(iii) *Examples.*—The rules of paragraph (e)(2) are illustrated by the following examples:

Example 1. A revenue agent issues a summons to A, an accountant for B, requiring production of records relating to B's income tax liabilities for 2002. The summons is served on A on March 1, 2004. B files a petition to quash the summons in district court on March 15, 2004. The district court dismisses B's petition on July 1, 2004. B fails to appeal this decision by filing a notice of appeal within 60 days from the date of the district court's order of dismissal. The revenue agent notifies A that B did not appeal the district court's order. A turns over all of the records requested in the summons. The periods of limitations applicable to B for 2002 under sections 6501 and 6531 are suspended under section 7609(e)(1) from March 15, 2004, the date B filed a petition to quash, until August 30, 2004, the last day on which B could have filed a notice of appeal.

Example 2. A revenue agent issues a summons to A, an accountant for B, requiring production of records relating to B's income tax liabilities for 2003. The summons is served on A on June 1, 2005. B files an untimely petition to quash the summons in district court on June 29, 2005. The district court dismisses B's petition on July 29, 2005. B does not file an appeal of the district court's order. The periods of limitations applicable to B for 2003 under sections 6501 and 6531 are suspended under section 7609(e)(1) from June 29, 2005, the date B filed an untimely petition to quash, until September 27, 2005, the last day on which B could have filed a notice of appeal.

(3) *Final resolution of the summoned third party's response to a summons.*—For purposes of section 7609(e)(2)(B), final resolution with respect to a summoned party's response to a third-party summons occurs when the summons or any order enforcing any part of the summons is fully complied with and all appeals or requests for further review are disposed of, the period in which an appeal may be taken has expired or the period in which a request for further review may be made has expired. The determination of whether there has been full compliance will be made within a reasonable time, given the volume and complexity of the records produced, after the later of the giving of all testimony or the production of all records requested by the summons or required by any order enforcing any part of the summons. If, following an enforce-

ment order, collateral proceedings are brought challenging whether the production made by the summoned party fully satisfied the court order and whether sanctions should be imposed against the summoned party for a failing to do so, the suspension of the periods of limitations shall continue until the summons or any order enforcing any part of the summons is fully complied with and the decision in the collateral proceeding becomes final. A decision in a collateral proceeding becomes final when all appeals are disposed of, the period in which an appeal may be taken has expired or the period in which a request for further review may be made has expired.

(f) *Effective/applicability date.*—This section is applicable on April 30, 2008. [Reg. § 301.7609-5.]

☐ [*T.D. 7899,* 7-18-83. *Amended by T.D.* 8091, 6-24-86 *and T.D. 9395,* 4-29-2008.]

[Reg. § 301.7610-1]

§ 301.7610-1. Fees and costs for witnesses.— (a) *Introduction.*—Section 7610 provides that the Internal Revenue Service may make payments to certain persons who are asked to give information to the Service. Under section 7610 witnesses generally will not be reimbursed for actual expenses incurred but instead will be paid in accordance with the payment rates established by regulations. Paragraph (b) of this section contains elaborations of certain terms found in section 7610 and definitions of other terms used in the regulations under section 7610(a)(2); and paragraphs (c) and (d) contain rules and rates applicable to payments under section 7610. Section 7610 and its regulations are effective for summonses issued after February 28, 1977, except as otherwise provided.

(b) *Definitions.*—(1) *Directly incurred costs.*— Directly incurred costs are costs incurred solely, immediately, and necessarily as a consequence of searching for, reproducing, or transporting records in order to comply with a summons. They do not include a proportionate allocation of fixed costs, such as overhead, equipment depreciation, etc. However, where a third party's records are stored at an independent storage facility that charges the third party a search fee to search for, reproduce, or transport particular records requested, these fees are considered to be directly incurred by the summoned third party.

(2) *Reproduction costs.*—Reproduction costs are costs incurred in making copies or duplicates of summoned documents, transcripts, and other similar material.

(3) *Search costs.*—Search costs include only the total cost of personnel time directly incurred in searching for records or information and the cost of retrieving information stored by computer. Salaries of persons locating and retrieving summoned material are not includible in search costs. Also, search costs do not include salaries, fees, or similar expenditures for analysis of material or for managerial or legal advice, expertise, or research, or time spent for these activities.

(4) *Third party.*—A third party is any person served with a summons, other than a person with respect to whose liability a summons is issued, or an officer, employee, agent, accountant, or attorney of that person.

(5) *Third party records.*—Third party records are books, papers, records or other data in which the person with respect to whose liability a summons is issued does not have a proprietary interest at the time the summons is served.

(6) *Transportation costs.*—Transportation costs include only costs incurred to transport personnel to search for records or information requested and costs incurred solely by the need to transport the summoned material to the place of examination. These costs do not include the cost of transporting the summoned witness for appearance at the place of examination. See paragraph (c)(2) of this section for payment of travel expenses.

(c) *Conditions and rates of payments.*—(1) *Basis for payment.*—Payment for search, reproduction, and transportation costs will be made only to third parties served with a summons to produce third party records or information and only for material requested by the summons. Payment will be made only for these costs that are both directly incurred and reasonably necessary. Search, reproduction, and transportation costs must be considered separately in determining whether costs are reasonably necessary. No payment will be made until the third party has satisfactorily complied with the summons and has submitted an itemized bill or invoice showing specific details concerning the costs to the Internal Revenue Service employee before whom the third party was summoned. If a third party charges any other person for any cost for which the third party is seeking payment from the Service, the amount charged to the other person must be subtracted from the amount the Internal Revenue Service may pay.

(2) *Payment rates.*—The following rates are established:

(i) *Search costs.*—(A) For the total amount of personnel time required to locate records or information, $8.50 per person hour for summonses issued after July 19, 1983. For summonses issued on or before such date, $5.00 per person hour.

(B) For retrieval of information stored by computer in the format in which it is normally produced, actual costs, based on computer time and necessary supplies, except that personnel time for computer search is payable only under subparagraph (2)(i)(A) of this paragraph.

(ii) *Reproductions costs.*—(A) For copies of documents, $.20 per page for summonses issued after July 19, 1983. For copies of documents issued on or before such date, $.10 per page.

(B) For photographs, films and other materials, actual cost, except that personnel time is payable only under subparagraph (2)(i)(A) of this paragraph.

(iii) *Transportation costs.*—For transportation costs, actual cost, except that personnel time is payable only under subparagraph (2)(i)(A) of this paragraph.

(d) *Appearance fees and allowances.*—(1) *In general.*—Under Section 7610(a)(1) and this paragraph, the Service shall pay a summoned person certain fees and allowances. No payments will be made until after the party summoned appears and has submitted any necessary receipts or other evidence of cost to the Service employee before whom the person was summoned. This paragraph is effective with respect to appearances made after October 26, 1978.

(2) *Attendance fees.*—A summoned person shall be paid an attendance fee for each day's attendance. A summoned person shall also be paid the attendance fee for the time necessarily occupied in going to and returning from the place of attendance at the beginning and end of the attendance or at any time during the attendance. The attendance fee is the higher of $30 per day or the amount paid under 28 U.S.C. 1821(b) to witnesses in attendance at courts of the United States at the time of the summoned person's appearance.

(3) *Travel allowances.*—A summoned person who travels by common carrier shall be paid for the actual expenses of travel on the basis of the means of transportation reasonably utilized and the distance necessarily traveled to and from the summoned person's residence by the shortest practical route in going to and returning from the place of attendance. Such a summoned person shall utilize a common carrier at the most economical rate reasonably available. A receipt or other evidence of actual cost shall be furnished. A travel allowance equal to the mileage allowance which the Administrator of General Services has prescribed, under 5 U.S.C. 5704, for official travel of employees of the Federal Government shall be paid to each summoned person who travels by privately owned vehicle. That rate is $.20 per mile as of April 20, 1980. Computation of mileage under this paragraph shall be made on the basis of a uniform table of distances adopted by the Administrator of General Services. Toll charges for toll roads, bridges, tunnels, and ferries, taxicab fares between places of lodging and carrier terminals, and parking fees (upon presentation of a valid parking receipt) shall be paid in full to a summoned person incurring those expenses.

(4) *Subsistence allowances.*—A subsistence allowance shall be paid to a summoned person (other than a summoned person who is incarcerated) when an overnight stay is required at the place of attendance because the place is so far removed from the residence of the summoned person as to prohibit return thereto from day to day. A subsistence allowance for a summoned person shall be paid in an amount not to exceed the maximum per diem allowance prescribed by the Administrator of General Services, under 5 U.S.C. 5702(a), for official travel in the area of

attendance by employees of the Federal Government. As of April 30, 1979, that maximum per diem allowance is $35 per day. A subsistence allowance for a summoned person attending in an area designated by the Administrator of General Services as a high-cost area shall be paid in an amount not to exceed the maximum actual subsistence allowance prescribed by the Administrator, under 5 U.S.C. 5702(c)(B), for official travel in that area by employees of the Federal Government. As of April 30, 1979, maximum rates of up to $50 per day have been prescribed by the Administrator for certain areas. An alien who has been paroled into the United States for prosecution, under section 212(d)(5) of the Immigration and Nationality Act (8 U.S.C. 1182(d)(5)), or an alien who either has admitted belonging to a class of aliens who are deportable or has been determined under section 242(b) of that Act (8 U.S.C. 1252(b)) to be deportable, shall be ineligible to receive the fees or allowances provided for under section 7610(a)(1). [Reg. § 301.7610-1.]

☐ [*T.D.* 7899, 7-18-83.]

[Reg. § 301.7611-1]

§ 301.7611-1. Questions and answers relating to church tax inquiries and examinations.—

Church tax inquiry

Q-1: When may the Internal Revenue Service begin an inquiry of a church's tax liability?

A-1: Under section 7611 of the Internal Revenue Code, the Internal Revenue Service may begin a church tax inquiry only when the appropriate Regional Commissioner (or higher Treasury official) reasonably believes, on the basis of facts and circumstances recorded in writing, that the organization (1) may not qualify for tax exemption as a church; (2) may be carrying on an unrelated trade or business (within the meaning of section 513); or (3) may be otherwise engaged in activities subject to tax. Information received by the Internal Revenue Service at its request may not be used to form the basis of a reasonable belief to begin a church tax inquiry, unless the Service's request is made within the procedures of section 7611, is a request permitted by these questions and answers to be made without application of the procedures of section 7611, or is a request to which the procedures of section 7611 do not apply.

Q-2: What is a church tax inquiry within the meaning of section 7611?

A-2: A church tax inquiry is any inquiry to a church (other than a routine request described in Q and A-4, an inquiry described in Q and A-5, an investigation described in Q and A-6 or an examination described in Qs and As 10 and 14), to serve as a basis for determining whether the organization qualifies for tax exemption as a church or whether it is carrying on an unrelated trade or business or is otherwise engaged in activities subject to tax. An inquiry is considered to commence when the Internal Revenue Service requests information or materials from a church of a type contained in church records. The term "church tax inquiry" does not include routine requests for information or inquiries regarding matters which do not primarily concern the tax status or liability of the church itself. See Q and A-4 with respect to routine requests regarding, among other things, withholding responsibilities for income tax or FICA (social security) tax liabilities. See Q and A-6 with respect to the types of investigations, other than routine requests, that are outside the scope of the procedures of section 7611. See Q and A-5 with respect to requests for third party records that are outside the scope of the procedures of section 7611.

Q-3: What is a "church" for purposes of the church tax inquiry and examination procedures of section 7611?

A-3: Solely for purposes of applying the procedures of section 7611, and as used in these questions and answers, the term "church" includes any organization claiming to be a church and any convention or association of churches. For purposes of the procedures of section 7611 and these questions and answers a church does not include separately incorporated church-supported schools or other organizations incorporated separately from the church.

Routine requests

Q-4: What is a routine request to a church that is outside the scope of and does not necessitate application of the procedures of the procedures set forth in section 7611?

A-4: Routine requests to a church will not be considered to commence a church tax inquiry and will not necessitate application of the procedures set forth in section 7611. Routine requests for this purpose include (but are not limited to) questions regarding (1) the filing or failure to file any tax return or information return by the church; (2) compliance with income tax or FICA (social security) tax withholding responsibilities by the church; (3) any supplemental information needed to complete the mechanical processing of any incomplete or incorrect return filed by the church; (4) information necessary to process applications for exempt status and letter ruling requests; (5) information necessary to process and update periodically a church's (i) registrations for tax-free transactions (excise tax), (ii)

elections for exemption from windfall profit tax, or (iii) employment tax exemption requests; (6) information identifying a church that is used to update the Cumulative List of Tax Exempt Organizations (Publication No. 78) and other computer files; and (7) confirmation that a specific business is or is not owned or operated by a church.

Third party records

Q-5: To what extent may the Internal Revenue Service gain access to third party records?

A-5: The Internal Revenue Service may request a church to provide information necessary to locate third-party records (for instance, bank records), including information regarding the church's chartered name, state and year of incorporation, and location of checking and savings accounts, without application of the procedures of section 7611.

Records (for instance, cancelled checks or other records in the possession of a bank) held by third party recordkeepers, as defined in section 7609, are not considered church records. Thus, subject to the provisions set forth in section 7609 regarding third party summonses, access is permitted to such records without regard to the requirements of the procedures set forth in section 7611. The Internal Revenue Service is generally required, under other rules, to inform a church of any Internal Revenue Service requests for materials.

Third party materials may be acquired without application of the procedures of section 7611; however, a determination that a church is not entitled to an exemption, or an assessment of tax for unrelated business income against a church, may not be made solely on the basis of third party records, without first complying with the requirements of two notices and offering of a conference (see Qs and As 9 and 10) pursuant to the procedures set forth in section 7611. This limitation does not apply to assessments of tax other than income tax resulting from loss of exemption or for unrelated business income (for instance, assessments of social security or other employment taxes). Third party bank records will not be used in a manner inconsistent with the procedures set forth in section 7611 or in these questions and answers.

Scope of section 7611

Q-6: What types of investigations, other than routine requests and requests for information necessary to locate and examine third party records, and examination of those records, are outside the scope of the procedures of section 7611?

A-6: The church inquiry and examination procedures described in section 7611 do not apply to (1) any inquiry or examination relating to the tax liability of any person other than a church; (2) any termination assessment under section 6851 or 6852, or jeopardy assessment under section 6861; or (3) any case involving a knowing failure to file a return or a willful attempt to defeat or evade tax (including but not limited to any case involving a failure by the church to withhold or pay social security or other employment taxes or income tax required to be withheld from wages). Additionally, the church inquiry and examination procedures do not apply to any criminal investigations.

The church tax inquiry and examination procedures also do not apply to inquiries or examinations which relate primarily to the tax status (including, but not limited to, social security or self-employment tax or income tax required to be withheld from wages) or liability of persons other than the church (including, but not limited to, the tax status or liability of a contributor or contributors to the church), rather than the tax status or liability of the church itself. These may include, but are not limited to: (1) inquiries or examinations regarding the inurement of church funds to a particular individual or individuals or to another organization, which may result in the denial of all or part of such individual's or organization's deduction for charitable contributions to a church; (2) inquiries or examinations regarding the assignment of income or services or contributions to a church; and (3) inquiries or examinations regarding a vow of poverty by an individual or individuals followed by a transfer of property or an assignment of income or services to a church. Inquiries may be made to a church regarding these matters without being considered to have commenced a church tax inquiry under section 7611, and an examination of church records may be made relating to these issues (including enforcement of a summons for access to such records) without application of the requirements contained in section 7611 applicable to church tax inquiries and examinations. Such examinations are subject to the general rules regarding examinations of taxpayer books and records.

Q-7: What action may be taken if the church or its agents fail to respond to routine requests, or questions regarding other individuals' or organizations' tax liabilities?

A-7: Repeated (two or more) failures by a church or its agents to reply to routine requests (see Q and A-4) will be considered by the appropriate Internal Revenue Service Regional Commissioner to be a reasonable basis for commencement of a church tax inquiry under the church tax inquiry and examination procedures of section 7611. The failure of a church to respond to repeated requests for information regarding individuals' or other organizations' tax liabilities (see Q and A-6) will be considered a reasonable basis for commencement of a church tax inquiry. Failure by a church to provide information necessary to locate third-party records (see Q and A-5) will be a factor, but not a conclusive factor, in determining if there is reasonable cause for commencing a church tax inquiry. For this purpose, a failure to respond to a request means either that no response has been made or that the response does not make a reasonable attempt to submit the information called for by the specific language of the request.

Q-8: Where an inquiry or examination is outside the scope of and does not necessitate application of the procedures of section 7611, what are the limitations on the Internal Revenue Service's actions?

A-8: Inquiries or examinations which are outside the scope of the procedures of section 7611 and therefore are conducted without application of the procedures of section 7611 (for instance, those addressed in Q and A-6) will be limited to the determination of facts and circumstances specifically relating to the tax liabilities of the individuals or other organizations in question. For example, in a case against an individual or other organization, information may be requested or church records examined, if pertinent, regarding amounts of money, property, or services transferred to the individual or individuals in question (including, but not limited to wages, loans, or noncontractual transfers), the use of church funds for personal expenses, or other similar matters, without having to follow the church tax inquiry and examination procedures. As one example, in an assignment of income case against an individual or other organization, information could be requested or church records examined if relevant to an individual's assignment of particular income, donation of property, or transfer of a business to a church. However, without following the church tax inquiry and examination procedures, no examination of a contributor or membership list in the possession of the church will be made, other than under the applicable procedures of section 7611, for the purpose of determining the overall financial structure of the church, merely because such structure was relevant to the church's qualification as a tax-exempt entity and therefore indirectly relevant to the validity of contributors' deductions in general. Inquiries or examinations regarding individuals' or other organizations' tax liabilities will not be used in a manner inconsistent with the procedures set forth in section 7611 or in these questions and answers.

Notice requirements

Q-9: What satisfies the inquiry notice requirement (first notice) upon commencement of a church tax inquiry?

A-9: Upon commencing a church tax inquiry, the appropriate Regional Commissioner is required to provide written notice to the church of the beginning of the inquiry. This notice will include (1) an explanation of the concerns which gave rise to the inquiry and the general subject matter of the inquiry, which is sufficiently specific to allow the church to understand the particular area of church activities or behavior which is at issue; (2) a general explanation of the provisions of the Internal Revenue Code which authorize the inquiry or which may otherwise be involved in the inquiry; and (3) a general explanation of applicable administrative and constitutional provisions with respect to the inquiry, including the right to a conference with the Internal Revenue Service before an examination of church records is commenced. The inquiry notice (first notice) will generally request information in an effort to alleviate the concerns which gave rise to the inquiry.

Reg. §301.7611-1

However, the Internal Revenue Service is not precluded from expanding its inquiry beyond the concerns expressed in the inquiry notice (first notice) as a result of facts and circumstances which subsequently come to its attention (including, where appropriate, an expansion of an unrelated business income inquiry to include questions of tax-exempt status, and vice-versa).

The inquiry notice requirement (first notice) does not require the Internal Revenue Service to share particular items of evidence with the church, or to identify its sources of information regarding church activities, if providing such information would be damaging to the inquiry or to the sources of information. For example, in an inquiry regarding unrelated business income, the Internal Revenue Service might state that its inquiry was prompted by a local newspaper advertisement regarding a church-owned business. However, the Internal Revenue Service would not be required to reveal the existence or identity of any so-called "informers" within a church (including present or former employees).

Q-10: What must be done to satisfy the examination notice requirement (second notice) before commencing an examination of church records or religious activities with respect to an examination conducted under section 7611?

A-10: Where an examination is conducted under section 7611, church records or religious activities of a church may be examined only if, at least 15 days prior to the examination, written notice of the proposed examination is provided to the church and to the appropriate Regional Counsel. This notice is in addition to the notice of commencement of inquiry (first notice) previously provided to the church.

The notice of examination (second notice) is required to include (1) a copy of the church tax inquiry notice (first notice) previously provided to the church; (2) a description of the church records and activities sought to be examined; and (3) a copy of all documents which were collected or prepared by the Internal Revenue Service for use in the examination, and which are required to be disclosed under the Freedom of Information Act (5 U.S.C. § 552) as supplemented by section 6103 of the Code (relating to disclosure and confidentiality of tax return information). The documents to be supplied under this provision will be limited to documents specifically concerning the church whose records are to be examined and will not include documents relating to other inquiries or examinations or to Internal Revenue Service practices and procedures in general. Disclosure to the church is subject to restrictions regarding the disclosure of the existence or identity of informants. Although a description of materials to be examined will be provided in the notice of examination (second notice), the description does not restrict the ability of the Internal Revenue Service to examine church records or religious activities which are not specifically mentioned in the notice of examination (second notice) but which are properly within the scope of the examination. Thus, the Internal Revenue Service is not precluded from

expanding its inquiry beyond the concerns expressed in the examination notice (second notice) as a result of facts and circumstances which subsequently come to its attention (including, where appropriate, an expansion of an unrelated business income examination to include questions of tax-exempt status, and vice versa).

At the time the notice of examination (second notice) is provided to the church, a copy of the same notice will be provided to the appropriate Regional Counsel. The Regional Counsel is then allowed 15 days from issuance of the second notice in which to file an advisory objection to the examination. (This is concurrent with the 15-day period during which an examination of church records is prohibited pending a request for a conference.)

As part of the notice of examination (second notice), the church will be offered an opportunity to meet with an Internal Revenue Service official to discuss the concerns which gave rise to the inquiry and the general subject matter of the inquiry. An examination will not begin until 15 days after the mailing of the notice of examination (second notice). The organization may request a conference at any time prior to beginning of the examination and a conference so requested will be scheduled within a reasonable time after the request is made.

The purpose of the conference is to remind the church, in general terms, of the stages of the church tax inquiry and examination procedures and to discuss the relevant issues that may arise as part of the inquiry, in an effort to resolve the issues of tax exemption or liability without the necessity of an examination of church records or activities. Information properly excludable from a written notice of examination (second notice) (including information regarding the identity of third-party witnesses or evidence provided by such witnesses) is not a subject for discussion at, and will not be revealed during, a conference.

Once a conference request is timely made, an examination will begin only following the conference. The conference requirement may not be utilized to delay an examination beyond the time reasonably necessary to prepare for and hold the conference. The holding of one conference with the church will be sufficient to satisfy the requirements of section 7611 and these questions and answers.

Action after issuance of notice

Q-11: What action may be taken after issuance of the examination notice (second notice)?

A-11: After the examination notice (second notice) is issued, the organization may request a conference as described in Q and A-10 (see Q and A-12 with respect to time for issuance of examination notice). If the matters of concern which gave rise to the issuance of the examination notice (second notice) are resolved at the conference, it may be determined that an examination is not necessary. If the matters of concern are not resolved at the conference, or if the organization does not request a conference, the examination will ordinarily begin.

The examination will be conducted under the Internal Revenue Service's general examination procedures and the procedures of section 7611. The outcome of such an examination will ordinarily be: (1) no change in tax-exempt status or tax liability; (2) no change in such status or liability, conditioned on compliance with a request to modify in future tax periods matters such as internal accounting practices and procedures or coupled with a caution to refrain from increasing certain activities limited by the Internal Revenue Code, such as lobbying programs aimed at influencing legislation; (3) a proposal to revoke tax-exempt status; (4) a proposal asserting unrelated business income tax liability; or (5) a proposal asserting liability for other taxes.

In certain exceptional circumstances the Internal Revenue Service may, in lieu of an examination, propose to revoke the organization's exemption based upon the facts and circumstances which form the basis for a reasonable belief to commence an inquiry under section 7611 and any other appropriate information that becomes apparent as a result of the inquiry, conference, or both.

Pursuant to section 7611(d), the Regional Counsel is required to approve, in writing, certain final determinations that are within the scope of section 7611 and adversely affect tax-exempt status or increase any tax liability. The Regional Counsel will review and approve (1) a determination that an organization is not entitled to tax-exempt status; (2) a determination that an organization is not entitled to receive tax-deductible contributions; or (3) the issuance of a notice of tax deficiency to a church arising out of an inquiry or examination or, in cases where deficiency procedures are inapplicable, the assessment of any underpayment of tax by the church arising out of an inquiry or examination. The Regional Counsel will also state in writing that there has been substantial compliance with section 7611, when applicable.

Procedural time limitations

Q-12: When may the notice of examination (second notice) be sent?

A-12: The notice of examination (second notice) may be mailed to a church not less than 15 days after the notice of commencement of a church tax inquiry (first notice). Thus, at least 30 days must pass between the first notice and the actual examination of church records since an examination may not begin until 15 days after the notice of examination (second notice). For example, if notice of commencement of an inquiry is mailed to a church on March 1st, the notice of proposed examination may be mailed to the church no earlier than the 15th day after the date of the inquiry notice, or March 16th. If the notice of examination (second notice) was mailed March 16th, no examination of church records may be made prior to day 30; thus, the earliest date the examination may commence is March 31st. If an organization does not request a conference prior to day 30, the Internal Revenue Service may proceed to examine church records

and complete its investigation or make a determination based on the information already in its possession.

Q-13: What is the limitation on the amount of time the Internal Revenue Service has to complete inquiries and examinations?

A-13: The Internal Revenue Service is required to complete any church inquiry or examination, and to make a final determination with respect thereto, not later than two years after the date on which the notice of examination (second notice) is mailed to the church. The running of this two-year period is suspended for any period during which (1) a judicial proceeding brought by the church or its officials or agents against the Internal Revenue Service with respect to the church tax inquiry or examination is pending or being appealed (even though section 7611 (e)(2) describes the exclusive remedy for a violation of the church tax inquiry and examination procedures; see Q and A-17); (2) a judicial proceeding brought by the Internal Revenue Service against the church (or any official or agent thereof) to compel compliance with any reasonable request for examination of church records or religious activities is pending or being appealed; or (3) the Internal Revenue Service is unable to take actions with respect to the church tax inquiry or examination by reason of an order issued in a suit under section 7609 involving access to records held by third-party recordkeepers. The two-year period is also suspended for any period in excess of 20 days (but not in excess of 6 months) in which the church or its agents fail to comply with any reasonable request for church records or other information. The two-year period may be extended by mutual agreement of the church and the Internal Revenue Service.

In cases where the inquiry is not followed by an examination notice (second notice), the inquiry must be concluded and a final determination made within 90 days of the date of the notice of inquiry (first notice). This 90-day period is suspended during any period for which the two year period for duration of a church examination would be suspended; except that the 90-day period will not be suspended because of the church's failure to comply with requests for information made prior to the notice of examination (second notice).

Q-13a: When do the church tax inquiry and church tax examination periods commence and conclude?

A-13a: A church tax inquiry commences when the church tax inquiry notice (first notice) is mailed. A church tax inquiry must be concluded not later than 90 days after the church tax inquiry notice (first notice) date. The period is counted from the day after the inquiry notice (first notice) is mailed. A church tax inquiry is concluded when the results of the inquiry or the notice of examination, as appropriate, is mailed. For example, if the inquiry notice (first notice) is mailed on November 1, 1985, the church tax inquiry must be concluded, in the absence of a permissible suspension of the period (see Q and A-13), on or before January 30, 1986.

A church tax examination commences when the church tax examination notice (second notice) is mailed. A church tax examination must be concluded not later than the date which is 2 years after the examination notice (second notice) date. The period is counted from the day after the examination notice (second notice) is mailed. A church tax examination is concluded when the final determination is mailed. For example, if the examination notice is mailed on November 16, 1985, the final determination must be made, in the absence of a permissible suspension of the period (see Q and A-13), on or before November 16, 1987.

Examination of records or religious activities

Q-14: To what extent may church records or religious activities of a church be examined?

A-14: In cases conducted under section 7611, an examination of church records may be made only after complying with the notice provisions of section 7611 (see Qs and As 9, 10 and 12) unless the church files a written waiver of the provisions of section 7611 or a part thereof. In cases conducted under section 7611 where no written waiver has been filed, church records may be examined only to the extent necessary to determine the liability for, and the amount of, any Federal tax. This includes examinations (1) to determine the initial or continuing qualification of the organization whose records are being examined as a tax-exempt church under section 501(c)(3); (2) to determine whether the organization qualifies to receive tax-deductible contributions under section 170(c); or (3) to determine the amount of tax (including unrelated business income tax), if any, which is to be imposed on the organization.

Church records include all regularly kept church corporate and financial records including (but not limited to) corporate minute books, contributor or membership lists, and any materials which qualified as church books of account under section 7605(c), as in effect on December 31, 1984. Church records include private correspondence between a church and its members that is in the possession of the church. However, church records do not include records previously filed with a public official or newspapers or newsletters distributed generally to church members.

The religious activities of an organization claiming to be a church (see Q and A-3 for a definition of the term "church" as used in section 7611 and in these questions and answers) may be examined only to the extent necessary to determine if the organization actually is a church exempt from tax. This includes a determination of the organization's qualification as a church for any period.

Limitations on period of assessment or proceedings for collections without assessment

Q-15: What are the special limitations on the period of assessment or proceedings for collection without assessment?

A-15: The special limitation periods for church tax liabilities are described below and are not to be construed to increase an otherwise applicable limitation period. Thus, a three-year limitation period would apply where a church filed a tax return before an examination was held and did not substantially understate income. No limitation period is to apply in any case of fraud, willful tax evasion, or knowing failure to file a return which should have been filed.

In the case of any church tax examination with respect to the revocation of tax-exempt status under section 501(a), any tax imposed by chapter 1 (other than section 511) may be assessed, or a proceeding in court for collection of such tax may be begun without assessment, only for the three most recently completed taxable years preceding the examination notice date (*i.e.*, the date the notice of examination is mailed to the church). If an organization is not a church exempt from tax under section 501(a) for any of the three years described in the preceding sentence, then the period of assessment will apply to the six most recently completed taxable years ending before the examination notice date.

For examinations concerning qualification for tax-exempt status, the examination is limited initially to an examination of church records which are relevant to a determination of tax status or liability for the three most recently completed taxable years ending before the examination notice date. If it is determined that an organization is not a church exempt from tax for one or more of the three most recently completed taxable years and no return has been filed for the three years ending before the three most recently completed taxable years, an examination of relevant records may be made, as part of the same examination, for the six most recently completed taxable years ending before the examination notice date. (This assumes that no returns were filed for any of the three years to which the examination is to be extended. If a return was timely filed for any such year, the filing of that return determines the applicable statute of limitations for that year in the absence of other factors, for example, fraud, willful tax evasion or substantial understatement, which ordinarily would extend the statute of limitations.)

For purposes of section 7611(d)(2)(A) and this question and answer, an organization is determined not to be a church exempt from tax for one or more of the three most recently completed taxable years ending before the examination notice date, when the appropriate Regional Commissioner approves, in writing, the completed findings of the examining agent that the organization is not a church exempt from tax for one or more of such years. Such approval may not be delegated by the Regional Commissioner to a subordinate official. The completed findings of the examining agent, as approved by the appropriate Regional Commissioner for this purpose, do not constitute a final revenue agent's report under section 7611(g).

Church records of a year earlier than the third or sixth completed taxable year, as applicable, may be examined if material to a determination of tax-exempt status during the applicable three or six year period.

For examinations concerning unrelated business taxable income, where no return has been filed by the church, tax may be assessed or collected for the six most recently completed taxable years ending before the examination notice date. Church records of a year earlier than the sixth year may be examined if material to a determination of unrelated business income tax liability during the six year period.

For examinations involving issues other than revocation of exempt status or unrelated business income (*e.g.*, examinations relating to social security or other employment taxes), no limitation period is to apply if no return has been filed.

The applicable limitation period may be extended by mutual agreement of the church and the Internal Revenue Service.

Multiple examinations

Q-16: What are the special multiple examination rules applicable to churches?

A-16: The Assistant Commissioner (Employee Plans and Exempt Organizations) is required to approve, in writing, any second inquiry or examination of a church, if the second inquiry or examination is to be undertaken within five years of an earlier inquiry or examination and if the earlier inquiry or examination did not result in either (1) revocation of tax exemption, notice of deficiency or an assessment of tax, or (2) a request for any significant changes in church operational practices (including the adequacy or sufficiency of records maintained to reflect income). The Assistant Commissioner's approval is required only if the second inquiry or examination involves the same or similar issues as the earlier inquiry or examination. The 5-year period is counted from the examination notice date of the earlier examination or, if no notice of examination was mailed, the inquiry notice date of the earlier examination. This 5-year period is to be suspended for periods during which the two-year period for completion of an examination is suspended (as described in Q and A-13) unless the prior examination was actually concluded within 2 years of the notice of examination.

In determining whether the second church tax inquiry or examination involves the same or similar issues as the preceding inquiry or examination, the substantive factual issues involved in the two examinations, rather than legal classifications, will govern. For example, where a prior examination and a current examination of unrelated business income involve income from different sources, the current examination involves different issues than the prior examination and the approval of the Assistant Commissioner (Employee Plans and Exempt Organizations) is not necessary.

Remedy for violations of section 7611

Q-17: What remedy is available for a violation of the church inquiry and examination procedures?

A-17: The exclusive remedy for any Internal Revenue Service violation of the church tax inquiry and examination procedures is as follows: Failure to comply substantially with the requirements that (1) two notices be sent to the church; (2) the Regional Commissioner approve the commencement of a church tax inquiry; or (3) an offer of a conference with the church be made (and a conference held if timely requested), will result in a stay of proceedings in a summons proceeding to gain access to church records (but not in dismissal of such proceeding), until these requirements are satisfied. The two-year limitation on duration of a church tax examination will not be suspended during stays of summons proceedings resulting from violations described above; however, violations may be corrected without regard to the otherwise applicable time limits prescribed under the procedures of section 7611. In determining whether a stay is necessary, a court must consider the good faith effort of the Internal Revenue Service and the effect of any violation of the proper examination procedures.

Section 7611(e)(2) provides that no suit may be maintained and no defense may be raised, other than a stay in a summons enforcement proceeding, by reason of any noncompliance with the requirements of section 7611. Thus, failure to comply with any of these requirements may not be raised as a defense or affirmative ground for relief in any judicial proceeding including, but not limited to, a summons proceeding to gain access to church records; a declaratory judgment proceeding involving a determination of tax-exempt status under section 7428; a proceeding to collect unpaid tax; or a deficiency or refund proceeding. Additionally, failure to substantially comply with the requirements that two notices be sent, that the Regional Commissioner approve an inquiry, and that a conference be offered (and the conference held if requested) may not be raised as a defense or as an affirmative ground for relief in a summons proceeding or any other judicial proceeding other than as specifically set forth above. Therefore, a church or its representatives will not be able to litigate the issue of the reasonableness of the appropriate Regional Commissioner's belief in approving the commencement of a church tax inquiry (*i.e.*, that the church may not be tax-exempt or may be engaged in taxable activities) in a summons proceeding or any other judicial proceeding. The church retains the right to raise any substantive or procedural argument which would be available to taxpayers generally in an appropriate proceeding.

Reg. §301.7611-1

Effective date

Q-18: What is the effective date of the church examination procedures?

A-18: The procedures set forth in section 7611 apply to all tax inquiries and examinations beginning after December 31, 1984. The procedures of section 7605 will apply to any examination commenced before January 1, 1985. Any activities commenced after December 31, 1984, that would constitute a new inquiry or new examination must comply with the procedures of section 7611.

Application to Section 4958

Q-19: When do the church tax inquiry and examination procedures described in section 7611 apply to a determination of whether there was an excess benefit transaction described in section 4958?

A-19: See § 53.4958-8(b) of this chapter for rules governing the interaction between section 4958 excise taxes on excess benefit transactions and section 7611 church tax inquiry and examination procedures. [Reg. § 301.7611-1.]

☐ [*T.D. 8013, 3-7-85. Amended by T.D. 8077,* 2-20-86; *T.D. 8628, 12-4-95; T.D. 8920, 1-9-2001* (*corrected* 3-1-2001) *and T.D. 8978, 1-22-2002* (*corrected* 3-18-2002).]

GENERAL POWERS AND DUTIES

[Reg. § 301.7621-1]

§ 301.7621-1. Internal revenue districts.—For delegation to the Secretary of authority to prescribe internal revenue districts for the purpose of administering the internal revenue laws, see Executive Order No. 10289, dated September 17, 1951 (16 F.R. 9499), as made applicable to the Code by Executive Order No. 10574, dated November 5, 1954 (19 F.R. 7249). [Reg. § 301.7621-1.]

☐ [*T.D. 6421, 10-23-59. Amended by T.D. 6498,* 10-24-60.]

[Reg. § 301.7622-1]

§ 301.7622-1. Authority to administer oaths and certify.—The officers and employees of the Internal Revenue Service whom the Commissioner has designated are authorized to administer such oaths or affirmations and to certify to such papers as may be necessary under the internal revenue laws or regulations issued thereunder, except that the authority to certify shall not be construed as applying to those papers or documents the certification of which is authorized by separate order or directive. [Reg. § 301.7622-1.]

☐ [*T.D. 6421, 10-23-59. Amended by T.D. 6498,* 10-24-60; *T.D. 6585, 12-27-61; T.D. 7188, 6-28-72; T.D. 7297, 12-18-73 and T.D. 7359, 5-30-75.]

[Reg. § 301.7623-1]

§ 301.7623-1. General rules, submitting information on underpayments of tax or violations of the internal revenue laws, and filing claims for award.—(a) *In general.*—In cases in which awards are not otherwise provided for by law, the Whistleblower Office may pay an award under section 7623(a), in a suitable amount, for information necessary for detecting underpayments of tax or detecting and bringing to trial and punishment persons guilty of violating the internal revenue laws or conniving at the same. In cases that satisfy the requirements of section 7623(b)(5) and (b)(6) and in which the Internal Revenue Service (IRS) proceeds with an administrative or judicial action based on information provided by an individual, the Whistleblower Office must determine and pay an award under section 7623(b)(1), (2), or (3). The awards provided for by section 7623 and this paragraph must be paid from collected proceeds, as defined in § 301.7623-2(d).

(b) *Eligibility to file claim for award.*—(1) *In general.*—Any individual, other than an individual described in paragraph (b)(2) of this section, is eligible to file a claim for award and to receive an award under section 7623 and §§ 301.7623-1 through 301.7623-4.

(2) *Ineligible whistleblowers.*—The Whistleblower Office will reject any claim for award filed by an ineligible whistleblower and will provide written notice of the rejection to the whistleblower. The following individuals are not eligible to file a claim for award or receive an award under section 7623 and §§ 301.7623-1 through 301.7623-4—

(i) An individual who is an employee of the Department of Treasury or was an employee of the Department of Treasury when the individual obtained the information on which the claim is based;

(ii) An individual who obtained the information through the individual's official duties as an employee of the Federal Government, or who is acting within the scope of those official duties as an employee of the Federal Government;

(iii) An individual who is or was required by Federal law or regulation to disclose the information or who is or was precluded by Federal law or regulation from disclosing the information;

(iv) An individual who obtained or had access to the information based on a contract with the Federal Government; or

(v) An individual who filed a claim for award based on information obtained from an ineligible whistleblower for the purpose of avoiding the rejection of the claim that would have resulted if the claim was filed by the ineligible whistleblower.

(c) *Submission of information and claims for award.*—(1) *Submitting information.*—To be eligible to receive an award under section 7623 and §§ 301.7623-1 through 301.7623-4, a whistleblower must submit to the IRS specific and credible information that the whistleblower believes will lead to collected proceeds from one or more persons whom the whistleblower believes have failed to comply with the internal revenue laws. In general, a whistleblower's submission should identify the person(s) believed to have failed to comply with the internal revenue laws and should provide substantive information, including all available documentation, that supports the whistleblower's allegations. Information that identifies a pass-through entity will be considered to also identify all persons with a direct or indirect interest in the entity. Information that identifies a member of a firm who promoted another identified person's participation in a transaction described and documented in the information provided will be considered to also identify the firm and all other members of the firm. Submissions that provide speculative information or that do not provide specific and credible information regarding tax underpayments or violations of internal revenue laws do not provide a basis for an award. If documents or supporting evidence are known to the whistleblower but are not in the whistleblower's control, then the whistleblower should describe the documents or supporting evidence and identify their location to the best of the whistleblower's ability. If all available information known to the whistleblower is not provided to the IRS by the whistleblower, then the whistleblower bears the risk that this information might not be considered by the Whistleblower Office for purposes of an award.

(2) *Filing claim for award.*—To claim an award under section 7623 and §§ 301.7623-1 through 301.7623-4 for information provided to the IRS, a whistleblower must file a formal claim for award by completing and sending Form 211, "Application for Award for Original Information," to the Internal Revenue Service, Whistleblower Office, at the address provided on the form, or by complying with other claim filing procedures as may be prescribed by the IRS in other published guidance. The Form 211 should be completed in its entirety and should include the following information—

(i) The date of the claim;

(ii) The whistleblower's name;

(iii) The whistleblower's address and telephone number;

(iv) The whistleblower's date of birth;

(v) The whistleblower's taxpayer identification number; and

(vi) An explanation of how the information on which the claim is based came to the attention and into the possession of the whistleblower, including, as available, the date(s) on which the whistleblower acquired the information and a complete description of the whistleblower's present or former relationship (if any) to person(s) identified on the Form 211.

(3) *Under penalty of perjury.*—No award may be made under section 7623(b) unless the infor-

mation on which the award is based is submitted to the IRS under penalty of perjury. All claims for award under section 7623 and §§ 301.7623-1 through 301.7623-4 must be accompanied by an original signed declaration under penalty of perjury, as follows: "I declare under penalty of perjury that I have examined this application, my accompanying statement, and supporting documentation and aver that such application is true, correct, and complete, to the best of my knowledge." This requirement precludes the filing of a claim for award by a person serving as a representative of, or in any way on behalf of, another individual. Claims filed by more than one whistleblower (joint claims) must be signed by each individual whistleblower under penalty of perjury.

(4) *Perfecting claim for award.*—If a whistleblower files a claim for award that does not include information described under paragraph (c)(2) of this section, does not contain specific and credible information as described in paragraph (c)(1) of this section, or is based on information that was not submitted under penalty of perjury as required by paragraph (c)(3) of this section, the Whistleblower Office may reject the claim or notify the whistleblower of the deficiencies and provide the whistleblower an opportunity to perfect the claim for award. If a whistleblower does not perfect the claim for award within the time period specified by the Whistleblower Office, then the Whistleblower Office may reject the claim. If the Whistleblower Office rejects a claim, then the Whistleblower Office will provide notice of the rejection to the whistleblower pursuant to the rules of § 301.7623-3(b)(3) or (c)(7). If the Whistleblower Office rejects a claim for the reasons described in this paragraph, then the whistleblower may perfect and resubmit the claim.

(d) *Request for assistance.*—(1) *In general.*—The Whistleblower Office, the IRS, or IRS Office of Chief Counsel may request the assistance of a whistleblower or the whistleblower's legal representative. Any assistance shall be at the direction and control of the Whistleblower Office, the IRS, or the IRS Office of Chief Counsel assigned to the matter. See § 301.6103(n)-2 for rules regarding written contracts among the IRS, whistleblowers, and legal representatives of whistleblowers.

(2) *No agency relationship.*—Submitting information, filing a claim for award, or responding to a request for assistance does not create an agency relationship between a whistleblower and the Federal Government, nor does a whistleblower or the whistleblower's legal representative act in any way on behalf of the Federal Government.

(e) *Confidentiality of whistleblowers.*—Under the informant's privilege, the IRS will use its best efforts to protect the identity of whistleblowers. In some circumstances, the IRS may need to reveal a whistleblower's identity, for example, when it is determined that it is in the best interests of the Government to use a whistleblower as a witness in a judicial proceeding. In those circumstances, the IRS will make every effort to notify the whistleblower before revealing the whistleblower's identity.

(f) *Effective/applicability date.*—This rule is effective on August 12, 2014. This rule applies to information submitted on or after August 12, 2014, and to claims for award under sections 7623(a) and 7623(b) that are open as of August 12, 2014. [Reg. § 301.7623-1.]

☐ [*T.D. 6421,* 10-23-59. *Amended by T.D. 6498,* 10-24-60; *T.D. 7188,* 6-28-72; *T.D. 7297,* 12-18-73; *T.D. 8737,* 10-10-97; *T.D. 8780,* 8-20-98; *T.D. 9580,* 2-21-2012 *and T.D. 9687,* 8-7-2014.]

[Reg. § 301.7623-2]

§ 301.7623-2. Definitions.—(a) *Action.*—(1) *In general.*—For purposes of section 7623(b) and §§ 301.7623-1 through 301.7623-4, the term *action* means an administrative or judicial action.

(2) *Administrative action.*—For purposes of section 7623(b) and §§ 301.7623-1 through 301.7623-4, the term *administrative action* means all or a portion of an Internal Revenue Service (IRS) civil or criminal proceeding against any person that may result in collected proceeds, as defined in paragraph (d) of this section, including, for example, an examination, a collection proceeding, a status determination proceeding, or a criminal investigation.

(3) *Judicial action.*—For purposes of section 7623(b) and §§ 301.7623-1 through 301.7623-4, the term *judicial action* means all or a portion of a proceeding against any person in any court that may result in collected proceeds, as defined in paragraph (d) of this section.

(b) *Proceeds based on.*—(1) *In general.*—For purposes of section 7623(b) and §§ 301.7623-1 through 301.7623-4, the IRS *proceeds based on* information provided by a whistleblower when the information provided substantially contributes to an action against a person identified by the whistleblower. For example, the IRS proceeds based on the information provided when the IRS initiates a new action, expands the scope of an ongoing action, or continues to pursue an ongoing action, that the IRS would not have initiated, expanded the scope of, or continued to pursue, but for the information provided. The IRS does not proceed based on information when the IRS analyzes the information provided or investigates a matter raised by the information provided.

(2) *Examples.*—The provisions of paragraph (b)(1) of this section may be illustrated by the following examples:

Example 1. Information provided to the IRS by a whistleblower, under section 7623 and § 301.7623-1, identifies a taxpayer, describes and documents specific facts relating to the taxpayer's foreign sales in Country A, and, based on those facts, alleges that the taxpayer was not entitled to a foreign tax credit relating to its foreign sales in Country A. The IRS receives the information after having already initiated an examination of the taxpayer. The IRS's audit plan includes foreign tax credit issues but focuses on taxpayer's foreign sales in Country B and does not specifically address the taxpayer's foreign sales in Country A. Based on the information provided, the IRS expands the examination of the foreign tax credit issue to include consideration of the amount of foreign tax credit relating to the taxpayer's foreign sales in Country A. For purposes of section 7623 and §§ 301.7623-1 through 301.7623-4, the portion of the IRS's examination of the taxpayer relating to the foreign tax credit issue with respect to Country A is an administrative action with which the IRS proceeds based on the information provided by the whistleblower because the information provided substantially contributed to the action by causing the expansion of the IRS's examination.

Example 2. Information provided to the IRS by a whistleblower, under section 7623 and § 301.7623-1, identifies a taxpayer, describes and documents specific facts relating to the taxpayer's activities, and, based on those facts, alleges that the taxpayer owed additional taxes in Year 1. The IRS proceeds with an examination of the taxpayer for Year 1 based on the information provided by the whistleblower. The IRS discovers that the taxpayer engaged in the same activities in Year 2 and expands the examination to Year 2. In the course of the examination, the IRS obtains, through the issuance of Information Document Requests (IDRs) and summonses, additional facts that are unrelated to the activities described in the information provided by the whistleblower. Based on these additional facts, the IRS expands the scope of the examination of the taxpayer for both Year 1 and Year 2. For purposes of section 7623 and §§ 301.7623-1 through 301.7623-4, the portion of the IRS's examination relating to the activities described and documented in the information provided is an administrative action with which the IRS proceeds based on information provided by the whistleblower because the information provided substantially contributed to the action by causing the expansion of the IRS's examination of Year 1 and Year 2. The portions of the IRS's examination of the taxpayer in both Year 1 and Year 2 relating to the additional facts obtained through the issuance of IDRs and summonses are not actions with which the IRS proceeds based on the information provided by the whistleblower because the information provided did not substantially contribute to the action.

Example 3. Information provided to the IRS by a whistleblower, under section 7623 and § 301.7623-1, identifies a taxpayer, describes and documents specific facts relating to the taxpayer's activities, and, based on those facts, alleges that the taxpayer owed additional taxes in Year 1. The IRS receives the information after having already initiated an examination of the taxpayer for Year 1. During the examination, the information is provided to the Exam team and the Exam team uses the information provided to confirm the correctness of adjustments made based on other information. Although the whistleblower's information confirms the correctness of the IRS's adjustments, the IRS does not rely on the whistleblower's information when it makes the adjustments, nor does the information cause the IRS to expand the scope of its examination. The whistleblower's information merely supports information independently obtained by the IRS. For purposes of section 7623 and §§ 301.7623-1 through 301.7623-4, the IRS's examination is not an administrative action with which the IRS proceeds based on information provided by the whistleblower because the information provided did not substantially contribute to the action.

Example 4. Same facts as *Example 3.* During the examination, however, the Exam team identifies inconsistencies between the information provided by the whistleblower and other information already in the Exam team's possession. The Exam team uses the information provided by the whistleblower to make additional adjustments that it would not have made based solely on the other information. For purposes of section 7623 and §§ 301.7623-1 through 301.7623-4, the portion of the IRS's examination relating to the additional adjustments is an administrative action with which the IRS proceeds based on information provided by the whistleblower because the information provided substantially contributed to the action.

(c) *Related action.*—(1) *In general.*—For purposes of section 7623(b) and §§ 301.7623-1 through 301.7623-4, the term *related action* means an action against a person other than the person(s) identified in the information provided and subject to the original action(s), when—

(i) The facts relating to the underpayment of tax or violations of the internal revenue laws by the other person are substantially the same as the facts described and documented in the information provided (with respect to the person(s) subject to the original action);

(ii) The IRS proceeds with the action against the other person based on the specific facts described and documented in the information provided; and

(iii) The other, unidentified person is related to the person identified in the information provided. For purposes of this paragraph, an unidentified person is related to the person identified in the information provided if the IRS can identify the unidentified person using the information provided (without first having to use the information provided to identify any other person or having to independently obtain additional information).

(2) *Examples.*—The provisions of paragraph (c)(1) of this section may be illustrated by the following examples:

Example 1. Information provided to the IRS by a whistleblower, under section 7623 and § 301.7623-1, identifies a taxpayer (Taxpayer 1), describes and documents specific facts relating to Taxpayer 1's activities, and, based on those facts, alleges tax underpayments by Taxpayer 1. The information provided also identifies an accountant (CPA 1) and describes and documents specific facts relating to CPA 1's contribution to the activities of Taxpayer 1 that the whistleblower alleges resulted in tax underpayments. The IRS proceeds with an examination of Taxpayer 1 based on the information provided by the whistleblower. Using the information provided, the IRS obtains CPA 1's client list and identifies two taxpayers/clients of CPA 1 (Taxpayer 2 and Taxpayer 3) that appear to have engaged in activities similar to Taxpayer 1. The IRS proceeds with an examination of Taxpayer 2 and finds that Taxpayer 2 engaged in the same activities as those described in the information provided with respect to Taxpayer 1. The IRS proceeds with an examination of Taxpayer 3 and finds that Taxpayer 3 engaged in different activities from those described in the information provided with respect to Taxpayer 1. For purposes of section 7623 and §§ 301.7623-1 through 301.7623-4, the examination of Taxpayer 2 is a related action because it satisfies the conditions of paragraph (c)(1) of this section. The examination of Taxpayer 3 is not a related action because the relevant facts are not substantially the same as the facts relevant to the examination of Taxpayer 1.

Example 2. Same facts as *Example 1.* Using the information provided by the whistleblower, the IRS identifies a co-promoter of CPA 1 (CPA 2) that appears to have engaged in activities similar to CPA 1. CPA 2 is not a member of CPA 1's firm. The IRS subsequently obtains the client list of CPA 2 and identifies a taxpayer/client of CPA 2 (Taxpayer 4) that appears to have engaged in activities similar to Taxpayer 1. The IRS proceeds with an examination of Taxpayer 4 and finds that Taxpayer 4 engaged in the same activities as those described in the information provided with respect to Taxpayer 1, and that CPA 2 contributed to the activities in the same way as described in the information provided with respect to CPA 1. The IRS proceeds with an examination of CPA 2's liability for promoter penalties under section 6700 in connection with the activities described in the information provided with respect to Taxpayer 1 and CPA 1. For purposes of section 7623 and §§ 301.7623-1 through 301.7623-4, the examination of CPA 2 is a related action because it satisfies the conditions of paragraph (c)(1) of this section. The examination of Taxpayer 4 is not a related action because Taxpayer 4 was not related to a person identified in the information provided. CPA 2 was not identified in the information provided and the IRS first had to identify CPA 2 before identifying Taxpayer 4 and proceeding with the examination of Taxpayer 4.

Example 3. Same facts as *Example 1.* An accountant (CPA 3) is a member of CPA 1's firm. Using the information provided by the whistleblower, the IRS obtains the client list of CPA 3 and identifies a taxpayer/client of CPA 3 (Taxpayer 5) that appears to have engaged in activities similar to Taxpayer 1. The IRS proceeds with an examination of Taxpayer 5 and finds that Taxpayer 5 engaged in the same activities as those described in the information provided with respect to Taxpayer 1, and that CPA 3 contributed to the activities in the same way as described in the information provided with respect to CPA 1. For purposes of section 7623 and §§ 301.7623-1 through 301.7623-4, the examination of Taxpayer 5 is a related action because Taxpayer 5 is related to CPA 3, a person considered to be identified in the information provided under § 301.7623-1(c)(1), and the facts relating to Taxpayer 5 are substantially the same as the facts described and documented in the information provided. An IRS examination of CPA 3's liability for promoter penalties under section 6700, based on the facts described and documented in the information provided with respect to Taxpayer 1 and CPA 1, is an administrative action based on the information provided.

Example 4. Information provided to the IRS by a whistleblower, under section 7623 and § 301.7623-1, identifies a taxpayer (Taxpayer 1), describes and documents specific facts relating to Taxpayer 1's activities, and, in particular, Taxpayer 1's participation in a transaction. Based on those facts, the whistleblower alleges that Taxpayer 1 owed additional taxes. The IRS proceeds with an examination of Taxpayer 1 based on the information provided by the whistleblower. The IRS identifies the other parties to the transaction described in the information provided (Taxpayer 2 and Taxpayer 3). The IRS proceeds with examinations of Taxpayer 2 and Taxpayer 3 relating to their participation in the transaction described in the information provided. For purposes of section 7623 and §§ 301.7623-1 through 301.7623-4, the IRS's examinations of Taxpayer 2 and Taxpayer 3 relating to the activities described and documented in the information provided are related actions because they satisfy the conditions of paragraph (c)(1) of this section.

(d) *Collected proceeds.*—(1) *In general.*—For purposes of section 7623 and §§ 301.7623-1 through 301.7623-4, the terms *proceeds of amounts collected* and *collected proceeds* (collectively, *collected proceeds*) include: tax, penalties, interest, additions to tax, and additional amounts collected because of the information provided; amounts collected prior to receipt of the information if the information provided results in the denial of a claim for refund that otherwise would have been paid; and a reduction of an overpayment credit balance used to satisfy a tax liability incurred because of the information provided. Collected proceeds are limited to amounts collected under the provisions of title 26, United States Code.

(2) *Refund netting.*—(i) *In general.*—If any portion of a claim for refund that is substantively unrelated to the information provided is—

(A) Allowed, and

(B) Used to satisfy a tax liability attributable to the information provided instead of refunded to the taxpayer, then the allowed but non-refunded amount constitutes collected proceeds.

(ii) *Example.*—The provisions of paragraph (d)(2)(i) of this section may be illustrated by the following example:

Example. Information provided to the IRS by a whistleblower, under section 7623 and § 301.7623-1, identifies a corporate taxpayer (Corporation), describes and documents specific facts relating to Corporation's activities, and, based on those facts, alleges that Corporation owed additional taxes. Based on the information provided by the whistleblower, the IRS proceeds with an examination of Corporation and determines adjustments that would result in an unpaid tax liability of $500,000. During the examination, Corporation informally claims a refund of $400,000 based on adjustments to items of income and expense that are wholly unrelated to the information provided by the whistleblower. The IRS agrees to the unrelated adjustments. The IRS nets the adjustments and determines a tax deficiency of $100,000. Thereafter, Corporation makes full payment of the $100,000 deficiency. For purposes of section 7623 and §§ 301.7623-1 through 301.7623-4, the collected proceeds include the $400,000 informally claimed as a refund and netted against the adjustments attributable to the information provided, as well as the $100,000 paid by Corporation.

(3) *Amended returns.*—Amounts collected based on amended returns constitute collected proceeds if—

(i) The IRS proceeds based on the information provided;

(ii) As a result, the person subject to the action(s) with which the IRS proceeds files amended returns; and

(iii) The amounts collected based on the amended returns relate to the activities or facts described in the information provided.

(4) *Criminal fines.*—Criminal fines deposited into the Crime Victims Fund are not collected proceeds and cannot be used for payment of awards.

(5) *Computation of collected proceeds.*—(i) *In general.*—Pursuant to § 301.7623-4(d)(1), the IRS cannot make an award payment until there has been a final determination of tax. For purposes of determining the amount of an award under section 7623 and §§ 301.7623-1 through 301.7623-4, after there has been a final determination of tax as defined in § 301.7623-4(d)(2), the IRS will compute the amount of collected proceeds based on all information known with respect to the taxpayer's account, including with respect to all tax attributes, as of the date the computation is made.

(ii) *Post-determination proceeds.*—If, based on all information known with respect to the taxpayer's account as of the date of the computation described in paragraph (d)(5)(i) of this section, there is a possibility that the IRS may collect additional proceeds, then the Whistleblower Office will continue to monitor the case. If the Whistleblower Office identifies additional collected proceeds, then the IRS will compute and pay accordingly.

(iii) *Partial collection.*—If the IRS does not collect the full amount of taxes, penalties, interest, additions to tax, and additional amounts assessed against the taxpayer, then any amounts that the IRS does collect will constitute collected proceeds in the same proportion that the adjustments attributable to the information provided bear to the total adjustments.

(e) *Amount in dispute and gross income.*—(1) *In general.*—Section 7623(b) applies with respect to any action against any taxpayer in which the tax, penalties, interest, additions to tax, and additional amounts in dispute exceed $2,000,000 but, if the taxpayer is an individual, then only if the taxpayer's gross income exceeds $200,000 in at least one taxable year subject to the action.

(2) *Amount in dispute.*—(i) *In general.*—For purposes of section 7623(b)(5) and §§ 301.7623-1 through 301.7623-4, the term *amount in dispute* means the greater of the maximum total of tax, penalties, interest, additions to tax, and additional amounts that resulted from the action(s) with which the IRS proceeded based on the information provided, or the maximum total of such amounts that were stated in formal positions taken by the IRS in the action(s). The IRS will compute the amount in dispute, for purposes of award determinations described in § 301.7623-3(c)(6), when there has been a final determination of tax as defined in § 301.7623-4(d)(2).

(ii) *Examples.*—The provisions of paragraph (e)(2)(i) of this section may be illustrated by the following examples:

Example 1. Information provided to the IRS by a whistleblower, under section 7623 and § 301.7623-1, identifies a corporate taxpayer, describes and documents specific facts relating to the taxpayer's activities, and, based on those facts, alleges that the taxpayer owed additional taxes. The IRS proceeds with an examination of the taxpayer based on the information provided by the whistleblower; makes adjustments to items of income and expense and allows certain credits; and, ultimately, determines a deficiency against the taxpayer of $1,900,000 and issues the taxpayer a statutory notice of deficiency. The taxpayer petitions the notice to the United States Tax Court. The Tax Court sustains the IRS's position resulting in a deficiency of $1,900,000. Following the final determination of tax, the IRS computes that the total of tax, penalties, interest, additions to tax, and additional amounts that resulted from the action was $2,500,000. For purposes of section 7623 and §§ 301.7623-1 through 301.7623-4, the amount in dispute is $2,500,000.

Example 2. Same facts as *Example 1*, except the IRS determines a deficiency of $1,500,000; the Tax Court sustains the deficiency of $1,500,000; and, following the final determination of tax, the IRS computes that the total of tax, penalties, interest, additions to tax, and additional amounts that resulted from the action was $1,750,000. For purposes of section 7623 and §§ 301.7623-1 through 301.7623-4, the amount in dispute is $1,750,000.

Example 3. Same facts as *Example 1*, except the IRS determines a deficiency of $2,100,000; the Tax Court redetermines a deficiency of $1,500,000; and, following the final determination of tax, the IRS computes that the total of tax, penalties, interest, additions to tax, and additional amounts that resulted from the action was $1,750,000. For purposes of section 7623 and §§ 301.7623-1 through 301.7623-4, the amount in dispute is $2,100,000.

(3) *Gross income.*—For purposes of section 7623(b)(5) and §§ 301.7623-1 through 301.7623-4, the term *gross income* has the same meaning as provided under section 61(a). The IRS will compute the individual taxpayer's gross income, for purposes of award determinations described in § 301.7623-3(c)(6), when there has been a final determination of tax as defined in § 301.7623-4(d)(2).

(f) *Effective/applicability date.*—This rule is effective on August 12, 2014. This rule applies to information submitted on or after August 12, 2014, and to claims for award under sections 7623(a) and 7623(b) that are open as of August 12, 2014. [Reg. § 301.7623-2.]

☐ [T.D. 9687, 8-7-2014 (*corrected* 9-25-2014).]

[Reg. § 301.7623-3]

§ 301.7623-3. Whistleblower administrative proceedings and appeals of award determinations.—(a) *In general.*—The Whistleblower Office will pay awards under section 7623(a) and determine and pay awards under section 7623(b) in whistleblower administrative proceedings pursuant to the rules of this section. The whistleblower administrative proceedings described in this section are administrative proceedings pertaining to tax administration for purposes of section 6103(h)(4). See § 301.6103(h)(4)-1 for additional rules regarding disclosures of return information in whistleblower administrative proceedings. The Whistleblower Office may determine awards for claims involving multiple actions in a single whistleblower administrative proceeding. For purposes of the whistleblower administrative proceedings for rejections and denials, described in paragraphs (b)(3), (c)(7), and (c)(8) of this section, the Internal Revenue Service (IRS) may rely on the whistleblower's description of the amount owed by the taxpayer(s). The IRS may, however, rely on other information as necessary (for example, when the alleged amount in dispute is below the $2 million threshold of section 7623(b)(5)(B), but the actual amount in dispute is above the threshold).

(b) *Awards under section 7623(a).*—(1) *Preliminary award recommendation.*—In cases in which the Whistleblower Office recommends payment of an award under section 7623(a), the Whistleblower Office will communicate a preliminary award recommendation under section 7623(a) and §§ 301.7623-1 through 301.7623-4 to the whistleblower by sending a preliminary award recommendation letter that states the Whistleblower Office's preliminary computation of the amount of collected proceeds, recommended award percentage, recommended award amount (even in cases when the application of § 301.7623-4 results in a reduction of the recommended award amount to zero), and a list of the factors that contributed to the recommended award percentage. The whistleblower administrative proceeding described in paragraphs (b)(1) and (2) of this section begins on the date the Whistleblower Office sends the preliminary award recommendation letter. If the whistleblower believes that the Whistleblower Office erred in evaluating the information provided, the whistleblower has 30 days from the date the Whistleblower Office sends the preliminary award recommendation to submit comments to the Whistleblower Office (this period may be extended at the sole discretion of the Whistleblower Office). The Whistleblower Office will review all comments submitted timely by the whistleblower (or the whistleblower's legal representative, if any) and pay an award, pursuant to paragraph (b)(2) of this section.

(2) *Decision letter.*—At the conclusion of the process described in paragraph (b)(1) of this section, and when there is a final determination of tax, as defined in § 301.7623-4(d)(2), the Whistleblower Office will pay an award under section 7623(a) and §§ 301.7623-1 through 301.7623-4. The Whistleblower Office will communicate the amount of the award to the whistleblower in a decision letter.

(3) *Rejections and denials.*—If the Whistleblower Office rejects a claim for award under section 7623(a), pursuant to § 301.7623-1(b) or (c), or if the IRS either did not proceed based on information provided by the whistleblower, as defined in § 301.7623-2(b), or did not collect proceeds, as defined in § 301.7623-2(d), then the Whistleblower Office will not apply the rules of paragraphs (b)(1) or (2) of this section. The Whistleblower Office will provide written notice to the whistleblower of the rejection or denial of any award and, in the case of a rejection, the written notice will state the basis for the rejection.

(c) *Awards under section 7623(b).*—(1) *Preliminary award recommendation.*—For claims under section 7623(b) other than those described in paragraphs (c)(7) and (c)(8) of this section (rejections and denials), the Whistleblower Office will prepare a preliminary award recommendation based on the Whistleblower Office's review of the administrative claim file and the application of the rules of section 7623 and §§ 301.7623-1 through 301.7623-4 to the facts of the case. See paragraph (e)(2) of this section for a description of the administrative claim file. The

whistleblower administrative proceeding described in paragraphs (c)(1) through (6) of this section begins on the date the Whistleblower Office sends the preliminary award recommendation letter. The preliminary award recommendation is not a determination letter within the meaning of paragraph (c)(6) of this section and cannot be appealed to Tax Court under section 7623(b)(4) and paragraph (d) of this section. The preliminary award recommendation will notify the whistleblower that the IRS cannot determine or pay any award until there is a final determination of tax, as defined in § 301.7623-4(d)(2).

(2) *Contents of preliminary award recommendation.*—The Whistleblower Office will communicate the preliminary award recommendation under section 7623(b) to the whistleblower by sending—

(i) A preliminary award recommendation letter that describes the whistleblower's options for responding to the preliminary award recommendation;

(ii) A summary report that states a preliminary computation of the amount of collected proceeds, the recommended award percentage, the recommended award amount (even in cases when the application of section 7623(b)(2) or section 7623(b)(3) results in a reduction of the recommended award amount to zero), and a list of the factors that contributed to the recommended award percentage;

(iii) An award consent form; and

(iv) A confidentiality agreement.

(3) *Opportunity to respond to preliminary award recommendation.*—The whistleblower will have 30 days (this period may be extended at the sole discretion of the Whistleblower Office) from the date the Whistleblower Office sends the preliminary award recommendation letter to respond to the preliminary award recommendation in one of the following ways—

(i) If the whistleblower takes no action, then the Whistleblower Office will make an award determination, pursuant to paragraph (c)(6) of this section;

(ii) If the whistleblower signs, dates, and returns the award consent form agreeing to the preliminary award recommendation and waiving any and all administrative and judicial appeal rights, then the Whistleblower Office will make an award determination, pursuant to paragraph (c)(6) of this section;

(iii) If the whistleblower signs, dates, and returns the confidentiality agreement, then the Whistleblower Office will provide the whistleblower with a detailed award report, and an opportunity to review documents supporting the report pursuant to paragraphs (c)(4) and (5) of this section, and any comments submitted by the whistleblower will be added to the administrative claim file; or

(iv) If the whistleblower submits comments on the preliminary award recommendation to the Whistleblower Office, but does not sign, date, and return the confidentiality agreement, then the comments will be added to the administrative claim file and reviewed by the Whistleblower Office in making an award determination, pursuant to paragraph (c)(6) of this section.

(4) *Detailed report.*—(i) *Contents of detailed report.*—If the whistleblower signs, dates, and returns the confidentiality agreement accompanying the preliminary award recommendation under section 7623(b), pursuant to paragraph (c)(3) of this section, then the Whistleblower Office will send the whistleblower—

(A) A detailed report that states a preliminary computation of the amount of collected proceeds, the recommended award percentage, and the recommended award amount, and provides a full explanation of the factors that contributed to the recommended award percentage;

(B) Instructions for scheduling an appointment for the whistleblower (and the whistleblower's legal representative, if any) to review information in the administrative claim file that is not protected by one or more common law or statutory privileges; and

(C) An award consent form.

(ii) *Opportunity to respond to detailed report.*—The whistleblower will have 30 days (this period may be extended at the sole discretion of the Whistleblower Office) from the date the Whistleblower Office sends the detailed report to respond in one of the following ways—

(A) If the whistleblower takes no action, then the Whistleblower Office will make an award determination, pursuant to paragraph (c)(6) of this section;

(B) If the whistleblower requests an appointment to review information from the administrative claim file that is not protected from disclosure by one or more common law or statutory privileges, then a meeting will be arranged pursuant to paragraph (c)(5) of this section;

(C) If the whistleblower does not request an appointment but does submit comments on the detailed report to the Whistleblower Office, then the comments will be added to the administrative claim file and reviewed by the Whistleblower Office in making an award determination pursuant to paragraph (c)(6) of this section; or

(D) If the whistleblower signs, dates, and returns the award consent form agreeing to the preliminary award recommendation and waiving any and all administrative and judicial appeal rights, then the Whistleblower Office will make an award determination, pursuant to paragraph (c)(6) of this section.

(iii) *Additional rules.*—The detailed report is not a determination letter within the meaning of paragraph (c)(6) of this section and cannot be appealed to Tax Court under section 7623(b)(4) and paragraph (d) of this section. The detailed report will notify the whistleblower that the IRS cannot determine or pay any award until there is a final determination of tax, as defined in §301.7623-4(d)(2).

(5) *Opportunity to review documents supporting award report recommendations.*—Appointments for the whistleblower (and the whistleblower's legal representative, if any) to review information from the administrative claim file that is not protected from disclosure by one or more common law or statutory privileges will be held at the Whistleblower Office in Washington, D.C., unless the Whistleblower Office, in its sole discretion, decides to hold the meeting at another location. At the appointment, the Whistleblower Office will provide for viewing the information from the administrative claim file. The Whistleblower Office will supervise the whistleblower's review of the information and the whistleblower will not be permitted to make copies of any documents or other information. The whistleblower will have 30 days (this period may be extended at the sole discretion of the Whistleblower Office) from the date of the appointment to submit comments on the detailed report and the documents reviewed at the appointment to the Whistleblower Office. All comments will be added to the administrative claim file and reviewed by the Whistleblower Office in making an award determination, pursuant to paragraph (c)(6) of this section.

(6) *Determination letter.*—After the whistleblower's participation in the whistleblower administrative proceeding, pursuant to paragraph (c) of this section, has concluded, and there is a final determination of tax, as defined in §301.7623-4(d)(2), a Whistleblower Office official will determine the amount of the award under section 7623(b)(1), (2), or (3), and §§301.7623-1 through 301.7623-4, based on the official's review of the administrative claim file. The Whistleblower Office will communicate the award to the whistleblower in a determination letter, stating the amount of the award. If, however, the whistleblower has executed an award consent form agreeing to the amount of the award and waiving the whistleblower's right to appeal the award determination, pursuant to section 7623(b)(4) and paragraph (d) of this section, then the Whistleblower Office will not send the whistleblower a determination letter and will make payment of the award as promptly as circumstances permit.

(7) *Rejections.*—A rejection is a determination that relates solely to the whistleblower and the information on the face of the claim that pertains to the whistleblower. If the Whistleblower Office rejects a claim for award under section 7623(b), pursuant to §301.7623-1(b) or (c), then the Whistleblower Office will not apply the rules of paragraphs (c)(1) through (6) of this section. The Whistleblower Office will send to the whistleblower a preliminary rejection letter that states the basis for the rejection of the claim. The whistleblower administrative proceeding described in this paragraph begins on the date the Whistleblower Office sends the preliminary rejection letter. If the whistleblower believes that the Whistleblower Office erred in evaluating the information pro-

vided, the whistleblower has 30 days from the date the Whistleblower Office sends the preliminary rejection letter to submit comments to the Whistleblower Office (this period may be extended at the sole discretion of the Whistleblower Office). The Whistleblower Office will review all comments submitted timely by the whistleblower (or the whistleblower's legal representative, if any) and, following that review, the Whistleblower Office will either provide written notice to the whistleblower of the rejection of the claim, including the basis for the rejection, or apply the rules of paragraphs (c)(1) through (c)(6) of this section.

(8) *Denials.*—A denial is a determination that relates to or implicates taxpayer information. If, with respect to a claim for award under section 7623(b), the IRS either did not proceed based on the information provided by the whistleblower, as defined in § 301.7623-2(b), or did not collect proceeds, as defined in § 301.7623-2(d), then the Whistleblower Office will not apply the rules of paragraphs (c)(1) through (6) of this section. The Whistleblower Office will send to the whistleblower a preliminary denial letter that states the basis for the denial of the claim. The whistleblower administrative proceeding described in this paragraph begins on the date the Whistleblower Office sends the preliminary denial letter. If the whistleblower believes that the Whistleblower Office erred in evaluating the information provided, the whistleblower has 30 days from the date the Whistleblower Office sends the preliminary denial letter to submit comments to the Whistleblower Office (this period may be extended at the sole discretion of the Whistleblower Office). The Whistleblower Office will review all comments submitted timely by the whistleblower (or the whistleblower's legal representative, if any) and, following that review, the Whistleblower Office will either provide written notice to the whistleblower of the denial of any award, including the basis for the denial, or apply the rules of paragraphs (c)(1) through (c)(6) of this section.

(d) *Appeal of award determination.*—Any determination regarding an award under section 7623(b)(1), (2), or (3) may, within 30 days of such determination, be appealed to the Tax Court.

(e) *Administrative record.*—(1) *In general.*—The administrative record comprises all information contained in the administrative claim file that is relevant to the award determination and not protected by one or more common law or statutory privileges.

(2) *Administrative claim file.*—The administrative claim file will include the following materials relating to the action(s) to which the determination relates—

(i) The Form 211, "Application for Award for Original Information," filed by the whistleblower and all information provided by the whistleblower (whether provided with the whistleblower's original submission or through a subsequent contact with the IRS).

(ii) Copies of all debriefing notes and recorded interviews held with the whistleblower (and the whistleblower's legal representative, if any).

(iii) Form(s) 11369, "Confidential Evaluation Report on Claim for Award," including narratives prepared by the relevant IRS office(s), explaining the whistleblower's contributions to the actions and documenting the actions taken by the IRS in the case(s). The Form 11369 will refer to and incorporate additional documents relating to the issues raised by the claim, as appropriate, including, for example, relevant portions of revenue agent reports, copies of agreements entered into with the taxpayer(s), tax returns, and activity records.

(iv) Copies of all contracts entered into among the IRS, the whistleblower, and the whistleblower's legal representative (if any), and an explanation of the cooperation provided by the whistleblower (or the whistleblower's legal representative, if any) under the contract.

(v) Any information that reflects actions by the whistleblower that may have had a negative impact on the IRS's ability to examine the taxpayer(s).

(vi) All correspondence and documents sent by the Whistleblower Office to the whistleblower.

(vii) All notes, memoranda, and other documents made by officers and employees of the Whistleblower Office and considered by the official making the award determination.

(viii) All correspondence and documents received by the Whistleblower Office from the whistleblower (and the whistleblower's legal representative, if any) in the course of the whistleblower administrative proceeding.

(ix) All other information considered by the official making the award determination.

(f) *Effective/applicability date.*—This rule is effective on August 12, 2014. This rule applies to information submitted on or after August 12, 2014, and to claims for award under sections 7623(a) and 7623(b) that are open as of August 12, 2014. [Reg. § 301.7623-3.]

☐ [*T.D.* 9687, 8-7-2014.]

[Reg. § 301.7623-4]

§ 301.7623-4. Amount and payment of award.—(a) *In general.*—The Whistleblower Office will pay all awards under section 7623(a) and determine and pay all awards under section 7623(b). For all awards under section 7623 and §§ 301.7623-1 through 301.7623-4, the Whistleblower Office will—

(1) Analyze the claim by applying the rules provided in paragraph (c) of this section to the information contained in the administrative claim file to determine an award percentage; and

(2) Multiply the award percentage by the amount of collected proceeds. If the award determination arises out of a single whistleblower

administrative proceeding involving multiple actions, the Whistleblower Office may determine separate award percentages on an action-by-action basis and apply the separate award percentages to the collected proceeds attributable to the corresponding actions. The Internal Revenue Service (IRS) will pay all awards in accordance with the rules provided in paragraph (d) of this section. All relevant factors will be taken into account by the Whistleblower Office in determining whether an award will be paid and, if so, the amount of the award. No person is authorized under this section to make any offer or promise or otherwise bind the Whistleblower Office with respect to the amount or payment of an award.

(b) *Factors used to determine award percentage.*— (1) *Positive factors.*—The application of the following non-exclusive factors may support increasing an award percentage under paragraphs (c)(1) or (2) of this section—

(i) The whistleblower acted promptly to inform the IRS or the taxpayer of the tax noncompliance.

(ii) The information provided identified an issue or transaction of a type previously unknown to the IRS.

(iii) The information provided identified taxpayer behavior that the IRS was unlikely to identify or that was particularly difficult to detect through the IRS's exercise of reasonable diligence.

(iv) The information provided thoroughly presented the factual details of tax noncompliance in a clear and organized manner, particularly if the manner of the presentation saved the IRS work and resources.

(v) The whistleblower (or the whistleblower's legal representative, if any) provided exceptional cooperation and assistance during the pendency of the action(s).

(vi) The information provided identified assets of the taxpayer that could be used to pay liabilities, particularly if the assets were not otherwise known to the IRS.

(vii) The information provided identified connections between transactions, or parties to transactions, that enabled the IRS to understand tax implications that might not otherwise have been understood by the IRS.

(viii) The information provided had an impact on the behavior of the taxpayer, for example by causing the taxpayer to promptly correct a previously-reported improper position.

(2) *Negative factors.*—The application of the following non-exclusive factors may support decreasing an award percentage under paragraphs (c)(1) or (2) of this section—

(i) The whistleblower delayed informing the IRS after learning the relevant facts, particularly if the delay adversely affected the IRS's ability to pursue an action or issue.

(ii) The whistleblower contributed to the underpayment of tax or tax noncompliance identified.

(iii) The whistleblower directly or indirectly profited from the underpayment of tax or tax noncompliance identified, but did not plan and initiate the actions that led to the underpayment of tax or actions described in section 7623(a)(2).

(iv) The whistleblower (or the whistleblower's legal representative, if any) negatively affected the IRS's ability to pursue the action(s), for example by disclosing the existence or scope of an enforcement activity.

(v) The whistleblower (or the whistleblower's legal representative, if any) violated instructions provided by the IRS, particularly if the violation caused the IRS to expend additional resources.

(vi) The whistleblower (or the whistleblower's legal representative, if any) violated the terms of the confidentiality agreement described in § 301.7623-3(c)(2)(iv).

(vii) The whistleblower (or the whistleblower's legal representative, if any) violated the terms of a contract entered into with the IRS pursuant to § 301.6103(n)-2.

(viii) The whistleblower provided false or misleading information or otherwise violated the requirements of section 7623(b)(6)(C) or § 301.7623-1(c)(3).

(c) *Amount of award percentage.*—(1) *Award for substantial contribution.*—(i) *In general.*—If the IRS proceeds with any administrative or judicial action based on information brought to the IRS's attention by a whistleblower, such whistleblower shall, subject to paragraphs (c)(2) and (3) of this section, receive as an award at least 15 percent but not more than 30 percent of the collected proceeds resulting from the action (including any related actions) or from any settlement in response to such action. The amount of any award under this paragraph depends on the extent of the whistleblower's substantial contribution to the action(s). See paragraph (c)(4) of this section for rules regarding multiple whistleblowers.

(ii) *Computational framework.*—Starting the analysis at 15 percent, the Whistleblower Office will analyze the administrative claim file using the factors listed in paragraph (b)(1) of this section to determine whether the whistleblower merits an increased award percentage of 22 percent or 30 percent. The Whistleblower Office may increase the award percentage based on the presence and significance of positive factors. The Whistleblower Office will then analyze the contents of the administrative claim file using the factors listed in paragraph (b)(2) of this section to determine whether the whistleblower merits a decreased award percentage of 15 percent, 18 percent, 22 percent, or 26 percent. The Whistleblower Office may decrease the award percentage based on the presence and significance of negative factors. Although the factors listed in paragraphs (b)(1) and (2) of this section are described as positive and negative factors, the Whistleblower Office's analysis cannot be reduced to a mathematical equation. The factors are not exclusive and are not weighted and, in a particular case, one factor may override several others. The presence and significance of positive factors may offset the presence and significance of negative factors. But the absence of negative factors does not constitute a positive factor.

(iii) *Examples.*—The operation of the provisions of paragraph (c)(1)(ii) of this section may be illustrated by the following examples. The examples are intended to illustrate the operation of the computational framework. The examples provide simplified descriptions of the facts relating to the claims for award, the information provided, and the facts relating to the underlying tax cases. The application of section 7623(b)(1) and paragraph (c)(1)(ii) of this section will depend on the specific facts of each case.

Example 1. Facts. Whistleblower A, an employee in Corporation's sales department, submitted to the IRS a claim for award under section 7623 and information indicating that Corporation improperly claimed a credit in tax year 2006. Whistleblower A's information consisted of numerous non-privileged documents relevant to Corporation's eligibility for the credit. Whistleblower A's original submission also included an analysis of the documents, as well as information about meetings in which the claim for credit was discussed. When interviewed by the IRS, Whistleblower A clarified ambiguities in the original submission, answered questions about Corporation's business and accounting practices, and identified potential sources to corroborate the information.

Some of the documents provided by Whistleblower A were not included in Corporation's general record-keeping system and their existence may not have been easily uncovered through normal IRS examination procedures. Corporation initially denied the facts revealed in the information provided by Whistleblower A, which were essential to establishing the impropriety of the claim for credit. IRS examination of Corporation's return confirmed that the credit was improperly claimed by Corporation in tax year 2006, as alleged by Whistleblower A. Corporation agreed to the ensuing assessments of tax and interest and paid the liabilities in full.

Analysis. In this case, Whistleblower A provided specific and credible information that formed the basis for action by the IRS. Whistleblower A provided information that was difficult to detect, provided useful assistance to the IRS, and helped the IRS sustain the assessment. Based on the presence and significance of these positive factors, viewed against all the specific facts relevant to Corporation's 2006 tax year, the Whistleblower Office could increase the award percentage to 22 percent of collected proceeds. If, however, Whistleblower A's claim reflected negative factors, for example Whistleblower A violated instructions provided by the IRS and the violation caused the IRS to expend additional resources, then the Whistleblower Office could, based on this nega-

tive factor, reduce the award percentage to 18 or 15 percent (but not to lower than 15 percent of collected proceeds).

Example 2. Facts. Whistleblower B, an employee of Financial Advisory Firm 1 (Firm 1), submitted to the IRS a claim for award under section 7623 and information indicating that Firm 1 helped clients engage in activities that were intended to, and did, result in substantial tax underpayments. The activities were designed to avoid detection by the IRS, and prior IRS audits of several clients of Firm 1 had failed to detect underpayments of tax. Whistleblower B learned of the activities after being reassigned to a new position with Firm 1. Whistleblower B provided the information to the IRS soon after he understood the scope, nature and impact of the activities. The information provided consisted of numerous documents containing client profiles and marketing strategies, as well as descriptions of the transactions and structures used by Firm 1 and its clients to obscure the clients' identities and to generate the substantial tax underpayments. Whistleblower B also provided an analysis of the documents, as well as information about meetings in which the transactions and structures were discussed. When interviewed by the IRS, Whistleblower B clarified ambiguities in the original submission, answered questions about Firm 1's execution of specific client transactions, and identified potential sources to corroborate the information provided. Whistleblower B also notified the IRS of steps taken by Firm 1 to limit the disclosure of information requested by the IRS, enabling the IRS to obtain full disclosure of the information through the targeted use of summonses.

Analysis. Ultimately, the IRS collected tax, penalties, and interest from Firm 1 and multiple clients. In addition, Treasury and the IRS issued a notice identifying the impropriety of the transactions and structures employed by Firm 1 and its clients. Whistleblower B provided specific and credible information that formed the basis for action by the IRS. The information provided identified transactions that were difficult to detect. Whistleblower B acted promptly after he understood the activities at issue and he provided useful assistance to the IRS. Whistleblower B's assistance, and the information he provided, helped the IRS overcome the efforts made to obscure the activities and the clients' identities. And the information provided by Whistleblower B contributed to the decision to issue the notice, which may have a positive effect on client behavior and save IRS resources. Based on the presence and significance of these positive factors, the Whistleblower Office could increase the award percentage to 30 percent of collected proceeds. If Whistleblower B directly or indirectly profited from Firm 1's and the clients' activities resulting in the tax underpayments, then the Whistleblower Office could, based on this negative factor, reduce the award percentage to 26, 22, 18 percent or 15 percent (but not to lower than 15 percent of collected proceeds).

(2) *Award for less substantial contribution.*—
(i) *In general.*—If the Whistleblower Office determines that the action described in paragraph (c)(1) of this section is based principally on disclosures of specific allegations resulting from a judicial or administrative hearing; a government report, hearing, audit, or investigation; or the news media, then the Whistleblower Office will determine an award of no more than 10 percent of the collected proceeds resulting from the action (including any related actions) or from any settlement in response to such action. If the whistleblower is the original source of the information from which the disclosures of specific allegations resulted, however, then the award percentage will be determined under paragraph (c)(1) of this section.

(ii) *Computational framework.*—The Whistleblower Office will analyze the administrative claim file to determine—

(A) Whether the claim involves specific allegations regarding a tax underpayment or a violation of the internal revenue laws that reasonably may be inferred to have resulted from a judicial or administrative hearing; a government report, hearing, audit, or investigation; or the news media;

(B) Whether the action described in paragraph (c)(1) of this section was based principally on the disclosure of the specific allegations; and

(C) Whether the whistleblower was the original source of the information that gave rise to the specific allegations. If the Whistleblower Office determines that the action was based principally on disclosures of specific allegations, as stated in paragraph (c)(2)(ii)(B) of this section, and that the whistleblower was not the original source of the information, then, starting at 1 percent, the Whistleblower Office will analyze the administrative claim file using the factors listed in paragraph (b)(1) of this section to determine whether the whistleblower merits an increased award percentage of 4 percent, 7 percent, or 10 percent. The Whistleblower Office will then determine whether the whistleblower merits a decreased award percentage of zero, 1 percent, 4 percent, or 7 percent using the factors listed in paragraph (b)(2) of this section. The Whistleblower Office may increase the award percentage based on the presence and significance of positive factors and may decrease (to zero) the award percentage based on the presence and significance of negative factors. Like the analysis described in paragraph (c)(1)(ii) of this section, the Whistleblower Office's analysis cannot be reduced to a mathematical equation. The factors are not exclusive and are not weighted and, in a particular case, one factor may override several others. The presence and significance of positive factors may offset the presence and significance of negative factors. But the absence of negative factors does not constitute a positive factor.

(iii) *Example.*—The operation of the provisions of paragraph (c)(2)(ii) of this section may be illustrated by the following example. The example is intended to illustrate the operation of the computational framework. The example provides a simplified description of the facts relating to the claim for award, the information provided, and the facts relating to the underlying tax case(s). The application of section 7623(b)(2) and paragraph (c)(2)(ii) of this section will depend on the specific facts of each case.

Example. Facts. Whistleblower A submitted to the IRS a claim for award under section 7623 and information indicating that Taxpayer B was the defendant in a criminal prosecution for embezzlement. Whistleblower A's information further indicated that evidence presented at Taxpayer B's trial revealed Taxpayer B's efforts to conceal the embezzled funds by depositing them in bank accounts of entities controlled by Taxpayer B. Taxpayer B's failure to pay tax on the embezzled funds was not explicitly stated during the judicial hearing, but could be reasonably inferred from the facts and circumstances, including Taxpayer B's efforts to conceal the funds.

Analysis. In this case, Whistleblower A's information is based principally on disclosures of specific allegations resulting from a judicial hearing. Absent information demonstrating that the investigation leading to the embezzlement charge was based on information provided by Whistleblower A, section 7623(b)(2) and paragraph (c)(2) of this section apply to the determination of Whistleblower A's award. In this case, there is no reason for the Whistleblower Office to increase the applicable award percentage above 1 percent, the starting point for its analysis, given the absence of positive factors. Accordingly, Whistleblower A may receive an award of 1 percent of collected proceeds.

(3) *Reduction in award and denial of award.*—
(i) *In general.*—If the Whistleblower Office determines that a claim for award is brought by a whistleblower who planned and initiated the actions, transaction, or events (underlying acts) that led to the underpayment of tax or actions described in section 7623(a)(2), then the Whistleblower Office may appropriately reduce the amount of the award percentage that would otherwise result under section 7623(b)(1) and paragraph (c)(1) of this section or section 7623(b)(2) and paragraph (c)(2) of this section, as applicable. The Whistleblower Office will deny an award if the whistleblower is convicted of criminal conduct arising from his or her role in planning and initiating the underlying acts.

(ii) *Threshold determination.*—A whistleblower *planned and initiated* the underlying acts if the whistleblower—

(A) Designed, structured, drafted, arranged, formed the plan leading to, or otherwise planned, an underlying act,

(B) Took steps to start, introduce, originate, set into motion, promote or otherwise initiate an underlying act, and

(C) Knew or had reason to know that an underpayment of tax or actions described in

Reg. § 301.7623-4(c)(3)(ii)(C)

section 7623(a)(2) could result from planning and initiating the underlying act.

(D) The whistleblower need not have been the sole person involved in planning and initiating the underlying acts. A whistleblower who merely furnishes typing, reproducing, or other mechanical assistance in implementing one or more underlying acts will not be treated as initiating any underlying act. A whistleblower who is a junior employee acting at the direction, and under the control, of a senior employee will not be treated as initiating any underlying act.

(E) If the Whistleblower Office determines that a whistleblower has satisfied this initial threshold of planning and initiating, the Whistleblower Office will then reduce the award amount based on the extent of the whistleblower's planning and initiating, pursuant to paragraph (c)(3)(iii) of this section.

(iii) *Computational framework.*—After determining the award percentage that would otherwise result from the application of section 7623(b)(1) and paragraph (c)(1) of this section or section 7623(b)(2) and paragraph (c)(2) of this section, as applicable, the Whistleblower Office will analyze the administrative claim file to make the threshold determination described in paragraph (c)(3)(ii) of this section. If the whistleblower is determined to have planned and initiated the underlying acts, then the Whistleblower Office will reduce the award based on the extent of the whistleblower's planning and initiating. The Whistleblower Office's analysis and the amount of the appropriate reduction determined in a particular case cannot be reduced to a mathematical equation. To determine the appropriate award reduction, the Whistleblower Office will—

(A) Categorize the whistleblower's role as a planner and initiator as primary, significant, or moderate; and

(B) Appropriately reduce the award percentage that would otherwise result from the application of section 7623(b)(1) and paragraph (c)(1) of this section or section 7623(b)(2) and paragraph (c)(2) of this section, as applicable, by 67 percent to 100 percent in the case of a primary planner and initiator, by 34 percent to 66 percent in the case of a significant planner and initiator, or by 0 percent to 33 percent in the case of a moderate planner and initiator. If the whistleblower is convicted of criminal conduct arising from his or her role in planning and initiating the underlying acts, then the Whistleblower Office will deny an award without regard to whether the Whistleblower Office categorized the whistleblower's role as a planner and initiator as primary, significant, or moderate.

(iv) *Factors demonstrating the extent of a whistleblower's planning and initiating.*—The application of the following non-exclusive factors may support a determination of the extent of a whistleblower's planning and initiating of the underlying acts—

(A) The whistleblower's role as a planner and initiator. Was the whistleblower the sole decision-maker or one of several contributing planners and initiators? To what extent was the whistleblower acting under the direction and control of a supervisor?

(B) The nature of the whistleblower's planning and initiating activities. Was the whistleblower involved in legitimate tax planning activities? Did the whistleblower take steps to hide the actions at the planning stage? Did the whistleblower commit any identifiable misconduct (legal, ethical, etc.)?

(C) The extent to which the whistleblower knew or should have known that tax noncompliance could result from the course of conduct.

(D) The extent to which the whistleblower acted in furtherance of the noncompliance, including, for example, efforts to conceal or disguise the transaction.

(E) The whistleblower's role in identifying and soliciting others to participate in the actions reported, whether as parties to a common transaction or as parties to separate transactions.

(v) *Examples.*—The operation of the provisions of paragraphs (c)(3)(ii) and (iii) of this section may be illustrated by the following examples. These examples are intended to illustrate the operation of the computational framework. The examples provide simplified descriptions of the facts relating to the claim for award, the information provided, and the facts relating to the underlying tax case. The application of section 7623(b)(3) and paragraph (c)(3) of this section will depend on the specific facts of each case.

Example 1. Facts. Whistleblower A is employed as a junior associate in a law firm and is responsible for performing research and drafting activities for, and under the direction and control of, partners of the law firm. Whistleblower A performed research on financial products for Partner B that Partner B used in advising a client (Corporation 1) on a financial strategy. After Corporation 1 executed the strategy, Whistleblower A submitted a claim for award under section 7623 along with information about the strategy to the IRS. The IRS initiated an examination of Corporation 1 based on Whistleblower A's information, determined deficiencies in tax and penalties, and ultimately assessed and collected the tax and penalties as determined.

Analysis. Whistleblower A did nothing to design or set into motion Corporation 1's activities. Whistleblower A did not know or have reason to know that an underpayment of tax or actions described in section 7623(a)(2) could result from the research and drafting activities. Accordingly, as a threshold matter, Whistleblower A was not a planner and initiator of Corporation 1's strategy, and the award that would otherwise be determined based on the application of section 7623(b)(1) and paragraph (c)(1) of this section is not subject to reduction under section 7623(b)(3) and paragraph (c)(3) of this section.

Example 2. Facts. Whistleblower C is employed in the human resources department of a corporation (Corporation 2). Corporation 2 tasked Whistleblower C with hiring a large number of temporary employees to meet Corporation 2's seasonal business demands. Whistleblower C organized, scheduled, and conducted job fairs and job interviews to hire the seasonal employees. Whistleblower C was not responsible for, had no knowledge of, and played no part in, classifying the seasonal employees for Federal income tax purposes. Whistleblower C later discovered, however, that Corporation 2 classified the seasonal employees as independent contractors. After discovering the misclassification, Whistleblower C submitted a claim for award under section 7623 along with non-privileged information describing the employee misclassification to the IRS. The IRS initiated an examination of Corporation 2 based on Whistleblower C's information, determined deficiencies in tax and penalties, and ultimately assessed and collected the tax and penalties as determined.

Analysis. The award that would otherwise be determined based on the application of section 7623(b)(1) and paragraph (c)(1) of this section would not be subject to a reduction under section 7623(b)(3) and paragraph (c)(3) of this section because Whistleblower C did not satisfy the requirements of the threshold determination of a planner and initiator. Whistleblower C did not know and had no reason to know that her actions could result in an underpayment of tax or actions described in section 7623(a)(2) or that Corporation 2 would misclassify the employees as independent contractors.

Example 3. Facts. Whistleblower D is employed as a supervisor in the finance department of a corporation (Corporation 3) and is responsible for planning Corporation 3's overall financial strategy. Pursuant to the overall financial strategy, Whistleblower D and others at Corporation 3, in good faith but incorrectly, planned tax-advantaged transactions. Whistleblower D and others at Corporation 3 prepared documents needed to execute the transactions. After Corporation 3 executed the transactions, Whistleblower D reached the conclusion that the tax consequences claimed were incorrect and Whistleblower D submitted a claim for award under section 7623 along with non-privileged information about the transactions to the IRS. The IRS initiated an examination of Corporation 3 based on Whistleblower D's information, determined deficiencies in tax and penalties, and ultimately assessed and collected the tax and penalties as determined.

Analysis. The award that would otherwise be determined based on the application of section 7623(b)(1) and paragraph (c)(1) of this section would be subject to an appropriate reduction under section 7623(b)(3) and paragraph (c)(3) of this section because Whistleblower D satisfies the requirements of the threshold determination of a planner and initiator. Whistleblower D planned the transactions, prepared the necessary documents, and knew that an underpayment of tax could result from the transactions. Whistleblower D was not the sole planner and initiator of Corporation 3's transactions. Whistleblower D did nothing to conceal Corporation 3's activities. Corporation 3 had a good faith basis for claiming the disallowed tax benefits. On the basis of those facts, Whistleblower D was a moderate-level planner and initiator. Accordingly, the Whistleblower Office will exercise its discretion to reduce Whistleblower D's award by 0 to 33 percent.

Example 4. Facts. Same facts as *Example 3,* except that Whistleblower D independently planned a high-risk tax avoidance transaction and prepared draft documents to execute the transaction. Whistleblower D presented the transaction, along with the draft documents, to Corporation 3's Chief Financial Officer. Without the further involvement of Whistleblower D, Corporation 3's Chief Financial Officer, Chief Executive Officer, and Board of Directors subsequently approved the execution of the transaction. After Corporation 3 executed the transaction, Whistleblower D submitted a claim for award under section 7623 along with non-privileged information about the transaction to the IRS. The IRS initiated an examination of Corporation 3 based on Whistleblower D's information, determined deficiencies in tax and penalties, and ultimately assessed and collected the tax and penalties as determined.

Analysis. The award that would otherwise be determined based on the application of section 7623(b)(1) and paragraph (c)(1) of this section would be subject to an appropriate reduction under section 7623(b)(3) and paragraph (c)(3) of this section because Whistleblower D satisfies the requirements of the threshold determination of a planner and initiator. Whistleblower D planned the transaction, prepared the necessary documents, and knew that an underpayment of tax or actions described in section 7623(a)(2) could result from the transaction. Working independently, Whistleblower D designed and took steps to effectuate the transaction while knowing that the planning and initiating of the transaction was likely to result in tax noncompliance. Whistleblower D, however, did not approve the execution of the transaction by Corporation 3 and, therefore, was not a decision-maker. On the basis of these facts, Whistleblower D was a significant-level planner and initiator. Accordingly, the Whistleblower Office will exercise its discretion to reduce Whistleblower D's award by 34 to 66 percent.

Example 5. Facts. Whistleblower E is a financial planner. Whistleblower E designed a financial product that the IRS identified as an abusive tax avoidance transaction. Whistleblower E marketed the transaction to taxpayers, facilitated their participation in the transaction, and, initially, took steps to disguise the transaction. After several taxpayers had participated in the transaction, Whistleblower E submitted a claim for award under section 7623 along with non-privileged information to the IRS about the transaction and the participating taxpayers. The IRS initiated an examination of the identified taxpayers based on Whistleblower E's information, determined deficiencies in tax and penalties, and ultimately assessed and collected the tax and penalties as determined. Whistleblower E was not criminally prosecuted.

Analysis. The award that would otherwise be determined based on the application of section 7623(b)(1) and paragraph (c)(1) of this section would be subject to an appropriate reduction under section 7623(b)(3) and paragraph (c)(3) of this section because Whistleblower E satisfies the requirements of the threshold determination of a planner and initiator. Whistleblower E designed the financial product, marketed and facilitated its use by taxpayers, and knew that an underpayment of tax or actions described in section 7623(a)(2) could result from the transaction. Whistleblower E was the sole designer of the transaction, solicited clients to participate in the transaction, and facilitated and attempted to conceal their participation in the transaction. Whistleblower E knew that the planning and initiating of the taxpayers' participation in the transaction was likely to result in an underpayment of tax or actions described in section 7623(a)(2). On the basis of these facts, Whistleblower E was a primary-level planner and initiator. Accordingly, the Whistleblower Office will exercise its discretion to reduce Whistleblower E's award by 67 to 100 percent.

(4) *Multiple whistleblowers.*—If two or more independent claims relate to the same collected proceeds, then the Whistleblower Office may evaluate the contribution of each whistleblower to the action(s) that resulted in collected proceeds. The Whistleblower Office will determine whether the information submitted by each whistleblower would have been obtained by the IRS as a result of the information previously submitted by any other whistleblower. If the Whistleblower Office determines that multiple whistleblowers submitted information that would not have been obtained based on a prior submission, then the Whistleblower Office will determine the amount of each whistleblower's award based on the extent to which each whistleblower contributed to the action(s). The aggregate award amount in cases involving two or more independent claims that relate to the same collected proceeds will not exceed the maximum award amount that could have resulted under section 7623(b)(1) or section 7623(b)(2), as applicable, subject to the award reduction provisions of section 7623(b)(3), if a single claim had been submitted.

(d) *Payment of Award.*—(1) *In general.*—The IRS will pay any award determined under section 7623 and §§ 301.7623-1 through 301.7623-4 to the whistleblower(s) that filed the corresponding claim for award. Payment of an award will be made as promptly as the circumstances permit, but not until there has been a final determination of tax with respect to the action(s), as defined in paragraph (d)(2) of this section, the Whistleblower Office has determined the award, and all appeals of the Whistleblower Office's determination are final or the whistleblower has executed an award consent form agreeing to the amount of the award and waiving the whistleblower's right to appeal the determination.

(2) *Final determination of tax.*—(i) *In general.*—For purposes of §§ 301.7623-1 through 301.7623-4, a *final determination of tax* means that the proceeds resulting from the action(s) subject to the award determination have been collected and either the statutory period for filing a claim for refund has expired or the taxpayer(s) subject to the action(s) and the IRS have agreed with finality to the tax or other liabilities for the period(s) at issue and the taxpayer(s) have waived the right to file a claim for refund. A final determination of tax does not preclude a subsequent final determination of tax if the IRS proceeds based on the information provided following the payment, denial, or rejection of an award.

(ii) *Example.*—The provisions of paragraph (d)(2)(i) of this section, regarding subsequent final determination of tax, may be illustrated by the following example:

Example. Information provided to the IRS by a whistleblower, under section 7623 and § 301.7623-1, identifies a taxpayer (Corporation 1), describes and documents specific facts relating to Corporation 1's activities, and, based on those facts, alleges that Corporation 1 owed additional taxes in Year 1. The Whistleblower Office processes the incoming claim and provides the information to an IRS Operating Division (Operating Division 1). Operating Division 1 reviews the claim and the allegations and ultimately decides not to proceed with an action against Corporation 1. Operating Division 1 conveys its determination not to proceed with an action against Corporation 1 to the Whistleblower Office on a Form 11369 along with all of the relevant supporting documents. The Whistleblower Office provides written notice to the whistleblower, denying any award pursuant to § 301.7623-3(c)(8), and the whistleblower does not appeal the notice to Tax Court within 30 days.

Two months after the Whistleblower Office denies the award, the Whistleblower Office recognizes a potential connection between the information provided and a recently-initiated, ongoing, examination of a second taxpayer by a second IRS Operating Division (Operating Division 2). The Whistleblower Office provides the information to Operating Division 2. Operating Division 2 evaluates the information and proceeds with an action against Taxpayer 2 based on the information provided. Ultimately, Operating Division 2 assesses and collects taxes resulting from the action and totaling $3 million. Following the conclusion of the whistleblower's participation in a whistleblower administrative proceeding described in §301.7623-3(c) and the expiration of the statutory period for filing a claim for refund by Taxpayer 2, the Whistleblower Office determines the amount of the award and communicates the award to the whistleblower in a determination letter. The whistleblower may appeal the notice to the Tax Court within 30 days.

(3) *Joint Whistleblowers.*—If multiple whistleblowers jointly submit a claim for award, the IRS will pay any award in equal shares to the joint whistleblowers unless the joint whistleblowers specify a different allocation in a written agreement, signed by all the joint whistleblowers and notarized, and submitted with the claim for award. The aggregate award payment in cases involving joint whistleblowers will be within the award percentage range of section 7623(b)(1) or section 7623(b)(2), as applicable, and subject to the award reduction provisions of section 7623(b)(3).

(4) *Deceased Whistleblower.*—If a whistleblower dies before or during the whistleblower administrative proceeding, the Whistleblower Office may substitute an executor, administrator, or other legal representative on behalf of the deceased whistleblower for purposes of conducting the whistleblower administrative proceeding.

(5) *Tax treatment of award.*—All awards are includible in gross income and subject to current Federal tax reporting and withholding requirements.

(e) *Effective/applicability date.*—This rule is effective on August 12, 2014. This rule applies to information submitted on or after August 12, 2014, and to claims for award under section 7623(b) that are open as of August 12, 2014. [Reg. §301.7623-4.]

☐ [*T.D. 9687, 8-7-2014.*]

[Reg. §301.7624-1]

§301.7624-1. Reimbursement to State and local law enforcement agencies.—(a) *In general.*—The Internal Revenue Service may reimburse a State or local law enforcement agency for expenses, such as salaries, overtime pay, per diem, and similar reasonable expenses, incurred in an investigation in which information is furnished to the Service that substantially contributes to the recovery of Federal taxes imposed with respect to illegal drug or related money laundering activities. The amount of reimbursement that may be paid shall not exceed the limits specified in paragraphs (e)(2) and (e)(3) of this section.

(b) *Information that substantially contributes to recovery of taxes.*—(1) *Definition.*—The Service generally will consider that information furnished by a State or local law enforcement agency substantially contributed to the recovery of taxes with respect to illegal drug or related money laundering activities provided the information was not already in the possession of the Service at the time the information is furnished by the State or local law enforcement agency, and

(i) concerns a taxpayer who is not under examination or investigation by the Service at the time the information is furnished or has not already been selected by the Service for examination or investigation in the near future, or

(ii) concerns a taxpayer who is under examination or has been selected for examination at the time the information is furnished but the information furnished would not normally have been discovered in the course of an ordinary investigation or examination by the Service. Also, information will generally be considered as substantially contributing to the recovery of taxes if it leads to the discovery of hidden assets owned by the taxpayer which are used to satisfy the taxpayer's assessed but otherwise uncollectable Federal tax liability with respect to illegal drug or related money laundering activities. For purposes of this paragraph (b), information includes, but is not limited to, tax years of violations, aliases, addresses, social security numbers and/or employer identification numbers, financial data (bank accounts, assets, etc.) and their location, and any documentation that substantiates allegations concerning tax liability (books and records) and its location.

(2) *Examples.*

Example (1). A local police department's narcotics division has been gathering information on a suspected local drug dealer for approximately six months. Because this person is very cautious when handling narcotics, the local police have been unsuccessful in catching this person in possession of drugs. Rather than drop the case, the narcotics detective turns over to the local IRS Criminal Investigation Division (CID) office information concerning this person. At the time the information is furnished, the Service is unaware of this person's suspected involvement in drugs and has no reason to suspect that this person's Federal income tax returns are incorrect. Upon examination of this person's returns for three open years, the Service determines that additional Federal income taxes and civil penalties of approximately $20,000 per year are due because of unreported income from drug dealing. Because the taxpayer was not under examination and was not reasonably anticipated to have been examined prior to receipt of the information, the Service will consider that the information furnished by the local police department substantially contributed to the recovery of approximately $60,000 in taxes with respect to illegal drug activities.

Example (2). Assume the same facts as example (1) except that at the time the information is turned over to the Service, the Service was already aware of the extent of this person's involvement in drug dealing, either through information developed in the course of examinations of other taxpayers or through information received from other sources, and had already selected this person's returns for examination although the person had not yet been contacted by the Service. In this case, the information provided by the local police department did not substantially contribute to the recovery of taxes from this person because the information was already known to the Service.

Example (3). A state or local police officer is conducting ordinary traffic patrol. The officer stops a vehicle for speeding and reckless driving. The officer recognizes the driver as a known narcotics dealer. In the vehicle is a brief case containing $75,000 in cash, but no trace of narcotics is found. The driver claims the cash was won in a high stakes poker game. The officer arrests the driver for traffic violations and takes the briefcase into custody for safe keeping. The local police department cannot seize the money because they cannot tie it to a narcotics transaction. Instead, they immediately inform the local CID office of their find. At the time this information is furnished to the Service, there is an unpaid assessed liability of $300,000 in Federal taxes and penalties owed by the dealer with respect to illegal drug activities that the Service has been unable to collect. Therefore, the Service immediately seizes the $75,000 in cash in partial payment of the tax liability. The Service will consider that the information furnished by the police department substantially contributed to the recovery of $75,000 in taxes with respect to drug related activities.

Example (4). Through information furnished by a reliable informant, a local police department learns that a known racketeer and suspected drug dealer maintains a second set of books and records in a safe at home. The local police obtain a search warrant and find a set of books revealing that this person has been using a legitimate business operation to launder money derived from both prostitution and drug dealing. At the time these records are turned over to the local CID office, the taxpayer is already under examination for tax evasion. However, based on the information contained in this second set of books, the Service is able to collect additional taxes and civil penalties in the amount of $1 million in connection with these illegal activities. The Service will consider that this information substantially contributed to the recovery of $1 million in taxes with respect to money laundering in connection with illegal drug activities because, even though the taxpayer was already under examination, the information provided by the local police would normally not have been discovered by the Service in the course of an ordinary investigation.

(c) *Application for reimbursement.*—An agency that intends to apply for reimbursement under the provisions of this section must indicate this intent to the Service at the time the information is first provided to the Service. A final application for reimbursement of expenses must be submitted on Form 211A, State or Local Law Enforcement Application for Reimbursement, to the Chief, Criminal Investigation Division of the Internal Revenue Service district in which the taxpayer is located. Copies of Forms 9061, DAG-71, or other claim for an equitable share of asset forfeitures in the case must also be furnished with Form 211A.

(d) *Time for filing application for reimbursement.*—An application for reimbursement may be filed by an agency at the time the information is first provided or as soon as practicable after submitting information to the Service. However, it must be filed not later than 30 days after the Service notifies the agency pursuant to section 7624(b) of the amount of taxes collected as a result of the information provided. If an application for reimbursement is filed by more than one agency with respect to taxes recovered from a taxpayer, the Service will use discretion in determining an equitable amount of reimbursement allocated to each agency based on all relevant factors. In no event, however, shall the aggregate of the amounts paid by the Service to two or more agencies exceed the amount specified in paragraph (e)(3) of this section.

(e) *Amount and payment of reimbursement.*—(1) *De minimis rule.*—No reimbursement shall be paid under section 7624 or this section to a State or local law enforcement agency in any case where the taxes recovered total less than $50,000.

(2) *Taxes recovered.*—For purposes of section 7624 and this section, the terms "taxes" recovered and "sum" recovered mean additional Federal taxes, civil penalties, and additions to tax collected (less any subsequent refund to the taxpayer) with respect to illegal drug or related money laundering activities, but not additional interest or criminal fines that may be collected.

(3) *Limitation on reimbursement.*—The amount of reimbursement payable under section 7624 and this section shall not exceed 10 percent of any taxes recovered.

(4) *No duplicate reimbursement.*—A State or local law enforcement agency shall not receive reimbursement under section 7624 or this section for any expenses incurred in the investigation of a taxpayer which have been or will be reimbursed under any other program or arrangement including, but not limited to, Federal or State forfeiture programs, State revenue laws, or Federal and State equitable sharing arrangements.

(5) *Time of payment.*—No payment of any reimbursement under this section will be made to a State or local law enforcement agency before the later of final expiration of the applicable period of limitations for filing a claim for refund by the taxpayer of the taxes recovered as provided in subchapter B of chapter 66 of the Code or the determination of the taxpayer's tax liability, as defined in section 1313(a). However, reimbursement may be made earlier but only if the agency provides adequate indemnification against loss by the Service due to a refund to the taxpayer of Federal taxes recovered.

(6) *Applicability.*—The provisions of section 7624 apply only to State and local law enforce-

ment agencies within the United States and the District of Columbia.

(f) *Effective date.*—This section applies with respect to information first provided to the Service by a State or local law enforcement agency after February 16, 1989. [Reg. §301.7624-1.]

☐ [*T.D.* 8415, 4-23-92.]

POSSESSIONS

[Reg. §301.7654-1]

§301.7654-1. Coordination of U.S. and Guam individual income taxes.—(a) *Application of section.*—(1) *Scope.*—Section 7654 and this section set forth the general procedures to be followed by the Government of the United States and the Government of Guam in the division between the two governments of revenue derived from collections of the income taxes imposed for any taxable year beginning after December 31, 1972, with respect to any individual described in subparagraph (2) of this paragraph and paragraph(e) of this section. To the extent that section 7654 and this section are inconsistent with the provisions of section 30 of the Organic Act of Guam (48 U.S.C. 1421h), relating to duties and taxes to be covered into the treasury of Guam and held in account for the Government of Guam, such section 30 is superseded.

(2) *Individuals covered.*—Paragraph (b) of this section applies only to an individual who, for a taxable year, is described in paragraph (a)(2) of §1.935-1 of this chapter (Income Tax Regulations) and has (or in the case of a joint return, such individual and his spouse have)—

(i) Adjusted gross income of $50,000 or more, and

(ii) Gross income of $5,000 or more from sources within the jurisdiction (either the United States or Guam) other than the jurisdiction with which the individual is required to file his income tax return under paragraph (b) of §1.935-1 of this chapter.

For the determination of gross income and adjusted gross income see sections 61 and 62, and the regulations thereunder, or, when applicable, the corresponding provisions as made applicable in Guam by the Guam Territorial income tax (48 U.S.C. 1421i). For purposes of this subparagraph, gross income consisting of compensation for military or naval service shall be taken into account notwithstanding section 514 of the Soldiers' and Sailors' Civil Relief Act of 1940 (50 App. U.S.C. 574). However, see paragraph (e) of this section.

(b) *Allocation of tax.*—(1) Net collections of income taxes imposed for each taxable year beginning after December 31, 1972, with respect to each individual described in paragraph (a)(2) of this section for such year shall be divided between the United States and Guam by the Commissioner of Internal Revenue and the Commissioner of Revenue and Taxation of Guam as follows:

(i) Net collections attributable to income from sources within the United States shall be covered into the Treasury of the United States,

(ii) Net collections attributable to income from sources within Guam shall be covered into the treasury of Guam, and

(iii) Net collections not described in subdivision (i) or (ii) of this subparagraph (i.e., net collections attributable to income from sources other than within the United States or Guam) shall be covered into the treasury of the jurisdiction (either the United States or Guam) with which the individual is required to file his return under paragraph (b) of §1.935-1 of this chapter for such year.

(2) The amount of tax of any individual for a taxable year which shall be allocated to Guam for purposes of determining the portion of the net collections from such individual which shall be covered into the treasury of Guam by the United States for such year shall be that amount which bears the same ratio to such amount of tax as the adjusted gross income of that individual for such year which is allocable to sources in Guam bears to the total adjusted gross income of such individual for such year. For purposes of such allocation by the United States, the adjusted gross income of the taxpayer shall be determined by taking into account any compensation of any member of the Armed Forces for services performed in Guam the withheld tax on which is paid into the treasury of Guam pursuant to paragraph (e) of this section. The amount of tax of any individual for any taxable year which shall be allocated to the United States for purposes of determining the portion of the net collections from such individual which shall be covered into the Treasury of the United States by Guam for such year shall be that amount which bears the same ratio to such amount of tax as the adjusted gross income of that individual for such year which is allocable to sources in the United States bears to the total adjusted gross income of such individual for such year.

(c) *Definitions and special rules.*—For purposes of this section—

(1) *Net collections.*—(i) In determining net collections for a taxable year, appropriate adjustment between the two jurisdictions shall be made on a proportionate basis for underpayments of income taxes for such taxable year, credits allowed against the income tax for such taxable year (other than the credit for taxes withheld under section 3402 on wages), and refunds made of income taxes paid with respect to such taxable year. Thus, if a net operating loss results in a carryback to an earlier taxable year which gives rise to a refund for that earlier year, an adjustment must be made based upon the proportion which the amount of tax covered by one jurisdiction into the treasury of the other juris-

diction for that earlier year bears to the total amount of tax paid for that earlier year, even though the loss may have resulted from activities in one jurisdiction and the income, against which the loss was offset, was earned in the other jurisdiction. Similar adjustments must be made for foreign tax credit carrybacks even though different jurisdictions are involved. If, for example, an individual pays income tax of $30,000 to the United States for 1974 and $10,000 of such tax is covered into the treasury of Guam, and if for 1975 such individual has a net operating loss attributable to a trade or business carried on in the United States which loss is carried back to 1974 and gives rise to a refund of $15,000 by the United States, Guam must cover into the Treasury of the United States the amount of $5,000 which is the adjustment based upon the refund ($15,000 × $10,000/$30,000 = $5,000).

(ii) Tax withheld from the compensation of any member of the Armed Forces described in paragraph (a)(2) of this section which is paid to Guam pursuant to section 7654(d) and paragraph (e) of this section shall be taken into account in determining the amount required to be covered into the treasury of Guam under paragraph (b)(1)(ii) of this section.

(iii) For purposes of this subparagraph, any underpayment of tax is treated as attributable on a pro rata basis to income from sources within the United States, Guam, and sources other than within the United States or Guam, respectively, and is divided between the United States and Guam under the rules in paragraph (b) of this section.

(2) *Income taxes.*—The term "income taxes" means—

(i) With respect to taxes imposed by the United States, the income taxes imposed by chapter 1 of the Code, and

(ii) With respect to taxes imposed by Guam, the Guam Territorial income tax (48 U.S.C. 1421i).

(3) *Source rules.*—The determination of the source of income shall be based on the principles contained in sections 861 through 863, and the regulations thereunder, or, when applicable, in those sections as made applicable in Guam by the Guam Territorial income tax. For such purposes the provisions of section 514 of the Soldiers' and Sailors' Civil Relief Act of 1940 (50 App. U.S.C. 574) relating to the determination of the source of income of members of the Armed Forces shall not be taken into account. For purposes of this subparagraph, the provisions in section 935(c) treating Guam as part of the United States, and vice versa, do not apply. For definition of the terms "United States" and "Guam" (see section 7701(a)(9) of the Code and section 2 of the Organic Act of Guam (48 U.S.C. 1421).

(d) *Information return.*—Each individual described in paragraph (a)(2) of this section for a taxable year who is required by paragraph (b)(1) of § 1.935-1 of this chapter to file his return of income for such year with the United States shall timely file a properly executed Form 5074 (Allocation of Individual Income Tax to Guam) by attaching such form to his income tax return. Each individual described in paragraph (a)(2) of this section for a taxable year who is required by paragraph (b)(1) of § 1.935-1 of this chapter to file his return of income for such year with Guam shall timely file such information as may be required by the Commissioner of Revenue and Taxation with respect to his income derived from sources within the United States. See section 6688 and § 301.6688-1 for the penalty for failure to comply with this paragraph.

(e) *Military personnel in Guam.*—The Commissioner of Internal Revenue shall arrange to pay to Guam the amount of the taxes deducted and withheld by the United States under section 3402 from wages paid to members of the Armed Forces who are stationed in Guam but who have no income tax liability to Guam with respect to such wages by reason of section 514 of the Soldiers' and Sailors' Civil Relief Act of 1940 (50 App. U.S.C. 574). Section 514 of that Act provides in effect that for purposes of the taxation of income by Guam a person shall not be deemed to have lost a residence or domicile in the United States solely by reason of being absent therefrom in compliance with military or naval orders and the compensation for military or naval service of such a person who is not a resident of, or domiciled in, Guam shall not be deemed income for services performed within, or from sources within, Guam. Any amount paid to Guam under this paragraph in respect of a member of the Armed Forces described in paragraph (a)(2) of this section shall be taken into account in determining the amount required to be covered into the treasury of Guam under paragraph (b)(1)(ii) of this section. For purposes of this paragraph, the term "Armed Forces of the United States" has the meaning provided by § 301.7701-8 of this chapter. This paragraph does not apply to wages for services performed in Guam by members of the Armed Forces of the United States which are not compensation for military or naval service. In determining the amount of tax to be covered into the treasury of Guam under this paragraph with respect to remuneration for services performed in Guam by members of the Armed Forces of the United States, the special procedure agreed upon with the Department of Defense in 1951 shall not apply to remuneration paid after December 31, 1974. Under that procedure the tax withheld under section 3402 upon such remuneration for services performed in Guam during April and October of each year was to be projected for the appropriate six-month period of which the base month is a part, thereby arriving at an estimated figure for semiannual withholding tax to be covered over.

(f) *Transfers of funds.*—The transfers of funds between the United States and Guam required to effectuate the provisions of this section shall be made when convenient for the two governments, but not less frequently than once in each calendar year. In complying with paragraph (b) of this section, only net balances will be transferred between the two governments. Further, amounts transferred pursuant to paragraph (b) of this section may be determined on the basis of estimates rather than the actual amounts derived from information furnished by taxpayers, except that the net collections for 1973 and every third calendar year thereafter are to be transferred on the basis of the information furnished by taxpay-

ers pursuant to paragraph (d) of this section. In order to facilitate the transfer of funds pursuant to this section, the Commissioner of Internal Revenue and the Commissioner of Revenue and Taxation of Guam shall exchange such information, including copies of income tax returns, as will ensure that the provisions of section 7654 and this section are being properly implemented. [Reg. § 301.7654-1.]

☐ [T.D. 7385, 10-18-75.]

Definitions

See p. 20,601 for regulations not amended to reflect law changes

[Reg. § 1.7701-1]

§ 1.7701-1. Definitions; spouse, husband and wife, husband, wife, marriage.—(a) *In general.*—For the definition of the terms spouse, husband and wife, husband, wife, and marriage, see § 301.7701-18 of this chapter.

(b) *Applicability date.*—The rules of this section apply to taxable years ending on or after September 2, 2016. [Reg. § 1.7701-1.]

☐ [T.D. 9785, 8-31-2016.]

[Reg. § 20.7701-1]

§ 20.7701-1. Tax return preparer.—(a) *In general.*—For the definition of a tax return preparer, see § 301.7701-15 of this chapter.

(b) *Effective/applicability date.*—This section is applicable to returns and claims for refund filed, and advice provided, after December 31, 2008. [Reg. § 20.7701-1.]

☐ [T.D. 9436, 12-15-2008.]

[Reg. § 25.7701-1]

§ 25.7701-1. Tax return preparer.—(a) *In general.*—For the definition of a tax return preparer, see § 301.7701-15 of this chapter.

(b) *Effective/applicability date.*—This section is applicable to returns and claims for refund filed, and advice provided, after December 31, 2008. [Reg. § 25.7701-1.]

☐ [T.D. 9436, 12-15-2008.]

[Reg. § 26.7701-1]

§ 26.7701-1. Tax return preparer.—(a) *In general.*—For the definition of a tax return preparer, see § 301.7701-15 of this chapter.

(b) *Effective/applicability date.*—This section is applicable to returns and claims for refund filed, and advice provided, after December 31, 2008. [Reg. § 26.7701-1.]

☐ [T.D. 9436, 12-15-2008.]

[Reg. § 31.7701-1]

§ 31.7701-1. Tax return preparer.—(a) *In general.*—For the definition of a tax return preparer, see § 301.7701-15 of this chapter.

(b) *Effective/applicability date.*—This section is applicable to returns and claims for refund filed,

and advice provided, after December 31, 2008. [Reg. § 31.7701-1.]

☐ [T.D. 9436, 12-15-2008.]

[Reg. § 40.7701-1]

§ 40.7701-1. Tax return preparer.—(a) *In general.*—For the definition of a tax return preparer, see § 301.7701-15 of this chapter.

(b) *Effective/applicability date.*—This section is applicable to returns and claims for refund filed, and advice provided, after December 31, 2008. [Reg. § 40.7701-1.]

☐ [T.D. 9436, 12-15-2008.]

[Reg. § 41.7701-1]

§ 41.7701-1. Tax return preparer.—(a) *In general.*—For the definition of a tax return preparer, see § 301.7701-15 of this chapter.

(b) *Effective/applicability date.*—This section is applicable to returns and claims for refund filed, and advice provided, after December 31, 2008. [Reg. § 41.7701-1.]

☐ [T.D. 9436, 12-15-2008.]

[Reg. § 44.7701-1]

§ 44.7701-1. Tax return preparer.—(a) *In general.*—For the definition of a tax return preparer, see § 301.7701-15 of this chapter.

(b) *Effective/applicability date.*—This section is applicable to returns and claims for refund filed, and advice provided, after December 31, 2008. [Reg. § 44.7701-1.]

☐ [T.D. 9436, 12-15-2008.]

[Reg. § 53.7701-1]

§ 53.7701-1. Tax return preparer.—(a) *In general.*—For the definition of a tax return preparer, see § 301.7701-15 of this chapter.

(b) *Effective/applicability date.*—This section is applicable to returns and claims for refund filed, and advice provided, after December 31, 2008. [Reg. § 53.7701-1.]

☐ [T.D. 9436, 12-15-2008.]

[Reg. § 54.7701-1]

§ 54.7701-1. Tax return preparer.—(a) *In general.*—For the definition of a tax return preparer, see § 301.7701-15 of this chapter.

(b) *Effective/applicability date.*—This section is applicable to returns and claims for refund filed, and advice provided, after December 31, 2008. [Reg. § 54.7701-1.]

☐ [*T.D.* 9436, 12-15-2008.]

[Reg. § 55.7701-1]

§ 55.7701-1. **Tax return preparer.**—(a) *In general.*—For the definition of a tax return preparer, see § 301.7701-15 of this chapter.

(b) *Effective/applicability date.*—This section is applicable to returns and claims for refund filed, and advice provided, after December 31, 2008. [Reg. § 55.7701-1.]

☐ [*T.D.* 9436, 12-15-2008.]

[Reg. § 56.7701-1]

§ 56.7701-1. **Tax return preparer.**—(a) *In general.*—For the definition of a tax return preparer, see § 301.7701-15 of this chapter.

(b) *Effective/applicability date.*—This section is applicable to returns and claims for refund filed, and advice provided, after December 31, 2008. [Reg. § 56.7701-1.]

☐ [*T.D.* 9436, 12-15-2008.]

[Reg. § 156.7701-1]

§ 156.7701-1. **Tax return preparer.**—(a) *In general.*—For the definition of a tax return preparer, see § 301.7701-15 of this chapter.

(b) *Effective/applicability date.*—This section is applicable to returns and claims for refund filed, and advice provided, after December 31, 2008. [Reg. § 156.7701-1.]

☐ [*T.D.* 9436, 12-15-2008.]

[Reg. § 157.7701-1]

§ 157.7701-1. **Tax return preparer.**—(a) *In general.*—For the definition of a tax return preparer, see § 301.7701-15 of this chapter.

(b) *Effective/applicability date.*—This section is applicable to returns and claims for refund filed, and advice provided, after December 31, 2008. [Reg. § 157.7701-1.]

☐ [*T.D.* 9436, 12-15-2008.]

[Reg. § 301.7701-1]

§ 301.7701-1. **Classification of organizations for federal tax purposes.**—(a) *Organizations for federal tax purposes.*—(1) *In general.*—The Internal Revenue Code prescribes the classification of various organizations for federal tax purposes. Whether an organization is an entity separate from its owners for federal tax purposes is a matter of federal tax law and does not depend on whether the organization is recognized as an entity under local law.

(2) *Certain joint undertakings give rise to entities for federal tax purposes.*—A joint venture or other contractual arrangement may create a separate entity for federal tax purposes if the participants carry on a trade, business, financial operation, or venture and divide the profits therefrom. For example, a separate entity exists for federal tax purposes if co-owners of an apartment building lease space and in addition provide services to the occupants either directly or through an agent. Nevertheless, a joint undertaking merely to share expenses does not create a separate entity for federal tax purposes. For example, if two or more persons jointly construct a ditch merely to drain surface water from their properties, they have not created a separate entity for federal tax purposes. Similarly, mere co-ownership of property that is maintained, kept in repair, and rented or leased does not constitute a separate entity for federal tax purposes. For example, if an individual owner, or tenants in common, of farm property lease it to a farmer for a cash rental or a share of the crops, they do not necessarily create a separate entity for federal tax purposes.

(3) *Certain local law entities not recognized.*—An entity formed under local law is not always recognized as a separate entity for federal tax purposes. For example, an organization wholly owned by a State is not recognized as a separate entity for federal tax purposes if it is an integral part of the State. Similarly, tribes incorporated under section 17 of the Indian Reorganization Act of 1934, as amended, 25 U.S.C. 477, or under section 3 of the Oklahoma Indian Welfare Act, as amended, 25 U.S.C. 503, are not recognized as separate entities for federal tax purposes.

(4) *Single owner organizations.*—Under §§ 301.7701-2 and 301.7701-3, certain organizations that have a single owner can choose to be recognized or disregarded as entities separate from their owners.

(b) *Classification of organizations.*—The classification of organizations that are recognized as separate entities is determined under §§ 301.7701-2, 301.7701-3, and 301.7701-4 unless a provision of the Internal Revenue Code (such as section 860A addressing Real Estate Mortgage Investment Conduits (REMICs)) provides for special treatment of that organization. For the classification of organizations as trusts, see § 301.7701-4. That section provides that trusts generally do not have associates or an objective to carry on business for profit. Sections 301.7701-2 and 301.7701-3 provide rules for classifying organizations that are not classified as trusts.

(c) *Cost sharing arrangements.*—A cost sharing arrangement that is described in § 1.482-7 of this chapter, including any arrangement that the Commissioner treats as a CSA under § 1.482-7(b)(5) of this chapter, is not recognized as a separate entity for purposes of the Internal Revenue Code. See § 1.482-7 of this chapter for the rules regarding CSAs.

(d) *Domestic and foreign business entities.*—See § 301.7701-5 for the rules that determine whether a business entity is domestic or foreign.

(e) *State.*—For purposes of this section and §301.7701-2, the term *State* includes the District of Columbia.

(f) *Effective/applicability dates.*—Except as provided in the following sentence, the rules of this section are applicable as of January 1, 1997. The rules of paragraph (c) of this section are applicable on January 5, 2009. [Reg. §301.7701-1.]

☐ [*T.D.* 6503, 11-15-80. *Amended by T.D.* 6797, 2-2-65; *T.D.* 7515, 10-17-77; *T.D.* 8697, 12-17-96; *T.D.* 9153, 8-11-2004; *T.D.* 9246, 1-27-2006; *T.D.* 9441, 12-31-2008 *and T.D.* 9568, 12-16-2011.]

[Reg. §305.7701-1]

§305.7701-1. Definition of Indian tribal government (Temporary).—(a) *Definition.*—A governing body of a tribe, band, pueblo, community, village, or group of native American Indians, or Alaska Natives, qualifies as an Indian tribal government upon determination by the Internal Revenue Service that the governing body exercises governmental functions. Designation of a governing body as an Indian tribal government will be by revenue procedure. If a governing body is not currently designated by the applicable revenue procedure as an Indian tribal government, and such governing body believes that it qualifies for such designation, the governing body may apply for a ruling from the Internal Revenue Service. In order to qualify as an Indian tribal government, for purposes of section 7701(a)(40) and this section, such governing body must receive a favorable ruling from the Internal Revenue Service. The request for a ruling shall be made in accordance with all applicable procedural rules set forth in the Statement of Procedural Rules (26 CFR Part 601) and any applicable revenue procedures relating to the submission of ruling requests. The request shall be submitted to the Internal Revenue Service, Associate Chief Counsel (Technical), Attention: CC:IND:S, Room 6545, 1111 Constitution Avenue, N.W., Washington, D.C. 20224.

(b) *Effective date.*—The provisions of this section are effective after December 31, 1982. [Temporary Reg. §305.7701-1.]

☐ [*T.D.* 7952, 5-4-84.]

[Reg. §20.7701-2]

§20.7701-2. Definitions; spouse, husband and wife, husband, wife, marriage.—(a) *In general.*—For the definition of the terms spouse, husband and wife, husband, wife, and marriage, see §301.7701-18 of this chapter.

(b) *Applicability date.*—The rules of this section apply to taxable years ending on or after September 2, 2016. [Reg. §20.7701-2.]

☐ [*T.D.* 9785, 8-31-2016.]

[Reg. §25.7701-2]

§25.7701-2. Definitions; spouse, husband and wife, husband, wife, marriage.—(a) *In general.*—For the definition of the terms spouse, husband and wife, husband, wife, and marriage, see §301.7701-18 of this chapter.

(b) *Applicability date.*—The rules of this section apply to taxable years ending on or after September 2, 2016. [Reg. §25.7701-2.]

☐ [*T.D.* 9785, 8-31-2016.]

[Reg. §26.7701-2]

§26.7701-2. Definitions; spouse, husband and wife, husband, wife, marriage.—(a) *In general.*—For the definition of the terms spouse, husband and wife, husband, wife, and marriage, see §301.7701-18 of this chapter.

(b) *Applicability date.*—The rules of this section apply to taxable years ending on or after September 2, 2016. [Reg. §26.7701-2.]

☐ [*T.D.* 9785, 8-31-2016.]

[Reg. §31.7701-2]

§31.7701-2. Definitions; spouse, husband and wife, husband, wife, marriage.—(a) *In general.*—For the definition of the terms spouse, husband and wife, husband, wife, and marriage, see §301.7701-18 of this chapter.

(b) *Applicability date.*—The rules of this section apply to taxable years ending on or after September 2, 2016. [Reg. §31.7701-2.]

☐ [*T.D.* 9785, 8-31-2016.]

[Reg. §301.7701-2]

§301.7701-2. Business entities; definitions.—(a) *Business entities.*—For purposes of this section and §301.7701-3, a *business entity* is any entity recognized for federal tax purposes (including an entity with a single owner that may be disregarded as an entity separate from its owner under §301.7701-3) that is not properly classified as a trust under §301.7701-4 or otherwise subject to special treatment under the Internal Revenue Code. A business entity with two or more members is classified for federal tax purposes as either a corporation or a partnership. A business entity with only one owner is classified as a corporation or is disregarded; if the entity is disregarded, its activities are treated in the same manner as a sole proprietorship, branch, or division of the owner. But see paragraphs (c)(2)(iii) through (vi) of this section for special rules that apply to an eligible entity that is otherwise disregarded as an entity separate from its owner.

(b) *Corporations.*—For federal tax purposes, the term *corporation* means—

(1) A business entity organized under a Federal or State statute, or under a statute of a federally recognized Indian tribe, if the statute describes or refers to the entity as incorporated or as a corporation, body corporate, or body politic;

(2) An association (as determined under §301.7701-3);

(3) A business entity organized under a State statute, if the statute describes or refers to the entity as a joint-stock company or joint-stock association;

(4) An insurance company;

(5) A State-chartered business entity conducting banking activities, if any of its deposits are insured under the Federal Deposit Insurance Act, as amended, 12 U.S.C. 1811 et seq., or a similar federal statute;

(6) A business entity wholly owned by a State or any political subdivision thereof, or a business entity wholly owned by a foreign government or any other entity described in §1.892-2T;

(7) A business entity that is taxable as a corporation under a provision of the Internal Revenue Code other than section 7701(a)(3); and

(8) *Certain foreign entities.*—(i) *In general.*— Except as provided in paragraphs (b)(8)(ii) and (d) of this section, the following business entities formed in the following jurisdictions:

American Samoa, Corporation
Argentina, Sociedad Anonima
Australia, Public Limited Company
Austria, Aktiengesellschaft
Barbados, Limited Company
Belgium, Societe Anonyme
Belize, Public Limited Company
Bolivia, Sociedad Anonima
Brazil, Sociedade Anonima
Bulgaria, Aktsionerno Druzhestvo
Canada, Corporation and Company
Chile, Sociedad Anonima
People's Republic of China, Gufen Youxian Gongsi
Republic of China (Taiwan), Ku-fen Yu-hsien Kung-szu
Colombia, Sociedad Anonima
Costa Rica, Sociedad Anonima
Cyprus, Public Limited Company
Czech Republic, Akciova Spolecnost
Denmark, Aktieselskab
Ecuador, Sociedad Anonima or Compania Anonima
Egypt, Sharikat Al-Mossahamah
El Salvador, Sociedad Anonima
Estonia, Aktsiaselts
European Economic Area/European Union, Societas Europaea
Finland, Julkinen Osakeyhtio/Publikt Aktiebolag
France, Societe Anonyme
Germany, Aktiengesellschaft
Greece, Anonymos Etairia
Guam, Corporation
Guatemala, Sociedad Anonima
Guyana, Public Limited Company
Honduras, Sociedad Anonima
Hong Kong, Public Limited Company
Hungary, Reszvenytarsasag
Iceland, Hlutafelag
India, Public Limited Company
Indonesia, Perseroan Terbuka
Ireland, Public Limited Company
Israel, Public Limited Company

Italy, Societa per Azioni
Jamaica, Public Limited Company
Japan, Kabushiki Kaisha
Kazakstan, Ashyk Aktsionerlik Kogham
Republic of Korea, Chusik Hoesa
Latvia, Akciju Sabiedriba
Liberia, Corporation
Liechtenstein, Aktiengesellschaft
Lithuania, Akcine Bendroves
Luxembourg, Societe Anonyme
Malaysia, Berhad
Malta, Public Limited Company
Mexico, Sociedad Anonima
Morocco, Societe Anonyme
Netherlands, Naamloze Vennootschap
New Zealand, Limited Company
Nicaragua, Compania Anonima
Nigeria, Public Limited Company
Northern Mariana Islands, Corporation
Norway, Allment Aksjeselskap
Pakistan, Public Limited Company
Panama, Sociedad Anonima
Paraguay, Sociedad Anonima
Peru, Sociedad Anonima
Philippines, Stock Corporation
Poland, Spolka Akcyjna
Portugal, Sociedade Anonima
Puerto Rico, Corporation
Romania, Societate pe Actiuni
Russia, Otkrytoye Aktsionernoy Obshchestvo
Saudi Arabia, Sharikat Al-Mossahamah
Singapore, Public Limited Company
Slovak Republic, Akciova Spolocnost
Slovenia, Delniska Druzba
South Africa, Public Limited Company
Spain, Sociedad Anonima
Surinam, Naamloze Vennootschap
Sweden, Publika Aktiebolag
Switzerland, Aktiengesellschaft
Thailand, Borisat Chamkad (Mahachon)
Trinidad and Tobago, Limited Company
Tunisia, Societe Anonyme
Turkey, Anonim Sirket
Ukraine, Aktsionerne Tovaristvo Vidkritogo Tipu
United Kingdom, Public Limited Company
United States Virgin Islands, Corporation
Uruguay, Sociedad Anonima
Venezuela, Sociedad Anonima or Compania Anonima

(ii) *Clarification of list of corporations in paragraph (b)(8)(i) of this section.*—(A) *Exceptions in certain cases.*—The following entities will not be treated as corporations under paragraph (b)(8)(i) of this section:

(1) With regard to Canada, a Nova Scotia Unlimited Liability Company (or any other company or corporation all of whose owners have unlimited liability pursuant to federal or provincial law).

(2) With regard to India, a company deemed to be a public limited company solely by operation of Section 43A(1) (relating to corporate ownership of the company), section 43A(1A) (relating to annual average turnover), or section 43A(1B) (relating to ownership interests in other companies) of the Companies Act, 1956 (or any combination of these), provided that the organizational documents of such deemed public limited company continue to meet the requirements of section 3(1)(iii) of the Companies Act, 1956.

(3) With regard to Malaysia, a Sendirian Berhad.

(B) *Inclusions in certain cases.*—With regard to Mexico, the term Sociedad Anonima includes a Sociedad Anonima that chooses to apply the variable capital provision of Mexican corporate law (Sociedad Anonima de Capital Variable).

(iii) *Public companies.*—For purposes of paragraph (b)(8)(i) of this section, with regard to Cyprus, Hong Kong, and Jamaica, the term Public Limited Company includes any Limited Company that is not defined as a private company under the corporate laws of those jurisdictions. In all other cases, where the term Public Limited Company is not defined, that term shall include any Limited Company defined as a public company under the corporate laws of the relevant jurisdiction.

(iv) *Limited companies.*—For purposes of this paragraph (b)(8), any reference to a Limited Company includes, as the case may be, companies limited by shares and companies limited by guarantee.

(v) *Multilingual countries.*—Different linguistic renderings of the name of an entity listed in paragraph (b)(8)(i) of this section shall be disregarded. For example, an entity formed under the laws of Switzerland as a Societe Anonyme will be a corporation and treated in the same manner as an Aktiengesellschaft.

(9) *Business entities with multiple charters.*— (i) An entity created or organized under the laws of more than one jurisdiction if the rules of this section would treat it as a corporation with reference to any one of the jurisdictions in which it is created or organized. Such an entity may elect its classification under § 301.7701-3, subject to the limitations of those provisions, only if it is created or organized in each jurisdiction in a manner that meets the definition of an eligible entity in § 301.7701-3(a). The determination of a business entity's corporate or non-corporate classification is made independently from the determination of whether the entity is domestic or foreign. See § 301.7701-5 for the rules that determine whether a business entity is domestic or foreign.

(ii) *Examples.*—The following examples illustrate the rule of this paragraph (b)(9):

Example 1. (i) *Facts.* X is an entity with a single owner organized under the laws of Country A as an entity that is listed in paragraph (b)(8)(i) of this section. Under the rules of this section, such an entity is a corporation for Federal tax purposes and under § 301.7701-3(a) is unable to elect its classification. Several years after its formation, X files a certificate of domestication in State B as a limited liability company (LLC). Under the laws of State B, X is considered to be created or organized in State B as an LLC upon the filing of the certificate of domestication and is therefore subject to the laws of State B. Under the rules of this section and § 301.7701-3, an LLC with a single owner organized only in State B is disregarded as an entity separate from its owner for Federal tax purposes (absent an election to be treated as an association). Neither Country A nor State B law requires X to terminate its charter in Country A as a result of the domestication, and in fact X does not terminate its Country A charter. Consequently, X is now organized in more than one jurisdiction.

(ii) *Result.* X remains organized under the laws of Country A as an entity that is listed in paragraph (b)(8)(i) of this section, and as such, it is an entity that is treated as a corporation under the rules of this section. Therefore, X is a corporation for Federal tax purposes because the rules of this section would treat X as a corporation with reference to one of the jurisdictions in which it is created or organized. Because X is organized in Country A in a manner that does not meet the definition of an eligible entity in § 301.7701-3(a), it is unable to elect its classification.

Example 2. (i) *Facts.* Y is an entity that is incorporated under the laws of State A and has two shareholders. Under the rules of this section, an entity incorporated under the laws of State A is a corporation for Federal tax purposes and under § 301.7701-3(a) is unable to elect its classification. Several years after its formation, Y files a certificate of continuance in Country B as an unlimited company. Under the laws of Country B, upon filing a certificate of continuance, Y is treated as organized in Country B. Under the rules of this section and § 301.7701-3, an unlimited company organized only in Country B that has more than one owner is treated as a partnership for Federal tax purposes (absent an election to be treated as an association). Neither State A nor Country B law requires Y to terminate its charter in State A as a result of the continuance, and in fact Y does not terminate its State A charter. Consequently, Y is now organized in more than one jurisdiction.

(ii) *Result.* Y remains organized in State A as a corporation, an entity that is treated as a corporation under the rules of this section. Therefore, Y is a corporation for Federal tax purposes because the rules of this section would treat Y as a corporation with reference to one of the jurisdictions in which it is created or organized. Because Y is organized in State A in a manner that does not meet the definition of an eligible entity in § 301.7701-3(a), it is unable to elect its classification.

Example 3. (i) *Facts.* Z is an entity that has more than one owner and that is recognized under the laws of Country A as an unlimited company organized in Country A. Z is organized in Country A in a manner that meets the definition of an eligible entity in § 301.7701-3(a). Under the rules of this section and § 301.7701-3, an unlimited company organized only in Country A with more than one owner is treated as a partnership for Federal tax purposes (absent an election to be treated as an association). At the time Z was formed, it was also organized as a private limited company under the laws of Country B. Z is organized in Country B in a manner that meets the definition of an eligible entity in § 301.7701-3(a). Under the rules of this section and § 301.7701-3, a private limited company organized only in Country B is treated as a corporation for Federal tax purposes (absent an election to be treated as a partnership). Thus, Z is organized in more than one jurisdiction. Z has not made any entity classification elections under § 301.7701-3.

(ii) *Result.* Z is organized in Country B as a private limited company, an entity that is treated (absent an election to the contrary) as a corporation under the rules of this section. However, because Z is organized in each jurisdiction in a manner that meets the definition of an eligible entity in § 301.7701-3(a), it may elect its classification under § 301.7701-3, subject to the limitations of those provisions.

Example 4. (i) *Facts.* P is an entity with more than one owner organized in Country A as a general partnership. Under the rules of this section and § 301.7701-3, an eligible entity with more than one owner in Country A is treated as a partnership for federal tax purposes (absent an election to be treated as an association). P files a certificate of continuance in Country B as an unlimited company. Under the rules of this section and § 301.7701-3, an unlimited company in Country B with more than one owner is treated as a partnership for federal tax purposes (absent an election to be treated as an association). P is not required under either the laws of Country A or Country B to terminate the general partnership in Country A, and in fact P does not terminate its Country A partnership. P is now organized in more than one jurisdiction. P has not made any entity classification elections under § 301.7701-3.

(ii) *Result.* P's organization in both Country A and Country B would result in P being classified as a partnership. Therefore, since the rules of this section would not treat P as a corporation with reference to any jurisdiction in which it is created or organized, it is not a corporation for federal tax purposes.

(c) *Other business entities.*—For federal tax purposes—

(1) The term *partnership* means a business entity that is not a corporation under paragraph (b) of this section and that has at least two members.

(2) *Wholly owned entities.*—(i) *In general.*— Except as otherwise provided in this paragraph

(c), a business entity that has a single owner and is not a corporation under paragraph (b) of this section is disregarded as an entity separate from its owner.

(ii) *Special rule for certain business entities.*—If the single owner of a business entity is a bank (as defined in section 581, or, in the case of a foreign bank, as defined in section 585(a)(2)(B) without regard to the second sentence thereof), then the special rules applicable to banks under the Internal Revenue Code will continue to apply to the single owner as if the wholly owned entity were a separate entity. For this purpose, the special rules applicable to banks under the Internal Revenue Code do not include the rules under sections 864(c), 882(c), and 884.

(iii) *Tax liabilities of certain disregarded entities.*—(A) *In general.*—An entity that is disregarded as separate from its owner for any purpose under this section is treated as an entity separate from its owner for purposes of—

(1) Federal tax liabilities of the entity with respect to any taxable period for which the entity was not disregarded;

(2) Federal tax liabilities of any other entity for which the entity is liable; and

(3) Refunds or credits of Federal tax.

(B) *Examples.*—The following examples illustrate the application of paragraph (c)(2)(iii)(A) of this section:

Example 1. In 2006, X, a domestic corporation that reports its taxes on a calendar year basis, merges into Z, a domestic LLC wholly owned by Y that is disregarded as an entity separate from Y, in a state law merger. X was not a member of a consolidated group at any time during its taxable year ending in December 2005. Under the applicable state law, Z is the successor to X and is liable for all of X's debts. In 2009, the Internal Revenue Service (IRS) seeks to extend the period of limitations on assessment for X's 2005 taxable year. Because Z is the successor to X and is liable for X's 2005 taxes that remain unpaid, Z is the proper party to sign the consent to extend the period of limitations.

Example 2. The facts are the same as in *Example 1,* except that in 2007, the IRS determines that X miscalculated and underreported its income tax liability for 2005. Because Z is the successor to X and is liable for X's 2005 taxes that remain unpaid, the deficiency may be assessed against Z and, in the event that Z fails to pay the liability after notice and demand, a general tax lien will arise against all of Z's property and rights to property.

(iv) *Special rule for employment tax purposes.*—(A) *In general.*—Except as provided in paragraph (c)(2)(iv)(C) of this section, paragraph (c)(2)(i) of this section (relating to certain wholly owned entities) does not apply to taxes imposed under Subtitle C—Employment Taxes and Collection of Income Tax (Chapters 21, 22, 23, 23A, 24, and 25 of the Internal Revenue Code).

(B) *Treatment of entity.*—Except as provided in paragraph (c)(2)(iv)(C) of this section, an entity that is disregarded as an entity separate from its owner for any purpose under this section is treated as a corporation with respect to taxes imposed under Subtitle C—Employment Taxes and Collection of Income Tax (Chapters 21, 22, 23, 23A, 24, and 25 of the Internal Revenue Code). For special rules regarding the application of certain employment tax exceptions, see §§ 31.3121(b)(3)-1(d), 31.3127-1(b), and 31.3306(c)(5)-1(d) of this chapter.

(C) *Special rules.*—(1) Paragraphs (c)(2)(iv)(A) and (B) of this section do not apply to withholding requirements imposed by section 3406 (backup withholding). Thus, in the case of an entity that is disregarded as an entity separate from its owner for any purpose under this section, the owner is subject to the withholding requirements imposed by section 3406 (backup withholding).

(2) [Reserved]. For further guidance, see § 301.7701-2T(c)(2)(iv)(C)(2).

(D) *Example.*—The following example illustrates the application of paragraph (c)(2)(iv) of this section:

Example. (i) LLCA is an eligible entity owned by individual A and is generally disregarded as an entity separate from its owner for Federal tax purposes. However, LLCA is treated as an entity separate from its owner for purposes of subtitle C of the Internal Revenue Code. LLCA has employees and pays wages as defined in sections 3121(a), 3306(b), and 3401(a).

(ii) LLCA is subject to the provisions of subtitle C of the Internal Revenue Code and related provisions under 26 CFR subchapter C, Employment Taxes and Collection of Income Tax at Source, parts 31 through 39. Accordingly, LLCA is required to perform such acts as are required of an employer under those provisions of the Internal Revenue Code and regulations thereunder that apply. All provisions of law (including penalties) and the regulations prescribed in pursuance of law applicable to employers in respect of such acts are applicable to LLCA. Thus, for example, LLCA is liable for income tax withholding, Federal Insurance Contributions Act (FICA) taxes, and Federal Unemployment Tax Act (FUTA) taxes. See sections 3402 and 3403 (relating to income tax withholding); 3102(b) and 3111 (relating to FICA taxes), and 3301 (relating to FUTA taxes). In addition, LLCA must file under its name and EIN the applicable Forms in the 94X series, for example, Form 941, "Employer's Quarterly Employment Tax Return," Form 940, "Employer's Annual Federal Unemployment Tax Return;" file with the Social Security Administration and furnish to LLCA's employees statements on Forms W-2, "Wage and Tax Statement;" and make timely employment tax deposits. See §§ 31.6011(a)-1, 31.6011(a)-3, 31.6051-1, 31.6051-2, and 31.6302-1 of this chapter.

(iii) A is self-employed for purposes of subtitle A, chapter 2, Tax on Self-Employment Income, of the Internal Revenue Code. Thus, A is subject to tax under section 1401 on A's net earnings from self-employment with respect to LLCA's activities. A is not an employee of LLCA for purposes of subtitle C of the Internal Revenue Code. Because LLCA is treated as a sole proprietorship of A for income tax purposes, A is entitled to deduct trade or business expenses paid or incurred with respect to activities carried on through LLCA, including the employer's share of employment taxes imposed under sections 3111 and 3301, on A's Form 1040, Schedule C, "Profit or Loss for Business (Sole Proprietorship)."

(v) *Special rule for certain excise tax purposes.*—(A) *In general.*—Paragraph (c)(2)(i) of this section (relating to certain wholly owned entities) does not apply for purposes of—

(1) Federal tax liabilities imposed by Chapters 31, 32 (other than section 4181), 33, 34, 35, 36 (other than section 4461), 38, and 49 of the Internal Revenue Code, or any floor stocks tax imposed on articles subject to any of these taxes;

(2) Collection of tax imposed by Chapters 33 and 49 of the Internal Revenue Code;

(3) Registration under sections 4101, 4222, and 4412;

(4) Claims of a credit (other than a credit under section 34), refund, or payment related to a tax described in paragraph (c)(2)(v)(A)(1) of this section or under section 6426 or 6427; and

(5) Assessment and collection of an assessable payment imposed by section 4980H and reporting required by section 6056.

(B) *Treatment of entity.*—An entity that is disregarded as an entity separate from its owner for any purpose under this section is treated as a corporation with respect to items described in paragraph (c)(2)(v)(A) of this section.

(C) *Example.*—The following example illustrates the provisions of this paragraph (c)(2)(v):

Example. (i) LLCB is an eligible entity that has a single owner, B. LLCB is generally disregarded as an entity separate from its owner. However, under paragraph (c)(2)(v) of this section, LLCB is treated as an entity separate from its owner for certain purposes relating to excise taxes.

(ii) LLCB mines coal from a coal mine located in the United States. Section 4121 of chapter 32 of the Internal Revenue Code imposes a tax on the producer's sale of such coal. Section 48.4121-1(a) of this chapter defines a "producer" generally as the person in whom is vested ownership of the coal under state law immediately after the coal is severed from the ground. LLCB is the person that owns the coal under state law immediately after it is severed from the ground. Under paragraph (c)(2)(v)(A)(1) of this section,

LLCB is the producer of the coal and is liable for tax on its sale of such coal under chapter 32 of the Internal Revenue Code. LLCB must report and pay tax on Form 720, "Quarterly Federal Excise Tax Return," under its own name and taxpayer identification number.

(iii) LLCB uses undyed diesel fuel in an earthmover that is not registered or required to be registered for highway use. Such use is an off-highway business use of the fuel. Under section 6427(l), the ultimate purchaser is allowed to claim an income tax credit or payment related to the tax imposed on diesel fuel used in an off-highway business use. Under paragraph (c)(2)(v) of this section, for purposes of the credit or payment allowed under section 6427(l), LLCB is the person that could claim the amount on its Form 720 or on a Form 8849, "Claim for Refund of Excise Taxes." Alternatively, if LLCB did not claim a payment during the time prescribed in section 6427(i)(2) for making a claim under section 6427, § 1.34-1 of this chapter provides that B, the owner of LLCB, could claim the income tax credit allowed under section 34 for the nontaxable use of diesel fuel by LLCB.

(iv) Assume the same facts as in paragraph (c)(2)(v)(C) *Example* (i) and (ii) of this section. If LLCB does not pay the tax on its sale of coal under chapter 32 of the Internal Revenue Code, any notice of lien the Internal Revenue Service files will be filed as if LLCB were a corporation.

(vi) *Special rule for reporting under section 6038A.*—(A) *In general.*—An entity that is disregarded as an entity separate from its owner for any purpose under this section is treated as an entity separate from its owner and classified as a corporation for purposes of section 6038A if—

(1) The entity is a domestic entity; and

(2) One foreign person has direct or indirect sole ownership of the entity.

(B) *Definitions.*—(1) *Indirect sole ownership.*—For purposes of paragraph (c)(2)(vi)(A)(2) of this section, indirect sole ownership means ownership by one person entirely through one or more other entities disregarded as entities separate from their owners or through one or more grantor trusts, regardless of whether any such disregarded entity or grantor trust is domestic or foreign.

(2) *Entity disregarded as separate from its owner.*—For purposes of paragraph (c)(2)(vi)(B)(1) of this section, an entity disregarded as an entity separate from its owner is an entity described in paragraph (c)(2)(i) of this section.

(3) *Grantor trust.*—For purposes of paragraph (c)(2)(vi)(B)(1) of this section, a grantor trust is any portion of a trust that is treated as owned by the grantor or another person under subpart E of subchapter J of chapter 1 of the Code.

(C) *Taxable year.*—The taxable year of an entity classified as a corporation for section 6038A purposes pursuant to paragraph (c)(2)(vi)(A) of this section is—

(1) The same as the taxable year of the foreign person described in paragraph (c)(2)(vi)(A)(2) of this section, if that foreign person has a U.S. income tax or information return filing obligation for its taxable year; or

(2) The calendar year, if paragraph (c)(2)(vi)(C)(1) of this section does not apply, unless otherwise provided in forms, instructions, or published guidance.

(d) *Special rule for certain foreign business entities.*—(1) *In general.*—Except as provided in paragraph (d)(3) of this section, a foreign business entity described in paragraph (b)(8)(i) of this section will not be treated as a corporation under paragraph (b)(8)(i) of this section if—

(i) The entity was in existence on May 8, 1996;

(ii) The entity's classification was relevant (as defined in § 301.7701-3(d)) on May 8, 1996;

(iii) No person (including the entity) for whom the entity's classification was relevant on May 8, 1996, treats the entity as a corporation for purposes of filing such person's federal income tax returns, information returns, and withholding documents for the taxable year including May 8, 1996;

(iv) Any change in the entity's claimed classification within the sixty months prior to May 8, 1996, occurred solely as a result of a change in the organizational documents of the entity, and the entity and all members of the entity recognized the federal tax consequences of any change in the entity's classification within the sixty months prior to May 8, 1996;

(v) A reasonable basis (within the meaning of section 6662) existed on May 8, 1996, for treating the entity as other than a corporation; and

(vi) Neither the entity nor any member was notified in writing on or before May 8, 1996, that the classification of the entity was under examination (in which case the entity's classification will be determined in the examination).

(2) *Binding contract rule.*—If a foreign business entity described in paragraph (b)(8)(i) of this section is formed after May 8, 1996, pursuant to a written binding contract (including an accepted bid to develop a project) in effect on May 8, 1996, and all times thereafter, in which the parties agreed to engage (directly or indirectly) in an active and substantial business operation in the jurisdiction in which the entity is formed, paragraph (d)(1) of this section will be applied to that entity by substituting the date of the entity's formation for May 8, 1996.

(3) *Termination of grandfather status.*—(i) *In general.*—An entity that is not treated as a corporation under paragraph (b)(8)(i) of this section by reason of paragraph (d)(1) or (d)(2) of this section will be treated permanently as a corporation under paragraph (b)(8)(i) of this section from the earliest of:

(A) The effective date of an election to be treated as an association under § 301.7701-3;

(B) A termination of the partnership under section 708(b)(1)(B) (regarding sale or exchange of 50 percent or more of the total interest in an entity's capital or profits within a twelve month period);

(C) A division of the partnership under section 708(b)(2)(B); or

(D) The date any person or persons, who were not owners of the entity as of November 29, 1999, own in the aggregate a 50 percent or greater interest in the entity.

(ii) *Special rule for certain entities.*—For purposes of paragraph (d)(2) of this section, paragraph (d)(3)(i)(B) of this section shall not apply if the sale or exchange of interests in the entity is to a related person (within the meaning of sections 267(b) and 707(b)) and occurs no later than twelve months after the date of the formation of the entity.

(e) *Effective/applicability date.*—(1) Except as otherwise provided in this paragraph (e), the rules of this section apply as of January 1, 1997, except that paragraph (b)(6) of this section applies on or after January 14, 2002, to a business entity wholly owned by a foreign government regardless of any prior entity classification, and paragraph (c)(2)(ii) of this section applies to taxable years beginning after January 12, 2001. The reference to the Finnish, Maltese, and Norwegian entities in paragraph (b)(8)(i) of this section is applicable on November 29, 1999. The reference to the Trinidadian entity in paragraph (b)(8)(i) of this section applies to entities formed on or after November 29, 1999. Any Maltese or Norwegian entity that becomes an eligible entity as a result of paragraph (b)(8)(i) of this section in effect on November 29, 1999, may elect by February 14, 2000, to be classified for Federal tax purposes as an entity other than a corporation retroactive to any period from and including January 1, 1997. Any Finnish entity that becomes an eligible entity as a result of paragraph (b)(8)(i) of this section in effect on November 29, 1999, may elect by February 14, 2000, to be classified for Federal tax purposes as an entity other than a corporation retroactive to any period from and including September 1, 1997. However, paragraph (d)(3)(i)(D) of this section applies on or after October 22, 2003.

(2) Paragraph (c)(2)(iii) of this section applies on and after September 14, 2009. For rules that apply before September 14, 2009, see 26 CFR part 301, revised as of April 1, 2009.

(3)(i) *General rule.*—Except as provided in paragraph (e)(3)(ii) of this section, the rules of paragraph (b)(9) of this section apply as of August 12, 2004, to all business entities existing on or after that date.

(ii) *Transition rule.*—For business entities created or organized under the laws of more than one jurisdiction as of August 12, 2004, the rules of paragraph (b)(9) of this section apply as of May 1, 2006. These entities, however, may rely on the rules of paragraph (b)(9) of this section as of August 12, 2004.

(4) The reference to the Estonian, Latvian, Liechtenstein, Lithuanian, and Slovenian entities in paragraph (b)(8)(i) of this section applies to such entities formed on or after October 7, 2004, and to any such entity formed before such date from the date any person or persons, who were not owners of the entity as of October 7, 2004, own in the aggregate a 50 percent or greater interest in the entity. The reference to the European Economic Area/European Union entity in paragraph (b)(8)(i) of this section applies to such entities formed on or after October 8, 2004.

(5)(i) Except as provided in this paragraph (e)(5), paragraph (c)(2)(iv) of this section applies with respect to wages paid on or after January 1, 2009.

(ii) Paragraph (c)(2)(iv)(B) applies with respect to wages paid on or after September 14, 2009. For rules that apply before September 14, 2009, see 26 CFR part 301 revised as of April 1, 2009.

(iii) Paragraph (c)(2)(iv)(C)(*1*) of this section applies with respect to wages paid on or after November 1, 2011. For rules that apply before November 1, 2011, see 26 CFR part 301, revised as of April 1, 2011. However, taxpayers may apply paragraph (c)(2)(iv)(C)(*1*) of this section with respect to wages paid on or after January 1, 2009.

(6)(i) Except as provided in this paragraph (e)(6), paragraph (c)(2)(v) of this section applies to liabilities imposed and actions first required or permitted in periods beginning on or after January 1, 2008.

(ii) Paragraphs (c)(2)(v)(B) and (c)(2)(v)(C) *Example* (iv) of this section apply on and after September 14, 2009.

(iii) Paragraph (c)(2)(v)(A)(*5*) of this section applies for periods after December 31, 2014.

(iv) References to Chapter 49 in paragraph (c)(2)(v) of this section apply to taxes imposed on amounts paid on or after July 1, 2012.

(7) The reference to the Bulgarian entity in paragraph (b)(8)(i) of this section applies to such entities formed on or after January 1, 2007, and to any such entity formed before such date from the date that, in the aggregate, a 50 percent or more interest in such entity is owned by any person or persons who were not owners of the entity as of January 1, 2007. For purposes of the preceding sentence, the term *interest* means—

(i) In the case of a partnership, a capital or profits interest; and

(ii) In the case of a corporation, an equity interest measured by vote or value.

(8) [Reserved]. For further guidance, see § 301.7701-2T(e)(8).

(9) *Reporting required under section 6038A.*—Paragraph (c)(2)(vi) of this section applies to taxable years of entities beginning after December 31, 2016, and ending on or after December 13, 2017. [Reg. § 301.7701-2.]

☐ [*T.D. 6503*, 11-15-60. *Amended by T.D. 6797*, 2-2-65; *T.D. 7515*, 10-17-77; *T.D. 7889*, 4-25-83; *T.D. 8475*, 5-13-93; *T.D. 8697*, 12-17-96 (*corrected* 4-3-2008); *T.D. 8844*, 11-26-99; *T.D. 9012*, 7-31-2002; *T.D. 9093*, 10-21-2003; *T.D. 9153*, 8-11-2004; *T.D. 9183*, 2-24-2005 *T.D. 9197*, 4-13-2005; *T.D. 9235*, 12-15-2005; *T.D. 9246*, 1-27-2006; *T.D. 9356*, 8-15-2007; *T.D. 9388*, 3-20-2008; *T.D. 9433*, 11-26-2008; *T.D. 9462*, 9-11-2009; *T.D. 9553*, 10-25-2011; *T.D. 9554*, 10-31-2011; *T.D. 9596*, 6-22-2012. *T.D. 9655*, 2-10-2014, *T.D. 9670*, 6-25-2014, *T.D. 9766*, 5-3-2016 *and T.D. 9796*, 12-12-2016.]

[Reg. §301.7701-2T]

§301.7701-2T. Business entities; definitions (temporary).—(a) through (c)(2)(iv)(C)(1) [Reserved]. For further guidance, see §301.7701-2(a) through (c)(2)(iv)(C)(1).

(2) Section 301.7701-2(c)(2)(i) applies to taxes imposed under subtitle A, including Chapter 2—Tax on Self-Employment Income. Thus, an entity that is treated in the same manner as a sole proprietorship under §301.7701-2(a) is not treated as a corporation for purposes of employing its owner; instead, the entity is disregarded as an entity separate from its owner for this purpose and is not the employer of its owner. The owner will be subject to self-employment tax on self-employment income with respect to the entity's activities. Also, if a partnership is the owner of an entity that is disregarded as an entity separate from its owner for any purpose under §301.7701-2, the entity is not treated as a corporation for purposes of employing a partner of the partnership that owns the entity; instead, the entity is disregarded as an entity separate from the partnership for this purpose and is not the employer of any partner of the partnership that owns the entity. A partner of a partnership that owns an entity that is disregarded as an entity separate from its owner for any purpose under §301.7701-2 is subject to the same self-employment tax rules as a partner of a partnership that does not own an entity that is disregarded as an entity separate from its owner for any purpose under §301.7701-2.

(c)(2)(iv)(D) through (e)(7) [Reserved]. For further guidance, see §301.7701-2(c)(2)(iv)(D) through (e)(7).

(8)(i) *Effective/applicability date.*—Paragraph (c)(2)(iv)(C)(2) of this section applies on the later of—

(A) August 1, 2016, or

(B) The first day of the latest-starting plan year following May 4, 2016, of an affected plan (based on the plans adopted before, and the plan years in effect as of, May 4, 2016) sponsored by an entity that is disregarded as an entity separate from its owner for any purpose under §301.7701-2. For rules that apply before the applicability date of these regulations, see 26 CFR part 301 revised as of April 1, 2016. For these purposes—

(1) An affected plan includes any qualified plan, health plan, or section 125 cafeteria plan if the plan benefits participants whose employment status is affected by paragraph (c)(2)(iv)(C)(2),

(2) A qualified plan means a plan, contract, pension, or trust described in paragraph (A) or (B) of section 219(g)(5) (other than paragraph (A)(iii)), and

(3) A health plan means an arrangement described under §1.105-5 of this chapter.

(ii) *Expiration date.*—The applicability of paragraph (c)(2)(iv)(C)(2) of this section expires on or before May 3, 2019, or such earlier date as may be determined under amendments to the regulations issued after May 3, 2016. [Temporary Reg. §301.7701-2T.]

☐ *T.D.* 9766, 5-3-2016 (*corrected* 7-1-2016).]

[Reg. §301.7701-3]

§301.7701-3. Classification of certain business entities.—(a) *In general.*—A business entity that is not classified as a corporation under §301.7701-2(b)(1), (3), (4), (5), (6), (7), or (8) (an *eligible entity*) can elect its classification for federal tax purposes as provided in this section. An eligible entity with at least two members can elect to be classified as either an association (and thus a corporation under §301.7701-2(b)(2)) or a partnership, and an eligible entity with a single owner can elect to be classified as an association or to be disregarded as an entity separate from its owner. Paragraph (b) of this section provides a default classification for an eligible entity that does not make an election. Thus, elections are necessary only when an eligible entity chooses to be classified initially as other than the default classification or when an eligible entity chooses to change its classification. An entity whose classification is determined under the default classification retains that classification (regardless of any changes in the members' liability that occurs at any time during the time that the entity's classification is relevant as defined in paragraph (d) of this section) until the entity makes an election to change that classification under paragraph (c)(1) of this section. Paragraph (c) of this section provides rules for making express elections. Paragraph (d) of this section provides special rules for foreign eligible entities. Paragraph (e) of this section provides special rules for classifying entities resulting from partnership terminations and divisions under section 708(b). Paragraph (f) of this section sets forth the effective date of this section and a special rule relating to prior periods.

(b) *Classification of eligible entities that do not file an election.*—(1) *Domestic eligible entities.*—Except as provided in paragraph (b)(3) of this section, unless the entity elects otherwise, a domestic eligible entity is—

(i) A partnership if it has two or more members; or

(ii) Disregarded as an entity separate from its owner if it has a single owner.

(2) *Foreign eligible entities.*—(i) *In general.*— Except as provided in paragraph (b)(3) of this section, unless the entity elects otherwise, a foreign eligible entity is—

(A) A partnership if it has two or more members and at least one member does not have limited liability;

(B) An association if all members have limited liability; or

(C) Disregarded as an entity separate from its owner if it has a single owner that does not have limited liability.

(ii) *Definition of limited liability.*—For purposes of paragraph (b)(2)(i) of this section, a member of a foreign eligible entity has limited liability if the member has no personal liability for the debts of or claims against the entity by reason of being a member. This determination is based solely on the statute or law pursuant to which the entity is organized, except that if the underlying statute or law allows the entity to specify in its organizational documents whether the members will have limited liability, the organizational documents may also be relevant. For purposes of this section, a member has personal liability if the creditors of the entity may seek satisfaction of all or any portion of the debts or claims against the entity from the member as such. A member has personal liability for purposes of this paragraph even if the member makes an agreement under which another person (whether or not a member of the entity) assumes such liability or agrees to indemnify that member for any such liability.

(3) *Existing eligible entities.*—(i) *In general.*— Unless the entity elects otherwise, an eligible entity in existence prior to the effective date of this section will have the same classification that the entity claimed under §§ 301.7701-1 through 301.7701-3 as in effect on the date prior to the effective date of this section; except that if an eligible entity with a single owner claimed to be a partnership under those regulations, the entity will be disregarded as an entity separate from its owner under this paragraph (b)(3)(i). For special rules regarding the classification of such entities prior to the effective date of this section, see paragraph (h)(2) of this section.

(ii) *Special rules.*—For purposes of paragraph (b)(3)(i) of this section, a foreign eligible entity is treated as being in existence prior to the effective date of this section only if the entity's classification was relevant (as defined in paragraph (d) of this section) at any time during the sixty months prior to the effective date of this section. If an entity claimed different classifications prior to the effective date of this section, the entity's classification for purposes of paragraph (b)(3)(i) of this section is the last classification claimed by the entity. If a foreign eligible entity's classification is relevant prior to the effective date of this section, but no federal tax or information return is filed or the federal tax or information return does not indicate the classification of the entity, the entity's classification for

the period prior to the effective date of this section is determined under the regulations in effect on the date prior to the effective date of this section.

(c) *Elections.*—(1) *Time and place for filing.*— (i) *In general.*—Except as provided in paragraphs (c)(1)(iv) and (v) of this section, an eligible entity may elect to be classified other than as provided under paragraph (b) of this section, or to change its classification, by filing Form 8832, Entity Classification Election, with the service center designated on Form 8832. An election will not be accepted unless all of the information required by the form and instructions, including the taxpayer identifying number of the entity, is provided on Form 8832. See § 301.6109-1 for rules on applying for and displaying Employer Identification Numbers.

(ii) *Further notification of elections.*—An eligible entity required to file a Federal tax or information return for the taxable year for which an election is made under § 301.7701-3(c)(1)(i) must attach a copy of its Form 8832 to its Federal tax or information return for that year. If the entity is not required to file a return for that year, a copy of its Form 8832 ("Entity Classification Election") must be attached to the Federal income tax or information return of any direct or indirect owner of the entity for the taxable year of the owner that includes the date on which the election was effective. An indirect owner of the entity does not have to attach a copy of the Form 8832 to its return if an entity in which it has an interest is already filing a copy of the Form 8832 with its return. If an entity, or one of its direct or indirect owners, fails to attach a copy of a Form 8832 to its return as directed in this section, an otherwise valid election under § 301.7701-3(c)(1)(i) will not be invalidated, but the non-filing party may be subject to penalties, including any applicable penalties if the Federal tax or information returns are inconsistent with the entity's election under § 301.7701-3(c)(1)(i). In the case of returns for taxable years beginning after December 31, 2002, the copy of Form 8832 attached to a return pursuant to this paragraph (c)(1)(ii) is not required to be a signed copy.

(iii) *Effective date of election.*—An election made under paragraph (c)(1)(i) of this section will be effective on the date specified by the entity on Form 8832 or on the date filed if no such date is specified on the election form. The effective date specified on Form 8832 can not be more than 75 days prior to the date on which the election is filed and can not be more than 12 months after the date on which the election is filed. If an election specifies an effective date more than 75 days prior to the date on which the election is filed, it will be effective 75 days prior to the date it was filed. If an election specifies an effective date more than 12 months from the date on which the election is filed, it will be effective 12 months after the date it was filed. If an election specifies an effective date before January 1, 1997, it will be effective as of January 1, 1997. If a purchasing corporation makes an election under section 338 regarding an acquired subsidiary, an election under paragraph (c)(1)(i) of this section for the acquired subsidiary can be effective no earlier than the day after the acquisition date (within the meaning of section 338(h)(2)).

(iv) *Limitation.*—If an eligible entity makes an election under paragraph (c)(1)(i) of this section to change its classification (other than an election made by an existing entity to change its classification as of the effective date of this section), the entity cannot change its classification by election again during the sixty months succeeding the effective date of the election. However, the Commissioner may permit the entity to change its classification by election within the sixty months if more than fifty percent of the ownership interests in the entity as of the effective date of the subsequent election are owned by persons that did not own any interests in the entity on the filing date or on the effective date of the entity's prior election. An election by a newly formed eligible entity that is effective on the date of formation is not considered a change for purposes of this paragraph (c)(1)(iv).

(v) *Deemed elections.*—(A) *Exempt organizations.*—An eligible entity that has been determined to be, or claims to be, exempt from taxation under section 501(a) is treated as having made an election under this section to be classified as an association. Such election will be effective as of the first day for which exemption is claimed or determined to apply, regardless of when the claim or determination is made, and will remain in effect unless an election is made under paragraph (c)(1)(i) of this section after the date the claim for exempt status is withdrawn or rejected or the date the determination of exempt status is revoked.

(B) *Real estate investment trusts.*—An eligible entity that files an election under section 856(c)(1) to be treated as a real estate investment trust is treated as having made an election under this section to be classified as an association. Such election will be effective as of the first day the entity is treated as a real estate investment trust.

(C) *S corporations.*—An eligible entity that timely elects to be an S corporation under section 1362(a)(1) is treated as having made an election under this section to be classified as an association, provided that (as of the effective date of the election under section 1362(a)(1)) the entity meets all other requirements to qualify as a small business corporation under section 1361(b). Subject to § 301.7701-3(c)(1)(iv), the deemed election to be classified as an association will apply as of the effective date of the S corporation election and will remain in effect until the entity makes a valid election, under § 301.7701-3(c)(1)(i), to be classified as other than an association.

(vi) *Examples.*—The following examples illustrate the rules of this paragraph (c)(1):

Example 1. On July 1, 1998, X, a domestic corporation, purchases a 10% interest in Y, an eligible entity formed under Country A law in 1990. The entity's classification was not relevant to any person for federal tax or information purposes prior to X's acquisition of an interest in Y. Thus, Y is not considered to be in existence on the effective date of this section for purposes of paragraph (b)(3) of this section. Under the applicable Country A statute, all members of Y have limited liability as defined in paragraph (b)(2)(ii) of this section. Accordingly, Y is classified as an association under paragraph (b)(2)(i)(B) of this section unless it elects under this paragraph (c) to be classified as a partnership. To be classified as a partnership as of July 1, 1998, Y must file a Form 8832 by September 14, 1998. See paragraph (c)(1)(i) of this section. Because an election cannot be effective more than 75 days prior to the date on which it is filed, if Y files its Form 8832 after September 14, 1998, it will be classified as an association from July 1, 1998, until the effective date of the election. In that case, it could not change its classification by election under this paragraph (c) during the sixty months succeeding the effective date of the election.

Example 2. (i) Z is an eligible entity formed under Country B law and is in existence on the effective date of this section within the meaning of paragraph (b)(3) of this section. Prior to the effective date of this section, Z claimed to be classified as an association. Unless Z files an election under this paragraph (c), it will continue to be classified as an association under paragraph (b)(3) of this section.

(ii) Z files a Form 8832 pursuant to this paragraph (c) to be classified as a partnership, effective as of the effective date of this section. Z can file an election to be classified as an association at any time thereafter, but then would not be permitted to change its classification by election during the sixty months succeeding the effective date of that subsequent election.

(2) *Authorized signatures.*—(i) *In general.*— An election made under paragraph (c)(1)(i) of this section must be signed by—

(A) Each member of the electing entity who is an owner at the time the election is filed; or

(B) Any officer, manager, or member of the electing entity who is authorized (under local law or the entity's organizational documents) to make the election and who represents to having such authorization under penalties of perjury.

(ii) *Retroactive elections.*—For purposes of paragraph (c)(2)(i) of this section, if an election under paragraph (c)(1)(i) of this section is to be effective for any period prior to the time that it is filed, each person who was an owner between the date the election is to be effective and the date the election is filed, and who is not an owner at the time the election is filed, must also sign the election.

(iii) *Changes in classification.*—For paragraph (c)(2)(i) of this section, if an election under paragraph (c)(1)(i) of this section is made to change the classification of an entity, each person who was an owner on the date that any transactions under paragraph (g) of this section are deemed to occur, and who is not an owner at the time the election is filed, must also sign the election. This paragraph (c)(2)(iii) applies to elections filed on or after November 29, 1999.

(d) *Special rules for foreign eligible entities.*— (1) *Definition of relevance.*—(i) *General rule.*—For purposes of this section, a foreign eligible entity's classification is relevant when its classification affects the liability of any person for federal tax or information purposes. For example, a foreign entity's classification would be relevant if U.S. income was paid to the entity and the determination by the withholding agent of the amount to be withheld under chapter 3 of the Internal Revenue Code (if any) would vary depending upon whether the entity is classified as a partnership or as an association. Thus, the classification might affect the documentation that the withholding agent must receive from the entity, the type of tax or information return to file, or how the return must be prepared. The date that the classification of a foreign eligible entity is relevant is the date an event occurs that creates an obligation to file a federal tax return, information return, or statement for which the classification of the entity must be determined. Thus, the classification of a foreign entity is relevant, for example, on the date that an interest in the entity is acquired which will require a U.S. person to file an information return on Form 5471.

(ii) *Deemed relevance.*—(A) *General rule.*—For purposes of this section, except as provided in paragraph (d)(1)(ii)(B) of this section, the classification for Federal tax purposes of a foreign eligible entity that files Form 8832, "Entity Classification Election", shall be deemed to be relevant only on the date the entity classification election is effective.

(B) *Exception.*—If the classification of a foreign eligible entity is relevant within the meaning of paragraph (d)(1)(i) of this section, then the rule in paragraph (d)(1)(ii)(A) of this section shall not apply.

(2) *Entities the classification of which has never been relevant.*—If the classification of a foreign eligible entity has never been relevant (as defined in paragraph (d)(1) of this section), then the entity's classification will initially be determined pursuant to the provisions of paragraph (b)(2) of this section when the classification of the entity first becomes relevant (as defined in paragraph (d)(1)(i) of this section).

(3) *Special rule when classification is no longer relevant.*—If the classification of a foreign eligible entity is not relevant (as defined in paragraph (d)(1) of this section) for 60 consecutive months, then the entity's classification will initially be determined pursuant to the provisions of paragraph (b)(2) of this section when the classifica-

tion of the foreign eligible entity becomes relevant (as defined in paragraph (d)(1)(i) of this section). The date that the classification of a foreign entity is not relevant is the date an event occurs that causes the classification to no longer be relevant, or, if no event occurs in a taxable year that causes the classification to be relevant, then the date is the first day of that taxable year.

(4) *Effective date.*—Paragraphs (d)(1)(ii), (d)(2), and (d)(3) of this section apply on or after October 22, 2003.

(e) *Coordination with section 708(b).*—Except as provided in §301.7701-2(d)(3) (regarding termination of grandfather status for certain foreign business entities), an entity resulting from a transaction described in section 708(b)(1)(B) (partnership termination due to sales or exchanges) or section 708(b)(2)(B) (partnership division) is a partnership.

(f) *Changes in number of members of an entity.*— (1) *Associations.*—The classification of an eligible entity as an association is not affected by any change in the number of members of the entity.

(2) *Partnerships and single member entities.*—An eligible entity classified as a partnership becomes disregarded as an entity separate from its owner when the entity's membership is reduced to one member. A single member entity disregarded as an entity separate from its owner is classified as a partnership when the entity has more than one member. If an elective classification change under paragraph (c) of this section is effective at the same time as a membership change described in this paragraph (f)(2), the deemed transactions in paragraph (g) of this section resulting from the elective change preempt the transactions that would result from the change in membership.

(3) *Effect on sixty month limitation.*—A change in the number of members of an entity does not result in the creation of a new entity for purposes of the sixty month limitation on elections under paragraph (c)(1)(iv) of this section.

(4) *Examples.*—The following examples illustrate the application of this paragraph (f):

Example 1. A, a U.S. person, owns a domestic eligible entity that is disregarded as an entity separate from its owner. On January 1, 1998, *B*, a U.S. person, buys a 50 percent interest in the entity from *A*. Under this paragraph (f), the entity is classified as a partnership when *B* acquires an interest in the entity. However, *A* and *B* elect to have the entity classified as an association effective on January 1, 1998. Thus, *B* is treated as buying shares of stock on January 1, 1998. (Under paragraph (c)(1)(iv) of this section, this election is treated as a change in classification so that the entity generally cannot change its classification by election again during the sixty months succeeding the effective date of the election.) Under paragraph (g)(1) of this section, *A* is treated as contributing the assets and liabilities of the entity to the newly formed association immediately before the close of December 31,

1997. Because *A* does not retain control of the association as required by section 351, *A*'s contribution will be a taxable event. Therefore, under section 1012, the association will take a fair market value basis in the assets contributed by *A*, and *A* will have a fair market value basis in the stock received. *A* will have no additional gain upon the sale of stock to *B*, and *B* will have a cost basis in the stock purchased from *A*.

Example 2. (i) On April 1, 1998, *A* and *B*, U.S. persons, form *X*, a foreign eligible entity. *X* is treated as an association under the default provisions of paragraph (b)(2)(i) of this section, and *X* does not make an election to be classified as a partnership. *A* subsequently purchases all of *B*'s interest in *X*.

(ii) Under paragraph (f)(1) of this section, *X* continues to be classified as an association. *X*, however, can subsequently elect to be disregarded as an entity separate from *A*. The sixty month limitation of paragraph (c)(1)(iv) of this section does not prevent *X* from making an election because *X* has not made a prior election under paragraph (c)(1)(i) of this section.

Example 3. (i) On April 1, 1998, *A* and *B*, U.S. persons, form *X*, a foreign eligible entity. *X* is treated as an association under the default provisions of paragraph (b)(2)(i) of this section, and *X* does not make an election to be classified as a partnership. On January 1, 1999, *X* elects to be classified as a partnership effective on that date. Under the sixty month limitation of paragraph (c)(1)(iv) of this section, *X* cannot elect to be classified as an association until January 1, 2004 (i.e., sixty months after the effective date of the election to be classified as a partnership).

(ii) On June 1, 2000, *A* purchases all of *B*'s interest in *X*. After *A*'s purchase of *B*'s interest, *X* can no longer be classified as a partnership because *X* has only one member. Under paragraph (f)(2) of this section, *X* is disregarded as an entity separate from *A* when *A* becomes the only member of *X*. *X*, however, is not treated as a new entity for purposes of paragraph (c)(1)(iv) of this section. As a result, the sixty month limitation of paragraph (c)(1)(iv) of this section continues to apply to *X*, and *X* cannot elect to be classified as an association until January 1, 2004 (i.e., sixty months after January 1, 1999, the effective date of the election by *X* to be classified as a partnership).

(5) *Effective date.*—This paragraph (f) applies as of November 29, 1999.

(g) *Elective changes in classification.*—(1) *Deemed treatment of elective change.*—(i) *Partnership to association.*—If an eligible entity classified as a partnership elects under paragraph (c)(1)(i) of this section to be classified as an association, the following is deemed to occur: The partnership contributes all of its assets and liabilities to the association in exchange for stock in the association, and immediately thereafter, the partnership liquidates by distributing the stock of the association to its partners.

(ii) *Association to partnership.*—If an eligible entity classified as an association elects under paragraph (c)(1)(i) of this section to be classified as a partnership, the following is deemed to occur: The association distributes all of its assets and liabilities to its shareholders in liquidation of the association, and immediately thereafter, the shareholders contribute all of the distributed assets and liabilities to a newly formed partnership.

(iii) *Association to disregarded entity.*—If an eligible entity classified as an association elects under paragraph (c)(1)(i) of this section to be disregarded as an entity separate from its owner, the following is deemed to occur: The association distributes all of its assets and liabilities to its single owner in liquidation of the association.

(iv) *Disregarded entity to an association.*—If an eligible entity that is disregarded as an entity separate from its owner elects under paragraph (c)(1)(i) of this section to be classified as an association, the following is deemed to occur: The owner of the eligible entity contributes all of the assets and liabilities of the entity to the association in exchange for stock of the association.

(2) *Effect of elective changes.*—(i) *In general.*—The tax treatment of a change in the classification of an entity for federal tax purposes by election under paragraph (c)(1)(i) of this section is determined under all relevant provisions of the Internal Revenue Code and general principles of tax law, including the step transaction doctrine.

(ii) *Adoption of plan of liquidation.*—For purposes of satisfying the requirement of adoption of a plan of liquidation under section 332, unless a formal plan of liquidation that contemplates the election to be classified as a partnership or to be disregarded as an entity separate from its owner is adopted on an earlier date, the making, by an association, of an election under paragraph (c)(1)(i) of this section to be classified as a partnership or to be disregarded as an entity separate from its owner is considered to be the adoption of a plan of liquidation immediately before the deemed liquidation described in paragraph (g)(1)(ii) or (iii) of this section. This paragraph (g)(2)(ii) applies to elections filed on or after December 17, 2001. Taxpayers may apply this paragraph (g)(2)(ii) retroactively to elections filed before December 17, 2001, if the corporate owner claiming treatment under section 332 and its subsidiary making the election take consistent positions with respect to the federal tax consequences of the election.

(3) *Timing of election.*—(i) *In general.*—An election under paragraph (c)(1)(i) of this section that changes the classification of an eligible entity for federal tax purposes is treated as occurring at the start of the day for which the election is effective. Any transactions that are deemed to occur under this paragraph (g) as a result of a change in classification are treated as occurring immediately before the close of the day before

the election is effective. For example, if an election is made to change the classification of an entity from an association to a partnership effective on January 1, the deemed transactions specified in paragraph (g)(1)(ii) of this section (including the liquidation of the association) are treated as occurring immediately before the close of December 31 and must be reported by the owners of the entity on December 31. Thus, the last day of the association's taxable year will be December 31 and the first day of the partnership's taxable year will be January 1.

(ii) *Coordination with section 338 election.*— A purchasing corporation that makes a qualified stock purchase of an eligible entity taxed as a corporation may make an election under section 338 regarding the acquisition if it satisfies the requirements for the election, and may also make an election to change the classification of the target corporation. If a taxpayer makes an election under section 338 regarding its acquisition of another entity taxable as a corporation and makes an election under paragraph (c) of this section for the acquired corporation (effective at the earliest possible date as provided by paragraph (c)(1)(iii) of this section), the transactions under paragraph (g) of this section are deemed to occur immediately after the deemed asset purchase by the new target corporation under section 338.

(iii) *Application to successive elections in tiered situations.*—When elections under paragraph (c)(1)(i) of this section for a series of tiered entities are effective on the same date, the eligible entities may specify the order of the elections on Form 8832. If no order is specified for the elections, any transactions that are deemed to occur in this paragraph (g) as a result of the classification change will be treated as occurring first for the highest tier entity's classification change, then for the next highest tier entity's classification change, and so forth down the chain of entities until all the transactions under this paragraph (g) have occurred. For example, Parent, a corporation, wholly owns all of the interest of an eligible entity classified as an association (S1), which wholly owns another eligible entity classified as an association (S2), which wholly owns another eligible entity classified as an association (S3). Elections under paragraph (c)(1)(i) of this section are filed to classify S1, S2, and S3 each as disregarded as an entity separate from its owner effective on the same day. If no order is specified for the elections, the following transactions are deemed to occur under this paragraph (g) as a result of the elections, with each successive transaction occurring on the same day immediately after the preceding transaction: S1 is treated as liquidating into Parent, then S2 is treated as liquidating into Parent, and finally S3 is treated as liquidating into Parent.

(4) *Effective date.*—Except as otherwise provided in paragraph (g)(2)(ii) of this section, this paragraph (g) applies to elections that are filed on or after November 29, 1999. Taxpayers may apply this paragraph (g) retroactively to elections filed before November 29, 1999 if all taxpayers affected by the deemed transactions file consistently with this paragraph (g).

(h) *Effective date.*—(1) *In general.*—Except as otherwise provided in this section, the rules of this section are applicable as of January 1, 1997.

(2) *Prior treatment of existing entities.*—In the case of a business entity that is not described in § 301.7701-2(b)(1), (3), (4), (5), (6), or (7), and that was in existence prior to January 1, 1997, the entity's claimed classification(s) will be respected for all periods prior to January 1, 1997, if—

(i) The entity had a reasonable basis (within the meaning of section 6662) for its claimed classification;

(ii) The entity and all members of the entity recognized the federal tax consequences of any change in the entity's classification within the sixty months prior to January 1, 1997; and

(iii) Neither the entity nor any member was notified in writing on or before May 8, 1996, that the classification of the entity was under examination (in which case the entity's classification will be determined in the examination).

(3) *Deemed elections for S corporations.*—Paragraph (c)(1)(v)(C) of this section applies to timely S corporation elections under section 1362(a) filed on or after July 20, 2004. Eligible entities that filed timely S elections before July 20, 2004 may also rely on the provisions of the regulation. [Reg. § 301.7701-3.]

☐ [*T.D.* 6503, 11-15-60. *Amended by T.D.* 8632, 12-19-95; *T.D.* 8697, 12-17-96; *T.D.* 8767, 3-23-98; *T.D.* 8827, 7-12-99 (*corrected* 10-29-99); *T.D.* 8844, 11-26-99; *T.D.* 8970, 12-14-2001; *T.D.* 9093, 10-21-2003; *T.D.* 9100, 12-18-2003; *T.D.* 9139, 7-19-2004; *T.D.* 9153, 8-11-2004; *T.D.* 9203, 5-20-2005 *and T.D.* 9300, 12-7-2006.]

[Reg. § 301.7701-4]

§ 301.7701-4. Trusts.—(a) *Ordinary trusts.*—In general, the term "trust" as used in the Internal Revenue Code refers to an arrangement created either by a will or by an inter vivos declaration whereby trustees take title to property for the purpose of protecting or conserving it for the beneficiaries under the ordinary rules applied in chancery or probate courts. Usually the beneficiaries of such a trust do no more than accept the benefits thereof and are not the voluntary planners or creators of the trust arrangement. However, the beneficiaries of such a trust may be the persons who create it and it will be recognized as a trust under the Internal Revenue Code if it was created for the purpose of protecting or conserving the trust property for beneficiaries who stand in the same relation to the trust as they would if the trust had been created by others for them. Generally speaking, an arrangement will be treated as a trust under the Internal Revenue Code if it can be shown that the purpose of the arrangement is to vest in trustees responsibility for the protection and conservation of property for beneficiaries who cannot share in the discharge of this responsibility and, therefore, are not associates in a joint enterprise for the conduct of business for profit.

(b) *Business trusts.*—There are other arrangements which are known as trusts because the legal title to property is conveyed to trustees for the benefit of beneficiaries, but which are not classified as trusts for purposes of the Internal Revenue Code because they are not simply arrangements to protect or conserve the property for the beneficiaries. These trusts, which are often known as business or commercial trusts, generally are created by the beneficiaries simply as a device to carry on a profit-making business which normally would have been carried on through business organizations that are classified as corporations or partnerships under the Internal Revenue Code. However, the fact that the corpus of the trust is not supplied by the beneficiaries is not sufficient reason in itself for classifying the arrangement as an ordinary trust rather than as an association or partnership. The fact that any organization is technically cast in the trust form, by conveying title to property to trustees for the benefit of persons designated as beneficiaries, will not change the real character of the organization if the organization is more properly classified as a business entity under § 301.7701-2.

(c) *Certain investment trusts.*—(1) An "investment" trust will not be classified as a trust if there is a power under the trust agreement to vary the investment of the certificate holders. *See Commissioner v. North American Bond Trust,* 122 F. 2d 545 [41-2 USTC ¶ 9644](2d Cir. 1941), *cert. denied,* 314 U.S. 701 (1942). An investment trust with a single class of ownership interests, representing undivided beneficial interests in the assets of the trust, will be classified as a trust if there is no power under the trust agreement to vary the investment of the certificate holders. An investment trust with multiple classes of ownership interests ordinarily will be classified as a business entity under § 301.7701-2; however, an investment trust with multiple classes of ownership interests, in which there is no power under the trust agreement to vary the investment of the certificate holders, will be classified as a trust if the trust is formed to facilitate direct investment in the assets of the trust and the existence of multiple classes of ownership interests is incidental to that purpose.

(2) The provisions of paragraph (c)(1) of this section may be illustrated by the following examples:

Example (1): A corporation purchases a portfolio of residential mortgages and transfers the mortgages to a bank under a trust agreement. At the same time, the bank as trustee delivers to the corporation certificates evidencing rights to payments from the pooled mortgages; the corporation sells the certificates to the public. The trustee holds legal title to the mortgages in the pool for the benefit of the certificate holders but has no power to reinvest proceeds attributable to the mortgages in the pool or to vary investments in the pool in any other manner. There are two classes of certificates. Holders of class A certificates are entitled to all payments of mortgage principal, both scheduled and prepaid, until their certificates are retired; holders of class B certificates receive payments of principal only after all class A certificates have been retired. The different rights of the class A and class B certificates serve to shift to the holders of the class A certificates, in addition to the earlier scheduled payments of principal, the risk that mortgages in the pool will be prepaid so that the holders of the class B certificates will have "call protection" (freedom from premature termination of their interests on account of prepayments). The trust thus serves to create investment interests with respect to the mortgages held by the trust that differ significantly from direct investment in the mortgages. As a consequence, the existence of multiple classes of trust ownership is not incidental to any purpose of the trust to facilitate direct investment, and, accordingly, the trust is classified as a business entity under § 301.7701-2.

Example (2): Corporation M is the originator of a portfolio of residential mortgages and transfers the mortgages to a bank under a trust agreement. At the same time, the bank as trustee delivers to M certificates evidencing rights to payments from the pooled mortgages. The trustee holds legal title to the mortgages in the pool for the benefit of the certificate holders, but has no power to reinvest proceeds attributable to mortgages in the pool or to vary investments in the pool in any other manner. There are two classes of certificates. Holders of class C certificates are entitled to receive 90 percent of the payments of principal and interest on the mortgages; class D certificate holders are entitled to receive the other ten percent. The two classes of certificates are identical except that, in the event of a default on the underlying mortgages, the payment rights of class D certificate holders are subordinated to the rights of class C certificate holders. M sells the class C certificates to investors and retains the class D certificates. The trust has multiple classes of ownership interests, given the greater security provided to holders of class C certificates. The interests of certificate holders, however, are substantially equivalent to undivided interests in the pool of mortgages, coupled with a limited recourse guarantee running from M to the holders of class C certificates. In such circumstances, the existence of multiple classes of ownership interests is incidental to the trust's purpose of facilitating direct investment in the assets of the trust. Accordingly, the trust is classified as a trust.

Example (3): A promoter forms a trust in which shareholders of a publicly traded corporation can deposit their stock. For each share of stock deposited with the trust, the participant receives two certificates that are initially attached, but may be separated and traded independently of each other. One certificate represents the right to dividends and the value of the underlying stock up to a specified amount;

the other certificate represents the right to appreciation in the stock's value above the specified amount. The separate certificates represent two different classes of ownership interest in the trust, which effectively separate dividend rights on the stock held by the trust from a portion of the right to appreciation in the value of such stock. The multiple classes of ownership interests are designed to permit investors, by transferring one of the certificates and retaining the other, to fulfill their varying investment objectives of seeking primarily either dividend income or capital appreciation from the stock held by the trust. Given that the trust serves to create investment interests with respect to the stock held by the trust that differ significantly from direct investment in such stock, the trust is not formed to facilitate direct investment in the assets of the trust. Accordingly, the trust is classified as a business entity under § 301.7701-2.

Example (4): Corporation N purchases a portfolio of bonds and transfers the bonds to a bank under a trust agreement. At the same time, the trustee delivers to N certificates evidencing interests in the bonds. These certificates are sold to public investors. Each certificate represents the right to receive a particular payment with respect to a specific bond. Under section 1286, stripped coupons and stripped bonds are treated as separate bonds for federal income tax purposes. Although the interest of each certificate holder is different from that of each other certificate holder, and the trust thus has multiple classes of ownership, the multiple classes simply provide each certificate holder with a direct interest in what is treated under section 1286 as a separate bond. Given the similarity of the interests acquired by the certificate holders to the interests that could be acquired by direct investment, the multiple classes of trust interests merely facilitate direct investment in the assets held by the trust. Accordingly, the trust is classified as a trust.

(d) *Liquidating trusts.*—Certain organizations which are commonly known as liquidating trusts are treated as trusts for purposes of the Internal Revenue Code. An organization will be considered a liquidating trust if it is organized for the primary purpose of liquidating and distributing the assets transferred to it, and if its activities are all reasonably necessary to, and consistent with, the accomplishment of that purpose. A liquidating trust is treated as a trust for purposes of the Internal Revenue Code because it is formed with the objective of liquidating particular assets and not as an organization having as its purpose the carrying on of a profit-making business which normally would be conducted through business organizations classified as corporations or partnerships. However, if the liquidation is unreasonably prolonged or if the liquidation purpose becomes so obscured by business activities that the declared purpose of liquidation can be said to be lost or abandoned, the status of the organization will no longer be that of a liquidating trust. Bondholders' protective committees, voting trusts, and other agencies formed to protect the interests of security holders during insolvency, bankruptcy, or corporate reorganization proceedings are analogous to liquidating trusts but if subsequently utilized to further the control or profitable operation of a going business on a permanent continuing basis, they will lose their classification as trusts for purposes of the Internal Revenue Code.

(e) *Environmental remediation trusts.*—(1) An environmental remediation trust is considered a trust for purposes of the Internal Revenue Code. For purposes of this paragraph (e), an organization is an environmental remediation trust if the organization is organized under state law as a trust; the primary purpose of the trust is collecting and disbursing amounts for environmental remediation of an existing waste site to resolve, satisfy, mitigate, address, or prevent the liability or potential liability of persons imposed by federal, state, or local environmental laws; all contributors to the trust have (at the time of contribution and thereafter) actual or potential liability or a reasonable expectation of liability under federal, state, or local environmental laws for environmental remediation of the waste site; and the trust is not a qualified settlement fund within the meaning of § 1.468B-1(a) of this chapter. An environmental remediation trust is classified as a trust because its primary purpose is environmental remediation of an existing waste site and not the carrying on of a profit-making business that normally would be conducted through business organizations classified as corporations or partnerships. However, if the remedial purpose is altered or becomes so obscured by business or investment activities that the declared remedial purpose is no longer controlling, the organization will no longer be classified as a trust. For purposes of this paragraph (e), environmental remediation includes the costs of assessing environmental conditions, remedying and removing environmental contamination, monitoring remedial activities and the release of substances, preventing future releases of substances, and collecting amounts from persons liable or potentially liable for the costs of these activities. For purposes of this paragraph (e), persons have potential liability or a reasonable expectation of liability under federal, state, or local environmental laws for remediation of the existing waste site if there is authority under a federal, state, or local law that requires or could reasonably be expected to require such persons to satisfy all or a portion of the costs of the environmental remediation.

(2) Each contributor (grantor) to the trust is treated as the owner of the portion of the trust contributed by that grantor under rules provided in section 677 and § 1.677(a)-1(d) of this chapter. Section 677 and § 1.677(a)-1(d) of this chapter provide rules regarding the treatment of a grantor as the owner of a portion of a trust applied in discharge of the grantor's legal obligation. Items of income, deduction, and credit attributable to an environmental remediation trust are not re-

ported by the trust on Form 1041, but are shown on a separate statement to be attached to that form. See §1.671-4(a) of this chapter. The trustee must also furnish to each grantor a statement that shows all items of income, deduction, and credit of the trust for the grantor's taxable year attributable to the portion of the trust treated as owned by the grantor. The statement must provide the grantor with the information necessary to take the items into account in computing the grantor's taxable income, including information necessary to determine the federal tax treatment of the items (for example, whether an item is a deductible expense under section 162(a) or a capital expenditure under section 263(a)) and how the item should be taken into account under the economic performance rules of section 461(h) and the regulations thereunder. See §1.461-4 of this chapter for rules relating to economic performance.

(3) All amounts contributed to an environmental remediation trust by a grantor (cash-out grantor) who, pursuant to an agreement with the other grantors, contributes a fixed amount to the trust and is relieved by the other grantors of any further obligation to make contributions to the trust, but remains liable or potentially liable under the applicable environmental laws, will be considered amounts contributed for remediation. An environmental remediation trust agreement may direct the trustee to expend amounts contributed by a cash-out grantor (and the earnings thereon) before expending amounts contributed by other grantors (and the earnings thereon). A cash-out grantor will cease to be treated as an owner of a portion of the trust when the grantor's portion is fully expended by the trust.

(4) The provisions of this paragraph (e) may be illustrated by the following example:

Example. (a) X, Y, and Z are calendar year corporations that are liable for the remediation of an existing waste site under applicable federal environmental laws. On June 1, 1996, pursuant to an agreement with the governing federal agency, X, Y, and Z create an environmental remediation trust within the meaning of paragraph (e)(1) of this section to collect funds contributed to the trust by X, Y, and Z and to carry out the remediation of the waste site to the satisfaction of the federal agency. X, Y, and Z are jointly and severally liable under the federal environmental laws for the remediation of the waste site, and the federal agency will not release X, Y, or Z from liability until the waste site is remediated to the satisfaction of the agency.

(b) The estimated cost of the remediation is $20,000,000. X, Y, and Z agree that, if Z contributes $1,000,000 to the trust, Z will not be required to make any additional contributions to the trust, and X and Y will complete the remediation of the waste site and make additional contributions if necessary.

(c) On June 1, 1996, X, Y, and Z each contribute $1,000,000 to the trust. The trust agreement directs the trustee to spend Z's contributions to the trust and the income allocable to Z's portion

before spending X's and Y's portions. On November 30, 1996, the trustee disburses $2,000,000 for remediation work performed from June 1, 1996, through September 30, 1996. For the six-month period ending November 30, 1996, the interest earned on the funds in the trust was $75,000, which is allocated in equal shares of $25,000 to X's, Y's, and Z's portions of the trust.

(d) Z made no further contributions to the trust. Pursuant to the trust agreement, the trustee expended Z's portion of the trust before expending X's and Y's portion. Therefore, Z's share of the remediation disbursement made in 1996 is $1,025,000 ($1,000,000 contribution by Z plus $25,000 of interest allocated to Z's portion of the trust). Z takes the $1,025,000 disbursement into account under the appropriate federal tax accounting rules. In addition, X's share of the remediation disbursement made in 1996 is $487,500, and Y's share of the remediation disbursement made in 1996 is $487,500. X and Y take their respective shares of the disbursement into account under the appropriate federal tax accounting rules.

(e) The trustee made no further remediation disbursements in 1996, and X and Y made no further contributions in 1996. From December 1, 1996, to December 31, 1996, the interest earned on the funds remaining in the trust was $5,000, which is allocated $2,500 to X's portion and $2,500 to Y's portion. Accordingly, for 1996, X and Y each had interest income of $27,500 from the trust and Z had interest income of $25,000 from the trust.

(5) This paragraph (e) is applicable to trusts meeting the requirements of paragraph (e)(1) of this section that are formed on or after May 1, 1996. This paragraph (e) may be relied on by trusts formed before May 1, 1996, if the trust has at all times met all requirements of this paragraph (e) and the grantors have reported items of income and deduction consistent with this paragraph (e) on original or amended returns. For trusts formed before May 1, 1996, that are not described in the preceding sentence, the Commissioner may permit by letter ruling, in appropriate circumstances, this paragraph (e) to be applied subject to appropriate terms and conditions.

(f) *Effective date.*—The rules of this section generally apply to taxable years beginning after December 31, 1960. Paragraph (e)(5) of this section contains rules of applicability for paragraph (e) of this section. In addition, the last sentences of paragraphs (b), (c)(1), and (c)(2) *Example 1* and *Example 3* of this section are effective as of January 1, 1997. [Reg. §301.7701-4.]

☐ [*T.D. 6503, 11-15-60. Amended by T.D. 8080, 3-21-86; T.D. 8668, 4-30-96 and T.D. 8697, 12-17-96.*]

[Reg. §301.7701-5]

§301.7701-5. Domestic and foreign business entities.—(a) *Domestic and foreign business entities.*—A business entity (including an entity that is disregarded as separate from its owner under

§ 301.7701-2(c)) is domestic if it is created or organized as any type of entity (including, but not limited to, a corporation, unincorporated association, general partnership, limited partnership, and limited liability company) in the United States, or under the law of the United States or of any State. Accordingly, a business entity that is created or organized both in the United States and in a foreign jurisdiction is a domestic entity. A business entity (including an entity that is disregarded as separate from its owner under § 301.7701-2(c)) is foreign if it is not domestic. The determination of whether an entity is domestic or foreign is made independently from the determination of its corporate or noncorporate classification. See §§ 301.7701-2 and 301.7701-3 for the rules governing the classification of entities.

(b) *Examples.*—The following examples illustrate the rules of this section:

Example 1. (i) *Facts.* Y is an entity that is created or organized under the laws of Country A as a public limited company. It is also an entity that is organized as a limited liability company (LLC) under the laws of State B. Y is classified as a corporation for Federal tax purposes under the rules of §§ 301.7701-2, and 301.7701-3.

(ii) *Result.* Y is a domestic corporation because it is an entity that is classified as a corporation and it is organized as an entity under the laws of State B.

Example 2. (i) *Facts.* P is an entity with more than one owner organized under the laws of Country A as an unlimited company. It is also an entity that is organized as a general partnership under the laws of State B. P is classified as a partnership for Federal tax purposes under the rules of §§ 301.7701-2, and 301.7701-3.

(ii) *Result.* P is a domestic partnership because it is an entity that is classified as a partnership and it is organized as an entity under the laws of State B.

(c) *Effective date.*—(1) *General rule.*—Except as provided in paragraph (c)(2) of this section, the rules of this section apply as of August 12, 2004, to all business entities existing on or after that date.

(2) *Transition rule.*—For business entities created or organized under the laws of more than one jurisdiction as of August 12, 2004, the rules of this section apply as of May 1, 2006. These entities, however, may rely on the rules of this section as of August 12, 2004. [Reg. § 301.7701-5.]

☐ [*T.D.* 6503, 11-15-60. *Amended by T.D.* 8813, 2-1-99; *T.D.* 9153, 8-11-2004 *and T.D.* 9246, 1-27-2006.]

[Reg. § 301.7701-6]

§ 301.7701-6. Definitions; person, fiduciary.—(a) *Person.*—The term *person* includes an individual, a corporation, a partnership, a trust or estate, a joint-stock company, an association, or a syndicate, group, pool, joint venture, or other unincorporated organization or group. The term also includes a guardian, committee, trustee, executor, administrator, trustee in bankruptcy, receiver, assignee for the benefit of creditors, conservator, or any person acting in a fiduciary capacity.

(b) *Fiduciary.*—(1) *In general.*—Fiduciary is a term that applies to persons who occupy positions of peculiar confidence toward others, such as trustees, executors, and administrators. A fiduciary is a person who holds in trust an estate to which another has a beneficial interest, or receives and controls income of another, as in the case of receivers. A committee or guardian of the property of an incompetent person is a fiduciary.

(2) *Fiduciary distinguished from agent.*—There may be a fiduciary relationship between an agent and a principal, but the word agent does not denote a fiduciary. An agent having entire charge of property, with authority to effect and execute leases with tenants entirely on his own responsibility and without consulting his principal, merely turning over the net profits from the property periodically to his principal by virtue of authority conferred upon him by a power of attorney, is not a fiduciary within the meaning of the Internal Revenue Code. In cases when no legal trust has been created in the estate controlled by the agent and attorney, the liability to make a return rests with the principal.

(c) *Effective date.*—The rules of this section are effective as of January 1, 1997. [Reg. § 301.7701-6.]

☐ [*T.D.* 6503, 11-15-60. *Amended by T.D.* 8697, 12-17-96.]

[Reg. § 301.7701-7]

§ 301.7701-7. Trusts—domestic and foreign.—(a) *In general.*—(1) A trust is a United States person if—

(i) A court within the United States is able to exercise primary supervision over the administration of the trust (court test); and

(ii) One or more United States persons have the authority to control all substantial decisions of the trust (control test).

(2) A trust is a United States person for purposes of the Internal Revenue Code (Code) on any day that the trust meets both the court test and the control test. For purposes of the regulations in this chapter, the term *domestic trust* means a trust that is a United States person. The term *foreign trust* means any trust other than a domestic trust.

(3) Except as otherwise provided in part I, subchapter J, chapter 1 of the Code, the taxable income of a foreign trust is computed in the same manner as the taxable income of a nonresident alien individual who is not present in the United States at any time. Section 641(b). Section 7701(b) is not applicable to trusts because it only applies to individuals. In addition, a foreign trust is not considered to be present in the United States at any time for purposes of section 871(a)(2), which deals with capital gains of non-

resident aliens present in the United States for 183 days or more.

(b) *Applicable law.*—The terms of the trust instrument and applicable law must be applied to determine whether the court test and the control test are met.

(c) *The court test.*—(1) *Safe harbor.*—A trust satisfies the court test if—

(i) The trust instrument does not direct that the trust be administered outside of the United States;

(ii) The trust in fact is administered exclusively in the United States; and

(iii) The trust is not subject to an automatic migration provision described in paragraph (c)(4)(ii) of this section.

(2) *Example.*—The following example illustrates the rule of paragraph (c)(1) of this section:

Example. A creates a trust for the equal benefit of *A*'s two children, *B* and *C*. The trust instrument provides that *DC*, a State *Y* corporation, is the trustee of the trust. State *Y* is a state within the United States. *DC* administers the trust exclusively in State *Y* and the trust instrument is silent as to where the trust is to be administered. The trust is not subject to an automatic migration provision described in paragraph (c)(4)(ii) of this section. The trust satisfies the safe harbor of paragraph (c)(1) of this section and the court test.

(3) *Definitions.*—The following definitions apply for purposes of this section:

(i) *Court.*—The term *court* includes any federal, state, or local court.

(ii) *The United States.*—The term *the United States* is used in this section in a geographical sense. Thus, for purposes of the court test, the United States includes only the States and the District of Columbia. See section 7701(a)(9). Accordingly, a court within a territory or possession of the United States or within a foreign country is not a court within the United States.

(iii) *Is able to exercise.*—The term *is able to exercise* means that a court has or would have the authority under applicable law to render orders or judgments resolving issues concerning administration of the trust.

(iv) *Primary supervision.*—The term *primary supervision* means that a court has or would have the authority to determine substantially all issues regarding the administration of the entire trust. A court may have primary supervision under this paragraph (c)(3)(iv) notwithstanding the fact that another court has jurisdiction over a trustee, a beneficiary, or trust property.

(v) *Administration.*—The term *administration* of the trust means the carrying out of the duties imposed by the terms of the trust instrument and applicable law, including maintaining the books and records of the trust, filing tax returns, managing and investing the assets of the trust, defending the trust from suits by creditors,

and determining the amount and timing of distributions.

(4) *Situations that cause a trust to satisfy or fail to satisfy the court test.*—(i) Except as provided in paragraph (c)(4)(ii) of this section, paragraphs (c)(4)(i)(A) through (D) of this section set forth some specific situations in which a trust satisfies the court test. The four situations described are not intended to be an exclusive list.

(A) *Uniform Probate Code.*—A trust meets the court test if the trust is registered by an authorized fiduciary or fiduciaries of the trust in a court within the United States pursuant to a state statute that has provisions substantially similar to Article VII, *Trust Administration*, of the Uniform Probate Code, 8 Uniform Laws Annotated 1 (West Supp. 1998), available from the National Conference of Commissioners on Uniform State Laws, 676 North St. Clair Street, Suite 1700, Chicago, Illinois 60611.

(B) *Testamentary trust.*—In the case of a trust created pursuant to the terms of a will probated within the United States (other than an ancillary probate), if all fiduciaries of the trust have been qualified as trustees of the trust by a court within the United States, the trust meets the court test.

(C) *Inter vivos trust.*—In the case of a trust other than a testamentary trust, if the fiduciaries and/or beneficiaries take steps with a court within the United States that cause the administration of the trust to be subject to the primary supervision of the court, the trust meets the court test.

(D) *A United States court and a foreign court are able to exercise primary supervision over the administration of the trust.*—If both a United States court and a foreign court are able to exercise primary supervision over the administration of the trust, the trust meets the court test.

(ii) *Automatic migration provisions.*—Notwithstanding any other provision in this section, a court within the United States is not considered to have primary supervision over the administration of the trust if the trust instrument provides that a United States court's attempt to assert jurisdiction or otherwise supervise the administration of the trust directly or indirectly would cause the trust to migrate from the United States. However, this paragraph (c)(4)(ii) will not apply if the trust instrument provides that the trust will migrate from the United States only in the case of foreign invasion of the United States or widespread confiscation or nationalization of property in the United States.

(5) *Examples.*—The following examples illustrate the rules of this paragraph (c):

Example 1. A, a United States citizen, creates a trust for the equal benefit of *A*'s two children, both of whom are United States citizens. The trust instrument provides that *DC*, a domestic corporation, is to act as trustee of the trust and that the trust is to be administered in Country *X*, a foreign country. *DC* maintains a branch office in Country *X* with personnel authorized to act as trustees in Country *X*. The trust instrument provides that the law of State *Y*, a state within the United States, is to govern the interpretation of the trust. Under the law of Country *X*, a court within Country *X* is able to exercise primary supervision over the administration of the trust. Pursuant to the trust instrument, the Country *X* court applies the law of State *Y* to the trust. Under the terms of the trust instrument the trust is administered in Country *X*. No court within the United States is able to exercise primary supervision over the administration of the trust. The trust fails to satisfy the court test and therefore is a foreign trust.

Example 2. A, a United States citizen, creates a trust for *A*'s own benefit and the benefit of *A*'s spouse, *B*, a United States citizen. The trust instrument provides that the trust is to be administered in State *Y*, a state within the United States, by *DC*, a State *Y* corporation. The trust instrument further provides that in the event that a creditor sues the trustee in a United States court, the trust will automatically migrate from State *Y* to Country *Z*, a foreign country, so that no United States court will have jurisdiction over the trust. A court within the United States is not able to exercise primary supervision over the administration of the trust because the United States court's jurisdiction over the administration of the trust is automatically terminated in the event the court attempts to assert jurisdiction. Therefore, the trust fails to satisfy the court test from the time of its creation and is a foreign trust.

(d) *Control test.*—(1) *Definitions.*—(i) *United States person.*—The term *United States person* means a United States person within the meaning of section 7701(a)(30). For example, a domestic corporation is a United States person, regardless of whether its shareholders are United States persons.

(ii) *Substantial decisions.*—The term *substantial decisions* means those decisions that persons are authorized or required to make under the terms of the trust instrument and applicable law and that are not ministerial. Decisions that are ministerial include decisions regarding details such as the bookkeeping, the collection of rents, and the execution of investment decisions. Substantial decisions include, but are not limited to, decisions concerning—

(A) Whether and when to distribute income or corpus;

(B) The amount of any distributions;

(C) The selection of a beneficiary;

(D) Whether a receipt is allocable to income or principal;

(E) Whether to terminate the trust;

(F) Whether to compromise, arbitrate, or abandon claims of the trust;

(G) Whether to sue on behalf of the trust or to defend suits against the trust;

(H) Whether to remove, add, or replace a trustee;

(I) Whether to appoint a successor trustee to succeed a trustee who has died, resigned, or otherwise ceased to act as a trustee, even if the power to make such a decision is not accompanied by an unrestricted power to remove a trustee, unless the power to make such a decision is limited such that it cannot be exercised in a manner that would change the trust's residency from foreign to domestic, or vice versa; and

(J) Investment decisions; however, if a United States person under section 7701(a)(30) hires an investment advisor for the trust, investment decisions made by the investment advisor will be considered substantial decisions controlled by the United States person if the United States person can terminate the investment advisor's power to make investment decisions at will.

(iii) *Control.*—The term *control* means having the power, by vote or otherwise, to make all of the substantial decisions of the trust, with no other person having the power to veto any of the substantial decisions. To determine whether United States persons have control, it is necessary to consider all persons who have authority to make a substantial decision of the trust, not only the trust fiduciaries.

(iv) *Safe harbor for certain employee benefit trusts and investment trusts.*—Notwithstanding the provisions of this paragraph (d), the trusts listed in this paragraph (d)(1)(iv) are deemed to satisfy the control test set forth in paragraph (a)(1)(ii) of this section, provided that United States trustees control all of the substantial decisions made by the trustees of the trust—

(A) A qualified trust described in section 401(a);

(B) A trust described in section 457(g);

(C) A trust that is an individual retirement account described in section 408(a);

(D) A trust that is an individual retirement account described in section 408(k) or 408(p);

(E) A trust that is a Roth IRA described in section 408A;

(F) A trust that is an education individual retirement account described in section 530;

(G) A trust that is a voluntary employees' beneficiary association described in section 501(c)(9);

(H) A group trust described in Rev. Rul. 81-100 (1981-1 C.B. 326) (See § 601.601(d)(2) of this chapter);

(I) An investment trust classified as a trust under § 301.7701-4(c), provided that the following conditions are satisfied—

(*1*) All trustees are United States persons and at least one of the trustees is a bank, as defined in section 581, or a United States Government-owned agency or United States Government-sponsored enterprise;

(*2*) All sponsors (persons who exchange investment assets for beneficial interests with a view to selling the beneficial interests) are United States persons; and

(3) The beneficial interests are widely offered for sale primarily in the United States to United States persons;

(J) Such additional categories of trusts as the Commissioner may designate in revenue procedures, notices, or other guidance published in the Internal Revenue Bulletin (see §601.601(d)(2)(ii)(*b*)).

(v) *Examples.*—The following examples illustrate the rules of paragraph (d)(1) of this section:

Example 1. Trust is a testamentary trust with three fiduciaries, *A*, *B*, and *C*. *A* and *B* are United States citizens, and *C* is a nonresident alien. No persons except the fiduciaries have authority to make any decisions of the trust. The trust instrument provides that no substantial decisions of the trust can be made unless there is unanimity among the fiduciaries. The control test is not satisfied because United States persons do not control all the substantial decisions of the trust. No substantial decisions can be made without *C*'s agreement.

Example 2. Assume the same facts as in *Example 1*, except that the trust instrument provides that all substantial decisions of the trust are to be decided by a majority vote among the fiduciaries. The control test is satisfied because a majority of the fiduciaries are United States persons and therefore United States persons control all the substantial decisions of the trust.

Example 3. Assume the same facts as in *Example 2*, except that the trust instrument directs that *C* is to make all of the trust's investment decisions, but that *A* and *B* may veto *C*'s investment decisions. *A* and *B* cannot act to make the investment decisions on their own. The control test is not satisfied because the United States persons, *A* and *B*, do not have the power to make all of the substantial decisions of the trust.

Example 4. Assume the same facts as in *Example 3*, except *A* and *B* may accept or veto *C*'s investment decisions and can make investments that *C* has not recommended. The control test is satisfied because the United States persons control all substantial decisions of the trust.

Example 5. *X*, a foreign corporation, conducts business in the United States through various branch operations. *X* has United States employees and has established a trust as part of a qualified employee benefit plan under section 401(a) for these employees. The trust is established under the laws of State *A*, and the trustee of the trust is *B*, a United States bank governed by the laws of State *A*. *B* holds legal title to the trust assets for the benefit of the trust beneficiaries. A plan committee makes decisions with respect to the plan and the trust. The plan committee can direct *B*'s actions with regard to those decisions and under the governing documents *B* is not liable for those decisions. Members of the plan committee consist of United States persons

and nonresident aliens, but nonresident aliens make up a majority of the plan committee. Decisions of the plan committee are made by majority vote. In addition, *X* retains the power to terminate the trust and to replace the United States trustee or to appoint additional trustees. This trust is deemed to satisfy the control test under paragraph (d)(1)(iv) of this section because *B*, a United States person, is the trust's only trustee. Any powers held by the plan committee or *X* are not considered under the safe harbor of paragraph (d)(1)(iv) of this section. In the event that *X* appoints additional trustees including foreign trustees, any powers held by such trustees must be considered in determining whether United States trustees control all substantial decisions made by the trustees of the trust.

(2) *Replacement of any person who had authority to make a substantial decision of the trust.*— (i) *Replacement within 12 months.*—In the event of an inadvertent change in any person that has the power to make a substantial decision of the trust that would cause the domestic or foreign residency of the trust to change, the trust is allowed 12 months from the date of the change to make necessary changes either with respect to the persons who control the substantial decisions or with respect to the residence of such persons to avoid a change in the trust's residency. For purposes of this section, an inadvertent change means the death, incapacity, resignation, change in residency or other change with respect to a person that has a power to make a substantial decision of the trust that would cause a change to the residency of the trust but that was not intended to change the residency of the trust. If the necessary change is made within 12 months, the trust is treated as retaining its pre-change residency during the 12-month period. If the necessary change is not made within 12 months, the trust's residency changes as of the date of the inadvertent change.

(ii) *Request for extension of time.*—If reasonable actions have been taken to make the necessary change to prevent a change in trust residency, but due to circumstances beyond the trust's control the trust is unable to make the modification within 12 months, the trust may provide a written statement to the district director having jurisdiction over the trust's return setting forth the reasons for failing to make the necessary change within the required time period. If the district director determines that the failure was due to reasonable cause, the district director may grant the trust an extension of time to make the necessary change. Whether an extension of time is granted is in the sole discretion of the district director and, if granted, may contain such terms with respect to assessment as may be necessary to ensure that the correct amount of tax will be collected from the trust, its owners, and its beneficiaries. If the district director does not grant an extension, the trust's residency changes as of the date of the inadvertent change.

Reg. §301.7701-7(d)(1)(iv)(I)(3)

(iii) *Examples.*—The following examples illustrate the rules of paragraphs (d)(2)(i) and (ii) of this section:

Example 1. A trust that satisfies the court test has three fiduciaries, *A*, *B*, and *C*. *A* and *B* are United States citizens and *C* is a nonresident alien. All decisions of the trust are made by majority vote of the fiduciaries. The trust instrument provides that upon the death or resignation of any of the fiduciaries, *D*, is the successor fiduciary. *A* dies and *D* automatically becomes a fiduciary of the trust. When *D* becomes a fiduciary of the trust, *D* is a nonresident alien. Two months after *A* dies, *B* replaces *D* with *E*, a United States person. Because *D* was replaced with *E* within 12 months after the date of *A*'s death, during the period after *A*'s death and before *E* begins to serve, the trust satisfies the control test and remains a domestic trust.

Example 2. Assume the same facts as in *Example 1* except that at the end of the 12-month period after *A*'s death, *D* has not been replaced and remains a fiduciary of the trust. The trust becomes a foreign trust on the date *A* died unless the district director grants an extension of the time period to make the necessary change.

(3) *Automatic migration provisions.*—Notwithstanding any other provision in this section, United States persons are not considered to control all substantial decisions of the trust if an attempt by any governmental agency or creditor to collect information from or assert a claim against the trust would cause one or more substantial decisions of the trust to no longer be controlled by United States persons.

(4) *Examples.*—The following examples illustrate the rules of this paragraph (d):

Example 1. A, a nonresident alien individual, is the grantor and, during *A*'s lifetime, the sole beneficiary of a trust that qualifies as an individual retirement account (IRA). *A* has the exclusive power to make decisions regarding withdrawals from the IRA and to direct its investments. The IRA's sole trustee is a United States person within the meaning of section 7701(a)(30). The control test is satisfied with respect to this trust because the special rule of paragraph (d)(1)(iv) of this section applies.

Example 2. A, a nonresident alien individual, is the grantor of a trust and has the power to revoke the trust, in whole or in part, and revest assets in *A*. *A* is treated as the owner of the trust under sections 672(f) and 676. *A* is not a fiduciary of the trust. The trust has one trustee, *B*, a United States person, and the trust has one beneficiary, *C*. *B* has the discretion to distribute corpus or income to *C*. In this case, decisions exercisable by *A* to have trust assets distributed to *A* are substantial decisions. Therefore, the trust is a foreign trust because *B* does not control all substantial decisions of the trust.

Example 3. A trust, Trust *T*, has two fiduciaries, *A* and *B*. Both *A* and *B* are United States persons. *A* and *B* hire *C*, an investment advisor who is a foreign person, and may terminate *C*'s

employment at will. The investment advisor makes the investment decisions for the trust. *A* and *B* control all other decisions of the trust. Although *C* has the power to make investment decisions, *A* and *B* are treated as controlling these decisions. Therefore, the control test is satisfied.

Example 4. G, a United States citizen, creates a trust. The trust provides for income to *A* and *B* for life, remainder to *A*'s and *B*'s descendants. *A* is a nonresident alien and *B* is a United States person. The trustee of the trust is a United States person. The trust instrument authorizes *A* to replace the trustee. The power to replace the trustee is a substantial decision. Because *A*, a nonresident alien, controls a substantial decision, the control test is not satisfied.

(e) *Effective date.*—(1) *General rule.*—Except for the election to remain a domestic trust provided in paragraph (f) of this section and except as provided in paragraph (e)(3) of this section, this section is applicable to taxable years ending after February 2, 1999. This section may be relied on by trusts for taxable years beginning after December 31, 1996, and also may be relied on by trusts whose trustees have elected to apply sections 7701(a)(30) and (31) to the trusts for taxable years ending after August 20, 1996, under section 1907(a)(3)(B) of the Small Business Job Protection Act of 1996, (the SBJP Act) Public Law 104-188, 110 Stat. 1755 (26 U.S.C. 7701 note).

(2) *Trusts created after August 19, 1996.*—If a trust is created after August 19, 1996, and before April 5, 1999, and the trust satisfies the control test set forth in the regulations project REG-251703-96 published under section 7701(a)(30) and (31) (1997-1 C.B. 795) (See § 601.601(d)(2) of this chapter), but does not satisfy the control test set forth in paragraph (d) of this section, the trust may be modified to satisfy the control test of paragraph (d) by December 31, 1999. If the modification is completed by December 31, 1999, the trust will be treated as satisfying the control test of paragraph (d) for taxable years beginning after December 31, 1996, (and for taxable years ending after August 20, 1996, if the election under section 1907(a)(3)(B) of the SBJP Act has been made for the trust).

(3) *Effective date of safe harbor for certain employee benefit trusts and investment trusts.*—Paragraphs (d)(1)(iv) and (v) *Examples 1* and *5* of this section apply to trusts for taxable years ending on or after August 9, 2001. Paragraphs (d)(1)(iv) and (v) *Examples 1* and *5* of this section may be relied on by trusts for taxable years beginning after December 31, 1996, and also may be relied on by trusts whose trustees have elected to apply sections 7701(a)(30) and (31) to the trusts for taxable years ending after August 20, 1996, under section 1907(a)(3)(B) of the SBJP Act.

(f) *Election to remain a domestic trust.*—(1) *Trusts eligible to make the election to remain domestic.*—A trust that was in existence on August 20, 1996, and that was treated as a domestic

Reg. § 301.7701-7(f)(1)

trust on August 19, 1996, as provided in paragraph (f)(2) of this section, may elect to continue treatment as a domestic trust notwithstanding section 7701(a)(30)(E). This election is not available to a trust that was wholly-owned by its grantor under subpart E, part I, subchapter J, chapter 1, of the Code on August 20, 1996. The election is available to a trust if only a portion of the trust was treated as owned by the grantor under subpart E on August 20, 1996. If a partially-owned grantor trust makes the election, the election is effective for the entire trust. Also, a trust may not make the election if the trust has made an election pursuant to section 1907(a)(3)(B) of the SBJP Act to apply the new trust criteria to the first taxable year of the trust ending after August 20, 1996, because that election, once made, is irrevocable.

(2) *Determining whether a trust was treated as a domestic trust on August 19, 1996.*—(i) *Trusts filing Form 1041 for the taxable year that includes August 19, 1996.*—For purposes of the election, a trust is considered to have been treated as a domestic trust on August 19, 1996, if: the trustee filed a Form 1041, "U.S. Income Tax Return for Estates and Trusts," for the trust for the period that includes August 19, 1996 (and did not file a Form 1040NR, "U.S. Nonresident Alien Income Tax Return," for that year); and the trust had a reasonable basis (within the meaning of section 6662) under section 7701(a)(30) prior to amendment by the SBJP Act (prior law) for reporting as a domestic trust for that period.

(ii) *Trusts not filing a Form 1041.*—Some domestic trusts are not required to file Form 1041. For example, certain group trusts described in Rev. Rul. 81-100 (1981-1 C.B. 326) (See § 601.601(d)(2) of this chapter) consisting of trusts that are parts of qualified retirement plans and individual retirement accounts are not required to file Form 1041. Also, a domestic trust whose gross income for the taxable year is less than the amount required for filing an income tax return and that has no taxable income is not required to file a Form 1041. Section 6012(a)(4). For purposes of the election, a trust that filed neither a Form 1041 nor a Form 1040NR for the period that includes August 19, 1996, will be considered to have been treated as a domestic trust on August 19, 1996, if the trust had a reasonable basis (within the meaning of section 6662) under prior law for being treated as a domestic trust for that period and for filing neither a Form 1041 nor a Form 1040NR for that period.

(3) *Procedure for making the election to remain domestic.*—(i) *Required Statement.*—To make the election, a statement must be filed with the Internal Revenue Service in the manner and time described in this section. The statement must be entitled "Election to Remain a Domestic Trust under Section 1161 of the Taxpayer Relief Act of 1997," be signed under penalties of perjury by at least one trustee of the trust, and contain the following information—

(A) A statement that the trust is electing to continue to be treated as a domestic trust under section 1161 of the Taxpayer Relief Act of 1997;

(B) A statement that the trustee had a reasonable basis (within the meaning of section 6662) under prior law for treating the trust as a domestic trust on August 19, 1996. (The trustee need not explain the reasonable basis on the election statement.);

(C) A statement either that the trust filed a Form 1041 treating the trust as a domestic trust for the period that includes August 19, 1996, (and that the trust did not file a Form 1040NR for that period), or that the trust was not required to file a Form 1041 or a Form 1040NR for the period that includes August 19, 1996, with an accompanying brief explanation as to why a Form 1041 was not required to be filed; and

(D) The name, address, and employer identification number of the trust.

(ii) *Filing the required statement with the Internal Revenue Service.*—(A) Except as provided in paragraphs (f)(3)(ii)(E) through (G) of this section, the trust must attach the statement to a Form 1041. The statement may be attached to either the Form 1041 that is filed for the first taxable year of the trust beginning after December 31, 1996 (1997 taxable year), or to the Form 1041 filed for the first taxable year of the trust beginning after December 31, 1997 (1998 taxable year). The statement, however, must be filed no later than the due date for filing a Form 1041 for the 1998 taxable year, plus extensions. The election will be effective for the 1997 taxable year, and thereafter, until revoked or terminated. If the trust filed a Form 1041 for the 1997 taxable year without the statement attached, the statement should be attached to the Form 1041 filed for the 1998 taxable year.

(B) If the trust has insufficient gross income and no taxable income for its 1997 or 1998 taxable year, or both, and therefore is not required to file a Form 1041 for either or both years, the trust must make the election by filing a Form 1041 for either the 1997 or 1998 taxable year with the statement attached (even though not otherwise required to file a Form 1041 for that year). The trust should only provide on the Form 1041 the trust's name, name and title of fiduciary, address, employer identification number, date created, and type of entity. The statement must be attached to a Form 1041 that is filed no later than October 15, 1999.

(C) If the trust files a Form 1040NR for the 1997 taxable year based on application of new section 7701(a)(30)(E) to the trust, and satisfies paragraph (f)(1) of this section, in order for the trust to make the election the trust must file an amended Form 1040NR return for the 1997 taxable year. The trust must note on the amended Form 1040NR that it is making an election under section 1161 of the Taxpayer Relief Act of 1997. The trust must attach to the amended Form 1040NR the statement required by paragraph (f)(3)(i) of this section and a completed Form 1041 for the 1997 taxable year. The items of income, deduction and credit of the trust must be excluded from the amended Form 1040NR and reported on the Form 1041. The amended Form 1040NR for the 1997 taxable year, with the statement and the Form 1041 attached, must be filed with the Philadelphia Service Center no later than the due date, plus extensions, for filing a Form 1041 for the 1998 taxable year.

(D) If a trust has made estimated tax payments as a foreign trust based on application of section 7701(a)(30)(E) to the trust, but has not yet filed a Form 1040NR for the 1997 taxable year, when the trust files its Form 1041 for the 1997 taxable year it must note on its Form 1041 that it made estimated tax payments based on treatment as a foreign trust. The Form 1041 must be filed with the Philadelphia Service Center (and not with the service center where the trust ordinarily would file its Form 1041).

(E) If a trust forms part of a qualified stock bonus, pension, or profit sharing plan, the election provided by this paragraph (f) must be made by attaching the statement to the plan's annual return required under section 6058 (information return) for the first plan year beginning after December 31, 1996, or to the plan's information return for the first plan year beginning after December 31, 1997. The statement must be attached to the plan's information return that is filed no later than the due date for filing the plan's information return for the first plan year beginning after December 31, 1997, plus extensions. The election will be effective for the first plan year beginning after December 31, 1996, and thereafter, until revoked or terminated.

(F) Any other type of trust that is not required to file a Form 1041 for the taxable year, but that is required to file an information return (for example, Form 5227) for the 1997 or 1998 taxable year must attach the statement to the trust's information return for the 1997 or 1998 taxable year. However, the statement must be attached to an information return that is filed no later than the due date for filing the trust's information return for the 1998 taxable year, plus extensions. The election will be effective for the 1997 taxable year, and thereafter, until revoked or terminated.

(G) A group trust described in Rev. Rul. 81-100 consisting of trusts that are parts of qualified retirement plans and individual retirement accounts (and any other trust that is not described above and that is not required to file a Form 1041 or an information return) need not attach the statement to any return and should file the statement with the Philadelphia Service Center. The trust must make the election provided by this paragraph (f) by filing the statement by October 15, 1999. The election will be effective for the 1997 taxable year, and thereafter, until revoked or terminated.

(iii) *Failure to file the statement in the required manner and time.*—If a trust fails to file the statement in the manner or time provided in paragraphs (f)(3)(i) and (ii) of this section, the trustee may provide a written statement to the district director having jurisdiction over the trust setting forth the reasons for failing to file the statement in the required manner or time. If the district director determines that the failure to file the statement in the required manner or time was due to reasonable cause, the district director may grant the trust an extension of time to file the statement. Whether an extension of time is granted shall be in the sole discretion of the district director. However, the relief provided by this paragraph (f)(3)(iii) is not ordinarily available if the statute of limitations for the trust's 1997 taxable year has expired. Additionally, if the district director grants an extension of time, it may contain terms with respect to assessment as may be necessary to ensure that the correct amount of tax will be collected from the trust, its owners, and its beneficiaries.

(4) *Revocation or termination of the election.*— (i) *Revocation of election.*—The election provided by this paragraph (f) to be treated as a domestic trust may only be revoked with the consent of the Commissioner. See sections 684, 6048, and 6677 for the federal tax consequences and reporting requirements related to the change in trust residence.

(ii) *Termination of the election.*—An election under this paragraph (f) to remain a domestic trust terminates if changes are made to the trust subsequent to the effective date of the election that result in the trust no longer having any reasonable basis (within the meaning of section 6662) for being treated as a domestic trust under section 7701(a)(30) prior to its amendment by the SBJP Act. The termination of the election will result in the trust changing its residency from a domestic trust to a foreign trust on the effective date of the termination of the election. See sections 684, 6048, and 6677 for the federal tax consequences and reporting requirements related to the change in trust residence.

(5) *Effective date.*—This paragraph (f) is applicable beginning on February 2, 1999. [Reg. § 301.7701-7.]

☐ [*T.D.* 8813, 2-1-99. *Amended by T.D.* 8962, 8-8-2001.]

[Reg. § 301.7701-8]

§ 301.7701-8. **Military or naval forces and Armed Forces of the United States.**—The term "military or naval forces of the United States" and the term "Armed Forces of the United States" each includes all regular and reserve components of the uniformed services which are subject to the jurisdiction of the Secretary of Defense, the Secretary of the Army, the Secretary of the Navy, or the Secretary of the Air Force. The terms also include the Coast Guard. The members of such forces include commissioned officers and the personnel below the grade of commissioned officer in such forces. [Reg. § 301.7701-8.]

☐ [*T.D.* 6503, 11-15-60.]

[Reg. § 301.7701-9]

§ 301.7701-9. **Secretary or his delegate.**— (a) The term "Secretary or his delegate" means the Secretary of the Treasury, or any officer, employee, or agency of the Treasury Department duly authorized by the Secretary (directly, or indirectly by one or more redelegations of authority) to perform the function mentioned or described in the context, and the term "or his delegate" when used in connection with any other official of the United States shall be similarly construed.

(b) In any case in which a function is vested by the Internal Revenue Code of 1954 or any other statute in the Secretary or his delegate, and Treasury regulations or Treasury decisions approved by the Secretary or his delegate provide that such function may be performed by the Commissioner, assistant commissioner, regional commissioner, assistant regional commissioner, district director, director of a regional service center, or by a designated officer or employee in the office of any such officer, such provision in the regulations or Treasury decision shall constitute a delegation by the Secretary of the authority to perform such function to the designated officer or employee. If such authority is delegated to any officer or employee performing services under the supervision and control of the Commissioner, such provision in the regulations or Treasury decision shall constitute a delegation by the Secretary to the Commissioner of the authority to perform such function and a redelegation thereof by the Commissioner to the designated officer or employee.

(c) An officer or employee, including the Commissioner, authorized by regulations or Treasury decision to perform a function shall have authority to redelegate the performance of such function to any officer or employee performing services under his supervision and control, unless such power to so redelegate is prohibited or restricted by proper order or directive. The Commissioner may also redelegate authority to perform such function to other officers or employees under his supervision and control and, to the extent he deems proper, may authorize further redelegation of such authority.

(d) The Commissioner may prescribe such limitations as he deems proper on the extent to which any officer or employee under his supervision and control shall perform any such function, but, in the case of an officer or employee designated in regulations or Treasury decision as authorized to perform such function, such limitations shall not render invalid any performance by such officer or employee of the function which, except for such limitations, such officer or employee is authorized to perform by such regulations or Treasury decision in effect at the time the function is performed. [Reg. § 301.7701-9.]

☐ [*T.D.* 6503, 11-15-60. *Amended by T.D.* 6585, 12-27-61.]

[Reg. § 301.7701-10]

§ 301.7701-10. District director.—The term "district director" means the district director of internal revenue for an internal revenue district. The term also includes the Assistant Commissioner(International). [Reg. § 301.7701-10.]

☐ [*T.D.* 6503, 11-15-60. *Amended by T.D.* 8411, 4-24-92.]

[Reg. § 301.7701-11]

§ 301.7701-11. Social security number.—For purposes of this chapter, the term "social security number" means the taxpayer identifying number of an individual or estate which is assigned pursuant to section 6011(b) or corresponding provisions of prior law, or pursuant to section 6109, and in which nine digits are separated by hyphens as follows: 000-00-0000. Such term does not include a number with a letter as a suffix which is used to identify an auxiliary beneficiary under the social security program. The terms "account number" and "social security number" refer to the same number. [Reg. § 301.7701-11.]

☐ [*T.D.* 6606, 8-24-62. *Amended by T.D.* 7306, 3-14-74.]

[Reg. § 301.7701-12]

§ 301.7701-12. Employer identification number.—For purposes of this chapter, the term "employer identification number" means the taxpayer identifying number of an individual or other person(whether or not an employer) which is assigned pursuant to section 6011(b) or corresponding provisions of prior law, or pursuant to section 6109, and in which nine digits are separated by a hyphen, as follows: 00-0000000. The terms "employer identification number" and "identification number" (defined in § 31.0-2(a)(11) of this chapter (Employment Tax Regulations)) refer to the same number. [Reg. § 301.7701-12.]

☐ [*T.D.* 6606, 8-24-62. *Amended by T.D.* 7306, 3-14-74.]

[Reg. § 301.7701-13A]

§ 301.7701-13A. Post-1969 domestic building and loan association.—(a) *In general.*—For taxable years beginning after July 11, 1969, the term "domestic building and loan association" means a domestic building and loan association, a domestic savings and loan association, a Federal savings and loan association, and any other savings institution chartered and supervised as a savings and loan or similar association under Federal or State law which meets the supervisory test (described in paragraph (b) of this section), the business operations test (described in paragraph (c) of this section), and the assets test (described in paragraph (d) of this section). For the definition of the term "domestic building and loan association" for taxable years beginning after October 16, 1962, and before July 12, 1969, see § 301.7701-13.

(b) *Supervisory test.*—A domestic building and loan association must be either (1) an insured institution within the meaning of section 401(a) of the National Housing Act (12 U.S.C. 1724(a)) or (2) subject by law to supervision and examination by State or Federal authority having supervision over such associations. An "insured institution" is one the accounts of which are insured by the Federal Savings and Loan Insurance Corporation.

(c) *Business operations test.*—(1) *In general.*— An association must utilize its assets so that its business consists principally of acquiring the savings of the public and investing in loans. The requirement of this paragraph is referred to in this section as the business operations test. The business of acquiring the savings of the public and investing in loans includes ancillary or incidental activities which are directly and primarily related to such acquisition and investment, such as advertising for savings, appraising property on which loans are to be made by the association, and inspecting the progress of construction in connection with construction loans. Even though an association meets the supervisory test described in paragraph (b) of this section and the assets test described in paragraph (d) of this section, it will nevertheless not qualify as a domestic building and loan association if it does not meet the requirements of both subparagraphs (2) and (3) of this paragraph, relating, respectively, to acquiring the savings of the public and investing in loans.

(2) *Acquiring the savings of the public.*—The requirement that an association's business (other than investing in loans) must consist principally of acquiring the savings of the public ordinarily will be considered to be met if savings are acquired in all material respects in conformity with the rules and regulations of the Federal Home Loan Bank Board or substantially equivalent rules of a State law or supervisory authority. Alternatively, such requirement will be considered to be met if more than 75 percent of the dollar amount of the total deposits, withdrawable shares, and other obligations of the association are held during the taxable year by the general public, as opposed to amounts deposited or held by family or related business groups or persons who are officers or directors of the association. However, the preceding sentence shall not apply if the dollar amount of other obligations of the association outstanding during the taxable year exceeds 25 percent of the dollar amount of the total deposits, withdrawable shares, and other obligations of the association outstanding during such year. For purposes of this subparagraph, the term "other obligations" means notes, bonds, debentures, or other obligations, or other securities (except capital stock), issued by an association in conformity with the rules and regulations of the Federal Home Loan Bank Board or substantially equivalent rules of a State law or supervisory authority. The term "other obligations" does not include an advance made by a Federal Home Loan Bank under the authority of section 10 or 10b of the Federal Home Loan Bank Act (12 U.S.C. 1430, 1430b) as amended and supplemented. Both percentages

specified in this subparagraph shall be computed either as of the close of the taxable year or, at the option of the taxpayer, on the basis of the average of the dollar amounts of the total deposits, withdrawable shares, and other obligations of the association held during the taxable year. Such averages shall be determined by computing each percentage specified either as of the close of each month, as of the close of each quarter, or semiannually during the taxable year and by using the yearly average of the monthly, quarterly, or semiannual percentages obtained. The method selected must be applied uniformly for the taxable year to both percentages, but the method may be changed from year to year.

(3) *Investing in loans.*—(i) *In general.*—The requirement that an association's business (other than acquiring the savings of the public) must consist principally of investing in loans will be considered to be met for a taxable year only if more than 75 percent of the gross income of the association consists of—

(*a*) Interest or dividends on assets defined in subparagraphs (1), (2), and (3) of paragraph (e) of this section,

(*b*) Interest on loans,

(*c*) Income attributable to the portion of property used in the association's business, as defined in paragraph (e)(11) of this section,

(*d*) So much of the amount of premiums, discounts, commissions, or fees (including late charges and penalties) on loans which have at some time been held by the association, or for which firm commitments have been issued, as is not in excess of 20 percent of the gross income of the association,

(*e*) Net gain from sales and exchanges of governmental obligations, as defined in paragraph (e)(2) of this section, or

(*f*) Income, gain or loss attributable to foreclosed property, as defined in paragraph (e)(9) of this section, but not including such income, gain or loss which, pursuant to section 595 and the regulations thereunder, is not included in gross income.
Examples of types of income which would cause an association to fail to meet the requirements of this subparagraph if, in the aggregate, they equal or exceed 25 percent of gross income, are: the excess of gains over losses from sales of real property (other than foreclosed property); rental income (other than on foreclosed property and the portion of property used in the association's business); premiums, commissions, and fees (other than commitment fees) on loans which have never been held by the association; and insurance brokerage fees.

(ii) *Computation of gross income.*—For purposes of this subparagraph, gross income is computed without regard to—

(*a*) Gain or loss on the sale or exchange of the portion of property used in the association's business as defined in paragraph (e)(11) of this section,

(*b*) Gain or loss on the sale or exchange of the rented portion of property used as the principal or branch office of the association, as defined in paragraph (e)(11) of this section, and

(c) Gains or losses on sales of participations and loans, other than governmental obligations defined in paragraph (e)(2) of this section.

For purposes of this subparagraph, gross income is also computed without regard to items of income which an association establishes arise out of transactions which are necessitated by exceptional circumstances and which are not undertaken as recurring business activities for profit. Thus, for example, an association would meet the investing in loans requirement if it can establish that it would otherwise fail to meet that requirement solely because of the receipt of a non-recurring item of income due to exceptional circumstances. For this purpose, transactions necessitated by an excess of demand for loans over savings capital in the association's area are not to be deemed to be necessitated by exceptional circumstances. For purposes of (c) of this subdivision, the term "sales of participations" means sales by an association of interests in loans, which sales meet the requirements of the regulations of the Federal Home Loan Bank Board relating to sale of participations, or which meet substantially equivalent requirements of State law or regulations relating to sales of participations.

(iii) *Reporting requirement.*—In the case of income tax returns for taxable years beginning after July 11, 1969, there is required to be filed with the return a statement showing the amount of gross income for the taxable year in each of the categories described in subdivision (i), of this subparagraph.

(d) *60 percent of assets test.*—At least 60 percent of the amount of the total assets of a domestic building and loan association must consist of the assets defined in paragraph (e) of this section. The percentage specified in this paragraph is computed as of the close of the taxable year or, at the option of the taxpayer, may be computed on the basis of the average assets outstanding during the taxable year. Such average is determined by making the appropriate computation described in this section either as of the close of each month, as of the close of each quarter, or semiannually during the taxable year and by using the yearly average of the monthly, quarterly, or semiannual percentage obtained for each category of assets defined in paragraph (e) of this section. The method selected must be applied uniformly for the taxable year to all categories of assets, but the method may be changed from year to year. For purposes of this paragraph, it is immaterial whether the association originated the loans defined in subparagraphs (4) through (8) and (10) of paragraph (e) of this section or purchased or otherwise acquired them in whole or in part from another. See paragraph (f) of this section for definition of certain terms used in this paragraph and in paragraph (e) of this section, and for the determination of amount and character of loans.

(e) *Assets defined.*—The assets defined in this paragraph are—

(1) *Cash.*—The term "cash" means cash on hand, and time or demand deposits with, or withdrawable accounts in, other financial institutions.

(2) *Governmental obligations.*—The term "governmental obligations" means—

(i) Obligations of the United States,

(ii) Obligations of a State or political subdivision of a State, and

(iii) Stock or obligations of a corporation which is an instrumentality of the United States, a State, or a political subdivision of a State,

other than obligations the interest on which is excludable from gross income under section 103 and the regulations thereunder.

(3) *Deposit insurance company securities.*—The term "deposit insurance company securities" means certificates of deposit in, or obligations of a corporation organized under a State law which specifically authorizes such corporation to insure the deposits or share accounts of member associations.

(4) *Passbook loan.*—The term "passbook loan" means a loan to the extent secured by a deposit, withdrawable share, or savings account in the association, or share of a member of the association, with respect to which a distribution is allowable as a deduction under section 591.

(5) *Residential real property loan.*—[Reserved]

(6) *Church loan.*—[Reserved]

(7) *Urban renewal loan.*—[Reserved]

(8) *Institutional loan.*—[Reserved]

(9) *Foreclosed property.*—[Reserved]

(10) *Educational loan.*—[Reserved]

(11) *Property used in the association's business.*—(i) *In general.*—The term "property used in the association's business" means land, buildings, furniture, fixtures, equipment, leasehold interests, leasehold improvements, and other assets used by the association in the conduct of its business of acquiring the savings of the public and investing in loans. Real property held for the purpose of being used primarily as the principal or branch office of the association constitutes property used in the association's business so long as it is reasonably anticipated that such property will be occupied for such use by the association, or that construction work preparatory to such occupancy will be commenced thereon, within 2 years after acquisition of the property. Stock of a wholly owned subsidiary corporation which has as its exclusive activity the ownership and management of property more than 50 percent of the fair rental value of which is used as the principal or branch office of

the association constitutes property used in such business. Real property held by an association for investment or sale, even for the purpose of obtaining mortgage loans thereon, does not constitute property used in the association's business.

(ii) *Property rented to others.*—Except as provided in the second sentence of subdivision (i) of this subparagraph, property or a portion thereof rented by the association to others does not constitute property used in the association's business. However, if the fair rental value of the rented portion of a single piece of real property (including appurtenant parcels) used as the principal or branch office of the association constitutes less than 50 percent of the fair rental value of such piece of property, or if such property has an adjusted basis of not more than $150,000, the entire property shall be considered used in such business. If such rented portion constitutes 50 percent or more of the fair rental value of such piece of property, and such property has an adjusted basis of more than $150,000, an allocation of its adjusted basis is required. The portion of the total adjusted basis of such piece of property which is deemed to be property used in the association's business shall be equal to an amount which bears the same ratio to such total adjusted basis as the amount of the fair rental value of the portion used as the principal or branch office of the association bears to the total fair rental value of such property. In the case of all property other than real property used or to be used as the principal or branch office of the association, if the fair rental value of the rented portion thereof constitutes less than 15 percent of the fair rental value of such property, the entire property shall be considered used in the association's business. If such rented portion constitutes 15 percent or more of the fair rental value of such property, an allocation of its adjusted basis (in the same manner as required for real property used as the principal or branch office) is required.

(12) *Regular or residual interest in a REMIC.*— (i) *In general.*—If for any calendar quarter at least 95 percent of a REMIC's assets (as determined in accordance with § 1.860F-4(e)(1)(ii) or § 1.6049-7(f)(3) of this chapter) are assets defined in paragraph (e)(1) through (e)(11) of this section, then for that calendar quarter all the regular and residual interests in that REMIC are treated as assets defined in this paragraph (e). If less than 95 percent of a REMIC's assets are assets defined in paragraph (e)(1) through (e)(11) of this section, the percentage of each REMIC regular or residual interest treated as an asset defined in this paragraph (e) is equal to the percentage of the REMIC's assets that are assets defined in paragraph (e)(1) through (e)(11) of this section. See § § 1.860F-4(e)(1)(ii)(B) and 1.6049-7(f)(3) of this chapter for information required to be provided to regular and residual interest holders if the 95 percent test is not met.

(ii) *Loans secured by manufactured housing.*—For purposes of paragraph (e)(12)(i) of this section, a loan secured by manufactured housing treated as a single family residence under section 25(e)(10) is an asset defined in paragraph (e)(1) through (e)(11) of this section.

(f) *Special rules.*—[Reserved][Reg. § 301.7701-13A.]

☐ [*T.D. 7622, 5-15-79. Amended by T.D. 8458, 12-23-92.*]

[Reg. § 301.7701-14]

§ 301.7701-14. Cooperative bank.—For taxable years beginning after October 16, 1962, the term "cooperative bank" means an institution without capital stock organized and operated for mutual purposes without profit which meets the supervisory test, the business operations test, and the various assets tests specified in paragraphs (d) through (h) of § 301.7701-13, employing the rules and definitions of paragraphs (j) through (l) of that section. In applying paragraphs (b) through (l) of such section any references to an "association" or to a "domestic building and loan association" shall be deemed to be a reference to a cooperative bank. [Reg. § 301.7701-14.]

☐ [*T.D. 6766, 10-30-64.*]

[Reg. § 301.7701-15]

§ 301.7701-15. Tax return preparer.—(a) *In general.*—A *tax return preparer* is any person who prepares for compensation, or who employs one or more persons to prepare for compensation, all or a substantial portion of any return of tax or any claim for refund of tax under the Internal Revenue Code (Code).

(b) *Definitions.*—(1) *Signing tax return preparer.*—A *signing tax return preparer* is the individual tax return preparer who has the primary responsibility for the overall substantive accuracy of the preparation of such return or claim for refund.

(2) *Nonsigning tax return preparer.*—(i) *In general.*—A *nonsigning tax return preparer* is any tax return preparer who is not a signing tax return preparer but who prepares all or a substantial portion of a return or claim for refund within the meaning of paragraph (b)(3) of this section with respect to events that have occurred at the time the advice is rendered. In determining whether an individual is a nonsigning tax return preparer, time spent on advice that is given after events have occurred that represents less than 5 percent of the aggregate time incurred by such individual with respect to the position(s) giving rise to the understatement shall not be taken into account. Notwithstanding the preceding sentence, time spent on advice before the events have occurred will be taken into account if all facts and circumstances show that the position(s) giving rise to the understatement is primarily attributable to the advice, the advice was substantially given before events occurred primarily to avoid treating the person giving the

advice as a tax return preparer, and the advice given before events occurred was confirmed after events had occurred for purposes of preparing a tax return. Examples of nonsigning tax return preparers are tax return preparers who provide advice (written or oral) to a taxpayer (or to another tax return preparer) when that advice leads to a position or entry that constitutes a substantial portion of the return within the meaning of paragraph(b)(3) of this section.

(ii) *Examples.*—The provisions of this paragraph (b)(2) are illustrated by the following examples:

Example 1. Attorney A, an attorney in a law firm, provides legal advice to a large corporate taxpayer regarding a completed corporate transaction. The advice provided by A is directly relevant to the determination of an entry on the taxpayer's return, and this advice leads to a position(s) or entry that constitutes a substantial portion of the return. A, however, does not prepare any other portion of the taxpayer's return and is not the signing tax return preparer of this return. A is considered a nonsigning tax return preparer.

Example 2. Attorney B, an attorney in a law firm, provides legal advice to a large corporate taxpayer regarding the tax consequences of a proposed corporate transaction. Based upon this advice, the corporate taxpayer enters into the transaction. Once the transaction is completed, the corporate taxpayer does not receive any additional advice from B with respect to the transaction. B did not provide advice with respect to events that have occurred and is not considered a tax return preparer.

Example 3. The facts are the same as *Example 2,* except that Attorney B provides supplemental advice to the corporate taxpayer on a phone call after the transaction is completed. Attorney B did not provide advice before the corporate transaction occurred with the primary intent to avoid being treated as a tax return preparer. The time incurred on this supplemental advice by B represented less than 5 percent of the aggregate amount of time spent by B providing tax advice on the position. B is not considered a tax return preparer.

(3) *Substantial portion.*—(i) Only a person who prepares all or a substantial portion of a return or claim for refund shall be considered to be a tax return preparer of the return or claim for refund. A person who renders tax advice on a position that is directly relevant to the determination of the existence, characterization, or amount of an entry on a return or claim for refund will be regarded as having prepared that entry. Whether a schedule, entry, or other portion of a return or claim for refund is a substantial portion is determined based upon whether the person knows or reasonably should know that the tax attributable to the schedule, entry, or other portion of a return or claim for refund is a substantial portion of the tax required to be shown on the return or claim for refund. A single tax entry may constitute a substantial portion of the tax required to be shown on a return. Factors to consider in determining whether a schedule, entry, or other portion of a return or claim for

refund is a substantial portion include but are not limited to—

(A) the size and complexity of the item relative to the taxpayer's gross income; and

(B) the size of the understatement attributable to the item compared to the taxpayer's reported tax liability.

(ii)(A) For purposes of applying the rules of paragraph (b)(3)(i) of this section to a nonsigning tax return preparer within the meaning of paragraph (b)(2) of this section only, the schedule or other portion is not considered to be a substantial portion if the schedule, entry, or other portion of the return or claim for refund involves amounts of gross income, amounts of deductions, or amounts on the basis of which credits are determined that are—

(1) Less than $10,000; or

(2) Less than $400,000 and also less than 20 percent of the gross income as shown on the return or claim for refund (or, for an individual, the individual's adjusted gross income).

(B) If more than one schedule, entry or other portion is involved, all schedules, entries or other portions shall be aggregated in applying the de minimis rule in paragraph (b)(3)(ii)(A) of this section.

(C) The de minimis rule in paragraph (b)(3)(ii)(A) of this section shall not apply to a signing tax return preparer within the meaning of paragraph (b)(1) of this section.

(iii) A tax return preparer with respect to one return is not considered to be a tax return preparer of another return merely because an entry or entries reported on the first return may affect an entry reported on the other return, unless the entry or entries reported on the first return are directly reflected on the other return and constitute a substantial portion of the other return. For example, the sole preparer of a partnership return of income or small business corporation income tax return is considered a tax return preparer of a partner's or a shareholder's return if the entry or entries on the partnership or small business corporation return reportable on the partner's or shareholder's return constitute a substantial portion of the partner's or shareholder's return.

(iv) *Examples.*—The provisions of this paragraph (b)(3) are illustrated by the following examples:

Example 1. Accountant C prepares a Form 8886, "Reportable Transaction Disclosure Statement", that is used to disclose reportable transactions. C does not prepare the tax return or advise the taxpayer regarding the tax return reporting position of the transaction to which the Form 8886 relates. The preparation of the Form 8886 is not directly relevant to the determination of the existence, characterization, or amount of an entry on a tax return or claim for refund. Rather, the Form 8886 is prepared by C to disclose a reportable transaction. C has not prepared a substantial portion of the tax return and is not considered a tax return preparer under section 6694.

Example 2. Accountant D prepares a schedule for an individual taxpayer's Form 1040,

"U.S. Individual Income Tax Return", reporting $4,000 in dividend income and gives oral or written advice about Schedule A, which results in a claim of a medical expense deduction totaling $5,000, but does not sign the tax return. D is not a nonsigning tax return preparer because the total aggregate amount of the deductions is less than $10,000.

(4) *Return and claim for refund.*— (i) *Return.*—For purposes of this section, a return of tax is a return (including an amended or adjusted return) filed by or on behalf of a taxpayer reporting the liability of the taxpayer for tax under the Code, if the type of return is identified in published guidance in the Internal Revenue Bulletin. A return of tax also includes any information return or other document identified in published guidance in the Internal Revenue Bulletin and that reports information that is or may be reported on another taxpayer's return under the Code if the information reported on the information return or other document constitutes a substantial portion of the taxpayer's return within the meaning of paragraph (b)(3) of this section.

(ii) *Claim for refund.*—For purposes of this section, a claim for refund of tax includes a claim for credit against any tax that is included in published guidance in the Internal Revenue Bulletin. A claim for refund also includes a claim for payment under section 6420, 6421, or 6427.

(c) *Mechanical or clerical assistance.*—A person who furnishes to a taxpayer or other tax return preparer sufficient information and advice so that completion of the return or claim for refund is largely a mechanical or clerical matter is considered a tax return preparer, even though that person does not actually place or review placement of information on the return or claim for refund. See also paragraph (b)(3) of this section.

(d) *Qualifications.*—A person may be a tax return preparer without regard to educational qualifications and professional status requirements.

(e) *Outside the United States.*—A person who prepares a return or claim for refund outside the United States is a tax return preparer, regardless of the person's nationality, residence, or the location of the person's place of business, if the person otherwise satisfies the definition of *tax return preparer*. Notwithstanding the provisions of § 301.6109-1(g), the person shall secure an employer identification number if the person is an employer of another tax return preparer, is a partnership in which one or more of the general partners is a tax return preparer, is a firm in which one or more of the equity holders is a tax return preparer, or is an individual not employed by another tax return preparer.

(f) *Persons who are not tax return preparers.*— (1) The following persons are not tax return preparers:

(i) An official or employee of the Internal Revenue Service (IRS) performing official duties.

(ii) Any individual who provides tax assistance under a Volunteer Income Tax Assistance (VITA) program established by the IRS, but only with respect to those returns prepared as part of the VITA program.

(iii) Any organization sponsoring or administering a VITA program established by the IRS, but only with respect to that sponsorship or administration.

(iv) Any individual who provides tax counseling for the elderly under a program established pursuant to section 163 of the Revenue Act of 1978, but only with respect to those returns prepared as part of that program.

(v) Any organization sponsoring or administering a program to provide tax counseling for the elderly established pursuant to section 163 of the Revenue Act of 1978, but only with respect to that sponsorship or administration.

(vi) Any individual who provides tax assistance as part of a qualified Low-Income Taxpayer Clinic (LITC), as defined by section 7526, subject to the requirements of paragraphs (f)(2) and (3) of this section, but only with respect to those returns and claims for refund prepared as part of the LITC program.

(vii) Any organization that is a qualified LITC, as defined by section 7526, subject to the requirements of paragraphs (f)(2) and (3) of this section.

(viii) An individual providing only typing, reproduction, or other mechanical assistance in the preparation of a return or claim for refund.

(ix) An individual preparing a return or claim for refund of a taxpayer, or an officer, a general partner, member, shareholder, or employee of a taxpayer, by whom the individual is regularly and continuously employed or compensated or in which the individual is a general partner.

(x) An individual preparing a return or claim for refund for a trust, estate, or other entity of which the individual either is a fiduciary or is an officer, general partner, or employee of the fiduciary.

(xi) An individual preparing a claim for refund for a taxpayer in response to—

(A) A notice of deficiency issued to the taxpayer; or

(B) A waiver of restriction on assessment after initiation of an audit of the taxpayer or another taxpayer if a determination in the audit of the other taxpayer affects, directly or indirectly, the liability of the taxpayer for tax.

(xii) A person who prepares a return or claim for refund for a taxpayer with no explicit or implicit agreement for compensation, even if the person receives an insubstantial gift, return service, or favor.

(2) Paragraphs (f)(1)(vi) and (vii) of this section apply only if any assistance with a return of

tax or claim for refund is directly related to a controversy with the IRS for which the qualified LITC is providing assistance or is an ancillary part of a LITC program to inform individuals for whom English is a second language about their rights and responsibilities under the Code.

(3) Notwithstanding paragraph (f)(2) of this section, paragraphs (f)(1)(vi) and (f)(1)(vii) of this section do not apply if an LITC charges a separate fee or varies a fee based on whether the LITC provides assistance with a return of tax or claim for refund under the Code or if the LITC charges more than a nominal fee for its services.

(4) For purposes of paragraph (f)(1)(ix) of this section, the employee of a corporation owning more than 50 percent of the voting power of another corporation, or the employee of a corporation more than 50 percent of the voting power of which is owned by another corporation, is considered the employee of the other corporation as well.

(5) For purposes of paragraph (f)(1)(x) of this section, an estate, guardianship, conservatorship, committee, or any similar arrangement for a taxpayer under a legal disability (such as a minor, an incompetent, or an infirm individual) is considered a trust or estate.

(6) *Examples.*—The mechanical assistance exception described in paragraph (f)(1)(viii) of this section is illustrated by the following examples:

Example 1. A reporting agent received employment tax information from a client from the client's business records. The reporting agent did not render any tax advice to the client or exercise any discretion or independent judgment on the client's underlying tax positions. The reporting agent processed the client's information, signed the return as authorized by the client pursuant to Form 8655, Reporting Agent Authorization, and filed the client's return using the information supplied by the client. The reporting agent is not a tax return preparer.

Example 2. A reporting agent rendered tax advice to a client on determining whether its workers are employees or independent contractors for Federal tax purposes. For compensation, the reporting agent received employment tax information from the client, processed the client's information and filed the client's return using the information supplied by the client. The reporting agent is a tax return preparer.

(g) *Effective/applicability date.*—This section is applicable to returns and claims for refund filed, and advice provided, after December 31, 2008. [Reg. § 301.7701-15.]

☐ [*T.D. 7519, 11-17-77. Amended by T.D. 7675, 2-20-80; T.D. 9026, 12-17-2002 and T.D. 9436, 12-15-2008 (corrected 1-28-2009).*]

[Reg. § 301.7701-16]

§ 301.7701-16. Other terms.—For a definition of the term "withholding agent" see § 1.1441-7(a). Any other terms that are defined in section 7701 and that are not defined in

§§ 301.7701-1 to 301.7701-15, inclusive, shall, when used in this chapter, have the meanings assigned to them in section 7701. [Reg. § 301.7701-16.]

☐ [*T.D. 6606, 8-24-62. Amended by T.D. 6766, 10-30-64, T.D. 7519, 11-17-77 and T.D. 7977, 9-19-84.*]

[Reg. § 301.7701-17T]

§ 301.7701-17T. Collective-bargaining plans and agreements (Temporary).—

Q-1: How did the Tax Reform Act of 1984 (TRA of 1984) change the laws with respect to plans that are maintained pursuant to collective bargaining agreements?

A-1: (a) Many of the requirements and rules applicable to deferred compensation and welfare benefit plans are different for plans maintained pursuant to a collective bargaining agreement. Prior to the TRA of 1984, the Internal Revenue Code provided no clear definition of an employee representative or whether there is a collective bargaining agreement between such employee representative and one or more employers.

(b) Section 526(c) of the TRA of 1984 added a new condition under a new section 7701(a)(46) that must be satisfied in order for a plan to be considered to be a plan maintained pursuant to a collective bargaining agreement between employee representatives and one or more employers for purposes of the Code after March 31, 1984. If more than one-half of the membership of an organization is comprised of owners, officers, and executives of employers covered by the plan, then such organization is not an employee representative for purposes of determining whether a plan is to be treated as maintained pursuant to a collective bargaining agreement between employee representatives and one or more employers. Whether an individual is an owner, officer or executive is to be determined separately with respect to each employer. Additionally, section 7701(a)(46) provides that the Internal Revenue Service shall make the determination for purposes of the Code as to whether there is a collective bargaining agreement between employee representatives and one or more employers.

Q-2: If an organization does not fail to be an employee representative under the 50 percent or less test of section 7701(a)(46), is a plan maintained pursuant to an agreement between such organization and one or more employers necessarily treated, under the Code, as a plan maintained pursuant to a collective bargaining agreement between an employee representative and one or more employers?

A-2: (a) No.

(b) Specific Code provisions generally require other conditions than that in section 7701(a)(46) to be satisfied in order for a plan to be considered to be collectively-bargained. For example, in order for a plan to be described in section 413(a), the Secretary of Labor must find that the plan is maintained pursuant to a collective bargaining agreement between employee representatives and one or more employers.

(c) Even if (1) the finding in the example in the preceding paragraph (b) is made by the Secretary of Labor, (2) the union has been recognized as exempt under section 501(c)(5), and (3) the percentage condition in section 7701(a)(46) is satisfied, the Internal Revenue Service has the authority, pursuant to section 7701(a)(46), to determine whether there is a collective bargaining agreement under the Code. [Temporary Reg. §301.7701-17T.]

☐ [*T.D. 8073, 1-29-86.*]

[Reg. §301.7701-18]

§301.7701-18. Definitions; spouse, husband and wife, husband, wife, marriage.—(a) *In general.*—For federal tax purposes, the terms *spouse, husband,* and *wife* mean an individual lawfully married to another individual. The term *husband and wife* means two individuals lawfully married to each other.

(b) *Persons who are lawfully married for federal tax purposes.*—(1) *In general.*—Except as provided in paragraph (b)(2) of this section regarding marriages entered into under the laws of a foreign jurisdiction, a marriage of two individuals is recognized for federal tax purposes if the marriage is recognized by the state, possession, or territory of the United States in which the marriage is entered into, regardless of domicile.

(2) *Foreign marriages.*—Two individuals who enter into a relationship denominated as marriage under the laws of a foreign jurisdiction are recognized as married for federal tax purposes if the relationship would be recognized as marriage under the laws of at least one state, possession, or territory of the United States, regardless of domicile.

(c) *Persons who are not lawfully married for federal tax purposes.*—The terms *spouse, husband,* and *wife* do not include individuals who have entered into a registered domestic partnership, civil union, or other similar formal relationship not denominated as a marriage under the law of the state, possession, or territory of the United States where such relationship was entered into, regardless of domicile. The term *husband and wife* does not include couples who have entered into such a formal relationship, and the term *marriage* does not include such formal relationships.

(d) *Applicability date.*—The rules of this section apply to taxable years ending on or after September 2, 2016. [Reg. §301.7701-18.]

☐ [*T.D. 9785, 8-31-2016.*]

[Reg. §301.7701(b)-0]

§301.7701(b)-0. Outline of regulations provisions for section 7701(b)-1 through (b)-9.—This section lists the paragraphs contained in §§301.7701(b)-1 through 301.7701(b)-9.

§301.7701(b)-1. Resident alien.
  (a) Scope.

  (b) Lawful permanent resident.
    (1) Green card test.
    (2) Rescission of resident status.
    (3) Administrative or judicial determination of abandonment of resident status.
  (c) Substantial presence test.
    (1) In general.
    (2) Determination of presence.
      (i) Physical presence.
      (ii) United States.
    (3) Current year.
    (4) Thirty-one day minimum.
  (d) Application of section 7701(b) to the possessions and territories.
    (1) Application to aliens.
    (2) Non-application to citizens.
  (e) Examples.

§301.7701(b)-2. Closer connection exception.
  (a) In general.
  (b) Foreign country.
  (c) Tax home.
    (1) Definition.
    (2) Duration and nature of tax home.
  (d) Closer connection to a foreign country.
    (1) In general.
    (2) Permanent home.
  (e) Special rule.
  (f) Closer connection exception unavailable.
  (g) Filing requirements.

§301.7701(b)-3. Days of presence in the United States that are excluded for purposes of section 7701(b).
  (a) In general.
  (b) Exempt individuals.
    (1) In general.
    (2) Foreign government-related individual.
      (i) In general.
      (ii) Definition of international organization.
      (iii) Full-time diplomatic or consular status.
    (3) Teacher or trainee.
    (4) Student.
    (5) Professional athlete.
    (6) Substantial compliance.
    (7) Limitation on teacher or trainee and student exemptions.
      (i) Teacher or trainee limitation in general.
      (ii) Special teacher or trainee limitation for section 872(b)(3) compensation.
      (iii) Limitation on student exemption.
      (iv) Transition rule.
      (v) Examples.
    (8) Immediate family.
  (c) Medical condition.
    (1) In general.
    (2) Intent to leave the United States.
    (3) Preexisting medical condition.
    (4) Examples.
  (d) Days in transit.

(e) Regular commuters from Mexico or Canada.
    (1) General rule.
    (2) Definitions.
    (3) Examples.
(f) Determination of excluded days applies beyond year of determination.

§ 301.7701(b)-4. Residency time periods.
    (a) First year of residency.
    (b) Last year of residency.
        (1) General rule.
        (2) Exceptions.
    (c) Rules relating to residency starting date and residency termination date.
        (1) De minimis presence.
        (2) Proration.
        (3) Residency starting date for certain individuals.
            (i) In general.
            (ii) Determination of presence.
            (iii) Thirty-one day period.
            (iv) Period of continuous presence.
            (v) Election procedure.
                (A) Filing requirements.
                (B) Election on behalf of a dependent child.
                (C) Statement.
            (vi) Penalty for failure to comply with filing requirements.
                (A) General rule.
                (B) Exception.
    (d) Examples.
    (e) No lapse.
        (1) Residency in prior year.
        (2) Residency in following year.
        (3) Special rule.
        (4) Example.

§ 301.7701(b)-5. Coordination with section 877.
    (a) General rule.
    (b) Tax imposed.
    (c) Example.

§ 301.7701(b)-6. Taxable year.
    (a) In general.
    (b) Examples.

§ 301.7701(b)-7. Coordination with income tax treaties.
    (a) Consistency requirement.
        (1) Application.
        (2) Computation of tax liability.
        (3) Other Internal Revenue Code purposes.
        (4) Special rules for S corporations. [Reserved]
    (b) Filing requirements.
    (c) Contents of statement.
        (1) In general.
            (i) Returns due after December 15, 1997.
            (ii) Earlier returns.
        (2) Controlled foreign corporation shareholders.

        (3) S corporation shareholders. [Reserved]
    (d) Relationship to section 6114(a) treaty-based return positions.
    (e) Examples.

§ 301.7701(b)-8. Procedural rules.
    (a) Who must file.
        (1) Closer connection exception.
        (2) Exempt individuals and individuals with a medical condition.
        (3) De minimis presence and residency starting and termination dates.
    (b) Contents of statement.
        (1) Closer connection exception.
            (i) Returns due after December 15, 1997.
            (ii) Earlier returns.
        (2) Exempt individuals and individuals with a medical condition.
            (i) Returns due after December 15, 1997.
            (ii) Earlier returns.
        (3) De minimis presence and residency starting and termination dates.
    (c) How to file.
    (d) Penalty for failure to file statement.
        (1) General rule.
        (2) Exception.
    (e) Filing requirement disregarded.

§ 301.7701(b)-9. Effective dates of
§§ 301.7701(b)-1 through 301.7701(b)-7.
    (a) In general.
    (b) Special rules.
        (1) Green card test-residency starting date.
        (2) Substantial presence test-years included.
        (3) Professional athletes.
        (4) Procedural rules and filing requirements. [Reg. § 301.7701(b)-0.]

    □ [*T.D. 8411, 4-24-92. Amended by T.D. 8733,* 10-6-97.]

[Reg. § 301.7701(b)-1]

    § 301.7701(b)-1. Resident alien.—(a) *Scope.*—Section 301.7701(b)-1(b) provides rules for determining whether an alien individual is a lawful permanent resident of the United States. Section 301.7701(b)-1(c) provides rules for determining if an alien individual satisfies the substantial presence test. Section 301.7701(b)-2 provides rules for determining when an alien individual will be considered to maintain a tax home in a foreign country and to have a closer connection to that foreign country. Section 301.7701(b)-3 provides rules for determining if an individual is an exempt individual because of his or her status as a foreign government-related individual, teacher, trainee, student, or professional athlete. Section 301.7701(b)-3 also provides rules for determining whether an individual may exclude days of presence in the United States because the individual was unable to leave the United States because of a medical condition. Section 301.7701(b)-4 provides rules for determining an individual's residency starting and termination dates. Section 301.7701(b)-5 provides rules for applying section 877 to a nonresident alien individual. Section 301.7701(b)-6 provides rules for determining the taxable year of an alien. Section 301.7701(b)-7 provides rules for determining the effect of these regulations on rules in tax conventions to which the United States is a party. Section 301.7701(b)-8 provides procedural rules for establishing that an individual is a nonresident alien. Section 301.7701(b)-9 provides the effective dates of section 7701(b) and the regulations under that section. Unless the context indicates otherwise, the regulations under § § 301.7701(b)-1 through 301.7701(b)-9 apply for purposes of determining whether a United States citizen is also a resident of the United States. (This determination may be relevant, for example, to the application of section 861(a)(1) which treats income from interest-bearing obligations of residents as income from sources within the United States.) The regulations do not apply and § § 1.871-2 and 1.871-5 of this chapter continue to apply for purposes of the bona fide residence test of section 911. See § 1.911-2(c) of this chapter. For purposes of determining whether an individual is a resident of the United States for estate and gift tax purposes, see § 20.0-1(b)(1) and (2) and § 25.2501-1(b) of this chapter, respectively.

(b) *Lawful permanent resident.*—(1) *Green card test.*—An alien is a resident alien with respect to a calendar year if the individual is a lawful permanent resident at any time during the calendar year. A lawful permanent resident is an individual who has been lawfully granted the privilege of residing permanently in the United States as an immigrant in accordance with the immigration laws. Resident status is deemed to continue unless it is rescinded or administratively or judicially determined to have been abandoned.

(2) *Rescission of resident status.*—Resident status is considered to be rescinded if a final administrative or judicial order of exclusion or deportation is issued regarding the alien individual. For purposes of this paragraph, the term "final judicial order" means an order that is no longer subject to appeal to a higher court of competent jurisdiction.

(3) *Administrative or judicial determination of abandonment of resident status.*—An administrative or judicial determination of abandonment of resident status may be initiated by the alien individual, the Immigration and Naturalization Service (INS), or a consular officer. If the alien initiates this determination, resident status is considered to be abandoned when the individual's application for abandonment (INS Form I-407) or a letter stating the alien's intent to abandon his or her resident status, with the Alien Registration Receipt Card (INS Form I-151 or Form I-551) enclosed, is filed with the INS or a consular officer. If INS replaces any of the form numbers referred to in this paragraph or

§ 301.7701(b)-2(f), refer to the comparable INS replacement form number. For purposes of this paragraph, an alien individual shall be considered to have filed a letter stating the intent to abandon resident status with the INS or a consular office if such letter is sent by certified mail, return receipt requested (or a foreign country's equivalent thereof). A copy of the letter, along with proof that the letter was mailed and received, should be retained by the alien individual. If the INS or a consular officer initiates this determination, resident status will be considered to be abandoned upon the issuance of a final administrative order of abandonment. If an individual is granted an appeal to a federal court of competent jurisdiction, a final judicial order is required.

(c) *Substantial presence test.*—(1) *In general.*—An alien individual is a resident alien if the individual meets the substantial presence test. An individual satisfies this test if he or she has been present in the United States on at least 183 days during a three year period that includes the current year. For purposes of this test, each day of presence in the current year is counted as a full day. Each day of presence in the first preceding year is counted as one-third of a day and each day of presence in the second preceding year is counted as one-sixth of a day. For purposes of this paragraph, any fractional days resulting from the above calculations will not be rounded to the nearest whole number. (See § 301.7701(b)-9(b)(2) for transitional rules for calendar years 1985 and 1986.)

(2) *Determination of presence.*—(i) *Physical presence.*—For purposes of the substantial presence test, an individual shall be treated as present in the United States on any day that he or she is physically present in the United States at any time during the day. (But see § 301.7701(b)-3 relating to days of presence that may be excluded.)

(ii) *United States.*—For purposes of section 7701(b) and the regulations thereunder, the term "United States" when used in a geographical sense includes the states and the District of Columbia. It also includes the territorial waters of the United States and the seabed and subsoil of those submarine areas which are adjacent to the territorial waters of the United States and over which the United States has exclusive rights, in accordance with international law, with respect to the exploration and exploitation of natural resources. It does not include the possessions and territories of the United States or the air space over the United States.

(3) *Current year.*—The term "current year" means any calendar year for which an alien individual is determining his or her resident status.

(4) *Thirty-one day minimum.*—If an individual is not physically present for more than 30 days during the current year, the substantial presence test will not be applied for that year even if the three-year total is 183 or more days.

Reg. § 301.7701(b)-1(c)(4)

For purposes of the substantial presence test, it is irrelevant that an individual was not present for more than 30 days in the first or second year preceding the current year.

(d) *Application of section 7701(b) to the possessions and territories.*—(1) *Application to aliens for purposes of mirror systems.*—Section 7701(b) provides the basis for determining whether an alien individual is a resident of a United States possession or territory that administers income tax laws that are identical (except for the substitution of the name of the possession or territory for the term "United States" where appropriate) to those in force in the United States, for purposes of applying such laws with respect to income tax liability incurred to such possession or territory.

(2) *Non-application for bona fide resident determination.*—Section 7701(b) does not provide the basis for determining whether an individual (including an alien individual) is a bona fide resident of a United States possession or territory for Federal income tax purposes. For the applicable rules for making this determination, see section 937(a) and § 1.937-1 of this chapter.

(e) *Examples.*—This section may be illustrated by the following examples:

Example 1. B, an alien individual, is present in the United States for 122 days in the current year. He was present in the United States for 122 days in the first preceding calendar year and for 122 days in the second preceding calendar year. In determining his status for the current year, B counts all 122 days in the United States in the current year plus $1/3$ of the 122 days in the United States in the first preceding calendar year ($40 \, 2/3$ days) and $1/6$ of the 122 days in the United States during the second preceding calendar year ($20 \, 1/3$ days). The total of $122 + 40 \, 2/3 + 20 \, 1/3$ equals 183 days. B meets the substantial presence test and is a resident alien for the current year.

Example 2. C, an alien individual, is present in the United States for 25 days during the current year. She was present in the United States for 365 days during the first preceding year and 365 days during the second preceding year. The substantial presence test does not apply because C is present in the United States for fewer than 31 days during the current year.

Example 3. D, an alien individual, is present in the United States for 170 days during the current year. He was present in the United States for 30 days during the first preceding year and 30 days during the second preceding year. In determining his status for the current year, D counts all 170 days in the United States in the current year plus $1/3$ of the 30 days in the United States in the first preceding calendar year (10 days) and $1/6$ of the 30 days in the United States during the second preceding calendar year (5 days). The total of $170 + 10 + 5$ equals 185 days. D meets the substantial presence test and is a resident alien for the current year notwithstanding the fact that he was present in the United States for fewer than 31 days in each of the two preceding years. [Reg. § 301.7701(b)-1.]

☐ [*T.D.* 8411, 4-24-92. *Amended by T.D.* 9194, 4-6-2005 *and T.D.* 9391, 4-4-2008.]

[Reg. § 301.7701(b)-2]

§ 301.7701(b)-2. Closer connection exception.—(a) *In general.*—An alien individual who meets the substantial presence test may nevertheless be considered a nonresident alien for the current year if the following conditions are satisfied—

(1) The individual is present in the United States for fewer than 183 days in the current year;

(2) The individual maintains a tax home in a foreign country during the current year; and

(3) Except as provided in paragraph (e) of this section, the individual has a closer connection during the current year to a single foreign country in which he or she maintains a tax home than to the United States.

(b) *Foreign country.*—For purposes of section 7701(b) and the regulations thereunder, the term "foreign country" when used in a geographical sense includes any territory under the sovereignty of the United Nations or a government other than that of the United States. It includes the territorial waters of the foreign country (determined in accordance with the laws of the United States), and the seabed and subsoil of those submarine areas which are adjacent to the territorial waters of the foreign country and over which the foreign country has exclusive rights, in accordance with international law, with respect to the exploration and exploitation of natural resources. It also includes the possessions and territories of the United States.

(c) *Tax home.*—(1) *Definition.*—For purposes of section 7701(b) and the regulations under that section, the term "tax home" has the same meaning that it has for purposes of section 162(a)(2) (relating to travel expenses while away from home). Thus, an individual's tax home is considered to be located at the individual's regular or principal (if more than one regular) place of business. If the individual has no regular or principal place of business because of the nature of the business, or because the individual is not engaged in carrying on any trade or business within the meaning of section 162(a), then the individual's tax home is the individual's regular place of abode in a real and substantial sense.

(2) *Duration and nature of tax home.*—The tax home maintained by the alien individual must be in existence for the entire current year. The tax home must be located in the same foreign country for which the individual is claiming to have the closer connection described in paragraph (d) of this section.

(d) *Closer connection to a foreign country.*—(1) *In general.*—For purposes of section 7701(b) and the regulations under that section, an alien individual will be considered to have a closer connection to a foreign country than the United States if the individual or the Commissioner establishes that the individual has maintained more significant contacts with the foreign country than with the United States. In determining whether an individual has maintained more significant contacts with a foreign country than the United States, the facts and circumstances to be considered include, but are not limited to, the following—

(i) The location of the individual's permanent home;

(ii) The location of the individual's family;

(iii) The location of personal belongings, such as automobiles, furniture, clothing and jewelry owned by the individual and his or her family;

(iv) The location of social, political, cultural or religious organizations with which the individual has a current relationship;

(v) The location where the individual conducts his or her routine personal banking activities;

(vi) The location where the individual conducts business activities (other than those that constitute the individual's tax home);

(vii) The location of the jurisdiction in which the individual holds a driver's license;

(viii) The location of the jurisdiction in which the individual votes;

(ix) The country of residence designated by the individual on forms and documents; and

(x) The types of official forms and documents filed by the individual, such as Form 1078 (Certificate of Alien Claiming Residence in the United States), Form W-8 (Certificate of Foreign Status) or Form W-9 (Payee's Request for Taxpayer Identification Number).

(2) *Permanent home.*—For purposes of paragraph (d)(1)(i) of this section, it is immaterial whether a permanent home is a house, an apartment, or a furnished room. It is also immaterial whether the home is owned or rented by the alien individual. It is material, however, that the dwelling be available at all times, continuously, and not solely for stays of short duration.

(e) *Special rule.*—An alien individual may demonstrate in one year that he or she has a closer connection to two foreign countries (but no more than two) if he or she satisfies all of the following conditions—

(1) The individual maintains a tax home beginning on the first day of the current year in one foreign country;

(2) The individual changes his or her tax home during the current year to a second foreign country;

(3) The individual continues to maintain his or her tax home in the second foreign country for the remainder of the current year;

(4) The individual has a closer connection to each foreign country than to the United States for the period during which the individual maintains a tax home in that foreign country; and

(5) The individual is subject to taxation as a resident pursuant to the internal laws of either foreign country for the entire year or subject to

taxation as a resident in both foreign countries for the period during which the individual maintains a tax home in each foreign country.

(f) *Closer connection exception unavailable.*—An alien individual who has personally applied, or taken other affirmative steps, to change his or her status to that of a permanent resident during the current year or has an application pending for adjustment of status during the current year will not be eligible for the closer connection exception. Affirmative steps to change status to that of a permanent resident include, but are not limited to, the following—

(1) The filing of Immigration and Naturalization Form I-508 (Waiver of Immunities) by the alien;

(2) The filing of Immigration and Naturalization Form I-485 (Application for Status as Permanent Resident) by the alien;

(3) The filing of Immigration and Naturalization Form I-130 (Petition for Alien Relative) on behalf of the alien;

(4) The filing of Immigration and Naturalization Form I-140 (Petition for Prospective Immigrant Employee) on behalf of the alien;

(5) The filing of Department of Labor Form ETA-750 (Application for Alien Employment Certification) on behalf of the alien; or

(6) The filing of Department of State Form OF-230 (Application for Immigrant Visa and Alien Registration) by the alien.

(g) *Filing requirements.*—See § 301.7701(b)-8 with regard to the statement that must be filed by an alien individual claiming the closer connection exception. [Reg. § 301.7701(b)-2.]

☐ [*T.D.* 8411, 4-24-92.]

[Reg. § 301.7701(b)-3]

§ 301.7701(b)-3. Days of presence in the United States that are excluded for purposes of section 7701(b).—(a) *In general.*—In computing days of presence in the United States, an alien is considered to be present if the individual is physically present in the United States at any time during the day (see § 301.7701(b)-1(c)(2)(i)). However, for purposes of section 7701(b) and the regulations under that section, the following days shall be excluded and will not count as days of presence in the United States—

(1) Any day that an individual is present in the United States as an exempt individual;

(2) Any day that an individual is prevented from leaving the United States because of a medical condition that arose while the individual was present in the United States—

(3) Any day that an individual is in transit between two points outside the United States; and

(4) Any day on which a regular commuter residing in Canada or Mexico commutes to and from employment in the United States.

(b) *Exempt individuals.*—(1) *In general.*—An exempt individual is an individual who is either a—

(i) Foreign government-related individual as defined in paragraph (b)(2) of this section;

(ii) Teacher or trainee as defined in paragraph (b)(3) of this section;

(iii) Student as defined in paragraph (b)(4) of this section; or

(iv) Professional athlete as defined in paragraph (b)(5) of this section.

(2) *Foreign government-related individual.*— (i) *In general.*—A foreign government-related individual is an individual (and that individual's immediate family) who is temporarily present in the United States—

(A) as a full-time employee of an international organization;

(B) by reason of diplomatic status; or

(C) by reason of a visa that the Secretary of the Treasury or his or her delegate (after consultation with the Secretary of State when appropriate) determines represents full-time diplomatic or consular status. An individual described in this paragraph shall be considered to be temporarily present in the United States if the individual is not a lawful permanent resident as described in § 301.7701(b)-1(b)(1), regardless of the actual amount of time that the individual is present in the United States.

(ii) *Definition of international organization.*—The term "international organization" means any public international organization that has been designated by the President by Executive Order as being entitled to enjoy the privileges, exemptions, and immunities provided for in the International Organizations Act (22 U.S.C. 288). An individual described in paragraph (b)(2)(i) of this section will be a full-time employee of an international organization if that individual's employment with the organization is consistent with an employment schedule of a person with a standard full-time work schedule with the organization.

(iii) *Full-time diplomatic or consular status.*—An individual is considered to have full-time diplomatic or consular status if—

(A) The individual has been accredited by a foreign government recognized de jure or de facto by the United States;

(B) The individual intends to engage primarily in official activities for that foreign government while in the United States; and

(C) The individual has been recognized by the President, or by the Secretary of State, or by a consular officer acting on behalf of the Secretary of State, as being entitled to such status.

(3) *Teacher or trainee.*—A teacher or trainee includes any individual (and that individual's immediate family), other than a student, who is admitted temporarily to the United States as a nonimmigrant under section 101(a)(15)(J) (relating to the admission of teachers and trainees into the United States) or section 101(a)(15)(Q) (relating to the admission of participants in international cultural exchange programs) of the Immigration and Nationality Act (8 U.S.C. 1101(a)(15)(J), (Q)) and who substantially complies with the requirements of being admitted.

(4) *Student.*—A student is any individual (and that individual's immediate family) who is admitted temporarily to the United States as a nonimmigrant under section 101(a)(15)(F) or (M) (relating to the admission of students into the United States) or as a student under section 101(a)(15)(J) (relating to the admission of teachers and trainees into the United States) or section 101(a)(15)(Q) (relating to the admission of participants in international cultural exchange programs) of the Immigration and Nationality Act (8 U.S.C. 1101(a)(15)(F), (J), (M), (Q)) who substantially complies with the requirements of being admitted. For rules concerning taxation of certain nonresident students or trainees, see section 871(c) and § 1.871-9(a) of this chapter.

(5) *Professional athlete.*—A professional athlete is an individual who is temporarily present in the United States to compete in a charitable sports event described in section 274(l)(1)(B). For purposes of computing the days of presence in the United States, only days on which the athlete actually competes in a charitable sports event described in section 274(l)(1)(B) shall be excluded. Thus, days on which the individual is present to practice for the event, to perform promotional or other activities related to the event, or to travel between events shall be included for purposes of the substantial presence test.

(6) *Substantial compliance.*—An individual described in paragraph (b)(3) or (4) of this section will be deemed to comply substantially with the visa requirements relevant to residence for tax purposes if the individual has not engaged in activities that are prohibited by the Immigration and Nationality Act and the regulations thereunder and could result in the loss of F, J or M visa status. An individual will not be deemed to comply substantially with the visa requirements relevant to residence for tax purposes merely by showing that the individual's visa has not been revoked. An independent determination of substantial compliance may be made by the Internal Revenue Service for any individual claiming to be an exempt individual under paragraph (b)(3) or (4) of this section. For example, if an individual with an F visa (student visa) is found to have accepted unauthorized employment or to have maintained a course of study that is not considered by the Internal Revenue Service to be full-time, the individual will not be considered to comply substantially with the individual's visa requirements regardless of whether the individual's visa has been revoked.

(7) *Limitation on teacher or trainee and student exemptions.*—(i) *Teacher or trainee limitation in general.*—Except as otherwise provided, an individual shall not exclude days of presence as a teacher or trainee if the individual has been exempt as a teacher, trainee, or student for any part of two of the six preceding calendar years.

(ii) *Special teacher or trainee limitation for section 872 (b)(3) compensation.*—If—

(A) A teacher or trainee receives compensation in the current year and all of that compensation is described in section 872(b)(3);

(B) That individual was present in the United States as a teacher or trainee in any prior year within the last 6 years; and

(C) During each prior year (within the 6 year period) in which the individual was present as a teacher or trainee, the individual received compensation all of which was described in section 872(b)(3);

then that individual shall include days of presence as a teacher or trainee in the current year only if the individual has been exempt as a teacher, trainee, or student for any part of four of the six preceding calendar years.

(iii) *Limitation on student exemption.*—An individual will not be able to exclude days of presence as a student if the individual has been exempt as a teacher, trainee, or student for any part of more than five calendar years, unless it is established to the satisfaction of the district director that the individual does not intend to reside permanently in the United States and has substantially complied with the requirements of the student visa providing for the individual's temporary presence in the United States. For purposes of this paragraph (b)(7), the facts and circumstances to be considered in determining if an individual has demonstrated an intent to reside permanently in the United States include (but are not limited to)—

(A) Whether the individual has maintained a closer connection with a foreign country as described in § 301.7701(b)-2; and

(B) Whether the individual has taken affirmative steps within the meaning of paragraph (f) of § 301.7701(b)-2 to adjust the individual's status from nonimmigrant to lawful permanent resident.

(iv) *Transition rule.*—The rules in this paragraph (b)(7) relating to stated periods of exempt status apply only for those stated periods that occur after 1984. Thus, for example, an alien who is present as a student during the calendar years 1982-1990 will not be subject to the five year rule for students until 1990.

(v) *Examples.*—The following examples illustrate the application of paragraphs (b)(7)(i) and (ii) of this section:

Example 1. B is temporarily present in the United States during the current year as a teacher, within the meaning of section 101(a)(15)(J) of the Immigration and Nationality Act. B does not receive compensation described in section 872(b)(3) in the current year. B has been treated as an exempt student for the past three years. Although this is the first year that B is seeking to be exempt as a teacher, he will not be considered an exempt individual for the year because he has been exempt as a student for at least two of the past six years.

Example 2. C is temporarily present in the United States during the current year as a teacher and receives compensation described in section 872(b)(3) in the current year. C has been treated as an exempt teacher for the past two years but C's compensation for those years was not described in section 872(b)(3). C will not be considered an exempt individual for the current year because she has been exempt as a teacher for at least two of the past six years.

Example 3. The facts are the same as in *Example 2*, except that all of C's compensation for the two preceding years was described in section 872(b)(3). C will be considered to be an exempt individual for the current year because she has not been exempt as a student, teacher or trainee for four of the six preceding calendar years.

Example 4. D is temporarily present in the United States during the current year as a teacher, within the meaning of section 101(a)(15)(J) of the Immigration and Nationality Act. D does not receive compensation described in section 872(b)(3) in the current year. D entered the United States in December of the second preceding year and intends to remain in the United States until June of the current year. D will not be considered an exempt individual for the current year because he has been exempt as a teacher for at least two of the past six years.

(8) *Immediate family.*—The immediate family of an exempt individual includes the individual's spouse and unmarried children (whether by blood or adoption) but only if the spouse's or unmarried children's visa status are derived from and dependent on the visa classification of the exempt individual. For the purposes of this paragraph, the term "unmarried children" means those children who are under 21 years of age, who reside regularly in the household of the exempt individual, and who are not members of some other household. The immediate family of an exempt individual does not include the attendants, servants, and personal employees of that individual.

(c) *Medical condition.*—(1) *In general.*—An individual will not be considered present on any day that the individual intends to leave and is unable to leave the United States because of a medical condition or medical problem that arose while the individual was present in the United States. A day of presence will not be excluded if the individual, who was initially prevented from leaving, is subsequently able to leave the United States and then remains in the United States beyond a reasonable period for making arrangements to leave the United States. A day will also not be excluded if the medical condition arose during a prior stay in the United States (whether or not days of presence during the prior stay were excluded) and the alien returns to the United States for treatment of the medical condition or medical problem that arose during the prior stay.

(2) *Intent to leave the United States.*—For purposes of paragraph (c)(1) of this section, whether

an individual intends to leave the United States on a particular day will be determined based on all the facts and circumstances. Thus, if at the time an individual's medical condition or medical problem arose, the individual was present in the United States for a definite purpose which by its nature could be accomplished within the United States during a period of time that would not cause the individual to be a resident under the substantial presence test, the individual may be able to establish that he or she intended to leave the United States. However, if the individual's purpose is of such a nature that an extended period of time would be required for its accomplishment (sufficient to cause the individual to be a resident under the substantial presence test), the individual would not be able to establish the requisite intent to leave the United States. If the individual is present in the United States for no particular purpose or a purpose by its nature that does not require a specific period of time to accomplish, the determination of whether the individual has the requisite intent to leave the United States will depend on all the surrounding facts and circumstances. In the case of an individual adjudicated mentally incompetent, proof of intent to leave the United States may be determined by analyzing the incompetent's pattern of behavior prior to the adjudication of incompetence. Generally, an individual will be presumed to have intended to leave during a period of illness if the individual leaves the United States within a reasonable period of time (time to make arrangements to leave) after becoming physically able to leave.

(3) *Pre-existing medical condition.*—A medical condition or problem will not be considered to arise while the individual is present in the United States, if the condition or problem existed prior to the individual's arrival in the United States, and the individual was aware of the condition or problem, regardless of whether the individual required treatment for the condition or problem when the individual entered the United States.

(4) *Examples.*—The following examples illustrate the application of this paragraph (c):

Example 1. B is in a serious automobile accident in the United States on March 25. B intended to leave the United States on March 31 (as evidenced by an airline ticket), but was unable to leave on that date as a result of the injuries suffered in the accident. B recovered from the injuries and was able to leave and did leave the United States on May 31. B's presence in the United States during the period from April 1 through May 31 will not be counted as days of presence in the United States.

Example 2. The facts are the same as in *Example 1*, except that B's return flight (as evidenced by an airline ticket) was scheduled for May 31. Because B did not intend to leave the United States until May 31, B may not exclude any days of presence in the United States.

(d) *Days in transit.*—An alien individual may exclude days of presence in the United States if the individual is in transit between two foreign points, and is physically present in the United States for fewer than 24 hours. For purposes of this paragraph, an individual will be considered to be in transit if the individual pursues activities that are substantially related to completing his or her travel to a foreign point of destination. For example, an alien who travels between airports in the United States in order to change planes en route to the individual's destination will be considered to be in transit. However, if the individual attends a business meeting while he or she is present in the United States, whether or not that meeting is within the confines of the airport, the individual will not be considered to be in transit. For purposes of this paragraph, the term "foreign point" means any areas that are not included within the definition of the term "United States" provided in § 301.7701(b)-1(c)(2)(ii).

(e) *Regular commuters from Mexico or Canada.*—(1) *General rule.*—An alien individual will not be considered to be present in the United States on days that the individual commutes to the United States from the individual's residence in Mexico or Canada if the individual regularly commutes from Mexico or Canada. An alien individual will be considered to commute regularly if the individual commutes to the individual's location of employment or self-employment in the United States from his or her residence in Mexico or Canada on more than 75% of the workdays during the working period.

(2) *Definitions.*—(i) The term "commutes" means to travel to employment or self-employment and to return to one's residence within a 24-hour period.

(ii) The term "workdays" means days on which the individual works in the United States or Canada or Mexico.

(iii) The term "working period" means the period beginning with the first day in the current year on which the individual is physically present in the United States for purposes of engaging in employment or self-employment and ending on the last day in the current year on which the individual is physically present in the United States for purposes of engaging in that employment or self-employment. If the nature of the employment or self-employment is such that it requires the individual to be present in the United States only on a seasonal or cyclical basis, the working period will begin with the first day of the season or cycle on which the individual is present in the United States for purposes of engaging in that employment or self-employment and end on the last day of the season or cycle on which the individual is present in the United States for the purpose of engaging in that employment or self-employment. Thus, there may be more than one working period in a calendar year and a working period may begin in one calendar year and end in the following calendar year.

Reg. § 301.7701(b)-3(c)(3)

(3) *Examples.*—The following examples illustrate the operation of this paragraph (e):

Example 1. B lives in Mexico and is employed by Corporation X in its office in Mexico. B was temporarily assigned to X's office in the United States. B's employment in the United States office began on February 1, 1988, and continued through June 1, 1988. On June 2, B resumed his employment in Mexico. On 59 days in the period beginning on February 1, 1988, and ending on June 1, 1988, B travelled each morning from his residence in Mexico to X Corporation's United States office for the purpose of engaging in his employment with X Corporation. B returned to his residence in Mexico on each of those evenings. On seven days in the period from February 1, 1988, through June 1, 1988, B worked in X's Mexico office. B is not considered to have been present in the United States on any of the days that he travelled to X's United States office for the purpose of engaging in employment with Corporation X because he commuted to his place of employment within the United States on more than 75% of the workdays during the working period (59 workdays in the United States/66 workdays in the working period = 89.4%).

Example 2. C, who lives in Canada, contracted with a resort located in the United States to provide snow-skiing instructions for the resort's customers for two skiing seasons, the first beginning on November 15, 1987, and ending on March 15, 1988, and the second beginning on November 15, 1988, and ending on March 15, 1989. On 90 days in each of the two skiing seasons, C travelled in the morning from Canada to the resort to provide skiing instructions pursuant to the contract. C returned to Canada on each of those evenings. On 20 days during each of the two skiing seasons, C worked in Canada. C is not considered to have been present in the United States on any of the days that she travelled to the United States to provide ski instructions in either the first working period beginning on November 15, 1987, and ending on March 15, 1988, or the second working period beginning on November 15, 1988, and ending on March 15, 1989, because she commuted to her employment within the United States on more than 75% of the workdays during each of the working periods (90 workdays in the United States / 110 workdays in the working period = 81.8%).

Example 3. D, who lives in Canada, is the sole proprietor of a wholesale lumber business with offices in both the United States and Canada. Beginning on January 4, 1988, and ending on February 12, 1988, D commuted to work in his United States office on 30 days. Beginning on February 15, 1988, and ending on March 25, 1988, D commuted to work in his Canadian office on 30 days. Beginning on March 28, 1988, and ending on May 27, 1988, D commuted to work in his United States office on 45 days. Subsequent to May 27, D did not commute to the United States on any other days in 1988. D is considered to have been present in the United States on each day that he travelled to his office

in the United States because D did not commute to the United States office on more than 75% of the workdays during the working period beginning on January 4, 1988, and ending on May 27, 1988 (75 workdays in the United States / 105 workdays in the working period = 71.4%).

(f) *Determination of excluded days applies beyond year of determination.*—If a day of presence is excluded under this section, then that day shall not be taken into account in the current year or the first or second preceding year. [Reg. §301.7701(b)-3.]

☐ [T.D. 8411, 4-24-92. *Amended by T.D.* 8733, 10-6-97.]

[Reg. §301.7701(b)-4]

§301.7701(b)-4. Residency time periods.—(a) *First year of residency.*—An alien individual who was not a United States resident during the preceding calendar year and who is a United States resident for the current year will begin to be a resident for tax purposes on the alien's residency starting date. The residency starting date for an alien who meets the substantial presence test is the first day during the calendar year on which the individual is present in the United States. The residency starting date for an alien who meets the lawful permanent resident test (green card test), described in paragraph (b)(1) of §301.7701(b)-1, is the first day during the calendar year in which the individual is physically present in the United States as a lawful permanent resident. The residency starting date for an alien who satisfies both the substantial presence test and the green card test will be the earlier of the first day the individual is physically present in the United States as a lawful permanent resident of the United States or the first day during the year that the individual is present for purposes of the substantial presence test. (See §301.7701(b)-9(b)(1) for the transitional rule relating to the residency starting date of an alien individual who was a lawful permanent resident in 1984. See also §301.7701(b)-3 for days that may be excluded.)

(b) *Last year of residency.*—(1) *General rule.*—An alien individual who is a United States resident during the current year but who is not a United States resident at any time during the following calendar year will cease to be a resident for tax purposes on the individual's residency termination date. Generally, the residency termination date will be the last day of the calendar year.

(2) *Exceptions.*—Notwithstanding paragraph (b)(1) of this section, the residency termination date for an alien individual who meets the substantial presence test is the last day during the calendar year that the individual is physically present in the United States if the individual establishes that, for the remainder of the calendar year, the individual's tax home was in a foreign country and he or she maintained a closer connection (within the meaning of §301.7701(b)-2(d)) to that foreign country than to

the United States. Similarly, the residency termination date for an alien who meets the green card test is the first day during the calendar year that the alien is no longer a lawful permanent resident if the individual establishes that, for the remainder of the calendar year, his or her tax home was in a foreign country and he or she maintained a closer connection to that foreign country than to the United States. The residency termination date for an alien who satisfies both the substantial presence test and the green card test for the current year, will be the later of the first day the individual is no longer a lawful permanent resident of the United States or the last day the individual was physically present in the United States if the alien establishes that, for the remainder of the calendar year, his or her tax home was in a foreign country and he or she maintained a closer connection to that foreign country than to the United States. It is immaterial whether the individual's tax home was in the United States, or that the individual had a closer connection to the United States than to the foreign country, prior to the date of his or her departure from the United States or the date on which the individual was no longer a lawful permanent resident, whichever is applicable.

(c) *Rules relating to residency starting date and residency termination date.*—(1) *De minimis presence.*—An alien individual may be present in the United States for up to 10 days without triggering the residency starting date (for purposes of the substantial presence test) or extending the residency termination date (for purposes of the substantial presence test) if the individual is able to establish that, during that period, the individual's tax home was in a foreign country and he or she maintained a closer connection to that foreign country than to the United States. Days from more than one period of presence may be disregarded for purposes of determining an individual's residency starting date or termination date so long as the total is not more than 10 days. However, an individual may not disregard any days that occur in a period of consecutive days of presence, if all the days that occur during that period cannot be excluded. An individual must include days of presence for purposes of determining whether the individual meets the substantial presence test even though the days may be disregarded for purposes of determining the individual's residency starting date or residency termination date.

(2) *Proration.*—If an individual's residency starting date does not fall on the first day of the tax year, or the individual's residency termination date does not fall on the last day of the tax year, the individual's income tax liability should be calculated in accordance with §1.871-13 of this chapter dealing with the taxation of individuals who change residence status during the taxable year.

(3) *Residency starting date for certain individuals.*—(i) *In general.*—If an alien individual (who otherwise does not meet the substantial presence test or the green card test for the current year) is physically present in the United States for at least 31 consecutive days during the current year, and also for a period of continuous presence beginning with the first day of that thirty-one day period (see paragraph (c)(3)(iii) of this section), then the individual may elect to be treated as a resident during the current year. The individual's residency starting date shall be the first day of that thirty-one day period, if—

(A) The individual was not a resident of the United States under the substantial presence test or the green card test in the year preceding the current year; and

(B) The individual is a resident of the United States in the subsequent year under the substantial presence test (whether or not the individual is also a resident of the United States under the green card test).

(ii) *Determination of presence.*—Except as otherwise provided in paragraph (c)(3)(iii) of this section, an individual shall be treated as present in the United States on any day that the individual is physically present in the United States at any time during the day.

(iii) *Thirty-one day period.*—For purposes of this paragraph (c)(3), the term "thirty-one day period" means any period of 31 consecutive days during which an individual is physically present in the United States during each day of the period.

(iv) *Period of continuous presence.*—For purposes of this paragraph (c)(3), the term "continuous presence" means a period of presence in the United States that includes 75 percent of the days in the current year beginning with (and including) the first day of the individual's thirty-one day period of presence. Only for purposes of the continuous presence requirement, an individual will be deemed to be present in the United States for up to 5 days on which the individual is absent from the United States. These days will not be deemed to be days of presence for purposes of the thirty-one day period of presence requirement. If an individual is present for more than one thirty-one day period of presence and satisfies the continuous presence requirement with regard to each period, the individual's residency starting date shall be the first day of the first thirty-one day period of presence. If an individual is present for more than one thirty-one day period of presence but satisfies the continuous presence requirement only for a later thirty-one day period, the individual's residency starting date shall be the first day of the later thirty-one day period of presence. For purposes of this paragraph (c)(3), days of presence that are otherwise excluded under section 7701(b)(3)(D)(i) and §301.7701(b)-3(a)(1) (exempt individual), (a)(2) (medical condition), (a)(3) (in transit between two foreign points), and (a)(4) (regular commuter) shall not be counted as days of presence for purposes of either the thirty-one day period or continuous presence requirement.

Reg. §301.7701(b)-4(c)

(v) *Election procedure.*—(A) *Filing requirements.*—An alien individual shall make an election to be treated as a resident under paragraph (c)(3) of this section by attaching a statement (described in paragraph (c)(3)(v)(C) of this section) to the individual's income tax return (Form 1040) for the taxable year for which the election is to be in effect (the election year). The alien individual may not make this election until such time as he has satisfied the substantial presence test for the year following the election year. If an alien individual has not satisfied the substantial presence test for the year following the election year as of the due date (not including extensions) of the tax return for the election year, the alien individual may request an extension of time for filing the return until a reasonable period after he or she has satisfied such test, provided that the individual pays with his or her extension application the amount of tax he or she expects to owe for the election year computed as if he or she were a nonresident alien throughout the election year. An election made under paragraph (c)(3) of this section may not be revoked without the approval of the Commissioner or his delegate.

(B) *Election on behalf of a dependent child.*—An individual may make an election on behalf of a dependent child (as defined in paragraphs (1) and (2) of section 152(a), without regard to section 152(b)(3)) if the individual is qualified to make an election on his or her own behalf, the child qualifies to make an election under this paragraph (c)(3), and the child is not required by section 6012 to file a United States income tax return for the year for which the election is to be effective.

(C) *Statement.*—The statement required by paragraph (c)(3)(v)(A) of this section shall include the name and address of the alien individual and contain a signed declaration that the election is being made. If the individual is also making an election on behalf of any dependent children, then the statement must include the required information with respect to those children. The statement must specify—

(1) That the alien individual was not a resident in the year immediately preceding the election year;

(2) That the alien individual is a resident under the substantial presence test in the year following the election year;

(3) The individual's number of days of presence in the United States during the year following the election year;

(4) The date or dates of the alien individual's thirty-one day period of presence and period of continuous presence in the United States during the election year; and

(5) The date or dates of absence from the United States during the election year that are deemed to be days of presence.

(vi) *Penalty for failure to comply with filing requirements.*—(A) *General rule.*—If an individual fails to comply with the election procedure of paragraph (c)(3)(v) of this section, the individual must file his or her income tax return for the current year as a nonresident alien.

(B) *Exception.*—The penalty described in paragraph (c)(3)(vi)(A) of this section shall not apply if the individual can show by clear and convincing evidence that he or she took reasonable actions to become aware of the filing requirements and significant affirmative steps to comply with the requirements. An individual who requests an extension of time to file his or her income tax return pursuant to paragraph (c)(3)(v) of this section will be considered to have taken significant affirmative steps to comply with the requirement that the individual pay his or her tax determined as if the individual were a nonresident alien if the individual paid with his or her extension application at least 90 percent of the amount of the tax the individual actually owed for the election year computed as if he or she were a nonresident alien throughout the election year.

(d) *Examples.*—The following examples illustrate the operation of this section:

Example 1. B, a citizen of foreign country X, is an alien who has never before been a United States resident for tax purposes. B comes to the United States on January 6, 1985, to attend a business meeting and returns to country X on January 10, 1985. B is able to establish a closer connection to country X for the period January 6-10. On March 1, 1985, B moves to the United States and resides here until August 20, 1985, when he returns to country X. On December 12, 1985, B comes to the United States for pleasure and stays here until December 16, 1985 when he returns to country X. B is able to establish a closer connection to country X for the period December 12-16. B is not a United States resident for tax purposes during the following year and can establish a closer connection to country X for the remainder of calendar year 1985. B is a resident of the United States under the substantial presence test because B is present in the United States for 183 days (5 days in January plus 173 days for the period March 1-August 20 plus 5 days in December). B's residency starting date is March 1, 1985, and his residency termination date is August 20, 1985.

Example 2. The facts are the same as in *Example 1*, except that B remains in the United States until December 17, 1985, and is able to establish a closer connection to country X for the period December 18 through 31. B's residency termination date is December 17, 1985.

Example 3. C, a citizen of foreign country Y, is an alien who has never before been a United States resident for tax purposes. C comes to the United States for the first time on February 10, 1985, and attends a business conference until February 24, 1985, when she returns to country Y. On April 20, 1985, C enters the United States as a lawful permanent resident. On November 10, 1985, C ceases to be a lawful permanent resident but stays on in the United States until November 20, 1985 when she returns to country

Y. On December 8, 1985, C comes to the United States and stays here until December 17, 1985 when she returns to country Y. She can establish a closer connection to country Y for that period. C is not a resident of the United States during the following calendar year and can establish a closer connection to country Y for the remainder of calendar year 1985. C qualifies as a United States resident under both the green card test and the substantial presence test. C's residency starting date under the green card test is April 20, 1985. Under the substantial presence test, C's residency starting date is February 10, 1985, because she is present for more than ten days in February and cannot take advantage of the de minimis presence rule. Therefore, C's residency starting date is February 10, 1985. C's residency termination date under the green card test is November 10, 1985. Her residency termination date under the substantial presence test is November 20, because B can disregard ten days of presence in December. Thus, her residency termination date is November 20, 1985, the later of her residency termination date under the substantial presence test or the green card test.

Example 4. The facts are the same as in *Example 3*, except that C is initially present in the United States on business from February 5 to February 9, 1985. C is able to establish a closer connection to country Y for that period. C may take advantage of only ten days of de minimis presence and may exclude days from a continuous period of presence only if she can exclude all the days that occur during that period. Thus, C may choose either of the following periods of residency: residency starting date February 5, 1985, and residency termination date November 20, 1985, or residency starting date April 20, 1985, and residency termination date December 17, 1985.

Example 5. D, a citizen of foreign country Z, is an alien who has never before been a United States resident for tax purposes. D comes to the United States on November 1, 1985 and is present in the United States on 31 consecutive days (from November 1 through December 1, 1985). D returns to country Z on December 1 and does not come back to the United States until December 17, 1985. He remains in the United States for the rest of the year. During 1986, D is a resident of the United States under the substantial presence test. D may elect to be treated as a resident of the United States for 1985 because he was present in the United States in 1985 for a 31 consecutive day period of presence (November 1 through December 1, 1985) and for at least 75 percent of the days following (and including) the first day of D's 31 consecutive day period of presence (46 total days of presence in the United States/61 days in the period from November 1 through December 31 = 75.4%). If D makes the election to be treated as a resident, his residency starting date will be November 1, 1985.

Example 6. The facts are the same as in *Example 5*, except that D is absent from the United States on December 24, 25, 29, 30 and 31. D may make the election to be treated as a resident for 1985 because up to five days of absence will be

deemed to be days of presence for purposes of the continuous presence requirement.

Example 7. F, a citizen of foreign country M, is an alien individual who has never before been a United States resident for tax purposes. F comes to the United States on January 1, 1985 and remains in the United States through January 31, 1985, when she returns to country M. F comes back to the United States on October 1, 1985 and is present in the United States through November 1, 1985. From November 1, 1985 through December 31, 1985, F is present in the United States for 38 days. Although F satisfies two 31 consecutive day periods of presence, (January 1 through January 31 and October 1 through November 1), she satisfies the continuous presence requirement only with regard to the later period of presence (69 total days of presence/92 days in the period from October 1 through December 31 = 75%). Thus, if F makes the election to be treated as a resident, his residency starting date is October 1, 1985.

(e) *No lapse.*—(1) *Residency in prior year.*—An alien individual who was a United States resident during any part of the preceding calendar year and who is a United States resident for any part of the current year will be considered to be taxable as a resident at the beginning of the current year. For purposes of this paragraph (e)(1), it is immaterial whether an individual is considered to be a resident under the substantial presence test or the green card test.

(2) *Residency in following year.*—An alien individual who is a United States resident for any part of the current year and who is also a United States resident for any part of the following year (regardless of whether the individual has a closer connection to a foreign country than the United States during the current year) will be taxable as a resident through the end of the current year. For purposes of this paragraph (e)(2), it is immaterial whether an individual is considered to be a resident under the substantial presence test or the green card test.

(3) *Special rule.*—If an individual meets the green card test for the current year but is not physically present in the United States during the current year, then the individual's residency starting date shall be the first day of the following year.

(4) *Example.*—The following example illustrates the application of this paragraph (e).

Example. B, an alien individual who is a citizen of foreign country M, comes to the United States for the first time on May 1, 1985, and remains in the United States until November 5, 1985, when he returns to country M. B comes back to the United States on March 5, 1986 as a lawful permanent resident and remains in the United States until September 10, 1986, when he ceases to be a lawful permanent resident and returns to country M. B is not a resident in calendar year 1987. B's United States residency in calendar year 1985 continues through December 31, 1985, because he is a United States resident in the following calendar year. In calendar year 1986, B's United States residency is deemed to begin on January 1, 1986 because B qualified as a resident in the preceding calendar year. Thus, B's residency period in the United States begins on May 1, 1985, and ends on September 10, 1986. [Reg. § 301.7701(b)-4.]

☐ [*T.D.* 8411, 4-24-92.]

[Reg. § 301.7701(b)-5]

§ 301.7701(b)-5. Coordination with section 877.—(a) *General rule.*—An alien individual will be subject to United States income tax in the manner provided by section 877, regardless of whether the individual has a tax avoidance motive, if—

(1) The alien individual is a resident alien of the United States for at least three consecutive calendar years (the initial residency period) beginning after December 31, 1984;

(2) The period of residence for each of the three consecutive calendar years includes at least 183 days;

(3) The alien is once again taxed as a nonresident (including an individual taxed as a nonresident under § 301.7701(b)-7(a)(1); and

(4) The alien then becomes a resident of the United States before the close of the third calendar year beginning after the individual's residency termination date in the initial residency period.

(b) *Tax imposed.*—The tax provided for under paragraph (a) of this section will be imposed for the intervening period of nonresidency only if the amount of tax would exceed the amount of tax that would be imposed under section 871, relating to the taxation of nonresident aliens.

(c) *Example.*—The following example illustrates the application of this section.

Example. B, a citizen of foreign country F, enters the United States on April 1, 1985, as a lawful permanent resident. On August 1, 1987, B ceases to be a lawful permanent resident and returns to country F. B meets the initial residency period requirement because he is a resident of the United States for at least 183 days in each of three consecutive years (1985, 1986 and 1987). B returns to the United States on October 5, 1990, as a lawful permanent resident. Because B became a resident of the United States before the close of the third calendar year (1990) beginning after the close of the initial residency period (August 1, 1987), he is subject to tax under section 877(b) for the intervening period of nonresidency, August 2, 1987 through October 4, 1990, if the amount of the tax imposed under section 877 is more than the tax imposed under section 871. [Reg. § 301.7701(b)-5.]

☐ [*T.D.* 8411, 4-24-92.]

[Reg. § 301.7701(b)-6]

§ 301.7701(b)-6. Taxable year.—(a) *In general.*—An alien individual who has not established a fiscal year as his or her taxable year prior to the period that the individual is subject to United States income tax as a resident or a nonresident shall adopt the calendar year as his or her taxable year. An alien who has established a fiscal year in a foreign country prior to the period that the individual is subject to United States income tax may adopt the calendar year as his or her taxable year for United States income tax purposes without requesting a change in accounting period. An individual will be considered to have established a fiscal year (whether in the United States or a foreign country) if the annual accounting period on which the individual computes his or her income is a fiscal year, the individual keeps his or her books in accordance with that fiscal year, and the requirements of section 441 and § 1.441-1(b) of this chapter are otherwise satisfied. An alien who has established a fiscal year and is a resident alien during the calendar year will be treated as a resident alien with respect to any portion of his or her taxable year (beginning with the individual's residency starting date and ending with the individual's residency termination date) that falls within such calendar year. Once the individual has established either a fiscal or calendar year taxable year for any period for which the individual is subject to United States income tax, the individual may not change that taxable year without the approval of the Secretary. See section 442.

(b) *Examples.*—The following examples illustrate the operation of this section:

Example 1. B, a citizen and resident of foreign country F, was engaged in a United States business during 1982 and filed a return on a fiscal year basis. B's fiscal year runs from October 1 to September 30. B comes to the United States on March 8, 1985 and remains in the United States until October 10, 1985, when he returns to country F. B maintains a closer connection to and his tax home in Country F for the remainder of calendar year 1985. B, who is not a United States resident at any time in 1986, is a United States resident for the period that begins on March 8, 1985, and ends on October 10, 1985. B has adopted a fiscal year taxable year for purposes of computing his United States income tax liability. For his fiscal year that ends on September 30, 1985, B will be taxed as a United States resident for the period that begins on March 8, 1985 and ends on September 30, 1985. For his fiscal year that ends on September 30, 1986, B will only be taxed as a United States resident for the period that begins on October 1, 1985 and ends on October 10, 1985.

Example 2. The facts are the same as in *Example 1*, except that B's 1982 business was a country F business established on a fiscal year basis and at no time prior to 1985 was B subject to United States income tax. B may adopt a calendar year as his taxable year for United States income tax purposes without requesting a change of accounting period. B continues to use a fiscal year as his taxable year. For his fiscal year that ends on September 30, 1985, B will be taxed as a United States resident for the period that begins on March 8, 1985 and ends September 30, 1985.

For his fiscal year that ends on September 30, 1986, B will be taxed as a United States resident for the period that begins on October 1, 1985 and ends on October 10, 1985.

Example 3. The facts are the same as in *Example 1*, except that B's 1982 business was a country F business established on a fiscal year basis and at no time prior to 1985 was B subject to United States income tax. B may adopt a calendar year as his taxable year for United States income tax purposes without requesting a change of accounting period. B adopts a calendar year as his taxable year for 1985. For his calendar year taxable year ending on December 31, 1985, B will be taxed as a United States resident for the period that begins on March 8, 1985, and ends on October 10, 1985. [Reg. § 301.7701(b)-6.]

☐ [*T.D. 8411, 4-24-92. Amended by T.D. 8996, 5-16-2002.*]

[Reg. § 301.7701(b)-7]

§ 301.7701(b)-7. Coordination with income tax treaties.—(a) *Consistency requirement.*— (1) *Application.*—The application of this section shall be limited to an alien individual who is a dual resident taxpayer pursuant to a provision of a treaty that provides for resolution of conflicting claims of residence by the United States and its treaty partner. A "dual resident taxpayer" is an individual who is considered a resident of the United States pursuant to the internal laws of the United States and also a resident of a treaty country pursuant to the treaty partner's internal laws. If the alien individual determines that he or she is a resident of the foreign country for treaty purposes, and the alien individual claims a treaty benefit (as a nonresident of the United States) so as to reduce the individual's United States income tax liability with respect to any item of income covered by an applicable tax convention during a taxable year in which the individual was considered a dual resident taxpayer, then that individual shall be treated as a nonresident alien of the United States for purposes of computing that individual's United States income tax liability under the provisions of the Internal Revenue Code and the regulations thereunder (including the withholding provisions of section 1441 and the regulations under that section in cases in which the dual resident taxpayer is the recipient of income subject to withholding) with respect to that portion of the taxable year the individual was considered a dual resident taxpayer.

(2) *Computation of tax liability.*—If an alien individual is a dual resident taxpayer, then the rules on residency provided in the convention shall apply for purposes of determining the individual's residence for all purposes of that treaty.

(3) *Other Code purposes.*—Generally, for purposes of the Internal Revenue Code other than the computation of the individual's United States income tax liability, the individual shall be treated as a United States resident. Therefore, for example, the individual shall be treated as a United States resident for purposes of determining whether a foreign corporation is a controlled foreign corporation under section 957 or whether a foreign corporation is a foreign personal holding company under section 552. In addition, the application of paragraph (a)(2) of this section does not affect the determination of the individual's residency time periods under § 301.7701(b)-4.

(4) *Special rules for S corporations.*— [Reserved]

(b) *Filing requirements.*—An alien individual described in paragraph (a) of this section who determines his or her U.S. tax liability as if he or she were a nonresident alien shall make a return on Form 1040NR on or before the date prescribed by law (including extensions) for making an income tax return as a nonresident. The individual shall prepare a return and compute his or her tax liability as a nonresident alien. The individual shall attach a statement (in the form required in paragraph (c) of this section) to the Form 1040NR. The Form 1040NR and the attached statement, shall be filed with the Internal Revenue Service Center, Philadelphia, PA 19255. The filing of a Form 1040NR by an individual described in paragraph (a) of this section may affect the determination by the Immigration and Naturalization Service as to whether the individual qualifies to maintain a residency permit.

(c) *Contents of statement.*—(1) *In general.*— (i) *Returns due after December 15, 1997.*—The statement filed by an individual described in paragraph (a)(1) of this section, for a return relating to a taxable year for which the due date (without extensions) is after December 15, 1997, must be in the form of a fully completed Form 8833 (Treaty-Based Return Position Disclosure Under Section 6114 or 7701(b)) or appropriate successor form. See section 6114 and § 301.6114-1 for rules relating to other treaty-based return positions taken by the same taxpayer.

(ii) *Earlier returns.*—For returns relating to taxable years for which the due date for filing returns (without extensions) is on or before December 15, 1997, the statement filed by the individual described in paragraph (a)(1) of this section must contain the information in accordance with paragraph (c)(1) of this section in effect prior to December 15, 1997 (see § 301.7701(b)-7(c)(1) as contained in 26 CFR part 301, revised April 1, 1997).

(2) *Controlled foreign corporation shareholders.*—If the taxpayer who claims a treaty benefit as a nonresident of the United States is a United States shareholder in a controlled foreign corporation (CFC), as defined in section 957 or section 953(c), and there are no other United States shareholders in that CFC, then for purposes of paragraph (c)(1) of this section, the approximate amount of subpart F income (as defined in section 952) that would have been included in the taxpayer's income may be determined based on the audited foreign financial statements of the CFC.

(3) *S corporation shareholders.*—[Reserved]

(d) *Relationship to section 6114(a) treaty-based return positions.*—The statement required by paragraph (b) of this section will be considered disclosure for purposes of section 6114 and § 301.6114-1(a), but only if the statement is in the form required by paragraph (c) of this section. If the taxpayer fails to file the statement required by paragraph (b) of this section on or before the date prescribed in paragraph (b) of this section, the taxpayer will be subject to the penalties imposed by section 6712. See section 6712 and § 301.6712-1.

(e) *Examples.*—The following examples illustrate the application of this section:

Example 1. B, an alien individual, is a resident of foreign country X, under X's internal law. Country X is a party to an income tax convention with the United States. B is also a resident of the United States under the Internal Revenue Code. B is considered to be a resident of country X under the convention. The convention does not specifically deal with characterization of foreign corporations as controlled foreign corporations or the taxability of United States shareholders on inclusions of subpart F income, but it provides, in an "Other Income" article similar to Article 21 of the 1981 draft of the United States Model Income Tax Convention (U.S. Model), that items of income of a resident of country X that are not specifically dealt with in the convention shall be taxable only in country X. B owns 80% of the one class of stock of foreign corporation R. The remaining 20% is owned by C, a United States citizen who is unrelated to B. In 1985, corporation R's only income is interest that is foreign personal holding company income under § 1.954A-2 of this chapter. Because the United States-X income tax convention does not deal with characterization of foreign corporations as controlled foreign corporations, United States internal income tax law applies. Therefore, B and C are United States shareholders within the meaning of § 1.951-1(g) of this chapter, corporation R is a controlled foreign corporation within the meaning of § 1.957-1 of this chapter, and corporation R's income is included in C's income as subpart F income under § 1.951-1 of this chapter. B may avoid current taxation on his share of the subpart F inclusion by filing as a nonresident (*i.e.*, by following the procedure in § 301.7701 (b)-7(b)).

Example 2. The facts are the same as in *Example 1*, except that B also earns United States source dividend income. The United States-X income tax convention provides that the rate of United States tax on United States source dividends paid to residents of country X shall not exceed 15 percent of the gross amount of the dividends. B's United States tax liability with respect to the dividends would be smaller if he were treated as a resident alien, subject to tax on a net basis (*i.e.*, after the allowance of deductions) than if he were treated as a nonresident alien. If, however, B chooses to file as a nonresident in order to claim treaty benefits with respect to his share of R's subpart F income, his overall United States tax liability, including the portion attributable to the dividends, must be determined as if he were a nonresident alien.

Example 3. C, a married alien individual with three children, is a resident of foreign country Y, under Y's internal law. Country Y is a party to an income tax convention with the United States. C is also a resident of the United States under the Internal Revenue Code. C is considered to be a resident of country Y under the convention. The convention specifically covers, among other items of income, personal services income, dividends and interest. C is sent by her country Y employer to work in the United States from January 1, 1985 until December 31, 1985. During 1985, C also earns United States source dividends and interest and incurs mortgage interest expenses on her personal residence. The United States-Y treaty provides that remuneration for personal services performed in the United States by a country Y resident is exempt from United States tax if, among other things, the individual performing such services is present in the United States for a period that is not in excess of 183 days. The treaty provides that the rate of United States tax on United States source dividends paid to residents of Y shall not exceed 15 percent of the gross amount of the dividends and it exempts residents of Y from United States tax on United States source interest. In filing her 1985 tax return, C may choose to file either as a resident alien without claiming any treaty benefits or as a nonresident alien if she desires to claim any treaty benefit. C files as a nonresident (*i.e.*, by following the procedure described in § 301.7701(b)-7(b)). Because C does not satisfy the requirements of the United States-Y treaty with regard to exempting personal services income from United States tax, C will be taxed on her personal services income at graduated rates under section 1 of the Code pursuant to section 871(b) of the Code. She will not be entitled to deduct her mortgage interest expenses or to claim more than one personal exemption because she is taxed as a nonresident alien under the Code by virtue of her decision to claim treaty benefits, and section 873 of the Code denies nonresidents the deduction for personal residence mortgage interest expense and generally limits them to only one personal exemption. C will be subject to a tax of 15 percent of the gross amount of her dividend income under section 871(a) of the Code as modified by the treaty, and she will be exempt from tax on her interest income. C is not entitled to file a joint return with her spouse even if he is a resident alien under the Code for 1985.

Example 4. The facts are the same as in *Example 3*, except that C does not choose to claim treaty benefits with respect to any items of income covered by the treaty (*i.e.*, she files as a resident). Therefore, she is taxed as a resident under the Code and pays tax at graduated rates on her personal services income, dividends, and interest. In addition, she is entitled to deduct her mortgage interest expenses and to take personal exemptions for her spouse and three children. C will be entitled to file a joint return with her spouse if he is a resident alien for 1985 or, if he is a nonresident alien, C and her spouse may elect to file a joint return pursuant to section 6013. [Reg. § 301.7701(b)-7.]

☐ [T.D. 8411, 4-24-92. Amended by T.D. 8733, 10-6-97.]

[Reg. § 301.7701(b)-8]

§ 301.7701(b)-8. Procedural rules.—(a) Who must file.—(1) Closer connection exception.—An alien individual who otherwise meets the substantial presence test must file a statement to explain the basis of the individual's claim that he or she is able to satisfy the closer connection exception described in § 301.7701(b)-2.

(2) Exempt individuals and individuals with a medical condition.—An alien individual must file a statement to explain the basis of the individual's claim that he or she is able to exclude days of presence in the United States because the individual—

(i) Is an exempt individual as described in § 301.7701(b)-3(b)(3) (teacher/trainee) or (b)(4) (student);

(ii) Is an exempt individual described in § 301.7701(b)-3(b)(5) (professional athlete); or

(iii) Has a medical condition or problem as described in § 301.7701(b)-3(c).

(3) De minimis presence and residency starting and termination dates.—A statement must be filed by an individual who is seeking to establish—

(i) That a period of de minimis presence of ten or fewer days should be disregarded for purposes of the individual's residency starting or termination date; or

(ii) A residency termination date.

(b) Contents of statement.—(1) Closer connection exception.—(i) Returns due after December 15, 1997.—The statement filed by an individual described in paragraph (a)(1) of this section, for a return relating to a taxable year for which the due date (without extensions) is after December 15, 1997, must be in the form of a fully completed Form 8840 (Closer Connection Exception Statement) or appropriate successor form.

(ii) Earlier returns.—For returns relating to taxable years for which the due date for filing returns (without extensions) is on or before December 15, 1997, the statement filed by the individual described in paragraph (a)(1) of this section must contain the information in accordance with paragraph (b)(1) of this section in effect prior to December 15, 1997 (see § 301.7701(b)-8(b)(1) as contained in 26 CFR Part 301, revised April 1, 1997).

(2) Exempt individuals and individuals with a medical condition.—(i) Returns due after December 15, 1997.—The statement filed by an individual described in paragraph (a)(2) of this section, for a

return relating to a taxable year for which the due date (without extensions) is after December 15, 1997, must be in the form of a fully completed Form 8843 (Statement for Exempt Individuals and Individuals with a Medical Condition) or appropriate successor form.

(ii) Earlier returns.—For returns relating to taxable years for which the due date for filing returns (without extensions) is on or before December 15, 1997, the statement filed by the individual described in paragraph (a)(2) of this section must contain the information in accordance with paragraph (b)(2) of this section in effect prior to December 15, 1997 (see § 301.7701(b)-8(b)(2) as contained in 26 CFR Part 301, revised April 1, 1997).

(3) De minimis presence and residency starting and termination dates.—The statement filed by an individual described in paragraph (a)(3) of this section shall be dated, signed by the individual seeking to exclude de minimis presence for purposes of the individual's residency starting or termination date or to establish a residency termination date, and verified by a declaration that the statement is made under the penalty of perjury. The statement shall contain the information described in paragraphs (b)(1)(i), (ii) and (iii) of this section and the following information (as applicable)—

(i) The first day that the individual was present in the United States during the current year;

(ii) The last day that the individual was present in the United States during the current year;

(iii) Dates of de minimis presence that the individual is seeking to exclude from his or her residency starting or termination dates;

(iv) Sufficient facts to establish that the individual has maintained his or her tax home in and a closer connection to a foreign country during a period of de minimis presence;

(v) Sufficient facts to establish that the individual has maintained his or her tax home in and a closer connection to a foreign country following the individual's last day of presence in the United States during the current year or following the abandonment or rescission of the individual's status as a lawful permanent resident during the current year;

(vi) Date that the individual's status as a lawful permanent resident was abandoned or rescinded; and

(vii) Sufficient facts (including copies of relevant documents) to establish that the individual's status as lawful permanent resident has been abandoned or rescinded.

(c) How to file.—Individuals described in paragraph (a) of this section who are required to make a return on Form 1040 or 1040NR pursuant to paragraph (a) or (b) of § 1.6012-1 of this chapter must attach the statement described in paragraph (b) of this section to their return for the taxable year for which the statement is relevant. An individual who is not required to file either

Form 1040 or 1040NR must file the statement with the Internal Revenue Service Center, Philadelphia, PA 19255 on or before the date prescribed by law (including extensions) for making an income tax return as a nonresident for the calendar year for which the statement applies. The statement may be signed and filed for the taxpayer by the taxpayer's agent in accordance with § 1.6061-1 of this chapter.

(d) *Penalty for failure to file statement.*—(1) *General rule.*—If an individual is required to file a statement pursuant to paragraph (a)(1), (a)(2)(ii), (a)(2)(iii) or (a)(3) of this section and fails to file such statement on or before the date prescribed by paragraph (c) of this section, the individual will not be eligible for the closer connection exception described in § 301.7701(b)-2 and will be required to include all days of presence in the United States (calculated without the benefit of §§ 301.7701(b)-3(b)(5), 301.7701(b)-3(c), and 301.7701(b)-4(c)(1)) for purposes of the substantial presence test and for determining the individual's residency starting and termination dates. If an individual is considered to be a resident because of this paragraph and the individual is also a resident of a country with which the United States has an income tax convention pursuant to that convention, the individual shall be treated in the manner provided in § 301.7701(b)-7(a) (relating to the treatment of individuals who are dual residents).

(2) *Exception.*—The penalty described in paragraph (d)(1) of this section shall not apply if the individual can show by clear and convincing evidence that he or she took reasonable actions to become aware of the filing requirements and significant affirmative steps to comply with those requirements.

(e) *Filing requirement disregarded.*—Notwithstanding paragraph (d) of this section, the Secretary or his or her delegate may in their sole discretion, when it is in the best interest of the government to do so and based on all of the facts and circumstances, disregard the individual's failure to file timely the statement described in paragraph (a) of this section in determining the individual's days of presence in the United States. [Reg. § 301.7701(b)-8.]

☐ [*T.D.* 8411, 4-24-92. *Amended by T.D.* 8733, 10-6-97.]

[Reg. § 301.7701(b)-9]

§ 301.7701(b)-9. Effective/applicability dates of §§ 301.7701(b)-1 through 301.7701(b)-7.— (a) *In general.*—Except as indicated in paragraph (b) of this section, §§ 301.7701(b)-1 through 301.7701(b)-7 apply to taxable years beginning after December 31, 1984. For the rules applicable to earlier taxable years, see §§ 1.871-2 through 1.871-5 of this chapter.

(b) *Special rules.*—(1) *Green card test-residency starting date.*—If an alien was a lawful permanent resident throughout 1984 (regardless of whether the individual was physically present in the United States), or was physically present in the United States at any time during 1984 while a lawful permanent resident, the individual will be considered to have been a resident of the United States during 1984 for purposes of applying the provisions of section 7701(b)(2)(A) and § 301.7701(b)-4 such that the individual will, if he meets the substantial presence or green card test in 1985, be considered a resident of the United States as of January 1, 1985, regardless of when the individual was first present in the United States in 1985.

(2) *Substantial presence test-years included.*— For purposes of applying the substantial presence test for calendar years 1985 and 1986, days of presence in 1984 will only be counted for aliens who had been residents under prior law (§§ 1.871-2 through 1.871-5 of this chapter) at the end of calendar year 1984. Days of presence in 1983 will only be counted for aliens who had been residents under prior law at the end of both calendar year 1983 and 1984.

(3) *Professional athletes.*—For purposes of applying the substantial presence test, only days of presence in the United States after October 22, 1986, shall be excluded for individuals described in § 301.7701(b)-3(b)(5) (professional athletes).

(4) *Procedural rules and filing requirements.*— The procedural rules and filing requirements described in §§ 301.7701(b)-7(b) and 301.7701(b)-8 shall apply to taxable years beginning after December 31, 1991.

(5) *Possessions and territories.*—For purposes of applying section 7701(b) and the regulations under that section, § 301.7701(b)-1(d) applies to taxable years ending after April 9, 2008. [Reg. § 301.7701(b)-9.]

☐ [*T.D.* 8411, 4-24-92. *Amended by T.D.* 9391, 4-4-2008.]

[Reg. § 301.7701(i)-0]

§ 301.7701(i)-0. Outline of taxable mortgage pool provisions.—
This section lists the major paragraphs contained in §§ 301.7701(i)-1 through 301.7701(i)-4.

§ 301.7701(i)-1. Definition of a taxable mortgage pool.

(a) Purpose.

(b) In general.

(c) Asset composition tests.

   (1) Determination of amount of assets.

   (2) Substantially all.

      (i) In general.

      (ii) Safe harbor.

   (3) Equity interests in pass-through arrangements.

   (4) Treatment of certain credit enhancement contracts.

      (i) In general.

      (ii) Credit enhancement contract defined.

   (5) Certain assets not treated as debt obligations.

      (i) In general.

(ii) Safe harbor.
(A) In general.
(B) Payments with respect to a mortgage defined.
(C) Entity treated as not anticipating payments.
(d) Real estate mortgages or interests therein defined.
(1) In general.
(2) Interests in real property and real property defined.
(i) In general.
(ii) Manufactured housing.
(3) Principally secured by an interest in real property.
(i) Tests for determining whether an obligation is principally secured.
(A) The 80 percent test.
(B) Alternative test.
(ii) Obligations secured by real estate mortgages (or interests therein), or by combinations of real estate mortgages (or interests therein) and other assets.
(A) In general.
(B) Example.
(e) Two or more maturities.
(1) In general.
(2) Obligations that are allocated credit risk unequally.
(3) Examples.
(f) Relationship test.
(1) In general.
(2) Payments on asset obligations defined.
(3) Safe harbor for entities formed to liquidate assets.
(g) Anti-avoidance rules.
(1) In general.
(2) Certain investment trusts.
(3) Examples.

§ 301.7701(i)-2. Special rules for portions of entities.
(a) Portion defined.
(b) Certain assets and rights to assets disregarded.
(1) Credit enhancement assets.
(2) Assets unlikely to service obligations.
(3) Recourse.
(c) Portion as obligor.
(1) In general.
(2) Example.

§ 301.7701(i)-3. Effective dates and duration of taxable mortgage pool classification.
(a) Effective dates.
(b) Entities in existence on December 31, 1991.
(1) In general.
(2) Special rule for certain transfers.
(3) Related debt obligation.
(4) Example.
(c) Duration of taxable mortgage pool classification.

(1) Commencement and duration.
(2) Testing day defined.

§ 301.7701(i)-4. Special rules for certain entities.
(a) States and municipalities.
(1) In general.
(2) Governmental purpose.
(3) Determinations by the Commissioner.
(b) REITs. [Reserved]
(c) Subchapter S corporations.
(1) In general.
(2) Portion of an S corporation treated as a separate corporation.
[Reg. § 301.7701(i)-0.]

□ [T.D. 8610, 8-4-95.]

[Reg. § 301.7701(i)-1]

§ 301.7701(i)-1. Definition of a taxable mortgage pool.—(a) *Purpose.*—This section provides rules for applying section 7701(i), which defines taxable mortgage pools. The purpose of section 7701(i) is to prevent income generated by a pool of real estate mortgages from escaping Federal income taxation when the pool is used to issue multiple class mortgage-backed securities. The regulations in this section and in § § 301.7701(i)-2 through 301.7701(i)-4 are to be applied in accordance with this purpose. The taxable mortgage pool provisions apply to entities or portions of entities that qualify for REMIC status but do not elect to be taxed as REMICs as well as to certain entities or portions of entities that do not qualify for REMIC status.

(b) *In general.*—(1) A taxable mortgage pool is any entity or portion of an entity (as defined in § 301.7701(i)-2) that satisfies the requirements of section 7701(i)(2)(A) and this section as of any testing day (as defined in § 301.7701(i)-3(c)(2)). An entity or portion of an entity satisfies the requirements of section 7701(i)(2)(A) and this section if substantially all of its assets are debt obligations, more than 50 percent of those debt obligations are real estate mortgages, the entity is the obligor under debt obligations with two or more maturities, and payments on the debt obligations under which the entity is obligor bear a relationship to payments on the debt obligations that the entity holds as assets.

(2) Paragraph (c) of this section provides the tests for determining whether substantially all of an entity's assets are debt obligations and for determining whether more than 50 percent of its debt obligations are real estate mortgages. Paragraph (d) of this section defines real estate mortgages for purposes of the 50 percent test. Paragraph (e) of this section defines two or more maturities and paragraph (f) of this section provides rules for determining whether debt obligations bear a relationship to the assets held by an entity. Paragraph (g) of this section provides anti-avoidance rules. Section 301.7701(i)-2 provides rules for applying section 7701(i) to portions of entities and § 301.7701(i)-3 provides effective dates. Section 301.7701(i)-4 provides special rules for certain entities. For purposes of the regulations under section 7701(i), the term

entity includes a portion of an entity (within the meaning of section 7701(i)(2)(B)), unless the context clearly indicates otherwise.

(c) *Asset composition tests.*—(1) *Determination of amount of assets.*—An entity must use the Federal income tax basis of an asset for purposes of determining whether substantially all of its assets consist of debt obligations (or interests therein) and whether more than 50 percent of those debt obligations (or interests) consist of real estate mortgages (or interests therein). For purposes of this paragraph, an entity determines the basis of an asset with the assumption that the entity is not a taxable mortgage pool.

(2) *Substantially all.*—(i) *In general.*—Whether substantially all of the assets of an entity consist of debt obligations (or interests therein) is based on all the facts and circumstances.

(ii) *Safe harbor.*—Notwithstanding paragraph (c)(2)(i) of this section, if less than 80 percent of the assets of an entity consist of debt obligations (or interests therein), then less than substantially all of the assets of the entity consist of debt obligations (or interests therein).

(3) *Equity interests in pass-through arrangements.*—The equity interest of an entity in a partnership, S corporation, trust, REIT, or other pass-through arrangement is deemed to have the same composition as the entity's share of the assets of the pass-through arrangement. For example, if an entity's stock interest in a REIT has an adjusted basis of $20,000, and the assets of the REIT consist of equal portions of real estate mortgages and other real estate assets, then the entity is treated as holding $10,000 of real estate mortgages and $10,000 of other real estate assets.

(4) *Treatment of certain credit enhancement contracts.*—(i) *In general.*—A credit enhancement contract (as defined in paragraph (c)(4)(ii) of this section) is not treated as a separate asset of an entity for purposes of the asset composition tests set forth in section 7701(i)(2)(A)(i), but instead is treated as part of the asset to which it relates. Furthermore, any collateral supporting a credit enhancement contract is not treated as an asset of an entity solely because it supports the guarantee represented by that contract.

(ii) *Credit enhancement contract defined.*—For purposes of this section, a credit enhancement contract is any arrangement whereby a person agrees to guarantee full or partial payment of the principal or interest payable on a debt obligation (or interest therein) or on a pool of such obligations (or interests), or full or partial payment on one or more classes of debt obligations under which an entity is the obligor, in the event of defaults or delinquencies on debt obligations, unanticipated losses or expenses incurred by the entity, or lower than expected returns on investments. Types of credit enhancement contracts may include, but are not limited to, pool insurance contracts, certificate guarantee

insurance contracts, letters of credit, guarantees, or agreements whereby an entity, a mortgage servicer, or other third party agrees to make advances (regardless of whether, under the terms of the agreement, the payor is obligated, or merely permitted, to make those advances). An agreement by a debt servicer to advance to an entity out of its own funds an amount to make up for delinquent payments on debt obligations is a credit enhancement contract. An agreement by a debt servicer to pay taxes and hazard insurance premiums on property securing a debt obligation, or other expenses incurred to protect an entity's security interests in the collateral in the event that the debtor fails to pay such taxes, insurance premiums, or other expenses, is a credit enhancement contract.

(5) *Certain assets not treated as debt obligations.*—(i) *In general.*—For purposes of section 7701(i)(2)(A), real estate mortgages that are seriously impaired are not treated as debt obligations. Whether a mortgage is seriously impaired is based on all the facts and circumstances including, but not limited to: the number of days delinquent, the loan-to-value ratio, the debt service coverage (based upon the operating income from the property), and the debtor's financial position and stake in the property. However, except as provided in paragraph (c)(5)(ii) of this section, no single factor in and of itself is determinative of whether a loan is seriously impaired.

(ii) *Safe harbor.*—(A) *In general.*—Unless an entity is receiving or anticipates receiving payments with respect to a mortgage, a single family residential real estate mortgage is seriously impaired if payments on the mortgage are more than 89 days delinquent, and a multi-family residential or commercial real estate mortgage is seriously impaired if payments on the mortgage are more than 59 days delinquent. Whether an entity anticipates receiving payments with respect to a mortgage is based on all the facts and circumstances.

(B) *Payments with respect to a mortgage defined.*—For purposes of paragraph (c)(5)(ii)(A) of this section, payments with respect to a mortgage mean any payments on the mortgage as defined in paragraph (f)(2)(i) of this section if those payments are substantial and relatively certain as to amount and any payments on the mortgage as defined in paragraph (f)(2)(ii) or (iii) of this section.

(C) *Entity treated as not anticipating payments.*—With respect to any testing day (as defined in § 301.7701(i)-3(c)(2)), an entity is treated as not having anticipated receiving payments on the mortgage as defined in paragraph (f)(2)(i) of this section if 180 days after the testing day, and despite making reasonable efforts to resolve the mortgage, the entity is not receiving such payments and has not entered into any agreement to receive such payments.

(d) *Real estate mortgages or interests therein defined.*—(1) *In general.*—For purposes of section

Reg. § 301.7701(i)-1(d)(1)

7701(i)(2)(A)(i), the term real estate mortgages (or interests therein) includes all—

(i) Obligations (including participations or certificates of beneficial ownership therein) that are principally secured by an interest in real property (as defined in paragraph (d)(3) of this section);

(ii) Regular and residual interests in a REMIC; and

(iii) Stripped bonds and stripped coupons (as defined in section 1286(e)(2) and (3)) if the bonds (as defined in section 1286(e)(1)) from which such stripped bonds or stripped coupons arose would have qualified as real estate mortgages or interests therein.

(2) *Interests in real property and real property defined.*—(i) *In general.*—The definition of interests in real property set forth in § 1.856-3(c) of this chapter and the definition of real property set forth in § 1.856-3(d) of this chapter apply to define those terms for purposes of paragraph (d) of this section.

(ii) *Manufactured housing.*—For purposes of this section, the definition of real property includes manufactured housing, provided the properties qualify as single family residences under section 25(e)(10) and without regard to the treatment of the properties under state law.

(3) *Principally secured by an interest in real property.*—(i) *Tests for determining whether an obligation is principally secured.*—For purposes of paragraph (d)(1) of this section, an obligation is principally secured by an interest in real property only if it satisfies either the test set out in paragraph (d)(3)(i)(A) of this section or the test set out in paragraph (d)(3)(i)(B) of this section.

(A) *The 80 percent test.*—An obligation is principally secured by an interest in real property if the fair market value of the interest in real property (as defined in paragraph (d)(2) of this section) securing the obligation was at least equal to 80 percent of the adjusted issue price of the obligation at the time the obligation was originated (that is, the issue date). For purposes of this test, the fair market value of the real property interest is first reduced by the amount of any lien on the real property interest that is senior to the obligation being tested, and is reduced further by a proportionate amount of any lien that is in parity with the obligation being tested.

(B) *Alternative test.*—An obligation is principally secured by an interest in real property if substantially all of the proceeds of the obligation were used to acquire, improve, or protect an interest in real property that, at the origination date, is the only security for the obligation. For purposes of this test, loan guarantees made by Federal, state, local governments or agencies, or other third party credit enhancement, are not viewed as additional security for a loan. An obligation is not considered to be secured by property other than real property solely because the obligor is personally liable on the obligation.

(ii) *Obligations secured by real estate mortgages (or interests therein), or by combinations of real estate mortgages (or interests therein) and other assets.*—(A) *In general.*—An obligation secured only by real estate mortgages (or interests therein), as defined in paragraph (d)(1) of this section, is treated as an obligation secured by an interest in real property to the extent of the value of the real estate mortgages (or interests therein). An obligation secured by both real estate mortgages (or interests therein) and other assets is treated as an obligation secured by an interest in real property to the extent of both the value of the real estate mortgages (or interests therein) and the value of so much of the other assets that constitute real property. Thus, under this paragraph, a collateralized mortgage obligation may be an obligation principally secured by an interest in real property. This section is applicable only to obligations issued after December 31, 1991.

(B) *Example.*—The following example illustrates the principles of this paragraph (d)(3)(ii):

Example. At the time it is originated, an obligation has an adjusted issue price of $300,000 and is secured by a $70,000 loan principally secured by an interest in a single family home, a fifty percent co-ownership interest in a $400,000 parcel of land, and $80,000 of stock. Under paragraph (d)(3)(ii)(A) of this section, the obligation is treated as secured by interests in real property and under paragraph (d)(3)(i)(A) of this section, the obligation is treated as principally secured by interests in real property.

(e) *Two or more maturities.*—(1) *In general.*—For purposes of section 7701(i)(2)(A)(ii), debt obligations have two or more maturities if they have different stated maturities or if the holders of the obligations possess different rights concerning the acceleration of or delay in the maturities of the obligations.

(2) *Obligations that are allocated credit risk unequally.*—Debt obligations that are allocated credit risk unequally do not have, by that reason alone, two or more maturities. Credit risk is the risk that payments of principal or interest will be reduced or delayed because of a default on an asset that supports the debt obligations.

(3) *Examples.*—The following examples illustrate the principles of this paragraph (e):

Example 1. (i) Corporation M transfers a pool of real estate mortgages to a trustee in exchange for Class A bonds and a certificate representing the residual beneficial ownership of the pool. All Class A bonds have a stated maturity of March 1, 2002, but if cash flows from the real estate mortgages and investments are sufficient, the trustee may select one or more bonds at random and redeem them earlier.

(ii) The Class A bonds do not have different maturities. Each outstanding Class A bond has an equal chance of being redeemed because the selection process is random. The holders of the Class A bonds, therefore, have identical rights concerning the maturities of their obligations.

Example 2. (i) Corporation N transfers a pool of real estate mortgages to a trustee in exchange for Class C bonds, Class D bonds, and a certificate representing the residual beneficial ownership of the pool. The Class D bonds are subordinate to the Class C bonds so that cash flow shortfalls due to defaults or delinquencies on the real estate mortgages are borne first by the Class D bond holders. The terms of the bonds are otherwise identical in all relevant aspects except that the Class D bonds carry a higher coupon rate because of the subordination feature.

(ii) The Class C bonds and the Class D bonds share credit risk unequally because of the subordination feature. However, neither this difference, nor the difference in interest rates, causes the bonds to have different maturities. The result is the same if, in addition to the other terms described in paragraph (i) of this *Example 2*, the Class C bonds are accelerated as a result of the issuer becoming unable to make payments on the Class C bonds as they become due.

(f) *Relationship test.*—(1) *In general.*—For purposes of section 7701(i)(2)(A)(iii), payments on debt obligations under which an entity is the obligor (liability obligations) bear a relationship to payments (as defined in paragraph (f)(2) of this section) on debt obligations an entity holds as assets (asset obligations) if under the terms of the liability obligations (or underlying arrangement) the timing and amount of payments on the liability obligations are in large part determined by the timing and amount of payments or projected payments on the asset obligations. For purposes of the relationship test, any payment arrangement, including a swap or other hedge, that achieves a substantially similar result is treated as satisfying the test. For example, any arrangement where the timing and amount of payments on liability obligations are determined by reference to a group of assets (or an index or other type of model) that has an expected payment experience similar to that of the asset obligations is treated as satisfying the relationship test.

(2) *Payments on asset obligations defined.*—For purposes of section 7701(i)(2)(A)(iii) and this section, payments on asset obligations include—

(i) A payment of principal or interest on an asset obligation, including a prepayment of principal, a payment under a credit enhancement contract (as defined in paragraph (c)(4)(ii) of this section) and a payment from a settlement at a discount (other than a substantial discount);

(ii) A payment from a settlement at a substantial discount, but only if the settlement is arranged, whether in writing or otherwise, prior to the issuance of the liability obligations; and

(iii) A payment from the foreclosure on or sale of an asset obligation, but only if the foreclo-

sure or sale is arranged, whether in writing or otherwise, prior to the issuance of the liability obligations.

(3) *Safe harbor for entities formed to liquidate assets.*—Payments on liability obligations of an entity do not bear a relationship to payments on asset obligations of the entity if—

(i) The entity's organizational documents manifest clearly that the entity is formed for the primary purpose of liquidating its assets and distributing proceeds of liquidation;

(ii) The entity's activities are all reasonably necessary to and consistent with the accomplishment of liquidating assets;

(iii) The entity plans to satisfy at least 50 percent of the total issue price of each of its liability obligations having a different maturity with proceeds from liquidation and not with scheduled payments on its asset obligations; and

(iv) The terms of the entity's liability obligations (or underlying arrangement) provide that within three years of the time it first acquires assets to be liquidated the entity either—

(A) Liquidates; or

(B) Begins to pass through without delay all payments it receives on its asset obligations (less reasonable allowances for expenses) as principal payments on its liability obligations in proportion to the adjusted issue prices of the liability obligations.

(g) *Anti-avoidance rules.*—(1) *In general.*—For purposes of determining whether an entity meets the definition of a taxable mortgage pool, the Commissioner can disregard or make other adjustments to a transaction (or series of transactions) if the transaction (or series) is entered into with a view to achieving the same economic effect as that of an arrangement subject to section 7701(i) while avoiding the application of that section. The Commissioner's authority includes treating equity interests issued by a non-REMIC as debt if the entity issues equity interests that correspond to maturity classes of debt.

(2) *Certain investment trusts.*—Notwithstanding paragraph (g)(1) of this section, an ownership interest in an entity that is classified as a trust under § 301.7701-4(c) will not be treated as a debt obligation of the trust.

(3) *Examples.*—The following examples illustrate the principles of this paragraph (g):

Example 1. (i) Partnership P, in addition to its other investments, owns $10,000,000 of mortgage pass-through certificates guaranteed by FNMA (FNMA Certificates). On May 15, 1997, Partnership P transfers the FNMA Certificates to Trust 1 in exchange for 100 Class A bonds and Certificate 1. The Class A bonds, under which Trust 1 is the obligor, have a stated principal amount of $5,000,000 and bear a relationship to the FNMA Certificates (within the meaning of § 301.7701(i)-1(f)). Certificate 1 represents the residual beneficial ownership of the FNMA Certificates.

Reg. § 301.7701(i)-1(g)(3)

(ii) On July 5, 1997, with a view to avoiding the application of section 7701(i), Partnership P transfers Certificate 1 to Trust 2 in exchange for 100 Class B bonds and Certificate 2. The Class B bonds, under which Trust 2 is the obligor, have a stated principal amount of $5,000,000, bear a relationship to the FNMA Certificates (within the meaning of §301.7701(i)-1(f)), and have a different maturity than the Class A bonds (within the meaning of §301.7701(i)-1(e)). Certificate 2 represents the residual beneficial ownership of Certificate 1.

(iii) For purposes of determining whether Trust 1 is classified as a taxable mortgage pool, the Commissioner can disregard the separate existence of Trust 2 and treat Trust 1 and Trust 2 as a single trust.

Example 2. (i) Corporation Q files a consolidated return with its two wholly-owned subsidiaries, Corporation R and Corporation S. Corporation R is in the business of building and selling single family homes. Corporation S is in the business of financing sales of those homes.

(ii) On August 10, 1998, Corporation S transfers a pool of its real estate mortgages to Trust 3, taking back Certificate 3 which represents beneficial ownership of the pool. On September 25, 1998, with a view to avoiding the application of section 7701(i), Corporation R issues bonds that have different maturities (within the meaning of §301.7701(i)-1(e)) and that bear a relationship (within the meaning of §301.7701(i)-1(f)) to the real estate mortgages in Trust 3. The holders of the bonds have an interest in a credit enhancement contract that is written by Corporation S and collateralized with Certificate 3.

(iii) For purposes of determining whether Trust 3 is classified as a taxable mortgage pool, the Commissioner can treat Trust 3 as the obligor of the bonds issued by Corporation R.

Example 3. (i) Corporation X, in addition to its other assets, owns $110,000,000 in Treasury securities. From time to time, Corporation X acquires pools of real estate mortgages, which it immediately uses to issue multiple-class debt obligations.

(ii) On October 1, 1996, Corporation X transfers $20,000,000 in Treasury securities to Trust 4 in exchange for Class C bonds, Class D bonds, Class E bonds, and Certificate 4. Trust 4 is the obligor of the bonds. The different classes of bonds have the same stated maturity date, but if cash flows from the Trust 4 assets exceed the amounts needed to make interest payments, the trustee uses the excess to retire the classes of bonds in alphabetical order. Certificate 4 represents the residual beneficial ownership of the Treasury securities.

(iii) With a view to avoiding the application of section 7701(i), Corporation X reserves the right to replace any Trust 4 asset with real estate mortgages or guaranteed mortgage pass-through certificates. In the event the right is exercised, cash flows on the real estate mortgages and guaranteed pass-through certificates will be used in the same manner as cash flows on the Trea-

sury securities. Corporation X exercises this right of replacement on February 1, 1997.

(iv) For purposes of determining whether Trust 4 is classified as a taxable mortgage pool, the Commissioner can treat February 1, 1997, as a testing day (within the meaning of §301.7701(i)-3(c)(2)). The result is the same if Corporation X has an obligation, rather than a right, to replace the Trust 4 assets with real estate mortgages and guaranteed pass-through certificates.

Example 4. (i) Corporation Y, in addition to its other assets, owns $1,900,000 in obligations secured by personal property. On November 1, 1995, Corporation Y begins negotiating a $2,000,000 loan to individual A. As security for the loan, A offers a first deed of trust on land worth $1,700,000.

(ii) With a view to avoiding the application of section 7701(i), Corporation Y induces A to place the land in a partnership in which A will have a 95 percent interest and agrees to accept the partnership interest as security for the $2,000,000 loan. Thereafter, the loan to A, together with the $1,900,000 in obligations secured by personal property, are transferred to Trust 5 and used to issue bonds that have different maturities (within the meaning of §301.7701(i)-1(e)) and that bear a relationship (within the meaning of §301.7701(i)-1(f)) to the $1,900,000 in obligations secured by personal property and the loan to A.

(iii) For purposes of determining whether Trust 5 is a taxable mortgage pool, the Commissioner can treat the loan to A as an obligation secured by an interest in real property rather than as an obligation secured by an interest in a partnership.

Example 5. (i) Corporation Z, in addition to its other assets, owns $3,000,000 in notes secured by interests in retail shopping centers. Partnership L, in addition to its other assets, owns $20,000,000 in notes that are principally secured by interests in single family homes and $3,500,000 in notes that are principally secured by interests in personal property.

(ii) On December 1, 1995, Partnership L asks Corporation Z for two separate loans, one in the amount of $9,375,000 and another in the amount of $625,000. Partnership L offers to collateralize the $9,375,000 loan with $10,312,500 of notes secured by interests in single family homes and the $625,000 loan with $750,000 of notes secured by interests in personal property. Corporation Z has made similar loans to Partnership L in the past.

(iii) With a view to avoiding the application of section 7701(i), Corporation Z induces Partnership L to accept a single $10,000,000 loan and to post as collateral $7,500,000 of the notes secured by interests in single family homes and all $3,500,000 of the notes secured by interests in personal property. Ordinarily, Corporation Z would not make a loan on these terms. Thereafter, the loan to Partnership L, together with the $3,000,000 in notes secured by interests in retail shopping centers, are transferred to Trust 6 and used to issue bonds that have different maturities (within the meaning of §301.7701(i)-1(e)) and that bear a relationship (within the meaning of §301.7701(i)-1(f)) to the loans secured by interests in retail shopping centers and the loan to Partnership L.

(iv) For purposes of determining whether Trust 6 is a taxable mortgage pool, the Commissioner can treat the $10,000,000 loan to Partnership L as consisting of a $9,375,000 obligation secured by interests in real property and a $625,000 obligation secured by interests in personal property. Under §301.7701(i)-1(d)(3)(ii)(A), the notes secured by single family homes are treated as $7,500,000 of interests in real property. Under §301.7701(i)-1(d)(3)(i)(A), $7,500,000 of interests in real property are sufficient to treat a $9,375,000 obligation as principally secured by an interest in real property ($7,500,000 equals 80 percent of $9,375,000). [Reg. §301.7701(i)-1.]

☐ [T.D. 8610, 8-4-95.]

[Reg. §301.7701(i)-2]

§301.7701(i)-2. Special rules for portions of entities.—(a) *Portion defined.*—Except as provided in paragraph (b) of this section and §301.7701(i)-1, a portion of an entity includes all assets that support one or more of the same issues of debt obligations. For this purpose, an asset supports a debt obligation if, under the terms of the debt obligation (or underlying arrangement), the timing and amount of payments on the debt obligation are in large part determined, either directly or indirectly, by the timing and amount of payments or projected payments on the asset or a group of assets that includes the asset. Indirect payment arrangements include, for example, a swap or other hedge, or arrangements where the timing and amount of payments on the debt obligations are determined by reference to a group of assets (or an index or other type of model) that has an expected payment experience similar to that of the assets. For purposes of this paragraph, the term payments includes all proceeds and receipts from an asset.

(b) *Certain assets and rights to assets disregarded.*—(1) *Credit enhancement assets.*—An asset that qualifies as a credit enhancement contract (as defined in §301.7701(i)-1(c)(4)(ii)) is not included in a portion as a separate asset, but is treated as part of the assets in the portion to which it relates under §301.7701(i)-1(c)(4)(i). An asset that does not qualify as a credit enhancement contract (as defined in §301.7701(i)-1(c)(4)(ii)), but that nevertheless serves the same function as a credit enhancement contract, is not included in a portion as a separate asset or otherwise.

(2) *Assets unlikely to service obligations.*—A portion does not include assets that are unlikely to produce any significant cash flows for the holders of the debt obligations. This paragraph applies even if the holders of the debt obligations are legally entitled to cash flows from the assets. Thus, for example, even if the sale of a

building would cause a series of debt obligations to be redeemed, the building is not included in a portion if it is not likely to be sold.

(3) *Recourse.*—An asset is not included in a portion solely because the holders of the debt obligations have recourse to the holder of that asset.

(c) *Portion as obligor.*—(1) *In general.*—For purposes of section 7701(i)(2)(A)(ii), a portion of an entity is treated as the obligor of all debt obligations supported by the assets in that portion.

(2) *Example.*—The following example illustrates the principles of this section:

Example. (i) Corporation Z owns $1,000,000,000 in assets including an office complex and $90,000,000 of real estate mortgages.

(ii) On November 30, 1998, Corporation Z issues eight classes of bonds, Class A through Class H. Each class is secured by a separate letter of credit and by a lien on the office complex. One group of the real estate mortgages supports Class A through Class D, another group supports Class E through Class G, and a third group supports Class H. It is anticipated that the cash flows from each group of mortgages will service its related bonds.

(iii) Each of the following constitutes a separate portion of Corporation Z: the group of mortgages supporting Class A through Class D; the group of mortgages supporting Class E through Class G; and the group of mortgages supporting Class H. No other asset is included in any of the three portions notwithstanding the lien of the bonds on the office complex and the fact that Corporation Z is the issuer of the bonds. The letters of credit are treated as incidents of the mortgages to which they relate.

(iv) For purposes of section 7701(i)(2)(A)(ii), each portion described above is treated as the obligor of the bonds of that portion, notwithstanding the fact that Corporation Z is the legal obligor with respect to the bonds. [Reg. §301.7701(i)-2.]

☐ [T.D. 8610, 8-4-95.]

[Reg. §301.7701(i)-3]

§301.7701(i)-3. Effective dates and duration of taxable mortgage pool classification.—(a) *Effective dates.*—Except as otherwise provided, the regulations under section 7701(i) are effective and applicable September 6, 1995.

(b) *Entities in existence on December 31, 1991.*—(1) *In general.*—For transitional rules concerning the application of section 7701(i) to entities in existence on December 31, 1991, see section 675(c) of the Tax Reform Act of 1986.

(2) *Special rule for certain transfers.*—A transfer made to an entity on or after September 6, 1995, is a substantial transfer for purposes of section 675(c)(2) of the Tax Reform Act of 1986 only if—

(i) The transfer is significant in amount; and

(ii) The transfer is connected to the entity's issuance of related debt obligations (as defined in paragraph (b)(3) of this section) that have different maturities (within the meaning of § 301.7701-1(e)).

(3) *Related debt obligation.*—A related debt obligation is a debt obligation whose payments bear a relationship (within the meaning of § 301.7701-1(f)) to payments on debt obligations that the entity holds as assets.

(4) *Example.*—The following example illustrates the principles of this paragraph (b):

Example. On December 31, 1991, Partnership Q holds a pool of real estate mortgages that it acquired through retail sales of single family homes. Partnership Q raises $10,000,000 on October 25, 1996, by using this pool to issue related debt obligations with multiple maturities. The transfer of the $10,000,000 to Partnership Q is a substantial transfer (within the meaning of § 301.7701(i)-3(b)(2)).

(c) *Duration of taxable mortgage pool classification.*—(1) *Commencement and duration.*—An entity is classified as a taxable mortgage pool on the first testing day that it meets the definition of a taxable mortgage pool. Once an entity is classified as a taxable mortgage pool, that classification continues through the day the entity retires its last related debt obligation.

(2) *Testing day defined.*—A testing day is any day on or after September 6, 1995, on which an entity issues a related debt obligation (as defined in paragraph (b)(3) of this section) that is significant in amount. [Reg. § 301.7701(i)-3.]

☐ [*T.D.* 8610, 8-4-95.]

[Reg. § 301.7701(i)-4]

§ 301.7701(i)-4. Special rules for certain entities.—(a) *States and municipalities.*—(1) *In general.*—Regardless of whether an entity satisfies any of the requirements of section 7701(i)(2)(A), an entity is not classified as a taxable mortgage pool if—

(i) The entity is a State, territory, a possession of the United States, the District of Columbia, or any political subdivision thereof (within the meaning of § 1.1031(b) of this chapter), or is empowered to issue obligations on behalf of one of the foregoing;

(ii) The entity issues the debt obligations in the performance of a governmental purpose; and

(iii) The entity holds the remaining interests in all assets that support those debt obligations until the debt obligations issued by the entity are retired.

(2) *Governmental purpose.*—The term governmental purpose means an essential governmental function within the meaning of section 115. A governmental purpose does not include the mere packaging of debt obligations for resale on the secondary market even if any profits from the sale are used in the performance of an essential governmental function.

(3) *Determinations by the Commissioner.*—If an entity is not described in paragraph (a)(1) of this section, but has a similar purpose, then the Commissioner may determine that the entity is not classified as a taxable mortgage pool.

(b) *REITs.*—[Reserved]

(c) *Subchapter S corporations.*—(1) *In general.*—An entity that is classified as a taxable mortgage pool may not elect to be an S corporation under section 1362(a) or maintain S corporation status.

(2) *Portion of an S corporation treated as a separate corporation.*—An S corporation is not treated as a member of an affiliated group under section 1361(b)(2)(A) solely because a portion of the S corporation is treated as a separate corporation under section 7701(i). [Reg. § 301.7701(i)-4.]

☐ [*T.D.* 8610, 8-4-95.]

[Reg. § 1.7701(l)-0]

§ 1.7701(l)-0. Table of contents.—This section lists captions that appear in § § 1.7701(l)-1 and 1.7701(l)-3:

§ 1.7701(l)-1 Conduit financing arrangements.

§ 1.7701(l)-3 Recharacterizing financing arrangements involving fast-pay stock.

(a) Purpose and scope.

(b) Definitions.

(1) Fast-pay arrangement.

(2) Fast-pay stock.

(i) Defined.

(ii) Determination.

(3) Benefited stock.

(c) Recharacterization of certain fast-pay arrangements.

(1) Scope.

(2) Recharacterization.

(i) Relationship between benefited shareholders and fast-pay shareholders.

(ii) Relationship between benefited shareholders and corporation.

(iii) Relationship between fast-pay shareholders and corporation.

(3) Other rules.

(i) Character of the financing instruments.

(ii) Multiple types of benefited stock.

(iii) Transactions affecting benefited stock.

(A) Sale of benefited stock.

(B) Transactions other than sales.

(iv) Adjustment to basis for amounts accrued or paid in taxable years ending before February 27, 1997.

(d) Prohibition against affirmative use of recharacterization by taxpayers.

(e) Examples.

(f) Reporting requirement.

(1) Filing requirements.

(i) In general.

(ii) Controlled foreign corporation.

(iii) Foreign personal holding company.

(iv) Passive foreign investment company.

(2) Statement.

(g) Effective date.

(1) In general.

(2) Election to limit taxable income attributable to a recharacterized fast-pay arrangement for periods before April 1, 2000.

(i) Limit.

(ii) Adjustment and statement.

(iii) Examples.

(3) Rule to comply with this section.

(4) Reporting requirements.

[Reg. § 1.7701(l)-0.]

☐ [T.D. 8853, 1-7-2000.]

[Reg. § 1.7701(l)-1]

§ 1.7701(l)-1. Conduit financing arrangements.—Section 7701(l) authorizes the issuance of regulations that recharacterize any multiple-party financing transaction as a transaction directly among any two or more of such parties where the Secretary determines that such recharacterization is appropriate to prevent avoidance of any tax imposed by title 26 of the United States Code. [Reg. § 1.7701(l)-1.]

☐ [T.D. 8611, 8-10-95. Amended by T.D. 8735, 10-6-97.]

[Reg. § 1.7701(l)-3]

§ 1.7701(l)-3. Recharacterizing financing arrangements involving fast-pay stock.— (a) *Purpose and scope.*—This section is intended to prevent the avoidance of tax by persons participating in fast-pay arrangements (as defined in paragraph (b)(1) of this section) and should be interpreted in a manner consistent with this purpose. This section applies to all fast-pay arrangements. Paragraph (c) of this section recharacterizes certain fast-pay arrangements to ensure the participants are taxed in a manner reflecting the economic substance of the arrangements. Paragraph (f) of this section imposes reporting requirements on certain participants.

(b) *Definitions.*—(1) *Fast-pay arrangement.*—A fast-pay arrangement is any arrangement in which a corporation has fast-pay stock outstanding for any part of its taxable year.

(2) *Fast-pay stock.*—(i) *Defined.*—Stock is fast-pay stock if it is structured so that dividends (as defined in section 316) paid by the corporation with respect to the stock are economically (in whole or in part) a return of the holder's investment (as opposed to only a return on the holder's investment). Unless clearly demonstrated otherwise, stock is presumed to be fast-pay stock if—

(A) It is structured to have a dividend rate that is reasonably expected to decline (as opposed to a dividend rate that is reasonably expected to fluctuate or remain constant); or

(B) It is issued for an amount that exceeds (by more than a de minimis amount, as determined under the principles of § 1.1273-1(d)) the amount at which the holder can be compelled to dispose of the stock.

(ii) *Determination.*—The determination of whether stock is fast-pay stock is based on all the facts and circumstances, including any related agreements such as options or forward contracts. A related agreement includes any direct or indirect agreement or understanding, oral or written, between the holder of the stock and the issuing corporation, or between the holder of the stock and one or more other shareholders in the corporation. To determine if it is fast-pay stock, stock is examined when issued, and, for stock that is not fast-pay stock when issued, when there is a significant modification in the terms of the stock or the related agreements or a significant change in the relevant facts and circumstances. Stock is not fast-pay stock solely because a redemption is treated as a dividend as a result of section 302(d) unless there is a principal purpose of achieving the same economic and tax effect as a fast-pay arrangement.

(3) *Benefited stock.*—With respect to any fast-pay stock, all other stock in the corporation (including other fast-pay stock having any significantly different characteristics) is benefited stock.

(c) *Recharacterization of certain fast-pay arrangements.*—(1) *Scope.*—This paragraph (c) applies to any fast-pay arrangement—

(i) In which the corporation that has outstanding fast-pay stock is a regulated investment company (RIC) (as defined in section 851) or a real estate investment trust (REIT) (as defined in section 856); or

(ii) If the Commissioner determines that a principal purpose for the structure of the fast-pay arrangement is the avoidance of any tax imposed by the Internal Revenue Code. Application of this paragraph (c)(1)(ii) is at the Commissioner's discretion, and a determination under this paragraph (c)(1)(ii) applies to all parties to the fast-pay arrangement, including transferees.

(2) *Recharacterization.*—A fast-pay arrangement described in paragraph (c)(1) of this section is recharacterized as an arrangement directly between the benefited shareholders and the fast-pay shareholders. The inception and resulting relationships of the recharacterized arrangement are deemed to be as follows:

(i) *Relationship between benefited shareholders and fast-pay shareholders.*—The benefited shareholders issue financial instruments (the financing instruments) directly to the fast-pay shareholders in exchange for cash equal to the fair market value of the fast-pay stock at the time of issuance (taking into account any related agreements). The financing instruments have the same terms (other than issuer) as the fast-pay stock. Thus, for example, the timing and amount of the payments made with respect to the financing instruments always match the timing and amount of the distributions made with respect to the fast-pay stock.

(ii) *Relationship between benefited shareholders and corporation.*—The benefited shareholders contribute to the corporation the cash they receive for issuing the financing instruments. Distributions made with respect to the fast-pay stock are distributions made by the corporation with respect to the benefited shareholders' benefited stock.

(iii) *Relationship between fast-pay shareholders and corporation.*—For purposes of determining the relationship between the fast-pay shareholders and the corporation, the fast-pay stock is ignored. The corporation is the paying agent of the benefited shareholders with respect to the financing instruments.

(3) *Other rules.*—(i) *Character of the financing instruments.*—The character of a financing instrument (for example, stock or debt) is determined under general tax principles and depends on all the facts and circumstances.

(ii) *Multiple types of benefited stock.*—If any benefited stock has any significantly different characteristics from any other benefited stock, the recharacterization rules of this paragraph (c) apply among the different types of benefited stock as appropriate to match the economic substance of the fast-pay arrangement.

(iii) *Transactions affecting benefited stock.*—(A) *Sale of benefited stock.*—If one person sells benefited stock to another—

(1) In addition to any consideration actually paid and received for the benefited stock, the buyer is deemed to pay and the seller is deemed to receive the amount necessary to terminate the seller's position in the financing instruments at fair market value; and

(2) The buyer is deemed to issue financing instruments to the fast-pay shareholders in exchange for the amount necessary to terminate the seller's position in the financing instruments.

(B) *Transactions other than sales.*—Except for transactions subject to paragraph (c)(3)(iii)(A) of this section, in the case of any transaction affecting benefited stock, the parties to the transaction must make appropriate adjustments to properly take into account the fast-pay arrangement as characterized under paragraph (c)(2) of this section.

(iv) *Adjustment to basis for amounts accrued or paid in taxable years ending before February 27, 1997.*—In the case of a fast-pay arrangement involving amounts accrued or paid in taxable years ending before February 27, 1997, and recharacterized under this paragraph (c), a benefited shareholder must decrease its basis in any benefited stock (as determined under paragraph (c)(2)(ii) of this section) by the amount (if any) that—

(A) Its income attributable to the benefited stock (reduced by deductions attributable

to the financing instruments) for taxable years ending before February 27, 1997, computed by recharacterizing the fast-pay arrangement under this paragraph (c) and by treating the financing instruments as debt; exceeds

(B) Its income attributable to such stock for taxable years ending before February 27, 1997, computed without applying the rules of this paragraph (c).

(d) *Prohibition against affirmative use of recharacterization by taxpayers.*—A taxpayer may not use the rules of paragraph (c) of this section if a principal purpose for using such rules is the avoidance of any tax imposed by the Internal Revenue Code. Thus, with respect to such taxpayer, the Commissioner may depart from the rules of this section and recharacterize (for all purposes of the Internal Revenue Code) the fast-pay arrangement in accordance with its form or its economic substance. For example, if a foreign person acquires fast-pay stock in a REIT and a principal purpose for acquiring such stock is to reduce United States withholding taxes by applying the rules of paragraph (c) of this section, the Commissioner may, for purposes of determining the foreign person's United States tax consequences (including withholding tax), depart from the rules of paragraph (c) of this section and treat the foreign person as holding fast-pay stock in the REIT.

(e) *Examples.*—The following examples illustrate the rules of paragraph (c) of this section:

Example 1. Decline in dividend rate—(i) *Facts.* Corporation X issues 100 shares of A Stock and 100 shares of B Stock for $1,000 per share. By its terms, a share of B Stock is reasonably expected to pay a $110 dividend in years 1 through 10 and a $30 dividend each year thereafter. If X liquidates, the holder of a share of B Stock is entitled to a preference equal to the share's issue price. Otherwise, the B Stock cannot be redeemed at either X's or the shareholder's option.

(ii) *Analysis.* When issued, the B Stock has a dividend rate that is reasonably expected to decline from an annual rate of 11 percent of its issue price to an annual rate of 3 percent of its issue price. Since the B Stock is structured to have a declining dividend rate, the B Stock is fast-pay stock, and the A Stock is benefited stock.

Example 2. Issued at a premium—(i) *Facts.* The facts are the same as in *Example 1* of this paragraph (e) except that a share of B Stock is reasonably expected to pay an annual $110 dividend as long as it is outstanding, and Corporation X has the right to redeem the B Stock for $400 a share at the end of year 10.

(ii) *Analysis.* The B Stock is structured so that the issue price of the B Stock ($1,000) exceeds (by more than a de minimis amount) the price at which the holder can be compelled to dispose of the stock ($400). Thus, the B Stock is fast-pay stock, and the A Stock is benefited stock.

Example 3. Planned section 302(d) redemptions—(i) *Facts.* Corporation L, a subchapter C corporation, issues 220 shares of common stock for $1,000 per share. No other stock is authorized, but L can issue warrants entitling the holder to acquire L common stock for $3,000 per share until such time as L adopts a plan of liquidation. L can adopt a plan of liquidation if approved by 90 percent of its shareholders. Half of L's stock is purchased by Corporation M, and half by Organization N, which is tax exempt. At the time of purchase, M and N agree that for a period of ten years L will annually redeem (and N will tender) ten shares of stock in exchange for $12,100 and ten warrants. It is anticipated that, under sections 302 and 301, the annual payment to N will be a distribution of property that is a dividend.

(ii) *Analysis.* Considering all the facts and circumstances, including the agreement between M and N, L's redemption of N's stock is undertaken with a principal purpose of achieving the same economic and tax effect as a fast-pay arrangement. Thus, N's stock is fast-pay stock, M's stock is benefited stock, and the parties have entered into a fast-pay arrangement. Because L is neither a RIC nor a REIT, whether this fast-pay arrangement is recharacterized under paragraph (c) of this section depends on whether the Commissioner determines, under paragraph (c)(1)(ii) of this section, that a principal purpose for the structure of the fast-pay arrangement is the avoidance of any tax imposed by the Internal Revenue Code.

Example 4. Recharacterization illustrated—(i) *Facts.* On formation, REIT Y issues 100 shares of C Stock and 100 shares of D Stock for $1,000 per share. By its terms, a share of D Stock is reasonably expected to pay a $110 dividend in years 1 through 10 and a $30 dividend each year thereafter. In years 1 through 10, persons holding a majority of the D Stock must consent before Y may take any action that would result in Y liquidating or dissolving, merging or consolidating, losing its REIT status, or selling substantially all of its assets. Thereafter, Y may take these actions without consent so long as the D Stock shareholders receive $400 in exchange for their D Stock.

(ii) *Analysis.* When issued, the D Stock has a dividend rate that is reasonably expected to decline from an annual rate of 11 percent of its issue price to an annual rate of 3 percent of its issue price. In addition, the $1,000 issue price of a share of D Stock exceeds the price at which the shareholder can be compelled to dispose of the stock ($400). Thus, the D Stock is fast-pay stock, and the C Stock is benefited stock. Because Y is a REIT, the fast-pay arrangement is recharacterized under paragraph (c) of this section.

(iii) *Recharacterization.* The fast-pay arrangement is recharacterized as follows:

(A) Under paragraph (c)(2)(i) of this section, the C Stock shareholders are treated as issuing financing instruments to the D Stock shareholders in exchange for $100,000 ($1,000, the fair market value of each share of D Stock, multiplied by 100, the number of shares).

(B) Under paragraph (c)(2)(ii) of this section, the C Stock shareholders are treated as contributing $200,000 to Y (the $100,000 received for the financing instruments, plus the $100,000 actually paid for the C Stock) in exchange for the C Stock.

(C) Under paragraph (c)(2)(ii) of this section, each distribution with respect to the D Stock is treated as a distribution with respect to the C Stock.

(D) Under paragraph (c)(2)(iii) of this section, the C Stock shareholders are treated as making payments with respect to the financing instruments, and Y is treated as the paying agent of the financing instruments for the C Stock shareholders.

Example 5. Transfer of benefited stock illustrated—(i) *Facts.* The facts are the same as in *Example 4* of this paragraph (e). Near the end of year 5, a person holding one share of C Stock sells it for $1,300. The buyer is unrelated to REIT Y or to any of the D Stock shareholders. At the time of the sale, the amount needed to terminate the seller's position in the financing instruments at fair market value is $747.

(ii) *Benefited shareholder's treatment on sale.* Under paragraph (c)(3)(iii)(A) of this section, the seller's amount realized is $2,047 ($1,300, the amount actually received, plus $747, the amount necessary to terminate the seller's position in the financing instruments at fair market value). The seller's gain on the sale of the common stock is $47 ($2,047, the amount realized, minus $2,000, the seller's basis in the common stock). The seller has no income or deduction with respect to terminating its position in the financing instruments.

(iii) *Buyer's treatment on purchase.* Under paragraph (c)(3)(iii)(A) of this section, the buyer's basis in the share of D Stock is $2,047 ($1,300, the amount actually paid, plus $747, the amount needed to terminate the seller's position in the financing instruments at fair market value). Under paragraph (c)(3)(iii)(B) of this section, simultaneous with the sale, the buyer is treated as issuing financing instruments to the fast-pay shareholders in exchange for $747, the amount necessary to terminate the seller's position in the financing instruments at fair market value.

Example 6. Fast-pay arrangement involving amounts accrued or paid in a taxable year ending before February 27, 1997—(i) *Facts.* Y is a calendar year taxpayer. In June 1996, Y acquires shares of REIT T benefited stock for $15,000. In December 1996, Y receives dividends of $100. Under the recharacterization rules of paragraph (c)(2) of this section, Y's 1996 income attributable to the benefited stock is $1,200, Y's 1996 deduction attributable to the financing instruments is $500, and Y's basis in the benefited stock is $25,000.

(ii) *Analysis.* Under paragraph (c)(3)(iv) of this section, Y's basis in the benefited stock is reduced by $600. This is the amount by which Y's 1996 income from the fast-pay arrangement as recharacterized under this section ($1,200 of income attributable to the benefited stock less $500 of deductions attributable to the financing instruments), exceeds Y's 1996 income from the fast-pay arrangement as not recharacterized under this section ($100 of income attributable to the benefited stock). Thus, in 1997 when the fast-pay arrangement is recharacterized, Y's basis in the benefited stock is $24,400.

(f) *Reporting requirement.*—(1) *Filing requirements.*—(i) *In general.*—A corporation that has fast-pay stock outstanding at any time during the taxable year must attach the statement described in paragraph (f)(2) of this section to its federal income tax return for such taxable year. This paragraph (f)(1)(i) does not apply to a corporation described in paragraphs (f)(1)(ii), (iii), or (iv) of this section.

(ii) *Controlled foreign corporation.*—In the case of a controlled foreign corporation (CFC), as defined in section 957, that has fast-pay stock outstanding at any time during its taxable year (during which time it was a CFC), each controlling United States shareholder (within the meaning of §1.964-1(c)(5)) must attach the statement described in paragraph (f)(2) of this section to the shareholder's Form 5471 for the CFC's taxable year. The provisions of section 6038 and the regulations under section 6038 apply to any statement required by this paragraph (f)(1)(ii).

(iii) *Foreign personal holding company.*—In the case of a foreign personal holding company (FPHC), as defined in section 552, that has fast-pay stock outstanding at any time during its taxable year (during which time it was a FPHC), each United States citizen or resident who is an officer, director, or 10-percent shareholder (within the meaning of section 6035(e)(1)) of such FPHC must attach the statement described in paragraph (f)(2) of this section to his or her Form 5471 for the FPHC's taxable year. The provisions of sections 6035 and 6679 and the regulations under sections 6035 and 6679 apply to any statement required by this paragraph (f)(1)(iii).

(iv) *Passive foreign investment company.*—In the case of a passive foreign investment company (PFIC), as defined in section 1297, that has fast-pay stock outstanding at any time during its taxable year (during which time it was a PFIC), each shareholder that has elected (under section 1295) to treat the PFIC as a qualified electing fund and knows or has reason to know that the PFIC has outstanding fast-pay stock must attach the statement described in paragraph (f)(2) of this section to the shareholder's Form 8621 for the PFIC's taxable year. Each shareholder owning 10 percent or more of the shares of the PFIC (by vote or value) is presumed to know that the PFIC has issued fast-pay stock. The provisions of sections 1295(a)(2) and 1298(f) and the regulations under those sections (including §1.1295-1T(f)(2)) apply to any statement required by this paragraph (f)(1)(iv).

(2) *Statement.*—The statement required under this paragraph (f) must say, "This fast-pay stock disclosure statement is required by §1.7701(l)-3(f) of the income tax regulations."

The statement must also identify the corporation that has outstanding fast-pay stock and must contain the date on which the fast-pay stock was issued, the terms of the fast-pay stock, and (to the extent the filing person knows or has reason to know such information) the names and taxpayer identification numbers of the shareholders of any stock that is not traded on an established securities market (as described in §1.7704-1(b)).

(g) *Effective date.*—(1) *In general.*—Except as provided in paragraph (g) (4) of this section (relating to reporting requirements), this section applies to taxable years ending after February 26, 1997. Thus, all amounts accrued or paid during the first taxable year ending after February 26, 1997, are subject to this section.

(2) *Election to limit taxable income attributable to a recharacterized fast-pay arrangement for periods before April 1, 2000.*—(i) *Limit.*—For periods before April 1, 2000, provided the shareholder recharacterizes the fast-pay arrangement consistently for all such periods, a shareholder may limit its taxable income attributable to a fast-pay arrangement recharacterized under paragraph (c) of this section to the taxable income that results if the fast-pay arrangement is recharacterized under either—

(A) Notice 97-21, 1997-1 C.B. 407, see §601.601(d)(2) of this chapter; or

(B) Paragraph (c) of this section, computed by assuming the financing instruments are debt.

(ii) *Adjustment and statement.*—A shareholder that limits its taxable income to the amount determined under paragraph (g)(2)(i)(A) of this section must include as an adjustment to taxable income the excess, if any, of the amount determined under paragraph (g)(2)(i)(B) of this section, over the amount determined under paragraph (g)(2)(i)(A) of this section. This adjustment to taxable income must be made in the shareholder's first taxable year that includes April 1, 2000. A shareholder to which this paragraph (g)(2)(ii) applies must include a statement in its books and records identifying each fast-pay arrangement for which an adjustment must be made and providing the amount of the adjustment for each such fast-pay arrangement.

(iii) *Examples.*—The following examples illustrate the rules of this paragraph (g)(2). For purposes of these examples, assume that a shareholder may limit its taxable income under this paragraph (g)(2) for periods before January 1, 2000.

Example 1. Fast-pay arrangement recharacterized under Notice 97-21; REIT holds third-party debt—(i) *Facts.* (A) REIT Y is formed on January 1, 1997, at which time it issues 1,000 shares of fast-pay stock and 1,000 shares of benefited stock for $100 per share. Y and all of its shareholders are U.S. persons and have calendar taxable years. All shareholders of Y have elected to accrue market discount based on a constant interest rate, to include the market discount in income as it accrues, and to amortize bond premium.

(B) For years 1 through 5, the fast-pay stock has an annual dividend rate of $17 per share ($17,000 for all fast-pay stock); in later years, the fast-pay stock has an annual dividend rate of $1 per share ($1,000 for all fast-pay stock). At the end of year 5, and thereafter, a share of fast-pay stock can be acquired by Y in exchange for $50 ($50,000 for all fast-pay stock).

(C) On the day Y is formed, it acquires a five-year mortgage note (the note) issued by an unrelated third party for $200,000. The note provides for annual interest payments on December 31 of $18,000 (a coupon interest rate of 9.00 percent, compounded annually), and one payment of principal at the end of 5 years. The note can be prepaid, in whole or in part, at any time.

(ii) *Recharacterization under Notice 97-21*— (A) *In general.* One way to recharacterize the fast-pay arrangement under Notice 97-21 is to treat the fast-pay shareholders and the benefited shareholders as if they jointly purchased the note from the issuer with the understanding that over the five-year term of the note the benefited shareholders would use their share of the interest to buy (on a dollar-for-dollar basis) the fast-pay shareholders' portion of the note. The benefited shareholders' and the fast-pay shareholders' yearly taxable income under Notice 97-21 can then be calculated after determining their initial portions of the note and whether those initial portions are purchased at a discount or premium.

(B) *Determining initial portions of the debt instrument.* The fast-pay shareholders' and the benefited shareholders' initial portions of the note can be determined by comparing the pre-sent values of their expected cash flows. As a group, the fast-pay shareholders expect to receive cash flows of $135,000 (five annual payments of $17,000, plus a final payment of $50,000). As a group, the benefited shareholders expect to receive cash flows of $155,000 (five annual payments of $1,000, plus a final payment of $150,000). Using a discount rate equal to the yield to maturity (as determined under § 1.1272-1(b)(1)(i)) of the mortgage note (9.00 percent, compounded annually), the present value of the fast-pay shareholders' cash flows is $98,620, and the present value of the benefited shareholders' cash flows is $101,380. Thus, the fast-pay shareholders initially acquire 49 percent of the note at a $1,380 premium (that is, they paid $100,000 for $98,620 of principal in the note). The benefited shareholders initially acquire 51 percent of the note at a $1,380 discount (that is, they paid $100,000 for $101,380 of principal in the note). Under section 171, the fast-pay shareholders' premium is amortizable based on their yield in their initial portion of the note (8.574 percent, compounded annually). The benefited shareholders' discount accrues based on the yield in their initial portion of the note (9.353 percent, compounded annually).

(C) *Taxable income under Notice 97-21*— (1) *Fast-pay shareholders.* Under Notice 97-21, the fast-pay shareholders compute their taxable income attributable to the fast-pay arrangement for periods before January 1, 2000, by subtracting the amortizable premium from the accrued interest on the fast-pay shareholders' portion of the note. For purposes of paragraph (g)(2)(i)(A) of this section, the fast-pay shareholders' taxable income as a group is as follows:

Taxable Period	Interest Income	Amortizable Premium	Taxable Income
1/1/97 - 12/31/97	$8,876	($302)	$8,574
1/1/98 - 12/31/98	$8,145	($293)	$7,852
1/1/99 - 12/31/99	$7,348	($281)	$7,067
	$24,369	($876)	$23,493

(2) *Benefited shareholders.* Under Notice 97-21, the benefited shareholders compute their taxable income attributable to the fast-pay arrangement for periods before January 1, 2000, by adding the accrued discount to the accrued interest on the benefited shareholders' portion of the note. For purposes of paragraph (g)(2)(i)(A) of this section, the benefited shareholders' taxable income as a group is as follows:

Taxable Period	Interest Income	Accrued Discount	Taxable Income
1/1/97 - 12/31/97	$9,124	$229	$9,353
1/1/98 - 12/31/98	$9,855	$251	$10,106
1/1/99 - 12/31/99	$10,652	$274	$10,926
	$29,631	$754	$30,385

(iii) *Taxable income under the recharacterization of this section*—(A) *Fast-pay shareholders.* Under paragraphs (c) and (g)(2)(i)(B) of this section, the fast-pay shareholders' taxable income attributable to the fast-pay arrangement for periods before January 1, 2000, is the interest deemed paid on the financing instruments. For purposes of paragraph (g)(2)(i)(B) of this section, the fast-pay shareholders' taxable income as a group is as follows:

Taxable Period	Taxable Income
1/1/97 - 12/31/97	$8,574
1/1/98 - 12/31/98	$7,852
1/1/99 - 12/31/99	$7,067
	$23,493

Reg. § 1.7701(l)-3(g)(2)(iii)

(B) *Benefited shareholders.* Under paragraphs (c) and (g)(2)(i)(B) of this section, the benefited shareholders compute their taxable income attributable to the fast-pay arrangement for periods before January 1, 2000, by subtracting the interest deemed paid on the financing instru- ments from the dividends actually and deemed paid on the benefited stock. For purposes of paragraph (g)(2)(i)(B) of this section, the bene- fited shareholders' taxable income as a group is as follows:

Taxable Period	Dividends Paid On Benefited Stock	Interest Paid On Financing Instruments	Taxable Income
1/1/97 - 12/31/97	$18,000	($8,574)	$9,426
1/1/98 - 12/31/98	$18,000	($7,852)	$10,148
1/1/99 - 12/31/99	$18,000	($7,067)	$10,933
	$54,000	($23,493)	$30,507

(iv) *Limit on taxable income under paragraph (g)(2)(i) of this section—(A) Fast-pay shareholders.* For periods before January 1, 2000, the fast-pay shareholders have the same taxable income under the recharacterization of Notice 97-21 and paragraph (g)(2)(i)(A) of this section ($23,493) as they have under the recharacterization of paragraphs (c) and (g)(2)(i)(B) of this section ($23,493). Thus, under paragraph (g)(2)(i) of this section, the fast-pay shareholders may limit their taxable income attributable to the fast-pay ar- rangement for periods before January 1, 2000, to $23,493 (as a group).

(B) *Benefited shareholders.* For periods before January 1, 2000, the benefited sharehold- ers have taxable income attributable to the fast- pay arrangement of $30,385 under the recharacterization of Notice 97-21 and paragraph (g)(2)(i)(A) of this section, and taxable income of $30,507 under the recharacterization of paragraphs (c) and (g)(2)(i)(B) of this section. Thus, under paragraph (g)(2)(i) of this section, the benefited shareholders may limit their taxa- ble income attributable to the fast-pay arrange- ment for periods before January 1, 2000, to either $30,385 (as a group) or $30,507 (as a group).

(v) *Adjustment to taxable income under para- graph (g)(2)(ii) of this section.* Under paragraph (g)(2)(ii) of this section, any benefited share- holder that limited its taxable income to the amount determined under paragraph (g)(2)(i)(A) of this section must include as an adjustment to taxable income the excess, if any, of the amount determined under paragraph (g)(2)(i)(B) of this section, over the amount determined under par- agraph (g)(2)(i)(A) of this section. If all benefited shareholders limited their taxable income to the amount determined under paragraph (g)(2)(i)(A) of this section, then as a group their adjustment to income is $122 ($30,507, minus $30,385). Each shareholder must include its adjustment in in- come for the taxable year that includes January 1, 2000.

Example 2. REIT holds debt issued by a bene- fited shareholder—(i) Facts. The facts are the same as in *Example 1* of this paragraph (g)(2) except that corporation Z holds 800 shares (80 percent) of the benefited stock, and Z, instead of a third party, issues the mortgage note acquired by Y.

(ii) *Recharacterization under Notice 97-21.* Because Y holds a debt instrument issued by Z, the fast-pay arrangement is recharacterized under Notice 97-21 as an arrangement in which Z issued one or more instruments directly to the fast-pay shareholders and the other benefited shareholders.

(A) *Fast-pay shareholders.* Consistent with this recharacterization, Z is treated as issuing a debt instrument to the fast-pay shareholders for $100,000. The debt instrument provides for five annual payments of $17,000 and an additional payment of $50,000 in year five. Thus, the debt instrument's yield to maturity is 8.574 percent per annum, compounded annually.

(B) *Benefited shareholders.* Z is also treated as issuing a debt instrument to the other bene- fited shareholders for $20,000 (200 shares multi- plied by $100, or 20 percent of the $100,000 paid to Y by the benefited shareholders as a group). This debt instrument provides for five annual payments of $200 and an additional payment of $30,000 in year five. The debt instrument's yield to maturity is 9.304 percent per annum, com- pounded annually.

(C) *Issuer's interest expense under Notice 97-21.* Under Notice 97-21, Z's interest expense attributable to the fast-pay arrangement for peri- ods before January 1, 2000, equals the interest accrued on the debt instrument held by the fast- pay shareholders, plus the interest accrued on the debt instrument held by the benefited share- holders other than Z. For purposes of paragraph (g)(2)(i)(A) of this section, Z's interest expense is as follows:

Taxable Period	Accrued Interest Fast-pay Shareholders	Accrued Interest Other Benefited Shareholders	Total Interest Expense
1/1/97 - 12/31/97	($8,574)	($1,861)	($10,435)
1/1/98 - 12/31/98	($7,852)	($2,015)	($9,867)
1/1/99 - 12/31/99	($7,067)	($2,184)	($9,251)
	($23,493)	($6,060)	($29,553)

Reg. § 1.7701(l)-3(g)(2)(iii)

(iii) *Recharacterization under this section.* Under paragraphs (c) and (g)(2)(i)(B) of this section, Z's taxable income attributable to the fast-pay arrangement for periods before January 1, 2000, equals Z's share of the dividends actually and deemed paid on the benefited stock (80 per-

cent of the outstanding benefited stock), reduced by the sum of the interest accrued on the note held by Y and the interest accrued on the financing instruments deemed to have been issued by Z. For purposes of paragraph (g)(2)(i)(B) of this section, Z's taxable income is as follows:

Taxable Period	Dividends Benefited Stock	Accrued Interest On Debt Held By Y	Accrued Interest Financing Instruments	Taxable Expense
1/1/97 - 12/31/97	$14,400	($18,000)	($6,859)	($10,459)
1/1/98 - 12/31/98	$14,400	($18,000)	($6,281)	($9,881)
1/1/99 - 12/31/99	$14,400	($18,000)	($5,654)	($9,254)
	$43,200	($54,000)	($18,794)	($29,594)

(iv) *Limit on taxable income under this paragraph (g)(2).* For periods before January 1, 2000, Z has a taxable loss attributable to the fast-pay arrangement of $29,553 under the recharacterization of Notice 97-21 and paragraph (g)(2)(i)(A) of this section, and a taxable loss of $29,594 under the recharacterization of paragraphs (c) and (g)(2)(i)(B) of this section. Thus, under paragraph (g)(2)(i) of this section, Z may report a taxable loss attributable to the fast-pay arrangement for periods before January 1, 2000, of either $29,553 or $29,594. Under paragraph (g)(2)(ii), Z has no adjustment to its taxable income for its taxable year that includes January 1, 2000.

(3) *Rule to comply with this section.*—To comply with this section for each taxable year in which it failed to do so, a taxpayer should file an amended return. For taxable years ending before January 10, 2000, a taxpayer that has complied with Notice 97-21, 1997-1 C.B. 407 (see §601.601(d)(2) of this chapter), for all such taxable years is considered to have complied with this section and limited its taxable income under paragraph (g)(2)(i)(A) of this section.

(4) *Reporting requirements.*—The reporting requirements of paragraph (f) of this section apply to taxable years (of the person required to file the statement) ending after January 10, 2000. [Reg. §1.7701(l)-3.]

☐ [*T.D.* 8853, 1-7-2000.]

[Reg. §1.7701(l)-4]

§1.7701(l)-4. Rules regarding inversion transactions.—(a) *Overview.*—This section provides rules applicable to United States shareholders of controlled foreign corporations after certain inversion transactions. Paragraph (b) of this section defines specified transactions and provides the scope of the rules in this section. Paragraph (c) of this section provides rules recharacterizing certain specified transactions. Paragraph (d) of this section sets forth rules governing transactions that affect the stock of an expatriated foreign subsidiary following a recharacterized specified transaction. Paragraph (e) of this section sets forth a rule concerning the treatment of amounts included in income as a result of a specified transaction as foreign personal holding company income. Paragraph (f) of this section sets forth definitions that apply for purposes of this section. Paragraph (g) of this

section sets forth examples illustrating these rules. Paragraph (h) of this section provides applicability dates. See §1.367(b)-4(e) and (f) for rules concerning certain other exchanges after an inversion transaction. See also §1.956-2(a)(4), (c)(5), and (d)(2) for additional rules applicable to United States property held by controlled foreign corporations after an inversion transaction.

(b) *Specified transaction.*—(1) *In general.*—Except as provided in paragraph (b)(2) of this section, paragraph (c) of this section applies to specified transactions. For purposes of this section, a *specified transaction* is, with respect to an expatriated foreign subsidiary, a transaction in which stock of the expatriated foreign subsidiary is issued or transferred to a person that immediately before the issuance or transfer is a specified related person, provided the transaction occurs during the applicable period. However, a specified transaction does not include a transaction in which stock of the expatriated foreign subsidiary is deemed issued pursuant to section 304.

(2) *Exceptions.*—Paragraph (c) of this section does not apply to a specified transaction—

(i) That is a fast-pay arrangement that is recharacterized under §1.7701(l)-3(c)(2);

(ii) In which the specified stock was transferred by a shareholder of the expatriated foreign subsidiary, and the shareholder either—

(A) Pursuant to §1.367(b)-4(e)(1), both—

(1) Included in gross income as a deemed dividend the section 1248 amount attributable to the specified stock; and

(2) After taking into account the increase in basis provided in §1.367(b)-2(e)(3)(ii) resulting from the deemed dividend (if any), recognized all realized gain with respect to the stock that otherwise would not have been recognized; or

(B) Included in gross income all of the gain recognized on the transfer of the specified stock (including gain included in gross income as a dividend pursuant to section 964(e), section 1248(a), or section 356(a)(2)); or

(iii) In which—

(A) Immediately after the specified transaction and any related transaction, the expatriated foreign subsidiary is a controlled foreign corporation;

Reg. §1.7701(l)-4(b)(2)(iii)(A)

(B) The post-transaction ownership percentage with respect to the expatriated foreign subsidiary is at least 90 percent of the pre-transaction ownership percentage with respect to the expatriated foreign subsidiary; and

(C) The post-transaction ownership percentage with respect to any lower-tier expatriated foreign subsidiary is at least 90 percent of the pre-transaction ownership percentage with respect to the lower-tier expatriated foreign subsidiary. See *Example 3* and *Example 4* of paragraph (g) of this section.

(c) *Recharacterization of specified transactions.*—(1) *In general.*—Except as otherwise provided, a specified transaction that is recharacterized under this paragraph (c) is recharacterized for all purposes of the Internal Revenue Code as of the date on which the specified transaction occurs, unless and until the rules of paragraph (d) of this section apply to alter or terminate the recharacterization. For purposes of paragraphs (c)(2) and (3) and (d) of this section, stock is considered owned by a section 958(a) U.S. shareholder if it is owned within the meaning of section 958(a) by the section 958(a) U.S. shareholder.

(2) *Specified transactions through stock issuance.*—A specified transaction in which the specified stock is issued by an expatriated foreign subsidiary to a specified related person is recharacterized as follows—

(i) The transferred property is treated as having been transferred by the specified related person to the persons that were section 958(a) U.S. shareholders of the expatriated foreign subsidiary immediately before the specified transaction, in proportion to the stock of the expatriated foreign subsidiary owned by each section 958(a) U.S. shareholder, in exchange for deemed instruments in the section 958(a) U.S. shareholders; and

(ii) The transferred property treated as transferred to the section 958(a) U.S. shareholders pursuant to paragraph (c)(2)(i) of this section is treated as having been contributed by the section 958(a) U.S. shareholders (through intermediate entities, if any, in exchange for equity in the intermediate entities) to the expatriated foreign subsidiary in exchange for deemed issued stock in the expatriated foreign subsidiary. See *Example 1, Example 2,* and *Example 6* of paragraph (g) of this section.

(3) *Specified transactions through shareholder transfer.*—A specified transaction in which specified stock is transferred by shareholders of the expatriated foreign subsidiary to a specified related person is recharacterized as follows—

(i) The transferred property is treated as having been transferred by the specified related person to the persons that were section 958(a) U.S. shareholders of the expatriated foreign subsidiary immediately before the specified transaction, in proportion to the specified stock owned by each section 958(a) U.S. shareholder, in ex-

change for deemed instruments in the section 958(a) U.S. shareholders; and

(ii) To the extent the section 958(a) U.S. shareholders are not the transferring shareholders, the transferred property treated as transferred to the section 958(a) U.S. shareholders pursuant to paragraph (c)(3)(i) of this section is treated as having been contributed by the section 958(a) U.S. shareholders (through intermediate entities, if any, in exchange for equity in the intermediate entities) to the transferring shareholder in exchange for equity in the transferring shareholder. See *Example 5* of paragraph (g) of this section.

(4) *Treatment of deemed instruments following a recharacterized specified transaction.*—(i) *Deemed instruments.*—The deemed instruments described in paragraphs (c)(2) and (3) of this section have the same terms as the specified stock issued or transferred pursuant to the specified transaction (that is, the disregarded specified stock), other than the issuer. When a distribution is made with respect to the disregarded specified stock, matching seriatim distributions with respect to the deemed issued stock are treated as made by the expatriated foreign subsidiary, through intermediate entities, if any, to the section 958(a) U.S. shareholders, which, in turn, then are treated as making corresponding payments with respect to the deemed instruments to the specified related person.

(ii) *Paying agent.*—The expatriated foreign subsidiary is treated as the paying agent of the section 958(a) U.S. shareholder with respect to the deemed instruments treated as issued by the section 958(a) U.S. shareholder to the specified related person.

(d) *Transactions affecting ownership of stock of an expatriated foreign subsidiary following a recharacterized specified transaction.*—(1) *Transfers of stock other than specified stock.*—When, after a specified transaction with respect to an expatriated foreign subsidiary that is recharacterized under paragraph (c)(2) or (3) of this section, stock of the expatriated foreign subsidiary, other than disregarded specified stock, that is owned by a section 958(a) U.S. shareholder is transferred, the deemed issued stock treated as owned by the section 958(a) U.S. shareholder as a result of the specified transaction continues to be treated as directly owned by the holder, as are the deemed instruments treated as issued to the specified related person as a result of the specified transaction.

(2) *Transactions in which the expatriated foreign subsidiary ceases to be a foreign related person.*—When, after a specified transaction with respect to an expatriated foreign subsidiary that is recharacterized under paragraph (c)(2) or (3) of this section, there is a transaction that affects the ownership of the stock (including disregarded specified stock) of the expatriated foreign subsidiary, and, immediately after the transaction, the expatriated foreign subsidiary is not a foreign related person (determined without tak-

ing into account the recharacterization under paragraph (c)(2) or (3) of this section), then, immediately before the transaction—

(i) Each section 958(a) U.S. shareholder that is treated as owning deemed issued stock in the expatriated foreign subsidiary under paragraph (c)(2) or (3) of this section is treated as transferring the deemed issued stock (after the deemed issued stock is deemed to be transferred to the section 958(a) U.S. shareholder through intermediate entities, if any, in redemption of equity deemed issued by the intermediate entities pursuant to paragraph (c)(2) or (3) of this section) to the specified related person that is treated as holding the deemed instruments issued by the section 958(a) U.S. shareholder under paragraph (c)(2) or (3) of this section, in redemption of the deemed instruments; and

(ii) The deemed issued stock that is treated as transferred pursuant to paragraph (d)(2)(i) of this section is treated as recapitalized into the disregarded specified stock actually held by the specified related person, which immediately thereafter is treated as specified stock owned by the specified related person for all purposes of the Internal Revenue Code. See *Example 8, Example 9,* and *Example 12* of paragraph (g) of this section.

(3) *Transfers in which disregarded specified stock ceases to be held by a foreign related person, specified related person, or expatriated entity.*— When, after a specified transaction with respect to an expatriated foreign subsidiary that is recharacterized under paragraph (c)(2) or (3) of this section, there is a direct or indirect transfer of the disregarded specified stock in the expatriated foreign subsidiary, and immediately after the transfer, the expatriated foreign subsidiary is a foreign related person, then, to the extent that, as a result of the transfer, the disregarded specified stock is actually held (determined without taking into account the recharacterization under paragraph (c)(2) or (3) of this section) by a person that is not a foreign related person, a specified related person, or an expatriated entity, immediately before the transfer—

(i) Each section 958(a) U.S. shareholder that is treated as owning all or a portion of the deemed issued stock in the expatriated foreign subsidiary is treated as transferring the deemed issued stock that is allocable to the transferred disregarded specified stock that is out-of-group transferred disregarded specified stock (after the deemed issued stock is deemed to be transferred to the section 958(a) U.S. shareholder through intermediate entities, if any, in redemption of equity deemed issued by the intermediate entities pursuant to paragraph (c)(2) or (3) of this section) to the specified related person that is treated as holding the deemed instruments allocable to the out-of-group transferred disregarded specified stock, in redemption of the deemed instruments that are allocable to the out-of-group transferred disregarded specified stock; and

(ii) The deemed issued stock that is treated as transferred pursuant to paragraph

(d)(3)(i) of this section is treated as recapitalized into the disregarded specified stock actually held by the specified related person, which immediately thereafter is treated as specified stock owned by the specified related person for all purposes of the Internal Revenue Code. See *Example 7* and *Example 11* of paragraph (g) of this section.

(4) *Certain direct transfers of disregarded specified stock to which unwind rules do not apply.*— When a specified related person directly transfers the disregarded specified stock of the expatriated foreign subsidiary and paragraphs (d)(2) and (3) of this section do not apply with respect to the transfer, the specified related person is deemed to transfer the deemed instruments allocable to the transferred disregarded specified stock, whether it is in-group transferred disregarded specified stock or out-of-group transferred disregarded specified stock, to the transferee of the specified stock, in lieu of the disregarded specified stock, in exchange for the consideration provided by the transferee for the disregarded specified stock. See *Example 10* of paragraph (g) of this section.

(5) *Determination of deemed issued stock and deemed instruments allocable to transferred disregarded specified stock.*—(i) *Out-of-group transfers of disregarded specified stock.*—For purposes of paragraphs (d)(3) and (4) of this section, the portion of the deemed issued stock treated as owned, and of the deemed instruments treated as issued, by each section 958(a) U.S. shareholder as a result of the specified transaction that is allocable to out-of-group transferred disregarded specified stock is the amount that is proportionate to the ratio of the amount of the out-of-group transferred disregarded specified stock to the amount of disregarded specified stock of the expatriated foreign subsidiary that is actually held by the specified related person immediately before the transfer referred to in paragraph (d)(3) or (4) of this section as a result of the specified transaction.

(ii) *In-group direct transfers of disregarded specified stock.*—For purposes of paragraph (d)(4) of this section, the portion of the deemed issued stock treated as owned by each section 958(a) U.S. shareholder as a result of the specified transaction that is allocable to in-group transferred disregarded specified stock is the amount that is proportionate to the ratio of the amount of the in-group transferred disregarded specified stock to the amount of disregarded specified stock of the expatriated foreign subsidiary that is actually held by the specified related person immediately before the transfer described in paragraph (d)(4) of this section as a result of the specified transaction.

(e) *Certain exception from foreign personal holding company income not available.*—An amount included in the gross income of a controlled foreign corporation as a dividend with respect to stock transferred in a specified transaction does not qualify for the exception from foreign per-

Reg. § 1.7701(I)-4(e)

sonal holding company income provided by section 954(c)(6) (to the extent in effect).

(f) *Definitions.*—In addition to the definitions in § 1.7874-12, the following definitions and special rules apply for purposes of this section:

(1) *Deemed instruments* mean, with respect to a specified transaction, instruments deemed issued by a section 958(a) U.S. shareholder in exchange for transferred property in the specified transaction.

(2) *Deemed issued stock* means, with respect to a specified transaction, stock of an expatriated foreign subsidiary deemed issued to a section 958(a) U.S. shareholder (or an intermediate entity) in the specified transaction.

(3) *Disregarded specified stock* means, with respect to a specified transaction, specified stock that is actually held by a specified related person but that is disregarded for all purposes of the Internal Revenue Code pursuant to paragraph (c)(2) or (3) of this section.

(4) *Indirect ownership.*—To determine indirect ownership of the stock of a corporation for purposes of calculating a pre-transaction ownership percentage or post-transaction ownership percentage with respect to that corporation, the principles of section 958(a) apply without regard to whether an intermediate entity is foreign or domestic. For this purpose, stock of the corporation that is directly or indirectly (applying the principles of section 958(a) without regard to whether an intermediate entity is foreign or domestic) owned by a domestic corporation that is an expatriated entity is not treated as indirectly owned by a non-EFS foreign related person.

(5) *In-group transferred disregarded specified stock* means disregarded specified stock that is directly transferred to a foreign related person, a specified related person, or an expatriated entity.

(6) A *lower-tier expatriated foreign subsidiary* means an expatriated foreign subsidiary, stock of which is directly or indirectly owned by an expatriated foreign subsidiary.

(7) *Out-of-group transferred disregarded specified stock* means disregarded specified stock that, as a result of a transfer of disregarded specified stock, is actually held by a person that is not a foreign related person, a specified related person, or an expatriated entity.

(8) *Pre-transaction ownership percentage* means, with respect to a corporation, 100 percent less the percentage of stock (by value) in the corporation that, immediately before a specified transaction and any related transaction, is owned, in the aggregate, directly or indirectly by non-EFS foreign related persons.

(9) *Post-transaction ownership percentage* means, with respect to a corporation, 100 percent less the percentage of stock (by value) in the corporation that, immediately after the specified transaction and any related transaction, is owned, in the aggregate, directly or indirectly by non-EFS foreign related persons.

(10) A *section 958(a) U.S. shareholder* means, with respect to an expatriated foreign subsidiary,

a United States shareholder with respect to the expatriated foreign subsidiary that owns (within the meaning of section 958(a)) stock of the expatriated foreign subsidiary and that is an expatriated entity.

(11) *Specified stock* means the stock of the expatriated foreign subsidiary that is issued or transferred to a specified related person in a specified transaction.

(12) *Transferred property* means the property transferred by the specified related person in exchange for specified stock in a specified transaction.

(g) *Examples.*—The following examples illustrate the regulations described in this section. Except as otherwise provided, FA, a foreign corporation, wholly owns DT, a domestic corporation, which, in turn, wholly owns FT, a foreign corporation that is a controlled foreign corporation. FA also wholly owns FS, a foreign corporation that is a controlled foreign corporation for its taxable year beginning January 1, 2017, but not for prior taxable years. FA acquired DT in an inversion transaction that was completed on January 1, 2015. Accordingly, DT is the domestic entity and a section 958(a) U.S. shareholder with respect to FT, FT is an expatriated foreign subsidiary, and FA and FS are non-EFS foreign related persons and specified related persons. All entities have a calendar year tax year for U.S. tax purposes.

Example 1. (i) *Facts.* On February 1, 2015, FA acquires $6x of FT stock, representing 60% of the total voting power and value of the stock of FT, from FT in a stock issuance, in exchange for $6x of cash.

(ii) *Analysis.* (A) Under paragraph (b) of this section, FA's acquisition of the FT specified stock from FT is a specified transaction because stock of an expatriated foreign subsidiary was issued to a specified related person (FA) during the applicable period. Furthermore, the exceptions to recharacterization in paragraph (b)(2) of this section do not apply to the transaction.

(B) FA's acquisition of the FT specified stock is recharacterized under paragraphs (c)(1) and (2) of this section as follows, with the result that FT continues to be a CFC even before its taxable year beginning January 1, 2017:

(*1*) DT is treated as having issued deemed instruments to FA in exchange for $6x of cash.

(*2*) DT is treated as having contributed the $6x of cash to FT in exchange for deemed issued stock of FT.

(C) Under paragraph (c)(4)(i) of this section, any distribution with respect to the FT specified stock issued to FA will be treated as a distribution to DT, which, in turn, will be treated as making a matching distribution with respect to the deemed instruments that DT is treated as having issued to FA. Under paragraph (c)(4)(ii) of this section, FT is treated as the paying agent of DT with respect to the deemed instruments issued by DT to FA.

Example 2. (i) *Facts.* DT owns stock of FT representing 60% of the total voting power and value of the stock of FT, and the remaining stock of FT, representing 40% of the total voting power and value, is owned by USP, a domestic corporation that is not an expatriated entity. On February 1, 2015, FA acquires $6x of FT stock, representing 60% of the total voting power and value of the stock of FT, from FT in a stock issuance, in exchange for $6x of cash.

(ii) *Analysis.* (A) Under paragraph (b) of this section, FA's acquisition of the FT specified stock from FT is a specified transaction because stock of an expatriated foreign subsidiary was issued to a specified related person (FA) during the applicable period. Furthermore, the exceptions to recharacterization in paragraph (b)(2) of this section do not apply to the transaction.

(B) FA's acquisition of the FT specified stock is recharacterized under paragraphs (c)(1) and (2) of this section as follows, with the result that FT continues to be a CFC even before its taxable year beginning January 1, 2017:

(*1*) DT is treated as having issued deemed instruments to FA in exchange for $6x of cash.

(*2*) DT is treated as having contributed the $6x of cash to FT in exchange for deemed issued stock of FT.

(*3*) DT is treated as owning $8.40x of the stock of FT, representing 84% of the total voting power and value of the stock of FT. USP owns $1.60x of the stock of FT, representing 16% of the total voting power and value of the stock of FT.

(C) Under paragraph (c)(4)(i) of this section, any distribution with respect to the FT specified stock issued to FA will be treated as a distribution to DT, which, in turn, will be treated as making a matching distribution with respect to the deemed instruments that DT is treated as having issued to FA. Under paragraph (c)(4)(ii) of this section, FT is treated as the paying agent of DT with respect to the deemed instruments issued by DT to FA.

Example 3. (i) *Facts.* DT owns stock of FT representing 50% of the total voting power and value of the $8x of stock of FT outstanding, and the remaining stock of FT, representing 50% of the total voting power and value, is owned by USP, a domestic corporation that is not an expatriated entity. On April 30, 2016, FA and USP each simultaneously acquire $1x of FT stock from FT in a stock issuance, in exchange for $1x of cash each.

(ii) *Analysis.* (A) Under paragraph (b) of this section, FA's acquisition of the FT specified stock from FT is a specified transaction because stock of an expatriated foreign subsidiary was issued to a specified related person (FA) during the applicable period.

(B) However, the specified transaction is not recharacterized under paragraphs (c)(1) and (2) of this section because the exception in paragraph (b)(2)(iii) of this section applies. The exception applies because FT remains a controlled foreign corporation immediately after the specified transaction and any related transaction, and the post-transaction ownership percentage with respect to FT is 90% (90%/100%), or at least 90%,

of the pre-transaction ownership percentage with respect to FT. The rule in paragraph (b)(2)(iii)(C) of this section does not apply because there is no lower-tier expatriated foreign subsidiary. Although FA (a non-EFS foreign related person) indirectly owns $4x of FT stock both immediately before and after the specified transaction and any related transaction, all of that stock is directly owned by DT (a domestic corporation), and as a result, under paragraph (f)(4) of this section, none of that stock is treated as directly or indirectly owned by FA for purposes of calculating the pre-transaction ownership percentage and the post-transaction ownership percentage with respect to FT. Accordingly, under paragraph (f)(8) of this section, the pre-transaction ownership percentage with respect to FT (100% less the percentage of stock (by value) in FT that, immediately before the specified transaction with respect to FT and any related transaction, is owned by non-EFS foreign related persons) is 100 (100% - 0%). Under paragraph (f)(9) of this section, the post-transaction ownership percentage with respect to FT (100% less the percentage of stock (by value) in FT that, immediately after the specified transaction with respect to FT and any related transaction, is owned by non-EFS foreign related persons) is 90 (100% - 10% ($1x/$10x)).

Example 4. (i) *Facts.* On February 1, 2015, FA acquires 60% of the FT stock owned by DT in exchange for $2.40x of cash in a fully taxable transaction. DT recognizes and includes in income all of the gain (including any gain treated as a deemed dividend pursuant to section 1248(a)) with respect to the FT stock transferred to FA.

(ii) *Analysis.* (A) Under paragraph (b) of this section, FA's acquisition of the FT specified stock is a specified transaction because stock of an expatriated foreign subsidiary was transferred to a specified related person (FA) during the applicable period.

(B) However, the specified transaction is not recharacterized under paragraphs (c)(1) and (c)(3) of this section because the exception in paragraph (b)(2)(ii) of this section applies. The exception applies because DT recognizes and includes in income all of the gain (including any gain treated as a deemed dividend pursuant to section 1248(a)) with respect to the FT specified stock transferred to FA.

Example 5. (i) *Facts.* On February 1, 2015, DT and FA organize FPRS, a foreign partnership, with nominal capital. DT transfers all of the stock of FT to FPRS in exchange for 40% of the capital and profits interests in the partnership. Furthermore, FA contributes property to FPRS in exchange for the other 60% of the capital and profits interests.

(ii) *Analysis.* (A) Under paragraph (b) of this section, DT's transfer of the FT specified stock is a specified transaction, because stock of an expatriated foreign subsidiary was transferred to a specified related person (FPRS) during the applicable period. The exceptions to recharacterization in paragraph (b)(2) of this section do not apply to the transaction.

(B) DT's transfer of the FT specified stock is recharacterized under paragraphs (c)(1) and (c)(3) of this section as follows, with the result that FT continues to be a CFC even before its taxable year beginning January 1, 2017:

(*1*) FPRS is treated as having issued 40% of its capital and profits interests to DT in exchange for deemed instruments treated as having been issued by DT.

(*2*) DT is treated as continuing to own all of the stock of FT, as well as the FPRS interests.

(C) Under paragraph (c)(4)(i) of this section, any distribution with respect to the FT specified stock transferred to FPRS will be treated as a distribution to DT, which, in turn, will be treated as making a matching distribution with respect to the deemed instruments that DT is treated as having issued to FPRS. Under paragraph (c)(4)(ii) of this section, FT is treated as the paying agent of DT with respect to the deemed instruments issued by DT to FPRS.

Example 6. (i) *Facts.* DT wholly owns FT2, a foreign corporation that is a controlled foreign corporation. FT and FT2 each own 50% of the capital and profits interests in DPRS, a domestic partnership. DPRS wholly owns FT3, a foreign corporation that is a controlled foreign corporation. FT2 and FT3 are expatriated foreign subsidiaries. On April 30, 2016, FS acquires $9x of the stock of each of FT and FT2, representing 9% of the total voting power and value of the stock of FT and FT2, from FT and FT2, respectively, in a stock issuance, in exchange for cash of $9x each. Also on April 30, 2016, in a related transaction, FS acquires $9x of the stock of FT3, representing 9% of the total voting power and value of the stock of FT3, from FT3 in a stock issuance, in exchange for cash of $9x.

(ii) *Analysis.* (A) Under paragraph (b) of this section, the acquisitions by FS of the specified stock of each of FT, FT2, and FT3 from FT, FT2, and FT3 are specified transactions with respect to each of FT, FT2, and FT3, respectively, because stock of an expatriated foreign subsidiary was issued to a specified related person (FS) during the applicable period.

(B) If FS had acquired only stock of FT and FT2, and had not acquired stock of FT3 in a related transaction, the specified transactions resulting from the acquisitions with respect to FT and FT2 would not have been recharacterized under paragraphs (c)(1) and (2) of this section, because the exception from recharacterization in paragraph (b)(2)(iii) of this section would have applied. FT and FT2 remain controlled foreign corporations immediately after each specified transaction and any related transaction. Under paragraph (f)(9) of this section, the post-transaction ownership percentage with respect to each of FT, FT2, and FT3 (a lower-tier expatriated foreign subsidiary of FT and FT2) would have been 91% ((100% - 9%)/(100% - 0%)), or at least 90%, of the pre-transaction ownership percentage determined under paragraph (f)(8) of this

section with respect to each of FT, FT2, and FT3 (100%).

(C) However, for the specified transactions with respect to FT, FT2, and FT3, the post-transaction ownership percentage determined under paragraph (f)(9) of this section with respect to FT3 (the lower-tier expatriated foreign subsidiary of FT and FT2), 100% less the percentage of stock (by value) in FT3 that, immediately after each of the specified transactions with respect to each of FT and FT2 and any related transaction, is owned by the non-EFS foreign related persons, is 82.81 (100%-(9%x50%x91%)-(9%x50%x91%)-9%). Accordingly, the post-transaction ownership percentage with respect to FT3 is 82.81% (82.81/(100%-0%)), which is less than 90%, of the pre-transaction ownership percentage determined under paragraph (f)(8) of this section with respect to FT3. Thus, the exception from recharacterization in paragraph (b)(2)(iii) of this section does not apply with respect to the specified transactions with respect to FT, FT2, or FT3.

(D) The specified transactions with respect to FT and FT2 are recharacterized under paragraphs (c)(1) and (2) of this section as follows:

(*1*) DT is treated as having issued 2 deemed instruments worth $9x each to FA in exchange for $18x ($9x + $9x) of cash.

(*2*) DT is treated as having contributed $9x of cash to each of FT and FT2 in exchange for deemed issued stock of FT and FT2.

(*3*) DT is treated as continuing to own all of the stock of FT and FT2.

(E) Under paragraph (c)(4)(i) of this section, any distribution with respect to the FT and FT2 specified stock issued to FS will be treated as a distribution to DT, which, in turn, will be treated as making a matching distribution with respect to the deemed instruments that DT is treated as having issued to FS. Under paragraph (c)(4)(ii) of this section, FT and FT2 are treated as the paying agents of DT with respect to the deemed instruments issued by DT to FS.

(F) The specified transaction with respect to FT3 is recharacterized under paragraphs (c)(1) and (2) of this section as follows:

(*1*) DPRS is treated as having issued a deemed instrument worth $9x to FA in exchange for $9x of cash.

(*2*) DPRS is treated as having contributed $9x of cash to FT3 in exchange for deemed issued stock of FT3.

(*3*) DPRS is treated as continuing to own all of the stock of FT3.

(G) Under paragraph (c)(4)(i) of this section, any distribution with respect to the FT3 specified stock issued to FS will be treated as a distribution to DPRS, which, in turn, will be treated as making a matching distribution with respect to the deemed instruments that DPRS is treated as having issued to FS. Under paragraph (c)(4)(ii) of this section, FT3 is treated as the paying agent of DPRS with respect to the deemed instrument issued by DPRS to FS.

Example 7. (i) *Facts.* The facts are the same as in *Example 1* of this paragraph (g). On April 30, 2016, FA transfers $4x of the FT disregarded specified stock that it acquired on February 1, 2015 to USP, a domestic corporation that is not an expatriated entity, in exchange for $4x of cash.

(ii) *Results.* After the transfer, FT remains a foreign related person. Therefore, paragraph (d)(2) of this section does not apply. However, the $4x of FT disregarded specified stock transferred to USP ceases to be held by a foreign related person, a specified related person, or an expatriated entity (determined without taking into account paragraph (c)(2) or (3) of this section). Therefore, under paragraph (d)(3) of this section, immediately before the transfer of the disregarded specified stock, DT is deemed to transfer $4x ($6x x ($4x/$6x)) of the FT deemed issued stock that it is treated as owning to FA, the specified related person, in redemption of $4x ($6x x ($4x/$6x)) of the DT deemed instruments that FA is treated as owning, and the $4x of FT deemed issued stock deemed transferred to FA is deemed recapitalized into disregarded specified stock actually held by FA, which is thereafter treated as owned by FA for all purposes of the Code until the transfer to USP.

Example 8. (i) *Facts.* The facts are the same as in *Example 7* of this paragraph (g), except that on April 30, 2016, FA transfers all $6x of the FT disregarded specified stock to USP in exchange for $6x of cash.

(ii) *Results.* After the transfer, FT ceases to be a foreign related person (determined without taking into account paragraph (c)(2) or (3) of this section). Therefore, under paragraph (d)(2) of this section, immediately before the transfer of the disregarded specified stock, DT is deemed to transfer the $6x of FT deemed issued stock that it is treated as owning to FA, the specified related person, in redemption of the $6x of DT deemed instruments that FA is treated as owning, and the $6x of FT deemed issued stock deemed transferred to FA is deemed recapitalized into disregarded specified stock actually held by FA, which is thereafter treated as owned by FA for all purposes of the Code until the transfer to USP.

Example 9. (i) *Facts.* The facts are the same as in *Example 7* of this paragraph (g), except that on April 30, 2016, FA transfers $5.5x of the FT disregarded specified stock to USP in exchange for $5.5x of cash.

(ii) *Results.* After the transfer, FT ceases to be a foreign related person (determined without taking into account paragraph (c)(2) or (3) of this section). Therefore, under paragraph (d)(2) of this section, immediately before the transfer of the disregarded specified stock, DT is deemed to transfer the $6x of FT deemed issued stock that it is treated as owning to FA, the specified related person, in redemption of the $6x of DT deemed instruments that FA is treated as owning, and the $6x of FT deemed issued stock deemed transferred to FA is deemed recapitalized into disre-

garded specified stock actually held by FA, which is thereafter treated as owned by FA for all purposes of the Code and $5.5x of which is transferred to USP. The remaining $0.5x of the specified stock continues to be treated as owned by FA for all purposes of the Code.

Example 10. (i) *Facts.* The facts are the same as in *Example 1* of this paragraph (g). On April 30, 2016, FA transfers $5x of the FT disregarded specified stock that it acquired on February 1, 2015 to DS, a domestic corporation wholly owned by DT, in exchange for $5x of cash.

(ii) *Results.* After the transfer, FT remains a foreign related person because DS is wholly owned by DT. Therefore, paragraph (d)(2) of this section does not apply. Furthermore, the $5x of FT disregarded specified stock is not, as a result of the transfer, held by a person that is not a foreign related person, a specified related person, or an expatriated entity. Therefore, paragraph (d)(3) of this section does not apply. Because FA, a specified related person, directly transferred disregarded specified stock of FT in a transaction to which paragraphs (d)(2) and (3) of this section do not apply, under paragraph (d)(4) of this section, FA is treated as transferring the $5x of deemed instruments of DT allocable to the $5x of in-group transferred disregarded specified stock ($6x x ($5x/$6x)) to DS.

Example 11. (i) *Facts.* On February 1, 2015, FS acquires $6x of FT stock, representing 60% of the total voting power and value of the stock of FT, from FT in a stock issuance, in exchange for $6x of cash. The $6x of FT stock is specified stock, and the transaction is recharacterized under paragraph (c)(2) of this section. See *Example 1* of this paragraph (g). On April 30, 2016, FA transfers stock of FS representing 60% of the total voting power and value of the stock of FS to USP, a domestic corporation that is not an expatriated entity. As a result of the transfer, FS ceases to be a foreign related person.

(ii) *Results.* After the February 1, 2015 transfer, FT remains a foreign related person because the FT stock is acquired by FS, a foreign related person with respect to DT at that time. Therefore, paragraph (d)(2) of this section does not apply. However, after the April 30, 2016 transfer, because FS ceases to be a foreign related person, it ceases to be a specified related person. Furthermore, the $6x of disregarded specified stock held before the transaction continues to be held by FS after the transaction, and therefore is not held by a foreign related person, a specified related person, or an expatriated entity after the transaction. Accordingly, under paragraph (d)(3) of this section, immediately before the transfer of FS disregarded specified stock, DT is deemed to transfer $6x ($6x x ($6x/$6x)) of the FT deemed issued stock that it is treated as owning to FS, the specified related person, in redemption of $6x ($6x x ($6x/$6x)) of the DT deemed instruments that FS is treated as owning, and the $6x of FT deemed issued stock deemed transferred to FS is deemed recapitalized into disregarded specified stock actually held by FS, which thereafter is treated as owned by FS for all purposes of the

Code, including after the transfer of 60% of the FS stock to USP.

Example 12. (i) *Facts.* The facts are the same as in *Example 1* of this paragraph (g). On April 30, 2016, FP, a foreign corporation that is not a foreign related person acquires $15x of FT stock, representing 60% of the total voting power and value of the stock of FT, from FT in a stock issuance, in exchange for $15x of cash.

(ii) *Results.* After the transaction, FT ceases to be a foreign related person. Therefore, under paragraph (d)(2) of this section, immediately before the issuance of FT stock to FP, DT is deemed to transfer the $6x of FT deemed issued stock that it is treated as owning to FA, the specified related person, in redemption of the $6x of DT deemed instruments that FA is treated as owning, and the $6x of FT deemed issued stock deemed transferred to FA is deemed recapitalized into disregarded specified stock actually held by FA, which thereafter is treated as owned by FA for all purposes of the Code.

Example 13. (i) *Facts.* The facts are the same as in *Example 1* of this paragraph (g). On April 30, 2016, FS acquires $4x of the FT stock owned by DT in exchange for $4x of cash in a fully taxable transaction. DT recognizes and includes in income all of the gain (including any gain treated as a deemed dividend pursuant to section 1248(a)) with respect to the FT stock transferred to FS.

(ii) *Results.* (A) The transfer of FT stock by DT to FS is a specified transaction, but it is not recharacterized under paragraphs (c)(1) and (3) of this section because the exception in paragraph (b)(2)(ii) of this section applies. See *Example 4* of this paragraph (g).

(B) After the transfer, FT remains a foreign related person. Therefore, paragraph (d)(2) of this section does not apply. The disregarded specified stock of FT is not, as a result of the transfer, held by a person that is not a foreign related person, a specified related person, or an expatriated entity. Therefore, paragraph (d)(3) of this section does not apply. There has been no direct transfer of specified stock. Therefore, paragraph (d)(4) of this section also does not apply.

(C) Under paragraph (d)(1) of this section, the $6x of deemed issued stock treated as owned by DT as a result of the specified transaction in which FA acquired FT stock continues to be treated as owned by DT, and the $6x of deemed instruments treated as issued by DT to FA continue to be treated as owned by FA.

(h) *Applicability date.*—Except as otherwise provided in this paragraph (h), this section applies to specified transactions completed on or after September 22, 2014, but only if the inversion transaction was completed on or after September 22, 2014. Paragraph (b)(2)(ii)(A)(2) of this section applies to specified transactions completed on or after November 19, 2015, but only if the inversion transaction was completed on or after September 22, 2014. Paragraphs (d) and (f)(5), (7), and (10) of this section apply to specified transactions completed on or after April 4, 2016, but only if the inversion transaction was completed on or after September 22, 2014. For inversion transactions completed on or after September 22, 2014, however, taxpayers may elect to apply paragraphs (d) and (f)(5), (7), and (10) of this section to specified transactions completed before April 4, 2016. In addition, for inversion transactions completed on or after September 22, 2014, in lieu of applying paragraphs (d) and (f)(5) and (7) of this section to specified transactions completed on or after September 22, 2014, and before April 4, 2016, taxpayers may elect to apply the principles of § 1.7701(l)-3(c)(3)(iii). Furthermore, for inversion transactions completed on or after September 22, 2014, in lieu of applying paragraph (f)(10) of this section to specified transactions completed on or after September 22, 2014, and before April 4, 2016, taxpayers may elect to define a section 958(a) U.S. shareholder as a United States shareholder with respect to the expatriated foreign subsidiary that owns (within the meaning of section 958(a)) stock in the expatriated foreign subsidiary, but only if such United States shareholder is related (within the meaning of section 267(b) or 707(b)(1)) to the specified related person or is under the same common control (within the meaning of section 482) as the specified related person. [Reg. § 1.7701(l)-4.]

☐ [T.D. 9834, 7-11-2018.]

[Reg. § 1.7702-0]

§ 1.7702-0. Table of contents.—This section lists the captions that appear in §§ 1.7702-1, 1.7702-2, and 1.7702-3.

§ 1.7702-1 Mortality charges.

(a) General rule.

(b) Reasonable mortality charges.

(1) Actually expected to be imposed.

(2) Limit on charges.

(c) Safe harbors.

(1) 1980 C.S.O. Basic Mortality Tables.

(2) Unisex tables and smoker/nonsmoker tables.

(3) Certain contracts based on 1958 C.S.O. table.

(d) Definitions.

(1) Prevailing commissioners' standard tables.

(2) Substandard risk.

(3) Nonparticipating contract.

(4) Charge reduction mechanism.

(5) Plan of insurance.

(e) Effective date.

§ 1.7702-2 Attained age of the insured under a life insurance contract.

(a) In general.

(b) Contract insuring a single life.

(c) Contract insuring multiple lives on a last-to-die basis.

(1) In general.

(2) Modifications to cash value and future mortality charges upon the death of insured.

(d) Contract insuring multiple lives on a first-to-die basis.

(e) Examples.

(f) Effective dates.

(1) In general.

(2) Contracts issued before the general effective date.

§ 1.7702-3 *Definitions.*

(a) In general.

(b) Cash value.

(1) In general.

(2) Amounts excluded from cash value.

(c) Death benefit.

(1) In general.

(2) Qualified accelerated death benefit treated as death benefit.

(d) Qualified accelerated death benefit.

(1) In general.

(2) Determination of present value of the reduction in death benefit.

(3) Examples.

(e) Terminally ill defined.

(f) Certain other additional benefits.

(1) In general.

(2) Examples.

(g) Adjustments under section 7702 (f) (7).

(h) Cash surrender value.

(1) In general.

(2) For purposes of section 7702 (f) (7).

(i) Net surrender value.

(j) Effective date and special rules.

(1) In general.

(2) Provision of certain benefits before July 1, 1993.

(i) Not treated as cash value.

(ii) No effect on date of issuance.

(iii) Special rule for addition of benefit or loan provision after December 15, 1992.

(3) Addition of qualified accelerated death benefit.

(4) Addition of other additional benefits.

[Reg. § 1.7702-0.]

☐ [*T.D. 9287, 9-12-2006.*]

[Reg. § 1.7702-2]

§ 1.7702-2. Attained age of the insured under a life insurance contract.—(a) *In general.*—This section provides guidance on determining the attained age of an insured under a contract that is a life insurance contract under the applicable law, for purposes of determining the guideline level premium of the contract under section 7702(c) (4), applying the cash value corridor of section 7702(d) or applying the computational rules of section 7702(e), as applicable.

(b) *Contract insuring a single life.*—(1) If a contract insures the life of a single individual, either of the following two ages may be treated as the attained age of the insured with respect to that contract—

(i) The insured's age determined by reference to the individual's actual birthday as of the date of determination (actual age); or

(ii) The insured's age determined by reference to contract anniversary (rather than the

individual's actual birthday), so long as the age assumed under the contract (contract age) is within 12 months of the actual age as of that date.

(2) Once determined under paragraph (b)(1) of this section, the attained age with respect to an individual insured under a contract changes annually. Moreover, the same attained age must be used for purposes of applying sections 7702(c) (4), 7702(d), and 7702(e), as applicable.

(c) *Contract insuring multiple lives on a last-to-die basis.*—(1) *In general.*—Except as provided in paragraph (c)(2) of this section, if a contract insures the lives of more than one individual on a last-to-die basis, the attained age of the insured is determined by applying paragraph (b) of this section as if the youngest individual were the only insured under the contract for purposes of sections 7702(c) (4), 7702(d), and 7702(e), as applicable.

(2) *Modifications to cash value and future mortality charges upon the death of insured.*—If both the cash value and future mortality charges under a contract change by reason of the death of one or more insureds to no longer take into account the attained age of the deceased insured or insureds, the youngest surviving insured shall thereafter be treated as the only insured under the contract.

(d) *Contract insuring multiple lives on a first-to-die basis.*—If a contract insures the lives of more than one individual on a first-to-die basis, the attained age of the insured is determined by applying paragraph (b) of this section as if the oldest individual were the only insured under the contract for purposes of sections 7702(c) (4), 7702(d), and 7702(e), as applicable.

(e) *Examples.*—The following examples illustrate the determination of the attained age of the insured for purposes of sections 7702(c)(4), 7702(d), and 7702(e), as applicable. The examples are as follows:

Example 1. (i) X was born on May 1, 1947. X became 60 years old on May 1, 2007. On January 1, 2008, X purchases from IC a contract insuring X's life. January 1 is the contract anniversary date for all future years. IC determines X's annual premiums on an age-last-birthday basis. Based on the method used by IC to determine age, X has an attained age of 60 for the first contract year, 61 for the second contract year, and so on.

(ii) Section 1.7702-2(b)(1) permits the determination of attained age under either of two alternative approaches. Section 1.7702-2(b)(1)(i) provides that, if a contract insures the life of a single insured individual, the attained age may be determined by reference to the individual's actual birthday as of the date of determination. Under this provision, X has an attained age of 60 for the first contract year, 61 for the second contract year, and so on. Alternatively, § 1.7702-2(b)(1)(ii) provides that the insured's age may be determined by reference to contract anniversary (rather than the individual's actual birthday), so long as the age assumed under the contract is within 12 months of the actual age as of that date. If IC determines X's attained age under § 1.7702-2(b)(1)(ii), X likewise has an attained age of 60 for the first contract year, 61 for the second contract year, and so on. Whichever provision IC uses to determine X's attained age must be used consistently from year to year for purposes of sections 7702 (c) (4), 7702(d), and 7702(e), as applicable.

Example 2. (i) The facts are the same as in *Example 1* except that, under the contract, X's annual premiums are determined on an age-nearest-birthday basis. X's nearest birthday to January 1, 2008, is May 1, 2008, when X will become 61 years old. Based on the method used by IC to determine age, X has an attained age of 61 for the first contract year, 62 for the second contract year, and so on.

(ii) Section 1.7702-2(b)(1) permits the determination of attained age under either of two alternative approaches. Section 1.7702-2(b)(1)(i) provides that, if a contract insures the life of a single insured individual, the attained age may be determined by reference to the individual's actual birthday as of the date of determination. Under this provision, X has an attained age of 60 for the first contract year, 61 for the second contract year, and so on. Alternatively, § 1.7702-2(b)(1)(ii) provides that the insured's age may be determined by reference to contract anniversary (rather than the individual's actual birthday), so long as the age assumed under the contract is within 12 months of the actual age as of that date. If IC determines X's attained age under § 1.7702-2(b)(1)(ii), X has an attained age of 61 for the first contract year, 62 for the second contract year, and so on. Whichever provision IC uses to determine X's attained age must be used consistently from year to year for purposes of sections 7702 (c) (4), 7702(d), and 7702(e), as applicable.

Example 3. (i) The facts are the same as in *Example 1* except that the face amount of the contract is increased on May 15, 2011. During the contract year beginning January 1, 2011, the age assumed under the contract on an age-last-birthday basis is 63 years. However, X has an actual age of 64 as of the date the face amount of the contract is increased.

(ii) Section 1.7702-2(b)(1)(ii) provides that the insured's age may be determined by reference to contract anniversary (rather than the individual's actual birthday), so long as the age assumed under the contract is within 12 months of the actual age. Section 1.7702-2(b)(2) provides that, once determined under paragraph (b)(1) of this section, the attained age with respect to an individual insured under a contract changes annually. Accordingly, X continues to be 63 years old throughout the contract year beginning January 1, 2011, for purposes of sections 7702(c)(4), 7702(d), and 7702 (e), as applicable.

Example 4. (i) The facts are the same as in *Example 1* except that in addition to X (born in 1947), the insurance contract also insures the life of Y, born on September 1, 1942. The death bene-

fit will be paid when the second of the two insureds dies.

(ii) Section 1.7702-2 (c) (1) provides that if a life insurance contract insures the lives of more than one individual on a last-to-die basis, the attained age of the insured is determined by applying § 1.7702-2(b) as if the youngest individual were the only insured under the contract. Because X is younger than Y, the attained age of X must be used for purposes of sections 7702 (c) (4), 7702(d), and 7702(e), as applicable.

Example 5. (i) The facts are the same as *Example 4* except that X (the younger of the two insureds) dies in 2012. After X's death, both the cash value and mortality charges of the life insurance contract are adjusted to take into account only the life of Y.

(ii) Section 1.7702-2 (c) (1) provides that if a life insurance contract insures the lives of more than one individual on a last-to-die basis, the attained age of the insured is determined by applying § 1.7702-2(b) as if the youngest individual were the only insured under the contract. Paragraph (c)(2) of this section provides that if both the cash value and future mortality charges under a contract change by reason of the death of an insured to no longer take into account the attained age of the deceased insured, the youngest surviving insured is thereafter treated as the only insured under the contract. Because both the cash value and mortality charges are adjusted after X's death to take into account only the life of Y, only the attained age of Y is taken into account after X's death for purposes of sections 7702(c) (4), 7702(d), and 7702 (e), as applicable.

Example 6. (i) The facts are the same as *Example 1* except that in addition to X (born in 1947), the insurance contract also insures the life of Z, born on September 1, 1952. The death benefit will be paid when the first of the two insureds dies.

(ii) Section 1.7702-2(d) provides that if a life insurance contract insures the lives of more than one individual on a first-to-die basis, the attained age of the insured is determined by applying § 1.7702-2(b) as if the oldest individual were the only insured under the contract. Because X is older than Z, the attained age of X must be used for purposes of sections 7702 (c) (4), 7702(d), and 7702 (e), as applicable.

(f) *Effective dates.*—(1) *In general.*—Except as provided in paragraph (f)(2) of this section, these regulations apply to all life insurance contracts that are either—

(i) Issued after December 31, 2008; or

(ii) Issued on or after October 1, 2007 and based upon the 2001 CSO tables.

(2) *Contracts issued before the general effective date.*—Pursuant to section 7805(b)(7), a taxpayer may apply these regulations retroactively for contracts issued before October 1, 2007, provided that the taxpayer does not later determine qualification of those contracts in a manner that is inconsistent with these regulations. [Reg. § 1.7702-2.]

□ [*T.D.* 9287, 9-12-2006.]

[Reg. § 1.7702B-1]

§ 1.7702B-1. Consumer protection provisions.—(a) *In general.*—Under sections 7702B(b)(1)(F), 7702B(g), and 4980C, qualified long-term care insurance contracts and issuers of those contracts are required to satisfy certain provisions of the Long-Term Care Insurance Model Act (Model Act) and Long-Term Care Insurance Model Regulation (Model Regulation) promulgated by the National Association of Insurance Commissioners (NAIC), as adopted as of January 1993. The requirements for qualified long-term care insurance contracts under section 7702B(b)(1)(F) and (g) relate to guaranteed renewal or noncancellability, prohibitions on limitations and exclusions, extension of benefits, continuation or conversion of coverage, discontinuance and replacement of policies, unintentional lapse, disclosure, prohibitions against post-claims underwriting, minimum standards, inflation protection, prohibitions against pre-existing conditions exclusions and probationary periods, and prior hospitalization. The requirements for qualified long-term care insurance contracts under section 4980C relate to application forms and replacement coverage, reporting requirements, filing requirements for marketing, standards for marketing, appropriateness of recommended purchase, standard format outline of coverage, delivery of a shopper's guide, right to return, outline of coverage, certificates under group plans, policy summary, monthly reports on accelerated death benefits, and incontestability period.

(b) *Coordination with State requirements.*—(1) *Contracts issued in a State that imposes more stringent requirements.*—If a State imposes a requirement that is more stringent than the analogous requirement imposed by section 7702B(g) or 4980C, then, under section 4980C(f), compliance with the more stringent requirement of State law is considered compliance with the parallel requirement of section 7702B(g) or 4980C. The principles of paragraph (b)(3) of this section apply to any case in which a State imposes a requirement that is more stringent than the analogous requirement imposed by section 7702B(g) or 4980C (as described in this paragraph (b)(1)), but in which there has been a failure to comply with that State requirement.

(2) *Contracts issued in a State that has adopted the model provisions.*—If a State imposes a requirement that is the same as the parallel requirement imposed by section 7702B(g) or 4980C, compliance with that requirement of State law is considered compliance with the parallel requirement of section 7702B(g) or 4980C, and failure to comply with that requirement of State law is considered failure to comply with the parallel requirement of section 7702B(g) or 4980C.

(3) *Contracts issued in a State that has not adopted the model provisions or more stringent requirements.*—If a State has not adopted the Model Act, the Model Regulation, or a requirement that is the same as or more stringent than the analogous requirement imposed by section 7702B(g) or 4980C, then the language, caption, format, and content requirements imposed by sections 7702B(g) and 4980C with respect to contracts, applications, outlines of coverage, policy summaries, and notices will be considered satisfied for a contract subject to the law of that State if the language, caption, format, and content are substantially similar to those required under the parallel provision of the Model Act or Model Regulation. Only nonsubstantive deviations are permitted in order for language, caption, format, and content to be considered substantially similar to the requirements of the Model Act or Model Regulation.

(c) *Effective date.*—This section applies with respect to contracts issued after December 10, 1999. [Reg. § 1.7702B-1.]

☐ [*T.D.* 8792, 12-9-98.]

[Reg. § 1.7702B-2]

§ 1.7702B-2. Special rules for pre-1997 long-term care insurance contracts.—(a) *Scope.*—The definitions and special provisions of this section apply solely for purposes of determining whether an insurance contract (other than a qualified long-term care insurance contract described in section 7702B(b) and any regulations issued thereunder) is treated as a qualified long-term care insurance contract for purposes of the Internal Revenue Code under section 321(f)(2) of the Health Insurance Portability and Accountability Act of 1996 (Public Law 104-191).

(b) *Pre-1997 long-term care insurance contracts.*—(1) *In general.*—A pre-1997 long-term care insurance contract is treated as a qualified long-term care insurance contract, regardless of whether the contract satisfies section 7702B(b) and any regulations issued thereunder.

(2) *Pre-1997 long-term care insurance contract defined.*—A pre-1997 long-term care insurance contract is any insurance contract with an issue date before January 1, 1997, that met the long-term care insurance requirements of the State in which the contract was sitused on the issue date. For this purpose, the long-term care insurance requirements of the State are the State laws (including statutory and administrative law) that are intended to regulate insurance coverage that constitutes "long-term care insurance" (as defined in section 4 of the National Association of Insurance Commissioners (NAIC) Long-Term Care Insurance Model Act, as in effect on August 21, 1996), regardless of the terminology used by the State in describing the insurance coverage.

(3) *Issue date of a contract.*—(i) *In general.*—Except as otherwise provided in this paragraph (b)(3), the issue date of a contract is the issue date assigned to the contract by the insurance company. In no event is the issue date earlier than the date the policyholder submitted a signed application for coverage to the insurance

Reg. § 1.7702B-2(b)(3)(i)

company. If the period between the date the signed application is submitted to the insurance company and the date coverage under the contract actually becomes effective is substantially longer than under the insurance company's usual business practice, then the issue date is the later of the date coverage under the contract becomes effective or the issue date assigned to the contract by the insurance company. A policyholder's right to return a contract within a free-look period following delivery for a full refund of any premiums paid is not taken into account in determining the contract's issue date.

(ii) *Special rule for group contracts.*—The issue date of a group contract (including any certificate issued thereunder) is the date on which coverage under the group contract becomes effective.

(iii) *Exchange of contract or certain changes in a contract treated as a new issuance.*—For purposes of this paragraph (b)(3)—

(A) A contract issued in exchange for an existing contract after December 31, 1996, is considered a contract issued after that date;

(B) Any change described in paragraph (b)(4) of this section is treated as the issuance of a new contract with an issue date no earlier than the date the change goes into effect; and

(C) If a change described in paragraph (b)(4) of this section occurs with regard to one or more, but fewer than all, of the certificates evidencing coverage under a group contract, then the insurance coverage under the changed certificates is treated as coverage under a newly issued group contract (and the insurance coverage provided by any unchanged certificate continues to be treated as coverage under the original group contract).

(4) *Changes treated as the issuance of a new contract.*—(i) *In general.*—For purposes of paragraph (b)(3) of this section, except as provided in paragraph (b)(4)(ii) of this section, the following changes are treated as the issuance of a new contract—

(A) A change in the terms of a contract that alters the amount or timing of an item payable by either the policyholder (or certificate holder), the insured, or the insurance company;

(B) A substitution of the insured under an individual contract; or

(C) A change (other than an immaterial change) in the contractual terms, or in the plan under which the contract was issued, relating to eligibility for membership in the group covered under a group contract.

(ii) *Exceptions.*—For purposes of this paragraph (b)(4), the following changes are not treated as the issuance of a new contract—

(A) A policyholder's exercise of any right provided under the terms of the contract as in effect on December 31, 1996, or a right required by applicable State law to be provided to the policyholder;

(B) A change in the mode of premium payment (for example, a change from monthly to quarterly premiums);

(C) In the case of a policy that is guaranteed renewable or noncancellable, a classwide increase or decrease in premiums;

(D) A reduction in premiums due to the purchase of a long-term care insurance contract by a family member of the policyholder;

(E) A reduction in coverage (with a corresponding reduction in premiums) made at the request of a policyholder;

(F) A reduction in premiums as a result of extending to an individual policyholder a discount applicable to similar categories of individuals pursuant to a premium rate structure that was in effect on December 31, 1996, for the issuer's pre-1997 long-term care insurance contracts of the same type;

(G) The addition, without an increase in premiums, of alternative forms of benefits that may be selected by the policyholder;

(H) The addition of a rider (including any similarly identifiable amendment) to a pre-1997 long-term care insurance contract in any case in which the rider, if issued as a separate contract of insurance, would itself be a qualified long-term care insurance contract under section 7702B and any regulations issued thereunder (including the consumer protection provisions in section 7702B(g) to the extent applicable to the addition of a rider);

(I) The deletion of a rider or provision of a contract that prohibited coordination of benefits with Medicare (often referred to as an HHS (Health and Human Services) rider);

(J) The effectuation of a continuation or conversion of coverage right that is provided under a pre-1997 group contract and that, in accordance with the terms of the contract as in effect on December 31, 1996, provides for coverage under an individual contract following an individual's ineligibility for continued coverage under the group contract; and

(K) The substitution of one insurer for another insurer in an assumption reinsurance transaction.

(5) *Examples.*—The following examples illustrate the principles of this paragraph (b):

Example 1. (i) On December 3, 1996, A, an individual, submits a signed application to an insurance company to purchase a nursing home contract that meets the long-term care insurance requirements of the State in which the contract is sitused. The insurance company decides on December 20, 1996, that it will issue the contract, and assigns December 20, 1996, as the issue date for the contract. Under the terms of the contract, A's insurance coverage becomes effective on January 1, 1997. The company delivers the contract to A on January 3, 1997. A has the right to return the contract within 15 days following delivery for a refund of all premiums paid.

(ii) Under paragraph (b)(3)(i) of this section, the issue date of the contract is December 20,

1996. Thus, the contract is a pre-1997 long-term care insurance contract that is treated as a qualified long-term care insurance contract.

Example 2. (i) The facts are the same as in *Example 1,* except that the insurance coverage under the contract does not become effective until March 1, 1997. Under the insurance company's usual business practice, the period between the date of the application and the date the contract becomes effective is 30 days or less.

(ii) Under paragraph (b)(3)(i) of this section, the issue date of the contract is March 1, 1997. Thus, the contract is not a pre-1997 long-term care insurance contract, and, accordingly, the contract must meet the requirements of section 7702B(b) and any regulations issued thereunder to be a qualified long-term care insurance contract.

Example 3. (i) B, an individual, is the policyholder under a long-term care insurance contract purchased in 1995. On June 15, 2000, the insurance coverage and premiums under the contract are increased by agreement between B and the insurance company.

(ii) Under paragraph (b)(4)(i)(A) of this section, a change in the terms of a contract that alters the amount or timing of an item payable by the policyholder or the insurance company is treated as the issuance of a new contract. Thus, B's coverage is treated as coverage under a contract issued on June 15, 2000, and, accordingly, the contract must meet the requirements of section 7702B(b) and any regulations issued thereunder in order to be a qualified long-term care insurance contract.

Example 4. (i) C, an individual, is the policyholder under a long-term care insurance contract purchased in 1994. At that time and through December 31, 1996, the contract met the long-term care insurance requirements of the State in which the contract was sitused. In 1996, the policy was amended to add a provision requiring the policyholder to be offered the right to increase dollar limits for inflation every three years (without the policyholder being required to pass a physical or satisfy any other underwriting requirements). During 2002, C elects to increase the amount of insurance coverage (with a resulting premium increase) pursuant to the inflation provision.

(ii) Under paragraph (b)(4)(ii)(A) of this section, an increase in the amount of insurance coverage at the election of the policyholder (without the insurance company's consent and without underwriting or other limitations on the policyholder's rights) pursuant to a pre-1997 inflation provision is not treated as the issuance of a new contract. Thus, C's contract continues to be a pre-1997 long-term care insurance contract that is treated as a qualified long-term care insurance contract.

(c) *Effective date.*—This section is applicable January 1, 1999. [Reg. § 1.7702B-2.]

□ [*T.D.* 8792, 12-9-98.]

[Reg. § 1.7703-1]

§ 1.7703-1. Determination of marital status.—

(a) *General rule.*—The determination of whether an individual is married shall be made as of the close of his taxable year unless his spouse dies during his taxable year, in which case such determination shall be made as of the time of such death; and, except as provided in paragraph (b) of this section, an individual shall be considered as married even though living apart from his spouse unless legally separated under a decree of divorce or separate maintenance. The provisions of this paragraph may be illustrated by the following examples:

Example (1). Taxpayer A and his wife B both make their returns on a calendar year basis. In July 1954, they enter into a separation agreement and thereafter live apart, but no decree of divorce or separate maintenance is issued until March 1955. If A itemizes and claims his actual deductions on his return for the calendar year 1954, B may not elect the standard deduction on her return since B is considered as married to A (although permanently separated by agreement) on the last day of 1954.

Example (2). Taxpayer A makes his returns on the basis of a fiscal year ending June 30. His wife B makes her returns on the calendar year basis. A died in October 1954. In such case, since A and B were married as of the date of death, B may not elect the standard deduction for the calendar year 1954 if the income of A for the short taxable year ending with the date of his death is determined without regard to the standard deduction.

(b) *Certain married individuals living apart.*—(1) For purposes of part IV of subchapter B of chapter 1 of the Code, an individual is not considered as married for taxable years beginning after December 31, 1969, if (i) such individual is married (within the meaning of paragraph (a) of this section) but files a separate return; (ii) such individual maintains as his home a household which constitutes for more than one-half of the taxable year the principal place of abode of a dependent (*a*) who (within the meaning of section 152 and the regulations thereunder) is a son, stepson, daughter, or stepdaughter of the individual, and (*b*) with respect to whom such individual is entitled to a deduction for the taxable year under section 151; (iii) such individual furnishes over half of the cost of maintaining such household during the taxable year; and (iv) during the entire taxable year such individual's spouse is not a member of such household.

(2) For purposes of subparagraph (1)(ii)(*a*) of this paragraph, a legally adopted son or daughter of an individual, a child (described in paragraph (c)(2) of § 1.152-2) who is a member of an individual's household if placed with such individual by an authorized placement agency (as defined in paragraph (c)(2) of § 1.152-2) for legal adoption by such individual, or a foster child (described in paragraph (c)(4) of § 1.152-2) of an individual if such child satisfies the requirements of section 152(a)(9) of the Code and paragraph (b) of § 1.152-1 with respect to such

individual, shall be treated as a son or daughter of such individual by blood.

(3) For purposes of subparagraph (1)(ii) of this paragraph, the household must actually constitute the home of the individual for his taxable year. However, a physical change in the location of such home will not prevent an individual from qualifying for the treatment provided in subparagraph (1) of this paragraph. It is not sufficient that the individual maintain the household without being its occupant. The individual and the dependent described in subparagraph (1)(ii)(a) of this paragraph must occupy the household for more than one-half of the taxable year of the individual. However, the fact that such dependent is born or dies within the taxable year will not prevent an individual from qualifying for such treatment if the household constitutes the principal place of abode of such dependent for the remaining or preceding part of such taxable year. The individual and such dependent will be considered as occupying the household during temporary absences from the household due to special circumstances. A nonpermanent failure to occupy the common abode by reason of illness, education, business, vacation, military service, or a custody agreement under which a child or stepchild is absent for less than 6 months in the taxable year of the taxpayer, shall be considered a temporary absence due to special circumstances. Such absence will not prevent an individual from qualifying for the treatment provided in subparagraph (1) of this paragraph if (i) it is reasonable to assume that such individual or the dependent will return to the household and (ii) such individual continues to maintain such household or a substantially equivalent household in anticipation of such return.

(4) An individual shall be considered as maintaining a household only if he pays more than one-half of the cost thereof for his taxable year. The cost of maintaining a household shall be the expenses incurred for the mutual benefit of the occupants thereof by reason of its operation as the principal place of abode of such occupants for such taxable year. The cost of maintaining a household shall not include expenses otherwise incurred. The expenses of maintaining a household include property taxes, mortgage interest, rent, utility charges, upkeep and repairs, property insurance, and food consumed on the premises. Such expenses do not include the cost of clothing, education, medical treatment, vacations, life insurance, and transportation. In addition, the cost of maintaining a household shall not include any amount which represents the value of services rendered in the household by the taxpayer or by a dependent described in subparagraph (1)(ii)(a) of this paragraph.

(5) For purposes of subparagraph (1)(iv) of this paragraph, an individual's spouse is not a member of the household during a taxable year if such household does not constitute such spouse's place of abode at any time during such year. An individual's spouse will be considered

to be a member of the household during temporary absences from the household due to special circumstances. A nonpermanent failure to occupy such household as his abode by reason of illness, education, business, vacation, or military service shall be considered a mere temporary absence due to special circumstances.

(6) The provisions of this paragraph may be illustrated by the following example:

Example. Taxpayer A, married to B at the close of the calendar year 1971, his taxable year, is living apart from B, but A is not legally separated from B under a decree of divorce or separate maintenance. A maintains a household as his home which is for 7 months of 1971 the principal place of abode of C, his son, with respect to whom A is entitled to a deduction under Section 151. A pays for more than one-half of the cost of maintaining that household. At no time during 1971 was B a member of the household occupied by A and C. A files a separate return for 1971. Under these circumstances, A is considered as not married under section 143(b) for purposes of the standard deduction. Even though A is married and files a separate return A may claim for 1971 as his standard deduction the larger of the low income allowance up to a maximum of $1,050 consisting of both the basic allowance and additional allowance (rather than the basic allowance only subject to the $500 limitation applicable to a separate return of a married individual) or the percentage standard deduction subject to the $1,500 limitation (rather than the $750 limitation applicable to a separate return of a married individual). See § 1.141-1. For purposes of the provisions of part IV of subchapter B of chapter 1 of the Code and the regulations thereunder, A is treated as unmarried. [Reg. § 1.7703-1.]

☐ [T.D. 6272, 11-25-57. *Amended by T.D. 7123, 6-8-71. Redesignated by T.D. 8712, 1-10-97.*]

[Reg. § 1.7704-1]

§ 1.7704-1. Publicly traded partnerships.—(a) *In general.—*(1) *Publicly traded partnership.—*A domestic or foreign partnership is a publicly traded partnership for purposes of section 7704(b) and this section if—

(i) Interests in the partnership are traded on an established securities market; or

(ii) Interests in the partnership are readily tradable on a secondary market or the substantial equivalent thereof.

(2) *Partnership interest.—*(i) *In general.—*For purposes of section 7704(b) and this section, an interest in a partnership includes—

(A) Any interest in the capital or profits of the partnership (including the right to partnership distributions); and

(B) Any financial instrument or contract the value of which is determined in whole or in part by reference to the partnership (including the amount of partnership distributions, the value of partnership assets, or the results of partnership operations).

(ii) *Exception for non-convertible debt.*—For purposes of section 7704(b) and this section, an interest in a partnership does not include any financial instrument or contract that—

(A) Is treated as debt for federal tax purposes; and

(B) Is not convertible into or exchangeable for an interest in the capital or profits of the partnership and does not provide for a payment of equivalent value.

(iii) *Exception for tiered entities.*—For purposes of section 7704(b) and this section, an interest in a partnership or a corporation (including a regulated investment company as defined in section 851 or a real estate investment trust as defined in section 856) that holds an interest in a partnership (lower-tier partnership) is not considered an interest in the lower-tier partnership.

(3) *Definition of transfer.*—For purposes of section 7704(b) and this section, a transfer of an interest in a partnership means a transfer in any form, including a redemption by the partnership or the entering into of a financial instrument or contract described in paragraph (a)(2)(i)(B) of this section.

(b) *Established securities market.*—For purposes of section 7704(b) and this section, an established securities market includes—

(1) A national securities exchange registered under section 6 of the Securities Exchange Act of 1934 (15 U.S.C. 78f);

(2) A national securities exchange exempt from registration under section 6 of the Securities Exchange Act of 1934 (15 U.S.C. 78f) because of the limited volume of transactions;

(3) A foreign securities exchange that, under the law of the jurisdiction where it is organized, satisfies regulatory requirements that are analogous to the regulatory requirements under the Securities Exchange Act of 1934 described in paragraph (b)(1) or (2) of this section (such as the London International Financial Futures Exchange; the Marche a Terme International de France; the International Stock Exchange of the United Kingdom and the Republic of Ireland, Limited; the Frankfurt Stock Exchange; and the Tokyo Stock Exchange);

(4) A regional or local exchange; and

(5) An interdealer quotation system that regularly disseminates firm buy or sell quotations by identified brokers or dealers by electronic means or otherwise.

(c) *Readily tradable on a secondary market or the substantial equivalent thereof.*—(1) *In general.*—For purposes of section 7704(b) and this section, interests in a partnership that are not traded on an established securities market (within the meaning of section 7704(b) and paragraph (b) of this section) are readily tradable on a secondary market or the substantial equivalent thereof if, taking into account all of the facts and circumstances, the partners are readily able to buy, sell, or exchange their partnership interests in a manner

that is comparable, economically, to trading on an established securities market.

(2) *Secondary market or the substantial equivalent thereof.*—For purposes of paragraph (c)(1) of this section, interests in a partnership are readily tradable on a secondary market or the substantial equivalent thereof if—

(i) Interests in the partnership are regularly quoted by any person, such as a broker or dealer, making a market in the interests;

(ii) Any person regularly makes available to the public (including customers or subscribers) bid or offer quotes with respect to interests in the partnership and stands ready to effect buy or sell transactions at the quoted prices for itself or on behalf of others;

(iii) The holder of an interest in the partnership has a readily available, regular, and ongoing opportunity to sell or exchange the interest through a public means of obtaining or providing information of offers to buy, sell, or exchange interests in the partnership; or

(iv) Prospective buyers and sellers otherwise have the opportunity to buy, sell, or exchange interests in the partnership in a time frame and with the regularity and continuity that is comparable to that described in the other provisions of this paragraph (c)(2).

(3) *Secondary market safe harbors.*—The fact that a transfer of a partnership interest is not within one or more of the safe harbors described in paragraph (e), (f), (g), (h), or (j) of this section is disregarded in determining whether interests in the partnership are readily tradable on a secondary market or the substantial equivalent thereof.

(d) *Involvement of the partnership required.*—For purposes of section 7704(b) and this section, interests in a partnership are not traded on an established securities market within the meaning of paragraph (b)(5) of this section and are not readily tradable on a secondary market or the substantial equivalent thereof within the meaning of paragraph (c) of this section (even if interests in the partnership are traded or readily tradable in a manner described in paragraph (b)(5) or (c) of this section) unless—

(1) The partnership participates in the establishment of the market or the inclusion of its interests thereon; or

(2) The partnership recognizes any transfers made on the market by—

(i) Redeeming the transferor partner (in the case of a redemption or repurchase by the partnership); or

(ii) Admitting the transferee as a partner or otherwise recognizing any rights of the transferee, such as a right of the transferee to receive partnership distributions (directly or indirectly) or to acquire an interest in the capital or profits of the partnership.

(e) *Transfers not involving trading.*—(1) *In general.*—For purposes of section 7704(b) and this section, the following transfers (private transfers) are disregarded in determining whether interests in a partnership are readily tradable on a secondary market or the substantial equivalent thereof—

(i) Transfers in which the basis of the partnership interest in the hands of the transferee is determined, in whole or in part, by reference to its basis in the hands of the transferor or is determined under section 732;

(ii) Transfers at death, including transfers from an estate or testamentary trust;

(iii) Transfers between members of a family (as defined in section 267(c)(4));

(iv) Transfers involving the issuance of interests by (or on behalf of) the partnership in exchange for cash, property, or services;

(v) Transfers involving distributions from a retirement plan qualified under section 401(a) or an individual retirement account;

(vi) Block transfers (as defined in paragraph (e)(2) of this section);

(vii) Transfers pursuant to a right under a redemption or repurchase agreement (as defined in paragraph (e) (3) of this section) that is exercisable only—

(A) Upon the death, disability, or mental incompetence of the partner; or

(B) Upon the retirement or termination of the performance of services of an individual who actively participated in the management of, or performed services on a full-time basis for, the partnership;

(viii) Transfers pursuant to a closed end redemption plan (as defined in paragraph (e)(4) of this section);

(ix) Transfers by one or more partners of interests representing in the aggregate 50 percent or more of the total interests in partnership capital and profits in one transaction or a series of related transactions; and

(x) Transfers not recognized by the partnership (within the meaning of paragraph (d)(2) of this section).

(2) *Block transfers.*—For purposes of paragraph (e)(1)(vi) of this section, a block transfer means the transfer by a partner and any related persons (within the meaning of section 267(b) or 707(b)(1)) in one or more transactions during any 30 calendar day period of partnership interests representing in the aggregate more than 2 percent of the total interests in partnership capital or profits.

(3) *Redemption or repurchase agreement.*—For purposes of section 7704(b) and this section, a redemption or repurchase agreement means a plan of redemption or repurchase maintained by a partnership whereby the partners may tender their partnership interests for purchase by the partnership, another partner, or a person related to another partner (within the meaning of section 267(b) or 707(b)(1)).

(4) *Closed end redemption plan.*—For purposes of paragraph (e)(1)(viii) of this section, a

redemption or repurchase agreement (as defined in paragraph (e)(3) of this section) is a closed end redemption plan only if—

(i) The partnership does not issue any interest after the initial offering (other than the issuance of additional interests prior to August 5, 1988); and

(ii) No partner or person related to any partner (within the meaning of section 267(b) or 707(b)(1)) provides contemporaneous opportunities to acquire interests in similar or related partnerships which represent substantially identical investments.

(f) *Redemption and repurchase agreements.*—For purposes of section 7704(b) and this section, the transfer of an interest in a partnership pursuant to a redemption or repurchase agreement (as defined in paragraph (e)(3) of this section) that is not described in paragraph (e)(1)(vii) or (viii) of this section is disregarded in determining whether interests in the partnership are readily tradable on a secondary market or the substantial equivalent thereof only if—

(1) The redemption or repurchase agreement provides that the redemption or repurchase cannot occur until at least 60 calendar days after the partner notifies the partnership in writing of the partner's intention to exercise the redemption or repurchase right;

(2) Either—

(i) The redemption or repurchase agreement requires that the redemption or repurchase price not be established until at least 60 calendar days after receipt of such notification by the partnership or the partner; or

(ii) The redemption or repurchase price is established not more than four times during the partnership's taxable year; and

(3) The sum of the percentage interests in partnership capital or profits transferred during the taxable year of the partnership (other than in private transfers described in paragraph (e) of this section) does not exceed 10 percent of the total interests in partnership capital or profits.

(g) *Qualified matching services.*—(1) *In general.*—For purposes of section 7704(b) and this section, the transfer of an interest in a partnership through a qualified matching service is disregarded in determining whether interests in the partnership are readily tradable on a secondary market or the substantial equivalent thereof.

(2) *Requirements.*—A matching service is a qualified matching service only if—

(i) The matching service consists of a computerized or printed listing system that lists customers' bid and/or ask quotes in order to match partners who want to sell their interests in a partnership (the selling partner) with persons who want to buy those interests;

(ii) Matching occurs either by matching the list of interested buyers with the list of interested sellers or through a bid and ask process that allows interested buyers to bid on the listed interest;

(iii) The selling partner cannot enter into a binding agreement to sell the interest until the 15th calendar day after the date information regarding the offering of the interest for sale is made available to potential buyers and such time period is evidenced by contemporaneous records ordinarily maintained by the operator at a central location;

(iv) The closing of the sale effected by virtue of the matching service does not occur prior to the 45th calendar day after the date information regarding the offering of the interest for sale is made available to potential buyers and such time period is evidenced by contemporaneous records ordinarily maintained by the operator at a central location;

(v) The matching service displays only quotes that do not commit any person to buy or sell a partnership interest at the quoted price (nonfirm price quotes) or quotes that express interest in partnership interest without an accompanying price (nonbinding indications of interest) and does not display quotes at which any person is committed to buy or sell a partnership interest at the quoted price (firm quotes);

(vi) The selling partner's information is removed from the matching service within 120 calendar days after the date information regarding the offering of the interest for sale is made available to potential buyers and, following any removal (other than removal by reason of a sale of any part of such interest) of the selling partner's information from the matching service, no offer to sell an interest in the partnership is entered into the matching service by the selling partner for at least 60 calendar days; and

(vii) The sum of the percentage interests in partnership capital or profits transferred during the taxable year of the partnership (other than in private transfers described in paragraph (e) of this section) does not exceed 10 percent of the total interests in partnership capital or profits.

(3) *Closing.*—For purposes of paragraph (g)(2)(iv) of this section, the closing of a sale occurs no later than the earlier of—

(i) The passage of title to the partnership interest;

(ii) The payment of the purchase price (which does not include the delivery of funds to the operator of the matching service or other closing agent to hold on behalf of the seller pending closing); or

(iii) The date, if any, that the operator of the matching service (or any person related to the operator within the meaning of section 267(b) or 707(b)(1)) loans, advances, or otherwise arranges for funds to be available to the seller in anticipation of the payment of the purchase price.

(4) *Optional features.*—A qualified matching service may be sponsored or operated by a partner of the partnership (either formally or informally), the underwriter that handled the issuance of the partnership interests, or an unre-

lated third party. In addition, a qualified matching service may offer the following features—

(i) The matching service may provide prior pricing information, including information regarding resales of interests and actual prices paid for interests; a description of the business of the partnership; financial and reporting information from the partnership's financial statements and reports; and information regarding material events involving the partnership, including special distributions, capital distributions, and refinancings or sales of significant portions of partnership assets;

(ii) The operator may assist with the transfer documentation necessary to transfer the partnership interest;

(iii) The operator may receive and deliver funds for completed transactions; and

(iv) The operator's fee may consist of a flat fee for use of the service, a fee or commission based on completed transactions, or any combination thereof.

(h) *Private placements.*—(1) *In general.*—For purposes of section 7704(b) and this section, except as otherwise provided in paragraph (h) (2) of this section, interests in a partnership are not readily tradable on a secondary market or the substantial equivalent thereof if—

(i) All interests in the partnership were issued in a transaction (or transactions) that was not required to be registered under the Securities Act of 1933 (15 U.S.C. 77a et seq.); and

(ii) The partnership does not have more than 100 partners at any time during the taxable year of the partnership.

(2) *Exception for certain offerings outside of the United States.*—Paragraph (h) (1) of this section does not apply to the offering and sale of interests in a partnership that was not required to be registered under the Securities Act of 1933 by reason of Regulation S (17 CFR 230.901 through 230.904) unless the offering and sale of the interests would not have been required to be registered under the Securities Act of 1933 if the interests had been offered and sold within the United States.

(3) *Anti-avoidance rule.*—For purposes of determining the number of partners in the partnership under paragraph (h)(1)(ii) of this section, a person (beneficial owner) owning an interest in a partnership, grantor trust, or S corporation (flow-through entity), that owns, directly or through other flow-through entities, an interest in the partnership, is treated as a partner in the partnership only if—

(i) Substantially all of the value of the beneficial owner's interest in the flow-through entity is attributable to the flow-through entity's interest (direct or indirect) in the partnership; and

(ii) A principal purpose of the use of the tiered arrangement is to permit the partnership to satisfy the 100partner limitation in paragraph (h)(1)(ii) of this section.

(i) [Reserved].

(j) *Lack of actual trading.*—(1) *General rule.*— For purposes of section 7704(b) and this section, interests in a partnership are not readily tradable on a secondary market or the substantial equivalent thereof if the sum of the percentage interests in partnership capital or profits transferred during the taxable year of the partnership (other than in transfers described in paragraph (e), (f), or (g) of this section) does not exceed 2 percent of the total interests in partnership capital or profits.

(2) *Examples.*—The following examples illustrate the rules of this paragraph (j):

Example 1. Calculation of percentage interest transferred. (i) ABC, a calendar year limited partnership formed in 1996, has 9,000 units of limited partnership interests outstanding at all times during 1997, representing in the aggregate 95 percent of the total interests in capital and profits of ABC. The remaining 5 percent is held by the general partner.

(ii) During 1997, the following transactions occur with respect to the units of ABC's limited partnership interests—

(A) 800 units are sold through the use of a qualified matching service that meets the requirements of paragraph (g) of this section;

(B) 50 units are sold through the use of a matching service that does not meet the requirements of paragraph (g) of this section; and

(C) 500 units are transferred as a result of private transfers described in paragraph (e) of this section.

(iii) The private transfers of 500 units and the sale of 800 units through a qualified matching service are disregarded under paragraph (j)(1) of this section for purposes of applying the 2 percent rule. As a result, the total percentage interests in partnership capital and profits transferred for purposes of the 2 percent rule is .528 percent, determined by—

(A) Dividing the number of units sold through a matching service that did not meet the requirements of paragraph (g) of this section (50) by the total number of outstanding limited partnership units (9,000); and

(B) Multiplying the result by the percentage of total interests represented by limited partnership units (95 percent) ([50/9,000]x .95 = .528 percent).

Example 2. Application of the 2 percent rule. (i) ABC operates a service consisting of computerized video display screens on which subscribers view and publish nonfirm price quotes that do not commit any person to buy or sell a partnership interest and unpriced indications of interest in a partnership interest without an accompanying price. The ABC service does not provide firm quotes at which any person (including the operator of the service) is committed to buy or sell a partnership interest. The service may provide prior pricing information, including information regarding resales of interests and actual prices paid for interests; transactional volume information; and information on special or capital distributions by a partnership. The operator's fee may consist of a flat fee for use of the service; a fee based on completed transactions, including, for example, the number of nonfirm quotes or unpriced indications of interest entered by users of the service; or any combination thereof.

(ii) The ABC service is not an established securities market for purposes of section 7704(b) and this section. The service is not an interdealer quotation system as defined in paragraph (b)(5) of this section because it does not disseminate firm buy or sell quotations. Therefore, partnerships whose interests are listed and transferred on the ABC service are not publicly traded for purposes of section 7704(b) and this section as a result of such listing or transfers if the sum of the percentage interests in partnership capital or profits transferred during the taxable year of the partnership (other than in transfers described in paragraph (e), (f), or (g) of this section) does not exceed 2 percent of the total interests in partnership capital or profits. In addition, assuming the ABC service complies with the necessary requirements, the service may qualify as a matching service described in paragraph (g) of this section.

(k) *Percentage interests in partnership capital or profits.*—(1) *Interests considered.*—(i) *General rule.*—Except as otherwise provided in this paragraph (k), for purposes of this section, the total interests in partnership capital or profits are determined by reference to all outstanding interests in the partnership.

(ii) *Exceptions.*—(A) *General partner with greater than 10 percent interest.*—If the general partners and any person related to the general partners (within the meaning of section 267(b) or 707(b)(1)) own, in the aggregate, more than 10 percent of the outstanding interests in partnership capital or profits at any one time during the taxable year of the partnership, the total interests in partnership capital or profits are determined without reference to the interests owned by such persons.

(B) *Derivative interests.*—Any partnership interests described in paragraph (a)(2)(i)(B) of this section are taken into account for purposes of determining the total interests in partnership capital or profits only if and to the extent that the partnership satisfies paragraph (d)(1) or (2) of this section.

(2) *Monthly determination.*—For purposes of this section, except in the case of block transfers (as defined in paragraph (e)(2) of this section), the percentage interests in partnership capital or profits represented by partnership interests that are transferred during a taxable year of the partnership is equal to the sum of the percentage interests transferred for each calendar month during the taxable year of the partnership in which a transfer of a partnership interest occurs (other than a private transfer as described in paragraph (e) of this section). The percentage interests in capital or profits of interests transferred during a calendar month is determined by

reference to the partnership interests outstanding during that month.

(3) *Monthly conventions.*—For purposes of paragraph (k) (2) of this section, a partnership may use any reasonable convention in determining the interests outstanding for a month, provided the convention is consistently used by the partnership from month to month during a taxable year and from year to year. Reasonable conventions include, but are not limited to, a determination by reference to the interests outstanding at the beginning of the month, on the 15th day of the month, or at the end of the month.

(4) *Block transfers.*—For purposes of paragraph (e)(2) of this section (defining block transfers), the partnership must determine the percentage interests in capital or profits for each transfer of an interest during the 30 calendar day period by reference to the partnership interests outstanding immediately prior to such transfer.

(5) *Example.*—The following example illustrates the rules of this paragraph (k):

Example. Conventions. (i) ABC limited partnership, a calendar year partnership formed in 1996, has 1,000 units of limited partnership interests outstanding on January 1, 1997, representing in the aggregate 95 percent of the total interests in capital and profits of ABC. The remaining 5 percent is held by the general partner.

(ii) The following transfers take place during 1997—

(A) On January 15, 10 units of limited partnership interests are sold in a transaction that is not a private transfer;

(B) On July 10, 1,000 additional units of limited partnership interests are issued by the partnership (the general partner's percentage interest is unchanged); and

(C) On July 20, 15 units of limited partnership interests are sold in a transaction that is not a private transfer.

(iii) For purposes of determining the sum of the percentage interests in partnership capital or profits transferred, ABC chooses to use the end of the month convention. The percentage interests in partnership capital and profits transferred during January is .95 percent, determined by dividing the number of transferred units (10) by the total number of limited partnership units (1,000) and multiplying the result by the percentage of total interests represented by limited partnership units ([10/1,000] x .95). The percentage interests in partnership capital and profits transferred during July is .7125 percent ([15/2,000] x .95). ABC is not required to make determinations for the other months during the year because no transfers of partnership interests occurred during such months. ABC may qualify for the 2 percent rule for its 1997 taxable year because less than 2 percent (.95 percent + .7125 percent = 1.6625 percent) of its total interests in partnership capital and profits was transferred during that year.

(iv) If ABC had chosen to use the beginning of the month convention, the interests in capital or profits sold during July would have been 1.425 percent ([15/1,000] x .95) and ABC would not have satisfied the 2 percent rule for its 1997 taxable year because 2.375 percent (.95 + 1.425) of ABC's interests in partnership capital and profits was transferred during that year.

(l) *Effective date.*—(1) *In general.*—Except as provided in paragraph (1)(2) of this section, this section applies to taxable years of a partnership beginning after December 31, 1995.

(2) *Transition period.*—For partnerships that were actively engaged in an activity before December 4, 1995, this section applies to taxable years beginning after December 31, 2005, unless the partnership adds a substantial new line of business after December 4, 1995, in which case this section applies to taxable years beginning on or after the addition of the new line of business. Partnerships that qualify for this transition period may continue to rely on the provisions of Notice 88-75 (1988-2 C.B. 386) (see § 601.601(d)(2) of this chapter) for guidance regarding the definition of readily tradable on a secondary market or the substantial equivalent thereof for purposes of section 7704(b).

(3) *Substantial new line of business.*—For purposes of paragraph (1)(2) of this section—

(i) Substantial is defined in § 1.7704-2(c); and

(ii) A new line of business is defined in § 1.7704-2(d), except that the applicable date is "December 4, 1995" instead of "December 17, 1987".

(4) *Termination under section 708(b)(1)(B).*—The termination of a partnership under section 708(b)(1)(B) due to the sale or exchange of 50 percent or more of the total interests in partnership capital and profits is disregarded in determining whether a partnership qualifies for the transition period provided in paragraph (1)(2) of this section. [Reg. § 1.7704-1.]

☐ [*T.D. 8629, 11-29-95.*]

[Reg. § 1.7704-2]

§ 1.7704-2. Transition   provisions.—
(a) *Transition rule.*—(1) *Statutory dates.*—Section 7704 generally applies to taxable years beginning after December 31, 1987. In the case of an existing partnership, however, section 7704 and the regulations thereunder apply to taxable years beginning after December 31, 1997.

(2) *Effective date of regulations.*—These regulations apply to taxable years beginning after December 31, 1991.

(b) *Existing partnership.*—(1) *In general.*—For purposes of § 1.7704-2, the term "existing partnership" means any partnership if:

(i) The partnership was a publicly traded partnership (within the meaning of section 7704(b)) on December 17, 1987;

(ii) A registration statement indicating that the partnership was to be a publicly traded partnership was filed with the Securities and Exchange Commission (SEC) with respect to the partnership on or before December 17, 1987; or

(iii) With respect to the partnership, an application was filed with a state regulatory commission on or before December 17, 1987, seeking permission to restructure a portion of a corporation as a publicly traded partnership.

(2) *Changed status of an existing partnership.*—A partnership will not qualify as an existing partnership after a new line of business is substantial.

(c) *Substantial.*—(1) *In general.*—A new line of business is substantial as of the earlier of—

(i) The taxable year in which the partnership derives more than 15 percent of its gross income from that line of business; or

(ii) The taxable year in which the partnership directly uses in that line of business more than 15 percent (by value) of its total assets.

(2) *Timing Rule.*—If a substantial new line of business is added during the taxable year (*e.g.*, by acquisition), the line of business is treated as substantial as of the date it is added; otherwise a substantial new line of business is treated as substantial as of the first day of the taxable year in which it becomes substantial.

(d) *New Line of Business.*—(1) *In general.*—A new line of business is any business activity of the partnership not closely related to a pre-existing business of the partnership to the extent that the activity generates income other than "qualifying income" within the meaning of section 7704 and the regulations thereunder.

(2) *Pre-existing business.*—A business activity is a pre-existing business of the partnership if—

(i) The partnership was actively engaged in the activity on or before December 17, 1987; or

(ii) The partnership is actively engaged in the business activity that was specifically described as a proposed business activity of the partnership in a registration statement or amendment thereto filed on behalf of the partnership with the SEC on or before December 17, 1987. For this purpose, a specific description does not include a general grant of authority to conduct any business.

(3) *Closely related.*—All of the facts and circumstances will determine whether a new business activity is closely related to a pre-existing business of the partnership. The following factors, among others, will help to establish that a new business activity is closely related to a pre-existing business of the partnership and therefore is not a new line of business:

(i) The activity provides products or services very similar to the products or services provided by the pre-existing business.

(ii) The activity markets products and services to the same class of customers as that of the pre-existing business.

(iii) The activity is of a type that is normally conducted in the same business location as the pre-existing business.

(iv) The activity requires the use of similar operating assets as those used in the pre-existing business.

(v) The activity's economic success depends on the success of the pre-existing business.

(vi) The activity is of a type that would normally be treated as a unit with the pre-existing business in the business, accounting records.

(vii) If the activity and the pre-existing business are regulated or licensed, they are regulated or licensed by the same or similar governmental authority.

(viii) The United States Bureau of the Census assigns the activity the same four-digit Industry Number Standard Identification Code ("Industry SIC Code") as the pre-existing business. Such Codes are set forth in the Executive Office of the President, Office of Management and Budget, Standard Industrial Classification Manual, prepared, and from time to time revised, by the Statistical Policy Division of the United States Office of Management and Budget. For example, if a partnership's pre-existing business is manufacturing steam turbines and then the partnership begins an activity manufacturing hydraulic turbines, both activities would be assigned the same Industry SIC Code, 3511—Steam, Gas, and Hydraulic Turbines, and Turbine Generator Set Units. In the case of a pre-existing business or activity that is listed under the Industry SIC Code, 9999—Nonclassifiable Establishments—or under a miscellaneous category (e.g., most Industry SIC Codes ending in a "9" are miscellaneous categories), the similarity of the SIC Codes is ignored as a factor in determining whether the activity is closely related to the pre-existing business. The dissimilarity of the SIC Codes is considered in determining whether the business activity is closely related to the pre-existing line of business.

(e) *Activities conducted through controlled corporations.*—(1) *In general.*—An activity conducted by a corporation controlled by an existing partnership may be treated as an activity of the existing partnership if the effect of the arrangement is to permit the partnership to engage in an activity the income from which is not subject to a corporate-level tax and which would be a new line of business if conducted directly by the partnership. This determination is based upon all facts and circumstances.

(2) *Safe harbor.*—(i) *In general.*—This paragraph (e)(2) provides a safe harbor for activities of a corporation controlled by an existing partnership. An activity conducted by a corporation controlled by an existing partnership is not deemed to be an activity of the partnership for

purposes of determining whether an existing partnership has added a new line of business if no more than 10% of the gross income that the partnership derives from the corporation during the taxable year is section 7704(d) qualifying income that is recharacterized as nonqualifying income under paragraphs (e)(2)(ii) and (iii) of this section. The Internal Revenue Service will not presume that an activity conducted through a corporation controlled by an existing partnership is an activity of the partnership solely because the partnership fails to satisfy the requirements of this paragraph (e)(2)(i).

(ii) *Recharacterization of qualifying income.*—Gross income received by a partnership from a controlled corporation that would be qualifying income under section 7704(d) is subject to recharacterization as nonqualifying income if the amount is deductible in computing the income of the controlled corporation.

(iii) *Extent of recharacterization.*—The amount of income described in paragraph (e)(2)(ii) of this section that is recharacterized as nonqualifying income is:

(A) The amount described in paragraph (e)(2)(ii) of this section; multiplied by

(B) The controlled corporation's taxable income (determined without regard to deductions for amounts paid to the partnership) that would not be qualifying income within the meaning of section 7704(d) if earned directly by the partnership; divided by

(C) The controlled corporation's taxable income (determined without regard to deductions for amounts paid to the partnership).

(3) *Control.*—For purposes of paragraphs (e)(1) and (2) of this section, control of a corporation is determined generally under the rules of section 304(c). However, the application of section 304(c) is modified to apply only to partners who own five percent or more by value (directly or indirectly) of the existing partnership unless a principal purpose of the arrangement is to avoid tax at the corporate level.

(4) *Example.*—The following example illustrates the application of this paragraph (e):

Example. (i) PTP, an existing partnership, acquired all the stock of X corporation on January 1, 1993. During PTP's 1993 taxable year it received $185,000 of dividends and $15,000 of interest from X. Determined without regard to interest paid to PTP, X's taxable income during that period was $500,000 none of which was "qualifying income" within the meaning of section 7704 and the regulations thereunder. In computing the income of X, the $15,000 of interest paid to PTP is deductible.

(ii) Under paragraph (e)(2)(ii) of this section, all $15,000 of PTP's interest income was nonqualifying income ($15,000 × 500,000/500,000). Under paragraph (e)(2) of this section, however, the activities of X will not be considered to be activities of PTP for the 1993 taxable year because no more than 10 percent of the gross in-

come that PTP derived from X would be treated as other than qualifying income (15,000/200,000 = 7.5%).

(f) *Activities conducted through tiered partnerships.*—An activity conducted by a partnership in which an existing partnership holds an interest (directly or through another partnership) will be considered an activity of the existing partnership.

(g) *Exceptions.*—(1) *Coordination with gross income requirements of section 7704(c)(2).*—A partnership that is either an existing partnership as of December 31, 1997, or an existing partnership that ceases to qualify as an existing partnership is subject to section 7704 and the regulations thereunder. Section 7704(a) does not apply to these partnerships, however, if these partnerships meet the gross income requirements of paragraphs (c)(1) and (2) of section 7704. For purposes of applying section 7704(c)(1) and (2) to these partnerships, the only taxable years that must be tested are those beginning on and after the earlier of—

(i) January 1, 1998; or

(ii) The day on which the partnership ceases to qualify as an existing partnership because of the addition of a new line of business; or

(iii) The first day of the first taxable year in which a new line of business becomes substantial (if the new line of business becomes substantial after the year in which it is added).

(2) *Specific exceptions.*—In determining whether a partnership is an existing partnership for purposes of section 7704, the following events do not in themselves terminate the status of existing partnerships:

(i) Termination of the partnership under section 708(b)(1)(B) due to the sale or exchange of 50 percent or more of the total interests in partnership capital and profits;

(ii) Issuance of additional partnership units; and

(iii) Dropping a line of business. This event, however, could affect an existing partnership's status indirectly. For example, dropping one line of business could change the composition of the partnership's gross income. The change in composition could make a new line of business "substantial," under paragraph (c) of this section, and terminate the partnership's status. *See* paragraph (b)(2) of this section.

(h) *Examples.*—The following examples illustrate the application of this section:

Example 1. (i) On December 17, 1987, PTP, a calendar-year publicly traded partnership, owned and operated citrus groves. On March 1, 1993, PTP purchased a processing business involving frozen citrus products. In the partnership's 1993 taxable year, the partnership directly used in the processing business more than 15 percent (by value) of its total assets.

(ii) The citrus grove activities provide different products from the processing activities, are marketed to customers different from the customers of the processing activities, require different types of operating assets, are not commonly conducted at the same location, are not commonly treated as a unit in accounting records, do not depend upon one another for economic success, and do not have the same Industry SIC Code. Under the facts and circumstances, the processing business is not closely related to the citrus grove operation and is a new line of business under paragraph (d)(1) of this section.

(iii) The assets of the partnership used in the new line of business are substantial under paragraph (c)(2) of this section. Because PTP added a substantial new line of business after December 17, 1987, paragraph (b)(2) of this section terminates PTP's status as an existing partnership on March 1, 1993.

Example 2. (i) On December 17, 1987, PTP, a calendar-year publicly traded partnership, owned and operated retirement centers that serve the elderly. Each center contains three sections—

(A) A residential section, which includes suites of rooms, dining facilities, lounges, and gamerooms;

(B) An assisted-living section, which provides laundry and housekeeping services, health monitoring, and emergency care; and

(C) A nursing section, which provides private and semiprivate rooms, dining facilities, examination and treatment rooms, drugs, medical equipment, and physical, speech, and occupational therapy.

(ii) The business activities of each section constitute pre-existing businesses of PTP under paragraph (d)(2) of this section, because PTP was actively engaged in the activities on or before December 17, 1987.

(iii) The nursing sections primarily furnish health care. They employ nurses and therapists, are subject to federal, state, and local licensing requirements, and may charge certain costs to government programs like Medicare and Medicaid.

(iv) In 1993, PTP acquired new nursing homes that treat inpatient adults of all ages. The nursing homes provide private and semiprivate rooms, dining facilities, examination and treatment rooms, drugs, medical equipment, and physical, speech, and occupational therapy. The nursing homes primarily furnish health care. They employ nurses and therapists, are subject to federal, state, and local licensing requirements, and may charge certain costs to government programs like Medicare and Medicaid.

(v) PTP's new nursing homes and old nursing sections provide very similar services, market to very similar customers, use similar types of property and personnel, and are licensed by the same regulatory agencies. The nursing homes and old nursing sections have the same Industry SIC Code. Under these facts and circumstances, the new nursing homes are closely related to a pre-existing business of the partnership. Accordingly, under paragraph (d)(1) of this section, the

acquisition of the new nursing homes is not the addition of a new line of business.

(vi) PTP was a publicly traded partnership on December 17, 1987, and was an existing partnership under paragraph (b)(1)(i) of this section. Because PTP has added no substantial new line of business after December 17, 1987, paragraph (b)(2) of this section does not terminate PTP's status as an existing partnership.

Example 3. (i) On December 17, 1987, PTP, a calendar-year publicly traded partnership, owned and operated cable television systems in the northeastern United States. PTP's registration statement described as its proposed business activities the ownership and operation of cable television systems, any ancillary operations, and any business permitted by the laws of the state in which PTP was formed.

(ii) PTP's cable systems include cables strung along telephone lines, converter boxes in subscribers' homes, other types of cable equipment, satellite dishes that receive programs broadcast by various television networks, and channels that carry public service announcements of local interest. Subscribers pay the systems a fee for the right to receive both the local announcements and the network signals relayed through the cables. Those fees constitute PTP's primary revenue. The systems operate under franchise agreements negotiated with each municipality in which they do business.

(iii) On September 1, 1993, PTP purchased a television station in the northwestern United States. The station owns broadcasting facilities, satellite dishes that receive programs broadcast by the station's network, and a studio that produces programs of interest to the area that receives the station's broadcasts. Fees from advertisers constitute the station's primary revenue. The station operates under a license from the Federal Communications Commission.

(iv) In the partnership's 1993 taxable year, the station generated less than 15 percent of PTP's gross income and constituted less than 15 percent of its total assets (by value). In PTP's 1994 taxable year, the station generated more than 15 percent of PTP's gross income.

(v) The cable systems relay signals through cables to subscribers and earn revenue from subscriber fees; the station broadcasts signals to the general public and earns revenue by selling air time for commercials. Despite certain similarities, the two types of activities generally require different operating assets and earn income from different sources. They are regulated by different agencies. They are not commonly conducted at the same location and do not generally depend upon one another for their economic success. They have different Industry SIC Codes. Under the facts and circumstances, the television station activities are not closely related to PTP's pre-existing business, the cable system activities.

(vi) As of December 17, 1987, PTP did not own and operate any television station. PTP's registration statement specifically described as its proposed business activities only the ownership and operation of cable television systems and any ancillary operations. For purposes of paragraph (d)(2) of this section, a specific description does not include PTP's general authority to carry on any business permitted by the state of its formation. Therefore, the television station line of business was not specifically described as a proposed business activity of PTP in its registration statement. PTP's acquisition of the television station business activity constitutes a new line of business under paragraph (d)(1) of this section.

(vii) PTP was a publicly traded partnership on December 17, 1987, and was an existing partnership under paragraph (b)(1)(i) of this section. PTP added a new line of business in 1993, but that line of business was not substantial under paragraph (c) of this section, and thus PTP remained an existing partnership for its 1993 taxable year. In 1994, the new line of business became substantial because it generated more than 15 percent of PTP's gross income. Paragraph (b)(2) of this section therefore terminates PTP's existing partnership status as of January 1, 1994, the first day of the first taxable year beginning after December 31, 1987, in which PTP's new line of business became substantial. [Reg. §1.7704-2.]

☐ [T.D. 8450, 12-10-92.]

[Reg. §301.7704-2]

§301.7704-2. Transition provisions.—See the regulations under section 7704 contained in part 1 of this chapter for a definition of the "substantial new line of business" that an "existing" publicly traded partnership cannot enter without forfeiting its partnership status under the transition provisions applicable to section 7704. [Reg. §301.7704-2.]

☐ [T.D. 8450,12-10-92.]

[Reg. §1.7704-3]

§1.7704-3. Qualifying income.—(a) *Certain investment income.*—(1) *In general.*—For purposes of section 7704(d)(1), qualifying income includes capital gain from the sale of stock, income from holding annuities, income from notional principal contracts (as defined in §1.446-3), and other substantially similar income from ordinary and routine investments to the extent determined by the Commissioner. Income from a notional principal contract is included in qualifying income only if the property, income, or cash flow that measures the amounts to which the partnership is entitled under the contract would give rise to qualifying income if held or received directly by the partnership.

(2) *Limitations.*—Qualifying income described in paragraph (a)(1) of this section does not include income derived in the ordinary course of a trade or business. For purposes of the preceding sentence, income derived from an asset with respect to which the partnership is a broker, market maker, or dealer is income derived in the ordinary course of a trade or business; income derived from an asset with respect to which the taxpayer is a trader or investor is

not income derived in the ordinary course of a trade or business.

(b) *Calculation of gross income and qualifying income.*—(1) *Treatment of losses.*—Except as otherwise provided in this section, in computing the gross income and qualifying income of a partnership for purposes of section 7704(c)(2) and this section, losses do not enter into the computation.

(2) *Certain positions that are marked to market.*—Gain recognized with respect to a position that is marked to market (for example, under section 475(f), 1256, 1259, or 1296) shall not fail to be qualifying income solely because there is no sale or disposition of the position.

(3) *Certain items of ordinary income.*—Gain recognized with respect to a capital asset shall not fail to be qualifying income solely because it is characterized as ordinary income under section 475(f), 988, 1258, or 1296.

(4) *Straddles.*—In computing the gross income and qualifying income of a partnership for purposes of section 7704(c)(2) and this section, a straddle (as defined in section 1092(c)) shall be treated as set forth in this paragraph (b)(4). For purposes of the preceding sentence, two or more straddles that are part of a larger straddle shall be treated as a single straddle. The amount of the gain from any straddle to be taken into account shall be computed as follows:

(i) *Straddles other than mixed straddle accounts.*—With respect to each straddle (whether or not a straddle during the taxable year) other than a mixed straddle account, the amount of gain taken into account shall be the excess, if any, of gain recognized during the taxable year with respect to property that was at any time a position in that straddle over any loss recognized during the taxable year with respect to property that was at any time a position in that straddle (including loss realized in an earlier taxable year).

(ii) *Mixed straddle accounts.*—With respect to each mixed straddle account (as defined in §1.1092(b)-4T(b)), the amount of gain taken into account shall be the annual account gain for that mixed straddle account, computed pursuant to §1.1092(b)-4T(c)(2).

(5) *Certain transactions similar to straddles.*—In computing the gross income and qualifying income of a partnership for purposes of section 7704(c)(2) and this section, related interests in property (whether or not personal property as defined in section 1092(d)(1)) that produce a substantial diminution of the partnership's risk of loss similar to that of a straddle (as defined in section 1092(c)) shall be combined so that the amount of gain taken into account by the partnership in computing its gross income shall be the excess, if any, of gain recognized during the taxable year with respect to such interests over any loss recognized during the taxable year with respect to such interests.

(6) *Wash sale rule.*—(i) *Gain not taken into account.*—Solely for purposes of section 7704(c)(2) and this section, if a partnership recognizes gain in a section 7704 wash sale transaction with respect to one or more positions in either a straddle (as defined in section 1092(c)) or an arrangement described in paragraph (b)(5) of this section, then the gain shall not be taken into account to the extent of the amount of unrecognized loss (as of the close of the taxable year) in one or more offsetting positions of the straddle or arrangement described in paragraph (b)(5) of this section.

(ii) *Section 7704 wash sale transaction.*—For purposes of this paragraph (b)(6), a section 7704 wash sale transaction is a transaction in which—

(A) A partnership disposes of one or more positions of a straddle (as defined in section 1092(c)) or one or more related positions described in paragraph (b)(5) of this section; and

(B) The partnership acquires a substantially similar position or positions within a period beginning 30 days before the date of the disposition and ending 30 days after such date.

(c) *Effective date.*—This section applies to taxable years of a partnership beginning on or after December 17, 1998. However, a partnership may apply this section in its entirety for all of the partnership's open taxable years beginning after any earlier date selected by the partnership. [Reg. § 1.7704-3.]

☐ [*T.D.* 8799, 12-16-98.]

[Reg. § 1.7704-4]

§ 1.7704-4. Qualifying income – mineral and natural resources.—(a) *In general.*—For purposes of section 7704(d)(1)(E), qualifying income is income and gains from qualifying activities with respect to minerals or natural resources as defined in paragraph (b) of this section. Qualifying activities are section 7704(d)(1)(E) activities (as described in paragraph (c) of this section) and intrinsic activities (as described in paragraph (d) of this section).

(b) *Mineral or natural resource.*—The term mineral or natural resource (including fertilizer, geothermal energy, and timber) means any product of a character with respect to which a deduction for depletion is allowable under section 611, except that such term does not include any product described in section 613(b)(7)(A) or (B) (soil, sod, dirt, turf, water, mosses, or minerals from sea water, the air, or other similar inexhaustible sources). For purposes of this section, the term mineral or natural resource does not include industrial source carbon dioxide, fuels described in section 6426(b) through (e), any alcohol fuel defined in section 6426(b)(4)(A), or any biodiesel fuel as defined in section 40A(d)(1).

(c) *Section 7704(d)(1)(E) activities.*—(1) *Definition.*—Section 7704(d)(1)(E) activities include the exploration, development, mining or production, processing, refining, transportation, or marketing of any mineral or natural resource. Solely for purposes of section 7704(d), such terms are defined as provided in this paragraph (c).

(2) *Exploration.*—An activity constitutes exploration if it is performed to ascertain the existence, location, extent, or quality of any deposit of mineral or natural resource before the beginning of the development stage of the natural deposit including by—

(i) Drilling an exploratory or stratigraphic type test well;

(ii) Conducting drill stem and production flow tests to verify commerciality of the deposit;

(iii) Conducting geological or geophysical surveys;

(iv) Interpreting data obtained from geological or geophysical surveys; or

(v) For minerals, testpitting, trenching, drilling, driving of exploration tunnels and adits, and similar types of activities described in Rev. Rul. 70-287 (1970-1 CB 146), (see § 601.601(d)(2)(ii)(*b*) of this chapter) if conducted prior to development activities with respect to the minerals.

(3) *Development.*—An activity constitutes development if it is performed to make accessible minerals or natural resources, including by—

(i) Drilling wells to access deposits of minerals or natural resources;

(ii) Constructing and installing drilling, production, or dual purpose platforms in marine locations, or any similar supporting structures necessary for extraordinary non-marine terrain (such as swamps or tundra);

(iii) Completing wells, including by installing lease and well equipment, such as pumps, flow lines, separators, and storage tanks, so that wells are capable of producing oil and gas, and the production can be removed from the premises;

(iv) Performing a development technique such as, for minerals other than oil and natural gas, stripping, benching and terracing, dredging by dragline, stoping, and caving or room-and-pillar excavation, and for oil and natural gas, fracturing; or

(v) Constructing and installing gathering systems and custody transfer stations.

(4) *Mining or production.*—An activity constitutes mining or production if it is performed to extract minerals or natural resources from the ground including by operating equipment to extract minerals or natural resources from mines and wells, or to extract minerals or natural resources from the waste or residue of prior mining or production allowable under this section. The recycling of scrap or salvaged metals or minerals from previously manufactured products or manufacturing processes is not considered to be the extraction of ores or minerals from waste or residue.

(5) *Processing.*—An activity constitutes processing if it is performed to convert raw mined or harvested products or raw well efflu-

ent to substances that can be readily transported or stored, as described in this paragraph (c)(5).

(i) *Natural gas.*—An activity constitutes processing of natural gas if it is performed to—

(A) Purify natural gas, including by removal of oil or condensate, water, or non-hydrocarbon gases (such as carbon dioxide, hydrogen sulfide, nitrogen, and helium); and

(B) Separate natural gas into its constituents which are normally recovered in a gaseous phase (methane and ethane) and those which are normally recovered in a liquid phase (propane, butane, pentane, and heavier streams).

(ii) *Crude oil.*—An activity constitutes processing of crude oil if it is performed to separate produced fluids by passing crude oil through mechanical separators to remove gas, placing crude oil in settling tanks to recover basic sediment and water, dehydrating crude oil, and operating heater-treaters that separate raw oil well effluent into crude oil, natural gas, and salt water.

(iii) *Ores and minerals other than natural gas or crude oil.*—An activity constitutes processing of ores and minerals other than natural gas or crude oil if it meets the definition of mining processes under §1.613-4(f)(1)(ii), without regard to §1.613-4(f)(2)(iv).

(iv) *Timber.*—An activity constitutes processing of timber if it is performed to modify the physical form of timber, including by the application of heat or pressure to timber, without adding any foreign substances. Processing of timber does not include activities that add chemicals or other foreign substances to timber to manipulate its physical or chemical properties, such as using a digester to produce pulp. Products that result from timber processing include wood chips, sawdust, rough lumber, kiln-dried lumber, veneers, wood pellets, wood bark, and rough poles. Products that are not the result of timber processing include pulp, paper, paper products, treated lumber, oriented strand board/plywood, and treated poles.

(6) *Refining.*—An activity constitutes refining if the activity is set forth in this paragraph (c)(6).

(i) *Natural gas and crude oil.*—(A) The refining of natural gas and crude oil includes the further physical or chemical conversion or separation processes of products resulting from activities listed in paragraph (c)(5)(i) and (ii) of this section, and the blending of petroleum hydrocarbons, to the extent they give rise to a product listed in paragraph (c)(5)(i) or (ii) of this section or to the products of a type produced in a petroleum refinery or natural gas processing plant listed in this paragraph (c)(6)(i)(A). Refining of natural gas and crude oil also includes the further physical or chemical conversion or separation processes and blending of the products listed in this paragraph (c)(6)(i)(A), to the extent that the resulting product is also listed in this paragraph (c)(6)(i)(A). The following products

are of a type produced in a petroleum refinery or natural gas processing plant:

(1) Ethane.
(2) Ethylene.
(3) Propane.
(4) Propylene.
(5) Normal butane.
(6) Butylene.
(7) Isobutane.
(8) Isobutene.
(9) Isobutylene.
(10) Pentanes plus.
(11) Unfinished naphtha.
(12) Unfinished kerosene and light gas oils.
(13) Unfinished heavy gas oils.
(14) Unfinished residuum.
(15) Reformulated gasoline with fuel ethanol.
(16) Reformulated other motor gasoline.
(17) Conventional gasoline with fuel ethanol – Ed55 and lower gasoline.
(18) Conventional gasoline with fuel ethanol – greater than Ed55 gasoline.
(19) Conventional gasoline with fuel ethanol – other conventional finished gasoline.
(20) Reformulated blendstock for oxygenate (RBOB).
(21) Conventional blendstock for oxygenate (CBOB).
(22) Gasoline treated as blendstock (GTAB).
(23) Other motor gasoline blending components defined as gasoline blendstocks as provided in §48.4081-1(c)(3) of this chapter.
(24) Finished aviation gasoline and blending components.
(25) Special naphthas (solvents).
(26) Kerosene-type jet fuel.
(27) Kerosene.
(28) Distillate fuel oil (heating oils, diesel fuel, and ultra-low sulfur diesel fuel).
(29) Residual fuel oil.
(30) Lubricants (lubricating base oils).
(31) Asphalt and road oil (atmospheric or vacuum tower bottom).
(32) Waxes.
(33) Petroleum coke.
(34) Still gas.
(35) Naphtha less than 401°F endpoint.
(36) Other products of a refinery that the Commissioner may identify through published guidance.

(B) For purposes of this section, the products listed in this paragraph (c)(6)(i)(B) are not products of refining:

(1) Heat, steam, or electricity produced by processing or refining.

(2) Products that are obtained from third parties or produced onsite for use in the refinery, such as hydrogen, if excess amounts are sold.

Reg. §1.7704-4(c)(6)(i)(B)(2)

(3) Any product that results from further chemical change of a product listed in paragraph (c)(6)(i)(A) of this section that does not result in the same or another product listed in paragraph (c)(6)(i)(A) of this section (for example, production of petroleum coke from heavy (refinery) residuum qualifies, but any upgrading of petroleum coke (such as to calcined coke) does not qualify because it is further chemically changed and does not result in the same or another product listed in paragraph (c)(6)(i)(A) of this section).

(4) Plastics or similar petroleum derivatives.

(ii) *Ores and minerals other than natural gas or crude oil.*—(A) An activity constitutes refining of ores and minerals other than natural gas or crude oil if it is one of the various processes performed subsequent to mining processes (as defined in paragraph (c)(5)(iii) of this section) to eliminate impurities or foreign matter and which are necessary steps in achieving a high degree of purity from metallic ores and minerals which are not customarily sold in the form of the crude mineral product, as specified in paragraph (c)(6)(ii)(B) of this section. Refining processes include: fine pulverization, electrowinning, electrolytic deposition, roasting, thermal or electric smelting, or substantially equivalent processes or combinations of processes used to separate or extract the specified metals listed in paragraph (c)(6)(ii)(B) of this section from the ore for the primary purpose of producing a purer form of the metal, as for example the smelting of concentrates to produce Dore bars or refining of blister copper.

(B) For purposes of this section, the specified metallic ores or minerals which are not customarily sold in the form of the crude mineral product are—

(1) Lead;

(2) Zinc;

(3) Copper;

(4) Gold;

(5) Silver; and

(6) Any other ores or minerals that the Commissioner may identify through published guidance.

(C) Refining does not include the introduction of additives that remain in the metal, for example, in the manufacture of alloys of gold. Also, the application of nonmining processes as defined in §1.613-4(g) in order to produce a specified metal that is considered a waste or by-product of production from a non-specified mineral deposit is not considered refining for purposes of this section.

(7) *Transportation.*—(i) *General rule.*—An activity constitutes transportation if it is performed to move minerals or natural resources, and products under paragraph (c)(4), (5), or (6) of this section, including by pipeline, marine vessel, rail, or truck. Except as provided in paragraph (c)(7)(ii) of this section, transportation does not

include the movement of minerals or natural resources, and products produced under paragraph (c)(4), (5), or (6) of this section, directly to retail customers or to a place that sells or dispenses to retail customers. Retail customers do not include a person who acquires oil or gas for refining or processing, or a utility. Transportation includes the following activities:

(A) Providing storage services.

(B) Providing terminalling services, including the following: receiving products from pipelines, marine vessels, railcars, or trucks; storing products; loading products to pipelines, marine vessels, railcars, or trucks for distribution; testing and treating, as well as blending and additization, if income from such activities would be qualifying income pursuant to paragraph (c)(10)(iv) and (v) of this section; and separating and selling excess renewable identification numbers acquired as part of additization services to comply with environmental regulations.

(C) Moving or carrying (whether by owner or operator) products via pipelines, gathering systems, and custody transfer stations.

(D) Operating marine vessels (including time charters), railcars, or trucks.

(E) Providing compression services to a pipeline.

(F) Liquefying or regasifying natural gas.

(ii) *Transportation to retail customers or to a place that sells to retail customers.*—Transportation includes the movement of minerals or natural resources, and products under paragraph (c)(4), (5), or (6) of this section, via pipeline to a place that sells to retail customers. Transportation also includes the movement of liquefied petroleum gas via trucks, rail cars, or pipeline to a place that sells to retail customers or directly to retail customers.

(8) *Marketing.*—(i) *General rule.*—An activity constitutes marketing if it is the bulk sale of minerals or natural resources, and products under paragraph (c)(4), (5), or (6) of this section. Except as provided in paragraph (c)(8)(ii) of this section, marketing does not include retail sales (sales made in small quantities directly to end users), which includes the operation of gasoline service stations, home heating oil delivery services, and local natural gas delivery services.

(ii) *Retail sales of liquefied petroleum gas.*—Retail sales of liquefied petroleum gas are included in marketing.

(iii) *Certain activities that facilitate sale.*—Marketing also includes certain activities that facilitate sales that constitute marketing under paragraphs (c)(8)(i) and (ii) of this section, including packaging, as well as and blending and additization, if income from blending and additization would be qualifying income pursuant to paragraph (c)(10)(iv) and (v) of this section.

(9) *Fertilizer.*—[Reserved]

(10) *Additional activities.*—The following types of income as described in paragraph (c)(10)(i) through (v) of this section will be considered derived from a section 7704(d)(1)(E) activity.

(i) *Cost reimbursements.*—If the partnership is in the trade or business of performing a section 7704(d)(1)(E) activity, qualifying income includes income received to reimburse the partnership for its costs in performing that section 7704(d)(1)(E) activity, whether imbedded in the rate the partnership charges or separately itemized. Reimbursable costs may include the cost of designing, constructing, installing, inspecting, maintaining, metering, monitoring, or relocating an asset used in that section 7704(d)(1)(E) activity, or providing office functions necessary to the operation of that section 7704(d)(1)(E) activity (such as staffing, purchasing supplies, billing, accounting, and financial reporting). For example, a pipeline operator that charges a customer for its cost to build, repair, or schedule flow on the pipelines that it operates will have qualifying income from such activity whether or not it itemizes those costs when it bills the customer.

(ii) *Hedging.*—[Reserved]

(iii) *Passive Interests.*—Qualifying income includes income and gains from a passive interest or non-operating interest, including production royalties, minimum annual royalties, net profits interests, delay rentals, and lease-bonus payments, if the interest is in a mineral or natural resource as defined in paragraph (b) of this section. Payments received on a production payment will not be qualifying income if they are properly treated as loan payments under section 636.

(iv) *Blending.*—Qualifying income includes income and gains from performing blending activities or services with respect to products under paragraph (c)(4), (5), or (6) of this section, so long as the products being blended are component parts of the same mineral or natural resource. For purposes of this paragraph (c)(10)(iv), products of oil and natural gas will be considered as from the same natural resource. Blending does not include combining different minerals or natural resources or products thereof together. However, see paragraph (c)(10)(v) of this section for rules concerning additization.

(v) *Additization.*—Qualifying income includes income and gains from providing additization services with respect to products under paragraph (c)(4), (5), or (6) of this section to the extent specifically permitted in this paragraph (c)(10)(v). The addition of additives described in paragraph (c)(10)(v)(A) through (C) of this section is permissible if the additives aid in the transportation of a product, enhance or protect the intrinsic properties of a product, or are necessary as required by federal, state, or local law (for example, to meet environmental standards), but only if such additives do not create a new product.

(A) The addition of additives to products of natural gas and crude oil is permissible, provided that such additives constitute less than 5 percent (except that ethanol or biodiesel may be up to 20 percent) of the total volume for products of natural gas and crude oil and are added into the product by the terminal operator or upstream of the terminal operator.

(B) In the case of ores and minerals other than natural gas or crude oil, the addition of incidental amounts of material such as paper dots to identify shipments, antifreeze to aid in shipping, or compounds to allay dust as required by law or reduce losses during shipping is permissible.

(C) In the case of timber, additization of incidental amounts to comply with government regulations is permissible, to the extent such additization does not create a new product. For example, the pressure treatment of wood is impermissible because it creates a new product.

(d) *Intrinsic activities.*—(1) *General requirements.*—An activity is an intrinsic activity only if the activity is specialized to support a section 7704(d)(1)(E) activity, is essential to the completion of the section 7704(d)(1)(E) activity, and requires the provision of significant services to support the section 7704(d)(1)(E) activity. Whether an activity is an intrinsic activity is determined on an activity-by-activity basis.

(2) *Specialization.*—An activity is a specialized activity if—

(i) The partnership provides personnel (including employees of the partnership, an affiliate, subcontractor, or independent contractor performing work on behalf of the partnership) to support a section 7704(d)(1)(E) activity and those personnel have received training in order to support the section 7704(d)(1)(E) activity that is unique to the mineral or natural resource industry and of limited utility other than to perform or support a section 7704(d)(1)(E) activity; and

(ii) To the extent that the activity involves the sale, provision, or use of specific property, either—

(A) The property is primarily tangible property that is dedicated to, and has limited utility outside of, section 7704(d)(1)(E) activities and is not easily converted (as determined based on all the facts and circumstances, including the cost to convert the property) to another use other than supporting or performing the section 7704(d)(1)(E) activities (except that the use of non-specialized property typically used incidentally in operating a business will not cause a partnership to fail this paragraph (d)(2)(ii)(A)); or

(B) If the property is used as an injectant to perform a section 7704(d)(1)(E) activity that is also commonly used outside of section 7704(d)(1)(E) activities (such as water and lubricants), the partnership provides the injectants exclusively to those engaged in section 7704(d)(1)(E) activities; the partnership is also in the trade or business of collecting, cleaning, recycling, or otherwise disposing of injectants after use in accordance with Federal, state, or local regulations concerning waste products from mining or production activities; and the partnership operates its injectant delivery and disposal services within the same geographic area.

(3) *Essential.*—(i) An activity is essential to the section 7704(d)(1)(E) activity if it is required to—

(A) Physically complete a section 7704(d)(1)(E) activity (including in a cost-effective manner, such as by making the activity economically viable), or

(B) Comply with Federal, state, or local law regulating the section 7704(d)(1)(E) activity.

(ii) Legal, financial, consulting, accounting, insurance, and other similar services do not qualify as essential to a section 7704(d)(1)(E) activity.

(4) *Significant services.*—(i) An activity requires significant services to support the section 7704(d)(1)(E) activity if those services must be conducted on an ongoing or frequent basis by the partnership's personnel at the site or sites of the section 7704(d)(1)(E) activities. Alternatively, those services may be conducted offsite if the services are performed on an ongoing or frequent basis and are offered to those engaged in one or more section 7704(d)(1)(E) activities. If the services are monitoring, those services must be offered exclusively to those engaged in one or more section 7704(d)(1)(E) activities. Whether services are conducted on an ongoing or frequent basis is determined based on all the facts and circumstances, including recognized best practices in the relevant industry.

(ii) Personnel perform significant services only if those services are necessary for the partnership to perform an activity that is essential to the section 7704(d)(1)(E) activity, or to support the section 7704(d)(1)(E) activity. Personnel include employees of the partnership, an affiliate, subcontractor, or independent contractor performing work on behalf of the partnership.

(iii) Services are not significant services with respect to a section 7704(d)(1)(E) activity if the services principally involve the design, construction, manufacturing, repair, maintenance, lease, rent, or temporary provision of property.

(e) *Interpretations of section 611 and section 613.*—This section and interpretations of this section have no effect on interpretations of sections 611 and 613, or other sections of the Code, or the regulations thereunder; however, this section incorporates some of the interpretations under section 611 and 613 and the regulations thereunder as provided in this section.

(f) *Examples.*—The following examples illustrate the provisions of this section:

Example 1. Petrochemical products sourced from an oil and gas well. (i) Z, a publicly traded partnership, chemically converts a mixture of ethane and propane (obtained from physical separation of natural gas) into ethylene and propylene

through use of a steam cracker. Z sells the ethylene and propylene in bulk to a third party.

(ii) Ethylene and propylene are products of refining as provided in paragraph (c)(6)(i) of this section; therefore, Z is engaged in a section 7704(d)(1)(E) activity. The income Z receives from the sale of ethylene and propylene is qualifying income for purposes of section 7704(d)(1)(E).

Example 2. Petroleum streams chemically converted into refinery grade olefins byproducts. (i) Y, a publicly traded partnership, owns a petroleum refinery. The refinery physically separates crude oil, obtaining heavy gas oil. The refinery then uses a catalytic cracking unit to chemically convert the heavy gas oil into a liquid stream suitable for gasoline blending and a gas stream containing ethane, ethylene, and other gases. The refinery also further physically separates the gas stream, resulting in refinery-grade ethylene. Y sells the ethylene in bulk to a third party.

(ii) Y's activities give rise to products of refining as provided in paragraph (c)(6)(i) of this section; therefore, Y is engaged in a section 7704(d)(1)(E) activity. The income Y receives from the sales of ethylene is qualifying income for purposes of section 7704(d)(1)(E).

Example 3. Converting methane gas into synthetic fuels through chemical change. (i) Y, a publicly traded partnership, chemically converts methane into methanol and synthesis gas, and further chemically converts those products into gasoline and diesel fuel. Y receives income from bulk sales of gasoline and diesel created during the conversion processes, as well as from sales of methanol.

(ii) With respect to the production of gasoline or diesel from methane, gasoline and diesel are products of refining as provided in paragraph (c)(6)(i) of this section; therefore, Y is engaged in a section 7704(d)(1)(E) activity. Y's income from the sale of gasoline and diesel is qualifying income for purposes of section 7704(d)(1)(E).

(iii) The income from the sale of methanol, an intermediate product in the conversion process, is not qualifying income for purposes of section 7704(d)(1)(E) because methanol is not a product of processing or refining as defined in paragraph (c)(5) and (6) of this section.

Example 4. Converting methanol into gasoline and diesel. (i) Assume the same facts as in *Example 3* of this paragraph (f), except Y purchases methanol and synthesis gas and chemically converts the methanol and synthesis gas into gasoline and diesel.

(ii) The chemical conversion of methanol and synthesis gas into gasoline and diesel is not refining as provided in paragraph (c)(6)(i) of this section because it is not the physical or chemical conversion or the separation or blending of products listed in paragraph (c)(6)(i)(A) of this section. Accordingly, the income from the sales of the gasoline and diesel is not qualifying income for purposes of section 7704(d)(1)(E).

Example 5. Delivery of refined products. (i) X, a publicly traded partnership, sells diesel to a government entity at wholesale prices and delivers those goods in bulk.

(ii) X's sale of a refined product to the government entity is a section 7704(d)(1)(E) activity because it is a bulk transportation and sale as described in paragraph (c)(7) and (8) of this section and is not a retail sale.

Example 6. Constructing a pipeline. (i) X, a publicly traded partnership, operates interstate and intrastate natural gas pipelines. Y, a corporation, is a construction firm. X pays Y to build a pipeline. X later seeks reimbursement for its cost to build the pipeline from A, a refiner who contracts with X to transport gasoline.

(ii) X, as an operator of pipelines, is engaged in transportation pursuant to paragraph (c)(7)(i)(C) of this section. The reimbursement X receives from A for X's cost to build the pipeline is qualifying income pursuant to paragraph (c)(10)(i) of this section because X receives the income to reimburse X for its costs in performing X's transportation activity and reimbursable costs may include construction costs. In contrast, Y is not in the trade or business of performing a 7704(d)(1)(E) activity, thus income Y received from X for building the pipeline is not qualifying income to Y.

Example 7. Delivery of water. (i) X, a publicly traded partnership, owns interstate and intrastate natural gas pipelines. X built a water delivery pipeline along the existing right of way for its natural gas pipeline to deliver water to A for use in A's fracturing activity. A uses the delivered water in fracturing to develop A's natural gas reserve in a cost-efficient manner. X earns income for transporting natural gas in the pipelines and for delivery of water.

(ii) X's income from transporting natural gas in its interstate and intrastate pipelines is qualifying income for purposes of section 7704(c) because transportation of natural gas is a section 7704(d)(1)(E) activity as provided in paragraph (c)(7)(i)(C) of this section.

(iii) The income X obtains from its water delivery services is not a section 7704(d)(1)(E) activity as provided in paragraph (c) of this section. However, because X's water delivery supports A's development of natural gas, a section 7704(d)(1)(E) activity, X's income from water delivery services may be qualifying income for purposes of section 7704(c) if the water delivery service is an intrinsic activity as provided in paragraph (d) of this section. An activity is an intrinsic activity if the activity is specialized to support the section 7704(d)(1)(E) activity, is essential to the completion of the section 7704(d)(1)(E) activity, and requires the provision of significant services to support the section 7704(d)(1)(E) activity. Under paragraph (d)(2)(ii)(B) of this section, the provision of water for use as an injectant in a section 7704(d)(1)(E) activity is specialized to that activity only if the partnership (1) provides the water exclusively to those engaged in section 7704(d)(1)(E) activities, (2) is also in the trade or business of cleaning, recycling, or otherwise disposing of water after

use in accordance with Federal, state, or local regulations concerning waste products from mining or production activities, and (3) operates these disposal services within the same geographic area as that in which it delivers water. Because X does not perform such disposal services, X's water delivery activities are not specialized to support the section 7704(d)(1)(E) activity. Thus, X's water delivery is not an intrinsic activity. Accordingly, X's income from the delivery of water is not qualifying income for purposes of section 7704(c).

Example 8. Delivery of water and recovery and recycling of flowback. (i) Assume the same facts as in *Example 7* of this paragraph (f), except that X also collects and treats flowback at the drilling site in accordance with state regulations as part of its water delivery services and transports the treated flowback away from the site. In connection with these services, X provides personnel to perform these services on an ongoing or frequent basis that is consistent with best industry practices. X has provided these personnel with specialized training regarding the recovery and recycling of flowback produced during the development of natural gas, and this training is of limited utility other than to perform or support the development of natural gas.

(ii) The income X obtains from its water delivery services is not a section 7704(d)(1)(E) activity as provided in paragraph (c) of this section. However, because X's water delivery supports A's development of natural gas, a section 7704(d)(1)(E) activity, X's income from water delivery services may be qualifying income for purposes of section 7704(c) if the water delivery service is an intrinsic activity as provided in paragraph (d) of this section.

(iii) An activity is an intrinsic activity if the activity is specialized to support the section 7704(d)(1)(E) activity, is essential to the completion of the section 7704(d)(1)(E) activity, and requires the provision of significant services to support the section 7704(d)(1)(E) activity. Under paragraph (d)(2)(ii)(B) of this section, the provision of water for use as an injectant in a section 7704(d)(1)(E) activity is specialized to that activity only if the partnership (1) provides the water exclusively to those engaged in section 7704(d)(1)(E) activities, (2) is also in the trade or business of cleaning, recycling, or otherwise disposing of water after use in accordance with Federal, state, or local regulations concerning waste products from mining or production activities, and (3) operates these disposal services within the same geographical area as where it delivers water. X's provision of personnel is specialized because those personnel received training regarding the recovery and recycling of flowback produced during the development of natural gas, and this training is of limited utility other than to perform or support the development of natural gas. The provision of water is also specialized because water is an injectant used to perform a section 7704(d)(1)(E) activity, and X also collects and treats flowback in accordance with state regulations as part of its water delivery services. Therefore, X meets the specialization requirement. The delivery of water is essential to support A's development activity because the water is needed for use in fracturing to develop A's natural gas reserve in a cost-efficient manner. Finally, the water delivery and recovery and recycling activities require significant services to support the development activity because X's personnel provide services necessary for the partnership to perform the support activity at the development site on an ongoing or frequent basis that is consistent with best industry practices. Because X's delivery of water and X's collection, transport, and treatment of flowback is a specialized activity, is essential to the completion of a section 7704(d)(1)(E) activity, and requires significant services, the delivery of water and the transport and treatment of flowback is an intrinsic activity. X's income from the delivery of water and the collection, treatment, and transport of flowback is qualifying income for purposes of section 7704(c).

(g) *Effective/applicability date and transition rule.*—(1) *In general.*—Except as provided in paragraph (g)(2) of this section, this section applies to income earned by a partnership in a taxable year beginning on or after January 19, 2017. Paragraph (g)(2) of this section applies during the period that ends on the last day of the partnership's taxable year that includes January 19, 2027 (Transition Period).

(2) *Income during Transition Period.*—A partnership may treat income from an activity as qualifying income during the Transition Period if—

(i) The partnership received a private letter ruling from the IRS holding that the income from that activity is qualifying income;

(ii) Prior to May 6, 2015, the partnership was publicly traded, engaged in the activity, and treated the activity as giving rise to qualifying income under section 7704(d)(1)(E), and that income was qualifying income under the statute as reasonably interpreted prior to May 6, 2015;

(iii) Prior to May 6, 2015, the partnership was publicly traded and had entered into a binding agreement for construction of assets to be used in such activity that would give rise to income that was qualifying income under the statute as reasonably interpreted prior to May 6, 2015; or

(iv) The partnership is publicly traded and engages in the activity after May 6, 2015 but before January 19, 2017, and the income from that activity is qualifying income under the proposed regulations (REG-132634-14) contained in the Internal Revenue Bulletin (IRB) 2015-21 (see https://www.irs.gov/pub/irs-irbs/irb15-21.pdf).

(3) *Relief from technical termination.*—In the event of a technical termination under section 708(b)(1)(B) of a partnership that satisfies the requirements of paragraph (g)(2) of this section without regard to the technical termination, the resulting partnership will be treated as the partnership that satisfies the requirements of paragraph (g)(2) of this section for purposes of applying the Transition Period. [Reg. § 1.7704-4.]

☐ [*T.D.* 9817, 1-19-2017.]

[Reg. § 301.7705-1T]

§ 301.7705-1T. Certified professional employer organization (temporary).— (a) *Application.*—The definitions set forth in this section apply for purposes of this section, § 301.7705-2T and sections 3302(h), 3303(a)(4), 3511, 6053(c)(8), and 7528(b)(4).

(b) *Definitions.*—(1) *Certified professional employer organization* (CPEO) means a person that applies to be certified as a CPEO in accordance with § 301.7705-2T(a) and has been certified by the Internal Revenue Service (IRS) as meeting the requirements of § 301.7705-2T. For purposes of § 301.7705-2T(g)(2), the term CPEO also includes the person before it applied for certification and while its application is pending with the IRS. For all other purposes, a person is a CPEO as of the effective date of its certification (as specified in the certification notice described in § 301.7705-2T(a)(2)) and until its certification is revoked by the IRS (as described in § 301.7705-2T(n)) or, if earlier and applicable, until the CPEO voluntarily terminates its certification in the time and manner prescribed by the Commissioner in further guidance.

(2) *CPEO applicant* means a person that has applied to be certified as a CPEO in accordance with § 301.7705-2T(a) and whose application is pending with the IRS.

(3) *CPEO contract.*—[Reserved]

(4) *Certified public accountant (CPA)* means a certified public accountant who—

(i) With respect to a CPEO applicant or CPEO, is independent of the CPEO applicant or CPEO (as prescribed by the American Institute of Certified Public Accountants' Professional Standards, Code of Professional Conduct, and its interpretations and rulings);

(ii) Is not currently under suspension or disbarment from practice before the IRS;

(iii) Is duly qualified to practice in any state;

(iv) Files with the IRS a written declaration that he or she is currently qualified as a CPA and authorized to represent the CPEO applicant or CPEO before the IRS; and

(v) Meets such other requirements as the Commissioner may prescribe in further guidance.

(5) *Covered employee.*—[Reserved]

(6) *Customer.*—[Reserved]

(7) *Federal employment taxes* means the taxes imposed by subtitle C of the Internal Revenue Code.

(8) *Guidance* includes guidance published in the Federal Register or Internal Revenue Bulletin, as well as administrative guidance such as forms, instructions, publications, or other guidance on the *IRS.gov* Web site.

(9) *Partnership* means a business entity (as described in §301.7701-2(a)) that is classified as a partnership for federal tax purposes under §§301.7701-1, 301.7701-2, and 301.7701-3. Accordingly, any references to a managing member or general partner of a partnership mean a managing member or general partner of an entity that is classified as a partnership for federal tax purposes.

(10) *Precursor entity.*—(i) *In general.*—A precursor entity means, with respect to a CPEO applicant, any related entity of the CPEO applicant that is or was a provider of employment-related services that—

(A) Has made a substantial asset transfer to the CPEO applicant during the calendar year that the CPEO applicant applies for certification or any of the three preceding calendar years or plans to make such a substantial asset transfer while the application for certification is pending or in the 12-month period following the date of the CPEO applicant's application for certification; or

(B) Has ceased operations or dissolved during the calendar year that the CPEO applicant applied for certification or any of the three preceding calendar years.

(ii) *Related.*—For purposes of this paragraph (b)(10), a provider of employment-related services is considered a related entity of a CPEO applicant if it is a related entity within the meaning of paragraph (b)(12) of this section or if it would be or would have been such a related entity based on the ownership and responsible individuals of the provider of employment-related services at the time of its substantial asset transfer, ceasing of operations, or dissolution, as applicable, and the ownership and responsible individuals of the CPEO applicant at the time of its application.

(11) *Provider of employment-related services* means a person that provides employment tax administration, payroll services, or other employment-related compliance services to clients, including, but not limited to, collecting, reporting, and paying employment taxes with respect to wages or compensation paid by the person to individuals performing services for the clients. A provider of employment-related services includes, but is not limited to, a CPEO.

(12) *Related entity* means, with respect to a CPEO applicant or CPEO, any person that meets one or more of the following criteria:

(i) The person is a member of a controlled group of which the CPEO applicant or CPEO is also a member. For purposes of this paragraph (b)(12)(i), controlled group has the meaning given to such term by sections 414(b) and (c) and the regulations thereunder, except that—

(A) With respect to a person that is not a provider of employment-related services "more than 50 percent" will be substituted for "at least 80 percent" each place it appears in section 1563(a) (which is cross-referenced in section 414(b)) and §1.414(c)-2 of this chapter); and

(B) With respect to a person that is a provider of employment-related services, "more than 5 percent" will be substituted for "at least 80 percent" each place it appears in section 1563(a) and §1.414(c)-2 of this chapter; or

(ii) The person is a provider of employment-related services and—

(A) A majority of the directors or a majority of the officers (as described in paragraph (b)(13)(ii) of this section) of the CPEO applicant or CPEO are directors or officers (as described in paragraph (b)(13)(ii) of this section), respectively, of the provider of employment-related services; or

(B) An individual is a responsible individual of both the provider of employment-related services and the CPEO applicant or CPEO by reason of paragraph (b)(13)(i) of this section.

(13) *Responsible individual* means, with respect to a CPEO applicant or CPEO, (or, for purposes of paragraphs (b)(10)(ii) or (b)(12)(ii) of this section, a provider of employment-related services), the following individuals:

(i) Any individual who owns, directly or indirectly and applying the constructive ownership rules of section 1563(e) with respect to stock ownership and by substituting the term "interest" for the term "stock" and the term "partnership" for the term "corporation" used in that section, as appropriate for purposes of determining whether an interest in a partnership is indirectly owned by any person, 33 percent or more of—

(A) In the case of a corporation, the total combined voting power of all classes of stock entitled to vote of such corporation or of the total value of shares of all classes of stock of such corporation; or

(B) In the case of a partnership, the capital interest or profits interest of such partnership.

(ii) Any individual who is a director or an officer. For purposes of this paragraph (b)(13)(ii), a director is a voting member of the governing body (that is, the board of directors or equivalent controlling body authorized under state law to make governance decisions on behalf of the organization), and the officers are determined by reference to the organizing document, bylaws, or resolutions of the governing body, or otherwise designated consistent with state law. Officers may include a president, vice-president, secretary, and treasurer.

(iii) Any individual who, regardless of title, has ultimate responsibility for implementing the decisions of the organization's governing body. An individual who serves with the title of chief executive officer, executive director, and/or president has this ultimate responsibility. An individual with this ultimate responsibility may include an individual who is not treated as an employee of the organization. If this ultimate responsibility resides with two or more individuals (for example, co-presidents), who may exercise such responsibility in concert or individually, then each individual is a responsible individual.

(iv) Any individual who, regardless of title, has ultimate responsibility for supervising the management, administration, or operation of the organization. An individual who serves with the title of chief operating officer has this ultimate responsibility. An individual with this ultimate responsibility may include an individual who is not treated as an employee of the organization. If this ultimate responsibility resides with two or more individuals, who may exercise such responsibility in concert or individually, then each individual is a responsible individual.

(v) Any individual who, regardless of title, has ultimate responsibility for managing the organization's finances. An individual who serves with the title of chief financial officer or treasurer has this ultimate responsibility. An individual with this ultimate responsibility may include an individual who is not treated as an employee of the organization. If this ultimate responsibility resides with two or more individuals who may exercise the responsibility in concert or individually, then each individual is a responsible individual.

(vi) In the case of a partnership, any individual who is a managing member or general partner.

(vii) In the case of a sole proprietorship, the sole proprietor.

(viii) Any other individual with primary responsibility for the organization's federal employment tax compliance.

(14) *Self-employed individual.*—[Reserved]

(15) *Substantial asset transfer* means any transfer of 35 percent or more of the value of the operating assets of the person making the transfer, whether through one or a series of transactions and whether accomplished through sale, lease, gift, assignment, succession, merger, consolidation, corporate separation, or any other means. For purposes of this paragraph (b)(15), operating assets include both tangible and intangible resources related to the conduct of the person's trade or business, including but not limited to such intangible assets as contracts, agreements, receivables, employees, and goodwill (which includes the value of a trade or business based on expected continued customer patronage due to its name, reputation, or any other factors). In the case of a contract described in section 7705(e)(2) or a service agreement described in § 31.3504-2(b)(2) of this chapter entered into by a provider of employment-related services, even if the contract or agreement is not sold, gifted, assigned, or otherwise formally transferred to a CPEO applicant, it will be considered transferred from the provider of employment-related services to the CPEO applicant if the CPEO applicant reports, withholds, or pays, under its employer identification number (EIN), any applicable federal employment taxes with respect to the wages of any individuals covered by the contract or agreement.

(c) *Effective/applicability date.*—(1) *In general.*— Except as provided in paragraph (c)(2) of this section, this section applies on and after July 1, 2016.

(2) *Definitions related to section 3511.*— [Reserved]

(3) *Expiration date.*—The applicability of this section expires on or before May 3, 2019. [Temporary Reg. § 301.7705-1T.]

☐ *T.D.* 9768, 5-4-2016.]

[Reg. § 301.7705-2T]

§ 301.7705-2T. CPEO certification requirements (temporary).—(a) *Application requirement and certification.*—(1) *Application.*—To be certified as a certified professional employer organization (CPEO), a person must submit a properly completed and executed application for certification as a CPEO in the time and manner prescribed by, and providing such information as required by, this section and any further guidance issued by the Commissioner. In addition, the applicant's responsible individuals must submit such information as is specified in this section and further guidance.

(2) *Notice.*—A CPEO applicant will be notified by the Internal Revenue Service (IRS) whether its application for certification has been approved or denied, and, if approved, the effective date of certification. If the IRS denies the application, the IRS will inform the CPEO applicant of the reason(s) for denial.

(3) *Public disclosure of certification.*—If the IRS approves a CPEO applicant's application for certification, the IRS will make available to the public the name and address of the CPEO, as well as the effective date of its certification, in the time and manner described in further guidance.

(4) *Effective date of certification.*—A CPEO's certification will be effective as of the effective date of certification specified in the notice described in paragraph (a)(2) of this section and in the public disclosure described in paragraph (a)(3) of this section and will continue in effect until the effective date of the revocation of the CPEO's certification, if any, as described in paragraph (n) of this section or, if earlier, the date that the CPEO voluntarily terminates its certification in the time and manner prescribed by the Commissioner in further guidance.

(b) *Requirements for certification.*—To receive and maintain certification, a CPEO applicant or CPEO must meet the requirements described in this section, as well as any additional requirements the Commissioner may prescribe in further guidance. In addition, any precursor entities, related entities, and responsible individuals (as defined in § § 301.7705-1T(b)(10), (12), and (13), respectively) of the CPEO applicant or CPEO must meet any requirements applicable to them described in this section and in further guidance. The IRS may deny an application for certification or revoke or suspend a CPEO's certification if a CPEO applicant or CPEO, or one or more of its precursor entities, related entities, or responsible individuals, fails to meet any applicable requirement described in this section or other applicable guidance, and the IRS will do so if the IRS determines, in its sole discretion, that such failure presents a material risk to the IRS's collection of federal employment taxes. In determining whether one or more failures to meet the requirements described in this section presents a material risk to the IRS's collection of federal employment taxes, the IRS generally will consider all relevant facts and circumstances, including the size, scope, nature, significance, recurrence, and timing of and reason for the failure and, in the case of a CPEO, any prior failures of the CPEO to meet the requirements of this section.

(c) *Suitability.*—(1) *In general.*—The IRS may deny an application for certification or revoke or suspend a CPEO's certification for any of the following reasons:

(i) The CPEO applicant or CPEO, or any of its precursor entities, related entities, or responsible individuals, has failed to pay any applicable federal, state, or local taxes or file any required federal, state, or local tax or information returns in a timely and accurate manner, unless the failure is determined to be due to reasonable cause and not due to willful neglect.

(ii) The CPEO applicant or CPEO, or any of its precursor entities, related entities, or responsible individuals, has been charged with or convicted of any criminal offense under the laws of the United States or of a state or political subdivision thereof, or is the subject of an active IRS criminal investigation.

(iii) The CPEO applicant or CPEO, or any of its precursor entities, related entities, or responsible individuals, has been sanctioned, or had a license, registration, or accreditation (including a license, registration, or accreditation relating to its status or ability to operate as a professional employer organization) denied, suspended, or revoked, by a court of competent jurisdiction, licensing board, assurance or other professional organization, or federal or state agency, court, body, board, or other authority for any misconduct that involves dishonesty, fraud, or breach of trust or that otherwise bears upon the suitability of the CPEO applicant or CPEO to perform its professional functions (including, but not limited to, any civil or criminal penalty described in 42 U.S.C. 503(k)(1)(D) imposed by state law).

(iv) The CPEO applicant or CPEO, or any of its precursor entities, related entities, or responsible individuals, is listed on any sanctions list compiled by the Office of Foreign Assets Control (OFAC) within the Department of Treasury, including, but not limited to the OFAC Consolidated Sanctions List and the OFAC Specially Designated Nationals (SDN) List.

(v) The CPEO applicant or CPEO, or any of its precursor entities, related entities, or re-

sponsible individuals, fails to demonstrate a history of financial responsibility, which the IRS may assess by checks on credit history and other similar indicators.

(vi) The CPEO applicant or CPEO and the responsible individuals of the CPEO applicant or CPEO fail to demonstrate adequate collective knowledge or experience with respect to:

(A) Federal or state employment tax reporting, depositing, and withholding requirements;

(B) Handling and accounting of payroll, tax payments, and other funds on behalf of others;

(C) Effective recordkeeping systems;

(D) Retention of qualified personnel and legal advisors as needed; and

(E) General business and risk management.

(vii) The CPEO applicant or CPEO, or any of its responsible individuals, gives false or misleading information (including by intentionally omitting relevant information), or participates in any way in the giving of false or misleading information, to the IRS, knowing, or having reason to know, that the information is false or misleading. For the purpose of this subsection, "information" includes (but is not limited to) facts or other matters contained in testimony, federal tax returns, and financial statements and opinions regarding such statements; applications for certification (and all accompanying documentation); affidavits, declarations, assertions, attestations, statements, and agreements; and periodic verifications that the requirements of this section continue to be met; and any other information that is required to be provided by this section, section 3511(g) and regulations thereunder, or further guidance.

(2) *Must be a business entity that is not a disregarded entity.*—A CPEO must be a business entity described in § 301.7701-2(a), except that a CPEO may not be a business entity that is disregarded as an entity separate from its owner for federal tax purposes under §§ 301.7701-2 and 301.7701-3 (without regard to the special rule in § 301.7701-2(c)(2)(iv) that provides that such entities are corporations for federal employment tax purposes). Accordingly, a CPEO may not be an individual or an entity classified as a trust under § 301.7701-4.

(3) *Authorization to investigate suitability.*—A CPEO applicant or CPEO, and each of its responsible individuals, must take such actions as are necessary to authorize the IRS to investigate the accuracy of statements and submissions, including waiving confidentiality and privilege when necessary, and to conduct comprehensive background checks, including, but not limited to, checks on tax compliance, criminal background, professional experience (including through the contact of third-party references), credit history, and professional sanctions. In addition, a CPEO applicant or CPEO, and any of its responsible individuals, must provide the IRS with such ad-

ditional information as the IRS may request to facilitate such background investigations. Each responsible individual of a CPEO applicant or CPEO must also submit fingerprints in the time and manner and under the circumstances prescribed by the Commissioner in further guidance.

(d) *Business location.*—(1) *State of organization.*—A CPEO applicant or CPEO must be created or organized in the United States or under the law of the United States or of any state.

(2) *Business location in the United States.*—A CPEO applicant or CPEO must have one or more established, physical business locations in the United States at which regular operations that constitute a trade or business within the United States (within the meaning of section 864(b)) take place and at which a significant portion of its CPEO-related functions are carried on and administrative records are kept.

(3) *United States responsible individuals.*—A majority of the CPEO applicant's or CPEO's responsible individuals must be citizens or residents of the United States.

(4) *Use of financial institution.*—A CPEO applicant or CPEO must use only financial institutions described in section 265(b)(5) to hold its cash and cash equivalents, receive payments from customers, and pay wages and federal employment taxes.

(e) *Financial statements.*—(1) *CPEOs.*—By the last day of the sixth month after the end of each fiscal year, and beginning with the first fiscal year that ends after the CPEO's effective date of certification, a CPEO must cause to be prepared and provided to the IRS a copy of its annual audited financial statements for the fiscal year and an opinion of a certified public accountant (CPA) that such financial statements—

(i) Are presented fairly in accordance with GAAP; and

(ii) Reflect positive working capital or, only if the CPEO satisfies the requirements of paragraph (e)(3) of this section, reflect negative working capital, with such opinion in either case setting forth in detail a calculation of the CPEO's working capital as reflected in the financial statements.

(2) *CPEO applicants.*—(i) *In general.*—A CPEO applicant must cause to be prepared and provided to the IRS, with its application, a copy of its annual audited financial statements and an opinion with respect to such financial statements (as described in paragraph (e)(1) of this section) for the most recently completed fiscal year as of the date it applies for certification. Notwithstanding the preceding sentence, if a CPEO applicant applies for certification before the last day of the sixth month following its most recently completed fiscal year, and the audit of the financial statements for this fiscal year has not yet been completed at the time of application, a CPEO applicant must provide to the IRS, with its application, the financial statements and opinion

described in paragraph (e)(1) of this section for the immediately preceding fiscal year, if any, and must subsequently provide to the IRS the financial statements and opinion described in paragraph (e)(1) of this section for the most recently completed fiscal year by the last day of the sixth month after such fiscal year ends. In addition, for any fiscal year that ends after the CPEO applicant applies for certification and on or before the effective date of certification, if applicable, the CPEO applicant must provide the audited financial statements and opinion described in paragraph (e)(1) of this section by the last day of the sixth month after such fiscal year ends. The obligation to provide the audited financial statements described in the preceding sentence continues to apply even if the CPEO applicant is certified as a CPEO prior to the date the audited financial statements are provided.

(ii) *Newly established CPEO applicants.*—In addition to the requirements in paragraph (e)(2)(i) of this section, a CPEO applicant that was not operating as a provider of employment-related services for all or part of the most recently completed fiscal year as of the date it applies for certification must provide a copy of the audited financial statements of any precursor entity, if one exists, and an opinion with respect to such financial statements (as described in paragraph (e)(1) of this section) for the precursor entity's most recently completed fiscal year as of the date of the application for certification in such time and manner as the Commissioner may prescribe in further guidance, as well as such additional information as the Commissioner may prescribe in further guidance.

(3) *Exception to positive working capital requirement.*—A CPEO applicant or CPEO with annual audited financial statements for a fiscal year that do not reflect positive working capital will not fail to meet the requirements of paragraph (e)(1)(ii) of this section if—

(i) The CPEO applicant or CPEO has negative working capital for no more than two consecutive fiscal quarters of that fiscal year, as demonstrated by the financial statements (for the final fiscal quarter in the fiscal year) and the statements described in paragraph (f)(1)(ii) of this section (for any other fiscal quarter);

(ii) The CPEO applicant or CPEO, or its CPA, provides, in such time and manner as the Commissioner may prescribe in further guidance, an explanation to the IRS describing the reason for the failure; and

(iii) The IRS determines, in its sole discretion, that the failure does not present a material risk to the IRS's collection of federal employment taxes.

(4) *Completed fiscal year.*—For purposes of this paragraph (e), a fiscal year will be considered completed once the last day of that fiscal year has ended, regardless of whether the CPEO applicant or CPEO was in operation or certified for all 12 months of the fiscal year or the fiscal year consisted of fewer than 12 months.

(f) *Quarterly assertions and attestations.*— (1) *CPEOs.*—By the last day of the second month after the end of each calendar quarter, and beginning with the first calendar quarter, that ends after the CPEO's effective date of certification, a CPEO must provide the following to the IRS:

(i) An assertion, signed by a responsible individual under penalties of perjury, stating that the CPEO has withheld and made deposits of all federal employment taxes (other than taxes imposed by chapter 23 of the Code) as required by subtitle C for such calendar quarter and an examination level attestation from a CPA stating that such assertion is fairly stated in all material respects.

(ii) A statement signed by a responsible individual under penalties of perjury verifying that the CPEO has positive working capital (as determined in accordance with GAAP) at the end of the most recently completed fiscal quarter, as well as such additional financial information that the Commissioner may specify in further guidance.

(2) *Exceptions.*—(i) *Immaterial failures.*—A CPEO will not fail to meet the requirements of paragraph (f)(1)(i) of this section if the CPA examination level attestation indicates that the CPEO has failed to withhold or make deposits in certain immaterial respects, provided that—

(A) The attestation provides a summary of the immaterial failures that were found;

(B) The attestation states that the failures were immaterial and isolated and do not reflect a meaningful lapse in compliance with federal employment tax withholding and deposit requirements; and

(C) The IRS determines, in its sole discretion, that the isolated and immaterial failures identified by the CPA do not present a material risk to the IRS's collection of federal employment taxes.

(ii) *Negative working capital.*—A CPEO with negative working capital at the end of a fiscal quarter will not fail to meet the requirements of paragraph (f)(1)(ii) of this section if—

(A) The CPEO does not have negative working capital at the end of the two fiscal quarters immediately preceding such fiscal quarter, as demonstrated by the financial statements described in paragraph (e)(1) of this section, if available, or the statements described in paragraph (f)(1)(ii) of this section;

(B) The CPEO provides an explanation to the IRS describing the reason for such negative working capital in such time and manner as the Commissioner may prescribe in further guidance; and

(C) The IRS determines, in its sole discretion, that the negative working capital does not present a material risk to the IRS's collection of federal employment taxes.

(3) *CPEO applicants.*—(i) *In general.*—By the last day of the second month after the end of each calendar quarter, beginning with the most recently completed calendar quarter as of the date of a CPEO applicant's application for certification and ending with the most recently completed calendar quarter as of the effective date of certification (if applicable), a CPEO applicant must provide to the IRS the assertion, examination level attestation, and working capital statement described in paragraph (f)(1) of this section, subject to the exceptions described in paragraph (f)(2) of this section (though substituting "CPEO applicant" for "CPEO").

(ii) *Newly established CPEO applicants.*—A CPEO applicant that was not operating as a provider of employment-related services during the most recently completed calendar quarter as of the date of its application for certification or during any calendar quarter that ends while its application for certification is pending must provide to the IRS the assertion, examination level attestation, and working capital statement described in paragraph (f)(1) of this section with respect to any precursor entity, if applicable, in such time and manner as the Commissioner may prescribe in further guidance, as well as such additional information as the Commissioner may prescribe in further guidance.

(g) *Bond.*—(1) *In general.*—A CPEO must post a bond for the payment of federal employment taxes issued in the form and containing the terms prescribed by the Commissioner in further guidance and in an amount described in paragraph (g)(2) of this section.

(2) *Bond amount.*—(i) *In general.*—The amount of the bond described in paragraph (g)(1) of this section must be, for each period beginning on April 1 of any calendar year and ending on March 31 of the following calendar year (or, in the case of a newly certified CPEO, beginning with the effective date of certification and ending on the subsequent March 31) (the bond period), at least equal to the greater of—

(A) Five percent of the CPEO's liability under section 3511 (or, if applicable, the liability described in paragraph (g)(2)(ii) of this section) during the calendar year preceding the beginning of the bond period, but not more than $1,000,000; or

(B) $50,000.

(ii) *Amount of bond in first and second year as a CPEO.*—If a CPEO does not have any liability under section 3511 for all or a portion of a preceding calendar year because the CPEO was not certified as a CPEO for all or a portion of that preceding calendar year, the liability applied for purposes of paragraph (g)(2)(i)(A) of this section for the entirety or portion of the preceding calendar year during which the CPEO was not certified will be the federal employment tax liability of the CPEO, and of any precursor entity of the CPEO described in §301.7705-1T(b)(10)(i)(A), that results from one or more service agreements described in §31.3504-2(b)(2) of this chapter. With respect to the federal employment tax liability of such precursor entity during a preceding calendar year, the liability will only be applied for purposes of paragraph (g)(2)(i)(A) of this section to the extent it results from service agreements that have been transferred or are intended to be transferred by the precursor entity to the CPEO at the time the bond amount is determined. For purposes of this paragraph (g)(2)(ii), an entity is considered a precursor entity of a CPEO described in §301.7705-1T(b)(10)(i)(A) if it was determined to be its precursor entity under that section at the time it was a CPEO applicant.

(3) *Cancellation.*—(i) *Notice.*—A bond required under this paragraph (g) must provide that it may be cancelled by the surety only after the surety gives written notice of such cancellation to the IRS and the CPEO in such time and manner as the Commissioner may prescribe in further guidance.

(ii) *Ongoing liability.*—A bond required under this paragraph (g) must provide that, if a surety cancels the bond without issuing a superseding bond to the CPEO, the surety will, notwithstanding the cancellation, remain liable for all federal employment tax liability accrued by the CPEO during the period beginning with the effective date of the first bond issued by the surety to the CPEO in any consecutive series of bonds issued by that surety prior to cancellation and ending with the cancellation of the bond (the total bond period), up to the penal amount of the bond at the time of the cancellation. A cancelling surety will remain liable as described in this paragraph (g)(3)(ii) for federal employment tax liability accrued during the total bond period up to the penal amount of the bond for as long as the Commissioner may assess and collect taxes for such period under sections 6501 and 6502.

(4) *Strengthening bonds to reflect CPEO adjustment or IRS assessment.*—In calculating five percent of its liability under section 3511 (or other applicable federal employment tax liability) for a preceding calendar year for purposes of determining a bond amount, a CPEO must base its calculation on the amount of applicable federal employment taxes that it reported and paid for that preceding calendar year. However, if the CPEO or the IRS subsequently determines during the period for which the bond amount applies that the applicable federal employment tax liability for the preceding calendar year was higher than the amount reported and paid (and makes an adjustment or assessment, respectively, reflecting such determination) and if the bond that the CPEO had posted was less than $1,000,000, the CPEO must post a strengthening bond that, together with the initially-posted bond, equals a total amount that reflects the adjusted applicable federal employment tax liability up to $1,000,000. Alternatively, such a CPEO could post a superseding bond in such adjusted amount.

(5) *No posting of collateral.*—A CPEO must meet the bond requirements of this paragraph (g) without posting collateral.

(6) *Requirements for surety.*—Any surety that issues a bond required by this paragraph (g) to a CPEO must be a surety company that holds a certificate of authority from the Secretary as an acceptable surety on federal bonds and meets such other requirements as the Commissioner may prescribe in further guidance.

(h) *Controlled group.*—All CPEO applicants and CPEOs that are members of a controlled group within the meaning of sections 414(b) and (c) will be treated as a single CPEO applicant or CPEO for purposes of paragraphs (e) (other than (e)(1)(ii)), (f) (other than (f)(1)(ii)), and (g) of this section.

(i) *Consents to disclose.*—To receive and maintain certification, a CPEO applicant or CPEO must provide such consents for the IRS to disclose confidential tax information to its customers, and to other persons as necessary to carry out the purposes of these regulations, that relates to its certification and obligations to report, deposit, and pay federal employment taxes as the Commissioner may require in further guidance.

(j) *Periodic verification.*—A CPEO must periodically verify that it continues to meet the requirements of this section in the time and manner prescribed by the Commissioner in further guidance.

(k) *Notification of material changes.*—A CPEO applicant or CPEO must notify the IRS, in the time and manner prescribed by the Commissioner in further guidance, of any change that materially affects the continuing accuracy of any agreement or information that was previously made or provided to the IRS.

(l) *Accrual method of accounting.*—A CPEO must compute its taxable income using an accrual method of accounting or, if applicable, another method that the Commissioner provides for in further guidance.

(m) *Compliance with reporting obligations.*—(1) *In general.*—A CPEO must agree to make reports to the IRS and to its clients as provided in section 3511(g) and the regulations thereunder, including filing all federal employment tax returns and information returns as required.

(2) *Filing on magnetic media.*—A CPEO must file all returns, schedules, reports, and other forms and documents on magnetic media when required by section 3511(g) and the regulations thereunder or other Treasury regulations.

(n) *Suspension and revocation.*—(1) *In general.*—The IRS may suspend or revoke the certification of any CPEO, in the time and manner and under the circumstances prescribed by the Commissioner in further guidance, as a result of one or more failures to meet any of the requirements for CPEOs described in this section, section 3511(g) and the regulations thereunder, and any further guidance and will suspend or revoke certification if the IRS determines, in its sole discretion, that such failure(s) present a material risk to the IRS's collection of federal employment taxes. See paragraph (b) of this section for the factors the IRS will consider in determining whether one or more failures to meet any of the requirements described in this section presents a material risk to the IRS's collection of federal employment taxes.

(2) *Suspension.*—Section 3511 will not apply to any contract described in section 7705(e)(2) into which the CPEO enters while its certification is suspended.

(3) *Revocation.*—If an organization's certification as a CPEO is revoked, the organization will not be considered a CPEO for purposes of section 3511 unless and until it again applies to be certified as a CPEO in accordance with paragraph (a) of this section and is again certified by the IRS as meeting the requirements of this section. An organization whose certification as a CPEO has been revoked may not re-apply to be certified as a CPEO until one year has passed since the effective date of its revocation.

(4) *Disclosure of suspension and revocation.*—(i) *Notification by the CPEO.*—An organization whose certification as a CPEO has been suspended or revoked must notify its customers of such suspension or revocation in the time and manner prescribed by the Commissioner in further guidance.

(ii) *Disclosure by the IRS.*—If the IRS suspends or revokes an organization's certification as a CPEO, the IRS will make available to the public the fact of such suspension or revocation in the time and manner described in further guidance. The IRS may also individually notify the organization's customers of such suspension or revocation.

(o) *Effective/applicability date.*—(1) *In general.*—This section applies on and after July 1, 2016.

(2) *Expiration date.*—The applicability of this section expires on or before May 3, 2019. [Temporary Reg. § 301.7705-2T.]

☐ *T.D. 9768, 5-4-2015.]*

General Rules

APPLICATION OF INTERNAL REVENUE LAWS

See p. 20,601 for regulations not amended to reflect law changes

[Reg. § 801.1]

§ 801.1. Balanced performance measurement system; in general.—(a) *In general.*—(1) The regulations in this part 801 implement the provisions of sections 1201 and 1204 of the Internal Revenue Service Restructuring and Reform Act of 1998 (Public Law 105-106, 112 Stat. 685, 715-716, 722) (the Act) and provide rules relating to the establishment by the Internal Revenue Service (IRS) of a balanced performance measurement system.

(2) Modern management practice and various statutory and regulatory provisions require the IRS to set performance goals for organizational units and to measure the results achieved by those units with respect to those goals. To fulfill these requirements, the IRS has established a balanced performance measurement system, composed of three elements: Customer Satisfaction Measures; Employee Satisfaction Measures; and Business Results Measures. The IRS is likewise required to establish a performance evaluation system for individual employees.

(b) [Reserved]. [Reg. § 801.1.]

☐ *[T.D. 9227, 10-14-2005. Redesignated and amended by T.D. 9426, 10-10-2008.]*

[Reg. § 801.2]

§ 801.2. Measuring organizational performance.—The performance measures that comprise the balanced measurement system will, to the maximum extent possible, be stated in objective, quantifiable, and measurable terms and will be used to measure the overall performance of various operational units within the IRS. In addition

to implementing the requirements of the Act, the measures described here will, where appropriate, be used in establishing performance goals and making performance evaluations established, inter alia, under Division E, National Defense Authorization Act for Fiscal Year 1996 (the Clinger-Cohen Act of 1996) (Public Law 104-106, 110 Stat. 186, 679); the Government Performance and Results Act of 1993 (Public Law 103-62, 107 Stat. 285); and the Chief Financial Officers Act of 1990 (Public Law 101-576, 108 Stat. 2838). Thus, organizational measures of customer satisfaction, employee satisfaction, and business results (including quality and quantity measures as described in § 801.6T) may be used to evaluate the performance of or to impose or suggest production goals for, any organizational unit. [Reg. § 801.2.]

☐ *[T.D. 9227, 10-14-2005. Redesignated and amended by T.D. 9426, 10-10-2008.]*

[Reg. § 801.3]

§ 801.3. Measuring employee performance.—(a) *In general.*—All employees of the IRS will be evaluated according to the critical elements and standards or such other performance criteria as may be established for their positions. In accordance with the requirements of 5 U.S.C. 4312, 4313, and 9508 and section 1201 of the Act, the performance criteria for each position as are appropriate to that position, will be composed of elements that support the organizational measures of Customer Satisfaction, Employee Satisfaction, and Business Results; however, such organizational measures will not directly determine the evaluation of individual employees.

(b) *Fair and equitable treatment of taxpayers.*—In addition to all other criteria required to be used in the evaluation of employee performance, all employees of the IRS will be evaluated on whether they provided fair and equitable treatment to taxpayers.

(c) *Senior Executive Service and special positions.*—Employees in the Senior Executive Service will be rated in accordance with the requirements of 5 U.S.C. 4312 and 4313 and employees selected to fill positions under 5 U.S.C. 9503 will be evaluated pursuant to workplans, employment agreements, performance agreements, or similar documents entered into between the IRS and the employee.

(d) *General workforce.*—The performance evaluation system for all other employees will—

(1) Establish one or more retention standards for each employee related to the work of the employee and expressed in terms of individual performance;

(2) Require periodic determinations of whether each employee meets or does not meet the employee's established retention standards;

(3) Require that action be taken in accordance with applicable laws and regulations, with respect to employees whose performance does not meet the established retention standards;

(4) Establish goals or objectives for individual performance consistent with the IRS's performance planning procedures;

(5) Use such goals and objectives to make performance distinctions among employees or groups of employees; and

(6) Use performance assessments as a basis for granting employee awards, adjusting an employee's rate of basic pay, and other appropriate personnel actions, in accordance with applicable laws and regulations.

(e) *Limitations.*—(1) No employee of the IRS may use records of tax enforcement results (as described in § 801.6) to evaluate any other employee or to impose or suggest production quotas or goals for any employee.

(i) For purposes of the limitation contained in this paragraph (e), *employee* has the meaning as defined in 5 U.S.C. 2105(a).

(ii) For purposes of the limitation contained in this paragraph (e), *evaluate* includes any process used to appraise or measure an employee's performance for purposes of providing the following:

(A) Any required or requested performance rating.

(B) A recommendation for an award covered by Chapter 45 of Title 5; 5 U.S.C. 5384; or section 1201(a) of the Act.

(C) An assessment of an employee's qualifications for promotion, reassignment, or other change in duties.

(D) An assessment of an employee's eligibility for incentives, allowances, or bonuses.

(E) Ranking of employees for release/recall and reductions in force.

(2) Employees who are responsible for exercising judgment with respect to tax enforcement results in cases concerning one or more taxpayers may be evaluated on work done on such cases only in the context of their critical elements and standards.

(3) Performance measures based in whole or in part on quantity measures (as described in § 801.6) will not be used to evaluate the performance of any non-supervisory employee who is responsible for exercising judgment with respect to tax enforcement results (as described in § 801.6). [Reg. § 801.3.]

☐ *[T.D. 9227, 10-14-2005. Redesignated and amended by T.D. 9426, 10-10-2008.]*

[Reg. § 801.4]

§ 801.4. Customer satisfaction measures.— The customer satisfaction goals and accomplishments of operating units within the IRS will be determined on the basis of information gathered through various methods. For example, questionnaires, surveys and other types of information gathering mechanisms may be employed to gather data regarding customer satisfaction. Information to measure customer satisfaction for a particular work unit will be gathered from a statistically valid sample of the customers served by that operating unit and will be used to measure, among other things, whether those customers believe that they received courteous, timely, and professional treatment by the IRS personnel with whom they dealt. Customers will be permitted to provide information requested for these purposes under conditions that guarantee them anonymity. For purposes of this section, customers may include individual taxpayers, organizational units, or employees within the IRS and external groups affected by the services performed by the IRS operating unit. [Reg. § 801.4.]

☐ *[T.D. 9227, 10-14-2005. Redesignated by T.D. 9426, 10-10-2008.]*

[Reg. § 801.5]

§ 801.5. Employee satisfaction measures.— (a) The employee satisfaction numerical ratings to be given to a Business Operating Division (BOD) or equivalent office within the IRS will be determined on the basis of information gathered through various methods. For example, questionnaires, surveys, and other information gathering mechanisms may be employed to gather data regarding satisfaction. The information gathered will be used to measure, among other factors bearing upon employee satisfaction, the quality of supervision, and the adequacy of training and support services. All full and part-time permanent employees of a BOD or equivalent office who are in pay and duty status will have an opportunity to provide information regarding employee satisfaction under conditions that guarantee them confidentiality.

(b) This section applies to the reporting of employee satisfaction information that occurs on or after March 7, 2018. [Reg. § 801.5.]

☐ [*T.D. 9227, 10-14-2005. Redesignated by T.D. 9426, 10-10-2008. Amended by T.D. 9703, 11-12-2014 and T.D. 9831, 3-6-2018.*]

[Reg. § 801.6]

§ 801.6. Business results measures.—(a) *In general.*—The business results measures will consist of numerical scores determined under the quality measures and the quantity measures described elsewhere in this section.

(b) *Quality measures.*—Quality measures will be determined on the basis of a review by a specially dedicated staff within the IRS of a statistically valid sample of work items handled by certain functions or organizational units determined by the Commissioner or his delegate such as the following:

(1) *Examination and collection units and Automated Collection System Units (ACS).*—The quality review of the handling of cases involving particular taxpayers will focus on such factors as whether IRS personnel devoted an appropriate amount of time to a matter, properly analyzed the facts, and complied with statutory, regulatory, and IRS procedures, including timeliness, adequacy of notifications, and required contacts with taxpayers.

(2) *Toll-free telephone sites.*—The quality review of telephone services will focus on such factors as whether IRS personnel provided accurate tax law and account information.

(3) *Other work units.*—The quality review of other work units will be determined according to criteria prescribed by the Commissioner or his delegate.

(c) *Quantity measures.*—Quantity measures will consist of outcome-neutral production and resource data that does not contain information regarding the tax enforcement result reached in any case that involves particular taxpayers. Examples of quantity measures include, but are not limited to—

(1) Cases started;

(2) Cases closed;

(3) Work items completed;

(4) Customer education, assistance, and outreach efforts completed;

(5) Time per case;

(6) Direct examination time/out of office time;

(7) Cycle time;

(8) Number or percentage of overage cases;

(9) Inventory information;

(10) Toll-free level of access; and

(11) Talk time.

(d) *Definitions.*—(1) *Tax enforcement results.*—A tax enforcement result is the outcome produced by an IRS employee's exercise of judgment in recommending or determining whether or how the IRS should pursue enforcement of the tax laws. Examples of tax enforcement results include a lien filed, a levy served, a seizure executed, the amount assessed, the amount col-lected, and a fraud referral. Examples of data that are not tax enforcement results include a quantity measure and data derived from a quality review or from a review of an employee's or a work unit's work on a case, such as the number or percentage of cases in which correct examination adjustments were proposed or appropriate lien determinations were made.

(2) *Records of tax enforcement results.*—Records of tax enforcement results are data, statistics, compilations of information or other numerical or quantitative recordations of the tax enforcement results reached in one or more cases. Such records may be used for purposes such as forecasting, financial planning, resource management, and the formulation of case selection criteria. Records of tax enforcement results may be used to develop methodologies and algorithms for use in selecting tax returns to audit. Records of tax enforcement results do not include tax enforcement results of individual cases when used to determine whether an employee exercised appropriate judgment in pursuing enforcement of the tax laws based upon a review of the employee's work on that individual case. [Reg. § 801.6.]

☐ [*T.D. 9227, 10-14-2005. Redesignated by T.D. 9426, 10-10-2008.*]

[Reg. § 801.7]

§ 801.7. Examples.—(a) The rules of § 801.3 are illustrated by the following examples:

Example 1. (i) Each year Division A's Examination and Collection functions develop detailed workplans that set goals for specific activities (e.g., number of audits or accounts closed) and for other quantity measures such as cases started, cycle time, overage cases, and direct examination time. These quantity measure goals are developed nationally and by Area Office based on budget allocations, available resources, historical experience, and planned improvements. These plans also include information on measures of quality, customer satisfaction, and employee satisfaction. Results are updated monthly to reflect how each organizational unit is progressing against its workplan, and this information is shared with all levels of management.

(ii) Although specific workplans are not developed at the Territory level, Headquarters management expects the Area Directors to use the information in the Area plans to guide the activity in their Territories. For 2005, Area Office 1's workplan has a goal to close 1,000 examinations of small business corporations and 120,000 taxpayer delinquent accounts (TDAs), and there are 10 Exam Territories and 12 Collection Territories in Area Office 1. While taking into account the mix and priority of workload, and available staffing and grade levels, the Examination Area Director communicates to the Territory Managers the expectation that, on average, each Territory should plan to close about 100 cases. The Collection Area Director similarly communicates to each Territory the expectation that, on average, they will close about 10,000 TDAs, subject to similar factors of workload mix and staffing.

(iii) Similar communications then occur at the next level of management between Territory Managers and their Group Managers, and between Group Managers and their employees. These communications will emphasize the overall goals of the organization and each employee's role in meeting those goals. The communications will include expectations regarding the average number of case closures that would have to occur to reach those goals, taking into account the fact that each employee's actual closures will vary based upon the facts and circumstances of specific cases.

(iv) Setting these quantity measure goals, and the communication of those goals, is permissible because case closures are a quantity measure. Case closures are an example of outcome-neutral production data that does not specify the outcome of any specific case such as the amount assessed or collected.

Example 2. In conducting a performance evaluation, a supervisor is permitted to take into consideration information the supervisor has developed showing that the employee failed to propose an appropriate adjustment to tax liability in one of the cases the employee examined, provided that information is derived from a review of the work done on the case. All information derived from such a review of individual cases handled by the employee, including time expended, issues raised, and enforcement outcomes reached should be considered and discussed with the employee and used in evaluating the employee.

Example 3. When assigning a case, a supervisor is permitted to discuss with the employee the merits, issues, and development of techniques of the case based upon a review of the case file.

Example 4. A supervisor is not permitted to establish a goal for proposed adjustments in a future examination.

(b) [Reserved].

[Reg. § 801.7.]

☐ [*T.D.* 9227, 10-14-2005. *Redesignated and amended by T.D.* 9426, 10-10-2008.]

[Reg. § 801.8]

§ 801.8. Effective/applicability dates.—The provisions of § § 801.1 through 801.7 apply on or after October 17, 2005. [Reg. § 801.8.]

☐ [*T.D.* 9227, 10-14-2005. *Redesignated and amended by T.D.* 9426, 10-10-2008.]

[Reg. § 31.7805-1]

§ 31.7805-1. Promulgation of regulations.—In pursuance of section 7805 of the Internal Revenue Code of 1954, the foregoing regulations are hereby prescribed. (See § 31.0-3 of Subpart A of the regulations in this part relating to the scope of the regulations.) [Reg. § 31.7805-1.]

☐ [*T.D.* 6472, 6-22-60.]

[Reg. § 301.7805-1]

§ 301.7805-1. Rules and regulations.—(a) *Issuance.*—The Commissioner, with the approval of the Secretary, shall prescribe all needful rules and regulations for the enforcement of the Code (except where this authority is expressly given by the Code to any person other than an officer or employee of the Treasury Department), including all rules and regulations as may be necessary by reason of any alteration of law in relation to internal revenue.

(b) *Retroactivity.*—The Commissioner, with the approval of the Secretary, may prescribe the extent, if any, to which any regulation or Treasury decision relating to the internal revenue laws shall be applied without retroactive effect. The Commissioner may prescribe the extent, if any, to which any ruling relating to the internal revenue laws, issued by or pursuant to authorization from him, shall be applied without retroactive effect.

(c) *Preparation and distribution of regulations, forms, stamps, and other matters.*—The Commissioner, under the direction of the Secretary, shall prepare and distribute all the instructions, regulations, directions, forms, blanks, stamps, and other matters pertaining to the assessment and collection of internal revenue. [Reg. § 301.7805-1.]

☐ [*T.D.* 6498, 10-24-60.]

[Reg. § 301.7811-1]

§ 301.7811-1. Authority to issue taxpayer assistance orders.—(a) *Authority to issue.*—(1) *In general.*—When an application for a taxpayer assistance order (TAO) is filed by the taxpayer or the taxpayer's authorized representative in the form, manner and time specified in paragraph (b) of this section, the National Taxpayer Advocate (NTA) may issue a TAO if, in the determination of the NTA, the taxpayer is suffering or is about to suffer a significant hardship as a result of the manner in which the internal revenue laws are being administered by the Internal Revenue Service (IRS), including action or inaction on the part of the IRS.

(2) *The National Taxpayer Advocate defined.*—The term *National Taxpayer Advocate* includes any designee of the NTA, such as a Local Taxpayer Advocate.

(3) *Issuance without a written application.*—The NTA may issue a TAO in the absence of a written application by the taxpayer under section 7811(a).

(4) *Significant hardship.*—(i) *Determination required.*—Before a TAO may be issued, the NTA is required to make a determination regarding significant hardship.

(ii) *Term defined.*—The term *significant hardship* means a serious privation caused or about to be caused to the taxpayer as the result of the particular manner in which the revenue laws are being administered by the IRS. Significant hardship includes situations in which a system or procedure fails to operate as intended or fails to resolve the taxpayer's problem or dispute with the IRS. A significant hardship also includes, but is not limited to:

(A) An immediate threat of adverse action;

(B) A delay of more than 30 days in resolving taxpayer account problems;

(C) The incurring by the taxpayer of significant costs (including fees for professional representation) if relief is not granted; or

(D) Irreparable injury to, or a long-term adverse impact on, the taxpayer if relief is not granted.

(iii) *A delay of more than 30 days in resolving taxpayer account problems is further defined.*—A delay of more than 30 days in resolving taxpayer account problems exists under the following conditions:

(A) When a taxpayer does not receive a response by the date promised by the IRS; or

(B) When the IRS has established a normal processing time for taking an action and the taxpayer experiences a delay of more than 30 days beyond the normal processing time.

(iv) *Examples of significant hardship.*—The provisions of this section are illustrated by the following examples:

Example 1. Immediate threat of adverse action. The IRS serves a levy on A's bank account. A needs the bank funds to pay for a medically necessary surgical procedure that is scheduled to take place in one week. If the levy is not released, A will lack the funds necessary to have the procedure. A is experiencing an immediate threat of adverse action.

Example 2. Delay of more than 30 days. B files a Form 4506, "Request for a Copy of Tax Return." B does not receive the photocopy of the tax return after waiting more than 30 days beyond the normal time for processing. B is experiencing a delay of more than 30 days.

Example 3. Significant costs. The IRS sends XYZ, Inc. a notice requesting payment of the outstanding employment taxes and penalties owed by XYZ, Inc. The notice indicates that XYZ, Inc. has small employment tax balances with respect to 12 employment tax quarters totaling $10X. XYZ, Inc. provides documentation to the IRS which it contends shows that if all payments were applied to each quarter correctly, there would be no balance due. The IRS requests additional records and documentation. Because there are 12 quarters involved, to comply with this request XYZ, Inc. asserts that it will need to hire an accountant, who estimates he will charge at least $5X to organize all the records and provide a detailed analysis of how to apply the deposits and payments. XYZ, Inc. is facing significant costs.

Example 4. Irreparable injury. D has arranged with a bank to refinance his mortgage to lower his monthly payment. D is unable to make the current monthly payment. Unless the monthly payment amount is lowered, D will lose his residence to foreclosure. The IRS refuses to subordinate the Federal tax lien, as permitted by section 6325(d), or discharge the property subject to the lien, as permitted by section 6325(b). As a result, the bank will not allow D to refinance. D is facing an irreparable injury if relief is not granted.

(5) *Distinction between significant hardship and the issuance of a TAO.*—A finding that a taxpayer is suffering or about to suffer a significant hardship as a result of the manner in which the internal revenue laws are being administered by the IRS will not automatically result in the issuance of a TAO. After making a determination of significant hardship, the NTA must determine whether the facts and the law support relief for the taxpayer. In cases where any IRS employee is not following applicable published administrative guidance (including the Internal Revenue Manual), the NTA shall construe the factors taken into account in determining whether to issue a TAO in the manner most favorable to the taxpayer.

(b) *Generally.*—A TAO is an order by the NTA to the IRS. The IRS will comply with a TAO unless it is appealed and then modified or rescinded by the NTA, the Commissioner, or the Deputy Commissioner. If a TAO is modified or rescinded by the Commissioner or the Deputy Commissioner, a written explanation of the reasons for the modification or rescission must be provided to the NTA. The NTA may not make a substantive determination of any tax liability. A TAO is also not intended to be a substitute for an established administrative or judicial review procedure, but rather is intended to supplement existing procedures if a taxpayer is about to suffer or is suffering a significant hardship. A request for a TAO shall be made on a Form 911, "Request for Taxpayer Advocate Service Assistance (And Application for Taxpayer Assistance Order)" (or other specified form) or in a written statement that provides sufficient information for the Taxpayer Advocate Service (TAS) to determine the nature of the harm or the need for assistance. A taxpayer's right to administrative or judicial review will not be diminished or expanded in any way as a result of the taxpayer's seeking assistance from TAS.

(c) *Contents of Taxpayer Assistance Orders.*—After establishing that the taxpayer is facing significant hardship and determining that the facts and law support relief to the taxpayer, the NTA may issue a TAO ordering the IRS within a specified time to—

(1) *Release a levy.*—Release levied property (to the extent that the IRS may by law release such property); or

(2) *Take certain other actions.*—Cease any action, take any action as permitted by law, or refrain from taking any action with respect to a taxpayer pursuant to—

(i) Chapter 64 (relating to collection);

(ii) Chapter 70, subchapter B (relating to bankruptcy and receiverships);

(iii) Chapter 78 (relating to discovery of liability and enforcement of title); or

(iv) Any other provision of the internal revenue laws specifically described by the NTA in the TAO.

(3) *Expedite, review, or reconsider an action at a higher level.*—Although the NTA may not make the substantive determination, a TAO may be issued to require the IRS to expedite, reconsider, or review at a higher level an action taken with respect to a determination or collection of a tax liability.

(4) *Examples.*—The following examples assume the existence of significant hardship:

Example 1. J contacts a Local Taxpayer Advocate because a wage levy is causing financial difficulties. The NTA determines that the levy should be released as it is causing economic hardship (within the meaning of section 6343(a)(1)(D) and § 301.6343-1(b)(4)). The NTA may issue a TAO ordering the IRS to release the levy in whole or in part by a specified date.

Example 2. The IRS rejects K's offer in compromise. K files a Form 911, "Request for Taxpayer Advocate Service Assistance (And Application for Taxpayer Assistance Order)." The NTA discovers facts that support acceptance of the offer in compromise. The NTA may issue a TAO ordering the IRS to reconsider its rejection of the offer or to review the rejection of the offer at a higher level. The TAO may include the NTA's analysis of and recommendation for resolving the case.

Example 3. L files a protest requesting Appeals consideration of IRS's proposed denial of L's request for innocent spouse relief. Appeals advises L that it is going to issue a Final Determination denying the request for innocent spouse relief. L files a Form 911, "Request for Taxpayer Advocate Service Assistance (And Application for Taxpayer Assistance Order)." The NTA reviews the administrative record and concludes that the facts support granting innocent spouse relief. The NTA may issue a TAO ordering Appeals to refrain from issuing a Final Determination and reconsider or review at a higher level its decision to deny innocent spouse relief. The TAO may include the NTA's analysis of and recommendation for resolving the case.

(d) *Issuance.*—A TAO may be issued to any office, operating division, or function of the IRS. A TAO shall apply to persons performing services under a qualified tax collection contract (as defined in section 6306(b)) to the same extent and in the same manner as the order applies to IRS employees. A TAO will not be issued to IRS Criminal Investigation division (CI), or any successor IRS division responsible for the criminal investigation function, if the action ordered in the TAO could reasonably be expected to impede a criminal investigation. CI will determine whether the action ordered in the TAO could reasonably be expected to impede an investiga-

tion. Generally, a TAO may not be issued to the Office of Chief Counsel.

(e) *Suspension of statutes of limitations.*—(1) *In general.*—The running of the applicable period of limitations for any action which is the subject of a taxpayer assistance order shall be suspended for the period beginning on the date the Ombudsman receives an application for a taxpayer assistance order in the form, manner, and time specified in paragraph (b) of this section and ending on the date on which the Ombudsman makes a determination with respect to the application, and for any additional period specified by the Ombudsman in an order issued pursuant to a taxpayer's application. For the purpose of computing the period suspended, all calendar days except the date of receipt of the application shall be included.

(2) *Date of decision.*—The "date on which the Ombudsman makes a decision with respect to the application" is the date on which the taxpayer's request for a taxpayer assistance order is denied, or agreement is reached with the involved function of the Service, or a taxpayer assistance order is issued (except that when the taxpayer assistance order is reviewed by an official who may modify or rescind the taxpayer assistance order as provided in paragraph (d) of this section, the decision date is the date on which such review is completed).

(3) *Periods suspended.*—The periods of limitations which are suspended under section 7811(d) are those which apply to the taxable periods to which the application for a taxpayer assistance order relate or the taxable periods specifically indicated in the terms of a taxpayer assistance order.

Example (1). On August 31, 1989, the Internal Revenue Service levies on funds in the taxpayer's checking account. On September 1, 1989, (at which time 7 months remain before the period of limitations on collection after assessment will expire on April 1, 1990) the Ombudsman receives the taxpayer's written application for a taxpayer assistance order. Subsequently, on September 6, 1989, the Ombudsman determines that the levy has caused a significant hardship and the Internal Revenue Service function which served the levy agrees to release the levy. The levy is released. As a result of the application and the decision by the Ombudsman and the involved function of the Service resolving the hardship, the statute of limitations on collection after assessment is suspended from the date the Ombudsman received the application, September 1, 1989, until the date on which the decision was made to release the levy, September 6, 1989. Therefore, the statute of limitations on collection after assessment will not expire until after April 6, 1990, which is 7 months plus 5 days after the date on which the application for a taxpayer assistance order was received by the Ombudsman.

Example (2). The facts are the same as in example (1) except that the Internal Revenue

Service function which served the levy does not agree to release the levy, and the Ombudsman, having made a determination that the levy is causing a significant hardship, issues a taxpayer assistance order on September 6, 1989, in which the levy is ordered to be released and specifies that the statute of limitations on collection after assessment is suspended for an additional 15 days. The period of limitations on collection after assessment will therefore not expire until after April 21, 1990, which is 7 months and 20 days (5 days plus 15 days) after the application for the taxpayer assistance order was received by the Ombudsman.

Example (3). The facts are the same as in example (2) except that the Ombudsman does not specifically suspend the statute of limitations on collection after assessment for an additional number of days in the taxpayer assistance order, but rather the function seeks modification or rescission of the taxpayer assistance order and the appropriate official charged with that re-

sponsibility completes his consideration of the assistance order on September 8, 1989. The period of limitations on collection after assessment will therefore not expire until after April 8, 1990, which is 7 months and 7 days after the application for the taxpayer assistance order was received by the Ombudsman.

(4) *Absence of a written application.*—The statute of limitations is not suspended in cases where the Ombudsman issues an order in the absence of a written application for relief by the taxpayer or the taxpayer's duly authorized representative.

(f) *Effective/applicability date.*—These regulations are applicable for TAOs issued on or after April 1, 2011 except that paragraph (e) of this section is applicable beginning March 20, 1992. [Reg. § 301.7811-1.]

☐ [*T.D. 8246, 3-21-89. Amended by T.D. 8403,* 3-20-92, *T.D. 9519, 4-1-2011.*]

PROVISIONS AFFECTING MORE THAN ONE SUBTITLE

[Reg. § 305.7871-1]

§ 305.7871-1. Indian tribal governments treated as States for certain purposes (Temporary).—(a) *In general.*—An Indian tribal government, as defined in section 7701(a)(40) and the regulations thereunder, shall be treated as a State, and a subdivision of an Indian tribal government, as determined under section 7871(d) and paragraph(e) of this section, shall be treated as a political subdivision of a State, under the following sections and regulations thereunder—

(1) Section 170 (relating to income tax deductions for charitable, etc., contributions and gifts), sections 2055 and 2106(a)(2) (relating to estate tax deductions for transfers of public, charitable and religious uses), and section 2522 (relating to gift tax deductions for charitable and similar gifts), for purposes of determining whether and in what amount any contribution or transfer to or for the use of an Indian tribal government (or subdivision thereof) is deductible;

(2) Section 164 (relating to deductions for taxes);

(3) Section 511 (a)(2)(B) (relating to the taxation of colleges and universities which are agencies or instrumentalities of governments or their political subdivisions);

(4) Section 37(e)(9)(A) (relating to certain public retirement systems);

(5) Section 41(c)(4) (defining "State" for purposes of credit for contributions to candidates for public offices);

(6) Section 117(b)(2)(A) (relating to scholarships and fellowship grants);

(7) Section 403(b)(1)(A)(ii) (relating to the taxation of contributions of certain employers for employee annuities);

(8) Chapter 41 of the Code (relating to tax on excess expenditures to influence legislation); and

(9) Subchapter A of chapter 42 of the Code (relating to private foundations).

(b) *Special rule for excise tax provisions.*—An Indian tribal government shall be treated as a State, and a subdivision of an Indian tribal government shall be treated as a political subdivision of a State, for purposes of any exemption from, credit or refund of, or payment with respect to, an excise tax imposed on a transaction under—

(1) Chapter 31 of the Code (relating to tax on special fuels);

(2) Chapter 32 of the Code (relating to manufacturers excise taxes);

(3) Subchapter B of chapter 33 of the Code (relating to communications excise tax); and

(4) Subchapter D of chapter 36 of the Code (relating to tax on use of certain highway vehicles),

if, in addition to satisfying all requirements applicable to a similar transaction involving a State (or political subdivision thereof) under the Code, the transaction involves the exercise of an essential governmental function of the Indian tribal government, as defined in paragraph (d) of this section.

(c) *Special rule for tax-exempt bonds.*—An Indian tribal government shall be treated as a State and a subdivision of an Indian tribal government shall be treated as a political subdivision of a State for purposes of any obligation issued by such government or subdivision under section 103 (relating to interest on certain governmental obligations) if such obligation is part of an issue substantially all of the proceeds of which are to be used in the exercise of an essential governmental function, as defined in paragraph (d) of this section. For purposes of section 7871 and this section, the "substantially all" test is the same as that provided in § 1.103-8(a)(1)(i). An Indian tribal government shall not be treated as a State and a subdivision of an Indian tribal government shall not be treated as a political subdivision of a State, however, for issues of the following private activity bonds—

(1) An industrial development bond (as defined in section 103(b)(2));

(2) An obligation described in section 103(l)(1)(A) (relating to scholarship bonds); or

(3) A mortgage subsidy bond (as defined in section 103A(b)(1), without regard to section 103A(b)(2)).

(d) *Essential governmental function.*—For purposes of section 7871 and this section, an essential governmental function of an Indian tribal government (or portion thereof) is a function of a type which is—

(1) Eligible for funding under 25 U.S.C. 13 and the regulations thereunder;

(2) Eligible for grants or contracts under 25 U.S.C. 450(f), (g), and (h) and the regulations thereunder; or

(3) An essential governmental function under section 115 and the regulations thereunder when conducted by a State or political subdivision thereof.

(e) *Treatment of subdivisions of Indian tribal governments as political subdivisions.*—A subdivision of an Indian tribal government shall be treated as a political subdivision of a State for purposes of section 7871 and this section if the Internal Revenue Service determines that the subdivision has been delegated the right to exercise one or more of the substantial governmental functions of the Indian tribal government. Designation of a subdivision of an Indian tribal government as a political subdivision of a State will be by revenue procedure. If a subdivision of an Indian tribal government is not currently designated by the applicable revenue procedure as a political subdivision of a State, and such subdivision believes that it qualifies for such designation, the subdivision may apply for a ruling from the Internal Revenue Service. In order to qualify as a political subdivision of a State, for purposes of section 7871 and this section, such subdivision must receive a favorable ruling from the Internal Revenue Service. The request for a ruling shall be made in accordance with all applicable procedural rules set forth in the Statement of Procedural Rules (26 CFR Part 601) and any applicable revenue procedures relating to submission of ruling requests. The request shall be submitted to the Internal Revenue Service, Associate Chief Counsel (Technical), Attention: CC:IND:S, Room 6545, 1111 Constitution Ave., N.W., Washington, D.C. 20224.

(f) *Effective dates.*—(1) *In general.*—Except as provided in paragraph (f)(2) of this section, the provisions of this section are effective after December 31, 1982.

(2) *Specific effective dates.*—Specific provisions of this section are effective as follows:

(i) Provisions relating to Chapter 1 of the Internal Revenue Code of 1954 (other than section 103 and section 37(e)(9)(A)) shall apply to taxable years beginning after December 31, 1982, and before January 1, 1985;

(ii) Provisions relating to section 37(e)(9)(A) shall apply to taxable years beginning after December 31, 1982, and before January 1, 1984;

(iii) Provisions relating to section 103 shall apply to obligations issued after December 31, 1982, and before January 1, 1985;

(iv) Provisions relating to chapter 11 of the Code shall apply to estates of decedents dying after December 31, 1982, and before January 1, 1985;

(v) Provisions relating to chapter 12 of the Code shall apply to gifts made after December 31, 1982, and before January 1, 1985; and

(vi) Provisions relating to taxes imposed by subtitle D of the Code shall take effect on January 1, 1983 and shall cease to apply at the close of December 31, 1984. [Temporary Reg. § 305.7871-1.]

☐ [*T.D.* 7952, 5-4-84.]

[Reg. § 1.7872-5]

§ 1.7872-5. Exempted loans.—(a) *In general.*—(1) *General rule.*—Except as provided in paragraph (a)(2) of this section, notwithstanding any other provision of section 7872 and the regulations under that section, section 7872 does not apply to the loans listed in paragraph (b) of this section because the interest arrangements do not have a significant effect on the Federal tax liability of the borrower or the lender.

(2) *No exemption for tax avoidance loans.*—If a taxpayer structures a transaction to be a loan described in paragraph (b) of this section and one of the principal purposes of so structuring the transaction is the avoidance of Federal tax, then the transaction will be recharacterized as a tax avoidance loan as defined in section 7872(c)(1)(D).

(b) *List of exemptions.*—Except as provided in paragraph (a) of this section, the following transactions are exempt from section 7872:

(1) through (15) [Reserved]. For further guidance, see § 1.7872-5T(b)(1) through (15).

(16) An exchange facilitator loan (within the meaning of § 1.468B-6(c)(1)) if the amount of the exchange funds (as defined in § 1.468B-6(b)(2)) treated as loaned does not exceed $2,000,000 and the duration of the loan is 6 months or less. The Commissioner may increase this $2,000,000 loan exemption amount in published guidance of general applicability, see § 601.601(d)(2) of this chapter.

(c) [Reserved]. For further guidance, see § 1.7872-5T(c).

(d) *Effective/applicability date.*—This section applies to exchange facilitator loans issued on or after October 8, 2008. [Reg. § 1.7872-5.]

☐ [*T.D.* 9413, 7-9-2008.]

[Reg. § 1.7872-5T]

§ 1.7872-5T. Exempted loans (temporary).— (a) *In general.*—(1) *General rule.*—Except as provided in paragraph (a) (2) of this section, notwithstanding any other provision of section 7872 and the regulations thereunder, section 7872 does not apply to the loans listed in paragraph (b) of this section because the interest arrangements do not have a significant effect on the Federal tax liability of the borrower or the lender.

(2) *No exemption for tax avoidance loans.*—If a taxpayer structures a transaction to be a loan described in paragraph (b) of this section and one of the principal purposes of so structuring the transaction is the avoidance of Federal tax, then the transaction will be recharacterized as a tax avoidance loan as defined in section 7872(c)(1)(D).

(b) *List of exemptions.*—Except as provided in paragraph (a) of this section, the following transactions are exempt from section 7872:

(1) Loans which are made available by the lender to the general public on the same terms and conditions and which are consistent with the lender's customary business practice;

(2) Accounts or withdrawable shares with a bank (as defined in section 581), or an institution to which section 591 applies, or a credit union, made in the ordinary course of its business;

(3) Acquisitions of publicly traded debt obligations for an amount equal to the public trading price at the time of acquisition;

(4) Loans made by a life insurance company (as defined in section 816(a)), in the ordinary course of its business, to an insured, under a loan right contained in a life insurance policy and in which the cash surrender values are used as collateral for the loans;

(5) Loans subsidized by the Federal, State (including the District of Columbia), or Municipal government (or any agency or instrumentality thereof), and which are made available under a program of general application to the public;

(6) Employee-relocation loans that meet the requirements of paragraph (c)(1) of this section;

(7) Obligations the interest on which is excluded from gross income under section 103;

(8) Obligations of the United States government;

(9) Gift loans to a charitable organization (described in section 170(c)), but only if at no time during the taxable year will the aggregate outstanding amount of loans by the lender to that organization exceed $250,000. Charitable organizations which are effectively controlled, within the meaning of section 1.482-1(a)(1), by the same person or persons shall be considered one charitable organization for purposes of this limitation.

(10) Loans made to or from a foreign person that meet the requirements of paragraph (c)(2) of this section;

(11) Loans made by a private foundation or other organization described in section 170(c), the primary purpose of which is to accomplish one or more of the purposes described in section 170(c)(2)(B);

(12) Indebtedness subject to section 482, but such indebtedness is exempt from the application of section 7872 only during the interest-free period, if any, determined under § 1.482-2(a)(1)(iii) with respect to intercompany trade receivables described in § 1.482-2(a)(1)(ii)(A)(*ii*). See also § 1.482-2(a)(3);

(13) All money, securities, and property—

(i) Received by a futures commission merchant or registered broker/dealer or by a clearing organization (A) to margin, guarantee or secure contracts for future delivery on or subject to the rules of a qualified board or exchange (as defined in section 1256(g)(7)), or (B) to purchase, margin, guarantee or secure options contracts traded on or subject to the rules of a qualified board or exchange, so long as the amounts so received to purchase, margin, guarantee or secure such contracts for future delivery or such options contracts are reasonably necessary for such purposes and so long as any commissions received by the futures commission merchant, registered broker/dealer, or clearing organization are not reduced for those making deposits of money, and all money accruing to account holders as the result of such futures and options contracts or

(ii) Received by a clearing organization from a member thereof as a required deposit to a clearing fund, guaranty fund, or similar fund maintained by the clearing organization to protect it against defaults by members.

(14) Loans the interest arrangements of which the taxpayer is able to show have no significant effect of any Federal tax liability of the lender or the borrower, as described in paragraph (c)(3) of this section; and

(15) Loans, described in revenue rulings or revenue procedures issued under section 7872(g)(1)(C), if the Commissioner finds that the factors justifying an exemption for such loans are sufficiently similar to the factors justifying the exemptions contained in this section.

(c) *Special rules.*—(1) *Employee-relocation loans.*—(i) *Mortgage loans.*—In the case of a compensation-related loan to an employee, where such loan is secured by a mortgage on the new principal residence (within the meaning of section 217 and the regulations thereunder) of the employee, acquired in connection with the transfer of that employee to a new principal place of work (which meets the requirements in section 217(c) and the regulations thereunder), the loan will be exempt from section 7872 if the following conditions are satisfied:

(A) The loan is a demand loan or is a term loan the benefits of the interest arrangements of which are not transferable by the em-

Reg. § 1.7872-5T(c)(1)(i)(A)

ployee and are conditioned on the future performance of substantial services by the employee;

(B) The employee certifies to the employer that the employee reasonably expects to be entitled to and will itemize deductions for each year the loan is outstanding; and

(C) The loan agreement requires that the loan proceeds be used only to purchase the new principal residence of the employee.

(ii) *Bridge loans.*—In the case of a compensation-related loan to an employee which is not described in paragraph (c)(1)(i) of this section, and which is used to purchase a new principal residence (within the meaning of section 217 and the regulations thereunder) of the employee acquired in connection with the transfer of that employee to a new principal place of work (which meets the requirements in section 217(c) and the regulations thereunder), the loan will be exempt from section 7872 if the following conditions are satisfied:

(A) The conditions contained in paragraphs (c)(1)(i)(A), (B), and (C) of this section;

(B) The loan agreement provides that the loan is payable in full within 15 days after the date of the sale of the employee's immediately former principal residence;

(C) The aggregate principal amount of all outstanding loans described in this paragraph (c)(1)(ii) to an employee is no greater than the employer's reasonable estimate of the amount of the equity of the employee and the employee's spouse in the employee's immediately former principal residence; and

(D) The employee's immediately former principal residence is not converted to business or investment use.

(2) *Below-market loans involving foreign persons.*—(i) Section 7872 shall not apply to a below-market loan (other than a compensation-related loan or a corporation-shareholder loan where the borrower is a shareholder that is not a C corporation as defined in section 1361(a)(2)) if the lender is a foreign person and the borrower is a U.S. person unless the interest income imputed to the foreign lender (without regard to this paragraph) would be effectively connected with the conduct of a U.S. trade or business within the meaning of section 864(c) and the regulations thereunder and not exempt from U.S. income taxation under an applicable income tax treaty.

(ii) Section 7872 shall not apply to a below-market loan where both the lender and the borrower are foreign persons unless the interest income imputed to the lender (without regard to this paragraph) would be effectively connected with the conduct of a U.S. trade or business within the meaning of section 864(c) and the regulations thereunder and not exempt from U.S. income taxation under an applicable income tax treaty.

(iii) For purposes of this section, the term "foreign person" means any person that is not a U.S. person.

(3) *Loans without significant tax effect.*— Whether a loan will be considered to be a loan the interest arrangements of which have a significant effect on any Federal tax liability of the lender or the borrower will be determined according to all of the facts and circumstances. Among the factors to be considered are—

(i) whether items of income and deduction generated by the loan offset each other;

(ii) the amount of such items;

(iii) the cost to the taxpayer of complying with the provisions of section 7872 if such section were applied; and

(iv) any non-tax reasons for deciding to structure the transaction as a below-market loan rather than a loan with interest at a rate equal to or greater than the applicable Federal rate and a payment by the lender to the borrower. [Temporary Reg. §1.7872-5T.]

☐ [T.D. 8045, 8-15-85. *Amended by* T.D. 8093, 7-9-86 *and* T.D. 8204, 5-20-88.]

[Reg. §1.7872-15]

§1.7872-15. Split-dollar loans.—(a) *General rules.*—(1) *Introduction.*—This section applies to split-dollar loans as defined in paragraph (b)(1) of this section. If a split-dollar loan is not a below-market loan, then, except as provided in this section, the loan is governed by the general rules for debt instruments (including the rules for original issue discount (OID) under sections 1271 through 1275 and the regulations thereunder). If a split-dollar loan is a below-market loan, then, except as provided in this section, the loan is governed by section 7872. The timing, amount, and characterization of the imputed transfers between the lender and borrower of a below-market split-dollar loan depend upon the relationship between the parties and upon whether the loan is a demand loan or a term loan. For additional rules relating to the treatment of split-dollar life insurance arrangements, see §1.61-22.

(2) *Loan treatment.*—(i) *General rule.*—A payment made pursuant to a split-dollar life insurance arrangement is treated as a loan for Federal tax purposes, and the owner and non-owner are treated, respectively, as the borrower and the lender, if—

(A) The payment is made either directly or indirectly by the non-owner to the owner (including a premium payment made by the non-owner directly or indirectly to the insurance company with respect to the policy held by the owner);

(B) The payment is a loan under general principles of Federal tax law or, if it is not a loan under general principles of Federal tax law (for example, because of the nonrecourse nature of the obligation or otherwise), a reasonable person nevertheless would expect the payment to be repaid in full to the non-owner (whether with or without interest); and

(C) The repayment is to be made from, or is secured by, the policy's death benefit proceeds, the policy's cash surrender value, or both.

(ii) *Payments that are only partially repayable.*—For purposes of § 1.61-22 and this section, if a non-owner makes a payment pursuant to a split-dollar life insurance arrangement and the non-owner is entitled to repayment of some but not all of the payment, the payment is treated as two payments: one that is repayable and one that is not. Thus, paragraph (a)(2)(i) of this section refers to the repayable payment.

(iii) *Treatment of payments that are not split-dollar loans.*—See § 1.61-22(b)(5) for the treatment of payments by a non-owner that are not split-dollar loans.

(iv) *Examples.*—The provisions of this paragraph (a)(2) are illustrated by the following examples:

Example 1. Assume an employee owns a life insurance policy under a split-dollar life insurance arrangement, the employer makes premium payments on this policy, there is a reasonable expectation that the payments will be repaid, and the repayments are secured by the policy. Under paragraph (a)(2)(i) of this section, each premium payment is a loan for Federal tax purposes.

Example 2. (i) Assume an employee owns a life insurance policy under a split-dollar life insurance arrangement and the employer makes premium payments on this policy. The employer is entitled to be repaid 80 percent of each premium payment, and the repayments are secured by the policy. Under paragraph (a)(2)(ii) of this section, the taxation of 20 percent of each premium payment is governed by § 1.61-22(b)(5). If there is a reasonable expectation that the remaining 80 percent of a payment will be repaid in full, then, under paragraph (a)(2)(i) of this section, the 80 percent is a loan for Federal tax purposes.

(ii) If less than 80 percent of a premium payment is reasonably expected to be repaid, then this paragraph (a)(2) does not cause any of the payment to be a loan for Federal tax purposes. If the payment is not a loan under general principles of Federal tax law, the taxation of the entire premium payment is governed by § 1.61-22(b)(5).

(3) *No de minimis exceptions.*—For purposes of this section, section 7872 is applied to a split-dollar loan without regard to the de minimis exceptions in section 7872(c)(2) and (3).

(4) *Certain interest provisions disregarded.*—(i) *In general.*—If a split-dollar loan provides for the payment of interest and all or a portion of the interest is to be paid directly or indirectly by the lender (or a person related to the lender), then the requirement to pay the interest (or portion thereof) is disregarded for purposes of this section. All of the facts and circumstances determine whether a payment to be made by the lender (or a person related to the lender) is sufficiently independent from the split-dollar loan for the payment to not be an indirect payment of the interest (or a portion thereof) by the lender (or a person related to the lender).

(ii) *Examples.*—The provisions of this paragraph (a)(4) are illustrated by the following examples:

Example 1—(i) On January 1, 2009, Employee *B* issues a split-dollar term loan to Employer *Y*. The split-dollar term loan provides for five percent interest, compounded annually. Interest and principal on the split-dollar term loan are due at maturity. On January 1, 2009, *B* and *Y* also enter into a fully vested non-qualified deferred compensation arrangement that will provide a payment to *B* in an amount equal to the accrued but unpaid interest due at the maturity of the split-dollar term loan.

(ii) Under paragraph (a)(4)(i) of this section, *B*'s requirement to pay interest on the split-dollar term loan is disregarded for purposes of this section, and the split-dollar term loan is treated as a loan that does not provide for interest for purposes of this section.

Example 2—(i) On January 1, 2004, Employee *B* and Employer *Y* enter into a fully vested non-qualified deferred compensation arrangement that will provide a payment to *B* equal to *B*'s salary in the three years preceding the retirement of *B*. On January 1, 2009, *B* and *Y* enter into a split-dollar life insurance arrangement and, under the arrangement, *B* issues a split-dollar term loan to *Y* on that date. The split-dollar term loan provides for five percent interest, compounded annually. Interest and principal on the split-dollar term loan are due at maturity. Over the period in which the non-qualified deferred compensation arrangement is effective, the terms and conditions of *B*'s non-qualified deferred compensation arrangement do not change in a way that indicates that the payment of the non-qualified deferred compensation is related to *B*'s requirement to pay interest on the split-dollar term loan. No other facts and circumstances exist to indicate that the payment of the non-qualified deferred compensation is related to *B*'s requirement to pay interest on the split-dollar term loan.

(ii) The facts and circumstances indicate that the payment by *Y* of non-qualified deferred compensation is independent from *B*'s requirement to pay interest under the split-dollar term loan. Under paragraph (a)(4)(i) of this section, the fully vested non-qualified deferred compensation does not cause *B*'s requirement to pay interest on the split-dollar term loan to be disregarded for purposes of this section. For purposes of this section, the split-dollar term loan is treated as a loan that provides for stated interest of five percent, compounded annually.

(b) *Definitions.*—For purposes of this section, the terms *split-dollar life insurance arrangement, owner,* and *non-owner* have the same meanings as provided in § 1.61-22(b) and (c). In addition, the following definitions apply for purposes of this section:

(1) A *split-dollar loan* is a loan described in paragraph (a)(2)(i) of this section.

(2) A *split-dollar demand loan* is any split-dollar loan that is payable in full at any time on the demand of the lender (or within a reasonable time after the lender's demand).

(3) A *split-dollar term loan* is any split-dollar loan other than a split-dollar demand loan. See paragraph (e)(5) of this section for special rules regarding certain split-dollar term loans payable on the death of an individual, certain split-dollar term loans conditioned on the future performance of substantial services by an individual, and gift split-dollar term loans.

(c) *Interest deductions for split-dollar loans.*—The borrower may not deduct any qualified stated interest, OID, or imputed interest on a split-dollar loan. See sections 163(h) and 264(a). In certain circumstances, an indirect participant may be allowed to deduct qualified stated interest, OID, or imputed interest on a deemed loan. See paragraph (e)(2)(iii) of this section (relating to indirect loans).

(d) *Treatment of split-dollar loans providing for nonrecourse payments.*—(1) *In general.*—Except as provided in paragraph (d)(2) of this section, if a payment on a split-dollar loan is nonrecourse to the borrower, the payment is a contingent payment for purposes of this section. See paragraph (j) of this section for the treatment of a split-dollar loan that provides for one or more contingent payments.

(2) *Exception for certain loans with respect to which the parties to the split-dollar life insurance arrangement make a representation.*— (i) *Requirement.*—An otherwise noncontingent payment on a split-dollar loan that is nonrecourse to the borrower is not a contingent payment under this section if the parties to the split-dollar life insurance arrangement represent in writing that a reasonable person would expect that all payments under the loan will be made.

(ii) *Time and manner for providing written representation.*—The Commissioner may prescribe the time and manner for providing the written representation required by paragraph (d)(2)(i) of this section. Until the Commissioner prescribes otherwise, the written representation that is required by paragraph (d)(2)(i) of this section must meet the requirements of this paragraph (d)(2)(ii). Both the borrower and the lender must sign the representation not later than the last day (including extensions) for filing the Federal income tax return of the borrower or lender, whichever is earlier, for the taxable year in which the lender makes the first split-dollar loan under the split-dollar life insurance arrangement. This representation must include the names, addresses, and taxpayer identification numbers of the borrower, lender, and any indirect participants. Unless otherwise stated therein, this representation applies to all subsequent split-dollar loans made pursuant to the split-dollar life insurance arrangement. Each party should retain an original of the representation as part of its books and records and should attach a copy of this representation to its Federal income tax return for any taxable year in which the lender makes a loan to which the representation applies.

(e) *Below-market split-dollar loans.*—(1) *Scope.*— (i) *In general.*—This paragraph (e) applies to below-market split-dollar loans enumerated under section 7872(c)(1), which include gift loans, compensation-related loans, and corporation-shareholder loans. The characterization of a split-dollar loan under section 7872(c)(1) and of the imputed transfers under section 7872(a)(1) and (b)(1) depends upon the relationship between the lender and the borrower or the lender, borrower, and any indirect participant. For example, if the lender is the borrower's employer, the split-dollar loan is generally a compensation-related loan, and any imputed transfer from the lender to the borrower is generally a payment of compensation. The loans covered by this paragraph (e) include indirect loans between the parties. See paragraph (e)(2) of this section for the treatment of certain indirect split-dollar loans. See paragraph (f) of this section for the treatment of any stated interest or OID on split-dollar loans. See paragraph (j) of this section for additional rules that apply to a split-dollar loan that provides for one or more contingent payments.

(ii) *Significant-effect split-dollar loans.*—If a direct or indirect below-market split-dollar loan is not enumerated in section 7872(c)(1)(A), (B), or (C), the loan is a significanteffect loan under section 7872(c)(1)(E).

(2) *Indirect split-dollar loans.*—(i) *In general.*—If, based on all the facts and circumstances, including the relationship between the borrower or lender and some third person (the indirect participant), the effect of a below-market split-dollar loan is to transfer value from the lender to the indirect participant and from the indirect participant to the borrower, then the below-market split-dollar loan is restructured as two or more successive below-market loans (the deemed loans) as provided in this paragraph (e)(2). The transfers of value described in the preceding sentence include (but are not limited to) a gift, compensation, a capital contribution, and a distribution under section 301 (or, in the case of an S corporation, under section 1368). The deemed loans are—

(A) A deemed below-market split-dollar loan made by the lender to the indirect participant; and

(B) A deemed below-market split-dollar loan made by the indirect participant to the borrower.

(ii) *Application.*—Each deemed loan is treated as having the same provisions as the original loan between the lender and borrower, and section 7872 is applied to each deemed loan. Thus, for example, if, under a split-dollar life insurance arrangement, an employer (lender) makes an interest-free split-dollar loan to an employee's child (borrower), the loan is restructured as a deemed compensation-related below-market split-dollar loan from the lender to the employee (the indirect participant) and a second deemed gift below-market split-dollar loan from the employee to the employee's child. In appropriate circumstances, section 7872(d)(1) may limit the interest that accrues on a deemed loan for Federal income tax purposes. For loan arrangements between husband and wife, see section 7872(f)(7).

(iii) *Limitations on investment interest for purposes of section 163(d)*.—For purposes of section 163(d), the imputed interest from the indirect participant to the lender that is taken into account by the indirect participant under this paragraph (e)(2) is not investment interest to the extent of the excess, if any, of—

(A) The imputed interest from the indirect participant to the lender that is taken into account by the indirect participant; over

(B) The imputed interest to the indirect participant from the borrower that is recognized by the indirect participant.

(iv) *Examples*.—The provisions of this paragraph (e)(2) are illustrated by the following examples:

Example 1. (i) On January 1, 2009, Employer X and Individual A enter into a split-dollar life insurance arrangement under which A is named as the policy owner. A is the child of B, an employee of X. On January 1, 2009, X makes a $30,000 premium payment, repayable upon demand without interest. Repayment of the premium payment is fully recourse to A. The payment is a below-market split-dollar demand loan. A's net investment income for 2009 is $1,100, and there are no other outstanding loans between A and B. Assume that the blended annual rate for 2009 is 5 percent, compounded annually.

(ii) Based on the relationships among the parties, the effect of the below-market split-dollar loan from X to A is to transfer value from X to B and then to transfer value from B to A. Under paragraph (e)(2) of this section, the below-market split-dollar loan from X to A is restructured as two deemed below-market split-dollar demand loans: a compensation-related below-market split-dollar loan between X and B and a gift below-market split-dollar loan between B and A. Each of the deemed loans has the same terms and conditions as the original loan.

(iii) Under paragraph (e)(3) of this section, the amount of forgone interest deemed paid to B by A in 2009 is $1,500 ([$30,000 × 0.05] – 0). Under section 7872(d)(1), however, the amount of forgone interest deemed paid to B by A is limited to $1,100 (A's net investment income for the year). Under paragraph (e)(2)(iii) of this section, B's deduction under section 163(d) in 2009 for interest deemed paid on B's deemed loan

from X is limited to $1,100 (the interest deemed received from A).

Example 2. (i) The facts are the same as the facts in *Example 1*, except that T, an irrevocable life insurance trust established for the benefit of A (B's child), is named as the policy owner. T is not a grantor trust.

(ii) Based on the relationships among the parties, the effect of the below-market split-dollar loan from X to T is to transfer value from X to B and then to transfer value from B to T. Under paragraph (e)(2) of this section, the below-market split-dollar loan from X to T is restructured as two deemed below-market split-dollar demand loans: a compensation-related below-market split-dollar loan between X and B and a gift below-market split-dollar loan between B and T. Each of the deemed loans has the same terms and conditions as the original loan.

(iii) Under paragraph (e)(3) of this section, the amount of forgone interest deemed paid to B by T in 2009 is $1,500 ([$30,000 × 0.05] – 0). Section 7872(d)(1) does not apply because T is not an individual. The amount of forgone interest deemed paid to B by T is $1,500. Under paragraph (e)(2)(iii) of this section, B's deduction under section 163(d) in 2009 for interest deemed paid on B's deemed loan from X is $1,500 (the interest deemed received from T).

(3) *Split-dollar demand loans*.—(i) *In general*.—This paragraph (e)(3) provides rules for testing split-dollar demand loans for sufficient interest, and, if the loans do not provide for sufficient interest, rules for the calculation and treatment of forgone interest on these loans. See paragraph (g) of this section for additional rules that apply to a split-dollar loan providing for certain variable rates of interest.

(ii) *Testing for sufficient interest*.—Each calendar year that a split-dollar demand loan is outstanding, the loan is tested to determine if the loan provides for sufficient interest. A split-dollar demand loan provides for sufficient interest for the calendar year if the rate (based on annual compounding) at which interest accrues on the loan's adjusted issue price during the year is no lower than the blended annual rate for the year. (The Internal Revenue Service publishes the blended annual rate in the Internal Revenue Bulletin in July of each year (see § 601.601(d)(2)(ii) of this chapter).) If the loan does not provide for sufficient interest, the loan is a below-market split-dollar demand loan for that calendar year. See paragraph (e)(3)(iii) of this section to determine the amount and treatment of forgone interest for each calendar year the loan is below-market.

(iii) *Imputations*.—(A) *Amount of forgone interest*.—For each calendar year, the amount of forgone interest on a split-dollar demand loan is treated as transferred by the lender to the borrower and as retransferred as interest by the borrower to the lender. This amount is the excess of—

(1) The amount of interest that would have been payable on the loan for the calendar year if interest accrued on the loan's adjusted issue price at the blended annual rate (determined in paragraph (e)(3)(ii) of this section) and were payable annually on the day referred to in paragraph (e)(3)(iii)(B) of this section; over

(2) Any interest that accrues on the loan during the year.

(B) *Timing of transfers of forgone interest.*—(1) *In general.*—Except as provided in paragraphs (e)(3)(iii)(B)(2) and (3) of this section, the forgone interest (as determined under paragraph (e)(3)(iii)(A) of this section) that is attributable to a calendar year is treated as transferred by the lender to the borrower (and retransferred as interest by the borrower to the lender) on the last day of the calendar year and is accounted for by each party to the split-dollar loan in a manner consistent with that party's method of accounting.

(2) Exception for death, liquidation, or termination of the borrower.—In the taxable year in which the borrower dies (in the case of a borrower who is a natural person) or is liquidated or otherwise terminated (in the case of a borrower other than a natural person), any forgone interest is treated, for both the lender and the borrower, as transferred and retransferred on the last day of the borrower's final taxable year.

(3) Exception for repayment of below-market split-dollar loan.—Any forgone interest is treated, for both the lender and the borrower, as transferred and retransferred on the day the split-dollar loan is repaid in full.

(4) *Split-dollar term loans.*—(i) *In general.*—Except as provided in paragraph (e)(5) of this section, this paragraph (e)(4) provides rules for testing split-dollar term loans for sufficient interest and, if the loans do not provide for sufficient interest, rules for imputing payments on these loans. See paragraph (g) of this section for additional rules that apply to a split-dollar loan providing for certain variable rates of interest.

(ii) *Testing a split-dollar term loan for sufficient interest.*—A split-dollar term loan is tested on the day the loan is made to determine if the loan provides for sufficient interest. A split-dollar term loan provides for sufficient interest if the imputed loan amount equals or exceeds the amount loaned. The imputed loan amount is the present value of all payments due under the loan, determined as of the date the loan is made, using a discount rate equal to the AFR in effect on that date. The AFR used for purposes of the preceding sentence must be appropriate for the loan's term (short-term, mid-term, or long-term) and for the compounding period used in computing the present value. See section 1274(d)(1). If the split-dollar loan does not provide for sufficient interest, the loan is a below-market split-dollar term loan subject to paragraph (e)(4)(iv) of this section.

(iii) *Determining loan term.*—This paragraph (e)(4)(iii) provides rules to determine the term of a split-dollar term loan for purposes of paragraph (e)(4)(ii) of this section. The term of the loan determined under this paragraph (e)(4)(iii) (other than paragraph (e)(4)(iii)(C) of this section) applies to determine the split-dollar loan's term, payment schedule, and yield for all purposes of this section.

(A) *In general.*—Except as provided in paragraph (e)(4)(iii)(B), (C), (D) or (E) of this section, the term of a split-dollar term loan is based on the period from the date the loan is made until the loan's stated maturity date.

(B) *Special rules for certain options.*—(1) *Payment schedule that minimizes yield.*—If a split-dollar term loan is subject to one or more unconditional options that are exercisable at one or more times during the term of the loan and that, if exercised, require payments to be made on the split-dollar loan on an alternative payment schedule (for example, an option to extend or an option to call a split-dollar loan), then the rules of this paragraph (e)(4)(iii)(B)(1) determine the term of the loan. However, this paragraph (e)(4)(iii)(B)(1) applies only if the timing and amounts of the payments that comprise each payment schedule are known as of the issue date. For purposes of determining a split-dollar loan's term, the borrower is projected to exercise or not exercise an option or combination of options in a manner that minimizes the loan's overall yield. Similarly, the lender is projected to exercise or not exercise an option or combination of options in a manner that minimizes the loan's overall yield. If different projected patterns of exercise or non-exercise produce the same minimum yield, the parties are projected to exercise or not exercise an option or combination of options in a manner that produces the longest term.

(2) Change in circumstances.—If the borrower (or lender) does or does not exercise the option as projected under paragraph (e)(4)(iii)(B)(1) of this section, the split-dollar loan is treated for purposes of this section as retired and reissued on the date the option is or is not exercised for an amount of cash equal to the loan's adjusted issue price on that date. The reissued loan must be retested using the appropriate AFR in effect on the date of reissuance to determine whether it is a below-market loan.

(3) Examples.—The following examples illustrate the rules of this paragraph (e)(4)(iii)(B):

Example 1. Employee *B* issues a 10-year split-dollar term loan to Employer *Y*. *B* has the right to prepay the loan at the end of year 5. Interest is payable on the split-dollar loan at 1 percent for the first 5 years and at 10 percent for the remaining 5 years. Under paragraph (e)(4)(iii)(B)(1) of this section, this arrangement is treated as a 5-year split-dollar term loan from *Y* to *B*, with interest payable at 1 percent.

Example 2. The facts are the same as the facts in *Example 1*, except that *B* does not in fact prepay the split-dollar loan at the end of year 5. Under paragraph (e)(4)(iii)(B)(2) of this section, the first loan is treated as retired at the end of year 5 and a new 5-year split-dollar term loan is issued at that time, with interest payable at 10 percent.

Example 3. Employee *A* issues a 10-year split-dollar term loan on which the lender, Employer *X*, has the right to demand payment at the end of year 2. Interest is payable on the split-dollar loan at 7 percent each year that the loan is outstanding. Under paragraph (e)(4)(iii)(B)(1) of this section, this arrangement is treated as a 10-year split-dollar term loan because the exercise of *X*'s put option would not reduce the yield of the loan (the yield of the loan is 7 percent, compounded annually, whether or not *X* demands payment).

(C) *Split-dollar term loans providing for certain variable rates of interest.*—If a split-dollar term loan is subject to paragraph (g) of this section (a split-dollar loan that provides for certain variable rates of interest), the term of the loan for purposes of paragraph (e)(4)(ii) of this section is determined under paragraph (g)(3)(ii) of this section.

(D) *Split-dollar loans payable upon the death of an individual.*—If a split-dollar term loan is described in paragraph (e)(5)(ii)(A) or (v)(A) of this section, the term of the loan for purposes of paragraph (e)(4)(ii) of this section is determined under paragraph (e)(5)(ii)(C) or (v)(B)(2) of this section, whichever is applicable.

(E) *Split-dollar loans conditioned on the future performance of substantial services by an individual.*—If a split-dollar term loan is described in paragraph (e)(5)(iii)(A)(1) or (v)(A) of this section, the term of the loan for purposes of paragraph (e)(4)(ii) of this section is determined under paragraph (e)(5)(iii)(C) or (v)(B)(2) of this section, whichever is applicable.

(iv) *Timing and amount of imputed transfer in connection with below-market split-dollar term loans.*—If a split-dollar term loan is a below-market loan, then the rules applicable to below-market term loans under section 7872 apply. In general, the loan is recharacterized as consisting of two portions: an imputed loan amount (as defined in paragraph (e)(4)(ii) of this section) and an imputed transfer from the lender to the borrower. The imputed transfer occurs at the time the loan is made (for example, when the lender makes a premium payment on a life insurance policy) and is equal to the excess of the amount loaned over the imputed loan amount.

(v) *Amount treated as OID.*—In the case of any below-market split-dollar term loan described in this paragraph (e)(4), for purposes of applying sections 1271 through 1275 and the regulations thereunder, the issue price of the loan is the amount determined under §1.1273-2, reduced by the amount of the imputed transfer described in paragraph (e)(4)(iv) of this section. Thus, the loan is generally treated as having OID

in an amount equal to the amount of the imputed transfer described in paragraph (e)(4)(iv) of this section, in addition to any other OID on the loan (determined without regard to section 7872(b)(2)(A) or this paragraph (e)(4)).

(vi) *Example.*—The provisions of this paragraph (e)(4) are illustrated by the following example:

Example. (i) On July 1, 2009, Corporation *Z* and Shareholder *A* enter into a split-dollar life insurance arrangement under which *A* is named as the policy owner. On July 1, 2009, *Z* makes a $100,000 premium payment, repayable without interest in 15 years. Repayment of the premium payment is fully recourse to *A*. The premium payment is a split-dollar term loan. Assume the long-term AFR (based on annual compounding) at the time the loan is made is 7 percent.

(ii) Based on a 15-year term and a discount rate of 7 percent, compounded annually (the long-term AFR), the present value of the payments under the loan is $36,244.60, determined as follows: $100,000/[1+(0.07/1)]^{15}$. This loan is a below-market split-dollar term loan because the imputed loan amount of $36,244.60 (the present value of the amount required to be repaid to *Z*) is less than the amount loaned ($100,000).

(iii) In accordance with section 7872(b)(1) and paragraph (e)(4)(iv) of this section, on the date that the loan is made, *Z* is treated as transferring to *A* $63,755.40 (the excess of $100,000 (amount loaned) over $36,244.60 (imputed loan amount)). Under section 7872 and paragraph (e)(1)(i) of this section, *Z* is treated as making a section 301 distribution to *A* on July 1, 2009, of $63,755.40. *Z* must take into account as OID an amount equal to the imputed transfer. See §1.1272-1 for the treatment of OID.

(5) *Special rules for certain split-dollar term loans.*—(i) *In general.*—This paragraph (e)(5) provides rules for split-dollar loans payable on the death of an individual, split-dollar loans conditioned on the future performance of substantial services by an individual, and gift term loans. These split-dollar loans are split-dollar term loans for purposes of determining whether the loan provides for sufficient interest. If, however, the loan is a below-market split-dollar loan, then, except as provided in paragraph (e)(5)(v) of this section, forgone interest is determined annually, similar to a demand loan, but using an AFR that is appropriate for the loan's term and that is determined when the loan is issued.

(ii) *Split-dollar loans payable not later than the death of an individual.*—(A) *Applicability.*—This paragraph (e)(5)(ii) applies to a split-dollar term loan payable not later than the death of an individual.

(B) *Treatment of loan.*—A split-dollar loan described in paragraph (e)(5)(ii)(A) of this section is tested under paragraph (e)(4)(ii) of this section to determine if the loan provides for sufficient interest. If the loan provides for sufficient interest, then section 7872 does not apply to the loan, and the interest on the loan is taken into account under paragraph (f) of this section. If the loan does not provide for sufficient interest, then section 7872 applies to the loan, and the loan is treated as a below-market demand loan subject to paragraph (e)(3)(iii) of this section. For each year that the loan is outstanding, however, the rate used in the determination of forgone interest under paragraph (e)(3)(iii) of this section is not the blended annual rate but rather is the AFR (based on annual compounding) appropriate for the loan's term as of the month in which the loan is made. See paragraph (e)(5)(ii)(C) of this section to determine the loan's term.

(C) *Term of loan.*—For purposes of paragraph (e)(5)(ii)(B) of this section, the term of a split-dollar loan payable on the death of an individual (including the death of the last survivor of a group of individuals) is the individual's life expectancy as determined under the appropriate table in §1.72-9 on the day the loan is made. If a split-dollar loan is payable on the earlier of the individual's death or another term determined under paragraph (e)(4)(iii) of this section, the term of the loan is whichever term is shorter.

(D) *Retirement and reissuance of loan.*—If a split-dollar loan described in paragraph (e)(5)(ii)(A) of this section remains outstanding longer than the term determined under paragraph (e)(5)(ii)(C) of this section because the individual outlived his or her life expectancy, the split-dollar loan is treated for purposes of this section as retired and reissued as a split-dollar demand loan at that time for an amount of cash equal to the loan's adjusted issue price on that date. However, the loan is not retested at that time to determine whether the loan provides for sufficient interest. For purposes of determining forgone interest under paragraph (e)(5)(ii)(B) of this section, the appropriate AFR for the reissued loan is the AFR determined under paragraph (e)(5)(ii)(B) of this section on the day the loan was originally made.

(iii) *Split-dollar loans conditioned on the future performance of substantial services by an individual.*—(A) *Applicability.*—(1) *In general.*—This paragraph (e)(5)(iii) applies to a split-dollar term loan if the benefits of the interest arrangements of the loan are not transferable and are conditioned on the future performance of substantial services (within the meaning of section 83) by an individual.

(2) *Exception.*—Notwithstanding paragraph (e)(5)(iii)(A)(1) of this section, this paragraph (e)(5)(iii) does not apply to a split-dollar loan described in paragraph (e)(5)(v)(A) of this section (regarding a split-dollar loan that is payable on the later of a term certain and the date on which the condition to perform substantial future services by an individual ends).

(B) *Treatment of loan.*—A split-dollar loan described in paragraph (e)(5)(iii)(A)(1) of this section is tested under paragraph (e)(4)(ii) of

this section to determine if the loan provides for sufficient interest. Except as provided in paragraph (e)(5)(iii)(D) of this section, if the loan provides for sufficient interest, then section 7872 does not apply to the loan and the interest on the loan is taken into account under paragraph (f) of this section. If the loan does not provide for sufficient interest, then section 7872 applies to the loan and the loan is treated as a below-market demand loan subject to paragraph (e)(3)(iii) of this section. For each year that the loan is outstanding, however, the rate used in the determination of forgone interest under paragraph (e)(3)(iii) of this section is not the blended annual rate but rather is the AFR (based on annual compounding) appropriate for the loan's term as of the month in which the loan is made. See paragraph (e)(5)(iii)(C) of this section to determine the loan's term.

(C) *Term of loan.*—The term of a split-dollar loan described in paragraph (e)(5)(iii)(A)(1) of this section is based on the period from the date the loan is made until the loan's stated maturity date. However, if a split-dollar loan described in paragraph (e)(5)(iii)(A)(1) of this section does not have a stated maturity date, the term of the loan is presumed to be seven years.

(D) *Retirement and reissuance of loan.*—If a split-dollar loan described in paragraph (e)(5)(iii)(A)(1) of this section remains outstanding longer than the term determined under paragraph (e)(5)(iii)(C) of this section because of the continued performance of substantial services, the split-dollar loan is treated for purposes of this section as retired and reissued as a split-dollar demand loan at that time for an amount of cash equal to the loan's adjusted issue price on that date. The loan is retested at that time to determine whether the loan provides for sufficient interest.

(iv) *Gift split-dollar term loans.*—(A) *Applicability.*—This paragraph (e)(5)(iv) applies to gift split-dollar term loans.

(B) *Treatment of loan.*—A split-dollar loan described in paragraph (e)(5)(iv)(A) of this section is tested under paragraph (e)(4)(ii) of this section to determine if the loan provides for sufficient interest. If the loan provides for sufficient interest, then section 7872 does not apply to the loan and the interest on the loan is taken into account under paragraph (f) of this section. If the loan does not provide for sufficient interest, then section 7872 applies to the loan and the loan is treated as a below-market demand loan subject to paragraph (e)(3)(iii) of this section. For each year that the loan is outstanding, however, the rate used in the determination of forgone interest under paragraph (e)(3)(iii) of this section is not the blended annual rate but rather is the AFR (based on annual compounding) appropriate for the loan's term as of the month in which the loan is made. See paragraph (e)(5)(iv)(C) of this section to determine the loan's term.

(C) *Term of loan.*—For purposes of paragraph (e)(5)(iv)(B) of this section, the term of a gift split-dollar term loan is the term determined under paragraph (e)(4)(iii) of this section.

(D) *Limited application for gift split-dollar term loans.*—The rules of paragraph (e)(5)(iv)(B) of this section apply to a gift split-dollar term loan only for Federal income tax purposes. For purposes of Chapter 12 of the Internal Revenue Code (relating to the gift tax), gift below-market split-dollar term loans are treated as term loans under section 7872(b) and paragraph (e)(4) of this section. See section 7872(d)(2).

(v) *Split-dollar loans payable on the later of a term certain and another specified date.*—(A) *Applicability.*—This paragraph (e)(5)(v) applies to any split-dollar term loan payable upon the later of a term certain or—

(1) The death of an individual; or

(2) For a loan described in paragraph (e)(5)(iii)(A)(1) of this section, the date on which the condition to perform substantial future services by an individual ends.

(B) *Treatment of loan.*—(1) *In general.*—A split-dollar loan described in paragraph (e)(5)(v)(A) of this section is a split-dollar term loan, subject to paragraph (e)(4) of this section.

(2) *Term of the loan.*—The term of a split-dollar loan described in paragraph (e)(5)(v)(A) of this section is the term certain.

(3) *Appropriate AFR.*—The appropriate AFR for a split-dollar loan described in paragraph (e)(5)(v)(A) of this section is based on a term of the longer of the term certain or the loan's expected term as determined under either paragraph (e)(5)(ii) or (iii) of this section, whichever is applicable.

(C) *Retirement and reissuance.*—If a split-dollar loan described in paragraph (e)(5)(v)(A) of this section remains outstanding longer than the term certain, the split-dollar loan is treated for purposes of this section as retired and reissued at the end of the term certain for an amount of cash equal to the loan's adjusted issue price on that date. The reissued loan is subject to paragraph (e)(5)(ii) or (iii) of this section, whichever is applicable. However, the loan is not retested at that time to determine whether the loan provides for sufficient interest. For purposes of paragraph (e)(5)(iii) of this section, the appropriate AFR for the reissued loan is the AFR determined under paragraph (e)(5)(v)(B)(3) of this section on the day the loan was originally made.

(vi) *Example.*—The provisions of this paragraph (e)(5) are illustrated by the following example:

Example. (i) On January 1, 2009, Corporation Y and Shareholder B, a 65 year-old male, enter into a split-dollar life insurance arrangement under which B is named as the policy owner. On January 1, 2009, Y makes a $100,000 premium payment, repayable, without interest, from the death benefits of the underlying con-

tract upon B's death. The premium payment is a split-dollar term loan. Repayment of the premium payment is fully recourse to B. Assume the long-term AFR (based on annual compounding) at the time of the loan is 7 percent. Both Y and B use the calendar year as their taxable years.

(ii) Based on Table 1 in § 1.72-9, the expected term of the loan is 15 years. Under paragraph (e)(5)(ii)(C) of this section, the long-term AFR (based on annual compounding) is the appropriate test rate. Based on a 15-year term and a discount rate of 7 percent, compounded annually (the long-term AFR), the present value of the payments under the loan is $36,244.60, determined as follows: $100,000/[1+(0.07/1)]^{15}$. Under paragraph (e)(5)(ii)(B) of this section, this loan is a below-market split-dollar term loan because the imputed loan amount of $36,244.60 (the present value of the amount required to be repaid to Y) is less than the amount loaned ($100,000).

(iii) Under paragraph (e)(5)(ii)(B) of this section, the amount of forgone interest for 2009 (and each subsequent full calendar year that the loan remains outstanding) is $7,000, which is the amount of interest that would have been payable on the loan for the calendar year if interest accrued on the loan's adjusted issue price ($100,000) at the long-term AFR (7 percent, compounded annually). Under section 7872 and paragraph (e)(1)(i) of this section, on December 31, 2009, Y is treated as making a section 301 distribution to B of $7,000. In addition, Y has $7,000 of imputed interest income for 2009.

(f) *Treatment of stated interest and OID for split-dollar loans.*—(1) *In general.*—If a split-dollar loan provides for stated interest or OID, the loan is subject to this paragraph (f), regardless of whether the split-dollar loan has sufficient interest. Except as otherwise provided in this section, split-dollar loans are subject to the same Internal Revenue Code and regulatory provisions for stated interest and OID as other loans. For example, the lender of a split-dollar loan that provides for stated interest must account for any qualified stated interest (as defined in § 1.1273-1(c)) under its regular method of accounting (for example, an accrual method or the cash receipts and disbursements method). See § 1.446-2 to determine the amount of qualified stated interest that accrues during an accrual period. In addition, the lender must account under § 1.1272-1 for any OID on a split-dollar loan. However, § 1.1272-1(c) does not apply to any split-dollar loan. See paragraph (h) of this section for a subsequent waiver, cancellation, or forgiveness of stated interest on a split-dollar loan.

(2) *Term, payment schedule, and yield.*—The term of a split-dollar term loan determined under paragraph (e)(4)(iii) of this section (other than paragraph (e)(4)(iii)(C) of this section) applies to determine the split-dollar loan's term, payment schedule, and yield for all purposes of this section.

(g) *Certain variable rates of interest.*—(1) *In general.*—This paragraph (g) provides rules for a split-dollar loan that provides for certain variable rates of interest. If this paragraph (g) does not apply to a variable rate split-dollar loan, the loan is subject to the rules in paragraph (j) of this section for split-dollar loans that provide for one or more contingent payments.

(2) *Applicability.*—(i) *In general.*—Except as provided in paragraph (g)(2)(ii) of this section, this paragraph (g) applies to a split-dollar loan that is a variable rate debt instrument (within the meaning of § 1.1275-5) and that provides for stated interest at a qualified floating rate (or rates).

(ii) *Interest rate restrictions.*—This paragraph (g) does not apply to a split-dollar loan if, as a result of interest rate restrictions (such as an interest rate cap), the expected yield of the loan taking the restrictions into account is significantly less than the expected yield of the loan without regard to the restrictions. Conversely, if reasonably symmetric interest rate caps and floors or reasonably symmetric governors are fixed throughout the term of the loan, these restrictions generally do not prevent this paragraph (g) from applying to the loan.

(3) *Testing for sufficient interest.*—(i) *Demand loan.*—For purposes of paragraph (e)(3)(ii) of this section (regarding testing a split-dollar demand loan for sufficient interest), a split-dollar demand loan is treated as if it provided for a fixed rate of interest for each accrual period to which a qualified floating rate applies. The projected fixed rate for each accrual period is the value of the qualified floating rate as of the beginning of the calendar year that contains the last day of the accrual period.

(ii) *Term loan.*—For purposes of paragraph (e)(4)(ii) of this section (regarding testing a split-dollar term loan for sufficient interest), a split-dollar term loan subject to this paragraph (g) is treated as if it provided for a fixed rate of interest for each accrual period to which a qualified floating rate applies. The projected fixed rate for each accrual period is the value of the qualified floating rate on the date the split-dollar term loan is made. The term of a split-dollar loan that is subject to this paragraph (g)(3)(ii) is determined using the rules in § 1.1274-4(c)(2). For example, if the loan provides for interest at a qualified floating rate that adjusts at varying intervals, the term of the loan is determined by reference to the longest interval between interest adjustment dates. See paragraph (e)(5) of this section for special rules relating to certain split-dollar term loans, such as a split-dollar term loan payable not later than the death of an individual.

(4) *Interest accruals and imputed transfers.*—For purposes of paragraphs (e) and (f) of this section, the projected fixed rate or rates determined under paragraph (g)(3) of this section are used for purposes of determining the accrual of interest each period and the amount of any im-

puted transfers. Appropriate adjustments are made to the interest accruals and any imputed transfers to take into account any difference between the projected fixed rate and the actual rate.

(5) *Example.*—The provisions of this paragraph (g) are illustrated by the following example:

Example. (i) On January 1, 2010, Employer *V* and Employee *F* enter into a split-dollar life insurance arrangement under which *F* is named as the policy owner. On January 1, 2010, *V* makes a $100,000 premium payment, repayable in 15 years. The premium payment is a split-dollar term loan. Under the arrangement between the parties, interest is payable on the split-dollar loan each year on January 1, starting January 1, 2011, at a rate equal to the value of 1-year LIBOR as of the payment date. The short-term AFR (based on annual compounding) at the time of the loan is 7 percent. Repayment of both the premium payment and the interest due thereon is nonrecourse to *F*. However, the parties made a representation under paragraph (d)(2) of this section. Assume that the value of 1-year LIBOR on January 1, 2010, is 8 percent, compounded annually.

(ii) The loan is subject to this paragraph (g) because the loan is a variable rate debt instrument that bears interest at a qualified floating rate. Because the interest rate is reset each year, under paragraph (g)(3)(ii) of this section, the short-term AFR (based on annual compounding) is the appropriate test rate used to determine whether the loan provides for sufficient interest. Moreover, under paragraph (g)(3)(ii) of this section, to determine whether the loan provides for sufficient interest, the loan is treated as if it provided for a fixed rate of interest equal to 8 percent, compounded annually. Based on a discount rate of 7 percent, compounded annually (the short-term AFR), the present value of the payments under the loan is $109,107.91. The loan provides for sufficient interest because the loan's imputed loan amount of $109,107.91 (the present value of the payments) is more than the amount loaned of $100,000. Therefore, the loan is not a below-market split-dollar term loan, and interest on the loan is taken into account under paragraph (f) of this section.

(h) *Adjustments for interest paid at less than the stated rate.*—(1) *Application.*—(i) *In general.*—To the extent required by this paragraph (h), if accrued but unpaid interest on a split-dollar loan is subsequently waived, cancelled, or forgiven by the lender, then the waiver, cancellation, or forgiveness is treated as if, on that date, the interest had in fact been paid to the lender and retransferred by the lender to the borrower. The amount deemed transferred and retransferred is determined under paragraph (h)(2) or (3) of this section. Except as provided in paragraph (h)(1)(iv) of this section, the amount treated as retransferred by the lender to the borrower under paragraph (h)(2) or (3) of this section is increased by the deferral charge determined under paragraph (h)(4) of this section. To determine the character of any retransferred amount, see paragraph (e)(1)(i) of this section. See § 1.61-22(b)(6) for the treatment of amounts other than interest on a split-dollar loan that are waived, cancelled, or forgiven by the lender.

(ii) *Certain split-dollar term loans.*—For purposes of this paragraph (h), a split-dollar term loan described in paragraph (e)(5) of this section (for example, a split-dollar term loan payable not later than the death of an individual) is subject to the rules of paragraph (h)(3) of this section.

(iii) *Payments treated as a waiver, cancellation, or forgiveness.*—For purposes of this paragraph (h), if a payment by the lender (or a person related to the lender) to the borrower is, in substance, a waiver, cancellation, or forgiveness of accrued but unpaid interest, the payment by the lender (or person related to the lender) is treated as an amount retransferred to the borrower by the lender under this paragraph (h) and is subject to the deferral charge in paragraph (h)(4) of this section to the extent that the payment is, in substance, a waiver, cancellation, or forgiveness of accrued but unpaid interest.

(iv) *Treatment of certain nonrecourse split-dollar loans.*—For purposes of this paragraph (h), if the parties to a split-dollar life insurance arrangement make the representation described in paragraph (d)(2) of this section and the interest actually paid on the split-dollar loan is less than the interest required to be accrued on the split-dollar loan, the excess of the interest required to be accrued over the interest actually paid is treated as waived, cancelled, or forgiven by the lender under this paragraph (h). However, the amount treated as retransferred under paragraph (h)(1)(i) of this section is not increased by the deferral charge in paragraph (h)(4) of this section.

(2) *Split-dollar term loans.*—In the case of a split-dollar term loan, the amount of interest deemed transferred and retransferred for purposes of paragraph (h)(1) of this section is determined as follows:

(i) If the loan's stated rate is less than or equal to the appropriate AFR (the AFR used to test the loan for sufficient interest under paragraph (e) of this section), the amount of interest deemed transferred and retransferred pursuant to this paragraph (h) is the excess of the amount of interest payable at the stated rate over the interest actually paid.

(ii) If the loan's stated rate is greater than the appropriate AFR (the AFR used to test the loan for sufficient interest under paragraph (e) of this section), the amount of interest deemed transferred and retransferred pursuant to this paragraph (h) is the excess, if any, of the amount of interest payable at the AFR over the interest actually paid.

(3) *Split-dollar demand loans.*—In the case of a split-dollar demand loan, the amount of interest deemed transferred and retransferred for purposes of paragraph (h)(1) of this section is equal to the aggregate of—

(i) For each year that the split-dollar demand loan was outstanding in which the loan was a below-market split-dollar demand loan, the excess of the amount of interest payable at the stated rate over the interest actually paid allocable to that year; plus

(ii) For each year that the split-dollar demand loan was outstanding in which the loan was not a below-market split-dollar demand loan, the excess, if any, of the amount of interest payable at the appropriate rate used for purposes of imputation for that year over the interest actually paid allocable to that year.

(4) *Deferral charge.*—The Commissioner may prescribe the method for determining the deferral charge treated as retransferred by the lender to the borrower under paragraph (h)(1) of this section. Until the Commissioner prescribes otherwise, the deferral charge is determined under paragraph (h)(4)(i) of this section for a split-dollar term loan subject to paragraph (h)(2) of this section and under paragraph (h)(4)(ii) of this section for a split-dollar demand loan subject to paragraph (h)(3) of this section.

(i) *Split-dollar term loan.*—The deferral charge for a split-dollar term loan subject to paragraph (h)(2) of this section is determined by multiplying the hypothetical underpayment by the applicable underpayment rate, compounded daily, for the period from the date the split-dollar loan was made to the date the interest is waived, cancelled, or forgiven. The hypothetical underpayment is equal to the amount determined under paragraph (h)(2) of this section, multiplied by the highest rate of income tax applicable to the borrower (for example, the highest rate in effect under section 1 for individuals) for the taxable year in which the split-dollar term loan was made. The applicable underpayment rate is the average of the quarterly underpayment rates in effect under section 6621(a)(2) for the period from the date the split-dollar loan was made to the date the interest is waived, cancelled, or forgiven.

(ii) *Split-dollar demand loan.*—The deferral charge for a split-dollar demand loan subject to paragraph (h)(3) of this section is the sum of the following amounts determined for each year the loan was outstanding (other than the year in which the waiver, cancellation, or forgiveness occurs): For each year the loan was outstanding, multiply the hypothetical underpayment for the year by the applicable underpayment rate, compounded daily, for the applicable period. The hypothetical underpayment is equal to the amount determined under paragraph (h)(3) of this section for each year, multiplied by the highest rate of income tax applicable to the borrower for that year (for example, the highest rate in effect under section 1 for individuals). The applicable underpayment rate is the average of the quarterly underpayment rates in effect under section 6621(a)(2) for the applicable period. The applicable period for a year is the period of time from the last day of that year until the date the interest is waived, cancelled, or forgiven.

(5) *Examples.*—The provisions of this paragraph (h) are illustrated by the following examples:

Example 1. (i) On January 1, 2009, Employer Y and Employee B entered into a split-dollar life insurance arrangement under which B is named as the policy owner. On January 1, 2009, Y made a $100,000 premium payment, repayable on December 31, 2011, with interest of 5 percent, compounded annually. The premium payment is a split-dollar term loan. Assume the short-term AFR (based on annual compounding) at the time the loan was made was 5 percent. Repayment of both the premium payment and the interest due thereon was fully recourse to B. On December 31, 2011, Y is repaid $100,000 but Y waives the remainder due on the loan ($15,762.50). Both Y and B use the calendar year as their taxable years.

(ii) When the split-dollar term loan was made, the loan was not a below-market loan under paragraph (e)(4)(ii) of this section. Under paragraph (f) of this section, Y was required to accrue compound interest of 5 percent each year the loan remained outstanding. B, however, was not entitled to any deduction for this interest under paragraph (c) of this section.

(iii) Under paragraph (h)(1) of this section, the waived amount is treated as if, on December 31, 2011, it had in fact been paid to Y and was then retransferred by Y to B. The amount deemed transferred to Y and retransferred to B equals the excess of the amount of interest payable at the stated rate ($15,762.50) over the interest actually paid ($0), or $15,762.50. In addition, the amount deemed retransferred to B is increased by the deferral charge determined under paragraph (h)(4) of this section. Because of the employment relationship between Y and B, the total retransferred amount is treated as compensation paid by Y to B.

Example 2. (i) On January 1, 2009, Employer Y and Employee B entered into a split-dollar life insurance arrangement under which B is named as the policy owner. On January 1, 2009, Y made a $100,000 premium payment, repayable on the demand of Y, with interest of 7 percent, compounded annually. The premium payment is a split-dollar demand loan. Assume the blended annual rate (based on annual compounding) in 2009 was 5 percent and in 2010 was 6 percent. Repayment of both the premium payment and the interest due thereon was fully recourse to B. On December 31, 2010, Y demands repayment and is repaid its $100,000 premium payment in full; however, Y waives all interest due on the loan. Both Y and B use the calendar year as their taxable years.

(ii) For each year that the split-dollar demand loan was outstanding, the loan was not a below-market loan under paragraph (e)(3)(ii) of this section. Under paragraph (f) of this section, Y was required to accrue compound interest of 7 percent each year the loan remained outstanding. B, however, was not entitled to any deduction for this interest under paragraph (c) of this section.

(iii) Under paragraph (h)(1) of this section, a portion of the waived interest is treated as if, on December 31, 2010, it had in fact been paid to Y and was then retransferred by Y to B. The amount of interest deemed transferred to Y and retransferred to B equals the excess, if any, of the amount of interest payable at the blended annual rate for each year the loan is outstanding over the interest actually paid with respect to that year. For 2009, the interest payable at the blended annual rate is $5,000 ($100,000 × 0.05). For 2010, the interest payable at the blended annual rate is $6,000 ($100,000 × 0.06). Therefore, the amount of interest deemed transferred to Y and retransferred to B equals $11,000. In addition, the amount deemed retransferred to B is increased by the deferral charge determined under paragraph (h)(4) of this section. Because of the employment relationship between Y and B, the total retransferred amount is treated as compensation paid by Y to B.

(i) [Reserved]

(j) *Split-dollar loans that provide for contingent payments.*—(1) *In general.*—Except as provided in paragraph (j)(2) of this section, this paragraph (j) provides rules for a split-dollar dollar loan that provides for one or more contingent payments. This paragraph (j), rather than § 1.1275-4, applies to split-dollar loans that provide for one or more contingent payments.

(2) *Exceptions.*—(i) *Certain contingencies.*—For purposes of this section, a split-dollar loan does not provide for contingent payments merely because—

(A) The loan provides for options described in paragraph (e)(4)(iii)(B) of this section (for example, certain call options, put options, and options to extend); or

(B) The loan is described in paragraph (e)(5) of this section (relating to certain split-dollar term loans, such as a split-dollar term loan payable not later than the death of an individual).

(ii) *Insolvency and default.*—For purposes of this section, a payment is not contingent merely because of the possibility of impairment by insolvency, default, or similar circumstances. However, if any payment on a split-dollar loan is nonrecourse to the borrower, the payment is a contingent payment for purposes of this paragraph (j) unless the parties to the arrangement make the written representation provided for in paragraph (d)(2) of this section.

(iii) *Remote and incidental contingencies.*—For purposes of this section, a payment is not a contingent payment merely because of a contingency that, as of the date the split-dollar loan is made, is either remote or incidental (within the meaning of § 1.1275-2(h)).

Reg. § 1.7872-15(h)(5)

(iv) *Exceptions for certain split-dollar loans.*—This paragraph (j) does not apply to a split-dollar loan described in § 1.1272-1(d) (certain debt instruments that provide for a fixed yield) or a split-dollar loan described in paragraph (g) of this section (relating to split-dollar loans providing for certain variable rates of interest).

(3) *Contingent split-dollar method.*—(i) *In general.*—If a split-dollar loan provides for one or more contingent payments, then the parties account for the loan under the contingent split-dollar method. In general, except as provided in this paragraph (j), this method is the same as the noncontingent bond method described in § 1.1275-4(b).

(ii) *Projected payment schedule.*—(A) *Determination of schedule.*—No comparable yield is required to be determined. The projected payment schedule for the loan includes all non-contingent payments and a projected payment for each contingent payment. The projected payment for a contingent payment is the lowest possible value of the payment. The projected payment schedule, however, must produce a yield that is not less than zero. If the projected payment schedule produces a negative yield, the schedule must be reasonably adjusted to produce a yield of zero.

(B) *Split-dollar term loans payable upon the death of an individual.*—If a split-dollar term loan described in paragraph (e)(5)(ii)(A) or (v)(A)(1) of this section provides for one or more contingent payments, the projected payment schedule is determined based on the term of the loan as determined under paragraph (e)(5)(ii)(C) or (v)(B)(2) of this section, whichever is applicable.

(C) *Certain split-dollar term loans conditioned on the future performance of substantial services by an individual.*—If a split-dollar term loan described in paragraph (e)(5)(iii)(A)(1) or (v)(A)(2) of this section provides for one or more contingent payments, the projected payment schedule is determined based on the term of the loan as determined under paragraph (e)(5)(iii)(C) or (v)(B)(2) of this section, whichever is applicable.

(D) *Demand loans.*—If a split-dollar demand loan provides for one or more contingent payments, the projected payment schedule is determined based on a reasonable assumption as to when the lender will demand repayment.

(E) *Borrower/lender consistency.*—Contrary to § 1.1275-4(b)(4)(iv), the lender rather than the borrower is required to determine the projected payment schedule and to provide the schedule to the borrower and to any indirect participant as described in paragraph (e)(2) of this section. The lender's projected payment schedule is used by the lender, the borrower, and any indirect participant to compute interest accruals and adjustments.

(iii) *Negative adjustments.*—If the issuer of a split-dollar loan is not allowed to deduct interest or OID (for example, because of section 163(h) or 264), then the issuer is not required to include in income any negative adjustment carryforward determined under § 1.1275-4(b)(6)(iii)(C) on the loan, except to the extent that at maturity the total payments made over the life of the loan are less than the issue price of the loan.

(4) *Application of section 7872.*—(i) *Determination of below-market status.*—The yield based on the projected payment schedule determined under paragraph (j)(3) of this section is used to determine whether the loan is a below-market split-dollar loan under paragraph (e) of this section.

(ii) *Adjustment upon the resolution of a contingent payment.*—To the extent that interest has accrued under section 7872 on a split-dollar loan and the interest would not have accrued under this paragraph (j) in the absence of section 7872, the lender is not required to recognize income under § 1.1275-4(b) for a positive adjustment and the borrower is not treated as having interest expense for a positive adjustment. To the same extent, there is a reversal of the tax consequences imposed under paragraph (e) of this section for the prior imputed transfer from the lender to the borrower. This reversal is taken into account in determining adjusted gross income.

(5) *Examples.*—The following examples illustrate the rules of this paragraph (j). For purposes of this paragraph (j)(5), assume that the contingent payments are neither remote nor incidental. The examples are as follows:

Example 1. (i) On January 1, 2010, Employer T and Employee G enter into a splitdollar life insurance arrangement under which G is named as the policy owner. On January 1, 2010, T makes a $100,000 premium payment. On December 31, 2013, T will be repaid an amount equal to the premium payment plus an amount based on the increase, if any, in the price of a specified commodity for the period the loan is outstanding. The premium payment is a split-dollar term loan. Repayment of both the premium payment and the interest due thereon is recourse to G. Assume that the appropriate AFR for this loan, based on annual compounding, is 7 percent. Both T and G use the calendar year as their taxable years.

(ii) Under this paragraph (j), the split-dollar term loan between T and G provides for a contingent payment. Therefore, the loan is subject to the contingent split-dollar method. Under this method, the projected payment schedule for the loan provides for a noncontingent payment of $100,000 and a projected payment of $0 for the contingent payment (because it is the lowest possible value of the payment) on December 31, 2013.

(iii) Based on the projected payment schedule and a discount rate of 7 percent, compounded annually (the appropriate AFR), the

Reg. § 1.7872-15(j)(5)

present value of the payments under the loan is $76,289.52. Under paragraphs (e)(4) and (j)(4)(i) of this section, the loan does not provide for sufficient interest because the loan's imputed loan amount of $76,289.52 (the present value of the payments) is less than the amount loaned of $100,000. Therefore, the loan is a below-market split-dollar term loan and the loan is recharacterized as consisting of two portions: an imputed loan amount of $76,289.52 and an imputed transfer of $23,710.48 (amount loaned of $100,000 minus the imputed loan amount of $76,289.52).

(iv) In accordance with section 7872(b)(1) and paragraph (e)(4)(iv) of this section, on the date the loan is made, T is treated as transferring to G $23,710.48 (the imputed transfer) as compensation. In addition, T must take into account as OID an amount equal to the imputed transfer. See § 1.1272-1 for the treatment of OID.

Example 2. (i) Assume, in addition to the facts in *Example 1*, that on December 31, 2013, T receives $115,000 (its premium payment of $100,000 plus $15,000).

(ii) Under the contingent split-dollar method, when the loan is repaid, there is a $15,000 positive adjustment ($15,000 actual payment minus $0 projected payment). Under paragraph (j)(4) of this section, because T accrued imputed interest under section 7872 on this split-dollar loan to G and this interest would not have accrued in the absence of section 7872, T is not required to include the positive adjustment in income, and G is not treated as having interest expense for the positive adjustment. To the same extent, T must include in income, and G is entitled to deduct, $15,000 to reverse their respective prior tax consequences imposed under paragraph (e) of this section (T's prior deduction for imputed compensation deemed paid to G and G's prior inclusion of this amount). G takes the reversal into account in determining adjusted gross income. That is, the $15,000 is an "above-the-line" deduction, whether or not G itemizes deductions.

Example 3. (i) Assume the same facts as in *Example 2*, except that on December 31, 2013, T receives $127,000 (its premium payment of $100,000 plus $27,000).

(ii) Under the contingent split-dollar method, when the loan is repaid, there is a $27,000 positive adjustment ($27,000 actual payment minus $0 projected payment). Under paragraph (j)(4) of this section, because T accrued imputed interest of $23,710.48 under section 7872 on this split-dollar loan to G and this interest would not have accrued in the absence of section 7872, T is not required to include $23,710.48 of the positive adjustment in income, and G is not treated as having interest expense for the positive adjustment. To the same extent, in 2013, T must include in income, and G is entitled to deduct, $23,710.48 to reverse their respective prior tax consequences imposed under paragraph (e) of this section (T's prior deduction for imputed compensation deemed paid to G and G's prior inclusion of this amount). G and T take

these reversals into account in determining adjusted gross income. Under the contingent split-dollar method, T must include in income $3,289.52 upon resolution of the contingency ($27,000 positive adjustment minus $23,710.48).

(k) *Payment ordering rule.*—For purposes of this section, a payment made by the borrower to or for the benefit of the lender pursuant to a split-dollar life insurance arrangement is applied to all direct and indirect split-dollar loans in the following order—

(1) A payment of interest to the extent of accrued but unpaid interest (including any OID) on all outstanding split-dollar loans in the order the interest accrued;

(2) A payment of principal on the outstanding split-dollar loans in the order in which the loans were made;

(3) A payment of amounts previously paid by a non-owner pursuant to a split-dollar life insurance arrangement that were not reasonably expected to be repaid by the owner; and

(4) Any other payment with respect to a split-dollar life insurance arrangement, other than a payment taken into account under paragraphs (k)(1), (2), and (3) of this section.

(l) [Reserved]

(m) *Repayments received by a lender.*—Any amount received by a lender under a life insurance contract that is part of a split-dollar life insurance arrangement is treated as though the amount had been paid to the borrower and then paid by the borrower to the lender. Any amount treated as received by the borrower under this paragraph (m) is subject to other provisions of the Internal Revenue Code as applicable (for example, sections 72 and 101(a)). The lender must take the amount into account as a payment received with respect to a split-dollar loan, in accordance with paragraph (k) of this section. No amount received by a lender with respect to a split-dollar loan is treated as an amount received by reason of the death of the insured.

(n) *Effective date.*—(1) *General rule.*—This section applies to any split-dollar life insurance arrangement entered into after September 17, 2003. For purposes of this section, an arrangement is entered into as determined under § 1.61-22(j)(1)(ii).

(2) *Modified arrangements treated as new arrangements.*—If an arrangement entered into on or before September 17, 2003 is materially modified (within the meaning of § 1.61-22(j)(2)) after September 17, 2003, the arrangement is treated as a new arrangement entered into on the date of the modification. [Reg. § 1.7872-15.]

☐ [*T.D.* 9092, 9-11-2003.]

[Reg. § 1.7872-16]

§ 1.7872-16. Loans to an exchange facilitator under § 1.468B-6.—(a) *Exchange facilitator loans.*—This section provides rules in applying section 7872 to an exchange facilitator loan (within the meaning of § 1.468B-6(c)(1)). For purposes of this section, the terms *deferred exchange, exchange agreement, exchange facilitator, exchange funds, qualified intermediary, replacement property,* and *taxpayer* have the same meanings as in § 1.468B-6(b).

(b) *Treatment as demand loans.*—For purposes of section 7872, except as provided in paragraph (d) of this section, an exchange facilitator loan is a demand loan.

(c) *Treatment as compensation-related loans.*—If an exchange facilitator loan is a below-market loan, the loan is a compensation-related loan under section 7872(c)(1)(B).

(d) *Applicable Federal rate (AFR) for exchange facilitator loans.*—For purposes of section 7872, in the case of an exchange facilitator loan, the applicable Federal rate is the lower of the short-term AFR in effect under section 1274(d)(1) (as of the day on which the loan is made), compounded semiannually, or the 91-day rate. For purposes of the preceding sentence, the 91-day rate is equal to the investment rate on a 13-week (generally 91-day) Treasury bill with an issue date that is the same as the date that the exchange facilitator loan is made or, if the two dates are not the same, with an issue date that most closely precedes the date that the exchange facilitator loan is made.

(e) *Use of approximate method permitted.*—The taxpayer and exchange facilitator may use the approximate method to determine the amount of forgone interest on any exchange facilitator loan.

(f) *Exemption for certain below-market exchange facilitator loans.*—If an exchange facilitator loan is a below-market loan, the loan is not eligible for the exemptions from section 7872 listed under § 1.7872-5T. However, the loan may be eligible for the exemption from section 7872 under § 1.7872-5(b)(16) (relating to exchange facilitator loans in which the amount treated as loaned does not exceed $2,000,000).

(g) *Effective/applicability date.*—This section applies to exchange facilitator loans issued on or after October 8, 2008.

(h) *Example.*—The provisions of this section are illustrated by the following example:

Example. (i) T enters into a deferred exchange with QI, a qualified intermediary. The exchange is governed by an exchange agreement. The exchange funds held by QI pursuant to the exchange agreement are treated as loaned to QI under § 1.468B-6(c)(1). The loan between T and QI is an exchange facilitator loan. The exchange agreement between T and QI provides that no earnings will be paid to T. On December 1, 2008, T transfers property to QI, QI transfers the property to a purchaser for $2,100,000, and QI deposits $2,100,000 in a money market account. On March 1, 2009, QI uses $2,100,000 of the funds in the account to purchase replacement property identified by T, and transfers the replacement property to T. The amount loaned for purposes of section 7872 is $2,100,000 and the loan is out-

standing for three months. For purposes of section 7872, under paragraph (d) of this section, T uses the 91-day rate, which is 4 percent, compounded semi-annually. T uses the approximate method for purposes of section 7872.

(ii) Under paragraphs (b) and (c) of this section, the loan from T to QI is a compensation-related demand loan. Because there is no interest payable on the loan from T to QI, the loan is a below-market loan under section 7872. The loan is not exempt under § 1.7872-5(b)(16) because the amount treated as loaned exceeds $2,000,000. Under section 7872(e)(2), the amount of forgone interest on the loan for 2008 is $7000 ($2,100,000*.04/2*1/6). Under section 7872(e)(2), the amount of forgone interest for 2009 is $14,000 ($2,100,000*.04/2*2/6). The $7000 for 2008 is deemed transferred as compensation by T to QI and retransferred as interest by QI to T on December 31, 2008. The $14,000 for 2009 is deemed transferred as compensation by T to QI and retransferred as interest by QI to T on March 1, 2009. [Reg. § 1.7872-16.]

☐ [*T.D.* 9413, 7-9-2008.]

[Reg. § 1.7874-1]

§ 1.7874-1. Disregard of affiliate-owned stock.—(a) *Scope.*—Section 7874(c)(2)(A) provides that stock of the foreign acquiring corporation held by members of the expanded affiliated group shall not be taken into account in determining ownership for purposes of section 7874(a)(2)(B)(ii). This section provides rules under section 7874(c)(2)(A). The rules provided in this section are also subject to section 7874(c)(4). For definitions that apply for purposes of this section, see 1.7874-12.

(b) *General rule.*—Except as provided in paragraph (c) of this section, for purposes of determining the ownership percentage described in section 7874(a)(2)(B)(ii), stock held by one or more members of the EAG is not included in either the numerator or the denominator of the ownership fraction.

(c) *Exceptions to general rule.*—(1) *Overview.*—Stock held by one or more members of the EAG shall be included in the denominator, but not in the numerator, of the ownership fraction, if the domestic entity acquisition qualifies as an *internal group restructuring* or results in a *loss of control*, as described in paragraph (c)(2) and (c)(3) of this section. For rules addressing the interaction of this section and other rules, see paragraph (d) of this section.

(2) *Internal group restructuring.*—For purposes of paragraph (c)(1) of this section, a domestic entity acquisition qualifies as an internal group restructuring if:

(i) Before the domestic entity acquisition, 80 percent or more of the stock (by vote and value) or the capital and profits interest, as applicable, of the domestic entity was held directly or indirectly by the corporation that is the common parent of the EAG after the acquisition; and

(ii) After the domestic entity acquisition, 80 percent or more of the stock (by vote and value) of the foreign acquiring corporation is held directly or indirectly by such common parent.

(iii) *Special rule.*—If § 1.7874-6(c)(2) applies for purposes of applying section 7874(c)(2)(A) and this section, then, for purposes of paragraph (c)(2) of this section (and so much of paragraph (c)(1) of this section as relates to paragraph (c)(2) of this section), the determination of the EAG after the domestic entity acquisition, as well as the determination of stock held by one or more members of the EAG after the domestic entity acquisition, is made without regard to one or more transfers (other than by issuance), in a transaction (or series of transactions) after and related to the acquisition, of stock of the acquiring foreign corporation by one or more members of the foreign-parented group described in § 1.7874-6(c)(2)(i).

(3) *Loss of control.*—For purposes of paragraph (c)(1) of this section, the domestic entity acquisition results in a loss of control if after the acquisition, the former domestic entity shareholders or former domestic entity partners do not hold, in the aggregate, directly or indirectly, more than 50 percent of the stock (by vote or value) of any member of the EAG.

(d) *Interaction of expanded affiliated group rules with other rules.*—(1) *Exclusion rules.*—Stock that is excluded from the denominator of the ownership fraction pursuant to § 1.7874-4(b), 1.7874-7(b), 1.7874-8(b), 1.7874-9(b), or section 7874(c)(4) is taken into account for purposes of determining whether an entity is a member of the expanded affiliated group for purposes of applying section 7874(c)(2)(A) and paragraph (b) of this section and determining whether a domestic entity acquisition qualifies as an internal group restructuring or results in a loss of control, as described in paragraphs (c)(2) and (3) of this section, respectively. However, such stock is excluded from the denominator of the ownership fraction regardless of whether it otherwise would be included in the denominator of the ownership fraction as a result of the application of paragraph (c) of this section. See *Example 8* and *Example 9* of § 1.7874-4(i) for illustrations of the application of this paragraph (d)(1).

(2) *NOCD rule.*—Stock of the foreign acquiring corporation treated as received by former domestic entity shareholders or former domestic entity partners, as applicable, under § 1.7874-10(b) is not taken into account for purposes of determining whether an entity is a member of the expanded affiliated group for purposes of applying section 7874(c)(2)(A) and paragraph (b) of this section and determining whether a domestic entity acquisition qualifies as an internal group restructuring or results in a loss of control, as described in paragraphs (c)(2) and (3) of this section, respectively. However, such stock is included in the numerator and denominator of the ownership fraction, except to the extent that it is treated as held by a member of the EAG and is excluded from the numerator or both the numerator and the denominator, as applicable, under section 7874(c)(2)(A) or paragraphs (b) or (c) of this section.

(e) *Treatment of certain hook stock.*—This paragraph applies to stock of a corporation that is held by an entity in which at least 50 percent of the stock (by vote or value) or at least 50 percent of the capital or profits interest, as applicable, in such entity, is held directly or indirectly by the corporation. The stock to which this paragraph applies shall not be included in either the numerator or denominator of any fraction for the following purposes:

(1) For applying paragraph (c)(1) of this section; and

(2) For determining whether the domestic entity acquisition qualifies as an internal group restructuring (described in paragraph (c)(2) of this section) or results in a loss of control (described in paragraph (c)(3) of this section).

(f) *Stock held by a partnership.*—For purposes of this section, each partner in a partnership shall be treated as holding its proportionate share of stock held by the partnership, as determined under the rules and principles of sections 701 through 777.

(g) *Treatment of transactions related to the acquisition.*—Except as provided in paragraph (c)(2)(iii) of this section, all transactions that are related to an acquisition are taken into account in applying this section.

(h) *Examples.*—The application of this section is illustrated by the following examples. It is assumed that all transactions in the examples occur after March 4, 2003. In all the examples, if an entity or other person is not described as either domestic or foreign, it may be either domestic or foreign. In addition, each entity has only a single class of equity outstanding. Finally, the analysis of the following examples is limited to a discussion of issues under section 7874, even though the examples may raise other issues (for example, under section 367).

Example 1. Disregard of hook stock—(i) *Facts.* USS, a domestic corporation, has 100 shares of stock outstanding. USS's stock is held by a group of individuals. Pursuant to a plan, USS forms FS, a foreign corporation, and transfers to FS the stock of several wholly owned foreign corporations, in exchange for 90 shares of FS stock. FS then forms Merger Sub, a domestic corporation. Under a merger agreement and state law, Merger Sub merges into USS, with USS surviving the merger. In exchange for their USS stock, the former shareholders of USS receive, in the aggregate, 100 shares of newly issued FS stock. As a result of the merger FS holds 100 percent of the USS stock. USS continues to hold 90 shares of FS stock.

(ii) *Analysis.* FS has indirectly acquired substantially all the properties held directly or indirectly by USS pursuant to a plan. After the acquisition, the former shareholders of USS hold 100 shares of FS stock by reason of holding stock in USS, and USS holds 90 shares of FS stock. Under paragraph (b) of this section, the 90 shares of FS stock held by USS, a member of the EAG, are not included in either the numerator or the denominator of the ownership fraction. Accordingly, the ownership fraction is 100/100. If the condition in section 7874(a)(2)(B)(iii) is satisfied, FS is a surrogate foreign corporation which is treated as a domestic corporation under section 7874(b).

Example 2. Internal group restructuring; wholly owned corporation—(i) *Facts.* P, a corporation, owns all 100 outstanding shares of USS, a domestic corporation. USS forms FS, a foreign corporation, and transfers all its assets to FS in exchange for all 100 shares of the stock of FS, in a reorganization described in section 368(a)(1). P exchanges its USS stock for FS stock under section 354.

(ii) *Analysis.* FS has directly acquired substantially all the properties held directly or indirectly by USS pursuant to a plan. The acquisition is an internal group restructuring described in paragraph (c)(2) of this section because P, the common parent of the EAG after the acquisition, held directly or indirectly 80 percent or more of the stock (by vote and value) of USS before the acquisition, and after the acquisition, P holds directly or indirectly 80 percent or more of the stock (by vote and value) of FS. Accordingly, under paragraph (c)(1) of this section, the FS stock held by P is included in the denominator, but not in the numerator of the ownership fraction. Therefore, the ownership fraction is 0/100. FS is not a surrogate foreign corporation.

Example 3. Internal group restructuring; wholly owned corporation—(i) *Facts.* The facts are the same as in *Example 2*, except that USS does not transfer any of its assets to FS. Instead, P transfers all 100 shares of USS stock to FS in exchange for all 100 shares of FS stock.

(ii) *Analysis.* FS has indirectly acquired substantially all the properties held directly or indirectly by USS pursuant to a plan. The acquisition is an internal group restructuring described in paragraph (c)(2) of this section because P, the common parent of the EAG after the acquisition, held directly or indirectly 80 percent or more of the stock (by vote and value) of USS before the acquisition, and after the acquisition, P holds directly or indirectly 80 percent or more of the stock (by vote and value) of FS. Accordingly, under paragraph (c)(1) of this section, the FS stock held by P is included in the denominator, but not in the numerator of the ownership fraction. Accordingly, the ownership fraction is 0/100. FS is not a surrogate foreign corporation.

Example 4. Internal group restructuring; less than wholly owned corporation—(i) *Facts.* The facts are the same as in *Example 3*, except that P holds 85 shares of USS stock. The remaining 15 shares of USS stock are held by A, a person unrelated to P. P and A transfer their shares of USS stock to FS

in exchange for 85 and 15 shares of FS stock, respectively.

(ii) *Analysis.* FS has indirectly acquired substantially all the properties held directly or indirectly by USS pursuant to a plan. The acquisition is an internal group restructuring described in paragraph (c)(2) of this section because P, the common parent of the EAG after the acquisition, held directly or indirectly 80 percent or more of the stock (by vote and value) of USS before the acquisition, and after the acquisition P holds directly or indirectly 80 percent or more of the stock (by vote and value) of FS. Therefore, under paragraph (c)(1) of this section, the FS stock held by P is included in the denominator, but not in the numerator of the ownership fraction. Accordingly, the ownership fraction is 15/100. FS is not a surrogate foreign corporation.

Example 5. Internal group restructuring exception not applicable; less than 80 percent owned corporation—(i) *Facts.* The facts are the same as in *Example 2*, except that P owns 55 shares of USS stock, and A, a person unrelated to P, holds 45 shares of USS stock. P and A exchange their shares of USS stock for 55 shares and 45 shares of FS stock, respectively.

(ii) *Analysis.* FS has acquired substantially all the properties held directly or indirectly by USS pursuant to a plan. P, the common parent of the EAG after the acquisition, did not hold directly or indirectly 80 percent or more of the stock (by vote and value) of USS before the acquisition, and after the acquisition P does not hold directly or indirectly 80 percent or more of the stock (by vote and value) of FS. Thus, the acquisition is not an internal group restructuring described in paragraph (c)(1) of this section, and the general rule of paragraph (b) of this section applies. Under paragraph (b) of this section, the FS stock held by P, a member of the EAG, is not included in either the numerator or the denominator of the ownership fraction. Accordingly, the ownership fraction is 45/45. If the condition in section 7874(a)(2)(B)(iii) is satisfied, FS is a surrogate foreign corporation which is treated as a domestic corporation under section 7874(b).

Example 6. Internal group restructuring; hook stock—(i) *Facts.* USS, a domestic corporation, has 100 shares of stock outstanding. P, a corporation, holds 80 shares of USS stock. The remaining 20 shares of USS stock are held by A, a person unrelated to P. USS owns all 30 outstanding shares of FS, a foreign corporation. Pursuant to a plan, FS forms Merger Sub, a domestic corporation. Under a merger agreement and state law, Merger Sub merges into USS, with USS surviving the merger as a subsidiary of FS. In exchange for their USS stock, P and A, the former shareholders of USS, respectively receive 56 and 14 shares of FS stock. USS continues to hold 30 shares of FS stock.

(ii) *Analysis.* FS has indirectly acquired substantially all the properties held directly or indirectly by USS pursuant to a plan. Under paragraph (b) of this section, the shares of FS stock held by P and USS, both of which are

Reg. § 1.7874-1(h)

members of the EAG, are not included in either the numerator or denominator of the ownership fraction, unless the acquisition results in an internal group restructuring or loss of control of USS such that the exception of paragraph (c)(1) of this section applies. In determining whether the acquisition of USS is an internal group restructuring, under paragraph (e)(2) of this section, the FS stock held by USS is disregarded. Because P held directly or indirectly 80 percent or more of the stock (by vote and value) of USS before the acquisition, and after the acquisition P holds directly or indirectly 80 percent or more of the stock (by vote and value) of FS (when disregarding the FS stock held by USS), the acquisition is an internal group restructuring and the exception of paragraph (c)(1) of this section applies. Accordingly, when determining whether FS is a surrogate foreign corporation, the FS stock held by P is included in the denominator, but not the numerator of the ownership fraction. However, under paragraph (b) of this section, the FS stock held by USS is not included in either the numerator or denominator of the ownership fraction. Accordingly, the ownership fraction is 14/70, or 20 percent, since only the stock held by A is included in the numerator, and the stock held by both P and A is included in the denominator. Accordingly, FS is not a surrogate foreign corporation.

Example 7. Loss of control—(i) *Facts.* P, a corporation, holds all the outstanding stock of USS, a domestic corporation. B, a corporation unrelated to P, holds all 60 outstanding shares of FS, a foreign corporation. P transfers to FS all the outstanding stock of USS in exchange for 40 newly issued shares of FS.

(ii) *Analysis.* FS has indirectly acquired substantially all the properties held directly or indirectly by USS pursuant to a plan. After the acquisition, B holds 60 percent of the outstanding shares of the FS stock. Accordingly, B, FS and USS are members of an EAG. After the acquisition, P does not hold directly or indirectly more than 50 percent of the stock (by vote or value) of any member of the EAG and, thus, the acquisition results in a loss of control described in paragraph (c)(3) of this section. Accordingly, under paragraph (c)(1) of this section, the FS stock owned by B is included in the denominator, but not in the numerator, of the ownership fraction. Therefore, the ownership fraction is 40/100. FS is not a surrogate foreign corporation.

Example 8. Internal group restructuring; partnership—(i) *Facts.* LLC, a Delaware limited liability company, is engaged in the conduct of a trade or business. P, a corporation, holds 90 percent of the interests of LLC. A, a person unrelated to P, holds 10 percent of the interests of LLC. LLC has not elected to be treated as an association taxable as a corporation. P and A transfer their interests in LLC to FS, a newly formed foreign corporation, in exchange for 90 shares and 10 shares, respectively, of FS's stock, which are all of the outstanding shares of FS. Accordingly, LLC becomes a disregarded entity.

(ii) *Analysis.* Prior to the FS's acquisition of the interests of LLC, LLC was a domestic partnership for Federal income tax purposes. FS has acquired substantially all the properties constituting a trade or business of LLC pursuant to a plan. After the acquisition, P holds 90 percent of FS's stock (by vote and value) by reason of holding a capital and profits interest in LLC, and A holds 10 percent of FS's stock (by vote and value) by reason of holding a capital and profits interest in LLC. The internal group restructuring exception under paragraph (c)(2) of this section applies, because before the acquisition, P held 80 percent or more of the capital and profits interest in LLC, and after the acquisition, P holds 80 percent or more of the stock (by vote and value) of FS. Under paragraph (c)(1) of this section, the FS stock held by P is included in the denominator, but not the numerator, of the ownership fraction. Accordingly, the ownership fraction is 10/100. FS is not a surrogate foreign corporation.

(i) *Applicability dates.*—(1) *In general.*—Except as otherwise provided, this section shall apply to domestic entity acquisitions completed on or after May 20, 2008. This section shall not, however, apply to a domestic entity acquisition that was completed on or after May 20, 2008, provided such acquisition was entered into pursuant to a written agreement which was (subject to customary conditions) binding prior to May 20, 2008, and at all times thereafter (binding commitment). For purposes of the preceding sentence, a binding commitment shall include entering into options and similar interests in connection with one or more written agreements described in the preceding sentence. Notwithstanding the general application of this paragraph, taxpayers may elect to apply this section to domestic entity acquisitions completed before May 20, 2008, but must apply it consistently to all acquisitions within its scope. Paragraph (f) of this section shall apply to acquisitions completed on or after June 7, 2012. See § 1.7874-1T(f), as contained in 26 CFR part 1 revised as of April 1, 2012, for domestic entity acquisitions completed before June 7, 2012.

(2) *Applicability date of certain provisions of this section.*—Except as provided in this paragraph (i)(2), paragraph (c)(2)(iii) of this section applies to domestic entity acquisitions completed on or after April 4, 2016. Except as provided in this paragraph (i)(2), paragraph (d) of this section (interaction of EAG rules with other rules) applies to domestic entity acquisitions completed on or after July 12, 2018. See §§ 1.7874-4(h) and 1.7874-7T(e), as contained in 26 CFR part 1 revised as of April 1, 2017, for certain coordination rules for domestic entity acquisitions completed before July 12, 2018. Except as provided in this paragraph (i)(2), paragraph (g) of this section applies to domestic entity acquisitions completed on or after September 22, 2014. For domestic entity acquisitions completed before April 4, 2016, however, taxpayers may elect to consistently apply paragraphs (c)(2)(iii) and (g) of this section, and § 1.7874-6(c)(2), (d)(2),

and (f)(2)(ii). In addition, for domestic entity acquisitions completed before July 12, 2018, taxpayers may elect to consistently apply paragraph (d) of this section. [Reg. § 1.7874-1.]

☐ [T.D. 9399, 5-19-2008. *Amended by T.D. 9453*, 6-9-2009; T.D. 9591, 6-7-2012, *T.D. 9654*, 1-16-2014, *T.D. 9761*, 4-4-2016; *T.D. 9812*, 1-13-2017 *and T.D. 9834*, 7-11-2018.]

[Reg. § 1.7874-2]

§ 1.7874-2. Surrogate foreign corporation.— (a) *Scope.*—This section provides rules for determining whether a foreign corporation is treated as a surrogate foreign corporation under section 7874(a)(2)(B). Paragraph (b) of this section provides definitions and special rules. Paragraph (c) of this section provides rules to determine whether a foreign corporation has acquired properties held by a domestic corporation (or a partnership). Paragraph (d) of this section provides rules that apply when two or more foreign corporations complete, in the aggregate, a domestic entity acquisition. Paragraph (e) of this section provides rules that apply when, pursuant to a plan, a single foreign corporation completes more than one domestic entity acquisition. Paragraph (f) of this section provides rules to identify the stock of a foreign corporation that is held by reason of holding stock in a domestic corporation (or an interest in a domestic partnership). Paragraph (g) of this section provides rules that treat certain publicly traded foreign partnerships as foreign corporations for purposes of section 7874. Paragraph (h) of this section provides rules concerning the treatment of certain options (or similar interests) for purposes of section 7874. Paragraph (i) of this section provides rules that treat certain interests (including debt, stock, or a partnership interest) as stock of a foreign corporation for purposes of section 7874. Paragraph (j) of this section provides rules concerning the conversion of a foreign corporation to a domestic corporation by reason of section 7874(b). Paragraph (k) of this section provides examples that illustrate the rules of this section. Paragraph (l) of this section provides the applicability dates of this section. For additional definitions that apply for purposes of this section, see § 1.7874-12.

(b) *Definitions and special rules.*—In addition to the definitions in § 1.7874-12, the following definitions and special rules apply for purposes of this section.

(1) The rules of this section are subject to section 7874(c)(4).

(2) References to *properties held* by a domestic corporation include properties held directly or indirectly by the domestic corporation.

(3) The rules and principles of sections 701 through 777 shall be applied for purposes of determining a proportionate amount (or share) of properties held by a partnership (such as stock).

(4) Any reference to the acquisition of properties held by a domestic corporation (or a partnership) includes a direct or indirect acquisition of such properties.

(5) In the case of an acquisition of stock of a domestic corporation or an interest in a partnership, the proportionate amount of properties held by the domestic corporation (or the partnership) that is treated as indirectly acquired shall, as applicable, be determined at the time of the acquisition based on the relative value of—

(i) The stock acquired compared to all outstanding stock of the domestic corporation; or

(ii) The interest acquired compared to all interests in the partnership.

(6) The determination of whether a foreign corporation is a surrogate foreign corporation is made after the domestic entity acquisition. A foreign corporation that is treated as a surrogate foreign corporation (including a surrogate foreign corporation treated as a domestic corporation described in section 7874(b)) shall continue to be treated as a surrogate foreign corporation (or a domestic corporation), even if the conditions of section 7874(a)(2)(B)(ii) and (iii) are not satisfied at a later date.

(7) A *former initial acquiring corporation shareholder* of an initial acquiring corporation means any person that held stock in the initial acquiring corporation before the subsequent acquisition, including any person that holds stock in the initial acquiring corporation both before and after the subsequent acquisition.

(8) An *initial acquisition* means, with respect to a subsequent acquisition, a domestic entity acquisition occurring, pursuant to a plan that includes the subsequent acquisition (or a series of related transactions), before the subsequent acquisition.

(9) An *initial acquiring corporation* means, with respect to an initial acquisition, the foreign acquiring corporation.

(10) A *subsequent acquisition* means, with respect to an initial acquisition, a transaction occurring, pursuant to a plan that includes the initial acquisition (or a series of related transactions), after the initial acquisition in which a foreign corporation directly or indirectly acquires (within the meaning of paragraph (c)(4)(ii) of this section) substantially all of the properties held directly or indirectly by the initial acquiring corporation.

(11) A *subsequent acquiring corporation* means, with respect to a subsequent acquisition, the foreign corporation that directly or indirectly acquires substantially all of the properties held directly or indirectly by the initial acquiring corporation.

(12) *Special rule regarding initial acquisitions.*—With respect to an initial acquisition, the determination of the ownership percentage described in section 7874(a)(2)(B)(ii) is made without regard to the subsequent acquisition and all related transactions occurring after the subsequent acquisition.

(13) *Special rule regarding subsequent acquisitions.*—With respect to a subsequent acquisition (or a similar acquisition under the principles of

paragraph (c)(4)(i) of this section) that is an inversion transaction, the applicable period begins on the first date that properties are acquired as part of the initial acquisition.

(c) *Acquisition of properties.*—(1) *Indirect acquisition of properties.*—For purposes of section 7874(a)(2)(B)(i), an indirect acquisition of properties held by a domestic corporation (or a partnership) includes, but is not limited to, the acquisitions described in paragraphs (c)(1)(i) through (iv) of this section. An acquisition of less than all of the stock of a domestic corporation (or interests in a partnership) shall constitute an indirect acquisition of a proportionate amount of the properties held by the domestic corporation or the partnership. See paragraph (b)(8) of this section for rules determining the proportionate amount of properties indirectly acquired.

(i) An acquisition of stock of a domestic corporation. See *Example 1* of paragraph (k) of this section for an illustration of the rules of this paragraph (c)(1)(i).

(ii) An acquisition of an interest in a partnership. See *Example 2* of paragraph (k) of this section for an illustration of the rules of this paragraph (c)(1)(ii).

(iii) An acquisition by a corporation (acquiring corporation) of properties held by a domestic corporation (or a partnership) in exchange for stock of a foreign corporation (foreign issuing corporation) that is part of the expanded affiliated group that includes the acquiring corporation after the acquisition shall be treated as an acquisition by the foreign issuing corporation. See *Example 3* of paragraph (k) of this section for an illustration of the rules of this paragraph (c)(1)(iii).

(iv) An acquisition by a partnership (acquiring partnership) of properties held by a domestic corporation (or a partnership) in exchange for stock of a foreign corporation that is part of the expanded affiliated group that would include the acquiring partnership after the acquisition (if the partnership were a corporation) shall be treated as an acquisition by the foreign issuing corporation.

(2) *Acquisition of stock of a foreign corporation.*—Except as provided in paragraph (c)(4) of this section, an acquisition of stock of a foreign corporation that owns directly or indirectly stock of a domestic corporation (or an interest in a partnership) shall not constitute an indirect acquisition of any properties held by the domestic corporation (or the partnership). See *Example 4* of paragraph (k) of this section for an illustration of the rules of this paragraph (c)(2).

(3) *Downstream transactions.*—An acquisition by a corporation of its stock from another corporation or a partnership (for example, as a result of a downstream merger) is an acquisition of the other corporation's or partnership's properties for purposes of section 7874(a)(2)(B)(i).

(4) *Multiple-step acquisitions.*—(i) *Rule.*—A subsequent acquisition is treated as a domestic entity acquisition, and the subsequent acquiring corporation is treated as a foreign acquiring corporation. See *Example 21* of paragraph (k) of this section for an illustration of this rule. See also paragraph (f)(1)(iv) of this section (treating certain stock of the subsequent acquiring corporation as stock of a foreign corporation that is held by reason of holding stock of, or a partnership interest in, the domestic entity).

(ii) *Acquisition of property pursuant to a subsequent acquisition.*—In determining whether a foreign corporation directly or indirectly acquires substantially all of the properties held directly or indirectly by an initial acquiring corporation, the principles of section 7874(a)(2)(B)(i) apply, including paragraph (c) of this section other than paragraph (c)(2) of this section. For this purpose, the principles of paragraph (c)(1) of this section, including paragraph (b)(5) of this section, apply by substituting the term "foreign" for "domestic" wherever it appears.

(iii) *Additional related transactions.*—If, pursuant to the same plan (or a series of related transactions), a foreign corporation directly or indirectly acquires (under the principles of paragraph (c)(4)(ii) of this section) substantially all of the properties directly or indirectly held by a subsequent acquiring corporation in a transaction occurring after the subsequent acquisition, then the principles of paragraph (c)(4)(i) of this section apply to such transaction (and any subsequent transaction or transactions occurring pursuant to the plan (or the series of related transactions)).

(d) *Acquisitions by multiple foreign corporations.*—If, pursuant to a plan (or a series of related transactions), two or more foreign corporations complete, in the aggregate, a domestic entity acquisition, then each foreign corporation shall be treated as completing the acquisition for purposes of determining whether such foreign corporation is treated as a surrogate foreign corporation. See *Examples 5* and 6 of paragraph (k) of this section for illustrations of the rules of this paragraph (d).

(e) *Acquisitions of multiple domestic entities.*—If, pursuant to a plan (or a series of related transactions), a foreign corporation completes two or more domestic entity acquisitions involving domestic corporations and/or domestic partnerships (domestic entities), then, for purposes of section 7874(a)(2)(B)(ii), the acquisitions shall be treated as a single acquisition and the domestic entities shall be treated as a single domestic entity. If the transaction involves one or more domestic corporations and one or more domestic partnerships, the stock of the foreign corporation held by former domestic entity shareholders and former domestic entity partners by reason of holding stock or a partnership interest in the domestic entities shall be aggregated for purposes of determining whether the ownership condition of section 7874(a)(2)(B)(ii) is satisfied.

See *Example 7* of paragraph (k) of this section for an illustration of the rules of this paragraph (e).

(f) *Stock held by reason of holding stock in a domestic corporation or an interest in a domestic partnership.*—(1) *Certain transactions.*—For purposes of section 7874(a)(2)(B)(ii), stock of a foreign corporation that is held by reason of holding stock in a domestic corporation (or an interest in a domestic partnership) includes, but is not limited to, the stock described in paragraphs (f)(1)(i) through (iv) of this section.

(i) Stock of a foreign corporation received in exchange for, or with respect to, stock of a domestic corporation.

(ii) Stock of a foreign corporation received in exchange for, or with respect to, an interest in a domestic partnership.

(iii) To the extent that paragraph (f)(1)(ii) of this section does not apply, stock of a foreign corporation received by a domestic partnership in exchange for all or part of its properties. In such a case, each partner in the domestic partnership shall be treated as holding its proportionate share of the stock of the foreign corporation by reason of holding an interest in the domestic partnership.

(iv) Stock of a subsequent acquiring corporation received by a former initial acquiring corporation shareholder pursuant to a subsequent acquisition in exchange for, or with respect to, stock of an initial acquiring corporation that is held by reason of holding stock of, or a partnership interest in, a domestic entity.

(2) *Transactions involving other property.*—(i) *Stock of a domestic corporation.*—If, pursuant to the same transaction, stock of a foreign corporation is received in exchange for, or with respect to, stock of a domestic corporation and other property, the stock of the foreign corporation that was received in exchange for, or with respect to, the stock of the domestic corporation shall be determined based on the relative value of the stock of the domestic corporation compared to the aggregate value of such stock and the other property.

(ii) *Interest in a domestic partnership.*—If, pursuant to the same transaction, stock of a foreign corporation is received in exchange for, or with respect to, an interest in a domestic partnership and other property, the stock of the foreign corporation that was received in exchange for, or with respect to, the interest in the domestic partnership shall be determined based on the relative value of the interest in the domestic partnership compared to the aggregate value of such interest and the other property.

(3) See *Examples 8* through *10* of paragraph (k) of this section for illustrations of the rules of this paragraph (f).

(g) *Publicly traded foreign partnerships.*—(1) *Treatment as a foreign corporation.*—For purposes of section 7874, a publicly traded foreign partnership described in paragraph (g)(2) of this section shall be treated as a foreign corporation that is organized in the foreign country in which, or under the law of which, the publicly traded foreign partnership was created or organized, and the partnership interests in the publicly traded foreign partnership shall be treated as stock of the foreign corporation. For purposes of determining whether the foreign corporation shall be treated as a surrogate foreign corporation, a deemed acquisition of assets and liabilities by reason of §1.708-1(b)(4) shall not constitute an acquisition described in section 7874(a)(2)(B)(i).

(2) *Publicly traded foreign partnership.*—A publicly traded foreign partnership described in this paragraph (g)(2) is any foreign partnership that would, but for section 7704(c), be treated as a corporation under section 7704(a)—

(i) At the time of the domestic entity acquisition; or

(ii) At any time after the domestic entity acquisition pursuant to a plan that existed at the time of the domestic entity acquisition. For this purpose, a plan shall be deemed to exist at the time of the domestic entity acquisition if the foreign partnership would, but for section 7704(c), be treated as a corporation under section 7704(a) at any time during the two-year period following the completion of the domestic entity acquisition.

(3) *Surrogate foreign corporation to which section 7874(b) applies.*—If paragraph (g)(1) of this section applies to a publicly traded foreign partnership and the foreign corporation is a surrogate foreign corporation to which section 7874(b) applies, the publicly traded foreign partnership shall be treated as a domestic corporation for purposes of the Internal Revenue Code (Code). See paragraph (g)(6) of this section for the timing and treatment of the conversion of the publicly traded foreign partnership to a domestic corporation. See *Example 11* of paragraph (k) of this section for an illustration of the rules of this paragraph (g)(3).

(4) *Surrogate foreign corporation to which section 7874(b) does not apply.*—If paragraph (g)(1) of this section applies to a publicly traded foreign partnership and the foreign corporation is a surrogate foreign corporation to which section 7874(b) does not apply, the publicly traded foreign partnership shall continue to be treated as a foreign partnership for purposes of the Code, but section 7874(a)(1) shall apply to any expatriated entity (as defined in section 7874(a)(2)(A)). See *Example 13* of paragraph (k) of this section for an illustration of the rules of this paragraph (g)(4).

(5) *Foreign corporation not treated as a surrogate foreign corporation.*—If paragraph (g)(1) of this section applies to a publicly traded foreign partnership and the foreign corporation is not treated as a surrogate foreign corporation, the status of the publicly traded foreign partnership as a foreign partnership shall not be affected by section 7874. See *Example 12* of paragraph (k) of this section for an illustration of the rules of this paragraph (g)(5).

(6) *Conversion to a domestic corporation.*—Except for purposes of determining whether the publicly traded foreign partnership is a surrogate foreign corporation, if paragraph (g)(1) of this section applies to a publicly traded foreign partnership and the foreign corporation is a surrogate foreign corporation to which section 7874(b) applies, then at the later of the end of the day immediately preceding the first date properties are acquired as part of the domestic entity acquisition or immediately after the formation of the publicly traded foreign partnership, the publicly traded foreign partnership shall be treated as transferring all of its assets and liabilities to a newly formed domestic corporation in exchange solely for stock of the domestic corporation, and then distributing such stock to its partners in proportion to their partnership interests in liquidation of the partnership. The treatment of the transfer of assets and liabilities to the domestic corporation and the distribution of the stock of the domestic corporation to the partners in liquidation of the partnership shall be determined under all relevant provisions of the Code and general tax principles.

(h) *Options.*—(1) *Value.*—Except to the extent otherwise provided in this paragraph (h), for purposes of section 7874, including for purposes of determining the membership of an expanded affiliated group under section 7874(c)(1), an option with respect to a corporation or partnership will be treated as stock in the corporation, or an interest in the partnership, as applicable, with a value equal to the holder's claim on the equity of the corporation or partnership. For this purpose, claim on the equity equals the value of the stock or partnership interest that may be acquired pursuant to the option, less the exercise price (but in no case is a claim on the equity less than zero). Also for this purpose, the equity of the corporation or partnership shall not include the amount of any property the holder of the option would be required to provide to the corporation or partnership under the terms of the option if such option were exercised. See *Example 14* and *Example 16* of paragraph (k) of this section for illustrations of the rules of this paragraph (h)(1).

(2) *Voting power.*—Except to the extent otherwise provided in this paragraph (h), for purposes of determining the voting power of a foreign corporation under section 7874, including for purposes of determining the membership of an expanded affiliated group under section 7874(c)(1), an option will be treated as exercised only if a principal purpose of the issuance or transfer of the option is to avoid the foreign corporation being treated as a surrogate foreign corporation.

(3) *Timing.*—For purposes of this paragraph (h), the value of the holder's claim on the equity is determined—

(i) In the case of a domestic corporation or a domestic partnership, immediately before the domestic entity acquisition.

(ii) In the case of a foreign corporation or foreign partnership, immediately after the domestic entity acquisition.

(4) *Certain options disregarded.*—The rules of paragraph (h)(1) of this section shall not apply to an option if—

(i) A principal purpose of the issuance or acquisition of the option is to avoid the foreign corporation being treated as a surrogate foreign corporation, or

(ii) At the time of the domestic entity acquisition, the probability of the option being exercised is remote.

(5) *Options and interests similar to an option.*—For purposes of this paragraph (h), an option includes an interest similar to an option. Examples of options (including interests similar to options) include, but are not limited to, a warrant, a convertible debt instrument, an instrument other than debt that is convertible into stock or a partnership interest, a put, stock or a partnership interest subject to risk of forfeiture, a contract to acquire or sell stock or a partnership interest, and an exchangeable share or exchangeable partnership interest.

(6) *Multiple claims on equity.*—Paragraph (h)(1) of this section shall not apply to an option to the extent treating the option as stock or a partnership interest would duplicate a shareholder's or partner's claim on the equity of the corporation or partnership by reason of holding stock in the corporation or an interest in the partnership. See *Example 15* of paragraph (k) of this section for an illustration of the rules of this paragraph (h)(6).

(i) *Interests treated as stock of a foreign corporation.*—(1) *Stock or other interests.*—If the conditions of paragraphs (i)(1)(i) and (ii) of this section are satisfied, then, for purposes of section 7874, any interest (including stock or a partnership interest) that is not otherwise treated as stock of a foreign corporation (including under paragraph (h) of this section) shall be treated as stock of the foreign corporation. See *Examples 17* and *18* of paragraph (k) of this section for illustrations of the rules of this paragraph (i)(1).

(i) The interest provides the holder distribution rights that are substantially similar in all material respects to the distribution rights provided by stock in the foreign corporation. For this purpose, distribution rights include rights to dividends (or partnership distributions), distributions in redemption of the interest (in whole or in part), distributions in liquidation, or other similar distributions that represent a return on, or of, the holder's investment in the interest.

(ii) Treating the interest as stock of the foreign corporation has the effect of treating the foreign corporation as a surrogate foreign corporation under section 7874(a)(2)(B).

(2) *Creditor claims.*—(i) *Domestic corporation.*—For purposes of section 7874, if, immediately prior to the first date properties are acquired as part of a domestic entity acquisition, a domestic corporation is in a title 11 or similar case (as defined in section 368(a)(3)), or the liabilities of the domestic corporation exceed the value of its assets, then each creditor of the domestic corporation shall be treated as a shareholder of the domestic corporation and any claim of the creditor against the domestic corporation shall be treated as stock of the domestic corporation. See *Example 19* of paragraph (k) of this section for an illustration of the rules of this paragraph (i)(2)(i).

(ii) *Domestic or foreign partnership.*—For purposes of section 7874, if, immediately prior to the first date properties are acquired as part of a domestic entity acquisition, a partnership (foreign or domestic) is in a title 11 or similar case (as defined in section 368(a)(3)), or the liabilities of the partnership exceed the value of its assets, then each creditor of the partnership shall be treated as a partner in the partnership and any claim of the creditor against the partnership shall be treated as an interest in the partnership.

(iii) *Treatment of creditor as shareholder or partner.*—A creditor that is treated as a shareholder or partner under paragraph (i)(2)(i) or (ii) of this section shall be treated as a shareholder or partner for all purposes of section 7874. See, for example, § 1.7874-1(c) and paragraph (f) of this section. See *Example 19* of paragraph (k) of this section for an illustration of the rules of this paragraph (i)(2)(iii).

(j) *Application of section 7874(b).*—(1) *Conversion to a domestic corporation.*—Except for purposes of determining whether a foreign corporation is treated as a surrogate foreign corporation, the conversion of a foreign corporation to a domestic corporation by reason of section 7874(b) shall constitute a reorganization described in section 368(a)(1)(F) that occurs at the later of the end of the day immediately preceding the first date properties are acquired as part of the domestic entity acquisition or immediately after the formation of the foreign corporation. See, for example, §§ 1.367(b)-2 and 1.367(b)-3 for certain consequences of the reorganization. The treatment of all other aspects of the conversion shall be determined under the relevant provisions of the Code and general tax principles. See *Example 20* of paragraph (k) of this section for an illustration of the rules of this paragraph (j)(1).

(2) *Entity classification.*—A foreign corporation that is treated as a domestic corporation under section 7874(b) is not an eligible entity as defined in §301.7701-3(a), and therefore may not elect to be classified as other than an association (and thus cannot be treated as other than a corporation) for Federal tax purposes.

(3) *Application of section 367.*—If a foreign corporation is treated as a domestic corporation under section 7874(b), section 367 shall not apply

to any transfer of property by a United States person to such foreign corporation as part of the domestic entity acquisition. However, section 367 shall apply to the conversion of the foreign corporation to a domestic corporation. See paragraph (j)(1) of this section. See *Example 20* of paragraph (k) of this section for an illustration of the rules of this paragraph (j)(3).

(k) *Examples.*—(1) *Assumed facts.*—Except as otherwise stated, assume the following for purposes of the examples included in paragraph (k)(2) of this section.

(i) DC1 and DC2 are domestic corporations.

(ii) FA, FP, F1, F2, F3, and F4 are foreign corporations organized in Country A.

(iii) DPS is a domestic partnership that conducts a trade or business.

(iv) FPS is a foreign partnership that is not publicly traded.

(v) Under the terms of the partnership agreements of DPS and FPS, each partner's share in the partnership's items of income, gain, deduction, and loss is determined in accordance with the partner's partnership interest percentage in the partnership, as stated in the examples.

(vi) A, B, and C are unrelated individuals.

(vii) Each entity has a single class of equity outstanding and is unrelated to all other entities.

(viii) All transactions are completed pursuant to a plan.

(ix) All acquisitions of properties are completed after March 4, 2003.

(x) Section 7874(c)(4) does not apply, and no option is issued or acquired with a principal purpose to avoid a foreign corporation being treated as a surrogate foreign corporation.

(2) *Examples.*—The following examples illustrate the rules of this section.

Example 1. Acquisition of stock of a domestic corporation. (i) *Facts.* FA acquires 25% of the outstanding stock of DC1.

(ii) *Analysis.* Under paragraph (c)(1)(i) of this section, for purposes of section 7874(a)(2)(B)(i), FA is treated as acquiring 25% of the properties held by DC1 on the date of the stock acquisition.

Example 2. Acquisition of a partnership interest. (i) *Facts.* DPS wholly owns DC1. FA acquires a 40% interest in DPS.

(ii) *Analysis.* Under paragraph (c)(1)(ii) of this section, for purposes of section 7874(a)(2)(B)(i), FA is treated as acquiring 40 percent of the DC1 stock held by DPS on the date of the acquisition of the partnership interest. Further, under paragraph (c)(1)(i) of this section, for purposes of section 7874(a)(2)(B)(i), FA is treated as acquiring 40% of the properties held by DC1 on the date of the acquisition of the partnership interest.

Example 3. Acquisition of stock by a subsidiary. (i) *Facts.* FP wholly owns FA. FA acquires all the outstanding stock of DC1 in exchange solely for

FP stock. FP and FA are members of the same expanded affiliated group after the acquisition.

(ii) *Analysis.* Under paragraph (c)(1)(i) of this section, for purposes of section 7874(a)(2)(B)(i), FA is treated as acquiring 100% of the properties held by DC1 on the date of the stock acquisition. Further, under paragraph (c)(1)(iii) of this section, for purposes of section 7874(a)(2)(B)(i), FP is also treated as acquiring 100% of the properties held by DC1 on the date of the stock acquisition. The result would be the same if instead FA had directly acquired all the properties held by DC1 in exchange for FP stock.

Example 4. Acquisition of stock of a foreign corporation. (i) *Facts.* FP wholly owns DC1. FA acquires all of the outstanding stock of FP.

(ii) *Analysis.* Under paragraph (c)(2) of this section, for purposes of section 7874(a)(2)(B)(i), FA is not treated as acquiring any properties held by DC1 on the date of the acquisition of the FP stock.

Example 5. Acquisition of stock by multiple foreign corporations. (i) *Facts.* Pursuant to the same plan, the shareholders of DC1 transfer all of their DC1 stock equally to F1, F2, F3, and F4 in exchange solely for stock of each foreign corporation.

(ii) *Analysis.* Under paragraph (c)(1)(i) of this section, in the aggregate F1, F2, F3, and F4 are treated as acquiring substantially all of the properties held by DC1. Because the acquisition was pursuant to the same plan, under paragraph (d) of this section, F1, F2, F3, and F4 are each treated as acquiring substantially all of the properties held by DC1 for purposes of determining whether each foreign corporation shall be treated as a surrogate foreign corporation.

Example 6. Acquisition of assets by multiple foreign corporations. (i) *Facts.* Individual A wholly owns DC1. DC1 forms F1, F2, F3, and F4, and transfers an equal portion of its properties to each corporation in exchange solely for stock of the corporation. Pursuant to the same plan DC1 then distributes the stock of each foreign corporation to individual A.

(ii) *Analysis.* Because pursuant to the same plan F1, F2, F3, and F4 acquired, in the aggregate, substantially all of the properties held by DC1, under paragraph (d) of this section, F1, F2, F3, and F4 are each treated as acquiring substantially all of the properties held by DC1 for purposes of determining whether each foreign corporation shall be treated as a surrogate foreign corporation.

Example 7. Acquisition of multiple domestic corporations. (i) *Facts.* Individual A wholly owns DC1, and individual B wholly owns DC2. Pursuant to the same plan, individuals A and B transfer all of their DC1 stock and DC2 stock to FA, a newly formed corporation, in exchange solely for all 100 shares of FA stock outstanding.

(ii) *Analysis.* Under paragraph (c)(1)(i) of this section, for purposes of section 7874(a)(2)(B)(i), FA is treated as acquiring all of the properties held by DC1 and DC2 on the date of the stock acquisition. Under paragraph (e) of this section, because pursuant to the same plan FA acquired substantially all of the properties held by DC1 and DC2, for purposes of determining whether FA shall be treated as a surrogate foreign corporation, DC1 and DC2 shall be treated as a single domestic corporation, of which individuals A and B are former domestic entity shareholders. Thus, individuals A and B are treated as holding all 100 shares of the FA stock by reason of holding stock of such domestic corporation, and the ownership fraction under section 7874(a)(2)(B)(ii) is 100/100, or 100%.

Example 8. Exchange of stock and other property. (i) *Facts.* Individual A wholly owns DC1 and F1. DC1 has a $40x value and F1 has a $60x value. Individual A transfers all of the DC1 stock and F1 stock to FA, a newly formed corporation, in exchange solely for FA stock.

(ii) *Analysis.* Under paragraphs (f)(1)(i) and (f)(2)(i) of this section, for purposes of section 7874(a)(2)(B)(ii), individual A is considered to hold 40% of the FA stock by reason of holding stock in DC1 ($100x FA stock multiplied by $40x/$100x, the relative value of the DC1 stock to all the property transferred by A to FA).

Example 9. Stock received as a distribution. (i) *Facts.* Pursuant to a divisive reorganization described in section 368(a)(1)(D), DC1 contributes substantially all of its properties to FA, a newly formed corporation, in exchange solely for FA stock and then distributes the FA stock to its shareholders in a transaction qualifying under section 355.

(ii) *Analysis.* Under paragraph (f)(1)(i) of this section, for purposes of section 7874(a)(2)(B)(ii), the FA stock received by the DC1 shareholders as a distribution with respect to the DC1 stock is considered held by reason of holding stock in DC1. The result would be the same if the transaction did not qualify as a reorganization (for example, if the distribution were subject to sections 301 and 311(b)).

Example 10. Incorporation of a partnership trade or business. (i) *Facts.* Individuals A and B equally own DPS. DPS transfers substantially all of its properties constituting a trade or business to FA, a newly formed corporation, solely in exchange for FA stock. DPS retains the FA stock after the transaction.

(ii) *Analysis.* Under paragraph (f)(1)(iii) of this section, for purposes of section 7874(a)(2)(B)(ii), individuals A and B are treated as holding a proportionate amount (that is, an equal amount) of the FA stock held by DPS by reason of holding an interest in DPS.

Example 11. Publicly traded foreign partnership treated as domestic corporation. (i) *Facts.* Pursuant to a plan, DC1 and individual B organize a limited liability company (HPS) under the law of Country A. DC1 owns 90% of the membership interests in HPS, and B owns 10% of the membership interests in HPS. HPS is a foreign eligible entity under §301.7701-2, and DC1 and B make an election under §301.7701-3 to treat HPS as a partnership for Federal tax purposes as of the date of the formation of HPS. HPS forms DC2. One day after the formation of HPS, DC2 merges with and into DC1. Pursuant to the merger agreement, the DC1 shareholders exchange their DC1 stock solely for membership interests in HPS. After the merger HPS wholly owns DC1, and the former domestic entity shareholders of DC1 own a greater than 80% interest in HPS by reason of holding stock of DC1. Public trading of the HPS ownership interests begins the day after the date on which the merger is completed. HPS is not treated as a corporation under section 7704(a) by reason of section 7704(c). If HPS were a corporation, the condition of section 7874(a)(2)(B)(iii) would be satisfied.

(ii) *Analysis.* HPS is a publicly traded foreign partnership that is described in paragraph (g)(2) of this section. Therefore, under paragraph (g)(1) of this section, for purposes of section 7874, HPS is treated as a foreign corporation organized under the law of Country A and the membership interests in HPS are treated as stock of the foreign corporation. The foreign corporation is treated as a surrogate foreign corporation under section 7874(a)(2)(B) because, pursuant to the merger, HPS acquired substantially all of the properties held by DC1, the former domestic entity shareholders of DC1 hold at least 60% of the stock of the foreign corporation by reason of holding stock of DC1, and the expanded affiliated group that includes the foreign corporation does not have substantial business activities in Country A when compared to the total business activities of the expanded affiliated group. Further, because the former domestic entity shareholders of DC1 hold at least 80% of the stock of the foreign corporation by reason of holding stock of DC1, section 7874(b) applies to the surrogate foreign corporation, and therefore HPS is treated as a domestic corporation for purposes of the Code. Under paragraph (g)(6) of this section, except for purposes of determining whether HPS is a surrogate foreign corporation, at the end of the day immediately preceding the date of the merger of DC2 with and into DC1, HPS is treated as transferring all of its assets and liabilities to a new domestic corporation in exchange solely for stock of the domestic corporation. HPS is then treated as proportionately distributing such stock to its membership interest holders in liquidation of the partnership. In addition, as a result of the merger of DC2 with and into DC1, the former domestic entity shareholders of DC1 shall be treated as receiving stock of a domestic corporation in exchange for their DC1 stock.

Example 12. Publicly traded foreign partnership not treated as a surrogate foreign corporation. (i) *Facts.* The facts are the same as in *Example 11* of this section, except that, after the domestic entity acquisition, the expanded affiliated group that includes HPS (treated as a foreign corporation for this purpose) has substantial business activities in Country A when compared to the total business activities of the expanded affiliated group.

(ii) *Analysis.* Under paragraph (g)(1) of this section, for purposes of section 7874, HPS is treated as a foreign corporation and the membership interests in HPS are treated as stock of the foreign corporation. However, the foreign corporation is not treated as a surrogate foreign corporation under section 7874(a)(2)(B) because, after the domestic entity acquisition, the expanded affiliated group that includes HPS has substantial business activities in Country A when compared to the total business activities of the expanded affiliated group. Therefore, under paragraph (g)(5) of this section, section 7874 does not apply and the status of HPS as a foreign partnership is not affected. In addition, DC1 is not treated as an expatriated entity under section 7874(a) by reason of the domestic entity acquisition.

Example 13. Publicly traded foreign partnership treated as a surrogate foreign corporation but not as a domestic corporation. (i) *Facts.* FPS is a publicly traded foreign partnership organized in Country A that, by reason of section 7704(c), is not treated as a corporation under section 7704(a). FPS acquires all the stock of DC1 in exchange for partnership interests in FPS. After the acquisition, the former domestic entity shareholders of DC1 hold a 75%-interest in FPS by reason of holding DC1 stock. After the acquisition, the expanded affiliated group that includes FPS (treated as a foreign corporation for this purpose) does not have substantial business activities in Country A when compared to the total business activities of the expanded affiliated group.

(ii) *Analysis.* Under paragraph (g)(1) of this section, for purposes of section 7874, FPS is treated as a foreign corporation and the partnership interests in FPS are treated as stock of the foreign corporation. FPS is treated as a surrogate foreign corporation because the conditions of section 7874(a)(2)(B) are satisfied. However, because the former domestic entity shareholders of DC1 hold less than an 80%-interest in FPS by reason of holding DC1 stock, section 7874(b) does not apply to FPS. Therefore, under paragraph (g)(4) of this section FPS continues to be treated as a foreign partnership for purposes of the Code, but section 7874(a)(1) applies to DC1 and any other expatriated entity.

Example 14. Warrant to acquire stock from the foreign corporation. (i) *Facts.* Individual A wholly owns DC1. DC1 has a $200x value. Individual B wholly owns FA. The value of B's FA stock is $400x. Individual C holds a warrant to acquire FA stock from FA at an exercise price of $20x. Individual A transfers all of its DC1 stock to FA in exchange solely for FA stock with a value of $200x. At the time of the transfer, the FA stock that individual C can acquire pursuant to the warrant has a $70x value.

(ii) *Analysis.* Under paragraphs (h)(1) of this section, for purposes of section 7874, individual C is treated as owning FA stock with a $50x value. This amount represents individual C's claim on the equity of FA after the domestic entity acquisition ($70x value of FA stock that may be acquired pursuant to the warrant, less the $20x exercise price), without taking into account the $20x individual C would be required

Reg. §1.7874-2(k)(2)

to provide to FA upon the exercise of the warrant. Thus, for purposes of section 7874, the value of the stock of FA immediately after the transaction is $650x ($600x of FA stock, plus C's $50x claim on the equity of FA). C's warrant is not taken into account for purposes of determining the voting power of FA under section 7874.

Example 15. Option to acquire stock from another shareholder. (i) *Facts.* The facts are the same as in *Example 14* except that, instead of holding a warrant issued by FA, individual C holds an option to acquire FA stock from individual B for an exercise price of $20x. At the time of the domestic entity acquisition, the FA stock that individual C can acquire under the option has a $70x value.

(ii) *Analysis.* Under paragraph (h)(6) of this section, for purposes of section 7874, individual C is not treated as owning FA stock by reason of holding the option because treating the option as FA stock would have the effect of partially duplicating individual B's claim on the equity of FA at the time of the domestic entity acquisition by reason of holding FA stock. However, all of the FA stock owned by individual B will be taken into account for purposes of section 7874. C's warrant is not taken into account for purposes of determining voting power of FA under section 7874.

Example 16. Warrant to acquire stock from the domestic corporation. (i) *Facts.* A DC1 employee holds a warrant to acquire DC1 stock from DC1. In connection with the domestic entity acquisition by FA of substantially all of the properties held by DC1, the DC1 employee receives a warrant from FA to acquire 15 shares of FA stock in exchange for the warrant to acquire DC1 stock.

(ii) *Analysis.* Under paragraphs (h)(1) of this section, for purposes of section 7874, the warrant held by the DC1 employee is treated as DC1 stock with a value equal to the employee's claim on the equity of DC1 immediately before the domestic entity acquisition. Further, for purposes of section 7874, the DC1 employee is treated as holding FA stock with a value equal to the employee's claim on the equity of FA after the domestic entity acquisition by reason of holding the warrant to acquire DC1 stock (treated as DC1 stock for this purpose). The option held by the DC1 employee is not taken into account for purposes of determining the voting power of FA under section 7874.

Example 17. Stock in a subsidiary treated as stock of a foreign parent corporation. (i) *Facts.* (A) Individuals A and B equally own DC1. FA, a newly formed corporation, issues stock in a public offering for cash. FA contributes part of the cash from the public offering to DC2, a newly formed corporation, in exchange for all the stock of DC2. DC2 merges with and into DC1 with DC1 surviving. Pursuant to the merger agreement, individuals A and B exchange their DC1 stock for cash and shares of class B stock of DC1. Following the merger FA owns all the class A stock of DC1. FA does not hold significant assets other than the class A stock of DC1. Individuals

A and B own all the class B stock of DC1. DC1 has no other class of stock outstanding.

(B) The class B stock entitles individuals A and B to dividend distributions approximately equal to any dividend distributions made by FA with respect to its publicly traded stock. In certain circumstances, the class B stock also permits individuals A and B to require DC1 to redeem the stock at fair market value. The class B stock does not provide individuals A and B voting rights with respect to FA.

(ii) *Analysis.* The dividend rights provided by the class B stock are substantially similar in all material respects to the dividend rights provided by the FA stock. In addition, because FA does not hold significant assets other than the class A stock, the value of the class B stock held by individuals A and B is approximately equal to the value of a corresponding amount of publicly traded FA stock. The distribution rights on liquidation (or redemption) provided by the class B stock, therefore, are substantially similar in all material respects to the distribution rights on liquidation (or redemption) provided by the FA stock. As a result, the distribution rights provided by the class B stock are substantially similar in all material respects to the distribution rights provided by the publicly traded FA stock. Thus, if treating the class B stock as FA stock would have the effect of treating FA as a surrogate foreign corporation, under paragraph (i)(1) of this section the class B stock will be treated as FA stock for purposes of section 7874.

Example 18. Partnership interest treated as stock of foreign acquiring corporation. (i) *Facts.* (A) Individuals A and B equally own DC1. FA, a newly formed corporation, issues stock in a public offering for cash. Individuals A and B and FA organize FPS. FA transfers part of the cash from the public offering to FPS in exchange for a class A partnership interest. FA does not hold any significant assets other than the class A partnership interest. Individuals A and B transfer their DC1 stock to FPS in exchange for class B partnership interests.

(B) The class B partnership interests entitle individuals A and B to cash distributions from FPS approximately equal to any dividend distributions made by FA with respect to its publicly traded stock. In certain circumstances, the class B partnership interests also permit individuals A and B to require FPS to redeem the interests in exchange for cash equal to the value of an amount of FA stock as determined on the redemption date. The class B partnership interests do not provide individuals A or B voting rights with respect to FA.

(ii) *Analysis.* The non-liquidating distribution rights provided by the class B partnership interests are substantially similar in all material respects to the dividend rights provided by the FA stock. Because FA does not hold any significant assets other than the class A partnership interest, the value of the class B partnership interests held by individuals A and B is approximately equal to a corresponding amount of FA stock. The distribution rights on liquidation (or redemption) provided by the class B partnership interests, therefore, are substantially similar in all material respects to distribution rights on liquidation (or redemption) provided by the FA stock. Thus, the distribution rights provided by the class B partnership interests are substantially similar in all material respects to the distribution rights provided by the publicly traded FA stock. As a result, if treating the class B partnership interests as FA stock would have the effect of treating FA as a surrogate foreign corporation, under paragraph (i)(1) of this section the class B partnership interests will be treated as FA stock for purposes of section 7874.

Example 19. Creditor treated as a shareholder. (i) *Facts.* Individuals A and B equally own DC1. The liabilities of DC1 exceed the value of its assets. Pursuant to a plan, FA, a newly formed corporation, acquires substantially all of the properties held by DC1 in exchange solely for FA stock. Pursuant to the plan, the DC1 stock held by individuals A and B is cancelled, and the creditors of DC1 receive all the FA stock in exchange for their claims against DC1.

(ii) *Analysis.* Because immediately before the first date on which properties are acquired as part of the domestic entity acquisition the liabilities of DC1 exceed the value of its assets, under paragraph (i)(2)(i) of this section, for purposes of section 7874, the creditors of DC1 are treated as shareholders of DC1 and the creditors' claims against DC1 are treated as DC1 stock. Therefore, for purposes of section 7874(a)(2)(B)(ii), the FA stock received by the creditors of DC1 by reason of their claims against DC1 is considered held by former domestic entity shareholders of DC1 by reason of holding DC1 stock.

Example 20. Conversion to a domestic corporation and application of section 367. (i) *Facts.* Individuals A and B are United States persons and equally own DC1. Pursuant to a plan, individuals A and B transfer their DC1 stock to FA in exchange solely for 80% of the outstanding FA stock. After the acquisition, the expanded affiliated group that includes FA does not have substantial business activities in Country A when compared to the total business activities of the expanded affiliated group.

(ii) *Analysis.* Under paragraph (c)(1)(i) of this section, for purposes of section 7874(a)(2)(B)(i), FA is treated as acquiring all of the properties held by DC1 on the date of the stock acquisition. After the acquisition, the former domestic entity shareholders of DC1 own 80% of the stock of FA by reason of holding DC1 stock. Therefore, FA is a surrogate foreign corporation that is treated as a domestic corporation under section 7874(b). Under paragraph (j)(1) of this section, except for purposes of determining whether FA is treated as a surrogate foreign corporation, the conversion of FA to a domestic corporation constitutes a reorganization described in section 368(a)(1)(F) that occurs at the end of the day immediately preceding the date of the stock acquisition. Section 367 applies to the conversion of FA to a domestic corporation.

See, for example, § § 1.367(b)-2 and 1.367(b)-3 for the consequences of the conversion. Under paragraph (j)(3) of this section, section 367 does not apply to the transfers of DC1 stock by individuals A and B to FA.

Example 21. Application of multiple-step acquisition rule—(i) *Facts.* Individual A owns all 70 shares of stock of DC1, a domestic corporation. Individual B owns all 30 shares of stock of F1, a foreign corporation that is a tax resident (as described in § 1.7874-3(d)(11)) of Country X. Pursuant to a reorganization described in section 368(a)(1)(D), DC1 transfers all of its properties to F1 solely in exchange for 70 newly issued voting shares of F1 stock (DC1 acquisition) and distributes the F1 stock to Individual A in liquidation pursuant to section 361(c)(1). Pursuant to a plan that includes the DC1 acquisition, F2, a newly formed foreign corporation that is also a tax resident of Country X, acquires 100 percent of the stock of F1 solely in exchange for 100 newly issued shares of F2 stock (F1 acquisition). After the F1 acquisition, Individual A owns 70 shares of F2 stock, Individual B owns 30 shares of F2 stock, F2 owns all 100 shares of F1 stock, and F1 owns all the properties held by DC1 immediately before the DC1 acquisition. In addition, the form of the transaction is respected for U.S. federal income tax purposes.

(ii) *Analysis*—(A) The DC1 acquisition is a domestic entity acquisition, and F1 is a foreign acquiring corporation, because F1 directly acquires 100 percent of the properties of DC1. In addition, the 70 shares of F1 stock received by A pursuant to the DC1 acquisition in exchange for Individual A's DC1 stock are stock of a foreign corporation that is held by reason of holding stock in DC1. As a result, those 70 shares are included in both the numerator and the denominator of the ownership fraction when applying section 7874 to the DC1 acquisition.

(B) The DC1 acquisition is also an initial acquisition because it is a domestic entity acquisition that, pursuant to a plan that includes the F1 acquisition, occurs before the F1 acquisition (which, as described in paragraph (ii)(C) of this *Example 21*, is a subsequent acquisition). Thus, F1 is the initial acquiring corporation.

(C) The F1 acquisition is a subsequent acquisition because it occurs, pursuant to a plan that includes the DC1 acquisition, after the DC1 acquisition and, pursuant to the F1 acquisition, F2 acquires 100 percent of the stock of F1 and therefore is treated under paragraph (c)(4)(ii) of this section (which applies the principles of section 7874(a)(2)(B)(i) with certain modifications) as indirectly acquiring substantially all of the properties held directly or indirectly by F1. Thus, F2 is the subsequent acquiring corporation.

(D) Under paragraph (c)(4)(i) of this section, the F1 acquisition is treated as a domestic entity acquisition, and F2 is treated as a foreign acquiring corporation. In addition, under paragraph (f)(1)(iv) of this section, the 70 shares of F2 stock received by Individual A (a former initial acquiring corporation shareholder) pursuant to the F1 acquisition in exchange for Individual A's F1 stock are stock of a foreign corporation that is held by reason of holding stock in DC1. As a result, those 70 shares are included in both the numerator and the denominator of the ownership fraction when applying section 7874 to the F1 acquisition.

(l) *Applicability date.*—(1) *In general.*—This section applies to domestic entity acquisitions completed on or after June 7, 2012. For domestic entity acquisitions completed prior to June 7, 2012, see §1.7874-2T(o), as contained in 26 CFR part 1, revised as of April 1, 2012.

(2) *Applicability date of certain provisions of this section.*—Paragraphs (a), (b)(7) through (13), (c)(2) and (4), and (f)(1)(iv) of this section, as well as the introductory text of paragraph (f)(1) and *Example 21* of paragraph (k)(2), apply to domestic entity acquisitions completed on or after April 4, 2016. [Reg. §1.7874-2.]

☐ [T.D. 9591, 6-7-2012. *Amended by T.D. 9761,* 4-4-2016 *and T.D. 9834,* 7-11-2018.]

[Reg. §1.7874-3]

§1.7874-3. Substantial business activities.— (a) *Scope.*—This section provides rules regarding when an expanded affiliated group will be considered to have substantial business activities in the relevant foreign country when compared to the total business activities of the expanded affiliated group for purposes of section 7874(a)(2)(B)(iii). Paragraph (b) of this section describes the general rule for determining whether the expanded affiliated group has substantial business activities in the relevant foreign country when compared to its total business activities. Paragraph (c) of this section describes certain items that are not taken into account as located or derived in the relevant foreign country. Paragraph (d) of this section provides definitions and certain rules of application. Paragraph (e) of this section provides rules regarding the treatment of partnerships for purposes of this section. Paragraph (f) of this section provides the effective/applicability dates.

(b) *General rule.*—The expanded affiliated group will be considered to have substantial business activities in the relevant foreign country on the completion date when compared to the total business activities of the expanded affiliated group only if, subject to paragraph (c) of this section, each of the requirements of this paragraph (b) are satisfied.

(1) *Group employees.*—(i) *Number of employees.*—The number of group employees based in the relevant foreign country is at least 25 percent of the total number of group employees on the applicable date.

(ii) *Employee compensation.*—The employee compensation incurred with respect to group employees based in the relevant foreign country is at least 25 percent of the total employee compensation incurred with respect to all group employees during the testing period.

(2) *Group assets.*—The value of the group assets located in the relevant foreign country is at least 25 percent of the total value of all group assets on the applicable date.

(3) *Group income.*—The group income derived in the relevant foreign country is at least 25 percent of the total group income during the testing period.

(4) *Tax residence of foreign acquiring corporation.*—The foreign acquiring corporation is a tax resident of the relevant foreign country. However, this paragraph (b)(4) does not apply if the relevant foreign country does not impose corporate income tax.

(c) *Items not to be considered.*—(1) *General rule.*—Except to the extent provided in paragraph (c)(2) of this section, the following items are not taken into account in the numerator, but are taken into account in the denominator, for each of the tests described in paragraphs (b)(1) through (3) of this section:

(i) Any group assets, group employees, or group income attributable to business activities that are associated with properties or liabilities the transfer of which is disregarded under section 7874(c)(4).

(ii) Any group assets or group employees located in, or group income derived in, the relevant foreign country as part of a plan with a principal purpose of avoiding the purposes of section 7874.

(iii) Any group assets or group employees located in, or group income derived in, the relevant foreign country if such group assets or group employees, or the business activities to which such group income is attributable, are subsequently transferred to another country in connection with a plan that existed at the time of the domestic entity acquisition.

(2) *Transfers of properties to the expanded affiliated group.*—Any group assets, group employees, or group income attributable to business activities that are associated with property that is transferred to the expanded affiliated group in a transfer that is disregarded under section 7874(c)(4) are not taken into account in the numerator or the denominator for each of the tests described in paragraphs (b)(1) through (3) of this section.

(d) *Definitions and special rules.*—In addition to the definitions in §1.7874-12, the following definitions and special rules apply for purposes of this section.

(1) The term *applicable date* means either of the following dates, applied consistently for all purposes of this section:

(i) The completion date; or

(ii) The last day of the month immediately preceding the month that includes the completion date.

(2) The term *employee compensation* means all amounts incurred by members of the expanded affiliated group that directly relate to services performed by group employees (includ-

ing, for example, wages, salaries, deferred compensation, employee benefits, and employer payroll taxes). Employee compensation with respect to a particular group employee is treated as incurred when it would be deductible by the employer as compensation, and the amount of employee compensation equals the amount that would be deductible by the employer as compensation. Both the timing and the amount of the deduction for employee compensation must be determined for all group employees under U.S. federal income tax principles or for all group employees based on the relevant tax laws. Employee compensation is determined in U.S. dollars, translated, if necessary, using the weighted average exchange rate (as defined in § 1.989(b)-1) for the testing period.

(3) The term *group assets* means tangible personal property or real property used or held for use in the active conduct of a trade or business by members of the expanded affiliated group, provided such property is either owned or, in the circumstances described below, rented by members of the expanded affiliated group at the close of the completion date. A group asset is considered to be located in the relevant foreign country only if the asset was physically present in such country at the close of the completion date and the asset was physically present in such country for more time than in any other country during the testing period. Notwithstanding the foregoing, a group asset that is mobile in nature and is used in a transportation activity, such as a vessel, an aircraft, or a motor vehicle, is considered to be located in the relevant foreign country if the asset was physically present in such country for more time than in any other country during the testing period, regardless of whether the asset was physically present in such country at the close of the completion date. Group assets must be valued on a gross basis (that is, not reduced by liabilities) by consistently using for all group assets of the expanded affiliated group either the adjusted tax basis or fair market value determined in U.S. dollars, translated, if necessary, at the spot rate determined under the principles of § 1.988-1(d)(1), (2), and (4). Tangible personal property or real property that is rented by members of the expanded affiliated group from a person other than a member of the expanded affiliated group is also treated as a group asset, provided such property is used in the active conduct of a trade or business and is being rented by members of the expanded affiliated group at the close of the completion date. For purposes of this section, a group asset that is rented is valued at eight times the net annual rent paid or accrued with respect to the property by members of the expanded affiliated group.

(4) The term *group employees* means all individuals who are employees of members of the expanded affiliated group. Whether individuals are employees must be determined for all members of the expanded affiliated group under U.S. federal tax principles or for all members of the expanded affiliated group based on the relevant tax laws. A group employee is considered to be

based in the relevant foreign country only if the employee spent more time providing services in such country than in any other single country during the testing period.

(5) The term *group income* means gross income of members of the expanded affiliated group from transactions occurring in the ordinary course of business with customers that are not related persons. Group income must be determined consistently for all members of the expanded affiliated group either under U.S. federal income tax principles or as reflected in the relevant financial statements. Group income is translated into U.S. dollars, if necessary, using the weighted average exchange rate (as defined in § 1.989(b)-1) for the testing period. Group income is considered derived in the relevant foreign country only if it is derived from a transaction with a customer located in such country.

(6) The term *net annual rent* means the annual rent paid or accrued with respect to property, less any payments received or accrued from subleasing such property (or other similar arrangement).

(7) The term *related person* has the meaning specified in section 954(d)(3), except that section 954(d)(3) is applied by substituting "one or more members of the expanded affiliated group" for "a controlled foreign corporation" and "the controlled foreign corporation" each place they appear.

(8) The term *relevant financial statements* means financial statements prepared consistently for all members of the expanded affiliated group in accordance with either U.S. Generally Accepted Accounting Principles (U.S. GAAP) or the International Financial Reporting Standards (IFRS) used for the expanded affiliated group's consolidated financial statements, but, if, after the domestic entity acquisition, financial statements will not be prepared consistently for all members of the expanded affiliated group in accordance with either U.S. GAAP or IFRS, then, for each member, financial statements prepared in accordance with either U.S. GAAP or IFRS. The relevant financial statements must take into account all items of income generated by all members of the expanded affiliated group for the entire testing period.

(9) The term *relevant foreign country* means the foreign country in which, or under the law of which, the foreign acquiring corporation was created or organized.

(10) The term *relevant tax law* means, for purposes of determining whether a particular individual who performs services for a member of the expanded affiliated group is an employee for purposes of paragraph (d)(6) of this section and the timing and amount of employee compensation for a particular employee of a member of the expanded affiliated group for purposes of paragraph (d)(3) of this section, the tax law to which the member is subject. Notwithstanding the foregoing, if the tax law to which a member is subject does not distinguish between whether an individual is an employee, or, for example, an

independent contractor, then for this purpose the relevant tax law is considered to be U.S. federal tax law.

(11) The term *tax resident* means, with respect to a foreign country, a body corporate liable to tax under the laws of the country as a resident.

(12) The term *testing period* means the one-year period ending on the applicable date.

(e) *Treatment of partnerships.*—(1) *Stock held by a partnership.*—In determining the members of the expanded affiliated group for purposes of this section, each partner in a partnership, as determined without regard to the application of paragraph (e)(2) of this section, shall be treated as holding its proportionate share of the stock held by the partnership, as determined under the rules and principles of sections 701 through 777.

(2) *Business activities of a partnership.*—For purposes of this section, if one or more members of the expanded affiliated group, as determined after the application of paragraph (e)(1) of this section, own, in the aggregate, more than 50 percent (by value) of the interests in a partnership, the partnership will be treated as a corporation that is a member of the expanded affiliated group. Thus, all items of such a partnership are taken into account for purposes of this section. No items of a partnership are taken into account for purposes of this section unless the partnership is treated as a member of the expanded affiliated group pursuant to this paragraph (e)(2).

(f) *Applicability dates.*—(1) *General rule.*—Except as otherwise provided in paragraph (f)(2) of this section, this section applies to domestic entity acquisitions that are completed on or after June 3, 2015. For domestic entity acquisitions completed before June 3, 2015, see §1.7874-3T as contained in 26 CFR part 1 revised as of April 1, 2016.

(2) *Paragraphs (b)(4), (d)(8), and (d)(11) of this section.*—The first sentence of paragraph (b)(4) of this section applies to domestic entity acquisitions completed on or after November 19, 2015, and the second sentence applies to domestic entity acquisitions completed on or after July 12, 2018. Paragraph (d)(8) of this section applies to domestic entity acquisitions completed on or after April 4, 2016. Paragraph (d)(11) of this section applies to domestic entity acquisitions completed on or after July 12, 2018. For domestic entity acquisitions completed on or after June 3, 2015, and before April 4, 2016, however, taxpayers may elect to apply paragraph (d)(8) of this section. For domestic entity acquisitions completed on or after November 19, 2015, and before July 12, 2018, taxpayers may elect to apply the second sentence of paragraph (b)(4) and paragraph (d)(11) of this section. [Reg. §1.7874-3.]

☐ [T.D. 9720, 6-3-2015. *Amended by T.D. 9761,* 4-4-2016 *and T.D. 9834,* 7-11-2018.]

[Reg. §1.7874-4]

§1.7874-4. Disregard of certain stock related to the domestic entity acquisition.—(a) *Scope.*—This section identifies certain stock of the foreign acquiring corporation that is disregarded in determining the ownership fraction and modifies the scope of section 7874(c)(2)(B). Paragraph (b) of this section sets forth the general rule that certain stock of the foreign acquiring corporation, and only such stock, is treated as stock described in section 7874(c)(2)(B) and therefore is excluded from the denominator of the ownership fraction. Paragraph (c) of this section identifies the stock of the foreign acquiring corporation that is subject to paragraph (b) of this section. Paragraph (d) of this section provides a de minimis exception to the application of the general exclusion rule of paragraph (b) of this section. Paragraph (e) of this section provides rules for transfers of stock of the foreign acquiring corporation in satisfaction of, or in exchange for the assumption of, one or more obligations of the transferor. Paragraph (f) of this section provides rules for certain transfers of stock of the foreign acquiring corporation involving multiple properties or obligations. Paragraph (g) of this section provides rules for the treatment of partnerships, and paragraph (h) of this section provides definitions. Paragraph (h) of this section provides definitions. Paragraph (i) of this section provides examples illustrating the application of the rules of this section. Paragraph (j) of this section provides dates of applicability. See §1.7874-1(d)(1) for rules addressing the interaction of this section with the expanded affiliated group rules of section 7874(c)(2)(A) and §1.7874-1.

(b) *Exclusion of disqualified stock under section 7874(c)(2)(B).*—Except as provided in paragraph (d) of this section, disqualified stock (as determined under paragraph (c) of this section) is treated as stock described in section 7874(c)(2)(B) and therefore is not included in the denominator of the ownership fraction. Section 7874(c)(2)(B) shall not apply to exclude stock from the denominator of the ownership fraction that is not disqualified stock.

(c) *Disqualified stock.*—(1) *General rule.*—Except as provided in paragraph (c)(2) of this section, disqualified stock is stock of the foreign acquiring corporation (other than stock described in §1.7874-2(f)) that is transferred in an exchange described in paragraph (c)(1)(i) or (ii) of this section that is related to the domestic entity acquisition. This paragraph (c) applies without regard to whether the stock of the foreign acquiring corporation is publicly traded at the time of the transfer or at any other time.

(i) *Exchanged for nonqualified property.*—The stock is transferred to a person other than the domestic entity in exchange for nonqualified property. See *Example 1, Example 2, Example 6, Example 8,* and *Example 9* of paragraph (i) of this section for illustrations of the application of this paragraph (c)(1)(i).

(ii) *Exchanged for property with associated obligations.*—(A) *General rule.*—Subject to the limitation provided in in paragraph (c)(1)(ii)(B) of this section, the stock is transferred by a person (transferor) to another person (transferee) in exchange for property (exchanged property) and, pursuant to the same plan (or series of related transactions), the transferee subsequently transfers such stock (or, if the transferee exchanges such stock for other property, such other property) in satisfaction of, or in exchange for the assumption of, one or more obligations of the transferee or a person related (within the meaning of section 267 or 707(b)) to the transferee. See *Example 6* and *Example 10* of paragraph (i) of this section for illustrations of the application of paragraph (c)(1)(ii) of this section.

(B) *Limitation.*—The amount of stock treated as transferred in an exchange described in paragraph (c)(2)(ii)(A) of this section shall not exceed—

(1) With respect to a transferee that is the domestic entity, the proportionate share of obligations associated with the exchanged property (determined based on the fair market value of the exchanged property relative to the fair market value of all properties with which the obligations are associated) that, pursuant to the same plan (or series of related transactions), is not assumed by the transferor.

(2) With respect to any other transferee, the proportionate share of obligations associated with the exchanged property (determined based on the fair market value of the exchanged property relative to the fair market value of all properties with which the obligations are associated) that, pursuant to the same plan (or series of related transactions), is not assumed by the transferor, multiplied by a fraction, the numerator of which is the amount of exchanged property that is qualified property, and the denominator of which is the total amount of exchanged property.

(C) *Associated obligations.*—For purposes of paragraph (c)(1)(ii) of this section, an obligation is associated with property if, for example, the obligation arose from the conduct of a trade or business in which the property has been used, regardless of whether the obligation is a non-recourse obligation.

(2) *Stock transferred in an exchange that does not increase the fair market value of the assets or decrease the amount of liabilities of the foreign acquiring corporation.*—Stock is disqualified stock only to the extent that the transfer of the stock in the exchange increases the fair market value of the assets of the foreign acquiring corporation or decreases the amount of its liabilities. This paragraph (c)(2) is applied to an exchange without regard to any other exchange described in paragraph (c)(1)(i) or (ii) of this section or any other transaction related to the domestic entity acquisition. See *Example 4* and *Example 7* of paragraph (i) of this section for illustrations of the application of this paragraph (c)(2).

(d) *Exception to exclusion of disqualified stock.*—(1) *De minimis ownership.*—Except as provided in paragraph (d)(2) of this section, paragraph (b) of this section does not apply if both:

(i) The ownership percentage described in section 7874(a)(2)(B)(ii), determined without regard to the application of paragraph (b) of this section and §§1.7874-7(b) and 1.7874-10(b), is less than five (by vote and value); and

(ii) On the completion date, each five percent former domestic entity shareholder or five percent former domestic entity partner, as applicable, owns (applying the attribution rules of section 318(a) with the modifications described in section 304(c)(3)(B)) less than five percent (by vote and value) of the stock of (or a partnership interest in) each member of the expanded affiliated group. For this purpose, a five percent former domestic entity shareholder (or five percent former domestic entity partner) is a former domestic entity shareholder (or former domestic entity partner) that, before the domestic entity acquisition, owned (applying the attribution rules of section 318(a) with the modifications described in section 304(c)(3)(B)) at least five percent (by vote and value) of the stock of (or a partnership interest in) the domestic entity. See *Example 5* of this paragraph (i) for an illustration of this paragraph (d).

(2) *Stock issued to avoid the purposes of section 7874.*—The exception in paragraph (d)(1) of this section does not apply to disqualified stock that is transferred in a transaction (or series of transactions) related to the domestic entity acquisition with a principal purpose of avoiding the purposes of section 7874.

(e) *Satisfaction or assumption of obligations.*—Except to the extent stock is treated as disqualified stock as a result of being described in paragraph (c)(1)(ii) of this section, this paragraph (e) applies if, in a transaction related to the domestic entity acquisition, stock of the foreign acquiring corporation is transferred to a person other than the domestic entity in exchange for the satisfaction or the assumption of one or more obligations of the transferor. In such a case, solely for purposes of this section, the stock of the foreign acquiring corporation is treated as if it is transferred in exchange for an amount of cash equal to the fair market value of such stock.

(f) *Transactions involving multiple properties.*—For purposes of this section, if stock and other property are exchanged for qualified property and nonqualified property, the stock is treated as transferred in exchange for the qualified property or nonqualified property, respectively, based on the relative fair market value of the property. See also §1.7874-2(f)(2) (allocating stock of a foreign acquiring corporation between an interest in the domestic entity and other property).

(g) *Treatment of partnerships.*—For purposes of this section, if one or more members of the expanded affiliated group own, in the aggregate, more than 50 percent (by value) of the interests in a partnership, such partnership is treated as a corporation that is a member of the expanded affiliated group.

(h) *Definitions.*—In addition to the definitions in § 1.7874-12, the following definitions apply for purposes of this section:

(1) *Marketable securities* has the meaning set forth in section 453(f)(2), except that the term marketable securities does not include stock of a corporation or an interest in a partnership that becomes a member of the expanded affiliated group in a transaction (or series of transactions) related to the domestic entity acquisition. See *Example 4* of paragraph (i) of this section for an illustration of this paragraph (h)(1).

(2) *Nonqualified property* is property described in paragraphs (h)(2)(i) through (iv) of this section. Thus, stock in a corporation or an interest in a partnership is nonqualified property to the extent provided in paragraph (h)(2)(ii) or (iv) of this section. Qualified property is property other than nonqualified property.

(i) Cash or cash equivalents.

(ii) Marketable securities, within the meaning of paragraph (h)(1) of this section.

(iii) An obligation owed by any of the following:

(A) A member of the expanded affiliated group, unless the holder of the obligation immediately before the domestic entity acquisition and any related transaction (or its successor) is a member of the expanded affiliated group after the domestic entity acquisition and all related transactions. See *Example 6* of paragraph (i) of this section for an illustration of this paragraph (h)(2)(iii)(A).

(B) A former domestic entity shareholder or former domestic entity partner of the domestic entity that owns (applying the attribution rules of section 318(a) with the modifications described in section 304(c)(3)(B)) at least five percent (by vote or value) of the stock of, or partnership interests in, the domestic entity before the domestic entity acquisition.

(C) A person, other than a member of the expanded affiliated group, that, before or after the domestic entity acquisition, either owns (applying the attribution rules of section 318(a) with the modifications described in section 304(c)(3)(B)) at least five percent (by vote or value) of the stock of (or partnership interests in) or is related (within the meaning of section 267 or 707(b)) to—

(1) A member of the expanded affiliated group; or

(2) A person described in paragraph (h)(2)(iii)(B) of this section.

(iv) Any other property acquired with a principal purpose of avoiding the purposes of section 7874, regardless of whether the transaction involves an indirect transfer of property described in paragraph (h)(2)(i), (ii), or (iii) of this section. See *Example 2* and *Example 3* of paragraph (i) of this section for illustrations of the application of this paragraph (h)(2)(iv).

(3) An *obligation* means any fixed or contingent obligation to make a payment or provide value without regard to whether the obligation is otherwise taken into account for purposes of the Internal Revenue Code. An obligation includes, but is not limited to, a debt obligation, an environmental obligation, a tort obligation, a contract obligation (including an obligation to provide goods or services), a pension obligation, an obligation under a short sale, and an obligation under derivative financial instruments such as options, forward contracts, futures contracts, and swaps. An obligation does not include any obligation treated as stock for purposes of section 7874 (see, for example, § 1.7874-2(i), which treats certain interests, including certain creditor claims, as stock).

(4) A *transfer* is, with respect to stock of the foreign acquiring corporation, an issuance, sale, distribution, exchange, or any other disposition of such stock.

(i) *Examples.*—The following examples illustrate the application of the rules of this section. For purposes of the examples, unless otherwise indicated, assume the following facts in addition to the facts stated in the examples:

(1) FA, FMS, FS, and FT are foreign corporations, all of which have only one class of stock issued and outstanding;

(2) DMS and DT are domestic corporations;

(3) P and R are corporations that may be either domestic or foreign;

(4) PRS is a partnership with individual partners;

(5) The de minimis ownership exception in paragraph (d)(1) of this section does not apply;

(6) None of the shareholders or partners in the entities described in the examples are related persons with respect to each other;

(7) All transactions described in each example occur pursuant to the same plan;

(8) No property is acquired with a principal purpose of avoiding the purposes of section 7874;

(9) FA, FMS, FS, and FT are tax residents in the same foreign country;

(10) For purposes of determining the ownership fraction, no shares of FA stock are excluded from the denominator pursuant to § 1.7874-7(b) (which disregards stock attributable to passive assets); and

(11) For purposes of determining the ownership fraction, no shares of FA stock are treated as received by former shareholders of DT pursuant to § 1.7874-10(b) (which disregards certain distributions).

Example 1. Stock transferred in exchange for marketable securities—(i) *Facts.* Individual A wholly owns DT. PRS transfers marketable securities (within the meaning of paragraph (h)(1) of this section) to FA, a newly formed corporation, in exchange solely for 25 shares of FA stock. Then Individual A transfers all the DT stock to FA in exchange solely for 75 shares of FA stock.

(ii) *Analysis.* Under paragraph (h)(2)(ii) of this section, the marketable securities constitute nonqualified property. Accordingly, the 25 shares of FA stock transferred by FA to PRS in exchange for the marketable securities constitute disqualified stock described in paragraph (c)(1) of this section by reason of paragraph (c)(1)(i) of this section. Paragraph (c)(2) of this section does not reduce the amount of disqualified stock described in paragraph (c)(1)(i) of this section because the transfer of FA stock in exchange for the marketable securities increases the fair market value of the assets of FA by the fair market value of the marketable securities transferred. Under paragraph (b) of this section, the 25 shares of FA stock transferred to PRS are not included in the denominator of the ownership fraction. See also section 7874(c)(4). Accordingly, the only FA stock included in the ownership fraction is the FA stock transferred to Individual A in exchange for the DT stock, and that FA stock is included in both the numerator and the denominator of the ownership fraction. Thus, the ownership fraction is 75/75.

Example 2. Stock transferred in exchange for property acquired with a principal purpose of avoiding the purposes of section 7874—(i) *Facts.* Individual A wholly owns DT. PRS transfers marketable securities (within the meaning of paragraph (h)(1) of this section) to FT, a newly formed corporation, in exchange solely for all the FT stock. Then PRS transfers the FT stock to FA, a newly formed corporation, in exchange solely for 25 shares of FA stock. Finally, Individual A transfers all the DT stock to FA in exchange solely for 75 shares of FA stock. FA acquires the FT stock with a principal purpose of avoiding the purposes of section 7874.

(ii) *Analysis.* Under paragraph (h)(2)(iv) of this section, the FT stock constitutes nonqualified property because a principal purpose of FA acquiring the FT stock is to avoid the purposes of section 7874. Accordingly, the 25 shares of FA stock transferred by FA to PRS in exchange for the FT stock constitute disqualified stock described in paragraph (c)(1) of this section by reason of paragraph (c)(1)(i) of this section. Paragraph (c)(2) of this section does not reduce the amount of disqualified stock described in paragraph (c)(1)(i) of this section because the transfer of FA stock in exchange for the FT stock increases the fair market value of FA's assets by the fair market value of the FT stock. Under paragraph (b) of this section, the 25 shares of FA stock transferred to PRS are not included in the denominator of the ownership fraction. Furthermore, even in the absence of paragraph (h)(2)(iv) of this section, the transfer of marketable securities to FT would be disregarded pursuant to section 7874(c)(4). Accordingly, the only FA stock included in the ownership fraction is the FA stock transferred to Individual A in exchange for the DT stock, and that FA stock is included in both the numerator and the denominator of the ownership fraction. Thus, the ownership fraction is 75/75.

Example 3. Stock transferred in exchange for property acquired with a principal purpose of avoiding the purposes of section 7874—(i) *Facts.* DT is a publicly traded corporation. PRS is a foreign partnership that is unrelated to DT. PRS transfers certain business assets (PRS properties) to FA, a newly formed foreign corporation, in exchange solely for 25 shares of FA stock. The shareholders of DT transfer all of their DT stock to FA in exchange solely for the remaining 75 shares of FA stock (DT acquisition). None of the PRS properties is property described in paragraph (h)(2)(i) through (iii) of this section, but FA acquires the PRS properties with a principal purpose of avoiding the purposes of section 7874.

(ii) *Analysis.* Under paragraph (h)(2)(iv) of this section, the PRS properties transferred to FA constitute nonqualified property, because FA acquires the PRS properties in a transaction related to the DT acquisition with a principal purpose of avoiding the purposes of section 7874. Accordingly, the 25 shares of FA stock transferred by FA to PRS in exchange for the PRS properties constitute disqualified stock described in paragraph (c)(1) of this section by reason of paragraph (c)(1)(i) of this section. Paragraph (c)(2) of this section does not apply to reduce the amount of disqualified stock described in paragraph (c)(1)(i) of this section because the transfer of FA stock in exchange for the PRS properties increases the fair market value of FA's assets by the fair market value of the PRS properties. Accordingly, pursuant to paragraph (b) of this section, the 25 shares of FA stock transferred to PRS in exchange for the PRS properties are not included in the denominator of the ownership fraction. Furthermore, even in the absence of paragraph (h)(2)(iv) of this section, the transfer of the PRS properties to FA would be disregarded pursuant to section 7874(c)(4). Therefore, the only FA stock included in the ownership fraction is the FA stock transferred to the former domestic entity shareholders of DT in exchange for their DT stock, and that FA stock is included in both the numerator and the denominator of the ownership fraction. Thus, the ownership fraction is 75/75.

Example 4. Stock transferred in exchange for stock of a foreign corporation that becomes a member of the expanded affiliated group—(i) *Facts.* FT, a publicly traded corporation, forms FA, and then FA forms DMS and FMS. FMS merges with and into FT, with FT surviving the merger (FMS-FT merger). Pursuant to the FMS-FT merger, the FT shareholders exchange their FT stock solely for 100 shares of FA stock and FT becomes a wholly owned subsidiary of FA. Following the FMS-FT merger, DMS merges with and into DT, also a publicly traded corporation, with DT surviving the merger (DT acquisition). Pursuant to the DT acquisition, the DT shareholders exchange their DT stock solely for the remaining 100 shares of FA stock, and DT becomes a wholly owned subsidiary of FA. After the completion of the plan, FA wholly owns FT and DT, DMS and FMS cease to exist, and the stock of FA is publicly traded.

Reg. §1.7874-4(i)(11)

(ii) *Analysis*. Because FT becomes a member of the expanded affiliated group that includes FA in a transaction related to the DT acquisition, the FT stock does not constitute marketable securities (within the meaning of paragraph (h)(1) of this section) and therefore does not constitute nonqualified property pursuant to paragraph (h)(2)(ii) of this section. Accordingly, no FA stock is disqualified stock described in paragraph (c)(1) of this section and therefore the FA stock transferred in exchange for the FT stock and DT stock is included in the denominator of the ownership fraction. Thus, the ownership fraction is 100/200.

(iii) *Alternative facts*. The facts are the same as in paragraph (i) of this *Example 4*, except that, instead of undertaking the FMS-FT merger, FT merges with and into FA with FA surviving the merger (FT-FA merger). Pursuant to the FT-FA merger, the FT shareholders exchange their FT stock solely for 100 shares of FA stock. At the time of the FT-FA merger, FT does not hold nonqualified property and has no obligations. Accordingly, FA stock transferred by FA to FT in exchange for the property of FT is not disqualified stock described in paragraph (c)(1) of this section. Furthermore, pursuant to paragraph (c)(2) of this section, the 100 shares of FA stock transferred by FT to the shareholders of FT in exchange for their FT stock do not constitute disqualified stock described in paragraph (c)(1) of this section. Although the FT stock is nonqualified property (the FT stock constitutes marketable securities within the meaning of paragraph (h)(2)(ii) of this section because the stock of FT is publicly traded and FT is not a member of the expanded affiliated group that includes FA after the DT acquisition), under paragraph (c)(2) of this section, the transfer of FA stock by FT to the shareholders of FT neither increases the fair market value of the assets of FA nor decreases the liabilities of FA. Accordingly, no FA stock is disqualified stock described in paragraph (c)(1) of this section and, therefore, the FA stock transferred in exchange for the assets of FT and the DT stock is included in the denominator of the ownership fraction. Thus, the ownership fraction is 100/200.

Example 5. De minimis exception—(i) *Facts*. Individual A wholly owns DT. The fair market value of the DT stock is $100x. PRS transfers $96x of cash to FA, a newly formed corporation, in exchange solely for 96 shares of FA stock. Then Individual A transfers the DT stock to FA in exchange for $96x of cash and 4 shares of FA stock (DT acquisition).

(ii) *Analysis*. Under paragraph (h)(2)(i) of this section, cash constitutes nonqualified property. Accordingly, the 96 shares of FA stock transferred by FA to PRS in exchange for $96x of cash constitute disqualified stock described in paragraph (c)(1) of this section by reason of paragraph (c)(1)(i) of this section. Furthermore, paragraph (c)(2) of this section does not reduce the amount of disqualified stock described in paragraph (c)(1)(i) of this section because the transfer of FA stock in exchange for $96x of cash increases the fair market value of the assets of FA by $96x. However, without regard to the application of paragraph (b) of this section and §§ 1.7874-7(b) and 1.7874-10T(b), the ownership percentage described in section 7874(a)(2)(B)(ii) would be less than 5 (by vote and value), or 4 (4/100, or 4 shares of FA stock held by Individual A by reason of owning the DT stock, determined under § 1.7874-2(f)(2), over 100 shares of FA stock outstanding after the DT acquisition). Furthermore, after the DT acquisition and all related transactions, Individual A owns less than 5% (by vote and value, applying the attribution rules of section 318(a) with the modifications described in section 304(c)(3)(B)) of the stock of FA and DT (the members of the expanded affiliated group that includes FA). Accordingly, the de minimis exception in paragraph (d)(1) of this section applies and therefore paragraph (b) of this section does not apply to exclude the FA stock transferred to PRS from the denominator of the ownership fraction. Therefore, the FA stock transferred to Individual A and PRS is included in the denominator of the ownership fraction. Thus, the ownership fraction is 4/100.

Example 6. Obligation of the expanded affiliated group satisfied with stock—(i) *Facts*. Individual A wholly owns DT. The stock of DT held by Individual A has a fair market value of $75x. Individual A also holds an obligation of DT with a value and face amount of $25x. DT holds property with a value of $100x, and the $25x obligation is associated with the property. FA, a newly formed corporation, transfers 100 shares of FA stock to Individual A in exchange for all the DT stock and the $25x obligation of DT.

(ii) *Analysis*. Under paragraph (h)(2)(iii)(A) of this section, the $25x obligation of DT constitutes nonqualified property because DT is a member of the expanded affiliated group that includes FA, and Individual A (the holder of the obligation immediately before the domestic entity acquisition and any related transaction) is not a member of the EAG after the domestic entity acquisition and all related transactions. Thus, the shares of FA stock transferred by FA to Individual A in exchange for the obligation of DT constitute disqualified stock described in paragraph (c)(1) of this section by reason of paragraph (c)(1)(i) of this section. Under § 1.7874-2(f)(2), Individual A is treated as receiving 75 shares of FA stock in exchange for the DT stock (100 x $75x/$100x) and 25 shares of FA stock in exchange for the obligation of DT (100 x $25x/$100x). Thus, 25 shares of FA stock constitute disqualified stock described in paragraph (c)(1) of this section by reason of paragraph (c)(1)(i) of this section. Paragraph (c)(2) of this section does not reduce the amount of disqualified stock described in paragraph (c)(1)(i) of this section because the transfer of FA stock for the $25x obligation increases the fair market value of FA's assets by $25x. Therefore, under paragraph (b) of this section, the 25 shares of FA stock transferred to Individual A in exchange for the obligation of DT are not included in the denominator of the ownership fraction. Accordingly, the only FA stock included in the ownership fraction is the 75 shares of FA stock transferred to Individual A in exchange for the DT stock, and that FA stock is included in both the numerator and the denominator of the ownership fraction. Thus, the ownership fraction is 75/75.

(iii) *Alternative facts.* The facts are the same as in paragraph (i) of this *Example 6*, except that instead of acquiring the stock of DT and the $25x obligation of DT, FA acquires the $100x of property from DT in exchange solely for 100 shares of FA stock. DT distributes 75 shares of FA stock to Individual A in exchange for Individual A's DT stock and transfers 25 shares of FA stock to Individual A in satisfaction of DT's obligation to Individual A, and liquidates. The 25 shares of FA stock transferred by FA to DT in exchange for the property of DT and then transferred by DT in satisfaction of DT's obligation to Individual A constitute disqualified stock described in paragraph (c)(1) of this section by reason of paragraph (c)(1)(ii) of this section. Paragraph (c)(2) of this section does not reduce the amount of disqualified stock described in paragraph (c)(1)(ii) of this section because the transfer of FA stock in exchange for the property of DT increases the fair market value of FA's assets by $100x (although the amount of disqualified stock is limited to 25 shares of FA stock in this case). Therefore, under paragraph (b) of this section, the 25 shares of FA stock that constitute disqualified stock are not included in the denominator of the ownership fraction. Accordingly, only 75 shares of FA stock are included in the ownership fraction, and that FA stock is included in both the numerator and the denominator of the ownership fraction. Thus, the ownership fraction is 75/75.

Example 7. "Over-the-top" stock transfer—(i) *Facts.* Individual A wholly owns DT. Individual B holds all 100 outstanding shares of FA stock. Individual C acquires 20 shares of FA stock from Individual B for cash, and then FA acquires all of the stock of DT from Individual A in exchange solely for 100 shares of FA stock.

(ii) *Analysis.* Under paragraph (h)(2)(i) of this section, cash constitutes nonqualified property. Accordingly, absent the application of paragraph (c)(2) of this section, the 20 shares of FA stock transferred by Individual B to Individual C in exchange for cash would constitute disqualified stock described in paragraph (c)(1) of this section by reason of paragraph (c)(1)(i) of this section. Nevertheless, because Individual B's sale of FA stock neither increases the assets of FA nor decreases the liabilities of FA, such FA stock is not disqualified stock by reason of paragraph (c)(2) of this section. Accordingly, paragraph (b) of this section does not apply to exclude the 20 shares of FA stock sold by Individual B to Individual C, and that FA stock is included in the denominator of the ownership fraction. The 100 shares of FA stock received by Individual A are the only shares included in the numerator of the ownership fraction. Thus, the ownership fraction is 100/200.

Example 8. Interaction with internal group restructuring rule—(i) *Facts.* P holds 85 shares of DT stock. The remaining 15 shares of DT stock are held by Individual A. P and Individual A transfer their shares of DT stock to FA, a newly formed corporation, in exchange for 85 and 15 shares of FA stock, respectively (DT acquisition), and PRS transfers $75x of cash to FA in exchange for the remaining 75 shares of FA stock.

(ii) *Analysis.* Under paragraph (h)(2)(i) of this section, cash constitutes nonqualified property. Accordingly, the 75 shares of FA stock transferred by FA to PRS in exchange for $75x of cash constitute disqualified stock described in paragraph (c)(1) of this section by reason of paragraph (c)(1)(i) of this section. Furthermore, paragraph (c)(2) of this section does not reduce the amount of disqualified stock described in paragraph (c)(1)(i) of this section because the transfer of FA stock in exchange for $75x of cash increases the fair market value of the assets of FA by $75x. Therefore, under paragraph (b) of this section, the 75 shares of FA stock transferred to PRS are not included in the denominator of the ownership fraction. Although PRS's shares of FA stock are excluded from the denominator of the ownership fraction under paragraph (b) of this section, under §1.7874-1(d)(1), such shares of FA stock nonetheless are taken into account for purposes of determining whether P is a member of the expanded affiliated group that includes FA and for purposes of determining whether the DT acquisition qualifies as an internal group restructuring. Because P holds 48.6% of the FA stock (85/175) after the DT acquisition and all transactions related to the DT acquisition, it is not a member of the expanded affiliated group that includes FA. In addition, the DT acquisition does not qualify as an internal group restructuring described in §1.7874-1(c)(2) because P does not hold, directly or indirectly, 80% or more of the shares of FA stock (by vote and value) after the DT acquisition and all transactions related to the DT acquisition. Therefore, the FA stock held by P (along with the FA stock held by Individual A) is included in the numerator and the denominator of the ownership fraction. Thus, the ownership fraction is 100/100.

Example 9. Interaction with loss of control rule—(i) *Facts.* P wholly owns DT. P transfers all of its shares of DT stock to FA, a newly formed corporation, in exchange for 49 shares of FA stock (DT acquisition), and R transfers marketable securities (within the meaning of paragraph (h)(1) of this section) to FA in exchange for the remaining 51 shares of FA stock.

(ii) *Analysis.* Under paragraph (h)(2)(ii) of this section, the marketable securities constitute nonqualified property. Accordingly, the shares of FA stock transferred by FA to R in exchange for the marketable securities constitute disqualified stock described in paragraph (c)(1) of this section by reason of paragraph (c)(1)(i) of this section. Paragraph (c)(2) of this section does not reduce the amount of disqualified stock described in paragraph (c)(1)(i) of this section because the transfer of FA stock in exchange for the marketable securities increases the fair market value of the assets of FA by the fair market value of the marketable securities transferred. Therefore, under paragraph (b) of this section, the shares of FA stock transferred to R are not included in the denominator of the ownership fraction. Although under paragraph (b) of this section R's shares of FA stock are excluded from the denominator of the ownership fraction, under § 1.7874-1(d)(1), such stock is taken into account for purposes of determining whether P or R is a member of the expanded affiliated group that includes FA. Because P holds 49% of the shares of FA stock (49/100), P is not a member of the expanded affiliated group that includes FA, and P's FA stock is included in both the numerator and the denominator of the ownership fraction. Because R holds 51% of the shares of FA stock (51/100), R is a member of the expanded affiliated group that includes FA and, before taking into account § 1.7874-1(c), R's FA stock would be excluded from the numerator and denominator of the ownership fraction under section 7874(c)(2)(A) and § 1.7874-1(b). However, the DT acquisition results in a loss of control described in § 1.7874-1(c)(3) because P does not hold, in the aggregate, directly or indirectly, more than 50% of the shares of stock (by vote or value) of R, FA, or DT after the acquisition. Accordingly, the FA stock held by R would be included in the denominator of the ownership fraction under § 1.7874-1(c)(1). Nevertheless, the FA stock held by R is excluded from the denominator of the ownership fraction under paragraph (b) of this section and § 1.7874-1(d)(1). Thus, the ownership fraction is 49/49.

(iii) *Alternative facts.* The facts are the same as in paragraph (i) of this *Example 9*, except that, in exchange for 51 shares of FA stock, R transfers marketable securities (within the meaning of paragraph (h)(1) of this section) with a value equal to that of 16 shares of FA stock and qualified property (within the meaning of paragraph (h)(2) of this section) with a value equal to that of 35 shares of FA stock. Accordingly, 16 of the 51 shares of FA stock transferred to R constitute disqualified stock described in paragraph (c)(1) of this section by reason of paragraph (c)(1)(i) of this section, and 35 of such shares do not constitute disqualified stock. Paragraph (c)(2) of this section does not reduce the amount of disqualified stock described in paragraph (c)(1)(i) of this section because the transfer of FA stock in exchange for the marketable securities increases the fair market value of the assets of FA by the fair market value of the marketable securities transferred. Therefore, under paragraph (b) of this section, 16 of the 51 shares of FA stock transferred to R are not included in the denominator of the ownership fraction. Although 16 of the 51 shares of FA stock that are transferred to R are excluded from the denominator of the ownership fraction, under § 1.7874-1(d)(1), all 51 of R's shares of FA stock are taken into account for purposes of determining whether P or R is a member of the expanded affiliated group that includes FA. Because P holds 49% of the shares

of FA stock (49/100), it is not a member of the expanded affiliated group that includes FA, and its FA stock is included in both the numerator and the denominator of the ownership fraction. Because R holds 51% of the shares of FA stock (51/100), it is a member of the expanded affiliated group that includes FA and, before taking into account § 1.7874-1(c), its FA stock is excluded from the numerator and denominator of the ownership fraction under section 7874(c)(2)(A) and § 1.7874-1(b). However, the DT acquisition results in a loss of control described in § 1.7874-1(c)(3) because P does not hold, in the aggregate, directly or indirectly, more than 50% of the shares of stock (by vote or value) of R, FA, or DT after the acquisition. Accordingly, the 51 shares of FA stock held by R would be included in the denominator of the ownership fraction under § 1.7874-1(c)(1). Nevertheless, the 16 shares of FA stock that constitute disqualified stock are excluded from the denominator of the ownership fraction under paragraph (b) of this section and § 1.7874-1(d)(1). In addition, the 35 shares of FA stock received by R that do not constitute disqualified stock are included in the denominator. Thus, the ownership fraction is 49/84.

Example 10. Stock issued in lieu of assuming associated obligation—(i) *Facts.* Individual A wholly owns DT. The stock of DT has a fair market value of $100x. Individual B wholly owns FT, a foreign corporation, which conducts two businesses, Business C and Business D. Business C comprises property with a gross fair market value of $70x and $20x of associated obligations. Business D comprises property with a gross fair market value of $45x and $35x of associated obligations. Individual A transfers all of the shares of DT stock to FA, a newly formed corporation, in exchange for $100x of FA stock (DT acquisition). In transactions related to the DT acquisition, FA acquires all of the Business C property from FT in exchange for $70x of FA stock and then FT transfers $30x of the FA stock to its creditors in satisfaction of $30x of its obligations. None of the Business C property is nonqualified property.

(ii) *Analysis.* Under paragraph (c)(1) of this section by reason of paragraph (c)(1)(ii) of this section, the $30x of FA stock transferred to FT (the transferee) in exchange for the Business C property (the exchanged property) and then transferred by FT in satisfaction of $30x of its obligations is disqualified stock, except to the extent limited by paragraph (c)(1)(ii)(B) of this section. Under paragraph (c)(1)(ii)(B)(1) of this section, the proportionate share of obligations associated with the exchanged property that is not assumed by FA must be determined. The proportionate share of obligations associated with the exchanged property is $20x, calculated as $20x (the obligations associated with the Business C properties) multiplied by $70x/$70x (the fair market value of the exchanged property, $70x, relative to the fair market value of all the Business C property, $70x). The proportionate share of obligations associated with the exchanged property that is not assumed by FA is $20x, calculated as the proportionate share of obligations associated with the exchanged property ($20x) less the obligations assumed by FA ($0x). Under paragraph (c)(1)(ii)(B)(2) of this section, the amount of disqualified stock is limited to the proportionate share of obligations associated with the exchanged property that is not assumed ($20x) multiplied by a fraction, which in this case is $70x/$70x (the amount of exchanged property that is qualified property, $70x, divided by the total amount of exchanged property, $70x). Accordingly, $20x of FA stock is disqualified stock under paragraph (c)(1) of this section by reason of paragraph (c)(1)(ii) of this section. Paragraph (c)(2) of this section does not reduce the amount of disqualified stock described in paragraph (c)(1)(ii) of this section because the transfer of the FA stock in exchange for the exchanged property increases the fair market value of FA's assets by $70x (although the amount of disqualified stock is limited to $20x of FA stock in this case). Therefore, under paragraph (b) of this section, the $20x of FA stock that constitutes disqualified stock is not included in the denominator of the ownership fraction. Accordingly, only $150x of FA stock is included in the denominator of the ownership fraction, calculated as the $100x of FA stock received by Individual A plus the $70x of FA stock received by FT less the $20x of FA stock that is disqualified stock. Thus, the ownership fraction is $100x/$150x. The result would be the same if, in transactions related to the DT acquisition, FT instead sold the $30x of FA stock for $30x cash and then transferred the cash in satisfaction of $30x of its obligations.

(iii) *Alternative facts*. The facts are the same as in paragraph (i) of this *Example 10*, except that FA acquires only $42x of the Business C property in exchange for $30x of FA stock and the assumption of $12x of the obligations associated with the Business C property. Under paragraph (c)(1) of this section by reason of paragraph (c)(1)(ii) of this section, the $30x of FA stock transferred to FT (the transferee) in exchange for the Business C property (the exchanged property) and then transferred by FT in satisfaction of $30x of its obligations is disqualified stock, except to the extent limited by paragraph (c)(1)(ii)(B) of this section. Under paragraph (c)(1)(ii)(B)(1) of this section, the proportionate share of obligations associated with the exchanged property that is not assumed by FA must be determined. The proportionate share of obligations associated with the exchanged property is $12x, calculated as $20x (the obligations associated with the Business C property) multiplied by $42x/$70x (the fair market value of the exchanged property, $42x, relative to the fair market value of all the Business C property, $70x). The proportionate share of obligations associated with the exchanged property that is not assumed by FA is $0, calculated as the proportionate share of obligations associated with the exchanged property ($12x) less the obligations

assumed by FA ($12x). Accordingly, as a result of the application of paragraph (c)(1)(ii)(B)(2) of this section, no FA stock is disqualified stock under paragraph (c)(1) of this section by reason of paragraph (c)(1)(ii) of this section. As a result, $130x of FA stock is included in the denominator of the ownership fraction, calculated as the $100x of FA stock received by Individual A plus the $30x of FA stock received by FT. Thus, the ownership fraction is $100x/$130x.

(j) *Applicability dates.*—(1) *General rule.*—Except to the extent otherwise provided in paragraph (j) of this section, this section applies to domestic entity acquisitions completed on or after September 17, 2009. Paragraphs (h)(1) and (h)(2)(iv) of this section apply to domestic entity acquisitions completed on or after November 19, 2015. Paragraph (d)(1)(i) of this section applies to domestic entity acquisitions completed on or after April 4, 2016. Paragraphs (c)(1)(ii), (h)(2)(iii), and (h)(3) of this section apply to domestic entity acquisitions completed on or after January 13, 2017. For domestic entity acquisitions completed before November 19, 2015, see § 1.7874-4T(i)(6) and (i)(7)(iv) (the predecessors of paragraphs (h)(1) and (h)(2)(iv) of this section) as contained in 26 CFR part 1 revised as of April 1, 2016. For domestic entity acquisitions completed on or after September 22, 2014, and before April 4, 2016, see § 1.7874-4T(d)(1)(i) as contained in 26 CFR part 1 revised as of April 1, 2016. For domestic entity acquisitions completed before January 13, 2017, see § 1.7874-4T(c)(1)(ii), (i)(7)(iii) (the predecessor of paragraph (h)(2)(iii) of this section), and (i)(8) (the predecessor of paragraph (h)(3) of this section) as contained in 26 CFR part 1 revised as of April 1, 2016. Paragraph (d)(1)(ii) of this section applies to domestic entity acquisitions completed on or after July 12, 2018, though taxpayers may elect to consistently apply paragraph (d)(1)(ii) of this section to domestic entity acquisitions completed before July 12, 2018. For domestic entity acquisitions completed before July 12, 2018, see § 1.7874-4(d)(1)(ii) as contained in 26 CFR part 1 revised as of April 1, 2017.

(2) *Transitional rules for domestic entity acquisitions completed on or after September 17, 2009, but before January 16, 2014.*—For domestic entity acquisitions completed on or after September 17, 2009, but before January 16, 2014, except as provided in paragraph (j)(3) of this section, this section shall be applied with the following modifications:

(i) Nonqualified property does not include property described in paragraph (h)(2)(iii) of this section.

(ii) A transfer is limited to an issuance of stock of the foreign acquiring corporation.

(iii) The determination of whether stock of the foreign acquiring corporation is described in paragraph (c)(1) of this section is made without regard to paragraphs (c)(1)(ii), (c)(2), and (e) of this section.

(iv) Paragraph (d) of this section and § 1.7874-1(d)(1) do not apply.

Reg. § 1.7874-4(j)(2)(iv)

(3) *Election for domestic entity acquisitions completed on or after September 17, 2009, and before January 13, 2017.*—If, pursuant to paragraph (j)(1) or (2) of this section, a paragraph of this section would not otherwise apply to a domestic entity acquisition completed on or after September 17, 2009, and before January 13, 2017 (transition period), a taxpayer may elect to apply the paragraph if the taxpayer applies the paragraph consistently to all acquisitions completed during the transition period. The election is made by applying the paragraph to all such acquisitions on a timely filed original return (including extensions) or an amended return filed no later than six months after January 13, 2017. A separate statement or form evidencing the election need not be filed. [Reg. § 1.7874-4.]

☐ [T.D. 9812, 1-13-2017 (*corrected* 9-6-2017). *Amended by T.D. 9834, 7-11-2018.*]

[Reg. § 1.7874-5]

§ 1.7874-5. Effect of certain transfers of stock related to the acquisition.—(a) *General rule.*— Stock of a foreign acquiring corporation that is described in section 7874(a)(2)(B)(ii) shall not cease to be so described as a result of any subsequent transfer of the stock by the former domestic entity shareholder or former domestic entity partner that received such stock, even if the subsequent transfer is related to the domestic entity acquisition.

(b) *Example.*—The rule of this section is illustrated by the following example:

Example. (i) *Facts.* Individual A wholly owns DT, a domestic corporation. FA, a newly formed foreign corporation, acquires all of the stock of DT from Individual A in exchange solely for 100 shares of FA stock. Pursuant to a binding commitment that was entered into in connection with FA's acquisition of the DT stock, Individual A sells 25 shares of FA stock to B, an unrelated person, in exchange for cash. For federal income tax purposes, the form of the steps of the transaction is respected.

(ii) *Analysis.* Under § 1.7874-2(f)(1), the 100 shares of FA stock received by Individual A are stock of a foreign corporation (FA) that is held by reason of holding stock in a domestic corporation (DT). Accordingly, such stock is described in section 7874(a)(2)(B)(ii). Under paragraph (a) of this section, all 100 shares of FA stock retain their status as being described in section 7874(a)(2)(B)(ii), even though Individual A sells 25 of the 100 shares in connection with the acquisition described in section 7874(a)(2)(B)(i) pursuant to the binding commitment. Therefore, all 100 of the shares of FA stock are included in both the numerator and denominator of the ownership fraction.

(c) *Certain transfers involving expanded affiliated group members.*—For rules addressing whether certain stock is treated as held by members of the expanded affiliated group for purposes of applying section 7874(c)(2)(A) and § 1.7874-1, see § 1.7874-6.

(d) *Definitions.*—The definitions provided in § 1.7874-12 apply for purposes of this section.

(e) *Applicability dates.*—This section applies to domestic entity acquisitions that are completed on or after January 16, 2014. [Reg. § 1.7874-5.]

☐ [T.D. 9812, 1-13-2017. *Amended by T.D. 9834, 7-11-2018.*]

[Reg. § 1.7874-6]

§ 1.7874-6. Stock transferred by members of the EAG.—(a) *Scope.*—This section provides rules regarding whether transferred stock is treated as held by members of the EAG for purposes of applying section 7874(c)(2)(A) and § 1.7874-1. Paragraph (b) of this section sets forth the general rule under which transferred stock is not treated as held by members of the EAG for purposes of applying section 7874(c)(2)(A) and § 1.7874-1. Paragraph (c) of this section provides exceptions to the general rule. Paragraph (d) of this section provides rules regarding the treatment of partnerships, and paragraph (e) of this section provides rules regarding transactions related to the acquisition. Paragraph (f) of this section provides definitions. Paragraph (g) of this section provides examples illustrating the application of the rules of this section. Paragraph (h) of this section provides dates of applicability.

(b) *General rule.*—Except as provided in paragraph (c) of this section, transferred stock is not treated as held by members of the EAG for purposes of applying section 7874(c)(2)(A) and § 1.7874-1. Transferred stock that is not treated as held by members of the EAG for purposes of applying section 7874(c)(2)(A) and § 1.7874-1 is included in the numerator and the denominator of the ownership fraction. See § 1.7874-5(a).

(c) *Exceptions.*—Transferred stock is treated as held by members of the EAG for purposes of applying section 7874(c)(2)(A) and § 1.7874-1 if paragraph (c)(1) or (2) of this section applies. Transferred stock that is treated as held by members of the EAG for purposes of applying section 7874(c)(2)(A) and § 1.7874-1 is excluded from the numerator of the ownership fraction and, depending upon the application of § 1.7874-1(c), may be excluded from the denominator of the ownership fraction. See § § 1.7874-1(b) and (c).

(1) *Transfers involving a U.S.-parented group.*—This paragraph (c)(1) applies if the following conditions are satisfied:

(i) Before the domestic entity acquisition, the transferring corporation is a member of a U.S.-parented group.

(ii) After the domestic entity acquisition, each of the transferring corporation (or its successor), any person that holds transferred stock, and the foreign acquiring corporation are members of a U.S.-parented group the common parent of which—

(A) Before the domestic entity acquisition, was a member of the U.S.-parented group described in paragraph (c)(1)(i) of this section; or

(B) Is a corporation that was formed in a transaction related to the domestic entity acquisition, provided that, immediately after the corporation was formed (and without regard to any related transactions), the corporation was a member of the U.S.-parented group described in paragraph (c)(1)(i) of this section.

(2) *Transfers involving a foreign-parented group.*—This paragraph (c)(2) applies if the following conditions are satisfied:

(i) Before the domestic entity acquisition, the transferring corporation and the domestic entity are members of the same foreign-parented group.

(ii) After the domestic entity acquisition, the transferring corporation—

(A) Is a member of the EAG; or

(B) Would be a member of the EAG absent one or more transfers (other than by issuance), in a transaction (or series of transactions) after and related to the domestic entity acquisition, of stock of the foreign acquiring corporation by one or more members of the foreign-parented group described in paragraph (c)(2)(i) of this section.

(d) *Treatment of partnerships.*—(1) *Stock held by a partnership.*—For purposes of this section, each partner in a partnership, as determined without regard to the application of paragraph (d)(2) of this section, is treated as holding its proportionate share of the stock held by the partnership, as determined under the rules and principles of sections 701 through 777.

(2) *Partnership treated as corporation.*—For purposes of this section, if one or more members of an affiliated group, as determined after the application of paragraph (d)(1) of this section, own, in the aggregate, more than 50 percent (by value) of the interests in a partnership, the partnership will be treated as a corporation that is a member of the affiliated group.

(e) *Treatment of transactions related to the acquisition.*—Except as provided in paragraphs (c)(1)(ii)(B) and (c)(2)(ii)(B) of this section, all transactions that are related to a domestic entity acquisition are taken into account in applying this section.

(f) *Definitions.*—In addition to the definitions provided in § 1.7874-12, the following definitions apply for purposes of this section.

(1) A *foreign-parented group* means an affiliated group that has a foreign corporation as the common parent corporation. A *member of the foreign-parented group* is an entity included in the foreign-parented group.

(2) *Transferred stock.*—(i) *In general.*—Transferred stock means stock of the foreign acquiring corporation described in section 7874(a)(2)(B)(ii) that is received by a transferring corporation and, in a transaction (or series of transactions) related to the domestic entity acquisition, is subsequently transferred.

(ii) *Special rule.*—This paragraph (f)(2)(ii) applies in certain cases in which a transferring corporation receives stock of the foreign acquiring corporation described in section 7874(a)(2)(B)(ii) that has the same terms as other stock of the foreign acquiring corporation that is received by the transferring corporation in a transaction (or series of transactions) related to the domestic entity acquisition or that is owned by the transferring corporation prior to the domestic entity acquisition (the stock described in this sentence, collectively, *fungible stock*). Pursuant to this paragraph (f)(2)(ii), if, in a transaction (or series of transactions) related to the domestic entity acquisition, the transferring corporation subsequently transfers less than all of the fungible stock, a pro rata portion of the stock subsequently transferred is treated as consisting of stock of the foreign acquiring corporation described in section 7874(a)(2)(B)(ii). The pro rata portion is based, at the time of the subsequent transfer, on the relative fair market value of the fungible stock that is stock of the foreign acquiring corporation described in section 7874(a)(2)(B)(ii) to the fair market value of all the fungible stock.

(3) A *transferring corporation* means a corporation that is a former domestic entity shareholder or former domestic entity partner.

(4) A *U.S.-parented group* means an affiliated group that has a domestic corporation as the common parent corporation. A *member of the U.S.-parented group* is an entity included in the U.S.-parented group, including the common parent corporation.

(g) *Examples.*—The following examples illustrate the application of this section.

Example 1. U.S.-parented group exception not available—(i) *Facts.* USP, a domestic corporation wholly owned by Individual A, owns all the stock of DT, a domestic corporation, as well as other property. The DT stock does not represent substantially all of the property of USP for purposes of section 7874. Pursuant to a reorganization described in section 368(a)(1)(D), USP transfers all the DT stock to FA, a newly formed foreign corporation, in exchange for 100 shares of FA stock (DT acquisition) and distributes the FA stock to Individual A pursuant to section 361(c)(1).

(ii) *Analysis.* The 100 FA shares received by USP are stock of a foreign acquiring corporation described in section 7874(a)(2)(B)(ii) and, under § 1.7874-5(a), the shares retain their status as such even though USP subsequently distributes the shares to Individual A pursuant to section 361(c)(1). Thus, the 100 FA shares are included in the ownership fraction, unless the shares are treated as held by members of the EAG for purposes of applying section 7874(c)(2)(A) and § 1.7874-1 and are excluded from the ownership fraction under those rules. For purposes of applying section 7874(c)(2)(A) and § 1.7874-1, the 100 FA shares, which constitute transferred stock under paragraph (f)(2) of this section, are treated as held by members of the EAG only if an exception in paragraph (c) of this section applies. See paragraph (b) of this section. The U.S.-parented group exception described in paragraph (c)(1) of this section does not apply. Although before the DT acquisition, USP (the transferring corporation) is a member of a U.S.-parented group of which USP is the common parent, after the DT acquisition, and taking into account all transactions related to the acquisition, each of USP, Individual A (the person that holds the transferred stock), and FA (the foreign acquiring corporation) are not members of a U.S.-parented group described in paragraph (c)(1)(ii)(A) or (B) of this section. Accordingly, because the 100 FA shares are not treated as held by members of the EAG, those shares are included in the numerator and the denominator of the ownership fraction. Therefore, the ownership fraction is 100/100.

Example 2. U.S.-parented group exception available—(i) *Facts.* USP, a domestic corporation wholly owned by Individual A, owns all the stock of USS, a domestic corporation, and USS owns all the stock of FT, a foreign corporation. FT owns all the stock of DT, a domestic corporation. FT does not own any other property and has no liabilities. Pursuant to a reorganization described in section 368(a)(1)(F), FT transfers all of its DT stock to FA, a newly formed foreign corporation, in exchange for 100 shares of FA stock (DT acquisition) and distributes the FA stock to USS in liquidation pursuant to section 361(c)(1). In a transaction after and related to the DT acquisition, USP sells 60 percent of the stock of USS (by vote and value) to Individual B.

(ii) *Analysis.* The 100 FA shares received by FT are stock of a foreign acquiring corporation described in section 7874(a)(2)(B)(ii) and, under § 1.7874-5(a), the shares retain their status as such even though FT subsequently distributes the shares to USS pursuant to section 361(c)(1). Thus, the 100 FA shares are included in the ownership fraction, unless the shares are treated as held by members of the EAG for purposes of applying section 7874(c)(2)(A) and § 1.7874-1 and are excluded from the ownership fraction under those rules. For purposes of applying section 7874(c)(2)(A) and § 1.7874-1, the 100 FA shares, which constitute transferred stock under paragraph (f)(2) of this section, are treated as held by members of the EAG only if an exception in paragraph (c) of this section applies. See paragraph (b) of this section. The U.S.-parented group exception described in paragraph (c)(1) of this section applies. The requirement set forth in paragraph (c)(1)(i) of this section is satisfied because before the DT acquisition, FT (the transferring corporation) is a member of a U.S.-parented group of which USP is the common parent (the USP group). The requirement set forth in paragraph (c)(1)(ii) of this section is satisfied because after the DT acquisition, and taking into account all transactions related to the acquisition, each of FA (which is both the successor to FT, the transferring corporation, and the foreign acquiring corporation) and USS (the person that holds the transferred stock) are members of a U.S.-parented group of which USS (a member of the

USP group before the DT acquisition) is the common parent. Moreover, the DT acquisition qualifies as an internal group restructuring under § 1.7874-1(c)(2). The requirement set forth in § 1.7874-1(c)(2)(i) is satisfied because before the DT acquisition, 80 percent or more of the stock (by vote and value) of DT was held directly or indirectly by USS (the corporation that after the acquisition, and taking into account all transactions related to the acquisition, is the common parent of the EAG). The requirement set forth in § 1.7874-1(c)(2)(ii) is satisfied because after the acquisition, and taking into account all transactions related to the acquisition, 80 percent or more of the stock (by vote and value) of FA (the foreign acquiring corporation) is held directly or indirectly by USS. Therefore, the 100 FA shares are excluded from the numerator, but included in the denominator, of the ownership fraction. Accordingly, the ownership fraction is 0/100.

Example 3. U.S.-parented group exception available—(i) *Facts.* USP, a domestic corporation wholly owned by Individual A, owns all the stock of USS, a domestic corporation, and USS owns all the stock of DT, also a domestic corporation. DT owns all the stock of FT, a foreign corporation. The FT stock represents substantially all of the property of DT for purposes of section 7874. Pursuant to a reorganization described in section 368(a)(1)(D), DT transfers all the FT stock to FA, a newly formed foreign corporation, in exchange for 100 shares of FA stock (DT acquisition) and distributes the FA stock to USS pursuant to section 361(c)(1). In a related transaction, USS distributes all the FA stock to USP under section 355(c)(1). Lastly, in another related transaction and pursuant to a divisive reorganization described in section 368(a)(1)(D), USP transfers all the stock of USS and FA to DP, a newly formed domestic corporation, in exchange for all the stock of DP and distributes the DP stock to Individual A pursuant to section 361(c)(1).

(ii) *Analysis.* The 100 FA shares received by USS are stock of a foreign acquiring corporation described in section 7874(a)(2)(B)(ii) and, under § 1.7874-5(a), the shares retain their status as such even though USS subsequently transfers the shares to USP. Thus, the 100 FA shares are included in the ownership fraction, unless the shares are treated as held by members of the EAG for purposes of applying section 7874(c)(2)(A) and § 1.7874-1 and are excluded from the ownership fraction under those rules. For purposes of applying section 7874(c)(2)(A) and § 1.7874-1, the 100 FA shares, which constitute transferred stock under paragraph (f)(2) of this section, are treated as held by members of the EAG only if an exception in paragraph (c) of this section applies. See paragraph (b) of this section. The U.S.-parented group exception described in paragraph (c)(1) of this section applies. The requirement set forth in paragraph (c)(1)(i) of this section is satisfied because before the DT acquisition, USS (the transferring corporation) is a member of a U.S.-parented group of which USP is the common parent (the USP group). The requirement set forth in paragraph (c)(1)(ii) of this section is satisfied because after the DT acquisition, and taking into account all transactions related to the acquisition, each of USS, DP (the person that holds the transferred stock), and FA (the foreign acquiring corporation) are members of a U.S.-parented group of which DP (a corporation that was formed in a transaction related to the DT acquisition and that, immediately after it was formed (but without regard to any related transactions) was a member of the USP group) is the common parent. Therefore, the 100 FA shares are excluded from the numerator and the denominator of the ownership fraction. Accordingly, the ownership fraction is 0/0.

Example 4. Foreign-parented group exception—(i) *Facts.* Individual A owns all the stock of FT, a foreign corporation, and FT owns all the stock of DT, a domestic corporation. FT does not own any other property and has no liabilities. Pursuant to a reorganization described in section 368(a)(1)(F), FT transfers all the stock of DT to FA, a newly formed foreign corporation, in exchange for 100 shares of FA stock (DT acquisition) and distributes the FA stock to Individual A in liquidation pursuant to section 361(c)(1).

(ii) *Analysis.* The 100 FA shares received by FT are stock of a foreign acquiring corporation described in section 7874(a)(2)(B)(ii) and, under § 1.7874-5(a), the shares retain their status as such even though FT subsequently distributes the shares to Individual A pursuant to section 361(c)(1). Thus, the 100 FA shares are included in the ownership fraction, unless the shares are treated as held by members of the EAG for purposes of applying section 7874(a)(2)(A) and § 1.7874-1 and are excluded from the ownership fraction under those rules. For purposes of applying section 7874(c)(2)(A) and § 1.7874-1, the 100 FA shares, which constitute transferred stock under paragraph (f)(2) of this section, are treated as held by members of the EAG only if an exception in paragraph (c) of this section applies. See paragraph (b) of this section. The foreign-parented group exception described in paragraph (c)(2) of this section applies. The requirement set forth in paragraph (c)(2)(i) of this section is satisfied because before the DT acquisition, FT (the transferring corporation) and DT are members of the foreign-parented group of which FT is the common parent. The requirement set forth in paragraph (c)(2)(ii) of this section is satisfied because after the acquisition, and taking into account all transactions related to the acquisition, FT would be a member of the EAG absent the distribution of the FA shares pursuant to section 361(c)(1). Moreover, the DT acquisition qualifies as an internal group restructuring under § 1.7874-1(c)(2). The requirement set forth in § 1.7874-1(c)(2)(i) is satisfied because before the acquisition, 80 percent or more of the stock (by vote and value) of DT was held directly or indirectly by FT, the corporation that, without regard to the distribution of the FA shares pursuant to section 361(c)(1), would be common parent of the EAG after the acquisition. See

§ 1.7874-1(c)(2)(iii). The requirement set forth in § 1.7874-1(c)(2)(ii) is satisfied because after the acquisition, but without regard to the distribution of the FA shares pursuant to the section 361(c)(1) distribution, FT would directly or indirectly hold 80 percent or more of the stock (by vote and value) of FA (the foreign acquiring corporation). See § 1.7874-1(c)(2)(iii). Therefore, the 100 FA shares are excluded from the numerator, but included in the denominator, of the ownership fraction. Accordingly, the ownership fraction is 0/100.

(iii) *Alternative facts.* The facts are the same as in paragraph (i) of this *Example 4,* except that in a transaction after and related to the DT acquisition, FA issues 200 shares of FA stock to Individual B in exchange for qualified property (within the meaning of § 1.7874-4(h)(2)). The foreign-parented group exception does not apply because after the acquisition, and taking into account FA's issuance of the 200 FA shares to Individual B, FT would not be a member of the EAG absent FT's distribution of the 100 FA shares pursuant to section 361(c)(1). Accordingly, the 100 FA shares received by FT are not treated as held by a member of the EAG for purposes of applying section 7874(c)(2)(A) and § 1.7874-1. As a result, the ownership fraction is 100/300.

(h) *Applicability dates.*—Except as otherwise provided in this paragraph (h), this section applies to domestic entity acquisitions completed on or after September 22, 2014. Paragraphs (d)(2) and (f)(2)(ii) of this section apply to domestic entity acquisitions completed on or after April 4, 2016. Taxpayers, however, may elect either to apply paragraph (c)(2) of this section to domestic entity acquisitions completed before September 22, 2014, or to consistently apply paragraphs (c)(2), (d)(2), and (f)(2)(ii) of this section and §§ 1.7874-1(c)(2)(iii) and (g) to domestic entity acquisitions completed before April 4, 2016. [Reg. § 1.7874-6.]

☐ [*T.D.* 9834, 7-11-2018.]

[Reg. § 1.7874-7]

§ 1.7874-7. Disregard of certain stock attributable to passive assets.—(a) *Scope.*—This section identifies certain stock of a foreign acquiring corporation that is attributable to passive assets and that is disregarded in determining the ownership fraction by value. Paragraph (b) of this section sets forth the general rule regarding when stock of a foreign acquiring corporation is excluded from the denominator of the ownership fraction under this section. Paragraph (c) of this section provides a de minimis exception to the application of the general rule of paragraph (b) of this section. Paragraph (d) of this section provides rules for the treatment of partnerships, and paragraph (e) of this section provides definitions. Paragraph (f) of this section provides examples illustrating the application of the rules of this section. Paragraph (g) of this section provides dates of applicability. The rules provided in this section are also subject to section

7874(c)(4). See §1.7874-1(d)(1) for rules addressing the interaction of this section with the expanded affiliated group rules of section 7874(c)(2)(A) and §1.7874-1.

(b) *General rule.*—If, on the completion date, more than fifty percent of the gross value of all foreign group property constitutes foreign group nonqualified property, then, for purposes of determining the ownership percentage by value (but not vote) described in section 7874(a)(2)(B)(ii), stock of the foreign acquiring corporation is excluded from the denominator of the ownership fraction in an amount equal to the product of—

(1) The value of the stock of the foreign acquiring corporation, other than stock that is described in section 7874(a)(2)(B)(ii) and stock that is excluded from the denominator of the ownership fraction under §1.7874-1(b), §1.7874-4(b), §1.7874-8(b), §1.7874-9(b), or section §7874(c)(4); and

(2) The foreign group nonqualified property fraction.

(c) *De minimis ownership.*—Paragraph (b) of this section does not apply if—

(1) The ownership percentage described in section 7874(a)(2)(B)(ii), determined without regard to the application of paragraph (b) of this section and §§1.7874-4(b) and 1.7874-10(b), is less than five (by vote and value); and

(2) On the completion date, each five percent former domestic entity shareholder or five percent former domestic entity partner, as applicable, owns (applying the attribution rules of section 318(a) with the modifications described in section 304(c)(3)(B)) less than five percent (by vote and value) of the stock of (or a partnership interest in) each member of the expanded affiliated group. For this purpose, a five percent former domestic entity shareholder (or five percent former domestic entity partner) is a former domestic entity shareholder (or former domestic entity partner) that, before the domestic entity acquisition, owned (applying the attribution rules of section 318(a) with the modifications described in section 304(c)(3)(B)) at least five percent (by vote and value) of the stock of (or a partnership interest in) the domestic entity.

(d) *Treatment of partnerships.*—For purposes of this section, if one or more members of the modified expanded affiliated group own, in the aggregate, more than 50 percent (by value) of the interests in a partnership, the partnership is treated as a corporation that is a member of the modified expanded affiliated group.

(e) *Definitions.*—In addition to the definitions provided in §1.7874-12, the following definitions apply for purposes of this section.

(1) *Foreign group nonqualified property.*—(i) *General rule.*—Foreign group nonqualified property means foreign group property described in §1.7874-4(h)(2), other than the following:

(A) Property that gives rise to income described in section 954(h), determined—

(1) In the case of property held by a foreign corporation, by substituting the term "foreign corporation" for the term "controlled foreign corporation;" and

(2) In the case of property held by a domestic corporation, by substituting the term "domestic corporation" for the term "controlled foreign corporation," without regard to the phrase "other than the United States" in section 954(h)(3)(A)(ii)(I), and without regard to any inference that the tests in section 954(h) should be calculated or determined without taking transactions with customers located in the United States into account.

(B) Property that gives rise to income described in section 954(i), determined by substituting the term "foreign corporation" for the term "controlled foreign corporation."

(C) Property that gives rise to income described in section 1297(b)(2)(A) or (B) (determined without regard to other passive foreign investment company rules).

(D) Property held by a domestic corporation that is subject to tax as an insurance company under subchapter L of chapter 1 of subtitle A of the Internal Revenue Code, provided that the property is required to support, or is substantially related to, the active conduct of an insurance business.

(ii) *Special rule.*—Foreign group nonqualified property also means any foreign group property that, in a transaction related to the domestic entity acquisition, is acquired in exchange for other property, including cash, if such other property would be described in paragraph (e)(1)(i) of this section had the transaction not occurred.

(2) *Foreign group property* means any property (including excluded property, as described in paragraph (e)(3)(ii) of this section)) held on the completion date by the modified expanded affiliated group, other than—

(i) Property that is directly or indirectly acquired in the domestic entity acquisition;

(ii) Stock or a partnership interest in a member of the modified expanded affiliated group; and

(iii) An obligation of a member of the modified expanded affiliated group.

(3) *Foreign group nonqualified property fraction.*—(i) *In general.*—Foreign group nonqualified property fraction means a fraction calculated with the following numerator and denominator:

(A) The numerator of the fraction is the gross value of all foreign group nonqualified property, other than excluded property (as described in paragraph (e)(3)(ii) of this section).

(B) The denominator of the fraction is the gross value of all foreign group property, other than excluded property (as described in paragraph (e)(3)(ii) of this section)

(ii) *Excluded property.*—For purposes of paragraph (e)(3) of this section, excluded property means property that gives rise to stock that is excluded from the ownership fraction with respect to the domestic entity acquisition under § 1.7874-4(b), § 1.7874-8(b), § 1.7874-9(b), or section 7874(c)(4). For this purpose, only property that was directly or indirectly acquired in a prior domestic entity acquisition (as described in § 1.7874-8(g)(4)) or covered foreign acquisition (as described in § 1.7874-9(d)(4)) with respect to the domestic entity acquisition may be considered to give rise to stock that is excluded from the ownership fraction with respect to the domestic entity acquisition under § 1.7874-8(b) or § 1.7874-9(b). If only a portion of the consideration provided in a prior domestic entity acquisition or covered foreign acquisition consisted of stock of the foreign acquiring corporation, then only a pro rata portion of a property directly or indirectly acquired in the prior domestic entity acquisition or covered foreign acquisition may be considered excluded property, based on a fraction the numerator of which is the amount of the consideration that consisted of stock of the foreign acquiring corporation and the denominator of which is the total amount of consideration.

(4) *Modified expanded affiliated group* means, with respect to a domestic entity acquisition, the group described in either paragraph (e)(4)(i) or paragraph (e)(4)(ii) of this section. A *member of the modified expanded affiliated group* is an entity included in the modified expanded affiliated group.

(i) When the foreign acquiring corporation is not the common parent corporation of the expanded affiliated group, the expanded affiliated group determined as if the foreign acquiring corporation was the common parent corporation.

(ii) When the foreign acquiring corporation is the common parent corporation of the expanded affiliated group, the expanded affiliated group.

(f) *Examples.*—The following examples illustrate the rules of this section.

Example 1. Application of general rule—(i) *Facts.* Individual A owns all 20 shares of the sole class of stock of FA, a foreign corporation. FA acquires all the stock of DT, a domestic corporation, solely in exchange for 76 shares of newly issued FA stock (DT acquisition). In a transaction related to the DT acquisition, FA issues 4 shares of stock to Individual A in exchange for Asset A, which has a gross value of $50x. On the completion date, in addition to the DT stock and Asset A, FA holds Asset B, which has a gross value of $150x, and Asset C, which has a gross value of $100x. Assets A and B, but not Asset C, are nonqualified property (within the meaning of § 1.7874-4(h)(2)). Further, Asset C was not acquired in a transaction related to the DT acquisition.

(ii) *Analysis.* The 4 shares of FA stock issued to Individual A in exchange for Asset A are disqualified stock under § 1.7874-4(c) and are ex-

cluded from the denominator of the ownership fraction pursuant to § 1.7874-4(b). Furthermore, additional shares of FA stock are excluded from the denominator of the ownership fraction pursuant to paragraph (b) of this section. This is because on the completion date, the gross value of all foreign group property is $300x (the sum of the gross values of Assets A, B, and C), the gross value of all foreign group nonqualified property is $200x (the sum of the gross values of Assets A and B), and thus 66.67% of the gross value of all foreign group property constitutes foreign group nonqualified property ($200x/$300x). Because FA has only one class of stock outstanding, the shares of FA stock that are excluded from the denominator of the ownership fraction pursuant to paragraph (b) of this section are calculated by multiplying 20 shares of FA stock (100 shares less the 76 shares described in section 7874(a)(2)(B)(ii) and the 4 shares of disqualified stock) by the foreign group nonqualified property fraction. The numerator of the foreign group nonqualified property fraction is $150x (the gross value of Asset B) and the denominator is $250x (the sum of the gross values of Assets B and C). Asset A is not taken into account for purposes of the foreign group nonqualified property fraction because it gives rise to FA stock that is excluded under § 1.7874-4(b) (4 shares) and, as a result, is excluded property. Accordingly, 12 shares of FA stock are excluded from the denominator of the ownership fraction pursuant to paragraph (b) of this section (20 shares multiplied by $150x/$250x). Thus, a total of 16 shares are excluded from the denominator of the ownership fraction (4 + 12). As a result, the ownership fraction by value is 76/84.

Example 2. Application of de minimis exception—(i) *Facts.* Individual A owns all 96 shares of the sole class of stock of FA, a foreign corporation. Individual B wholly owns DT, a domestic corporation. Individuals A and B are not related. FA acquires all the stock of DT solely in exchange for 4 shares of newly issued FA stock (DT acquisition). On the completion date, in addition to all of the stock of DT, FA holds Asset A, which is nonqualified property (within the meaning of § 1.7874-4(h)(2)).

(ii) *Analysis.* Without regard to the application of § § 1.7874-4(b) and 1.7874-10(b) as well as paragraph (b) of this section, the ownership percentage described in section 7874(a)(2)(B)(ii) would be less than 5 (by vote and value), or 4 (4/100, or 4 shares of FA stock held by Individual B by reason of owning the DT stock, determined under § 1.7874-2(f)(2), over 100 shares of FA stock outstanding after the DT acquisition). Furthermore, on the completion date, Individual B owns less than 5% (by vote and value) of the stock of FA and DT (the members of the expanded affiliated group). Accordingly, the de minimis exception in paragraph (c) of this section applies. Therefore, paragraph (b) of this section does not apply and the ownership fraction is 4/100.

Example 3. Foreign acquiring corporation not common parent of EAG—(i) *Facts.* FP, a foreign corporation, owns all 85 shares of the sole class of stock of FA, a foreign corporation. FA acquires all the stock of DT, a domestic corporation, solely in exchange for 65 shares of newly issued FA stock (DT acquisition). On the completion date, FA, in addition to all of the stock of DT, owns Asset A, which has a gross value of $40x, and Asset B, which has a gross value of $45x. Moreover, on the completion date, in addition to the 85 shares of FA stock, FP owns Asset C, which has a gross value of $10x. Assets A and C, but not Asset B, are nonqualified property (within the meaning of § 1.7874-4(h)(2)). Further, Asset B was not acquired in a transaction related to the DT acquisition in exchange for nonqualified property.

(ii) *Analysis.* Under paragraph (e)(2) of this section, Assets A and B, but not Asset C, are foreign group property. Although Asset C is held on the completion date by FP, a member of the expanded affiliated group, Asset C is not foreign group property because FP is not a member of the modified expanded affiliated group. This is the case because if the expanded affiliated group were determined based on FA as the common parent corporation, FP would not be a member of such expanded affiliated group (see paragraph (e)(4)(i) of this section). Under paragraph (e)(1) of this section, Asset A, but not Asset B, is foreign group nonqualified property. Therefore, on the completion date, the gross value of all foreign group property is $85x (the sum of the gross values of Assets A and B), and the gross value of all foreign group nonqualified property is $40x (the gross value of Asset A). Accordingly, on the completion date, only 47.06% of the gross value of all foreign group property constitutes foreign group nonqualified property ($40x/$85x). Consequently, paragraph (b) of this section does not apply to exclude any FA stock from the denominator of the ownership fraction.

Example 4. Coordination with serial acquisition rule—(i) *Facts.* Individual A owns all 30 shares of the sole class of stock of FA, a foreign corporation. In Year 1, FA acquires all the stock of DT1, a domestic corporation, solely in exchange for 40 shares of newly issued FA stock (DT1 acquisition). In Year 2, FA acquires all the stock of DT2, a domestic corporation, solely in exchange for 50 shares of newly issued FA stock (DT2 acquisition). On the completion date for the DT2 acquisition, in addition to the DT2 stock, FA holds Asset A, which has a gross value of $15x, Asset B, which has a gross value of $15x, and all the stock of DT1, which has a gross value of $40x. At all times, DT1 holds only Asset C, which has a gross value of $30x, and Asset D, which has a gross value of $10x. Assets A and C, but not Assets B and D, are nonqualified property (within the meaning of § 1.7874-4(h)(2)). In addition, at all times, the fair market value of each share of FA stock is $1x. Further, there have been no redemptions of FA stock subsequent to the DT1 acquisition. Lastly, under § 1.7874-8, the DT1 acquisition is a prior domestic entity acquisition with respect to the DT2 acquisition and

$40x of FA stock is excluded from the denominator of the ownership fraction with respect to the DT2 acquisition.

(ii) *Analysis.* Shares of FA stock are excluded from the denominator of the ownership fraction pursuant to paragraph (b) of this section. This is because on the completion date, the gross value of all foreign group property is $70x (the sum of the gross values of Assets A, B, C, and D), the gross value of all foreign group nonqualified property is $45x (the sum of the gross values of Assets A and C), and thus 64.29% of the gross value of all foreign group property constitutes foreign group nonqualified property ($45x/$70x). The shares of FA stock that are excluded from the denominator of the ownership fraction pursuant to paragraph (b) of this section are calculated by multiplying $30x (the value of all the shares of FA stock, less $50x, the value of the stock described in section 7874(a)(2)(B)(ii), less $40x, the value of the stock excluded under § 1.7874-8(b)) by the foreign group nonqualified property fraction. The property taken into account for purposes of determining the foreign group nonqualified property fraction is Asset A and Asset B. Asset C and Asset D are not taken into account for purposes of the foreign group nonqualified property fraction because they are excluded property. This is because FA indirectly acquired the Assets in the DT1 acquisition (a prior domestic entity acquisition with respect to the DT2 acquisition) and, as a result of that acquisition, $40x of FA stock is excluded from the denominator of the ownership fraction with respect to the DT2 acquisition under § 1.7874-8(b). Thus, the numerator of the foreign group nonqualified property fraction is $15x (the gross value of Asset A) and the denominator is $30x (the sum of the gross values of Asset A, $15x, and Asset B, $15x). Accordingly, $15x of FA stock is excluded from the denominator of the ownership fraction pursuant to paragraph (b) of this section ($30x multiplied by $15x/$30x). Thus, a total of $55x of FA stock is excluded from the denominator of the ownership fraction ($40x + $15x), making the denominator $65x ($120x - $55x). As a result, the ownership percentage with respect to the DT2 acquisition by value is 76.92 ($50x/$65x).

(iii) *Alternative facts.* The facts are the same as in paragraph (i) of this *Example 4,* except as follows. Initially, there are 40 shares of FA stock outstanding, all of which are owned by Individual A. At all times, the gross value of asset D is $20x. In the DT1 acquisition, FA acquires all the stock of DT1 ($50x fair market value) solely in exchange for 40 shares of newly issued FA stock and $10x of other property. As in paragraph (i) of this *Example 4,* shares of FA stock are excluded from the denominator of the ownership fraction pursuant to paragraph (b) of this section. This is because on the completion date, the gross value of all foreign group property is $80x (the sum of the gross values of Assets A, B, C, and D), the gross value of all foreign group nonqualified property is $45x (the sum of the gross values of Assets A and C), and thus 56.25%

of the gross value of all foreign group property constitutes foreign group nonqualified property ($45x/$80x). The shares of FA stock that are excluded from the denominator of the ownership fraction pursuant to paragraph (b) of this section are calculated by multiplying $40x ($130x, the value of all the shares of FA stock, less $50x, the value of the stock described in section 7874(a)(2)(B)(ii), less $40x, the value of the stock excluded under §1.7874-8(b)) by the foreign group nonqualified property fraction. The property taken into account for purposes of determining the foreign group nonqualified property fraction is Asset A, Asset B, and the portion of Asset C and Asset D that is not excluded property. Eighty percent of each of Asset C and Asset D are considered excluded property because FA indirectly acquired Asset C and Asset D in the DT1 acquisition (a prior domestic entity acquisition with respect to the DT2 acquisition); as a result of that acquisition, $40x of FA stock is excluded from the denominator of the ownership fraction with respect to the DT2 acquisition under §1.7874-8(b); and 80% of the consideration provided in the DT1 acquisition consisted of stock of FA ($40x/$50x). Thus, the numerator of the foreign group nonqualified property fraction is $21x (the sum of the gross values of Asset A, $15x, and the portion of Asset C that is not excluded property, $6x) and the denominator is $40x (the sum of the gross values of Asset A, $15x, Asset B, $15x, and the portion of Asset C and Asset D that is not excluded property, $6x and $4x, respectively). Accordingly, $21x of FA stock is excluded from the denominator of the ownership fraction pursuant to paragraph (b) of this section ($40x multiplied by $21x/$40x). Thus, a total of $61x of FA stock is excluded from the denominator of the ownership fraction pursuant to paragraph (b) of this section ($40x + $21x), making the denominator $69x ($130x - $61x). As a result, the ownership percentage with respect to D2 acquisition by value is 72.46 ($50x/$69x).

(g) *Applicability dates.*—This section applies to domestic entity acquisitions completed on or after July 12, 2018. For domestic entity acquisitions completed before July 12, 2018, see §1.7874-7T, as contained in 26 CFR part 1 revised as of April 1, 2017. However, to the extent this section differs from §1.7874-7T, as contained in 26 CFR part 1 revised as of April 1, 2017, taxpayers may elect to consistently apply the differences to domestic entity acquisitions completed before July 12, 2018. [Reg. §1.7874-7.]

☐ [T.D. 9834, 7-11-2018.]

[Reg. §1.7874-8]

§1.7874-8. Disregard of certain stock attributable to serial acquisitions.—(a) *Scope.*—This section identifies stock of a foreign acquiring corporation that is disregarded in determining an ownership fraction by value because it is attributable to certain prior domestic entity acquisitions. Paragraph (b) of this section sets forth

the general rule regarding the amount of stock of a foreign acquiring corporation that is excluded from the denominator of the ownership fraction by value under this section, and paragraphs (c) through (f) of this section provide rules for determining this amount. Paragraph (g) provides definitions. Paragraph (h) of this section provides examples illustrating the application of the rules of this section. Paragraph (i) of this section provides dates of applicability. This section applies after taking into account §1.7874-2(e). See §1.7874-1(d)(1) for rules addressing the interaction of this section with the expanded affiliated group rules of section 7874(c)(2)(A) and §1.7874-1.

(b) *General rule.*—This paragraph (b) applies to a domestic entity acquisition (relevant domestic entity acquisition) when the foreign acquiring corporation (including a predecessor, as defined in §1.7874-10(f)(1)) has completed one or more prior domestic entity acquisitions. When this paragraph (b) applies, then, for purposes of determining the ownership percentage by value (but not vote) described in section 7874(a)(2)(B)(ii), stock of the foreign acquiring corporation is excluded from the denominator of the ownership fraction in an amount equal to the sum of the excluded amounts computed separately with respect to each prior domestic entity acquisition and each relevant share class.

(c) *Computation of excluded amounts.*—With respect to each prior domestic entity acquisition and each relevant share class, the excluded amount is the product of—

(1) The total number of prior acquisition shares, reduced by the sum of the number of allocable redeemed shares for all redemption testing periods; and

(2) The fair market value of a single share of stock of the relevant share class on the completion date of the relevant domestic entity acquisition.

(d) *Computation of allocable redeemed shares.*—(1) *In general.*—With respect to each prior domestic entity acquisition and each relevant share class, the allocable redeemed shares, determined separately for each redemption testing period, is the product of the number of redeemed shares during the redemption testing period and the redemption fraction.

(2) *Redemption fraction.*—The redemption fraction is determined separately with respect to each prior domestic entity acquisition, each relevant share class, and each redemption testing period, as follows:

(i) The numerator is the total number of prior acquisition shares, reduced by the sum of the number of allocable redeemed shares for all prior redemption testing periods.

(ii) The denominator is the sum of—

(A) The number of outstanding shares of the foreign acquiring corporation stock as of the end of the last day of the redemption testing period; and

(B) The number of redeemed shares during the redemption testing period.

(e) *Rules for determining redemption testing periods.*—(1) *In general.*—Except as provided in paragraph (e)(2) of this section, a redemption testing period with respect to a prior domestic entity acquisition is the period beginning on the day after the completion date of the prior domestic entity acquisition and ending on the day prior to the completion date of the relevant domestic entity acquisition.

(2) *Election to use multiple redemption testing periods.*—A foreign acquiring corporation may establish a reasonable method for dividing the period described in paragraph (e)(1) of this section into shorter periods (each such shorter period, a redemption testing period). A reasonable method would include a method based on a calendar convention (for example, daily, monthly, quarterly, or yearly), or on a convention that triggers the start of a new redemption testing period whenever a share issuance occurs that exceeds a certain threshold. In order to be reasonable, the method must be consistently applied with respect to all prior domestic entity acquisitions and all relevant share classes.

(f) *Appropriate adjustments required to take into account share splits and similar transactions.*—For purposes of this section, appropriate adjustments must be made to take into account changes in a foreign acquiring corporation's capital structure, including, for example, stock splits, reverse stock splits, stock distributions, recapitalizations, and similar transactions. Thus, for example, in determining the total number of prior acquisition shares with respect to a relevant share class, appropriate adjustments must be made to take into account a stock split with respect to that relevant share class that occurs after the completion date with respect to a prior domestic entity acquisition.

(g) *Definitions.*—In addition to the definitions provided in § 1.7874-12, the following definitions apply for purposes of this section.

(1) A *binding contract* means an instrument enforceable under applicable law against the parties to the instrument. The presence of a condition outside the control of the parties (including, for example, regulatory agency approval) does not prevent an instrument from being a binding contract. Further, the fact that insubstantial terms remain to be negotiated by the parties to the contract, or that customary conditions remain to be satisfied, does not prevent an instrument from being a binding contract. A tender offer that is subject to section 14(d) of the Securities and Exchange Act of 1934, (15 U.S.C. 78n(d)(1)), and Regulation 14D (17 CFR 240.14d-1 through 240.14d-103) and that is not pursuant to a binding contract, is treated as a binding contract made on the date of its announcement, notwithstanding that it may be modified by the offeror or that it is not enforceable against the offerees.

(2) A *relevant share class* means, with respect to a prior domestic entity acquisition, each separate legal class of shares in the foreign acquiring corporation from which prior acquisition shares were issued. See also paragraph (f) of this section (requiring appropriate adjustments in certain cases).

(3) *Total number of prior acquisition shares* means, with respect to a prior domestic entity acquisition and each relevant share class, the total number of shares of stock of the foreign acquiring corporation that were described in section 7874(a)(2)(B)(ii) as a result of that acquisition (without regard to whether the 60 percent test of section 7874(a)(2)(B)(ii) was satisfied), other than stock treated as received by former domestic entity shareholders or former domestic entity partners under § 1.7874-10(b) or section 7874(c)(4), adjusted as appropriate under paragraph (f) of this section.

(4) A *prior domestic entity acquisition.*—(i) *General rule.*—Except as provided in this paragraph (g)(4), a prior domestic entity acquisition means, with respect to a relevant domestic entity acquisition, a domestic entity acquisition that occurred within the 36-month period ending on the signing date of the relevant domestic entity acquisition.

(ii) *Exception.*—A domestic entity acquisition is not a prior domestic entity acquisition if it is described in paragraph (g)(4)(ii)(A) or (B) of this section.

(A) *De minimis.*—A domestic entity acquisition is described in this paragraph (g)(4)(ii)(A) if—

(1) The ownership percentage described in section 7874(a)(2)(B)(ii) with respect to the domestic entity acquisition was less than five (by vote and value); and

(2) The fair market value of the stock of the foreign acquiring corporation described in section 7874(a)(2)(B)(ii) as a result of the domestic entity acquisition (without regard to whether the 60 percent test of section 7874(a)(2)(B)(ii) was satisfied) did not exceed $50 million, as determined on the completion date with respect to the domestic entity acquisition.

(B) *Foreign-parented group.*—A domestic entity acquisition is described in this paragraph (g)(4)(ii)(B) if—

(1) Before the domestic entity acquisition and any related transaction, the domestic entity was a member of a foreign-parented group (as described in § 1.7874-6(f)(1)); and

(2) The domestic entity acquisition qualified for the internal group restructuring exception under § 1.7874-1(c)(2).

(5) A *redeemed share* means a share of stock in a relevant share class that was redeemed (within the meaning of section 317(b)).

(6) A *signing date* means the first date on which the contract to effect the relevant domestic entity acquisition is a binding contract, or if another binding contract to effect a substantially

similar acquisition was terminated with a principal purpose of avoiding section 7874, the first date on which such other contract was a binding contract.

(h) *Examples.*—The following examples illustrate the rules of this section.

Example 1. Application of general rule—(i) *Facts.* Individual A wholly owns DT1, a domestic corporation. Individual B owns all 100 shares of the sole class of stock of FA, a foreign corporation. In Year 1, FA acquires all the stock of DT1 solely in exchange for 100 shares of newly issued FA stock (DT1 acquisition). On the completion date with respect to the DT1 acquisition, the fair market value of each share of FA stock is $1x. In Year 3, FA enters into a binding contract to acquire all the stock of DT2, a domestic corporation wholly owned by Individual C. Thereafter, FA acquires all the stock of DT2 solely in exchange for 150 shares of newly issued FA stock (DT2 acquisition). On the completion date with respect to the DT2 acquisition, the fair market value of each share of FA stock is $1.50x. FA did not complete the DT1 acquisition and DT2 acquisition pursuant to a plan (or series of related transactions) for purposes of applying § 1.7874-2(e). In addition, there have been no redemptions of FA stock subsequent to the DT1 acquisition.

(ii) *Analysis.* The DT1 acquisition is a prior domestic entity acquisition with respect to the DT2 acquisition (the relevant domestic entity acquisition) because the DT1 acquisition occurred within the 36-month period ending on the signing date with respect to the DT2 acquisition. Accordingly, paragraph (b) of this section applies to the DT2 acquisition. As a result, and because there were no redemptions of FA stock, the excluded amount is $150x, calculated as 100 (the total number of prior acquisition shares) multiplied by $1.50x (the fair market value of a single share of FA stock on the completion date with respect to the DT2 acquisition). Accordingly, the numerator of the ownership fraction by value is $225x (the fair market value of the stock of FA that, with respect to the DT2 acquisition, is described in section 7874(a)(2)(B)(ii)) (150 shares x $1.50x per share). In addition, the denominator of the ownership fraction is $375x (calculated as $525x, the fair market value of all 350 shares of FA stock as of the completion date with respect to the DT2 acquisition, less $150x, the excluded amount). Therefore, the ownership percentage by value is 60 ($225x divided by $375x).

Example 2. Effect of certain redemptions—(i) *Facts.* The facts are the same as in paragraph (i) of *Example 1* of this paragraph (h), except that in Year 2 FA redeems 50 shares of its stock (the Year 2 redemption).

(ii) *Analysis.* As is the case in paragraph (ii) of *Example 1* of this paragraph (h), the DT1 acquisition is a prior domestic entity acquisition with respect to the DT2 acquisition (the relevant domestic entity acquisition), and paragraph (b) of this section thus applies to the DT2 acquisition. Because of the Year 2 redemption, the allocable

redeemed shares, and thus the redemption fraction, must be calculated. For this purpose, the redemption testing period is the period beginning on the day after the completion date with respect to the DT1 acquisition and ending on the day prior to the completion date with respect to the DT2 acquisition. The redemption fraction for the redemption testing period is thus 100/200, calculated as 100 (the total number of prior acquisition shares) divided by 200 (150, the number of outstanding shares of FA stock on the last day of the redemption testing period, plus 50, the number of redeemed shares during the redemption testing period), and the allocable redeemed shares for the redemption testing period is 25, calculated as 50 (the number of redeemed shares during the redemption testing period) multiplied by 100/200 (the redemption fraction for the redemption testing period). As a result, the excluded amount is $112.50x, calculated as 75 (100, the total number of prior acquisition shares, less 25, the allocable redeemed shares) multiplied by $1.50x (the fair market value of a single share of FA stock on the completion date with respect to the DT2 acquisition). Accordingly, the numerator of the ownership fraction by value is $225x (the fair market value of the stock of FA that, with respect to the DT2 acquisition, is described in section 7874(a)(2)(B)(ii)) (150 shares x $1.50x per share), and the denominator of the ownership fraction is $337.50x (calculated as $450x, the fair market value of all 300 shares of FA stock as of the completion date with respect to the DT2 acquisition, less $112.50x, the excluded amount). Therefore, the ownership percentage by value is 66.67 ($225x divided by $337.50x).

Example 3. Stock split—(i) *Facts.* The facts are the same as in paragraph (i) of *Example 2* of this paragraph (h), except as follows. After the Year 2 redemption, but before the DT2 acquisition, FA undergoes a stock split and, as a result, each of the 150 shares of FA stock outstanding are converted into two shares (Year 2 stock split). Further, pursuant to the DT2 acquisition, FA acquires all the stock of DT2 solely in exchange for 300 shares of newly issued FA stock. Moreover, on the completion date with respect to the DT2 acquisition, the fair market value of each share of FA stock is $0.75x.

(ii) *Analysis.* As is the case in paragraph (ii) of *Example 1* of this paragraph (h), the DT1 acquisition is a prior domestic entity acquisition with respect to the DT2 acquisition (the relevant domestic entity acquisition), and paragraph (b) of this section thus applies to the DT2 acquisition. In addition, as is the case in paragraph (ii) of *Example 2* of this paragraph (h), the redemption testing period is the period beginning on the day after the completion date with respect to the DT1 acquisition and ending on the day prior to the completion date with respect to the DT2 acquisition. To calculate the redemption fraction, the total number of prior acquisition shares and the number of redeemed shares during the redemption testing period must be appropriately adjusted to take into account the Year 2 stock split.

See paragraph (f) of this section. In this case, the appropriate adjustment is to increase the total number of prior acquisition shares from 100 to 200 and to increase the number of redeemed shares during the redemption testing period from 50 to 100. Thus, the redemption fraction for the redemption testing period is 200/400, calculated as 200 (the total number of prior acquisition shares) divided by 400 (300, the number of outstanding shares of FA stock on the last day of the redemption testing period, plus 100, the number of redeemed shares during the redemption testing period), and the allocable redeemed shares for the redemption testing period is 50, calculated as 100 (the number of redeemed shares during the redemption testing period) multiplied by 200/400 (the redemption fraction for the redemption testing period). In addition, for purposes of calculating the excluded amount, the total number of prior acquisition shares must be adjusted from 100 to 200. See paragraph (f) of this section. Accordingly, the excluded amount is $112.50x, calculated as 150 (200, the total number of prior acquisition shares, less 50, the allocable redeemed shares) multiplied by $0.75x (the fair market value of a single share of FA stock on the completion date with respect to the DT2 acquisition). Consequently, the numerator of the ownership fraction by value is $225x (the fair market value of the stock of FA that, with respect to the DT2 acquisition, is described in section 7874(a)(2)(B)(ii)) (300 shares x $0.75x per share), and the denominator of the ownership fraction is $337.50x (calculated as $450x, the fair market value of all 600 shares of FA stock as of the completion date with respect to the DT2 acquisition, less $112.50x, the excluded amount). Therefore, the ownership percentage by value is 66.67 ($225 divided by $337.50x).

(i) *Applicability dates.*—Except as provided in this paragraph (i), this section applies to domestic entity acquisitions completed on or after April 4, 2016, regardless of when a prior domestic entity acquisition was completed. Paragraphs (g)(3) and (g)(4)(ii) of this section apply to domestic entity acquisitions completed on or after July 12, 2018. However, taxpayers may elect to consistently apply paragraphs (g)(3) and (g)(4)(ii) of this section to domestic entity acquisitions completed on or after April 4, 2016, and before July 12, 2018. For domestic entity acquisitions completed on or after April 4, 2016, and before July 12, 2018, see §1.7874-8T(g)(3) and (g)(4)(ii) as contained in 26 CFR part 1 revised as of April 1, 2017. [Reg. §1.7874-8.]

☐ [*T.D.* 9834, 7-11-2018.]

[Reg. §1.7874-9]

§1.7874-9. Disregard of certain stock in third-country transactions.—(a) *Scope.*—This section identifies certain stock of a foreign acquiring corporation that is disregarded in determining the ownership fraction. Paragraph (b) of this section provides a rule that, in a third-country transaction, excludes from the denominator of the ownership fraction stock in the foreign

acquiring corporation held by former shareholders of an acquired foreign corporation by reason of holding certain stock in that foreign corporation. Paragraph (c) of this section defines a third-country transaction, and paragraph (d) of this section provides other definitions. Paragraph (e) of this section provides operating rules. Paragraph (f) of this section provides an example illustrating the application of the rules of this section. Paragraph (g) of this section provides the dates of applicability. See §1.7874-1(d)(1) for rules addressing the interaction of this section with the expanded affiliated group rules of section 7874(c)(2)(A) and §1.7874-1.

(b) *Exclusion of certain stock of a foreign acquiring corporation from the ownership fraction.*—When a domestic entity acquisition is a third-country transaction, stock of the foreign acquiring corporation held by reason of holding stock in the acquired foreign corporation (within the meaning of paragraph (e)(4) of this section) is, to the extent the stock otherwise would be included in the denominator of the ownership fraction, excluded from the denominator of the ownership fraction pursuant to this paragraph.

(c) *Third-country transaction.*—A domestic entity acquisition is a third-country transaction if the following requirements are satisfied:

(1) The foreign acquiring corporation completes a covered foreign acquisition pursuant to a plan (or series of related transactions) that includes the domestic entity acquisition.

(2) After the covered foreign acquisition and all related transactions are complete, the foreign acquiring corporation is not a tax resident of the foreign country in which the acquired foreign corporation was a tax resident before the covered foreign acquisition and all related transactions.

(3) The ownership percentage described in section 7874(a)(2)(B)(ii), determined without regard to the application of paragraph (b) of this section, is at least 60.

(d) *Definitions.*—In addition to the definitions provided in §1.7874-12, the following definitions apply for purposes of this section.

(1) A *foreign acquisition* means a transaction in which a foreign acquiring corporation directly or indirectly acquires substantially all of the properties held directly or indirectly by an acquired foreign corporation (within the meaning of paragraph (e)(2) of this section).

(2) An *acquired foreign corporation* means a foreign corporation whose properties are acquired in a foreign acquisition.

(3) *Foreign ownership percentage* means, with respect to a foreign acquisition, the percentage of stock (by vote or value) of the foreign acquiring corporation held by reason of holding stock in the acquired foreign corporation (within the meaning of paragraph (e)(3) of this section).

(4) *Covered foreign acquisition.*—(i) *In general.*—Except as provided in paragraphs (d)(4)(ii) and (iii) of this section, a covered foreign acquisi-

tion means a foreign acquisition in which, after the acquisition and all related transactions are complete, the foreign ownership percentage is at least 60.

(ii) *Substantial business activities exception.*—A foreign acquisition is not a covered foreign acquisition if, on the completion date, the following requirements are satisfied:

(A) The foreign acquiring corporation is a tax resident of a foreign country.

(B) The expanded affiliated group has substantial business activities in the country in which the foreign acquiring corporation is a tax resident when compared to the total business activities of the expanded affiliated group. For this purpose, the principles of § 1.7874-3 apply and the determination of whether there are substantial business activities is made without regard to the domestic entity acquisition.

(iii) *No income tax exception.*—A foreign acquisition is not a covered foreign acquisition if—

(A) Before the acquisition and all related transactions, the acquired foreign corporation was created or organized in, or under the law of, a foreign country that does not impose corporate income tax and was not a tax resident of any other foreign country; and

(B) After the acquisition and all related transactions are complete, the foreign acquiring corporation is created or organized in, or under the law of, a foreign country that does not impose corporate income tax and is not a tax resident of any other foreign country.

(5) A *tax resident* of a foreign country has the meaning set forth in § 1.7874-3(d)(11).

(e) *Operating rules.*—The following rules apply for purposes of this section.

(1) *Acquisition of multiple foreign corporations that are tax residents of the same foreign country.*—When multiple foreign acquisitions occur pursuant to the same plan (or a series of related transactions) and two or more of the acquired foreign corporations were tax residents of the same foreign country before the foreign acquisitions and all related transactions, then those foreign acquisitions are treated as a single foreign acquisition and those acquired foreign corporations are treated as a single acquired foreign corporation for purposes of this section.

(2) *Acquisition of properties of an acquired foreign corporation.*—For purposes of determining whether a foreign acquisition occurs, the principles of section 7874(a)(2)(B)(i) and § 1.7874-2(c) and (d) (regarding acquisitions of properties of a domestic entity and acquisitions by multiple foreign corporations) apply with the following modifications:

(i) The principles of § 1.7874-2(c)(1) (providing rules for determining whether there is an indirect acquisition of properties of a domestic entity), including § 1.7874-2(b)(5) (providing rules for determining the proportionate amount of properties indirectly acquired), apply by sub-stituting the term "foreign" for "domestic" wherever it appears.

(ii) The principles of § 1.7874-2(c)(2) (regarding acquisitions of stock of a foreign corporation that owns a domestic entity) apply by substituting the term "domestic" for "foreign" wherever it appears.

(3) *Computation of foreign ownership percentage.*—For purposes of determining a foreign ownership percentage, the principles of all rules applicable to calculating an ownership percentage apply (including § § 1.7874-2, 1.7874-4, 1.7874-5, 1.7874-7, and section 7874(c)(4)) with the following modifications:

(i) Stock of a foreign acquiring corporation described in section 7874(a)(2)(B)(ii) is not taken into account.

(ii) The principles of this section, section 7874(c)(2)(A), and § § 1.7874-1, 1.7874-6, 1.7874-8, and 1.7874-10 do not apply.

(iii) The principles of § 1.7874-7 apply by, in addition to the exclusions listed in § 1.7874-7(e)(2)(i) through (iii), also excluding from the definition of foreign group property any property held directly or indirectly by the acquired foreign corporation immediately before the foreign acquisition and directly or indirectly acquired in the foreign acquisition.

(4) *Stock held by reason of holding stock in an acquired foreign corporation.*—For purposes of determining stock of a foreign acquiring corporation held by reason of holding stock in an acquired foreign corporation, the principles of section 7874(a)(2)(B)(ii) and § § 1.7874-2(f) and 1.7874-5 apply.

(5) *Change in the tax residency of a foreign corporation.*—For purposes of this section, a change in a country in which a foreign corporation is a tax resident is treated as a transaction. Further, for purposes of this section, if a foreign acquiring corporation changes the country in which it is a tax resident in a manner that would not otherwise be considered to result in a foreign acquisition (for example, by changing where it is managed and controlled), then the foreign acquiring corporation is treated as—

(i) Both an acquired foreign corporation and a foreign acquiring corporation; and

(ii) Directly or indirectly acquiring all of the properties held directly or indirectly by the acquired foreign corporation solely in exchange for stock of the foreign acquiring corporation.

(f) *Example.*—The following example illustrates the rules of this section.

Example. Third-country transaction—(i) *Facts.* FA, a newly formed foreign corporation that is a tax resident of Country Y, acquires all the stock of DT, a domestic corporation that is wholly owned by Individual A, solely in exchange for 65 shares of newly issued FA stock (DT acquisition). Pursuant to a plan that includes the DT acquisition, FA acquires all the stock of FT, a foreign corporation that is a tax resident of Country X and wholly owned by Individual B, solely in exchange for the remaining 35 shares of newly issued FA stock (FT acquisition). After the FT acquisition and all related transactions, the expanded affiliated group does not have substantial business activities in Country Y when compared to the total business activities of the expanded affiliated group, as determined under the principles of § 1.7874-3 and without regard to the DT acquisition.

(ii) *Analysis.* As described in paragraphs (A) through (C) of this *Example*, the requirements set forth in paragraphs (c)(1) through (3) of this section are satisfied and, as result, the DT acquisition is a third-country transaction.

(A) The FT acquisition is a foreign acquisition because, pursuant to the FT acquisition, FA (a foreign acquiring corporation) acquires 100 percent of the stock of FT and is thus treated as indirectly acquiring 100 percent of the properties held by FT (an acquired foreign corporation). See § 1.7874-2(c)(1) and paragraph (e)(2) of this section. Moreover, Individual B is treated as receiving 35 shares of FA stock by reason of holding stock in FT. See § 1.7874-2(f)(1)(i) and paragraph (e)(4) of this section. As a result, not taking into account the 65 shares of FA stock held by Individual A (a former domestic entity shareholder), 100 percent (35/35) of the stock of FA is held by reason of holding stock in FT and, thus, the foreign ownership percentage is 100. See paragraph (e)(3) of this section. Accordingly, the FT acquisition is a covered foreign acquisition. Therefore, because the FT acquisition occurs pursuant to a plan that includes the DT acquisition, the requirement set forth in paragraph (c)(1) of this section is satisfied.

(B) The requirement set forth in paragraph (c)(2) of this section is satisfied because, after the FT acquisition and all related transactions, the foreign country in which FA is a tax resident (Country Y) is different than the foreign country in which FT was a resident (Country X) before the FT acquisition and all related transactions.

(C) The requirement set forth in paragraph (c)(3) of this section is satisfied because, not taking into account paragraph (b) of this section, the ownership fraction is 65/100 and the ownership percentage is 65.

(D) Because the DT acquisition is a third-country transaction, the 35 shares of FA stock held by reason of holding stock in FT are excluded from the denominator of the ownership fraction. See paragraph (b) of this section. As a result, the ownership fraction is 65/65 and the ownership percentage is 100. The result would be the same if instead FA had directly acquired all of the properties held by FT in exchange for FA stock, for example, in a transaction that would qualify for U.S. federal income tax purposes as an asset reorganization under section 368.

(iii) *Alternative facts.* The facts are the same as in paragraph (i) of this example, except that before the FT acquisition, but in a transaction related to the FT acquisition, FT becomes a tax resident of Country Y by reincorporating in Country Y. As is the case in paragraph (ii) of this

Example, the requirements set forth in paragraphs (c)(1) and (3) of this section are satisfied. The requirement set forth in paragraph (c)(2) of this section is satisfied because, after the FT acquisition and any related transactions, the foreign country of which FA is a tax resident (Country Y) is different than the foreign country of which FT was a tax resident (Country X) before the FT acquisition and the reincorporation. See paragraph (e)(5) of this section. Accordingly, the DT acquisition is a third-country transaction and the consequences are the same as in paragraph (ii)(D) of this *Example*.

(iv) *Alternative facts.* The facts are the same as in paragraph (i) of this *Example*, except that, instead of FA acquiring all of the stock of FT, FS, a newly formed foreign corporation that is wholly owned by FA and that is a tax resident of Country X, acquires all the stock of FT solely in exchange for 35 shares of newly issued FA stock (FT acquisition). As a result of the FT acquisition, FS and FA are each treated as indirectly acquiring 100 percent of the properties held by FT. See § 1.7874-2(c)(1)(i) and (iii) and paragraph (e)(2) of this section. Accordingly, each of FS's and FA's indirect acquisition of properties of FT (an acquired foreign corporation) is a foreign acquisition. However, FS's indirect acquisition of FT's properties is not a covered foreign acquisition because no shares of FS stock are held by reason of holding stock in FT; thus, with respect to this foreign acquisition, the foreign ownership percentage is zero. See § 1.7874-2(f) and paragraphs (e)(3) and (4) of this section. FA's indirect acquisition of FT's properties is a covered foreign acquisition because 35 shares of FA stock (the shares received by Individual B) are held by reason of holding stock in FT; thus, the foreign ownership percentage is 100 percent (35/35). See § 1.7874-2(f)(1)(i) and paragraphs (e)(3) and (4) of this section. Accordingly, because the FT acquisition occurs pursuant to a plan that includes the DT acquisition, the requirement set forth in paragraph (c)(1) of this section is satisfied. Further, as is the case in paragraphs (ii)(B) through (C) of this *Example*, the requirements set forth in paragraphs (c)(2) and (3) of this section are satisfied. Therefore, the DT acquisition is a third-country transaction and the consequences are the same as in paragraph (ii)(D) of this *Example*.

(g) *Applicability dates.*—This section applies to domestic entity acquisitions completed on or after July 12, 2018. For domestic entity acquisitions completed before July 12, 2018, see § 1.7874-9T, as contained in 26 CFR part 1 revised as of April 1, 2017. However, to the extent this section differs from § 1.7874-9T, as contained in 26 CFR part 1 revised as of April 1, 2017, taxpayers may elect to consistently apply the differences to domestic entity acquisitions completed before July 12, 2018. [Reg. § 1.7874-9.]

☐ [*T.D.* 9834, 7-11-2018.]

[Reg. § 1.7874-10]

§ 1.7874-10. Disregard of certain distributions.—(a) *Scope.*—This section identifies distributions made by a domestic entity that are disregarded in determining an ownership fraction. Paragraph (b) of this section provides the general rule that former domestic entity shareholders or former domestic entity partners are treated as receiving additional stock of the foreign acquiring corporation when the domestic entity has made non-ordinary course distributions (NOCDs). Paragraph (c) of this section identifies distributions that, in whole or in part, are outside the scope of this section. Paragraph (d) of this section provides a de minimis exception to the application of the general rule in paragraph (b) of this section. Paragraph (e) of this section provides rules concerning the treatment of distributions made by a predecessor, and paragraph (f) of this section provides rules for identifying a predecessor. Paragraph (g) of this section provides a special rule for certain distributions described in section 355. Paragraph (h) of this section provides rules regarding the allocation of NOCD stock. Paragraph (i) of this section addresses cases in which there are multiple foreign acquiring corporations, and paragraph (j) of this section addresses cases in which multiple domestic entities are treated as a single domestic entity. Paragraph (k) of this section provides definitions. Paragraph (l) of this section provides dates of applicability. See § 1.7874-1(d)(2) for rules addressing the interaction of this section with the expanded affiliated group rules of section 7874(c)(2)(A) and § 1.7874-1.

(b) *General rule regarding NOCDs.*—Except as provided in paragraph (d) of this section, for purposes of determining the ownership percentage by value (but not vote) described in section 7874(a)(2)(B)(ii), former domestic entity shareholders or former domestic entity partners, as applicable, are treated as receiving, by reason of holding stock or partnership interests in a domestic entity, stock of the foreign acquiring corporation with a fair market value equal to the amount of the non-ordinary course distributions (NOCDs), determined as of the date of the distributions, made by the domestic entity during the look-back period. The stock of the foreign acquiring corporation treated as received under this paragraph (b) (NOCD stock) is in addition to stock of the foreign acquiring corporation otherwise treated as received by the former domestic entity shareholders or former domestic entity partners by reason of holding stock or partnership interests in the domestic entity.

(c) *Distributions that are not NOCDs.*—If only a portion of a distribution is an NOCD, section 7874(c)(4) may apply to the remainder of the distribution. This section does not, however, create a presumption that section 7874(c)(4) applies to the remainder of the distribution.

(d) *De minimis exception to the general rule.*— Paragraph (b) of this section does not apply if—

(1) The ownership percentage described in section 7874(a)(2)(B)(ii), determined without regard to the application of paragraph (b) of this

section and §§ 1.7874-4(b) and 1.7874-7(b), is less than five (by vote and value); and

(2) On the completion date, each five percent former domestic entity shareholder or five percent former domestic entity partner, as applicable, owns (applying the attribution rules of section 318(a) with the modifications described in section 304(c)(3)(B)) less than five percent (by vote and value) of the stock of (or a partnership interest in) each member of the expanded affiliated group. For this purpose, a five percent former domestic entity shareholder (or five percent former domestic entity partner) is a former domestic entity shareholder (or former domestic entity partner) that, before the domestic entity acquisition, owned (applying the attribution rules of section 318(a) with the modifications described in section 304(c)(3)(B)) at least five percent (by vote and value) of the stock of (or a partnership interest in) the domestic entity.

(e) *Treatment of distributions made by a predecessor.*—For purposes of this section, a corporation or a partnership (relevant entity), including a domestic entity, is treated as making the following distributions made by a predecessor with respect to the relevant entity:

(1) A distribution made before the predecessor acquisition with respect to the predecessor; and

(2) A distribution made in connection with the predecessor acquisition to the extent the property distributed is directly or indirectly provided by the predecessor. See paragraph (k)(1)(iv) of this section.

(f) *Rules for identifying a predecessor.*—(1) *Definition of predecessor.*—A corporation or a partnership (tentative predecessor) is a predecessor with respect to a relevant entity if—

(i) The relevant entity completes a predecessor acquisition; and

(ii) After the predecessor acquisition and all related transactions are complete, the tentative predecessor ownership percentage is at least 10.

(2) *Definition of predecessor acquisition.*— (i) *In general.*—Predecessor acquisition means a transaction in which a relevant entity directly or indirectly acquires substantially all of the properties held directly or indirectly by a tentative predecessor.

(ii) *Acquisition of properties of a tentative predecessor.*—For purposes of determining whether a predecessor acquisition occurs, the principles of section 7874(a)(2)(B)(i) apply, including § 1.7874-2(c) other than § 1.7874-2(c)(2) and (4) (regarding acquisitions of properties of a domestic entity), without regard to whether the tentative predecessor is domestic or foreign.

(iii) *Lower-tier entities of a predecessor.*—If, before a predecessor acquisition and all related transactions, the predecessor held directly or indirectly stock in a corporation or an interest in a partnership, then, for purposes of this section, the relevant entity is not considered to directly or indirectly acquire the properties held directly or indirectly by the corporation or partnership.

(3) *Definition of tentative predecessor ownership percentage.*—Tentative predecessor ownership percentage means, with respect to a predecessor acquisition, the percentage of stock or partnership interests (by value) in a relevant entity held by reason of holding stock or partnership interests in the tentative predecessor. For purposes of computing the tentative predecessor ownership percentage, the following rules apply:

(i) For purposes of determining the stock or partnership interests in a relevant entity held by reason of holding stock or partnership interests in the tentative predecessor, the principles of section 7874(a)(2)(B)(ii) and §§ 1.7874-2(f)(1)(i) through (iii) and 1.7874-5 apply.

(ii) For purposes of determining the stock or partnership interests in a relevant entity included in the numerator of the fraction used to compute the tentative predecessor ownership percentage, the rules of paragraph (f)(3)(i) of this section apply, and all the rules applicable to calculating the numerator of an ownership fraction with respect to a domestic entity acquisition apply, except that—

(A) The principles of section 7874(c)(2)(A) and §§ 1.7874-1 and 1.7874-6 do not apply; and

(B) The principles of paragraph (b) of this section do not apply.

(iii) For purposes of determining stock or partnership interests in a relevant entity included in the denominator of the fraction used to compute the tentative predecessor ownership percentage, the principles of section 7874(a)(2)(B)(ii) and all rules applicable to calculating the denominator of an ownership fraction with respect to a domestic entity acquisition apply, except that—

(A) The principles of section 7874(c)(2)(A) and §§ 1.7874-1 and 1.7874-6 do not apply; and

(B) The principles of §§ 1.7874-4 and 1.7874-7 through 1.7874-9 do not apply.

(g) *Rule regarding direction of a section 355 distribution.*—For purposes of this section, if a domestic corporation (distributing corporation) distributes the stock of another domestic corporation (controlled corporation) pursuant to a transaction described in section 355, and, immediately before the distribution, the fair market value of the stock of the controlled corporation owned by the distributing corporation and any related person (determined under section 7874(d)(3), without regard to whether the person is foreign) represents more than 50 percent of the fair market value of the stock of the distributing corporation, then, the controlled corporation is deemed, on the date of the distribution, to have distributed the stock of the distributing corporation. The deemed distribution is equal to the fair market value of the stock of the distributing corporation (but not taking into account the fair market value of the stock of the controlled corporation) on the date of the distribution.

(h) *Allocation of NOCD stock.*—NOCD stock is allocated among the former domestic entity shareholders or former domestic entity partners, as applicable, based on the amount of NOCDs that the former domestic entity shareholders or former domestic entity partners, as applicable, are treated as having received under this paragraph (h). Under this paragraph (h), a pro rata portion of each distribution during a look-back year is treated as comprising an NOCD with respect to the look-back year, based on a fraction the numerator of which is the amount of NOCDs during the look-back year and the denominator of which is the amount of distributions during the look-back year. Thus, each former domestic entity shareholder or former domestic entity partner, as applicable, is treated as receiving an amount of NOCD stock equal to the amount of NOCDs treated as received by the former domestic entity shareholder or former domestic entity partner, as applicable.

(i) *Multiple foreign acquiring corporations.*—If there are multiple foreign acquiring corporations with respect to a domestic entity acquisition, then the foreign acquiring corporation or corporations as to which NOCD stock is considered comprised is based on the proportion of consideration directly or indirectly provided by a foreign acquiring corporation in the domestic entity acquisition relative to the total amount of consideration directly or indirectly provided by the foreign acquiring corporations in the domestic entity acquisition. For purposes of this paragraph (i), consideration is not considered directly provided by a foreign acquiring corporation if it was indirectly provided by another foreign acquiring corporation. In addition, for purposes of this paragraph (i), consideration provided in the domestic entity acquisition does not include money or other property described in paragraph (k)(1)(iii) of this section.

(j) *Multiple domestic entities.*—If pursuant to § 1.7874-2(e) two or more domestic entities are treated as a single domestic entity, then the determination of the amount of NOCDs made by the single domestic entity is made by—

(1) Applying the rules of this section to each domestic entity on a separate basis, with the result that the amount of NOCDs made by each domestic entity is separately computed; and

(2) Treating the amount of NOCDs made by the single domestic entity as the sum of the separately computed NOCDs made by each domestic entity.

(k) *Definitions.*—In addition to the definitions provided in § 1.7874-12, the following definitions apply for purposes of this section.

(1) A *distribution* means the following:

(i) Any distribution made by a corporation with respect to its stock other than—

(A) A distribution to which section 305 applies;

(B) A distribution to which section 304(a)(1) applies; and

(C) Except as provided in paragraphs (k)(1)(iii) and (iv) of this section, a distribution pursuant to section 361(c)(1) (other than a distribution to which section 355 applies).

(ii) Any distribution by a partnership (other than a distribution pursuant to section 752(b) to the extent that the transaction giving rise to such distribution does not reduce the partnership's value).

(iii) In the case of a domestic entity, a transfer of money or other property to the former domestic entity shareholders or former domestic entity partners that is made in connection with the domestic entity acquisition to the extent the money or other property is directly or indirectly provided by the domestic entity.

(iv) In the case of a predecessor, a transfer of money or other property to the former owners of the predecessor that is made in connection with the predecessor acquisition to the extent the money or other property is directly or indirectly provided by the predecessor.

(2) *Distribution history period.*—(i) *In general.*—Except as provided in paragraph (k)(2)(ii) or (iii) of this section, a distribution history period means, with respect to a look-back year, the 36-month period preceding the start of the look-back year.

(ii) *Formation date less than 36 months but at least 12 months before look-back year.*—If the formation date is less than 36 months, but at least 12 months, before the start of a look-back year, then the distribution history period with respect to that look-back year means the entire period, starting with the formation date, that precedes the start of the look-back year.

(iii) *Formation date less than 12 months before look-back year.*—If the formation date is less than 12 months before the start of a look-back year, then there is no distribution history period with respect to that look-back year.

(3) *Formation date* means, with respect to a domestic entity, the date that the domestic entity was created or organized, or, if earlier, the earliest date that any predecessor of the domestic entity was created or organized.

(4) *Look-back period* means, with respect to a domestic acquisition, the 36-month period ending on the completion date or, if shorter, the entire period, starting with the formation date, that ends on the completion date.

(5) *Look-back year* means, with respect to a look-back period, the following:

(i) If the look-back period is 36 months, the three consecutive 12-month periods that comprise the look-back period.

(ii) If the look-back period is less than 36 months, but at least 24 months-

(A) The 12-month period that ends on the completion date;

(B) The 12-month period that immediately precedes the period described in paragraph (k)(5)(ii)(A) of this section; and

(C) The period, if any, that immediately precedes the period described in paragraph (k)(5)(ii)(B) of this section.

(iii) If the look-back period is less than 24 months, but at least 12 months—

(A) The 12-month period that ends on the completion date; and

(B) The period, if any, that immediately precedes the period described in paragraph (k)(5)(iii)(A) of this section.

(iv) If the look-back period is less than 12 months, the entire period, starting with the formation date, that ends on the completion date.

(6) *NOCDs* mean, with respect to a look-back year, the excess of all distributions made during the look-back year over the NOCD threshold for the look-back year.

(7) *NOCD threshold* means, with respect to a look-back year, the following:

(i) If the look-back year has at least a 12-month distribution history period, 110 percent of the sum of all distributions made during the distribution history period multiplied by a fraction. The numerator of the fraction is the number of days in the look-back year and the denominator is the number of days in the distribution history period with respect to the look-back year.

(ii) If the look-back year has no distribution history period, zero.

(l) *Applicability date.*—This section applies to domestic entity acquisitions completed on or after July 12, 2018. For domestic entity acquisitions completed before July 12, 2018, see §1.7874-10T, as contained in 26 CFR part 1 revised as of April 1, 2017. However, to the extent this section differs from §1.7874-10T, as contained in 26 CFR part 1 revised as of April 1, 2017, taxpayers may elect to consistently apply the differences to domestic entity acquisitions completed before July 12, 2018. [Reg. §1.7874-10.]

☐ [T.D. 9834, 7-11-2018.]

[Reg. §1.7874-11]

§1.7874-11. Rules regarding inversion gain.—(a) *Scope.*—This section provides rules for determining the inversion gain of an expatriated entity for purposes of section 7874. Paragraph (b) of this section provides rules for determining the inversion gain of an expatriated entity. Paragraph (c) of this section provides special rules with respect to certain foreign partnerships in which an expatriated entity owns an interest. Paragraph (d) of this section provides additional definitions. Paragraph (e) of this section provides an example that illustrates the rules of this section. Paragraph (f) of this section provides the applicability dates.

(b) *Inversion gain.*—(1) *General rule.*—Except as provided in paragraphs (b)(2) and (3) of this section, inversion gain includes income (including an amount treated as a dividend under section 78) or gain recognized by an expatriated entity for any taxable year that includes any portion of the applicable period by reason of a direct or indirect transfer of stock or other properties or license of any property either as part of the domestic entity acquisition, or after such acquisition if the transfer or license is to a specified related person.

(2) *Exception for property described in section 1221(a)(1).*—Inversion gain does not include income or gain recognized by reason of the transfer or license, after the domestic entity acquisition, of property that is described in section 1221(a)(1) in the hands of the transferor or licensor.

(3) *Treatment of partnerships.*—Except to the extent provided in paragraph (c) of this section and section 7874(e)(2), inversion gain does not include income or gain recognized by reason of the transfer or license of property by a partnership.

(c) *Transfers and licenses by partnerships.*—If a partnership that is a foreign related person transfers or licenses property, a partner of the partnership shall be treated as having transferred or licensed its proportionate share of that property, as determined under the rules and principles of sections 701 through 777, for purposes of determining the inversion gain of an expatriated entity. See section 7874(e)(2) for rules regarding the treatment of transfers and licenses by domestic partnerships and transfers of interests in certain domestic partnerships.

(d) *Definitions.*—The definitions provided in § 1.7874-12 apply for purposes of this section.

(e) *Example.*—The following example illustrates the rules of this section.

Example—(i) *Facts.* On July 1, 2016, FA, a foreign corporation, acquires all the stock of DT, a domestic corporation, in an inversion transaction. When the inversion transaction occurred, DT wholly owned FS, a foreign corporation that is a controlled foreign corporation (within the meaning of section 957(a)). During the applicable period, FS sells to FA property that is not described in section 1221(a)(1) in the hands of FS. Under section 951(a)(1)(A), DT has a $80x gross income inclusion that is attributable to FS's gain from the sale of the property. Under section 960(a)(1), DT is deemed to have paid $20x of the post-1986 foreign income taxes of FS by reason of this income inclusion and includes $20x in gross income as a deemed dividend under section 78. Accordingly, DT recognizes $100x ($80x + $20x) of gross income because of FS's sale of property to FA.

(ii) *Analysis.* Pursuant to section 7874(a)(2)(A), DT is an expatriated entity. Under paragraph (b)(1) of this section, DT's $100x gross income recognized under sections 951(a)(1)(A) and 78 is inversion gain, because it is income recognized by an expatriated entity during the applicable period by reason of an indirect transfer of property by DT (through its wholly-owned CFC, FS)

after the inversion transaction to a specified related person (FA). Sections 7874(a)(1) and (e) therefore prevent the use of certain tax attributes (such as net operating losses) to reduce the U.S. tax owed with respect to DT's $100x gross income recognized under sections 951(a)(1)(A) and 78.

(f) *Applicability dates.*—Except as otherwise provided in this paragraph (f), this section applies to transfers and licenses of property completed on or after November 19, 2015, but only if the inversion transaction was completed on or after September 22, 2014. For inversion transactions completed on or after September 22, 2014, however, taxpayers may elect to apply paragraph (b) of this section by excluding the phrase "(including an amount treated as a dividend under section 78)" for transfers and licenses of property completed on or after November 19, 2015, and before April 4, 2016. [Reg. § 1.7874-11.]

☐ [*T.D.* 9834, 7-11-2018.]

[Reg. § 1.7874-12]

§ 1.7874-12. Definitions.—(a) *Definitions.*— Except as otherwise provided, the following definitions apply for purposes of this section and §§ 1.367(b)-4, 1.956-2, 1.7701(l)-4, and 1.7874-1 through 1.7874-11.

(1) An *affiliated group* has the meaning set forth in section 1504(a) but without regard to section 1504(b)(3), except that section 1504(a) is applied by substituting "more than 50 percent" for "at least 80 percent" each place it appears. A *member of the affiliated group* is an entity included in the affiliated group.

(2) The *applicable period* means, with respect to an inversion transaction, the period described in section 7874(d)(1). However, see also § 1.7874-2(b)(13) in the case of a subsequent acquisition (or a similar acquisition under the principles of § 1.7874-2(c)(4)(i)) that is an inversion transaction.

(3) The *completion date* means, with respect to a domestic entity acquisition, the date that the domestic entity acquisition and all transactions related to the domestic entity acquisition are complete.

(4) A *controlled foreign corporation* (or *CFC*) has the meaning provided in section 957.

(5) A *domestic entity acquisition* means an acquisition described in section 7874(a)(2)(B)(i).

(6) A *domestic entity* means, with respect to a domestic entity acquisition, a domestic corporation or domestic partnership described in section 7874(a)(2)(B)(i). A reference to a domestic entity includes a successor to such domestic corporation or domestic partnership, including a corporation that succeeds to and takes into account amounts with respect to the domestic entity pursuant to section 381.

(7) An *expanded affiliated group* (or *EAG*) means, with respect to a domestic entity acquisition, an affiliated group that includes the foreign acquiring corporation, determined as of the completion date. A *member of the EAG* is an entity

included in the EAG, and a reference to a member of the EAG includes a predecessor with respect to such member.

(8) An *expatriated entity* means, with respect to an inversion transaction—

(i) The domestic entity; and

(ii) A United States person that, on any date on or after the completion date, is or was related (within the meaning of section 267(b) or 707(b)(1)) to the domestic entity.

(9) *Expatriated foreign subsidiary.*—(i) *General rule.*—Except as provided in paragraph (a)(9)(ii) of this section, an expatriated foreign subsidiary means a foreign corporation that is a CFC (determined without applying subparagraphs (A), (B), and (C) of section 318(a)(3) so as to consider a United States person as owning stock which is owned by a person who is not a United States person) and in which an expatriated entity is a United States shareholder (determined without applying subparagraphs (A), (B), and (C) of section 318(a)(3) so as to consider a United States person as owning stock which is owned by a person who is not a United States person).

(ii) *Exception to the general rule.*—A foreign corporation is not an expatriated foreign subsidiary if, with respect to the inversion transaction as a result of which the foreign corporation otherwise would be an expatriated foreign subsidiary—

(A) On the completion date, the foreign corporation was both a CFC (determined without applying subparagraphs (A), (B), and (C) of section 318(a)(3) so as to consider a United States person as owning stock which is owned by a person who is not a United States person) and a member of the EAG; and

(B) On or before the completion date, the domestic entity was not a United States shareholder (determined without applying subparagraphs (A), (B), and (C) of section 318(a)(3) so as to consider a United States person as owning stock which is owned by a person who is not a United States person) with respect to the foreign corporation.

(10) A *foreign acquiring corporation* means, with respect to a domestic entity acquisition, the foreign corporation described in section 7874(a)(2)(B). A reference to a foreign acquiring corporation includes a successor to the foreign acquiring corporation, including a corporation that succeeds to and takes into account amounts with respect to the foreign acquiring corporation pursuant to section 381.

(11) A *foreign related person* means, with respect to an inversion transaction, a foreign person that is related (within the meaning of section 267(b) or 707(b)(1)) to, or under the same common control as (within the meaning of section 482), a person that is an expatriated entity with respect to the inversion transaction.

(12) A *former domestic entity partner* of a domestic entity that is a domestic partnership is any person that held an interest in the partnership before the domestic entity acquisition, including any person that holds an interest in the partnership both before and after the domestic entity acquisition.

(13) A *former domestic entity shareholder* of a domestic entity that is a domestic corporation is any person that held stock in the domestic corporation before the domestic entity acquisition, including any person that holds stock in the domestic corporation both before and after the domestic entity acquisition.

(14) An *interest in a partnership* includes a capital or profits interest.

(15) An *inversion transaction* means a domestic entity acquisition in which the foreign acquiring corporation is treated as a surrogate foreign corporation under section 7874(a)(2)(B), taking into account section 7874(a)(3).

(16) A *non-EFS foreign related person* means, with respect to an inversion transaction, a foreign related person that is not an expatriated foreign subsidiary.

(17) The *ownership fraction* means, with respect to a domestic entity acquisition, the ownership percentage described in section 7874(a)(2)(B)(ii), expressed as a fraction.

(18) A *specified related person* means, with respect to an inversion transaction—

(i) A non-EFS foreign related person;

(ii) A domestic partnership in which a non-EFS foreign related person is a partner; and

(iii) A domestic trust of which a non-EFS foreign related person is a beneficiary.

(19) A *United States person* means a person described in section 7701(a)(30).

(20) A *United States shareholder* has the meaning provided in section 951(b).

(b) *Applicability dates.*—Except as otherwise provided in this paragraph (b), this section applies to domestic entity acquisitions completed on or after September 22, 2014. The following apply to domestic entity acquisitions completed on or after April 4, 2016: paragraph (a)(8) of this section; in paragraph (a)(6) of this section, the phrase ", including a corporation that succeeds to and takes into account amounts with respect to the domestic entity pursuant to section 381"; and the second sentence of paragraph (a)(10) of this section. For domestic entity acquisitions completed on or after September 22, 2014, and before April 4, 2016, however, taxpayers may elect to apply the provisions in the immediately prior sentence. [Reg. § 1.7874-12.]

☐ [*T.D. 9834, 7-11-2018.*]

Regulations Not Issued Under Specific Code Sections
IRS PROCEDURE ON REQUESTS FOR DISCLOSURE

See p. 20,601 for regulations not amended to reflect law changes

[Reg. §301.9000-1]

§301.9000-1. Definitions when used in §§ 301.9000-1 through 301.9000-6.—(a) *IRS records or information* means any material (including copies thereof) contained in the files (including paper, electronic or other media files) of the Internal Revenue Service (IRS), any information relating to material contained in the files of the IRS, or any information acquired by an IRS officer or employee, while an IRS officer or employee, as a part of the performance of official duties or because of that IRS officer's or employee's official status with respect to the administration of the internal revenue laws or any other laws administered by or concerning the IRS. IRS records or information includes, but is not limited to, returns and return information as those terms are defined in section 6103(b)(1) and (2) of the Internal Revenue Code (Code), tax convention information as defined in section 6105 of the Code, information gathered during Bank Secrecy Act and money laundering investigations, and personnel records and other information pertaining to IRS officers and employees. IRS records and information also includes information received, generated or collected by an IRS contractor pursuant to the contractor's contract or agreement with the IRS. The term does not include records or information obtained by IRS officers and employees, solely for the purpose of a federal grand jury investigation, while under the direction and control of the United States Attorney's Office. The term IRS records or information nevertheless does include records or information obtained by the IRS before, during, or after a Federal grand jury investigation if the records or information are obtained—

(1) At the administrative stage of a criminal investigation (prior to the initiation of the grand jury);

(2) From IRS files (such as transcripts or tax returns); or

(3) For use in a subsequent civil investigation.

(b) *IRS officers and employees* means all officers and employees of the United States appointed by, employed by, or subject to the directions, instructions, or orders of the Commissioner or IRS Chief Counsel and also includes former officers and employees.

(c) *IRS contractor* means any person, including the person's current and former employees, maintaining IRS records or information pursuant to a contract or agreement with the IRS, and also includes former contractors.

(d) A *request* is any request for testimony of an IRS officer, employee or contractor or for production of IRS records or information, oral or written, by any person, which is not a demand.

(e) A *demand* is any subpoena or other order of any court, administrative agency or other authority, or the Congress, or a committee or subcommittee of the Congress, and any notice of deposition (either upon oral examination or written questions), request for admissions, request for production of documents or things, written interrogatories to parties, or other notice of, request for, or service for discovery in a matter before any court, administrative agency or other authority.

(f) An *IRS matter* is any matter before any court, administrative agency or other authority in which the United States, the Commissioner, the IRS, or any IRS officer or employee acting in an official capacity, or any IRS officer or employee (including an officer or employee of IRS Office of Chief Counsel) in his or her individual capacity if the United States Department of Justice or the IRS has agreed to represent or provide representation to the IRS officer or employee, is a party and that is directly related to official business of the IRS or to any law administered by or concerning the IRS, including, but not limited to, judicial and administrative proceedings described in section 6103(h)(4) and (I)(4) of the Internal Revenue Code.

(g) An *IRS congressional matter* is any matter before the Congress, or a committee or subcommittee of the Congress, that is related to the administration of the internal revenue laws or any other laws administered by or concerning the IRS, or to IRS records or information.

(h) A *non-IRS matter* is any matter that is not an IRS matter or an IRS congressional matter.

(i) A *testimony authorization* is a written instruction or oral instruction memorialized in writing within a reasonable period by an authorizing official that sets forth the scope of and limitations on proposed testimony and/or disclosure of IRS records or information issued in response to a request or demand for IRS records or information. A testimony authorization may grant or deny authorization to testify or disclose IRS records or information and may make an authorization effective only upon the occurrence of a precedent condition, such as the receipt of a consent complying with the provisions of section 6103(c) of the Internal Revenue Code. To authorize testimony means to issue the instruction described in this paragraph (i).

(j) An *authorizing official* is a person with delegated authority to authorize testimony and the disclosure of IRS records or information. [Reg. §301.9000-1.]

☐ [*T.D.* 6920, 6-7-67. *Amended by* 37 F.R. 2481, 2-1-72; *T.D.* 7188, 6-28-72; *T.D.* ATF-33, 10-6-76 *and T.D.* 9178, 2-11-2005.]

[Reg. § 301.9000-2]

§ 301.9000-2. Considerations in responding to a request or demand for IRS records or information.—(a) *Situations in which disclosure shall not be authorized.*—Authorizing officials shall not permit testimony or disclosure of IRS records or information in response to requests or demands if testimony or disclosure of IRS records or information would—

(1) Violate a Federal statute including, but not limited to, sections 6103 or 6105 of the Internal Revenue Code (Code), the Privacy Act of 1974 (5 U.S.C. 552a), or a rule of procedure, such as the grand jury secrecy rule, Fed. R. Crim. P. 6(e);

(2) Violate a specific Federal regulation, including, but not limited to, 31 CFR 103.53;

(3) Reveal classified national security information, unless property declassified;

(4) Reveal the identity of an informant; or

(5) Reveal investigatory records or information compiled for law enforcement purposes that would permit interference with law enforcement proceedings or would disclose investigative techniques and procedures, the effectiveness of which could thereby be impaired.

(b) *Assertion of privileges.*—Any applicable privilege or protection under law may be asserted in response to a request or demand for testimony or disclosure of IRS records or information, including, but not limited to, the following—

(1) Attorney-client privilege;

(2) Attorney work product doctrine; and

(3) Deliberative process (executive) privilege.

(c) *Non-IRS matters.*—If any person makes a request or demand for IRS records or information in connection with a non-IRS matter, authorizing officials shall take into account the following additional factors in responding to the request or demand—

(1) Whether the requester is a Federal agency, or a state or local government or agency thereof;

(2) Whether the demand was issued by a Federal or state court, administrative agency or other authority;

(3) The potential effect of the case on the administration of the internal revenue laws or any other laws administered by or concerning the IRS;

(4) The importance of the legal issues presented;

(5) Whether the IRS records or information are available from other sources;

(6) The IRS's anticipated commitment of time and anticipated expenditure of funds necessary to comply with the request or demand;

(7) The number of similar requests and their cumulative effect on the expenditure of IRS resources;

(8) Whether the request or demand allows a reasonable time for compliance (generally, at least fifteen business days);

(9) Whether the testimony or disclosure is appropriate under the rules of procedure governing the case or matter in which the request or demand arises;

(10) Whether the request or demand involves expert witness testimony;

(11) Whether the request or demand is for the testimony of an IRS officer, employee or contractor who is without personal knowledge of relevant facts;

(12) Whether the request or demand is for the testimony of a presidential appointee or senior executive and whether the testimony of a lower-level official would suffice;

(13) Whether the procedures in § 301.9000-5 have been followed; and

(14) Any other relevant factors that may be brought to the attention of the authorizing official. [Reg. § 301.9000-2.]

☐ [*T.D.* 9178, 2-11-2005.]

[Reg. § 301.9000-3]

§ 301.9000-3. Testimony authorizations.—(a) *Prohibition on disclosure of IRS records or information without testimony authorization.*—Except as provided in paragraph (b) of this section, when a request or demand for IRS records or information is made, no IRS officer, employee or contractor shall testify or disclose IRS records or information to any court, administrative agency or other authority, or to the Congress, or to a committee or subcommittee of the Congress without a testimony authorization. However, an IRS officer, employee or contractor may appear in person to advise that he or she is awaiting instructions from an authorizing official with respect to the request or demand.

(b) *Exceptions.*—No testimony authorization is required in the following circumstances—

(1) To respond to a request or demand for IRS records or information by the attorney or other government representative representing the IRS in a particular IRS matter;

(2) To respond solely in writing, under the direction of the attorney or other government representative, to requests and demands in IRS matters, including, but not limited to, admissions, document production, and written interrogatories to parties;

(3) To respond to a request or demand issued to a former IRS officer, employee or contractor for expert or opinion testimony if the testimony sought from the former IRS officer, employee or contractor involves general knowledge (such as information contained in published procedures of the IRS or the IRS Office of Chief Counsel) gained while the former IRS officer, employee or contractor was employed or under contract with the IRS; or

(4) If a more specific procedure established by the Commissioner governs the disclosure of IRS records or information. These procedures

include, but are not limited to, those relating to: procedures pursuant to §601.702(d) of this chapter; Freedom of Information Act requests pursuant to 5 U.S.C. 552; Privacy Act of 1974 requests pursuant to 5 U.S.C. 552a; disclosures to state tax agencies pursuant to section 6103(d) of the Internal Revenue Code (Code) and disclosures to the United States Department of Justice pursuant to an ex parte order under section 6103(i)(1) of the Code.

(c) *Disclosures of IRS records or information with or without testimony authorization must be permitted under other applicable law.*—Any disclosure of IRS records or information that is otherwise permissible under this section must not be prohibited under applicable law. For example, in a case in which returns and return information may be disclosed, the disclosure must be authorized under section 6103, even if any required testimony authorization is obtained. If tax convention information (as defined under section 6105) may be disclosed, in deciding whether the disclosure is authorized, the authorizing official must coordinate the disclosure with the U.S. Competent Authority. [Reg. § 301.9000-3.]

☐ [*T.D.* 9178, 2-11-2005.]

[Reg. § 301.9000-4]

§ 301.9000-4. Procedure in the event of a request or demand for IRS records or information.—(a) *Purpose and scope.*—This section prescribes procedures to be followed by IRS officers, employees and contractors upon receipt of a request or demand in matters in which a testimony authorization is or may be required.

(b) *Notification of the Disclosure Officer.*—Except as provided in paragraphs (c), (d), and (e) of this section, an IRS officer, employee or contractor who receives a request or demand for IRS records or information for which a testimony authorization is or may be required shall notify promptly the disclosure officer servicing the IRS officer's, employee's or contractor's geographic area. The IRS officer, employee or contractor shall await instructions from the authorizing official concerning the response to the request or demand. An IRS officer, employee, or contractor who receives a request or demand in one of the following matters should not notify the disclosure officer, but should follow the instructions in paragraph (c), (d), or (e) of this section, as applicable:

(1) United States Tax Court cases.

(2) Personnel matters, labor relations matters, government contract matters, matters related to informant claims or matters related to the rules of *Bivens v. Six Unknown Named Agents of Federal Bureau of Narcotics*, 403 U.S. 388 (1971) (Bivens matters), or matters under the Federal Tort Claims Act (FTCA).

(3) IRS congressional matters.

(c) *Requests or demands in United States Tax Court cases.*—An IRS officer, employee or contractor who receives a request or demand for IRS records or Information on behalf of a petitioner in a United States Tax Court case shall notify promptly the IRS Office of Chief Counsel attorney assigned to the case. The IRS Office of Chief Counsel attorney shall notify promptly the authorizing official. The IRS officer, employee or contractor who received the request or demand shall await instructions from the authorizing official.

(d) *Requests or demands in personnel, labor relations, government contract, Bivens or FTCA matters, or matters related to informant claims.*—An IRS officer, employee or contractor who receives a request or demand, on behalf of an appellant, grievant, complainant or representative, for IRS records or information in a personnel, labor relations, government contract, Bivens or FTCA matter, or matter related to informant claims, shall notify promptly the IRS Associate Chief Counsel (General Legal Services) attorney assigned to the case. If no IRS Associate Chief Counsel (General Legal Services) attorney is assigned to the case, the IRS officer, employee or contractor shall notify promptly the IRS Associate Chief Counsel (General Legal Services) attorney servicing the geographic area. The IRS Associate Chief Counsel (General Legal Services) attorney shall notify promptly the authorizing official. The IRS officer, employee or contractor who received the request or demand shall await instructions from the authorizing official.

(e) *Requests or demands in IRS congressional matters.*—An IRS officer, employee or contractor who receives a request or demand in an IRS congressional matter shall notify promptly the IRS Office of Legislative Affairs. The IRS officer, employee or contractor who received the request or demand shall await instructions from the authorizing official.

(f) *Opposition to a demand for IRS records or information in IRS and non-IRS matters.*—If, in response to a demand for IRS records or information, an authorizing official has not had a sufficient opportunity to issue a testimony authorization, or determines that the demand for IRS records or information should be denied, the authorizing official shall request the government attorney or other representative of the government to oppose the demand and respectfully inform the court, administrative agency or other authority, by appropriate action, that the authorizing official either has not yet issued a testimony authorization, or has issued a testimony authorization to the IRS officer, employee or contractor that denies permission to testify or disclose the IRS records or information. If the authorizing official denies authorization in whole or in part, the government attorney or other representative of the government shall inform the court, administrative agency or other authority of the reasons the authorizing official gives for not authorizing the testimony or the disclosure of the IRS records or information or take other action in opposition as may be appropriate (including, but not limited to, filing a motion to quash or a motion to remove to Federal court).

(g) Procedure in the event of an adverse ruling.—In the event the court, administrative agency, or other authority rules adversely with respect to the refusal to disclose the IRS records or information pursuant to the testimony authorization, or declines to defer a ruling until a testimony authorization has been received, the IRS officer, employee or contractor who has received the request or demand shall, pursuant to this section, respectfully decline to testify or disclose the IRS records or information.

(h) Penalties.—Any IRS officer or employee who discloses IRS records or information without following the provisions of this section or § 301.9000-3, may be subject to administrative discipline, up to and including dismissal. Any IRS officer, employee or contractor may be subject to applicable contractual sanctions and civil or criminal penalties, including prosecution under 5 U.S.C. 552a(i), for willful disclosure in an unauthorized manner of information protected by the Privacy Act of 1974, or under section 7213 of the Internal Revenue Code, for willful disclosure in an unauthorized manner of return information.

(i) No creation of benefit or separate privilege.—Nothing in §§ 301.9000-1 through 301.9000-3, this section, and §§ 301.9000-5 and 301.9000-6, creates, is intended to create, or may be relied upon to create, any right or benefit, substantive or procedural, enforceable at law by a party against the United States. Nothing in these regulations creates a separate privilege or basis to withhold IRS records or information. [Reg. § 301.9000-4.]

□ [*T.D.* 9178, 2-11-2005.]

[Reg. § 301.9000-5]

§ 301.9000-5. Written statement required for requests or demands in non-IRS matters.—(a) *Written statement.*—A request or demand for IRS records or information for use in a non-IRS matter shall be accompanied by a written statement made by or on behalf of the party seeking the testimony or disclosure of IRS records or information, setting forth—

(1) A brief description of the parties to and subject matter of the proceeding and the issues;

(2) A summary of the testimony, IRS records or information sought, the relevance to the proceeding, and the estimated volume of IRS records involved;

(3) The time that will be required to present the testimony (on both direct and cross examination);

(4) Whether any of the IRS records or information is a return or is return information (as defined in section 6103(b) of the Internal Revenue Code (Code)), or tax convention information (as defined in section 6105(c)(1) of the Code), and the statutory authority for the disclosure of the return or return information (and, if no consent to disclose pursuant to section 6103(c) of the

Code accompanies the request or demand, the reason consent is not necessary);

(5) Whether a declaration of an IRS officer, employee or contractor under penalties of perjury pursuant to 28 U.S.C. 1746 would suffice in lieu of deposition or trial testimony;

(6) Whether deposition or trial testimony is necessary in a situation in which IRS records may be authenticated without testimony under applicable rules of evidence and procedure;

(7) Whether IRS records or information are available from other sources; and

(8) A statement that the request or demand allows a reasonable time (generally at least fifteen business days) for compliance.

(b) Permissible waiver of statement.—The requirement of a written statement in paragraph (a) of this section may be waived by the authorizing official for good cause. [Reg. § 301.9000-5.]

□ [*T.D.* 9178, 2-11-2005.]

[Reg. § 301.9000-6]

§ 301.9000-6. Examples.—The following examples illustrate the provisions of §§ 301.9000-1 through 301.9000-5:

Example 1. A taxpayer sues a practitioner in state court for malpractice in connection with the practitioner's preparation of a Federal income tax return. The taxpayer subpoenas an IRS employee to testify concerning the IRS employee's examination of the taxpayer's Federal income tax return. The taxpayer provides the statement required by § 301.9000-5. This is a non-IRS matter. A testimony authorization would be required for the IRS employee to testify. (In addition, the taxpayer would be required to execute an appropriate consent under section 6103(c) of the Code). The IRS would oppose the IRS employee's appearance in this case because the IRS is a disinterested party with respect to the dispute and would consider the commitment of resources to comply with the subpoena inappropriate.

Example 2. In a state judicial proceeding concerning child support, the child's custodiel parent subpoenas for a deposition an IRS agent who is examining certain post-divorce Federal income tax returns of the non-custodial parent. This is a non-IRS matter. The custodial parent submits with the subpoena the statement required by § 301.9000-5 stating as the reason for the lack of taxpayer consent to disclosure that the non-custodial parent has refused to provide the consent (both a consent from the taxpayer complying with section 6103(c) and a testimony authorization would be required prior to the IRS agent testifying at the deposition). If taxpayer consent is obtained, the IRS may provide a declaration or certified return information of the taxpayer. A deposition would be unnecessary under the circumstances.

Example 3. The chairperson of a congressional committee requests the appearance of an IRS employee before the committee and committee staff to submit to questioning by committee staff concerning the procedures for processing Federal employment tax returns. This is an IRS congressional matter. Even though questioning would not involve the disclosure of returns or return information, the questioning would involve the disclosure of IRS records or information; therefore, a testimony authorization would be required. The IRS employee must contact the IRS Office of Legislative Affairs for instructions before appearing.

Example 4. The IRS opens a criminal investigation as to the tax liabilities of a taxpayer. This is an IRS matter. During the criminal investigation, the IRS refers the matter to the United States Department of Justice, requesting the institution of a Federal grand jury to investigate further potential criminal tax violations. The United States Department of Justice approves the request and initiates a grand jury investigation. The grand jury indicts the taxpayer. During the taxpayer's trial, the taxpayer subpoenas an IRS special agent for testimony regarding the investigation. The records and information collected during the administrative stage of the investigation, including the taxpayer's tax returns from IRS files, are IRS records and information. A testimony authorization is required for the IRS special agent to testify regarding this information. However, no IRS testimony authorization is required regarding the information collected by the IRS special agent when the IRS special agent was acting under the direction and control of the United States Attorney's Office in the Federal grand jury investigation. That information is not IRS records or information within the meaning of § 301.9000-1(a). Disclosure of that information should be coordinated with the United States Attorney's Office.

Example 5. The United States Department of Justice attorney representing the IRS in a suit for refund requests testimony from an IRS revenue agent. This is an IRS matter. A testimony authorization would not be required for the IRS revenue agent to testify because the testimony was requested by the government attorney.

Example 6. In response to a request by the taxpayer's counsel to interview an IRS revenue agent who was involved in a case at the administrative level, the United States Department of Justice attorney representing the IRS in a suit for refund asks that the IRS revenue agent be made available to be interviewed. This is an IRS matter. A testimony authorization would be required for the IRS agent to testify because the testimony was first requested by taxpayer's counsel.

Example 7. A state assistant attorney general, acting in accordance with a recommendation from his state's department of revenue, is prosecuting a taxpayer under a state criminal law proscribing the intentional failure to file a state income tax return. The assistant attorney general serves an IRS employee with a subpoena to testify concerning the taxpayer's Federal income tax return filing history. This is a non-IRS matter. This is also a state judicial proceeding pertaining to tax administration within the meaning of section 6103(h)(4) and (b)(4). As such, the requirements of section 6103(h)(4) apply. A testimony authorization would be required for the testimony demand in the subpoena.

Example 8. A former IRS revenue agent is requested to testify in a divorce proceeding. The request seeks testimony explaining the meaning of entries appearing on one party's transcript of account, which is already in the possession of the parties. This is a non-IRS matter. No testimony authorization is required because the testimony requested from the former IRS employee involves general knowledge gained while the former IRS revenue agent was employed with the IRS.

Example 9. A Department of Justice attorney requests an IRS employee to testify in a refund suit involving Taxpayer A. The testimony may include tax convention information, as defined in section 6105, which was originally obtained by the IRS from a treaty partner in connection with a tax case against Taxpayer B. While no testimony authorization is necessary, because the testimony is being requested by government counsel in a tax matter, the IRS employee may not testify (or otherwise disclose IRS records or information) without coordinating with the U.S. Competent Authority, as disclosure of tax convention information is governed by section 6105. The disclosure must also meet the requirements in section 6103(h)(4).

Example 10. In a state court tort action, Defendant subpoenas IRS for Plaintiff's federal income tax returns for particular taxable years. This is a non-IRS matter. The Disclosure Officer instructs Defendant that the IRS has established procedures for obtaining copies of Federal income tax returns. Section 601.702(d)(1) of this chapter establishes the procedures for obtaining Federal tax returns by requiring written requests for copies of tax returns using IRS Form 4506, "Request for Copy of Tax Return." At Defendant's request, Plaintiff executes Form 4506, naming Defendant's counsel as designee, and the form is properly submitted to IRS. A testimony authorization would not be required to disclose Plaintiff's returns to Defendant's counsel.
[Reg. § 301.9000-6.]
☐ [*T.D.* 9178, 2-11-2005.]

[Reg. § 301.9000-7]

§ 301.9000-7. Effective date.—These regulations are applicable on February 14, 2005.
☐ [*T.D.* 9178, 2-11-2005.]

EXTENSION OF TIME FOR MAKING ELECTIONS

[Reg. § 301.9100-0]

§ 301.9100-0. Outline of regulations.—This section lists the paragraphs in §§ 301.9100-1 through 301.9100-3.

§ 301.9100-1. Extensions of time to make elections.
  (a) Introduction.
  (b) Terms.
  (c) General standards for relief.
  (d) Exceptions.

(e) Effective dates.

§ 301.9100-2. *Automatic extensions.*

(a) Automatic 12-month extension.

(1) In general.

(2) Elections eligible for automatic 12-month extension.

(b) Automatic 6-month extension.

(c) Corrective action.

(d) Procedural requirements.

(e) Examples.

§ 301.9100-3. *Other extensions.*

(a) In general.

(b) Reasonable action and good faith.

(1) In general.

(2) Reasonable reliance on a qualified tax professional.

(3) Taxpayer deemed to have not acted reasonably or in good faith.

(c) Prejudice to the interests of the Government.

(1) In general.

(i) Lower tax liability.

(ii) Closed years.

(2) Special rules for accounting method regulatory elections.

(3) Special rules for accounting period regulatory elections.

(d) Effect of amended returns.

(1) Second examination under section 7605(b).

(2) Suspension of the period of limitations under section 6501(a).

(e) Procedural requirements.

(1) In general.

(2) Affidavit and declaration from taxpayer.

(3) Affidavits and declarations from other parties.

(4) Other information.

(5) Filing instructions.

(f) Examples.

[Reg. § 301.9100-0.]

☐ [*T.D. 8742, 12-30-97.*]

[Reg. § 301.9100-1]

§ 301.9100-1. Extensions of time to make elections.—(a) *Introduction.*—The regulations under this section and §§ 301.9100-2 and 301.9100-3 provide the standards the Commissioner will use to determine whether to grant an extension of time to make a regulatory election. The regulations under this section and § 301.9100-2 also provide an automatic extension of time to make certain statutory elections. An extension of time is available for elections that a taxpayer is otherwise eligible to make. However, the granting of an extension of time is not a determination that the taxpayer is otherwise eligible to make the election. Section 301.9100-2 provides automatic extensions of time for making regulatory and statutory elections when the deadline for making the election is the due date of the return or the due date of the return including extensions. Section 301.9100-3 provides extensions of time for

making regulatory elections that do not meet the requirements of § 301.9100-2.

(b) *Terms.*—The following terms have the meanings provided below—

Election includes an application for relief in respect of tax; a request to adopt, change, or retain an accounting method or accounting period; but does not include an application for an extension of time for filing a return under section 6081.

Regulatory election means an election whose due date is prescribed by a regulation published in the Federal Register, or a revenue ruling, revenue procedure, notice, or announcement published in the Internal Revenue Bulletin (see § 601.601(d)(2) of this chapter).

Statutory election means an election whose due date is prescribed by statute.

Taxpayer means any person within the meaning of section 7701(a)(1).

(c) *General standards for relief.*—The Commissioner in exercising the Commissioner's discretion may grant a reasonable extension of time under the rules set forth in §§ 301.9100-2 and 301.9100-3 to make a regulatory election, or a statutory election (but no more than 6 months except in the case of a taxpayer who is abroad), under all subtitles of the Internal Revenue Code except subtitles E, G, H, and I.

(d) *Exceptions.*—Notwithstanding the provisions of paragraph (c) of this section, an extension of time will not be granted—

(1) For elections under section 4980A(f)(5); or

(2) For elections that are expressly excepted from relief or where alternative relief is provided by a statute, a regulation published in the Federal Register, or a revenue ruling, revenue procedure, notice, or announcement published in the Internal Revenue Bulletin (see § 601.601(d)(2) of this chapter).

(e) *Effective dates.*—In general, this section and §§ 301.9100-2 and 301.9100-3 apply to all requests for an extension of time submitted to the Internal Revenue Service (IRS) on or after December 31, 1997. However, the automatic 12-month and 6-month extensions provided in § 301.9100-2 apply to elections for which corrective action is taken on or after December 31, 1997. For other requests for an extension of time, see §§ 301.9100-1T through 301.9100-3T in effect prior to December 31, 1997. (§§ 301.9100-1T through 301.9100-3T as contained in the 26 CFR part 1 edition revised as of April 1, 1997). [Reg. § 301.9100-1.]

☐ [*T.D. 8378, 12-21-91. Amended by T.D. 8481, 6-29-93 and T.D. 8742, 12-30-97.*]

[Reg. § 301.9100-2]

§ 301.9100-2. Automatic extensions.—(a) *Automatic 12-month extension .*—(1) *In general .*—An automatic extension of 12 months from the due date for making a regulatory election is granted to make elections described in paragraph (a) of this section provided the taxpayer takes corrective action as defined in paragraph (c) of this section within that 12-month extension period. For purposes of this paragraph (a), the due date for making a regulatory election is the extended due date of the return if the due date of the election is the due date of the return or the due date of the return including extensions and the taxpayer has obtained an extension of time to file the return. This extension is available regardless of whether the taxpayer timely filed its return for the year the election should have been made.

(2) *Elections eligible for automatic 12-month extension* .—The following regulatory elections are eligible for the automatic 12-month extension described in paragraph (a)(1) of this section—

(i) The election to use other than the required taxable year under section 444;

(ii) The election to use the last-in, first-out (LIFO) inventory method under section 472;

(iii) The 15-month rule for filing an exemption application for a section 501(c)(9), 501(c)(17), or 501(c) (20) organization under section 505;

(iv) The 15-month rule for filing an exemption application for a section 501(c)(3) organization under section 508;

(v) The election to be treated as a homeowners association under section 528;

(vi) The election to adjust basis on partnership transfers and distributions under section 754;

(vii) The estate tax election to specially value qualified real property (where the Internal Revenue Service (IRS) has not yet begun an examination of the filed return) under section 2032A(d)(1)

(viii) The chapter 14 gift tax election to treat a qualified payment right as other than a qualified payment under section 2701(c)(3)(C)(i); and

(ix) The chapter 14 gift tax election to treat any distribution right as a qualified payment under section 2701(c)(3)(C)(ii).

(b) *Automatic 6-month extension* .—An automatic extension of 6 months from the due date of a return excluding extensions is granted to make regulatory or statutory elections whose due dates are the due date of the return or the due date of the return including extensions provided the taxpayer timely filed its return for the year the election should have been made and the taxpayer takes corrective action as defined in paragraph (c) of this section within that 6-month extension period. This paragraph (b) does not apply to regulatory or statutory elections that must be made by the due date of the return excluding extensions.

(c) *Corrective action* .—For purposes of this section, corrective action means taking the steps required to file the election in accordance with the statute or the regulation published in the Federal Register, or the revenue ruling, revenue procedure, notice, or announcement published in the Internal Revenue Bulletin (see §601.601(d)(2) of this chapter). For those elections required to be filed with a return, corrective action includes filing an original or an amended return for the year the regulatory or statutory election should have been made and attaching the appropriate form or statement for making the election. Taxpayers who make an election under an automatic extension (and all taxpayers whose tax liability would be affected by the election) must file their return in a manner that is consistent with the election and comply with all other requirements for making the election for the year the election should have been made and for all affected years; otherwise, the IRS may invalidate the election.

(d) *Procedural requirements* .—Any return, statement of election, or other form of filing that must be made to obtain an automatic extension must provide the following statement at the top of the document: "FILED PURSUANT TO §301.9100-2". Any filing made to obtain an automatic extension must be sent to the same address that the filing to make the election would have been sent had the filing been timely made. No request for a letter ruling is required to obtain an automatic extension. Accordingly, user fees do not apply to taxpayers taking corrective action to obtain an automatic extension.

(e) *Examples* .—The following examples illustrate the provisions of this section:

Example 1. Automatic 12-month extension. Taxpayer A fails to make an election described in paragraph (a)(2) of this section when filing A's 1997 income tax return on March 16, 1998, the due date of the return. This election does not affect the tax liability of any other taxpayer. The applicable regulation requires that the election be made by attaching the appropriate form to a timely filed return including extensions. In accordance with paragraphs (a) and (c) of this section, A may make the regulatory election by taking the corrective action of filing an amended return with the appropriate form by March 15, 1999 (12 months from the March 16, 1998 due date of the return). If A obtained a 6-month extension to file its 1997 income tax return, A may make the regulatory election by taking the corrective action of filing an amended return with the appropriate form by September 15, 1999 (12 months from the September 15, 1998 extended due date of the return).

Example 2. Automatic 6-month extension. Taxpayer B fails to make an election not described in paragraph (a)(2) of this section when filing B's 1997 income tax return on March 16, 1998, the due date of the return. This election does not affect the tax liability of any other taxpayer. The applicable regulation requires that the election be made by attaching the appropriate form to a timely filed return including extensions. In accordance with paragraphs (b) and (c) of this section, B may make the regulatory election by taking the corrective action of filing an amended return with the appropriate form by September 15, 1998 (6 months from the March 16, 1998 due date of the return).

[Reg. § 301.9100-2.]

☐ [*T.D.* 8742, 12-30-97.]

[Reg. § 301.9100-3]

§ 301.9100-3. Other extensions.—(a) *In general.*—Requests for extensions of time for regulatory elections that do not meet the requirements of § 301.9100-2 must be made under the rules of this section. Requests for relief subject to this section will be granted when the taxpayer provides the evidence (including affidavits described in paragraph (e) of this section) to establish to the satisfaction of the Commissioner that the taxpayer acted reasonably and in good faith, and the grant of relief will not prejudice the interests of the Government.

(b) *Reasonable action and good faith.*—(1) *In general.*—Except as provided in paragraphs (b)(3)(i) through (iii) of this section, a taxpayer is deemed to have acted reasonably and in good faith if the taxpayer—

(i) Requests relief under this section before the failure to make the regulatory election is discovered by the Internal Revenue Service (IRS);

(ii) Failed to make the election because of intervening events beyond the taxpayer's control;

(iii) Failed to make the election because, after exercising reasonable diligence (taking into account the taxpayer's experience and the complexity of the return or issue), the taxpayer was unaware of the necessity for the election;

(iv) Reasonably relied on the written advice of the Internal Revenue Service (IRS); or

(v) Reasonably relied on a qualified tax professional, including a tax professional employed by the taxpayer, and the tax professional failed to make, or advise the taxpayer to make, the election.

(2) *Reasonable reliance on a qualified tax professional.*—For purposes of this paragraph (b), a taxpayer will not be considered to have reasonably relied on a qualified tax professional if the taxpayer knew or should have known that the professional was not—

(i) Competent to render advice on the regulatory election; or

(ii) Aware of all relevant facts.

(3) *Taxpayer deemed to have not acted reasonably or in good faith.*—For purposes of this paragraph (b), a taxpayer is deemed to have not acted reasonably and in good faith if the taxpayer—

(i) Seeks to alter a return position for which an accuracy-related penalty has been or could be imposed under section 6662 at the time the taxpayer requests relief (taking into account any qualified amended return filed within the meaning of § 1.6664-2(c)(3) of this chapter) and the new position requires or permits a regulatory election for which relief is requested;

(ii) Was informed in all material respects of the required election and related tax consequences, but chose not to file the election; or

(iii) Uses hindsight in requesting relief. If specific facts have changed since the due date for making the election that make the election advantageous to a taxpayer, the IRS will not ordinarily grant relief. In such a case, the IRS will grant relief only when the taxpayer provides strong proof that the taxpayer's decision to seek relief did not involve hindsight.

(c) *Prejudice to the interests of the Government.*—(1) *In general.*—The Commissioner will grant a reasonable extension of time to make a regulatory election only when the interests of the Government will not be prejudiced by the granting of relief. This paragraph (c) provides the standards the Commissioner will use to determine when the interests of the Government are prejudiced.

(i) *Lower tax liability.*—The interests of the Government are prejudiced if granting relief would result in a taxpayer having a lower tax liability in the aggregate for all taxable years affected by the election than the taxpayer would have had if the election had been timely made (taking into account the time value of money). Similarly, if the tax consequences of more than one taxpayer are affected by the election, the Government's interests are prejudiced if extending the time for making the election may result in the affected taxpayers, in the aggregate, having a lower tax liability than if the election had been timely made.

(ii) *Closed years.*—The interests of the Government are ordinarily prejudiced if the taxable year in which the regulatory election should have been made or any taxable years that would have been affected by the election had it been timely made are closed by the period of limitations on assessment under section 6501(a) before the taxpayer's receipt of a ruling granting relief under this section. The IRS may condition a grant of relief on the taxpayer providing the IRS with a statement from an independent auditor (other than an auditor providing an affidavit pursuant to paragraph (e)(3) of this section) certifying that the interests of the Government are not prejudiced under the standards set forth in paragraph (c)(1)(i) of this section.

(2) *Special rules for accounting method regulatory elections.*—The interests of the Government are deemed to be prejudiced except in unusual and compelling circumstances if the accounting method regulatory election for which relief is requested—

(i) Is subject to the procedure described in § 1.4461(e)(3)(i) of this chapter (requiring the advance written consent of the Commissioner);

(ii) Requires an adjustment under section 481(a) (or would require an adjustment under section 481(a) if the taxpayer changed to the method of accounting for which relief is requested in a taxable year subsequent to the taxable year the election should have been made);

(iii) Would permit a change from an impermissible method of accounting that is an issue under consideration by examination, an appeals office, or a federal court and the change would provide a more favorable method or more favorable terms and conditions than if the change were made as part of an examination; or

(iv) Provides a more favorable method of accounting or more favorable terms and conditions if the election is made by a certain date or taxable year.

(3) *Special rules for accounting period regulatory elections.*—The interests of the Government are deemed to be prejudiced except in unusual and compelling circumstances if an election is an accounting period regulatory election (other than the election to use other than the required taxable year under section 444) and the request for relief is filed more than 90 days after the due date for filing the Form 1128, Application to Adopt, Change, or Retain a Tax Year (or other required statement).

(d) *Effect of amended returns-.*—(1) *Second examination under section 7605(b).*—Taxpayers requesting and receiving an extension of time under this section waive any objections to a second examination under section 7605(b) for the issue(s) that is the subject of the relief request and any correlative adjustments.

(2) *Suspension of the period of limitations under section 6501(a).*—A request for relief under this section does not suspend the period of limitations on assessment under section 6501(a). Thus, for relief to be granted, the IRS may require the taxpayer to consent under section 6501(c)(4) to an extension of the period of limitations on assessment for the taxable year in which the regulatory election should have been made and any taxable years that would have been affected by the election had it been timely made.

(e) *Procedural requirements.*—(1) *In general.*—Requests for relief under this section must provide evidence that satisfies the requirements in paragraphs (b) and (c) of this section, and must provide additional information as required by this paragraph (e).

(2) *Affidavit and declaration from taxpayer.*—The taxpayer, or the individual who acts on behalf of the taxpayer with respect to tax matters, must submit a detailed affidavit describing the events that led to the failure to make a valid regulatory election and to the discovery of the failure. When the taxpayer relied on a qualified tax professional for advice, the taxpayer's affidavit must describe the engagement and responsibilities of the professional as well as the extent to which the taxpayer relied on the professional. The affidavit must be accompanied by a dated declaration, signed by the taxpayer, which states: "Under penalties of perjury, I declare that I have examined this request, including accompanying documents, and, to the best of my knowledge and belief, the request contains all the relevant facts relating to the request, and such facts are true, correct, and complete." The individual who signs for an entity must have personal knowledge of the facts and circumstances at issue.

(3) *Affidavits and declarations from other parties.*—The taxpayer must submit detailed affidavits from the individuals having knowledge or information about the events that led to the failure to make a valid regulatory election and to the discovery of the failure. These individuals must include the taxpayer's return preparer, any individual (including an employee of the taxpayer) who made a substantial contribution to the preparation of the return, and any accountant or attorney, knowledgeable in tax matters, who advised the taxpayer with regard to the election. An affidavit must describe the engagement and responsibilities of the individual as well as the advice that the individual provided to the taxpayer. Each affidavit must include the name, current address, and taxpayer identification number of the individual, and be accompanied by a dated declaration, signed by the individual, which states: "Under penalties of perjury, I declare that I have examined this request, including accompanying documents, and, to the best of my knowledge and belief, the request contains all the relevant facts relating to the request, and such facts are true, correct, and complete."

(4) *Other information.*—The request for relief filed under this section must also contain the following information—

(i) The taxpayer must state whether the taxpayer's return(s) for the taxable year in which the regulatory election should have been made or any taxable years that would have been affected by the election had it been timely made is being examined by a district director, or is being considered by an appeals office or a federal court. The taxpayer must notify the IRS office considering the request for relief if the IRS starts an examination of any such return while the taxpayer's request for relief is pending;

(ii) The taxpayer must state when the applicable return, form, or statement used to make the election was required to be filed and when it was actually filed;

(iii) The taxpayer must submit a copy of any documents that refer to the election;

(iv) When requested, the taxpayer must submit a copy of the taxpayer's return for any taxable year for which the taxpayer requests an extension of time to make the election and any return affected by the election; and

(v) When applicable, the taxpayer must submit a copy of the returns of other taxpayers affected by the election.

(5) *Filing instructions.*—A request for relief under this section is a request for a letter ruling. Requests for relief should be submitted in accordance with the applicable procedures for requests for a letter ruling and must be accompanied by the applicable user fee.

(f) *Examples.*—The following examples illustrate the provisions of this section:

Example 1. Taxpayer discovers own error. Taxpayer A prepares A's 1997 income tax return. A is unaware that a particular regulatory election is available to report a transaction in a particular manner. A files the 1997 return without making the election and reporting the transaction in a different manner. In 1999, A hires a qualified tax professional to prepare A's 1999 return. The professional discovers that A did not make the election. A promptly files for relief in accordance with this section. Assume paragraphs (b)(3)(i) through (iii) of this section do not apply. Under paragraph (b)(3)(i) of this section, A is deemed to have acted reasonably and in good faith because A requested relief before the failure to make the regulatory election was discovered by the IRS.

Example 2. Reliance on qualified tax professional. Taxpayer B hires a qualified tax professional to advise B on preparing B's 1997 income tax return. The professional was competent to render advice on the election and B provided the professional with all the relevant facts. The professional fails to advise B that a regulatory election is necessary in order for B to report income on B's 1997 return in a particular manner. Nevertheless, B reports this income in a manner that is consistent with having made the election. In 2000, during the examination of the 1997 return by the IRS, the examining agent discovers that the election has not been filed. B promptly files for relief in accordance with this section, including attaching an affidavit from B's professional stating that the professional failed to advise B that the election was necessary. Assume paragraphs (b)(3)(i) through (iii) of this section do not apply. Under paragraph (b)(1)(v) of this section, B is deemed to have acted reasonably and in good faith because B reasonably relied on a qualified tax professional and the tax professional failed to advise B to make the election.

Example 3. Accuracy-related penalty. Taxpayer C reports income on its 1997 income tax return in a manner that is contrary to a regulatory provision. In 2000, during the examination of the 1997 return, the IRS raises an issue regarding the reporting of this income on C's return and asserts the accuracy-related penalty under section 6662. C requests relief under this section to elect an alternative method of reporting the income. Under paragraph (b)(3)(i) of this section, C is deemed to have not acted reasonably and in good faith because C seeks to alter a return position for which an accuracy-related penalty could be imposed under section 6662.

Example 4. Election not requiring adjustment under section 481(a). Taxpayer D prepares D's 1997 income tax return. D is unaware that a particular accounting method regulatory election is available. D files D's 1997 return without making the election and uses another permissible method of accounting. The applicable regulation

provides that the election is made on a cut-off basis (without an adjustment under section 481(a)). In 1998, D requests relief under this section to make the election under the regulation. If D were granted an extension of time to make the election, D would pay no less tax than if the election had been timely made. Assume that paragraphs (c)(2)(i), (iii), and (iv) of this section do not apply. Under paragraph (c)(2)(ii) of this section, the interests of the Government are not deemed to be prejudiced because the election does not require an adjustment under section 481(a).

Example 5. Election requiring adjustment under section 481(a). The facts are the same as in *Example 4* of this paragraph (f) except that the applicable regulation provides that the election requires an adjustment under section 481(a). Under paragraph (c)(2)(ii) of this section, the interests of the Government are deemed to be prejudiced except in unusual or compelling circumstances.

Example 6. Under examination by the IRS. A regulation permits an automatic change in method of accounting for an item on a cut-off basis. Taxpayer E reports income on E's 1997 income tax return using an impermissible method of accounting for the item. In 2000, during the examination of the 1997 return by the IRS, the examining agent notifies E in writing that its method of accounting for the item is an issue under consideration. Any change from the impermissible method made as part of an examination is made with an adjustment under section 481(a). E requests relief under this section to make the change pursuant to the regulation for 1997. The change on a cut-off basis under the regulation would be more favorable than if the change were made with an adjustment under section 481(a) as part of an examination. Under paragraph (c)(2)(iii) of this section, the interests of the Government are deemed to be prejudiced except in unusual and compelling circumstances because E seeks to change from an impermissible method of accounting that is an issue under consideration in the examination on a basis that is more favorable than if the change were made as part of an examination.

[Reg. § 301.9100-3.]

☐ [*T.D.* 8742, 12-30-97.]

ELECTIONS UNDER ECONOMIC RECOVERY TAX ACT OF 1981

[Reg. § 301.9100-4T]

§ 301.9100-4T. Time and manner of making certain elections under the Economic Recovery Tax Act of 1981 (Temporary).—(a) *Miscellaneous*

elections.—(1) *Elections to which this paragraph applies.*—This paragraph applies to the following elections provided under the Economic Recovery Tax Act of 1981:

Section of Act	Section of Code	Description of Election	Availability of Election
201(a)	168(b)(3)	Different recovery period.	Property placed in service after 1980.
201(a)	168(d)(2)(A)	Inclusion in income of entire proceeds of disposition.	Property placed in service after 1980.
201(a)	168(e)(2)	Exclusion of property from recovery system.	Property placed in service after 1980.
201(a)	168(f)(2)(C)	Different recovery period for property used outside U.S.	Property placed in service after 1980.

Section of Act	Section of Code	Description of Election	Availability of Election
202(a)	179	Expensing certain depreciable property.	Taxable years beginning after 1981.
237	474	For small business to use one inventory pool when LIFO is elected.	Taxable years beginning after 1981.
266(a)		Deferral of commencement of amortization period for motor carrier operating authority.	Taxable years ending after June 30, 1980.
508(c)		Application of Title V of the Act to all regulated futures contracts or positions held on June 23, 1981.	Property held on June 23, 1981.
509		Application of Code sec. 1256 and extension of time for payment of tax for all regulated futures contracts held at any time during taxable year that includes June 23, 1981.	Property held during taxable year that includes June 23, 1981.

(2) *Time for making elections.*—(i) *In general.*—Except as otherwise provided in this paragraph (a)(2), the elections specified in paragraph (a)(1) of this section shall be made by the later of—

    (A) The due date (taking extensions into account) of the income tax return for the taxable year for which the election is to be effective, or

    (B) April 15, 1982.

    (ii) *No extension of time for payment.*—Payments of tax due shall be made in accordance with chapter 62 of the Code.

    (iii) *Elections under section 508(c) or 509 of the Act.*—Elections under section 508(c) or 509 of the Act shall be made by the due date (taking extensions into account) of the income tax return for the taxable year for which the election is to be effective.

(3) *Manner of making elections.*—The elections specified in paragraph (a)(1) of this section shall be made by attaching a statement to the income tax return (or amended return) for the taxable year for which the election is made. Except as otherwise provided in the return or in the instructions accompanying the return for the taxable year, the statement shall—

    (i) Contain the name, address, and taxpayer identification number of the electing taxpayer,

    (ii) Identify the election,

    (iii) Indicate the section of the Code (or, if the provision is not codified, the section of the Act) under which the election is being made,

    (iv) Specify the period for which the election is being made and the property to which the election is to apply, and

    (v) Provide any information required by the relevant statutory provisions and any information necessary to show that the taxpayer is entitled to make the election.

(b) *Designation of principal campaign committee.*—This paragraph applies to the designation of a principal campaign committee under section 527(h) of the Code, as added by section 128 of the Act. References in this section to "elections" include designations under section 527 (h). Under that provision a candidate for Congress may designate one committee as the candidate's principal campaign committee. The political organization taxable income of that committee shall be taxed at the appropriate rates under section 11(b); that income is ordinarily taxed at the highest rate specified in section 11(b). The candidate shall designate the principal campaign committee by filing a statement of designation with the income tax return of the committee for the first taxable year of the committee ending after 1981 for which the designation is to be effective. The return and the statement shall be filed by the due date (taking extensions into account) of the return. The rules of section 21 (relating to effects of changes in rates during a taxable year) shall apply in the case of any taxable year beginning before 1982 for which a designation is made. The statement of designation shall be signed by the candidate and shall—

(1) Contain the name, address, and taxpayer identification number of the candidate and of the committee,

(2) Identify the statement as a designation under section 527(h) of the Code, and

(3) Designate the committee as the principal campaign committee of the candidate.

The candidate shall attach to the statement a copy of the statement of designation filed with the Federal Election Commission.

(c) *Election to be treated as a qualified fund for purposes of the research credit.*—This paragraph applies to the election provided under section 44F(e)(4) of the Code, as added by section 221(a) of the Act. The election to be treated as a qualified fund for purposes of the research credit may be made effective as of any date after June 30, 1981, and before January 1, 1986. An organization shall make this election by filing with the service center with which it files its annual return a statement signed by a person authorized to act on behalf of the organization. That statement shall—

(1) Contain the name, address, and taxpayer identification number of the electing organization and of the organization that established and maintains the electing organization,

(2) Identify the election as an election under section 44F(e)(4) of the Code,

(3) Specify the date on which the election is to become effective (in the case of elections filed before February 1, 1982, not earlier than the date that is 7 months before the date on which the election is filed; in the case of elections filed after January 31, 1982, not earlier than the date on which the election is filed), and

(4) Provide all information necessary to show that the organization is entitled to make the election.

(d) *Election to treat qualified subchapter S trust as grantor trust.*—This paragraph applies to the election provided under section 1371(g)(2) of the Code, as added by section 234(b) of the Act. The election to treat a qualified subchapter S trust as a grantor trust described in section 1371(e)(1)(A) of the Code is available for taxable years beginning after 1981. The beneficiary of the trust (or the legal representative of the beneficiary) shall make this election by signing and filing with the service center with which the subchapter S corporation files its income tax return a statement that—

(1) Contains the name, address, and taxpayer identification number of the beneficiary, the trust, and the subchapter S corporation,

(2) Identifies the election as an election under section 1371(g)(2) of the Code,

(3) Specifies the date on which the election is to become effective (not earlier than 60 days before the date on which the election is filed), and

(4) Provides all information necessary to show that the beneficiary is entitled to make the election.

Note that this election does not itself constitute an election as to the status of the corporation; the corporation must make the election provided in section 1372(a) to be treated as an electing small business corporation.

(e) *Election to have Code section 422A apply to options granted before 1981.*—This paragraph applies to the election provided under section 251(c)(1)(B) of the Act to have Code section 422A apply to certain options granted before 1981. A corporation may make only one election under this provision. Thus, a corporation that makes an election under this provision with respect to certain options granted before 1981 may not make any subsequent election under this provision with respect to other options granted before 1981. An election under this provision shall be made no later than the due date (taking extensions into account) of the income tax return of the corporation for its first taxable year during which either an option subject to the election or an option subject to the rules of section 422A of the Code is exercised. In any event, no election under this provision will be permitted after the due date (taking extensions into account) of the income tax return for the taxable year including December 31, 1982. A corporation shall make this election by attaching to its income tax return (or amended return) a statement that—

(1) Contains the name, address, and taxpayer identification number of the corporation,

(2) Identifies the election as an election under section 251(c)(1)(B) of the Economic Recovery Tax Act of 1981,

(3) Specifies the options to which the election applies, and

(4) Provides all information necessary to show that the corporation is entitled to make the election.

(f) *Election to increase basis of property on which additional estate tax is imposed.*—This paragraph applies to the election provided under section 1016 (c) of the Code, as amended by section 421(g) of the Act. The election to increase the basis of property on which additional estate tax is imposed is available with respect to the estates of decedents dying after 1981. The qualified heir shall make this election by filing with the Form 706-A (Additional Estate Tax Return) a statement that—

(1) Contains the name, address, and taxpayer identification number of the qualified heir and of the estate,

(2) Identifies the election as an election under section 1016(c) of the Code,

(3) Specifies the property with respect to which the election is made, and

(4) Provides any additional information required by the instructions accompanying Form 706-A.

A qualified heir making an election under this paragraph must pay interest on the additional estate tax from the date that is 9 months after the date of the decedent's death to the date of the payment of the additional estate tax.

(g) *Revocation of elections.*—Elections under paragraph (f) of this section are irrevocable. Other elections made under this section may be revoked only with the consent of the Commissioner. An application for consent to revoke an election shall be signed by the applicant and filed with the service center with which the election was filed and shall—

(1) Contain the name, address, and taxpayer identification number of all parties identified in connection with the election,

(2) Identify the election being revoked by reference to the section of the Code or Act under which the election was made,

(3) Specify the scope of the election, and

(4) Explain why the applicant seeks to revoke the election.

(h) *Additional information required.*—If later regulations issued under the section of the Code or Act under which the election was made require the furnishing of information in addition to that which was furnished with the statement of election and an office of the Internal Revenue Service requests the taxpayer to provide the additional information, the taxpayer shall furnish the additional information in a statement filed with that office of the Internal Revenue Service within 60 days after the request is made. This statement shall also—

(1) Contain the name, address, and taxpayer identification numbers of all parties identified in connection with the election,

(2) Identify the election by reference to the section of the Code or Act under which the election was made, and

(3) Specify the scope of the election.

If the additional information is not provided within 60 days after the request is made, the election may, at the discretion of the Commissioner, be held invalid.

(i) *Effective date.*—This section applies to elections made after August 12, 1981. [Temporary Reg. § 301.9100-4T.]

☐ [*T.D.* 7793, 10-29-81. *Redesignated by T.D.* 8435, 9-18-92. *Amended by T.D.* 9481, 4-7-2010.]

ELECTIONS UNDER TAX EQUITY AND FISCAL RESPONSIBILITY ACT OF 1982

[Reg. § 301.9100-5T]

§ 301.9100-5T. Time and manner of making certain elections under the Tax Equity and Fiscal Responsibility Act of 1982 (Temporary).—

(a) *Miscellaneous elections.*—(1) *Elections to which this paragraph applies.*—This paragraph applies to the following elections provided under the Tax Equity and Fiscal Responsibility Act of 1982.

Section of Act	Section of Code	Description of Election	Availability of Election
201(c)	58(i)(1)	Optional 10-year write off of certain tax preferences.	Taxable years beginning after Dec. 31, 1982.
201(c)(1)	58(i)(4)	Intangible drilling and development costs.	Taxable years beginning after Dec. 31, 1982.
205(a)	48(q)	Reduced investment credit in lieu of basis adjustment.	Generally to period beginning after Dec. 31, 1982.
256(f)	820	Insurance company revocation of election under section 820.	Contracts which took effect in 1980 or 1981.

(2) *Time for making elections.*—(i) *In general.*—Except as otherwise provided in paragraph (a)(2) of this section, the elections specified in paragraph (a)(1) of this section shall be made by the later of—

(A) The due date (taking extensions into account) of the income tax return for the taxable year for which the election is to be effective, or

(B) April 15, 1983.

(ii) *No extensions of time for payment.*—Payments of tax due shall be made in accordance with chapter 62 of the Code.

(iii) *Election by insurance companies relating to repeal of section 820.*—Elections under section 256(f) of the Act, relating to special rule allowing reinsured insurance company to revoke an election under section 820, must be made before March 5, 1983.

(3) *Manner of making elections.*—The elections specified in paragraph (a)(1) of this section shall be made by attaching a statement to the income tax return (or amended return) for the taxable year for which the election is made. Except as otherwise provided in the return or in the instructions accompanying the return for the taxable year, the statement shall—

(i) Contain the name, address, and taxpayer identification number of the electing taxpayer,

(ii) Identify the election,

(iii) Indicate the section of the Code (or, if the provision is not codified, the section of the Act) under which the election is being made,

(iv) Specify the period for which the election is being made and the property to which the election is to apply, and

(v) Provide any information required by the relevant statutory provisions and any information necessary to show that the taxpayer is entitled to make the election.

(b) *Special rules for reduced investment credit in lieu of basis adjustment.*—(1) *Appropriate return.*—

For purposes of section 48(q) of the Code and paragraph (a)(2)(i)(A) and (3) of this section the term "income tax return for the taxable year for which the election is effective" with respect to any property is the tax return for the taxable year in which such property is placed in service, or in the case of property to which an election under section 46(d) (relating to qualified progress expenditures) applies, the appropriate return is the return for the first taxable year for which qualified progress expenditures were taken into account with respect to such property.

(2) *Applicability of election.*—In general, the election under section 48(q) is applicable to periods beginning after December 31, 1982 under rules similar to the rules of section 48(m) of the Code. However, the election does not apply to property excepted by section 205(c)(1)(B) of the Act.

(c) *Election by a reinsurer to make installment payments of taxes owed resulting from the repeal of section 820.*—This paragraph applies to the election by an insurance company provided under section 256(e) of the Act. A reinsurer that is a calendar year taxpayer shall be considered to have made an election under section 256(e) of the Act if by March 15, 1983 it files its income tax return (or an application on Form 7004 for an automatic extension of time to file its income tax return), with the statement required to be filed under this paragraph attached and, unless the reinsurer is making a further election under section 256(e)(2)(B) of the Act, pays one-third of the amount described in section 256(e)(1) of the Act by March 15, 1983. A reinsurer making an election under section 256(e)(2)(B) of the Act must pay one-sixth of the amount described in section 256(e)(1) of the Act by March 15, 1983 and one-sixth of such amount by June 15, 1983. The statement required to be filed under this paragraph shall—

(1) Contain the name, address, and taxpayer identification number of the corporation,

(2) Identify the election as an election under section 256(e) of the Act, and section 256(e)(2)(B) if applicable, and

(3) Provide all information necessary to show the taxpayer is entitled to make the election.

For provisions relating to the use of authorized financial institutions in depositing the taxes, see §1.6302-1.

(d) [Reserved].

(e) *Additional information required.*—If later regulations issued under the section of the Code or Act under which the election was made require the furnishing of information in addition to that which was furnished with the statement of election and an office of the Internal Revenue Service requests the taxpayer to provide the additional information, the taxpayer shall furnish the additional information in a statement filed with that office of the Internal Revenue Service within 60 days after the request is made. This statement shall also—

(1) Contain the name, address, and taxpayer identification numbers of all parties identified in connection with the election,

(2) Identify the election by reference to the section of the Code or Act under which the election was made, and

(3) Specify the scope of the election.

If the additional information is not provided within 60 days after the request is made, the election may, at the discretion of the Commissioner, be held valid.

[(f)] *Effective date.*—This section applies to elections made after September 3, 1982. [Temporary Reg. §301.9100-5T.]

☐ [*T.D. 7870, 1-12-83. Redesignated by T.D. 8435, 9-18-92. Amended by T.D. 8952, 6-25-2001.*]

ELECTIONS UNDER DEFICIT REDUCTION ACT OF 1984

[Reg. §301.9100-6T]

§301.9100-6T. Time and manner of making certain elections under the Deficit Reduction Act of 1984 (Temporary).—(a) *Miscellaneous elec-*tions.—(1) *Elections to which this paragraph applies.*—This paragraph applies to the following elections provided under the Deficit Reduction Act of 1984 (the Act):

Section of Act	Section of Code	Description of Election	Availability of Election
31(a) and 31(g)(16)	168(j)(4)(E)(ii)	Election by certain 501(c)(12) organizations to be treated as taxable organizations and to have certain arbitrage profits taxed	Generally for property placed in service after May 23, 1983, or leased after such date
31(f)	46(e)(4)(C)	Election by section 593 organizations not to apply section 46(e)(4)(A)	Generally for property placed in service after November 5, 1983, or leased after such date
41(a)	1282(b)(2)	Election to have section 1281 apply to all short-term obligations acquired on or after the first day of the first taxable year to which the election relates (but not to obligations acquired before July 19, 1984)	Taxable years ending after July 18, 1984, with respect to obligations acquired after such date

Section of Act	Section of Code	Description of Election	Availability of Election
41(a)	1283(c)(2)	Election to have section 1283(c)(1) not apply to all obligations acquired on or after the first day of the first taxable year to which the election relates (but not to obligations acquired before July 19, 1984)	Taxable years ending after July 18, 1984, with respect to obligations acquired after such date
113	48(r)	Election by all persons having an ownership interest in a sound recording to treat such recording as 3-year recovery property	Property placed in service after March 15, 1984
211	806(d)(4)	Election with respect to loss from operations of member of group	Taxable years beginning after December 31, 1983
211	807(d)(4)(C)	Election to use preceding year's interest rate for nonannuity reserves	Taxable years beginning after December 31, 1983
211	810(b)(3)	Election to forgo carryback period by life insurance companies	Losses from operations for taxable years beginning after December 31, 1983
216(c)(1)		Election not to have reserves recomputed	First taxable year beginning after December 31, 1983
216(c)(2)		Election to use adjusted statutory reserves for certain contracts	Generally for contracts issued after 1983 and before 1989 by certain companies that make an election under section 261(c)(1) of the Act
217(i)		Election to treat individual non-cancellable accident and health contracts as cancellable	First taxable year beginning after December 31, 1983
217(l)(2)(b)		Treatment of losses from certain guaranteed interest contracts	Taxable years beginning after December 31, 1983, and before January 1, 1988
431(e)(2)	46(c)(8) and (9), 48(d)(6), 47(d)(1) and (2)	Election to apply the investment tax credit at risk rules as modified by the Tax Reform Act of 1984 to all transactions covered by section 211(f) of the Economic Recovery Tax Act of 1981	Generally to property placed in service between February 18, 1981, and July 19, 1984
712(l)(7)(B)	304	Election to apply certain technical corrections of section 304 to all transfers covered by the changes made to section 304 by the Tax Equity and Fiscal Responsibility Act of 1982	Stock acquired after August 31, 1982, and before June 19, 1984
712(l)(7)(C)(ii)	304	Election with respect to bank holding companies to apply certain technical corrections of section 304 to stock acquired after June 18, 1984	Generally to transfers to bank holding companies formed pursuant to application filed with Federal Reserve Board before June 18, 1984
1066	163(d)	Elections to treat certain income from S corporations, for purposes of section 163(d), as such income would have been treated prior to the Subchapter S Revision Act of 1982	With respect to S corporation taxable years beginning in 1983 or 1984

Section of Act	Section of Code	Description of Election	Availability of Election
1078		Election to exclude from gross income payments from U.S. Forest Service as result of restricting motorized traffic in the Boundary Waters Canoe Area	Payments in taxable years beginning after December 31, 1979

(2) *Time for making elections.*—(i) *In general.*—Except as otherwise provided in this paragraph (a)(2), the elections specified in paragraph (a)(1) of this section shall be made by the later of—

(A) The due date (taking extensions into account) of the tax return for the first taxable year for which the election is to be effective, or

(B) April 15, 1985 (in which case the election generally must be made by amended return).

(ii) *No extension of time for payment.*—Payments of tax due shall be made in accordance with chapter 62 of the Code.

(iii) *Time for making certain life insurance company elections.*—(A) *Election to use preceding year's interest rate for non-annuity reserves.*—The election under section 807(d)(4)(C) to use the preceding year's interest rate for non-annuity reserves applies on a contract-by-contract basis. For contracts issued before the first day of the first taxable year beginning after December 31, 1983, the election shall be made by the due date (including extensions) of the income tax return for the first taxable year beginning after December 31, 1983. For contracts issued on or after the first day of the first taxable year beginning after December 31, 1983, the election shall be made by the due date (including extensions) of the income tax return for the taxable year in which the contract is issued.

(B) *Election not to have reserves recomputed.*—The election under section 216(c)(1) of the Act not to have reserves recomputed shall be made by the due date (including extensions) of the income tax return for the taxable year beginning after December 31, 1983.

(C) *Election to use adjusted statutory reserves for certain contracts.*—The election under section 216(c)(2) of the Act to use adjusted statutory reserves for certain contracts may be made only by life insurance companies that make an election under section 216(c)(1) of the Act and that meet the other requirements of section 216(c)(2). The election, if made, applies to all contracts issued on or after the first day of the first taxable year beginning after December 31, 1983, and before January 1, 1989. The election shall be made by the due date (including extensions) of the income tax return for the taxable year beginning after December 31, 1983.

(D) *Election to treat individual non-cancellable accident and health contracts as cancellable.*—The election under section 217(i) of the Act to treat individual non-cancellable accident and health contracts as cancellable shall be made by the due date (including extensions) of the income tax return for the taxable year beginning after December 31, 1983.

(E) *Treatment of losses from certain guaranteed interest contracts.*—The election under section 217(l)(2)(B) of the Act with respect to the treatment of losses from certain guaranteed interest contracts shall be made by the due date (including extensions) of the income tax return for the taxable year beginning after December 31, 1983.

(iv) *Time for making the election to exclude from gross income payments received from the U.S. Forest Service as a result of the restriction of motorized traffic in the Boundary Waters Canoe Area.*—Elections under section 1078 of the Act shall be made by the later of the expiration of the period for making a claim for credit or refund of the tax imposed by chapter 1 of the Code for the taxable year in which the reinvestment of the payment occurred, or July 18, 1985. Amended returns for years after the year for which the election is made must be filed if making this election affects the tax liability for such years.

(3) *Manner of making elections.*—(i) *In general.*—The elections specified in paragraph (a)(1) of this section shall be made by attaching a statement to the tax return for the taxable year in which the election is made. If because of paragraph (a)(2)(i)(B) the election may be filed after the due date of the tax return for the first taxable year for which the election is to be effective, such election must be attached to a tax return or amended return for the taxable year to which the election relates. Except as otherwise provided in the return or in the instructions accompanying the return for the taxable year, the statement shall—

(A) Contain the name, address, and taxpayer identification number of the electing taxpayer,

(B) Identify the election,

(C) Indicate the section of the Code (or, if the provision is not codified, the section of the Act) under which the election is made,

(D) Specify, as applicable, the period for which the election is being made and/or the property or other items to which the election is to apply, and

(E) Provide any information required by the relevant statutory provisions and any information necessary to show that the taxpayer is entitled to make the election.

(ii) *Special rules for making the election with respect to sound recordings.*—The election under section 48(r), as amended by section 113 of the Act, shall be made separately for each sound recording and must be made by all persons hav-

Reg. §301.9100-6T(a)(3)(ii)

ing an ownership interest in the sound recording. In the case of an ownership interest held by a partnership or an S corporation, the partnership or S corporation shall make the election. Each person making the election shall do so in accordance with paragraph (a)(2) and (3) of this section, and shall identify in the statement described in paragraph (a)(3) of this section the persons with ownership interests in the sound recording, and shall state that each such person is making the election with respect to that sound recording.

(iii) *Special rules for making the election with respect to redemption through use of related corporations.*—For either election available under section 712(l)(7) of the Act (relating to redemptions through related corporations) to be effective, such election must be made jointly by both the issuing and acquiring corporations. The election is made jointly when both the issuing and acquiring corporations make the election in accordance with paragraph (a)(2) and (3) of this section.

(iv) *Special rules for making the election for investment tax credit at risk rules.*—The election under section 431(e)(2) of the Act is made by filing an amended return for the first taxable year ending after February 18, 1981, during which taxable year property, to which the amendments made by section 211(f) of the Economic Recovery Tax Act of 1981 apply, was placed in service. If that taxable year is a closed year, the election is made by filing an amended return for the first succeeding open taxable year, but in such event this election can be made only if the aggregate amount of the investment tax credit that would have been allowable in the closed years had the election been effective for those years is greater than or equal to the amount of the investment tax credits actually claimed in the closed years. In the case of partnerships and S corporations, the election under section 431(e) is made, respectively, at the partner or the shareholder level. Any election made under section 431(e) shall apply to all property of the taxpayer to which the amendments made by section 211(f) of the Economic Recovery Tax Act of 1981 apply. Amended returns must be filed for any year the tax liability for which is affected by making this election.

(v) *Special rules for certain elections by life insurance companies.*—(A) *Election with respect to loss from operations of member of group.*—Any life insurance company that makes an election under section 806(d)(4) must include on the statement described in paragraph (a)(3) of this section the name, address and taxpayer identification number of the members of the controlled group that did not file a consolidated return with the life insurance company for the taxable year to which the election applies, the amount of loss subject to the limitation provided by section 806(d)(4)(B), and a computation showing how such amount was derived.

(B) *Election to use preceding year's interest rate for non-annuity reserves.*—If the election

under section 807(d)(4)(C) is not made for all non-annuity contracts issued by the life insurance company before the end of the taxable year in which the election is made, the company must reasonably identify, in the statement described in paragraph (a)(3) of this section, the contracts or groups of contracts for which the election is made. The statement, however, need not specify each individual contract for which the election is made.

(4) *Revocation.*—The elections under Act sections 31(a), 31(g)(16), 31(f), 41(a) (Code section 1283(b)(2)), 113, 211 (Code section 810(b)(3)), 216(c)(1) and (2), 217(l), 431(e)(2), and 712(l)(7)(B) and (C)(ii) are irrevocable. Elections under Act sections 41(a) (Code sections 1282(b)(2) and 1283(c)(2)), 211 (Code sections 806(d)(4), and 807(d)(4)(C)), 217(i), 1066, and 1078 are revocable only with the consent of the Commissioner. A revocation under Act section 211 (Code section 807(d)(4)(C)) shall be treated as a change in basis of computing reserves that is subject to the adjustment provided in section 807(f) of the Code.

(b) *Church or qualified church-controlled organization's election of exemption from social security taxes under chapter 21.*—(1) *In general.*—This paragraph applies to the election under section 3121(w) of the Code, as added by section 2603(b) of the Act, by a church or qualified church-controlled organization (as defined in section 3121(w)(3)) that service performed in the employ of such church or organization shall be excluded from employment for purposes of title II of the Social Security Act and chapter 21 of the Internal Revenue Code. Any election made under section 3121(w) shall apply to all service performed on or after January 1, 1984, by employees of such church or organization (whether or not they were employees on that date or on the date the election is made). Employees of the electing church or organization are subject to the provisions of chapter 2 of the Code (relating to the tax on self-employment income) as amended by section 2603(c)(2) and (d)(2) of the Act for service performed for such church or organization on or after January 1, 1984.

(2) *Time for making the election.*—Any election under section 3121(w) by a church or qualified church-controlled organization for which a quarterly employment tax return for the tax imposed under section 3111 is due (or would be due but for the election) on October 31, 1984, must be made on or before October 30, 1984. Any election under section 3121(w) by a church or organization for which the first quarterly employment tax return for the tax imposed under section 3111 is due (or would be due but for this election) after October 31, 1984, must be made on or before the day before the first date that such tax return would be due from the church or organization (disregarding any extension of such due date). A purported election filed after the date prescribed in this paragraph (b)(2) shall be void.

(3) *Manner of making the election.*—To make an election under section 3121(w), a church or

qualified church-controlled organization must certify that it is opposed for religious reasons to the payment of the tax imposed by section 3111 (relating to the employer tax) of the Code. The election and certification are made by executing and filing Form 8274 in accordance with the form and its instructions. The form shall be signed by an official authorized to sign tax returns for the church or organization. Where tax imposed by section 3111 is reported (or would be reported but for this election) with respect to more than one church or organization on a single quarterly employment tax return, and the election under section 3121(w) is made, then all of the churches and organizations covered by the last such return filed before such election was made for which the time for making the election has not expired shall be covered by the election unless specifically excluded by stating such exclusion in the election.

(4) *Refunds of FICA taxes paid.*—Where a church or qualified church-controlled organization makes a timely election under section 3121(w), a refund, without interest, shall be made to such church or organization of any taxes paid under sections 3101 and 3111 with respect to service performed after December 31, 1983, covered by the election. However, the refund will be made only if the church or organization agrees on its claim for the refund to pay to each employee covered by the election the portion of the refund attributable to the tax imposed on the wages of the employee by section 3101. The employee may not receive any other refund of such taxes. The claim for refund shall be made by the church or organization by filing Form 843 with the service center where the Form 941 on which the taxes subject to refund was filed. Form 843 shall be executed in accordance with the form and its instructions, and also in accordance with the instructions to Form 8274 that relate to Form 843.

(5) *Irrevocability of election except by Commissioner.*—An election under section 3121 shall be irrevocable by the electing church or organization. The Commissioner, however, shall permanently revoke the election if the church or organization fails to furnish the information required under section 6051 to the Internal Revenue Service for a period of 2 years or more and also fails to furnish such information within 60 days after a written request therefor is made by the Internal Revenue Service.

(c) *Election to issue taxable student loan bonds.*—This paragraph applies to the election by an issuer to issue taxable student loan bonds under section 625(c) of the Act. The election is available for obligations issued after December 31, 1983, and is made by filing a statement and necessary attachments with the Internal Revenue Service Center, Philadelphia, PA 19255, prior to the issuance of such taxable bonds. The statement shall identify the election as made under section

625(c) of the Tax Reform Act of 1984 and shall contain the name, address and taxpayer identification number of the issuer, and the total purchase price, face amount and interest rate of the issue, bond issuance costs, amounts allocated to reasonably required reserve or replacement funds, and the date of issue. The issuer shall attach to the statement of election a copy of previous Internal Revenue Service correspondence relating to the tax exempt status of the issuing authority and a statement containing the total purchase price, face amount, interest rate, bond issuance costs, amounts allocated to reasonably required reserve or replacement funds, and the date of issuance of outstanding tax exempt issues of student loan bonds of the issuer. With respect to outstanding tax exempt issues of student loan bonds of the issuer issued after December 31, 1982, the issuer may alternatively attach copies of the Form 8038 filed with respect to such issues. Each taxable student loan bond must state on its face that the interest paid on such bond is subject to federal income taxation. An election with respect to an issue is irrevocable once made.

(d) [Reserved.]

(e) *Election not to claim the credit for alcohol used as fuel.*—The election under section 40(f) (as added by section 474(k) of the Act) not to claim the alcohol fuels credit is available for taxable years beginning after December 31, 1983, and shall be made for the taxable year, in which such credit is determined by not claiming such credit on an original return or amended return at any time before the expiration of the 3-year period beginning on the last date prescribed by law for filing the return for the taxable year (determined without regard for extensions). The election may be revoked within the 3-year period by filing an amended return and claiming the credit on the return.

(f) *Protective election to adopt LIFO method.*—(1) *Time for making the election.*—A protective election in connection with the enactment of section 95 of the Act to adopt the LIFO method of accounting for inventory under section 472 of the Code can only be made for the taxpayer's first taxable year beginning after July 18, 1984, and must be made on or before the due date (including extensions) of the tax return for such taxable year. Once made, the election is irrevocable unless the Commissioner authorizes the use of another inventory method (see §1.472-5).

(2) *Manner for making a protective election.*—The protective election is made by completing all line items on a current Form 970 and indicating that the election is a protective election filed in connection with the enactment of section 95 of the Tax Reform Act of 1984. The Form 970 must be attached to the taxpayer's income tax return for the taxable year for which the protective election is made. The LIFO method adopted under the protective election must be consistent

Reg. §301.9100-6T(f)(2)

in all respects with the taxpayer's LIFO method used in the taxpayer's most recently completed taxable year for which the LIFO method was used. In completing the current Form 970, the taxpayer shall specify the method of inventory valuation that the taxpayer would have used, the opening LIFO inventory for the taxable year for which the protective election is made, and the section 481 adjustment that would be required, as if the taxpayer were not on the LIFO method for the taxable year immediately preceding the taxable year for which the protective election is made.

(g) *Election by an estate or trust to recognize gain or loss on the distribution of property (other than cash) to a beneficiary.*—This paragraph applies to the election made by a trust or estate to recognize gain or loss on the distribution of property (other than cash) to a beneficiary under section 643(d) of the Code as amended by section 81 of the Act. The election is available for distributions made after June 1, 1984, in taxable years ending after such date. The election must be made by the fiduciary who is required to make the return of the estate or trust under section 641 and § 1.641(b)-2. The election shall be made by such fiduciary on the tax return of the estate or trust for the taxable year with respect to which the distribution of property was made and must be filed by the due date (including extensions) of such return. Until the Form 1041, U.S. Fiduciary Income Tax Return is revised, the election should be made by including the gain or loss on the Schedule D (or other appropriate schedule, if applicable) of the Form 1041 and attaching the statement described in paragraph (a)(3) of this section to the tax return on which the election is made and including on that statement the name and taxpayer identification number of the distributee. For distributions made after June 1, 1984, and before July 18, 1984, the election must be filed by the later of the due date (including extensions) of the tax return of the estate or trust for the taxable year with respect to which the distribution was made or January 1, 1985. For those distributions, the fiduciary may make the election in the manner described above on a tax return, or amended return, for the year with respect to which the distribution was made. An election under section 643(d) may be revoked only with the consent of the Commissioner. The request for revocation of an election should be made by the fiduciary in the form of a ruling request and must contain the information required by regulations and revenue procedures pertaining thereto.

(h) *Election to treat a stapled foreign entity as a subsidiary.*—This paragraph applies to the election, provided under section 136(c)(6) of the Act, to treat a foreign corporation which was a stapled entity with a domestic corporation as of June 30, 1983, as being owned (to the extent of its stapled interests) by the domestic corporation with which it is stapled. This treatment, if so elected, is in lieu of the treatment prescribed in section 269B(a)(1) of the Code, as added by the Act. This election may be made by the domestic corporation with which the foreign entity is stapled. The election may not be made by the foreign entity or by shareholders of the domestic corporation. This election must be made no later than January 14, 1985, and may be revoked only with the consent of the Commissioner. This election shall be effective after December 31, 1986. The domestic corporation shall make this election by filing with the service center with which the domestic corporation files its income tax return a statement that—

(1) Contains the name, address, and taxpayer identification number of the domestic corporation,

(2) Identifies the election as made under section 136(c)(6) of the Tax Reform Act of 1984, and

(3) Identifies the foreign entity and the interests in the foreign entity which constitute stapled interests with respect to the stock of the domestic corporation, and specifies the date on which those interests became stapled interests.

If this election is not made, the foreign corporation (interests in which were stapled interests as of June 30, 1983) will be treated as a domestic corporation, effective January 1, 1987, under section 269B(a)(1) of the Code.

(i) *Election to treat certain section 1248 amounts as included in gross income under section 951(a)(1)(A).*—This paragraph applies to the elections, provided under section 133(d)(3) of the Act, to treat amounts included in the gross income of any person as a dividend by reason of section 1248(a) or (f) after October 9, 1975, and before July 19, 1985, as an amount included in the gross income of such person under section 951(a)(1)(A). The election with respect to transactions to which section 1248(a) applies may be made by the foreign corporation described in section 1248(a) (or its successor in interest). The election with respect to transactions to which section 1248(f) applies may be made by the domestic corporation described in section 1248(f)(1) (or its successor in interest). Neither election may be made by an affected shareholder of any such corporation (unless the shareholder is the successor in interest). This election must be made no later than January 14, 1985, and shall apply with respect to all transactions to which section 1248(a) or (f) applies that occurred after October 9, 1975, and before July 19, 1984. Once made, the election may be revoked only with the consent of the Commissioner. A foreign corporation shall make this election by filing the statement described in this paragraph with the Internal Revenue Service Center, Philadelphia, PA 19255. A domestic corporation shall make this election by filing the statement described in this paragraph with the service center with which the domestic corporation files its income tax return. In either case, the statement shall—

(1) Contain the name, address, and taxpayer identification number (if any) of the corporation making the election,

(2) Identify the election as made under section 133(d)(3) of the Tax Reform Act of 1984, and

(3) Identify all of the transactions (including the date of each transaction), shareholders involved in those transactions, and amounts to which the election applies.

(j) *Special election for computing investment company taxable income.*—This paragraph applies to the election by a regulated investment company provided under section 1071(b) of the Act, which added section 852(b)(2)(F) to the Code. Under section 852(b)(2)(F), the taxable income of a regulated investment company shall be computed without regard to Section 454(b) (relating to short-term obligations issued on a discount basis) if the company so elects. The election may be made only for taxable years beginning after December 31, 1978. A regulated investment company shall make the election by computing taxable income without regard to section 454(b) on its return for the first taxable year for which it desires the election to apply and shall attach the statement described in paragraph (a)(3) of this section to the return on which the election is made. A regulated investment company shall make the election by the time set forth in paragraph (a)(2) of this section. Once made, the election applies to the first taxable year for which it is made and to all subsequent taxable years and cannot be revoked without the consent of the Commissioner.

(k) *Election of extension of time for payment of estate tax for interests in certain holding companies.*—An election under section 6166(b)(8), as added by section 1021(a) of the Act, or under section 1021(d)(2) of the Act, shall be made by including on the notice of election under section 6166 required by § 20.6166-1(b) a statement that an election is being made under section 6166(b)(8) or section 1021(d)(2) of the Act (whichever is applicable) and the facts which formed the basis for the executor's conclusion that the estate qualified for such election. If a taxpayer makes an election described in this paragraph (k), then the special 4-percent interest rate of section 6601(j) and the 5-year deferral of principal payments of section 6166(a)(3) are not available. Thus, the first installment of tax is due on the date prescribed by section 6151(a) and subsequent installments bear interest at the rate determined under section 6621. If the executor makes an election described in this paragraph (k) and the notice of election under section 6166 fails to state the amount of tax to be paid in installments or the number of installments, then the election is presumed to be for the maximum amount so payable and for payment thereof in 10 equal annual installments, beginning on the date prescribed in section 6151(a). The elections described under this paragraph (k) are available for estates of decedents dying after July 18, 1984.

(l) *Subchapter S election by commodities dealers and options dealers.*—This paragraph applies to a commodities dealer or options dealer referred to in section 102(d)(3) of the Act (relating to the election by such a dealer to be an S corporation) whose taxable year is the calendar year and that was a small business corporation (as defined in section 1361(b) of the Code) as of January 1, 1984. The election by such a dealer under section 102(d)(3) of the Act shall be made in the manner prescribed by section 1362 and the regulations thereunder, except that the election under section 102(d)(3) must be made before October 2, 1984. In addition to making the election in the manner prescribed under such section 1362 and the regulations thereunder, the commodities dealer or options dealer must indicate on Form 2553 that the election is made under section 102(d)(3) of the Act. Although section 102(d)(3) of the Act applies to dealers not covered by this paragraph, and such dealers may make an election under such section 102(d)(3), guidelines for making such an election are not provided in this paragraph and are forthcoming.

(m) *Election with respect to treatment of S termination year.*—For the election provided under section 1362(e)(3), as amended by section 721(h) of the Act, see § 18.1362-4 of this chapter.

(n) *Election to be an S corporation; certain short taxable years.*—For the election provided under section 1362(b), as amended by section 721(l) of the Act, see § 18.1362-1(b) of this chapter.

(o) *Election with respect to subchapter S passive investment income rules.*—For the election provided under 721(i) of the Act which amends section 6(b) of the Subchapter S Revision Act of 1982, see § 18.1362-5 of this chapter.

(p) *Election with respect to subchapter S distributions during certain post-termination transition periods.*—For the election provided under section 1371(e), as amended by section 721(o) of the Act, see § 18.1371-1 of this chapter.

(q) *No elections for closed year.*—Any election under this section which is allowed to be made by filing an amended return may only be made if the period for making a claim for refund or credit with respect to the taxable year for which such election is to be effective has not expired. This paragraph shall not apply to the election under paragraph (a)(2)(iv) of this section with respect to the election under section 1078 of the Act.

(r) *Additional information required.*—Later regulations or revenue procedures issued under provisions of the Code or Act covered by this section may require the furnishing of information in addition to that which was furnished with the statement of election described herein. In such event the later regulations or revenue procedures will provide guidance with respect to the furnishing of such additional information. [Temporary Reg. § 301.9100-6T.]

☐ [T.D. 7976, 9-5-84. *Amended by T.D. 8062,* 11-5-85. *Redesignated by T.D. 8435, 9-18-92. Amended by T.D. 9172, 1-3-2005.*]

ELECTIONS UNDER TAX REFORM ACT OF 1986

[Reg. §301.9100-7T]

§301.9100-7T. Time and manner of making certain elections under the Tax Reform Act of 1986 (Temporary).—(a) *Miscellaneous elections.*—(1) *Elections to which this paragraph applies.*—This paragraph applies to the elections set forth below provided under the Tax Reform Act of 1986 (the Act). General rules regarding the time for making the elections are provided in paragraph(a)(2) of this section. General rules regarding the manner for making the elections are

provided in paragraph (a)(3) of this section. Special rules regarding the time and manner for making certain elections are contained in paragraphs (a)—(i) of this section. If a special rule applies to one of the elections listed below, a cross-reference to the special rule is shown in brackets at the end of the description of the "Availability of Election." Paragraph (j) of this section provides that additional information with respect to elections may be required by future regulations or revenue procedures.

Section of Act	Section of Code	Description of Election	Availability of Election
201(a)	168(b)(5)	Election to depreciate property using the straight line method of recovery with respect to one or more classes of property for any taxable year.	Property placed in service after 12-31-86. Election must be made for taxable year in which property is placed in service. Election shall apply to all property in the class placed in service during the taxable year for which the election is made.
201(a)	168(f)(1)	Election to exclude certain property from the accelerated cost recovery system.	Property placed in service after 12-31-86. Election must be made for taxable year in which property is placed in service.
201(a)	168(g)(7)	Election to use alternative depreciation system with respect to one or more classes of property for any taxable year (except for residential rental or nonresidential real property where the election may be made separately with respect to each property).	Property placed in service after 12-31-86. Election must be made for taxable year in which property is placed in service. Except for residential rental or nonresidential real property, election shall apply to all property in the class placed in service during the taxable year for which the election is made.
201(a), 1802(a)	168(h)(6)(F)(ii), 168(j) (as in effect before October 22, 1986)	Election by a tax-exempt controlled entity to treat any gain recognized by the tax-exempt parent on any disposition of an interest in the tax-exempt controlled entity (and to treat any dividends or interest received or accrued from the tax-exempt controlled entity) as unrelated business taxable income under Code section 511 in order for the tax-exempt controlled entity to not be treated as a tax-exempt entity (or as a successor to a tax-exempt entity).	Property placed in service after 9-27-85, but can apply to property placed in service before such date if the tax-exempt controlled entity so elects. [See paragraph (a)(3)(ii) of this section.]
203(a)(1)(B)	—	Election to apply Act section 201 (including all elections within section 201).	Property placed in service after 7-31-86 and before 1-1-87.
204(e)	—	Election to have Act section 201 either (i) not apply to any property placed in service during 1987 or 1988 which is replacement property for property lost, damaged or destroyed in a flood which occurred 11-3-85 through 11-7-85 and which was declared a natural disaster area by the President of the United States, or (ii) apply to all such replacement property placed in service during 1985 or 1986.	(i) Property placed in service during 1987 or 1988; or (ii) property placed in service during 1985 or 1986.

Section of Act	Section of Code	Description of Election	Availability of Election
243(a)	—	Election to begin the 60 month amortization period with the first month of the taxpayer's first taxable year beginning after 11-19-82 in lieu of the 11-19-82 date or the bus operating authority acquisition date.	Bus operating authorities held on 11/19/82, or acquired after that date under a written contract that was binding on that date.
243(b)	—	Election to begin the 60 month amortization period on the first month of the taxpayer's first taxable year beginning after the deregulation month in lieu of the deregulation month.	Freight forwarder operating authorities held at the beginning of the 60 month period applicable to the taxpayer (*i.e.,* the deregulation date or the first month of the first taxable year beginning after the deregulation date).
243(a), (b)	—	Election by a qualified corporate taxpayer to allocate a portion of the cost basis of a qualified acquiring corporation in the stock of an acquired corporation to the basis of the authority.	For bus operating authorities: authorities held on 11/19/82, or acquired after that date under a written contract that was binding on that date. For freight forwarders: authorities held at the beginning of the 60-month period applicable to the taxpayer.
252(a)	42(f)(1)	Election concerning beginning of credit period for low-income housing credit.	Buildings placed in service after 12-31-86 and before 1-1-90 (before 1-1-91 for buildings described in Code section 42(n)(2)(B)). [See paragraph (b) of this section.]
252(a)	42(g)(1)	Election concerning qualified low-income housing project to either satisfy the 20-50 or the 40-60 occupancy test.	Buildings placed in service after 12-31-86 and before 1-1-90 (before 1-1-91 for buildings described in Code section 42(n)(2)(B)). [See paragraph (b) of this section.]
252(a)	42(i)(2)	Election to reduce eligible basis by outstanding balance of Federal loan subsidy.	Buildings placed in service after 12-31-86 and before 1-1-90 (before 1-1-91 for buildings described in Code section 42(n)(2)(B)). [See paragraph (b) of this section.]
252(a)	42(j)(5)	Election to have certain partnerships treated as the taxpayer eligible for low-income housing credit.	Buildings placed in service after 12-31-86 and before 1-1-90 (before 1-1-91 for buildings described in Code section 42(n)(2)(B)). [See paragraph (b) of this section.]
311(d)(2)	—	Revocation of prior election under Code section 631(a).	Election for taxable years beginning before 1-1-87 may be revoked for taxable years ending after 12-31-86.
411(b)(1)	263(i)	For intangible drilling and development costs paid or incurred with respect to an oil, gas, or geothermal well located outside the United States, election to include such costs in adjusted basis for purposes of computing the amount of any deduction under Code section 611 (without regard to section 613).	Costs paid or incurred after 12-31-86 in taxable years ending after such date. [See paragraph (a)(2)(iii) of this section.]

Section of Act	Section of Code	Description of Election	Availability of Election
411(b)(2)	616(d)	For expenditures paid or incurred with respect to the development of a mine or other natural deposit (other than an oil, gas, or geothermal well) located outside the United States, election to include such expenditures paid or incurred during the taxable year for which made in adjusted basis for purposes of computing the amount of any deduction under Code section 611 (without regard to section 613).	Costs paid or incurred after 12-31-86 in taxable years ending after such date. [See paragraph (a)(2)(iv) of this section.]
411(b)(2)	617(h)	For expenditures paid or incurred before the development stage for the purpose of ascertaining the existence, location, extent or quality of any deposit of ore or other mineral deposit (other than an oil, gas or geothermal well) located outside the United States, election to include all such expenditures, paid or incurred during the taxable year or any subsequent taxable year with respect to any such deposit, in adjusted basis for purposes of computing the amount of any deduction under Code section 611 (without regard to section 613).	Costs paid or incurred after 12-31-86 in taxable years ending after such date. [See paragraph (a)(2)(v) of this section.]
501(a)	469(j)(9)	Election to increase basis of property by amount of disallowed credit for purposes of determining gain or loss from a disposition of property used in a passive activity.	Taxable years beginning after 12-31-86. [See paragraph (a)(3)(iii) of this section.]
614(b)	1059(c)(4)	Election to determine whether a dividend is extraordinary by reference to the fair market value of the share of stock with respect to which the dividend was received.	Dividends declared after July 18, 1986 in taxable years ending after such date.
644(d)	216(b)(3)	Election by a cooperative housing corporation to allocate real estate taxes or interest or both to each tenant- stockholder's dwelling unit in a manner which reasonably reflects the cost to the corporation of the tenant-stockholder's dwelling unit.	Taxable years beginning after 12-31-86. [See paragraph (a)(3)(iv) of this section.]
646	—	Election by an entity to be treated as a trust under the Internal Revenue Code if such entity was created in 1906 as a common law trust and governed by the trust laws of the State of Minnesota, receives royalties from iron ore leases, and income interests in the entity are publicly traded on a national stock exchange.	The election is effective beginning on first day of the first taxable year beginning after October 22, 1986 and following the year in which the election is made. Such election must be made by the board of trustees of such entity and must be accompanied by a written agreement signed by the board of trustees of the entity.
651	4982(e)(4)	Election by a regulated investment company to use taxable years ending on 11-30 or 12-31 for purposes of computing capital gain net income under Code section 4982.	Calendar years beginning after 12/31/86. [See paragraph (a)(2)(vi) of this section.]

Section of Act	Section of Code	Description of Election	Availability of Election
701(a)	56(f)(3)(B)	Election to have amount of net book income be equal to amount of earnings and profits.	Taxable years beginning after 12-31-86.
801(a)	448(d)(4)	Election of common parent of an affiliated group that all members of such group be treated as one taxpayer if substantially all the activities of all members of the affiliated group involve performance of services in the same field.	Taxable years beginning after 12-31-86.
801(d)(2)	—	Election to continue using the cash method of accounting for loans, leases and related party transactions.	Loans, leases and related party transactions entered into before 9-26-85.
802	474	Election by certain small businesses to use the simplified dollar-value LIFO method.	Taxable years beginning after 12-31-86. [See paragraph (a)(3)(v) of this section.]
803(a)	263A(d)(3)	Election to have rules of Code section 263A (relating to capitalization and inclusion in inventory costs of certain expenses) not apply to any plant or animal produced in any farming business conducted by the electing taxpayer.	Unless consent is obtained from the Commissioner, the first taxable year beginning after 12-31-86 during which the taxpayer engages in a farming business. [See paragraph (c) of this section.]
806(e)(2)(C)	—	Election to have net income for the short taxable year of a partnership or S corporation which results from the required change in accounting period included entirely in income for such short taxable year.	Partner and shareholder taxable years beginning after 12-31-86 with or within which the short taxable year created under section 806 of the Act ends. [See paragraph (d) of this section.]
—	—	Election to reduce partnership or S corporation income for the short taxable year resulting from a required change in accounting period under section 806 of the Act by an unamortized adjustment amount existing as of October 22, 1986, where such adjustment was required to effectuate a previous accounting period change under Rev. Proc. 72-51, 1972-2 C.B. 832 or Rev. Proc. 83-25, 1983-1 C.B. 689.	Short taxable years of partnerships or S corporations beginning after 12-31-86. [See paragraph (e) of this section.]
811(a)	453C(b)(2)(B)	Election to compute adjusted bases using depreciation deduction used under Code section 312(k).	Taxable years ending after 12-31-86 with respect to dispositions made after 2-28-86.
811(a)	453C(e)(4)	Election to have Code section 453C not apply to obligations arising from sales of timeshares and unimproved residential lots to individuals.	Taxable years ending after 12-31-86 with respect to dispositions made after 2-28-86. [See paragraph (a)(3)(vi) of this section.]
905(a)	165(l)(1)	Election to treat amount of reasonably estimated loss on a deposit in insolvent or bankrupt qualified financial institution as a loss described in Code section 165(c)(3) and incurred in the taxable year.	Taxable years beginning after 12-31-82. [See paragraph (f) of this section.]
905(c)	—	Election to apply Code section 451(f) (relating to treatment of interest on frozen deposits in certain financial institutions).	Taxable years beginning after 12-31-82 and before 1-1-87.

Reg. §301.9100-7T(a)(1)

Section of Act	Section of Code	Description of Election	Availability of Election
1301(b)	141(b)(9)	Election by issuer of tax-exempt bonds to treat a portion of an issue as a qualified 501(c)(3) bond if such portion would have qualified as a 501(c)(3) bond had it been issued separately.	Bonds issued after 8-15-86. [See paragraph (g) of this section.]
1301(b)	142(d)(1)	Election by issuer of tax-exempt bonds for residential rental property to satisfy either the 20-50 or the 40-60 occupancy test.	Bonds issued after 8-15-86. [See paragraph (g) of this section.]
1301(b)	142(d)(4)(B)	Election by issuer of tax-exempt bonds for residential rental property to treat the project as a deep rent skewed project.	Bonds issued after 8-15-86. [See paragraph (g) of this section.]
1301(b)	143(k)(9)(D)(iii)	Election to treat limited equity cooperative housing as residential rental property and not as owner-occupied housing.	Bonds issued after 8-15-86 and before 1-1-89. [See paragraph (g) of this section.]
1301(b)	145(d)	Election by issuer of tax-exempt bonds to have Code section 145 not apply to the issue if the issue is an issue of exempt facility bonds or qualified redevelopment bonds, to which the volume cap applies.	Bonds issued after 8-15-86. [See paragraph (g) of this section.]
1301(b)	147(b)(4)(A)	Election by issuer of qualified 501(c)(3) bonds to have such bonds treated as meeting the limitation on maturity requirements of Code section 147(b)(1) if the requirements of section 147(b)(4)(B) are met.	Bonds issued after 8-15-86. [See paragraph (g) of this section.]
1704(b)	—	Election to revoke prior election under Code section 1402(e) (relating to exemption from social security taxes for certain clergy).	Remuneration received in taxable years ending on or after October 22, 1986. [See paragraph (h) of this section.]
1801(a)	168(i) (as in effect before October 22, 1986)	Election to make finance leasing rules inapplicable to property which would otherwise be subject to them under the transitional rules of section 12(c)(1) of the Tax Reform Act of 1984.	Personal property leased under certain lease agreements effective on or after 1-1-84. [See paragraph (a)(3)(vii) of this section.]
1804(e)(4)	—	Election by a common parent of an affiliated group to apply amendments made by the Tax Reform Act of 1984 for taxable years beginning after 12-31-83.	Groups which include a corporation which on 6-22-84 is a member of the group which files a consolidated return for such corporation's taxable year which includes 6-22-84.
1807(a)(7)	468B	Election to treat a qualified payment made to a court-ordered fund as a payment made to a designated settlement fund.	Generally, liabilities arising out of personal injury, death or property damage that are incurred after 7-18-84 under law in effect before the enactment of Code section 461(h). Election is made for the taxable year in which qualified payments are made to a designated settlement fund.

Section of Act	Section of Code	Description of Election	Availability of Election
1809(e)(2)	48(b)(2)	Election by lessee and lessor not to apply the rule of Code section 48(b)(2) concerning the date leased property is treated as originally placed in service.	Property originally placed in service after 4-11-84 (as determined under Code section 48(b) prior to its amendment by section 114(a) of the Tax Reform Act of 1984). [See paragraph (a)(3)(viii) of this section.]
1810(l)(4)	7701(b)	Election to be treated as a resident alien.	Taxable years beginning after December 31, 1984. [See paragraph (a)(3)(ix) of this section.]
1879(p)(1)	83(c)(3)	Election to treat certain stock acquired upon the exercise of nonqualified stock options as subject to a substantial risk of forfeiture by reason of Code section 83(c)(3) even though the transfer of stock pursuant to such exercise occurred before 1-1-82, the effective date of section 83(c)(3).	Transfers of stock described in section 1879(p)(1) of the Act. [See paragraphs (a)(2)(vii) and (a)(3)(x) of this section.]
1882(c)	3121(w)(2)	Election to revoke prior election under Code section 3121(w) (relating to exemption from social security taxes for certain churches and qualified church-controlled organizations).	Remuneration paid after 12-31-86 unless such electing church or church-controlled organization had withheld and paid over all employment taxes due, as if such election had never been in effect during the period from the stated effective date of the election being revoked through 12-31-86. [See paragraph (i) of this section.]

(2) *Time for making elections.*—(i) *In general.*—Except as otherwise provided in this section, the elections specified in paragraph (a)(1) of this section shall be made by the later of—

(A) The due date (taking extensions into account) of the tax return for the first taxable year for which the election is to be effective, or

(B) April 15, 1987 (in which case the election generally must be made by amended return).

(ii) *No extension of time for payment.*—Payments of tax due shall be made in accordance with chapter 62 of the Code.

(iii) *Time for making the election with respect to foreign intangible drilling costs.*—With respect to the election under Act section 411(b)(1) (Code section 263(i)(2)(A)), the election shall be made on a property-by-property basis for each oil, gas, or geothermal property (as defined in Code section 614). The election shall be made by the due date (taking extensions into account) of the income tax return for the first taxable year in which the taxpayer pays or incurs any cost with respect to the development of such property for which the election is available.

(iv) *Time for making the election with respect to foreign development expenditures.*—With respect to the election under Act section 411(b)(2) (Code section 616(d)(2)(A)), the election shall be made for each mine or other natural deposit not later than the time prescribed by law for filing the income tax return (taking extensions into account) for the taxable year to which such election is applicable.

(v) *Time for making the election with respect to foreign exploration expenditures.*—With respect to the election under Act section 411(b)(2) (Code section 617(h)(2)(A)), the election may be made at any time before the expiration of the period prescribed for filing a claim for credit or refund of the tax imposed by chapter 1 of the Code for the first taxable year for which the taxpayer desires the election to be applicable.

(vi) *Time for making certain elections by regulated investment companies.*—The election under Act section 651 (Code section 4982(e)(4)) shall be made on a statement attached to the form prescribed by the Internal Revenue Service which is used to report and pay the excise tax liability under section 4982. The election shall be filed on or before the later of—

(A) March 15 of the first calendar year beginning after the end of the first excise tax period for which the election is to be effective, or

(B) If the regulated investment company has been granted an extension of time to file a return for the excise tax under Code section 4982 for such excise tax period, the due date (including extensions thereof) for such return.

The statement of election under section 4982(e)(4) shall be attached to the prescribed form regardless of whether the regulated investment company is liable for the excise tax imposed by section 4982 for the excise tax period in question.

(vii) *Time for making the election with respect to certain nonqualified stock options.*—The election under section 1879(p)(1) of the Act (Code section 83(c)(3)) shall be made—

(A) By April 21, 1987, in any case in which the operation of any law or rule of law on or before such date would prevent the credit or refund of any overpayment of tax resulting from such election, and

(B) By no later than any date after April 21, 1987 on which the operation of any law or rule of law would prevent the credit or refund of any overpayment of tax resulting from such election.

(3) *Manner of making elections.*—(i) *In general.*—Except as otherwise provided in this section, the elections specified in paragraph (a)(1) of this section shall be made by attaching a statement to the tax return for the taxable year for which the election is to be effective. If because of paragraph (a)(2)(i)(B) of this section the election may be filed after the due date of the tax return for the first taxable year for which the election is to be effective, such statement must be attached to a tax return or amended return for the taxable year to which the election relates. Except as otherwise provided in the return or in the instructions accompanying the return for the taxable year, the statement shall—

(A) Contain the name, address and taxpayer identification number of the electing taxpayer,

(B) Identify the election,

(C) Indicate the section of the Code (or, if the provision is not codified, the section of the Act) under which the election is made,

(D) Specify, as applicable, the period for which the election is being made and/or the property or other items to which the election is to apply, and

(E) Provide any information required by the relevant statutory provisions and any information necessary to show that the taxpayer is entitled to make the election.

(ii) *Special rules for making the transitional rule elections with respect to certain tax-exempt controlled entities.*—The irrevocable election under Act sections 201(a) and 1802(a) (Code sections 168(h)(6)(F)(ii) and 168(j)), as in effect before October 22, 1986, shall be made by the tax-exempt controlled entity at the time and in the manner described in paragraphs (a)(2) and (a)(3)(i) of this section. A copy of the election statement filed by the tax-exempt controlled entity shall also be attached to the Federal tax returns (*e.g.*, Form 990 or 5500) of each of the tax-exempt shareholders or beneficiaries of the controlled entity.

(iii) *Special rule for making the election with respect to gain or loss from a disposition of property used in a passive activity.*—The election under Act section 501(a) (Code section 469(j)(9)) shall be made on the form prescribed by the Internal Revenue Service for computing the taxpayer's passive activity loss and credit for the taxable year in which the property is disposed.

(iv) *Special rules for making the election with respect to cooperative housing corporations.*—The election under Act section 644(d) (Code section 216(b)(3)(B)(ii)) may be made by a cooperative housing corporation with respect to its real estate taxes or interest or both. The election is available for any taxable year beginning after December 31, 1986, if the cooperative housing corporation has, by January 31 of the year following the first calendar year that includes any period to which the election applies, furnished to each tenant-stockholder during that period a written statement showing the amount of the allocation (or allocations) under section 216(b)(3)(B)(i) attributable to such tenant-stockholder's dwelling unit (or units) for that period. Any cooperative housing corporation making the election shall do so in accordance with paragraph (a)(2) and (3) of this section and shall identify in the statement described in paragraph (a)(3) of this section whether the election is for real estate taxes or interest or both.

(v) *Special rules for making the election with respect to the simplified dollar-value LIFO method.*—The election under Act section 802 (Code section 474) may be made only if the taxpayer files with the taxpayer's income tax return for the taxable year as of the close of which the method is first to be used a statement of the taxpayer's election to use the simplified dollar-value LIFO inventory method. The statement shall be on Form 970 pursuant to the instructions to the form and to the requirements of the regulations under section 474, or in such other manner as may be acceptable to the Commissioner.

(vi) *Special rules for making election to have section 453C not apply to obligations arising from sales of timeshares and unimproved residential lots to individuals.*—The election under Act section 811(a) (Code section 453C(e)(4)) to have section 453C not apply to obligations arising from sales of timeshares and unimproved residential lots to individuals may be made with respect to any obligation, or with respect to a class of such obligations. In the case of an election made with respect to a class of obligations, such election shall describe the class of obligations with such specificity as to make the class readily identifiable.

(vii) *Special rules for making certain finance leasing transitional rule elections.*—The election relating to finance leases under Act section 1801(a)(1) (Code section 168(i) as in effect before October 22, 1986) shall be made by the lessor under a lease agreement subject to the finance lease rules of section 168(i) of the Code, as in effect before October 22, 1986, by noting this election in the books and records relating to the lease agreement within 12 months after February 5, 1987.

(viii) *Special rules for making the election relating to the date leased property is treated as originally placed in service.*—The election under Act section 1809(e)(2) (Code section 48(b)(2)) must be made jointly by the lessee and the lessor. The

Reg. §301.9100-7T(a)(2)(vii)(A)

election is made jointly when both the lessee and the lessor make the election in accordance with paragraphs (a)(2) and (a)(3)(i) of this section. In addition to the other information required to be provided under paragraph (a)(3)(i) of this section, the statement described therein shall include a copy of the lease agreement and shall be signed by both the lessee and the lessor.

(ix) *Special rules for making the election to be treated as a resident alien.*—The election under Act section 1810 (l)(4) (Code section 7701(b)) to be treated as a resident under Code section 7701(b) shall be made by an alien individual by attaching a statement to the individual's income tax return (Form 1040), for the taxable year for which the election is to be in effect (the election year). The alien individual may not make this election until such time as he has satisfied the substantial presence test of Code section 7701(b)(1)(A)(ii) for the year following the election year. If an alien individual has not satisfied the substantial presence test for the year following the election year as of the due date (without regard to extensions) of the tax return for the election year, the alien individual may request an extension of time for filing the return until after he has satisfied such test, provided that he pays with his extension application the amount of tax he expects to owe for the election year, computed as if he were a nonresident alien throughout the election year. The statement shall include the name and address of the alien individual and contain a signed declaration that the election is being made. It must specify—

(A) That the alien individual was not a resident in the year immediately preceding the election year;

(B) That the alien individual is a resident in the year immediately following the election year under the substantial presence test and the individual's number of days of presence in the United States during such year;

(C) The date or dates of the alien individual's 31 consecutive day period of presence and continuous presence in the United States during the election year; and

(D) The date or dates of absence from the United States during the election year that are deemed to be days of presence.

(x) *Special rules for making the election with respect to the treatment of the exercise of certain nonqualified stock options.*—The election under Act section 1879(p)(1) (Code section 83(c)(3)) is made by filing on Form 1040X a claim for credit or refund of the overpayment of tax resulting from the election. In order to satisfy the requirements of § 301.6402-2(b)(1) (relating to grounds set forth in claim), the claim for credit or refund must set forth—

(A) The date on which the option was granted,

(B) The name of the corporation which granted the option,

(C) The date on which the stock was transferred pursuant to the exercise of the option,

(D) The fair market value of such stock on December 4, 1973,

(E) The fair market value on July 1, 1974 of the stock received upon the reorganization of the corporation which granted the option, and

(F) The date on which the taxpayer sold substantially all of the stock received in such reorganization.

The taxpayer shall file a single claim for credit or refund of the entire overpayment of tax resulting from the election under Act section 1879(p)(1).

(4) *Revocation.*—(i) *Irrevocable elections.*—The elections described in this section under Act sections 201(a) (Code sections 168(b)(5), 168(f)(1), 168(g)(7), and 168(h)(6)(F)(ii)), 203(a)(1)(B), 252(a) (Code sections 42(f)(1), 42(g)(1), 42(i)(2), and 42(j)(5)), 411(b)(1) (Code section 263(i)), 411(b)(2)(A) (Code section 616(d)(2)(A)), 501(a) (Code section 469(j)(9)), 801(d)(2), 905(c), 1301(b) (Code sections 141(b)(9), 142(d)(1), 142(d)(4)(B), 143(k)(9)(D)(iii), 145(d), and 147(b)(4)(A)), 1704(b), 1802(a) (Code section 168(j) as in effect before October 22, 1986), 1804(e)(4), 1879(p)(1) (Code section 83(c)(3)), and 1882(c) (Code section 3121(w)(2)) are irrevocable.

(ii) *Elections revocable with the consent of the Commissioner.*—The elections described in this section under Act sections 204(e), 243(a), 243(b), 243(a)(b), 411(b)(2)(B) (Code section 617(h)(2)(A)), 614(b) (Code section 1059(c)(4)), 644(d) (Code section 216(b)(3)), 646, 651 (Code section 4982(e)(4)(B)), 701(a) (Code section 56(f)(3)(B)), 801(a) (Code section 448(d)(4)), 802 (Code section 474), 803(a) (Code section 263A(d)(3)), 806(e)(2)(C) (and the election described in H.R. Rep. No. 99-841 at II-320), 811(a) (Code sections 453C(b)(2)(B)(i) and 453C(e)(4)), (Code sections 585(c)(3)(B)(ii) and 585(c)(4)), 905(a) (Code section 165(l)(1)), 1801(a) (Code section 168(i) as in effect before October 22, 1986), 1807(a)(7) (Code section 468B), 1809(e)(2) (Code section 48(b)(2)), and 1810(l)(4) (Code section 7701(b)) are revocable only with the consent of the Commissioner.

(iii) *Freely revocable elections.*—The election described in this section under Act section 311(d)(2) is freely revocable.

(b) *Elections with respect to low-income housing credit.*—The elections under Act section 252(a) (Code sections 42(f)(1), 42(g)(1), 42(i)(2), and 42(j)(5)) must be made for the taxable year in which the project is placed in service and shall be made in the certification required to be filed pursuant to section 42(l)(1).

(c) *Election to have the rules of section 263A (relating to capitalization and inclusion in inventory costs of certain expenses) not apply to any plant or animal produced in any farming business conducted by the electing taxpayer.*—(1) *In general.*—This paragraph applies to the election under Act section 803(a) (Code section 263A(d)(3)) to have the rules of section 263A (relating to capitalization and inclusion in inventory costs of certain expenses) not apply to any plant or animal produced in any farming business conducted by the electing taxpayer. The election is available to taxpayers engaged in the business of farming, including producers of agricultural crops, livestock, nursery stock, sod, trees bearing fruit, nuts or other crops, and ornamental trees (for purposes of section 263A, an evergreen tree that is more than 6 years old at the time it is severed from the roots shall not be treated as an ornamental tree). The election is not available to a corporation, partnership, or tax shelter that is required to use the accrual method of accounting under section 447 or section 448(a)(3), or farming syndicates (as defined in section 464(c)), or with respect to the planting, cultivation, maintenance or development of pistachio trees. In addition, the election does not apply with respect to costs incurred for the planting, cultivation, maintenance or development of any citrus or almond grove incurred during the 4-taxable-year period beginning with the taxable year in which such grove was planted. If a citrus or almond grove is planted in more than one taxable year, the portion of the grove planted in one taxable year is treated as a separate grove for this purpose.

(2) *Time and manner of making the election.*— Unless consent is obtained from the Commissioner, the election may only be made for the taxpayer's first taxable year that begins after December 31, 1986, and during which the taxpayer engages in a farming business. The election shall be made on the Schedule E, F or other schedule required to be attached to the income tax return for the first taxable year for which the election is effective. In the case of a partnership or S corporation, the election must be made at the partner or shareholder level.

(3) *Election treated as if made if certain requirements satisfied.*—A taxpayer eligible to make the election under section 263A(d)(3) shall be treated as having made the election if such taxpayer reports income and expenses in accordance with the rules under the election on a timely filed income tax return.

(4) *Revocation.*—Once the election is made, it is revocable only with the consent of the Commissioner.

(5) *Special rules for treatment of expenses.*—If the election is made, the plant or animal produced is treated as section 1245 property and gain is recaptured (treated as ordinary income) in the amount of deductions which, but for the election, would have been required to be capitalized with respect to the plant or animal. If the taxpayer or a related person makes the election, a non-accelerated method of depreciation (as defined in section 168(g)(2)) shall be applied to all property used predominantly in any farming business of the taxpayer or related person and placed in service in any taxable year during which the election is in effect. For purposes of

this election, related party means: (i) the members of the taxpayer's family (defined for this purpose to include the spouse of the taxpayer and any of his or her children who have not reached the age of 18 as of the last day of the taxable year); (ii) any corporation (including an S corporation) 50 percent or more of the value of which is owned directly or indirectly (through the application of section 318) by the taxpayer or members of the taxpayer's family; (iii) any corporation that is a member of the same controlled group (within the meaning of section 1563) as the taxpayer; and (iv) any partnership if 50 percent or more of the value of the interests in such partnership is owned directly or indirectly (through the application of section 318) by the taxpayer or members of the taxpayer's family.

(d) *Election with respect to the treatment of net income for the short taxable year resulting from a required change in accounting period.*—This paragraph applies to the election under section 806(e)(2)(C) of the Act. Net income for the short taxable year resulting from a required change in accounting period under the provisions of section 806 of the Act which is to be included ratably in the partners' and S corporation shareholders' income for the first four taxable years (including the short taxable year) beginning after December 31, 1986, or included entirely in income for the short taxable year at the election of the partner or shareholder, shall be taken into account in accordance with section 702 (with respect to partners) and section 1366 (with respect to S corporation shareholders).

(e) *Election with respect to reducing partnership or S corporation income for the short taxable year resulting from a required change in accounting period under section 806 of the Act by an unamortized adjustment amount existing as of October 22, 1986.*—(1) *In general.*—This paragraph applies to the election described in H.R. Rep. No. 99-841 at II-320.

(2) *Partnerships or S corporations that make the election to reduce income for the short taxable year by an unamortized adjustment amount existing as of October 22, 1986.*—Where a partnership or S corporation elects to reduce its income for the short taxable year required under the provisions of section 806 of the Act by the unamortized adjustment amount existing as of October 22, 1986, in accordance with paragraph (a) of this section, the income for the short taxable year (reduced by the unamortized adjustment amount) may then be subject to the election, under section 806(e)(2)(C) of the Act, by partners and S corporation shareholders to include all the net income for the short taxable year entirely in income for the partners' or shareholders' taxable year with or within which the short taxable year ends.

(3) *Partnership or S corporations that do not make the election to reduce income for the short taxable year by an unamortized adjustment amount existing as of October 22, 1986.*—Where a partnership or S corporation does not elect to reduce its income for the short taxable year created by the

provisions of section 806 of the Act by the unamortized adjustment amount existing as of October 22, 1986, as provided in paragraph (a) of this section, the short taxable year required under the provisions of section 806 of the Act shall be considered one taxable year for purposes of amortizing the adjustment amount under the requirements of Rev. Proc. 72-51, 1972-2 C.B. 832, or Rev. Proc. 83-25, 1983-1 C.B. 689. The net income of the partnership or S corporation after reduction by the adjustment amount for the short taxable year may then be subject to the election under section 806(e)(2)(C) of the Act by partners or S corporation shareholders to include all the net income for the short taxable year entirely in income for the partners' or shareholders' taxable year with or within which the short taxable year of the partnership or S corporation ends.

(f) *Cross-reference.*—See § 301.9100-8(d) for rules on both the election under section 905(a) of the Act, relating to section 165(l)(1), and the related election under section 165(l)(5), added by section 1009(d) of the Technical and Miscellaneous Revenue Act of 1988, 102 Stat. 3342. An election under section 165(l) is available only to qualified individuals and, in general, applies to reasonably estimated losses on deposits in an insolvent or bankrupt financial institution.

(g) *Elections with respect to certain bonds.*—The elections under Act section 1301(b) (Code sections 141(b)(9), 142(d)(1), 142(d)(4)(B), 143(k)(9)(D)(iii), 145(d), and 147(b)(4)(A)) must be made in the bond indenture or a related document (as defined in § 1.103-13(b)(8)) on or before the date of issue. With respect to obligations issued on or before March 9, 1987, these elections must be made on or before March 9, 1987, and need not be made in the bond indenture or a related document, but must be made in writing and retained as part of the issuer's books and records.

(h) *Revocation of the election for exemption from social security taxes by certain clergy.*—(1) *In general.*—This paragraph applies to the election under Act section 1704(b) to revoke an election under section 1402(e)(1) of the Code by a duly ordained, commissioned, or licensed minister of a church, a member of a religious order (other than a member of a religious order who has taken a vow of poverty as a member of such order), or a Christian Science practitioner. Only elections which are effective for the taxable year containing October 22, 1986 may be revoked under this paragraph.

(2) *Time for revoking the election.*—The election shall be revoked by filing Form 2031 before the date on which the individual becomes entitled to benefits under section 202(a) or 223 of the Social Security Act (without regard to section 202(j)(1) or 223(b) of such Act), and no later than the due date of the Federal income tax return (including any extension thereof) for the individual's first taxable year beginning after October 22, 1986.

(3) *Manner of revoking the election.*—To revoke an election under section 1402(e)(1), the individual shall file Form 2031 in accordance with the instructions accompanying that form. The revocation shall be made effective, as designated by the individual on the form, either with respect to the individual's first taxable year ending on or after October 22, 1986, or with respect to the individual's first taxable year beginning after October 22, 1986.

(4) *Special rules for payment of self-employment taxes with respect to certain taxable years ending on or after October 22, 1986.*—(i) *Elections filed after the due date of the Federal income tax return.*—If Form 2031 is filed on or after the due date of the Federal income tax return (including any extension thereof) for the individual's first taxable year ending on or after October 22, 1986, and the election made therein is effective with respect to that taxable year, Form 2031 shall be accompanied by an amended Federal income tax return for such taxable year together with payment in full of an amount equal to the total of the taxes that would have been imposed by section 1401 of the Code with respect to all of the individual's income derived in that taxable year which would have constituted net earnings from self-employment for purposes of chapter 2 of subtitle A of the Code (notwithstanding paragraph (4) or (5) of section 1402(c)) but for the exemption under section 1402(e)(1).

(ii) *Elections filed before the due date of the Federal income tax return.*—If Form 2031 is filed before the due date of the Federal income tax return (including any extension thereof) for the individual's first taxable year ending on or after October 22, 1986, and the election is effective with respect to that taxable year, payment in full of an amount equal to the total of the taxes that would have been imposed by section 1401 of the Code with respect to all of the individual's income derived in that taxable year which would have constituted net earnings from self-employment for purposes of chapter 2 of subtitle A of the Code (notwithstanding paragraph (4) or (5) of section 1402(c)) but for the exemption under section 1402(e)(1) shall be made:

(A) In the case of Forms 2031 that are filed on or before the date on which the individual's Federal income tax return for such first taxable year is filed, with the individual's Federal income tax return for such taxable year; and

(B) In the case of Forms 2031 that are filed after the date on which the individual's Federal income tax return for such first taxable year is filed, with an amended Federal income tax return for that taxable year filed on or before the due date for the individual's Federal income tax return (including any extension thereof) for such taxable year.

(iii) *Interest on amounts paid after the due date of the Federal income tax return.*—If any amount of tax imposed by section 1401 for an individual's taxable year with respect to which an election under this paragraph (h) is effective is paid after the due date of the individual's Federal income tax return (without regard to extensions) for such taxable year, interest will be assessed on such tax from the due date of such return (without regard to extensions) to the date on which such tax is paid.

(5) *Revocability of the revocation of the election.*—Once having filed Form 2031, the individual may not thereafter file an application for an exemption under section 1402(e)(1).

(6) *Effective date of this provision.*—This provision shall apply with respect to remuneration received in the taxable years for which the individual designates the revocation to be effective, as described in paragraph (h)(3) of this section, and with respect to monthly insurance benefits payable under title II of the Social Security Act on the basis of the wages and self-employment income of any individual for months in or after the calendar year in which such individual's application for revocation is effective (and lumpsum death payments payable under such title on the basis of such wages and self-employment income in the case of deaths occurring in or after such calendar year).

(i) *Revocation of the election for exemption from social security taxes by certain churches or qualified church-controlled organizations.*—(1) *In general.*— This paragraph applies to the election under Act section 1882 (Code section 3121(w)(2)) to revoke an election under section 3121(w) by a church or qualified church-controlled organization (as defined in section 3121(w)(3)).

(2) *Time and manner of revoking the election.*— The revocation described in this paragraph (i) shall be made by filing a Form 941 on or before the due date for filing Form 941 (without regard to extensions) for the first quarter for which the revocation is to be effective, accompanied by payment in full of the taxes that would be due for that quarter had there been no election under section 3121(w). See paragraph (i)(4) of this section for the effective date of revocations made under this paragraph (i).

(3) *Revocability of the revocation of the election.*—Once an election under section 3121(w) is revoked under this paragraph (i), a new election under section 3121(w) may not be made.

(4) *Effective date of this paragraph.*—A revocation made under this paragraph (i) shall be effective for the quarter of the calendar year covered by the Form 941 on which the revocation is made in accordance with paragraph (i)(2) of this section and all subsequent quarters. However, no revocation shall be effective prior to January 1, 1987 unless such electing church or church-controlled organization had withheld and paid over all employment taxes due, as if such election had never been in effect, during the period from the effective date of the election being revoked through December 31, 1986.

(j) *Additional information required.*—Later regulations or revenue procedures issued under provisions of the Code or Act covered by this section may require the furnishing of information in addition to that which was furnished with the statement of election described in this section. In such event, the later regulations or revenue procedures will provide guidance with respect to the furnishing of such additional information. (26 U.S.C. 7805). [Temporary Reg. § 301.9100-7T.]

☐ [*T.D. 8124, 2-4-87. Amended by T.D. 8180, 2-29-88 and T.D. 8267, 9-21-89. Redesignated and amended by T.D. 8435, 9-18-92. Amended by T.D. 8513, 12-28-93; T.D. 8530, 3-17-94 and T.D. 8644, 12-26-95.*]

ELECTIONS UNDER TECHNICAL AND MISCELLANEOUS REVENUE ACT OF 1988

[Reg. § 301.9100-8]

§ 301.9100-8. Time and manner of making certain elections under the Technical and Miscellaneous Revenue Act of 1988.— (a) *Miscellaneous elections.*—(1) *Elections to which this paragraph applies.*—This paragraph applies to the elections set forth below provided under the Technical and Miscellaneous Revenue Act of 1988, 102 Stat. 3342 (the Act). General rules regarding the time for making the elections are provided in paragraph (a)(2) of this section. General rules regarding the manner for making the elections are provided in paragraph (a)(3) of this section. Special rules regarding the time and manner for making certain elections are contained in paragraphs (a) through (i) of this section. In this paragraph (a)(1), a cross-reference to a special rule applicable to an election is shown in brackets at the end of the description of the "Availability of Election." Paragraph (j) of this section lists certain elections provided under the Act that are not addressed in this section. Paragraph (k) of this section provides that additional information with respect to elections may be required by future regulations or revenue procedures.

Section of Act	Section of Code	Description of Election	Availability of Election
1002(a) (11)(A)	168(b)(2)	Election to depreciate property using the 150 percent declining balance method for one or more classes of property for any taxable year.	For property placed in service after December 31, 1986, the election must be made for the taxable year in which the property is placed in service. For taxable years ending before January 1, 1989, taxpayers have until January 22, 1990 to amend their returns to elect the 150 percent declining balance method, regardless of whether the taxpayer had used or elected to use a different method for property placed in service during those taxable years. The election will apply to all property in the class placed in service during the taxable year for which the election is made.
1002(a) (23)(B)	168(d) (3)(B)	Election to disregard property placed in service and disposed of in the same taxable year in applying the 40 percent test to determine if the mid- quarter convention applies.	Available for property placed in service in taxable years beginning on or before March 31, 1988. Election will apply to all property placed in service and disposed of during the taxable year for which the election is made.
1002(l) (1)(A)	42(b)(2) (A)(ii)	Election to use the applicable percentage for a month other than the month in which a building is placed in service.	Available for qualified buildings placed in service after December 31, 1987 and with respect to which either a binding agreement is made as to the allocable credit dollar amount or tax-exempt bonds are issued. [See paragraph (b) of this section.]
1002(l) (2)(B)	42(f)(1)	Election to defer the beginning of the credit period for the low-income housing credit.	Available for qualified buildings placed in service after December 31, 1986.
1002(l) (4)	42(d)(3) (B)	Election to exclude excess costs of disproportionate units.	Available for qualified buildings placed in service after December 31, 1986.
1002(l) (12)	42(g)(3) (B)(i)	Election to aggregate buildings in a low-income housing project to satisfy the minimum set-aside requirement elected under section 42(g)(1) of the Code.	Available for qualified buildings placed in service after December 31, 1986.
1002(l) (19)(B)	42(i) (2)(B)	Election to reduce eligible basis by outstanding balance of Federal loan subsidy or proceeds of tax- exempt obligation.	Available for qualified buildings placed in service after December 31, 1986.
1005(c) (11)	469, 163	Election to treat certain carryovers of disallowed investment interest expense as passive activity deductions for the first taxable year beginning after December 31, 1986.	Available for investment interest that is disallowed for the last taxable year beginning before January 1, 1987, and is properly allocable to a passive activity for the first taxable year beginning after December 31, 1986. [See paragraph (c) of this section.]
1006(d) (15)	382	As a general rule, a firm commitment underwriter of an offering of a loss corporation's stock made before September 19, 1986 (January 1, 1989, for an institution described in section 591) is not treated as acquiring underwritten stock if it is disposed of pursuant to the offering on or before 60 days after the initial offering. The loss corporation may elect not to apply the general rule.	Available to any loss corporation to which the general rule would otherwise apply. The election is to be made by filing a statement with the District Director with whom the loss corporation would file its Federal income tax return. The statement must identify the election as an election under section 1006(d)(15) of the Act and must (1) contain the taxpayer's name, address, and employee identification number, (2) identify the transaction to which the election relates, (3) represent that the conditions for making the election have been satisfied, and (4) be signed by a person authorized to sign the Federal income tax return of the loss corporation.

Section of Act	Section of Code	Description of Election	Availability of Election
1006(j) (1)(C)	171(e)	Election to reduce interest payments received on certain bonds by allocable bond premium in accordance with section 171(e) of the Code.	Available for obligations acquired after October 22, 1986, and before January 1, 1988.
1006(t) (18)(B)	860F(e)	Election not to treat a REMIC (real estate mortgage investment conduit) as a partnership for purposes of determining who may sign the REMIC return.	Available for REMICs with a start-up date (as defined in section 860G(a)(9) of the Code, as in effect on November 9, 1988) before November 10, 1988. The election is made by attaching a statement to the amended tax return for tax year 1987 or to the tax return for the first taxable year for which the election is to be effective.
1008(c) (4)(A)	460(b)(3)	Election not to discount an amount received or accrued after completion of a contract to its value as of the completion of the contract for purposes of applying the look-back method.	Effective as if included in the Tax Reform Act of 1986 (1986 Act) (available for contracts entered into after February 28, 1986). The election must be made on a contract-by-contract basis by attaching a statement to the tax return for the first year after completion in which the taxpayer includes in income any adjustments to the contract price or deducts any adjustments to contract costs (or, if later, the first tax return filed after October 23, 1989).
1009(d)	165(l)	Election to treat amount of reasonably estimated loss on a deposit in an insolvent or bankrupt qualified financial institution as a loss described in either section 165(c)(2) or (3) of the Code and incurred in the taxable year for which the election is made.	Available for taxable years beginning after December 31, 1981. [See paragraph (d) of this section.]
1010(f) (1)	831(b) (2)(A)	Election for insurance companies other than life to use alternative tax under certain circumstances.	Available for taxable years beginning after December 31, 1986.
1010(f) (2)	835(a)	Election for an interinsurer or reciprocal under- writer mutual insurance company subject to section 831(a) of the Code to be subject to section 835(b) limitation.	Available for taxable years beginning after December 31, 1986.
1011(a)	219(g)(4)	Election to treat a married individual as not married for purposes of certain contributions made to an individual retirement plan for 1987.	Available to a married individual who (1) was an active participant during 1987, (2) lived apart from the other spouse during the entire 1987 calendar year, (3) filed a separate income tax return for 1987, (4) had adjusted gross income of not more than $35,000 for 1987, and (5) made a contribution to an individual retirement plan for 1987.
1012(d) (4)	865(f)	Election to treat an affiliate and its wholly-owned subsidiaries as one corporation.	Shareholder-level election, available, subject to certain conditions, to United States residents selling stock in an affiliate which is a foreign corporation. Available for taxable years beginning after December 31, 1986.
1012(d) (6)	865(g)(3)	Election to treat a corporation and its wholly- owned subsidiaries as one corporation.	Shareholder-level election, available only to individual bona fide residents of Puerto Rico, if the corporate group is engaged in active trade or business in Puerto Rico and meets a gross income test. Available for taxable years beginning after December 31, 1986.

Reg. §301.9100-8(a)(1)

Technical and Miscellaneous Revenue Act Elections
See p. 20,601 for regulations not amended to reflect law changes

67,697

Section of Act	Section of Code	Description of Election	Availability of Election
1012(d) (8)	865(h)(2)	Election to apply treaty source rule to treat gain from a sale of an intangible or of stock in a foreign corporation as foreign source.	Taxpayer election for treatment of gain on the disposition of certain stocks and intangibles. Available for taxable years beginning after December 31, 1986.
1012(l) (2)	245(a) (10)	Election to apply treaty source rules to treat dividends received from a qualified 10-percent owned foreign corporation as foreign source.	Available to corporations for distributions out of earnings and profits for taxable years beginning after December 31, 1986.
1012(n) (3)	936	Election to reduce the amount of qualified possession source investment income for certain corporations that fail the 75 percent active trade or business income requirement of section 936(a)(2)(B) of the Code due to section 1231(d) of the 1986 Act.	Corporate-level election, available for any taxable year beginning in 1987 or 1988.
1012(bb) (4)	904(g) (10)	Election to apply treaty source rules (in lieu of rules in section 904(g) of the Code) to treat an amount derived from a U.S.-owned foreign corporation as foreign source.	Available generally beginning July 18, 1984 (the amendment is to take effect as if included in the amendment made in section 121 of the Tax Reform Act of 1984).
1014(c) (1)	664(b)	Election by a beneficiary of a trust to which section 664 of the Code applies to obtain certain benefits of section 1403(c)(2) of the 1986 Act, relating to the ratable inclusion of certain income over 4 taxable years.	Available for taxable years beginning after December 31, 1986, provided the trust was required to change its taxable year under section 1403(a) of the 1986 Act. Election is made by attaching a statement to an amended return for the trust beneficiary's first taxable year beginning after December 31, 1986. Amended return must be filed on or before January 22, 1990. If no such election is filed, the benefits of section 1403(c)(2) are waived.
1014(c) (2)	652 662	Election by any trust beneficiary (other than a beneficiary of a trust to which section 664 of the Code applies), to waive the benefits of section 1403(c)(2) of the 1986 Act.	Available for taxable years beginning after December 31, 1986. Election is made by attaching a statement to an amended return for the trust beneficiary's first taxable year beginning after December 31, 1986. Amended return must be filed on or before January 22, 1990.
1014(d) (3)(B); 1014(d) (4)	643(g) (2)	Election to have certain payments of estimated tax made by a trust or estate treated as paid by the beneficiary.	Available for taxable years beginning after December 31, 1986. In the case of an estate, the election is available only for a taxable year reasonably expected to be the estate's last taxable year. Election must be made by the fiduciary of the trust or estate on or before the 65th day after the close of the taxable year for which the election is made. The election must be made by that date by filing Form 1041-T with the Internal Revenue Service Center where the trust's return for such taxable year is required to be filed. The trust's return (or amended return) for that year must include a copy of the Form 1041-T.

Section of Act	Section of Code	Description of Election	Availability of Election
2004(j) (1)	1503(e)	Election, made by an affiliated group filing a consolidated return upon the disposition of intragroup stock on or before December 15, 1987, to reduce the disposing member's basis in the indebtedness of the subsidiary member whose stock has been disposed of, in lieu of taking into account as negative basis the "unrecaptured amount" allocable to the stock disposed of.	Available to an affiliated group filing a consolidated return in which a member disposes of intragroup stock on or before December 15, 1987.
2004(m) (5)	384	Election to have amendments (to the limitation on use of preacquisition losses to offset corporate built-in gains) made by section 2004(m) of the Act not apply in any case where the acquisition date is before March 31, 1988.	Available when the acquisition date is before March 31, 1988. Election must be made not later than the later of the due date (including extensions) for filing the return for the taxable year of the acquiring corporation in which the acquisition date occurs or March 10, 1989.
4004(a)	42(j) (5)(B)	Election to have certain partnerships not treated as the taxpayer to which the low-income housing credit is allowable.	Available for qualified buildings placed in service after December 31, 1986, and owned by partnerships with 35 or more partners. [See paragraph (b) of this section.]
4008(b)	41(h)	Election to have the research credit under section 41 of the Code not apply for any taxable year.	Available in any taxable year beginning after December 31, 1988. The election is made by not claiming the research credit on an original return, or by filing an amended return on which no research credit is claimed, at any time before the expiration of the 3-year period beginning on the last day prescribed by law for filing the return for the taxable year (determined without regard to extensions). The election may be revoked within the above-described 3-year period by filing an amended return on which the credit is claimed.
5012(e) (4)	7702A (c)(3) 72(e)	Election to recognize gain on exchange of life insurance contracts to avoid the characterization of life insurance contract as a modified endowment contract.	Available for contracts entered into after June 20, 1988, and before November 6, 1988, which are exchanged before February 10, 1989.
5031(a)	7520(a)	Election to use 120 percent of the Applicable Federal Midterm rate for either of the two months preceding a valuation date in valuing certain interests transferred to charity for which an income, estate, or gift tax charitable deduction is allowable.	Available in cases where the valuation date occurs on or after May 1, 1989. The election is made by attaching a statement to the last income, estate, or gift tax return filed before the due date, or if a timely return is not filed, the first return filed after the due date. The statement shall contain the following: (1) a statement that an election under section 7520(a) is being made; (2) the transferor's name and taxpayer identification number as they appear on the return; (3) a description of the interest being valued; (4) the recipients, beneficiaries, or donees of the transferred interest; (5) the date of the transfer; (6) the Applicable Federal Midterm rate that is used to value the transferred interest and the month to which the rate pertains.

Section of Act	Section of Code	Description of Election	Availability of Election
5033(a) (2)	2056A(d)	Election to treat a trust for the benefit of a surviving spouse who is not a U.S. citizen as a Qualified Domestic Trust, transfers to which are deductible under section 2056(a) of the Code.	Available in the case of estates of decedents dying after November 11, 1988. The election is made by the executor on the last Federal estate tax return filed by the executor before the due date of the return, or if a timely return is not filed by the executor, on the first estate tax return filed by the executor after the due date. However, elections made on or after May 5, 1991, may not be made on any return filed more than one year after the time prescribed for filing the return (including extensions).
6006(a)	1(i)(7)	Election to include certain unearned income of a child on the parent's return.	Available for taxable years beginning after December 31, 1988. The election must be made in the manner prescribed by the appropriate forms for the parent's return for the year for which the election is effective. The election must be made by the due date (taking extensions into account) of such tax return.
6011	121(d)(9)	Election to exclude gain on the sale of a principal residence by certain incapacitated taxpayers age 55 or over.	Election may be made for a sale or exchange after September 30, 1988, by a taxpayer who becomes physically or mentally incapable of self-care and meets the required use rule provided in section 121(d)(9) of the Code. For the time and manner of making the election see § 1.121-4 of the Income Tax Regulations.
6026(a)	263A(h)	Election for certain authors, photographers, and artists to apply the exemption from the uniform capitalization rules for the first taxable year ending after November 10, 1988.	Available for the first taxable year ending after November 10, 1988. An eligible taxpayer will be treated as having made the election if the taxpayer reports income and expenses for the first taxable year ending after November 10, 1988 in accordance with the exemption from section 263A of the Code.
6026(b) (1)	263A(d) (1)	Revocation of prior election under section 263A(d)(3) of the Code (relating to the capitalization of certain expenses for the production of animals).	Election for any taxable year beginning before January 1, 1989, may be revoked for the first taxable year beginning after December 31, 1988.
6026(c)	263A(d) (3)(B)	Election by eligible taxpayers not to have section 263A of the Code apply to costs incurred in the planting, cultivation, maintenance, or development of pistachio trees.	Available without the consent of the Commissioner for the first taxable year beginning after December 31, 1986, during which the taxpayer engages in the planting, cultivation, maintenance, or development of pistachio trees. Consent must be obtained from the Commissioner for the election to be made for any subsequent taxable year.
6152(a) 6152(c) (3)	2056(b) (7)(C) (ii)	Election to treat a survivor annuity payable to a surviving spouse that is otherwise deductible under section 2056(b)(7)(C) of the Code as a nondeductible terminable interest.	Available in the case of estates of decedents dying after December 31, 1981, and in no event will the time for making the election expire before November 11, 1990. [See paragraph (e) of this section.]
6152(b) 6152(c) (3)	2523(f) (6)(B)	Election to treat a joint and survivor annuity in which the donee spouse has a survivorship interest that is otherwise deductible under section 2523(f)(6)(A) of the Code as a nondeductible terminable interest.	Available in the case of transfers made after December 31, 1981, and in no event will the time for making the election expire before November 11, 1990. [See paragraph (f) of this section.]

Section of Act	Section of Code	Description of Election	Availability of Election
6152(c) (2)	2056(b) (7)(C) (ii) 2523(f) (6)(B)	Election to treat as deductible for estate or gift tax purposes under sections 2056(b)(7)(C) or 2523(f)(6) of the Code, respectively, a survivor's annuity payable to a surviving spouse reported on an estate or gift tax return filed prior to November 11, 1988, as a nondeductible terminable interest.	Available to estates of decedents dying after December 31, 1981, or to transfers made after December 31, 1981, where: (1) the estate or gift tax return was filed prior to November 11, 1988; (2) the annuity was not deducted on the return as qualified terminable interest property under sections 2056(b)(7) or 2523(f) of the Code; and (3) the executor or donor elects to treat the interest as a deductible terminable interest under sections 2056(b)(7)(C) or 2523(f)(6) prior to November 11, 1990. [See paragraph (g) of this section.]
6180(b) (1)	142(i)(2)	Election by a nongovernmental owner of a highspeed intercity rail facility not to claim any deduction under section 167 or 168 of the Code and any credit under subtitle A, in order for the facility to be described in section 142(a)(11).	Available for bonds issued after November 10, 1988. [See paragraph (h) of this section.]
6181(c) (2)	148(f) (4)(A)	One-time election by the issuer of tax-exempt bonds outstanding as of November 11, 1988, other than private activity bonds, to apply the amendments made by section 148(b) of the Code to amounts deposited after such date in bona fide debt service funds.	Available for bonds outstanding as of November 11, 1988. The election must be made in writing on the later of March 21, 1990 or the first date any payment is required under section 148(f) of the Code. The election should be retained as part of the issuer's books and records (as defined in § 1.103-10(b)(2)(vi) of the regulations) of the bond issue to which it relates.
6277	382 383	Election by a loss corporation that otherwise qualifies for the exception of section 621(f)(5) of the 1986 Act not to apply that exception. That exception provides for the inapplicability, in certain situations, of the amendments to sections 382 and 383 of the Code made by the 1986 Act (relating to limitation of corporate attributes after an ownership change). That exception applies with respect to a loss corporation's ownership change resulting from a reorganization described in section 368(a)(1)(G) of the Code or from an exchange of debt for stock in a Title 11 or similar case if a petition was filed with the court before August 14, 1986.	Available for ownership changes described in section 621(f)(5) of the 1986 Act, if a petition was filed with the court before August 14, 1986. The election is to be made by filing a statement with the District Director with whom the loss corporation would file its Federal income tax return. The statement must identify the election as an election under section 6277 of the Act and must (1) contain the taxpayer's name, address, and employee identification number, (2) identify the transaction to which the election relates, (3) represent that the conditions for making the election have been satisfied, and (4) be signed by a person authorized to sign the Federal income tax return of the loss corporation.
8007(a) (1)	3127	Election to be exempted from the taxes imposed by sections 3101 and 3111 of the Code.	An individual employer and an employee, both of whom are members of a recognized religious sect or a division thereof described in section 1402(g)(1) of the Code and adherents of established tenets or teachings of such sect or division, may, if both qualify and make elections, obtain exemptions from the taxes imposed by sections 3101 and 3111. [See paragraph (i) of this section.]

(2) *Time for making elections.*—(i) *In general.*—Except as otherwise provided in this section, the elections described in paragraph (a)(1) of this section must be made by the later of—

(A) The due date (taking into account any extensions of time to file obtained-by the taxpayer) of the tax return for the first taxable year for which the election is effective, or

Reg. §301.9100-8(a)(2)(i)

(B) January 22, 1990 (in which case the election generally must be made by amended return).

(ii) *No extension of time for payment.*—Payments of tax due must be made in accordance with chapter 62 of the Code.

(3) *Manner of making elections.*—Except as otherwise provided in this section, the elections described in paragraph (a)(1) of this section must be made by attaching a statement to the tax return for the first taxable year for which the election is to be effective. If such tax return is filed prior to the making of the election, the statement must be attached to an amended tax return of the first taxable year for which the election is to be effective. Except as otherwise provided in the return or in the instructions accompanying the return for the taxable year, the statement must—

(i) Contain the name, address and taxpayer identification number of the electing taxpayer;

(ii) Identify the election;

(iii) Indicate the section of the Code (or, if the provision is not codified, the section of the Act) under which the election is made;

(iv) Specify, as applicable, the period for which the election is being made and the property or other items to which the election is to apply; and

(v) Provide any information required by the relevant statutory provisions and any information requested in applicable forms and instructions, such as the information necessary to show that the taxpayer is entitled to make the election.

Notwithstanding the foregoing, an amended return need not be filed for an election made prior to October 23, 1989 if the taxpayer made the election in a reasonable manner.

(4) *Revocation.*—(i) *Irrevocable elections.*—The elections described in this section that are made under the following sections of the Act are irrevocable: 1002(a)(11)(A) (Code section 168(b)(2)), 1002(a)(23)(B), 1002(l)(1)(A) (Code section 42(b)(2)(A)(ii)), 1002(l)(2)(B) (Code section 42(f)(1)), 1005(c)(11), 1008(c)(4)(A) (Code section 460(b)(3)), 1014(c)(1), 1014(c)(2), 1014(d)(3)(B) and 1014(d)(4) (Code section 643(g)(2)), 2004(m)(5), 4004(a) (Code section 42(j)(5)(B)), 5033(a)(2) (Code section 2056A(d)), 6006(a) (Code section 1(i)(7)), 6026(a) (Code section 263A(h)), 6026(b)(1) (Code section 263A(d)(1)), 6152(a) and 6152(c)(3) (Code section 2056(b)(7)(C)(ii)), 6152(b) and 6152(c)(3) (Code section 2523(f)(6)(B)), 6152(c)(2) (Code sections 2056(b)(7)(C)(ii) and 2523(f)(6)(B)), and 6180(b)(1) (Code section 142(i)(2)).

(ii) *Elections revocable with the consent of the Commissioner.*—The elections described in this section that are made under the following sections of the Act are revocable only with the consent of the Commissioner: 1006(d)(15), 1006(j)(1)(C), 1006(t)(18)(B), 1009(d) (Code section 165(l)), 1010(f)(1) (Code section 831(b)(2)(A)), 1010(f)(2) (Code section 835(a)), 1012(d)(4) (Code section 865(f)), 1012(d)(6) (Code section 865(g)(3)), 1012(d)(8) (Code section 865(h)(2)), 1012(l)(2) (Code section 245(a)(10)), 1012(n)(3), 1012(bb)(4) (Code section 904(g)(10)), 2004(j)(1), 5031(a) (Code section 7520(a)), 6026(c) (Code section 263A(d)(3)(B)), and 6277.

(iii) *Freely revocable elections.*—The election described in this section that is made under section 6011 of the Act is revocable without the consent of the Commissioner. (See section 121(c) of the Code and § 1.121-4 of the regulations.)

(b) *Elections with respect to the low-income housing credit.*—The elections under sections 42(d)(3)(B), 42(f)(1), 42(g)(3)(B)(i), 42(i)(2)(B), and 42(j)(5)(B) of the Code generally must be made for the taxable year in which the building is placed in service, or the succeeding taxable year if the section 42(f)(1) election is made to defer the start of the credit period, and must be made in the certification required to be filed pursuant to section 42(l)(1) and (2), as amended by the Act. The election under section 42(j)(5)(B) of the Code must be made by the later of the due date of the certification or January 22, 1990. The election under section 42(b)(2)(A)(ii) must be made in accordance with the requirements of Notice 89-1, 1989-2 I.R.B. 10.

(c) *Election to treat certain carryovers of disallowed investment interest expense as passive activity deductions.*—The requirements of paragraphs (a)(2) and (3) of this section do not apply to an election under section 1005(c)(11) of the Act. Instead, the election must be made at the time and in the manner prescribed in Notice 89-36, 1989-13 I.R.B. 6. Thus, the election must be made before the filing deadline specified in Notice 89-36 by amending previously filed returns to reflect any change in the computation of tax liability that results from the election.

(d) *Election with respect to the treatment of reasonably estimated losses in an insolvent or bankrupt financial institution.*—(1) *In general.*—This paragraph (d) applies to an election under section 905(a) of the 1986 Act, and to an election under section 1009(d) of the Act, both relating to section 165(l) of the Code. If—

(i) As of the close of the taxable year, it can reasonably be estimated that there is a loss on a deposit (within the meaning of section 165(l)(4)) of a qualified individual (as defined in section 165(l)(2)) in a qualified financial institution (as defined in section 165(l)(3)), and

(ii) Such loss is on account of the bankruptcy or insolvency of such institution, then the qualified individual may elect under either section 165(l)(1) or (5) (but not both), to treat the amount (subject to the applicable limitations if under section 165(l)(5)) so estimated for that taxable year as a loss described in either section 165(c)(3), relating to casualty losses, or section 165(c)(2), relating to transactions entered into for profit, and incurred during the taxable year.

The election will apply to all losses of the qualified individual on deposits in the institution with respect to which an election is made. For additional information and examples of the application of the election rules, see Notice 89-28, 1989-12 I.R.B. 72. This paragraph (d) includes the procedural and the principal substantive rules first issued in Notice 89-28. For specific rules relating to an election under section 165(l)(5), see paragraph (d)(2) of this section.

(2) *Specific rules relating to the section 165(l)(5) election.*—(i) *Applicability.*—An election under section 165(l)(5) of the Code may be made only if no part of the taxpayer's deposits in the financial institution is federally insured. Generally, this requirement will be met only in cases in which none of the deposits in the financial institution are federally insured.

(ii) *Dollar limitations.*—An election under section 165(l)(5) of the Code is limited to $20,000 ($10,000 in the case of a separate return by a married individual) in aggregate losses on deposits in any one financial institution. The applicable dollar limit must be reduced by the amount of any insurance proceeds that can reasonably be expected to be received under any state law.

(3) *Time and manner of determining loss and making the election.*—(i) *Year of election and determination of loss.*—A qualified individual may make an election under section 165(l) of the Code either for the first taxable year in which a reasonable estimate of the loss can be made or for a later taxable year that is prior to the taxable year in which the loss is sustained. The amount of the loss is determined by the difference between a taxpayer's basis in the deposits and the amount that is reasonably estimated to be recovered, taking into account all facts and circumstances reasonably available to the taxpayer as of the date the election is made. A reasonable estimate might be based, for example, on the percentage of total deposits likely to be recovered by the depositors according to a determination made by the regulatory authority or trustee having responsibility over the institution. In addition, the taxpayer's basis in the deposits must be reduced to the extent that a loss is claimed.

(ii) *Time and manner of making election.*—A qualified individual may make an election under section 165(l) of the Code on—

(A) The income tax return for the taxable year with respect to which the taxpayer made a reasonable estimate of the loss;

(B) An amended income tax return for a taxable year described in paragraph (d)(3)(ii)(A) of this section, if the period prescribed for filing a claim for refund or credit for that taxable year has not yet expired; or, if applicable,

(C) An amended income tax return for a taxable year (beginning after December 31, 1981) described in paragraph (d)(3)(ii)(A) of this section, whether or not the claim for refund or credit is barred by another provision of law, but only if the amended return is properly filed on or before November 9, 1989.

(iii) *Information to include with election.*—The election should include any information requested in the applicable forms and instructions (e.g., Form 4684, Casualties and Thefts). If the applicable form(s) and instructions do not make reference to or request information concerning this election, the taxpayer should, on an appropriate line or space clearly indicate the name of the financial institution, include the following language: "Insolvent Financial Institution Election," and include the calculation of the reasonably estimated loss claimed.

(4) *Revocability of the election.*—(i) *In general.*—If a taxpayer desires to revoke an election under section 165(l) of the Code, the taxpayer must request, in writing, the consent of the Secretary setting forth the pertinent facts surrounding the election and the reasons for requesting a revocation.

(ii) *Exception.*—With respect to an election made under section 165(l)(1) of the Code prior to November 9, 1989, a qualified individual may revoke such election without securing the prior consent of the Secretary but only if the taxpayer makes an election under section 165(l)(5) by November 9, 1989, in the manner prescribed in paragraph (d)(3) of this section.

(5) *Effective date.*—Paragraph (d) of this section is generally effective for elections made under section 165(l) of the Code on or after November 10, 1988. However, an election filed prior to February 24, 1989, that is made in any reasonable manner will be effective.

(e) *Election to treat a survivor annuity payable to a surviving spouse as a nondeductible terminable interest.*—Where the time for making the election under section 2056(b)(7)(C)(ii) of the Code to treat the survivor annuity as nondeductible otherwise expires before November 11, 1990, the election may be made before November 11, 1990, by filing with the Service Center where the original return was filed supplemental information under § 20.6081-1(c) of the Estate Tax Regulations containing:

(1) A statement that the election under section 2056(b)(7)(C)(ii) of the Code is being made;

(2) The applicable revised schedules;

(3) A recomputation of the tax due; and

(4) Payment of any additional tax due.

(f) *Election to treat a joint and survivor annuity in which the donee spouse has a survivor interest as a nondeductible terminable interest.*—Where the time for making the election under section 2523(f)(6)(B) of the Code to treat the interest as nondeductible otherwise expires before November 11, 1990, the election may be made before November 11, 1990, by filing with the appropriate Service Center an original return (or an amended return if an original return was filed) containing:

(1) A statement that the election under section 2523(f)(6)(B) is being made;

(2) A recomputation of the tax due; and

(3) Payment of any additional tax due.

(g) *Election to treat survivor's annuity payable to the surviving spouse as qualified terminable interest property deductible under sections 2056(b)(7)(C) or 2523(f)(6) of the Code in the case of a return filed prior to November 11, 1988.*—(1) In the case of an estate tax election under section 2056(b)(7)(C) the election is made by filing with the Service Center where the estate tax return was filed supplemental information under §20.6081-1(c) of the Estate Tax Regulations (and timely claim for refund under section 6511 of the Code, if applicable) containing:

(i) A statement that the election under section 6152(c)(2) of the Technical and Miscellaneous Revenue Act of 1988 is being made;

(ii) The applicable revised schedules; and

(iii) A recomputation of the estate's tax liability showing the amount of any refund due.

(2) In the case of a gift tax election under section 2523(f)(6) of the Code, the election is made by filing with the Service Center where the original return was filed an amended return (and timely claim for refund under section 6511, if applicable) containing:

(i) A statement that the election under section 6152(c)(2) of the Technical and Miscellaneous Revenue Act of 1988 is being made;

(ii) The applicable revised schedules; and

(iii) A recomputation of the gift tax liability showing the amount of any refund due.

(h) *Elections with respect to certain nongovernmentally owned rail facilities.*—(1) *In general.*—This paragraph applies to the election under section 6180(b)(1) of the Act (Code section 142(i)(2)) not to claim a deduction under section 167 or 168 of the Code or any credit with respect to certain bond-financed property. An electing owner that is not a governmental unit must make the election at the time the loan agreement with the issuer of the bond is executed. The election must be signed by the owner and include—

(i) A description of the property with respect to which the election is being made;

(ii) The name, address, and taxpayer identification number of the issuing authority;

(iii) The name, address, and taxpayer identification number of the electing owner; and

(iv) The date and face amount of the issue used to provide the property.

(2) *Other requirements.*—The electing owner must provide a copy of the election to the issuing authority and to any person purchasing the facilities during the period the bonds are outstanding or within 6 years after the last bond that is part of the issue is retired. The electing owner, purchaser, and all successors in interest to the electing owner or purchaser must each retain the original election document or a copy thereof in its records until 6 years after the later of the date the last bond that is part of the issue is retired or the date such owner, purchaser or successor in interest ceases to own the facilities. The issuer must retain a copy of the election until 6 years after the date the last bond that is part of the issue is retired. In addition, while the facilities are nongovernmentally owned, any publicly recorded document with respect to the facilities must state that neither the electing owner, nor any person purchasing the facilities during the period the bonds are outstanding or within 6 years after the date the last bond that is part of the issue is retired, nor any successor in interest to the electing owner or such purchaser, may claim any deduction under section 167 or 168 of the Code or any credit with respect to the facilities.

(3) *Election is binding on purchasers and successors.*—The election is binding at all times on any person purchasing the facilities during the period the bonds are outstanding or within 6 years after the date the last bond that is part of the issue is retired and on all successors in interest to the electing owner and such purchaser.

(i) *Election under section 3127 of the Code to be exempted from the taxes imposed by sections 3111 and 3101.*—(1) *Application for exemption.*—To be exempt from the taxes imposed under section 3111 and 3101 of the Code with regard to wages paid after December 31, 1988, an individual who is an employer and his or her employee must each file an application on the prescribed form with the Internal Revenue Service office designated in the instructions relating to the application for exemption.

(2) *Approval of application for exemption.*—The application for exemption by the individual employer or the employee will be approved only if:

(i) The application contains or is accompanied by the evidence described in section 1402(g)(1)(A) of the Code and a waiver described in section 1402(g)(1)(B);

(ii) The Secretary of Health and Human Services makes the findings described in section 1402(g)(1)(C), (D), and (E) with respect to the religious sect or division described in section 1402(g)(1) of which the individual employer and employee are members; and

(iii) No benefit or other payment referred to in section 1402(g)(1)(B) became payable (or, but for sections 203 or 222(b) of the Social Security Act, would have become payable) to the employee filing the application at or before the time of the filing.

(3) *Effective period of exemption.*—The election provided in paragraph (h)(1) of this section will apply with respect to wages paid by such individual employer during the period commencing with the first day of the first calendar quarter, after the quarter in which such application is filed, throughout which such individual employer or employee meets the applicable requirements specified in paragraphs (h)(2) and (h)(3).

(4) *Termination of election.*—The exemption granted under section 3127 of the Code will end on the last day of the calendar quarter preceding the first calendar quarter thereafter in which:

(i) Such individual employer or the employee involved ceases to meet the applicable requirements of paragraphs (h)(2) and (h)(3), or

(ii) The sect or division thereof of which such individual employer or employee is a member is found by the Secretary of Health and Human Services to have failed to meet the requirements of section 3127(b)(2).

(5) *Both the individual employer and employee must qualify and elect.*—The exemption from the taxes imposed under sections 3101 and 3111 of the Code is applicable only if both the individual employer and the employee qualify and make the election under the provisions of section 3127.

(j) *Certain elections not addressed in this section.*—Elections under the Act that are not addressed in this section include:

(1) An election relating to the effective date of certain source rules under section 861(a) of the Code (section 1012(g)(1) of the Act);

(2) An election relating to transitional rules for interest allocation under 864(e) of the Code (section 1012(h)(7) of the Act);

(3) An election relating to the chain deficit rules under section 952(c)(1)(C) of the Code (section 1012(i)(25) of the Act);

(4) An election relating to the definition of a passive foreign investment company in section 1296 of the Code (section 1012(p)(27) of the Act);

(5) An election by a shareholder of a qualified electing fund under section 1291(d)(2)(B) of the Code (section 1012(p)(28) of the Act);

(6) An election to be treated as a qualified electing fund under section 1295 of the Code (section 6127 of the Act);

(7) An election relating to treatment of an insurance branch as a separate corporation

under section 964(d) of the Code (section 6129 of the Act);

(8) An election relating to certain regulated futures contracts and nonequity options under section 988(c)(1)(D) of the Code (section 6130(b) of the Act);

(9) An election relating to certain qualified funds under section 988(c)(1)(E) of the Code (section 6130(b) of the Act);

(10) An election under section 952(c)(1)(B) of the Code to apply section 953(a) without regard to the same country exception (section 6131(a) of the Act);

(11) An election relating to treatment of a foreign insurance company as a domestic corporation under section 953(d) of the Code (section 6135 of the Act).

Guidance concerning the elections described in this paragraph (j) will generally be provided in regulations to be issued under the relevant Code sections. With respect to certain elections described in this paragraph (j), preliminary guidance has been published. See Notice 88-125, 1988-52 I.R.B. 4, for guidance with respect to the election described in paragraph (j)(6) of this section, relating to the qualified electing fund election. See Notice 88-124, 1988-51 I.R.B. 6, for guidance with respect to the elections described in paragraph (j)(8) and (9) of this section, relating to section 988(c)(1)(D) and (E) of the Code.

(k) *Additional information required.*—Later regulations or revenue procedures issued under provisions of the Code or Act covered by this section may require the furnishing of information in addition to that which was furnished with the statement of election described in this section. In that event, the later regulations or revenue procedures will provide guidance with respect to the furnishing of additional information. [Reg. § 301.9100-8.]

☐ [*T.D. 8267, 9-21-89. Redesignated and amended by T.D. 8435, 9-18-92.*]

ELECTIONS UNDER THE BANK HOLDING COMPANY ACT OF 1976

[Reg. § 301.9100-9T]

§ 301.9100-9T. Election by a bank holding company to forego grandfather provision for all property representing pre-June 30, 1968, activities (Temporary).—(a) *In general.*—For purposes of sections 1101 through 1103 and 6158 of the Code, a bank holding company may elect under section 1103(g) to have the determination of whether property is prohibited property or is property eligible to be distributed without recognition of gain under section 1101(b)(1) made under the Bank Holding Company Act (12 U.S.C. 1841 et seq.) as if the Act did not contain the proviso of section 4(a)(2) thereof.

(b) *Manner of making election.*—The election under section 1103(g) shall be made in a written statement filed with the Federal Reserve Board

indicating that by resolution of its board of directors, the bank holding company is electing to apply the provisions of section 1103(g). In addition, the bank holding company shall indicate on its income tax return for each taxable year in which the election applies to a distribution or sale of property (in the manner specified in the Internal Revenue Service's instructions for the preparation of the return) that it has made the election under section 1103(g). The election shall be considered to be made on the date on which the written statement is received by the Federal Reserve Board.

(c) *Scope of election.*—The election under section 1103(g) applies to all determinations of whether property is prohibited property or is property eligible to be distributed without recognition of gain under section 1101(b)(1).

(d) *Election; binding effect.*—An election made under section 1103(g) is irrevocable.

(e) *Final certification.*—An election under section 1103(g) shall not apply unless the final certification referred to in section 1101(e) or section 6158(c)(2), as the case may be, includes a certification by the Federal Reserve Board that the bank holding company has disposed of either all banking property or all nonbanking property (including property described in the proviso of section 4(a)(2) of the Bank Holding Company Act).

(f) *Conditional certification.*—A certification by the Federal Reserve Board under section 1101(a)(1)(B), 1101(b)(1)(B), 1101(c)(2)(C), 1101(c)(3)(C), or 6158(a) that is conditioned upon the bank holding company's making an election under section 1103(g) shall not be considered to be made before the distribution or sale unless the certification and the election are made before the distribution or sale. [Temporary Reg. § 301.9100-9T.]

☐ [*T.D. 7570, 11-7-78. Redesignated by T.D. 8435, 9-18-92.*]

[Reg. § 301.9100-10T]

§ 301.9100-10T. Election by certain family-owned bank holding companies to divest all banking or nonbanking property (Temporary).—(a) *In general.*—For purposes of sections 1101 through 1103 and 6158 of the Code, a bank holding company may elect under section 1103(h) to have the determination of whether property is prohibited property or is property eligible to be distributed without recognition of gain under section 1101(b)(1) made under the Bank Holding Company Act (12 U.S.C. 1841 et seq.) as if the Act did not contain clause (ii) of section 4(c) thereof.

(b) *Manner of making election.*—The election under section 1103(h) shall be made in a written statement filed with the Federal Reserve Board indicating that by resolution of its board of directors, the bank holding company is electing to apply the provisions of section 1103(h). In addition, the bank holding company shall indicate on its income tax return for each taxable year in which the election applies to a distribution or sale of property (in the manner specified in the Internal Revenue Service's instructions for the preparation of the return) that it has made the election under section 1103(h). The election shall be considered to be made on the date on which the written statement is received by the Federal Reserve Board.

(c) *Scope of election.*—The election under section 1103(h) applies to all determinations of whether property is prohibited property or is property eligible to be distributed without recognition of gain under section 1101(b)(1).

(d) *Election; binding effect.*—An election made under section 1103(h) is irrevocable.

(e) *Final certification.*—An election under section 1103(h) shall not apply unless the final certification referred to in section 1101(e) or section 6158(c)(2), as the case may be, includes a certification by the Federal Reserve Board that the bank holding company has disposed of either all banking property or all nonbanking property.

(f) *Conditional certification.*—A certification by the Federal Reserve Board under section 1101(a)(1)(B), 1101(b)(1)(B), 1101(c)(2)(C), 1101(c)(3)(C), or 6158(a) that is conditioned upon the bank holding company's making an election under section 1103(h) shall not be considered to be made before the distribution or sale unless the certification and the election are made before the distribution or sale. [Temporary Reg. § 301.9100-10T.]

☐ [*T.D. 7570, 11-7-78. Redesignated by T.D. 8435, 9-18-92.*]

[Reg. § 301.9100-11T]

§ 301.9100-11T. Election by a qualified bank holding corporation to pay in installments the tax attributable to sales under the Bank Holding Company Act (Temporary).—(a) *In general.*—Under section 6158(a) of the Code, a qualified bank holding corporation may elect to pay in installments the tax under chapter 1 of the Code attributable to the sale of bank property or prohibited property (as those terms are defined in section 6158(f)(2) and (3)) if—

(1) It meets the conditions described in paragraph (b) of this section, and

(2) It files an election in accordance with the rules set forth in paragraph (c) of this section.

(b) *Conditions.*—(1) The sale of bank property or prohibited property must take place after July 7, 1970.

(2) The Federal Reserve Board must certify before the sale of the bank property or prohibited property that the divestiture of such property is necessary or appropriate to effectuate section 4 or the policies of the Bank Holding Company Act (12 U.S.C. 1841 et seq.).

(3) If bank property is sold, the qualified bank holding corporation (or a corporation having control of it or a subsidiary of it) must not have—

(i) Previously elected to apply section 6158 to a sale of prohibited property, or

(ii) Previously distributed prohibited property under section 1101(a).

(4) If prohibited property is sold, the qualified bank holding corporation (or a corporation having control of it or a subsidiary of it) must not have—

(i) Previously elected to apply section 6158 to a sale of bank property, or

(ii) Previously distributed bank property under section 1101(b).

(5) The qualified bank holding corporation must not have elected to return the income from the sale under the installment provisions of section 453.

Reg. § 301.9100-11T(b)(5)

(c) *Time and manner of making election.*—(1) Except as provided in paragraph (c)(2) of this section, a qualified bank holding corporation shall make the election under section 6158(a) by—

(i) Attaching a statement to its income tax return for the taxable year in which the prohibited property or bank property is sold showing the tax computation under paragraph (f) of this section and the amount of the installment paid with the return, and

(ii) Entering the amount of the installment payment followed by the words "computed under section 6158" in the appropriate place on the tax return.

(2) If the qualified bank holding corporation filed its income tax return for the year of sale before February 6, 1979 (without electing under section 6158(a)), then it shall make the election under section 6158(a) by attaching a statement to its claim for credit or refund (amended tax return) for its overpayment of income tax attributable to the application of section 6158 showing the tax computation under paragraph (f) of this section and entering the amount of the credit or refund followed by the words "attributable to the application of section 6158" in the appropriate place on the claim. In order for the election to be effective, the claim must be filed before the earlier of—

(i) The expiration of the period of limitation for the filing of the claim, or

(ii) February 6, 1979.

(d) *Scope of election.*—An election under section 6158 will apply only to the particular sale or sales of property with respect to which the election is being made.

(e) *Special rule for certifying sales.*—For purposes of section 6158(a) and paragraph (b)(2) of this section, in the case of a sale which takes place after July 7, 1970, and before January 1, 1977, a certification by the Federal Reserve Board shall be treated as made before the sale if application for such certification was made before January 1, 1977.

(f) *Tax attributable to sales.*—The tax under chapter 1 of the Code attributable to sales with respect to which an election under section 6158 has been made shall be the amount, if any, by which the tax under chapter 1 on the taxable income of the qualified bank holding corporation (computed without regard to section 6158) for the taxable year during which the sales occur exceeds the greater of—

(1) The tax under chapter 1 for such year on the taxable income of the corporation exclusive of gains on sales of property with respect to which an election under section 6158 has been made, or

(2) The tax under chapter 1 for such year on the taxable income of the corporation exclusive of gains and losses on all sales of the type of property (either bank property or prohibited property) with respect to which an election under section 6158 has been made. [Temporary Reg. § 301.9100-11T.]

☐ [*T.D. 7570, 11-7-78. Redesignated by T.D. 8435, 9-18-92.*]

ELECTIONS UNDER TAX REFORM ACT OF 1976

[Reg. § 301.9100-12T]

§ 301.9100-12T. Various elections under the Tax Reform Act of 1976 (Temporary).— (a) *Elections covered by temporary rules.*—The sections of the Internal Revenue Code of 1954, or of the Tax Reform Act of 1976, to which this section applies and under which an election or notification may be made pursuant to the procedures described in paragraphs (b) and (d) are as follows:

Section	Description of Election	Availability of Election
(1) First Category		
167(o) of Code	Substantially rehabilitated historic property.	Additions to capital account occurring after June 30, 1976, and before July 1, 1981.
172(b)(3)(E)[(C)] of Code	Forego of carryback period.	Any taxable year ending after December 31, 1975.
402(e)(4)(L) of Code	Lump sum distributions from qualified plans.	Distributions and payments made after December 31, 1975, in taxable years beginning after such date.
451(e) of Code	Livestock sold on account of drought.	Any taxable year beginning after December 31, 1975.
812(b)(3) of Code	Forego of carryback period by life insurance companies.	Any taxable year ending after December 31, 1975.
819A of Code	Contiguous country branches of domestic life insurance companies.	All taxable years beginning after December 31, 1975.
825(d)(2) of Code	Forego of carryback period by mutual insurance companies.	Any taxable year ending after December 31, 1975.

Section	Description of Election	Availability of Election
911(e) of Code	Foregoing of benefits of section 911.	All taxable years beginning after December 31, 1975.
(2) *Second Category*		
185(d) of Code	Amortization of railroad grading and tunnel bores.	All taxable years beginning after December 31, 1974.
1057 of Code	Transfer to foreign trusts etc.	Any transfer of property after October 2, 1975.

(b) *Time for making election or serving notice.*— (1) *Category (1).*—A taxpayer may make an election under any section referred to in paragraph (a)(1) of this section for the first taxable year for which the election is required to be made or for the taxable year selected by the taxpayer when the choice of the taxable year is optional. The election must be made by the later of the time, including extensions thereof, prescribed by law for filing income tax returns for such taxable year or March 8, 1977.

(2) *Category (2).*—A taxpayer may make an election under any section referred to in paragraph (a)(2) for the first taxable year for which the election is allowed or for the taxable year selected by the taxpayer when the choice of the taxable year is optional. The election must be made (i) for any taxable year ending before December 31, 1976, for which a return has been filed before January 31, 1977, by filing an amended return, provided that the period of limitation for filing claim for credit or refund of overpayment of tax, determined from the time the return was filed, has not expired or (ii) for all other years by filing the income tax return for the year for which the election is made not later than the time, including extensions thereof, prescribed by law for filing income tax returns for such year.

(c) *Certain other elections.*—The elections described in this paragraph shall be made in the manner and within the time prescribed herein and in paragraph (d) of this section.

(1) The following elections under the Tax Reform Act of 1976 shall be made:

(i)	Sec. 207 (c)(3) of Act.	Change from static value method of accounting.	All taxable years beginning after December 31, 1976.

by filing Form 3115 with the National Office of the Internal Revenue Service before October 5, 1977.

(ii)	Sec. 604 of Act.	Travel expenses of State legislators.	All taxable years beginning before January 1, 1976.

by filing an amended return for any taxable year for which the period for assessing or collecting a deficiency has not expired before October 4, 1976, by the last day for filing a claim for refund or credit for the taxable year but in no event shall such day be earlier than October 4, 1977.

(iii)	Sec. 804(e)(2) of Act.	Retroactive applications of amendments to property described in section 50(a) of Code.	Certain taxable years beginning before January 1, 1975.

by filing amended returns before October 5, 1977, for all taxable years to which applicable for which the period of limitation for filing claim for credit or refund for overpayment of tax has not expired.

(iv)	Sec. 1608(d)(2) of Act.	Election as a result of determination as defined in section 859(c) of the Code.	Determinations made after October 4, 1976.

by filing a statement with the district director for the district in which the taxpayer maintains its principal place of business within 60 days after such determination.

(v)	Sec. 2103 of Act.	Treatment of certain 1972 disaster losses.	Any taxable year in which payment is received or indebtedness is forgiven.

by filing a return for the taxable year or an amended return by the last day for making a claim for credit or refund for the taxable year but in no event shall such day be earlier than October 4, 1977.

(2) [Deleted].

(3) The election provided for in section 167(e)(3) of the Code shall be made in accordance with § 1.167(e)-1(d) except that the election shall be applicable for the first taxable year of the taxpayer beginning after December 31, 1975.

(d) *Manner of making election.*—Unless otherwise provided in the return or in a form accompanying a return for the taxable year, the elections described in paragraphs (a) and (c) (except paragraphs (c)(1)(i) and (c)(5)) shall be made by a statement attached to the return (or amended return) for the taxable year. The statement required when making an election pursuant to this section shall indicate the section under which the election is being made and shall set forth information to identify the election, the period for which it applies, and the taxpayer's basis or entitlement for making the election.

(e) *Effect of election.*—(1) *Consent to revoke required.*—Except where otherwise provided by statute or except as provided in subparagraph

(2) of this paragraph, an election to which this section applies made in accordance with this section shall be binding unless consent to revoke the election is obtained from the Commissioner. An application for consent to revoke the election will not be accepted before the promulgation of the permanent regulations relating to the section of the Code or Act under which the election is made. Such regulations will provide a reasonable period of time within which taxpayers will be permitted to apply for consent to revoke the election.

(2) *Revocation without consent.*—An election to which this section applies, made in accordance with this section, may be revoked without the consent of the Commissioner not later than 90 days after the permanent regulations relating to the section of the Code or Act under which the election is made are filed with the office of the Federal Register, provided such regulations grant taxpayers blanket permission to revoke that election within such time without the consent of the Commissioner. Such blanket permission to revoke an election will be provided by the permanent regulations in the event of a de-

termination by the Secretary or his delegate that such regulations contain provisions that may not reasonably have been anticipated by taxpayers at the time of making such election.

(f) *Furnishing of supplementary information required.*—If the permanent regulations which are issued under the section of the Code or Act referred to in this section to which the election relates require the furnishing of information in addition to that which was furnished with the statement of election filed pursuant to paragraph (d) of this section, the taxpayer must furnish such additional information in a statement addressed to the district director, or the director of the regional service center, with whom the election was filed. This statement must clearly identify the election and the taxable year for which it was made. If such information is not provided the election may, at the discretion of the Commissioner, be held invalid. [Temporary Reg. § 301.9100-12T.]

☐ [*T.D.* 7459, 1-4-77. *Amended by T.D.* 7478, 4-5-77; *T.D.* 7670, 1-30-80; *T.D.* 7673, 2-7-80; *T.D.* 7692, 4-7-80; *T.D.* 7743, 12-19-80 *and T.D.* 8308, 8-30-90. *Redesignated by T.D.* 8435, 9-18-92.]

ELECTIONS UNDER THE BANKRUPTCY TAX ACT OF 1980

[Reg. § 301.9100-14T]

§ 301.9100-14T. Individual's election to terminate taxable year when case commences (Temporary).—(a) *Scope.*—The regulations prescribed in this section provide rules for making the election under section 1398(d)(2) to terminate the taxable year of an individual taxpayer.

(b) *Availability of election.*—This election is available to an individual taxpayer in a case commenced after March 24, 1981, under chapter 7 (relating to liquidations) or chapter 11 (relating to reorganizations) of title 11 of the United States Code. If the case is dismissed, the taxpayer cannot make the election, and an election previously made will be void. For purposes of this section, a partnership is not treated as an individual. If the taxpayer making the election is married (within the meaning of section 143), the election is available to the taxpayer's spouse, but only if the spouse is eligible to file, and does file, a joint return with the taxpayer for the taxable year ended as a result of the election.

(c) *Effect of election.*—The election terminates the taxable year of the taxpayer (and of a spouse who joins in the election) on the day before the commencement date of the case. A new taxable year begins on the commencement date and (unless terminated earlier) ends on the date on which the taxpayer's taxable year in which the case commenced would have ended if the election had not been made.

(d) *Time and manner.*—A taxpayer to whom the election is available makes the election by filing a return for the short taxable year ending the day before commencement of the case (the "first short taxable year") on or before the 15th

day of the fourth full month following the end of that first short taxable year. The spouse of such a taxpayer makes the election by making a joint return with the taxpayer for that first short taxable year within the time prescribed in the preceding sentence. To facilitate processing, the taxpayer should write "SECTION 1398 ELECTION" at the top of the return. A taxpayer may also make the election by attaching a statement of election to an application for extension of time for filing a return that satisfies the requirements under section 6081 for the first short taxable year. The application for extension must be submitted under section 6081 on or before the due date of the return for the first short taxable year. The statement must state that the taxpayer elects under section 1398(d)(2) to close his or her taxable year as of the day before commencement of the case. If the taxpayer's spouse elects to close his or her taxable year, the spouse must join in the application for extension and in the statement of election. If a joint return is not filed for the first short taxable year, the election of the spouse made with the application is void.

(e) *Irrevocability of election.*—The election is irrevocable.

(f) *Subsequent bankruptcy case of debtor's spouse.*—If a case under chapter 7 or chapter 11 of title 11 of the United States Code commences with respect to the spouse of a debtor to whom an election under this section was available, the spouse can make an election under this section even if the spouse's case commences in the same taxable year in which the debtor's case commences. The spouse can make the election whether or not the spouse previously joined in the debtor's election. If the spouse joined in the debtor's election, or if the debtor did not make the election, the debtor may join in the spouse's election, assuming the debtor is otherwise eligible to file a joint return with the spouse.

(g) *Example.*—(1) Assume that husband and wife are calendar-year taxpayers, that a bankruptcy case involving only the husband commences on March 1, 1982, and that a bankruptcy case involving only the wife commences on October 10, 1982.

(2) If the husband does not make an election, his taxable year would not be affected; *i.e.*, it does not terminate on February 28. If the husband does make an election, his first short taxable year would be January 1 through February 28; his second short taxable year would begin March 1. The tax return for his first short taxable year would be due on June 15. The wife could join in the husband's election, but only if they file a joint return for the taxable year January 1 through February 28.

(3) The wife could elect to terminate her taxable year on October 9. If she did, and if the husband had not made an election or if the wife had not joined in the husband's election, she would have two taxable years in 1982—the first from January 1 through October 9, and the second from October 10 through December 31. The tax return for her first short taxable year would be due on February 15, 1983. If the husband had not made an election to terminate his taxable year on February 28, the husband could join in an election by his wife, but only if they file a joint return for the taxable year January 1 through October 9. If the husband had made an election but the wife had not joined in the husband's election, the husband could not join in an election by the wife to terminate her taxable year on October 9, since they could not file a joint return for such year.

(4) If the wife makes the election relating to her own bankruptcy case, and had joined the husband in making an election relating to his case, she would have two additional taxable years with respect to her 1982 income and deductions—the second short taxable year would be March 1 through October 9, and the third short taxable year would be October 10 through December 31. The husband could join in the wife's election if they file a joint return for the second short taxable year. If the husband joins in the wife's election, they could file joint returns for the short taxable year ending December 31, but would not be required to do so. [Temporary Reg. §301.9100-14T.]

☐ [*T.D. 7775, 5-1-81. Redesignated by T.D. 8435, 9-18-92.*]

[Reg. §301.9100-15T]

§301.9100-15T. Election to use retroactive effective date (Temporary).—(a) *Scope.*—The regulations prescribed in this section provide rules for making the election to use a retroactive effective date under section 7(f) of the Bankruptcy Tax Act of 1980.

(b) *Availability of election.*—The election is available to the debtor (or debtors) in a case under title 11 of the United States Code (or a receivership, foreclosure, or similar proceeding in a Federal or State court) that commences after September 30, 1979, and before January 1, 1981. The court must approve the election. For purposes of this paragraph (b), a receivership, foreclosure, or similar proceeding before a Federal or State agency involving a financial institution to which section 585 or 593 applies shall be treated as a proceeding before a court.

(c) *Effect of election.*—(1) *In general.*—An election under this section changes the effective date of certain amendments to the Code made by the Bankruptcy Tax Act of 1980. The amendments affected by an election under this section are listed in paragraph (c)(2) and (3) of this section. If the election is made, all of the amendments listed in paragraph (c)(2) and (3) of this section apply to all transactions in the case (or similar proceeding) and to all parties in respect of all transactions in the case (or similar proceeding). Thus, the debtor may not elect to have only certain of the amendments apply to transactions in the case (or similar proceeding) and may not elect to have the amendments apply only to certain transactions in the case (or similar proceeding). An election under this section will not make the amendments listed in paragraph (c)(2) and (3) applicable to transactions occurring prior to commencement of the case (or similar proceeding) or transactions not in the case (or similar proceeding).

(2) *Amendments affected.*—An election under this section changes the effective date of the amendments to the following sections:

(i) 111, relating to recovery of bad debts, prior taxes and delinquency amounts,

(ii) 302, relating to the repeal of special treatment for certain railroad redemptions,

(iii) 312, relating to the effect of debt discharge on earnings and profits,

(iv) 337, relating to the application of the 12-month liquidation rule,

(v) 351, relating to certain transfers to controlled corporations,

(vi) 354 (other than the amendment made by section 6(i)(2) of the Bankruptcy Tax Act of 1980), 355, 357, 368, and 381, relating to corporate reorganizations,

(vii) 382, relating to special limitations on net operating loss carryover,

(viii) 542, relating to the personal holding company tax, and

(ix) 703, relating to elections of partnerships.

(3) *Other amendments affected in part.*—Subject to the transitional rule of section 7(a)(2) of the Bankruptcy Tax Act of 1980, an election under this section changes the effective date of the amendments to sections 108 and 1017, relating to the tax treatment of discharge of indebtedness.

Reg. §301.9100-15T(c)(3)

(4) *Substitution of effective dates.*—The election under this section changes the effective date of the amendments listed in paragraph (c)(2) and (3) of this section by substituting "September 30, 1979" for "December 31, 1980" wherever it appears in section 7(a), (c), and (d) of the Bankruptcy Tax Act of 1980.

(d) *Time and manner.*—(1) *Time and place.*—A debtor makes the election under this section by filing the written statement and evidence of court approval required under paragraph (d)(2) and (3) of this section on or before November 2, 1981, with the District Director or the Director of the Internal Revenue Service Center with whom an income tax return for the debtor would be filed if it were due on the date the election is filed. The election shall be considered to be made on the date on which the written statement and evidence of court approval is filed. The debtor should attach a copy of the statement and evidence of court approval to the next income tax return filed on or after the date the election is made.

(2) *Statement.*—The written statement must be signed by the debtor (or a person duly authorized to sign the income tax return of the debtor) and must contain the following:

(i) the name, address, and taxpayer identification number of the debtor,

(ii) a statement that the debtor is making the election under section 7(f) of the Bankruptcy Tax Act of 1980, and

(iii) information (including the date of commencement) sufficient to identify the bankruptcy case or similar proceeding.

(3) *Evidence of court approval.*—The evidence of court approval (or of approval of an agency in certain proceedings described in paragraph (b) of this section) must be a copy of an order or other document properly signed by the judge or other presiding officer. In addition to information identifying the debtor and the case or proceeding over which the officer presides, the order or other document must state that the court (or agency, as the case may be) approves the election of the debtor under section 7(f) of the Bankruptcy Tax Act of 1980.

(e) *Revocability.*—An election under this section may be revoked only with the consent of the Commissioner. A request for revocation can be made only with approval of the court (or agency). [Temporary Reg. § 301.9100-15T.]

☐ *[T.D. 7775, 5-1-81. Redesignated by T.D. 8435, 9-18-92.]*

[Reg. § 301.9100-21]

§ 301.9100-21. **References to other temporary elections under various tax acts.**—Regulations regarding elections under various other tax acts are found at the following sections in title 26 of the Code of Federal Regulations:

Section of 26 CFR	Description of Election
5c.168(f)(8)-2	Election to characterize transaction as a section 168(f)(8) lease, under the Economic Recovery Tax Act of 1981.
5c.1256-1	Election with respect to property held on June 23, 1981, under section 508(c) of the Economic Recovery Tax Act of 1981.
5c.1256-2	Election with respect to taxable years beginning before June 23, 1981, and ending after June 22, 1981, under section 509 of the Economic Recovery Tax Act of 1981.
7.48-1	Election to have investment credit for movie and television films determined in accordance with previous litigation, under the Tax Reform Act of 1976.
7.48-2	Election of forty-percent method of determining investment credit for movie and television films placed in service in a taxable year beginning before January 1, 1975, under the Tax Reform Act of 1976.
7.48-3	Election to apply the amendments made by sections 804(a) and (b) of the Tax Reform Act of 1976 to property described in section 50(a) of the Code.
7.57(d)-1	Election with respect to straight line recovery of intangibles, under the Tax Reform Act of 1976.
11.402(a)(4)(B)-1	Election to treat an amount as a lump sum distribution, under the Employee Retirement Income Security Act of 1974.
11.410-1	Election by church to have participation, vesting, funding, etc., provisions apply, under the Employee Retirement Income Security Act of 1974.
11.412(c)-7	Election to treat certain retroactive plan amendments as made on the first day of the plan year, under the Employee Retirement Income Security Act of 1974.
11.412(c)-11	Election with respect to bonds, under the Employee Retirement Income Security Act of 1974.

[Reg. § 301.9100-21.]

☐ [*T.D.* 8435, 9-18-92.]

[Reg. § 301.9100-22]

§ 301.9100-22. Time, form, and manner of making the election under section 1101(g)(4) of the Bipartisan Budget Act of 2015 for returns filed for partnership taxable years beginning after November 2, 2015 and before January 1, 2018.—(a) *Election.*—Pursuant to section 1101(g)(4) of the Bipartisan Budget Act of 2015, Public Law 114-74 (BBA), a partnership may elect at the time and in such form and manner as described in this section for amendments made by section 1101 of the BBA, except section 6221(b) as added by the BBA, to apply to any return of the partnership filed for an eligible taxable year as defined in paragraph (d) of this section. An election is valid only if made in accordance with this section. Once made, an election may only be revoked with the consent of the Internal Revenue Service (IRS). An election is not valid if it frustrates the purposes of section 1101 of the BBA. A partnership may not request an extension of time under § 301.9100-3 for an election described in this section.

(b) *Election on notification by the IRS.*—(1) *Time for making the election.*—Except as described in paragraph (c) of this section, an election under this section must be made within 30 days of the date of notification to a partnership, in writing, that a return of the partnership for an eligible taxable year has been selected for examination (a notice of selection for examination).

(2) *Form and manner of making the election.*—(i) *In general.*—The partnership makes an election under this section by providing a written statement with the words "Election under Section 1101(g)(4)" written at the top that satisfies the requirements of paragraph (b)(2) of this section to the individual identified in the notice of selection for examination as the IRS contact regarding the examination.

(ii) *Statement requirements.*—A statement making an election under this section must be in writing and be dated and signed by the tax matters partner, as defined under section 6231(a)(7) (prior to amendment by the BBA), and the applicable regulations, or an individual who has the authority to sign the partnership return for the taxable year under section 6063, the regulations thereunder, and applicable forms and instructions. The fact that an individual dates and signs the statement making the election described in this paragraph (b) shall be prima facie evidence that the individual is authorized to make the election on behalf of the partnership. A statement making an election must include—

(A) The partnership's name, taxpayer identification number, and the partnership taxable year for which the election described in this paragraph (b) is being made;

(B) The name, taxpayer identification number, address, and daytime telephone number of the individual who signs the statement;

(C) Language indicating that the partnership is electing application of section 1101(c) of the BBA for the partnership return for the eligible taxable year identified in the notice of selection for examination;

(D) The information required to properly designate the partnership representative as defined by section 6223 as amended by the BBA, which must include the name, taxpayer identification number, address, and daytime telephone number of the partnership representative and any additional information required by applicable regulations, forms and instructions, and other guidance issued by the IRS;

(E) The following representations—

(1) The partnership is not insolvent and does not reasonably anticipate becoming insolvent before resolution of any adjustment with respect to the partnership taxable year for which the election described in this paragraph (b) is being made;

(2) The partnership has not filed, and does not reasonably anticipate filing, voluntarily a petition for relief under title 11 of the United States Code;

(3) The partnership is not subject to, and does not reasonably anticipate becoming subject to, an involuntary petition for relief under title 11 of the United States Code; and

(4) The partnership has sufficient assets, and reasonably anticipates having sufficient assets, to pay a potential imputed underpayment with respect to the partnership taxable year that may be determined under subchapter C of chapter 63 of the Internal Revenue Code as amended by the BBA; and

(F) A representation, signed under penalties of perjury, that the individual signing the statement is duly authorized to make the election described in this paragraph (b) and that, to the best of the individual's knowledge and belief, all of the information contained in the statement is true, correct, and complete.

(iii) *Notice of Administrative Proceeding.*—Upon receipt of the election described in this paragraph (b), the IRS will promptly mail a notice of administrative proceeding to the partnership and the partnership representative, as required under section 6231(a)(1) as amended by the BBA. Notwithstanding the preceding sentence, the IRS will not mail the notice of administrative proceeding before the date that is 30 days after receipt of the election described in paragraph (b) of this section.

(c) *Election for the purpose of filing an administrative adjustment request (AAR) under section 6227 as amended by the BBA.*—(1) *In general.*—A partnership that has not been issued a notice of selection for examination as described in paragraph (b)(1) of this section may make an election with respect to a partnership return for an eligible taxable year for the purpose of filing an AAR under section 6227 as amended by the BBA. Once an election under this paragraph (c) is made, all of the amendments made by section 1101 of the BBA, except section 6221(b) as added by the BBA, apply with respect to the partnership taxable year for which such election is made.

(2) *Time for making the election.*—No election under this paragraph (c) may be made before January 1, 2018.

(3) *Form and manner of making an election.*—An election under this paragraph (c) must be made in the manner prescribed by the IRS for that purpose in accordance with applicable regulations, forms and instructions, and other guidance issued by the IRS.

(4) *Effect of filing an AAR before January 1, 2018.*—Except in the case of an election made in accordance with paragraph (b) of this section, an AAR filed on behalf of a partnership before January 1, 2018, is deemed for purposes of paragraph (d)(2) of this section, to be an AAR filed under section 6227(c) (prior to amendment by the BBA) or an amended return of partnership income, as applicable.

(d) *Eligible taxable year.*—(1) *In general.*—For purposes of this section, the term *eligible taxable year* means any partnership taxable year beginning after November 2, 2015 and before January 1, 2018, except as provided in paragraph (d)(2) of this section.

(2) *Exception if AAR or amended return filed or deemed filed.*—Notwithstanding paragraph (d)(1) of this section, a partnership taxable year is not an eligible taxable year for purposes of this section if for the partnership taxable year—

(i) The tax matters partner has filed an AAR under section 6227(c) (prior to amendment by the BBA),

(ii) The partnership is deemed to have filed an AAR under section 6227(c) (prior to the amendment by the BBA) in accordance with paragraph (c)(4) of this section, or

(iii) An amended return of partnership income has been filed or has been deemed to be filed under paragraph (c)(4) of this section.

(e) *Applicability date.*—These regulations are applicable to returns filed for partnership taxable years beginning after November 2, 2015 and before January 1, 2018. [Reg. § 301.9100-22.]

☐ [*T.D.* 9839, 8-6-2018.]

USE OF MAGNETIC TAPES

[Reg. § 1.9101-1]

§ 1.9101-1. Permission to submit information required by certain returns and statements on magnetic tape.—In any case where the use of a Form 1087 or 1099 is required by the regulations under this part for the purpose of making a return or reporting information, such requirement may be satisfied by submitting the information required by such form on magnetic tape or by other media, provided that the prior consent of the Commissioner or other authorized officer or employee of the Internal Revenue Service has been obtained. Applications for such

consent must be filed in accordance with procedures established by the Internal Revenue Service. In any case where the use of Form W-2 is required for the purpose of making a return or reporting information, such requirement may be satisfied by submitting the information required by such form on magnetic tape or other approved media, provided that the prior consent of the Commissioner of Social Security (or other authorized officer or employee thereof) has been obtained. [Reg. § 1.9101-1.]

☐ [*T.D.* 6883, 5-2-66. *Amended by T.D.* 7580, 12-20-78.]

GROUP HEALTH PLAN REQUIREMENTS

[Reg. § 54.9801-1]

§ 54.9801-1. Basis and scope.—(a) *Statutory basis.*—This section and sections 54.9801-2 through 54.9801-6, 54.9802-1, 54.9802-2, 54.9802-3T, 54.9811-1, 54.9812-1T, 54.9831-1, and 54.9833-1 (portability sections) implement Chapter 100 of Subtitle K of the Internal Revenue Code of 1986.

(b) *Scope.*—A group health plan or health insurance issuer offering group health insurance coverage may provide greater rights to participants and beneficiaries than those set forth in the portability and market reform sections of this part 54. This part 54 sets forth minimum requirements for group health plans and group health insurance issuers offering group health insurance coverage concerning certain consumer protections of the Health Insurance Portability and Accountability Act (HIPAA), including special enrollment periods and the prohibition against discrimination based on a health factor, as amended by the Patient Protection and Affordable Care Act (Affordable Care Act). Other consumer protection provisions, including other protections provided by the Affordable Care Act and the Mental Health Parity and Addiction Equity Act, are set forth in this part 54.

(c) *Similar Requirements under the Employee Retirement Income Security Act and the Public Health Service Act.*—Sections 701, 702, 703, 711, 712, 732, and 733 of the Employee Retirement Income Security Act of 1974 and sections 2701, 2702, 2704, 2705, 2721, and 2791 of the Public Health Service Act impose requirements similar to those imposed under Chapter 100 of Subtitle K with respect to health insurance issuers offering group health insurance coverage. See 29 CFR Part 2590 and 45 CFR Parts 144, 146, and 148. See also Part B of Title XXVII of the Public Health Service Act and 45 CFR Part 148 for other rules applicable to

health insurance offered in the individual market (defined in § 54.9801-2). [Reg. § 54.9801-1.]

☐ [*T.D.* 9166, 12-29-2004. *Amended by T.D.* 9299, 12-12-2006; *T.D.* 9427, 10-17-2008; *T.D.* 9464, 10-1-2009 *and T.D.* 9656, 2-20-2014.]

[Reg. § 54.9801-2]

§ 54.9801-2. Definitions.—Unless otherwise provided, the definitions in this section govern in applying the provisions of sections 9801 through 9815 and 9831 through 9833.

Affiliation period means a period of time that must expire before health insurance coverage provided by an HMO becomes effective, and during which the HMO is not required to provide benefits.

COBRA definitions:

(1) *COBRA* means Title X of the Consolidated Omnibus Budget Reconciliation Act of 1985, as amended.

(2) *COBRA continuation coverage* means coverage, under a group health plan, that satisfies an applicable COBRA continuation provision.

(3) *COBRA continuation provision* means section 4980B (other than paragraph (f)(1) of section 4980B insofar as it relates to pediatric vaccines), sections 601-608 of ERISA, or Title XXII of the PHS Act.

(4) *Exhaustion of COBRA continuation coverage* means that an individual's COBRA continuation coverage ceases for any reason other than either failure of the individual to pay premiums on a timely basis, or for cause (such as making a fraudulent claim or an intentional misrepresentation of a material fact in connection with the plan). An individual is considered to have exhausted COBRA continuation coverage if such coverage ceases —

(i) Due to the failure of the employer or other responsible entity to remit premiums on a timely basis;

(ii) When the individual no longer resides, lives, or works in the service area of an HMO or similar program (whether or not within the choice of the individual) and there is no other COBRA continuation coverage available to the individual; or

(iii) When the individual incurs a claim that would meet or exceed a lifetime limit on all benefits and there is no other COBRA continuation coverage available to the individual.

Condition means a *medical condition.*

Creditable coverage means *creditable coverage* within the meaning of § 54.9801-4(a).

Dependent means any individual who is or may become eligible for coverage under the terms of a group health plan because of a relationship to a participant.

Employee Retirement Income Security Act of 1974 (ERISA) means the Employee Retirement Income Security Act of 1974, as amended (29 U.S.C. 1001 et seq.).

Enroll means to become covered for benefits under a group health plan (that is, when coverage becomes effective), without regard to when the individual may have completed or filed any forms that are required in order to become covered under the plan. For this purpose, an individual who has health coverage under a group health plan is enrolled in the plan regardless of whether the individual elects coverage, the individual is a dependent who becomes covered as a result of an election by a participant, or the individual becomes covered without an election.

Enrollment date means the first day of coverage or, if there is a waiting period, the first day of the waiting period. If an individual receiving benefits under a group health plan changes benefit packages, or if the plan changes group health insurance issuers, the individual's enrollment date does not change.

Excepted benefits means the benefits described as excepted in § 54.9831(c).

First day of coverage means, in the case of an individual covered for benefits under a group health plan, the first day of coverage under the plan and, in the case of an individual covered by health insurance coverage in the individual market, the first day of coverage under the policy or contract.

Genetic information has the meaning given the term in § 54.9802-3T(a)(3).

Group health insurance coverage means health insurance coverage offered in connection with a group health plan.

Group health plan or *plan* means a *group health plan* within the meaning of § 54.9831-1(a).

Group market means the market for health insurance coverage offered in connection with a group health plan. (However, certain very small plans may be treated as being in the individual market, rather than the group market; see the definition of *individual market* in this section.)

Health insurance coverage means benefits consisting of medical care (provided directly, through insurance or reimbursement, or otherwise) under any hospital or medical service policy or certificate, hospital or medical service plan contract, or HMO contract offered by a health insurance issuer. Health insurance coverage includes group health insurance coverage, individual health insurance coverage, and short-term, limited-duration insurance. However, benefits described in § 54.9831(c)(2) are not treated as benefits consisting of medical care.

Health insurance issuer or *issuer* means an insurance company, insurance service, or insurance organization (including an HMO) that is required to be licensed to engage in the business of insurance in a state and that is subject to state law that regulates insurance (within the meaning of section 514(b)(2) of ERISA). Such term does not include a group health plan.

Health maintenance organization or *HMO* means—

(1) A federally qualified health maintenance organization (as defined in section 1301(a) of the PHS Act);

(2) An organization recognized under state law as a health maintenance organization; or

(3) A similar organization regulated under state law for solvency in the same manner and to the same extent as such a health maintenance organization.

Individual health insurance coverage means health insurance coverage offered to individuals in the individual market, but does not include short-term, limited-duration insurance. Individual health insurance coverage can include dependent coverage.

Individual market means the market for health insurance coverage offered to individuals other than in connection with a group health plan. Unless a state elects otherwise in accordance with section 2791(e)(1)(B)(ii) of the PHS Act, such term also includes coverage offered in connection with a group health plan that has fewer than two participants who are current employees on the first day of the plan year.

Issuer means a *health insurance issuer.*

Late enrollee means an individual whose enrollment in a plan is a late enrollment.

Late enrollment means enrollment of an individual under a group health plan other than on the earliest date on which coverage can become effective for the individual under the terms of the plan; or through special enrollment. (For rules relating to special enrollment, see § 54.9801-6.) If an individual ceases to be eligible for coverage under a plan, and then subsequently becomes eligible for coverage under the plan, only the individual's most recent period of eligibility is taken into account in determining whether the individual is a late enrollee under the plan with respect to the most recent period of coverage. Similar rules apply if an individual again becomes eligible for coverage following a suspension of coverage that applied generally under the plan.

Medical care has the meaning given such term by section 213(d), determined without regard to section 213(d)(1)(C) and so much of section 213(d)(1)(D) as relates to qualified long-term care insurance.

Medical condition or *condition* means any condition, whether physical or mental, including, but not limited to, any condition resulting from illness, injury (whether or not the injury is accidental), pregnancy, or congenital malformation. However, genetic information is not a condition.

Participant means *participant* within the meaning of section 3(7) of ERISA.

Placement, or being placed, for adoption means the assumption and retention of a legal obligation for total or partial support of a child by a person with whom the child has been placed in anticipation of the child's adoption. The child's placement for adoption with such person ends upon the termination of such legal obligation.

Plan year means the year that is designated as the plan year in the plan document of a group health plan, except that if the plan document does not designate a plan year or if there is no plan document, the plan year is —

(1) The deductible or limit year used under the plan;

(2) If the plan does not impose deductibles or limits on a yearly basis, then the plan year is the policy year;

(3) If the plan does not impose deductibles or limits on a yearly basis, and either the plan is not insured or the insurance policy is not renewed on an annual basis, then the plan year is the employer's taxable year; or

(4) In any other case, the plan year is the calendar year.

Preexisting condition exclusion means a limitation or exclusion of benefits (including a denial of coverage) based on the fact that the condition was present before the effective date of coverage (or if coverage is denied, the date of the denial) under a group health plan or group or individual health insurance coverage (or other coverage provided to Federally eligible individuals pursuant to 45 CFR part 148), whether or not any medical advice, diagnosis, care, or treatment was recommended or received before that day. A preexisting condition exclusion includes any limitation or exclusion of benefits (including a denial of coverage) applicable to an individual as a result of information relating to an individual's health status before the individual's effective date of coverage (or if coverage is denied, the date of the denial) under a group health plan, or group or individual health insurance coverage (or other coverage provided to Federally eligible individuals pursuant to 45 CFR part 148), such as a condition identified as a result of a pre-enrollment questionnaire or physical examination given to the individual, or review of medical records relating to the pre-enrollment period.

Public health plan means *public health plan* within the meaning of § 54.9801-4(a)(1)(ix).

Public Health Service Act (PHS Act) means the Public Health Service Act (42 U.S.C. 201, *et seq.*).

Short-term, limited-duration insurance means health insurance coverage provided pursuant to a contract with an issuer that:

(1) Has an expiration date specified in the contract that is less than 12 months after the original effective date of the contract and, taking into account renewals or extensions, has a duration of no longer than 36 months in total;

(2) With respect to policies having a coverage start date before January 1, 2019, displays prominently in the contract and in any application materials provided in connection with enrollment in such coverage in at least 14 point type the language in the following Notice 1, excluding the heading "Notice 1," with any additional information required by applicable state law:

Notice 1:

This coverage is not required to comply with certain federal market requirements for health insurance, principally those contained in the Affordable Care Act. Be sure to check your policy carefully to make sure you are aware of any exclusions or limitations regarding coverage of preexisting conditions or health benefits (such as hospitalization, emergency services, maternity care, preventive care, prescription drugs, and mental health and substance use disorder services). Your policy might also have lifetime and/or annual dollar limits on health benefits. If this coverage expires or you lose eligibility for this coverage, you might have to wait until an open enrollment period to get other health insurance coverage. Also, this coverage is not "minimum essential coverage." If you don't have minimum essential coverage for any month in 2018, you may have to make a payment when you file your tax return unless you qualify for an exemption from the requirement that you have health coverage for that month.;

(3) With respect to policies having a coverage start date on or after January 1, 2019, displays prominently in the contract and in any application materials provided in connection with enrollment in such coverage in at least 14 point type the language in the following Notice 2, excluding the heading "Notice 2," with any additional information required by applicable state law:

Notice 2:

This coverage is not required to comply with certain federal market requirements for health insurance, principally those contained in the Affordable Care Act. Be sure to check your policy carefully to make sure you are aware of any exclusions or limitations regarding coverage of preexisting conditions or health benefits (such as hospitalization, emergency services, maternity care, preventive care, prescription drugs, and mental health and substance use disorder services). Your policy might also have lifetime and/or annual dollar limits on health benefits. If this coverage expires or you lose eligibility for this coverage, you might have to wait until an open enrollment period to get other health insurance coverage.

(4) If a court holds the 36-month maximum duration provision set forth in paragraph (1) of this definition or its applicability to any person

or circumstances invalid, the remaining provisions and their applicability to other people or circumstances shall continue in effect.

Significant break in coverage means a *significant break in coverage* within the meaning of § 54.9801-4(b)(2)(iii).

Special enrollment means enrollment in a group health plan under the rights described in § 54.9801-6 or in group health insurance coverage under the rights described in 29 CFR 2590.701-6 or 45 CFR 146.117.

State health benefits risk pool means a *state health benefits risk pool* within the meaning of § 54.9801-4(a)(1)(vii).

Travel insurance means insurance coverage for personal risks incident to planned travel, which may include, but is not limited to, interruption or cancellation of trip or event, loss of baggage or personal effects, damages to accommodations or rental vehicles, and sickness, accident, disability, or death occurring during travel, provided that the health benefits are not offered on a stand-alone basis and are incidental to other coverage. For this purpose, the term travel insurance does not include major medical plans that provide comprehensive medical protection for travelers with trips lasting 6 months or longer, including, for example, those working overseas as an expatriate or military personnel being deployed.

Waiting period means *waiting period* within the meaning of § 54.9815-2708(b).

[Reg. § 54.9801-2.]

☐ [*T.D.* 9166, 12-29-2004. *Amended by T.D.* 9299, 12-12-2006; *T.D.* 9427, 10-17-2008; *T.D.* 9464, 10-1-2009; *T.D.* 9491, 6-22-2010, *T.D.* 9656, 2-20-2014, *T.D.* 9744, 11-13-2015, *T.D.* 9791, 10-28-2016 *and T.D.* 9837, 8-1-2018.]

[Reg. § 54.9801-3]

§ 54.9801-3. Limitations on preexisting condition exclusion period.—(a) *Preexisting condition exclusion defined.*—(1) A *preexisting condition exclusion* means a *preexisting condition exclusion* within the meaning of § 54.9801-2.

(2) *Examples.*—The rules of this paragraph (a)(1) are illustrated by the following examples:

Example 1. (i) *Facts.* A group health plan provides benefits solely through an insurance policy offered by Issuer S. At the expiration of the policy, the plan switches coverage to a policy offered by Issuer T. Issuer T's policy excludes benefits for any prosthesis if the body part was lost before the effective date of coverage under the policy.

(ii) *Conclusion.* In this *Example 1,* the exclusion of benefits for any prosthesis if the body part was lost before the effective date of coverage is a preexisting condition exclusion because it operates to exclude benefits for a condition based on the fact that the condition was present before the effective date of coverage under the

policy. The exclusion of benefits, therefore, is prohibited.

Example 2. (i) *Facts.* A group health plan provides coverage for cosmetic surgery in cases of accidental injury, but only if the injury occurred while the individual was covered under the plan.

(ii) *Conclusion.* In this *Example 2,* the plan provision excluding cosmetic surgery benefits for individuals injured before enrolling in the plan is a preexisting condition exclusion because it operates to exclude benefits relating to a condition based on the fact that the condition was present before the effective date of coverage. The plan provision, therefore, is prohibited.

Example 3. (i) *Facts.* A group health plan provides coverage for the treatment of diabetes, generally not subject to any requirement to obtain an approval for a treatment plan. However, if an individual was diagnosed with diabetes before the effective date of coverage under the plan, diabetes coverage is subject to a requirement to obtain approval of a treatment plan in advance.

(ii) *Conclusion.* In this *Example 3,* the requirement to obtain advance approval of a treatment plan is a preexisting condition exclusion because it limits benefits for a condition based on the fact that the condition was present before the effective date of coverage. The plan provision, therefore, is prohibited.

Example 4. (i) *Facts.* A group health plan provides coverage for three infertility treatments. The plan counts against the three-treatment limit benefits provided under prior health coverage.

(ii) *Conclusion.* In this *Example 4,* counting benefits for a specific condition provided under prior health coverage against a treatment limit for that condition is a preexisting condition exclusion because it operates to limit benefits for a condition based on the fact that the condition was present before the effective date of coverage. The plan provision, therefore, is prohibited.

Example 5. (i) *Facts.* When an individual's coverage begins under a group health plan, the individual generally becomes eligible for all benefits. However, benefits for pregnancy are not available until the individual has been covered under the plan for 12 months.

(ii) *Conclusion.* In this *Example 5,* the requirement to be covered under the plan for 12 months to be eligible for pregnancy benefits is a subterfuge for a preexisting condition exclusion because it is designed to exclude benefits for a condition (pregnancy) that arose before the effective date of coverage. The plan provision, therefore, is prohibited.

Example 6. (i) *Facts.* A group health plan provides coverage for medically necessary items and services, generally including treatment of heart conditions. However, the plan does not cover those same items and services when used for treatment of congenital heart conditions.

(ii) *Conclusion.* In this *Example 6*, the exclusion of coverage for treatment of congenital heart conditions is a preexisting condition exclusion because it operates to exclude benefits relating to a condition based on the fact that the condition was present before the effective date of coverage. The plan provision, therefore, is prohibited.

Example 7. (i) *Facts.* A group health plan generally provides coverage for medically necessary items and services. However, the plan excludes coverage for the treatment of cleft palate.

(ii) *Conclusion.* In this *Example 7*, the exclusion of coverage for treatment of cleft palate is not a preexisting condition exclusion because the exclusion applies regardless of when the condition arose relative to the effective date of coverage. The plan provision, therefore, is not prohibited. (But see 45 CFR 147.150, which may require coverage of cleft palate as an essential health benefit for health insurance coverage in the individual or small group market, depending on the essential health benefits benchmark plan as defined in 45 CFR 156.20).

Example 8. (i) *Facts.* A group health plan provides coverage for treatment of cleft palate, but only if the individual being treated has been continuously covered under the plan from the date of birth.

(ii) *Conclusion.* In this *Example 8*, the exclusion of coverage for treatment of cleft palate for individuals who have not been covered under the plan from the date of birth operates to exclude benefits in relation to a condition based on the fact that the condition was present before the effective date of coverage. The plan provision, therefore, is prohibited.

(b) *General rules.—See* section 2704 of the Public Health Service Act, incorporated into section 9815 of the Code, and its implementing regulations for rules prohibiting the imposition of a preexisting condition exclusion. [Reg. §54.9801-3.]

☐ *[T.D. 9166, 12-29-2004. Amended by T.D. 9491, 6-22-2010, T.D. 9656, 2-20-2014 and T.D. 9744, 11-13-2015.]*

[Reg. §54.9801-4]

§54.9801-4. Rules relating to creditable coverage.—(a) *General rules.*—(1) *Creditable coverage.*—For purposes of this section, except as provided in paragraph (a)(2) of this section, the term *creditable coverage* means coverage of an individual under any of the following:

(i) A group health plan as defined in §54.9831-1(a).

(ii) Health insurance coverage as defined in §54.9801-2 (whether or not the entity offering the coverage is subject to Chapter 100 of Subtitle K, and without regard to whether the coverage is offered in the group market, the individual market, or otherwise).

(iii) Part A or B of Title XVIII of the Social Security Act (Medicare).

(iv) Title XIX of the Social Security Act (Medicaid), other than coverage consisting solely of benefits under section 1928 of the Social Security Act (the program for distribution of pediatric vaccines).

(v) Title 10 U.S.C. Chapter 55 (medical and dental care for members and certain former members of the uniformed services, and for their dependents; for purposes of Title 10 U.S.C. Chapter 55, *uniformed services* means the armed forces and the Commissioned Corps of the National Oceanic and Atmospheric Administration and of the Public Health Service).

(vi) A medical care program of the Indian Health Service or of a tribal organization.

(vii) A state health benefits risk pool. For purposes of this section, a *state health benefits risk pool* means —

(A) An organization qualifying under section 501(c)(26);

(B) A qualified high risk pool described in section 2744(c)(2) of the PHS Act; or

(C) Any other arrangement sponsored by a state, the membership composition of which is specified by the state and which is established and maintained primarily to provide health coverage for individuals who are residents of such state and who, by reason of the existence or history of a medical condition —

(1) Are unable to acquire medical care coverage for such condition through insurance or from an HMO, or

(2) Are able to acquire such coverage only at a rate which is substantially in excess of the rate for such coverage through the membership organization.

(viii) A health plan offered under Title 5 U.S.C. Chapter 89 (the Federal Employees Health Benefits Program).

(ix) A public health plan. For purposes of this section, a *public health plan* means any plan established or maintained by a state, the U.S. government, a foreign country, or any political subdivision of a state, the U.S. government, or a foreign country that provides health coverage to individuals who are enrolled in the plan.

(x) A health benefit plan under section 5(e) of the Peace Corps Act (22 U.S.C. 2504(e)).

(xi) Title XXI of the Social Security Act (State Children's Health Insurance Program).

(2) *Excluded coverage.*—Creditable coverage does not include coverage of solely excepted benefits (described in §54.9831-1).

(b) *Counting creditable coverage rules superseded by prohibition on preexisting condition exclusion.*— *See* section 2704 of the Public Health Service Act, incorporated into section 9815 of the Code, and its implementing regulations for rules prohibiting the imposition of a preexisting condition exclusion. [Reg. §54.9801-4.]

☐ *[T.D. 9166, 12-29-2004. Amended by T.D. 9656, 2-20-2014.]*

>>→ *Caution: Reg. §54.9801-5, below, prior to amendment by T.D. 9656, applies before December 31, 2014.*

[Reg. §54.9801-5]

§54.9801-5. Evidence of creditable coverage.—(a) *Certificate of creditable coverage.*—(1) *Entities required to provide certificate.*—(i) *In general.*—A group health plan is required to furnish certificates of creditable coverage in accordance with this paragraph (a). (See section 701(e) of ERISA and section 2701(e) of the PHS Act, under which this obligation is also imposed on each health insurance issuer offering group health insurance coverage under the plan.)

(ii) *Duplicate certificates not required.*—An entity required to provide a certificate under this paragraph (a) with respect to an individual satisfies that requirement if another party provides the certificate, but only to the extent that the certificate contains the information required in paragraph (a)(3) of this section. For example, a group health plan is deemed to have satisfied the certification requirement with respect to a participant or beneficiary if any other entity actually provides a certificate that includes the information required under paragraph (a)(3) of this section with respect to the participant or beneficiary.

(iii) *Special rule for group health plans.*—To the extent coverage under a plan consists of group health insurance coverage, the plan satisfies the certification requirements under this paragraph (a) if any issuer offering the coverage is required to provide the certificates pursuant to an agreement between the plan and the issuer. For example, if there is an agreement between an issuer and an employer sponsoring a plan under which the issuer agrees to provide certificates for individuals covered under the plan, and the issuer fails to provide a certificate to an individual when the plan would have been required to provide one under this paragraph (a), then the plan does not violate the certification requirements of this paragraph (a) (though the issuer would have violated the certification requirements pursuant to section 701(e) of ERISA and section 2701(e) of the PHS Act).

(iv) *Special rules relating to issuers providing coverage under a plan.*—(A)(1) *Responsibility of issuer for coverage period.*—See 29 CFR 2590.701-5 and 45 CFR 146.115, under which an issuer is not required to provide information regarding coverage provided to an individual by another party.

(2) *Example.*—The rule referenced by this paragraph (a)(1)(iv)(A) is illustrated by the following example:

Example. (i) *Facts.* A plan offers coverage with an HMO option from one issuer and an indemnity option from a different issuer. The HMO has not entered into an agreement with the plan to provide certificates as permitted under paragraph (a)(1)(iii) of this section.

(ii) *Conclusion.* In this *Example,* if an employee switches from the indemnity option to the HMO option and later ceases to be covered

under the plan, any certificate provided by the HMO is not required to provide information regarding the employee's coverage under the indemnity option.

(B)(1) *Cessation of issuer coverage prior to cessation of coverage under a plan.*—If an individual's coverage under an issuer's policy or contract ceases before the individual's coverage under the plan ceases, the issuer is required (under section 701(e) of ERISA and section 2701(e) of the PHS Act) to provide sufficient information to the plan (or to another party designated by the plan) to enable the plan (or other party), after cessation of the individual's coverage under the plan, to provide a certificate that reflects the period of coverage under the policy or contract. By providing that information to the plan, the issuer satisfies its obligation to provide an automatic certificate for that period of creditable coverage with respect to the individual under paragraph (a)(2)(ii) of this section. The issuer, however, must still provide a certificate upon request as required under paragraph (a)(2)(iii) of this section. In addition, the issuer is required to cooperate with the plan in responding to any request made under paragraph (b)(2) of this section (relating to the alternative method of counting creditable coverage). Moreover, if the individual's coverage under the plan ceases at the time the individual's coverage under the issuer's policy or contract ceases, the issuer must still provide an automatic certificate under paragraph (a)(2)(ii) of this section. If an individual's coverage under an issuer's policy or contract ceases on the effective date for changing enrollment options under the plan, the issuer may presume (absent information to the contrary) that the individual's coverage under the plan continues. Therefore, the issuer is required to provide information to the plan in accordance with this paragraph (a)(1)(iv)(B)(1) (and is not required to provide an automatic certificate under paragraph (a)(2)(ii) of this section).

(2) *Example.*—The rule of this paragraph (a)(1)(iv)(B) is illustrated by the following example:

Example. (i) *Facts.* A group health plan provides coverage under an HMO option and an indemnity option through different issuers, and only allows employees to switch on each January 1. Neither the HMO nor the indemnity issuer has entered into an agreement with the plan to provide certificates as permitted under paragraph (a)(1)(iii) of this section.

(ii) *Conclusion.* In this *Example,* if an employee switches from the indemnity option to the HMO option on January 1, the indemnity issuer must provide the plan (or a person designated by the plan) with appropriate information with respect to the individual's coverage with the indemnity issuer. However, if the individual's coverage with the indemnity issuer ceases at a date other than January 1, the issuer is

>>>→ *Caution: Reg. §54.9801-5, below, prior to amendment by T.D. 9656, applies before December 31, 2014.*

instead required to provide the individual with an automatic certificate.

(2) *Individuals for whom certificate must be provided; timing of issuance.*—(i) *Individuals.*—A certificate must be provided, without charge, for participants or dependents who are or were covered under a group health plan upon the occurrence of any of the events described in paragraph (a)(2)(ii) or (iii) of this section.

(ii) *Issuance of automatic certificates.*—The certificates described in this paragraph (a)(2)(ii) are referred to as automatic certificates.

(A) *Qualified beneficiaries upon a qualifying event.*—In the case of an individual who is a qualified beneficiary (as defined in section 4980B(g)(3)) entitled to elect COBRA continuation coverage, an automatic certificate is required to be provided at the time the individual would lose coverage under the plan in the absence of COBRA continuation coverage or alternative coverage elected instead of COBRA continuation coverage. A plan satisfies this requirement if it provides the automatic certificate no later than the time a notice is required to be furnished for a qualifying event under section 4980B(f)(6) (relating to notices required under COBRA).

(B) *Other individuals when coverage ceases.*—In the case of an individual who is not a qualified beneficiary entitled to elect COBRA continuation coverage, an automatic certificate must be provided at the time the individual ceases to be covered under the plan. A plan satisfies the requirement to provide an automatic certificate at the time the individual ceases to be covered if it provides the automatic certificate within a reasonable time after coverage ceases (or after the expiration of any grace period for nonpayment of premiums).

(1) The cessation of temporary continuation coverage (TCC) under Title 5 U.S.C. Chapter 89 (the Federal Employees Health Benefit Program) is a cessation of coverage upon which an automatic certificate must be provided.

(2) In the case of an individual who is entitled to elect to continue coverage under a state program similar to COBRA and who receives the automatic certificate not later than the time a notice is required to be furnished under the state program, the certificate is deemed to be provided within a reasonable time after coverage ceases under the plan.

(3) If an individual's coverage ceases due to the operation of a lifetime limit on all benefits, coverage is considered to cease for purposes of this paragraph (a)(2)(ii)(B) on the earliest date that a claim is denied due to the operation of the lifetime limit.

(C) *Qualified beneficiaries when COBRA ceases.*—In the case of an individual who is a qualified beneficiary and has elected COBRA continuation coverage (or whose coverage has continued after the individual became entitled to elect COBRA continuation coverage), an automatic certificate is to be provided at the time the individual's coverage under the plan ceases. A plan satisfies this requirement if it provides the automatic certificate within a reasonable time after coverage ceases (or after the expiration of any grace period for nonpayment of premiums). An automatic certificate is required to be provided to such an individual regardless of whether the individual has previously received an automatic certificate under paragraph (a)(2)(ii)(A) of this section.

(iii) *Any individual upon request.*—A certificate must be provided in response to a request made by, or on behalf of, an individual at any time while the individual is covered under a plan and up to 24 months after coverage ceases. Thus, for example, a plan in which an individual enrolls may, if authorized by the individual, request a certificate of the individual's creditable coverage on behalf of the individual from a plan in which the individual was formerly enrolled. After the request is received, a plan or issuer is required to provide the certificate by the earliest date that the plan, acting in a reasonable and prompt fashion, can provide the certificate. A certificate is required to be provided under this paragraph (a)(2)(iii) even if the individual has previously received a certificate under this paragraph (a)(2)(iii) or an automatic certificate under paragraph (a)(2)(ii) of this section.

(iv) *Examples.*—The rules of this paragraph (a)(2) are illustrated by the following examples:

Example 1. (i) *Facts.* Individual *A* terminates employment with Employer *Q*. *A* is a qualified beneficiary entitled to elect COBRA continuation coverage under Employer *Q's* group health plan. A notice of the rights provided under COBRA is typically furnished to qualified beneficiaries under the plan within 10 days after a covered employee terminates employment.

(ii) *Conclusion.* In this *Example 1*, the automatic certificate may be provided at the same time that *A* is provided the COBRA notice.

Example 2. (i) *Facts.* Same facts as *Example 1*, except that the automatic certificate for *A* is not completed by the time the COBRA notice is furnished to *A*.

(ii) *Conclusion.* In this *Example 2*, the automatic certificate may be provided after the COBRA notice but must be provided within the period permitted by law for the delivery of notices under COBRA.

Example 3. (i) *Facts.* Employer *R* maintains an insured group health plan. *R* has never had 20 employees and thus *R's* plan is not subject to the COBRA continuation provisions. However, *R* is in a state that has a state program similar to COBRA. *B* terminates employment with *R* and loses coverage under *R's* plan.

⋙→ *Caution: Reg. §54.9801-5, below, prior to amendment by T.D. 9656, applies before December 31, 2014.*

(ii) *Conclusion.* In this *Example 3*, the automatic certificate must be provided not later than the time a notice is required to be furnished under the state program.

Example 4. (i) *Facts.* Individual *C* terminates employment with Employer *S* and receives both a notice of *C's* rights under COBRA and an automatic certificate. *C* elects COBRA continuation coverage under Employer *S's* group health plan. After four months of COBRA continuation coverage and the expiration of a 30-day grace period, *S's* group health plan determines that *C's* COBRA continuation coverage has ceased due to a failure to make a timely payment for continuation coverage.

(ii) *Conclusion.* In this *Example 4*, the plan must provide an updated automatic certificate to *C* within a reasonable time after the end of the grace period.

Example 5. (i) *Facts.* Individual *D* is currently covered under the group health plan of Employer *T*. *D* requests a certificate, as permitted under paragraph (a)(2)(iii) of this section. Under the procedure for *T's* plan, certificates are mailed (by first class mail) 7 business days following receipt of the request. This date reflects the earliest date that the plan, acting in a reasonable and prompt fashion, can provide certificates.

(ii) *Conclusion.* In this *Example 5*, the plan's procedure satisfies paragraph (a)(2)(iii) of this section.

(3) *Form and content of certificate.*— (i) *Written certificate.*—(A) *In general.*—Except as provided in paragraph (a)(3)(i)(B) of this section, the certificate must be provided in writing (including any form approved by the Secretary as a writing).

(B) *Other permissible forms.*—No written certificate is required to be provided under this paragraph (a) with respect to a particular event described in paragraph (a)(2)(ii) or (iii) of this section, if —

(1) An individual who is entitled to receive the certificate requests that the certificate be sent to another plan or issuer instead of to the individual;

(2) The plan or issuer that would otherwise receive the certificate agrees to accept the information in this paragraph (a)(3) through means other than a written certificate (such as by telephone); and

(3) The receiving plan or issuer receives the information from the sending plan or issuer through such means within the time required under paragraph (a)(2) of this section.

(ii) *Required information.*—The certificate must include the following —

(A) The date the certificate is issued;

(B) The name of the group health plan that provided the coverage described in the certificate;

(C) The name of the participant or dependent with respect to whom the certificate applies, and any other information necessary for the plan providing the coverage specified in the certificate to identify the individual, such as the individual's identification number under the plan and the name of the participant if the certificate is for (or includes) a dependent;

(D) The name, address, and telephone number of the plan administrator or issuer required to provide the certificate;

(E) The telephone number to call for further information regarding the certificate (if different from paragraph (a)(3)(ii)(D) of this section);

(F) Either —

(1) A statement that an individual has at least 18 months (for this purpose, 546 days is deemed to be 18 months) of creditable coverage, disregarding days of creditable coverage before a significant break in coverage, or

(2) The date any waiting period (and affiliation period, if applicable) began and the date creditable coverage began;

(G) The date creditable coverage ended, unless the certificate indicates that creditable coverage is continuing as of the date of the certificate; and

(H) An educational statement regarding HIPAA, which explains:

(1) The restrictions on the ability of a plan or issuer to impose a preexisting condition exclusion (including an individual's ability to reduce a preexisting condition exclusion by creditable coverage);

(2) Special enrollment rights;

(3) The prohibitions against discrimination based on any health factor;

(4) The right to individual health coverage;

(5) The fact that state law may require issuers to provide additional protections to individuals in that state; and

(6) Where to get more information.

(iii) *Periods of coverage under the certificate.*—If an automatic certificate is provided pursuant to paragraph (a)(2)(ii) of this section, the period that must be included on the certificate is the last period of continuous coverage ending on the date coverage ceased. If an individual requests a certificate pursuant to paragraph (a)(2)(iii) of this section, the certificate provided must include each period of continuous coverage ending within the 24-month period ending on the date of the request (or continuing on the date of the request). A separate certificate may be provided for each such period of continuous coverage.

(iv) *Combining information for families.*—A certificate may provide information with respect to both a participant and the participant's dependents if the information is identical for each indi-

⟫⟫→ *Caution: Reg. §54.9801-5, below, prior to amendment by T.D. 9656, applies before December 31, 2014.*

vidual. If the information is not identical, certificates may be provided on one form if the form provides all the required information for each individual and separately states the information that is not identical.

(v) *Model certificate.*—The requirements of paragraph (a)(3)(ii) of this section are satisfied if the plan provides a certificate in accordance with a model certificate authorized by the Secretary.

(vi) *Excepted benefits; categories of benefits.*—No certificate is required to be furnished with respect to excepted benefits described in § 54.9831-1(c). In addition, the information in the certificate regarding coverage is not required to specify categories of benefits described in § 54.9801-4(c) (relating to the alternative method of counting creditable coverage). However, if excepted benefits are provided concurrently with other creditable coverage (so that the coverage does not consist solely of excepted benefits), information concerning the benefits may be required to be disclosed under paragraph (b) of this section.

(4) *Procedures.*—(i) *Method of delivery.*—The certificate is required to be provided to each individual described in paragraph (a)(2) of this section or an entity requesting the certificate on behalf of the individual. The certificate may be provided by first-class mail. If the certificate or certificates are provided to the participant and the participant's spouse at the participant's last known address, then the requirements of this paragraph (a)(4) are satisfied with respect to all individuals residing at that address. If a dependent's last known address is different than the participant's last known address, a separate certificate is required to be provided to the dependent at the dependent's last known address. If separate certificates are being provided by mail to individuals who reside at the same address, separate mailings of each certificate are not required.

(ii) *Procedure for requesting certificates.*—A plan or issuer must establish a written procedure for individuals to request and receive certificates pursuant to paragraph (a)(2)(iii) of this section. The written procedure must include all contact information necessary to request a certificate (such as name and phone number or address).

(iii) *Designated recipients.*—If an automatic certificate is required to be provided under paragraph (a)(2)(ii) of this section, and the individual entitled to receive the certificate designates another individual or entity to receive the certificate, the plan or issuer responsible for providing the certificate is permitted to provide the certificate to the designated individual or entity. If a certificate is required to be provided upon request under paragraph (a)(2)(iii) of this section and the individual entitled to receive the certificate designates another individual or entity to receive the certificate, the plan or issuer respon-

sible for providing the certificate is required to provide the certificate to the designated individual or entity.

(5) *Special rules concerning dependent coverage.*—(i)(A) *Reasonable efforts.*—A plan is required to use reasonable efforts to determine any information needed for a certificate relating to dependent coverage. In any case in which an automatic certificate is required to be furnished with respect to a dependent under paragraph (a)(2)(ii) of this section, no individual certificate is required to be furnished until the plan knows (or making reasonable efforts should know) of the dependent's cessation of coverage under the plan.

(B) *Example.*—The rules of this paragraph (a)(5)(i) are illustrated by the following example:

Example. (i) *Facts.* A group health plan covers employees and their dependents. The plan annually requests all employees to provide updated information regarding dependents, including the specific date on which an employee has a new dependent or on which a person ceases to be a dependent of the employee.

(ii) *Conclusion.* In this *Example*, the plan has satisfied the standard in this paragraph (a)(5)(i) of this section that it make reasonable efforts to determine the cessation of dependents' coverage and the related dependent coverage information.

(ii) *Special rules for demonstrating coverage.*—If a certificate furnished by a plan or issuer does not provide the name of any dependent covered by the certificate, the procedures described in paragraph (c)(5) of this section may be used to demonstrate dependent status. In addition, these procedures may be used to demonstrate that a child was covered under any creditable coverage within 30 days after birth, adoption, or placement for adoption. See also § 54.9801-3(b), under which such a child cannot be subject to a preexisting condition exclusion.

(6) *Special certification rules for entities not subject to Chapter 100 of Subtitle K.*—(i) *Issuers.*—For rules requiring that issuers in the group and individual markets provide certificates consistent with the rules in this section, see section 701(e) of ERISA and sections 2701(e), 2721(b)(1)(B), and 2743 of the PHS Act.

(ii) *Other entities.*—For special rules requiring that certain other entities not subject to Chapter 100 of Subtitle K provide certificates consistent with the rules in this section, see section 2791(a)(3) of the PHS Act applicable to entities described in sections 2701(c)(1)(C), (D), (E), and (F) of the PHS Act (relating to Medicare, Medicaid, TRICARE, and Indian Health Service), section 2721(b)(1)(A) of the PHS Act applicable to nonfederal governmental plans generally, and section 2721(b)(2)(C)(ii) of the PHS Act applicable to nonfederal governmental plans that elect

⟫⟫→ *Caution: Reg. §54.9801-5, below, prior to amendment by T.D. 9656, applies before December 31, 2014.*

to be excluded from the requirements of Subparts 1 through 3 of Part A of Title XXVII of the PHS Act.

(b) *Disclosure of coverage to a plan or issuer using the alternative method of counting creditable coverage.*—(1) *In general.*—After an individual provides a certificate of creditable coverage to a plan (or issuer) using the alternative method under §54.9801-4(c), that plan (or issuer) (requesting entity) must request that the entity that issued the certificate (prior entity) disclose the information set forth in paragraph (b)(2) of this section. The prior entity is required to disclose this information promptly.

(2) *Information to be disclosed.*—The prior entity is required to identify to the requesting entity the categories of benefits with respect to which the requesting entity is using the alternative method of counting creditable coverage, and the requesting entity may identify specific information that the requesting entity reasonably needs in order to determine the individual's creditable coverage with respect to any such category.

(3) *Charge for providing information.*—The prior entity may charge the requesting entity for the reasonable cost of disclosing such information.

(c) *Ability of an individual to demonstrate creditable coverage and waiting period information.*—(1) *Purpose.*—The rules in this paragraph (c) implement section 9801(c)(4), which permits individuals to demonstrate the duration of creditable coverage through means other than certificates, and section 9801(e)(3), which requires the Secretary to establish rules designed to prevent an individual's subsequent coverage under a group health plan or health insurance coverage from being adversely affected by an entity's failure to provide a certificate with respect to that individual.

(2) *In general.*—If the accuracy of a certificate is contested or a certificate is unavailable when needed by an individual, the individual has the right to demonstrate creditable coverage (and waiting or affiliation periods) through the presentation of documents or other means. For example, the individual may make such a demonstration when —

(i) An entity has failed to provide a certificate within the required time;

(ii) The individual has creditable coverage provided by an entity that is not required to provide a certificate of the coverage pursuant to paragraph (a) of this section;

(iii) The individual has an urgent medical condition that necessitates a determination before the individual can deliver a certificate to the plan; or

(iv) The individual lost a certificate that the individual had previously received and is unable to obtain another certificate.

(3) *Evidence of creditable coverage.*—(i) *Consideration of evidence.*—(A) A plan is required to take into account all information that it obtains or that is presented on behalf of an individual to make a determination, based on the relevant facts and circumstances, whether an individual has creditable coverage. A plan shall treat the individual as having furnished a certificate under paragraph (a) of this section if —

(1) The individual attests to the period of creditable coverage;

(2) The individual also presents relevant corroborating evidence of some creditable coverage during the period; and

(3) The individual cooperates with the plan's efforts to verify the individual's coverage.

(B) For purposes of this paragraph (c)(3)(i), cooperation includes providing (upon the plan's or issuer's request) a written authorization for the plan to request a certificate on behalf of the individual, and cooperating in efforts to determine the validity of the corroborating evidence and the dates of creditable coverage. While a plan may refuse to credit coverage where the individual fails to cooperate with the plan's or issuer's efforts to verify coverage, the plan may not consider an individual's inability to obtain a certificate to be evidence of the absence of creditable coverage.

(ii) *Documents.*—Documents that corroborate creditable coverage (and waiting or affiliation periods) include explanations of benefits (EOBs) or other correspondence from a plan or issuer indicating coverage, pay stubs showing a payroll deduction for health coverage, a health insurance identification card, a certificate of coverage under a group health policy, records from medical care providers indicating health coverage, third party statements verifying periods of coverage, and any other relevant documents that evidence periods of health coverage.

(iii) *Other evidence.*—Creditable coverage (and waiting or affiliation periods) may also be corroborated through means other than documentation, such as by a telephone call from the plan or provider to a third party verifying creditable coverage.

(iv) *Example.*—The rules of this paragraph (c)(3) are illustrated by the following example:

Example. (i) *Facts.* Individual F terminates employment with Employer W and, a month later, is hired by Employer X. X's group health plan imposes a preexisting condition exclusion of 12 months on new enrollees under the plan and uses the standard method of determining creditable coverage. F fails to receive a certificate of prior coverage from the self-insured group health plan maintained by F's prior employer, W, and requests a certificate. However, F (and X's plan, on F's behalf and with F's cooperation)

⟫⟫→ *Caution: Reg. §54.9801-5, below, prior to amendment by T.D. 9656, applies before December 31, 2014.*

is unable to obtain a certificate from W's plan. F attests that, to the best of F's knowledge, F had at least 12 months of continuous coverage under W's plan, and that the coverage ended no earlier than F's termination of employment from W. In addition, F presents evidence of coverage, such as an explanation of benefits for a claim that was made during the relevant period.

(ii) *Conclusion.* In this *Example,* based solely on these facts, F has demonstrated creditable coverage for the 12 months of coverage under W's plan in the same manner as if F had presented a written certificate of creditable coverage.

(4) *Demonstrating categories of creditable coverage.*—Procedures similar to those described in this paragraph (c) apply in order to determine the duration of an individual's creditable coverage with respect to any category under paragraph (b) of this section (relating to determining creditable coverage under the alternative method).

(5) *Demonstrating dependent status.*—If, in the course of providing evidence (including a certificate) of creditable coverage, an individual is required to demonstrate dependent status, the group health plan or issuer is required to treat the individual as having furnished a certificate showing the dependent status if the individual attests to such dependency and the period of such status and the individual cooperates with the plan's or issuer's efforts to verify the dependent status. [Reg. §54.9801-5.]

☐ [T.D. 9166, 12-29-2004.]

⟫⟫→ *Caution: Reg. §54.9801-5, below, as amended by T.D. 9656, applies beginning December 31, 2014.*

[Reg. §54.9801-5]

§54.9801-5. Evidence of creditable coverage.—(a) *In general.*—The rules for providing certificates of creditable coverage and demonstrating creditable coverage have been superseded by the prohibition on preexisting condition exclusions. *See* section 2704 of the Public Health Service Act, incorporated into section 9815 of the Code, and its implementing regulations for rules prohibiting the imposition of a preexisting condition exclusion.

(b) *Applicability.*—The provisions of this section apply beginning December 31, 2014. [Reg. §54.9801-5.]

☐ [T.D. 9166, 12-29-2004. *Amended by T.D.* 9656, 2-20-2014.]

[Reg. §54.9801-6]

§54.9801-6. Special enrollment periods.—(a) *Special enrollment for certain individuals who lose coverage.*—(1) *In general.*—A group health plan is required to permit current employees and dependents (as defined in §54.9801-2) who are described in paragraph (a)(2) of this section to enroll for coverage under the terms of the plan if the conditions in paragraph (a)(3) of this section are satisfied. The special enrollment rights under this paragraph (a) apply without regard to the dates on which an individual would otherwise be able to enroll under the plan. (See section 701(f)(1) of ERISA and section 2701(f)(1) of the PHS Act, under which this obligation is also imposed on a health insurance issuer offering group health insurance coverage.)

(2) *Individuals eligible for special enrollment.*—(i) *When employee loses coverage.*—A current employee and any dependents (including the employee's spouse) each are eligible for special enrollment in any benefit package under the plan (subject to plan eligibility rules conditioning dependent enrollment on enrollment of the employee) if —

(A) The employee and the dependents are otherwise eligible to enroll in the benefit package;

(B) When coverage under the plan was previously offered, the employee had coverage under any group health plan or health insurance coverage; and

(C) The employee satisfies the conditions of paragraph (a)(3)(i), (ii), or (iii) of this section and, if applicable, paragraph (a)(3)(iv) of this section.

(ii) *When dependent loses coverage.*—(A) A dependent of a current employee (including the employee's spouse) and the employee each are eligible for special enrollment in any benefit package under the plan (subject to plan eligibility rules conditioning dependent enrollment on enrollment of the employee) if —

(1) The dependent and the employee are otherwise eligible to enroll in the benefit package;

(2) When coverage under the plan was previously offered, the dependent had coverage under any group health plan or health insurance coverage; and

(3) The dependent satisfies the conditions of paragraph (a)(3)(i), (ii), or (iii) of this section and, if applicable, paragraph (a)(3)(iv) of this section.

(B) However, the plan is not required to enroll any other dependent unless that dependent satisfies the criteria of this paragraph (a)(2)(ii), or the employee satisfies the criteria of paragraph (a)(2)(i) of this section.

(iii) *Examples.*—The rules of this paragraph (a)(2) are illustrated by the following examples:

Example 1. (i) *Facts.* Individual A works for Employer X. A, A's spouse, and A's dependent children are eligible but not enrolled for coverage under X's group health plan. A's spouse works for Employer Y and at the time coverage was offered under X's plan, A was enrolled in coverage under Y's plan. Then, A loses eligibility for coverage under Y's plan.

(ii) *Conclusion.* In this *Example 1*, because A satisfies the conditions for special enrollment under paragraph (a)(2)(i) of this section, A, A's spouse, and A's dependent children are eligible for special enrollment under X's plan.

Example 2. (i) *Facts.* Individual A and A's spouse are eligible but not enrolled for coverage under Group Health Plan P maintained by A's employer. When A was first presented with an opportunity to enroll A and A's spouse, they did not have other coverage. Later, A and A's spouse enroll in Group Health Plan Q maintained by the employer of A's spouse. During a subsequent open enrollment period in P, A and A's spouse did not enroll because of their coverage under Q. They then lose eligibility for coverage under Q.

(ii) *Conclusion.* In this *Example 2*, because A and A's spouse were covered under Q when they did not enroll in P during open enrollment, they satisfy the conditions for special enrollment under paragraphs (a)(2)(i) and (ii) of this section. Consequently, A and A's spouse are eligible for special enrollment under P.

Example 3. (i) *Facts.* Individual B works for Employer X. B and B's spouse are eligible but not enrolled for coverage under X's group health plan. B's spouse works for Employer Y and at the time coverage was offered under X's plan, B's spouse was enrolled in self-only coverage under Y's group health plan. Then, B's spouse loses eligibility for coverage under Y's plan.

(ii) *Conclusion.* In this *Example 3*, because B's spouse satisfies the conditions for special enrollment under paragraph (a)(2)(ii) of this section, both B and B's spouse are eligible for special enrollment under X's plan.

Example 4. (i) *Facts.* Individual A works for Employer X. X maintains a group health plan with two benefit packages — an HMO option and an indemnity option. Self-only and family coverage are available under both options. A enrolls for self-only coverage in the HMO option. A's spouse works for Employer Y and was enrolled for self-only coverage under Y's plan at the time coverage was offered under X's plan. Then, A's spouse loses coverage under Y's plan. A requests special enrollment for A and A's spouse under the plan's indemnity option.

(ii) *Conclusion.* In this *Example 4*, because A's spouse satisfies the conditions for special enrollment under paragraph (a)(2)(ii) of this section, both A and A's spouse can enroll in either benefit package under X's plan. Therefore, if A requests enrollment in accordance with the requirements of this section, the plan must allow A and A's spouse to enroll in the indemnity option.

(3) *Conditions for special enrollment.*—(i) *Loss of eligibility for coverage.*—In the case of an employee or dependent who has coverage that is not COBRA continuation coverage, the conditions of this paragraph (a)(3)(i) are satisfied at the time the coverage is terminated as a result of loss of eligibility (regardless of whether the individual is eligible for or elects COBRA continua-

tion coverage). Loss of eligibility under this paragraph (a)(3)(i) does not include a loss due to the failure of the employee or dependent to pay premiums on a timely basis or termination of coverage for cause (such as making a fraudulent claim or an intentional misrepresentation of a material fact in connection with the plan). Loss of eligibility for coverage under this paragraph (a)(3)(i) includes (but is not limited to) —

(A) Loss of eligibility for coverage as a result of legal separation, divorce, cessation of dependent status (such as attaining the maximum age to be eligible as a dependent child under the plan), death of an employee, termination of employment, reduction in the number of hours of employment, and any loss of eligibility for coverage after a period that is measured by reference to any of the foregoing;

(B) In the case of coverage offered through an HMO, or other arrangement, in the individual market that does not provide benefits to individuals who no longer reside, live, or work in a service area, loss of coverage because an individual no longer resides, lives, or works in the service area (whether or not within the choice of the individual);

(C) In the case of coverage offered through an HMO, or other arrangement, in the group market that does not provide benefits to individuals who no longer reside, live, or work in a service area, loss of coverage because an individual no longer resides, lives, or works in the service area (whether or not within the choice of the individual), and no other benefit package is available to the individual; and

(D) A situation in which a plan no longer offers any benefits to the class of similarly situated individuals (as described in § 54.9802-1(d)) that includes the individual.

(ii) *Termination of employer contributions.*— In the case of an employee or dependent who has coverage that is not COBRA continuation coverage, the conditions of this paragraph (a)(3)(ii) are satisfied at the time employer contributions towards the employee's or dependent's coverage terminate. Employer contributions include contributions by any current or former employer that was contributing to coverage for the employee or dependent.

(iii) *Exhaustion of COBRA continuation coverage.*—In the case of an employee or dependent who has coverage that is COBRA continuation coverage, the conditions of this paragraph (a)(3)(iii) are satisfied at the time the COBRA continuation coverage is exhausted. For purposes of this paragraph (a)(3)(iii), an individual who satisfies the conditions for special enrollment of paragraph (a)(3)(i) of this section, does not enroll, and instead elects and exhausts COBRA continuation coverage satisfies the conditions of this paragraph (a)(3)(iii). (*Exhaustion of COBRA continuation coverage* is defined in § 54.9801-2.)

(iv) *Written statement.*—A plan may require an employee declining coverage (for the employee or any dependent of the employee) to state in writing whether the coverage is being declined due to other health coverage only if, at or before the time the employee declines coverage, the employee is provided with notice of the requirement to provide the statement (and the consequences of the employee's failure to provide the statement). If a plan requires such a statement, and an employee does not provide it, the plan is not required to provide special enrollment to the employee or any dependent of the employee under this paragraph (a)(3). A plan must treat an employee as having satisfied the plan requirement permitted under this paragraph (a)(3)(iv) if the employee provides a written statement that coverage was being declined because the employee or dependent had other coverage; a plan cannot require anything more for the employee to satisfy the plan's requirement to provide a written statement. (For example, the plan cannot require that the statement be notarized.)

(v) The rules of this paragraph (a)(3) are illustrated by the following examples:

Example 1. (i) *Facts.* Individual *D* enrolls in a group health plan maintained by Employer *Y.* At the time *D* enrolls, *Y* pays 70 percent of the cost of employee coverage and *D* pays the rest. *Y* announces that beginning January 1, *Y* will no longer make employer contributions towards the coverage. Employees may maintain coverage, however, if they pay the total cost of the coverage.

(ii) *Conclusion.* In this *Example 1,* employer contributions towards *D*'s coverage ceased on January 1 and the conditions of paragraph (a)(3)(ii) of this section are satisfied on this date (regardless of whether *D* elects to pay the total cost and continue coverage under *Y*'s plan).

Example 2. (i) *Facts.* A group health plan provides coverage through two options — Option 1 and Option 2. Employees can enroll in either option only within 30 days of hire or on January 1 of each year. Employee *A* is eligible for both options and enrolls in Option 1. Effective July 1 the plan terminates coverage under Option 1 and the plan does not create an immediate open enrollment opportunity into Option 2.

(ii) *Conclusion.* In this *Example 2, A* has experienced a loss of eligibility for coverage that satisfies paragraph (a)(3)(i) of this section, and has satisfied the other conditions for special enrollment under paragraph (a)(2)(i) of this section. Therefore, if *A* satisfies the other conditions of this paragraph (a), the plan must permit *A* to enroll in Option 2 as a special enrollee. (*A* may also be eligible to enroll in another group health plan, such as a plan maintained by the employer of *A*'s spouse, as a special enrollee.) The outcome would be the same if Option 1 was terminated by an issuer and the plan made no other coverage available to *A.*

Example 3. (i) *Facts.* Individual *C* is covered under a group health plan maintained by Employer *X.* While covered under *X*'s plan, *C* was eligible for but did not enroll in a plan

maintained by Employer *Z,* the employer of *C*'s spouse. *C* terminates employment with *X* and loses eligibility for coverage under *X*'s plan. *C* has a special enrollment right to enroll in *Z*'s plan, but *C* instead elects COBRA continuation coverage under *X*'s plan. *C* exhausts COBRA continuation coverage under *X*'s plan and requests special enrollment in *Z*'s plan.

(ii) *Conclusion.* In this *Example 3, C* has satisfied the conditions for special enrollment under paragraph (a)(3)(iii) of this section, and has satisfied the other conditions for special enrollment under paragraph (a)(2)(i) of this section. The special enrollment right that *C* had into *Z*'s plan immediately after the loss of eligibility for coverage under *X*'s plan was an offer of coverage under *Z*'s plan. When *C* later exhausts COBRA coverage under *X*'s plan, *C* has a second special enrollment right in *Z*'s plan.

(4) *Applying for special enrollment and effective date of coverage.*—(i) A plan or issuer must allow an employee a period of at least 30 days after an event described in paragraph (a)(3) of this section to request enrollment (for the employee or the employee's dependent).

(ii) Coverage must begin no later than the first day of the first calendar month beginning after the date the plan or issuer receives the request for special enrollment.

(b) *Special enrollment with respect to certain dependent beneficiaries.*—(1) *In general.*—A group health plan that makes coverage available with respect to dependents is required to permit individuals described in paragraph (b)(2) of this section to be enrolled for coverage in a benefit package under the terms of the plan. Paragraph (b)(3) of this section describes the required special enrollment period and the date by which coverage must begin. The special enrollment rights under this paragraph (b) apply without regard to the dates on which an individual would otherwise be able to enroll under the plan. (See 29 CFR 2590.701-6(b) and 45 CFR 146.117(b), under which this obligation is also imposed on a health insurance issuer offering group health insurance coverage.)

(2) *Individuals eligible for special enrollment.*— An individual is described in this paragraph (b)(2) if the individual is otherwise eligible for coverage in a benefit package under the plan and if the individual is described in paragraph (b)(2)(i), (ii), (iii), (iv), (v), or (vi) of this section.

(i) *Current employee only.*—A current employee is described in this paragraph (b)(2)(i) if a person becomes a dependent of the individual through marriage, birth, adoption, or placement for adoption.

(ii) *Spouse of a participant only.*—An individual is described in this paragraph (b)(2)(ii) if either —

(A) The individual becomes the spouse of a participant; or

(B) The individual is a spouse of a participant and a child becomes a dependent of the participant through birth, adoption, or placement for adoption.

(iii) *Current employee and spouse.*—A current employee and an individual who is or becomes a spouse of such an employee, are described in this paragraph (b)(2)(iii) if either —

(A) The employee and the spouse become married; or

(B) The employee and spouse are married and a child becomes a dependent of the employee through birth, adoption, or placement for adoption.

(iv) *Dependent of a participant only.*—An individual is described in this paragraph (b)(2)(iv) if the individual is a dependent (as defined in §54.9801-2) of a participant and the individual has become a dependent of the participant through marriage, birth, adoption, or placement for adoption.

(v) *Current employee and a new dependent.*—A current employee and an individual who is a dependent of the employee, are described in this paragraph (b)(2)(v) if the individual becomes a dependent of the employee through marriage, birth, adoption, or placement for adoption.

(vi) *Current employee, spouse, and a new dependent.*—A current employee, the employee's spouse, and the employee's dependent are described in this paragraph (b)(2)(vi) if the dependent becomes a dependent of the employee through marriage, birth, adoption, or placement for adoption.

(3) *Applying for special enrollment and effective date of coverage.*—(i) *Request.*—A plan must allow an individual a period of at least 30 days after the date of the marriage, birth, adoption, or placement for adoption (or, if dependent coverage is not generally made available at the time of the marriage, birth, adoption, or placement for adoption, a period of at least 30 days after the date the plan makes dependent coverage generally available) to request enrollment (for the individual or the individual's dependent).

(ii) *Reasonable procedures for special enrollment.*—[Reserved.]

(iii) *Date coverage must begin.*—(A) *Marriage.*—In the case of marriage, coverage must begin no later than the first day of the first calendar month beginning after the date the plan (or any issuer offering health insurance coverage under the plan) receives the request for special enrollment.

(B) *Birth, adoption, or placement for adoption.*—Coverage must begin in the case of a dependent's birth on the date of birth and in the case of a dependent's adoption or placement for adoption no later than the date of such adoption or placement for adoption (or, if dependent coverage is not made generally available at the time of the birth, adoption, or placement for adoption, the date the plan makes dependent coverage available).

(4) *Examples.*—The rules of this paragraph (b) are illustrated by the following examples:

Example 1. (i) *Facts.* An employer maintains a group health plan that offers all employees employee-only coverage, employee-plus-spouse coverage, or family coverage. Under the terms of the plan, any employee may elect to enroll when first hired (with coverage beginning on the date of hire) or during an annual open enrollment period held each December (with coverage beginning the following January 1). Employee *A* is hired on September 3. *A* is married to *B*, and they have no children. On March 15 in the following year a child *C* is born to *A* and *B*. Before that date, *A* and *B* have not been enrolled in the plan.

(ii) *Conclusion.* In this *Example 1*, the conditions for special enrollment of an employee with a spouse and new dependent under paragraph (b)(2)(vi) of this section are satisfied. If *A* satisfies the conditions of paragraph (b)(3) of this section for requesting enrollment timely, the plan will satisfy this paragraph (b) if it allows *A* to enroll either with employee-only coverage, with employee-plus-spouse coverage (for *A* and *B*), or with family coverage (for *A*, *B*, and *C*). The plan must allow whatever coverage is chosen to begin on March 15, the date of *C*'s birth.

Example 2. (i) *Facts.* Individual *D* works for Employer *X*. *X* maintains a group health plan with two benefit packages - an HMO option and an indemnity option. Self-only and family coverage are available under both options. *D* enrolls for self-only coverage in the HMO option. Then, a child, *E*, is placed for adoption with *D*. Within 30 days of the placement of *E* for adoption, *D* requests enrollment for *D* and *E* under the plan's indemnity option.

(ii) *Conclusion.* In this *Example 2*, *D* and *E* satisfy the conditions for special enrollment under paragraphs (b)(2)(v) and (b)(3) of this section. Therefore, the plan must allow *D* and *E* to enroll in the indemnity coverage, effective as of the date of the placement for adoption.

(c) *Notice of special enrollment.*—At or before the time an employee is initially offered the opportunity to enroll in a group health plan, the plan must furnish the employee with a notice of special enrollment that complies with the requirements of this paragraph (c).

(1) *Description of special enrollment rights.*— The notice of special enrollment must include a description of special enrollment rights. The following model language may be used to satisfy this requirement:

> If you are declining enrollment for yourself or your dependents (including your spouse) because of other health insurance or group health plan coverage, you may be able to enroll yourself and your dependents in this plan if you or your dependents lose eligibility for that other coverage (or if the employer stops contributing towards your or your dependents' other coverage).

However, you must request enrollment within [insert "30 days" or any longer period that applies under the plan] after your or your dependents' other coverage ends (or after the employer stops contributing toward the other coverage).

In addition, if you have a new dependent as a result of marriage, birth, adoption, or placement for adoption, you may be able to enroll yourself and your dependents. However, you must request enrollment within [insert "30 days" or any longer period that applies under the plan] after the marriage, birth, adoption, or placement for adoption.

To request special enrollment or obtain more information, contact [insert the name, title, telephone number, and any additional contact information of the appropriate plan representative].

(2) *Additional information that may be required.*—The notice of special enrollment must also include, if applicable, the notice described in paragraph (a)(3)(iv) of this section (the notice required to be furnished to an individual declining coverage if the plan requires the reason for declining coverage to be in writing).

(d) *Treatment of special enrollees.*—(1) If an individual requests enrollment while the individual is entitled to special enrollment under either paragraph (a) or (b) of this section, the individual is a special enrollee, even if the request for enrollment coincides with a late enrollment opportunity under the plan. Therefore, the individual cannot be treated as a late enrollee.

(2) Special enrollees must be offered all the benefit packages available to similarly situated individuals who enroll when first eligible. For this purpose, any difference in benefits or cost-sharing requirements for different individuals constitutes a different benefit package. In addition, a special enrollee cannot be required to pay more for coverage than a similarly situated individual who enrolls in the same coverage when first eligible.

(3) The rules of this section are illustrated by the following example:

Example. (i) *Facts.* Employer *Y* maintains a group health plan that has an enrollment period for late enrollees every November 1 through November 30 with coverage effective the following January 1. On October 18, Individual *B* loses coverage under another group health plan and satisfies the requirements of paragraphs (a)(2), (3), and (4) of this section. *B* submits a completed application for coverage on November 2.

(ii) *Conclusion.* In this *Example*, *B* is a special enrollee. Therefore, even though *B*'s request for enrollment coincides with an open enrollment period, *B*'s coverage is required to be made effective no later than December 1 (rather than the plan's January 1 effective date for late enrollees). [Reg. § 54.9801-6.]

☐ [*T.D.* 9166, 12-29-2004. *Amended by T.D.* 9656, 2-20-2014.]

[Reg. § 54.9802-1]

§ 54.9802-1. Prohibiting discrimination against participants and beneficiaries based on a health factor.—(a) *Health factors.*—(1) The term *health factor* means, in relation to an individual, any of the following health status-related factors:

(i) Health status;

(ii) Medical condition (including both physical and mental illnesses), as defined in § 54.9801-2;

(iii) Claims experience;

(iv) Receipt of health care;

(v) Medical history;

(vi) Genetic information, as defined in § 54.9802-3T.

(vii) Evidence of insurability; or

(viii) Disability.

(2) Evidence of insurability includes —

(i) Conditions arising out of acts of domestic violence; and

(ii) Participation in activities such as motorcycling, snowmobiling, all-terrain vehicle riding, horseback riding, skiing, and other similar activities.

(3) The decision whether health coverage is elected for an individual (including the time chosen to enroll, such as under special enrollment or late enrollment) is not, itself, within the scope of any health factor. (However, under § 54.9801-6, a plan must treat special enrollees the same as similarly situated individuals who are enrolled when first eligible.)

(b) *Prohibited discrimination in rules for eligibility.*—(1) *In general.*—(i) A group health plan, and a health insurance issuer offering health insurance coverage in connection with a group health plan, may not establish any rule for eligibility (including continued eligibility) of any individual to enroll for benefits under the terms of the plan or group health insurance coverage that discriminates based on any health factor that relates to that individual or a dependent of that individual. This rule is subject to the provisions of paragraph (b)(2) of this section (explaining how this rule applies to benefits), paragraph (d) of this section (containing rules for establishing groups of similarly situated individuals), paragraph (e) of this section (relating to nonconfinement, actively-at-work, and other service requirements), paragraph (f) of this section (relating to wellness programs), and paragraph (g) of this section (permitting favorable treatment of individuals with adverse health factors).

(ii) For purposes of this section, rules for eligibility include, but are not limited to, rules relating to—

(A) Enrollment;

(B) The effective date of coverage;

(C) Waiting (or affiliation) periods;

(D) Late and special enrollment;

(E) Eligibility for benefit packages (including rules for individuals to change their selection among benefit packages);

(F) Benefits (including rules relating to covered benefits, benefit restrictions, and cost-sharing mechanisms such as coinsurance, copayments, and deductibles), as described in paragraphs (b)(2) and (3) of this section;

(G) Continued eligibility; and

(H) Terminating coverage (including disenrollment) of any individual under the plan.

(iii) The rules of this paragraph (b)(1) are illustrated by the following examples:

Example 1. (i) *Facts.* An employer sponsors a group health plan that is available to all employees who enroll within the first 30 days of their employment. However, employees who do not enroll within the first 30 days cannot enroll later unless they pass a physical examination.

(ii) *Conclusion.* In this *Example 1*, the requirement to pass a physical examination in order to enroll in the plan is a rule for eligibility that discriminates based on one or more health factors and thus violates this paragraph (b)(1).

Example 2. (i) *Facts.* Under an employer's group health plan, employees who enroll during the first 30 days of employment (and during special enrollment periods) may choose between two benefit packages: an indemnity option and an HMO option. However, employees who enroll during late enrollment are permitted to enroll only in the HMO option and only if they provide evidence of good health.

(ii) *Conclusion.* In this *Example 2*, the requirement to provide evidence of good health in order to be eligible for late enrollment in the HMO option is a rule for eligibility that discriminates based on one or more health factors and thus violates this paragraph (b)(1). However, if the plan did not require evidence of good health but limited late enrollees to the HMO option, the plan's rules for eligibility would not discriminate based on any health factor, and thus would not violate this paragraph (b)(1), because the time an individual chooses to enroll is not, itself, within the scope of any health factor.

Example 3. (i) *Facts.* Under an employer's group health plan, all employees generally may enroll within the first 30 days of employment. However, individuals who participate in certain recreational activities, including motorcycling, are excluded from coverage.

(ii) *Conclusion.* In this *Example 3*, excluding from the plan individuals who participate in recreational activities, such as motorcycling, is a rule for eligibility that discriminates based on one more health factors and thus violates this paragraph (b)(1).

Example 4. (i) *Facts.* A group health plan applies for a group health policy offered by an issuer. As part of the application, the issuer receives health information about individuals to be covered under the plan. Individual *A* is an employee of the employer maintaining the plan. *A* and *A*'s dependents have a history of high health claims. Based on the information about *A* and

A's dependents, the issuer excludes *A* and *A*'s dependents from the group policy it offers to the employer.

(ii) *Conclusion.* See *Example 4* in 29 CFR 2590.702(b)(1) and 45 CFR 146.121(b)(1) for a conclusion that the exclusion by the issuer of *A* and *A*'s dependents from coverage is a rule for eligibility that discriminates based on one or more health factors and violates rules under 29 CFR 2590.702(b)(1) and 45 CFR 146.121(b)(1) similar to the rules under this paragraph (b)(1). (If the employer is a small employer under 45 CFR 144.103 (generally, an employer with 50 or fewer employees), the issuer also may violate 45 CFR 146.150, which requires issuers to offer all the policies they sell in the small group market on a guaranteed available basis to all small employers and to accept every eligible individual in every small employer group.) If the plan provides coverage through this policy and does not provide equivalent coverage for *A* and *A*'s dependents through other means, the plan violates this paragraph (b)(1).

(2) *Application to benefits.*—(i) *General rule.*—(A) Under this section, a group health plan is not required to provide coverage for any particular benefit to any group of similarly situated individuals.

(B) However, benefits provided under a plan must be uniformly available to all similarly situated individuals (as described in paragraph (d) of this section). Likewise, any restriction on a benefit or benefits must apply uniformly to all similarly situated individuals and must not be directed at individual participants or beneficiaries based on any health factor of the participants or beneficiaries (determined based on all the relevant facts and circumstances). Thus, for example, a plan may limit or exclude benefits in relation to a specific disease or condition, limit or exclude benefits for certain types of treatments or drugs, or limit or exclude benefits based on a determination of whether the benefits are experimental or not medically necessary, but only if the benefit limitation or exclusion applies uniformly to all similarly situated individuals and is not directed at individual participants or beneficiaries based on any health factor of the participants or beneficiaries. In addition, a plan or issuer may require the satisfaction of a deductible, copayment, coinsurance, or other cost-sharing requirement in order to obtain a benefit if the limit or cost-sharing requirement applies uniformly to all similarly situated individuals and is not directed at individual participants or beneficiaries based on any health factor of the participants or beneficiaries. In the case of a cost-sharing requirement, see also paragraph (b)(2)(ii) of this section, which permits variances in the application of a cost-sharing mechanism made available under a wellness program. (Whether any plan provision or practice with respect to benefits complies with this paragraph (b)(2)(i) does not affect whether the provision or practice is permitted under ERISA, the Affordable Care Act (including the requirements related to essential health benefits), the Americans with Disabilities Act, or any other law, whether State or Federal.)

(C) For purposes of this paragraph (b)(2)(i), a plan amendment applicable to all individuals in one or more groups of similarly situated individuals under the plan and made effective no earlier than the first day of the first plan year after the amendment is adopted is not considered to be directed at any individual participants or beneficiaries.

(D) The rules of this paragraph (b)(2)(i) are illustrated by the following examples:

Example 1. (i) *Facts.* A group health plan applies a $10,000 annual limit on a specific covered benefit that is not an essential health benefit to each participant or beneficiary covered under the plan. The limit is not directed at individual participants or beneficiaries.

(ii) *Conclusion.* In this *Example 1*, the limit does not violate this paragraph (b)(2)(i) because coverage of the specific, non-essential health benefit up to $10,000 is available uniformly to each participant and beneficiary under the plan and because the limit is applied uniformly to all participants and beneficiaries and is not directed at individual participants or beneficiaries.

Example 2. (i) *Facts.* A group health plan has a $500 deductible on all benefits for participants covered under the plan. Participant *B* files a claim for the treatment of AIDS. At the next corporate board meeting of the plan sponsor, the claim is discussed. Shortly thereafter, the plan is modified to impose a $2,000 deductible on benefits for the treatment of AIDS, effective before the beginning of the next plan year.

(ii) *Conclusion.* The facts of this *Example 2* strongly suggest that the plan modification is directed at *B* based on *B*'s claim. Absent outweighing evidence to the contrary, the plan violates this paragraph (b)(2)(i).

Example 3. (i) A group health plan applies for a group health policy offered by an issuer. Individual *C* is covered under the plan and has an adverse health condition. As part of the application, the issuer receives health information about the individuals to be covered, including information about *C*'s adverse health condition. The policy form offered by the issuer generally provides benefits for the adverse health condition that *C* has, but in this case the issuer offers the plan a policy modified by a rider that excludes benefits for *C* for that condition. The exclusionary rider is made effective the first day of the next plan year.

(ii) *Conclusion.* See *Example 3* in 29 CFR 2590.702(b)(2)(i) and 45 CFR 146.121(b)(2)(i) for a conclusion that the issuer violates rules under 29 CFR 2590.702(b)(2)(i) and 45 CFR 146.121(b)(2)(i) similar to the rules under this paragraph (b)(2)(i) because benefits for *C*'s condition are available to other individuals in the group of similarly situated individuals that includes *C* but are not available to *C*. Thus, the benefits are not uni-

formly available to all similarly situated individuals. Even though the exclusionary rider is made effective the first day of the next plan year, because the rider does not apply to all similarly situated individuals, the issuer violates the rules under 29 CFR 2590.702(b)(2)(i) and 45 CFR 146.121(b)(2)(i). If the plan provides coverage through this policy and does not provide equivalent coverage for *C* through other means, the plan violates this paragraph (b)(2)(i).

Example 4. (i) *Facts.* A group health plan has a $2,000 lifetime limit for the treatment of temporomandibular joint syndrome (TMJ). The limit is applied uniformly to all similarly situated individuals and is not directed at individual participants or beneficiaries.

(ii) *Conclusion.* In this *Example 4*, the limit does not violate this paragraph (b)(2)(i) because $2,000 of benefits for the treatment of TMJ are available uniformly to all similarly situated individuals and a plan may limit benefits covered in relation to a specific disease or condition if the limit applies uniformly to all similarly situated individuals and is not directed at individual participants or beneficiaries. (However, applying a lifetime limit on TMJ may violate PHS Act section 2711 and its implementing regulations, if TMJ coverage is an essential health benefit, depending on the essential health benefits benchmark plan as defined in 45 CFR 156.20. This example does not address whether the plan provision is permissible under any other applicable law, including PHS Act section 2711 or the Americans with Disabilities Act.)

Example 5. (i) *Facts.* A group health plan applies a $2 million lifetime limit on all benefits. However, the $2 million lifetime limit is reduced to $10,000 for any participant or beneficiary covered under the plan who has a congenital heart defect.

(ii) *Conclusion.* In this *Example 5*, the lower lifetime limit for participants and beneficiaries with a congenital heart defect violates this paragraph (b)(2)(i) because benefits under the plan are not uniformly available to all similarly situated individuals and the plan's lifetime limit on benefits does not apply uniformly to all similarly situated individuals. Additionally, this plan provision is prohibited under PHS Act section 2711 and its implementing regulations because it imposes a lifetime limit on essential health benefits.

Example 6. (i) *Facts.* A group health plan limits benefits for prescription drugs to those listed on a drug formulary. The limit is applied uniformly to all similarly situated individuals and is not directed at individual participants or beneficiaries.

(ii) *Conclusion.* In this *Example 6*, the exclusion from coverage of drugs not listed on the drug formulary does not violate this paragraph (b)(2)(i) because benefits for prescription drugs listed on the formulary are uniformly available to all similarly situated individuals and because the exclusion of drugs not listed on the formulary applies uniformly to all similarly situated individuals and is not directed at individual participants or beneficiaries.

Example 7. (i) *Facts.* Under a group health plan, doctor visits are generally subject to a $250 annual deductible and 20 percent coinsurance requirement. However, prenatal doctor visits are not subject to any deductible or coinsurance requirement. These rules are applied uniformly to all similarly situated individuals and are not directed at individual participants or beneficiaries.

(ii) *Conclusion.* In this *Example 7,* imposing different deductible and coinsurance requirements for prenatal doctor visits and other visits does not violate this paragraph (b)(2)(i) because a plan may establish different deductibles or coinsurance requirements for different services if the deductible or coinsurance requirement is applied uniformly to all similarly situated individuals and is not directed at individual participants or beneficiaries.

(ii) *Exception for wellness programs.*—A group health plan may vary benefits, including cost-sharing mechanisms (such as a deductible, copayment, or coinsurance), based on whether an individual has met the standards of a wellness program that satisfies the requirements of paragraph (f) of this section.

(iii) *Specific rule relating to source-of-injury exclusions.*—(A) If a group health plan generally provides benefits for a type of injury, the plan may not deny benefits otherwise provided for treatment of the injury if the injury results from an act of domestic violence or a medical condition (including both physical and mental health conditions). This rule applies in the case of an injury resulting from a medical condition even if the condition is not diagnosed before the injury.

(B) The rules of this paragraph (b)(2)(iii) are illustrated by the following examples:

Example 1. (i) *Facts.* A group health plan generally provides medical/surgical benefits, including benefits for hospital stays, that are medically necessary. However, the plan excludes benefits for self-inflicted injuries or injuries sustained in connection with attempted suicide. Because of depression, Individual *D* attempts suicide. As a result, *D* sustains injuries and is hospitalized for treatment of the injuries. Under the exclusion, the plan denies *D* benefits for treatment of the injuries.

(ii) *Conclusion.* In this *Example 1,* the suicide attempt is the result of a medical condition (depression). Accordingly, the denial of benefits for the treatments of *D's* injuries violates the requirements of this paragraph (b)(2)(iii) because the plan provision excludes benefits for treatment of an injury resulting from a medical condition.

Example 2. (i) *Facts.* A group health plan provides benefits for head injuries generally. The plan also has a general exclusion for any injury sustained while participating in any of a number of recreational activities, including bungee jumping. However, this exclusion does not apply to

any injury that results from a medical condition (nor from domestic violence). Participant *E* sustains a head injury while bungee jumping. The injury did not result from a medical condition (nor from domestic violence). Accordingly, the plan denies benefits for *E's* head injury.

(ii) *Conclusion.* In this *Example 2,* the plan provision that denies benefits based on the source of an injury does not restrict benefits based on an act of domestic violence or any medical condition. Therefore, the provision is permissible under this paragraph (b)(2)(iii) and does not violate this section. (However, if the plan did not allow *E* to enroll in the plan (or applied different rules for eligibility to *E*) because *E* frequently participates in bungee jumping, the plan would violate paragraph (b)(1) of this section.)

(c) *Prohibited discrimination in premiums or contributions.*—(1) *In general.*—(i) A group health plan may not require an individual, as a condition of enrollment or continued enrollment under the plan, to pay a premium or contribution that is greater than the premium or contribution for a similarly situated individual (described in paragraph (d) of this section) enrolled in the plan based on any health factor that relates to the individual or a dependent of the individual.

(ii) Discounts, rebates, payments in kind, and any other premium differential mechanisms are taken into account in determining an individual's premium or contribution rate. (For rules relating to cost-sharing mechanisms, see paragraph (b)(2) of this section (addressing benefits).)

(2) *Rules relating to premium rates.*—(i) *Group rating based on health factors not restricted under this section.*—Nothing in this section restricts the aggregate amount that an employer may be charged for coverage under a group health plan. But see § 54.9802-3T(b), which prohibits adjustments in group premium or contribution rates based on genetic information.

(ii) *List billing based on a health factor prohibited.*—However, a group health plan may not quote or charge an employer (or an individual) a different premium for an individual in a group of similarly situated individuals based on a health factor. (But see paragraph (g) of this section permitting favorable treatment of individuals with adverse health factors.)

(iii) *Examples.*—The rules of this paragraph (c)(2) are illustrated by the following examples:

Example 1. (i) *Facts.* An employer sponsors a group health plan and purchases coverage from a health insurance issuer. In order to determine the premium rate for the upcoming plan year, the issuer reviews the claims experience of individuals covered under the plan. The issuer finds that Individual *F* had significantly higher claims experience than similarly situated individuals in the plan. The issuer quotes the plan a higher per-participant rate because of *F's* claims experience.

(ii) *Conclusion.* See *Example 1* in 29 CFR 2590.702(c)(2) and 45 CFR 146.121(c)(2) for a conclusion that the issuer does not violate the provisions of 29 CFR 2590.702(c)(2) and 45 CFR 146.121(c)(2) similar to the provisions of this paragraph (c)(2) because the issuer blends the rate so that the employer is not quoted a higher rate for F than for a similarly situated individual based on F's claims experience. (However, those examples conclude that if the issuer used genetic information in computing the group rate, it would violate 29 CFR 2590.702-1(b) or 45 CFR 146.122(b).)

Example 2. (i) *Facts.* Same facts as *Example 1*, except that the issuer quotes the employer a higher premium rate for *F*, because of *F*'s claims experience, than for a similarly situated individual.

(ii) *Conclusion.* See *Example 2* in 29 CFR 2590.702(c)(2) and 45 CFR 146.121(c)(2) for a conclusion that the issuer violates provisions of 29 CFR 2590.702(c)(2) and 45 CFR 146.121(c)(2) similar to the provisions of this paragraph (c)(2). Moreover, even if the plan purchased the policy based on the quote but did not require a higher participant contribution for F than for a similarly situated individual, see *Example 2* in 29 CFR 2590.702(c)(2) and 45 CFR 146.121(c)(2) for a conclusion that the issuer would still violate 29 CFR 2590.702(c)(2) and 45 CFR 146.121(c)(2) (but in such a case the plan would not violate this paragraph (c)(2)).

(3) *Exception for wellness programs.*—Notwithstanding paragraphs (c)(1) and (2) of this section, a plan may vary the amount of premium or contribution it requires similarly situated individuals to pay based on whether an individual has met the standards of a wellness program that satisfies the requirements of paragraph (f) of this section.

(d) *Similarly situated individuals.*—The requirements of this section apply only within a group of individuals who are treated as similarly situated individuals. A plan may treat participants as a group of similarly situated individuals separate from beneficiaries. In addition, participants may be treated as two or more distinct groups of similarly situated individuals and beneficiaries may be treated as two or more distinct groups of similarly situated individuals in accordance with the rules of this paragraph (d). Moreover, if individuals have a choice of two or more benefit packages, individuals choosing one benefit package may be treated as one or more groups of similarly situated individuals distinct from individuals choosing another benefit package.

(1) *Participants.*—Subject to paragraph (d)(3) of this section, a plan may treat participants as two or more distinct groups of similarly situated individuals if the distinction between or among the groups of participants is based on a bona fide employment-based classification consistent with the employer's usual business practice. Whether an employment-based classification is bona fide

is determined on the basis of all the relevant facts and circumstances. Relevant facts and circumstances include whether the employer uses the classification for purposes independent of qualification for health coverage (for example, determining eligibility for other employee benefits or determining other terms of employment). Subject to paragraph (d)(3) of this section, examples of classifications that, based on all the relevant facts and circumstances, may be bona fide include full-time versus part-time status, different geographic location, membership in a collective bargaining unit, date of hire, length of service, current employee versus former employee status, and different occupations. However, a classification based on any health factor is not a bona fide employment-based classification, unless the requirements of paragraph (g) of this section are satisfied (permitting favorable treatment of individuals with adverse health factors).

(2) *Beneficiaries.*—(i) Subject to paragraph (d)(3) of this section, a plan may treat beneficiaries as two or more distinct groups of similarly situated individuals if the distinction between or among the groups of beneficiaries is based on any of the following factors:

(A) A bona fide employment-based classification of the participant through whom the beneficiary is receiving coverage;

(B) Relationship to the participant (for example, as a spouse or as a dependent child);

(C) Marital status;

(D) With respect to children of a participant, age or student status; or

(E) Any other factor if the factor is not a health factor.

(ii) Paragraph (d)(2)(i) of this section does not prevent more favorable treatment of individuals with adverse health factors in accordance with paragraph (g) of this section.

(3) *Discrimination directed at individuals.*—Notwithstanding paragraphs (d)(1) and (2) of this section, if the creation or modification of an employment or coverage classification is directed at individual participants or beneficiaries based on any health factor of the participants or beneficiaries, the classification is not permitted under this paragraph (d), unless it is permitted under paragraph (g) of this section (permitting favorable treatment of individuals with adverse health factors). Thus, if an employer modified an employment-based classification to single out, based on a health factor, individual participants and beneficiaries and deny them health coverage, the new classification would not be permitted under this section.

(4) *Examples.*—The rules of this paragraph (d) are illustrated by the following examples:

Example 1. (i) *Facts.* An employer sponsors a group health plan for full-time employees only. Under the plan (consistent with the employer's usual business practice), employees who normally work at least 30 hours per week are considered to be working full-time. Other

Reg. §54.9802-1(d)(4)

employees are considered to be working part-time. There is no evidence to suggest that the classification is directed at individual participants or beneficiaries.

(ii) *Conclusion.* In this *Example 1*, treating the full-time and part-time employees as two separate groups of similarly situated individuals is permitted under this paragraph (d) because the classification is bona fide and is not directed at individual participants or beneficiaries.

Example 2. (i) *Facts.* Under a group health plan, coverage is made available to employees, their spouses, and their children. However, coverage is made available to a child only if the child is under age 26 (or under age 29 if the child is continuously enrolled full-time in an institution of higher learning (full-time students)). There is no evidence to suggest that these classifications are directed at individual participants or beneficiaries.

(ii) *Conclusion.* In this Example 2, treating spouses and children differently by imposing an age limitation on children, but not on spouses, is permitted under this paragraph (d). Specifically, the distinction between spouses and children is permitted under paragraph (d)(2) of this section and is not prohibited under paragraph (d)(3) of this section because it is not directed at individual participants or beneficiaries. It is also permissible to treat children who are under age 26 (or full-time students under age 29) as a group of similarly situated individuals separate from those who are age 26 or older (or age 29 or older if they are not full-time students) because the classification is permitted under paragraph (d)(2) of this section and is not directed at individual participants or beneficiaries.

Example 3. (i) *Facts.* A university sponsors a group health plan that provides one health benefit package to faculty and another health benefit package to other staff. Faculty and staff are treated differently with respect to other employee benefits such as retirement benefits and leaves of absence. There is no evidence to suggest that the distinction is directed at individual participants or beneficiaries.

(ii) *Conclusion.* In this *Example 3*, the classification is permitted under this paragraph (d) because there is a distinction based on a bona fide employment-based classification consistent with the employer's usual business practice and the distinction is not directed at individual participants and beneficiaries.

Example 4. (i) *Facts.* An employer sponsors a group health plan that is available to all current employees. Former employees may also be eligible, but only if they complete a specified number of years of service, are enrolled under the plan at the time of termination of employment, and are continuously enrolled from that date. There is no evidence to suggest that these distinctions are directed at individual participants or beneficiaries.

(ii) *Conclusion.* In this *Example 4*, imposing additional eligibility requirements on former em-

ployees is permitted because a classification that distinguishes between current and former employees is a bona fide employment-based classification that is permitted under this paragraph (d), provided that it is not directed at individual participants or beneficiaries. In addition, it is permissible to distinguish between former employees who satisfy the service requirement and those who do not, provided that the distinction is not directed at individual participants or beneficiaries. (However, former employees who do not satisfy the eligibility criteria may, nonetheless, be eligible for continued coverage pursuant to a COBRA continuation provision or similar State law.)

Example 5. (i) *Facts.* An employer sponsors a group health plan that provides the same benefit package to all seven employees of the employer. Six of the seven employees have the same job title and responsibilities, but Employee G has a different job title and different responsibilities. After G files an expensive claim for benefits under the plan, coverage under the plan is modified so that employees with G's job title receive a different benefit package that includes a higher deductible than in the benefit package made available to the other six employees.

(ii) *Conclusion.* Under the facts of this *Example 5*, changing the coverage classification for G based on the existing employment classification for G is not permitted under this paragraph (d) because the creation of the new coverage classification for G is directed at G based on one or more health factors.

(e) *Nonconfinement and actively-at-work provisions.*—(1) *Nonconfinement provisions.*—(i) *General rule.*—Under the rules of paragraphs (b) and (c) of this section, a plan may not establish a rule for eligibility (as described in paragraph (b)(1)(ii) of this section) or set any individual's premium or contribution rate based on whether an individual is confined to a hospital or other health care institution. In addition, under the rules of paragraphs (b) and (c) of this section, a plan may not establish a rule for eligibility or set any individual's premium or contribution rate based on an individual's ability to engage in normal life activities, except to the extent permitted under paragraphs (e)(2)(ii) and (3) of this section (permitting plans, under certain circumstances, to distinguish among employees based on the performance of services).

(ii) *Examples.*—The rules of this paragraph (e)(1) are illustrated by the following examples:

Example 1. (i) *Facts.* Under a group health plan, coverage for employees and their dependents generally becomes effective on the first day of employment. However, coverage for a dependent who is confined to a hospital or other health care institution does not become effective until the confinement ends.

(ii) *Conclusion.* In this *Example 1*, the plan violates this paragraph (e)(1) because the plan delays the effective date of coverage for dependents based on confinement to a hospital or other health care institution.

Example 2. (i) *Facts.* In previous years, a group health plan has provided coverage through a group health insurance policy offered by Issuer *M.* However, for the current year, the plan provides coverage through a group health insurance policy offered by Issuer *N.* Under Issuer *N's* policy, items and services provided in connection with the confinement of a dependent to a hospital or other health care institution are not covered if the confinement is covered under an extension of benefits clause from a previous health insurance issuer.

(ii) *Conclusion.* See *Example 2* in 29 CFR 2590.702(e)(1) and 45 CFR 146.121(e)(1) for a conclusion that Issuer *N* violates provisions of 29 CFR 2590.702(e)(1) and 45 CFR 146.121(e)(1) similar to the provisions of this paragraph (e)(1) because the group health insurance coverage restricts benefits based on whether a dependent is confined to a hospital or other health care institution that is covered under an extension of benefits from a previous issuer. See *Example 2* in 29 CFR 2590.702(e)(1) and 45 CFR 146.121(e)(1) for the additional conclusions that under State law Issuer *M* may also be responsible for providing benefits to such a dependent; and that in a case in which Issuer *N* has an obligation under 29 CFR 2590.702(e)(1) or 45 CFR 146.121(e)(1) to provide benefits and Issuer *M* has an obligation under State law to provide benefits, any State laws designed to prevent more than 100% reimbursement, such as State coordination-of-benefits laws, continue to apply.

(2) *Actively-at-work and continuous service provisions.*—(i) *General rule.*—(A) Under the rules of paragraphs (b) and (c) of this section and subject to the exception for the first day of work described in paragraph (e)(2)(ii) of this section, a plan may not establish a rule for eligibility (as described in paragraph (b)(1)(ii) of this section) or set any individual's premium or contribution rate based on whether an individual is actively at work (including whether an individual is continuously employed), unless absence from work due to any health factor (such as being absent from work on sick leave) is treated, for purposes of the plan, as being actively at work.

(B) The rules of this paragraph (e)(2)(i) are illustrated by the following examples:

Example 1. (i) *Facts.* Under a group health plan, an employee generally becomes eligible to enroll 30 days after the first day of employment. However, if the employee is not actively at work on the first day after the end of the 30-day period, then eligibility for enrollment is delayed until the first day the employee is actively at work.

(ii) *Conclusion.* In this *Example 1,* the plan violates this paragraph (e)(2) (and thus also violates paragraph (b) of this section). However, the plan would not violate paragraph (e)(2) or (b) of this section if, under the plan, an absence due to any health factor is considered being actively at work.

Example 2. (i) *Facts.* Under a group health plan, coverage for an employee becomes effective after 90 days of continuous service; that is, if an employee is absent from work (for any reason) before completing 90 days of service, the beginning of the 90-day period is measured from the day the employee returns to work (without any credit for service before the absence).

(ii) *Conclusion.* In this Example 2, the plan violates this paragraph (e)(2) (and thus also paragraph (b) of this section) because the 90-day continuous service requirement is a rule for eligibility based on whether an individual is actively at work. However, the plan would not violate this paragraph (e)(2) or paragraph (b) of this section if, under the plan, an absence due to any health factor is not considered an absence for purposes of measuring 90 days of continuous service. (In addition, any eligibility provision that is time-based must comply with the requirements of PHS Act section 2708 and its implementing regulations.)

(ii) *Exception for the first day of work.*—(A) Notwithstanding the general rule in paragraph (e)(2)(i) of this section, a plan may establish a rule for eligibility that requires an individual to begin work for the employer sponsoring the plan (or, in the case of a multiemployer plan, to begin a job in covered employment) before coverage becomes effective, provided that such a rule for eligibility applies regardless of the reason for the absence.

(B) The rules of this paragraph (e)(2)(ii) are illustrated by the following examples:

Example 1. (i) *Facts.* Under the eligibility provision of a group health plan, coverage for new employees becomes effective on the first day that the employee reports to work. Individual *H* is scheduled to begin work on August 3. However, *H* is unable to begin work on that day because of illness. *H* begins working on August 4, and *H's* coverage is effective on August 4.

(ii) *Conclusion.* In this *Example 1,* the plan provision does not violate this section. However, if coverage for individuals who do not report to work on the first day they were scheduled to work for a reason unrelated to a health factor (such as vacation or bereavement) becomes effective on the first day they were scheduled to work, then the plan would violate this section.

Example 2. (i) *Facts.* Under a group health plan, coverage for new employees becomes effective on the first day of the month following the employee's first day of work, regardless of whether the employee is actively at work on the first day of the month. Individual *J* is scheduled to begin work on March 24. However, *J* is unable to begin work on March 24 because of illness. *J* begins working on April 7 and *J's* coverage is effective May 1.

(ii) *Conclusion.* In this *Example 2,* the plan provision does not violate this section. However, as in *Example 1,* if coverage for individuals absent from work for reasons unrelated to a health factor became effective despite their absence, then the plan would violate this section.

(3) *Relationship to plan provisions defining similarly situated individuals.*— (i) Notwithstanding the rules of paragraphs (e)(1) and (2) of this section, a plan may establish rules for eligibility or set any individual's premium or contribution rate in accordance with the rules relating to similarly situated individuals in paragraph (d) of this section. Accordingly, a plan may distinguish in rules for eligibility under the plan between full-time and part-time employees, between permanent and temporary or seasonal employees, between current and former employees, and between employees currently performing services and employees no longer performing services for the employer, subject to paragraph (d) of this section. However, other Federal or State laws (including the COBRA continuation provisions and the Family and Medical Leave Act of 1993) may require an employee or the employee's dependents to be offered coverage and set limits on the premium or contribution rate even though the employee is not performing services.

(ii) The rules of this paragraph (e)(3) are illustrated by the following examples:

Example 1. (i) *Facts.* Under a group health plan, employees are eligible for coverage if they perform services for the employer for 30 or more hours per week or if they are on paid leave (such as vacation, sick, or bereavement leave). Employees on unpaid leave are treated as a separate group of similarly situated individuals in accordance with the rules of paragraph (d) of this section.

(ii) *Conclusion.* In this *Example 1*, the plan provisions do not violate this section. However, if the plan treated individuals performing services for the employer for 30 or more hours per week, individuals on vacation leave, and individuals on bereavement leave as a group of similarly situated individuals separate from individuals on sick leave, the plan would violate this paragraph (e) (and thus also would violate paragraph (b) of this section) because groups of similarly situated individuals cannot be established based on a health factor (including the taking of sick leave) under paragraph (d) of this section.

Example 2. (i) *Facts.* To be eligible for coverage under a bona fide collectively bargained group health plan in the current calendar quarter, the plan requires an individual to have worked 250 hours in covered employment during the three-month period that ends one month before the beginning of the current calendar quarter. The distinction between employees working at least 250 hours and those working less than 250 hours in the earlier three-month period is not directed at individual participants or beneficiaries based on any health factor of the participants or beneficiaries.

(ii) *Conclusion.* In this *Example 2*, the plan provision does not violate this section because, under the rules for similarly situated individuals allowing full-time employees to be treated differently than part-time employees, employees who work at least 250 hours in a three-month period can be treated differently than employees who fail to work 250 hours in that period. The result would be the same if the plan permitted individuals to apply excess hours from previous periods to satisfy the requirement for the current quarter.

Example 3. (i) *Facts.* Under a group health plan, coverage of an employee is terminated when the individual's employment is terminated, in accordance with the rules of paragraph (d) of this section. Employee *B* has been covered under the plan. *B* experiences a disabling illness that prevents *B* from working. *B* takes a leave of absence under the Family and Medical Leave Act of 1993. At the end of such leave, *B* terminates employment and consequently loses coverage under the plan. (This termination of coverage is without regard to whatever rights the employee (or members of the employee's family) may have for COBRA continuation coverage.)

(ii) *Conclusion.* In this *Example 3*, the plan provision terminating *B*'s coverage upon *B*'s termination of employment does not violate this section.

Example 4. (i) *Facts.* Under a group health plan, coverage of an employee is terminated when the employee ceases to perform services for the employer sponsoring the plan, in accordance with the rules of paragraph (d) of this section. Employee *C* is laid off for three months. When the layoff begins, *C*'s coverage under the plan is terminated. (This termination of coverage is without regard to whatever rights the employee (or members of the employee's family) may have for COBRA continuation coverage.)

(ii) *Conclusion.* In this *Example 4*, the plan provision terminating *C*'s coverage upon the cessation of *C*'s performance of services does not violate this section.

⟫⟩→ *Caution: Reg. §54.9802-1(f), below, prior to amendment by T.D. 9620, generally applies to group health plans and group health insurance issuers, for plan years beginning before January 1, 2014.*

(f) *Wellness programs.*—A wellness program is any program designed to promote health or prevent disease. Paragraphs (b)(2)(ii) and (c)(3) of this section provide exceptions to the general prohibitions against discrimination based on a health factor for plan provisions that vary benefits (including cost-sharing mechanisms) or the premium or contribution for similarly situated individuals in connection with a wellness pro-

gram that satisfies the requirements of this paragraph (f). If none of the conditions for obtaining a reward under a wellness program is based on an individual satisfying a standard that is related to a health factor, paragraph (f)(1) of this section clarifies that the wellness program does not violate this section if participation in the program is made available to all similarly situated individuals. If any of the conditions for obtaining a re-

►►► *Caution: Reg. §54.9802-1(f), below, prior to amendment by T.D. 9620, generally applies to group health plans and group health insurance issuers, for plan years beginning before January 1, 2014.*

ward under a wellness program is based on an individual satisfying a standard that is related to a health factor, the wellness program does not violate this section if the requirements of paragraph (f)(2) of this section are met.

(1) *Wellness programs not subject to requirements.*—If none of the conditions for obtaining a reward under a wellness program are based on an individual satisfying a standard that is related to a health factor (or if a wellness program does not provide a reward), the wellness program does not violate this section, if participation in the program is made available to all similarly situated individuals. Thus, for example, the following programs need not satisfy the requirements of paragraph (f)(2) of this section, if participation in the program is made available to all similarly situated individuals:

(i) A program that reimburses all or part of the cost for memberships in a fitness center.

(ii) A diagnostic testing program that provides a reward for participation and does not base any part of the reward on outcomes.

(iii) A program that encourages preventive care through the waiver of the copayment or deductible requirement under a group health plan for the costs of, for example, prenatal care or well-baby visits.

(iv) A program that reimburses employees for the costs of smoking cessation programs without regard to whether the employee quits smoking.

(v) A program that provides a reward to employees for attending a monthly health education seminar.

(2) *Wellness programs subject to requirements.*—If any of the conditions for obtaining a reward under a wellness program is based on an individual satisfying a standard that is related to a health factor, the wellness program does not violate this section if the requirements of this paragraph (f)(2) are met.

(i) The reward for the wellness program, coupled with the reward for other wellness programs with respect to the plan that require satisfaction of a standard related to a health factor, must not exceed 20 percent of the cost of employee-only coverage under the plan. However, if, in addition to employees, any class of dependents (such as spouses or spouses and dependent children) may participate in the wellness program, the reward must not exceed 20 percent of the cost of the coverage in which an employee and any dependents are enrolled. For purposes of this paragraph (f)(2), the cost of coverage is determined based on the total amount of employer and employee contributions for the benefit package under which the employee is (or the employee and any dependents are) receiving coverage. A reward can be in the form of a discount or rebate of a premium or contribution, a waiver of all or part of a cost-sharing mecha-

nism (such as deductibles, copayments, or coinsurance), the absence of a surcharge, or the value of a benefit that would otherwise not be provided under the plan.

(ii) The program must be reasonably designed to promote health or prevent disease. A program satisfies this standard if it has a reasonable chance of improving the health of or preventing disease in participating individuals and it is not overly burdensome, is not a subterfuge for discriminating based on a health factor, and is not highly suspect in the method chosen to promote health or prevent disease.

(iii) The program must give individuals eligible for the program the opportunity to qualify for the reward under the program at least once per year.

(iv) The reward under the program must be available to all similarly situated individuals.

(A) A reward is not available to all similarly situated individuals for a period unless the program allows—

(1) A reasonable alternative standard (or waiver of the otherwise applicable standard) for obtaining the reward for any individual for whom, for that period, it is unreasonably difficult due to a medical condition to satisfy the otherwise applicable standard; and

(2) A reasonable alternative standard (or waiver of the otherwise applicable standard) for obtaining the reward for any individual for whom, for that period, it is medically inadvisable to attempt to satisfy the otherwise applicable standard.

(B) A plan or issuer may seek verification, such as a statement from an individual's physician, that a health factor makes it unreasonably difficult or medically inadvisable for the individual to satisfy or attempt to satisfy the otherwise applicable standard.

(v)(A) The plan must disclose in all plan materials describing the terms of the program the availability of a reasonable alternative standard (or the possibility of waiver of the otherwise applicable standard) required under paragraph (f)(2)(iv) of this section. However, if plan materials merely mention that a program is available, without describing its terms, this disclosure is not required.

(B) The following language, or substantially similar language, can be used to satisfy the requirement of this paragraph (f)(2)(v): "If it is unreasonably difficult due to a medical condition for you to achieve the standards for the reward under this program, or if it is medically inadvisable for you to attempt to achieve the standards for the reward under this program, call us at [insert telephone number] and we will work with you to develop another way to qualify for the reward." In addition, other examples of language that would satisfy this requirement are set forth in *Examples 3, 4,* and *5* of paragraph (f)(3) of this section.

>>>→ *Caution: Reg. §54.9802-1(f), below, prior to amendment by T.D. 9620, generally applies to group health plans and group health insurance issuers, for plan years beginning before January 1, 2014.*

(3) *Examples.*—The rules of paragraph (f)(2) of this section are illustrated by the following examples:

Example 1. (i) *Facts.* An employer sponsors a group health plan. The annual premium for employee-only coverage is $3,600 (of which the employer pays $2,700 per year and the employee pays $900 per year). The annual premium for family coverage is $9,000 (of which the employer pays $4,500 per year and the employee pays $4,500 per year). The plan offers a wellness program with an annual premium rebate of $360. The program is available only to employees.

(ii) *Conclusion.* In this *Example 1*, the program satisfies the requirements of paragraph (f)(2)(i) of this section because the reward for the wellness program, $360, does not exceed 20 percent of the total annual cost of employee-only coverage, $720. ($3,600 × 20% = $720.) If any class of dependents is allowed to participate in the program and the employee is enrolled in family coverage, the plan could offer the employee a reward of up to 20 percent of the cost of family coverage, $1,800. ($9,000 × 20% = $1,800.)

Example 2. (i) *Facts.* A group health plan gives an annual premium discount of 20 percent of the cost of employee-only coverage to participants who adhere to a wellness program. The wellness program consists solely of giving an annual cholesterol test to participants. Those participants who achieve a count under 200 receive the premium discount for the year.

(ii) *Conclusion.* In this *Example 2*, the program fails to satisfy the requirement of being available to all similarly situated individuals because some participants may be unable to achieve a cholesterol count of under 200 and the plan does not make available a reasonable alternative standard or waive the cholesterol standard. (In addition, plan materials describing the program are required to disclose the availability of a reasonable alternative standard (or the possibility of waiver of the otherwise applicable standard) for obtaining the premium discount. Thus, the premium discount violates paragraph (c) of this section because it may require an individual to pay a higher premium based on a health factor of the individual than is required of a similarly situated individual under the plan.

Example 3. (i) *Facts.* Same facts as *Example 2*, except that the plan provides that if it is unreasonably difficult due to a medical condition for a participant to achieve the targeted cholesterol count (or if it is medically inadvisable for a participant to attempt to achieve the targeted cholesterol count) within a 60-day period, the plan will make available a reasonable alternative standard that takes the relevant medical condition into account. In addition, all plan materials describing the terms of the program include the following statement: "If it is unreasonably difficult due to a medical condition for you to achieve a cholesterol count under 200, or if it is medically inadvisable for you to attempt to

achieve a count under 200, call us at the number below and we will work with you to develop another way to get the discount." Individual *D* begins a diet and exercise program but is unable to achieve a cholesterol count under 200 within the prescribed period. *D*'s doctor determines *D* requires prescription medication to achieve a medically advisable cholesterol count. In addition, the doctor determines that *D* must be monitored through periodic blood tests to continually reevaluate *D*'s health status. The plan accommodates *D* by making the discount available to *D*, but only if *D* follows the advice of *D*'s doctor's regarding medication and blood tests.

(ii) *Conclusion.* In this *Example 3*, the program is a wellness program because it satisfies the five requirements of paragraph (f)(2) of this section. First, the program complies with the limits on rewards under a program. Second, it is reasonably designed to promote health or prevent disease. Third, individuals eligible for the program are given the opportunity to qualify for the reward at least once per year. Fourth, the reward under the program is available to all similarly situated individuals because it accommodates individuals for whom it is unreasonably difficult due to a medical condition to achieve the targeted count (or for whom it is medically inadvisable to attempt to achieve the targeted count) in the prescribed period by providing a reasonable alternative standard. Fifth, the plan discloses in all materials describing the terms of the program the availability of a reasonable alternative standard. Thus, the premium discount does not violate this section.

Example 4. (i) *Facts.* A group health plan will waive the $250 annual deductible (which is less than 20 percent of the annual cost of employee-only coverage under the plan) for the following year for participants who have a body mass index between 19 and 26, determined shortly before the beginning of the year. However, any participant for whom it is unreasonably difficult due to a medical condition to attain this standard (and any participant for whom it is medically inadvisable to attempt to achieve this standard) during the plan year is given the same discount if the participant walks for 20 minutes three days a week. Any participant for whom it is unreasonably difficult due to a medical condition to attain either standard (and any participant for whom it is medically inadvisable to attempt to achieve either standard) during the year is given the same discount if the individual satisfies an alternative standard that is reasonable in the burden it imposes and is reasonable taking into consideration the individual's medical situation. All plan materials describing the terms of the wellness program include the following statement: "If it is unreasonably difficult due to a medical condition for you to achieve a body mass index between 19 and 26 (or if it is medically inadvisable for you to attempt to achieve this body mass index) this year, your deductible will be waived

>>>→ *Caution: Reg. §54.9802-1(f), below, prior to amendment by T.D. 9620, generally applies to group health plans and group health insurance issuers, for plan years beginning before January 1, 2014.*

if you walk for 20 minutes three days a week. If you cannot follow the walking program, call us at the number above and we will work with you to develop another way to have your deductible waived." Due to a medical condition, Individual E is unable to achieve a BMI of between 19 and 26 and is also unable to follow the walking program. E proposes a program based on the recommendations of E's physician. The plan agrees to make the discount available to E if E follows the physician's recommendations.

(ii) *Conclusion.* In this *Example 4*, the program satisfies the five requirements of paragraph (f)(2) of this section. First, the program complies with the limits on rewards under a program. Second, it is reasonably designed to promote health or prevent disease. Third, individuals eligible for the program are given the opportunity to qualify for the reward at least once per year. Fourth, the reward under the program is available to all similarly situated individuals because it generally accommodates individuals for whom it is unreasonably difficult due to a medical condition to achieve (or for whom it is medically inadvisable to attempt to achieve) the targeted body mass index by providing a reasonable alternative standard (walking) and it accommodates individuals for whom it is unreasonably difficult due to a medical condition (or for whom it is medically inadvisable to attempt) to walk by providing an alternative standard that is reasonable for the individual. Fifth, the plan discloses in all materials describing the terms of the program the availability of a reasonable alternative standard for every individual. Thus, the waiver of the deductible does not violate this section.

Example 5. (i) *Facts.* In conjunction with an annual open enrollment period, a group health plan provides a form for participants to certify that they have not used tobacco products in the preceding twelve months. Participants who do not provide the certification are assessed a surcharge that is 20 percent of the cost of employee-only coverage. However, all plan materials describing the terms of the wellness program include the following statement: "If it is unrea-

sonably difficult due to a health factor for you to meet the requirements under this program (or if it is medically inadvisable for you to attempt to meet the requirements of this program), we will make available a reasonable alternative standard for you to avoid this surcharge." It is unreasonably difficult for Individual F to stop smoking cigarettes due to an addiction to nicotine (a medical condition). The plan accommodates F by requiring F to participate in a smoking cessation program to avoid the surcharge. F can avoid the surcharge for as long as F participates in the program, regardless of whether F stops smoking (as long as F continues to be addicted to nicotine).

(ii) *Conclusion.* In this *Example 5*, the premium surcharge is permissible as a wellness program because it satisfies the five requirements of paragraph (f)(2) of this section. First, the program complies with the limits on rewards under a program. Second, it is reasonably designed to promote health or prevent disease. Third, individuals eligible for the program are given the opportunity to qualify for the reward at least once per year. Fourth, the reward under the program is available to all similarly situated individuals because it accommodates individuals for whom it is unreasonably difficult due to a medical condition (or for whom it is medically inadvisable to attempt) to quit using tobacco products by providing a reasonable alternative standard. Fifth, the plan discloses in all materials describing the terms of the program the availability of a reasonable alternative standard. Thus, the premium surcharge does not violate this section.

Example 6. (i) *Facts.* Same facts as *Example 5*, except the plan accommodates F by requiring F to view, over a period of 12 months, a 12-hour video series on health problems associated with tobacco use. F can avoid the surcharge by complying with this requirement.

(ii) *Conclusion.* In this *Example 6*, the requirement to watch the series of video tapes is a reasonable alternative method for avoiding the surcharge.

>>>→ *Caution: Reg. §54.9802-1(f), below, as amended by T.D. 9620, generally applies to group health plans and group health insurance issuers, for plan years beginning on or after January 1, 2014.*

(f) *Nondiscriminatory wellness programs - in general.*—A wellness program is a program of health promotion or disease prevention. Paragraphs (b)(2)(ii) and (c)(3) of this section provide exceptions to the general prohibitions against discrimination based on a health factor for plan provisions that vary benefits (including cost-sharing mechanisms) or the premium or contribution for similarly situated individuals in connection with a wellness program that satisfies the requirements of this paragraph (f).

(1) *Definitions.*—The definitions in this paragraph (f)(1) govern in applying the provisions of this paragraph (f).

(i) *Reward.*—Except where expressly provided otherwise, references in this section to an individual obtaining a reward include both obtaining a reward (such as a discount or rebate of a premium or contribution, a waiver of all or part of a cost-sharing mechanism, an additional benefit, or any financial or other incentive) and avoiding a penalty (such as the absence of a premium surcharge or other financial or nonfinancial disincentive). References in this section to a plan providing a reward include both providing a reward (such as a discount or rebate of a premium or contribution, a waiver of all or part of a cost-sharing mechanism, an additional benefit, or any financial or other incentive) and im-

Reg. §54.9802-1(f)(1)(i)

>>>→ *Caution: Reg. §54.9802-1(f), below, as amended by T.D. 9620, generally applies to group health plans and group health insurance issuers, for plan years beginning on or after January 1, 2014.*

posing a penalty (such as a surcharge or other financial or nonfinancial disincentive).

(ii) *Participatory wellness programs.*—If none of the conditions for obtaining a reward under a wellness program is based on an individual satisfying a standard that is related to a health factor (or if a wellness program does not provide a reward), the wellness program is a participatory wellness program. Examples of participatory wellness programs are:

(A) A program that reimburses employees for all or part of the cost for membership in a fitness center.

(B) A diagnostic testing program that provides a reward for participation in that program and does not base any part of the reward on outcomes.

(C) A program that encourages preventive care through the waiver of the copayment or deductible requirement under a group health plan for the costs of, for example, prenatal care or well-baby visits. (Note that, with respect to non-grandfathered plans, § 54.9815-2713T requires benefits for certain preventive health services without the imposition of cost sharing.)

(D) A program that reimburses employees for the costs of participating, or that otherwise provides a reward for participating, in a smoking cessation program without regard to whether the employee quits smoking.

(E) A program that provides a reward to employees for attending a monthly, no-cost health education seminar.

(F) A program that provides a reward to employees who complete a health risk assessment regarding current health status, without any further action (educational or otherwise) required by the employee with regard to the health issues identified as part of the assessment. (*See also* § 54.9802-3T for rules prohibiting collection of genetic information.)

(iii) *Health-contingent wellness programs.*—A health-contingent wellness program is a program that requires an individual to satisfy a standard related to a health factor to obtain a reward (or requires an individual to undertake more than a similarly situated individual based on a health factor in order to obtain the same reward). A health-contingent wellness program may be an activity-only wellness program or an outcome-based wellness program.

(iv) *Activity-only wellness programs.*—An activity-only wellness program is a type of health-contingent wellness program that requires an individual to perform or complete an activity related to a health factor in order to obtain a reward but does not require the individual to attain or maintain a specific health outcome. Examples include walking, diet, or exercise programs, which some individuals may be unable to participate in or complete (or have difficulty participating in or completing) due to a health factor, such as severe asthma, pregnancy, or a recent surgery. *See* paragraph (f)(3) of this section for requirements applicable to activity-only wellness programs.

(v) *Outcome-based wellness programs.*—An outcome-based wellness program is a type of health-contingent wellness program that requires an individual to attain or maintain a specific health outcome (such as not smoking or attaining certain results on biometric screenings) in order to obtain a reward. To comply with the rules of this paragraph (f), an outcome-based wellness program typically has two tiers. That is, for individuals who do not attain or maintain the specific health outcome, compliance with an educational program or an activity may be offered as an alternative to achieve the same reward. This alternative pathway, however, does not mean that the overall program, which has an outcome-based component, is not an outcome-based wellness program. That is, if a measurement, test, or screening is used as part of an initial standard and individuals who meet the standard are granted the reward, the program is considered an outcome-based wellness program. For example, if a wellness program tests individuals for specified medical conditions or risk factors (including biometric screening such as testing for high cholesterol, high blood pressure, abnormal body mass index, or high glucose level) and provides a reward to individuals identified as within a normal or healthy range for these medical conditions or risk factors, while requiring individuals who are identified as outside the normal or healthy range (or at risk) to take additional steps (such as meeting with a health coach, taking a health or fitness course, adhering to a health improvement action plan, complying with a walking or exercise program, or complying with a health care provider's plan of care) to obtain the same reward, the program is an outcome-based wellness program. *See* paragraph (f)(4) of this section for requirements applicable to outcome-based wellness programs.

(2) *Requirement for participatory wellness programs.*—A participatory wellness program, as described in paragraph (f)(1)(ii) of this section, does not violate the provisions of this section only if participation in the program is made available to all similarly situated individuals, regardless of health status.

(3) *Requirements for activity-only wellness programs.*—A health-contingent wellness program that is an activity-only wellness program, as described in paragraph (f)(1)(iv) of this section, does not violate the provisions of this section only if all of the following requirements are satisfied:

(i) *Frequency of opportunity to qualify.*—The program must give individuals eligible for the program the opportunity to qualify for the reward under the program at least once per year.

➤➤➤ *Caution: Reg. §54.9802-1(f), below, as amended by T.D. 9620, generally applies to group health plans and group health insurance issuers, for plan years beginning on or after January 1, 2014.*

(ii) *Size of reward.*—The reward for the activity-only wellness program, together with the reward for other health-contingent wellness programs with respect to the plan, must not exceed the applicable percentage (as defined in paragraph (f)(5) of this section) of the total cost of employee-only coverage under the plan. However, if, in addition to employees, any class of dependents (such as spouses, or spouses and dependent children) may participate in the wellness program, the reward must not exceed the applicable percentage of the total cost of the coverage in which an employee and any dependents are enrolled. For purposes of this paragraph (f)(3)(ii), the cost of coverage is determined based on the total amount of employer and employee contributions towards the cost of coverage for the benefit package under which the employee is (or the employee and any dependents are) receiving coverage.

(iii) *Reasonable design.*—The program must be reasonably designed to promote health or prevent disease. A program satisfies this standard if it has a reasonable chance of improving the health of, or preventing disease in, participating individuals, and it is not overly burdensome, is not a subterfuge for discriminating based on a health factor, and is not highly suspect in the method chosen to promote health or prevent disease. This determination is based on all the relevant facts and circumstances.

(iv) *Uniform availability and reasonable alternative standards.*—The full reward under the activity-only wellness program must be available to all similarly situated individuals.

(A) Under this paragraph (f)(3)(iv), a reward under an activity-only wellness program is not available to all similarly situated individuals for a period unless the program meets both of the following requirements:

(1) The program allows a reasonable alternative standard (or waiver of the otherwise applicable standard) for obtaining the reward for any individual for whom, for that period, it is unreasonably difficult due to a medical condition to satisfy the otherwise applicable standard; and

(2) The program allows a reasonable alternative standard (or waiver of the otherwise applicable standard) for obtaining the reward for any individual for whom, for that period, it is medically inadvisable to attempt to satisfy the otherwise applicable standard.

(B) While plans and issuers are not required to determine a particular reasonable alternative standard in advance of an individual's request for one, if an individual is described in either paragraph (f)(3)(iv)(A)(1) or (2) of this section, a reasonable alternative standard must be furnished by the plan or issuer upon the individual's request or the condition for obtaining the reward must be waived.

(C) All the facts and circumstances are taken into account in determining whether a plan or issuer has furnished a reasonable alternative standard, including but not limited to the following:

(1) If the reasonable alternative standard is completion of an educational program, the plan or issuer must make the educational program available or assist the employee in finding such a program (instead of requiring an individual to find such a program unassisted), and may not require an individual to pay for the cost of the program.

(2) The time commitment required must be reasonable (for example, requiring attendance nightly at a one-hour class would be unreasonable).

(3) If the reasonable alternative standard is a diet program, the plan or issuer is not required to pay for the cost of food but must pay any membership or participation fee.

(4) If an individual's personal physician states that a plan standard (including, if applicable, the recommendations of the plan's medical professional) is not medically appropriate for that individual, the plan or issuer must provide a reasonable alternative standard that accommodates the recommendations of the individual's personal physician with regard to medical appropriateness. Plans and issuers may impose standard cost sharing under the plan or coverage for medical items and services furnished pursuant to the physician's recommendations.

(D) To the extent that a reasonable alternative standard under an activity-only wellness program is, itself, an activity-only wellness program, it must comply with the requirements of this paragraph (f)(3) in the same manner as if it were an initial program standard. (Thus, for example, if a plan or issuer provides a walking program as a reasonable alternative standard to a running program, individuals for whom it is unreasonably difficult due to a medical condition to complete the walking program (or for whom it is medically inadvisable to attempt to complete the walking program) must be provided a reasonable alternative standard to the walking program.) To the extent that a reasonable alternative standard under an activity-only wellness program is, itself, an outcome-based wellness program, it must comply with the requirements of paragraph (f)(4) of this section, including paragraph (f)(4)(iv)(D).

(E) If reasonable under the circumstances, a plan or issuer may seek verification, such as a statement from an individual's personal physician, that a health factor makes it unreasonably difficult for the individual to satisfy, or medically inadvisable for the individual to attempt to satisfy, the otherwise applicable standard of an activity-only wellness program. Plans and issuers may seek verification with respect to requests for a reasonable alternative

>>>→ *Caution: Reg. §54.9802-1(f), below, as amended by T.D. 9620, generally applies to group health plans and group health insurance issuers, for plan years beginning on or after January 1, 2014.*

standard for which it is reasonable to determine that medical judgment is required to evaluate the validity of the request.

(v) *Notice of availability of reasonable alternative standard.*—The plan or issuer must disclose in all plan materials describing the terms of an activity-only wellness program the availability of a reasonable alternative standard to qualify for the reward (and, if applicable, the possibility of waiver of the otherwise applicable standard), including contact information for obtaining a reasonable alternative standard and a statement that recommendations of an individual's personal physician will be accommodated. If plan materials merely mention that such a program is available, without describing its terms, this disclosure is not required. Sample language is provided in paragraph (f)(6) of this section, as well as in certain examples of this section.

(vi) *Example.*—The provisions of this paragraph (f)(3) are illustrated by the following example:

Example. (i) *Facts.* A group health plan provides a reward to individuals who participate in a reasonable specified walking program. If it is unreasonably difficult due to a medical condition for an individual to participate (or if it is medically inadvisable for an individual to attempt to participate), the plan will waive the walking program requirement and provide the reward. All materials describing the terms of the walking program disclose the availability of the waiver.

(ii) *Conclusion.* In this *Example,* the program satisfies the requirements of paragraph (f)(3)(iii) of this section because the walking program is reasonably designed to promote health and prevent disease. The program satisfies the requirements of paragraph (f)(3)(iv) of this section because the reward under the program is available to all similarly situated individuals. It accommodates individuals for whom it is unreasonably difficult to participate in the walking program due to a medical condition (or for whom it would be medically inadvisable to attempt to participate) by providing them with the reward even if they do not participate in the walking program (that is, by waiving the condition). The plan also complies with the disclosure requirement of paragraph (f)(3)(v) of this section. Thus, the plan satisfies paragraphs (f)(3)(iii), (iv), and (v) of this section.

(4) *Requirements for outcome-based wellness programs.*—A health-contingent wellness program that is an outcome-based wellness program, as described in paragraph (f)(1)(v) of this section, does not violate the provisions of this section only if all of the following requirements are satisfied:

(i) *Frequency of opportunity to qualify.*—The program must give individuals eligible for the program the opportunity to qualify for the reward under the program at least once per year.

(ii) *Size of reward.*—The reward for the outcome-based wellness program, together with the reward for other health-contingent wellness programs with respect to the plan, must not exceed the applicable percentage (as defined in paragraph (f)(5) of this section) of the total cost of employee-only coverage under the plan. However, if, in addition to employees, any class of dependents (such as spouses, or spouses and dependent children) may participate in the wellness program, the reward must not exceed the applicable percentage of the total cost of the coverage in which an employee and any dependents are enrolled. For purposes of this paragraph (f)(4)(ii), the cost of coverage is determined based on the total amount of employer and employee contributions towards the cost of coverage for the benefit package under which the employee is (or the employee and any dependents are) receiving coverage.

(iii) *Reasonable design.*—The program must be reasonably designed to promote health or prevent disease. A program satisfies this standard if it has a reasonable chance of improving the health of, or preventing disease in, participating individuals, and it is not overly burdensome, is not a subterfuge for discriminating based on a health factor, and is not highly suspect in the method chosen to promote health or prevent disease. This determination is based on all the relevant facts and circumstances. To ensure that an outcome-based wellness program is reasonably designed to improve health and does not act as a subterfuge for underwriting or reducing benefits based on a health factor, a reasonable alternative standard to qualify for the reward must be provided to any individual who does not meet the initial standard based on a measurement, test, or screening that is related to a health factor, as explained in paragraph (f)(4)(iv) of this section.

(iv) *Uniform availability and reasonable alternative standards.*—The full reward under the outcome-based wellness program must be available to all similarly situated individuals.

(A) Under this paragraph (f)(4)(iv), a reward under an outcome-based wellness program is not available to all similarly situated individuals for a period unless the program allows a reasonable alternative standard (or waiver of the otherwise applicable standard) for obtaining the reward for any individual who does not meet the initial standard based on the measurement, test, or screening, as described in this paragraph (f)(4)(iv).

(B) While plans and issuers are not required to determine a particular reasonable alternative standard in advance of an individual's request for one, if an individual is described in paragraph (f)(4)(iv)(A) of this section, a reasonable alternative standard must be furnished by

⋙→ *Caution: Reg. §54.9802-1(f), below, as amended by T.D. 9620, generally applies to group health plans and group health insurance issuers, for plan years beginning on or after January 1, 2014.*

the plan or issuer upon the individual's request or the condition for obtaining the reward must be waived.

(C) All the facts and circumstances are taken into account in determining whether a plan or issuer has furnished a reasonable alternative standard, including but not limited to the following:

(1) If the reasonable alternative standard is completion of an educational program, the plan or issuer must make the educational program available or assist the employee in finding such a program (instead of requiring an individual to find such a program unassisted), and may not require an individual to pay for the cost of the program.

(2) The time commitment required must be reasonable (for example, requiring attendance nightly at a one-hour class would be unreasonable).

(3) If the reasonable alternative standard is a diet program, the plan or issuer is not required to pay for the cost of food but must pay any membership or participation fee.

(4) If an individual's personal physician states that a plan standard (including, if applicable, the recommendations of the plan's medical professional) is not medically appropriate for that individual, the plan or issuer must provide a reasonable alternative standard that accommodates the recommendations of the individual's personal physician with regard to medical appropriateness. Plans and issuers may impose standard cost sharing under the plan or coverage for medical items and services furnished pursuant to the physician's recommendations.

(D) To the extent that a reasonable alternative standard under an outcome-based wellness program is, itself, an activity-only wellness program, it must comply with the requirements of paragraph (f)(3) of this section in the same manner as if it were an initial program standard. To the extent that a reasonable alternative standard under an outcome-based wellness program is, itself, another outcome-based wellness program, it must comply with the requirements of this paragraph (f)(4), subject to the following special rules:

(1) The reasonable alternative standard cannot be a requirement to meet a different level of the same standard without additional time to comply that takes into account the individual's circumstances. For example, if the initial standard is to achieve a BMI less than 30, the reasonable alternative standard cannot be to achieve a BMI less than 31 on that same date. However, if the initial standard is to achieve a BMI less than 30, a reasonable alternative standard for the individual could be to reduce the individual's BMI by a small amount or small percentage, over a realistic period of time, such as within a year.

(2) An individual must be given the opportunity to comply with the recommendations of the individual's personal physician as a second reasonable alternative standard to meeting the reasonable alternative standard defined by the plan or issuer, but only if the physician joins in the request. The individual can make a request to involve a personal physician's recommendations at any time and the personal physician can adjust the physician's recommendations at any time, consistent with medical appropriateness.

(E) It is not reasonable to seek verification, such as a statement from an individual's personal physician, under an outcome-based wellness program that a health factor makes it unreasonably difficult for the individual to satisfy, or medically inadvisable for the individual to attempt to satisfy, the otherwise applicable standard as a condition of providing a reasonable alternative to the initial standard. However, if a plan or issuer provides an alternative standard to the otherwise applicable measurement, test, or screening that involves an activity that is related to a health factor, then the rules of paragraph (f)(3) of this section for activity-only wellness programs apply to that component of the wellness program and the plan or issuer may, if reasonable under the circumstances, seek verification that it is unreasonably difficult due to a medical condition for an individual to perform or complete the activity (or it is medically inadvisable to attempt to perform or complete the activity). (For example, if an outcome-based wellness program requires participants to maintain a certain healthy weight and provides a diet and exercise program for individuals who do not meet the targeted weight, a plan or issuer may seek verification, as described in paragraph (f)(3)(iv)(D) of this section, if reasonable under the circumstances, that a second reasonable alternative standard is needed for certain individuals because, for those individuals, it would be unreasonably difficult due to a medical condition to comply, or medically inadvisable to attempt to comply, with the diet and exercise program, due to a medical condition.)

(v) *Notice of availability of reasonable alternative standard.*—The plan or issuer must disclose in all plan materials describing the terms of an outcome-based wellness program, and in any disclosure that an individual did not satisfy an initial outcome-based standard, the availability of a reasonable alternative standard to qualify for the reward (and, if applicable, the possibility of waiver of the otherwise applicable standard), including contact information for obtaining a reasonable alternative standard and a statement that recommendations of an individual's personal physician will be accommodated. If plan materials merely mention that such a program is available, without describing its terms, this disclosure is not required. Sample language is pro-

⋙→ *Caution: Reg. §54.9802-1(f), below, as amended by T.D. 9620, generally applies to group health plans and group health insurance issuers, for plan years beginning on or after January 1, 2014.*

vided in paragraph (f)(6) of this section, as well as in certain examples of this section.

(vi) *Examples.*—The rules of this paragraph (f)(4) are illustrated by the following examples:

Example 1 - Cholesterol screening with reasonable alternative standard to work with personal physician. (i) *Facts.* A group health plan offers a reward to participants who achieve a count under 200 on a total cholesterol test. If a participant does not achieve the targeted cholesterol count, the plan allows the participant to develop an alternative cholesterol action plan in conjunction with the participant's personal physician that may include recommendations for medication and additional screening. The plan allows the physician to modify the standards, as medically necessary, over the year. (For example, if a participant develops asthma or depression, requires surgery and convalescence, or some other medical condition or consideration makes completion of the original action plan inadvisable or unreasonably difficult, the physician may modify the original action plan.) All plan materials describing the terms of the program include the following statement: "Your health plan wants to help you take charge of your health. Rewards are available to all employees who participate in our Cholesterol Awareness Wellness Program. If your total cholesterol count is under 200, you will receive the reward. If not, you will still have an opportunity to qualify for the reward. We will work with you and your doctor to find a Health Smart program that is right for you." In addition, when any individual participant receives notification that his or her cholesterol count is 200 or higher, the notification includes the following statement: "Your plan offers a Health Smart program under which we will work with you and your doctor to try to lower your cholesterol. If you complete this program, you will qualify for a reward. Please contact us at [contact information] to get started."

(ii) *Conclusion.* In this *Example 1*, the program is an outcome-based wellness program because the initial standard requires an individual to attain or maintain a specific health outcome (a certain cholesterol level) to obtain a reward. The program satisfies the requirements of paragraph (f)(4)(iii) of this section because the cholesterol program is reasonably designed to promote health and prevent disease. The program satisfies the requirements of paragraph (f)(4)(iv) of this section because it makes available to all participants who do not meet the cholesterol standard a reasonable alternative standard to qualify for the reward. Lastly, the plan also discloses in all materials describing the terms of the program and in any disclosure that an individual did not satisfy the initial outcome-based standard the availability of a reasonable alternative standard (including contact information and the individual's ability to involve his or her personal physician), as required by paragraph (f)(4)(v) of

this section. Thus, the program satisfies the requirements of paragraphs (f)(4)(iii), (iv), and (v) of this section.

Example 2 - Cholesterol screening with plan alternative and no opportunity for personal physician involvement. (i) *Facts.* Same facts as *Example 1*, except that the wellness program's physician or nurse practitioner (rather than the individual's personal physician) determines the alternative cholesterol action plan. The plan does not provide an opportunity for a participant's personal physician to modify the action plan if it is not medically appropriate for that individual.

(ii) *Conclusion.* In this *Example 2*, the wellness program does not satisfy the requirements of paragraph (f)(4)(iii) of this section because the program does not accommodate the recommendations of the participant's personal physician with regard to medical appropriateness, as required under paragraph (f)(4)(iv)(C)(3) of this section. Thus, the program is not reasonably designed under paragraph (f)(4)(iii) of this section and is not available to all similarly situated individuals under paragraph (f)(4)(iv) of this section. The notice also does not provide all the content required under paragraph (f)(4)(v) of this section.

Example 3 - Cholesterol screening with plan alternative that can be modified by personal physician. (i) *Facts.* Same facts as *Example 2*, except that if a participant's personal physician disagrees with any part of the action plan, the personal physician may modify the action plan at any time, and the plan discloses this to participants.

(ii) *Conclusion.* In this *Example 3*, the wellness program satisfies the requirements of paragraph (f)(4)(iii) of this section because the participant's personal physician may modify the action plan determined by the wellness program's physician or nurse practitioner at any time if the physician states that the recommendations are not medically appropriate, as required under paragraph (f)(4)(iv)(C)(3) of this section. Thus, the program is reasonably designed under paragraph (f)(4)(iii) of this section and is available to all similarly situated individuals under paragraph (f)(4)(iv) of this section. The notice, which includes a statement that recommendations of an individual's personal physician will be accommodated, also complies with paragraph (f)(4)(v) of this section.

Example 4 - BMI screening with walking program alternative. (i) *Facts.* A group health plan will provide a reward to participants who have a body mass index (BMI) that is 26 or lower, determined shortly before the beginning of the year. Any participant who does not meet the target BMI is given the same discount if the participant complies with an exercise program that consists of walking 150 minutes a week. Any participant for whom it is unreasonably difficult due to a medical condition to comply with this walking program (and any participant for whom it is medically inadvisable to attempt to comply with

>>>→ *Caution: Reg. §54.9802-1(f), below, as amended by T.D. 9620, generally applies to group health plans and group health insurance issuers, for plan years beginning on or after January 1, 2014.*

the walking program) during the year is given the same discount if the participant satisfies an alternative standard that is reasonable taking into consideration the participant's medical situation, is not unreasonably burdensome or impractical to comply with, and is otherwise reasonably designed based on all the relevant facts and circumstances. All plan materials describing the terms of the wellness program include the following statement: "Fitness is Easy! Start Walking! Your health plan cares about your health. If you are considered overweight because you have a BMI of over 26, our Start Walking program will help you lose weight and feel better. We will help you enroll. (**If your doctor says that walking isn't right for you, that's okay too. We will work with you (and, if you wish, your own doctor) to develop a wellness program that is.)" Participant E is unable to achieve a BMI that is 26 or lower within the plan's timeframe and receives notification that complies with paragraph (f)(4)(v) of this section. Nevertheless, it is unreasonably difficult due to a medical condition for E to comply with the walking program. E proposes a program based on the recommendations of E's physician. The plan agrees to make the same discount available to E that is available to other participants in the BMI program or the alternative walking program, but only if E actually follows the physician's recommendations.

(ii) *Conclusion*. In this *Example 4*, the program is an outcome-based wellness program because the initial standard requires an individual to attain or maintain a specific health outcome (a certain BMI level) to obtain a reward. The program satisfies the requirements of paragraph (f)(4)(iii) of this section because it is reasonably designed to promote health and prevent disease. The program also satisfies the requirements of paragraph (f)(4)(iv) of this section because it makes available to all individuals who do not satisfy the BMI standard a reasonable alternative standard to qualify for the reward (in this case, a walking program that is not unreasonably burdensome or impractical for individuals to comply with and that is otherwise reasonably designed based on all the relevant facts and circumstances). In addition, the walking program is, itself, an activity-only standard and the plan complies with the requirements of paragraph (f)(3) of this section (including the requirement of paragraph (f)(3)(iv) that, if there are individuals for whom it is unreasonably difficult due to a medical condition to comply, or for whom it is medically inadvisable to attempt to comply, with the walking program, the plan provide a reasonable alternative to those individuals). Moreover, the plan satisfies the requirements of paragraph (f)(4)(v) of this section because it discloses, in all materials describing the terms of the program and in any disclosure that an individual did not satisfy the initial outcome-based standard, the availability of a reasonable alternative standard (including contact information and the individ-

ual's option to involve his or her personal physician) to qualify for the reward or the possibility of waiver of the otherwise applicable standard. Thus, the program satisfies the requirements of paragraphs (f)(4)(iii), (iv), and (v) of this section.

Example 5 - BMI screening with alternatives available to either lower BMI or meet personal physician's recommendations. (i) Facts. Same facts as *Example 4* except that, with respect to any participant who does not meet the target BMI, instead of a walking program, the participant is expected to reduce BMI by one point. At any point during the year upon request, any individual can obtain a second reasonable alternative standard, which is compliance with the recommendations of the participant's personal physician regarding weight, diet, and exercise as set forth in a treatment plan that the physician recommends or to which the physician agrees. The participant's personal physician is permitted to change or adjust the treatment plan at any time and the option of following the participant's personal physician's recommendations is clearly disclosed.

(ii) *Conclusion*. In this *Example 5*, the reasonable alternative standard to qualify for the reward (the alternative BMI standard requiring a one-point reduction) does not make the program unreasonable under paragraph (f)(4)(iii) or (iv) of this section because the program complies with paragraph (f)(4)(iv)(C)(4) of this section by allowing a second reasonable alternative standard to qualify for the reward (compliance with the recommendations of the participant's personal physician, which can be changed or adjusted at any time). Accordingly, the program continues to satisfy the applicable requirements of paragraph (f) of this section.

Example 6 - Tobacco use surcharge with smoking cessation program alternative. (i) *Facts*. In conjunction with an annual open enrollment period, a group health plan provides a premium differential based on tobacco use, determined using a health risk assessment. The following statement is included in all plan materials describing the tobacco premium differential: "Stop smoking today! We can help! If you are a smoker, we offer a smoking cessation program. If you complete the program, you can avoid this surcharge." The plan accommodates participants who smoke by facilitating their enrollment in a smoking cessation program that requires participation at a time and place that are not unreasonably burdensome or impractical for participants, and that is otherwise reasonably designed based on all the relevant facts and circumstances, and discloses contact information and the individual's option to involve his or her personal physician. The plan pays for the cost of participation in the smoking cessation program. Any participant can avoid the surcharge for the plan year by participating in the program, regardless of whether the participant stops smoking, but the plan can require a participant who wants to avoid the

⋙→ *Caution: Reg. §54.9802-1(f), below, as amended by T.D. 9620, generally applies to group health plans and group health insurance issuers, for plan years beginning on or after January 1, 2014.*

surcharge in a subsequent year to complete the smoking cessation program again.

(ii) *Conclusion.* In this *Example 6*, the premium differential satisfies the requirements of paragraphs (f)(4)(iii), (iv), and (v). The program is an outcome-based wellness program because the initial standard for obtaining a reward is dependent on the results of a health risk assessment (a measurement, test, or screening). The program is reasonably designed under paragraph (f)(4)(iii) because the plan provides a reasonable alternative standard (as required under paragraph (f)(4)(iv) of this section) to qualify for the reward to all tobacco users (a smoking cessation program). The plan discloses, in all materials describing the terms of the program, the availability of the reasonable alternative standard (including contact information and the individual's option to involve his or her personal physician). Thus, the program satisfies the requirements of paragraphs (f)(4)(iii), (iv), and (v) of this section.

Example 7 - Tobacco use surcharge with alternative program requiring actual cessation. (i) *Facts.* Same facts as *Example 6*, except the plan does not provide participant F with the reward in subsequent years unless *F* actually stops smoking after participating in the tobacco cessation program.

(ii) *Conclusion.* In this *Example 7*, the program is not reasonably designed under paragraph (f)(4)(iii) of this section and does not provide a reasonable alternative standard as required under paragraph (f)(4)(iv) of this section. The plan cannot cease to provide a reasonable alternative standard merely because the participant did not stop smoking after participating in a smoking cessation program. The plan must continue to offer a reasonable alternative standard whether it is the same or different (such as a new recommendation from F's personal physician or a new nicotine replacement therapy).

Example 8 - Tobacco use surcharge with smoking cessation program alternative that is not reasonable. (i) *Facts.* Same facts as *Example 6*, except the plan does not facilitate participant F's enrollment in a smoking cessation program. Instead the plan advises F to find a program, pay for it, and provide a certificate of completion to the plan.

(ii) *Conclusion.* In this *Example 8*, the requirement for *F* to find and pay for F's own smoking cessation program means that the alternative program is not reasonable. Accordingly, the plan has not offered a reasonable alternative standard that complies with paragraphs (f)(4)(iii) and (iv) of this section and the program fails to satisfy the requirements of paragraph (f) of this section.

(5) *Applicable percentage.*—(i) For purposes of this paragraph (f), the applicable percentage is 30 percent, except that the applicable percentage is increased by an additional 20 percentage points (to 50 percent) to the extent that the additional percentage is in connection with a program designed to prevent or reduce tobacco use.

(ii) The provisions of this paragraph (f)(5) are illustrated by the following examples:

Example 1. (i) *Facts.* An employer sponsors a group health plan. The annual premium for employee-only coverage is $6,000 (of which the employer pays $4,500 per year and the employee pays $1,500 per year). The plan offers employees a health-contingent wellness program with several components, focused on exercise, blood sugar, weight, cholesterol, and blood pressure. The reward for compliance is an annual premium rebate of $600.

(ii) *Conclusion.* In this *Example 1*, the reward for the wellness program, $600, does not exceed the applicable percentage of 30 percent of the total annual cost of employee-only coverage, $1,800. ($6,000 × 30% = $1,800.)

Example 2. (i) *Facts.* Same facts as *Example 1*, except the wellness program is exclusively a tobacco prevention program. Employees who have used tobacco in the last 12 months and who are not enrolled in the plan's tobacco cessation program are charged a $1,000 premium surcharge (in addition to their employee contribution towards the coverage). (Those who participate in the plan's tobacco cessation program are not assessed the $1,000 surcharge.)

(ii) *Conclusion.* In this *Example 2*, the reward for the wellness program (absence of a $1,000 surcharge), does not exceed the applicable percentage of 50 percent of the total annual cost of employee-only coverage, $3,000. ($6,000 × 50% = $3,000.)

Example 3. (i) *Facts.* Same facts as *Example 1*, except that, in addition to the $600 reward for compliance with the health-contingent wellness program, the plan also imposes an additional $2,000 tobacco premium surcharge on employees who have used tobacco in the last 12 months and who are not enrolled in the plan's tobacco cessation program. (Those who participate in the plan's tobacco cessation program are not assessed the $2,000 surcharge.)

(ii) *Conclusion.* In this *Example 3*, the total of all rewards (including absence of a surcharge for participating in the tobacco program) is $2,600 ($600 + $2,000 = $2,600), which does not exceed the applicable percentage of 50 percent of the total annual cost of employee-only coverage ($3,000); and, tested separately, the $600 reward for the wellness program unrelated to tobacco use does not exceed the applicable percentage of 30 percent of the total annual cost of employee-only coverage ($1,800).

Example 4. (i) *Facts.* An employer sponsors a group health plan. The total annual premium for employee-only coverage (including both employer and employee contributions towards the coverage) is $5,000. The plan provides a $250 reward to employees who complete a health risk assessment, without regard to the health issues identified as part of the assessment. The plan also offers a Healthy Heart program, which is a

>>>→ *Caution: Reg. §54.9802-1(f), below, as amended by T.D. 9620, generally applies to group health plans and group health insurance issuers, for plan years beginning on or after January 1, 2014.*

health-contingent wellness program, with an opportunity to earn a $1,500 reward.

(ii) *Conclusion.* In this *Example 4*, even though the total reward for all wellness programs under the plan is $1,750 ($250 + $1,500 = $1,750, which exceeds the applicable percentage of 30 percent of the cost of the annual premium for employee-only coverage ($5,000 × 30% = $1,500)), only the reward offered for compliance with the health-contingent wellness program ($1,500) is taken into account in determining whether the rules of this paragraph (f)(5) are met. (The $250 reward is offered in connection with a participatory wellness program and therefore is not taken into account.) Accordingly, the health-contingent wellness program offers a reward that does not exceed the applicable percentage of 30 percent of the total annual cost of employee-only coverage.

(6) *Sample language.*—The following language, or substantially similar language, can be used to satisfy the notice requirement of paragraphs (f)(3)(v) or (f)(4)(v) of this section: "Your health plan is committed to helping you achieve your best health. Rewards for participating in a wellness program are available to all employees. If you think you might be unable to meet a standard for a reward under this wellness program, you might qualify for an opportunity to earn the same reward by different means. Contact us at [insert contact information] and we will work with you (and, if you wish, with your doctor) to find a wellness program with the same reward that is right for you in light of your health status."

(g) *More favorable treatment of individuals with adverse health factors permitted.*—(1) *In rules for eligibility.*—(i) Nothing in this section prevents a group health plan from establishing more favorable rules for eligibility (described in paragraph (b)(1) of this section) for individuals with an adverse health factor, such as disability, than for individuals without the adverse health factor. Moreover, nothing in this section prevents a plan from charging a higher premium or contribution with respect to individuals with an adverse health factor if they would not be eligible for the coverage were it not for the adverse health factor. (However, other laws, including State insurance laws, may set or limit premium rates; these laws are not affected by this section.)

(ii) The rules of this paragraph (g)(1) are illustrated by the following examples:

Example 1. (i) *Facts.* An employer sponsors a group health plan that generally is available to employees, spouses of employees, and dependent children until age 26. However, dependent children who are disabled are eligible for coverage beyond age 26.

(ii) *Conclusion.* In this Example 1, the plan provision allowing coverage for disabled dependent children beyond age 26 satisfies this para-

graph (g)(1) (and thus does not violate this section).

Example 2. (i) *Facts.* An employer sponsors a group health plan, which is generally available to employees (and members of the employee's family) until the last day of the month in which the employee ceases to perform services for the employer. The plan generally charges employees $50 per month for employee-only coverage and $125 per month for family coverage. However, an employee who ceases to perform services for the employer by reason of disability may remain covered under the plan until the last day of the month that is 12 months after the month in which the employee ceased to perform services for the employer. During this extended period of coverage, the plan charges the employee $100 per month for employee-only coverage and $250 per month for family coverage. (This extended period of coverage is without regard to whatever rights the employee (or members of the employee's family) may have for COBRA continuation coverage.)

(ii) *Conclusion.* In this *Example 2*, the plan provision allowing extended coverage for disabled employees and their families satisfies this paragraph (g)(1) (and thus does not violate this section). In addition, the plan is permitted, under this paragraph (g)(1), to charge the disabled employees a higher premium during the extended period of coverage.

Example 3. (i) *Facts.* To comply with the requirements of a COBRA continuation provision, a group health plan generally makes COBRA continuation coverage available for a maximum period of 18 months in connection with a termination of employment but makes the coverage available for a maximum period of 29 months to certain disabled individuals and certain members of the disabled individual's family. Although the plan generally requires payment of 102 percent of the applicable premium for the first 18 months of COBRA continuation coverage, the plan requires payment of 150 percent of the applicable premium for the disabled individual's COBRA continuation coverage during the disability extension if the disabled individual would not be entitled to COBRA continuation coverage but for the disability.

(ii) *Conclusion.* In this *Example 3*, the plan provision allowing extended COBRA continuation coverage for disabled individuals satisfies this paragraph (g)(1) (and thus does not violate this section). In addition, the plan is permitted, under this paragraph (g)(1), to charge the disabled individuals a higher premium for the extended coverage if the individuals would not be eligible for COBRA continuation coverage were it not for the disability. (Similarly, if the plan provided an extended period of coverage for disabled individuals pursuant to State law or plan provision rather than pursuant to a COBRA continuation coverage provision, the plan could likewise charge the disabled individuals a higher premium for the extended coverage.)

(2) *In premiums or contributions.*—(i) Nothing in this section prevents a group health plan from charging individuals a premium or contribution that is less than the premium (or contribution) for similarly situated individuals if the lower charge is based on an adverse health factor, such as disability.

(ii) The rules of this paragraph (g)(2) are illustrated by the following example:

Example. (i) *Facts.* Under a group health plan, employees are generally required to pay $50 per month for employee-only coverage and $125 per month for family coverage under the plan. However, employees who are disabled receive coverage (whether employee-only or family coverage) under the plan free of charge.

(ii) *Conclusion.* In this *Example,* the plan provision waiving premium payment for disabled employees is permitted under this paragraph (g)(2) (and thus does not violate this section).

(h) *No effect on other laws.*—Compliance with this section is not determinative of compliance with any provision of ERISA (including the CO-BRA continuation provisions) or any other State or Federal law, such as the Americans with Disabilities Act. Therefore, although the rules of this section would not prohibit a plan from treating one group of similarly situated individuals differently from another (such as providing different benefit packages to current and former employees), other Federal or State laws may require that two separate groups of similarly situated individuals be treated the same for certain purposes (such as making the same benefit package available to COBRA qualified beneficiaries as is made available to active employees). In addition, although this section generally does not impose new disclosure obligations on plans, this section does not affect any other laws, including those that require accurate disclosures and prohibit intentional misrepresentation.

(i) *Applicability dates.*—This section applies for plan years beginning on or after July 1, 2007. [Reg. § 54.9802-1.]

☐ [T.D. 8931, 1-5-2001 (*corrected* 3-8-2001). *Amended by* T.D. 9298, 12-12-2006 (*corrected* 2-21-2007); T.D. 9464, 10-1-2009; T.D. 9620, 5-29-2013 *and* T.D. 9656, 2-20-2014.]

[Reg. § 54.9802-2]

§ 54.9802-2. Special rules for certain church plans.—(a) *Exception for certain church plans.*—(1) *Church plans in general.*—A church plan described in paragraph (b) of this section is not treated as failing to meet the requirements of section 9802 or § 54.9802-1 solely because the plan requires evidence of good health for coverage of individuals under plan provisions described in paragraph (b)(2) or (3) of this section.

(2) *Health insurance issuers.*—See sections 2702 and 2721(b)(1)(B) of the Public Health Ser-

vice Act (42 U.S.C. 300gg-2 and 300gg-21(b)(1)(B)) and 45 CFR 146.121, which require health insurance issuers providing health insurance coverage under a church plan that is a group health plan to comply with nondiscrimination requirements similar to those that church plans are required to comply with under section 9802 and § 54.9802-1 except that those nondiscrimination requirements do not include an exception for health insurance issuers comparable to the exception for church plans under section 9802(c) and this section.

(b) *Church plans to which this section applies.*—(1) *Church plans with certain coverage provisions in effect on July 15, 1997.*—This section applies to any church plan (as defined in section 414(e)) for a plan year if, on July 15, 1997 and at all times thereafter before the beginning of the plan year, the plan contains either the provisions described in paragraph (b)(2) of this section or the provisions described in paragraph (b)(3) of this section.

(2) *Plan provisions applicable to individuals employed by employers of 10 or fewer employees and self-employed individuals.*—(i) A plan contains the provisions described in this paragraph (b)(2) if it requires evidence of good health of both—

(A) Any employee of an employer of 10 or fewer employees (determined without regard to section 414(e)(3)(C), under which a church or convention or association of churches is treated as the employer); and

(B) Any self-employed individual.

(ii) A plan does not contain the provisions described in this paragraph (b)(2) if the plan contains only one of the provisions described in this paragraph (b)(2). Thus, for example, a plan that requires evidence of good health of any self-employed individual, but not of any employee of an employer with 10 or fewer employees, does not contain the provisions described in this paragraph (b)(2). Moreover, a plan does not contain the provision described in paragraph (b)(2)(i)(A) of this section if the plan requires evidence of good health of any employee of an employer of fewer than 10 (or greater than 10) employees. Thus, for example, a plan does not contain the provision described in paragraph (b)(2)(i)(A) of this section if the plan requires evidence of good health of any employee of an employer with five or fewer employees.

(3) *Plan provisions applicable to individuals who enroll after the first 90 days of initial eligibility.*—(i) A plan contains the provisions described in this paragraph (b)(3) if it requires evidence of good health of any individual who enrolls after the first 90 days of initial eligibility under the plan.

(ii) A plan does not contain the provisions described in this paragraph (b)(3) if it provides for a longer (or shorter) period than 90 days. Thus, for example, a plan requiring evidence of good health of any individual who enrolls after the first 120 days of initial eligibility under the plan does not contain the provisions described in this paragraph (b)(3).

(c) *Examples.*—The rules of this section are illustrated by the following examples:

Example 1. (i) *Facts.* A church organization maintains two church plans for entities affiliated with the church. One plan is a group health plan that provides health coverage to all employees (including ministers and lay workers) of any affiliated church entity that has more than 10 employees. The other plan is Plan *O*, which is a group health plan that is not funded through insurance coverage and that provides health coverage to any employee (including ministers and lay workers) of any affiliated church entity that has 10 or fewer employees and any self-employed individual affiliated with the church (including a self-employed minister of the church). Plan *O* requires evidence of good health in order for any individual of a church entity that has 10 or fewer employees to be covered and in order for any self-employed individual to be covered. On July 15, 1997 and at all times thereafter before the beginning of the plan year, Plan *O* has contained all the preceding provisions.

(ii) *Conclusion.* In this *Example 1*, because Plan *O* contains the plan provisions described in paragraph (b)(2) of this section and because those provisions were in the plan on July 15, 1997 and at all times thereafter before the beginning of the plan year, Plan *O* will not be treated as failing to meet the requirements of section 9802 or

§ 54.9802-1 for the plan year solely because the plan requires evidence of good health for coverage of the individuals described in those plan provisions.

Example 2. (i) *Facts.* A church organization maintains Plan *P*, which is a church plan that is not funded through insurance coverage and that is a group health plan providing health coverage to individuals employed by entities affiliated with the church and self-employed individuals affiliated with the church (such as ministers). On July 15, 1997 and at all times thereafter before the beginning of the plan year, Plan *P* has required evidence of good health for coverage of any individual who enrolls after the first 90 days of initial eligibility under the plan.

(ii) *Conclusion.* In this *Example 2*, because Plan *P* contains the plan provisions described in paragraph (b)(3) of this section and because those provisions were in the plan on July 15, 1997 and at all times thereafter before the beginning of the plan year, Plan *P* will not be treated as failing to meet the requirements of section 9802 or § 54.9802-1 for the plan year solely because the plan requires evidence of good health for coverage of individuals enrolling after the first 90 days of initial eligibility under the plan.

(d) *Applicability date.*—This section is applicable to plan years beginning on or after July 1, 2007. [Reg. § 54.9802-2.]

☐ [T.D. 9299, 12-12-2006.]

⫸→ *Caution: Temporary Reg. § 54.9802-3T, below, applies for plan years beginning on or after December 7, 2009.*

[Reg. § 54.9802-3T]

§ 54.9802-3T. Standards relating to benefits for mothers and newborns (temporary).—(a) *Definitions.*—Unless otherwise provided, the definitions in this paragraph (a) govern in applying the provisions of this section.

(1) *Collect* means, with respect to information, to request, require, or purchase such information.

(2) *Family member* means, with respect to an individual —

(i) A dependent (as defined for purposes of § 54.9801-2) of the individual; or

(ii) Any other person who is a first-degree, second-degree, third-degree, or fourthdegree relative of the individual or of a dependent of the individual. Relatives by affinity (such as by marriage or adoption) are treated the same as relatives by consanguinity (that is, relatives who share a common biological ancestor). In determining the degree of the relationship, relatives by less than full consanguinity (such as half-siblings, who share only one parent) are treated the same as relatives by full consanguinity (such as siblings who share both parents).

(A) First-degree relatives include parents, spouses, siblings, and children.

(B) Second-degree relatives include grandparents, grandchildren, aunts, uncles, nephews, and nieces.

(C) Third-degree relatives include great-grandparents, great-grandchildren, great aunts, great uncles, and first cousins.

(D) Fourth-degree relatives include great-great grandparents, great-great grandchildren, and children of first cousins.

(3) *Genetic information* means—

(i) Subject to paragraphs (a)(3)(ii) and (a)(3)(iii) of this section, with respect to an individual, information about—

(A) The individual's genetic tests (as defined in paragraph (a)(5) of this section);

(B) The genetic tests of family members of the individual;

(C) The manifestation (as defined in paragraph (a)(6) of this section) of a disease or disorder in family members of the individual; or

(D) Any request for, or receipt of, genetic services (as defined in paragraph (a)(4) of this section), or participation in clinical research which includes genetic services, by the individual or any family member of the individual.

(ii) The term *genetic information* does not include information about the sex or age of any individual.

(iii) The term *genetic information* includes—

(A) With respect to a pregnant woman (or a family member of the pregnant woman), genetic information of any fetus carried by the pregnant woman; and

Reg. § 54.9802-3T(a)(3)(iii)(A)

⟫⟩→ *Caution: Temporary Reg. §54.9802-3T, below, applies for plan years beginning on or after December 7, 2009.*

(B) With respect to an individual (or a family member of the individual) who is utilizing an assisted reproductive technology, genetic information of any embryo legally held by the individual or family member.

(4) *Genetic services* means—

(i) A genetic test, as defined in paragraph (a)(5) of this section;

(ii) Genetic counseling (including obtaining, interpreting, or assessing genetic information); or

(iii) Genetic education.

(5)(i) *Genetic test* means an analysis of human DNA, RNA, chromosomes, proteins, or metabolites, if the analysis detects genotypes, mutations, or chromosomal changes. However, a genetic test does not include an analysis of proteins or metabolites that is directly related to a manifested disease, disorder, or pathological condition. Accordingly, a test to determine whether an individual has a BRCA1 or BRCA2 variant is a genetic test. Similarly, a test to determine whether an individual has a genetic variant associated with hereditary nonpolyposis colorectal cancer is a genetic test. However, an HIV test, complete blood count, cholesterol test, liver function test, or test for the presence of alcohol or drugs is not a genetic test.

(ii) The rules of this paragraph (a)(5) are illustrated by the following example:

Example. (i) *Facts.* Individual A is a newborn covered under a group health plan. A undergoes a phenylketonuria (PKU) screening, which measures the concentration of a metabolite, phenylalanine, in A's blood. In PKU, a mutation occurs in the phenylalanine hydroxylase (PAH) gene which contains instructions for making the enzyme needed to break down the amino acid phenylalanine. Individuals with the mutation, who have a deficiency in the enzyme to break down phenylalanine, have high concentrations of phenylalanine.

(ii) *Conclusion.* In this *Example,* the PKU screening is a genetic test with respect to A because the screening is an analysis of metabolites that detects a genetic mutation.

(6)(i) *Manifestation* or *manifested* means, with respect to a disease, disorder, or pathological condition, that an individual has been or could reasonably be diagnosed with the disease, disorder, or pathological condition by a health care professional with appropriate training and expertise in the field of medicine involved. For purposes of this section, a disease, disorder, or pathological condition is not manifested if a diagnosis is based principally on genetic information.

(ii) The rules of this paragraph (a)(6) are illustrated by the following examples:

Example 1. (i) *Facts.* Individual A has a family medical history of diabetes. A begins to experience excessive sweating, thirst, and fatigue. A's physician examines A and orders blood glucose testing (which is not a genetic test). Based on the physician's examination, A's symptoms, and test results that show elevated levels of blood glucose, A's physician diagnoses A as having adult onset diabetes mellitus (Type 2 diabetes).

(ii) *Conclusion.* In this *Example 1,* A has been diagnosed by a health care professional with appropriate training and expertise in the field of medicine involved. The diagnosis is not based principally on genetic information. Thus, Type 2 diabetes is manifested with respect to A.

Example 2. (i) *Facts.* Individual B has several family members with colon cancer. One of them underwent genetic testing which detected a mutation in the MSH2 gene associated with hereditary nonpolyposis colorectal cancer (HNPCC). B's physician, a health care professional with appropriate training and expertise in the field of medicine involved, recommends that B undergo a targeted genetic test to look for the specific mutation found in B's relative to determine if B has an elevated risk for cancer. The genetic test with respect to B showed that B also carries the mutation and is at increased risk to develop colorectal and other cancers associated with HNPCC. B has a colonoscopy which indicates no signs of disease, and B has no symptoms.

(ii) *Conclusion.* In this *Example 2,* because B has no signs or symptoms of colorectal cancer, B has not been and could not reasonably be diagnosed with HNPCC. Thus, HNPCC is not manifested with respect to B.

Example 3. (i) *Facts.* Same facts as *Example 2,* except that B's colonoscopy and subsequent tests indicate the presence of HNPCC. Based on the colonoscopy and subsequent test results, B's physician makes a diagnosis of HNPCC.

(ii) *Conclusion.* In this *Example 3,* HNPCC is manifested with respect to B because a health care professional with appropriate training and expertise in the field of medicine involved has made a diagnosis that is not based principally on genetic information.

Example 4. (i) *Facts.* Individual C has a family member that has been diagnosed with Huntington's Disease. A genetic test indicates that C has the Huntington's Disease gene variant. At age 42, C begins suffering from occasional moodiness and disorientation, symptoms which are associated with Huntington's Disease. C is examined by a neurologist (a physician with appropriate training and expertise for diagnosing Huntington's Disease). The examination includes a clinical neurological exam. The results of the examination do not support a diagnosis of Huntington's Disease.

(ii) *Conclusion.* In this *Example 4,* C is not and could not reasonably be diagnosed with Huntington's Disease by a health care professional with appropriate training and expertise. Therefore, Huntington's Disease is not manifested with respect to C.

➤➤➤ *Caution: Temporary Reg. §54.9802-3T, below, applies for plan years beginning on or after December 7, 2009.*

Example 5. (i) *Facts.* Same facts as *Example 4,* except that C exhibits additional neurological and behavioral symptoms, and the results of the examination support a diagnosis of Huntington's Disease with respect to C.

(ii) *Conclusion.* In this *Example 5,* C could reasonably be diagnosed with Huntington's Disease by a health care professional with appropriate training and expertise. Therefore, Huntington's Disease is manifested with respect to C.

(7) *Underwriting purposes* has the meaning given in paragraph (d)(1) of this section.

(b) *No group-based discrimination based on genetic information.*—(1) *In general.*—For purposes of this section, a group health plan must not adjust premium or contribution amounts for any employer, or any group of similarly situated individuals under the plan, on the basis of genetic information. For this purpose, "similarly situated individuals" are those described in §54.9802-1(d).

(2) *Rule of construction.*—Nothing in paragraph (b)(1) of this section (or in paragraph (d)(1) or (d)(2) of this section) limits the ability of a group health plan to increase the premium for an employer or for a group of similarly situated individuals under the plan based on the manifestation of a disease or disorder of an individual who is enrolled in the plan. In such a case, however, the manifestation of a disease or disorder in one individual cannot also be used as genetic information about other group members to further increase the premium for an employer or a group of similarly situated individuals under the plan.

(3) *Examples.*—The rules of this paragraph (b) are illustrated by the following examples:

Example 1. (i) *Facts.* An employer sponsors a group health plan that provides coverage through a health insurance issuer. In order to determine the premium rate for the upcoming plan year, the issuer reviews the claims experience of individuals covered under the plan and other health status information of the individuals, including genetic information. The issuer finds that three individuals covered under the plan had unusually high claims experience. In addition, the issuer finds that the genetic information of two other individuals indicates the individuals have a higher probability of developing certain illnesses although the illnesses are not manifested at this time. The issuer quotes the plan a higher per-participant rate because of both the genetic information and the higher claims experience.

(ii) *Conclusion.* See *Example 1* in 29 CFR 2590.702-1(b)(3) or 45 CFR 146.122(b)(3) for a conclusion that the issuer violates the provisions of 29 CFR 2590.702-1(b) or 45 CFR 146.122(b) similar to the requirements of this paragraph (b) because the issuer adjusts the premium based on genetic information. However, if the adjustment

related solely to claims experience, the adjustment would not violate the requirements of 29 CFR 2590.702-1 or 45 CFR 146.122 similar to the requirements of this section (nor would it violate the requirements of paragraph (c) of 29 CFR 2590.702 or 45 CFR 146.121 similar to the requirements of paragraph (c) of §54.9802-1, which prohibits discrimination in individual premiums or contributions based on a health factor but permits increases in the group rate based on a health factor).

Example 2. (i) *Facts.* An employer sponsors a group health plan that provides coverage through a health insurance issuer. In order to determine the premium rate for the upcoming plan year, the issuer reviews the claims experience of individuals covered under the plan and other health status information of the individuals, including genetic information. The issuer finds that Employee A has made claims for treatment of polycystic kidney disease. A also has two dependent children covered under the plan. The issuer quotes the plan a higher per-participant rate because of both A's claims experience and the family medical history of A's children (that is, the fact that A has the disease).

(ii) *Conclusion.* See *Example 2* in 29 CFR 2590.702-1(b)(3) or 45 CFR 146.122(b)(3) for a conclusion that the issuer violates the provisions of 29 CFR 2590.702-1(b) or 45 CFR 146.122(b) similar to the requirements of this paragraph (b) because, by taking the likelihood that A's children may develop polycystic kidney disease into account in computing the rate for the plan, the issuer adjusts the premium based on genetic information relating to a condition that has not been manifested in A's children. However, the issuer does not violate the requirements of 29 CFR 2590.702-1(b) or 45 CFR 146.122(b) similar to the requirements of this paragraph (b) by increasing the premium based on A's claims experience.

(c) *Limitation on requesting or requiring genetic testing.*—(1) *General rule.*—Except as otherwise provided in this paragraph (c), a group health plan must not request or require an individual or a family member of the individual to undergo a genetic test.

(2) *Health care professional may recommend a genetic test.*—Nothing in paragraph (c)(1) of this section limits the authority of a health care professional who is providing health care services to an individual to request that the individual undergo a genetic test.

(3) *Examples.*—The rules of paragraphs (c)(1) and (c)(2) of this section are illustrated by the following examples:

Example 1. (i) *Facts.* Individual A goes to a physician for a routine physical examination. The physician reviews A's family medical history and A informs the physician that A's mother has been diagnosed with Huntington's Disease. The physician advises A that Hunting-

»»→ Caution: Temporary Reg. §54.9802-3T, below, applies for plan years beginning on or after December 7, 2009.

ton's Disease is hereditary and recommends that A undergo a genetic test.

(ii) *Conclusion.* In this *Example 1,* the physician is a health care professional who is providing health care services to A. Therefore, the physician's recommendation that A undergo the genetic test does not violate this paragraph (c).

Example 2. (i) *Facts.* Individual B is covered by a health maintenance organization (HMO). *B* is a child being treated for leukemia. B's physician, who is employed by the HMO, is considering a treatment plan that includes six-mercaptopurine, a drug for treating leukemia in most children. However, the drug could be fatal if taken by a small percentage of children with a particular gene variant. B's physician recommends that B undergo a genetic test to detect this variant before proceeding with this course of treatment.

(ii) *Conclusion.* In this *Example 2,* even though the physician is employed by the HMO, the physician is nonetheless a health care professional who is providing health care services to B. Therefore, the physician's recommendation that B undergo the genetic test does not violate this paragraph (c).

(4) *Determination regarding payment.*—(i) *In general..*—As provided in this paragraph (c)(4), nothing in paragraph (c)(1) of this section precludes a plan from obtaining and using the results of a genetic test in making a determination regarding payment. For this purpose, "payment" has the meaning given such term in 45 CFR 164.501 of the privacy regulations issued under the Health Insurance Portability and Accountability Act. Thus, if a plan conditions payment for an item or service based on its medical appropriateness and the medical appropriateness of the item or service depends on the genetic makeup of a patient, then the plan is permitted to condition payment for the item or service on the outcome of a genetic test. The plan may also refuse payment if the patient does not undergo the genetic test.

(ii) *Limitation.*—A plan is permitted to request only the minimum amount of information necessary to make a determination regarding payment. The minimum amount of information necessary is determined in accordance with the minimum necessary standard in 45 CFR 164.502(b) of the privacy regulations issued under the Health Insurance Portability and Accountability Act.

(iii) *Examples.*—See paragraph (e) of this section for examples illustrating the rules of this paragraph (c)(4), as well as other provisions of this section.

(5) *Research exception.*—Notwithstanding paragraph (c)(1) of this section, a plan may request, but not require, that a participant or beneficiary undergo a genetic test if all of the conditions of this paragraph (c)(5) are met:

(i) *Research in accordance with Federal regulations and applicable State or local law or regulations.*—The plan makes the request pursuant to research, as defined in 45 CFR 46.102(d), that complies with 45 CFR Part 46 or equivalent Federal regulations, and any applicable State or local law or regulations for the protection of human subjects in research.

(ii) *Written request for participation in research.*—The plan makes the request in writing, and the request clearly indicates to each participant or beneficiary (or, in the case of a minor child, to the legal guardian of the beneficiary) that—

(A) Compliance with the request is voluntary; and

(B) Noncompliance will have no effect on eligibility for benefits (as described in §54.9802-1(b)(1)) or premium or contribution amounts.

(iii) *Prohibition on underwriting.*—No genetic information collected or acquired under this paragraph (c)(5) can be used for underwriting purposes (as described in paragraph (d)(1) of this section).

(iv) *Notice to Federal agencies.*—The plan completes a copy of the "Notice of Research Exception under the Genetic Information Nondiscrimination Act" authorized by the Secretary and provides the notice to the address specified in the instructions thereto.

(d) *Prohibitions on collection of genetic information.*—(1) *For underwriting purposes.*—(i) *General rule.*—A group health plan must not collect (as defined in paragraph (a)(1) of this section) genetic information for underwriting purposes. See paragraph (e) of this section for examples illustrating the rules of this paragraph (d)(1), as well as other provisions of this section.

(ii) *Underwriting purposes defined.*—Subject to paragraph (d)(1)(iii) of this section, *underwriting purposes* means, with respect to any group health plan, or health insurance coverage offered in connection with a group health plan—

(A) Rules for, or determination of, eligibility (including enrollment and continued eligibility) for benefits under the plan or coverage as described in §54.9802-1(b)(1)(ii) (including changes in deductibles or other cost-sharing mechanisms in return for activities such as completing a health risk assessment or participating in a wellness program);

(B) The computation of premium or contribution amounts under the plan or coverage (including discounts, rebates, payments in kind, or other premium differential mechanisms in return for activities such as completing a health risk assessment or participating in a wellness program);

⋙→ *Caution: Temporary Reg. §54.9802-3T, below, applies for plan years beginning on or after December 7, 2009.*

(C) The application of any preexisting condition exclusion under the plan or coverage; and

(D) Other activities related to the creation, renewal, or replacement of a contract of health insurance or health benefits.

(iii) *Medical appropriateness.*—If an individual seeks a benefit under a group health plan, the plan may limit or exclude the benefit based on whether the benefit is medically appropriate, and the determination of whether the benefit is medically appropriate is not within the meaning of underwriting purposes. Accordingly, if an individual seeks a benefit under the plan and the plan conditions the benefit based on its medical appropriateness and the medical appropriateness of the benefit depends on genetic information of the individual, then the plan is permitted to condition the benefit on the genetic information. A plan is permitted to request only the minimum amount of genetic information necessary to determine medical appropriateness. The plan may deny the benefit if the patient does not provide the genetic information required to determine medical appropriateness. If an individual is not seeking a benefit, the medical appropriateness exception of this paragraph (d)(1)(iii) to the definition of underwriting purposes does not apply. See paragraph (e) of this section for examples illustrating the medical appropriateness provisions of this paragraph (d)(1)(iii), as well as other provisions of this section.

(2) *Prior to or in connection with enrollment.*—(i) *In general.*—A group health plan must not collect genetic information with respect to any individual prior to that individual's effective date of coverage under that plan, nor in connection with the rules for eligibility (as defined in §54.9802-1(b)(1)(ii)) that apply to that individual. Whether or not an individual's information is collected prior to that individual's effective date of coverage is determined at the time of collection.

(ii) *Incidental collection exception.*—(A) *In general.*—If a group health plan obtains genetic information incidental to the collection of other information concerning any individual, the collection is not a violation of this paragraph (d)(2), as long as the collection is not for underwriting purposes in violation of paragraph (d)(1) of this section.

(B) *Limitation.*—The incidental collection exception of this paragraph (d)(2)(ii) does not apply in connection with any collection where it is reasonable to anticipate that health information will be received, unless the collection explicitly states that genetic information should not be provided.

(3) *Examples.*—The rules of this paragraph (d) are illustrated by the following examples:

Example 1. (i) *Facts.* A group health plan provides a premium reduction to enrollees who complete a health risk assessment. The health risk assessment is requested to be completed after enrollment. Whether or not it is completed or what responses are given on it has no effect on an individual's enrollment status, or on the enrollment status of members of the individual's family. The health risk assessment includes questions about the individual's family medical history.

(ii) *Conclusion.* In this *Example 1*, the health risk assessment includes a request for genetic information (that is, the individual's family medical history). Because completing the health risk assessment results in a premium reduction, the request for genetic information is for underwriting purposes. Consequently, the request violates the prohibition on the collection of genetic information in paragraph (d)(1) of this section.

Example 2. (i) *Facts.* The same facts as *Example 1*, except there is no premium reduction or any other reward for completing the health risk assessment.

(ii) *Conclusion.* In this *Example 2*, the request is not for underwriting purposes, nor is it prior to or in connection with enrollment. Therefore, it does not violate the prohibition on the collection of genetic information in this paragraph (d).

Example 3. (i) *Facts.* A group health plan requests that enrollees complete a health risk assessment prior to enrollment, and includes questions about the individual's family medical history. There is no reward or penalty for completing the health risk assessment.

(ii) *Conclusion.* In this *Example 3*, because the health risk assessment includes a request for genetic information (that is, the individual's family medical history), and requests the information prior to enrollment, the request violates the prohibition on the collection of genetic information in paragraph (d)(2) of this section. Moreover, because it is a request for genetic information, it is not an incidental collection under paragraph (d)(2)(ii) of this section.

Example 4. (i) *Facts.* The facts are the same as in *Example 1*, except there is no premium reduction or any other reward given for completion of the health risk assessment. However, certain people completing the health risk assessment may become eligible for additional benefits under the plan by being enrolled in a disease management program based on their answers to questions about family medical history. Other people may become eligible for the disease management program based solely on their answers to questions about their individual medical history.

(ii) *Conclusion.* In this *Example 4*, the request for information about an individual's family medical history could result in the individual being eligible for benefits for which the individual would not otherwise be eligible. Therefore, the questions about family medical history on

Reg. §54.9802-3T(d)(3)

»»→ *Caution: Temporary Reg. §54.9802-3T, below, applies for plan years beginning on or after December 7, 2009.*

the health risk assessment are a request for genetic information for underwriting purposes and are prohibited under this paragraph (d). Although the plan conditions eligibility for the disease management program based on determinations of medical appropriateness, the exception for determinations of medical appropriateness does not apply because the individual is not seeking benefits.

Example 5. (i) *Facts.* A group health plan requests enrollees to complete two distinct health risk assessments (HRAs) after and unrelated to enrollment. The first HRA instructs the individual to answer only for the individual and not for the individual's family. The first HRA does not ask about any genetic tests the individual has undergone or any genetic services the individual has received. The plan offers a reward for completing the first HRA. The second HRA asks about family medical history and the results of genetic tests the individual has undergone. The plan offers no reward for completing the second HRA and the instructions make clear that completion of the second HRA is wholly voluntary and will not affect the reward given for completion of the first HRA.

(ii) *Conclusion.* In this *Example 5*, no genetic information is collected in connection with the first HRA, which offers a reward, and no benefits or other rewards are conditioned on the request for genetic information in the second HRA. Consequently, the request for genetic information in the second HRA is not for underwriting purposes, and the two HRAs do not violate the prohibition on the collection of genetic information in this paragraph (d).

Example 6. (i) *Facts.* A group health plan waives its annual deductible for enrollees who complete an HRA. The HRA is requested to be completed after enrollment. Whether or not the HRA is completed or what responses are given on it has no effect on an individual's enrollment status, or on the enrollment status of members of the individual's family. The HRA does not include any direct questions about the individual's genetic information (including family medical history). However, the last question reads, "Is there anything else relevant to your health that you would like us to know or discuss with you?"

(ii) *Conclusion.* In this *Example 6*, the plan's request for medical information does not explicitly state that genetic information should not be provided. Therefore, any genetic information collected in response to the question is not within the incidental collection exception and is prohibited under this paragraph (d).

Example 7. (i) *Facts.* Same facts as *Example 6*, except that the last question goes on to state, "In answering this question, you should not include any genetic information. That is, please do not include any family medical history or any information related to genetic testing, genetic services, genetic counseling, or genetic diseases for which you believe you may be at risk."

(ii) *Conclusion.* In this *Example 7*, the plan's request for medical information explicitly states that genetic information should not be provided. Therefore, any genetic information collected in response to the question is within the incidental collection exception. However, the plan may not use any genetic information it obtains incidentally for underwriting purposes.

Example 8. (i) *Facts.* Issuer M acquires Issuer N. M requests N's records, stating that N should not provide genetic information and should review the records to excise any genetic information. N assembles the data requested by M and, although N reviews it to delete genetic information, the data from a specific region included some individuals' family medical history. Consequently, M receives genetic information about some of N's covered individuals.

(ii) *Conclusion.* In this *Example 8*, M's request for health information explicitly stated that genetic information should not be provided. See *Example 8* in 29 CFR 2590.702-1(d)(3) or 45 CFR 146.122(d)(3) for a conclusion that the collection of genetic information was within the incidental collection exception of 29 CFR 2590.702-1(d)(2)(ii) or 45 CFR 146.122(d)(ii) similar to the incidental exception of paragraph (d)(2)(ii) of this section. See *Example 8* in 29 CFR 2590.702-1(d)(3) or 45 CFR 146.122(d)(3) also for a caveat that M may not use the genetic information it obtained incidentally for underwriting purposes.

(e) *Examples regarding determinations of medical appropriateness.*—The application of the rules of paragraphs (c) and (d) of this section to plan determinations of medical appropriateness is illustrated by the following examples:

Example 1. (i) *Facts.* Individual A's group health plan covers genetic testing for celiac disease for individuals who have family members with this condition. After A's son is diagnosed with celiac disease, A undergoes a genetic test and promptly submits a claim for the test to A's issuer for reimbursement. The issuer asks A to provide the results of the genetic test before the claim is paid.

(ii) *Conclusion.* See *Example 1* in 29 CFR 2590.702-1(e) or 45 CFR 146.122(e) for a conclusion under the rules of paragraph (c)(4) of 29 CFR 2590.702-1 or 45 CFR 146.122 similar to the rules of paragraph (c)(4) of this section that the issuer is permitted to request only the minimum amount of information necessary to make a decision regarding payment. Because the results of the test are not necessary for the issuer to make a decision regarding the payment of A's claim, the conclusion in *Example 1* in 29 CFR 2590.702-1(e) or 45 CFR 146.122(e) concludes that the issuer's request for the results of the genetic test violates paragraph (c) of 29 CFR 2590.702-1 or 45 CFR 146.122 similar to paragraph (c) of this section.

Example 2. (i) *Facts.* Individual B's group health plan covers a yearly mammogram for participants and beneficiaries starting at age 40,

>>>→ *Caution: Temporary Reg. §54.9802-3T, below, applies for plan years beginning on or after December 7, 2009.*

or at age 30 for those with increased risk for breast cancer, including individuals with BRCA1 or BRCA2 gene mutations. B is 33 years old and has the BRCA2 mutation. B undergoes a mammogram and promptly submits a claim to B's plan for reimbursement. Following an established policy, the plan asks B for evidence of increased risk of breast cancer, such as the results of a genetic test or a family history of breast cancer, before the claim for the mammogram is paid. This policy is applied uniformly to all similarly situated individuals and is not directed at individuals based on any genetic information.

(ii) *Conclusion.* In this *Example 2*, the plan does not violate paragraphs (c) or (d) of this section. Under paragraph (c), the plan is permitted to request and use the results of a genetic test to make a determination regarding payment, provided the plan requests only the minimum amount of information necessary. Because the medical appropriateness of the mammogram depends on the genetic makeup of the patient, the minimum amount of information necessary includes the results of the genetic test. Similarly, the plan does not violate paragraph (d) of this section because the plan is permitted to request genetic information in making a determination regarding the medical appropriateness of a claim if the genetic information is necessary to make the determination (and if the genetic information is not used for underwriting purposes).

Example 3. (i) *Facts.* Individual C was previously diagnosed with and treated for breast cancer, which is currently in remission. In accordance with the recommendation of C's physician, C has been taking a regular dose of tamoxifen to help prevent a recurrence. C's group health plan adopts a new policy requiring patients taking tamoxifen to undergo a genetic test to ensure that tamoxifen is medically appropriate for their genetic makeup. In accordance with, at the time, the latest scientific research, tamoxifen is not helpful in up to 7 percent of breast cancer patients, those with certain variations of the gene for making the CYP2D6 enzyme. If a patient has a gene variant making tamoxifen not medically appropriate, the plan does not pay for the tamoxifen prescription.

(ii) *Conclusion.* In this *Example 3*, the plan does not violate paragraph (c) of this section if it conditions future payments for the tamoxifen prescription on C's undergoing a genetic test to determine what genetic markers C has for making the CYP2D6 enzyme. Nor does the plan violate paragraph (c) of this section if the plan refuses future payment if the results of the genetic test indicate that tamoxifen is not medically appropriate for C.

Example 4. (i) *Facts.* A group health plan offers a diabetes disease management program to all similarly situated individuals for whom it is medically appropriate based on whether the individuals have or are at risk for diabetes. The program provides enhanced benefits related only to diabetes for individuals who qualify for the program. The plan sends out a notice to all participants that describes the diabetes disease management program and explains the terms for eligibility. Individuals interested in enrolling in the program are advised to contact the plan to demonstrate that they have diabetes or that they are at risk for diabetes. For individuals who do not currently have diabetes, genetic information may be used to demonstrate that an individual is at risk.

(ii) *Conclusion.* In this *Example 4*, the plan may condition benefits under the disease management program upon a showing by an individual that the individual is at risk for diabetes, even if such showing may involve genetic information, provided that the plan requests genetic information only when necessary to make a determination regarding whether the disease management program is medically appropriate for the individual and only requests the minimum amount of information necessary to make that determination.

Example 5. (i) *Facts.* Same facts as *Example 4*, except that the plan includes a questionnaire that asks about the occurrence of diabetes in members of the individual's family as part of the notice describing the disease management program.

(ii) *Conclusion.* In this *Example 5*, the plan violates the requirements of paragraph (d)(1) of this section because the requests for genetic information are not limited to those situations in which it is necessary to make a determination regarding whether the disease management program is medically appropriate for the individuals.

Example 6. (i) *Facts.* Same facts as *Example 4*, except the disease management program provides an enhanced benefit in the form of a lower annual deductible to individuals under the program; the lower deductible applies with respect to all medical expenses incurred by the individual. Thus, whether or not a claim relates to diabetes, the individual is provided with a lower deductible based on the individual providing the plan with genetic information.

(ii) *Conclusion.* In this *Example 6*, because the enhanced benefits include benefits not related to the determination of medical appropriateness, making available the enhanced benefits is within the meaning of underwriting purposes. Accordingly, the plan may not request or require genetic information (including family history information) in determining eligibility for enhanced benefits under the program because such a request would be for underwriting purposes and would violate paragraph (d)(1) of this section.

(f) *Effective/applicability date.*—This section applies for plan years beginning on or after December 7, 2009.

Reg. §54.9802-3T(f)

≫→ *Caution: Temporary Reg. §54.9802-3T, below, applies for plan years beginning on or after December 7, 2009.*

(g) *Expiration date.*—This section expires on or before October 1, 2012. [Temporary Reg. § 54.9802-3T.]

☐ [T.D. 9464, 10-1-2009.]

≫→ *Caution: Reg. §54.9811-1, below, as added by T.D. 9427, applies to group health plans for plan years beginning on or after January 1, 2009.*

[Reg. § 54.9811-1]

§ 54.9811-1. Standards relating to benefits for mothers and newborns.—(a) *Hospital length of stay.*—(1) *General rule.*—Except as provided in paragraph (a)(5) of this section, a group health plan that provides benefits for a hospital length of stay in connection with childbirth for a mother or her newborn may not restrict benefits for the stay to less than—

(i) 48 hours following a vaginal delivery; or

(ii) 96 hours following a delivery by cesarean section.

(2) *When stay begins.*—(i) *Delivery in a hospital.*—If delivery occurs in a hospital, the hospital length of stay for the mother or newborn child begins at the time of delivery (or in the case of multiple births, at the time of the last delivery).

(ii) *Delivery outside a hospital.*—If delivery occurs outside a hospital, the hospital length of stay begins at the time the mother or newborn is admitted as a hospital inpatient in connection with childbirth. The determination of whether an admission is in connection with childbirth is a medical decision to be made by the attending provider.

(3) *Examples.*—The rules of paragraphs (a)(1) and (2) of this section are illustrated by the following examples. In each example, the group health plan provides benefits for hospital lengths of stay in connection with childbirth and is subject to the requirements of this section, as follows:

Example 1. (i) *Facts.* A pregnant woman covered under a group health plan goes into labor and is admitted to the hospital at 10 p.m. on June 11. She gives birth by vaginal delivery at 6 a.m. on June 12.

(ii) *Conclusion.* In this *Example 1*, the 48-hour period described in paragraph (a)(1)(i) of this section ends at 6 a.m. on June 14.

Example 2. (i) *Facts.* A woman covered under a group health plan gives birth at home by vaginal delivery. After the delivery, the woman begins bleeding excessively in connection with the childbirth and is admitted to the hospital for treatment of the excessive bleeding at 7 p.m. on October 1.

(ii) *Conclusion.* In this *Example 2*, the 48-hour period described in paragraph (a)(1)(i) of this section ends at 7 p.m. on October 3.

Example 3. (i) *Facts.* A woman covered under a group health plan gives birth by vaginal delivery at home. The child later develops pneumonia and is admitted to the hospital. The attending provider determines that the admission is not in connection with childbirth.

(ii) *Conclusion.* In this *Example 3*, the hospital length-of-stay requirements of this section do not apply to the child's admission to the hospital because the admission is not in connection with childbirth.

(4) *Authorization not required.*—(i) *In general.*—A plan may not require that a physician or other health care provider obtain authorization from the plan, or from a health insurance issuer offering health insurance coverage under the plan, for prescribing the hospital length of stay specified in paragraph (a)(1) of this section. (See also paragraphs (b)(2) and (c)(3) of this section for rules and examples regarding other authorization and certain notice requirements.)

(ii) *Example.*—The rule of this paragraph (a)(4) is illustrated by the following example:

Example. (i) *Facts.* In the case of a delivery by cesarean section, a group health plan subject to the requirements of this section automatically provides benefits for any hospital length of stay of up to 72 hours. For any longer stay, the plan requires an attending provider to complete a certificate of medical necessity. The plan then makes a determination, based on the certificate of medical necessity, whether a longer stay is medically necessary.

(ii) *Conclusion.* In this *Example*, the requirement that an attending provider complete a certificate of medical necessity to obtain authorization for the period between 72 hours and 96 hours following a delivery by cesarean section is prohibited by this paragraph (a)(4).

(5) *Exceptions.*—(i) *Discharge of mother.*—If a decision to discharge a mother earlier than the period specified in paragraph (a)(1) of this section is made by an attending provider, in consultation with the mother, the requirements of paragraph (a)(1) of this section do not apply for any period after the discharge.

(ii) *Discharge of newborn.*—If a decision to discharge a newborn child earlier than the period specified in paragraph (a)(1) of this section is made by an attending provider, in consultation with the mother (or the newborn's authorized representative), the requirements of paragraph (a)(1) of this section do not apply for any period after the discharge.

(iii) *Attending provider defined.*—For purposes of this section, attending provider means an individual who is licensed under applicable state law to provide maternity or pediatric care and who is directly responsible for providing maternity or pediatric care to a mother or new-

⋙→ *Caution: Reg. §54.9811-1, below, as added by T.D. 9427, applies to group health plans for plan years beginning on or after January 1, 2009.*

born child. Therefore, a plan, hospital, managed care organization, or other issuer is not an attending provider.

    (iv) *Example.*—The rules of this paragraph (a)(5) are illustrated by the following example:

    Example. (i) *Facts.* A pregnant woman covered under a group health plan subject to the requirements of this section goes into labor and is admitted to a hospital. She gives birth by cesarean section. On the third day after the delivery, the attending provider for the mother consults with the mother, and the attending provider for the newborn consults with the mother regarding the newborn. The attending providers authorize the early discharge of both the mother and the newborn. Both are discharged approximately 72 hours after the delivery. The plan pays for the 72-hour hospital stays.

    (ii) *Conclusion.* In this *Example*, the requirements of this paragraph (a) have been satisfied with respect to the mother and the newborn. If either is readmitted, the hospital stay for the readmission is not subject to this section.

    (b) *Prohibitions.*—(1) *With respect to mothers.*— (i) *In general.*—A group health plan may not—

    (A) Deny a mother or her newborn child eligibility or continued eligibility to enroll or renew coverage under the terms of the plan solely to avoid the requirements of this section; or

    (B) Provide payments (including payments-in-kind) or rebates to a mother to encourage her to accept less than the minimum protections available under this section.

    (ii) *Examples.*—The rules of this paragraph (b)(1) are illustrated by the following examples. In each example, the group health plan is subject to the requirements of this section, as follows:

    Example 1. (i) *Facts.* A group health plan provides benefits for at least a 48-hour hospital length of stay following a vaginal delivery. If a mother and newborn covered under the plan are discharged within 24 hours after the delivery, the plan will waive the copayment and deductible.

    (ii) *Conclusion.* In this *Example 1*, because waiver of the copayment and deductible is in the nature of a rebate that the mother would not receive if she and her newborn remained in the hospital, it is prohibited by this paragraph (b)(1). (In addition, the plan violates paragraph (b)(2) of this section because, in effect, no copayment or deductible is required for the first portion of the stay and a double copayment and a deductible are required for the second portion of the stay.)

    Example 2. (i) *Facts.* A group health plan provides benefits for at least a 48-hour hospital length of stay following a vaginal delivery. In the event that a mother and her newborn are discharged earlier than 48 hours and the dis-

charges occur after consultation with the mother in accordance with the requirements of paragraph (a)(5) of this section, the plan provides for a follow-up visit by a nurse within 48 hours after the discharges to provide certain services that the mother and her newborn would otherwise receive in the hospital.

    (ii) *Conclusion.* In this *Example 2*, because the follow-up visit does not provide any services beyond what the mother and her newborn would receive in the hospital, coverage for the follow-up visit is not prohibited by this paragraph (b)(1).

    (2) *With respect to benefit restrictions.*—(i) *In general.*—Subject to paragraph (c)(3) of this section, a group health plan may not restrict the benefits for any portion of a hospital length of stay specified in paragraph (a) of this section in a manner that is less favorable than the benefits provided for any preceding portion of the stay.

    (ii) *Example.*—The rules of this paragraph (b)(2) are illustrated by the following example:

    Example. (i) *Facts.* A group health plan subject to the requirements of this section provides benefits for hospital lengths of stay in connection with childbirth. In the case of a delivery by cesarean section, the plan automatically pays for the first 48 hours. With respect to each succeeding 24-hour period, the participant or beneficiary must call the plan to obtain precertification from a utilization reviewer, who determines if an additional 24-hour period is medically necessary. If this approval is not obtained, the plan will not provide benefits for any succeeding 24-hour period.

    (ii) *Conclusion.* In this *Example*, the requirement to obtain precertification for the two 24-hour periods immediately following the initial 48-hour stay is prohibited by this paragraph (b)(2) because benefits for the latter part of the stay are restricted in a manner that is less favorable than benefits for a preceding portion of the stay. (However, this section does not prohibit a plan from requiring precertification for any period after the first 96 hours.) In addition, the requirement to obtain precertification from the plan based on medical necessity for a hospital length of stay within the 96-hour period would also violate paragraph (a) of this section.

    (3) *With respect to attending providers.*—A group health plan may not directly or indirectly—

    (i) Penalize (for example, take disciplinary action against or retaliate against), or otherwise reduce or limit the compensation of, an attending provider because the provider furnished care to a participant or beneficiary in accordance with this section; or

    (ii) Provide monetary or other incentives to an attending provider to induce the provider to furnish care to a participant or beneficiary in a manner inconsistent with this section, including

>>>→ *Caution: Reg. §54.9811-1, below, as added by T.D. 9427, applies to group health plans for plan years beginning on or after January 1, 2009.*

providing any incentive that could induce an attending provider to discharge a mother or newborn earlier than 48 hours (or 96 hours) after delivery.

(c) *Construction.*—With respect to this section, the following rules of construction apply:

(1) *Hospital stays not mandatory.*—This section does not require a mother to—

(i) Give birth in a hospital; or

(ii) Stay in the hospital for a fixed period of time following the birth of her child.

(2) *Hospital stay benefits not mandated.*—This section does not apply to any group health plan that does not provide benefits for hospital lengths of stay in connection with childbirth for a mother or her newborn child.

(3) *Cost-sharing rules.*—(i) *In general.*—This section does not prevent a group health plan from imposing deductibles, coinsurance, or other cost-sharing in relation to benefits for hospital lengths of stay in connection with childbirth for a mother or a newborn under the plan or coverage, except that the coinsurance or other cost-sharing for any portion of the hospital length of stay specified in paragraph (a) of this section may not be greater than that for any preceding portion of the stay.

(ii) *Example.*—The rules of this paragraph (c)(3) are illustrated by the following examples. In each example, the group health plan is subject to the requirements of this section, as follows:

Example 1. (i) *Facts.* A group health plan provides benefits for at least a 48-hour hospital length of stay in connection with vaginal deliveries. The plan covers 80 percent of the cost of the stay for the first 24-hour period and 50 percent of the cost of the stay for the second 24-hour period. Thus, the coinsurance paid by the patient increases from 20 percent to 50 percent after 24 hours.

(ii) *Conclusion.* In this *Example 1*, the plan violates the rules of this paragraph (c)(3) because coinsurance for the second 24-hour period of the 48-hour stay is greater than that for the preceding portion of the stay. (In addition, the plan also violates the similar rule in paragraph (b)(2) of this section.)

Example 2. (i) *Facts.* A group health plan generally covers 70 percent of the cost of a hospital length of stay in connection with childbirth. However, the plan will cover 80 percent of the cost of the stay if the participant or beneficiary notifies the plan of the pregnancy in advance of admission and uses whatever hospital the plan may designate.

(ii) *Conclusion.* In this *Example 2*, the plan does not violate the rules of this paragraph (c)(3) because the level of benefits provided (70 percent or 80 percent) is consistent throughout the 48-hour (or 96-hour) hospital length of stay required under paragraph (a) of this section. (In addition, the plan does not violate the rules in paragraph (a)(4) or (b)(2) of this section.)

(4) *Compensation of attending provider.*—This section does not prevent a group health plan from negotiating with an attending provider the level and type of compensation for care furnished in accordance with this section (including paragraph (b) of this section).

(d) *Notice requirement.*—See 29 CFR 2520.102-3(u) for rules relating to a disclosure requirement imposed under section 711(d) of ERISA (29 U.S.C. 1181) on certain group health plans that provide benefits for hospital lengths of stay in connection with childbirth.

(e) *Applicability in certain states.*—(1) *Health insurance coverage.*—The requirements of section 9811 and this section do not apply with respect to health insurance coverage offered in connection with a group health plan if there is a state law regulating the coverage that meets any of the following criteria:

(i) The state law requires the coverage to provide for at least a 48-hour hospital length of stay following a vaginal delivery and at least a 96-hour hospital length of stay following a delivery by cesarean section.

(ii) The state law requires the coverage to provide for maternity and pediatric care in accordance with guidelines that relate to care following childbirth established by the American College of Obstetricians and Gynecologists, the American Academy of Pediatrics, or any other established professional medical association.

(iii) The state law requires, in connection with the coverage for maternity care, that the hospital length of stay for such care is left to the decision of (or is required to be made by) the attending provider in consultation with the mother. State laws that require the decision to be made by the attending provider with the consent of the mother satisfy the criterion of this paragraph (e)(1)(iii).

(2) *Group health plans.*—(i) *Fully-insured plans.*—For a group health plan that provides benefits solely through health insurance coverage, if the state law regulating the health insurance coverage meets any of the criteria in paragraph (e)(1) of this section, then the requirements of section 9811 and this section do not apply.

(ii) *Self-insured plans.*—For a group health plan that provides all benefits for hospital lengths of stay in connection with childbirth other than through health insurance coverage, the requirements of section 9811 and this section apply.

(iii) *Partially-insured plans.*—For a group health plan that provides some benefits through health insurance coverage, if the state law regulating the health insurance coverage meets any of the criteria in paragraph (e)(1) of this section,

⫸→ *Caution: Reg. §54.9811-1, below, as added by T.D. 9427, applies to group health plans for plan years beginning on or after January 1, 2009.*

then the requirements of section 9811 and this section apply only to the extent the plan provides benefits for hospital lengths of stay in connection with childbirth other than through health insurance coverage.

(3) *Preemption provisions under section 731(a) of ERISA.*—See 29 CFR 2590.711(e)(3) for a rule providing that the preemption provisions contained in section 731(a)(1) of ERISA and 29 CFR 2590.731(a) do not supersede a state law if the state law is described in paragraph (e)(1) of 29 CFR 2590.711 (which is substantially similar to paragraph (e)(1) of this section).

(4) *Examples.*—The rules of this paragraph (e) are illustrated by the following examples:

Example 1. (i) *Facts.* A group health plan buys group health insurance coverage in a state that requires that the coverage provide for at least a 48-hour hospital length of stay following a vaginal delivery and at least a 96-hour hospital length of stay following a delivery by cesarean section.

(ii) *Conclusion.* In this *Example 1,* the coverage is subject to state law, and the requirements of section 9811 and this section do not apply.

Example 2. (i) *Facts.* A self-insured group health plan covers hospital lengths of stay in connection with childbirth in a state that requires health insurance coverage to provide for maternity and pediatric care in accordance with guidelines that relate to care following childbirth established by the American College of Obstetricians and Gynecologists and the American Academy of Pediatrics.

(ii) *Conclusion.* In this *Example 2,* even though the state law satisfies the criterion of paragraph (e)(1)(ii) of this section, because the plan provides benefits for hospital lengths of stay in connection with childbirth other than through health insurance coverage, the plan is subject to the requirements of section 9811 and this section.

(f) *Effective/applicability date.*—This section applies to group health plans for plan years beginning on or after January 1, 2009. [Reg. §54.9811-1.]

☐ [T.D. 9427, 10-17-2008.]

⫸→ *Caution: Temporary Reg. §54.9811-1T, below, was removed by T.D. 9427 but applies to group heath plans for plan years beginning before January 1, 2009.*

[Reg. §54.9811-1T]

§54.9811-1T. Standards relating to benefits for mothers and newborns (temporary).—(a) *Hospital length of stay.*—(1) *General rule.*—Except as provided in paragraph (a)(5) of this section, a group health plan that provides benefits for a hospital length of stay in connection with childbirth for a mother or her newborn may not restrict benefits for the stay to less than—

(i) 48 hours following a vaginal delivery; or

(ii) 96 hours following a delivery by cesarean section.

(2) *When stay begins.*—(i) *Delivery in a hospital.*—If delivery occurs in a hospital, the hospital length of stay for the mother or newborn child begins at the time of delivery (or in the case of multiple births, at the time of the last delivery).

(ii) *Delivery outside a hospital.*—If delivery occurs outside a hospital, the hospital length of stay begins at the time the mother or newborn is admitted as a hospital inpatient in connection with childbirth. The determination of whether an admission is in connection with childbirth is a medical decision to be made by the attending provider.

(3) *Examples.*—The rules of paragraphs (a)(1) and (2) of this section are illustrated by the following examples. In each example, the group health plan provides benefits for hospital lengths of stay in connection with childbirth and is subject to the requirements of this section, as follows:

Example 1. (i) A pregnant woman covered under a group health plan goes into labor and is admitted to the hospital at 10 p.m. on June 11. She gives birth by vaginal delivery at 6 a.m. on June 12.

(ii) In this *Example 1,* the 48-hour period described in paragraph (a)(1)(i) of this section ends at 6 a.m. on June 14.

Example 2. (i) A woman covered under a group health plan gives birth at home by vaginal delivery. After the delivery, the woman begins bleeding excessively in connection with the childbirth and is admitted to the hospital for treatment of the excessive bleeding at 7 p.m. on October 1.

(ii) In this *Example 2,* the 48-hour period described in paragraph (a)(1)(i) of this section ends at 7 p.m. on October 3.

Example 3. (i) A woman covered under a group health plan gives birth by vaginal delivery at home. The child later develops pneumonia and is admitted to the hospital. The attending provider determines that the admission is not in connection with childbirth.

(ii) In this *Example 3,* the hospital length-of-stay requirements of this section do not apply to the child's admission to the hospital because the admission is not in connection with childbirth.

(4) *Authorization not required.*—(i) *In general.*—A plan may not require that a physician or other health care provider obtain authorization from the plan, or from a health insurance issuer offering health insurance coverage under the plan, for prescribing the hospital length of stay required under paragraph (a)(1) of this section.

⨠→ *Caution: Temporary Reg. §54.9811-1T, below, was removed by T.D. 9427 but applies to group heath plans for plan years beginning before January 1, 2009.*

(See also paragraphs (b)(2) and (c)(3) of this section for rules and examples regarding other authorization and certain notice requirements.)

(ii) *Example.*—The rule of this paragraph (a)(4) is illustrated by the following example:

Example. (i) In the case of a delivery by cesarean section, a group health plan subject to the requirements of this section automatically provides benefits for any hospital length of stay of up to 72 hours. For any longer stay, the plan requires an attending provider to complete a certificate of medical necessity. The plan then makes a determination, based on the certificate of medical necessity, whether a longer stay is medically necessary.

(ii) In this *Example*, the requirement that an attending provider complete a certificate of medical necessity to obtain authorization for the period between 72 hours and 96 hours following a delivery by cesarean section is prohibited by this paragraph (a)(4).

(5) *Exceptions.*—(i) *Discharge of mother.*—If a decision to discharge a mother earlier than the period specified in paragraph (a)(1) of this section is made by an attending provider, in consultation with the mother, the requirements of paragraph (a)(1) of this section do not apply for any period after the discharge.

(ii) *Discharge of newborn.*—If a decision to discharge a newborn child earlier than the period specified in paragraph (a)(1) of this section is made by an attending provider, in consultation with the mother (or the newborn's authorized representative), the requirements of paragraph (a)(1) of this section do not apply for any period after the discharge.

(iii) *Attending provider defined.*—For purposes of this section, *attending provider* means an individual who is licensed under applicable State law to provide maternity or pediatric care and who is directly responsible for providing maternity or pediatric care to a mother or newborn child.

(iv) *Example.*—The rules of this paragraph (a)(5) are illustrated by the following example:

Example. (i) A pregnant woman covered under a group health plan subject to the requirements of this section goes into labor and is admitted to a hospital. She gives birth by cesarean section. On the third day after the delivery, the attending provider for the mother consults with the mother, and the attending provider for the newborn consults with the mother regarding the newborn. The attending providers authorize the early discharge of both the mother and the newborn. Both are discharged approximately 72 hours after the delivery. The plan pays for the 72-hour hospital stays.

(ii) In this *Example*, the requirements of this paragraph (a) have been satisfied with respect to the mother and the newborn. If either is readmitted, the hospital stay for the readmission is not subject to this section.

(b) *Prohibitions.*—(1) *With respect to mothers.*—(i) *In general.*—A group health plan may not—

(A) Deny a mother or her newborn child eligibility or continued eligibility to enroll or renew coverage under the terms of the plan solely to avoid the requirements of this section; or

(B) Provide payments (including payments-in-kind) or rebates to a mother to encourage her to accept less than the minimum protections available under this section.

(ii) *Examples.*—The rules of this paragraph (b)(1) are illustrated by the following examples. In each example, the group health plan is subject to the requirements of this section, as follows:

Example 1. (i) A group health plan provides benefits for at least a 48-hour hospital length of stay following a vaginal delivery. If a mother and newborn covered under the plan are discharged within 24 hours after the delivery, the plan will waive the copayment and deductible.

(ii) In this *Example 1*, because waiver of the copayment and deductible is in the nature of a rebate that the mother would not receive if she and her newborn remained in the hospital, it is prohibited by this paragraph (b)(1). (In addition, the plan violates paragraph (b)(2) of this section because, in effect, no copayment or deductible is required for the first portion of the stay and a double copayment and a deductible are required for the second portion of the stay.)

Example 2. (i) A group health plan provides benefits for at least a 48-hour hospital length of stay following a vaginal delivery. In the event that a mother and her newborn are discharged earlier than 48 hours and the discharges occur after consultation with the mother in accordance with the requirements of paragraph (a)(5) of this section, the plan provides for a follow-up visit by a nurse within 48 hours after the discharges to provide certain services that the mother and her newborn would otherwise receive in the hospital.

(ii) In this *Example 2*, because the follow-up visit does not provide any services beyond what the mother and her newborn would receive in the hospital, coverage for the follow-up visit is not prohibited by this paragraph (b)(1).

(2) *With respect to benefit restrictions.*—(i) *In general.*—Subject to paragraph (c)(3) of this section, a group health plan may not restrict the benefits for any portion of a hospital length of stay required under paragraph (a) of this section in a manner that is less favorable than the benefits provided for any preceding portion of the stay.

(ii) *Example.*—The rules of this paragraph (b)(2) are illustrated by the following example:

➤➤➤ *Caution: Temporary Reg. §54.9811-1T, below, was removed by T.D. 9427 but applies to group heath plans for plan years beginning before January 1, 2009.*

Example. (i) A group health plan subject to the requirements of this section provides benefits for hospital lengths of stay in connection with childbirth. In the case of a delivery by cesarean section, the plan automatically pays for the first 48 hours. With respect to each succeeding 24-hour period, the participant or beneficiary must call the plan to obtain precertification from a utilization reviewer, who determines if an additional 24-hour period is medically necessary. If this approval is not obtained, the plan will not provide benefits for any succeeding 24-hour period.

(ii) In this *Example,* the requirement to obtain precertification for the two 24-hour periods immediately following the initial 48-hour stay is prohibited by this paragraph (b)(2) because benefits for the latter part of the stay are restricted in a manner that is less favorable than benefits for a preceding portion of the stay. (However, this section does not prohibit a plan from requiring precertification for any period after the first 96 hours.) In addition, if the plan's utilization reviewer denied any mother or her newborn benefits within the 96-hour stay, the plan would also violate paragraph (a) of this section.

(3) *With respect to attending providers.*—A group health plan may not directly or indirectly—

(i) Penalize (for example, take disciplinary action against or retaliate against), or otherwise reduce or limit the compensation of, an attending provider because the provider furnished care to a participant or beneficiary in accordance with this section; or

(ii) Provide monetary or other incentives to an attending provider to induce the provider to furnish care to a participant or beneficiary in a manner inconsistent with this section, including providing any incentive that could induce an attending provider to discharge a mother or newborn earlier than 48 hours (or 96 hours) after delivery.

(c) *Construction.*—With respect to this section, the following rules of construction apply:

(1) *Hospital stays not mandatory.*—This section does not require a mother to—

(i) Give birth in a hospital; or

(ii) Stay in the hospital for a fixed period of time following the birth of her child.

(2) *Hospital stay benefits not mandated.*—This section does not apply to any group health plan that does not provide benefits for hospital lengths of stay in connection with childbirth for a mother or her newborn child.

(3) *Cost-sharing rules.*—(i) *In general.*—This section does not prevent a group health plan from imposing deductibles, coinsurance, or other cost-sharing in relation to benefits for hospital lengths of stay in connection with childbirth for

a mother or a newborn under the plan or coverage, except that the coinsurance or other cost-sharing for any portion of the hospital length of stay required under paragraph (a) of this section may not be greater than that for any preceding portion of the stay.

(ii) *Examples.*—The rules of this paragraph (c)(3) are illustrated by the following examples. In each example, the group health plan is subject to the requirements of this section, as follows:

Example 1. (i) A group health plan provides benefits for at least a 48-hour hospital length of stay in connection with vaginal deliveries. The plan covers 80 percent of the cost of the stay for the first 24-hour period and 50 percent of the cost of the stay for the second 24-hour period. Thus, the coinsurance paid by the patient increases from 20 percent to 50 percent after 24 hours.

(ii) In this *Example 1,* the plan violates the rules of this paragraph (c)(3) because coinsurance for the second 24-hour period of the 48-hour stay is greater than that for the preceding portion of the stay. (In addition, the plan also violates the similar rule in paragraph (b)(2) of this section.)

Example 2. (i) A group health plan generally covers 70 percent of the cost of a hospital length of stay in connection with childbirth. However, the plan will cover 80 percent of the cost of the stay if the participant or beneficiary notifies the plan of the pregnancy in advance of admission and uses whatever hospital the plan may designate.

(ii) In this *Example 2,* the plan does not violate the rules of this paragraph (c)(3) because the level of benefits provided (70 percent or 80 percent) is consistent throughout the 48-hour (or 96-hour) hospital length of stay required under paragraph (a) of this section. (In addition, the plan does not violate the rules in paragraph (a)(4) or (b)(2) of this section.)

(4) *Compensation of attending provider.*—This section does not prevent a group health plan from negotiating with an attending provider the level and type of compensation for care furnished in accordance with this section (including paragraph (b) of this section).

(d) *Notice requirement.*—See 29 CFR 2520.102-3(u) and (v)(2) for rules relating to a notice requirement imposed under section 711 of the Employee Retirement Income Security Act of 1974 (29 U.S.C. 1181) on certain group health plans that provide benefits for hospital lengths of stay in connection with childbirth.

(e) *Applicability in certain States.*—(1) *Health insurance coverage.*—The requirements of section 9811 and this section do not apply with respect to health insurance coverage offered in connection with a group health plan if there is a State

⋙→ Caution: *Temporary Reg. §54.9811-1T, below, was removed by T.D. 9427 but applies to group heath plans for plan years beginning before January 1, 2009.*

law regulating the coverage that meets any of the following criteria:

(i) The State law requires the coverage to provide for at least a 48-hour hospital length of stay following a vaginal delivery and at least a 96-hour hospital length of stay following a delivery by cesarean section.

(ii) The State law requires the coverage to provide for maternity and pediatric care in accordance with guidelines established by the American College of Obstetricians and Gynecologists, the American Academy of Pediatrics, or any other established professional medical association.

(iii) The State law requires, in connection with the coverage for maternity care, that the hospital length of stay for such care is left to the decision of (or is required to be made by) the attending provider in consultation with the mother. State laws that require the decision to be made by the attending provider with the consent of the mother satisfy the criterion of this paragraph (e)(1)(iii).

(2) *Group health plans.*—(i) *Fully-insured plans.*—For a group health plan that provides benefits solely through health insurance coverage, if the State law regulating the health insurance coverage meets any of the criteria in paragraph (e)(1) of this section, then the requirements of section 9811 and this section do not apply.

(ii) *Self-insured plans.*—For a group health plan that provides all benefits for hospital lengths of stay in connection with childbirth other than through health insurance coverage, the requirements of section 9811 and this section apply.

(iii) *Partially-insured plans.*—For a group health plan that provides some benefits through health insurance coverage, if the State law regulating the health insurance coverage meets any of the criteria in paragraph (e)(1) of this section, then the requirements of section 9811 and this section apply only to the extent the plan provides benefits for hospital lengths of stay in con-

nection with childbirth other than through health insurance coverage.

(3) *Preemption provisions under ERISA.*—See 29 CFR 2590.711(e)(3) regarding how rules parallel to those under paragraph (e)(1) of this section relate to other preemption provisions under the Employee Retirement Income Security Act of 1974.

(4) *Examples.*—The rules of this paragraph (e) are illustrated by the following examples:

Example 1. (i) A group health plan buys group health insurance coverage in a State that requires that the coverage provide for at least a 48-hour hospital length of stay following a vaginal delivery and at least a 96-hour hospital length of stay following a delivery by cesarean section.

(ii) In this *Example 1*, the coverage is subject to State law, and the requirements of section 9811 and this section do not apply.

Example 2. (i) A self-insured group health plan covers hospital lengths of stay in connection with childbirth in a State that requires health insurance coverage to provide for maternity care in accordance with guidelines established by the American College of Obstetricians and Gynecologists and to provide for pediatric care in accordance with guidelines established by the American Academy of Pediatrics.

(ii) In this *Example 2*, even though the State law satisfies the criterion of paragraph (e)(1)(ii) of this section, because the plan provides benefits for hospital lengths of stay in connection with childbirth other than through health insurance coverage, the plan is subject to the requirements of section 9811 and this section.

(f) *Effective date.*—Section 9811 applies to group health plans for plan years beginning on or after January 1, 1998. This section applies to group health plans for plan years beginning on or after January 1, 1999. [Temporary Reg. §54.9811-1T.]

☐ [*T.D.* 8788, 10-26-98. *Removed by T.D.* 9427, 10-17-2008.]

⋙→ Caution: *Reg. §54.9812-1, below, as added by T.D. 9640, is generally applicable to group health plans and health insurance issuers for plan or policy years beginning on or after July 1, 2014.*

[Reg. §54.9812-1]

§54.9812-1. Parity in mental health and substance use disorder benefits.—(a) *Meaning of terms.*—For purposes of this section, except where the context clearly indicates otherwise, the following terms have the meanings indicated:

Aggregate lifetime dollar limit means a dollar limitation on the total amount of specified benefits that may be paid under a group health plan (or health insurance coverage offered in connection with such a plan) for any coverage unit.

Annual dollar limit means a dollar limitation on the total amount of specified benefits that may be paid in a 12-month period under a group

health plan (or health insurance coverage offered in connection with such a plan) for any coverage unit.

Coverage unit means coverage unit as described in paragraph (c)(1)(iv) of this section.

Cumulative financial requirements are financial requirements that determine whether or to what extent benefits are provided based on accumulated amounts and include deductibles and out-of-pocket maximums. (However, cumulative financial requirements do not include aggregate lifetime or annual dollar limits because these two terms are excluded from the meaning of financial requirements.)

>>>→ *Caution: Reg. §54.9812-1, below, as added by T.D. 9640, is generally applicable to group health plans and health insurance issuers for plan or policy years beginning on or after July 1, 2014.*

Cumulative quantitative treatment limitations are treatment limitations that determine whether or to what extent benefits are provided based on accumulated amounts, such as annual or lifetime day or visit limits.

Financial requirements include deductibles, copayments, coinsurance, or out-of-pocket maximums. Financial requirements do not include aggregate lifetime or annual dollar limits.

Medical/surgical benefits means benefits with respect to items or services for medical conditions or surgical procedures, as defined under the terms of the plan or health insurance coverage and in accordance with applicable Federal and State law, but does not include mental health or substance use disorder benefits. Any condition defined by the plan or coverage as being or as not being a medical/surgical condition must be defined to be consistent with generally recognized independent standards of current medical practice (for example, the most current version of the International Classification of Diseases (ICD) or State guidelines).

Mental health benefits means benefits with respect to items or services for mental health conditions, as defined under the terms of the plan or health insurance coverage and in accordance with applicable Federal and State law. Any condition defined by the plan or coverage as being or as not being a mental health condition must be defined to be consistent with generally recognized independent standards of current medical practice (for example, the most current version of the Diagnostic and Statistical Manual of Mental Disorders (DSM), the most current version of the ICD, or State guidelines).

Substance use disorder benefits means benefits with respect to items or services for substance use disorders, as defined under the terms of the plan or health insurance coverage and in accordance with applicable Federal and State law. Any disorder defined by the plan as being or as not being a substance use disorder must be defined to be consistent with generally recognized independent standards of current medical practice (for example, the most current version of the DSM, the most current version of the ICD, or State guidelines).

Treatment limitations include limits on benefits based on the frequency of treatment, number of visits, days of coverage, days in a waiting period, or other similar limits on the scope or duration of treatment. Treatment limitations include both quantitative treatment limitations, which are expressed numerically (such as 50 outpatient visits per year), and nonquantitative treatment limitations, which otherwise limit the scope or duration of benefits for treatment under a plan or coverage. (See paragraph (c)(4)(ii) of this section for an illustrative list of nonquantitative treatment limitations.) A permanent exclusion of all benefits for a particular condition or disorder, however, is not a treatment limitation for purposes of this definition.

(b) *Parity requirements with respect to aggregate lifetime and annual dollar limits.*—This paragraph (b) details the application of the parity requirements with respect to aggregate lifetime and annual dollar limits. This paragraph (b) does not address the provisions of PHS Act section 2711, as incorporated in ERISA section 715 and Code section 9815, which prohibit imposing lifetime and annual limits on the dollar value of essential health benefits.

(1) *General.*—(i) *General parity requirement.*—A group health plan (or health insurance coverage offered by an issuer in connection with a group health plan) that provides both medical/surgical benefits and mental health or substance use disorder benefits must comply with paragraph (b)(2), (b)(3), or (b)(5) of this section.

(ii) *Exception.*—The rule in paragraph (b)(1)(i) of this section does not apply if a plan (or health insurance coverage) satisfies the requirements of paragraph (f) or (g) of this section (relating to exemptions for small employers and for increased cost).

(2) *Plan with no limit or limits on less than one-third of all medical/surgical benefits.*—If a plan (or health insurance coverage) does not include an aggregate lifetime or annual dollar limit on any medical/surgical benefits or includes an aggregate lifetime or annual dollar limit that applies to less than one-third of all medical/surgical benefits, it may not impose an aggregate lifetime or annual dollar limit, respectively, on mental health or substance use disorder benefits.

(3) *Plan with a limit on at least two-thirds of all medical/surgical benefits.*—If a plan (or health insurance coverage) includes an aggregate lifetime or annual dollar limit on at least two-thirds of all medical/surgical benefits, it must either—

(i) Apply the aggregate lifetime or annual dollar limit both to the medical/surgical benefits to which the limit would otherwise apply and to mental health or substance use disorder benefits in a manner that does not distinguish between the medical/surgical benefits and mental health or substance use disorder benefits; or

(ii) Not include an aggregate lifetime or annual dollar limit on mental health or substance use disorder benefits that is less than the aggregate lifetime or annual dollar limit, respectively, on medical/surgical benefits. (For cumulative limits other than aggregate lifetime or annual dollar limits, see paragraph (c)(3)(v) of this section prohibiting separately accumulating cumulative financial requirements or cumulative quantitative treatment limitations.)

(4) *Determining one-third and two-thirds of all medical/surgical benefits.*—For purposes of this paragraph (b), the determination of whether the portion of medical/surgical benefits subject to an aggregate lifetime or annual dollar limit represents one-third or two-thirds of all medical/surgical benefits is based on the dollar amount of all

Reg. §54.9812-1(b)(4)

⋙→ *Caution: Reg. §54.9812-1, below, as added by T.D. 9640, is generally applicable to group health plans and health insurance issuers for plan or policy years beginning on or after July 1, 2014.*

plan payments for medical/surgical benefits expected to be paid under the plan for the plan year (or for the portion of the plan year after a change in plan benefits that affects the applicability of the aggregate lifetime or annual dollar limits). Any reasonable method may be used to determine whether the dollar amount expected to be paid under the plan will constitute one-third or two-thirds of the dollar amount of all plan payments for medical/surgical benefits.

(5) *Plan not described in paragraph (b)(2) or (b)(3) of this section.*—(i) *In general.*—A group health plan (or health insurance coverage) that is not described in paragraph (b)(2) or (b)(3) of this section with respect to aggregate lifetime or annual dollar limits on medical/surgical benefits, must either—

(A) Impose no aggregate lifetime or annual dollar limit, as appropriate, on mental health or substance use disorder benefits; or

(B) Impose an aggregate lifetime or annual dollar limit on mental health or substance use disorder benefits that is no less than an average limit calculated for medical/surgical benefits in the following manner. The average limit is calculated by taking into account the weighted average of the aggregate lifetime or annual dollar limits, as appropriate, that are applicable to the categories of medical/surgical benefits. Limits based on delivery systems, such as inpatient/outpatient treatment or normal treatment of common, low-cost conditions (such as treatment of normal births), do not constitute categories for purposes of this paragraph (b)(5)(i)(B). In addition, for purposes of determining weighted averages, any benefits that are not within a category that is subject to a separately-designated dollar limit under the plan are taken into account as a single separate category by using an estimate of the upper limit on the dollar amount that a plan may reasonably be expected to incur with respect to such benefits, taking into account any other applicable restrictions under the plan.

(ii) *Weighting.*—For purposes of this paragraph (b)(5), the weighting applicable to any category of medical/surgical benefits is determined in the manner set forth in paragraph (b)(4) of this section for determining one-third or two-thirds of all medical/surgical benefits.

(c) *Parity requirements with respect to financial requirements and treatment limitations.*—(1) *Clarification of terms.*—(i) *Classification of benefits.*— When reference is made in this paragraph (c) to a classification of benefits, the term "classification" means a classification as described in paragraph (c)(2)(ii) of this section.

(ii) *Type of financial requirement or treatment limitation.*—When reference is made in this paragraph (c) to a type of financial requirement or treatment limitation, the reference to type means its nature. Different types of financial re-

quirements include deductibles, copayments, co-insurance, and out-of-pocket maximums. Different types of quantitative treatment limitations include annual, episode, and lifetime day and visit limits. See paragraph (c)(4)(ii) of this section for an illustrative list of nonquantitative treatment limitations.

(iii) *Level of a type of financial requirement or treatment limitation.*—When reference is made in this paragraph (c) to a level of a type of financial requirement or treatment limitation, level refers to the magnitude of the type of financial requirement or treatment limitation. For example, different levels of coinsurance include 20 percent and 30 percent; different levels of a copayment include $15 and $20; different levels of a deductible include $250 and $500; and different levels of an episode limit include 21 inpatient days per episode and 30 inpatient days per episode.

(iv) *Coverage unit.*—When reference is made in this paragraph (c) to a coverage unit, coverage unit refers to the way in which a plan (or health insurance coverage) groups individuals for purposes of determining benefits, or premiums or contributions. For example, different coverage units include self-only, family, and employee-plus-spouse.

(2) *General parity requirement.*—(i) *General rule.*—A group health plan (or health insurance coverage offered by an issuer in connection with a group health plan) that provides both medical/surgical benefits and mental health or substance use disorder benefits may not apply any financial requirement or treatment limitation to mental health or substance use disorder benefits in any classification that is more restrictive than the predominant financial requirement or treatment limitation of that type applied to substantially all medical/surgical benefits in the same classification. Whether a financial requirement or treatment limitation is a predominant financial requirement or treatment limitation that applies to substantially all medical/surgical benefits in a classification is determined separately for each type of financial requirement or treatment limitation. The application of the rules of this paragraph (c)(2) to financial requirements and quantitative treatment limitations is addressed in paragraph (c)(3) of this section; the application of the rules of this paragraph (c)(2) to nonquantitative treatment limitations is addressed in paragraph (c)(4) of this section.

(ii) *Classifications of benefits used for applying rules.*—(A) *In general.*—If a plan (or health insurance coverage) provides mental health or substance use disorder benefits in any classification of benefits described in this paragraph (c)(2)(ii), mental health or substance use disorder benefits must be provided in every classification in which medical/surgical benefits are provided. In determining the classification in which a particular benefit belongs, a plan (or health insur-

⟫→ *Caution: Reg. §54.9812-1, below, as added by T.D. 9640, is generally applicable to group health plans and health insurance issuers for plan or policy years beginning on or after July 1, 2014.*

ance issuer) must apply the same standards to medical/surgical benefits and to mental health or substance use disorder benefits. To the extent that a plan (or health insurance coverage) provides benefits in a classification and imposes any separate financial requirement or treatment limitation (or separate level of a financial requirement or treatment limitation) for benefits in the classification, the rules of this paragraph (c) apply separately with respect to that classification for all financial requirements or treatment limitations (illustrated in examples in paragraph (c)(2)(ii)(C) of this section. The following classifications of benefits are the only classifications used in applying the rules of this paragraph (c):

(1) Inpatient, in-network.—Benefits furnished on an inpatient basis and within a network of providers established or recognized under a plan or health insurance coverage. See special rules for plans with multiple network tiers in paragraph (c)(3)(iii) of this section.

(2) Inpatient, out-of-network.—Benefits furnished on an inpatient basis and outside any network of providers established or recognized under a plan or health insurance coverage. This classification includes inpatient benefits under a plan (or health insurance coverage) that has no network of providers.

(3) Outpatient, in-network.—Benefits furnished on an outpatient basis and within a network of providers established or recognized under a plan or health insurance coverage. See special rules for office visits and plans with multiple network tiers in paragraph (c)(3)(iii) of this section.

(4) Outpatient, out-of-network.—Benefits furnished on an outpatient basis and outside any network of providers established or recognized under a plan or health insurance coverage. This classification includes outpatient benefits under a plan (or health insurance coverage) that has no network of providers. See special rules for office visits in paragraph (c)(3)(iii) of this section.

(5) Emergency care.—Benefits for emergency care.

(6) Prescription drugs.—Benefits for prescription drugs. See special rules for multitiered prescription drug benefits in paragraph (c)(3)(iii) of this section.

(B) *Application to out-of-network providers.*—See paragraph (c)(2)(ii)(A) of this section, under which a plan (or health insurance coverage) that provides mental health or substance use disorder benefits in any classification of benefits must provide mental health or substance use disorder benefits in every classification in which medical/surgical benefits are provided, including out-of-network classifications.

(C) *Examples.*—The rules of this paragraph (c)(2)(ii) are illustrated by the following

examples. In each example, the group health plan is subject to the requirements of this section and provides both medical/surgical benefits and mental health and substance use disorder benefits.

Example 1. (i) *Facts.* A group health plan offers inpatient and outpatient benefits and does not contract with a network of providers. The plan imposes a $500 deductible on all benefits. For inpatient medical/surgical benefits, the plan imposes a coinsurance requirement. For outpatient medical/surgical benefits, the plan imposes copayments. The plan imposes no other financial requirements or treatment limitations.

(ii) *Conclusion.* In this *Example 1,* because the plan has no network of providers, all benefits provided are out-of-network. Because inpatient, out-of-network medical/surgical benefits are subject to separate financial requirements from outpatient, out-of-network medical/surgical benefits, the rules of this paragraph (c) apply separately with respect to any financial requirements and treatment limitations, including the deductible, in each classification.

Example 2. (i) *Facts.* A plan imposes a $500 deductible on all benefits. The plan has no network of providers. The plan generally imposes a 20 percent coinsurance requirement with respect to all benefits, without distinguishing among inpatient, outpatient, emergency care, or prescription drug benefits. The plan imposes no other financial requirements or treatment limitations.

(ii) *Conclusion.* In this *Example 2,* because the plan does not impose separate financial requirements (or treatment limitations) based on classification, the rules of this paragraph (c) apply with respect to the deductible and the coinsurance across all benefits.

Example 3. (i) *Facts.* Same facts as *Example 2,* except the plan exempts emergency care benefits from the 20 percent coinsurance requirement. The plan imposes no other financial requirements or treatment limitations.

(ii) *Conclusion.* In this *Example 3,* because the plan imposes separate financial requirements based on classifications, the rules of this paragraph (c) apply with respect to the deductible and the coinsurance separately for—

(A) Benefits in the emergency care classification; and

(B) All other benefits.

Example 4. (i) *Facts.* Same facts as *Example 2,* except the plan also imposes a preauthorization requirement for all inpatient treatment in order for benefits to be paid. No such requirement applies to outpatient treatment.

(ii) *Conclusion.* In this *Example 4,* because the plan has no network of providers, all benefits provided are out-of-network. Because the plan imposes a separate treatment limitation based on classifications, the rules of this para-

Reg. §54.9812-1(c)(2)(ii)(C)

⋙⟶ Caution: *Reg. §54.9812-1, below, as added by T.D. 9640, is generally applicable to group health plans and health insurance issuers for plan or policy years beginning on or after July 1, 2014.*

graph (c) apply with respect to the deductible and coinsurance separately for—

(A) Inpatient, out-of-network benefits; and

(B) All other benefits.

(3) *Financial requirements and quantitative treatment limitations.*—(i) *Determining "substantially all" and "predominant".*—(A) *Substantially all.*—For purposes of this paragraph (c), a type of financial requirement or quantitative treatment limitation is considered to apply to substantially all medical/surgical benefits in a classification of benefits if it applies to at least two-thirds of all medical/surgical benefits in that classification. (For this purpose, benefits expressed as subject to a zero level of a type of financial requirement are treated as benefits not subject to that type of financial requirement, and benefits expressed as subject to a quantitative treatment limitation that is unlimited are treated as benefits not subject to that type of quantitative treatment limitation.) If a type of financial requirement or quantitative treatment limitation does not apply to at least two-thirds of all medical/surgical benefits in a classification, then that type cannot be applied to mental health or substance use disorder benefits in that classification.

(B) *Predominant.*—(1) If a type of financial requirement or quantitative treatment limitation applies to at least two-thirds of all medical/surgical benefits in a classification as determined under paragraph (c)(3)(i)(A) of this section, the level of the financial requirement or quantitative treatment limitation that is considered the predominant level of that type in a classification of benefits is the level that applies to more than one-half of medical/surgical benefits in that classification subject to the financial requirement or quantitative treatment limitation.

(2) If, with respect to a type of financial requirement or quantitative treatment limitation that applies to at least two-thirds of all medical/surgical benefits in a classification, there is no single level that applies to more than one-half of medical/surgical benefits in the classification subject to the financial requirement or quantitative treatment limitation, the plan (or health insurance issuer) may combine levels until the combination of levels applies to more than one-half of medical/surgical benefits subject to the financial requirement or quantitative treatment limitation in the classification. The least restrictive level within the combination is considered the predominant level of that type in the classification. (For this purpose, a plan may combine the most restrictive levels first, with each less restrictive level added to the combination until the combination applies to more than one-half of the benefits subject to the financial requirement or treatment limitation.)

(C) *Portion based on plan payments.*—For purposes of this paragraph (c), the determination of the portion of medical/surgical benefits in a classification of benefits subject to a financial requirement or quantitative treatment limitation (or subject to any level of a financial requirement or quantitative treatment limitation) is based on

the dollar amount of all plan payments for medical/surgical benefits in the classification expected to be paid under the plan for the plan year (or for the portion of the plan year after a change in plan benefits that affects the applicability of the financial requirement or quantitative treatment limitation).

(D) *Clarifications for certain threshold requirements.*—For any deductible, the dollar amount of plan payments includes all plan payments with respect to claims that would be subject to the deductible if it had not been satisfied. For any out-of-pocket maximum, the dollar amount of plan payments includes all plan payments associated with out-of-pocket payments that are taken into account towards the out-of-pocket maximum as well as all plan payments associated with out-of-pocket payments that would have been made towards the out-of-pocket maximum if it had not been satisfied. Similar rules apply for any other thresholds at which the rate of plan payment changes. (See also PHS Act section 2707(b) and Affordable Care Act section 1302(c), which establish limitations on annual deductibles for non-grandfathered health plans in the small group market and annual limitations on out-of-pocket maximums for all non-grandfathered health plans.)

(E) *Determining the dollar amount of plan payments.*—Subject to paragraph (c)(3)(i)(D) of this section, any reasonable method may be used to determine the dollar amount expected to be paid under a plan for medical/surgical benefits subject to a financial requirement or quantitative treatment limitation (or subject to any level of a financial requirement or quantitative treatment limitation).

(ii) *Application to different coverage units.*—If a plan (or health insurance coverage) applies different levels of a financial requirement or quantitative treatment limitation to different coverage units in a classification of medical/surgical benefits, the predominant level that applies to substantially all medical/surgical benefits in the classification is determined separately for each coverage unit.

(iii) *Special rules.*—(A) *Multi-tiered prescription drug benefits.*—If a plan (or health insurance coverage) applies different levels of financial requirements to different tiers of prescription drug benefits based on reasonable factors determined in accordance with the rules in paragraph (c)(4)(i) of this section (relating to requirements for nonquantitative treatment limitations) and without regard to whether a drug is generally prescribed with respect to medical/surgical benefits or with respect to mental health or substance use disorder benefits, the plan (or health insurance coverage) satisfies the parity requirements of this paragraph (c) with respect to prescription drug benefits. Reasonable factors include cost, efficacy, generic versus brand name, and mail order versus pharmacy pick-up.

(B) *Multiple network tiers.*—If a plan (or health insurance coverage) provides benefits through multiple tiers of in-network providers

>>>→ *Caution: Reg. §54.9812-1, below, as added by T.D. 9640, is generally applicable to group health plans and health insurance issuers for plan or policy years beginning on or after July 1, 2014.*

(such as an in-network tier of preferred providers with more generous cost-sharing to participants than a separate in-network tier of participating providers), the plan may divide its benefits furnished on an in-network basis into sub-classifications that reflect network tiers, if the tiering is based on reasonable factors determined in accordance with the rules in paragraph (c)(4)(i) of this section (such as quality, performance, and market standards) and without regard to whether a provider provides services with respect to medical/surgical benefits or mental health or substance use disorder benefits. After the sub-classifications are established, the plan or issuer may not impose any financial requirement or treatment limitation on mental health or substance use disorder benefits in any sub-classification that is more restrictive than the predominant financial requirement or treatment limitation that applies to substantially all medical/surgical benefits in the sub-classification using the methodology set forth in paragraph (c)(3)(i) of this section.

(C) *Sub-classifications permitted for office visits, separate from other outpatient services.*—For purposes of applying the financial requirement and treatment limitation rules of this paragraph (c), a plan or issuer may divide its benefits furnished on an outpatient basis into the two sub-classifications described in this paragraph (c)(3)(iii)(C). After the sub-classifications are established, the plan or issuer may not impose any

financial requirement or quantitative treatment limitation on mental health or substance use disorder benefits in any sub-classification that is more restrictive than the predominant financial requirement or quantitative treatment limitation that applies to substantially all medical/surgical benefits in the sub-classification using the methodology set forth in paragraph (c)(3)(i) of this section. Sub-classifications other than these special rules, such as separate sub-classifications for generalists and specialists, are not permitted. The two sub-classifications permitted under this paragraph (c)(3)(iii)(C) are:

(1) Office visits (such as physician visits), and

(2) All other outpatient items and services (such as outpatient surgery, facility charges for day treatment centers, laboratory charges, or other medical items).

(iv) *Examples.*—The rules of paragraphs (c)(3)(i), (c)(3)(ii), and (c)(3)(iii) of this section are illustrated by the following examples. In each example, the group health plan is subject to the requirements of this section and provides both medical/surgical benefits and mental health and substance use disorder benefits.

Example 1. (i) *Facts.* For inpatient, out-of-network medical/surgical benefits, a group health plan imposes five levels of coinsurance. Using a reasonable method, the plan projects its payments for the upcoming year as follows:

Coinsurance rate	0 %	10%	15%	20%	30%	Total
Projected payments	$200x	$100x	$450x	$100x	$150x	$1,000x
Percent of total plan costs	20%	10%	45%	10%	15%	
Percent subject to coinsurance level	N/A	12.5% (100x/800x)	56.25% (450x/800x)	12.5% (100x/800x)	18.75% (150x/800x)	

The plan projects plan costs of $800x to be subject to coinsurance ($100x + $450x + $100x + $150x = $800x). Thus, 80 percent ($800x/$1,000x) of the benefits are projected to be subject to coinsurance, and 56.25 percent of the benefits subject to coinsurance are projected to be subject to the 15 percent coinsurance level.

(ii) *Conclusion.* In this *Example 1*, the two-thirds threshold of the substantially all standard is met for coinsurance because 80 percent of all inpatient, out-of-network medical/surgical benefits are subject to coinsurance. Moreover, the 15 percent coinsurance is the predominant level be-

cause it is applicable to more than one-half of inpatient, out-of-network medical/surgical benefits subject to the coinsurance requirement. The plan may not impose any level of coinsurance with respect to inpatient, out-of-network mental health or substance use disorder benefits that is more restrictive than the 15 percent level of coinsurance.

Example 2. (i) *Facts.* For outpatient, in-network medical/surgical benefits, a plan imposes five different copayment levels. Using a reasonable method, the plan projects payments for the upcoming year as follows:

Copayment amount	$0	$10	$15	$20	$50	Total
Projected payments	$200x	$200x	$200x	$300x	$100x	$1,000x
Percent of total plan costs	20%	20%	20%	30%	10%	
Percent subject to copayments	N/A	25% (200x/800x)	25% (200x/800x)	37.5% (300x/800x)	12.5% (100x/800x)	

Reg. §54.9812-1(c)(3)(iv)

⫸➤ *Caution: Reg. §54.9812-1, below, as added by T.D. 9640, is generally applicable to group health plans and health insurance issuers for plan or policy years beginning on or after July 1, 2014.*

The plan projects plan costs of $800x to be subject to copayments ($200x + $200x +$300x + $100x = $800x). Thus, 80 percent ($800x/$1,000x) of the benefits are projected to be subject to a copayment.

(ii) *Conclusion*. In this *Example 2*, the two-thirds threshold of the substantially all standard is met for copayments because 80 percent of all outpatient, in-network medical/surgical benefits are subject to a copayment. Moreover, there is no single level that applies to more than one-half of medical/surgical benefits in the classification subject to a copayment (for the $10 copayment, 25%; for the $15 copayment, 25%; for the $20 copayment, 37.5%; and for the $50 copayment, 12.5%). The plan can combine any levels of copayment, including the highest levels, to determine the predominant level that can be applied to mental health or substance use disorder benefits. If the plan combines the highest levels of copayment, the combined projected payments for the two highest copayment levels, the $50 copayment and the $20 copayment, are not more than one-half of the outpatient, in-network medical/surgical benefits subject to a copayment because they are exactly one-half ($300x + $100x = $400x; $400x/$800x = 50%). The combined projected payments for the three highest copayment levels - the $50 copayment, the $20 copayment, and the $15 copayment - are more than one-half of the outpatient, in-network medical/surgical benefits subject to the copayments ($100x + $300x + $200x = $600x; $600x/$800x = 75%). Thus, the plan may not impose any copayment on outpatient, in-network mental health or substance use disorder benefits that is more restric-

tive than the least restrictive copayment in the combination, the $15 copayment.

Example 3. (i) *Facts*. A plan imposes a $250 deductible on all medical/surgical benefits for self-only coverage and a $500 deductible on all medical/surgical benefits for family coverage. The plan has no network of providers. For all medical/surgical benefits, the plan imposes a coinsurance requirement. The plan imposes no other financial requirements or treatment limitations.

(ii) *Conclusion*. In this *Example 3*, because the plan has no network of providers, all benefits are provided out-of-network. Because self-only and family coverage are subject to different deductibles, whether the deductible applies to substantially all medical/surgical benefits is determined separately for self-only medical/surgical benefits and family medical/surgical benefits. Because the coinsurance is applied without regard to coverage units, the predominant coinsurance that applies to substantially all medical/surgical benefits is determined without regard to coverage units.

Example 4. (i) *Facts*. A plan applies the following financial requirements for prescription drug benefits. The requirements are applied without regard to whether a drug is generally prescribed with respect to medical/surgical benefits or with respect to mental health or substance use disorder benefits. Moreover, the process for certifying a particular drug as "generic", "preferred brand name", "non-preferred brand name", or "specialty" complies with the rules of paragraph (c)(4)(i) of this section (relating to requirements for nonquantitative treatment limitations).

	Tier 1	Tier 2	Tier 3	Tier 4
Tier description	Generic drugs	Preferred brand name drugs	Non-preferred brand name drugs (which may have Tier 1 or Tier 2 alternatives)	Specialty drugs
Percent paid by plan	90%	80%	60%	50%

(ii) *Conclusion*. In this *Example 4*, the financial requirements that apply to prescription drug benefits are applied without regard to whether a drug is generally prescribed with respect to medical/surgical benefits or with respect to mental health or substance use disorder benefits; the process for certifying drugs in different tiers complies with paragraph (c)(4) of this section;

and the bases for establishing different levels or types of financial requirements are reasonable. The financial requirements applied to prescription drug benefits do not violate the parity requirements of this paragraph (c)(3).

Example 5. (i) *Facts*. A plan has two-tiers of network of providers: a preferred provider tier and a participating provider tier. Providers are

>>→ *Caution: Reg. §54.9812-1, below, as added by T.D. 9640, is generally applicable to group health plans and health insurance issuers for plan or policy years beginning on or after July 1, 2014.*

placed in either the preferred tier or participating tier based on reasonable factors determined in accordance with the rules in paragraph (c)(4)(i) of this section, such as accreditation, quality and performance measures (including customer feedback), and relative reimbursement rates. Furthermore, provider tier placement is determined without regard to whether a provider specializes in the treatment of mental health conditions or substance use disorders, or medical/surgical conditions. The plan divides the in-network classifications into two sub-classifications (in-network/preferred and in-network/participating). The plan does not impose any financial requirement or treatment limitation on mental health or substance use disorder benefits in either of these sub-classifications that is more restrictive than the predominant financial requirement or treatment limitation that applies to substantially all medical/surgical benefits in each sub-classification.

(ii) *Conclusion.* In this *Example 5*, the division of in-network benefits into sub-classifications that reflect the preferred and participating provider tiers does not violate the parity requirements of this paragraph (c)(3).

Example 6. (i) *Facts.* With respect to outpatient, in-network benefits, a plan imposes a $25 copayment for office visits and a 20 percent coinsurance requirement for outpatient surgery. The plan divides the outpatient, in-network classification into two sub-classifications (in-network office visits and all other outpatient, in-network items and services). The plan or issuer does not impose any financial requirement or quantitative treatment limitation on mental health or substance use disorder benefits in either of these sub-classifications that is more restrictive than the predominant financial requirement or quantitative treatment limitation that applies to substantially all medical/surgical benefits in each sub-classification.

(ii) *Conclusion.* In this *Example 6*, the division of outpatient, in-network benefits into sub-classifications for office visits and all other outpatient, in-network items and services does not violate the parity requirements of this paragraph (c)(3).

Example 7. (i) *Facts.* Same facts as *Example 6*, but for purposes of determining parity, the plan divides the outpatient, in-network classification into outpatient, in-network generalists and outpatient, in-network specialists.

(ii) *Conclusion.* In this *Example 7*, the division of outpatient, in-network benefits into any

sub-classifications other than office visits and all other outpatient items and services violates the requirements of paragraph (c)(3)(iii)(C) of this section.

(v) *No separate cumulative financial requirements or cumulative quantitative treatment limitations.*—(A) A group health plan (or health insurance coverage offered in connection with a group health plan) may not apply any cumulative financial requirement or cumulative quantitative treatment limitation for mental health or substance use disorder benefits in a classification that accumulates separately from any established for medical/surgical benefits in the same classification.

(B) The rules of this paragraph (c)(3)(v) are illustrated by the following examples:

Example 1. (i) *Facts.* A group health plan imposes a combined annual $500 deductible on all medical/surgical, mental health, and substance use disorder benefits.

(ii) *Conclusion.* In this *Example 1*, the combined annual deductible complies with the requirements of this paragraph (c)(3)(v).

Example 2. (i) *Facts.* A plan imposes an annual $250 deductible on all medical/surgical benefits and a separate annual $250 deductible on all mental health and substance use disorder benefits.

(ii) *Conclusion.* In this *Example 2*, the separate annual deductible on mental health and substance use disorder benefits violates the requirements of this paragraph (c)(3)(v).

Example 3. (i) *Facts.* A plan imposes an annual $300 deductible on all medical/surgical benefits and a separate annual $100 deductible on all mental health or substance use disorder benefits.

(ii) *Conclusion.* In this *Example 3*, the separate annual deductible on mental health and substance use disorder benefits violates the requirements of this paragraph (c)(3)(v).

Example 4. (i) *Facts.* A plan generally imposes a combined annual $500 deductible on all benefits (both medical/surgical benefits and mental health and substance use disorder benefits) except prescription drugs. Certain benefits, such as preventive care, are provided without regard to the deductible. The imposition of other types of financial requirements or treatment limitations varies with each classification. Using reasonable methods, the plan projects its payments for medical/surgical benefits in each classification for the upcoming year as follows:

Classification	Benefits Subject to Deductible	Total Benefits	Percent Subject to Deductible
Inpatient, in-network	$1,800x	$2,000x	90%
Inpatient, out-of-network	$1,000x	$1,000x	100%
Outpatient, in-network	$1,400x	$2,000x	70%
Outpatient, out-of-network	$1,880x	$2,000x	94%
Emergency care	$300x	$500x	60%

»»→ *Caution: Reg. §54.9812-1, below, as added by T.D. 9640, is generally applicable to group health plans and health insurance issuers for plan or policy years beginning on or after July 1, 2014.*

(ii) *Conclusion.* In this *Example 4,* the two-thirds threshold of the substantially all standard is met with respect to each classification except emergency care because in each of those other classifications at least two-thirds of medical/surgical benefits are subject to the $500 deductible. Moreover, the $500 deductible is the predominant level in each of those other classifications because it is the only level. However, emergency care mental health and substance use disorder benefits cannot be subject to the $500 deductible because it does not apply to substantially all emergency care medical/surgical benefits.

(4) *Nonquantitative treatment limitations.*— (i) *General rule.*—A group health plan (or health insurance coverage) may not impose a nonquantitative treatment limitation with respect to mental health or substance use disorder benefits in any classification unless, under the terms of the plan (or health insurance coverage) as written and in operation, any processes, strategies, evidentiary standards, or other factors used in applying the nonquantitative treatment limitation to mental health or substance use disorder benefits in the classification are comparable to, and are applied no more stringently than, the processes, strategies, evidentiary standards, or other factors used in applying the limitation with respect to medical/surgical benefits in the classification.

(ii) *Illustrative list of nonquantitative treatment limitations.*—Nonquantitative treatment limitations include—

(A) Medical management standards limiting or excluding benefits based on medical necessity or medical appropriateness, or based on whether the treatment is experimental or investigative;

(B) Formulary design for prescription drugs;

(C) For plans with multiple network tiers (such as preferred providers and participating providers), network tier design;

(D) Standards for provider admission to participate in a network, including reimbursement rates;

(E) Plan methods for determining usual, customary, and reasonable charges;

(F) Refusal to pay for higher-cost therapies until it can be shown that a lower-cost therapy is not effective (also known as fail-first policies or step therapy protocols);

(G) Exclusions based on failure to complete a course of treatment; and

(H) Restrictions based on geographic location, facility type, provider specialty, and other criteria that limit the scope or duration of benefits for services provided under the plan or coverage.

(iii) *Examples.*—The rules of this paragraph (c)(4) are illustrated by the following examples. In each example, the group health plan is subject to the requirements of this section and provides both medical/surgical benefits and mental health and substance use disorder benefits.

Example 1. (i) *Facts.* A plan requires prior authorization from the plan's utilization reviewer that a treatment is medically necessary for all inpatient medical/surgical benefits and for all inpatient mental health and substance use disorder benefits. In practice, inpatient benefits for medical/surgical conditions are routinely approved for seven days, after which a treatment plan must be submitted by the patient's attending provider and approved by the plan. On the other hand, for inpatient mental health and substance use disorder benefits, routine approval is given only for one day, after which a treatment plan must be submitted by the patient's attending provider and approved by the plan.

(ii) *Conclusion.* In this Example 1, the plan violates the rules of this paragraph (c)(4) because it is applying a stricter nonquantitative treatment limitation in practice to mental health and substance use disorder benefits than is applied to medical/surgical benefits.

Example 2. (i) *Facts.* A plan applies concurrent review to inpatient care where there are high levels of variation in length of stay (as measured by a coefficient of variation exceeding 0.8). In practice, the application of this standard affects 60 percent of mental health conditions and substance use disorders, but only 30 percent of medical/surgical conditions.

(ii) *Conclusion.* In this *Example 2,* the plan complies with the rules of this paragraph (c)(4) because the evidentiary standard used by the plan is applied no more stringently for mental health and substance use disorder benefits than for medical/surgical benefits, even though it results in an overall difference in the application of concurrent review for mental health conditions or substance use disorders than for medical/surgical conditions.

Example 3. (i) *Facts.* A plan requires prior approval that a course of treatment is medically necessary for outpatient, in-network medical/surgical, mental health, and substance use disorder benefits and uses comparable criteria in determining whether a course of treatment is medically necessary. For mental health and substance use disorder treatments that do not have prior approval, no benefits will be paid; for med-

⋙→ *Caution: Reg. §54.9812-1, below, as added by T.D. 9640, is generally applicable to group health plans and health insurance issuers for plan or policy years beginning on or after July 1, 2014.*

ical/surgical treatments that do not have prior approval, there will only be a 25 percent reduction in the benefits the plan would otherwise pay.

(ii) *Conclusion.* In this *Example 3*, the plan violates the rules of this paragraph (c)(4). Although the same nonquantitative treatment limitation—medical necessity—is applied both to mental health and substance use disorder benefits and to medical/surgical benefits for outpatient, in-network services, it is not applied in a comparable way. The penalty for failure to obtain prior approval for mental health and substance use disorder benefits is not comparable to the penalty for failure to obtain prior approval for medical/surgical benefits.

Example 4. (i) *Facts.* A plan generally covers medically appropriate treatments. For both medical/surgical benefits and mental health and substance use disorder benefits, evidentiary standards used in determining whether a treatment is medically appropriate (such as the number of visits or days of coverage) are based on recommendations made by panels of experts with appropriate training and experience in the fields of medicine involved. The evidentiary standards are applied in a manner that is based on clinically appropriate standards of care for a condition.

(ii) *Conclusion.* In this *Example 4*, the plan complies with the rules of this paragraph (c)(4) because the processes for developing the evidentiary standards used to determine medical appropriateness and the application of these standards to mental health and substance use disorder benefits are comparable to and are applied no more stringently than for medical/surgical benefits. This is the result even if the application of the evidentiary standards does not result in similar numbers of visits, days of coverage, or other benefits utilized for mental health conditions or substance use disorders as it does for any particular medical/surgical condition.

Example 5. (i) *Facts.* A plan generally covers medically appropriate treatments. In determining whether prescription drugs are medically appropriate, the plan automatically excludes coverage for antidepressant drugs that are given a black box warning label by the Food and Drug Administration (indicating the drug carries a significant risk of serious adverse effects). For other drugs with a black box warning (including those prescribed for other mental health conditions and substance use disorders, as well as for medical/surgical conditions), the plan will provide coverage if the prescribing physician obtains authorization from the plan that the drug is medically appropriate for the individual, based on clinically appropriate standards of care.

(ii) *Conclusion.* In this *Example 5*, the plan violates the rules of this paragraph (c)(4). Although the standard for applying a nonquantitative treatment limitation is the same for both mental health and substance use disorder bene-

fits and medical/surgical benefits—whether a drug has a black box warning—it is not applied in a comparable manner. The plan's unconditional exclusion of antidepressant drugs given a black box warning is not comparable to the conditional exclusion for other drugs with a black box warning.

Example 6. (i) *Facts.* An employer maintains both a major medical plan and an employee assistance program (EAP). The EAP provides, among other benefits, a limited number of mental health or substance use disorder counseling sessions. Participants are eligible for mental health or substance use disorder benefits under the major medical plan only after exhausting the counseling sessions provided by the EAP. No similar exhaustion requirement applies with respect to medical/surgical benefits provided under the major medical plan.

(ii) *Conclusion.* In this *Example 6*, limiting eligibility for mental health and substance use disorder benefits only after EAP benefits are exhausted is a nonquantitative treatment limitation subject to the parity requirements of this paragraph (c). Because no comparable requirement applies to medical/surgical benefits, the requirement may not be applied to mental health or substance use disorder benefits.

Example 7. (i) *Facts.* Training and State licensing requirements often vary among types of providers. A plan applies a general standard that any provider must meet the highest licensing requirement related to supervised clinical experience under applicable State law in order to participate in the plan's provider network. Therefore, the plan requires master's-level mental health therapists to have post-degree, supervised clinical experience but does not impose this requirement on master's-level general medical providers because the scope of their licensure under applicable State law does require clinical experience. In addition, the plan does not require post-degree, supervised clinical experience for psychiatrists or PhD level psychologists since their licensing already requires supervised training.

(ii) *Conclusion.* In this *Example 7*, the plan complies with the rules of this paragraph (c)(4). The requirement that master's-level mental health therapists must have supervised clinical experience to join the network is permissible, as long as the plan consistently applies the same standard to all providers even though it may have a disparate impact on certain mental health providers.

Example 8. (i) *Facts.* A plan considers a wide array of factors in designing medical management techniques for both mental health and substance use disorder benefits and medical/surgical benefits, such as cost of treatment; high cost growth; variability in cost and quality; elasticity of demand; provider discretion in determining diagnosis, or type or length of treatment; clinical efficacy of any proposed treatment or

Reg. §54.9812-1(c)(4)(iii)

⋙→ Caution: *Reg. §54.9812-1, below, as added by T.D. 9640, is generally applicable to group health plans and health insurance issuers for plan or policy years beginning on or after July 1, 2014.*

service; licensing and accreditation of providers; and claim types with a high percentage of fraud. Based on application of these factors in a comparable fashion, prior authorization is required for some (but not all) mental health and substance use disorder benefits, as well as for some medical/surgical benefits, but not for others. For example, the plan requires prior authorization for: outpatient surgery; speech, occupational, physical, cognitive and behavioral therapy extending for more than six months; durable medical equipment; diagnostic imaging; skilled nursing visits; home infusion therapy; coordinated home care; pain management; high-risk prenatal care; delivery by cesarean section; mastectomy; prostate cancer treatment; narcotics prescribed for more than seven days; and all inpatient services beyond 30 days. The evidence considered in developing its medical management techniques includes consideration of a wide array of recognized medical literature and professional standards and protocols (including comparative effectiveness studies and clinical trials). This evidence and how it was used to develop these medical management techniques is also well documented by the plan.

(ii) *Conclusion.* In this *Example 8*, the plan complies with the rules of this paragraph (c)(4). Under the terms of the plan as written and in operation, the processes, strategies, evidentiary standards, and other factors considered by the plan in implementing its prior authorization requirement with respect to mental health and substance use disorder benefits are comparable to, and applied no more stringently than, those applied with respect to medical/surgical benefits.

Example 9. (i) *Facts.* A plan generally covers medically appropriate treatments. The plan automatically excludes coverage for inpatient substance use disorder treatment in any setting outside of a hospital (such as a freestanding or residential treatment center). For inpatient treatment outside of a hospital for other conditions (including freestanding or residential treatment centers prescribed for mental health conditions, as well as for medical/surgical conditions), the plan will provide coverage if the prescribing physician obtains authorization from the plan that the inpatient treatment is medically appropriate for the individual, based on clinically appropriate standards of care.

(ii) *Conclusion.* In this *Example 9*, the plan violates the rules of this paragraph (c)(4). Although the same nonquantitative treatment limitation—medical appropriateness—is applied to both mental health and substance use disorder benefits and medical/surgical benefits, the plan's unconditional exclusion of substance use disorder treatment in any setting outside of a hospital is not comparable to the conditional exclusion of inpatient treatment outside of a hospital for other conditions.

Example 10. (i) *Facts.* A plan generally provides coverage for medically appropriate medical/surgical benefits as well as mental health and substance use disorder benefits. The plan excludes coverage for inpatient, out-of-network treatment of chemical dependency when obtained outside of the State where the policy is written. There is no similar exclusion for medical/surgical benefits within the same classification.

(ii) *Conclusion.* In this *Example 10*, the plan violates the rules of this paragraph (c)(4). The plan is imposing a nonquantitative treatment limitation that restricts benefits based on geographic location. Because there is no comparable exclusion that applies to medical/surgical benefits, this exclusion may not be applied to mental health or substance use disorder benefits.

Example 11. (i) *Facts.* A plan requires prior authorization for all outpatient mental health and substance use disorder services after the ninth visit and will only approve up to five additional visits per authorization. With respect to outpatient medical/surgical benefits, the plan allows an initial visit without prior authorization. After the initial visit, the plan pre-approves benefits based on the individual treatment plan recommended by the attending provider based on that individual's specific medical condition. There is no explicit, predetermined cap on the amount of additional visits approved per authorization.

(ii) *Conclusion.* In this *Example 11*, the plan violates the rules of this paragraph (c)(4). Although the same nonquantitative treatment limitation—prior authorization to determine medical appropriateness—is applied to both mental health and substance use disorder benefits and medical/surgical benefits for outpatient services, it is not applied in a comparable way. While the plan is more generous with respect to the number of visits initially provided without pre-authorization for mental health benefits, treating all mental health conditions and substance use disorders in the same manner, while providing for individualized treatment of medical conditions, is not a comparable application of this nonquantitative treatment limitation.

(5) *Exemptions.*—The rules of this paragraph (c) do not apply if a group health plan (or health insurance coverage) satisfies the requirements of paragraph (f) or (g) of this section (relating to exemptions for small employers and for increased cost).

(d) *Availability of plan information.*—(1) *Criteria for medical necessity determinations.*—The criteria for medical necessity determinations made under a group health plan with respect to mental health or substance use disorder benefits (or health insurance coverage offered in connection with the plan with respect to such benefits) must be made available by the plan administrator (or the health insurance issuer offering such cover-

➤➤➤ Caution: *Reg. §54.9812-1, below, as added by T.D. 9640, is generally applicable to group health plans and health insurance issuers for plan or policy years beginning on or after July 1, 2014.*

age) to any current or potential participant, beneficiary, or contracting provider upon request.

(2) *Reason for any denial.*—The reason for any denial under a group health plan (or health insurance coverage offered in connection with such plan) of reimbursement or payment for services with respect to mental health or substance use disorder benefits in the case of any participant or beneficiary must be made available by the plan administrator (or the health insurance issuer offering such coverage) to the participant or beneficiary in accordance with this paragraph (d)(2).

(i) *Plans subject to ERISA.*—If a plan is subject to ERISA, it must provide the reason for the claim denial in a form and manner consistent with the requirements of 29 CFR 2560.503-1 for group health plans.

(ii) *Plans not subject to ERISA.*—If a plan is not subject to ERISA, upon the request of a participant or beneficiary the reason for the claim denial must be provided within a reasonable time and in a reasonable manner. For this purpose, a plan that follows the requirements of 29 CFR 2560.503-1 for group health plans complies with the requirements of this paragraph (d)(2)(ii).

(3) *Provisions of other law.*—Compliance with the disclosure requirements in paragraphs (d)(1) and (d)(2) of this section is not determinative of compliance with any other provision of applicable Federal or State law. In particular, in addition to those disclosure requirements, provisions of other applicable law require disclosure of information relevant to medical/surgical, mental health, and substance use disorder benefits. For example, ERISA section 104 and 29 CFR 2520.104b-1 provide that, for plans subject to ERISA, instruments under which the plan is established or operated must generally be furnished to plan participants within 30 days of request. Instruments under which the plan is established or operated include documents with information on medical necessity criteria for both medical/surgical benefits and mental health and substance use disorder benefits, as well as the processes, strategies, evidentiary standards, and other factors used to apply a nonquantitative treatment limitation with respect to medical/surgical benefits and mental health or substance use disorder benefits under the plan. In addition, 29 CFR 2560.503-1 and 29 CFR 2590.715-2719 set forth rules regarding claims and appeals, including the right of claimants (or their authorized representative) upon appeal of an adverse benefit determination (or a final internal adverse benefit determination) to be provided upon request and free of charge, reasonable access to and copies of all documents, records, and other information relevant to the claimant's claim for benefits. This includes documents with information on medical necessity criteria for both medical/surgical benefits and mental health and substance use disorder benefits, as well as the processes, strategies, evidentiary standards, and other factors used to apply a nonquantitative treatment limitation with respect to medical/surgical benefits and mental health or substance use disorder benefits under the plan.

(e) *Applicability.*—(1) *Group health plans.*—The requirements of this section apply to a group health plan offering medical/surgical benefits and mental health or substance use disorder benefits. If, under an arrangement or arrangements to provide medical care benefits by an employer or employee organization (including for this purpose a joint board of trustees of a multiemployer trust affiliated with one or more multiemployer plans), any participant (or beneficiary) can simultaneously receive coverage for medical/surgical benefits and coverage for mental health or substance use disorder benefits, then the requirements of this section (including the exemption provisions in paragraph (g) of this section) apply separately with respect to each combination of medical/surgical benefits and of mental health or substance use disorder benefits that any participant (or beneficiary) can simultaneously receive from that employer's or employee organization's arrangement or arrangements to provide medical care benefits, and all such combinations are considered for purposes of this section to be a single group health plan.

(2) *Health insurance issuers.*—The requirements of this section apply to a health insurance issuer offering health insurance coverage for mental health or substance use disorder benefits in connection with a group health plan subject to paragraph (e)(1) of this section.

(3) *Scope.*—This section does not—

(i) Require a group health plan (or health insurance issuer offering coverage in connection with a group health plan) to provide any mental health benefits or substance use disorder benefits, and the provision of benefits by a plan (or health insurance coverage) for one or more mental health conditions or substance use disorders does not require the plan or health insurance coverage under this section to provide benefits for any other mental health condition or substance use disorder;

(ii) Require a group health plan (or health insurance issuer offering coverage in connection with a group health plan) that provides coverage for mental health or substance use disorder benefits only to the extent required under PHS Act section 2713 to provide additional mental health or substance use disorder benefits in any classification in accordance with this section; or

(iii) Affect the terms and conditions relating to the amount, duration, or scope of mental health or substance use disorder benefits under the plan (or health insurance coverage) except as specifically provided in paragraphs (b) and (c) of this section.

Reg. §54.9812-1(e)(3)(iii)

⮞⮞➤ *Caution: Reg. §54.9812-1, below, as added by T.D. 9640, is generally applicable to group health plans and health insurance issuers for plan or policy years beginning on or after July 1, 2014.*

(4) *Coordination with EHB requirements.*— Nothing in paragraph (f) or (g) of this section changes the requirements of 45 CFR 147.150 and 45 CFR 156.115, providing that a health insurance issuer offering non-grandfathered health insurance coverage in the individual or small group market providing mental health and substance use disorder services, including behavioral health treatment services, as part of essential health benefits required under 45 CFR 156.110(a)(5) and 156.115(a), must comply with the provisions of 45 CFR 146.136 to satisfy the requirement to provide essential health benefits.

(f) *Small employer exemption.*—(1) *In general.*— The requirements of this section do not apply to a group health plan (or health insurance issuer offering coverage in connection with a group health plan) for a plan year of a small employer. For purposes of this paragraph (f), the term *small employer* means, in connection with a group health plan with respect to a calendar year and a plan year, an employer who employed an average of at least two (or one in the case of an employer residing in a State that permits small groups to include a single individual) but not more than 50 employees on business days during the preceding calendar year. See section 9831(a) and §54.9831-1(b), which provide that this section (and certain other sections) does not apply to any group health plan for any plan year if, on the first day of the plan year, the plan has fewer than two participants who are current employees.

(2) *Rules in determining employer size.*—For purposes of paragraph (f)(1) of this section—

(i) All persons treated as a single employer under subsections (b), (c), (m), and (o) of section 414 are treated as one employer;

(ii) If an employer was not in existence throughout the preceding calendar year, whether it is a small employer is determined based on the average number of employees the employer reasonably expects to employ on business days during the current calendar year; and

(iii) Any reference to an employer for purposes of the small employer exemption includes a reference to a predecessor of the employer.

(g) *Increased cost exemption.*—(1) *In general.*—If the application of this section to a group health plan (or health insurance coverage offered in connection with such plans) results in an increase for the plan year involved of the actual total cost of coverage with respect to medical/surgical benefits and mental health and substance use disorder benefits as determined and certified under paragraph (g)(3) of this section by an amount that exceeds the applicable percentage described in paragraph (g)(2) of this section of the actual total plan costs, the provisions of this section shall not apply to such plan (or

coverage) during the following plan year, and such exemption shall apply to the plan (or coverage) for one plan year. An employer or issuer may elect to continue to provide mental health and substance use disorder benefits in compliance with this section with respect to the plan or coverage involved regardless of any increase in total costs.

(2) *Applicable percentage.*—With respect to a plan or coverage, the applicable percentage described in this paragraph (g) is—

(i) 2 percent in the case of the first plan year in which this section is applied to the plan or coverage; and

(ii) 1 percent in the case of each subsequent plan year.

(3) *Determinations by actuaries.*— (i) Determinations as to increases in actual costs under a plan or coverage that are attributable to implementation of the requirements of this section shall be made and certified by a qualified and licensed actuary who is a member in good standing of the American Academy of Actuaries. All such determinations must be based on the formula specified in paragraph (g)(4) of this section and shall be in a written report prepared by the actuary.

(ii) The written report described in paragraph (g)(3)(i) of this section shall be maintained by the group health plan or health insurance issuer, along with all supporting documentation relied upon by the actuary, for a period of six years following the notification made under paragraph (g)(6) of this section.

(4) *Formula.*—The formula to be used to make the determination under paragraph (g)(3)(i) of this section is expressed mathematically as follows:

$$[(E_1 - E_0)/T_0] - D > k$$

(i) E_1 is the actual total cost of coverage with respect to mental health and substance use disorder benefits for the base period, including claims paid by the plan or issuer with respect to mental health and substance use disorder benefits and administrative costs (amortized over time) attributable to providing these benefits consistent with the requirements of this section.

(ii) E_0 is the actual total cost of coverage with respect to mental health and substance use disorder benefits for the length of time immediately before the base period (and that is equal in length to the base period), including claims paid by the plan or issuer with respect to mental health and substance use disorder benefits and administrative costs (amortized over time) attributable to providing these benefits.

(iii) T_0 is the actual total cost of coverage with respect to all benefits during the base period.

(iv) k is the applicable percentage of increased cost specified in paragraph (g)(2) of this

>>> *Caution: Reg. §54.9812-1, below, as added by T.D. 9640, is generally applicable to group health plans and health insurance issuers for plan or policy years beginning on or after July 1, 2014.*

section that will be expressed as a fraction for purposes of this formula.

(v) D is the average change in spending that is calculated by applying the formula $(E_1 - E_0)/T_0$ to mental health and substance use disorder spending in each of the five prior years and then calculating the average change in spending.

(5) *Six month determination.*—If a group health plan or health insurance issuer seeks an exemption under this paragraph (g), determinations under paragraph (g)(3) of this section shall be made after such plan or coverage has complied with this section for at least the first 6 months of the plan year involved.

(6) *Notification.*—A group health plan or health insurance issuer that, based on the certification described under paragraph (g)(3) of this section, qualifies for an exemption under this paragraph (g), and elects to implement the exemption, must notify participants and beneficiaries covered under the plan, the Secretary, and the appropriate State agencies of such election.

(i) *Participants and beneficiaries.*—(A) *Content of notice.*—The notice to participants and beneficiaries must include the following information:

(1) A statement that the plan or issuer is exempt from the requirements of this section and a description of the basis for the exemption.

(2) The name and telephone number of the individual to contact for further information.

(3) The plan or issuer name and plan number (PN).

(4) The plan administrator's name, address, and telephone number.

(5) For single-employer plans, the plan sponsor's name, address, and telephone number (if different from paragraph (g)(6)(i)(A)(3) of this section) and the plan sponsor's employer identification number (EIN).

(6) The effective date of such exemption.

(7) A statement regarding the ability of participants and beneficiaries to contact the plan administrator or health insurance issuer to see how benefits may be affected as a result of the plan's or issuer's election of the exemption.

(8) A statement regarding the availability, upon request and free of charge, of a summary of the information on which the exemption is based (as required under paragraph (g)(6)(i)(D) of this section).

(B) *Use of summary of material reductions in covered services or benefits.*—A plan or issuer may satisfy the requirements of paragraph (g)(6)(i)(A) of this section by providing participants and beneficiaries (in accordance with paragraph (g)(6)(i)(C) of this section) with a summary of material reductions in covered services or benefits consistent with 29 CFR 2520.104b-3(d) that also includes the information specified in paragraph (g)(6)(i)(A) of this section. However, in all cases, the exemption is not effective until 30 days after notice has been sent.

(C) *Delivery.*—The notice described in this paragraph (g)(6)(i) is required to be provided to all participants and beneficiaries. The notice may be furnished by any method of delivery that satisfies the requirements of section 104(b)(1) of ERISA (29 U.S.C. 1024(b)(1)) and its implementing regulations (for example, first-class mail). If the notice is provided to the participant and any beneficiaries at the participant's last known address, then the requirements of this paragraph (g)(6)(i) are satisfied with respect to the participant and all beneficiaries residing at that address. If a beneficiary's last known address is different from the participant's last known address, a separate notice is required to be provided to the beneficiary at the beneficiary's last known address.

(D) *Availability of documentation.*—The plan or issuer must make available to participants and beneficiaries (or their representatives), on request and at no charge, a summary of the information on which the exemption was based. (For purposes of this paragraph (g), an individual who is not a participant or beneficiary and who presents a notice described in paragraph (g)(6)(i) of this section is considered to be a representative. A representative may request the summary of information by providing the plan a copy of the notice provided to the participant under paragraph (g)(6)(i) of this section with any personally identifiable information redacted.) The summary of information must include the incurred expenditures, the base period, the dollar amount of claims incurred during the base period that would have been denied under the terms of the plan or coverage absent amendments required to comply with paragraphs (b) and (c) of this section, the administrative costs related to those claims, and other administrative costs attributable to complying with the requirements of this section. In no event should the summary of information include any personally identifiable information.

(ii) *Federal agencies.*—(A) *Content of notice.*—The notice to the Secretary must include the following information:

(1) A description of the number of covered lives under the plan (or coverage) involved at the time of the notification, and as applicable, at the time of any prior election of the cost exemption under this paragraph (g) by such plan (or coverage);

(2) For both the plan year upon which a cost exemption is sought and the year prior, a description of the actual total costs of coverage with respect to medical/surgical benefits and mental health and substance use disorder benefits; and

Reg. §54.9812-1(g)(6)(ii)(A)(2)

>>>→ *Caution: Reg. §54.9812-1, below, as added by T.D. 9640, is generally applicable to group health plans and health insurance issuers for plan or policy years beginning on or after July 1, 2014.*

(3) For both the plan year upon which a cost exemption is sought and the year prior, the actual total costs of coverage with respect to mental health and substance use disorder benefits under the plan.

(B) *Reporting with respect to church plans.*—A church plan (as defined in section 414(e)) claiming the exemption of this paragraph (g) for any benefit package, must provide notice to the Department of the Treasury. This requirement is satisfied if the plan sends a copy, to the address designated by the Secretary in generally applicable guidance, of the notice described in paragraph (g)(6)(ii)(A) of this section identifying the benefit package to which the exemption applies.

(C) *Reporting with respect to ERISA plans.*—See 29 CFR 2590.712(g)(6)(ii) for delivery with respect to ERISA plans.

(iii) *Confidentiality.*—A notification to the Secretary under this paragraph (g)(6) shall be confidential. The Secretary shall make available, upon request and not more than on an annual basis, an anonymous itemization of each notification that includes—

(A) A breakdown of States by the size and type of employers submitting such notification; and

(B) A summary of the data received under paragraph (g)(6)(ii) of this section.

(iv) *Audits.*—The Secretary may audit the books and records of a group health plan or a health insurance issuer relating to an exemption, including any actuarial reports, during the 6 year period following notification of such exemption under paragraph (g)(6) of this section. A State agency receiving a notification under paragraph (g)(6) of this section may also conduct such an audit with respect to an exemption covered by such notification.

(h) *Sale of nonparity health insurance coverage.*— A health insurance issuer may not sell a policy, certificate, or contract of insurance that fails to comply with paragraph (b) or (c) of this section, except to a plan for a year for which the plan is exempt from the requirements of this section because the plan meets the requirements of paragraph (f) or (g) of this section.

(i) *Applicability dates.*—(1) *In general.*—Except as provided in paragraph (i)(2) of this section, this section applies to group health plans and health insurance issuers offering group health insurance coverage on the first day of the first plan year beginning on or after July 1, 2014.

(2) *Special effective date for certain collectively-bargained plans.*—For a group health plan maintained pursuant to one or more collective bargaining agreements ratified before October 3, 2008, the requirements of this section do not apply to the plan (or health insurance coverage offered in connection with the plan) for plan years beginning before the date on which the last of the collective bargaining agreements terminates (determined without regard to any extension agreed to after October 3, 2008). [Reg. §54.9812-1.]

☐ [*T.D. 9640*, 11-8-2013.]

>>>→ *Caution: Temporary Reg. §54.9812-1T, below, as removed by T.D. 9640, is generally applicable to group health plans and health insurance issuers for plan or policy years beginning before July 1, 2014.*

[Reg. §54.9812-1T]

§54.9812-1T. Parity in the application of certain limits to mental health benefits (temporary).—(a) *Meaning of terms.*—For purposes of this section, except where the context clearly indicates otherwise, the following terms have the meanings indicated:

Aggregate lifetime dollar limit means a dollar limitation on the total amount of specified benefits that may be paid under a group health plan for any coverage unit.

Annual dollar limit means a dollar limitation on the total amount of specified benefits that may be paid in a 12-month period under a group health plan for any coverage unit.

Coverage unit means coverage unit as described in paragraph (c)(1)(iv) of this section.

Cumulative financial requirements are financial requirements that determine whether or to what extent benefits are provided based on accumulated amounts and include deductibles and out-of-pocket maximums. (However, cumulative financial requirements do not include aggregate lifetime or annual dollar limits because these two terms are excluded from the meaning of financial requirements.)

Cumulative quantitative treatment limitations are treatment limitations that determine whether or to what extent benefits are provided based on accumulated amounts, such as annual or lifetime day or visit limits.

Financial requirements include deductibles, copayments, coinsurance, or out-of-pocket maximums. Financial requirements do not include aggregate lifetime or annual dollar limits.

Medical/surgical benefits means benefits for medical or surgical services, as defined under the terms of the plan, but does not include mental health or substance use disorder benefits. Any condition defined by the plan as being or as not being a medical/surgical condition must be defined to be consistent with generally recognized independent standards of current medical practice (for example, the most current version of the International Classification of Diseases (ICD) or State guidelines).

Mental health benefits means benefits with respect to services for mental health conditions, as defined under the terms of the plan and in accor-

»»→ *Caution: Temporary Reg. §54.9812-1T, below, as removed by T.D. 9640, is generally applicable to group health plans and health insurance issuers for plan or policy years beginning before July 1, 2014.*

dance with applicable Federal and State law. Any condition defined by the plan as being or as not being a mental health condition must be defined to be consistent with generally recognized independent standards of current medical practice (for example, the most current version of the Diagnostic and Statistical Manual of Mental Disorders (DSM), the most current version of the ICD, or State guidelines).

Substance use disorder benefits means benefits with respect to services for substance use disorders, as defined under the terms of the plan and in accordance with applicable Federal and State law. Any disorder defined by the plan as being or as not being a substance use disorder must be defined to be consistent with generally recognized independent standards of current medical practice (for example, the most current version of the DSM, the most current version of the ICD, or State guidelines).

Treatment limitations include limits on benefits based on the frequency of treatment, number of visits, days of coverage, days in a waiting period, or other similar limits on the scope or duration of treatment. Treatment limitations include both quantitative treatment limitations, which are expressed numerically (such as 50 outpatient visits per year), and nonquantitative treatment limitations, which otherwise limit the scope or duration of benefits for treatment under a plan. (See paragraph (c)(4)(ii) of this section for an illustrative list of nonquantitative treatment limitations.) A permanent exclusion of all benefits for a particular condition or disorder, however, is not a treatment limitation.

(b) *Parity requirements with respect to aggregate lifetime and annual dollar limits.*—(1) *General.*— (i) *General parity requirement.*—A group health plan that provides both medical/surgical benefits and mental health or substance use disorder benefits must comply with paragraph (b)(2), (b)(3), or (b)(6) of this section.

(ii) *Exception.*—The rule in paragraph (b)(1)(i) of this section does not apply if a plan satisfies the requirements of paragraph (f) or (g) of this section (relating to exemptions for small employers and for increased cost).

(2) *Plan with no limit or limits on less than one-third of all medical/surgical benefits.*—If a plan does not include an aggregate lifetime or annual dollar limit on any medical/surgical benefits or includes an aggregate lifetime or annual dollar limit that applies to less than one-third of all medical/surgical benefits, it may not impose an aggregate lifetime or annual dollar limit, respectively, on mental health or substance use disorder benefits.

(3) *Plan with a limit on at least two-thirds of all medical/surgical benefits.*—If a plan includes an aggregate lifetime or annual dollar limit on at least two-thirds of all medical/surgical benefits, it must either—

(i) Apply the aggregate lifetime or annual dollar limit both to the medical/surgical benefits to which the limit would otherwise apply and to mental health or substance use disorder benefits in a manner that does not distinguish between the medical/surgical benefits and mental health or substance use disorder benefits; or

(ii) Not include an aggregate lifetime or annual dollar limit on mental health or substance use disorder benefits that is less than the aggregate lifetime or annual dollar limit, respectively, on medical/surgical benefits. (For cumulative limits other than aggregate lifetime or annual dollar limits, see paragraph (c)(3)(v) of this section prohibiting separately accumulating cumulative financial requirements or cumulative quantitative treatment limitations.)

(4) *Examples.*—The rules of paragraphs (b)(2) and (b)(3) of this section are illustrated by the following examples:

Example 1. (i) *Facts.* A group health plan has no annual limit on medical/surgical benefits and a $10,000 annual limit on mental health and substance use disorder benefits. To comply with the requirements of this paragraph (b), the plan sponsor is considering each of the following options:

(A) Eliminating the plan's annual dollar limit on mental health and substance use disorder benefits;

(B) Replacing the plan's annual dollar limit on mental health and substance use disorder benefits with a $500,000 annual limit on all benefits (including medical/surgical and mental health and substance use disorder benefits); and

(C) Replacing the plan's annual dollar limit on mental health and substance use disorder benefits with a $250,000 annual limit on medical/surgical benefits and a $250,000 annual limit on mental health and substance use disorder benefits.

(ii) *Conclusion.* In this *Example 1,* each of the three options being considered by the plan sponsor would comply with the requirements of this paragraph (b).

Example 2. (i) *Facts.* A plan has a $100,000 annual limit on medical/surgical inpatient benefits and a $50,000 annual limit on medical/surgical outpatient benefits. To comply with the parity requirements of this paragraph (b), the plan sponsor is considering each of the following options:

(A) Imposing a $150,000 annual limit on mental health and substance use disorder benefits; and

(B) Imposing a $100,000 annual limit on mental health and substance use disorder inpatient benefits and a $50,000 annual limit on mental health and substance use disorder outpatient benefits.

»»→ *Caution: Temporary Reg. §54.9812-1T, below, as removed by T.D. 9640, is generally applicable to group health plans and health insurance issuers for plan or policy years beginning before July 1, 2014.*

(ii) *Conclusion.* In this *Example 2*, each option under consideration by the plan sponsor would comply with the requirements of this section.

(5) *Determining one-third and two-thirds of all medical/surgical benefits.*—For purposes of this paragraph (b), the determination of whether the portion of medical/surgical benefits subject to an aggregate lifetime or annual dollar limit represents one-third or two-thirds of all medical/surgical benefits is based on the dollar amount of all plan payments for medical/surgical benefits expected to be paid under the plan for the plan year (or for the portion of the plan year after a change in plan benefits that affects the applicability of the aggregate lifetime or annual dollar limits). Any reasonable method may be used to determine whether the dollar amount expected to be paid under the plan will constitute one-third or two-thirds of the dollar amount of all plan payments for medical/surgical benefits.

(6) *Plan not described in paragraph (b)(2) or (b)(3) of this section.*—(i) *In general.*—A group health plan that is not described in paragraph (b)(2) or (b)(3) of this section with respect to aggregate lifetime or annual dollar limits on medical/surgical benefits, must either—

(A) Impose no aggregate lifetime or annual dollar limit, as appropriate, on mental health or substance use disorder benefits; or

(B) Impose an aggregate lifetime or annual dollar limit on mental health or substance use disorder benefits that is no less than an average limit calculated for medical/surgical benefits in the following manner. The average limit is calculated by taking into account the weighted average of the aggregate lifetime or annual dollar limits, as appropriate, that are applicable to the categories of medical/surgical benefits. Limits based on delivery systems, such as inpatient/outpatient treatment or normal treatment of common, low-cost conditions (such as treatment of normal births), do not constitute categories for purposes of this paragraph (b)(6)(i)(B). In addition, for purposes of determining weighted averages, any benefits that are not within a category that is subject to a separately-designated dollar limit under the plan are taken into account as a single separate category by using an estimate of the upper limit on the dollar amount that a plan may reasonably be expected to incur with respect to such benefits, taking into account any other applicable restrictions under the plan.

(ii) *Weighting.*—For purposes of this paragraph (b)(6), the weighting applicable to any category of medical/surgical benefits is determined in the manner set forth in paragraph (b)(5) of this section for determining one-third or two-thirds of all medical/surgical benefits.

(iii) *Example.*—The rules of this paragraph (b)(6) are illustrated by the following example:

Example. (i) *Facts.* A group health plan that is subject to the requirements of this section includes a $100,000 annual limit on medical/surgical benefits related to cardio-pulmonary diseases. The plan does not include an annual dollar limit on any other category of medical/surgical benefits. The plan determines that 40 percent of the dollar amount of plan payments for medical/surgical benefits are related to cardio-pulmonary diseases. The plan determines that $1,000,000 is a reasonable estimate of the upper limit on the dollar amount that the plan may incur with respect to the other 60 percent of payments for medical/surgical benefits.

(ii) *Conclusion.* In this *Example*, the plan is not described in paragraph (b)(3) of this section because there is not one annual dollar limit that applies to at least two-thirds of all medical/surgical benefits. Further, the plan is not described in paragraph (b)(2) of this section because more than one-third of all medical/surgical benefits are subject to an annual dollar limit. Under this paragraph (b)(6), the plan sponsor can choose either to include no annual dollar limit on mental health or substance use disorder benefits, or to include an annual dollar limit on mental health or substance use disorder benefits that is not less than the weighted average of the annual dollar limits applicable to each category of medical/surgical benefits. In this example, the minimum weighted average annual dollar limit that can be applied to mental health or substance use disorder benefits is $640,000 (40% × $100,000 + 60% × $1,000,000 = $640,000).

(c) *Parity requirements with respect to financial requirements and treatment limitations.*—(1) *Clarification of terms.*—(i) *Classification of benefits.*—When reference is made in this paragraph (c) to a classification of benefits, the term "classification" means a classification as described in paragraph (c)(2)(ii) of this section.

(ii) *Type of financial requirement or treatment limitation.*—When reference is made in this paragraph (c) to a type of financial requirement or treatment limitation, the reference to type means its nature. Different types of financial requirements include deductibles, copayments, coinsurance, and out-of-pocket maximums. Different types of quantitative treatment limitations include annual, episode, and lifetime day and visit limits. See paragraph (c)(4)(ii) of this section for an illustrative list of nonquantitative treatment limitations.

(iii) *Level of a type of financial requirement or treatment limitation.*—When reference is made in this paragraph (c) to a level of a type of financial requirement or treatment limitation, level refers to the magnitude of the type of financial requirement or treatment limitation. For example, dif-

⟫⟫→ *Caution: Temporary Reg. §54.9812-1T, below, as removed by T.D. 9640, is generally applicable to group health plans and health insurance issuers for plan or policy years beginning before July 1, 2014.*

ferent levels of coinsurance include 20 percent and 30 percent; different levels of a copayment include $15 and $20; different levels of a deductible include $250 and $500; and different levels of an episode limit include 21 inpatient days per episode and 30 inpatient days per episode.

(iv) *Coverage unit.*—When reference is made in this paragraph (c) to a coverage unit, coverage unit refers to the way in which a plan groups individuals for purposes of determining benefits, or premiums or contributions. For example, different coverage units include self-only, family, and employee-plus-spouse.

(2) *General parity requirement.*—(i) *General rule.*—A group health plan that provides both medical/surgical benefits and mental health or substance use disorder benefits may not apply any financial requirement or treatment limitation to mental health or substance use disorder benefits in any classification that is more restrictive than the predominant financial requirement or treatment limitation of that type applied to substantially all medical/surgical benefits in the same classification. Whether a financial requirement or treatment limitation is a predominant financial requirement or treatment limitation that applies to substantially all medical/surgical benefits in a classification is determined separately for each type of financial requirement or treatment limitation. The application of the rules of this paragraph (c)(2) to financial requirements and quantitative treatment limitations is addressed in paragraph (c)(3) of this section; the application of the rules of this paragraph (c)(2) to nonquantitative treatment limitations is addressed in paragraph (c)(4) of this section.

(ii) *Classifications of benefits used for applying rules.*—(A) *In general.*—If a plan provides mental health or substance use disorder benefits in any classification of benefits described in this paragraph (c)(2)(ii), mental health or substance use disorder benefits must be provided in every classification in which medical/surgical benefits are provided. In determining the classification in which a particular benefit belongs, a plan must apply the same standards to medical/surgical benefits and to mental health or substance use disorder benefits. To the extent that a plan provides benefits in a classification and imposes any separate financial requirement or treatment limitation (or separate level of a financial requirement or treatment limitation) for benefits in the classification, the rules of this paragraph (c) apply separately with respect to that classification for all financial requirements or treatment limitations. The following classifications of benefits are the only classifications used in applying the rules of this paragraph (c):

(1) *Inpatient, in-network.*—Benefits furnished on an inpatient basis and within a network of providers established or recognized under a plan.

(2) *Inpatient, out-of-network.*—Benefits furnished on an inpatient basis and outside any network of providers established or recognized under a plan. This classification includes inpatient benefits under a plan that has no network of providers.

(3) *Outpatient, in-network.*—Benefits furnished on an outpatient basis and within a network of providers established or recognized under a plan.

(4) *Outpatient, out-of-network.*—Benefits furnished on an outpatient basis and outside any network of providers established or recognized under a plan. This classification includes outpatient benefits under a plan that has no network of providers.

(5) *Emergency care.*—Benefits for emergency care.

(6) *Prescription drugs.*—Benefits for prescription drugs. See special rules for multitiered prescription drug benefits in paragraph (c)(3)(iii) of this section.

(B) *Application to out-of-network providers.*—See paragraph (c)(2)(ii)(A) of this section, under which a plan that provides mental health or substance use disorder benefits in any classification of benefits must provide mental health or substance use disorder benefits in every classification in which medical/surgical benefits are provided, including out-of-network classifications.

(C) *Examples.*—The rules of this paragraph (c)(2)(ii) are illustrated by the following examples. In each example, the group health plan is subject to the requirements of this section and provides both medical/surgical benefits and mental health and substance use disorder benefits.

Example 1. (i) *Facts.* A group health plan offers inpatient and outpatient benefits and does not contract with a network of providers. The plan imposes a $500 deductible on all benefits. For inpatient medical/surgical benefits, the plan imposes a coinsurance requirement. For outpatient medical/surgical benefits, the plan imposes copayments. The plan imposes no other financial requirements or treatment limitations.

(ii) *Conclusion.* In this *Example 1*, because the plan has no network of providers, all benefits provided are out-of-network. Because inpatient, out-of-network medical/surgical benefits are subject to separate financial requirements from outpatient, out-of-network medical/surgical benefits, the rules of this paragraph (c) apply separately with respect to any financial requirements and treatment limitations, including the deductible, in each classification.

Reg. §54.9812-1T(c)(2)(ii)(C)

⟫⟫→ Caution: *Temporary Reg. §54.9812-1T, below, as removed by T.D. 9640, is generally applicable to group health plans and health insurance issuers for plan or policy years beginning before July 1, 2014.*

Example 2. (i) *Facts.* A plan imposes a $500 deductible on all benefits. The plan has no network of providers. The plan generally imposes a 20 percent coinsurance requirement with respect to all benefits, without distinguishing among inpatient, outpatient, emergency, or prescription drug benefits. The plan imposes no other financial requirements or treatment limitations.

(ii) *Conclusion.* In this *Example 2,* because the plan does not impose separate financial requirements (or treatment limitations) based on classification, the rules of this paragraph (c) apply with respect to the deductible and the coinsurance across all benefits.

Example 3. (i) *Facts.* Same facts as *Example 2,* except the plan exempts emergency care benefits from the 20 percent coinsurance requirement. The plan imposes no other financial requirements or treatment limitations.

(ii) *Conclusion.* In this *Example 3,* because the plan imposes separate financial requirements based on classifications, the rules of this paragraph (c) apply with respect to the deductible and the coinsurance separately for—

(A) Benefits in the emergency classification; and

(B) All other benefits.

Example 4. (i) *Facts.* Same facts as *Example 2,* except the plan also imposes a preauthorization requirement for all inpatient treatment in order for benefits to be paid. No such requirement applies to outpatient treatment.

(ii) *Conclusion.* In this *Example 4,* because the plan has no network of providers, all benefits provided are out-of-network. Because the plan imposes a separate treatment limitation based on classifications, the rules of this paragraph (c) apply with respect to the deductible and coinsurance separately for—

(A) Inpatient, out-of-network benefits; and

(B) All other benefits.

(3) *Financial requirements and quantitative treatment limitations.*—(i) *Determining "substantially all" and "predominant".*—(A) *Substantially all.*—For purposes of this paragraph (c), a type of financial requirement or quantitative treatment limitation is considered to apply to substantially all medical/surgical benefits in a classification of benefits if it applies to at least two-thirds of all medical/surgical benefits in that classification. (For this purpose, benefits expressed as subject to a zero level of a type of financial requirement are treated as benefits not subject to that type of financial requirement, and benefits expressed as subject to a quantitative treatment limitation that is unlimited are treated as benefits not subject to that type of quantitative treatment limitation.) If a type of financial requirement or quantitative treatment limitation does not apply to at least

two-thirds of all medical/surgical benefits in a classification, then that type cannot be applied to mental health or substance use disorder benefits in that classification.

(B) *Predominant.*—(1) If a type of financial requirement or quantitative treatment limitation applies to at least two-thirds of all medical/surgical benefits in a classification as determined under paragraph (c)(3)(i)(A) of this section, the level of the financial requirement or quantitative treatment limitation that is considered the predominant level of that type in a classification of benefits is the level that applies to more than one-half of medical/surgical benefits in that classification subject to the financial requirement or quantitative treatment limitation.

(2) If, with respect to a type of financial requirement or quantitative treatment limitation that applies to at least two-thirds of all medical/surgical benefits in a classification, there is no single level that applies to more than one-half of medical/surgical benefits in the classification subject to the financial requirement or quantitative treatment limitation, the plan may combine levels until the combination of levels applies to more than one-half of medical/surgical benefits subject to the financial requirement or quantitative treatment limitation in the classification. The least restrictive level within the combination is considered the predominant level of that type in the classification. (For this purpose, a plan may combine the most restrictive levels first, with each less restrictive level added to the combination until the combination applies to more than one-half of the benefits subject to the financial requirement or treatment limitation.)

(C) *Portion based on plan payments.*—For purposes of this paragraph (c), the determination of the portion of medical/surgical benefits in a classification of benefits subject to a financial requirement or quantitative treatment limitation (or subject to any level of a financial requirement or quantitative treatment limitation) is based on the dollar amount of all plan payments for medical/surgical benefits in the classification expected to be paid under the plan for the plan year (or for the portion of the plan year after a change in plan benefits that affects the applicability of the financial requirement or quantitative treatment limitation).

(D) *Clarifications for certain threshold requirements.*—For any deductible, the dollar amount of plan payments includes all plan payments with respect to claims that would be subject to the deductible if it had not been satisfied. For any out-of-pocket maximum, the dollar amount of plan payments includes all plan payments associated with out-of-pocket payments that are taken into account towards the out-of-pocket maximum as well as all plan payments associated with out-of-pocket payments that

⟫→ Caution: *Temporary Reg. §54.9812-1T, below, as removed by T.D. 9640, is generally applicable to group health plans and health insurance issuers for plan or policy years beginning before July 1, 2014.*

would have been made towards the out-of-pocket maximum if it had not been satisfied. Similar rules apply for any other thresholds at which the rate of plan payment changes.

    (E) *Determining the dollar amount of plan payments.*—Subject to paragraph (c)(3)(i)(D) of this section, any reasonable method may be used to determine the dollar amount expected to be paid under a plan for medical/surgical benefits subject to a financial requirement or quantitative treatment limitation (or subject to any level of a financial requirement or quantitative treatment limitation).

    (ii) *Application to different coverage units.*—If a plan applies different levels of a financial requirement or quantitative treatment limitation to different coverage units in a classification of medical/surgical benefits, the predominant level that applies to substantially all medical/surgical benefits in the classification is determined separately for each coverage unit.

    (iii) *Special rule for multi-tiered prescription drug benefits.*—If a plan applies different levels of financial requirements to different tiers of pre-scription drug benefits based on reasonable factors determined in accordance with the rules in paragraph (c)(4)(i) of this section (relating to requirements for nonquantitative treatment limitations) and without regard to whether a drug is generally prescribed with respect to medical/surgical benefits or with respect to mental health or substance use disorder benefits, the plan satisfies the parity requirements of this paragraph (c) with respect to prescription drug benefits. Reasonable factors include cost, efficacy, generic versus brand name, and mail order versus pharmacy pick-up.

    (iv) *Examples.*—The rules of paragraphs (c)(3)(i), (c)(3)(ii), and (c)(3)(iii) of this section are illustrated by the following examples. In each example, the group health plan is subject to the requirements of this section and provides both medical/surgical benefits and mental health and substance use disorder benefits.

    Example 1. (i) *Facts.* For inpatient, out-of-network medical/surgical benefits, a group health plan imposes five levels of coinsurance. Using a reasonable method, the plan projects its payments for the upcoming year as follows:

Coinsurance rate	0 %	10%	15%	20%	30%	Total
Projected payments	$200x	$100x	$450x	$100x	$150x	$1,000x
Percent of total plan costs	20%	10%	45%	10%	15%	
Percent subject to coinsurance level	N/A	12.5% (100x/800x)	56.25% (450x/800x)	12.5% (100x/800x)	18.75% (150x/800x)	

The plan projects plan costs of $800x to be subject to coinsurance ($100x + $450x + $100x + $150x = $800x). Thus, 80 percent ($800x/$1,000x) of the benefits are projected to be subject to coinsurance, and 56.25 percent of the benefits subject to coinsurance are projected to be subject to the 15 percent coinsurance level.

    (ii) *Conclusion.* In this *Example 1*, the two-thirds threshold of the substantially all standard is met for coinsurance because 80 percent of all inpatient, out-of-network medical/surgical benefits are subject to coinsurance. Moreover, the 15 percent coinsurance is the predominant level be-cause it is applicable to more than one-half of inpatient, out-of-network medical/surgical benefits subject to the coinsurance requirement. The plan may not impose any level of coinsurance with respect to inpatient, out-of-network mental health or substance use disorder benefits that is more restrictive than the 15 percent level of coinsurance.

    Example 2. (i) *Facts.* For outpatient, in-network medical/surgical benefits, a plan imposes five different copayment levels. Using a reasonable method, the plan projects payments for the upcoming year as follows:

Copayment amount	$0	$10	$15	$20	$50	Total
Projected payments	$200x	$200x	$200x	$300x	$100x	$1,000x
Percent of total plan costs	20%	20%	20%	30%	10%	
Percent subject to copayments	N/A	25% (200x/800x)	25% (200x/800x)	37.5% (300x/800x)	12.5% (100x/800x)	

⫸→ *Caution: Temporary Reg. §54.9812-1T, below, as removed by T.D. 9640, is generally applicable to group health plans and health insurance issuers for plan or policy years beginning before July 1, 2014.*

The plan projects plan costs of $800x to be subject to copayments ($200x + $200x +$300x + $100x = $800x). Thus, 80 percent ($800x/$1,000x) of the benefits are projected to be subject to a copayment.

(ii) *Conclusion.* In this *Example 2*, the two-thirds threshold of the substantially all standard is met for copayments because 80 percent of all outpatient, in-network medical/surgical benefits are subject to a copayment. Moreover, there is no single level that applies to more than one-half of medical/surgical benefits in the classification subject to a copayment (for the $10 copayment, 25 percent; for the $15 copayment, 25 percent; for the $20 copayment, 37.5 percent; and for the $50 copayment, 12.5 percent). The plan can combine any levels of copayment, including the highest levels, to determine the predominant level that can be applied to mental health or substance use disorder benefits. If the plan combines the highest levels of copayment, the combined projected payments for the two highest copayment levels, the $50 copayment and the $20 copayment, are not more than one-half of the outpatient, in-network medical/surgical benefits subject to a copayment because they are exactly one-half ($300x + $100x = $400x; $400x/$800x = 50%). The combined projected payments for the three highest copayment levels — the $50 copayment, the $20 copayment, and the $15 copayment — are more than one-half of the outpatient, in-network medical/surgical benefits subject to the copayments ($100x + $300x + $200x = $600x; $600x/$800x = 75%). Thus, the plan may not impose any copayment on outpatient, in-network mental health or substance use disorder benefits that is more restrictive than the least restrictive copayment in the combination, the $15 copayment.

Example 3. (i) *Facts.* A plan imposes a $250 deductible on all medical/surgical benefits for self-only coverage and a $500 deductible on all medical/surgical benefits for family coverage. The plan has no network of providers. For all medical/surgical benefits, the plan imposes a coinsurance requirement. The plan imposes no other financial requirements or treatment limitations.

(ii) *Conclusion.* In this *Example 3*, because the plan has no network of providers, all benefits are provided out-of-network. Because self-only and family coverage are subject to different deductibles, whether the deductible applies to substantially all medical/surgical benefits is determined separately for self-only medical/surgical benefits and family medical/surgical benefits. Because the coinsurance is applied without regard to coverage units, the predominant coinsurance that applies to substantially all medical/surgical benefits is determined without regard to coverage units.

Example 4. (i) *Facts.* A plan applies the following financial requirements for prescription drug benefits. The requirements are applied without regard to whether a drug is generally prescribed with respect to medical/surgical benefits or with respect to mental health or substance use disorder benefits. Moreover, the process for certifying a particular drug as "generic", "preferred brand name", "non-preferred brand name", or "specialty" complies with the rules of paragraph (c)(4)(i) of this section (relating to requirements for nonquantitative treatment limitations).

	Tier 1	Tier 2	Tier 3	Tier 4
Tier description	Generic drugs	Preferred brand name drugs	Non-preferred brand name drugs (which may have Tier 1 or Tier 2 alternatives)	Specialty drugs
Percent paid by plan	90%	80%	60%	50%

(ii) *Conclusion.* In this *Example 4*, the financial requirements that apply to prescription drug benefits are applied without regard to whether a drug is generally prescribed with respect to medical/surgical benefits or with respect to mental health or substance use disorder benefits; the process for certifying drugs in different tiers complies with paragraph (c)(4) of this section; and the bases for establishing different levels or types of financial requirements are reasonable. The financial requirements applied to prescription drug benefits do not violate the parity requirements of this paragraph (c)(3).

(v) *No separate cumulative financial requirements or cumulative quantitative treatment limitations.*—(A) A group health plan may not apply any cumulative financial requirement or cumulative quantitative treatment limitation for mental health or substance use disorder benefits in a classification that accumulates separately from any established for medical/surgical benefits in the same classification.

(B) The rules of this paragraph (c)(3)(v) are illustrated by the following examples:

Example 1. (i) *Facts.* A group health plan imposes a combined annual $500 deductible on all medical/surgical, mental health, and substance use disorder benefits.

⟫⟶ *Caution: Temporary Reg. §54.9812-1T, below, as removed by T.D. 9640, is generally applicable to group health plans and health insurance issuers for plan or policy years beginning before July 1, 2014.*

(ii) *Conclusion.* In this *Example 1*, the combined annual deductible complies with the requirements of this paragraph (c)(3)(v).

Example 2. (i) *Facts.* A plan imposes an annual $250 deductible on all medical/surgical benefits and a separate annual $250 deductible on all mental health and substance use disorder benefits.

(ii) *Conclusion.* In this *Example 2*, the separate annual deductible on mental health and substance use disorder benefits violates the requirements of this paragraph (c)(3)(v).

Example 3. (i) *Facts.* A plan imposes an annual $300 deductible on all medical/surgical benefits and a separate annual $100 deductible on all mental health or substance use disorder benefits.

(ii) *Conclusion.* In this *Example 3*, the separate annual deductible on mental health and substance use disorder benefits violates the requirements of this paragraph (c)(3)(v).

Example 4. (i) *Facts.* A plan generally imposes a combined annual $500 deductible on all benefits (both medical/surgical benefits and mental health and substance use disorder benefits) except prescription drugs. Certain benefits, such as preventive care, are provided without regard to the deductible. The imposition of other types of financial requirements or treatment limitations varies with each classification. Using reasonable methods, the plan projects its payments for medical/surgical benefits in each classification for the upcoming year as follows:

Classification	Benefits Subject to Deductible	Total Benefits	Percent Subject to Deductible
Inpatient, in-network	$1,800x	$2,000x	90%
Inpatient, out-of-network	$1,000x	$1,000x	100%
Outpatient, in-network	$1,400x	$2,000x	70%
Outpatient, out-of-network	$1,880x	$2,000x	94%
Emergency care	$300x	$500x	60%

(ii) *Conclusion.* In this *Example 4*, the two-thirds threshold of the substantially all standard is met with respect to each classification except emergency care because in each of those other classifications at least two-thirds of medical/surgical benefits are subject to the $500 deductible. Moreover, the $500 deductible is the predominant level in each of those other classifications because it is the only level. However, emergency care mental health and substance use disorder benefits cannot be subject to the $500 deductible because it does not apply to substantially all emergency care medical/surgical benefits.

(4) *Nonquantitative treatment limitations.—* (i) *General rule.—*A group health plan may not impose a nonquantitative treatment limitation with respect to mental health or substance use disorder benefits in any classification unless, under the terms of the plan as written and in operation, any processes, strategies, evidentiary standards, or other factors used in applying the nonquantitative treatment limitation to mental health or substance use disorder benefits in the classification are comparable to, and are applied no more stringently than, the processes, strategies, evidentiary standards, or other factors used in applying the limitation with respect to medical surgical/benefits in the classification, except to the extent that recognized clinically appropriate standards of care may permit a difference.

(ii) *Illustrative list of nonquantitative treatment limitations.—*Nonquantitative treatment limitations include—

(A) Medical management standards limiting or excluding benefits based on medical necessity or medical appropriateness, or based on whether the treatment is experimental or investigative;

(B) Formulary design for prescription drugs;

(C) Standards for provider admission to participate in a network, including reimbursement rates;

(D) Plan methods for determining usual, customary, and reasonable charges;

(E) Refusal to pay for higher-cost therapies until it can be shown that a lower-cost therapy is not effective (also known as fail-first policies or step therapy protocols); and

(F) Exclusions based on failure to complete a course of treatment.

(iii) *Examples.—*The rules of this paragraph (c)(4) are illustrated by the following examples. In each example, the group health plan is subject to the requirements of this section and provides both medical/surgical benefits and mental health and substance use disorder benefits.

Example 1. (i) *Facts.* A group health plan limits benefits to treatment that is medically necessary. The plan requires concurrent review for inpatient, in-network mental health and sub-

⋙→ *Caution: Temporary Reg. §54.9812-1T, below, as removed by T.D. 9640, is generally applicable to group health plans and health insurance issuers for plan or policy years beginning before July 1, 2014.*

stance use disorder benefits but does not require it for any inpatient, in-network medical/surgical benefits. The plan conducts retrospective review for inpatient, in-network medical/surgical benefits.

(ii) *Conclusion.* In this *Example 1*, the plan violates the rules of this paragraph (c)(4). Although the same nonquantitative treatment limitation - medical necessity - applies to both mental health and substance use disorder benefits and to medical/surgical benefits for inpatient, in-network services, the concurrent review process does not apply to medical/surgical benefits. The concurrent review process is not comparable to the retrospective review process. While such a difference might be permissible in certain individual cases based on recognized clinically appropriate standards of care, it is not permissible for distinguishing between all medical/surgical benefits and all mental health or substance use disorder benefits.

Example 2. (i) *Facts.* A plan requires prior approval that a course of treatment is medically necessary for outpatient, in-network medical/surgical, mental health, and substance use disorder benefits. For mental health and substance use disorder treatments that do not have prior approval, no benefits will be paid; for medical/surgical treatments that do not have prior approval, there will only be a 25 percent reduction in the benefits the plan would otherwise pay.

(ii) *Conclusion.* In this *Example 2*, the plan violates the rules of this paragraph (c)(4). Although the same nonquantitative treatment limitation - medical necessity - is applied both to mental health and substance use disorder benefits and to medical/surgical benefits for outpatient, in-network services, the penalty for failure to obtain prior approval for mental health and substance use disorder benefits is not comparable to the penalty for failure to obtain prior approval for medical/surgical benefits.

Example 3. (i) *Facts.* A plan generally covers medically appropriate treatments. For both medical/surgical benefits and mental health and substance use disorder benefits, evidentiary standards used in determining whether a treatment is medically appropriate (such as the number of visits or days of coverage) are based on recommendations made by panels of experts with appropriate training and experience in the fields of medicine involved. The evidentiary standards are applied in a manner that may differ based on clinically appropriate standards of care for a condition.

(ii) *Conclusion.* In this *Example 3*, the plan complies with the rules of this paragraph (c)(4) because the nonquantitative treatment limitation - medical appropriateness - is the same for both medical/surgical benefits and mental health and substance use disorder benefits, and the processes for developing the evidentiary standards and the application of them to mental health and substance use disorder benefits are comparable to and are applied no more stringently than for medical/surgical benefits. This is the result even if, based on clinically appropriate standards of care, the application of the evidentiary standards does not result in similar numbers of visits, days of coverage, or other benefits utilized for mental health conditions or substance use disorders as it does for any particular medical/surgical condition.

Example 4. (i) *Facts.* A plan generally covers medically appropriate treatments. In determining whether prescription drugs are medically appropriate, the plan automatically excludes coverage for antidepressant drugs that are given a black box warning label by the Food and Drug Administration (indicating the drug carries a significant risk of serious adverse effects). For other drugs with a black box warning (including those prescribed for other mental health conditions and substance use disorders, as well as for medical/surgical conditions), the plan will provide coverage if the prescribing physician obtains authorization from the plan that the drug is medically appropriate for the individual, based on clinically appropriate standards of care.

(ii) *Conclusion.* In this *Example 4*, the plan violates the rules of this paragraph (c)(4). Although the same nonquantitative treatment limitation - medical appropriateness - is applied to both mental health and substance use disorder benefits and medical/surgical benefits, the plan's unconditional exclusion of antidepressant drugs given a black box warning is not comparable to the conditional exclusion for other drugs with a black box warning.

Example 5. (i) *Facts.* An employer maintains both a major medical program and an employee assistance program (EAP). The EAP provides, among other benefits, a limited number of mental health or substance use disorder counseling sessions. Participants are eligible for mental health or substance use disorder benefits under the major medical program only after exhausting the counseling sessions provided by the EAP. No similar exhaustion requirement applies with respect to medical/surgical benefits provided under the major medical program.

(ii) *Conclusion.* In this *Example 5*, limiting eligibility for mental health and substance use disorder benefits only after EAP benefits are exhausted is a nonquantitative treatment limitation subject to the parity requirements of this paragraph (c). Because no comparable requirement applies to medical/surgical benefits, the requirement may not be applied to mental health or substance use disorder benefits.

(5) *Exemptions.*—The rules of this paragraph (c) do not apply if a group health plan satisfies the requirements of paragraph (f) or (g) of this section (relating to exemptions for small employers and for increased cost).

≫→ *Caution: Temporary Reg. §54.9812-1T, below, as removed by T.D. 9640, is generally applicable to group health plans and health insurance issuers for plan or policy years beginning before July 1, 2014.*

(d) *Availability of plan information.*—(1) *Criteria for medical necessity determinations.*—The criteria for medical necessity determinations made under a group health plan with respect to mental health or substance use disorder benefits must be made available by the plan administrator to any current or potential participant, beneficiary, or contracting provider upon request.

(2) *Reason for denial.*—The reason for any denial under a group health plan of reimbursement or payment for services with respect to mental health or substance use disorder benefits in the case of any participant or beneficiary must be made available by the plan administrator to the participant or beneficiary in accordance with this paragraph (d)(2).

(i) *Plans subject to ERISA.*—If a plan is subject to ERISA, it must provide the reason for the claim denial in a form and manner consistent with the requirements of 29 CFR 2560.503-1 for group health plans.

(ii) *Plans not subject to ERISA.*—If a plan is not subject to ERISA, upon the request of a participant or beneficiary the reason for the claim denial must be provided within a reasonable time and in a reasonable manner. For this purpose, a plan that follows the requirements of 29 CFR 2560.503-1 for group health plans complies with the requirements of this paragraph (d)(2)(ii).

(e) *Applicability.*—(1) *Group health plans.*—The requirements of this section apply to a group health plan offering medical/surgical benefits and mental health or substance use disorder benefits. If, under an arrangement or arrangements to provide health care benefits by an employer or employee organization (including for this purpose a joint board of trustees of a multiemployer trust affiliated with one or more multiemployer plans), any participant (or beneficiary) can simultaneously receive coverage for medical/surgical benefits and coverage for mental health or substance use disorder benefits, then the requirements of this section (including the exemption provisions in paragraph (g) of this section) apply separately with respect to each combination of medical/surgical benefits and of mental health or substance use disorder benefits that any participant (or beneficiary) can simultaneously receive from that employer's or employee organization's arrangement or arrangements to provide health care benefits, and all such combinations are considered for purposes of this section to be a single group health plan.

(2) *Health insurance issuers.*—See 29 CFR 2590.712(e)(2) and 45 CFR 146.136(e)(2), under which a health insurance issuer offering health insurance coverage for mental health or substance use disorder benefits is subject to requirements similar to those applicable to group health plans under this section if the health insurance coverage is offered in connection with a group health plan subject to requirements under 29 CFR 2590.712 or 45 CFR 146.136 similar to those applicable to group health plans under this section.

(3) *Scope.*—This section does not—

(i) Require a group health plan to provide any mental health benefits or substance use disorder benefits, and the provision of benefits by a plan for one or more mental health conditions or substance use disorders does not require the plan under this section to provide benefits for any other mental health condition or substance use disorder; or

(ii) Affect the terms and conditions relating to the amount, duration, or scope of mental health or substance use disorder benefits under the plan except as specifically provided in paragraphs (b) and (c) of this section.

(f) *Small employer exemption.*—(1) *In general.*—The requirements of this section do not apply to a group health plan for a plan year of a small employer. For purposes of this paragraph (f), the term *small employer* means, in connection with a group health plan with respect to a calendar year and a plan year, an employer who employed an average of at least two (or one in the case of an employer residing in a state that permits small groups to include a single individual) but not more than 50 employees on business days during the preceding calendar year. See section 9831(a)(2) and §54.9831-1(b), which provide that this section (and certain other sections) does not apply to any group health plan for any plan year if, on the first day of the plan year, the plan has fewer than two participants who are current employees.

(2) *Rules in determining employer size.*—For purposes of paragraph (f)(1) of this section—

(i) All persons treated as a single employer under subsections (b), (c), (m), and (o) of section 414 are treated as one employer;

(ii) If an employer was not in existence throughout the preceding calendar year, whether it is a small employer is determined based on the average number of employees the employer reasonably expects to employ on business days during the current calendar year; and

(iii) Any reference to an employer for purposes of the small employer exemption includes a reference to a predecessor of the employer.

(g) *Increased cost exemption.*—[Reserved].

(h) *Sale of nonparity health insurance coverage.*—See 29 CFR 2590.712(h) and 45 CFR 146.136(h), under which a health insurance issuer may not sell a policy, certificate, or contract of insurance that fails to comply with requirements similar to those under paragraph (b) or (c) of this section, except to a plan for a year for which the plan is

Reg. §54.9812-1T(h)

»»→ Caution: *Temporary Reg. §54.9812-1T, below, as removed by T.D. 9640, is generally applicable to group health plans and health insurance issuers for plan or policy years beginning before July 1, 2014.*

exempt from requirements similar to those under paragraph (b) or (c) of this section because the plan meets requirements under paragraph (f) or (g) of 29 CFR 2590.712 or 45 CFR 146.136 similar to those under paragraph (f) or (g) of this section.

(i) *Effective/applicability dates.*—(1) *In general.*— Except as provided in paragraph (i)(2) of this section, the requirements of this section are applicable for plan years beginning on or after July 1, 2010.

(2) *Special effective date for certain collectively-bargained plans.*—For a group health plan maintained pursuant to one or more collective bar-

gaining agreements ratified before October 3, 2008, the requirements of this section do not apply to the plan for plan years beginning before the later of either—

(i) The date on which the last of the collective bargaining agreements relating to the plan terminates (determined without regard to any extension agreed to after October 3, 2008); or

(ii) July 1, 2010.

(j) *Expiration date.*—This section expires on or before *January 29, 2013.* [Temporary Reg. §54.9812-1T.]

☐ [*T.D. 8741, 12-19-97. Amended by T.D. 9479, 1-29-2010. Removed by T.D. 9640, 11-8-2013.*]

»»→ Caution: *Reg. §54.9815-1251, below, as added by T.D. 9744, is applicable to group health plans and health insurance issuers beginning on the first day of the plan year (or, in the individual market, the first day of the first policy year) beginning on or after January 1, 2017.*

[Reg. §54.9815-1251]

§54.9815-1251. Preservation of right to maintain existing coverage.—(a) *Definition of grandfathered health plan coverage.*—(1) *In general.*—(i) *Grandfathered health plan coverage* means coverage provided by a group health plan, or a health insurance issuer, in which an individual was enrolled on March 23, 2010 (for as long as it maintains that status under the rules of this section). A group health plan or group health insurance coverage does not cease to be grandfathered health plan coverage merely because one or more (or even all) individuals enrolled on March 23, 2010 cease to be covered, provided that the plan or group health insurance coverage has continuously covered someone since March 23, 2010 (not necessarily the same person, but at all times at least one person). In addition, subject to the limitation set forth in paragraph (a)(1)(ii) of this section, a group health plan (and any health insurance coverage offered in connection with the group health plan) does not cease to be a grandfathered health plan merely because the plan (or its sponsor) enters into a new policy, certificate, or contract of insurance after March 23, 2010 (for example, a plan enters into a contract with a new issuer or a new policy is issued with an existing issuer). For purposes of this section, a plan or health insurance coverage that provides grandfathered health plan coverage is referred to as a grandfathered health plan. The rules of this section apply separately to each benefit package made available under a group health plan or health insurance coverage. Accordingly, if any benefit package relinquishes grandfather status, it will not affect the grandfather status of the other benefit packages.

(ii) *Changes in group health insurance coverage.*—Subject to paragraphs (f) and (g)(2) of this section, if a group health plan (including a group health plan that was self-insured on March 23, 2010) or its sponsor enters into a new policy, certificate, or contract of insurance after March

23, 2010 that is effective before November 15, 2010, then the plan ceases to be a grandfathered health plan.

(2) *Disclosure of grandfather status.*—(i) To maintain status as a grandfathered health plan, a plan or health insurance coverage must include a statement that the plan or coverage believes it is a grandfathered health plan within the meaning of section 1251 of the Patient Protection and Affordable Care Act, and must provide contact information for questions and complaints, in any summary of benefits provided under the plan.

(ii) The following model language can be used to satisfy this disclosure requirement:

> This [group health plan or health insurance issuer] believes this [plan or coverage] is a "grandfathered health plan" under the Patient Protection and Affordable Care Act (the Affordable Care Act). As permitted by the Affordable Care Act, a grandfathered health plan can preserve certain basic health coverage that was already in effect when that law was enacted. Being a grandfathered health plan means that your [plan or policy] may not include certain consumer protections of the Affordable Care Act that apply to other plans, for example, the requirement for the provision of preventive health services without any cost sharing. However, grandfathered health plans must comply with certain other consumer protections in the Affordable Care Act, for example, the elimination of lifetime dollar limits on benefits.
>
> Questions regarding which protections apply and which protections do not apply to a grandfathered health plan and what might cause a plan to change from

⋙→ *Caution: Reg. §54.9815-1251, below, as added by T.D. 9744, is applicable to group health plans and health insurance issuers beginning on the first day of the plan year (or, in the individual market, the first day of the first policy year) beginning on or after January 1, 2017.*

grandfathered health plan status can be directed to the plan administrator at [insert contact information]. [For ERISA plans, insert: You may also contact the Employee Benefits Security Administration, U.S. Department of Labor at 1-866-444-3272 or www.dol.gov/ebsa/healthreform. This Web site has a table summarizing which protections do and do not apply to grandfathered health plans.] [For individual market policies and nonfederal governmental plans, insert: You may also contact the U.S. Department of Health and Human Services at www.healthcare.gov.]

(3)(i) *Documentation of plan or policy terms on March 23, 2010.*—To maintain status as a grandfathered health plan, a group health plan, or group health insurance coverage, must, for as long as the plan or health insurance coverage takes the position that it is a grandfathered health plan—

(A) Maintain records documenting the terms of the plan or health insurance coverage in connection with the coverage in effect on March 23, 2010, and any other documents necessary to verify, explain, or clarify its status as a grandfathered health plan; and

(B) Make such records available for examination upon request.

(ii) *Change in group health insurance coverage.*—To maintain status as a grandfathered health plan, a group health plan that enters into a new policy, certificate, or contract of insurance must provide to the new health insurance issuer (and the new health insurance issuer must require) documentation of plan terms (including benefits, cost sharing, employer contributions, and annual dollar limits) under the prior health coverage sufficient to determine whether a change causing a cessation of grandfathered health plan status under paragraph (g)(1) of this section has occurred.

(4) *Family members enrolling after March 23, 2010.*—With respect to an individual who is enrolled in a group health plan or health insurance coverage on March 23, 2010, grandfathered health plan coverage includes coverage of family members of the individual who enroll after March 23, 2010 in the grandfathered health plan coverage of the individual.

(b) *Allowance for new employees to join current plan.*—(1) *In general.*—Subject to paragraph (b)(2) of this section, a group health plan (including health insurance coverage provided in connection with the group health plan) that provided coverage on March 23, 2010 and has retained its status as a grandfathered health plan (consistent with the rules of this section, includ-

ing paragraph (g) of this section) is grandfathered health plan coverage for new employees (whether newly hired or newly enrolled) and their families enrolling in the plan after March 23, 2010. Further, the addition of a new contributing employer or new group of employees of an existing contributing employer to a grandfathered multiemployer health plan will not affect the plan's grandfather status.

(2) *Anti-abuse rules.*—(i) *Mergers and acquisitions.*—If the principal purpose of a merger, acquisition, or similar business restructuring is to cover new individuals under a grandfathered health plan, the plan ceases to be a grandfathered health plan.

(ii) *Change in plan eligibility.*—A group health plan or health insurance coverage (including a benefit package under a group health plan) ceases to be a grandfathered health plan if—

(A) Employees are transferred into the plan or health insurance coverage (the transferee plan) from a plan or health insurance coverage under which the employees were covered on March 23, 2010 (the transferor plan);

(B) Comparing the terms of the transferee plan with those of the transferor plan (as in effect on March 23, 2010) and treating the transferee plan as if it were an amendment of the transferor plan would cause a loss of grandfather status under the provisions of paragraph (g)(1) of this section; and

(C) There was no bona fide employment-based reason to transfer the employees into the transferee plan. For this purpose, changing the terms or cost of coverage is not a bona fide employment-based reason.

(iii) *Illustrative list of bona fide employment-based reasons.*—For purposes of paragraph (b)(2)(ii)(C) of this section, bona fide employment-based reasons include—

(A) When a benefit package is being eliminated because the issuer is exiting the market;

(B) When a benefit package is being eliminated because the issuer no longer offers the product to the employer;

(C) When low or declining participation by plan participants in the benefit package makes it impractical for the plan sponsor to continue to offer the benefit package;

(D) When a benefit package is eliminated from a multiemployer plan as agreed upon as part of the collective bargaining process; or

(E) When a benefit package is eliminated for any reason and multiple benefit packages covering a significant portion of other employees remain available to the employees being transferred.

(3) *Examples.*—The rules of this paragraph (b) are illustrated by the following examples:

Reg. §54.9815-1251(b)(3)

»»→ *Caution: Reg. §54.9815-1251, below, as added by T.D. 9744, is applicable to group health plans and health insurance issuers beginning on the first day of the plan year (or, in the individual market, the first day of the first policy year) beginning on or after January 1, 2017.*

Example 1. (i) *Facts.* A group health plan offers two benefit packages on March 23, 2010, Options *F* and *G.* During a subsequent open enrollment period, some of the employees enrolled in Option *F* on March 23, 2010 switch to Option *G.*

(ii) *Conclusion.* In this *Example 1*, the group health coverage provided under Option *G* remains a grandfathered health plan under the rules of paragraph (b)(1) of this section because employees previously enrolled in Option *F* are allowed to enroll in Option *G* as new employees.

Example 2. (i) *Facts.* A group health plan offers two benefit packages on March 23, 2010, Options *H* and *I.* On March 23, 2010, Option *H* provides coverage only for employees in one manufacturing plant. Subsequently, the plant is closed, and some employees in the closed plant are moved to another plant. The employer eliminates Option *H* and the employees that are moved are transferred to Option *I.* If instead of transferring employees from Option *H* to Option *I,* Option *H* was amended to match the terms of Option *I,* then Option *H* would cease to be a grandfathered health plan.

(ii) *Conclusion.* In this *Example 2*, the plan has a bona fide employment-based reason to transfer employees from Option *H* to Option *I.* Therefore, Option *I* does not cease to be a grandfathered health plan.

(c) *General grandfathering rule.*—(1) Except as provided in paragraphs (d) and (e) of this section, subtitles A and C of title I of the Patient Protection and Affordable Care Act (and the amendments made by those subtitles, and the incorporation of those amendments into ERISA section 715 and Internal Revenue Code section 9815) do not apply to grandfathered health plan coverage. Accordingly, the provisions of PHS Act sections 2701, 2702, 2703, 2705, 2706, 2707, 2709 (relating to coverage for individuals participating in approved clinical trials, as added by section 10103 of the Patient Protection and Affordable Care Act), 2713, 2715A, 2716, 2717, 2719, and 2719A, as added or amended by the Patient Protection and Affordable Care Act, do not apply to grandfathered health plans. (In addition, *see* 45 CFR 147.140(c), which provides that the provisions of PHS Act section 2704, and PHS Act section 2711 insofar as it relates to annual dollar limits, do not apply to grandfathered health plans that are individual health insurance coverage.)

(2) To the extent not inconsistent with the rules applicable to a grandfathered health plan, a grandfathered health plan must comply with the requirements of the PHS Act, ERISA, and the Internal Revenue Code applicable prior to the changes enacted by the Patient Protection and Affordable Care Act.

(d) *Provisions applicable to all grandfathered health plans.*—The provisions of PHS Act section 2711 insofar as it relates to lifetime dollar limits, and the provisions of PHS Act sections 2712, 2714, 2715, and 2718, apply to grandfathered health plans for plan years beginning on or after September 23, 2010. The provisions of PHS Act section 2708 apply to grandfathered health plans for plan years beginning on or after January 1, 2014.

(e) *Applicability of PHS Act sections 2704, 2711, and 2714 to grandfathered group health plans and group health insurance coverage.*—(1) The provisions of PHS Act section 2704 as it applies with respect to enrollees who are under 19 years of age, and the provisions of PHS Act section 2711 insofar as it relates to annual dollar limits, apply to grandfathered health plans that are group health plans (including group health insurance coverage) for plan years beginning on or after September 23, 2010. The provisions of PHS Act section 2704 apply generally to grandfathered health plans that are group health plans (including group health insurance coverage) for plan years beginning on or after January 1, 2014.

(2) For plan years beginning before January 1, 2014, the provisions of PHS Act section 2714 apply in the case of an adult child with respect to a grandfathered health plan that is a group health plan only if the adult child is not eligible to enroll in an eligible employer-sponsored health plan (as defined in section 5000A(f)(2) of the Internal Revenue Code) other than a grandfathered health plan of a parent. For plan years beginning on or after January 1, 2014, the provisions of PHS Act section 2714 apply with respect to a grandfathered health plan that is a group health plan without regard to whether an adult child is eligible to enroll in any other coverage.

(f) *Effect on collectively bargained plans—In general.*—In the case of health insurance coverage maintained pursuant to one or more collective bargaining agreements between employee representatives and one or more employers that was ratified before March 23, 2010, the coverage is grandfathered health plan coverage at least until the date on which the last of the collective bargaining agreements relating to the coverage that was in effect on March 23, 2010 terminates. Any coverage amendment made pursuant to a collective bargaining agreement relating to the coverage that amends the coverage solely to conform to any requirement added by subtitles A and C of title I of the Patient Protection and Affordable Care Act (and the amendments made by those subtitles, and the incorporation of those amendments into ERISA section 715 and Internal Revenue Code section 9815) is not treated as a termination of the collective bargaining agreement. After the date on which the last of the collective bargaining agreements relating to the coverage that was in effect on March 23, 2010 terminates, the determination of whether health

>>>→ *Caution: Reg. §54.9815-1251, below, as added by T.D. 9744, is applicable to group health plans and health insurance issuers beginning on the first day of the plan year (or, in the individual market, the first day of the first policy year) beginning on or after January 1, 2017.*

insurance coverage maintained pursuant to a collective bargaining agreement is grandfathered health plan coverage is made under the rules of this section other than this paragraph (f) (comparing the terms of the health insurance coverage after the date the last collective bargaining agreement terminates with the terms of the health insurance coverage that were in effect on March 23, 2010).

(g) *Maintenance of grandfather status.—* (1) *Changes causing cessation of grandfather status.—*Subject to paragraph (g)(2) of this section, the rules of this paragraph (g)(1) describe situations in which a group health plan or health insurance coverage ceases to be a grandfathered health plan. A plan or coverage will cease to be a grandfathered health plan when an amendment to plan terms that results in a change described in this paragraph (g)(1) becomes effective, regardless of when the amendment was adopted. Once grandfather status is lost, it cannot be regained.

(i) *Elimination of benefits.—*The elimination of all or substantially all benefits to diagnose or treat a particular condition causes a group health plan or health insurance coverage to cease to be a grandfathered health plan. For this purpose, the elimination of benefits for any necessary element to diagnose or treat a condition is considered the elimination of all or substantially all benefits to diagnose or treat a particular condition. Whether or not a plan or coverage has eliminated substantially all benefits to diagnose or treat a particular condition must be determined based on all the facts and circumstances, taking into account the items and services provided for a particular condition under the plan on March 23, 2010, as compared to the benefits offered at the time the plan or coverage makes the benefit change effective.

(ii) *Increase in percentage cost-sharing requirement.—*Any increase, measured from March 23, 2010, in a percentage cost-sharing requirement (such as an individual's coinsurance requirement) causes a group health plan or health insurance coverage to cease to be a grandfathered health plan.

(iii) *Increase in a fixed-amount cost-sharing requirement other than a copayment.—*Any increase in a fixed-amount cost-sharing requirement other than a copayment (for example, deductible or out-of-pocket limit), determined as of the effective date of the increase, causes a group health plan or health insurance coverage to cease to be a grandfathered health plan, if the total percentage increase in the cost-sharing requirement measured from March 23, 2010 exceeds the maximum percentage increase (as defined in paragraph (g)(3)(ii) of this section).

(iv) *Increase in a fixed-amount copayment.—*Any increase in a fixed-amount copayment, de-

termined as of the effective date of the increase, and determined for each copayment level if a plan has different copayment levels for different categories of services, causes a group health plan or health insurance coverage to cease to be a grandfathered health plan, if the total increase in the copayment measured from March 23, 2010 exceeds the greater of:

(A) An amount equal to $5 increased by medical inflation, as defined in paragraph (g)(3)(i) of this section (that is, $5 times medical inflation, plus $5), or

(B) The maximum percentage increase (as defined in paragraph (g)(3)(ii) of this section), determined by expressing the total increase in the copayment as a percentage.

(v) *Decrease in contribution rate by employers and employee organizations.—*(A) *Contribution rate based on cost of coverage.—*A group health plan or group health insurance coverage ceases to be a grandfathered health plan if the employer or employee organization decreases its contribution rate based on cost of coverage (as defined in paragraph (g)(3)(iii)(A) of this section) towards the cost of any tier of coverage for any class of similarly situated individuals (as described in §54.9802(d)) by more than 5 percentage points below the contribution rate for the coverage period that includes March 23, 2010.

(B) *Contribution rate based on a formula.—*A group health plan or group health insurance coverage ceases to be a grandfathered health plan if the employer or employee organization decreases its contribution rate based on a formula (as defined in paragraph (g)(3)(iii)(B) of this section) towards the cost of any tier of coverage for any class of similarly situated individuals (as described in §54.9802(d)) by more than 5 percent below the contribution rate for the coverage period that includes March 23, 2010.

(C) *Special rules regarding decreases in contribution rates.—*An insured group health plan (or a multiemployer plan) that is a grandfathered health plan will not cease to be a grandfathered health plan based on a change in the employer contribution rate unless the issuer (or multiemployer plan) knows, or should know, of the change, provided:

(1) Upon renewal (or, in the case of a multiemployer plan, before the start of a new plan year), the issuer (or multiemployer plan) requires relevant employers, employee organizations, or plan sponsors, as applicable, to make a representation regarding its contribution rate for the plan year covered by the renewal, as well as its contribution rate on March 23, 2010 (if the issuer, or multiemployer plan, does not already have it); and

(2) The relevant policies, certificates, contracts of insurance, or plan documents disclose in a prominent and effective manner that employers, employee organizations, or plan

Reg. §54.9815-1251(g)(1)(v)(C)(2)

>>> *Caution: Reg. §54.9815-1251, below, as added by T.D. 9744, is applicable to group health plans and health insurance issuers beginning on the first day of the plan year (or, in the individual market, the first day of the first policy year) beginning on or after January 1, 2017.*

sponsors, as applicable, are required to notify the issuer (or multiemployer plan) if the contribution rate changes at any point during the plan year.

(D) *Application to plans with multi-tiered coverage structures.*—The standards for employer contributions in this paragraph (g)(1)(v) apply on a tier-by-tier basis. Therefore, if a group health plan modifies the tiers of coverage it had on March 23, 2010 (for example, from self-only and family to a multi-tiered structure of self-only, self-plus-one, self-plus-two, and self-plus-three-or-more), the employer contribution for any new tier would be tested by comparison to the contribution rate for the corresponding tier on March 23, 2010. For example, if the employer contribution rate for family coverage was 50 percent on March 23, 2010, the employer contribution rate for any new tier of coverage other than self-only (i.e., self-plus-one, self-plus-two, self-plus-three or more) must be within 5 percentage points of 50 percent (i.e., at least 45 percent). If, however, the plan adds one or more new coverage tiers without eliminating or modifying any previous tiers and those new coverage tiers cover classes of individuals that were not covered previously under the plan, the new tiers would not be analyzed under the standards for changes in employer contributions. For example, if a plan with self-only as the sole coverage tier added a family coverage tier, the level of employer contributions toward the family coverage would not cause the plan to lose grandfather status.

(E) *Group health plans with fixed-dollar employee contributions or no employee contributions.*—A group health plan that requires either fixed-dollar employee contributions or no employee contributions will not cease to be a grandfathered health plan solely because the employer contribution rate changes so long as there continues to be no employee contributions or no increase in the fixed-dollar employee contributions towards the cost of coverage.

(vi) *Changes in annual limits.*—(A) *Addition of an annual limit.*—A group health plan, or group health insurance coverage, that, on March 23, 2010, did not impose an overall annual or lifetime limit on the dollar value of all benefits ceases to be a grandfathered health plan if the plan or health insurance coverage imposes an overall annual limit on the dollar value of benefits. (But see § 54.9815-2711, which prohibits all annual dollar limits on essential health benefits for plan years beginning on or after January 1, 2014).

(B) *Decrease in limit for a plan or coverage with only a lifetime limit.*—A group health plan, or group health insurance coverage, that, on March 23, 2010, imposed an overall lifetime limit on the dollar value of all benefits but no overall annual

limit on the dollar value of all benefits ceases to be a grandfathered health plan if the plan or health insurance coverage adopts an overall annual limit at a dollar value that is lower than the dollar value of the lifetime limit on March 23, 2010. (But see § 54.9815-2711, which prohibits all annual dollar limits on essential health benefits for plan years beginning on or after January 1, 2014).

(C) *Decrease in limit for a plan or coverage with an annual limit.*—A group health plan, or group health insurance coverage, that, on March 23, 2010, imposed an overall annual limit on the dollar value of all benefits ceases to be a grandfathered health plan if the plan or health insurance coverage decreases the dollar value of the annual limit (regardless of whether the plan or health insurance coverage also imposed an overall lifetime limit on March 23, 2010 on the dollar value of all benefits). (But see § 54.9815-2711, which prohibits all annual dollar limits on essential health benefits for plan years beginning on or after January 1, 2014).

(2) *Transitional rules.*—(i) *Changes made prior to March 23, 2010.*—If a group health plan or health insurance issuer makes the following changes to the terms of the plan or health insurance coverage, the changes are considered part of the terms of the plan or health insurance coverage on March 23, 2010 even though they were not effective at that time and such changes do not cause a plan or health insurance coverage to cease to be a grandfathered health plan:

(A) Changes effective after March 23, 2010 pursuant to a legally binding contract entered into on or before March 23, 2010;

(B) Changes effective after March 23, 2010 pursuant to a filing on or before March 23, 2010 with a State insurance department; or

(C) Changes effective after March 23, 2010 pursuant to written amendments to a plan that were adopted on or before March 23, 2010.

(ii) *Changes made after March 23, 2010 and adopted prior to issuance of regulations.*—If, after March 23, 2010, a group health plan or health insurance issuer makes changes to the terms of the plan or health insurance coverage and the changes are adopted prior to June 14, 2010, the changes will not cause the plan or health insurance coverage to cease to be a grandfathered health plan if the changes are revoked or modified effective as of the first day of the first plan year (in the individual market, policy year) beginning on or after September 23, 2010, and the terms of the plan or health insurance coverage on that date, as modified, would not cause the plan or coverage to cease to be a grandfathered health plan under the rules of this section, including paragraph (g)(1) of this section. For this purpose, changes will be considered to have been adopted prior to June 14, 2010 if:

⋙→ *Caution: Reg. §54.9815-1251, below, as added by T.D. 9744, is applicable to group health plans and health insurance issuers beginning on the first day of the plan year (or, in the individual market, the first day of the first policy year) beginning on or after January 1, 2017.*

(A) The changes are effective before that date;

(B) The changes are effective on or after that date pursuant to a legally binding contract entered into before that date;

(C) The changes are effective on or after that date pursuant to a filing before that date with a State insurance department; or

(D) The changes are effective on or after that date pursuant to written amendments to a plan that were adopted before that date.

(3) *Definitions.*—(i) *Medical inflation defined.*—For purposes of this paragraph (g), the term *medical inflation* means the increase since March 2010 in the overall medical care component of the Consumer Price Index for All Urban Consumers (CPI-U) (unadjusted) published by the Department of Labor using the 1982 – 1984 base of 100. For this purpose, the increase in the overall medical care component is computed by subtracting 387.142 (the overall medical care component of the CPI-U (unadjusted) published by the Department of Labor for March 2010, using the 1982 – 1984 base of 100) from the index amount for any month in the 12 months before the new change is to take effect and then dividing that amount by 387.142.

(ii) *Maximum percentage increase defined.*— For purposes of this paragraph (g), the term *maximum percentage increase* means medical inflation (as defined in paragraph (g)(3)(i) of this section), expressed as a percentage, plus 15 percentage points.

(iii) *Contribution rate defined.*—For purposes of paragraph (g)(1)(v) of this section:

(A) *Contribution rate based on cost of coverage.*—The term *contribution rate based on cost of coverage* means the amount of contributions made by an employer or employee organization compared to the total cost of coverage, expressed as a percentage. The total cost of coverage is determined in the same manner as the applicable premium is calculated under the COBRA continuation provisions of section 604 of ERISA, section 4980B(f)(4) of the Internal Revenue Code, and section 2204 of the PHS Act. In the case of a self-insured plan, contributions by an employer or employee organization are equal to the total cost of coverage minus the employee contributions towards the total cost of coverage.

(B) *Contribution rate based on a formula.*—The term *contribution rate based on a formula* means, for plans that, on March 23, 2010, made contributions based on a formula (such as hours worked or tons of coal mined), the formula.

(4) *Examples.*—The rules of this paragraph (g) are illustrated by the following examples:

Example 1. (i) *Facts.* On March 23, 2010, a grandfathered health plan has a coinsurance re-

quirement of 20% for inpatient surgery. The plan is subsequently amended to increase the coinsurance requirement to 25%.

(ii) *Conclusion.* In this *Example 1*, the increase in the coinsurance requirement from 20% to 25% causes the plan to cease to be a grandfathered health plan.

Example 2. (i) *Facts.* Before March 23, 2010, the terms of a group health plan provide benefits for a particular mental health condition, the treatment for which is a combination of counseling and prescription drugs. Subsequently, the plan eliminates benefits for counseling.

(ii) *Conclusion.* In this *Example 2*, the plan ceases to be a grandfathered health plan because counseling is an element that is necessary to treat the condition. Thus the plan is considered to have eliminated substantially all benefits for the treatment of the condition.

Example 3. (i) *Facts.* On March 23, 2010, a grandfathered health plan has a copayment requirement of $30 per office visit for specialists. The plan is subsequently amended to increase the copayment requirement to $40. Within the 12-month period before the $40 copayment takes effect, the greatest value of the overall medical care component of the CPI-U (unadjusted) is 475.

(ii) *Conclusion.* In this *Example 3*, the increase in the copayment from $30 to $40, expressed as a percentage, is 33.33% (40 - 30 = 10; 10 ÷ 30 = 0.3333; 0.3333 = 33.33%). Medical inflation (as defined in paragraph (g)(3)(i) of this section) from March 2010 is 0.2269 (475 – 387.142 = 87.858; 87.858 ÷ 387.142 = 0.2269). The maximum percentage increase permitted is 37.69% (0.2269 = 22.69%; 22.69% + 15% = 37.69%). Because 33.33% does not exceed 37.69%, the change in the copayment requirement at that time does not cause the plan to cease to be a grandfathered health plan.

Example 4. (i) *Facts.* Same facts as *Example 3*, except the grandfathered health plan subsequently increases the $40 copayment requirement to $45 for a later plan year. Within the 12-month period before the $45 copayment takes effect, the greatest value of the overall medical care component of the CPI-U (unadjusted) is 485.

(ii) *Conclusion.* In this *Example 4*, the increase in the copayment from $30 (the copayment that was in effect on March 23, 2010) to $45, expressed as a percentage, is 50% (45 - 30 = 15; 15 ÷ 30 = 0.5; 0.5 = 50%). Medical inflation (as defined in paragraph (g)(3)(i) of this section) from March 2010 is 0.2527 (485 – 387.142 = 97.858; 97.858 ÷ 387.142 = 0.2527). The increase that would cause a plan to cease to be a grandfathered health plan under paragraph (g)(1)(iv) of this section is the greater of the maximum percentage increase of 40.27% (0.2527 = 25.27%; 25.27% + 15% = 40.27%), or $6.26 ($5 x 0.2527 = $1.26; $1.26 + $5 = $6.26). Because 50% exceeds 40.27% and $15 exceeds $6.26, the change in the copayment re-

>>> Caution: *Reg. §54.9815-1251, below, as added by T.D. 9744, is applicable to group health plans and health insurance issuers beginning on the first day of the plan year (or, in the individual market, the first day of the first policy year) beginning on or after January 1, 2017.*

quirement at that time causes the plan to cease to be a grandfathered health plan.

Example 5. (i) *Facts.* On March 23, 2010, a grandfathered health plan has a copayment of $10 per office visit for primary care providers. The plan is subsequently amended to increase the copayment requirement to $15. Within the 12-month period before the $15 copayment takes effect, the greatest value of the overall medical care component of the CPI-U (unadjusted) is 415.

(ii) *Conclusion.* In this *Example 5,* the increase in the copayment, expressed as a percentage, is 50% (15 - 10 = 5; 5 ÷ 10 = 0.5; 0.5 = 50%). Medical inflation (as defined in paragraph (g)(3) of this section) from March 2010 is 0.0720 (415.0 - 387.142 = 27.858; 27.858 ÷ 387.142 = 0.0720). The increase that would cause a plan to cease to be a grandfathered health plan under paragraph (g)(1)(iv) of this section is the greater of maximum percentage increase of 22.20% (0.0720 = 7.20%; 7.20% + 15% = 22.20), or $5.36 ($5 x 0.0720 = $0.36; $0.36 + $5 = $5.36). The $5 increase in copayment in this *Example 5* would not cause the plan to cease to be a grandfathered health plan pursuant to paragraph (g)(1)(iv)this section, which would permit an increase in the copayment of up to $5.36.

Example 6. (i) *Facts.* The same facts as *Example 5,* except on March 23, 2010, the grandfathered health plan has no copayment ($0) for office visits for primary care providers. The plan is subsequently amended to increase the copayment requirement to $5.

(ii) *Conclusion.* In this *Example 6,* medical inflation (as defined in paragraph (g)(3)(i) of this section) from March 2010 is 0.0720 (415.0 - 387.142 = 27.858; 27.858 ÷ 387.142 = 0.0720). The increase that would cause a plan to cease to be a grandfathered health plan under paragraph (g)(1)(iv)(A) of this section is $5.36 ($5 x 0.0720 = $0.36; $0.36 + $5 = $5.36). The $5 increase in copayment in this *Example 6* is less than the amount calculated pursuant to paragraph (g)(1)(iv)(A) of this section of $5.36. Thus, the $5 increase in copayment does not cause the plan to cease to be a grandfathered health plan.

Example 7. (i) *Facts.* On March 23, 2010, a self-insured group health plan provides two tiers of coverage — self-only and family. The employer contributes 80% of the total cost of coverage for self-only and 60% of the total cost of coverage for family. Subsequently, the employer reduces the contribution to 50% for family coverage, but keeps the same contribution rate for self-only coverage.

(ii) *Conclusion.* In this *Example 7,* the decrease of 10 percentage points for family coverage in the contribution rate based on cost of coverage causes the plan to cease to be a grandfathered health plan. The fact that the contribution rate for self-only coverage remains the same does not change the result.

Example 8. (i) *Facts.* On March 23, 2010, a self-insured grandfathered health plan has a COBRA premium for the 2010 plan year of $5000 for self-only coverage and $12,000 for family coverage. The required employee contribution for the coverage is $1000 for self-only coverage and $4000 for family coverage. Thus, the contribution rate based on cost of coverage for 2010 is 80% ((5000 − 1000)/5000) for self-only coverage and 67% ((12,000 − 4000)/12,000) for family coverage. For a subsequent plan year, the COBRA premium is $6000 for self-only coverage and $15,000 for family coverage. The employee contributions for that plan year are $1200 for self-only coverage and $5000 for family coverage. Thus, the contribution rate based on cost of coverage is 80% ((6000 − 1200)/6000) for self-only coverage and 67% ((15,000 − 5000)/15,000) for family coverage.

(ii) *Conclusion.* In this *Example 8,* because there is no change in the contribution rate based on cost of coverage, the plan retains its status as a grandfathered health plan. The result would be the same if all or part of the employee contribution was made pre-tax through a cafeteria plan under section 125 of the Internal Revenue Code.

Example 9. (i) *Facts.* A group health plan not maintained pursuant to a collective bargaining agreement offers three benefit packages on March 23, 2010. Option *F* is a self-insured option. Options *G* and *H* are insured options. Beginning July 1, 2013, the plan increases coinsurance under Option *H* from 10% to 15%.

(ii) *Conclusion.* In this *Example 9,* the coverage under Option *H* is not grandfathered health plan coverage as of July 1, 2013, consistent with the (rule in paragraph (g)(1)(ii) of this section. Whether the coverage under Options *F* and *G* is grandfathered health plan coverage is determined separately under the rules of this paragraph (g). [Reg. § 54.9815-1251.]

☐ [T.D. 9744, 11-13-2015.]

>>> Caution: *Temporary Reg. §54.9815-1251T, below, was removed by T.D. 9744 and is inapplicable under Code Sec. 7805(e)(2). However, until final Reg. §54.9815-1251 is applicable on the first day of the plan or policy year beginning after January 1, 2017, taxpayers may comply with the corresponding interim final regulation at 29 CFR part 2590 that is substantially similar to the temporary reg below.*

[Reg. § 54.9815-1251T]

§ 54.9815-1251T. Preservation of right to maintain existing coverage (temporary).— (a) *Definition of grandfathered health plan cover-* age.—(1) *In general.*—(i) *Grandfathered health plan coverage.*—Grandfathered health plan coverage means coverage provided by a group health plan, or a health insurance issuer, in which an individual was enrolled on March 23, 2010 (for

⫸→ *Caution: Temporary Reg. §54.9815-1251T, below, was removed by T.D. 9744 and is inapplicable under Code Sec. 7805(e)(2). However, until final Reg. §54.9815-1251 is applicable on the first day of the plan or policy year beginning after January 1, 2017, taxpayers may comply with the corresponding interim final regulation at 29 CFR part 2590 that is substantially similar to the temporary reg below.*

as long as it maintains that status under the rules of this section). A group health plan or group health insurance coverage does not cease to be grandfathered health plan coverage merely because one or more (or even all) individuals enrolled on March 23, 2010 cease to be covered, provided that the plan has continuously covered someone since March 23, 2010 (not necessarily the same person, but at all times at least one person). In addition, subject to the limitation set forth in paragraph (a)(1)(ii) of this section, a group health plan (and any health insurance coverage offered in connection with the group health plan) does not cease to be a grandfathered health plan merely because the plan (or its sponsor) enters into a new policy, certificate, or contract of insurance after March 23, 2010 (for example, a plan enters into a contract with a new issuer or a new policy is issued with an existing issuer). For purposes of this section, a plan or health insurance coverage that provides grandfathered health plan coverage is referred to as a grandfathered health plan. The rules of this section apply separately to each benefit package made available under a group health plan or health insurance coverage.

(ii) *Changes in group health insurance coverage.*—Subject to paragraphs (f) and and (g)(2) of this section, if a group health plan (including a group health plan that was self-insured on March 23, 2010) or its sponsor enters into a new policy, certificate, or contract of insurance after March 23, 2010 that is effective before November 15, 2010, then the plan ceases to be a grandfathered health plan.

(2) *Disclosure of grandfather status.*—(i) To maintain status as a grandfathered health plan, a plan or health insurance coverage must include a statement, in any plan materials provided to a participant or beneficiary describing the benefits provided under the plan or health insurance coverage, that the plan or coverage believes it is a grandfathered health plan within the meaning of section 1251 of the Patient Protection and Affordable Care Act and must provide contact information for questions and complaints.

(ii) The following model language can be used to satisfy this disclosure requirement:

This [group health plan or health insurance issuer] believes this [plan or coverage] is a "grandfathered health plan" under the Patient Protection and Affordable Care Act (the Affordable Care Act). As permitted by the Affordable Care Act, a grandfathered health plan can preserve certain basic health coverage that was already in effect when that law was enacted. Being a grandfathered health plan means that your [plan or policy] may not include certain consumer protections of the Affordable Care Act

that apply to other plans, for example, the requirement for the provision of preventive health services without any cost sharing. However, grandfathered health plans must comply with certain other consumer protections in the Affordable Care Act, for example, the elimination of lifetime limits on benefits.

Questions regarding which protections apply and which protections do not apply to a grandfathered health plan and what might cause a plan to change from grandfathered health plan status can be directed to the plan administrator at [insert contact information]. [For ERISA plans, insert: You may also contact the Employee Benefits Security Administration, U.S. Department of Labor at 1-866-444-3272 or *www.dol.gov/ebsa/healthreform*. This website has a table summarizing which protections do and do not apply to grandfathered health plans.] [For individual market policies and nonfederal governmental plans, insert: You may also contact the U.S. Department of Health and Human Services at *www.healthreform.gov*.]

(3)(i) *Documentation of plan or policy terms on March 23, 2010.*—To maintain status as a grandfathered health plan, a group health plan, or group health insurance coverage, must, for as long as the plan or health insurance coverage takes the position that it is a grandfathered health plan -

(A) Maintain records documenting the terms of the plan or health insurance coverage in connection with the coverage in effect on March 23, 2010, and any other documents necessary to verify, explain, or clarify its status as a grandfathered health plan; and

(B) Make such records available for examination upon request.

(ii) *Change in group health insurance coverage.*—To maintain status as a grandfathered health plan, a group health plan that enters into a new policy, certificate, or contract of insurance must provide to the new health insurance issuer (and the new health insurance issuer must require) documentation of plan terms (including benefits, cost sharing, employer contributions, and annual limits) under the prior health coverage sufficient to determine whether a change causing a cessation of grandfathered health plan status under paragraph (g)(1) of this section has occurred.

(4) *Family members enrolling after March 23, 2010.*—With respect to an individual who is enrolled in a group health plan or health insurance coverage on March 23, 2010, grandfathered health plan coverage includes coverage of family members of the individual who enroll after March 23, 2010 in the grandfathered health plan coverage of the individual.

>>>→ *Caution: Temporary Reg. §54.9815-1251T, below, was removed by T.D. 9744 and is inapplicable under Code Sec. 7805(e)(2). However, until final Reg. §54.9815-1251 is applicable on the first day of the plan or policy year beginning after January 1, 2017, taxpayers may comply with the corresponding interim final regulation at 29 CFR part 2590 that is substantially similar to the temporary reg below.*

(b) *Allowance for new employees to join current plan.*—(1) *In general.*—Subject to paragraph (b)(2) of this section, a group health plan (including health insurance coverage provided in connection with the group health plan) that provided coverage on March 23, 2010 and has retained its status as a grandfathered health plan (consistent with the rules of this section, including paragraph (g) of this section) is grandfathered health plan coverage for new employees (whether newly hired or newly enrolled) and their families enrolling in the plan after March 23, 2010.

(2) *Anti-abuse rules.*—(i) *Mergers and acquisitions.*—If the principal purpose of a merger, acquisition, or similar business restructuring is to cover new individuals under a grandfathered health plan, the plan ceases to be a grandfathered health plan.

(ii) *Change in plan eligibility.*—A group health plan or health insurance coverage (including a benefit package under a group health plan) ceases to be a grandfathered health plan if—

(A) Employees are transferred into the plan or health insurance coverage (the transferee plan) from a plan or health insurance coverage under which the employees were covered on March 23, 2010 (the transferor plan);

(B) Comparing the terms of the transferee plan with those of the transferor plan (as in effect on March 23, 2010) and treating the transferee plan as if it were an amendment of the transferor plan would cause a loss of grandfather status under the provisions of paragraph (g)(1) of this section; and

(C) There was no bona fide employment-based reason to transfer the employees into the transferee plan. For this purpose, changing the terms or cost of coverage is not a bona fide employment-based reason.

(3) *Examples.*—The rules of this paragraph (b) are illustrated by the following examples:

Example 1. (i) *Facts.* A group health plan offers two benefit packages on March 23, 2010, Options F and G. During a subsequent open enrollment period, some of the employees enrolled in Option F on March 23, 2010 switch to Option G.

(ii) *Conclusion.* In this *Example 1,* the group health coverage provided under Option G remains a grandfathered health plan under the rules of paragraph (b)(1) of this section because employees previously enrolled in Option F are allowed to enroll in Option G as new employees.

Example 2. (i) *Facts.* Same facts as *Example 1,* except that the plan sponsor eliminates Option F because of its high cost and transfers employees covered under Option F to Option G. If instead of transferring employees from Option F to Op-

tion G, Option F was amended to match the terms of Option G, then Option F would cease to be a grandfathered health plan.

(ii) *Conclusion.* In this *Example 2,* the plan did not have a bona fide employment-based reason to transfer employees from Option F to Option G. Therefore, Option G ceases to be a grandfathered health plan with respect to all employees. (However, any other benefit package maintained by the plan sponsor is analyzed separately under the rules of this section.)

Example 3. (i) *Facts.* A group health plan offers two benefit packages on March 23, 2010, Options H and I. On March 23, 2010, Option H provides coverage only for employees in one manufacturing plant. Subsequently, the plant is closed, and some employees in the closed plant are moved to another plant. The employer eliminates Option H and the employees that are moved are transferred to Option I. If instead of transferring employees from Option H to Option I, Option H was amended to match the terms of Option I, then Option H would cease to be a grandfathered health plan.

(ii) *Conclusion.* In this *Example 3,* the plan has a bona fide employment-based reason to transfer employees from Option H to Option I. Therefore, Option I does not cease to be a grandfathered health plan.

(c) *General grandfathering rule.*—(1) Except as provided in paragraphs (d) and (e) of this section, subtitles A and C of title I of the Patient Protection and Affordable Care Act (and the amendments made by those subtitles, and the incorporation of those amendments into section 9815 and ERISA section 715) do not apply to grandfathered health plan coverage. Accordingly, the provisions of PHS Act sections 2701, 2702, 2703, 2705, 2706, 2707, 2709 (relating to coverage for individuals participating in approved clinical trials, as added by section 10103 of the Patient Protection and Affordable Care Act), 2713, 2715A, 2716, 2717, 2719, and 2719A, as added or amended by the Patient Protection and Affordable Care Act, do not apply to grandfathered health plans. (In addition, see 45 CFR 147.140(c), which provides that the provisions of PHS Act section 2704, and PHS Act section 2711 insofar as it relates to annual limits, do not apply to grandfathered health plans that are individual health insurance coverage.)

(2) To the extent not inconsistent with the rules applicable to a grandfathered health plan, a grandfathered health plan must comply with the requirements of the Code, the PHS Act, and ERISA applicable prior to the changes enacted by the Patient Protection and Affordable Care Act.

(d) *Provisions applicable to all grandfathered health plans.*—The provisions of PHS Act section

>>>→ *Caution: Temporary Reg. §54.9815-1251T, below, was removed by T.D. 9744 and is inapplicable under Code Sec. 7805(e)(2). However, until final Reg. §54.9815-1251 is applicable on the first day of the plan or policy year beginning after January 1, 2017, taxpayers may comply with the corresponding interim final regulation at 29 CFR part 2590 that is substantially similar to the temporary reg below.*

2711 insofar as it relates to lifetime limits, and the provisions of PHS Act sections 2712, 2714, 2715, and 2718, apply to grandfathered health plans for plan years beginning on or after September 23, 2010. The provisions of PHS Act section 2708 apply to grandfathered health plans for plan years beginning on or after January 1, 2014.

(e) *Applicability of PHS Act sections 2704, 2711, and 2714 to grandfathered group health plans and group health insurance coverage.*—(1) The provisions of PHS Act section 2704 as it applies with respect to enrollees who are under 19 years of age, and the provisions of PHS Act section 2711 insofar as it relates to annual limits, apply to grandfathered health plans that are group health plans (including group health insurance coverage) for plan years beginning on or after September 23, 2010. The provisions of PHS Act section 2704 apply generally to grandfathered health plans that are group health plans (including group health insurance coverage) for plan years beginning on or after January 1, 2014.

(2) For plan years beginning before January 1, 2014, the provisions of PHS Act section 2714 apply in the case of an adult child with respect to a grandfathered health plan that is a group health plan only if the adult child is not eligible to enroll in an eligible employer-sponsored health plan (as defined in section 5000A(f)(2)) other than a grandfathered health plan of a parent. For plan years beginning on or after January 1, 2014, the provisions of PHS Act section 2714 apply with respect to a grandfathered health plan that is a group health plan without regard to whether an adult child is eligible to enroll in any other coverage.

(f) *Effect on collectively bargained plans.*—In the case of health insurance coverage maintained pursuant to one or more collective bargaining agreements between employee representatives and one or more employers that was ratified before March 23, 2010, the coverage is grandfathered health plan coverage at least until the date on which the last of the collective bargaining agreements relating to the coverage that was in effect on March 23, 2010 terminates. Any coverage amendment made pursuant to a collective bargaining agreement relating to the coverage that amends the coverage solely to conform to any requirement added by subtitles A and C of title I of the Patient Protection and Affordable Care Act (and the amendments made by those subtitles, and the incorporation of those amendments into section 9815 and ERISA section 715) is not treated as a termination of the collective bargaining agreement. After the date on which the last of the collective bargaining agreements relating to the coverage that was in effect on March 23, 2010 terminates, the determination of whether health insurance coverage maintained

pursuant to a collective bargaining agreement is grandfathered health plan coverage is made under the rules of this section other than this paragraph (f) (comparing the terms of the health insurance coverage after the date the last collective bargaining agreement terminates with the terms of the health insurance coverage that were in effect on March 23, 2010).

(g) *Maintenance of grandfather status.*— (1) *Changes causing cessation of grandfather status.*—Subject to paragraph (g)(2) of this section, the rules of this paragraph (g)(1) describe situations in which a group health plan or health insurance coverage ceases to be a grandfathered health plan.

(i) *Elimination of benefits.*—The elimination of all or substantially all benefits to diagnose or treat a particular condition causes a group health plan or health insurance coverage to cease to be a grandfathered health plan. For this purpose, the elimination of benefits for any necessary element to diagnose or treat a condition is considered the elimination of all or substantially all benefits to diagnose or treat a particular condition.

(ii) *Increase in percentage cost-sharing requirement.*—Any increase, measured from March 23, 2010, in a percentage cost-sharing requirement (such as an individual's coinsurance requirement) causes a group health plan or health insurance coverage to cease to be a grandfathered health plan.

(iii) *Increase in a fixed-amount cost-sharing requirement other than a copayment.*—Any increase in a fixed-amount cost-sharing requirement other than a copayment (for example, deductible or out-of-pocket limit), determined as of the effective date of the increase, causes a group health plan or health insurance coverage to cease to be a grandfathered health plan, if the total percentage increase in the cost-sharing requirement measured from March 23, 2010 exceeds the maximum percentage increase (as defined in paragraph (g)(3)(ii) of this section).

(iv) *Increase in a fixed-amount copayment.*— Any increase in a fixed-amount copayment, determined as of the effective date of the increase, causes a group health plan or health insurance coverage to cease to be a grandfathered health plan, if the total increase in the copayment measured from March 23, 2010 exceeds the greater of:

(A) An amount equal to $5 increased by medical inflation, as defined in paragraph (g)(3)(i) of this section (that is, $5 times medical inflation, plus $5), or

(B) The maximum percentage increase (as defined in paragraph (g)(3)(ii) of this section),

⟫⟫→ Caution: Temporary Reg. §54.9815-1251T, below, was removed by T.D. 9744 and is inapplicable under Code Sec. 7805(e)(2). However, until final Reg. §54.9815-1251 is applicable on the first day of the plan or policy year beginning after January 1, 2017, taxpayers may comply with the corresponding interim final regulation at 29 CFR part 2590 that is substantially similar to the temporary reg below.

determined by expressing the total increase in the copayment as a percentage.

(v) *Decrease in contribution rate by employers and employee organizations.*—(A) *Contribution rate based on cost of coverage.*—A group health plan or group health insurance coverage ceases to be a grandfathered health plan if the employer or employee organization decreases its contribution rate based on cost of coverage (as defined in paragraph (g)(3)(iii)(A) of this section) towards the cost of any tier of coverage for any class of similarly situated individuals (as described in §54.9802-1(d)) by more than 5 percentage points below the contribution rate for the coverage period that includes March 23, 2010.

(B) *Contribution rate based on a formula.*—A group health plan or group health insurance coverage ceases to be a grandfathered health plan if the employer or employee organization decreases its contribution rate based on a formula (as defined in paragraph (g)(3)(iii)(B) of this section) towards the cost of any tier of coverage for any class of similarly situated individuals (as described in §54.9802-1(d)) by more than 5 percent below the contribution rate for the coverage period that includes March 23, 2010.

(vi) *Changes in annual limits.*—(A) *Addition of an annual limit.*—A group health plan, or group health insurance coverage, that, on March 23, 2010, did not impose an overall annual or lifetime limit on the dollar value of all benefits ceases to be a grandfathered health plan if the plan or health insurance coverage imposes an overall annual limit on the dollar value of benefits.

(B) *Decrease in limit for a plan or coverage with only a lifetime limit.*—A group health plan, or group health insurance coverage, that, on March 23, 2010, imposed an overall lifetime limit on the dollar value of all benefits but no overall annual limit on the dollar value of all benefits ceases to be a grandfathered health plan if the plan or health insurance coverage adopts an overall annual limit at a dollar value that is lower than the dollar value of the lifetime limit on March 23, 2010.

(C) *Decrease in limit for a plan or coverage with an annual limit.*—A group health plan, or group health insurance coverage, that, on March 23, 2010, imposed an overall annual limit on the dollar value of all benefits ceases to be a grandfathered health plan if the plan or health insurance coverage decreases the dollar value of the annual limit (regardless of whether the plan or health insurance coverage also imposed an overall lifetime limit on March 23, 2010 on the dollar value of all benefits).

(2) *Transitional rules.*—(i) *Changes made prior to March 23, 2010.*—If a group health plan or health insurance issuer makes the following changes to the terms of the plan or health insurance coverage, the changes are considered part of the terms of the plan or health insurance coverage on March 23, 2010 even though they were not effective at that time and such changes do not cause a plan or health insurance coverage to cease to be a grandfathered health plan:

(A) Changes effective after March 23, 2010 pursuant to a legally binding contract entered into on or before March 23, 2010;

(B) Changes effective after March 23, 2010 pursuant to a filing on or before March 23, 2010 with a State insurance department; or

(C) Changes effective after March 23, 2010 pursuant to written amendments to a plan that were adopted on or before March 23, 2010.

(ii) *Changes made after March 23, 2010 and adopted prior to issuance of regulations.*—If, after March 23, 2010, a group health plan or health insurance issuer makes changes to the terms of the plan or health insurance coverage and the changes are adopted prior to June 14, 2010, the changes will not cause the plan or health insurance coverage to cease to be a grandfathered health plan if the changes are revoked or modified effective as of the first day of the first plan year (in the individual market, policy year) beginning on or after September 23, 2010, and the terms of the plan or health insurance coverage on that date, as modified, would not cause the plan or coverage to cease to be a grandfathered health plan under the rules of this section, including paragraph (g)(1) of this section. For this purpose, changes will be considered to have been adopted prior to June 14, 2010 if:

(A) The changes are effective before that date;

(B) The changes are effective on or after that date pursuant to a legally binding contract entered into before that date;

(C) The changes are effective on or after that date pursuant to a filing before that date with a State insurance department; or

(D) The changes are effective on or after that date pursuant to written amendments to a plan that were adopted before that date.

(3) *Definitions.*—(i) *Medical inflation defined.*—For purposes of this paragraph (g), the term *medical inflation* means the increase since March 2010 in the overall medical care component of the Consumer Price Index for All Urban Consumers (CPI-U) (unadjusted) published by the Department of Labor using the 1982 - 1984 base of 100. For this purpose, the increase in the overall medical care component is computed by subtracting 387.142 (the overall medical care component of the CPI-U (unadjusted) published

⋙→ *Caution: Temporary Reg. §54.9815-1251T, below, was removed by T.D. 9744 and is inapplicable under Code Sec. 7805(e)(2). However, until final Reg. §54.9815-1251 is applicable on the first day of the plan or policy year beginning after January 1, 2017, taxpayers may comply with the corresponding interim final regulation at 29 CFR part 2590 that is substantially similar to the temporary reg below.*

by the Department of Labor for March 2010, using the 1982 - 1984 base of 100) from the index amount for any month in the 12 months before the new change is to take effect and then dividing that amount by 387.142.

(ii) *Maximum percentage increase defined.*— For purposes of this paragraph (g), the term *maximum percentage increase* means medical inflation (as defined in paragraph (g)(3)(i) of this section), expressed as a percentage, plus 15 percentage points.

(iii) *Contribution rate defined.*—For purposes of paragraph (g)(1)(v) of this section:

(A) *Contribution rate based on cost of coverage.*—The term *contribution rate based on cost of coverage* means the amount of contributions made by an employer or employee organization compared to the total cost of coverage, expressed as a percentage. The total cost of coverage is determined in the same manner as the applicable premium is calculated under the COBRA continuation provisions of section 4980B(f)(4), section 604 of ERISA, and section 2204 of the PHS Act. In the case of a self-insured plan, contributions by an employer or employee organization are equal to the total cost of coverage minus the employee contributions towards the total cost of coverage.

(B) *Contribution rate based on a formula.*—The term *contribution rate based on a formula* means, for plans that, on March 23, 2010, made contributions based on a formula (such as hours worked or tons of coal mined), the formula.

(4) *Examples.*—The rules of this paragraph (g) are illustrated by the following examples:

Example 1. (i) *Facts.* On March 23, 2010, a grandfathered health plan has a coinsurance requirement of 20% for inpatient surgery. The plan is subsequently amended to increase the coinsurance requirement to 25%.

(ii) *Conclusion.* In this *Example 1*, the increase in the coinsurance requirement from 20% to 25% causes the plan to cease to be a grandfathered health plan.

Example 2. (i) *Facts.* Before March 23, 2010, the terms of a group health plan provide benefits for a particular mental health condition, the treatment for which is a combination of counseling and prescription drugs. Subsequently, the plan eliminates benefits for counseling.

(ii) *Conclusion.* In this *Example 2*, the plan ceases to be a grandfathered health plan because counseling is an element that is necessary to treat the condition. Thus the plan is considered to have eliminated substantially all benefits for the treatment of the condition.

Example 3. (i) *Facts.* On March 23, 2010, a grandfathered health plan has a copayment requirement of $30 per office visit for specialists. The plan is subsequently amended to increase the copayment requirement to $40. Within the 12-month period before the $40 copayment takes effect, the greatest value of the overall medical care component of the CPI-U (unadjusted) is 475.

(ii) *Conclusion.* In this *Example 3*, the increase in the copayment from $30 to $40, expressed as a percentage, is 33.33% (40 - 30 = 10; 10 ÷ 30 = 0.3333; 0.3333 = 33.33%). Medical inflation (as defined in paragraph (g)(3)(i) of this section) from March 2010 is 0.2269 (475 - 387.142 = 87.858; 87.858 ÷ 387.142 = 0.2269). The maximum percentage increase permitted is 37.69% (0.2269 = 22.69%; 22.69% + 15% = 37.69%). Because 33.33% does not exceed 37.69%, the change in the copayment requirement at that time does not cause the plan to cease to be a grandfathered health plan.

Example 4. (i) *Facts.* Same facts as *Example 3*, except the grandfathered health plan subsequently increases the $40 copayment requirement to $45 for a later plan year. Within the 12-month period before the $45 copayment takes effect, the greatest value of the overall medical care component of the CPI-U (unadjusted) is 485.

(ii) *Conclusion.* In this *Example 4*, the increase in the copayment from $30 (the copayment that was in effect on March 23, 2010) to $45, expressed as a percentage, is 50% (45 - 30 = 15; 15 ÷ 30 = 0.5; 0.5 = 50%). Medical inflation (as defined in paragraph (g)(3)(i) of this section) from March 2010 is 0.2527 (485 - 387.142 = 97.858; 97.858 ÷ 387.142 = 0.2527). The increase that would cause a plan to cease to be a grandfathered health plan under paragraph (g)(1)(iv) of this section is the greater of the maximum percentage increase of 40.27% (0.2527 = 25.27%; 25.27% + 15% = 40.27%), or $6.26 ($5 × 0.2527 = $1.26; $1.26 + $5 = $6.26). Because 50% exceeds 40.27% and $15 exceeds $6.26, the change in the copayment requirement at that time causes the plan to cease to be a grandfathered health plan.

Example 5. (i) *Facts.* On March 23, 2010, a grandfathered health plan has a copayment of $10 per office visit for primary care providers. The plan is subsequently amended to increase the copayment requirement to $15. Within the 12-month period before the $15 copayment takes effect, the greatest value of the overall medical care component of the CPI-U (unadjusted) is 415.

(ii) *Conclusion.* In this *Example 5*, the increase in the copayment, expressed as a percentage, is 50% (15 - 10 = 5; 5 ÷ 10 = 0.5; 0.5 = 50%). Medical inflation (as defined in paragraph (g)(3) of this section) from March 2010 is 0.0720 (415.0 - 387.142 = 27.858; 27.858 ÷ 387.142 = 0.0720). The increase that would cause a plan to cease to be a grandfathered health plan under paragraph (g)(1)(iv) of this section is the greater of the

Reg. §54.9815-1251T(g)(4)

>>>→ *Caution: Temporary Reg. §54.9815-1251T, below, was removed by T.D. 9744 and is inapplicable under Code Sec. 7805(e)(2). However, until final Reg. §54.9815-1251 is applicable on the first day of the plan or policy year beginning after January 1, 2017, taxpayers may comply with the corresponding interim final regulation at 29 CFR part 2590 that is substantially similar to the temporary reg below.*

maximum percentage increase of 22.20% (0.0720 = 7.20%; 7.20% + 15% = 22.20), or $5.36 ($5 × 0.0720 = $0.36; $0.36 + $5 = $5.36). The $5 increase in copayment in this *Example 5* would not cause the plan to cease to be a grandfathered health plan pursuant to paragraph (g)(1)(iv)this section, which would permit an increase in the copayment of up to $5.36.

Example 6. (i) *Facts*. The same facts as *Example 5*, except on March 23, 2010, the grandfathered health plan has no copayment ($0) for office visits for primary care providers. The plan is subsequently amended to increase the copayment requirement to $5.

(ii) *Conclusion*. In this *Example 6*, medical inflation (as defined in paragraph (g)(3)(i) of this section) from March 2010 is 0.0720 (415.0 - 387.142 = 27.858; 27.858 ÷ 387.142 = 0.0720). The increase that would cause a plan to cease to be a grandfathered health plan under paragraph (g)(1)(iv)(A) of this section is $5.36 ($5 × 0.0720 = $0.36; $0.36 + $5 = $5.36). The $5 increase in copayment in this *Example 6* is less than the amount calculated pursuant to paragraph (g)(1)(iv)(A) of this section of $5.36. Thus, the $5 increase in copayment does not cause the plan to cease to be a grandfathered health plan.

Example 7. (i) *Facts*. On March 23, 2010, a self-insured group health plan provides two tiers of coverage — self-only and family. The employer contributes 80% of the total cost of coverage for self-only and 60% of the total cost of coverage for family. Subsequently, the employer reduces the contribution to 50% for family coverage, but keeps the same contribution rate for self-only coverage.

(ii) *Conclusion*. In this *Example 7*, the decrease of 10 percentage points for family coverage in the contribution rate based on cost of coverage causes the plan to cease to be a grandfathered health plan. The fact that the contribution rate for self-only coverage remains the same does not change the result.

Example 8. (i) *Facts*. On March 23, 2010, a self-insured grandfathered health plan has a CO-BRA premium for the 2010 plan year of $5000 for self-only coverage and $12,000 for family coverage. The required employee contribution for the coverage is $1000 for self-only coverage and $4000 for family coverage. Thus, the contribution rate based on cost of coverage for 2010 is 80% ((5000 - 1000)/5000) for self-only coverage and 67% ((12,000 - 4000)/12,000) for family coverage. For a subsequent plan year, the COBRA premium is $6000 for self-only coverage and $15,000 for family coverage. The employee contributions for that plan year are $1200 for selfonly coverage and $5000 for family coverage. Thus, the contribution rate based on cost of coverage is 80% ((6000 -1200)/6000) for self-only coverage and 67% ((15,000 - 5000)/15,000) for family coverage.

(ii) *Conclusion*. In this *Example 8*, because there is no change in the contribution rate based on cost of coverage, the plan retains its status as a grandfathered health plan. The result would be the same if all or part of the employee contribution was made pre-tax through a cafeteria plan under section 125 of the Internal Revenue Code.

Example 9. (i) *Facts*. A group health plan not maintained pursuant to a collective bargaining agreement offers three benefit packages on March 23, 2010. Option F is a selfinsured option. Options G and H are insured options. Beginning July 1, 2013, the plan increases coinsurance under Option H from 10% to 15%.

(ii) *Conclusion*. In this *Example 9*, the coverage under Option H is not grandfathered health plan coverage as of July 1, 2013, consistent with the rule in paragraph (g)(1)(ii) of this section. Whether the coverage under Options F and G is grandfathered health plan coverage is determined separately under the rules of this paragraph (g).

(h) *Expiration date.*—This section expires on or before June 14, 2013. [Temporary Reg. §54.9815-1251T.]

☐ [*T.D. 9489, 6-14-2010. Amended by T.D. 9506, 11-15-2010. Removed by T.D. 9744, 11-13-2015.*]

>>>→ *Caution: Reg. §54.9815-2704, below, as added by T.D. 9744, is applicable to group health plans and health insurance issuers beginning on the first day of the plan year (or, in the individual market, the first day of the first policy year) beginning on or after January 1, 2017.*

[Reg. §54.9815-2704]

§54.9815-2704. Prohibition of preexisting condition exclusions.—(a) *No preexisting condition exclusions.*—A group health plan, or a health insurance issuer offering group health insurance coverage, may not impose any preexisting condition exclusion (as defined in §54.9801-2).

(b) *Examples.*—The rules of paragraph (a) of this section are illustrated by the following examples (for additional examples illustrating the definition of a preexisting condition exclusion, see §54.9801-3(a)(2)):

Example 1. (i) *Facts*. A group health plan provides benefits solely through an insurance policy offered by Issuer *P*. At the expiration of the policy, the plan switches coverage to a policy offered by Issuer *N*. *N*'s policy excludes benefits for oral surgery required as a result of a traumatic injury if the injury occurred before the effective date of coverage under the policy.

(ii) *Conclusion*. In this *Example 1*, the exclusion of benefits for oral surgery required as a result of

⫸→ Caution: Reg. §54.9815-2704, below, as added by T.D. 9744, is applicable to group health plans and health insurance issuers beginning on the first day of the plan year (or, in the individual market, the first day of the first policy year) beginning on or after January 1, 2017.

a traumatic injury if the injury occurred before the effective date of coverage is a preexisting condition exclusion because it operates to exclude benefits for a condition based on the fact that the condition was present before the effective date of coverage under the policy. Therefore, such an exclusion is prohibited.

Example 2. (i) *Facts.* Individual C applies for individual health insurance coverage with Issuer M. M denies C's application for coverage because a pre-enrollment physical revealed that C has type 2 diabetes.

(ii) *Conclusion. See Example 2* in 45 CFR 147.108(a)(2) for a conclusion that M's denial of C's application for coverage is a preexisting condition exclusion because a denial of an application for coverage based on the fact that a condition was present before the date of denial is an exclusion of benefits based on a preexisting condition. Therefore, such an exclusion is prohibited.

(c) *Applicability date.*—The provisions of this section are applicable to group health plans and health insurance issuers for plan years beginning on or after January 1, 2017. Until the applicability date for this regulation, plans and issuers are required to continue to comply with the interim final regulations promulgated by the Department of Labor at 29 CFR part 2590, contained in the 29 CFR, parts 1927 to end, edition revised as of July 1, 2015. [Reg. § 54.9815-2704.]

□ [T.D. 9744, 11-13-2015.]

⫸→ Caution: Temporary Reg. §54.9815-2704T, below, was removed by T.D. 9744 and is inapplicable under Code Sec. 7805(e)(2). However, until final Reg. §54.9815-2704 is applicable on the first day of the plan or policy year beginning after January 1, 2017, taxpayers may comply with the corresponding interim final regulation at 29 CFR part 2590 that is substantially similar to the temporary reg below.

[Reg. § 54.9815-2704T]

§ 54.9815-2704T. Prohibition of preexisting condition exclusions (temporary).—(a) *No preexisting condition exclusions.*—(1) *In general.*—A group health plan, or a health insurance issuer offering group health insurance coverage, may not impose any preexisting condition exclusion (as defined in § 54.9801-2).

(2) *Examples.*—The rules of this paragraph (a) are illustrated by the following examples (for additional examples illustrating the definition of a preexisting condition exclusion, see § 54.9801-3(a)(1)(ii)):

Example 1. (i) *Facts.* A group health plan provides benefits solely through an insurance policy offered by Issuer P. At the expiration of the policy, the plan switches coverage to a policy offered by Issuer N. N's policy excludes benefits for oral surgery required as a result of a traumatic injury if the injury occurred before the effective date of coverage under the policy.

(ii) *Conclusion.* In this *Example 1*, the exclusion of benefits for oral surgery required as a result of a traumatic injury if the injury occurred before the effective date of coverage is a preexisting condition exclusion because it operates to exclude benefits for a condition based on the fact that the condition was present before the effective date of coverage under the policy.

Example 2. (i) *Facts.* Individual C applies for individual health insurance coverage with Issuer M. M denies C's application for coverage because a pre-enrollment physical revealed that C has type 2 diabetes.

(ii) *Conclusion. See Example 2* in 45 CFR 147.108(a)(2) for a conclusion that M's denial of C's application for coverage is a preexisting condition exclusion because a denial of an application for coverage based on the fact that a condition was present before the date of denial is an exclusion of benefits based on a preexisting condition.

(b) *Effective/applicability date.*—(1) *General applicability date.*—Except as provided in paragraph (b)(2) of this section, the rules of this section apply for plan years beginning on or after January 1, 2014.

(2) *Early applicability date for children.*—The rules of this section apply with respect to enrollees, including applicants for enrollment, who are under 19 years of age for plan years beginning on or after September 23, 2010.

(3) *Applicability to grandfathered health plans.*—See § 54.9815-1251T for determining the application of this section to grandfathered health plans (providing that a grandfathered health plan that is a group health plan or group health insurance coverage must comply with the prohibition against preexisting condition exclusions).

(4) *Example.*—The rules of this paragraph (b) are illustrated by the following example:

Example. (i) *Facts.* Individual F commences employment and enrolls F and F's 16-yearold child in the group health plan maintained by F's employer, with a first day of coverage of October 15, 2010. F's child had a significant break in coverage because of a lapse of more than 63 days without creditable coverage immediately prior to enrolling in the plan. F's child was treated for asthma within the six-month period prior to the enrollment date and the plan imposes a 12-month preexisting condition exclusion for coverage of asthma. The next plan year begins on January 1, 2011.

(ii) *Conclusion.* In this *Example*, the plan year beginning January 1, 2011 is the first plan year of the group health plan beginning on or after September 23, 2010. Thus, beginning on January 1,

»»→ *Caution: Temporary Reg. §54.9815-2704T, below, was removed by T.D. 9744 and is inapplicable under Code Sec. 7805(e)(2). However, until final Reg. §54.9815-2704 is applicable on the first day of the plan or policy year beginning after January 1, 2017, taxpayers may comply with the corresponding interim final regulation at 29 CFR part 2590 that is substantially similar to the temporary reg below.*

2011, because the child is under 19 years of age, the plan cannot impose a preexisting condition exclusion with respect to the child's asthma regardless of the fact that the preexisting condition exclusion was imposed by the plan before the applicability date of this provision.

(c) *Expiration date.*—This section expires on June 21, 2013. [Temporary Reg. § 54.9815-2704T.]

☐ [*T.D. 9491, 6-22-2010. Removed by T.D. 9744, 11-13-2015.*]

[Reg. § 54.9815-2705]

§ 54.9815-2705. Special rules for certain church plans.—(a) *In general.*—A group health plan and a health insurance issuer offering group health insurance coverage must comply with the requirements of § 54.9802-1.

(b) *Applicability date.*—This section is applicable to group health plans and health insurance issuers offering group health insurance coverage for plan years beginning on or after January 1, 2014. [Reg. § 54.9815-2705.]

☐ [*T.D. 9620, 5-29-2013.*]

»»→ *Caution: Reg. §54.9815-2708, below, as added by T.D. 9656, is applicable for plan years beginning on or after January 1, 2015.*

[Reg. § 54.9815-2708]

§ 54.9815-2708. Prohibition on waiting periods that exceed 90 days.—(a) *General rule.*—A group health plan, and a health insurance issuer offering group health insurance coverage, must not apply any waiting period that exceeds 90 days, in accordance with the rules of this section. If, under the terms of a plan, an individual can elect coverage that would begin on a date that is not later than the end of the 90-day waiting period, this paragraph (a) is considered satisfied. Accordingly, in that case, a plan or issuer will not be considered to have violated this paragraph (a) solely because individuals take, or are permitted to take, additional time (beyond the end of the 90-day waiting period) to elect coverage.

(b) *Waiting period defined.*—For purposes of this part, a waiting period is the period that must pass before coverage for an individual who is otherwise eligible to enroll under the terms of a group health plan can become effective. If an individual enrolls as a late enrollee (as defined under § 54.9801-2) or special enrollee (as described in § 54.9801-6), any period before such late or special enrollment is not a waiting period.

(c) *Relation to a plan's eligibility criteria.*—(1) *In general.*—Except as provided in paragraphs (c)(2) and (c)(3) of this section, being otherwise eligible to enroll under the terms of a group health plan means having met the plan's substantive eligibility conditions (such as, for example, being in an eligible job classification, achieving job-related licensure requirements specified in the plan's terms, or satisfying a reasonable and bona fide employment-based orientation period). Moreover, except as provided in paragraphs (c)(2) and (c)(3) of this section, nothing in this section requires a plan sponsor to offer coverage to any particular individual or class of individuals (including, for example, part-time employees). Instead, this section prohibits requiring otherwise eligible individuals to wait more than 90 days

before coverage is effective. *See also* section 4980H of the Code and its implementing regulations for an applicable large employer's shared responsibility to provide health coverage to full-time employees.

(2) *Eligibility conditions based solely on the lapse of time.*—Eligibility conditions that are based solely on the lapse of a time period are permissible for no more than 90 days.

(3) *Other conditions for eligibility.*—Other conditions for eligibility under the terms of a group health plan are generally permissible under PHS Act section 2708, unless the condition is designed to avoid compliance with the 90-day waiting period limitation, determined in accordance with the rules of this paragraph (c)(3).

(i) *Application to variable-hour employees in cases in which a specified number of hours of service per period is a plan eligibility condition.*—If a group health plan conditions eligibility on an employee regularly having a specified number of hours of service per period (or working full-time), and it cannot be determined that a newly-hired employee is reasonably expected to regularly work that number of hours per period (or work full-time), the plan may take a reasonable period of time, not to exceed 12 months and beginning on any date between the employee's start date and the first day of the first calendar month following the employee's start date, to determine whether the employee meets the plan's eligibility condition. Except in cases in which a waiting period that exceeds 90 days is imposed in addition to a measurement period, the time period for determining whether such an employee meets the plan's eligibility condition will not be considered to be designed to avoid compliance with the 90-day waiting period limitation if coverage is made effective no later than 13 months from the employee's start date plus, if the employee's start date is not the first day of a calendar month, the time remaining until the first day of the next calendar month.

>>>→ *Caution: Reg. §54.9815-2708, below, as added by T.D. 9656, is applicable for plan years beginning on or after January 1, 2015.*

(ii) *Cumulative service requirements.*—If a group health plan or health insurance issuer conditions eligibility on an employee's having completed a number of cumulative hours of service, the eligibility condition is not considered to be designed to avoid compliance with the 90-day waiting period limitation if the cumulative hours-of-service requirement does not exceed 1,200 hours.

(iii) *Limitation on orientation periods.*—To ensure that an orientation period is not used as a subterfuge for the passage of time, or designed to avoid compliance with the 90-day waiting period limitation, an orientation period is permitted only if it does not exceed one month. For this purpose, one month is determined by adding one calendar month and subtracting one calendar day, measured from an employee's start date in a position that is otherwise eligible for coverage. For example, if an employee's start date in an otherwise eligible position is May 3, the last permitted day of the orientation period is June 2. Similarly, if an employee's start date in an otherwise eligible position is October 1, the last permitted day of the orientation period is October 31. If there is not a corresponding date in the next calendar month upon adding a calendar month, the last permitted day of the orientation period is the last day of the next calendar month. For example, if the employee's start date is January 30, the last permitted day of the orientation period is February 28 (or February 29 in a leap year). Similarly, if the employee's start date is August 31, the last permitted day of the orientation period is September 30.

(d) *Application to rehires.*—A plan or issuer may treat an employee whose employment has terminated and who then is rehired as newly eligible upon rehire and, therefore, required to meet the plan's eligibility criteria and waiting period anew, if reasonable under the circumstances (for example, the termination and rehire cannot be a subterfuge to avoid compliance with the 90-day waiting period limitation).

(e) *Counting days.*—Under this section, all calendar days are counted beginning on the enrollment date (as defined in §54.9801-2), including weekends and holidays. A plan or issuer that imposes a 90-day waiting period may, for administrative convenience, choose to permit coverage to become effective earlier than the 91st day if the 91st day is a weekend or holiday.

(f) *Examples.*—The rules of this section are illustrated by the following examples:

Example 1. (i) *Facts.* A group health plan provides that full-time employees are eligible for coverage under the plan. Employee *A* begins employment as a full-time employee on January 19.

(ii) *Conclusion.* In this *Example 1*, any waiting period for *A* would begin on January 19 and may not exceed 90 days. Coverage under the plan must become effective no later than April 19 (assuming February lasts 28 days).

Example 2. (i) *Facts.* A group health plan provides that only employees with job title *M* are eligible for coverage under the plan. Employee *B* begins employment with job title *L* on January 30.

(ii) *Conclusion.* In this *Example 2*, *B* is not eligible for coverage under the plan, and the period while *B* is working with job title *L* and therefore not in an eligible class of employees, is not part of a waiting period under this section.

Example 3. (i) *Facts.* Same facts as in *Example 2*, except that *B* transfers to a new position with job title *M* on April 11.

(ii) *Conclusion.* In this *Example 3*, *B* becomes eligible for coverage on April 11, but for the waiting period. Any waiting period for *B* begins on April 11 and may not exceed 90 days; therefore, coverage under the plan must become effective no later than July 10.

Example 4. (i) *Facts.* A group health plan provides that only employees who have completed specified training and achieved specified certifications are eligible for coverage under the plan. Employee *C* is hired on May 3 and meets the plan's eligibility criteria on September 22.

(ii) *Conclusion.* In this *Example 4*, *C* becomes eligible for coverage on September 22, but for the waiting period. Any waiting period for *C* would begin on September 22 and may not exceed 90 days; therefore, coverage under the plan must become effective no later than December 21.

Example 5. (i) *Facts.* A group health plan provides that employees are eligible for coverage after one year of service.

(ii) *Conclusion.* In this *Example 5*, the plan's eligibility condition is based solely on the lapse of time and, therefore, is impermissible under paragraph (c)(2) of this section because it exceeds 90 days.

Example 6. (i) *Facts.* Employer *V*'s group health plan provides for coverage to begin on the first day of the first payroll period on or after the date an employee is hired and completes the applicable enrollment forms. Enrollment forms are distributed on an employee's start date and may be completed within 90 days. Employee *D* is hired and starts on October 31, which is the first day of a pay period. *D* completes the enrollment forms and submits them on the 90th day after *D*'s start date, which is January 28. Coverage is made effective 7 days later, February 4, which is the first day of the next pay period.

(ii) *Conclusion.* In this *Example 6*, under the terms of *V*'s plan, coverage may become effective as early as October 31, depending on when *D* completes the applicable enrollment forms. Under the terms of the plan, when coverage becomes effective depends solely on the length of time taken by *D* to complete the enrollment materials. Therefore, under the terms of the plan,

>>>→ *Caution: Reg. §54.9815-2708, below, as added by T.D. 9656, is applicable for plan years
beginning on or after January 1, 2015.*

D may elect coverage that would begin on a date that does not exceed the 90-day waiting period limitation, and the plan complies with this section.

Example 7. (i) *Facts.* Under Employer *W*'s group health plan, only employees who are full-time (defined under the plan as regularly averaging 30 hours of service per week) are eligible for coverage. Employee *E* begins employment for Employer *W* on November 26 of Year 1. *E*'s hours are reasonably expected to vary, with an opportunity to work between 20 and 45 hours per week, depending on shift availability and *E*'s availability. Therefore, it cannot be determined at *E*'s start date that *E* is reasonably expected to work full-time. Under the terms of the plan, variable-hour employees, such as *E*, are eligible to enroll in the plan if they are determined to be a full-time employee after a measurement period of 12 months that begins on the employee's start date. Coverage is made effective no later than the first day of the first calendar month after the applicable enrollment forms are received. *E*'s 12-month measurement period ends November 25 of Year 2. *E* is determined to be a full-time employee and is notified of *E*'s plan eligibility. If *E* then elects coverage, *E*'s first day of coverage will be January 1 of Year 3.

(ii) *Conclusion.* In this *Example 7*, the measurement period is permissible because it is not considered to be designed to avoid compliance with the 90-day waiting period limitation. The plan may use a reasonable period of time to determine whether a variable-hour employee is a full-time employee, provided that (a) the period of time is no longer than 12 months; (b) the period of time begins on a date between the employee's start date and the first day of the next calendar month (inclusive); (c) coverage is made effective no later than 13 months from *E*'s start date plus, if the employee's start date is not the first day of a calendar month, the time remaining until the first day of the next calendar month; and (d) in addition to the measurement period, no more than 90 days elapse prior to the employee's eligibility for coverage.

Example 8. (i) *Facts.* Employee *F* begins working 25 hours per week for Employer *X* on January 6 and is considered a part-time employee for purposes of *X*'s group health plan. *X* sponsors a group health plan that provides coverage to part-time employees after they have completed a cumulative 1,200 hours of service. *F* satisfies the plan's cumulative hours of service condition on December 15.

(ii) *Conclusion.* In this *Example 8*, the cumulative hours of service condition with respect to part-time employees is not considered to be designed to avoid compliance with the 90-day waiting period limitation. Accordingly, coverage for *F* under the plan must begin no later than the 91st day after *F* completes 1,200 hours. (If the plan's cumulative hours-of-service requirement was more than 1,200 hours, the requirement

would be considered to be designed to avoid compliance with the 90-day waiting period limitation.)

Example 9. (i) *Facts.* A multiemployer plan operating pursuant to an arms-length collective bargaining agreement has an eligibility provision that allows employees to become eligible for coverage by working a specified number of hours of covered employment for multiple contributing employers. The plan aggregates hours in a calendar quarter and then, if enough hours are earned, coverage begins the first day of the next calendar quarter. The plan also permits coverage to extend for the next full calendar quarter, regardless of whether an employee's employment has terminated.

(ii) *Conclusion.* In this *Example 9*, these eligibility provisions are designed to accommodate a unique operating structure, and, therefore, are not considered to be designed to avoid compliance with the 90-day waiting period limitation, and the plan complies with this section.

Example 10. (i) *Facts.* Employee *G* retires at age 55 after 30 years of employment with Employer *Y* with no expectation of providing further services to Employer *Y*. Three months later, *Y* recruits *G* to return to work as an employee providing advice and transition assistance for *G*'s replacement under a one-year employment contract. *Y*'s plan imposes a 90-day waiting period from an employee's start date before coverage becomes effective.

(ii) *Conclusion.* In this *Example 10*, *Y*'s plan may treat *G* as newly eligible for coverage under the plan upon rehire and therefore may impose the 90-day waiting period with respect to *G* for coverage offered in connection with *G*'s rehire.

Example 11. (i) *Facts.* Employee *H* begins working full time for Employer *Z* on October 16. *Z* sponsors a group health plan, under which full time employees are eligible for coverage after they have successfully completed a bona fide one-month orientation period. *H* completes the orientation period on November 15.

(ii) *Conclusion.* In this *Example 11*, the orientation period is not considered a subterfuge for the passage of time and is not considered to be designed to avoid compliance with the 90-day waiting period limitation. Accordingly, plan coverage for *H* must begin no later than February 14, which is the 91st day after *H* completes the orientation period. (If the orientation period was longer than one month, it would be considered to be a subterfuge for the passage of time and designed to avoid compliance with the 90-day waiting period limitation. Accordingly it would violate the rules of this section.)

(g) *Special rule for health insurance issuers.*—To the extent coverage under a group health plan is insured by a health insurance issuer, the issuer is permitted to rely on the eligibility information reported to it by the employer (or other plan sponsor) and will not be considered to violate the requirements of this section with respect to

>>>→ *Caution: Reg. §54.9815-2708, below, as added by T.D. 9656, is applicable for plan years beginning on or after January 1, 2015.*

its administration of any waiting period, if both of the following conditions are satisfied:

(1) The issuer requires the plan sponsor to make a representation regarding the terms of any eligibility conditions or waiting periods imposed by the plan sponsor before an individual is eligible to become covered under the terms of the plan (and requires the plan sponsor to update this representation with any changes), and

(2) The issuer has no specific knowledge of the imposition of a waiting period that would exceed the permitted 90-day period.

(h) *No effect on other laws.*—Compliance with this section is not determinative of compliance with any other provision of State or Federal law (including ERISA, the Code, or other provisions of the Patient Protection and Affordable Care Act). *See e.g.,* §54.9802-1, which prohibits discrimination in eligibility for coverage based on a health factor and section 4980H, which generally requires applicable large employers to offer coverage to full-time employees and their dependents or make an assessable payment.

(i) *Applicability date.*—The provisions of this section apply for plan years beginning on or after January 1, 2015. *See* section 1251 of the Affordable Care Act, as amended by section 10103 of the Affordable Care Act and section 2301 of the Health Care and Education Reconciliation Act, and its implementing regulations providing that the prohibition on waiting periods exceeding 90 days applies to all group health plans and group health insurance issuers, including grandfathered health plans. [Reg. §54.9815-2708.]

☐ [*T.D. 9656, 2-20-2014. Amended by T.D. 9671, 6-20-2014.*]

>>>→ *Caution: Reg. §54.9815-2711, below, as added by T.D. 9744, is applicable to group health plans and health insurance issuers beginning on the first day of the plan year (or, in the individual market, the first day of the first policy year) beginning on or after January 1, 2017.*

[Reg. §54.9815-2711]

§54.9815-2711. No lifetime or annual limits.—(a) *Prohibition.*—(1) *Lifetime limits.*—Except as provided in paragraph (b) of this section, a group health plan, or a health insurance issuer offering group health insurance coverage, may not establish any lifetime limit on the dollar amount of essential health benefits for any individual, whether provided in-network or out-of-network.

(2) *Annual limits.*—(i) *General rule.*—Except as provided in paragraphs (a)(2)(ii) and (b) of this section, a group health plan, or a health insurance issuer offering group health insurance coverage, may not establish any annual limit on the dollar amount of essential health benefits for any individual, whether provided in-network or out-of-network.

(ii) *Exception for health flexible spending arrangements.*—A health flexible spending arrangement (as defined in section 106(c)(2) of the Internal Revenue Code) offered through a cafeteria plan pursuant to section 125 of the Internal Revenue Code is not subject to the requirement in paragraph (a)(2)(i) of this section.

(b) *Construction.*—(1) *Permissible limits on specific covered benefits.*—The rules of this section do not prevent a group health plan, or a health insurance issuer offering group health insurance coverage, from placing annual or lifetime dollar limits with respect to any individual on specific covered benefits that are not essential health benefits to the extent that such limits are otherwise permitted under applicable Federal or State law. (The scope of essential health benefits is addressed in paragraph (c) of this section).

(2) *Condition-based exclusions.*—The rules of this section do not prevent a group health plan, or a health insurance issuer offering group health insurance coverage, from excluding all benefits for a condition. However, if any benefits are provided for a condition, then the requirements of this section apply. Other requirements of Federal or State law may require coverage of certain benefits.

(c) *Definition of essential health benefits.*—The term "essential health benefits" means essential health benefits under section 1302(b) of the Patient Protection and Affordable Care Act and applicable regulations. For this purpose, a group health plan or a health insurance issuer that is not required to provide essential health benefits under section 1302(b) must define "essential health benefits" in a manner that is consistent with—

(1) One of the EHB-benchmark plans applicable in a State under 45 CFR 156.110, and includes coverage of any additional required benefits that are considered essential health benefits consistent with 45 CFR 155.170(a)(2); or

(2) One of the three Federal Employees Health Benefits Program (FEHBP) plan options as defined by 45 CFR 156.100(a)(3), supplemented, as necessary, to meet the standards in 45 CFR 156.110.

(d) *Special rule for health reimbursement arrangements (HRAs) and other account-based plans.*—(1) *In general.*—If an HRA or other account-based plan is integrated with other coverage under a group health plan and the other group health plan coverage alone satisfies the requirements in paragraph (a)(2) of this section, the fact that the benefits under the HRA or other account-based plan are limited does not mean that the HRA or other account-based plan fails to meet the requirements of paragraph (a)(2) of this section. Similarly, if an HRA or other account-based plan is integrated with other coverage

>>>→ *Caution: Reg. §54.9815-2711, below, as added by T.D. 9744, is applicable to group health plans and health insurance issuers beginning on the first day of the plan year (or, in the individual market, the first day of the first policy year) beginning on or after January 1, 2017.*

under a group health plan and the other group health plan coverage alone satisfies the requirements in PHS Act section 2713 and section 54.9815-2713(a)(1), the HRA or other account-based plan will not fail to meet the requirements of PHS Act section 2713 and §54.9815-2713(a)(1).

(2) *Integration requirements.*—An HRA or other account-based plan is integrated with a group health plan for purposes of paragraph (a)(2) of this section if it meets the requirements under either the integration method set forth in paragraph (d)(2)(i) of this section or the integration method set forth in paragraph (d)(2)(ii) of this section. Integration does not require that the HRA (or other account-based plan) and the group health plan with which it is integrated share the same plan sponsor, the same plan document, or governing instruments, or file a single Form 5500, if applicable. The term "excepted benefits" is used throughout the integration methods; for a definition of the term "excepted benefits" see Code section 9832(c), ERISA section 733(c), and PHS Act section 2791(c).

(i) *Integration Method: Minimum value not required.*—An HRA or other account-based plan is integrated with another group health plan for purposes of this paragraph if:

(A) The plan sponsor offers a group health plan (other than the HRA or other account-based plan) to the employee that does not consist solely of excepted benefits;

(B) The employee receiving the HRA or other account-based plan is actually enrolled in a group health plan (other than the HRA or other account-based plan) that does not consist solely of excepted benefits, regardless of whether the plan is offered by the same plan sponsor (referred to as non-HRA group coverage);

(C) The HRA or other account-based plan is available only to employees who are enrolled in non-HRA group coverage, regardless of whether the non-HRA group coverage is offered by the plan sponsor of the HRA or other account-based plan (for example, the HRA may be offered only to employees who do not enroll in an employer's group health plan but are enrolled in other non-HRA group coverage, such as a group health plan maintained by the employer of the employee's spouse);

(D) The benefits under the HRA or other account-based plan are limited to reimbursement of one or more of the following—co-payments, co-insurance, deductibles, and premiums under the non-HRA group coverage, as well as medical care (as defined under section 213(d) of the Code) that does not constitute essential health benefits as defined in paragraph (c) of this section; and

(E) Under the terms of the HRA or other account-based plan, an employee (or former employee) is permitted to permanently opt out of and waive future reimbursements from the HRA or other account-based plan at least annually and, upon termination of employment, either the remaining amounts in the HRA or other account-based plan are forfeited or the employee is permitted to permanently opt out of and waive future reimbursements from the HRA or other account-based plan.

(ii) *Integration Method: Minimum value required.*—An HRA or other account-based plan is integrated with another group health plan for purposes of this paragraph if:

(A) The plan sponsor offers a group health plan (other than the HRA or other account-based plan) to the employee that provides minimum value pursuant to Code section 36B(c)(2)(C)(ii) (and its implementing regulations and applicable guidance);

(B) The employee receiving the HRA or other account-based plan is actually enrolled in a group health plan that provides minimum value pursuant to section 36B(c)(2)(C)(ii) of the Code (and applicable guidance), regardless of whether the plan is offered by the plan sponsor of the HRA or other account-based plan (referred to as non-HRA MV group coverage);

(C) The HRA or other account-based plan is available only to employees who are actually enrolled in non-HRA MV group coverage, regardless of whether the non-HRA MV group coverage is offered by the plan sponsor of the HRA or other account-based plan (for example, the HRA may be offered only to employees who do not enroll in an employer's group health plan but are enrolled in other non-HRA MV group coverage, such as a group health plan maintained by an employer of the employee's spouse); and

(D) Under the terms of the HRA or other account-based plan, an employee (or former employee) is permitted to permanently opt out of and waive future reimbursements from the HRA or other account-based plan at least annually, and, upon termination of employment, either the remaining amounts in the HRA or other account-based plan are forfeited or the employee is permitted to permanently opt out of and waive future reimbursements from the HRA or other account-based plan.

(3) *Forfeiture.*—For purpose of integration under paragraphs (d)(2)(i)(E) and (d)(2)(ii)(D) of this section, forfeiture or waiver occurs even if the forfeited or waived amounts may be reinstated upon a fixed date, a participant's death, or the earlier of the two events (the reinstatement event). For this purpose coverage under an HRA or other account-based plan is considered forfeited or waived prior to a reinstatement event only if the participant's election to forfeit or waive is irrevocable, meaning that, beginning on the effective date of the election and through the date of the reinstatement event, the participant and the participant's beneficiaries have no access

⮞⮞⮞ *Caution: Reg. §54.9815-2711, below, as added by T.D. 9744, is applicable to group health plans and health insurance issuers beginning on the first day of the plan year (or, in the individual market, the first day of the first policy year) beginning on or after January 1, 2017.*

to amounts credited to the HRA or other account-based plan. This means that upon and after reinstatement, the reinstated amounts under the HRA or other account-based plan may not be used to reimburse or pay medical expenses incurred during the period after forfeiture and prior to reinstatement.

(4) *No integration with individual market coverage.*—A group health plan, including an HRA or other account-based plan, used to purchase coverage on the individual market is not integrated with that individual market coverage for purposes of paragraph (a)(2) of this section (or for purposes of the requirements of PHS Act section 2713).

(5) *Integration with Medicare parts B and D.*—For employers that are not required to offer their non-HRA group health plan coverage to employees who are Medicare beneficiaries, an HRA or other account-based plan that may be used to reimburse premiums under Medicare part B or D may be integrated with Medicare (and deemed to comply with PHS Act sections 2711 and 2713) if the following requirements are satisfied with respect to employees who would be eligible for the employer's non-HRA group health plan but for their eligibility for Medicare (and the integration rules under paragraphs (d)(2)(i) and (ii) of this section continue to apply to employees who are not eligible for Medicare):

(i) The plan sponsor offers a group health plan (other than the HRA or other account-based plan and that does not consist solely of excepted benefits) to employees who are not eligible for Medicare;

(ii) The employee receiving the HRA or other account-based plan is actually enrolled Medicare part B or D;

(iii) The HRA or other account-based plan is available only to employees who are enrolled in Medicare part B or D; and

(iv) The HRA or other account-based plan complies with paragraphs (d)(2)(i)(E) and (d)(2)(ii)(D) of this section.

(6) *Account-based plan.*—An account-based plan for purposes of this section is an employer-provided group health plan that provides reimbursements of medical expenses other than individual market policy premiums with the reimbursement subject to a maximum fixed dollar amount for a period. An HRA is a type of account-based plan.

(e) *Applicability date.*—The provisions of this section are applicable to group health plans and health insurance issuers for plan years beginning on or after January 1, 2017. Until the applicability date for this regulation, plans and issuers are required to continue to comply with the interim final regulations promulgated by the Department of Labor at 29 CFR part 2590, contained in the 29 CFR, parts 1927 to end, edition revised as of July 1, 2015. [Reg. § 54.9815-2711.]

☐ [*T.D. 9744, 11-13-2015. Amended by T.D. 9791, 10-28-2016.*]

⮞⮞⮞ *Caution: Temporary Reg. §54.9815-2711T, below, was removed by T.D. 9744 and is inapplicable under Code Sec. 7805(e)(2). However, until final Reg. §54.9815-2711 is applicable on the first day of the plan or policy year beginning after January 1, 2017, taxpayers may comply with the corresponding interim final regulation at 29 CFR part 2590 that is substantially similar to the temporary reg below.*

[Reg. § 54.9815-2711T]

§ 54.9815-2711T. No lifetime or annual limits (temporary).—(a) *Prohibition.*—(1) *Lifetime limits.*—Except as provided in paragraph (b) of this section, a group health plan, or a health insurance issuer offering group health insurance coverage, may not establish any lifetime limit on the dollar amount of benefits for any individual.

(2) *Annual limits.*—(i) *General rule.*—Except as provided in paragraphs (a)(2)(ii), (b), and (d) of this section, a group health plan, or a health insurance issuer offering group health insurance coverage, may not establish any annual limit on the dollar amount of benefits for any individual.

(ii) *Exception for health flexible spending arrangements.*—A health flexible spending arrangement (as defined in section 106(c)(2)) is not subject to the requirement in paragraph (a)(2)(i) of this section.

(b) *Construction.*—(1) *Permissible limits on specific covered benefits.*—The rules of this section do not prevent a group health plan, or a health insurance issuer offering group health insurance coverage, from placing annual or lifetime dollar limits with respect to any individual on specific covered benefits that are not essential health benefits to the extent that such limits are otherwise permitted under applicable Federal or State law. (The scope of essential health benefits is addressed in paragraph (c) of this section).

(2) *Condition-based exclusions.*—The rules of this section do not prevent a group health plan, or a health insurance issuer offering group health insurance coverage, from excluding all benefits for a condition. However, if any benefits are provided for a condition, then the requirements of this section apply. Other requirements of Federal or State law may require coverage of certain benefits.

(c) *Definition of essential health benefits.*—The term "essential health benefits" means essential health benefits under section 1302(b) of the Patient Protection and Affordable Care Act and applicable regulations.

>>→ *Caution: Temporary Reg. §54.9815-2711T, below, was removed by T.D. 9744 and is inapplicable under Code Sec. 7805(e)(2). However, until final Reg. §54.9815-2711 is applicable on the first day of the plan or policy year beginning after January 1, 2017, taxpayers may comply with the corresponding interim final regulation at 29 CFR part 2590 that is substantially similar to the temporary reg below.*

(d) *Restricted annual limits permissible prior to 2014.*—(1) *In general.*—With respect to plan years beginning prior to January 1, 2014, a group health plan, or a health insurance issuer offering group health insurance coverage, may establish, for any individual, an annual limit on the dollar amount of benefits that are essential health benefits, provided the limit is no less than the amounts in the following schedule:

(i) For a plan year beginning on or after September 23, 2010, but before September 23, 2011, $750,000.

(ii) For a plan year beginning on or after September 23, 2011, but before September 23, 2012, $1,250,000.

(iii) For plan years beginning on or after September 23, 2012, but before January 1, 2014, $2,000,000.

(2) *Only essential health benefits taken into account.*—In determining whether an individual has received benefits that meet or exceed the applicable amount described in paragraph (d)(1) of this section, a plan or issuer must take into account only essential health benefits.

(3) *Waiver authority of the Secretary of Health and Human Services.*—For plan years beginning before January 1, 2014, the Secretary of Health and Human Services may establish a program under which the requirements of paragraph (d)(1) of this section relating to annual limits may be waived (for such period as is specified by the Secretary of Health and Human Services) for a group health plan or health insurance coverage that has an annual dollar limit on benefits below the restricted annual limits provided under paragraph (d)(1) of this section if compliance with paragraph (d)(1) of this section would result in a significant decrease in access to benefits under the plan or health insurance coverage or would significantly increase premiums for the plan or health insurance coverage.

(e) *Transitional rules for individuals whose coverage or benefits ended by reason of reaching a lifetime limit.*—(1) *In general.*—The relief provided in the transitional rules of this paragraph (e) applies with respect to any individual—

(i) Whose coverage or benefits under a group health plan or group health insurance coverage ended by reason of reaching a lifetime limit on the dollar value of all benefits for any individual (which, under this section, is no longer permissible); and

(ii) Who becomes eligible (or is required to become eligible) for benefits not subject to a lifetime limit on the dollar value of all benefits under the group health plan or group health insurance coverage on the first day of the first plan year beginning on or after September 23, 2010, by reason of the application of this section.

(2) *Notice and enrollment opportunity requirements.*—(i) If an individual described in paragraph (e)(1) of this section is eligible for benefits (or is required to become eligible for benefits) under the group health plan — or group health insurance coverage — described in paragraph (e)(1) of this section, the plan and the issuer are required to give the individual written notice that the lifetime limit on the dollar value of all benefits no longer applies and that the individual, if covered, is once again eligible for benefits under the plan. Additionally, if the individual is not enrolled in the plan or health insurance coverage, or if an enrolled individual is eligible for but not enrolled in any benefit package under the plan or health insurance coverage, then the plan and issuer must also give such an individual an opportunity to enroll that continues for at least 30 days (including written notice of the opportunity to enroll). The notices and enrollment opportunity required under this paragraph (e)(2)(i) must be provided beginning not later than the first day of the first plan year beginning on or after September 23, 2010.

(ii) The notices required under paragraph (e)(2)(i) of this section may be provided to an employee on behalf of the employee's dependent. In addition, the notices may be included with other enrollment materials that a plan distributes to employees, provided the statement is prominent. For either notice, if a notice satisfying the requirements of this paragraph (e)(2) is provided to an individual, the obligation to provide the notice with respect to that individual is satisfied for both the plan and the issuer.

(3) *Effective date of coverage.*—In the case of an individual who enrolls under paragraph (e)(2) of this section, coverage must take effect not later than the first day of the first plan year beginning on or after September 23, 2010.

(4) *Treatment of enrollees in a group health plan.*—Any individual enrolling in a group health plan pursuant to paragraph (e)(2) of this section must be treated as if the individual were a special enrollee, as provided under the rules of §54.9801-6(d). Accordingly, the individual (and, if the individual would not be a participant once enrolled in the plan, the participant through whom the individual is otherwise eligible for coverage under the plan) must be offered all the benefit packages available to similarly situated individuals who did not lose coverage by reason of reaching a lifetime limit on the dollar value of all benefits. For this purpose, any difference in benefits or cost-sharing requirements constitutes a different benefit package. The individual also cannot be required to pay more for coverage than similarly situated individuals who did not lose coverage by reason of reaching a lifetime limit on the dollar value of all benefits.

>>>→ *Caution: Temporary Reg. §54.9815-2711T, below, was removed by T.D. 9744 and is inapplicable under Code Sec. 7805(e)(2). However, until final Reg. §54.9815-2711 is applicable on the first day of the plan or policy year beginning after January 1, 2017, taxpayers may comply with the corresponding interim final regulation at 29 CFR part 2590 that is substantially similar to the temporary reg below.*

(5) *Examples.*—The rules of this paragraph (e) are illustrated by the following examples:

Example 1. (i) *Facts.* Employer Y maintains a group health plan with a calendar year plan year. The plan has a single benefit package. For plan years beginning before September 23, 2010, the plan has a lifetime limit on the dollar value of all benefits. Individual B, an employee of Y, was enrolled in Y's group health plan at the beginning of the 2008 plan year. On June 10, 2008, B incurred a claim for benefits that exceeded the lifetime limit under Y's plan and ceased to be enrolled in the plan. B is still eligible for coverage under Y's group health plan. On or before January 1, 2011, Y's group health plan gives B written notice informing B that the lifetime limit on the dollar value of all benefits no longer applies, that individuals whose coverage ended by reason of reaching a lifetime limit under the plan are eligible to enroll in the plan, and that individuals can request such enrollment through February 1, 2011 with enrollment effective retroactively to January 1, 2011.

(ii) *Conclusion.* In this *Example 1*, the plan has complied with the requirements of this paragraph (e) by providing a timely written notice and enrollment opportunity to B that lasts at least 30 days.

Example 2. (i) *Facts.* Employer Z maintains a group health plan with a plan year beginning October 1 and ending September 30. Prior to October 1, 2010, the group health plan has a lifetime limit on the dollar value of all benefits. Individual D, an employee of Z, and Individual E, D's child, were enrolled in family coverage under Z's group health plan for the plan year beginning on October 1, 2008. On May 1, 2009, E incurred a claim for benefits that exceeded the lifetime limit under Z's plan. D dropped family coverage but remains an employee of Z and is still eligible for coverage under Z's group health plan.

(ii) *Conclusion.* In this *Example 2*, not later than October 1, 2010, the plan must provide D and E an opportunity to enroll (including written notice of an opportunity to enroll) that continues for at least 30 days, with enrollment effective not later than October 1, 2010.

Example 3. (i) *Facts.* Same facts as *Example 2*, except that Z's plan had two benefit packages (a low-cost and a high-cost option). Instead of dropping coverage, D switched to the low-cost benefit package option.

(ii) *Conclusion.* In this *Example 3*, not later than October 1, 2010, the plan must provide D and E an opportunity to enroll in any benefit package available to similarly situated individuals who enroll when first eligible. The plan would have to provide D and E the opportunity to enroll in any benefit package available to similarly situated individuals who enroll when first eligible, even if D had not switched to the low-cost benefit package option.

Example 4. (i) *Facts.* Employer Q maintains a group health plan with a plan year beginning October 1 and ending September 30. For the plan year beginning on October 1, 2009, Q has an annual limit on the dollar value of all benefits of $500,000.

(ii) *Conclusion.* In this *Example 4*, Q must raise the annual limit on the dollar value of essential health benefits to at least $750,000 for the plan year beginning October 1, 2010. For the plan year beginning October 1, 2011, Q must raise the annual limit to at least $1.25 million. For the plan year beginning October 1, 2012, Q must raise the annual limit to at least $2 million. Q may also impose a restricted annual limit of $2 million for the plan year beginning October 1, 2013. After the conclusion of that plan year, Q cannot impose an overall annual limit.

Example 5. (i) *Facts.* Same facts as *Example 4*, except that the annual limit for the plan year beginning on October 1, 2009 is $1 million and Q lowers the annual limit for the plan year beginning October 1, 2010 to $750,000.

(ii) *Conclusion.* In this *Example 5*, Q complies with the requirements of this paragraph (e). However, Q's choice to lower its annual limit means that under §54.9815-1251T(g)(1)(vi)(C), the group health plan will cease to be a grandfathered health plan and will be generally subject to all of the provisions of PHS Act sections 2701 through 2719A.

(f) *Effective/applicability date.*—The provisions of this section apply for plan years beginning on or after September 23, 2010. See §54.9815-1251T for determining the application of this section to grandfathered health plans (providing that the prohibitions on lifetime and annual limits apply to all grandfathered health plans that are group health plans and group health insurance coverage, including the special rules regarding restricted annual limits).

(g) *Expiration date.*—This section expires on June 21, 2013. [Temporary Reg. §54.9815-2711T.]

☐ [T.D. 9491, 6-22-2010. *Removed by T.D. 9744*, 11-13-2015.]

➤➤➤ *Caution: Reg. §54.9815-2712, below, as added by T.D. 9744, is applicable to group health plans and health insurance issuers beginning on the first day of the plan year (or, in the individual market, the first day of the first policy year) beginning on or after January 1, 2017.*

[Reg. §54.9815-2712]

§54.9815-2712. Rules regarding rescissions.—(a) *Prohibition on rescissions.*—(1) A group health plan, or a health insurance issuer offering group health insurance coverage, must not rescind coverage under the plan, or under the policy, certificate, or contract of insurance, with respect to an individual (including a group to which the individual belongs or family coverage in which the individual is included) once the individual is covered under the plan or coverage, unless the individual (or a person seeking coverage on behalf of the individual) performs an act, practice, or omission that constitutes fraud, or makes an intentional misrepresentation of material fact, as prohibited by the terms of the plan or coverage. A group health plan, or a health insurance issuer offering group health insurance coverage, must provide at least 30 days advance written notice to each participant who would be affected before coverage may be rescinded under this paragraph (a)(1), regardless of whether the coverage is insured or self-insured, or whether the rescission applies to an entire group or only to an individual within the group. (The rules of this paragraph (a)(1) apply regardless of any contestability period that may otherwise apply.)

(2) For purposes of this section, a rescission is a cancellation or discontinuance of coverage that has retroactive effect. For example, a cancellation that treats a policy as void from the time of the individual's or group's enrollment is a rescission. As another example, a cancellation that voids benefits paid up to a year before the cancellation is also a rescission for this purpose. A cancellation or discontinuance of coverage is not a rescission if

(i) The cancellation or discontinuance of coverage has only a prospective effect;

(ii) The cancellation or discontinuance of coverage is effective retroactively to the extent it is attributable to a failure to timely pay required premiums or contributions (including COBRA premiums) towards the cost of coverage;

(iii) The cancellation or discontinuance of coverage is initiated by the individual (or by the individual's authorized representative) and the sponsor, employer, plan, or issuer does not, directly or indirectly, take action to influence the individual's decision to cancel or discontinue coverage retroactively or otherwise take any adverse action or retaliate against, interfere with, coerce, intimidate, or threaten the individual; or

(iv) The cancellation or discontinuance of coverage is initiated by the Exchange pursuant to 45 CFR 155.430 (other than under paragraph (b)(2)(iii)).

(3) The rules of this paragraph (a) are illustrated by the following examples:

Example 1. (i) *Facts.* Individual *A* seeks enrollment in an insured group health plan. The plan terms permit rescission of coverage with respect to an individual if the individual engages in fraud or makes an intentional misrepresentation of a material fact. The plan requires *A* to complete a questionnaire regarding *A's* prior medical history, which affects setting the group rate by the health insurance issuer. The questionnaire complies with the other requirements of this part. The questionnaire includes the following question: "Is there anything else relevant to your health that we should know?" *A* inadvertently fails to list that *A* visited a psychologist on two occasions, six years previously. *A* is later diagnosed with breast cancer and seeks benefits under the plan. On or around the same time, the issuer receives information about *A's* visits to the psychologist, which was not disclosed in the questionnaire.

(ii) *Conclusion.* In this *Example 1*, the plan cannot rescind *A's* coverage because *A's* failure to disclose the visits to the psychologist was inadvertent. Therefore, it was not fraudulent or an intentional misrepresentation of material fact.

Example 2. (i) *Facts.* An employer sponsors a group health plan that provides coverage for employees who work at least 30 hours per week. Individual *B* has coverage under the plan as a full-time employee. The employer reassigns *B* to a part-time position. Under the terms of the plan, *B* is no longer eligible for coverage. The plan mistakenly continues to provide health coverage, collecting premiums from *B* and paying claims submitted by *B*. After a routine audit, the plan discovers that *B* no longer works at least 30 hours per week. The plan rescinds *B's* coverage effective as of the date that *B* changed from a full-time employee to a part-time employee.

(ii) *Conclusion.* In this *Example 2*, the plan cannot rescind *B's* coverage because there was no fraud or an intentional misrepresentation of material fact. The plan may cancel coverage for *B* prospectively, subject to other applicable Federal and State laws.

(b) *Compliance with other requirements.*—Other requirements of Federal or State law may apply in connection with a rescission of coverage.

(c) *Applicability date.*—The provisions of this section are applicable to group health plans and health insurance issuers for plan years beginning on or after January 1, 2017. Until the applicability date for this regulation, plans and issuers are required to continue to comply with the interim final regulations promulgated by the Department of Labor at 29 CFR part 2590, contained in the 29 CFR, parts 1927 to end, edition revised as of July 1, 2015. [Reg. §54.9815-2712.]

☐ [*T.D. 9744*, 11-13-2015.]

>>>→ *Caution: Temporary Reg. §54.9815-2712T, below, was removed by T.D. 9744 and is inapplicable under Code Sec. 7805(e)(2). However, until final Reg. §54.9815-2712 is applicable on the first day of the plan or policy year beginning after January 1, 2017, taxpayers may comply with the corresponding interim final regulation at 29 CFR part 2590 that is substantially similar to the temporary reg below.*

[Reg. §54.9815-2712T]

§54.9815-2712T. Rules regarding rescissions (temporary).—(a) *Prohibition on rescissions.*— (1) A group health plan, or a health insurance issuer offering group health insurance coverage, must not rescind coverage under the plan, or under the policy, certificate, or contract of insurance, with respect to an individual (including a group to which the individual belongs or family coverage in which the individual is included) once the individual is covered under the plan or coverage, unless the individual (or a person seeking coverage on behalf of the individual) performs an act, practice, or omission that constitutes fraud, or unless the individual makes an intentional misrepresentation of material fact, as prohibited by the terms of the plan or coverage. A group health plan, or a health insurance issuer offering group health insurance coverage, must provide at least 30 days advance written notice to each participant who would be affected before coverage may be rescinded under this paragraph (a)(1), regardless of whether the coverage is insured or self-insured, or whether the rescission applies to an entire group or only to an individual within the group. (The rules of this paragraph (a)(1) apply regardless of any contestability period that may otherwise apply.)

(2) For purposes of this section, a rescission is a cancellation or discontinuance of coverage that has retroactive effect. For example, a cancellation that treats a policy as void from the time of the individual's or group's enrollment is a rescission. As another example, a cancellation that voids benefits paid up to a year before the cancellation is also a rescission for this purpose. A cancellation or discontinuance of coverage is not a rescission if—

(i) The cancellation or discontinuance of coverage has only a prospective effect; or

(ii) The cancellation or discontinuance of coverage is effective retroactively to the extent it is attributable to a failure to timely pay required premiums or contributions towards the cost of coverage.

(3) The rules of this paragraph (a) are illustrated by the following examples:

Example 1. (i) *Facts.* Individual A seeks enrollment in an insured group health plan. The plan terms permit rescission of coverage with respect to an individual if the individual engages in fraud or makes an intentional misrepresentation of a material fact. The plan requires A to complete a questionnaire regarding A's prior medical history, which affects setting the group rate by the health insurance issuer. The questionnaire complies with the other requirements of this part. The questionnaire includes the following question: "Is there anything else relevant to your health that we should know?" A inadvertently fails to list that A visited a psychologist on two occasions, six years previously. A is later diagnosed with breast cancer and seeks benefits under the plan. On or around the same time, the issuer receives information about A's visits to the psychologist, which was not disclosed in the questionnaire.

(ii) *Conclusion.* In this *Example 1*, the plan cannot rescind A's coverage because A's failure to disclose the visits to the psychologist was inadvertent. Therefore, it was not fraudulent or an intentional misrepresentation of material fact.

Example 2. (i) *Facts.* An employer sponsors a group health plan that provides coverage for employees who work at least 30 hours per week. Individual B has coverage under the plan as a full-time employee. The employer reassigns B to a part-time position. Under the terms of the plan, B is no longer eligible for coverage. The plan mistakenly continues to provide health coverage, collecting premiums from B and paying claims submitted by B. After a routine audit, the plan discovers that B no longer works at least 30 hours per week. The plan rescinds B's coverage effective as of the date that B changed from a full-time employee to a part-time employee.

(ii) *Conclusion.* In this *Example 2*, the plan cannot rescind B's coverage because there was no fraud or an intentional misrepresentation of material fact. The plan may cancel coverage for B prospectively, subject to other applicable Federal and State laws.

(b) *Compliance with other requirements.*—Other requirements of Federal or State law may apply in connection with a rescission of coverage.

(c) *Effective/applicability date.*—The provisions of this section apply for plan years beginning on or after September 23, 2010. See §54.9815-1251T for determining the application of this section to grandfathered health plans (providing that the rules regarding rescissions and advance notice apply to all grandfathered health plans).

(d) *Expiration date.*—This section expires on June 21, 2013. [Temporary Reg. §54.9815-2712T.]

☐ [T.D. 9491, 6-22-2010. *Removed by T.D. 9744,* 11-13-2015.]

[Reg. §54.9815-2713]

§54.9815-2713. Coverage of preventive health services.—(a) *Services.*—(1) *In general.*— [Reserved]. For further guidance, see §54.9815-2713T(a)(1) introductory text.

(i) Evidence-based items or services that have in effect a rating of A or B in the current recommendations of the United States Preventive Services Task Force with respect to the individual involved (except as otherwise provided in paragraph (c) of this section);

(ii) Immunizations for routine use in children, adolescents, and adults that have in effect a recommendation from the Advisory Committee on Immunization Practices of the Centers for Disease Control and Prevention with respect to the individual involved (for this purpose, a recommendation from the Advisory Committee on Immunization Practices of the Centers for Disease Control and Prevention is considered in effect after it has been adopted by the Director of the Centers for Disease Control and Prevention, and a recommendation is considered to be for routine use if it is listed on the Immunization Schedules of the Centers for Disease Control and Prevention);

(iii) With respect to infants, children, and adolescents, evidence-informed preventive care and screenings provided for in comprehensive guidelines supported by the Health Resources and Services Administration; and

(iv) [Reserved]. For further guidance, see §54.9815-2713T(a)(1)(iv).

(2) *Office visits.*—(i) If an item or service described in paragraph (a)(1) of this section is billed separately (or is tracked as individual encounter data separately) from an office visit, then a plan or issuer may impose cost-sharing requirements with respect to the office visit.

(ii) If an item or service described in paragraph (a)(1) of this section is not billed separately (or is not tracked as individual encounter data separately) from an office visit and the primary purpose of the office visit is the delivery of such an item or service, then a plan or issuer may not impose cost-sharing requirements with respect to the office visit.

(iii) If an item or service described in paragraph (a)(1) of this section is not billed separately (or is not tracked as individual encounter data separately) from an office visit and the primary purpose of the office visit is not the delivery of such an item or service, then a plan or issuer may impose cost-sharing requirements with respect to the office visit.

(iv) The rules of this paragraph (a)(2) are illustrated by the following examples:

Example 1. (i) *Facts.* An individual covered by a group health plan visits an in-network health care provider. While visiting the provider, the individual is screened for cholesterol abnormalities, which has in effect a rating of A or B in the current recommendations of the United States Preventive Services Task Force with respect to the individual. The provider bills the plan for an office visit and for the laboratory work of the cholesterol screening test.

(ii) *Conclusion.* In this *Example 1*, the plan may not impose any cost-sharing requirements with respect to the separately-billed laboratory work of the cholesterol screening test. Because the office visit is billed separately from the cholesterol screening test, the plan may impose cost-sharing requirements for the office visit.

Example 2. (i) *Facts.* Same facts as *Example 1* of this section. As the result of the screening, the individual is diagnosed with hyperlipidemia and is prescribed a course of treatment that is not included in the recommendations under paragraph (a)(1) of this section.

(ii) *Conclusion.* In this *Example 2*, because the treatment is not included in the recommendations under paragraph (a)(1) of this section, the plan is not prohibited from imposing cost-sharing requirements with respect to the treatment.

Example 3. (i) *Facts.* An individual covered by a group health plan visits an in-network health care provider to discuss recurring abdominal pain. During the visit, the individual has a blood pressure screening, which has in effect a rating of A or B in the current recommendations of the United States Preventive Services Task Force with respect to the individual. The provider bills the plan for an office visit.

(ii) *Conclusion.* In this *Example 3*, the blood pressure screening is provided as part of an office visit for which the primary purpose was not to deliver items or services described in paragraph (a)(1) of this section. Therefore, the plan may impose a cost-sharing requirement for the office visit charge.

Example 4. (i) *Facts.* A child covered by a group health plan visits an in-network pediatrician to receive an annual physical exam described as part of the comprehensive guidelines supported by the Health Resources and Services Administration. During the office visit, the child receives additional items and services that are not described in the comprehensive guidelines supported by the Health Resources and Services Administration, nor otherwise described in paragraph (a)(1) of this section. The provider bills the plan for an office visit.

(ii) *Conclusion.* In this *Example 4*, the service was not billed as a separate charge and was billed as part of an office visit. Moreover, the primary purpose for the visit was to deliver items and services described as part of the comprehensive guidelines supported by the Health Resources and Services Administration. Therefore, the plan may not impose a cost-sharing requirement with respect to the office visit.

(3) *Out-of-network providers.*—(i) Subject to paragraph (a)(3)(ii) of this section, nothing in this section requires a plan or issuer that has a network of providers to provide benefits for items or services described in paragraph (a)(1) of this section that are delivered by an out-of-network provider. Moreover, nothing in this section precludes a plan or issuer that has a network of providers from imposing cost-sharing requirements for items or services described in paragraph (a)(1) of this section that are delivered by an out-of-network provider.

(ii) If a plan or issuer does not have in its network a provider who can provide an item or service described in paragraph (a)(1) of this section, the plan or issuer must cover the item or service when performed by an out-of-network provider, and may not impose cost-sharing with respect to the item or service.

(4) Reasonable medical management.—Nothing prevents a plan or issuer from using reasonable medical management techniques to determine the frequency, method, treatment, or setting for an item or service described in paragraph (a)(1) of this section to the extent not specified in the relevant recommendation or guideline. To the extent not specified in a recommendation or guideline, a plan or issuer may rely on the relevant clinical evidence base and established reasonable medical management techniques to determine the frequency, method, treatment, or setting for coverage of a recommended preventive health service.

(5) Services not described.—Nothing in this section prohibits a plan or issuer from providing coverage for items and services in addition to those recommended by the United States Preventive Services Task Force or the Advisory Committee on Immunization Practices of the Centers for Disease Control and Prevention, or provided for by guidelines supported by the Health Resources and Services Administration, or from denying coverage for items and services that are not recommended by that task force or that advisory committee, or under those guidelines. A plan or issuer may impose cost-sharing requirements for a treatment not described in paragraph (a)(1) of this section, even if the treatment results from an item or service described in paragraph (a)(1) of this section.

(b) Timing.—(1) *In general.*—A plan or issuer must provide coverage pursuant to paragraph (a)(1) of this section for plan years that begin on or after September 23, 2010, or, if later, for plan years that begin on or after the date that is one year after the date the recommendation or guideline is issued.

(2) Changes in recommendations or guidelines.—(i) A plan or issuer that is required to provide coverage for any items and services specified in any recommendation or guideline described in paragraph (a)(1) of this section on the first day of a plan year must provide coverage through the last day of the plan year, even if the recommendation or guideline changes is or is no longer described in paragraph (a)(1) of this section, during the plan year.

(ii) Notwithstanding paragraph (b)(2)(i) of this section, to the extent a recommendation or guideline described in paragraph (a)(1)(i) of this section that was in effect on the first day of a plan year is downgraded to a "D" rating, or any item or service associated with any recommendation or guideline specified in paragraph (a)(1) of this section is subject to a safety recall or is otherwise determined to pose a significant safety concern by a federal agency authorized to regulate the item or service during a plan year, there is no requirement under this section to cover these items and services through the last day of the plan year.

(c) Recommendations not current.—For purposes of paragraph (a)(1)(i) of this section, and

for purposes of any other provision of law, recommendations of the United States Preventive Services Task Force regarding breast cancer screening, mammography, and prevention issued in or around November 2009 are not considered to be current.

(d) Effective/applicability date.—April 16, 2012. [Reg. § 54.9815-2713.]

☐ [*T.D.* 9578, 2-10-2012. *Amended by T.D.* 9624, 6-28-2013, *T.D.* 9726, 7-10-2015 *and T.D.* 9827, 10-6-2017.]

[Reg. § 54.9815-2713T]

§ 54.9815-2713T. Coverage of preventive health services (temporary).—(a) *Services.*—(1) *In general.*—Beginning at the time described in paragraph (b) of § 54.9815–2713 and subject to § 54.9815-2713A, a group health plan, or a health insurance issuer offering group health insurance coverage, must provide coverage for and must not impose any cost-sharing requirements (such as a copayment, coinsurance, or a deductible) for—

(i) – (iii) [Reserved]. For further guidance, see § 54.9815-2713(a)(1)(i) through (iii).

(iv) With respect to women, such additional preventive care and screenings not described in paragraph (a)(1)(i) of § 54.9815–2713 as provided for in comprehensive guidelines supported by the Health Resources and Services Administration for purposes of section 2713(a)(4) of the Public Health Service Act, subject to 45 CFR 147.131, 147.132, and 147.133.

(2) – (c) [Reserved]. For further guidance, see § 54.9815-2713(a)(2) through (c).

(d) Effective/Applicability date.—(1) Paragraphs (a) through (c) of this section are applicable beginning on April 16, 2012, except—

(2) Paragraphs (a)(1) introductory text and (a)(1)(iv) of this section are effective on October 6, 2017.

(e) Expiration date.—This section expires on October 6, 2020. [Temporary Reg. § 54.9815-2713T.]

☐ [*T.D.* 9827, 10-6-2017. *Amended by T.D.* 9828, 10-6-2017.]

[Reg. § 54.9815-2713A]

§ 54.9815-2713A. Accommodations in connection with coverage of preventive health services.—(a) through (f) [Reserved]. For further guidance, see § 54.9815-2713AT. [Reg. § 54.9815-2713A.]

☐ [*T.D.* 9624, 6-28-2013. *Amended by T.D.* 9690, 8-22-2014, *T.D.* 9726, 7-10-2015 *and T.D.* 9827, 10-6-2017.]

[Reg. § 54.9815-2713AT]

§ 54.9815-2713AT. Accommodations in connection with coverage of preventive health services (temporary).—(a) *Eligible organizations for optional accommodation.*—An eligible organization is an organization that meets the criteria of paragraphs (a)(1) through (4) of this section.

Reg. § 54.9815-2713AT(a)

(1) The organization is an objecting entity described in 45 CFR 147.132(a)(1)(i) or (ii), or 45 CFR 147.133(a)(1)(i) or (ii);

(2) Notwithstanding its status under paragraph (a)(1) of this section and under 45 CFR 147.132(a) or 147.133(a), the organization voluntarily seeks to be considered an eligible organization to invoke the optional accommodation under paragraph (b) or (c) of this section as applicable; and

(3) [Reserved]

(4) The organization self-certifies in the form and manner specified by the Secretary of Labor or provides notice to the Secretary of the Department of Health and Human Services as described in paragraph (b) or (c) of this section. To qualify as an eligible organization, the organization must make such self-certification or notice available for examination upon request by the first day of the first plan year to which the accommodation in paragraph (b) or (c) of this section applies. The self-certification or notice must be executed by a person authorized to make the certification or provide the notice on behalf of the organization, and must be maintained in a manner consistent with the record retention requirements under section 107 of ERISA.

(5) An eligible organization may revoke its use of the accommodation process, and its issuer or third party administrator must provide participants and beneficiaries written notice of such revocation as specified in guidance issued by the Secretary of the Department of Health and Human Services. If contraceptive coverage is currently being offered by an issuer or third party administrator through the accommodation process, the revocation will be effective on the first day of the first plan year that begins on or after 30 days after the date of the revocation (to allow for the provision of notice to plan participants in cases where contraceptive benefits will no longer be provided). Alternatively, an eligible organization may give sixty-days notice pursuant to section 2715(d)(4) of the PHS Act and § 54.9815-2715(b), if applicable, to revoke its use of the accommodation process.

(b) *Optional accommodation - self-insured group health plans.*—(1) A group health plan established or maintained by an eligible organization that provides benefits on a self-insured basis may voluntarily elect an optional accommodation under which its third party administrator(s) will provide or arrange payments for all or a subset of contraceptive services for one or more plan years. To invoke the optional accommodation process:

(i) The eligible organization or its plan must contract with one or more third party administrators.

(ii) The eligible organization must provide either a copy of the self-certification to each third party administrator or a notice to the Secretary of the Department of Health and Human Services that it is an eligible organization and of its objection as described in 45 CFR 147.132 or 147.133 to coverage of all or a subset of contraceptive services.

(A) When a copy of the self-certification is provided directly to a third party administrator, such self-certification must include notice that obligations of the third party administrator are set forth in 29 CFR 2510.3-16 and this section.

(B) When a notice is provided to the Secretary of Health and Human Services, the notice must include the name of the eligible organization; a statement that it objects as described in 45 CFR 147.132 or 147.133 to coverage of some or all contraceptive services (including an identification of the subset of contraceptive services to which coverage the eligible organization objects, if applicable), but that it would like to elect the optional accommodation process; the plan name and type (that is, whether it is a student health insurance plan within the meaning of 45 CFR 147.145(a) or a church plan within the meaning of section 3(33) of ERISA); and the name and contact information for any of the plan's third party administrators. If there is a change in any of the information required to be included in the notice, the eligible organization must provide updated information to the Secretary of the Department of Health and Human Services for the optional accommodation process to remain in effect. The Department of Labor (working with the Department of Health and Human Services), will send a separate notification to each of the plan's third party administrators informing the third party administrator that the Secretary of the Department of Health and Human Services has received a notice under paragraph (b)(1)(ii) of this section and describing the obligations of the third party administrator under 29 CFR 2510.3-16 and this section.

(2) If a third party administrator receives a copy of the self-certification from an eligible organization or a notification from the Department of Labor, as described in paragraph (b)(1)(ii) of this section, and is willing to enter into or remain in a contractual relationship with the eligible organization or its plan to provide administrative services for the plan, then the third party administrator will provide or arrange payments for contraceptive services, using one of the following methods—

(i) Provide payments for the contraceptive services for plan participants and beneficiaries without imposing any cost-sharing requirements (such as a copayment, coinsurance, or a deductible), premium, fee, or other charge, or any portion thereof, directly or indirectly, on the eligible organization, the group health plan, or plan participants or beneficiaries; or

(ii) Arrange for an issuer or other entity to provide payments for the contraceptive services for plan participants and beneficiaries without imposing any cost-sharing requirements (such as a copayment, coinsurance, or a deductible), premium, fee, or other charge, or any portion thereof, directly or indirectly, on the eligible organization, the group health plan, or plan participants or beneficiaries.

(3) If a third party administrator provides or arranges payments for contraceptive services in accordance with either paragraph (b)(2)(i) or (ii) of this section, the costs of providing or arranging such payments may be reimbursed through an adjustment to the Federally facilitated Exchange user fee for a participating issuer pursuant to 45 CFR 156.50(d).

(4) A third party administrator may not require any documentation other than a copy of the self-certification from the eligible organization or notification from the Department of Labor described in paragraph (b)(1)(ii) of this section.

(5) Where an otherwise eligible organization does not contract with a third party administrator and files a self-certification or notice under paragraph (b)(1)(ii) of this section, the obligations under paragraph (b)(2) of this section do not apply, and the otherwise eligible organization is under no requirement to provide coverage or payments for contraceptive services to which it objects. The plan administrator for that otherwise eligible organization may, if it and the otherwise eligible organization choose, arrange for payments for contraceptive services from an issuer or other entity in accordance with paragraph (b)(2)(ii) of this section, and such issuer or other entity may receive reimbursements in accordance with paragraph (b)(3) of this section.

(6) Where an otherwise eligible organization is an ERISA-exempt church plan within the meaning of section 3(33) of ERISA and it files a self-certification or notice under paragraph (b)(1)(ii) of this section, the obligations under paragraph (b)(2) of this section do not apply, and the otherwise eligible organization is under no requirement to provide coverage or payments for contraceptive services to which it objects. The third party administrator for that otherwise eligible organization may, if it and the otherwise eligible organization choose, provide or arrange payments for contraceptive services in accordance with paragraphs (b)(2)(i) or (ii) of this section, and receive reimbursements in accordance with paragraph (b)(3) of this section.

(c) *Optional accommodation - insured group health plans.*—(1) *General rule.*—A group health plan established or maintained by an eligible organization that provides benefits through one or more group health insurance issuers may voluntarily elect an optional accommodation under which its health insurance issuer(s) will provide payments for all or a subset of contraceptive services for one or more plan years. To invoke the optional accommodation process—

(i) The eligible organization or its plan must contract with one or more health insurance issuers.

(ii) The eligible organization must provide either a copy of the self-certification to each issuer providing coverage in connection with the plan or a notice to the Secretary of the Department of Health and Human Services that it is an eligible organization and of its objection as described in 45 CFR 147.132 or 147.133 to coverage for all or a subset of contraceptive services.

(A) When a self-certification is provided directly to an issuer, the issuer has sole responsibility for providing such coverage in accordance with § 54.9815-2713.

(B) When a notice is provided to the Secretary of the Department Health and Human Services, the notice must include the name of the eligible organization; a statement that it objects as described in 45 CFR 147.132 or 147.133 to coverage of some or all contraceptive services (including an identification of the subset of contraceptive services to which coverage the eligible organization objects, if applicable) but that it would like to elect the optional accommodation process; the plan name and type (that is, whether it is a student health insurance plan within the meaning of 45 CFR 147.145(a) or a church plan within the meaning of section 3(33) of ERISA); and the name and contact information for any of the plan's health insurance issuers. If there is a change in any of the information required to be included in the notice, the eligible organization must provide updated information to the Secretary of Department of Health and Human Services for the optional accommodation process to remain in effect. The Department of Health and Human Services will send a separate notification to each of the plan's health insurance issuers informing the issuer that the Secretary of the Department Health and Human Services has received a notice under paragraph (c)(2)(ii) of this section and describing the obligations of the issuer under this section.

(2) If an issuer receives a copy of the self-certification from an eligible organization or the notification from the Department of Health and Human Services as described in paragraph (c)(2)(ii) of this section and does not have its own objection as described in 45 CFR 147.132 or 147.133 to providing the contraceptive services to which the eligible organization objects, then the issuer will provide payments for contraceptive services as follows—

(i) The issuer must expressly exclude contraceptive coverage from the group health insurance coverage provided in connection with the group health plan and provide separate payments for any contraceptive services required to be covered under § 54.9815-2713(a)(1)(iv) for plan participants and beneficiaries for so long as they remain enrolled in the plan.

(ii) With respect to payments for contraceptive services, the issuer may not impose any cost-sharing requirements (such as a copayment, coinsurance, or a deductible), or impose any premium, fee, or other charge, or any portion thereof, directly or indirectly, on the eligible organization, the group health plan, or plan participants or beneficiaries. The issuer must segregate premium revenue collected from the eligible organization from the monies used to provide payments for contraceptive services. The issuer must provide payments for contraceptive

Reg. § 54.9815-2713AT(c)(2)(ii)

services in a manner that is consistent with the requirements under sections 2706, 2709, 2711, 2713, 2719, and 2719A of the PHS Act, as incorporated into section 9815 of the PHS Act. If the group health plan of the eligible organization provides coverage for some but not all of any contraceptive services required to be covered under §54.9815-2713(a)(1)(iv), the issuer is required to provide payments only for those contraceptive services for which the group health plan does not provide coverage. However, the issuer may provide payments for all contraceptive services, at the issuer's option.

(3) A health insurance issuer may not require any documentation other than a copy of the self-certification from the eligible organization or the notification from the Department of Health and Human Services described in paragraph (c)(1)(ii) of this section.

(d) *Notice of availability of separate payments for contraceptive services - self-insured and insured group health plans.*—For each plan year to which the optional accommodation in paragraph (b) or (c) of this section is to apply, a third party administrator required to provide or arrange payments for contraceptive services pursuant to paragraph (b) of this section, and an issuer required to provide payments for contraceptive services pursuant to paragraph (c) of this section, must provide to plan participants and beneficiaries written notice of the availability of separate payments for contraceptive services contemporaneous with (to the extent possible), but separate from, any application materials distributed in connection with enrollment (or reenrollment) in group health coverage that is effective beginning on the first day of each applicable plan year. The notice must specify that the eligible organization does not administer or fund contraceptive benefits, but that the third party administrator or issuer, as applicable, provides or arranges separate payments for contraceptive services, and must provide contact information for questions and complaints. The following

model language, or substantially similar language, may be used to satisfy the notice requirement of this paragraph (d): "Your employer has certified that your group health plan qualifies for an accommodation with respect to the Federal requirement to cover all Food and Drug Administration-approved contraceptive services for women, as prescribed by a health care provider, without cost sharing. This means that your employer will not contract, arrange, pay, or refer for contraceptive coverage. Instead, [name of third party administrator/health insurance issuer] will provide or arrange separate payments for contraceptive services that you use, without cost sharing and at no other cost, for so long as you are enrolled in your group health plan. Your employer will not administer or fund these payments. If you have any questions about this notice, contact [contact information for third party administrator/health insurance issuer]."

(e) *Definition.*—For the purposes of this section, reference to "contraceptive" services, benefits, or coverage includes contraceptive or sterilization items, procedures, or services, or related patient education or counseling, to the extent specified for purposes of §54.9815-2713(a)(1)(iv).

(f) *Severability.*—Any provision of this section held to be invalid or unenforceable by its terms, or as applied to any person or circumstance, shall be construed so as to continue to give maximum effect to the provision permitted by law, unless such holding shall be one of utter invalidity or unenforceability, in which event the provision shall be severable from this section and shall not affect the remainder thereof or the application of the provision to persons not similarly situated or to dissimilar circumstances.

(g) *Expiration date.*—This section expires on October 6, 2020. [Temporary Reg. §54.9815-2713AT.]

☐ [T.D. 9827, 10-6-2017. *Amended by T.D. 9828*, 10-6-2017.]

⋙→ *Caution: Reg. §54.9815-2714, below, as added by T.D. 9744, is applicable to group health plans and health insurance issuers beginning on the first day of the plan year (or, in the individual market, the first day of the first policy year) beginning on or after January 1, 2017.*

[Reg. §54.9815-2714]

§54.9815-2714. Eligibility of children until at least age 26.—(a) *In general.*—(1) A group health plan, or a health insurance issuer offering group health insurance coverage, that makes available dependent coverage of children must make such coverage available for children until attainment of 26 years of age.

(2) The rule of this paragraph (a) is illustrated by the following example:

Example. (i) *Facts* For the plan year beginning January 1, 2011, a group health plan provides health coverage for employees, employees' spouses, and employees' children until the child turns 26. On the birthday of a child of an employee, July 17, 2011, the child turns 26. The last day the plan covers the child is July 16, 2011.

(ii) *Conclusion* In this *Example*, the plan satisfies the requirement of this paragraph (a) with respect to the child.

(b) *Restrictions on plan definition of dependent.*—(1) *In general.*—With respect to a child who has not attained age 26, a plan or issuer may not define dependent for purposes of eligibility for dependent coverage of children other than in terms of a relationship between a child and the participant. Thus, for example, a plan or issuer may not deny or restrict dependent coverage for a child who has not attained age 26 based on the presence or absence of the child's financial dependency (upon the participant or any other person); residency with the participant or with any other person; whether the child lives, works, or resides in an HMO's service area or other network service area; marital status; student sta-

>>>→ *Caution: Reg. §54.9815-2714, below, as added by T.D. 9744, is applicable to group health plans and health insurance issuers beginning on the first day of the plan year (or, in the individual market, the first day of the first policy year) beginning on or after January 1, 2017.*

tus; employment; eligibility for other coverage; or any combination of those factors. (Other requirements of Federal or State law, including section 609 of ERISA or section 1908 of the Social Security Act, may require coverage of certain children.)

(2) *Construction.*—A plan or issuer will not fail to satisfy the requirements of this section if the plan or issuer limits dependent child coverage to children under age 26 who are described in section 152(f)(1). For an individual not described in section 152(f)(1), such as a grandchild or niece, a plan may impose additional conditions on eligibility for dependent child health coverage, such as a condition that the individual be a dependent for income tax purposes.

(c) *Coverage of grandchildren not required.*— Nothing in this section requires a plan or issuer to make coverage available for the child of a child receiving dependent coverage.

(d) *Uniformity irrespective of age.*—The terms of the plan or health insurance coverage providing dependent coverage of children cannot vary based on age (except for children who are age 26 or older).

(e) *Examples.*—The rules of paragraph (d) of this section are illustrated by the following examples:

Example 1. (i) *Facts.* A group health plan offers a choice of self-only or family health coverage. Dependent coverage is provided under family health coverage for children of participants who have not attained age 26. The plan imposes an additional premium surcharge for children who are older than age 18.

(ii) *Conclusion.* In this *Example 1,* the plan violates the requirement of paragraph (d) of this section because the plan varies the terms for dependent coverage of children based on age.

Example 2. (i) *Facts.* A group health plan offers a choice among the following tiers of health coverage: self-only, self-plus-one, self-plus-two, and self-plus-three-or-more. The cost of coverage increases based on the number of covered individuals. The plan provides dependent coverage of children who have not attained age 26.

(ii) *Conclusion.* In this *Example 2,* the plan does not violate the requirement of paragraph (d) of this section that the terms of dependent coverage for children not vary based on age. Although the

cost of coverage increases for tiers with more covered individuals, the increase applies without regard to the age of any child.

Example 3. (i) *Facts.* A group health plan offers two benefit packages — an HMO Option and an indemnity option. Dependent coverage is provided for children of participants who have not attained age 26. The plan limits children who are older than age 18 to the HMO option.

(ii) *Conclusion.* In this *Example 3,* the plan violates the requirement of paragraph (d) of this section because the plan, by limiting children who are older than age 18 to the HMO option, varies the terms for dependent coverage of children based on age.

Example 4. (i) *Facts.* A group health plan sponsored by a large employer normally charges a copayment for physician visits that do not constitute preventive services. The plan charges this copayment to individuals age 19 and over, including employees, spouses, and dependent children, but waives it for those under age 19.

(ii) *Conclusion.* In this *Example 4,* the plan does not violate the requirement of paragraph (d) of this section that the terms of dependent coverage for children not vary based on age. While the requirement of paragraph (d) of this section generally prohibits distinctions based upon age in dependent coverage of children, it does not prohibit distinctions based upon age that apply to all coverage under the plan, including coverage for employees and spouses as well as dependent children. In this *Example 4,* the copayments charged to dependent children are the same as those charged to employees and spouses. Accordingly, the arrangement described in this *Example 4* (including waiver, for individuals under age 19, of the generally applicable copayment) does not violate the requirement of paragraph (d) of this section.

(f) *Applicability date.*—The provisions of this section are applicable to group health plans and health insurance issuers for plan years beginning on or after January 1, 2017. Until the applicability date for this regulation, plans and issuers are required to continue to comply with the interim final regulations promulgated by the Department of Labor at 29 CFR part 2590, contained in the 29 CFR, parts 1927 to end, edition revised as of July 1, 2015. [Reg. § 54.9815-2714.]

☐ [T.D. 9744, 11-13-2015.]

>>>→ *Caution: Temporary Reg. §54.9815-2714T, below, was removed by T.D. 9744 and is inapplicable under Code Sec. 7805(e)(2). However, until final Reg. §54.9815-2714 is applicable on the first day of the plan or policy year beginning after January 1, 2017, taxpayers may comply with the corresponding interim final regulation at 29 CFR part 2590 that is substantially similar to the temporary reg below.*

[Reg. § 54.9815-2714T]

§ 54.9815-2714T. Eligibility of children until at least age 26 (temporary).—(a) *In general.*— (1) A group health plan, or a health insurance issuer offering group health insurance coverage,

that makes available dependent coverage of children must make such coverage available for children until attainment of 26 years of age.

(2) The rule of this paragraph (a) is illustrated by the following example:

»»→ *Caution: Temporary Reg. §54.9815-2714T, below, was removed by T.D. 9744 and is inapplicable under Code Sec. 7805(e)(2). However, until final Reg. §54.9815-2714 is applicable on the first day of the plan or policy year beginning after January 1, 2017, taxpayers may comply with the corresponding interim final regulation at 29 CFR part 2590 that is substantially similar to the temporary reg below.*

Example. (i) *Facts.* For the plan year beginning January 1, 2011, a group health plan provides health coverage for employees, employees' spouses, and employees' children until the child turns 26. On the birthday of a child of an employee, July 17, 2011, the child turns 26. The last day the plan covers the child is July 16, 2011.

(ii) *Conclusion.* In this *Example*, the plan satisfies the requirement of this paragraph (a) with respect to the child.

(b) *Restrictions on plan definition of dependent.*— With respect to a child who has not attained age 26, a plan or issuer may not define dependent for purposes of eligibility for dependent coverage of children other than in terms of a relationship between a child and the participant. Thus, for example, a plan or issuer may not deny or restrict coverage for a child who has not attained age 26 based on the presence or absence of the child's financial dependency (upon the participant or any other person), residency with the participant or with any other person, student status, employment, or any combination of those factors. In addition, a plan or issuer may not deny or restrict coverage of a child based on eligibility for other coverage, except that paragraph (g) of this section provides a special rule for plan years beginning before January 1, 2014 for grandfathered health plans that are group health plans. (Other requirements of Federal or State law, including section 609 of ERISA or section 1908 of the Social Security Act, may mandate coverage of certain children.)

(c) *Coverage of grandchildren not required.*— Nothing in this section requires a plan or issuer to make coverage available for the child of a child receiving dependent coverage.

(d) *Uniformity irrespective of age.*—The terms of the plan or health insurance coverage providing dependent coverage of children cannot vary based on age (except for children who are age 26 or older).

(e) *Examples.*—The rules of paragraph (d) of this section are illustrated by the following examples:

Example 1. (i) *Facts.* A group health plan offers a choice of self-only or family health coverage. Dependent coverage is provided under family health coverage for children of participants who have not attained age 26. The plan imposes an additional premium surcharge for children who are older than age 18.

(ii) *Conclusion.* In this *Example 1*, the plan violates the requirement of paragraph (d) of this section because the plan varies the terms for dependent coverage of children based on age.

Example 2. (i) *Facts.* A group health plan offers a choice among the following tiers of health coverage: self-only, self-plus-one, self-plus-two, and self-plus-three-or-more. The cost of coverage increases based on the number of covered individuals. The plan provides dependent coverage of children who have not attained age 26.

(ii) *Conclusion.* In this *Example 2*, the plan does not violate the requirement of paragraph (d) of this section that the terms of dependent coverage for children not vary based on age. Although the cost of coverage increases for tiers with more covered individuals, the increase applies without regard to the age of any child.

Example 3. (i) *Facts.* A group health plan offers two benefit packages — an HMO option and an indemnity option. Dependent coverage is provided for children of participants who have not attained age 26. The plan limits children who are older than age 18 to the HMO option.

(ii) *Conclusion.* In this *Example 3*, the plan violates the requirement of paragraph (d) of this section because the plan, by limiting children who are older than age 18 to the HMO option, varies the terms for dependent coverage of children based on age.

(f) *Transitional rules for individuals whose coverage ended by reason of reaching a dependent eligibility threshold.*—(1) *In general.*—The relief provided in the transitional rules of this paragraph (f) applies with respect to any child—

(i) Whose coverage ended, or who was denied coverage (or was not eligible for coverage) under a group health plan or group health insurance coverage because, under the terms of the plan or coverage, the availability of dependent coverage of children ended before the attainment of age 26 (which, under this section, is no longer permissible); and

(ii) Who becomes eligible (or is required to become eligible) for coverage under a group health plan or group health insurance coverage on the first day of the first plan year beginning on or after September 23, 2010 by reason of the application of this section.

(2) *Opportunity to enroll required.*—(i) If a group health plan, or group health insurance coverage, in which a child described in paragraph (f)(1) of this section is eligible to enroll (or is required to become eligible to enroll) is the plan or coverage in which the child's coverage ended (or did not begin) for the reasons described in paragraph (f)(1)(i) of this section, and if the plan, or the issuer of such coverage, is subject to the requirements of this section, the plan and the issuer are required to give the child an opportunity to enroll that continues for at least 30 days (including written notice of the opportunity to enroll). This opportunity (including the written notice) must be provided beginning not later than the first day of the first plan year beginning on or after September 23, 2010.

>>>→ *Caution: Temporary Reg. §54.9815-2714T, below, was removed by T.D. 9744 and is inapplicable under Code Sec. 7805(e)(2). However, until final Reg. §54.9815-2714 is applicable on the first day of the plan or policy year beginning after January 1, 2017, taxpayers may comply with the corresponding interim final regulation at 29 CFR part 2590 that is substantially similar to the temporary reg below.*

(ii) The written notice must include a statement that children whose coverage ended, or who were denied coverage (or were not eligible for coverage), because the availability of dependent coverage of children ended before attainment of age 26 are eligible to enroll in the plan or coverage. The notice may be provided to an employee on behalf of the employee's child. In addition, the notice may be included with other enrollment materials that a plan distributes to employees, provided the statement is prominent. If a notice satisfying the requirements of this paragraph (f)(2) is provided to an employee whose child is entitled to an enrollment opportunity under this paragraph (f), the obligation to provide the notice of enrollment opportunity under this paragraph (f)(2) with respect to that child is satisfied for both the plan and the issuer.

(3) *Effective date of coverage.*—In the case of an individual who enrolls under paragraph (f)(2) of this section, coverage must take effect not later than the first day of the first plan year beginning on or after September 23, 2010.

(4) *Treatment of enrollees in a group health plan.*—Any child enrolling in a group health plan pursuant to paragraph (f)(2) of this section must be treated as if the child were a special enrollee, as provided under the rules of §54.9801-6(d). Accordingly, the child (and, if the child would not be a participant once enrolled in the plan, the participant through whom the child is otherwise eligible for coverage under the plan) must be offered all the benefit packages available to similarly situated individuals who did not lose coverage by reason of cessation of dependent status. For this purpose, any difference in benefits or cost-sharing requirements constitutes a different benefit package. The child also cannot be required to pay more for coverage than similarly situated individuals who did not lose coverage by reason of cessation of dependent status.

(5) *Examples.*—The rules of this paragraph (f) are illustrated by the following examples:

Example 1. (i) *Facts.* Employer Y maintains a group health plan with a calendar year plan year. The plan has a single benefit package. For the 2010 plan year, the plan allows children of employees to be covered under the plan until age 19, or until age 23 for children who are full-time students. Individual B, an employee of Y, and Individual C, B's child and a full-time student, were enrolled in Y's group health plan at the beginning of the 2010 plan year. On June 10, 2010, C turns 23 years old and loses dependent coverage under Y's plan. On or before January 1, 2011, Y's group health plan gives B written notice that individuals who lost coverage by reason of ceasing to be a dependent before attainment of age 26 are eligible to enroll in the plan, and that individuals may request enrollment for such

children through February 14, 2011 with enrollment effective retroactively to January 1, 2011.

(ii) *Conclusion.* In this *Example 1*, the plan has complied with the requirements of this paragraph (f) by providing an enrollment opportunity to C that lasts at least 30 days.

Example 2. (i) *Facts.* Employer Z maintains a group health plan with a plan year beginning October 1 and ending September 30. Prior to October 1, 2010, the group health plan allows children of employees to be covered under the plan until age 22. Individual D, an employee of Z, and Individual E, D's child, are enrolled in family coverage under Z's group health plan for the plan year beginning on October 1, 2008. On May 1, 2009, E turns 22 years old and ceases to be eligible as a dependent under Z's plan and loses coverage. D drops coverage but remains an employee of Z.

(ii) *Conclusion.* In this *Example 2*, not later than October 1, 2010, the plan must provide D and E an opportunity to enroll (including written notice of an opportunity to enroll) that continues for at least 30 days, with enrollment effective not later than October 1, 2010.

Example 3. (i) *Facts.* Same facts as *Example 2*, except that D did not drop coverage. Instead, D switched to a lower-cost benefit package option.

(ii) *Conclusion.* In this *Example 3*, not later than October 1, 2010, the plan must provide D and E an opportunity to enroll in any benefit package available to similarly situated individuals who enroll when first eligible.

Example 4. (i) *Facts.* Same facts as *Example 2*, except that E elected COBRA continuation coverage.

(ii) *Conclusion.* In this *Example 4*, not later than October 1, 2010, the plan must provide D and E an opportunity to enroll other than as a COBRA qualified beneficiary (and must provide, by that date, written notice of the opportunity to enroll) that continues for at least 30 days, with enrollment effective not later than October 1, 2010.

Example 5. (i) *Facts.* Employer X maintains a group health plan with a calendar year plan year. Prior to 2011, the plan allows children of employees to be covered under the plan until the child attains age 22. During the 2009 plan year, an individual with a 22-year old child joins the plan; the child is denied coverage because the child is 22.

(ii) *Conclusion.* In this *Example 5*, notwithstanding that the child was not previously covered under the plan, the plan must provide the child, not later than January 1, 2011, an opportunity to enroll (including written notice to the employee of an opportunity to enroll the child) that continues for at least 30 days, with enrollment effective not later than January 1, 2011.

Reg. §54.9815-2714T(f)(5)

>>>→ *Caution: Temporary Reg. §54.9815-2714T, below, was removed by T.D. 9744 and is inapplicable under Code Sec. 7805(e)(2). However, until final Reg. §54.9815-2714 is applicable on the first day of the plan or policy year beginning after January 1, 2017, taxpayers may comply with the corresponding interim final regulation at 29 CFR part 2590 that is substantially similar to the temporary reg below.*

(g) *Special rule for grandfathered group health plans.*—(1) For plan years beginning before January 1, 2014, a group health plan that qualifies as a grandfathered health plan under section 1251 of the Patient Protection and Affordable Care Act and that makes available dependent coverage of children may exclude an adult child who has not attained age 26 from coverage only if the adult child is eligible to enroll in an eligible employer-sponsored health plan (as defined in section 5000A(f)(2)) other than a group health plan of a parent.

(2) For plan years beginning on or after January 1, 2014, a group health plan that qualifies as a grandfathered health plan under section 1251 of the Patient Protection and Affordable Care Act must comply with the requirements of paragraphs (a) through (f) of this section.

(h) *Applicability date.*—The provisions of this section apply for plan years beginning on or after September 23, 2010. *See* § 54.9815-1251T for determining the application of this section to grandfathered health plans.

(i) *Expiration date.*—This section expires on or before May 10, 2013. [Temporary Reg. § 54.9815-2714T.]

☐ [*T.D.* 9482, 5-10-2010. *Amended by T.D.* 9489, 6-14-2010. *Removed by T.D.* 9744, 11-13-2015.]

[Reg. § 54.9815-2715]

§ 54.9815-2715. Summary of benefits and coverage and uniform glossary.—(a) *Summary of benefits and coverage.*—(1) *In general.*—A group health plan (and its administrator as defined in section 3(16)(A) of ERISA)), and a health insurance issuer offering group health insurance coverage, is required to provide a written summary of benefits and coverage (SBC) for each benefit package without charge to entities and individuals described in this paragraph (a)(1) in accordance with the rules of this section.

(i) *SBC provided by a group health insurance issuer to a group health plan.*—(A) *Upon application.*—A health insurance issuer offering group health insurance coverage must provide the SBC to a group health plan (or its sponsor) upon application for health coverage, as soon as practicable following receipt of the application, but in no event later than seven business days following receipt of the application. If an SBC was provided before application pursuant to paragraph (a)(1)(i)(D) of this section (relating to SBCs upon request), this paragraph (a)(1)(i)(A) is deemed satisfied, provided there is no change to the information required to be in the SBC. However, if there has been a change in the information required, a new SBC that includes the changed information must be provided upon application pursuant to this paragraph (a)(1)(i)(A).

(B) *By first day of coverage (if there are changes).*—If there is any change in the information required to be in the SBC that was provided upon application and before the first day of coverage, the issuer must update and provide a current SBC to the plan (or its sponsor) no later than the first day of coverage.

(C) *Upon renewal, reissuance, or reenrollment.*—If the issuer renews or reissues a policy, certificate, or contract of insurance for a succeeding policy year, or automatically re-enrolls the policyholder or its participants and beneficiaries in coverage, the issuer must provide a new SBC as follows:

(1) If written application is required (in either paper or electronic form) for renewal or reissuance, the SBC must be provided no later than the date the written application materials are distributed.

(2) If renewal, reissuance, or reenrollment is automatic, the SBC must be provided no later than 30 days prior to the first day of the new plan or policy year; however, with respect to an insured plan, if the policy, certificate, or contract of insurance has not been issued or renewed before such 30-day period, the SBC must be provided as soon as practicable but in no event later than seven business days after issuance of the new policy, certificate, or contract of insurance, or the receipt of written confirmation of intent to renew, whichever is earlier.

(D) *Upon request.*—If a group health plan (or its sponsor) requests an SBC or summary information about a health insurance product from a health insurance issuer offering group health insurance coverage, an SBC must be provided as soon as practicable, but in no event later than seven business days following receipt of the request.

(ii) *SBC provided by a group health insurance issuer and a group health plan to participants and beneficiaries.*—(A) *In general.*—A group health plan (including its administrator, as defined under section 3(16) of ERISA), and a health insurance issuer offering group health insurance coverage, must provide an SBC to a participant or beneficiary (as defined under sections 3(7) and 3(8) of ERISA), and consistent with the rules of paragraph (a)(1)(iii) of this section, with respect to each benefit package offered by the plan or issuer for which the participant or beneficiary is eligible.

(B) *Upon application.*—The SBC must be provided as part of any written application materials that are distributed by the plan or issuer for enrollment. If the plan or issuer does not distribute written application materials for enrollment, the SBC must be provided no later than the first date on which the participant is eligible to enroll in coverage for the participant or any beneficiaries. If an SBC was provided before application pursuant to paragraph (a)(1)(ii)(F) of this section (relating to SBCs upon request), this paragraph (a)(1)(ii)(B) is deemed satisfied, provided there is no change to the information required to be in the SBC. However, if there has been a change in the information that is required to be in the SBC, a new SBC that includes the changed information must be provided upon application pursuant to this paragraph (a)(1)(ii)(B).

(C) *By first day of coverage (if there are changes).*—(1) If there is any change to the information required to be in the SBC that was provided upon application and before the first day of coverage, the plan or issuer must update and provide a current SBC to a participant or beneficiary no later than the first day of coverage.

(2) If the plan sponsor is negotiating coverage terms after an application has been filed and the information required to be in the SBC changes, the plan or issuer is not required to provide an updated SBC (unless an updated SBC is requested) until the first day of coverage.

(D) *Special enrollees.*—The plan or issuer must provide the SBC to special enrollees (as described in § 54.9801-6) no later than the date by which a summary plan description is required to be provided under the timeframe set forth in ERISA section 104(b)(1)(A) and its implementing regulations, which is 90 days from enrollment.

(E) *Upon renewal, reissuance, or reenrollment.*—If the plan or issuer requires participants or beneficiaries to renew in order to maintain coverage (for example, for a succeeding plan year), or automatically re-enrolls participants and beneficiaries in coverage, the plan or issuer must provide a new SBC, as follows:

(1) If written application is required for renewal, reissuance, or reenrollment (in either paper or electronic form), the SBC must be provided no later than the date on which the written application materials are distributed.

(2) If renewal, reissuance, or reenrollment is automatic, the SBC must be provided no later than 30 days prior to the first day of the new plan or policy year; however, with respect to an insured plan, if the policy, certificate, or contract of insurance has not been issued or renewed before such 30-day period, the SBC must be provided as soon as practicable but in no event later than seven business days after issuance of the new policy, certificate, or contract of insurance, or the receipt of written confirmation of intent to renew, whichever is earlier.

(F) *Upon request.*—A plan or issuer must provide the SBC to participants or beneficiaries upon request for an SBC or summary information about the health coverage, as soon as practicable, but in no event later than seven business days following receipt of the request.

(iii) *Special rules to prevent unnecessary duplication with respect to group health coverage.*—

(A) An entity required to provide an SBC under this paragraph (a)(1) with respect to an individual satisfies that requirement if another party provides the SBC, but only to the extent that the SBC is timely and complete in accordance with the other rules of this section. Therefore, for example, in the case of a group health plan funded through an insurance policy, the plan satisfies the requirement to provide an SBC with respect to an individual if the issuer provides a timely and complete SBC to the individual. An entity required to provide an SBC under this paragraph (a)(1) with respect to an individual that contracts with another party to provide such SBC is considered to satisfy the requirement to provide such SBC if:

(1) The entity monitors performance under the contract;

(2) If the entity has knowledge that the SBC is not being provided in a manner that satisfies the requirements of this section and the entity has all information necessary to correct the noncompliance, the entity corrects the noncompliance as soon as practicable; and

(3) If the entity has knowledge the SBC is not being provided in a manner that satisfies the requirements of this section and the entity does not have all information necessary to correct the noncompliance, the entity communicates with participants and beneficiaries who are affected by the noncompliance regarding the noncompliance, and begins taking significant steps as soon as practicable to avoid future violations.

(B) If a single SBC is provided to a participant and any beneficiaries at the participant's last known address, then the requirement to provide the SBC to the participant and any beneficiaries is generally satisfied. However, if a beneficiary's last known address is different than the participant's last known address, a separate SBC is required to be provided to the beneficiary at the beneficiary's last known address.

(C) With respect to a group health plan that offers multiple benefit packages, the plan or issuer is required to provide a new SBC automatically to participants and beneficiaries upon renewal or reenrollment only with respect to the benefit package in which a participant or beneficiary is enrolled (or will be automatically re-enrolled under the plan); SBCs are not required to be provided automatically upon renewal or reenrollment with respect to benefit packages in which the participant or beneficiary is not enrolled (or will not automatically be enrolled). However, if a participant or beneficiary requests an SBC with respect to another benefit package (or more than one other benefit package) for which the participant or beneficiary is eligible, the SBC (or SBCs, in the case of a request for SBCs relating to more than one benefit package) must be provided upon request as soon as practicable, but in no event later than seven business days following receipt of the request.

(D) Subject to paragraph (a)(2)(ii) of this section, a plan administrator of a group health plan that uses two or more insurance products provided by separate health insurance issuers with respect to a single group health plan may synthesize the information into a single SBC or provide multiple partial SBCs provided that all the SBC include the content in paragraph (a)(2)(iii) of this section.

(2) *Content.*—(i) *In general.*—Subject to paragraph (a)(2)(iii) of this section, the SBC must include the following:

(A) Uniform definitions of standard insurance terms and medical terms so that consumers may compare health coverage and understand the terms of (or exceptions to) their coverage, in accordance with guidance as specified by the Secretary;

(B) A description of the coverage, including cost sharing, for each category of benefits identified by the Secretary in guidance;

(C) The exceptions, reductions, and limitations of the coverage;

(D) The cost-sharing provisions of the coverage, including deductible, coinsurance, and copayment obligations;

(E) The renewability and continuation of coverage provisions;

(F) Coverage examples, in accordance with the rules of paragraph (a)(2)(ii) of this section;

(G) With respect to coverage beginning on or after January 1, 2014, a statement about whether the plan or coverage provides minimum essential coverage as defined under section 5000A(f) and whether the plan's or coverage's share of the total allowed costs of benefits provided under the plan or coverage meets applicable requirements;

(H) A statement that the SBC is only a summary and that the plan document, policy, certificate, or contract of insurance should be consulted to determine the governing contractual provisions of the coverage;

(I) Contact information for questions;

(J) For issuers, an Internet web address where a copy of the actual individual coverage policy or group certificate of coverage can be reviewed and obtained;

(K) For plans and issuers that maintain one or more networks of providers, an Internet address (or similar contact information) for obtaining a list of network providers;

(L) For plans and issuers that use a formulary in providing prescription drug coverage, an Internet address (or similar contact information) for obtaining information on prescription drug coverage; and

(M) An Internet address for obtaining the uniform glossary, as described in paragraph (c) of this section, as well as a contact phone number to obtain a paper copy of the uniform glossary, and a disclosure that paper copies are available.

(ii) *Coverage examples.*—The SBC must include coverage examples specified by the Secretary in guidance that illustrate benefits provided

under the plan or coverage for common benefits scenarios (including pregnancy and serious or chronic medical conditions) in accordance with this paragraph (a)(2)(ii).

(A) *Number of examples.*—The Secretary may identify up to six coverage examples that may be required in an SBC.

(B) *Benefits scenarios.*—For purposes of this paragraph (a)(2)(ii), a benefits scenario is a hypothetical situation, consisting of a sample treatment plan for a specified medical condition during a specific period of time, based on recognized clinical practice guidelines as defined by the National Guideline Clearinghouse, Agency for Healthcare Research and Quality. The Secretary will specify, in guidance, the assumptions, including the relevant items and services and reimbursement information, for each claim in the benefits scenario.

(C) *Illustration of benefit provided.*—For purposes of this paragraph (a)(2)(ii), to illustrate benefits provided under the plan or coverage for a particular benefits scenario, a plan or issuer simulates claims processing in accordance with guidance issued by the Secretary to generate an estimate of what an individual might expect to pay under the plan, policy, or benefit package. The illustration of benefits provided will take into account any cost sharing, excluded benefits, and other limitations on coverage, as specified by the Secretary in guidance.

(iii) *Coverage provided outside the United States.*—In lieu of summarizing coverage for items and services provided outside the United States, a plan or issuer may provide an Internet address (or similar contact information) for obtaining information about benefits and coverage provided outside the United States. In any case, the plan or issuer must provide an SBC in accordance with this section that accurately summarizes benefits and coverage available under the plan or coverage within the United States.

(3) *Appearance.*—(i) A group health plan and a health insurance issuer must provide an SBC in the form, and in accordance with the instructions for completing the SBC, that are specified by the Secretary in guidance. The SBC must be presented in a uniform format, use terminology understandable by the average plan enrollee, not exceed four double-sided pages in length, and not include print smaller than 12-point font.

(ii) A group health plan that utilizes two or more benefit packages (such as major medical coverage and a health flexible spending arrangement) may synthesize the information into a single SBC, or provide multiple SBCs.

(4) *Form.*—(i) An SBC provided by an issuer offering group health insurance coverage to a plan (or its sponsor), may be provided in paper form. Alternatively, the SBC may be provided electronically (such as by email or an Internet posting) if the following three conditions are satisfied—

(A) The format is readily accessible by the plan (or its sponsor);

(B) The SBC is provided in paper form free of charge upon request; and

(C) If the electronic form is an Internet posting, the issuer timely advises the plan (or its sponsor) in paper form or email that the documents are available on the Internet and provides the Internet address.

(ii) An SBC provided by a group health plan or health insurance issuer to a participant or beneficiary may be provided in paper form. Alternatively, the SBC may be provided electronically (such as by email or an Internet posting) if the requirements of this paragraph (a)(4)(ii) are met.

(A) With respect to participants and beneficiaries covered under the plan or coverage, the SBC may be provided electronically as described in this paragraph (a)(4)(ii)(A). However, in all cases, the plan or issuer must provide the SBC in paper form if paper form is requested.

(1) In accordance with the Department of Labor's disclosure regulations at 29 CFR 2520.104b-1;

(2) In connection with online enrollment or online renewal of coverage under the plan; or

(3) In response to an online request made by a participant or beneficiary for the SBC.

(B) With respect to participants and beneficiaries who are eligible but not enrolled for coverage, the SBC may be provided electronically if:

(1) The format is readily accessible;

(2) The SBC is provided in paper form free of charge upon request; and

(3) In a case in which the electronic form is an Internet posting, the plan or issuer timely notifies the individual in paper form (such as a postcard) or email that the documents are available on the Internet, provides the Internet address, and notifies the individual that the documents are available in paper form upon request.

(5) *Language.*—A group health plan or health insurance issuer must provide the SBC in a culturally and linguistically appropriate manner. For purposes of this paragraph (a)(5), a plan or issuer is considered to provide the SBC in a culturally and linguistically appropriate manner if the thresholds and standards of 29 CFR 2590.715-2719(e) are met as applied to the SBC.

(b) *Notice of modification.*—If a group health plan, or health insurance issuer offering group health insurance coverage, makes any material modification (as defined under section 102 of ERISA) in any of the terms of the plan or coverage that would affect the content of the SBC, that is not reflected in the most recently provided SBC, and that occurs other than in connection with a renewal or reissuance of coverage, the plan or issuer must provide notice of the modification to enrollees not later than 60 days prior to the date on which the modification will become effective. The notice of modification must be provided in a form that is consistent with the rules of paragraph (a)(4) of this section.

(c) *Uniform glossary.*—(1) *In general.*—A group health plan, and a health insurance issuer offering group health insurance coverage, must make available to participants and beneficiaries the uniform glossary described in paragraph (c)(2) of this section in accordance with the appearance and form and manner requirements of paragraphs (c)(3) and (4) of this section.

(2) *Health-coverage-related terms and medical terms.*—The uniform glossary must provide uniform definitions, specified by the Secretary in guidance, of the following health-coverage-related terms and medical terms:

(i) Allowed amount, appeal, balance billing, co-insurance, complications of pregnancy, co-payment, deductible, durable medical equipment, emergency medical condition, emergency medical transportation, emergency room care, emergency services, excluded services, grievance, habilitation services, health insurance, home health care, hospice services, hospitalization, hospital outpatient care, in-network co-insurance, in-network co-payment, medically necessary, network, non-preferred provider, out-of-network co-insurance, out-of-network co-payment, out-of-pocket limit, physician services, plan, preauthorization, preferred provider, premium, prescription drug coverage, prescription drugs, primary care physician, primary care provider, provider, reconstructive surgery, rehabilitation services, skilled nursing care, specialist, usual customary and reasonable (UCR), and urgent care; and

(ii) Such other terms as the Secretary determines are important to define so that individuals and employers may compare and understand the terms of coverage and medical benefits (including any exceptions to those benefits), as specified in guidance.

(3) *Appearance.*—A group health plan, and a health insurance issuer, must provide the uniform glossary with the appearance specified by the Secretary in guidance to ensure the uniform glossary is presented in a uniform format and uses terminology understandable by the average plan enrollee.

(4) *Form and manner.*—A plan or issuer must make the uniform glossary described in this paragraph (c) available upon request, in either paper or electronic form (as requested), within seven business days after receipt of the request.

(d) *Preemption.*—State laws that conflict with this section (including a state law that requires a health insurance issuer to provide an SBC that supplies less information than required under paragraph (a) of this section) are preempted.

(e) *Failure to provide.*—A group health plan that willfully fails to provide information required under this section to a participant or beneficiary is subject to a fine of not more than $1,000 for each such failure. A failure with respect to each participant or beneficiary constitutes a separate offense for purposes of this paragraph (e). The Department will enforce this section using a process and procedure consistent with section 4980D of the Code.

(f) *Applicability to Medicare Advantage benefits.*—The requirements of this section do not apply to a group health plan benefit package that provides Medicare Advantage benefits pursuant to or 42 U.S.C. Chapter 7, Subchapter XVIII, Part C.

(g) *Applicability date.*—(1) This section is applicable to group health plans and group health insurance issuers in accordance with this paragraph (g). (See 29 CFR 2590.715-1251(d), providing that this section applies to grandfathered health plans.)

(i) For disclosures with respect to participants and beneficiaries who enroll or re-enroll

through an open enrollment period (including re-enrollees and late enrollees), this section applies beginning on the first day of the first open enrollment period that begins on or after September 1, 2015; and

(ii) For disclosures with respect to participants and beneficiaries who enroll in coverage other than through an open enrollment period (including individuals who are newly eligible for coverage and special enrollees), this section applies beginning on the first day of the first plan year that begins on or after September 1, 2015.

(2) For disclosures with respect to plans, this section is applicable to health insurance issuers beginning September 1, 2015. [Reg. § 54.9815-2715.]

☐ [*T.D.* 9575, 2-9-2012. *Amended by T.D.* 9724, 6-12-2015.]

>>>→ *Caution: Reg. §54.9815-2719, below, as added by T.D. 9744, is applicable to group health plans and health insurance issuers beginning on the first day of the plan year (or, in the individual market, the first day of the first policy year) beginning on or after January 1, 2017.*

[Reg. § 54.9815-2719]

§ 54.9815-2719. Internal claims and appeals and external review processes.—(a) *Scope and definitions.*—(1) *Scope.*—This section sets forth requirements with respect to internal claims and appeals and external review processes for group health plans and health insurance issuers that are not grandfathered health plans under § 54.9815-1251. Paragraph (b) of this section provides requirements for internal claims and appeals processes. Paragraph (c) of this section sets forth rules governing the applicability of State external review processes. Paragraph (d) of this section sets forth a Federal external review process for plans and issuers not subject to an applicable State external review process. Paragraph (e) of this section prescribes requirements for ensuring that notices required to be provided under this section are provided in a culturally and linguistically appropriate manner. Paragraph (f) of this section describes the authority of the Secretary to deem certain external review processes in existence on March 23, 2010 as in compliance with paragraph (c) or (d) of this section.

(2) *Definitions.*—For purposes of this section, the following definitions apply

(i) *Adverse benefit determination.*—An *adverse benefit determination* means an adverse benefit determination as defined in 29 CFR 2560.503-1, as well as any rescission of coverage, as described in § 54.9815-2712(a)(2) (whether or not, in connection with the rescission, there is an adverse effect on any particular benefit at that time).

(ii) *Appeal (or internal appeal).*—An *appeal* or *internal appeal* means review by a plan or issuer of an adverse benefit determination, as required in paragraph (b) of this section.

(iii) *Claimant.*—Claimant means an individual who makes a claim under this section. For purposes of this section, references to claimant include a claimant's authorized representative.

(iv) *External review.*—External review means a review of an adverse benefit determination (including a final internal adverse benefit determination) conducted pursuant to an applicable State external review process described in paragraph (c) of this section or the Federal external review process of paragraph (d) of this section.

(v) *Final internal adverse benefit determination.*—A *final internal adverse benefit determination* means an adverse benefit determination that has been upheld by a plan or issuer at the completion of the internal appeals process applicable under paragraph (b) of this section (or an adverse benefit determination with respect to which the internal appeals process has been exhausted under the deemed exhaustion rules of paragraph (b)(2)(ii)(F) of this section).

(vi) *Final external review decision.*—A *final external review decision* means a determination by an independent review organization at the conclusion of an external review.

(vii) *Independent review organization (or IRO).*—An *independent review organization (or IRO)* means an entity that conducts independent external reviews of adverse benefit determinations and final internal adverse benefit determinations pursuant to paragraph (c) or (d) of this section.

(viii) *NAIC Uniform Model Act.*—The *NAIC Uniform Model Act* means the Uniform Health Carrier External Review Model Act promulgated by the National Association of Insurance Commissioners in place on July 23, 2010.

(b) *Internal claims and appeals process.*—(1) *In general.*—A group health plan and a health insur-

⟫→ *Caution: Reg. §54.9815-2719, below, as added by T.D. 9744, is applicable to group health plans and health insurance issuers beginning on the first day of the plan year (or, in the individual market, the first day of the first policy year) beginning on or after January 1, 2017.*

ance issuer offering group health insurance coverage must implement an effective internal claims and appeals process, as described in this paragraph (b).

(2) *Requirements for group health plans and group health insurance issuers.*—A group health plan and a health insurance issuer offering group health insurance coverage must comply with all the requirements of this paragraph (b)(2). In the case of health insurance coverage offered in connection with a group health plan, if either the plan or the issuer complies with the internal claims and appeals process of this paragraph (b)(2), then the obligation to comply with this paragraph (b)(2) is satisfied for both the plan and the issuer with respect to the health insurance coverage.

(i) *Minimum internal claims and appeals standards.*—A group health plan and a health insurance issuer offering group health insurance coverage must comply with all the requirements applicable to group health plans under 29 CFR 2560.503–1, except to the extent those requirements are modified by paragraph (b)(2)(ii) of this section. Accordingly, under this paragraph (b), with respect to health insurance coverage offered in connection with a group health plan, the group health insurance issuer is subject to the requirements in 29 CFR 2560.503-1 to the same extent as the group health plan.

(ii) *Additional standards.*—In addition to the requirements in paragraph (b)(2)(i) of this section, the internal claims and appeals processes of a group health plan and a health insurance issuer offering group health insurance coverage must meet the requirements of this paragraph (b)(2)(ii).

(A) *Clarification of meaning of adverse benefit determination.*—For purposes of this paragraph (b)(2), an "adverse benefit determination" includes an adverse benefit determination as defined in paragraph (a)(2)(i) of this section. Accordingly, in complying with 29 CFR 2560.503–1, as well as the other provisions of this paragraph (b)(2), a plan or issuer must treat a rescission of coverage (whether or not the rescission has an adverse effect on any particular benefit at that time) as an adverse benefit determination. (Rescissions of coverage are subject to the requirements of § 54.9815-2712.)

(B) *Expedited notification of benefit determinations involving urgent care.*—The requirements of 29 CFR 2560.503-1(f)(2)(i) (which generally provide, among other things, in the case of urgent care claims for notification of the plan's benefit determination (whether adverse or not) as soon as possible, taking into account the medical exigencies, but not later than 72 hours after the receipt of the claim) continue to apply to the plan and issuer. For purposes of this para-

graph (b)(2)(ii)(B), a claim involving urgent care has the meaning given in 29 CFR 2560.503-1(m)(1), as determined by the attending provider, and the plan or issuer shall defer to such determination of the attending provider.

(C) *Full and fair review.*—A plan and issuer must allow a claimant to review the claim file and to present evidence and testimony as part of the internal claims and appeals process. Specifically, in addition to complying with the requirements of 29 CFR 2560.503-1(h)(2) —

(1) The plan or issuer must provide the claimant, free of charge, with any new or additional evidence considered, relied upon, or generated by the plan or issuer (or at the direction of the plan or issuer) in connection with the claim; such evidence must be provided as soon as possible and sufficiently in advance of the date on which the notice of final internal adverse benefit determination is required to be provided under 29 CFR 2560.503-1(i) to give the claimant a reasonable opportunity to respond prior to that date; and

(2) Before the plan or issuer can issue a final internal adverse benefit determination based on a new or additional rationale, the claimant must be provided, free of charge, with the rationale; the rationale must be provided as soon as possible and sufficiently in advance of the date on which the notice of final internal adverse benefit determination is required to be provided under 29 CFR 2560.503-1(i) to give the claimant a reasonable opportunity to respond prior to that date. Notwithstanding the rules of 29 CFR 2560.503-1(i), if the new or additional evidence is received so late that it would be impossible to provide it to the claimant in time for the claimant to have a reasonable opportunity to respond, the period for providing a notice of final internal adverse benefit determination is tolled until such time as the claimant has a reasonable opportunity to respond. After the claimant responds, or has a reasonable opportunity to respond but fails to do so, the plan administrator shall notify the claimant of the plan's benefit determination as soon as a plan acting in a reasonable and prompt fashion can provide the notice, taking into account the medical exigencies.

(D) *Avoiding conflicts of interest.*—In addition to the requirements of 29 CFR 2560.503-1(b) and (h) regarding full and fair review, the plan and issuer must ensure that all claims and appeals are adjudicated in a manner designed to ensure the independence and impartiality of the persons involved in making the decision. Accordingly, decisions regarding hiring, compensation, termination, promotion, or other similar matters with respect to any individual (such as a claims adjudicator or medical expert) must not be made based upon the likelihood that the individual will support the denial of benefits.

Reg. §54.9815-2719(b)(2)(ii)(D)

>>→ *Caution: Reg. §54.9815-2719, below, as added by T.D. 9744, is applicable to group health plans and health insurance issuers beginning on the first day of the plan year (or, in the individual market, the first day of the first policy year) beginning on or after January 1, 2017.*

(E) *Notice.*—A plan and issuer must provide notice to individuals, in a culturally and linguistically appropriate manner (as described in paragraph (e) of this section) that complies with the requirements of 29 CFR 2560.503-1(g) and (j). The plan and issuer must also comply with the additional requirements of this paragraph (b)(2)(ii)(E).

(1) The plan and issuer must ensure that any notice of adverse benefit determination or final internal adverse benefit determination includes information sufficient to identify the claim involved (including the date of service, the health care provider, the claim amount (if applicable), and a statement describing the availability, upon request, of the diagnosis code and its corresponding meaning, and the treatment code and its corresponding meaning).

(2) The plan and issuer must provide to participants and beneficiaries, as soon as practicable, upon request, the diagnosis code and its corresponding meaning, and the treatment code and its corresponding meaning, associated with any adverse benefit determination or final internal adverse benefit determination. The plan or issuer must not consider a request for such diagnosis and treatment information, in itself, to be a request for an internal appeal under this paragraph (b) or an external review under paragraphs (c) and (d) of this section.

(3) The plan and issuer must ensure that the reason or reasons for the adverse benefit determination or final internal adverse benefit determination includes the denial code and its corresponding meaning, as well as a description of the plan's or issuer's standard, if any, that was used in denying the claim. In the case of a notice of final internal adverse benefit determination, this description must include a discussion of the decision.

(4) The plan and issuer must provide a description of available internal appeals and external review processes, including information regarding how to initiate an appeal.

(5) The plan and issuer must disclose the availability of, and contact information for, any applicable office of health insurance consumer assistance or ombudsman established under PHS Act section 2793 to assist individuals with the internal claims and appeals and external review processes.

(F) Deemed exhaustion of internal claims and appeals processes.—*(1)* In the case of a plan or issuer that fails to strictly adhere to all the requirements of this paragraph (b)(2) with respect to a claim, the claimant is deemed to have exhausted the internal claims and appeals process of this paragraph (b), except as provided in paragraph (b)(2)(ii)(F)(2) of this section. Accordingly the claimant may initiate an external review under paragraph (c) or (d) of this section, as applicable. The claimant is also entitled to pursue any available remedies under section 502(a)

of ERISA or under State law, as applicable, on the basis that the plan or issuer has failed to provide a reasonable internal claims and appeals process that would yield a decision on the merits of the claim. If a claimant chooses to pursue remedies under section 502(a) of ERISA under such circumstances, the claim or appeal is deemed denied on review without the exercise of discretion by an appropriate fiduciary.

(2) Notwithstanding paragraph (b)(2)(ii)(F)(1) of this section, the internal claims and appeals process of this paragraph (b) will not be deemed exhausted based on *de minimis* violations that do not cause, and are not likely to cause, prejudice or harm to the claimant so long as the plan or issuer demonstrates that the violation was for good cause or due to matters beyond the control of the plan or issuer and that the violation occurred in the context of an ongoing, good faith exchange of information between the plan and the claimant. This exception is not available if the violation is part of a pattern or practice of violations by the plan or issuer. The claimant may request a written explanation of the violation from the plan or issuer, and the plan or issuer must provide such explanation within 10 days, including a specific description of its bases, if any, for asserting that the violation should not cause the internal claims and appeals process of this paragraph (b) to be deemed exhausted. If an external reviewer or a court rejects the claimant's request for immediate review under paragraph (b)(2)(ii)(F)(1) of this section on the basis that the plan met the standards for the exception under this paragraph (b)(2)(ii)(F)(2), the claimant has the right to resubmit and pursue the internal appeal of the claim. In such a case, within a reasonable time after the external reviewer or court rejects the claim for immediate review (not to exceed 10 days), the plan shall provide the claimant with notice of the opportunity to resubmit and pursue the internal appeal of the claim. Time periods for re-filing the claim shall begin to run upon claimant's receipt of such notice.

(iii) Requirement to provide continued coverage pending the outcome of an appeal.—A plan and issuer subject to the requirements of this paragraph (b)(2) are required to provide continued coverage pending the outcome of an appeal. For this purpose, the plan and issuer must comply with the requirements of 29 CFR 2560.503-1(f)(2)(ii), which generally provides that benefits for an ongoing course of treatment cannot be reduced or terminated without providing advance notice and an opportunity for advance review.

(c) *State standards for external review.*—(1) *In general.*—(i) If a State external review process that applies to and is binding on a health insurance issuer offering group health insurance coverage includes at a minimum the consumer

>>>→ *Caution: Reg. §54.9815-2719, below, as added by T.D. 9744, is applicable to group health plans and health insurance issuers beginning on the first day of the plan year (or, in the individual market, the first day of the first policy year) beginning on or after January 1, 2017.*

protections in the NAIC Uniform Model Act, then the issuer must comply with the applicable State external review process and is not required to comply with the Federal external review process of paragraph (d) of this section. In such a case, to the extent that benefits under a group health plan are provided through health insurance coverage, the group health plan is not required to comply with either this paragraph (c) or the Federal external review process of paragraph (d) of this section.

(ii) To the extent that a group health plan provides benefits other than through health insurance coverage (that is, the plan is self-insured) and is subject to a State external review process that applies to and is binding on the plan (for example, is not preempted by ERISA) and the State external review process includes at a minimum the consumer protections in the NAIC Uniform Model Act, then the plan must comply with the applicable State external review process and is not required to comply with the Federal external review process of paragraph (d) of this section. Where a self-insured plan is not subject to an applicable State external review process, but the State has chosen to expand access to its process for plans that are not subject to the applicable State laws, the plan may choose to comply with either the applicable State external review process or the Federal external review process of paragraph (d) of this section.

(iii) If a plan or issuer is not required under paragraph (c)(1)(i) or (c)(1)(ii) of this section to comply with the requirements of this paragraph (c), then the plan or issuer must comply with the Federal external review process of paragraph (d) of this section, except to the extent, in the case of a plan, the plan is not required under paragraph (c)(1)(i) of this section to comply with paragraph (d) of this section.

(2) *Minimum standards for State external review processes.*—An applicable State external review process must meet all the minimum consumer protections in this paragraph (c)(2). The Department of Health and Human Services will determine whether State external review processes meet these requirements.

(i) The State process must provide for the external review of adverse benefit determinations (including final internal adverse benefit determinations) by issuers (or, if applicable, plans) that are based on the issuer's (or plan's) requirements for medical necessity, appropriateness, health care setting, level of care, or effectiveness of a covered benefit.

(ii) The State process must require issuers (or, if applicable, plans) to provide effective written notice to claimants of their rights in connection with an external review for an adverse benefit determination.

(iii) To the extent the State process requires exhaustion of an internal claims and appeals process, exhaustion must be unnecessary

where the issuer (or, if applicable, the plan) has waived the requirement; the issuer (or the plan) is considered to have exhausted the internal claims and appeals process under applicable law (including by failing to comply with any of the requirements for the internal appeal process, as outlined in paragraph (b)(2) of this section); or the claimant has applied for expedited external review at the same time as applying for an expedited internal appeal.

(iv) The State process provides that the issuer (or, if applicable, the plan) against which a request for external review is filed must pay the cost of the IRO for conducting the external review. Notwithstanding this requirement, a State external review process that expressly authorizes, as of November 18, 2015, a nominal filing fee may continue to permit such fees. For this purpose, to be considered nominal, a filing fee must not exceed $25; it must be refunded to the claimant if the adverse benefit determination (or final internal adverse benefit determination) is reversed through external review; it must be waived if payment of the fee would impose an undue financial hardship; and the annual limit on filing fees for any claimant within a single plan year must not exceed $75.

(v) The State process may not impose a restriction on the minimum dollar amount of a claim for it to be eligible for external review. Thus, the process may not impose, for example, a $500 minimum claims threshold.

(vi) The State process must allow at least four months after the receipt of a notice of an adverse benefit determination or final internal adverse benefit determination for a request for an external review to be filed.

(vii) The State process must provide that IROs will be assigned on a random basis or another method of assignment that assures the independence and impartiality of the assignment process (such as rotational assignment) by a State or independent entity, and in no event selected by the issuer, plan, or the individual.

(viii) The State process must provide for maintenance of a list of approved IROs qualified to conduct the external review based on the nature of the health care service that is the subject of the review. The State process must provide for approval only of IROs that are accredited by a nationally recognized private accrediting organization.

(ix) The State process must provide that any approved IRO has no conflicts of interest that will influence its independence. Thus, the IRO may not own or control, or be owned or controlled by a health insurance issuer, a group health plan, the sponsor of a group health plan, a trade association of plans or issuers, or a trade association of health care providers. The State process must further provide that the IRO and the clinical reviewer assigned to conduct an external review may not have a material profes-

Reg. §54.9815-2719(c)(2)(ix)

»»→ *Caution: Reg. §54.9815-2719, below, as added by T.D. 9744, is applicable to group health plans and health insurance issuers beginning on the first day of the plan year (or, in the individual market, the first day of the first policy year) beginning on or after January 1, 2017.*

sional, familial, or financial conflict of interest with the issuer or plan that is the subject of the external review; the claimant (and any related parties to the claimant) whose treatment is the subject of the external review; any officer, director, or management employee of the issuer; the plan administrator, plan fiduciaries, or plan employees; the health care provider, the health care provider's group, or practice association recommending the treatment that is subject to the external review; the facility at which the recommended treatment would be provided; or the developer or manufacturer of the principal drug, device, procedure, or other therapy being recommended.

(x) The State process allows the claimant at least five business days to submit to the IRO in writing additional information that the IRO must consider when conducting the external review, and it requires that the claimant is notified of the right to do so. The process must also require that any additional information submitted by the claimant to the IRO must be forwarded to the issuer (or, if applicable, the plan) within one business day of receipt by the IRO.

(xi) The State process must provide that the decision is binding on the plan or issuer, as well as the claimant except to the extent the other remedies are available under State or Federal law, and except that the requirement that the decision be binding shall not preclude the plan or issuer from making payment on the claim or otherwise providing benefits at any time, including after a final external review decision that denies the claim or otherwise fails to require such payment or benefits. For this purpose, the plan or issuer must provide benefits (including by making payment on the claim) pursuant to the final external review decision without delay, regardless of whether the plan or issuer intends to seek judicial review of the external review decision and unless or until there is a judicial decision otherwise.

(xii) The State process must require, for standard external review, that the IRO provide written notice to the issuer (or, if applicable, the plan) and the claimant of its decision to uphold or reverse the adverse benefit determination (or final internal adverse benefit determination) within no more than 45 days after the receipt of the request for external review by the IRO.

(xiii) The State process must provide for an expedited external review if the adverse benefit determination (or final internal adverse benefit determination) concerns an admission, availability of care, continued stay, or health care service for which the claimant received emergency services, but has not been discharged from a facility; or involves a medical condition for which the standard external review time frame would seriously jeopardize the life or health of the claimant or jeopardize the claimant's ability to regain maximum function. As expeditiously

as possible but within no more than 72 hours after the receipt of the request for expedited external review by the IRO, the IRO must make its decision to uphold or reverse the adverse benefit determination (or final internal adverse benefit determination) and notify the claimant and the issuer (or, if applicable, the plan) of the determination. If the notice is not in writing, the IRO must provide written confirmation of the decision within 48 hours after the date of the notice of the decision.

(xiv) The State process must require that issuers (or, if applicable, plans) include a description of the external review process in or attached to the summary plan description, policy, certificate, membership booklet, outline of coverage, or other evidence of coverage it provides to participants, beneficiaries, or enrollees, substantially similar to what is set forth in section 17 of the NAIC Uniform Model Act.

(xv) The State process must require that IROs maintain written records and make them available upon request to the State, substantially similar to what is set forth in section 15 of the NAIC Uniform Model Act.

(xvi) The State process follows procedures for external review of adverse benefit determinations (or final internal adverse benefit determinations) involving experimental or investigational treatment, substantially similar to what is set forth in section 10 of the NAIC Uniform Model Act.

(3) *Transition period for external review processes.*—(i) Through December 31, 2017, an applicable State external review process applicable to a health insurance issuer or group health plan is considered to meet the requirements of PHS Act section 2719(b). Accordingly, through December 31, 2017, an applicable State external review process will be considered binding on the issuer or plan (in lieu of the requirements of the Federal external review process). If there is no applicable State external review process, the issuer or plan is required to comply with the requirements of the Federal external review process in paragraph (d) of this section.

(ii) An applicable State external review process must apply for final internal adverse benefit determinations (or, in the case of simultaneous internal appeal and external review, adverse benefit determinations) provided on or after January 1, 2018. The Federal external review process will apply to such internal adverse benefit determinations unless the Department of Health and Human Services determines that a State law meets all the minimum standards of paragraph (c)(2) of this section. Through December 31, 2017, a State external review process applicable to a health insurance issuer or group health plan may be considered to meet the minimum standards of paragraph (c)(2) of this section, if it meets the temporary standards

⋙→ *Caution: Reg. §54.9815-2719, below, as added by T.D. 9744, is applicable to group health plans and health insurance issuers beginning on the first day of the plan year (or, in the individual market, the first day of the first policy year) beginning on or after January 1, 2017.*

established by the Secretary in guidance for a process similar to the NAIC Uniform Model Act.

(d) *Federal external review process.*—A plan or issuer not subject to an applicable State external review process under paragraph (c) of this section must provide an effective Federal external review process in accordance with this paragraph (d) (except to the extent, in the case of a plan, the plan is described in paragraph (c)(1)(i) of this section as not having to comply with this paragraph (d)). In the case of health insurance coverage offered in connection with a group health plan, if either the plan or the issuer complies with the Federal external review process of this paragraph (d), then the obligation to comply with this paragraph (d) is satisfied for both the plan and the issuer with respect to the health insurance coverage. A Multi State Plan or MSP, as defined by 45 CFR 800.20, must provide an effective Federal external review process in accordance with this paragraph (d). In such circumstances, the requirement to provide external review under this paragraph (d) is satisfied when a Multi State Plan or MSP complies with standards established by the Office of Personnel Management.

(1) *Scope.*—(i) *In general.*—The Federal external review process established pursuant to this paragraph (d) applies to the following:

(A) An adverse benefit determination (including a final internal adverse benefit determination) by a plan or issuer that involves medical judgment (including, but not limited to, those based on the plan's or issuer's requirements for medical necessity, appropriateness, health care setting, level of care, or effectiveness of a covered benefit; its determination that a treatment is experimental or investigational; its determination whether a participant or beneficiary is entitled to a reasonable alternative standard for a reward under a wellness program; or its determination whether a plan or issuer is complying with the nonquantitative treatment limitation provisions of Code section 9812 and § 54.9812, which generally require, among other things, parity in the application of medical management techniques), as determined by the external reviewer. (A denial, reduction, termination, or a failure to provide payment for a benefit based on a determination that a participant or beneficiary fails to meet the requirements for eligibility under the terms of a group health plan or health insurance coverage is not eligible for the Federal external review process under this paragraph (d)); and

(B) A rescission of coverage (whether or not the rescission has any effect on any particular benefit at that time).

(ii) *Examples.*—The rules of paragraph (d)(1)(i) of this section are illustrated by the following examples:

Example 1. (i) *Facts.* A group health plan provides coverage for 30 physical therapy visits generally. After the 30th visit, coverage is provided only if the service is preauthorized pursuant to an approved treatment plan that takes into account medical necessity using the plan's definition of the term. Individual *A* seeks coverage for a 31st physical therapy visit. *A*'s health care provider submits a treatment plan for approval, but it is not approved by the plan, so coverage for the 31st visit is not preauthorized. With respect to the 31st visit, *A* receives a notice of final internal adverse benefit determination stating that the maximum visit limit is exceeded.

(ii) *Conclusion.* In this *Example 1*, the plan's denial of benefits is based on medical necessity and involves medical judgment. Accordingly, the claim is eligible for external review under paragraph (d)(1)(i) of this section. Moreover, the plan's notification of final internal adverse benefit determination is inadequate under paragraphs (b)(2)(i) and (b)(2)(ii)(E)(3) of this section because it fails to make clear that the plan will pay for more than 30 visits if the service is preauthorized pursuant to an approved treatment plan that takes into account medical necessity using the plan's definition of the term. Accordingly, the notice of final internal adverse benefit determination should refer to the plan provision governing the 31st visit and should describe the plan's standard for medical necessity, as well as how the treatment fails to meet the plan's standard.

Example 2. (i) *Facts.* A group health plan does not provide coverage for services provided out of network, unless the service cannot effectively be provided in network. Individual *B* seeks coverage for a specialized medical procedure from an out-of-network provider because *B* believes that the procedure cannot be effectively provided in network. *B* receives a notice of final internal adverse benefit determination stating that the claim is denied because the provider is out-of-network.

(ii) *Conclusion.* In this *Example 2*, the plan's denial of benefits is based on whether a service can effectively be provided in network and, therefore, involves medical judgment. Accordingly, the claim is eligible for external review under paragraph (d)(1)(i) of this section. Moreover, the plan's notice of final internal adverse benefit determination is inadequate under paragraphs (b)(2)(i) and (b)(2)(ii)(E)(3) of this section because the plan does provide benefits for services on an out-of-network basis if the services cannot effectively be provided in network. Accordingly, the notice of final internal adverse benefit determination is required to refer to the exception to the out-of-network exclusion and should describe the plan's standards for determining effectiveness of services, as well as how services available to the claimant within the

>>> *Caution: Reg. §54.9815-2719, below, as added by T.D. 9744, is applicable to group health plans and health insurance issuers beginning on the first day of the plan year (or, in the individual market, the first day of the first policy year) beginning on or after January 1, 2017.*

plan's network meet the plan's standard for effectiveness of services.

(2) *External review process standards.*—The Federal external review process established pursuant to this paragraph (d) is considered similar to the process set forth in the NAIC Uniform Model Act and, therefore satisfies the requirements of paragraph (d)(2), if such process provides the following.

(i) *Request for external review.*—A group health plan or health insurance issuer must allow a claimant to file a request for an external review with the plan or issuer if the request is filed within four months after the date of receipt of a notice of an adverse benefit determination or final internal adverse benefit determination. If there is no corresponding date four months after the date of receipt of such a notice, then the request must be filed by the first day of the fifth month following the receipt of the notice. For example, if the date of receipt of the notice is October 30, because there is no February 30, the request must be filed by March 1. If the last filing date would fall on a Saturday, Sunday, or Federal holiday, the last filing date is extended to the next day that is not a Saturday, Sunday, or Federal holiday.

(ii) *Preliminary review.*—(A) *In general.*— Within five business days following the date of receipt of the external review request, the group health plan or health insurance issuer must complete a preliminary review of the request to determine whether:

(1) The claimant is or was covered under the plan or coverage at the time the health care item or service was requested or, in the case of a retrospective review, was covered under the plan or coverage at the time the health care item or service was provided;

(2) The adverse benefit determination or the final adverse benefit determination does not relate to the claimant's failure to meet the requirements for eligibility under the terms of the group health plan or health insurance coverage (e.g., worker classification or similar determination);

(3) The claimant has exhausted the plan's or issuer's internal appeal process unless the claimant is not required to exhaust the internal appeals process under paragraph (b)(1) of this section; and

(4) The claimant has provided all the information and forms required to process an external review.

(B) Within one business day after completion of the preliminary review, the plan or issuer must issue a notification in writing to the claimant. If the request is complete but not eligible for external review, such notification must include the reasons for its ineligibility and current contact information, including the phone number, for the Employee Benefits Security Administration. If the request is not complete, such notification must describe the information or materials needed to make the request complete, and the plan or issuer must allow a claimant to perfect the request for external review within the four-month filing period or within the 48 hour period following the receipt of the notification, whichever is later.

(iii) *Referral to Independent Review Organization.*—(A) *In general.*—The group health plan or health insurance issuer must assign an IRO that is accredited by URAC or by similar nationally-recognized accrediting organization to conduct the external review. The IRO referral process must provide for the following:

(1) The plan or issuer must ensure that the IRO process is not biased and ensures independence;

(2) The plan or issuer must contract with at least three (3) IROs for assignments under the plan or coverage and rotate claims assignments among them (or incorporate other independent, unbiased methods for selection of IROs, such as random selection); and

(3) The IRO may not be eligible for any financial incentives based on the likelihood that the IRO will support the denial of benefits.

(4) The IRO process may not impose any costs, including filing fees, on the claimant requesting the external review.

(B) *IRO contracts.*—A group health plan or health insurance issuer must include the following standards in the contract between the plan or issuer and the IRO:

(1) The assigned IRO will utilize legal experts where appropriate to make coverage determinations under the plan or coverage.

(2) The assigned IRO will timely notify a claimant in writing whether the request is eligible for external review. This notice will include a statement that the claimant may submit in writing to the assigned IRO, within ten business days following the date of receipt of the notice, additional information. This additional information must be considered by the IRO when conducting the external review. The IRO is not required to, but may, accept and consider additional information submitted after ten business days.

(3) Within five business days after the date of assignment of the IRO, the plan or issuer must provide to the assigned IRO the documents and any information considered in making the adverse benefit determination or final internal adverse benefit determination. Failure by the plan or issuer to timely provide the documents and information must not delay the conduct of the external review. If the plan or issuer fails to timely provide the documents and information, the assigned IRO may terminate the external review and make a decision to reverse

>>>→ *Caution: Reg. §54.9815-2719, below, as added by T.D. 9744, is applicable to group health plans and health insurance issuers beginning on the first day of the plan year (or, in the individual market, the first day of the first policy year) beginning on or after January 1, 2017.*

the adverse benefit determination or final internal adverse benefit determination. Within one business day after making the decision, the IRO must notify the claimant and the plan.

(4) Upon receipt of any information submitted by the claimant, the assigned IRO must within one business day forward the information to the plan or issuer. Upon receipt of any such information, the plan or issuer may reconsider its adverse benefit determination or final internal adverse benefit determination that is the subject of the external review. Reconsideration by the plan or issuer must not delay the external review. The external review may be terminated as a result of the reconsideration only if the plan decides, upon completion of its reconsideration, to reverse its adverse benefit determination or final internal adverse benefit determination and provide coverage or payment. Within one business day after making such a decision, the plan must provide written notice of its decision to the claimant and the assigned IRO. The assigned IRO must terminate the external review upon receipt of the notice from the plan or issuer.

(5) The IRO will review all of the information and documents timely received. In reaching a decision, the assigned IRO will review the claim de novo and not be bound by any decisions or conclusions reached during the plan's or issuer's internal claims and appeals process applicable under paragraph (b). In addition to the documents and information provided, the assigned IRO, to the extent the information or documents are available and the IRO considers them appropriate, will consider the following in reaching a decision:

(i) The claimant's medical records;

(ii) The attending health care professional's recommendation;

(iii) Reports from appropriate health care professionals and other documents submitted by the plan or issuer, claimant, or the claimant's treating provider;

(iv) The terms of the claimant's plan or coverage to ensure that the IRO's decision is not contrary to the terms of the plan or coverage, unless the terms are inconsistent with applicable law;

(v) Appropriate practice guidelines, which must include applicable evidence-based standards and may include any other practice guidelines developed by the Federal government, national or professional medical societies, boards, and associations;

(vi) Any applicable clinical review criteria developed and used by the plan or issuer, unless the criteria are inconsistent with the terms of the plan or coverage or with applicable law; and

(vii) To the extent the final IRO decision maker is different from the IRO's clinical reviewer, the opinion of such clinical reviewer, after considering information described in this notice, to the extent the information or documents are available and the clinical reviewer or reviewers consider such information or documents appropriate.

(6) The assigned IRO must provide written notice of the final external review decision within 45 days after the IRO receives the request for the external review. The IRO must deliver the notice of the final external review decision to the claimant and the plan or issuer.

(7) The assigned IRO's written notice of the final external review decision must contain the following:

(i) A general description of the reason for the request for external review, including information sufficient to identify the claim (including the date or dates of service, the health care provider, the claim amount (if applicable), and a statement describing the availability, upon request, of the diagnosis code and its corresponding meaning, the treatment code and its corresponding meaning, and the reason for the plan's or issuer's denial);

(ii) The date the IRO received the assignment to conduct the external review and the date of the IRO decision;

(iii) References to the evidence or documentation, including the specific coverage provisions and evidence-based standards, considered in reaching its decision;

(iv) A discussion of the principal reason or reasons for its decision, including the rationale for its decision and any evidence-based standards that were relied on in making its decision;

(v) A statement that the IRO's determination is binding except to the extent that other remedies may be available under State or Federal law to either the group health plan or health insurance issuer or to the claimant, or to the extent the health plan or health insurance issuer voluntarily makes payment on the claim or otherwise provides benefits at any time, including after a final external review decision that denies the claim or otherwise fails to require such payment or benefits;

(vi) A statement that judicial review may be available to the claimant; and

(vii) Current contact information, including phone number, for any applicable office of health insurance consumer assistance or ombudsman established under PHS Act section 2793.

(viii) After a final external review decision, the IRO must maintain records of all claims and notices associated with the external review process for six years. An IRO must make such records available for examination by the claimant, plan, issuer, or State or Federal oversight agency upon request, except where such disclosure would violate State or Federal privacy laws.

See p. 20,601 for regulations not amended to reflect law changes

Caution: Reg. §54.9815-2719, below, as added by T.D. 9744, is applicable to group health plans and health insurance issuers beginning on the first day of the plan year (or, in the individual market, the first day of the first policy year) beginning on or after January 1, 2017.

(iv) *Reversal of plan's or issuer's decision.*—Upon receipt of a notice of a final external review decision reversing the adverse benefit determination or final adverse benefit determination, the plan or issuer immediately must provide coverage or payment (including immediately authorizing care or immediately paying benefits) for the claim.

(3) *Expedited external review.*—A group health plan or health insurance issuer must comply with the following standards with respect to an expedited external review:

(i) *Request for external review.*—A group health plan or health insurance issuer must allow a claimant to make a request for an expedited external review with the plan or issuer at the time the claimant receives:

(A) An adverse benefit determination if the adverse benefit determination involves a medical condition of the claimant for which the timeframe for completion of an expedited internal appeal under paragraph (b) of this section would seriously jeopardize the life or health of the claimant or would jeopardize the claimant's ability to regain maximum function and the claimant has filed a request for an expedited internal appeal; or

(B) A final internal adverse benefit determination, if the claimant has a medical condition where the timeframe for completion of a standard external review would seriously jeopardize the life or health of the claimant or would jeopardize the claimant's ability to regain maximum function, or if the final internal adverse benefit determination concerns an admission, availability of care, continued stay, or health care item or service for which the claimant received emergency services, but has not been discharged from the facility.

(ii) *Preliminary review.*—Immediately upon receipt of the request for expedited external review, the plan or issuer must determine whether the request meets the reviewability requirements set forth in paragraph (d)(2)(ii) of this section for standard external review. The plan or issuer must immediately send a notice that meets the requirements set forth in paragraph (d)(2)(ii)(B) for standard review to the claimant of its eligibility determination.

(iii) *Referral to independent review organization.*—(A) Upon a determination that a request is eligible for expedited external review following the preliminary review, the plan or issuer will assign an IRO pursuant to the requirements set forth in paragraph (d)(2)(iii) of this section for standard review. The plan or issuer must provide or transmit all necessary documents and information considered in making the adverse benefit determination or final internal adverse benefit determination to the assigned IRO electronically or by telephone or facsimile or any other available expeditious method.

(B) The assigned IRO, to the extent the information or documents are available and the IRO considers them appropriate, must consider the information or documents described above under the procedures for standard review. In reaching a decision, the assigned IRO must review the claim de novo and is not bound by any decisions or conclusions reached during the plan's or issuer's internal claims and appeals process.

(iv) *Notice of final external review decision.*—The plan's or issuer's contract with the assigned IRO must require the IRO to provide notice of the final external review decision, in accordance with the requirements set forth in paragraph (d)(2)(iii)(B) of this section, as expeditiously as the claimant's medical condition or circumstances require, but in no event more than 72 hours after the IRO receives the request for an expedited external review. If the notice is not in writing, within 48 hours after the date of providing that notice, the assigned IRO must provide written confirmation of the decision to the claimant and the plan or issuer.

(4) *Alternative, Federally-administered external review process.*—Insured coverage not subject to an applicable State external review process under paragraph (c) of this section may elect to use either the Federal external review process, as set forth under paragraph (d) of this section or the Federally-administered external review process, as set forth by HHS in guidance. In such circumstances, the requirement to provide external review under this paragraph (d) is satisfied.

(e) *Form and manner of notice.*—(1) *In general.*—For purposes of this section, a group health plan and a health insurance issuer offering group health insurance coverage are considered to provide relevant notices in a culturally and linguistically appropriate manner if the plan or issuer meets all the requirements of paragraph (e)(2) of this section with respect to the applicable non-English languages described in paragraph (e)(3) of this section.

(2) *Requirements.*—(i) The plan or issuer must provide oral language services (such as a telephone customer assistance hotline) that includes answering questions in any applicable non-English language and providing assistance with filing claims and appeals (including external review) in any applicable non-English language;

(ii) The plan or issuer must provide, upon request, a notice in any applicable non-English language; and

(iii) The plan or issuer must include in the English versions of all notices, a statement prominently displayed in any applicable non-English language clearly indicating how to access the language services provided by the plan or issuer.

»»→ *Caution: Reg. §54.9815-2719, below, as added by T.D. 9744, is applicable to group health plans and health insurance issuers beginning on the first day of the plan year (or, in the individual market, the first day of the first policy year) beginning on or after January 1, 2017.*

(3) *Applicable non-English language.*—With respect to an address in any United States county to which a notice is sent, a non-English language is an applicable non-English language if ten percent or more of the population residing in the county is literate only in the same non-English language, as determined in guidance published by the Secretary.

(f) *Secretarial authority.*—The Secretary may determine that the external review process of a group health plan or health insurance issuer, in operation as of March 23, 2010, is considered in compliance with the applicable process established under paragraph (c) or (d) of this section

if it substantially meets the requirements of paragraph (c) or (d) of this section, as applicable.

(g) *Applicability date.*—The provisions of this section are applicable to group health plans and health insurance issuers for plan years beginning on or after January 1, 2017. Until the applicability date for this regulation, plans and issuers are required to continue to comply with the interim final regulations promulgated by the Department of Labor at 29 CFR part 2590, contained in the 29 CFR, parts 1927 to end, edition revised as of July 1, 2015. [Reg. § 54.9815-2719.]

☐ [*T.D.* 9744, 11-13-2015.]

»»→ *Caution: Temporary Reg. §54.9815-2719T, below, was removed by T.D. 9744 and is inapplicable under Code Sec. 7805(e)(2). However, until final Reg. §54.9815-2719 is applicable on the first day of the plan or policy year beginning after January 1, 2017, taxpayers may comply with the corresponding interim final regulation at 29 CFR part 2590 that is substantially similar to the temporary reg below.*

[Reg. § 54.9815-2719T]

§ 54.9815-2719T. Internal claims and appeals and external review processes (temporary).— (a) *Scope and definitions.*—(1) *Scope.*—This section sets forth requirements with respect to internal claims and appeals and external review processes for group health plans and health insurance issuers that are not grandfathered health plans under § 54.9815-1251T. Paragraph (b) of this section provides requirements for internal claims and appeals processes. Paragraph (c) of this section sets forth rules governing the applicability of State external review processes. Paragraph (d) of this section sets forth a Federal external review process for plans and issuers not subject to an applicable State external review process. Paragraph (e) of this section prescribes requirements for ensuring that notices required to be provided under this section are provided in a culturally and linguistically appropriate manner. Paragraph (f) of this section describes the authority of the Secretary to deem certain external review processes in existence on March 23, 2010 as in compliance with paragraph (c) or (d) of this section. Paragraph (g) of this section sets forth the applicability date for this section.

(2) *Definitions.*—For purposes of this section, the following definitions apply -

(i) *Adverse benefit determination.*—An *adverse benefit determination* means an adverse benefit determination as defined in 29 CFR 2560.503-1, as well as any rescission of coverage, as described in § 54.9815-2712T(a)(2) (whether or not, in connection with the rescission, there is an adverse effect on any particular benefit at that time).

(ii) *Appeal (or internal appeal).*—An *appeal* or *internal appeal* means review by a plan or issuer of an adverse benefit determination, as required in paragraph (b) of this section.

(iii) *Claimant.*—*Claimant* means an individual who makes a claim under this section. For

purposes of this section, references to claimant include a claimant's authorized representative.

(iv) *External review.*—*External review* means a review of an adverse benefit determination (including a final internal adverse benefit determination) conducted pursuant to an applicable State external review process described in paragraph (c) of this section or the Federal external review process of paragraph (d) of this section.

(v) *Final internal adverse benefit determination.*—A *final internal adverse benefit determination* means an adverse benefit determination that has been upheld by a plan or issuer at the completion of the internal appeals process applicable under paragraph (b) of this section (or an adverse benefit determination with respect to which the internal appeals process has been exhausted under the deemed exhaustion rules of paragraph (b)(2)(ii)(F) of this section).

(vi) *Final external review decision.*—A *final external review decision*, as used in paragraph (d) of this section, means a determination by an independent review organization at the conclusion of an external review.

(vii) *Independent review organization (or IRO).*—An *independent review organization (or IRO)* means an entity that conducts independent external reviews of adverse benefit determinations and final internal adverse benefit determinations pursuant to paragraph (c) or (d) of this section.

(viii) *NAIC Uniform Model Act.*—The *NAIC Uniform Model Act* means the Uniform Health Carrier External Review Model Act promulgated by the National Association of Insurance Commissioners in place on [INSERT DATE OF PUBLICATION IN THE FEDERAL REGISTER].

(b) *Internal claims and appeals process.*—(1) *In general.*—A group health plan and a health insur-

»»→ *Caution: Temporary Reg. §54.9815-2719T, below, was removed by T.D. 9744 and is inapplicable under Code Sec. 7805(e)(2). However, until final Reg. §54.9815-2719 is applicable on the first day of the plan or policy year beginning after January 1, 2017, taxpayers may comply with the corresponding interim final regulation at 29 CFR part 2590 that is substantially similar to the temporary reg below.*

ance issuer offering group health insurance coverage must implement an effective internal claims and appeals process, as described in this paragraph (b).

(2) *Requirements for group health plans and group health insurance issuers.*—A group health plan and a health insurance issuer offering group health insurance coverage must comply with all the requirements of this paragraph (b)(2). In the case of health insurance coverage offered in connection with a group health plan, if either the plan or the issuer complies with the internal claims and appeals process of this paragraph (b)(2), then the obligation to comply with this paragraph (b)(2) is satisfied for both the plan and the issuer with respect to the health insurance coverage.

(i) *Minimum internal claims and appeals standards.*—A group health plan and a health insurance issuer offering group health insurance coverage must comply with all the requirements applicable to group health plans under 29 CFR 2560.503-1, except to the extent those requirements are modified by paragraph (b)(2)(ii) of this section. Accordingly, under this paragraph (b), with respect to health insurance coverage offered in connection with a group health plan, the group health insurance issuer is subject to the requirements in 29 CFR 2560.503-1 to the same extent as the group health plan.

(ii) *Additional standards.*—In addition to the requirements in paragraph (b)(2)(i) of this section, the internal claims and appeals processes of a group health plan and a health insurance issuer offering group health insurance coverage must meet the requirements of this paragraph (b)(2)(ii).

(A) *Clarification of meaning of adverse benefit determination.*—For purposes of this paragraph (b)(2), an "adverse benefit determination" includes an adverse benefit determination as defined in paragraph (a)(2)(i) of this section. Accordingly, in complying with 29 CFR 2560.503-1, as well as the other provisions of this paragraph (b)(2), a plan or issuer must treat a rescission of coverage (whether or not the rescission has an adverse effect on any particular benefit at that time) as an adverse benefit determination. (Rescissions of coverage are subject to the requirements of § 54.9815-2712T.)

(B) *Expedited notification of benefit determinations involving urgent care.*—The requirements of 29 CFR 2560.503-1(f)(2)(i) (which generally provide, among other things, in the case of urgent care claims for notification of the plan's benefit determination (whether adverse or not) as soon as possible, taking into account the

medical exigencies, but not later than 72 hours after receipt of the claim) continue to apply to the plan and issuer. For purposes of this paragraph (b)(2)(ii)(B), a claim involving urgent care has the meaning given in 29 CFR 2560.503-1(m)(1), as determined by the attending provider, and the plan or issuer shall defer to such determination of the attending provider.

(C) *Full and fair review.*—A plan and issuer must allow a claimant to review the claim file and to present evidence and testimony as part of the internal claims and appeals process. Specifically, in addition to complying with the requirements of 29 CFR 2560.503-1(h)(2) —

(1) The plan or issuer must provide the claimant, free of charge, with any new or additional evidence considered, relied upon, or generated by the plan or issuer (or at the direction of the plan or issuer) in connection with the claim; such evidence must be provided as soon as possible and sufficiently in advance of the date on which the notice of final internal adverse benefit determination is required to be provided under 29 CFR 2560.503-1(i) to give the claimant a reasonable opportunity to respond prior to that date; and

(2) Before the plan or issuer can issue a final internal adverse benefit determination based on a new or additional rationale, the claimant must be provided, free of charge, with the rationale; the rationale must be provided as soon as possible and sufficiently in advance of the date on which the notice of final internal adverse benefit determination is required to be provided under 29 CFR 2560.503-1(i) to give the claimant a reasonable opportunity to respond prior to that date.

(D) *Avoiding conflicts of interest.*—In addition to the requirements of 29 CFR 2560.503-1(b) and (h) regarding full and fair review, the plan and issuer must ensure that all claims and appeals are adjudicated in a manner designed to ensure the independence and impartiality of the persons involved in making the decision. Accordingly, decisions regarding hiring, compensation, termination, promotion, or other similar matters with respect to any individual (such as a claims adjudicator or medical expert) must not be made based upon the likelihood that the individual will support the denial of benefits.

(E) *Notice.*—A plan and issuer must provide notice to individuals, in a culturally and linguistically appropriate manner (as described in paragraph (e) of this section) that complies with the requirements of 29 CFR 2560.503-1(g) and (j). The plan and issuer must also comply

>>>→ *Caution: Temporary Reg. §54.9815-2719T, below, was removed by T.D. 9744 and is inapplicable under Code Sec. 7805(e)(2). However, until final Reg. §54.9815-2719 is applicable on the first day of the plan or policy year beginning after January 1, 2017, taxpayers may comply with the corresponding interim final regulation at 29 CFR part 2590 that is substantially similar to the temporary reg below.*

with the additional requirements of this paragraph (b)(2)(ii)(E).

(1) The plan and issuer must ensure that any notice of adverse benefit determination or final internal adverse benefit determination includes information sufficient to identify the claim involved (including the date of service, the health care provider, the claim amount (if applicable), and a statement describing the availability, upon request, of the diagnosis code and its corresponding meaning, and the treatment code and its corresponding meaning).

(2) The plan and issuer must provide to participants and beneficiaries, as soon as practicable, upon request, the diagnosis code and its corresponding meaning, and the treatment code and its corresponding meaning, associated with any adverse benefit determination or final internal adverse benefit determination. The plan or issuer must not consider a request for such diagnosis and treatment information, in itself, to be a request for an internal appeal under this paragraph (b) or an external review under paragraphs (c) and (d) of this section.

(3) The plan and issuer must ensure that the reason or reasons for the adverse benefit determination or final internal adverse benefit determination includes the denial code and its corresponding meaning, as well as a description of the plan's or issuer's standard, if any, that was used in denying the claim. In the case of a notice of final internal adverse benefit determination, this description must include a discussion of the decision.

(4) The plan and issuer must provide a description of available internal appeals and external review processes, including information regarding how to initiate an appeal.

(5) The plan and issuer must disclose the availability of, and contact information for, any applicable office of health insurance consumer assistance or ombudsman established under PHS Act section 2793 to assist individuals with the internal claims and appeals and external review processes.

(F) Deemed exhaustion of internal claims and appeals processes.—*(1)* In the case of a plan or issuer that fails to adhere to all the requirements of this paragraph (b)(2) with respect to a claim, the claimant is deemed to have exhausted the internal claims and appeals process of this paragraph (b), except as provided in paragraph (b)(2)(ii)(F)(2) of this section. Accordingly, the claimant may initiate an external review under paragraph (c) or (d) of this section, as applicable. The claimant is also entitled to pursue any available remedies under section 502(a) of ERISA or under State law, as applicable, on the basis that the plan or issuer has failed to provide a reasonable internal claims and appeals process that would yield a decision on the merits of the claim. If a claimant chooses to pursue remedies under section 502(a) of ERISA under such circumstances, the claim or appeal is deemed denied on review without the exercise of discretion by an appropriate fiduciary.

(2) Notwithstanding paragraph (b)(2)(ii)(F)(1) of this section, the internal claims and appeals process of this paragraph (b) will not be deemed exhausted based on *de minimis* violations that do not cause, and are not likely to cause, prejudice or harm to the claimant so long as the plan or issuer demonstrates that the violation was for good cause or due to matters beyond the control of the plan or issuer and that the violation occurred in the context of an ongoing, good faith exchange of information between the plan and the claimant. This exception is not available if the violation is part of a pattern or practice of violations by the plan or issuer. The claimant may request a written explanation of the violation from the plan or issuer, and the plan or issuer must provide such explanation within 10 days, including a specific description of its bases, if any, for asserting that the violation should not cause the internal claims and appeals process of this paragraph (b) to be deemed exhausted. If an external reviewer or a court rejects the claimant's request for immediate review under paragraph (b)(2)(ii)(F)(1) of this section on the basis that the plan met the standards for the exception under this paragraph (b)(2)(ii)(F)(2), the claimant has the right to resubmit and pursue the internal appeal of the claim. In such a case, within a reasonable time after the external reviewer or court rejects the claim for immediate review (not to exceed 10 days), the plan shall provide the claimant with notice of the opportunity to resubmit and pursue the internal appeal of the claim. Time periods for re-filing the claim shall begin to run upon claimant's receipt of such notice.

(iii) Requirement to provide continued coverage pending the outcome of an appeal.—A plan and issuer subject to the requirements of this paragraph (b)(2) are required to provide continued coverage pending the outcome of an appeal. For this purpose, the plan and issuer must comply with the requirements of 29 CFR 2560.503-1(f)(2)(ii), which generally provides that benefits for an ongoing course of treatment cannot be reduced or terminated without providing advance notice and an opportunity for advance review.

(c) State standards for external review.—*(1) In general.*—(i) If a State external review process that applies to and is binding on a health insurance issuer offering group health insurance coverage includes at a minimum the consumer protections in the NAIC Uniform Model Act, then the issuer must comply with the applicable

>>>→ *Caution: Temporary Reg. §54.9815-2719T, below, was removed by T.D. 9744 and is inapplicable under Code Sec. 7805(e)(2). However, until final Reg. §54.9815-2719 is applicable on the first day of the plan or policy year beginning after January 1, 2017, taxpayers may comply with the corresponding interim final regulation at 29 CFR part 2590 that is substantially similar to the temporary reg below.*

State external review process and is not required to comply with the Federal external review process of paragraph (d) of this section. In such a case, to the extent that benefits under a group health plan are provided through health insurance coverage, the group health plan is not required to comply with either this paragraph (c) or the Federal external review process of paragraph (d) of this section.

(ii) To the extent that a group health plan provides benefits other than through health insurance coverage (that is, the plan is self-insured) and is subject to a State external review process that applies to and is binding on the plan (for example, is not preempted by ERISA) and the State external review process includes at a minimum the consumer protections in the NAIC Uniform Model Act, then the plan must comply with the applicable State external review process and is not required to comply with the Federal external review process of paragraph (d) of this section.

(iii) If a plan or issuer is not required under paragraph (c)(1)(i) or (c)(1)(ii) of this section to comply with the requirements of this paragraph (c), then the plan or issuer must comply with the Federal external review process of paragraph (d) of this section, except to the extent, in the case of a plan, the plan is not required under paragraph (c)(1)(i) of this section to comply with paragraph (d) of this section.

(2) *Minimum standards for State external review processes.*—An applicable State external review process must meet all the minimum consumer protections in this paragraph (c)(2). The Department of Health and Human Services will determine whether State external review processes meet these requirements.

(i) The State process must provide for the external review of adverse benefit determinations (including final internal adverse benefit determinations) by issuers (or, if applicable, plans) that are based on the issuer's (or plan's) requirements for medical necessity, appropriateness, health care setting, level of care, or effectiveness of a covered benefit.

(ii) The State process must require issuers (or, if applicable, plans) to provide effective written notice to claimants of their rights in connection with an external review for an adverse benefit determination.

(iii) To the extent the State process requires exhaustion of an internal claims and appeals process, exhaustion must be unnecessary where the issuer (or, if applicable, the plan) has waived the requirement, the issuer (or the plan) is considered to have exhausted the internal claims and appeals process under applicable law (including by failing to comply with any of the requirements for the internal appeal process, as outlined in paragraph (b)(2) of this section), or

the claimant has applied for expedited external review at the same time as applying for an expedited internal appeal.

(iv) The State process provides that the issuer (or, if applicable, the plan) against which a request for external review is filed must pay the cost of the IRO for conducting the external review. Notwithstanding this requirement, the State external review process may require a nominal filing fee from the claimant requesting an external review. For this purpose, to be considered nominal, a filing fee must not exceed $25, it must be refunded to the claimant if the adverse benefit determination (or final internal adverse benefit determination) is reversed through external review, it must be waived if payment of the fee would impose an undue financial hardship, and the annual limit on filing fees for any claimant within a single plan year must not exceed $75.

(v) The State process may not impose a restriction on the minimum dollar amount of a claim for it to be eligible for external review. Thus, the process may not impose, for example, a $500 minimum claims threshold.

(vi) The State process must allow at least four months after the receipt of a notice of an adverse benefit determination or final internal adverse benefit determination for a request for an external review to be filed.

(vii) The State process must provide that IROs will be assigned on a random basis or another method of assignment that assures the independence and impartiality of the assignment process (such as rotational assignment) by a State or independent entity, and in no event selected by the issuer, plan, or the individual.

(viii) The State process must provide for maintenance of a list of approved IROs qualified to conduct the external review based on the nature of the health care service that is the subject of the review. The State process must provide for approval only of IROs that are accredited by a nationally recognized private accrediting organization.

(ix) The State process must provide that any approved IRO has no conflicts of interest that will influence its independence. Thus, the IRO may not own or control, or be owned or controlled by a health insurance issuer, a group health plan, the sponsor of a group health plan, a trade association of plans or issuers, or a trade association of health care providers. The State process must further provide that the IRO and the clinical reviewer assigned to conduct an external review may not have a material professional, familial, or financial conflict of interest with the issuer or plan that is the subject of the external review; the claimant (and any related parties to the claimant) whose treatment is the subject of the external review; any officer, direc-

>>>→ *Caution: Temporary Reg. §54.9815-2719T, below, was removed by T.D. 9744 and is inapplicable under Code Sec. 7805(e)(2). However, until final Reg. §54.9815-2719 is applicable on the first day of the plan or policy year beginning after January 1, 2017, taxpayers may comply with the corresponding interim final regulation at 29 CFR part 2590 that is substantially similar to the temporary reg below.*

tor, or management employee of the issuer; the plan administrator, plan fiduciaries, or plan employees; the health care provider, the health care provider's group, or practice association recommending the treatment that is subject to the external review; the facility at which the recommended treatment would be provided; or the developer or manufacturer of the principal drug, device, procedure, or other therapy being recommended.

(x) The State process allows the claimant at least five business days to submit to the IRO in writing additional information that the IRO must consider when conducting the external review and it requires that the claimant is notified of the right to do so. The process must also require that any additional information submitted by the claimant to the IRO must be forwarded to the issuer (or, if applicable, the plan) within one business day of receipt by the IRO.

(xi) The State process must provide that the decision is binding on the plan or issuer, as well as the claimant, except to the extent other remedies are available under State or Federal law, and except that the requirement that the decision be binding shall not preclude the plan or issuer from making payment on the claim or otherwise providing benefits at any time, including after a final external review decision that denies the claim or otherwise fails to require such payment or benefits. For this purpose, the plan or issuer must provide benefits (including by making payment on the claim) pursuant to the final external review decision without delay, regardless of whether the plan or issuer intends to seek judicial review of the external review decision and unless or until there is a judicial decision otherwise.

(xii) The State process must require, for standard external review, that the IRO provide written notice to the claimant and the issuer (or, if applicable, the plan) of its decision to uphold or reverse the adverse benefit determination (or final internal adverse benefit determination) within no more than 45 days after the receipt of the request for external review by the IRO.

(xiii) The State process must provide for an expedited external review if the adverse benefit determination (or final internal adverse benefit determination) concerns an admission, availability of care, continued stay, or health care service for which the claimant received emergency services, but has not been discharged from a facility; or involves a medical condition for which the standard external review time frame would seriously jeopardize the life or health of the claimant or jeopardize the claimant's ability to regain maximum function. As expeditiously as possible but within no more than 72 hours after the receipt of the request for expedited external review by the IRO, the IRO must make

its decision to uphold or reverse the adverse benefit determination (or final internal adverse benefit determination) and notify the claimant and the issuer (or, if applicable, the plan) of the determination. If the notice is not in writing, the IRO must provide written confirmation of the decision within 48 hours after the date of the notice of the decision.

(xiv) The State process must require that issuers (or, if applicable, plans) include a description of the external review process in or attached to the summary plan description, policy, certificate, membership booklet, outline of coverage, or other evidence of coverage it provides to participants, beneficiaries, or enrollees, substantially similar to what is set forth in section 17 of the NAIC Uniform Model Act.

(xv) The State process must require that IROs maintain written records and make them available upon request to the State, substantially similar to what is set forth in section 15 of the NAIC Uniform Model Act.

(xvi) The State process follows procedures for external review of adverse benefit determinations (or final internal adverse benefit determinations) involving experimental or investigational treatment, substantially similar to what is set forth in section 10 of the NAIC Uniform Model Act.

(3) *Transition period for external review processes.*—(i) Through December 31, 2011, an applicable State external review process applicable to a health insurance issuer or group health plan is considered to meet the requirements of PHS Act section 2719(b). Accordingly, through December 31, 2011, an applicable State external review process will be considered binding on the issuer or plan (in lieu of the requirements of the Federal external review process). If there is no applicable State external review process, the issuer or plan is required to comply with the requirements of the Federal external review process in paragraph (d) of this section.

(ii) For final internal adverse benefit determinations (or, in the case of simultaneous internal appeal and external review, adverse benefit determinations) provided on or after January 1, 2012, the Federal external review process will apply unless the Department of Health and Human Services determines that a State law meets all the minimum standards of paragraph (c)(2) of this section.

(d) *Federal external review process.*—A plan or issuer not subject to an applicable State external review process under paragraph (c) of this section must provide an effective Federal external review process in accordance with this paragraph (d) (except to the extent, in the case of a plan, the plan is described in paragraph (c)(1)(i) of this section as not having to comply with this

>>>→ *Caution: Temporary Reg. §54.9815-2719T, below, was removed by T.D. 9744 and is inapplicable under Code Sec. 7805(e)(2). However, until final Reg. §54.9815-2719 is applicable on the first day of the plan or policy year beginning after January 1, 2017, taxpayers may comply with the corresponding interim final regulation at 29 CFR part 2590 that is substantially similar to the temporary reg below.*

paragraph (d)). In the case of health insurance coverage offered in connection with a group health plan, if either the plan or the issuer complies with the Federal external review process of this paragraph (d), then the obligation to comply with this paragraph (d) is satisfied for both the plan and the issuer with respect to the health insurance coverage.

(1) *Scope.*—(i) *In general.*—Subject to the suspension provision in paragraph (d)(1)(ii) of this section and except to the extent provided otherwise by the Secretary in guidance, the Federal external review process established pursuant to this paragraph (d) applies to any adverse benefit determination or final internal adverse benefit determination (as defined in paragraphs (a)(2)(i) and (a)(2)(v) of this section), except that a denial, reduction, termination, or a failure to provide payment for a benefit based on a determination that a participant or beneficiary fails to meet the requirements for eligibility under the terms of a group health plan is not eligible for the Federal external review process under this paragraph (d).

(ii) *Suspension of general rule.*—Unless or until this suspension is revoked in guidance by the Secretary, with respect to claims for which external review has not been initiated before September 20, 2011, the Federal external review process established pursuant to this paragraph (d) applies only to:

(A) An adverse benefit determination (including a final internal adverse benefit determination) by a plan or issuer that involves medical judgment (including, but not limited to, those based on the plan's or issuer's requirements for medical necessity, appropriateness, health care setting, level of care, or effectiveness of a covered benefit; or its determination that a treatment is experimental or investigational), as determined by the external reviewer; and

(B) A rescission of coverage (whether or not the rescission has any effect on any particular benefit at that time).

(iii) *Examples.*—This rules of paragraph (d)(1)(ii) of this section are illustrated by the following examples:

Example 1. (i) *Facts.* A group health plan provides coverage for 30 physical therapy visits generally. After the 30th visit, coverage is provided only if the service is preauthorized pursuant to an approved treatment plan that takes into account medical necessity using the plan's definition of the term. Individual *A* seeks coverage for a 31st physical therapy visit. *A*'s health care provider submits a treatment plan for approval, but it is not approved by the plan, so coverage for the 31st visit is not preauthorized. With respect to the 31st visit, *A* receives a notice of final

internal adverse benefit determination stating that the maximum visit limit is exceeded.

(ii) *Conclusion.* In this *Example 1*, the plan's denial of benefits is based on medical necessity and involves medical judgment. Accordingly, the claim is eligible for external review during the suspension period under paragraph (d)(1)(ii) of this section. Moreover, the plan's notification of final internal adverse benefit determination is inadequate under paragraphs (b)(2)(i) and (b)(2)(ii)(E)(3) of this section because it fails to make clear that the plan will pay for more than 30 visits if the service is preauthorized pursuant to an approved treatment plan that takes into account medical necessity using the plan's definition of the term. Accordingly, the notice of final internal adverse benefit determination should refer to the plan provision governing the 31st visit and should describe the plan's standard for medical necessity, as well as how the treatment fails to meet the plan's standard.

Example 2. (i) *Facts.* A group health plan does not provide coverage for services provided out of network, unless the service cannot effectively be provided in network. Individual *B* seeks coverage for a specialized medical procedure from an out-of-network provider because *B* believes that the procedure cannot be effectively provided in network. *B* receives a notice of final internal adverse benefit determination stating that the claim is denied because the provider is out-of-network.

(ii) *Conclusion.* In this *Example 2*, the plan's denial of benefits is based on whether a service can effectively be provided in network and, therefore, involves medical judgment. Accordingly, the claim is eligible for external review during the suspension period under paragraph (d)(1)(ii) of this section. Moreover, the plan's notice of final internal adverse benefit determination is inadequate under paragraphs (b)(2)(i) and (b)(2)(ii)(E)(3) of this section because the plan does provide benefits for services on an out-of-network basis if the services cannot effectively be provided in network. Accordingly, the notice of final internal adverse benefit determination is required to refer to the exception to the out-of-network exclusion and should describe the plan's standards for determining effectiveness of services, as well as how services available to the claimant within the plan's network meet the plan's standard for effectiveness of services.

(2) *External review process standards.*—The Federal external review process established pursuant to this paragraph (d) will be similar to the process set forth in the NAIC Uniform Model Act and will meet standards issued by the Secretary. These standards will comply with all of the requirements described in this paragraph (d)(2).

(i) These standards will describe how a claimant initiates an external review, procedures

>>>→ *Caution: Temporary Reg. §54.9815-2719T, below, was removed by T.D. 9744 and is inapplicable under Code Sec. 7805(e)(2). However, until final Reg. §54.9815-2719 is applicable on the first day of the plan or policy year beginning after January 1, 2017, taxpayers may comply with the corresponding interim final regulation at 29 CFR part 2590 that is substantially similar to the temporary reg below.*

for preliminary reviews to determine whether a claim is eligible for external review, minimum qualifications for IROs, a process for approving IROs eligible to be assigned to conduct external reviews, a process for random assignment of external reviews to approved IROs, standards for IRO decision-making, and rules for providing notice of a final external review decision.

(ii) These standards will provide an expedited external review process for —

(A) An adverse benefit determination, if the adverse benefit determination involves a medical condition of the claimant for which the timeframe for completion of an expedited internal appeal under paragraph (b) of this section would seriously jeopardize the life or health of the claimant, or would jeopardize the claimant's ability to regain maximum function and the claimant has filed a request for an expedited internal appeal under paragraph (b) of this section; or

(B) A final internal adverse benefit determination, if the claimant has a medical condition where the timeframe for completion of a standard external review pursuant to paragraph (d)(3) of this section would seriously jeopardize the life or health of the claimant or would jeopardize the claimant's ability to regain maximum function, or if the final internal adverse benefit determination concerns an admission, availability of care, continued stay, or health care service for which the claimant received emergency services, but has not been discharged from a facility.

(iii) With respect to claims involving experimental or investigational treatments, these standards will also provide additional consumer protections to ensure that adequate clinical and scientific experience and protocols are taken into account as part of the external review process.

(iv) These standards will provide that an external review decision is binding on the plan or issuer, as well as the claimant, except to the extent other remedies are available under State or Federal law, and except that the requirement that the decision be binding shall not preclude the plan or issuer from making payment on the claim or otherwise providing benefits at any time, including after a final external review decision that denies the claim or otherwise fails to require such payment or benefits. For this purpose, the plan or issuer must provide any benefits (including by making payment on the claim) pursuant to the final external review decision without delay, regardless of whether the plan or issuer intends to seek judicial review of the external review decision and unless or until there is a judicial decision otherwise.

(v) These standards may establish external review reporting requirements for IROs.

(vi) These standards will establish additional notice requirements for plans and issuers regarding disclosures to participants and beneficiaries describing the Federal external review procedures (including the right to file a request for an external review of an adverse benefit determination or a final internal adverse benefit determination in the summary plan description, policy, certificate, membership booklet, outline of coverage, or other evidence of coverage it provides to participants or beneficiaries).

(vii) These standards will require plans and issuers to provide information relevant to the processing of the external review, including, but not limited to, the information considered and relied on in making the adverse benefit determination or final internal adverse benefit determination.

(e) *Form and manner of notice.*—(1) *In general.*—For purposes of this section, a group health plan and a health insurance issuer offering group health insurance coverage are considered to provide relevant notices in a culturally and linguistically appropriate manner if the plan or issuer meets all the requirements of paragraph (e)(2) of this section with respect to the applicable non-English languages described in paragraph (e)(3) of this section.

(2) *Requirements.*—(i) The plan or issuer must provide oral language services (such as a telephone customer assistance hotline) that include answering questions in any applicable non- English language and providing assistance with filing claims and appeals (including external review) in any applicable non-English language;

(ii) The plan or issuer must provide, upon request, a notice in any applicable non-English language; and

(iii) The plan or issuer must include in the English versions of all notices, a statement prominently displayed in any applicable non-English language clearly indicating how to access the language services provided by the plan or issuer.

(3) *Applicable non-English language.*—With respect to an address in any United States county to which a notice is sent, a non-English language is an applicable non-English language if ten percent or more of the population residing in the county is literate only in the same non-English language, as determined in guidance published by the Secretary.

(f) *Secretarial authority.*—The Secretary may determine that the external review process of a group health plan or health insurance issuer, in operation as of March 23, 2010, is considered in compliance with the applicable process established under paragraph (c) or (d) of this section

»»→ *Caution: Temporary Reg. §54.9815-2719T, below, was removed by T.D. 9744 and is inapplicable under Code Sec. 7805(e)(2). However, until final Reg. §54.9815-2719 is applicable on the first day of the plan or policy year beginning after January 1, 2017, taxpayers may comply with the corresponding interim final regulation at 29 CFR part 2590 that is substantially similar to the temporary reg below.*

if it substantially meets the requirements of paragraph (c) or (d) of this section, as applicable.

(g) *Applicability/effective date.*—The provisions of this section apply for plan years beginning on or after September 23, 2010. See § 54.9815-1251T for determining the application of this section to grandfathered health plans (providing that these rules regarding internal claims and appeals and

external review processes do not apply to grandfathered health plans).

(h) *Expiration date.*—The applicability of this section expires on July 22, 2013 or on such earlier date as may be provided in final regulations or other action published in the **Federal Register**. [Temporary Reg. § 54.9815-2719T.]

☐ [*T.D. 9494, 7-22-2010. Amended by T.D. 9532, 6-22-2011. Removed by T.D. 9744, 11-13-2015.*]

»»→ *Caution: Reg. §54.9815-2719A, below, as added by T.D. 9744, is applicable to group health plans and health insurance issuers beginning on the first day of the plan year (or, in the individual market, the first day of the first policy year) beginning on or after January 1, 2017.*

[Reg. § 54.9815-2719A]

§ 54.9815-2719A. Patient protections.— (a) *Choice of health care professional.*—(1) *Designation of primary care provider.*—(i) *In general.*—If a group health plan, or a health insurance issuer offering group health insurance coverage, requires or provides for designation by a participant or beneficiary of a participating primary care provider, then the plan or issuer must permit each participant or beneficiary to designate any participating primary care provider who is available to accept the participant or beneficiary. In such a case, the plan or issuer must comply with the rules of paragraph (a)(4) of this section by informing each participant of the terms of the plan or health insurance coverage regarding designation of a primary care provider.

(ii) *Construction.*—Nothing in paragraph (a)(1)(i) of this section is to be construed to prohibit the application of reasonable and appropriate geographic limitations with respect to the selection of primary care providers, in accordance with the terms of the plan or coverage, the underlying provider contracts, and applicable State law.

(iii) *Example.*—The rules of this paragraph (a)(1) are illustrated by the following example:

Example. (i) *Facts.* A group health plan requires individuals covered under the plan to designate a primary care provider. The plan permits each individual to designate any primary care provider participating in the plan's network who is available to accept the individual as the individual's primary care provider. If an individual has not designated a primary care provider, the plan designates one until one has been designated by the individual. The plan provides a notice that satisfies the requirements of paragraph (a)(4) of this section regarding the ability to designate a primary care provider.

(ii) *Conclusion* In this *Example*, the plan has satisfied the requirements of paragraph (a) of this section.

(2) *Designation of pediatrician as primary care provider.*—(i) *In general.*—If a group health plan,

or a health insurance issuer offering group health insurance coverage, requires or provides for the designation of a participating primary care provider for a child by a participant or beneficiary, the plan or issuer must permit the participant or beneficiary to designate a physician (allopathic or osteopathic) who specializes in pediatrics (including pediatric subspecialties, based on the scope of that provider's license under applicable State law) as the child's primary care provider if the provider participates in the network of the plan or issuer and is available to accept the child. In such a case, the plan or issuer must comply with the rules of paragraph (a)(4) of this section by informing each participant of the terms of the plan or health insurance coverage regarding designation of a pediatrician as the child's primary care provider.

(ii) *Construction.*—Nothing in paragraph (a)(2)(i) of this section is to be construed to waive any exclusions of coverage under the terms and conditions of the plan or health insurance coverage with respect to coverage of pediatric care.

(iii) *Examples.*—The rules of this paragraph (a)(2) are illustrated by the following examples:

Example 1. (i) *Facts.* A group health plan's HMO designates for each participant a physician who specializes in internal medicine to serve as the primary care provider for the participant and any beneficiaries. Participant *A* requests that Pediatrician *B* be designated as the primary care provider for *A*'s child. *B* is a participating provider in the HMO's network and is available to accept the child.

(ii) *Conclusion.* In this *Example 1*, the HMO must permit *A*'s designation of *B* as the primary care provider for *A*'s child in order to comply with the requirements of this paragraph (a)(2).

Example 2. (i) *Facts.* Same facts as *Example 1*, except that *A* takes *A*'s child to *B* for treatment of the child's severe shellfish allergies. *B* wishes to refer *A*'s child to an allergist for treatment. The HMO, however, does not provide coverage for treatment of food allergies, nor does it have an allergist participating in its network, and it therefore refuses to authorize the referral.

≫→ *Caution: Reg. §54.9815-2719A, below, as added by T.D. 9744, is applicable to group health plans and health insurance issuers beginning on the first day of the plan year (or, in the individual market, the first day of the first policy year) beginning on or after January 1, 2017.*

(ii) *Conclusion.* In this *Example 2*, the HMO has not violated the requirements of this paragraph (a)(2) because the exclusion of treatment for food allergies is in accordance with the terms of *A*'s coverage.

(3) *Patient access to obstetrical and gynecological care.*—(i) *General rights.*—(A) *Direct access.*—A group health plan, or a health insurance issuer offering group health insurance coverage, described in paragraph (a)(3)(ii) of this section may not require authorization or referral by the plan, issuer, or any person (including a primary care provider) in the case of a female participant or beneficiary who seeks coverage for obstetrical or gynecological care provided by a participating health care professional who specializes in obstetrics or gynecology. In such a case, the plan or issuer must comply with the rules of paragraph (a)(4) of this section by informing each participant that the plan may not require authorization or referral for obstetrical or gynecological care by a participating health care professional who specializes in obstetrics or gynecology. The plan or issuer may require such a professional to agree to otherwise adhere to the plan's or issuer's policies and procedures, including procedures regarding referrals and obtaining prior authorization and providing services pursuant to a treatment plan (if any) approved by the plan or issuer. For purposes of this paragraph (a)(3), a health care professional who specializes in obstetrics or gynecology is any individual (including a person other than a physician) who is authorized under applicable State law to provide obstetrical or gynecological care.

(B) *Obstetrical and gynecological care.*—A group health plan or health insurance issuer described in paragraph (a)(3)(ii) of this section must treat the provision of obstetrical and gynecological care, and the ordering of related obstetrical and gynecological items and services, pursuant to the direct access described under paragraph (a)(3)(i)(A) of this section, by a participating health care professional who specializes in obstetrics or gynecology as the authorization of the primary care provider.

(ii) *Application of paragraph.*—A group health plan, or a health insurance issuer offering group health insurance coverage, is described in this paragraph (a)(3) if the plan or issuer—

(A) Provides coverage for obstetrical or gynecological care; and

(B) Requires the designation by a participant or beneficiary of a participating primary care provider.

(iii) *Construction.*—Nothing in paragraph (a)(3)(i) of this section is to be construed to—

(A) Waive any exclusions of coverage under the terms and conditions of the plan or health insurance coverage with respect to coverage of obstetrical or gynecological care; or

(B) Preclude the group health plan or health insurance issuer involved from requiring that the obstetrical or gynecological provider notify the primary care health care professional or the plan or issuer of treatment decisions.

(iv) *Examples.*—The rules of this paragraph (a)(3) are illustrated by the following examples:

Example 1. (i) *Facts.* A group health plan requires each participant to designate a physician to serve as the primary care provider for the participant and the participant's family. Participant *A*, a female, requests a gynecological exam with Physician *B*, an in-network physician specializing in gynecological care. The group health plan requires prior authorization from *A*'s designated primary care provider for the gynecological exam.

(ii) *Conclusion.* In this *Example 1*, the group health plan has violated the requirements of this paragraph (a)(3) because the plan requires prior authorization from *A*'s primary care provider prior to obtaining gynecological services.

Example 2. (i) *Facts.* Same facts as *Example 1* except that *A* seeks gynecological services from *C*, an out-of-network provider.

(ii) *Conclusion.* In this *Example 2*, the group health plan has not violated the requirements of this paragraph (a)(3) by requiring prior authorization because *C* is not a participating health care provider.

Example 3. (i) *Facts.* Same facts as *Example 1* except that the group health plan only requires *B* to inform *A*'s designated primary care physician of treatment decisions.

(ii) *Conclusion.* In this *Example 3*, the group health plan has not violated the requirements of this paragraph (a)(3) because *A* has direct access to *B* without prior authorization. The fact that the group health plan requires notification of treatment decisions to the designated primary care physician does not violate this paragraph (a)(3).

Example 4. (i) *Facts.* A group health plan requires each participant to designate a physician to serve as the primary care provider for the participant and the participant's family. The group health plan requires prior authorization before providing benefits for uterine fibroid embolization.

(ii) *Conclusion.* In this *Example 4*, the plan requirement for prior authorization before providing benefits for uterine fibroid embolization does not violate the requirements of this paragraph (a)(3) because, though the prior authorization requirement applies to obstetrical services, it does not restrict access to any providers specializing in obstetrics or gynecology.

(4) *Notice of right to designate a primary care provider.*—(i) *In general.*—If a group health plan or health insurance issuer requires the designation by a participant or beneficiary of a primary

>>>→ *Caution: Reg. §54.9815-2719A, below, as added by T.D. 9744, is applicable to group health plans and health insurance issuers beginning on the first day of the plan year (or, in the individual market, the first day of the first policy year) beginning on or after January 1, 2017.*

care provider, the plan or issuer must provide a notice informing each participant of the terms of the plan or health insurance coverage regarding designation of a primary care provider and of the rights—

(A) Under paragraph (a)(1)(i) of this section, that any participating primary care provider who is available to accept the participant or beneficiary can be designated;

(B) Under paragraph (a)(2)(i) of this section, with respect to a child, that any participating physician who specializes in pediatrics can be designated as the primary care provider; and

(C) Under paragraph (a)(3)(i) of this section, that the plan may not require authorization or referral for obstetrical or gynecological care by a participating health care professional who specializes in obstetrics or gynecology.

(ii) *Timing.*—The notice described in paragraph (a)(4)(i) of this section must be included whenever the plan or issuer provides a participant with a summary plan description or other similar description of benefits under the plan or health insurance coverage.

(iii) *Model language.*—The following model language can be used to satisfy the notice requirement described in paragraph (a)(4)(i) of this section:

(A) For plans and issuers that require or allow for the designation of primary care providers by participants or beneficiaries, insert:
[Name of group health plan or health insurance issuer] generally [requires/allows] the designation of a primary care provider. You have the right to designate any primary care provider who participates in our network and who is available to accept you or your family members. [If the plan or health insurance coverage designates a primary care provider automatically, insert: Until you make this designation, [name of group health plan or health insurance issuer] designates one for you.] For information on how to select a primary care provider, and for a list of the participating primary care providers, contact the [plan administrator or issuer] at [insert contact information].

(B) For plans and issuers that require or allow for the designation of a primary care provider for a child, add:

For children, you may designate a pediatrician as the primary care provider.

(C) For plans and issuers that provide coverage for obstetric or gynecological care and require the designation by a participant or beneficiary of a primary care provider, add:
You do not need prior authorization from [name of group health plan or issuer] or from any other person (including a primary care provider) in order to obtain access to obstetrical or gynecological care from a health care professional in our network who specializes in obstetrics or gynecology. The health care professional, however, may be required to comply with certain procedures, including obtaining prior authorization for certain services, following a pre-approved treatment plan, or procedures for making referrals. For a list of participating health care professionals who specialize in obstetrics or gynecology, contact the [plan administrator or issuer] at [insert contact information].

(b) *Coverage of emergency services.*—(1) *Scope.*—If a group health plan, or a health insurance issuer offering group health insurance coverage, provides any benefits with respect to services in an emergency department of a hospital, the plan or issuer must cover emergency services (as defined in paragraph (b)(4)(ii) of this section) consistent with the rules of this paragraph (b).

(2) *General rules.*—A plan or issuer subject to the requirements of this paragraph (b) must provide coverage for emergency services in the following manner—

(i) Without the need for any prior authorization determination, even if the emergency services are provided on an out-of-network basis;

(ii) Without regard to whether the health care provider furnishing the emergency services is a participating network provider with respect to the services;

(iii) If the emergency services are provided out of network, without imposing any administrative requirement or limitation on coverage that is more restrictive than the requirements or limitations that apply to emergency services received from in-network providers;

(iv) If the emergency services are provided out of network, by complying with the cost-sharing requirements of paragraph (b)(3) of this section; and

(v) Without regard to any other term or condition of the coverage, other than—

(A) The exclusion of or coordination of benefits;

Reg. §54.9815-2719A(a)(4)(i)(A)

⟫⟫→ *Caution: Reg. §54.9815-2719A, below, as added by T.D. 9744, is applicable to group health plans and health insurance issuers beginning on the first day of the plan year (or, in the individual market, the first day of the first policy year) beginning on or after January 1, 2017.*

(B) An affiliation or waiting period permitted under part 7 of ERISA, part A of title XXVII of the PHS Act, or chapter 100 of the Internal Revenue Code; or

(C) Applicable cost sharing.

(3) *Cost-sharing requirements.*— (i) *Copayments and coinsurance.*—Any cost-sharing requirement expressed as a copayment amount or coinsurance rate imposed with respect to a participant or beneficiary for out-of-network emergency services cannot exceed the cost-sharing requirement imposed with respect to a participant or beneficiary if the services were provided in network. However, a participant or beneficiary may be required to pay, in addition to the in-network cost sharing, the excess of the amount the out-of-network provider charges over the amount the plan or issuer is required to pay under this paragraph (b)(3)(i). A group health plan or health insurance issuer complies with the requirements of this paragraph (b)(3) if it provides benefits with respect to an emergency service in an amount at least equal to the greatest of the three amounts specified in paragraphs (b)(3)(i)(A), (B), and (C) of this section (which are adjusted for in-network cost-sharing requirements).

(A) The amount negotiated with in-network providers for the emergency service furnished, excluding any in-network copayment or coinsurance imposed with respect to the participant or beneficiary. If there is more than one amount negotiated with in-network providers for the emergency service, the amount described under this paragraph (b)(3)(i)(A) is the median of these amounts, excluding any in-network copayment or coinsurance imposed with respect to the participant or beneficiary. In determining the median described in the preceding sentence, the amount negotiated with each in-network provider is treated as a separate amount (even if the same amount is paid to more than one provider). If there is no per-service amount negotiated with in-network providers (such as under a capitation or other similar payment arrangement), the amount under this paragraph (b)(3)(i)(A) is disregarded.

(B) The amount for the emergency service calculated using the same method the plan generally uses to determine payments for out-of-network services (such as the usual, customary, and reasonable amount), excluding any in-network copayment or coinsurance imposed with respect to the participant or beneficiary. The amount in this paragraph (b)(3)(i)(B) is determined without reduction for out-of-network cost sharing that generally applies under the plan or health insurance coverage with respect to out-of-network services. Thus, for example, if a plan generally pays 70 percent of the usual, customary, and reasonable amount for out-of-network services, the amount in this paragraph (b)(3)(i)(B) for an emergency service is the total

(that is, 100 percent) of the usual, customary, and reasonable amount for the service, not reduced by the 30 percent coinsurance that would generally apply to out-of-network services (but reduced by the in-network copayment or coinsurance that the individual would be responsible for if the emergency service had been provided in-network).

(C) The amount that would be paid under Medicare (part A or part B of title XVIII of the Social Security Act, 42 U.S.C. 1395 *et seq.*) for the emergency service, excluding any in-network copayment or coinsurance imposed with respect to the participant or beneficiary.

(ii) *Other cost sharing.*—Any cost-sharing requirement other than a copayment or coinsurance requirement (such as a deductible or out-of-pocket maximum) may be imposed with respect to emergency services provided out of network if the cost-sharing requirement generally applies to out-of-network benefits. A deductible may be imposed with respect to out-of-network emergency services only as part of a deductible that generally applies to out-of-network benefits. If an out-of-pocket maximum generally applies to out-of-network benefits, that out-of-pocket maximum must apply to out-of-network emergency services.

(iii) *Special rules regarding out-of-network minimum payment standards.*—(A) The minimum payment standards set forth under paragraph (b)(3) of this section do not apply in cases where State law prohibits a participant or beneficiary from being required to pay, in addition to the in-network cost sharing, the excess of the amount the out-of-network provider charges over the amount the plan or issuer provides in benefits, or where a group health plan or health insurance issuer is contractually responsible for such amounts. Nonetheless, in such cases, a plan or issuer may not impose any copayment or coinsurance requirement for out-of-network emergency services that is higher than the copayment or coinsurance requirement that would apply if the services were provided in network.

(B) A group health plan and health insurance issuer must provide a participant or beneficiary adequate and prominent notice of their lack of financial responsibility with respect to the amounts described under this paragraph (b)(3)(iii), to prevent inadvertent payment by the participant or beneficiary.

(iv) *Examples.*—The rules of this paragraph (b)(3) are illustrated by the following examples. In all of these examples, the group health plan covers benefits with respect to emergency services.

Example 1.(i) *Facts.* A group health plan imposes a 25% coinsurance responsibility on individuals who are furnished emergency services, whether provided in network or out of network. If a covered individual notifies the plan within

>>→ *Caution: Reg. §54.9815-2719A, below, as added by T.D. 9744, is applicable to group health plans and health insurance issuers beginning on the first day of the plan year (or, in the individual market, the first day of the first policy year) beginning on or after January 1, 2017.*

two business days after the day an individual receives treatment in an emergency department, the plan reduces the coinsurance rate to 15%.

(ii) *Conclusion.* In this *Example 1*, the requirement to notify the plan in order to receive a reduction in the coinsurance rate does not violate the requirement that the plan cover emergency services without the need for any prior authorization determination. This is the result even if the plan required that it be notified before or at the time of receiving services at the emergency department in order to receive a reduction in the coinsurance rate.

Example 2. (i) *Facts.* A group health plan imposes a $60 copayment on emergency services without preauthorization, whether provided in network or out of network. If emergency services are preauthorized, the plan waives the copayment, even if it later determines the medical condition was not an emergency medical condition.

(ii) *Conclusion.* In this *Example 2*, by requiring an individual to pay more for emergency services if the individual does not obtain prior authorization, the plan violates the requirement that the plan cover emergency services without the need for any prior authorization determination. (By contrast, if, to have the copayment waived, the plan merely required that it be notified rather than a prior authorization, then the plan would not violate the requirement that the plan cover emergency services without the need for any prior authorization determination.)

Example 3. (i) *Facts.* A group health plan covers individuals who receive emergency services with respect to an emergency medical condition from an out-of-network provider. The plan has agreements with in-network providers with respect to a certain emergency service. Each provider has agreed to provide the service for a certain amount. Among all the providers for the service: one has agreed to accept $85, two have agreed to accept $100, two have agreed to accept $110, three have agreed to accept $120, and one has agreed to accept $150. Under the agreement, the plan agrees to pay the providers 80% of the agreed amount, with the individual receiving the service responsible for the remaining 20%.

(ii) *Conclusion.* In this *Example 3*, the values taken into account in determining the median are $85, $100, $100, $110, $110, $120, $120, $120, and $150. Therefore, the median amount among those agreed to for the emergency service is $110, and the amount under paragraph (b)(3)(i)(A) of this section is 80% of $110 ($88).

Example 4. (i) *Facts.* Same facts as *Example 3*. Subsequently, the plan adds another provider to its network, who has agreed to accept $150 for the emergency service.

(ii) *Conclusion.* In this *Example 4*, the median amount among those agreed to for the emergency service is $115. (Because there is no one middle amount, the median is the average of the two middle amounts, $110 and $120.) Accordingly, the amount under paragraph (b)(3)(i)(A) of this section is 80% of $115 ($92).

Example 5. (i) *Facts.* Same facts as *Example 4*. An individual covered by the plan receives the emergency service from an out-of-network provider, who charges $125 for the service. With respect to services provided by out-of-network providers generally, the plan reimburses covered individuals 50% of the reasonable amount charged by the provider for medical services. For this purpose, the reasonable amount for any service is based on information on charges by all providers collected by a third party, on a zip code by zip code basis, with the plan treating charges at a specified percentile as reasonable. For the emergency service received by the individual, the reasonable amount calculated using this method is $116. The amount that would be paid under Medicare for the emergency service, excluding any copayment or coinsurance for the service, is $80.

(ii) *Conclusion.* In this *Example 5*, the plan is responsible for paying $92.80, 80% of $116. The median amount among those agreed to for the emergency service is $115 and the amount the plan would pay is $92 (80% of $115); the amount calculated using the same method the plan uses to determine payments for out-of-network services — $116 — excluding the in-network 20% coinsurance, is $92.80; and the Medicare payment is $80. Thus, the greatest amount is $92.80. The individual is responsible for the remaining $32.20 charged by the out-of-network provider.

Example 6. (i) *Facts.* Same facts as *Example 5*. The group health plan generally imposes a $250 deductible for in-network health care. With respect to all health care provided by out-of-network providers, the plan imposes a $500 deductible. (Covered in-network claims are credited against the deductible.) The individual has incurred and submitted $260 of covered claims prior to receiving the emergency service out of network.

(ii) *Conclusion.* In this *Example 6*, the plan is not responsible for paying anything with respect to the emergency service furnished by the out-of-network provider because the covered individual has not satisfied the higher deductible that applies generally to all health care provided out of network. However, the amount the individual is required to pay is credited against the deductible.

(4) *Definitions.*—The definitions in this paragraph (b)(4) govern in applying the provisions of this paragraph (b).

(i) *Emergency medical condition.*—The term *emergency medical condition* means a medical condition manifesting itself by acute symptoms of sufficient severity (including severe pain) so that a prudent layperson, who possesses an average

>>>→ *Caution: Reg. §54.9815-2719A, below, as added by T.D. 9744, is applicable to group health plans and health insurance issuers beginning on the first day of the plan year (or, in the individual market, the first day of the first policy year) beginning on or after January 1, 2017.*

knowledge of health and medicine, could reasonably expect the absence of immediate medical attention to result in a condition described in clause (i), (ii), or (iii) of section 1867(e)(1)(A) of the Social Security Act (42 U.S.C. 1395dd(e)(1)(A)). (In that provision of the Social Security Act, clause (i) refers to placing the health of the individual (or, with respect to a pregnant woman, the health of the woman or her unborn child) in serious jeopardy; clause (ii) refers to serious impairment to bodily functions; and clause (iii) refers to serious dysfunction of any bodily organ or part.)

(ii) *Emergency services.*—The term *emergency services* means, with respect to an emergency medical condition—

(A) A medical screening examination (as required under section 1867 of the Social Security Act, 42 U.S.C. 1395dd) that is within the capability of the emergency department of a hospital, including ancillary services routinely available to the emergency department to evaluate such emergency medical condition, and

(B) Such further medical examination and treatment, to the extent they are within the capabilities of the staff and facilities available at the hospital, as are required under section 1867 of the Social Security Act (42 U.S.C. 1395dd) to stabilize the patient.

(iii) *Stabilize.*—The term *to stabilize*, with respect to an emergency medical condition (as defined in paragraph (b)(4)(i) of this section) has the meaning given in section 1867(e)(3) of the Social Security Act (42 U.S.C. 1395dd(e)(3)).

(c) *Applicability date.*—The provisions of this section are applicable to group health plans and health insurance issuers for plan years beginning on or after January 1, 2017. Until the applicability date for this regulation, plans and issuers are required to continue to comply with the interim final regulations promulgated by the Department of Labor at 29 CFR part 2590, contained in the 29 CFR, parts 1927 to end, edition revised as of July 1, 2015. [Reg. §54.9815-2719A.]

☐ [T.D. 9744, 11-13-2015.]

>>>→ *Caution: Temporary Reg. §54.9815-2719AT, below, was removed by T.D. 9744 and is inapplicable under Code Sec. 7805(e)(2). However, until final Reg. §54.9815-2719A is applicable on the first day of the plan or policy year beginning after January 1, 2017, taxpayers may comply with the corresponding interim final regulation at 29 CFR part 2590 that is substantially similar to the temporary reg below.*

[Reg. §54.9815-2719AT]

§54.9815-2719AT. Patient protections (temporary).—(a) *Choice of health care professional.*— (1) *Designation of primary care provider.*—(i) *In general.*—If a group health plan, or a health insurance issuer offering group health insurance coverage, requires or provides for designation by a participant or beneficiary of a participating primary care provider, then the plan or issuer must permit each participant or beneficiary to designate any participating primary care provider who is available to accept the participant or beneficiary. In such a case, the plan or issuer must comply with the rules of paragraph (a)(4) of this section by informing each participant of the terms of the plan or health insurance coverage regarding designation of a primary care provider.

(ii) *Example.*—The rules of this paragraph (a)(1) are illustrated by the following example:

Example. (i) *Facts.* A group health plan requires individuals covered under the plan to designate a primary care provider. The plan permits each individual to designate any primary care provider participating in the plan's network who is available to accept the individual as the individual's primary care provider. If an individual has not designated a primary care provider, the plan designates one until one has been designated by the individual. The plan provides a notice that satisfies the requirements of paragraph (a)(4) of this section regarding the ability to designate a primary care provider.

(ii) *Conclusion.* In this *Example*, the plan has satisfied the requirements of paragraph (a) of this section.

(2) *Designation of pediatrician as primary care provider.*—(i) *In general.*—If a group health plan, or a health insurance issuer offering group health insurance coverage, requires or provides for the designation of a participating primary care provider for a child by a participant or beneficiary, the plan or issuer must permit the participant or beneficiary to designate a physician (allopathic or osteopathic) who specializes in pediatrics as the child's primary care provider if the provider participates in the network of the plan or issuer and is available to accept the child. In such a case, the plan or issuer must comply with the rules of paragraph (a)(4) of this section by informing each participant of the terms of the plan or health insurance coverage regarding designation of a pediatrician as the child's primary care provider.

(ii) *Construction.*—Nothing in paragraph (a)(2)(i) of this section is to be construed to waive any exclusions of coverage under the terms and conditions of the plan or health insurance coverage with respect to coverage of pediatric care.

(iii) *Examples.*—The rules of this paragraph (a)(2) are illustrated by the following examples:

Example 1. (i) *Facts.* A group health plan's HMO designates for each participant a physician who specializes in internal medicine to serve as

>>>→ *Caution: Temporary Reg. §54.9815-2719AT, below, was removed by T.D. 9744 and is inapplicable under Code Sec. 7805(e)(2). However, until final Reg. §54.9815-2719A is applicable on the first day of the plan or policy year beginning after January 1, 2017, taxpayers may comply with the corresponding interim final regulation at 29 CFR part 2590 that is substantially similar to the temporary reg below.*

the primary care provider for the participant and any beneficiaries. Participant A requests that Pediatrician B be designated as the primary care provider for A's child. B is a participating provider in the HMO's network.

(ii) *Conclusion.* In this *Example 1*, the HMO must permit A's designation of B as the primary care provider for A's child in order to comply with the requirements of this paragraph (a)(2).

Example 2. (i) *Facts.* Same facts as *Example 1*, except that A takes A's child to B for treatment of the child's severe shellfish allergies. B wishes to refer A's child to an allergist for treatment. The HMO, however, does not provide coverage for treatment of food allergies, nor does it have an allergist participating in its network, and it therefore refuses to authorize the referral.

(ii) *Conclusion.* In this *Example 2*, the HMO has not violated the requirements of this paragraph (a)(2) because the exclusion of treatment for food allergies is in accordance with the terms of A's coverage.

(3) *Patient access to obstetrical and gynecological care.*—(i) *General rights.*—(A) *Direct access.*— A group health plan, or a health insurance issuer offering group health insurance coverage, described in paragraph (a)(3)(ii) of this section may not require authorization or referral by the plan, issuer, or any person (including a primary care provider) in the case of a female participant or beneficiary who seeks coverage for obstetrical or gynecological care provided by a participating health care professional who specializes in obstetrics or gynecology. In such a case, the plan or issuer must comply with the rules of paragraph (a)(4) of this section by informing each participant that the plan may not require authorization or referral for obstetrical or gynecological care by a participating health care professional who specializes in obstetrics or gynecology. The plan or issuer may require such a professional to agree to otherwise adhere to the plan's or issuer's policies and procedures, including procedures regarding referrals and obtaining prior authorization and providing services pursuant to a treatment plan (if any) approved by the plan or issuer. For purposes of this paragraph (a)(3), a health care professional who specializes in obstetrics or gynecology is any individual (including a person other than a physician) who is authorized under applicable State law to provide obstetrical or gynecological care.

(B) *Obstetrical and gynecological care.*—A group health plan or health insurance issuer described in paragraph (a)(3)(ii) of this section must treat the provision of obstetrical and gynecological care, and the ordering of related obstetrical and gynecological items and services, pursuant to the direct access described under paragraph (a)(3)(i)(A) of this section, by a participating health care professional who specializes in obstetrics or gynecology as the authorization of the primary care provider.

(ii) *Application of paragraph.*—A group health plan, or a health insurance issuer offering group health insurance coverage, is described in this paragraph (a)(3) if the plan or issuer—

(A) Provides coverage for obstetrical or gynecological care; and

(B) Requires the designation by a participant or beneficiary of a participating primary care provider.

(iii) *Construction.*—Nothing in paragraph (a)(3)(i) of this section is to be construed to—

(A) Waive any exclusions of coverage under the terms and conditions of the plan or health insurance coverage with respect to coverage of obstetrical or gynecological care; or

(B) Preclude the group health plan or health insurance issuer involved from requiring that the obstetrical or gynecological provider notify the primary care health care professional or the plan or issuer of treatment decisions.

(iv) *Examples.*—The rules of this paragraph (a)(3) are illustrated by the following examples:

Example 1. (i) *Facts.* A group health plan requires each participant to designate a physician to serve as the primary care provider for the participant and the participant's family. Participant A, a female, requests a gynecological exam with Physician B, an in-network physician specializing in gynecological care. The group health plan requires prior authorization from A's designated primary care provider for the gynecological exam.

(ii) *Conclusion.* In this *Example 1*, the group health plan has violated the requirements of this paragraph (a)(3) because the plan requires prior authorization from A's primary care provider prior to obtaining gynecological services.

Example 2. (i) *Facts.* Same facts as *Example 1* except that A seeks gynecological services from C, an out-of-network provider.

(ii) *Conclusion.* In this *Example 2*, the group health plan has not violated the requirements of this paragraph (a)(3) by requiring prior authorization because C is not a participating health care provider.

Example 3. (i) *Facts.* Same facts as *Example 1* except that the group health plan only requires B to inform A's designated primary care physician of treatment decisions.

(ii) *Conclusion.* In this *Example 3*, the group health plan has not violated the requirements of this paragraph (a)(3) because A has direct access to B without prior authorization. The fact that the group health plan requires notification of treatment decisions to the designated primary care physician does not violate this paragraph (a)(3).

⋙→ *Caution: Temporary Reg. §54.9815-2719AT, below, was removed by T.D. 9744 and is inapplicable under Code Sec. 7805(e)(2). However, until final Reg. §54.9815-2719A is applicable on the first day of the plan or policy year beginning after January 1, 2017, taxpayers may comply with the corresponding interim final regulation at 29 CFR part 2590 that is substantially similar to the temporary reg below.*

Example 4. (i) *Facts.* A group health plan requires each participant to designate a physician to serve as the primary care provider for the participant and the participant's family. The group health plan requires prior authorization before providing benefits for uterine fibroid embolization.

(ii) *Conclusion.* In this *Example 4,* the plan requirement for prior authorization before providing benefits for uterine fibroid embolization does not violate the requirements of this paragraph (a)(3) because, though the prior authorization requirement applies to obstetrical services, it does not restrict access to any providers specializing in obstetrics or gynecology.

(4) *Notice of right to designate a primary care provider.*—(i) *In general.*—If a group health plan or health insurance issuer requires the designation by a participant or beneficiary of a primary care provider, the plan or issuer must provide a notice informing each participant of the terms of the plan or health insurance coverage regarding designation of a primary care provider and of the rights—

(A) Under paragraph (a)(1)(i) of this section, that any participating primary care provider who is available to accept the participant or beneficiary can be designated;

(B) Under paragraph (a)(2)(i) of this section, with respect to a child, that any participating physician who specializes in pediatrics can be designated as the primary care provider; and

(C) Under paragraph (a)(3)(i) of this section, that the plan may not require authorization or referral for obstetrical or gynecological care by a participating health care professional who specializes in obstetrics or gynecology.

(ii) *Timing.*—The notice described in paragraph (a)(4)(i) of this section must be included whenever the plan or issuer provides a participant with a summary plan description or other similar description of benefits under the plan or health insurance coverage.

(iii) *Model language.*—The following model language can be used to satisfy the notice requirement described in paragraph (a)(4)(i) of this section:

(A) For plans and issuers that require or allow for the designation of primary care providers by participants or beneficiaries, insert:

[Name of group health plan or health insurance issuer]generally [requires/allows] the designation of a primary care provider. You have the right to designate any primary care provider who

participates in our network and who is available to accept you or your family members. [If the plan or health insurance coverage designates a primary care provider automatically, insert: Until you make this designation, [name of group health plan or health insurance issuer]designates one for you.] For information on how to select a primary care provider, and for a list of the participating primary care providers, contact the [plan administrator or issuer] at [insert contact information].

(B) For plans and issuers that require or allow for the designation of a primary care provider for a child, add:

For children, you may designate a pediatrician as the primary care provider.

(C) For plans and issuers that provide coverage for obstetric or gynecological care and require the designation by a participant or beneficiary of a primary care provider, add:

You do not need prior authorization from [name of group health plan or issuer] or from any other person (including a primary care provider) in order to obtain access to obstetrical or gynecological care from a health care professional in our network who specializes in obstetrics or gynecology. The health care professional, however, may be required to comply with certain procedures, including obtaining prior authorization for certain services, following a pre-approved treatment plan, or procedures for making referrals. For a list of participating health care professionals who specialize in obstetrics or gynecology, contact the [plan administrator or issuer] at [insert contact information].

(b) *Coverage of emergency services.*—(1) *Scope.*—If a group health plan, or a health insurance issuer offering group health insurance coverage, provides any benefits with respect to services in an emergency department of a hospital, the plan or issuer must cover emergency services (as defined in paragraph (b)(4)(ii) of this section) consistent with the rules of this paragraph (b).

≫→ *Caution: Temporary Reg. §54.9815-2719AT, below, was removed by T.D. 9744 and is inapplicable under Code Sec. 7805(e)(2). However, until final Reg. §54.9815-2719A is applicable on the first day of the plan or policy year beginning after January 1, 2017, taxpayers may comply with the corresponding interim final regulation at 29 CFR part 2590 that is substantially similar to the temporary reg below.*

(2) *General rules.*—A plan or issuer subject to the requirements of this paragraph (b) must provide coverage for emergency services in the following manner—

(i) Without the need for any prior authorization determination, even if the emergency services are provided on an out-of-network basis;

(ii) Without regard to whether the health care provider furnishing the emergency services is a participating network provider with respect to the services;

(iii) If the emergency services are provided out of network, without imposing any administrative requirement or limitation on coverage that is more restrictive than the requirements or limitations that apply to emergency services received from in-network providers;

(iv) If the emergency services are provided out of network, by complying with the costsharing requirements of paragraph (b)(3) of this section; and

(v) Without regard to any other term or condition of the coverage, other than -

(A) The exclusion of or coordination of benefits;

(B) An affiliation or waiting period permitted under part 7 of ERISA, part A of title XXVII of the PHS Act, or chapter 100 of the Internal Revenue Code; or

(C) Applicable cost sharing.

(3) *Cost-sharing requirements.*—(i) *Copayments and coinsurance.*—Any cost-sharing requirement expressed as a copayment amount or coinsurance rate imposed with respect to a participant or beneficiary for out-of-network emergency services cannot exceed the cost-sharing requirement imposed with respect to a participant or beneficiary if the services were provided in-network. However, a participant or beneficiary may be required to pay, in addition to the innetwork cost sharing, the excess of the amount the out-of-network provider charges over the amount the plan or issuer is required to pay under this paragraph (b)(3)(i). A group health plan or health insurance issuer complies with the requirements of this paragraph (b)(3) if it provides benefits with respect to an emergency service in an amount equal to the greatest of the three amounts ·specified in paragraphs (b)(3)(i)(A), (b)(3)(i)(B), and (b)(3)(i)(C) of this section (which are adjusted for in-network cost-sharing requirements).

(A) The amount negotiated with in-network providers for the emergency service furnished, excluding any in-network copayment or coinsurance imposed with respect to the participant or beneficiary. If there is more than one amount negotiated with in-network providers for the emergency service, the amount described under this paragraph (b)(3)(i)(A) is the median

of these amounts, excluding any in-network copayment or coinsurance imposed with respect to the participant or beneficiary. In determining the median described in the preceding sentence, the amount negotiated with each in-network provider is treated as a separate amount (even if the same amount is paid to more than one provider). If there is no per-service amount negotiated with in-network providers (such as under a capitation or other similar payment arrangement), the amount under this paragraph (b)(3)(i)(A) is disregarded.

(B) The amount for the emergency service calculated using the same method the plan generally uses to determine payments for out-of-network services (such as the usual, customary, and reasonable amount), excluding any in-network copayment or coinsurance imposed with respect to the participant or beneficiary. The amount in this paragraph (b)(3)(i)(B) is determined without reduction for out-of-network cost sharing that generally applies under the plan or health insurance coverage with respect to out-of-network services. Thus, for example, if a plan generally pays 70 percent of the usual, customary, and reasonable amount for out-of-network services, the amount in this paragraph (b)(3)(i)(B) for an emergency service is the total (that is, 100 percent) of the usual, customary, and reasonable amount for the service, not reduced by the 30 percent coinsurance that would generally apply to out-of-network services (but reduced by the in-network copayment or coinsurance that the individual would be responsible for if the emergency service had been provided in-network).

(C) The amount that would be paid under Medicare (part A or part B of title XVIII of the Social Security Act, 42 U.S.C. 1395 *et seq.*) for the emergency service, excluding any in-network copayment or coinsurance imposed with respect to the participant or beneficiary.

(ii) *Other cost sharing.*—Any cost-sharing requirement other than a copayment or coinsurance requirement (such as a deductible or out-of-pocket maximum) may be imposed with respect to emergency services provided out of network if the cost-sharing requirement generally applies to out-of-network benefits. A deductible may be imposed with respect to out-of-network emergency services only as part of a deductible that generally applies to out-of-network benefits. If an out-of-pocket maximum generally applies to out-of-network benefits, that out-of-pocket maximum must apply to out-of-network emergency services.

(iii) *Examples.*—The rules of this paragraph (b)(3) are illustrated by the following examples. In all of these examples, the group health plan covers benefits with respect to emergency services.

>>>→ *Caution: Temporary Reg. §54.9815-2719AT, below, was removed by T.D. 9744 and is inapplicable under Code Sec. 7805(e)(2). However, until final Reg. §54.9815-2719A is applicable on the first day of the plan or policy year beginning after January 1, 2017, taxpayers may comply with the corresponding interim final regulation at 29 CFR part 2590 that is substantially similar to the temporary reg below.*

Example 1. (i) *Facts.* A group health plan imposes a 25% coinsurance responsibility on individuals who are furnished emergency services, whether provided in network or out of network. If a covered individual notifies the plan within two business days after the day an individual receives treatment in an emergency department, the plan reduces the coinsurance rate to 15%.

(ii) *Conclusion.* In this *Example 1,* the requirement to notify the plan in order to receive a reduction in the coinsurance rate does not violate the requirement that the plan cover emergency services without the need for any prior authorization determination. This is the result even if the plan required that it be notified before or at the time of receiving services at the emergency department in order to receive a reduction in the coinsurance rate.

Example 2. (i) *Facts.* A group health plan imposes a $60 copayment on emergency services without preauthorization, whether provided in network or out of network. If emergency services are preauthorized, the plan waives the copayment, even if it later determines the medical condition was not an emergency medical condition.

(ii) *Conclusion.* In this *Example 2,* by requiring an individual to pay more for emergency services if the individual does not obtain prior authorization, the plan violates the requirement that the plan cover emergency services without the need for any prior authorization determination. (By contrast, if, to have the copayment waived, the plan merely required that it be notified rather than a prior authorization, then the plan would not violate the requirement that the plan cover emergency services without the need for any prior authorization determination.)

Example 3. (i) *Facts.* A group health plan covers individuals who receive emergency services with respect to an emergency medical condition from an out-of-network provider. The plan has agreements with in-network providers with respect to a certain emergency service. Each provider has agreed to provide the service for a certain amount. Among all the providers for the service: one has agreed to accept $85, two have agreed to accept $100, two have agreed to accept $110, three have agreed to accept $120, and one has agreed to accept $150. Under the agreement, the plan agrees to pay the providers 80% of the agreed amount, with the individual receiving the service responsible for the remaining 20%.

(ii) *Conclusion.* In this *Example 3,* the values taken into account in determining the median are $85, $100, $100, $110, $110, $120, $120, $120, and $150. Therefore, the median amount among those agreed to for the emergency service is $110, and the amount under paragraph (b)(3)(i)(A) of this section is 80% of $110 ($88).

Example 4. (i) *Facts.* Same facts as *Example 3.* Subsequently, the plan adds another provider to its network, who has agreed to accept $150 for the emergency service.

(ii) *Conclusion.* In this *Example 4,* the median amount among those agreed to for the emergency service is $115. (Because there is no one middle amount, the median is the average of the two middle amounts, $110 and $120.) Accordingly, the amount under paragraph (b)(3)(i)(A) of this section is 80% of $115 ($92).

Example 5. (i) *Facts.* Same facts as *Example 4.* An individual covered by the plan receives the emergency service from an out-of-network provider, who charges $125 for the service. With respect to services provided by out-of-network providers generally, the plan reimburses covered individuals 50% of the reasonable amount charged by the provider for medical services. For this purpose, the reasonable amount for any service is based on information on charges by all providers collected by a third party, on a zip-code-by-zip-code basis, with the plan treating charges at a specified percentile as reasonable. For the emergency service received by the individual, the reasonable amount calculated using this method is $116. The amount that would be paid under Medicare for the emergency service, excluding any copayment or coinsurance for the service, is $80.

(ii) *Conclusion.* In this *Example 5,* the plan is responsible for paying $92.80, 80% of $116. The median amount among those agreed to for the emergency service is $115 and the amount the plan would pay is $92 (80% of $115); the amount calculated using the same method the plan uses to determine payments for out-of-network services — $116 — excluding the in-network 20% coinsurance, is $92.80; and the Medicare payment is $80. Thus, the greatest amount is $92.80. The individual is responsible for the remaining $32.20 charged by the out-of-network provider.

Example 6. (i) *Facts.* Same facts as *Example 5.* The group health plan generally imposes a $250 deductible for in-network health care. With respect to all health care provided by out-ofnetwork providers, the plan imposes a $500 deductible. (Covered in-network claims are credited against the deductible.) The individual has incurred and submitted $260 of covered claims prior to receiving the emergency service out of network.

(ii) *Conclusion.* In this *Example 6,* the plan is not responsible for paying anything with respect to the emergency service furnished by the out-of-network provider because the covered individual has not satisfied the higher deductible that applies generally to all health care provided

>>>→ *Caution: Temporary Reg. §54.9815-2719AT, below, was removed by T.D. 9744 and is inapplicable under Code Sec. 7805(e)(2). However, until final Reg. §54.9815-2719A is applicable on the first day of the plan or policy year beginning after January 1, 2017, taxpayers may comply with the corresponding interim final regulation at 29 CFR part 2590 that is substantially similar to the temporary reg below.*

out of network. However, the amount the individual is required to pay is credited against the deductible.

(4) *Definitions.*—The definitions in this paragraph (b)(4) govern in applying the provisions of this paragraph (b).

(i) *Emergency medical condition.*—The term *emergency medical condition* means a medical condition manifesting itself by acute symptoms of sufficient severity (including severe pain) so that a prudent layperson, who possesses an average knowledge of health and medicine, could reasonably expect the absence of immediate medical attention to result in a condition described in clause (i), (ii), or (iii) of section 1867(e)(1)(A) of the Social Security Act (42 U.S.C. 1395dd(e)(1)(A)). (In that provision of the Social Security Act, clause (i) refers to placing the health of the individual (or, with respect to a pregnant woman, the health of the woman or her unborn child) in serious jeopardy; clause (ii) refers to serious impairment to bodily functions; and clause (iii) refers to serious dysfunction of any bodily organ or part.)

(ii) *Emergency services.*—The term *emergency services* means, with respect to an emergency medical condition—

(A) A medical screening examination (as required under section 1867 of the Social Security Act, 42 U.S.C. 1395dd) that is within the capability of the emergency department of a hospital, including ancillary services routinely available to the emergency department to evaluate such emergency medical condition, and

(B) Such further medical examination and treatment, to the extent they are within the capabilities of the staff and facilities available at the hospital, as are required under section 1867 of the Social Security Act (42 U.S.C. 1395dd) to stabilize the patient.

(iii) *Stabilize.*—The term *to stabilize*, with respect to an emergency medical condition (as defined in paragraph (b)(4)(i) of this section) has the meaning given in section 1867(e)(3) of the Social Security Act (42 U.S.C. 1395dd(e)(3)).

(c) *Effective/applicability date.*—The provisions of this section apply for plan years beginning on or after September 23, 2010. See §54.9815-1251T for determining the application of this section to grandfathered health plans (providing that these rules regarding patient protections do not apply to grandfathered health plans).

(d) *Expiration date.*—This section expires on June 21, 2013. [Temporary Reg. §54.9815-2719AT.]

☐ [T.D. 9491, 6-22-2010. *Removed by T.D. 9744*, 11-13-2015.]

[Reg. §54.9831-1]

§54.9831-1. **Special rules relating to group health plans.**—(a) *Group health plan.*—(1) *Defined.*—A group health plan means a plan (including a self-insured plan) of, or contributed to by, an employer (including a self-employed person) or employee organization to provide health care (directly or otherwise) to the employees, former employees, the employer, others associated or formerly associated with the employer in a business relationship, or their families.

(2) *Determination of number of plans.*—[Reserved.]

(b) *General exception for certain small group health plans.*—(1) Subject to paragraph (b)(2) of this section, the requirements of §§54.9801-1 through 54.9801-6, 54.9802-1, 54.9802-2, 54.9811-1, 54.9812-1, 54.9815-1251 through 54.9815-2719A, and 54.9833-1 do not apply to any group health plan for any plan year if, on the first day of the plan year, the plan has fewer than two participants who are current employees.

(2) The exception of paragraph (b)(1) of this section does not apply with respect to the following requirements:

(i) Section 54.9802-1(b), as such paragraph applies with respect to genetic information as a health factor.

(ii) Section 54.9802-1(c), as such paragraph applies with respect to genetic information as a health factor.

(iii) Section 54.9802-1(e), as such paragraph applies with respect to genetic information as a health factor.

(iv) Section 54.9802-3T(b).

(v) Section 54.9802-3T(c).

(vi) Section 54.9802-3T(d).

(vii) Section 54.9802-3T(e).

(c) *Excepted benefits.*—(1) *In general.*—The requirements of §§54.9801-1 through 54.9801-6, 54.9802-1, 54.9802-2, 54.9811-1, 54.9812-1, 54.9815-1251 through 54.9815-2719A, and 54.9833-1 do not apply to any group health plan in relation to its provision of the benefits described in paragraph (c)(2), (3), (4), or (5) of this section (or any combination of these benefits).

(2) *Benefits excepted in all circumstances.*—The following benefits are excepted in all circumstances —

(i) Coverage only for accident (including accidental death and dismemberment);

(ii) Disability income coverage;

(iii) Liability insurance, including general liability insurance and automobile liability insurance;

(iv) Coverage issued as a supplement to liability insurance;

(v) Workers' compensation or similar coverage;

(vi) Automobile medical payment insurance;

(vii) Credit-only insurance (for example, mortgage insurance);

(viii) Coverage for on-site medical clinics; and

(ix) Travel insurance, within the meaning of § 54.9801–2.

(3) *Limited excepted benefits.*—(i) *In general.*—Limited-scope dental benefits, limited-scope vision benefits, or long-term care benefits are excepted if they are provided under a separate policy, certificate, or contract of insurance, or are otherwise not an integral part of a group health plan as described in paragraph (c)(3)(ii) of this section. In addition, benefits provided under a health flexible spending arrangement are excepted benefits if they satisfy the requirements of paragraph (c)(3)(v) of this section. Furthermore, benefits provided under an employee assistance program are excepted benefits if they satisfy the requirements of paragraph (c)(3)(vi) of this section.

(ii) *Not an integral part of a group health plan.*—For purposes of this paragraph (c)(3), benefits are not an integral part of a group health plan (whether the benefits are provided through the same plan or a separate plan) only if the following two requirements are satisfied—

(A) Participants must have the right to elect not to receive coverage for the benefits; and

(B) If a participant elects to receive coverage for the benefits, the participant must pay an additional premium or contribution for that coverage.

(ii) *Not an integral part of a group health plan.*—For purposes of this paragraph (c)(3), benefits are not an integral part of a group health plan (whether the benefits are provided through the same plan, a separate plan, or as the only plan offered to participants) if either paragraph (c)(3)(ii)(A) or (B) are satisfied.

(A) Participants may decline coverage. For example, a participant may decline coverage if the participant can opt out of the coverage upon request, whether or not there is a participant contribution required for the coverage.

(B) Claims for the benefits are administered under a contract separate from claims administration for any other benefits under the plan.

(iii) *Limited scope.*—(A) *Dental benefits.*— Limited scope dental benefits are benefits substantially all of which are for treatment of the mouth (including any organ or structure within the mouth).

(B) *Vision benefits.*—Limited scope vision benefits are benefits substantially all of which are for treatment of the eye.

(iv) *Long-term care.*—Long-term care benefits are benefits that are either—

(A) Subject to state long-term care insurance laws;

(B) For qualified long-term care services, as defined in section 7702B(c)(1), or provided under a qualified long-term care insurance contract, as defined in section 7702B(b); or

(C) Based on cognitive impairment or a loss of functional capacity that is expected to be chronic.

(v) *Health flexible spending arrangements.*— Benefits provided under a health flexible spending arrangement (as defined in section 106(c)(2)) are excepted for a class of participants only if they satisfy the following two requirements—

(A) Other group health plan coverage, not limited to excepted benefits, is made available for the year to the class of participants by reason of their employment; and

(B) The arrangement is structured so that the maximum benefit payable to any participant in the class for a year cannot exceed two times the participant's salary reduction election under the arrangement for the year (or, if greater, cannot exceed $500 plus the amount of the participant's salary reduction election). For this purpose, any amount that an employee can elect to receive as taxable income but elects to apply to the health flexible spending arrangement is considered a salary reduction election (regardless of whether the amount is characterized as salary or as a credit under the arrangement).

(vi) *Employee assistance programs.*—Benefits provided under employee assistance programs are excepted if they satisfy all of the requirements of this paragraph (c)(3)(vi).

(A) The program does not provide significant benefits in the nature of medical care. For this purpose, the amount, scope and duration of covered services are taken into account.

(B) The benefits under the employee assistance program are not coordinated with benefits under another group health plan, as follows:

(1) Participants in the other group health plan must not be required to use and exhaust benefits under the employee assistance program (making the employee assistance program a gatekeeper) before an individual is eligible for benefits under the other group health plan; and

(2) Participant eligibility for benefits under the employee assistance program must not be dependent on participation in another group health plan.

(C) No employee premiums or contributions are required as a condition of participation in the employee assistance program.

(D) There is no cost sharing under the employee assistance program.

(vii) *Limited wraparound coverage.*—Limited benefits provided through a group health plan that wrap around eligible individual health insurance (or Basic Health Plan coverage described in section 1331 of the Patient Protection and Affordable Care Act); or that wrap around coverage under a Multi-State Plan described in section 1334 of the Patient Protection and Affordable Care Act, collectively referred to as "limited wraparound coverage," are excepted benefits if all of the following conditions are satisfied. For this purpose, eligible individual health insurance is individual health insurance coverage that is not a grandfathered health plan (as described in section 1251 of the Patient Protection and Affordable Care Act and 29 CFR 2590.715-1251), not a transitional individual health insurance plan (as described in the March 5, 2014 Insurance Standards Bulletin Series – Extension of Transitional Policy through October 1, 2016), and does not consist solely of excepted benefits (as defined in paragraph (c) of this section).

(A) *Covers additional benefits.*—The limited wraparound coverage provides meaningful benefits beyond coverage of cost sharing under either the eligible individual health insurance, Basic Health Program coverage, or Multi-State Plan coverage. The limited wraparound coverage must not provide benefits only under a coordination-of-benefits provision and must not consist of an account-based reimbursement arrangement.

(B) *Limited in amount.*—The annual cost of coverage per employee (and any covered dependents, as defined in §54.9801-2) under the limited wraparound coverage does not exceed the greater of the amount determined under either paragraph (c)(3)(vii)(B)(1) or (2) of this section. Making a determination regarding the annual cost of coverage per employee must occur on an aggregate basis relying on sound actuarial principles.

(1) The maximum permitted annual salary reduction contribution toward health flexible spending arrangements, indexed in the manner prescribed under section 125(i)(2). For this purpose, the cost of coverage under the limited wraparound includes both employer and employee contributions towards coverage and is determined in the same manner as the applicable premium is calculated under a COBRA continuation provision.

(2) Fifteen percent of the cost of coverage under the primary plan. For this purpose, the cost of coverage under the primary plan and under the limited wraparound coverage includes both employer and employee contributions towards the coverage and each is determined in the same manner as the applicable premium is calculated under a COBRA continuation provision.

(C) *Nondiscrimination.*—All of the conditions of this paragraph (c)(3)(vii)(C) are satisfied.

(1) *No preexisting condition exclusion.*—The limited wraparound coverage does not impose any preexisting condition exclusion, consistent with the requirements of section 2704

of the PHS Act (incorporated by reference into section 9815) and 29 CFR 2590.715-2704.

(2) *No discrimination based on health status.*—The limited wraparound coverage does not discriminate against individuals in eligibility, benefits, or premiums based on any health factor of an individual (or any dependent of the individual, as defined in §54.9801-2), consistent with the requirements of section 9802 and section 2705 of the PHS Act (incorporated by reference into section 9815).

(3) *No discrimination in favor of highly compensated individuals.*—Neither the limited wraparound coverage, nor any other group health plan coverage offered by the plan sponsor, fails to comply with section 2716 of the PHS Act (incorporated by reference into section 9815) or fails to be excludible from income for any individual due to the application of section 105(h)(as applicable).

(D) *Plan eligibility requirements.*—Individuals eligible for the wraparound coverage are not enrolled in excepted benefit coverage under paragraph (c)(3)(v) of this section (relating to health FSAs). In addition, the conditions set forth in either paragraph (c)(3)(vii)(D)(1) or (2) of this section are met.

(1) *Limited wraparound coverage that wraps around eligible individual insurance for persons who are not full-time employees.*—Coverage that wraps around eligible individual health insurance (or that wraps around Basic Health Plan coverage) must satisfy all of the conditions of this paragraph (c)(3)(vii)(D)(1).

(i) For each year for which limited wraparound coverage is offered, the employer that is the sponsor of the plan offering limited wraparound coverage, or the employer participating in a plan offering limited wraparound coverage, offers to its full-time employees coverage that is substantially similar to coverage that the employer would need to offer to its full-time employees in order not to be subject to a potential assessable payment under the employer shared responsibility provisions of section 4980H(a), if such provisions were applicable; provides minimum value (as defined in section 36B(c)(2)(C)(ii)); and is reasonably expected to be affordable (applying the safe harbor rules for determining affordability set forth in §54.4980H-5(e)(2)). If a plan or issuer providing limited wraparound coverage takes reasonable steps to ensure that employers disclose to the plan or issuer necessary information regarding their coverage offered and affordability information, the plan or issuer is permitted to rely on reasonable representations by employers regarding this information, unless the plan or issuer has specific knowledge to the contrary. In the event that the employer that is the sponsor of the plan offering wraparound coverage, or the employer participating in a plan offering wraparound coverage, has no full-time employees for any plan year limited wraparound coverage is offered, the requirement of this paragraph (c)(3)(vii)(D)(1)(i) is considered satisfied.

(ii) Eligibility for the limited wraparound coverage is limited to employees who are reasonably determined at the time of enrollment to not be full-time employees (and their dependents, as defined in § 54.9801-2), or who are retirees (and their dependents, as defined in § 54.9801-2). For this purpose, full-time employees are employees who are reasonably expected to work at least an average of 30 hours per week.

(iii) Other group health plan coverage, not limited to excepted benefits, is offered to the individuals eligible for the limited wraparound coverage. Only individuals eligible for the other group health plan coverage are eligible for the limited wraparound coverage.

(2) *Limited coverage that wraps around Multi-State Plan coverage.*—Coverage that wraps around Multi-State Plan coverage must satisfy all of the conditions of this paragraph (c)(3)(vii)(D)(2). For this purpose, the term "full-time employee" means a "full-time employee" as defined in § 54.4980H-1(a)(21). who is not in a limited non-assessment period for certain employees (as defined in § 54.4980H-1(a)(26)). Moreover, if a plan or issuer providing limited wraparound coverage takes reasonable steps to ensure that employers disclose to the plan or issuer necessary information regarding their coverage offered and contribution levels for 2013 or 2014 (as applicable), and for any year in which limited wraparound coverage is offered, the plan or issuer is permitted to rely on reasonable representations by employers regarding this information, unless the plan or issuer has specific knowledge to the contrary. Consistent with the reporting and evaluation criteria of paragraph (c)(3)(vii)(E) of this section, the Office of Personnel Management may verify that plans and issuers have reasonable mechanisms in place to ensure that contributing employers meet these standards.

(i) The limited wraparound coverage is reviewed and approved by the Office of Personnel Management, consistent with the reporting and evaluation criteria of paragraph (c)(3)(vii)(E) of this section, to provide benefits in conjunction with coverage under a Multi-State Plan authorized under section 1334 of the Patient Protection and Affordable Care Act. The Office of Personnel Management may revoke approval if it determines that continued approval is inconsistent with the reporting and evaluation criteria of paragraph (c)(3)(vii)(E) of this section.

(ii) The employer offered coverage in the plan year that began in either 2013 or 2014 that is substantially similar to coverage that the employer would need to have offered to its full-time employees in order to not be subject to an assessable payment under the employer shared responsibility provisions of section 4980H(a), if such provisions had been applicable. In the event that a plan that offered coverage in 2013 or 2014 has no full-time employees for any plan year limited wraparound coverage is offered, the

requirement of this paragraph (c)(3)(vii)(D)(2)(ii) is considered satisfied.

(iii) In the plan year that began in either 2013 or 2014, the employer offered coverage to a substantial portion of full-time employees that provided minimum value (as defined in section 36B(c)(2)(C)(ii)) and was affordable (applying the safe harbor rules for determining affordability set forth in § 54.4980H-5(e)(2)). In the event that the plan that offered coverage in 2013 or 2014 has no full-time employees for any plan year limited wraparound coverage is offered, the requirement of this paragraph (c)(3)(vii)(D)(2)(iii) is considered satisfied.

(iv) For the duration of the pilot program, as described in paragraph (c)(3)(vii)(F) of this section, the employer's annual aggregate contributions for both primary and limited wraparound coverage are substantially the same as the employer's total contributions for coverage offered to full-time employees in 2013 or 2014.

(E) *Reporting.*—(1) *Reporting by group health plans and group health insurance issuers.*—A self-insured group health plan, or a health insurance issuer, offering or proposing to offer limited wraparound coverage in connection with Multi-State Plan coverage pursuant to paragraph (c)(3)(vii)(D)(2) of this section reports to the Office of Personnel Management (OPM), in a form and manner specified in guidance, information OPM reasonably requires to determine whether the plan or issuer qualifies to offer such coverage or complies with the applicable requirements of this section.

(2) *Reporting by group health plan sponsors.*—The plan sponsor of a group health plan offering limited wraparound coverage under paragraph (c)(3)(vii) of this section, must report to the Department of Health and Human Services (HHS), in a form and manner specified in guidance, information HHS reasonably requires.

(F) *Pilot program with sunset.*—The provisions of paragraph (c)(3)(vii) of this section apply to limited wraparound coverage that is first offered no earlier than January 1, 2016 and no later than December 31, 2018 and that ends no later than on the later of:

(1) The date that is three years after the date limited wraparound coverage is first offered; or

(2) The date on which the last collective bargaining agreement relating to the plan terminates after the date limited wraparound coverage is first offered (determined without regard to any extension agreed to after the date limited wraparound coverage is first offered).

(4) *Noncoordinated benefits.*—(i) *Excepted benefits that are not coordinated.*—Coverage for only a specified disease or illness (for example, cancer-only policies) or hospital indemnity or other fixed indemnity insurance is excepted only if it meets each of the conditions specified in paragraph (c)(4)(ii) of this section. To be hospital

indemnity or other fixed indemnity insurance, the insurance must pay a fixed dollar amount per day (or per other period) of hospitalization or illness (for example, $100/day) regardless of the amount of expenses incurred.

(ii) *Conditions.*—Benefits are described in paragraph (c)(4)(i) of this section only if—

(A) The benefits are provided under a separate policy, certificate, or contract of insurance;

(B) There is no coordination between the provision of the benefits and an exclusion of benefits under any group health plan maintained by the same plan sponsor; and

(C) The benefits are paid with respect to an event without regard to whether benefits are provided with respect to the event under any group health plan maintained by the same plan sponsor.

(iii) *Example.*—The rules of this paragraph (c)(4) are illustrated by the following example:

Example. (i) *Facts.* An employer sponsors a group health plan that provides coverage through an insurance policy. The policy provides benefits only for hospital stays at a fixed percentage of hospital expenses up to a maximum of $100 a day.

(ii) *Conclusion.* In this *Example,* even though the benefits under the policy satisfy the conditions in paragraph (c)(4)(ii) of this section, because the policy pays a percentage of expenses incurred rather than a fixed dollar amount, the benefits under the policy are not excepted benefits under this paragraph (c)(4). This is the result even if, in practice, the policy pays the maximum of $100 for every day of hospitalization.

(5) *Supplemental benefits.*—(i) The following benefits are excepted only if they are provided under a separate policy, certificate, or contract of insurance—

(A) Medicare supplemental health insurance (as defined under section 1882(g)(1) of the Social Security Act; also known as Medigap or MedSupp insurance);

(B) Coverage supplemental to the coverage provided under Chapter 55, Title 10 of the United States Code (also known as TRICARE supplemental programs); and

(C) *Similar supplemental coverage provided to coverage under a group health plan.*—To be similar supplemental coverage, the coverage must be specifically designed to fill gaps in the primary coverage. The preceding sentence is satisfied if the coverage is designed to fill gaps in cost sharing in the primary coverage, such as coinsurance or deductibles, or the coverage is designed to provide benefits for items and services not covered by the primary coverage and that are not essential health benefits (as defined under section 1302(b) of the Patient Protection and Affordable Care Act) in the State where the

coverage is issued, or the coverage is designed to both fill such gaps in cost sharing under, and cover such benefits not covered by, the primary coverage. Similar supplemental coverage does not include coverage that becomes secondary or supplemental only under a coordination-of-benefits provision.

(ii) The rules of this paragraph (c)(5) are illustrated by the following example:

Example. (i) *Facts.* An employer sponsors a group health plan that provides coverage for both active employees and retirees. The coverage for retirees supplements benefits provided by Medicare, but does not meet the requirements for a supplemental policy under section 1882(g)(1) of the Social Security Act.

(ii) *Conclusion.* In this *Example,* the coverage provided to retirees does not meet the definition of supplemental excepted benefits under this paragraph (c)(5) because the coverage is not Medicare supplemental insurance as defined under section 1882(g)(1) of the Social Security Act, is not a TRICARE supplemental program, and is not supplemental to coverage provided under a group health plan.

(d) *Treatment of partnerships.*—For purposes of this part:

(1) *Treatment as a group health plan.*—(See 29 CFR 2590.732(d)(1) and 45 CFR 146.145(d)(1), under which a plan providing medical care, maintained by a partnership, and usually not treated as an employee welfare benefit plan under ERISA is treated as a group health plan for purposes of Part 7 of Subtitle B of Title I of ERISA and Title XXVII of the PHS Act.)

(2) *Employment relationship.*—In the case of a group health plan, the term *employer* also includes the partnership in relation to any bona fide partner. In addition, the term *employee* also includes any bona fide partner. Whether or not an individual is a bona fide partner is determined based on all the relevant facts and circumstances, including whether the individual performs services on behalf of the partnership.

(3) *Participants of group health plans.*—In the case of a group health plan, the term *participant* also includes any individual described in paragraph (d)(3)(i) or (ii) of this section if the individual is, or may become, eligible to receive a benefit under the plan or the individual's beneficiaries may be eligible to receive any such benefit.

(i) In connection with a group health plan maintained by a partnership, the individual is a partner in relation to the partnership.

(ii) In connection with a group health plan maintained by a self-employed individual (under which one or more employees are participants), the individual is the self-employed individual.

(e) *Determining the average number of employees.*—[Reserved.]

[Reg. § 54.9831-1.]

☐ [*T.D.* 9166, 12-29-2004 (*corrected* 4-25-2005). *Amended by T.D.* 9299, 12-12-2006; *T.D.* 9427, 10-17-2008; *T.D.* 9464, 10-1-2009; *T.D.* 9656, 2-20-2014, *T.D.* 9697, 9-26-2014, *T.D.* 9714, 3-16-2015 *and T.D.* 9791, 10-28-2016.]

[Reg. § 54.9833-1]

§ 54.9833-1. Applicability dates.—Sections 54.9801-1 through 54.9801-6, 54.9831-1, and this section are applicable for plan years beginning on or after July 1, 2005. Notwithstanding the previous sentence, the definition of "short-term, limited-duration insurance" in § 54.9801–2 applies October 2, 2018. [Reg. § 54.9833-1.]

☐ [*T.D.* 9166, 12-29-2004. *Amended by T.D.* 9791, 10-28-2016 *and T.D.* 9837, 8-1-2018.]

[The next page is 72,301.]

STATEMENT OF PROCEDURAL RULES

(26 C.F.R., Part 601)

Subpart A—General Procedural Rules

[Reg. § 601.101]

§ 601.101. Introduction.—(a) *General.*—The Internal Revenue Service is a bureau of the Department of the Treasury under the immediate direction of the Commissioner of Internal Revenue. The Commissioner has general superintendence of the assessment and collection of all taxes imposed by any law providing internal revenue. The Internal Revenue Service is the agency by which these functions are performed. Within an internal revenue district the internal revenue laws are administered by a district director of internal revenue. The Director, Foreign Operations District, administers the internal revenue laws applicable to taxpayers residing or doing business abroad, foreign taxpayers deriving income from sources within the United States, and taxpayers who are required to withhold tax on certain payments to nonresident aliens and foreign corporations, provided the books and records of those taxpayers are located outside the United States. For purposes of these procedural rules any reference to a district director or a district office includes the Director, Foreign Operations District, or the District Office, Foreign Operations District, if appropriate. Generally, the procedural rules of the Service are based on the Internal Revenue Code of 1939 and the Internal Revenue Code of 1954, and the procedural rules in this part apply to the taxes imposed by both Codes except to the extent specifically stated or where the procedure under one Code is incompatible with the procedure under the other Code. References to sections of the Code are references to the Internal Revenue Code of 1954, unless otherwise expressly indicated.

(b) *Scope.*—This part sets forth the procedural rules of the Internal Revenue Service respecting all taxes administered by the Service, and supersedes the previously published statement (26 CFR (1949 ed., Part 300-End) Parts 600 and 601) with respect to such procedural rules. Subpart A provides a descriptive statement of the general course and method by which the Service's functions are channeled and determined, insofar as such functions relate generally to the assessment, collection, and enforcement of internal revenue taxes. Certain provisions special to particular taxes are separately described in Subpart D of this part. Conference and practice requirements of the Internal Revenue Service are contained in Subpart E of this part. Specific matters not generally involved in the assessment, collection, and enforcement functions are separately described in Subpart B of this part. A description of the rulemaking functions of the Department of the Treasury with respect to internal revenue tax matters is contained in Subpart F of this part. Subpart G of this part relates to matters of official record in the Internal Revenue Service and the extent to which records and documents are subject to publication or open to public inspection. This part does not contain a detailed discussion of the substantive provisions pertaining to any particular tax or the procedures relating thereto, and for such information it is necessary that reference be made to the applicable provisions of law and the regulations promulgated thereunder. The regulations relating to the taxes administered by the Service are contained in Title 26 of the Code of Federal Regulations. The regulations administered by the Bureau of Alcohol, Tobacco and Firearms are contained in Title 27 of the Code of Federal Regulations. [Reg. § 601.101.]

☐ [38 FR 4955, Feb. 23, 1973 and 41 FR 20880, May 21, 1976, as amended at 45 FR 7251, Feb. 1, 1980; 49 FR 36498, Sept. 18, 1984; T.D. 8685, 61 FR 58008, Nov. 12, 1996.]

[Reg. § 601.102]

§ 601.102. Classification of taxes collected by the Internal Revenue Service.—(a) *Principal divisions.*—Internal Revenue taxes fall generally into the following principal divisions:

(1) Taxes collected by assessment.

(2) Taxes collected by means of revenue stamps.

(b) *Assessed taxes.*—Taxes collected principally by assessment fall into the following two main classes—

(1) Taxes within the jurisdiction of the United States Tax Court. These include:

(i) Income and profits taxes imposed by chapters 1 and 2 of the 1939 Code and taxes imposed by subtitle A of the 1954 Code, relating to income taxes.

(ii) Estate taxes imposed by chapter 3 of the 1939 Code and chapter 11 of the 1954 Code.

(iii) Gift tax imposed by chapter 4 of the 1939 Code and chapter 12 of the 1954 Code.

(iv) The tax on generation-skipping transfers imposed by chapter 13 of the 1954 Code.

(v) Taxes imposed by chapters 41 through 44 of the 1954 Code.

(2) Taxes not within the jurisdiction of the United States Tax Court. Taxes not imposed by chapter 1, 2, 3, or 4 of the 1939 Code or subtitle A or chapter 11 or 12 of the 1954 Code are within this class, such as—

(i) Employment taxes.

(ii) Miscellaneous excise taxes collected by return.

(3) The difference between these two main classes is that only taxes described in subparagraph (1) of this paragraph, i.e., those within the jurisdiction of the Tax Court, may be contested before an independent tribunal prior to pay-

ment. Taxes of both classes may be contested by first making payment, filing claim for refund, and then bringing suit to recover if the claim is disallowed or no decision is rendered thereon within six months. [Reg. § 601.102.]

☐ [32 FR 15990, Nov. 22, 1967, as amended at 35 FR 7111, May 6, 1970; 46 FR 26053, May 11, 1981; T.D. 8685, 61 FR 58008, Nov. 12, 1996.]

[Reg. § 601.103]

§ 601.103. Summary of general tax procedure.—(a) *Collection procedure.*—The Federal tax system is basically one of self-assessment. In general each taxpayer (or person required to collect and pay over the tax) is required to file a prescribed form of return which shows the facts upon which tax liability may be determined and assessed. Generally, the taxpayer must compute the tax due on the return and make payment thereof on or before the due date for filing the return. If the taxpayer fails to pay the tax when due, the district director of internal revenue or the director of the regional service center after assessment issues a notice and demands payment within 10 days from the date of the notice. In the case of wage earners, annuitants, pensioners, and nonresident aliens, the income tax is collected in large part through withholding at the source. Another means of collecting the income tax is through payments of estimated tax which are required by law to be paid by certain individual and corporate taxpayers. Neither withholding nor payments of estimated tax relieves a taxpayer from the duty of filing a return otherwise required. Certain excise taxes are collected by the sale of internal revenue stamps.

(b) *Examination and determination of tax liability.*—After the returns are filed and processed in internal revenue service centers, some returns are selected for examination. If adjustments are proposed with which the taxpayer does not agree, ordinarily the taxpayer is afforded certain appeal rights. If the taxpayer agrees to the proposed adjustments and the tax involved is an income, profits, estate, gift, generation-skipping transfer, or chapter 41, 42, 43, or 44 tax, and if the taxpayer waives restrictions on the assessment and collection of the tax (see § 601.105(b)(4)), the deficiency will be immediately assessed.

(c) *Disputed liability.*—(1) *General.*—The taxpayer is given an opportunity to request that the case be considered by an Appeals Office provided that office has jurisdiction (see § 601.106(a)(3)). If the taxpayer requests such consideration, the case will be referred to the Appeals Office, which will afford the taxpayer the opportunity for a conference. The determination of tax liability by the Appeals Office is final insofar as the taxpayer's appeal rights within the Services are concerned. Upon protest of cases under the jurisdiction of the Director, Foreign Operations District, exclusive settlement authority is vested in the Appeals Office having jurisdiction of the place where the taxpayer requests the conference. If the taxpayer does not specify a location for the conference, or if the location specified is outside the territorial limits of the

United States, the Washington, D.C. Appeals Office of the Mid-Atlantic Region assumes jurisdiction.

(2) *Petition to the U.S. Tax Court.*—In the case of income, profits, estate, and gift taxes imposed by subtitles A and B, and excise taxes under chapters 41 through 44 of the 1954 Code, before a deficiency may be assessed a statutory notice of deficiency (commonly called a "90-day letter") must be sent to the taxpayer by certified mail or registered mail unless the taxpayer waives this restriction on assessment. See, however, §§ 601.105(h) and 601.109 for exceptions. The taxpayer may then file a petition for a redetermination of the proposed deficiency with the U.S. Tax Court within 90 days from the date of the mailing of the statutory notice. If the notice is addressed to a person outside the States of the Union and the District of Columbia, the period within which a petition may be filed in the Tax Court is 150 days in lieu of 90 days. In other words, the taxpayer has the right in respect of these taxes to contest any proposed deficiency before an independent tribunal prior to assessment or payment of the deficiency. Unless the taxpayer waives the restrictions on assessment and collection after the date of the mailing of the statutory notice, no assessment or collection of a deficiency (not including the correction of a mathematical error) may be made in respect of these taxes until the expiration of the applicable period or, if a petition is filed with the Tax Court, until the decision of the Court has become final. If, however, the taxpayer makes a payment with respect to a deficiency, the amount of such payment may be assessed. See, however, § 601.105(h). If the taxpayer fails to file a petition with the Tax Court within the applicable period, the deficiency will be assessed upon the expiration of such period and notice and demand for payment of the amount thereof will be mailed to the taxpayer. If the taxpayer files a petition with the Tax Court, the entire amount redetermined as the deficiency by a final decision of the Tax Court will be assessed and is payable upon notice and demand. There are no restrictions on the timely assessment and collection of the amount of any deficiency determined by the Tax Court, and a notice of appeal of the Court's decision will not stay the assessment and collection of the deficiency so determined, unless on or before the time the notice of appeal is filed the taxpayer files with the Tax Court a bond in a sum fixed by the Court not exceeding twice the portion of the deficiency in respect of which the notice of appeal is filed. No part of an amount determined as a deficiency but disallowed as such by a decision of the Tax Court which has become final may be assessed or collected by levy or by proceeding in court with or without assessment.

(3) *Claims for refund.*—After payment of the tax a taxpayer may, within the applicable period of limitations, contest the assessment by filing with the district director a claim for refund of all or any part of the amount paid, except with respect to certain taxes determined by the Tax Court, the decision of which has become final. If

the claim is allowed, the overpayment of tax and allowable interest thereon will be credited against other liabilities of the taxpayer, or will be refunded to the taxpayer. Generally, if the claim for refund is rejected in whole or in part, the taxpayer is notified of the rejection by certified mail or registered mail. The taxpayer may then bring suit in the United States District Court or in the United States Claims Court for recovery of the tax. Suit may not be commenced before the expiration of six months from the date of filing of the claim for refund, unless a decision is rendered thereon within that time, nor after the expiration of two years from the date of mailing by certified mail or registered mail to the taxpayer of a notice of the disallowance of the part of the claim to which the suit relates. Under the 1954 Code, the 2-year period of limitation for bringing suit may be extended for such period as may be agreed upon in a properly executed Form 907. Also, under the 1954 Code, if the taxpayer files a written waiver of the requirement that the taxpayer be sent a notice of disallowance, the 2-year period for bringing suit begins to run on the date such waiver is filed. See section 6532(a) of the Code. [Reg. § 601.103.]

☐ [32 FR 15990, Nov. 22, 1967, as amended at 38 FR 4955, Feb. 23, 1973; 43 FR 44497, Sept. 28, 1978; 45 FR 7251, Feb. 1, 1980; 46 FR 26053, May 11, 1981; 49 FR 36498, Sept. 18, 1984.]

[Reg. § 601.104]

§ 601.104. Collection functions.— (a) *Collection methods.*—(1) *Returns.*—Generally, an internal revenue tax assessment is based upon a return required by law or regulations to be filed by the taxpayer upon which the taxpayer computes the tax in the manner indicated by the return. Certain taxpayers who choose to use the Optional Tax Tables may elect to have the Internal Revenue Service compute the tax and mail them a notice stating the amount of tax due. If a taxpayer fails to make a return it may be made for the taxpayer by a district director or other duly authorized officer or employee. See section 6020 of the Code and the regulations thereunder. Returns must be made on the forms prescribed by the Internal Revenue Service. Forms are obtainable at the principal and branch offices of district directors of internal revenue. Taxpayers overseas may also obtain forms from any United States Embassy or consulate. Forms are generally mailed to persons whom the Service has reason to believe may be required to file returns, but failure to receive a form does not excuse failure to comply with the law or regulations requiring a return. Returns, supplementary returns, statements or schedules, and the time for filing them, may sometimes be prescribed by regulations issued under authority of law by the Commissioner with the approval of the Secretary of the Treasury or the Secretary's delegate. A husband and wife may make a single income tax return jointly. Certain affiliated groups of corporations may file consolidated income tax returns. See section 1501 of the Code and the regulations thereunder.

(2) *Withholding of tax at source.*—Withholding at the source of income payments is an important method used in collecting taxes. For example, in the case of wage earners, the income tax is collected in large part through the withholding by employers of taxes on wages paid to their employees. The tax withheld at the source on wages is applied as a credit in payment of the individual's income tax liability for the taxable year. In no case does withholding of the tax relieve an individual from the duty of filing a return otherwise required by law. The chief means of collecting the income tax due from nonresident alien individuals and foreign corporations having United States source gross income which is not effectively connected with the conduct of a trade or business in the United States is the withholding of the tax by persons paying or remitting the income to the recipients. The tax withheld is allowed as a credit in payment of the tax imposed on such nonresident alien individuals and foreign corporations.

(3) *Payments of estimated tax.*—Any individual who may reasonably expect to receive gross income for the taxable year from wages or from sources other than wages, in excess of amounts specified by law, and who can reasonably expect his or her estimated tax to be at least $200 in 1982, $300 in 1983, $400 in 1984, and $500 in 1985 and later is required to make estimated tax payments. Payments of estimated tax are applied in payment of the tax for the taxable year. A husband and wife may jointly make a single payment which may be applied in payment of the income tax liability of either spouse in any proportion they may specify. For taxable years ending on or after December 31, 1955, the law requires payments of estimated tax by certain corporations. See section 6154 of the Code.

(b) *Extension of time for filing returns.*—(1) *General.*—Under certain circumstances the district directors or directors of service centers are authorized to grant a reasonable extension of time for filing a return or declaration. The maximum period for extensions cannot be in excess of 6 months, except in the case of taxpayers who are abroad. With an exception in the case of estate tax returns, written application for extension must be received by the appropriate director on or before the date prescribed by law for filing the return or declaration.

(2) *Corporations.*—On or before the date prescribed by law for filing its income tax return, a corporation may obtain an automatic 6-month extension of time (a 3-month extension in the case of taxable years ending before December 31, 1982) for filing the income tax return by filing Form 7004 and paying the full amount of the properly estimated unpaid tax liability. For taxable years beginning before 1983, however, the corporation must remit with Form 7004 an estimated amount not less than would be assessed as the first installment of tax should the corporation elect to pay the tax in installments.

(3) *Individuals.*—On or before the date prescribed for the filing of the return of an individ-

ual, such individual may obtain an automatic 4-month extension of time for filing his or her return by filing Form 4868 accompanied by payment of the full amount of the estimated unpaid tax liability.

(c) *Enforcement procedure.*—(1) *General.*—Taxes shown to be due on returns, deficiencies in taxes, additional or delinquent taxes to be assessed, and penalties, interest, and additions to taxes, are recorded by the district director or the director of the appropriate service center as "assessments." Under the law an assessment is prima facie correct for all purposes. Generally, the taxpayer bears the burden of disproving the correctness of an assessment. Upon assessment, the district director is required to effect collection of any amounts which remain due and unpaid. Generally, payment within 10 days from the date of the notice and demand for payment is requested; however, payment may be required in a shorter period if collection of the tax is considered to be in jeopardy. When collection of income tax is in jeopardy, the taxpayer's taxable period may be terminated under section 6851 of the Code and assessment of the tax made expeditiously under section 6201 of the Code.

(2) *Levy.*—If a taxpayer neglects or refuses to pay any tax within the period provided for its payment, it is lawful for the district director to make collection by levy on the taxpayer's property. However, unless collection is in jeopardy, the taxpayer must be furnished written notice of intent to levy no fewer than 10 days before the date of the levy. See section 6331 of the Code. No suit for the purpose of restraining the assessment or collection of an internal revenue tax may be maintained in any court, except to restrain the assessment or collection of income, estate, chapters 41 through 44, or gift taxes during the period within which the assessment or collection of deficiencies in such taxes is prohibited. See section 7421 of the Code. Property taken under authority of any revenue law of the United States is irrepleviable. 28 U.S.C. 2463. If the Service sells property, and it is subsequently determined that the taxpayer had no interest in the property or that the purchaser was misled by the Service as to the value of the taxpayer's interest, immediate action will be taken to refund any money wrongfully collected if a claim is made and the pertinent facts are present. The mere fact that a taxpayer's interest in property turns out to be less valuable than the purchaser expected will not be regarded as giving the purchaser any claim against the Government.

(3) *Liens.*—The United States' claim for taxes is a lien on the taxpayer's property at the time of assessment. Such lien is not valid as against any purchaser, holder of a security interest, mechanic's lienor, or judgment lien creditor until notice has been filed by the district director. Despite such filing, the lien is not valid with respect to certain securities as against any purchaser of such security who, at the time of purchase, did not have actual notice or knowledge of the existence of such lien and as against

a holder of a security interest in such security who, at the time such interest came into existence, did not have actual notice or knowledge of the existence of such lien. Certain motor vehicle purchases are similarly protected. Even though a notice of lien has been filed, certain other categories are afforded additional protection. These categories are: Retain purchases, casual sales, possessory liens, real property taxes and property assessments, small repairs and improvements, attorneys' liens, certain insurance contracts and passbook loans. A valid lien generally continues until the liability is satisfied; becomes unenforceable by reason of lapse of time or is discharged in bankruptcy. A certificate of release of lien will be issued not later than 30 days after the taxpayer furnishes proper bond in lieu of the lien, or 30 days after it is determined that the liability has been satisfied, has become unenforceable by reason of lapse of time, or has been discharged in bankruptcy. If a certificate has not been issued and one of the foregoing criteria for release has been met, a certificate of release of lien will be issued within 30 days after a written request by a taxpayer, specifying the grounds upon which the issuance of release is sought. The Code also contains additional provisions with respect to the discharge of specific property from the effect of the lien. Also, under certain conditions, a lien may be subordinated. The Code also contains additional provisions with respect to liens in the case of estate and gift taxes. For the specific rules with respect to liens, see subchapter C of chapter 64 of the Code and the regulations thereunder.

(4) *Penalties.*—In the case of failure to file a return within the prescribed time, a certain percentage of the amount of tax (or a minimum penalty) is, pursuant to statute, added to the tax unless the failure to file the return within the prescribed time is shown to the satisfaction of the district director or the director of the appropriate service center to be due to reasonable cause and not neglect. In the case of failure to file an exempt organization information return within the prescribed time, a penalty of $10 a day for each day the return is delinquent is assessed unless the failure to file the return within the prescribed time is shown to be due to reasonable cause and not neglect. In the case of failure to pay or deposit taxes due within the prescribed time, a certain percentage of the amount of tax due is, pursuant to statute, added to the tax unless the failure to pay or deposit the tax due within the prescribed time is shown to the satisfaction of the district director or the director of the appropriate service center to be due to reasonable cause and not neglect. Civil penalties are also imposed for fraudulent returns; in the case of income and gift taxes, for intentional disregard of rules and regulations or negligence; and additions to the tax are imposed for the failure to comply with the requirements of law with respect to the estimated income tax. There are also civil penalties for filing false withholding certificates, for substantial understatement of income tax, for filing a frivolous return, for or-

ganizing or participating in the sale of abusive tax shelters, and for aiding and abetting in the understatement of tax liability. See chapter 68 of the Code. A 50 percent penalty, in addition to the personal liability incurred, is imposed upon any person who fails or refuses without reasonable cause to honor a levy. Criminal penalties are imposed for willful failure to make returns, keep records, supply information, etc. See chapter 75 of the Code.

(5) *Informants' rewards.*—Payments to informers are authorized for detecting and bringing to trial and punishment persons guilty of violating the internal revenue laws. See section 7623 of the Code and the regulations thereunder. Claims for rewards should be made on Form 211. Relevant facts should be stated on the form, which after execution should be forwarded to the district director of internal revenue for the district in which the informer resides, or the Commissioner of Internal Revenue, Washington, D.C. 20224. [Reg. § 601.104.]

☐ [32 FR 15990, Nov. 22, 1967, as amended at 32 FR 20645, Dec. 21, 1967; 33 FR 17234, Nov. 21, 1968; 34 FR 6424, Apr. 12, 1969; 35 FR 7112, May 6, 1970; 36 FR 7584, Apr. 22, 1971; 38 FR 4956, Feb. 23, 1973; 45 FR 7251, Feb. 1, 1980; 49 FR 36499, Sept. 18, 1984; 49 FR 40809, Oct. 18, 1984; T.D. 8685, 61 FR 58008, Nov. 12, 1996.]

[Reg. § 601.105]

§ 601.105. Examination of returns and claims for refund, credit or abatement; determination of correct tax liability.—(a) *Processing of returns.*—When the returns are filed in the office of the district director of internal revenue or the office of the director of a regional service center, they are checked first for form, execution, and mathematical accuracy. Mathematical errors are corrected and a correction notice of any such error is sent to the taxpayer. Notice and demand is made for the payment of any additional tax so resulting, or refund is made of any overpayment. Returns are classified for examination at regional service centers. Certain individual income tax returns with potential unallowable items are delivered to Examination Divisions at regional service centers for correction by correspondence. Otherwise, returns with the highest examination potential are delivered to district Examination Divisions based on workload capacities. Those most in need of examination are selected for office or field examination.

(b) *Examination of returns.*—(1) *General.*—The original examination of income (including partnership and fiduciary), estate, gift, excise, employment, exempt organization, and information returns is a primary function of examiners in the Examination Division of the office of each district director of internal revenue. Such examiners are organized in groups, each of which is under the immediate supervision of a group supervisor designated by the district director. Revenue agents (and such other officers or employees of the Internal Revenue Service as may be designated for this purpose by the Commissioner) are authorized to examine any books, papers,

records, or memoranda bearing upon matters required to be included in Federal tax returns and to take testimony relative thereto and to administer oaths. See section 7602 of the Code and the regulations thereunder. There are two general types of examination. These are commonly called "office examination" and "field examination". During the examination of a return a taxpayer may be represented before the examining officer by an attorney, certified public accountant, or other representative. See Subpart E of this part for conference and practice requirements.

(2) *Office examination.*—(i) *Adjustments by Examination Division at service center.*—Certain individual income tax returns identified as containing potential unallowable items are examined by Examination Divisions at regional service centers. Correspondence examination techniques are used. If the taxpayer requests an interview to discuss the proposed adjustments, the case is transferred to the taxpayer's district office. If the taxpayer does not agree to the proposed adjustments, regular appeals procedures apply.

(ii) *Examinations at district office.*—Certain returns are examined at district offices by office examination techniques. These returns include some business returns, besides the full range of nonbusiness individual income tax returns. Office examinations are conducted primarily by the interview method. Examinations are conducted by correspondence only when warranted by the nature of the questionable items and by the convenience and characteristics of the taxpayer. In a correspondence examination, the taxpayer is asked to explain or send supporting evidence by mail. In an office interview examination the taxpayer is asked to come to the district director's office for an interview and to bring certain records with the taxpayer in support of the return. During the interview examination, the taxpayer has the right to point out to the examining officer any amounts included in the return which are not taxable, or any deductions which the taxpayer failed to claim on the return. If it develops that a field examination is necessary, the examiner may conduct such examination.

(3) *Field examination.*—Certain returns are examined by field examination which involves an examination of the taxpayer's books and records on the taxpayer's premises. An examiner will check the entire return filed by the taxpayer and will examine all books, papers, records, and memoranda dealing with matters required to be included in the return. If the return presents an engineering or appraisal problem (e.g., depreciation or depletion deductions, gains or losses upon the sale or exchange of property, or losses on account of abandonment, exhaustion, or obsolescence), it may be investigated by an engineer agent who makes a separate report.

(4) *Conclusion of examination.*—At the conclusion of an office or field examination, the taxpayer is given an opportunity to agree with the findings of the examining officer. If the tax-

payer does not agree, the examining officer will inform the taxpayer of the taxpayer's appeal rights. If the taxpayer does agree with the proposed changes the examining officer will invite the taxpayer to execute either Form 870 or another appropriate agreement form. When the taxpayer agrees with the proposed changes but does not offer to pay any deficiency or additional tax which may be due, the examining officer will also invite payment (by check or money order), together with any applicable interest or penalty. If the agreed case involves income, profits, estate, gift, generation-skipping transfer or chapter 41, 42, 43 or 44 taxes, the agreement is evidenced by a waiver by the taxpayer of restrictions on assessment and collection of the deficiency, or an acceptance of a proposed overassessment. If the case involves excise or employment taxes or 100 percent penalty, the agreement is evidenced in the form of a consent to assessment and collection of additional tax or penalty and waiver of right to file claim for abatement, or the acceptance of the proposed overassessment. Even though the taxpayer signs an acceptance of a proposed overassessment the district director or the director of the regional service center remains free to assess a deficiency. On the other hand, the taxpayer who has given a waiver may still claim a refund of any part of the deficiency assessed against, and paid by, the taxpayer or any part of the tax originally assessed and paid by the taxpayer. The taxpayer's acceptance of an agreed overassessment does not prevent the taxpayer from filing a claim and bringing a suit for an additional sum, nor does it preclude the Government from maintaining suit to recover an erroneous refund. As a matter of practice, however, waivers or acceptances ordinarily result in the closing of a case insofar as the Government is concerned.

(5) *Technical advice from the National Office.*— (i) *Definition and nature of technical advice.*— (a) As used in this subparagraph, "technical advice" means advice or guidance as to the interpretation and proper application of internal revenue laws, related statutes, and regulations, to a specific set of facts, furnished by the National Office upon request of a district office in connection with the examination of a taxpayer's return or consideration of a taxpayer's return claim for refund or credit. It is furnished as a means of assisting Service personnel in closing cases and establishing and maintaining consistent holdings in the several districts. It does not include memorandums on matters of general technical application furnished to district offices where the issues are not raised in connection with the examination of the return of a specific taxpayer.

(b) The consideration or examination of the facts relating to a request for a determination letter is considered to be in connection with the examination or consideration of a return of the taxpayer. Thus, a district director may, in his discretion, request technical advice with respect to the consideration of a request for a determination letter.

(c) If a district director is of the opinion that a ruling letter previously issued to a taxpayer should be modified or revoked, and requests the National Office to reconsider the ruling, the reference of the matter to the National Office is treated as a request for technical advice and the procedures specified in subdivision (iii) of this subparagraph should be followed in order that the National Office may consider the district director's recommendation.

Only the National Office can revoke a ruling letter. Before referral to the National Office, the district director should inform the taxpayer of his opinion that the ruling letter should be revoked. The district director, after development of the facts and consideration of the taxpayer's arguments, will decide whether to recommend revocation of the ruling to the National Office. For procedures relating to a request for a ruling, see § 601.201.

(d) The Assistant Commissioner (Technical), acting under a delegation of authority from the Commissioner of Internal Revenue, is exclusively responsible for providing technical advice in any issue involving the establishment of basic principles and rules for the uniform interpretation and application of tax laws other than those which are under the jurisdiction of the Bureau of Alcohol, Tobacco, and Firearms. This authority has been largely redelegated to subordinate officials.

(e) The provisions of this subparagraph apply only to a case under the jurisdiction of a district director, but do not apply to the Employee Plans case under the jurisdiction of a key district director as provided in § 601.201(o) or to an Exempt Organization case under the jurisdiction of a key district director as provided in § 601.201(n). The technical advice provisions applicable to Employee Plans and Exempt Organization cases are set forth in § 601.201(n)(9). The provisions of this subparagraph do not apply to a case under the jurisdiction of the Bureau of Alcohol, Tobacco, and Firearms. They also do not apply to a case under the jurisdiction of an Appeals office, including a case previously considered by Appeals. The technical advice provisions applicable to a case under the jurisdiction of an Appeals office, other than Employee Plans and Exempt Organizations cases, are set forth in § 601.106(f)(10). A case remains under the jurisdiction of the district director even though an Appeals office has the identical issue under consideration in the case of another taxpayer (not related within the meaning of section 267 of the Code) in an entirely different transaction. Technical advice may not be requested with respect to a taxable period if a prior Appeals disposition of the same taxable period of the same taxpayer's case was based on mutual concessions (ordinarily with a Form 870-AD, Offer of Waiver of Restrictions on Assessment and Collection of Deficiency in Tax and of Acceptance of Overassessment). However, technical advice may be requested by a district director on issues previously considered in a prior Appeals disposition, not based on mutual concessions, of the same taxable periods of the same taxpayer with the concurrence of the Appeals office that had the case.

(ii) *Areas in which technical advice may be requested.*—*(a)* District directors may request technical advice on any technical or procedural question that develops during the audit or examination of a return, or claim for refund or credit, of a taxpayer. These procedures are applicable as provided in subdivision (i) of this subparagraph.

(b) District directors are encouraged to request technical advice on any technical or procedural question arising in connection with any case of the type described in subdivision (i) of this subparagraph which cannot be resolved on the basis of law, regulations, or a clearly applicable revenue ruling or other precedent issued by the National Office. This request should be made at the earliest possible stage of the examination process.

(iii) *Requesting technical advice.*—*(a)* It is the responsibility of the district office to determine whether technical advice is to be requested on any issue before that office. However, while the case is under the jurisdiction of the district director, a taxpayer or his/her representative may request that an issue be referred to the National Office for technical advice on the grounds that a lack of uniformity exists as to the disposition of the issue, or that the issue is so unusual or complex as to warrant consideration by the National Office. This request should be made at the earliest possible stage of the examination process. While taxpayers are encouraged to make written requests setting forth the facts, law, and argument with respect to the issue, and reason for requesting National Office advice, a taxpayer may make the request orally. If, after considering the taxpayer's request, the examiner is of the opinion that the circumstances do not warrant referral of the case to the National Office, he/she will so advise the taxpayer. (See subdivision (iv) of this subparagraph for taxpayer's appeal rights where the examiner declines to request technical advice.)

(b) When technical advice is to be requested, whether or not upon the request of the taxpayer, the taxpayer will be so advised, except as noted in (g) of this subdivision. If the examiner initiates the action, the taxpayer will be furnished a copy of the statement of the pertinent facts and the question or questions proposed for submission to the National Office. The request for advice submitted by the district director should be so worded as to avoid possible misunderstanding, in the National Office, of the facts or of the specific point or points at issue.

(c) After receipt of the statement of facts and specific questions from the district office, the taxpayer will be given 10 calendar days in which to indicate in writing the extent, if any, to which he may not be in complete agreement. An extension of time must be justified by the taxpayer in writing and approved by the Chief, Audit Division. Every effort should be made to reach agreement as to the facts and specific point at issue. If agreement cannot be reached, the taxpayer may submit, within 10 calendar days

after receipt of notice from the district office, a statement of his understanding as to the specific point or points at issue which will be forwarded to the National Office with the request for advice. An extension of time must be justified by the taxpayer in writing and approved by the Chief, Examination Division.

(d) If the taxpayer initiates the action to request advice, and his statement of the facts and point or points at issue are not wholly acceptable to the district officials, the taxpayer will be advised in writing as to the areas of disagreement. The taxpayer will be given 10 calendar days after receipt of the written notice to reply to the district official's letter. An extension of time must be justified by the taxpayer in writing and approved by the Chief, Examination Division. If agreement cannot be reached, both the statements of the taxpayer and the district official will be forwarded to the National Office.

(e)(1) In the case of requests for technical advice the taxpayer must also submit, within the 10-day period referred to in (c) and (d) of this subdivision, whichever applicable (relating to agreement by the taxpayer with the statement of facts submitted in connection with the request for technical advice), the statement described in (f) of this subdivision of proposed deletions pursuant to section 6110(c) of the Code. If the statement is not submitted, the taxpayer will be informed by the district director that such a statement is required. If the district director does not receive the statement within 10 days after the taxpayer has been informed of the need for such statement, the district director may decline to submit the request for technical advice. If the district director decides to request technical advice in a case where the taxpayer has not submitted the statement of proposed deletions, the National Office will make those deletions which in the judgment of the Commissioner are required by section 6110(c) of the Code.

(2) The requirements included in §601.105(b)(5) with respect to submissions of statements and other material with respect to proposed deletions to be made from technical advice memoranda before public inspection is permitted to take place do not apply to requests made by the district director before November 1, 1976, or requests for any document to which section 6104 of the Code applies.

(f) In order to assist the Internal Revenue Service in making the deletions, required by section 6110(c) of the Code, from the text of technical advice memoranda which are open to public inspection pursuant to section 6110(a) of the Code, there must accompany requests for such technical advice either a statement of the deletions proposed by the taxpayer and the statutory basis for each proposed deletion, or a statement that no information other than names, addresses, and taxpayer identifying numbers need be deleted. Such statements shall be made in a separate document. The statement of proposed deletions shall be accompanied by a copy of all statements of facts and supporting documents which are submitted to the National Office pursuant to (c) or (d) of this subdivision, on which shall be indicated, by the use of brackets, the material which the taxpayer indicates should be deleted pursuant to section 6110(c) of the Code. The statement of proposed deletions shall indicate the statutory basis, under section 6110(c) of the Code, for each proposed deletion. The statement of proposed deletions shall not appear or be referred to anywhere in the request for technical advice. If the taxpayer decides to request additional deletions pursuant to section 6110(c) of the Code prior to the time the National Office replies to the request for technical advice, additional statements may be submitted.

(g) If the taxpayer has not already done so, the taxpayer may submit a statement explaining the taxpayer's position on the issues, citing precedents which the taxpayer believes will bear on the case. This statement will be forwarded to the National Office with the request for advice. If it is received at a later date, it will be forwarded for association with the case file.

(h) At the time the taxpayer is informed that the matter is being referred to the National Office, the taxpayer will also be informed of the right to a conference in the National Office in the event an adverse decision is indicated, and will be asked to indicate whether such a conference is desired.

(i) Generally, prior to replying to the request for technical advice, the National Office shall inform the taxpayer orally or in writing of the material likely to appear in the technical advice memorandum which the taxpayer proposed be deleted but which the Internal Revenue Service determined should not be deleted. If so informed, the taxpayer may submit within 10 days any further information, arguments or other material in support of the position that such material be deleted. The Internal Revenue Service will attempt, if feasible, to resolve all disagreements with respect to proposed deletions prior to the time the National Office replies to the request for technical advice. However, in no event shall the taxpayer have the right to a conference with respect to resolution of any disagreements concerning material to be deleted from the text of the technical advice memorandum, but such matters may be considered at any conference otherwise scheduled with respect to the request.

(j) The provisions of (a) through (i) of this subdivision, relating to the referral of issues upon request of the taxpayer, advising taxpayers of the referral of issues, the submission of proposed deletions, and the granting of conferences in the National Office, are not applicable to technical advice memoranda described in section 6110(g)(5)(A) of the Code, relating to cases involving criminal or civil fraud investigations and jeopardy or termination assessments. However, in such cases the taxpayer shall be allowed to provide the statement of proposed deletions to the National Office upon the completion of all proceedings with respect to the investigations or assessments, but prior to the date on which the Commissioner mails the notice pursuant to section 6110(f)(1) of the Code of intention to disclose the technical advice memorandum.

(k) Form 4463, Request for Technical Advice, should be used for transmitting requests for technical advice to the National Office.

(iv) *Appeal by taxpayers of determinations not to seek technical advice.*—(a) If the taxpayer has requested referral of an issue before a district office to the National Office for technical advice, and after consideration of the request the examiner is of the opinion that the circumstances do not warrant such referral, the examiner will so advise the taxpayer.

(b) The taxpayer may appeal the decision of the examining officer not to request technical advice by submitting to that official, within 10 calendar days after being advised of the decision, a statement of the facts, law, and arguments with respect to the issue, and the reasons why he believes the matter should be referred to the National Office for advice. An extension of time must be justified by the taxpayer in writing and approved by the Chief, Examination Division.

(c) The examining officer will submit the statement of the taxpayer through channels to the Chief, Examination Division, accompanied by a statement of his reasons why the issue should not be referred to the National Office. The Chief, Examination Division, will determine, on the basis of the statements submitted, whether technical advice will be requested. If he determines that technical advice is not warranted, he will inform the taxpayer in writing that he proposes to deny the request. In the letter to the taxpayer the Chief, Examination Division, will (except in unusual situations where such action would be prejudicial to the best interests of the Government) state specifically the reasons for the proposed denial. The taxpayer will be given 15 calendar days after receipt of the letter in which to notify the Chief, Examination Division, whether he agrees with the proposed denial. The taxpayer may not appeal the decision of the Chief, Examination Division, not to request technical advice from the National Office. However, if he does not agree with the proposed denial, all data relating to the issue for which technical advice has been sought, including taxpayer's written request and statements, will be submitted to the National Office, Attention: Director, Examination Division, for review. After review in the National Office, the district office will be notified whether the proposed denial is approved or disapproved.

(d) While the matter is being reviewed in the National Office, the district office will suspend action on the issue (except where the delay would prejudice the Government's interests) until it is notified of the National Office decision. This notification will be made within 30 days after receipt of the data in the National Office. The review will be solely on the basis of the written record and no conference will be held in the National Office.

(v) *Conference in the National Office.*—(a) If, after a study of the technical advice request, it appears that advice adverse to the taxpayer should be given and a conference has been requested, the taxpayer will be notified of the time and place of the conference. If conferences are being arranged with respect to more than one request for advice involving the same taxpayer, they will be so scheduled as to cause the least inconvenience to the taxpayer. The conference will be arranged by telephone, if possible, and must be held within 21 calendar days after contact has been made. Extensions of time will be granted only if justified in writing by the taxpayer and approved by the appropriate Technical branch chief.

(b) A taxpayer is entitled, as a matter of right, to only one conference in the National Office unless one of the circumstances discussed in (c) of this subdivision exists. This conference will usually be held at the branch level in the appropriate division (Corporation Tax Division or Individual Tax Division) in the office of the Assistant Commissioner (Technical), and will usually be attended by a person who has authority to act for the branch chief. In appropriate cases the examining officer may also attend the conference to clarify the facts in the case. If more than one subject is discussed at the conference, the discussion constitutes a conference with respect to each subject. At the request of the taxpayer or his representative, the conference may be held at an earlier stage in the consideration of the case than the Service would ordinarily designate. A taxpayer has no "right" of appeal from an action of a branch to the director of a division or to any other National Office official.

(c) In the process of review of a holding proposed by a branch, it may appear that the final answer will involve a reversal of the branch proposal with a result less favorable to the taxpayer. Or it may appear that an adverse holding proposed by a branch will be approved, but on a new or different issue or on different grounds than those on which the branch decided the case. Under either of these circumstances, the taxpayer or his representative will be invited to another conference. The provisions of this subparagraph limiting the number of conferences to which a taxpayer is entitled will not foreclose inviting a taxpayer to attend further conferences when, in the opinion of National Office personnel, such need arises. All additional conferences of this type discussed are held only at the invitation of the Service.

(d) It is the responsibility of the taxpayer to furnish to the National Office, within 21 calendar days after the conference, a written record of any additional data, line of reasoning, precedents, etc., that were proposed by the taxpayer and discussed at the conference but were not previously or adequately presented in writing. Extensions of time will be granted only if justified in writing by the taxpayer and approved by the appropriate Technical branch chief. Any additional material and a copy thereof should be addressed to and sent to the National Office which will forward the copy to the appropriate district director. The district director will be requested to give the matter his prompt attention. He may verify the additional facts and data

and comment upon it to the extent he deems it appropriate.

(e) A taxpayer or a taxpayer's representative desiring to obtain information as to the status of the case may do so by contacting the following offices with respect to matters in the areas of their responsibility:

Official	Telephone Numbers (Area Code 202)
Director, Corporation Tax Division	566-4504 or 566-4505
Director, Individual Tax Division	566-3767 or 566-3788

(vi) *Preparation of technical advice memorandum by the National Office.*—(a) Immediately upon receipt in the National Office, the technical employee to whom the case is assigned will analyze the file to ascertain whether it meets the requirements of subdivision (iii) of this subparagraph. If the case is not complete with respect to any requirement in subdivision (iii) (a) through (d) of this subparagraph, appropriate steps will be taken to complete the file. If any request for technical advice does not comply with the requirements of subdivision (iii) (e) of this subparagraph, relating to the statement of proposed deletions, the National Office will make those deletions from the technical advice memorandum which in the judgment of the Commissioner are required by section 6110(c) of the Code.

(b) If the taxpayer has requested a conference in the National Office, the procedures in subdivision (v) of this subparagraph will be followed.

(c) Replies to requests for technical advice will be addressed to the district director and will be drafted in two parts. Each part will identify the taxpayer by name, address, identification number, and year or years involved. The first part (hereafter called the "Technical Advice Memorandum") will contain (1) a recitation of the pertinent facts having a bearing on the issue; (2) a discussion of the facts, precedents, and reasoning of the National Office; and (3) the conclusions of the National Office. The conclusions will give direct answers, whenever possible, to the specific questions of the district office. The discussion of the issues will be in such detail that the district officials are apprised of the reasoning underlying the conclusion. There shall accompany the technical advice memorandum a notice pursuant to section 6110(f)(l) of the Code of intention to disclose the technical advice memorandum (including a copy of the version proposed to be open to public inspection and notations of third party communications pursuant to section 6110(d) of the Code) which the district director shall forward to the taxpayer at such time that the district director furnishes a copy of the technical advice memorandum to the taxpayer pursuant to (e) of this subdivision.

(d) The second part of the reply will consist of a transmittal memorandum. In the unusual cases it will serve as a vehicle for providing the district office administrative information or other information which, under the nondisclosure statutes, or for other reasons, may not be discussed with the taxpayer.

Reg. § 601.105(b)(5)(vi)(d)

(e) It is the general practice of the Service to furnish a copy of the technical advice memorandum to the taxpayer after it has been adopted by the district director. However, in the case of technical advice memoranda described in section 6110(g)(5)(A) of the Code, relating to cases involving criminal or civil fraud investigations and jeopardy or termination assessments, a copy of the technical advice memorandum shall not be furnished the taxpayer until all proceedings with respect to the investigations or assessments are completed.

(f) After receiving the notice pursuant to section 6110(f)(1) of the Code of intention to disclose the technical advice memorandum, if the taxpayer desires to protest the disclosure of certain information in the technical advice memorandum, the taxpayer must within 20 days after the notice is mailed submit a written statement identifying those deletions not made by the Internal Revenue Service which the taxpayer believes should have been made. The taxpayer shall also submit a copy of the version of the technical advice memorandum proposed to be open to public inspection on which the taxpayer indicates, by the use of brackets, the deletions proposed by the taxpayer but which have not been made by the Internal Revenue Service. Generally, the Internal Revenue Service will not consider the deletion under this subparagraph of any material which the taxpayer did not, prior to the time when the National Office sent its reply to the request for technical advice to the district director, propose be deleted. The Internal Revenue Service shall, within 20 days after receipt of the response by the taxpayer to the notice pursuant to section 6110(f)(1) of the Code, mail to the taxpayer its final administrative conclusion with respect to the deletions to be made.

(vii) *Action on technical advice in district offices.*—(a) Unless the district director feels that the conclusions reached by the National Office in a technical advice memorandum should be reconsidered and promptly requests such reconsideration, his office will proceed to process the taxpayer's case on the basis of the conclusions expressed in the technical advice memorandum.

(b) The district director will furnish to the taxpayer a copy of the technical advice memorandum described in subdivision (vi) (c) of this subparagraph and the notice pursuant to section 6110(f)(1) of the Code of intention to disclose the technical advice memorandum (including a copy of the version proposed to be open to public inspection and notations of third party communications pursuant to section 6110(d) of the Code). The preceding sentence shall not apply to technical advice memoranda involving civil fraud or criminal investigations, or jeopardy or termination assessments, as described in subdivision (iii) (j) of this subparagraph or to documents to which section 6104 of the Code applies.

(c) In those cases in which the National Office advises the district director that he should not furnish a copy of the technical memorandum to the taxpayer, the district director will so inform the taxpayer if he requests a copy.

(viii) *Effect of technical advice.*—(a) A technical advice memorandum represents an expression of the views of the Service as to the application of law, regulations, and precedents to the facts of a specific case, and is issued primarily as a means of assisting district officials in the examination and closing of the case involved.

(b) Except in rare or unusual circumstances, a holding in a technical advice memorandum that is favorable to the taxpayer is applied retroactively. Moreover, since technical advice, as described in subdivision (i) of this subparagraph, is issued only on closed transactions, a holding in a technical advice memorandum that is adverse to the taxpayer is also applied retroactively unless the Assistant Commissioner (Technical) exercises the discretionary authority under section 7805(b) of the Code to limit the retroactive effect of the holding. Likewise, a holding in a technical advice memorandum that modifies or revokes a holding in a prior technical advice memorandum will also be applied retroactively, with one exception. If the new holding is less favorable to the taxpayer, it will generally not be applied to the period in which the taxpayer relied on the prior holding in situations involving continuing transactions of the type described in § 601.201(l)(7) and § 601.201(l)(8).

(c) Technical advice memoranda often form the basis for revenue rulings. For the description of revenue rulings and the effect thereof, see § 601.601(d)(2)(i)(a) and § 601.601(d)(2)(v).

(d) A district director may raise an issue in any taxable period, even though he or she may have asked for and been furnished technical advice with regard to the same or a similar issue in any other taxable period.

(c) *District procedure.*—(1) *Office examination.*—(i) In a correspondence examination the taxpayer is furnished with a report of the examiner's findings by a form letter. The taxpayer is asked to sign and return an agreement if the taxpayer accepts the findings. The letter also provides a detailed explanation of the alternatives available if the taxpayer does not accept the findings, including consideration of the case by an Appeals office, and requests the taxpayer to inform the district director, within the specified period, of the choice of action. An Appeals office conference will be granted to the taxpayer upon request without submission of a written protest.

(ii) If, at the conclusion of an office interview examination, the taxpayer does not agree with the adjustments proposed, the examiner will fully explain the alternatives available which include, if practicable, an immediate interview with a supervisor or an immediate conference with an Appeals Officer. If an immediate interview or Appeals office conference is not practicable, or is not requested by the taxpayer, the examination report will be mailed to the taxpayer under cover of an appropriate transmittal letter. This letter provides a detailed explanation of the alternatives available, including consideration of the case by an Appeals office, and requests the taxpayer to inform the district director, within the specified period, of the choice of action. An Appeals office conference will be granted to the taxpayer upon request without submission of a written protest.

(2) *Field examination.*—(i) If, at the conclusion of an examination, the taxpayer does not agree with the adjustments proposed, the examiner will prepare a complete examination report fully explaining all proposed adjustments. Before the report is sent to the taxpayer, the case file will be submitted to the district Centralized Services and, in some cases, Quality Review function for appropriate review. Following such review, the taxpayer will be sent a copy of the examination report under cover of a transmittal (30-day) letter, providing a detailed explanation of the alternatives available, including consideration of the case by an Appeals office, and requesting the taxpayer to inform the district director, within the specified period, of the choice of action.

(ii) If the total amount of proposed additional tax, proposed overassessment, or claimed refund (or, in an offer in compromise, the total amount of assessed tax, penalty, and interest sought to be compromised) does not exceed $2,500 for any taxable period, the taxpayer will be granted an Appeals office conference on request. A written protest is not required.

(iii) If for any taxable period the total amount of proposed additional tax including penalties, proposed overassessment, or claimed refund (or, in an offer in compromise, the total amount of assessed tax, penalty, and interest sought to be compromised) exceeds $2,500 but does not exceed $10,000, the taxpayer, on request, will be granted an Appeals office conference, provided a brief written statement of disputed issues is submitted.

(iv) If for any taxable period the total amount of proposed additional tax including penalties, proposed overassessment, or claimed refund (or, in an offer in compromise, the total amount of assessed tax, penalty, and interest sought to be compromised) exceeds $10,000, the taxpayer, on request, will be granted an Appeals office conference, provided a written protest is filed.

(d) *Thirty-day letters and protests.*—(1) *General.*—The report of the examiner, as approved after review, recommends one of four determinations:

(i) Acceptance of the return as filed and closing of the case;

(ii) Assertion of a given deficiency or additional tax;

(iii) Allowance of a given overassessment, with or without a claim for refund, credit, or abatement;

(iv) Denial of a claim for refund, credit, or abatement which has been filed and is found wholly lacking in merit.

When a return is accepted as filed (as in (i) above), the taxpayer is notified by appropriate "no change" letter. In an unagreed case, the district director sends to the taxpayer a preliminary or "30-day letter" if any one of the last three determinations is made (except a full allowance of a claim in respect of any tax). The 30-day letter is a form letter which states the determination proposed to be made. It is accompanied by a copy of the examiner's report explaining the basis of the proposed determination. It suggests to the taxpayer that if the taxpayer concurs in the recommendation, he or she indicate agreement by executing and returning a waiver or acceptance. The preliminary letter also informs the taxpayer of appeal rights available if he or she disagrees with the proposed determination. If the taxpayer does not respond to the letter within 30 days, a statutory notice of deficiency will be issued or other appropriate action taken, such as the issuance of a notice of adjustment, the denial of a claim in income, profits, estate, and gift tax cases, or an appropriate adjustment of the tax liability or denial of a claim in excise and employment tax cases.

(2) *Protests.*—(i) No written protest or brief written statement of disputed issues is required to obtain an Appeals office conference in office interview and correspondence examination cases.

(ii) No written protest or brief written statement of disputed issues is required to obtain an Appeals office conference in a field examination case if the total amount of proposed additional tax including penalties, proposed overassessment, or claimed refund (or, in an offer in compromise, the total amount of assessed tax, penalty, and interest sought to be compromised) is $2,500 or less for any taxable period.

(iii) A written protest is required to obtain an Appeals consideration in a field examination case if the total amount of proposed tax including penalties, proposed overassessment, or claimed refund (or, in an offer in compromise, the total amount of assessed tax, penalty, and interest sought to be compromised) exceeds $10,000 for any taxable period.

(iv) A written protest is optional (although a brief written statement of disputed issues is required) to obtain Appeals consideration in a field examination case if for any taxable period the total amount of proposed additional tax including penalties, proposed overassessment, or claimed refund (or, in an offer in compromise, the total amount of assessed tax, penalty, and interest sought to be compromised) exceeds $2,500 but does not exceed $10,000.

(v) Instructions for preparation of written protests are sent to the taxpayer with the transmittal (30-day) letter.

(e) *Claims for refund or credit.*—(1) After payment of the tax a taxpayer may (unless he has executed an agreement to the contrary) contest the assessment by filing a claim for refund or credit for all or any part of the amount paid, except as provided in section 6512 of the Code with respect to certain taxes determined by the Tax Court, the decision of which has become final. A claim for refund or credit of income taxes shall be made on Form 1040X, 1120X, or an amended income tax return, in accordance with §301.6402-3. In the case of taxes other than income taxes, a claim for refund or credit shall be made on Form 843. The appropriate forms are obtainable from district directors or directors of service centers. Generally, the claim, together with appropriate supporting evidence, must be filed at the location prescribed in §301.6402-2(a)(2). A claim for refund or credit must be filed within the applicable statutory period of limitation. In certain cases, a properly executed income tax return may operate as a claim for refund or credit of the amount of the overpayment disclosed by such return. (See §301.6402-3.)

(2) When claims for refund or credit are examined by the Examination Division, substantially the same procedure is followed (including appeal rights afforded to taxpayers) as when taxpayers' returns are originally examined. But see §601.108 for procedure for reviewing proposed overpayment exceeding $200,000 of income, estate, and gift taxes.

(3) As to suits for refund, see §601.103(c).

(4) [Reserved.]

(5) There is also a special procedure applicable to applications for tentative carryback adjustments under section 6411 of the Code (consult Forms 1045 and 1139).

(6) For special procedure applicable to claims for payment or credit in respect of gasoline used on a farm for farming purposes, for certain nonhighway purposes, for use in commercial aircraft, or used by local transit systems, see sections 39, 6420, and 6421 of the Code and §601.402(c)(3). For special procedure applicable to claims for payment or credit in respect of lubricating oil used otherwise than in a highway motor vehicle, see sections 39 and 6424 of the Code and §601.402(c)(3). For special procedure applicable for credit or refund of aircraft use tax, see section 6426 of the Code and §601.402(c)(4). For special procedure applicable for payment or credit in respect of special fuels not used for taxable purposes, see sections 39 and 6427 of the Code and §601.402(c)(5).

(7) For special procedure applicable in certain cases to adjustment of overpayment of estimated tax by a corporation see section 6425 of the Code.

(f) *Interruption of examination procedure.*—The process of field examinations and the course of the administrative procedure described in this section and in the following section may be interrupted in some cases by the imminent expiration of the statutory period of limitations for assessment of the tax. To protect the Government's interests in such a case, the district director of internal revenue or other designated officer may be required to dispatch a statutory notice of deficiency (if the case is within jurisdiction of United States Tax Court), or take other appropriate action to assess the tax even though the case may be in examination status. In order to avoid interruption of the established procedure (except in estate tax cases), it is suggested

to the taxpayer that he execute an agreement on Form 872 (or such other form as may be prescribed for this purpose). To be effective this agreement must be entered into by the taxpayer and the district director or other appropriate officer concerned prior to the expiration of the time otherwise provided for assessment. Such a consent extends the period for assessment of any deficiency, or any additional or delinquent tax, and extends the period during which the taxpayer may claim a refund or credit to a date 6 months after the agreed time of extension of the assessment period. When appropriate, a consent may be entered into restricted to certain issues.

(g) *Fraud.*—The procedure described in this section does not apply in any case in which criminal prosecution is under consideration. Such procedure does obtain, however, in cases involving the assertion of the civil fraud penalty after the criminal aspects of the case have been closed.

(h) *Jeopardy assessments.*—If the district director believes that the assessment or collection of a tax will be jeopardized by delay, he/she is authorized and required to assess the tax immediately, together with interest and other additional amounts provided by law, notwithstanding the restrictions on assessment or collection of income, estate, gift, generation-skipping transfer or chapter 41, 42, 43, or 44 taxes contained in section 6213(a) of the Code. A jeopardy assessment does not deprive the taxpayer of the right to file a petition with the Tax Court. Collection of a tax in jeopardy may be immediately enforced by the district director upon notice and demand. To stay collection, the taxpayer may file with the district director a bond equal to the amount for which the stay is desired. The taxpayer may request a review in the Appeals office of whether the making of the assessment was reasonable under the circumstances and whether the amount assessed or demanded was appropriate under the circumstances. See section 7429. This request shall be made, in writing, within 30 days after the earlier of—

(1) The day on which the taxpayer is furnished the written statement described in section 7429(a)(1); or

(2) The last day of the period within which this statement is required to be furnished.

An Appeals office conference will be granted as soon as possible and a decision rendered without delay.

(i) *Regional post review of examined cases.*—Regional commissioners review samples of the examined cases closed in their district offices to ensure uniformity throughout their districts in applying Code provisions, regulations, and rulings, as well as the general policies of the Service.

(j) *Reopening of cases closed after examination.*—(1) The Service does not reopen any case closed after examination by a district office or service center to make an adjustment unfavorable to the taxpayer unless:

(i) There is evidence of fraud, malfeasance, collusion, concealment or misrepresentation of a material fact; or

(ii) The prior closing involved a clearly defined substantial error based on an established Service position existing at the time of the previous examination; or

(iii) Other circumstances exist which indicate failure to reopen would be a serious administrative omission.

(2) All reopenings are approved by the Chief, Examination Division (District Director in streamlined districts), or by the Chief, Compliance Division, for cases under his/her jurisdiction. If an additional inspection of the taxpayer's books of account is necessary, the notice to the taxpayer required by Code section 7605(b) will be delivered to the taxpayer at the time the reexamination is begun.

(k) *Transfer of returns between districts.*—When a request is received to transfer returns to another district for examination or the closing of a case, the district director having jurisdiction may transfer the case, together with pertinent records, to the district director of such other district. The Service will determine the time and place of the examination. In determining whether a transfer should be made, circumstances such as the following will be considered:

(1) Change of the taxpayer's domicile, either before or during examination.

(2) Discovery that taxpayer's books and records are kept in another district.

(3) Change of domicile of an executor or administrator to another district before or during examination.

(4) The effective administration of the tax laws.

(l) *Special procedures for crude oil windfall profit tax cases.*—For special procedures relating to crude oil windfall profit tax cases, see § 601.405. [Reg. § 601.105.]

☐ [32 FR 15990, Nov. 22, 1967, as amended at 33 FR 6819, May 4, 1968; 34 FR 6424, Apr. 12, 1969; 35 FR 7112, May 6, 1970; 35 FR 15916, Oct. 9. 1970; 36 FR 7584, Apr. 22, 1971; 38 FR 4956, Feb. 23, 1973; 38 FR 7458, Mar. 22, 1973; 38 FR 33300, Dec. 3, 1973; 41 FR 20880, May 21, 1976; 41 FR 48740, Nov. 5, 1976; 42 FR 34280, July 5, 1977; 43 FR 17817, Apr. 26, 1978; 43 FR 44497, Sept. 28, 1978; 43 FR 53029, Nov. 15, 1978; 45 FR 7252, Feb. 1, 1980; 46 FR 26053, May 11, 1981; 48 FR 15623, Apr. 12, 1983; 48 FR 24670, June 2, 1983; 49 FR 19649, May 9, 1984; 52 FR 38406, Oct. 16, 1987.]

[Reg. § 601.106]

§ 601.106. Appeals functions.—(a) *General.*—(1)(i) There are provided in each region Appeals offices with office facilities within the region. Unless they otherwise specify, taxpayers living outside the United States use the facilities of the Washington, D.C., Appeals Office of the Mid-Atlantic Region. Subject to the limitations set forth in subparagraphs (2) and (3) of this paragraph, the Commissioner has delegated to cer-

tain officers of the Appeals offices authority to represent the regional commissioner in those matters set forth in subdivisions (ii) through (v) of this subparagraph. If a statutory notice of deficiency was issued by a district director or the Director, Foreign Operations District, the Appeals office may waive jurisdiction to the director who issued the statutory notice during the 90-day (or 150-day) period for filing a petition with the Tax Court, except where criminal prosecution has been recommended and not finally disposed of, or the statutory notice includes the ad valorem fraud penalty. After the filing of a petition in the Tax Court the Appeals office will have exclusive settlement jurisdiction, subject to the provisions of subparagraph(2) of this paragraph, for a period of 4 months (but no later than the receipt of the trial calendar in regular cases and no later than 15 days before the calendar call in S cases), over cases docketed in the Tax Court. Subject to the exceptions and limitations set forth in subparagraph(2) of this paragraph, there is also vested in the Appeals offices authority to represent the regional commissioner in his/her exclusive authority to settle (*a*) all cases docketed in the Tax Court and designated for trial at any place within the territory comprising the region, and (*b*) all docketed cases originating in the office of any district director situated within the region, or in which jurisdiction has been transferred to the region, which are designated for trial at Washington, D.C., unless the petitioner resides in, and his/her books and records are located or can be made available in, the region which includes Washington, D.C.

(ii) Certain officers of the Appeals offices may represent the regional commissioner in his/her exclusive and final authority for the determination of—

(*a*) Federal income, profits, estate (including extensions for payment under section 6161(a)(2)), gift, generation-skipping transfer or chapter 41, 42, 43, or 44 tax liability (whether before or after the issuance of a statutory notice of deficiency);

(*b*) Employment or certain Federal excise tax liability; and

(*c*) Liability for additions to the tax, additional amounts, and assessable penalties provided under chapter 68 of the Code.

in any case originating in the office of any district director situated in the region, or in any case in which jurisdiction has been transferred to the region.

(iii) The taxpayer must request Appeals consideration.

(*a*) An oral request is sufficient to obtain Appeals consideration in (*1*) all office interview or correspondence examination cases or (*2*) a field examination case if the total amount of proposed additional tax including penalties, proposed overassessment, or claimed refund (or, in an offer in compromise, the total amount of assessed tax, penalty, and interest sought to be compromised) is $2,500 or less for any taxable period. No written protest or brief statement of disputed issues is required.

(b) A brief written statement of disputed issues is required (a written protest is optional) to obtain Appeals consideration in a field examination case if the total amount of proposed additional tax including penalties, proposed overassessment, or claimed refund (or, in an offer in compromise, the total amount of assessed tax, penalty, and interest sought to be compromised) exceeds $2,500 but does not exceed $10,000 for any taxable period.

(c) A written protest is required to obtain Appeals consideration in a field examination case if the total amount of proposed additional tax including penalties, proposed overassessment, or claimed refund (or, in an offer in compromise, the total amount of assessed tax, penalty, and interest sought to be compromised) exceeds $10,000 for any taxable period.

(d) A written protest is required to obtain Appeals consideration in all employee plan and exempt organization cases.

(e) A written protest is required to obtain Appeals consideration in all partnership and S corporation cases.

(iv) Sections 6659(a)(1) and 6671(a) provide that additions to the tax, additional amounts, penalties and liabilities (collectively referred to in this subdivision as "penalties") provided by chapter 68 of the Code shall be paid upon notice and demand and shall be assessed and collected in the same manner as taxes. Certain chapter 68 penalties may be appealed after assessment to the Appeals office. This postassessment appeal procedure applies to all but the following chapter 68 penalties:

(a) Penalties that are not subject to a reasonable cause or reasonable basis determination (examples are additions to the tax for failure to pay estimated income tax under sections 6654 and 6655);

(b) Penalties that are subject to the deficiency procedures of subchapter B of chapter 63 of the Code (because the taxpayer has the right to appeal such penalties, such as those provided under section 6653(a) and (b), prior to assessment);

(c) Penalties that are subject to an administratively granted preassessment appeal procedure such as that provided in § 1.6694-2(a)(1) because taxpayers are able to protest such penalties prior to assessment;

(d) The penalty provided in section 6700 for promoting abusive tax shelters (because the penalty is subject to the procedural rules of section 6703 which provide for an extension of the period of collection of the penalty when a person pays not less than 15% of the amount of such penalty); and

(e) The 100 percent penalty provided under section 6672 (because the taxpayer has the opportunity to appeal this penalty prior to assessment).

The appeal may be made before or after payment, but shall be made before the filing of a claim for refund. Technical advice procedures are not applicable to an appeal made under this subdivision.

(v) The Appeals office considers cases involving the initial or continuing recognition of tax exemption and foundation classification. See § 601.201(n)(5) and (n)(6). The Appeals office also considers cases involving the initial or continuing determination of employee plan qualification under subchapter D of chapter 1 of the Code. See § 601.201(o)(6). However, the jurisdiction of the Appeals office in these cases is limited as follows:

(a) In cases under the jurisdiction of a key district director (or the National Office) which involve an application for, or the revocation or modification of, the recognition of exemption or the determination of qualification, if the determination concerning exemption is made by a National Office ruling, or if National Office technical advice is furnished concerning exemption or qualification, the decision of the National Office is final. The organization/plan has no right of appeal to the Appeals office or any other avenue of administrative appeal. See § 601.201(n)(5)(i), (n)(6)(ii)(b), (n)(9)(viii)(a), (o)(2)(iii), and (o)(6)(i).

(b) In cases already under the jurisdiction of an Appeals office, if the proposed disposition by that office is contrary to a National Office ruling concerning exemption, or to a National Office technical advice concerning exemption or qualification, issued prior to the case, the proposed disposition will be submitted, through the Office of the Regional Director of Appeals, to the Assistant Commissioner (Employee Plans and Exempt Organizations) or, in section 521 cases, to the Assistant Commissioner (Technical). The decision of the Assistant Commissioner will be followed by the Appeals office. See § 601.201(n)(5)(iii), (n)(6)(ii)(d), (n)(6)(iv), and (o)(6)(iii).

(2) The authority described in subparagraph (1) of this paragraph does not include the authority to:

(i) Negotiate or make a settlement in any case docketed in the Tax Court if the notice of deficiency, liability or other determination was issued by Appeals officials;

(ii) Negotiate or make a settlement in any docketed case if the notice of deficiency, liability or other determination was issued after appeals consideration of all petitioned issues by the Employee Plans/Exempt Organizations function;

(iii) Negotiate or make a settlement in any docketed case if the notice of deficiency, liability or final adverse determination letter was issued by a District Director and is based upon a National Office ruling or National Office technical advice in that case involving a qualification of an employee plan or tax exemption and/or foundation status of an organization (but only to the extent the case involves such issue);

(iv) Negotiate or make a settlement if the case was docketed under Code sections 6110, 7477, or 7478;

(v) Eliminate the ad valorem fraud penalty in any case in which the penalty was determined by the district office or service center office in connection with a tax year or period, or which is related to or affects such year or period, for which criminal prosecution against the taxpayer (or related taxpayer involving the same transaction) has been recommended to the Department of Justice for willful attempt to evade or defeat tax, or for willful failure to file a return, except upon the recommendation or concurrence of Counsel; or

(vi) Act in any case in which a recommendation for criminal prosecution is pending, except with the concurrence of Counsel.

(3) The authority vested in the Appeals does not extend to the determination of liability for any excise tax imposed by subtitle E or by subchapter D of chapter 78, to the extent it relates to subtitle E.

(4) In cases under Appeals jurisdiction, the Appeals official has the authority to make and subscribe to a return under the provisions under section 6020 of the Code where taxpayer fails to make a required return.

(b) *Initiation of proceedings before the official Appeals.*—In any case in which the district director has issued a preliminary or "30-day letter" and the taxpayer requests Appeals consideration and files a written protest when required (see paragraph (c)(1) of §§601.103, (c)(1) and (c)(2) of 601.105, and 601.507) against the proposed determination of tax liability, except as to those taxes described in paragraph (a)(3) of this section, the taxpayer has the right (and will be so advised by the district director) of administrative appeal to the Appeals organization. However, the appeal procedures do not extend to cases involving solely the failure or refusal to comply with the tax laws because of moral, religious, political, constitutional, conscientious, or similar grounds. Organizations such as labor unions and trade associations which have been examined by the district director to determine the amounts expended by the organization for purposes of lobbying, promotion or defeat of legislation, political campaigns, or propaganda related to those purposes are treated as "taxpayers" for the purpose of this right of administrative appeal. Thus, upon requesting appellate consideration and filing a written protest, when required, to the district director's findings that a portion of member dues is to be disallowed as a deduction to each member because expended for such purposes, the organization will be afforded full rights of administrative appeal to the Appeals activity similar to those rights afforded to taxpayers generally. After review of any required written protest by the district director, the case and its administrative record are referred to the Appeals. Appeals may refuse to accept a protested nondocketed case where preliminary review indicates it requires further consideration or development. No taxpayer is required to submit the case to the Appeals for consideration. Appeal is at the option of the taxpayer. After the issuance by the district director of a statutory notice of deficiency, upon the taxpayer's request, the Appeals may take up the case for settlement and may grant the taxpayer a conference thereon.

(c) *Nature of proceedings before Appeals.*—Proceedings before the Appeals are informal. Testimony under oath is not taken, although matters alleged as facts may be required to be submitted in the form of affidavits, or declared to be true under the penalties of perjury. Taxpayers may represent themselves or designate a qualified representative to act for them. See Subpart E of this part for conference and practice requirements. At any conference granted by the Appeals on a nondocketed case, the district director will be represented if the Appeals official having settlement authority and the district director deem it advisable. At any such conference on a case involving the ad valorem fraud penalty for which criminal prosecution against the taxpayer (or a related taxpayer involving the same transaction) has been recommended to the Department of Justice for willful attempt to evade or defeat tax, or for willful failure to file a return, the District Counsel will be represented if he or she so desires.

(d) *Disposition and settlement of cases before the Appeals.*—(1) *General.*—During consideration of a case, the Appeals office should neither reopen an issue as to which the taxpayer and the office of the district director are in agreement nor raise a new issue, unless the ground for such action is a substantial one and the potential effect upon the tax liability is material. If the Appeals raises a new issue, the taxpayer or the taxpayer's representative should be so advised and offered an opportunity for discussion prior to the taking of any formal action, such as the issuance of a statutory notice of deficiency.

(2) *Cases not docketed in the Tax Court.*—(i) If after consideration of the case by the Appeals a satisfactory settlement of some or all the issues is reached with the taxpayer, the taxpayer will be requested to sign Form 870-AD or other appropriate agreement form waiving restrictions on the assessment and collection of any deficiency and accepting any overassessment resulting from the agreed settlement. In addition, in partially unagreed cases, a statutory notice of deficiency will be prepared and issued in accordance with subdivision (ii) of this subparagraph with respect to the unagreed issue or issues.

(ii) If after consideration of the case by Appeals it is determined that there is a deficiency in income, profits, estate, generation-skipping transfer gift tax, or chapter 41, 42, 43, or 44 tax liability to which the taxpayer does not agree, a statutory notice of deficiency will be prepared and issued by Appeals. Officers of the Appeals office having authority for the administrative determination of tax liabilities referred to in paragraph (a) of this section are also authorized to prepare, sign on behalf of the Commissioner, and send to the taxpayer by registered or certified mail any statutory notice of deficiency prescribed in sections 6212 and 6861 of the Code, and in corresponding provisions of the Internal Revenue Code of 1939. Within 90 days, or 150 days if the notice is addressed to a person outside of the States of the Union and the District of Columbia, after such a statutory notice of deficiency is mailed (not counting Saturday, Sunday, or a legal holiday in the District of Columbia as the last day), the taxpayer may file a petition with the U.S. Tax Court for a redetermination of the deficiency. In addition, if a claim for refund is disallowed in full or in part by the Appelate Division and the taxpayer does not sign Form 2297, Appeals will prepare the statutory notice of claim disallowance and send it to the taxpayer by certified mail (or registered mail if the taxpayer is outside the United States), with a carbon copy to the taxpayer's representative by regular mail, if appropriate. In any other unagreed case, the case and its administrative file will be forwarded to the appropriate function with directions to take action with respect to the tax liability determined in Appeals. Administrative appeal procedures will apply to 100-percent penalty cases, except where an assessment is made because of Chief Counsel's request to support a third-party action in a pending refund suit. See Rev. Proc. 69-26.

(iii) Taxpayers desiring to further contest unagreed excise (other than those under chapters 41 through 44 of the Code) and employment tax cases and 100-percent penalty cases must pay the additional tax (or portion thereof of divisible taxes) when assessed, file claim for refund within the applicable statutory period of limitations (ordinarily three years from time return was required to be filed or two years from payment, whichever expires later), and upon disallowance of claim or after six months from date claim was filed, file suit in U.S. District Court or U.S. Claims Court. Suits for refund of taxes paid are under the jurisdiction of the Department of Justice.

(3) *Cases docketed in the Tax Court.*—(i) If the case under consideration in the Appeals is docketed in the Tax Court and agreement is reached with the taxpayer with respect to the issues involved, the disposition of the case is effected by a stipulation of agreed deficiency or overpayment to be filed with the Tax Court and in conformity with which the Court will enter its order.

(ii) If the case under consideration in Appeals is docketed in the Tax Court and the issues remain unsettled after consideration and conference in Appeals, the case will be referred to the appropriate district counsel for the region for defense of the tax liability determined.

(iii) If the deficiency notice in a case docketed in the Tax Court was not issued by the Appeals office and no recommendation for criminal prosecution is pending, the case will be referred by the district counsel to the Appeals office for settlement as soon as it is at issue in the Tax Court. The settlement procedure shall be governed by the following rules:

(a) The Appeals office will have exclusive settlement jurisdiction for a period of 4 months over certain cases docketed in the Tax Court. The 4-month period will commence at the time Appeals receives the case from Counsel, which will be after the case is at issue. Appeals will arrange settlement conferences in such cases within 45 days of receipt of the case. In the event

of a settlement, Appeals will prepare and forward to Counsel the necessary computations and any stipulation decisions secured. Counsel will prepare any needed settlement documents for execution by the parties and filing with the Tax Court. Appeals will also have authority to settle less than all the issues in the case and to refer the unsettled issues to Counsel for disposition. In the event of a partial settlement, Appeals will inform Counsel of the agreement of the petitioner(s) and Appeals may secure and forward to Counsel a stipulation covering the agreed issues. Counsel will, if necessary, prepare documents reflecting settlement of the agreed issues for execution by the parties and filing with the Tax Court at the appropriate time.

(b) At the end of the 4-month period, or before that time if Appeals determines the case is not suceptible of settlement, the case will be returned to Counsel. Thereafter, Counsel will have exclusive authority to dispose of the case. If, at the end of the 4-month period, there is substantial likelihood that a settlement of the entire case can be effected in a reasonable period of time, Counsel may extend Appeals settlement jurisdiction for a period not to exceed 60 days, but not beyond the date of the receipt of a trial calendar upon which the case appears. Extensions beyond the 60-day period or after the event indicated will be granted only with the personal approval of regional counsel and will be made only in those cases in which the probability of settlement of the case in its entirety by Appeals clearly outweighs the need to commence trial preparation.

(c) During the period of Appeals jurisdiction, Appeals will make available such files and information as may be necessary for Counsel to take any action required by the Court or which is in the best interests of the Government. When a case is referred by Counsel to Appeals, Counsel may indicate areas of needed factual development or areas of possible technical uncertainties. In referring a case to Counsel, Appeals will furnish its summary of the facts and the pertinent legal authorities.

(d) The Appeals office may specify that proposed Counsel settlements be referred back to Appeals for its views. Appeals may protest the proposed Counsel settlements. If Counsel disagrees with Appeals, the Regional Counsel will determine the disposition of the cases.

(e) If an offer is received at or about the time of trial in a case designated by the Appeals office for settlement consultation, Counsel will endeavor to have the case placed on a motions calendar to permit consultation with and review by Appeals in accordance with the foregoing procedures.

(f) For issues in docketed and nondocketed cases pending with Appeals which are related to issues in docketed cases over which Counsel has jurisdiction, no settlement offer will be accepted by either Appeals or Counsel unless both agree that the offer is acceptable. The protest procedure will be available to Appeals and regional counsel will have authority to resolve the issue with respect to both the Appeals and

Counsel cases. If settlement of the docketed case requires approval by regional counsel or Chief Counsel, the final decision with respect to the issues under the jurisdiction of both Appeals and Counsel will be made by regional counsel or Chief Counsel. See Rev. Proc. 79-59.

(g) Cases classified as "Small Tax" cases by the Tax Court are given expeditious consideration because such cases are not included on a Trial Status Request. These cases are considered by the Court as ready for placing on a trial calendar as soon as the answer has been filed and are given priority by the Court for trial over other docketed cases. These cases are designated by the Court as small tax cases upon request of petitioners and will include letter "S" as part of the docket number.

(e) *Transfer and centralization of cases.*—(1) An Appeals office is authorized to transfer settlement jurisdiction in a non-docketed case or in an excise or employment tax case to another region, if the taxpayer resides in and the taxpayer's books and records are located (or can be made available) in such other region. Otherwise, transfer to another region requires the approval of the Director of the Appeals Division.

(2) An Appeals office is authorized to transfer settlement jurisdiction in a docketed case to another region if the location for the hearing by the Tax Court has been set in such other region, except that if the place of hearing is Washington, D.C., settlement jurisdiction shall not be transferred to the region in which Washington, D.C., is located unless the petitioner resides in and the petitioner's books and records are located (or can be made available) in that region. Otherwise, transfer to another region requires the approval of the Director of the Appeals Division. Likewise, the Chief Counsel has corresponding authority to transfer the jurisdiction, authority, and duties of the regional counsel for any region to the regional counsel of another region within which the case has been designated for trial before the Tax Court.

(3) Should a regional commissioner determine that it would better serve the interests of the Government, he or she may, by order in writing, withdraw any case not docketed before the Tax Court from the jurisdiction of the Appeals office of the region, and provide for its disposition under his or her personal direction.

(f) *Conference and practice requirements.*—Practice and conference procedure before Appeals is governed by Treasury Department Circular 230 as amended (31 CFR Part 10) [¶44,500 et seq.], and the requirements of Subpart E of this part [¶44,408 et seq.]. In addition to such rules but not in modification of them, the following rules are also applicable to practice before Appeals:

(1) *Rule I.*—An exaction by the U.S. Government, which is not based upon law, statutory or otherwise, is a taking of property without due process of law, in violation of the Fifth Amendment to the U.S. Constitution. Accordingly, an Appeals representative in his or her conclusions of fact or application of the law, shall hew to the law and the recognized standards of legal construction. It shall be his or her duty to determine the correct amount of the tax, with strict impartiality as between the taxpayer and the Government, and without favoritism or discrimination as between taxpayers.

(2) *Rule II.*—Appeals will ordinarily give serious consideration to an offer to settle a tax controversy on a basis which fairly reflects the relative merits of the opposing views in light of the hazards which would exist if the case were litigated. However, no settlement will be made based upon nuisance value of the case to either party. If the taxpayer makes an unacceptable proposal of settlement under circumstances indicating a good-faith attempt to reach an agreed disposition of the case on a basis fair both to the Government and the taxpayer, the Appeals official generally should give an evaluation of the case in such a manner as to enable the taxpayer to ascertain the kind of settlement that would be recommended for acceptance. Appeals may defer action on or decline to settle some cases or issues (for example, issues on which action has been suspended nationwide) in order to achieve greater uniformity and enhance overall voluntary compliance with the tax laws.

(3) *Rule III.*—Where the Appeals officer recommends acceptance of the taxpayer's proposal of settlement, or, in the absence of a proposal, recommends action favorable to the taxpayer, and said recommendation is disapproved in whole or in part by a reviewing officer in the Appeals, the taxpayer shall be so advised and upon written request shall be accorded a conference with such reviewing officer. The Appeals may disregard this rule where the interest of the Government would be injured by delay, as for example, in a case involving the imminent expiration of limitation or the dissipation of assets.

(4) *Rule IV.*—Where the Appeals official having settlement authority and the district director deem it advisable, the district director may be represented at any Appeals conferences on a non-docketed case. This rule is also applicable to the Director, Foreign Operations District, in the event his or her office issued the preliminary or "30-day letter."

(5) *Rule V.*—In order to bring an unagreed income, profits, estate, gift, or chapter 41, 42, 43, or 44 tax case in prestatutory notice status, an employment or excise tax case, a penalty case, an Employee Plans and Exempt Organization case, a termination of taxable year assessment case, a jeopardy assessment case, or an offer in compromise before the Appeals office, the taxpayer or the taxpayer's representative should first request Appeals consideration and, when required, file with the district office (including the Foreign Operations District) or service center a written protest setting forth specifically the reasons for the refusal to accept the findings. If the protest includes a statement of facts upon which the taxpayer relies, such statement should be declared to be true under the penalties of perjury. The protest and any new facts, law, or argu-

ments presented therewith will be reviewed by the receiving office for the purpose of deciding whether further development or action is required prior to referring the case to the Appeals. Where the Appeals has an issue under consideration it may, with the concurrence of the taxpayer, assume jurisdiction in a related case, after the office having original jurisdiction has completed any necessary action. The Director, Appeals Division, may authorize the regional Appeals office to accept jurisdiction (after any necessary action by office having original jurisdiction) in specified classes of cases without written protests provided written or oral requests for Appeals consideration are submitted by or for each taxpayer.

(6) *Rule VI.*—A taxpayer cannot withhold evidence from the district director of internal revenue and expect to introduce it for the first time before the Appeals, at a conference in nondocketed status, without being subject to having the case returned to the district director for reconsideration. Where newly discovered evidence is submitted for the first time to the Appeals, in a case pending in nondocketed status, that office, in the reasonable exercise of its discretion, may transmit same to the district director for his or her consideration and comment.

(7) *Rule VII.*—Where the taxpayer has had the benefit of a conference before the Appeals office in the prestatutory notice status, or where the opportunity for such a conference was accorded but not availed of, there will be no conference granted before the Appeals office in the 90-day status after the mailing of the statutory notice of deficiency, in the absence of unusual circumstances.

(8) *Rule VIII.*—In cases not docketed in the United States Tax Court on which a conference is being conducted by the Appeals office, the district counsel may be requested to attend and to give legal advice in the more difficult cases, or on matters of legal or litigating policy.

(9) *Rule IX—Technical advice from the National Office.*—(i) *Definition and nature of technical advice.*—(a) As used in this subparagraph, "technical advice" means advice or guidance as to the interpretation and proper application of internal revenue laws, related statutes, and regulations, to a specific set of facts, furnished by the National Office upon request of an Appeals office in connection with the processing and consideration of a nondocketed case. It is furnished as a means of assisting Service personnel in closing cases and establishing and maintaining consistent holdings in the various regions. It does not include memorandum on matters of general technical application furnished to Appeals offices where the issues are not raised in connection with the consideration and handling of a specific taxpayer's case.

(b) The provisions of this subparagraph do not apply to a case under the jurisdiction of a district director or the Bureau of Alcohol, Tobacco, and Firearms, to Employee Plans, Exempt Organization, or certain penalty cases being considered by an Appeals office, or to any case previously considered by an Appeals office. The technical advice provisions applicable to cases under the jurisdiction of a district director, other than Employee Plans and Exempt Organization cases, are set forth in § 601.105(b)(5). The technical advice provisions applicable to Employee Plans and Exempt Organization cases are set forth in § 601.201(n)(9). Technical advice may not be requested with respect to a taxable period if a prior Appeals disposition of the same taxable period of the same taxpayer's case was based on mutual concessions (ordinarily with a form 870-AD, Offer of Waiver of Restrictions on Assessment and Collection of Deficiency in Tax and of Acceptance of Overassessment). However, technical advice may be requested by a district director on issues previously considered in a prior Appeals disposition, not based on mutual concessions, of the same taxable periods of the same taxpayer with the concurrence of the Appeals office that had the case.

(c) The consideration or examination of the facts relating to a request for a determination letter is considered to be in connection with the consideration and handling of a taxpayer's case. Thus, an Appeals office may, under this subparagraph, request technical advice with respect to the consideration of a request for a determination letter. The technical advice provisions applicable to a request for a determination letter in Employee Plans and Exempt Organization cases are set forth in § 601.201(n)(9).

(d) If an Appeals office is of the opinion that a ruling letter previously issued to a taxpayer should be modified or revoked and it requests the National Office to reconsider the ruling, the reference of the matter to the National Office is treated as a request for technical advice. The procedures specified in subdivision (iii) of this subparagraph should be followed in order that the National Office may consider the recommendation. Only the National Office can revoke a ruling letter. Before referral to the National Office, the Appeals office should inform the taxpayer of its opinion that the ruling letter should be revoked. The Appeals office, after development of the facts and consideration of the taxpayer's arguments, will decide whether to recommend revocation of the ruling to the National Office. For procedures relating to a request for a ruling, see § 601.201.

(e) The Assistant Commissioner (Technical), acting under a delegation of authority from the Commissioner of Internal Revenue, is exclusively responsible for providing technical advice in any issue involving the establishment of basic principles and rules for the uniform interpretation and application of tax laws in cases under this subparagraph. This authority has been largely redelegated to subordinate officials.

(ii) *Areas in which technical advice may be requested.*—(a) Appeals offices may request technical advice on any technical or procedural question that develops during the processing and consideration of a case. These procedures are applicable as provided in subdivision (i) of this subparagraph.

(b) As provided in §601.105(b)(5)(ii)(b) and (iii)(a), requests for technical advice should be made at the earliest possible stage of the examination process. However, if identification of an issue on which technical advice is appropriate is not made until the case is in Appeals, a decision to request such advice (in nondocketed cases) should be made prior to or at the first conference.

(c) Subject to the provisions of (b) of this subdivision, Appeals Offices are encouraged to request technical advice on any technical or procedural question arising in connection with a case described in subdivision (i) of this subparagraph which cannot be resolved on the basis of law, regulations, or a clearly applicable revenue ruling or other precedent issued by the National Office.

(iii) *Requesting technical advice.—(a)* It is the responsibility of the Appeals Office to determine whether technical advice is to be requested on any issue being considered. However, while the case is under the jurisdiction of the Appeals Office, a taxpayer or his/her representative may request that an issue be referred to the National Office for technical advice on the grounds that a lack of uniformity exists as to the disposition of the issue, or that the issue is so unusual or complex as to warrant consideration by the National Office. While taxpayers are encouraged to make written requests setting forth the facts, law, and argument with respect to the issue, and reason for requesting National Office advice, a taxpayer may make the request orally. If, after considering the taxpayer's request, the Appeals Officer is of the opinion that the circumstances do not warrant referral of the case to the National Office, he/she will so advise the taxpayer. (See subdivision (iv) of this subparagraph for taxpayer's appeal rights where the Appeals Officer declines to request technical advice.)

(b) When technical advise is to be requested, whether or not upon the request of the taxpayer, the taxpayer will be so advised, except as noted in (j) of this subdivision. If the Appeals Office initiates the action, the taxpayer will be furnished a copy of the statement of the pertinent facts and the question or questions proposed for submission to the National Office. The request for advice should be so worded as to avoid possible misunderstanding, in the National Office, of the facts or of the specific point or points at issue.

(c) After receipt of the statement of facts and specific questions, the taxpayer will be given 10 calendar days in which to indicate in writing the extent, if any, to which he/she may not be in complete agreement. An extension of time must be justified by the taxpayer in writing and approved by the Chief, Appeals Office. Every effort should be made to reach agreement as to the facts and specific points at issue. If agreement cannot be reached, the taxpayer may submit, within 10 calendar days after receipt of notice from the Appeals Office, a statement of his/her understanding as to the specific point or points at issue which will be forwarded to the National Office with the request for advice. An extension of time must be justified by the taxpayer in writing and approved by the Chief, Appeals Office.

(d) If the taxpayer initiates the action to request advice, and his/her statement of the facts and point or points at issue are not wholly acceptable to the Appeals Office, the taxpayer will be advised in writing as to the areas of disagreement. The taxpayer will be given 10 calendar days after receipt of the written notice to reply to such notice. An extension of time must be justified by the taxpayer in writing and approved by the Chief, Appeals Office. If agreement cannot be reached, both the statements of the taxpayer and the Appeals Office will be forwarded to the National Office.

(e)(1) In the case of requests for technical advice, the taxpayer must also submit, within the 10-day period referred to in (c) and (d) of this subdivision, whichever is applicable (relating to agreement by the taxpayer with the statement of facts and points submitted in connection with the request for technical advice), the statement described in (f) of this subdivision of proposed deletions pursuant to section 6110(c) of the Code. If the statement is not submitted, the taxpayer will be informed by the Appeals Office that the statement is required. If the Appeals Office does not receive the statement within 10 days after the taxpayer has been informed of the need for the statement, the Appeals Office may decline to submit the request for technical advice. If the Appeals Office decides to request technical advice in a case where the taxpayer has not submitted the statement of proposed deletions, the National Office will make those deletions which in the judgment of the Commissioner are required by section 6110(c) of the Code.

(2) The requirements included in this subparagraph relating to the submission of statements and other material with respect to proposed deletions to be made from technical advice memoranda before public inspection is permitted to take place do not apply to requests for any document to which section 6104 of the Code applies.

(f) In order to assist the Internal Revenue Service in making the deletions required by section 6110(c) of the Code, from the text of technical advice memoranda which are open to public inspection pursuant to section 6110(a) of the Code, there must accompany requests for such technical advice either a statement of the deletions proposed by the taxpayer, or a statement that no information other than names, addresses, and taxpayer identifying numbers need be deleted. Such statements shall be made in a separate document. The statement of proposed deletions shall be accompanied by a copy of all statements of facts and supporting documents which are submitted to the National Office pursuant to (c) or (d) of this subdivision, on which shall be indicated, by the use of brackets, the material which the taxpayer indicates should be deleted pursuant to section 6110(c) of the Code.

The statement of proposed deletions shall indicate the statutory basis for each proposed deletion. The statement of proposed deletions shall not appear or be referred to anywhere in the request for technical advice. If the taxpayer decides to request additional deletions pursuant to section 6110(c) of the Code prior to the time the National Office replies to the request for technical advice, additional statements may be submitted.

(g) If the taxpayer has not already done so, he/she may submit a statement explaining his/her position on the issues, citing precedents which the taxpayer believes will bear on the case. This statement will be forwarded to the National Office with the request for advice. If it is received at a later date, it will be forwarded for association with the case file.

(h) At the time the taxpayer is informed that the matter is being referred to the National Office, he/she will also be informed of the right to a conference in the National Office in the event an adverse decision is indicated, and will be asked to indicate whether a conference is desired.

(i) Generally, prior to replying to the request for technical advice, the National Office shall inform the taxpayer orally or in writing of the material likely to appear in the technical advice memorandum which the taxpayer proposed be deleted but which the Internal Revenue Service determined should not be deleted. If so informed, the taxpayer may submit within 10 days any further information, arguments, or other material in support of the position that such material be deleted. The Internal Revenue Service will attempt, if feasible, to resolve all disagreements with respect to proposed deletions prior to the time the National Office replies to the request for technical advice. However, in no event shall the taxpayer have the right to a conference with respect to resolution of any disagreements concerning material to be deleted from the text of the technical advice memorandum, but such matters may be considered at any conference otherwise scheduled with respect to the request.

(j) The provisions of (a) through (i) of this subdivision, relating to the referral of issues upon request of the taxpayer, advising taxpayers of the referral of issues, the submission of proposed deletions, and the granting of conferences in the National Office, are not applicable to technical advice memoranda described in section 6110(g)(5)(A) of the Code, relating to cases involving criminal or civil fraud investigations and jeopardy or termination assessments. However, in such cases, the taxpayer shall be allowed to provide the statement of proposed deletions to the National Office upon the completion of all proceedings with respect to the investigations or assessments, but prior to the date on which the Commissioner mails the notice pursuant to section 6110(f)(1) of the Code of intention to disclose the technical advice memorandum.

(k) Form 4463, Request for Technical Advice, should be used for transmitting requests for technical advice to the National Office.

(iv) *Appeal by taxpayers of determinations not to seek technical advice.*—(a) If the taxpayer has requested referral of an issue before an Appeals Office to the National Office for technical advice, and after consideration of the request, the Appeals Officer is of the opinion that the circumstances do not warrant such referral, he/she will so advise the taxpayer.

(b) The taxpayer may appeal the decision of the Appeals Officer not to request technical advice by submitting to that official, within 10 calendar days after being advised of the decision, a statement of the facts, law, and arguments with respect to the issue, and the reasons why the taxpayer believes the matter should be referred to the National Office for advice. An extension of time must be justified by the taxpayer in writing and approved by the Chief, Appeals Office.

(c) The Appeals Officer will submit the statement of the taxpayer to the chief, Appeals Office, accompanied by a statement of the officer's reasons why the issue should not be referred to the National Office. The Chief will determine, on the basis of the statements submitted, whether technical advice will be requested. If the Chief determines that technical advice is not warranted, that official will inform the taxpayer in writing that he/she proposes to deny the request. In the letter to the taxpayer the Chief will (except in unusual situations where such action would be prejudicial to the best interests of the Government) state specifically the reasons for the proposed denial. The taxpayer will be given 15 calendar days after receipt of the letter in which to notify the Chief whether the taxpayer agrees with the proposed denial. The taxpayer may not appeal the decision of the Chief, Appeals Office not to request technical advice from the National Office. However, if the taxpayer does not agree with the proposed denial, all data relating to the issue for which technical advice has been sought, including the taxpayer's written request and statements, will be submitted to the National Office, Attention: Director, Appeals Division, for review. After review in the National Office, the Appeals Office will be notified whether the proposed denial is approved or disapproved.

(d) While the matter is being reviewed in the National Office, the Appeals Office will suspend action on the issue (except where the delay would prejudice the Government's interests) until it is notified of the National Office decision. This notification will be made within 30 days after receipt of the data in the National Office. The review will be solely on the basis of the written record and no conference will be held in the National Office.

(v) *Conference in the National Office.*—(a) If, after a study of the technical advice request, it appears that advice adverse to the taxpayer should be given and a conference has been requested, the taxpayer will be notified of the time and place of the conference. If conferences are being arranged with respect to more than one request for advice involving the same taxpayer, they will be so scheduled as to cause the least inconvenience to the taxpayer. The conference will be arranged by telephone, if possible, and must be held within 21 calendar days after contact has been made. Extensions of time will be granted only if justified in writing by the taxpayer and approved by the appropriate Technical branch chief.

(b) A taxpayer is entitled, as a matter of right, to only one conference in the National Office unless one of the circumstances discussed in (c) of this subdivision exists. This conference will usually be held at the branch level in the appropriate division (Corporation Tax Division or Individual Tax Division) in the Office of the Assistant Commissioner (Technical), and will usually be attended by a person who has authority to act for the branch chief. In appropriate cases the Appeals Officer may also attend the conference to clarify the facts in the case. If more than one subject is discussed at the conference, the discussion constitutes a conference with respect to each subject. At the request of the taxpayer or the taxpayer's representative, the conference may be held at an earlier stage in the consideration of the case than the Service would ordinarily designate. A taxpayer has no "right" of appeal from an action of a branch to the director of a division or to any other National Office official.

(c) In the process of review of a holding proposed by a branch, it may appear that the final answer will involve a reversal of the branch proposal with a result less favorable to the taxpayer. Or it may appear that an adverse holding proposed by a branch will be approved, but on a new or different issue or on different grounds than those on which the branch decided the case. Under either of these circumstances, the taxpayer or the taxpayer's representative will be invited to another conference. The provisions of this subparagraph limiting the number of conferences to which a taxpayer is entitled will not foreclose inviting a taxpayer to attend further conferences when, in the opinion of National Office personnel, such need arises. All additional conferences of this type discussed are held only at the invitation of the Service.

(d) It is the responsibility of the taxpayer to furnish to the National Office, within 21 calendar days after the conference, a written record of any additional data, line of reasoning, precedents, etc., that were proposed by the taxpayer and discussed at the conference but were not previously or adequately presented in writing. Extensions of time will be granted only if justified in writing by the taxpayer and approved by the appropriate Technical branch chief. Any additional material and a copy thereof should be addressed to and sent to the National Office which will forward the copy to the appropriate Appeals Office. The Appeals Office will be requested to give the matter prompt attention, will verify the additional facts and data, and will comment on it to the extent deemed appropriate.

(e) A taxpayer or the taxpayer's representative desiring to obtain information as to the status of the case may do so by contacting the following offices with respect to matters in the areas of their responsibility:

Official	Telephone Numbers (Area Code 202)
Director, Corporation Tax Division	566-4504 or 566-4505
Director, Individual Tax Division	566-3767 or 566-3788

(vi) *Preparation of technical advice memorandum by the National Office..*—(a) Immediately upon receipt in the National Office, the technical employee to whom the case is assigned will analyze the file to ascertain whether it meets the requirements of subdivision (iii) of this subparagraph. If the case is not complete with respect to any requirement in subdivision (iii) (a) through (d) of this subparagraph, appropriate steps will be taken to complete the file. If any request for technical advice does not comply with the requirements of subdivision (iii)(e) of this subparagraph, relating to the statement of proposed deletions, the National Office will make those deletions from the technical advice memorandum which in the judgment of the Commissioner are required by section 6110(c) of the Code.

(b) If the taxpayer has requested a conference in the National Office, the procedures in subdivision (v) of this subparagraph will be followed.

(c) Replies to requests for technical advice will be addressed to the Appeals office and will be drafted in two parts. Each part will identify the taxpayer by name, address, identification number, and year or years involved. The first part (hereafter called the "technical advice memorandum") will contain (1) a recitation of the pertinent facts having a bearing on the issue; (2) a discussion of the facts, precedents, and reasoning of the National Office; and (3) the conclusions of the National Office. The conclusions will give direct answers, whenever possible, to the specific questions of the Appeals office. The discussion of the issues will be in such detail that the Appeals office is apprised of the reasoning underlying the conclusion. There shall accompany the technical advice memorandum a notice, pursuant to section 6110(f)(1) of the Code, of intention to disclose the technical advice memorandum (including a copy of the version proposed to be open to public inspection and notations of third party communications pursuant to section 6110(d) of the Code) which the Appeals office shall forward to the taxpayer at such time that it furnishes a copy of the technical advice memorandum to the taxpayer pursuant to (e) of this subdivision and subdivision (vii)(b) of this subparagraph.

(d) The second part of the reply will consist of a transmittal memorandum. In the unusual cases it will serve as a vehicle for providing the Appeals office administrative information or other information which, under the nondisclosure statutes, or for other reasons, may not be discussed with the taxpayer.

(e) It is the general practice of the Service to furnish a copy of the technical advice memorandum to the taxpayer after it has been adopted by the Appeals office. However, in the case of technical advice memorandums described in section 6110(g)(5)(A) of the Code, relating to cases involving criminal or civil fraud investigations and jeopardy or termination assessments, a copy of the technical advice memorandum shall not be furnished the taxpayer until all proceedings with respect to the investigations or assessments are completed.

(f) After receiving the notice pursuant to section 6110(f)(1) of the Code of intention to disclose the technical advice memorandum, the taxpayer, if desiring to protest the disclosure of certain information in the memorandum, must, with 20 days after the notice is mailed, submit a written statement identifying those deletions not made by the Internal Revenue Service which the taxpayer believes should have been made. The taxpayer shall also submit a copy of the version of the technical advice memorandum proposed to be open to public inspection on which the taxpayer indicates, by the use of brackets, the deletions proposed by the taxpayer but which have not been made by the Internal Revenue Service. Generally, the Internal Revenue Service will not consider the deletion of any material which the taxpayer did not, prior to the time when the National Office sent its reply to the request for technical advice to the Appeals office, propose be deleted. The Internal Revenue Service shall, within 20 days after receipt of the response by the taxpayer to the notice pursuant to section 6110(f)(1) of the Code, mail to the taxpayer its final administrative conclusion regarding the deletions to be made.

(vii) *Action on technical advice in Appeals offices..—(a)* Unless the Chief, Appeals Office, feels that the conclusions reached by the National Office in a technical advice memorandum should be reconsidered and promptly requests such reconsideration, the Appeals office will proceed to process the taxpayer's case taking into account the conclusions expressed in the technical advice memorandum. The effect of technical advice on the taxpayer's case is set forth in subdivision (viii) of this subparagraph.

(b) The Appeals office will furnish the taxpayer a copy of the technical advice memorandum described in subdivision (vi)(c) of this subparagraph and the notice pursuant to section 6110(f)(1) of the Code of intention to disclose the technical advice memorandum (including a copy of the version proposed to be open to public inspection and notations of third-party communications pursuant to section 6110(d) of the Code). The preceding sentence shall not apply to technical advice memorandums involving civil fraud or criminal investigations, or jeopardy or termination assessments, as described in subdivision (iii)(j) of this subparagraph (except to the extent provided in subdivision (vi)(e) of this subparagraph) or to documents to which section 6104 of the Code applies.

(c) In those cases in which the National Office advises the Appeals office that it should not furnish a copy of the technical advice memorandum to the taxpayer, the Appeals office will so inform the taxpayer if he/she requests a copy.

(viii) *Effect of technical advice.—(a)* A technical advice memorandum represents an expression of the views of the Service as to the application of law, regulations, and precedents to the facts of a specific case, and is issued primarily as a means of assisting Service officials in the closing of the case involved.

(b) Except in rare or unusual circumstances, a holding in a technical advice memorandum that is favorable to the taxpayer is applied retroactively. Moreover, since technical advice, as described in subdivision (i) of this subparagraph, is issued only on closed transactions, a holding in a technical advice memorandum that is adverse to the taxpayer is also applied retroactively unless the Assistant Commissioner or Deputy Assistant Commissioner (Technical) exercises the discretionary authority under section 7805(b) of the Code to limit the retroactive effect of the holding. Likewise, a holding in a technical advice memorandum that modifies or revokes a holding in a prior technical advice memorandum will also be applied retroactively, with one exception. If the new holding is less favorable to the taxpayer, it will generally not be applied to the period in which the taxpayer relied on the prior holding in situations involving continuing transactions of the type described in § 601.201(1)(7) and § 601.201(1)(8).

(c) The Appeals office is bound by technical advice favorable to the taxpayer. However, if the technical advice is unfavorable to the taxpayer, the Appeals office may settle the issue in the usual manner under existing authority. For the effect of the technical advice in Employee Plans and Exempt Organization cases see § 601.201(n)(9)(viii).

(d) In connection with section 446 of the Code, taxpayers may request permission from the Assistant Commissioner (Technical) to change a method of accounting and obtain a 10-year (or less) spread of the resulting adjustments. Such a request should be made prior to or at the first Appeals conference. The Appeals office has authority to allow a change and the resulting spread without referring the case to Technical.

(e) Technical advice memorandums often form the basis for revenue rulings. For the description of revenue rulings and the effect thereof, see § § 601.601(d)(2)(i)(a) and 601.601(d)(2)(v).

(f) An Appeals office may raise an issue in a taxable period, even though technical advice may have been asked for and furnished with regard to the same or a similar issue in any other taxable period.

(g) *Limitation on the jurisdiction and function of Appeals.—(1) Overpayment of more than $200,000.—*If Appeals determines that there is an overpayment of income, war profits, excess profits, estate, generation-skipping transfer or gift tax, or any tax imposed by chapters 41 through 44, including penalties and interest, in excess of $200,000, such determination will be considered by the Joint Committee on Taxation, See section 601.108.

Reg. § 601.106(f)(9)(vi)(f)

(2) *Offers in compromise.*—For jurisdiction of Appeals with respect to offers in compromise of tax liabilities, see § 601.203.

(3) *Closing agreements.*—For jurisdiction of Appeals with respect to closing agreements under section 7121 of the Code relating to any internal revenue tax liability, see § 601.202.

(h) *Reopening closed cases not docketed in the Tax Court.*—(1) A case not docketed in the Tax Court and closed by Appeals on the basis of concessions made by both Appeals and the taxpayer will not be reopened by action initiated by the Service unless the disposition involved fraud, malfeasance, concealment or misrepresentation of material fact, or an important mistake in mathematical calculation, and then only with the approval of the Regional Director of Appeals.

(2) Under certain unusual circumstances favorable to the taxpayer, such as retroactive legislation, a case not docketed in the Tax Court and closed by Appeals on the basis of concessions made by both Appeals and the taxpayer may be reopened upon written application from the taxpayer, and only with the approval of the Regional Director of Appeals. The processing of an application for a tentative carryback adjustment or of a claim for refund or credit for an overassessment (for a year involved in the prior closing) attributable to a claimed deduction or credit for a carryback provided by law, and not included in a previous Appeals determination, shall not be considered a reopening requiring approval. A subsequent assessment of an excessive tentative allowance shall likewise not be considered such a reopening. The Director of Appeals may authorize, in advance, the reopening of similar classes of cases where legislative enactments or compelling administrative reasons require such advance approval.

(3) A case not docketed in the Tax Court and closed by Appeals on a basis not involving concessions made by both Appeals and the taxpayer will not be reopened by action initiated by the Service unless the disposition involved fraud, malfeasance, concealment or misrepresentation of material fact, an important mistake in mathematical calculation, or such other circumstance that indicates that failure to take such action would be a serious administrative omission, and then only with the approval of the Regional Director of Appeals.

(4) A case not docketed in the Tax Court and closed by Appeals on a basis not involving concessions made by both Appeals and the taxpayer may be reopened by the taxpayer by any appropriate means, such as by the filing of a timely claim for refund.

(i) *Special procedures for crude oil windfall profit tax cases.*—For special procedures relating to crude oil windfall profit tax cases, see § 601.405. [Reg. § 601.106.]

☐ [32 FR 15990, Nov. 22, 1967, as amended at 32 FR 20646, Dec. 21, 1967; 33 FR 6820, May 4, 1968; 34 FR 14600, Sept. 19, 1969; 35 FR 7113, May 6, 1970; 35 FR 15917, Oct. 9, 1970; 36 FR 7584, Apr. 22, 1971; 38 FR 4959, Feb. 23, 1973; 38 FR 33301, Dec. 3, 1973; 39 FR 8917, Mar. 7, 1974; 41 FR 20880, May 21, 1976; 41 FR 40103, Sept. 17, 1976; 42 FR 46519, Sept. 16, 1977; 42 FR 48336, Sept. 23, 1977; 43 FR 17817, Apr. 26, 1978; 43 FR 44498, Sept. 28, 1978; 43 FR 53029, Nov. 15, 1978; 45 FR 7253, Feb. 1, 1980; 46 FR 26053, May 11, 1981; 48 FR 24670, June 2, 1983; 49 FR 26499, Sept. 18, 1984; 52 FR 38406, Oct. 16, 1987.]

[Reg. § 601.107]

§ 601.107. Criminal Investigation functions.—(a) *General.*—Each district has a Criminal Investigation function whose mission is to encourage and achieve the highest possible degree of voluntary compliance with the internal revenue laws by: enforcing the statutory sanctions applicable to income, estate, gift, employment, and certain excise taxes through the investigation of possible criminal violations of such laws and the recommendation (when warranted) of prosecution and/or assertion of the 50 percent ad valorem addition to the tax; developing information concerning the extent of criminal violations of all Federal tax laws (except those relating to alcohol, tobacco, narcotics, and firearms); measuring the effectiveness of the investigation process; and providing protection of persons and of property and other enforcement coordination as required.

(b) *Investigative procedure.*—(1) A witness when questioned in an investigation conducted by the Criminal Investigation Division may have counsel present to represent and advise him. Upon request, a copy of an affidavit or transcript of a question and answer statement will be furnished a witness promptly, except in circumstances deemed by the Regional Commissioner to necessitate temporarily withholding a copy.

(2) A taxpayer who may be the subject of a criminal recommendation will be afforded a district Criminal Investigation conference when he requests one or where the Chief, Criminal Investigation Division, makes a determination that such a conference will be in the best interests of the Government. At the conference, the IRS representative will inform the taxpayer by a general oral statement of the alleged fraudulent features of the case, to the extent consistent with protecting the Government's interests, and, at the same time, making available to the taxpayer sufficient facts and figures to acquaint him with the basis, nature, and other essential elements of the proposed criminal charges against him.

(c) *Processing of cases after investigation.*—The Chief, Criminal Investigation Division, shall ordinarily notify the subject of an investigation and his authorized representative, if any, when he forwards a case to the Regional Counsel with a recommendation for prosecution. The rule will not apply if the case is with a United States Attorney. [Reg. § 601.107.]

☐ [33 FR 17325, Nov. 21, 1968, as amended at 38 FR 9227, Apr. 12, 1973; 39 FR 8917, Mar. 7, 1974; 43 FR 53029, Nov. 15, 1978.]

[Reg. §601.108]

§601.108. **Review of overpayments exceeding $200,000.**—(a) *General.*—Section 6405(a) of the Code provides that no refund or credit of income, war profits, excess profits, estate, or gift taxes, or any tax imposed by chapters 41 through 44, including penalties and interest, in excess of $200,000 may be made until after the expiration of 30 days from the date a report is made to the Joint Committee on Taxation. Taxpayers in cases requiring review by the Joint Committee are afforded the same appeal rights as other taxpayers. In general, these cases follow regular procedures, except for preparation of reports to and review by the Joint Committee.

(b) *Reports to Joint Committee.*—In any case in which no protest is made to Appeals and no petition docketed in the Tax Court, the report to the Joint Committee is prepared by a Joint Committee Coordinator, who is an Examination Division regional specialist. In cases in which a protest has been made, the report to the Joint Committee is prepared by an Appeals officer; in cases in which a petition is docketed, either an Appeals officer or a Counsel attorney prepares the report, depending on the circumstances.

(c) *Procedure after report to Joint Committee.*—After compliance with section 6405 of the Code, the case is processed for issuance of a certificate of overassessment, and payment or credit of any overpayment. If the final determination involves a rejection of a claimed overpayment in whole or in part, a statutory notice of disallowance will be sent by certified or registered mail to the taxpayer, except where the taxpayer has filed a written waiver of such notice of disallowance. [Reg. §601.108.]

☐ [32 FR 15990, Nov. 22, 1967, as amended at 42 FR 46519, Sept. 16, 1977; 43 FR 44503, Sept. 28, 1978; 43 FR 53030, Nov. 15, 1978; 45 FR 7255, Feb. 1, 1980.]

[Reg. §601.109]

§601.109. **Bankruptcy and receivership cases.**—(a) *General.*—(1) Upon the adjudication of bankruptcy of any taxpayer in any liquidating proceeding, the filing or (where approval is required by the Bankruptcy Act) the approval of a petition of, or the approval of a petition against, any taxpayer in any other proceeding under the Bankruptcy Act or the appointment of a receiver for any taxpayer in any receivership proceeding before a court of the United States or of any State or Territory or of the District of Columbia, the assessment of any deficiency in income, profits, estate, or gift tax (together with all interest, additional amounts, or additions to the tax provided for by law) shall be made immediately. See section 6871 of the Code. In such cases the restrictions imposed by section 6213(a) of the Code upon assessments are not applicable. (In the case of an assignment for the benefit of creditors, the assessment will be made under section 6861, relating to jeopardy assessments. See §601.105(h).) Cases in which immediate assessment will be made include those of taxpayers in receivership or in bankruptcy, reorganization, arrangement, or wage earner proceedings under chapters I to VII, section 77, chapters X, XI, XII, and XIII of the Bankruptcy Act. The term "approval of a petition in any other proceeding under the Bankruptcy Act" includes the filing of a petition under chapters XI to XIII of the Bankruptcy Act with a court of competent jurisdiction. A fiduciary in any proceeding under the Bankruptcy Act (including a trustee, receiver-debtor in possession, or other person designated by the court as in control of the assets or affairs of a debtor) or a receiver in any receivership proceeding may be required, as provided in regulations prescribed under section 6036 of the Code, to give notice in writing to the district director of his qualification as such. Failure on the part of such fiduciary in a receivership proceeding or a proceeding under the Bankruptcy Act to give such notice, when required, results in the suspension of the running of the period of limitations on the making of assessments from the date of the institution of the proceeding to the date upon which such notice is received by the district director, and for an additional 30 days thereafter. However, in no case where the required notice is not given shall the suspension of the running of the period of limitations on assessment exceed 2 years. See section 6872 of the Code.

(2) Except in cases where departmental instructions direct otherwise, the district director will, promptly after ascertaining the existence of any outstanding Federal tax liability against a taxpayer in any proceeding under the Bankruptcy Act or receivership proceeding, and in any event within the time limited by appropriate provisions of law or the appropriate orders of the court in which such proceeding is pending, file a proof of claim covering such liability in the court in which the proceeding is pending. Such a claim may be filed regardless of whether the unpaid taxes involved have been assessed. Whenever an immediate assessment is made of any income, estate, or gift tax after the commencement of a proceeding, the district director will send to the taxpayer notice and demand for payment together with a copy of such claim.

(b) *Procedure in office of district director.*—(1) While the district director is required by section 6871 of the Code to make immediate assessment of any deficiency in income, estate, or gift taxes, such assessment is not made as a jeopardy assessment (see paragraph (h) of §601.105), and the provisions of section 6861 of the Code do not apply to any assessment made under section 6871. Therefore, the notice of deficiency provided for in section 6861(b) will not be mailed to the taxpayer. Nevertheless, Letter 1005 (DO) will be prepared and addressed in the name of the taxpayer, immediately followed by the name of the trustee, receiver, debtor in possession, or other person designated to be in control of the assets or affairs of the debtor by the court in which the bankruptcy or receivership proceeding is pending. Such letter will state how the deficiency was computed, advise that within 30 days a written protest under penalties of perjury may be filed with the district director showing wherein the deficiency is claimed to be incorrect, and advise that upon request an Appeals office conference will be granted with respect to such deficiency. If, after protest is filed (in triplicate) and an Appeals office conference is held, adjustment appears necessary in the deficiency, appropriate action will be taken. Except where the interests of the Government require otherwise, Letters 1005 (DO) are issued by the office of the district director.

(2) The immediate assessment required by section 6871 of the Code represents an exception to the usual restrictions on the assessment of Federal income, estate, and gift taxes. Since there are no restrictions on the assessment of Federal excise or employment taxes, immediate assessment of such taxes will be made in any case where section 6871 of the Code would require immediate assessment of income, estate, or gift taxes.

(3) If after such assessment a claim for abatement is filed and such claim is accompanied by a request in writing for a conference, an Appeals office conference will be granted. Ordinarily, only one conference will be held, unless it develops that additional information can be furnished which has a material bearing upon the tax liability in which event the conference will be continued to a later date.

(c) *Procedure before the Appeals office.*—If an income, estate, or gift tax case is under consideration by an Appeals office (whether before or after issuance of a statutory notice of deficiency) at the time of either: (i) The adjudication of bankruptcy of the taxpayer in any liquidating proceeding; (ii) the filing with a court of competent jurisdiction or (where approval is required by the Bankruptcy Act) the approval of a petition of, or against, the taxpayer in any other proceeding under the Bankruptcy Act; or (iii) the appointment of any receiver, then the case will be returned to the district director for assessment (if not previously made), for issuance of the Letter 1005 (DO), and for filing proof of claim in the proceeding. Excise and employment tax cases pending in the Appeals office at such time will likewise be returned to the district director for assessment (if not previously made) and for filing proof of claim in the proceeding. A petition for redetermination of a deficiency may not be filed in the Tax Court after the adjudication of bankruptcy, the filing or (where approval is required by the Bankruptcy Act) the approval of a petition of, or the approval of a petition against, the taxpayer in any other bankruptcy proceeding, or the appointment of a receiver. See section 6871(b) of the Code. However, the Tax Court is not deprived of jurisdiction where the adjudication of bankruptcy, the filing or (where approval is required by the Bankruptcy Act) the approval of a petition of, or the approval of a petition against, the taxpayer in any other bankruptcy proceeding, or the appointment of a receiver, occurred after the filing of the petition. In such a case, the jurisdiction of the bankruptcy or receivership court and the Tax Court is concurrent.

(d) *Priority of claims.*—Under Section 3466 of the Revised Statutes and Section 3467 of the Revised Statutes, as amended, taxes are entitled to priority over other claims therein stated and the receiver or other person designated as in control of the assets or affairs of the debtor by the court in which the receivership proceeding is pending may be held personally liable for failure on his part to protect the priority of the Government respecting taxes of which he has notice. Under Section 64 of the Bankruptcy Act, taxes may be entitled to priority over other claims therein stated and the trustee, receiver, debtor in possession or other person designated as in control of the assets or affairs of the debtor by the court in which the bankruptcy proceeding is pending may be held personally liable for any failure on his part to protect a priority of the Government respecting taxes of which he has notice and which are entitled to priority under the Bankruptcy Act. Sections 77(e), 199, 337(2), 455 and 659(6) of the Bankruptcy Act also contain provisions with respect to the rights of the United States relative to priority of payment. Bankruptcy courts have jurisdiction under the Bankruptcy Act to determine all disputes regarding the amount and the validity of tax claims against a bankrupt or a debtor in a proceeding under the Bankruptcy Act. A receivership proceeding or an assignment for the benefit of creditors does not discharge any portion of a claim of the United States for taxes and any portion of such claim allowed by the court in which the proceeding is pending and which remains unsatisfied after the termination of the proceeding shall be collected with interest in accordance with law. A bankruptcy proceeding under Chapters I through VII of the Bankruptcy Act does discharge that portion of a claim of the United States which became legally due and owing more than three years preceding bankruptcy, with certain exceptions [as] provided in the Bankruptcy Act, as does a proceeding under Section 77 or Chapter X of the Bankruptcy Act. Any taxes which are dischargeable under the Bankruptcy Act which remain unsatisfied after the termination of the proceeding may be collected only from exempt or abandoned property. [Reg. § 601.109.]

☐ [32 FR 15990, Nov. 22, 1967, as amended at 33 FR 6821, May 4, 1968; 35 FR 15917, Oct. 9, 1970; 43 FR 44503, Sept. 28, 1978; 45 FR 7255, Feb. 1, 1980.]

Subpart B—Rulings and Other Specific Matters

[Reg. § 601.201]

§ 601.201. Rulings and determination letters.—(a) *General practice and definitions.*—(1) It is the practice of the Internal Revenue Service to answer inquiries of individuals and organizations, whenever appropriate in the interest of sound tax administration, as to their status for tax purposes and as to the tax effects of their acts or transactions. One of the functions of the National Office of the Internal Revenue Service is to issue rulings in such matters. If a taxpayer's request for a ruling concerns an action that may have an impact on the environment, compliance by the Service with the requirements of the National Environmental Policy Act of 1969 (Public Law 91-190) may result in delay in issuing the ruling. Accordingly, taxpayers requesting rulings should take this factor into account. District directors apply the statutes, regulations, Revenue Rulings, and other precedents published in the Internal Revenue Bulletin in the determination of tax liability, the collection of taxes, and the issuance of determination letters in answer to taxpayers' inquiries or requests. For purposes of this section any reference to district director or district office also includes, where appropriate, the office of the Director, Office of International Operations.

(2) A "ruling" is a written statement issued to a taxpayer or his authorized representative by the National Office which interprets and applies the tax laws to a specific set of facts. Rulings are issued only by the National Office. The issuance of rulings is under the general supervision of the Assistant Commissioner (Technical) and has been largely redelegated to the Director, Corporation Tax Division and Director, Individual Tax Division.

(3) A "determination letter" is a written statement issued by a district director in response to a written inquiry by an individual or an organization that applies to the particular facts involved, the principles and precedents previously announced by the National Office. A determination letter is issued only where a determination can be made on the basis of clearly established rules as set forth in the statute, Treasury decision, or regulation, or by a ruling, opinion, or court decision published in the Internal Revenue Bulletin. Where such a determination cannot be made, such as where the question presented involves a novel issue or the matter is excluded from the jurisdiction of a district director by the provisions of paragraph (c) of this section, a determination letter will not be issued. However, with respect to determination letters in the pension trust area, see paragraph (o) of this section.

(4) An "opinion letter" is a written statement issued by the National Office as to the acceptability of the form of a master or prototype plan and any related trust or custodial account under sections 401 and 501(a) of the Internal Revenue Code of 1954.

(5) An "information letter" is a statement issued either by the National Office or by a district director which does no more than call attention to a well-established interpretation or principle of tax law, without applying it to a specific set of facts. An information letter may be issued when the nature of the request from the individual or the organization suggests that it is seeking general information, or where the request does not meet all the requirements of paragraph (e) of this section, and it is believed that such general information will assist the individual or organization.

(6) A "Revenue Ruling" is an official interpretation by the Service which has been published in the Internal Revenue Bulletin. Revenue Rulings are issued only by the National Office and are published for the information and guidance of taxpayers, Internal Revenue Service officials, and others concerned.

(7) A "closing agreement," as the term is used herein, is an agreement between the Commissioner of Internal Revenue or his delegate and a taxpayer with respect to a specific issue or issues entered into pursuant to the authority contained in section 7121 of the Internal Revenue Code. Such a closing agreement is based on a ruling which has been signed by the Commissioner or his delegate and in which it is indicated that a closing agreement will be entered into on the basis of the holding of the ruling letter. Closing agreements are final and conclusive except upon a showing of fraud, malfeasance, or misrepresentation of material fact. They may be entered into where it is advantageous to have the matter permanently and conclusively closed, or where a taxpayer can show good and sufficient reasons for an agreement and the Government will sustain no disadvantage by its consummation. In appropriate cases, taxpayers may be required to enter into a closing agreement as a condition to the issuance of a ruling. Where in a single case, closing agreements are requested on behalf of each of a number of taxpayers, such agreements are not entered into if the number of such taxpayers exceeds 25. However, in a case where the issue and holding are identical as to all of the taxpayers and the number of taxpayers is in excess of 25, a Mass Closing Agreement will be entered into with the taxpayer who is authorized by the others to represent the entire group. See, for example, Rev. Proc. 78-15, 1978-2 C.B. 488, and Rev. Proc. 78-16, 1978-2 C.B. 489.

(b) *Rulings issued by the National Office.*—(1) In income and gift tax matters and matters involving taxes imposed under Chapter 42 of the Code, the National Office issues rulings on prospective transactions and on completed transactions before the return is filed. However, rulings will not ordinarily be issued if the identical issue is present in a return of the taxpayer for a prior year which is under active examination or audit by a district office, or is being considered by a branch office of the Appellate Division. The National Office issues rulings involving the exempt status of organizations under section 501 or 521 of the Code, only to the extent provided in paragraph (n) of this section, Revenue Procedure 72-5, Internal Revenue Bulletin No. 1972-1, 19, and Revenue Procedure 68-13, C.B. 1968-1, 764.

The National Office issues rulings as to the foundation status of certain organizations under sections 509(a) and 4942(j)(3) of the Code only to the extent provided in paragraph (r) of this section. The National Office issues rulings involving qualification of plans under section 401 of the Code only to the extent provided in paragraph (o) of this section. The National Office issues opinion letters as to the acceptability of the form of master or prototype plans and any related trusts or custodial accounts under sections 401 and 501(a) of the Code only to the extent provided in paragraphs (p) and (q) of this section. The National Office will not issue rulings with respect to the replacement of involuntarily converted property, even though replacement has not been made, if the taxpayer has filed a return for the taxable year in which the property was converted. However, see paragraph (c)(6) of this section as to the authority of district directors to issue determination letters in this connection.

(2) In estate tax matters, the National Office issues rulings with respect to transactions affecting the estate tax of a decedent before the estate tax return is filed. It will not rule with respect to such matters after the estate tax return has been filed, nor will it rule on matters relating to the application of the estate tax to property or the estate of a living person.

(3) In employment and excise tax matters (except taxes imposed under Chapter 42 of the Code), the National Office issues rulings with respect to prospective transactions and to completed transactions either before or after the return is filed. However, the National Office will not ordinarily rule with respect to an issue, whether related to a prospective or a completed transaction, if it knows or has reason to believe that the same or an identical issue is before any field office (including any branch office of the Appellate Division) in connection with an examination or audit of the liability of the same taxpayer for the same or a prior period.

(4) The Service will not issue rulings to business, trade, or industrial associations or to other similar groups relating to the application of the tax laws to members of the group. However, rulings may be issued to such groups or associations relating to their own tax status or liability provided such tax status or liability is not an issue before any field office (including any branch office or the Appellate Division) in connection with an examination or audit of the liability of the same taxpayer for the same or a prior period.

(5) Pending the adoption of regulations (either temporary or final) that reflect the provisions of any Act, consideration will be given to the issuance of rulings under the conditions set forth below.

(i) If an inquiry presents an issue on which the answer seems to be clear from an application of the provisions of the statute to the facts described, a ruling will be issued in accordance with usual procedures.

(ii) If an inquiry presents an issue on which the answer seems reasonably certain but not entirely free from doubt, a ruling will be issued only if it is established that a business emergency requires a ruling or that unusual hardship will result from failure to obtain a ruling.

(iii) If an inquiry presents an issue that cannot be reasonably resolved prior to the issuance of regulations, a ruling will not be issued.

(iv) In any case in which the taxpayer believes that a business emergency exists or that an unusual hardship will result from failure to obtain a ruling, he should submit with the request a separate letter setting forth the facts necessary for the Service to make a determination in this regard. In this connection, the Service will not deem a "business emergency" to result from circumstances within the control of the taxpayer such as, for example, scheduling within an inordinately short time the closing date for a transaction or a meeting of the board of directors or the shareholders of a corporation.

(c) *Determination letters issued by district directors.*—(1) In income and gift tax matters, and in matters involving taxes imposed under Chapter 42 of the Code, district directors issue determination letters in response to taxpayers' written requests submitted to their offices involving completed transactions which affect returns over which they have audit jurisdiction, but only if the answer to the question presented is covered specifically by statute, Treasury Decision or regulation, or specifically by a ruling, opinion, or court decision published in the Internal Revenue Bulletin. A determination letter will not usually be issued with respect to a question which involves a return to be filed by the taxpayer if the identical question is involved in a return or returns already filed by the taxpayer. District directors may not issue determination letters as to the tax consequence of prospective or proposed transactions, except as provided in subparagraphs (5) and (6) of this paragraph.

(2) In estate and gift tax matters, district directors issue determination letters in response to written requests submitted to their offices affecting the estate tax returns of decedents that will be audited by their offices, but only if the answer to the questions presented are specifically covered by statute, Treasury decision or regulation, or by a ruling, opinion, or court decision published in the Internal Revenue Bulletin. District directors will not issue determination letters relating to matters involving the application of the estate tax to property or the estate of a living person.

(3) In employment and excise tax matters (except excise taxes imposed under Chapter 42 of the Code), district directors issue determination letters in response to written requests from taxpayers who have filed or who are required to file returns over which they have audit jurisdiction, but only if the answers to the questions presented are covered specifically by statute, Treasury decision or regulation, or a ruling, opinion, or court decision published in the Internal Revenue Bulletin. Because of the impact of these taxes upon the business operation of the

taxpayer and because of special problems of administration both to the Service and to the taxpayer, district directors may take appropriate action in regard to such requests, whether they relate to completed or prospective transactions or returns previously filed or to be filed.

(4) Notwithstanding the provisions of subparagraphs (1), (2), and (3), of this paragraph, a district director will not issue a determination letter in response to an inquiry which presents a question specifically covered by statute, regulations, rulings, etc., published in the Internal Revenue Bulletin, where (i) it appears that the taxpayer has directed a similar inquiry to the National Office, (ii) the identical issue involving the same taxpayer is pending in a case before the Appellate Division, (iii) the determination letter is requested by an industry, trade association, or similar group, or (iv) the request involves an industrywide problem. Under no circumstances will a district director issue a determination letter unless it is clearly indicated that the inquiry is with regard to a taxpayer or taxpayers who have filed or are required to file returns over which his office has or will have audit jurisdiction. Notwithstanding the provisions of subparagraph (3), of this paragraph, a district director will not issue a determination letter on an employment tax question when the specific question involved has been or is being considered by the Central Office of the Social Security Administration. Nor will district directors issue determination letters on excise tax questions if a request is for a determination of a constructive sales price under section 4216(b) or 4218(e) of the Code. However, the National Office will issue rulings in this area. See paragraph (d)(2) of this section.

(5) District directors issue determination letters as to the qualification of plans under sections 401 and 405(a) of the Code, and as to the exempt status of related trusts under section 501 of the Code, to the extent provided in paragraphs (o) and (q) of this section. Selected district directors also issue determination letters as to the qualification of certain organizations for exemption from Federal income tax under sections 501 and 521 of the Code, to the extent provided in paragraph (n) of this section. Selected district directors also issue determination letters as to the qualification of certain organizations for foundation status under sections 509(a) and 4942(j)(3) of the Code, to the extent provided in paragraph (r) of this section.

(6) District directors issue determination letters with regard to the replacement of involuntarily converted property under section 1033 of the Code even though the replacement has not been made, if the taxpayer has filed his income tax return for the year in which the property was involuntarily converted.

(7) A request received by a district director with respect to a question involved in an income, estate, or gift tax return already filed will, in general, be considered in connection with the examination of the return. If response is made to such inquiry prior to an examination or audit, it will be considered a tentative finding in any subsequent examination or audit of the return.

(d) *Discretionary authority to issue rulings and determination letters.*—(1) It is the practice of the Service to answer inquiries of individuals and organizations, whenever appropriate in the interest of sound tax administration, as to their status for tax purposes and the tax effect of their acts or transactions.

(2) There are, however, certain areas where, because of the inherently factual nature of the problem involved, or for other reasons, the Service will not issue rulings or determination letters. A ruling or determination letter is not issued on alternative plans of proposed transactions or on hypothetical situations. A specific area or a list of these areas is published from time to time in the Internal Revenue Bulletin. Such list is not all inclusive since the Service may decline to issue rulings or determination letters on other questions whenever warranted by the facts or circumstances of a particular case. The National Office and district directors may, when it is deemed appropriate and in the best interest of the Service, issue information letters calling attention to well-established principles of tax law.

(3) The National Office will issue rulings in all cases on prospective or future transactions when the law or regulations require a determination of the effect of a proposed transaction for tax purposes, as in the case of a transfer coming within the provisions of sections 1491 and 1492 of the Code, or an exchange coming within the provisions of section 367 of the Code. The National Office will issue rulings in all cases involving the determination of a constructive sales price under section 4216(b) or 4218(e) of the Code.

(e) *Instructions to taxpayers.*—(1) A request for a ruling or determination letter is to be submitted in duplicate if (i) more than one issue is presented in the request or (ii) a closing agreement is requested with respect to the issue presented. There shall accompany the request a declaration in the following form: "Under penalties of perjury, I declare that I have examined this request, including accompanying documents, and to the best of my knowledge and belief, the facts presented in support of the requested ruling or determination letter are true, correct, and complete". The declaration must accompany requests that are postmarked or hand delivered to the Internal Revenue Service after October 31, 1976. The declaration must be signed by the person or persons on whose behalf the request is made.

(2) Each request for a ruling or a determination letter must contain a complete statement of all relevant facts relating to the transaction. Such facts include names, addresses and taxpayer identifying numbers of all interested parties; the location of the district office that has or will have audit jurisdiction over the return or report of each party; a full and precise statement of the business reasons for the transaction; and a carefully detailed description of the transaction. In

addition, true copies of all contracts, wills, deeds, agreements, instruments, and other documents involved in the transaction must be submitted with the request. However, relevant facts reflected in documents submitted must be included in the taxpayer's statement and not merely incorporated by reference, and must be accompanied by an analysis of their bearing on the issue or issues, specifying the pertinent provisions. (The term "all interested parties" is not to be construed as requiring a list of all shareholders of a widely held corporation requesting a ruling relating to a reorganization, or a list of employees where a large number may be involved in a plan.) The request must contain a statement whether, to the best of the knowledge of the taxpayer or his representative, the identical issue is being considered by any field office of the Service in connection with an active examination or audit of a tax return of the taxpayer already filed or is being considered by a branch office by the Appellate Division. Where the request pertains to only one step of a larger integrated transaction, the facts, circumstances, etc., must be submitted with respect to the entire transaction. The following list contains references to revenue procedures for advance ruling requests under certain sections of the Code.

(i) For ruling requests under section 103 of the Code, see Rev. Proc. 79-4, 1979-1 C.B. 483, as amplified by Rev. Proc. 79-12, 1979-1 C.B. 492. Revenue Procedure 79-12 sets forth procedures for submitting ruling requests to which sections 103 and 7478 of the Code apply.

(ii) For ruling requests under section 367 of the Code, see Rev. Proc. 68-23, 1968-1 C.B. 821, as amplified by Rev. Proc. 76-20, 1976-1 C.B. 560, Rev. Proc. 77-5, 1977-1 C.B. 536, Rev. Proc. 78-27, 1978-2 C.B. 526, and Rev. Proc. 78-28, 1978-2 C.B. 526. Revenue Procedure 68-23 contains guidelines for taxpayers and their representatives in connection with issuing rulings under section 367. Revenue Procedure 76-20 explains the effect of Rev. Rul. 75-561, 1975-2 C.B. 129, on transactions described in section 3.03(1)(c) of Rev. Proc. 68-23. Revenue Procedure 77-5 sets forth procedures for submitting ruling requests under section 367, and the administrative remedies available to a taxpayer within the Service after such rulings have been issued. Revenue Procedure 78-27 relates to the notice requirement set forth in the section 367(b) temporary regulations. Revenue Procedure 78-28 relates to the timely filing of a section 367(a) ruling request.

(iii) For ruling requests under section 351 of the Code, see Rev. Proc. 73-10, 1973-1 C.B. 760, and Rev. Proc. 69-19, 1969-2 C.B. 301. Revenue Procedure 73-10 sets forth the information to be included in the ruling request. Revenue Procedure 69-19 sets forth the conditions and circumstances under which an advance ruling will be issued under section 367 of the Code that an agreement which purports to furnish technical know-how in exchange for stock is a transfer of property within the meaning of section 351.

(iv) For ruling requests under section 332, 334(b)(1), or 334(b)(2) of the Code, see Rev. Proc. 73-17, 1973-2 C.B. 465. Revenue Procedure 73-17

sets forth the information to be included in the ruling request.

(v) See Rev. Proc. 77-30, 1977-2 C.B. 539, and Rev. Proc. 78-18, 1978-2 C.B. 491, relating to rules for the issuance of an advance ruling that a proposed sale of employer stock to a related qualified defined contribution plan of deferred compensation will be a sale of the stock rather than a distribution of property.

(vi) For ruling requests under section 302 or section 311 of the Code, see Rev. Proc. 73-35, 1973-2 C.B. 490. Revenue Procedure 73-35 sets forth the information to be included in the ruling request.

(vii) For ruling requests under section 337 of the Code (and related section 331) see Rev. Proc. 75-32, 1975-2 C.B. 555. Revenue Procedure 75-32 sets forth the information to be included in the ruling request.

(viii) For ruling requests under section 346 of the Code (and related sections 331 and 336), see Rev. Proc. 73-36, 1973-2 C.B. 496. Revenue Procedure 73-36 sets forth the information to be included in the ruling request.

(ix) For ruling requests under section 355 of the Code, see Rev. Proc. 75-35, 1975-2 C.B. 561. Revenue Procedure 75-35 sets forth the information to be included in the ruling request.

(x) For ruling requests under section 368(a)(1)(E) of the Code, see Rev. Proc. 78-33, 1978-2 C.B. 532. Revenue Procedure 78-33 sets forth the information to be included in the ruling request.

(xi) For ruling requests concerning the classification of an organization as a limited partnership where a corporation is the sole general partner, see Rev. Proc. 72-13, 1972-1 C.B. 735. See also Rev. Proc. 74-17, 1974-1 C.B. 438, and Rev. Proc. 75-16, 1975-1 C.B. 676. Revenue Procedure 74-17 announces certain operating rules of the Service relating to the issuance of advance ruling letters concerning the classification of organizations formed as limited partnerships. Revenue Procedure 75-16 sets forth a checklist outlining required information frequently omitted from requests for rulings relating to classification of organizations for Federal tax purposes.

(xii) For ruling requests concerning the creditability of a foreign tax under section 901 or 903 of the Code, see Rev. Rul. 67-308, 1967-2 C.B. 254, which sets forth requirements for establishing that translations of foreign law are satisfactory as evidence for purposes of determining the creditability of a particular foreign tax. Original documents should not be submitted because documents and exhibits become a part of the Internal Revenue Service file which cannot be returned. If the request is with respect to a corporate distribution, reorganization, or other similar or related transaction, the corporate balance sheet nearest the date of the transaction should be submitted. (If the request relates to a prospective transaction, the most recent balance sheet should be submitted.) In the case of requests for rulings or determination letters, other than those to which section 6104 of the Code applies, postmarked or hand delivered to the Internal Revenue Service after October 31, 1976, there must accompany such requests a statement, described in subparagraph (5) of this paragraph, of proposed deletions pursuant to section 6110(c) of the Code. Such statement is not required if the request is to secure the consent of the Commissioner with respect to the adoption of or change in accounting or funding periods or methods pursuant to section 412, 442, 446(e), or 706 of the Code. If, however, the person seeking the consent of the Commissioner receives from the Internal Revenue Service a notice that proposed deletions should be submitted because the resulting ruling will be open to public inspection under section 6110, the statement of proposed deletions must be submitted within 20 days after such notice is mailed.

(3) As an alternative procedure for the issuance of rulings on prospective transactions, the taxpayer may submit a summary statement of the facts he considers controlling the issue, in addition to the complete statement required for ruling requests by subparagraph (2) of this paragraph. Assuming agreement with the taxpayer's summary statement, the Service will use it as the basis for the ruling. Any taxpayer wishing to adopt this procedure should submit with the request for ruling:

(i) A complete statement of facts relating to the transaction, together with related documents, as required by subparagraph (2) of this paragraph; and

(ii) A summary statement of the facts which he believes should be controlling in reaching the requested conclusion.

Where the taxpayer's statement of controlling facts is accepted, the ruling will be based on those facts and only this statement will ordinarily be incorporated in the ruling letter. It is emphasized, however, that:

(a) This procedure for a "two-part" ruling request is elective with the taxpayer and is not to be considered a required substitute for the regular procedure contained in paragraphs (a) through (m) of this section;

(b) Taxpayers' rights and responsibilities are the same under the "two-part" ruling request procedure as those provided in paragraphs (a) through (m) of this section;

(c) The Service reserves the right to rule on the basis of a more complete statement of facts it considers controlling and to seek further information in developing facts and restating them for ruling purposes; and

(d) The "two-part" ruling request procedure will not apply where it is inconsistent with other procedures applicable to specific situations such as: requests for permission to change accounting method or period; application for recognition of exempt status under section 501 or 521; or rulings on employment tax status.

(4) If the taxpayer is contending for a particular determination, he must furnish an explanation of the grounds for his contentions, together with a statement of relevant authorities in support of his views. Even though the taxpayer is urging no particular determination with regard to a proposed or prospective transaction, he must state his views as to the tax results of the proposed action and furnish a statement of relevant authorities to support such views.

(5) In order to assist the Internal Revenue Service in making the deletions, required by section 6110(c) of the Code, from the text of rulings and determination letters, which are open to public inspection pursuant to section 6110(a) of the Code, there must accompany requests for such rulings or determination letters either a statement of the deletions proposed by the person requesting the ruling or determination letter and the statutory basis for each proposed deletion, or a statement that no information other than names, addresses, and taxpayer identifying numbers need be deleted. Such statement shall be made in a separate document. The statement of proposed deletions shall be accompanied by a copy of the request for a ruling or determination letter and supporting documents, on which shall be indicated, by the use of brackets, the material which the person making such request indicates should be deleted pursuant to section 6110(c) of the Code. The statement of proposed deletions shall indicate the statutory basis, under section 6110(c) of the Code, for each proposed deletion. The statement of proposed deletions shall not appear or be referred to anywhere in the request for a ruling of determination letter. If the person making the request decides to request additional deletions pursuant to section 6110(c) of the Code prior to the time the ruling or determination letter is issued, additional statements may be submitted.

(6) If the request is with respect to the qualification of a plan under section 401 or 405(a) of the Code, see paragraphs (o) and (p) of this section. If the request is with respect to the qualification of an organization for exemption from Federal income tax under section 501 or 521 of the Code, see paragraph (n) of this section, Revenue Procedure 72-5, Internal Revenue Bulletin No. 1972-1, 19 [1972-1 C.B. 709], and Revenue Procedure 68-13, C.B. 1968-1, 764.

(7) A request by or for a taxpayer must be signed by the taxpayer or his authorized representative. If the request is signed by a representative of the taxpayer, or if the representative is to appear before the Internal Revenue Service in connection with the request, he must either be:

(i) An attorney who is a member in good standing of the bar of the highest court of any State, possession, territory, Commonwealth, or the District of Columbia, and who files with the Service a written declaration that he is currently qualified as an attorney and he is authorized to represent the principal,

(ii) A certified public accountant who is duly qualified to practice in any State, possession, territory, Commonwealth, or the District of Columbia, and who files with the Service a written declaration that he is currently qualified as a certified public accountant and he is authorized to represent the principal, or

(iii) A person, other than an attorney or certified public accountant, enrolled to practice before the Service, and who files with the Service a written declaration that he is currently enrolled (including in the declaration either his enrollment number or the expiration date of his enrollment card) and that he is authorized to represent the principal. (See Treasury Department Circular No. 230, as amended, C.B. 1966-2, 1171, for the rules on who may practice before the Service. See § 601.503(c) for the statement required as evidence of recognition as an enrollee.)

(8) A request for a ruling or an opinion letter by the National Office should be addressed to the Commissioner of Internal Revenue, Attention: T:PP:T, Washington, D.C. 20224. A request for a determination letter should be addressed to the district director of internal revenue whose office has or will have audit jurisdiction of the taxpayer's return. See also paragraphs (n) through (q) of this section.

(9) Any request for a ruling or determination letter that does not comply with all the provisions of this paragraph will be acknowledged, and the requirements that have not been met will be pointed out. If a request for a ruling lacks essential information, the taxpayer or his representative will be advised that if the information is not forthcoming within 30 days, the request will be closed. If the information is received after the request is closed, the request will be reopened and treated as a new request as of the date of the receipt of the essential information. Priority treatment of such request will be granted only in rare cases upon the approval of the division director.

(10) A taxpayer or his representative who desires an oral discussion of the issue or issues involved should indicate such desire in writing when filing the request or soon thereafter in order that the conference may be arranged at that stage of consideration when it will be most helpful.

(11) Generally, prior to issuing the ruling or determination letter, the National Office or district director shall inform the person requesting such ruling or determination letter orally or in writing of the material likely to appear in the ruling or determination letter which such person proposed be deleted but which the Internal Revenue Service determines should not be deleted. If so informed, the person requesting the ruling or determination letter may submit within 10 days any further information, arguments or other material in support of the position that such material be deleted. The Internal Revenue Service will attempt, if feasible, to resolve all disagreements with respect to proposed deletions prior to the issuance of the ruling or determination letter. However, in no event shall the person requesting the ruling or determination letter have the right to a conference with respect to resolution of any disagreements concerning material to be deleted from the text of the ruling or determination letter, but such matters may be considered at any conference otherwise scheduled with respect to the request.

(12) It is the practice of the Service to process requests for rulings, opinion letters, and determination letters in regular order and as ex-

peditiously as possible. Compliance with a request for consideration of a particular matter ahead of its regular order, or by a specified time, tends to delay the disposition of other matters. Requests for processing ahead of the regular order, made in writing in a separate letter submitted with the request or subsequent thereto and showing clear need for such treatment, will be given consideration as the particular circumstances warrant. However, no assurance can be given that any letter will be processed by the time requested. For example, the scheduling of a closing date for a transaction or a meeting of the Board of Directors or shareholders of a corporation without due regard to the time it may take to obtain a ruling, opinion letter, or determination letter will not be deemed sufficient reason for handling a request ahead of its regular order. Neither will the possible effect of fluctuation in the market price of stocks on a transaction be deemed sufficient reason for handling a request out of order. Requests by telegram will be treated in the same manner as requests by letter. Rulings, opinion letters, and determination letters ordinarily will not be issued by telegram. A taxpayer or his representative desiring to obtain information as to the status of his case may do so by contacting the appropriate division in the office of the Assistant Commissioner, Technical).

(13) The Director, Corporation Tax Division, has responsibility for issuing rulings in areas involving the application of Federal income tax to taxpayers; those involving income tax conventions or treaties with foreign countries; those involving depreciation, depletion, and valuation issues; and those involving the taxable status of exchanges and distributions in connection with corporate reorganizations, organizations, liquidations, etc.

(14) The Director, Individual Tax Division, has responsibility for issuing rulings with respect to the application of Federal income tax to taxpayers (including individuals, partnerships, estates and trusts); areas involving the application of Federal estate and gift taxes including estate and gift tax conventions or treaties with foreign countries; areas involving certain excise taxes; the provisions of the Internal Revenue Code dealing with procedure and administration; and areas involving employment taxes.

(15) A taxpayer or the taxpayer's representative desiring to obtain information as to the status of the taxpayer's case may do so by contacting the following offices with respect to matters in the areas of their responsibility:

Official	Telephone Numbers (Area Code 202)
Director, Corporation Tax Division	566-4504 or 566-4505
Director, Individual Tax Division	566-3767 or 566-3788

(16) After receiving the notice pursuant to section 6110(f)(1) of the Code of intention to disclose the ruling or determination letter (including a copy of the version proposed to be open to public inspection and notations of third-party communications pursuant to section

6110(d) of the Code), if the person requesting the ruling or determination letter desires to protest the disclosure of certain information in the ruling or determination letter, such person must within 20 days after the notice is mailed submit a written statement identifying those deletions not made by the Internal Revenue Service which such person believes should have been made. Such person shall also submit a copy of the version of the ruling or determination letter proposed to be open to public inspection on which such person indicates, by the use of brackets, the deletions proposed by the taxpayer but which have not been made by the Internal Revenue Service. Generally, the Internal Revenue Service will not consider the deletion under this subparagraph of any material which the taxpayer did not, prior to the issuance of the ruling or determination letter, propose be deleted. The Internal Revenue Service shall, within 20 days after receipt of the response by the person requesting the ruling or determination letter to the notice pursuant to section 6110(f)(1) of the Code, mail to such person its final administrative conclusion with respect to the deletions to be made.

(17) After receiving the notice pursuant to section 6110(f)(1) of the Code of intention to disclose (but no later than 60 days after such notice is mailed), the person requesting a ruling or determination letter may submit a request for delay of public inspection pursuant to either section 6110(g)(3) or section 6110(g)(3) and (4) of the Code. The request for delay shall be submitted to the office to which the request for a ruling or determination letter was submitted. A request for delay shall contain the date on which it is expected that the underlying transaction will be completed. The request for delay pursuant to section 6110(g)(4) of the Code shall contain a statement from which the Commissioner may determine that good cause exists to warrant such delay.

(18) When a taxpayer receives a ruling or determination letter prior to the filing of his return with respect to any transaction that has been consummated and that is relevant to the return being filed, he should attach a copy of the ruling or determination letter to the return.

(19) A taxpayer may protest an adverse ruling letter, or the terms and conditions contained in a ruling letter, issued after January 30, 1977, under section 367(a)(1) of the Code (including a ruling with respect to an exchange described in section 367(b) which begins before January 1, 1978) or section 1042(e)(2) of the Tax Reform Act of 1976, not later than 45 days after the date of the ruling letter. (For rulings issued under these sections prior to January 31, 1977, see section 4.01 of Revenue Procedure 77-5.) The Assistant Commissioner (Technical) will establish an ad hoc advisory board to consider each protest, whether or not a conference is requested. A protest is considered made on the date of the postmark of a letter of protest or the date that such letter is hand delivered to any Internal Revenue Service office, including the National Office. The protest letter must be addressed to the Assistant Commissioner (Technical), Attention: T:FP:T.

The taxpayer will be granted one conference upon request. Whether or not the request is made the board may request one or more conferences or written submissions. The taxpayer will be notified of the time, date, and place of the conference, and the names of the members of the board. The board will consider all materials submitted in writing by the taxpayer and oral arguments presented at the conference. Any oral arguments made at a conference by the taxpayer, which have not previously been submitted to the Service in writing, may be submitted to the Service in writing if postmarked not later than seven days after the day of the conference.

The Board will make its recommendation to the Assistant Commissioner (Technical) and the Assistant Commissioner will make the decision. The taxpayer will be informed of the decision of the Assistant Commissioner by certified or registered mail. The specific procedures to be used by a taxpayer in protesting an adverse ruling letter, or the terms and conditions contained in a ruling letter, under section 367 will be published from time to time in the Internal Revenue Bulletin (see, for example, Revenue Procedure 77-5).

(f) *Conferences in the National Office.*—(1) If a conference has been requested, the taxpayer will be notified of the time and place of the conference. A conference is normally scheduled only when the Service deems it will be helpful in deciding the case or an adverse decision is indicated. If conferences are being arranged with respect to more than one request for a ruling involving the same taxpayer, they will be so scheduled as to cause the least inconvenience to the taxpayer.

(2) A taxpayer is entitled, as a matter of right, to only one conference in the National Office unless one of the circumstances discussed in subparagraph (3) of this paragraph develops. This conference will usually be held at the branch level of the appropriate division in the office of the Assistant Commissioner (Technical) and will usually be attended by a person who has authority to act for the branch chief. (See § 601.201(a)(2) for the divisions involved.) If more than one subject is to be discussed at the conference, the discussion will constitute a conference with respect to each subject. In order to promote a free and open discussion of the issues, the conference will usually be held after the branch has had an opportunity to study the case. However, at the request of the taxpayer or his representative, the conference may be held at an earlier stage in the consideration of the case than the Service would ordinarily designate. No taxpayer has a "right" to appeal the action of a branch to a division director or to any other official of the Service, nor is a taxpayer entitled, as a matter of right, to a separate conference in the Chief Counsel's office on a request for a ruling.

(3) In the process of review in Technical of a holding proposed by a branch, it may appear that the final answer will involve a reversal of the branch proposal with a result less favorable to the taxpayer. Or it may appear that an adverse

holding proposed by a branch will be approved, but on a new or different issue or on different grounds than those on which the branch decided the case. Under either of these circumstances, the taxpayer or his representative will be invited to another conference. The provisions of this section limiting the number of conferences to which a taxpayer is entitled will not foreclose the invitation of a taxpayer to attend further conferences when, in the opinion of National Office personnel, such need arises. All additional conferences of the type discussed in this paragraph are held only at the invitation of the Service.

(4) It is the responsibility of the taxpayer to add to the case file a written record of any additional data, lines of reasoning, precedents, etc., which are proposed by the taxpayer and discussed at the conference but which were not previously or adequately presented in writing.

(g) *Referral of matters to the National Office.*—(1) Requests for determination letters received by the district directors that, in accordance with paragraph (c) of this section, may not be acted upon by a district office, will be forwarded to the National Office for reply and the taxpayer advised accordingly. District directors also refer to the National Office any request for a determination letter that in their judgment warrants the attention of the National Office. See also the provisions of paragraphs (o), (p), and (q) of this section, with respect to requests relating to qualification of a plan under sections 401 and 405(a) of the Code, and paragraph (n) of this section, Revenue Procedure 72-5, Internal Revenue Bulletin No. 1972-1, 19, and Revenue Procedure 68-13, C.B. 1968-1, 764, with respect to application for recognition of exempt status under section 501 and 521 of the Code.

(2) If the request is with regard to an issue or an area with respect to which the Service will not issue a ruling or a determination letter, such request will not be forwarded to the National Office, but the district office will advise the taxpayer that the Service will not issue a ruling or a determination letter on the issue. See paragraph (d)(2) of this section.

(h) *Referral of matters to district offices.*—Requests for rulings received by the National Office that, in accordance with the provisions of paragraph (b) of this section, may not be acted upon by the National Office will be forwarded for appropriate action to the district office that has or will have audit jurisdiction of the taxpayer's return and the taxpayer advised accordingly. If the request is with respect to an issue or an area of the type discussed in paragraph (d)(2) of this section, the taxpayer will be so advised and the request may be forwarded to the appropriate district office for association with the related return or report of the taxpayer.

(i) *Review of determination letters.*—(1) Determination letters issued with respect to the types of inquiries authorized by paragraph (c)(1), (2), and (3) of this section are not generally reviewed by the National Office as they merely inform a taxpayer of a position of the Service which has

been previously established either in the regulations or in a ruling, opinion, or court decision published in the Internal Revenue Bulletin. If a taxpayer believes that a determination letter of this type is in error, he may ask the district director to reconsider the matter. He may also ask the district director to request advice from the National Office. In such event, the procedures in paragraph (b)(5) of § 601.105 will be followed.

(2) The procedures for review of determination letters relating to the qualification of employers' plans under section 401(a) of the Code are provided in paragraph (o) of this section.

(3) The procedures for review of determination letters relating to the exemption from Federal income tax of certain organizations under sections 501 and 521 of the Code are provided in paragraph (n) of this section.

(j) *Withdrawals of requests.*—The taxpayer's request for a ruling or a determination letter may be withdrawn at any time prior to the signing of the letter of reply. However, in such a case, the National Office may furnish its views to the district director whose office has or will have audit jurisdiction of the taxpayer's return. The information submitted will be considered by the district director in a subsequent audit or examination of the taxpayer's return. Even though a request is withdrawn, all correspondence and exhibits will be retained in the Service and may not be returned to the taxpayer.

(k) *Oral advice to taxpayers.*—(1) The Service does not issue rulings or determination letters upon oral requests. Furthermore, National Office officials and employees ordinarily will not discuss a substantive tax issue with a taxpayer or his representative prior to the receipt of a request for a ruling, since oral opinions or advice are not binding on the Service. This should not be construed as preventing a taxpayer or his representative from inquiring whether the Service will rule on a particular question. In such cases, however, the name of the taxpayer and his identifying number must be disclosed. The Service will also discuss questions relating to procedural matters with regard to submitting a request for a ruling, including the application of the provisions of paragraph (e) to the particular case.

(2) A taxpayer may, of course, seek oral technical assistance from a district office in the preparation of his return or report, pursuant to other established procedures. Such oral advice is advisory only and the Service is not bound to recognize it in the examination of the taxpayer's return.

(l) *Effect of rulings.*—(1) A taxpayer may not rely on an advance ruling issued to another taxpayer. A ruling, except to the extent incorporated in a closing agreement, may be revoked or modified at any time in the wise administration of the taxing statutes. See paragraph (a)(6) of this section for the effect of a closing agreement. If a ruling is revoked or modified, the revocation or modification applies to all open years under the statutes, unless the Commissioner or his delegate exercises the discretionary authority under section 7805(b) of the Code to limit the retroactive effect of the revocation or modification. The manner in which the Commissioner or his delegate generally will exercise this authority is set forth in this section. With reference to rulings relating to the sale or lease of articles subject to the manufacturers excise tax and the retailers excise tax, see specifically subparagraph (8) of this paragraph.

(2) As part of the determination of a taxpayer's liability, it is the responsibility of the district director to ascertain whether any ruling previously issued to the taxpayer has been properly applied. It should be determined whether the representations upon which the ruling was based reflected an accurate statement of the material facts and whether the transaction actually was carried out substantially as proposed. If, in the course of the determination of the tax liability, it is the view of the district director that a ruling previously issued to the taxpayer should be modified or revoked, the findings and recommendations of that office will be forwarded to the National Office for consideration prior to further action. Such reference to the National Office will be treated as a request for technical advice and the procedures of paragraph (b)(5) of § 601.105 will be followed. Otherwise, the ruling is to be applied by the district office in its determination of the taxpayer's liability.

(3) Appropriate coordination with the National Office will be undertaken in the event that any other field official having jurisdiction of a return or other matter proposes to reach a conclusion contrary to a ruling previously issued to the taxpayer.

(4) A ruling found to be in error or not in accord with the current views of the Service may be modified or revoked. Modification or revocation may be effected by a notice to the taxpayer to whom the ruling originally was issued, or by a Revenue Ruling or other statement published in the Internal Revenue Bulletin.

(5) Except in rare or unusual circumstances, the revocation or modification of a ruling will not be applied retroactively with respect to the taxpayer to whom the ruling was originally issued or to a taxpayer whose tax liability was directly involved in such ruling if (i) there has been no misstatement or omission of material facts, (ii) the facts subsequently developed are not materially different from the facts on which the ruling was based, (iii) there has been no change in the applicable law, (iv) the ruling was originally issued with respect to a prospective or proposed transaction, and (v) the taxpayer directly involved in the ruling acted in good faith in reliance upon the ruling and the retroactive revocation would be to his detriment. To illustrate, the tax liability of each employee covered by a ruling relating to a pension plan of an employer is directly involved in such ruling. Also, the tax liability of each shareholder is directly involved in a ruling related to the reorganization of a corporation. However, the tax liability of members of an industry is not directly involved in a ruling issued to one of the members, and the position taken in a revocation or modification of ruling to one member of an industry may be retroactively applied to other members of that industry. By the same reasoning, a tax practitioner may not obtain the nonretroactive application to one client of a modification or revocation of a ruling previously issued to another client. Where a ruling to a taxpayer is revoked with retroactive effect, the notice to such taxpayer will, except in fraud cases, set forth the grounds upon which the revocation is being made and the reasons why the revocation is being applied retroactively.

(6) A ruling issued to a taxpayer with respect to a particular transaction represents a holding of the Service on that transaction only. However, the application of that ruling to the transaction will not be affected by the subsequent issuance of regulations (either temporary or final), if the conditions specified in subparagraph (5) of this paragraph are met. If the ruling is later found to be in error or no longer in accord with the holding of the Service, it will afford the taxpayer no protection with respect to a like transaction in the same or subsequent year, except to the extent provided in subparagraphs (7) and (8) of this paragraph.

(7) If a ruling is issued covering a continuing action or a series of actions and it is determined that the ruling was in error or no longer in accord with the position of the Service, the Assistant Commissioner (Technical) ordinarily will limit the retroactivity of the revocation or modification to a date not earlier than that on which the original ruling was modified or revoked. To illustrate, if a taxpayer rendered service or provided a facility which is subject to the excise tax on services or facilities, and in reliance on a ruling issued to the same taxpayer did not pass the tax on to the user of the service or the facility, the Assistant Commissioner (Technical) ordinarily will restrict the retroactive application of the revocation or modification of the ruling. Likewise, if an employer incurred liability under the Federal Insurance Contributions Act, but in reliance on a ruling made to the same employer neither collected the employee tax nor paid the employee and employer taxes under the Act, the Assistant Commissioner (Technical) ordinarily will restrict the retroactive application of the revocation or modification of the ruling with respect to both the employer tax and the employee tax. In the latter situation, however, the restriction of retroactive application ordinarily will be conditioned on the furnishing by the employer of wage data, or of such corrections of wage data as may be required by § 31.6011(a)-1(c) of the Employment Tax Regulations. Consistent with these provisions, if a ruling relates to a continuing action or a series of actions, the ruling will be applied until the date of issuance of applicable regulations or the publication of a Revenue Ruling holding otherwise, or until specifically withdrawn. Publication of a notice of proposed rulemaking will not affect the application of any ruling issued under the procedures set forth herein. (As to the effective date in cases involving revocation or modification of rulings or de-

termination letters recognizing exemption, see paragraph (n)(1) of this section.

(8) A ruling holding that the sale or lease of a particular article is subject to the manufacturers excise tax or the retailers excise tax may not revoke or modify retroactively a prior ruling holding that the sale or lease of such article was not taxable, if the taxpayer to whom the ruling was issued, in reliance upon such prior ruling, parted with possession or ownership of the article without passing the tax on to his customer. Section 1108(b), Revenue Act of 1926.

(9) In the case of rulings involving completed transactions, other than those described in subparagraphs (7) and (8) of this paragraph, taxpayers will not be afforded the protection against retroactive revocation provided in subparagraph (5) of this paragraph in the case of proposed transactions since they will not have entered into the transactions in reliance on the rulings.

(m) *Effect of determination letters.*—A determination letter issued by a district director in accordance with this section will be given the same effect upon examination of the return of the taxpayer to whom the determination letter was is-

sued as is described in paragraph (l) of this section, in the case of a ruling issued to a taxpayer, except that reference to the National Office is not necessary where, upon examination of the return, it is the opinion of the district director that a conclusion contrary to that expressed in the determination letter is indicated. A district director may not limit the modification or revocation of a determination letter but may refer the matter to the National Office for exercise by the Commissioner or his delegate of the authority to limit the modification or revocation. In this connection see also paragraphs (n) and (o) of this section.

(n) *Organization claiming exemption under section 501 or 521 of the Code.*—(1) *Filing applications for exemption.*—(i) An organization seeking recognition of exempt status under section 501 or section 521 of the Code is required to file an application with the key district director for the Internal Revenue district in which the principal place of business or principal office of the organization is located. Following are the 19 key district offices that process the applications and the Internal Revenue districts covered by each:

Key District(s)	*IRS Districts Covered*
	Central Region
Cincinnati	Cincinnati, Louisville, Indianapolis.
Cleveland	Cleveland, Parkersburg.
Detroit	Detroit.
	Mid-Atlantic Region
Baltimore	Baltimore (which includes the District of Columbia and Office of International Operations), Pittsburgh, Richmond.
Philadelphia	Philadelphia, Wilmington.
Newark	Newark.
	Midwest Region
Chicago	Chicago.
St. Paul	St. Paul, Fargo, Aberdeen, Milwaukee.
St. Louis	St. Louis, Springfield, Des Moines, Omaha.
	North-Atlantic Region
Boston	Boston, Augusta, Burlington, Providence, Hartford, Portsmouth.
Manhattan	Manhattan.
Brooklyn	Brooklyn, Albany, Buffalo.
	Southeast Region
Atlanta	Atlanta, Greensboro, Columbia, Nashville.
Jacksonville	Jacksonville, Jackson, Birmingham.
	Southwest Region
Austin	Austin, New Orleans, Albuquerque, Denver, Cheyenne.
Dallas	Dallas, Oklahoma City, Little Rock, Wichita.
	Western Region
Los Angeles	Los Angeles, Phoenix, Honolulu.
San Francisco	San Francisco, Salt Lake City, Reno.
Seattle	Seattle, Portland, Anchorage, Boise, Helena.

(ii) A ruling or determination letter will be issued to an organization provided its application and supporting documents establish that it meets the particular requirements of the section under which exemption is claimed. Exempt status will be recognized in advance of operations if proposed operations can be described in sufficient detail to permit a conclusion that the organization will meet the particular requirements of the section under which exemption is claimed. A mere restatement of purposes or a statement that proposed activities will be in furtherance of such purposes will not satisfy these requirements. The organization must fully describe the activities in which it expects to engage, including the standards, criteria, procedures, or other means adopted or planned for carrying out the activities; the anticipated sources of receipts; and the nature of contemplated expenditures. Where the Service considers it warranted, a record of actual operations may be required before a ruling or determination letter will be issued.

(iii) Where an application for recognition of exemption does not contain the required information, the application may be returned to the applicant without being considered on its merits with an appropriate letter of explanation. In the case of an application under section 501(c)(3) of the Code, the applicant will also be informed of the time within which the completed application must be resubmitted in order for the application to be considered as timely notice within the meaning of section 508(a) of the Code.

(iv) A ruling or determination letter recognizing exemption will not ordinarily be issued if an issue involving the organization's exempt status under section 501 or 521 of the Code is pending in litigation or on appeal within the Service.

(2) *Processing applications.*—(i) Under the general procedures outlined in paragraphs (a) through (m) of this section, key district directors are authorized to issue determination letters involving applications for exemption under sections 501 and 521 of the Code, and requests for foundation status under sections 509 and 4942(j)(3).

(ii) A key district director will refer to the National Office those applications that present questions the answers to which are not specifically covered by statute, Treasury decision or regulation, or by a ruling, opinion, or court decision published in the Internal Revenue Bulletin. The National Office will consider each such application, issue a ruling directly to the organization, and send a copy of the ruling to the key district director. Where the issue of exemption under section 501(c)(3) of the Code is referred to the National Office for decision under this subparagraph, the foundation status issue will also be the subject of a National Office ruling. In the event of a conclusion unfavorable to the applicant, it will be informed of the basis for the conclusion and of its rights to file a protest and to a conference in the National Office. If a conference is requested, the conference procedures set forth in subparagraph (9)(v) of this paragraph will be followed. After reconsideration of the application in the light of the protest and any information developed in conference, the National Office will affirm, modify, or reverse the original conclusion, issue a ruling to the organization, and send a copy of the ruling to the key district director.

(iii) Key district directors will issue determination letters on foundation status. All adverse determinations issued by key district directors (including adverse determinations on the foundation status under section 509(a) of the Code of nonexempt charitable trusts described in section 4947(a)(1)) are subject to the protest and conference procedures outlined in subparagraph (5) of this paragraph. Key district directors will issue such determinations in response to applications for recognition of exempt status under section 501(c)(3). They will also issue such determinations in response to requests for determination of foundation status by organizations presumed to be private foundations under section 508(b), requests for new determinations of foundation status by organizations previously classified as other than private foundations, and, subject to the conditions set forth in subdivision (vi) of subparagraph (6) of this paragraph, requests to reconsider status. The requests described in the preceding sentence must be made in writing. For information relating to the circumstances under which an organization presumed to be a private foundation under section 508(b) may request a determination of its status as other than a private foundation, see Revenue Ruling 73-504, 1973-2 C.B. 190. All requests for determinations referred to in this paragraph should be made to the key district director for the district in which the principal place of business or principal office of the organization is located.

(iv) If the exemption application or request for foundation status involves an issue which is not covered by published precedent or on which there may be nonuniformity between districts, or if the National Office had issued a previous contrary ruling or technical advice on the issue, the key district director must request technical advice from the National Office. If, during the consideration of its application or request by a key district director, the organization believes that the case involves an issue with respect to which referral for technical advice is appropriate, the organization may ask the district director to request technical advice from the National Office. The district director shall advise the organization of its right to request referral of the issue to the National Office for technical advice. The technical advice provisions applicable to these cases are set forth in subparagraph (9) of this paragraph. The effect on an organization's appeal rights of technical advice or a National Office ruling issued under this subparagraph are set forth in § 601.106(a)(1)(iv)(a) and in subparagraph (5)(i) of this paragraph.

(3) *Effect of exemption rulings or determination letters.*—(i) A ruling or determination letter recognizing exemption is usually effective as of the date of formation of an organization, if its purposes and activities during the period prior to the date of the ruling or determination letter were consistent with the requirements for exemption. However, with respect to organizations formed after October 9, 1969, applying for recognition of exemption under section 501(c)(3) of the Code, the provisions of section 508(a) apply. If the organization is required to alter its activi-

ties or make substantive amendments to its enabling instrument, the ruling or determination letter recognizing its exemption will be effective as of the date specified therein.

(ii) A ruling or determination letter recognizing exemption may not be relied upon if there is a material change inconsistent with exemption in the character, the purpose, or the method of operation of the organization.

(iii)(a) When an organization that has been listed in IRS Publication No. 78, "Cumulative List of Organizations described in Section 170(c) of the Internal Revenue Code of 1954," as an organization contributions to which are deductible under section 170 of the Code subsequently ceases to qualify as such, and the ruling or determination letter issued to it is revoked, contributions made to the organization by persons unaware of the change in the status of the organization generally will be considered allowable until (1) the date of publication of an announcement in the Internal Revenue Bulletin that contributions are no longer deductible, or (2) a date specified in such an announcement where deductibility is terminated as of a different date.

(b) In appropriate cases, however, this advance assurance of deductibility of contributions made to such an organization may be suspended pending verification of continuing qualification under section 170 of the Code. Notice of such suspension will be made in a public announcement by the Service. In such cases allowance of deductions for contributions made after the date of the announcement will depend upon statutory qualification of the organization under section 170.

(c) If an organization, whose status under Section 170(c)(2) of the Code is revoked, initiates within the statutory time limit a proceeding for declaratory judgment under section 7428, special reliance provisions apply. If the decision of the court is adverse to the organization, it shall nevertheless be treated as having been described in section 170(c)(2) for purposes of deductibility of contributions from other organizations described in section 170(c)(2) and individuals (up to a maximum of $1,000), for the period beginning on the date that notice of revocation was published and ending on the date the court first determines that the organization is not described in section 170(c)(2).

(d) In any event, the Service is not precluded from disallowing any contributions made after an organization ceases to qualify under section 170 of the Code where the contributor (1) had knowledge of the revocation of the ruling or determination letter, (2) was aware that such revocation was imminent, or (3) was in part responsible for, or was aware of, the activities or deficiencies on the part of the organization which gave rise to the loss of qualification.

(4) *National Office review of determination letters.*—The National Office will review determination letters on exemption issued under sections 501 and 521 of the Code and foundation status under sections 509(a) and 4942(j)(3) to as-

sure uniformity in the application of the established principles and precedents of the Service. Where the National Office takes exception to a determination letter the key district director will be advised. If the organization protests the exception taken, the file and protest will be returned to the National Office. The referral will be treated as a request for technical advice and the procedures of subparagraph (9) of this paragraph will be followed.

(5) *Protest of adverse determination letters.*—(i) Upon the issuance of an adverse determination letter, the key district director will advise the organization of its right to protest the determination by requesting Appeals office consideration. However, if the determination was made on the basis of National Office technical advice the organization may not appeal the determination to the Appeals office. See § 601.106(a)(1)(iv)(a). To request Appeals consideration, the organization shall submit to the key district director, within 30 days from the date of the letter, a statement of the facts, law, and arguments in support of its position. The organization must also state whether it wishes an Appeals office conference. Upon receipt of an organization's request for Appeals consideration, the key district director will, if it maintains its position, forward the request and the case file to the Appeals office.

(ii) Except as provided in subdivisions (iii) and (iv) of this subparagraph, the Appeals office, after considering the organization's protest and any additional information developed, will advise the organization of its decision and issue an appropriate determination letter. Organizations should make full presentation of the facts, circumstances, and arguments at the initial level of consideration, since submission of additional facts, circumstances, and arguments at the Appeals office may result in suspension of Appeals procedures and referral of the case back to the key district for additional consideration.

(iii) If the proposed disposition by the Appeals office is contrary to a National Office technical advice or ruling concerning tax exemption, issued prior to the case, the proposed disposition will be submitted, through the Office of the Regional Director of Appeals, to the Assistant Commissioner (Employee Plans and Exempt Organizations) or, in a section 521 case, to the Assistant Commissioner (Technical). The decision of the Assistant Commissioner will be followed by the Appeals office. See § 601.106(a)(1)(iv)(b).

(iv) If the case involves an issue that is not covered by published precedent or on which there may be nonuniformity between regions, and on which the National Office has not previously ruled, the Appeals office must request technical advice from the National Office. If, during the consideration of its case by Appeals, the organization believes that the case involves an issue with respect to which referral for technical advice is appropriate, the organization may ask the Appeals office to request technical advice from the National Office. The Appeals office shall advise the organization of its right to request referral of the issue to the National Office for technical advice. If the Appeals office requests technical advice, the decision of the Assistant Commissioner (Employee Plans and Exempt Organizations) or, in a section 521 case, the decision of the Assistant Commissioner (Technical), in a technical advice memorandum is final and the Appeals office must dispose of the case in accordance with that decision. See subparagraph (9)(viii)(*a*) of this paragraph.

(6) *Revocation or modification of rulings or determination letters on exemption and foundation status.*—(i) An exemption ruling or determination letter may be revoked or modified by a ruling or determination letter addressed to the organization, or by a revenue ruling or other statement published in the Internal Revenue Bulletin. The revocation or modification may be retroactive if the organization omitted or misstated a material fact, operated in a manner materially different from that originally represented, or engaged in a prohibited transaction of the type described in subdivision (vii) of this subparagraph. In any event, revocation or modification will ordinarily take effect no later than the time at which the organization received written notice that its exemption ruling or determination letter might be revoked or modified.

(ii)(*a*) If a key district director concludes as a result of examining an information return, or considering information from any other source, that an exemption ruling or determination letter should be revoked or modified, the organization will be advised in writing of the proposed action and the reasons therefor. If the case involves an issue not covered by published precedent or on which there may be nonuniformity between districts, or if the National Office had issued a previous contrary ruling or technical advice on the issue, the district director must seek technical advice from the National Office. If the organization believes that the case involves an issue with respect to which referral for technical advice is appropriate, the organization may ask the district director to request technical advice from the National Office. The district director shall advise the organization of its right to request referral of the issue to the National Office for technical advice.

(*b*) The key district director will advise the organization of its right to protest the proposed revocation or modification by requesting Appeals office consideration. However, if National Office technical advice was furnished concerning revocation or modification under (*a*) of this subdivision, the decision of the Assistant Commissioner in the technical advice memorandum is final and the organization has no right of appeal to the Appeals office. See § 601.106(a)(1)(iv)(*a*). To request Appeals consideration, the organization must submit to the key district director, within 30 days from the date of the letter, a statement of the facts, law, and arguments in support of its continued exemption. The organization must also state whether it wishes an Appeals office conference. Upon re-

ceipt of an organization's request for Appeals consideration, the key district office, will, if it maintains its position, forward the request and the case file to the Appeals office.

(*c*) Except as provided in (*d*) and (*e*) of this subdivision, the Appeals office, after considering the organization's protest and any additional information developed, will advise the organization of its decision and issue an appropriate determination letter. Organizations should make full presentation of the facts, circumstances, and arguments at the initial level of consideration, since submission of additional facts, circumstances, and arguments at the Appeals office may result in suspension of Appeals procedures and referral of the case back to the key district for additional consideration.

(*d*) If the proposed disposition by the Appeals office is contrary to a National Office technical advice or ruling concerning tax exemption, issued prior to the case, the proposed disposition will be submitted, through the Office of the Regional Director of Appeals, to the Assistant Commissioner (Employee Plans and Exempt Organizations) or, in a section 521 case, to the Assistant Commissioner (Technical). The decision of the Assistant Commissioner will be followed by the Appeals office. See § 601.106(a)(1)(iv)(*b*).

(*e*) If the case involves an issue that is not covered by published precedent or on which there may be nonuniformity between regions, and on which the National Office has not previously ruled, the Appeals office must request technical advice from the National Office. If the organization believes that the case involves an issue with respect to which referral for technical advice is appropriate, the organization may ask the Appeals office to request technical advice from the National Office. The Appeals office shall advise the organization of its right to request referral of the issue to the National Office for technical advice.

(iii) A ruling or determination letter respecting private foundation or operating foundation status may be revoked or modified by a ruling or determination letter addressed to the organization, or by a revenue ruling or other statement published in the Internal Revenue Bulletin. If a key district director concludes, as a result of examining an information return or considering information from any other source, that a ruling or determination letter concerning private foundation status (including foundation status under section 509(a)(3) of the Code of a nonexempt charitable trust described in section 4947(a)(1)) or operating foundation status should be modified or revoked, the procedures in subdivision (iv) or (v) of this subparagraph should be followed depending on whether the revocation or modification is adverse or non-adverse to the affected organization. Where there is a proposal by the Service to change foundation status classification from one particular paragraph of section 509(a) to another paragraph of that section, the procedures described in subdivision (iv) of this subparagraph will be followed to modify the ruling or determination letter.

(iv) If a key district director concludes that a ruling or determination letter concerning private foundation or operating foundation status should be revoked or modified, the organization will be advised in writing of the proposed adverse action, the reasons therefor, and the proposed new determination of foundation status. The procedures set forth in subdivision (ii) of this subparagraph apply to a proposed revocation or modification under this subdivision. Unless the effective date of revocation or modification of a ruling or determination letter concerning private foundation or operating foundation status is expressly covered by statute or regulations, the effective date generally is the same as the effective date of revocation or modification of exemption rulings or determination letters as provided in subdivision (i) of this subparagraph.

(v) If the key district director concludes that a ruling or determination letter concerning private foundation or operating foundation status should be revoked or modified and that such revocation or modification will not be adverse to the organization, the key district director will issue a determination letter revoking or modifying foundation status. The determination letter will also serve to notify the organization of its foundation status as redetermined. A nonadverse revocation or modification as to private foundation or operating foundation status will ordinarily be retroactive if the initial ruling or determination letter was incorrect.

(vi) In cases where an organization believes that it received an incorrect ruling or determination letter as to its private foundation or operating foundation status, the organization may request a key district director to reconsider such ruling or determination letter. Except in rare circumstances, the key district director will only consider such requests where the organization had not exercised any protest or conference rights with respect to the issuance of such ruling or determination letter. If a key district director decides that reconsideration is warranted, the request will be treated as an initial request for a determination of foundation status, and the key district director will issue a determination on foundation status or operating foundation status under the procedures of subparagraph (2) of this paragraph. If a nonadverse determination is issued, it will also inform the organization that the prior ruling or determination letter is revoked or modified. Adverse determinations are subject to the procedures set out in subparagraph (5) of this paragraph. If the key district director decides that reconsideration is not warranted, the organization will be notified accordingly. The organization does not have a right to protest the key district director's decision not to reconsider.

(vii) If it is concluded that an organization that is subject to the provisions of section 503 of the Code entered into a prohibited transaction for the purpose of diverting corpus or income from its exempt purpose, and if the transaction involved a substantial part of the corpus or income of the organization, its exemption is revoked effective as of the beginning of the taxable year during which the prohibited transaction was commenced.

(viii) The provisions of this subparagraph relating to protests, conferences, and the rights of organizations to ask that technical advice be requested before a revocation (or modification) notice is issued are not applicable to matters where delay would be prejudicial to the interests of the Internal Revenue Service (such as in cases involving fraud, jeopardy, the imminence of the expiration of the period of limitations, or where immediate action is necessary to protect the interests of the Government).

(7) *Declaratory judgments relating to status and classification of organizations under section 501(c)(3) of the Code.*—(i) An organization seeking recognition of exempt status under section 501(c)(3) of the Code must follow the procedures of subparagraph (1) of this paragraph regarding the filing of Form 1023, Application for Recognition of Exemption. The 270-day period referred to in section 7428(b)(2) will be considered by the Service to begin on the date a substantially completed Form 1023 is sent to the appropriate key district director. A substantially completed Form 1023 is one that:

(*a*) Is signed by an authorized individual;

(*b*) Includes an Employer Identification Number (EIN) or a completed Form SS-4, Application for Employer Identification Number;

(*c*) Includes a statement of receipts and expenditures and a balance sheet for the current year and the three preceding years or the years the organization was in existence, if less than four years (if the organization has not yet commenced operations, a proposed budget for two full accounting periods and a current statement of assets and liabilities will be acceptable);

(*d*) Includes a statement of proposed activities and a description of anticipated receipts and contemplated expenditures;

(*e*) Includes a copy of the organizing or enabling document that is signed by a principal officer or is accompanied by a written declaration signed by an officer authorized to sign for the organization certifying that the document is a complete and accurate copy of the original; and

(*f*) If the organization is a corporation or unincorporated association and it has adopted bylaws, includes a copy that is signed or otherwise verified as current by an authorized officer. If an application does not contain all of the above items, it will not be further processed and may be returned to the applicant for completion. The 270-day period will not be considered as starting until the date the application is remailed to the Service with the requested information, or, if a postmark is not evident, on the date the Service receives a substantially completed application.

(ii) Generally, rulings and determination letters in cases subject to declaratory judgment are issued under the procedures outlined in this paragraph. In National Office exemption application cases, proposed adverse rulings will be issued by the rulings sections in the Exempt Organizations Technical Branch. Applicants shall appeal these proposed adverse rulings to the Conference and Review Staff of the Exempt Organizations Technical Branch. In those cases where an organization is unable to describe fully its purposes and activities (see subparagraph (1)(ii) of this paragraph), a refusal to rule will be considered an adverse determination for which administrative appeal rights will be afforded. Any oral representation of additional facts or modification of the facts as represented or alleged in the application for a ruling or determination letter must be reduced to writing.

(iii) If an organization withdraws in writing its request for a ruling or determination letter, the withdrawal will not be considered by the Service as either a failure to make a determination within the meaning of section 7428(a)(2) of the Code or as an exhaustion of administrative remedies within the meaning of section 7428(b)(2).

(iv) Section 7428(b)(2) of the Code requires that an organization must exhaust its administrative remedies by taking timely, reasonable steps to secure a determination. Those steps and administrative remedies that must be exhausted within the Internal Revenue Service are:

(a) The filing of a substantially completed application Form 1023 pursuant to subdivision (i) of this subparagraph, or the filing of a request for a determination of foundation status pursuant to subparagraph (2) of this paragraph;

(b) The timely submission of all additional information requested to perfect an exemption application or request for determination of private foundation status; and

(c) Exhaustion of all administrative appeals available within the Service pursuant to subparagraphs (5) and (6) of this paragraph, as well as appeal of a proposed adverse ruling to the Conference and Review Staff of the Exempt Organizations Technical Branch in National Office original jurisdiction exemption application cases.

(v) An organization will in no event be deemed to have exhausted its administrative remedies prior to the completion of the steps described in subdivision (iv) of this subparagraph and the earlier of:

(a) The sending by certified or registered mail of a notice of final determination; or

(b) The expiration of the 270-day period described in section 7428(b)(2) of the Code, in a case in which the Service has not issued a notice of final determination and the organization has taken, in a timely manner, all reasonable steps to secure a ruling or determination.

(vi) The steps described in subdivision (iv) of this subparagraph will not be considered completed until the Internal Revenue Service has had a reasonable time to act upon the appeal or request for consideration, as the case may be.

(vii) A notice of final determination to which section 7428 of the Code applies is a ruling or determination letter, sent by certified or registered mail, which holds that the organization is not described in section 501(c)(3) or section 170(c)(2), is a private foundation as defined

in section 509(a), or is not a private operating foundation as defined in section 4942(j)(3).

(8) *Group exemption letters.*—(i) *General.*—(a) A group exemption letter is a ruling issued to a central organization recognizing on a group basis the exemption under section 501(c) of the Code of subordinate organizations on whose behalf the central organization has applied for exemption in accordance with this subparagraph.

(b) A central organization is an organization which has one or more subordinates under its general supervision or control.

(c) A subordinate is a chapter, local, post, or unit of a central organization. It may or may not be incorporated. A central organization may be a subordinate itself, such as a state organization which has subordinate units and is itself affiliated with a national organization.

(d) A subordinate included in a group exemption letter should not apply separately for an exemption letter, unless it no longer wants to be included in the group exemption letter.

(e) A subordinate described in section 501(c)(3) of the Code may not be included in a group exemption letter if it is a private foundation as defined in section 509(a) of the Code. Such an organization should apply separately for exempt status under the procedures outlined in subparagraph (1) of this paragraph.

(ii) *Requirements for inclusion in a group exemption letter.*—(a) A central organization applying for a group exemption letter must establish its own exempt status.

(b) It must also establish that the subordinates to be included in the group exemption letter are:

(1) Affiliated with it;

(2) Subject to its general supervision or control;

(3) Exempt under the same paragraph of section 501(c) of the Code, though not necessarily the paragraph under which the central organization is exempt; and

(4) Not private foundations if application for a group exemption letter involves section 501(c)(3) of the Code.

(c) Each subordinate must authorize the central organization to include it in the application for the group exemption letter. The authorization must be signed by a duly authorized officer of the subordinate and retained by the central organization while the group exemption letter is in effect.

(iii) *Filing application for a group exemption letter.*—(a) A central organization seeking a group exemption letter for its subordinates must obtain recognition of its own exemption by filing an application with the District Director of Internal Revenue for the district in which is located the principal place of business or the principal office of the organization. For the form of organization see section 1.501(a)-1 of the Income Tax Regulations. Any application received by the National Office or by a district director other than as provided above will be forwarded, without any action thereon, to the appropriate district director.

(b) If the central organization has previously established its own exemption, it must indicate its employer identification number, the date of the exemption letter, and the Internal Revenue Office that issued it. It need not resubmit documents already submitted. However, if it has not already done so, it must submit a copy of any amendments to its governing instruments or internal regulations as well as any information regarding any change in its character, purposes, or method of operation.

(c) In addition to the information required to establish its own exemption, the central organization must submit to the district director the following information, in duplicate, on behalf of those subordinates to be included in the group exemption letter:

(1) A letter signed by a principal officer of the central organization setting forth or including as attachments;

(i) Information verifying the existence of the relationships required by subdivision (ii)(b) of this subparagraph;

(ii) A description of the principal purposes and activities of the subordinates;

(iii) A sample copy of a uniform governing instrument (charter, trust indenture, articles of association, etc.), if such an instrument has been adopted by the subordinates; or, in the absence of a uniform governing instrument, copies of representative instruments;

(iv) An affirmation to the effect that, to the best of his knowledge, the subordinates are operating in accordance with the stated purposes;

(v) A statement that each subordinate to be included in the group exemption letter has furnished written authorization to the central organization as described in subdivision (ii)(c) of this subparagraph; and

(vi) A list of subordinates to be included in the group exemption letter to which the Service has issued an outstanding ruling or determination letter relating to exemption.

(vii) If the application for a group exemption letter involves section 501(c)(3) of the Code, an affirmation to the effect that, to the best of his knowledge and belief, no subordinate to be included in the group exemption letter is a private foundation as defined in section 509(a) of the Code.

(2) A list of the names, mailing addresses (including Postal ZIP Codes), and employer identification numbers (if required for group exemption letter purposes by (e) of this subdivision) of subordinates to be included in the group exemption letter. A current directory of subordinates may be furnished in lieu of the list if it includes the required information and if the subordinates not to be included in the group exemption letter are identified.

(d) If the central organization does not have an employer identification number, it must submit a completed Form SS-4, Application for Employer Identification Number, with its exemption application. See Rev. Rul. 63-247, C.B. 1963-2, 612.

(e) Each subordinate required to file an annual information return, Form 990 or 990-A, must have its own employer identification number, even if it has no employees. The central organization must submit with the exemption application a completed Form SS-4 on behalf of each subordinate not having a number. Although subordinates not required to file annual information returns, Form 990 or 990-A, need not have employer identification numbers for group exemption letter purposes, they may need such numbers for other purposes.

(iv) *Information required annually to maintain a group exemption letter.*—(a) The central organization must submit annually within 45 days after the close of its annual accounting period the information set out below to the Philadelphia Service Center, 11601 Roosevelt Boulevard, Philadelphia, Pennsylvania 19155, Attention: EO:R Branch:

(1) Information regarding all changes in the purposes, character, or method of operation of subordinates included in the group exemption letter.

(2) Lists of (i) subordinates which have changed their names or addresses during the year, (ii) subordinates no longer to be included in the group exemption letter because they have ceased to exist, disaffiliated, or withdrawn the authorization to the central organization, and (iii) subordinates to be added to the group exemption letter because they are newly organized or affiliated or they have newly authorized the central organization to include them. A separate list must be submitted for each of the three categories set out above. Each list must show the names, mailing addresses (including Postal ZIP Codes), and employer identification numbers of the affected subordinates. An annotated directory of subordinates will not be acceptable for this purpose. If there were none of the above changes, the central organization must submit a statement to that effect.

(3) The information required by subdivision (iii)(c)(1) of this subparagraph, with respect to subordinates to be added to the group exemption letter. However, if the information upon which the group exemption letter was based is applicable in all material respects to such subordinates, a statement to this effect may be submitted in lieu of the information required by subdivision (iii)(c)(1)(i) through (v) of this subparagraph.

(b) Submission of the information required by this subdivision does not relieve the central organization or any of its subordinates of the duty to submit such additional information as a key district director may require to enable him to determine whether the conditions for continued exemption are being met. See sections 6001 and 6033 of the Code and the regulations thereunder.

(v) *Termination of a group exemption letter.*—(a) Termination of a group exemption letter will result in non-recognition of the exempt status of all included subordinates. To reestablish an exempt status in such cases, each subordinate must file an exemption application under the procedures outlined in subparagraph (1) of this paragraph, or a new group exemption letter must be applied for under this subparagraph.

(b) If a central organization dissolves or ceases to exist, the group exemption letter will be terminated, notwithstanding that the subordinates continue to exist and operate independently.

(c) Failure of the central organization to submit the information required by subdivision (iv) of this subparagraph, or to file a required information return, Form 990 or 990-A, or to otherwise comply with section 6001 or 6033 of the Code and the regulations thereunder, may result in termination of the group exemption letter on the grounds that the conditions required for the continuance of the group exemption letter have not been met. See Rev. Rul. 59-95, C.B. 1959-1, 627.

(d) The dissolution of a subordinate included in a group exemption letter will not affect the exempt status of the other included subordinates.

(e) If a subordinate covered by a group exemption letter fails to comply with section 6001 or 6033 of the Code and the regulations thereunder (for example, by failing to file a required information return) and the Service terminates its recognition of the subordinate's status, a copy of the termination letter to the subordinate will be furnished to the central organization. The group exemption letter will no longer be applicable to such subordinate, but will otherwise remain in effect. (It should be noted that if Form 990 is required to be filed, failure to file such return on time may also result in the imposition of a penalty of $10 for each day the return is late, up to a maximum of $5,000. See section 6652 of the Code and the regulations thereunder.)

(vi) *Revocation of a group exemption letter.*—(a) If the Service determines, under the procedures described in subparagraph (6) of this paragraph, that a central organization no longer qualifies for exemption under section 501(c) of the Code, the group exemption letter will be revoked. The revocation will result in nonrecognition of the exempt status of all included subordinates. To reestablish an exempt status in such cases, each subordinate must file an exemption application under the procedures outlined in subparagraph (1) of this paragraph or a new group exemption letter must be applied for under this subparagraph.

(b) If the Service determines, under the procedures described in subparagraph (6) of this paragraph, that a subordinate included in a group exemption letter no longer qualifies for exemption under section 501(c) of the Code, the central organization and the subordinate will be notified accordingly, and the group exemption letter will no longer apply to such subordinate, but will otherwise remain in effect.

(c) Where a subordinate organization has been disqualified for inclusion in a group

exemption letter as described in (b) of this subdivision, and thereafter wishes to reestablish its exempt status, the central organization should, at the time it submits the information required by subdivision (iv) of this subparagraph, submit detailed information relating to the subordinate's qualification for reinclusion in the group exemption letter.

(vii) *Instrumentalities or agencies of political subdivisions.*—An instrumentality or agency of a political subdivision that exercises control or supervision over a number of organizations similar in purposes and operations, each of which may qualify for exemption under the same paragraph of section 501(c) of the Code, may obtain a group exemption letter covering those organizations in the same manner as a central organization. However, the instrumentality or agency must furnish evidence that it is a qualified governmental agency. Examples of organizations over which governmental agencies exercise control or supervision are Federal credit unions, State chartered credit unions, and Federal land bank associations.

(viii) *Listing in cumulative list of organizations to which charitable contributions are deductible.*—If a central organization to which a group exemption letter has been issued is eligible to receive deductible charitable contributions as provided in section 170 of the Code, it will be listed in Publication No. 78, Cumulative List— Organizations Described in Section 170(c) of the Internal Revenue Code of 1954. The names of the subordinates covered by the group exemption letter will not be listed individually. However, the identification of the central organization will indicate whether contributions to its subordinates are also deductible.

(9) *Technical advice from the National Office.*— (i) *Definition and nature of technical advice.*— (a) As used in this subparagraph, "technical advice" means advice or guidance as to the interpretation and proper application of internal revenue laws, related statutes, and regulations, to a specific set of facts, in Employee Plans and Exempt Organization matters, furnished by the National Office upon request of a key district office or Appeals office in connection with the processing and consideration of a nondocketed case. It is furnished as a means of assisting Service personnel in closing cases and establishing and maintaining consistent holdings. It does not include memorandums on matters of general technical application furnished to key district offices or to Appeals offices where the issues are not raised in connection with the consideration and handling of a specific case.

(b) The provisions of this subparagraph only apply to Employee Plans and Exempt Organization cases being considered by a key district director or Appeals office. They do not apply to any other case under the jurisdiction of a district director or Appeals office or to a case under the jurisdiction of the Bureau of Alcohol, Tobacco, and Firearms. The technical advice provisions applicable to cases under the jurisdiction of a district director, other than Employee Plans and Exempt Organization cases, are set forth in § 601.105(b)(5). The technical advice provisions applicable to cases under the jurisdiction of an Appeals office, other than Employee Plans and Exempt Organization cases are set forth in § 601.106(f)(10).

(c) A key district director or an Appeals office may, under this subparagraph, request technical advice with respect to the consideration of a request for a determination letter. If the case involves certain Exempt Organization issues that are not covered by published precedent or on which there may be nonuniformity, requesting technical advice is mandatory rather than discretionary. See subparagraphs (2)(iv) and (5)(iii) of this paragraph.

(d) If a key district director is of the opinion that a National Office ruling letter or technical advice previously issued should be modified or revoked and it requests the National Office to reconsider the ruling or technical advice, the reference of the matter to the National Office is treated as a request for technical advice. The procedures specified in subdivision (iii) of this subparagraph should be followed in order that the National Office may consider the recommendation. Only the National Office can revoke a National Office ruling letter or technical advice. Before referral to the National Office, the key district director should inform the plan/organization of its opinion that the ruling letter or technical advice should be revoked. The key district director, after development of the facts and consideration of the arguments, will decide whether to recommend revocation of the ruling or technical advice to the National Office.

(e) The Assistant Commissioner (Employee Plans and Exempt Organizations) and, in section 521 cases, the Assistant Commissioner (Technical), acting under a delegation of authority from the Commissioner of Internal Revenue, are exclusively responsible for providing technical advice in any issue involving the establishment of basic principles and rules for the uniform interpretation and application of tax laws in cases under this subparagraph. This authority has been largely redelegated to subordinate officials.

(ii) *Areas in which technical advice may be requested.*—(a) Key district directors and Appeals offices may request technical advice on any technical or procedural question that develops during the processing and consideration of a case. These procedures are applicable as provided in subdivision (i) of this subparagraph.

(b) Key district directors and Appeals offices are encouraged to request technical advice on any technical or procedural question arising in connection with any case described in subdivision (i) of this subparagraph which cannot be resolved on the basis of law, regulations, or a clearly applicable revenue ruling or other precedent issued by the National Office. However, in Exempt Organization cases concerning qualification for exemption or foundation status,

key district directors and Appeals offices must request technical advice on any issue that is not covered by published precedent or on which nonuniformity may exist. Requests for technical advice should be made at the earliest possible stage of the proceedings.

(iii) *Requesting technical advice.*—(a) It is the responsibility of the key district office or the Appeals office to determine whether technical advice is to be requested on any issue before that office. However, while the case is under the jurisdiction of the key district director or the Appeals office, an employee plan/organization or its representative may request that an issue be referred to the National Office for technical advice on the grounds that a lack of uniformity exists as to the disposition of the issue, or that the issue is so unusual or complex as to warrant consideration by the National Office. This request should be made at the earliest possible stage of the proceedings. While plans/organizations are encouraged to make written requests setting forth the facts, law, and argument with respect to the issue, and reason for requesting National Office advice, a plan/organization may make the request orally. If, after considering the plan's/organization's request, the examiner or the Appeals Officer is of the opinion that the circumstances do not warrant referral of the case to the National Office, he/she will so advise the plan/organization. (See subdivision (iv) of this subparagraph for a plan's/organization's appeal rights where the examiner or Appeal Officer declines to request technical advice.)

(b) When technical advice is to be requested, whether or not upon the request of the plan/organization, the plan/organization will be so advised, except as noted in (j) of this subdivision. If the key district office or the Appeals office initiates the action, the plan/organization will be furnished a copy of the statement of the pertinent facts and the question or questions proposed for submission to the National Office. The request for advice should be so worded as to avoid possible misunderstanding, in the National Office, of the facts or of the specific point or points at issue.

(c) After receipt of the statement of facts and specific questions, the plan/organization will be given 10 calendar days in which to indicate in writing the extent, if any, to which it may not be in complete agreement. An extension of time must be justified by the plan/organization in writing and approved by the Chief, Employee Plans and Exempt Organizations Division (in the district office) or the Chief, Appeals Office, as the case may be. Every effort should be made to reach agreement as to the facts and specific points at issue. If agreement cannot be reached, the plan/organization may submit, within 10 calendar days after receipt of notice from the key district director or the Appeals office, a statement of its understanding as to the specific point or points at issue which will be forwarded to the National Office with the request for advice. An extension of time must be justified by the plan/organization in writing and approved by the Chief, Employee Plans and Exempt Organizations Division or the Chief, Appeals Office.

(d) If the plan/organization initiates the action to request advice, and its statement of the facts and point or points at issue are not wholly acceptable to the key district office or the Appeals office, the plan/organization will be advised in writing as to the areas of disagreement. The plan/organization will be given 10 calendar days after receipt of the written notice to reply to such notice. An extension of time must be justified by the plan/organization in writing and approved by the Chief, Employee Plans and Exempt Organizations Division or the Chief, Appeals Office. If agreement cannot be reached, both the statements of the plan/organization and the key district office or the Appeals office will be forwarded to the National Office.

(e)(1) In the case of requests for technical advice subject to the disclosure provisions of section 6110 of the Code, the plan/organization must also submit, within the 10-day period referred to in (c) and (d) of this subdivision, whichever applicable (relating to agreement by the plan/organization with the statement of facts and points submitted in connection with the request for technical advice) the statement described in (f) of this subdivision of proposed deletions pursuant to section 6110(c) of the Code. If the statement is not submitted, the plan/organization will be informed by the key district director or the Appeals office that the statement is required. If the key district director or the Appeals office does not receive the statement within 10 days after the plan/organization has been informed of the need for the statement, the key district director or the Appeals office may decline to submit the request for technical advice. If the key district director or the Appeals office decides to request technical advice in a case where the plan/organization has not submitted the statement of proposed deletions, the National Office will make those deletions which in the judgment of the Commissioner are required by section 6110(c) of the Code.

(2) The requirements included in this subparagraph, relating to the submission of statements and other material with respect to proposed deletions to be made from technical advise memoranda before public inspection is permitted to take place, do not apply to requests made by the key district director before November 1, 1976, or requests for any document to which section 6104 of the Code applies.

(f) In order to assist the Internal Revenue Service in making the deletions, required by section 6110(c) of the Code, from the text of technical advice memoranda which are open to public inspection pursuant to section 6110(a) of the Code, there must accompany requests for such technical advice either a statement of the deletions proposed by the plan/organization, or a statement that no information other than names, addresses, and identifying numbers need be deleted. Such statements shall be made in a separate document. The statement of proposed deletions shall be accompanied by a copy of all statements of facts and supporting documents which are submitted to the National Office pursuant to (c) or (d) of this subdivision, on which shall be indicated, by the use of brackets, the material which the plan/organization indicates should be deleted pursuant to section 6110(c) of the Code. The statement of proposed deletions shall indicate the statutory basis for each proposed deletion. The statement of proposed deletions shall not appear or be referred to anywhere in the request for technical advice. If the plan/organization decides to request additional deletions pursuant to section 6110(c) of the Code prior to the time the National Office replies to the request for technical advice, additional statements may be submitted.

(g) If the plan/organization has not already done so, it may submit a statement explaining its position on the issues, citing precedents which it believes will bear on the case. This statement will be forwarded to the National Office with the request for advice. If it is received at a later date, it will be forwarded for association with the case file.

(h) At the time the plan/organization is informed that the matter is being referred to the National Office, it will also be informed of the right to a conference in the National Office in the event an adverse decision is indicated, and will be asked to indicate whether a conference is desired.

(i) Generally, prior to replying to the request for technical advice, the National Office shall inform the plan/organization orally or in writing of the material likely to appear in the technical advice memorandum which the plan/organization proposed be deleted but which the Internal Revenue Service determined should not be deleted. If so informed, the plan/organization may submit within 10 days any further information, arguments, or other material in support of the position that such material be deleted. The Internal Revenue Service will attempt, if feasible, to resolve all disagreements with respect to proposed deletions prior to the time the National Office replies to the request for technical advice. However, in no event shall the plan/organization have the right to a conference with respect to resolution of any disagreements concerning material to be deleted from the text of the technical advice memorandum, but such matters may be considered at any conference otherwise scheduled with respect to the request.

(j) The provisions of (a) through (i) of this subdivision, relating to the referral of issues upon request of the plan/organization, advising plans/organizations of the referral of issues, the submission of proposed deletions, and the granting of conferences in the National Office, are not applicable to technical advice memoranda described in section 6110(g)(5)(A) of the Code, relating to cases involving criminal or civil fraud investigations and jeopardy or termination assessments. However, in such cases the plan/organization shall be allowed to provide the statement of proposed deletions to the National Office upon the completion of all proceedings with respect to the investigations or assessments, but prior to the date on which the Commissioner mails the notice pursuant to section 6110(f)(1) of the Code of intention to disclose the technical advice memorandum.

(k) Form 4463, Request for Technical Advice, should be used for transmitting requests for technical advice to the National Office.

(iv) *Appeal by plans/organizations of determinations not to seek technical advice.*—(a) If the plan/organization has requested referral of an issue before a key district office or an Appeals office to the National Office for technical advice, and after consideration of the request the examiner or the Appeals Officer is of the opinion that the circumstances do not warrant such referral, he/she will so advise the plan/organization.

(b) The plan/organization may appeal the decision of the examiner or the Appeals Officer not to request technical advice by submitting to the relevant official, within 10 calendar days after being advised of the decision, a statement of the facts, law, and arguments with respect to the issue, and the reasons why the plan/organization believes the matter should be referred to the National Office for advice. An extension of time must be justified by the plan/organization in writing and approved by the Chief, Employee Plans and Exempt Organizations Division of the Chief, Appeals Office.

(c) The examiner or the Appeals Officer will submit the statement of the plan/organization to the Chief, Employee Plans and Exempt Organizations Division or the Chief, Appeals Office, accompanied by a statement of the official's reasons why the issue should not be referred to the National Office. The Chief will determine, on the basis of the statements submitted, whether technical advice will be requested. If the Chief determines that technical advice is not warranted, that official will inform the plan/organization in writing that he/she proposes to deny the request. In the letter to the plan/organization the Chief will (except in unusual situations where such action would be prejudicial to the best interests of the Government) state specifically the reasons for the proposed denial. The plan/organization will be given 15 calendar days after receipt of the letter in which to notify the Chief whether it agrees with the proposed denial. The plan/organization may not appeal the decision of the Chief, Employee Plans and Exempt Organizations Division, or of the Chief, Appeals Office, not to request technical advice from the National Office. However, if the plan/organization does not agree with the proposed denial, all data relating to the issue for which technical advice has been sought, including the plan's/organization's written request and statements, will be submitted to the National Office, Attention: Director, Exempt Organizations or Employee Plans Division or Actuarial Division or, in a section 521 case, Attention: Director, Corporation Tax Division for review. After review in the National Office, the submitting office will be notified whether the proposed denial is approved or disapproved.

(d) While the matter is being reviewed in the National Office, the key district office or the Appeals office will suspend action on the issue (except where the delay would prejudice the Government's interests) until it is notified of the National Office decision. This notification will be made within 30 days after receipt of the data in the National Office. The review will be solely on the basis of the written record and no conference will be held in the National Office.

(v) *Conference in the National Office.*— (a) If, after a study of the technical advice request, it appears that advice adverse to the plan/organization should be given and a conference has been requested, the plan/organization will be notified of the time and place of the conference. If conferences are being arranged with respect to more than one request for advice involving the same plan/organization, they will be so scheduled as to cause the least inconvenience to the plan/organization. The conference will be arranged by telephone, if possible, and must be held within 21 calendar days after contact has been made. Extensions of time will be granted only if justified in writing by the plan/organization and approved by the appropriate branch chief.

(b) A plan/organization is entitled, as a matter of right, to only one conference in the National Office unless one of the circumstances discussed in (c) of this subdivision exists. This conference will usually be held at the branch level in the appropriate division in the Office of the Assistant Commissioner (Employee Plans and Exempt Organizations) or, in section 521 cases, in the Office of the Assistant Commissioner (Technical), and will usually be attended by a person who has authority to act for the branch chief. In appropriate cases the examiner or the Appeals Officer may also attend the conference to clarify the facts in the case. If more than one subject is discussed at the conference, the discussion constitutes a conference with respect to each subject. At the request of the plan/organization or its representative, the conference may be held at an earlier stage in the consideration of the case than the Service would ordinarily designate. A plan/organization has no "right" of appeal from an action of a branch to the director of a division or to any other National Office official.

(c) In the process of review of a holding proposed by a branch, it may appear that the final answer will involve a reversal of the branch proposal with a result less favorable to the plan/organization. Or it may appear that an adverse holding proposed by a branch will be approved, but on a new or different issue or on different grounds than those on which the branch decided the case. Under either of these circumstances, the plan/organization or its representative will be invited to another conference. The provisions of this subparagraph limiting the number of conferences to which a plan/organization is entitled will not foreclose inviting the plan/organization to attend further conferences when, in the opinion of National Office personnel, such need arises. All additional conferences of this type discussed are held only at the invitation of the Service.

(d) It is the responsibility of the plan/organization to furnish to the National Office, within 21 calendar days after the conference, a written record of any additional data, line of reasoning, precedents, etc., that were proposed by the plan/organization and discussed at the conference but were not previously or adequately presented in writing. Extensions of time will be granted only if justified in writing by the plan/organization and approved by the appropriate branch chief. Any additional material and a copy thereof should be addressed to and sent to the National Office which will forward the copy to the appropriate key district director or Appeals office. The key district director or the Appeals office will be requested to give the matter prompt attention, will verify the additional facts and data, and will comment on it to the extent deemed appropriate.

(e) A plan/organization or its representative desiring to obtain information as to the status of its case (other than a section 521 case) may do so by contacting the following offices with respect to matters in the areas of their responsibility:

Official	Telephone Numbers (Area Code 202)
Chief, Employee Plans Technical Branch	566-3871
Chief, Exempt Organizations Technical Branch	566-3856 or 566-3593
Director, Actuarial Division	566-4311

An organization or its representative desiring to obtain information as to the status of its section 521 case may do so by contacting the Director, Corporation Tax Division (202-566-4504 or 566-4505).

(vi) Preparation of technical advice memorandum by the National Office.—(a) Immediately upon receipt in the National Office, the employee to whom the case is assigned will analyze the file to ascertain whether it meets the requirements of subdivision (iii) of this subparagraph. If the case is not complete with respect to any requirement in subdivision (iii)(*a*) through (*d*) of this subparagraph, appropriate steps will be taken to complete the file. If any request for technical advice does not comply with the requirements of subdivision (iii)(*e*) of this subparagraph, if applicable, relating to the statement of proposed deletions, the National Office will make those deletions from the technical advice memorandum which in the judgment of the Commissioner are required by section 6110(c) of the Code.

(b) If the plan/organization has requested a conference in the National Office, the procedures in subdivision (v) of this subparagraph will be followed.

(c) Replies to requests for technical advice will be addressed to the key district director or to the Appeals office and will be drafted in two parts. Each part will identify the plan/organization by name, address, identification number, and year or years involved. The first part

(hereafter called the "technical advice memorandum") will contain (1) a recitation of the pertinent facts having a bearing on the issue; (2) a discussion of the facts, precedents, and reasoning of the National Office; and (3) the conclusions of the National Office. The conclusions will give direct answers, whenever possible, to the specific questions of the key district director or the Appeals office. The discussion of the issues will be in such detail that the key district director or the Appeals office is apprised of the reasoning underlying the conclusion. There shall accompany the technical advice memorandum, where applicable, a notice, pursuant to section 6110(f)(1) of the Code, of intention to disclose the technical advice memorandum (including a copy of the version proposed to be open to public inspection and notations of third party communications pursuant to section 6110(d) of the Code) which the key district director or the Appeals office will forward to the plan/organization at such time that it furnishes a copy of the technical advice memorandum to the plan/organization pursuant to (e) of this subdivision and subdivision (vii)(*b*) of this subparagraph.

(d) The second part of the reply will consist of a transmittal memorandum. In the unusual cases it will serve as a vehicle for providing the key district office or Appeals office administrative information or other information which, under the nondisclosure statutes, or for other reasons, may not be discussed with the plan/organization.

(e) It is the general practice of the Service to furnish a copy of the technical advice memorandum to the plan/organization after it has been adopted by the key district director or the Appeals office. However, in the case of technical advice memoranda described in section 6110(g)(5)(A) of the Code, relating to cases involving criminal or civil fraud investigations and jeopardy or termination assessments, a copy of the technical advice memorandum shall not be furnished the plan/organization until all proceedings with respect to the investigations or assessments are completed.

(f) After receiving the notice, pursuant to section 6110(f)(1) of the Code, of intention to disclose the technical advice memorandum (if applicable), the plan/organization, if desiring to protest the disclosure of certain information in the memorandum, must, within 20 days after the notice is mailed, submit a written statement identifying those deletions not made by the Internal Revenue Service which the plan/organization believes should have been made. The plan/organization shall also submit a copy of the version of the technical advice memorandum proposed to be open to public inspection on which it indicates, by the use of brackets, the deletions proposed by the plan/organization but which have not been made by the Internal Revenue Service. Generally, the Internal Revenue Service will not consider the deletion of any material which the plan/organization did not, prior to the time when the National Office sent its reply to the request for technical advice to the key district

director or the Appeals office, propose be deleted. The Internal Revenue Service shall, within 20 days after receipt of the response by the plan/organization to the notice pursuant to section 6110(f)(1) of the Code (if applicable), mail to the plan/organization its final administrative conclusion regarding the deletions to be made.

(vii) *Action on technical advice in key district offices and in Appeals offices.*—(a) Unless the key district director or the Chief, Appeals office, feels that the conclusions reached by the National Office in a technical advice memorandum should be reconsidered and promptly requests such reconsideration, the key district office or the Appeals office will proceed to process the case on the basis of the conclusions expressed in the technical advice memorandum. The effect of technical advice on the plan's/organization's case once the technical advice memorandum is adopted is set forth in subdivision (viii) of this subparagraph.

(b) The key district director or the Appeals office will furnish the plan/organization a copy of the technical advice memorandum described in subdivision (vi)(c) of this subparagraph and the notice pursuant to section 6110(f)(1) of the Code (if applicable) of intention to disclose the technical advice memorandum (including a copy of the version proposed to be open to public inspection and notations of third party communications pursuant to section 6110(d) of the Code). The preceding sentence shall not apply to technical advice memoranda involving civil fraud or criminal investigations, or jeopardy or termination assessments, as described in subdivision (iii)(j) of this subparagraph (except to the extent provided in subdivision (vi)(e) of this subparagraph) or to documents to which section 6104 of the Code applies.

(c) In those cases in which the National Office advises the key district director or the Appeals office that it should not furnish a copy of the technical advice memorandum to the plan/organization, the key district director or the Appeals office will so inform the plan/organization if it requests a copy.

(viii) *Effect of technical advice.*—(a) A technical advice memorandum represents an expression of the views of the Service as to the application of law, regulations, and precedents to the facts of a specific case, and is issued primarily as a means of assisting Service officials in the examination and closing of the case involved. In cases under this subparagraph concerning a plan's/organization's qualification or an organization's status, the conclusions expressed in a technical advice memorandum are final and will be followed by the key district office or the Appeals office.

(b) Unless otherwise stated, a holding in a technical advice memorandum will be applied retroactively. Moreover, where the plan/organization had previously been issued a favorable ruling or determination letter (whether or not it was based on a previous technical advice memorandum) concerning that transaction, its purpose, or method of operation, the holding in a technical advice memorandum that is adverse to the plan/organization is also applied retroactively unless the Assistant Commissioner or Deputy Assistant Commissioner (Employee Plans and Exempt Organizations) or, in a section 521 case, the Assistant Commissioner or Deputy Assistant Commissioner (Technical) exercises the discretionary authority under section 7805(b) of the Code to limit the retroactive effect of the holding as illustrated, in the case of rulings, in paragraph (1)(5) of this section.

(c) Technical advice memoranda often form the basis for revenue rulings. For the description of revenue rulings and the effect thereof, see §§ 601.601 (d)(2)(i)(a) and 601.601 (d)(2)(v).

(d) A key district director or an Appeals office may raise an issue in a taxable period, even though technical advice may have been asked for and furnished with regard to the same or a similar issue in any other taxable period. However, if the proposal by the key district director or the Appeals office is contrary to a prior technical advice or ruling issued to the same plan/organization, the proposal must be submitted to the National Office. See § 601.106(a)(1)(iv)(b) and subdivision (i)(d) of this subparagraph.

(o) *Employees' trusts or plans.*—(1) *In general.*—Paragraph (o) provides procedures relating to the issuance of determination letters with respect to the qualification of retirement plans. Paragraph (o)(2) of this section sets forth the authority of key district directors to issue determination letters. Paragraph (o)(3) provides instructions to applicants, including which forms to file, where such forms must be filed, and requirements for giving notice to interested parties. Paragraph (o)(5) describes the administrative remedies available to interested parties and the Pension Benefit Guaranty Corporation. Paragraph (o)(6) describes the administrative appeal rights available to applicants. Paragraph (o)(7) provides for the issuance of notice of final determination. Paragraph (o)(8) describes the documents which will make up the administrative record. Paragraph (o)(9) describes the notice of final determination. Paragraph (o)(10) sets forth the actions that will be necessary on the part of applicants, interested parties, and the Pension Benefit Guaranty Corporation in order for each to exhaust the administrative remedies within the meaning of section 7476(b)(3) of the Code.

(2) *Determination letters.*—(i) The district directors of the key district offices (described in paragraph (o)(4) of this section) shall have the authority to issue determination letters involving the provisions of sections 401, 403(a), 405, and 501(a) of the Internal Revenue Code of 1954 with respect to:

(a) Initial qualification of stock bonus, pension, profit-sharing, annuity, and bond purchase plans;

(b) Initial exemption from Federal income tax under section 501(a) of trusts forming a part of such plans, provided that the determination does not involve application of section 502 (feeder organizations) or section 511 (unrelated business income), or the question of whether a proposed transaction will be a prohibited transaction under section 503;

(c) Compliance with the applicable requirements of foreign situs trusts as to taxability of beneficiaries (section 402(c)) and deductions for employer contributions (section 404(a)(4)) in connection with a request for a determination letter as to the qualification of a retirement plan;

(d) Amendments, curtailments, or terminations of such plans and trusts.

(ii) Determination letters authorized by paragraph (o)(2)(i) of this section do not include determinations or opinions relating to other inquiries with respect to plans or trusts. Thus, except as specifically provided in paragraph (o)(2)(i) of this section, key district directors may not issue determination letters relating to issues under other sections of the Code, such as sections 72, 402 through 404, 412, 502, 503, and 511 through 515, unless such determination letters are otherwise authorized under paragraph (c) of this section.

(iii) If, during the consideration of a case described in paragraph (o)(2)(i) of this section by a key district director, the applicant believes that the case involves an issue with respect to which referral for technical advice is appropriate, the applicant may ask the district director to request technical advice from the National Office. The district director shall advise the applicant of its right to request referral of the issue to the National Office for technical advice. The technical advice provisions applicable in these cases are set forth in paragraph (n)(9) of this section. If technical advice is issued, the decision of the National Office is final and the applicant may not thereafter appeal the issue to the Appeals office. See § 601.106(a)(1)(iv)(a) and paragraph (o)(6) of this section.

(3) *Instructions to taxpayers.*—(i) If an applicant for a determination letter does not comply with all the provisions of this paragraph, the district director, in his discretion, may return the application and point out to the applicant those provisions which have not been met. If such a request is returned to the applicant, the 270 day period described in section 7476(b)(3) will not begin to run until such time as the provisions of this paragraph are complied with.

(ii) An applicant requesting a determination letter must file with the appropriate district director specified in paragraph (o)(3)(xii) of this section the application form required by paragraphs (o)(3)(iii) through (x) of this section including all information and documents required by such form. (See section 6104 and the regulations thereunder for provisions relating to the extent to which information submitted to the Internal Revenue Service in connection with the application for determination may be subject to public inspection.) However, before filing such application, the applicant must comply with the provisions of paragraphs (o)(3)(xiv) through (xx) of this section (relating to notification of inter-

ested parties). (See paragraph (o)(5)(vi) of this section with respect to the effective date of paragraphs (o)(3)(xiv) through (xx) of this section.)

(iii) Paragraphs (o)(3)(iv)-(vi), (viii), and (ix) apply only to applications for determinations in respect of plan years to which section 410 of the Code does not apply. Paragraph (o)(3)(x) applies only to applications for determinations in respect of plan years to which section 410 applies. Paragraph (o)(3)(vii) applies whether or not the application is for a determination in respect of plan years to which section 410 applies. For this purpose, section 410 will be considered to apply with respect to a plan year if an election has been made under section 1017(d) of the Employee Retirement Income Security Act of 1974 to have section 410 apply to such plan year, whether or not the election is conditioned upon the issuance by the Commissioner of a favorable determination. For purposes of this paragraph (o)(3), in the case of an organization described in section 410(c)(1), section 410 will be considered to apply to a plan year of such organization for any plan year to which section 410(c)(2) applies to such plan.

(iv) If the request relates to the initial qualification of an individually designed plan, a subsequent amendment thereto, or compliance with the requirements for a foreign situs trust, the employer should (a) if the plan does not include self-employed individuals, file Form 4573, Application for Determination—Individually Designed Plan (not covering self-employed individuals), or (b) if the plan includes self-employed individuals, file Form 4574, Application for Determination—Individually Designed Plan Covering Self-Employed Individuals, except that where a bond purchase plan includes a self-employed individual, file Form 4578, Application for Approval of Bond Purchase Plan. (See paragraph (o)(3)(iii) for plan years to which this paragraph (o)(3)(iv) applies.)

(v) If the request involves a curtailment or termination of the plan (or complete discontinuance of contributions), the applicant should file Form 4576, Application for Determination—Termination or Curtailment of Plan. This form will also be applicable to the termination of a plan that includes self-employed individuals. (See paragraph (o)(3)(iii) of this section for plan years to which this paragraph (o)(3)(v) applies.)

(vi) An association of employers or a board of trustees should file Form 4577, Application for Determination—Industry-Wide Plan and Trust, if the request relates to the initial qualification or subsequent amendments of an industry-wide or area-wide union negotiated plan. (See paragraph (o)(3)(iii) of this section for plan years to which this paragraph (o)(3)(vi) applies.)

(vii) If the request relates to the qualification of a bond purchase plan, which includes self-employed individuals, the applicant should file, in duplicate, Form 4578, Application for Approval of Bond Purchase Plan that includes Self-Employed Individuals. When properly completed, Form 4578 will constitute a bond purchase plan. (See paragraph (o)(3)(iii) for plan years to which this section (o)(3)(vii) applies.)

(viii) An employer who desires a determination letter on his adoption of a master or prototype plan which is designed to satisfy section 401(a) or 403(a) but which is not designed to include self-employed individuals within the meaning of section 401(c)(1) must file Form 4462, Employer Application—Determination as to Qualification of Pension, Annuity, or Profit-Sharing Plan and Trust, and furnish a copy of the adoption agreement or other evidence of adoption of the plan and such additional information as the district director may require. (See paragraph (o)(3)(iii) of this section for plan years to which this paragraph (o)(3)(viii) applies.)

(ix) An applicant who amends his adoption agreement under a master or prototype plan may request a determination letter as to the effect of such amendment by filing Form 4462 with his district director, together with a copy of the amendment and a summary of the changes. However, in the event an applicant desires to amend his adoption agreement under a master or prototype plan, and such amendment is not contemplated or permitted under the plan, then such amendment will in effect substitute an individually designed plan for the master or prototype plan. (See paragraph (o)(3)(iii) of this section for plan years to which this paragraph (o)(3)(ix) applies.)

(x) An applicant requesting a determination letter relating to a defined contribution plan, other than a letter on the qualification of a bond purchase plan, shall file in duplicate, Form 5301, Application for Determination of Defined Contribution Plan, and Form 5302, Employee Census. Those forms are to be filed in accordance with the instructions therefor and accompanied by any schedules or additional material prescribed in those instructions. (See paragraph (o)(3)(iii) of this section for plan years to which this paragraph (o)(3)(x) applies.)

(xi) When, in connection with an application for a determination on the qualification of the plan, it is necessary to determine whether an organization (including a professional service organization) is a corporation or an association classified as a corporation under § 301.7701-2 of this chapter of the Regulations on Procedure and Administration, and whether an employer-employee relationship exists between it and its associates, the district director will make such determination. In such cases, the application with respect to the qualification of the plan should be filed in accordance with the provisions herein set forth and should contain the information and documents specified in the application. It should also be accompanied by such information and copies of documents as the organization deems appropriate to establish its status. The Service may, in addition, require any further information that is considered necessary to determine the status of the organization, the employment status of the individuals involved, or the qualification of the plan. After the taxable status of the organizations and the employer-employee relationship have been determined, the key district director may issue a determination letter as to the qualification of the plan.

(xii) Requests for determination letters on matters authorized by paragraph (o)(2) of this section, and the necessary supporting data, are to be addressed to the district director (whether or not such district director is the director of a key district) specified below (determined without regard to the application of section 414(b) or (c) to the plan):

(a) In the case of a plan for a single employer, the request shall be addressed to the district director for the district in which such employer's principal place of business is located.

(b) In the case of a single plan for a parent company and its subsidiaries, the request shall be addressed to the district director for the district in which the principal place of business of the parent company is located, whether separate or consolidated returns are filed.

(c) In the case of a plan established or proposed for an industry by all subscribing employers whose principal places of business are located within more than one district, the request shall be addressed to the district director for the district in which is located the principal place of business of the trustee, or if more than one trustee, the usual meeting place of the trustees.

(d) In the case of a pooled fund arrangement (individual trusts under separate plans pooling their funds for investment purposes through a master trust), the request on behalf of the master trust shall be addressed to the district director for the district where the principal place of business of such trust is located. Requests on behalf of the participating trusts and related plans will be addressed as otherwise provided herein.

(e) In the case of a plan of multiple employers (other than a master or prototype plan) not otherwise herein provided for, the request shall be addressed to the district director for the district in which is located the principal place of business of the trustee, or if not trusteed or if more than one trustee, the principal or usual meeting place of the trustees or plan supervisors.

(xiii) The applicant's request for a determination letter may be withdrawn by a written request at any time prior to appealing a proposed determination to the regional office as described in paragraph (o)(6) of this section. In the case of such a withdrawal the Service will not render a determination of any type. A failure to render a determination as a result of such a withdrawal will not be considered a failure of the Secretary or his delegate to make a determination within the meaning of section 7476. In the case of a withdrawal the district director may consider the information submitted in connection with the withdrawn request in a subsequent audit or examination.

(xiv) In the case of an application for a determination for plan years to which section 410 applies (see paragraph (o)(5)(vi) of this section), notice that an application for an advance determination regarding the qualification of plans described in section 401(a), 403(a), or

405(a) is to be made must be given to all interested parties in the manner set forth in the regulations under section 7476 of the Code.

(xv) When the notice referred to in paragraph (o)(3)(xiv) of this section is given in the manner set forth in §1.7476-2(c) of this chapter, such notice must be given not less than 10 days nor more than 24 days prior to the date the application for a determination is made. See paragraph (o)(3)(xxi) of this section for determining when an application is made. If, however, an application is returned to the applicant for failure to adequately satisfy the notification requirement with respect to a particular group or class of interested parties, the applicant need not cause notice to be given to those groups or classes of interested parties with respect to which the notice requirement was already satisfied merely because, as a result of the resubmission of the application, the time limitations of this paragraph (o)(3)(xv) would not be met.

(xvi) The notice referred to in paragraph (o)(3)(xiv) of this section shall be given in the manner prescribed in §1.7476-2 of this chapter and shall contain the following information:

(a) a brief description identifying the class or classes of interested parties to whom the notice is addressed (e.g., all present employees of the employer, all present employees eligible to participate);

(b) the name of the plan, the plan identification number, and the name of the plan administrator;

(c) the name and taxpayer identification number of the applicant;

(d) that an application for a determination as to the qualified status of the plan is to be made to the Internal Revenue Service, stating whether the application relates to an initial qualification, a plan amendment or a plan termination, and the address of the district director to whom the application will be submitted;

(e) a description of the class of employees eligible to participate under the plan;

(f) whether or not the Service has issued a previous determination as to the qualified status of the plan;

(g) a statement that any person to whom the notice is addressed is entitled to submit, or request the Department of Labor to submit, to the district director described in paragraph (o)(3)(xvi)(d) of this section, a comment on the question of whether the plan meets the requirements for qualification under part I of Subchapter D of Chapter 1 of the Internal Revenue Code of 1954; that two or more such persons may join in a single comment or request; and that if such a person or persons request the Department of Labor to submit a comment and that department declines to do so in respect of one or more matters raised in the request, the person or persons so requesting may submit a comment to the district director in respect of the matters on which the Department of Labor declines to comment;

(h) that a comment to the district director or a request of the Department of Labor must be made according to the following procedures:

(1) a comment to the district director must be received on or before the 45th day (specified by date) after the day on which the application for determination is received by the district director;

(2) or if the comment is being submitted on a matter on which the Department of Labor was first requested but declined to comment, on or before the later of such 45th day or the 15th day after the day on which the Department of Labor notifies such person or persons that it declines to comment, but in no event later than the 60th day (specified by date) after the day the application is received by the district director; and

(3) a request of the Department of Labor to submit such a comment must be received by such department on or before the 25th day (specified by date) (or if the person or persons requesting the Department of Labor to submit such a comment wish to preserve their right to submit a comment to the district director in the event the Department of Labor declines to comment, on or before the 15th day (specified by date)) after the day the application is received by the district director;

(i) except to the extent there is included in the notice the additional informational materials which paragraphs (o)(3)(xviii), (xix), and (xx) of this section require be made available to interested parties, a description of a reasonable procedure whereby such additional informational material will be made available to them (see paragraph (o)(3)(xvii) of this section).

(xvii) The procedure referred to in paragraph (o)(3)(xvi)(i) of this ection whereby the additional informational material required by paragraphs (o)(3)(xviii), (xix), and (xx) of this section will (to the extent not included in this notice) be made available to interested parties, may consist of making such material available for inspection and copying by interested parties at a place or places reasonably accessible to such parties, or supplying such material by using a method of delivery or a combination thereof that is reasonably calculated to ensure that all interested parties will have access to the materials. The procedure referred to in paragraph (o)(3)(xvi)(i) of this section must be immediately available to all interested parties and must be designed to supply them with such additional informational material in time for them to pursue their rights within the time period prescribed, and must be available until the earlier of the filing of a pleading commencing a declaratory judgment action under section 7476 with respect to the qualification of the plan or the ninety-second day after the day the notice of final determination is mailed to the applicant.

(xviii) Unless provided in the notice, the following materials shall be made available to interested parties under a procedure described in paragraph (o)(3)(xvii) of this section:

(a) An updated copy of the plan and the related trust agreement (if any);

(b) The application for determination;

provided, however, that if there would be less than 26 participants in the plan, as described in the application (including, as participants, retired employees and beneficiaries of deceased employees who have a nonforfeitable right to benefits under the plan and employees who would be eligible to participate upon making mandatory employee contributions, if any), then in lieu of making such materials available to interested parties who are not participants (as described above), there may be made available to such interested parties a document containing the following information: a description of the plan's requirements respecting eligibility for participation and benefits; a description of the provisions providing for nonforfeitable benefits; a description of the circumstances which may result in ineligibility, or denial or loss of benefits; a description of the source of financing of the plan and the identity of any organization through which benefits are provided; whether the applicant is claiming in his application that the plan meets the requirements of section 410(b)(1)(A) of the Code, and, if not, the coverage schedule required by the application in the case of plans not meeting the requirements of such section. However, once such an interested party or his designated representative receives a notice of final determination, the applicant must, upon request, make available to such interested party (regardless of whether or not the interested party is a participant in the plan and regardless of whether or not the plan has less than 26 participants) an updated copy of the plan and related trust agreement (if any) and the application for determination. Information of the type described in section 6104(a)(1)(D) of the Code should not be included in the application, plan, or related trust agreement submitted to the Internal Revenue Service. Accordingly, such information should not be included in any of the materials required by this paragraph (o)(3) to be available to interested parties. There may be excluded from such material information contained in Form 5302 (Employee Census). However, information showing the number of individuals covered and not covered in the plan, listed by compensation range, shall not be excluded.

(xix) Unless provided in the notice, there shall be made available to interested parties under a procedure described in paragraph (o)(3)(xvii) of this section, any additional document dealing with the application which is submitted by or for the applicant to the Internal Revenue Service, or furnished by the Internal Revenue Service to the applicant; provided, however, if there would be less than 26 participants in the plan as described in the application (including, as participants, retired employees and beneficiaries of deceased employees who have a nonforfeitable right to benefits under the plan and employees who would be eligible to participate upon making mandatory employee contributions, if any), such additional documents need not be made available to interested parties who are not participants (as described above) until they or their designated representative, receive a notice of final determination. The applicant may also withhold from such inspection and copying, information described in section 6104(a)(1)(C) and (D) of the Code which may be contained in such additional documents.

(xx) Unless provided in the notice, there shall be made available to all interested parties under a procedure described in paragraph (o)(3)(xvii) of this section, material setting forth the following information:

(a) the rights of interested parties described in paragraph (o)(5)(i) of this section; and

(b) the information provided in paragraph (o)(5)(ii), (iii), (iv) and (v) of this section.

(xxi) An application for an advance determination, a comment to the district director, or a request to the Department of Labor, shall be deemed made when it is received by the district director, or the Department of Labor. The notice to interested parties required by paragraph (o)(3)(xiv) of this section shall be deemed given when it is given in person, posted as prescribed in the regulations under section 7476 or received through the mail. In any case where such an application, request, comment, or notice is sent by mail, it shall be deemed received as of the date of the postmark (or if sent by certified or registered mail, the date of certification or registration), if it is deposited in the mail in the United States in an envelope, or other appropriate wrapper first class postage prepaid, properly addressed. However, if such an application, request or comment is not received within a reasonable period from the date of postmark, the immediately preceding sentence shall not apply.

(4) *Key district offices.*—Following are the 19 key district offices that issue determination letters and the area covered:

Key District(s)	IRS Districts Covered
Central Region	
Cincinnati	Cincinnati, Louisville, Indianapolis
Cleveland	Cleveland, Parkersburg
Detroit	Detroit
Mid-Atlantic Region	
Baltimore	Baltimore (which includes the District of Columbia and Office of International Operations), Pittsburgh, Richmond
Philadelphia	Philadelphia, Wilmington
Newark	Newark

Key District(s)	IRS Districts Covered
Midwest Region	
Chicago	Chicago
St. Paul	St. Paul, Fargo, Aberdeen, Milwaukee
St. Louis	St. Louis, Springfield, Des Moines, Omaha
North-Atlantic Region	
Boston	Boston, Augusta, Burlington, Providence, Hartford, Portsmouth
Manhattan	Manhattan
Brooklyn	Brooklyn, Albany, Buffalo
Southeast Region	
Atlanta	Atlanta, Greensboro, Columbia, Nashville
Jacksonville	Jacksonville, Jackson, Birmingham
Southwest Region	
Austin	Austin, New Orleans, Albuquerque, Denver, Cheyenne
Dallas	Dallas, Oklahoma City, Little Rock, Wichita
Western Region	
Los Angeles	Los Angeles, Phoenix, Honolulu
San Francisco	San Francisco, Salt Lake City, Reno
Seattle	Seattle, Portland, Anchorage, Boise, Helena

(5) *Administrative remedies of interested parties and the Pension Benefit Guaranty Corporation.*— (i) With respect to plan years to which section 410 applies (see paragraph (o)(5)(vi) of this section), persons who qualify as interested parties under the regulations issued under section 7476 and the Pension Benefit Guaranty Corporation shall have the following rights:

(a) To submit to the district director for the district where an application for determination is filed, by the 45th day after the day on which the application is received by the district director, a written comment on said application, with respect to the qualification of the plan under subchapter D of chapter 1 of the Internal Revenue Code.

(b) To request the Administrator of Pension and Welfare Benefit Programs, Department of Labor, 200 Constitution Avenue, N.W., Washington, D.C. 20210, to submit to such district director such a written comment under the provisions of section 3001(b)(2) of the Employee Retirement Income Security Act of 1974. Such a request, if made by an interested party or parties, must be received by such department on or before the 25th day after the day said application is received by the district director. However, if such party or parties requesting the Department of Labor to submit such a comment wish to preserve their rights to submit a comment to the district director in the event the Department of Labor declines to comment (pursuant to paragraph (o)(5)(i)(c) of this section), such request must be received by such department on or before the 15th day after the day the application is received by the district director.

(c) If a request described in paragraph (o)(5)(i)(b) of this section is made and the Department of Labor notifies the interested party or parties making the request that it declines to submit a comment on a matter concerning qualification of the plan which was raised in such request, to submit a written comment to the district director on such matter by the later of the 45th day after the day the application for determination is received by the district director or the 15th day after the day on which the Department of Labor notifies such party or parties that it declines to submit a comment on such matter, but, in no event later than the 60th day after the application for determination was received. (See paragraph (o)(5)(iii) of this section for determining when notice that the Department of Labor declines to comment is received by an interested party or parties.)

Such a comment must comply with the requirements of paragraph (o)(5)(ii) of this section, and include a statement that the comment is being submitted on matters raised in a request to the Department of Labor on which that department declined to comment.

(ii) A comment submitted by an interested party or parties to the district director must be in writing, signed by such party or parties or by an authorized representative of such party or parties (as provided in paragraph (e)(6) of this section), be addressed to the district director described in paragraph (o)(3)(xvi)(d) of this section, and contain the following:

(a) The name or names of the interested party or parties making the comment;

(b) The name and taxpayer identification number of the applicant making the application;

(c) The name of the plan and the plan identification number;

(d) Whether the party or parties submitting the comments are—

(1) Employees eligible to participate under the plan,

(2) Former employees or beneficiaries of deceased former employees who have a vested right to benefits under the plan, or

(3) Employees not eligible to participate under the plan;

Reg. §601.201(o)(5)

(e) The specific matter or matters raised by the interested party or parties on the question of whether the plan meets the requirements for qualification under Part I of Subchapter D of the Code, and how such matter or matters relate to the interests of such party or parties making such comment.

(f) The address of the interested party submitting the comment to which all correspondence, including a notice of the Internal Revenue Service's final determination with respect to qualification, should be sent. (See section 7476(b)(5) of the Code.) If more than one interested party submits the comment, they must designate a representative for receipt of such correspondence and notice on behalf of all interested parties submitting the said comment, and state the address of such representative. Such representative shall be one of the interested parties submitting the comment or the authorized representative.

(iii) For purposes of paragraph (o)(3)(xvi)(h) and (o)(5)(i)(c), notice by the Department of Labor that it declines to comment shall be deemed given to the interested party designated to receive such notice when received by him.

(iv) A request of the Department of Labor to submit a comment to the district director must be in writing, signed, and in addition to the information prescribed in paragraph (o)(5)(ii) of this section must also contain the address of the district director to whom the application was, or will be, submitted. The address designated for notice by the Internal Revenue Serivce will be used by the Department of Labor in communicating with the party or parties submitting the request.

(v) The contents of written comments submitted by interested parties to the Internal Revenue Service pursuant to paragraphs (o)(5)(i)(a) and (c) will not be treated as confidential material and may be inspected by persons outside the Internal Revenue Service, including the applicant for the determination. Accordingly, designations of material as confidential or not to be disclosed, contained in such comments, will not be accepted. Thus, a person submitting a written comment should not include therein material that he considers to be confidential or inappropriate for disclosure to the public. It will be presumed by the Internal Revenue Service that every written comment submitted to it is intended by the party or parties submitting it to be subject in its entirety to public inspection and copying.

(vi)(a) Paragraphs (o)(3)(xiv) through (xxi) and (o)(5) of this section apply to an application for an advance determination in respect of a plan year or years to which section 410 applies to the plan, whether or not such application is received by the district director before the first date on which such section applies to the plan.

(b) For purposes of paragraph (o)(5)(vi)(a) of this section, section 410 shall be considered to apply to a plan year if an election has been made under section 1017(d) of the Employee Retirement Income Security Act of 1974 to have section 410 apply to such plan year, whether or not the election is conditioned upon the issuance by the Commissioner of a favorable determination.

(c) For purposes of paragraph (o)(5)(vi)(a) of this section, in the case of an organization described in section 410(c)(1), section 410 will be considered to apply to a plan year of such organization for any plan year to which section 410(c)(2) applies to such plan.

(vii) The Internal Revenue Service will provide to the applicant a copy of all comments on the application submitted pursuant to paragraph (o)(5)(i) (a), (b) or (c) of this section. In addition, the Internal Revenue Service will provide to the applicant a copy of all correspondence in respect of a comment between the Internal Revenue Service and a person submitting the comment.

(6) *Reference of matters to the Appeals office.*— (i) Where issues arise in a district director's office on matters within the contemplation of paragraph (o)(2)(i) of this section, and the key district director issues a notice of proposed determination which is adverse to the applicant, the applicant may appeal the proposed determination to the Appeals office. However, the applicant may not appeal a determination that is based on a National Office technical advice. See § 601.106(a)(1)(iv)(a) and paragraph (o)(2)(iii) of this section. The applicant shall notify the key district director that it intends to request Appeals office consideration by submitting the request, in writing, to the key district director within 30 days from issuance of the notice of proposed determination. The key district director will forward the request and the administrative record to the Appeals office and will so notify the applicant in writing. A failure by the applicant to request Appeals office consideration will constitute a failure to exhaust available administrative remedies as required by section 7476(b)(3) and will thus preclude the applicant from seeking a declaratory judgment as provided under section 7476. (See paragraph (o)(10)(i)(c) of this section.)

(ii) The request for Appeals office consideration must show the following:

(a) Date of application for determination letter;

(b) Name and address of the applicant and the name and address of the representative, if any, who has been authorized to represent the applicant as provided in paragraph (c)(6) of this section;

(c) The key district office in which the case is pending;

(d) Type of plan (pension, annuity, profit-sharing, stock bonus, bond purchase, and foreign situs trusts), and type of action involved (initial qualification, amendment, curtailment, or termination);

(e) Date of filing this request with the key district director and the date and symbols of the letter referred to in paragraph (o)(6)(i) of this section;

(f) A complete statement of the issues and a presentation of the arguments in support of the applicant's position; and

(g) Whether a conference is desired.

(iii) After receipt of the administrative record in the Appeals office, the applicant will be afforded the opportunity for a conference, if a conference was requested. After full consideration of the entire administrative record, the Appeals office will notify the applicant in writing of the proposed decision and the reasons therefor and will issue a notice of final determination in accordance with the decision. However, if the proposed disposition by the Appeals office is contrary to a National Office technical advice concerning qualification, issued prior to the case, the proposed disposition will be submitted to the Assistant Commissioner (Employee Plans and Exempt Organizations) and the decision of that official will be followed by the Appeals office. See § 601.106(a)(1)(iv)(b). Additionally, if the applicant believes that the case involves an issue with respect to which referral for technical advice is appropriate, the applicant may ask the Appeals office to request technical advice from the National Office. The Appeals office shall advise the applicant of its right to request referral of the issue to the National Office for technical advice. The technical advice provisions applicable to these cases are set forth in paragraph (n)(9) of this section. If technical advice is issued, the decision of the National Office will be followed by the Appeals office. See paragraph (n)(9)(viii)(a) of this section.

(iv) Applicants are advised to make full presentation of the facts, circumstances, and arguments at the initial level of consideration, since submission of additional facts, circumstances, and arguments at the Appeals office may result in suspension of Appeals procedures and referral of the case back to the key district for additional consideration.

(7) *Issuance of the notice of final determination.*—The key district director or Appeals office will send notice of the final determination to the applicant. The key district director will send notice of the final determination to the interested parties who have previously submitted comments on the application to the Internal Revenue Service pursuant to paragraph (o)(5)(i)(a) or (c) of this section (or to the persons designated by them to receive such notice), to the Department of Labor in the case of a comment submitted by that department upon the request of interested parties or the Pension Benefit Guaranty Corporation pursuant to paragraph (o)(5)(i)(b) of this section, and to the Pension Benefit Guaranty Corporation if it has filed a comment pursuant to paragraph (o)(5)(i)(a) of this section.

(8) *Administrative record.*—(i) In the case of a request for an advance determination in respect of a retirement plan, the determination of the district director or Appeals office on the qualification or nonqualification of the retirement plan shall be based solely on the facts contained in the administrative record. Such administrative record shall consist of the following:

(a) The request for determination, the retirement plan and any related trust instruments, and any written modifications or amendments thereof made by the applicant during the proceedings within the Internal Revenue Service;

(b) All other documents submitted to the Internal Revenue Service by or on behalf of the applicant in respect of the request for determination;

(c) All written correspondence between the Internal Revenue Service and the applicant in respect of the request for determination and any other documents issued to the applicant from the Internal Revenue Service;

(d) All written comments submitted to the Internal Revenue Service pursuant to paragraphs (o)(5)(i)(a), (b), and (c) of this section, and all correspondence in respect of comments submitted between the Internal Revenue Service and persons (including the Pension Benefit Guaranty Corporation and the Department of Labor) submitting comments pursuant to paragraphs (o)(5)(i)(a), (b), and (c) of this section;

(e) In any case in which the Internal Revenue Service makes an investigation regarding the facts as represented or alleged by the applicant in his request for determination or in comments submitted pursuant to paragraphs (o)(5)(i)(a), (b), and (c) of this section, a copy of the official report of such investigation;

(ii) The administrative record shall be closed upon the earlier of the following events:

(a) The date of mailing of a notice of final determination by the Internal Revenue Service in respect of the application for determination; or

(b) The filing of a petition with the United States Tax Court seeking a declaratory judgment in respect of the retirement plan.

Any oral representation or modification of the facts as represented or alleged in the application for determination or in a comment filed by an interested party, which is not reduced to writing and submitted to the Service shall not become a part of the administrative record and shall not be taken into account in the determination of the qualified status of the retirement plan by the district director or Appeals office.

(9) *Notice of final determination.*—For purposes of this paragraph (o), the notice of final determination shall be—

(i) In the case of a final determination which is favorable to the applicant, the letter issued by the key district director or Appeals office (whether or not by certified or registered mail) which states that the applicant's plan satisfies the qualification requirements of the Internal Revenue Code.

(ii) In the case of a final determination which is adverse to the applicant, the letter issued by certified or registered mail by the key district director or Appeals office, subsequent to a letter of proposed determination, stating that the applicant's plan fails to satisfy the qualification requirements of the Internal Revenue Code.

(10) *Exhaustion of administrative remedies.*— For purposes of section 7476(b)(3), a petitioner shall be deemed to have exhausted the administrative remedies available to him in the Internal Revenue Service upon the completion of the steps described in paragraph (o)(10)(i), (ii), or (iii) of this section, subject, however, to paragraphs (o)(10)(iv) and (v) of this section. If an applicant, interested party, or the Pension Benefit Guaranty Corporation does not complete the applicable steps described below, such applicant, interested party, or the Pension Benefit Guaranty Corporation will not have exhausted available administrative remedies as required by section 7476(b)(3) and will thus be precluded from seeking a declaratory judgment under section 7476 except to the extent that paragraph (o)(10)(iv)(b) or (v) of this section applies.

(i) The administrative remedies of an applicant with respect to any matter relating to the qualification of a plan are:

(a) Filing a completed application with the appropriate district director pursuant to paragraphs (o)(3)(iii) through (xii) of this section;

(b) Compliance with the requirements pertaining to notice to interested parties as set forth in paragraphs (o)(3)(xiv) through (o)(3)(xxi) of this section; and

(c) An appeal to the Appeals office pursuant to paragraph (o)(6) of this section, in the event of a notice of proposed adverse determination from the district director.

(ii) The administrative remedy of an interested party with respect to any matter relating to the qualification of the plan is submission to the district director of a comment raising such matter in accordance with paragraph (o)(5)(i)(a) of this section or requesting the Department of Labor to submit to the district director a comment with respect to such matter in accordance with paragraph (o)(5)(i)(b) of this section, and, if such department declines to comment, submission of such a comment in accordance with paragraph (o)(5)(i)(c) of this section, so that such comment may be considered by the Internal Revenue Service through the administrative process.

(iii) The administrative remedy of the Pension Benefit Guaranty Corporation with respect to any matter relating to the qualification of the plan is submission to the district director of a comment raising such matter in accordance with paragraph (o)(5)(i)(a) of this section or requesting the Department of Labor to submit to the district director a comment with respect to such matter in accordance with paragraph (o)(5)(i)(b) of this section, and, if such department declines to comment, submission of such a comment to the Internal Revenue Service directly, so that such comment may be considered by the Internal Revenue Service through the administrative process.

(iv) An applicant, or an interested party, or the Pension Benefit Guaranty Corporation shall in no event be deemed to have exhausted his (its) administrative remedies prior to the earlier of:

(a) The completion of all the steps described in paragraph (o)(11)(i), (ii), or (iii) of this section, whichever is applicable, subject, however, to paragraph (o)(11)(v), or

(b) The expiration of the 270 day period described in section 7476(b)(3), in a case where the completion of the steps referred to in paragraph (o)(10)(iv)(a) of this section shall not have occurred before the expiration of such 270 day period because of the failure of the Internal Revenue Service to proceed with due diligence.

The step described in paragraph (o)(10)(i)(c) of this section will not be considered completed until the Internal Revenue Service has had a reasonable time to act upon the appeal. In addition, the administrative remedies described in paragraphs (o)(10)(ii) and (iii) will not be considered completed until the Internal Revenue Service has had a reasonable time to consider the comments submitted pursuant to such paragraphs at each step of the Administrative process described in paragraph (o)(10)(i).

(v) The administrative remedy described in paragraph (o)(10)(i)(c) of this section will not be available to an applicant with respect to any issue on which technical advice from the National Office has been obtained.

(p) *Pension plans of self-employed individuals.*— (1) *Rulings, determination letters, and opinion letters.*—(i) The National Office of the Service, upon request, will furnish a written opinion as to the acceptability (for the purpose of sections 401 and 501(a) of the Code) of the form of any master or prototype plan designed to include groups of self-employed individuals who may adopt the plan, where the plan is submitted by a sponsor that is a trade or professional association, bank, insurance company, or regulated investment company as defined in section 851 of the Code. Each opinion letter will bear an identifying plan serial number. If the trustee or custodian has been designated at the time of approval of a plan as to form, a ruling will be issued as to the exempt status of such trust or custodial account which forms part of the master or prototype plan. As used here, the term "master plan" refers to a standardized form of plan, with a related trust or custodial agreement, where indicated, administered by the sponsoring organization for the purpose of providing plan benefits on a standardized basis. The term "prototype plan" refers to a standardized form of plan, with or without a related form of trust or custodial agreement, that is made available by the sponsoring organization, for use without change by employers who wish to adopt such a plan, and which will not be administered by the sponsoring organization that makes such form available. The degree of relationship among the separate employers adopting either a master plan or a prototype plan or to the sponsoring organization is immaterial.

(ii) Since a determination as to the qualification of a particular employer's plan can be made only with regard to facts peculiar to that employer, a letter expressing the opinion of the Service as to the acceptability of the form of a master or prototype plan will not constitute a ruling or determination as to the qualification of a plan as adopted by any individual employer or as to the exempt status of a related trust or custodial account. However, where an employer adopts a master or prototype plan and any related prototype trust or custodial account previously approved as to form, and observes the provisions thereof, such plan and trust or custodial account will be deemed to satisfy the requirements of sections 401 and 501(a) of the Code, provided the eligibility requirements and contributions on benefits under the plan for owner-employees are not more favorable than for other employees, including those required to be covered under plans of all businesses controlled by such owner-employees.

(iii) Although district directors no longer make advance determinations on plans of self-employed individuals who have adopted previously approved master or prototype plans, they will continue, upon request, to issue determination letters as to the qualification of individually designed plans (those not utilizing a master or prototype plan) and the exempt status of a related trust or custodial account, if any, in accordance with the procedures set forth in paragraph (o) of this section.

(2) *Determination letters as to qualified bond purchase plans.*—A determination as to the qualification of a bond purchase plan will, upon request, be made by the appropriate district director. Form 4578, Application for Approval of Bond Purchase Plan, must be used for this purpose. When properly completed, this form will constitute a bond purchase plan.

(3) *Instructions to sponsoring organizations and employers.*—(i) A sponsoring organization of the type referred to in subparagraph (1)(i) of this paragraph, that desires a written opinion as to the acceptability of the form of a master or prototype plan (or as to the exempt status of a related trust or custodial account) should submit its request to the National Office. Copies of all documents, including the plan and trust instruments and all amendments thereto, together with specimen insurance contracts (where applicable) must be submitted with the request. The request must be submitted to the Commissioner of Internal Revenue Service, Washington, D.C. 20224, Attn: T:MS:PT. Form 3672, Application for Approval of Master or Prototype Plan for Self-Employed Individuals, is to be used for this purpose.

(ii) If, subsequent to obtaining approval of the form of a master or prototype plan, an amendment is to be made, the procedure will depend on whether the sponsor is authorized to act on behalf of the subscribers.

(a) If the plan provides that each employer has delegated to the sponsor the power to amend the plan and that each employer shall be deemed to have consented thereto, the plan may be amended by the sponsor. If the plan contains no specific provision permitting the sponsor to amend such plan, but all employers consent in writing to permit such amendment, the sponsor may then amend the plan. However, where a sponsor is unable to secure the consent of each employer, the plan cannot be amended by the sponsor. In such cases, any change will have to be effected by the adoption of a new plan and the submission of a new Form 3672. The new plan will be complete and separate from the old plan and individual employers may, if they desire, substitute the new plan for the old plan.

(b) In the first two instances mentioned above, where the plan has been properly amended, the sponsor must submit Form 3672, a copy of the amendment and, if required, copies of the signed consent of each participating employer.

(c) Upon approval of the amendment by the Service, an opinion letter will be issued to the sponsor containing the serial number of the original plan followed by a suffix: "A-1" for the first amendment, "A-2" for the second amendment, etc. Employers adopting the form of plan subsequent to the date of the amendment will use the revised serial number.

(d) If a new plan is submitted, together with form 3672 and copies of all documents evidencing the plan, an opinion letter bearing a new serial number will be issued to the sponsor and all employers who adopt the new plan shall use the new serial number. Employers who adopted the old plan will continue to use the original serial number.

(4) *Applicability.*—The general procedures of paragraphs (a) through (m) and paragraph (o) of this section, relating to the issuance of rulings and determination letters, are applicable to requests relating to the qualification of plans covering self-employed individuals under sections 401 and 405(a) of the Code and the exempt status of related trusts or custodial accounts under section 501(a), to the extent that the matter is not covered by the specific procedures and instructions contained in this paragraph.

(q) *Corporate master and prototype plans.*—(1) *Scope and definitions.*—(i) The general procedures set forth in this paragraph pertain to the issuance of rulings, determination letters, and opinion letters relating to master and prototype pension, annuity, and profit-sharing plans (except those covering self-employed individuals) under section 401(a) of the Code, and the status for exemption of related trusts or custodial accounts under section 501(a). (A custodial account described in section 401(f) of the Code is treated as a qualified trust for purposes of the Code.) These procedures are subject to the general procedures set forth in paragraph (o) of this section, and relate only to master plans and prototype plans that do not include self-employed individuals and are sponsored by trade or professional associations, banks, insurance companies, or regulated investment companies. These plans are further identified as "variable form" and "standardized form" plans.

(ii) A "master plan" is a form of plan in which the funding organization (trust, custodial account, or insurer) is specified in the sponsor's application, and a "prototype plan" is a form of plan in which the funding organization is specified in the adopting employer's application.

(iii) A "variable form" plan is either a master or prototype plan that permits an employer to select various options relating to such basic provisions as employee coverage, contributions, benefits, and vesting. These options must be set forth in the body of the plan or in a separate document. Such plan, however, is not complete until all provisions necessary for qualification under section 401(a) of the Code are appropriately included.

(iv) A "standardized form" plan is either a master or prototype plan that meets the requirements of subparagraph (2) of this paragraph.

(2) *Standardized form plan requirements.*—A standardized form plan must be complete in all respects (except for choices permissible under subdivisions (i) and (iv) of this subparagraph) and contain among other things provisions as to the following requirements:

(i) *Coverage.*—The percentage coverage requirements set forth in section 401(a)(3)(A) of the Code must be satisfied. Provisions may be made, however, for an adopting employer to designate such eligibility requirements as are permitted under that section.

(ii) *Nonforfeitable rights.*—Each employee's rights to or derived from the contributions under the plan must be nonforfeitable at the time the contributions are paid to or under the plan, except to the extent that the limitations set forth in § 1.401-4(c) of the Income Tax Regulations, regarding early termination of a plan, may be applicable.

(iii) *Bank trustee.*—In the case of a trusteed plan, the trustee must be a bank.

(iv) *Definite contribution formula.*—In the case of a profit-sharing plan, there must be a definite formula for determining the employer contributions to be made. Provision may be made, however, for an adopting employer to specify his rate of contribution.

(3) *Rulings, determination letters, and opinion letters.*—(i) A favorable determination letter as to the qualification of a pension or profit-sharing plan and the exempt status of any related trust or custodial account, is not required as a condition for obtaining the tax benefits pertaining thereto. However, paragraph (c)(5) of this section authorizes district directors to issue determination letters as to the qualification of plans and the exempt status of related trusts or custodial accounts.

(ii) In addition, the National Office upon request from a sponsoring organization will furnish a written opinion as to the acceptability of the form of a master or prototype plan and any related trust or custodial account, under sections 401(a) and 501(a) of the Code. Each opinion letter will bear an identifying plan serial number. However, opinion letters will not be issued under this paragraph as to (a) plans of a parent company and its subsidiaries, (b) pooled fund arrangements contemplated by Revenue Ruling 56-267, C.B. 1956-1, 206, (c) industry-wide or area-wide union negotiated plans, (d) plans that include self-employed individuals, (e) stock bonus plans, and (f) bond purchase plans.

(iii) A ruling as to the exempt status of a trust or custodial account under section 501(a) of the Code will be issued to the trustee or custodian by the National Office where such trust or custodial account forms part of a plan described in subparagraph (1) of this paragraph and the trustee or custodian is specified on Form 4461, Sponsor Application—Approval of Master or Prototype Plan. Where not so specified, a determination letter as to the exempt status of a trust or custodial account will be issued by the district director for the district in which is located the principal place of business of an employer who adopts such trust or custodial account after he furnishes the name of the trustee or custodian.

(iv) Since a determination as to the qualification of a particular employer's plan can be made only with regard to facts peculiar to such employer, a letter expressing the opinion of the Service as to the acceptability of the form of a master or prototype plan will not constitute a ruling or determination as to the qualification of a plan as adopted by any individual employer nor as to the exempt status of a related trust or custodial account.

(v) A determination as to the qualification of a plan as it relates to a particular employer will be made by the district director for the district in which each employer's principal place of business is located, if the employer has adopted a master or prototype plan that has been previously approved as to form. An employer who desires such a determination must file Form 4462, Employer Application—Determination as to Qualification of Pension, Annuity, or Profit-Sharing Plan and Trust, and furnish a copy of the adoption agreement or other evidence of adoption of the plan and such additional information as the district director may require.

(vi) Where master or prototype plans involve integration with Social Security benefits, it is impossible to determine in advance whether in an individual case a particular restrictive definition of the compensation (such as basic compensation) on which contributions or benefits are based would result in discrimination in contributions or benefits in favor of employees who are officers, shareholders, persons whose principal duties consist in supervising the work of other employees, or highly compensated employees. See Revenue Ruling 69-503 C.B. 1969-2, 94. Accordingly, opinion letters relating to master or prototype plans that involve integration with Social Security benefits will not be issued except for those plans where annual compensation, for the purposes of §§ 3.01, 5.02, 6.02, 6.03, 13.01, 13.02, and 14.02 of Revenue Ruling 69-4, C.B. 1969-1, 118, is defined to be all of each employee's compensation that would be subject to tax under section 3101(a) of the Code without the dollar limitation of section 3121(a)(1) of the Code.

(4) *Request by sponsoring organizations and employers.*—(i) The National Office will consider the request of a sponsoring organization desiring a written opinion as to the acceptability of the form of a master or prototype plan and any related trust or custodial account. Such request is to be made on Form 4461 and filed with the Commissioner of Internal Revenue, Washington, D.C. 20224, attention T:MS:PT. Copies of all documents, including the plan and trust or custodial agreement, together with specimen insurance contracts, if applicable, are to be submitted with the request. In making its determination, the National Office may require additional information as appropriate.

(ii) Each district director, in whose jurisdiction there are employers who adopt the form of plan, must be furnished a copy of the previously approved form of plan and related documents by the sponsoring organization. The sponsoring organization must also furnish such district director a copy of all amendments subsequently approved as to form by the National Office.

(iii) The sponsoring organization must furnish copies of opinion letters as to the acceptability of the form of plan, including amendments (see subparagraph (5) of this paragraph), to all adopting employers.

(5) *Amendments.*—(i) Subsequent to obtaining approval of the form of a master or prototype plan, a sponsoring organization may wish to amend the plan. Whether a sponsoring organization may effect an amendment depends on the plan's administrative provisions.

(ii) If the plan provides that each subscribing employer has delegated authority to the sponsor to amend the plan and that each such employer shall be deemed to have consented thereto, the plan may be amended by the sponsor acting on behalf of the subscribers. If the plan does not contain such provision but all subscribing employers consent in a collateral document to permit amendment, the sponsor, acting on their behalf, may amend the plan. However, where a sponsor is unable to secure the consent of each such employer, the plan cannot be amended. In such cases any change can only be effected by the establishment of a new plan and the submission of a new Form 4461 by the sponsor. The new plan must be complete and separate from the old plan, and individual employers may, if they desire, substitute the new plan for the old plan.

(iii) Where the plan has been amended pursuant to subdivision (ii) of this subparagraph, the sponsor is to submit an application, Form 4461, a copy of the amendment, a description of the changes, and a statement indicating the provisions in the original plan authorizing amendments, or a statement that each participating employer's consent has been obtained.

(iv) Upon approval of the amendment by the National Office, an opinion letter will be issued to the sponsor containing the serial number of the original plan, followed by a suffix: "A-1" for the first amendment, "A-2" for the second amendment, etc. Employers adopting the form of plan subsequent to the date of the amendment must use the revised serial number.

(v) If a new plan is submitted, together with Form 4461 and copies of all documents evidencing the plan, an opinion letter bearing a new serial number will be issued to the sponsor, and all employers who adopt the new plan are to use the new serial number. Employers who adopted the old plan continue to use the original serial number. However, any employer who wishes to change to the new plan may do so by filing with his district director a new Form 4462, indicating the change.

(vi) An employer who amends his adoption agreement may request a determination letter as to the effect of such amendment by filing Form 4462 with his district director, together with a copy of the amendment and a summary of the changes. However, in the event an employer desires to amend his adoption agreement under a master or prototype plan, and such amendment is not contemplated or permitted under the plan, then such amendment will in effect substitute an individually designed plan for the master or prototype plan and the amendment procedure described in paragraph (o) of this section will be applicable.

(6) *Effect on other plans.*—Determination letters previously issued by district directors specified in paragraph (o)(2)(viii) of this section are not affected by these procedures even though the plans covered by the determination letters were designed by organizations described in subparagraph (1)(i) of this paragraph. However, such organizations may avail themselves of these procedures with respect to any subsequent action regarding such plans if they otherwise come within the scope of this paragraph.

(r) *Rulings and determination letters with respect to foundation status classification.*—(1) *Rulings and determination letters on private and operating foundation status.*—The procedures relating to the issuance of rulings and determination letters on private foundation status under section 509(a), and operating foundation status under section 4942(j)(3), of organizations exempt from Federal Income Tax under section 501(c)(3) of the Code will be published from time to time in the Internal Revenue Bulletin (see for example, Rev. Proc. 76-34, 1976-2 C.B. 656, as modified by Rev. Proc. 80-25, 1980-1 C.B. 667. These procedures apply in connection with notices filed by the organizations on Form 4653, Notification Concerning Foundation Status, or with applications for recognition of exempt status under section 501(c)(3) of the Code. Such notices and statements are filed by organizations in accordance with section 508(a) of the Code in order for an organization to avoid the presumption of private foundation status or to claim status as an operating foundation. In addition, these procedures also relate to National Office review of determination letters on foundation status under sections 509(a) and 4942(j)(3) of the Code and protest of adverse determination letters regarding foundation status.

(2) *Nonexempt charitable trusts claiming nonprivate foundation status under section 509(a)(3) of the Code.*—A trust described in section 4947(a)(1) of the Code is one that is not exempt from tax under section 501(a) of the Code, has all of its unexpired interests devoted to one or more of the purposes described in section 170(c)(2)(B) of the Code, and is a trust for which a charitable deduction was allowed. These trusts are subject to the private foundation provisions (Part II of subchapter F of chapter 1 and chapter 42 of the Code) except section 508(a), (b), and (c) of the Code. The procedures to be used by nonexempt charitable trusts to obtain determinations of their foundation status under section 509(a)(3) of the Code will be published from time to time in the Internal Revenue Bulletin (see, for example, Rev. Proc. 72-50, 1972-2 C.B. 830).

(s) *Advance rulings or determination letters.*—(1) *General.*—It is the practice of the Service to answer written inquiries, when appropriate and in the interest of sound tax administration, as to the tax effects of acts or transactions of individuals and organizations and as to the status of certain organizations for tax purposes prior to the filing of returns or reports as required by the Revenue laws.

(2) *Exceptions.*—There are, however, certain areas where because of the inherently factual nature of the problems involved or for other reasons, the Service will not issue advance rulings or determination letters. Ordinarily, an advance ruling or determination letter is not issued on any matter where the determination requested is primarily one of fact (e.g., market value of property), or on the tax effect of any transaction to be consummated at some indefinite future time or of any transaction or matter having as a major purpose the reduction of Federal taxes. A specific area or a list of these areas is published from time to time in the Internal Revenue Bulletin (see, for example, Rev. Proc. 80-22, 1980-1 C.B. 654). Such list is not all inclusive. Whenever a particular item is added to or deleted from the list, however, appropriate notice thereof will be published in the Internal Revenue Bulletin. The authority and general procedures of the National Office of the Internal Revenue Service and of the offices of the district directors of internal revenue with respect to the issuance of advance rulings and determination letters are outlined in paragraphs (b) and (c) of this section.

(t) *Alternative method of depletion.*—(1) *In general.*—Section 1.613-4(d)(1)(i) of the regulations, adopted by T.D. 7170, March 10, 1972, provides that, in those cases where it is impossible to determine a representative market or field price under the provisions of § 1.613-4(c), gross income from mining shall be computed by use of the proportionate profits method set forth in § 1.613-4(d)(4).

(2) *Exception.*—An exception is provided in § 1.613-4(d)(1)(ii) where, upon application, the Office of the Assistant Commissioner (Technical) approves the use of an alternative method that is more appropriate than the proportionate profits method or the alternative method being used by the taxpayer.

(3) *Procedure.*—The procedure for making application for approval to compute gross income from mining by use of an alternative method, other than the proportionate profits method; the conditions for approval and use of an alternative method; changes in an approved method; and other pertinent information with respect thereto, will be published from time to time in the Cumulative Bulletin (see, for example, Rev. Proc. 74-43, 1974-2 C.B. 496).

(u) *Conditions for issuing rulings involving bonuses and advanced royalties of lessors under § 631(c) of IRC of 1954.*—(1) *In general.*—Rev. Proc. 77-11, 1977-1 C.B. 568, provides that the tax liability of a lessor who received a bonus or an advance royalty is required to be recomputed for the taxable year or years in which such payment or payments were received if the right to mine coal or iron ore under the lease expires, terminates, or is abandoned before (with respect to bonuses) any coal or iron ore has been mined; or (with respect to advance royalties) the coal or iron ore that has been paid for in advance is mined. In such recomputation, the lessor is required to treat the bonus payment or payments or any portion of the advance royalty payment or payments attributable to unmined coal or iron ore, as ordinary income and not as received from the sale of coal or iron ore under section 631(c) of the Code.

(2) *Condition for issuing rulings.*—Prior to issuing a ruling to lessors who request a ruling that they may treat bonuses or advance royalties received under a lease for coal or iron ore as received from a.sale of coal or iron under section 631(c) of the Code, the Internal Revenue Service will require that the lessor enter a closing agreement in which the lessor agrees that—

(i) If the lease under which the lessor received a bonus or an advance royalty expires, terminates, or is abandoned before (with respect to a bonus) any coal or iron ore has been mined or (with respect to an advance royalty) the coal or iron ore that has been paid for in advance is mined, the tax liability of the lessor will be recomputed for the taxable year or years of receipt of (A) the bonus by treating the bonus payment or payments as ordinary income or (B) the advance royalty by treating any portion of the advance royalty payment or payments attributable to unmined coal or iron ore as ordinary income;

(ii) If the recomputation described in paragraph (u)(2)(i) of this section is required, the lessor will pay the additional amount, if any, of all federal income tax finally determined as due and payable by the lessor for the taxable year or years of the receipt of the bonus or advance royalty; and

(iii) If any of the described events has occurred, the lessor will notify the appropriate district director of such event in writing within 90 days of the close of the taxable year in which the lease expires, terminates, or is abandoned. [Reg. § 601.201.]

☐ [32 FR 15990, Nov. 22, 1967, as amended at 33 FR 6821, May 4, 1968; 33 FR 17236, Nov. 21, 1968; 34 FR 6425, Apr. 12, 1969; 34 FR 14601, Sept. 19, 1969; 35 FR 7114, May 6, 1970; 35 FR 15918, Oct. 9, 1970; 36 FR 7585, Apr. 22, 1971; 38 FR 4960, Feb. 23, 1973; 38 FR 33301, Dec. 3, 1973; 39 FR 8917, Mar. 7, 1974; 40 FR 32323, Aug. 1, 1975; 41 FR 20881, 20884, May 21, 1976; 41 FR 48741, Nov. 5, 1976; 42 FR 34280, July 5, 1977; 42 FR 46519, Sept. 16, 1977; 42 FR 48336, Sept. 23, 1977; 43 FR 17817, Apr. 26, 1978; 43 FR 44504, Sept. 28, 1978; 45 FR 7255, Feb. 1, 1980; 46 FR 26053, May 11, 1981; 48 FR 15624, Apr. 12, 1983; T.D. 8685, 61 FR 58008, Nov. 12, 1996; T.D. 9006, July 18, 2002.]

[Reg. §601.202]

§601.202. Closing   agreements.—
(a) *General.*—(1) Under section 7121 of the Code and the regulations and delegations thereunder, the Commissioner, or any officer or employee of the Internal Revenue Service authorized in writing by the Commissioner, may enter into and approve a written agreement with a person relating to the liability of such person (or of the person or estate for whom he acts) in respect of any internal revenue tax for any taxable period. Such agreement, except upon a showing of fraud or malfeasance, or misrepresentation of a material fact, shall be final and conclusive.

(2) Closing agreements under section 7121 of the Code may relate to any taxable period ending prior or subsequent to the date of the agreement. With respect to taxable periods ended prior to the date of the agreement, the matter agreed upon may relate to the total tax liability of the taxpayer or it may relate to one or more separate items affecting the tax liability of the taxpayer. A closing agreement may also be entered into in order to provide a "determination", as defined in section 1313 of the Code, and for the purpose of allowing a deficiency dividend deduction under section 547 of the Code. But see also sections 547(c)(3) and 1313(a)(4) of the Code and the regulations thereunder as to other types of "determination" agreements. With respect to taxable periods ending subsequent to the date of the agreement, the matter agreed upon may relate to one or more separate items affecting the tax liability of the taxpayer. A closing agreement with respect to any taxable period ending subsequent to the date of the agreement is subject to any change in or modification of the law enacted subsequent to the date of the agreement and applicable to such taxable period, and each such closing agreement shall so recite. Closing agreements may be entered into even though under the agreement the taxpayer is not liable for any tax for the period to which the agreement relates. There may be a series of agreements relating to the tax liability for a single period. A closing agreement may be entered into in any case in which there appears to be an advantage in having the case permanently and conclusively closed, or where good and sufficient reasons are shown by the taxpayer for desiring a closing agreement and it is determined by the Commissioner or his representatives that the Govern-ment will sustain no disadvantage through consummation of such an agreement.

(b) *Use of prescribed forms.*—In cases in which it is proposed to close conclusively the total tax liability for a taxable period ending prior to the date of the agreement, Form 866, Agreement as to Final Determination of Tax Liability, generally will be used. In cases in which agreement has been reached as to the disposition of one or more issues and a closing agreement is considered necessary to insure consistent treatment of such issues in any other taxable period Form 906, Closing Agreement as to Final Determination Covering Specific Matters, generally will be used. A request for a closing agreement which determines tax liability may be submitted and entered into at any time before the determination of such liability becomes a matter within the province of a court of competent jurisdiction and may thereafter be entered into in appropriate circumstances when authorized by the court (e.g., in certain bankruptcy situations). The request should be submitted to the district director of internal revenue with whom the return for the period involved was filed. However, if the matter to which the request relates is pending before an office of the Appellate Division, the request should be submitted to that office. A request for a closing agreement which relates only to a subsequent period should be submitted to the Commissioner of Internal Revenue, Washington, D.C. 20224.

(c) *Approval.*—(1) Closing agreements relating to alcohol, tobacco, and firearms taxes in respect of any prospective transactions or completed transactions affecting returns to be filed may be entered into and approved by the Director, Bureau of Alcohol, Tobacco and Firearms.

(2) Closing agreements relating to taxes other than those taxes covered in subparagraph (1) of this paragraph in respect of any prospective transactions or completed transactions affecting returns to be filed may be entered into and approved by the Assistant Commissioner (Technical).

(3) Closing agreements for a taxable period or periods ended prior to the date of agreement and related specific items affecting other taxable periods (including those covering competent authority determinations in the administration of the operating provisions of the tax conventions of the United States) may be entered into and approved by the Assistant Commissioner (Compliance).

(4) Regional commissioners, assistant regional commissioners (appellate), assistant regional commissioners (examination), district directors (including the Director, Foreign Operations District), chiefs and assistant chiefs of appellate branch offices may enter into and approve closing agreements on cases under their jurisdiction (but excluding cases docketed before the U.S. Tax Court) for a taxable period or periods which end prior to the date of agreement and related specific items affecting other taxable periods.

(5) Regional commissioners, assistant regional commissioners (examination) and (appel-

late), chiefs and assistant chiefs of appellate branch offices are authorized to enter into and approve closing agreements in cases under their jurisdiction docketed in the U.S. Tax Court but only in respect to related specific items affecting other taxable periods.

(6) Closing agreements providing for the mitigation of economic double taxation under section 3 of Revenue Procedure 64-54, C.B. 1964-2, 1008, or under Revenue Procedure 69-13, C.B. 1969-1, 402 or for such mitigation and relief under Revenue Procedure 65-17, C.B. 1965-1, 833, may be entered into and approved by the Director, Foreign Operations District.

(7) Closing agreements in cases under the jurisdiction of a district director providing that the taxability of earnings from a deposit or account of the type described in Revenue Procedure 64-24, C.B. 1964-1 (Part 1), 693, opened prior to November 15, 1962, will be determined on the basis that earnings on such deposits or accounts are not includible in gross income until maturity or termination, whichever occurs earlier, and that the full amount of earnings on the deposit or account will constitute gross income in the year the plan matures, is assigned, or is terminated, whichever occurs first, may be entered into and approved by such district director.

(d) *Applicability of ruling requirements.*—The requirements relating to requests for rulings (see § 601.201) shall be applicable with respect to requests for closing agreements pertaining to prospective transactions or completed transactions affecting returns to be filed (see paragraph (c)(2) of this section). [Reg. § 601.202.]

☐ [32 FR 15990, Nov. 22, 1967, as amended at 32 FR 20647, Dec. 21, 1967; 33 FR 17237, Nov. 21, 1968; 34 FR 14601, Sept. 19, 1969; 35 FR 15920, Oct. 9, 1970; 38 FR 4967, Feb. 23, 1973; 42 FR 46520, Sept. 16, 1977; 43 FR 53030, Nov. 15, 1978; 49 FR 36499, Sept. 18, 1984; T.D. 8685, 61 FR 58008, Nov. 12, 1996.]

[Reg. § 601.203]

§ 601.203. Offers in compromise.— (a) *General.*—(1) The Commissioner may compromise, in accordance with the provisions of section 7122 of the Code, any civil or criminal case arising under the internal revenue laws prior to reference to the Department of Justice for prosecution or defense. Certain functions of the Commissioner with respect to compromise of civil cases involving liability of $100,000 or more, based solely on doubt as to liability, have been delegated to regional commissioners and, for cases arising in the District Office, Foreign Operations District, to the Assistant Commissioner (Compliance). The authority concerning liability of $100,000 or more based on doubt as to collectibility or doubt as to both collectibility and liability has been delegated to the Director, Collection Division, and regional commissioners. The authority with respect to compromise of civil cases involving liability under $100,000, and of certain specific penalties has been delegated to

district directors, assistant district directors, and (including the District Director and Assistant District Director, Foreign Operations District), regional directors of Appeals, and chiefs and associate chiefs, Appeals offices. The authority concerning offers in compromise of penalties based solely on doubt as to liability, if the liability is less than $100,000, has also been delegated to service center directors and assistant service center directors. In civil cases involving liability of $500 or over and in criminal cases the functions of the General Counsel are performed by the Chief Counsel for the Internal Revenue Service. These functions are performed in the District Counsel, Regional Counsel, or National Office as appropriate. (See also paragraph (c) of this section.) In cases arising under chapters 51, 52, and 53 of the Code, offers are acted upon by the Bureau of Alcohol, Tobacco and Firearms.

(2) An offer in compromise of taxes, interest, delinquency penalties, or specific penalties may be based on either inability to pay or doubt as to liability. Offers in compromise arise usually when payments of assessed liabilities are demanded, penalties for delinquency in filing returns are asserted, or specific civil or criminal penalties are incurred by taxpayers. A criminal liability will not be compromised unless it involves only the regulatory provisions of the Internal Revenue Code and related statutes. However, if the violations involving the regulatory provisions are deliberate and with intent to defraud, the criminal liabilities will not be compromised.

(b) *Use of prescribed form.*—Offers in compromise are required to be submitted on Form 656, properly executed, and accompanied by a financial statement on Form 433 (if based on inability to pay). Form 656 is used in all cases regardless of whether the amount of the offer is tendered in full at the time the offer is filed or the amount of the offer is to be paid by deferred payment or payments. Copies of Form 656 and Form 433 may be obtained from district directors. An offer in compromise should be filed with the district director or service center director.

(c) *Consideration of offer.*—(1) An offer in compromise is first considered by the director having jurisdiction. Except in certain penalty cases, an investigation of the basis of the offer is required. The examining officer makes a written recommendation for acceptance or rejection of the offer. If the director has jurisdiction over the processing of the offer he or she will:

(i) Reject the offer, or

(ii) Accept the offer if it involves a civil liability under $500, or

(iii) Accept the offer if it involves a civil liability of $500 or more, but less than $100,000, or involves a specific penalty, and the District Counsel concurs in the acceptance of the offer, or

(iv) Recommend to the National Office the acceptance of the offer if it involves a civil liability of $100,000 or over.

(2)(i) If the district director does not have jurisdiction over the entire processing of the offer, the offer is transmitted to the appropriate District Counsel if the case is one in which:

(a) Recommendations for prosecution are pending in the Office of the Chief Counsel, the Department of Justice, or in an office of a United States attorney, including cases in which criminal proceedings have been instituted but not disposed of and related cases in which offers in compromise have been submitted or are pending;

(b) The taxpayer is in receivership or is involved in a proceeding under any provision of the Bankruptcy Act;

(c) The taxpayer is deceased; in joint liability cases, where either taxpayer is deceased;

(d) A proposal is made to discharge property from the effect of a tax lien or to subordinate the lien or liens;

(e) An insolvent bank is involved;

(f) An assignment for the benefit of creditors is involved;

(g) A liquidation proceeding is involved; or

(h) Court proceedings are pending, except Tax Court cases.

(ii) The District Counsel considers and processes offers submitted in cases described in paragraph (c)(2)(i)(a) through (h) of this section and forwards those offers to the district director, service center director, Regional Counsel, or Office of Chief Counsel in Washington, as appropriate.

(iii) In those cases described in (a) of subdivision (i) of this subparagraph no investigation will be made unless specifically requested by the office having jurisdiction of the criminal case.

(iv) In those cases described in (b) through (h) of subdivision (i) of this subparagraph the district director retains the duplicate copy of the offer and the financial statement for investigation. After investigation, the district director transmits to the appropriate District Counsel for consideration and processing his or her recommendation for acceptance or rejection of the offer together with the examining officer's report of the investigation.

(3) The district directors, assistant district directors (including the District Director and Assistant District Director, Foreign Operations District), service center directors, assistant service center directors, Regional Directors of appeals, and Chiefs and Associate Chiefs, Appeals Offices are authorized to reject any offer in compromise referred for their consideration. Unacceptable offers considered by the District Counsel, Regional Counsel, or Office of Chief Counsel in Washington, or the Appeals office are also rejected by the district directors (including the Director, Foreign Operations District) as applicable. If an offer is not acceptable, the taxpayer is promptly notified of the rejection of that offer. If an offer is rejected, the sum submitted with the offer is returned to the proponent, unless the taxpayer authorizes application of the sum offered to the tax liability. Each Regional Commissioner will perform a post review of offers accepted, rejected, or withdrawn by the district director's office if the offer covers liabilities of $5,000 or more. The post review will cover a sampling of cases processed by the Collection function and all cases processed by the Examination function.

(4) If an offer involving unpaid liability of $100,000 or more is considered acceptable by the office having jurisdiction over the offer, a recommendation for acceptance is forwarded to the National Office or Regional Office, as appropriate, for review. If the recommendation for acceptance is approved, the offer is forwarded to the Regional Counsel or Office of Chief Counsel in Washington, as appropriate, for approval. After approval by the Regional Counsel or Office of Chief Counsel in Washington, as appropriate, it is forwarded to the Assistant Commissioner (Compliance), Director, Collection Division, or Regional Commissioner, as appropriate, for acceptance. The taxpayer is notified of the acceptance of the offer in accordance with its terms. Acceptance of an offer in compromise of civil liabilities does not remit criminal liabilities, nor does acceptance of an offer in compromise of criminal liabilities remit civil liabilities.

(d) *Conferences.*—Before filing a formal offer in compromise, a taxpayer may request a meeting in the office which would have jurisdiction over the offer to explore the possibilities of compromising unpaid tax liability. After all investigations have been made, the taxpayer may also request a meeting in the office having jurisdiction of the offer to determine the amount which may be accepted as a compromise. If agreement is not reached at such meeting and the district director has processing jurisdiction over the offer, the taxpayer will be informed that the taxpayer may request consideration of the case by an Appeals office. The request may be in writing or oral. If the tax, penalty, and assessed (but not accrued) interest sought to be compromised exceeds $2,500 for any return, taxable year or taxable period, a written protest is required. Taxpayers and their representatives are required to comply with the applicable conference and practice requirements. See subpart E of this part. [Reg. § 601.203.]

☐ [32 FR 15990, Nov. 22, 1967, as amended at 33 FR 17238, Nov. 21, 1968; 35 FR 7116, May 6, 1970; 35 FR 15920, Oct. 9, 1970; 43 FR 44510, Sept. 28, 1978; 45 FR 7255, Feb. 1, 1980; 46 FR 26054, May 11, 1981; 49 FR 36499, Sept. 18, 1984; T.D. 8685, 61 FR 58008, Nov. 12, 1996.]

[Reg. § 601.204]

§ 601.204. Changes in accounting periods and in methods of accounting.—(a) *Accounting periods.*—A taxpayer who changes his accounting period shall, before using the new period for income tax purposes, comply with the provisions of the income tax regulations relating to changes in accounting periods. In cases where the regulations require the taxpayer to secure the consent of the Commissioner to the change, the application for permission to change the accounting period shall be made on Form 1128 and shall be submitted to the Commissioner of Internal Revenue, Washington, D.C. 20224, within the period of time prescribed in such regulations. See section 442 of the Code and regulations thereunder. If the change is approved by the Commissioner, the taxpayer shall thereafter make his returns and compute his net income upon the basis of the new accounting period. A request for permission to change the accounting period will be considered by the Corporation Tax Division. However, in certain instances, Form 1128 may be filed with the Director of the Internal Revenue Service Center in which the taxpayer files its return. See, for example, Rev. Proc. 66-13, 1966-1 C.B. 626; Rev. Proc. 66-50, 1966-2 C.B. 1260, and Rev. Proc. 68-41, 1968-2 C.B. 943. With respect to partnership adoption, see § 1.706-1(b) of the Income Tax Regulations.

(b) *Methods of accounting.*—A taxpayer who changes the method of accounting employed in keeping his books shall, before computing his income upon such method for purposes of income taxation, comply with the provisions of the income tax regulations relating to changes in accounting methods. The regulations require that, in the ordinary case, the taxpayer secure the consent of the Commissioner to the change. See section 446 of the Code and the regulations thereunder. Application for permission to change the method of accounting employed shall be made on Form 3115 and shall be submitted to the Commissioner of Internal Revenue, Washington, D.C. 20224, during the taxable year in which it is desired to make the change. Permission to change the method of accounting will not be granted unless the taxpayer and the Commissioner agree to the terms and conditions under which the change will be effected. The request will be considered by the Corporation Tax Division. However, in certain instances, Form 3115 may be filed with the Director of the Internal Revenue Service Center. See, for example, Rev. Proc. 74-11, 1974-1 C.B. 420.

(c) *Verification of changes.*—Written permission to a taxpayer by the National Office consenting to a change in his annual accounting period or to a change in his accounting method is a "ruling." Therefore, in the examination of returns involving changes of annual accounting periods and methods of accounting, district directors must determine whether the representations upon which the permission was granted reflect an accurate statement of the material facts, and whether the agreed terms, conditions, and adjustments have been substantially carried out as proposed. An application, Form 3115, filed with the Director of the Internal Revenue Service Center is also subject to similar verification.

(d) *Instructions to taxpayers.*—The person seeking to secure the consent of the Commissioner with respect to a change of accounting periods or methods pursuant to section 442 or 446(e) of the Code need not submit the statement of proposed deletions described in § 601.201(e)(5) at the time the request is made. If, however, the person seeking the consent of the Commissioner receives from the National Office a notice that proposed deletions should be submitted because the resulting ruling will be open to public inspection under section 6110, the statement of proposed deletions must be submitted within 20 days after such notice is mailed. [Reg. § 601.204.]

☐ [41 FR 20882, May 21, 1976, as amended at 41 FR 48742, Nov. 5, 1976; 42 FR 34280, July 5, 1977; T.D. 8719, May 15, 1997; T.D. 8742, Dec. 30, 1997.]

[Reg. § 601.205]

§ 601.205. Tort claims.—Claims for property loss or damage, personal injury, or death caused by the negligent or wrongful act or omission of any employee of the Service, acting within the scope of his office or employment, filed under the Federal Tort Claims Act, as amended, must be prepared and filed in accordance with Treasury Department regulations entitled "Central Office Procedures" and "Claims Regulations" (31 CFR, Parts 1 and 3). Such regulations contain the procedural and substantive requirements relative to such claims, and set forth the manner in which they are handled. The claims should be filed with the Commissioner of Internal Revenue, Washington, D.C. 20224, and must be filed within two years after the accident or incident occurred. [Reg. § 601.205.]

☐ [32 FR 15990, Nov. 22, 1967.]

[Reg. § 601.206]

§ 601.206. Certification required to obtain reduced foreign tax rates under income tax treaties.—(a) *Basis of certification.*—Most of the income tax treaties between the United States and foreign countries provide for either a reduction in the statutory rate of tax or an exemption from tax on certain types of income received from sources within the foreign treaty country by citizens, domestic corporations, and residents of the United States. Some of the treaty countries reduce the withholding tax on such types of income or exempt the income from withholding tax after the claimant furnishes evidence that he is entitled to the benefits of the treaty. Other countries initially withhold the tax at statutory rates and refund the excess tax withheld after satisfactory evidence of U.S. residence has been accepted. As part of the proof that the applicant is a resident of the United States and thus entitled to the benefits of the treaty, he must usually furnish a certification from the U.S. Government that he has filed a U.S. income tax return as a citizen, domestic corporation, or resident of the U.S.

(b) *Procedure for obtaining the certification.*—Most of the treaty countries which require certification have printed special forms. The forms contain a series of questions to be answered by the taxpayer claiming the benefits of the treaty, followed by a statement which the foreign governments use for the U.S. taxing authority's certification. This certification may be obtained from the office of the district director of the district in which the claimant filed his latest income tax return. Some certification forms are acceptable for Service execution; however, others cannot be executed by the Service without revision. In these instances the office of the district director will prepare its own document of certification in accordance with internal instructions. This procedure has been accepted by most treaty countries as a satisfactory substitute.

(c) *Obtaining the official certification forms.*—The forms may be obtained from the foreign payor, the tax authority of the treaty country involved, or the District Office, Foreign Operations District. [Reg. § 601.206.]

☐ [34 FR 14601, Sept. 19, 1969, as amended at 49 FR 36500, Sept. 18, 1984.]

Subpart C—[Reserved]

Subpart D—Provisions Special to Certain Employment Taxes

[Reg. § 601.401]

§ 601.401. Employment taxes.—(a) *General.*— (1) *Description of taxes.*—Federal employment taxes are imposed by Subtitle C of the Internal Revenue Code. Chapter 21 (Federal Insurance Contributions Act) imposes a tax on employers of one or more individuals and also a tax on employees, with respect to "wages" paid and received. Chapter 22 (Railroad Retirement Tax Act) imposes (i) an employer tax and employee tax with respect to "compensation" paid and received,(ii) an employee representative tax with respect to "compensation" received, and (iii) a supplemental tax on employers, measured by man-hours for which "compensation" is paid. Chapter 23 (Federal Unemployment Tax Act) imposes a tax on employers of one or more individuals with respect to "wages" paid. Chapter 24 (collection of income tax at source on wages) requires every employer making payment of "wages" to deduct and withhold upon such wages the tax computed or determined as provided therein. The tax so deducted and withheld is allowed as a credit against the income tax liability of the employee receiving such wages.

(2) *Applicable regulations.*—The descriptive terms used in this section to designate the various classes of taxes are intended only to indicate their general character. Specific information relative to the scope of each tax, the forms used, and the functioning of the Service with respect thereto is contained in the applicable regulations. Copies of all necessary forms, and instructions as to their preparation and filing, may be obtained from the district director of internal revenue.

(3) *Collection methods.*—Employment taxes are collected by means of returns and by withholding by employers. Employee tax must be deducted and withheld by employers from "wages" or "compensation" (including tips reported in writing to employers) paid to employees, and the employer is liable for the employee tax whether or not it is so deducted. For special rules relating to tips see §§ 31.3102-3 and 31.3402(k)-1. Rev. Proc. 81-48, 1981-2 C.B. 623, provides guidelines for determining wages when the employer pays the employee tax imposed by chapter 21 without deducting the amount from the employee's pay. Employee representatives (as defined in the Railroad Retirement Act) are required to file returns. Employment tax returns must be filed with the district director or, if so provided in instructions

applicable to a return, with the service center designated in the instructions. The return of the Federal unemployment tax is required to be filed annually on Form 940 with respect to wages paid during the calendar year. All other returns of Federal employment taxes (with the exception of returns filed for agricultural employees) are required to be filed for each calendar quarter except that if pursuant to regulations the district director so notifies the employer, returns on Form 941 are required to be filed on a monthly basis. In the case of certain employers required to report withheld income tax but not required to report employer and employee taxes imposed by chapter 21 (for example, state and local government employers), Form 941E is prescribed for reporting on a quarterly basis. The employer and employee taxes imposed by chapter 21 (other than the employer and employee taxes on wages paid for agricultural labor) and the tax required to be deducted and withheld upon wages by chapter 24 are combined in a single return on Form 941. In the case of wages paid by employers for domestic service performed in a private home not on a farm operated for profit, the return of both the employee tax and the employer tax imposed by chapter 21 is on Form 942. However, if the employer is required to file a return for the same quarter on Form 941, the employer may elect to include the taxes with respect to such domestic service on Form 941. The employer and employee taxes imposed by chapter 21 with respect to wages paid for agricultural labor are required to be reported annually on Form 943. Under the Railroad Retirement Tax Act, the return required of the employer is on Form CT-1, and the return required of each employee representative is on Form CT-2. An employee is not required to file a return of employee tax, except that the employee must include in his or her income tax return (as provided in the applicable instructions) any amount of employee tax (i) due with respect to tips that the employee failed to report to the employer or (ii) shown on the employee's Form W-2 as "Uncollected Employee Tax on Tips".

(4) *Receipts for employees.*—Employers are required to furnish each employee a receipt or statement, in duplicate, showing the total wages subject to income tax withholding, the amount of income tax withheld, the amount of wages subject to tax under the Federal Insurance Contributions Act, and the amount of employee tax withheld. See section 6051 of the Code.

(5) *Use of authorized commercial banks and trust companies in connection with payment of Federal employment taxes.*—Most employers are required to deposit employment taxes either on a monthly basis, a semimonthly basis or a quarter-monthly period basis as follows:

(i) *Quarter-monthly period deposits.*—With respect to wages paid after January 31, 1971, (March 31, 1971 in the case of wages paid for agricultural labor), if at the close of any quarter-monthly period (that ends on the 7th, 15th, 22nd, or the last day of any month) the aggregate amount of undeposited taxes, exclusive of taxes reportable on Form 942, is $2,000 or more, the employer shall deposit such taxes within 3 banking days after the close of such quarter-monthly period.

(ii) *Monthly deposits.*—With respect to employers not required to make deposits under subdivision (i) of this subparagraph, if after January 31, 1971 (March 31, 1971, in the case of income tax withheld from wages paid for agricultural labor) (a) during any calendar month, other than the last month of a calendar quarter, the aggregate amount of the employee tax deducted and the employer tax under chapter 21 and the income tax withheld at source on wages under chapter 24, exclusive of taxes reportable on Form 942, exceeds $200, or (b) at the end of any month or period of 2 or more months and prior to December 1 of any calendar year, the total amount of undeposited taxes imposed by chapter 21, with respect to wages paid for agricultural labor, exceeds $200, it is the duty of the employer to deposit such amount within 15 days after the close of such calendar month.

(iii) *Quarterly and year-end deposits.*—Whether or not an employer is required to make deposits under subdivisions (i) and (ii) of this subparagraph, if the amount of such taxes reportable on Form 941 or 943 (reduced by any previous deposits) exceeds $200, the employer shall, on or before the last day of the first calendar month following the period for which the return is required to be filed, deposit such amount with an authorized financial institution. However, if the amount of such taxes (reduced by any previous deposits) does not exceed $200, the employer may either include with his return a direct remittance for the amount of such taxes or, on or before the last day of the first calendar month following the period for which the return is required to be filed, voluntarily deposit such amount with an authorized financial institution.

(iv) *Additional rules.*—Deposits under subdivisions (i), (ii) and (iii) of this subparagraph are made with an authorized financial institution. The remittance of such amount must be accompanied by a Federal Tax Deposit form. Each employer making deposits shall report on the return for the period with respect to which such deposits are made information regarding such deposits in accordance with the instructions applicable to such return and pay therewith (or deposit by the due date of such return) the balance, if any, of the taxes due for such period.

(v) *Employers under chapter 22 of the Code.*—Depository procedures similar to those prescribed in this subparagraph are prescribed for employers as defined by the Railroad Retirement Tax Act, except that railroad retirement taxes are not requested to be deposited semimonthly or quarter-monthly. Such taxes must be deposited by using a Federal Tax Deposit form.

(vi) *Employers under chapter 23 of the Code.*—Every person who is an employer as defined by the Federal Unemployment Tax Act shall deposit the tax imposed under chapter 23 on or before the last day of the first calendar month following the quarterly period in which the amount of such tax exceeds $100.

(6) *Separate accounting.*—If an employer fails to withhold and pay over income, social security, or railroad retirement tax due on wages of employees, the employer may be required by the district director to collect such taxes and deposit them in a separate banking account in trust for the United States not later than the second banking day after such taxes are collected.

(b) *Provisions special to the Federal Insurance Contributions Act.*—(1) *Employers' identification numbers.*—For purposes of the Federal Insurance Contributions Act each employer who files Form 941 or Form 943 must have an identification number. Any such employer who does not have an identification number must secure a Form SS-4 from the district director of internal revenue or from a district office of the Social Security Administration and, after executing the form in accordance with the instructions contained thereon, file it with the district director or the district office of the Social Security Administration. At a subsequent date the district director will assign the employer a number which must appear in the appropriate space on each tax return, Form 941 or Form 943, filed thereafter. The requirement to secure an identification number does not apply to an employer who employs only employees who are engaged exclusively in the performance of domestic service in the employer's private home not on a farm operated for profit.

(2) *Employees' account numbers.*—Each employee (or individual making a return of net earnings from self-employment) who does not have an account number must file an application on Form SS-5), a copy of which may be obtained from any district office of the Social Security Administration or from a district director of internal revenue. The form, after execution in accordance with the instructions thereon, must be filed with the district office of the Social Security Administration, and at a later date the employee will be furnished an account number. The employee must furnish such number to each employer for whom the employee works, in order that such number may be entered on each tax return filed thereafter by the employer.

(3) *Reporting of wages.*—Forms 941, 942, and 943 each require, as a part of the return, that the wages of each employee paid during the period

covered by the return be reported thereon. Form 941a is available to employers who need additional space for the listing of employees. Employers who meet the requirements of the Social Security Administration may, with the approval of the Commissioner of Internal Revenue, submit wage information on reels of magnetic tape in lieu of Form 941a. It is necessary at times that employers correct wage information previously reported. A special form, Form 941c, has been adopted for use in correcting erroneous wage information or omissions of such wage information on Forms 941, 942, or 943. Instructions on Forms 941, 941c, 942, and 943 explain the manner of preparing and filing the forms. Any further instructions should be obtained from the district director.

(c) *Adjustments by employers.*—(1) *Undercollections and underpayments.*—(i) *Employer tax or employee tax.*—If a return is filed by an employer under the Federal Insurance Contributions Act or the Railroad Retirement Tax Act, and the employer reports and pays less than the correct amount of employer tax or employee tax, the employer is required to report and pay the additional amount due. The reporting will be an adjustment without interest only if the employer reports and pays the additional amount on or before the last day on which the return is required to be filed for the return period in which the error is ascertained. The employer may so report the additional amount either on the return for that period or on a supplemental return for the period for which the underpayment was made. If the employer fails to report the additional amount due within the time so fixed for making an interest-free adjustment, the employer nevertheless is required to report the additional amount in the same manner, but interest will be due. No adjustment of an underpayment may be made under this section or §31.6205-1(b)(2) if the employer is sent a notice and demand for payment of the additional tax.

(ii) *Income tax withholding.*—If an employer files a return reporting and paying less than the correct amount of income tax required to be withheld from wages paid during the return period, the employer is required to report and pay the additional amount due, either (a) on a return for any return period in the calendar year in which the wages were paid, or (b) on a supplemental return for the return period in which the wages were paid. The reporting will be an adjustment without interest only if the employer reports and pays the additional amount on or before the last day on which the return is required to be filed for the return period in which the error was ascertained. If an employer reports and pays less than the correct amount of income tax required to be withheld in a calendar year, and the employer does not correct the underpayment in the same calendar year, the employer should consult the district director of internal revenue as to the manner of correcting the error.

(2) *Overcollections from employees.*—(i) *Employee tax.*—If an employer collects from an employee more than the correct amount of employee tax under the Federal Insurance Contributions Act or the Railroad Retirement Act, and the error is ascertained within the applicable period of limitation on credit or refund, the employer is required either to repay the amount to the employee, or to reimburse the employee by applying the amount of the overcollection against employee tax which otherwise would be collected from the employee after the error is ascertained. If the overcollection is repaid to the employee, the employer is required to obtain and keep the employee's written receipt showing the date and amount of the repayment. In addition, if the employer repays or reimburses an employee in any calendar year for an overcollection which occurred in a prior calendar year, the employer is required to obtain and keep the employee's written statement (a) that the employee has not claimed refund or credit of the amount of the overcollection, or if so, such claim has been rejected, and (b) that the employee will not claim refund or credit of such amount.

(ii) *Income tax withholding.*—If, in any return period in a calendar year, an employer withholds more than the correct amount of income tax, and pays over to the Internal Revenue Service the amount withheld, the employer may repay or reimburse the employee in the excess amount in any subsequent return period in the same calendar year. If the amount is so repaid, the employer is required to obtain and keep the employee's written receipt showing the date and amount of the repayment.

(3) *Employer's claims for credit or refund of overpayments.*—(i) *Employee tax.*—If an employer repays or reimburses an employee for an overcollection of employee tax, as described in subparagraph (2)(i) of this paragraph, the employer may claim credit on a return in accordance with the instructions applicable to the return. In lieu of claiming credit the employer may claim refund by filing Form 843, but the employer may not thereafter claim credit for the same overpayment.

(ii) *Income tax withholding.*—If an employer repays or reimburses an employee for an excess amount withheld as income tax, as described in subparagraph (2)(ii) of this paragraph, the employer may claim credit on a return for a return period in the calendar year in which the excess amount was withheld. The employer is not otherwise permitted to claim credit or refund for any overpayment of income tax that the employer deducted or withheld from an employee.

(d) *Special refunds of employee social security tax.*—(1) An employee who receives wages from more than one employer during a calendar year may, under certain conditions, receive a "special refund" of the amount of employee social security tax (*i.e.*, employee tax under the Federal Insurance Contributions Act) deducted and withheld from wages that exceed the following amounts: calendar years 1968 through 1971,

$7,800; calendar year 1972, $9,000; calendar year 1973, $10,800; calendar year 1974, $13,200; calendar years after 1974, an amount equal to the contribution and benefit base (as determined under section 230 of the Social Security Act) effective with respect to that year. An employee who is entitled to a special refund of employee tax with respect to wages received during a calendar year, and who is required to file an income tax return for such calendar year (or for his last taxable year beginning in such calendar year), may obtain the benefits of such special refund only by claiming credit for such special refund on such income tax return in the same manner as if such special refund were an amount deducted and withheld as income tax at source on wages.

(2) The amount of the special refund allowed as a credit shall be considered as an amount deducted and withheld as income tax at source on wages. If the amount of such special refund when added to amounts deducted and withheld as income tax under chapter 24 exceeds the income tax imposed by chapter 1, the amount of the excess constitutes an overpayment of income tax, and interest on such overpayment is allowed to the extent provided under section 6611 of the Code upon an overpayment of income tax resulting from a credit for income tax withheld at source on wages.

(3) If an employee entitled to a special refund of employee social security tax is not required to file an income tax return for the year in which such special refund may be claimed as a credit, the employee may file a claim for refund of the excess social security tax on Form 843. Claims must be filed with the district director of internal revenue for the district in which the employee resides.

(4) Employee taxes under the Federal Insurance Contributions Act and the Railroad Retirement Tax Act include a percentage rate for hospital insurance. If in 1968 or any calendar year thereafter employee taxes under both Acts are deducted from an employee's wages and compensation aggregating more than $7,800, the "special refund" provisions may apply to the portion of the tax that is deducted for hospital insurance. The employee may take credit on Form 1040 for the amount allowable, in accordance with the instructions applicable to that form. [Reg. § 601.401.]

☐ [32 FR 15990, Nov. 22, 1967, as amended at 33 FR 6825, May 4, 1968; 33 FR 17239, Nov. 21, 1968; 36 FR 7586, Apr. 22, 1971; 38 FR 4970, Feb. 23, 1973; 39 FR 8918, Mar. 7, 1974; 41 FR 20883, May 21, 1976; 45 FR 7257, Feb. 1, 1980; 49 FR 19648, 19649, May 9, 1984; 49 FR 25239, June 20, 1984; 49 FR 36500, Sept. 18, 1984; 66 FR 33830, June 26, 2001.]

Subpart E—Conference and Practice Requirements

[Reg. § 601.501]

§ 601.501. Scope of rules; definitions.— (a) *Scope of rules.*—The rules prescribed in this subpart concern, among other things, the representation of taxpayers before the Internal Revenue Service under the authority of a power of attorney. These rules apply to all offices of the Internal Revenue Service in all matters under the jurisdiction of the Internal Revenue Service and apply to practice before the Internal Revenue Service (as defined in 31 CFR 10.2(a) and 10.7(a)(7)). For special provisions relating to alcohol, tobacco, and firearms activities, see §§ 601.521 through 601.527. These rules detail the means by which a recognized representative is authorized to act on behalf of a taxpayer. Such authority must be evidenced by a power of attorney and declaration of representative filed with the appropriate office of the Internal Revenue Service. In general, a power of attorney must contain certain information concerning the taxpayer, the recognized representative, and the specific tax matter(s) for which the recognized representative is authorized to act. (See § 601.503(a).) A "declaration of representative" is a written statement made by a recognized representative that he/she is currently eligible to practice before the Internal Revenue Service and is authorized to represent the particular party on whose behalf he/she acts. (See § 601.502(c).)

(b) *Definitions.*—(1) *Attorney-in-fact.*—An agent authorized by a principal under a power of attorney to perform certain specified act(s) or kinds of act(s) on behalf of the principal.

(2) *Centralized Authorization File (CAF) system.*—An automated file containing information regarding the authority of a person appointed under a power of attorney or designated under a tax information authorization.

(3) *Circular No. 230.*—Treasury Department Circular No. 230 codified at 31 CFR part 10, which sets forth the regulations governing practice before the Internal Revenue Service.

(4) *Declaration of representative.*—(See § 601.502(c).)

(5) *Delegation of authority.*—An act performed by a recognized representative whereby authority given under a power of attorney is delegated to another recognized representative. After a delegation is made, both the original recognized representative and the recognized representative to whom a delegation is made will be recognized to represent the taxpayer. (See § 601.505(b)(2).)

(6) *Form 2848, "Power of Attorney and Declaration of Representative.".*—The Internal Revenue Service power of attorney form which may be used by a taxpayer who wishes to appoint an individual to represent him/her before the Internal Revenue Service. (See § 601.503(b)(1).)

(7) *Matter.*—The application of each tax imposed by the Internal Revenue Code and the

regulations thereunder for each taxable period constitutes a (separate) matter.

(8) *Office of the Internal Revenue Service.*— The office of each district director, the office of each service center, the office of each compliance center, the office of each regional commissioner, and the National Office constitute separate offices of the Internal Revenue Service.

(9) *Power of attorney.*—A document signed by the taxpayer, as principal, by which an individual is appointed as attorney-in-fact to perform certain specified act(s) or kinds of act(s) on behalf of the principal. Specific types of powers of attorney include the following—

(i) *General power of attorney.*—The attorney-in-fact is authorized to perform any or all acts the taxpayer can perform.

(ii) *Durable power of attorney.*—A power of attorney which specifies that the appointment of the attorney-in-fact will not end due to either the passage of time (i.e., the authority conveyed will continue until the death of the taxpayer) or the incompetency of the principal (e.g., the principal becomes unable or is adjudged incompetent to perform his/her business affairs).

(iii) *Limited power of attorney.*—A power of attorney which is limited in any facet (i.e., a power of attorney authorizing the attorney-in-fact to perform only certain specified acts as contrasted to a general power of attorney authorizing the representative to perform any and all acts the taxpayer can perform).

(10) *Practice before the Internal Revenue Service.*—Practice before the Internal Revenue Service encompasses all matters connected with presentation to the Internal Revenue Service or any of its personnel relating to a taxpayer's rights, privileges, or liabilities under laws or regulations administered by the Internal Revenue Service. Such presentations include the preparation and filing of necessary documents, correspondence with and communications to the Internal Revenue Service, and the representation of a taxpayer at conferences, hearings, and meetings. (See 31 CFR 10.2(a) and 10.7(a)(7).)

(11) *Principal.*—A person (i.e., taxpayer) who appoints an attorney-in-fact under a power of attorney.

(12) *Recognized representative.*—An individual who is recognized to practice before the Internal Revenue Service under the provisions of § 601.502.

(13) *Representation.*—Acts performed on behalf of a taxpayer by a representative in practice before the Internal Revenue Service. (See § 601.501(b)(10).) Representation does not include the furnishing of information at the request of the Internal Revenue Service or any of its officers or employees (See 31 CFR 10.7(c).)

(14) *Substitution of representative.*—An act performed by an attorney-in-fact whereby authority given under a power of attorney is transferred to another recognized representative. After a substitution is made, only the newly recognized representative will be considered the taxpayer's representative. (See § 601.505(b)(2).)

(15) *Tax information authorization.*—A document signed by the taxpayer authorizing any individual or entity (e.g., corporation, partnership, trust or organization) designated by the taxpayer to receive and/or inspect confidential tax information in a specified matter. (See section 6103 of the Internal Revenue Code and the regulations thereunder.)

(c) *Conferences.*—(1) *Scheduling.*—The Internal Revenue Service encourages the discussion of any Federal tax matter affecting a taxpayer. Conferences may be offered only to taxpayers and/ or their recognized representative(s) acting under a valid power of attorney. As a general rule, such conferences will not be held without previous arrangement. However, if a compelling reason is shown by the taxpayer that an immediate conference should be held, the Internal Revenue Service official(s) responsible for the matter has the discretion to make an exception to the general rule.

(2) *Submission of information.*—Every written protest, brief, or other statement the taxpayer or recognized representative wishes to be considered at any conference should be submitted to or filed with the appropriate Internal Revenue Service official(s) at least five business days before the date of the conference. If the taxpayer or the representative is unable to meet this requirement, arrangement should be made with the appropriate Internal Revenue Service official for a postponement of the conference to a date mutually agreeable to the parties. The taxpayer or the representative remains free to submit additional or supporting facts or evidence within a reasonable time after the conference. [Reg. § 601.501.]

☐ [56 FR 24003, May 28, 1991; amended at 57 FR 27356, June 19, 1992.]

[Reg. § 601.502]

§ 601.502. Recognized representative.—(a) A recognized representative is an individual who is

(1) Appointed as an attorney-in-fact under a power of attorney, and a

(2) Member of one of the categories described in § 601.502(b) and who files a declaration of representative, as described in § 601.502(c).

(b) *Categories.*—(1) *Attorney.*—Any individual who is a member in good standing of the bar of the highest court of any state, possession, territory, commonwealth, or the District of Columbia;

(2) *Certified public accountant.*—Any individual who is duly qualified to practice as a certified public accountant in any state, possession, territory, commonwealth, or the District of Columbia;

(3) *Enrolled agent.*—Any individual who is enrolled to practice before the Internal Revenue Service and is in active status pursuant to the requirements of Circular No. 230;

(4) *Enrolled actuary.*—Any individual who is enrolled as an actuary by and is in active status with the Joint Board for the Enrollment of Actuaries pursuant to 29 U.S.C. 1242.

(5) *Other individuals.*—(i) *Temporary recognition.*—Any individual who is granted temporary recognition as an enrolled agent by the Director of Practice (31 CFR 10.5(c)).

(ii) *Practice based on a relationship or special status with a taxpayer.*—Any individual authorized to represent a taxpayer with whom/which a special relationship exists (31 CFR 10.7(a)(1)-(6)). (For example, an individual may represent another individual who is his/her regular full-time employer or a member of his/her immediate family; an individual who is a bona fide officer or regular full-time employee of a corporation or certain other organizations may represent that entity.)

(iii) *Unenrolled return preparer.*—Any individual who signs a return as having prepared it for a taxpayer, or who prepared a return with respect to which the instructions or regulations do not require that the return be signed by the preparer. The acts which an unenrolled return preparer may perform are limited to representation of a taxpayer before revenue agents and examining officers of the Examination Division in the offices of District Director with respect to the tax liability of the taxpayer for the taxable year or period covered by a return prepared by the unenrolled return preparer (31 CFR 10.7(a)(7)).

(iv) *Special appearance.*—Any individual who, upon written application, is authorized by the Director of Practice to represent a taxpayer in a particular matter (31 CFR 10.7(b)).

(c) *Declaration of representative.*—A recognized representative must attach to the power of attorney a written declaration (e.g., Part II of Form 2848) stating the following—

(1) I am not currently under suspension or disbarment from practice before the Internal Revenue Service or other practice of my profession by any other authority;

(2) I am aware of the regulations contained in Treasury Department Circular No. 230 (31 C.F.R., part 10), concerning the practice of attorneys, certified public accountants, enrolled agents, enrolled actuaries, and others);

(3) I am authorized to represent the taxpayer(s) identified in the power of attorney; and

(4) I am an individual described in § 601.502(b).
If an individual is unable to make such declaration, he/she may not engage in representation of a taxpayer before the Internal Revenue Service or perform the acts described in § § 601.504(a)(2) through (6). [Reg. § 601.502.]

☐ [56 FR 24004, May 28, 1991; amended at 57 FR 27356, June 19, 1992.]

[Reg. § 601.503]

§ 601.503. **Requirements of power of attorney, signatures, fiduciaries and Commissioner's authority to substitute other requirements.**—(a) *Requirements.*—A power of attorney must contain the following information—

(1) name and mailing address of the taxpayer;

(2) identification number of the taxpayer (i.e., social security number and/or employer identification number);

(3) employee plan number (if applicable);

(4) name and mailing address of the recognized representative(s);

(5) description of the matter(s) for which representation is authorized which, if applicable, must include—

(i) the type of tax involved;

(ii) the Federal tax form number;

(iii) the specific year(s)/period(s) involved; and

(iv) in estate matters, decedent's date of death; and

(6) a clear expression of the taxpayer's intention concerning the scope of authority granted to the recognized representative(s).

(b) *Acceptable power of attorney documents.*—(1) *Form 2848.*—A properly completed Form 2848 satisfies the requirements for both a power of attorney (as described in § 601.503(a)) and a declaration of representative (as described in § 601.502(c)).

(2) *Other documents.*—The Internal Revenue Service will accept a power of attorney other than Form 2848 provided such document satisfies the requirements of § 601.503(a). However, for purposes of processing such documents onto the Centralized Authorization File (see § 601.506(d)), a completed Form 2848 must be attached. (In such situations, Form 2848 is not the operative power of attorney and need not be signed by the taxpayer. However, the Declaration of Representative must be signed by the representative.)

(3) *Special provision.*—The Internal Revenue Service will not accept a power of attorney which fails to include the information required by § § 601.503(a)(1) through (5). If a power of attorney fails to include some or all of the information required by such section, the attorney-in-fact can cure this defect by executing a Form 2848 (on behalf of the taxpayer) which includes the missing information. Attaching a Form 2848 to a copy of the original power of attorney will validate the original power of attorney (and will be treated in all circumstances as one signed and filed by the taxpayer) provided the following conditions are satisfied—

(i) The original power of attorney contemplates authorization to handle, among other things, Federal tax matters (e.g., the power of attorney includes language to the effect that the attorney-in-fact has the authority to perform any and all acts).

(ii) The attorney-in-fact attaches a statement (signed under penalty of perjury) to the Form 2848 which states that the original power of attorney is valid under the laws of the governing jurisdiction.

(4) *Other categories of powers of attorney.*— Categories of powers of attorney not addressed in these rules (e.g., durable powers of attorney and limited powers of attorney) will be accepted by the Internal Revenue Service provided such documents satisfy the requirements of § 601.503(b)(2) or (3).

(c) *Signatures.*—Internal Revenue Service officials may require a taxpayer (or such individual(s) required or authorized to sign on behalf of a taxpayer) to submit appropriate identification or evidence of authority. Except when Form 2848 (or its equivalent) is executed by an attorney-in-fact under the provisions of § 601.503(b)(3), the individual who must execute a Form 2848 depends on the type of taxpayer involved—

(1) *Individual taxpayer.*—In matter(s) involving an individual taxpayer, a power of attorney must be signed by such individual.

(2) *Husband and wife.*—In matters involving a joint return the following rules apply—

(i) *Joint representation.*—In the case of any matter concerning a joint return in which both husband and wife are to be represented by the same representative(s), the power of attorney must be executed by both husband and wife.

(ii) *Individual representation.*—In the case of any matter concerning a joint return in which both husband and wife are not to be represented by the same recognized representative(s), the power of attorney must be executed by the spouse who is to be represented. However, the recognized representative of such spouse cannot perform any act with respect to a tax matter that the spouse being represented cannot perform alone.

(3) *Corporation.*—In the case of a corporation, a power of attorney must be executed by an officer of the corporation having authority to legally bind the corporation, who must certify that he/she has such authority.

(4) *Association.*—In the case of an association, a power of attorney must be executed by an officer of the association having authority to legally bind the association, who must certify that he/she has such authority.

(5) *Partnership.*—In the case of a partnership, a power of attorney must be executed by all partners, or if executed in the name of the partnership, by the partner or partners duly authorized to act for the partnership, who must certify that he/she has such authority.

(6) *Dissolved partnership.*—In the case of a dissolved partnership, each of the former partners must execute a power of attorney. However, if one or more of the former partners is deceased, the following provisions apply—

(i) The legal representative of each deceased partner(s) (or such person(s) having legal control over the disposition of partnership interest(s) and/or the share of partnership asset(s) of the deceased partner(s)) must execute a power of attorney in the place of such deceased partner(s). (See § 601.503(c)(6)(ii).)

(ii) Notwithstanding § 601.503(c)(6)(i), if the laws of the governing jurisdiction provide that such partner(s) has exclusive right to control or possession of the firm's assets for the purpose of winding up its affairs, the signature(s) of the surviving partner(s) alone will be sufficient. (If the surviving partner(s) claims exclusive right to control or possession of the firm's assets for the purpose of winding up its affairs, Internal Revenue Service officials may require the submission of a copy of or a citation to the pertinent provisions of the law of the governing jurisdiction upon which the surviving partner(s) relies.)

(d) *Fiduciaries.*—In general, when a fiduciary is involved in a tax matter, a power of attorney is not required. Instead Form 56, "Notice Concerning Fiduciary Relationship," should be filed. Types of taxpayer for which fiduciaries act are—

(1) *Dissolved corporation.*—(i) *Appointed trustee.*—In the case of a dissolved corporation, Form 56, "Notice Concerning Fiduciary Relationship," should be filed by the liquidating trustee(s), if one or more have been appointed, or by the trustee(s) deriving authority under a law of the jurisdiction in which the corporation was organized. If there is more than one trustee, all must join unless it is established that fewer than all have authority to act in the matter under consideration. Internal Revenue Service officials may require the submission of a properly authenticated copy of the instrument and/or citation to the law under which the trustee derives his/her authority. If the authority of the trustee is derived under the law of a jurisdiction, Internal Revenue Service officials may require a statement (signed under penalty of perjury) setting forth the facts required by the law as a condition precedent to the vesting of authority in said trustee and stating that the authority of the trustee has not been terminated.

(ii) *No appointed trustee.*—If there is no appointed trustee, a Form 56, "Notice Concerning Fiduciary Relationship," should be filed by the stockholder(s) holding a majority of the voting stock of the corporation as of the date of dissolution. Internal Revenue Service officials may require submission of a statement showing the total number of outstanding shares of voting stock as of the date of dissolution, the number of shares held by each signatory to a power of attorney, the date of dissolution, and a representation that no trustee has been appointed.

(2) *Insolvent taxpayer.*—In the case of an insolvent taxpayer, Form 56, "Notice Concerning Fiduciary Relationship," should be filed by the trustee, receiver, or attorney appointed by the court. Internal Revenue Service officials may re-

quire the submission of a certified order or document from the court having jurisdiction over the insolvent taxpayer which shows the appointment and qualification of the trustee, receiver, or attorney and that his/her authority has not been terminated. In cases pending before a court of the United States (e.g., U.S. District Court or U.S. Bankruptcy Court), an authenticated copy of the order approving the bond of the trustee, receiver, or attorney will meet this requirement.

(3) *Deceased taxpayers.*—(i) *Executor, personal representative or administrator.*—In the case of a deceased taxpayer, a Form 56, "Notice Concerning Fiduciary Relationship," should be filed by the executor, personal representative or administrator if one has been appointed and is responsible for disposition of the matter under consideration. Internal Revenue Service officials may require the submission of a short-form certificate (or authenticated copy of letters testamentary or letters of administration) showing that such authority is in full force and effect at the time the Form 56, "Notice Concerning Fiduciary Relationship," is filed.

(ii) *Testamentary trustee(s).*—In the event that a trustee is acting under the provisions of the will, a Form 56, "Notice Concerning Fiduciary Relationship," should be filed by the trustee, unless the executor, personal representative or administrator has not been discharged and is responsible for disposition of the matter. Internal Revenue Service officials may require either the submission of evidence of the discharge of the executor and appointment of the trustee or other appropriate evidence of the authority of the trustee.

(iii) *Residuary legatee(s).*—If no executor, administrator, or trustee named under the will is acting or responsible for disposition of the matter and the estate has been distributed to the residuary legatee(s), a Form 56, "Notice Concerning Fiduciary Relationship," should be filed by the residuary legatee(s). Internal Revenue Service officials may require the submission of a statement from the court certifying that no executor, administrator, or trustee named under the will is acting or responsible for disposition of the matter, naming the residuary legatee(s), and indicating the proper share to which each is entitled.

(iv) *Distributee(s).*—In the event that the decedent died intestate and the administrator has been discharged and is not responsible for disposition of the matter (or none was ever appointed), a Form 56, "Notice Concerning Fiduciary Relationship," should be filed by the distributee(s). Internal Revenue Service officials may require the submission of evidence of the discharge of the administrator (if one had been appointed) and evidence that the administrator is not responsible for disposition of the matter. It also may require a statement(s) signed under penalty of perjury (and such other appropriate evidence as can be produced) to show the relationship of the individual(s) who sign the Form 56, "Notice Concerning Fiduciary Relationship,"

to the decedent and the right of each signer to the respective shares of the assets claimed under the law of the domicile of the decedent.

(4) *Taxpayer for whom a guardian or other fiduciary has been appointed.*—In the case of a taxpayer for whom a guardian or other fiduciary has been appointed by a court of record, a Form 56, "Notice Concerning Fiduciary Relationship," should be filed by the fiduciary. Internal Revenue Service officials may require the submission of a court certificate or court order showing that the individual who executes the Form 56, "Notice Concerning Fiduciary Relationship," has been appointed and that his/her appointment has not been terminated.

(5) *Taxpayer who has appointed a trustee.*—In the case of a taxpayer who has appointed a trustee, a Form 56, "Notice Concerning Fiduciary Relationship," should be filed by the trustee. If there is more than one trustee appointed, all should join unless it is shown that fewer than all have authority to act. Internal Revenue Service officials may require the submission of documentary evidence of the authority of the trustee to act. Such evidence may be either a copy of a properly executed trust instrument or a certified copy of extracts from the trust instruments, showing—

(i) The date of the instrument;

(ii) That it is or is not of record in any court;

(iii) The names of the beneficiaries;

(iv) The appointment of the trustee, the authority granted, and other information as may be necessary to show that such authority extends to Federal tax matters; and

(v) That the trust has not been terminated and the trustee appointed therein is still legally acting as such.

In the event that the trustee appointed in the original trust instrument has been replaced by another trustee, documentary evidence of the appointment of the new trustee must be submitted.

(e) *Commissioner's authority to substitute other requirements for power of attorney.*—Upon application of a taxpayer or a recognized representative, the Commissioner of Internal Revenue may substitute a requirement(s) other than provided herein for a power of attorney as evidence of the authority of the representative. [Reg. § 601.503.]

☐ [56 FR 24005, May 28, 1991; 57 FR 27356, June 19, 1992.]

[Reg. § 601.504]

§ 601.504. Requirements for filing power of attorney.—(a) *Situations in which a power of attorney is required.*—Except as otherwise provided in § 601.504(b), a power of attorney is required by the Internal Revenue Service when the taxpayer wishes to authorize a recognized representative to perform one or more of the following acts on behalf of the taxpayer—

(1) *Representation.*—(See § § 601.501(b)(10) and 601.501(b)(13).)

(2) *Waiver.*—Offer and/or execution of either (i) a waiver of restriction on assessment or collection of a deficiency in tax, or (ii) a waiver of notice of disallowance of a claim for credit or refund.

(3) *Consent.*—Execution of a consent to extend the statutory period for assessment or collection of a tax.

(4) *Closing agreement.*—Execution of a closing agreement under the provisions of the Internal Revenue Code and the regulations thereunder.

(5) *Check drawn on the United States Treasury.*—The authority to receive (but not endorse or collect) a check drawn on the United States Treasury must be specifically granted in a power of attorney. (The endorsement and payment of a check drawn on the United States Treasury are governed by Treasury Department Circular No. 21, as amended, 31 CFR part 240. Endorsement and payment of such check by any person other than the payee must be made under one of the special types of powers of attorney prescribed by Circular No. 21, 31 CFR Part 240. For restrictions on the assignment of claims, see Revised Statute section 3477, as amended (31 U.S.C. 3727).)

(6) *Signing tax returns.*—The filing of a power of attorney does not authorize the recognized representative to sign a tax return on behalf of the taxpayer unless such act is both—

(i) permitted under the Internal Revenue Code and the regulations thereunder (e.g., the authority to sign income tax returns is governed by the provisions of § 1.6012-1(a)(5) of the Income Tax Regulations); and

(ii) specifically authorized in the power of attorney.

(b) *Situations in which a power of attorney is not required.*—(1) *Disclosure of confidential tax information.*—The submission of a tax information authorization to request a disclosure of confidential tax information does not constitute practice before the Internal Revenue Service. (Such procedure is governed by the provisions of § 6103 of the Internal Revenue Code and the regulations thereunder.) Nevertheless, if a power of attorney is properly filed, the recognized representative also is authorized to receive and/or inspect confidential tax information concerning the matter(s) specified (provided the power of attorney places no limitations upon such disclosure).

(2) *Estate matter.*—A power of attorney is not required at a conference concerning an estate tax matter if the individual seeking to act as a recognized representative presents satisfactory evidence to Internal Revenue Service officials that he/she is—

(i) an individual described in § 601.502(b); and

(ii) the attorney of record for the executor, personal representative, or administrator before the court where the will is probated or the estate is administered.

(3) *Bankruptcy matters.*—A power of attorney is not required in the case of a trustee, receiver, or an attorney (designated to represent a trustee, receiver, or debtor in possession) appointed by a court having jurisdiction over a debtor. In such a case, Internal Revenue Service officials may require the submission of a certificate from the court having jurisdiction over the debtor showing the appointment and qualification of the trustee, receiver, or attorney and that his/her authority has not been terminated. In cases pending before a court of the United States (e.g., U.S. District Court or U.S. Bankruptcy Court), an authenticated copy of the order approving the bond of the trustee, receiver, or attorney will meet this requirement.

(c) *Administrative requirements of filing.*—(1) *General.*—Except as provided in this section, a power of attorney (including the declaration of representative and any other required statement(s)) must be filed in each office of the Internal Revenue Service in which the recognized representative desires to perform one or more of the acts described in § 601.504(a).

(2) *Regional offices.*—If a power of attorney (including the declaration of representative and any other required statement(s)) is filed with the office of a district director or with a service center which has the matter under consideration, it is not necessary to file a copy with the office of a regional commissioner which subsequently has the matter under consideration unless requested.

(3) *National Office.*—In case of a request for a ruling or other matter to be considered in the National Office, a power of attorney, including the declaration of representative and any other required statement(s), must be submitted with each request or matter.

(4) *Copy of power of attorney.*—The Internal Revenue Service will accept either the original or a copy of a power of attorney. A copy of a power of attorney received by facsimile transmission (FAX) also will be accepted.

(d) *Practice by correspondence.*—If an individual desires to represent a taxpayer through correspondence with the Internal Revenue Service, such individual must submit a power of attorney, including the declaration of representative and any other required statement(s), even though no personal appearance is contemplated. [Reg. § 601.504.]

☐ [56 FR 24007, May 28, 1991; 57 FR 27356, June 19, 1992.]

[Reg. § 601.505]

§ 601.505. Revocation, change in representation and substitution or delegation of representative.—(a) *By the taxpayer.*—(1) *New power of attorney filed.*—A new power of attorney revokes a prior power of attorney if it is granted by the taxpayer to another recognized representative with respect to the same matter. However, a new power of attorney does not revoke a prior power of attorney if it contains a clause stating that it does not revoke such prior power of attorney and there is attached to the new power of attorney either—

(i) a copy of the unrevoked prior power of attorney; or

(ii) a statement signed by the taxpayer listing the name and address of each recognized representative authorized under the prior unrevoked power of attorney.

(2) *Statement of revocation filed.*—A taxpayer may revoke a power of attorney without authorizing a new representative by filing a statement of revocation with those offices of the Internal Revenue Service where the taxpayer has filed the power of attorney to be revoked. The statement of revocation must indicate that the authority of the first power of attorney is revoked and must be signed by the taxpayer. Also, the name and address of each recognized representative whose authority is revoked must be listed (or a copy of the power of attorney to be revoked must be attached).

(b) *By the recognized representative.*—(1) *Revocation of power of attorney.*—A recognized representative may withdraw from representation in a matter in which a power of attorney has been filed by filing a statement with those offices of the Internal Revenue Service where the power of attorney to be revoked was filed. The statement must be signed by the representative and must identify the name and address of the taxpayer(s) and the matter(s) from which the representative is withdrawing.

(2) *Substitution or delegation of recognized representative.*—Any recognized representative appointed in a power of attorney may substitute or delegate authority under the power of attorney to another recognized representative if substitution or delegation is specifically permitted under the power of attorney. Unless otherwise provided in the power of attorney, a recognized representative may make a substitution or delegation without the consent of any other recognized representative appointed to represent the taxpayer in the same matter. A substitution or delegation is effected by filing the following items with offices of the Internal Revenue Service where the power of attorney has been filed—

(i) *Notice of substitution or delegation.*—A Notice of Substitution or Delegation is a statement signed by the recognized representative appointed under the power of attorney. The statement must contain the name and mailing address of the new recognized representative and, if more than one individual is to represent the taxpayer in the matter, a designation of which recognized representative is to receive notices and other written communications;

(ii) *Declaration of representative.*—A written declaration which is made by the new representative as required by § 601.502(c); and

(iii) *Power of attorney.*—A power of attorney which specifically authorizes the substitution or delegation.

An employee of a recognized representative may not be substituted for his/her employer with respect to the representation of a taxpayer before the Internal Revenue Service unless the employee is a recognized representative in his/her own capacity under the provisions of § 601.502(b). However, even if such employee is not a recognized representative in his/her own capacity under the provisions of § 601.502(b), that individual may be authorized by the taxpayer under a tax information authorization to receive and/or inspect confidential tax information under the provisions of section 6103 of the Internal Revenue Code and the regulations thereunder. [Reg. § 601.505.]

☐ [56 FR 24007, May 28, 1991, amended at 57 FR 27356, June 19, 1992.]

[Reg. § 601.506]

§ 601.506. Notices to be given to recognized representative; direct contact with taxpayer; delivery of a check drawn on the United States Treasury to recognized representative.—(a) *General.*—Any notice or other written communication (or a copy thereof) required or permitted to be given to a taxpayer in any matter before the Internal Revenue Service must be given to the taxpayer and, unless restricted by the taxpayer, to the representative according to the following procedures—

(1) If the taxpayer designates more than one recognized representative to receive notices and other written communications, it will be the practice of the Internal Revenue Service to give copies of such to two (but not more than two) individuals so designated.

(2) In a case in which the taxpayer does not designate which recognized representative is to receive notices, it will be the practice of the Internal Revenue Service to give notices and other communications to the first recognized representative appointed on the power of attorney.

(3) Failure to give notice or other written communication to the recognized representative of a taxpayer will not affect the validity of any notice or other written communication delivered to a taxpayer.

Unless otherwise indicated in the document, a power of attorney other than Form 2848 will be presumed to grant the authority to receive notices or other written communication (or a copy thereof) required or permitted to be given to a taxpayer in any matter(s) before the Internal Revenue Service to which the power of attorney pertains.

(b) *Cases where taxpayer may be contacted directly.*—Where a recognized representative has unreasonably delayed or hindered an examination, collection or investigation by failing to furnish, after repeated request, nonprivileged information necessary to the examination, collection or investigation, the Internal Revenue Service employee conducting the examination, collection or investigation may request the permission of his/her immediate supervisor to contact the taxpayer directly for such information.

(1) *Procedure.*—If such permission is granted, the case file will be documented with sufficient facts to show how the examination, collection or investigation was being delayed or hindered. Written notice of such permission, briefly stating the reason why it was granted, will be given to both the recognized representative and the taxpayer together with a request of the taxpayer to supply such nonprivileged information. (See 7521(c) of the Internal Revenue Code and the regulations thereunder.)

(2) *Effect of direct notification.*—Permission to by-pass a recognized representative and contact a taxpayer directly does not automatically disqualify an individual to act as the recognized representative of a taxpayer in a matter. However, such information may be referred to the Director of Practice for possible disciplinary proceedings under Circular No. 230, 31 CFR Part 10.

(c) *Delivery of a check drawn on the United States Treasury.*—(1) *General.*—A check drawn on the United States Treasury (e.g., a check in payment of refund of internal revenue taxes, penalties, or interest, see § 601.504(a)(5)) will be mailed to the recognized representative of a taxpayer provided that a power of attorney is filed containing specific authorization for this to be done.

(2) *Address of recognized representative.*—The check will be mailed to the address of the recognized representative listed on the power of attorney unless such recognized representative notifies the Internal Revenue Service in writing that his/her mailing address has been changed.

(3) *Authorization of more than one recognized representative.*—In the event a power of attorney authorizes more than one recognized representative to receive a check on the taxpayer's behalf, and such representatives have different addresses, the Internal Revenue Service will mail the check directly to the taxpayer, unless a statement (signed by all of the recognized representatives so authorized) is submitted which indicates the address to which the check is to be mailed.

(4) *Cases in litigation.*—The provisions of § 601.506(c) concerning the issuance of a tax refund do not apply to the issuance of a check in payment of claims which have been either reduced to judgment or settled in the course (or as a result) of litigation.

(d) *Centralized Authorization File (CAF) system.*—(1) *Information recorded onto the CAF system.*—Information from both powers of attorney and tax information authorizations is recorded onto the CAF system. Such information enables Internal Revenue Service personnel who do not have access to the actual power of attorney or tax information authorizations to—

(i) determine whether a recognized representative or an appointee is authorized by a taxpayer to receive and/or inspect confidential tax information;

(ii) determine, in the case of a recognized representative, whether that representative is authorized to perform the acts set forth in § 601.504(a); and

(iii) send copies of computer generated notices and communications to an appointee or recognized representative so authorized by the taxpayer.

(2) *CAF number.*—A Centralized Authorization File (CAF) number generally will be issued to

(i) a recognized representative who files a power of attorney and a written declaration of representative; or

(ii) an appointee authorized under a tax information authorization.

The issuance of a CAF number does not indicate that a person is either recognized or authorized to practice before the Internal Revenue Service. Such determination is made under the provisions of Circular No. 230, 31 CFR Part 10. The purpose of the CAF number is to facilitate the processing of a power of attorney or a tax information authorization submitted by a recognized representative or an appointee. A recognized representative or an appointee should include the same CAF number on every power of attorney or tax information authorization filed. However, because the CAF number is not a substantive requirement (i.e., as listed in § 601.503(a)), a tax information authorization or power of attorney which does not include such number will not be rejected based on the absence of a CAF number.

(3) *Tax matters recorded on CAF.*—Although a power of attorney or tax information authorization may be filed in all matters under the jurisdiction of the Internal Revenue Service, only those documents which meet each of the following criteria will be recorded onto the CAF system—

(i) *Specific tax period.*—Only documents which concern a matter(s) relating to a specific tax period will be recorded onto the CAF system. A power of attorney or tax information authorization filed in a matter unrelated to a specific period (e.g., the 100% penalty for failure to pay over withholding taxes imposed by § 6672 of the Internal Revenue Code, applications for an employer identification number, and requests for a private letter ruling request pertaining to a proposed transaction) cannot be recorded onto the CAF system.

(ii) *Future three-year limitation.*—Only documents which concern a tax period that ends no later than three years after the date on a power of attorney is received by the Internal Revenue Service will be recorded onto the CAF system. For example, a power of attorney received by the Internal Revenue Service on August 1, 1990, which indicates that the authorization applies to Form 941 for the quarters ended December 31, 1990 through December 31, 2000, will be recorded onto the CAF system for the applicable tax periods which end no later than July 31, 1993 (i.e., three years after the date of receipt by the Internal Revenue Service).

(iii) *Documents for prior tax periods.*—Documents which concern any tax period which has ended prior to the date on which a power of attorney is received by the Internal Revenue Service will be recorded onto the CAF system provided that matters concerning such years are under consideration by the Internal Revenue Service.

(iv) *Limitation on representatives recorded onto the CAF system.*—No more than three representatives appointed under a power of attorney or three persons designated under a tax information authorization will be recorded onto the CAF system. If more than three representatives are appointed under a power of attorney or more than three persons designated under a tax information authorization, only the first three names will be recorded onto the CAF system.

The fact that a power of attorney or tax information authorization cannot be recorded onto the CAF system is not determinative of the (current or future) validity of such document. (For example, documents which concern tax periods that end more than three years from the date of receipt by the IRS are not invalid for the period(s) not recorded onto the CAF system, but can be resubmitted at a later date.) [Reg. § 601.506.]

☐ [56 FR 24008, May 28, 1991.]

[Reg. § 601.507]

§ 601.507. Evidence required to substantiate facts alleged by a recognized representative.—The Internal Revenue Service may require a recognized representative to submit all evidence, except that of a supplementary or incidental character, over a declaration (signed under penalty of perjury) that the recognized representative prepared such submission and that the facts contained therein are true. In any case in which a recognized representative is unable or unwilling to declare his/her own knowledge that the facts are true and correct, the Internal Revenue Service may require the taxpayer to make such a declaration under penalty of perjury. [Reg. § 601.507.]

☐ [56 FR 24009, May 28, 1991.]

[Reg. § 601.508]

§ 601.508. Dispute between recognized representatives of a taxpayer.—Where there is a dispute between two or more recognized representatives concerning who is entitled to represent a taxpayer in a matter pending before the Internal Revenue Service (or to receive a check drawn on the United States Treasury), the Internal Revenue Service will not recognize any party. However, if the contesting recognized representatives designate one or more of their number under the terms of an agreement signed by all, the Internal Revenue Service will recognize such designated recognized representatives upon receipt of a copy of such agreement according to the terms of the power of attorney. [Reg. § 601.508.]

☐ [56 FR 24009, May 28, 1991.]

[Reg. § 601.509]

§ 601.509. Power of attorney not required in cases docketed in the Tax Court of the United States.—The petitioner and the Commissioner of Internal Revenue stand in the position of parties litigant before a judicial body in a case docketed in the Tax Court of the United States. The Tax Court has its own rules of practice and procedure and its own rules respecting admission to practice before it. Accordingly, a power of attorney is not required to be submitted by an attorney of record in a case which is docketed in the Tax Court. Correspondence in connection with cases docketed in the Tax Court will be addressed to counsel of record before the Court. However, a power of attorney is required to be submitted by an individual other than the attorney of record in any matter before the Internal Revenue Service concerning a docketed case. [Reg. § 601.509.]

☐ [56 FR 24009, May 28, 1991.]

Subpart F—Rules, Regulations, and Forms

[Reg. § 601.601]

§ 601.601. Rules and regulations.—(a) *Formulation.*—(1) Internal Revenue rules take various forms. The most important rules are issued as regulations and Treasury decisions prescribed by the Commissioner and approved by the Secretary or his delegate. Other rules may be issued over the signature of the Commissioner or the signature of any other official to whom authority has been delegated. Regulations and Treasury decisions are prepared in the Office of the Chief Counsel. After approval by the Commissioner, regulations and Treasury decisions are forwarded to the Secretary or his delegate for further consideration and final approval.

(2) Where required by 5 U.S.C. 553 and in such other instances as may be desirable, the Commissioner publishes in the FEDERAL REGISTER general notice of proposed rules (unless all persons subject thereto are named and either personally served or otherwise have actual notice thereof in accordance with law). This notice includes (i) a statement of the time, place, and nature of public rule-making proceedings; (ii) reference to the authority under which the rule is proposed; and (iii) either the terms or substance of the proposed rule or a description of the subjects and issues involved.

(3)(i) This subparagraph shall apply where the rules of this subparagraph are incorporated by reference in a notice of hearing with respect to a notice of proposed rule making.

(ii) A person wishing to make oral comments at a public hearing to which this subparagraph applies shall file his written comments within the time prescribed by the notice of proposed rule making (including any extensions thereof) and submit the outline referred to in subdivision (iii) of this subparagraph within the time prescribed by the notice of hearing. In lieu of the reading of a prepared statement at the hearing, such person's oral comments shall ordinarily be limited to a discussion of matters relating to such written comments and to questions and answers in connection therewith. However, the oral comments shall not be merely a restatement of matters the person has submitted in writing. Persons making oral comments should be prepared to answer questions not only on the topics listed in his outline but also in connection with the matters relating to his written comments. Except as provided in paragraph (b) of this section, in order to be assured of the availability of copies of such written comments or outlines on or before the beginning of such hearing, any person who desires such copies should make such a request within the time prescribed in the notice of hearing and shall agree to pay reasonable costs for copying. Persons who make such a request after the time prescribed in the notice of hearing will be furnished copies as soon as they are available, but it may not be possible to furnish the copies on or before the beginning of the hearing. Except as provided in the preceding sentences, copies of written comments regarding the rules proposed shall not be made available at the hearing.

(iii) A person who wishes to be assured of being heard shall submit, within the time prescribed in the notice of hearing, an outline of the topics he or she wishes to discuss, and the time he or she wishes to devote to each topic. An agenda will then be prepared containing the order of presentation of oral comments and the time allotted to such presentation. A period of 10 minutes will be the time allotted to each person for making his or her oral comments.

(iv) At the conclusion of the presentations of comments of persons listed in the agenda, to the extent time permits, other persons may be permitted to present oral comments provided they have notified, either the Commissioner of Internal Revenue (Attention: CC:LR:T) before the hearing, or the representative of the Internal Revenue Service stationed at the entrance to the hearing room at or before commencement of the hearing, of their desire to be heard.

(v) In the case of unusual circumstances or for good cause shown, the application of rules contained in this subparagraph, including the 10-minute rule in subdivision (iii), above, may be waived.

(vi) To the extent resources permit, the public hearings to which this subparagraph applies may be transcribed.

(b) *Comments on proposed rules.*—(1) *In general.*—Interested persons are privileged to submit any data, views, or arguments in response to a notice of proposed rule making published pursuant to 5 U.S.C. 553. Further, procedures are provided in paragraph (d)(9) of § 601.702 for members of the public to inspect and to obtain copies of written comments submitted in response to such notices. Designations of material as confidential or not to be disclosed, contained in such comments, will not be accepted. Thus, a person submitting written comments in response to a notice of proposed rule making should not

include therein material that he considers to be confidential or inappropriate for disclosure to the public. It will be presumed by the Internal Revenue Service that every written comment submitted to it in response to a notice of proposed rule making is intended by the person submitting it to be subject in its entirety to public inspection and copying in accordance with the procedures of paragraph (d)(9) of § 601.702. The name of any person requesting a public hearing and hearing outlines described in paragraph (a)(3)(iii) of this section are not exempt from disclosure.

(2) *Effective date.*—This paragraph (b) applies only to comments submitted in response to notices of proposed rule making of the Internal Revenue Service published in the Federal Register after June 5, 1974.

(c) *Petition to change rules.*—Interested persons are privileged to petition for the issuance, amendment, or repeal of a rule. A petition for the issuance of a rule should identify the section or sections of law involved; and a petition for the amendment or repeal of a rule should set forth the section or sections of the regulations involved. The petition should also set forth the reasons for the requested action. Such petitions will be given careful consideration and the petitioner will be advised of the action taken thereon. Petitions should be addressed to the Commissioner of Internal Revenue, Attention: CC:LR:T, Washington, D.C. 20224. However, in the case of petitions to amend the regulations pursuant to subsection (c)(4)(A)(viii) or (5)(A)(i) of section 23 or former section 44C, follow the procedure outlined in paragraph (a) of § 1.23-6.

(d) *Publication of rules and regulations.*—(1) *General.*—All internal revenue regulations and Treasury decisions are published in the FEDERAL REGISTER and in the Code of Federal Regulations. See paragraph (a) of § 601.702. The Treasury decisions are also published in the weekly Internal Revenue Bulletin and the semiannual Cumulative Bulletin. The Internal Revenue Bulletin is the authoritative instrument of the Commissioner for the announcement of official rulings, decisions, opinions, and procedures, and for the publication of Treasury decisions, Executive orders, tax conventions, legislation, court decisions, and other items pertaining to internal revenue matters. It is the policy of the Internal Revenue Service to publish in the Bulletin all substantive and procedural rulings of importance or general interest, the publication of which is considered necessary to promote a uniform application of the laws administered by the Service. Procedures set forth in Revenue Procedures published in the Bulletin which are of general applicability and which have continuing force and effect are incorporated as amendments to the Statement of Procedural Rules. It is also the policy to publish in the Bulletin all rulings which revoke, modify, amend, or affect any published ruling. Rules relating solely to matters of internal practices and procedures are not published; however, statements of internal practices and procedures affecting rights or duties of taxpayers, or industry regulation, which appear in internal management documents, are published in the Bulletin. No unpublished ruling or decision will be relied on, used, or cited by any officer or employee of the Internal Revenue Service as a precedent in the disposition of other cases.

(2) *Objectives and standards for publication of Revenue Rulings and Revenue Procedures in the Internal Revenue Bulletin.*—(i)(a) A "Revenue Ruling" is an official interpretation by the Service that has been published in the Internal Revenue Bulletin. Revenue Rulings are issued only by the National Office and are published for the information and guidance of taxpayers, Internal Revenue Service officials, and others concerned.

(b) A "Revenue Procedure" is a statement of procedure that affects the rights or duties of taxpayers or other members of the public under the Code and related statutes or information that, although not necessarily affecting the rights and duties of the public, should be a matter of public knowledge.

(ii)(a) The Internal Revenue Bulletin is the authoritative instrument of the Commissioner of Internal Revenue for the publication of official rulings and procedures of the Internal Revenue Service, including all rulings and statements of procedure which supersede, revoke, modify, amend, or affect any previously published ruling or procedure. The Service also announces in the Bulletin the Commissioner's acquiescences and non-acquiescences in decisions of the United States Tax Court (other than decisions in memorandum opinions), and publishes Treasury decisions, Executive orders, tax conventions, legislation, court decisions, and other items considered to be of general interest. The Assistant Commissioner (Technical) administers the Bulletin program.

(b) The Bulletin is published weekly. In order to provide a permanent reference source, the contents of the Bulletin are consolidated semiannually into an indexed Cumulative Bulletin. The Bulletin Index-Digest System provides a research and reference guide to matters appearing in the Cumulative Bulletins. These materials are sold by the Superintendent of Documents, U.S. Government Printing Office, Washington, D.C. 20402.

(iii) The purpose of publishing revenue rulings and revenue procedures in the Internal Revenue Bulletin is to promote correct and uniform application of the tax laws by Internal Revenue Service employees and to assist taxpayers in attaining maximum voluntary compliance by informing Service personnel and the public of National Office interpretations of the internal revenue laws, related statutes, treaties, regulations, and statements of Service procedures affecting the rights and duties of taxpayers. Therefore, issues and answers involving substantive tax law under the jurisdiction of the Internal Revenue Service will be published in the Internal Revenue Bulletin, except those involving:

(a) Issues answered by statute, treaty, or regulations;

(b) Issues answered by rulings, opinions, or court decisions previously published in the Bulletin;

(c) Issues that are of insufficient importance or interest to warrant publication;

(d) Determinations of fact rather than interpretations of law;

(e) Informers and informers' rewards; or

(f) Disclosure of secret formulas, processes, business practices, and similar information.

Procedures affecting taxpayers' rights or duties that relate to matters under the jurisdiction of the Service will be published in the Bulletin.

(iv) [Reserved].

(v)(a) Rulings and other communications involving substantive tax law published in the Bulletin are published in the form of Revenue Rulings. The conclusions expressed in Revenue Rulings will be directly responsive to and limited in scope by the pivotal facts stated in the revenue ruling. Revenue Rulings arise from various sources, including rulings to taxpayers, technical advice to district offices, studies undertaken by the Office of the Assistant Commissioner (Technical), court decisions, suggestions from tax practitioner groups, publications, etc.

(b) It will be the practice of the Service to publish as much of the ruling or communication as is necessary for an understanding of the position stated. However, in order to prevent unwarranted invasions of personal privacy and to comply with statutory provisions, such as 18 U.S.C. 1905 and 26 U.S.C. 7213, dealing with disclosure of information obtained from members of the public, identifying details, including the names and addresses of persons involved, and information of a confidential nature are deleted from the ruling.

(c) Revenue Rulings, other than those relating to the qualification of pension, annuity, profit-sharing, stock bonus, and bond purchase plans, apply retroactively unless the Revenue Ruling includes a specific statement indicating, under the authority of section 7805(b) of the Internal Revenue Code of 1954, the extent to which it is to be applied without retroactive effect. Where Revenue Rulings revoke or modify rulings previously published in the Bulletin the authority of section 7805(b) of the Code ordinarily is invoked to provide that the new rulings will not be applied retroactively to the extent that the new rulings have adverse tax consequences to taxpayers. Section 7805(b) of the Code provides that the Secretary of the Treasury or his delegate may prescribe the extent to which any ruling is to be applied without retroactive effect. The exercise of this authority requires an affirmative action. For the effect of Revenue Rulings on determination letters and opinion letters issued with respect to the qualification of pension, annuity, profit-sharing, stock bonus, and bond purchase plans, see paragraph (o) of §601.201.

(d) Revenue Rulings published in the Bulletin do not have the force and effect of Treasury Department Regulations (including Treasury decisions), but are published to provide precedents to be used in the disposition of other cases, and may be cited and relied upon for that purpose. No unpublished ruling or decision will be relied on, used, or cited, by an officer or employee of the Service as a precedent in the disposition of other cases.

(e) Taxpayers generally may rely upon Revenue Rulings published in the Bulletin in determining the tax treatment of their own transactions and need not request specific rulings applying the principles of a published Revenue Ruling to the facts of their particular cases. However, since each Revenue Ruling represents the conclusion of the Service as to the application of the law to the entire state of facts involved, taxpayers, Service personnel, and others concerned are cautioned against reaching the same conclusion in other cases unless the facts and circumstances are substantially the same. They should consider the effect of subsequent legislation, regulations, court decisions, and revenue rulings.

(f) Comments and suggestions from taxpayers or taxpayer groups on Revenue Rulings being prepared for publication in the Bulletin may be solicited, if justified by special circumstances. Conferences on Revenue Rulings being prepared for publication will not be granted except where the Service determines that such action is justified by special circumstances.

(vi) Statements of procedures which affect the rights or duties of taxpayers or other members of the public under the Code and related statutes will be published in the Bulletin in the form of Revenue Procedures. Revenue Procedures usually reflect the contents of internal management documents, but, where appropriate, they are also published to announce practices and procedures for guidance of the public. It is Service practice to publish as much of the internal management document or communication as is necessary for an understanding of the procedure. Revenue Procedures may also be based on internal management documents which should be a matter of public knowledge even though not necessarily affecting the rights or duties of the public. When publication of the substance of a Revenue Procedure in the Federal Register is required pursuant to 5 U.S.C. 552, it will usually be accomplished by an amendment of the Statement of Procedural Rules (26 CFR Part 601).

(vii)(a) The Assistant Commissioner (Technical) is responsible for administering the system for the publication of Revenue Rulings and Revenue Procedures in the Bulletin, including the standards for style and format.

(b) In accordance with the standards set forth in subdivision (iv) of this subparagraph, each Assistant Commissioner is responsible for the preparation and appropriate referral for publication of Revenue Rulings reflecting interpretations of substantive tax law made by his office

and communicated in writing to taxpayers or field offices. In this connection, the Chief Counsel is responsible for the referral to the appropriate Assistant Commissioner, for consideration for publication as Revenue Rulings, of interpretations of substantive tax law made by his Office.

(c) In accordance with the standards set forth in subdivision (iv) of this subparagraph, each Assistant Commissioner and the Chief Counsel is responsible for determining whether procedures established by any office under his jurisdiction should be published as Revenue Procedures and for the initiation, content, and appropriate referral for publication of such Revenue Procedures.

(e) *Foreign tax law.*—(1) The Service will accept the interpretation placed by a foreign tax convention country on its revenue laws which do not affect the tax convention. However, when such interpretation conflicts with a provision in the tax convention, reconsideration of that interpretation may be requested.

(2) Conferences in the National Office of the Service will be granted to representatives of American firms doing business abroad and of American citizens residing abroad, in order to discuss with them foreign tax matters with respect to those countries with which we have tax treaties in effect. [Reg. § 601.601.]

☐ [32 FR 15990, Nov. 22, 1967, as amended at 33 FR 6826, May 4, 1968; 35 FR 16593, Oct. 24, 1970; 38 FR 4971, Feb. 23, 1973; 39 FR 15755, May 6, 1974; 41 FR 13611, Mar. 31, 1976; 41 FR 20883, May 21, 1976; 43 FR 17821, Apr. 26, 1978; 47 FR 56333, Dec. 16, 1982; 48 FR 15624, Apr. 12, 1983; 52 FR 26673, July 16, 1987.]

[Reg. § 601.602]

§ 601.602. Tax forms and instructions.— (a) *Tax return forms and instructions.*—The Internal Revenue Service develops forms and instructions that explain the requirements of the Internal Revenue Code and regulations. The Service distributes the forms and instructions to help taxpayers comply with the law. The tax system is based on voluntary compliance, and the taxpayers complete and return the forms with payment of any tax owed.

(b) *Other forms and instructions.*—In addition to tax return forms, the Internal Revenue Service furnishes the public copies of other forms and instructions developed for use in complying with the laws and regulations. These forms and instructions lead the taxpayer step-by-step through data needed to accurately report information required by law.

(c) *Where to get forms and instructions.*—The Internal Revenue Service mails tax return forms to taxpayers who have previously filed returns. However, taxpayers can call or write to district directors or directors of service centers for copies of any forms they need. These forms are described in Publication 676 *Catalog of Federal Tax Forms, Form Letters, and Notices,* which the public can buy from the Superintendent of Documents, U.S. Government Printing Office, Washington, D.C. 20402. [Reg. § 601.602.]

☐ [46 FR 26055, May 11, 1981.]

Subpart G—Records

[Reg. § 601.702]

§ 601.702. Publication, public inspection, and specific requests for records.—(a) *Publication in the Federal Register.*—(1) *Requirement.*—(i) Subject to the application of the exemptions and exclusions described in the Freedom of Information Act, 5 U.S.C. 552(b) and (c), and subject to the limitations provided in paragraph (a)(2) of this section, the IRS is required under 5 U.S.C. 552(a)(1), to state separately and publish currently in the Federal Register for the guidance of the public the following information—

(A) Descriptions of its central and field organization and the established places at which, the persons from whom, and the methods whereby, the public may obtain information, make submittals or requests, or obtain decisions, from the IRS;

(B) Statement of the general course and method by which its functions are channeled and determined, including the nature and requirements of all formal and informal procedures which are available;

(C) Rules of procedure, descriptions of forms available or the places at which forms may be obtained, and instructions as to the scope and contents of all papers, reports, or examinations;

(D) Substantive rules of general applicability adopted as authorized by law, and statements of general policy or interpretations of general applicability formulated and adopted by the IRS; and

(E) Each amendment, revision, or repeal of matters referred to in paragraphs (a)(1)(i)(A) through (D) of this section.

(ii) Pursuant to the foregoing requirements, the Commissioner publishes in the Federal Register from time to time a statement, which is not codified in this chapter, on the organization and functions of the IRS, and such amendments as are needed to keep the statement on a current basis. In addition, there are published in the Federal Register the rules set forth in this Part 601 (Statement of Procedural Rules), such as those in paragraph E of this section, relating to conference and practice requirements of the IRS; the regulations in Part 301 of this chapter (Procedure and Administration Regulations); and the various substantive regulations under the Internal Revenue Code of 1986, such as the regulations in Part 1 of this chapter (Income Tax Regulations), in Part 20 of this chapter (Estate Tax Regulations) and, in Part 31 of this chapter (Employment Tax Regulations).

(2) *Limitations.*—(i) *Incorporation by reference in the Federal Register.*—Matter which is reasonably available to the class of persons affected thereby, whether in a private or public publication, shall be deemed published in the Federal

Register for purposes of paragraph (a)(1) of this section when it is incorporated by reference therein with the approval of the Director of the Office of the Federal Register. The matter which is incorporated by reference must be set forth in the private or public publication substantially in its entirety and not merely summarized or printed as a synopsis. Matter, the location and scope of which are familiar to only a few persons having a special working knowledge of the activities of the IRS, may not be incorporated in the Federal Register by reference. Matter may be incorporated by reference in the Federal Register only pursuant to the provisions of 5 U.S.C. 552(a)(1) and 1 CFR Part 20.

(ii) *Effect of failure to publish.*—Except to the extent that a person has actual and timely notice of the terms of any matter referred to in paragraph (a)(1) of this section which is required to be published in the Federal Register, such person is not required in any manner to resort to, or be adversely affected by, such matter if it is not so published or is not incorporated by reference therein pursuant to paragraph (a)(2)(i) of this section. Thus, for example, any such matter which imposes an obligation and which is not so published or incorporated by reference shall not adversely change or affect a person's rights.

(b) *Public inspection and copying.*—(1) *In general.*—(i) Subject to the application of the exemptions described in 5 U.S.C. 552(b) and the exclusions described in 5 U.S.C. 552(c), the IRS is required under 5 U.S.C. 552(a)(2) to make available for public inspection and copying or, in the alternative, to promptly publish and offer for sale the following information:

(A) Final opinions, including concurring and dissenting opinions, and orders, if such opinions and orders are made in the adjudication of cases;

(B) Those statements of policy and interpretations which have been adopted by the IRS but are not published in the Federal Register;

(C) Its administrative staff manuals and instructions to staff that affect a member of the public; and

(D) Copies of all records, regardless of form or format, which have been released to any person under 5 U.S.C. 552(a)(3) and which, because of the nature of their subject matter, the IRS determines have become or are likely to become the subject of subsequent requests for substantially the same records. The determination that records have become or may become the subject of subsequent requests shall be based on the following criteria:

(1) The subject matter is clearly of interest to the public at large or to special interest groups from which more than one request is expected to be received; or

(2) When more than four requests for substantially the same records have already been received.

(ii) The IRS is also required by 5 U.S.C. 552(a)(2) to maintain and make available for public inspection and copying current indexes identifying any matter described in paragraphs (b)(1)(i)(A) through (C) of this section which is issued, adopted, or promulgated after July 4, 1967, and which is required to be made available for public inspection or published. In addition, the IRS shall also promptly publish, quarterly or more frequently, and distribute (by sale or otherwise) copies of each index or supplements thereto unless it determines by order published in the Federal Register that the publication would be unnecessary and impracticable, in which case the IRS shall nonetheless provide copies of such indexes on request at a cost not to exceed the direct cost of duplication. No matter described in paragraphs (b)(1)(i)(A) through (C) of this section which is required by this section to be made available for public inspection or published may be relied upon, used, or cited as precedent by the IRS against a party other than an agency unless such party has actual and timely notice of the terms of such matter or unless the matter has been indexed and either made available for inspection or published, as provided by this paragraph (b). This paragraph (b) applies only to matters which have precedential significance. It does not apply, for example, to any ruling or advisory interpretation issued to a taxpayer or to a particular transaction or set of facts which applies only to that transaction or set of facts. Rulings, determination letters, technical advice memorandums, and Chief Counsel advice are open to public inspection and copying pursuant to 26 U.S.C. 6110. This paragraph (b) does not apply to matters which have been made available pursuant to paragraph (a) of this section.

(iii) For records required to be made available for public inspection and copying pursuant to 5 U.S.C. 552(a)(2) and paragraphs (b)(1)(i)(A) through (D) of this section, which are created on or after November 1, 1996, the IRS shall make such records available on the Internet within one year after such records are created.

(iv) The IRS shall make the index referred to in paragraph (b)(1)(ii) of this section available on the Internet.

(2) *Deletion of identifying details.*—To prevent a clearly unwarranted invasion of personal privacy, the IRS shall, in accordance with 5 U.S.C. 552(a)(2), delete identifying details contained in any matter described in paragraphs (b)(1)(i)(A) through (D) of this section before making such matter available for inspection or publication. Such matters shall also be subject to any applicable exemption set forth in 5 U.S.C. 552(b). In every case where identifying details or other matters are so deleted, the justification for the deletion shall be explained in writing. The extent of such deletion shall be indicated on the portion of the record which is made available or published, unless including that indication would

harm an interest protected by the exemption in 5 U.S.C. 552(b) under which the deletion is made. If technically feasible, the extent of the deletion shall be indicated at the place in the record where the deletion was made.

(3) *Freedom of Information Reading Room.*— (i) *In general.*—The Headquarters Disclosure Office of the IRS shall provide a reading room where the matters described in paragraphs (b)(1)(i)(A) through (D) of this section which are required to be made available for public inspection, and the current indexes to such matters, shall be made available to the public for inspection and copying. The Freedom of Information Reading Room shall contain other matters determined to be helpful for the guidance of the public, including a complete set of rules and regulations (except those pertaining to alcohol, tobacco, firearms, and explosives) contained in this title, any Internal Revenue matters which may be incorporated by reference in the Federal Register (but not a copy of the Federal Register so doing) pursuant to paragraph (a)(2)(i) of this section, a set of Cumulative Bulletins, and copies of various IRS publications. The public shall not be allowed to remove any record from the Freedom of Information Reading Room.

(ii) *Location of Freedom of Information Reading Room.* The location of the Headquarters Disclosure Office Freedom of Information Reading Room is: IRS, 1111 Constitution Avenue, N.W., Room 1621, Washington, D.C.

(iii) *Copying facilities.* The Headquarters Disclosure Office shall provide facilities whereby a person may obtain copies of material located on the shelves of the Freedom of Information Reading Room.

(c) *Specific requests for other records.*—(1) *In general.*—(i) Subject to the application of the exemptions described in 5 U.S.C. 552(b) and the exclusions described in 5 U.S.C. 552(c), the IRS shall, in conformance with 5 U.S.C. 552(a)(3), make reasonably described records available to a person making a request for such records which conforms in every respect with the rules and procedures set forth in this section. Any request or any appeal from the initial denial of a request that does not comply with the requirements set forth in this section shall not be considered subject to the time constraints of paragraphs (c)(9), (10), and (11) of this section, unless and until the request or appeal is amended to comply. The IRS shall promptly advise the requester in what respect the request or appeal is deficient so that it may be resubmitted or amended for consideration in accordance with this section. If a requester does not resubmit a perfected request or appeal within 35 days from the date of a communication from the IRS, the request or appeal file shall be closed. When the resubmitted request or appeal conforms with the requirements of this section, the time constraints of paragraphs (c) (9), (10), and (11) of this section shall begin.

(ii) Requests for the continuing production of records created or for records created after the date of receipt of the request shall not be honored.

(iii) Specific requests under paragraph (a) (3) for material described in paragraph (a) (2) (A) through (C) and which is in the Freedom of Information Reading Room shall not be honored.

(2) *Electronic format records.*—(i) The IRS shall provide the responsive record or records in the form or format requested if the record or records are readily reproducible by the IRS in that form or format. The IRS shall make reasonable efforts to maintain its records in forms or formats that are reproducible for the purpose of disclosure. For purposes of this paragraph, the term *readily reproducible* means, with respect to electronic format, a record or records that can be downloaded or transferred intact to a floppy disk, computer disk (CD), tape, or other electronic medium using equipment currently in use by the office or offices processing the request. Even though some records may initially be readily reproducible, the need to segregate exempt from nonexempt records may cause the releasable material to be not readily reproducible.

(ii) In responding to a request for records, the IRS shall make reasonable efforts to search for the records in electronic form or format, except where such efforts would significantly interfere with the operation of the agency's automated information system(s). For purposes of this paragraph (c), the term *search* means to locate, manually or by automated means, agency records for the purpose of identifying those records which are responsive to a request.

(iii) Searches for records maintained in electronic form or format may require the application of codes, queries, or other minor forms of programming to retrieve the requested records.

(3) *Requests for records not in control of the IRS.*—(i) Where the request is for a record which is determined to be in the possession or under the control of a constituent unit of the Department of the Treasury other than the IRS, the request for such record shall immediately be transferred to the appropriate constituent unit and the requester notified to that effect. Such referral shall not be deemed a denial of access within the meaning of these regulations. The constituent unit of the Department to which such referral is made shall treat such request as a new request addressed to it and the time limits for response set forth in paragraphs (c)(9) and (c)(10) of this section shall commence when the referral is received by the designated office or officer of the constituent unit. Where the request is for a record which is of a type that is not maintained by any constituent unit of the Department of the Treasury, the requester shall be so advised.

(ii) Where the record requested was created by another agency or constituent unit of the Department of the Treasury and a copy thereof is in the possession of the IRS, the IRS official to whom the request is delivered shall refer the request to the agency or constituent unit which originated the record for direct reply to the requester. The requester shall be informed of such referral. This referral shall not be considered a denial of access within the meaning of these regulations. Where the record is determined to

be exempt from disclosure under 5 U.S.C. 552, the referral need not be made, but the IRS shall inform the originating agency or constituent unit of its determination. Where notifying the requester of its referral may cause a harm to the originating agency or constituent unit which would enable the originating agency or constituent unit to withhold the record under 5 U.S.C. 552, then such referral need not be made. In both of these circumstances, the IRS official to whom the request is delivered shall process the request in accordance with the procedures set forth in this section.

(iii) When a request is received for a record created by the IRS (*i.e.,* in its possession and control) that includes information originated by another agency or constituent unit of the Department of the Treasury, the record shall be referred to the originating agency or constituent unit for review, coordination, and concurrence prior to being released to a requester. The IRS official to whom the request is delivered may withhold the record without prior consultation with the originating agency or constituent unit.

(4) *Form of request.*—(i) Requesters are advised that only requests for records which fully comply with the requirements of this section can be processed in accordance with this section. Requesters shall be notified promptly in writing of any requirements which have not been met or any additional requirements to be met. Every effort shall be made to comply with the requests as written. The initial request for records must—

(A) Be made in writing and signed by the individual making the request;

(B) State that it is made pursuant to the Freedom of Information Act, 5 U.S.C. 552, or regulations thereunder;

(C) Be addressed to and mailed to the office of the IRS official who is responsible for the control of the records requested (see paragraph (h) of this section for the responsible officials and their addresses), regardless of where such records are maintained. Generally, requests for records pertaining to the requester, or other matters of local interest, should be directed to the office servicing the requester's geographic area of residence. Requests for records maintained in the Headquarters of the IRS and its National Office of Chief Counsel, concerning matters of nationwide applicability, such as published guidance (regulations and revenue rulings), program management, operations, or policies, should be directed to the Headquarters Disclosure Office. If the person making the request does not know the official responsible for the control of the records being requested, the person making the request may contact, by telephone or in writing, the disclosure office servicing the requester's geographic area of residence to ascertain the identity of the official having control of the records being requested so that the request can be addressed, and delivered, to the appropriate responsible official. Misdirected requests that otherwise satisfy the requirements of this section shall be immediately transferred to the appropriate responsible IRS official and the

Reg. §601.702(c)(4)(i)(C)

requester notified to that effect. Such transfer shall not be deemed a denial of access within the meaning of these regulations. The IRS official to whom the request is redirected shall treat such request as a new request addressed to it and the time limits for response set forth in paragraphs (c)(9) and (c)(11) of this section shall commence when the transfer is received by the designated office;

(D) Reasonably describe the records in accordance with paragraph (c)(5)(i) of this section;

(E) In the case of a request for records the disclosure of which is limited by statute or regulations (as, for example, the Privacy Act of 1974 (5 U.S.C. 552a) or section 6103 and the regulations thereunder), establish the identity and the right of the person making the request to the disclosure of the records in accordance with paragraph (c)(5)(iii) of this section;

(F) Set forth the address where the person making the request desires to be notified of the determination as to whether the request shall be granted;

(G) State whether the requester wishes to inspect the records or desires to have a copy made and furnished without first inspecting them;

(H) State the firm agreement of the requester to pay the fees for search, duplication, and review ultimately determined in accordance with paragraph (f) of this section, or, in accordance with paragraph (c)(4)(ii) of this section, place an upper limit for such fees that the requester is willing to pay, or request that such fees be reduced or waived and state the justification for such request; and

(I) Identify the category of the requester and, with the exception of "other requesters," state how the records shall be used, as required by paragraph (f)(3) of this section.

(ii) As provided in paragraph (c)(4)(i)(H) of this section, rather than stating a firm agreement to pay the fee ultimately determined in accordance with paragraph (f) of this section or requesting that such fees be reduced or waived, the requester may place an upper limit on the amount the requester agrees to pay. If the requester chooses to place an upper limit and the estimated fee is deemed to be greater than the upper limit, or where the requester asks for an estimate of the fee to be charged, the requester shall be promptly advised of the estimate of the fee and asked to agree to pay such amount. Where the initial request includes a request for reduction or waiver of the fee, the IRS officials responsible for the control of the requested records (or their delegates) shall determine whether to grant the request for reduction or waiver in accordance with paragraph (f) of this section and notify the requester of their decisions and, if their decisions result in the requester being liable for all or part of the fee normally due, ask the requester to agree to pay the amount so determined. The requirements of this paragraph shall not be deemed met until the requester has explicitly agreed to pay the fee applicable to the request for records, if any, or

has made payment in advance of the fee estimated to be due. If the requester has any outstanding balance of search, review, or duplication fees, the requirements of this paragraph shall not be deemed met until the requester has remitted the outstanding balance due.

(5) *Reasonable description of records; identity and right of the requester.*—(i) The request for records must describe the records in reasonably sufficient detail to enable the IRS employees who are familiar with the subject matter of the request to locate the records without placing an unreasonable burden upon the IRS. While no specific formula for a reasonable description of a record can be established, the requirement shall generally be satisfied if the requester gives the name, taxpayer identification number (*e.g.*, social security number or employer identification number), subject matter, location, and years at issue, of the requested records. If the request seeks records pertaining to pending litigation, the request shall indicate the title of the case, the court in which the case was filed, and the nature of the case. It is suggested that the person making the request furnish any additional information which shall more clearly identify the requested records. Where the requester does not reasonably describe the records being sought, the requester shall be afforded an opportunity to refine the request. Such opportunity may involve a conference with knowledgeable IRS personnel at the discretion of the disclosure officer. The reasonable description requirement shall not be used by officers or employees of the Internal Revenue as a device for improperly withholding records from the public.

(ii) The IRS shall make a reasonable effort to comply fully with all requests for access to records subject only to any applicable exemption set forth in 5 U.S.C. 552(b) or any exclusion described in 5 U.S.C. 552(c). In any situation in which it is determined that a request for voluminous records would unduly burden and interfere with the operations of the IRS, the person making the request shall be asked to be more specific and to narrow the request, or to agree on an orderly procedure for the production of the requested records, in order to satisfy the request without disproportionate adverse effect on IRS operations.

(iii) *Statutory or regulatory restrictions.*—(A) In the case of records containing information with respect to particular persons the disclosure of which is limited by statute or regulations, persons making requests shall establish their identity and right to access to such records. Persons requesting access to such records which pertain to themselves may establish their identity by—

(1) The presentation of a single document bearing a photograph (such as a passport or identification badge), or the presentation of two items of identification which do not bear a photograph but do bear both a name and signature (such as a credit card or organization membership card), in the case of a request made in person,

(2) The submission of the requester's signature, address, and one other identifier (such as a photocopy of a driver's license) bearing the requester's signature, in the case of a request by mail, or

(3) The presentation in person or the submission by mail of a notarized statement, or a statement made under penalty of perjury in accordance with 28 U.S.C. 1746, swearing to or affirming such person's identity.

(B) Additional proof of a person's identity shall be required before the requests shall be deemed to have met the requirement of paragraph (c)(4)(i)(E) of this section if it is determined that additional proof is necessary to protect against unauthorized disclosure of information in a particular case. Persons who have identified themselves to the satisfaction of IRS officials pursuant to this paragraph (c) shall be deemed to have established their right to access records pertaining to themselves. Persons requesting records on behalf of or pertaining to another person must provide adequate proof of the legal relationship under which they assert the right to access the requested records before the requirement of paragraph (c)(4)(i)(E) of this section shall be deemed met.

(C) In the case of an attorney-in-fact, or other person requesting records on behalf of or pertaining to other persons, the requester shall furnish a properly executed power of attorney, Privacy Act consent, or tax information authorization, as appropriate. In the case of a corporation, if the requester has the authority to legally bind the corporation under applicable state law, such as its corporate president or chief executive officer, then a written statement or tax information authorization certifying as to that person's authority to make a request on behalf of the corporation shall be sufficient. If the requester is any other officer or employee of the corporation, then such requester shall furnish a written statement certifying as to that person's authority to make a request on behalf of the corporation by any principal officer and attested to by the secretary or other officer (other than the requester) that the person making the request on behalf of the corporation is properly authorized to make such a request. If the requester is other than one of the above, then such person may furnish a resolution by the corporation's board of directors or other governing body which provides that the person making the request on behalf of the corporation is properly authorized to make such a request, or shall otherwise satisfy the requirements set forth in section 6103(e). A person requesting access to records of a partnership or a subchapter S Corporation shall provide a notarized statement, or a statement made under penalty of perjury in accordance with 28 U.S.C. 1746, that the requester was a member of the partnership or subchapter S corporation for a part of each of the years included in the request.

(6) Requests for expedited processing.— (i) When a requester demonstrates compelling need, a request shall be taken out of order and given expedited treatment. A compelling need involves—

(A) Circumstances in which the lack of expedited treatment could reasonably be expected to pose an imminent threat to the life or physical safety of an individual;

(B) An urgency to inform the public concerning actual or alleged Federal government activity, if made by a person primarily engaged in disseminating information. A person primarily engaged in disseminating information, if not a fulltime representative of the news media, as defined in paragraph (f)(3)(ii)(B) of this section, must establish that he or she is a person whose main professional activity or occupation is information dissemination, though it need not be his or her sole occupation. A person primarily engaged in disseminating information does not include individuals who are engaged only incidentally in the dissemination of information. The standard of urgency to inform requires that the records requested pertain to a matter of current exigency to the American public, beyond the public's right to know about government activity generally, and that delaying a response to a request for records would compromise a significant recognized interest to and throughout the American general public;

(C) The loss of substantial due process rights.

(ii) A requester who seeks expedited processing must submit a statement, certified to be true and correct to the best of his or her knowledge and belief, explaining in detail why there is a compelling need for expedited processing.

(iii) A request for expedited processing may be made at the time of the initial request for records or at any later time. For a prompt determination, requests for expedited processing must be submitted to the responsible official of the IRS who maintains the records requested except that a request for expedited processing under paragraph (c)(6)(i)(B) of this section shall be submitted directly to the Director, Communications Division, whose address is Office of Media Relations, CL:C:M, Internal Revenue Service, Room 7032, 1111 Constitution Avenue, N.W., Washington, D.C. 20224.

(iv) Upon receipt by the responsible official in the IRS, a request for expedited processing shall be considered and a determination as to whether to grant or deny the request shall be made, and the requester notified, within ten days of the date of the request; provided that in no event shall the IRS have less than five days (excluding Saturdays, Sundays, and legal public holidays) from the date of the responsible official's receipt of the request for such processing. The determination to grant or deny a request for expedited processing shall be made solely on the information initially provided by the requester.

(v) An appeal of an initial determination to deny expedited processing must be made within ten days of the date of the initial determination to deny expedited processing, and must

Reg. §601.702(c)(6)(v)

otherwise comply with the requirements of paragraph (c)(10) of this section. Both the envelope and the appeal itself shall be clearly marked, "Appeal for Expedited Processing."

(vi) IRS action to deny or affirm denial of a request for expedited processing pursuant to this paragraph, and IRS failure to respond in a timely manner to such a request shall be subject to judicial review, except that judicial review shall be based on the record before the IRS at the time of the determination. A district court of the United States shall not have jurisdiction to review the IRS's denial of expedited processing of a request for records after the IRS has provided a complete response to the request.

(7) *Date of receipt of request.*—(i) Requests for records and any separate agreement to pay, final notification of waiver of fees, or letter transmitting payment, shall be promptly stamped with the date of delivery to or dispatch by the office of the IRS official responsible for the control of the records requested. A request for records shall be considered to have been received on the date on which a complete request containing the information required by paragraphs (c)(4)(i)(A) through (I) has been received by the IRS official responsible for the control of the records requested. A determination that a request is deficient in any respect is not a denial of access, and such determinations are not subject to administrative appeal.

(ii) The latest of such stamped dates shall be deemed for purposes of this section to be the date of receipt of the request, provided that the requirements of paragraphs (c)(4)(i)(A) through (I) of this section have been satisfied, and, where applicable—

(A) The requester has agreed in writing, by executing a separate contract or otherwise, to pay the fees for search, duplication, and review determined due in accordance with paragraph (f) of this section, or

(B) The fees have been waived in accordance with paragraph (f) of this section, or

(C) Payment in advance has been received from the requester.

(8) *Search for records requested.*—(i) Upon the receipt of a request, search services shall be performed by IRS personnel to identify and locate the requested records. Search time includes any and all time spent looking for material responsive to the request, including page-by-page or line-by-line identification of material within records. Where duplication of an entire record would be less costly than a line-by-line identification, duplication should be substituted for this kind of search. With respect to records maintained in computerized form, a search shall include services functionally analogous to a search for records which are maintained on paper.

(ii) In determining which records are responsive to a request, the IRS official responsible for the control of the records requested shall include only those records within the official's possession and control as of the date of the re-

ceipt of the request by the appropriate disclosure officer.

(9) *Initial determination.*—(i) *Responsible official.*—(A) The Associate Director, Personnel Security or delegate shall have the sole authority to make initial determinations with respect to requests for records under that office's control.

(B) The Director of the Office of Governmental Liaison and Disclosure or delegate shall have the sole authority to make initial determinations with respect to all other requests for records of the IRS maintained in the Headquarters and its National Office of the Chief Counsel. For all other records within the control of the IRS, the initial determination with respect to requests for records may be made either by the Director, Office of Governmental Liaison and Disclosure, or by the IRS officials responsible for the control of the records requested, or their delegates (see paragraph (h) of this section).

(ii) *Processing of request.*—The appropriate responsible official or delegate shall respond in the approximate order of receipt of the requests, to the extent consistent with sound administrative practice. In any event, the initial determination shall be made and notification thereof mailed within twenty days (excepting Saturdays, Sundays, and legal public holidays) after the date of receipt of the request, as determined in accordance with paragraph (c)(7) of this section, unless the responsible official invokes an extension pursuant to paragraph (c)(11) of this section, the requester otherwise agrees to an extension of the twenty day time limitation, or the request is an expedited request.

(iii) *Granting of request.*—If the request is granted in full or in part, and if the requester wants a copy of the records, a statement of the applicable fees, if there are any, shall be mailed to the requester either at the time of the determination or shortly thereafter. In the case of a request for inspection, the records shall be made available promptly for inspection, at the time and place stated, normally at the appropriate office where the records requested are controlled. If the person making the request has expressed a desire to inspect the records at another office of the IRS, a reasonable effort shall be made to comply with the request. Records shall be made available for inspection at such reasonable and proper times so as not to interfere with their use by the IRS or to exclude other persons from making inspections. In addition, reasonable limitations may be placed on the number of records which may be inspected by a person on any given date. The person making the request shall not be allowed to remove the records from the office where inspection is made. If, after making inspection, the person making the request desires copies of all or a portion of the requested records, copies shall be furnished upon payment of the established fees prescribed by paragraph (f) of this section.

(iv) *Denial of request.*—If it is determined that some records shall be denied, the person making the request shall be so notified by mail.

The letter of notification shall specify the city or other location where the requested records are situated, contain a brief statement of the grounds for not granting the request in full including the exemption(s) relied upon, the name and any title or position of the official responsible for the denial, and advise the person making the request of the right to appeal to the Commissioner in accordance with paragraph (c)(10) of this section.

(A) In denying a request for records, in whole or in part, the IRS shall include the date that the request was received in the appropriate disclosure office, and shall provide an estimate of the volume of the denied matter to the person making the request, unless providing such estimate would harm an interest protected by an exemption in 5 U.S.C. 552(b) or (c) pursuant to which the denial is made; and

(B) The amount of information deleted shall be indicated on the released portion of the record, unless including that indication would harm an interest protected by an exemption in 5 U.S.C. 552(b) under which the deletion is made. If technically feasible, the amount of the information deleted and the asserted exemption shall be indicated at the place in the record where such deletion is made.

(v) *Inability to locate and evaluate within time limits.*—Where the records requested cannot be located and evaluated within the initial twenty day period or any extension thereof in accordance with paragraph (c)(11) of this section, the search for the records or evaluation shall continue, but the requester shall be notified, and advised that the requester may consider such notification a denial of the request for records. The requester shall be provided with a statement of judicial rights along with the notification letter. The requester may also be invited, in the alternative, to agree to a voluntary extension of time in which to locate and evaluate the records. Such voluntary extension of time shall not constitute a waiver of the requester's right to appeal or seek judicial review of any denial of access ultimately made or the requester's right to seek judicial review in the event of failure to comply with the time extension granted.

(10) *Administrative appeal.*—(i) The requester may submit an administrative appeal to the Commissioner of Internal Revenue by letter that is postmarked within 35 days after the later of the date of any letter of notification described in paragraph (c)(9)(iv) of this section, the date of any letter of notification of an adverse determination of the requester's category described in paragraph (f)(3) of this section, the date of any letter of notification of an adverse determination of the requester's fee waiver or reduction request described in paragraph (f)(2) of this section, the date of any letter determining that no responsive records exist, or the date of the last transmission of the last records released. An administrative appeal for denial of a request for expedited processing must be made to the Commissioner of Internal Revenue by letter that is postmarked within ten days after the date of any letter of notification discussed in paragraph (c)(6)(iv) of this section.

(ii) The letter of appeal shall

(A) Be made in writing and signed by the requester;

(B) Be addressed to the Commissioner and mailed to IRS Appeals, 6377A Riverside Avenue, Suite 110, Riverside, California 92506-FOIA Appeal;

(C) Reasonably describe the records requested to which the appeal pertains in accordance with paragraph (c)(5)(i) of this section;

(D) Set forth the address where the appellant desires to be notified of the determination on appeal;

(E) Specify the date of the request, the office to which the request was submitted, and where possible, enclose a copy of the initial request and the initial determination being appealed; and

(F) Ask the Commissioner to grant the request for records, fee waiver, expedited processing, or favorable fee category, as applicable, or verify that an appropriate search was conducted and the responsive records were either produced or an appropriate exemption asserted. The person submitting the appeal may submit any argument in support of the appeal in the letter of appeal.

(iii) Appeals shall be stamped promptly with the date of their receipt in the Office of Appeals, and the later of this stamped date or the stamped date of a document submitted subsequently which supplements the original appeal so that the appeal satisfies the requirements set forth in paragraphs (c)(10)(ii)(A) through (F) of this section shall be deemed by the IRS to be the date of receipt of the appeal for all purposes of this section. The Commissioner or a delegate shall acknowledge receipt of the appeal and advise the requester of the date of receipt and the date a response is due in accordance with this paragraph. If an appeal fails to satisfy any of the requirements of paragraph (c)(10)(ii)(A) through (F) of this section, the person making the request shall be advised promptly in writing of the additional requirements to be met. Except for appeals of denials of expedited processing, the determination to affirm the initial denial (in whole or in part) or to grant the request for records shall be made and notification of the determination shall be mailed within twenty days (exclusive of Saturdays, Sundays, and legal public holidays) after the date of receipt of the appeal unless extended pursuant to paragraph (c)(11)(i) of this section. Appeals of initial determinations to deny expedited processing must be made within ten calendar days of the determination to deny the expedited processing. If it is determined that the appeal from the initial denial is to be denied (in whole or in part), the requester shall be notified in writing of the denial, the reasons therefor, the name and title or position of the official responsible for the denial on appeal, and the provisions of 5 U.S.C. 552(a)(4) for judicial review of that determination.

(11) *Time extensions.*—(i) *Unusual circumstances.*—(A) In unusual circumstances, the time limitations specified in paragraphs (c)(9) and (10) of this section may be extended by written notice from the official charged with the duty of making the determinations to the person making the request or appeal setting forth the reasons for this extension and the date on which the determination is expected to be sent. As used in this paragraph, the term *unusual circumstances* means, but only to the extent reasonably necessary to the proper processing of the particular request:

(1) The need to search for and collect the requested records from field facilities or other establishments that are separate from the office processing the request;

(2) The need to search for, collect, and appropriately examine a voluminous amount of separate and distinct records which are demanded in a single request;

(3) The need for consultation, which shall be conducted with all practicable speed, with another agency having a substantial interest in the determination of the request or among two or more constituent units of the Department of the Treasury having substantial subject matter interest therein; and

(4) The need for consultation with business submitters to determine the nature and extent of proprietary information in accordance with this section.

(B) Any extension or extensions of time for unusual circumstances shall not cumulatively total more than ten days (exclusive of Saturday, Sunday and legal public holidays). If additional time is needed to process the request, the IRS shall notify the requester and provide the requester an opportunity to limit the scope of the request or arrange for an alternative time frame for processing the request or a modified request. The requester shall retain the right to define the desired scope of the request, as long as it meets the requirements contained in this section.

(ii) *Aggregation of requests.*—If more than one request is received from the same requester, or from a group of requesters acting in concert, and the IRS believes that such requests constitute a single request which would otherwise satisfy the unusual circumstances specified in subparagraph (c)(11)(i) of this section, and the requests involve clearly related matters, the IRS may aggregate these requests for processing purposes. Multiple requests involving unrelated matters shall not be aggregated.

(12) *Failure to comply.*—If the IRS fails to comply with the time limitations specified in paragraphs (c)(9), (10), or paragraph (c)(11)(i) of this section, any person making a request for records satisfying the requirements of paragraphs (c)(4)(i)(A) through (I) of this section, shall be deemed to have exhausted administrative remedies with respect to such request. Accordingly, this person may initiate suit in accordance with paragraph (c)(13) of this section.

(13) *Judicial review.*—If an administrative appeal pursuant to paragraph (c)(10) of this section for records or fee waiver or reduction is denied, or if a request for expedited processing is denied and there has been no determination as to the release of records, or if a request for a favorable fee category under paragraph (f)(3) of this section is denied, or a determination is made that there are no responsive records, or if no determination is made within the twenty day periods specified in paragraphs (c)(9) and (10) of this section, or the period of any extension pursuant to paragraph (c)(11)(i) of this section, or by grant of the requester, respectively, the person making the request may commence an action in a United States district court in the district in which the requester resides, in which the requester's principal place of business is located, in which the records are situated, or in the District of Columbia, pursuant to 5 U.S.C. 552(a)(4)(B). The statute authorizes an action only against the agency. With respect to records of the IRS, the agency is the IRS, not an officer or an employee thereof. Service of process in such an action shall be in accordance with the Federal Rules of Civil Procedure (28 U.S.C. App.) applicable to actions against an agency of the United States. Delivery of process upon the IRS shall be directed to the Commissioner of Internal Revenue, Attention: CC:PA, 1111 Constitution Avenue, N.W., Washington, D.C. 20224. The IRS shall serve an answer or otherwise plead to any complaint made under this paragraph within 30 days after service upon it, unless the court otherwise directs for good cause shown. The district court shall determine the matter *de novo*, and may examine the contents of the IRS records in question *in camera* to determine whether such records or any part thereof shall be withheld under any of the exemptions described in 5 U.S.C. 552(b) and the exclusions described in 5 U.S.C. 552(c). The burden shall be upon the IRS to sustain its action in not making the requested records available. The court may assess against the United States reasonable attorney fees and other litigation costs reasonably incurred by the person making the request in any case in which the complainant has substantially prevailed.

(14) *Preservation of records.*—All correspondence relating to the requests received by the IRS under this chapter, and all records processed pursuant to such requests, shall be preserved, until such time as the destruction of such correspondence and records is authorized pursuant to Title 44 of the United States Code. Under no circumstances shall records be destroyed while they are the subject of a pending request, appeal, or lawsuit under 5 U.S.C. 552.

(d) *Rules for disclosure of certain specified matters.*—Requests for certain specified categories of records shall be processed by the IRS in accordance with other established procedures.

(1) *Inspection of tax returns and attachments or transcripts.*—The inspection of returns and attachments is governed by the provisions of the internal revenue laws and regulations thereun-

der promulgated by the Secretary of the Treasury. *See* section 6103 and the regulations thereunder. Written requests for a copy of a tax return and attachments or a transcript of a tax return shall be made using IRS Form 4506, "Request for Copy or Transcript of Tax Form." A reasonable fee, as the Commissioner may from time to time establish, may be charged for such copies.

(2) *Record of seizure and sale of real estate.*— Subject to the rules on disclosure set forth in section 6103, Record 21, Part 2, "Record of seizure and sale of real estate", is available for public inspection in the local IRS office where the real estate is located. Copies of Record 21, Part 2 shall be furnished upon written request. Members of the public may call the toll-free IRS Customer Service number, 1-800-829-1040, to obtain the address of the appropriate local office. Record 21 does not list real estate seized for use in violation of the internal revenue laws (*see* section 7302).

(3) *Public inspection of certain information returns, notices, and reports furnished by certain tax-exempt organizations and certain trusts.*—Subject to the rules on disclosure set forth in section 6104: Information furnished on any Form 990 series or Form 1041-A returns, pursuant to sections 6033 and 6034, shall be made available for public inspection and copying, upon written request; information furnished by organizations exempt from tax under section 527 on Forms 8871, Political Organization Notice of Section 527 Status, and Forms 8872, Political Organization Report of Contributions and Expenditures, are available for public inspection and copying from the IRS website at *www.eforms.irs.gov.* In addition, Forms 8871 and 8872 shall be made available for public inspection and copying, upon written request; and information furnished by organizations exempt from tax under section 527 on Form 1120-POL pursuant to section 6012(a)(6) shall be made available for public inspection and copying upon written request. Written requests to inspect or obtain copies of any of the information described in this paragraph (d)(3) shall be made using Form 4506-A, "Request for Public Inspection or Copy of Exempt or Political Organization IRS Form," and be directed to the appropriate address listed on Form 4506-A.

(4) *Public inspection of applications and determinations of certain organizations for tax exemption.*—Subject to the rules on disclosure set forth in section 6104, applications, including Forms 1023 and 1024, and certain papers submitted in support of such applications, filed by organizations described in section 501(c) or (d) and determined to be exempt from taxation under section 501(a), and any letter or other document issued by the IRS with respect to such applications, shall be made available for public inspection and copying, upon written request. Written requests to inspect or obtain copies of this information shall be made using Form 4506-A, "Request for Public Inspection or Copy of Exempt or Political

Organization IRS Form" and be directed to the appropriate address listed on Form 4506-A.

(5) *Public inspection of applications and annual returns with respect to certain deferred compensation plans and accounts and employee plans.*—Subject to the rules on disclosure set forth in section 6104; forms, applications, and papers submitted in support of such applications, with respect to the qualification of a pension, profit sharing, or stock bonus plan under sections 401(a), 403(a), or 405(a), an individual retirement account described in section 408(a), an individual retirement annuity described in section 408(b), or with respect to the exemption from tax of an organization forming part of such a plan or account, and any document issued by the IRS dealing with such qualification or exemption, shall be open to public inspection and copying upon written request. This paragraph shall not apply with respect to plans with no more than 25 plan participants. Written requests to inspect or obtain copies of such material shall be directed to IRS Customer Service—Tax Exempt & Government Entities Division (TEGE), P.O. Box 2508, Room 2023, Cincinnati, Ohio 45201; and information furnished on the Form 5500 series of returns, pursuant to section 6058, shall be made available for public inspection and copying upon written request. Except for requests for Form 5500-EZ, written requests to inspect or to obtain a copy of this information shall be directed to the Department of Labor, Public Disclosure, Room N-5638, 200 Constitution Avenue, N.W., Washington, D.C. 20210. Written requests to inspect or to obtain a copy of Form 5500-EZ shall be directed to the Internal Revenue Service Center, P.O. Box 9941, Stop 6716, Ogden, Utah 84409.

(6) *Publication of statistics of income.*—Statistics with respect to the operation of the income tax laws are published annually in accordance with section 6108 and § 301.6108-1.

(7) *Comments received in response to a notice of proposed rulemaking, a solicitation for public comments, or prepublication comments.*—Written comments received in response to a notice of proposed rulemaking, a solicitation for public comments, or prepublication comments, may be inspected, upon written request, by any person upon compliance with the provisions of this paragraph. Comments may be inspected in the Freedom of Information Reading Room, IRS, 1111 Constitution Avenue, N.W., Room 1621, Washington, D.C. The request to inspect comments must be in writing and signed by the person making the request and shall be addressed to the Commissioner of Internal Revenue, Attn: CC:ITA:RU, P.O. Box 7604, Ben Franklin Station, Washington, D.C. 20044. The person submitting the written request may inspect the comments that are the subject of the request during regular business hours. If the requester wishes to inspect the documents, the requester shall be contacted by IRS Freedom of Information Reading Room personnel when the documents are available for inspection. Copies of comments may be made in the Freedom of Information Reading Room by

Reg. § 601.702(d)(7)

the person making the request or may be requested, in writing, to the Commissioner of Internal Revenue, Attn: CC:ITA:RU, P.O. Box 7604, Ben Franklin Station, Washington, D.C. 20044. The IRS shall comply with requests for records under the paragraph within a reasonable time. The provisions of paragraph (f)(5)(iii) of this section, relating to fees for duplication, shall apply with respect to requests made in accordance with this paragraph.

(8) *Accepted offers in compromise.*—For one year after the date of execution, a copy of the Form 7249, "Offer Acceptance Report," for each accepted offer in compromise with respect to any liability for a tax imposed by Title 26 shall be made available for inspection and copying in the location designated by the Compliance Area Director or Compliance Services Field Director within the Small Business and Self-Employed Division (SBSE) of the taxpayer's geographic area of residence.

(9) *Public inspection of written determinations.*—Certain rulings, determination letters, technical advice memorandums, and Chief Counsel advice are open to public inspection pursuant to section 6110.

(e) *Other disclosure procedures.*—For procedures to be followed by officers and employees of the IRS upon receipt of a request or demand for certain internal revenue records or information the disclosure procedure for which is not covered by this section, see § 301.9000-1.

(f) *Fees for services.*—(1) *In general.*—Except as otherwise provided, the fees to be charged for search, duplication, and review services performed by the IRS, with respect to the processing of Freedom of Information Act requests, shall be determined and collected in accordance with provisions of this subsection. A fee shall not be charged for monitoring a requester's inspection of records which contains exempt matter. The IRS may recover the applicable fees even if there is ultimately no disclosure of records. Should services other than the services described in this paragraph be requested and rendered, which are not required by the Freedom of Information Act, fees shall be charged to recover the actual direct cost to the IRS.

(2) *Waiver or reduction of fees.*—(i) The fees authorized by this paragraph may be waived or reduced on a case-by-case basis in accordance with this subsection by any IRS official who is authorized to make the initial determination pursuant to paragraph (c)(9) of this section. Fees shall be waived or reduced by such official when it is determined that disclosure of the requested information is in the public interest because it is likely to contribute significantly to public understanding of the operations or activities of the IRS and is not primarily in the commercial interest of the requester. Such officials shall consider several factors, including, but not limited to, paragraphs (f)(2)(i) through (vi), in determining requests for waiver or reduction of fees—

(A) Whether the subject of the releasable records concerns the agency's operations or activities;

(B) Whether the releasable records are likely to contribute to an understanding of the agency's operations or activities;

(C) Whether the releasable records are likely to contribute to the general public's understanding of the agency's operations or activities (*e.g.*, how will the requester convey the information to the general public);

(D) The significance of the contribution to the general public's understanding of the agency's operations or activities (*e.g.*, is the information contained in the releasable records already available to the general public);

(E) The existence and magnitude of the requester's commercial interest, as that term is used in paragraph (f)(3)(i)(A) of this section, being furthered by the releasable records; and

(F) Whether the magnitude of the requester's commercial interest is sufficiently large in comparison to the general public's interest.

(ii) Requesters asking for reduction or waiver of fees must state the reasons why they believe disclosure meets the standards set forth in paragraph (f)(2)(ii) of this section in a written request signed by the requester.

(iii) The indigence of the requester shall not be considered as a factor to determine if the requester is entitled to a reduction or waiver of fees.

(iv) Normally, no charge shall be made for providing records to federal, state, local, or foreign governments, or agencies or offices thereof, or international governmental organizations.

(v) The initial request for waiver or reduction of fees shall be addressed to the official of the IRS to whose office the request for disclosure is delivered pursuant to paragraph (c)(4)(i)(C) of this section. Appeals from denials of requests for waiver or reduction of fees shall be decided by the Commissioner's delegate in accordance with the criteria set forth in paragraph (f)(2)(ii) of this section. Appeals shall be received by the Commissioner's delegate within 35 days of the date of the letter of notification denying the initial request for waiver or reduction and shall be decided promptly. See paragraph (c)(10)(ii)(B) of this section for the appropriate address. Upon receipt of the determination on appeal to deny a request for waiver of fees, the requester may initiate an action in a United States district court to review the request for waiver of fees. In such action, the court shall consider the matter *de novo*, except that the court's review of the matter shall be limited to the record before the IRS official to whose office the request for waiver is delivered. In such action, the court shall consider the matter under the arbitrary and capricious standard.

(3) *Categories of requesters.*—(i) *Attestation.*— A request for records under this section shall include an attestation as to the status of the requester for use by the IRS official to whose office the request is delivered in determining the

appropriate fees to be assessed. No attestation is required for a requester who falls within paragraph (f)(3)(ii)(E) (an "other requester").

(ii) *Categories.*—(A) *Commercial use requester.*—Any person who seeks information for a use or purpose that furthers the commercial, trade, or profit interests of the requester or the person on whose behalf the request is made.

(B) *News media requester.*—Any person actively gathering news for an entity that is organized and operated to publish or broadcast news (*i.e.,* information about current events or of current interest to the public) to the public. News media entities include, but are not limited to, television or radio stations broadcasting to the public at large, publishers of periodicals, to the extent they disseminate news, who make their periodicals available for purchase or subscription by the general public, computerized news services and telecommunications. Free lance journalists shall be included as media requesters if they can demonstrate a solid basis for expecting publication through a qualifying news entity (*e.g.,* publication contract, past publication record). Specialized periodicals, although catering to a narrower audience, may be considered media requesters so long as they are available to the public generally, via newsstand or subscription.

(C) *Educational institution requester.*—Any person who, on behalf of a preschool, public or private elementary or secondary school, institution of undergraduate or graduate higher education, institution of professional or vocational education, which operates a program or programs of scholarly research, seeks records in furtherance of the institution's scholarly research and is not for a commercial use. This category does not include requesters wanting records for use in meeting individual academic research or study requirements.

(D) *Noncommercial scientific institution requester.*—Any person on behalf of an institution that is not operated on a commercial basis, that is operated solely for the purpose of conducting scientific research whose results are not intended to promote any particular product or industry.

(E) *Other requester.*—Any requester who does not fall within the categories described in paragraphs (f)(3)(ii)(A) through (D).

(iii) *Determination of proper category.*—Where the IRS has reasonable cause to doubt the use to which a requester shall put the records sought, or where that use is not clear from the record itself, the IRS shall seek additional clarification from the requester before assigning the request to a specific category. In any event, a determination of the proper category of requester shall be based upon a review of the requester's submission and may also be based upon the IRS' own records.

(iv) *Allowable charges.*—(A) *Commercial use requesters.*—Records shall be provided to commercial use requesters for the cost of search, duplication, and review (including doing all that is necessary to excise and otherwise prepare records for release) of records. Commercial use requesters are not entitled to two hours of free search time or 100 pages of free duplication.

(B) *News media, educational institution, and noncommercial scientific institution requesters.*—Records shall be provided to news media, educational institution, and noncommercial scientific institution requesters for the cost of duplication alone, excluding fees for the first 100 pages.

(C) *Other requesters.*—Requesters who do not fit into any of the above categories shall be charged fees that shall cover the full actual direct cost of searching for and duplicating records, except that the first two hours of search time and first 100 pages of duplication shall be furnished without charge. Requests from individuals for records about themselves maintained in the IRS's systems of records shall continue to be treated under the fee provisions of the Privacy Act of 1974, which permits fees only for duplication after the first 100 pages are furnished free of charge.

(4) *Avoidance of unexpected fees.*—(i) In order to protect requesters from unexpected fees, all requests for records shall state the agreement of the requesters to pay the fees determined in accordance with paragraph (f)(5) of this section or state the upper limit they are willing to pay to cover the costs of processing their requests.

(ii) When the fees for processing requests are estimated by the IRS to exceed the upper limit agreed to by a requester, or when a requester has failed to state a limit and the costs are estimated to exceed $250, and the IRS has not then determined to waive or reduce the fees, a notice shall be sent to the requester. This notice shall—

(A) Inform the requester of the estimated costs;

(B) Extend an offer to the requester to confer with agency personnel in an attempt to reformulate the request in a manner which shall reduce the fees and still meet the needs of the requester;

(C) If the requester is not amenable to reformulation, which would reduce fees to under $250, then advance payment of the estimated fees shall be required; and

(D) Inform the requester that the time period, within which the IRS is obliged to make a determination on the request, shall not begin to run, pending a reformulation of the request or the receipt of advance payment from the requester, as appropriate.

(5) *Fees for services.*—The fees for services performed by the IRS shall be imposed and collected as set forth in this paragraph. No fees shall be charged if the costs of routine collecting and processing the fees allowable under 5 U.S.C. 552(a)(4)(A) are likely to equal or exceed the amount of the fee.

(i) *Search services.*—Fees charged for search services are as follows:

(A) *Searches for records other than computerized records.*—The IRS shall charge for search services at the salary rate(s) (*i.e.*, basic pay plus 16 percent) of the employee(s) making the search. An average rate for the range of grades typically involved may be established. Fees may be charged for search time as prescribed in this section even if the time spent searching does not yield any records, or if records are denied.

(B) *Searches for computerized records.*—Actual direct cost of the search, including computer search time, runs, and the operator's salary. The fee for computer output shall be actual direct costs. For requesters in the "other requester" category, the charge for the computer search shall begin when the cost of the search (including the operator time and the cost of operating the computer) equals the equivalent dollar amount of two hours of the salary of the person performing the search.

(C) *Searches requiring travel or transportation.*—Shipping charges to transport records from one location to another, or for the transportation of an employee to the site of requested records when it is necessary to locate rather than examine the records, shall be at the rate of actual cost of such shipping or transportation.

(ii) *Review Services.*—(A) *Review defined.*—Review is the process of examining records in response to a commercial use requester, as that term is defined in paragraph (f)(3)(i)(A), upon initial consideration of the applicability of an exemption described in 5 U.S.C. 552(b) or an exclusion described in 5 U.S.C. 552(c) to the requested records, be it at the initial request or administrative appeal level, to determine whether any portion of any record responsive to the request is permitted to be withheld. Review includes doing all that is necessary to excise and otherwise prepare the records for release. Review does not include the time spent on resolving general legal or policy issues regarding the applicability of exemptions to the requested records.

(B) *Fees charged for review services.*—The IRS shall charge commercial use requesters for review of records at the initial determination stage at the salary rate(s) (*i.e.*, basic pay plus 16 percent) of the employee(s) making the review. An average rate for the range of grades typically involved may be established by the Commissioner.

(iii) *Duplication other than for tax returns and attachments.*—(A) Duplication fees charged for copies of paper records shall be a reasonable fee, as the Commissioner may from time to time establish.

(B) The actual direct cost of duplication for photographs, films, videotapes, audiotapes, compact disks, and other materials shall be charged.

(C) Records may be provided to a private contractor for copying and the requester shall be charged for the actual cost of duplication charged by the private contractor.

(D) When other duplication processes not specifically identified above are requested and provided pursuant to the Freedom of Information Act, their actual direct cost to the IRS shall be charged.

(E) Where the condition of the record does not enable the IRS to make legible copies, the IRS shall not attempt to reconstruct it. The official having jurisdiction over the record shall furnish the best copy that is available and advise the requester of this fact.

(iv) *Charges for copies of tax returns and attachments, and transcripts of tax returns.*—A charge shall be made for each copy of a tax return and its attachments, and transcripts of tax returns, supplied in response to a Form 4506, "Request for Copy of Tax Form." The amount of the charge shall be a reasonable fee as computed by the Commissioner from time to time, and as set forth on Form 4506.

(v) *Other services.*—Other services and materials requested (*e.g.*, certification, express mailing) which are not specifically covered by this part and/or not required by the Freedom of Information Act are provided at the discretion of the IRS and are chargeable at the actual direct cost to the IRS.

(6) *Printed material.*—Certain relevant government publications which shall be placed on the shelves of the Freedom of Information Reading Room shall not be sold at that location. Copies of pages of these publications may be duplicated on the premises and a fee for such service may be charged in accordance with paragraph (f)(5)(iii) of this section. A person desiring to purchase the complete publication, for example, an Internal Revenue Bulletin, should contact the Superintendent of Documents, U.S. Government Printing Office, Washington, D.C. 20402.

(7) *Search, duplication, and deletion services with respect to records open to public inspection pursuant to section 6110.*—Fees charged for searching for, making deletions in, and copies of records subject to public inspection pursuant to section 6110 only upon written request shall be at the actual cost, as the Commissioner may from time to time establish.

(8) *Form of payment.*—Payment shall be made by check or money order, payable to the order of the Treasury of the United States.

(9) *Advance payments.*—(i) If previous fees have not been paid in a timely fashion, as defined in paragraph (f)(10) of this section, or where the estimated fees exceed $250, the IRS shall require payment in full of any outstanding fees and all estimated fees prior to processing a request. Additionally, the IRS reserves the right to require payment of fees after a request is processed and before any records are released to a requester. For purposes of this paragraph, a requester is the individual in whose name a request is made; however, where a request is made on behalf of another individual, and previous

fees have not been paid within the designated time period by either the requester or the individual on whose behalf the request is made, then the IRS shall require payment in full of all outstanding fees and all estimated fees before processing the request.

(ii) When the IRS acts pursuant to paragraph (f)(9) (i) of this section, the administrative time limits prescribed in paragraphs (c)(9) and (10) of this section, plus permissible extensions of these time limits as prescribed in paragraph (c)(11)(i) of this section, shall begin only after the IRS official to whom the request is delivered has received the fees described above in paragraph (f)(9)(i) of this section.

(10) *Interest.*—Interest shall be charged to requesters who fail to pay the fees in a timely fashion; that is, within 30 days following the day on which the statement of fees as set forth in paragraph (c)(9)(i) of this section was sent by the IRS official to whom the request was delivered. Whenever interest is charged, the IRS shall begin assessing interest on the 31st day following the date the statement of fees was mailed to the requester. Interest shall be at the rate prescribed in 31 U.S.C. 3717. In addition, the IRS shall take all steps authorize by the Debt Collection Act of 1982, including administrative offset, disclosure to consumer reporting agencies, and use of collection agencies, as otherwise authorized by law to effect payment.

(11) *Aggregating requests.*—When the IRS official to whom a request is delivered reasonably believes that a requester or group of requesters is attempting to break down a request into a series of requests for the purpose of evading the assessment of fees, the IRS shall aggregate such requests and charge accordingly, upon notification to the requester and/or requesters.

(g) *Business information and contractor proposal procedures.*—(1) *In general.*—Business information provided to the IRS by a business submitter shall not be disclosed pursuant to a Freedom of Information Act request except in accordance with this section.

(2) *Definition.*—Business information is any trade secret or other confidential financial or commercial (including research) information.

(3) *Notice to business submitters.*—Except where it is determined that the information is covered by paragraph (g)(9), the official having control over the requested records, which includes business information, shall provide a business submitter with prompt written notice of a request encompassing its business information whenever required in accordance with paragraph (g)(4) of this section. Such written notice shall either describe the exact nature of the business information requested or provide copies of the records or portions thereof containing the business information.

(4) *When notice is required.*—(i) For business information submitted to the IRS prior to October 13, 1987, the official having control over the

requested records shall provide a business submitter with notice of a request whenever—

(A) The business information was submitted to the IRS upon a commitment of confidentiality; or

(B) The business information was voluntarily submitted and it is of a kind that would customarily not be released to the public by the person from whom it was obtained; or

(C) The official has reason to believe that disclosure of the information may result in commercial or financial injury to the business submitter.

(ii) For business information submitted to the IRS on or after October 13, 1987, the IRS shall provide a business submitter with notice of a request whenever—

(A) The business submitter has designated the information as commercially or financially sensitive information; or

(B) The official has reason to believe that disclosure of the information may result in commercial or financial injury to the business submitter.

(iii) The business submitter's designation that the information is commercially or financially sensitive information should be supported by a statement or certification by an officer or authorized representative of the business providing specific justification that the information in question is, in fact, confidential commercial or financial information and has not been disclosed to the public.

(iv) Notice of a request for business information falling within paragraph (g)(4)(ii)(A) of this section shall be required for a period of not more than ten years after the date of submission unless the business submitter requests, and provides acceptable justification for, a specific notice period of greater duration.

(5) *Opportunity to object to disclosure.*—Through the notice described in paragraph (g)(3) of this section, the official having control over the requested records shall afford a business submitter ten days (excepting Saturdays, Sundays and legal public holidays) within which to provide the official with a detailed statement of any objection to disclosure. Such statement shall specify all grounds for withholding any of the information, with particular attention to why the information is claimed to be trade secret or commercial or financial information that is privileged and confidential. Information provided by a business submitter pursuant to this paragraph may itself be subject to disclosure under 5 U.S.C. 552.

(6) *Notice of intent to disclose.*—The IRS shall consider a business submitter's objections and specific grounds for nondisclosure prior to determining whether to disclose business information. Whenever the official having control over the requested records decides to disclose business information over the objection of a business submitter, the official shall forward to the business submitter a written notice which shall include—

Reg. §601.702(g)(6)

(i) A statement of the reasons for which the business submitter's disclosure objections were not sustained;

(ii) A description of the business information to be disclosed; and

(iii) A specified disclosure date, which is ten days (excepting Saturdays, Sundays and legal public holidays) after the notice of the final decision to release the requested records has been mailed to the submitter. Except as otherwise prohibited by law, a copy of the disclosure notice shall be forwarded to the requester at the same time.

(7) *Judicial review.*—(i) *In general.*—The IRS' disposition of the request and the submitter's objections shall be subject to judicial review under paragraph (c)(14) of this section. A requester is not required to exhaust administrative remedies if a complaint has been filed under this paragraph by a business submitter of the information contained in the requested records. Likewise, a business submitter is not required to exhaust administrative remedies if a complaint has been filed by the requester of these records.

(ii) *Notice of FOIA lawsuit.*—Whenever a requester brings suit seeking to compel disclosure of business information covered by paragraph (g)(4) of this section, the official having control over the requested records shall promptly provide the business submitter with written notice thereof.

(iii) *Exception to notice requirement.*—The notice requirements of this paragraph shall not apply if—

(A) The official having control over the records determines that the business information shall not be disclosed;

(B) The information lawfully has been published or otherwise made available to the public; or

(C) Disclosure of the information is required by law (other than 5 U.S.C. 552).

(8) *Appeals.*—Procedures for administrative appeals from denials of requests for business information are to be processed in accordance with paragraph (c)(10) of this section.

(9) *Contractor Proposals.*—(i) Pursuant to 41 U.S.C. 253b(m), the IRS shall not release under the Freedom of Information Act any proposal submitted by a contractor in response to the requirements of a solicitation for a competitive proposal, unless that proposal is set forth or incorporated by reference in a contract entered into between the IRS and the contractor that submitted the proposal. For purposes of this paragraph, the term *proposal* means any proposal, including a technical, management, or cost proposal, submitted by a contractor in response to the requirements of a solicitation for a competitive proposal.

(ii) A copy of the FOIA request for information protected from disclosure under this paragraph shall be furnished to the contractor who submitted the proposal.

(h) *Responsible officials and their addresses.*—For purposes of this section, the IRS officials in the disclosure offices listed below are responsible for the control of records within their geographic area. In the case of records of the Headquarters Office (including records of the National Office of the Office of Chief Counsel), except as provided in paragraph (c)(9)(i)(A), the Director, Office of Governmental Liaison and Disclosure, or delegate, is the responsible official. Requests for these records should be sent to:

IRS FOIA Request
Headquarters Disclosure Office
CL:GLD:D
1111 Constitution Avenue, N.W.
Washington, D.C. 20224

(1) For Personnel Background Investigation Records, the address of the responsible official is:

Internal Revenue Service
Attn: Associate Director, Personnel Security
Room 4244, A:PS:PSO
1111 Constitution Avenue N.W.
Washington, D.C. 20224

(2) For records of the Office of Chief Counsel other than those located in the Headquarters or Division Counsel immediate offices, records shall be deemed to be under the jurisdiction of the local area Disclosure Office. Requesters seeking records under this section should send their requests to the local area Disclosure Office address listed for the state where the requester resides or any activity associated with the records occurred (for states with multiple offices, the request should be sent to the nearest office):

Alabama
IRS FOIA Request
New Orleans Disclosure Office
Mail Stop 40
600 S. Maestri Place
New Orleans, LA 70130

Alaska
IRS FOIA Request
Oakland Disclosure Office
1301 Clay Street, Suite 840-S
Oakland, CA 94612-5210

Arkansas
IRS FOIA Request
Nashville Disclosure Office
MDP 44
801 Broadway, Room 480
Nashville, TN 37203

Arizona
IRS FOIA Request
Phoenix Disclosure Office
Mail Stop 7000 PHX
210 E. Earll Drive
Phoenix, AZ 85012

California
IRS FOIA Request
Laguna Niguel Disclosure Office
24000 Avila Road, M/S 2201
Laguna Niguel, CA 92677-0207
IRS FOIA Request
Los Angeles Disclosure Office
Mail Stop 1020
300 N. Los Angeles Street

Los Angeles, CA 90012-3363
IRS FOIA Request
Oakland Disclosure Office
1301 Clay Street, Suite 840-S
Oakland, CA 94612
IRS FOIA Request
San Jose Disclosure Office
Mail Stop HQ-4603
55 South Market Street
San Jose, CA 95113
Colorado
IRS FOIA Request
Denver Disclosure Office
Mail Stop 7000 DEN
600 17th Street
Denver, CO 80202-2490
Connecticut
IRS FOIA Request
Hartford Disclosure Office
William R. Cotter F.O.B.
Mail Stop 140
135 High Street
Hartford, CT 06103
Delaware
IRS FOIA Request
Baltimore Disclosure Office
George Fallon Fed. Bldg.
31 Hopkins Plaza, Room 1210
Baltimore, MD 21201
District of Columbia
IRS FOIA Request
Baltimore Disclosure Office
George Fallon Fed. Bldg.
31 Hopkins Plaza, Room 1210
Baltimore, MD 21201
Florida
IRS FOIA Request
Fort Lauderdale Disclosure Off.
Mail Stop 4030
7850 SW 6th Court, Rm. 260
Plantation, FL 33324-3202
IRS FOIA Request
Jacksonville Disclosure Office
MS 4030
400 West Bay Street
Jacksonville, FL 32202-4437
Georgia
IRS FOIA Request
Atlanta Disclosure Office
Mail Stop 602D, Room 1905
401 W. Peachtree Street, NW
Atlanta, GA 30308
Hawaii
IRS FOIA Request
Laguna Niguel Disclosure Office
24000 Avila Road, M/S 2201
Laguna Niguel, CA 92677-0207
Idaho
IRS FOIA Request
Seattle Disclosure Office
Mail Stop W625
915 2nd Avenue
Seattle, WA 98174
Illinois
IRS FOIA Request
Chicago Disclosure Office
Mail Stop 7000 CHI, Room 2820

230 S. Dearborn Street
Chicago, IL 60604
Indiana
IRS FOIA Request
Indianapolis Disclosure Office
Mail Stop CL 658
575 N. Penn. Street
Indianapolis, IN 46204
Iowa
IRS FOIA Request
St. Paul Disclosure Office
Stop 7000
316 N. Robert Street
St. Paul, MN 55101
Kansas
IRS FOIA Request
St. Louis Disclosure Office
Mail Stop 7000 STL
P.O. Box 66781
St. Louis, MO 63166
Kentucky
IRS FOIA Request
Cincinnati Disclosure Office
Post Office Box 1818, Rm. 7019
Cincinnati, OH 45201
Louisiana
IRS FOIA Request
New Orleans Disclosure Office
Mail Stop 40
600 S. Maestri Place
New Orleans, LA 70130
Maine
IRS FOIA Request
Boston Disclosure Office
Mail Stop 41150
Post Office Box 9112
JFK Building
Boston, MA 02203
Maryland
IRS FOIA Request
Baltimore Disclosure Office
George Fallon Fed. Bldg.
31 Hopkins Plaza, Room 1210
Baltimore, MD 21201
Massachusetts
IRS FOIA Request
Boston Disclosure Office
Mail Stop 41150
JFK Building
Post Office Box 9112
Boston, MA 02203
Michigan
IRS FOIA Request
Detroit Disclosure Office
Mail Stop 11
Post Office Box 330500
Detroit, MI 48232-6500
Minnesota
IRS FOIA Request
St. Paul Disclosure Office
Stop 7000
316 N. Robert Street
St. Paul, MN 55101
Mississippi
IRS FOIA Request
New Orleans Disclosure Office
Mail Stop 40

600 S. Maestri Place
New Orleans, LA 70130
Missouri
IRS FOIA Request
St. Louis Disclosure Office
Mail Stop 7000 STL
P.O. Box 66781
St. Louis, MO 63166
Montana
IRS FOIA Request
Denver Disclosure Office
Mail Stop 7000 DEN
600 17th Street
Denver, CO 80202-2490
Nebraska
IRS FOIA Request
St. Paul Disclosure Office
Stop 7000
316 N. Robert Street
St. Paul, MN 55101
Nevada
IRS FOIA Request
Phoenix Disclosure Office
Mail Stop 7000 PHX
210 E. Earll Drive
Phoenix, AZ 85012
New Hampshire
IRS FOIA Request
Boston Disclosure Office
Mail Stop 41150
Post Office Box 9112
JFK Building
Boston, MA 02203
New Mexico
IRS FOIA Request
Phoenix Disclosure Office
Mail Stop 7000 PHX
210 E. Earll Drive
Phoenix, AZ 85012
New Jersey
IRS FOIA Request
Springfield Disclosure Office
P.O. Box 748
Springfield, N.J. 07081-0748
New York (Brooklyn, Queens, and the counties of Nassau and Suffolk)
IRS FOIA Request
Brooklyn Disclosure Office
10 Metro Tech Center
625 Fulton Street
4th Floor, Suite 611
Brooklyn, N.Y. 11201-5404
New York (Manhattan, Staten Island, the Bronx, and the counties of Rockland and Westchester)
IRS FOIA Request
Manhattan Disclosure Office
110 W. 44th Street
New York, N.Y. 10036
New York (all other counties)
IRS FOIA Request
Buffalo Disclosure Office
111 West Huron St., Room 505
Buffalo, N.Y. 14202
North Carolina
IRS FOIA Request
Greensboro Disclosure Office

320 Federal Place, Room 409
Greensboro, N.C. 27401
North Dakota
IRS FOIA Request
St. Paul Disclosure Office
Stop 7000
316 N. Robert Street
St. Paul, MN 55101
Ohio
IRS FOIA Request
Cincinnati Disclosure Office
Post Office Box 1818, Rm. 7019
Cincinnati, OH 45201
Oklahoma
IRS FOIA Request
Oklahoma City Disclosure Office
Mail Stop 7000 OKC
55 N. Robinson
Oklahoma City, OK 73102
Oregon
IRS FOIA Request
Seattle Disclosure Office
Mail Stop W625
915 2nd Avenue
Seattle, WA 98174
Pennsylvania
IRS FOIA Request
Philadelphia Disclosure Office
600 Arch Street, Room 3214
Philadelphia, PA 19106
Rhode Island
IRS FOIA Request
Hartford Disclosure Office
William R. Cotter F.O.B.
Mail Stop 140
135 High Street
Hartford, CT 06103
South Carolina
IRS FOIA Request
Greensboro Disclosure Office
320 Federal Place, Room 409
Greensboro, N.C. 27401
South Dakota
IRS FOIA Request
St. Paul Disclosure Office
Stop 7000
316 N. Robert Street
St. Paul, MN 55101
Tennessee
IRS FOIA Request
Nashville Disclosure Office
MDP 44
801 Broadway, Room 480
Nashville, TN 37203
Texas
IRS FOIA Request
Austin Disclosure Office
Mail Stop 7000 AUS
300 East 8th Street, Room 262
Austin, TX 78701
IRS FOIA Request
Dallas Disclosure Office
Mail Stop 7000 DAL
1100 Commerce Street
Dallas, TX 75242
IRS FOIA Request
Houston Disclosure Office

Mail Stop 7000 HOU
1919 Smith Street
Houston, TX 77002
Utah
IRS FOIA Request
Denver Disclosure Office
Mail Stop 7000 DEN
600 17th Street
Denver, CO 80202-2490
Vermont
IRS FOIA Request
Boston Disclosure Office
Mail Stop 41150
Post Office Box 9112
JFK Building
Boston, MA 02203
Virginia
IRS FOIA Request
Richmond Disclosure Office
P.O. Box 10107
Richmond, VA 23240
Washington
IRS FOIA Request
Seattle Disclosure Office
Mail Stop 625
915 2nd Avenue
Seattle, WA 98174
West Virginia
IRS FOIA Request
Cincinnati Disclosure Office
Post Office Box 1818, Rm. 7019
Cincinnati, OH 45201

Wisconsin
IRS FOIA Request
Milwaukee Disclosure Office
Mail Stop 7000 MIL
310 W. Wisconsin Avenue
Milwaukee, WI 53203-2221
Wyoming
IRS FOIA Request
Denver Disclosure Office
Mail Stop 7000 DEN
600 17th Street
Denver, CO 80202-2490
All APO and FPO addresses
IRS FOIA Request
Headquarters Disclosure Office
GL:GLD:D
1111 Constitution Avenue, N.W.
Washington, D.C. 20224
[Reg. § 601.702.]

☐ [32 FR 15990, Nov. 22, 1967, as amended at 33 FR 6826, May 4, 1968; 34 FR 6433, Apr. 12, 1969; 34 FR 14604, Sept. 19, 1969; 35 FR 7117, May 6, 1970; 36 FR 7587, Apr. 22, 1971; 36 FR 8149, Apr. 30, 1970; 38 FR 4973, Feb. 23, 1973; 39 FR 15755, May 6, 1974; 41 FR 19937, May 14, 1976; 41 FR 24704, June 18, 1976; 41 FR 48472, Nov. 5, 1976; 43 FR 53030, Nov. 15, 1978; 45 FR 7259, Feb. 1, 1980; 48 FR 15624, Apr. 12, 1983; 49 FR 12702, Mar. 30, 1984; 49 FR 19651, May 9, 1984; 49 FR 36500, Sept. 18, 1984; 51 FR 7442, Mar. 4, 1986; 52 FR 30996, Aug. 18, 1987; 52 FR 37940, Oct. 13, 1987; 67 FR 69673, Nov. 19, 2002.]

Subpart H—Tax Counseling for the Elderly

[Reg. § 601.801]

§ 601.801. Purpose and statutory authority.— (a) This Subpart H contains the rules for implementation of the Tax Counseling for the Elderly assistance program under Section 163 of the Revenue Act of 1978, Public Law 95-600, November 6, 1978 (92 Stat. 2810). Section 163 authorizes the Secretary of the Treasury, through the Internal Revenue Service, to enter into agreements with private or public non-profit agencies or organizations for the purpose of providing training and technical assistance to prepare volunteers to provide tax counseling assistance for elderly individuals, age 60 and over, in the preparation of their Federal income tax returns.

(b) Section 163 provides that the Secretary may provide:

(1) Preferential access to Internal Revenue Service taxpayer service representatives for the purpose of making available technical information needed during the course of the volunteers' work;

(2) Publicity for making elderly persons aware of the availability of volunteer taxpayer return preparation assistance programs under this section; and

(3) Technical materials and publications to be used by such volunteers.

(c) In carrying out responsibilities under Section 163, the Secretary, through the Internal Revenue Service is also authorized:

(1) To provide assistance to organizations which demonstrate, to the satisfaction of the Secretary, that their volunteers are adequately trained and competent to render effective tax counseling to the elderly in the preparation of Federal income tax returns;

(2) To provide for the training of such volunteers, and to assist in such training, to ensure that such volunteers are qualified to provide tax counseling assistance to elderly individuals in the preparation of Federal income tax returns;

(3) To provide reimbursement to volunteers through such organizations for transportation, meals, and other expenses incurred by them in training or providing tax counseling assistance in the preparation of Federal income tax returns under this section, and such other support and assistance determined to be appropriate in carrying out the provisions of the section;

(4) To provide for the use of services, personnel, and facilities of Federal executive agencies and State and local public agencies with their consent, with or without reimbursement; and

(5) To prescribe rules and regulations necessary to carry out the provisions of the section.

(d) With regard to the employment status of volunteers, section 163 also provides that service as a volunteer in any program carried out under this section shall not be considered service as an employee of the United States. Volunteers under such a program shall not be subject to the provisions of law relating to Federal employment, except that the provisions relating to the illegal disclosure of income or other information punishable under Section 1905 of Title 18, United States Code, shall apply to volunteers as if they were employees of the United States. [Reg. § 601.801.]

☐ [44 FR 72113, Dec. 13, 1979.]

[Reg. § 601.802]

§ 601.802. Cooperative agreements.— (a) *General.*—Tax Counseling for the Elderly programs will be administered by sponsor organizations under cooperative agreements with the Internal Revenue Service. Use of cooperative agreements is in accordance with the Federal Grant and Cooperative Agreement Act of 1977, Public Law 95-224, February 3, 1978 (92 Stat. 3, 41 U.S.C. 501-509). Cooperative agreements will be legally binding agreements in document form.

(b) *Nature and contents of cooperative agreements.*—Each cooperative agreement will provide for implementation of the program in specified geographic areas. Cooperative agreements will set forth:

(1) The functions and duties to be performed by the Internal Revenue Service and the functions and duties to be performed by the program sponsor,

(2) The maximum amount of the award available to the program sponsor,

(3) The services to be provided for each geographical area, and

(4) Other requirements specified in the application.

(c) *Entry into cooperative agreements.*—The Commissioner of Internal Revenue, the Director, Taxpayer Service Division, or any other individual designated by the Commissioner may enter into a cooperative agreement for the Internal Revenue Service.

(d) *Competitive award of cooperative agreements.*—Cooperative agreements will generally be entered into based upon competition among eligible applicants.

(1) To be eligible to enter into a cooperative agreement, an organization must be a private or public non-profit agency or organization with experience in coordinating volunteer programs. Federal, state, and local governmental agencies and organizations will not be eligible to become program sponsors.

(2) Eligible applicants will be selected to enter into cooperative agreements based on an evaluation by the Internal Revenue Service of material provided in their applications. The Service will set forth the evaluative criteria in the application instructions.

(3) Determinations as to the eligibility and selection of agencies and organizations to enter into cooperative agreements will be made solely by the Internal Revenue Service and will not be subject to appeal.

(e) *Noncompetitive award of cooperative agreements.*—If appropriations to implement the Tax Counseling for the Elderly program are received at a time close to when tax return preparation assistance must be provided or when other factors exist which make the use of competition to select agencies and organizations to enter into cooperative agreements impracticable, cooperative agreements will be entered into without competition with eligible agencies and organizations selected by the Internal Revenue Service. Determination of when the use of competition is impracticable will be made solely by the Internal Revenue Service and will not be subject to appeal.

(f) *Renegotiation, suspension, termination and modification.*

(1) Cooperative agreements will be subject to renegotiation (including the maximum amount of the award available to a sponsor), suspension, or termination if performance reports required by the cooperative agreement and/or other evaluations by or audits by the Internal Revenue Service or others indicate that planned performance goals or other provisions of the cooperative agreement, the regulations, or Section 163 of the Revenue Act of 1978 are not being satisfactorily met. The necessity for renegotiation, suspension, or termination, will be determined solely by the Internal Revenue Service and will not be subject to appeal.

(2) Cooperative agreements may be modified in writing by mutual agreement between the Internal Revenue Service and the program sponsor at any time. Modifications will be based upon factors such as an inability to utilize all funds available under a cooperative agreement, the availability of additional funds and an ability to effectively utilize additional funds, and interference of some provisions with the efficient operation of the program.

(g) *Negotiation.*—If the proposed program of an eligible applicant does not warrant award of an agreement, the Internal Revenue Service may negotiate with the applicant to bring the application up to a standard that will be adequate for award. If more than one inadequate application has been received for the geographic area involved, negotiation to bring all such applications up to standard will be conducted with all such applicants unless time does not permit negotiations with all. [Reg. § 601.802.]

☐ [44 FR 72113, Dec. 13, 1979.]

[Reg. § 601.803]

§ 601.803. Program operations and requirements.— (a) *Objective.*—The objective of the Tax Counseling for the Elderly program is to provide free assistance in the preparation of Federal income tax returns to elderly taxpayers age 60 and over, by providing training, technical and administrative support to volunteers under the direction of non-profit agencies and organizations that have cooperative agreements with the Internal Revenue Service.

(b) *Period of program operations.*—Most tax return preparation assistance will be provided to elderly taxpayers during the period for filing Federal income tax returns, from January 1 to April 15 each year. However, the program activities required to ensure elderly taxpayers efficient and quality tax assistance will normally be conducted year round. Program operations will generally be divided into the following segments each year: October—recruit volunteers; November and December—set training and testing schedules for volunteers, identify assistance sites, complete publicity plans for sites; December and January—train and test volunteers, set volunteer assistance schedules; January through May—provide tax assistance, conduct publicity for sites; May and June—prepare final report and evaluate program; July and August—prepare for next year's program.

(c) *Assistance requirements.*—All tax return preparation assistance provided under Tax Counseling for the Elderly programs must be provided free of charge to taxpayers and must be provided only to elderly individuals. An elderly individual is an individual age 60 or over at the close of the individual's taxable year with respect to which tax return preparation assistance is to be provided. Where a joint return is involved, assistance may be provided where only one spouse satisfies the 60 year age requirement.

(d) *Training and testing of volunteers.*—Volunteers will normally be provided training and will normally be required to pass tests designed to measure their understanding of Federal tax subjects on which they will provide tax return assistance. Volunteers who do not receive a satisfactory score will not be eligible to participate in the program.

(e) *Confidentiality of tax information.*—Program sponsors must obtain written assurance from all volunteers and all other individuals involved in the program, to respect the confidentiality of income and financial information known as a result of preparation of a return or of providing tax counseling assistance in the preparation of Federal income tax returns. [Reg. § 601.803.]

☐ [44 FR 72113, Dec. 13, 1979.]

[Reg. § 601.804]

§ 601.804. Reimbursements.—(a) *General.*—When provided for in cooperative agreements, the Internal Revenue Service will provide amounts to program sponsors for reimbursement to volunteers for transportation, meals, and other expenses incurred in training or providing tax return assistance and to program sponsors for reimbursement of overhead expenses. Cooperative agreements will establish the items for which reimbursements will be allowed and the method of reimbursement, e.g. stipend versus actual expenses for meals, as well as developing necessary procedures, forms, and accounting and financial control systems.

(b) *Direct, reasonable, and prudent expenses.*—Reimbursements will be allowed only for direct, reasonable, and prudent expenses incurred as a part of a volunteer's service or as a part of the program's sponsor's overhead.

(c) *Limitation.*—Total reimbursements provided to a program sponsor shall not exceed the total amount specified in the cooperative agreement. The Internal Revenue Service shall not be liable for additional amounts to program sponsors, volunteers, or anyone else.

(d) *Availability of appropriated funds.*—Expense reimbursements and other assistance to be provided by the Internal Revenue Service under cooperative agreements are contingent upon the availability of appropriated funds for the Tax Counseling for the Elderly program. [Reg. § 601.804.]

☐ [44 FR 72113, Dec. 13, 1979.]

[Reg. § 601.805]

§ 601.805. Miscellaneous administrative provisions.—(a) *Responsibilities and relationship of Internal Revenue and program sponsor.*—Substantial involvement is anticipated between the Internal Revenue Service and the program sponsors in conducting this program. Specific responsibilities and obligations of the Internal Revenue Service and the program sponsors will be set forth in each cooperative agreement.

(b) *Administrative requirements set forth in OMB and Treasury Circulars.*

(1) The basic administrative requirements applicable to individual cooperative agreements are contained in Office of Management and Budget Circular No. A-110, Grants and Agreements with Institutions of Higher Education, Hospitals and Other Nonprofit Organizations (41 F.R. 32016). All applicable provisions of this circular and any existing and further supplements and revisions are incorporated into these regulations and into all cooperative agreements entered into between the Internal Revenue Service and program sponsors.

(2) Additional operating procedures and instructions may be developed by the Internal Revenue Service to direct recipient organizations in carrying out the provisions of this subpart, such as instructions for using letters of credit. Any such operating procedures or instructions will be incorporated into each cooperative agreement.

(c) *Joint funding.*—Tax Counseling for the Elderly programs will not be eligible for joint funding. Accordingly, the Joint Funding Simplification Act of 1974, Public Law 93-510, December 5, 1974 (88 Stat. 1604, 42 U.S.C. 4251-4261) and Office of Management and Budget Circular No. A-111, Jointly Funded Assistance to State and Local Governments and Nonprofit Organizations (41 F.R. 32039), will not apply.

(d) *Discrimination.*—No program sponsor shall discriminate against any person providing tax return assistance on the basis of age, sex, race, religion or national origin in conducting program operations. No program sponsor shall discriminate against any person in providing such assistance on the basis of sex, race, religion or national origin. [Reg. § 601.805.]

☐ [44 FR 72113, Dec. 13, 1979, as amended at 49 FR 36500, Sept. 18, 1984.]

[Reg. § 601.806]

§ 601.806. Solicitation of applications.— (a) *Solicitation.*—The Commissioner of Internal Revenue or the Commissioner's delegate may, at any time, solicit eligible agencies and organizations to submit applications. Generally, applications will be solicited and accepted in June and July of each year. Deadlines for submitting applications and the schedule for selecting program sponsors will be provided with application documents.

(1) Before preparing and submitting an unsolicited application, organizations are strongly encouraged to contact the Internal Revenue Service at the address provided in (b)(2) of this section.

(2) A solicitation of an application is not an assurance or commitment that the Internal Revenue Service will enter into a cooperative agreement. The Internal Revenue Service will not pay any expenses or other costs incurred by the applicant in considering, preparing or submitting an application.

(b) *Application.*

(1) In the application documents, the Commissioner or the Commissioner's delegate will specify program requirements which the applicant must meet.

(2) Eligible organizations interested in participating in the Internal Revenue Service Tax Counseling for the Elderly program should request an application from the:

Program Manager
Tax Counseling for the Elderly
Taxpayer Service Division TX:T:I
Internal Revenue Service
1111 Constitution Ave., N.W.
Washington, D.C. 20224
(202) 566-4904

[Reg. § 601.806.]

☐ [44 FR 72113, Dec. 13, 1979.]

Subpart I—Use of Penalty Mail in the Location and Recovery of Missing Children

[Reg. § 601.901]

§ 601.901. Missing children shown on penalty mail.—(a) *Purpose.*—To support the national effort to locate and recover missing children, the Internal Revenue Service (IRS) joins other executive departments and agencies of the Government of the United States in using official mail to disseminate photographs and biographical information on hundreds of missing children.

(b) *Procedures for obtaining and disseminating data.*—(1) The IRS shall publish pictures and biographical data related to missing children in domestic penalty mail containing annual tax forms and instructions, taxpayer information publications, and other IRS products directed to members of the public in the United States and its territories and possessions.

(2) Missing children information shall not be placed on the "Penalty Indicia," "OCR Read Area," "Bar Code Read Area," and "Return Address" areas of letter-size envelopes.

(3) The IRS shall accept photographic and biographical materials solely from the National Center for Missing and Exploited Children (National Center). Photographs that were reasonably current as of the time of the child's disappearance, or those which have been updated to reflect a missing child's current age through computer enhancement technique, shall be the only acceptable form of visual media or pictorial likeness used in penalty mail.

(c) *Withdrawal of data.*—The shelf life of printed penalty mail is limited to 3 months for missing child cases. The IRS shall follow those guidelines whenever practicable. For products with an extended shelf life, such as those related to filing and paying taxes, the IRS will not print any pictures or biographical data relating to missing children without obtaining from the National Center a waiver of the 3-month shelf-life guideline.

(d) *Reports and contact official.*—IRS shall compile and submit to OJJDP reports on its experience in implementing Public Law 99-87, 99 Stat. 290, as required by that office. The IRS contact person is: Chief, Business Publications Section (or successor office), Tax Forms and Publications Division, Technical Publications Branch, OP:FS:FP:P:3, Room 5613, Internal Revenue Service, 1111 Constitution Ave., N.W., Washington, DC 20224.

(e) *Period of applicability.*—This section is applicable December 13, 1999 through December 31, 2002. [Reg. § 601.901.]

☐ [*T.D.* 8848, 12-10-99.]